A Concordance to the Writings of

WILLIAM BLAKE

THE CORNELL CONCORDANCES

Supervisory Committee
M. H. Abrams
Ephim G. Fogel
William R. Keast
James A. Painter, *Computer Programmer*
S. M. Parrish, *General Editor*

POEMS OF MATTHEW ARNOLD
Edited by S. M. Parrish

POEMS OF W. B. YEATS
Edited by S. M. Parrish

POEMS OF EMILY DICKINSON
Edited by S. P. Rosenbaum

WRITINGS OF WILLIAM BLAKE
Edited by D. V. Erdman

A Concordance to the Writings of

WILLIAM BLAKE

Edited by

DAVID V. ERDMAN

With the assistance of

JOHN E. THIESMEYER AND RICHARD J. WOLFE

Also G. E. Bentley, Jr., Palmer Brown, Robert F. Gleckner,

George Mills Harper, Karl Kiralis, Martin K. Nurmi, and Paul M. Zall

VOLUME I

Cornell University Press

ITHACA, NEW YORK

Library of Congress Catalog Card Number: 66–18608

PRINTED IN THE UNITED STATES OF AMERICA

BY VALLEY OFFSET, INC.

BOUND BY VAIL-BALLOU PRESS, INC.

To Oothoon

PREFACE

EACH new concordance brings its particular surprises, those most immediately accessible being some of the words that come out at the top of the frequency count—or at the bottom. We may have expected to find MAN, LOVE, ETERNAL, and EARTH among Blake's most used words, but not DEATH so near the top or NIGHT so far ahead of DAY. And among those used only once we may be struck to see how many were memorably effective in their single impacts: ABRUPT, AMALGAMATING (a climactic word in *Jerusalem*), FOOLISHER, GEM (but there are seventeen GEMS, commonly in the tag GEMS & GOLD), INLETS, LAPSED, REGALE. There even emerges a category of abstract plurals which Blake was plainly fond of yet never repeated: KINDNESSES, GOODNESSES, FORGIVENESSES, HAPPI-NESSES, SELF-RIGHTEOUSNESSES.

Every concordance of English poetry added to the shelf multiplies the uses of the ones there already; a double concordance of prose and verse is both more entire in itself as an index and a richer resource for linguistic and stylistic comparisons. When we pursue the language of Spenser, Shakespeare, Milton, and the English Bible, Blake's avowed sources, we need not halt within the bounds of his lyrics and prophecies but can enter Steelyard's study and Blake's exhibition "Catalogue" and "Public Address," even his marginalia and his correspondence. The distinctions between Blake's vocabularies for poetry and for prose can be investigated—also the points where such distinctions change or vanish. But the user can always ignore the added material and concentrate on the poetry.

Comparisons can now be made in a forward direction, with the Yeats concordance in the present series, to test impressions of Blake's influence on the poetry of his interpreter and follower. Some verbal echoes will quickly be discovered under such index words in both concordances as ARISE and GO and JOY. Nevertheless we may find that the vocabularies of

the two poets have very few words in common, if Blake's twenty-eight and Yeats's twenty-two epithets for atmospheric AIR constitute a representative sample. AIR in Blake's poetry is sometimes THIN, MILD, NOURISHING, SERENE, JOYFUL, or BRIGHT, TRANSPARENT, or simply OUTWARD or EXPECTING, or KEEN OPEN, but more often BURNING, SECRET, SOUNDING, CAVERND, BOSOMD, or HUMID, HEAVY, BURDEND, LEADEN, DISMAL, DIM, TROUBLED, RED, or DARK BLUE, PURPLE, FURIOUS, DARKSOM, DARK. (In his prose it is OPEN, MILD, SWEET, HAMPSTEAD, or MORNING, or THO WARM . . . UNHEALTHY.) Blake's FRESH AIRS and GENTLE AIRS also refer to atmosphere, not song. In the poetry of Yeats, AIR is MISTY or MIST-COLD, MORTAL, CLINGING, WINTRY, BREATHLESS, STARLIT, DREAMING, NIGHT, WASTE, DARK, or DELIGHTED, WHIRLING, BRIGHTENING, VIOLET, LIGHT, GREEN, HIGH, UPPER, STILL, SEA, MIDDLE, ODOROUS, FLOWING. Besides DARK the only approximately overlapping terms are BRIGHT/BRIGHTENING and PURPLE/VIOLET. The differences are vastly greater than can be accounted for by differences of climate.

Basic Text of the Concordance

The basic text for this concordance is the 1957 edition of *The Complete Writings of William Blake: With All the Variant Readings*, edited by Geoffrey Keynes (London: Nonesuch Press; New York: Random House). Revisions and additions made to this text are listed and explained in an Appendix to the concordance, and all revised or added lines are starred with asterisks in the main body of the work. Publication of the Keynes edition made a Blake concordance possible, and through the courtesy of the editor and publishers a supply of unbound copies was made available at cost to Mr. Wolfe and myself. It was originally our intention, on becoming aware of a sprinkling of errors in the text, some of which were called to our attention by Sir Geoffrey himself, simply to make a rapid collation of readily available sources. Among those who combined forces for this task were Palmer Brown, who had made a fresh transcription of *An Island in the Moon* from photostats, and Gerald E. Bentley, Jr., who was finishing a new transcription of the manuscript of *The Four Zoas*. Plans were soon made for inclusion in the Cornell University series of a concordance of these *"Complete Writings,"* but Blake's lines would not fit comfortably into a standard format; other complications arose that delayed the programming and processing, and during the time that thus became available it was possible to consult original manuscripts and books and to accumulate film copies of them—and to devise methods for deciphering doubtful and deleted passages. (See my report on the "Sup-

pressed and Altered Passages in Blake's *Jerusalem*," in *Studies in Bibliography*, XVII, 1964, pp. 1–54.) My original collaborators continued to help with a good deal of hard work, including the proofreading of the basic print-out from the computer, and with valuable criticism and suggestions; but they are not to be held accountable for the readings of the text as modified for the final keypunching of revisions in the summer of 1965. My own scrutiny of the manuscripts, even of *An Island in the Moon* and *The Four Zoas,* has gradually led me to overrule several of the earlier readings.

The concordance text remains that of the Keynes edition of 1957 in pagination, lineation, and arrangement, and in these respects Keynes's 1966 revision published in the Oxford Standard Authors series stands unchanged; printed by offset from the 1957 Nonesuch, the text has been mended here and there to incorporate some of our salient minor corrections, while a part of the supplementary matter and major revisions of our Appendix are placed at the end to spare the original pagination.

A thorough textual revision, departing in punctuation, capitalization, and arrangement from these editions, will inevitably differ also in pagination and lineation. Users of this concordance may sometimes, nevertheless, wish to consult my revised and rearranged edition of *The Poetry and Prose of William Blake*, published in the autumn of 1965 by Doubleday & Company, with a full apparatus of deletions and variants, and a commentary by Harold Bloom. (Second printing, 1966, extensively revised.)

Inclusiveness

Once embarked on the inclusion of prose as well as verse in this concordance we have not wished to make any exclusions that would limit its value as an index. From Geoffrey Keynes's edition of Blake's *Letters* we have drawn proper names and significant words in addresses, receipts, and lists which were omitted from the *Complete Writings*. We have included the few authentic titles of pictures, as well as titles of writings, and have only been prevented from incorporating an authoritative list of the subjects of Blake's paintings and engravings by the fact that none exists.

We have omitted quoted matter occurring in large blocks but have included quotations that are brief and integral (clearly setting them apart by the insertion of quotation marks). We should have included the series of biblical inscriptions in the borders of the *Illustrations of the Book of Job,* if we had recognized in time that they often depart from verbatim quotation. We do include the legends under the emblem drawings in Blake's Notebook, quoted from Spenser and Shakespeare and

others, partly because these are the raw material from which Blake evolved *The Gates of Paradise*. Such inclusions permit the index itself to initiate the exploration of associations and influences. For example, FORTH-WITH, in a legend drawn from *Paradise Lost,* "Forthwith upright he rears from off the pool," heralds the resurgence of Satan; the word has a similar function in each of the three passages in which Blake used it for himself—in *Urizen, Ahania,* and *Jerusalem.* On the other hand he echoed INFLUX four times in his notes on Swedenborg but never adopted the word. Again, the legend "At length for hatching ripe he breaks the shell—Dryden" contains words that reverberate widely in Blake, and anyone who looks up the whole passage in Dryden's *Palamon and Arcite,* Book III, will find that the discussion of Man, the creation, and the golden chain contains a number of terms that seem worth investigating singly or in clusters for their development in Blake's poetry.

Still further we have reached out to include, with highly selective indexing, some of the words which supply the context for marginal notes by Blake which are so brief as to be otherwise enigmatic. Such excerpts, often condensed without marks of elision, are carefully marked off by parentheses around quotation marks. For example, the following line, consisting of an excerpt from Reynolds and a marginal note by Blake,

("ERROR IS ON THE SIDE OF MINUTENESS") HERE IS NONSENSE

will be found in the concordance under ERROR and MINUTENESS as well as under NONSENSE. The word SIDE was not relevant here, and it was possible before key-punching to mark it for omission from the indexing. Editorial decisions of this sort were made in passing, however, and the passages in question varied greatly in the degree to which they lent themselves to this treatment; so I cannot claim to have been wholly consistent either in the selecting or in the marking of excerpts. I assume merely that inclusions in this category may have value while omissions can do no harm.

The inclusion of quoted matter has produced a few index words which prove never to have been directly used by Blake; their index value is usually self-evident. DAPHNE, for example, will lead to the location of Blake's drawing of that subject, under which he inscribed the legend we print thus:

"AS DAPHNE WAS ROOT BOUND" MILTON

yet this line provides the only occurrence of DAPHNE or of ROOT BOUND (to which the computer has automatically produced a cross reference from BOUND).

It has also seemed useful to include partly conjectural restorations of deleted words or incomplete words, duly provided with question marks. Thus under ROMAN will be found a line in which "Ron" was written and then deleted, in a context where "Roman" is the evident intention. In the concordance line the word is given as [(?ROMAN)]; in the Appendix the explanation is [?Ron(?Roman)]. Undeciphered erasures and deletions are recorded by the use of "X's" within brackets, but these, of course, are not indexed. Catchwords are included only when they do not appear in the following page or plate and hence are relics of something lost. Restricted to uppercase letters, we cannot record Blake's sometimes frequent shifts of case such as the correction of "man" to "Man." We have omitted passages in Greek and Hebrew, except for a few transliterations.

At the beginnings and ends of segments of prose (gathered by clauses or phrases when possible, to supply meaningful contexts) we sometimes saved space by omitting nonsignificant words from the key-punching, since they would not be indexed anyway; but this does mean that the frequency counts for omitted words are slightly short. Frequency counts for the indexed words are sometimes reduced from true totals because of the programming feature which omits the second or third occurrence of a word within the same line.

A feature of the Blake concordance is the retention of words previously ruled out as common or "nonsignificant," so long as they are not of prohibitively high frequency. We exclude DO and DID but retain DOTH and DOST, partly on the ground that these uncommon forms of common words are of stylistic interest. Words omitted in previous concordances in this series but kept here include AGAIN, ALTHO, ALTHOUGH, ANOTHER, ANOTHER'S, BOTH, CANST, COULDST, DIDST, DONT, DOST, DOTH, EITHER, HADST, HAST, HATH, HAVENT, HOWEVER, ITSELF, MUST, NEITHER, NO, OTHER, OTHER'S, OTHERS, SHALT, SHANT, SHOULDNT, SHOULDST, THAT'S, THEIRS, THEMSELVES, THERE'S, THEY'D, THEY'LL, THRO, THROUGH, THYSELF, TIS, TWAS, 'TWILL, TWOULD, WAS'T, WERT, WHAT'S, WHENEER, WHENEVER, WHEREER, WHEREVER, WHETHER, WHO'D, WHOEVER, WHOSE, WILT, WON'T, WOULDST. And there are several similar words not specifically omitted from the other volumes because they did not occur in the texts concorded.

We follow the fresh tradition of the Cornell Concordances in including LIKE and AS, for the comparison of comparisons, although limitations of space compelled us to weed out the less significant uses of AS. The "nonsignificant" forms of several other words or homographs were also removed. Words in the first list, below, were omitted when used as indicated; high-frequency words considered nonsignificant and omitted from the index appear in the second list with their frequencies.

A	2	(4406 occurrences as article omitted)
AN	2	(529 occurrences as article omitted)
ART	244	(172 occurrences as verb omitted)
AS	682	(833 occurrences not in simile or other special use omitted)
HAD	101	(161 occurrences as auxiliary verb omitted)
HAS	112	(329 occurrences as auxiliary verb omitted)
HAVE	244	(674 occurrences as auxiliary verb omitted)
HAVING	21	(29 occurrences as auxiliary verb omitted)
I AM (the)	1	
WILL	89	(661 occurrences as auxiliary verb omitted)

OMITTED WORDS

AM	402	HERE	223	SHALL	502	THY	835
AND	4775	HIM	679	SHE	505	TO	5442
ARE	1436	HIS	3154	SHOULD	234	TOO	104
AT	808	HOW	282	SO	609	US	209
BE	1287	I	3651	THAT	2184	WAS	1017
BECAUSE	195	IF	572	THE	18365	WE	542
BEEN	180	IN	6303	THEE	400	WERE	388
BUT	1601	INTO	822	THEIR	1065	WHAT	596
BY	1215	IS	3371	THEM	582	WHEN	655
CAN	471	IT	1417	THEN	688	WHERE	422
CANNOT	226	ITS	411	THERE	302	WHICH	714
COULD	222	ME	1017	THEREFORE	90	WHO	960
DID	179	MY	2159	THESE	444	WHOM	83
DO	369	NOR	268	THEY	1458	WHY	182
DOES	206	NOT	1640	THIS	1192	WITH	2314
EACH	189	NOW	519	THO	178	WOULD	229
FOR	1781	OF	10114	THOSE	290	YET	191
FROM	1753	ON	1932	THOU	854	YOU	1257
HE	2231	OR	943	THOUGH	20	YOUR	516
HER	952	OUR	499	THUS	214		

Also omitted entirely, for various reasons, were ALB (6) and ALBERT (8), to be found under DURER, ETC (4), MR (313), MRS (76), and all Roman numerals. Arabic numerals were not even printed in the text line (since numerals are lacking from the print wheel) but were sometimes written out (within parentheses) and sometimes elided.

Discrimination of Homographs; Grouping of Compounds

Blake's use of capital letters is irregular but does not concern us in a program restricted to solid capitals. His punctuation is also irregular, when not lacking altogether, and has some importance for us. It was not available in a printed text when we began, however, and for the concordance we restricted our collation of punctuation to the hyphens. The text now indexed follows Blake exactly in the matter of hyphenation of

compound words (with silent correction of Keynes). In the use of apostrophes it follows neither Blake nor Keynes but has been systematized to enable the computer to sort out possessive forms (e.g., to distinguish LOS's from LOSS, ROSE's from ROSES and ROSES') and to separate contractions from their homographs (e.g., SHE'D from SHED). When Blake used an apostrophe for a plural (e.g., "the Lewis's" and "they are named Life's [Zoas]"), we have had to remove it (LEWISS, LIFES). We have removed the apostrophe contracting "is" to "'s" but not closed up the space: "Edward's afraid of Philip" is punched EDWARD S AFRAID OF PHILIP SO that the line is indexed under EDWARD and s (IS) and not under the possessive EDWARD's.

A few ambiguous possessives, uncertainly singular or plural, ANGELS WINGS, LIONS GORE, THE PHILOSOPHERS HOUSE, were not supplied with apostrophes and so have been indexed among the simple plurals. Our apostrophizing of contractions has not been entirely consistent. When the lines were first marked for key-punching, apostrophes needed for sorting were not always inserted; unnecessary ones were usually but not always omitted. Correct groupings were later achieved, but not all the lines were repunched.

Homographs have generally been left together—even such ill-sorted ones as "Lear" and "lear (leer)" or "hail" and "Hail!" But many groups were discriminated in the final editing. Proper names such as GATES, GREEN, GRACE, HUNTER, ROSE, and the symbolic name HAND were distinguished from their homographs. We separated BEING (noun) from BEING (verb), also MAY (noun from verb), MIGHT (noun from verb), MINE (noun from pronoun; verb lacking), OUGHT (verb from noun or adverb), and ROSE (noun from verb).

Blake's hyphens assisted in the segregation of compound words, but invisible hyphens were inserted to enable the computer to index, for example, CORN-FIELD and CORN FIELD together, or BRICK-KILN and BRICK KILN —with, of course, appropriate cross references. This method led to some inconsistencies. Blake's ROSE-TREE suggested the grouping with it of ROSE TREE as a compound. But MIRTLE and TREE were not compounded, no instance of hyphenation having turned up. HOLY GHOST was given a separate listing with one HOLY-GHOST. FOUR ZOAS, difficult to find under FOUR, might have been separated except that occurrences are already conveniently isolated under ZOAS. As Blake's compounding proclivities became familiar, I risked treating as compounds several pairs of words not hyphenated by Blake. Preceding and following SELF (with cross reference to HERSELF, HIMSELF, ITSELF, MYSELF, MY SELF, THYSELF, THY SELF) we now have sixty compound words beginning with SELF. Twenty-five, as

we can see, were never hyphenated by the author, but there are clear advantages in having these all in one place. Similarly I have separated such terms as ONCE SAVAGE and ONCE STUPID from the long list under ONCE. Nor in the matter of inclusions has it seemed advisable to respect all Blake's hyphenations as normative. All LITTLE ONES, for example, do not appear to belong under LITTLE-ONES.

One side effect of the grouping of pairs of words as compounds, it should be noted, is a reduction of the frequency count for each of the components. The grouping of ROSE TREE with ROSE-TREE reduces the counts for ROSE and TREE; recognition of MIRTLE TREE as a compound would have reduced the count for TREE still further. The frequencies are also subdivided by the discrimination of homographs and by the recognition of variant spellings; yet it is well to be aware that the totals given in the various concordances can never be closely comparable without normalization. They are data, not statistics.

Variant Spellings

No attempt has been made to consolidate variant spellings, even when assignable to printed as against manuscript sources, but most variants have been cross-referred, except when alphabetically near each other. INQUIRE and ENQUIRE, INTREAT and ENTREAT have been given cross references in both directions. AKEING and AKING, though sufficiently close to each other, require mutual cross reference to ACHEING. Of these, ENQUIRE and INTREAT and all three forms of "aching" go back to manuscript; INQUIRE and ENTREAT are pre-Keynesian transcriptions of letters now lost. Blake wrote AX and GREEN WOOD, his printer AXE and GREENWOOD. ASTONISHED occurs once, in a lost letter; Blake wrote ASTONISHD 42 times. PERSWADE is his consistent spelling, deriving from Milton (as we see from a quoted emblem); PERSUADE(D) occurs only in two lost letters. In short, many of the variant spellings cannot be traced to Blake himself; a revised concordance might well dispense with these, as might a revised text. Yet Blake's own practice is not constant. Some spellings hold his allegiance throughout a long life; some he maintains up to a certain time and then corrects. (SEPERATE was his spelling, if not his printer's, up into the books of *Urizen* and *Los;* with *Urizen* he corrected to SEPARATE, to which he held thereafter.) GHIOTTO is invariant, so the name was apparently not intentionally misspelled in *An Island.* On the other hand, CORREGGIO is spelled three ways, to no particular purpose, and BARTOLOZZI four within one document, with an obvious sneer in BARTOLLOZE and a probable one in BARTOLOUZZI. One of the words his spelling made his own is BEASTIAL. TYGER(S) roam and burn throughout his writings, and the spelling is obviously a chosen

one, for he could write TIGERS (once in 1794) or TIGER (once in 1807). DESART and SLUMBEROUS are spellings maintained except in printed sources.

Chronological Arrangement

The lines under each index word are arranged in the order of their occurrence in the Keynes text, which is roughly chronological, with the letters forming a separate sequence at the end. "A Divine Image" belongs to 1791 rather than 1794; the Reynolds marginalia were probably written from 1798 to 1810 rather than all "about 1808"; the three epics may or may not overlap by several years; the "Note in Cennini's 'Tratto . . .'" perhaps should read "Cellini's" and be dated much earlier than 1822. And in the concordance the added matter designated SUPP(lement) has been irregularly inserted at the front or back of the Keynes lines, or in approximate position in his sequence. With due precaution, nevertheless, it is possible to make some observations of the broadly chronological distribution of words and idiom. In the early *Poetical Sketches* archaisms abound; of these, the Spenserian ones tend to drop away (it would be instructive to look up the archaic words in the line "In lucent words my darkling verses dight"), while the biblical ones persist. With some sifting and comparing it should be possible to categorize some of the words that drop from Blake's vocabulary after 1795 (a sampling produces BLAZING, BLEACHD, BLEAK, CRAWL); to distinguish the language of *The Four Zoas;* to characterize the words that first appear in *Milton* or *Jerusalem.*

Subject matter may account for the relative prominence of EAGLE(S) in early work, for the occurrence of the ELECT thirteen times in *Milton* and never elsewhere, of ETERNALS fourteen times in *Urizen* and *Ahania,* only thrice in *The Four Zoas,* once each in *Milton* and *Jerusalem.* The author of *Jerusalem,* however, draws heavily on the language of his earliest work as from a fond rereading; such terms as DAMPS OF DEATH and COUCH OF DEATH lay unemployed since *Poetical Sketches;* to go through the concordance with attention to *Jerusalem* is to accumulate a strong impression that Blake's last epic is an intentional culmination and amalgamation of all his styles. To his own declaration that his poetry was now freed from the fetters of rhyme and cadence, he might have added that it was shedding some distinctions in diction as well. Up through *The Four Zoas* OFT and OFTEN reign respectively in verse and prose; in *Milton* and *Jerusalem* they are distributed almost equally. The exclusively poetic OER reigns through *The Four Zoas,* where it is used twenty-two times, and then dramatically gives way to OVER. OER occurs only thrice in *Milton,* not at all in *Jerusalem,* once in *The Everlasting Gospel* (as an intentional revision of

OVER). OH is dropped very early in favor of O.

This kind of evidence, carefully sifted, may help answer the question whether the epics overlap in composition; the shifts from OFT and OER seem to put a space between *The Four Zoas* and *Milton,* and a number of highly significant words cease before or begin in *Milton:* SELFHOOD begins there, as do SEX(ES) and SEXUAL in their Blakean senses. Further study of the concordance may clarify other problems of chronology, such as the relation of Night VII and Night VIIb in *The Four Zoas.* Vocabulary changes, for example, such as the shift from OFT to OFTEN, would appear to support the hypothesis that Night VII was written later than Night VIIb. One notes that the important later terms ANNIHILATE and EMANA-TION first occur in VII, and that SPECTRE, occurring once in VIIb as an adjective ("took the Spectre form"), first occurs as a noun and with full symbolic meaning in VII—not once but eighteen times in the singular and six times in the plural, as though upon the fresh discovery of a new term and concept.

Acknowledgments

Our greatest debt is to Sir Geoffrey Keynes, for having established the basic text of Blake's writings, for generous help and encouragement in the work of its revision and concording, indeed for cooperation at every step of the way. We are also indebted to Sir Geoffrey for access to unique Blake materials in his collection, and, for the same courtesy extended, to the owners and curators of the other Blake collections cited in the notes in our Appendix. In this connection we must particularly thank Frederick B. Adams, Jr., Lady Cunliffe and the late Lord Rolf Cunliffe, David Fox-on, John D. Gordan, Mrs. Esther Harvey, the late William A. Jackson, William H. McCarthy, Paul Mellon, Kerrison Preston, Mrs. Landon K. Thorne, Charles J. Rosenbloom, Lessing J. Rosenwald, Lord Rothschild, T. C. Skeat, Lewis M. Stark, Willis Van Devanter, and Marjorie Wynne.

For a variety of favors we are grateful to Ruth Aldrich, F. W. Bateson, John Beer, Morchard Bishop, Sir Anthony Blunt, Edward E. Bostetter, Fredson Bowers, Martin Butlin, S. Foster Damon, Robert Carl Elliott, William Elton, Martha Winburn England, Wendy Erdman, the late Peter F. Fisher, John Fleming, Northrop Frye, George Goyder, John E. Grant, Jean Hagstrum, Désirée Hirst, Arthur Hudd, Anne T. Kostelantz, Lewis and Heidi Lichterman, Paul Miner, Genevieve Oswald, David H. Stam, W. H. Stevenson, Irene Tayler, Craig Thompson, Michael J. Tolley, and Lucyle Werkmeister.

The undersigned has particular indebtedness to acknowledge to Rich-ard J. Wolfe, for the initial daring that launched this undertaking as a

manual compilation; to Stephen M. Parrish, for generously welcoming it into the Cornell series under his patient editorship; to James A. Painter, for returning to the special problems of an unusual program again and again; to John E. Thiesmeyer, for forcing the terrible Sentences of Blake right through the electronic gates; to the members of the Cornell supervisory committee, including at a crucial stage the late Stephen E. Whicher, for guidance, encouragement, and fortitude. And to my wife Virginia for critical aid and tolerant sympathy.

DAVID V. ERDMAN

Princeton, New Jersey
November 1966

CONTENTS

VOLUME I

Preface   vii

Explanation of References and Symbols   xxi

Abbreviations and Short Titles   xxiii

Concordance to the Writings of William Blake (A–LOVE)   1

VOLUME II

Concordance (LOVED–Z)   1147

Appendixes

  Appendix A: Word Frequencies (Verse and Prose)   2181

  Appendix B: Corrections and Additions to the Keynes Text   2245

EXPLANATION OF
REFERENCES AND SYMBOLS

PAGE and line numbers refer to *The Complete Writings of William Blake: With All the Variant Readings,* edited by Geoffrey Keynes (London: The Nonesuch Press; New York: Random House, 1957). For prose, the quarter of the page (divided horizontally) is shown by the letters A, B, C, D, following the page number, and PROSE is printed in place of the line number. SUPP refers to new or supplementary matter not easily assignable to pages in Keynes; precise locations are given in Appendix B. All additions to and corrections of the Keynes text are specified in the Appendix; all lines containing additions or corrections are marked with asterisks in the concordance proper.

* A line (or segment of prose) so marked differs in some respect from the Keynes text; see Appendix B for explanation of correction or addition.

XXX An illegible passage; so marked, whether a single letter or several words.

[ ] Deletion.

[[ ]] Deletion within deletion.

( ) Editorial emendation or insertion. Parentheses enclose the whole word even when emendation is of a letter only. When emendation is new or is not clearly shown in Keynes, asterisk refers user to Appendix for explanation where parentheses may enclose only exact letters (or whole words) not to be found in Blake's original text.

? Doubtful reading.

(?) Doubtful emendation.

(" ") Words quoted by or annotated by Blake, included in concordance to supply context of marginalia—or to index emblematic use of quotations.

. . . Elision of last or first portion of a line of verse too long to be punched on a single card.

... Elision of digits (when not spelled out within parentheses) or
elision within quoted matter.

Two or more double-spaced periods (never one) at the end of a line are
simply fillers added mechanically to facilitate reference.

Verse and Prose

All lines of verse will show numbers in the line-number position (except
the few added as SUPP). Prose is designated as TITLE (main and sub titles,
captions, inscriptions, section headings), MARG (marginalia), or simply
PROSE.

When one deletion extends beyond a single line or segment of prose,
each line or segment is enclosed within a pair of deletion marks [   ].

For inclusion in the concordance, prose passages were cut into arbi-
trary segments, but no elision marks were used to mark the severed ends;
Keynes will have to be consulted to discover the beginnings and endings
of clauses and sentences.

Punctuation

The punctuation in Keynes or in Blake's original texts has been omitted
—except for hyphens, which follow Blake rather than Keynes. Apostrophes (given by Keynes but nearly always omitted by Blake) have been
inserted to distinguish possessives from plurals (or "Los's" from "loss")
and certain contractions from homographs ("she'd" from "shed").

ABBREVIATIONS AND SHORT TITLES

Short Abbreviations for Inclusive Titles

Abbreviation	Title
BT	*The Book of Thel*
GP	*The Gates of Paradise*
IM	(*An Island in the Moon*)
J	*Jerusalem*
L	(*Letter*)
M	Milton
N	(Notebook) (the so-called Rossetti Manuscript)
PA	(Public Address) (in the Notebook)
PS	*Poetical Sketches*
SE	*Songs of Experience*
SI	*Songs of Innocence*

Short Titles

Short Title	Title or first line	Page (Keynes)	Page (Erdman & Bloom)
A DREAM/SI	A Dream	111	16
A FAIRY SKIPD	"A fairy skipd upon my knee" (MS)	188	473
ABSTINENCE/N	"Abstinence sows sand all over"(N 105)	178	465
ADDRESS/L	(Address on Letter, followed by letter number)	SUPP	
ADDRESSES/L	(Address on several letters; see Appendix B)	SUPP	
AH SUNFLOWR/SE	Ah! Sun-Flower	215	25
AHANIA	The Book of Ahania	249	83
ALBION ROSE	"Albion rose from where he labourd . . ."	160	660
ALL PICTURES/N	"All Pictures thats Painted . . ." (N 40)	548	502
ALL RELIGIONS	All Religions are One	98	2
ALWAYS THOT/N	"I always thought that Jesus Christ . . ." (N 64)	555	672

xxiii

AMERICA	America a Prophecy	195	51
AMERICA CANC	(America, cancelled plates *a, b, c*)	203	57
AMERICA PREL	America, Preludium	195	50
AN EPITAPH/N	An Epitaph (N 37)	545	494
ANCNT PROVRB/N	An ancient Proverb (N 107)	176	466
AND HIS LEGS/N	"And his legs carried it like a long fork" (N 22)	536	494
ANGEL PRESID/N	"The Angel that presided oer my birth" (N 32)	541	493
ANGER WRATH/N	"Anger & Wrath my bosom rends" (N 23)	538	494
ANNO BACON	(Annotations to *Essays Moral, Economical and Political* by Francis Bacon)	396	609
ANNO BERKELEY	(Annotations to Berkeley's *Siris*)	731	652
ANNO BOYD	(Annotations to Boyd's Translation of Dante's *Inferno*)	411	622
ANNO CELLINI	(Note probably in Cellini's *Tratto dell' Oreficeria*)	779	659
ANNO LAVATER	(Annotations to Lavater's *Aphorisms on Man*)	65	572
ANNO REYNOLDS	(Annotations to Sir Joshua Reynolds' *Works*)	445	625
ANNO SPURZHEIM	(Annotations to Spurzheim's *Observations*)	772	652
ANNO SWED HELL	(Annotations to Swedenborg's *Of Heaven and Hell*)	SUPP	590
ANNO SWED LOVE	(Annotations to Swedenborg's *Divine Love*)	89	591
ANNO SWED PROV	(Annotations to Swedenborg's *Divine Providence*)	131	599
ANNO THORNTON	(Annotations to Thornton's *New Translation of the Lord's Prayer*)	786	656
ANNO WATSON	(Annotations to Watson's *Apology for the Bible*)	383	601
ANNO WW EXCUR	(Annotations to *The Excursion*, by William Wordsworth)	784	655
ANNO WW POEMS	(Annotations to *Poems* by William Wordsworth)	782	654
ANOTHER/N 1	Another (Epitaph) ("I was buried . . .") (N 37)	546	494
ANOTHER/N 2	Another (Epitaph) ("Here lies John Trot . . .") (N 37)	546	494
ANSWR PARSON/N	An answer to the parson (N 103)	181	461
ARE NOT JOYS/N	"Are not the joys of morning sweeter" (N 109)	172	463

ARGUMENT V DAU	The Argument (pl. iii, Visions of the Daughters of Albion)	189	44
ART HAS LOST/N	"Now Art has lost its mental Charms" (N 79)	557	471
ASK GODS/IM	"Honor & Genius is all I ask" (IM chaps 3, 9)	47	443
		55	449
ASKD PRIGG/N	"I askd my dear Friend, Orator Prigg" (N 60–61)	553	506
ASKED THIEF/N	"I asked a thief to steal me a peach" (N 114)	163	769
ASKED THIEF	"I asked a .thief to steal me a peach" (MS)	261	459
AUGURIES	Auguries of Innocence (Pickering MS)	431	481
BELLS WEEKLY/N	From Bell's Weekly Messenger, Augst 4, 1811 (N 59)	553	672
BENEATH/N	"Beneath the white thorn lovely May" (N 14)	421	777
BENEATH AD/N	"Wings they had that soft inclose" (additional passage deleted) (N 14)	422	777
BENEATH REWR/N	"Beneath the white thorn, lovely may" (rewritten and deleted) (N 14)	422	777
BLAKES APL/N 1	Blake's apology for his Catalogue ("Dryden in Rhyme cries") (N 62–63)	554	496
BLAKES APL/N 2	(Blake's apology for his Catalogue) ("Having given great offense") (N 65)	555	783
BLAKES APOL/PA	(Blake's apology for his Catalogue) ("Dryden in Rhyme cries") (N 62)	595	783
BLAKES MEMORAN	Blake's Memorandum (August 1803)	437	700
BLIND-MANS/PS	Blind-Man's Buff	15	413
BLOCKHEAD/N	"He's a Blockhead who wants a proof" (N 28)	540	499
BOOK OF LOS	The Book of Los	255	89
BOOK OF THEL	The Book of Thel	127	3
CAN THERE BE/N	"Can there be any thing more mean" (N 26)	539	503
CHAUCER 1	(Prospectus of the Engraving of Chaucer's Canterbury Pilgrims) May 15th, 1809	586	556
CHAUCER 2	(Prospectus of the Engraving of Chaucer's Canterbury Pilgrims) (about 1810)	589	557
CHAUCER/N	(Draft for the Prospectus of the Engraving of Chaucer's Canterbury Pilgrims) (N 117–119)	587	557
CHIMNEY SWP/N	The Chimney Sweeper (N 106, 103)	180	716

CHIMNEY SWP/SE	The Chimney Sweeper	212	22
CHIMNEY SWP/SI	The Chimney Sweeper	117	10
CHRISTN FORB/N	Christian Forbearance (N 114)	165	721
CLOD PEBBLE/N	"Love seeketh not itself to please" (N 115)	162	19
CLOD PEBBLE/SE	The Clod & the Pebble	211	19
COCK WOULD/N	"He is a Cock would" (N 29)	540	494
COLOR PRT TATE	(Color print in the Tate Gallery)	SUPP	
CONTEMPLATN/PS	Contemplation	36	433
COSWAY FRAZR/N	"Cosway Frazer & Baldwin of Egypts Lake" (N 37)	545	496
COUCH DEATH/PS	The Couch of Death	35	432
CR LOVES ART/N	"Cromek loves artists as he loves his Meat" (N 29)	540	500
CRADLE SONG/N	A cradle song (N 114)	164	459
CRADLE SONG/SI	A Cradle Song	120	11
CRIPPLE EVRY/N	"The Cripple every Step . . ." (N 39)	548	504
CROMEK SPEAK/N	Cromek Speaks (N 41)	549	501
CROWND KING/IM	"A crowned king" (IM chap 11)	62	455
CRY MATCHES/IM	"I cry my matches . . ." (IM chap 9)	55	449
CRYSTL CABINET	The Crystal Cabinet (Pickering MS)	429	479
CUNNING SURE/N	"The Cunning sures & . . ." (N 40)	548	502
DAY/N	Day (N 105)	177	464
DEDICATN BLAIR	(Dedication to the Illustrations to Blair's *Grave*)	442	471
DELICATE/N	"Delicate Hands & Heads . . ." (N 46)	551	506
DESC CAT	A Descriptive Catalogue of Pictures . . . 1809	563	520
DESC CAT ADV	(Advertisement of) A Descriptive Catalogue . . .	562	519
DIVNE IMAGE/SE	A Divine Image	221	32
DIVNE IMAGE/SI	The Divine Image	117	12
DONT BELIEVE/N	"You dont believe —" (N 21)	536	492
DR CLASH/IM	"Theres Doctor Clash" (IM chap 11)	61	455
DRAWING HEH	(A drawing in H. E. Huntington Library)	SUPP	
DRAWING WGR	(A drawing in the W. Graham Robertson collection)	SUPP	
EACH MAN/J	"Each Man is in his Spectre's power" (J 41 [37])	669	731
EACH MAN/N	"Each Man is in his Spectres power" (N 12)	421	732
EARTHS ANSR/SE	Earths Answer	210	18
EARTHS ANSWR/N	Earths Answer (N 111)	168	715

ECCHOING GR/SI	The Ecchoing Green	116	8
EDW FOURTH/PS	Prologue Intended for a Dramatic Piece of King Edward the Fourth	33	430
EDW THIRD/PS	King Edward the Third	17	415
ENGL ENCOU/N 1	English Encouragement of Art . . . (First reading) (N 41)	549	501
ENGL ENCOU/N 2	English Encouragement of Art . . . (Second reading) (N 41)	549	501
ENGLISH CONN/N	To English Connoisseurs (N 38)	546	505
ENGLND AWAKE/J	"England! awake! . . . " (J 77)	718	231
EPILOGUE/GP	(Epilogue) "To the Accuser . . . "	771	266
ETERNITY/N	Eternity (N 105)	179	461
EUROPE	Europe a Prophecy	239	60
EUROPE INTRO	Europe (Introductory Poem, plate iii)	237	58
EUROPE PREL	Europe, Preludium	238	59
EV GOSPEL/N	The Everlasting Gospel (prose, and verse sections 1, 2; MS fragment)	757	792
EV GOSPEL( )/N	The Everlasting Gospel (sections a [N 33], b [N 100–101], c [N 98], d [N 52–54], e [N 48–52], f [N 54], g [N 52], h [N 48], i [N 120])	748	510 793
EVNING STAR/PS	To the Evening Star	3	402
EXHIBITION ADV	(Advertisement of) Exhibition of Paintings in Fresco, Poetical and Historical Inventions, by Wm. Blake (May 15, 1809)	560	517
EXODUS/N	(Subjects from) Exodus (N 116)	SUPP	661
FA RA SO BO/IM	"Fa ra so bo ro" (IM chap 9)	56	450
FAIR ELENOR/PS	Fair Elenor	4	402
FIELDS FROM/J	"The fields from Islington to Marybone" (J 27)	649	170
F(LAXMAN)/N 1	To F(laxman) (N 26)	539	499
F(LAXMAN)/N 2	To F(laxman) (N 35)	544	499
FLORENTINE/N	Florentine Ingratitude (N 32)	541	503
FOR CHILDRN/GP	For Children: The Gates of Paradise	209	32
FOR SEXES/GP	For the Sexes: The Gates of Paradise	760	256
FOUND WORD/N	"23 May 1810 found the Word Golden" (N 67)	556	672
FOUR ZOAS	The Four Zoas	263	296
FOUR ZOAS AD	The Four Zoas (Additional Fragments) (1) "Beneath this veil of Vala . . . "	380	763
	(2) "The ocean calm, the clouds . . ."	381	764
	(3) "The womb impress'd, Enion fled . . . "	381	764

	(4) "From Enion pours the seed . . . "	381	764
	(5) "Opening in rifted rocks . . . "	381	299
	(6) "The Lamb of God stood . . . "	382	759
FOUR ZOAS NOTE	(Notes Written on pages 56, 70, 88, 93)	380	753
			754
			757
			763
FRENCH REVOLTN	The French Revolution (1791)	134	282
FRESH FROM/PS	Song ("Fresh from the dewy hill . . .")	9	407
FRM CRATELOS/N	From Cratelos (N 64)	555	493
GARDEN LOVE/N	"I went to the garden of love" (N 115)	162	718
GARDEN LOVE/SE	The Garden of Love	215	26
GHOST ABEL	The Ghost of Abel (1822)	779	268
GIVE PENSION/N	"Give pensions to the Learned Pig" (N 40)	548	506
GIVE YOU END/N	"I give you the end·of a golden string" (N 46)	551	229
GOLDEN RULE/N	"He has observd the Golden Rule" (N 30)	540	499
GREAT MEN/N	"Great Men & Fools do often me Inspire" (N 63)	554	507
GREAT THINGS/N	"Great things are done when Men . . . " (N 43)	550	502
GREY MONK	The Grey Monk (Pickering MS)	430	480
GROWN OLD IN/N	"Grown old in Love from Seven . . . " (N 54)	552	508
GWIN KING/PS	Gwin, King of Norway	11	409
H PICK THANK/N	On H(ayley) the Pick thank (N 41)	549	498
HAIL MATRIM/IM	"Hail Matrimony, made of Love" (IM chap 9)	56	450
HAPPINESS/L	"With happiness stretchd across the hills" (L 24, 22 November 1802)	816	692
HAST LAP/N	"Thou hast a lap full of seed" (N 111)	168	461
HEARD ANGEL/N	"I heard an Angel singing" (N 114)	164	461
HEBREW NATN/N	"The Hebrew Nation did not write it" (N 39)	187	508
HER LIFE IS/N	"Her whole Life is an Epigram . . ." (N 100)	184	508
HOLY THURS/IM	"Upon a holy thursday . . ." (IM chap 11)	59	453
HOLY THURS/N	Holy Thursday (N 103)	181	716
HOLY THURS/SE	Holy Thursday	211	19
HOLY THURS/SI	Holy Thursday	121	13
HOMERS HERO/N	"I am no Homers Hero . . . " (N 31)	541	493

HOMERS POETRY	On Homers Poetry	778	267
HOW CAME/N	"How came pride in Man" (N 107)	173	463
HOW SWEET/PS	Song ("How sweet I roam'd from field to field")	6	404
HOW TO KNOW/N	How to know Love from Deceit (N 107)	175	463
HS FRENDSHIP/N	On H(ayle)ys Friendship (N 35)	544	497
HUMAN ABSTR/SE	The Human Abstract	217	27
HUMAN IMAGE/N	The Human Image (N 107)	174	719
I FEARD FURY/N	"I feard the fury of my wind" (N 113)	166	458
I GIVE YOU/J	"I give you the end of a golden string" (J 77)	716	229
I ROSE UP AT/N	"I rose up at the dawn of day" (N 89)	558	472
I SAW A MONK/J	"I saw a Monk of Charlemaine" (J 52)	683	199
I SAW A MONK/N	"I saw a Monk of Charlemaine" (N 12)	418	732
I SAW CHAPEL/N	"I saw a chapel all of gold" (N 115)	163	458
I SAW MNK AD/N	"When Satan first . . . " (Additional stanzas) (N 12)	420	200
IF I GROW/N	"If I eer Grow to Mans Estate" (N 39)	547	493
IF MEN ACT/N	"If Men will act like a maid . . . " (N 65)	556	493
IF TRUE/N	"If it is True what the Prophets write" (N 33)	543	492
IF YOU PLAY/N	"If you play a Game of Chance . . . " (N 47)	551	502
IF YOU TRAP/N	"If you trap the moment" (N 105)	179	461
ILLUS CHAUCER	(Engraved plate) Chaucer's Canterbury Pilgrims	SUPP	663
ILLUS DANTE	(Notes on the Illustrations to Dante)	SUPP 785	667
ILLUS GENESIS	(Illustrated MS of) Genesis	SUPP	667
ILLUS GRAY	(Lines for the illustrations to Gray's Poems)	414	473
ILLUS HISTORY	(Inscriptions on a group of historical pictures)	SUPP	
ILLUS MILTON	(Descriptions of the Illustrations to Milton's "L'Allegro" and "Il Penseroso")	617	663
IMIT POPE/N	Imitation of Pope A Compliment to the Ladies (N 37)	545	498
IMIT SPEN/PS	An Imitation of Spen(s)er	14	412
IN A WIFE/N	"In a wife I would desire" (N 105)	178	465
IN CHILDHOOD/N	"S(tothard) in Childhood on the Nursery Floor" (N 27)	539	499

IN HARMONY/N	"Every thing which is in harmony with me . . . " (N 92) SUPP		673
IN HEAVEN/J	"In Heaven the only Art of Living" (J 81)	724	733
INFANT JOY/SI	Infant Joy	118	16
INFANT SORW/N	Infant Sorrow (N 113)	166	719
INFANT SORW/SE	Infant Sorrow	217	28
INSC ARIMATHEA	(Inscription on engraving) Joseph of Arimathea	604	660
INSC FALL MAN	(Inscription on back of) The Fall of Man	441	662
INSC HERVEY	(Inscription on Epitome of Hervey's Meditations) SUPP		
INSC JOSEPH	(Inscription on a proof of) Joseph of Arimathea SUPP		660
INSC LAOCOON	(Inscriptions on engraving, The Laocoön)	775	270
INSC OUR END	(Inscriptions on various states of engraving) Our End is Come SUPP		660
INSC UPCOTT	(Inscription in Autograph Album of William Upcott)	781	674
INSCR CHAINING	(Inscription on etched) Chaining of Orc SUPP		663
INSCRIPTION	(See Appendix B) SUPP		
INTRODUCTN/SE	Introduction, Songs of Experience	210	18
INTRODUCTN/SI	Introduction, Songs of Innocence	111	7
ISLAND MOON	(An Island in the Moon)	44	440
JERUSALEM	Jerusalem	620	143
JESUS NOT/N	"Jesus does not treat . . . " (N 72)	556	673
KING JOHN/PS	Prologue to King John	34	430
LACEDEMONIAN/N	Lacedemonian Instruction (N 103)	180	465
LAID ME DOWN/N	"I laid me down upon a bank" (N 115)	162	459
LAND OF DREAMS	The Land of Dreams (Pickering MS)	427	478
LARGE BK DSGNS	(Legend in a Large Book of Designs)	262	662
LAST JUDGMNT/L	(Description of a Vision of The Last Judgment) (in letter to Humphry, 1808)	442	542
LAUGHING/SI	Laughing Song	124	11
LEAVE O/IM	"Leave O leave (me) to my sorrows" (IM chap 11)	61	454
LEGEND/N	(Legend under drawing; number after N refers to page) SUPP		722
LET BE TOLD/N	"Let it be told" (N 38) ("These are the Idiots")	547	505
LET BROTHELS/N	"Let the Brothels of Paris be opened" (N 99)	185	490

LETTER	(The Letters) (as numbered in Keynes; additional letters numbered 6A &c.) SUPP		
		790	
LIT BLK BOY/SI	The Little Black Boy	125	9
LIT BOY FND/SI	The Little Boy found	121	11
LIT BOY LST/IM	"O father father where are you going" (IM chap 11)	60	454
LIT BOY LST/N	"Nought loves another as itself" (N 106)	176	721
LIT BOY LST/SE	A Little Boy Lost	218	28
LIT BOY LST/SI	The Little Boy lost	120	11
LIT GRL FND/SI	The Little Girl Found	113	21
LIT GRL LST/SE	A Little Girl Lost	219	29
LIT GRL LST/SI	The Little Girl Lost	112	20
LIT VAGABND/SE	The Little Vagabond	216	26
LIT VAGABOND/N	The little Vagabond (N 105)	179	718
LO THE BAT/IM	"Lo the Bat with Leathern wing" (IM chap 9)	54	448
LONDON/N	London (N 109)	170	718
LONDON/SE	London	216	26
LONG JOHN BRWN	Long John Brown & Little Mary Bell (Pickering MS)	434	487
LOOK OF LOVE/N	"The look of love alarms" (N 103)	182	465
LOVE HARMNY/PS	Song ("Love and harmony combine")	7	405
LOVE JOCUND/PS	Song ("I love the jocund dance")	7	406
MAD SONG/PS	Mad Song	8	407
MADMAN CALLD/N	"Madman I have been calld . . . " (N 25)	538	499
MARRIAGE HH	The Marriage of Heaven and Hell	148	33
MARY	Mary (Pickering MS)	428	478
MEMORANDUM/N	(Memoranda from N 10, as numbered by Keynes)	440	672
MEMORY COME/PS	Song ("Memory, hither come")	8	406
MENTAL TRAVLER	The Mental Traveler (Pickering MS)	424	475
MERLNS PROPH/N	Merlins prophecy (N 106)	177	464
MILTON	Milton	480	94
MIRTH AND COMP	Mirth and Her Companions (inscription)	773	667
MIRTLE SHADE/N	in a mirtle shade (N 111)	169	460
MOCK ON/N	"Mock on Mock on Voltaire Rousseau" (N 7)	418	468
MORNING/N	Morning (N 12)	421	469
MOTTO SONGS/N	Motto to the Songs of Innocence & of Experience (N 101)	183	490
MR CROMEK/N	Mr Cromek to Mr Stothard (N 31)	541	500
MR STOTHARD/N	Mr Stothard to Mr Cromek (N 31)	541	500

MRS FLAXMAN/L	To My Dear Friend, Mrs Anna Flaxman (L 12, 14 September 1800)	800	680
MY SILKS/PS	Song ("My silks and fine array")	6	405
MY SPECTR AD/N	"Oer my Sins Thou sit & moan" (Additional stanzas "My Spectre . . ." N 2)	417	468
MY SPECTRE/N	"My Spectre around me night & day" (N 3, 2)	415	467
MY TITLE AS/N	"My title as a(n) Genius . . . " (N 38)	546	497
NAIL NECK/N	"Nail his neck to the Cross . . . " (N 79)	557	509
NAT RELIGION 1	There is No Natural Religion (First Draft)	97	1
NAT RELIGION 2	There is No Natural Religion (Second Draft)	97	2
NEVER PAIN/N	"Never pain to tell thy love" (N 115)	161	458
NIGHT/SI	Night	118	13
NO REAL STYL/N	"No real Style of Colouring ever appears" (N 21)	536	502
NOTE NINE HEAD	(Note on a Pencil Drawing of Nine Grotesque Heads)	773	667
NURSES SONG/IM	"When the tongues of children . . . " (IM chap 11)	60	15
NURSES SONG/N	"When the voices of children . . . " (N 109)	171	716
NURSES SONG/SE	Nurses Song	212	23
NURSES SONG/SI	Nurse's Song	121	15
O I CANNOT/N	"O I cannot find" ("An old maid . . . ") (N 100)	184	465
O LAPWING/N	"O lapwing thou fliest around the heath" (N 113)	168	460
O WHY BORN/L	"O why was I born with a different face" (L 28, 16 August 1803)	828	700
OF GATES/GP	Of the Gates	770	265
OF HS BIRTH/N	"Of H(ayley)s birth this was the happy lot" (N 27)	539	497
OLD ACQUAINT/N	"old acquaintance well renew" (N 24)	538	500
ON ANOTHERS/SI	On Anothers Sorrow	122	17
ON F AND S/N	On F(laxman) & S(tothard) (N 34)	543	500
ON GREAT ENC/N	On the Great Encouragement . . . (N 40)	548	506
ON PLATE/N101	On 1 Plate (memorandum in N 101)	SUPP	673
ON S(TOTHRD)/N	On S(tothard) (N 36)	545	500

xxxii

ON VIRGINITY/N	On the Virginity of the Virgin Mary . . . (N 6)	418	492
ONLY MAN/N	"The only Man that eer I knew" (N 50)	551	498
P LOVED NOT/N	"P(hillips) loved me not . . . " (N 34)	544	497
PENC DRAW	(Inscriptions on drawings in *Pencil Drawings,* ed. G. Keynes, by volume and plate number)	SUPP	
PETTY SNEAK/N	"A petty sneaking Knave I knew" (N 29)	540	501
PHEBE DREST/IM	"Phebe drest like beauties Queen" (IM chap 8)	53	448
PILGRIMS/N	" . . . Pilgrims Engravd . . . " (N 51)	SUPP	560
PITIFUL CASE/N	A Pitiful Case (N 33)	542	504
POISON TREE/SE	A Poison Tree	218	28
PRETTY EPIGR/N	A Pretty Epigram for those . . . (N 38)	547	505
PRSPECTUS 1793	Prospectus October 10, 1793	207	670
PUB ADDR AD/N	(Public Address) (additional passages, N 38 . . . 47)	602	564
PUB ADDRESS/N	(Public Address) (N 1 . . . 86)	591	560
PUBLC VOICE/PA	"Call that the Public Voice . . . " (from Public Address, N 66)	597	567
QUESTN ANSRD/N	The Question Answerd (N 103)	180	466
RAFAEL SUBLI/N	"Rafael Sublime Majestic Graceful Wise" (N 39)	547	505
READER LOVER/J	"Reader! lover of books! lover of heaven" (J 3)	621	144
RECEIPTS LINNL	(Receipts for Linnell)	SUPP	
REMARKS MALKIN	(Remarks on Malkin's Drawings)	439	671
RICHES/N	Riches (N 103)	181	461
ROSE TREE/N	"A flower was offered to me" (N 115)	161	718
ROSE TREE/SE	My pretty Rose Tree	215	25
RUBENS HAD/N	"Rubens had been a Statesman . . . " (N 38)	546	505
SAMSON/PS	Samson	37	434
SAY I SHANT/N	"I say I shant live five years . . . " (N 10)	187	672
SAY PICTURES/N	"You say their Pictures well Painted be" (N 42)	550	502
SAY YOU JOE/IM	"O I say you Joe" (IM chap 11)	60	454
SCHOOL BOY/SI	The School Boy	124	31
SEVRL QUESTN/N	Several Questions Answered (N 99)	184	465
SHEPHERD/SI	The Shepherd	118	7
SHEPHERD FIRST	Song 1st by a Shepherd	63	457

SHEPHERD OLD	Song by an Old Shepherd	64	457
SHEPHERD YOUNG	Song 2nd by a Young Shepherd	63	715
SICK ROSE/N	The sick rose (N 107)	175	716
SICK ROSE/SE	The Sick Rose	213	23
SILENT NIGHT/N	"Silent Silent Night" (N 113)	168	462
SINCE RICHES/N	"Since all the Riches of this World" (N 73)	557	508
SIR JOSH MIC/N	"Sir Joshua Praises Michael Angelo" (N 28)	539	503
SIR JOSH RUB/N	"Sir Joshua praised Rubens with a Smile" (N 29)	540	503
SLEPT DARK/N	"I slept in the dark" (N 109)	170	772
SMALL BK DSGNS	(Legends in a Small Book of Designs)	261	662
SOFT SNOW/N	Soft Snow (N 107)	176	464
SOME MEN/N	"Some Men created for destruction come" (N 36)	544	493
SOME PEOPLE/N	"Some people admire the work of a Fool" (N 70)	556	508
SONG LIBERTY	A Song of Liberty	159	43
SONG OF LOS	The Song of Los	245	65
SONGS OF EXPER	Songs of Experience	210	18
SONGS OF INNOC	Songs of Innocence	111	7
SPRING/SI	Spring	123	14
STOOD AMONG/J	"I stood among my valleys of the south" (J 77)	717	230
S(TOTHAR)D/N	To S(tothar)d (N 30)	540	499
SUBJCTS HIST/N	(Subjects for) The History of England, a small book of Engravings (N 116)	208	661
SUCH VISIONS/J	"Such Visions Have Appeared to Me" (J 26)	649	169
SUSSEX MEN/N	"The Sussex Men are Noted Fools" (N 24)	538	497
SWELLD LIMBS/N	"Swelld limbs with no outline . . . " (N 38)	546	505
SWORD SUNG/N	"The sword sung on the barren heath" (N 105)	178	464
TELL YOU WHA/N	"I will tell you what Joseph of Arimathea" (N 52)	552	470
TERROR IN/N	"Terror in the house does roar" (N 12)	421	469
THE ANGEL/N	The Angel (N 103)	182	717
THE ANGEL/SE	The Angel	213	24
THE BIRDS/N	The Birds (N 14)	422	469
THE BLOSSOM/SI	The Blossom	115	10
THE CAVERNS/N	"The Caverns of the Grave Ive seen" (N 87)	558	472

THE FAIRY/N	The Fairy (N 105)	178	466
THE FLY/N	"Woe alas my guilty hand" (N 101)	182	716
THE FLY/SE	The Fly	213	23
THE GOLDEN NET	The Golden Net (Pickering MS)	424	474
THE KEYS/GP	The Keys	770	265
THE KID/N	The Kid (N 105)	179	466
THE LAMB/SI	The Lamb	115	8
THE LILLY/N	"The modest rose puts forth a thorn" (N 109)	171	718
THE LILLY/SE	The Lilly	215	25
THE SMILE	The Smile (Pickering MS)	423	474
THE TYGER/N 1	The Tyger (first draft, N 109–108)	172	717
THE TYGER/N 2	(The Tyger) (second draft, N 108)	173	717
THE TYGER/SE	The Tyger	214	24
THELS MOTTO/BT	Thel's Motto	127	3
THEN SHE BORE	"then she bore Pale desire . . ." (Berg MS)	40	437
THIRALATHA	"As when a dream of Thiralatha . . ." (Fragment)	206	58
THIS CITY/IM	"This city & this country . . ." (IM chap 9)	58	452
THIS FROG/IM	"This frog he would a wooing ride" (IM chap 9)	55	450
TIRIEL	Tiriel	99	273
TO AUTUMN/PS	To Autumn	2	401
TO BE OR/IM	"To be, or not to be" (IM chap 9)	57	451
TO BUTTS/L	"To my Friend Butts I write" (L 16, 2 October 1800)	804	683
TO CHLOES/N	"To Chloe's breast young Cupid slily stole" (N 78)	557	508
TO FLAXMAN/L	To My Dearest Friend, John Flaxman, these lines (L 11, 12 September 1800)	799	680
TO FORGIVE/N	"To forgive Enemies H(ayley) does pretend" (N 34)	544	497
TO GOD/N	To God (N 73)	557	408
TO H(AYLEY)/N	To H(ayley) (N 37)	545	498
TO H(UNT)/N	To H(unt) (N 25)	538	497
TO MORNING/PS	To Morning	3	402
TO MRS BUTTS/L	To Mrs Butts (L 16, 2 October 1800)	806	685
TO MRS FLAXMAN	To Mrs Ann Flaxman (with illustrations to Gray's *Poems*)	414	473
TO MUSES/PS	To the Muses	10	408
TO MY MIRTLE/N	To my Mirtle (N 106)	176	460
TO NANCY F/N	To Nancy F(laxman) (N 27)	539	499

TO NOBODADDY/N	To Nobodaddy (N 109)	171	462
TO ROYL ACAD/ N	To the Royal Academy (N 33)	543	504
TO SPRING/PS	To Spring	1	400
TO SUMMER/PS	To Summer	1	400
TO TIRZAH/SE	To Tirzah	220	30
TO VENETIAN/N	To Venetian Artists (N 60–61)	554	507
TO WINTER/PS	To Winter	2	401
URIZEN	The [First] Book of Urizen	222	69
V DAU ALBION	Visions of the Daughters of Albion	189	44
V LAST JUDG/N	(A Vision of the Last Judgment) (N 68 . . . 95)	604	544
VOICE BARD/SI	The Voice of the Ancient Bard	126	31
WAR SONG/PS	A War Song to Englishmen	34	431
WAS I ANGRY/N	"Was I angry with Hayley . . ." (N 23)	538	496
WASHERWOMANS/N	The Washer Womans Song (N 42)	550	509
WHEN CORRUP/IM	"When old corruption first begun" (IM chap 6)	50	445
WHEN EARLY/PS	Song ("When early morn walks forth in sober grey")	10	408
WHEN I SEE/N	"When I see a Rubens . . . " (N 43)	550	506
WHEN KLOPSTK/N	"When Klopstock England defied" (N 5)	186	491
WHEN LOOK AT/N	"When you look at a picture . . . " (N 41)	550	501
WHEN MAN HAS/N	"When a Man has Married a Wife" (N 4)	418	508
WHICH ARE/N	"Which are beauties sweetest dress" (N 103)	182	466
WHY CARE FOR/N	"Why should I care for the men of thames" (N 113)	166	464
WHY CUPID/N	"Why was Cupid a Boy" (N 56)	552	470
WILD FLOWERS/N	The wild flowers song (N 107)	175	463
WILLIAM BOND	William Bond (Pickering MS)	434	487
WILLM COWPER/N	William Cowper Esqre (N 50)	551	498
WOE CRIED MUSE	"Woe cried the muse . . . " (Berg MS)	43	439
WOMAN SCALY/N	"A Woman Scaly & a Man all Hairy" (N 93)	559	509

A Concordance to the Writings of

WILLIAM BLAKE

```
                                                                    PAGE      TITLE        LINE
A    SEE THOMAS A BECKET
     GREAT A LITTLE A . . . . . . . . . . . . . . . .     62 DR CLASH/IM          8
     ONCE A DID SO WHEN I PRAYD IN THE GARDEN  . . . . .   753 EV GOSPEL(D)/N     89
AARON
     PROTECTING ANGEL AARON ABRAHAM BELIEVED GOD  . . . . .  SUPP INSC HERVEY    *TITLE
     ?EXODUS AARON XXX ?MOSES XXX RIVER XXX FROGS LICE  . .  SUPP EXODUS/N       *PROSE
AARON'S
     WHAT WE CALL ANTIQUE GEMS ARE THE GEMS OF AARON'S BREAST  777D INSC LAOCOON  PROSE
        PLATE
ABANDON
     WHICH I HID MY FACE FOR NOT BEING ABLE TO ABANDON   . . . 798C LETTER 10     PROSE
ABARIM
     ARE HOR & PEOR & BASHAN & ABARIM & LEBANON & HERMON . . . 498 MILTON 17       16
ABASEMENT    SEE SELF ABASEMENT
ABASHD
     SHOOK THE CHAMBER HE CEASD ABASHD THEN ORLEANS SPOKE ALL  142 FRENCH REVOLTN  178
        WAS SILENT
ABASHED
     A LIAR HE NEVER WAS ABASHED IN HIS LIFE & NEVER FELT HIS  447D ANNO REYNOLDS  MARG
        IGNORANCE
ABBE
     THE ABBE DE (SIEYES) FROM THE NATION'S ASSEMBLY . . . . .  141 FRENCH REVOLTN * 163
     . . . THEN THE ABBE DE (SIEYES) RAISD HIS FEET  . . . .   143 FRENCH REVOLTN * 201
     . . . LIKE A VOICE OF GOD FOLLOWING A STORM THE ABBE      143 FRENCH REVOLTN   202
        FOLLOWD
ABBESS
     THE PROCESSION NEXT FOLLOW THE YOUTHFUL ABBESS HER NUN . . 566D DESC CAT 3     PROSE
     THE PROCESSION THEN THE YOUTHFUL ABBESS HER NUN  . . . .   588B CHAUCER/N      PROSE
     THE PROCESSION THEN THE YOUTHFUL ABBESS HER NUN  . . . .   589D CHAUCER 2      PROSE
ABBEY
     WESTMINSTER ABBEY SUCH IS THE PROJECT & MR ADDINGTON   . . 824D LETTER 27      PROSE
ABBEYS
     MY GROANING IS HEARD IN THE ABBEYS . . .  . . . . . . .    140 FRENCH REVOLTN  137
     IN WINDS DRIVEN OUT OF THE ABBEYS . . . . . . . . . . .    146 FRENCH REVOLTN  275
     OUR CHURCHES & ABBEYS ARE TREASURES OF [SPIRITUAL RICHES]  601A PUB ADDRESS/N *PROSE
ABBOT
     SAYS WAS THE LODGING OF THE ABBOT OF HYDE BY WINCHESTER    567B DESC CAT 3      PROSE
     SAYS WAS THE LODGING OF THE ABBOT OF HYDE BY WINCHESTER    588D CHAUCER/N       PROSE
     SAYS WAS THE LODGING OF THE ABBOT OF HYDE DY WINCHESTER    590C CHAUCER 2       PROSE
ABDOMEN
     AND OF THE PRIEST'S OERGORGED ABDOMEN & OF THE MERCHANT'S  363 FOUR ZOAS 9      247
        THIN
A-BED
     OF THE STATE OF THE DEPARTED I CAN DRAW AS WELL A-BED AS   869A LETTER 68       PROSE
        UP
ABEL
     NUMBER XI THE BODY OF ABEL FOUND BY ADAM AND EVE    . . .  584A DESC CAT 11     TITLE
     JUDGMENT SEAT IN HUMILIATION ABEL SURROUNDED BY INNOCENTS  606B V LAST JUDG/N   PROSE
     ON THE RIGHT BENEATH THE CLOUD ON WHICH ABEL KNEELS . . .  606C V LAST JUDG/N   PROSE
     ABEL KNEELS ON A BLOODY CLOUD &C . . . . . . . .  . . .    606D V LAST JUDG/N   PROSE
     ABEL KNEELS ON A BLOODY CLOUD DESCRIPTIVE OF THOSE CHURCHES 606D V LAST JUDG/N  PROSE
     THE GHOST OF ABEL  . . . . . . . . . . . . .  . . . .     779B GHOST ABEL 1     TITLE
     EVE FAINTED OVER THE DEAD BODY OF ABEL WHICH LAYS NEAR     779C GHOST ABEL 1     PROSE
        A GRAVE
     ENTER THE GHOST OF ABEL . . . . . . . . . . . . .  . .    780A GHOST ABEL 1     PROSE
     EVE THOU VISIONARY PHANTASM THOU ART NOT THE REAL ABEL . . 780 GHOST ABEL 1       9
     ABEL AMONG THE ELOHIM A HUMAN VICTIM I WANDER I AM THEIR   780 GHOST ABEL 1      10
        HOUSE
     OF BLOOD O EARTH COVER NOT THOU THE BLOOD OF ABEL   . . .  780 GHOST ABEL 1      13
     ABEL LIFE FOR LIFE LIFE FOR LIFE . . . . . . . . . . .     780 GHOST ABEL 1      14
     JEHOVAH HE WHO SHALL TAKE CAIN'S LIFE MUST ALSO DIE O ABEL 780 GHOST ABEL 1      15
     ABEL IS DEAD & CAIN SLEW HIM WE SHALL ALSO DIE A DEATH . . 780 GHOST ABEL 1      19
     AND THEN WHAT THEN BE AS POOR ABEL A THOUGHT OR AS  . . .  780 GHOST ABEL 1      20
     EVE I SEE HIM PLAINLY WITH MY MIND'S EYE I SEE ALSO ABEL   780 GHOST ABEL 1      23
        LIVING
     ABEL ARE THESE THE SACRIFICES OF ETERNITY O JEHOVAH       780 GHOST ABEL 2        4
        A BROKEN SPIRIT
     ABEL COMPELLED I CRY O EARTH COVER NOT THE BLOOD OF ABEL   780 GHOST ABEL 2      12
     ABEL SINKS DOWN INTO THE GRAVE FROM WHICH ARISES SATAN . . 780C GHOST ABEL 2    PROSE
     CAIN SERPENT ABEL EVE ADAM  . . . . . . . . . . . .       SUPP INSC HERVEY     *TITLE
ABEL'S
     THE VOICE OF ABEL'S BLOOD  . . . . . . . . . . .  . .     781B GHOST ABEL 2    *PROSE
ABERDEEN     SEE ABRDEEN
ABERNETHY'S
     P S FINCHAM IS A PUPIL OF ABERNETHY'S   . . . . . . . .    874C LETTER 79       PROSE
ABETTOR
     DOES FORGIVE SIN IS CRUCIFIED AS AN ABETTOR OF CRIMINALS   616C V LAST JUDG/N   PROSE
ABHOR
     IF HE IS GOOD HE WILL ABHOR WICKEDNESS IN DAVID OR ABRAHAM 393B ANNO WATSON     MARG
     TO IMITATE I ABHOR I OBSTINATELY ADHERE TO THE TRUE STYLE  600B PUB ADDRESS/N   PROSE
     TO BE THEIR INFERIORS OR SUPERIORS WE EQUALLY ABHOR . . .  686 JERUSALEM 55      7
ABHORRD
     HOW MUCH BY US CONTEMND ABHORRD . . . . . . . . . .       188 A FAIRY SKIPD     10
     DARK VIRGIN SAID THE HAIRY YOUTH THY FATHER STERN ABHORRD  196 AMERICA PREL 1    11
     HOPELESS ABHORRD A DEATH-SHADOW  . . . . . . . . . . .     250 AHANIA 2          41
     [WANDERING DESOLATE A WONDER ABHORRD BY GODS & MEN] . . .  269 FOUR ZOAS 1      190
     ABHORRD ACCURSED EVER DYING AN ETERNAL DEATH  . . . . .    347 FOUR ZOAS 8    * 256
     QUALITIES WHICH MICHAEL ANGELO ABHORRD &  . . . . . . .    452A ANNO REYNOLDS   MARG
     AND WORSHIPPD THEM [TO] THAT THEY MIGHT MAKE INSPIRD ART   543 IF TRUE/N         10
        ABHORRD
     AND NOT TREMBLE HOW CAN I BE BEHELD & NOT ABHORRD  . . .   630 JERUSALEM 10      59
     THE KENNELS OF THE STREETS & LANES AS IF THEY WERE ABHORRD 657 JERUSALEM 31      18
```

1

```
                                                              PAGE     TITLE          LINE
ABHORRED
    TO THE ABHORRED BIRTH OF CHERUBS IN THE HUMAN FORM    .  .  .   193  V DAU ALBION 5      28
    WRITHING IN PANGS OF ABHORRED BIRTH RED FLAMES THE CREST       199  AMERICA 9          17
      REBELLIOUS
    THOU RASH ABHORRED DEMON IN THY FURY HAST OERTHROWN   .  .  .   299  FOUR ZOAS 4        52
    AND NOW HE CAME INTO THE ABHORRED WORLD OF DARK URTHONA        319  FOUR ZOAS 6       281
    FLED WITH THEIR SISTER MOAB INTO THAT ABHORRED VOID   .  .  .   508  MILTON 24          15
    NAY ABHORRED AS VASARI TELLS US   .  .  .  .  .  .  .  .  .  . 597C PUB ADDRESS/N     PROSE
    ALBION REPLIED GO HAND & HYLE SIEZE THE ABHORRED FRIEND        670  JERUSALEM 42       47
ABHORRENCE
    OF STONE ONCE A MAN WHO REFUSD TO SIGN PAPERS OF ABHORRENCE    135  FRENCH REVOLTN     34
      .  .  .
    DOES HE WHO CONTEMNS POVERTY AND HE WHO TURNS WITH            192  V DAU ALBION 5     10
      ABHORRENCE
    ARE MY ABHORRENCE WHEREFORE HAST THOU TAKEN THAT FAIR FORM    295  FOUR ZOAS 3      * 119
    THE DAY OF TERROR & ABHORRENCE [ETERNAL]   .  .  .  .  .  .   299  FOUR ZOAS 4      *  85
    GO FORTH SONS OF MY CURSE GO FORTH DAUGHTERS OF              313  FOUR ZOAS 6        46
      MY ABHORRENCE
    SIMILAR I FELT THE SAME CONTEMPT & ABHORRENCE THEN THAT      477A  ANNO REYNOLDS     MARG
      I DO
    I WILL CAST THEE INTO FORMS OF ABHORRENCE & TORMENT IF THOU  627   JERUSALEM 8        11
    CONDENSING THEM INTO SOLID ROCKS WITH CRUELTY AND           641   JERUSALEM 19       25
      ABHORRENCE
    .  .  .  ON ONE-ANOTHER FOR ABHORRENCE THE BLUE   .  .  .  . 647   JERUSALEM 24        7
    OF UNBELIEF ENVY HOVERS OVER HIM HIS FRIENDS ARE           667   JERUSALEM 40       14
      HIS ABHORRENCE
    BY LAWS OF CHASTITY & ABHORRENCE I AM WITHERD UP  .  .  .  . 679   JERUSALEM 49       26
    AND JEALOUSY & ABHORRENCE & REVENGE & DEADLY MURDER  .  .  . 707   JERUSALEM 69       13
ABIDE
    WE CAN ABIDE LIFE'S PELTING STORM  .  .  .  .  .  .  .  .  .   64   SHEPHERD OLD        3
    WE CAN ABIDE LIFE'S PELTING STORM  .  .  .  .  .  .  .  .  .   64   SHEPHERD OLD        7
    SO GLAD WE'LL ABIDE LIFE'S PELTING STORM  .  .  .  .  .  .    64   SHEPHERD OLD       11
    DARE THY MOST TERRIBLE WRATH ABIDE BOUND HERE TO WASTE      321   FOUR ZOAS 7        47
      IN PAIN
    I ALONE DARE THE LASH ABIDE TO SIT BENEATH THE BLAST  .  .  344   FOUR ZOAS 8       148
    .  .  .  OR THE SUMMER PESTILENCE FOR A TENT TO ABIDE IN  .  . 353  FOUR ZOAS 8       494
ABILITIES
    OH I WAS AT MRS ?SICKNAKER'S & I WAS SPEAKING OF            62D   ISLAND MOON 11   *PROSE
      MY ABILITIES
    THEY ENVY ME MY ABILITIES & ALL THE WOMEN ENVY YOUR         63A   ISLAND MOON 11    PROSE
      ABILITIES
    MY DEAR THEY HATE PEOPLE WHO ARE OF HIGHER ABILITIES  .  .   63A   ISLAND MOON 11    PROSE
    WHICH SPRANG FROM SIR ISAAC NEWTON'S GREAT ABILITIES  .  .  542   FLORENTINE/N       31
    ABILITIES AS ALSO FOR THE D(DEAN) OF C(CANTERBURY) BUT  .  . 868D  LETTER 68         PROSE
ABJECT
    ("A KING IS A MORTAL GOD") O CONTEMPTIBLE & ABJECT SLAVE    401A   ANNO BACON        MARG
    TREMBLING & FEAR TERROR CONSTRICTION ABJECT SELFISHNESS     530   MILTON 38          39
ABJECTNESS
    AND DEADLY CUNNING & MEAN ABJECTNESS ONLY SHALL ENJOY THEM  734   JERUSALEM 88       38
ABLE
    HE IS NOT ABLE TO HURT ME SAID HE MORE THAN MAKING ME  .   52A   ISLAND MOON 8     PROSE
    IT IS MAN'S FAULT IF GOD IS NOT ABLE TO DO HIM GOOD FOR HE 392B   ANNO WATSON        MARG
    OR IS ABLE & AFTERWARDS GO AND SWEAR OUR LIVES AWAY  .  .  439A   BLAKES MEMORAN    PROSE
    TO THE CONTRARY TO BE BETTER ABLE THAN ANY OTHER  .  .  .  586D   CHAUCER 1         PROSE
    SHOULD HE BE ABLE TO MAKE USE OF EITHER LABOUR OR CARE  .  593A   PUB ADDRESS/N     PROSE
    I HAVE NOT BEEN ABLE TO SEND A PROOF OF THE BATH THO  .  .  791A   LETTER 2          PROSE
    WHICH I HID MY FACE FOR NOT BEING ABLE TO ABANDON  .  .  .  798C   LETTER 10         PROSE
    THIS -- CITY I SHALL NOT BE ABLE TO AVAIL MYSELF OF THE    801B   LETTER 13         PROSE
    THAT TILL NOW I HAVE NOT BEEN ABLE TO DO THIS DUTY THE  .  811B   LETTER 22         PROSE
    ABLE TO SEND ANY MORE BEFORE MY RETURN THO PERHAPS I MAY   826D   LETTER 28         PROSE
    BEEN ABLE TO CONSULT MR FLAXMAN ABOUT THE DESIGNS OF MR    838B   LETTER 37         PROSE
    HAS NOT YET BEEN ABLE TO GO WITH ME AM SORRY TO INFORM YOU 839C   LETTER 38         PROSE
    YET BEEN ABLE TO MEET MR BRAITHWAITE AT HOME DUT INTEND    849B   LETTER 45         PROSE
    IMMEDIATELY ON RECEIPT OF IT BUT HOPED TO BE ABLE TO SEND  851B   LETTER 50         PROSE
    I HAVE NOT YET BEEN ABLE TO MEET PHILLIPS  .  .  .  .  .  . 853A   LETTER 51        *PROSE
    FOR NOT BEING ABLE TO FURNISH ANY DESIGNS YOU WILL READILY 853A   LETTER 51        *PROSE
    SHOULD NOT BE ABLE TO DO THEM JUSTICE BUT THAT HE WILL  .  853A   LETTER 51        *PROSE
    MY FEET IT WILL NOT BE LONG BEFORE I SHALL BE ABLE        862D   LETTER 60         PROSE
      TO PRESENT
    I SHALL BE ABLE TO SETTLE WITH HIM SOON WHAT IS BETWEEN US 863B   LETTER 60         PROSE
    INTENDED BUT I HAVE NEVER BEEN ABLE TO PRODUCE A SUFFICIENT 867C  LETTER 66         PROSE
    GRATEFUL THO NOT ABLE ON ACCOUNT OF THIS ABOMINABLE AGUE   868D   LETTER 68         PROSE
    FEEL MYSELF WEAKER THAN I WAS AWARE BEING NOT ABLE AS YET  872D   LETTER 76         PROSE
ABODE
    THRO THE ORBED ABODE OF THE HOLY DEAD .  .  .  .  .  .  .   140   FRENCH REVOLTN    142
    WHEN FOURTEEN SUNS HAD FAINTLY JOURNEYD OER HIS DARK ABODE 195   AMERICA PREL 1      2
    THE ETERNAL ABODE IN MY HOLINESS  .  .  .  .  .  .  .  .  . 224   URIZEN 4           7
    IN AN ALLEGORICAL ABODE WHERE EXISTENCE HATH NEVER COME    240   EUROPE 5           7
    SO SPOKE LOS AS WE WENT ALONG TO HIS SUPREME ABODE  .  .   505   MILTON 22         26
    HERE IN THESE CHAOSES THE SONS OF OLOLON TOOK THEIR ABODE  524   MILTON 34         40
ABODES
    .  .  .  & ROUND THE ABODES OF MEN  .  .  .  .  .  .  .  .  203   AMERICA 16        23
    WAR CEASD & ALL THE TROOPS LIKE SHADOWS FLED TO THEIR      239   EUROPE 4           4
      ABODES
ABOLISH
    WHEREFORE DID CHRIST COME WAS IT NOT TO ABOLISH THE JEWISH 387B   ANNO WATSON      * MARG
      IMPOSTURE
    [TO GOVERN THE EVIL BY GOOD AND ?STATES ABOLISH ?SYSTEMS]  662   JERUSALEM 35      *  18
ABOMINABLE
    WHY WHY I THINK IT VERY ABOMINABLE  .  .  .  .  .  .  .  .   44D  ISLAND MOON 1     PROSE
    PREDESTINATION AFTER THIS LIFE IS MORE ABOMINABLE THAN     133A   ANNO SWED PROV    MARG
      CALVIN'S
```

2

ABOMINABLE   (CONTINUED)
```
    HATH FORMD THIS ABOMINABLE VOID  . . . . . . . .  222 URIZEN 3          4
    THE PETRIFIC ABOMINABLE CHAOS  . . . . . . . . . .  223 URIZEN 3         26
    WITHIN AS IN A TABERNACLE ABOMINABLE DEADLY  . . .  343 FOUR ZOAS 8     106
    BY DEVILISH ARTS ABOMINABLE UNLAWFUL UNUTTERABLE . .  348 FOUR ZOAS 8    288
    ABOMINABLE TO THE EYES OF MORTALS WHO EXPLORE HIS BOOKS  352 FOUR ZOAS 8  430
    FROM GOD IS ALTOGETHER ABOMINABLE & BLASPHEMOUS  . . .  387B ANNO WATSON  MARG
    WITH MANY ABOMINABLE IMPRECATIONS & WITH SOME . . . .  827A LETTER 28    PROSE
    GRATEFUL THO NOT ABLE ON ACCOUNT OF THIS ABOMINABLE AGUE  868D LETTER 68  PROSE
ABOMINATION
    IS THAT ABOMINATION WHICH LIKE THE JEWISH CEREMONIES  . .  389C ANNO WATSON   MARG
    CHRIST PRONOUNCD THEM THE ABOMINATION THAT MAKETH DESOLATE  393D ANNO WATSON  * MARG
    BABYLON THE GREAT THE ABOMINATION OF DESOLATION  . . . .  506 MILTON 22        49
    THESE ARE THE SEXUAL GARMENTS THE ABOMINATION OF DESOLATION  533 MILTON 41     25
    WHERE THEY DESIRE TO PLACE THE ABOMINATION OF DESOLATION  626 JERUSALEM 7      70
    AND IN ITS HOLINESS IS CLOSED THE ABOMINATION OF DESOLATION  629 JERUSALEM 10  16
    MYSTERY BABYLON THE GREAT THE ABOMINATION OF DESOLATION  716 JERUSALEM 75      19
ABOUND
    EACH SHALL BEHOLD THE ETERNAL FATHER & LOVE & JOY ABOUND  374 FOUR ZOAS 9     642
    BY CARICATURE PRINTS WHICH OUGHT NOT TO ABOUND SO MUCH .  793C LETTER 5     PROSE
    HEAVEN HAVILAH EDEN & ALL THE COUNTRIES WHERE JEWELS ABOUND  837D LETTER 36  PROSE
ABOUNDED
    WENT DOWN THE HUMAN HEART WHERE PARADISE & ITS JOYS  294 FOUR ZOAS 3        95
        ABOUNDED
    WENT DOWN THE HUMAN HEART WHERE PARADISE & ITS JOYS  655 JERUSALEM 29       74
        ABOUNDED
ABOUNDING
    REMAINS & IN THE VINEYARDS STAND THE ABOUNDING SHEAVES  375 FOUR ZOAS 9     697
        BENEATH
ABOUT
    A WET NAPKIN WRAPD ABOUT THEN RUSHD  . . . . . . . .    4 FAIR ELENOR/PS     26
    FEARS THE SMALL FIRE THAT PLAYS ABOUT THE FEN . . . . .   24 EDW THIRD/PS 3  117
    WHILE VACANT YOUTH DOTH CRAVE AND SEEK ABOUT  . . . .   27 EDW THIRD/PS 3   252
    ITS A NEW SONG ABOUT THE FRENCH AND ENGLISH  . . . . .   29B EDW THIRD/PS 4  PROSE
    AND HE IS TO WRITE ANOTHER ABOUT ALL US THAT ARE TO DIE   29C EDW THIRD/PS 4  PROSE
    WHEN MEN SLEEP IN THEIR BEDS WALKETH ABOUT  . . . . .   30 EDW THIRD/PS 5     7
    HER CITIZENS SHALL THRONG ABOUT HER GATES . . . . . .   34C KING JOHN/PS    PROSE
    I WILL GO MAD AND TEAR MY CRISPED HAIR I'LL RUN ABOUT .   38C SAMSON/PS     PROSE
    I TURND MYSELF ABOUT WITH GREAT CONTEMPT SAID I GO ALONG   45A ISLAND MOON 1  PROSE
        YOU FOOL
    OF A VAST NUMBER OF PAPERS TURNED ABOUT & SAT DOWN  . .   45B ISLAND MOON 1  PROSE
    THE CYNIC ANSWERD THEY ARE ONLY QUARRELING ABOUT VOLTAIRE   45C ISLAND MOON 1  PROSE
    WITH DOUBLE VIOLENCE IT IS NOT WORTH QUARRELING ABOUT .   45D ISLAND MOON 1  PROSE
    WHY SIR SAID HE THE GENTLEMAN THAT THE SONG WAS ABOUT .   47A ISLAND MOON 3  PROSE
    YOU HAVE READ ABOUT THAT IN THE BIBLE  . . . . . . .   47B ISLAND MOON 3  PROSE
    WHAT WAS IT YOU WAS TALKING ABOUT . . . . . . . . .   47C ISLAND MOON 3  PROSE
    FOR YOU NEVER SAY ANY THING ABOUT THE SCRIPTURES  . . .   48A ISLAND MOON 4  PROSE
    & SET HIS [HEAD] HAIR ALL IN A FLAME & RAN ABOUT THE ROOM   48C ISLAND MOON 4  PROSE
    AND RAN ABOUT WITH BLOODY HANDS  . . . . . . . . . .   50 WHEN CORRUP/IM   15
    THE FATHER GRIN'D & SKIPT ABOUT  . . . . . . . . . .   51 WHEN CORRUP/IM   23
    AND NEVER THINK AT ALL ABOUT IT IM HANGD IF I DONT GET UP   51D ISLAND MOON 7  PROSE
    O AY LOCK SAID SCOPPRELL [XXX ?ABOUT]  . . . . . . . .   52D ISLAND MOON 8  *PROSE
    THEN SHE REPEATED THESE VERSES WHILE STEELYARD WALKD ABOUT   53C ISLAND MOON 8  PROSE
        THE ROOM
    VERY PRITTY & FUNNY [ABOUT LONDON O NO] ABOUT MATCHES  . .   54D ISLAND MOON 9  *PROSE
    IN THE CIRCUMFERENCE THEY CAST A BOUND ABOUT THE INFINITE   92A ANNO SWED LOVE  MARG
    THEY EXIST LITERALLY ABOUT THE SUN & NOT ABOUT THE EARTH   92B ANNO SWED LOVE  MARG
    PIPE A SONG ABOUT A LAMB . . . . . . . . . . . . .  111 INTRODUCTN/SI      5
    AT LAST TO THE EAST DISTANT ABOUT THREE DEGREES APPEARD  156C MARRIAGE HH 17  PROSE
    A MAN CARRIED A MONKEY ABOUT FOR A SHEW &  . . . . . .  157C MARRIAGE HH 21  PROSE
    [ABOUT THE FRUITFUL LAND]  . . . . . . . . . . . .  185 LET BROTHELS/N    30
    AND THREW THE NETS ROUND ABOUT . . . . . . . . . .  227 URIZEN 8           8
    WHIRLING ABOUT IN FURIOUS CIRCLES ROUND THE IMMORTAL FIEND  240 EUROPE 4       30
    WHIRLING ABOUT IN THE DEEP . . . . . . . . . . . .  259 BOOK OF LOS 5     17
    WHERE THOU & I IN UNDIVIDED ESSENCE WALKD ABOUT  . . .  327 FOUR ZOAS 7     271
    RAVING ABOUT THE UPPER ELEMENTS IN MADDNING FURY . . . .  328 FOUR ZOAS 7  *  322
    DART FORTH UPON THE WIND IN PIPES WRITHING ABOUT IN THE  353 FOUR ZOAS 8     473
        ABYSS
    THE ROCKS GROAN HORRIBLE & RUN ABOUT THE MOUNTAINS &  . .  358 FOUR ZOAS 9     53
    INCOMPREHENSIBLE PERVADING ALL AMIDST & ROUND ABOUT  . .  364 FOUR ZOAS 9    282
    THAT CREEP ABOUT THE OBSCURE PLACES SHEW THEIR VARIOUS  377 FOUR ZOAS 9     765
        LIMBS
    HE WHO THINKS THAT HONESTY IS CHANGEABLE KNOWS NOTHING  386B ANNO WATSON    MARG
        ABOUT IT
    HOW SHOULD ONE SO FOOLISH KNOW ABOUT RICHES  . . . . .  409A ANNO BACON     MARG
    THE FAIRY SKIPD ABOUT IN HIS GLORY JOY & PRIDE . . . .  434 LONG JOHN BRWN   15
    I DESIRED THE GENTLEMAN TO SET GAINSBOROUGH ABOUT  . . .  465C ANNO REYNOLDS  MARG
    KNEW NOTHING AT ALL ABOUT ART AS AN OBJECT OF IMITATION  467B ANNO REYNOLDS  MARG
    SAY FIRST WHAT MOVD MILTON WHO WALKD ABOUT IN ETERNITY .  481 MILTON 2        16
    IN MOMENTS NEW CREATED FOR DELUSION INTERWOVEN ROUND ABOUT  494 MILTON 13      39
    AND THOU O MILTON ART A STATE ABOUT TO BE CREATED  . . .  521 MILTON 32       26
    ABOUT FREEDOM & JENNY SUCK AWA . . . . . . . . . .  550 WHEN LOOK AT/N     4
    A THING THATS TIED ABOUT THE EXAMINER'S'NECK . . . . .  555 BLAKES APL/N 1   11
    ABOUT JOHN OF BRUGES INVENTING OIL COLOURS  . . . . .  565B DESC CAT 2     PROSE
    HOW SPOTS OF BROWN AND YELLOW SMEARED ABOUT AT RANDOM  .  575A DESC CAT 3    PROSE
    THE PAINTER THOUGHT HE WOULD GIVE THEM A RIDE ROUND ABOUT  575B DESC CAT 3    PROSE
    THAT ABOUT IT WHICH MAY BE WORTHY THE ATTENTION  . . .  581C DESC CAT 7     PROSE
    ABOUT CORREGGIO BEING POOR AND BUT BADLY PAID  . . . .  583B DESC CAT 9     PROSE
    AND KNOCKED ABOUT WITHOUT MERCY TO TRY ALL EXPERIMENTS .  583D DESC CAT 9     PROSE
    CAIN WHO WAS ABOUT TO BURY IT  . . . . . . . . . .  584A DESC CAT 11    TITLE
    TROUBLE THEIR HEADS VERY LITTLE ABOUT ART & SCIENCE & THAT  592C PUB ADDRESS/N  PROSE
    IMMEDIATELY SET ABOUT SEARCHING FOR POINTS OF LIGHT  . . .  599A PUB ADDRESS/N  PROSE
```

```
                                                              PAGE      TITLE      LINE
ABOUT    (CONTINUED)
     SORRY TO SEE MY COUNTRYMEN TROUBLE THEMSELVES ABOUT      600A  PUB ADDRESS/N   PROSE
        POLITICS
     ABSURD NONSENSE ABOUT DOTS & LOZENGES & CLEAN STROKES  . . 602A PUB ADDRESS/N  PROSE
     WANDERING ABOUT IN SHEEP SKINS & GOAT SKINS OF WHOM THE   604A  INSC ARIMATHEA PROSE
     WITH THEIR HAMMER & TONGS ABOUT TO NEW CREATE  . . . . .  609B  V LAST JUDG/N  PROSE
     [ JERUSALEM WHO IS ABOUT TO BE RECIEVD LIKE THE BRIDE     609C  V LAST JUDG/N  *PROSE
        OF THE]
     IN CLOUD OF SECRET GLOOM WHICH BEHOLD INVOLVE ME ROUND    660   JERUSALEM 33    47
        ABOUT
     AT THY WORD & AT THY LOOK DEATH ENROBES ME ABOUT  . . .   660   JERUSALEM 34     5
     TO PREVENT ALBION WALKING ABOUT IN THE FOUR COMPLEXIONS   671   JERUSALEM 43     5
     THAT WALKS ABOUT AMONG THE STONES OF FIRE IN BLISS & WOE  680   JERUSALEM 49    73
     THEN FAR THE GREATEST NUMBER WERE ABOUT TO MAKE A         686   JERUSALEM 55    30
        SEPARATION
     JERUSALEM IN RUINS WANDERING ABOUT FROM HOUSE TO HOUSE . . 714  JERUSALEM 74    17
     ABOUT HIS FATHER'S BUSINESS  . . . . . . . . . . . .      752   EV GOSPEL(D)/N  54
     AS TO MYSELF ABOUT WHOM YOU ARE SO KINDLY INTERESTED I .  . 795C LETTER 6       PROSE
     & STUDY OF ARCHANGELS WHY THEN SHOULD I BE ANXIOUS ABOUT  802C  LETTER 14      PROSE
        THE
     ARE GENUINE SAXONS HANDSOMER THAN THE PEOPLE [AR ] ABOUT  806B  LETTER 16      *PROSE
        LONDON
     TELL ME ABOUT YOUR SIGHT AFFLICTED ME NOT A LITTLE & THAT 811C  LETTER 22      PROSE
     ABOUT YOUR HEALTH IN ANOTHER PART OF YOUR LETTER MAKES ME 811C  LETTER 22      PROSE
     THINK OF TROUBLING YOU ABOUT IT OR ANY OF MY REAL FRIENDS 815C  LETTER 23      PROSE
     I ALSO TOLD YOU WHAT I WAS ABOUT & THAT I WAS NOT IGNORANT 820C LETTER 25      PROSE
     ABOUT VARIOUS PROJECTED WORKS & PARTICULARLY A WORK NOW   821C  LETTER 25      PROSE
     THIS I BELIEVE ABOUT BALANCES OUR ACCOUNT  . . . . . .    826B  LETTER 28      PROSE
     BUT HE TURNING ABOUT PUT HIMSELF INTO A POSTURE OF DEFIANCE 827A LETTER 28     PROSE
     PUSHED HIM FORWARDS DOWN THE ROAD ABOUT FIFTY YARDS  . .  827B  LETTER 28      PROSE
     PERHAPS IT WILL BE IN YOUR POWER TO LEARN SOMEWHAT ABOUT  828B  LETTER 28      PROSE
     IF YOU CAN LEARN NOTHING ABOUT HIM & WHAT I AS WELL KNOW  828B  LETTER 28      PROSE
     BURN WHAT I HAVE PEEVISHLY WRITTEN ABOUT ANY FRIEND  . .  828C  LETTER 28      PROSE
     YOUR GENEROUS & TENDER SOLICITUDE ABOUT YOUR DEVOTED REBEL 829C LETTER 30      PROSE
     IN HAND BUT WHO RIDES ABOUT THE PARKS OR SAUNTERS ABOUT   830A  LETTER 30      PROSE
     P S MY WIFE IS BETTER WE ARE VERY ANXIOUS ABOUT MISS      833A  LETTER 32      PROSE
        POOLE'S
     AT ABOUT (TWELVE) OCLOCK . . . . . . . . . . .           836B  LETTER 35      PROSE
     YET HAD AN OPPORTUNITY OF CONSULTING ABOUT IT BUT SOON WILL 836C LETTER 35     PROSE
     BUT I HASTEND TO WRITE TO YOU ABOUT MR BRAITHWAITE HOPE   837A  LETTER 35      PROSE
     BEEN ABLE TO CONSULT MR FLAXMAN ABOUT THE DESIGNS OF MR   838B  LETTER 37      PROSE
     ABOUT IT MONEY IN THESE TIMES IS NOT TO BE TRIFLED WITH   841A  LETTER 40      PROSE
        I HAVE
     ON A CANVAS ABOUT TWO FEET BY ONE AND A HALF  . . . . .   843A  LETTER 43      PROSE
     FIVE SHILLINGS AT A BROKER'S SHOP IT IS ABOUT FIVE FEET   843D  LETTER 43      PROSE
        BY FOUR
     IN WESTMORELAND PROMISES TO MAKE EVERY INQUIRY ABOUT IT   844C  LETTER 43      PROSE
     SUPPOSES THAT ROMNEY WAS ABOUT EIGHTEEN WHEN HE PAINTED IT 845D LETTER 44      PROSE
     I SPOKE TO MR FLAXMAN ABOUT CHOOSING OUT PROPER SUBJECTS  846A  LETTER 44      PROSE
     TO ENGRAVE ONE IN EACH MANNER THE SIZE TO BE ABOUT (SEVEN) 848B LETTER 45      PROSE
        INCHES
     I WAS ABOUT TO HAVE WRITTEN TO YOU TO EXPRESS MY WISH THAT 853A LETTER 51      *PROSE
     BEING AT FLAXMAN'S TAKING HIS ADVICE ABOUT OUR ENGRAVINGS 853A  LETTER 51      *PROSE
     WHAT YOU HAD SAID ABOUT THE DESIGNS FOR EDWARD THE FIRST & 853A LETTER 51      *PROSE
     I WILL SOON SPEAK WITH PHILLIPS ABOUT IT IF YOU WILL  .   853A  LETTER 51      *PROSE
     ABOUT IT IMMEDIATELY AND HAS DESIRED THAT I  . . . . .    858D  LETTER 55      PROSE
     IN CONSEQUENCE OF THIS I PRODUCED ABOUT TWENTY DESIGNS .  861C  LETTER 59      PROSE
     WHICH HE SET ME ABOUT THE DRAWINGS HAS NOW SET ME TO  .   861D  LETTER 59      PROSE
     WHICH IS BUT OF ABOUT TWO MONTHS DATE  . . . . . . .      862A  LETTER 59      PROSE
     (TWELVE) LARGE PRINTS SIZE OF EACH ABOUT (TWO) FEET BY... 867B  LETTER 66      PROSE
     SOON GET ABOUT AGAIN GREAT MEN DIE EQUALLY WITH THE LITTLE 868D LETTER 68      PROSE
     BEGAN PAIN OF MIND & THAT NOT A SMALL ONE IT IS ABOUT  .  874B  LETTER 79      PROSE
     WHAT I WAS ABOUT I HAVE GOT ON VERY FORWARD WITH (FOUR)   876D  LETTER 84      PROSE
        PLATES
     ABOUT AT THE SAME TIME  . . . . . . . . . . .            877C  LETTER 86      PROSE
     WHICH IS ALL I CARE ABOUT  . . . . . . . . . . .         877D  LETTER 88      PROSE
ABOVE
     ABOVE HEROIC HAVING SUCH EXAMPLES . . . . . . . . .       23   EDW THIRD/PS 3   80
     WITH STOCKINGS ROLLD ABOVE THEIR KNEES & SHOES AS BLACK   58   THIS CITY/IM  *  6
        AS [GIT] JET
     THIS IS TRUE CHRISTIAN PHILOSOPHY FAR ABOVE ALL ABSTRACTION 65C ANNO LAVATER   MARG
     THE MERCY SEAT IS ABOVE UPON THE ARK CHERUBIMS  . . . .   82A  ANNO LAVATER   MARG
     THUS FOOLS QUOTE SHAKESPEARE THE ABOVE IS THESEUS'S OPINION SUPP ANNO SWED HELL * MARG
     LIKE THE MORNING STAR ARISING ABOVE THE BLACK WAVES . . .  145  FRENCH REVOLTN  255
     A FIERY CREST ABOVE THE WAVES SLOWLY IT REARED LIKE A RIDGE 156C MARRIAGE HH 17 PROSE
     & RED GILLS HANG JUST ABOVE THE RAGING FOAM  . . . . .    156C  MARRIAGE HH 17  PROSE
     TILL WE WERE ELEVATED ABOVE THE EARTH'S SHADOW  . . .     156D  MARRIAGE HH 17  PROSE
     AT THE LABOUR THAT IS ABOVE PAYMENT AND WILT THOU TAKE    192   V DAU ALBION 5   8
        THE APE
     DARK IS THE HEAVEN ABOVE & COLD & HARD THE EARTH BENEATH  201   AMERICA 14       7
     ABOVE ALL HEAVENS IN THUNDERS WRAPD EMERGD HIS LEPROUS HEAD 203  AMERICA 16       3
     THEY SAW THE SERPENT TEMPLE LIFTED ABOVE SHADOWING THE    242   EUROPE 12       11
        ISLAND WHITE
     ABOVE THE REST THE HOWL WAS HEARD FROM WESTMINSTER LOUDER  242   EUROPE 12       14
        & LOUDER
     WENT ENORMOUS ABOVE THE RED FLAMES  . . . . . . . .      248   SONG OF LOS 7    11
     FROM HIS WOVEN DARKNESS ABOVE  . . . . . . . . . .       248   SONG OF LOS 7    25
     AROSE LIKE A PILLAR OF FIRE ABOVE THE ALPS  . . . . .     248   SONG OF LOS 7    27
     EFFLUVIA VAPORD ABOVE  . . . . . . . . . . . . .         253   AHANIA 4        17
     AND I HAVE MURDERED THEM WITH CRUELTY ABOVE ATONEMENT  .  268   FOUR ZOAS 1   * 166
     [SHRIEKING] ABOVE THE OCEAN . . . . . . . . . . .        269   FOUR ZOAS 1     183
     THEY STOOD ABOVE THE HEAVENS FORSAKEN DESOLATE SUSPENDED  274   FOUR ZOAS 1     361
        IN BLOOD
```

```
                                                              PAGE      TITLE         LINE
ABOVE    (CONTINUED)
     ETERNITY APPEARD ABOVE THEM AS ONE MAN INFOLDED    . . . .   274  FOUR ZOAS 1     363
     CONSULTING AS ONE MAN ABOVE [MOUNT GILEAD]. . . . . .       277  FOUR ZOAS 1     475
     ABOVE [MOUNT GILEAD] HIGH SNOWDON. . . . . . . . . .        279  FOUR ZOAS 1     552
     TERRIFIC URIZEN STRODE ABOVE IN FEAR & PALE DISMAY         280  FOUR ZOAS 2      19
     ABOVE HIM ROSE A SHADOW FROM HIS WEARIED INTELLECT         293  FOUR ZOAS 3      50
     THEY STROVE TOGETHER ABOVE THE BODY WHERE VALA WAS INCLOSD 294  FOUR ZOAS 3      80
     THEY ROSE IN STRENGTH ABOVE THE HEAVING DELUGE IN MIGHTY   297  FOUR ZOAS 4       4
       SCORN
     WEAVE SOFT DELUSIVE FORMS OF MAN ABOVE MY WATRY WORLD  . . 298  FOUR ZOAS 4      29
     SWAM IN RED TEARS HE REARD HIS WAVES ABOVE THE HEAD OF LOS 298  FOUR ZOAS 4      45
     THEY POURD THEIR RADIANCE ABOVE ALL THE DAUGHTERS OF LUVAH 312  FOUR ZOAS 6      33
       ENVIED
     ABOVE BENEATH ON ALL SIDES ROUND IN THE VAST DEEP         318  FOUR ZOAS 6     275
       OF IMMENSITY
     BENEATH THEE & AROUND ABOVE A SHOWER OF FIRE NOW BEATS  . . 321  FOUR ZOAS 7      51
     IN THE DIM AIR THEY TOOK THE BOOK OF IRON & PLACD ABOVE    322  FOUR ZOAS 7      97
     WHILE THE ENORMOUS SCROLLS ROLLD DREADFUL IN THE HEAVENS   322  FOUR ZOAS 7     105
       ABOVE
     BURST FORTH UPON THE WINDS ABOVE THE TREE OF MYSTERY   . . 324  FOUR ZOAS 7     168
     AND TREMBLED THRO THE WORLDS ABOVE LOS WEPT . . . .        328  FOUR ZOAS 7     318
     LOS REARD HIS MIGHTY [FOREHEAD] STATURE ON EARTH STOOD     334  FOUR ZOAS 7B     40
       HIS FEET ABOVE
     APPEAR ABOVE THE (CRUMBLING) MOUNTAIN SILENCE WAITS AROUND 336  FOUR ZOAS 7B   * 130
       HIM
     LIKE TO A RUSHING TORRENT BENEATH & A FALLING ROCK ABOVE   340  FOUR ZOAS 7B    267
     [THEIR WINGS TOUCHD THE HEAVENS THEIR FAIR FEET HOVERD     341  FOUR ZOAS 8      12
       ABOVE]
     FLATTEN ABOVE & BENEATH & STRETCH OUT INTO BEASTIAL LENGTH 344  FOUR ZOAS 8     128
     SHE STOOD BEFORE LOS IN HER PRIDE [ABOVE] AMONG THE        350  FOUR ZOAS 8   * 345
       FURNACES
     SHE TENDERLY LOVD HIM ABOVE ALL HIS BRETHREN HE GREW UP    351  FOUR ZOAS 8     385
     THARMAS [ABOVE] ON HIGH RODE FURIOUS THRO THE AFFLICTED    353  FOUR ZOAS 8     485
       WORLDS
     OF ALL BENEATH & ALL ABOVE & IN THE GENTLE WEST  . . .    355  FOUR ZOAS 8     569
     ABOVE UPON ITS VOLUMES IS BEHELD [AS] A THRONE & [AS ]     364  FOUR ZOAS 9     279
       A PAVEMENT
     IF GODS COMBINE AGAINST MAN SETTING THEIR DOMINION ABOVE   366  FOUR ZOAS 9     366
     ABOVE ON THE BRIGHT HEAVENS IN PEACE THE SPIRITS OF MEN    372  FOUR ZOAS 9     574
       BENEATH
     ABOVE VEERD ROUND BY THE VIOLENT WHIRLWIND DRIVEN WEST     374  FOUR ZOAS 9   * 655
       & SOUTH
     SHRIEKING ABOVE THE OCEAN A BRIGHT WONDER THAT NATURE      381  FOUR ZOAS AD 5    3
       SHUDDERD AT
     EVER DOUBT CHRIST'S IN THE ABOVE SENSE OF THE WORD MIRACLE 391D ANNO WATSON   MARG
     HOW CAN WATSON EVER BELIEVE THE ABOVE SENSE OF A MIRACLE   391D ANNO WATSON   MARG
     WORSHIPD IN THIS WORLD AS GOD & SET ABOVE ALL THAT IS CALLD 394C ANNO WATSON   MARG
       GOD
     ABOVE THE LIGHT OF THE MORNING STAR . . . . . . .          427  LAND OF DREAMS   20
     & ABOVE HIS [CAVERNS] CAVERN ON THE EARTH'S SURFACE . . . 443A LAST JUDGMNT/L PROSE
     & ABOVE THESE [THERE ARE] SEVEN ANGELS WITH THE . . . .   444A LAST JUDGMNT/L PROSE
     IS NO ARTIST ARTISTS WHO ARE ABOVE A PLAIN UNDERSTANDING   458C ANNO REYNOLDS  MARG
     BUT GENIUS (IS ALWAYS ABOVE THE AGE) . . . . . . .        461A ANNO REYNOLDS * MARG
     THAT GAINSBOROUGH HAD IN MAKING THE ABOVE ASSERTION NAMELY 465D ANNO REYNOLDS  MARG
     HE CALLS THE ABOVE PROCEEDING WITH METHOD . . . . .       475B ANNO REYNOLDS  MARG
     IMAGINATION NOT TO BE ABOVE THE MORTAL & PERISHING NATURE  475D ANNO REYNOLDS  MARG
     THICK FIRES CONTENDING WITH THE RAIN THUNDER ABOVE ROLLING 488  MILTON 8         28
     FLAMD ABOVE ALL THE PLOWED FURROWS ANGRY RED AND FURIOUS   488  MILTON 8         36
     BEING CALLD GOD SETTING HIMSELF ABOVE ALL THAT IS CALLED   491  MILTON 11        12
       GOD
     SATAN ASTONISHD AND WITH POWER ABOVE HIS OWN CONTROLL  . . 492  MILTON 12        16
     THE HARROW CAST THICK FLAMES JEHOVAH THUNDERD ABOVE  . . . 493  MILTON 12        20
     JEHOVAH THUNDERD ABOVE SATAN IN PRIDE OF HEART . . .      493  MILTON 12        24
     TO THE BOSOM OF DEATH WHAT WAS UNDERNEATH SOON SEEMD ABOVE 497  MILTON 15        42
     BUT MILTON'S HUMAN SHADOW CONTINUD JOURNEYING ABOVE  . . . 498  MILTON 17        18
     HIS REAL HUMAN WALKD ABOVE IN POWER AND MAJESTY . . . .   502  MILTON 20        13
     OF LOS AND HERE HE LAYS HIS WORDS IN ORDER ABOVE THE MORTAL 513 MILTON 27         9
       BRAIN
     THE RIVER RISES ABOVE HIS BANKS TO WASH THE WOOF . . . .  518  MILTON 29        60
     MILD SHADOW ABOVE BENEATH & ON ALL SIDES ROUND . . . .    519  MILTON 30        33
     BESIDE THE FOUNT ABOVE THE LARK'S NEST IN GOLGONOOZA  . . 526  MILTON 35        58
     THE EAST TOWARD JERUSALEM'S GATES GROANING HE SAT ABOVE    531  MILTON 39        34
     FOR ABOVE TIME'S TROUBLED FOUNTAINS . . . . . . . .       558  THE CAVERNS/N    17
     ARE SEEN ABOVE THE HORIZON SOME BUILDINGS AND SPIRES  . . 567B DESC CAT 3     PROSE
     CHARACTERS LIKELY TO RIDE IN COMPANY ALL BEING ABOVE THE   568C DESC CAT 3     PROSE
     ABOVE THE SHADOWS OF GENERATION AND DEATH . . . . .       578C DESC CAT 5     PROSE
     BY PLACING LEARNING ABOVE INSPIRATION O ARTIST . . . .    582A DESC CAT 8     PROSE
     THE ABOVE FOUR DRAWINGS THE ARTIST WISHES WERE IN FRESCO   584B DESC CAT 14    PROSE
     THIS DRAWING WAS DONE ABOVE THIRTY YEARS AGO AND PROVES    585D DESC CAT 16    PROSE
     ARE SEEN ABOVE THE HORIZON SOME BUILDINGS & SPIRES . . .  588D CHAUCER/N     PROSE
     ARE SEEN ABOVE THE HORRIZON SOME BUILDINGS AND SPIRES  . . 590C CHAUCER 2    *PROSE
     [TO ELEVATE ME ABOVE THE MEDIOCRITY TO WHICH I HAVE        591F PUB ADDRESS/N  PROSE
       HITHERTO]
     THEIR HISTORY SHEWS FOR THE ABOVE REASON . . . . . .      593D PUB ADDRESS/N  PROSE
     WOULD MAKE A NOBLE FINISH PLACED ABOVE THE GREAT PUBLIC    601A PUB ADDRESS/N  PROSE
     QUERY THE ABOVE OUGHT TO FOLLOW THE DESCRIPTION . . . .   606A V LAST JUDG/N  PROSE
     ABRAHAM HOVERS ABOVE HIS POSTERITY WHICH APPEAR . . . .   607C V LAST JUDG/N  PROSE
     ABOVE HIM ARE TWO FIGURES ELEVATED ON A CLOUD . . . .     607D V LAST JUDG/N  PROSE
     ABOVE THE GATE A FIEND WITH WINGS [DR] URGES [THEM] . . . 608B V LAST JUDG/N *PROSE
     WHICH THE FLOOD DID NOT SWEEP AWAY ABOVE NOAH IS . . . .  609D V LAST JUDG/N  PROSE
     EMBRACING ABOVE THE GRAVES & REPRESENT RELIGION . . . .   610C V LAST JUDG/N  PROSE
     JUST ABOVE THE GRAVES & ABOVE THE SPOT . . . . . . .      610C V LAST JUDG/N  PROSE
```

5

```
                                                                      PAGE      TITLE          LINE
ABOVE   (CONTINUED)
     ABOVE THE HEAD OF NOAH IS SETH THIS STATE CALLD    .   .   . 611C  V LAST JUDG/N    PROSE
     WHERE THE MAN IS EITHER IN AFFLUENCE OR IS ABOVE THE CARE    612C  V LAST JUDG/N    PROSE
        OF IT
     & THEIR INCAPABILITY OF ART THO ART IS ABOVE EITHER    .   . 612C  V LAST JUDG/N    PROSE
     THE DAWN WITH HER DAPPLED HORSES ARISES ABOVE THE EARTH      618A  ILLUS MILTON     PROSE
     HIS REASON HIS SPECTROUS POWER COVERS THEM ABOVE   .   .   . 620   JERUSALEM 1          5
     OUT FROM THE FURNACES OF LOS ABOVE THE HEAD OF LOS           624   JERUSALEM 5         50
     WHICH REVOLVE HEAVILY IN THE MIGHTY VOID ABOVE THE FURNACES  624   JERUSALEM 5         53
     FORMING THE MUNDANE SHELL ABOVE BENEATH ON ALL SIDES         634   JERUSALEM 13        54
        SURROUNDING
     AND IN THE NON ENTITY NOR SHALL THAT WHICH IS ABOVE   .   .  639   JERUSALEM 17        43
     STANDING ABOVE THAT MIGHTY RUIN   .   .   .   .   .   .   .  650   FIELDS FROM/J       27
     THEN THE DIVINE VISION LIKE A SILENT SUN APPEARD ABOVE   .   653   JERUSALEM 29         1
     ABOVE HIM ROSE A SHADOW FROM HIS WEARIED INTELLECT   .   .   654   JERUSALEM 29        37
     THEY STROVE TOGETHER ABOVE THE BODY WHERE VALA WAS INCLOSD   655   JERUSALEM 29        62
     BY THE WAVES OF DESPAIR WHOSE EMANATION ROSE ABOVE    .   .  667   JERUSALEM 40        49
     JEHOVAH IS BEFORE BEHIND ABOVE BENEATH AROUND   .   .   .   .680   JERUSALEM 49        53
     JERUSALEM & VALA APPEARD & ABOVE BETWEEN THE WINGS           685   JERUSALEM 54        31
        MAGNIFICENT
     SO CRIED THEY AT THE PLOW ALBION'S ROCK FROWNED ABOVE   .   .687   JERUSALEM 55        67
     AND THE GREAT VOICE OF ETERNITY ROLLED ABOVE TERRIBLE IN     687   JERUSALEM 55        68
        CLOUDS
     URIZEN WRATHFUL STRODE ABOVE DIRECTING THE AWFUL BUILDING    690   JERUSALEM 58        21
     SO SPOKE THE LAMB OF GOD WHILE LUVAH'S CLOUD REDDENING       696   JERUSALEM 62        30
        ABOVE
     HE BLEEDS IN TORRENTS OF BLOOD AS HE ROLLS THRO HEAVEN       703   JERUSALEM 66        77
        ABOVE
     THUNDER ABOVE WHEN THEY SEE THE TWELVE PANTING VICTIMS   .   706   JERUSALEM 68        40
     AND ABOVE ALBION'S LAND WAS SEEN THE HEAVENLY CANAAN    .   .709   JERUSALEM 71         1
     AS THE SUBSTANCE IS TO THE SHADOW AND ABOVE ALBION'S TWELVE  709   JERUSALEM 71         2
        SONS
     WHAT IS ABOVE IS WITHIN FOR EVERY-THING IN ETERNITY IS       709   JERUSALEM 71         6
        TRANSLUCENT
     ABOVE THE MOUNTAINS OF ALBION ABOVE THE HEAD OF LOS    .   . 711   JERUSALEM 71    *   55
     THESE CRUEL DRUID TEMPLES O VALA HUMANITY IS FAR ABOVE   .   721   JERUSALEM 79        73
     AND HER DELUSIVE LIGHT BEAMD FIERCE ABOVE THE MOUNTAIN   .   723   JERUSALEM 80        59
     MINGLED ABOVE THE MOUNTAIN WHAT SHALL WE DO TO KEEP    .   . 723   JERUSALEM 80        84
     LOS SAW THE ENVIOUS BLIGHT ABOVE HIS SEVENTH FURNACE    .   .726   JERUSALEM 82        56
     ABOVE HIS HEAD HIGH ARCHING WINGS BLACK FILLD WITH EYES      735   JERUSALEM 89        28
     CONWENNA SAT ABOVE WITH SOLEMN CADENCES SHE DREW    .   .   .736   JERUSALEM 90        21
     STRUGGLING TO RISE ABOVE THE MOUNTAINS IN HIS BURNING HAND   742   JERUSALEM 95        12
     AND THE DIM CHAOS BRIGHTEND BENEATH ABOVE AROUND EYED AS     745   JERUSALEM 98        14
        THE PEACOCK
     EARTH GROANID BENEATH & HEAVEN ABOVE   .   .   .   .   .   . 753   EV GOSPEL(E)/N       5
     THAT HE MIGHT LIVE ABOVE CONTROLL   .   .   .   .   .   .   .757   EV GOSPEL(I)/N      44
     ADAM KNEELS BY HER JEHOVAH STANDS ABOVE   .   .   .   .   .  779C  GHOST ABEL 1     PROSE
     THE ABOVE WAS WRITTEN & THE DRAWING ANNEXED BY THE DESIRE    781D  INSC UPCOTT      PROSE
     WHO LOVE & ADMIRE YOUR WORKS BUT ABOVE ALL FOR THE SAKE      795B  LETTER 6         PROSE
        OF THE ARTS
     AFTER ANOTHER ARTIST BUT ABOVE ALL I FEEL MYSELF HAPPY &     795C  LETTER 6         PROSE
     .  .  .  TERRORS APPEARD IN THE HEAVENS ABOVE   .   .   .   .799   TO FLAXMAN/L         7
     THE ILL DRAWN & UGLY YOUNG WOMEN & ABOVE ALL    .   .   .   .815A  LETTER 23        PROSE
     & RESPECT THEY WERE COMPOSED ABOVE A TWELVE-MONTH AGO   .   .816D  LETTER 24        PROSE
     WIND SINGING ABOVE OUR ROOF & THE SEA ROARING AT A DISTANCE  820B  LETTER 25        PROSE
     TO PRAY THAT MY FRIENDS & YOU ABOVE THE REST MAY BE MADE     830B  LETTER 30        PROSE
     ABOVE ALL YOU MY DEAR FRIEND & BENEFACTOR IN THE LORD    .   834A  LETTER 33        PROSE
     OTHER BOTH HELD ABOVE HER HEAD & A FIGURE KNEELING AT HER    839C  LETTER 38        PROSE
        FEET
     IT IS THE FIRST PORTRAIT ROMNEY EVER PAINTED BUT ABOVE ALL   843D  LETTER 43        PROSE
     I WRITE IMMEDIATELY ON RECIEVING THE ABOVE INFORMATION   .   849A  LETTER 45        PROSE
     WHICH I HAVE NOT BEEN FOR THE ABOVE LONG PERIOD    .   .   . 852D  LETTER 50        PROSE
     HE ADVISED IT TO BE DONE AS ABOVE RELATED   .   .   .   .   .853A  LETTER 51       *PROSE
     PROJECTED WORK IT BIDS FAIR TO SET ME ABOVE                  862C  LETTER 60        PROSE
        THE DIFFICULTIES
     ON THE ABOVE TERMS & I WILL TAKE CARE THAT THEY SHALL BE     867C  LETTER 66        PROSE
        DONE
     YOUR SUCCESS IN YOUR PROFESSION IS ABOVE ALL THINGS TO ME    876C  LETTER 83        PROSE
     YESTERDAY HE SAT WITH ME ABOVE AN HOUR & LOOKD OVER    .   . 877A  LETTER 85        PROSE
ABRAHAM
     IF HE IS GOOD HE WILL ABHOR WICKEDNESS IN DAVID OR ABRAHAM   393B  ANNO WATSON       MARG
     ABRAHAM & MOSES KNEEL ON EACH SIDE BENEATH THEM    .   .   . 443B  LAST JUDGMNT/L   PROSE
     ABRAHAM MOSES SOLOMON PAUL CONSTANTINE CHARLEMAINE    .   .  528   MILTON 37           41
     ALSO ABRAHAM WAS CALLED TO SUCCEED THE DRUIDICAL AGE    .   .578A  DESC CAT 5       PROSE
     IS ABRAHAM WITH SARAH & ISAAC ALSO HAGAR & ISHMAEL    .   .  606D  V LAST JUDG/N    PROSE
     MOSES & ABRAHAM ARE NOT HERE MEANT BUT THE STATES   .   .   .607B  V LAST JUDG/N    PROSE
     ABRAHAM HOVERS ABOVE HIS POSTERITY WHICH APPEAR    .   .   . 607C  V LAST JUDG/N    PROSE
     FEET OF ABRAHAM & RECIEVE THEIR CHILDREN FROM THE EARTH      607C  V LAST JUDG/N    PROSE
     THE CHILDREN OF ABRAHAM OR HEBREW CHURCH ARE    .   .   .   .610B  V LAST JUDG/N    PROSE
     FROM WHENCE ABRAHAM WAS TAKEN ALSO ON THE RIGHT HAND OF      610D  V LAST JUDG/N    PROSE
        NOAH
     NEITHER CAN SETH ENVY NOAH OR ELIJAH ENVY ABRAHAM    .   .   616B  V LAST JUDG/N    PROSE
     AS ABRAHAM FLEES FROM CHALDEA SHAKING HIS GOARY LOCKS   .   .636   JERUSALEM 15        28
     ABRAHAM HEBER SHEM AND NOAH WHO WERE DRUIDS    .   .   .   . 649C  JERUSALEM 27     PROSE
     IN THE LOINS OF ABRAHAM & DAVID   .   .   .   .   .   .   .  652B  JERUSALEM 27     PROSE
     ADAM NOAH ABRAHAM MOSES SAMUEL DAVID EZEKIEL    .   .   .   .714   JERUSALEM 73        41
     ABRAHAM MOSES SOLOMON PAUL CONSTANTINE CHARLEMAINE    .   .  716   JERUSALEM 75        16
     BUT JESUS AS ALSO ABRAHAM & DAVID CONSIDERD GOD    .   .   . 774A  ANNO BERKELEY     MARG
     PROTECTING ANGEL AARON ABRAHAM BELIEVED GOD    .   .   .   . SUPP  INSC HERVEY      *TITLE
ABRAHAM'S
     & VAPOUR OF SMOKE EVEN TILL ABRAHAM'S TIME THE VAPOR    .   .606D  V LAST JUDG/N    PROSE
```

```
                                                               PAGE      TITLE         LINE
ABRAM
     ABRAM FLED IN FIRES FROM CHALDEA  . . . . . . . . .  .  .  245 SONG OF LOS 3       16
     FROM THE LIMIT NOAH TO THE LIMIT ABRAM IN WHOSE LOINS  . .  636 JERUSALEM 15       26
ABRDEEN
     LEVI EDINBURH ROXBRO ROSS JUDAH ABRDEEN BERWIK DUMFRIES    638 JERUSALEM 16   *   54
ABROAD
     LIKE LIONS' WHELPS ROARING ABROAD  . . . . . . . . .       11 GWIN KING/PS        19
     THE MOON I WALKD ABROAD WHEN ALL HAD PITCHD  . . . . .     25 EDW THIRD/PS 3      161
     LIKE SHOULDRING FIRE OR IN THE BUZZ OF CITIES FLIES ABROAD 42C THEN SHE BORE     PROSE
     NOW THEY LOOK ABROAD TO SEE  . . . . . . . . . . . . .    112 A DREAM/SI          11
     AND THE PALACE APPEARD LIKE A CLOUD DRIVEN ABROAD . . .   145 FRENCH REVOLTN      246
     I WALKED ABROAD IN A SNOWY DAY  . . . . . . . . . . .     176 SOFT SNOW/N          1
     THAT STONY LAW I STAMP TO DUST AND SCATTER RELIGION ABROAD 198 AMERICA 8           5
     AND THOU DOST STAMP THEM WITH A SIGNET THEN THEY          238 EUROPE PREL 2       10
        ROAM ABROAD
     WHY [HOWLS] HOWL THE LION & THE WOLF WHY DO THEY          276 FOUR ZOAS 1    *  451
        ROAM ABROAD
     WAS THIS WIDE EARTH SPREAD ALL ABROAD NOT FOR WILD BEASTS 283 FOUR ZOAS 2       125
        TO ROAM
     CASTING THEIR SPARKLES DIRE ABROAD INTO THE DISMAL DEEP   283 FOUR ZOAS 2       140
     THEY BEAR THE WOVEN DRAPERIES ON GOLDEN HOOKS THEY HANG   284 FOUR ZOAS 2       152
        ABROAD
     THEY DUG THE CHANNELS FOR THE RIVERS & THEY POURD ABROAD  286 FOUR ZOAS 2       250
     DO I NOT STRETCH THEM ABROAD OR FOLD THEM UP LIKE        294 FOUR ZOAS 3       107
        A GARMENT
     THOU SHALT HAVE REST IF THOU REFUSEST DASHD ABROAD ON ALL 299 FOUR ZOAS 4        73
     SETTLED LIKE BATS INNUMERABLE READY TO FLY ABROAD   . . . 306 FOUR ZOAS 5        35
     SHE ANSWERD NOT BUT FILLD HER URN & POURD IT FORTH ABROAD 312 FOUR ZOAS 6        11
     SHE ANSWERD NOT BUT STRETCHD HER ARMS & THREW HER LIMBS   312 FOUR ZOAS 6    *   16
        ABROAD
     YET THROW THY LIMBS THESE FIRES ABROAD THAT BACK RETURN   321 FOUR ZOAS 7        60
        UPON THEE
     WHICH NOW OPEND WITHIN THE CENTER WE BEHOLD SPREAD ABROAD 331 FOUR ZOAS 7       442
     GIRT AS A SOWER WITH HIS SEED TO SCATTER LIFE ABROAD  . . 338 FOUR ZOAS 7B      199
     TO SEE IF HUNGRY WINDS ARE ABROAD WITH THEIR INVISIBLE ARMY 355 FOUR ZOAS 8     560
     ROAMING ABROAD ON ALL THE WINDS RAGING INTENSE REDDENING  358 FOUR ZOAS 9        36
     LAMBETH MOURNS CALLING JERUSALEM SHE WEEPS & LOOKS ABROAD 511 MILTON 25          54
     JUST IN THIS MOMENT WHEN THE MORNING ODOURS RISE ABROAD   526 MILTON 35          48
     WHILE IN THE LABOURS OF HIS CALLING SENDS HIS THOUGHT     531 MILTON 39          55
        ABROAD
     & THEN THEY ARE SCATTERD ABROAD TO THE FOUR WINDS   . . . 594A PUB ADDRESS/N   PROSE
     IN A COMMERCIAL NATION IMPOSTORS ARE ABROAD   . . . . .   601C PUB ADDRESS/N   PROSE
     WHO DRIVES ABROAD ALL THOSE WHO REBELL AGAINST THEIR      608B V LAST JUDG/N   PROSE
        SAVIOUR
     JERUSALEM IS SCATTERD ABROAD LIKE A CLOUD OF SMOKE THRO   623 JERUSALEM 5        13
        NON-ENTITY
     FROM THESE TWELVE ALL THE FAMILIES OF ENGLAND SPREAD ABROAD 623 JERUSALEM 5     33
     . . . SENDING HIM ABROAD OVER THE FOUR POINTS OF HEAVEN   638 JERUSALEM 17       11
     ABROAD INTO THE INDEFINITE SPECTRE WHO IS THE RATIONAL    698 JERUSALEM 64        5
        POWER
     GIRT AS A SOWER WITH HIS SEED TO SCATTER LIFE ABROAD OVER 700 JERUSALEM 65       45
        ALBION
     GWENDOLEN & CAMBEL WHO IS BOADICEA THEY GO ABROAD & RETURN 710 JERUSALEM 71      23
     BE SCATTERD ABROAD AND LET THE NAME OF ALBION BE FORGOTTEN 725 JERUSALEM 82      23
     (DEFORMITY) SHE GAVE HER BEAUTY TO ANOTHER BEARING ABROAD 726 JERUSALEM 82       69
     AND SOMETIMES SPREAD ABROAD REVEAL THE FLAMES OF HOLINESS 731 JERUSALEM 86       23
     WHICH STRETCHD ABROAD EXPANDING EAST & WEST & NORTH & SOUTH 733 JERUSALEM 88     32
     AND ROME IN SWEET HESPERIA THERE ISRAEL SCATTERD ABROAD   735 JERUSALEM 89       39
     AND WASHD INCESSANT BY THE FOR-EVER RESTLESS SEA-WAVES    741 JERUSALEM 94        6
        FOAMING ABROAD
     DO YOU SLEEP ROUZE UP ROUZE UP ETERNAL DEATH IS ABROAD    744 JERUSALEM 96       34
     AND THY REVENGE ABROAD DISPLAY  . . . . . . . . . . .     750 EV GOSPEL(C)/N     43
     AND THY REVENGE ABROAD DISPLAY  . . . . . . . . . . .     753 EV GOSPEL(D)/N     79
     BROUGHT INTO ENGLAND OR CAN BE PURCHASD ABROAD AS ITS  .  797D LETTER 10       *PROSE
     CANNOT TELL WHERE IT NOW IS AS THEY WERE SCATTERED ABROAD 844C LETTER 43        PROSE
ABROGATION
     TO THE INTIRE ABROGATION OF EXPERIMENTAL THEORY  . . . .  682B JERUSALEM 52     PROSE
ABRUPT
     BLEAK DARK ABRUPT IT STANDS & OVERSHADOWS LONDON CITY  . .242 EUROPE 12           9
ABSENCE
     IS THE ABSENCE FROM HEAT & LIGHT  . . . . . . . . . . .   94D ANNO SWED LOVE    MARG
     FEMALE'S LIMBS IN HIS ABSENCE & HER DAUGHTERS OFT UPON .  285 FOUR ZOAS 2       189
     HER COLD LIMBS IN THE ABSENCE OF HER LORD ALSO HER SONS   285 FOUR ZOAS 2       193
     DELECTABLE REPOSEST RUDDY IN MY ABSENCE FLAMING WITH BEAUTY 325 FOUR ZOAS 7     187
     IN THE ABSENCE OF THE MORN  . . . . . . . . . . . . .     753 EV GOSPEL(D)/N     92
     HAVE LEARND TO VALUE BY ABSENCE NO LESS PERHAPS THAN WE DID 824B LETTER 27      PROSE
     SAYS HE LAMENTS YOUR ABSENCE FROM LONDON AS YOUR ADVICE   844A LETTER 43        PROSE
ABSOLUTE
     WHICH SUM I AM IN ABSOLUTE WANT OF AS WELL AS THAT I  . . 861B LETTER 58        PROSE
ABSOLUTELY
     MAKES IT ABSOLUTELY NECESSARY THAT HE SHOULD TROUBLE YOU  829C LETTER 30        PROSE
ABSORB
     HOW CAN ONE JOY ABSORB ANOTHER ARE NOT DIFFERENT JOYS  .  192 V DAU ALBION 5      5
     AND LEARN WHAT TIS TO ABSORB THE MAN YOU SPIRITS OF PITY  294 FOUR ZOAS 3        90
        & LOVE
     OIL WILL NOT DRINK OR ABSORB COLOUR ENOUGH TO STAND THE   561A EXHIBITION ADV   PROSE
        TEST
     OIL WILL NOT DRINK OR ABSORB COLOUR ENOUGH TO STAND THE   565A DESC CAT 2       PROSE
        TEST
     ITSELF WILL DRINK OR ABSORB VERY LITTLE COLOUR  . . . .   566B DESC CAT 2       PROSE
     AND LEARN WHAT TIS TO ABSORB THE MAN YOU SPIRITS OF PITY  655 JERUSALEM 29       71
        & LOVE
```

7

	PAGE	TITLE	LINE
ABSORB (CONTINUED)			
ABSORB ME NOT IN SUCH DIRE GRIEF O ALBION MY BROTHER . .	727	JERUSALEM 83	6
ABSORBD			
OF LOS ABSORBD IN DIRE REVENGE HE DRANK WITH JOY THE CRIES	302	FOUR ZOAS 4	191
THEY SAW THAT WRATH NOW SWAYD AND NOW PITY ABSORBD HIM . .	509	MILTON 24	46
[FOR MY SAVIOUR AND LORD FOR THEY WERE WHOLLY ABSORBD IN	621A	JERUSALEM 3	*PROSE
THEIR GODS]			
CONDENSD HAND HAS ABSORBD ALL HIS BRETHREN IN HIS MIGHT	628	JERUSALEM 8	43
SOON HAND MIGHTILY DEVOURD & ABSORBD ALBION'S TWELVE SONS	641	JERUSALEM 18	39
THEY BECOME ONE WITH THE ANTICHRIST & ARE ABSORBD IN HIM	736	JERUSALEM 89	62
ABSORBED			
SUCH WORKS AS HAVE WHOLLY ABSORBED THE MAN OF GENIUS .	207B	PRSPECTUS 1793	PROSE
ABSORBED BY THE POETS MILTON HOMER CAMOENS ERCILLA ARIOSTO	806D	LETTER 17	PROSE
ABSORBING			
SOFT EXULTING IN EXISTENCE ALL THE MAN ABSORBING	293	FOUR ZOAS 3	53
THEY PROPAGATED THE DEADLY [WORLD] WORDS THE SHADOWY FEMALE	344	FOUR ZOAS 8	* 143
ABSORBING			
SOFT EXULTING IN EXISTENCE ALL THE MAN ABSORBING	654	JERUSALEM 29	40
ABSTAIN			
STILL ABSTAIN FROM PLEASURE & REST IN THE LABOURS	511	MILTON 25	46
OF ETERNITY			
O THAT I COULD ABSTAIN FROM WRATH O THAT THE LAMB . . .	626	JERUSALEM 7	59
THOU ABSTAIN RAVENING I WILL CREATE AN ETERNAL HELL FOR	627	JERUSALEM 8	38
THEE			
WE ARE TOLD TO ABSTAIN FROM FLESHLY DESIRES	716D	JERUSALEM 77	PROSE
ABSTINENCE			
ABSTINENCE SOWS SAND ALL OVER	178	ABSTINENCE/N	1
WHAT CRAWLING VILLAIN PREACHES ABSTINENCE & WRAPS HIMSELF	200	AMERICA 11	14
WITH LABOUR & ABSTINENCE SAY HE LOOKS HEALTHY & HAPPY .	323	FOUR ZOAS 7	119
IMPOSSIBILITIES CHASTITY & ABSTINENCE GODS OF THE HEATHEN	776C	INSC LAOCOON	PROSE
THAT ENJOYMENT & NOT ABSTINENCE IS THE FOOD OF INTELLECT	790D	LETTER 2	PROSE
THEY KNEW MY INDUSTRY AND ABSTINENCE FROM EVERY PLEASURE	852B	LETTER 50	PROSE
ABSTRACT			
ENSLAVD THE VULGAR BY ATTEMPTING TO REALIZE OR ABSTRACT THE	153A	MARRIAGE HH 11	PROSE
THE HUMAN ABSTRACT	217A	HUMAN ABSTR/SE	TITLE
WHEN RINTRAH GAVE ABSTRACT PHILOSOPHY TO BRAMA IN THE EAST	245	SONG OF LOS 3	11
TO TRISMEGISTUS PALAMABRON GAVE AN ABSTRACT LAW	246	SONG OF LOS 3	18
SAID FUZON THIS ABSTRACT NON-ENTITY	249	AHANIA 2	11
IN ABSTRACT FALSE EXPANSES THAT HE MAY NOT HEAR THE VOICE	353	FOUR ZOAS 8	487
("REDUCED VARIETY OF NATURE TO ABSTRACT IDEA") WHAT FOLLY	460D	ANNO REYNOLDS	MARG
REFUSING ALL DEFINITE FORM THE ABSTRACT HORROR ROOFD STONY	482	MILTON 3	9
HARD			
ABSTRACT PHILOSOPHY WARRING IN ENMITY AGAINST IMAGINATION	624	JERUSALEM 5	58
FROM THEM THEY MAKE AN ABSTRACT WHICH IS A NEGATION . . .	629	JERUSALEM 10	10
AN ABSTRACT OBJECTING POWER THAT NEGATIVES EVERY THING . .	629	JERUSALEM 10	14
AND THE ABSTRACT VOIDS BETWEEN THE STARS ARE THE SATANIC	633	JERUSALEM 13	37
WHEELS			
BROODING ABSTRACT PHILOSOPHY TO DESTROY	709	JERUSALEM 70	19
INTO THE ABSTRACT VOID IT IS CALLED THE DIVINE MERCY .	784B	MANO WW EXCUR	MARG
& PROVE TO THE ABSTRACT PHILOSOPHERS	790D	LETTER 2	PROSE
I INTEND BECAUSE MY ABSTRACT FOLLY HURRIES ME OFTEN AWAY	809A	LETTER 20	PROSE
DID NOT HE IS ALSO A HAPPY ABSTRACT KNOWN BY ALL	809C	LETTER 20	PROSE
HIS FRIENDS			
THE CHIMNEY SWEEPER A LITTLE BLACK THING &C THE HUMAN	SUPP	LETTER 66A	*PROSE
ABSTRACT			
ABSTRACTED			
IT IS URIZEN BUT UNKNOWN ABSTRACTED	222	URIZEN 3	6
ABSTRACTED FROM THE ROOTS OF [NATURE] SCIENCE THEN INCLOSD	374	FOUR ZOAS 9	631
AROUND			
BUT THESE ARE NOT ABSTRACTED NOR COMPOUNDED FROM NATURE	459C	ANNO REYNOLDS	MARG
I NEVER SAW THEE TILL THIS TIME NOR BEHELD LIFE ABSTRACTED	659	JERUSALEM 33	31
("THE AEGYPTIANS") THEY ALSO CONSIDERD GOD AS ABSTRACTED	774A	ANNO BERKELEY	* MARG
ABSTRACTING			
HER ALSO INTIRELY ABSTRACTING HIMSELF FROM FEMALE LOVES	522	MILTON 33	16
ABSTRACTION			
THIS IS TRUE CHRISTIAN PHILOSOPHY FAR ABOVE ALL ABSTRACTION	65C	ANNO LAVATER	MARG
("ALL ABSTRACTION IS TEMPORARY FOLLY ") UNEASY	86D	ANNO LAVATER	MARG
WITH COLD FLOODS OF ABSTRACTION AND WITH FORESTS	193	V DAU ALBION 5	19
OF SOLITUDE			
FOR IN URIZEN'S SLUMBERS OF ABSTRACTION	252	AHANIA 4	11
AND TURNING [WISDOM] AFFECTION INTO FURY & THOUGHT INTO	324	FOUR ZOAS 7	155
ABSTRACTION			
COME FORTH FROM SLUMBERS OF THY COLD ABSTRACTION COME	360	FOUR ZOAS 9	129
FORTH			
AND BY ABSTRACTION OPPOSED TO THE VISIONS OF IMAGINATION	715	JERUSALEM 74	26
WHICH ARE NOT REAL IN A LAND OF ABSTRACTION WHERE SPECTRES	809A	LETTER 20	PROSE
SPIRIT OF ABSTRACTION & IMPROVIDENCE SUCH MY DEAR SIR .	809B	LETTER 20	PROSE
ABSTRUSE			
ABSTRUSE IN THOUGHT AND CONTEMPLATION NAKED SIMPLE . . .	577C	DESC CAT 5	PROSE
ABSURD			
("NATURAL IDEAS") HOW ABSURD THEN WOULD IT BE TO SAY . .	94C	ANNO SWED LOVE	MARG
HOW ABSURD MUST MEN BE TO UNDERSTAND HIM AS IF HE . . .	94C	ANNO SWED LOVE	MARG
HOW ABSURD	405D	ANNO BACON	MARG
HE STATES ABSURDITIES IN COMPANY WITH TRUTHS & CALLS BOTH	474A	ANNO REYNOLDS	MARG
ABSURD			
THIS ABSURD ASSERTION HAS DONE ME & MAY STILL DO ME .	602A	PUB ADDRESS/N	PROSE
ABSURD NONSENSE ABOUT DOTS & LOZENGES & CLEAN STROKES .	602A	PUB ADDRESS/N	PROSE
P S I DO NOT BELIEVE THAT THIS ABSURD OPINION EVER WAS .	602B	PUB ADDRESS/N	PROSE
SO HONEST AS TO EXPOSE TO YOU HIS WHOLE ABSURD PREJUDICE	838C	LETTER 37	PROSE
ABSURDITIES			
HE STATES ABSURDITIES IN COMPANY WITH TRUTHS & CALLS BOTH	474A	ANNO REYNOLDS	MARG
ABSURD			

		PAGE	TITLE	LINE

ABSURDITY
THIS NATURAL RELIGION THIS IMPOSSIBLE ABSURDITY . . . 532 MILTON 40 13
THESE MEN HAVE REPEATEDLY ASSERTED THIS ABSURDITY TO ME 592B PUB ADDRESS/N PROSE
ABUNDANCE
AN ABUNDANCE OF ENQUIRIES TO NO PURPOSE SAT HIMSELF DOWN 44B ISLAND MOON 1 PROSE
"PRIDE FULLNESS OF BREAD & ABUNDANCE OF IDLENESS" WAS THE 79D ANNO LAVATER MARG
SIN
FOR I PERCEIVE THOU HAST ABUNDANCE WHICH I CLAIM AS MINE 273 FOUR ZOAS 1 334
ABUNDANCE OF STUPIDITY . . . . 478A ANNO REYNOLDS MARG
WORK IN ABUNDANCE & IF GOD BLESSES ME WITH HEALTH . . . 835A LETTER 34 PROSE
ABUNDANT
OUTSPREAD WITH ABUNDANT RICHES AND HIS EMANATIONS . . . 668 JERUSALEM 40 54
WHERE THE HUMAN HARVEST WAVES ABUNDANT IN THE BEAMS OF EDEN 678 JERUSALEM 48 34
INDEED WITH SUCH ABUNDANT FELICITY IN THE MEETING HIM . 854B LETTER 53 PROSE
ABUNDANTLY
TO BUILD HER BOWERS FOR THE ELEMENTS BROUGHT FORTH 340 FOUR ZOAS 7B 277
ABUNDANTLY
ABUSE
THE GLITTERING DISSIMULATION ACHILLES' WRATH IS BLUNT ABUSE 384D ANNO WATSON MARG
ABUSIVE
THOUGHT THE SOLDIER ABUSIVE & IN AN INTOXICATION OF MIND 438D BLAKES MEMORAN PROSE
AFTER MANY ABUSIVE THREATS [FROM THEM] AGAINST ME & . . . 827B LETTER 28 PROSE
ABYSS
. . . TO PLANT BEAUTY IN THE DESERT CRAVING ABYSS THEY 136 FRENCH REVOLTN 55
GLEAM
& FORMED A HEAVEN OF WHAT HE STOLE FROM THE ABYSS . . . 150A MARRIAGE HH 5 PROSE
WHEN I CAME HOME ON THE ABYSS OF THE FIVE SENSES . . . . 150C MARRIAGE HH 6 PROSE
BY DEGREES WE BEHELD THE INFINITE ABYSS FIERY AS THE SMOKE 156A MARRIAGE HH 17 PROSE
AND SUNK MY HEART INTO THE ABYSS A RED ROUND GLOBE HOT 191 V DAU ALBION 2 33
BURNING
THE RAGING FATHOMLESS ABYSS ANON A SERPENT FOLDING . . . 196 AMERICA PREL 1 15
ARMD WITH DISEASES OF THE EARTH TO CAST UPON THE ABYSS . . 201 AMERICA 13 15
DEEP DOWN INTO THE ABYSS . . . . 228 URIZEN 11 4
AND HIS FEET STAMPD THE NETHER ABYSS . . . . 229 URIZEN 13 16
THE ABYSS OF LOS STRETCHD IMMENSE . . . . 230 URIZEN 15 5
IN THE ENDLESS ABYSS OF SPACE . . . . 231 URIZEN 15 10
TO DIVIDE THE ABYSS BENEATH . . . . 233 URIZEN 20 34
AND BEGAN TO EXPLORE THE ABYSS . . . . 234 URIZEN 20 40
SITTING IN FATHOMLESS ABYSS OF MY IMMORTAL SHRINE . . . 238 EUROPE PREL 2 2
OF NON-ENTITY HOW WIDE THE ABYSS . . . . 254 AHANIA 4 54
AND HIS FEET WHICH THE NETHER ABYSS . . . . 257 BOOK OF LOS 3 47
THEN ALOFT HIS HEAD REARD IN THE ABYSS . . . . 258 BOOK OF LOS 4 41
PALE HE BEHELD FUTURITY PALE HE BEHELD THE ABYSS . . . 280 FOUR ZOAS 2 15
TO BIND THE BODY OF MAN TO HEAVEN FROM FALLING INTO THE 287 FOUR ZOAS 2 267
ABYSS
THE NETHER ABYSS & GNASHING IN FIERCE DESPAIR PANTING 296 FOUR ZOAS 3 * 155
IN SOBS
FOR HER BRIGHT EYES BEHOLD THE ABYSS SOMETIMES A LITTLE 297 FOUR ZOAS 3 209
SLEEP
BUT THARMAS RODE ON THE DARK ABYSS THE VOICE OF THARMAS 297 FOUR ZOAS 4 1
ROLLD
IN STRENGTH & BRIGHTNESS FROM THE ABYSS HIS BOWELS YEARND 297 FOUR ZOAS 4 3
OVER THEM
BUT URIZEN SLEPT IN A STONED STUPOR IN THE NETHER ABYSS 302 FOUR ZOAS 4 170
A RED ROUND GLOBE HOT BURNING DEEP DEEP DOWN INTO THE 303 FOUR ZOAS 4 224
ABYSS
AND HIS FEET STAMPD THE NETHER ABYSS IN TREMBLING HOWLING 303 FOUR ZOAS 4 245
& DISMAY
INTO UNUSUAL FORMS DANCING & HOWLING STAMPING THE ABYSS 305 FOUR ZOAS 4 295
SOON AS HIS BURNING EYES WERE OPEND ON THE ABYSS . . . . 306 FOUR ZOAS 5 39
THAT DREW THE BODY OF MAN FROM HEAVEN INTO THIS DARK ABYSS 306 FOUR ZOAS 5 47
[AROUND THE ABYSS (DEFIANTLY) ?SHOUTING ALL HIS DEMONS] SUPP FOUR ZOAS 5 *
FOR URIZEN BEHELD THE TERRORS OF THE ABYSS WANDRING AMONG 314 FOUR ZOAS 6 * 87
[FOR URIZEN BEHELD THE TERRORS OF THE ABYSS WANDRING AMONG] 314 FOUR ZOAS 6 * 102
THEN DARTING INTO THE ABYSS OF NIGHT HIS VENTUROUS LIMBS 316 FOUR ZOAS 6 184
. . . & OVER THE SONS & DAUGHTERS OF LUVAH IN THE HORRIBLE 317 FOUR ZOAS 6 237
ABYSS
BUT THEY REFUSD BECAUSE THEIR OUTWARD FORMS WERE IN THE 318 FOUR ZOAS 6 253
ABYSS
OF ALL HIS WANDERING EXPERIMENTS IN THE HORRIBLE ABYSS . . 324 FOUR ZOAS 7 160
BENEATH THE TREE OF MYSTERY WHICH IN THE DISMAL ABYSS . . 325 FOUR ZOAS 7 212
INTO THE TEMPLE OF URIZEN TO GIVE LIGHT TO THE ABYSS . . 333 FOUR ZOAS 7B 35
MINGLED WITH HER DOLOROUS MEMBERS STREWN THRO THE ABYSS 338 FOUR ZOAS 7B 212
INTO A FORMLESS INDEFINITE & STREWING HER ON THE ABYSS . . 338 FOUR ZOAS 7B 217
WHERE HAST THOU HID HIM WHOM I LOVE IN WHAT REMOTE ABYSS 345 FOUR ZOAS 8 155
AND HIS IMMENSE TAIL LASHD THE ABYSS HIS HUMAN FORM A STONE 352 FOUR ZOAS 8 428
AND STILL HIS STONY FORM REMAIND IN THE ABYSS IMMENSE . . 352 FOUR ZOAS 8 432
HIS NECK FLAMES WITH WRATH & MAJESTY HE LASHES THE ABYSS 352 FOUR ZOAS 8 442
OFT DOTH HIS EYES EMERGE FROM THE ABYSS INTO THE REALMS 352 FOUR ZOAS 8 * 454
AND URIZEN REPENTANT FORGETS HIS WISDOM IN THE ABYSS . . 353 FOUR ZOAS 8 463
DART FORTH UPON THE WIND IN PIPES WRITHING ABOUT IN THE 353 FOUR ZOAS 8 473
ABYSS
REJOICE TO ONE ANOTHER LOUD THEIR VOICES SHAKE THE ABYSS 378 FOUR ZOAS 9 813
ARE DESCENDING INTO THE ABYSS IN WAILING & DESPAIR . . . 443A LAST JUDGMNT/L PROSE
THE ABYSS OF HELL WHICH OPENS [TO RECIEVE THEM] BENEATH 443C LAST JUDGMNT/L PROSE
DEEP DOWN INTO THE ABYSS PANTING CONGLOBING TREMBLING . . 482 MILTON 3 12
THE EYES BEHELD THE ABYSS LEST BONES OF SOLIDNESS FREEZE 482 MILTON 3 15
OVER ALL
STAMPD THE NETHER ABYSS IN TREMBLING & HOWLING & DISMAY 483 MILTON 3 26
TERRIFIED LOS STOOD IN THE ABYSS & HIS IMMORTAL LIMBS . . 483 MILTON 3 28
THE NETHER ABYSS IN TREMBLINGS HE WEPT OVER IT HE CHERISHD 483 MILTON 3 32
IT

<pre>
                                                                PAGE   TITLE   LINE
ABYSS   (CONTINUED)
        A BLUE FLUID EXUDED IN SINEWS HARDENING IN THE ABYSS   .   . 483 MILTON 3   35
        OF THE ASSEMBLY IN SATAN'S BOSOM A VAST UNFATHOMABLE ABYSS   490 MILTON 9   35
        FALLING INTO THE ABYSS SIN IS ALSO REPRESENTED AS A FEMALE 606C V LAST JUDG/N   PROSE
        PRECIPITATING HIMSELF INTO THE ABYSS . . . . 606C V LAST JUDG/N   PROSE
        AND DRAW THEE DOWN INTO THIS ABYSS OF SORROW AND TORTURE   646 JERUSALEM 23   39
        AND BUILD A WORLD OF PHANTASY UPON MY GREAT ABYSS .   .   . 685 JERUSALEM 54   23
        A LONG SERPENT IN THE ABYSS OF THE SPECTRE WHICH AUGMENTED   685 JERUSALEM 54   29
        AND SOMETIMES THE EARTH SHALL ROLL IN THE ABYSS & SOMETIMES   728 JERUSALEM 83   40
        INTO THE BOTTOMLESS ABYSS WHOSE TORMENT ARISES FOR EVER   781 GHOST ABEL 2   21
           & EVER
        WHICH I BELIEVE IS NOW FOR EVER FALLEN INTO THE ABYSS   . . 835A LETTER 34   PROSE
ABYSSAL
        A CONCAVE EARTH WONDROUS CHASMAL ABYSSAL INCOHERENT   .   .   634 JERUSALEM 13   53
        NOT YET FORMED BUT A WRETCHED TORMENT UNFORMED & ABYSSAL   692 JERUSALEM 60   4
ABYSSES
        THE ENORMOUS WONDERS OF THE ABYSSES ONCE HIS BRIGHTEST JOY   314 FOUR ZOAS 6   86
        BY ROCKY MASSES FROWNING IN THE ABYSSES REVOLVING ERRATIC   316 FOUR ZOAS 6   178
        WITHIN THE DARK HORRORS OF THE ABYSSES LION OR TYGER OR   318 FOUR ZOAS 6   251
           SCORPION
        RAN THRO THE ABYSSES RENDING THE WEB TORMENT ON TORMENT   .   318 FOUR ZOAS 6   259
        FROM DARK ABYSSES OF THE TIMES REMOTE FATED TO BE .   .   . 345 FOUR ZOAS 8   150
        AMONG THE STARS THE EARTH & ALL THE ABYSSES FEEL ?HIS FURY   352 FOUR ZOAS 8   *   448
        INTO THE ABYSSES OF HIS BOSOM THE VESSELS OF HIS BLOOD   .   353 FOUR ZOAS 8   *   472
        STRENGTH FROM THE EARTHS CONSUMD & HEAVENS & ALL HIDDEN   358 FOUR ZOAS 9   *   38
           ABYSSES
        IN CHASMS & ABYSSES OF SORROW ENLARGD WITHOUT DIMENSION   623 JERUSALEM 5   5
           TERRIBLE
        & IN THE ABYSSES OF THE ACCUSER MY ENTHUSIASM IS STILL   .   816A LETTER 23   PROSE
ACADEMICAL
        I INCLOSE LIKEWISE THE ACADEMICAL CORRESPONDENCE OF .   .   836D LETTER 35   PROSE
ACADEMY
        & MICHAEL ANGELO IN THE LIBRARY OF THE ROYAL ACADEMY   .   449C ANNO REYNOLDS   MARG
        I CONSIDER REYNOLDS'S DISCOURSES TO THE ROYAL ACADEMY   .   452A ANNO REYNOLDS   MARG
        TO THE ROYAL ACADEMY   .   .   .   . 543A TO ROYL ACAD/N   TITLE
        ARE REGULARLY REFUSED TO BE EXHIBITED BY THE ROYAL ACADEMY 561B EXHIBITION ADV   PROSE
           AND
        TO THE ROYAL ACADEMY WILL SHEW THAT THE VENETIAN FINESSE   814B LETTER 23   PROSE
        FUSELI IS MADE MASTER OF THE ROYAL ACADEMY .   .   .   .   859D LETTER 56   PROSE
        AT THE ROYAL ACADEMY ON THE OCCASION OF BANKS'S DEATH   .   859D LETTER 56   *PROSE
        YOU WILL BE PLEASED TO SEE THAT THE ROYAL ACADEMY HAVE .   861D LETTER 59   PROSE
        COUNT UGOLINO BY MR FUSELI IN THE ROYAL ACADEMY EXHIBITION 863D LETTER 61   PROSE
ACADEMYS
        AND THE ROYAL ACADEMY'S DIRECTORS . . . . 543 TO ROYL ACAD/N   4
ACCENTS
        [FROM HIS DRY TONGUE THESE ACCENTS FLOW] .   .   .   .   . 419 I SAW A MONK/N *   25
        AND IN MELODIOUS ACCENTS I .   .   .   . 600 MELODIOUS/PA   1
ACCEPT
        ACCEPT THEM YOURSELF & BELIEVE ME FOR EVER .   .   .   .   803C LETTER 15   PROSE
        ACCEPT MINE ALSO & BELIEVE ME TO REMAIN YOUR DEVOTED   .   808C LETTER 19   PROSE
        WELFARE OF YOUR FAMILY ACCEPT MY SINCERE LOVE & RESPECT   816A LETTER 23   PROSE
        ACCEPT OF MY THANKS FOR YOUR KIND & HEARTENING LETTER   .   822B LETTER 26   PROSE
        EXCUSE MY PERHAPS TOO GREAT ENTHUSIASM PLEASE TO ACCEPT OF 823C LETTER 26   PROSE
        PRAY GIVE MY & MY WIFE'S DUTIES TO MISS POOLE ACCEPT THEM   834A LETTER 33   PROSE
        ACCEPT ALSO OF MY THANKS FOR COWPER'S THIRD VOLUME .   .   844C LETTER 43   PROSE
        PRAY ACCEPT MY & MY WIFE'S SINCEREST AFFECTION & BELIEVE   857C LETTER 54   PROSE
        PRAY ACCEPT MY AND MY WIFE'S SINCEREST LOVE AND GRATITUDE   861B LETTER 58   PROSE
        MISS DENMAN'S SERVICE IF SHE WILL ACCEPT OF THEM WHAT   .   877B LETTER 86   PROSE
ACCEPTABLE
        WOULD BE ACCEPTABLE AT ALL TIMES BUT ESPECIALLY AT THE   844A LETTER 43   PROSE
           PRESENT
ACCEPTED
        NOR HIS ACCEPTED BRETHREN WHOM TYRANT HE CALLS FREE   .   . 160A SONG LIBERTY   PROSE
        YOU HAD ACCEPTED THE SPIRIT OF P'S(PHILLIPS') INTENTION   842C LETTER 42   PROSE
ACCIDENT
        IT IS NOT HIS GENIUS BUT AN ACCIDENT ACQUIRED FOR HOW   .   81D ANNO LAVATER   MARG
        CAN SUBSTANCE AND ACCIDENT BE PREDICATED OF THE SAME   81D ANNO LAVATER   MARG
           ESSENCE
        I CANNOT CONCIEVE BUT SUBSTANCE GIVES TINCTURE TO   81D ANNO LAVATER   MARG
           THE ACCIDENT
        & THAT IS HE MAKES EVERY THING ORIGINATE IN ITS ACCIDENT   88C ANNO LAVATER   MARG
        & ITS OWN EFFECT ACCIDENT IS THE OMISSION OF ACT IN SELF &   88D ANNO LAVATER   MARG
        ACCIDENT BROUGHT ON BY A MAN'S OWN CARELESSNESS .   .   . 388B ANNO WATSON   MARG
        WHAT IS FORTUNE BUT AN OUTWARD ACCIDENT FOR A FEW YEARS   409B ANNO BACON   MARG
        FOR THE COUNTESS OF EGREMONT [BY A HAPPY ACCIDENT] .   .   442D LAST JUDGMNT/L   PROSE
        BUT IN THE NERVES OF THE NOSTRILS ACCIDENT BEING FORMED   517 MILTON 29   35
        NOTHING NEW OCCURS IN IDENTICAL EXISTENCE ACCIDENT EVER   567C DESC CAT 3   PROSE
           VARIES
        LAMENTABLE ACCIDENT AND ERROR OF THE MORTAL AND .   .   . 579D DESC CAT 5   PROSE
        NOTHING NEW OCCURS IN IDENTICAL EXISTENCE ACCIDENT EVER   589A CHAUCER/N   PROSE
           VARIES
        TO BE THE SPORT OF ACCIDENT TO WASTE IN WRATH & LOVE A   647 JERUSALEM 24   15
           WEARY
        AND ACCIDENT & CHANCE WERE FOUND HIDDEN IN LENGTH BREDTH   663 JERUSALEM 36   35
           & HIGHTH
        TO EXCEPTION & NOT TO RULE TO ACCIDENT & NOT TO SUBSTANCE   778C HOMERS POETRY   PROSE
        WITHOUT ACCIDENT OR HINDRANCE THO IT WAS BETWEEN ELEVEN   803A LETTER 15   PROSE
ACCIDENTAL
        MINUTE DISCRIMINATION IS NOT ACCIDENTAL .   .   .   .   . 453B ANNO REYNOLDS   MARG
ACCIDENTALLY
        WITH WHOM I ACCIDENTALLY MET IN THE STRAND HE SAYS .   .   850B LETTER 49   PROSE
</pre>

```
                                                              PAGE    TITLE         LINE
ACCIDENTS
      AGE & YOUTH ARE NOT CLASSES BUT [ACCIDENTS] [SITUATIONS]  460C ANNO REYNOLDS  * MARG
        PROPERTIES
ACCOMODATE
      AT HIS HOUSE LET US ACCOMODATE HIM IN WHAT IS INDIFFERENT  868B LETTER 67      PROSE
ACCOMODATED
      I HAVE HOWEVER SOMEWHAT ACCOMODATED MY FIGURE OF TIME  . . 614D V LAST JUDG/N  PROSE
ACCOMODATION
      ACCOMODATION OF THOSE WHO GIVE IT THE HONOR OF ATTENTION   442D LAST JUDGMNT/L PROSE
      ACCOMODATION IN MY POWER TO RECIEVE YOU & MRS BUTTS . . .  808B LETTER 19      PROSE
      MY HEARTIEST THANKS FOR YOUR CARE IN MY ACCOMODATION  . . 872D LETTER 76      PROSE
ACCOMODATIONS
      NECESSARIES ACCOMODATIONS & ORNAMENTS ARE THE WHOLE OF LIFE 446C ANNO REYNOLDS  MARG
      SATAN TOOK AWAY ORNAMENT FIRST NEXT HE TOOK AWAY          446C ANNO REYNOLDS  MARG
        ACCOMODATIONS
      NOT SO DESTITUTE OF ACCOMODATIONS TO OUR WANTS AS         806B LETTER 16      PROSE
        I EXPECTED
      & ROOMS & ACCOMODATIONS ARE EASILY PROCURD BY ONE  . . . 808B LETTER 19      PROSE
      [NECESSARIES ACCOMODATIONS & ORNAMENTS ARE LIFE'S WANTS]  SUPP ANNO REYNOLDS  * MARG
ACCOMPANIED
      NOT UNBECOMING IN HER BEING ACCOMPANIED WITH  . . . . .   568B DESC CAT 3      PROSE
      THE UGLY LIKEWISE WHEN ACCOMPANIED AND  . . . . . . .     580A DESC CAT 5      PROSE
      PECULIAR TO MR B'S(BLAKE'S) PRINTS WILL BE HERE FOUND     588A CHAUCER/N      PROSE
        ACCOMPANIED
      FOR INVENTION & DRAWING HAS GENERALLY BEEN ACCOMPANIED BY  602A PUB ADDRESS/N  PROSE
      LEARNING & SCIENCE WHICH ACCOMPANIED ADAM OUT OF EDEN  . . 611D V LAST JUDG/N  PROSE
      A VERY COMFORTABLE COACH & I MAY SAY I ACCOMPANIED HIM PART 869C LETTER 70     PROSE
      ACCOMPANIED BY ALL THE OLD SYMPTOMS I AM DEAR SIR YOURS    880A LETTER 90      PROSE
        SINCERELY
ACCOMPANIMENT
      WOULD BE AN APPROPRIATE ACCOMPANIMENT TO THE LIFE OF ROMNEY 832C LETTER 32     PROSE
ACCOMPANIMENTS
      BEING WITH THEIR ACCOMPANIMENTS TERRIFIC AND  . . . . .   565D DESC CAT 2      PROSE
      WITH CERTAIN HUMOUROUS ACCOMPANIMENTS IN HIS CHARACTER  . . 568D DESC CAT 3     *PROSE
      BUT ALSO WITH OTHER ACCOMPANIMENTS NOT SO RESPECTABLE  . . 568D DESC CAT 3      PROSE
ACCOMPANY
      ACCOMPANY THEM DOWN TO THE ULRO WITH SOFT MELODIOUS TEARS   524 MILTON 34        21
      WILL NONE ACCOMPANY ME IN MY DEATH OR BE A RANSOM FOR ME    666 JERUSALEM 39     19
      PORTRAITS WHICH ACCOMPANY THE LIFE OF COWPER  . . . . .   860C LETTER 56      PROSE
      BEST THINGS FOR THEY WHEN PRINTED PERFECT ACCOMPANY  . .  867A LETTER 66      PROSE
ACCOMPANYING
      OF SOUNDS OF SPIRITUAL MUSIC AND ITS ACCOMPANYING  . . .  576B DESC CAT 4      PROSE
      ARE UNACQUAINTED WITH DRAWING [& THE ACCOMPANYING]  . . . 591B PUB ADDRESS/N   PROSE
      ACCOMPANYING DEATHLY FEEL I GOT AGAIN INTO A PERSPIRATION  872B LETTER 75      PROSE
ACCOMPLISH
      I LABOUR INCESSANTLY & ACCOMPLISH NOT ONE HALF OF WHAT  . . 809A LETTER 20      PROSE
      & AM HARD AT IT TO ACCOMPLISH IN TIME WHAT I INTEND  . .  859B LETTER 56      PROSE
ACCOMPLISHD
      (VENETIANS) THEY ACCOMPLISHD NOTHING  . . . . . . . .     462D ANNO REYNOLDS   MARG
      ACCOMPLISHD IN THIS WORLD OF SORROW MILTON'S ANGEL KNEW    504 MILTON 21        52
      DEAR FLAXMAN I REJOICE TO HEAR THAT YOUR GREAT WORK IS    810C LETTER 21      PROSE
        ACCOMPLISHD
      OF REAL CONSEQUENCE I HAVE ACCOMPLISHD BY COMING  . . .   812A LETTER 22      PROSE
      TILL MY THREE YEARS SHOULD BE ALMOST ACCOMPLISHD  . . .   825D LETTER 27      PROSE
      OF EMPLOYMENT THIS WISH I FEAR IS NOT TO BE ACCOMPLISHD    830B LETTER 30      PROSE
      & ROMAN CANNOT EXIST THIS WILL BE SHORTLY ACCOMPLISHD  . . 866B LETTER 64      PROSE
ACCOMPLISHMENTS
      HUMANE & POLITE ACCOMPLISHMENTS SUCH HAVE  . . . . . .    810D LETTER 21      PROSE
ACCORD
      AROUND THE STARRY EIGHT WITH ONE ACCORD THE STARRY EIGHT   534 MILTON 42        10
        BECAME
      THE HORSES HE HAS ALSO VARIED TO ACCORD TO THEIR RIDERS   567D DESC CAT 3      PROSE
      THE HORSES HE HAS VARIED TO ACCORD TO THEIR RIDERS  . .   590D CHAUCER 2       PROSE
      WITH ONE ACCORD IN LOVE SUBLIME & AS ON CHERUBS WINGS  .   674 JERUSALEM 44      1
      AND FEELING THE DAMPS OF DEATH THEY WITH ONE ACCORD        674 JERUSALEM 44     28
        DELEGATED LOS
ACCORDANT
      ACCORDANT WITH THE HORRID LABOURS MAKE SWEET MELODY  . .   509 MILTON 24        57
ACCORDING
      EACH CLAD IN GLORY ACCORDING TO HIS SPHERE  . . . . . .    18 EDW THIRD/PS 1    34
      SIR SAID THE ANTIQUARIAN ACCORDING TO MY OPINION  . . . .  44D ISLAND MOON 1   PROSE
      GOD DESCENDING ACCORDING TO THE WEAKNESS OF MAN  . . . .   87B ANNO LAVATER    MARG
      FALSE PHILOSOPHY ACCORDING TO THE LETTER  . . . . . . .    92B ANNO SWED LOVE  MARG
      BUT TRUE ACCORDING TO THE SPIRIT  . . . . . . . . .       92B ANNO SWED LOVE  MARG
      THIS IS CERTAINLY NOT TO BE UNDERSTOOD ACCORDING TO THE    92D ANNO SWED LOVE  MARG
        LETTER
      ACCORDING TO THE PROVERB THE WEAK IN COURAGE IS STRONG    155A MARRIAGE HH 15  PROSE
        IN CUNNING
      EACH ACCORDING TO HIS GENIUS AND LOVING THE GREATEST MEN  158B MARRIAGE HH 22  PROSE
        BEST
      THE ANCIENT BRITONS ACCORDING TO CAESAR [THE FRONTISPIECE] 208C SUBJCTS HIST/N TITLE
      ACCORDING TO THEIR VARIOUS POWERS SUBORDINATE TO URIZEN    287 FOUR ZOAS 2     270
      ACCORDING TO THE WILL OF LUVAH WHO ASSUMD THE PLACE  . .   326 FOUR ZOAS 7     263
      IN HEAD OR HEART OR REINS ACCORDING TO THE FITTEST ORDER   342 FOUR ZOAS 8      59
      MIGHT ACT ACCORDING TO THEIR FORMS BY INNATE CRUELTY  .    344 FOUR ZOAS 8     134
      TO EACH ACCORDING TO TO THE MULTIPLICATION OF THEIR        350 FOUR ZOAS 8   * 367
        MULTITUDES
      IN HEAD OR HEART OR REINS ACCORDING TO THE FITTEST ORDER   382 FOUR ZOAS AD 6   28
      DOES GOD LOVE THE RIGHTEOUS ACCORDING TO THE GOSPEL  . .  396A ANNO WATSON     MARG
      ACCORDING TO REYNOLDS MICH ANGELO WAS WORSE STILL &  . .  467B ANNO REYNOLDS   MARG
      PRINCIPLES ACCORDING TO SR JOSHUA BECOME DEFECTS  . . .   477A ANNO REYNOLDS   MARG
      ACCORDING TO THE INSPIRATION OF THE POETIC GENIUS  . .    495 MILTON 14          1
```

	PAGE	TITLE	LINE

ACCORDING   (CONTINUED)

YOU SHALL BIND THEM IN THREE CLASSES ACCORDING TO THEIR   510 MILTON 25   27
CLASSES
THE COSTUME IS CORRECT ACCORDING TO AUTHENTIC MONUMENTS   567D DESC CAT 3   PROSE
AND IS SERVED BY NONE HE IS ACCORDING TO CHRIST'S   570B DESC CAT 3   PROSE
DEFINITION
ACCORDING TO HIS PROSPECTUS HE HAS THREE MONKS THESE HE   574A DESC CAT 3   PROSE
THE COSTUME IS CORRECT ACCORDING TO AUTHENTIC MONUMENTS   590D CHAUCER 2   PROSE
UNDERSTAND DRAWING & WHICH ACCORDING TO HEATH & STOTHARD   592B PUB ADDRESS/N   PROSE
ACCORDING TO THE SITUATION HE HOLDS   604C V LAST JUDG/N   PROSE
RETURNS [ACCORDING TO] BY THE SEED OF CONTEMPLATIVE THOUGHT 605B V LAST JUDG/N   PROSE
ACCORDING TO [THEIR AGGREGATE IMAGINATIONS] A CERTAIN ORDER 606A V LAST JUDG/N   *PROSE
PERSONAGES ACCORDING TO THE DESCRIPTIONS IN THE PROPHETS   608C V LAST JUDG/N   PROSE
FORMING THE SPECTRES OF ALBION ACCORDING TO HIS RAGE   . . 626 JERUSALEM 7   41
TO WEAVE JERUSALEM A BODY ACCORDING TO HER WILL .   .   .   722 JERUSALEM 80   35
ACCORDING TO HIS CHANGES SHE ROLLD HIS KIDNEYS ROUND   . . 723 JERUSALEM 80   72
THE INVISIBLE LOVELY ONE GIVING HIM A FORM ACCORDING TO   723 JERUSALEM 80   78
TO FORM THE MIGHTY FORM OF HAND ACCORDING TO HER WILL   . . 726 JERUSALEM 82   63
FORMING THE FLUCTUATING GLOBE ACCORDING TO THEIR WILL   . . 727 JERUSALEM 83   34
ACCORDING AS THEY WEAVE THE LITTLE EMBRYON NERVES & VEINS   728 JERUSALEM 83   35
ACCORDING TO THE WILL OF THE LOVELY DAUGHTERS OF ALBION   728 JERUSALEM 83   42
ACCORDING TO THEIR WILL THE OUTSIDE SURFACE OF THE EARTH   728 JERUSALEM 83   46
IN OTHER MEN & LOVING THE GREATEST MEN BEST EACH ACCORDING   738 JERUSALEM 91   9
LIKE TO A CURTAIN & FOLDING THEM ACCORDING TO HIS WILL . . 738 JERUSALEM 91   34
THEN THOU WILT CREATE ANOTHER FEMALE ACCORDING TO THY WILL   739 JERUSALEM 92   12
ACCORDING TO THE HUMAN NERVES OF SENSATION .   .   .   . . 745 JERUSALEM 98   15
CREATING SPACE CREATING TIME ACCORDING TO THE WONDERS   746 JERUSALEM 98   31
DIVINE
ACCORDING TO THE SUBJECT OF DISCOURSE & EVERY WORD & EVERY   746 JERUSALEM 98   35
CHARACTER
WAS HUMAN ACCORDING TO THE EXPANSION OR CONTRACTION .   .   746 JERUSALEM 98   36
WHICH VARY ACCORDING AS THE ORGANS OF PERCEPTION VARY   746 JERUSALEM 98   38
& THEY WALKED
AND SEEING ACCORDING TO FITNESS & ORDER AND I HEARD JEHOVAH 746 JERUSALEM 98   40
SPEAK
. . . ACCORDING TO [THY] THE COVENANT [OF] JEHOVAH THEY CRY 746 JERUSALEM 98   *   45
US & WITH US ACCORDING TO HIS DIVINE WILL FOR OUR GOOD . . 802C LETTER 14   PROSE
ACCORDING TO YOUR DESIRE I SEND PROOFS OF THE   .   .   . . 838A LETTER 37   PROSE
ITS DEFICIENCY OR TO NEW CREATE IT ACCORDING TO YOUR WISH   860C LETTER 56   PROSE
EACH ACCORDING TO ITS RANK & THAT THEY WOULD KNOW THAT . . 863A LETTER 60   PROSE

ACCORDINGLY

OUGHT TO BE CONTEMND & I ACCORDINGLY HOLD REYNOLDS   .   . . 467A ANNO REYNOLDS   MARG
ACCORDINGLY CHAUCER HAS MADE HIS MONK A GREAT TRAGEDIAN . . 569A DESC CAT 3   PROSE
ACCORDINGLY THE PAINTER HAS GIVEN IN HIS BEAUTIFUL MAN   . . 580A DESC CAT 5   PROSE
& DISGUST [A] & ACCORDINGLY .   .   .   . 596B PUB ADDRESS/N   *PROSE
HE IS THE WATER OF LIFE ACCORDINGLY   .   .   .   . 612D V LAST JUDG/N   PROSE
GOD AS TO GET OUT & HAVE ACCORDINGLY BEEN TO MR WALKER'S   834B LETTER 34   PROSE
& THAT YOU HAD ACCORDINGLY NOMINATED ONE OF YOUR FRIENDS   842C LETTER 42   *PROSE
MEN & ACCORDINGLY HAVE GIVEN A LOOK OVER MY ACCOUNT BOOK   854C LETTER 53   PROSE
ACCORDINGLY I DID NOT SAY THAT I KNEW OF ANY POEM BUT   . . 857A LETTER 54   PROSE

ACCORDS

IN WHICH HE SAYS IT ACCORDS NOT WITH HIS INTENTIONS .   . . 794D LETTER 6   PROSE

ACCOST

NOW DIREFUL PAINS ACCOST HER AND STILL PREGNANT   .   .   . . 41C THEN SHE BORE   PROSE
& GOLDEN PLEASURES BEAM AROUND MY HEAD WHY GRIEF DOST THOU   43B WOE CRIED MUSE   PROSE
ACCOST ME

ACCOUNT

SEE N...WORLDS IN UNIVERSE FOR ACCOUNT OF INSTRUCTING   SUPP ANNO SWED HELL * MARG
SPIRITS
BUT THE DEVIL'S ACCOUNT IS THAT THE MESSIAH FELL .   .   . . 150A MARRIAGE HH 5   PROSE
AND UNPOLLUTED & WILL BRING TO RIGID STRICT ACCOUNT .   .   . 268 FOUR ZOAS 1   152
OF SUN MOON OR STARS IS STRANGE ON A CONTRARY ACCOUNT   .   . 390A ANNO WATSON   MARG
IT IS NECESSARY TO GIVE SOME ACCOUNT OF   .   .   .   .   . . 442D LAST JUDGMNT/L   PROSE
IF YOU ACCOUNT IT WISDOM WHEN YOU ARE ANGRY TO BE SILENT   483 MILTON 4   6
AND
NOT TO SHEW IT I DO NOT ACCOUNT THAT WISDOM BUT FOLLY   . . 483 MILTON 4   7
BE WORTHY OF ATTENTION NOT ONLY ON ACCOUNT OF ITS   582B DESC CAT 9   PROSE
COMPOSITION
BY RESPECTABLE MEN OF OTHER COUNTRIES ON ACCOUNT OF ART   584B DESC CAT 14   PROSE
I ACCOUNT IT A PUBLIC DUTY RESPECTFULLY TO ADDRESS MYSELF   591C PUB ADDRESS/N   PROSE
& TAKING ACCOUNT OF THE NUMBERS WHO ARISE IS THAT   .   . . 610A V LAST JUDG/N   PROSE
ON ACCOUNT OF OUR LEAVING THE DIVINE HARVEST TO THE ENEMY   716C JERUSALEM 77   *PROSE
ON ACCOUNT OF NOT ACKNOWLEDGING YOUR FRIENDSHIP TO ME   . . 791A LETTER 3   PROSE
WHICH WILL ACCOUNT FOR THE DIFFERENCE OF PRICE AS ALSO THAT   794B LETTER 5   PROSE
ACCOUNT & WHATEVER ELSE I CAN FINISH .   .   .   . 803D LETTER 15   PROSE
VERY BEAUTIFUL & ENCOURAGING VERSES WHICH I ACCOUNT .   . . 804A LETTER 16   PROSE
NOT ONLY ON ACCOUNT OF MR HAYLEY'S COMPOSITION BUT ALSO   810A LETTER 20   PROSE
BUT I SHOULD NOT HAVE TROUBLED YOU WITH THIS ACCOUNT OF   813A LETTER 22   PROSE
I HAVE INCLOSED THE ACCOUNT OF MONEY RECIEVD & WORK DONE   816A LETTER 23   PROSE
ACCOUNT THAT THE REMAINING NUMBER OF DRAWINGS .   .   .   . . 816C LETTER 24   PROSE
DEAR BROTHER YOUR LETTER MENTIONING MR BUTTS'S ACCOUNT OF   819B LETTER 25   *PROSE
MY AGUE
BE NOT THEN UNEASY ON ANY ACCOUNT & TELL MY SISTER NOT   819D LETTER 25   PROSE
TO BE
THIS I BELIEVE ABOUT BALANCES OUR ACCOUNT   .   .   .   .   . . 826B LETTER 28   PROSE
TROUBLE YOU TAKE ON MY ACCOUNT I TRUST WILL BE RECOMPENSED   826C LETTER 28   PROSE
ON ACCOUNT OF SEDITION WAS UTTERD AT THAT TIME   .   .   . . 827B LETTER 28   PROSE
NO EXPRESSION OF THREATENING ON ACCOUNT OF SEDITION .   . . 827C LETTER 28   PROSE
WITH AN ACCOUNT OF HIS SAFE ARRIVAL WHICH WILL EXCUSE HIS   829C LETTER 30   PROSE
YOU HAVE & MUST SUFFER MORE ON MY ACCOUNT THAN I SHALL EVER   829C LETTER 30   PROSE
THEM ON A SMALLER SCALE WHICH HE DECLINED ON ACCOUNT OF ITS   831C LETTER 31   PROSE
I WISH I COULD GIVE YOU A PLEASANT ACCOUNT OF OUR BELOVED   836B LETTER 35   PROSE

	PAGE	TITLE	LINE

ACCOUNT   (CONTINUED)
```
    I SEND MY PROOFS TO GIVE AS GOOD AN ACCOUNT OF MR WALKER        837B LETTER 35        PROSE
    HEAR THE SAME GOOD ACCOUNT OF OUR MOST ADMIRABLE  .  .  .  .    838C LETTER 37        PROSE
    THAT HIS MULTIPLICITY OF BUSINESS MAY VERY WELL ACCOUNT FOR     842D LETTER 42        PROSE
    ACCOUNT OF ITS EXPANDED MEADOWS BUT ALSO ON ACCOUNT OF ITS      847C LETTER 44        PROSE
    EXPECT A FULL ACCOUNT OF ALL HE CAN COLLECT MR SANDERS  .  .    847D LETTER 44        PROSE
    THIS IS MR PARKER'S ACCOUNT OF THE MATTER & PERHAPS MAY         848C LETTER 45        PROSE
    OF SINCERE SORROW ON ACCOUNT OF THE BELOVED COUNCILLOR  .  .  . 851C LETTER 50        PROSE
    MEN & ACCORDINGLY HAVE GIVEN A LOOK OVER MY ACCOUNT BOOK        854C LETTER 53        PROSE
    RECIEVD FROM YOU & THO I NEVER CAN BALANCE THE ACCOUNT  .  .    854C LETTER 53        PROSE
    ACCOUNT I AM THEREFORE THAT (TWELVE) GUINEAS IN YOUR DEBT       854D LETTER 53        PROSE
    PROPOSING THE BALLADS TO HIM ON MY ACCOUNT AND INFORM YOU       858B LETTER 55        PROSE
    I CANNOT GIVE YOU ANY ACCOUNT OF OUR BALLADS  .  .  .  .  .     862A LETTER 59        PROSE
    ON ACCOUNT OF THAT VERY COLOURING WHICH OUR CRITIC CALLS        864C LETTER 61        PROSE
      BLACK
    BEGUN TO PRINT AN ACCOUNT OF MY VARIOUS INVENTIONS IN ART       865D LETTER 63        PROSE
    GRATEFUL THO NOT ABLE ON ACCOUNT OF THIS ABOMINABLE AGUE        868D LETTER 68        PROSE
    ON ACCOUNT I HAVE RECIEVD A LETTER FROM MR CUMBERLAND  .  .  .  876D LETTER 85        PROSE
    ON ACCOUNT OF TEACHING YOUR SON AT...TO COMMENCE THIS DAY       SUPP LETTER 56A      *PROSE
    RECIEVED MARCH...THE SUM OF...ON ACCOUNT  .  .  .  .  .  .      SUPP LETTER 61E      *PROSE
    RECIEVD...OF MR LINNELL THE SUM OF FIVE POUNDS ON ACCOUNT       SUPP LETTER 66C      *PROSE
    THE BALANCE OF ACCOUNT OF MR UPTON'S PLATE  .  .  .  .  .       SUPP LETTER 66F      *PROSE
ACCOUNTED
    VOLUPTUOUSNESS AND FOLLY BEGAN TO BE ACCOUNTED BEAUTIFUL        568B DESC CAT 3       PROSE
    ACCOUNTED IGNORANT OF THAT EPIGRAMMATIC WIT IN ART  .  .  .     599A PUB ADDRESS/N    PROSE
    STATES IN WHICH ALL VISIONARY MEN ARE ACCOUNTED MAD MEN         777B INSC LAOCOON     PROSE
ACCOUNTS
    THE ACCOUNTS OF NORTH AMERICAN SAVAGES AS THEY ARE CALLD        389C ANNO WATSON      MARG
    PLACE YET I DO NOT REPENT OF COMING ON A THOUSAND ACCOUNTS      811C LETTER 22        PROSE
    ON TWO ACCOUNTS FIRST I OMITTED TO DESIRE YOU WOULD COME        870C LETTER 72        PROSE
    I BEGIN TO AGAIN FEEL RETURNING STRENGTH ON THESE ACCOUNTS      874D LETTER 80        PROSE
ACCT
    CASH ON ACCT OF PLATES IN THE FOREGOING AGREEMENT  .  .  .      SUPP LETTER 67D      *PROSE
ACCUMULATE
    SCOFELD & KOX ARE LET LOOSE UPON MY SAXONS THEY ACCUMULATE      673 JERUSALEM 43        51
    YOU ACCUMULATE PARTICULARS & MURDER BY ANALYZING THAT YOU       738 JERUSALEM 91        27
    IT WILL ROB & PLUNDER & ACCUMULATE INTO ONE PLACE  .  .         778D HOMERS POETRY    PROSE
ACCUMULATED
    IN FORTUITOUS CONCOURSE OF MEMORYS ACCUMULATED & LOST  .  .     659 JERUSALEM 33         8
ACCUMULATES
    A BLACK WATER ACCUMULATES RETURN ALBION RETURN  .  .  .  .      622 JERUSALEM 4         10
    SURPASSED BUT EVERY MOMENT IT ACCUMULATES MORE & MORE  .  .     630 JERUSALEM 10        45
ACCUMULATING
    IT CONTINUES ACCUMULATING TO ETERNITY THE JOYS OF              630 JERUSALEM 10        46
      GOD ADVANCE
    ACCUMULATING WITHOUT END HERE LOS WHO IS OF THE ELOHIM  .  .    713 JERUSALEM 73        24
ACCUMULATION
    STRENGTH CONSISTS IN ACCUMULATION OF POWER TO THE  .  .  .     580B DESC CAT 5       PROSE
ACCURSD
    ENQUIRE OF MY DAUGHTERS WHO ACCURSD IN THE DARK DEPTHS  .  .    322 FOUR ZOAS 7         92
ACCURSED
    WAS REFT OF LIFE BY THE ACCURSED DUKE  .  .  .  .  .  .  .        5 FAIR ELENOR/PS      63
    ACCURSED RACE OF TIRIEL BEHOLD YOUR [ AGED ] FATHER  .  .  .     99 TIRIEL 1             7
    COME FORTH & LOOK ON HER THAT BORE YOU COME YOU ACCURSED         99 TIRIEL 1             8
      SONS
    WHY SHOULD THY SONS CARE FOR THY CURSES THOU ACCURSED MAN        99 TIRIEL 1            16
    LISTEN & HEAR YOUR MOTHER'S GROANS NO MORE ACCURSED SONS         99 TIRIEL 1            24
    AND WHEN THE SHAKING CEAST A FOG POSSEST THE ACCURSED CLIME     106 TIRIEL 5            17
    O LEAGUED WITH EVIL SPIRITS THOU ACCURSED MAN OF SIN  .  .      107 TIRIEL 6            13
    .  .  . THE HOLY BESIDE THE ACCURSED  .  .  .  .  .  .  .       141 FRENCH REVOLTN     149
    FATHER OF JEALOUSY BE THOU ACCURSED FROM THE EARTH  .  .  .     194 V DAU ALBION 7      12
    WHY HAST THOU TAUGHT MY THEOTORMON THIS ACCURSED THING  .       194 V DAU ALBION 7      13
    THE TERROR ANSWERD I AM ORC WREATHD ROUND THE ACCURSED TREE     198 AMERICA 8            1
    THEN WHY SHOULDST THOU ACCURSED MOTHER BRING ME INTO LIFE       238 EUROPE PREL 1       11
    ON THE ACCURSED TREE OF MYSTERY  .  .  .  .  .  .  .  .  .      252 AHANIA 4             6
    [ WHAT HAVE I DONE SAID ENION ACCURSED WRETCH WHAT DEED]        267 FOUR ZOAS 1        109
    THE [ DISMAL ] ACCURSED CHAIN O HOW BRIGHT ENITHARMON HOWLD     308 FOUR ZOAS 5        102
      & CRIED
    STRUCK THRO THE ROCK THE ROOT OF MYSTERY ACCURSED SHOOTING      321 FOUR ZOAS 7         32
      UP
    IN ALL THE DISEASES OF MAN FALLING UPON THY GREY ACCURSED       322 FOUR ZOAS 7         89
      FRONT
    THAT SWAGGD HEAVY WITH THE ACCURSED DOUGH THE HOAR FROST        322 FOUR ZOAS 7        100
      RAGD
    ABHORRD ACCURSED EVER DYING AN ETERNAL DEATH  .  .  .  .  .     347 FOUR ZOAS 8     *  256
    AS NOW I REND THIS ACCURSED FAMILY FROM MY COVERING  .  .       490 MILTON 9            29
    THE DEAD DESPISE & SCORN THEE & CAST THEE OUT AS ACCURSED       626 JERUSALEM 7         68
    THESE HILLS & VALLEYS ARE ACCURSED WITNESSES OF SIN  .  .  .    652 JERUSALEM 28         9
    AND BE THOU FOR EVER ACCURSED THAT ALBION MAY ARISE AGAIN       662 JERUSALEM 35        14
    HE SAW THAT THE ACCURSED THINGS WERE HIS OWN AFFECTIONS         669 JERUSALEM 42         3
    MY DAUGHTERS ARE HARLOTS MY SONS ARE ACCURSED BEFORE ME         670 JERUSALEM 42        14
    ENITHARMON IS MY DAUGHTER ACCURSED WITH A FATHER'S CURSE        670 JERUSALEM 42        15
    THY SELFHOOD IS FOR EVER ACCURSED FROM THE DIVINE PRESENCE      670 JERUSALEM 42        45
    AN OPINION OF FATAL & ACCURSED CONSEQUENCE TO MAN  .  .  .      682A JERUSALEM 52      PROSE
    OF SELFHOOD BODY PUT OFF THE ANTICHRIST ACCURSED  .  .  .  .    734 JERUSALEM 89        10
ACCURST      SEE SELF ACCURST
ACCUSATION      SEE SELF ACCUSATION
    INGRATITUDE & LOS BELIEVE THE ACCUSATION THRO SATAN'S          486 MILTON 7            14
      EXTREME
    THE LAST JUDGMENT A DELIVERANCE FROM SATAN'S ACCUSATION        615C V LAST JUDG/N     PROSE
    IN JEALOUS FEAR IN STERN ACCUSATION WITH CRUEL STRIPES  .      644 JERUSALEM 21        29
    THE SEXUAL DEATH LIVING ON ACCUSATION OF SIN & JUDGMENT        699 JERUSALEM 64        22
```

13

	PAGE	TITLE	LINE

ACCUSATION   (CONTINUED)
WHAT IS THE ACCUSATION OF SIN . . . . 758 EV GOSPEL (2)   7
THE ROOT OF GOOD & EVIL IN THE ACCUSATION OF SIN . . . 776B INSC LAOCOON   PROSE
[HIS JUDGMENT] THE ACCUSATION SHALL BE FORGIVENESS . . . 788A ANNO THORNTON   * MARG
WROTE DOWN THE ACCUSATION TOLD ME IN PRIVATE ARE COMPELLD   827D LETTER 28   PROSE
TO EVERY ONE THAT THE WHOLE ACCUSATION IS A WILFUL PERJURY   828A LETTER 28   PROSE
SUCH IS THE PRESENT STATE OF THINGS THIS FOOLISH ACCUSATION   828B LETTER 28   PROSE
ACCUSATIONS
HOWLINGS FILLD ALL THE DESOLATE PLACES IN ACCUSATIONS OF   500 MILTON 18   43
  SIN
[WHO] HE HAS SATAN'S BOOK OF ACCUSATIONS . . . . . . 609B V LAST JUDG/N   PROSE
THE ACCUSATIONS OF SIN THAT EACH MAY BE . . . . 697 JERUSALEM 63   29
WHEN ALL THEIR CRIMES THEIR PUNISHMENTS THEIR ACCUSATIONS   739 JERUSALEM 92   15
  OF SIN
IN THE ACCUSATIONS OF SIN . . . . 759 EV GOSPEL (2)   35
ACCUSD
BUT SATAN ACCUSD PALAMABRON BEFORE [LOS] HIS BRETHREN ALSO   350 FOUR ZOAS 8   368
  HE MADDEND
WHEREFORE [RINTRAH &] PALAMABRON BEING ACCUSD BY SATAN   351 FOUR ZOAS 8   * 388
  TO LOS
THE GNOMES ACCUSD SATAN WITH INDIGNATION FURY AND FIRE . . 487 MILTON 7   21
AND MILDLY CURSING PALAMABRON HIM ACCUSD OF CRIMES . . 487 MILTON 7   36
ACCUSD PALAMABRON BEFORE THE ASSEMBLY OF INGRATITUDE OF   489 MILTON 9   20
  MALICE
ACCUSE
THEY SHEW THEIR WOUNDS THEY ACCUSE . . . . 363 FOUR ZOAS 9   250
PALAMABRON FEARD TO BE ANGRY LEST SATAN SHOULD ACCUSE HIM   486 MILTON 7   13
  OF
INTO SIN THAT HE MAY ACCUSE HIM SUCH IS . . . . . . 615B V LAST JUDG/N   PROSE
PARTICULARLY OF YOUR OWN THAT YOU MAY ACCUSE OTHERS . . . 682D JERUSALEM 52   PROSE
WHO SHALL ACCUSE THEE COME YE FORTH . . . . 754 EV GOSPEL(E)/N   49
ACCUSED
AGAINST HER LITTLE ONES THE INNOCENT ACCUSED BEFORE THE   364 FOUR ZOAS 9   267
  JUDGES
OF MORTAL LIFE TO CONDEMN THE ACCUSED WHO AT SATAN'S BAR   507 MILTON 23   42
HE COMES TO DELIVER MAN THE [FORGIVEN] ACCUSED . . . 615B V LAST JUDG/N   *PROSE
WE DO NOT FIND ANY WHERE THAT SATAN IS ACCUSED OF SIN . 615B V LAST JUDG/N   PROSE
HE IS ONLY ACCUSED OF UNBELIEF & THEREBY DRAWING MAN . 615B V LAST JUDG/N   PROSE
ACCUSER
THE ACCUSER OF SINS BY MY SIDE DOES STAND . . . . . 558 I ROSE UP AT/N   15
& NOT SATAN THE ACCUSER . . . . 615B V LAST JUDG/N   PROSE
OF JESUS THE SAVIOUR WHERE THE ACCUSER IS CAST OUT NOT . 616D V LAST JUDG/N   PROSE
FOR SIN IN WAR & IN THE DRUID TEMPLES OF THE ACCUSER OF   746 JERUSALEM 98   49
  SIN BENEATH
THE ACCUSER HOLY GOD OF ALL . . . . 758 EV GOSPEL (2)   13
AND THE ACCUSER STANDING BY . . . . 759 EV GOSPEL (2)   30
TO THE ACCUSER WHO IS THE GOD OF THIS WORLD . . . . 771D EPILOGUE/GP   TITLE
VAIN IS THY COVENANT O JEHOVAH I AM THE ACCUSER & AVENGER   780 GHOST ABEL 1   12
AND A CONTRITE HEART O I CANNOT FORGIVE THE ACCUSER HATH   780 GHOST ABEL 2   5
BUT OF SATAN THE ACCUSER & FATHER OF HELL . . . . 785B ILLS DANTE 101   PROSE
WHO IS THE GOD OF THIS WORLD THE ACCUSER LET HIS JUDGMENT   788A ANNO THORNTON   MARG
& IN THE ABYSSES OF THE ACCUSER MY ENTHUSIASM IS STILL . 816A LETTER 23   PROSE
THE TROUBLE & EXPENSE I HAVE HEARD THAT MY ACCUSER IS A   828B LETTER 28   PROSE
SATAN'S HOLY TRINITY THE ACCUSER THE JUDGE & THE   SUPP INSC OUR END   *TITLE
  EXECUTIONER
ACCUSER'S
AGAINST THE ACCUSER'S CHIEF DESIRE . . . . 761 FOR SEXES/GP   3
ACCUSERS
ALL WARRIORS THE MORAL VIRTUES ARE CONTINUAL ACCUSERS . 774D ANNO BERKELEY   MARG
THE ACCUSERS OF THEFT ADULTERY MURDER A SCENE IN THE LAST   SUPP INSC OUR END   *TITLE
  JUDGMENT
ACCUSES
("TO AVERT SUSPICION ACCUSES THE INNOCENT") DAMN HIM . . 78A ANNO LAVATER   MARG
ACCUSING
AND GHOSTS ACCUSING GROAN . . . . 13 GWIN KING/PS   100
NAKED OF THEIR CLOTHING THE POOR SPECTRES BEFORE   346 FOUR ZOAS 8   219
  THE ACCUSING HEAVENS
MEAN WHILE WEPT SATAN BEFORE LOS ACCUSING PALAMABRON . 487 MILTON 8   1
WITH THUNDERS UTTERD FROM HIS HIDDEN WHEELS ACCUSING LOUD   490 MILTON 9   41
ACCUSTOMD
OF ACCUSTOMD FRIENDSHIP IF YOU WERE NOT . . . . . . 816D LETTER 24   PROSE
ACCUSTOMED
A CIVILIZED MAN WHO HAS BEEN ACCUSTOMED TO GO NAKED . . 580D DESC CAT 5   PROSE
PARTICULAR TO YOU AND YOUR ACCUSTOMED FORGIVENESS OF MY   808A LETTER 19   PROSE
  WANT
ACHIEVE   SEE ATCHIEVD,ATCHIEVEMENT
ACHILLES
AS ENEAS IS HERE SHEWN A WORSE MAN THAN ACHILLES IN LEAVING   412A ANNO BOYD   MARG
  DIDO
ACHILLES'
THE GLITTERING DISSIMULATION ACHILLES' WRATH IS BLUNT ABUSE   384D ANNO WATSON   MARG
ACHING   SEE AKEING,AKING
RUNS ACHING COLD INTO THE SCEPTER TOO HEAVY FOR MORTAL   134 FRENCH REVOLTN   4
  GRASP NO MORE
FLOWD INTO THE ACHING FIBRES OF LOS YET CONTENDING AGAINST   733 JERUSALEM 88   29
  HIM
ACHITOPHEL
ACHITOPHEL IS ALSO HERE WITH THE CORD IN HIS HAND . . . 608D V LAST JUDG/N   PROSE
ACKNOWLEDGD
ON ALL HANDS ACKNOWLEDGD IT ONLY REMAINS TO BE CERTIFIED   591C PUB ADDRESS/N   PROSE
I OUGHT TO HAVE ACKNOWLEDGD THE RECEIT OF FIVE POUNDS . . 875D LETTER 82   PROSE
YOU DESIRED I WOULD SEND AN ACKNOWLEDGD IT I DID NOT . . 875D LETTER 82   PROSE

```
                                                            PAGE     TITLE        LINE
ACKNOWLEDGE
       [ TO THE FULL AS ENTHUSIASTICALLY AS I HAVE WHO ACKNOWLEDGE  621A JERUSALEM 3    *PROSE
         MINE ]
       IT IS EASY TO ACKNOWLEDGE A MAN TO BE GREAT & GOOD WHILE WE  673 JERUSALEM 43       56
ACKNOWLEDGED
       AN OLD WELL-KNOWN AND ACKNOWLEDGED ENGRAVER    . . . . . .586D CHAUCER 1         PROSE
ACKNOWLEDGEMENT
       HERE IS AN ACKNOWLEDGEMENT OF ALL THAT I COULD WISH  . . . 448D ANNO REYNOLDS     MARG
ACKNOWLEDGING
       ON ACCOUNT OF NOT ACKNOWLEDGING YOUR FRIENDSHIP TO ME    . 791A LETTER 3         PROSE
ACKNOWLEDGMENTS
       ACKNOWLEDGMENTS TO EXPRESS PARTICULARLY FOR YOUR TENS WHICH 832B LETTER 32       PROSE
       ACKNOWLEDGMENTS TO YOU AS DO MY BROTHER & SISTER  . . . . 849C LETTER 45         PROSE
       ACKNOWLEDGMENTS FOR THE KIND RECEPTION YOU HAVE GIVEN MY    862C LETTER 60       PROSE
         NEW
A-COLD
       AND THE NIGHT IS A-COLD  . . . . . . . . . . . .   8 MAD SONG/PS             2
A-COMING
       WITH DESIRE AND CURIOSITY BUT HOWEVER CHRISTMAS IS A-COMING 851D LETTER 50       PROSE
ACOURTING
       ALL THE COUNTRY FOLKS ACOURTING   . . . . . . . .  53 PHEBE DREST/IM         6
A COURTING
       THAT I MUST GO A COURTING WHICH I SHALL DO AWKWARDLY IN     829D LETTER 30      PROSE
         THE MEAN TIME
ACQUAINTANCE
       UNLESS YOU FIND IT TO BE HIS ALSO PREVIOUS TO YOUR         87D ANNO LAVATER     MARG
         ACQUAINTANCE
       ACQUAINTANCE WITH KNAVES     . . . . . . . . . . .405B ANNO BACON      MARG
       [ LOOK XXX FLAXMAN & STOTHARD DO] OLD ACQUAINTANCE WE'LL    538 OLD ACQUAINT/N *    1
         RENEW
       ADVANTAGEOUS ACQUAINTANCE I GO ON WITHOUT DARING TO COUNT   879C LETTER 89      PROSE
ACQUAINTED
       SAID HE YOU MUST BE ACQUAINTED WITH A GREAT MANY SONGS  .  . 61C ISLAND MOON 11 PROSE
       SUCH MEN AS GOLDSMITH OUGHT NOT TO HAVE BEEN ACQUAINTED     450D ANNO REYNOLDS  MARG
         WITH
       THO HE IS IN TOWN MR PLAXMAN IS NOT AT ALL ACQUAINTED   . .834D LETTER 34       PROSE
       A HISTORY OF THE REVIEWING BUSINESS AS FAR AS I            845C LETTER 44       PROSE
         AM ACQUAINTED
ACQUIRABLE
       I SAY TASTE & GENIUS ARE NOT TEACHABLE OR ACQUIRABLE    . .474B ANNO REYNOLDS   MARG
ACQUIRE
       FROM ALREADY ACQUIRED KNOWLEDGE MAN COULD NOT ACQUIRE MORE  98C ALL RELIGIONS   PROSE
ACQUIRED
       IT IS NOT HIS GENIUS BUT AN ACCIDENT ACQUIRED FOR HOW   . . 81D ANNO LAVATER    MARG
       BECAUSE IT REPROACHES HIM WITH THE ERRORS OF ACQUIRED FOLLY 87C ANNO LAVATER    MARG
       ACQUIRED BY MEANS OF SUFFERING & DISTRESS I E EXPERIENCE    89B ANNO SWED LOVE * MARG
       AFFECTIONS ARE NATURAL BUT UNDERSTANDING IS ACQUIRED BUT    89B ANNO SWED LOVE * MARG
         OBSERVE
       FROM ALREADY ACQUIRED KNOWLEDGE MAN COULD NOT ACQUIRE MORE  98C ALL RELIGIONS   PROSE
       ALL THIS CONCESSION IS TO PROVE THAT GENIUS IS ACQUIRED     448A ANNO REYNOLDS  MARG
       KNOWLEDGE OF IDEAL BEAUTY IS NOT TO BE ACQUIRED   . . . .459B ANNO REYNOLDS     MARG
       BY WHICH THEY ACQUIRED PUBLIC PATRONAGE . . . . . . .572D DESC CAT 3           PROSE
       THE OTHER NEVER CAN BE ACQUIRED BUT MUST BE BORN  . . . .602D PUB ADDR AD/N     PROSE
       ("RELISH FOR EXCELLENCIES AN ACQUIRED TASTE") [FOOL]   . . SUPP ANNO REYNOLDS  * MARG
ACQUIREMENT
       OR INTELLECTUAL ACQUIREMENT . . . . . . . . . . . .402C ANNO BACON       MARG
ACQUIRES
       THE MAN EITHER PAINTER OR PHILOSOPHER WHO LEARNS           449B ANNO REYNOLDS   MARG
         OR ACQUIRES
ACQUIRING
       WHEN A MAN TALKS OF ACQUIRING INVENTION &   . . . . . .469D ANNO REYNOLDS      MARG
ACQUISITION
       OBJECTS OF ACQUISITION SUCH IS THE PLAN AS I AM TOLD & SUCH 798A LETTER 10       PROSE
       & WHICH WILL BE A MOST VALUABLE ACQUISITION TO LITERATURE   809D LETTER 20       PROSE
ACQUIT
       WHILE YOU ACQUIT & FLATTER THE ALEXANDERS & CAESARS  . . . 683A JERUSALEM 52    PROSE
ACRES
       HIS CORN-FIELDS AND HIS VALLEYS OF FIVE HUNDRED ACRES      497 MILTON 15          31
         SQUARE
ACROS
       THRO MALDEN & ACROS THE SEA . . . . . . . . . . . 650 FIELDS FROM/J        43
ACROSS
       FROM HIS EYES ACROSS THE FIELD I HAVE SEEN HIM    . . . .  22 EDW THIRD/PS 3      28
       AND BLOOD SHALL FLOW LIKE STREAMS ACROSS THE MEADOWS  . .  31 EDW THIRD/PS 5      54
       HER SHIPS SHALL SING ACROSS THE FOAMING SEA    . . . . .  31 EDW THIRD/PS 5      58
       HOVERD AND STRETCHD ACROSS THE CITY . . . . . . . . .  146 FRENCH REVOLTN    272
       . . . AND ACROSS THE ARMY AND ACROSS THE LOUVRE    . . .  146 FRENCH REVOLTN    272
       AND MUTTER ACROSS THE OCEAN FRANCE REND DOWN THY DUNGEON   159A SONG LIBERTY    PROSE
       [BRUSHD ACROSS THY SUMMER JOY] . . . . . . . . . .  182 THE FLY/N            2
       [BUT THE BLOODTHIRSTY PEOPLE ACROSS THE WATER] . . . .  185 LET BROTHELS/N      22
       SULLEN FIRES ACROSS THE ATLANTIC GLOW TO AMERICA'S SHORE   197 AMERICA 3          2
       DESCENDS LINK BY LINK FROM ALBION'S CLIFFS ACROSS THE      197 AMERICA 3          8
         SEA TO BIND
       OF TRUMPETS BLEW A LOUD ALARM ACROSS THE ATLANTIC DEEP  .  200 AMERICA 10         2
       THE EASTERN SKY SPREADING HIS AWFUL WINGS ACROSS          201 AMERICA 13         12
         THE HEAVENS
       ACROSS THE LIMBS OF ALBION'S GUARDIAN . . . . . . .  202 AMERICA 15          2
       SULLEN FIRES ACROSS THE ATLANTIC GLOW TO AMERICA'S SHORE   203 AMERICA CANC A     2
       DESCENDS LINK BY LINK FROM ALBION'S CLIFFS ACROSS THE      204 AMERICA CANC A     8
         SEA TO BIND
       AND ITS ROOFS CRACK ACROSS DOWN FALLING ON TH ANGELIC SEATS 204 AMERICA CANC B   24
       RANGD IN GLOOMD ABRAY STRETCH OUT ACROSS   . . . . . .  223 URIZEN 3           29
```

15

		PAGE	TITLE	LINE

ACROSS   (CONTINUED)
```
        ACROSS THE VOID MANY A MILE  . . . . . . . . . .     249 AHANIA 2          22
        CRACKD ACROSS INTO NUMBERLESS FRAGMENTS . . . . . . .  257 BOOK OF LOS 4     18
        WEARIED WITH SEEKING FOOD ACROSS THE SNOWY WASTE THE LITTLE  276 FOUR ZOAS 1   448
        ACROSS EUROPE & ASIA TO CHINA & JAPAN LIKE LIGHTENINGS  . .  281 FOUR ZOAS 2  *  59
        AT WILL TO STRETCH ACROSS THE HEAVENS & STEP FROM STAR   288 FOUR ZOAS 2      298
            TO STAR
        I STILL KEEP WATCH ALTHO I TREMBLE & WITHER ACROSS THE   288 FOUR ZOAS 2      330
            HEAVENS
        [[OF] IN A SOFT CLOUD OUTSTRETCHD ACROSS & LUVAH DWELT   292 FOUR ZOAS 3       48
            IN THE CLOUD ]
        THRO THE CONFUSION LIKE A CRACK ACROSS FROM IMMENSE TO   295 FOUR ZOAS 3      149
            IMMENSE
        THE WINTER SPREAD HIS WIDE BLACK WINGS ACROSS FROM POLE  306 FOUR ZOAS 5       32
            TO POLE
        THARMAS HEARD THE DEADLY SCREAM ACROSS HIS WATRY WORLD  . .  313 FOUR ZOAS 6   47
        SHIVERING ACROSS FROM VORTEX TO VORTEX . . . . . . . .  318 FOUR ZOAS 6      245
        STRIDING ACROSS THE NARROW VALE THE [SHADE] SHADOW      319 FOUR ZOAS 6   *  297
            OF URTHONA
        HIS SWIFT WINGD DAUGHTERS SWEEP ACROSS THE VAST BLACK OCEAN  320 FOUR ZOAS 7   26
        WITH A CRASH BREAKING ACROSS THE HORRIBLE MASS COMES DOWN  322 FOUR ZOAS 7     78
        TERRIFIC WITH THEIR IRON VESSELS DRIVING THEM ACROSS  . .  322 FOUR ZOAS 7     96
        . . . CRACKING THE HEAVENS ACROSS FROM IMMENSE TO IMMENSE   357 FOUR ZOAS 9     9
        THAT LINE OF BLOOD THAT STRETCHD ACROSS THE WINDOWS OF   361 FOUR ZOAS 9      160
            THE MORNING
        RESHONE ACROSS THE FIELD IMMENSE WHERE ALL THE NATIONS  . .  364 FOUR ZOAS 9  293
        [ SHINING ACROSS THE OCEAN . . . . . . . . .            381 FOUR ZOAS AD 5    14
        STRATFORD & OLD BOW & ACROSS TO THE GARDENS OF KENSINGTON  485 MILTON 6        10
        IN ALL THEIR BEAUTY TO ENTICE MILTON ACROSS THE RIVER  . .  501 MILTON 19      31
        OF DEATH ACROSS THE ATLANTIC TO AMERICA NORTH & SOUTH  . .  525 MILTON 35      17
        EASTWARD UPON THE PAVED WORK ACROSS EUROPE & ASIA  . . .  532 MILTON 40        18
        FROM YORK ALL ACROSS SCOTLAND TO THE SEA  . . . . . .  536 AND HIS LEGS/N      3
        THRO HEAVEN THE DISTANT STEEPLE SEEN ACROSS A WIDE WATER  619B ILLUS MILTON  PROSE
        UPON THE DARKNING THAMES ACROSS THE WHOLE ISLAND WESTWARD  625 JERUSALEM 7      3
        ACROSS ALL EUROPE & ASIA HE SAW THE TORTURES OF THE VICTIMS  627 JERUSALEM 8   24
        IN SOLEMN POMP INTO CHALDEA ACROSS THE BREDTHS OF EUROPE  644 JERUSALEM 21     43
        OF SURREY ACROSS MIDDLESEX & ACROSS ALBION'S HOUSE  . . .  658 JERUSALEM 31    69
        BENDING ACROSS THE ROAD OF OXFORD STREET IT FROM HYDE PARK  665 JERUSALEM 38   57
        AND MANY SORROWS OBLIQUE ACROSS THE ATLANTIC VALE  . . .  678 JERUSALEM 48     32
        TILL CANAAN ROLLD APART FROM ALBION ACROSS THE RHINE ALONG  698 JERUSALEM 63   41
            THE DANUBE
        ACROSS EUROPE ACROSS AFRICA IN HOWLINGS & DEADLY WAR  . .  706 JERUSALEM 68    20
        ACROSS THE HILLS OF EPHRAIM & DOWN MOUNT OLIVET TO  . .  706 JERUSALEM 68      22
        LO THEY SHOOT FORTH IN TENDER NERVES ACROSS EUROPE & ASIA  706 JERUSALEM 68    26
        AND SWORD FAINT IN HIS HAND FROM ALBION ACROSS GREAT   706 JERUSALEM 68        52
            TARTARY
        HE RAN IN TENDER NERVES ACROSS EUROPE TO JERUSALEM'S SHADE  723 JERUSALEM 80   64
        TO BROCKLEY HILLS ACROSS THE THAMES HE WITH DOUBLE BOADICEA  736 JERUSALEM 90  24
        ACROSS THE ATLANTIC TO FRANCE . . . . . . . . . . .  799 TO FLAXMAN/L         10
        WITH HAPPINESS STRETCHD ACROSS THE HILLS  . . . . . .  816 HAPPINESS/L         1
        WITH SILVER ANGELS ACROSS MY WAY . . . . . . . . .  817 HAPPINESS/L           11
        WITH MY OUTWARD A THISTLE ACROSS MY WAY . . . . . . .  817 HAPPINESS/L         30
        AND ARE LAID ACROSS BEAMS AT THE TOP  . . . . . . .  831B LETTER 31          PROSE
        ACROSS THE COUNTRY TO FELPHAM AS HE ALWAYS KEEPS A HORSE  843A LETTER 42      PROSE
ACT
        BUT I MUST TELL YOU THAT GUILT BEING AN ACT OF THE MIND   29A EDW THIRD/PS 4  PROSE
        AND TIS A SIN TO ACT WITHOUT SOME REASON  . . . . . .   29A EDW THIRD/PS 4    PROSE
        AN ACT OF PARLIAMENT IN HIS HAND SAID THAT IT WAS       46A ISLAND MOON 1     PROSE
            A SHAMEFUL
        NO OMNIPOTENCE CAN ACT AGAINST ORDER  . . . . . . . .   78A ANNO LAVATER      MARG
        & ITS OWN EFFECT ACCIDENT IS THE OMISSION OF ACT IN SELF &   88D ANNO LAVATER MARG
        THE HINDERING OF ACT IN ANOTHER THIS IS VICE  . . . . .   88D ANNO LAVATER    MARG
        BUT ALL ACT [FROM INDIVIDUAL PROPENSITY] IS VIRTUE  . . .   88D ANNO LAVATER  MARG
        TO HINDER ANOTHER IS NOT AN ACT IT IS THE CONTRARY  . . .   88D ANNO LAVATER  MARG
        THE FATHER FORMS A WHIP TO ROUZE THE SLUGGISH SENSES TO ACT  110 TIRIEL 8      30
        THE MOST SUBLIME ACT IS TO SET ANOTHER BEFORE YOU  . .  151B MARRIAGE HH 7    PROSE
        THINK IN THE MORNING ACT IN THE NOON  . . . . . . . .  152A MARRIAGE HH 9     PROSE
        MIGHT ACT ACCORDING TO THEIR FORMS BY INNATE CRUELTY  . .  344 FOUR ZOAS 8    134
        WHO CONSIDERS IT AS AN ARBITRARY ACT OF THE AGENT  . . .  391D ANNO WATSON    MARG
        DO OR ACT TO DO GOOD OR TO DO EVIL  . . . . . . . .  396A ANNO WATSON         MARG
        THOUGHT IS ACT CHRIST'S ACTS WERE NOTHING TO CAESAR'S IF  400C ANNO BACON     MARG
            THIS IS NOT
        NONE BUT A FOOL CAN ACT SO . . . . . . . . . . .  406A ANNO BACON            MARG
        IF WELL REGULATED GOVERNMENTS ACT SO WHO CAN TELL SO WELL  413D ANNO BOYD     MARG
            AS
        HOWLING & [DESCENDING INTO THE FLAMES & IN THE ACT OF]  . .  443C LAST JUDGMNT/L  PROSE
        ACT MORE TERRIFIC IN THE CENTRAL CITIES OF THE NATIONS  . .  510 MILTON 25      4
        DRIVEN FROM ETERNITY HIM I SEEK TERRIFIED AT MY ACT  . .  527 MILTON 37         2
        AND THOSE WHO ACT WITH BENEVOLENCE & VIRTUE THEY MURDER  533 MILTON 41         20
            TIME ON TIME
        [TO [SAY] SPEAK MICHAEL ANGELO [ANY OTHER WORD] & [MEAN]  542 FLORENTINE/N  *  11
            ACT REMBRANT]
        TO SPEAK MICHAEL ANGELO & ACT REMBRANDT . . . . . . .  542 FLORENTINE/N       21
        AND WHEN HE COULD NOT ACT UPON MY WIFE . . . . . . .  544 HS FRENDSHIP/N       5
        IF MEN WILL ACT LIKE A MAID SMILING OVER A CHURN . . .  556 IF MEN ACT/N       1
        I AM AWARE OF YOU BECAUSE I KNOW THAT YOU ACT NOT FROM  . .  573A DESC CAT 3  PROSE
        ETERNITY INDEPENDENT OF CREATION WHICH WAS AN ACT OF MERCY  614B V LAST JUDG/N  PROSE
        I AM INSPIRED I ACT NOT FOR MYSELF FOR ALBION'S SAKE  . .  627 JERUSALEM 8      17
        PERMANENT & NOT LOST NOT LOST NOR VANISHD & EVERY LITTLE  634 JERUSALEM 13      60
            ACT
        AND EVERY ACT A CRIME AND ALBION THE PUNISHER & JUDGE  . .  652 JERUSALEM 28    4
        NEITHER DARING TO PUT IN ACT ITS COUNCILS FEARING      708 JERUSALEM 70         6
            EACH-OTHER
```

	PAGE	TITLE	LINE
ACT (CONTINUED)			
TO PUT IN ACT WHAT HER HEART WILLS O WHO CAN WITHSTAND HER POWER	709	JERUSALEM 70	30
I ACT WITH BENEVOLENCE & VIRTUE & GET MURDERD TIME AFTER TIME	738	JERUSALEM 91	26
OR ANGEL TO FOLLOW WHERE HE LED IF I WERE TO ACT OTHERWISE	791D	LETTER 4	PROSE
BECAUSE IT ROUZES THE FACULTIES TO ACT	793B	LETTER 5	PROSE
ACTED			
JESUS WAS ALL VIRTUE AND ACTED FROM IMPULSE NOT FROM RULES	158D	MARRIAGE HH 22	PROSE
ALL THINGS ACTED ON EARTH ARE SEEN IN THE BRIGHT SCULPTURES OF	638	JERUSALEM 16	61
"SENDS OVER TO IMAGINATION BEFORE THE DECREE CAN BE ACTED"	794A	LETTER 5	PROSE
ACTEON			
THE "VIEWS IN KEW GARDENS" "FOOTS CRAY" & "DIANA" & "ACTEON"	594A	PUB ADDRESS/N	PROSE
ACTING			
LOS BUILT THE STUBBORN STRUCTURE OF THE LANGUAGE ACTING AGAINST	668	JERUSALEM 40	59
AS TO REAL ACTING IT IS LIKE HISTORICAL PAINTING NO BOY'S WORK	859C	LETTER 56	PROSE
ACTION			
BY RIGHT OF NATURE THUS SET IN ACTION	26	EDW THIRD/PS 3	199
I SHALL WITH PLEASURE VIEW A GLORIOUS ACTION	27	EDW THIRD/PS 3	280
IT IS A RESTRAINT ON ACTION BOTH IN OURSELVES &	88D	ANNO LAVATER	MARG
NO MAN CAN DO A VICIOUS ACTION & THINK IT TO BE VIRTUOUS	386C	ANNO WATSON	MARG
IF HE DOES NOT SHEW THE MAN AS WELL AS THE ACTION	462B	ANNO REYNOLDS	* MARG
ACTION AND REALITY REASONS AND OPINIONS CONCERNING ACTS	579A	DESC CAT 5	PROSE
ALL THAT IS NOT ACTION IS NOT WORTH READING TELL ME THE WHAT	579A	DESC CAT 5	PROSE
& THAT TO ME IT IS HINDRANCE & NOT ACTION	617B	V LAST JUDG/N	PROSE
OF ACTION FOR OBEDIENCE TO DESTROY THE CONTRARIES OF MAN	653	JERUSALEM 29	15
REVOLUTIONS OF ACTION & PASSION THRO THE FOUR ELEMENTS ON ALL SIDES	742	JERUSALEM 95	10
ACTIONS			
IF I CAN JUDGE OF ACTIONS BUT YOUR HEAT	27	EDW THIRD/PS 3	245
TO KNOW THE MOTIVES OF THEIR OWN ACTIONS	29A	EDW THIRD/PS 4	PROSE
AND FROM AN IDIOT'S ACTIONS FORM MY RULE	547	RAFAEL SUBLI/N	6
LINE OF RECTITUDE AND CERTAINTY IN THE ACTIONS AND INTENTIONS	585C	DESC CAT 15	PROSE
ACTIVE			
NOBLE BUT MARK ACTIVE EVIL IS BETTER THAN PASSIVE GOOD	77B	ANNO LAVATER	MARG
THE WHOLE OF THE NEW CHURCH IS IN THE ACTIVE LIFE	92D	ANNO SWED LOVE	MARG
EVIL IS THE ACTIVE SPRINGING FROM ENERGY	149B	MARRIAGE HH 3	PROSE
SET HERSELF UP TO GIVE HER LAWS TO THE ACTIVE MASCULINE VIRTUE	295	FOUR ZOAS 3	116
NONE NEEDS BE ACTIVE MEAN TIME PALAMABRON'S HORSES	487	MILTON 7	45
SPIRIT OF TITIAN WAS PARTICULARLY ACTIVE IN RAISING DOUBTS	582C	DESC CAT 9	PROSE
WITH MY ACTIVE PHYSIOGNOMY HAD DONE ME MUCH MISCHIEF	828C	LETTER 28	PROSE
ACTIVITY			
& THE SOURCES OF ALL ACTIVITY BUT THE CHAINS ARE THE CUNNING OF	155A	MARRIAGE HH 15	PROSE
DARK REVOLVING IN SILENT ACTIVITY	223	URIZEN 3	18
AN ACTIVITY UNKNOWN AND HORRIBLE	223	URIZEN 3	20
RUINS ACTIVITY & ARE THE GREATEST HURT TO AN ARTIST SUCH AS I AM	879C	LETTER 89	PROSE
ACTOR			
BUT THE ACTOR SUCH ARE MOST OF THE ACTS OF MOSES	390D	ANNO WATSON	MARG
MUST EITHER BE THE ACTOR OR A FABLE WRITER OR A LIAR	390D	ANNO WATSON	MARG
FOR THE FACTS ARE SUCH AS NONE BUT THE ACTOR COULD TELL	392D	ANNO WATSON	MARG
NOT AN ERROR BUT IT HAS A MAN FOR ITS [ACTOR] AGENT	615A	V LAST JUDG/N	PROSE
ACTORS			
ITS ACTORS BUT THE RELIGION OF JESUS FORGIVENESS OF SIN	683A	JERUSALEM 52	PROSE
ACTS			
AND NOT ACTS WHEN NEITHER WARBLING VOICE	28	EDW THIRD/PS 3	283
AND WHOEVER ACTS WITHOUT REASON	29A	EDW THIRD/PS 4	PROSE
THING THAT ACTS OF PARLIAMENT SHOULD BE IN A FREE STATE IT HAD	46A	ISLAND MOON 1	PROSE
HE WHO DESIRES BUT ACTS NOT BREEDS PESTILENCE	151A	MARRIAGE HH 7	PROSE
GOD ONLY ACTS & IS IN EXISTING BEINGS OR MEN	155B	MARRIAGE HH 15	PROSE
CALL THAT VIRGINITY THAT WISHES BUT ACTS NOT	160B	SONG LIBERTY	PROSE
IS IT BECAUSE ACTS ARE NOT LOVELY THAT THOU SEEKEST SOLITUDE	194	V DAU ALBION 7	10
THE HUMAN NATURE SHALL NO MORE REMAIN NOR HUMAN ACTS	272	FOUR ZOAS 1	310
THE PERVERSIONS OF CHRIST'S WORDS & ACTS ARE ATTACKD	383B	ANNO WATSON	MARG
DEFEND EITHER THE ACTS OF CHRIST OR THE BIBLE UNPERVERTED	383B	ANNO WATSON	MARG
BUT THE ACTOR SUCH ARE MOST OF THE ACTS OF MOSES	390D	ANNO WATSON	MARG
IF MOSES DID NOT WRITE THE HISTORY OF HIS ACTS IT	390D	ANNO WATSON	MARG
THOUGHT IS ACT CHRIST'S ACTS WERE NOTHING TO CAESAR'S IF THIS IS NOT	400C	ANNO BACON	MARG
OF GUILT OTHERS SAID IF IT IS TRUE IF THE ACTS HAVE BEEN PERFORMD	495	MILTON 13	49
OF THAT MILD VISION WONDROUS WERE THEIR ACTS BY ME UNKNOWN	532	MILTON 40	2
WHO IN EVERY AGE IS BORN TO RECORD AND ETERNIZE ITS ACTS	569A	DESC CAT 3	PROSE
PLAIN IN THEIR ACTS AND MANNERS WISER THAN AFTER-AGES	577C	DESC CAT 5	PROSE
THE STORIES OF ARTHUR ARE THE ACTS OF ALBION APPLIED	578C	DESC CAT 5	PROSE
ACTION AND REALITY REASONS AND OPINIONS CONCERNING ACTS	579A	DESC CAT 5	PROSE
ARE NOT HISTORY ACTS THEMSELVES ALONE ARE HISTORY AND	579A	DESC CAT 5	PROSE
TELL ME THE ACTS O HISTORIAN AND LEAVE ME TO REASON UPON	579A	DESC CAT 5	PROSE
THE STRONG MAN ACTS FROM CONSCIOUS SUPERIORITY	580B	DESC CAT 5	PROSE
THE BEAUTIFUL MAN ACTS FROM DUTY AND ANXIOUS SOLICITUDE	580B	DESC CAT 5	PROSE
UGLY MAN ACTS FROM LOVE OF CARNAGE AND DELIGHT IN	580C	DESC CAT 5	PROSE
BUT HE ACTS WITH TRIUMPHANT HONEST PRIDE	750	EV GOSPEL(C)/N	23

17

```
                                                               PAGE      TITLE           LINE
ACTS     (CONTINUED)
     FOR HE ACTS WITH HONEST TRIUMPHANT PRIDE    . . . . . .  751 EV GOSPEL(D)/N      29
     MR HAYLEY ACTS LIKE A PRINCE I AM AT COMPLETE EASE BUT  . 808A LETTER 19         PROSE
     AT THE TASKS SET BEFORE US IF WE REFUSE TO DO SPIRITUAL  813A LETTER 22         PROSE
        ACTS
     NONE CAN KNOW THE SPIRITUAL ACTS OF MY THREE YEARS' SLUMBER 823A LETTER 26      PROSE
     OR UNLESS HE SHOULD READ MY LONG POEM DESCRIPTIVE OF THOSE 823A LETTER 26       PROSE
        ACTS
     POETICAL PERSONIFICATIONS & ACTS WITHOUT WHICH POEMS   . . 867A LETTER 66       PROSE
ACTUAL
     THE ACTUAL CAUSE OF MY UNEASINESS INTO WHICH YOU ARE SO   813A LETTER 22        PROSE
        KIND
ACUTE
     HE PERCIEVES MORE THAN SENSE THO EVER SO ACUTE CAN DISCOVER 97C NAT RELIGION 2  PROSE
     ACUTE [& OBLONG] SCALENE IN SIMPLE PATHS BUT OTHERS MOVE   287 FOUR ZOAS 2       283
ADA
     CAINAH & ADA & ZILLAH & NAAMAH WIFE OF NOAH  . . . . .    696 JERUSALEM 62         9
ADAH
     ADAH ZILLAH CAINA NAAMAH TAMAR RAHAB TIRZAH MARY  . . . .  350 FOUR ZOAS 8       365
ADAM     SEE UDAN ADAM
     & THE RETURN OF ADAM INTO PARADISE SEE ISAIAH XXXIV & XXXV 149B MARRIAGE HH 3   PROSE
        CHAP
     ADAM STOOD IN THE GARDEN OF EDEN . . . . . . . . . .      245 SONG OF LOS 3        6
     ADAM SHUDDERD NOAH FADED BLACK GREW THE SUNNY AFRICAN  . . 245 SONG OF LOS 3       10
     FOR ADAM A MOULDERING SKELETON . . . . . . . . . . .      248 SONG OF LOS 7       20
     AND NEXT HE FOUND THE LIMIT OF CONTRACTION & NAMD IT ADAM  304 FOUR ZOAS 4       273
     BUT YET HAVING A LIMIT TWOFOLD NAMED SATAN & ADAM   . . .  329 FOUR ZOAS 7       383
     HAR OCHIM IJIM ADAM REUBEN SIMEON LEVI JUDAH DAN NAPHTALI  350 FOUR ZOAS 8       360
     MOLECH IMPATIENT THEY SENT ELOHIM WHO CREATED ADAM  . . .  351 FOUR ZOAS 8       401
     TO DIE FOR SATAN ADAM REFUSD BUT WAS COMPELLD TO DIE   . . 351 FOUR ZOAS 8       402
     AT THE FALL OF ADAM & THAT . . . . . . . . . . . . .      390A ANNO WATSON      MARG
     IMMEDIATELY BEFORE THE THRONE OF CHRIST IS ADAM & EVE  . . 443B LAST JUDGMNT/L   PROSE
     OPACITY WAS NAMED SATAN CONTRACTION WAS NAMED ADAM   . . . 494 MILTON 13          21
     HE NAMED THE OPAKE SATAN HE NAMED THE SOLID ADAM   . . .   517 MILTON 29          39
     SATAN & ADAM ARE STATES CREATED INTO TWENTY-SEVEN CHURCHES 521 MILTON 32          25
     ADAM SATAN MILTON'S TRACK  . . . . . . . . . . . . .      523B MILTON 33         TITLE
     ADAM SETH ENOS CAINAN MAHALALEEL JARED ENOCH  . . . . .   528 MILTON 37           36
     HIGHEST ANTIQUITY ADAM WAS A DRUID AND NOAH  . . . . .    578A DESC CAT 5        PROSE
     AND THE WORLD OF SATAN AND OF ADAM . . . . . . . . .      578B DESC CAT 5        PROSE
     NUMBER XI THE BODY OF ABEL FOUND BY ADAM AND EVE   . . .  584A DESC CAT 11       TITLE
     ADAM & EVE APPEAR FIRST BEFORE THE [THRONE]  . . . . .    606B V LAST JUDG/N     PROSE
     BETWEEN THE FIGURES OF ADAM & EVE APPEARS A FIERY GULPH    609A V LAST JUDG/N    PROSE
     LEARNING & SCIENCE WHICH ACCOMPANIED ADAM OUT OF EDEN  . . 611D V LAST JUDG/N    PROSE
     MANY SUPPOSE THAT BEFORE [ADAM] THE CREATION ALL   . . .  614B V LAST JUDG/N     PROSE
     FROM ENOCH TO ADAM SCHOFIELD IS ADAM WHO WAS NEW-CREATED   625 JERUSALEM 7         25
        . . .
     TO PREPARE THE SPECTRE SONS OF ADAM WHO IS SCOFIELD THE    626 JERUSALEM 7         42
        NINTH
     IN ALL THE TWENTY-SEVEN HEAVENS NUMBERD FROM ADAM TO LUTHER 633 JERUSALEM 13      32
     AND THENCE I SEE THE CHAOS OF SATAN & THE WORLD OF ADAM    636 JERUSALEM 15        31
     SATAN & ADAM & THE WHOLE WORLD WAS CREATED BY THE ELOHIM   649D JERUSALEM 27     PROSE
     THEN THE DIVINE HAND FOUND THE TWO LIMITS SATAN AND ADAM   662 JERUSALEM 35         1
     REUBEN SLEPT IN THE CAVE OF ADAM AND LOS FOLDED HIS TONGUE 662 JERUSALEM 36         5
     IS NAMED SATAN AND THE LIMIT OF CONTRACTION IS NAMED ADAM  670 JERUSALEM 42        31
     FORBIDDING US THAT VEIL WHICH SATAN PUTS BETWEEN EVE & ADAM 686 JERUSALEM 55      11
     THEY WERE AS ADAM BEFORE ME UNITED INTO ONE MAN  . . . .  692 JERUSALEM 60        16
     ADAM WHO IS PELEG & JOKTAN & ESAU & JACOB & SAUL & DAVID   713 JERUSALEM 73        28
     ADAM NOAH ABRAHAM MOSES SAMUEL DAVID EZEKIEL  . . . . .   714 JERUSALEM 73        41
     ADAM SETH ENOS CAINAN MAHALALEEL JARED ENOCH  . . . . .   716 JERUSALEM 75        11
     AND WHERE LUTHER ENDS ADAM BEGINS AGAIN IN ETERNAL CIRCLE  716 JERUSALEM 75        24
     (YHWH) & HIS TWO SONS SATAN & ADAM AS THEY  . . . . .    775D INSC LAOCOON       TITLE
     HE REPENTED THAT HE HAD MADE ADAM OF THE FEMALE THE ADAMAH 776C INSC LAOCOON     PROSE
     ADAM IS ONLY THE NATURAL MAN & NOT THE SOUL OR IMAGINATION 776C INSC LAOCOON     PROSE
     ADAM KNEELS BY HER JEHOVAH STANDS ABOVE  . . . . . . .    779C GHOST ABEL 1      PROSE
     JEHOVAH ADAM . . . . . . . . . . . . . . . . . .         779 GHOST ABEL 1          1
     ADAM I WILL NOT HEAR THEE MORE THOU SPIRITUAL VOICE  . . . 779 GHOST ABEL 1         1
     JEHOVAH ADAM . . . . . . . . . . . . . . . . . .         779 GHOST ABEL 1          2
     ADAM IT IS IN VAIN I WILL NOT HEAR THEE  . . . . . . .    779 GHOST ABEL 1          2
     AND WHO IS HE ADAM WILT THOU OR EVE THOU DO THIS  . . .   780 GHOST ABEL 1         16
     ADAM IT IS ALL A VAIN DELUSION OF THE ALL CREATIVE   . .  780 GHOST ABEL 1         17
        IMAGINATION
     ADAM EVE THOU HAST SPOKEN TRULY LET US KNEEL BEFORE HIS    780 GHOST ABEL 2          3
        FEET
     CLOTHING ADAM & EVE WITH COATS OF SKINS  . . . . . .     824A LETTER 27          PROSE
     ELOHIM CREATING ADAM  . . . . . . . . . . . . .         SUPP COLOR PRT TATE     *TITLE
     CAIN SERPENT ABEL EVE ADAM   . . . . . . . . . .        SUPP INSC HERVEY        *TITLE
     GOD SPEAKING TO ADAM  . . . . . . . . . . . .           SUPP INSCRIPTION        *TITLE
     GOOD & EVIL ANGEL HOUSE OF DEATH GOD JUDGING ADAM LAMECH SUPP LETTER 56A        *PROSE
     GOD CREATING ADAM CHRIST APPEARING TOUCHG UP CHRIST     SUPP LETTER 56A         *PROSE
        BAPTIZING
     ADAM & EVE  . . . . . . . . . . . . . . . .             SUPP PENC DRAW 2.13     *TITLE
ADAMAH
     HE REPENTED THAT HE HAD MADE ADAM OF THE FEMALE THE ADAMAH 776C INSC LAOCOON     PROSE
     "GROUND" ADAMAH  . . . . . . . . . . . . . .            SUPP ILLUS GENESIS      *PROSE
ADAMANT
     BUT SILKEN NETS AND TRAPS OF ADAMANT WILL OOTHOON SPREAD   194 V DAU ALBION 7      23
     WITHOUT FLUCTUATION HARD AS ADAMANT  . . . . . . . .      257 BOOK OF LOS 4        5
     A HAMMER OF ADAMANT THEN BEGAN . . . . . . . . . .        259 BOOK OF LOS 5        22
     HIS KNEES ARE ROCKS OF ADAMANT & RUBIE & EMERALD  . . .   308 FOUR ZOAS 5      *  139
     FOR EVERY HUMAN HEART HAS GATES OF BRASS & BARS OF ADAMANT 502 MILTON 20           34
     AND EVERY DAY & NIGHT HAS WALLS OF BRASS & GATES OF ADAMANT 516 MILTON 28          52
     HIS HAMMER OF GOLD HE SIEZD AND HIS ANVIL OF ADAMANT   . . 628 JERUSALEM 9          3
```

	PAGE	TITLE	LINE

ADAMANTINE
    O WINTER BAR THINE ADAMANTINE DOORS . . . .   2 TO WINTER/PS   1
    RATTLING THE ADAMANTINE CHAINS & HOOKS HEAVE UP THE ORE   282 FOUR ZOAS 2   66
    CAN WRITE AND ADAMANTINE LEAVES RECIEVE NOR CAN THE MAN   316 FOUR ZOAS 6   174
        WHO GOES
    IN FORESTS OF AFFLICTION THE ADAMANTINE SCALES OF JUSTICE   320 FOUR ZOAS 7   10
ADAN   SEE UDAN-ADAN,UDAN ADAN
ADAPTED
    ADAPTED TO THE WEAKNESSES OF EVERY INDIVIDUAL . . . . .   98C ALL RELIGIONS   PROSE
    MORE ADAPTED TO SOLEMN ORNAMENT THAN [DEAD] MARBLE CAN BE   601A PUB ADDRESS/N   *PROSE
    THE PRESENT PROPOSAL AS PECULIARLY ADAPTED TO YOUR IDEAS   841D LETTER 41   PROSE
ADD
    FOR THY RIGHTEOUSNESS BUT I ADD MERCY ALSO AND BIND . . .   670 JERUSALEM 42   20
    WE MIGHT ADD TO THE NUMBER OF PLATES IN A SECOND EDITION   858B LETTER 55   PROSE
        AND HE
ADDED
    CORREGGIO'S REFLECTIONS AND REFRACTIONS TO BE ADDED TO IT   583C DESC CAT 9   PROSE
    EXPECTATION & GLADNESS ADDED TO LABOUR IN OUR REMOVAL THAT   801B LETTER 13   PROSE
    IF I HAVE SUCCEEDED IN THESE MORE MAY BE ADDED AT PLEASURE   860C LETTER 56   PROSE
    HAVE ADDED UPON A PROOF BEFORE I PARTED WITH THE PICTURE   863C LETTER 60   PROSE
ADDER
    . . . IN FOLDS OF THE ROBE THE CROWND ADDER BUILDS AND   147 FRENCH REVOLTN   299
        HISSES
ADDERS
    WHERE NOUGHT BUT ENVIOUS HISSING ADDERS DWELL . . . . .   15 IMIT SPEN/PS   28
ADDING
    & ADDING ORNAMENTS & NOT PRINCIPALS NOTHING CAN BE . . .   801D LETTER 14   PROSE
ADDINGTON
    WESTMINSTER ABBEY SUCH IS THE PROJECT & MR ADDINGTON . .   824D LETTER 27   PROSE
ADDITION
    GOOD HELP & WITH YOUR REMARKS ON IT IN ADDITION I HOPE TO   855B LETTER 53   PROSE
    I HAVE BEEN EVER SINCE TAKING DR YOUNG'S ADDITION TO . .   874B LETTER 79   PROSE
    MR FINCHAM'S PRACTISE WITH ME THE ADDITION IS DANDELION   874B LETTER 79   PROSE
ADDITIONAL
    FLAXMAN'S HOMER WITH ADDITIONAL DESIGNS TWO OF WHICH . .   841A LETTER 40   PROSE
ADDITIONS
    FOR THE YEAR...ADDITIONS TO BLAKE'S CATALOGUE OF PICTURES   604B V LAST JUDG/N   TITLE
        &C
ADDLED
    AND [ALL MY] STEWHARD'S EGGS ARE ADDLED & DECAYD . . . .   537 AND HIS LEGS/N   15
ADDRESS
    I ACCOUNT IT A PUBLIC DUTY RESPECTFULLY TO ADDRESS MYSELF   591C PUB ADDRESS/N   PROSE
    IN THIS PUBLIC ADDRESS . . . .   594D PUB ADDRESS/N   PROSE
    TO THE SOCIETY FOR ENCOURAGEMENT OF ARTS I ADDRESS MYSELF   601A PUB ADDRESS/N   PROSE
    MR EDWARDS KNOW LADY HAMILTON'S ADDRESS THE . . . . .   836B LETTER 35   PROSE
    AGO MR EDWARDS WILL PROCURE HER ADDRESS FOR YOU . . . .   836C LETTER 35   PROSE
    MR HOARE'S ADDRESS IS TO PRINCE HOARE ESQRE BUCKINGHAM   842B LETTER 41   PROSE
        STREET STRAND
    HIS ADDRESS IS THIS TO JOHN HAWKINS ESQR DALLINGTON . . .   855B LETTER 53   PROSE
ADDRESSD
    HE ADDRESSD THE COMPANY IN THESE WORDS . . . .   53B ISLAND MOON 8   PROSE
    URIZEN KNEW THEM NOT & THUS ADDRESSD THE SPIRITS   311 FOUR ZOAS 6   *   7
        OF DARKNESS
    THE VIRGIN OLOLON & ADDRESSD HER AS A DAUGHTER OF BEULAH   527 MILTON 36   27
    ALLEGORY ADDRESSD TO THE INTELLECTUAL POWERS WHILE IT IS   825A LETTER 27   PROSE
ADDRESSED
    IS IT NOT BECAUSE THEY ARE ADDRESSED TO THE IMAGINATION   794A LETTER 5   PROSE
        WHICH
ADDRESSES
    CHRIST ADDRESSES HIMSELF TO THE MAN NOT TO HIS REASON . .   774C ANNO BERKELEY   MARG
ADEQUATE
    OUR INCESSANT LABOUR FULLY ADEQUATE TO [IT] THEM AT PRESENT   811D LETTER 22   PROSE
ADERS
    RECIEVED...OF MRS ADERS BY THE HANDS OF MR LINNELL THE SUM   SUPP LETTER 80A   *PROSE
    MR BLAKE'S RESPECTFUL COMPLIMENTS TO MRS (ADERS) IS SORRY TO   SUPP LETTER 81A   *PROSE
ADHERE
    TO IMITATE I ABHOR I OBSTINATELY ADHERE TO THE TRUE STYLE   600B PUB ADDRESS/N   PROSE
ADHERED
    ADHERED AND GREW ONE WITH HIS FLESH AND NERVES & VEINS   242 EUROPE 12   17
        SHOT THRO THEM
ADHERES
    ("WHO ADHERES TO TRUTH NOR BETRAYS TRUST IS NEAR SUMMIT")   67B ANNO LAVATER   MARG
        EXCELLENT
ADJOIND
    AND IF UGLINESS IS ADJOIND TO BEAUTY . . . .   81D ANNO LAVATER   MARG
    A LIVING MANTLE ADJOIND TO HIS LIFE & GROWING FROM HIS SOUL   318 FOUR ZOAS 6   *   246
    COBAN'S SON IS NIMROD HIS SON CUSH IS ADJOIND TO ARAM . .   625 JERUSALEM 7   19
    MAN IS ADJOIND TO MAN BY HIS EMANATIVE PORTION . . . .   675 JERUSALEM 44   38
    BY INVISIBLE HATREDS ADJOIND THEY SEEM REMOTE AND SEPARATE   703 JERUSALEM 66   53
    HE WHO WILL NOT COMINGLE IN LOVE MUST BE ADJOIND BY HATE   703 JERUSALEM 66   56
    SHE ADJOIND WITH GWANTOKE'S CHILDREN SOON LOVELY CORDELLA   710 JERUSALEM 71   28
        AROSE
    IS RAGAN SHE ADJOIND TO SLADE & PRODUCED GONORILL   710 JERUSALEM 71   33
        FAR BEAMING
    SO YOU SEE HE IS SPIRITUALLY ADJOIND WITH US . . . . .   841C LETTER 41   PROSE
ADJUNCT
    DIGNITY AN ADJUNCT . . . .   477C ANNO REYNOLDS   MARG
ADMINISTER
    THEIR SWEET INSPIRITING LYRES THY LABOURS SHALL ADMINISTER   301 FOUR ZOAS 4   *   154
ADMINISTERD
    & ON THE LEFT HAND THE LORD'S SUPPER IS ADMINISTERD . . .   444B LAST JUDGMNT/L   PROSE

ADMIRABLE

CONNOISSEURS WHO SAID THAT THEY WERE VERY ADMIRABLE . . .	585A	DESC CAT 15	PROSE
HOWEVER ADMIRABLE THAT TRACK MAY BE AT ANY RATE MY EXCUSE	792A	LETTER 4	PROSE
WHO WITH HER ADMIRABLE HUSBAND PRESENT THEIR BEST . . .	836C	LETTER 35	PROSE
HEAR THE SAME GOOD ACCOUNT OF OUR MOST ADMIRABLE	838C	LETTER 37	PROSE
I THANK YOU SINCERELY FOR FALCONER AN ADMIRABLE POET .	843B	LETTER 43	PROSE
ADMIRABLE PRINTS TO IT BY FITTLER WHETHER YOU INTENDED	843B	LETTER 43	PROSE
IT OR			
AND KENT AND THE OTHER ATTENDANT ARE ADMIRABLE	843D	LETTER 43	PROSE
& ADMIRABLE PRESENT IN HOPES TO SEND PROOFS OF MY PLATES	853A	LETTER 51	*PROSE

ADMIRABLY

THIS IS ADMIRABLY SAID WHY DOES HE NOT ALWAYS ALLOW AS MUCH	454D	ANNO REYNOLDS	MARG
FOR I AM BECOME A LIKENESS TAKER & SUCCEED ADMIRABLY WELL	824B	LETTER 27	PROSE
THO ADMIRABLY CONTRIVED FOR AN EFFECT EQUAL TO REMBRANDT	855A	LETTER 53	PROSE

ADMIRATION

ENTHUSIASTIC ADMIRATION IS THE FIRST PRINCIPLE OF KNOWLEDGE	458B	ANNO REYNOLDS	MARG
DELUSORY LOVE TO PALAMABRON ADMIRATION JOIND WITH ENVY . .	492	MILTON 12	7
ATTENDING HIS LOUD HARMONY WITH ADMIRATION & LOVE . . .	520	MILTON 31	44
LOSES ALL ADMIRATION OF ANY OTHER ARTIST BUT RUBENS . .	583A	DESC CAT 9	PROSE
CAN IT BE WORTHY OF ADMIRATION TO ANY BODY OF UNDERSTANDING	597B	PUB ADDRESS/N	PROSE
AND THEY STOOD AROUND TERRIFIED WITH ADMIRATION AT ERIN'S	631	JERUSALEM 12	22
SPACES			
OF THE PLATES FOR COWPER'S WORK WHICH SHE DOES TO	821A	LETTER 25	PROSE
ADMIRATION			
MY ADMIRATION OF FLAXMAN'S GENIUS IS MORE AND MORE . . .	829B	LETTER 29	PROSE
OBJECT OF HIS LOVE & ADMIRATION	838C	LETTER 37	PROSE
MANY YEARS UNDER THE PRETENCE OF ADMIRATION OF THE ARTS	864A	LETTER 61	PROSE
FUSELI'S COUNT UGOLINO IS A MAN OF WONDER AND ADMIRATION	864B	LETTER 61	PROSE

ADMIRD

AND ALL ADMIRD HIS PRIESTLY CARE	177	LIT BOY LST/N	15
AND ALL ADMIRD THE PRIESTLY CARE	218	LIT BOY LST/SE	12
STILL ADMIRD BY [WORTHY] NOBLE MINDS	558	THE CAVERNS/N	11
WE ALL ADMIRD & LOVD WHOSE ALL BENEVOLENT COUNTENANCE SEEN	675	JERUSALEM 45	5

ADMIRE

NOT ADMIRE RAFAEL'S EXECUTION DOES NOT EVEN SEE RAFAEL .	467A	ANNO REYNOLDS	MARG
HE WHO ADMIRES RAFAEL MUST ADMIRE RAFAEL'S EXECUTION . .	472A	ANNO REYNOLDS	MARG
HE WHO DOES NOT ADMIRE RAFAEL'S EXECUTION CANNOT ADMIRE	472A	ANNO REYNOLDS	MARG
RAFAEL			
[TO LEARN TO ADMIRE THE WORKS OF A FOOL]	550	SAY PICTURES/N	4
SOME PEOPLE ADMIRE THE WORK OF A FOOL	556	SOME PEOPLE/N	1
WHICH THEY ADMIRE IN GREEK STATUES	576C	DESC CAT 4	PROSE
[AP] ADMIRE ONLY THE WORK OF THE JOURNEYMAN	596C	PUB ADDRESS/N	*PROSE
DESTROYING BY SELFISH AFFECTIONS THE THINGS THAT THEY MOST	669	JERUSALEM 41	28
ADMIRE			
THOSE ALONE ARE HIS FRIENDS WHO ADMIRE HIS MINUTEST POWERS	673	JERUSALEM 43	58
WHO LOVE & ADMIRE YOUR WORKS BUT ABOVE ALL FOR THE SAKE	795B	LETTER 6	PROSE
OF THE ARTS			

ADMIRED

IF REYNOLDS HAD REALLY ADMIRED MICH ANGELO	450C	ANNO REYNOLDS	MARG
& ADVERTISED FOR EVER IT WILL ONLY BE ADMIRED BY FOOLS . .	466A	ANNO REYNOLDS	MARG
IN A VERY SUPERIOR STYLE TO THOSE JUSTLY ADMIRED COPIES	565D	DESC CAT 2	PROSE
LOOK HOW THEY SCORN THY ONCE ADMIRED PALACES NOW IN RUINS	625	JERUSALEM 7	16
I HAVE MOCKD THOSE WHO REFUSED CRUELTY & I HAVE ADMIRED	723	JERUSALEM 81	1
MY MUCH ADMIRED & RESPECTED EDWARD THE BARD OF OXFORD . .	835A	LETTER 34	PROSE
AND ADMIRED WITHOUT ANY PREFACE MY PRINT OF ROMNEY AND .	843C	LETTER 43	PROSE
I MUCH ADMIRED HIS MILD AND GENTLE BENEVOLENT MANNERS .	844A	LETTER 43	PROSE
DOING JUSTICE TO OUR ADMIRED SUBLIME ROMNEY I HAVE NOT .	849B	LETTER 45	PROSE

ADMIRER

I OWN MYSELF AN ADMIRER OF OSSIAN EQUALLY	783C	ANNO WW POEMS	MARG

ADMIRERS

WILL AT ALL TIMES MAKE THEM HIS ADMIRERS	473A	ANNO REYNOLDS	MARG
INVITES THE ADMIRERS OF OLD ENGLISH PORTRAITS TO LOOK AT	596C	PUB ADDRESS/N	PROSE
HIS PRINT			

ADMIRES

HE WHO ADMIRES RAFAEL MUST ADMIRE RAFAEL'S EXECUTION . .	472A	ANNO REYNOLDS	MARG
ADMIRES ALL HIS COLOURS BROWN & WARM	597	PUBLC VOICE/PA	3

ADMIRING SEE SELF ADMIRING

THE GODS ADMIRING LOADED HER WITH GIFTS AS ONCE PANDORA	42D	THEN SHE BORE	PROSE
FORM IMMORTAL WITH GOLDEN PEN SUCH AS THE SPECTRE ADMIRING	515	MILTON 28	17
ON LONDON STONE & THE DAUGHTERS OF ALBION RAN AROUND	715	JERUSALEM 74	34
ADMIRING			

ADMISSION

I INCLOSE A TICKET OF ADMISSION IF YOU SHOULD HONOUR .	866B	LETTER 64	PROSE

ADMIT

WILL NOT ADMIT OF GRAND COLOURING IN MR B'S (BLAKE'S)	581A	DESC CAT 5	PROSE
BRITONS			

ADMITS

AS POETRY ADMITS NOT A LETTER THAT IS INSIGNIFICANT . . .	611B	V LAST JUDG/N	PROSE
SO PAINTING ADMITS NOT A GRAIN OF SAND OR A BLADE OF GRASS	611B	V LAST JUDG/N	PROSE
HIDDEN IN ALBION'S FORESTS HE LURKS HE ADMITS OF NO REPLY	653	JERUSALEM 29	13
TO TYBURN'S DEATHFUL SHADES ADMITS THE WANDERING SOULS .	665	JERUSALEM 38	58

ADMITTANCE

ADMITTANCE...EACH PERSON A DISCRIPTIVE CATALOGUE INCLUDED	560C	EXHIBITION ADV	PROSE
ADMITTANCE TO THE EXHIBITION (ONE) SHILLING	562C	DESC CAT ADV	PROSE

ADMITTED

MEN ARE ADMITTED INTO HEAVEN NOT BECAUSE THEY	615C	V LAST JUDG/N	PROSE

ADMONISHERS

AND THE PRIVY ADMONISHERS OF MEN	247	SONG OF LOS 6	19

ADONA

DOWN BY THE RIVER OF ADONA HER SOFT VOICE IS HEARD . . .	127	BOOK OF THEL 1	4

ADOPT

WHO IN HOPES OF A GOOD LIVING ADOPT THE STATE RELIGION .	390D	ANNO WATSON	MARG

ADOPT   (CONTINUED)
        AND ROMAN PRACTICE AND ADOPT THE VENETIAN AND FLEMISH   . . 583A DESC CAT 9   PROSE
        I THINK THE MANNER I ADOPT MORE PERFECT THAN ANY OTHER   . . 815B LETTER 23   PROSE
        RESPECT WHICH YOU WILL BE PLEASED WITH & I HOPE WILL ADOPT 841B LETTER 41   PROSE
        HIS MANNER OF WORKING IS WHAT I SHALL ENDEAVOUR TO ADOPT   843B LETTER 43   PROSE
ADOPTED
        FOR THIS HISTORY HAS BEEN ADOPTED BY BOTH PARTIES   . . .   150A MARRIAGE HH 5   PROSE
        THAT THEY MAY CURSE THARMAS THEIR GOD & LOS HIS ADOPTED SON 313 FOUR ZOAS 6   43
        & THAT BAD ART WILL BE ADOPTED & MIXED WITH GOOD ART   . . 617A V LAST JUDG/N   PROSE
ADOPTS
        ADOPTS THE VENETIAN PRACTICE OR DOES AS MR B(BLAKE) HAS   582D DESC CAT 9   PROSE
          DONE
ADORATION
        SHE SAW THE WORLD FALL DOWN IN ADORATION [NOR COULD   41B THEN SHE BORE   PROSE
          REFRAIN]
        WHEN LOVE & JOY WERE ADORATION . . . .   256 BOOK OF LOS 3   8
        IN TORMENTS OF FIERCE JEALOUSY & PANGS OF ADORATION . . . 289 FOUR ZOAS 2   351
        WITH HOLY RAPTURES OF ADORATION RAPD SUBLIME IN THE VISIONS 720 JERUSALEM 79   44
          OF GOD
ADORD
        AND SECRET ASSASINATIONS NOT WORSHIPD NOR ADORD BUT . . . 528 MILTON 37   31
        WHO ALMOST ADORD HER COUSIN THE POET & THOUGHT HIM . . . 820D LETTER 25   PROSE
ADORE
        ("WHOSE RULING PASSION IS NOT VANITY") SUCH A WOMAN I   78D ANNO LAVATER   MARG
          ADORE
        [THAT NOUGHT BUT ENION COULD BE FOUND TO PRAISE ADORE &   267 FOUR ZOAS 1   133
          LOVE]
        THE BIRDS ADORE THE SUN THE BEASTS RISE UP & PLAY IN HIS   367 FOUR ZOAS 9   406
          BEAMS
        [AS DO ?FOOLS THAT ADORE THINGS & ?IDEAS XXX OF GENERAL   451A ANNO REYNOLDS   * MARG
          KNOWLEDGE]
        AND FRANCE SHALL FALL DOWN & ADORE . . . .   557 ART HAS LOST/N   6
        THEY CALL THE ROCKS PARENTS OF MEN & ADORE THE FROWNING   704 JERUSALEM 67   15
          CHAOS
        THEY ADORE & HIS REVENGE CHERISH WITH THE BLOOD OF THE   704 JERUSALEM 67   21
          INNOCENT
        THINE OWN HUMANITY LEARN TO ADORE . . . .   750 EV GOSPEL(C)/N   42
        THY OWN HUMANITY LEARN TO ADORE . . . .   752 EV GOSPEL(D)/N   76
        CHRISTIANITY AND ADORE HIM WHO IS THE EXPRESS IMAGE OF GOD 815D LETTER 23   PROSE
        AS THE FRENCH NOW ADORE BUONAPARTE AND THE ENGLISH OUR   845B LETTER 44   PROSE
          POOR GEORGE
ADORES
        SHE WHO ADORES NOT YOUR FROWNS WILL ONLY LOATHE YOUR SMILES 743 JERUSALEM 95   24
ADORING
        REJOICING IN HIS INDIGNATION ADORING HIS WRATHFUL REBUKE   743 JERUSALEM 95   23
ADORN
        AND THE WILD SNAKE THE PESTILENCE TO ADORN HIM WITH GEMS   195 V DAU ALBION 8   7
          & GOLD
        AND YOU BIRDS THAT SING & ADORN THE SKY YOU ARE MY SISTERS 368 FOUR ZOAS 9   444
        WHY DID HEAVEN ADORN ME WITH BOUNTIFUL HAND . . . . .   428 MARY   23
        WHEN GOLD & GEMS ADORN THE PLOW . . . .   433 AUGURIES   101
        [?O ?WHAT ?WISDOM ?& ?LEARNING ?ADORN ?HIS ?SUPERIORITY]   472A ANNO REYNOLDS   * MARG
ADORND
        EVERY ART & SCIENCE ADORND HIM AS BEADS ROUND HIS NECK . . 46D ISLAND MOON/3   PROSE
        ADORND IN YELLOW VEST . . . .   50 WHEN CORRUP/IM   2
ADORNED   SEE WELL ADORNED
        . . . NOW BEAMING WITH KNOWLEDGE WITH GENTLE AWE ADORNED   144 FRENCH REVOLTN   230
ADORNING
        OR GENIUSES CALLING THEM BY THE NAMES AND ADORNING THEM   153A MARRIAGE HH 11   PROSE
        AND OTHERS ADORNING IT WITH GOLD SILVER AND PRECIOUS STONES 154D MARRIAGE HH 15   PROSE
        ON WHOM I POURD THE BEAUTIES OF MY LIGHT ADORNING THEM . . 312 FOUR ZOAS 6   26
        HEAVEN'S MOUNTAINS ADORNING . . . .   804 TO BUTTS/L   14
ADORNS
        THE JEWEL HEALTH ADORNS HER NECK . . . .   63 SHEPHERD FIRST   8
ADULTERATE
        AND FOLDED HIS BLACK JEALOUS WATERS ROUND THE ADULTERATE   190 V DAU ALBION 2   4
          PAIR
ADULTERESS
        MARRY A HARLOT & AN ADULTERESS MARY ANSWERD ART THOU MORE   694 JERUSALEM 61   6
          PURE
        THE REAPERS SAYING AM I JERUSALEM THE LOST ADULTERESS OR   695 JERUSALEM 61   34
          AM I
        AND FROM THE ADULTERESS TURND AWAY . . . .   757 EV GOSPEL(I)/N   47
ADULTERIES
        THENCE ROSE SECRET ADULTERIES . . . .   755 EV GOSPEL(E)/N   73
ADULTEROUS
        MARY WAS FOUND IN ADULTEROUS BED . . . .   753 EV GOSPEL(E)/N   4
ADULTERY
        TURN AWAY THE LAW FROM THE WOMAN TAKEN IN ADULTERY . . . 158C MARRIAGE HH 22   PROSE
        THE ACCUSERS OF THEFT ADULTERY MURDER A SCENE IN THE LAST SUPP INSC OUR END   *TITLE
          JUDGMENT
ADVANCD
        AND CHOSE HER ARROWS THEN ADVANCD TO MEET THE TERRIBLE PAIR 109 TIRIEL 7   24
        THRO CAVES OF DEATH INTO EXISTENCE THE BEECH LONG LIMBD   335 FOUR ZOAS 7B   *   100
          ADVANCD
        YOU SHALL SOON SEE A PROOF OF HIM IN A VERY ADVANCD STATE   851A LETTER 49   PROSE
ADVANCE
        GROW LARGER AS WE ADVANCE AND SOME PERHAPS . . . . .   18 EDW THIRD/PS 1   37
        TO TWINKLE IN THEIR SPHERE MAY SO ADVANCE . . . . .   18 EDW THIRD/PS 1   39
        THEY SLOW ADVANCE TO SHUT THE FIVE GATES OF THEIR LAW-BUILT 203 AMERICA 16   19
          HEAVEN
        IT CONTINUES ACCUMULATING TO ETERNITY THE JOYS OF   630 JERUSALEM 10   46
          GOD ADVANCE

```
                                                                PAGE    TITLE        LINE
ADVANCE    (CONTINUED)
      BUT MY GRIEFS ADVANCE ALSO FOR EVER & EVER WITHOUT END    630 JERUSALEM 10      50
      HOW WE ADVANCE WITH ROMNEY HIS BEST WORKS ONLY    . . . . 857C LETTER 54       PROSE
ADVANCEMENT
      UNDERSTANDING & BACON'S (ADVANCEMENT) OF LEARNING    . . . 476D ANNO REYNOLDS  * MARG
ADVANCEMT
      SEE ADVANCEMT OF LEARNING PART...P...OF FIRST EDITION  .   794A LETTER 5       PROSE
ADVANCES
      LOOK HOW THE OPENING DAWN ADVANCES WITH VOCAL HARMONY  .    367 FOUR ZOAS 9      397
      UNWAKEND AND THE COVERING CHERUB ADVANCES FROM THE EAST     506 MILTON 23        10
ADVANCING
      ADVANCING TOWARD US WITH ALL THE FURY OF A SPIRITUAL       156C MARRIAGE HH 17 PROSE
        EXISTENCE
      OF ADVANCING FINE ART IN PROTESTANT COMMUNITIES    . . . . 601B PUB ADDRESS/N  PROSE
ADVANTAGE
      TILL A SYSTEM WAS FORMED WHICH SOME TOOK ADVANTAGE OF &    153A MARRIAGE HH 11 PROSE
      ON THE INN IS INSCRIBED ITS TITLE AND A PROPER ADVANTAGE   567B DESC CAT 3     PROSE
      ON THE INN IS INSCRIBED ITS TITLE & A PROPER ADVANTAGE  .  588D CHAUCER/N      PROSE
      ON THE INN IS INSCRIBED ITS TITLE AND A PROPER ADVANTAGE   590C CHAUCER 2      PROSE
      THE ADVANTAGE OF SO EXTENSIVE A DIFFUSAL AS WOULD          856C LETTER 54      PROSE
        BE PROMOTED
      OF ADVANTAGE TO OUR FRIEND SEAGRAVE THE IDEA OF SEEING  .  859C LETTER 56      PROSE
ADVANTAGEOUS
      PERMANENT I TAKE THE ADVANTAGEOUS OPPORTUNITY    . . . . . 863D LETTER 61      PROSE
      ADVANTAGEOUS ACQUAINTANCE I GO ON WITHOUT DARING TO COUNT  879C LETTER 89      PROSE
ADVANTAGES
      HE MAKES LITTLE CONCESSIONS THAT HE MAY TAKE GREAT         463C ANNO REYNOLDS   MARG
        ADVANTAGES
ADVENT
      SINCE ITS ADVENT THE ETERNAL HELL REVIVES AND LO  . . . . 149A MARRIAGE HH 3   PROSE
ADVENTURE
      WITHOUT SOME ADVENTURE IT HAS STRUCK A CONSTERNATION THRO  828A LETTER 28      PROSE
      GIVE ME YOUR ADVICE IN MY PERILOUS ADVENTURE    . . . . . 828C LETTER 28      PROSE
ADVERSARY
      TO HIS ADVERSARY AND THEY SENT FORTH ALL THEIR SONS        501 MILTON 19         30
        & DAUGHTERS
ADVERSARYS
      IT WOULD HAVE BEEN AS DULL AS HIS ADVERSARY'S    . . . . . 576C DESC CAT 4     *PROSE
ADVERSE
      AS COGS ARE FORMD IN A WHEEL TO TURN THE COGS OF           513 MILTON 27         10
        THE ADVERSE WHEEL
      ARE FORMD IN A WHEEL TO FIT THE COGS OF THE ADVERSE WHEEL  633 JERUSALEM 13      14
ADVERSITIES
      ("ADVERSITIES") A LIE  .  .  .  .  .  .  .  .  .  .  .  .  403D ANNO BACON      MARG
ADVERT
      THE SHIPWRECK WHICH IT WAS BUT I DID NOT ADVERT TO THE  .  854D LETTER 53      PROSE
ADVERTISED
      & ADVERTISED FOR EVER IT WILL ONLY BE ADMIRED BY FOOLS  .  466A ANNO REYNOLDS  MARG
ADVERTISEMENT
      ADVERTISEMENT THE REMAINING BOOKS OF THIS POEM ARE FINISHED 134A FRENCH REVOLTN TITLE
      P S YOUR DESIRE THAT I SHOULD WRITE A LITTLE ADVERTISEMENT 860B LETTER 56      PROSE
      ADVERTISEMENT CALLING IT AN APPEAL TO CHARITY AND SAYS IT  861B LETTER 58      PROSE
ADVERTISING
      BUT ADVERTISING IN THE NEWS PAPERS  .  .  .  .  .  .  .  . 536 NO REAL STYL/N    2
ADVERTIZEMENTS
      THIS DAY IS PUBLISHD ADVERTIZEMENTS TO BLAKE'S CANTERBURY  591B PUB ADDRESS/N  PROSE
      ADVERTIZEMENTS IN NEWSPAPERS  .  .  .  .  .  .  .  .  .  . 593C PUB ADDRESS/N  *PROSE
ADVERTIZING
      EXPENSIVE ADVERTIZING BOASTS THAT THEY MAKE OF SUCH WORKS  480C MILTON 1       PROSE
ADVICE
      BY YOUR ADVICE WE LANDED HERE IN BRITTANY    .  .  .  .  .  18 EDW THIRD/PS 1    46
      MY LORDS I HAVE BY THE ADVICE OF HER  .  .  .  .  .  .  .   19 EDW THIRD/PS 2     1
      NOW BY THE QUEEN'S ADVICE I ASK YOUR LEAVE .  .  .  .  .  . 20 EDW THIRD/PS 2    41
      LORD PERCY'S ADVICE I HAVE BEEN USED SO MUCH .  .  .  .  .  20 EDW THIRD/PS 2    60
      WATER HIM WITH THY ADVICE AND HEAVN  .  .  .  .  .  .  .  . 26 EDW THIRD/PS 3   214
      FOR A LETTER OF ADVICE TO A KING .  .  .  .  .  .  .  .  . 136 FRENCH REVOLTN    51
      GOOD ADVICE FOR SATAN'S KINGDOM  .  .  .  .  .  .  .  .  . 396D ANNO BACON      MARG
      GOOD ADVICE FOR THE DEVIL  .  .  .  .  .  .  .  .  .  .  . 402D ANNO BACON      MARG
      THE CONTRARY IS THE BEST ADVICE  .  .  .  .  .  .  .  .  . 405A ANNO BACON      MARG
      IF THIS IS ADVICE TO THE POOR IT IS MOCKING THEM  .  .  . 406D ANNO BACON      MARG
      IF TO THE MIDDLE CLASS IT IS THE DIRECT CONTRARY          406D ANNO BACON      MARG
        TO CHRIST'S ADVICE
      VERY PERNICIOUS ADVICE  .  .  .  .  .  .  .  .  .  .  .  . 408B ANNO BACON      MARG
      ADVICE OF THE POPES WHO SUCCEEDED THE AGE OF RAFAEL  .  .  445B ANNO REYNOLDS  MARG
      HE WAS TOO WISE TO TAKE THIS ADVICE  .  .  .  .  .  .  .  452C ANNO REYNOLDS  MARG
      GOOD ADVICE  .  .  .  .  .  .  .  .  .  .  .  .  .  .  .  . 456D ANNO REYNOLDS  MARG
      OF EXECUTION IN ART LET HIM WHO WILL FOLLOW SUCH ADVICE    461C ANNO REYNOLDS  MARG
      FOR A MAN CAN ONLY REJECT ERROR BY THE ADVICE OF A FRIEND  614A V LAST JUDG/N  PROSE
      I HEAR HIS ADVICE & EVEN NOW WRITE FROM HIS DICTATE  .  .  797B LETTER 9       PROSE
      THRO THE PETWORTH ROAD WHICH BY YOUR FORTUNATE ADVICE I    801B LETTER 13      PROSE
        MEAN
      YOUR ADVICE I SEE THE FACE OF MY HEAVENLY FATHER HE LAYS   823B LETTER 26      PROSE
        HIS
      GIVE ME YOUR ADVICE IN MY PERILOUS ADVENTURE    .  .  .  .  828C LETTER 28      PROSE
      SAYS HE LAMENTS YOUR ABSENCE FROM LONDON AS YOUR ADVICE    844A LETTER 43      PROSE
      SEND YOU FLAXMAN'S ADVICE UPON THIS ARTICLE WHEN I REPEATED 846B LETTER 44      PROSE
      BEING AT FLAXMAN'S TAKING HIS ADVICE ABOUT OUR ENGRAVINGS  853A LETTER 51      *PROSE
      WITH FLAXMAN'S ADVICE WHICH HE GIVES  .  .  .  .  .  .  .  853B LETTER 52      PROSE
      OF HIS ADVICE CONCERNING THEM AND HE THINKS THAT THEY  .  858B LETTER 55      PROSE
      I ENTREAT YOUR IMMEDIATE ADVICE WHAT I AM TO DO FOR I  .  858C LETTER 55      PROSE
ADVISE
      BUT I WILL NOT ADVISE ANY THING TILL FLAXMAN SEES THEM  .  839C LETTER 38      PROSE
```

22

ADVISE   (CONTINUED)
    OVERLOOK & ADVISE & DO ALL THAT HE CAN TO MAKE MY DESIGNS   853A LETTER 51   *PROSE
ADVISED   SEE WELL ADVISED
    IF THE LION WAS ADVISED BY THE FOX HE WOULD BE CUNNING . . 152D MARRIAGE HH 10 PROSE
    LEO X WAS ADVISED NOT TO ENCOURAGE THE ARTS . . . . 452C ANNO REYNOLDS   MARG
    IS IMPROVED THE LIP I HAVE AGAIN LESSENED AS YOU ADVISED   797A LETTER 9   PROSE
    HAS ADVISED THAT (FOUR) SHOULD BE DONE . . . . . 848B LETTER 45   PROSE
    HE ADVISED IT TO BE DONE AS ABOVE RELATED . . . . 853A LETTER 51   *PROSE
ADVISER
    CELSUS WAS A BAD ADVISER . . . . 408D ANNO BACON   MARG
ADVISES
    AUTHORS AND CURIOUS BOOKS IN GENERAL HE ADVISES THAT SOME   831C LETTER 31   PROSE
    MR FLAXMAN ADVISES THAT THE DRAWING OF MR ROMNEY'S . . 840D LETTER 40   PROSE
    MR FLAXMAN ADVISES THAT THE BEST ENGRAVERS SHOULD BE . . 848C LETTER 45   PROSE
ADVOCATE
    FULFILLED IN ME & IN FUTURE I AM THE DETERMINED ADVOCATE   804A LETTER 16   PROSE
    THE DEATH OF SO EXCELLENT A MAN AS MY GENEROUS ADVOCATE   854B LETTER 53   PROSE
AEGYPTIANS   SEE EGYPTIANS
    ("THE AEGYPTIANS") THEY ALSO CONSIDERD GOD AS ABSTRACTED   774A ANNO BERKELEY * MARG
AERIAL
    THE OTHER FLOWS THRO THE AERIAL VOID & ALL THE CHURCHES   526 MILTON 35   52
AERY
    OF ALPINE HILLS ROUND HIS HIGH AERY . . . . . . 15 INIT SPEN/PS   39
AFAR
    THE KING IS SEEN RAGING AFAR . . . . 13 GWIN KING/PS   81
    BLOOD CRIES AFAR THE LAND DOTH SOW ITSELF . . . . . 34B KING JOHN/PS   PROSE
    AND DREADFUL THUNDER OF THE BATTLE HEARD AFAR . . . . 34B KING JOHN/PS   PROSE
    BUT CLOUDS OBSCURE MY AGED SIGHT A VISION FROM AFAR . . 199 AMERICA 9   12
    AH VISION FROM AFAR AH REBEL FORM THAT RENT THE ANCIENT   199 AMERICA 9   14
    PARENTS WERE AFAR . . . . 219 LIT GRL LST/SE   17
    AFAR OFF RUSHING BACK REDDNING WITH RAGE THE [ETERNAL]   275 FOUR ZOAS 1   * 413
      MIGHTY FATHER
    AFAR INTO THE ZENITH HIGH BENDING THY FURIOUS COURSE . . 278 FOUR ZOAS 1   495
    THE EVIL DAY AFAR & IF PERCHANCE WITH IRON POWER . . . 282 FOUR ZOAS 2   75
    FALL OFF AFAR FROM THARMAS COME NOT TOO NEAR MY STRONG FURY   296 FOUR ZOAS 3   173
    ROUND LOS AFAR HIS WATERS BORE ON ALL SIDES ROUND WITH   301 FOUR ZOAS 4   159
      NOISE
    [SEDITIOUS] THOU LAZY MONK [SAID CHARLEMAINE] THEY SOUND   419 I SAW A MONK/N   10
      AFAR
    TO WHOM THE ANCIENTS LOOKD AND SAW HIS DAY AFAR OFF . . 621A JERUSALEM 3   PROSE
    I AM NOT A GOD AFAR OFF I AM A BROTHER AND FRIEND . . . 622 JERUSALEM 4   18
    A PILLAR OF SMOKE WRITHING AFAR INTO NON-ENTITY REDOUNDING   624 JERUSALEM 5   51
    TILL THE CLOUD REACHES AFAR OUTSTRETCHD AMONG THE STARRY   624 JERUSALEM 5   52
      WHEELS
    LOS HEARD HER LAMENTATIONS IN THE DEEPS AFAR HIS TEARS FALL   624 JERUSALEM 5   66
    THE EVIL DAY AFAR AND IF PERCHANCE WITH IRON POWER . . . 626 JERUSALEM 7   33
    THOU LAZY MONK THEY SOUND AFAR . . . . 683 I SAW A MONK/J   9
    AFAR INTO THE UNKNOWN NIGHT THE MOUNTAINS FLED AWAY . . 702 JERUSALEM 66   44
    IN VAIN HE IS HURRIED AFAR INTO AN UNKNOWN NIGHT . . . 703 JERUSALEM 66   76
    FROM ALBION'S TOMB AFAR AND FROM THE FOUR-FOLD WONDERS   721 JERUSALEM 79   62
      OF GOD
    ARE MEN SEEN AFAR . . . . 805 TO BUTTS/L   32
AFFAIR
    WHICH WAS TO LEAVE THE WHOLE CONDUCT OF THE AFFAIR TO YOU   842C LETTER 42   PROSE
    & MORE CEREMONY ALSO IN SO SERIOUS AN AFFAIR AS THE CALLING   854D LETTER 53   PROSE
      ON
    MY DESIRE IS THAT YOU WOULD ENQUIRE INTO THIS AFFAIR & . . 865B LETTER 62   PROSE
AFFAIRS
    THE FOLLOWING AFFAIRS HAPPEND . . . . 58C ISLAND MOON 10   PROSE
    & THE AFFAIRS OF LIFE & DEATH TRIFLES SPORTS OF TIME . . 383C ANNO WATSON   MARG
AFFECT
    & WHENEVER ANY THING APPEARS TO AFFECT THAT INTEREST . . 812D LETTER 22   PROSE
AFFECTATION
    ("AFFECTATION OF SANCTITY IS A BLOTCH ON FACE OF PIETY")   71B ANNO LAVATER   MARG
      BRAVO
    AFFECTATION & FOPPERY HE WHO COPIES DOES NOT EXECUTE . . 596B PUB ADDRESS/N   PROSE
AFFECTATIONS
    SHE HAS CERTAIN PECULIARITIES AND LITTLE DELICATE   568B DESC CAT 3   PROSE
      AFFECTATIONS
AFFECTED
    NOT HIS AFFECTED CONTEMPT THAT CAN MOVE ME TO ANY THING BUT   825C LETTER 27   PROSE
    FIRMNESS I HAVE BROUGHT DOWN HIS AFFECTED LOFTINESS . . . 825C LETTER 27   PROSE
AFFECTING
    A MASTER OF ART AND LEARNING THOUGH AFFECTING TO DESPISE IT   569C DESC CAT 3   PROSE
AFFECTION
    ("FORWARDNESS NIPS AFFECTION IN THE BUD") THE MORE IS THE   85A ANNO LAVATER   MARG
      PITY
    THOUGHT WITHOUT AFFECTION MAKES A DISTINCTION BETWEEN . . 90D ANNO SWED LOVE   MARG
    AS FROM ONE AFFECTION MAY PROCEED MANY THOUGHTS . . . . 91A ANNO SWED LOVE   MARG
    MUCH LESS CAN INTELLECT TEACH AFFECTION HOW FOOLISH THEN   93A ANNO SWED LOVE   MARG
    LAUGHS AT AFFECTION GLORIES IN REBELLION SCOFFS AT LOVE   107 TIRIEL 6   18
    AND TURNING [WISDOM] AFFECTION INTO FURY & THOUGHT INTO   324 FOUR ZOAS 7   155
      ABSTRACTION
    KNOWING THE ARTS OF URIZEN WERE PITY & MEEK [LOVE]   336 FOUR ZOAS 7B   134
      AFFECTION
    ENRAPTURD WITH AFFECTION SWEET AND MILD BENEVOLENCE . . . 518 MILTON 30   7
    AFFECTION OR LOVE BECOMES A STATE WHEN DIVIDED FROM   522 MILTON 32   33
      IMAGINATION
    GOING IN AND OUT BEFORE HIM IN HIS LOVE AND SWEET AFFECTION   642 JERUSALEM 20   10
    ALBION THEY CURSE THEIR HUMAN KINDNESS & AFFECTION . . . 671 JERUSALEM 42   60
    ALL POWERFUL PARENTAL AFFECTION FILLS ALBION FROM HEAD   685 JERUSALEM 54   10
      TO FOOT

```
                                                                   PAGE       TITLE              LINE
AFFECTION    (CONTINUED)
      CORD OF AFFECTION THRILLING EXTATIC ON THE IRON REEL     .   .   688  JERUSALEM 56          12
      IS DIVIDED IN THE INTOXICATIONS OF PLEASURE & AFFECTION      690  JERUSALEM 58          14
      JERUSALEM HUNGERS IN THE DESERT AFFECTION TO HER CHILDREN    727  JERUSALEM 83           7
      LEST HAND THE TERRIBLE DESTROY HIS AFFECTION THOU HIDEST     727  JERUSALEM 83          30
         HER
      OF TENDER AFFECTION THAT NO MORE THE MASCULINE MINGLES   .   .   736  JERUSALEM 90          10
      "REMEMBER WITH AFFECTION EVEN THE HEM OF YOUR GARMENT"   .   .  800A  LETTER 12         PROSE
      "RECIEVE MY & MY HUSBAND'S LOVE & AFFECTION &"   .   .   .   .  801A  LETTER 12         PROSE
      MR HAYLEY RECIEVD US WITH HIS USUAL BROTHERLY AFFECTION      802A  LETTER 14         PROSE
      MR HAYLEY RECIEVD ME WITH HIS USUAL BROTHERLY AFFECTION      803B  LETTER 15         PROSE
      PAST THE TURRET MY WIFE JOINS WITH ME IN DUTY AND AFFECTION  807B  LETTER 17         PROSE
      WITH FAVOUR & AFFECTION PERHAPS THE SIMPLICITY OF MYSELF     828C  LETTER 28         PROSE
      IN HIGH SPIRITS & WELCOMD ME WITH KIND AFFECTION &   .   .   .  833C  LETTER 33         PROSE
      PANG OF AFFECTION & GRATITUDE IS THE GIFT OF GOD FOR GOOD    833D  LETTER 33         PROSE
      YOU BOTH WITH GREAT AFFECTION MR FLAXMAN HAS ALSO PROMISED   846A  LETTER 44         PROSE
      THIS PHILLIPS SPOKE WITH REAL AFFECTION  .   .   .   .   .   .  846B  LETTER 44         PROSE
      AT LAVANT I REMAIN WITH MY WIFE'S JOINT AFFECTION            852D  LETTER 50         PROSE
      & TO THOSE WHO HAVE AN AFFECTION FOR HIM LIKE YOURS IS   .   854B  LETTER 53         PROSE
      IN THIS WORLD AS EASY AS I CAN IN THAT OF AFFECTION &    .   857C  LETTER 54         PROSE
      PRAY ACCEPT MY & MY WIFE'S SINCEREST AFFECTION & BELIEVE     857C  LETTER 54         PROSE
      PRAYER AND PARENTAL AFFECTION FILLS THE FIGURE FROM HEAD     864B  LETTER 61        *PROSE
         TO FOOT
AFFECTIONATE
      BUT HERE THE AFFECTIONATE TOUCH OF THE TONGUE .   .   .   .   .  672  JERUSALEM 43          24
      & BELIEVE ME FOR EVER TO REMAIN YOUR GRATEFUL               802D  LETTER 14          PROSE
         & AFFECTIONATE
      YOUR AFFECTIONATE & OBLIGED FRIEND   .   .   .   .   .   .   .  803C  LETTER 15         PROSE
      MR AND MRS FLAXMAN AND BELIEVE ME TO BE YOUR AFFECTIONATE    807B  LETTER 17         PROSE
      YOUR VERY KIND & AFFECTIONATE LETTER & THE MANY KIND        811B  LETTER 22         PROSE
         THINGS
      & WE BOTH REMAIN YOUR AFFECTIONATE   .   .   .   .   .   .   .  837D  LETTER 36         PROSE
      MOST UNPROFITABLE OF HURRIES YOUR SINCERE & AFFECTIONATE     840C  LETTER 39         PROSE
      I AM DEAR SIR YOUR SINCERELY AFFECTIONATE  .   .   .   .   .   .  841A  LETTER 40         PROSE
      MY AFFECTIONATE COMPLIMENTS TO HIM   .   .   .   .   .   .   .  850C  LETTER 49         PROSE
      AND AFFECTIONATE COMPLIMENTS TO HIM ALSO TO OUR KIND FRIEND  852D  LETTER 50         PROSE
      I REMAIN DEAR SIR YOUR OBLIGED AND AFFECTIONATE  .   .   .   .  858D  LETTER 55         PROSE
      THE SITUATIONS OF OUR BEAUTIFUL AFFECTIONATE BALLADS I KNOW  863B  LETTER 60         PROSE
      YOUR AFFECTIONATE WILL BLAKE & HIS WIFE CATHERINE BLAKE      863C  LETTER 60         PROSE
AFFECTIONATELY
      MOST SUPERLATIVELY BEAUTIFUL & MOST AFFECTIONATELY HOLY       82D  ANNO LAVATER        MARG
      "BELIEVE ME TO BE YOURS AFFECTIONATELY CATHERINE BLAKE"      801A  LETTER 12         PROSE
      & BELIEVE ME TO BE EVER YOURS AFFECTIONATELY  .   .   .   .   .  823C  LETTER 26         PROSE
      TO MY BROTHER & REMAIN SINCERELY & AFFECTIONATELY YOURS      829B  LETTER 28         PROSE
      REMEMBER US BOTH AFFECTIONATELY & GRATEFULLY TO MISS POOLE   840A  LETTER 38         PROSE
      IT IS NOW BETTER HE DESIRES TO BE MOST AFFECTIONATELY    .   842D  LETTER 42         PROSE
      REMEMBERD IN SUSSEX I AM DEAR SIR YOURS EVER AFFECTIONATELY  862B  LETTER 59         PROSE
      I AM DEAR SIR YOURS AFFECTIONATELY   .   .   .   .   .   .   .  879A  LETTER 88         PROSE
AFFECTIONS
      AFFECTIONS ARE NATURAL BUT UNDERSTANDING IS ACQUIRED BUT      89B  ANNO SWED LOVE  *  MARG
         OBSERVE
      OF HOLINESS DISTINCT FROM MAN IS IMPOSSIBLE TO THE           90C  ANNO SWED LOVE      MARG
         AFFECTIONS
      THOUGHT ALONE CAN MAKE MONSTERS BUT THE AFFECTIONS CANNOT    90C  ANNO SWED LOVE      MARG
      ASTONISHD SAT HER SISTERS OF BEULAH TO SEE HER SOFT         270  FOUR ZOAS 1     *    227
         AFFECTIONS
      THEN DRAWING INTO WIRES THE TERRIFIC PASSIONS & AFFECTIONS   346  FOUR ZOAS 8         208
      HER LOOMS VIBRATE WITH SOFT AFFECTIONS WEAVING THE WEB       486  MILTON 6             28
         OF LIFE
      A POLYPUS OF SOFT AFFECTIONS WITHOUT THOUGHT OR VISION  .   .  509  MILTON 24            38
      AND TAKE POSSESSION OF HIS AFFECTIONS  .   .   .   .   .   .   .  583B  DESC CAT 9        PROSE
      I LABOUR DAY AND NIGHT I BEHOLD THE SOFT AFFECTIONS  .   .   .  628  JERUSALEM 9          26
      THE STONES ARE PITY AND THE BRICKS WELL WROUGHT AFFECTIONS   632  JERUSALEM 12         30
      ALL HIS AFFECTIONS NOW APPEAR WITHOUTSIDE ALL HIS SONS       641  JERUSALEM 19         17
      MY HOUSES ARE THOUGHTS MY INHABITANTS AFFECTIONS  .   .   .   .  665  JERUSALEM 38         33
      DESTROYING BY SELFISH AFFECTIONS THE THINGS THAT THEY MOST   669  JERUSALEM 41         28
         ADMIRE
      HE SAW THAT THE ACCURSED THINGS WERE HIS OWN AFFECTIONS      669  JERUSALEM 42          3
      AMONG THE INFANT LOVES & AFFECTIONS AND THE DIVINE VISION    669  JERUSALEM 42          7
         WEPT
      .  .  .  FROM THE MINGLED AFFECTIONS OF THE BROTHERS     .   .  710  JERUSALEM 71         24
      HOW HYLE ROOFD LOS IN ALBION'S CLIFFS BY THE AFFECTIONS      715  JERUSALEM 74         28
         RENT
      AND ON HIS ANVILS LEST THEY DESTROY THE FEMININE AFFECTIONS  719  JERUSALEM 78          8
      DOWN FLOWING INTO ENTUTHON'S VALES GLISTENS WITH            728  JERUSALEM 83         74
         SOFT AFFECTIONS
      IN GOOD LUCK AT LAST & SHALL BE FORGOT BY MY AFFECTIONS &    824D  LETTER 27         PROSE
      MY WIFE JOINS ME IN BEST AFFECTIONS TO YOU  .   .   .   .   .  839A  LETTER 37         PROSE
      PLEASE TO PRESENT OUR SINCEREST AFFECTIONS TO HER MY WIFE    849C  LETTER 45         PROSE
AFFINITIES
      IN BOWLAHOOLA & AS THE SPECTRES CHOOSE THEIR AFFINITIES      512  MILTON 26            38
AFFINITY
      WHICH SMALL ISLAND SEEMS TO HAVE SOME AFFINITY TO ENGLAND    44A  ISLAND MOON 1    *PROSE
      EVERY AFFINITY OF PARENTS MARRIAGES & FRIENDSHIPS ARE HERE   638  JERUSALEM 16         65
AFFIRM
      & I DO AFFIRM THAT THERE ARE NO SUCH THING  .   .   .   .   .  44D  ISLAND MOON 1     PROSE
      UNDERSTAND & CAN ASSUREDLY AFFIRM THAT THE  .   .   .   .   .  814D  LETTER 23         PROSE
AFFIRMD
      THE ANCIENTS DID NOT MEAN TO IMPOSE WHEN THEY AFFIRMD    .   473D  ANNO REYNOLDS       MARG
AFFIXD
      MR PARKER HAS AFFIXD TO EACH IS EXACTLY WHAT I MYSELF    .   .  848C  LETTER 45         PROSE
```

24

PAGE   TITLE   LINE

AFFLICTED
```
    OR DOES TH AFFLICTED MAN THY HEAVNLY BOSOM MOVE   . . .  .   15 IMIT SPEN/PS        53
    IT IS AN EASY THING TO TALK OF PATIENCE TO THE AFFLICTED     290 FOUR ZOAS 2       404
    THARMAS [ABOVE] ON HIGH RODE FURIOUS THRO THE AFFLICTED      353 FOUR ZOAS 8       485
      WORLDS
    I WILL LAMENT OVER MILTON IN THE LAMENTATIONS OF            499 MILTON 18            5
      THE AFFLICTED
    THE EMANATIONS OF THE GRIEVOUSLY AFFLICTED FRIENDS          678 JERUSALEM 48        27
      OF ALBION
    TO FEED THE AFFLICTED IN THE FURNACES SHE MINDED NOT   . .  726 JERUSALEM 82        66
    WHOM GOD HAS AFFLICTED FOR SECRET ENDS                      755 EV GOSPEL(E)/N      89
    THO TERRIBLY AFFLICTED AS WE ALSO ARE YET JEHOVAH SEES HIM  780 GHOST ABEL 1        24
    TELL ME ABOUT YOUR SIGHT AFFLICTED ME NOT A LITTLE & THAT   811C LETTER 22       PROSE
```
AFFLICTION
```
    . . . HIS BROWS FOLDED HEAVY HIS FOREHEAD WAS IN AFFLICTION  137 FRENCH REVOLTN      79
    IF THOU RETURNEST TO THE PRESENT MOMENT OF AFFLICTION   . .  192 V DAU ALBION 4       9
    . . . WITH MUCH CARE & AFFLICTION . . . . . . . . .         270 FOUR ZOAS 1        223
    LUVAH WAS CAST INTO THE FURNACES OF AFFLICTION & SEALED     282 FOUR ZOAS 2         72
    DISCORDANT PRINCIPLES OF LOVE & HATE I SUFFER AFFLICTION    282 FOUR ZOAS 2        103
    IN FORESTS OF AFFLICTION                                    289 FOUR ZOAS 2        372
    IN FORESTS OF AFFLICTION THE ADAMANTINE SCALES OF JUSTICE   320 FOUR ZOAS 7         10
    SPARKLES OF DIRE AFFLICTION ISSUD [FROM] ROUND HIS FROZEN   343 FOUR ZOAS 8      *  91
      LIMBS
    AND ALL NATIONS WEPT IN AFFLICTION FAMILY BY FAMILY  . . .  519 MILTON 31           12
    IS IT AGAIN TO PLUNGE INTO DEEPER AFFLICTION BEHOLD ME  . .  527 MILTON 36           30
    ITS FURNACES OF AFFLICTION IN WHICH HIS ANGELS & EMANATIONS  529 MILTON 38           20
    LUVAH WAS CAST INTO THE FURNACES OF AFFLICTION AND SEALED   625 JERUSALEM 7         30
    OF AFFLICTION AND LOS DREW THEM FORTH COMPELLING THE HARSH  628 JERUSALEM 9         35
      SPECTRE
    AND AS DARK ROOTS AND STEMS A FOREST OF AFFLICTION GROWING  634 JERUSALEM 14         8
    WORSHIPPING MERCY & BEHOLDING THY FRIEND IN SUCH AFFLICTION 669 JERUSALEM 42        10
    THEY RAGE LIKE WILD BEASTS IN THE FORESTS OF AFFLICTION     671 JERUSALEM 42        61
    TO BE POUNDED TO DUST & MELTED IN THE FURNACES OF           687 JERUSALEM 55        59
      AFFLICTION
    OF AFFLICTION OF LOVE OF SWEET DESPAIR OF TORMENT           705 JERUSALEM 67        51
      UNENDURABLE
    OPENS THE FURNACES OF AFFLICTION IN THE EMANATION   . . .   713 JERUSALEM 73        25
    I WALK IN AFFLICTION I AM A WORM AND NO LIVING SOUL  . . .  721 JERUSALEM 80         3
    BEGAN TO GIVE THEIR SOULS AWAY IN THE (FURNACES)            727 JERUSALEM 82        79
      OF AFFLICTION
    WITHOUT BECOMING HIS CHILDREN IN THE FURNACES OF AFFLICTION 732 JERUSALEM 86        49
    SO ALBION SPOKE & THREW HIMSELF INTO THE FURNACES           744 JERUSALEM 96        35
      OF AFFLICTION
    FELT AFFLICTION & SORROW & SICKNESS & DEARTH   . . . . .    818 HAPPINESS/L         76
```
AFFLICTIONS
```
    ON MY AMERICAN PLAINS I FEEL THE STRUGGLING AFFLICTIONS     196 AMERICA PREL 2      10
    SMILE SON OF MY AFFLICTIONS                                 244 EUROPE 14           30
    IN (LUVAH'S) ROBES OF BLOOD & BEARING ALL HIS AFFLICTIONS   274 FOUR ZOAS 1      * 364
    THESE WERE THE WORDS OF LUVAH PATIENT IN AFFLICTIONS   .    283 FOUR ZOAS 2        111
    O LORD WILT THOU NOT LOOK UPON OUR SORE AFFLICTIONS  . .    285 FOUR ZOAS 2        218
    THEY LABOUR INCESSANT WITH MANY TEARS & AFFLICTIONS  . .    515 MILTON 28            6
    A MOMENT OF TIME DRAWING IT OUT WITH MANY TEARS &          678 JERUSALEM 48        31
      AFFLICTIONS
    THEY MEND THEM SORROWING WITH MANY TEARS & AFFLICTIONS  .   692 JERUSALEM 59        41
```
AFFLICTIVE
```
    ARE A MOST SORE PLAGUE & ON A WEAK BODY TRULY AFFLICTIVE    874D LETTER 80       PROSE
```
AFFLUENCE
```
    WHERE THE MAN IS EITHER IN AFFLUENCE OR IS ABOVE THE CARE   612C V LAST JUDG/N    PROSE
      OF IT
    THE ARGUMENT IS BETTER FOR AFFLUENCE THAN POVERTY   . . .   612C V LAST JUDG/N    PROSE
```
AFFORD
```
    HE CAN AFFORD FLATTER HIS WIFE PITY HIS CHILDREN TILL WE    323 FOUR ZOAS 7        128
      CAN
    & I CANNOT AFFORD TO DO IT FOR LESS I HAD TWELVE FOR THE    794B LETTER 5        PROSE
      HEAD
    HE PROPOSES TO COMMENCE WITH YOUR ASSISTANCE HE CAN AFFORD  841C LETTER 41       PROSE
    BEAUTIFUL POEM MUST NOW AFFORD YOU THEIR FULL REWARD   .    854B LETTER 53       PROSE
```
AFFORDS
```
    LONDON AFFORDS OF SEEING FINE PICTURES AND THE VARIOUS  .   823A LETTER 26       PROSE
```
AFFRAY
```
    SOUND WITHOUT SENSE YET IN HIS RUDE AFFRAY  . . . . . .     14 IMIT SPEN/PS        12
```
AFFRIGHT
```
    WHY A NOSTRIL WIDE INHALING TERROR TREMBLING & AFFRIGHT     130 BOOK OF THEL 6      18
    AFFRIGHT THE COASTS . . . . . . . . . .                     147 FRENCH REVOLTN     281
    COULDST THOU BUT CEASE FROM TERROR & TREMBLING & AFFRIGHT   330 FOUR ZOAS 7        418
    DOES THE RISING SUN AFFRIGHT   . . . . . . . .              431 AUGURIES            18
```
AFFRIGHTED
```
    TILL LOS ROUZD HIS HIS FIRES AFFRIGHTED  . . . . . . .      226 URIZEN 7         *   8
    THE ENORMOUS WARP & WOOF RAGE DIREFUL IN THE AFFRIGHTED     284 FOUR ZOAS 2        149
      DEEP
    THARMAS REARD UP HIS HANDS & STOOD ON THE AFFRIGHTED OCEAN  296 FOUR ZOAS 3        160
    BORE ON THRO THE AFFRIGHTED VALES ASCENDING & DESCENDING    319 FOUR ZOAS 6        287
    INTO THE VERY TEETH OF THE AFFRIGHTED ENEMY   . . . . .     580C DESC CAT 5     *PROSE
```
AFFRONT
```
    CALLD DEATH A MADMAN [DEADLY THE AFFRONT] TREMBLING FOR THE 537 AND HIS LEGS/N      17
      AFFRONT
```
AFFRONTED
```
    CONTEMPT FOR MY PERSON IT AFFRONTED MY FOOLISH PRIDE   .    827A LETTER 28       PROSE
```
AFFRONTING
```
    FOR AFFRONTING HIM THRICE IN THE WILDERNESS   . . . . .     752 EV GOSPEL(D)/N      38
```
AFRAID
```
    I THINK YOU DO NOT KNOW EDWARD S AFRAID OF PHILIP   . . .   21 EDW THIRD/PS 3        8
```

```
                                                              PAGE      TITLE        LINE
AFRAID    (CONTINUED)
     HE IS AFRAID HE MAKES US ALL AFRAID  . . . . . . . .      21  EDW THIRD/PS 3      19
     PERHAPS YOU THINK THE PRINCE TOO IS AFRAID  . . . . .      22  EDW THIRD/PS 3      24
     IM SURE HES NOT AFRAID NOR WARWICK NOR NONE  . . . .       22  EDW THIRD/PS 3      32
     NONE OF US BUT ME AND I AM VERY MUCH AFRAID  . . . .       22  EDW THIRD/PS 3      33
     AR  YOU AFRAID TOO SIR THOMAS . . . . . . . . .            22  EDW THIRD/PS 3      34
     THE KING S AFRAID BUT WHAT ARE YOU AFRAID OF  . . . .      22  EDW THIRD/PS 3      36
     AND IF YOUR MAJESTY S AFRAID OF PHILIP  . . . . . .        24  EDW THIRD/PS 3     130
     THEN I CAN NEVER BE AFRAID OF PHILIP  . . . . . . .        25  EDW THIRD/PS 3     153
     BEFORE THE PUBLIC WORKS HE IS NOT AFRAID TO SAY  . . .    207C PRSPECTUS 1793   PROSE
     WHY SHOULDST THOU REMEMBER & BE AFRAID I SURELY HAVE DIED  330 FOUR ZOAS 7       420
       IN PAIN
     A LIE EVERY BODY HATES A KING BACON WAS AFRAID TO SAY THAT 400B ANNO BACON      MARG
     WHOSE TERRORS THIS MORNING MADE THEM AFRAID  . . . .      803B LETTER 15        PROSE
     I AM NOT ASHAMED AFRAID OR AVERSE TO TELL YOU WHAT OUGHT  812A LETTER 22        PROSE
     AND HIS DISMAL TERRORS MAKE ME AFRAID  . . . . . .        818  HAPPINESS/L        52
     THY TERRORS SHALL NOT MAKE ME AFRAID  . . . . . . .       818  HAPPINESS/L        70
     THAT HE IS VERY AFRAID OF LOSING ME  . . . . . . .        820D LETTER 25        PROSE
     & ALSO VERY AFRAID THAT MY FRIENDS IN LONDON SHOULD HAVE  820D LETTER 25        PROSE
     ALL THE VILLAGES ROUND EVERY MAN IS NOW AFRAID OF SPEAKING 828A LETTER 28       PROSE
AFRESH
     TO COMFORT ORC IN HIS DIRE SUFFERINGS LOOK MY FIRES ENLUME 331 FOUR ZOAS 7       444
       AFRESH
AFRICA
     THOU ART THE IMAGE OF GOD WHO DWELLS IN DARKNESS OF AFRICA 196 AMERICA PREL 2      8
     AFRICA ITS NAME WAS THEN EGYPT . . . . . . . . .          236  URIZEN 28          10
     AFRICA  . . . . . . . . . . . . . . . . . . .            245C SONG OF LOS 3     TITLE
     IN HEART-FORMED AFRICA  . . . . . . . . . . .            245  SONG OF LOS 3       3
     OF ASIA & ON THE DESARTS OF AFRICA ROUND THE FALLEN ANGELS 246 SONG OF LOS 4      20
     HOW SOON HIS LOT MAY BE OUR OWN WHEN AFRICA IN SLEEP  .   675  JERUSALEM 45       19
     ACROSS EUROPE ACROSS AFRICA IN HOWLINGS & DEADLY WAR  .   706  JERUSALEM 68       20
     EUROPE & ASIA & AFRICA & AMERICA IN FURY FOURFOLD  . .    712  JERUSALEM 72       31
AFRICAN
     O AFRICAN BLACK AFRICAN GO WINGED THOUGHT WIDEN          159C SONG LIBERTY      PROSE
       HIS FOREHEAD
     ADAM SHUDDERD NOAH FADED BLACK GREW THE SUNNY AFRICAN  .  245  SONG OF LOS 3      10
     COMPOSED BY AN AFRICAN BLACK FROM THE LITTLE EARTH OF SOTHA 375 FOUR ZOAS 9      686
AFRICANUS
     TO SCIPIO AFRICANUS  . . . . . . . . . . . . .            54  LO THE BAT/IM       7
     SAID SCIPIO AFRICANUS  . . . . . . . . . . . .            54  LO THE BAT/IM      11
AFRICAS
     LIKE AFRICA'S AND HIS MACHINES ARE WOVEN WITH HIS LIFE  . 675  JERUSALEM 45       25
AFRICS
     THAN ALL THE GOLD ON AFRIC'S SHORE  . . . . . . .        432  AUGURIES           80
AFTER
     HES DEAD AND HOWLING AFTER ME FOR BLOOD . . . . . . .       4  FAIR ELENOR/PS     24
     AFTER NIGHT I DO CROUD  . . . . . . . . . . . .             9  MAD SONG/PS        19
     YOU YET ARE WHOLE BUT AFTER A FEW MORE  . . . . . . .      23  EDW THIRD/PS 3      63
     HAS TO GET BEFORE ANOTHER IN ANY PURSUIT AFTER GLORY  .    28  EDW THIRD/PS 4      15
     I LOOK BEHIND THERE IS NO RETURNING DEATH FOLLOWS AFTER ME 35D COUCH DEATH/PS   PROSE
     NERVOUS ARMS AND AFTER THAT WHEN I HAD FOUND THY FALSHOOD  38D SAMSON/PS       *PROSE
     ENQUIRE NOT AFTER IT SEEING IT IS A SECRET  . . . . .     40C SAMSON/PS         PROSE
     A VIRGIN EVER YOUNG AND AFTER LEADEN SLOTH . . . . .      40D THEN SHE BORE      PROSE
     IN COMES ETRUSCAN COLUMN THE ANTIQUARIAN & AFTER . . .    44B ISLAND MOON 1      PROSE
     AFTER SUPPER STEELYARD & OBTUSE ANGLE  . . . . . .        59A ISLAND MOON 11     PROSE
     AFTER THIS THEY ALL SAT SILENT FOR A QUARTER OF AN HOUR    59D ISLAND MOON 11    PROSE
     WHO SHALL DARE TO SAY AFTER THIS THAT ALL ELEVATION IS     94B ANNO SWED LOVE    MARG
       OF SELF
     THAT NO MAN ON EARTH HAS A SPIRITUAL IDEA AFTER READING    94C ANNO SWED LOVE    MARG
       N...
     PLAYING WITH FLOWERS & RUNNING AFTER BIRDS THEY SPENT THE 100 TIRIEL 2            8
       DAY
     AND AFTER DINNER WE WILL WALK INTO THE CAGE OF HAR  . .   102  TIRIEL 3           14
     THEY THREW DIRT AFTER THEM TILL TO THE COVERT OF A WOOD    109  TIRIEL 7          15
     GRASE AFTER THEE AND WEEP  . . . . . . . . . .           119  NIGHT/SI         *  44
     PREDESTINATION AFTER THIS LIFE IS MORE ABOMINABLE THAN   133A ANNO SWED PROV     MARG
       CALVIN'S
     AND BRIGHT CHILDREN LOOK AFTER HIM INTO THE GRAVE . . .   139  FRENCH REVOLTN    108
     KNOW THAT AFTER CHRIST'S DEATH HE BECAME JEHOVAH  . . .  150B MARRIAGE HH 5     PROSE
     AFTER DINNER I ASKD ISAIAH TO FAVOUR THE WORLD WITH  . . 154A MARRIAGE HH 12    PROSE
     CRAWLING AFTER THEIR PREY  . . . . . . . . . .          156A MARRIAGE HH 17    PROSE
     WAS LEFT A HELPLESS TRUNK THIS AFTER GRINNING & KISSING IT 157B MARRIAGE HH 17  PROSE
     AND I [GREW] [SMILD] SOOTHD DAY AFTER DAY  . . . . .      167  INFANT SORW/N      14
     AND I [GREW] SMILD NIGHT AFTER NIGHT  . . . . . . .       167  INFANT SORW/N      16
     SEEKING AFTER THAT SWEET GOLDEN CLIME  . . . . . .        215  AH SUNFLOWR/SE      3
     TIMES ROLLED ON OER ALL THE SONS OF HAR TIME AFTER TIME   246  SONG OF LOS 3      20
     DAY AFTER DAY SHE FED UPON THE MOUNTAINS IN LUVAH'S SIGHT  282 FOUR ZOAS 2        86
     AND WHEN LUVAH AGE AFTER AGE WAS QUITE MELTED WITH WOE     283  FOUR ZOAS 2       113
     TWELVE HALLS AFTER THE NAMES OF HIS TWELVE SONS COMPOSD    284  FOUR ZOAS 2       173
     . . . THREE CENTRAL DOMES AFTER THE NAMES  . . . .        284  FOUR ZOAS 2       174
     IT STOOD ON TWELVE STEPS NAMD AFTER THE NAMES OF HER TWELVE 285 FOUR ZOAS 2      199
       SONS
     I LAID MY HEAD IN THE HOT NOON AFTER THE BROKEN CLODS  .  295  FOUR ZOAS 3       123
     WHERE LUVAH STRIVES SCORNED BY VALA AGE AFTER AGE  . .    295  FOUR ZOAS 3      * 128
       WANDERING
     [WE FLED FROM ?JERUSALEM ?AFTER ?THE MERCIFUL           SUPP FOUR ZOAS 3        *
       LORD & SAVIOUR]
     THE LINKS OF FATE LINK AFTER LINK AN ENDLESS CHAIN OF     302  FOUR ZOAS 4       207
       SORROWS
     WHERE THE HERDS LOW AFTER THE SHADOW & AFTER THE WATER    308  FOUR ZOAS 5       137
       SPRING
     I WRITE NOT HERE BUT ALL THEIR AFTER LIFE WAS LAMENTATION  309  FOUR ZOAS 5      175
```

	PAGE	TITLE	LINE

AFTER   (CONTINUED)

LIGHTNINGS WHICH BLAZED AFTER THEM UPON THEIR SHOULDERS   314 FOUR ZOAS 6   108

TIME AFTER TIME FOR SUCH A JOURNEY NONE BUT IRON PENS . .   316 FOUR ZOAS 6   173
THE JOURNEY OBSTINATE REFUSE TO WRITE TIME AFTER TIME . .   316 FOUR ZOAS 6   175
PULSE AFTER PULSE BEAT ON HIS FETTERS PULSE AFTER PULSE   320 FOUR ZOAS 7   21
    HIS SPIRIT
AGE AFTER AGE TILL UNDERNEATH HIS HEEL A DEADLY ROOT . .   321 FOUR ZOAS 7   31
NOR FELT THE STINGINGS OF DESIRE NOR LONGINGS AFTER LIFE   325 FOUR ZOAS 7   203
AND POLISH BRASS & IRON HOUR AFTER HOUR LABORIOUS   337 FOUR ZOAS 7B   182
    WORKMANSHIP
THE ENORMOUS SCIENCES OF URIZEN AGES AFTER AGES EXPLORING   344 FOUR ZOAS 8   144
TO PUT OFF MYSTERY TIME AFTER TIME & AS A MAN . . . .   347 FOUR ZOAS 8   261
TIMES AFTER TIMES AND THOSE IN EDEN SENT LUCIFER FOR THEIR   351 FOUR ZOAS 8   398
    GUARD
TIME AFTER TIME BY THE DIVINE LAMB WHO DIED FOR ALL . .   353 FOUR ZOAS 8   483
. . . TIMES AFTER TIMES BESIDE JERUSALEM'S GATE] . . .   356 FOUR ZOAS 8   588
AND AFTER THE FLAMES APPEARS THE CLOUD OF THE SON OF MAN   364 FOUR ZOAS 9   272
REAR ON THE MOUNTAINS STEM AFTER STEM THE SCALY   373 FOUR ZOAS 9   606
    NEWT CREEPS
AFTER THEIR SIN . . . .   380 FOUR ZOAS AD 1 *   10
THIS THE DAY AFTER MY TURNING HIM OUT OF THE GARDEN . . . 437B BLAKES MEMORAN PROSE
THE SOLDIER AFTER HE AND HIS COMRADE CAME TOGETHER INTO THE 438C BLAKES MEMORAN PROSE
WERE SAVAGE FIRST TO FRANCE & AFTER SLAVES . . . . . .   451 ANNO REYNOLDS   2
AFTER HAVING BEEN A FOOL A STUDENT IS TO AMASS A STOCK . 455B ANNO REYNOLDS   MARG
THIS TO PREVENT ENTERING THE DOORS OF SATAN'S BRAIN NIGHT   492 MILTON 12   4
    AFTER NIGHT
FOLLOW AFTER THE DETESTABLE GODS OF PRIAM IN POMP . . .   495 MILTON 14   15
OF PHILISTEA INTO TWELVE DIVIDED CALLD AFTER THE NAMES . . 532 MILTON 40   25
REENGRAVD TIME AFTER TIME . . . .   558 THE CAVERNS/N   13
IT WAS NEVER GENERALLY USED TILL AFTER VANDYKE'S TIME .   561A EXHIBITION ADV PROSE
TWO YEARS BEFORE MICHAEL ANGELO AND TITIAN BUT FOUR YEARS 563C DESC CAT   PROSE
    AFTER
EXCEPT BY BLUNDERING IGNORANCE TILL AFTER VANDYKE'S TIME   566C DESC CAT 2   PROSE
THE PARDONER AND THE SOMNER AND MANCIPLE AFTER THESE . . 566D DESC CAT 3   PROSE
AFTER THE HOST FOLLOW THE SHIPMAN THE HABERDASHER . . . 566D DESC CAT 3   *PROSE
WAS THE BEAUTY OF OUR ANCESTORS TILL AFTER ELIZABETH'S TIME 568B DESC CAT 3   PROSE
CHAUCER'S CHARACTERS LIVE AGE AFTER AGE . . . . . .   570D DESC CAT 3   PROSE
AND REMAIN FOR EVER UNSUBDUED AGE AFTER AGE . . . . .   577D DESC CAT 5   PROSE
CONTINUE TO GOVERN MANKIND AFTER DEATH . . . .   581D DESC CAT 8   PROSE
EASY FOR HIM TO SNATCH AWAY THE VISION TIME AFTER TIME FOR 582C DESC CAT 9   PROSE
THE PARDONER THE SOMPNOUR & THE MANCIPLE AFTER THESE .   588B CHAUCER/N   PROSE
AFTER THE HOST FOLLOW THE SHIPMAN THE HABERDASHER . . . 588C CHAUCER/N   *PROSE
THE PARDONER THE SOMPNOUR AND THE MANICIPLE AFTER THESE . 589D CHAUCER 2   PROSE
AFTER THE HOST FOLLOW THE SHIPMAN THE HABERDASHER . . . 589D CHAUCER 2   PROSE
OF HUMAN CHARACTERS AS THEY APPEAR AGE AFTER AGE . . .   591A PUB ADDRESS/N TITLE
WHICH I ENGRAVED AFTER HIM FIVE & TWENTY YEARS AGO . .   592B PUB ADDRESS/N PROSE
AFTER HOGARTH [COGAR] COOKE WISHED TO GIVE TO HOGARTH .   594B PUB ADDRESS/N *PROSE
AFTER THE DEATH OF THE VEGETATED BODY . . . .   605D V LAST JUDG/N PROSE
UNDER THE NAMES OF THE FATHERS BEFORE & AFTER THE FLOOD   609D V LAST JUDG/N PROSE
AS YOU [PREP] PRETEND TILL AFTER THE LAST JUDGMENT . .   616A V LAST JUDG/N *PROSE
THEY ARE NOT ALWAYS PRYING AFTER GOOD & EVIL IN ONE ANOTHER 616D V LAST JUDG/N PROSE
AFTER MY THREE YEARS SLUMBER ON THE BANKS OF THE OCEAN . 620D JERUSALEM 3   PROSE
THIS THEME CALLS ME IN SLEEP NIGHT AFTER NIGHT & EVRY MORN 622 JERUSALEM 4   3
DIVIDED INTO MALE AND FEMALE FORMS TIME AFTER TIME . . .   623 JERUSALEM 5   32
THAT WE MAY PRY AFTER HIM AS AFTER A STOLEN TREASURE . .   661 JERUSALEM 34   34
AND MANY OF THE ETERNAL ONES LAUGHED AFTER THEIR MANNER   663 JERUSALEM 36   43
THEY ENQUIRE AFTER JERUSALEM IN THE REGIONS OF THE DEAD   671 JERUSALEM 42   68
CLIFF AFTER CLIFF & OVER VALLEYS OF DESPAIR & DEATH . .   674 JERUSALEM 44   13
IN ERIN'S LAND TOWARD THE NORTH JOINT AFTER JOINT   674 JERUSALEM 44   26
    & BURNING
MAY BE DELIVERD TIME AFTER TIME EVERMORE AMEN . . . .   680 JERUSALEM 49   71
INCLOSING ALL THE CHILDREN OF LOS TIME AFTER TIME . . .   684 JERUSALEM 53   7
HOUR AFTER HOUR LABOURING AT THE WHIRLING WHEEL . . . .   691 JERUSALEM 59   32
AND POLISH BRASS & IRON HOUR AFTER HOUR LABORIOUS TASK   700 JERUSALEM 65   24
DRIVN FORTH BY LOS TIME AFTER TIME FROM ALBION'S CLIFFY   707 JERUSALEM 69   8
    SHORE
AGE AFTER AGE DRAWING THEM AWAY TOWARDS BABYLON . . . .   715 JERUSALEM 74   31
THE RAGING FLAMES THO SHE RETURND [CONSUMD DAY AFTER DAY] 726 JERUSALEM 82   67
AWAY & MIGHTY HYLE & AFTER THEM JERUSALEM IS GONE AWAKE   729 JERUSALEM 83   87
AND HEALD AFTER THE SEPARATION HIS PAINS HE SOON FORGOT   732 JERUSALEM 86   59
I ACT WITH BENEVOLENCE & VIRTUE & GET MURDERD TIME AFTER   738 JERUSALEM 91   26
    TIME
HE ACTED TIME AFTER TIME WITH DIRE PAIN & MANY TEARS . .   739 JERUSALEM 91   52
WHEN AFTER THREE DAYS' SORROW FOUND . . . .   748 EV GOSPEL(B)/N   5
WHO FOLLOW AFTER THE HEATHEN SCHOOLS . . . .   751 EV GOSPEL(D)/N   22
AFTER THEY HAVE PASSED THE CENTER . . . .   785D ILLS DANTE 101 PROSE
AGES AFTER AGES IN THY DESCENDENTS . . . .   789A ANNO THORNTON * MARG
TO ENGRAVE AFTER ANOTHER PAINTER IS INFINITELY MORE   794B LETTER 5   PROSE
    LABORIOUS
I SENT YOU AS A SPECIMEN BUT AFTER MY OWN DESIGNS I COULD   794B LETTER 5   PROSE
    DO
I HAVE NO OBJECTION TO ENGRAVING AFTER ANOTHER ARTIST .   794C LETTER 5   PROSE
THUS IF I AM A PAINTER IT IS NOT TO BE ATTRIBUTED   794C LETTER 5   PROSE
    TO SEEKING AFTER
AFTER ANOTHER ARTIST BUT ABOVE ALL I FEEL MYSELF HAPPY &   795C LETTER 6   PROSE
THE FIRST MORNING AFTER MY ARRIVAL & THE PLOWBOY SAID . . 803C LETTER 15   PROSE
YOU THRO LIFE & AFTER DEATH SHAME & CONFUSION OF FACE .   813B LETTER 22   PROSE
AFTER I HAD FINISHD MY LETTER I FOUND THAT I HAD NOT SAID   816C LETTER 24   PROSE
A MONTH AFTER MY ARRIVAL HERE I SHOULD HAVE DONE SO BUT   825D LETTER 27   PROSE
AFTER MANY ABUSIVE THREATS [FROM THEM] AGAINST ME & . .   827B LETTER 28   PROSE
AFTER THEY HAD GOT TOGETHER INTO THE STABLE THIS IS THE   827C LETTER 28   PROSE
    WHOLE

27

```
                                                               PAGE      TITLE           LINE
AFTER    (CONTINUED)
    WHICH IS AFTER MICHAELMASS SO I SHALL HAVE THE SATISFACTION  828A LETTER 28          PROSE
    AFTER ALL & CERTAINLY DOES NOT LEAD ME INTO SCRAPES  . . .   830D LETTER 30          PROSE
    ROMNEY'S PICTURES THAT REMAINED AFTER THE SALE AT HAMPSTEAD   831A LETTER 31          PROSE
    I HAVE GOT TO WORK AFTER FUSELI FOR A LITTLE SHAKESPEARE      831B LETTER 31          PROSE
    VERIFIED THE MORNING AFTER I RECEIVED YOUR KIND LETTER  .  .  831B LETTER 31          PROSE
    I SENT OFF THE MORNING AFTER I RECIEVD IT FROM YOU BEING      834C LETTER 34          PROSE
    HIS WORK & THE DAY AFTER I RECIEVD IT WITH THE NOTE  .  .     836D LETTER 35          PROSE
    I HAVE AT LENGTH SEEN MR HOARE AFTER HAVING REPEATEDLY  .     842B LETTER 42          PROSE
    THE HEAD OF COWPER AFTER LAWRENCE THE HEADS TO BE FINISHD     850D LETTER 49          PROSE
    STRENGTH I NOW ENJOY SUDDENLY ON THE DAY AFTER VISITING       852A LETTER 50          PROSE
    ON THE PLATES I AM NOW ENGRAVING AFTER ROMNEY WHOSE  .  .     852B LETTER 50          PROSE
    THE HONOUR TO ENQUIRE AFTER UNPROFITABLE ENOUGH TO ME THO     867A LETTER 66          PROSE
    UP THE DAY AFTER & SOMETIMES TWO OR THREE DAYS  .  .  .       871A LETTER 72          PROSE
    FOR SOME TIME AFTER SR FRANCIS BACON WOULD SAY IT IS WANT     871A LETTER 72          PROSE
        OF
    YESTERDAY AFTERNOON AFTER AS GOOD A MORNING AS I EVER  .  .   872B LETTER 75          PROSE
    AFTER MRS LINNELL'S FATHER IT WILL BE BRUTAL NOT TO SAY       874B LETTER 79          PROSE
    I PROPOSE TO SET OUT FROM HERE AS SOON AFTER TEN AS WE        875B LETTER 81          PROSE
        CAN ON
    A BREACH IN A CITY THE MORNING AFTER THE BATTLE  .  .  .  .   SUPP ILLUS HISTORY     *TITLE
    FROM A DRAWING BY SALVIATI AFTER MICHAEL ANGELO  .  .  .  .   SUPP INSC JOSEPH       *TITLE
AFTER-AGES
    PLAIN IN THEIR ACTS AND MANNERS WISER THAN AFTER-AGES  .  .   577C DESC CAT 5         PROSE
AFTERNOON
    [AND] WHO WITH IRON HAND CUFFD IN THE AFTERNOON  .  .  .  .   537 AND HIS LEGS/N       24
    SUNDAY AFTERNOON TO CALL ON MRS FLAXMAN AT HAMPSTEAD I SEND   799A LETTER 11          PROSE
    "ON SUNDAY AFTERNOON IN HAMPSTEAD TO TAKE FAREWELL ALL"       800A LETTER 12          PROSE
    THE PRINTERS [BEING] HAVING BEEN THIS AFTERNOON UNABLE  .  .  833A LETTER 32          PROSE
    AFTERNOON MY POOR WIFE HAS BEEN NEAR THE GATE OF DEATH  .     833D LETTER 33          PROSE
    YESTERDAY AFTERNOON AFTER AS GOOD A MORNING AS I EVER  .  .   872B LETTER 75          PROSE
AFTERWARD
    AFTERWARD EXECUTED FOR A LADY OF HIGH RANK AN EXPERIMENT      582B DESC CAT 9         TITLE
        PICTURE
AFTERWARDS
    BUT AFTERWARDS I THOUGHT HE WAS NOT  .  .  .  .  .  .  .  .   48D ISLAND MOON 5       PROSE
    & THEN AFTERWARDS WHEN I SAID HE WAS NOT  .  .  .  .  .  .    48D ISLAND MOON 5       PROSE
    .  .  .  FAIRIES OF ALBION AFTERWARDS GODS OF THE HEATHEN  .  264 FOUR ZOAS 1          19
    CHARGE MUST HAVE BEEN FABRICATED IN THE STABLE AFTERWARDS     437C BLAKES MEMORAN     PROSE
    OR IS ABLE & AFTERWARDS GO AND SWEAR OUR LIVES AWAY  .  .  .  439A BLAKES MEMORAN     PROSE
    & TIME WILL NOT BE WASTED IN SEEKING THEM AFTERWARDS  .  .    440B MEMORANDUM/N 2     PROSE
    UNCULTIVATED LIFE COMES AFTERWARDS FROM SATAN'S HIRELINGS     446C ANNO REYNOLDS      MARG
    THE FUN AFTERWARDS EXHIBITED ON THE ROAD MAY BE SEEN  .  .    588C CHAUCER/N         PROSE
    SELSEY TRUE FRIEND WHO AFTERWARDS SUBMITTED TO BE DEVOURD     667 JERUSALEM 40         48
    HER TWO COVERING CHERUBS AFTERWARDS NAMED VOLTAIRE  .  .  .   702 JERUSALEM 66         12
        & ROUSSEAU
AGAG
    CONSTRICTING INTO DRUID ROCKS ROUND CANAAN AGAG & ARAM        685 JERUSALEM 54         26
        & PHAROH
AGAIN
    AND HODGE AGAIN HOLDS UP HIS HEAD  .  .  .  .  .  .  .  .  .   17 BLIND-MANS/PS         60
    AND SEPARATE MARCH BUT JOIN AGAIN AT NIGHT  .  .  .  .  .  .   19 EDW THIRD/PS 1        51
    AND WOULD AGAIN WERE I NOT FORBID  .  .  .  .  .  .  .  .  .   23 EDW THIRD/PS 3       100
    TILL PHILIP SPRINGS THE TIMROUS COVEY AGAIN  .  .  .  .  .  .  24 EDW THIRD/PS 3       112
    O YET MAY ALBION SMILE AGAIN AND STRETCH HER PEACEFUL ARMS    34C KING JOHN/PS        PROSE
    ERE ONCE AGAIN THE CHANGING MOON HER CIRCUIT HATH PERFORMED   38A SAMSON/PS           PROSE
    AND LO AGAIN THE ANGEL CAME  .  .  .  .  .  .  .  .  .  .  .   40B SAMSON/PS           PROSE
    THE CLOUD OER PAST & ROME NOW SHONE AGAIN MITERD AND  .  .    41B THEN SHE BORE       PROSE
    I'LL BEGIN AGAIN SAID THE CYNIC  .  .  .  .  .  .  .  .  .  .  46C ISLAND MOON 3       PROSE
    & BEGD TO HAVE IT SUNG OVER AGAIN & AGAIN  .  .  .  .  .  .    57D ISLAND MOON 9       PROSE
    THE WISE MAN FALLETH (SEVEN) TIMES IN A DAY AND RISETH        83D ANNO LAVATER        MARG
        AGAIN &C
    TO DO OTHER THAN REPEAT THE SAME DULL ROUND OVER AGAIN  .  .  97B NAT RELIGION 1      PROSE
    PIPER PIPE THAT SONG AGAIN  .  .  .  .  .  .  .  .  .  .  .   111 INTRODUCTN/SI         7
    SO I SUNG THE SAME AGAIN  .  .  .  .  .  .  .  .  .  .  .  .  111 INTRODUCTN/SI        11
    AGAIN THE LOUD VOICE OF FRANCE CRIES TO THE MORNING .  .  .  134 FRENCH REVOLTN       15
    APPEARD AND SUNK AGAIN THE SCALY FOLD OF A MONSTROUS         156B MARRIAGE HH 17  PROSE
        SERPENT
    SOON MY ANGEL CAME AGAIN  .  .  .  .  .  .  .  .  .  .  .  .  182 THE ANGEL/N          13
    THEN AGAIN OLD NOBODADDY SWORE  .  .  .  .  .  .  .  .  .  .  187 WHEN KLOPSTK/N       21
    AND SO FEELING HE BEGD HIM TO TURN AGAIN  .  .  .  .  .  .    187 WHEN KLOPSTK/N *     27
    THRICE [AGAIN] BLUSHING HE REDEND ROUND  .  .  .  .  .  .  .  187 WHEN KLOPSTK/N *     29
    AND WHEN WILL THEY RENEW AGAIN & THE NIGHT OF OBLIVION PAST   192 V DAU ALBION 4       5
    SOON MY ANGEL CAME AGAIN  .  .  .  .  .  .  .  .  .  .  .  .  214 THE ANGEL/SE         13
    AGAIN HE BURST IT AGAIN  .  .  .  .  .  .  .  .  .  .  .  .   233 URIZEN 20            14
    AGAIN THE NIGHT IS COME  .  .  .  .  .  .  .  .  .  .  .  .   239 EUROPE 4              9
    AND AGAIN SPRUNG TO MANY A TREE  .  .  .  .  .  .  .  .  .  .  252 AHANIA 3            67
    THEN SURVEYD THE ALL BRIGHT MASS AGAIN  .  .  .  .  .  .  .   260 BOOK OF LOS 5        36
    SHE SHOULD ARISE AGAIN TO LIFE EMBALMD IN ENION'S BOSOM       278 FOUR ZOAS 1        527
    O I AM NOTHING & TO NOTHING MUST RETURN AGAIN  .  .  .  .  .  293 FOUR ZOAS 3         64
    ARE THOSE WHO LOVE LIKE THOSE WHO DIED RISEN AGAIN FROM       298 FOUR ZOAS 4         19
        DEATH
    IS IT NOT POSSIBLE THAT ONE RISEN AGAIN FROM DEATH  .  .  .   298 FOUR ZOAS 4         21
    LEST HE SHOULD RISE AGAIN FROM DEATH IN ALL HIS [DISMAL]      300 FOUR ZOAS 4    *   121
        DREARY POWER
    SAYING IF YE WILL BELIEVE YOUR BROTHER SHALL RISE AGAIN       304 FOUR ZOAS 4        270
    .  .  .  BURST OPEN & AGAIN CLOSE WITH A [?DISMAL] DEADLY PAIN  309 FOUR ZOAS 5    *   178
    ART THOU LIKE ME RISEN AGAIN FROM DEATH OR ART THOU           313 FOUR ZOAS 6         56
        DEATHLESS
    TAKE ROOT AGAIN WHEREEVER THEY TOUCH AGAIN BRANCHING FORTH    321 FOUR ZOAS 7         34
    AGAIN HE TOOK HIS SEAT & RANGD HIS [BOOKS] BOOKS AROUND       321 FOUR ZOAS 7    *    40
    TILL ONCE AGAIN THE MORN OF AGES SHALL RENEW UPON US  .  .    326 FOUR ZOAS 7        269
```

28

```
                                                        PAGE     TITLE            LINE
AGAIN     (CONTINUED)
      THAT BODY I CREATED THEN SHALL WE UNITE AGAIN IN BLISS  . .  327 FOUR ZOAS 7        301
      [ I HAVE THEE IN MY ARMS & AM AGAIN UNITED TO LOS ]  .  .  .  327 FOUR ZOAS 7        308
      NOR COULD THEY EVER BE CLOSD AGAIN THE GOLDEN HINGES WERE    328 FOUR ZOAS 7        324
        BROKEN
      THAT VANISH AGAIN INTO MY BOSOM BUT IF THOU MY LOS   .  .  .  331 FOUR ZOAS 7        452
      WITH DARTS OF WINTRY HAIL AGAIN THE BLACK BOW DRAW   .  .  .  337 FOUR ZOAS 7B       156
      AGAIN THE ELEMENTAL STRINGS TO YOUR RIGHT BREASTS DRAW   .  337 FOUR ZOAS 7B       157
      THESE WORDS IF YE WILL BELIEVE YOUR BROTHER SHALL RISE      340 FOUR ZOAS 7B       293
        AGAIN
      A TEAR OF BLOOD DROPPED FROM EITHER EYE AGAIN HE REPOSD     341 FOUR ZOAS 8         18
      BABYLON AGAIN IN INFANCY CALLD NATURAL RELIGION   .  .  .  .  357 FOUR ZOAS 8        620
      AND MY HEAD FAINT YET WILL I LOOK AGAIN UNTO THE MORNING    360 FOUR ZOAS 9        120
      THEN WRATH BURST ROUND THE ETERNAL MAN WAS WRATH AGAIN      360 FOUR ZOAS 9        137
        HE CRIED
      AND THESE AGAIN SURROUNDED [OF] BY FOUR WONDERS OF THE      364 FOUR ZOAS 9     *  281
        ALMIGHTY
      AGAIN REORGANIZE TILL THEY RESUME THE IMAGE OF THE HUMAN    366 FOUR ZOAS 9        372
      I SHALL CAST OFF MY DEATH CLOTHES & EMBRACE THARMAS AGAIN   373 FOUR ZOAS 9        599
      HOW LOVELY THE DELIGHTS OF THOSE RISEN AGAIN FROM DEATH     376 FOUR ZOAS 9        729
      WHEN WILT THOU RETURN AGAIN  .  .  .  .  .  .  .  .  .  .  .  416 MY SPECTRE/N       30
      [THE] AND THE WIND BLOWS IT BACK AGAIN   .  .  .  .  .  .  .  418 MOCK ON/N      *   4
      O WHEN SHALL I AGAIN RETURN   .  .  .  .  .  .  .  .  .  .  .  427 LAND OF DREAMS     12
      OR AGAIN DOES RETURN THE GOLDEN TIMES   .  .  .  .  .  .  .  428 MARY                6
      AND IN THE OUTWARD AIR AGAIN   .  .  .  .  .  .  .  .  .  .  .  430 CRYSTL CABINET     27
      GENERAL PRINCIPLE AGAIN UNLESS YOU CONSULT PARTICULARS   .  456B ANNO REYNOLDS  *  MARG
      BACON IS ONLY EPICURUS OVER AGAIN   .  .  .  .  .  .  .  .  .  456C ANNO REYNOLDS    MARG
      HERE HE COMES AGAIN TO HIS CENTRAL FORM   .  .  .  .  .  .  .  460B ANNO REYNOLDS    MARG
      GENERAL IDEAS AGAIN  .  .  .  .  .  .  .  .  .  .  .  .  .  .  461D ANNO REYNOLDS    MARG
      & COMES NOT AGAIN TILL ANOTHER IS BORN WITH IT   .  .  .  .  470D ANNO REYNOLDS    MARG
      MUST BE A BLANK IN NATURE FOLLOW WITH ME AND TOMORROW AGAIN 488 MILTON 8          21
      AND WERE TROUBLED AND AGAIN THE DIVINE FAMILY GROANED IN    504 MILTON 21         44
        SPIRIT
      BUT AS TO THIS ELECTED FORM WHO IS RETURND AGAIN   .  .  .  509 MILTON 24         41
      THE NIGHTINGALE AGAIN ASSAYS HIS SONG & THRO THE DAY   .  .  520 MILTON 31         42
      MEETING AGAIN IN GOLGONOOZA BEYOND SATAN'S SEAT   .  .  .  .  526 MILTON 35         53
      THUS ARE THE MESSENGERS DISPATCHD TILL THEY REACH THE EARTH 526 MILTON 36          8
        AGAIN
      IS IT AGAIN TO PLUNGE INTO DEEPER AFFLICTION BEHOLD ME   .  .  527 MILTON 36         30
      WITH CAVERNS WHOSE REMOTEST BOTTOMS MEET AGAIN WITH     .  .  529 MILTON 37         55
      BECOME LEAD AGAIN THIS IS AN AWFUL THING TO SAY TO OIL      566B DESC CAT 2       PROSE
        PAINTERS
      THE SAME CHARACTERS REPEATED AGAIN AND AGAIN IN ANIMALS     567C DESC CAT 3       PROSE
      ARISE AGAIN WITH TENFOLD SPLENDOR WHEN ARTHUR SHALL AWAKE   577B DESC CAT 5       TITLE
      AND ITS ANCIENT GLORY WHEN IT WAS AS IT AGAIN SHALL BE   .  577C DESC CAT 5       PROSE
      OF HIS DEATH OR SLEEP AND PROMISE TO RETURN AGAIN    .  .  .  577D DESC CAT 5       PROSE
      TO BE OPENED AGAIN TO HEAVEN THROUGH EDEN   .  .  .  .  .  .  578A DESC CAT 5       PROSE
      WHICH THE ROMANS NEVER AGAIN RECOVERED IN THIS PICTURE   .  578C DESC CAT 5       PROSE
      IT WAS WITH DIFFICULTY BROUGHT BACK AGAIN TO A CERTAIN      582B DESC CAT 9       PROSE
        EFFECT
      I SAY AGAIN O ARTIST YOU MAY DISBELIEVE ALL THIS   .  .  .  583C DESC CAT 9       PROSE
      ALL IS CHAOS AGAIN AND THE LINE OF THE ALMIGHTY MUST BE     585C DESC CAT 15      PROSE
      THE SAME CHARACTERS REPEATED AGAIN & AGAIN IN ANIMALS   .  589A CHAUCER/N        PROSE
      I AGAIN DISPLAY MY GIANT FORMS TO THE PUBLIC MY FORMER   .  620D JERUSALEM 3      PROSE
      AGAIN HE SPEAKS IN THUNDER AND IN FIRE  .  .  .  .  .  .  .  621 READER LOVER/J      5
      AGAIN THEY LAMENT O WHAT SHALL WE DO FOR LOVELY JERUSALEM   631 JERUSALEM 11        17
      AND THERE IT MEETS ETERNITY AGAIN BOTH WITHIN AND WITHOUT   633 JERUSALEM 13        36
      BURSTING THEIR ARKS THEY RISE AGAIN TO LIFE THEY           644 JERUSALEM 21        46
        PLAY BEFORE
      ALBION AGAIN UTTERD HIS VOICE BENEATH THE SILENT MOON   .  .  645 JERUSALEM 22        16
      HAST THOU AGAIN KNITTED THE VEIL OF VALA WHICH I FOR THEE   645 JERUSALEM 23         5
      THEY BENT DOWN THEY FELT THE EARTH AND AGAIN ENROOTING  .  .  653 JERUSALEM 28        18
      FEAR NOT O LITTLE FLOCK I COME ALBION SHALL RISE AGAIN   .  653 JERUSALEM 29        26
      O I AM NOTHING AND TO NOTHING MUST RETURN AGAIN   .  .  .  .  654 JERUSALEM 29        51
      AND BE THOU FOR EVER ACCURSED THAT ALBION MAY ARISE AGAIN   662 JERUSALEM 35        14
      AND LENGTH BREDTH HIGHTH AGAIN OBEY THE DIVINE VISION       664 JERUSALEM 36        56
        HALLELUJAH
      AGAIN HE JOIND THE DIVINE BODY FOLLOWING MERCIFUL          664 JERUSALEM 37        11
      OF REDEMPTION & OF AWAKING AGAIN INTO ETERNITY   .  .  .  .  691 JERUSALEM 59         9
      THAN THY MAKER WHO FORGIVETH SINS & CALLS AGAIN HER THAT    694 JERUSALEM 61         7
        IS LOST
      THO SHE HATES HE CALLS HER AGAIN IN LOVE I LOVE MY DEAR     694 JERUSALEM 61         8
        JOSEPH
      DOES THE VOICE OF MY LORD CALL ME AGAIN AM I PURE THRO      695 JERUSALEM 61        36
        HIS MERCY
      I MUST RUSH AGAIN TO WAR FOR THE VIRGIN HAS FROWND & REFUSD 707 JERUSALEM 68        63
      AND WHERE LUTHER ENDS ADAM BEGINS AGAIN IN ETERNAL CIRCLE   716 JERUSALEM 75        24
      TO AWAKE THE PRISONERS OF DEATH TO BRING ALBION AGAIN   .  716 JERUSALEM 75        25
      AND NOW THE TIME RETURNS AGAIN  .  .  .  .  .  .  .  .  .  .  718 ENGLND AWAKE/J      9
      TILL SWEET JERUSALEM EMANATES AGAIN INTO ETERNITY   .  .  .  728 JERUSALEM 83        60
      HOW THEN CAN I EVER AGAIN BE UNITED AS MAN WITH MAN   .  .  733 JERUSALEM 88        12
      THEN LOS AGAIN TOOK UP HIS SPEECH AS ENITHARMON CEAST   .  741 JERUSALEM 93        17
      HIS STONY MEMBERS HE SAW ENGLAND AH SHALL THE DEAD LIVE     742 JERUSALEM 95         4
        AGAIN
      BUT IF I DIE I SHALL ARISE AGAIN & THOU WITH ME   .  .  .  .  743 JERUSALEM 96        15
      HE WROTE YE MUST BE BORN AGAIN   .  .  .  .  .  .  .  .  .  .  750 EV GOSPEL(C)/N     14
      HE WROTE YE MUST BE BORN AGAIN   .  .  .  .  .  .  .  .  .  .  751 EV GOSPEL(D)/N     14
      BECAUSE YOU MURDER HIM HE ARISES AGAIN   .  .  .  .  .  .  .  757D EV GOSPEL       PROSE
      IS IMPROVED THE LIP I HAVE AGAIN LESSENED AS YOU ADVISED    797A LETTER 9        PROSE
      IS ARRIVD WHEN MEN SHALL AGAIN CONVERSE IN HEAVEN & WALK    799B LETTER 11       PROSE
        WITH
      WE MEAN TO BEGIN PRINTING AGAIN TO-MORROW  .  .  .  .  .  .  807A LETTER 17       PROSE
```

29

AGAIN   (CONTINUED)

	PAGE	TITLE	LINE
I THANK YOU AGAIN & AGAIN FOR YOUR GENEROUS FORBEARANCE	809C	LETTER 20	PROSE
& THIS FROM MR H(HAYLEY) WILL BRING ME BACK AGAIN	812C	LETTER 22	PROSE
& NOW GO ON AGAIN WITH MY TASK FEARLESS AND THO MY	813B	LETTER 22	PROSE
COULD UNITE AGAIN IN SOCIETY & HOPE THAT THE TIME IS NOT	813C	LETTER 22	PROSE
A PICTURE TILL I HAD AGAIN RECONSIDERD MY NOTIONS OF ART	815A	LETTER 23	PROSE
THEM OVER AGAIN THEY WOULD LOSE AS MUCH AS THEY GAIND	815C	LETTER 23	PROSE
BEEN VERY UNHAPPY I AM SO NO LONGER I AM AGAIN EMERGED	815D	LETTER 23	PROSE
OF SOON SEEING YOU AGAIN I OFTEN OMIT TO ENQUIRE OF YOU	816A	LETTER 23	PROSE
& I MEAN TO TRY MANY BUT I AGAIN SAY AS I SAID BEFORE WE ARE	820B	LETTER 25	PROSE
PRESSURE OF OTHER BUSINESS BUT THEY WILL GO ON AGAIN SOON	822B	LETTER 26	PROSE
TO LONDON AGAIN APPLAUDS IT AS THE ONLY COURSE FOR THE	822D	LETTER 26	PROSE
TOWARD OUR MEETING AGAIN IN LONDON WITH THOSE WHOM WE	824B	LETTER 27	PROSE
MEETING AGAIN WITH YOU IS ONE OF OUR GREATEST PLEASURES	826B	LETTER 28	PROSE
TOOK HIM AGAIN BY THE ELBOWS & KEEPING HIS BACK TO ME	827B	LETTER 28	PROSE
YOU & MRS BUTTS & ALL YOUR FAMILY I AGAIN TAKE THE LIBERTY	829A	LETTER 28	PROSE
THE FLAME SOON DIES AGAIN & I AM LEFT STUPIFIED AND ASTONISHD	830B	LETTER 30	PROSE
THAT WICKED HORSE AGAIN NOR AGAIN TRUST TO ONE WHO HAS BEEN	833C	LETTER 33	PROSE
GOOD WOMAN AGAIN BEGINS TO RESUME HER HEALTH & STRENGTH	833D	LETTER 33	PROSE
HIS SON WAS LIKEWISE NOT AT HOME BUT I WILL AGAIN CALL ON	834B	LETTER 34	PROSE
BUT I WILL CALL AGAIN IN A DAY OR TWO NEITHER MR FLAXMAN NOR	836B	LETTER 35	PROSE
NEVER SEE HIM AGAIN BUT WHEN I CALL ON HIM FOR HE HAS	836C	LETTER 35	PROSE
ENTER AGAIN WITH GREAT PLEASURE AND HOPE SOON TO SHOW YOU	841A	LETTER 40	PROSE
& THAT MISS POOLE IS AGAIN IN SUCH HEALTH	843A	LETTER 42	*PROSE
IMMEDIATELY TO LADY HAMILTON MR WALKER I HAVE AGAIN SEEN	845D	LETTER 44	PROSE
VERY SOON TO CALL AGAIN & AS YOU WISH TO WRITE ALL I CAN	849B	LETTER 45	PROSE
TRUCHSESSIAN GALLERY OF PICTURES I WAS AGAIN ENLIGHTENED	852B	LETTER 50	PROSE
I AM AGAIN IN WANT OF TEN POUNDS HOPE THAT THE SIZE AND	853C	LETTER 52	PROSE
MIGHT AGAIN CALL I HAVE HOWEVER SEEN HIM THIS MORNING	856A	LETTER 54	PROSE
MAY TURN OUT SO AGAIN NOTWITHSTANDING APPEARANCES	862C	LETTER 60	PROSE
A CIRCUMSTANCE HAS OCCURRED WHICH HAS AGAIN RAISED MY INDIGNATION	865A	LETTER 62	PROSE
HOPING THAT I MAY MEET YOU AGAIN IN PERFECT HEALTH & HAPPINESS	868B	LETTER 67	PROSE
SOON GET ABOUT AGAIN GREAT MEN DIE EQUALLY WITH THE LITTLE	868D	LETTER 68	PROSE
FOR I AM AGAIN LAID UP BY A COLD IN MY STOMACH THE	870B	LETTER 72	PROSE
I HAVE BEEN VERY ILL SINCE I SAW YOU BUT AM AGAIN WELL	871D	LETTER 74	PROSE
SHIVERING FIT ATTACKED ME AGAIN & THE PAIN WITH ITS	872B	LETTER 75	PROSE
ACCOMPANYING DEATHLY FEEL I GOT AGAIN INTO A PERSPIRATION	872B	LETTER 75	PROSE
SUNDAY AT HAMPSTEAD AS I FEAR THE ATTACK AGAIN	872C	LETTER 75	PROSE
SAYING DO NOT VENTURE TILL SUMMER APPEARS AGAIN I ALSO	872D	LETTER 76	PROSE
YOUR HAPPY FAMILY ONCE AGAIN & THAT FOR A LONGER PERIOD	873A	LETTER 76	PROSE
I BEGIN TO AGAIN FEEL RETURNING STRENGTH ON THESE ACCOUNTS	874D	LETTER 80	PROSE
THAT HE IS DEPRIVED OF THE HAPPINESS OF VISITING AGAIN &	SUPP	LETTER 81A	*PROSE
ALSO OF SEEING AGAIN THOSE PICTURES OF THE OLD MASTERS BUT	SUPP	LETTER 81A	*PROSE

AGAINST

	PAGE	TITLE	LINE
NOR LAUREL WREATHS AGAINST THE SULTRY HEAT	2	TO SUMMER/PS	19
CAN IF THEY WILL DEFEND THEMSELVES AGAINST	21	EDW THIRD/PS 2	87
I FEEL IT COMING UPON ME SO I STRIVE AGAINST IT	22	EDW THIRD/PS 3	62
AND SHOOK HIS MORTAL DART AGAINST MY HEAD	25	EDW THIRD/PS 3	176
WHOSE EYES DO GLARE AGAINST THE STORMY FIRES	32	EDW THIRD/PS 6	9
OLD AGE MUST WORK THE WORK OF DEATH AGAINST THEIR PROGENY	34B	KING JOHN/PS	PROSE
EAGER SONG GOES ON TELLING HOW PRIDE AGAINST HER FATHER WARRD	42B	THEN SHE BORE	PROSE
NO OMNIPOTENCE CAN ACT AGAINST ORDER	78A	ANNO LAVATER	MARG
[HE STROVE AGAINST HIS RISING PASSIONS BUT STILL HE COULD NOT SPEAK]	101	TIRIEL 2	45
[HATH WORKD OUR RUIN WE SUBMIT NOR STRIVE AGAINST STERN FATE]	105	TIRIEL 4	80
ESCAPE YE FIENDS FOR IJIM WILL NOT LIFT HIS HAND AGAINST YE	106	TIRIEL 4	88
THEY DASH LIKE FOAM AGAINST THE RIDGES OF THE ARMY	146	FRENCH REVOLTN	277
AGAINST SUCH AS REFUSED TO LODGE THEM I TELL YOU	158C	MARRIAGE HH 22	PROSE
STRIVING AGAINST MY SWADDLING BANDS	166	INFANT SORW/N	6
[HIS HARP ALOFT SOUNDING THEN DASHD ITS SHINING FRAME AGAINST]	196	AMERICA PREL 2	19
BOADICEA INSPIRING THE BRITONS AGAINST THE ROMANS	208D	SUBJCTS HIST/N	TITLE
STRIVING AGAINST MY SWADLING BANDS	217	INFANT SORW/SE	6
TURND OUTWARD BARRD AND PETRIFYD AGAINST THE INFINITE	241	EUROPE 10	15
AGAINST ONE ANOTHER SO LET THEM WAR ON SLAVES TO THE ETERNAL ELEMENTS	245	SONG OF LOS 3	14
TO FOREGO EACH HIS OWN DELIGHT TO WAR AGAINST HIS SPECTRE	273	FOUR ZOAS 1	340
DARING MY POWER WILT ARM MY SONS AGAINST ME IN THE [DEEP] ATLANTIC	278	FOUR ZOAS 1	510
AGAINST ME WHO THEE GUARDED IN THE NIGHT OF DEATH FROM HARM	300	FOUR ZOAS 4	110
THY ETERNAL FORM SHALL NEVER RENEW MY UNCERTAIN PREVAILS AGAINST THEE	301	FOUR ZOAS 4	136
AGAINST THE MONSTROUS FORMS THAT BREED AMONG MY SILENT WAVES	301	FOUR ZOAS 4	145
NOW THOU DOST KNOW WHAT TIS TO STRIVE AGAINST THE GOD OF WATERS	301	FOUR ZOAS 4	156
RAGING AGAINST THARMAS HIS GOD & UTTERING	302	FOUR ZOAS 4	204
STEMMING HIS DOWNWARD FALL LABOURING UP AGAINST FUTURITY	316	FOUR ZOAS 6	186
IN [ANGUISH FOR] RAGE AGAINST THE DARK DESPAIR THE HOWLING MELANCHOLY	340	FOUR ZOAS 7B *	287
LOS BUILDS THE WALLS OF GOLGONOOZA AGAINST THE STIRRING BATTLE	343	FOUR ZOAS 8	109
AGAINST THE DIVINE IMAGE CONGREGATED ASSEMBLIES OF WICKED MEN	347	FOUR ZOAS 8	258

	PAGE	TITLE	LINE
AGAINST (CONTINUED)			
THE SYNAGOGUE OF SATAN THEREFORE UNITING AGAINST MYSTERY	357	FOUR ZOAS 8	614
SATAN DIVIDED AGAINST SATAN RESOLVD IN OPEN SANHEDRIM . .	357	FOUR ZOAS 8	615
AGAINST THEE TO ETERNITY & NEVER RECIEVE THEE MORE . .	361	FOUR ZOAS 9	149
MY ANGER AGAINST THEE IS GREATER THAN AGAINST THIS LUVAH	361	FOUR ZOAS 9	151
IN SILKEN GARMENTS SPUN BY HER OWN HANDS AGAINST HER FUNERAL	362	FOUR ZOAS 9	213
THEY MAGNIFY THEMSELVES NO MORE AGAINST JERUSALEM NOR . .	364	FOUR ZOAS 9	266
AGAINST HER LITTLE ONES THE INNOCENT ACCUSED BEFORE THE JUDGES	364	FOUR ZOAS 9	267
EXPENDING ALL HIS ENERGY AGAINST THE FUEL OF FIRE . . .	366	FOUR ZOAS 9	359
IF GODS COMBINE AGAINST MAN SETTING THEIR DOMINION ABOVE	366	FOUR ZOAS 9	366
AGAINST FRANCE IS IT NOT TO STATE RELIGION BLUSH FOR SHAME	385C	ANNO WATSON	MARG
SPEAKS A WORD AGAINST THE SON OF MAN SHALL BE FORGIVEN .	387C	ANNO WATSON	MARG
NOT SPOKEN AGAINST THE HOLY GHOST WHO IN PAINE STRIVES .	387C	ANNO WATSON	MARG
OF GOD WILL BE A LASTING WITNESS AGAINST THEM	389A	ANNO WATSON	MARG
& THE SAME WILL IT BE AGAINST [OF] CHRISTIANS	389B	ANNO WATSON	MARG
LETTERS ARE SUCH AS DO NOTHING AGAINST PAINE'S ARGUMENTS	390C	ANNO WATSON	MARG
AN ATHEIST PRETENDING TO TALK AGAINST ATHEISM	404A	ANNO BACON	MARG
INDIGNANT AGAINST KNAVERY	414A	ANNO BOYD	MARG
WHILE EITHER COUNTRY HINDS ARE AS INDIGNANT AGAINST HONESTY	414A	ANNO BOYD	MARG
[I SIN AGAINST [HER] THEE MORE & MORE]	415	MY SPECTRE/N	6
YOU THROW THE SAND AGAINST THE WIND	418	MOCK ON/N	3
AGAINST THIS IMAGE OF HIS LORD	420	I SAW MNK AD/N	9
AND THAT NOT ONE WORD OF CHARGE AGAINST ME WAS UTTERED .	437B	BLAKES MEMORAN	PROSE
BROUGHT AGAINST US THAT WERE NOT THERE	438B	BLAKES MEMORAN	PROSE
AND SWEAR AGAINST ME WILLIAM SAID THAT HE WOULD NOT TAKE	438C	BLAKES MEMORAN	PROSE
REYNOLDS & GAINSBOROUGH BLOTTED & BLURRED ONE AGAINST THE	445C	ANNO REYNOLDS	MARG
THEY MILITATE AGAINST INDIVIDUAL CHARACTER	453B	ANNO REYNOLDS	MARG
ARE SET UP BY ARTIFICE AGAINST THE SUBLIME OF THE BIBLE	480B	MILTON 1	PROSE
AGAINST THE IGNORANT HIRELINGS FOR	480C	MILTON 1	PROSE
WERE LEAGUED TOGETHER AGAINST SATAN THRO ANCIENT ENMITY	487	MILTON 7	40
MICHAEL CONTENDED AGAINST SATAN IN THE ROLLING THUNDER .	488	MILTON 8	32
WHICH NOW FLAMD HIGH & FURIOUS IN SATAN AGAINST PALAMBRON	489	MILTON 9	11
OPAKE AGAINST THE DIVINE VISION THE PAVED TERRACES OF .	490	MILTON 9	31
A MIGHTY FIEND AGAINST THE DIVINE HUMANITY MUSTRING TO WAR	491	MILTON 10	11
HE SET HIS FACE AGAINST JERUSALEM TO DESTROY THE EON OF ALBION	491	MILTON 11	1
AGAINST THE ROCK WHICH WAS INWRAPPED WITH THE WEEDS OF DEATH	497	MILTON 15	40
HIS LIMBS SHOT FORTH LIKE ROOTS OF TREES AGAINST THE FORWARD PATH	498	MILTON 17	35
BURNS TO THE TOP OF HEAVEN AGAINST THEE IN JEALOUSY & FEAR	499	MILTON 18	32
GLOWD ON HIS ROCKY COUCH AGAINST THE DARKNESS LOUD THUNDERS	500	MILTON 18	47
BROODED OVER HIS BODY IN HOREB AGAINST THE RESURRECTION	502	MILTON 20	22
ASSERTING THE SELF-RIGHTEOUSNESS AGAINST THE UNIVERSAL SAVIOUR	506	MILTON 22	42
ARISE O SONS GIVE ALL YOUR STRENGTH AGAINST ETERNAL DEATH	509	MILTON 24	34
WHO SET PLEASURE AGAINST DUTY WHO CREATE OLYMPIC CROWNS	511	MILTON 25	51
FOR LOS AGAINST THE EAST HIS FORCE CONTINUALLY BENDS . .	512	MILTON 26	18
HERE THE SONS OF LOS LABOUR AGAINST DEATH ETERNAL THROUGH ALL	514	MILTON 27	44
OZOTH HERE BUILDS WALLS OF ROCKS AGAINST THE SURGING SEA	515	MILTON 28	39
AND CRUEL OPPOSITION ELEMENT AGAINST ELEMENT OPPOSED IN WAR	520	MILTON 31	24
REECHOING AGAINST THE LOVELY BLUE & SHINING HEAVENLY SHELL	520	MILTON 31	33
IN WHICH MAN LIVETH ETERNALLY MADNESS & BLASPHEMY AGAINST	521	MILTON 32	20
GORGEOUS & BEAUTIFUL LOUD HIS THUNDERS AGAINST MILTON	529	MILTON 38	12
AGAINST HIS PRICE BUT DEATH WAS IN THE POT	537	AND HIS LEGS/N	29
[YE] COME ARTISTS KNOCK YOUR HEADS AGAINST THIS STONE .	537	AND HIS LEGS/N	46
THIS LIFE IS A WARFARE AGAINST EVILS	545	COSWAY FRAZR/N	3
COME KNOCK YOUR HEADS AGAINST THIS STONE	545	AN EPITAPH/N	1
OF MAN AGAINST THE OPPRESSOR HIS SON IS LIKE HIM . . .	568A	DESC CAT 3	PROSE
WHICH WAS PAINTED IN SELF-DEFENCE AGAINST THE INSOLENT .	572C	DESC CAT 3	PROSE
ENDEAVOUR TO RAISE UP A STYLE AGAINST RAFAEL MICH ANGELO	573B	DESC CAT 3	PROSE
[AGAINST A CERTAIN IMPOSTOR WHO C] IN [OUR ART] THE ART OF	601C	PUB ADDRESS/N	*PROSE
AGAINST THESE VILLAINS I AM LIKE OTHERS	602A	PUB ADDRESS/N	PROSE
& AGAINST WHICH WE SHOULD ALL WATCH	608A	V LAST JUDG/N	PROSE
WHO DRIVES ABROAD ALL THOSE WHO REBELL AGAINST THEIR SAVIOUR	608B	V LAST JUDG/N	PROSE
THESE ARE ONLY EMPLOYD AGAINST THE JUST	616B	V LAST JUDG/N	PROSE
ABSTRACT PHILOSOPHY WARRING IN ENMITY AGAINST IMAGINATION	624	JERUSALEM 5	58
TO ALBION SUGGESTING MURDEROUS THOUGHTS AGAINST ALBION .	624	JERUSALEM 6	7
ROSE UP AGAINST ME THUNDERING FROM THE BROOK OF ALBION'S RIVER	627	JERUSALEM 8	1
AND THOU MY SPECTRE ART DIVIDED AGAINST ME BUT MARK . .	627	JERUSALEM 8	14
THY HOLY WRATH & DEEP DECEIT CANNOT AVAIL AGAINST ME . .	627	JERUSALEM 8	33
O SPECTRE OF URTHONA REASON NOT AGAINST THEIR DEAR APPROACH	629	JERUSALEM 10	32
SELF-RIGHTEOUSNESSES CONGLOMERATING AGAINST THE DIVINE VISION	634	JERUSALEM 13	* 52
HAVING A WALL BUILDED AGAINST IT AND THEREBY THE GATES . .	635	JERUSALEM 14	27
BUT LOS HIMSELF AGAINST ALBION'S SONS HIS FURY BENDS FOR HE	638	JERUSALEM 17	6
RAGING AGAINST THEIR HUMAN NATURES RAVNING TO GORMANDIZE	641	JERUSALEM 19	23
WHICH HARDEND AGAINST THEM MORE AND MORE AS HE BUILDED ONWARDS	641	JERUSALEM 19	30
APPEARD A ROCKY FORM AGAINST THE DIVINE HUMANITY . . .	642	JERUSALEM 19	35
TWO BLEEDING CONTRARIES EQUALLY TRUE ARE HIS WITNESSES AGAINST ME	646	JERUSALEM 24	3
FORTIFICATION AGAINST THE DIVINE HUMANITY AND MERCY . . .	653	JERUSALEM 28	26
FEARING THAT ALBION SHOULD TURN HIS BACK AGAINST THE DIVINE VISION	656	JERUSALEM 31	2

31

		PAGE	TITLE	LINE

AGAINST   (CONTINUED)

LEANING AGAINST THE PILLARS & HIS DISEASE ROSE FROM HIS   658 JERUSALEM 32   1
SKIRTS
THE RIVER OF LIFE TO FLOW AGAINST MY WALLS & AMONG MY TREES   660 JERUSALEM 33   38
WHY DOST THOU THUNDER WITH FROZEN SPECTROUS WRATH AGAINST   664 JERUSALEM 37   3
US
THOU WILT CERTAINLY PROVOKE MY SPECTRE AGAINST THINE IN   664 JERUSALEM 37   5
FURY
HIS COLD AGAINST THE WARMTH OF EDEN RAGD WITH LOUD   . . .   664 JERUSALEM 38   8
IF WE HAVE OFFENDED FORGIVE US TAKE NOT VENGEANCE AGAINST   665 JERUSALEM 38   26
US
SEEING ALBION HAD TURND HIS BACK AGAINST THE DIVINE VISION   666 JERUSALEM 39   14
AND CURSES WITH HIS MIGHTY ARMS BRANDISHD AGAINST   667 JERUSALEM 40   37
THE HEAVENS
LOS BUILT THE STUBBORN STRUCTURE OF THE LANGUAGE ACTING   668 JERUSALEM 40   59
AGAINST
WINCHESTER IN HIS DEN & CAVERN THEY LAMENT AGAINST   . . .   671 JERUSALEM 42   59
THEY SAW THEIR WHEELS RISING UP POISONOUS AGAINST ALBION   671 JERUSALEM 43   1
VICTIMS TO ONE ANOTHER & DREADFULLY PLOTTING AGAINST EACH   671 JERUSALEM 43   4
OTHER
AGAINST HIS WILL THRO LOS'S GATE TO EDEN FOUR-FOLD LOUD   674 JERUSALEM 44   3
OF BLACK DESPAIR THAT THE IMMORTAL WINGS LABOURD AGAINST   674 JERUSALEM 44   12
AGAINST THIS IMAGE OF HIS LORD . . . .   683 I SAW A MONK/J   24
WHERE IS THAT FRIEND OF SINNERS THAT REBEL AGAINST MY LAWS   685 JERUSALEM 54   19
BUT SHE STRETCHD OUT HER STARRY NIGHT IN SPACES AGAINST   685 JERUSALEM 54   28
HIM LIKE
RIVERS THUNDERD AGAINST THEIR BANKS LOUD WINDS FURIOUS   686 JERUSALEM 55   24
FOUGHT
TWO CONTRARIES WAR AGAINST EACH OTHER IN FURY & BLOOD   . .   690 JERUSALEM 58   15
MARY LEANED HER SIDE AGAINST JERUSALEM JERUSALEM RECIEVED   695 JERUSALEM 61   47
AGAINST THE DIVINE VISION & FALL OVER THE PRECIPICE OF   711 JERUSALEM 71   59
ETERNAL DEATH
AND DEADLY STUPOR TURND AGAINST EACH OTHER LOUD & FIERCE   714 JERUSALEM 74   6
FROM WEST TO EAST AGAINST THE CURRENT OF . . . . . .   717 STOOD AMONG/J   4
AGAINST THE CURRENT OF THIS WHEEL ITS NAME . . . . . .   718 STOOD AMONG/J   17
IN TERRIBLE ARMOUR RAGING AGAINST THE LAMB & AGAINST   719 JERUSALEM 78   13
JERUSALEM
THE FIFTY-TWO COUNTIES OF ENGLAND ARE HARDEND AGAINST ME   720 JERUSALEM 79   20
THY MASCULINE FROM THY FEMININE HARDENING AGAINST   721 JERUSALEM 79   71
THE HEAVENS
AGAINST JERUSALEM THEY RAGE THRO ALL THE NATIONS OF EUROPE   722 JERUSALEM 80   46
COMPELLD INTO A SHAPE OF MORAL VIRTUE AGAINST THE LAMB . .   723 JERUSALEM 80   77
HIS LAW A FORM AGAINST THE LAMB OF GOD OPPOSD TO MERCY . .   723 JERUSALEM 80   79
AGAINST THE PATRIARCHAL POMP AND CRUELTY LABOURING   727 JERUSALEM 83   4
INCESSANT
FLOWD INTO THE ACHING FIBRES OF LOS YET CONTENDING AGAINST   733 JERUSALEM 88   29
HIM
HOWLING WINDS COVER HIM ROARING SEAS DASH FURIOUS AGAINST   741 JERUSALEM 94   3
HIM
MARCHES AGAINST THEE DECEITFUL FROM SINAI & FROM EDOM   . .   743 JERUSALEM 96   9
SHOOTING OUT AGAINST THE LIGHT . . . .   753 EV GOSPEL(D)/N   95
AGAINST RELIGION & GOVERNMENT . . . .   757 EV GOSPEL(I)/N   38
WHO AGAINST SINNERS HEAVEN CLOSE . . . .   758 EV GOSPEL (1)   12
AGAINST THE ACCUSER'S CHIEF DESIRE . . . .   761 FOR SEXES/GP   3
EMPIRE AGAINST ART SEE VIRGIL'S ENEID LIB VI...   777A INSC LAOCOON   PROSE
WHETHER HE SHALL [?RIM] RUN AGAINST A POST . . . .   782A INSC UPCOTT   *PROSE
RISING UP AGAINST THE SPIRITUAL MAN CONTINUALLY . . . .   782D ANNO WW POEMS   MARG
AT ENMITY AGAINST ALL TRUE POETRY OR INSPIRATION . . .   782D ANNO WW POEMS   MARG
& TO ITS LAWS OF GOOD & EVIL & ITS ENMITIES AGAINST MIND   784D ANNO WW EXCUR   MARG
BOOK IS AGAINST THE FORGIVENESS OF SINS IS NOT OF   785D ILLS DANTE 101 PROSE
THE FATHER
IS HERESY & REBELLION AGAINST CAESAR VIRGIL'S ONLY GOD .   789B ANNO THORNTON   * MARG
PERMIT ME IN RETURN TO DEFEND IT AGAINST A MISTAKEN ONE   793B LETTER 5   PROSE
WHEN MY HEART KNOCKD AGAINST THE ROOT OF MY TONGUE . . .   817 HAPPINESS/L   8
"ME IS AGAINST ME" THERE IS NO MEDIUM OR MIDDLE STATE &   822D LETTER 26   PROSE
AGAINST MY WILL THE TIME IT HAS TAKEN IN WRITING WAS THUS   823B LETTER 26   PROSE
BUT IF ALL THE WORLD SHOULD SET THEIR FACES AGAINST THIS   825B LETTER 27   PROSE
AGAINST THEIR FACES & MY FOREHEAD AGAINST THEIR FOREHEADS   825B LETTER 27   PROSE
AGAINST FORMER CONDUCT & TO DEMAND JUSTICE & TRUTH . .   825D LETTER 27   PROSE
TO DEFEND MYSELF AGAINST A VERY UNWARRANTABLE WARRANT .   826D LETTER 28   PROSE
AGAINST ME BY A PRIVATE IN CAPTN LEATHES'S TROOP OF (FIRST)   826D LETTER 28   PROSE
OR
AFTER MANY ABUSIVE THREATS [FROM THEM] AGAINST ME & . . .   827B LETTER 28   PROSE
IS THE ORIGIN OF ALL OFFENCES COMMITTED AGAINST ME IF I   828C LETTER 28   PROSE
HAVE
IT MAY BE CALLD A DEFENCE OF LITERATURE AGAINST THOSE PESTS   841D LETTER 41   PROSE
OF
HAS TAKEN CARE WHEN I HAVE SEEN HIM TO RAIL AGAINST   846C LETTER 44   PROSE
SEAGRAVE
IN LONDON EVERY CALUMNY AND FALSEHOOD UTTERD AGAINST   847B LETTER 44   PROSE
ANOTHER
MEET TO CONSULT AGAINST THE OTHER NOTHING CAN BE GREATER   859B LETTER 56   PROSE
THAN
AGAINST TRUE ART SUCH AS IT EXISTED . . . .   864A LETTER 61   PROSE
SHOULDER AND WHOLE STRENGTH AGAINST THOSE WRETCHES WHO .   864A LETTER 61   PROSE
OF RESENTMENT AGAINST MAN AND DEVIL AND OF HUMILIATION   864B LETTER 61   PROSE
BEFORE GOD
AGAINST THEIR ETERNAL EXISTENCE ITSELF BECAUSE IT IS .   871A LETTER 72   PROSE
MENTAL REBELLION AGAINST THE HOLY SPIRIT . . . . .   871B LETTER 72   PROSE
"& THAT THOU SHOULDST SET THINE HEART AGAINST HIM" JOB .   SUPP LEGEND/N68   *TITLE

AGAMEMNON

AS WOULD HAVE CALLED FOR THE SCEPTRE OF AGAMEMNON   . . .   847B LETTER 44   PROSE

AGE
```
                                                               PAGE    TITLE          LINE

  AGE IS CONTEMPLATIVE EACH ROLLING YEAR    . . . . . . .    27 EDW THIRD/PS 3      250
  THAT YOUTH HAS NEED OF AGE TO POINT FIT PREY   . . . . .   27 EDW THIRD/PS 3      269
  CONSIDERATE AGE MY LORD VIEWS MOTIVES   . . . . . . . .    27 EDW THIRD/PS 3      282
  WITH TREMBLING AGE THE VOICE OF CONSCIENCE THEN   . . .    28 EDW THIRD/PS 3      285
  OLD AGE MUST WORK THE WORK OF DEATH AGAINST THEIR PROGENY  34B KING JOHN/PS      PROSE
  TILL VENERABLE AGE CAME ON HIS FLOCKS INCREASED   . .     39C SAMSON/PS         PROSE
  THE SON OF HIS OLD AGE SHALL SET IT FREE THE   . . . . .  39C SAMSON/PS         PROSE
  TILL YOUR WHITE BONES ARE BLEACHD WITH AGE FOR A MEMORIAL 100 TIRIEL 1             47
  TO SMITE (THEE) IN THE FORM OF HELPLESS AGE & EYELESS     104 TIRIEL 4          *  18
     POLICY
  THE FIVE SENSES THE CHIEF INLETS OF SOUL IN THIS AGE   .  149D MARRIAGE HH 4    PROSE
  LET AGE & SICKNESS SILENT ROB   . . . . . . . . .         172 ARE NOT JOYS/N        5
  TO SPIN A WEB OF AGE AROUND HIM GREY AND HOARY DARK   . . 194 V DAU ALBION 7       19
  OF ANY AGE OR COUNTRY AMONG WHICH ARE TWO LARGE   . . .   207C PRSPECTUS 1793   PROSE
  CHILDREN OF THE FUTURE AGE   . . . . . . . . . .          219 LIT GRL LST/SE        1
  IN THE AGE OF GOLD   . . . . . . . . . . . . . .          219 LIT GRL LST/SE        5
  AGE ON AGES HE LAY CLOSD UNKNOWN   . . . . . . . . .      223 URIZEN 3             24
  AND A FIRST AGE PASSED OVER   . . . . . . . . . .         228 URIZEN 10            42
  AND A SECOND AGE PASSED OVER   . . . . . . . . . .        228 URIZEN 11             8
  AND A THIRD AGE PASSED OVER   . . . . . . . . . .         228 URIZEN 11            17
  AS THEY GREW AND A FOURTH AGE PASSED   . . . . . . .      229 URIZEN 11            24
  AND A FIFTH AGE PASSED OVER   . . . . . . . . . .         229 URIZEN 13             2
  AND A SIXTH AGE PASSED OVER   . . . . . . . . . .         229 URIZEN 13            10
  AND A SEVENTH AGE PASSED OVER   . . . . . . . . . .       229 URIZEN 13            18
  THO THOU HAST NOT PITID MY AGE O URIZEN PRINCE OF LIGHT   280 FOUR ZOAS 2          8
  AND WHEN LUVAH AGE AFTER AGE WAS QUITE MELTED WITH WOE    283 FOUR ZOAS 2        113
  WHERE LUVAH STRIVES SCORNED BY VALA AGE AFTER AGE         295 FOUR ZOAS 3      *  128
     WANDERING
  A FIRST AGE PASSED A STATE OF DISMAL WOE   . . . . . .    303 FOUR ZOAS 4        222
  AROUND HIS SOLID BONES & A SECOND AGE PASSED OVER   . .   303 FOUR ZOAS 4        226
  AND A THIRD AGE PASSED A STATE OF DISMAL WOE   . . . .    303 FOUR ZOAS 4        231
  AGE PASSED OVER & A STATE OF DISMAL WOE   . . . . . .     303 FOUR ZOAS 4        235
  AND A FIFTH AGE PASSED & A STATE OF DISMAL WOE   . . .    303 FOUR ZOAS 4        238
  AND THIRST APPEARD AND A SIXTH AGE PASSED OF DISMAL WOE   303 FOUR ZOAS 4      *  242
  AND A SEVENTH AGE PASSED OVER & A STATE OF DISMAL WOE  .  303 FOUR ZOAS 4        246
  AGE AFTER AGE TILL UNDERNEATH HIS HEEL A DEADLY ROOT  .   321 FOUR ZOAS 7         31
  AND THUS THEIR ANCIENT GOLDEN AGE RENEWD FOR LUVAH SPOKE  367 FOUR ZOAS 9        386
  AND TO ALLAY HIS [XXX] FREEZING AGE   . . . . . . . .     426 MENTAL TRAVLER   *  57
  SHALL BE MOCKD IN AGE & DEATH   . . . . . . . . . .       433 AUGURIES             86
  ADVICE OF THE POPES WHO SUCCEEDED THE AGE OF RAPAEL  . .  445B ANNO REYNOLDS     MARG
  CHILDHOOD AND AGE ARE EQUALLY BELONGING TO EVERY CLASS .  460B ANNO REYNOLDS     MARG
  AGE & YOUTH ARE NOT CLASSES BUT [ACCIDENTS] [SITUATIONS]  460C ANNO REYNOLDS   *  MARG
     PROPERTIES
  FIRST PAINTERS OF HIS AGE ALBERT DURER IS NOT WOULD HAVE  461A ANNO REYNOLDS     MARG
     BEEN
  & NOT TALK OF DARK AGES OR OF ANY AGE AGES ARE ALL EQUAL  461A ANNO REYNOLDS     MARG
  BUT GENIUS (IS ALWAYS ABOVE THE AGE)   . . . . . . .      461A ANNO REYNOLDS   *  MARG
  BUT WHEN THE NEW AGE IS AT LEISURE TO PRONOUNCE   . . .   480B MILTON 1          PROSE
  ROUZE UP O YOUNG MEN OF THE NEW AGE SET YOUR FOREHEADS .  480C MILTON 1          PROSE
  AND A FIRST AGE PASSED OVER & A STATE OF DISMAL WOE   . . 482 MILTON 3             10
  AND A SECOND AGE PASSED OVER & A STATE OF DISMAL WOE  . . 482 MILTON 3             13
  AND A THIRD AGE PASSED OVER & A STATE OF DISMAL WOE   . . 482 MILTON 3             16
  AND A FOURTH AGE PASSED OVER & A STATE OF DISMAL WOE  . . 482 MILTON 3             19
  AND A FIFTH AGE PASSED OVER & A STATE OF DISMAL WOE   . . 482 MILTON 3             21
  AND A SIXTH AGE PASSED OVER & A STATE OF DISMAL WOE   . . 482 MILTON 3             23
  AND A SEVENTH AGE PASSED OVER & A STATE OF DISMAL WOE  .  483 MILTON 3             27
  AND EVERY AGE IS MOATED DEEP WITH BRIDGES OF SILVER & GOLD 516 MILTON 28           56
  AND WHAT IS THE THIRD SHE PUT OFF OLD AGE   . . . . .     554 ASKD PRIGG/N         20
  POETS IN ANY AGE OR COUNTRY AND THESE IN A CORRUPT STATE  561C EXHIBITION ADV   PROSE
  NOW LOST OR PERHAPS BURIED TILL SOME HAPPIER AGE THE   .  565C DESC CAT 2        PROSE
  AS ONE AGE FALLS ANOTHER RISES DIFFERENT TO MORTAL SIGHT  567C DESC CAT 3        PROSE
  OF THOSE WHO WOULD HAVE BEEN MONKS IN THE AGE OF MONKERY  567C DESC CAT 3        PROSE
  WHO IN THIS DEISTICAL AGE ARE DEISTS   . . . . . . .      567D DESC CAT 3        PROSE
  WHICH IN EVERY AGE STANDS AS THE GUARDIAN   . . . . .     568A DESC CAT 3        PROSE
  HE IS A LEADER OF THE AGE   . . . . . . . . . .           568C DESC CAT 3        PROSE
  WHO IN EVERY AGE IS BORN TO RECORD AND ETERNIZE ITS ACTS  569A DESC CAT 3        PROSE
  OUR HOST WAS ALSO A LEADER OF THE AGE   . . . . . .       569D DESC CAT 3        PROSE
  IS SENT IN EVERY AGE FOR A ROD AND SCOURGE AND FOR   . .  570A DESC CAT 3        PROSE
  AN APOSTLE A REAL MESSENGER OF HEAVEN SENT IN EVERY AGE   570B DESC CAT 3        PROSE
  GREATEST OF HIS AGE YET HE IS A POOR PARSON OF A TOWN  .  570C DESC CAT 3        PROSE
  THE HEAD AND THE KNEE TO HIM WHO IN EVERY AGE SENDS US .  570C DESC CAT 3        PROSE
  SHALL THE GOLDEN AGE RETURN BUT ALAS YOU WILL NOT EASILY  570C DESC CAT 3        PROSE
  A JUDGE AND A REAL MASTER OF THE JURISPRUDENCE OF HIS AGE  570D DESC CAT 3        PROSE
  CHAUCER'S CHARACTERS LIVE AFTER AGE   . . . . . . .       570D DESC CAT 3        PROSE
  EVERY AGE IS A CANTERBURY PILGRIMAGE WE   . . . . . .     570D DESC CAT 3        PROSE
  AND NOT WITH OLD AGE AS SOME HAVE SUPPOSED   . . . . .    571B DESC CAT 3        PROSE
  CALLS THE SQUIRE THE FOP OF CHAUCER'S AGE NOW HEAR CHAUCER 573C DESC CAT 3        PROSE
  WORN OUT WITH AGE AND LABOUR AS THE PROSPECTUS HAS   . .  575A DESC CAT 3        PROSE
  HE IS WORN DOWN WITH LABOUR BUT NOT WITH AGE   . . . .    575A DESC CAT 3        PROSE
  AND REMAIN FOR EVER UNSUBDUED AGE AFTER AGE   . . . . .   577D DESC CAT 5        PROSE
  ALSO ABRAHAM WAS CALLED TO SUCCEED THE DRUIDICAL AGE  . . 578A DESC CAT 5        PROSE
  AND HELD THE EMPIRE OF THE WORLD IN THE DARK AGE   . . .  578C DESC CAT 5        PROSE
  LIMBS THAT DEVIATES OR ALTERS LEAST FROM INFANCY TO OLD AGE 580A DESC CAT 5       PROSE
  THAT THE PRODUCTIONS OF OUR YOUTH AND OF OUR MATURER AGE  585D DESC CAT 16       PROSE
  AS ONE AGE FALLS ANOTHER RISES DIFFERENT TO MORTAL SIGHT  589A CHAUCER/N         PROSE
  OF HUMAN CHARACTERS AS THEY APPEAR AGE AFTER AGE   . . .  591A PUB ADDRESS/N     TITLE
  AN IRON AGE & BEGAT ON MNEMOSYNE OR MEMORY   . . . . .    605C V LAST JUDG/N     PROSE
  ENDEAVOUR TO RESTORE WHAT THE ANCIENTS CALLD THE GOLDEN AGE 605D V LAST JUDG/N    PROSE
  BECAUSE IGNORANT OF CRIME IN THE MIDST OF A CORRUPTED AGE 610B V LAST JUDG/N     PROSE
  MILTON IN HIS OLD AGE SITTING IN HIS MOSSY CELL   . . . . 619C ILLUS MILTON      PROSE
  AND EVERY ONE HAS THE THREE REGIONS CHILDHOOD MANHOOD & AGE 635 JERUSALEM 14       25
```

AGE   (CONTINUED)

	PAGE	TITLE	LINE
LOS'S HALLS & EVERY AGE RENEWS ITS POWERS FROM THESE WORKS	638	JERUSALEM 16	62
OF AGE AND YOUTH AND BOY AND GIRL AND ANIMAL AND HERB . .	640	JERUSALEM 18	17
AND CHAMBERS OF TREMBLING & SUSPITION HATREDS OF AGE & YOUTH	640	JERUSALEM 18	24
AGE AFTER AGE DRAWING THEM AWAY TOWARDS BABYLON	715	JERUSALEM 74	31
OF CHILDHOOD MANHOOD & OLD AGE	746	JERUSALEM 98	33
SUCH THINGS AS THESE DEPEND ON THE FASHION OF THE AGE . .	787A	ANNO THORNTON	MARG
SINCE THE AGE OF RAFAEL ALL SR J REYNOLDS'S DISCOURSES . .	814B	LETTER 23	PROSE
POVERTY ENVY OLD AGE & FEAR	817	HAPPINESS/L	37
HOW IS IT POSSIBLE THAT A MAN ALMOST (FIFTY) YEARS OF AGE	830A	LETTER 30	PROSE
A VERY STOUT MAN AT EIGHTY-FIVE WHICH AGE HE TELLS ME HE	844B	LETTER 43	PROSE
WILL BE ?REVISED IN AN AGE OR TWO	845B	LETTER 44	PROSE
OF ROMNEY'S AGE MR W(WALKER) SAYS ROMNEY WAS TWO YEARS OLDER	847D	LETTER 44	PROSE
HE DIED AT THE AGE OF (SEVENTY-FIVE) OF A PARALYTIC STROKE	860A	LETTER 56	PROSE
FOR I HAVE HEARD NOTHING OF PHILLIPS THIS AGE I HEAR . .	862A	LETTER 59	PROSE
VIRGIN WIFE INFANCY OLD AGE HUSBAND ANGEL OF PROVIDENCE	SUPP	INSC HERVEY	*TITLE

AGE-BENT

	PAGE	TITLE	LINE
[AND] ENION BLIND & AGE-BENT WEPT UPON THE DESOLATE WIND	276	FOUR ZOAS 1	* 444
WHERE ENION BLIND & AGE BENT WEPT IN DIREFUL HUNGER CRAVING	280	FOUR ZOAS 2	16
INSTEAD OF LOVE TO ENION BLIND & AGE BENT	296	FOUR ZOAS 3	178
WHERE ENION BLIND & AGE BENT WANDERD AHANIA WANDERS NOW	297	FOUR ZOAS 3	207
OFT BLIND & AGE-BENT SORE DISTREST	426	MENTAL TRAVLER	55
I SEE LONDON BLIND & AGE-BENT BEGGING THRO THE STREETS . .	729	JERUSALEM 84	11
REPELLING WEEPING ENION BLIND & AGE-BENT INTO THE FOURFOLD	732	JERUSALEM 87	1

AGE-BROKE

	PAGE	TITLE	LINE
TILL HOARY AND AGE-BROKE AND AGED	225	URIZEN 5	26

AGED

	PAGE	TITLE	LINE
THY AGED FATHERS GIRD THEMSELVES FOR WAR	34B	KING JOHN/PS	PROSE
THE AGED SENATORS THEIR ANCIENT SWORDS ASSUME THE TREMBLING SINEWS OF	34B	KING JOHN/PS	PROSE
THE AGED WOMAN RAISED HER VOICE O MY SON MY SON . . .	36A	COUCH DEATH/PS	PROSE
THE AGED WOMAN RAISED HER CRY AND SAID	36B	COUCH DEATH/PS	PROSE
THEIR HELMED YOUTH AND AGED WARRIORS IN DUST TOGETHER LY(LIE)	37D	SAMSON/PS	PROSE
THUS PRAYED MANOA THE AGED WOMAN WALKED INTO THE FIELD . .	40B	SAMSON/PS	PROSE
FOR AGED MEN & YOUTH	57	TO BE OR/IM	8
AND AGED TIRIEL STOOD BEFORE THE GATES OF HIS BEAUTIFUL PALACE	99	TIRIEL 1	1
OF AGED TIRIEL AROSE THAT HIS SONS MIGHT HEAR IN THEIR GATES	99	TIRIEL 1	6
ACCURSED RACE OF TIRIEL BEHOLD YOUR [AGED] FATHER . .	99	TIRIEL 1	7
IN MY WEAK [AGED] ARMS I HERE HAVE BORNE YOUR DYING MOTHER	99	TIRIEL 1	9
HIS SONS RAN FROM THEIR GATES & SAW THEIR AGED PARENTS STAND	99	TIRIEL 1	11
HE CEAST THE AGED MAN [XXX] RAISD UP HIS RIGHT HAND TO THE HEAVENS	99	TIRIEL 1	* 19
YE WORMS OF DEATH FEASTING UPON YOUR AGED PARENTS FLESH	99	TIRIEL 1	23
SO SAYING HE BEGAN TO DIG A GRAVE WITH HIS AGED HANDS . .	100	TIRIEL 1	34
OER MOUNTAINS & THRO VALES OF WOE THE BLIND & AGED MAN . .	100	TIRIEL 2	3
MNETHA NOW AGED WAITED ON THEM & BROUGHT THEM FOOD & CLOTHING	100	TIRIEL 2	6
[THE AGED FATHER & MOTHER SAW HIM AS THEY SAT AT PLAY] . .	100	TIRIEL 2	11
[THE AGED TIRIEL COULD NOT SPEAK HIS HEART WAS FULL OF GRIEF]	101	TIRIEL 2	44
MNETHA SAID COME IN AGED WANDERER TELL US OF THY NAME . .	101	TIRIEL 2	46
I AM AN AGED WANDERER ONCE FATHER OF A RACE	102	TIRIEL 2	50
AND SAW THEIR AGED FATHER BORNE UPON HIS MIGHTY SHOULDERS	105	TIRIEL 4	46
[DESIRES OUR DEATHS O IJIM [?TIS ?ONE ?WHOSE AGED TONGUE]	105	TIRIEL 4	78
[SET AGED TIRIEL IN DEEP THOUGHT WHETHER THESE THINGS WERE SO]	106	TIRIEL 4	82
THEN IS IT TRUE HEUXOS THAT THOU HAST TURND THY AGED PARENT	106	TIRIEL 4	83
AND AGED TIRIEL STOOD & SAID WHERE DOES THE THUNDER SLEEP	106	TIRIEL 5	1
FOR THOU HAST LAUGHED AT MY TEARS & CURST THY AGED FATHER	108	TIRIEL 6	42
OR WHEREFORE DOST THOU CRY AH WRETCH TO CURSE THY AGED FATHER	108	TIRIEL 6	47
THE AGED WANDERER LED TOWARDS THE TENTS SHE TOOK HER BOW	109	TIRIEL 7	23
RAN TO THE DOOR WHEN TIRIEL FELT THE ANKLES OF AGED HAR	109	TIRIEL 8	1
BENEATH THEM SIT THE AGED MEN WISE GUARDIANS OF THE POOR	122	HOLY THURS/SI	11
. . . THE OLD MOUNTAINS OF FRANCE LIKE AGED MEN FADING AWAY	134	FRENCH REVOLTN	9
AN AGED FORM WHITE AS SNOW HOVRING IN MIST	140	FRENCH REVOLTN	131
. . . FROM THE GLOOM WHERE THE AGED FORM WEPT	140	FRENCH REVOLTN	135
. . . WHOSE AGED TREES UTTER AN AWFUL VOICE AND THEIR BRANCHES	145	FRENCH REVOLTN	242
THE AGED SUN RISES APPALLD FROM DARK MOUNTAINS . . .	146	FRENCH REVOLTN	270
BUT CLOUDS OBSCURE MY AGED SIGHT A VISION FROM AFAR . .	199	AMERICA 9	12
THE COUNCIL SAT ALL ROSE BEFORE THE AGED APPARITION . . .	204	AMERICA CANC B	15
AND ON HIS [SHINING] AGED LIMBS	205	AMERICA CANC C	6
[OVER THE] A FROWNING SHADOW LIKE [A] AN AGED KING IN ARMS OF GOLD	205	AMERICA CANC C	* 25
ALAS MY SON MY SON I WANT I WANT HELP HELP AGED IGNORANCE	209C	FOR CHILDRN/GP	TITLE
TILL HOARY AND AGE-BROKE AND AGED	225	URIZEN 5	26
UPON THE AGED HEAVENS	235	URIZEN 25	8
THEIR PARENTS BROUGHT THEM FORTH & AGED IGNORANCE PREACHES CANTING	242	EUROPE 12	7
ENO AGED MOTHER	255	BOOK OF LOS 3	1
THE SONG OF THE AGED MOTHER WHICH SHOOK THE HEAVENS WITH WRATH	264	FOUR ZOAS 1	2
CLOTHED IN AGED VENERABLENESS OBSTINATELY RESOLVD . . .	318	FOUR ZOAS 6	242

AGED   (CONTINUED)
    THE FLEECY WHITE RENEWD HE SHOOK HIS AGED MANTLES OFF . .   362 FOUR ZOAS 9   190
    AND HIS PALE WIFE THE AGED SNOW THEY WATCH OVER THE FIRES   378 FOUR ZOAS 9   815
    AN AGED SHADOW SOON HE FADES   . . . .   425 MENTAL TRAVLER   29
    THEY SOON DRIVE OUT THE AGED HOST . . . .   426 MENTAL TRAVLER   51
    APPROACH THE FIGURE OF AN AGED APOSTLE WHICH REPRESENTS   444B LAST JUDGMNT/L PROSE
        BAPTISM
    BY ANGELS FROM THE HANDS OF ANOTHER [AGED] APOSTLE   . . . 444B LAST JUDGMNT/L PROSE
    FOR ALL ARE BORN POOR AGED SIXTY THREE . . . . . .   452 ANNO REYNOLDS   4
    AN AGED WOMAN RAVING ALONG THE STREETS THE SPACE IS NAMED   490 MILTON 10   4
    BUT THEY DEPICT HIM BALD & AGED WHO IS IN ETERNAL YOUTH   509 MILTON 24   69
    AN AGED PATRIARCH IS AWAKED BY HIS AGED WIFE HE IS ALBION   609C V LAST JUDG/N   PROSE
    THEIR HEAD THE AGED WOMAN IS BRITTANNICA THE WIFE OF ALBION 609C V LAST JUDG/N   PROSE
    THE AGED FIGURE WITH WINGS HAVING A WRITING TABLET   . .   610A V LAST JUDG/N   PROSE
    THESE ARE CAUGHT UP BY THREE AGED MEN WHO APPEAR . . .   610D V LAST JUDG/N   PROSE
    THESE THREE AGED MEN REPRESENT DIVINE PROVIDENCE . . .   611A V LAST JUDG/N   PROSE
    REPRESENTED BY THREE AGED MEN ON THE SIDE OF THE PICTURE   611A V LAST JUDG/N   PROSE
    THE GREEKS REPRESENT CHRONOS OR TIME AS A VERY AGED MAN   614D V LAST JUDG/N   PROSE
        THIS IS FABLE
    & MY VISIONS ALSO INFECTED & I SEE TIME AGED ALAS TOO MUCH   614D V LAST JUDG/N   PROSE
        SO
    HER LITTLE-ONES SHE MUST SLAY UPON OUR ALTARS AND HER AGED   640 JERUSALEM 18   33
    FORMING A SEXUAL MACHINE AN AGED VIRGIN FORM . . . .   674 JERUSALEM 44   25
    CONCENTER IN ONE FEMALE FORM AN AGED PENSIVE WOMAN . .   678 JERUSALEM 48   28
    HIS AGED PARENTS SOUGHT ME OUT IN EVERY CITY & VILLAGE .   720 JERUSALEM 79   27
    AGED IGNORANCE PERCEPTIVE ORGANS CLOSED THEIR OBJECTS   767D FOR SEXES/GP   TITLE
        CLOSE
    IN AGED IGNORANCE PROFOUND . . . .   771 OF GATES/GP   34
    AGED IGNORANCE . . . .   SUPP LEGEND/N52   *TITLE
AGENCY
    HIS OPINIONS WHO DOES NOT SEE SPIRITUAL AGENCY   . . . . 579B DESC CAT 5   PROSE
    THESE I SUPPOSE TO HAVE THE CHIEF AGENCY IN   . . . . . 612A V LAST JUDG/N   PROSE
AGENT
    TEACH MAN TO THINK HES A FREE AGENT . . . .   25 EDW THIRD/PS 3   195
    CONSIDERED AS AN ARBITRARY COMMAND OF THE AGENT . . . . 391C ANNO WATSON   MARG
    WHO CONSIDERS IT AS AN ARBITRARY ACT OF THE AGENT . . . 391D ANNO WATSON   MARG
    IS NO LESS AN AGENT OF RELIGION THAN HE WHO IS IN IT . . 613A V LAST JUDG/N   PROSE
    NOT AN ERROR BUT IT HAS A MAN FOR ITS [ACTOR] AGENT . . 615A V LAST JUDG/N   PROSE
AGE'S
    THE PARDONER THE AGE'S KNAVE WHO ALWAYS COMMANDS . . . 570A DESC CAT 3   PROSE
AGES   SEE AFTER-AGES
    OBTUSE ANGLE ANSWERD THE HEATHENS IN THE OLD AGES . . . 47B ISLAND MOON 3   *PROSE
    TO CREATE A LITTLE FLOWER IS THE LABOUR OF AGES . . . . 152C MARRIAGE HH 9   PROSE
    AGES OF IMAGINATION THIS FIRM PERSWASION REMOVED MOUNTAINS 153C MARRIAGE HH 12   PROSE
    AGES ON AGES ROLLD OVER HIM . . . . 227 URIZEN 10   1
    IN STONY SLEEP AGES ROLLD OVER HIM . . . . 227 URIZEN 10   2
    ON AGES ROLLD AGES IN GHASTLY   . . . . 227 URIZEN 10   5
    AGES ON AGES ROLLD OVER THEM . . . .   230 URIZEN 13   41
    IN THE INFINITE AGES OF ETERNITY . . . . 252 AHANIA 4   12
    YEARS ON YEARS AND AGES ON AGES   . . . . 258 BOOK OF LOS 4   31
    MANY AGES OF GROANS TILL THERE GREW . . . . 258 BOOK OF LOS 4   43
    NINE AGES COMPLETED THEIR CIRCLES . . . . 260 BOOK OF LOS 5   41
    UPON THE ROCK OF AGES WATCHING OVER HIM WITH LOVE & CARE . 277 FOUR ZOAS 1   468
    CUT BY THE PLOW OF AGES HELD IN URIZEN'S STRONG HAND   . . 283 FOUR ZOAS 2   119
    LABOUR OF AGES IN THE DARKNESS & THE WAR OF THARMAS . .   301 FOUR ZOAS 4   167
    A LABOURER OF AGES A DIRE DISCONTENT A LIVING WOE   . . . 317 FOUR ZOAS 6   226
    THE PLOW OF AGES & THE GOLDEN HARROW WADE THRO FIELDS   .   320 FOUR ZOAS 7   14
    TILL ONCE AGAIN THE MORN OF AGES SHALL RENEW UPON US   . . 326 FOUR ZOAS 7   269
    THE ENORMOUS SCIENCES OF URIZEN AGES AFTER AGES EXPLORING   344 FOUR ZOAS 8   144
    BUT I THE LABOURER OF AGES WHOSE UNWEARIED HANDS . . .   361 FOUR ZOAS 9   174
    AND THE FALLN MAN WHO WAS ARISEN UPON THE ROCK OF AGES .   364 FOUR ZOAS 9   285
    FROM RUST OF AGES ALL ITS ORNAMENTS OF GOLD & SILVER &   364 FOUR ZOAS 9   292
        IVORY
    THRO DISMAL DARKNESS DRAVE THE PLOW OF AGES OVER CITIES . 365 FOUR ZOAS 9   312
    IN DARK OBLIVION WITH INCESSANT PANGS AGES ON AGES   . .   366 FOUR ZOAS 9   369
    AS HE AROSE FROM THE BRIGHT FEAST DRUNK WITH THE WINE OF   376 FOUR ZOAS 9   710
        AGES
    AND TOOK AWAY THE WINE OF AGES WITH SOLEMN SONGS & JOY . . 378 FOUR ZOAS 9   794
    URTHONA MADE THE BREAD OF AGES & HE PLACED IT . . . . . 379 FOUR ZOAS 9   822
    FUTURE AGES THEY WILL AND SHALL FOOLISH MEN . . . . . 452C ANNO REYNOLDS   MARG
    & NOT TALK OF DARK AGES OR OF ANY AGE AGES ARE ALL EQUAL   461A ANNO REYNOLDS   MARG
    THEY BUILDED GREAT GOLGONOOZA TIMES ON TIMES AGES ON AGES   483 MILTON 3   39
    FIRST MILTON SAW ALBION UPON THE ROCK OF AGES . . . .   497 MILTON 15   36
    AND DAYS & MONTHS & YEARS & AGES & PERIODS WONDROUS   516 MILTON 28   45
        BUILDINGS
    AND EVERY SEVEN AGES IS INCIRCLED WITH A FLAMING FIRE   .   516 MILTON 28   57
    NOW SEVEN AGES IS AMOUNTING TO TWO HUNDRED YEARS . . .   516 MILTON 28   58
    AND THE ETERNAL MAN EVEN ALBION UPON THE ROCK OF AGES   .   524 MILTON 34   46
    TO DESTROY THE WISDOM OF AGES TO GRATIFY RAVENOUS ENVY .   533 MILTON 41   17
    WHICH COMPOSE ALL AGES AND NATIONS . . . . 567B DESC CAT 3   PROSE
    A DESCRIPTION OF THE ETERNAL PRINCIPLES THAT EXIST IN ALL   571A DESC CAT 3   PROSE
        AGES
    CHARACTERS OF HUMAN LIFE APPEAR TO POETS IN ALL AGES   .   571B DESC CAT 3   PROSE
    ARE NOT THESE LEADERS OF THE AGES OF MEN . . . . . . 572B DESC CAT 3   PROSE
    THE LADY PRIORESS IN SOME AGES PREDOMINATES AND IN SOME   572B DESC CAT 3   PROSE
    AND BUNGLING GREAT INVENTORS IN ALL AGES KNEW THIS . .   585B DESC CAT 15   PROSE
    THAT COMPOSE ALL AGES & NATIONS . . . . 589A CHAUCER/N   PROSE
    THEIR PRODUCING FOR AGES BACK WHILE PAINTING IS EXCLUDED   601A PUB ADDRESS/N   PROSE
    IN WHAT WE CALL THE DARK AGES . . . . 604A INSC ARIMATHEA PROSE
    WORLD WAS NOT WORTHY SUCH WERE THE CHRISTIANS IN ALL AGES   604A INSC ARIMATHEA PROSE
    OF TRUE ART CALLD GOTHIC IN ALL AGES BY THOSE . . . .   610D V LAST JUDG/N   PROSE
    GUIDE THOU MY HAND WHICH TREMBLES EXCEEDINGLY UPON THE   623 JERUSALEM 5   23
        ROCK OF AGES

```
                                                          PAGE      TITLE          LINE
AGES    (CONTINUED)
      UPON THE ROCK OF AGES THEN SURROUNDED WITH A CLOUD   . . .   677 JERUSALEM 48      4
      TILL HE CAME TO THE ROCK OF AGES & HE TOOK HIS SEAT UPON     689 JERUSALEM 57      16
          THE ROCK
      OF AGES & GENERATIONS FOLDING & UNFOLDING IT LIKE A VEIL     698 JERUSALEM 64       3
          OF CHERUBIM
      THE LABOURER OF AGES IN THE VALLEYS OF DESPAIR    . . . .    728 JERUSALEM 83      53
      A MAN & THEY CONVERSED AS MAN WITH MAN IN AGES               743 JERUSALEM 96       6
          OF ETERNITY
      AGES AFTER AGES IN THY DESCENDENTS   . . . . . . . . .     789A ANNO THORNTON    * MARG
      BOOKS & PICTURES OF OLD WHICH I WROTE & PAINTED IN AGES     802B LETTER 14         PROSE
AGGRAVATING
      TO MR JOHNSON'S AGGRAVATING LETTERS HAVE BEEN REPRESENTED    847A LETTER 44        PROSE
AGGREGATE
      THESE THEY NAMD SATANS & IN THE AGGREGATE THEY NAMD THEM     340 FOUR ZOAS 7B      301
          SATAN
      SEEN IN THE AGGREGATE A VAST HERMAPHRODITIC FORM   . . . .   347 FOUR ZOAS 8       248
      WITH BITTER WAILING THESE IN THE AGGREGATE ARE NAMED SATAN   519 MILTON 31          18
      WHO IN THE AGGREGATE ARE CALLD JERUSALEM FABLE IS ALLEGORY  604D V LAST JUDG/N     PROSE
      ACCORDING TO [THEIR AGGREGATE IMAGINATIONS] A CERTAIN ORDER 606A V LAST JUDG/N    *PROSE
      SUCH FORM THE AGGREGATE OF THE TWELVE SONS OF ALBION TOOK    708 JERUSALEM 70       10
          & SUCH
      MAY TAKE THE AGGREGATE & YOU CALL THE AGGREGATE MORAL LAW    738 JERUSALEM 91       28
AGGRIEVD
      MUST BE AGGRIEVD IF BUT ONE MEMBER SUFFER   . . . . . .      21 EDW THIRD/PS 2      85
AGHAST
      WITH TREMBLING HORROR PALE AGHAST THE CHILDREN OF MAN   . .  283 FOUR ZOAS 2       121
      TO ETERNITY EVERY ONE IN ETERNITY WILL LEAVE YOU AGHAST     813B LETTER 22        PROSE
AGITATION
      AND EDDYING FIERCE REJOICE IN THE FIERCE AGITATION OF        378 FOUR ZOAS 9       811
          THE WHEELS
AGITATIONS
      BUT IF THE EMANATIONS MINGLE NOT WITH STORMS & AGITATIONS    733 JERUSALEM 88       8
AGO
      I AM THAT SHADOWY PROPHET WHO SIX THOUSAND YEARS AGO   . .   350 FOUR ZOAS 8       351
      I AM THAT SHADOWY PROPHET WHO SIX THOUSAND YEARS AGO   . .   505 MILTON 22          15
      THIS PICTURE WAS DONE MANY YEARS AGO AND WAS ONE OF . .     581B DESC CAT 6        PROSE
      THIS DRAWING WAS DONE ABOVE THIRTY YEARS AGO AND PROVES     585D DESC CAT 16       PROSE
      WHICH I ENGRAVED AFTER HIM FIVE & TWENTY YEARS AGO   . .    592B PUB ADDRESS/N     PROSE
      OR NEAR SO GOOD TILL A FEW YEARS AGO . . . . . . . .       602C PUB ADDRESS/N     PROSE
      I OUGHT LONG AGO TO HAVE WRITTEN TO YOU TO THANK YOU FOR    794D LETTER 6          PROSE
          YOUR
      THIRTEEN YEARS AGO I LOST A BROTHER & WITH HIS SPIRIT I     797A LETTER 9          PROSE
      WHICH I OUGHT LONG AGO TO HAVE SENT YOU . . . . . .         816C LETTER 23         PROSE
      & RESPECT THEY WERE COMPOSED ABOVE A TWELVE-MONTH AGO   .   816D LETTER 24         PROSE
      YEARS AGO & THIS IS ONE OF THE NUMEROUS BENEFITS I HAVE     820A LETTER 25         PROSE
      AGO MR EDWARDS WILL PROCURE HER ADDRESS FOR YOU   . . .     836C LETTER 35         PROSE
      AGO BY HIS DESIRE I WRITE TO HIM BY THIS POST TO INQUIRE    841A LETTER 40         PROSE
      REMEMBERD TO YOU HAD BEGUN A LETTER TO YOU A WEEK AGO   .   842D LETTER 42        *PROSE
      FROM RHEUMATISM AS SHE WAS FIVE YEARS AGO AND WE HAVE   .   851C LETTER 50         PROSE
      [WHO DARES ?WORSHIP ?ONE WHOD HAVE DRIVEN YOU LONG AGO      SUPP ANNO REYNOLDS   * MARG
          INSANE]
A-GONE
      STAND IN HIS STEAD AS LONG A-GONE . . . . . . . .           17 BLIND-MANS/PS       65
AGONIES
      ("WILL BORN UNDER AGONIES OF SELF-DENIAL") REGENERATION     66C ANNO LAVATER       MARG
      FELL SHAKING AGONIES & IN EACH WRINKLE OF THAT FACE . . .   108 TIRIEL 6           38
      THEY LIE IN TWISTING AGONIES BENEATH THE COVRING HEAVENS     381 FOUR ZOAS AD 2 *   5
      AND IN GRINDING AGONIES IN THREATS STIFLINGS & DIREFUL       639 JERUSALEM 17      58
          STRUGGLINGS
AGONIZING
      AND THE TWELVE FEMALE EMANATIONS FLED WITH THEM AGONIZING    663 JERUSALEM 36      20
      HIS EMANATION SEPARATES IN MILKY FIBRES AGONIZING   . . .   731 JERUSALEM 86      39
      BUT DARK OPAKE TENDER TO TOUCH & PAINFUL & AGONIZING   . .   736 JERUSALEM 90       8
AGONY
      SWALLOWING UP THE HORRIBLE DIN IN AGONY ON AGONY   . . .    295 FOUR ZOAS 3       148
      CREATED TO BE THE GREAT EXAMPLE OF HORROR & AGONY ALSO MY    630 JERUSALEM 10      52
      HE WEPT IN DEADLY WRATH OF THE SPECTRE                       699 JERUSALEM 64      27
          IN SELF-CONTRADICTING AGONY
      IN THE MOMENT OF HIS AGONY BUT WOULD RATHER RETIRE AND DIE  864B LETTER 61         PROSE
AGREE
      FOR FLESH & HE COULD NEER AGREE   . . . . . . . .           50 WHEN CORRUP/IM      11
      I DO NOT UNDERSTAND THIS OR ELSE I DO NOT AGREE TO IT  . .  78D ANNO LAVATER       MARG
      ("BUT ONE SCALE") THIS IS MOST TRUE BUT HOW DOES THIS AGREE 83D ANNO LAVATER       MARG
          WITH...
      THAT THERE IS BUT ONE OMNIPOTENT UNCREATE & GOD I AGREE     91A ANNO SWED LOVE     MARG
      THEY AGREE TO MEET   . . . . . . . . . . . .               219 LIT GRL LST/SE     21
      LET US AGREE TO GIVE UP LOVE   . . . . . . . .             417 MY SPECTRE/N        67
      HE MAKES THE LAME TO WALK WE ALL AGREE   . . . . . . .     463 ANNO REYNOLDS        1
      YOU MUST AGREE THAT RUBENS WAS A FOOL   . . . . . .        546 ENGLISH CONN/N       1
      AND YET THEY ARE BLOCKHEADS YOU ALL AGREE   . . . . .      550 SAY PICTURES/N       2
      CORPOREAL DISEASE TO WHICH I READILY AGREE . . . . .       772B ANNO SPURZHEIM     MARG
      NOT AGREE GOD KEEP ME FROM THE DIVINITY OF YES & NO TOO     878B LETTER 88         PROSE
AGREEABLE
      [& HE DOES NOT] & HIS WIFE IS THE MOST AGREEABLE WOMAN  . .  53A ISLAND MOON 8     PROSE
      IF YOU APPROVE OF MY MANNER & IT IS AGREEABLE TO YOU   . .  792C LETTER 4          PROSE
      AS IS MOST AGREEABLE TO YOU IF YOU & MRS BUTTS SHOULD THINK 808C LETTER 19         PROSE
      THO NOT SO AGREEABLE BECAUSE WE WISH NATURALLY FOR   . . .  821A LETTER 25         PROSE
      THAT MR H(HAYLEY) IS QUITE AGREEABLE TO OUR RETURN   . . .  824C LETTER 27         PROSE
      THE FIRST IN INTERNAL VALUE I THEN SAID IS IT AGREEABLE     856D LETTER 54         PROSE
          TO YOU
      HE IS AGREEABLE TO EVERY PROPOSAL YOU HAVE MADE AND WILL    857D LETTER 55         PROSE
```

		PAGE	TITLE	LINE

AGREED
| & AGREED TO NOMINATE OTHERS BUT IF P (PHILLIPS) MEANT | . | 842C LETTER 42 | *PROSE |
| I HAVE I BELIEVE DONE NEARLY ALL THAT WE AGREED ON &C | . | 870B LETTER 71 | PROSE |

AGREEMENT
CERTAINLY A HAPPY STATE OF AGREEMENT TO WHICH I FOR ONE DO		878B LETTER 88	PROSE
MEMORANDUM OF AGREEMENT BETWEEN WILLIAM BLAKE AND JOHN LINNELL		SUPP LETTER 67D	*PROSE
CASH ON ACCT OF PLATES IN THE FOREGOING AGREEMENT	. . .	SUPP LETTER 67D	*PROSE

AGREEMENTS
| TO CONSIST IN THE AGREEMENTS & (DISAGREEMENTS) OF IDEAS | | 708 JERUSALEM 70 | 8 |

AGREES
| THAT IS TILL HE AGREES TO THE PRIESTS INTEREST | . . . | 131C ANNO SWED PROV | MARG |
| MR FLAXMAN AGREES WITH ME THAT SOMEWHAT MORE THAN OUTLINE | | 844B LETTER 43 | PROSE |

AGRICULTURE
MY LORD BISHOP YOU WOULD RECOMMEND US AGRICULTURE	. . .	19 EDW THIRD/PS 2	17
FOR COMMERCE THO THE CHILD OF AGRICULTURE	. . . . .	19 EDW THIRD/PS 2	31
NOTHING OF ARTS OR ARTISTS OR LEARNED MEN OR OF AGRICULTURE		404D ANNO BACON	* MARG

AGROUND
| WHILE REASON RUNS AGROUND AS WE HAVE RUN OUR ARGUMENT | . | 29A EDW THIRD/PS 4 | PROSE |

AGUE
AGUE & RHEUMATISM HAVE BEEN ALMOST HER CONSTANT ENEMIES		811B LETTER 22	PROSE
DEAR BROTHER YOUR LETTER MENTIONING MR BUTTS'S ACCOUNT OF MY AGUE		819B LETTER 25	*PROSE
SURPRIZED ME BECAUSE I HAVE NO AGUE BUT HAVE HAD A COLD		819B LETTER 25	PROSE
GRATEFUL THO NOT ABLE ON ACCOUNT OF THIS ABOMINABLE AGUE		868D LETTER 68	PROSE

AGUES
| NOR MY FRIENDS UNEASY IF I CAN HELP IT MY WIFE HAS HAD AGUES | | 819C LETTER 25 | PROSE |

AH
AH WOMAN'S FEAR SHE CRYD AH CURSED DUKE	. . . . . .	5 FAIR ELENOR/PS	39
AH MY DEAR LORD AH WRETCHED ELENOR	. . . .	5 FAIR ELENOR/PS	40
OF LUSTY MAY AH LIFE AS FRAIL AS FLOWER	. . . . . .	5 FAIR ELENOR/PS	42
AH SAID TILLY LALLY I DID NOT HEAR IT WHAT WAS IT OBTUSE ANGLE		47A ISLAND MOON 3	PROSE
AH THAT WAS THE GENTLEMAN SAID ARADOBO		47B ISLAND MOON 3	PROSE
AH SAID ARADOBO I THOUGHT I HAD READ OF PHEBUS IN THE BIBLE		47B ISLAND MOON 3	PROSE
HANG PHAROH AH SAID MRS SINAGAIN	. . . .	48A ISLAND MOON 4	*PROSE
AH MR HUFFCAP WOULD KICK THE BOTTOM OF THE PULPIT OUT	. .	48B ISLAND MOON 4	PROSE
AH SAID THE PYTHAGOREAN ARADOBO WILL MAKE A VERY CLEVER FELLOW .		49D ISLAND MOON 6	PROSE
AH HANG YOUR REASONING SAID THE EPICUREAN	. . . . .	50A ISLAND MOON 6	PROSE
I HATE REASONING I DO EVERYTHING BY MY FEELINGS AH SAID SIPSOP I ONLY		50A ISLAND MOON 6	PROSE
AH SAID SIPSOP YOU THINK WE ARE RASCALS	. . . . .	51C ISLAND MOON 6	PROSE
("SPEAKS SOFTLY AND WRITES SHARPLY") AH ROGUE I COULD BE THY HANGMAN		83B ANNO LAVATER	MARG
OR WHEREFORE DOST THOU CRY AH WRETCH TO CURSE THY AGED FATHER		108 TIRIEL 6	47
AH THEN AT TIMES I DROOPING SIT	. . . .	124 SCHOOL BOY/SI	11
AH THEL IS LIKE A WATRY BOW AND LIKE A PARTING CLOUD	. .	127 BOOK OF THEL 1	8
AH GENTLE MAY I LAY ME DOWN AND GENTLE REST MY HEAD	. .	127 BOOK OF THEL 1	12
THEN WE SHALL SEEK THEE BUT NOT FIND AH THEL IS LIKE TO THEE		128 BOOK OF THEL 3	3
AH WEEP NOT LITTLE VOICE THOU CANST NOT SPEAK BUT THOU CANST WEEP		129 BOOK OF THEL 4	4
AH SHE DOTH DEPART	. . . .	161 NEVER PAIN/N	8
[AH THAT SWEET LOVE SHOULD BE THOUGHT A CRIME]	. . . .	176 SOFT SNOW/N	4
AH ARE THERE OTHER WARS BESIDE THE WARS OF SWORD AND FIRE		192 V DAU ALBION 4	19
AH VISION FROM AFAR AH REBEL FORM THAT RENT THE ANCIENT		199 AMERICA 9	14
AH TERRIBLE BIRTH A YOUNG ONE BURSTING WHERE IS THE WEEPING MOUTH		199 AMERICA 9	22
AH SUN-FLOWER	. . . .	215B AH SUNFLOWR/SE	TITLE
AH SUN-FLOWER WEARY OF TIME	. . . .	215 AH SUNFLOWR/SE	1
AH MOTHER ENITHARMON	. . . .	238 EUROPE PREL 2	7
AH I AM DROWND IN SHADY WOE AND VISIONARY JOY	. . . . .	238 EUROPE PREL 2	12
AND THE VOICE CRIED AH URIZEN LOVE	. . . .	254 AHANIA 4	52
I WISH & FEEL & WEEP & GROAN AH TERRIBLE TERRIBLE	. . .	265 FOUR ZOAS 1	63
HIS SECRET LOVES & GRACES AH ME WRETCHED WHAT HAVE I DONE		268 FOUR ZOAS 1	164
IN THIS THY WORLD [FOR AH HOW] NOT MINE	. . . . . .	268 FOUR ZOAS 1	172
AH HAPPY BLINDNESS [SHE] ENION SEES NOT THE TERRORS OF THE UNCERTAIN		290 FOUR ZOAS 2	* 385
WHERE ART THOU ENION THOU ART NEAR TO CUNNING TOO FAR OFF		296 FOUR ZOAS 3	169
AH ENION AH ENION AH LOVELY LOVELY ENION	. . . . .	297 FOUR ZOAS 4	8
FLOW DOWN INTO THE SEA & SLUMBER IN OBLIVION AH ENION	.	298 FOUR ZOAS 4	23
AH HOW SHALL URIZEN THE KING SUBMIT TO THIS DARK MANSION		310 FOUR ZOAS 5	190
AH HOW IS THIS ONCE ON THE HEIGHTS I STRETCHD MY THRONE SUBLIME		310 FOUR ZOAS 5	191
THOU & THAT DEMON LOS [WERE] WERT BORN AH JEALOUSY & WOE		327 FOUR ZOAS 7	* 295
AH POOR DIVIDED DARK URTHONA NOW A SPECTRE WANDERING	.	327 FOUR ZOAS 7	* 296
AH WEAK & WIDE ASTRAY AH SHUT IN NARROW DOLEFUL FORM	. .	484 MILTON 5	19
SATAN AH ME IS GONE TO HIS OWN PLACE SAID LOS THEIR GOD		491 MILTON 10	12
TO SIEZE HER NEW BORN SON AH ME THE WRETCHED LEUTHA	. .	492 MILTON 12	3
TILL TWO ETERNITIES MEET TOGETHER AH LOST LOST LOST FOR EVER		494 MILTON 13	11
AND HELL & THE GRAVE STATES THAT ARE NOT BUT AH SEEM TO BE		522 MILTON 32	29
BUT AH MORE WONDROUS STILL THE CHARMING FAIR	. . . .	545 IMIT POPE/N	4
BE LOST & LEST HE SHOULD DEVOUR ENITHARMON AH ME	. . .	638 JERUSALEM 17	18
ART THOU BROKEN AH ME SABRINA RUNNING BY MY SIDE	. . .	644 JERUSALEM 21	22
THIS OUTRAGE AH ME HOW SICK & PALE YOU ALL STAND ROUND ME		673 JERUSALEM 43	72
AH ME PITIABLE ONES DO YOU ALSO GO TO DEATH'S VALE	. . .	673 JERUSALEM 43	73
AH WEAK & WIDE ASTRAY AH SHUT IN NARROW DOLEFUL FORM	. .	679 JERUSALEM 49	32
AND ROCK THE CRADLE WHILE AH ME OF THAT ETERNAL MAN	. .	688 JERUSALEM 56	33

		PAGE	TITLE	LINE
A	(CONTINUED)			
	AH THAT IT COULD BE AS THE DAUGHTERS OF BEULAH WISH . . .	692	JERUSALEM 59	44
	AH MY MARY SAID JOSEPH WEEPING OVER & EMBRACING HER CLOSELY IN	694	JERUSALEM 61	14
	AH ALAS AT THE SIGHT OF THE VICTIM	702	JERUSALEM 66	35
	IN MARTYRDOMS & SLAVERY I BEHOLD AH VISION OF SORROW . .	735	JERUSALEM 89	40
	AH THEN I HEARD MY LITTLE ONES WEEPING ALONG THE VALLEY	740	JERUSALEM 93	11
	AH THEN I SAW MY BELOVED ONES FLEEING FROM MY TENT . .	740	JERUSALEM 93	12
	IN DREAMS OF (CHASTITY) & MORAL LAW I HAVE MURDERED ALBION AH	742	JERUSALEM 94	23
	HIS STONY MEMBERS HE SAW ENGLAND AH SHALL THE DEAD LIVE AGAIN	742	JERUSALEM 95	4
	SHOULD BRUISE THE SERPENT'S HEAD IS THIS THE SERPENT AH	779	GHOST ABEL 1	4
	SEVEN TIMES O EVE THOU HAST FAINTED OVER THE DEAD AH AH	779	GHOST ABEL 1	5
	WITHOUT A WORD AND SHE IMMEDIATELY SAID AH ROMNEY . .	843C	LETTER 43	PROSE
	"AH LUCKLESS BABE BORN UNDER CRUEL STAR" (SPENSER) . . .	SUPP	LEGEND/N19	*
AHA				
	AHA AHA HOW CAME I HERE SO SOON IN MY SWEET NATIVE LAND	375	FOUR ZOAS 9	687
A HA				
	A HA TO DOCTOR JOHNSON	54	LO THE BAT/IM *	10
AHANIA				
	THE BOOK OF AHANIA LAMBETH PRINTED BY W BLAKE... . .	249A	AHANIA	TITLE
	AHANIA SO NAME HIS PARTED SOUL	249	AHANIA 2	32
	THE LAMENTING VOICE OF AHANIA	253	AHANIA 4	45
	BETWEEN AHANIA AND THEE	254	AHANIA 4	55
	WHY DIDST THOU DESPISE AHANIA	254	AHANIA 4	62
	O ETERNAL BIRTHS SUNG ROUND AHANIA	255	AHANIA 5	22
	TO AHANIA RETURND IN EVENING	255	AHANIA 5	36
	AND OF AHANIA HIS PURE BRIDE BUT SHE WAS DISTANT FAR	276	FOUR ZOAS 1	438
	HE DRAVE THE MALE SPIRITS ALL AWAY FROM AHANIA . . .	285	FOUR ZOAS 2	209
	TO PLANT DIVISIONS IN THE SOUL OF URIZEN & AHANIA	286	FOUR ZOAS 2	239
	TO PLANT DIVISIONS IN THE SOUL OF URIZEN & AHANIA	287	FOUR ZOAS 2	289
	THEN JEALOUSY SHALL SHADOW ALL HIS MOUNTAINS & AHANIA	289	FOUR ZOAS 2	338
	AHANIA HEARD THE LAMENTATION & A SWIFT VIBRATION . . .	291	FOUR ZOAS 2	419
	AND BRIGHT AHANIA BOWD HERSELF BEFORE HIS SPLENDID FEET	291	FOUR ZOAS 3	2
	O BRIGHT [AHANIA] [SHADOW] A BOY IS BORN OF THE DARK OCEAN	292	FOUR ZOAS 3	* 14
	AHANIA BOWD HER HEAD & WEPT SEVEN DAYS BEFORE THE KING . .	292	FOUR ZOAS 3	24
	THEN O MY DEAR LORD LISTEN TO AHANIA LISTEN TO THE VISION	292	FOUR ZOAS 3	41
	THE VISION OF AHANIA IN THE SLUMBERS OF URIZEN . . .	292	FOUR ZOAS 3	42
	O URIZEN WHY ART THOU PALE AT THE VISIONS OF AHANIA . .	294	FOUR ZOAS 3	91
	TO CAST AHANIA TO THE EARTH HE SIEZD HER BY THE HAIR . .	294	FOUR ZOAS 3	111
	AND THREW AHANIA FROM HIS BOSOM OBDURATE SHE FELL LIKE LIGHTNING	295	FOUR ZOAS 3	132
	A WORLD OF DARKNESS AHANIA FELL FAR INTO NON ENTITY . .	295	FOUR ZOAS 3	144
	WHERE ENION BLIND & AGE BENT WANDERD AHANIA WANDERS NOW	297	FOUR ZOAS 3	207
	WHERE BRIGHT AHANIA WEPT SHE ALSO SAW THE INFERNAL ROOTS	309	FOUR ZOAS 5	181
	SHALL SEE HIM ENITHARMON & AHANIA COMBIND WITH ENION . .	339	FOUR ZOAS 7B	248
	OF AHANIA WAILING ON THE WINDS IN VAIN HE FLIES FOR STILL	353	FOUR ZOAS 8	488
	AND THUS AHANIA CRIES ALOUD TO THE CAVERNS OF THE GRAVE	353	FOUR ZOAS 8	492
	BUT LISTEN TO AHANIA O YE SONS OF THE MURDERED ONE . .	354	FOUR ZOAS 8	503
	THESE ARE THE VISIONS OF MY EYES THE VISIONS OF AHANIA	354	FOUR ZOAS 8	532
	THUS CRIES AHANIA ENION REPLIES FROM THE CAVERNS OF THE GRAVE	354	FOUR ZOAS 8	533
	SUCH ARE THE WORDS OF AHANIA & ENION LOS HEARS & WEEPS . .	356	FOUR ZOAS 8	584
	BUT WHEN SHE SAW THE FORM OF AHANIA WEEPING ON THE VOID	356	FOUR ZOAS 8	604
	WITH HARPS & SONGS WHERE BRIGHT AHANIA SANG BEFORE THY FACE	360	FOUR ZOAS 9	* 126
	WHEN VOCAL MAY COMES DANCING FROM THE EAST AHANIA CAME . .	362	FOUR ZOAS 9	194
	ON TO THE SURFACE OF A LAKE AHANIA ROSE IN JOY	362	FOUR ZOAS 9	196
	SHALL REFLOURISH THEN BRIGHT AHANIA SHALL AWAKE FROM DEATH	362	FOUR ZOAS 9	210
	EXPECTING TO RECIEVE AHANIA IN THE SPRING WITH JOY . . .	362	FOUR ZOAS 9	215
	AND LO LIKE THE HARVEST MOON AHANIA CAST OFF HER DEATH CLOTHES	366	FOUR ZOAS 9	344
	AND BRIGHT AHANIA TOOK HER SEAT BY URIZEN IN SONGS & JOY	366	FOUR ZOAS 9	353
	THEN ENION & AHANIA & VALA & THE WIFE OF DARK URTHONA	377	FOUR ZOAS 9	778
	BECAUSE AHANIA RENT APART INTO A DESOLATE NIGHT	501	MILTON 19	41
	AHANIA AND ENION AND VALA AND ENITHARMON LOVELY	634	JERUSALEM 14	10
	AHANIA & ENION & VALA ARE THREE EVANESCENT SHADES . . .	635	JERUSALEM 14	12
	[?THEN AHANIA XXX ENDED WITH XXX THY LOVE FOR VALA] . . .	SUPP	FOUR ZOAS 3	*
AHANIA'S				
	TO EMBRACE AHANIA'S JOY	254	AHANIA 5	11
	TO CONDUCT THE VOICE OF ENION TO AHANIA'S MIDNIGHT PILLOW	287	FOUR ZOAS 2	290
	NOW TAKING ON AHANIA'S FORM & NOW THE FORM OF ENION . .	288	FOUR ZOAS 2	324
	AHANIA'S IMAGE I DECIEVD THEE & WILL STILL DECIEVE . . .	288	FOUR ZOAS 2	328
	THAT HE MAY ALSO DRAW AHANIA'S SPIRIT INTO HER VORTEX . .	290	FOUR ZOAS 2	384
	TRIUMPHING EVEN TO THE STARS AT BRIGHT AHANIA'S FALL . .	295	FOUR ZOAS 3	138
	THE THREE DAUGHTERS OF URIZEN GUARD AHANIA'S DEATH COUCH	362	FOUR ZOAS 9	201
AHOLIAB				
	AND IF BEZALEEL & AHOLIAB DREW	543	IF TRUE/N	5
AID				
	WITHOUT THINE AID THE TWISTED MAIL AND SPEAR	17	EDW THIRD/PS 1	3
	THE MERCHANTS DO COMPLAIN AND BEG OUR AID	20	EDW THIRD/PS 2	69
	HIS GENEROUS AID TO PUT IT INTO PRACTICE	21	EDW THIRD/PS 2	90
	UPON THE VALLEYS OF MIDDLESEX SHOUTING LOUD FOR AID DIVINE	658	JERUSALEM 32	9
	HIS IMMORTAL CHEEKS REARING HIS HANDS TO HEAVEN FOR AID DIVINE	711	JERUSALEM 71	57
	SPIRITUAL AID HAS NOT A LITTLE CONDUCED TO MY RESTORATION TO	852B	LETTER 50	PROSE
AIM				
	TO MAKE OUT THE PARTS IS THE WISE MAN'S AIM	547	LET BE TOLD/N	8
AIM AT YOURS	(AMATEURS)			
	THE CUNNING SURES & THE AIM AT YOURS	548	CUNNING SURE/N	1

	PAGE	TITLE	LINE

AIR   SEE MID-AIR

Entry	PAGE	TITLE	LINE
THE SPIRITS OF THE AIR LIVE ON THE SMELLS	2	TO AUTUMN/PS	13
MY SMILES AND LANGUISHD AIR	6	MY SILKS/PS	2
THY SWEET BOUGHS PERFUME THE AIR	7	LOVE HARMNY/PS	11
AND THROW ALL PITY ON THE BURNING AIR	10	WHEN EARLY/PS	18
OR THE BLUE REGIONS OF THE AIR	10	TO MUSES/PS	7
PERHAPS THE AIR OF THE COUNTRY IS THE CAUSE	22	EDW THIRD/PS 3	61
AND BREATHE MY HOPES INTO THE BURNING AIR	26	EDW THIRD/PS 3	221
FIGHT IN THE TROUBLED AIR THAT RAGES WHO CAN STAND . .	33	EDW FOURTH/PS	5
GREEN GRASS SPRINGS IN JOY AND THE NIMBLE AIR KISSES THE LEAVES	37B	CONTEMPLATN/PS	PROSE
I HAVE GOT A BOTTLE OF AIR THAT WOULD SPREAD A PLAGUE .	46A	ISLAND MOON 1	PROSE
THY FATHER CALLS THY FATHER LIFTS HIS HAND UNTO THE [AIR] HEAVENS	108	TIRIEL 6	41
WHEN THE AIR DOES LAUGH WITH OUR MERRY WIT	124	LAUGHING/SI	3
ALL BUT THE YOUNGEST IN PALENESS SOUGHT THE SECRET AIR	127	BOOK OF THEL 1	2
LIKE THE DOVE'S VOICE LIKE TRANSIENT DAY LIKE MUSIC IN THE AIR	127	BOOK OF THEL 1	11
AND WHY IT SCATTERS ITS BRIGHT BEAUTY THRO THE HUMID AIR	128	BOOK OF THEL 2	15
HOVERING AND GLITTERING ON THE AIR BEFORE THE FACE OF THEL	128	BOOK OF THEL 3	6
AND I COMPLAIND IN THE MILD AIR BECAUSE I FADE AWAY . .	130	BOOK OF THEL 5	12
THE LAW AND GOSPEL FROM FIRE AND AIR AND ETERNAL REASON AND SCIENCE	138	FRENCH REVOLTN	95
IN WHITE ROBES STREWN IN AIR CENSERS AND HARPS	140	FRENCH REVOLTN	133
. . . THEIR NAKED SOULS SHIVER IN KEEN OPEN AIR	146	FRENCH REVOLTN	275
RINTRAH ROARS & SHAKES HIS FIRES IN THE BURDEND AIR . . .	148	MARRIAGE HH 2	1
RINTRAH ROARS & SHAKES HIS FIRES IN THE BURDEND AIR . . .	149	MARRIAGE HH 2	21
THE EYES OF FIRE THE NOSTRILS OF AIR	152B	MARRIAGE HH 9	PROSE
AS THE AIR TO A BIRD OR THE SEA TO A FISH	152D	MARRIAGE HH 10	PROSE
OF AIR HE CAUSED THE INSIDE OF THE CAVE TO BE INFINITE .	154D	MARRIAGE HH 15	PROSE
& THE AIR WAS FULL OF THEM & SEEMD COMPOSED OF THEM . .	156B	MARRIAGE HH 17	PROSE
THESE ARE DEVILS AND ARE CALLED POWERS OF THE AIR . . .	156B	MARRIAGE HH 17	PROSE
I CALL WITH HOLY VOICE KINGS OF THE SOUNDING AIR . . .	190	V DAU ALBION 2	14
THEIR AWFUL FOLDS IN THE DARK AIR SILENT SHE STOOD AS NIGHT	196	AMERICA PREL 1	8
LET HIM LOOK UP INTO THE HEAVENS & LAUGH IN THE BRIGHT AIR	198	AMERICA 6	7
IN THE RED AIR BEFORE THE DEMON [SEEN EVEN BY MORTAL MEN]	205	AMERICA CANC C	21
WATER EARTH AIR FIRE	209C	FOR CHILDRN/GP	TITLE
APPEARD TRANSPARENT AIR FOR THEIR EYES	236	URIZEN 25	35
FIVE WINDOWS LIGHT THE CAVERND MAN THRO ONE HE BREATHES THE AIR	237	EUROPE INTRO	1
FLOTING UPON THE BOSOMD AIR	244	EUROPE 14	* 18
SOME IN VALES SOME ALOFT FLEW IN AIR	250	AHANIA 3	12
A WHITE LAKE ON THE DARK BLUE AIR	252	AHANIA 4	14
SIDELONG ON THE PURPLE AIR WAFTING	258	BOOK OF LOS 4	47
THE BANDS OF HEAVEN FLEW THRO THE AIR SINGING & SHOUTING TO URIZEN	281	FOUR ZOAS 2	26
STOOD ON THE INFINITE EARTH & SAW THESE VISIONS IN THE AIR	283	FOUR ZOAS 2	122
AND MANY SAID WE SEE NO VISIONS IN THE DARKSOM AIR . . .	283	FOUR ZOAS 2	127
FOR NOW NO MORE REMAIND OF ENION IN THE DISMAL AIR . .	297	FOUR ZOAS 3	205
RENEW THESE RUIND SOULS OF MEN THRO EARTH SEA AIR & FIRE	298	FOUR ZOAS 4	30
OF ENION I ISSUED INTO THE AIR DIVIDED FROM ENITHARMON . .	300	FOUR ZOAS 4	106
WHIRLING UP BROKEN ROCKS ON HIGH INTO THE DISMAL AIR . .	301	FOUR ZOAS 4	163
MELT INTO THIN AIR WHILE THE SEED DRIVN BY THE FURIOUS WIND	305	FOUR ZOAS 5	10
SHADOWS OF ETERNAL DEATH SIT IN THE LEADEN AIR	305	FOUR ZOAS 5	22
LOUD & MORE LOUD THE LIVING MUSIC FLOATS UPON THE AIR . .	306	FOUR ZOAS 5	26
HE THREW HIS FLIGHT THRO THE DARK AIR TO WHERE A RIVER FLOWD	311	FOUR ZOAS 6	2
THE MIDST BETWEEN AN EQUILIBRIUM GREY OF AIR SERENE . .	316	FOUR ZOAS 6	194
OF WINDS & WATERS OR THENCE FALL INTO A VOID WHERE AIR .	317	FOUR ZOAS 6	219
ALL THRO THE CAVERNS OF FIRE & AIR & EARTH SEEKING . . .	318	FOUR ZOAS 6	272
IN THE DIM AIR THEY TOOK THE BOOK OF IRON & PLACD ABOVE	322	FOUR ZOAS 7	97
AND WHET THEIR BEAKS & SNUFF THE AIR & WATCH THE OPENING DAWN	325	FOUR ZOAS 7	206
FOR HE BEHELD NEW FEMALE FORMS BORN FORTH UPON THE AIR . .	332	FOUR ZOAS 7	487
BE NOT PERSUADED THAT THE AIR KNOWS THIS OR THE FALLING DEW	339	FOUR ZOAS 7B	231
TREMBLING BEFORE ME LIKE A SHADOW LIKE A MIST LIKE AIR	339	FOUR ZOAS 7B	238
HAST THOU FORGOT THAT THE AIR LISTENS THRO ALL ITS DISTRICTS TELLING	339	FOUR ZOAS 7B	242
AND NOW HE BEATS THE HEAVY AIR WITH HIS ENORMOUS WINGS . .	354	FOUR ZOAS 8	526
ON RIFTED ROCKS SUSPENDED IN THE AIR BY INWARD FIRES . .	363	FOUR ZOAS 9	241
STANDS IN THE FURIOUS AIR HE CRIES THE CHILDREN OF SIX THOUSAND YEARS	363	FOUR ZOAS 9	252
NAKED & PALE STANDING ON THE EXPECTING AIR TO BE DELIVERD	363	FOUR ZOAS 9	254
WEAK WAILING IN THE TROUBLED AIR EAST WEST & NORTH & SOUTH	365	FOUR ZOAS 9	318
. . . IN THE VOICE OF THE NOURISHING AIR	367	FOUR ZOAS 9	393
THAT SING & FLY IN THE BRIGHT AIR BUT YOU DO LICK MY FEET	368	FOUR ZOAS 9	431
I SAW HIM LUVAH LIKE A SPIRIT STAND IN THE BRIGHT AIR . .	369	FOUR ZOAS 9	465
LET HIM LOOK UP INTO THE HEAVENS & LAUGH IN THE BRIGHT AIR	375	FOUR ZOAS 9	671
IN WATERS STIFLING OR IN AIR CORRODING OR IN EARTH SHUT UP	377	FOUR ZOAS 9	741
THE WORLD OF SHADOWS THRO THE AIR TILL WINTER IS OVER & GONE	378	FOUR ZOAS 9	798
WHO HAS THE POWER OF THE AIR	388A	ANNO WATSON	MARG
AND IN THE OUTWARD AIR AGAIN	430	CRYSTL CABINET	27
THE BEGGAR'S RAGS FLUTTERING IN AIR	432	AUGURIES	75
IN VARIOUS ATTITUDES OF DESPAIR & HORROR FALL THRO THE AIR	443C	LAST JUDGMNT/L	PROSE
HUMILIATION & IN EXULTATION RISE THRO THE AIR WITH THEIR CHILDREN	443D	LAST JUDGMNT/L	PROSE
THEY ARISE UPON THE AIR REJOICING	444A	LAST JUDGMNT/L	PROSE
WHEN GRAPES & FIGS BURST THEIR COVERING TO THE JOYFUL AIR	485	MILTON 5	33
LIGHT SPRINGING ON THE AIR LEAD THE SWEET DANCE THEY WAKE	520	MILTON 31	53
AND FLOWER & HERB SOON FILL THE AIR WITH AN INNUMERABLE DANCE	521	MILTON 31	61

39

```
                                                              PAGE      TITLE        LINE
AIR    (CONTINUED)
       SWEET FEMALE FORMS WINGED OR FLOATING IN THE AIR       524 MILTON 34          11
          SPONTANEOUS
       VERY LITTLE TIME AND OF THE AIR IT GROWS YELLOW AND AT 561A EXHIBITION ADV  PROSE
          LENGTH BROWN
       OF VERY LITTLE TIME AND OF THE AIR IT DEADENS EVERY COLOUR  565A DESC CAT 2  PROSE
       THE FLUSH OF HEALTH IN FLESH EXPOSED TO THE OPEN AIR  .  580D DESC CAT 5     PROSE
       INTO THE AIR AMONG THESE ARE THREE FEMALES  . . . . . . 610A V LAST JUDG/N   PROSE
       MEET THE LORD IN THE AIR & THEN HE WOULD BE HAPPY   . . 611A V LAST JUDG/N   PROSE
       AIR WATER & EARTH SURROUND MILTON'S CHAIR  . . . . . .  619B ILLUS MILTON    PROSE
       NETS & WEBS UNFOLDED BY SPIRITS IN THE AIR & IN THE BROOK  619C ILLUS MILTON PROSE
       AROUND MILTON ARE SIX SPIRITS OR FAIRIES HOVERING ON THE  619C ILLUS MILTON PROSE
          AIR
       TO LABOUR IN THE FIRE IN THE WATER IN THE EARTH IN THE AIR  638 JERUSALEM 17     2
       THAT EVERY LITTLE PARTICLE OF LIGHT & AIR BECAME OPAKE    674 JERUSALEM 44      10
       AIR ON CLOUDY DOUBTS & REASONING CARES  . . . . . . . 763C FOR SEXES/GP     TITLE
       NAKED IN AIR IN SHAME & FEAR  . . . . . . . . . .       770 OF GATES/GP          9
       PRINCE OF THE AIR & OUR DIMENSIONS COMPASS ZENITH & NADIR  780 GHOST ABEL 1     11
       THE LADDER OF ANGELS DESCENDS THRO THE AIR  . . . .     800 MRS FLAXMAN/L       6
       MODEST HEAT IS CHEAPER THAN IN LONDON BUT THE SWEET AIR &  803B LETTER 15     PROSE
       INTO REGIONS OF AIR                                    804 TO BUTTS/L          9
       BEAUTIFUL AND THO THE WEATHER IS WET THE AIR IS VERY MILD  806A LETTER 16     PROSE
       MAY YET SHINE & THEN THEY WILL BE BROUGHT INTO OPEN AIR   812B LETTER 22      PROSE
       PERSWADED AS I AM NOW THAT THE AIR THO WARM IS UNHEALTHY  820C LETTER 25      PROSE
       HAMPSTEAD AIR AS IT ALWAYS DID SO I FEAR IT ALWAYS WILL DO  870D LETTER 72    PROSE
       THIS EXCEPT IT BE THE MORNING AIR & THAT IN MY COUSIN'S   870D LETTER 72      PROSE
          TIME
       AIR YET I LOSE NOTHING BY IT DANTE GOES ON THE BETTER  .  877D LETTER 88      PROSE
AIRPUMP
       WERE PUMPING AT THE AIRPUMP SMACK WENT THE GLASS  . . .  58D ISLAND MOON 10   PROSE
AIRS
       FLOW ON YE GENTLE AIRS & BEAR THE VOICE OF MY REJOICING  368 FOUR ZOAS 9      435
       THE SUN ARISES FROM HIS DEWY BED & THE FRESH AIRS   . . . 379 FOUR ZOAS 9      846
AIRY
       AND THRO HEAVN'S HALLS THY AIRY FLIGHT DOST THROW   . .   15 IMIT SPEN/PS      21
       WHILE THE AIRY MUSIC FILLS THE WORLD WITH JOYFUL SOUNDS   37B CONTEMPLATN/PS PROSE
       THE CLOUD RECLIND UPON HIS AIRY THRONE AND ANSWERD THUS  129 BOOK OF THEL 3    24
       HOW DO YOU KNOW BUT EVRY BIRD THAT CUTS THE AIRY WAY  .  150D MARRIAGE HH 6  PROSE
       GIVING TO AIRY NOTHING A NAME AND A HABITATION  . . . .  514 MILTON 28          3
AJOIND
       AND WAS AJOIND TO BEULAH AS THE POLYPUS TO THE ROCK  . .  340 FOUR ZOAS 7B     289
AKE
       IF HER HEART DOES AKE . . . . . . . . . . . . .        113 LIT GRL LST/SI     25
       THY FRIENDSHIP OFT HAS MADE MY HEART TO AKE   . . . . . 545 TO H(AYLEY)/N       1
AKEING    SEE ACHING,AKING
       THE COUNTLESS GOLD OF THE AKEING HEART   . . . . . . .  425 MENTAL TRAVLER     35
AKING
       HE DROPD HIS HAMMER DIVIDING FROM HIS AKING BOSOM FLED .  278 FOUR ZOAS 1      523
       BIND AROUND MY AKING HEAD  . . . . . . . . . . . .     417 MY SPECTR AD/N      12
ALACK
       AND WOE & ALACK FOR PRETTY MARY BELL . . . . . . .     434 LONG JOHN BRWN      18
       HE MADE THEM PAY HIS PRICE ALACK A DAY  . . . . . .    537 AND HIS LEGS/N      30
ALARM
       SOUND SOUND MY LOUD WAR-TRUMPETS & ALARM MY THIRTEEN    199 AMERICA 9           1
          ANGELS
       SOUND SOUND MY LOUD WAR-TRUMPETS & ALARM MY THIRTEEN    199 AMERICA 9          13
          ANGELS
       SOUND SOUND MY LOUD WAR TRUMPETS & ALARM MY THIRTEEN    199 AMERICA 9          21
          ANGELS
       SOUND SOUND MY LOUD WAR-TRUMPETS & ALARM MY THIRTEEN    199 AMERICA 9          26
          ANGELS
       OF TRUMPETS BLEW A LOUD ALARM ACROSS THE ATLANTIC DEEP .  . 200 AMERICA 10      2
       SILENT THE COLONIES REMAIN AND REFUSE THE LOUD ALARM   . . 200 AMERICA 10      4
       ALL THIS I LEARND WITH SOME ALARM & HEARD ALSO WHAT  . . . 833C LETTER 33    PROSE
ALARMD
       ALARMD WITH THESE GLOOMY VISIONS  . . . . . . . . .     232 URIZEN 19          38
ALARMING
       RECOVERED AS YOU ARE SILENT ON THAT MOST ALARMING AND  .  841A LETTER 40      PROSE
ALARMS
       THE VILLAGE BELL ALARMS AWAY I GO . . . . . . . .        10 WHEN EARLY/PS       5
       THE LOOK OF LOVE ALARMS  . . . . . . . . . . .         182 LOOK OF LOVE/N      1
       THE LOOK OF LOVE ALARMS  . . . . . . . . . . .         184 SEVRL QUESTN/N      5
ALAS
       BUT DOWN HE CAME ALAS HOW FRAIL  . . . . . . . .         17 BLIND-MANS/PS      51
       ALAS MY LORD WHAT AM I CALLING THEE THOU ART MY GOD  . . . 38B SAMSON/PS     PROSE
       I AM BUT A WEAK WOMAN ALAS I AM WEDDED TO YOUR ENEMY   . . 38C SAMSON/PS     PROSE
       I KNEW THOU DIDST BUT MOCK ME ALAS WHEN IN THY SLEEP  . . 39A SAMSON/PS     PROSE
       ALAS IN CITIES WHERES THE MAN WHOSE FACE IS NOT A MASK   42D THEN SHE BORE   PROSE
          UNTO HIS HEART
       AND YOU WILL LOSE YOUR ONCE LOVD TIRIEL ALAS HOW FAINT I AM  104 TIRIEL 4     36
       AND SAID ALAS I KNEW NOT THIS AND THEREFORE DID I WEEP . . 130 BOOK OF THEL 5   8
       [WOE ALAS MY GUILTY HAND]  . . . . . . . . . .         182 THE FLY/N           1
       ALAS MY SON MY SON I WANT I WANT HELP HELP AGED        209C FOR CHILDRN/GP  TITLE
          IGNORANCE
       ALAS MY RINTRAH BRING THE LOVELY JEALOUS OCALYTHRON  . . . 240 EUROPE 8        7
       ALAS FOR ME WHAT WILL BECOME OF ME AT THAT DREAD TIME  . . 292 FOUR ZOAS 3    23
       AND SHRUNK UP TO THE BONES ALAS THAT MAN SHOULD COME TO   354 FOUR ZOAS 8     516
          THIS
       ALAS AM I BUT AS A FLOWER THEN WILL I SIT ME DOWN   . . . 368 FOUR ZOAS 9     410
       ALAS FOR WO ALAS FOR WO ALAS FOR WO  . . . . . . . .    421 BENEATH/N           4
       ALAS FOR WOE ALAS FOR WOE  . . . . . . . . . . .        424 THE GOLDEN NET      3
       CAN SUCH GROSS LIPS PERCIEVE ALAS FOLDED WITHIN THEMSELVES  485 MILTON 5       36
```

		PAGE	TITLE	LINE

ALAS (CONTINUED)

	PAGE	TITLE	LINE
LOS GAVE TO HIM THE HARROW OF THE ALMIGHTY ALAS BLAMABLE	486	MILTON 7	12
NOT SO THE SICK-ONE ALAS WHAT SHALL BE DONE HIM TO RESTORE	493	MILTON 13	4
BUT ONCE ALAS COMMITTING A MISTAKE	536	AND HIS LEGS/N	10
WE THOUGHT ALAS THAT SUCH A THOUGHT SHOULD BE . . .	537	AND HIS LEGS/N	34
AND I ALAS LIVE TO WEEP OUT MINE EYES	537	AND HIS LEGS/N	41
SHALL THE GOLDEN AGE RETURN BUT ALAS YOU WILL NOT EASILY	570C	DESC CAT 3	PROSE
WHICH ALAS EVERY ONE ON EARTH IS LIABLE TO ENTER INTO .	608A	V LAST JUDG/N	PROSE
& MY VISIONS ALSO INFECTED & I SEE TIME AGED ALAS TOO MUCH SO	614D	V LAST JUDG/N	PROSE
AND MALICE & ENVY BUT MY EMANATION ALAS WILL BECOME . . .	639	JERUSALEM 17	38
JESUS ALONE CAN SAVE HIM FOR ALAS WE NONE CAN KNOW . . .	675	JERUSALEM 45	18
ALAS THE TIME WILL COME WHEN A MAN'S WORST ENEMIES . . .	676	JERUSALEM 46	25
AH ALAS AT THE SIGHT OF THE VICTIM	702	JERUSALEM 66	35
TILL THY AWAKING YET ALAS I SHALL FORGET ETERNITY . . .	727	JERUSALEM 83	3
WHERE THE OLD PARENT STILL RETAINS HIS YOUTH AS I ALAS . .	728	JERUSALEM 83	51
WHAT ARE THESE ALAS THE FEMALE MARTYR	765D	FOR SEXES/GP	TITLE
ONE DIES ALAS THE LIVING & DEAD	771	OF GATES/GP	25
MY MOCK & SCORN ALAS WRETCHED HAPPY INEFFECTUAL LABOURER OF	809B	LETTER 20	PROSE
PROMISE BUT ALAS NOW I MAY SAY TO YOU WHAT PERHAPS . . .	822C	LETTER 26	PROSE
COUNCELLOR HE ALAS WAS ILL IN BED WHEN I CALLD YESTERDAY	836B	LETTER 35	*PROSE

ALBION

	PAGE	TITLE	LINE
OF ALBION THEY KISSD THE ROCKY SHORE	32	EDW THIRD/PS 6	14
LIBERTY SHALL STAND UPON THE CLIFFS OF ALBION	33	EDW THIRD/PS 6	55
O YET MAY ALBION SMILE AGAIN AND STRETCH HER PEACEFUL ARMS	34C	KING JOHN/PS	PROSE
ALBION ROSE FROM WHERE HE LABOURD AT THE MILL WITH SLAVES	160	ALBION ROSE	1
VISIONS OF THE DAUGHTERS OF ALBION	189A	V DAU ALBION	TITLE
ENSLAVD THE DAUGHTERS OF ALBION WEEP A TREMBLING LAMENTATION	189	V DAU ALBION 1	1
THE DAUGHTERS OF ALBION HEAR HER WOES & ECCHO BACK HER SIGHS	190	V DAU ALBION 2	20
THE DAUGHTERS OF ALBION HEAR HER WOES & ECCHO BACK HER SIGHS	192	V DAU ALBION 5	2
THE DAUGHTERS OF ALBION HEAR HER WOES & ECCHO BACK HER SIGHS	195	V DAU ALBION 8	13
THE GUARDIAN PRINCE OF ALBION BURNS IN HIS NIGHTLY TENT	197	AMERICA 3	1
AND FLAMD RED METEORS ROUND THE LAND OF ALBION BENEATH . .	197	AMERICA 3	16
ALBION IS SICK AMERICA FAINTS ENRAGD THE ZENITH GREW . .	197	AMERICA 4	4
HID IN HIS CAVES THE BARD OF ALBION FELT THE ENORMOUS PLAGUES	202	AMERICA 15	16
IN TERROR VIEWD THE BANDS OF ALBION AND THE ANCIENT GUARDIANS	203	AMERICA 16	17
THE GUARDIAN PRINCE OF ALBION BURNS IN HIS NIGHTLY TENT	203	AMERICA CANC A	1
AND FLAMD FIERCE METEORS ROUND THE LAND OF ALBION BENEATH	204	AMERICA CANC A *	16
FROM THE FOUR CLIFFS OF ALBION RISE	205	AMERICA CANC C	17
OVER THE RUGGED OCEAN SO THE ANGELS OF ALBION HUNG . . .	205	AMERICA CANC C	24
VISION OF THE DAUGHTERS OF ALBION IN ILLUMINATED PRINTING .	207D	PRSPECTUS 1793	PROSE
IN COUNCIL GATHER THE SMITTEN ANGELS OF ALBION	241	EUROPE 9	11
ARISE AROUND HIM IN THE CLOUDY HEAVENS OF ALBION FURIOUS	243	EUROPE 12	35
A MIGHTY SPIRIT LEAPD FROM THE LAND OF ALBION	243	EUROPE 13	4
THE GUARDIAN PRINCE OF ALBION BURNS IN HIS NIGHTLY TENT	246	SONG OF LOS 4	21
THE DEATH AND JUDGEMENT OF ALBION THE ANCIENT MAN . . .	263C	FOUR ZOAS	TITLE
. . . FAIRIES OF ALBION AFTERWARDS GODS OF THE HEATHEN . .	264	FOUR ZOAS 1	19
SAYING [SHILOH] IS IN RUINS OUR BROTHER IS SICK [SHILOH] ALBION HE	277	FOUR ZOAS 1	* 477
EVEN [SHILOH] ALBION WHOM THOU LOVEST WEPT IN PAIN HIS FAMILY	277	FOUR ZOAS 1	* 485
[XXX ?LIVING JOY FILLS ?ALBION]	SUPP	FOUR ZOAS 1	*
RISING UPON HIS COUCH OF DEATH ALBION BEHELD HIS SONS . .	280	FOUR ZOAS 2	1
[THE MAN] ALBION CALLD URIZEN & SAID BEHOLD THESE SICKNING SPHERES	280	FOUR ZOAS 2	* 3
BUILD WE THE MUNDANE SHELL AROUND THE ROCK OF ALBION . .	280	FOUR ZOAS 2	25
AMONG THE DRUID TEMPLES ALBION GROAND ON TYBURN'S BROOK	281	FOUR ZOAS 2	40
ALBION GAVE HIS LOUD DEATH GROAN THE ATLANTIC MOUNTAINS TREMBLED	281	FOUR ZOAS 2	41
THE DAUGHTERS OF ALBION GIRDED AROUND THEIR GARMENTS OF NEEDLEWORK	281	FOUR ZOAS 2	57
THEY GO FORTH & RETURN TO ALBION ON HIS ROCKY COUCH . . .	281	FOUR ZOAS 2	60
. . . OF THE [ETERNAL] FALLEN ONE ALBION	293	FOUR ZOAS 3	* 68
. . . [THE ETERNAL MAN] AROSE IN TERROR ALBION ROSE . .	293	FOUR ZOAS 3	* 69
. . . THE [ETERNAL] [FALLN ONE] ALBION STARTING FROM HIS SLEEP	293	FOUR ZOAS 3	* 71
. . . THE [ETERNAL] ANCIENT MAN MIGHTY ALBION	293	FOUR ZOAS 3	* 79
AND THE DARK BODY OF [MAN] ALBION LEFT PROSTRATE	294	FOUR ZOAS 3	81
THEN FROWND THE [ETERNAL] FALLEN MAN ALBION	294	FOUR ZOAS 3	* 83
ALBION CLOSD THE WESTERN GATE & SHUT AMERICA OUT BY THE . . .	294	FOUR ZOAS 3	105
THE CORSE OF [MAN] ALBION LAY ON THE ROCK THE SEA OF TIME & SPACE	304	FOUR ZOAS 4	265
[HE IS THE (SHEPHERD) OF ALBION HE IS ALL IN ALL] . . .	SUPP	FOUR ZOAS 8	*
FOR DEATH ETERNAL IN THE HEAVENS OF ALBION & BEFORE THE GATES	481	MILTON 2	14
TERRIFIC AMONG THE SONS OF ALBION IN CHORUS SOLEMN & LOUD	482	MILTON 2	23
BY ENITHARMON'S LOOMS WHEN ALBION WAS SLAIN UPON HIS MOUNTAINS	482	MILTON 3	1
AND THIS IS THE MANNER OF THE DAUGHTERS OF ALBION IN THEIR BEAUTY	484	MILTON 5	5
AMONG THE DAUGHTERS OF ALBION AMONG THE ROCKS OF THE DRUIDS	485	MILTON 5	42
OF ENITHARMON'S LOOM PLAY LULLING CADENCES ON THE WINDS OF ALBION	485	MILTON 6	6
THE SPECTRE OF ALBION FROWND OVER THE NATIONS IN GLORY & WAR	486	MILTON 6	24

41

	PAGE	TITLE	LINE
ALBION (CONTINUED)			
BUT NOW THE STARRY HEAVENS ARE FLED FROM THE MIGHTY LIMBS OF ALBION	486	MILTON 6	26
UPON THE MOUNTAINS OF ALBION AMONG THE CLIFFS OF THE DEAD	488	MILTON 8	26
BENEATH THE COUCH OF ALBION ON THE SEVEN (MOUNTAINS) OF ROME	490	MILTON 9	50
HE SET HIS FACE AGAINST JERUSALEM TO DESTROY THE EON OF ALBION	491	MILTON 11	1
WHERE BEULAH LOVELY TERMINATES IN ROCKY ALBION . . .	491	MILTON 11	4
TO DEVOUR ALBION AND JERUSALEM THE EMANATION OF ALBION . .	493	MILTON 12	27
OF ALBION O VALA O LUVAH O ALBION O LOVELY JERUSALEM	494	MILTON 13	9
THEN THERE WAS MURMURING IN THE HEAVENS OF ALBION . . .	495	MILTON 14	4
THE LAMB THE SAVIOUR ALBION TREMBLED TO ITALY GREECE & EGYPT	495	MILTON 14	6
THEN MILTON ROSE UP FROM THE HEAVENS OF ALBION ARDOROUS	495	MILTON 14	10
FIRST MILTON SAW ALBION UPON THE ROCK OF AGES	497	MILTON 15	36
IS THIS MAN COME SATAN SHALL BE UNLOOSD UPON ALBION . .	498	MILTON 17	33
OVER THE DEEPS OUTSTRETCHING HER TWENTY SEVEN HEAVENS OVER ALBION	499	MILTON 18	3
AND ALBION WAS SLAIN UPON HIS MOUNTAINS & IN HIS TENT . .	500	MILTON 19	20
WITHIN HER BOSOM ALBION LIES EMBALMD NEVER TO AWAKE . . .	501	MILTON 19	57
WHICH IS THE SPIRITUAL FOURFOLD LONDON IN THE LOINS OF ALBION	502	MILTON 20	40
THAT MILTON OF THE LAND OF ALBION SHOULD UP ASCEND . . .	503	MILTON 20	59
UPON THE BODY OF ALBION FOR THIS HE IS COME BEHOLD IT WRITTEN	505	MILTON 22	34
IN ALBION & TO DENY THE VALUE OF THE SAVIOUR'S BLOOD . .	506	MILTON 22	54
AWAKE THOU SLEEPER ON THE ROCK OF ETERNITY ALBION AWAKE	506	MILTON 23	3
BUT THOU ART STILL HEAVY AND DULL AWAKE ALBION AWAKE . .	506	MILTON 23	5
GLOW ON AMERICA'S SHORE ALBION TURNS UPON HIS COUCH . . .	506	MILTON 23	7
SUNG TO THE HARP THAT MILTON OF THE LAND OF ALBION . . .	507	MILTON 23	36
TILL ALBION IS ARISEN THEN PATIENT WAIT A LITTLE WHILE . .	508	MILTON 23	54
LAZARUS WHO IS THE VEHICULAR BODY OF ALBION THE REDEEMD	508	MILTON 24	27
ARISE INTO THE COVERING CHERUB WHO IS THE SPECTRE OF ALBION	508	MILTON 24	28
THE ANCIENT MAN UPON THE ROCK OF ALBION AWAKES	510	MILTON 25	23
AWAKING OF ALBION OUR FRIEND AND ANCIENT COMPANION . . .	511	MILTON 25	62
AND THE SHADOWS OF BEULAH TERMINATE IN ROCKY ALBION . . .	519	MILTON 31	11
COMPELLD TO COMBINE INTO FORM BY SATAN THE SPECTRE OF ALBION	521	MILTON 32	12
AND THE ETERNAL MAN EVEN ALBION UPON THE ROCK OF AGES . .	524	MILTON 34	46
EVEN OF LOS & ENITHARMON & ALL THE SONS OF ALBION . . .	525	MILTON 35	27
THESE TWELVE GODS ARE THE TWELVE SPECTRE SONS OF THE DRUID ALBION	528	MILTON 37	34
THE SPECTRE OF ALBION IN WHICH THE SPECTRE OF LUVAH INHABITS	528	MILTON 37	45
AWAKE ALBION AWAKE RECLAIM THY REASONING SPECTRE SUBDUE	530	MILTON 39	10
STRETCHING FROM SOUTH TO NORTH OVER THE MOUNTAINS OF ALBION	531	MILTON 39	15
THEN ALBION ROSE UP IN THE NIGHT OF BEULAH ON HIS COUCH	531	MILTON 39	32
THE FOUR ZOAS OF ALBION & THY SPIRIT WITH THEM STRIVING	532	MILTON 40	7
BECOMES A WOMB & IS THIS THE DEATH COUCH OF ALBION . . .	534	MILTON 42	1
AND I BEHELD THE TWENTY-FOUR CITIES OF ALBION	534	MILTON 42	16
THE GIANT ALBION WAS PATRIARCH OF THE ATLANTIC	578C	DESC CAT 5	PROSE
THE STORIES OF ARTHUR ARE THE ACTS OF ALBION APPLIED . .	578C	DESC CAT 5	PROSE
JOSEPH OF ARIMATHEA AMONG THE ROCKS OF ALBION	604A	INSC ARIMATHEA	TITLE
AN AGED PATRIARCH IS AWAKED BY HIS AGED WIFE HE IS ALBION	609C	V LAST JUDG/N	PROSE
THEIR HEAD THE AGED WOMAN IS BRITTANNICA THE WIFE OF ALBION	609C	V LAST JUDG/N	PROSE
NAME OF JEHOVAH ELOHIM THE I AM OF THE OAKS OF ALBION . .	610A	V LAST JUDG/N	PROSE
JERUSALEM THE EMANATION OF THE GIANT ALBION	620A	JERUSALEM	TITLE
O [XXX ?BEHOLD ?PITYING] BEHOLD THE VISION OF ALBION	620	JERUSALEM 1	* 7
A BLACK WATER ACCUMULATES RETURN ALBION RETURN	622	JERUSALEM 4	10
SO SPOKE ALBION IN JEALOUS FEARS HIDING HIS EMANATION . .	622	JERUSALEM 4	33
THE BANKS OF THE THAMES ARE CLOUDED THE ANCIENT PORCHES OF ALBION ARE	623	JERUSALEM 5	1
OF THE TERRIBLE SONS & DAUGHTERS OF ALBION AND THEIR GENERATIONS	623	JERUSALEM 5	26
AND TO DEVOUR THE SLEEPING HUMANITY OF ALBION IN RAGE & HUNGER	623	JERUSALEM 5	30
UPON THE EMANATIONS OF ALBION'S SONS THE DAUGHTERS OF ALBION	624	JERUSALEM 5	37
ESTRILD MEHETABEL & RAGAN LOVELY DAUGHTERS OF ALBION . .	624	JERUSALEM 5	44
THEY ARE THE BEAUTIFUL EMANATIONS OF THE TWELVE SONS OF ALBION	624	JERUSALEM 5	45
AMONG THE DAUGHTERS OF ALBION AMONG THE STARRY WHEELS . .	624	JERUSALEM 5	64
LAMENTING FOR HER CHILDREN FOR THE SONS & DAUGHTERS OF ALBION	624	JERUSALEM 5	65
TO ALBION SUGGESTING MURDEROUS THOUGHTS AGAINST ALBION .	624	JERUSALEM 6	7
BECAUSE OF ALBION BECAUSE OF DECEIT AND FRIENDSHIP FOR LO	625	JERUSALEM 7	17
TO PREPARE THE SPECTRE OF ALBION TO REIGN OVER THEE O LOS	626	JERUSALEM 7	40
FORMING THE SPECTRES OF ALBION ACCORDING TO HIS RAGE . .	626	JERUSALEM 7	41
INVOLVD THE EIGHT SUCH ARE THE GENERATIONS OF THE GIANT ALBION	626	JERUSALEM 7	49
I KNOW THAT ALBION HATH DIVIDED ME AND THAT THOU O MY SPECTRE	626	JERUSALEM 7	52
OF GOD TO DESTROY JERUSALEM & TO DEVOUR THE BODY OF ALBION	628	JERUSALEM 9	10
AND THIS IS THE MANNER OF THE SONS OF ALBION IN THEIR STRENGTH	629	JERUSALEM 10	7
WAS BUILT IN FROM ETERNITY IN THE CLIFFS OF ALBION . . .	631	JERUSALEM 11	15
ALBION IS DEAD HIS EMANATION IS DIVIDED FROM HIM	631	JERUSALEM 12	6
AND FROM THEM ALL THE LOVELY BEAMING DAUGHTERS OF ALBION	635	JERUSALEM 14	11
IN EVERY NATION OF THE EARTH TILL THE TWELVE SONS OF ALBION	635	JERUSALEM 15	3
FROM ALBION OVER THE WHOLE EARTH SUCH IS MY AWFUL VISION	635	JERUSALEM 15	5
THAT I MAY AWAKE ALBION FROM HIS LONG & COLD REPOSE . . .	635	JERUSALEM 15	10

42

		PAGE	TITLE	LINE
ALBION (CONTINUED)				
LIKE IRON SCOURGES OVER ALBION REASONINGS LIKE VAST SERPENTS		635	JERUSALEM 15	12
BUT FIRST ALBION MUST SLEEP DIVIDED FROM THE NATIONS	. .	636	JERUSALEM 15	29
I SEE ALBION SITTING UPON HIS ROCK IN THE FIRST WINTER	.	636	JERUSALEM 15	30
WHEN THE DIVINE HAND WENT FORTH ON ALBION IN THE MID WINTER		636	JERUSALEM 15	32
AND AT THE PLACE OF DEATH WHEN ALBION SAT IN ETERNAL DEATH		636	JERUSALEM 15	33
GIVES TO THE CHILDREN OF ALBION & TO THE CHILDREN OF JERUSALEM		637	JERUSALEM 16	24
ALBION GROANS IN THE DEEP SLUMBERS OF DEATH UPON HIS ROCK		637	JERUSALEM 16	27
TO FOLLOW THE DAUGHTERS OF ALBION AS THE HOUND FOLLOWS THE SCENT		638	JERUSALEM 17	3
TORMENTED WITH SWEET DESIRE FOR THESE BEAUTIES OF ALBION		639	JERUSALEM 17	22
ENITHARMON VALA WOULD NEVER HAVE SOUGHT & LOVED ALBION	. .	639	JERUSALEM 17	24
HERE THE TWELVE SONS OF ALBION JOIND IN DARK ASSEMBLY		640	JERUSALEM 18	5
SETTLED AROUND ALBION AND AROUND LUVAH IN HIS SECRET CLOUD		641	JERUSALEM 19	27
AND ALBION FLED INWARD AMONG THE CURRENTS OF HIS RIVERS		642	JERUSALEM 19	39
BUT WHEN THEY SAW ALBION FALLN UPON MILD LAMBETH'S VALE		642	JERUSALEM 20	1
WHEN ALBION RENT THY BEAUTIFUL NET OF GOLD AND SILVER TWINE		643	JERUSALEM 20	30
OF LOVE THOU REFUSEDST TO LET ME GO ALBION BEHELD THY BEAUTY		643	JERUSALEM 20	32
THE VEIL SHONE WITH THY BRIGHTNESS IN THE EYES OF ALBION		643	JERUSALEM 20	34
ALBION LOVD THEE HE RENT THY VEIL HE EMBRACD THEE HE LOVD THEE		643	JERUSALEM 20	36
HE MADE ME HIS BRIDE & WIFE HE GAVE THEE TO ALBION	. . .	643	JERUSALEM 20	40
THEN ALBION BROKE SILENCE AND WITH GROANS REPLYD	. .	643	JERUSALEM 20	42
SHAME DIVIDES FAMILIES SHAME HATH DIVIDED ALBION IN SUNDER		643	JERUSALEM 21	6
THEN VALA ANSWERD SPREADING HER SCARLET VEIL OVER ALBION		644	JERUSALEM 21	50
ALBION THY FEAR HAS MADE ME TREMBLE THY TERRORS HAVE SURROUNDED ME		644	JERUSALEM 22	1
ALBION AGAIN UTTERD HIS VOICE BENEATH THE SILENT MOON	. .	645	JERUSALEM 22	16
THEN SPOKE JERUSALEM O ALBION MY FATHER ALBION	. . .	645	JERUSALEM 22	19
THEN ALBION TURND HIS FACE TOWARD JERUSALEM & SPOKE	. .	645	JERUSALEM 22	25
LOUD GROAND ALBION FROM MOUNTAIN TO MOUNTAIN & REPLIED		645	JERUSALEM 22	36
JERUSALEM JERUSALEM DELUDING SHADOW OF ALBION	. .	645	JERUSALEM 23	1
TREMBLING STOOD ALBION AT HER WORDS IN JEALOUS DARK DESPAIR		646	JERUSALEM 23	13
WHICH STAND UPON THE EDGE OF BEULAH AND THERE ALBION SUNK		646	JERUSALEM 23	25
STRETCHING THEIR WINGS SUBLIME OVER THE LITTLE-ONES OF ALBION		647	JERUSALEM 24	22
BUT ALBION IS CAST FORTH TO THE POTTER HIS CHILDREN TO THE BUILDERS		647	JERUSALEM 24	29
THEY CAME UP TO JERUSALEM THEY WALKED BEFORE ALBION	. . .	647	JERUSALEM 24	41
ALBION COVERD THE WHOLE EARTH ENGLAND ENCOMPASSD THE NATIONS		648	JERUSALEM 24	44
WHY DID YOU TAKE VENGEANCE O YE SONS OF THE MIGHTY ALBION		648	JERUSALEM 25	3
AS THE SONS OF ALBION HAVE DONE TO LUVAH SO THEY HAVE IN HIM		648	JERUSALEM 25	6
THUS WEPT THEY IN BEULAH OVER THE FOUR REGIONS OF ALBION		648	JERUSALEM 25	14
AMONG THE SONS OF ALBION	. . . .	649	SUCH VISIONS/J	4
JERUSALEM THE EMANATION OF THE GIANT ALBION CAN IT BE	.	649B	JERUSALEM 27	PROSE
THAT JERUSALEM WAS & IS THE EMANATION OF THE GIANT ALBION		649B	JERUSALEM 27	PROSE
BUT NOW THE STARRY HEAVENS ARE FLED FROM THE MIGHTY LIMBS OF ALBION		649C	JERUSALEM 27	PROSE
ALBION WAS THE PARENT OF THE DRUIDS	. . . .	649D	JERUSALEM 27	PROSE
WHERE ALBION SLEPT BENEATH THE FATAL TREE	. . . . . .	650	FIELDS FROM/J	29
ALBION GAVE HIS DEADLY GROAN	. . . .	650	FIELDS FROM/J	35
SPECTRE OF ALBION WARLIKE FIEND		651	FIELDS FROM/J	73
AND EVERY ACT A CRIME AND ALBION THE PUNISHER & JUDGE	. .	652	JERUSALEM 28	4
AND ALBION SPOKE FROM HIS SECRET SEAT AND SAID	. .	652	JERUSALEM 28	5
THE TREE SPREAD OVER HIM ITS COLD SHADOWS ALBION GROAND		653	JERUSALEM 28	17
FOR ATONEMENT ALBION BEGAN TO ERECT TWELVE ALTARS	. .	653	JERUSALEM 28	21
AND THUS THE VOICE DIVINE WENT FORTH UPON THE ROCKS OF ALBION		653	JERUSALEM 29	5
I ELECTED ALBION FOR MY GLORY I GAVE TO HIM THE NATIONS		653	JERUSALEM 29	6
ALBION'S REACTOR MUST HAVE A PLACE PREPARD ALBION MUST SLEEP		653	JERUSALEM 29	11
FROM ALBION BUT HATH FOUNDED HIS REACTION INTO A LAW	. .	653	JERUSALEM 29	14
HE HATH COMPELLD ALBION TO BECOME A PUNISHER & HATH POSSESSD		653	JERUSALEM 29	16
FEAR NOT O LITTLE FLOCK I COME ALBION SHALL RISE AGAIN	. .	653	JERUSALEM 29	26
ALBION WALKD ON THE STEPS OF FIRE BEFORE HIS HALLS	. . .	654	JERUSALEM 29	33
THEN ALBION ASCENDED MOURNING INTO THE PORCHES OF HIS PALACE		654	JERUSALEM 29	36
A SWEET ENTRANCING SELF-DELUSION A WATRY VISION OF ALBION		654	JERUSALEM 29	39
ALBION FELL UPON HIS FACE PROSTRATE BEFORE THE WATRY SHADOW		654	JERUSALEM 29	41
WE HEARD THE VOICE OF SLUMBEROUS ALBION AND THUS HE SPAKE		654	JERUSALEM 29	45
AND LO THAT SON OF MAN THAT SHADOWY SPIRIT OF MILD ALBION		654	JERUSALEM 29	55
LUVAH DESCENDED FROM THE CLOUD IN TERROR ALBION ROSE	.	654	JERUSALEM 29	56
WE HEARD THE VOICE OF ALBION STARTING FROM HIS SLEEP	. .	654	JERUSALEM 29	58
AND LUVAH STROVE TO GAIN DOMINION OVER ALBION	. . . . .	655	JERUSALEM 29	61
AND THE DARK BODY OF ALBION LEFT PROSTRATE UPON THE CRYSTAL PAVEMENT		655	JERUSALEM 29	63
. . . THEY JOIND THE DIVINE FAMILY [?ALBION ?SLEPT] TREMBLING		655	JERUSALEM 29	* 83
INTO HIS BOSOM FROM WHICH ALBION SHRUNK IN DISMAL PAIN	. .	656	JERUSALEM 30	17
FOLLOWING ALBION INTO HIS CENTRAL VOID AMONG HIS OAKS	. .	656	JERUSALEM 30	20
UPON THE MOUNTAINS OF ALBION AS IN ANCIENT TIME BEHOLD	. .	656	JERUSALEM 30	22
THE CITIES OF ALBION SEEK THY FACE LONDON GROANS IN PAIN		656	JERUSALEM 30	23
THE TWENTY-EIGHT CITIES OF ALBION STRETCH THEIR HANDS TO THEE		656	JERUSALEM 30	26
BECAUSE OF THE OPRESSORS OF ALBION IN EVERY CITY & VILLAGE		656	JERUSALEM 30	27
ALBION HATH ENTERD THE LOINS THE PLACE OF THE LAST JUDGMENT		656	JERUSALEM 30	38

43

	PAGE	TITLE	LINE

ALBION   (CONTINUED)

AND LUVAH HATH DRAWN THE CURTAINS AROUND ALBION IN VALA'S BOSOM	656	JERUSALEM 30	39
SO LOS IN LAMENTATIONS FOLLOWD ALBION ALBION COVERD . .	656	JERUSALEM 30	41
FEARING THAT ALBION SHOULD TURN HIS BACK AGAINST THE DIVINE VISION	656	JERUSALEM 31	2
AND SAW EVERY MINUTE PARTICULAR OF ALBION DEGRADED & MURDERD	656	JERUSALEM 31	7
AND SAW EVERY MINUTE PARTICULAR THE JEWELS OF ALBION RUNNING DOWN	657	JERUSALEM 31	17
O ALBION IF THOU TAKEST VENGEANCE IF THOU REVENGEST THY WRONGS	657	JERUSALEM 31	36
OF ALBION FROM TAKING VENGEANCE OR HOW SHALL I THEM PERSWADE	657	JERUSALEM 31	38
ALBION I CANNOT BE THY WIFE THINE OWN MINUTE PARTICULARS	657	JERUSALEM 31	44
VALA REPLYD ALBION IS MINE LUVAH GAVE ME TO ALBION . . .	658	JERUSALEM 31	50
AND IS THIS FAITH BEHOLD THE STRIFE OF ALBION & LUVAH . .	658	JERUSALEM 31	55
URIZEN IS THE CHAMPION OF ALBION THEY WILL SLAY MY LUVAH .	658	JERUSALEM 31	57
HERE IS THE HOUSE OF ALBION & HERE IS THY SECLUDED PLACE	658	JERUSALEM 31	60
OF ETERNITY PALE STOOD ALBION AT HIS EASTERN GATE . . .	658	JERUSALEM 31	70
HE SAW ALSO THE FOUR POINTS OF ALBION REVERSD INWARDS . .	658	JERUSALEM 32	7
THEN SPOKE THE SPECTROUS CHAOS TO ALBION DARKNING COLD . .	659	JERUSALEM 33	3
I AM YOUR RATIONAL POWER O ALBION & THAT HUMAN FORM . . .	659	JERUSALEM 33	5
SO SPOKE THE SPECTRE TO ALBION HE IS THE GREAT SELFHOOD	659	JERUSALEM 33	17
REFLECTING BACK TO ALBION IN SEXUAL REASONING HERMAPHRODITIC	659	JERUSALEM 33	28
ALBION SPOKE WHO ART THOU THAT APPEAREST IN GLOOMY POMP	659	JERUSALEM 33	29
KNOW ME NOW ALBION LOOK UPON ME I ALONE AM BEAUTY . . .	660	JERUSALEM 33	48
BORN OF THE WOMAN TO OBEY THE WOMAN O ALBION THE MIGHTY	660	JERUSALEM 33	51
ART THOU VALA REPLIED ALBION IMAGE OF MY REPOSE	660	JERUSALEM 34	2
ALBION THE HIGH CLIFF OF THE ATLANTIC IS BECOME A BARREN LAND	660	JERUSALEM 34	16
HE OPEND HIS FURNACES BEFORE VALA THEN ALBION FROWND IN ANGER	660	JERUSALEM 34	19
TO THE SONS OF ALBION & TO HAND THE ELDEST SON OF ALBION	660	JERUSALEM 34	22
ALBION IS THE TABERNACLE OF VALA & HER TEMPLE	661	JERUSALEM 34	29
O ALBION WHY WILT THOU CREATE A FEMALE WILL	661	JERUSALEM 34	31
IS THIS THE FEMALE WILL O YE LOVELY DAUGHTERS OF ALBION TO	661	JERUSALEM 34	39
WHILE THE DAUGHTERS OF ALBION DIVIDED LUVAH INTO THREE BODIES	661	JERUSALEM 34	46
ALBION GOES TO ETERNAL DEATH IN ME ALL ETERNITY	662	JERUSALEM 35	9
ALBION HATH ENTERD THE STATE SATAN BE PERMANENT O STATE	662	JERUSALEM 35	13
AND BE THOU FOR EVER ACCURSED THAT ALBION MAY ARISE AGAIN	662	JERUSALEM 35	14
ALBION GROANS HE SEES THE ELEMENTS DIVIDE BEFORE HIS FACE	663	JERUSALEM 36	27
BECAME FOUR ELEMENTS SEPARATING FROM THE LIMBS OF ALBION	663	JERUSALEM 36	32
AND THE SEA POURED IN AMAIN UPON THE GIANTS OF ALBION . .	663	JERUSALEM 36	40
ZOAS OF ALBION WHERE A MAN DARE HARDLY TO EMBRACE . . .	663	JERUSALEM 36	45
I FEEL MY SPECTRE RISING UPON ME ALBION AROUZE THYSELF . .	664	JERUSALEM 37	2
WHILE ALBION FLED MORE INDIGNANT REVENGEFUL COVERING . .	664	JERUSALEM 37	12
SAYING ALBION OUR WARS ARE WARS OF LIFE & WOUNDS OF LOVE	664	JERUSALEM 38	14
HE IS THE SHEPHERD OF ALBION HE IS ALL IN ALL	565	JERUSALEM 38	24
THUS SPEAKING THE DIVINE FAMILY FOLLOW ALBION	665	JERUSALEM 38	27
HE SAYS RETURN ALBION RETURN I GIVE MYSELF FOR THEE . .	665	JERUSALEM 38	30
AWAKE ALBION AWAKE AND LET US AWAKE UP TOGETHER	665	JERUSALEM 38	32
I GIVE MYSELF AND THESE MY BRETHREN GIVE THEMSELVES FOR ALBION	665	JERUSALEM 38	39
IN FELPHAM I HEARD AND SAW THE VISIONS OF ALBION	665	JERUSALEM 38	41
THERE IS IN ALBION A GATE OF PRECIOUS STONES AND GOLD . .	665	JERUSALEM 38	55
ALBION FLED THRO THE GATE OF LOS AND HE STOOD IN THE GATE	666	JERUSALEM 39	11
LOS WAS THE FRIEND OF ALBION WHO MOST LOVD HIM IN CAMBRIDGESHIRE	666	JERUSALEM 39	12
SEEING ALBION HAD TURND HIS BACK AGAINST THE DIVINE VISION	666	JERUSALEM 39	14
LOS SAID TO ALBION WHITHER FLEEST THOU ALBION REPLYD . .	666	JERUSALEM 39	15
LOS SHUDDERD AT BEHOLDING ALBION FOR HIS DISEASE	666	JERUSALEM 40	1
THE FRIENDS OF ALBION TREMBLING AT THE SIGHT OF ETERNAL DEATH	666	JERUSALEM 40	3
ALBION IS SICK SAID EVERY VALLEY EVERY MOURNFUL HILL . .	667	JERUSALEM 40	11
AND EVERY RIVER OUR BROTHER ALBION IS SICK TO DEATH . . .	667	JERUSALEM 40	12
ARISE AWAKE O FRIENDS OF THE GIANT ALBION	667	JERUSALEM 40	18
FOR HAD THE BODY OF ALBION FALLN DOWN AND FROM ITS DREADFUL RUINS	667	JERUSALEM 40	31
HER LAMBS BLEAT TO THE SEA-FOWLS CRY LAMENTING STILL FOR ALBION	667	JERUSALEM 40	51
WINCHESTER STOOD DEVOTING HIMSELF FOR ALBION HIS TENTS . .	668	JERUSALEM 40	53
THEY SAW ALBION ENDEAVOURING TO DESTROY THEIR EMANATIONS	669	JERUSALEM 41	31
THUS ALBION SAT STUDIOUS OF OTHERS IN HIS PALE DISEASE . .	669	JERUSALEM 42	1
ALBION SPOKE IN HIS DISMAL DREAMS O THOU DECEITFUL FRIEND	669	JERUSALEM 42	9
SO SPOKE ALBION IN GLOOMY MAJESTY AND DEEPEST NIGHT . . .	670	JERUSALEM 42	17
SO LOS SPOKE THEN TURND HIS FACE & WEPT FOR ALBION . . .	670	JERUSALEM 42	46
ALBION REPLIED GO HAND & HYLE SIEZE THE ABHORRED FRIEND	670	JERUSALEM 42	47
UPON THE HILLS OF ALBION OXFORD GROANS IN HIS IRON FURNACE	671	JERUSALEM 42	58
ALBION THEY CURSE THEIR HUMAN KINDNESS & AFFECTION . . .	671	JERUSALEM 42	60
O GOD OF ALBION WHERE ART THOU PITY THE WATCHERS	671	JERUSALEM 42	74
AND AS ALBION BUILT HIS FROZEN ALTARS LOS BUILT THE MUNDANE SHELL	671	JERUSALEM 42	78
THEY SAW THEIR WHEELS RISING UP POISONOUS AGAINST ALBION	671	JERUSALEM 43	1
TO PREVENT ALBION WALKING ABOUT IN THE FOUR COMPLEXIONS	671	JERUSALEM 43	5
IF WE ARE WRATHFUL ALBION WILL DESTROY JERUSALEM WITH ROOTY GROVES	672	JERUSALEM 43	8
O GOD OF ALBION DESCEND DELIVER JERUSALEM FROM THE OAKEN GROVES	672	JERUSALEM 43	11
BEHOLDING ALBION UPON THE PRECIPICE READY TO FALL INTO NON-ENTITY	672	JERUSALEM 43	15

	PAGE	TITLE	LINE
ALBION (CONTINUED)			
JERUSALEM'S CHILDREN HARK HEAR THE GIANTS OF ALBION CRY AT NIGHT	673	JERUSALEM 43	47
FOR BREAD OF THE SONS OF ALBION OF THE GIANTS HAND & SCOFIELD	673	JERUSALEM 43	50
THEY ALBION SURROUND WITH KINDEST VIOLENCE TO BEAR HIM BACK	674	JERUSALEM 44	2
THEIR AWFUL CHARGE BACK TO HIS NATIVE HOME BUT ALBION DARK	674	JERUSALEM 44	5
LOUD ROLL THE STARRY WHEELS OF ALBION INTO THE WORLD OF DEATH	674	JERUSALEM 44	7
THE NARROW SEA BETWEEN ALBION & THE ATLANTIC CONTINENT . .	674	JERUSALEM 44	14
THE FAMILY DIVINE HOVER AROUND THE DARKEND ALBION . . .	674	JERUSALEM 44	20
FROM HYDE PARK SPREAD THEIR VEGETATING ROOTS BENEATH ALBION	674	JERUSALEM 44	23
THEY ASSIMILATE WITH ALBION IN PITY & COMPASSION	674	JERUSALEM 44	33
AMONG THE FURNACES OF LOS AMONG THE OAKS OF ALBION . . .	674	JERUSALEM 44	37
O ALBION MILDEST SON OF EDEN CLOSD IS THY WESTERN GATE . .	675	JERUSALEM 45	3
THAT THY IMMORTAL TONGUE INSPIRES PRESENT THEM TO ALBION	675	JERUSALEM 45	31
SO SPOKE UNHEARD BY ALBION THE MERCIFUL SON OF HEAVEN . .	676	JERUSALEM 45	33
AROUND ALBION BUT ALBION HEARD HIM NOT OBDURATE HARD . .	676	JERUSALEM 45	35
DIVINE HE WEPT OVER ALBION SPEAKING THE WORDS OF GOD . .	676	JERUSALEM 46	8
THOU ART IN ERROR ALBION THE LAND OF ULRO	676	JERUSALEM 46	10
BUT ALBION TURND AWAY REFUSING COMFORT	676	JERUSALEM 46	16
[WHEN ALBION UTTERD HIS LAST WORDS HOPE IS BANISHD FROM ME]	677	JERUSALEM 47	* 1
HARK THE MINGLING CRIES OF LUVAH WITH THE SONS OF ALBION	677	JERUSALEM 47	13
WEPT FOR THEIR SISTER THE DAUGHTER OF ALBION JERUSALEM . .	678	JERUSALEM 48	22
THE EMANATIONS OF THE GRIEVOUSLY AFFLICTED FRIENDS OF ALBION	678	JERUSALEM 48	27
WHEN WITH A DREADFUL GROAN THE EMANATION MILD OF ALBION	678	JERUSALEM 48	47
ALBION THE VORTEX OF THE DEAD ALBION THE GENEROUS . . .	678	JERUSALEM 48	54
ALBION THE MILDEST SON OF HEAVEN THE PLACE OF HOLY SACRIFICE	678	JERUSALEM 48	55
THE SECRET COVERTS OF ALBION & THE HIDDEN PLACES OF AMERICA	679	JERUSALEM 49	1
COME & MOURN OVER ALBION THE WHITE CLIFF OF THE ATLANTIC	679	JERUSALEM 49	6
THE MOUNTAIN OF GIANTS ALL THE GIANTS OF ALBION ARE BECOME	679	JERUSALEM 49	7
WEAK WITHERD DARKEND & JERUSALEM IS CAST FORTH FROM ALBION	679	JERUSALEM 49	8
THE GIGANTIC ROOTS & TWIGS OF THE VEGETATING SONS OF ALBION	679	JERUSALEM 49	10
LO SHILOH DWELLS OVER FRANCE AS JERUSALEM DWELLS OVER ALBION	680	JERUSALEM 49	48
RUSH ON RUSH ON RUSH ON YE VEGETATING SONS OF ALBION	680	JERUSALEM 49	50
HE HATH PLACED OG & ANAK THE GIANTS OF ALBION FOR THEIR GUARDS	600	JERUSALEM 49	56
REMOVE FROM ALBION FAR REMOVE THESE TERRIBLE SURFACES . .	680	JERUSALEM 49	60
THEREFORE REMOVE FROM ALBION THESE TERRIBLE SURFACES . .	680	JERUSALEM 49	76
ALBION IS NOW POSSESSD BY THE WAR OF BLOOD THE SACRIFICE	681	JERUSALEM 50	8
OF ENVY ALBION IS BECOME AND HIS EMANATION CAST OUT . . .	681	JERUSALEM 50	9
IF THOU HADST BEEN HERE OUR BROTHER ALBION HAD NOT DIED	681	JERUSALEM 50	11
OF STARS FOR ALL THE SONS OF ALBION APPEARD DISTANT STARS	681	JERUSALEM 50	20
WEPT VEHEMENTLY OVER ALBION WHERE THAMES' CURRENTS SPRING	684	JERUSALEM 53	2
IN THE MIDST OF THE ROCKS OF THE ALTARS OF ALBION IN FEARS	684	JERUSALEM 53	17
THE TWENTYFOUR FRIENDS OF ALBION AND ROUND THE AWFUL FOUR	684	JERUSALEM 53	22
AND JERUSALEM IS CALLED LIBERTY AMONG THE CHILDREN OF ALBION	684	JERUSALEM 54	5
BUT ALBION FELL DOWN A ROCKY FRAGMENT FROM ETERNITY HURLD	685	JERUSALEM 54	6
ALL POWERFUL PARENTAL AFFECTION FILLS ALBION FROM HEAD TO FOOT	685	JERUSALEM 54	10
BUT THE SPECTRE LIKE A HOAR FROST & A MILDEW ROSE OVER ALBION	685	JERUSALEM 54	15
THEN ALBION DREW ENGLAND INTO HIS BOSOM IN GROANS & TEARS	685	JERUSALEM 54	27
CONTENDING FOR ALBION & FOR JERUSALEM HIS EMANATION . . .	686	JERUSALEM 55	28
ON CIRCUMCISION NOT ON VIRGINITY O REASONERS OF ALBION	687	JERUSALEM 55	66
AND THUS HE CHAUNTED HIS SONG THE DAUGHTERS OF ALBION REPLY	687	JERUSALEM 56	2
ENTUNE DAUGHTERS OF ALBION YOUR HYMNING CHORUS MILDLY . .	688	JERUSALEM 56	11
WHERE DWELLS THE SPECTRE OF ALBION DESTROYER OF DEFINITE FORM	688	JERUSALEM 56	17
OVER THESE DESOLATE ROCKS OF ALBION O DAUGHTERS OF DESPAIR	688	JERUSALEM 56	21
THEN THE RESPONSE CAME WARBLING FROM TRILLING LOOMS IN ALBION	688	JERUSALEM 56	38
THE CROSS O ALBION WHY DIDST THOU A FEMALE WILL CREATE . .	688	JERUSALEM 56	43
OVER THE PLOW OF NATIONS IN THE STRONG HAND OF ALBION . . .	689	JERUSALEM 57	2
BUT ALBION FLED FROM THE DIVINE VISION	689	JERUSALEM 57	12
THE LIVING CREATURES MADDEND AND ALBION FELL INTO THE FURROW AND	689	JERUSALEM 57	13
. . . ALBION FLED BENEATH THE PLOW	689	JERUSALEM 57	15
IN BEAUTY THE DAUGHTERS OF ALBION DIVIDE & UNITE AT WILL	689	JERUSALEM 58	1
AMONG THE INHABITANTS OF ALBION THE PEOPLE FALL AROUND .	689	JERUSALEM 58	4
THE DAUGHTERS OF ALBION DIVIDE & UNITE IN JEALOUSY & CRUELTY	689	JERUSALEM 58	5
THE INHABITANTS OF ALBION AT THE HARVEST & THE VINTAGE .	689	JERUSALEM 58	6
AND WHILE THE SONS OF ALBION BY SEVERE WAR & JUDGMENT BONIFY	689	JERUSALEM 58	10
FURIOUS IN PRIDE OF SELFHOOD THE TERRIBLE SPECTRES OF ALBION	690	JERUSALEM 58	48
FOR THE VEIL OF VALA WHICH ALBION CAST INTO THE ATLANTIC DEEP	691	JERUSALEM 59	2
AROUND THE EARTH OF ALBION AMONG THE ROOTS OF HIS TREE .	691	JERUSALEM 59	4
AND ALBION WAS SLAIN UPON HIS MOUNTAINS & IN HIS TENT . .	691	JERUSALEM 59	16
A SHEPHERD IN THE NIGHT OF ALBION WHICH OVERSPREAD ALL THE EARTH	692	JERUSALEM 60	9
I GAVE THEE HAND & SCOFIELD & THE COUNTIES OF ALBION .	692	JERUSALEM 60	14
AND IN MY LOVE I WILL LEAD THEE LOVELY SHADOW OF SLEEPING ALBION	693	JERUSALEM 60	37
THE STARS OF ALBION CRUEL RISE THOU BINDEST TO SWEET INFLUENCES	693	JERUSALEM 60	60

45

		PAGE	TITLE		LINE
ALBION	**(CONTINUED)**				
THY BROTHER WHO SLEEPETH IN ALBION FEAR NOT TREMBLING SHADE		694	JERUSALEM 60		69
JERUSALEM REPLIED I AM AN OUTCAST ALBION IS DEAD		695	JERUSALEM 62		2
SHALL ALBION ARISE I KNOW HE SHALL ARISE AT THE LAST DAY		696	JERUSALEM 62		15
ON DEATH ETERNAL IN FIERCE SHUDDERS UPON THE MOUNTAINS OF ALBION		696	JERUSALEM 62		40
WHEN THE FOUR ZOAS OF ALBION THE FOUR LIVING CREATURES THE CHERUBIM		696	JERUSALEM 63		2
OF ALBION TREMBLE BEFORE THE SPECTRE		697	JERUSALEM 63		3
LUVAH SLEW THARMAS THE ANGEL OF THE TONGUE & ALBION BROUGHT HIM		697	JERUSALEM 63		5
THEN VALA THE WIFE OF ALBION WHO IS THE DAUGHTER OF LUVAH		697	JERUSALEM 63		7
THE GIANTS & THE WITCHES & THE GHOSTS OF ALBION DANCE WITH		697	JERUSALEM 63		13
THE CITIES & VILLAGES OF ALBION BECAME ROCK & SAND UNHUMANIZED		697	JERUSALEM 63		18
THE DRUID SONS OF ALBION & THE HEAVENS A VOID AROUND UNFATHOMABLE		697	JERUSALEM 63		19
INSTEAD OF HUMAN VICTIMS BY THE DAUGHTERS OF ALBION & CANAAN		697	JERUSALEM 63		31
IN VISIONS OF THE DREAMS OF BEULAH AMONG THE DAUGHTERS OF ALBION		698	JERUSALEM 63		37
TILL CANAAN ROLLD APART FROM ALBION ACROSS THE RHINE ALONG THE DANUBE		698	JERUSALEM 63		41
THE VAST EXPANSE WHERE THE DAUGHTERS OF ALBION WEAVE THE WEB		698	JERUSALEM 64		2
THEN ALL THE DAUGHTERS OF ALBION BECAME ONE BEFORE LOS EVEN VALA		698	JERUSALEM 64		6
ART THOU VALA THE WIFE OF ALBION O THOU LOVELY DAUGHTER OF LUVAH		698	JERUSALEM 64		19
AS REUBEN FLED BEFORE THE DAUGHTERS OF ALBION TAXING THE NATIONS		699	JERUSALEM 64		34
THAT DROP WITH CRIMSON GORE WITH THE LOVES OF ALBION & CANAAN		⸢99	JERUSALEM 64		37
TO CAST LUVAH INTO THE WRATH AND ALBION INTO THE PITY . .		699	JERUSALEM 65		3
AND ALL THE ARTS OF LIFE THEY CHANGD INTO THE ARTS OF DEATH IN ALBION		700	JERUSALEM 65		16
TO PERPLEX YOUTH IN THEIR OUTGOINGS & TO BIND TO LABOURS IN ALBION		700	JERUSALEM 65		22
GIRT AS A SOWER WITH HIS SEED TO SCATTER LIFE ABROAD OVER ALBION		700	JERUSALEM 65		45
SO SANG THE SPECTRE SONS OF ALBION ROUND LUVAH'S STONE OF TRIAL		701	JERUSALEM 65		56
FOR LUVAH IS FRANCE THE VICTIM OF THE SPECTRES OF ALBION		702	JERUSALEM 66		15
THE DAUGHTERS OF ALBION CLOTHED IN GARMENTS OF NEEDLE WORK		702	JERUSALEM 66		17
GUSHES & STAINS THE FAIR SIDE OF THE FAIR (DAUGHTERS) OF ALBION		702	JERUSALEM 66		21
THE HUMAN FORM BEGAN TO BE ALTERD BY THE DAUGHTERS OF ALBION		703	JERUSALEM 66		46
RED RUN THE STREAMS OF ALBION THAMES IS DRUNK WITH BLOOD		703	JERUSALEM 66		61
SCATTERING HER LEPROUS SNOWS IN FLAKES OF DISEASE OVER ALBION		703	JERUSALEM 66		80
AND THE TWELVE DAUGHTERS OF ALBION UNITED IN RAHAB & TIRZAH		704	JERUSALEM 67		2
SONS WITHOUT TO FEED WITH THEIR SOULS THE SPECTRES OF ALBION		704	JERUSALEM 67		18
LOOK THE BEAUTIFUL DAUGHTER OF ALBION SITS NAKED UPON THE STONE		705	JERUSALEM 68		11
THO HER BRAIN IS NOT DRUNK WITH WINE SHE GOES FORTH FROM ALBION		705	JERUSALEM 68		13
OF ALBION DELIGHTS THE EYES OF THE KINGS THEIR HEARTS & THE		706	JERUSALEM 68		16
THE HEAVENS ARE CUT LIKE A MANTLE AROUND FROM THE CLIFFS OF ALBION		706	JERUSALEM 68		19
TO THE BEAUTIFUL DAUGHTERS OF ALBION THEY SPORT BEFORE THE KINGS		706	JERUSALEM 68		32
ON THE TWELVE STONES OF POWER & THE BEAUTIFUL DAUGHTERS OF ALBION		706	JERUSALEM 68		41
AND SWORD FAINT IN HIS HAND FROM ALBION ACROSS GREAT TARTARY		706	JERUSALEM 68		52
O BEAUTIFUL DAUGHTER OF ALBION CRUELTY IS THY DELIGHT . .		706	JERUSALEM 68		53
BEFORE THE FACE OF ALBION A MIGHTY THREATNING FORM . . .		708	JERUSALEM 70		2
SUCH FORM THE AGGREGATE OF THE TWELVE SONS OF ALBION TOOK & SUCH		708	JERUSALEM 70		10
IN THE OAK GROVES OF ALBION WHICH OVERSPREAD ALL THE EARTH		708	JERUSALEM 70		16
THE STARRY HEAVENS ALL WERE FLED FROM THE MIGHTY LIMBS OF ALBION		709	JERUSALEM 70		32
OVER ALBION AS THE SOUL IS TO THE BODY SO JERUSALEM'S SONS		709	JERUSALEM 71		4
ARE TO THE SONS OF ALBION AND JERUSALEM IS ALBION'S EMANATION		709	JERUSALEM 71		5
BUT NOW ALBION IS DARKENED & JERUSALEM LIES IN RUINS . .		711	JERUSALEM 71		54
ABOVE THE MOUNTAINS OF ALBION ABOVE THE HEAD OF LOS . .		711	JERUSALEM 71	*	55
BUT HE SPOKE NOT TO ALBION FEARING LEST ALBION SHOULD TURN HIS BACK		711	JERUSALEM 71		58
BUT HE RECEDED BEFORE ALBION & BEFORE VALA WEAVING THE VEIL		711	JERUSALEM 71		60
WITH THE IRON SHUTTLE OF WAR AMONG THE ROOTED OAKS OF ALBION		711	JERUSALEM 71		61
FOR ALBION IN ETERNITY HAS SIXTEEN GATES AMONG HIS PILLARS		711	JERUSALEM 72		5
RETURN O ALBION LET JERUSALEM OVERSPREAD ALL NATIONS . .		712	JERUSALEM 72		35
AS IN THE TIMES OF OLD O ALBION AWAKE REUBEN WANDERS . .		712	JERUSALEM 72		36
IN MIRACLES & WONDERS IN THE FOUR-FOLD DESART OF ALBION		713	JERUSALEM 73		33
TO DEVOUR THE BODY OF ALBION HUNGRING & THIRSTING & RAVNING		714	JERUSALEM 73		48
THE FOUR ZOAS CLOUDED RAGE URIZEN STOOD BY ALBION . . .		714	JERUSALEM 74		1
DRAVE THE SONS & DAUGHTERS OF ALBION FROM THEIR ANCIENT MOUNTAINS		714	JERUSALEM 74		21

		PAGE	TITLE	LINE
ALBION	(CONTINUED)			
THE SONS OF ALBION ARE TWELVE THE SONS OF JERUSALEM SIXTEEN		715	JERUSALEM 74	23
ON LONDON STONE & THE DAUGHTERS OF ALBION RAN AROUND ADMIRING		715	JERUSALEM 74	34
HOW LOS DRAVE THEM FROM ALBION & THEY BECAME DAUGHTERS OF CANAAN		715	JERUSALEM 74	38
HENCE ALBION WAS CALLD THE CANAANITE & ALL HIS GIANT SONS		715	JERUSALEM 74	39
TO AWAKE THE PRISONERS OF DEATH TO BRING ALBION AGAIN	. .	716	JERUSALEM 75	25
BUT NOW THE STARRY HEAVENS ARE FLED FROM THE MIGHTY LIMBS OF ALBION		716	JERUSALEM 75	27
ALBION [JESUS]	. . . .	716C	JERUSALEM 76	*TITLE
HOW DISTANT FAR FROM ALBION HIS HILLS & HIS VALLEYS NO MORE		720	JERUSALEM 79	15
AND ALBION IS HIMSELF SHRUNK TO A NARROW ROCK IN THE MIDST OF THE SEA		720	JERUSALEM 79	17
AND ALL THE NATIONS OF THE EARTH WERE SEEN IN THE CITIES OF ALBION		720	JERUSALEM 79	23
ALBION GAVE ME TO THE WHOLE EARTH TO WALK UP & DOWN TO POUR		720	JERUSALEM 79	36
TILL ALBION IS SHUT OUT FROM EVERY NATION UNDER HEAVEN	. .	721	JERUSALEM 79	80
MY FATHER GAVE TO ME COMMAND TO MURDER ALBION	. . . . .	722	JERUSALEM 80	16
TO MURDER ALBION THE KING OF MEN HE FOUGHT IN BATTLES FIERCE		722	JERUSALEM 80	18
THE CLOUD OF RAHAB VIBRATING WITH THE DAUGHTERS OF ALBION		722	JERUSALEM 80	40
AMONG THE FOUR FORESTS OF ALBION WHICH OVERSPREAD ALL THE EARTH		722	JERUSALEM 80	43
THE CRUEL-ONE OF ALBION TO CLOTHE HIM IN GEMS OF MY ZONE		724	JERUSALEM 81	12
THE TWELVE DAUGHTERS OF ALBION ATTENTIVE LISTEN IN SECRET SHADES		725	JERUSALEM 82	10
SPOKE TO THE DAUGHTERS OF ALBION STANDING ON SKIDDAW'S TOP		725	JERUSALEM 82	16
I HEARD ENITHARMON SAY TO LOS LET THE DAUGHTERS OF ALBION		725	JERUSALEM 82	22
BE SCATTERED ABROAD AND LET THE NAME OF ALBION BE FORGOTTEN		725	JERUSALEM 82	23
LET ALBION REMAIN A DESOLATION WITHOUT AN INHABITANT	. .	725	JERUSALEM 82	25
DISCOVERING HER OWN PERFECT BEAUTY TO THE DAUGHTERS OF ALBION		726	JERUSALEM 82	46
BECOME A FOUNTAIN OF VEINY PIPES O ALBION MY BROTHER	. .	727	JERUSALEM 82	84
ABSORB ME NOT IN SUCH DIRE GRIEF O ALBION MY BROTHER	. .	727	JERUSALEM 83	6
ACCORDING TO THE WILL OF THE LOVELY DAUGHTERS OF ALBION		728	JERUSALEM 83	42
ALBION MUST BE A ROCK OF BLOOD MARK YE THE POINTS	. . .	728	JERUSALEM 83	56
THE SONS OF ALBION GO FORTH I FOLLOW FROM MY FURNACES	. .	728	JERUSALEM 83	62
THE NIGHT FALLS THICK HAND COMES FROM ALBION IN HIS STRENGTH		729	JERUSALEM 84	20
TERRIFIED AT THE SONS OF ALBION THEY TOOK THE FALSHOOD WHICH		729	JERUSALEM 84	* 31
HIS VOICE IS HEARD FROM ALBION THE ALPS & APPENINES	. . .	730	JERUSALEM 85	16
. . . IN THE HILLS & VALLEYS OF ALBION	. . . .	730	JERUSALEM 85	26
TO SPRING UP FOR JERUSALEM LOVELY SHADOW OF SLEEPING ALBION		730	JERUSALEM 85	29
ALBION BELOVED LAND I SEE THY MOUNTAINS & THY HILLS	. . .	731	JERUSALEM 86	11
I SEE THE SPECTRES OF THY DEAD O EMANATION OF ALBION		731	JERUSALEM 86	13
OF ALBION DRANK & IMBIBED THE LIFE & ETERNAL FORM OF LUVAH		736	JERUSALEM 90	17
LOUD SCREAM THE DAUGHTERS OF ALBION BENEATH THE TONGS & HAMMER		737	JERUSALEM 90	44
SO LOS SPOKE AND THE GIANTS OF ALBION TERRIFIED & ASHAMED		737	JERUSALEM 90	58
PLOTTING TO DEVOUR ALBION & LOS THE FRIEND OF ALBION	. .	737	JERUSALEM 90	63
THESE BEAUTIFUL WITCHCRAFTS OF ALBION ARE GRATIFYD BY CRUELTY		737	JERUSALEM 90	68
LOS READS THE STARS OF ALBION THE SPECTRE READS THE VOIDS		738	JERUSALEM 91	37
IN THE LOINS OF ALBION THE CANAANITE UNITED WITH THE FUGITIVE		739	JERUSALEM 92	3
THIS SINFUL NATION CREATED IN OUR FURNACES & LOOMS IS ALBION		739	JERUSALEM 92	6
FOR IF HE BE THAT ALBION I CAN NEVER WEAVE HIM IN MY LOOMS		739	JERUSALEM 92	9
TO BE WHEN ALBION ARISES FROM HIS DREAD REPOSE O LOVELY ENITHARMON		739	JERUSALEM 92	14
MERLIN WAS LIKE THEE RINTRAH AMONG THE GIANTS OF ALBION		740	JERUSALEM 93	13
ALBION COLD LAYS ON HIS ROCK STORMS & SNOWS BEAT ROUND HIM		741	JERUSALEM 94	1
AND THE BODY OF ALBION WAS CLOSED APART FROM ALL NATIONS		741	JERUSALEM 94	14
AROUND THE WORMY GARMENTS OF ALBION THEN PAUSING IN DEATHLIKE SILENCE		741	JERUSALEM 94	17
TIME WAS FINISHED THE BREATH DIVINE BREATHED OVER ALBION		742	JERUSALEM 94	18
SHE AWOKE PALE & COLD SHE FAINTED SEVEN TIMES ON THE BODY OF ALBION		742	JERUSALEM 94	21
IN DREAMS OF (CHASTITY) & MORAL LAW I HAVE MURDERED ALBION AH		742	JERUSALEM 94	23
THE BREATH DIVINE WENT FORTH UPON THE MORNING HILLS ALBION MOVD		742	JERUSALEM 95	2
THE BREATH DIVINE WENT FORTH OVER THE MORNING HILLS ALBION ROSE		742	JERUSALEM 95	5
THEN JESUS APPEARED STANDING BY ALBION AS THE GOOD SHEPHERD		743	JERUSALEM 96	3
BY THE LOST SHEEP THAT HE HATH FOUND & ALBION KNEW THAT IT		743	JERUSALEM 96	4
WAS THE LORD THE UNIVERSAL HUMANITY & ALBION SAW HIS FORM		743	JERUSALEM 96	5
ALBION SAID O LORD WHAT CAN I DO MY SELFHOOD CRUEL	. . .	743	JERUSALEM 96	8
JESUS REPLIED FEAR NOT ALBION UNLESS I DIE THOU CANST NOT LIVE		743	JERUSALEM 96	14
ALBION REPLYD CANNOT MAN EXIST WITHOUT MYSTERIOUS	. . .	743	JERUSALEM 96	20
ALBION STOOD IN TERROR NOT FOR HIMSELF BUT FOR HIS FRIEND		743	JERUSALEM 96	30
SO ALBION SPOKE & THREW HIMSELF INTO THE FURNACES OF AFFLICTION		744	JERUSALEM 96	35
AND ALL THE CITIES OF ALBION ROSE FROM THEIR SLUMBERS AND ALL		744	JERUSALEM 96	38
THE SONS & DAUGHTERS OF ALBION ON SOFT CLOUDS WAKING FROM SLEEP		744	JERUSALEM 96	39
ALBION'S BOSOM THEN ALBION STOOD BEFORE JESUS IN THE CLOUDS		744	JERUSALEM 96	42

	PAGE	TITLE	LINE
ALBION (CONTINUED)			
AWAKE AWAKE JERUSALEM O LOVELY EMANATION OF ALBION . . .	744	JERUSALEM 97	1
SO SPAKE THE VISION OF ALBION & IN HIM SO SPAKE IN MY HEARING	744	JERUSALEM 97	5
THE UNIVERSAL FATHER THEN ALBION STRETCHD HIS HAND INTO INFINITUDE	744	JERUSALEM 97	6
THE OAK GROVES OF ALBION	746	JERUSALEM 98	50
OF ALBION TAXED THE NATIONS INTO DESOLATION	746	JERUSALEM 98	53
EMANATION OF THE GIANT ALBION BUT FIND THAT TO PRINT IT WILL	878C	LETTER 88	PROSE
ALBION'S			
FAIR ALBION'S SHORE AND ALL HER FAMILIES	33	EDW THIRD/PS 6	60
JUSTICE HATH HEAVED A SWORD TO PLUNGE IN ALBION'S BREAST	34A	KING JOHN/PS	PROSE
FOR ALBION'S SINS ARE CRIMSON DYD	34A	KING JOHN/PS	PROSE
TYRANNY HATH STAIND FAIR ALBION'S BREAST WITH HER OWN CHILDREN'S GORE	34A	KING JOHN/PS	PROSE
ALBION'S COAST IS SICK SILENT THE AMERICAN MEADOWS FAINT	159A	SONG LIBERTY	PROSE
ARE SUCH THINGS [ARE] DONE ON ALBION'S SHORE	177	LIT BOY LST/N	* 29
MEET ON THE COAST GLOWING WITH BLOOD FROM ALBION'S FIERY PRINCE	197	AMERICA 3	5
DESCENDS LINK BY LINK FROM ALBION'S CLIFFS ACROSS THE SEA TO BIND	197	AMERICA 3	8
THE EASTERN CLOUD RENT ON HIS CLIFFS STOOD ALBION'S WRATHFUL PRINCE	197	AMERICA 3	14
ALBION'S ANGEL STOOD BESIDE THE STONE OF NIGHT AND SAW . .	197	AMERICA 5	1
IN THUNDERS ENDS THE VOICE THEN ALBION'S ANGEL WRATHFUL BURNT	198	AMERICA 7	1
ON THOSE VAST SHADY HILLS BETWEEN AMERICA & ALBION'S SHORE	200	AMERICA 10	5
IN SIGHT OF ALBION'S GUARDIAN AND ALL THE THIRTEEN ANGELS	200	AMERICA 12	2
OF ALBION'S ANGEL WHO ENRAGD HIS SECRET CLOUDS OPEND . .	201	AMERICA 13	10
BENEATH HIM ROLLD HIS NUMROUS HOSTS ALL ALBION'S ANGELS CAMPD	201	AMERICA 13	13
AND HEARD THE VOICE OF ALBION'S ANGEL GIVE THE THUNDEROUS COMMAND	201	AMERICA 14	3
ON ALBION'S ANGELS THEN THE PESTILENCE BEGAN IN STREAKS OF RED	202	AMERICA 15	1
ACROSS THE LIMBS OF ALBION'S GUARDIAN	202	AMERICA 15	2
ALBION'S GUARDIAN WRITHED IN TORMENT ON THE EASTERN SKY	202	AMERICA 15	6
MEET ON THE COAST GLOWING WITH BLOOD FROM ALBION'S FIERY PRINCE	203	AMERICA CANC A	5
DESCENDS LINK BY LINK FROM ALBION'S CLIFFS ACROSS THE SEA TO BIND	204	AMERICA CANC A	8
THE EASTERN CLOUD RENT ON HIS CLIFFS STOOD ALBION'S FIERY PRINCE	204	AMERICA CANC A	14
[THEN ALBION'S ANGEL] ROSE RESOLVD TO THE COVE OF ARMOURY	205	AMERICA CANC C	1
ARE SUCH THINGS DONE ON ALBION'S SHORE	219	LIT BOY LST/SE	24
TILL ALBION'S ANGEL SMITTEN WITH HIS OWN PLAGUES FLED WITH HIS BANDS	241	EUROPE 9	8
THE CLOUD BEARS HARD ON ALBION'S SHORE	241	EUROPE 9	9
ON THE HEADS OF ALBION'S ANGELS	241	EUROPE 9	13
ALBION'S ANGEL ROSE UPON THE STONE OF NIGHT	242	EUROPE 11	1
ROUND ALBION'S CLIFFS & LONDON'S WALLS STILL ENITHARMON SLEPT	242	EUROPE 12	2
INTO THE DEADLY NIGHT TO SEE THE FORM OF ALBION'S ANGEL	242	EUROPE 12	6
THEY HEARD THE VOICE OF ALBION'S ANGEL HOWLING IN FLAMES OF ORC	242	EUROPE 12	12
AROUND THE LIMBS OF ALBION'S GUARDIAN HIS FLESH CONSUMING	243	EUROPE 12	33
FROM ALBION'S LOINS FLED ALL PEOPLES AND NATIONS OF THE EARTH [FLED]	281	FOUR ZOAS 2	* 43
IN EVERY PILLARD HALL & ARCHED ROOF OF ALBION'S SKIES . .	281	FOUR ZOAS 2	48
IN ALBION'S BOSOM FOR IN EVERY HUMAN BOSOM THESE LIMITS STAND	304	FOUR ZOAS 4	272
THRO ALBION'S FOUR FORESTS WHICH OVERSPREAD ALL THE EARTH	485	MILTON 6	3
ALL THINGS BEGIN & END IN ALBION'S ANCIENT DRUID ROCKY SHORE	486	MILTON 6	25
AMONG ALBION'S DRUIDS & BARDS IN THE CAVES EENEATH ALBION'S	489	MILTON 9	2
STANDING ON ALBION'S ROCKS AMONG HIGH-REARD DRUID TEMPLES	489	MILTON 9	14
BECAME CANAAN CLOSING LOS FROM ETERNITY IN ALBION'S CLIFFS	491	MILTON 10	10
AMONG THE ROCKS OF ALBION'S TEMPLES AND SATAN'S DRUID SONS	491	MILTON 11	7
OFFER THE HUMAN VICTIMS THROUGHOUT ALL THE EARTH AND ALBION'S	491	MILTON 11	8
GLORYING TO INVOLVE ALBION'S BODY IN FIRES OF ETERNAL WAR	493	MILTON 13	6
THE ELECT SHALL MEET THE REDEEMD ON ALBION'S ROCKS THEY SHALL MEET	494	MILTON 13	30
THUS THEY WEEP UPON THE FATAL BROOK OF ALBION'S RIVER . .	494	MILTON 13	35
REACHD TO THE DEPTHS OF (DIREST) HELL & THENCE TO ALBION'S LAND	496	MILTON 14	* 40
NOW ALBION'S SLEEPING HUMANITY BEGAN TO TURN UPON HIS COUCH	502	MILTON 20	25
THUS MILTON FELL THRO ALBION'S HEART TRAVELLING OUTSIDE OF HUMANITY	502	MILTON 20	41
ALBION'S DREAD SONS HAND HYLE & COBAN SURROUND HIM AS . .	507	MILTON 23	15
SINCE ALBION'S DEATH & SATAN'S CUTTING-OFF FROM OUR AWFUL FIELDS	510	MILTON 25	30
ON ALBION'S ROCK LOS STANDS CREATING THE GLORIOUS SUN EACH MORNING	517	MILTON 29	41
CIRCLING ALBION'S CLIFFS IN WHICH THE FOUR-FOLD WORLD RESIDES	532	MILTON 39	60
TO CAST OFF BACON LOCKE & NEWTON FROM ALBION'S COVERING	533	MILTON 41	5
AROSE AROUND ALBION'S BODY JESUS WEPT & WALKED FORTH . .	534	MILTON 42	19
ALBION'S BOSOM THE BOSOM OF DEATH & THE FOUR SURROUNDED HIM	534	MILTON 42	21
ENGLOBES ITSELF & BECOMES A WOMB SUCH WAS ALBION'S COUCH	620	JERUSALEM 1	2

48

		PAGE	TITLE	LINE
ALBION'S (CONTINUED)				
A PLEASANT SHADOW OF REPOSE CALLD ALBION'S LOVELY LAND . .		620	JERUSALEM 1	3
AS HE ENTERD THE DOOR OF DEATH FOR ALBION'S SAKE INSPIRED		620	JERUSALEM 1	9
FIBRES OF LOVE FROM MAN TO MAN THRO ALBION'S PLEASANT LAND		622	JERUSALEM 4	8
ALBION'S MOUNTAINS RUN WITH BLOOD THE CRIES OF WAR & OF TUMULT		623	JERUSALEM 5	6
UPON THE EMANATIONS OF ALBION'S SONS THE DAUGHTERS OF ALBION		624	JERUSALEM 5	37
HIS SPECTRE DRIVN BY THE STARRY WHEELS OF ALBION'S SONS BLACK AND		624	JERUSALEM 6	1
IS HOWLING IN THE FURNACES IN FLAMES AMONG ALBION'S SPECTRES		626	JERUSALEM 7	39
OF ALBION'S SONS & THE FATHER OF ALL HIS BRETHREN IN THE SHADOWY		626	JERUSALEM 7	43
RELIGION TO INVOLVE ALL ALBION'S SONS AND WHEN THEY HAD		626	JERUSALEM 7	45
WHEN ALL ALBION'S INJURIES SHALL CEASE AND WHEN WE SHALL		626	JERUSALEM 7	55
ROSE UP AGAINST ME THUNDERING FROM THE BROOK OF ALBION'S RIVER		627	JERUSALEM 8	1
I AM INSPIRED I ACT NOT FOR MYSELF FOR ALBION'S SAKE . .		627	JERUSALEM 8	17
NOR SHALT THOU EVER ASSUME THE TRIPLE-FORM OF ALBION'S SPECTRE		627	JERUSALEM 8	34
ALBION'S DREAD SPECTRES STORMING LOUD THUNDEROUS & MIGHTY		629	JERUSALEM 10	5
TO PROTECT THE EMANATIONS OF ALBION'S MIGHTY ONES FROM CRUELTY		631	JERUSALEM 11	18
UPON MY FURNACES FROM WITHIN THE WHEELS OF ALBION'S SONS		631	JERUSALEM 12	11
THE STARRY WHEELS OF ALBION'S SONS WITH SPACES FOR JERUSALEM		631	JERUSALEM 12	18
ULRO IS THE SPACE OF THE TERRIBLE STARRY WHEELS OF ALBION'S SONS		632	JERUSALEM 12	51
TURNING UPON THE WHEELS OF ALBION'S SONS WITH ENORMOUS POWER		632	JERUSALEM 12	65
TAKING THEIR FORMS FROM THE WHEELS OF ALBION'S SONS AS COGS		633	JERUSALEM 13	13
STAND ROUND HIM CUTTING THE FIBRES FROM ALBION'S HILLS . . .		636	JERUSALEM 15	23
THAT ALBION'S SONS MAY ROLL APART OVER THE NATIONS . . .		636	JERUSALEM 15	24
AND TWEED & TYNE ANXIOUS GIVE UP THEIR SOULS FOR ALBION'S SAKE		636	JERUSALEM 16	17
FOR THE PROTECTION OF THE TWELVE EMANATIONS OF ALBION'S SONS		637	JERUSALEM 16	42
BUT LOS HIMSELF AGAINST ALBION'S SONS HIS FURY BENDS FOR HE		638	JERUSALEM 17	6
OUR FATHER ALBION'S SIN AND SHAME BUT FATHER NOW NO MORE		640	JERUSALEM 18	13
SO CRY HAND & HYLE THE ELDEST OF THE FATHERS OF ALBION'S		641	JERUSALEM 18	36
SOON HAND MIGHTILY DEVOURD & ABSORBD ALBION'S TWELVE SONS		641	JERUSALEM 18	39
HOARSE TURND THE STARRY WHEELS RENDING A WAY IN ALBION'S LOINS		641	JERUSALEM 18	44
WILLING THE FRIENDS ENDURD FOR ALBION'S SAKE AND FOR . .		641	JERUSALEM 19	28
AND LOS WAS ROOFD IN FROM ETERNITY IN ALBION'S CLIFFS . .		642	JERUSALEM 19	33
ALBION'S CIRCUMFERENCE WAS CLOSD HIS CENTER BEGAN DARKNING		642	JERUSALEM 19	36
I REDOUNDED FROM ALBION'S BOSOM IN MY VIRGIN LOVELINESS		643	JERUSALEM 20	38
DAUGHTER OF MY PHANTASY UNLAWFUL PLEASURE ALBION'S CURSE		645	JERUSALEM 23	2
IN AN ETERNAL DEATH FOR ALBION'S SAKE OUR BEST BELOVED . .		646	JERUSALEM 23	10
BUT A MEER PHANTASY HEAR DYING ALBION'S CURSE		646	JERUSALEM 23	37
ALL THINGS BEGIN & END IN ALBION'S ANCIENT DRUID ROCKY SHORE		649B	JERUSALEM 27	PROSE
ALBION'S SPECTRE FROM HIS LOINS		650	FIELDS FROM/J	37
ART THOU RETURND TO ALBION'S LAND		651	FIELDS FROM/J	67
HE NAMD THEM JUSTICE AND TRUTH AND ALBION'S SONS		653	JERUSALEM 28	23
ALBION'S DARK ROCKS SETTING BEHIND THE GARDENS OF KENSINGTON		653	JERUSALEM 29	2
THE SONS OF GOD WERE ALBION'S SONS AND JERUSALEM WAS MY JOY		653	JERUSALEM 29	8
ALBION'S REACTOR MUST HAVE A PLACE PREPARD ALBION MUST SLEEP		653	JERUSALEM 29	11
HIDDEN IN ALBION'S FORESTS HE LURKS HE ADMITS OF NO REPLY		653	JERUSALEM 29	13
HIMSELF OF ALBION'S FORESTS & WILDS AND JERUSALEM IS TAKEN		653	JERUSALEM 29	17
FORTHWITH FROM ALBION'S DARKNING LOCKS CAME TWO IMMORTAL FORMS		654	JERUSALEM 29	28
WE FLEE FROM THE INTERIORS OF ALBION'S HILLS AND MOUNTAINS		654	JERUSALEM 29	30
NOT WHERE TO FLEE THEY HAD BEEN ON A VISIT TO ALBION'S CHILDREN		655	JERUSALEM 30	5
OF ALBION'S CHILDREN FLEEING THRO ALBION'S VALES IN STREAMS OF GORE		655	JERUSALEM 30	8
LOS TOOK HIS GLOBE OF FIRE TO SEARCH THE INTERIORS OF ALBION'S		656	JERUSALEM 31	3
ALBION'S ROCKS & PRECIPICES CAVES OF SOLITUDE & DARK DESPAIR		656	JERUSALEM 31	6
AND THUS HE SPOKE LOOKING ON ALBION'S CITY WITH MANY TEARS		657	JERUSALEM 31	28
OF SURREY ACROSS MIDDLESEX & ACROSS ALBION'S HOUSE . . .		658	JERUSALEM 31	69
OF LONDON BUT THE INTERIORS OF ALBION'S FIBRES & NERVES WERE HIDDEN		658	JERUSALEM 32	4
IN STERN DEFIANCE CAME FROM ALBION'S BOSOM HAND HYLE KOBAN		658	JERUSALEM 32	10
BOWEN ALBION'S SONS THEY BORE HIM A GOLDEN COUCH INTO THE PORCH		658	JERUSALEM 32	12
ALL THINGS BEGIN & END IN ALBION'S ANCIENT DRUID ROCKY SHORE		658	JERUSALEM 32	15
AND SHALL ALBION'S CITIES REMAIN WHEN I PASS OVER THEM . .		659	JERUSALEM 33	15
ALBION'S EMANATION WHICH HE HAD HIDDEN IN JEALOUSY . . .		659	JERUSALEM 33	26
VALA REPLIED IN CLOUDS OF TEARS ALBION'S GARMENT EMBRACING		659	JERUSALEM 33	35
I WAS A CITY & A TEMPLE BUILT BY ALBION'S CHILDREN . . .		659	JERUSALEM 33	36
VALA WAS ALBION'S BRIDE & WIFE IN GREAT ETERNITY		660	JERUSALEM 33	39
OF DEATH IN ALBION'S CLOUDS DREADFUL UTTERD OVER ALL THE EARTH		661	JERUSALEM 34	24
CUT OFF FROM ALBION'S MOUNTAINS & FROM ALL THE EARTH'S SUMMITS		661	JERUSALEM 34	44

	PAGE	TITLE	LINE
ALBION'S (CONTINUED)			
IN ALBION'S BOSOM FOR IN EVERY HUMAN BOSOM THOSE LIMITS STAND	662	JERUSALEM 35	2
THE ATLANTIC CONTINENT SUNK ROUND ALBION'S CLIFFY SHORE	663	JERUSALEM 36	39
SO LOS SPOKE BUT WHEN HE SAW [PALE] BLUE DEATH IN ALBION'S FEET	664	JERUSALEM 37	10
FOR ALBION'S SAKE AND FOR JERUSALEM THY EMANATION . .	665	JERUSALEM 38	38
CHARIOTS BLACK THEIR FIRES ROLL BEHOLDING ALBION'S HOUSE OF ETERNITY	666	JERUSALEM 40	5
DESCENDED AND FELL DOWN UPON THEIR KNEES ROUND ALBION'S KNEES	666	JERUSALEM 40	8
WENT ALONG ALBION'S ROADS TILL THEY ARRIVD AT ALBION'S HOUSE	667	JERUSALEM 40	24
ALBION'S MELANCHOLY WHO MUST ELSE HAVE BEEN A DUMB DESPAIR	668	JERUSALEM 40	60
WHOSE SPECTRE FIRST ASSIMILATED WITH LUVAH IN ALBION'S MOUNTAINS	668	JERUSALEM 41	3
DRINKING THE SHUDDERING FEARS & LOVES OF ALBION'S FAMILIES	669	JERUSALEM 41	27
AND LOS DREW HIS SEVEN FURNACES AROUND ALBION'S ALTARS . .	671	JERUSALEM 42	77
INSTEAD OF ALBION'S LOVELY MOUNTAINS & THE CURTAINS OF JERUSALEM	673	JERUSALEM 43	59
AWAY FROM ALBION'S MOUNTAINS FAR AWAY FROM LONDON'S SPIRES	673	JERUSALEM 43	70
AMONG REARED ROCKS OF ALBION'S SONS AT LENGTH THEY ROSE	673	JERUSALEM 43	82
ALBION'S DREAD WHEELS STRETCHING OUT SPACES IMMENSE BETWEEN	674	JERUSALEM 44	9
AND ALBION'S SONS ASCENDING & DESCENDING IN THE HORRID VOID	674	JERUSALEM 44	17
STRUCKEN WITH ALBION'S DISEASE THEY BECOME WHAT THEY BEHOLD	674	JERUSALEM 44	32
ALBION'S WESTERN GATE IS CLOSD HIS DEATH IS COMING APACE	675	JERUSALEM 45	17
FOR THEIR WELL TIMED WRATH BUT ALBION'S SLEEP IS NOT . .	675	JERUSALEM 45	24
ASSIMILATED AND EMBRACD ETERNAL DEATH FOR ALBION'S SAKE	676	JERUSALEM 45	39
LUVAH TORE FORTH FROM ALBION'S LOINS IN FIBROUS VEINS IN RIVERS	677	JERUSALEM 47	4
LOUD THE CRIES OF WAR ON THE RHINE & DANUBE WITH ALBION'S SONS	677	JERUSALEM 47	9
THEREFORE I WRITE ALBION'S LAST WORDS HOPE IS BANISHD FROM ME	677	JERUSALEM 47	18
ALBION'S DREAD TOMB EIGHT THOUSAND AND FIVE HUNDRED YEARS	678	JERUSALEM 48	36
OF SUBLIME MERCY IN REPHAIM'S VALE PERUSING ALBION'S TOMB	678	JERUSALEM 48	41
TO HIDE THEM FROM THE WRATH OF ALBION'S LAW THAT FREEZES SORE	679	JERUSALEM 48	60
DRAW YE JERUSALEM AWAY FROM ALBION'S MOUNTAINS . . .	679	JERUSALEM 48	62
HE HAS BUILT THE ARCHES OF ALBION'S TOMB BINDING THE STARS	680	JERUSALEM 49	54
BEHOLD THE FOGGY MORNINGS OF THE DEAD ON ALBION'S CLIFFS	681	JERUSALEM 50	13
AND WE ALSO & ALL BEULAH CONSUME BENEATH ALBION'S CURSE	681	JERUSALEM 50	17
ASCENDING AND DESCENDING INTO ALBION'S SEA OF DEATH . .	681	JERUSALEM 50	21
AND ERIN'S LOVELY BOW ENCLOSD THE WHEELS OF ALBION'S SONS	681	JERUSALEM 50	22
AND THE ROOTS OF ALBION'S TREE ENTERD THE SOUL OF LOS . .	684	JERUSALEM 53	4
FOR THE PROTECTION OF THE TWELVE EMANATIONS OF ALBION'S SONS	684	JERUSALEM 53	23
THEY NAMD THE EIGHTH HE CAME NOT HE HID IN ALBION'S FORESTS	686	JERUSALEM 55	33
SO CRIED THEY AT THE PLOW ALBION'S ROCK FROWNED ABOVE . .	687	JERUSALEM 55	67
GENTLE TO ALBION'S WATCHMAN ON ALBION'S MOUNTAINS REECCHO	688	JERUSALEM 56	32
OF ALBION'S & LUVAH'S SPECTRES WAS HERMAPHRODITIC . . .	690	JERUSALEM 58	20
OF WEEPING & THE PALM OF SUFFERING BENEATH ALBION'S TOMB	691	JERUSALEM 59	6
WEAVING THE SHUDDRING FEARS & LOVES OF ALBION'S FAMILIES	692	JERUSALEM 59	52
THE CLOUDS OF ALBION'S DRUID TEMPLES RAGE IN THE EASTERN HEAVEN	692	JERUSALEM 60	1
WHILE LOS SAT TERRIFIED BEHOLDING ALBION'S SPECTRE WHO IS LUVAH	692	JERUSALEM 60	2
ON ALBION'S HILLS OFTEN WALKING FROM THE FURNACES IN CLOUDS	692	JERUSALEM 60	6
AND BY THESE VISIONS OF PITY & LOVE BECAUSE OF ALBION'S DEATH	693	JERUSALEM 60	64
INVOLVD JERUSALEM & THE WHEELS OF ALBION'S SONS TURND HOARSE	696	JERUSALEM 62	32
OF ALBION'S SPECTRES THAT LOS IN DESPAIR OFT SAT & OFTEN PONDERD	696	JERUSALEM 62	39
AROUND IN THE CLOUDS OF THE FEMALE ON ALBION'S CLIFFS OF THE DEAD	697	JERUSALEM 63	22
OVER THE PLOW OF NATIONS THUNDRING IN THE HAND OF ALBION'S SPECTRE	699	JERUSALEM 64	30
FOR IN THE DEPTHS OF ALBION'S BOSOM IN THE EASTERN HEAVEN	699	JERUSALEM 65	5
. . . & THEY NAILD HIM TO ALBION'S TREE IN BATH	699	JERUSALEM 65	8
OVER ALBION'S MOUNTAINS A FEMININE INDEFINITE CRUEL DELUSION	701	JERUSALEM 65	67
THEY KNEW NOT THIS VALA WAS THEIR BELOVED MOTHER VALA ALBION'S WIFE	701	JERUSALEM 65	71
THE TREMBLINGS OF VALA VIBRATE THRO THE LIMBS OF ALBION'S SONS	701	JERUSALEM 65	73
A MIGHTY POLYPUS NAMD ALBION'S TREE THEY TIE THE VEINS . .	703	JERUSALEM 66	48
AS THE MISTLETOE GROWS ON THE OAK SO ALBION'S TREE ON ETERNITY LO	703	JERUSALEM 66	55
IN THE HANDS OF ALBION'S DAUGHTERS AMONG THE DRUID TEMPLES	703	JERUSALEM 66	84
BY THE ATHEISTICAL EPICUREAN PHILOSOPHY OF ALBION'S TREE	704	JERUSALEM 67	13
HIDING ALBION'S SONS WITHIN THE VEIL CLOSING JERUSALEM'S	704	JERUSALEM 67	17
OF HOREB STILL EYEING ALBION'S CLIFFS EAGERLY SIEZING & TWISTING	704	JERUSALEM 67	27
GOING FORTH & RETURNING FROM ALBION'S ROCKS TO CANAAN . .	707	JERUSALEM 69	4
DRIVN FORTH BY LOS TIME AFTER TIME FROM ALBION'S CLIFFY SHORE	707	JERUSALEM 69	8
AND THIS THE FORM OF MIGHTY HAND SITTING ON ALBION'S CLIFFS	708	JERUSALEM 70	1
PLOTTING TO DEVOUR ALBION'S BODY OF HUMANITY & LOVE . . .	708	JERUSALEM 70	9
AND ABOVE ALBION'S LAND WAS SEEN THE HEAVENLY CANAAN . .	709	JERUSALEM 71	1
AS THE SUBSTANCE IS TO THE SHADOW AND ABOVE ALBION'S TWELVE SONS	709	JERUSALEM 71	2

	PAGE	TITLE	LINE

ALBION'S   (CONTINUED)
ARE TO THE SONS OF ALBION AND JERUSALEM IS ALBION'S   709 JERUSALEM 71   5
EMANATION
AND THESE THE NAMES OF ALBION'S TWELVE SONS . . . .   709 JERUSALEM 71   10
IN ALBION'S TOMB THE WONDROUS CREATION & THE FOUR-FOLD GATE 712 JERUSALEM 72   49
PERUSING ALBION'S TOMB IN THE STARRY CHARACTERS OF OG &   13 JERUSALEM 73   16
ANAK
IN THE TERRIBLE FAMILY FEUDS OF ALBION'S CITIES & VILLAGES   714 JERUSALEM 73   47
I TELL HOW ALBION'S SONS BY HARMONIES OF CONCORDS   715 JERUSALEM 74   24
& DISCORDS
HOW HYLE ROOFD LOS IN ALBION'S CLIFFS BY THE AFFECTIONS   715 JERUSALEM 74   28
RENT
IN BASHAN TERROR-STRUCK ALBION'S SONS LOOK TOWARD BASHAN   715 JERUSALEM 74   43
OF ALBION'S DAUGHTERS IN PHILISTEA BY THE SIDE OF AMALEK   715 JERUSALEM 74   46
THE SPECTRES OF ALBION'S TWELVE SONS REVOLVE MIGHTILY   . . 718 JERUSALEM 78   1
DASHING IN PIECES SELF-RIGHTEOUSNESSES DRIVING THEM FROM   719 JERUSALEM 78   6
ALBION'S
ALBION'S TWELVE SONS SURROUND THE FORTY-TWO GATES OF ERIN   719 JERUSALEM 78   12
FROM ALBION'S TOMB AFAR AND FROM THE FOUR-FOLD WONDERS   721 JERUSALEM 79   62
OF GOD
BEFORE IN ALBION'S LAND . . . .   722 JERUSALEM 80   24
DRAWING OUT FIBRE BY FIBRE RETURNING TO ALBION'S TREE . .   723 JERUSALEM 80   61
INTO TWO IRREGULAR FORMS AND LOOKING ON ALBION'S DREAD TREE 723 JERUSALEM 80   73
BY THE FRUIT OF ALBION'S TREE I HAVE FED HIM WITH SWEET   726 JERUSALEM 82   40
MILK
BENEATH ALBION'S FATAL TREE BEFORE THE GATE OF LOS   . . . 726 JERUSALEM 82   60
SEPARATE ALBION'S SONS GENTLY FROM THEIR EMANATIONS . . . 728 JERUSALEM 83   49
IT MUST LIE IN CONFUSION TILL ALBION'S TIME OF AWAKING . . 728 JERUSALEM 83   58
AND THUS HE HEARD THE VOICE OF ALBION'S DAUGHTERS   729 JERUSALEM 83   84
ON EUPHRATES
OUR FATHER ALBION'S LAND O IT WAS A LOVELY LAND . . . . .   729 JERUSALEM 83   85
TO ISLINGTON & PADDINGTON & THE BROOK OF ALBION'S RIVER   729 JERUSALEM 84   2
ON ALBION'S ROCKS & LET THY VOICE BE HEARD UPON EUPHRATES   729 JERUSALEM 84   28
WHO STRETCHD ON ALBION'S ROCKS REPOSES AMIDST HIS   730 JERUSALEM 85   25
TWENTY-EIGHT
OF ALBION'S CLOUDS HE FED IT WITH HIS TEARS & BITTER GROANS 732 JERUSALEM 86   53
I HAVE LOVES OF MY OWN I WILL WEAVE THEM IN ALBION'S   732 JERUSALEM 87   18
SPECTRE
YOU ARE ALBION'S VICTIM HE HAS SET HIS DAUGHTER IN YOUR   733 JERUSALEM 87   24
PATH
IN THE LITTLE LOVELY ALLEGORIC NIGHT OF ALBION'S DAUGHTERS   733 JERUSALEM 88   31
FROWN OVER EACH RIVER STUPENDOUS WORKS OF ALBION'S DRUID   735 JERUSALEM 89   22
SONS
AND ALBION'S FORESTS OF OAKS COVERD THE EARTH FROM POLE   735 JERUSALEM 89   23
TO POLE
BETWEEN THE STARS AMONG THE ARCHES OF ALBION'S TOMB SUBLIME 738 JERUSALEM 91   38
AND ENGLAND WHO IS BRITTANNIA AWOKE FROM DEATH ON ALBION'S   742 JERUSALEM 94   20
BOSOM
HER VOICE PIERCD ALBION'S CLAY COLD EAR HE MOVED UPON THE   742 JERUSALEM 95   1
ROCK
ENGLAND WHO IS BRITTANNIA ENTERD ALBION'S BOSOM REJOICING   743 JERUSALEM 95   22
ENGLAND WHO IS BRITTANNIA ENTERED ALBION'S BOSOM REJOICING   743 JERUSALEM 96   2
ALBION'S BOSOM THEN ALBION STOOD BEFORE JESUS IN THE CLOUDS 744 JERUSALEM 96   42
OF ALBION'S SPECTRE THE PATRIARCH DRUID . . . .   746 JERUSALEM 98   48
THE FRUIT OF ALBION'S POVERTY TREE . . . .   746 JERUSALEM 98   52
ALCHYMIST
I HAVE NOW SENT THEM TO YOU TO BE TRANSMUTED THOU REAL   791B LETTER 3   PROSE
ALCHYMIST
ALDEGRAVE
COPPER PLATES OF ALBERT DURER LUCAS HISBEN ALDEGRAVE AND   586D CHAUCER 1   PROSE
ALDERMAN
I HAVE ALSO SEEN ALDERMAN BOYDEL WHO HAS PROMISED   . . . . 844A LETTER 43   PROSE
ALDERMEN
GOD BLESS THE DUKE & HIS ALDERMEN ALL   . . . .   55 CRY MATCHES/IM * 2
THUS SITTING AT THE TABLE WIDE THE MAYOR & ALDERMEN . . .   58 THIS CITY/IM   9
ALE
THE MERRY CAN OF NUT-BROWN ALE . . . .   16 BLIND-MANS/PS   9
WITH FACE AS BROWN AS ANY NUT WITH DRINKING OF STRONG ALE   58 THIS CITY/IM   3
THE HUNGRY POOR ENTERD THE HALL TO EAT GOOD BEEF & ALE . .   58 THIS CITY/IM   11
BUT IF AT THE CHURCH THEY WOULD GIVE US SOME ALE . . . .   179 LIT VAGABOND/N   6
BUT IF AT THE CHURCH THEY WOULD GIVE US SOME ALE . . . .   216 LIT VAGABND/SE   5
ALEHOUSE
BUT THE ALEHOUSE IS HEALTHY & PLEASANT & WARM . . . . .   179 LIT VAGABOND/N   2
ALE-HOUSE
BUT THE ALE-HOUSE IS HEALTHY & PLEASANT & WARM . . . . .   216 LIT VAGABND/SE   2
ALEPH
VERY EASY AM NOW LEARNING MY HEBREW (ALEPH BETH GIMMEL)   821D LETTER 25   PROSE
ALEXANDERS
WHILE YOU ACQUIT & FLATTER THE ALEXANDERS & CAESARS . . .   683A JERUSALEM 52   PROSE
ALFRED
ALFRED SHALL SMILE AND MAKE HIS HARP REJOICE . . . . .   35 WAR SONG/PS   26
ALFRED IN THE COUNTRYMAN'S HOUSE . . . .   208D SUBJCTS HIST/N TITLE
ARTHUR ALFRED THE NORMAN CONQUEROR RICHARD JOHN . . . .   713 JERUSALEM 73   36
ALIAMET
STRANGE'S PRINTS WERE WHEN I KNEW HIM ALL DONE BY ALIAMET   594A PUB ADDRESS/N   PROSE
[ALIAMET] GRAVELOT ONCE SAID TO MY MASTER BASIRE [YOU]   594D PUB ADDRESS/N *PROSE
DE ENGLISH
ALIGHTED
ALIGHTED WHERE THIS LITTLE FLOWER WAS   . . . .   414 TO MRS FLAXMAN   6
ALIGHTING
[ALIGHTING DOWN FROM] ALIGHTING IN HIS DRUNKEN JOY   . . .   266 FOUR ZOAS 1   * 93

ALIKE

& WHAT IS MORE EXTRAORDINARY THE PEOPLE ARE SO MUCH ALIKE . . . . 44A ISLAND MOON 1   PROSE
AS ALL MEN ARE ALIKE IN OUTWARD FORM SO AND WITH THE . .   98C ALL RELIGIONS   PROSE
SAME INFINITE VARIETY ALL ARE ALIKE IN THE POETIC GENIUS   98C ALL RELIGIONS   PROSE
AS ALL MEN ARE ALIKE THO INFINITELY VARIOUS   . . . . .   98D ALL RELIGIONS   PROSE
TO HIM THE DAY & NIGHT ALIKE WAS DARK & DESOLATE . . . . 103 TIRIEL 4   2
[DOST THOU NOT SEE THAT MEN CANNOT BE FORMED ALL ALIKE]   109 TIRIEL 8   11
ARE BOTH ALIKE A NIGHT OF SIGHS A MORNING OF FRESH TEARS   191 V DAU ALBION 2   38
FROM USURY FEEL THE SAME PASSION OR ARE THEY MOVED ALIKE   193 V DAU ALBION 5   11
WHAT HAVE I DONE BOTH RAGE & MERCY ARE ALIKE TO ME . . . 297 FOUR ZOAS 3   196
BACON SUPPOSES ALL MEN ALIKE . . . . 398C ANNO BACON   MARG
CONTRARY OPINIONS CAN NEVER BY ANY LANGUAGE BE MADE ALIKE   474B ANNO REYNOLDS   MARG
ALL GENIUS VARIES THUS DEVILS ARE VARIOUS ANGELS ARE ALL   773A NOTE NINE HEAD   PROSE
    ALIKE
BUT EVERY BODY DOES NOT SEE ALIKE TO THE EYES OF A MISER   793D LETTER 5   PROSE

ALIVE

ALL THAT REMAIN ALIVE . . . .   14 GWIN KING/PS   110
I'LL SING TO YOU TO THIS SOFT LUTE AND SHEW YOU ALL ALIVE   237 EUROPE INTRO   17
BUT OF THOSE FOUND ALIVE AT THE LAST JUDGMENT . . . . . 610B V LAST JUDG/N   PROSE
AND THE EMANATIONS BURIED ALIVE IN THE EARTH WITH POMP   628 JERUSALEM 9   15
    OF RELIGION
DOST THOU FORGIVE ME THOU WHO WAST DEAD & ART ALIVE . . . 648 JERUSALEM 24   58
ART THOU ALIVE & LIVEST THOU FOR-EVERMORE OR ART THOU . . 693 JERUSALEM 60   54
ALIVE & NOT DEAD WERE IT NOT BETTER TO BELIEVE VISION . . 780 GHOST ABEL 2   1
THAT I EXPECT NOTHING I WAS ALIVE & IN HEALTH & WITH THE   862C LETTER 60   PROSE

ALL   SEE AT-ALL,HALL

VALLIES HEAR ALL OUR LONGING EYES ARE TURNED . . . . .   1 TO SPRING/PS   6
AND ALL THE DAUGHTERS OF THE YEAR SHALL DANCE . . . . .   2 TO AUTUMN/PS   5
HE WITHERS ALL IN SILENCE AND [IN] HIS HAND . . . . . .   3 TO WINTER/PS   11
AND ALL IS SILENT BUT THE SIGHING VAULTS . . . .   4 FAIR ELENOR/PS   8
OF HER DEAR LORD ALL GHASTLY PALE CLOTTED . . . . 5 FAIR ELENOR/PS   59
AND TASTED ALL THE SUMMER'S PRIDE . . . .   6 HOW SWEET/PS   2
WHERE ALL HIS GOLDEN PLEASURES GROW . . . . 6 HOW SWEET/PS   8
WHERE ALL LOVE'S PILGRIMS COME . . . .   6 MY SILKS/PS   12
WHERE ALL THE OLD VILLAGERS MEET . . . . 8 LOVE JOCUND/PS   15
I LOVE OUR NEIGHBOURS ALL . . . .   8 LOVE JOCUND/PS   17
BUT THOU ART ALL TO ME . . . .   8 LOVE JOCUND/PS   20
AND THROW ALL PITY ON THE BURNING AIR . . . . 10 WHEN EARLY/PS   18
AND ALL HIS SPEARMEN BOLD . . . . 12 GWIN KING/PS   58
WITH ALL HIS MEN OF MIGHT . . . . 13 GWIN KING/PS   82
ALL THAT REMAIN ALIVE . . . .   14 GWIN KING/PS   110
ALL WHILE THE JOCUND HOURS IN THY TRAIN . . . . 14 IMIT SPEN/PS   6
THE BLUSHING BANK IS ALL MY CARE . . . .   15 BLIND-MANS/PS   3
CONFUSION STARTLES ALL AROUND . . . .   17 BLIND-MANS/PS   54
BY WHOLESOME LAWS SUCH AS ALL THOSE . . . .   17 BLIND-MANS/PS   63
IS IN HIS HAND TO WHOM ALL MEN ARE EQUAL . . . . . .   18 EDW THIRD/PS 1   31
EACH KNOWS HIS RANK AND HEAVN MARSHAL ALL . . . . . .   19 EDW THIRD/PS 1   52
LIKE SUMMER BEES AND ALL THE GOLDEN CITIES . . . . . . 19 EDW THIRD/PS 2   13
INFEST OUR ENGLISH SEAS DEVOURING ALL . . . .   20 EDW THIRD/PS 2   67
HE IS AFRAID HE MAKES US ALL AFRAID . . . .   21 EDW THIRD/PS 3   19
RETREATS WE ALL SHALL KNOW HOW TO RETREAT . . . . . .   23 EDW THIRD/PS 3   64
THEM ALL GENERALS . . . .   23 EDW THIRD/PS 3   91
AND SET ALL HEARTS ON FIRE TO BE WITH US . . . . . .   24 EDW THIRD/PS 3   139
IF ALL MY SOLDIERS ARE AS PLEASD AS YOU . . . . 25 EDW THIRD/PS 3   151
THE MOON I WALKD ABROAD WHEN ALL HAD PITCHD . . . . . . 25 EDW THIRD/PS 3   161
THEIR TENTS AND ALL WERE STILL . . . . 25 EDW THIRD/PS 3   162
IN THAT ENLARGED BREAST OF HIS THAT ALL . . . . 25 EDW THIRD/PS 3   187
WHILE THE POOR SLAVE DRUDGES ALL DAY IN HOPE . . . . . 26 EDW THIRD/PS 3   202
THY CARE PRUNE ALL EXTRAVAGANT SHOOTS AND GUIDE . . . . 26 EDW THIRD/PS 3   212
THYSELF AS WE MAY ALL EACH PREFER OTHER . . . . 26 EDW THIRD/PS 3   217
DOES RISE SO HIGH TO OVERFLOW ALL BOUNDS . . . . . .   26 EDW THIRD/PS 3   235
SHALL FLEE AWAY AND LEAVE [THEM] HIM ALL FORLORN . . . . 28 EDW THIRD/PS 3   292
ALL BE WRONG OF COURSE TIS BEST TO KNOW A LITTLE . . . . 28D EDW THIRD/PS 4   PROSE
THEN IF AMBITION IS A SIN WE ARE ALL GUILTY . . . . . . 28D EDW THIRD/PS 4   PROSE
ONLY REMEMBER WILLIAM ALL HAVE IT IN THEIR POWER . . . . 29A EDW THIRD/PS 4   PROSE
WHETHER HE DONT MENTION US ALL ONE BY ONE . . . . . . 29C EDW THIRD/PS 4   PROSE
AND HE IS TO WRITE ANOTHER ABOUT ALL US THAT ARE TO DIE   29C EDW THIRD/PS 4   PROSE
FOR ALL OUR BLOOD AND BONES ARE IN FRANCE AND A . . . . 29C EDW THIRD/PS 4   PROSE
GREAT DEAL MORE THAT WE SHALL ALL HEAR BY AND BY AND I CAME 29C EDW THIRD/PS 4   PROSE
THE WISE MAN THAT KNOWS US ALL AS WELL AS YOUR HONOUR . . 29C EDW THIRD/PS 4   PROSE
FAIR ALBION'S SHORE AND ALL HER FAMILIES . . . . . .   33 EDW THIRD/PS 6   60
ALL IS SILENT WHEN NATURE TAKES HER REPOSE . . . . . . 35C COUCH DEATH/PS   PROSE
AND A RAY OF LIGHT BEAMED AROUND HIS HEAD ALL WAS STILL   36C COUCH DEATH/PS   PROSE
LORD OF THYSELF THOU THEN ART LORD OF ALL . . . . . . 37A CONTEMPLATN/PS   PROSE
THAT ALL WHO PASS MAY READ NOW NIGHT NOON-TIDE OF DAMNED   37D SAMSON/PS   PROSE
    SPIRITS
AND ALL YE GODS OF PALESTINE WITHDRAW YOUR HAND . . . . 38C SAMSON/PS   PROSE
THOUGH I SHOULD TELL HER ALL MY HEART WHAT CAN I FEAR . . 38D SAMSON/PS   PROSE
FOR SORROW IS THE LOT OF ALL OF WOMAN BORN . . . . . . 39B SAMSON/PS   PROSE
SHE KNEW THEM NOT YET THEY ALL WAR WITH SHAME . . . . . 40D THEN SHE BORE   PROSE
PRIDE BEARS IT IN HER BOSOM AND THE GODS ALL BOW TO IT . . 41A THEN SHE BORE   PROSE
PROPHETIC SAW THE KINGDOMS OF THE WORLD & ALL THEIR GLORY   41A THEN SHE BORE   PROSE
AS WELL AS THIS [FOR ALL SHE XXX FEAR AND XXX THE XXX]   41A THEN SHE BORE   *PROSE
THE GODS ALL SERVE HER AT HER WILL SO GREAT HER POWER IS   41D THEN SHE BORE   PROSE
LORD OF ALL [HUMILITY HER DAUGHTER] . . . .   42A THEN SHE BORE   PROSE
AND SWELLING SIGHS BURST FORTH HIS CHILDREN ALL IN ARMS   42B THEN SHE BORE   PROSE
    APPEAR
NOW ALL THE GODS IN BLACKNING RANKS APPEAR . . . . . . 42C THEN SHE BORE   PROSE
PRIDE BOUND HIM THEN USURPD OER ALL THE GODS . . . . . 42C THEN SHE BORE   PROSE
SHE RODE UPON THE SWELLING WIND AND SCATTERD ALL . . . . 42C THEN SHE BORE   PROSE
INDEED HATE CONTROLS ALL THE GODS AT WILL . . . . . . 42D THEN SHE BORE   PROSE
WHEN ALL AROUND SUMMER HATH SPRED HER PLUMES . . . . . 43B WOE CRIED MUSE   PROSE

		PAGE	TITLE	LINE

ALL   (CONTINUED)

	PAGE	TITLE	LINE
MY NERVES WITH TREMBLING CURDLE ALL MY BLOOD	43C	WOE CRIED MUSE	PROSE
TO BE SURE WE ARE ALL POOR CREATURES WELL	44B	ISLAND MOON 1	PROSE
BY THE SLEEVE CRIES PRAY SIR WHO DO ALL THEY BELONG TO . .	45A	ISLAND MOON 1	PROSE
PHO NONSENSE HANG PHAROH & ALL HIS HOST SAID THE PYTHAGOREAN	47C	ISLAND MOON 3	PROSE
HONOUR & GENIUS IS ALL I ASK	47	ASK GODS/IM 1	1
SAID INFLAMMABLE GASS ID SEE THE PARSONS ALL HANGD A PARCEL OF LYING	48A	ISLAND MOON 4	PROSE
I WOULD RUN LIKE THE DICKINS TILL I WAS ALL IN A HEAT . .	48B	ISLAND MOON 4	PROSE
& STAMP & KICK & SWEAT AND ALL FOR THE GOOD OF THEIR SOULS	48B	ISLAND MOON 4	PROSE
& SET HIS [HEAD] HAIR ALL IN A FLAME & RAN ABOUT THE ROOM	48C	ISLAND MOON 4	PROSE
OBTUSE ANGLE SCOPPRELL ARADOBO & TILLY LALLY ARE ALL . .	48C	ISLAND MOON 5	PROSE
SO ALL THE PEOPLE IN THE BOOK ENTERD INTO THE ROOM . . .	49C	ISLAND MOON 5	PROSE
THEY ALL WENT HOME & LEFT THE PHILOSOPHERS THEN SUCTION ASKD	49D	ISLAND MOON 6	PROSE
AND THRUST HIS FIST IN AND ALL IN THE SPACE OF A QUARTER OF AN HOUR	50A	ISLAND MOON 6	PROSE
& STOPT UP ALL ITS VENTS	51	WHEN CORRUP/IM	28
AND CUT OUT ALL ITS SPOTS	51	WHEN CORRUP/IM	34
IF I DONT KNOCK THEM ALL UP NEXT YEAR IN THE EXHIBITION	51D	ISLAND MOON 7	PROSE
I WOULD NOT GIVE A FARTHING FOR IT DO ALL BY YOUR FEELINGS	51D	ISLAND MOON 7	PROSE
AND NEVER THINK AT ALL ABOUT IT IM HANGD IF I DONT GET UP	51D	ISLAND MOON 7	PROSE
SITTING ALL BENEATH A GROT	53	PHEBE DREST/IM	3
ALL THE COUNTRY FOLKS ACOURTING	53	PHEBE DREST/IM	6
[THAT WAS ALL FOR] HERE THEY RECEIVD A SUMMONS	54A	ISLAND MOON 8	PROSE
THIS EVENING [WE'D] WE'LL ALL GET DRUNK I SAY DASH AN ANTHEM	54B	ISLAND MOON 9	*PROSE
GOD BLESS THE DUKE & HIS ALDERMEN ALL	55	CRY MATCHES/IM *	2
FORMED TO SUCKLE ALL MANKIND	56	HAIL MATRIM/IM	9
COME & BE EASED OF ALL YOUR PAINS	56	HAIL MATRIM/IM	26
AND ALL HIS OWN	57	TO BE OR/IM	12
AND ALL THE WAY HE PAVD	57	TO BE OR/IM	23
THIS WILL SPREAD A PLAGUE ALL THRO THE ISLAND	59A	ISLAND MOON 10	PROSE
ON THE BACK OF HIM CAME ALL THE OTHERS IN A HEAP . . .	59A	ISLAND MOON 10	PROSE
SEATED IN COMPANIES THEY SIT WITH RADIANCE ALL THEIR OWN	59	HOLY THURS/IM	6
[AND ALL IN ORDER SIT WAITING THE CHIEF CHANTER'S COMMANDS]	59	HOLY THURS/IM	8
AFTER THIS THEY ALL SAT SILENT FOR A QUARTER OF AN HOUR	59D	ISLAND MOON 11	PROSE
AND ALL THE HILLS ECCHOED	60	NURSES SONG/IM	17
AND LEAVE YOU ALL	60	SAY YOU JOE/IM	4
THE LAWGIVER ALL THE WHILE SAT	61D	ISLAND MOON 11	PROSE
THEY ALL DECLINED & HE WAS FORCED TO SING HIMSELF . . .	61D	ISLAND MOON 11	PROSE
THEN SAID HE I WOULD HAVE ALL THE WRITING ENGRAVED INSTEAD	62D	ISLAND MOON 11	PROSE
ALL IN THREE VOLUMES FOLIO & SELL THEM	62D	ISLAND MOON 11	PROSE
THEY ENVY ME MY ABILITIES & ALL THE WOMEN ENVY YOUR ABILITIES	63A	ISLAND MOON 11	PROSE
& FRIGHTEN ALL THE PEOPLE THERE & SHOW THEM WHAT TRUTH IS	63A	ISLAND MOON 11	PROSE
THIS IS TRUE CHRISTIAN PHILOSOPHY FAR ABOVE ALL ABSTRACTION	65C	ANNO LAVATER	MARG
("AS MAN SO HIS GOD AS HIS GOD SO HE") ALL GOLD . . .	65D	ANNO LAVATER	MARG
ALL THIS MAY BE MIMICKED VERY WELL	68D	ANNO LAVATER	MARG
FOR WHAT ARE ALL CRAWLERS BUT MIMICKERS OF HUMILITY & LOVE	68D	ANNO LAVATER	MARG
("ANSWER THIS...AND YOU WILL KNOW YOURSELF ") ALL GOLD	73C	ANNO LAVATER	MARG
WHICH SHORTLY WEARY THE MAN FOR ALL LIFE IS HOLY . . .	74B	ANNO LAVATER	MARG
HETEROGENEOUS WHICH ALL EXTRAVAGANCE IS BUT EXUBERANCE NOT	81D	ANNO LAVATER	MARG
& PURE WOULD TO GOD THAT ALL MEN WOULD CONSIDER IT . .	82D	ANNO LAVATER	MARG
& GOD WHO LOVES ALL HONEST MEN	85C	ANNO LAVATER	MARG
IT IS THE GOD IN ALL THAT IS OUR COMPANION & FRIEND . .	87A	ANNO LAVATER	MARG
AND AS ALL OF US ON EARTH ARE UNITED IN THOUGHT FOR IT IS	88B	ANNO LAVATER	MARG
THEREFORE ALL WHO CONVERSE IN THE SPIRIT CONVERSE WITH SPIRITS	88B	ANNO LAVATER	MARG
OF THE MAN BUT THE STAMINA ON WHICH ALL HIS VIRTUES GROW	88C	ANNO LAVATER	MARG
AS IT HAS ALL HIS COTEMPORARIES EACH THING IS ITS OWN CAUSE	88C	ANNO LAVATER	MARG
BUT ALL ACT [FROM INDIVIDUAL PROPENSITY] IS VIRTUE . .	88D	ANNO LAVATER	MARG
IN CONSEQUENCE ALL THE LOVES & GRACES WITH THEM ARE SIN	88D	ANNO LAVATER *	MARG
WILL DESIRE LOVE RAGE ENVY & ?ALL ?OTHER	89B	ANNO SWED LOVE *	MARG
BUT THAT THERE IS BUT ONE INFINITE I DO NOT FOR IF ALL BUT GOD	91A	ANNO SWED LOVE	MARG
FOR IT IS FALSE BY ALL EXPERIENCE	92D	ANNO SWED LOVE	MARG
& NOT IN CEREMONIES AT ALL	92D	ANNO SWED LOVE	MARG
WHO SHALL DARE TO SAY AFTER THIS THAT ALL ELEVATION IS OF SELF	94B	ANNO SWED LOVE	MARG
SAID THE ANGELS COULD NOT EXPRESS THEMSELVES AT ALL TO HIM	94C	ANNO SWED LOVE	MARG
WOULD SOON BE AT THE RATIO OF ALL THINGS & STAND STILL UNABLE	97B	NAT RELIGION 1	PROSE
REASON OR THE RATIO OF ALL WE HAVE ALREADY KNOWN	97C	NAT RELIGION 2	PROSE
LESS THAN ALL CANNOT SATISFY MAN	97D	NAT RELIGION 2	PROSE
APPLICATION HE WHO SEES THE INFINITE IN ALL THINGS SEES GOD	98A	NAT RELIGION 2	PROSE
ALL RELIGIONS ARE ONE	98B	ALL RELIGIONS	TITLE
THAT THE FORMS OF ALL THINGS ARE DERIVED FROM THEIR GENIUS	98B	ALL RELIGIONS	PROSE
AS ALL MEN ARE ALIKE IN OUTWARD FORM SO AND WITH THE . .	98C	ALL RELIGIONS	PROSE
SAME INFINITE VARIETY ALL ARE ALIKE IN THE POETIC GENIUS	98C	ALL RELIGIONS	PROSE
THUS ALL SECTS OF PHILOSOPHY ARE FROM THE POETIC GENIUS	98C	ALL RELIGIONS	PROSE
THE (RELIGIONS) OF ALL NATIONS ARE DERIVED	98C	ALL RELIGIONS	*PROSE
AS ALL MEN ARE ALIKE THO INFINITELY VARIOUS	98D	ALL RELIGIONS	PROSE
SO ALL RELIGIONS & AS ALL SIMILARS HAVE ONE SOURCE . .	98D	ALL RELIGIONS	PROSE
WITH MYRATANA ONCE THE QUEEN OF ALL THE WESTERN PLAINS .	99	TIRIEL 1	3
LOOK AT MY BALD HEAD HARK LISTEN YE SERPENTS [?ALL] LISTEN	99	TIRIEL 1 *	29
AND NOT A BONE OF ALL THE SONS OF TIRIEL REMAIN	100	TIRIEL 1	50
WANDERD TILL HE THAT LEADETH ALL LED HIM TO THE VALES OF HAR	100	TIRIEL 2	4
TIRIEL IS KING OF ALL THE WEST WHO ART THOU I AM MNETHA	101	TIRIEL 2	19
FAR IN THE NORTH BUT THEY WERE WICKED & WERE ALL DESTROYD	102	TIRIEL 2	51

<pre>
                                                        PAGE   TITLE   LINE

ALL   (CONTINUED)
       AND I THEIR FATHER SENT AN OUTCAST I HAVE TOLD YOU ALL . . 102 TIRIEL 2   52
       NO MORE SAID TIRIEL BUT I REMAIN ON ALL THIS GLOBE   . . .   102 TIRIEL 2   56
       MY HAIR IS VERY LONG MY BEARD DOTH COVER ALL MY BREAST . . 102 TIRIEL 3   4
       ALL DAY THEY WALKD & ALL THE NIGHT BENEATH THE PLEASANT   104 TIRIEL 4   30
          MOON
       ALL DAY HE BORE HIM & WHEN EVENING DREW HER SOLEMN CURTAIN   104 TIRIEL 4   41
       THE [GLOOM] SECRET FORESTS & ALL NIGHT WANDERD IN DESOLATE   106 TIRIEL 4   * 90
          WAYS
       AYE NOW YOU FEEL THE CURSE YOU CRY BUT MAY ALL EARS BE DEAF 106 TIRIEL 5   20
       AS TIRIEL'S & ALL EYES AS BLIND AS TIRIEL'S TO YOUR WOES   106 TIRIEL 5   21
       IN HASTE THEY FLED WHILE ALL THE SONS & DAUGHTERS OF TIRIEL 107 TIRIEL 5   27
       CHAIND IN THICK DARKNESS UTTERD CRIES OF MOURNING ALL THE   107 TIRIEL 5   28
          NIGHT
       THE FOUR DAUGHTERS [& ALL THE CHILDREN IN THEIR SILENT   107 TIRIEL 5   30
          BEDS]
       [XXX] STRETCHD ON THE MARBLE PAVEMENT SILENT ALL . . . .   107 TIRIEL 5   31
       AND ALL THE CHILDREN IN THEIR BEDS WERE CUT OFF IN ONE   107 TIRIEL 5   33
          NIGHT
       NOW THAT THE CURSE SHALL CLEAN DEVOUR ALL THOSE GUILTY SONS 107 TIRIEL 6   4
       AND ALL THAT TIME WE WAITED FOR THE FIRE TO FALL   107 TIRIEL 6   9
          FROM HEAVEN
       OR FOR THE TORRENTS OF THE SEA TO OVERWHELM YOU ALL . . .   107 TIRIEL 6   10
       BUT NOW MY WIFE IS DEAD & ALL THE TIME OF GRACE IS PAST   107 TIRIEL 6   11
       TRUE [?HILI] HELA THIS IS THE DESERT OF ALL THOSE CRUEL   107 TIRIEL 6   * 16
          ONES
       ALL NIGHT THEY WANDERD THRO THE WOOD & WHEN THE SUN AROSE   109 TIRIEL 7   18
       [DOST THOU NOT SEE THAT MEN CANNOT BE FORMED ALL ALIKE]   109 TIRIEL 8   11
       AND SCOURGES OFF ALL YOUTHFUL FANCIES FROM THE NEW-BORN MAN 110 TIRIEL 8   31
       BLACK BERRIES APPEAR THAT POISON ALL AROUND HIM SUCH [IS]   110 TIRIEL 8   * 34
          WAS TIRIEL
       CONSUMING ALL BOTH FLOWERS & FRUITS INSECTS & WARBLING   110 TIRIEL 8   38
          BIRDS
       IN A BOOK THAT ALL MAY READ . . . .   111 INTRODUCTN/SI   14
       ALL HEART-BROKE I HEARD HER SAY . . . .   111 A DREAM/SI   8
       ALL THE NIGHT IN WOE . . . .   113 LIT GRL FND/SI   1
       GONE WAS ALL THEIR CARE . . . .   114 LIT GRL FND/SI   40
       MAKING ALL THE VALES REJOICE . . . .   115 THE LAMB/SI   8
       AND SOON THEY ALL SAY . . . .   116 ECCHOING GR/SI   16
       WHEN WE ALL GIRLS & BOYS . . . .   116 ECCHOING GR/SI   18
       ALL PRAY IN THEIR DISTRESS . . . .   117 DIVNE IMAGE/SI   2
       AND ALL MUST LOVE THE HUMAN FORM . . . .   117 DIVNE IMAGE/SI   17
       WERE ALL OF THEM LOCKD UP IN COFFINS OF BLACK . . . . . .   117 CHIMNEY SWP/SI   12
       AND HE OPEND THE COFFINS & SET THEM ALL FREE . . . . . .   117 CHIMNEY SWP/SI   14
       THEN NAKED & WHITE ALL THEIR BAGS LEFT BEHIND . . . . .   118 CHIMNEY SWP/SI   17
       SO IF ALL DO THEIR DUTY THEY NEED NOT FEAR HARM . . . .   118 CHIMNEY SWP/SI   24
       HE SHALL FOLLOW HIS SHEEP ALL THE DAY . . . .   118 SHEPHERD/SI   3
       TO KEEP THEM ALL FROM HARM . . . .   119 NIGHT/SI   20
       ALL THE LIVELONG NIGHT BEGUILES . . . .   120 CRADLE SONG/SI   12
       ALL THE DOVELIKE MOANS BEGUILES . . . .   120 CRADLE SONG/SI   16
       ALL CREATION SLEPT AND SMILD . . . .   120 CRADLE SONG/SI   18
       WEPT FOR ME FOR THEE FOR ALL . . . .   120 CRADLE SONG/SI   25
       SMILES ON THEE ON ME ON ALL . . . .   120 CRADLE SONG/SI   29
       AND THE HILLS ARE ALL COVERD WITH SHEEP . . . .   121 NURSES SONG/SI   12
       AND ALL THE HILLS ECCHOED . . . .   121 NURSES SONG/SI   16
       SEATED IN COMPANIES THEY SIT WITH RADIANCE ALL THEIR OWN   122 HOLY THURS/SI   6
       AND CAN HE WHO SMILES ON ALL . . . .   122 ON ANOTHERS/SI   13
       WIPING ALL OUR TEARS AWAY . . . .   122 ON ANOTHERS/SI   22
       HE DOTH GIVE HIS JOY TO ALL . . . .   122 ON ANOTHERS/SI   25
       O IT DRIVES ALL JOY AWAY . . . .   124 SCHOOL BOY/SI   7
       THEY STUMBLE ALL NIGHT OVER BONES OF THE DEAD . . . . .   126 VOICE BARD/SI   9
       ALL BUT THE YOUNGEST SHE IN PALENESS SOUGHT THE SECRET AIR 127 BOOK OF THEL 1   2
       YET I AM VISITED FROM HEAVEN AND HE THAT SMILES ON ALL . . 127 BOOK OF THEL 1   19
       WIPING HIS MILD AND MEEKIN MOUTH FROM ALL CONTAGIOUS TAINTS 128 BOOK OF THEL 2   7
       BUT WALK UNITED BEARING FOOD TO ALL OUR TENDER FLOWERS . . 128 BOOK OF THEL 3   16
       AND ALL SHALL SAY WITHOUT A USE THIS SHINING WOMAN LIVD   129 BOOK OF THEL 3   22
       AND ALL THY MOANS FLEW OER MY ROOF BUT I HAVE CALLD THEM   130 BOOK OF THEL 5   15
          DOWN
       FOR ALL KINGS ARE UNIVERSAL IN THEIR GOVERNMENT . . . .   132C ANNO SWED PROV MARG
       ("THAT MEN LIVE AFTER DEATH") IT WAS NOT KNOWN & YET ALL   132D ANNO SWED PROV MARG
          KNOW
       SICK THE MOUNTAINS AND ALL THEIR VINEYARDS WEEP . . . . .   134 FRENCH REVOLTN   6
       . . . ALL CHILDREN NEW-BORN FIRST BEHOLD THEM TEARS ARE   136 FRENCH REVOLTN   56
          FLED
       . . . KINGS ARE SICK THROUGHOUT ALL THE EARTH . . . . .   137 FRENCH REVOLTN   61
       . . . MOW DOWN ALL THIS GREAT STARRY HARVEST OF SIX   138 FRENCH REVOLTN   90
          THOUSAND YEARS
       WHAT DAMP ALL OUR FIRES O SPECTRE OF HENRY . . . .   142 FRENCH REVOLTN 171
       SHOOK THE CHAMBER HE CEASD ABASHD THEN ORLEANS SPOKE ALL   142 FRENCH REVOLTN 178
          WAS SILENT
       . . . LEARN TO CONSIDER ALL MEN AS THY EQUALS . . . . .   143 FRENCH REVOLTN 193
       BREATHE FIRES BUT TEN MILES FROM PARIS LET ALL BE PEACE   145 FRENCH REVOLTN 240
          . . .
       BUT SILENT HE STOOD TILL ALL THE OFFICERS RUSH ROUND HIM   146 FRENCH REVOLTN 279
          LIKE WAVES
       ALL BIBLES OR SACRED CODES HAVE BEEN THE CAUSES . . . .   149C MARRIAGE HH 4   PROSE
       ALL WHOLSOM FOOD IS CAUGHT WITHOUT A NET OR A TRAP . . . 151A MARRIAGE HH 7 *PROSE
       THE ANCIENT POETS ANIMATED ALL SENSIBLE OBJECTS WITH GODS 153A MARRIAGE HH 11 PROSE
       THUS MEN FORGOT THAT ALL DEITIES RESIDE IN THE HUMAN BREAST 153B MARRIAGE HH 11 PROSE
       HE REPLIED ALL POETS BELIEVE THAT IT DOES & IN   . . . .   153C MARRIAGE HH 12 PROSE
       WAS THE FIRST PRINCIPLE AND ALL THE OTHERS MERELY   153D MARRIAGE HH 12 PROSE
          DERIVATIVE
</pre>

ALL   (CONTINUED)

		PAGE	TITLE		LINE
OF OTHER COUNTRIES AND PROPHECYING THAT ALL GODS WOULD	. .	153D	MARRIAGE HH	12	PROSE
AND WE SO LOVED OUR GOD THAT WE CURSED IN HIS NAME ALL	. .	153D	MARRIAGE HH	12	PROSE
CAME TO THINK THAT ALL NATIONS WOULD AT LAST BE SUBJECT		154A	MARRIAGE HH	12	PROSE
TO THE JEWS					
THIS SAID HE LIKE ALL FIRM PERSWASIONS IS COME TO PASS	. .	154A	MARRIAGE HH	12	PROSE
FOR ALL NATIONS BELIEVE THE JEWS' CODE AND	. . . . .	154A	MARRIAGE HH	12	PROSE
FOR MAN HAS CLOSED HIMSELF UP TILL HE SEES ALL THINGS	. .	154C	MARRIAGE HH	14	PROSE
& THE SOURCES OF ALL ACTIVITY BUT THE CHAINS ARE		155A	MARRIAGE HH	15	PROSE
THE CUNNING OF					
DUNGEON THOU ART PREPARING FOR THYSELF TO ALL ETERNITY	. .	155C	MARRIAGE HH	17	PROSE
FIRE BURST AND ROLLED THRO THE DEEP BLACKNING ALL BENEATH		156B	MARRIAGE HH	17	PROSE
ADVANCING TOWARD US WITH ALL THE FURY OF A SPIRITUAL		156C	MARRIAGE HH	17	PROSE
EXISTENCE					
I ANSWERD ALL THAT WE SAW WAS OWING TO YOUR METAPHYSICS		156D	MARRIAGE HH	17	PROSE
AND PASSED ALL THE PLANETS TILL WE CAME TO SATURN	. . .	157A	MARRIAGE HH	17	PROSE
& ALL OF THAT SPECIES CHAIND BY THE MIDDLE GRINNING	. .	157A	MARRIAGE HH	17	PROSE
& EXPOSES HYPOCRITES TILL HE IMAGINES THAT ALL ARE		157D	MARRIAGE HH	21	PROSE
RELIGIOUS					
NOW HEAR ANOTHER HE HAS WRITTEN ALL THE OLD FALSHOODS	. .	157D	MARRIAGE HH	21	*PROSE
ARE ALL RELIGIOUS & CONVERSED NOT WITH DEVILS WHO ALL		157D	MARRIAGE HH	21	PROSE
HATE RELIGION					
OF ALL SUPERFICIAL OPINIONS		158A	MARRIAGE HH	21	PROSE
AND ARE NOT ALL OTHER MEN FOOLS SINNERS & NOTHINGS	. . .	158B	MARRIAGE HH	22	PROSE
JESUS WAS ALL VIRTUE AND ACTED FROM IMPULSE NOT FROM RULES		158D	MARRIAGE HH	22	PROSE
THE ETERNAL FEMALE GROAND IT WAS HEARD OVER ALL THE EARTH		159A	SONG LIBERTY		PROSE
ALL NIGHT BENEATH THE RUINS THEN		159D	SONG LIBERTY		PROSE
I TOLD HER ALL MY HEART	. . . .	161	NEVER PAIN/N		6
I SAW A CHAPEL ALL OF GOLD	. . . . . .	163	I SAW CHAPEL/N		1
ALL HIS SLIMY LENGTH HE DREW	. . . . . .	163	I SAW CHAPEL/N		12
THUS HE SUNG ALL DAY	. . . .	164	HEARD ANGEL/N		5
IF ALL WERE AS HAPPY AS WE	. . . . . .	164	HEARD ANGEL/N		14
WOULD BLIGHT ALL BLOSSOMS FAIR & TRUE	. . .	166	I FEARD FURY/N		4
FOR ALL BLOSSOMS GREW & GREW	. . . . . .	166	I FEARD FURY/N		7
[BLOSSOMS SHOWRING ALL AROUND]	. . . . .	169	MIRTLE SHADE/N		2
IN ALL THY WORDS & LAWS	. . . .	171	TO NOBODADDY/N		6
IF ALL WERE AS HAPPY AS WE	. . . . . .	174	HUMAN IMAGE/N		5
BUT THEIR SEARCH WAS ALL IN (VAIN)	. . . .	174	HUMAN IMAGE/N	*	24
AND BREAKS ALL CHAINS FROM EVERY MIND	. . .	175	HOW TO KNOW/N		4
SHE PLAYD & SHE MELTED IN ALL HER PRIME	. . .	176	SOFT SNOW/N		3
BLOSSOMS SHOWRING ALL AROUND	. . . . . .	176	TO MY MIRTLE/N		6
AND ALL ADMIRD HIS PRIESTLY CARE	. . . . .	177	DAY/N		15
ALL AROUND HIS [ANCLES] BOSOM ROLLD	. . . .	177	DAY/N		4
ABSTINENCE SOWS SAND ALL OVER	. . . . . .	178	ABSTINENCE/N		1
[SUCH USAGE IN HEAVEN MAKES ALL GO TO HELL]	. .	179	LIT VAGABOND/N		4
WE'D SING AND WE'D PRAY ALL THE LIVELONG DAY	. .	179	LIT VAGABOND/N		8
[ALL THY GILDED PAINTED PRIDE]	. . . . . .	182	THE FLY/N		3
AND ALL HIS GOOD FRIENDS SHEW THEIR PRIVATE ENDS	. .	183	MOTTO SONGS/N		7
AND A GREAT MANY SUCKERS GROW ALL AROUND	. . .	185	LET BROTHELS/N		26
AND ALL THE DEVILS THAT WERE IN HELL	. . . .	187	WHEN KLOPSTK/N		13
AND ALL HIS BOWELS BEGAN TO [BURN] CHURN	. . .	187	WHEN KLOPSTK/N		16
THEY TOLD ME THAT THE NIGHT & DAY WERE ALL THAT I COULD SEE		191	V DAU ALBION 2		30
TILL ALL FROM LIFE I WAS OBLITERATED AND ERASED	. . .	191	V DAU ALBION 2		34
SILENT I HOVER ALL THE NIGHT AND ALL DAY COULD BE SILENT		191	V DAU ALBION 3		14
THEN OOTHOON WAITED SILENT ALL THE DAY AND ALL THE NIGHT		192	V DAU ALBION 4		25
OVER HER SHRINKING SHOULDERS ALL THE DAY & ALL THE NIGHT		193	V DAU ALBION 5		26
WHEN THOU AWAKEST WILT THOU DISSEMBLE ALL THY SECRET JOYS		193	V DAU ALBION 6		8
OR WERT THOU NOT AWAKE WHEN ALL THIS MYSTERY WAS DISCLOSD		193	V DAU ALBION 6		9
THEN IS OOTHOON A WHORE INDEED AND ALL THE VIRGIN JOYS	. .	194	V DAU ALBION 6		18
THAT CLOUDS WITH JEALOUSY HIS NIGHTS WITH WEEPINGS ALL		194	V DAU ALBION 7		18
THE DAY					
SUCH IS SELF-LOVE THAT ENVIES ALL A CREEPING SKELETON	. .	194	V DAU ALBION 7		21
AS HUMAN BLOOD SHOOTING ITS VEINS ALL ROUND THE ORBED		197	AMERICA 4		5
HEAVEN					
IN SIGHT OF ALBION'S GUARDIAN AND ALL THE THIRTEEN ANGELS		200	AMERICA 12		2
THEY GROVEL ON THE SAND AND WRITHING LIE WHILE ALL	. . .	201	AMERICA 13		5
BENEATH HIM ROLLD HIS NUMROUS HOSTS ALL ALBION'S ANGELS		201	AMERICA 13		13
CAMPD					
BUT ALL RUSH TOGETHER IN THE NIGHT IN WRATH AND RAGING FIRE		202	AMERICA 14		19
AND THE LEPROSY LONDON'S SPIRIT SICKENING ALL THEIR BANDS		202	AMERICA 15		3
. . . ALL HIS ANGELS FRIGHT THEIR ANCIENT HEAVENS	. . .	202	AMERICA 15		18
ABOVE ALL HEAVENS IN THUNDERS WRAPD EMERGD HIS LEPROUS HEAD		203	AMERICA 16		3
LEPROUS HIS LIMBS ALL OVER WHITE AND HOARY WAS HIS VISAGE		203	AMERICA 16		11
THE COUNCIL SAT ALL ROSE BEFORE THE AGED APPARITION	. . .	204	AMERICA CANC B		15
BY THE WISE SPIRIT OF LONDON'S RIVER ALL IN XXX?WITH XXX		205	AMERICA CANC C	*	5
?LOOK . . .					
PROVIDED THAT IT EXCEEDS IN ELEGANCE ALL FORMER METHODS		207B	PRSPECTUS 1793		PROSE
WE'D SING AND WE'D PRAY ALL THE LIVE-LONG DAY	. . . .	216	LIT VAGABND/SE		7
IF ALL WERE AS HAPPY AS WE	. . . .	217	HUMAN ABSTR/SE		4
BUT THEIR SEARCH WAS ALL IN VAIN	. . . . .	217	HUMAN ABSTR/SE		23
AND ALL ADMIRD THE PRIESTLY CARE	. . . . .	218	LIT BOY LST/SE		12
ALL HER TENDER LIMBS WITH TERROR SHOOK	. . .	219	LIT GRL LST/SE		29
BROODING SHUT IN THE DEEP ALL AVOID	. . . .	223	URIZEN 3		25
WHICH THE BOSOMS OF ALL INHABIT	. . . . .	224	URIZEN 4		29
ALL THE SEVEN DEADLY SINS OF THE SOUL	. . .	225	URIZEN 4		49
MOUNTAINOUS ALL AROUND	. . . .	225	URIZEN 5		7
HANGING FROWNING CLIFFS & ALL BETWEEN	. . .	225	URIZEN 5		10
FIRES POUR THRO THE VOID ON ALL SIDES	. . .	225	URIZEN 5		15
BUT NO LIGHT FROM THE FIRES ALL WAS DARKNESS	. .	225	URIZEN 5		17
ON ALL SIDES [THEY] HE FRAMD LIKE A WOMB	. . .	225	URIZEN 5	*	29
OVER ALL HIS NERVES OF JOY	. . . . . .	228	URIZEN 10		41
ALL THE MYRIADS OF ETERNITY	. . . . . .	230	URIZEN 13		28

55

	PAGE	TITLE	LINE
ALL (CONTINUED)			
ALL THE WISDOM & JOY OF LIFE	230	URIZEN 13	29
ALL ETERNITY SHUDDERD AT SIGHT	231	URIZEN 18	9
ALL DAY THE WORM LAY ON HER BOSOM	232	URIZEN 19	24
ALL NIGHT WITHIN HER WOMB	232	URIZEN 19	25
ALL THINGS HEARD THE VOICE OF THE CHILD	233	URIZEN 20	28
ALL HIS ETERNAL SONS IN LIKE MANNER	234	URIZEN 23	19
HE IN DARKNESS CLOSD VIEWD ALL HIS RACE	235	URIZEN 23	22
TILL A WEB DARK & COLD THROUGHOUT ALL	235	URIZEN 25	15
AND ALL CALLD IT THE NET OF RELIGION	235	URIZEN 25	22
THRO ALL THE COASTS TILL WEAKEND	236	URIZEN 25	28
SO FUZON CALLD ALL TOGETHER	237	URIZEN 28	19
I'LL SING TO YOU TO THIS SOFT LUTE AND SHEW YOU ALL ALIVE	237	EUROPE INTRO	17
AND ALL THE OVERFLOWING STARS RAIN DOWN PROLIFIC PAINS .	238	EUROPE PREL 1	15
WAR CEASD & ALL THE TROOPS LIKE SHADOWS FLED TO THEIR ABODES	239	EUROPE 4	4
TILL ALL THE SONS OF URIZEN LOOK OUT AND ENVY LOS . .	239	EUROPE 4	16
SIEZE ALL THE SPIRITS OF LIFE AND BIND	239	EUROPE 4	17
BIND ALL THE NOURISHING SWEETS OF EARTH	239	EUROPE 4	19
FORBID ALL JOY & FROM HER CHILDHOOD SHALL THE LITTLE FEMALE	240	EUROPE 5	8
ARISE MY SON BRING ALL THY BRETHREN O THOU KING OF FIRE	240	EUROPE 8	8
INTO TWO STATIONARY ORBS CONCENTRATING ALL THINGS . .	241	EUROPE 10	12
IN FORESTS OF NIGHT THEN ALL THE ETERNAL FORESTS WERE DIVIDED	241	EUROPE 10	18
AND OVERWHELMED ALL EXCEPT THIS FINITE WALL OF FLESH . .	241	EUROPE 10	20
. . . ALL THE SOLDIERS	242	EUROPE 12	19
AND RINTRAH HUNG WITH ALL HIS LEGIONS IN THE NETHER DEEP	242	EUROPE 12	24
STILL ALL YOUR THUNDERS GOLDEN HOOFD & BIND YOUR HORSES BLACK	244	EUROPE 14	28
SHE CEASD [AND] FOR ALL [WENT] WERE FORTH [TO] AT SPORT . . .	244	EUROPE 14	* 32
THAT NATURE FELT THRO ALL HER PORES THE ENORMOUS REVELRY	244	EUROPE 14	34
AND WITH A CRY THAT SHOOK ALL NATURE TO THE UTMOST POLE	245	EUROPE 15	10
CALLD ALL HIS SONS TO THE STRIFE OF BLOOD	245	EUROPE 15	11
TIMES ROLLED ON OER ALL THE SONS OF HAR TIME AFTER TIME	246	SONG OF LOS 3	20
AND ALL THE REST A DESERT	246	SONG OF LOS 4	3
AND ALL THE VAST OF NATURE SHRUNK	246	SONG OF LOS 4	11
AND ALL FLESH NAKED STANDS FATHERS AND FRIENDS . . .	248	SONG OF LOS 7	33
BROUGHT HIS BOOKS ALL BUT THE BOOK	252	AHANIA 3	73
ENROOTING ITSELF ALL AROUND	252	AHANIA 4	3
RAN THRO ALL HIS DISMAL WORLD	253	AHANIA 4	39
FORTY YEARS ALL HIS SONS & DAUGHTERS	253	AHANIA 4	40
AND ROUND ON ALL SIDES MAKING THEIR WAY	256	BOOK OF LOS 3	41
BUT NO LIGHT FROM THE FIRES ALL WAS	257	BOOK OF LOS 3	49
HURLD APART ON ALL SIDES AS A FALLING	257	BOOK OF LOS 4	23
BENEATH HIM & ON ALL SIDES ROUND	257	BOOK OF LOS 4	26
FOR AS YET WERE ALL OTHER PARTS FORMLESS	258	BOOK OF LOS 4	55
ON ALL SIDES AND LEFT AN UNFORMD	260	BOOK OF LOS 5	49
WAIT SISTERS THO ALL IS LOST	262A	SMALL BK DSGNS	TITLE
WITH ALL THEIR WOODS THE STREAMS & VALLEYS [WAIL] . . .	264	FOUR ZOAS 1	* 8
. . . KNOWETH [NOT] NOR CAN KNOW IN ALL ETERNITY	264	FOUR ZOAS 1	13
ALL LOVE IS LOST TERROR SUCCEEDS & HATRED INSTEAD OF LOVE	265	FOUR ZOAS 1	36
ON ALL SIDES WITHIN & WITHOUT THE UNIVERSAL MAN . . .	266	FOUR ZOAS 1	98
. . . IN ALL THEIR [WANDERINGS] DREAMS	267	FOUR ZOAS 1	* 99
[ALREADY ARE MY EYES REVERTED ALL THAT I BEHOLD]	267	FOUR ZOAS 1	115
[SUCH WONDROUS BEAUTY REPINING IN THE MIDST OF ALL HIS GLORY]	267	FOUR ZOAS 1	132
ALL THY PAST DEEDS HEAR WHAT I TELL THEE MARK IT WELL REMEMBER	268	FOUR ZOAS 1	153
[BUT] FOR NOW I FIND THAT ALL THOSE EMANATIONS	268	FOUR ZOAS 1	* 165
. . . ALL THY SOFT DELUSIVE BEAUTY CANNOT	268	FOUR ZOAS 1	170
TIS THOU HAST DARKEND ALL MY WORLD O WOMAN LOVELY BANE . .	269	FOUR ZOAS 1	178
[THUS THEY CONTENDED ALL THE DAY AMONG THE CAVES OF THARMAS]	269	FOUR ZOAS 1	179
. . . ALL HIS LOVELY CHANGING COLOURS MIX	269	FOUR ZOAS 1	184
[BEAUTY ALL BLUSHING WITH DESIRE MOCKING HER FELL DESPAIR]	269	FOUR ZOAS 1	189
THUS ENION GAVE THEM ALL HER SPECTROUS LIFE [IN DEEP DESPAIR]	270	FOUR ZOAS 1	221
SHE DRAVE THE FEMALES ALL AWAY FROM LOS	271	FOUR ZOAS 1	243
[?&] AND LOS DRAVE ALL THE MALES FROM HER AWAY	271	FOUR ZOAS 1	* 244
WHILE THY MILD VOICE FILLS ALL THESE CAVERNS WITH SWEET HARMONY	271	FOUR ZOAS 1	250
DRIVING THE FEMALE EMANATIONS ALL AWAY FROM LOS	271	FOUR ZOAS 1	273
[IF THOU DRIVST ALL THE [MALES] FEMALES AWAY	272	FOUR ZOAS 1	* 276
. . . FROM [VALA] LUVAH I WILL DRIVE ALL]	272	FOUR ZOAS 1	* 276
. . . NOW BORN TO DRINK UP ALL HIS POWERS	272	FOUR ZOAS 1	278
REFUSING TO BEHOLD THE DIVINE IMAGE WHICH ALL BEHOLD . .	272	FOUR ZOAS 1	290
AND THAT HE MUST BE BORN IS CERTAIN FOR ONE MUST BE ALL	272	FOUR ZOAS 1	294
AND COMPREHEND WITHIN HIMSELF ALL THINGS BOTH SMALL & GREAT	272	FOUR ZOAS 1	* 295
WE THEREFORE FOR WHOSE SAKE ALL THINGS ASPIRE TO BE & LIVE	272	FOUR ZOAS 1	296
THO THIS BRIGHT WORLD OF ALL OUR JOY IS IN THE HUMAN BRAIN	272	FOUR ZOAS 1	303
WHERE URIZEN & ALL HIS HOSTS HANG THEIR IMMORTAL LAMPS . .	272	FOUR ZOAS 1	304
BUT THE BRIGHT SUN WAS NOT AS YET HE FILLING ALL THE EXPANSE	273	FOUR ZOAS 1	349
ARISE IN ALL HIS VEINS HE THREW HIS ARMS AROUND HER LOINS	274	FOUR ZOAS 1	353
IN (LUVAH'S) ROBES OF BLOOD & BEARING ALL HIS AFFLICTIONS	274	FOUR ZOAS 1	* 364
THE NUPTIAL SONG AROSE FROM ALL THE THOUSAND THOUSAND SPIRITS	274	FOUR ZOAS 1	375
AND WITH IMMORTAL VOICE SOFT WARBLING FILL ALL EARTH & HEAVEN	274	FOUR ZOAS 1	381
HARROW BURN ALL THESE CORN FIELDS THROW DOWN ALL THESE FENCES	274	FOUR ZOAS 1	388

56

```
                                                             PAGE    TITLE        LINE
ALL    (CONTINUED)
     THAN ALL THESE LABOURS OF THE HARVEST & THE VINTAGE SEE    275 FOUR ZOAS 1       390
       THE RIVER
     CALL TO THY DARK ARMD HOSTS FOR ALL THE SONS OF MEN MUSTER 275 FOUR ZOAS 1       406
       TOGETHER
     THERE IS NO CITY NOR CORN FIELD NOR ORCHARD ALL IS ROCK    276 FOUR ZOAS 1       426
       & SAND
     FROM ALL THE TURNING WHEELS OF HEAVEN & THE CHARIOTS OF    276 FOUR ZOAS 1       441
       THE SLAIN
     HIS WEB IS LEFT ALL DESOLATE THAT HIS LITTLE ANXIOUS HEART 277 FOUR ZOAS 1       459
     AS ONE MAN ALL THE UNIVERSAL FAMILY & THAT ONE MAN   . . . 277 FOUR ZOAS 1       472
     ON ALL HER SONS & ON THY SONS O LUVAH & ON MINE       .  . 278 FOUR ZOAS 1       499
     THE PRINCE OF ALL THE HOSTS OF MEN NOR EQUAL KNOW IN HEAVEN 278 FOUR ZOAS 1      505
     GLOWD FURIOUS ON THE ANVIL PREPARD FOR SPADES & COULTERS   278 FOUR ZOAS 1       520
       ALL
     BUT URIZEN WITH DARKNESS OVERSPREADING ALL THE ARMIES   .  . 279 FOUR ZOAS 1     535
     RETREAT FROM THE FIERCE CONFLICT ALL THE SONS OF URIZEN    279 FOUR ZOAS 1       538
       AT ONCE
     SUDDEN DOWN FELL THEY ALL TOGETHER INTO AN UNKNOWN SPACE   279 FOUR ZOAS 1       541
     . . . SCATTERD INTO [ALL NATIONS] THE INDEFINITE  . . .  . 279 FOUR ZOAS 1       547
     HIS INWARD EYES CLOSING FROM THE DIVINE VISION & ALL   .  . 279 FOUR ZOAS 1      558
     [TILL ?FAR DISMAL XXX ?FOUR XXX ALL XXX]  .   .   .   .  . SUPP FOUR ZOAS 1     *
     AND ALL ITS GOLDEN PORCHES GREW PALE WITH HIS SICKENING    280 FOUR ZOAS 2        13
       LIGHT
     ALL RAVNING LIKE THE HUNGRY WORM & LIKE THE SILENT GRAVE   280 FOUR ZOAS 2        17
     PETRIFYING ALL THE HUMAN IMAGINATION INTO ROCK & SAND   .  . 281 FOUR ZOAS 2      38
     FROM ALBION'S LOINS FLED ALL PEOPLES AND NATIONS OF THE    281 FOUR ZOAS 2     *  43
       EARTH [FLED ]
     JERUSALEM CAME DOWN IN A DIRE RUIN OVER ALL THE EARTH   .  . 281 FOUR ZOAS 2      45
     THE FURNACES A TIME & TIMES ALL THE WHILE BLEW THE NORTH   282 FOUR ZOAS 2        68
     AND ALL THE WHILE THE PLOW OF IRON CUT THE DREADFUL FURROWS 282 FOUR ZOAS 2       70
     I OPEND ALL THE FLOODGATES OF THE HEAVENS TO QUENCH HER    282 FOUR ZOAS 2        90
       THIRST
     I LOVED HER I GAVE HER ALL MY SOUL & MY DELIGHT     .  .  . 282 FOUR ZOAS 2       94
     OF DEATH ETERNAL THAT WE ALL GO TO ETERNAL DEATH      .  . 282 FOUR ZOAS 2       101
     THAT HUMAN [TERROR] DELUSION TO DELIVER ALL THE SONS OF GOD 282 FOUR ZOAS 2      107
     WAS THIS WIDE EARTH SPREAD ALL ABROAD NOT FOR WILD BEASTS  283 FOUR ZOAS 2       125
       TO ROAM
     COMMANDING ALL THE WORK WITH CARE & POWER & SEVERITY    .  . 283 FOUR ZOAS 2     134
     AND ALL THE TIME IN CAVERNS SHUT THE GOLDEN LOOMS ERECTED  284 FOUR ZOAS 2       145
     PLIED THE WINGD SHUTTLE PIPING SHRILL THRO ALL THE LISTNING 284 FOUR ZOAS 2      147
       THREADS
     UNFOLDS THE WONDROUS SCAFFOLD REARD ALL ROUND THE INFINITE 284 FOUR ZOAS 2       167
     HE DRAVE THE MALE SPIRITS ALL AWAY FROM AHANIA     .  .  . 285 FOUR ZOAS 2       209
     AND SHE DRAVE ALL THE FEMALES FROM HIM AWAY      .   .   . 285 FOUR ZOAS 2       210
     AT ALL OUR SORROW WE ARE MADE TO TURN THE WHEEL FOR WATER  285 FOUR ZOAS 2       220
     [FROM ALL THE SORROW OF LUVAH & THE LABOUR OF URIZEN]   .  . 286 FOUR ZOAS 2     237
     . . . IMMOVEABLE WITHIN ITS [ARCHES ALL] WALLS & CIELINGS  286 FOUR ZOAS 2       245
     THEY WEIGHD & ORDERD ALL & URIZEN [?IN ?COMFORT SAW]    287 FOUR ZOAS 2     *     259
       COMFORTED SAW
     PERMITTED ALL LEST MAN SHOULD FALL INTO ETERNAL DEATH   .  . 287 FOUR ZOAS 2     262
     IN SEVENS & TENS & FIFTIES HUNDREDS THOUSANDS NUMBERD ALL  287 FOUR ZOAS 2       269
     IT RISES UP ON HIGH ALL SUMMER TILL ITS WEARIED COURSE  .  . 287 FOUR ZOAS 2     280
     THEN JEALOUSY SHALL SHADOW ALL HIS MOUNTAINS & AHANIA   .  . 289 FOUR ZOAS 2     338
     OF ALL THAT A MAN HATH HIS HOUSE HIS WIFE HIS CHILDREN  .  . 290 FOUR ZOAS 2  *  399
     [THOU SITST IN HARMONY FOR GOD HATH SET THEE OVER ALL]   .  . 291 FOUR ZOAS 3     10
     ALL THIS IS MINE YET I MUST SERVE & THAT PROPHETIC BOY  .  . 292 FOUR ZOAS 3      18
     . . . [& ALL MY KINGLY POWER] BUT HEAR MY DETERMIND DECREE 292 FOUR ZOAS 3       19
     LEAVE ALL FUTURITY TO HIM RESUME THY FIELDS OF LIGHT    .  . 292 FOUR ZOAS 3      30
     SOFT EXULTING IN EXISTENCE ALL THE MAN ABSORBING   .   .  . 293 FOUR ZOAS 3       53
     LIKE A DARK LAMP ETERNAL DEATH HAUNTS ALL MY EXPECTATION  293 FOUR ZOAS 3        75
     ALL IS CONFUSION ALL IS TUMULT & WE ALONE ARE ESCAPED   .  . 294 FOUR ZOAS 3     103
     REFLECTING ALL MY INDOLENCE MY WEAKNESS & MY DEATH    .  . 295 FOUR ZOAS 3       126
     A DOLOROUS GROAN THAT STRUCK WITH DUMBNESS ALL CONFUSION  295 FOUR ZOAS 3        147
     THAN ALL THE WRACKING ELEMENTS DEAFEND & RENDED WORSE   .  195 FOUR ZOAS 3       151
     THAN URIZEN & ALL HIS HOSTS IN CURST DESPAIR DOWN RUSHING  296 FOUR ZOAS 3       152
     IN ALL MY RIVERS & ON DRIED SHELLS THAT THE FISH   .   .  . 296 FOUR ZOAS 3      167
     A WORLD OF DEEP DARKNESS WHERE ALL THINGS IN HORRORS ARE   296 FOUR ZOAS 3       181
       ROOTED
     WHERE NEVER YET EXISTENCE CAME THERE LOSING ALL MY LIFE   296 FOUR ZOAS 3       189
     CONSUMING ALL TO THE END CONSUMING LOVE AND [JOY] HOPE    297 FOUR ZOAS 3       204
       ARE ENDED
     HOW IS THIS ALL MY HOPE IS GONE [ENION] FOR EVER FLED   .  . 297 FOUR ZOAS 4      9
     AND LOS REMAINS GOD OVER ALL WEAK FATHER OF WORMS & CLAY   298 FOUR ZOAS 4        41
     O HOW LOS HOWLD AT THE RENDING ASUNDER ALL THE FIBRES RENT 299 FOUR ZOAS 4        59
     BUILD HER A BOWER IN THE MIDST OF ALL MY DASHING WAVES  .  . 299 FOUR ZOAS 4      71
     THOU SHALT HAVE REST IF THOU REFUSEST DASHD ABROAD ON ALL  299 FOUR ZOAS 4        73
     BECOME A PREY TO ALL MY DEMONS OF DESPAIR & HOPE   .   .  . 299 FOUR ZOAS 4       75
     A TERROR TO ALL LIVING THINGS THINK NOT THAT I AM IGNORANT 299 FOUR ZOAS 4        82
     DREWST ALL THE SONS OF BEULAH INTO THY [GREAT] DREAD VORTEX 299 FOUR ZOAS 4       88
       FOLLOWING
     THY EDDYING SPIRIT DOWN THE HILLS OF BEULAH ALL MY SONS   300 FOUR ZOAS 4        89
     HEARING THE SYMPHONIES OF WAR LOUD SOUNDING ALL MY SONS   300 FOUR ZOAS 4        92
     LEST HE SHOULD RISE AGAIN FROM DEATH IN ALL HIS [DISMAL]   300 FOUR ZOAS 4  *    121
       DREARY POWER
     NOW ALL COMES INTO THE POWER OF THARMAS URIZEN IS FALLN    301 FOUR ZOAS 4       129
     YET THO I RAGE GOD OVER ALL A PORTION OF MY LIFE    .   .  . 301 FOUR ZOAS 4     137
     AND ALL THE ELEMENTS SHALL SERVE THEE TO THEIR SOOTHING    301 FOUR ZOAS 4       153
       FLUTES
     ROUND LOS AFAR HIS WATERS BORE ON ALL SIDES ROUND WITH     301 FOUR ZOAS 4       159
       NOISE
     AND FLUCTUATING ALL BENEATH IN EDDIES OF MOLTEN FLUID   .  . 301 FOUR ZOAS 4     164
```

57

ALL   (CONTINUED)
FREEZING TO SOLID ALL BENEATH HIS GREY OBLIVIOUS FORM . .   302 FOUR ZOAS 4   172
AND BONES OF SOLIDNESS FROZE OVER ALL HIS NERVES OF JOY   303 FOUR ZOAS 4   221
THE EMPYREAN GROAND THROUGHOUT ALL EDEN WAS DARKEND . . .   304 FOUR ZOAS 4   264
[AND THARMAS ?SAID ALL MY HOPE I THOUGHT ENION FOR EVER   SUPP FOUR ZOAS 4   *
   GONE]
[THEN ALL THE SPACE OF ?EMPYREAN ?PLAYD IN XXX SONG] . . SUPP FOUR ZOAS 4   *
AND ENITHARMON SHRUNK UP ALL THEIR FIBRES WITHRING BENEATH   305 FOUR ZOAS 5   8
BUT ALL THE FURNACES WERE OUT & THE BELLOWS HAD CEAST TO   305 FOUR ZOAS 5   17
   BLOW
CALL [VALAN] VALA FROM HER CLOSE RECESS IN ALL HER DARK   307 FOUR ZOAS 5   *   64
   DECEIT
HIS BOSOM IS LIKE STARRY HEAVEN EXPANDED ALL THE STARS . . 308 FOUR ZOAS 5   130
FELT ALL THE SORROW PARENTS FEEL THEY WEPT TOWARD   309 FOUR ZOAS 5   144
   ONE ANOTHER
NOR ALL URTHONA'S STRENGTH NOR ALL THE POWER OF LUVAH'S   309 FOUR ZOAS 5   164
   BULLS
RUBBING THEIR TEMPLES HE REVIVD THEM ALL THEIR LAMENTATIONS 309 FOUR ZOAS 5   174
I WRITE NOT HERE BUT ALL THEIR AFTER LIFE WAS LAMENTATION   309 FOUR ZOAS 5   175
AND DARKEN ALL MY PALACE WALLS WITH ENVYINGS & HATE . . .   310 FOUR ZOAS 5   213
[AROUND THE ABYSS (DEFIANTLY) ?SHOUTING ALL HIS DEMONS]   SUPP FOUR ZOAS 5   *
DRAWS ALL INTO A FOUNTAIN AT THE ROCK OF THY ATTRACTION   312 FOUR ZOAS 6   14
THEY POURD THEIR RADIANCE ABOVE ALL THE DAUGHTERS OF LUVAH   312 FOUR ZOAS 6   33
   ENVIED
FROM THEE THY FOOD SO SHALL WE CEASE TO BE & ALL   313 FOUR ZOAS 6   65
   OUR SORROWS
THE EVER PITYING ONE WHO SEETH ALL THINGS SAW HIS FALL . . 316 FOUR ZOAS 6   157
FROM WHENCE HE CAME TWAS UPWARD ALL & IF HE TURND AND VIEWD 316 FOUR ZOAS 6   192
WHERE SELF SUSTAINING I MAY VIEW ALL THING BENEATH MY FEET   317 FOUR ZOAS 6   198
TIS UPWARD ALL WHICH WAY SOEVER I MY COURSE BEGIN . . .   317 FOUR ZOAS 6   203
AND WEARINESS BEGINS ON ALL MY LIMBS THEN SLEEP REVIVES   317 FOUR ZOAS 6   205
MY WEARIED SPIRITS WAKING THEN TIS DOWNWARD ALL WHICH WAY   317 FOUR ZOAS 6   206
SO EVER I MY SPIRITS TURN NO END I FIND OF ALL . . .   317 FOUR ZOAS 6   207
THOU HORRIBLE RUIN ONCE LIKE ME THOU WAST ALL GLORIOUS . . 317 FOUR ZOAS 6   210
OF ALL & ALL FUTURITY BE BOUND IN HIS VAST CHAIN . . .   317 FOUR ZOAS 6   233
ON ALL THE SONS OF MEN & EVERY HUMAN SOUL TERRIFIED . . .   317 FOUR ZOAS 6   235
GAINING A NEW DOMINION OVER ALL HIS SONS & DAUGHTERS . . .   317 FOUR ZOAS 6   237
AND THE WING LIKE TENT OF THE UNIVERSE BEAUTIFUL   318 FOUR ZOAS 6   254
   SURROUNDING ALL
ALL THRO THE CAVERNS OF FIRE & AIR & EARTH SEEKING . . .   318 FOUR ZOAS 6   272
ABOVE BENEATH ON ALL SIDES ROUND IN THE VAST DEEP   318 FOUR ZOAS 6   275
   OF IMMENSITY
ALL THESE AROUND THE WORLD OF LOS CAST FORTH THEIR   318 FOUR ZOAS 6   278
   MONSTROUS BIRTHS
REVOLVING ROUND IN WHIRLPOOLS FIERCE ALL ROUND THE CAVERND 320 FOUR ZOAS 7   4
   WORLDS
THE HOLY OIL RAGES THRO ALL THE CAVERND ROCKS FIERCE FLAMES 320 FOUR ZOAS 7   12
HIS BOOKS OUT OF THE DISMAL SHADE ALL BUT THE BOOK OF IRON   321 FOUR ZOAS 7   39
IN ALL THIS CHASM I BEHOLD NO OTHER LIVING THING . . .   321 FOUR ZOAS 7   46
YET THOU DOST LAUGH AT ALL THESE TORTURES & THIS HORRIBLE   321 FOUR ZOAS 7   59
   PLACE
AND DIM OBLIVION OF ALL WOE & DESPERATE REPOSE . . . .   321 FOUR ZOAS 7   67
IN ALL THE DISEASES OF MAN FALLING UPON THY GREY ACCURSED   322 FOUR ZOAS 7   89
   FRONT
OF ALL THIS DREADFUL RUIN RISE O DAUGHTERS AT MY STERN   322 FOUR ZOAS 7   94
   COMMAND
SO SHALL (?YOU) GOVERN OVER ALL LET MORAL DUTY TUNE YOUR   323 FOUR ZOAS 7   * 111
   TONGUE
IN STRONG DRINK THO YOU KNOW THAT BREAD & WATER ARE ALL   323 FOUR ZOAS 7   127
REDUCE ALL TO OUR WILL AS SPANIELS ARE TAUGHT WITH ART . . 323 FOUR ZOAS 7   129
LOS WITH AMBITIOUS FURY THAT HIS RACE SHALL ALL DEVOUR . . 323 FOUR ZOAS 7   134
THOU WILT NOT CEASE FROM RAGE GREY DEMON SILENCE ALL THY   323 FOUR ZOAS 7   144
   STORMS
OF ALL HIS WANDERING EXPERIMENTS IN THE HORRIBLE ABYSS . . 324 FOUR ZOAS 7   160
HE SUFFERD HIM TO CLIMB THAT HE MIGHT DRAW ALL HUMAN FORMS   324 FOUR ZOAS 7   164
[SHE SAID I AM AVENGD FOR ALL MY SUFFERINGS OF OLD] . . .   324 FOUR ZOAS 7   178
ALL THINGS BESIDE THE WOFUL LOS ENJOY THE DELIGHTS   325 FOUR ZOAS 7   198
   OF BEAUTY
ALL HEAVEN THEY SAW HIM DARK THEY BUILT A GOLDEN WALL . .   326 FOUR ZOAS 7   242
FROM ITS HINGES UTTERING ITS FINAL GROAN ALL BEULAH FELL   326 FOUR ZOAS 7   258
OPENING ITS GATES & IN IT ALL THE REAL SUBSTANCES . . .   329 FOUR ZOAS 7   365
ALL THINGS SUBSIST ON ONE ANOTHER THENCEFORTH IN DESPAIR   330 FOUR ZOAS 7   391
I ALSO TREMBLE AT MYSELF & AT ALL MY FORMER LIFE . . . .   330 FOUR ZOAS 7   423
OF EXISTENCE TO BE A SIGN & TERROR TO ALL WHO BEHOLD . .   331 FOUR ZOAS 7   429
THY WORKS ARE ALL MY JOY & IN THY FIRES MY SOUL DELIGHTS   331 FOUR ZOAS 7   448
THE TIME OF PROPHECY IS NOW REVOLVD & ALL . . . . .   333 FOUR ZOAS 7B   4
AND ALL THE SONS OF ?EVERLASTING SHALL BOW DOWN AT MY FEET   333 FOUR ZOAS 7B   10
OF DIRE NECESSITY STILL LABORING DAY & NIGHT TILL ALL . .   333 FOUR ZOAS 7B   14
AND URIZEN LAID THE FIRST STONE & ALL HIS MYRIADS . . .   333 FOUR ZOAS 7B   19
THEY FORMD THE SECRET PLACE REVERSING ALL THE ORDER OF   333 FOUR ZOAS 7B   22
   DELIGHT
ALL NIGHT AMONG THE SLAIN & MOCK THE WOUNDED THAT GROAN   334 FOUR ZOAS 7B   48
   IN THE FIELD
CRYING AS I WILL I REND THE NATIONS ALL ASUNDER RENDING   334 FOUR ZOAS 7B   50
AND I WILL GIVE THEE ALL THE ENDS OF HEAVEN FOR THY   334 FOUR ZOAS 7B   56
   POSSESSION
IN SIGHS & SOBBINGS [TILL] ALL DIVIDING TILL I WAS DIVIDED   334 FOUR ZOAS 7B   * 64
BEAT ROUND HER HEAD ALL NIGHT ALL DAY SHE RIOTS IN EXCESS   334 FOUR ZOAS 7B   74
THRO ALL THE HEAVENS URIZEN'S WEB VIBRATED TORMENT   336 FOUR ZOAS 7B   122
   ON TORMENT
WHEN ALL THE ELEMENTAL GODS JOIND IN THE WONDROUS SONG . . 336 FOUR ZOAS 7B   146
THE ARROWS FLEW FROM CLOUDY BOW ALL DAY TILL BLOOD . . .   337 FOUR ZOAS 7B   159

	PAGE	TITLE		LINE

ALL   (CONTINUED)

AND ALL THE ARTS OF LIFE THEY CHANGD INTO THE ARTS OF   337 FOUR ZOAS 7B   174
    DEATH
IN IGNORANCE TO VIEW A SMALL PORTION & THINK THAT ALL . .   337 FOUR ZOAS 7B   185
AND CALL IT DEMONSTRATION BLIND TO ALL THE SIMPLE RULES   337 FOUR ZOAS 7B   186
    OF LIFE
NOW SMILE AMONG THY BITTER TEARS NOW PUT ON ALL THY BEAUTY   337 FOUR ZOAS 7B   188
REMEMBER ALL THY FEIGNED TERRORS ON THE SECRET COUCH   . .   338 FOUR ZOAS 7B   196
SHE JOYD IN ALL THE CONFLICT . . . .   338 FOUR ZOAS 7B   213
AMONG THE APPLE TREES & ALL THE GARDENS OF DELIGHT   . . .   339 FOUR ZOAS 7B *   234
I HEAR THY VOICE BUT NOT THY FORM SEE THOU & ALL DELIGHT   339 FOUR ZOAS 7B   240
HAST THOU FORGOT THAT THE AIR LISTENS THRO ALL ITS   339 FOUR ZOAS 7B   242
    DISTRICTS TELLING
AND WHENCE THEY NEVER CAN BE BROUGHT IN ALL ETERNITY   . .   339 FOUR ZOAS 7B   245
IS HIDDEN FROM ME & I NEVER IN ALL ETERNITY   . . . . .   339 FOUR ZOAS 7B   247
FOR ALL MY SECRET FAULTS WHICH HE BRINGS FORTH UPON THE   339 FOUR ZOAS 7B   250
    LIGHT
HOWLING IN ALL THE NOTES OF WOE TO STAY HIS FURIOUS RAGE   339 FOUR ZOAS 7B   262
THO ALL THOSE FAIR PERFECTIONS WHICH MEN KNOW ONLY BY NAME   340 FOUR ZOAS 7B   274
FOR FAR & WIDE SHE STRETCHD THRO ALL THE WORLDS OF URIZEN'S   340 FOUR ZOAS 7B   288
    JOURNEY
THEY WROTE ON ALL THEIR TOMBS & PILLARS & ON EVERY URN   340 FOUR ZOAS 7B   292
AND ALL THE SONGS OF BEULAH SOUNDED COMFORTABLE NOTES   . . 340 FOUR ZOAS 7B   296
THEN ALL IN GREAT ETERNITY [WHICH IS CALLED] . . . . .   341 FOUR ZOAS 8   1
SUCH IS A VISION OF ALL BEULAH HOVRING OVER THE SLEEPER   341 FOUR ZOAS 8   15
ALL BEULAH STOOD ASTONISHD LOOKING DOWN TO ETERNAL DEATH   342 FOUR ZOAS 8   47
SURROUNDING THEM ON ALL SIDES BEYOND SIN & DEATH & HELL   342 FOUR ZOAS 8   51
SHE SPREAD HERSELF THRO ALL THE BRANCHES IN THE POWER OF   343 FOUR ZOAS 8   85
    ORC
AND WHEN ALL THINGS WERE FINISHD . . . .   343 FOUR ZOAS 8   87
AND ALL THE HOLLOW DEEP REBELLOWD WITH THE WONDEROUS WAR   343 FOUR ZOAS 8 *   89
AND CHAINS & PULLIES FABRICATED ALL ROUND THE HEAVENS OF   343 FOUR ZOAS 8   95
    LOS
TO THE FOUR WINDS HOPELESS OF FUTURE ALL FUTURITY   . . .   343 FOUR ZOAS 8   99
TO ALL HIS ENGINES OF DECEIT THAT LINKED CHAINS MIGHT RUN   344 FOUR ZOAS 8   132
THE SPIRITS OF LIFE TO PERVERT ALL THE FACULTIES OF SENSE   344 FOUR ZOAS 8   137
MY LUVAH THEN COULD I DELIVER ALL THE SONS OF GOD   . . .   345 FOUR ZOAS 8   157
WE ARE ALL SERVANTS TO THY WILL O KING OF LIGHT RELENT   .   345 FOUR ZOAS 8   162
SHE SPREAD HERSELF THRO ALL THE BRANCHES IN THE POWER OF   345 FOUR ZOAS 8   174
    ORC
FROM HEAVEN TO HEAVN THRO ALL ITS MESHES ALTERING   345 FOUR ZOAS 8   177
    THE VORTEXES
BUT [ALL] THOU O UNIVERSAL HUMANITY WHO IS ONE MAN BLESSED   347 FOUR ZOAS 8   232
    FOR EVER
THE VICTIMS FLED FROM PUNISHMENT FOR ALL HIS WORDS WERE   348 FOUR ZOAS 8   271
    PEACE
EPHRAIM WAS A WILDERNESS OF JOY WHERE ALL MY WILD BEASTS   349 FOUR ZOAS 8   309
    RAN
BEARING HIS SORROWS & (?RECIEVING) ALL HIS CRUEL WOUNDS   349 FOUR ZOAS 8 *   324
DEATH GOD OF ALL FROM WHOM WE RISE TO WHOM WE ALL RETURN   349 FOUR ZOAS 8   335
AND LET ALL NATIONS [IN] OF THE EARTH WORSHIP AT   349 FOUR ZOAS 8 *   336
    THE SEPULCHER
THE LAMB OF GOD IT ROLLD APART REVEALING TO ALL IN HEAVEN   350 FOUR ZOAS 8   342
AND ALL ON EARTH THE TEMPLE & THE SYNAGOGUE OF SATAN &   350 FOUR ZOAS 8   343
    MYSTERY
EVEN RAHAB IN ALL HER TURPITUDE RAHAB DIVIDED HERSELF   . . 350 FOUR ZOAS 8   344
THE STATE NAMD SATAN NEVER CAN BE REDEEMD IN ALL ETERNITY   351 FOUR ZOAS 8   381
SHE TENDERLY LOVD HIM ABOVE ALL HIS BRETHREN HE GREW UP   351 FOUR ZOAS 8   385
MUST HAVE GIVEN SATAN BY THESE MILD ARTS DOMINION OVER ALL   351 FOUR ZOAS 8   387
DARKNESS & SORROW COVERD ALL FLESH ETERNITY WAS DARKEND   351 FOUR ZOAS 8   414
HIS WISDOM STILL REMAIND & ALL HIS MEMORY STORD WITH WOE   352 FOUR ZOAS 8   431
ARISING IN HIS PRIDE ENLIGHTEN ALL THE GRIZLY DEEPS   . . . 352 FOUR ZOAS 8   440
AMONG THE STARS THE EARTH & ALL THE ABYSSES FEEL ?HIS FURY   352 FOUR ZOAS 8 *   448
THEN WEEPING HE DESCENDS IN WRATH DRAWING ALL THINGS IN   353 FOUR ZOAS 8   456
    HIS FURY
REPINING IN HIS HEART & SPIRIT THAT ORC REIGND OVER ALL   353 FOUR ZOAS 8   465
THUS IN A LIVING DEATH THE NAMELESS SHADOW ALL THINGS BOUND   353 FOUR ZOAS 8   481
ALL MORTAL THINGS MADE PERMANENT THAT THEY MAY BE PUT OFF   353 FOUR ZOAS 8   482
TIME AFTER TIME BY THE DIVINE LAMB WHO DIED FOR ALL   . .   353 FOUR ZOAS 8   483
AND ALL IN HIM DIES & HE PUT OFF ALL MORTALITY   . . . .   353 FOUR ZOAS 8   484
THE VOICE INCESSANT CALLS ON ALL THE CHILDREN OF MEN   . .   353 FOUR ZOAS 8   489
FOR SHE SPOKE OF ALL IN HEAVEN & ALL UPON THE EARTH   . .   353 FOUR ZOAS 8   490
AND A FOUNTAIN FROM MY BREASTS TO ME COME ALL MULTITUDES   354 FOUR ZOAS 8   501
NOR SILENT MOON NOR ALL THE HOSTS OF HEAVEN MOVE IN HIS   354 FOUR ZOAS 8   508
    BODY
FEAST ON HIS DEATH TILL UNIVERSAL DEATH DEVOURS ALL   . .   354 FOUR ZOAS 8   528
MORE HAPPY IS THE DARK CONSUMER HOPE DROWNS ALL MY TORMENT   355 FOUR ZOAS 8   544
OF ALL BENEATH & ALL ABOVE & IN THE GENTLE WEST   . . . .   355 FOUR ZOAS 8   569
AND ALL HIS SORROWS TILL HE REASSUMES HIS ANCIENT BLISS   356 FOUR ZOAS 8   583
RAHAB TRIUMPHS OVER ALL SHE TOOK JERUSALEM . . . . . .   356 FOUR ZOAS 8   597
FOR GOD PUT IT INTO THEIR HEART TO FULFILL ALL HIS WILL   357 FOUR ZOAS 8   617
[HE IS THE (SHEPHERD) OF ALBION HE IS ALL IN ALL]   . . .   SUPP FOUR ZOAS 8 *
ISSUD ON ALL SIDES GATHRING STRENGTH IN ANIMATING VOLUMES   358 FOUR ZOAS 9 *   35
ROAMING ABROAD ON ALL THE WINDS RAGING INTENSE REDDENING   358 FOUR ZOAS 9   36
STRENGTH FROM THE EARTHS CONSUMD & HEAVENS & ALL HIDDEN   358 FOUR ZOAS 9 *   38
    ABYSSES
AND ALL THE WHILE THE TRUMPET SOUNDS [AWAKE YE DEAD & COME]   358 FOUR ZOAS 9   42
AND ALL THE SONS OF ETERNITY DESCENDED INTO BEULAH   . . .   359 FOUR ZOAS 9   66
OF FOAMING BLOOD BENEATH THE BLACK INCESSANT SKY TILL ALL   359 FOUR ZOAS 9   78
AND WHEN ALL TYRANNY WAS CUT OFF FROM THE FACE OF EARTH   359 FOUR ZOAS 9 *   80
AND ALL EXILED FROM THE FACE OF LIGHT & SHINE OF MORNING   360 FOUR ZOAS 9   112
O WEARY LIFE WHY SIT I HERE & GIVE UP ALL MY POWERS   . . . 360 FOUR ZOAS 9   116

		PAGE	TITLE	LINE
ALL	(CONTINUED)			
	AND ALL THY SONS & DAUGHTERS GATHERD ROUND MY AMPLE TABLE	360	FOUR ZOAS 9	127
	SEE YOU NOT ALL THIS WRACKING FURIOUS CONFUSION	360	FOUR ZOAS 9	128
	THY CROWN & SCEPTER I WILL SIEZE & REGULATE ALL MY MEMBERS	360	FOUR ZOAS 9	145
	ERROR CAN NEVER BE REDEEMD IN ALL ETERNITY	361	FOUR ZOAS 9 *	158
	UNGRATIFIED GIVE ALL MY JOY INTO THIS LUVAH & VALA . . .	361	FOUR ZOAS 9 *	179
	ALL STRENGTH TO LOS & ENITHARMON & LET LOS SELF CURSD . .	362	FOUR ZOAS 9	185
	THE TIMES REVOLVE THE TIME IS COMING WHEN ALL THESE DELIGHTS	362	FOUR ZOAS 9	208
	SHALL BE RENEWD & ALL THESE ELEMENTS THAT NOW CONSUME . .	362	FOUR ZOAS 9	209
	IMMORTAL THOU REGENERATE SHE & ALL THE LOVELY SEX . . .	362	FOUR ZOAS 9	216
	ALL THINGS REVERSD FLEW FROM THEIR CENTERS RATTLING BONES [TO BONES]	363	FOUR ZOAS 9	231
	ALL SPIRITS DECEASD LET LOOSE FROM REPTILE PRISONS COME IN SHOALS	363	FOUR ZOAS 9	235
	AND ALL THE MARKS REMAIN OF THE SLAVE'S SCOURGE & TYRANT'S CROWN	363	FOUR ZOAS 9	246
	ALL NATIONS LOOK UP TO THE CLOUD & BEHOLD HIM WHO WAS CRUCIFIED	364	FOUR ZOAS 9	274
	INCOMPREHENSIBLE PERVADING ALL AMIDST & ROUND ABOUT . . .	364	FOUR ZOAS 9	282
	FROM RUST OF AGES ALL ITS ORNAMENTS OF GOLD & SILVER & IVORY	364	FOUR ZOAS 9	292
	RESHONE ACROSS THE FIELD IMMENSE WHERE ALL THE NATIONS . .	364	FOUR ZOAS 9	293
	AND ALL THEIR VILLAGES OVER MOUNTAINS & ALL THEIR VALLIES	365	FOUR ZOAS 9	313
	THE TREMBLING SOULS OF ALL THE DEAD STOOD BEFORE URIZEN	365	FOUR ZOAS 9	317
	AND ALL THE WHILE THE FLAMES OF ORC FOLLOW THE VENTROUS FEET	365	FOUR ZOAS 9	330
	OF URIZEN & ALL THE WHILE THE TRUMP OF THARMAS SOUNDS . .	365	FOUR ZOAS 9	331
	THEN URIZEN SITS DOWN TO REST & ALL HIS WEARIED SONS . .	366	FOUR ZOAS 9	340
	A TIME THEY GIVE TO SWEET REPOSE TILL ALL THE HARVEST IS RIPE	366	FOUR ZOAS 9	343
	EXPENDING ALL HIS ENERGY AGAINST THE FUEL OF FIRE . . .	366	FOUR ZOAS 9	359
	THEY HEARD NOT SAW NOT FELT NOT ALL THE TERRIBLE CONFUSION	367	FOUR ZOAS 9	381
	BENEATH HER ROSE A DOWNY BED & A CIELING COVERD ALL . . .	369	FOUR ZOAS 9	463
	AND DARKNESS COVERD ALL THE DEEP THE LIGHT OF ENION FADED	370	FOUR ZOAS 9	496
	ENLIGHTEN ALL THE CRYSTAL HOUSE OF VALA AWAKE AWAKE . . .	371	FOUR ZOAS 9	520
	HE SAID O VALA I AM SICK & ALL THIS GARDEN OF PLEASURE . .	371	FOUR ZOAS 9	538
	DARKNESS WAS ALL BENEATH THE HEAVENS ONLY A LITTLE LIGHT	372	FOUR ZOAS 9	560
	THRO ALL THE IMMENSE BORNE DOWN BY CLOUDS SWAGGING IN AUTUMNAL HEAT	372	FOUR ZOAS 9	563
	DOWN POUR THE TORRENT FLOODS OF HEAVEN ON ALL THE HUMAN HARVEST	372	FOUR ZOAS 9	566
	HE POURD HIS LIGHT & ALL HIS SONS & DAUGHTERS POURD THEIR LIGHT	372	FOUR ZOAS 9	569
	IN ALL THEIR ANCIENT INNOCENCE THE FLOODS DEPART THE CLOUDS	372	FOUR ZOAS 9	572
	AND WENT FORTH & BEGAN TO REAP & ALL HIS JOYFUL SONS . .	372	FOUR ZOAS 9	583
	WAS SERVD ROUND BY THE FLAMES OF LUVAH ALL DAY & ALL THE NIGHT	372	FOUR ZOAS 9	589
	AND ALL THE BLACK MOULD SINGS SHE SPEAKS TO HER INFANT RACE HER MILK	373	FOUR ZOAS 9	601
	JOY THRILLD THRO ALL THE FURIOUS FORM OF THARMAS HUMANIZING	373	FOUR ZOAS 9 *	613
	WAS SERVD ROUND BY THE FLAMES OF LUVAH ALL DAY & ALL THE NIGHT	373	FOUR ZOAS 9	620
	. . . BUT BORN TO DRINK UP ALL HIS POWERS	373	FOUR ZOAS 9	623
	AND ONE OF THE ETERNALS SPOKE ALL WAS SILENT AT THE FEAST	374	FOUR ZOAS 9	626
	AND HEARTHS PROTECT THE SELFISH TERROR TILL DIVIDED ALL	374	FOUR ZOAS 9	636
	SOUNDS ON THE FLOOR HEARD TERRIBLE BY ALL BENEATH THE HEAVENS	374	FOUR ZOAS 9	651
	AND ALL NATIONS WERE THRESHED OUT	374	FOUR ZOAS 9	653
	WHERE SHALL THE GRAVES RECIEVE THEM ALL & WHERE SHALL BE THEIR PLACE	375	FOUR ZOAS 9	668
	THE GOOD OF ALL THE LAND IS BEFORE YOU FOR MYSTERY IS NO MORE	375	FOUR ZOAS 9	681
	THEN ALL THE SLAVES FROM EVERY EARTH IN THE WIDE UNIVERSE	375	FOUR ZOAS 9	682
	AND ALL THY SONS O LUVAH BEAR AWAY THE FAMILIES OF EARTH	375	FOUR ZOAS 9	695
	THEN LUVAH STOOD BEFORE THE WINE PRESS ALL HIS FIERY SONS	376	FOUR ZOAS 9	716
	TO THE GOLDEN WHEELS CIRCLING UPON THE PAVEMENT OF HEAVEN & ALL	376	FOUR ZOAS 9	719
	ALL ROUND THE HEAVENLY ARCHES & THE ODORS ROSE SINGING THIS SONG	376	FOUR ZOAS 9	727
	. . . THERE ALL THE IDLE WEEDS	377	FOUR ZOAS 9	764
	NAKED IN ALL THEIR BEAUTY DANCING ROUND THE WINE PRESSES	377	FOUR ZOAS 9	766
	RANG SWEET THE PRAISE OF INDUSTRY THRO ALL THE GOLDEN ROOMS	378	FOUR ZOAS 9	781
	HEAVEN RANG WITH WINGED EXULTATION ALL BENEATH HOWLD LOUD	378	FOUR ZOAS 9	782
	OF GLASS & PRECIOUS STONES THEY LOADED ALL THE WAGGONS OF HEAVEN	378	FOUR ZOAS 9	793
	LUVAH & VALA WOKE & ALL THE SONS & DAUGHTERS OF LUVAH . .	378	FOUR ZOAS 9	795
	BUT THE HUMAN WINE STOOD WONDERING IN ALL THEIR DELIGHTFUL EXPANSES	378	FOUR ZOAS 9	799
	THEN LOS WHO IS URTHONA ROSE IN ALL HIS REGENERATE POWER	378	FOUR ZOAS 9	801
	VOMITED OUT & GAVE UP ALL THE FLOODS LIFT UP THEIR HANDS	378	FOUR ZOAS 9	803
	OF ALL THE NATIONS OF EARTH GROUND IN THE MILLS OF URTHONA	378	FOUR ZOAS 9	808
	AND MAN WALKS FORTH FROM MIDST OF THE FIRES THE EVIL IS ALL CONSUMD	379	FOUR ZOAS 9	827
	HOW IS IT THAT ALL THINGS CHANGD EVEN AS IN ANCIENT TIMES	379	FOUR ZOAS 9	845
	IN ALL HIS ANCIENT STRENGTH TO FORM THE GOLDEN ARMOUR OF SCIENCE	379	FOUR ZOAS 9	853
	TO LOVE DEVOTED FEMALE ALL ASTONISHD STOOD THE HOSTS . .	380	FOUR ZOAS AD 1	13
	FROM ENION POURS THE SEED OF LIFE & DEATH IN ALL HER LIMBS	381	FOUR ZOAS AD 4	1
	. . . ALL HIS [LOVELY CHANGING] DARKLY WAVING COLOURS MIX	381	FOUR ZOAS AD 5	4
	BEAUTY ALL BLUSHING WITH DESIRE A SELF ENJOYING WONDER . .	381	FOUR ZOAS AD 5	9

```
                                                        PAGE    TITLE       LINE
ALL    (CONTINUED)
     THE VICTIMS FLED FROM PUNISHMENT [THAT] FOR ALL HIS WORDS   382 FOUR ZOAS AD 6      4
        WERE PEACE
     . . . ALL THE SYNAGOGUE OF SATAN IN DARK SANHEDRIM  . . .   382 FOUR ZOAS AD 6      5
     IN ALL ITS TURPITUDE BENEATH THE DIVINE LIGHT & OF LUVAH'S  382 FOUR ZOAS AD 6     22
        ROBES
     DARKNESS & SORROW COVERD ALL FLESH ETERNITY WAS DARKEND     382 FOUR ZOAS AD 6     30
     ("ALL CHRISTIAN STATES") PAINE HAS NOT ATTACKED            383D ANNO WATSON      MARG
        CHRISTIANITY
     NEVER READ ONE THAT IS TO ME IT IS ALL DAGGERS & POISON    384C ANNO WATSON      MARG
     ALL MEN & WAS THEIR FATHER & FORBAD ALL CONTENTION  . . .  387B ANNO WATSON      MARG
     THE POSSIBILITY OF HUMAN BEASTLINESS IN ALL ITS BRANCHES   387C ANNO WATSON      MARG
     LET ALL THEIR WORKS WITNESS  . . . . . . . . . .           388D ANNO WATSON      MARG
     THAT THE BIBLE IS ALL A STATE TRICK  . . . . . . .         390C ANNO WATSON      MARG
     THRO WHICH THO THE PEOPLE AT ALL TIMES COULD SEE  . .      390C ANNO WATSON      MARG
     ANOTHER ARGUMENT IS THAT ALL THE COMMENTATORS  . . .       390C ANNO WATSON      MARG
     OVERTHROW ALL THE ARMIES OF EUROPE WITH A SMALL PAMPHLET   391C ANNO WATSON      MARG
     ALL FALSE IN THE EYES OF ONE MAN & TRUE IN THE EYES OF     393B ANNO WATSON      MARG
     TO ALL & EQUALLY PLAIN TO ALL NONE CAN DOUBT  . . . .      393B ANNO WATSON      MARG
     ALL PENAL LAWS COURT TRANSGRESSION & THEREFORE ARE CRUELTY 393C ANNO WATSON      MARG
        &
     ALL OTHER CODES GIVEN UNDER PRETENCE OF DIVINE COMMAND     393C ANNO WATSON      MARG
     I E STATE RELIGION WHICH IS THE SOURCE OF ALL CRUELTY  . . 393D ANNO WATSON      MARG
     OF ALL THE WRITINGS OF THE NEW TESTAMENT  . . . . .        394B ANNO WATSON      MARG
     WORSHIPD IN THIS WORLD AS GOD & SET ABOVE ALL THAT IS CALLD 394C ANNO WATSON     MARG
        GOD
     FOR WHO IS REALLY RIGHTEOUS IT IS ALL PRETENSION  . . .    396B ANNO WATSON      MARG
     & ALL MEN OF SENSE HAVE DESPISED THE BOOK AS MUCH AS I DO  397A ANNO BACON       MARG
     BACON SUPPOSES ALL MEN ALIKE  . . . . . . . . .            398C ANNO BACON       MARG
     WHEN IT IS FOUND REVERENCE IS ALL FOR REVERENCE  . . .     401D ANNO BACON       MARG
     A TYRANT IS THE WORST DISEASE & THE CAUSE OF ALL OTHERS    402B ANNO BACON       MARG
     ALL FALSE  . . . . . . . . . . . . . . . .                 402C ANNO BACON       MARG
     HE DID NOT PERHAPS DISBELIEVE FOR ALL THAT BACON DID       403C ANNO BACON       MARG
     ATHEISM IS THUS THE BEST OF ALL BACON FOOLS US  . . .      404B ANNO BACON       MARG
     ARE ALL THE TRUMPERY HE COULD RAKE TOGETHER  . . . .       404D ANNO BACON       MARG
     BACON HATED TALENTS OF ALL KINDS ELOQUENCE IS DISCRETION   409A ANNO BACON       MARG
        OF SPEECH
     FALSE ALL POETRY GIVES THE LIE TO THIS  . . . . .          411C ANNO BOYD        MARG
     THEY ARE ALL GREATER VILLAINS THAN THE IMPERFECT  . .      412A ANNO BOYD        MARG
     HOW VERY FOOLISH ALL THIS IS  . . . . . . . . .            413C ANNO BOYD        MARG
     [DRIVING ALL MY LOVES AWAY]  . . . . . . . . .             415 MY SPECTRE/N        22
     FILL WITH TEMPESTS ALL MY MORN  . . . . . . . .            416 MY SPECTRE/N        32
     PITYING & FORGIVING ALL  . . . . . . . . . .               416 MY SPECTRE/N        45
     & THROUGHOUT ALL ETERNITY  . . . . . . . . .               417 MY SPECTRE/N        71
     MOCK ON MOCK ON TIS ALL IN VAIN  . . . . . . .             418 MOCK ON/N            2
     HE TOLD ME THAT ALL I WROTE SHOULD PROVE  . . . .          419 I SAW A MONK/N      30
     THE BANE OF ALL THAT ON EARTH I LOVE  . . . . .            419 I SAW A MONK/N      31
     MELTED ALL MY SOUL AWAY  . . . . . . . . . .               422 BENEATH/N           17
     THERES AN END TO ALL MISERY  . . . . . . . . .             424 THE SMILE           16
     MELTED ALL MY SOUL AWAY  . . . . . . . . . .               424 THE GOLDEN NET      16
     HE PLANTS HIMSELF IN ALL HER NERVES  . . . . . .           425 MENTAL TRAVLER      25
     FULL FILLED ALL WITH GEMS & GOLD  . . . . . . .            425 MENTAL TRAVLER      31
     AND SHE IS ALL OF SOLID FIRE  . . . . . . . .              425 MENTAL TRAVLER      45
     FOR THE EYE ALTERING ALTERS ALL  . . . . . . .            426 MENTAL TRAVLER      62
     THE STARS SUN MOON ALL SHRINK AWAY  . . . . . .            426 MENTAL TRAVLER      65
     AND A DARK DESART ALL AROUND  . . . . . . . .              426 MENTAL TRAVLER      68
     TO ALL WHO IN THE DESART ROAM  . . . . . . . .             427 MENTAL TRAVLER      90
     LIONS BOARS WOLVES ALL HOWLING FLEE  . . . . . .           427 MENTAL TRAVLER      99
     AND ALL IS DONE AS I HAVE TOLD  . . . . . . . .            427 MENTAL TRAVLER     104
     HAVE WANDERD ALL NIGHT IN THE LAND OF DREAMS  . . . .      427 LAND OF DREAMS      14
     TO AUGMENT WITH SWEET SMILES ALL THE JOYS OF THE NIGHT . . 428 MARY                10
     A DAMP COLD CAME OER HER HER BLUSHES ALL FLED  . . . .     428 MARY                19
     ALL FACES HAVE ENVY SWEET MARY BUT THINE  . . . . .        429 MARY                44
     THE BANE OF ALL THAT ON EARTH I LOVD  . . . . . .          430 GREY MONK           16
     PUTS ALL HEAVEN IN A RAGE  . . . . . . . . .               431 AUGURIES             6
     SHUDDERS HELL THRO ALL ITS REGIONS  . . . . . .            431 AUGURIES             8
     BEATS ALL THE LIES YOU CAN INVENT  . . . . . .             432 AUGURIES            54
     THROUGHOUT ALL THESE HUMAN LANDS  . . . . . . .            432 AUGURIES            64
     THAN ALL THE GOLD ON AFRIC'S SHORE  . . . . . .            432 AUGURIES            80
     BUT ALL HE COULD DO HE GREW THINNER & THINNER  . . . .     434 LONG JOHN BRWN      11
     DOWN THE ROAD & ALL THE WHILE WE WERE AT THE STABLE DOOR  437B BLAKES MEMORAN   PROSE
     ALL HE DID WAS SWEARING AND THREATENING  . . . . . . .    437B BLAKES MEMORAN   PROSE
     (DAMN) THE (KING) NOW I HAVE ALL THE PERSONS WHO WERE  .  437C BLAKES MEMORAN   PROSE
     IT IS NECESSARY TO LEARN THE NAMES OF ALL THAT WERE PRESENT 438B BLAKES MEMORAN PROSE
     ALL THE PERSONS PRESENT AT THE STABLE DOOR WERE  . . .    438B BLAKES MEMORAN   PROSE
     MRS GRINDER AND HER DAUGHTER ALL THE TIME  . . . . .      438B BLAKES MEMORAN   PROSE
     MRS HAYNES & HER DAUGHTER ALL THE TIME MR GRINDER  . . .  438B BLAKES MEMORAN   PROSE
     ALL THE REST OF THE TIME WHAT PASSED IN THE GARDEN THERE IS 438B BLAKES MEMORAN PROSE
     THEY ARE ALL FIRM DETERMINATE OUTLINE OR IDENTICAL FORM   439C REMARKS MALKIN   PROSE
     DETERMINATE ALL HIS EFFORTS PROVE THIS LITTLE BOY TO HAVE 439C REMARKS MALKIN   PROSE
        HAD
     THAT GREATEST OF ALL BLESSINGS A STRONG IMAGINATION  . .  439D REMARKS MALKIN   PROSE
     THE READER MUST EXPECT TO READ IN ALL MY REMARKS  . . .   445B ANNO REYNOLDS    MARG
     OTHER & DIVIDED ALL THE ENGLISH WORLD BETWEEN THEM  . .   445C ANNO REYNOLDS    MARG
     ALL THIS CONCESSION IS TO PROVE THAT GENIUS IS ACQUIRED   448A ANNO REYNOLDS    MARG
     HERE IS AN ACKNOWLEDGEMENT OF ALL THAT I COULD WISH  . .  448D ANNO REYNOLDS    MARG
     ALL HE KNOWS FROM OTHERS MUST BE FULL OF CONTRADICTIONS   449B ANNO REYNOLDS    MARG
     ALL NATURE WAS DEGRADED  . . . . . . . . . .              451 ANNO REYNOLDS        2
     AND ALL HIS PICTURES FADED  . . . . . . . . .             451 ANNO REYNOLDS        4
     ARE AT ALL TIMES HIRED BY THE SATANS FOR THE DEPRESSION   452B ANNO REYNOLDS    MARG
        OF ART
     FOR ALL ARE BORN POOR AGED SIXTY THREE  . . . . . .       452 ANNO REYNOLDS        4
```

<table>
<tr><td></td><td></td><td>PAGE</td><td>TITLE</td><td>LINE</td></tr>
</table>

ALL (CONTINUED)

	PAGE	TITLE	LINE
& THAT ALL PRETENCE TO INSPIRATION IS A LIE & A DECEIT . .	452D	ANNO REYNOLDS	MARG
ALL SUBLIMITY IS FOUNDED ON MINUTE DISCRIMINATION . . .	453B	ANNO REYNOLDS	MARG
THIS IS ALL FALSE & SELF-CONTRADICTORY	454A	ANNO REYNOLDS	MARG
ALL SELF-CONTRADICTORY TRUTH & FALSHOOD JUMBLED TOGETHER	454B	ANNO REYNOLDS	* MARG
TITIAN VERONESE & ALL THE VENETIANS OUGHT NOT TO BE SHEWN	455A	ANNO REYNOLDS	MARG
THAN COLOURING WITHOUT ANY MEANING AT ALL	455D	ANNO REYNOLDS	MARG
[DAMN THE FOOL] MEER ENTHUSIASM IS THE ALL IN ALL . . .	456C	ANNO REYNOLDS	* MARG
("RUBENS VANDYCK") ALL THE PICTURES SAID TO BE BY THESE MEN	457A	ANNO REYNOLDS	MARG
HE CALLS ALL OTHERS VAGUE ENTHUSIASTS OR MADMEN	458C	ANNO REYNOLDS	MARG
ONE CENTRAL FORM COMPOSED OF ALL OTHER FORMS BEING GRANTED	459C	ANNO REYNOLDS	MARG
IT DOES NOT THEREFORE FOLLOW THAT ALL OTHER FORMS ARE DEFORMITY	459C	ANNO REYNOLDS	MARG
ALL FORMS ARE PERFECT IN THE POET'S MIND	459C	ANNO REYNOLDS	MARG
[STRICTLY SPEAKING] ALL KNOWLEDGE IS PARTICULAR . . .	459D	ANNO REYNOLDS	MARG
& NOT TALK OF DARK AGES OR OF ANY AGE AGES ARE ALL EQUAL	461A	ANNO REYNOLDS	MARG
A NOBLE SENTENCE HERE IS A SENTENCE WHICH OVERTHROWS ALL HIS BOOK	461B	ANNO REYNOLDS	MARG
ALL BUT NAMES OF PERSONS & PLACES IS INVENTION	461D	ANNO REYNOLDS	MARG
DESTRUCTION OF ALL FORM OR OUTLINE PURPOSELY & INTENTIONALLY	463D	ANNO REYNOLDS	MARG
HE MAKES THE LAME TO WALK WE ALL AGREE	463	ANNO REYNOLDS	1
MICH ANG KNEW & DESPISED ALL THAT TITIAN COULD DO . . .	464A	ANNO REYNOLDS	MARG
VENETIAN ALL THY COLOURING IS NO MORE	464	ANNO REYNOLDS	1
ALL EQUIVOCATION & SELF-CONTRADICTION	465C	ANNO REYNOLDS	MARG
KNEW NOTHING AT ALL ABOUT ART AS AN OBJECT OF IMITATION	467B	ANNO REYNOLDS	MARG
IF ALL THIS IS TRUE WHY DOES NOT REYNOLDS RECOMMEND . .	468A	ANNO REYNOLDS	MARG
THE GREAT STYLE IS ALWAYS NOVEL OR NEW IN ALL ITS OPERATIONS	468A	ANNO REYNOLDS	MARG
HANDLING IS ALL THAT HE HAS & WE ALL KNOW THIS HANDLING IS	468D	ANNO REYNOLDS	MARG
ALL RUBENS'S PICTURES ARE PAINTED BY JOURNEYMEN & . . .	468D	ANNO REYNOLDS	MARG
SO FAR FROM BEING ALL OF A PIECE ARE THE MOST WRETCHED BUNGLES	468D	ANNO REYNOLDS	MARG
HIS LIGHTS ARE ALL THE COLOURS OF THE RAINBOW	469A	ANNO REYNOLDS	MARG
BUT HE OUGHT TO PUT ALL MEN OF GENIUS WHO EVER PAINTED .	469A	ANNO REYNOLDS	MARG
BACON'S (PHILOSOPHY) HAS DESTROYD (ALL) ART & SCIENCE .	470A	ANNO REYNOLDS	* MARG
REYNOLDS THINKS THAT MAN LEARNS ALL THAT HE KNOWS . . .	471A	ANNO REYNOLDS	MARG
MAN BRINGS ALL THAT HE HAS OR CAN HAVE INTO THE WORLD WITH HIM	471A	ANNO REYNOLDS	MARG
OF ALL THINGS & INEXHAUSTIBLE	471A	ANNO REYNOLDS	MARG
IF SO THEY KNEW ALL THAT TITIAN & CORREGGIO KNEW	471C	ANNO REYNOLDS	MARG
WHY THEN IMITATE AT ALL	471C	ANNO REYNOLDS	MARG
THAT ALL WHO HAVE SUPPOSED THAT THEY ARE SO	473A	ANNO REYNOLDS	MARG
OBLIGATIONS REYNOLDS HAS LAID ON BAD ARTISTS OF ALL CLASSES	473A	ANNO REYNOLDS	MARG
WILL AT ALL TIMES MAKE THEM HIS ADMIRERS	473A	ANNO REYNOLDS	MARG
TO CALL ALL OTHER OPINIONS UNSOLID	474A	ANNO REYNOLDS	MARG
HERE IS A GREAT DEAL TO DO TO PROVE THAT ALL TRUTH IS PREJUDICE	475A	ANNO REYNOLDS	MARG
FOR ALL THAT IS VALUABLE IN [KNOWLEDGES] KNOWLEDGE IS SUPERIOR TO	475A	ANNO REYNOLDS	* MARG
THINKS HE HAS PROVED THAT GENIUS & INSPIRATION ARE ALL A HUM	475A	ANNO REYNOLDS	MARG
REASON OR A [RATION] RATIO OF ALL WE HAVE KNOWN	475B	ANNO REYNOLDS	* MARG
HIS ASSERTIONS IN ALL HIS DISCOURSES	476D	ANNO REYNOLDS	MARG
POUSSIN KNEW BETTER THAT(THAN) TO MAKE ALL HIS PICTURES	477C	ANNO REYNOLDS	MARG
TO PLEASE ALL IS IMPOSSIBLE	478A	ANNO REYNOLDS	MARG
OF ALL ART BECAUSE IT TAKES AWAY THE POSSIBILITY OF VARIETY	478C	ANNO REYNOLDS	MARG
ONE SPECIES OF GENERAL HUE OVER ALL IS THE CURSED THING	478D	ANNO REYNOLDS	MARG
ALL THIS IS DESTRUCTIVE OF ART	479A	ANNO REYNOLDS	MARG
OF PLATO & CICERO WHICH ALL MEN OUGHT TO CONTEMN	480B	MILTON 1	PROSE
ALL WILL BE SET RIGHT & THOSE GRAND WORKS OF	480B	MILTON 1	PROSE
"WOULD TO GOD THAT ALL THE LORD'S PEOPLE WERE PROPHETS" NUMBERS XI...	481B	MILTON 1	PROSE
A BARD BROKE FORTH ALL SAT ATTENTIVE TO THE AWFUL MAN . .	482	MILTON 2	24
REFUSING ALL DEFINITE FORM THE ABSTRACT HORROR ROOFD STONY HARD	482	MILTON 3	9
THE EYES BEHELD THE ABYSS LEST BONES OF SOLIDNESS FREEZE OVER ALL	482	MILTON 3	15
AS THE CLOUD THAT BRINGS THE SNOW ALL THE WHILE FROM HIS BACK	483	MILTON 3	34
FIRST ORC WAS BORN THEN THE SHADOWY FEMALE THEN ALL LOS'S FAMILY	483	MILTON 3	40
WITH ALL COLOURS OF PRECIOUS STONES & THEIR INMOST PALACES	484	MILTON 4	24
ALL PITIED THE PITEOUS & WAS WRATH WITH THE WRATHFUL & LOS HEARD IT	484	MILTON 5	4
ALL MELODIES & COMPREHENDING ONLY DISCORD AND HARMONY .	484	MILTON 5	24
THRO ALBION'S FOUR FORESTS WHICH OVERSPREAD ALL THE EARTH	485	MILTON 6	3
WHEN SHALL JERUSALEM RETURN & OVERSPREAD ALL THE NATIONS	485	MILTON 6	18
ALL THINGS BEGIN & END IN ALBION'S ANCIENT DRUID ROCKY SHORE	486	MILTON 6	25
MILDNESS SATAN LABOURD ALL DAY IT WAS A THOUSAND YEARS .	486	MILTON 7	15
WOULD I HAD TOLD LOS ALL MY HEART BUT PATIENCE O MY FRIENDS	487	MILTON 7	31
ALL MAY BE WELL SILENT REMAIN WHILE I CALL LOS AND SATAN	487	MILTON 7	32
THE MILLS OF SATAN AS THE EASIER TASK FOUND ALL CONFUSION	488	MILTON 8	5
HIS ARM LEAND TREMBLINGLY OBSERVING ALL THESE THINGS . .	488	MILTON 8	15
THEY MOURND ALL DAY THIS MOURNFUL DAY OF SATAN & PALAMABRON	488	MILTON 8	24
AND ALL THE ELECT & ALL THE REDEEMD MOURND ONE TOWARD ANOTHER	488	MILTON 8	25
FLAMD ABOVE ALL THE PLOWED FURROWS ANGRY RED AND FURIOUS	488	MILTON 8	36
AND ALL EDEN DESCENDED INTO PALAMABRON'S TENT	489	MILTON 9	1

		PAGE	TITLE	LINE

ALL   (CONTINUED)

AND PALAMABRON APPEALD TO ALL EDEN AND RECIEVD	489 MILTON 9	9
BUT HE CLOSD UP ENITHARMON FROM THE SIGHT OF ALL THESE THINGS	489 MILTON 9	18
THERE IS NO OTHER LET ALL OBEY MY PRINCIPLES OF MORAL INDIVIDUALITY	490 MILTON 9	26
BUT LOS HID ENITHARMON FROM THE SIGHT OF ALL THESE THINGS	491 MILTON 11	2
OFFER THE HUMAN VICTIMS THROUGHOUT ALL THE EARTH AND ALBION'S	491 MILTON 11	8
BEING CALLD GOD SETTING HIMSELF ABOVE ALL THAT IS CALLED GOD	491 MILTON 11	12
AND ALL THE SPECTRES OF THE DEAD CALLING THEMSELVES SONS OF GOD	491 MILTON 11	13
AND ONE MUST DIE FOR ANOTHER THROUGHOUT ALL ETERNITY . .	491 MILTON 11	18
IN ALL MY BEAUTY THAT I MIGHT UNLOOSE THE FLAMING STEEDS	492 MILTON 12	11
THE GNOMES IN ALL THAT DAY SPARD NOT THEY CURSD SATAN BITTERLY	493 MILTON 12	31
FOR ELYNITTRIA MET SATAN WITH ALL HER SINGING WOMEN . . .	493 MILTON 12	42
I HUMBLY BOW IN ALL MY SIN BEFORE THE THRONE DIVINE . .	493 MILTON 13	3
ALL IS MY FAULT WE ARE THE SPECTRE OF LUVAH THE MURDERER	494 MILTON 13	8
THE BARD CEASD ALL CONSIDERD AND A LOUD RESOUNDING MURMUR	495 MILTON 13	45
ITS VORTEX AND THE NORTH & SOUTH WITH ALL THEIR STARRY HOST	497 MILTON 15	29
HARDEND SHADOW OF ALL THINGS UPON OUR VEGETATED EARTH . .	498 MILTON 17	22
IN TWENTY-SEVEN HEAVENS AND ALL THEIR HELLS WITH CHAOS	498 MILTON 17	24
CALLD ALL HER DAUGHTERS SAYING SURELY TO UNLOOSE MY BOND	498 MILTON 17	32
I WILL HAVE WRITINGS WRITTEN ALL OVER IT IN HUMAN WORDS	499 MILTON 18	12
AND ALL MY ORNAMENTS SHALL BE OF THE GOLD OF BROKEN HEARTS	499 MILTON 18	22
HOWLINGS FILLD ALL THE DESOLATE PLACES IN ACCUSATIONS OF SIN	500 MILTON 18	43
ALL FELL TOWARDS THE CENTER IN DIRE RUIN SINKING DOWN . .	500 MILTON 19	21
TO HIS ADVERSARY AND THEY SENT FORTH ALL THEIR SONS & DAUGHTERS	501 MILTON 19	30
IN ALL THEIR BEAUTY TO ENTICE MILTON ACROSS THE RIVER . .	501 MILTON 19	31
THEREFORE BRIGHT TIRZAH TRIUMPHS PUTTING ON ALL BEAUTY . .	501 MILTON 19	44
AND ALL PERFECTION IN HER CRUEL SPORTS AMONG THE VICTIMS	501 MILTON 19	45
REGIONS OF THE IMAGINATION ALSO ALL MEN ON EARTH	503 MILTON 21	5
AND ALL IN HEAVEN SAW IN THE NETHER REGIONS OF THE IMAGINATION	503 MILTON 21	6
AND ALL THIS VEGETABLE WORLD APPEARD ON MY LEFT FOOT . .	503 MILTON 21	12
THAT WORK ALL NIGHT AT THE STARRY HARNESS STRONG AND VIGOROUS	504 MILTON 21	22
THEY DRAG THE UNWILLING ORB AT THIS TIME ALL THE FAMILY	504 MILTON 21	23
AND WHEN NIGHT CAME ALL WAS SILENT IN OLOLON & ALL REFUSD TO LAMENT	504 MILTON 21	26
HE HEARD THEM CALL IN PRAYER ALL THE DIVINE FAMILY . . .	504 MILTON 21	35
BUT ALL THE FAMILY DIVINE COLLECTED AS FOUR SUNS . . .	504 MILTON 21	37
IN A DARK TOMB SO ALL THE FAMILY DIVINE WEPT OVER OLOLON	504 MILTON 21	42
BUT ALL REMAIN EVERY FABRIC OF SIX THOUSAND YEARS . . .	505 MILTON 22	20
FELL AND WAS CUT OFF ALL THINGS VANISH & ARE SEEN NO MORE	505 MILTON 22	22
AND ALL THE DAUGHTERS OF LOS PROPHETIC WAIL YET IN DECEIT	506 MILTON 22	37
NO FAITH IS IN ALL THE EARTH THE BOOK OF GOD IS TRODDEN UNDER FOOT	506 MILTON 22	60
THE TRUMPET OF JUDGMENT HATH TWICE SOUNDED ALL NATIONS ARE AWAKE	506 MILTON 23	4
DELUGE ALL THE COUNTRY ROUND SUCH IS A VISION OF LOS . .	507 MILTON 23	27
OF JEALOUSY FROM ALL ITS ROOTS BE PATIENT THEREFORE O MY SONS	507 MILTON 23	38
ONE THOUSAND YEARS AND ALL THE EARTH WAS IN A WATRY DELUGE	508 MILTON 24	5
ARISE O SONS GIVE ALL YOUR STRENGTH AGAINST ETERNAL DEATH	509 MILTON 24	34
MUST TREMBLE IN THE HEAVENS & EARTHS THRO ALL THE ULRO SPACE	509 MILTON 24	39
THROW ALL THE VEGETATED MORTALS INTO BOWLAHOOLA	509 MILTON 24	40
NOR VEGETATION MAY GO ON TILL ALL THE EARTH IS REAPD . .	509 MILTON 24	43
BOWLAHOOLA THRO ALL ITS PORCHES FEELS THO TOO FAST FOUNDED	509 MILTON 24	54
ALL POWERFUL AND HIS LOCKS FLOURISH LIKE THE BROWS OF MORNING	509 MILTON 24	70
WHICH IS THE SWIFTEST OF ALL THINGS ALL WERE ETERNAL TORMENT	510 MILTON 24	73
ALL THE GODS OF THE KINGDOMS OF EARTH LABOUR IN LOS'S HALLS	510 MILTON 24	74
THE WINE-PRESS ON THE RHINE GROANS LOUD BUT ALL ITS CENTRAL BEAMS	510 MILTON 25	3
THERE LOS PUTS ALL INTO THE PRESS THE OPRESSOR & THE OPRESSED	510 MILTON 25	6
SHALL NO MORE BE SOWN UPON EARTH TILL ALL THE VINTAGE IS OVER	510 MILTON 25	9
AND ALL GATHERD IN TILL THE PLOW HAS PASSD OVER THE NATIONS	510 MILTON 25	10
BUT LOS REFUSED TILL ALL THE VINTAGE OF EARTH WAS GATHERD IN	510 MILTON 25	* 15
ALL THE WISDOM WHICH WAS HIDDEN IN CAVES & DENS FROM ANCIENT	510 MILTON 25	20
WHEN UNDER PRETENCE TO BENEVOLENCE THE ELECT SUBDUD ALL	510 MILTON 25	31
ALL IS THE SAME & EVERY ONE REMAINS IN HIS OWN ENERGY . .	511 MILTON 25	43
FOR THE LORD'S COMING THAT JERUSALEM MAY OVERSPREAD ALL NATIONS	511 MILTON 25	55
SO LOS SPOKE BUT LIGHTNINGS OF DISCONTENT BROKE ON ALL SIDES ROUND	511 MILTON 25	63
THERE ARE TWO GATES THRO WHICH ALL SOULS DESCEND ONE SOUTHWARD	512 MILTON 26	13
FOR THE VARIOUS CLASSES OF MEN ARE ALL MARKD OUT DETERMINATE	512 MILTON 26	37
AND ALL ARE CLASSD BY SPIRITUAL & NOT BY NATURAL POWER . .	513 MILTON 26	43
THE FLEA LOUSE BUG THE TAPE-WORM ALL THE ARMIES OF DISEASE	513 MILTON 27	17

63

		PAGE	TITLE	LINE
ALL	(CONTINUED)			
	WHO FEEDS ON CONTEMPT OF HIS NEIGHBOUR THERE ALL THE IDLE WEEDS	513	MILTON 27	27
	NAKED IN ALL THEIR BEAUTY DANCING ROUND THE WINE-PRESSES	513	MILTON 27	29
	HERE THE SONS OF LOS LABOUR AGAINST DEATH ETERNAL THROUGH ALL	514	MILTON 27	44
	HERE ARE THE STARS CREATED & THE SEEDS OF ALL THINGS PLANTED	514	MILTON 27	53
	IN RUGGED COVERING IN THE MINE IS OPEN ALL WITHIN	515	MILTON 28	37
	ALL ARE THE WORK OF FAIRY HANDS OF THE FOUR ELEMENTS	516	MILTON 28	60
	FOR IN THIS PERIOD THE POET'S WORK IS DONE AND ALL THE GREAT	516	MILTON 29	1
	ON ALL SIDES & THE TWO POLES TURN ON THEIR VALVES OF GOLD	516	MILTON 29	11
	WHEREER HE GOES & ALL HIS NEIGHBOURHOOD BEWAIL HIS LOSS	516	MILTON 29	13
	DEATH TO DELUDE WHO ALL IN TERROR AT THEIR SPLENDOR LEAVES	517	MILTON 29	43
	TO THE INHABITANTS OF EDEN AROUND THEM ON ALL SIDES	518	MILTON 30	9
	WALKS AMONG ALL HIS AWFUL FAMILY SEEN IN EVERY FACE	519	MILTON 30	17
	MILD SHADOW ABOVE BENEATH & ON ALL SIDES ROUND	519	MILTON 30	33
	INTO THIS PLEASANT SHADOW ALL THE WEAK & WEARY	519	MILTON 31	1
	A SHADOW TO REPOSE IN ALL THE DAYS OF HAPPY ETERNITY	519	MILTON 31	7
	INTO THIS PLEASANT SHADOW BEULAH ALL OLOLON DESCENDED	519	MILTON 31	8
	ALL BEULAH WEPT FOR THEY SAW THE LORD COMING IN THE CLOUDS	519	MILTON 31	10
	AND ALL NATIONS WEPT IN AFFLICTION FAMILY BY FAMILY	519	MILTON 31	12
	AND ALL THE LIVING CREATURES OF THE FOUR ELEMENTS WAILD	519	MILTON 31	17
	ORC HOWLS ON THE ATLANTIC ENITHARMON TREMBLES ALL BEULAH WEEPS	520	MILTON 31	27
	ALL NATURE LISTENS SILENT TO HIM & THE AWFUL SUN	520	MILTON 31	36
	THEN LOUD FROM THEIR GREEN COVERT ALL THE BIRDS BEGIN THEIR SONG	520	MILTON 31	39
	YET ALL IN ORDER SWEET & LOVELY MEN ARE SICK WITH LOVE	521	MILTON 31	62
	WHEN I FIRST MARRIED YOU I GAVE YOU ALL MY WHOLE SOUL	522	MILTON 33	2
	HIMSELF THAT SEEING ALL HIS LOVES BY HER CUT OFF HE LEAVES	522	MILTON 33	15
	AND ALL THE SONGS OF BEULAH SOUNDED COMFORTABLE NOTES	523	MILTON 34	1
	CAN FROM THOSE GATES VIEW ALL THESE WONDROUS IMAGINATIONS	524	MILTON 34	18
	ALL FELL TOWARDS THE CENTER SINKING DOWNWARD IN DIRE RUIN	524	MILTON 34	39
	IN CHASMS OF THE MUNDANE SHELL WHICH OPEN ON ALL SIDES ROUND	524	MILTON 34	41
	ON ALL SIDES ROUND TO THE FOUR QUARTERS OF THE WORLD EASTWARD ON	525	MILTON 35	15
	IT IS VIEWED ON ALL SIDES ROUND BY A FOUR-FOLD VISION	525	MILTON 35	23
	AND OLOLON EXAMINED ALL THE COUCHES OF THE DEAD	525	MILTON 35	26
	EVEN OF LOS & ENITHARMON & ALL THE SONS OF ALBION	525	MILTON 35	27
	THEY THUNDEROUS UTTERD ALL A UNIVERSAL GROAN FALLING DOWN	525	MILTON 35	31
	AND THROUGH BEULAH AND ALL SILENT FORBORE TO CONTEND	526	MILTON 35	40
	THE OTHER FLOWS THRO THE AERIAL VOID & ALL THE CHURCHES	526	MILTON 35	52
	THRO ALL THE TWENTY-SEVEN HEAVENS MAY NOT SLUMBER NOR SLEEP	526	MILTON 35	65
	TO THEIR RESPECTIVE EARTHS & THERE ALL NIGHT CONSULT WITH ANGELS	526	MILTON 36	4
	OF PROVIDENCE & WITH THE EYES OF GOD ALL NIGHT IN SLUMBERS	526	MILTON 36	5
	AND AS ONE FEMALE OLOLON AND ALL ITS MIGHTY HOSTS	527	MILTON 36	16
	COTTAGE FOR ME THAT IN THREE YEARS I MIGHT WRITE ALL THESE VISIONS	527	MILTON 36	24
	THAT MILTON'S SHADOW HEARD & CONDENSING ALL HIS FIBRES	527	MILTON 37	6
	ALL THESE ARE SEEN IN MILTON'S SHADOW WHO IS THE COVERING CHERUB	528	MILTON 37	44
	INTO ETERNITY THAT WAY BUT ALL DESCEND TO LOS	529	MILTON 37	58
	AND MILTON COLLECTING ALL HIS FIBRES INTO IMPREGNABLE STRENGTH	529	MILTON 38	5
	DESCENDED DOWN A PAVED WORK OF ALL KINDS OF PRECIOUS STONES	529	MILTON 38	6
	IN ALL ITS HYPOCRITIC TURPITUDE OPENING TO EVERY EYE	530	MILTON 38	44
	EXPLORE IN ALL ITS SELFISH NATURAL VIRTUE & PUT OFF	530	MILTON 38	47
	IN SELF ANNIHILATION ALL THAT IS NOT OF GOD ALONE	530	MILTON 38	48
	TO PUT OFF SELF & ALL I HAVE EVER & EVER AMEN	530	MILTON 38	49
	SAYING I AM GOD THE JUDGE OF ALL THE LIVING & THE DEAD	530	MILTON 38	51
	OF ALL THAT LIVE DARE UTTER THIS OTHERS TREMBLE & BOW	530	MILTON 38	57
	TILL ALL THINGS BECOME ONE GREAT SATAN IN HOLINESS	530	MILTON 39	1
	AND ANCIENT NIGHT SPREAD OVER ALL THE HEAVN HIS MANTLE OF LAWS	531	MILTON 39	30
	AND ALL BENEATH THE NATIONS INNUMERABLE OF ULRO	532	MILTON 40	23
	ALL THAT CAN BE ANN BE ANNIHILATED MUST BE ANNIHILATED	532	MILTON 40	* 30
	TO CAST ASIDE FROM POETRY ALL THAT IS NOT INSPIRATION	533	MILTON 41	7
	HENCE AROSE ALL OUR TERRORS IN ETERNITY & NOW REMEMBRANCE	534	MILTON 41	34
	THOU GOEST TO ETERNAL DEATH & ALL MUST GO WITH THEE	534	MILTON 42	2
	DOLOROUS THAT RAN THRO ALL CREATION A DOUBLE SIX-FOLD WONDER	534	MILTON 42	4
	ALL ANIMALS UPON THE EARTH ARE PREPARD IN ALL THEIR STRENGTH	535	MILTON 42	39
	LOOK AT HIS PICTURES [TIS QUITE ANOTHER THING] ALL HAS TAKEN WING	536	NO REAL STYL/N	4
	AYE THATS THE WAY TO MAKE ALL NATURE OUT	536	DONT BELIEVE/N	8
	REACHD ALL THE WAY FROM CHICHESTER TO YORK	536	AND HIS LEGS/N	2
	FROM YORK ALL ACROSS SCOTLAND TO THE SEA	536	AND HIS LEGS/N	3
	AND [ALL MY] STEWHARD'S EGGS ARE ADDLED & DECAYD	537	AND HIS LEGS/N	15
	HERE LIES STEWHARD THE [LORD OF] FRIEND OF ALL &C	537	AND HIS LEGS/N *	52
	[MIRTH S ALL YOUR SUFFERINGS CONVEY SIR]	538	WAS I ANGRY/N *	7
	BUT ALL MY LIMBS WITH WARMTH GLOW	538	ANGER WRATH/N	3
	BUT TWOULD BE MADNESS [THAT WE ALL MUST]	539	SIR JOSH MIC/N	5
	. . . ALL THE WORLD [SHOULD] WOULD SAY	539	SIR JOSH MIC/N *	5
	[HE] YOU ALL [HIS] YOUR YOUTH [OBSERVES] OBSERVD THE GOLDEN RULE	540	S(TOTHAR)D/N *	1
	TURN BACK TURN BACK YOU TRAVEL ALL IN VAIN	541	MR CROMEK/N	3
	I AM NO HOMER'S HERO YOU ALL KNOW	541	HOMERS HERO/N	1

```
                                                            PAGE     TITLE          LINE
ALL    (CONTINUED)
     IT WILL SET HIS DUTCH FRIENDS ALL IN A ROAR      . . . . .  542 FLORENTINE/N        24
     A STRANGE ERRATUM IN ALL THE EDITIONS      . . . . . .  543 TO ROYL ACAD/N       1
     IN ALL THAT HE HAS WRIT      . . . . . . . . . .  543 TO ROYL ACAD/N      10
     THAT THE HEATHEN GODS ARE ALL STOCKS & STONES    . . . .  543 IF TRUE/N            2
     ALL THE ATONEMENTS OF JEHOVAH SPURND     . . . . . .  543 IF TRUE/N           13
     [BUT] HE LOVED ME [BUT] AND FOR NO GAIN AT ALL   . . . .  544 P LOVED NOT/N        3
     AND ALL THE [RIGHTEOUS] VIRTUOUS HAVE SHEWN THEIR BACKSIDES  545 COSWAY FRAZR/N       8
     HERE LIES JOHN TROT THE FRIEND OF ALL MANKIND    . . . .  546 ANOTHER/N  2         1
     BUT ALL THE PULP WASHD PAINTED FINISHD WITH LABOUR   . . .  546 SWELLD LIMBS/N       3
     MAY I GOVERN ALL BOTH GREAT & SMALL      . . . . . .  547 IF I GROW/N          3
     HE IS ALL EXPERIMENTS FROM LAST TO FIRST     . . . .  548 CRIPPLE EVRY/N       7
     ALL PICTURES THATS PANTED WITH SENSE & WITH THOUGHT  . .  548 ALL PICTURES/N  *    1
     [BECAUSE WE KNOW] AMIABLE STATE HE CANNOT FEEL AT ALL  . .  549 CROMEK SPEAK/N       4
     SAY ALL WAS OWING TO THE SKILFUL MAN     . . . . . .  549 ENGL ENCOU/N 1      10
     SO EEN LET IGNORANCE DO IT ALL     . . . . . . .  549 ENGL ENCOU/N 1      12
     FOR ITS ALL SHEER LOSS AS IT SEEMS TO ME     . . . .  550 ENGL ENCOU/N 2       7
     AND YET THEY ARE BLOCKHEADS YOU ALL AGREE    . . . .  550 SAY PICTURES/N       2
     PERHAPS THIS IS ALL A PAINTER CAN WANT   . . . . . .  553 ASKD PRIGG/N        13
     AND THE DEVIL IS A BLACK OUTLINE ALL OF US KNOW  . . . .  554 TO VENETIAN/N        2
     ALL IS CHIARO SCURO POCO PEN [&] ITS ALL COLORING  . . .  554 TO VENETIAN/N  *    11
     BUT NOBODY [AT ALL] SEES ANY HARM IN RHYMING     . . . .  555 BLAKES APL/N 1       9
     WHO CRIES ALL ART IS A FRAUD & GENIUS A TRICK    . . . .  555 BLAKES APL/N 1      20
     IS HE INFIRM IS ALL THAT HE DOES     . . . . . . .  555 FRM CRATELOS/N       2
     KNOWING & FEELING THAT WE ALL HAVE NEED OF BUTTER    . . .  556 IF MEN ACT/N         4
     SINCE ALL THE RICHES OF THIS [EARTH] WORLD   . . . . .  557 SINCE RICHES/N       1
     NAIL HIS NECK TO THE CROSS YE ALL HAVE POWER OVER HIS TAIL  557 NAIL NECK/N          2
     IVE ALL BUT RICHES BODILY      . . . . . . . .  558 I ROSE UP AT/N      12
     FOR [ALL THAT] MY WORLDLY THINGS GOD MAKES HIM PAY   . .  559 I ROSE UP AT/N      17
     A WOMAN SCALY & A MAN ALL HAIRY      . . . . . . .  559 WOMAN SCALY/N        1
     ALL THE LITTLE OLD PICTURES CALLED CABINET PICTURES  . . .  561A EXHIBITION ADV      PROSE
     BEING ALL IN WATER-COLOURS THAT IS IN FRESCO     . . . .  561B EXHIBITION ADV      PROSE
     BY ARTISTS AND CONNOISSEURS OF ALL RANKS     . . . .  562B DESC CAT ADV       PROSE
     CONTEMNED AND REJECTED ALL HE DID WITH THE UTMOST DISDAIN   563C DESC CAT          PROSE
     AND ALL DEPENDS ON FORM OR OUTLINE ON WHERE THAT IS PUT     563D DESC CAT          PROSE
     BECOMES A YELLOW MASK OVER ALL THAT IT TOUCHES   . . . .  565B DESC CAT 2         PROSE
     AND IN HIS TIME ALL THE GENUINE PICTURES     . . . .  565B DESC CAT 2         PROSE
     AND ALL THE GRAND WORKS OF ANCIENT ART THEY WERE EXECUTED   565D DESC CAT 2         PROSE
     ALL THE REST ARE EVIDENTLY COPIES THOUGH FINE ONES   . .  565D DESC CAT 2         PROSE
     STATUES ALL CONTAINING MYTHOLOGICAL AND RECONDITE MEANING   566A DESC CAT 2         PROSE
     ALL FRESCOES ARE AS HIGH FINISHED AS MINIATURES OR ENAMELS  566B DESC CAT 2         PROSE
     ALL THE GENUINE OLD LITTLE PICTURES CALLED CABINET PICTURES 566B DESC CAT 2         PROSE
     AS THEY ARE IN ALL THE OLD PICTURES AND IN MR B'S(BLAKE'S) 566C DESC CAT 2         PROSE
          FRESCOS
     WHICH COMPOSE ALL AGES AND NATIONS     . . . . . .  567B DESC CAT 3         PROSE
     OF HIS PERSONAGES INTO ALL NATURE'S VARIETIES    . . . .  567D DESC CAT 3         PROSE
     WITHOUT OSTENTATION AND WITH ALL THE TRUE GRANDEUR   . .  568A DESC CAT 3         PROSE
     HER COMPANION AND HER THREE PRIESTS WERE NO DOUBT ALL   .  568C DESC CAT 3         PROSE
     CHARACTERS LIKELY TO RIDE IN COMPANY ALL BEING ABOVE THE    568C DESC CAT 3         PROSE
     TO MAKE HIM A MASTER OF ALL THE PLEASURES OF THE WORLD  .  568D DESC CAT 3         PROSE
     VENERATED BY ALL AND NEGLECTED BY ALL HE SERVES ALL    .  570B DESC CAT 3         PROSE
     AND TAKE THEIR COUNSEL ESPECIALLY IN ALL DIFFICULT POINTS   570D DESC CAT 3         PROSE
     ALL PASS ON EACH SUSTAINING ONE OR OTHER OF THESE          570D DESC CAT 3         PROSE
          CHARACTERS
     A DESCRIPTION OF THE ETERNAL PRINCIPLES THAT EXIST IN ALL   571A DESC CAT 3         PROSE
          AGES
     CHARACTERS OF HUMAN LIFE APPEAR TO POETS IN ALL AGES   .  571B DESC CAT 3         PROSE
     A TERRIBLE FELLOW SUCH AS EXISTS IN ALL TIMES AND PLACES    571C DESC CAT 3         PROSE
     SCHOLAR OF INSPIRATION AND ALL WILL BE HAPPY     . . . .  572C DESC CAT 3         PROSE
     I ANSWER OF NONE AT ALL BUT THE CONTRARY AS YOU WELL KNOW   573A DESC CAT 3         PROSE
     AND TO KEEP IT HIS ARTS ARE OPPOSITE TO THEIRS IN         573B DESC CAT 3         PROSE
          ALL THINGS
     IS SOON KNOWN "BY THEIR WORKS YE SHALL KNOW THEM" ALL WHO   573B DESC CAT 3         PROSE
     IT IS THE SAME WITH ALL HIS CHARACTERS HE HAS DONE ALL  .  574A DESC CAT 3         PROSE
     "AND VERY ORDINARY FORMS" WHICH IS THE TRUEST PART OF ALL   574D DESC CAT 3         PROSE
     BUT IT APPEARS IN ALL THE WRITINGS OF CHAUCER    . . . .  575A DESC CAT 3         PROSE
     MUST BE THE DESTRUCTION OF ALL CHARACTER AND EXPRESSION     575B DESC CAT 3         PROSE
     ALL IS MISCONCEIVED      . . . . . . . . . .  575D DESC CAT 3         PROSE
     WHO OWE TO ME ALL THAT THEY HAVE IT SHALL BE SO NO LONGER   575D DESC CAT 3         PROSE
     ARE ALL OF THEM REPRESENTATIONS OF SPIRITUAL EXISTENCES     576C DESC CAT 4         PROSE
     MR B(BLAKE) REQUIRES THE SAME LATITUDE AND ALL IS WELL  .  576D DESC CAT 4         PROSE
     AND MINUTELY ARTICULATED BEYOND ALL THAT THE MORTAL AND     576D DESC CAT 4         PROSE
     DOES NOT IMAGINE AT ALL THE PAINTER OF THIS WORK ASSERTS    576D DESC CAT 4         PROSE
     THAT ALL HIS IMAGINATIONS APPEAR TO HIM  . . . . . .  576D DESC CAT 4         PROSE
     THEY WERE OVERWHELMED BY BRUTAL ARMS ALL BUT A SMALL   .  577C DESC CAT 5         PROSE
     ALL HIS VISIONARY CONTEMPLATIONS RELATING TO HIS          577D DESC CAT 5         PROSE
          OWN COUNTRY
     OF THE NORTH POLE AND ALL THE FABLES OF ARTHUR AND HIS  .  577D DESC CAT 5         PROSE
     WOULD HAVE DEPOPULATED THE EARTH ALL THESE THINGS         578A DESC CAT 5         PROSE
          ARE WRITTEN
     MR B(BLAKE) HAS DONE AS ALL THE ANCIENTS DID     . . . .  578C DESC CAT 5         PROSE
     AND AS ALL THE MODERNS WHO ARE WORTHY OF FAME    . . . .  578C DESC CAT 5         PROSE
     CANNOT SEE EITHER MIRACLE OR PRODIGY ALL IS TO THEM   . .  578D DESC CAT 5         PROSE
     BUT THE HISTORY OF ALL TIMES AND PLACES IS NOTHING ELSE     578D DESC CAT 5         PROSE
     SAME THING AS JACOB BRYANT AND ALL ANTIQUARIES HAVE PROVED  578D DESC CAT 5         PROSE
     AND THE DIVINE ALL HAD ORIGINALLY ONE LANGUAGE AND   . .  579A DESC CAT 5         PROSE
     SUCH AS HUME GIBBON AND VOLTAIRE CANNOT WITH ALL THEIR  .  579A DESC CAT 5         PROSE
     ALL THAT IS NOT ACTION IS NOT WORTH READING TELL ME THE     579A DESC CAT 5         PROSE
          WHAT
     IT IS IMPROBABLE MUST REJECT ALL HISTORY AND RETAIN DOUBTS  579B DESC CAT 5         PROSE
          ONLY
     HENCE RUBENS TITIAN CORREGGIO AND ALL OF THAT CLASS ARE     581A DESC CAT 5         PROSE
```

```
                                                         PAGE     TITLE         LINE

ALL   (CONTINUED)
      YOU MAY DISBELIEVE ALL THIS BUT IT SHALL BE AT YOUR OWN    582A DESC CAT 9      PROSE
      PERIL
      WHICH IT HAD AT FIRST WHEN ALL THE LINEAMENTS WERE PERFECT 582B DESC CAT 9      PROSE
      AND TO ALL ARTISTS WHO STUDY IN THE FLORENTINE AND  .  .   582C DESC CAT 9      PROSE
      THEY CAUSE THAT THE EXECUTION SHALL BE ALL BLOCKED UP  .   582C DESC CAT 9      PROSE
      HINDERS ALL POWER OF INDIVIDUAL THOUGHT   .  .  .  .       582D DESC CAT 9      PROSE
      LOSES ALL ADMIRATION OF ANY OTHER ARTIST BUT RUBENS  .  .  583A DESC CAT 9      PROSE
      THOUGH THE ORIGINAL CONCEPTION WAS ALL FIRE AND ANIMATION  583A DESC CAT 9      PROSE
      AND BLOCKS UP ALL ITS GATES OF LIGHT EXCEPT ONE  .  .  .   583A DESC CAT 9      PROSE
      THE STORY THAT IS TOLD IN ALL LIVES OF THE PAINTERS  .  .  583A DESC CAT 9      PROSE
      AND HINDER ALL CORRECT DRAWING FROM APPEARING TO BE CORRECT 583C DESC CAT 9     PROSE
      I SAY AGAIN O ARTIST YOU MAY DISBELIEVE ALL THIS  .  .  .  583C DESC CAT 9      PROSE
      AND KNOCKED ABOUT WITHOUT MERCY TO TRY ALL EXPERIMENTS  .  583D DESC CAT 9      PROSE
      FLANDERS IT LOSES ALL CHARACTER AND LEAVES WHAT SOME PEOPLE 585A DESC CAT 15    PROSE
      AND BUNGLING GREAT INVENTORS IN ALL AGES KNEW THIS  .  .   585B DESC CAT 15     PROSE
      MIND AND THE PRETENCE OF THE PLAGIARY IN ALL ITS BRANCHES  585C DESC CAT 15     PROSE
      ALL IS CHAOS AGAIN AND THE LINE OF THE ALMIGHTY MUST BE    585C DESC CAT 15     PROSE
      ARE EQUAL IN ALL ESSENTIAL POINTS   .  .  .  .  .  .  .    585D DESC CAT 16     PROSE
      AND TIME AWAIT TO GIVE HIM ALL THAT THE WORLD CAN GIVE  .  586A DESC CAT 16     PROSE
      AS IT IS IN THIS PICTURE WHERE ALL THE LINEAMENTS          586D CHAUCER 1       PROSE
      ARE DISTINCT
      THAT COMPOSE ALL AGES & NATIONS   .  .  .  .  .  .  .  .   589A CHAUCER/N       PROSE
      OF HIS PERSONAGES INTO ALL NATURE'S VARIETIES  .  .  .  .  590D CHAUCER 2       PROSE
      ON ALL HANDS ACKNOWLEDGD IT ONLY REMAINS TO BE CERTIFIED   591C PUB ADDRESS/N   PROSE
      ENGRAVING BY LOSING DRAWING HAS LOST ALL CHARACTER  .  .   592A PUB ADDRESS/N   *PROSE
      & ALL EXPRESSION WITHOUT WHICH THE ART IS LOST   .  .  .   592A PUB ADDRESS/N   PROSE
      IN BEAUFORT BUILDINGS WE ALL KNOW THAT EDITORS OF          592C PUB ADDRESS/N   PROSE
      NEWSPAPERS
      ALL THE WORLD OVER BUT HAVE NEVER BEEN SO GOOD AN          592C PUB ADDRESS/N   PROSE
      SINCE I HAVE PRACTISED PAINTING I HAVE LOST ALL IDEA OF    592D PUB ADDRESS/N   PROSE
      ALL HIS STUDY WAS CLEAN STROKES & MOSSY TINTS HOW THEN  .  593A PUB ADDRESS/N   PROSE
      TO ALL THE CONTINENT WHO LAUGH AT THE CONTEMPTIBLE  .  .   593C PUB ADDRESS/N   PROSE
      SHEW THAT IT IS ONLY SOME ENGLISHMEN AND NOT ALL   .  .  . 593C PUB ADDRESS/N   PROSE
      ITS INSATIABLE MAW MUST BE FED BY WHAT ALL CAN DO   .  .   593D PUB ADDRESS/N   PROSE
      TO EMPIRE THAT IT IS DESTRUCTIVE OF BOTH AS ALL  .  .  .   593D PUB ADDRESS/N   *PROSE
      STRANGE'S PRINTS WERE WHEN I KNEW HIM ALL DONE BY ALIAMET  594A PUB ADDRESS/N   PROSE
      & IN SHORT ALL THAT ARE CALLD WOOLETT'S WERE ETCHD   .  .  594A PUB ADDRESS/N   PROSE
      BY JACK BROWNE & IN WOOLETT'S WORKS THE ETCHING IS ALL  .  594A PUB ADDRESS/N   PROSE
      COLOUR BUT HE COULD[NT ] NOT [& HOGARTH WITH ALL HIS MERIT 594B PUB ADDRESS/N   *PROSE
      NEVER G ]
      & ALL BECAUSE I UNDERSTAND DRAWING WHICH THEY UNDERSTOOD   594C PUB ADDRESS/N   PROSE
      NOT
      & ALL THE COPIES OR PRETENDED COPIERS OF NATURE  .  .  .   594D PUB ADDRESS/N   PROSE
      COPIERS OF IMAGINATION ARE CORRECT THIS IS MANIFEST TO ALL 595A PUB ADDRESS/N   PROSE
      ALL THE BEAUTIES PICKD OUT [BUT] & BLURRD & BLOTTED  .  .  595C PUB ADDRESS/N   *PROSE
      BUT DRAWN WITH A FIRM & DECIDED HAND AT ONCE [WITH ALL ITS] 595C PUB ADDRESS/N  PROSE
      BUT NOBODY AT ALL SEES HARM IN RHYMING   .  .  .  .  .  .  595 BLAKES APOL/PA    6
      UNAPPROPRIATE EXECUTION IS THE MOST NAUSEOUS OF ALL  .  .  596B PUB ADDRESS/N   PROSE
      SUCH THING AS GENEROUS CONTENTION I KNOW THAT ALL THOSE    596D PUB ADDRESS/N   PROSE
      WITH
      [ALL] MOST OF THEM SUCH SILLY FELLOWS AS TO BELIEVE THIS   597B PUB ADDRESS/N   PROSE
      ALL THE ARTICLES OF PAINTING HE PUTS A MODEL BEFORE HIM    597B PUB ADDRESS/N   PROSE
      ADMIRES ALL HIS COLOURS BROWN & WARM  .  .  .  .  .  .  .  597 PUBLC VOICE/PA    3
      BY ALL THE MEANS IN THEIR POWER   .  .  .  .  .  .  .  .   598B PUB ADDRESS/N   PROSE
      THE PAINTER BEGS PUBLIC PROTECTION & ALL WILL BE WELL  .   598B PUB ADDRESS/N   PROSE
      THE PUBLIC INDIGNATION OF MEN OF SENSE IN ALL PROFESSIONS  598D PUB ADDRESS/N   PROSE
      WHEN YOU HAVE SEEN ONE OF THEIR PICTURES YOU HAVE SEEN ALL 598D PUB ADDRESS/N   PROSE
      A POINT OF LIGHT IS A WITTICISM MANY ARE DESTRUCTIVE OF    599A PUB ADDRESS/N   PROSE
      ALL ART
      HAS INTIRELY PUT AN END TO ALL GENUINE & APPROPRIATE EFFECT 599B PUB ADDRESS/N *PROSE
      ALL BOTH MORNING & NIGHT IS NOW A DARK CAVERN XXX WHEN     599B PUB ADDRESS/N   *PROSE
      YOU VIEW
      RUBENS'S LUXEMBOURG GALLERY IS CONFESSD ON ALL HANDS  .  . 599C PUB ADDRESS/N   *PROSE
      AWKWARD FRENCH PALACE ARE [ALL] THROWN TOGETHER AROUND  .  599C PUB ADDRESS/N   *PROSE
      IS ALLOWD ON ALL HANDS TO BE THE PRODUCTION OF A MAN  .  . 599D PUB ADDRESS/N   *PROSE
      IF ALL THE PRINCES IN EUROPE LIKE LOUIS XIV  .  .  .  .  . 599D PUB ADDRESS/N   PROSE
      MUSIC TRADERS & RHIME TRADERS TO THE DESTRUCTION OF ALL    600B PUB ADDRESS/N   PROSE
      TRUE
      [CLLLLLNNN AOOJLMM ALL ALLS HANDS BRITISH ALLS WWWNDJ      601A PUB ADDRESS/N   *PROSE
      BLUUUU]
      OF ALL THE RUBBISH OF THE CONTINENT BROUGHT HERE BY  .  .  601C PUB ADDRESS/N   PROSE
      IN ALL PROFESSIONS THESE ARE THE GREATEST ENEMIES OF GENIUS 601C PUB ADDRESS/N  PROSE
      AS DESTRUCTIVE OF THE TRUE ARTIST AS IT IS FALSE BY ALL    601D PUB ADDRESS/N   PROSE
      EXPERIENCE
      MY CONCEPTION & INVENTION ARE ON ALL HANDS ALLOWD   .  .   601D PUB ADDRESS/N   PROSE
      THE LAVISH PRAISE I HAVE RECIEVED FROM ALL QUARTERS  .  .  601D PUB ADDRESS/N   PROSE
      MADE TO OCCUPY THE ATTENTION TO THE NEGLECT OF ALL REAL ART 602A PUB ADDRESS/N  PROSE
      LIKE ALL THAT THEY SAY FOR THERE IS EVERY LINE IN NATURE   603B PUB ADDR AD/N   PROSE
      WORLD WAS NOT WORTHY SUCH WERE THE CHRISTIANS IN ALL AGES  604A INSC ARIMATHEA  PROSE
      THE LAST JUDGMENT WHEN ALL THOSE ARE CAST AWAY   .  .  .   604C V LAST JUDG/N   PROSE
      WHICH HINDER THE VISION OF GOD TURNING ALL INTO A CONSUMING 604C V LAST JUDG/N  PROSE
      FIRE
      WHEN IMAGINATION ART & SCIENCE & ALL INTELLECTUAL GIFTS    604C V LAST JUDG/N   PROSE
      ALL THE GIFTS OF THE HOLY GHOST ARE [DESPISD] LOOKD UPON   604C V LAST JUDG/N   PROSE
      BUT ETERNAL VISION OR IMAGINATION OF ALL THAT EXISTS  .  . 604D V LAST JUDG/N   PROSE
      ARE LESS PERMANENT THAN A SHADOW AS WE ALL KNOW TOO WELL   605A V LAST JUDG/N   PROSE
      IT IS THE DIVINE BOSOM INTO WHICH WE SHALL ALL GO   .  .   605D V LAST JUDG/N   PROSE
      ALL THINGS ARE COMPREHENDED IN THEIR ETERNAL FORMS   .  .  605D V LAST JUDG/N   PROSE
      & AGAINST WHICH WE SHOULD ALL WATCH   .  .  .  .  .  .  .  608A V LAST JUDG/N   PROSE
      WHO DRIVES ABROAD ALL THOSE WHO REBELL AGAINST THEIR       608B V LAST JUDG/N   PROSE
      SAVIOUR
```

ALL   (CONTINUED)

THESE ARE CAIPHAS & PILATE TWO STATES WHERE ALL THOSE   . . 608D V LAST JUDG/N   PROSE
OF TRUE ART CALLD GOTHIC IN ALL AGES BY THOSE   . . . . 610D V LAST JUDG/N   PROSE
& IN HIM SEES ALL REFLECTED AS IN A GLASS OF ETERNAL   610D V LAST JUDG/N   PROSE
    DIAMOND
THE [EXPRESSION] CHARACTERS IN ALL THEIR BRANCHES   . . . 611B V LAST JUDG/N   PROSE
& ON THIS DISCRIMINATION ALL ART IS FOUNDED I INTREAT THEN   611B V LAST JUDG/N   PROSE
ALL DESCRIPTIVE OF CHARACTER & NOT A LINE IS DRAWN   . . . 611B V LAST JUDG/N   PROSE
HE COMPREHENDS ALL THE PROPHETIC CHARACTERS   . . . . 611C V LAST JUDG/N   PROSE
ALL THESE ARISE TOWARD THE OPENING CLOUD BEFORE THE THRONE   611D V LAST JUDG/N   PROSE
ALL SPRINGING FROM THE DIVINE HUMANITY   . . . . . . 612D V LAST JUDG/N   PROSE
ALL BEAMS FROM HIM [& [BECAUSE] AS HE HIMSELF HAS SAID]   612D V LAST JUDG/N   PROSE
[ALL DWELLS IN HIM] HE IS THE BREAD & THE WINE   . . . 612D V LAST JUDG/N   PROSE
ALL LIFE CONSISTS OF THESE TWO THROWING OFF ERROR & KNAVES   612D V LAST JUDG/N   PROSE
FOUNDATION OF SOCIETY [ALL] WHICH IS HUMANITY ITSELF   . . 613A V LAST JUDG/N   PROSE
WHAT ARE ALL THE GIFTS OF THE SPIRIT BUT MENTAL GIFTS   . . 613A V LAST JUDG/N   PROSE
JESUS IS SURROUNDED BY BEAMS OF GLORY IN WHICH ARE SEEN ALL 613D V LAST JUDG/N   PROSE
MANY SUPPOSE THAT BEFORE [ADAM] THE CREATION ALL   . . . 614B V LAST JUDG/N   PROSE
THAT CAN ENTER THE MIND AS IT TAKES AWAY ALL SUBLIMITY   . . 614B V LAST JUDG/N   PROSE
FROM THE BIBLE & LIMITS ALL EXISTENCE TO CREATION & TO   614B V LAST JUDG/N   PROSE
    CHAOS
OF UNBELIEVING DEMONS ETERNITY EXISTS AND ALL THINGS IN   614B V LAST JUDG/N   PROSE
& THE GIVING ALL UP TO INSPIRATION BY THIS IT WILL BE SEEN   614C V LAST JUDG/N   PROSE
BUT REALITIES OF INTELLECT FROM WHICH ALL THE PASSIONS   . . 615C V LAST JUDG/N   PROSE
THOSE WHO ARE CAST OUT ARE ALL THOSE WHO   . . . . 615D V LAST JUDG/N   PROSE
BY THE VARIOUS ARTS OF POVERTY & CRUELTY OF ALL KINDS   . . 615D V LAST JUDG/N   PROSE
OF ALL THE MISCHIEFS IN THE WORLD ARE HERE DEPICTED   . . 616B V LAST JUDG/N   PROSE
IN HELL ALL IS SELF RIGHTEOUSNESS   . . . . 616C V LAST JUDG/N   PROSE
THESE PERSONIFICATIONS ARE ALL BROUGHT TOGETHER IN THE   618A ILLUS MILTON   PROSE
    FIRST DESIGN
THESE PERSONIFICATIONS ARE ALL BROUGHT TOGETHER   . . . 619A ILLUS MILTON   PROSE
AND OF THAT GOD FROM WHOM [ALL BOOKS ARE GIVEN]   . . . 621 READER LOVER/J *   2
& SHAKSPEARE & ALL WRITERS OF ENGLISH BLANK VERSE   . . 621C JERUSALEM 3   PROSE
PROSAIC FOR INFERIOR PARTS ALL ARE NECESSARY TO EACH OTHER   621D JERUSALEM 3   PROSE
IN ALL THE DARK ATLANTIC VALE DOWN FROM THE HILLS OF SURREY 622 JERUSALEM 4   9
LO WE ARE ONE FORGIVING ALL EVIL NOT SEEKING RECOMPENSE   622 JERUSALEM 4   20
ANNIHILATE THE SELFHOOD IN ME BE THOU ALL MY LIFE   . . . 623 JERUSALEM 5   22
FROM THESE TWELVE ALL THE FAMILIES OF ENGLAND SPREAD ABROAD 623 JERUSALEM 5   33
BUT ALL WITHIN IS OPEND INTO THE DEEPS OF ENTUTHON BENYTHON 624 JERUSALEM 5   56
TILL THY LIFE IS ALL TAKEN AWAY BY THIS DECEITFUL   625 JERUSALEM 7   10
    FRIENDSHIP
IS HIS GARDEN OF PLEASURE ALL THE SPECTRES OF HIS SONS   625 JERUSALEM 7   15
    MOCK THEE
OF ALBION'S SONS & THE FATHER OF ALL HIS BRETHREN IN THE   626 JERUSALEM 7   43
    SHADOWY
RELIGION TO INVOLVE ALL ALBION'S SONS AND WHEN THEY HAD   626 JERUSALEM 7   45
WHEN ALL ALBION'S INJURIES SHALL CEASE AND WHEN WE SHALL   626 JERUSALEM 7   55
POISONS ROSE UP & HIS SWEET DECEITS COVERD THEM ALL OVER   627 JERUSALEM 8   5
ACROSS ALL EUROPE & ASIA HE SAW THE TORTURES OF THE VICTIMS 627 JERUSALEM 8   24
THOU ART REVEALD BEFORE ME IN ALL THY MAGNITUDE & POWER   627 JERUSALEM 8   31
IN THE WARS OF BABEL & SHINAR ALL THEIR EMANATIONS WERE   628 JERUSALEM 8   42
CONDENSD HAND HAS ABSORBD ALL HIS BRETHREN IN HIS MIGHT   628 JERUSALEM 8   43
ALL THE INFANT LOVES & GRACES WERE LOST FOR THE MIGHTY HAND 628 JERUSALEM 8   44
AND I WILL BE MERCIFUL TO THEE BE THOU INVISIBLE TO ALL   629 JERUSALEM 10   30
TO BE ALL EVIL ALL REVERSED & FOR EVER DEAD KNOWING   . . 630 JERUSALEM 10   57
THEN ERIN CAME FORTH FROM THE FURNACES & ALL THE DAUGHTERS   630 JERUSALEM 11   8
    OF BEULAH
LOS WEPT WITH EXCEEDING JOY & ALL WEPT WITH JOY TOGETHER   631 JERUSALEM 13   13
BUT ALL CLOSD UP TILL THE LAST DAY . . . . 633 JERUSALEM 13   11
IN ALL THE TWENTY-SEVEN HEAVENS NUMBERED FROM ADAM TO LUTHER 633 JERUSALEM 13   32
FORMING THE MUNDANE SHELL ABOVE BENEATH ON ALL SIDES   634 JERUSALEM 13   54
    SURROUNDING
AND ALL THAT HAS EXISTED IN THE SPACE OF SIX THOUSAND YEARS 634 JERUSALEM 13   59
WORD WORK & WISH THAT HAS EXISTED ALL REMAINING STILL   . . 634 JERUSALEM 13   61
OF ALL THE INHABITANTS OF EARTH WAILING TO BE CREATED   . . 634 JERUSALEM 13   63
AND FROM THEM ALL THE LOVELY BEAMING DAUGHTERS OF ALBION   635 JERUSALEM 14   11
AND EVERY ONE A GATE OF RUBIES & ALL SORTS OF PRECIOUS   635 JERUSALEM 14   21
    STONES
I SEE THE PAST PRESENT & FUTURE EXISTING ALL AT ONCE   . . 635 JERUSALEM 15   8
AND THENCE TO ALL THE KINGDOMS & NATIONS & FAMILIES OF   637 JERUSALEM 16   34
    THE EARTH
GOVERNING ALL BY THE SWEET DELIGHTS OF SECRET AMOROUS   638 JERUSALEM 16   59
    GLANCES
ALL THINGS ACTED ON EARTH ARE SEEN IN THE BRIGHT SCULPTURES 638 JERUSALEM 16   61
    OF
IN ALL THEIR VARIOUS COMBINATIONS WROUGHT WITH WONDROUS ART 638 JERUSALEM 16   66
ALL THAT CAN HAPPEN TO MAN IN HIS PILGRIMAGE OF SEVENTY   638 JERUSALEM 16   67
    YEARS
FATHER AND SON AND LIGHT AND LOVE ALL BOLD ASPERITIES   . . 640 JERUSALEM 18   21
ALL HIS AFFECTIONS NOW APPEAR WITHOUTSIDE ALL HIS SONS   641 JERUSALEM 19   17
WHICH STAND UPON THE ENDS OF BEULAH AND WITHOUTSIDE ALL   642 JERUSALEM 19   34
ASK ME NOT OF MY GRIEFS THOU KNOWEST ALL MY GRIEFS   . . . 642 JERUSALEM 20   20
ALL IS ETERNAL DEATH UNLESS YOU CAN WEAVE A CHASTE   . . . 643 JERUSALEM 21   11
AND ALL MY CHILDREN FOLLOWD HIS LOUD HOWLINGS INTO THE DEEP 643 JERUSALEM 21   17
ALL LOVE IS LOST TERROR SUCCEEDS & [RATRED] HATRED INSTEAD   645 JERUSALEM 22 *   10
    OF LOVE
DISPLAYING OUR GIANT LIMBS TO ALL THE WINDS OF HEAVEN   647 JERUSALEM 24   6
    SUDDEN
OF OUR IMMORTAL VEINS & ALL THEIR HOSTS FLED FROM OUR LIMBS 647 JERUSALEM 24   8
SCANDINAVIA FLED WITH ALL HIS MOUNTAINS PILLD WITH GROANS   647 JERUSALEM 24   11
THY SEVERE JUDGE ALL THE DAY LONG PROVES THEE O BABYLON   647 JERUSALEM 24   27
AND THERE WAS HEARD A GREAT LAMENTING IN BEULAH ALL THE   648 JERUSALEM 25   1
    REGIONS

		PAGE	TITLE	LINE
ALL	(CONTINUED)			
	IN ALL ITS REGIONS & ITS FATHER & SAVIOUR NOT PITY AND WEEP	648	JERUSALEM 25	9
	ALL THINGS BEGIN & END IN ALBION'S ANCIENT DRUID ROCKY SHORE	649B	JERUSALEM 27	PROSE
	IN HIS MIGHTY LIMBS ALL THINGS IN HEAVEN & EARTH	649C	JERUSALEM 27	PROSE
	AND ALL THE ATLANTIC MOUNTAINS SHOOK	650	FIELDS FROM/J	36
	TORE FORTH IN ALL THE POMP OF WAR	650	FIELDS FROM/J	38
	BUT O TRANSLUCENT ALL WITHIN	651	FIELDS FROM/J	56
	DESTROYING ALL THE WORLD BESIDE	651	FIELDS FROM/J	80
	IF YOUR TRADITION THAT MAN CONTAINED IN HIS LIMBS ALL ANIMALS	652B	JERUSALEM 27	PROSE
	IN ALL THE GARDEN OF EDEN & IN ALL THE GOLDEN MOUNTAINS	652	JERUSALEM 28	2
	ALL THESE ORNAMENTS ARE CRIMES THEY ARE MADE BY THE LABOURS	652	JERUSALEM 28	6
	HORRID TO THINK OF WHEN ENQUIRED DEEPLY INTO AND ALL . .	652	JERUSALEM 28	8
	OF THE WHOLE EARTH HE WAS THE ANGEL OF MY PRESENCE AND ALL	653	JERUSALEM 29	7
	SOFT EXULTING IN EXISTENCE ALL THE MAN ABSORBING	654	JERUSALEM 29	40
	ALL IS CONFUSION ALL IS TUMULT & WE ALONE ARE ESCAPED .	655	JERUSALEM 29	82
	BOSOM IN ALL THE TERRORS OF FRIENDSHIP ENTERING THE CAVES	656	JERUSALEM 31	4
	AND ALL THE TENDERNESSES OF THE SOUL CAST FORTH AS FILTH & MIRE	657	JERUSALEM 31	21
	I COULD NOT DARE TO TAKE VENGEANCE FOR ALL THINGS ARE SO CONSTRUCTED	657	JERUSALEM 31	30
	BELONG TO GOD ALONE AND ALL THY LITTLE ONES ARE HOLY .	657	JERUSALEM 31	45
	AND THOU O HARLOT DAUGHTER DAUGHTER OF DESPAIR ART ALL	658	JERUSALEM 31	58
	FOR ALL TO AVOID THEE TO BE ASTONISHD AT THEE FOR THY SINS	658	JERUSALEM 31	62
	LOS WAS ALL ASTONISHMENT & TERROR HE TREMBLED SITTING ON THE STONE	658	JERUSALEM 32	3
	ALL THINGS BEGIN & END IN ALBION'S ANCIENT DRUID ROCKY SHORE	658	JERUSALEM 32	15
	IS AS NOTHING BEFORE THEE FADED IS ALL LIFE AND JOY . .	659	JERUSALEM 33	34
	A DEWY GARMENT COVERS ME ALL OVER ALL MANHOOD IS GONE .	660	JERUSALEM 34	4
	ART THOU NATURE MOTHER OF ALL IS JERUSALEM THY DAUGHTER	660	JERUSALEM 34	9
	OF DEATH IN ALBION'S CLOUDS DREADFUL UTTERD OVER ALL THE EARTH	661	JERUSALEM 34	24
	CUT OFF FROM ALBION'S MOUNTAINS & FROM ALL THE EARTH'S SUMMITS	661	JERUSALEM 34	44
	OVER JORDAN ALL TERRIFIED FLED THEY BECAME WHAT THEY BEHELD	661	JERUSALEM 34	54
	ALBION GOES TO ETERNAL DEATH IN ME ALL ETERNITY	662	JERUSALEM 35	9
	ALL THAT BEHELD HIM FLED HOWLING AND GNAWED THEIR TONGUES .	662	JERUSALEM 36	8
	BY THE NAME OF MORALITY THEIR DAUGHTERS GOVERN ALL . . .	663	JERUSALEM 36	47
	MUTUAL IN ONE ANOTHER'S LOVE AND WRATH ALL RENEWING . .	664	JERUSALEM 38	16
	AS ONE MAN ALL THE UNIVERSAL FAMILY AND THAT ONE MAN . .	664	JERUSALEM 38	19
	HE IS THE SHEPHERD OF ALBION HE IS ALL IN ALL	665	JERUSALEM 38	24
	THEY HAVE SOWN ERRORS OVER ALL HIS FRUITFUL FIELDS . . .	667	JERUSALEM 40	20
	MERCIFUL TO THEE AND CRUEL TO ALL THAT THOU HATEST . . .	670	JERUSALEM 42	22
	CONSIDER ME AS THINE ENEMY ON ME TURN ALL THY FURY . . .	670	JERUSALEM 42	40
	ALL THAT THEY HAVE IS MINE FROM MY FREE GENROUS GIFT . .	671	JERUSALEM 42	52
	THEY NOW HOLD ALL THEY HAVE INGRATITUDE TO ME	671	JERUSALEM 42	53
	COME UP BUILD BABYLON RAHAB IS OURS & ALL HER MULTITUDES	671	JERUSALEM 42	63
	TO WHICH ALL LINEAMENTS TEND & SEEK WITH LOVE & SYMPATHY	672	JERUSALEM 43	21
	ALL BROAD & GENERAL PRINCIPLES BELONG TO BENEVOLENCE . .	672	JERUSALEM 43	22
	THIS OUTRAGE AH ME HOW SICK & PALE YOU ALL STAND ROUND ME	673	JERUSALEM 43	72
	ALL YOU MY FRIENDS & BROTHERS ALL YOU MY BELOVED COMPANIONS	673	JERUSALEM 43	74
	ME SOME COMFORT WHY DO YOU ALL STAND SILENT I ALONE . .	673	JERUSALEM 43	77
	REMAIN IN PERMANENT STRENGTH OR IS ALL THIS GOODNESS & PITY ONLY	673	JERUSALEM 43	78
	AND ALL THE GATE OF LOS CLOUDED WITH CLOUDS REDOUNDING FROM	674	JERUSALEM 44	8
	WE ALL ADMIRD & LOVD WHOSE ALL BENEVOLENT COUNTENANCE SEEN	675	JERUSALEM 45	5
	HE FROWND ON ALL HIS FRIENDS COUNTING THEM ENEMIES IN HIS SORROW	676	JERUSALEM 45	36
	WEEPING WAS IN ALL BEULAH AND ALL THE DAUGHTERS OF BEULAH	678	JERUSALEM 48	21
	THE MOUNTAIN OF GIANTS ALL THE GIANTS OF ALBION ARE BECOME	679	JERUSALEM 49	7
	AND THE BODIES IN WHICH ALL ANIMALS & VEGETATIONS THE EARTH & HEAVEN	679	JERUSALEM 49	13
	THE GOLDEN GATE OF HAVILAH AND ALL THE GARDEN OF GOD . .	679	JERUSALEM 49	15
	STRIVING TO CREATE A HEAVEN IN WHICH ALL SHALL BE PURE & HOLY	679	JERUSALEM 49	27
	IN WHOSE SIGHT ALL ARE AS THE DUST	679	JERUSALEM 49	31
	AND WE ALSO & ALL BEULAH CONSUME BENEATH ALBION'S CURSE	681	JERUSALEM 50	17
	OF STARS FOR ALL THE SONS OF ALBION APPEARD DISTANT STARS	681	JERUSALEM 50	20
	THE SPIRITUAL STATES OF THE SOUL ARE ALL ETERNAL	681D	JERUSALEM 52	PROSE
	CALLING THE PRINCE OF THIS WORLD GOD AND DESTROYING ALL	682B	JERUSALEM 52	PROSE
	BUT CONFESSED HIS SINS BEFORE ALL THE WORLD	682D	JERUSALEM 52	PROSE
	ALL THE DESTRUCTION THEREFORE IN CHRISTIAN EUROPE . . .	683A	JERUSALEM 52	PROSE
	INCLOSING ALL THE CHILDREN OF LOS TIME AFTER TIME . . .	684	JERUSALEM 53	7
	WHICH OVERSPREAD ALL THE EARTH HE GROANS AMONG HIS RUIND PORCHES	685	JERUSALEM 54	14
	WHEN THOSE WHO DISREGARD ALL MORTAL THINGS SAW A MIGHTY-ONE	686	JERUSALEM 55	1
	SUPERIOR NONE WE KNOW INFERIOR NONE ALL EQUAL SHARE . .	686	JERUSALEM 55	8
	WALKETH AMONG US GIVE DECISION BRING FORTH ALL YOUR FIRES	686	JERUSALEM 55	18
	BY HIS OWN WORKS LET ALL INDEFINITES BE THROWN INTO DEMONSTRATIONS	687	JERUSALEM 55	58
	THIS WORLD IS ALL A CRADLE FOR THE ERRED WANDERING PHANTOM	688	JERUSALEM 56	8
	WONDER SIEZD ALL IN ETERNITY TO BEHOLD THE DIVINE VISION OPEN	689	JERUSALEM 57	17
	THE FOUR ZOAS RUSH AROUND ON ALL SIDES IN DIRE RUIN . . .	690	JERUSALEM 58	47
	ALL FELL TOWARDS THE CENTER SINKING DOWNWARDS IN DIRE RUIN	691	JERUSALEM 59	17
	A SHEPHERD IN THE NIGHT OF ALBION WHICH OVERSPREAD ALL THE EARTH	692	JERUSALEM 60	9
	HER FORM WAS HELD BY BEULAH'S DAUGHTERS BUT ALL WITHIN UNSEEN	693	JERUSALEM 60	40

```
                                                            PAGE      TITLE        LINE
ALL    (CONTINUED)
    ALL NIGHT VALA HEARS SHE TRIUMPHS IN PRIDE OF HOLINESS  . .   693 JERUSALEM 60    45
    THAT THOU O HUMAN IMAGINATION O DIVINE BODY ART ALL     . .   693 JERUSALEM 60    57
    COME NOW WITH ME INTO THE VILLAGES WALK THRO ALL THE CITIES   696 JERUSALEM 62    23
    MULTITUDINOUS IN THE LOOKING GLASS OF ENITHARMON ON ALL       697 JERUSALEM 63    21
        SIDES
    WHEN THE DRUIDS DEMANDED CHASTITY FROM WOMAN & ALL WAS LOST   697 JERUSALEM 63    25
    LOS KNEW NOT YET WHAT WAS DONE HE THOUGHT IT WAS ALL IN       698 JERUSALEM 63    36
        VISION
    AND ALL THE LAND OF CANAAN SUSPENDED OVER THE VALLEY OF       698 JERUSALEM 63    42
        CHEVIOT
    OF THE MUNDANE SHELL WHICH FROZE ON ALL SIDES ROUND CANAAN    698 JERUSALEM 64     1
        ON
    THEN ALL THE DAUGHTERS OF ALBION BECAME ONE BEFORE LOS        698 JERUSALEM 64     6
        EVEN VALA
    ALL QUARRELS ARISE FROM REASONING THE SECRET MURDER AND       699 JERUSALEM 64    20
    AND ALL THE ARTS OF LIFE THEY CHANGD INTO THE ARTS OF DEATH   700 JERUSALEM 65    16
        IN ALBION
    IN IGNORANCE TO VIEW A SMALL PORTION & THINK THAT ALL   . .   700 JERUSALEM 65    27
    AND CALL IT DEMONSTRATION BLIND TO ALL THE SIMPLE RULES       700 JERUSALEM 65    28
        OF LIFE
    NOW SMILE AMONG THY BITTER TEARS NOW PUT ON ALL THY BEAUTY    700 JERUSALEM 65    30
    REMEMBER ALL THY FEIGNED TERRORS . . . . .  . . .  . . .      700 JERUSALEM 65    42
    IN AWFUL POMP & GOLD IN ALL THE PRECIOUS UNHEWN STONES        701 JERUSALEM 66     1
        OF EDEN
    ALL WHO SEE BECOME WHAT THEY BEHOLD THEIR EYES ARE COVERD     702 JERUSALEM 66    36
    AND ALL THE MOUNTAINS & HILLS SHRINK UP LIKE A WITHERING      703 JERUSALEM 66    82
        GOURD
    THE ROCKS ARE OPAKE HARDNESSES COVERING ALL VEGETATED         704 JERUSALEM 67     5
        THINGS
    EPHRAIM WAS A WILDERNESS OF JOY WHERE ALL MY WILD BEASTS      705 JERUSALEM 67    56
        RAN
    BUT THEY FROWN & DELIGHT IN CRUELTY REFUSING ALL OTHER JOY    706 JERUSALEM 68    29
    THEN ALL THE MALES [CONJOINED] COMBINED INTO ONE MALE &       707 JERUSALEM 69  *  1
        EVERY ONE
    IN ALL ITS MEMBERS IN ETERNAL TORMENT OF LOVE & JEALOUSY      707 JERUSALEM 69     7
    AND FEEDS HER WITH THE FOOD OF EDEN HENCE ALL HER BEAUTY      707 JERUSALEM 69    18
        BEAMS
    FOR ALL THINGS EXIST IN THE HUMAN IMAGINATION . . . . .       707 JERUSALEM 69    25
    HENCE ROSE THE TABERNACLE IN THE WILDERNESS & ALL            707 JERUSALEM 69    28
        ITS OFFERINGS
    AND NOW THE SPECTRES OF THE DEAD AWAKE IN BEULAH ALL    . .   708 JERUSALEM 69    32
    THEREFORE REJECTING IDEAS AS NOTHING & HOLDING ALL WISDOM     708 JERUSALEM 70     7
    IN THE OAK GROVES OF ALBION WHICH OVERSPREAD ALL THE EARTH    708 JERUSALEM 70    16
    BEAMS MILD ALL LOVE AND ALL PERFECTION THAT WHEN THE LIPS     709 JERUSALEM 70    24
    THE STARRY HEAVENS ALL WERE FLED FROM THE MIGHTY LIMBS        709 JERUSALEM 70    32
        OF ALBION
    WERE SEEN JERUSALEM'S SONS AND ALL THE TWELVE TRIBES          709 JERUSALEM 71     3
        SPREADING
    AND KENT & MIDDLESEX ALL THEIR RIVERS & THEIR HILLS OF        709 JERUSALEM 71    12
        FLOCKS & HERDS
    ALL WERE HIS FRIENDS & THEIR SONS & DAUGHTERS INTERMARRY      709 JERUSALEM 71    14
        IN BEULAH
    FOR ALL ARE MEN IN ETERNITY RIVERS MOUNTAINS CITIES           709 JERUSALEM 71    15
        VILLAGES
    ALL ARE HUMAN & WHEN YOU ENTER INTO THEIR BOSOMS YOU WALK     709 JERUSALEM 71    16
    AND EARTH & ALL YOU BEHOLD THO IT APPEARS WITHOUT IT IS       709 JERUSALEM 71    18
        WITHIN
    GWANTOKE FORGAVE & JOYD OVER SOUTH WALES & ALL ITS            710 JERUSALEM 71    29
        MOUNTAINS
    BEAUTIFUL SHE BEAMS TOWARDS THE EAST ALL KINDS OF PRECIOUS    710 JERUSALEM 71    40
        STONES
    BOWEN HAD ALL SCOTLAND THE ISLES NORTHUMBERLAND &             710 JERUSALEM 71    46
        CUMBERLAND
    ALL THESE CENTER IN LONDON & IN GOLGONOOZA FROM WHENCE  . .   712 JERUSALEM 72    28
    AND FROM THEM ARE CREATED ALL THE NATIONS OF THE EARTH  . .   712 JERUSALEM 72    30
    RETURN O ALBION LET JERUSALEM OVERSPREAD ALL NATIONS    . .   712 JERUSALEM 72    35
    ALL THE NATIONS PEOPLES & TONGUES THROUGHOUT ALL THE EARTH    712 JERUSALEM 72    44
    WHITEFIELD & HERVEY GUARD THAT GATE WITH ALL THE GENTLE       712 JERUSALEM 72    51
        SOULS
    THRO ALL THE FOUR POINTS LO THE LABOURERS AT THE FURNACES     713 JERUSALEM 73     4
    AND ALL THE KINGS & NOBLES OF THE EARTH & ALL THEIR           713 JERUSALEM 73    38
        GLORIES
    HENCE ALBION WAS CALLD THE CANAANITE & ALL HIS GIANT SONS     715 JERUSALEM 74    39
    FROM ALL THE NATIONS OF THE EARTH TO DISSIPATE INTO NON       715 JERUSALEM 74    51
        ENTITY
    AND ALL HER TWENTY-SEVEN HEAVENS NOW HID & NOW REVEALD  . .   715 JERUSALEM 75     4
    ALL THE TORTURES OF REPENTANCE ARE TORTURES                  716D JERUSALEM 77  PROSE
        OF SELF-REPROACH
    WHAT WERE ALL THEIR SPIRITUAL GIFTS WHAT IS THE DIVINE       717A JERUSALEM 77  PROSE
        SPIRIT
    WHAT ARE ALL THE GIFTS OF THE GOSPEL ARE THEY NOT ALL        717A JERUSALEM 77  PROSE
        MENTAL GIFTS
    CAN YOU THINK AT ALL & NOT PRONOUNCE HEARTILY . . . . . .    717C JERUSALEM 77  PROSE
    ENGAGE HIMSELF OPENLY & PUBLICLY BEFORE ALL THE WORLD   . .  717C JERUSALEM 77  PROSE
    OF FIRE SURROUNDING ALL THE HEAVENS IT WENT    . . . . .      717 STOOD AMONG/J    3
    CREATION AND DEVOURD ALL THINGS IN ITS LOUD    . . . . .      717 STOOD AMONG/J    5
    THE HILL OF GIANTS ALL HER FOUNDATIONS LEVELLD WITH THE       719 JERUSALEM 78    22
        DUST
    AND ALL THE NATIONS OF THE EARTH WERE SEEN IN THE CITIES      720 JERUSALEM 79    23
        OF ALBION
    MY GATES IN ALL THEIR MOUNTAINS & MY CURTAINS IN ALL THEIR    720 JERUSALEM 79    46
        VALES
```

69

		PAGE	TITLE	LINE
ALL	**(CONTINUED)**			
	FROM ALL MY MYRIADS ONCE THE FOUR-FOLD WORLD REJOICD AMONG	721	JERUSALEM 79	58
	WHICH OVERSPREAD ALL THE EARTH IN PATRIARCHAL POMP & CRUEL PRIDE	721	JERUSALEM 79	67
	AMONG THE FOUR FORESTS OF ALBION WHICH OVERSPREAD ALL THE EARTH	722	JERUSALEM 80	43
	AGAINST JERUSALEM THEY RAGE THRO ALL THE NATIONS OF EUROPE	722	JERUSALEM 80	46
	REFUSD TO TAKE A DEFINITE FORM SHE HOVERD OVER ALL THE EARTH	723	JERUSALEM 80	52
	THAT APPARENT TO ALL IN ETERNITY GLOWS LIKE THE SUN IN THE BREAST	723	JERUSALEM 80	68
	BEFORE THE FURNACES LABOURING WHILE LOS ALL NIGHT WATCHES	729	JERUSALEM 83	80
	IN ALL THE CITIES OF THE NATIONS PARIS MADRID AMSTERDAM	729	JERUSALEM 84	14
	TO GREAT QUEEN STREET & LINCOLNS INN ALL IS DISTRESS & WOE	729	JERUSALEM 84	16
	BUT WE WOO HIM ALL THE NIGHT IN SONGS O LOS COME FORTH O LOS	729	JERUSALEM 84	25
	TWELVE-FOLD HERE ALL THE TRIBES OF ISRAEL I BEHOLD . . .	731	JERUSALEM 86	17
	OF BLOOD THRO ALL MY NERVOUS LIMBS SOON OVERGROWN IN ROOTS	732	JERUSALEM 87	6
	WHEN SOULS MINGLE & JOIN THRO ALL THE FIBRES OF BROTHERHOOD	733	JERUSALEM 88	14
	THRO ALL THE WORLD OF ERIN & OF LOS & ALL THEIR CHILDREN	733	JERUSALEM 88	33
	YOU SHALL WANT ALL THE MINUTE PARTICULARS OF LIFE . . .	734	JERUSALEM 88	43
	THE FOUR ZOAS IN ALL THEIR FADED MAJESTY BURST OUT IN FURY	734	JERUSALEM 88	55
	OF EDEN ALL PERVERTED EGYPT ON THE GIHON MANY TONGUED . .	734	JERUSALEM 89	15
	TWELVE RIDGES OF STONE FROWN OVER ALL THE EARTH IN TYRANT PRIDE	735	JERUSALEM 89	21
	OF JAVAN THRO THE ISLES OF GRECIA & ALL EUROPE'S KINGS . .	735	JERUSALEM 89	34
	INTO THE SEA OF REPHAIM BUT THE SEA OERWHELD THEM ALL	735	JERUSALEM 89	51
	THEN HE SENT FORTH THE SPECTRE ALL HIS PYRAMIDS WERE GRAINS	739	JERUSALEM 91	48
	I CARE NOT WHETHER A MAN IS GOOD OR EVIL ALL THAT I CARE	739	JERUSALEM 91	55
	WHEN ALL THEIR CRIMES THEIR PUNISHMENTS THEIR ACCUSATIONS OF SIN	739	JERUSALEM 92	15
	ALL THEIR JEALOUSIES REVENGES MURDERS HIDINGS OF CRUELTY IN DECEIT	739	JERUSALEM 92	16
	ENITHARMON'S NAME IS NOTHING BEFORE YOU YOU FORGET ALL MY LOVE	740	JERUSALEM 93	3
	AND THE BODY OF ALBION WAS CLOSED APART FROM ALL NATIONS	741	JERUSALEM 94	14
	O ALL YE NATIONS OF THE EARTH BEHOLD YE THE JEALOUS WIFE	742	JERUSALEM 94	26
	IN ANGER THE WRATH OF GOD BREAKING BRIGHT FLAMING ON ALL SIDES AROUND	742	JERUSALEM 95	6
	REVOLUTIONS OF ACTION & PASSION THRO THE FOUR ELEMENTS ON ALL SIDES	742	JERUSALEM 95	10
	ALL WAS A VISION ALL A DREAM THE FURNACES BECAME . . .	744	JERUSALEM 96	36
	AND ALL THE CITIES OF ALBION ROSE FROM THEIR SLUMBERS AND ALL	744	JERUSALEM 96	38
	SOON ALL AROUND REMOTE THE HEAVENS BURNT WITH FLAMING FIRES	744	JERUSALEM 96	40
	AWAKE AND OVERSPREAD ALL NATIONS AS IN ANCIENT TIME . . .	744	JERUSALEM 97	2
	A SUN OF BLOOD RED WRATH SURROUNDING HEAVEN ON ALL SIDES AROUND	745	JERUSALEM 98	10
	OF HUMAN IMAGINATION THROUGHOUT ALL THE THREE REGIONS IMMENSE	746	JERUSALEM 98	32
	. . . WHERE ARE ALL HIS HUMAN SACRIFICES	746	JERUSALEM 98	* 48
	. . . ALL THEIR GLORY THAT GREW ON DESOLATION	746	JERUSALEM 98	51
	SUCH IS THE CRY FROM ALL THE EARTH	746	JERUSALEM 98	54
	ALL HUMAN FORMS IDENTIFIED EVEN TREE METAL EARTH & STONE ALL	747	JERUSALEM 99	1
	THINE IS THE FRIEND OF ALL MANKIND	748	EV GOSPEL(A)/N	5
	SATAN & ALL HIS HELLISH CREW	749	EV GOSPEL(B)/N	51
	OR OF CHRIST & HIS FATHER ITS ALL A BOAST . . . . .·.	752	EV GOSPEL(D)/N	46
	WHAT WAS HE DOING ALL THAT TIME	752	EV GOSPEL(D)/N	51
	[[ALL] THIS CORPOREAL LIFE S A] [ALL LIFE S A FICTION]	753	EV GOSPEL(D)/N *	85
	THE BURIED SOUL & ALL ITS GEMS	753	EV GOSPEL(D)/N	102
	ALL AWAY BEGAN TO ROLL	754	EV GOSPEL(E)/N	14
	[THOU] THO THOU DIDST ALL TO CHAOS ROLL	754	EV GOSPEL(E)/N *	39
	ALL MENTAL POWERS BY DISEASES WE BIND	755	EV GOSPEL(E)/N	87
	I MADE MY VOICE HEARD ALL OVER THE NATION	756	EV GOSPEL(G)/N	2
	CHRIST'S PRETENSIONS WERE ALL VANITY	758	EV GOSPEL (1)	2
	THE HEATHEN DEITIES WROTE THEM ALL	758	EV GOSPEL (2)	5
	THE ACCUSER HOLY GOD OF ALL	758	EV GOSPEL (2)	13
	THY SINS ARE ALL FORGIVEN THEE	758	EV GOSPEL (2)	18
	THY SINS ARE ALL FORGIVEN THEE	758	EV GOSPEL (2)	23
	THRO ALL THE WORLD IN JESUS' NAME	758	EV GOSPEL (2)	25
	FOR MORAL VIRTUES ALL BEGIN	759	EV GOSPEL (2)	34
	AND [MORAL] ALL THE HEROIC VIRTUES [ALL] END	759	EV GOSPEL (2)	36
	OF ALL SUBLUNARY THINGS	771	OF GATES/GP	36
	STICK TO THIS ALL IS RIGHT BUT SEE PAGE...	772B	ANNO SPURZHEIM	MARG
	YOU RETAIN HEALTH AND YET ARE AS MAD AS ANY OF US ALL .	772D	ANNO SPURZHEIM	MARG
	OVER US ALL MAD AS A REFUGE FROM UNBELIEF	772D	ANNO SPURZHEIM	MARG
	ALL GENIUS VARIES THUS DEVILS ARE VARIOUS ANGELS ARE ALL ALIKE	773A	NOTE NINE HEAD	PROSE
	SOLOMON SAYS "VANITY OF VANITIES ALL IS VANITY "	773B	MIRTH AND COMP	PROSE
	THE ALL IN MAN THE DIVINE IMAGE OR IMAGINATION . . .	773D	ANNO BERKELEY	MARG
	ALL WARRIORS THE MORAL VIRTUES ARE CONTINUAL ACCUSERS .	774D	ANNO BERKELEY	MARG
	MAN IS ALL IMAGINATION GOD IS MAN & EXISTS IN US & WE IN HIM	775A	ANNO BERKELEY	MARG
	FASTING &C ALL RELATE TO ART	776A	INSC LAOCOON	PROSE
	IN ETERNITY ALL IS VISION	776B	INSC LAOCOON	PROSE
	ALL THAT WE SEE IS VISION	776D	INSC LAOCOON	PROSE
	STATES IN WHICH ALL VISIONARY MEN ARE ACCOUNTED MAD MEN	777B	INSC LAOCOON	PROSE
	JESUS & HIS APOSTLES & DISCIPLES WERE ALL ARTISTS . .	777B	INSC LAOCOON	PROSE
	THE WHOLE BUSINESS OF MAN IS THE ARTS & ALL THINGS COMMON	777C	INSC LAOCOON	PROSE
	ALL IS NOT SIN THAT SATAN CALLS SO	777D	INSC LAOCOON	PROSE
	ALL THE LOVES & GRACES OF ETERNITY	777D	INSC LAOCOON	PROSE

		PAGE	TITLE	LINE
ALL	**(CONTINUED)**			
	& SCIENCES AS THEY PRETEND WERE DESTROYERS OF ALL ART . .	778C	HOMERS POETRY	PROSE
	EVE IS THIS THE PROMISE OF JEHOVAH O IT IS ALL A VAIN DELUSION	779	GHOST ABEL 1	6
	ADAM IT IS ALL A VAIN DELUSION OF THE ALL CREATIVE IMAGINATION	780	GHOST ABEL 1	17
	WITH ALL OUR MIGHT & STRENGTH THO WE ARE FALLEN & LOST . .	780	GHOST ABEL 2	2
	. . . IN THE MIDST OF THE DARKNESS OF THE OATH ALL CLOTHED	781	GHOST ABEL 2	23
	AT ENMITY AGAINST ALL TRUE POETRY OR INSPIRATION	782D	ANNO WW POEMS	MARG
	("TO HC SIX YEARS OLD") THIS IS ALL IN THE HIGHEST DEGREE IMAGINATIVE	783A	ANNO WW POEMS	MARG
	THE FOUNDATION OF ALL & THE GODDESS NATURE	785A	ILLUS DANTE 7	*PROSE
	SO THAT HOMER IS THE CENTER OF ALL I MEAN THE POETRY OF THE HEATHEN	785B	ILLUS DANTE 7	PROSE
	TO CONSIDER THIS TO ALL ETERNITY WILL BE COMMENT ENOUGH	787A	ANNO THORNTON	MARG
	IN A BOOK WHERE ALL MAY READ &	787A	ANNO THORNTON	MARG
	IN A BOOK WHICH ALL MAY READ &	787A	ANNO THORNTON	MARG
	IN A BOOK THAT ALL MAY READ ARE EQUALLY RIGHT	787A	ANNO THORNTON	MARG
	OR TAX UPON WHAT IS COMMON TO ALL IN THY KINGDOM	788A	ANNO THORNTON	MARG
	WE HAVE ALL THINGS COMMON [ALL THINGS COMMON] AMONG US	788B	ANNO THORNTON	* MARG
	FOR ALL IS DEBTS & TAXES BETWEEN [XXX] CAESAR & US . . .	788D	ANNO THORNTON	* MARG
	WEIGHED & TAXED & MEASURED ALL ELSE	789B	ANNO THORNTON	MARG
	SEE ECLOGUE I FOR ALL THIS WE THANK DR THORNTON	789B	ANNO THORNTON	MARG
	NOTE THE DANGER IS IN NOT COVERING THE PLATE ALL OVER . .	790C	LETTER 2	PROSE
	NOW YOU I HOPE SHEW ALL THE FAMILY OF ANTIQUE BORERS	790D	LETTER 2	PROSE
	I HAVE LIKEWISE HAD BY ME ALL THE SUMMER (SIX) PLATES	791B	LETTER 3	PROSE
	WHOSE PLATES WERE OR THAT THEY WERE [THERE] AT ALL . . .	791B	LETTER 3	PROSE
	HOW ALL YOUR BRETHREN SAY THE SOUND OF HIS HARP	791B	LETTER 3	PROSE
	HOPED YOUR PLAN COMPREHENDED ALL SPECIES OF THIS ART . .	793A	LETTER 5	PROSE
	AS THEY DO FUN I LOVE BUT TOO MUCH FUN IS OF ALL THINGS	793C	LETTER 5	PROSE
	IN THE WAY SOME SEE NATURE ALL RIDICULE & DEFORMITY & .	793D	LETTER 5	PROSE
	SEE NATURE AT ALL BUT TO THE EYES OF THE MAN OF IMAGINATION	793D	LETTER 5	PROSE
	TO ME THIS WORLD IS ALL ONE CONTINUED VISION OF FANCY OR	793D	LETTER 5	PROSE
	WHICH ARE TO REJECT ALL FANCY FROM HIS WORK	794D	LETTER 6	PROSE
	IT IS THE ONLY SOURCE OF PLEASURE ALL YOUR OTHER PLEASURES	795B	LETTER 6	PROSE
	WHO LOVE & ADMIRE YOUR WORKS BUT ABOVE ALL FOR THE SAKE OF THE ARTS	795B	LETTER 6	PROSE
	AFTER ANOTHER ARTIST BUT ABOVE ALL I FEEL MYSELF HAPPY &	795C	LETTER 6	PROSE
	WITH ALL POSSIBLE EXPEDITION I SEND YOU A PROOF OF MY .	796C	LETTER 8	PROSE
	OF WHAT ALL FEEL IN THIS VALLEY OF MISERY & HAPPINESS MIXED	797A	LETTER 9	PROSE
	ALL TO PARTAKE OF SINCE IT IS TO ME A SOURCE OF IMMORTAL JOY	797B	LETTER 9	PROSE
	ALL YOUR WISHES SHALL IN DUE TIME BE FULFILLED	797C	LETTER 10	PROSE
	MUST BE THE PLAN IF ENGLAND WISHES TO CONTINUE AT ALL WORTH	798A	LETTER 10	PROSE
	GOD KEEP YOU FROM & ALL GOOD MEN OUR ARTISTS OF ALL RANKS	798A	LETTER 10	PROSE
	MY DEAREST FRIEND IT IS TO YOU I OWE ALL MY PRESENT . .	799A	LETTER 11	PROSE
	THE AMERICAN WAR BEGAN ALL ITS DARK HORRORS PASSED BEFORE MY FACE	799	TO FLAXMAN/L	9
	"ON SUNDAY AFTERNOON IN HAMPSTEAD TO TAKE FAREWELL ALL"	800A	LETTER 12	PROSE
	DO ALL THAT YOU CAN OR ALL THAT YOU MAY	800	MRS FLAXMAN/L	3
	DISPENSING UNCEASING TO ALL THE WHOLE LAND	800	MRS FLAXMAN/L	16
	HEAVEN OPENS HERE ON ALL SIDES HER GOLDEN GATES . . .	802A	LETTER 14	PROSE
	ALL WAS CHEARFULNESS & GOOD HUMOUR ON THE ROAD & YET WE	802B	LETTER 14	PROSE
	CHAISES & AS MANY DIFFERENT DRIVERS ALL UPON THE ROAD WAS	803A	LETTER 15	PROSE
	THERE WAS NO GRUMBLING AT ALL WE TRAVELD THRO	803A	LETTER 15	PROSE
	AWAY FROM ALL CARE	804	TO BUTTS/L	10
	ALL MY MIRE & MY CLAY	805	TO BUTTS/L	56
	ALL I EVER HAD KNOWN	806	TO BUTTS/L	73
	WE DETERMINE THEREFORE TO BE HAPPY AND DO ALL THAT WE CAN	807A	LETTER 17	PROSE
	THO NOT ALL THAT WE WOULD	807A	LETTER 17	PROSE
	I SHALL BE ENABLED TO THROW OFF ALL OBSTRUCTIONS TO SUCCESS	808A	LETTER 19	PROSE
	MENTAL DISTRESS & I KNOW THAT ALL DISTRESS INFLICTED BY	809B	LETTER 20	PROSE
	HEAVEN IS A MERCY A FIG FOR ALL CORPOREAL SUCH DISTRESS IS	809B	LETTER 20	PROSE
	DID NOT HE IS ALSO A HAPPY ABSTRACT KNOWN BY ALL HIS FRIENDS	809C	LETTER 20	PROSE
	AS ALL MY FRIENDS TELL ME BUT MY PRINCIPAL LABOUR . . .	809C	LETTER 20	PROSE
	WITH ALL HIS MATCHLESS INDUSTRY	809D	LETTER 20	PROSE
	WILL NEXT SUMMER JOKE US FACE TO FACE GOD BLESS YOU ALL	810C	LETTER 20	PROSE
	& MR H(HAYLEY) I DOUBT NOT WILL DO ULTIMATELY ALL . . .	811D	LETTER 22	PROSE
	& I DOUBT NOT THAT ALL YOUR KIND WISHES IN MY BEHALF	811D	LETTER 22	PROSE
	NAMELY I HAVE RECOLLECTED ALL MY SCATTERED THOUGHTS ON ART	812A	LETTER 22	PROSE
	& I FIND ON ALL HANDS GREAT OBJECTIONS TO MY DOING ANY THING	812C	LETTER 22	PROSE
	YOU WILL UNDERSTAND BY THIS THE SOURCE OF ALL MY UNEASINESS	812C	LETTER 22	PROSE
	THE THING I HAVE MOST AT HEART MORE THAN LIFE OR ALL .	812D	LETTER 22	PROSE
	WE ARE RICHLY CLOTHD IN SPIRITUAL & SUFFER ALL THE REST GLADLY	813C	LETTER 22	PROSE
	SINCE THE AGE OF RAFAEL ALL SR J REYNOLDS'S DISCOURSES . .	814B	LETTER 23	PROSE
	TO PLEASE BECAUSE YOU AMONG ALL MEN HAVE ENABLED ME . .	815A	LETTER 23	PROSE
	THE ILL DRAWN & UGLY YOUNG WOMEN & ABOVE ALL	815A	LETTER 23	PROSE
	BUT YOU WILL JUSTLY ENQUIRE WHY I HAVE NOT WRITTEN ALL THIS	815C	LETTER 23	PROSE
	PAINT PORTRAIT & IF YOU HAVE NATURE BEFORE YOU AT ALL .	815D	LETTER 23	PROSE
	EXPECT A LIKENESS BUT NOW I HAVE DONE ALL I COULD & KNOW	815D	LETTER 23	PROSE
	WITH ALL POSSIBLE EXPEDITION IF INDEED I HAVE NOT TIRED YOU	816C	LETTER 24	PROSE
	AND ALL MY FRIENDS BE WITH DOUBTS BEGUILD	818	HAPPINESS/L	48
	THEN LOS APPEARD IN ALL HIS POWER	818	HAPPINESS/L	55
	ALL THE DEVILS IN HELL WILL NEVER DO I MUST OWN THAT SEEING	819C	LETTER 25	PROSE
	BUT IF SICKNESS COMES ALL IS UNPLEASANT	820B	LETTER 25	PROSE
	ALL PERFECTION & SHE WRITES THAT SHE IS QUITE SATISFIED WITH	820D	LETTER 25	PROSE
	ONLY ILLNESS MAKES ALL UNCOMFORTABLE	821B	LETTER 25	PROSE
	HAVE SOLD ALL THAT WE HAVE HAD TIME TO PRINT	821B	LETTER 25	PROSE

		PAGE	TITLE	LINE
ALL	(CONTINUED)			
INTEREST OF ALL CONCERND IN MY WORKS OBSERVING THAT	. . .	822D	LETTER 26	PROSE
WHICH SEEMS TO BE THE LABOUR OF A LONG LIFE ALL PRODUCD		823B	LETTER 26	PROSE
HAND UPON MY HEAD & GIVES A BLESSING TO ALL MY WORKS	.	823B	LETTER 26	PROSE
THESE ARE ALL IN GREAT FORWARDNESS & I AM SATISFIED THAT		824A	LETTER 27	PROSE
WITHOUT THE ORIGINAL SITTING BEFORE YOU FOR EVERY TOUCH ALL		824B	LETTER 27	PROSE
& THAT THERE IS ALL THE APPEARANCE IN THE WORLD OF OUR	.	824C	LETTER 27	PROSE
& TO CONSIST OF ALL MILTON'S POEMS WITH COWPER'S NOTES AND		824C	LETTER 27	PROSE
SIX GUINEAS THUS I HOPE THAT ALL OUR THREE YEARS' TROUBLE ENDS		824D	LETTER 27	PROSE
BUT IF ALL THE WORLD SHOULD SET THEIR FACES AGAINST THIS		825B	LETTER 27	PROSE
I AM NOT TO REGARD IT AT ALL BUT MR H(HAYLEY)	. . . .	825C	LETTER 27	PROSE
I WAS COMMANDED BY MY SPIRITUAL FRIENDS TO BEAR ALL TO BE SILENT		825D	LETTER 27	PROSE
& TO GO THRO ALL WITHOUT MURMURING & IN FIRM HOPE	. .	825D	LETTER 27	*PROSE
& WILL RELINQUISH ANY ENGAGEMENT OF DESIGNING AT ALL	.	826A	LETTER 27	PROSE
HE ALL THE WHILE ENDEAVOURING TO TURN ROUND & STRIKE ME		827B	LETTER 28	PROSE
ALL THAT HAPPEND AT THE GATE OF THE INN WHO EVIDENCES THAT		827C	LETTER 28	PROSE
ALL THE WHILE & HE WAS THE ONLY PERSON I THOUGHT NECESSARY		827D	LETTER 28	PROSE
ALL THE VILLAGES ROUND EVERY MAN IS NOW AFRAID OF SPEAKING		828A	LETTER 28	PROSE
TO CLEAR THEMSELVES OF ALL IMPUTATION IF A MAN OFFENDS ME		828C	LETTER 28	PROSE
IS THE ORIGIN OF ALL OFFENCES COMMITTED AGAINST ME IF I HAVE		828C	LETTER 28	PROSE
ALL IS COME FROM THE SPIRITUAL WORLD FOR GOOD & NOT FOR EVIL		828C	LETTER 28	PROSE
BUT IF IT ALL ARISE FROM MY OWN FAULT I OUGHT TO BLAME MYSELF		828D	LETTER 28	PROSE
ALL MY TALENTS I BURY AND DEAD IS MY FAME	. . . . .	829	O WHY BORN/L	8
GOD TO KEEP YOU & ALL MEN FROM IT & TO DELIVER ME IN HIS		829A	LETTER 28	PROSE
YOU & MRS BUTTS & ALL YOUR FAMILY I AGAIN TAKE THE LIBERTY		829A	LETTER 28	PROSE
AFTER ALL & CERTAINLY DOES NOT LEAD ME INTO SCRAPES	. .	830D	LETTER 30	PROSE
AS HE WAS OUT OF THE WAY ALL THE TIME ON OTHER EMPLOYMENT		830D	LETTER 30	PROSE
BEEN WITH MR SAUNDERS WHO HAS NOW IN HIS POSSESSION ALL MR		831A	LETTER 31	PROSE
FEMALE HEAD HE HAS PROMISED TO WRITE A LIST OF ALL THAT HE		831A	LETTER 31	PROSE
HAS IN HIS POSSESSION AND OF ALL THAT HE REMEMBERS OF	.	831A	LETTER 31	PROSE
GOING ON WOULD BE A CERTAIN LOSS OF ALMOST ALL THE EXPENSES		831C	LETTER 31	PROSE
EVERY BODY COMPLAINS YET ALL GO ON CHEERFULLY AND WITH SPIRIT		831D	LETTER 31	PROSE
THE HEALTH OF MISS POOLE AND FOR ALL OUR FRIENDS IN SUSSEX		832A	LETTER 31	PROSE
ALL THIS I LEARND WITH SOME ALARM & HEARD ALSO WHAT	. .	833C	LETTER 33	PROSE
MORNING YOUR PRESENT TO HIS SCHOLAR HE & HIS ARE ALL WELL &		833C	LETTER 33	PROSE
ALL THE ATTENTION THAT A DAUGHTER COULD PAY TO A MOTHER		833D	LETTER 33	PROSE
ABOVE ALL YOU MY DEAR FRIEND & BENEFACTOR IN THE LORD	.	834A	LETTER 33	PROSE
THO HE IS IN TOWN MR FLAXMAN IS NOT AT ALL ACQUAINTED	.	834D	LETTER 34	PROSE
I WRITE NOW TO SATISFY YOU THAT ALL IS IN A GOOD TRAIN I AM		835A	LETTER 34	PROSE
BLESSING AMEN GOD BLESS YOU ALL O PEOPLE OF SUSSEX	. .	835B	LETTER 34	PROSE
HEAVEN HAVILAH EDEN & ALL THE COUNTRIES WHERE JEWELS ABOUND		837D	LETTER 36	PROSE
WITH ALL THE FIDELITY I COULD & WILL FINISH WITH EQUAL CARE		838A	LETTER 37	PROSE
IN ALL THINGS MY WIFE JOINS ME IN THIS PRAYER	. . . .	841A	LETTER 40	PROSE
IT IS THE FIRST PORTRAIT ROMNEY EVER PAINTED BUT ABOVE ALL		843D	LETTER 43	PROSE
AND MR WALKER PROMISES TO COLLECT ALL HE CAN OF INFORMATION		844A	LETTER 43	PROSE
IT SEEMS AS IF ALL ROMNEY'S INTIMATE FRIENDS	. . . .	844A	LETTER 43	PROSE
TO GET THE NUMBER AND PRICES OF ALL ROMNEY'S PRINTS AS	.	844A	LETTER 43	PROSE
YOU DESIRED HE HAS SENT A CATALOGUE OF ALL HIS COLLECTION		844A	LETTER 43	PROSE
WOULD BE ACCEPTABLE AT ALL TIMES BUT ESPECIALLY AT THE PRESENT		844A	LETTER 43	PROSE
THAT WASHINGTON DID ALL THAT WAS DONE BEFORE HE WAS BORN		845B	LETTER 44	PROSE
HEARTILY DEVOTE HIMSELF TO THE BUSINESS IN ALL ITS LABORIOUS		845C	LETTER 44	PROSE
TO WRITE ALL HE KNOWS OR CAN COLLECT CONCERNING ROMNEY	.	846A	LETTER 44	PROSE
SELECT FOR THAT PURPOSE DOUBTS NOT AT ALL OF MR ROMNEY'S		846A	LETTER 44	PROSE
IF THIS CAN BE DONE IT WILL BE ALL THAT COULD BE WISHED		846A	LETTER 44	PROSE
BUT TO BALANCE ALL THIS I MUST IN DUTY TO MY FRIEND SEAGRAVE		846C	LETTER 44	PROSE
EXPECT A FULL ACCOUNT OF ALL HE CAN COLLECT MR SANDERS	.	847D	LETTER 44	PROSE
LODGINGS & FIND THEM ALL TOO GRAND AS WELL AS	. . . .	848A	LETTER 45	PROSE
ENGAGED IN THE WORK AS ITS MAGNITUDE DEMANDS ALL THE	.	848D	LETTER 45	PROSE
VERY SOON TO CALL AGAIN & AS YOU WISH TO WRITE ALL I CAN		849B	LETTER 45	PROSE
IT YET WANTS ALL ITS LAST & FINISHING TOUCHES BUT I HOPE YOU		850B	LETTER 49	PROSE
YET OF TRUE ART WHICH IS ALL	. . . . . .	850C	LETTER 49	PROSE
& HER & TO ALL WHOM WE LOVE THAT IS TO ALL SUSSEX	. .	851A	LETTER 49	PROSE
OVERLOOK & ADVISE & DO ALL THAT HE CAN TO MAKE MY DESIGNS		853A	LETTER 51	*PROSE
FRIENDS AT LAVANT & IN ALL SUSSEX I REMAIN DEAR SIR	. .	853A	LETTER 51	*PROSE
WITH ALL THE WARMTH OF FRIENDSHIP BOTH TO YOU AND ME		853B	LETTER 52	PROSE
OF OBLIGATIONS WITH YOU I OUGHT TO DO MY BEST AT ALL TIMES &		854C	LETTER 53	PROSE
IN ALL CIRCUMSTANCES I FIND THAT YOU WAS RIGHT IN SUPPOSING		854C	LETTER 53	PROSE
THAT I HAD BEEN PAID FOR ALL I HAVE DONE BUT WHEN I WROTE		854D	LETTER 53	PROSE
ALL THE ENGRAVER'S NICEST ATTENTION INDEED IT IS MORE FINISHD		855A	LETTER 53	PROSE
INTO ALL PARTS TO A VERY GREAT AMOUNT HE THEN SAID IF MR		856C	LETTER 54	PROSE
LEFT ALL TO YOU INTIRELY I DO THINK FROM THE LIBERALITY OF		857A	LETTER 54	*PROSE
THIS ENTERPRIZING MAN THAT ALL PARTIES I MEAN OUR FRIEND		857A	LETTER 54	PROSE
SHOULD BE PUBLISHED ALL TOGETHER IN A VOLUME THE SIZE OF THE		858B	LETTER 55	PROSE
ALL THAT HAS BEEN PRINTED AS LOST AND BEGIN ANEW UNLESS		858B	LETTER 55	PROSE
THE TOWN IS MAD YOUNG ROSCIUS LIKE ALL PRODIGIES IS THE		859C	LETTER 56	PROSE
SHOULD LOSE ALL THE LABOUR I HAVE BEEN AT ON THAT PLATE		861B	LETTER 58	PROSE
MATTERS AND LEAVE ALL TO YOUR DECISION	. . . . . .	861B	LETTER 58	PROSE
AS I KNOW THAT YOU WILL DO WHAT IS RIGHT ON ALL HANDS	.	861B	LETTER 58	PROSE
[OF] ALL OUR FRIENDS TO WHOM WE ARE GRATEFUL & DESIRE TO BE		862A	LETTER 59	PROSE

```
                                                              PAGE    TITLE        LINE
ALL    (CONTINUED)
       SAME TALENTS I NOW HAVE ALL THE TIME OF BOYDELL'S MACKLIN'S  862C LETTER 60    PROSE
       ALL HITHERTO YOU DEAR SIR ARE ONE WHO HAS MY PARTICULAR      862C LETTER 60    PROSE
       I THROW MYSELF & ALL THAT I HAVE ON OUR SAVIOUR'S DIVINE     863A LETTER 60    PROSE
       WISHING YOU & ALL FRIENDS IN SUSSEX A MERRY &  . . . . .     863C LETTER 60    PROSE
       WE ARE ALL SUBJECT TO ERROR . . . . . . . . .               865B LETTER 62    PROSE
       THAT WE ARE NOT ALL SUBJECT TO CRIME . . . . . . .          865B LETTER 62    PROSE
       THAT PRECLUDE ALL POSSIBILITY OF PROMISING ANY THING I HAVE  865D LETTER 63    PROSE
       COURAGE TO SAY SO PUBLICKLY & TO DARE ALL THE POWER ON       866B LETTER 64    PROSE
          EARTH
       IT WILL BE MORE CONVENIENT TO ME TO MAKE ALL THE DRAWINGS    866C LETTER 65    PROSE
       ANY OR ALL OF THEM SHOULD SEND ME THEIR ORDER TO PRINT THEM  867C LETTER 66    PROSE
       BUT NOT AT ALL IN WHAT IS OF WEIGHT & MOMENT TO OUR          868B LETTER 67    PROSE
          DECISION
       SEEMS TO BE ALL THAT I WANT I SEND THE  . . . . . . .        869B LETTER 69    PROSE
       WHEN AT LENGTH WE FOUND THAT WE WERE ALL THREE PROCEEDING    869C LETTER 70    PROSE
       I HAVE I BELIEVE DONE NEARLY ALL THAT WE AGREED ON &C   .    870B LETTER 71    PROSE
       LAST TIME WE MET I HAVE NO DOUBT THAT THE PLATES WOULD       870B LETTER 71    PROSE
          BE ALL
       EVEN ISLINGTON & ALL PLACES NORTH OF LONDON ALWAYS LAID ME   871A LETTER 72    PROSE
       FOR ALL SUCH WHO MAY BE LED TO SUCH OSTENTATIOUS EXERTION    871A LETTER 72    PROSE
       & SOON SPREAD A DEATHLY FEEL ALL OVER THE LIMBS WHICH   .    872B LETTER 75    PROSE
       ALL MY HOPES BY THE ROOTS EVERY ONE WHO KNOWS OF OUR   .     872D LETTER 76    PROSE
       I SUPPOSED AS TO PLEASANTNESS OF PROSPECT IT IS ALL          873A LETTER 76    PROSE
          PLEASANT
       SHUT UP IN THE BOOK ALL WILL GO VERY WELL IN THE COACH       873A LETTER 76    PROSE
          WHICH
       RETURN PRAY LET YOUR OWN HEALTH & CONVENIENCE PUT ALL   .    873C LETTER 77    PROSE
       TWO OR THREE DAYS MAY BE SUFFICIENT OR NOT ALL NOW WILL      875A LETTER 80    PROSE
          DEPEND
       BONES & SINEWS ALL STRINGS & BOBBINS LIKE A WEAVER'S LOOM    875B LETTER 81    PROSE
       TOTTERING THO ALL THE SYMPTOMS OF MY COMPLAINT SEEM ALMOST   876A LETTER 83    PROSE
       YOUR SUCCESS IN YOUR PROFESSION IS ABOVE ALL THINGS TO ME    876C LETTER 83    PROSE
       & AM GETTING BETTER OR I COULD NOT HAVE COME AT ALL YOURS    876D LETTER 84    PROSE
       PROOFS HE HAS REMAINING [ALL] ARE ALL PRINTED ON BOTH SIDES  877B LETTER 86   *PROSE
          OF
       WHICH IS ALL I CARE ABOUT  . . . . . . . . . .              877D LETTER 88    PROSE
       ENGLISHMEN ARE ALL INTERMEASURABLE ONE BY ANOTHER   . .      878B LETTER 88    PROSE
       TO BE THE SAME THING AS ALL EXPERIMENTALISTS MUST SUPPOSE    878B LETTER 88    PROSE
       TO MAKE THEM PLEASIN I AM OBLIGED TO YOU & TO ALL WHO DO SO  878B LETTER 88    PROSE
       BUT HAVING NONE REMAINING OF ALL THAT I HAD PRINTED I   .    878C LETTER 88    PROSE
       FLAXMAN IS GONE & WE MUST ALL SOON FOLLOW EVERY ONE TO HIS   879A LETTER 88    PROSE
       LAWS TO GET INTO FREEDOM FROM ALL LAW OF THE MEMBERS INTO    879A LETTER 88    PROSE
       ACCOMPANIED BY ALL THE OLD SYMPTOMS I AM DEAR SIR YOURS      880A LETTER 90    PROSE
          SINCERELY
       IS ALL JOY FORBIDDEN . . . . . . . . . .     SUPP PENC DRAW 1.7 *TITLE
ALLA
       THE SECOND STATE IS ALLA & THE THIRD STATE AL-ULRO   . . .   524 MILTON 34      12
       FOR MULTITUDES OF THOSE WHO SLEEP IN ALLA DESCEND   . . .    736 JERUSALEM 89   58
ALLAMANDA
       A WEB OF DEATH & WERE IT NOT FOR BOWLAHOOLA & ALLAMANDA      509 MILTON 24      36
       SO LOS SPOKE FURIOUS THEY DESCENDED TO BOWLAHOOLA            509 MILTON 24      44
          & ALLAMANDA
       AND THESE THE LABOURS OF THE SONS OF LOS IN ALLAMANDA   .    512 MILTON 26      23
       BUILT BY THE SONS OF LOS IN BOWLAHOOLA & ALLAMANDA   . . .   512 MILTON 26      33
       BUT ALLAMANDA CALLD ON EARTH COMMERCE IS THE CULTIVATED      514 MILTON 27      42
          LAND
       AND SCIENCE IS DIVIDED INTO BOWLAHOOLA & ALLAMANDA   . .     514 MILTON 27      63
       BOWLAHOOLA & ALLAMANDA ARE PLACED ON EACH SIDE   . . . .     517 MILTON 29      25
       IN ALLAMANDA & ENTUTHON BENYTHON WHERE SOULS WAIL   . .      517 MILTON 29      28
       TO BOWLAHOOLA & ALLAMANDA & TO ENTUTHON BENYTHON   . . . .   529 MILTON 37      59
       IN BOWLAHOOLA & ALLAMANDA WHERE THE DEAD WAIL NIGHT & DAY    668 JERUSALEM 40   57
ALLAN
       WITH SR ALLAN CHAMBRE RECOMMENDS ME TO ENQUIRE CONCERNING    834D LETTER 34    PROSE
       HIM OF MR ROSE MY BROTHER SAYS HE BELIEVES SR ALLAN IS  .    834D LETTER 34    PROSE
ALLAY
       THY STRENGTH CURB THY FIERCE STEEDS ALLAY THE HEAT   . . .     1 TO SUMMER/PS    2
       BUT THEIR FEARS ALLAY . . . . . . . . . . .                114 LIT GRL FND/SI  30
       AND TO ALLAY HIS [XXX] FREEZING AGE  . . . . . . . .        426 MENTAL TRAVLER * 57
ALL BENEVOLENT
       WE ALL ADMIRD & LOVD WHOSE ALL BENEVOLENT COUNTENANCE SEEN   675 JERUSALEM 45    5
ALL BRIGHT
       THEN SURVEYD THE ALL BRIGHT MASS AGAIN  . . . . . . .       260 BOOK OF LOS 5   36
ALL CREATIVE
       ADAM IT IS ALL A VAIN DELUSION OF THE ALL CREATIVE          780 GHOST ABEL 1    17
          IMAGINATION
ALL DEVOURING
       AND BRING FORTH HOWLING TERRORS ALL DEVOURING FIERY KINGS    238 EUROPE PREL 2   4
       ENVYING EACH OTHER YET DESIRING IN ALL DEVOURING LOVE   .    732 JERUSALEM 86   64
ALLEDGE
       TO ALLEDGE FOR OUR IMITATION & APPROVAL . . . . . . .       406D ANNO BACON    MARG
ALLEDGED
       THE REASON ALLEDGED BY PRIESTS FOR MIRACLES IS FALSE   .     391D ANNO WATSON   MARG
       SUFFICIENT FOR ME TO HAVE UTTERED THE THINGS THAT           438A BLAKES MEMORAN PROSE
          HE ALLEDGED
       BE ALLEDGED AS THE CAUSE OF HIS THIEVERY FOR  . . . . .     793B LETTER 5     *PROSE
ALLEGORIC
       TO INVENT ALLEGORIC RICHES  . . . . . . . . . .            247 SONG OF LOS 6    18
       THE HIDDEN WONDERS ALLEGORIC OF THE GENERATIONS  . . .  .   333 FOUR ZOAS 7B    24
       UNFOLDS IN ALLEGORIC FRUIT WHEN SHALL THE DEAD REVIVE   .    345 FOUR ZOAS 8    169
       WHICH BEGAN TO TURN ALLEGORIC AND MENTAL SIGNIFICATION  . .  578A DESC CAT 5    PROSE
       BETWEEN ALLEGORIC FABLE & SPIRITUAL MYSTERY LET IT HERE BE   605C V LAST JUDG/N PROSE
```

```
                                                             PAGE     TITLE            LINE
ALLEGORIC    (CONTINUED)
      NOW GIVEN TO STONY DRUIDS AND ALLEGORIC GENERATION   . .   681 JERUSALEM 50          2
      IN THE LITTLE LOVELY ALLEGORIC NIGHT OF ALBION'S DAUGHTERS  733 JERUSALEM 88         31
      TWELVEFOLD IN ALLEGORIC POMP IN SELFISH HOLINESS  . . . .   734 JERUSALEM 89          5
      OF THREEFOLD WORKMANSHIP IN ALLEGORIC DELUSION & WOE   .    735 JERUSALEM 89         45
      FOR THINE IS THE KINGSHIP OR ALLEGORIC GODSHIP   . . . . 789A ANNO THORNTON    * MARG
ALLEGORICAL
      IN AN ALLEGORICAL ABODE WHERE EXISTENCE HATH NEVER COME     240 EUROPE 5              7
      THE SAME ALLEGORICAL PERSONAGES BUT THE   . . . . . .  779A ANNO CELLINI       MARG
ALLEGORIES
      ALLEGORIES ARE THINGS THAT RELATE TO MORAL VIRTUES   .  614D V LAST JUDG/N      PROSE
      MORAL VIRTUES DO NOT EXIST THEY ARE [ EL ] ALLEGORIES & .  614D V LAST JUDG/N     *PROSE
      RENDING THE FIBRES OF BROTHERHOOD & IN FEMININE ALLEGORIES  656 JERUSALEM 30     *   18
      AND NOT THE SHEEPFOLD ALLEGORIES  . . . . . . . .    758 EV GOSPEL (1)          5
ALLEGORY
      THE LAST JUDGMENT IS NOT FABLE OR ALLEGORY BUT VISION   .  604D V LAST JUDG/N      PROSE
      FABLE OR ALLEGORY ARE A TOTALLY DISTINCT & INFERIOR KIND   604D V LAST JUDG/N      PROSE
      FABLE OR ALLEGORY IS FORMD BY THE DAUGHTERS OF MEMORY   .  604D V LAST JUDG/N      PROSE
      WHO IN THE AGGREGATE ARE CALLD JERUSALEM FABLE IS ALLEGORY 604D V LAST JUDG/N      PROSE
      THE HEBREW BIBLE & THE GOSPEL OF JESUS ARE NOT ALLEGORY    604D V LAST JUDG/N      PROSE
      NOTE HERE THAT FABLE OR (ALLEGORY) IS SELDOM WITHOUT   .   604D V LAST JUDG/N     *PROSE
      THE SAME BUT [FABLE & ALLEGORY] ALLEGORY & VISION   . .  604D V LAST JUDG/N      PROSE
      IN FABLE & ALLEGORY [WHICH]  . . . . . . . . .      605C V LAST JUDG/N      PROSE
      BECAME A SPACE & AN ALLEGORY AROUND THE WINDING WORM  .    730 JERUSALEM 85          1
      FOR GOD IS ONLY AN ALLEGORY OF KINGS & NOTHING ELSE AMEN  789A ANNO THORNTON    MARG
      TO COME & TO SPEAK TO FUTURE GENERATIONS BY A SUBLIME     825A LETTER 27        PROSE
         ALLEGORY
      ALLEGORY ADDRESSD TO THE INTELLECTUAL POWERS WHILE IT IS  825A LETTER 27        PROSE
      AN ALLEGORY OF IDOLATRY OR POLITICS  . . . . . .    SUPP ILLUS CHAUCER    *TITLE
ALLEGRO
      MIRTH ALLEGRO   . . . . . . . . . . . . .       617D ILLUS MILTON     TITLE
ALLEN
      WASHINGTON FRANKLIN PAINE & WARREN ALLEN GATES & LEE   .   201 AMERICA 14            2
ALLESTONE
      THE MAP OF ALLESTONE HAS THE SAME CHARACTER OF THE FIRM AND 439C REMARKS MALKIN   PROSE
ALL FLEXIBLE
      OR CONTRACTED HIS ALL FLEXIBLE SENSES  . . . . . .     223 URIZEN 3             38
      CONTRACTING OR EXPANDING THEIR ALL FLEXIBLE SENSES   . . .  288 FOUR ZOAS 2          296
ALL GLORIOUS
      WERE CONTAIND IN THE ALL GLORIOUS IMAGINATION ARE WITHERD  679 JERUSALEM 49         14
         & DARKEND
ALLOTTED
      THE SWEETEST TIME THAT GOD HAS ALLOTTED MORTAL MAN   . .   40A SAMSON/PS         PROSE
ALLOW
      I DO NOT ALLOW THAT THERE IS SUCH A THING AS SUPERSTITION   75A ANNO LAVATER     MARG
      UNLESS WE ALLOW IT TO BE POETRY & THAT POETRY INSPIRED     392D ANNO WATSON      MARG
      WHAT MUST OUR CLERGY BE WHO ALLOW BACON TO BE EITHER WISE  404B ANNO BACON       MARG
      THIS IS ADMIRABLY SAID WHY DOES HE NOT ALWAYS ALLOW AS MUCH 454D ANNO REYNOLDS    MARG
      WHY DOES HE NOT ALWAYS ALLOW THIS  . . . . . . .     461D ANNO REYNOLDS    MARG
      FINE & JUST NOTIONS WHY DOES HE NOT ALWAYS ALLOW AS MUCH   462C ANNO REYNOLDS    MARG
      HOW MUCH OF HIS HOMER & DANTE HE WILL ALLOW TO BE MINE  .  592D PUB ADDRESS/N    PROSE
      I ALLOW THAT THERE IS SUCH A THING AS HIGH FINISHD        593B PUB ADDRESS/N    PROSE
         IGNORANCE
      BUT AT THE SAME TIME I WILL ALLOW THAT  . . . . . .    600D PUB ADDRESS/N    PROSE
      ARE COMPELLD TO ALLOW IS NOT DONE IN PASSION   . . . .   615D V LAST JUDG/N      PROSE
ALLOWD
      THE LANGUAGE OF PAINTERS CANNOT BE ALLOWD THEM   . . .    463B ANNO REYNOLDS    MARG
      IS ALLOWD ON ALL HANDS TO BE THE PRODUCTION OF A MAN   .  599D PUB ADDRESS/N   *PROSE
      MY CONCEPTION & INVENTION ARE ON ALL HANDS ALLOWD   . .   601D PUB ADDRESS/N    PROSE
ALLOWED
      IT IS HOPED THAT THE PAINTER WILL BE ALLOWED BY THE PUBLIC  586D CHAUCER 1        PROSE
ALLOWS
      HERE HE ALLOWS AN ANALYSIS OF CIRCUMSTANCES   . . . .    462B ANNO REYNOLDS    MARG
      AT PAGE...HE ALLOWS THAT THE VENETIAN  . . . . . .     468A ANNO REYNOLDS    MARG
ALL PIERCING
      O FOOL TO THINK THAT I COULD HIDE FROM HIS ALL PIERCING    310 FOUR ZOAS 5          214
         EYES
ALL-PITEOUS-ONE
      SUCH THING WAS NEVER KNOWN O PITY ME THOU ALL-PITEOUS-ONE  631 JERUSALEM 12          8
ALL-POWERFUL,ALL POWERFUL
      THE ALL POWERFUL CURSE OF AN HONEST MAN BE UPON URIZEN     298 FOUR ZOAS 4           25
         & LUVAH
      BUT NOW I AM ALL POWERFUL LOS & URTHONA IS BUT MY SHADOW   298 FOUR ZOAS 4           43
      WHAT HAVE I SAID WHAT HAVE I DONE O ALL-POWERFUL HUMAN     646 JERUSALEM 24          1
         WORDS
      ALL POWERFUL PARENTAL AFFECTION FILLS ALBION FROM HEAD     685 JERUSALEM 54         10
         TO FOOT
ALL-PROTECTING
      WHO IS THE ETERNAL ALL-PROTECTING DIVINE HUMANITY   . .   495 MILTON 14             2
ALL-REPELLING
      SELF-CLOSD ALL-REPELLING WHAT DEMON  . . . . . . .     222 URIZEN 3               3
ALL TREMENDOUS
      . . . & THE ALL TREMENDOUS UNFATHOMABLE NON ENS   . . .   746 JERUSALEM 98          33
ALLUDES
      LOT'S WIFE BEING CHANGED INTO (A) PILLAR OF SALT ALLUDES  607A V LAST JUDG/N      PROSE
ALLURED
      I WAS A GARDEN PLANTED WITH BEAUTY I ALLURED ON HILL &     659 JERUSALEM 33         37
         VALLEY
ALLURING
      CALL THINE ALLURING ARTS AND HONEST-SEEMING BROW   . . .   38A SAMSON/PS         PROSE
      WITH MANY AN ALLURING DANCE  . . . . . . . . . .     185 LET BROTHELS/N         2
```

ALL WONDROUS
   AND THE ALL WONDROUS SERPENT CLOTHED IN GEMS & RICH ARRAY   746 JERUSALEM 98   44
ALL WORSHIPD
ALLWORSHIPD
   HIS BREAST IS LOVE'S ALL WORSHIPD TOMB . . . .   6 MY SILKS/PS   11
ALMIGHTIE'S
   IS AN ARROW FROM THE ALMIGHTIE'S BOW . . . . 420 I SAW A MONK/N   61
   IS AN ARROW FROM THE ALMIGHTIE'S BOW . . . . 430 GREY MONK   32
   IS AN ARROW FROM THE ALMIGHTIE'S BOW . . . . 683 I SAW A MONK/J   28
ALMIGHTY
   ARMD WITH THE TERRORS OF ALMIGHTY JOVE . . . . . .   15 IMIT SPEN/PS   45
   TH ALMIGHTY TO STRETCH OUT MY SPAN OF LIFE . . . . .   27 EDW THIRD/PS 3 279
   THE ARROWS OF ALMIGHTY GOD ARE DRAWN . . . .   35 WAR SONG/PS   16
   FROM PRESENCE OF THE ALMIGHTY FATHER . . . . 37D SAMSON/PS PROSE
   EYES OF GOD & THE SEVEN LAMPS OF THE ALMIGHTY . . . . 279 FOUR ZOAS 1 554
   BECAUSE THOU GAVEST URIZEN THE WINE OF THE ALMIGHTY . . 311 FOUR ZOAS 5 234
   AND THESE AGAIN SURROUNDED [OF] BY FOUR WONDERS OF THE   364 FOUR ZOAS 9 * 281
     ALMIGHTY
   THE SEVEN LAMPS OF THE ALMIGHTY BURNING BEFORE THE THRONE 443C LAST JUDGMNT/L PROSE
   BENEATH THE PLOW OF RINTRAH & THE HARROW OF THE ALMIGHTY 483 MILTON 4   1
   LOS GAVE TO HIM THE HARROW OF THE ALMIGHTY ALAS BLAMABLE 486 MILTON 7   12
   AS THE BREATH OF THE ALMIGHTY SUCH ARE THE WORDS OF MAN 519 MILTON 30   18
     TO MAN
   OF FORTY-EIGHT DEFORMED HUMAN WONDERS OF THE ALMIGHTY . . 529 MILTON 37   54
   ALL IS CHAOS AGAIN AND THE LINE OF THE ALMIGHTY MUST BE 585C DESC CAT 15 PROSE
   FIRST GOD ALMIGHTY COMES WITH A THUMP ON THE HEAD . . . 617A V LAST JUDG/N PROSE
   CRYING HOLY HOLY IS THE [G] LORD GOD ALMIGHTY . . . . 617B V LAST JUDG/N *PROSE
   CONSUMING & THE ALMIGHTY HATH MADE ME HIS CONTRARY . . . 630 JERUSALEM 10   56
   THE ARROWS OF THE ALMIGHTY POUR UPON ME & MY CHILDREN . . 719 JERUSALEM 78   32
   THE INNUMERABLE CHARIOTS OF THE ALMIGHTY APPEARD IN HEAVEN 745 JERUSALEM 98   8
   READING IN THE BIBLE OF THE EYES OF THE ALMIGHTY . . . . 860D LETTER 57 PROSE
ALMIGHTY'S   SEE ALMIGHTIE'S
   HELD IN TH ALMIGHTY'S HAND . . . .   13 GWIN KING/PS   66
   THAT ANGEL WHO PLEASED TO PERFORM THE ALMIGHTY'S ORDERS 565A DESC CAT 2 TITLE
ALMOST
   WHEN ALMOST SINGLY HE DROVE SIX THOUSAND . . . . .   21 EDW THIRD/PS 3   11
   DIM THE FORM ALMOST FADED. . . . . 140 FRENCH REVOLTN 132
   THE ANGEL HEARING THIS BECAME ALMOST BLUE . . . . . 158B MARRIAGE HH 22 PROSE
   I AM ALMOST EXTINCT & SOON SHALL BE A SHADOW IN OBLIVION 265 FOUR ZOAS 1   40
   FUSELI INDIGNANT ALMOST HID HIMSELF I [?WAS] AM HID . . . 445C ANNO REYNOLDS * MARG
   WHICH HE ALMOST ALWAYS APPROVES & RECOMMENDS . . . . 448C ANNO REYNOLDS MARG
   HIMSELF HAD WROUGHT LOS TREMBLED SATAN'S BLANDISHMENTS 487 MILTON 7   37
     ALMOST
   AT LAST WHEN DESPERATION ALMOST TORE HIS HEART IN TWAIN 503 MILTON 20   56
   WHO DID NOT MAKE ME ALMOST SPEW . . . . 551 ONLY MAN/N   2
   OUR ALMOST ONLY PUBLIC WORKS [WHILE] YET IT IS . . . . 601A PUB ADDRESS/N PROSE
   CAM IS A LITTLE STREAM ELY IS ALMOST SWALLOWD UP . . . 623 JERUSALEM 5   9
   AGUE & RHEUMATISM HAVE BEEN ALMOST HER CONSTANT ENEMIES 811B LETTER 22 PROSE
   & RHEUMATISM ALMOST EVER SINCE SHE HAS BEEN HERE . . . 819C LETTER 25 PROSE
   BUT OUR TIME IS ALMOST OUT THAT WE TOOK THE COTTAGE FOR 819C LETTER 25 PROSE
     I DID
   TEN POUNDS & ITS ALMOST CERTAIN PROFITS ARE...G I AM . . 820A LETTER 25 PROSE
   WHO ALMOST ADORD HER COUSIN THE POET & THOUGHT HIM . . 820D LETTER 25 PROSE
   THE ENGLISH TRANSLATION IT IS ALMOST WORD FOR WORD & . . 821D LETTER 25 PROSE
   TILL MY THREE YEARS SHOULD BE ALMOST ACCOMPLISHD . . . 825D LETTER 27 PROSE
   HOW IS IT POSSIBLE THAT A MAN ALMOST (FIFTY) YEARS OF AGE 830A LETTER 30 PROSE
   GOING ON WOULD BE A CERTAIN LOSS OF ALMOST ALL THE EXPENSES 831C LETTER 31 PROSE
   EVEN SNOW HILL IS BECOME ALMOST LEVEL . . . . 831D LETTER 31 PROSE
   ENGRAVING IS ETERNAL WORK THE TWO PLATES ARE ALMOST FINISHD 837C LETTER 36 PROSE
   ALMOST WELL IF I CAN POSSIBLY I WILL BE AT MR LAHEE'S . . 869B LETTER 69 *PROSE
   TOTTERING THO ALL THE SYMPTOMS OF MY COMPLAINT SEEM ALMOST 876A LETTER 83 PROSE
ALMS-HOUSES
   FROM HYDE PARK TO THE ALMS-HOUSES OF MILE-END & OLD BOW 486 MILTON 6   31
ALOFT
   DOST MOUNT ALOFT INTO THE YIELDING SKY . . . . . .   15 IMIT SPEN/PS   20
   THE SPEARY HAND BURNED ALOFT UNBUCKLED WAS THE SHIELD . . 159B SONG LIBERTY PROSE
   [THEN OLD NOBODADDY ALOFT] . . . . 185 LET BROTHELS/N   9
   FOR OLD NOBODADDY ALOFT . . . . 186 WHEN KLOPSTK/N   3
   [HIS HARP ALOFT SOUNDING THEN DASHD ITS SHINING FRAME 196 AMERICA PREL 2   19
     AGAINST]
   SOME IN VALES SOME ALOFT FLEW IN AIR . . . . 250 AHANIA 3   12
   THEN ALOFT HIS HEAD REARD IN THE ABYSS . . . . . . 258 BOOK OF LOS 4   41
   [HE SPURND ENION WITH HIS FOOT HE SPRANG ALOFT IN CLOUDS] 266 FOUR ZOAS 1   92
   ALOFT THE MOON FLED WITH A CRY THE SUN WITH STREAMS OF 281 FOUR ZOAS 2   42
     BLOOD
   UPON THE IRON CRAG OF URIZEN THENCE SPRINGING UP ALOFT . . 332 FOUR ZOAS 7 465
   HOVERS WITH BLASTED WINGS ALOFT WATCHING WITH EAGER EYE 354 FOUR ZOAS 8 523
   BORE THE GOLDEN NET ALOFT . . . . 422 BENEATH/N   20
   BORE THE GOLDEN NET ALOFT . . . . 424 THE GOLDEN NET   19
ALONE
   NOW WE ARE ALONE SIR JOHN I WILL UNBURDEN . . . . .   26 EDW THIRD/PS 3 220
   ALONE AND COMFORTLESS . . . . 35D COUCH DEATH/PS PROSE
   PENSIVE ALONE SHE SAT WITHIN THE HOUSE . . . . . . 39D SAMSON/PS PROSE
   THEN [THEY] QUID & SUCTION WERE LEFT ALONE . . . . . 51D ISLAND MOON 7 PROSE
   KITTY ALONE KITTY ALONE . . . .   55 THIS FROG/IM   2
   KITTY ALONE & I . . . .   55 THIS FROG/IM   4
   [THIS FROG] SING COCK I CARY KITTY ALONE . . . . .   55 THIS FROG/IM * 5
   KITTY ALONE KITTY ALONE . . . .   55 THIS FROG/IM   6
   COCK I CARY KITTY ALONE . . . .   55 THIS FROG/IM   7
   KITTY ALONE KITTY ALONE . . . .   55 THIS FROG/IM   8
   THOUGHT ALONE CAN MAKE MONSTERS BUT THE AFFECTIONS CANNOT 90C ANNO SWED LOVE MARG
   [?BUT] AND MNETHA SAID THOU MUST NOT GO TO WANDER DARK 103 TIRIEL 3 * 33
     ALONE

ALONE   (CONTINUED)

		PAGE	TITLE	LINE
LIVES NOT ALONE NOR FOR ITSELF FEAR NOT AND I WILL CALL		129	BOOK OF THEL 3	27
AWE SURROUNDED ALONE THRO THE ARMY		141	FRENCH REVOLTN *	162
THAT ENERGY CALLD EVIL IS ALONE FROM THE BODY		149C	MARRIAGE HH 4	PROSE
& THAT REASON CALLD GOOD IS ALONE FROM THE SOUL		149C	MARRIAGE HH 4	PROSE
SOME WILL SAY IS NOT GOD ALONE THE PROLIFIC I ANSWER . .		155B	MARRIAGE HH 15	PROSE
I REMAIND ALONE & THEN THIS APPEARANCE WAS NO MORE . . .		156C	MARRIAGE HH 17	PROSE
I ALONE EVEN I THE WINDS MERCILESS		224	URIZEN 4	19
HERE ALONE I IN BOOKS FORMD OF METALS		224	URIZEN 4	24
THE OBSCURE SEPARATION ALONE		226	URIZEN 5	40
ALONE I SEE THEE CRYSTAL FORM		244	EUROPE 14	17
BUT NOW ALONE OVER ROCKS MOUNTAINS		255	AHANIA 5	39
. . . [WHERE WE MAY REMAIN FOR EVER ALONE] ALSO O PITY ME O ENION		265	FOUR ZOAS 1	28
. . . [?ALONE ?POSSESSD BY DEADLY FEARS] LOVE IS CHANGD TO DEADLY HATE		267	FOUR ZOAS 1	* 111
[A LIFE IS BLOTTED OUT & I ALONE REMAIN POSSESSD WITH FEARS]		267	FOUR ZOAS 1	112
ON HIGH REMAIND ALONE FORSAKEN IN FIERCE JEALOUSY . . .		274	FOUR ZOAS 1	360
REPOSD ON BEDS LET THEM SLEEP ON DO THOU ALONE DEPART . .		277	FOUR ZOAS 1	489
IN THE BRIGHT SANDS OF LOS EVADING MY EMBRACE THEN I ALONE		288	FOUR ZOAS 2	305
ALL IS CONFUSION ALL IS TUMULT & WE ALONE ARE ESCAPED . .		294	FOUR ZOAS 3	103
NOR KNEW THAT I ALONE EXEMPTED FROM THE JOYS OF LOVE . .		325	FOUR ZOAS 7	200
ALONE & THEY REFUSD TO RETURN FROM THE FIELDS OF THE MIGHTY		334	FOUR ZOAS 7B	67
AND SHE IS GONE & HERE ALONE I WAR WITH DARKNESS & DEATH		339	FOUR ZOAS 7B	239
I ALONE DARE THE LASH ABIDE TO SIT BENEATH THE BLAST . .		344	FOUR ZOAS 8	148
DEPENDS ALONE UPON THE UNIVERSAL HAND & NOT IN US . . .		346	FOUR ZOAS 8	198
ALONE ENJOY NOT I ALONE IN MISERY SUPREME		361	FOUR ZOAS 9	178
TO FEEL THY HEAT & SEE THY LIGHT & WANDER HERE ALONE . .		368	FOUR ZOAS 9	416
I AM NOT HERE ALONE MY FLOCKS YOU ARE MY BRETHREN . . .		368	FOUR ZOAS 9	443
THEY ROSE THEY WENT OUT WANDRING SOMETIMES TOGETHER SOMETIMES ALONE		371	FOUR ZOAS 9	529
MAN LIVETH NOT BY SELF ALONE BUT IN HIS BROTHER'S FACE . .		374	FOUR ZOAS 9	641
WHO DARE TO JUDGE BUT GOD ALONE		396A	ANNO WATSON	MARG
LIVING THEE ALONE I'LL HAVE		416	MY SPECTRE/N	53
ALONE CAN FREE THE [WOLD] WORLD FROM FEAR		419	I SAW A MONK/N *	43
BUT ONLY ONE SMILE ALONE		423	THE SMILE	12
ALONE CAN FREE THE WORLD FROM FEAR		430	GREY MONK	28
TO PARTICULARIZE IS THE ALONE DISTINCTION OF MERIT . .		451A	ANNO REYNOLDS	MARG
SOFTNESS IS PRODUCED ALONE BY COMPARATIVE STRENGTH & .		457B	ANNO REYNOLDS	MARG
THE DRAPERY IS FORMED ALONE BY THE SHAPE OF THE NAKED .		462D	ANNO REYNOLDS	MARG
PUNISHMENTS & DEATHS MUSTERD & NUMBERD SAYING I AM GOD ALONE		490	MILTON 9	25
MERCY ALONE OF FREE GIFT AND ELECTION THAT WE LIVE . .		494	MILTON 13	33
O SONS WE LIVE NOT BY WRATH BY MERCY ALONE WE LIVE . . .		507	MILTON 23	34
FOR SUCH ALONE SLEEPERS REMAIN MEER PASSION & APPETITE .		512	MILTON 26	29
BUT NOT BY NATURAL BUT BY SPIRITUAL POWER ALONE BECAUSE .		512	MILTON 26	40
AND THEN & THEN ALONE BEGINS THE HAPPY FEMALE JOY . . .		522	MILTON 33	19
IN SELF ANNIHILATION ALL THAT IS NOT OF GOD ALONE . . .		530	MILTON 38	48
BUT I ALONE AM GOD & I ALONE IN HEAVN & EARTH . . .		530	MILTON 38	56
ARE NOT HISTORY ACTS THEMSELVES ALONE ARE HISTORY AND .		579A	DESC CAT 5	PROSE
THIS ALONE THE WANT OF THIS DETERMINATE AND BOUNDING FORM		585B	DESC CAT 15	PROSE
AND DESIGNING WHOSE METHOD ALONE CAN DELINEATE CHARACTER		586D	CHAUCER 1	PROSE
IF MEN OF WEAK CAPACITIES [IN ART] HAVE ALONE THE POWER		591B	PUB ADDRESS/N	PROSE
IS THE ALONE WISE OR SENSIBLE MAN		611B	V LAST JUDG/N	PROSE
MENTAL THINGS ARE ALONE REAL		617A	V LAST JUDG/N	PROSE
BY DEMONSTRATION MAN ALONE CAN LIVE AND NOT BY FAITH .		622	JERUSALEM 4	28
PLANTING THY FAMILY ALONE		651	FIELDS FROM/J	79
SAYING WE ALONE ARE ESCAPED O MERCIFUL LORD AND SAVIOUR		654	JERUSALEM 29	29
ALL IS CONFUSION ALL IS TUMULT & WE ALONE ARE ESCAPED .		655	JERUSALEM 29	82
AND HE WHO TAKES VENGEANCE ALONE IS THE CRIMINAL OF PROVIDENCE		657	JERUSALEM 31	32
BELONG TO GOD ALONE AND ALL THY LITTLE ONES ARE HOLY .		657	JERUSALEM 31	45
KNOW ME NOW ALBION LOOK UPON ME I ALONE AM BEAUTY . .		660	JERUSALEM 33	48
THOSE ALONE ARE HIS FRIENDS WHO ADMIRE HIS MINUTEST POWERS		673	JERUSALEM 43	58
I WILL NOT ENDURE THIS THING I ALONE WITHSTAND TO DEATH		673	JERUSALEM 43	71
ME SOME COMFORT WHY DO YOU ALL STAND SILENT I ALONE . .		673	JERUSALEM 43	77
JESUS ALONE CAN SAVE HIM FOR ALAS WE NONE CAN KNOW . .		675	JERUSALEM 45	18
THE LEWISS & FREDERICKS WHO ALONE ARE ITS CAUSES & . .		683A	JERUSALEM 52	*PROSE
THE INFINITE ALONE RESIDES IN DEFINITE & DETERMINATE IDENTITY		687	JERUSALEM 55	64
OVERWEARIED WITH HOWLING WALES & SCOTLAND ALONE SUSTAIN THE FIGHT		703	JERUSALEM 66	67
WHICH ALONE ARE THE LABOURS OF THE GOSPEL		717B	JERUSALEM 77	PROSE
THOU ART GOOD & THOU ALONE		754	EV GOSPEL(E)/N	25
THIS ALONE IS THE GOSPEL & THIS IS THE LIFE & IMMORTALITY		757D	EV GOSPEL	PROSE
ONE POWER ALONE MAKES A POET IMAGINATION THE DIVINE VISION		782D	ANNO WW POEMS	MARG
IT WOULD NOT FULFILL THE PURPOSE FOR WHICH ALONE I LIVE WHICH		791D	LETTER 4	PROSE
ALONE VALUED BY THE GREEKS & THE BEST MODERN ARTISTS . .		794A	LETTER 5	PROSE
ALONE IS THE GOVERNOR OF WORLDLY RICHES & WHEN IT IS FIT		796A	LETTER 6	PROSE
I SHOULD NOT DARE TO SAY TO ANY ONE ELSE THAT I CAN ALONE		822C	LETTER 26	PROSE
BREAD ALONE I SHALL LIVE ALTHO I SHOULD WANT BREAD NOTHING		830B	LETTER 30	PROSE
& THIS ALONE WILL PAY ITS LABOUR BY SUCCESS IF NOT OF MONEY		850C	LETTER 49	PROSE
ARE ALONE TO BE FOUND IN RELIGION THE SUN & THE MOON OF OUR		854B	LETTER 53	PROSE
EVER TO LAMENT YOUR DISTANCE FROM LONDON AS THAT ALONE .		861D	LETTER 59	PROSE
WITHOUT DISARRANGING MY TIME WHICH IN FUTURE MUST ALONE		865D	LETTER 63	PROSE
BE DEVOTED TO DESIGNING & PAINTING [ALONE] WHEN I HAVE GOT		866A	LETTER 63	PROSE
THAT MUST BE MYSELF ALONE SHUT UP IN MYSELF OR REDUCED TO NOTHING		876B	LETTER 83	PROSE
MY WIFE ALONE IS ANSWERABLE FOR THEIR HAVING EXISTED IN ANY		879C	LETTER 89	PROSE

ALONG

	PAGE	TITLE	LINE
THERE HE SPORTS ALONG THE DAY	7	LOVE HARMNY/PS	19
THE DAY ALONG	8	MEMORY COME/PS	12
WALKING ALONG THE DARKEND VALLEY	8	MEMORY COME/PS	15
CLAMOUR BRAWLS ALONG THE STREETS	37A	CONTEMPLATN/PS	PROSE
THE BROOK STRETCHES ITS ARMS ALONG THE VELVET MEADOW	37B	CONTEMPLATN/PS	PROSE
EXAMPLE FOR YOUR REASON AS I WAS WALKING ALONG THE STREET	45A	ISLAND MOON 1	PROSE
I TURND MYSELF ABOUT WITH GREAT CONTEMPT SAID I GO ALONG YOU FOOL	45A	ISLAND MOON 1	PROSE
JOE BRADLEY & I WAS GOING ALONG ONE DAY IN THE SUGAR HOUSE	55B	ISLAND MOON 9	PROSE
THEN IF CHANCE ALONG THIS FOREST	61	LEAVE O/IM	5
. . . MOVE ALONG THE DUSKY ROAD TO VERSAILLES THERE . . .	145	FRENCH REVOLTN	251
RUSHING ALONG IRON RANKS GLITTERING THE OFFICERS EACH TO HIS STATION	147	FRENCH REVOLTN	287
. . . ALONG THE ROADS GLITTER LIKE FIRE	147	FRENCH REVOLTN	292
THE JUST MAN KEPT HIS COURSE ALONG	148	MARRIAGE HH 2	4
SHADOWS OF PROPHECY SHIVER ALONG BY THE LAKES AND THE RIVERS	159A	SONG LIBERTY	PROSE
AND ALONG THE PAVEMENT SWEET	163	I SAW CHAPEL/N	10
ALONG THE VALES OF LEUTHA SEEKING FLOWERS TO COMFORT HER	189	V DAU ALBION 1	4
TREMBLING SUNK AN EARTHQUAKE ROLLD ALONG THE MOSSY PILE	205	AMERICA CANC C	12
I TOOK HIM HOME IN MY WARM BOSOM AS WE WENT ALONG	238	EUROPE INTRO	19
THAT STRETCHES OUT ITS SHADY LENGTH ALONG THE ISLAND WHITE	241	EUROPE 10	3
ALONG THE INFINITE SHORES OF THAMES TO GOLDEN VERULAM	241	EUROPE 10	5
GROVELING ALONG GREAT GEORGE STREET THRO THE PARK GATE . . .	242	EUROPE 12	19
BEATEN ALONG ITS SIGHTLESS WAY GROWING ENORMOUS IN ITS MOTION TO	269	FOUR ZOAS 1	194
GROANS RAN ALONG TYBURN'S BROOK AND ALONG THE RIVER OF OXFORD	281	FOUR ZOAS 2	39
WEAVING MAZES OF DELIGHT ALONG THE SUNNY PARADISE . . .	282	FOUR ZOAS 2	96
TRAVELLING IN SILENT MAJESTY ALONG THEIR ORDERD WAYS	287	FOUR ZOAS 2	272
AND MEASURE MATHEMATIC MOTION WONDROUS ALONG THE DEEP .	287	FOUR ZOAS 2	274
OF FIRE FAR SHINING TRAVELLING ALONG EVEN TO ITS DESTIND END	287	FOUR ZOAS 2	276
THE NUMROUS FLOCKS COVER THE MOUNTAIN & SHINE ALONG THE VALLEY	308	FOUR ZOAS 5	* 138
LOS TAKING ENITHARMON BY THE HAND LED HER ALONG . . .	309	FOUR ZOAS 5	150
COMMUNING WITH THE SPECTRE WHO REJOICD ALONG THE VALE	319	FOUR ZOAS 6	303
SHUT UP WITHIN THEMSELVES DESCENDING DOWN I SUNK ALONG .	327	FOUR ZOAS 7	286
WITH WHIPS ALONG THE SULTRY [ROADS] SANDS I HEARD THOSE WHOM I LOVD	334	FOUR ZOAS 7B	61
ALONG THE RANKS CRYING LISTEN TO THE PRIEST OF GOD YE WARRIORS	336	FOUR ZOAS 7B	114
SOUND OF LOUD TRUMPET THUNDERING ALONG FROM HEAVEN TO HEAVEN	357	FOUR ZOAS 9	11
MUTTERING ALONG FROM HEAVEN TO HEAVEN HOARSE ROLL THE HUMAN FORMS	372	FOUR ZOAS 9	* 564
ARE THESE THE SLAVES THAT GROAND ALONG THE STREETS OF MYSTERY	375	FOUR ZOAS 9	677
EACH DAY I MOURN ALONG THE WOOD . . .	423	THE BIRDS/N	11
SO LOS SPOKE SATAN TREMBLING OBEYD WEEPING ALONG THE WAY	484	MILTON 4	19
AN AGED WOMAN RAVING ALONG THE STREETS THE SPACE IS NAMED	490	MILTON 10	4
ELYNITTRIA WHENCE IS THIS JEALOUSY RUNNING ALONG THE MOUNTAINS	491	MILTON 10	14
ALONG THE ROCKY ISLAND & THENCE THROUGHOUT THE WHOLE EARTH	499	MILTON 18	9
SO SPOKE LOS AS WE WENT ALONG TO HIS SUPREME ABODE .	505	MILTON 22	26
ALONG THE VALLEYS OF MIDDLESEX FROM HOUNSLOW TO BLACKHEATH	512	MILTON 26	19
REVELS ALONG UPON THE WIND THE WHITE-THORN LOVELY MAY . .	520	MILTON 31	55
AMONG THE SPIRITUAL FIRES LOUD THE CORN FIELDS THUNDER ALONG	636	JERUSALEM 16	5
FEEDS THE DREAD FORGE TREMBLING & SHUDDERING ALONG THE VALLEYS	636	JERUSALEM 16	15
I SEE THEM DISTANT FROM MY BOSOM SCOURGD ALONG THE ROADS	644	JERUSALEM 21	40
GREAT IS THE CRY OF THE HOUNDS OF NIMROD ALONG THE VALLEY	644	JERUSALEM 22	8
FROM HILL TO HILL & THE THAMES LAMENTS ALONG THE VALLEYS	656	JERUSALEM 30	24
WENT ALONG ALBION'S ROADS TILL THEY ARRIVD AT ALBION'S HOUSE	667	JERUSALEM 40	24
FROM CAMBERWELL TO HIGHGATE WHERE THE MIGHTY THAMES SHUDDERS ALONG	677	JERUSALEM 47	2
. . . THUNDERING ALONG	689	JERUSALEM 57	2
THE CHARIOT WHEELS FILLED WITH EYES RAGE ALONG THE HOWLING VALLEY	697	JERUSALEM 63	11
THOR & FRIGA & THE FAIRIES LEAD THE MOON ALONG THE VALLEY OF CHERUBIM	697	JERUSALEM 63	14
TILL CANAAN ROLLD APART FROM ALBION ACROSS THE RHINE ALONG THE DANUBE	698	JERUSALEM 63	41
HUMAN MISERIES TURND FIERCE WITH THE LIVES OF MEN ALONG THE VALLEY	699	JERUSALEM 64	33
OPENING ALONG THE VALLEY OF REPHAIM	699	JERUSALEM 64	38
AND GREECE & ALONG THE SEA OF REPHAIM INTO JUDEA	704	JERUSALEM 67	39
ALONG THE VALLEY OF DESTRUCTION AMONG THESE DRUID TEMPLES	721	JERUSALEM 79	66
ALONG THE ISLAND WHITE AMONG THE DRUID TEMPLES WHILE GWENDOLEN	725	JERUSALEM 82	15
THEY ARE RED HOT WITH CRUELTY RAVING ALONG THE BANKS OF THAMES	737	JERUSALEM 90	47
OF THE DRUID ALONG THE VALLEY OF REPHAIM FROM CAMBERWELL TO GOLGOTHA	740	JERUSALEM 92	26
UPON EAST MOOR IN DERBYSHIRE & ALONG THE VALLEYS OF CHEVIOT	740	JERUSALEM 93	6
AH THEN I HEARD MY LITTLE ONES WEEPING ALONG THE VALLEY	740	JERUSALEM 93	11
HOW CAN I HEAR MY LITTLE ONES WEEPING ALONG THE VALLEY . .	740	JERUSALEM 93	15

		PAGE	TITLE	LINE

ALOUD
```
    SHE SHRIEKD ALOUD AND SUNK UPON THE STEPS . . . . . .      4 FAIR ELENOR/PS      5
    HE SHOUTED OUT ALOUD . . . . . . . . . . . . . .          51 WHEN CORRUP/IM     30
    ENTERD THE GATES OF TIRIEL'S PALACE & STOOD & CALLD ALOUD 104 TIRIEL 4           42
    . . . AND CRIED OUT ALOUD . . . . . . . . . .            146 FRENCH REVOLTN    260
    AND CALLD ALOUD TO ENGLISH BLAKE . . . . . . .           187 WHEN KLOPSTK/N      6
    AND BOSTON'S ANGEL CRIED ALOUD AS THEY FLEW THRO THE DARK 200 AMERICA 11          3
        NIGHT
    HE LAUGHD ALOUD TO SEE THEM WHIMPER BECAUSE THEY         238 EUROPE INTRO       21
        WERE PLUCKD
    THEN THE THUNDERS OF URIZEN BELLOWD ALOUD . . . . . .    248 SONG OF LOS 7      24
    WHY DOES THE RAVEN CRY ALOUD AND NO EYE PITIES HER . . . 276 FOUR ZOAS 1       445
    HIS WOES ALOUD TO ENITHARMON SINCE HE COULD NOT HIDE . . 307 FOUR ZOAS 5        96
    AND THUS AHANIA CRIES ALOUD TO THE CAVERNS OF THE GRAVE  353 FOUR ZOAS 8       492
    RAHAB & TIRZAH WAIL ALOUD IN THE WILD FLAMES . . . . .   358 FOUR ZOAS 9        32
    GIBBON ALOUD HIS LASH DOES PLY . . . . . . . . . .       420 I SAW MNK AD/N     16
    IN SOLEMN DEATH THE SEA OF TIME & SPACE THUNDERD ALOUD   497 MILTON 15          39
    THUS ALOUD [WAS HEARD TO] DID HOWL & CRY . . . . . .     542 PITIFUL CASE/N *    7
    THEY GROAND ALOUD ON LONDON STONE . . . . . . . . .      650 FIELDS FROM/J      33
    THEY GROAND ALOUD ON TYBURN'S BROOK . . . . . . . .      650 FIELDS FROM/J      34
    FROM HIS AWFUL MEMBERS AND THUS LOS CRIED ALOUD . . . .  660 JERUSALEM 34       21
    OF HUMAN MAJESTY THE LIVING CREATURES WEPT ALOUD AS THEY 667 JERUSALEM 40       23
    TO ME THEIR BENEFACTOR CALLS ALOUD FOR VENGEANCE DEEP . . 671 JERUSALEM 42      54
```
ALPINE
```
    OF ALPINE HILLS ROUND HIS HIGH AERY . . . . . . . . .     15 IMIT SPEN/PS       38
```
ALPS
```
    CLOUDS ROLL HEAVY UPON THE ALPS ROUND ROUSSEAU & VOLTAIRE 246 SONG OF LOS 4      18
    AROSE LIKE A PILLAR OF FIRE ABOVE THE ALPS . . . . .     248 SONG OF LOS 7      27
    HIS VOICE IS HEARD FROM ALBION THE ALPS & APPENINES . .  730 JERUSALEM 85       16
```
ALREADY
```
    ID FIND IT OUT IN A MINUTE BUT IVE FOUND IT OUT ALREADY   51D ISLAND MOON 7    PROSE
    OF WHAT HE HAS ALREADY PERCIEVD . . . . . . . . . .       97A NAT RELIGION 1   PROSE
    REASON OR THE RATIO OF ALL WE HAVE ALREADY KNOWN . . . .  97C NAT RELIGION 2   PROSE
    FROM ALREADY ACQUIRED KNOWLEDGE MAN COULD NOT ACQUIRE MORE 98C ALL RELIGIONS   PROSE
    MY SONS HAVE SMITTEN ME ALREADY AND IF THOU SMITEST ME . 104 TIRIEL 4           13
    IT IS ONLY THE CONTENTS OR INDEX OF ALREADY PUBLISHD BOOKS 157C MARRIAGE HH 21 PROSE
    I AM ALREADY DISTRACTED AT THEIR DEEDS & IF I LOOK . . . 265 FOUR ZOAS 1        55
    [ALREADY ARE MY EYES REVERTED ALL THAT I BEHOLD] . . . . 267 FOUR ZOAS 1       115
    . . . ALREADY ROUND THY TREE . . . . . . . . . .        323 FOUR ZOAS 7       135
    BY REASON'S POWER EVEN I ALREADY FEEL A WORLD WITHIN . . 329 FOUR ZOAS 7       364
    BEGUN ALREADY IN ETERNITY COME THEN O LAMB OF GOD . .    347 FOUR ZOAS 8       244
    HE WHO SAYS THERE ARE SECOND CAUSES HAS ALREADY DENIED   403B ANNO BACON       MARG
        A FIRST
    THUS IS THE HEAVEN A VORTEX PASSD ALREADY AND THE EARTH  497 MILTON 15          34
    HE ONLY IMITATES WHAT IS ALREADY EXECUTED . . . . .      596B PUB ADDRESS/N    PROSE
    LET THEM ENCOURAGE WHAT EXISTS ALREADY . . . . . . .     597A PUB ADDR AD/N    PROSE
    BY SUCH PRACTISE & HAVE ALREADY DONE SO THAT YOU WILL RAGE 603B PUB ADDR AD/N  PROSE
    HIMSELF CAST OUT BY THOSE WHO HAVE ALREADY EMBRACED TRUE 613A V LAST JUDG/N   PROSE
        ART
    THE ASSISTANCE & COUNTENANCE OF THOSE ALREADY IN THE TRUTH 614A V LAST JUDG/N PROSE
    IN WAY OF VENGEANCE I PUNISH THE ALREADY PUNISHD O WHOM  657 JERUSALEM 31        34
    OR AS IT IS POLITELY CALLD BORED YOU TOO MUCH ALREADY .  816C LETTER 24        PROSE
    ALREADY INDEBTED TO MY WIFE TWENTY GUINEAS FOR WORK . .  821A LETTER 25        PROSE
    & MR PITT ARE BOTH AMONG THE SUBSCRIBERS WHICH ARE ALREADY 824D LETTER 27      PROSE
    I HAVE SEEN FLAXMAN ALREADY AS I TOOK TO HIM EARLY THIS  833C LETTER 33        PROSE
    & THE HEAD OF ROMNEY FOR WHICH I AM ALREADY PAID . . .   851A LETTER 49        PROSE
    FINISHED THOUGH FLAXMAN HAS ALREADY PRONOUNCED IT SO .   853C LETTER 52        PROSE
    THE SUBJECTS I CANNOT DO BETTER THAN THOSE ALREADY CHOSEN 859A LETTER 56       PROSE
    TEMPTING THAT I HAVE ALREADY INVOLVED MYSELF IN ENGAGEMENTS 865C LETTER 63     PROSE
```
ALSO
```
    WIDOWS & MAIDS & YOUTHS ALSO . . . . . . . . . .          56 HAIL MATRIM/IM      4
    THAT WHICH IS CAPABLE OF GOOD IS NOT ALSO CAPABLE OF EVIL 80A ANNO LAVATER     MARG
        BUT
    THAT WHICH IS CAPABLE OF EVIL IS ALSO CAPABLE OF GOOD    80A ANNO LAVATER      MARG
        THIS APHORISM
    UNLESS YOU FIND IT TO BE HIS ALSO PREVIOUS TO YOUR       87D ANNO LAVATER      MARG
        ACQUAINTANCE
    THEY ALSO PERCIEVE THIS FROM KNOWLEDGE BUT NOT WITH THE  89C ANNO SWED LOVE    MARG
        NATURAL PART
    IS IT NOT ALSO EVIDENT THAT ONE DEGREE WILL NOT OPEN THE 93A ANNO SWED LOVE    MARG
        OTHER
    QUERY DOES HE ALSO OCCUPY THAT PLACE IN HEAVEN SEE N...AT 131D ANNO SWED PROV  MARG
        THE END
    SEE ALSO...WHERE HE SAYS THAT A PLACE FOR EACH MAN       133D ANNO SWED PROV   MARG
        IS FORESEEN
    EZEKIEL SAID THE SAME OF HIS I ALSO ASKED ISAIAH WHAT .  154A MARRIAGE HH 12   PROSE
    SEE WHETHER PROVIDENCE IS HERE ALSO IF YOU WILL NOT I WILL 155D MARRIAGE HH 17 PROSE
    I HAVE ALSO THE BIBLE OF HELL WHICH THE WORLD SHALL HAVE 158D MARRIAGE HH 22   PROSE
    . . . [WHERE WE MAY REMAIN FOR EVER ALONE] ALSO O PITY   265 FOUR ZOAS 1        28
        ME O ENION
    [TO SMITE ME WITH THY TONGUE BEWARE LEST I STING ALSO THEE] 268 FOUR ZOAS 1    148
    SHE ALSO TOOK AN ATOM OF SPACE & OPEND ITS CENTER . . .  270 FOUR ZOAS 1    *  225
    MEAN MISCHIEF MOST IF YOU ARE SUCH LO I AM ALSO SUCH . . 273 FOUR ZOAS 1       332
    ONE MUST BE MASTER [?THY] TRY THY ARTS I ALSO WILL TRY   273 FOUR ZOAS 1    *  333
        MINE
    HER COLD LIMBS IN THE ABSENCE OF HER LORD ALSO HER SONS  285 FOUR ZOAS 2       193
    SO SAYING IN DEEP SOBS HE LANGUISHD TILL DEAD HE ALSO FELL 289 FOUR ZOAS 2     340
    THAT HE MAY ALSO DRAW AHANIA'S SPIRIT INTO HER VORTEX .  290 FOUR ZOAS 2       384
    LISTEN TO HER WHO LOVES THEE LEST WE ALSO ARE DRIVEN AWAY 294 FOUR ZOAS 3       92
    SAYING ART THOU ALSO BECOME LIKE VALA THUS I CAST THEE OUT 295 FOUR ZOAS 3     113
    AND ART THOU ALSO BECOME LIKE VALA THUS I CAST THEE OUT  295 FOUR ZOAS 3       130
    BEWARE LEST WE ALSO DRINK UP THEE ROUGH DEMON OF THE WATERS 298 FOUR ZOAS 4     37
```

		PAGE	TITLE	LINE
ALSO   (CONTINUED) | | | | |
WHERE BRIGHT AHANIA WEPT SHE ALSO SAW THE INFERNAL ROOTS | | 309 | FOUR ZOAS 5 | 181 |
HER ONCE LOVD LORD NOW BUT A SHADE HERSELF ALSO A SHADE | | 327 | FOUR ZOAS 7 | 313 |
TO BEAR THIS SELF CONVICTION TAKE THEN EAT THOU ALSO OF | | 330 | FOUR ZOAS 7 | 393 |
I ALSO TREMBLE AT MYSELF & AT ALL MY FORMER LIFE . . . . | | 330 | FOUR ZOAS 7 | 423 |
ALSO THE VEGETATED BODIES WHICH ENITHARMON WOVE . . . . | | 342 | FOUR ZOAS 8 | 54 |
HE FORMED ALSO HARSH INSTRUMENTS OF SOUND . . . . . . | | 344 | FOUR ZOAS 8 | 135 |
OF PRIDE AND I ALSO HAVE PIERCD THE LAMB OF GOD IN PRIDE & WRATH | | 350 | FOUR ZOAS 8 | 355 |
HEAR ME REPEAT MY GENERATIONS THAT THOU MAYST ALSO REPENT | | 350 | FOUR ZOAS 8 | * 356 |
BUT SATAN ACCUSD PALAMABRON BEFORE [LOS] HIS BRETHREN ALSO HE MADDEND | | 350 | FOUR ZOAS 8 | 368 |
LET US FLEE ALSO TO THE NORTH THEY FLED THE SONS OF MEN | | 359 | FOUR ZOAS 9 | 64 |
THE ETERNAL MAN ALSO SAT DOWN UPON THE COUCHES OF BEULAH | | 366 | FOUR ZOAS 9 | 354 |
I SEE THE HAND THAT LEADETH ME DOTH ALSO LEAD MY FLOCKS | | 369 | FOUR ZOAS 9 | 474 |
ALSO THE VEGETATED BODIES WHICH ENITHARMON WOVE IN HER LOOMS | | 382 | FOUR ZOAS AD 6 | 24 |
BY PAINE & ALSO THE PERVERSIONS OF THE BIBLE WHO DARE . . | | 383B | ANNO WATSON | MARG |
LUTHER ALSO LEFT THE PRIEST & JOIND THE SOLDIER . . . . | | 413B | ANNO BOYD | MARG |
DEAR CHILD I ALSO BY PLEASANT STREAMS . . . . | | 427 | LAND OF DREAMS | 13 |
IS THE HARLOT ALSO SIEZED & BOUND [CHAIND] BY TWO ANGELS | | 443A | LAST JUDGMNT/L | PROSE |
HOW I DID SECRETLY RAGE I ALSO SPOKE MY MIND XXX . . . . | | 449C | ANNO REYNOLDS | MARG |
ARE ARTFUL OPINIONS & FALLACIOUS ALSO . . . . | | 474C | ANNO REYNOLDS | MARG |
IN LIKENESS OF HIMSELF TELL ALSO OF THE FALSE TONGUE VEGETATED | | 481 | MILTON 2 | 10 |
EMBRACD SOFT WITH A BROTHER'S TEARS PALAMABRON WHO ALSO WEPT | | 486 | MILTON 7 | 17 |
BUT WE MUST NOT BE TYRANTS ALSO HE HATH ASSUMD MY PLACE | | 487 | MILTON 7 | 27 |
THEY BIT IN THEIR WILD FURY WHO ALSO MADDEND LIKE WILDEST BEASTS | | 487 | MILTON 7 | 49 |
LOS WEPT BUT RINTRAH ALSO CAME AND ENITHARMON ON . . . | | 488 | MILTON 8 | 14 |
YOUR LABOURS CALL YOU PALAMABRON IS ALSO IN SAD DILEMMA | | 488 | MILTON 8 | 17 |
THULLOH THE FRIEND OF SATAN ALSO REPROVD HIM FAINT THEIR REPROOF | | 488 | MILTON 8 | 33 |
ALSO THE RISING SUN & SETTING MOON HE VIEWS SURROUNDING | | 497 | MILTON 15 | 30 |
IN THE DARK ULRO TILL THE JUDGMENT ALSO MILTON KNEW THEY AND | | 498 | MILTON 17 | 5 |
TERROR UPON THEE BEHOLD HOW I AM & TREMBLE LEST THOU ALSO | | 499 | MILTON 18 | 27 |
AND HE ALSO DARKEND HIS BROWS FREEZING DARK ROCKS BETWEEN | | 500 | MILTON 19 | 1 |
UPON THE CLAY NOW CHANGD TO MARBLE ALSO URIZEN ROSE . . . | | 500 | MILTON 19 | 4 |
REGIONS OF THE IMAGINATION ALSO ALL MEN ON EARTH . . . . | | 503 | MILTON 21 | 5 |
AND OLOLON SAID LET US DESCEND ALSO AND LET US GIVE . . | | 504 | MILTON 21 | 45 |
THE UNIVERSAL DICTATE AND YOU ALSO FEEL THIS DICTATE . . | | 504 | MILTON 21 | 53 |
LOS STOOD IN THAT FIERCE GLOWING FIRE & HE ALSO STOOPD DOWN | | 505 | MILTON 22 | 8 |
GUARD ROUND THEM BUT I THE FOURTH ZOA AM ALSO SET . . . | | 508 | MILTON 24 | 8 |
AND IF YOU ALSO FLEE AWAY AND LEAVE YOUR FATHER'S SIDE . | | 508 | MILTON 24 | 22 |
SURELY YOU ALSO SHALL BECOME POOR MORTAL VEGETATIONS . . | | 508 | MILTON 24 | 24 |
FORTH IN YOUR WRATH LEST YOU ALSO ARE VEGETATED BY TIRZAH | | 511 | MILTON 25 | 58 |
URIZEN'S SONS HERE LABOUR ALSO & HERE ARE SEEN THE MILLS | | 514 | MILTON 27 | 49 |
AND IF HE MOVE HIS DWELLING-PLACE HIS HEAVENS ALSO MOVE | | 516 | MILTON 29 | 12 |
HER ALSO INTIRELY ABSTRACTING HIMSELF FROM FEMALE LOVES | | 522 | MILTON 33 | 16 |
I ALSO STOOD IN SATAN'S BOSOM & BEHELD ITS DESOLATIONS . | | 529 | MILTON 38 | 15 |
BUT MY SOUL ALSO WOULD HE BEAR AWAY . . . . | | 536 | AND HIS LEGS/N | 6 |
I'LL ALSO WRITE MY OWN DEAR EPITAPH . . . . | | 537 | AND HIS LEGS/N | 49 |
HAYLEY FLAXMAN & STOTHARD ARE ALSO IN DOUBT . . . . . | | 545 | COSWAY FRAZR/N | 5 |
"THAT RETURND AND THE MOST STRONG ANOTHER WITH THEM ALSO RETURND" | | 560B | EXHIBITION ADV | PROSE |
THIS PICTURE ALSO IS A PROOF OF THE POWER OF COLOURS UNSULLIED | | 565A | DESC CAT 2 | PROSE |
THE HORSES HE HAS ALSO VARIED TO ACCORD TO THEIR RIDERS | | 567D | DESC CAT 3 | PROSE |
AS CHAUCER HAS ALSO PLACED THEM FIRST IN HIS PROLOGUE . | | 567D | DESC CAT 3 | PROSE |
THE SQUIRE'S YEOMAN IS ALSO A GREAT CHARACTER . . . . | | 568A | DESC CAT 3 | PROSE |
LADY IS DESCRIBED ALSO AS OF THE FIRST RANK RICH AND HONOURED | | 568B | DESC CAT 3 | PROSE |
THE PAINTER HAS ALSO GROUPED WITH THESE THE PARDONER . . | | 568C | DESC CAT 3 | PROSE |
HAS HERE ALSO INTRODUCED ONE OF THE RICH CITIZENS OF LONDON | | 568C | DESC CAT 3 | PROSE |
BUT ALSO WITH OTHER ACCOMPANIMENTS NOT SO RESPECTABLE . | | 568D | DESC CAT 3 | PROSE |
THE FRIAR IS A CHARACTER ALSO OF A MIXED KIND . . . . . | | 568D | DESC CAT 3 | PROSE |
OUR HOST WAS ALSO A LEADER OF THE AGE . . . . | | 569D | DESC CAT 3 | PROSE |
SHAKSPEARE'S FAIRIES ALSO ARE THE RULERS OF THE VEGETABLE WORLD | | 570A | DESC CAT 3 | PROSE |
AND HAS ALSO HIS GREAT USE AND HIS GRAND LEADING DESTINY | | 570A | DESC CAT 3 | PROSE |
HIS COMPANION THE SOMPNOUR IS ALSO A DEVIL . . . . . . | | 570A | DESC CAT 3 | PROSE |
THEY ALSO ARE "FULL SOLEMN MEN" AND THEIR COUNSEL . . | | 570C | DESC CAT 3 | PROSE |
THIS GROUPE IS ALSO WOULD FURNISH SUBSTANTIAL MATTER . . | | 571A | DESC CAT 3 | PROSE |
MINUTE AND EXACT BECAUSE SHE IS ALSO A SCOURGE AND A BLIGHT | | 572B | DESC CAT 3 | PROSE |
EXECUTION OF THIS PICTURE IS ALSO IN WATER COLOURS OR FRESCO | | 577B | DESC CAT 4 | PROSE |
ALSO ABRAHAM WAS CALLED TO SUCCEED THE DRUIDICAL AGE . . | | 578A | DESC CAT 5 | PROSE |
IT IS ALSO CALLED THE BARREN WASTE OF LOCKE AND NEWTON . | | 581B | DESC CAT 6 | TITLE |
DEMONS BUT HE WAS ALSO COMPELLED TO LEAVE IT UNFINISHED | | 581B | DESC CAT 6 | PROSE |
I ALSO KNEW SOMETHING OF TOM COOKE WHO ENGRAVED . . . | | 594B | PUB ADDRESS/N | PROSE |
FALLING INTO THE ABYSS SIN IS ALSO REPRESENTED AS A FEMALE | | 606C | V LAST JUDG/N | PROSE |
IS ABRAHAM WITH SARAH & ISAAC ALSO HAGAR & ISHMAEL . . . | | 606D | V LAST JUDG/N | PROSE |
& INTO BLOOD BY MOSES RELATES TO VEGETABLE NATURE ALSO . | | 607B | V LAST JUDG/N | PROSE |
ACHITOPHEL IS ALSO HERE WITH THE CORD IN HIS HAND . . | | 608D | V LAST JUDG/N | PROSE |
GREEK LEARNED & WISE ALSO OF THOSE OF OTHER NATIONS . . | | 610B | V LAST JUDG/N | PROSE |
FROM WHENCE ABRAHAM WAS TAKEN ALSO ON THE RIGHT HAND OF NOAH | | 610D | V LAST JUDG/N | PROSE |
TO THE COMMON OPINION AS I MYSELF AM ALSO INFECTED WITH IT | | 614D | V LAST JUDG/N | PROSE |
& MY VISIONS ALSO INFECTED & I SEE TIME AGED ALAS TOO MUCH SO | | 614D | V LAST JUDG/N | PROSE |

		PAGE	TITLE	LINE

ALSO   (CONTINUED)

	PAGE	TITLE	LINE
THAT IS IT IS A MAN THERE IS NOT A TRUTH BUT IT HAS ALSO A MAN	615A	V LAST JUDG/N	PROSᴱ
I ALSO HOPE THE READER WILL BE WITH ME WHOLLY ONE IN JESUS	621A	JERUSALEM 3	PROSE
FOR AS HIS EMANATION DIVIDED HIS SPECTRE ALSO DIVIDED . .	624	JERUSALEM 6	3
A MURDERER OF ITS OWN BODY BUT ALSO A MURDERER	629	JERUSALEM 10	12
FOR THINE ARE ALSO MINE I HAVE KEPT SILENT HITHERTO . .	629	JERUSALEM 10	40
O THOU MY ENEMY WHERE IS MY GREAT SIN SHE IS ALSO THINE	630	JERUSALEM 10	43
BUT MY GRIEFS ADVANCE ALSO FOR EVER & EVER WITHOUT END	630	JERUSALEM 10	50
CREATED TO BE THE GREAT EXAMPLE OF HORROR & AGONY ALSO MY	630	JERUSALEM 10	52
BUT I AM LIVING YET I FEEL MY EMANATION ALSO DIVIDING .	631	JERUSALEM 12	7
HE VIEWS THE CHERUB AT THE TREE OF LIFE ALSO THE SERPENT	634	JERUSALEM 14	2
IN SEAS OF SORROW LOS ALSO VIEWS THE FOUR FEMALES . . .	634	JERUSALEM 14	9
TO THOSE I HATE FOR I CAN HATE ALSO AS WELL AS THEY .	640	JERUSALEM 17	63
THOU ART MY SISTER AND MY DAUGHTER THY SHAME IS MINE ALSO	642	JERUSALEM 20	19
FOR NOT ONE SPARROW CAN SUFFER & THE WHOLE UNIVERSE NOT SUFFER ALSO	648	JERUSALEM 25	8
IF IT IS TRUE MY TITLE-PAGE IS ALSO TRUE	649B	JERUSALEM 27	PROSE
HE SAW ALSO THE FOUR POINTS OF ALBION REVERSD INWARDS .	658	JERUSALEM 32	7
IF THE PERCEPTIVE ORGANS CLOSE THEIR OBJECTS SEEM TO CLOSE ALSO	661	JERUSALEM 34	56
ARE ALSO MEN EVERY THING IS HUMAN MIGHTY SUBLIME . . .	665	JERUSALEM 38	48
ALSO LOS SICK & TERRIFIED BEHELD THE FURNACES OF DEATH .	669	JERUSALEM 42	5
FOR THY RIGHTEOUSNESS BUT I ADD MERCY ALSO AND BIND . .	670	JERUSALEM 42	20
AH ME PITIABLE ONES DO YOU ALSO GO TO DEATH'S VALE . . .	673	JERUSALEM 43	73
HAVE YOU ALSO CAUGHT THE INFECTION OF SIN & STERN REPENTANCE	673	JERUSALEM 43	75
SHE ALSO TOOK AN ATOM OF SPACE WITH DIRE PAIN OPENING IT A CENTER	678	JERUSALEM 48	38
LOS ALSO SAW HER IN HIS SEVENTH FURNACE HE ALSO TERRIFIED	678	JERUSALEM 48	44
AND WE ALSO & ALL BEULAH CONSUME BENEATH ALBION'S CURSE	681	JERUSALEM 50	17
AND YOU ARE SO YOU ARE ALSO THE ENEMIES OF THE HUMAN RACE	682A	JERUSALEM 52	PROSE
BUT YOU ALSO CHARGE THE POOR MONKS & RELIGIOUS . . .	683A	JERUSALEM 52	PROSE
FOR THOU ALSO SUFFEREST WITH ME ALTHO I BEHOLD THEE NOT	693	JERUSALEM 60	61
SHALL VALA BRING THEE FORTH SHALL THE CHASTE BE ASHAMED ALSO	696	JERUSALEM 62	7
DIVIDING IN FIERCE PAIN ALSO THE VISION OF GOD WAS CLOSD IN CLOUDS	696	JERUSALEM 62	38
THEY HAVE DIVIDED SIMEON HE ALSO ROLLD APART IN BLOOD . .	715	JERUSALEM 74	44
REPENTANT AND SHE ALSO IN THE EDDYING WIND OF LOS'S BELLOWS	726	JERUSALEM 82	74
A ROUND WOMB BENEATH MY BOSOM LEST I ALSO BE OVERWOVEN .	732	JERUSALEM 87	14
KNOW THAT I NEVER WILL BE THINE ALSO THOU HIDEST VALA . .	733	JERUSALEM 87	22
THE HUMAN FOUR-FOLD FORMS MINGLE ALSO IN THUNDERS OF INTELLECT	733	JERUSALEM 88	7
HE ALSO WILL RECIEVE IT GO SPECTRE OBEY MY MOST SECRET DESIRE	737	JERUSALEM 91	4
[THOU ALSO DWELST IN ETERNITY]	750	EV GOSPEL(C)/N	38
THOU ALSO DWELST IN ETERNITY	750	EV GOSPEL(C)/N	40
THOU ALSO DWELLST IN ETERNITY	752	EV GOSPEL(D)/N	74
AND THENCE DID COVET ALSO RISE	755	EV GOSPEL(E)/N	74
IS SHE ALSO THE DIVINE IMAGE	765D	FOR SEXES/GP	TITLE
("THE AEGYPTIANS") THEY ALSO CONSIDERED GOD AS ABSTRACTED	774A	ANNO BERKELEY	* MARG
BUT JESUS AS ALSO ABRAHAM & DAVID CONSIDERD GOD . . .	774A	ANNO BERKELEY	MARG
HE SAYS THE SPIRITUAL BODY OR ANGEL AS LITTLE CHILDREN	774A	ANNO BERKELEY	MARG
JEHOVAH HE WHO SHALL TAKE CAIN'S LIFE MUST ALSO DIE O ABEL	780	GHOST ABEL 1	15
ABEL IS DEAD & CAIN SLEW HIM WE SHALL ALSO DIE A DEATH . .	780	GHOST ABEL 1	19
THAT APPEAREST TO MY SPIRITUAL VISION EVE SEEST THOU ALSO	780	GHOST ABEL 1	22
EVE I SEE HIM PLAINLY WITH MY MIND'S EYE I SEE ALSO ABEL LIVING	780	GHOST ABEL 1	23
THO TERRIBLY AFFLICTED AS WE ALSO ARE YET JEHOVAH SEES HIM	780	GHOST ABEL 1	24
WITH ANY OTHER POET WHATEVER ROWLEY & CHATTERTON ALSO . .	783C	ANNO WW POEMS	MARG
HE ALSO PASSED HIM BY UNALARMD & WAS PERMITTED	784B	ANNO WW EXCUR	MARG
AS ALSO PRIDE & HUMILITY BUT	792B	LETTER 4	PROSE
& BEING ALSO IN THE PREDICAMENT OF THAT PROPHET WHO SAYS	792C	LETTER 4	PROSE
WHICH WILL ACCOUNT FOR THE DIFFERENCE OF PRICE AS ALSO THAT	794B	LETTER 5	PROSE
I HAVE ALSO SENT A PROOF OF PERICLES FOR YOUR REMARKS .	797B	LETTER 9	PROSE
& MY COTTAGE IS ALSO A SHADOW OF THEIR HOUSES MY . . .	802A	LETTER 14	PROSE
COTTAGE IS MORE BEAUTIFUL THAN I THOUGHT IT & ALSO MORE CONVENIENT	803B	LETTER 15	PROSE
A CROWN OF LAURELS & I ALSO THANK YOU FOR YOUR REPREHENSION	804A	LETTER 16	PROSE
ACCEPT MINE ALSO & BELIEVE ME TO REMAIN YOUR DEVOTED .	808C	LETTER 19	PROSE
I OUGHT ALSO TO MENTION MY EXTREME DISAPPOINTMENT AT .	809C	LETTER 20	PROSE
DID NOT HE IS ALSO A HAPPY ABSTRACT KNOWN BY ALL HIS FRIENDS	809C	LETTER 20	PROSE
NOT ONLY ON ACCOUNT OF MR HAYLEY'S COMPOSITION BUT ALSO	810A	LETTER 20	PROSE
HOPING THAT HER JOY IS NOW INCREASED & YOURS ALSO . . .	810A	LETTER 20	PROSE
PERMITTED HER TO SEND IT TO YOU ALSO WE OFTEN WISH THAT WE	813C	LETTER 22	PROSE
THAT I CAN CONFESS MYSELF IGNORANT OF I ALSO KNOW & . .	814D	LETTER 23	PROSE
ALSO LET ME OBSERVE THAT THE YELLOW LEATHER FLESH OF OLD MEN	815A	LETTER 23	PROSE
LET ME ALSO NOTICE THAT CARRACHE'S PICTURES ARE NOT LIKE	815B	LETTER 23	PROSE
I ALSO INCLOSE YOU SOME BALLADS BY MR HAYLEY WITH PRINTS	819A	LETTER 24	PROSE
I ALSO TOLD YOU WHAT I WAS ABOUT & THAT I WAS NOT IGNORANT	820C	LETTER 25	PROSE
SAKE OF CONVENIENCE I ALSO OUGHT TO INFORM YOU THAT I READ	820D	LETTER 25	PROSE
& ALSO VERY AFRAID THAT MY FRIENDS IN LONDON SHOULD HAVE	820D	LETTER 25	PROSE
AM ALSO GRATEFUL TO THE KIND HAND THAT ENDEAVOURS TO LIFT ME	822C	LETTER 26	PROSE
& TO BE ENGRAVD ALSO BY THE LAST MENTIOND THE . . .	824C	LETTER 27	PROSE
IT IS ALSO SOMEWHAT IN THE SAME MANNER DEFIND BY PLATO .	825A	LETTER 27	PROSE
YOU THAT I AM SAFE ARRIVD BUT ALSO TO INFORM YOU THAT IN A	833B	LETTER 33	PROSE
ALL THIS I LEARND WITH SOME ALARM & HEARD ALSO WHAT . .	833C	LETTER 33	PROSE
YOUR USE AS ALSO THE CATALOGUE OF HAMPSTEAD SALE . . .	836A	LETTER 35	PROSE

		PAGE	TITLE	LINE

ALSO   (CONTINUED)

& IN HIS BEST STYLE HE ALSO DESIRES ME TO EXPRESS TO YOU   836A LETTER 35   PROSE
  HIS
TO CALL ON ME MRS FLAXMAN & HER SISTERS GAVE ALSO THEIR   836C LETTER 35   PROSE
MR HOARE THE PAINTER WHOSE NOTE TO ME I ALSO INCLOSE FOR   836D LETTER 35   PROSE
I ENCLOSE ALSO NO...OF THE SHAKSPEARE   . . . . . .   839A LETTER 37   PROSE
AS ALSO FOR OMITTING TO MENTION MR HOARE'S GRATEFUL . .   839B LETTER 38   PROSE
TO BRING THEM TO PERFECTION HAS CAUSED THIS DELAY AS ALSO   840B LETTER 39   PROSE
BUT HE IS ALSO A LABORIOUS VOTARY OF ENDLESS WORK   . .   842D LETTER 42   PROSE
ON THE BACK IS WRITTEN...HE SHEWD ME ALSO   . . . .   843C LETTER 43   PROSE
MR WALKER ALSO SHEWD ME A PORTRAIT OF HIMSELF W WHOLE   843D LETTER 43   PROSE
  LENGTH
I HAVE ALSO SEEN ALDERMAN BOYDEL WHO HAS PROMISED   . . .   844A LETTER 43   PROSE
THE BEST OF WHICH I HAVE I SEND ALSO THE FRENCH MONUMENTS   844C LETTER 43   PROSE
ACCEPT ALSO OF MY THANKS FOR COWPER'S THIRD VOLUME . . .   844C LETTER 43   PROSE
MUST BE SO TO A MAN JUST OUT OF SO DREADFUL A FEVER I ALSO   844D LETTER 43   PROSE
YOU BOTH WITH GREAT AFFECTION MR FLAXMAN HAS ALSO PROMISED   846A LETTER 44   PROSE
AND WILL ALSO RESPECT JOHNSON THE MORE FOR SUCH TESTIMONY   846C LETTER 44   PROSE
AND BETTER TYPE THAN THE TWO EXTREMITIES ALSO IT   847A LETTER 44   PROSE
  IS CAREFULLY
ACCOUNT OF ITS EXPANDED MEADOWS BUT ALSO ON ACCOUNT OF ITS   847C LETTER 44   PROSE
SHALL HAVE A PROOF OF IT FOR YOUR REMARKS ALSO I HOPE BY   849B LETTER 45   PROSE
AND AFFECTIONATE COMPLIMENTS TO HIM ALSO TO OUR KIND FRIEND   852D LETTER 50   PROSE
OF THE SHIPWRECK MRS FLAXMAN ALSO WHO IS A GOOD . . .   853B LETTER 52   PROSE
I BEG YOUR REMARKS ALSO ON BOTH MY PERFORMANCES AS IN THEIR   853C LETTER 52   PROSE
CELESTIAL CITY I ALSO HAVE BUT A FEW MORE MOUNTAINS TO PASS   854C LETTER 53   PROSE
& MORE CEREMONY ALSO IN SO SERIOUS AN AFFAIR AS THE CALLING   854D LETTER 53   PROSE
  ON
MAKE IT A SUPERNACULUM THE SHIPWRECK ALSO WILL BE   . . .   855B LETTER 53   PROSE
SEAGRAVE TOGETHER WITH THE AUTHOR & PUBLISHER & ALSO THE   857A LETTER 54   PROSE
& IF ANY OTHERS ARE DISPLEASD IT IS ALSO AN ARGUMENT OF   862A LETTER 59   PROSE
  THEIR
JESUS PRESENT ALSO MY THANKS TO THE GENEROUS SEAGRAVE IN   863B LETTER 60   PROSE
AS THAT PAPER AND AS IT ALSO MUST FROM ITS NATURE BE MORE   863D LETTER 61   PROSE
ALSO TO REGULATE A SYSTEM OF WORKING THAT WILL BE UNIFORM   866C LETTER 65   PROSE
ABILITIES AS ALSO FOR THE D(DEAN) OF C(ANTERBURY) BUT .   868D LETTER 68   PROSE
& I WILL GO WITH YOU TO THE COACH ALSO I WILL GO . .   870D LETTER 72   PROSE
SAYING DO NOT VENTURE TILL SUMMER APPEARS AGAIN I ALSO .   872D LETTER 76   PROSE
TO SIT UP LONGER THAN SIX HOURS AT A TIME & ALSO FEEL THE   872D LETTER 76   PROSE
  COLD
THESE PILES HAVE NOW ALSO AS I HOPE RUN THEIR PERIOD & . .   874D LETTER 80   PROSE
ALSO OF SEEING AGAIN THOSE PICTURES OF THE OLD MASTERS BUT   SUPP LETTER 81A   *PROSE
& MORE SO WISHES ALSO YOURS SINCERELY   . . . . . .   876C LETTER 83   PROSE
BEST USE AS ALSO FOR THE PROSPECT OF MR OTTLEY'S . . .   879C LETTER 89   PROSE

ALTAR

THE CHURCH & I TOOK HIM TO THE ALTAR AND OPEND THE BIBLE   157A MARRIAGE HH 17   PROSE
TILL UPON THE ALTAR WHITE . . . .   163 I SAW CHAPEL/N   13
AND STANDING ON THE ALTAR HIGH . . . .   177 LIT BOY LST/N   16
AND STANDING ON THE ALTAR HIGH . . . .   218 LIT BOY LST/SE   13
A GOLDEN ALTAR BURNT PERFUMES WITH ART CELESTIAL FORMD .   285 FOUR ZOAS 2   190
WITH LIVES OF VICTIMS SACRIFICED UPON AN ALTAR OF BRASS   285 FOUR ZOAS 2   194
SLAIN ON THE ALTAR UP ASCENDING INTO HER CLOUDY BOSOM .   285 FOUR ZOAS 2   196
OF TERRIBLE WORKMANSHIP THE ALTAR LABOUR OF TEN THOUSAND   285 FOUR ZOAS 2   197
  SLAVES
. . . AND AN ALTAR OF VICTIMS TO SIN AND REPENTANCE . . .   294 FOUR ZOAS 3   105
UPON THE BLOODY ALTAR JOHN SAW THESE THINGS REVEALD IN   356 FOUR ZOAS 8   600
  HEAVEN
AND HIS BRIGHT FEET FIRM AS A BRAZEN ALTAR BUT THE PARTS   380 FOUR ZOAS AD 1   12
THAT THEY BE OFFERED UPON HIS ALTAR O CRUELTY & TORMENT   629 JERUSALEM 10   39
IN MANY TEARS & THERE THEY ERECT A TEMPLE & AN ALTAR .   702 JERUSALEM 66   29
ENQUIRING FOR JERUSALEM HE LED THEM UP MY STEPS TO MY ALTAR   721 JERUSALEM 79   52
BUT HIDE AMERICA FOR A CURSE AN ALTAR OF VICTIMS & A HOLY   725 JERUSALEM 82   29
  PLACE
EARTHAM WILL BE MY FIRST TEMPLE & ALTAR . . . . . .   801B LETTER 13   PROSE

ALTARS

ON AN ENLARGED SCALE TO ORNAMENT THE ALTARS OF CHURCHES   584B DESC CAT 14   PROSE
HER LITTLE-ONES SHE MUST SLAY UPON OUR ALTARS AND HER AGED   640 JERUSALEM 18   33
HIS FIRES REDOUND FROM HIS DRAGON ALTARS IN ERRORS   646 JERUSALEM 23   21
  RETURNING
FOR ATONEMENT ALBION BEGAN TO ERECT TWELVE ALTARS . . .   653 JERUSALEM 28   21
AND LOS DREW HIS SEVEN FURNACES AROUND ALBION'S ALTARS .   671 JERUSALEM 42   77
AND AS ALBION BUILT HIS FROZEN ALTARS LOS BUILT   671 JERUSALEM 42   78
  THE MUNDANE SHELL
AND THARMAS DASHD ON THE ROCKS OF THE ALTARS OF VICTIMS   672 JERUSALEM 43   7
  IN MEXICO
. . . WE DELIGHT IN THEIR BLOOD ON OUR ALTARS . . . . .   673 JERUSALEM 43   49
FILLD WITH THE LITTLE-ONES ARE CONSUMED IN THE FIRES OF   679 JERUSALEM 49   11
  THEIR ALTARS
IN THE MIDST OF THE ROCKS OF THE ALTARS OF ALBION IN FEARS   684 JERUSALEM 53   17
AND THE GREAT VOICE OF THE ATLANTIC HOWLED OVER THE DRUID   689 JERUSALEM 57   5
  ALTARS
OVER THE MOUNTAINS & THE FIRES BLAZD ON DRUID ALTARS .   696 JERUSALEM 62   33
HOWLING THE VICTIMS ON THE DRUID ALTARS YIELD THEIR SOULS   701 JERUSALEM 65   63
THE BUILDING IS NATURAL RELIGION & ITS ALTARS NATURAL   702 JERUSALEM 66   8
  MORALITY
TOGETHER AMONG MY LITTLE-ONES BUT NOW MY ALTARS RUN WITH   721 JERUSALEM 79   55
  BLOOD
ON THEIR ENORMOUS ALTARS BUILT IN THE TERRIBLE NORTH . .   727 JERUSALEM 83   20
OF JERUSALEM'S CHERUBIMS & TO FORGE THEM SWORDS OF HER   729 JERUSALEM 84   10
  ALTARS
YOU REAR IT ON YOUR ALTARS HIGH . . . .   761 FOR SEXES/GP   13

ALTAR-TABLE
    THEIR BREAD THEIR ALTAR-TABLE THEIR INCENSE & THEIR OATH   738 JERUSALEM 91   14
ALTER
    THE MICROSCOPE KNOWS NOT OF THIS NOR THE TELESCOPE THEY   516 MILTON 29   17
        ALTER
    NAMES ALTER THINGS NEVER ALTER I HAVE KNOWN MULTITUDES   567C DESC CAT 3   PROSE
ALTERD
    THARMAS I KNOW THEE HOW ARE WE ALTERD OUR BEAUTY DECAYD   299 FOUR ZOAS 4   79
    HE ALTERD THE POLES OF THE WORLD EAST WEST & NORTH & SOUTH   489 MILTON 9   17
    THE HUMAN FORM BEGAN TO BE ALTERD BY THE DAUGHTERS   703 JERUSALEM 66   46
        OF ALBION
    THUS LOS ALTERD HIS SPECTRE & EVERY RATIO OF HIS REASON   739 JERUSALEM 91   51
    HE ALTERD TIME AFTER TIME WITH DIRE PAIN & MANY TEARS . . 739 JERUSALEM 91   52
ALTERED
    SOME OF THE NAMES OR TITLES ARE ALTERED BY TIME . . . . 567C DESC CAT 3   PROSE
    SOME OF THE NAMES ARE ALTERED BY TIME . . . . 590D CHAUCER 2   PROSE
    PROMISE YOU OCULAR DEMONSTRATION OF MY ALTERED STATE . . 852B LETTER 50   PROSE
    I SEND TWO MORE DRAWINGS WITH THE FIRST THAT I DID ALTERED 866C LETTER 65   PROSE
ALTERING
    FROM HEAVEN TO HEAVN THRO ALL ITS MESHES ALTERING   345 FOUR ZOAS 8   177
        THE VORTEXES
    FOR THE EYE ALTERING ALTERS ALL . . . . 426 MENTAL TRAVLER   62
    OF MAGNIFICENCE ONLY ENLARGING NOT ALTERING ITS PROPORTIONS 801D LETTER 14   PROSE
ALTERNATE
    AND THEY ALTERNATE KEPT WATCH OVER THE YOUTHFUL TERRORS   270 FOUR ZOAS 1   229
    ALTERNATE LOVE & HATE HIS BREAST HERS SCORN & JEALOUSY   270 FOUR ZOAS 1   237
    WHAT THOU FORGETTEST THEY IN US & WE IN THEM ALTERNATE LIVD 327 FOUR ZOAS 7   276
    IN INFANT SORROW & JOY ALTERNATE ENION & THARMAS PLAYD . 372 FOUR ZOAS 9   554
    TAKE THOU THESE TONGS STRIKE THOU ALTERNATE WITH ME LABOUR 627 JERUSALEM 8   40
        OBEDIENT
    ALTERNATE FROM THOSE STATES OR WORLDS IN WHICH THE SPIRIT   680 JERUSALEM 49   74
        TRAVELS
    ALTERNATE THEY WATCH IN NIGHT ALTERNATE LABOUR IN DAY . . 729 JERUSALEM 83   79
    SHE SPOKE IN SCORN & JEALOUSY ALTERNATE TORMENTS AND . . 733 JERUSALEM 88   22
ALTERNATELY
    LEANING ON ONE ANOTHER'S NECKS ALTERNATELY . . . . . 35D COUCH DEATH/PS   PROSE
    SO IF BOTH POETS & PAINTERS SHOULD ALTERNATELY DISLIKE . 825B LETTER 27   PROSE
    I CURSE & BLESS ENGRAVING ALTERNATELY BECAUSE IT TAKES   837D LETTER 36   PROSE
        SO MUCH TIME
ALTERS
    & HIS THEME WAS THE MAN WHO NEVER ALTERS HIS OPINION . . 156D MARRIAGE HH 17 PROSE
    FOR THE EYE ALTERING ALTERS ALL . . . . 426 MENTAL TRAVLER   62
    LIMBS THAT DEVIATES OR ALTERS LEAST FROM INFANCY TO OLD AGE 580A DESC CAT 5   PROSE
ALTHO
    I STILL KEEP WATCH ALTHO I TREMBLE & WITHER ACROSS THE   288 FOUR ZOAS 2   330
        HEAVENS
    OF BITTER HOPE ALTHO I CONSUME IN THESE RAGING WATERS . . 355 FOUR ZOAS 8 * 547
    FOLLOWING MILTON INTO ULRO ALTHO YOUR POWER IS GREAT . 508 MILTON 24   23
    ALTHO OUR HUMAN POWER CAN SUSTAIN THE SEVERE CONTENTIONS   533 MILTON 41   32
    LOS ANSWERD ALTHO I KNOW NOT THIS I KNOW FAR WORSE THAN   626 JERUSALEM 7   51
        THIS
    FOR THOU ALSO SUFFEREST WITH ME ALTHO I BEHOLD THEE NOT   693 JERUSALEM 60   61
    AND ALTHO I SIN & BLASPHEME THY HOLY NAME THOU PITIEST ME   693 JERUSALEM 60   62
    ALTHO THEY MUST KNOW & IT IS MANIFEST THAT THE WHOLE IS   827D LETTER 28   PROSE
    BREAD ALONE I SHALL LIVE ALTHO I SHOULD WANT BREAD NOTHING 830B LETTER 30   PROSE
    TILL THEN I REMAIN YOUR GRATEFUL ALTHO SEEMINGLY OTHERWISE 866B LETTER 64   PROSE
ALTHOUGH
    OR ENAMEL ALTHOUGH IN WORKS LARGER THAN LIFE . . . . 561A EXHIBITION ADV PROSE
    ALTHOUGH MOLESTED CONTINUALLY BY BLOTTING AND BLURRING . 581B DESC CAT 6   PROSE
    ALTHOUGH IN EVERY BOSOM THEY CONTROLL OUR VEGETATIVE POWERS 624 JERUSALEM 5   39
    [I NOW DESPISE & MOCK IN TURN ?ALTHOUGH SUFFRING ?POVERTY] SUPP ANNO REYNOLDS * MARG
ALTOGETHER
    FROM GOD IS ALTOGETHER ABOMINABLE & BLASPHEMOUS . . . 387B ANNO WATSON   MARG
    TAKES AWAY THE AUTHORITY ALTOGETHER IT CEASES TO BE HISTORY 390D ANNO WATSON   MARG
    INVENTION DEPENDS ALTOGETHER UPON EXECUTION . . . . . 446D ANNO REYNOLDS   MARG
    ON MICHAEL ANGELO'S EXECUTION ALTOGETHER . . . . . 447A ANNO REYNOLDS   MARG
    WHICH ALTOGETHER DEPENDS ON DISTINCTNESS OF FORM . . . 463A ANNO REYNOLDS   MARG
    ALTOGETHER HIS COLOURING (IS) CONTRARY . . . . . . 469A ANNO REYNOLDS * MARG
    FOR HIS PICTURES IS ALTOGETHER FALSE HE WAS A . . . . 583B DESC CAT 9   PROSE
    AND FALSE BOWELS ALTOGETHER COMPOSING THE FALSE TONGUE   634 JERUSALEM 14   6
    IS ALTOGETHER AN EVIL & REQUIRES A NEW SELFHOOD CONTINUALLY 682A JERUSALEM 52   PROSE
    AY & THE FINEST PICTURES I ALTOGETHER REJECT AS . . . 815B LETTER 23   PROSE
    ALTOGETHER HIDDEN FROM THE CORPOREAL UNDERSTANDING . . 825A LETTER 27   PROSE
    UNLESS ALTOGETHER LEFT TO MY OWN JUDGMENT . . . . . 826A LETTER 27   PROSE
    THE PROPOSAL ALTOGETHER I TOOK THE LIBERTY TO TELL HIM THAT 842C LETTER 42   PROSE
    HAD TWENTY THANK GOD I WAS NOT ALTOGETHER A BEAST AS HE WAS 852A LETTER 50   PROSE
    MR PHILLIPS OBJECTS ALTOGETHER TO THE INSERTION OF MY . 861B LETTER 58   PROSE
AL-ULRO
    THE SECOND STATE IS ALLA & THE THIRD STATE AL-ULRO . . 524 MILTON 34   12
ALWAY
    RENEW IT TO ETERNAL LIFE LO I AM WITH YOU ALWAY . . . 504 MILTON 21   56
    SPIRIT A SELFHOOD WHICH MUST BE PUT OFF & ANNIHILATED ALWAY 533 MILTON 40   36
ALWAYS
    DEAR SIR A PRINCE SHOULD ALWAYS KEEP HIS STATE . . . 20 EDW THIRD/PS 2   46
    NOW I ALWAYS THOUGHT THAT A MAN MIGHT BE . . . . . 29A EDW THIRD/PS 4   PROSE
    AS SIR JOHN CHANDOS THAT THE PRINCE IS ALWAYS WITH . . 29C EDW THIRD/PS 4   PROSE
    OBTUSE ANGLE SHUTTING HIS EYES & SAYING THAT HE ALWAYS . 45D ISLAND MOON 1   PROSE
    ALWAYS PLAYING WITH ITS OWN TAIL . . . . 46A ISLAND MOON 1   PROSE
    ARADOBO YOU SHOULD ALWAYS THINK [OF WHAT YOU SP] BEFORE   47B ISLAND MOON 3 *PROSE
        YOU SPEAK
    YOU MUST ALWAYS THINK FOR YOURSELF HOW SIR SAID ARADOBO   49B ISLAND MOON 5   PROSE
    AND THIS HE ALWAYS KEPT IN MIND . . . . 50 WHEN CORRUP/IM   13

```
                                                                  PAGE      TITLE      LINE
ALWAYS    (CONTINUED)
     WHAT IS IT TO ANY BODY WHAT I DO I AM ALWAYS UNHAPPY TOO        51C ISLAND MOON 6   PROSE
     IN MY LIFE YOU ARE ALWAYS TALKING OF YOUR BOOKS   . . . .      52D ISLAND MOON 8   PROSE
     SUCH A LIAR AS QUID THINKS HE IS [BUT HE IS ALWAYS ENVYING]     53A ISLAND MOON 8   PROSE
     A GIRL HAS ALWAYS MORE TONGUE THAN A BOY I HAVE SEEN   .       53B ISLAND MOON 8   PROSE
     [ALWAYS SPOILS GOOD COMPANY IN THIS MANNER & ITS A SHAME]       57A ISLAND MOON 9   PROSE
     ("ALL FINERY IS A SIGN OF LITTLENESS") NOT ALWAYS     . . .    71B ANNO LAVATER    MARG
     THERE CAN BE NO GOOD-WILL WILL IS ALWAYS EVIL  . . . . .       89A ANNO SWED LOVE  MARG
     ALWAYS BE READY TO SPEAK YOUR MIND AND A BASE MAN WILL         151D MARRIAGE HH 8  PROSE
          AVOID YOU
     THESE TWO CLASSES OF MEN ARE ALWAYS UPON EARTH    . . . .     155B MARRIAGE HH 15  PROSE
     I HAVE ALWAYS FOUND THAT ANGELS HAVE THE VANITY TO SPEAK      157C MARRIAGE HH 21  PROSE
     LOVE TO FAULTS IS ALWAYS BLIND . . . . . . . . . .            175 HOW TO KNOW/N       1
     ALWAYS IS TO JOY INCLIND . . . . . . . . . . . .              175 HOW TO KNOW/N       2
     [ALWAYS] LAWLESS WINGD & UNCONFIND  . . . . . . . .           175 HOW TO KNOW/N       3
     WHAT IN WHORES IS ALWAYS FOUND . . . . . . . . . .            178 IN A WIFE/N         2
     AND MODEST DAME LURCH WHO IS ALWAYS AT CHURCH  . . . .        179 LIT VAGABOND/N     12
     AND MODEST DAME LURCH WHO IS ALWAYS AT CHURCH  . . . .        216 LIT VAGABND/SE     11
     CRAVING & DEVOURING BUT MY EYES ARE ALWAYS UPON THEE O        327 FOUR ZOAS 7      306
          LOVELY
     SEEKING THE ETERNAL WHICH IS ALWAYS PRESENT TO THE WISE       361 FOUR ZOAS 9      171
     ("ON ALL OCCASIONS ACT RIGHT ") ALWAYS OR THE BIBLE          386B ANNO WATSON     MARG
          IS FALSE
     WILL [ALWAYS BE FOUND TO BE NEITHER COLD NOR HOT & WILL]      386C ANNO WATSON     MARG
     THAT GOD DOES & ALWAYS DID CONVERSE WITH HONEST MEN  . .      389A ANNO WATSON     MARG
     BACON WAS ALWAYS A POOR DEVIL IF HISTORY SAYS TRUE  . .       409A ANNO BACON     * MARG
     HEARD PEOPLE QUARREL BUT THEY ALWAYS CHARGED EACH OTHER       437C BLAKES MEMORAN PROSE
     ARE ALWAYS CLUMSY AND INDEFINITE THE EFFECT OF RUBBING OUT    439C REMARKS MALKIN PROSE
     WHICH HE ALMOST ALWAYS APPROVES & RECOMMENDS  . . . . .       448C ANNO REYNOLDS   MARG
     I ALWAYS CONSIDERD TRUE ART & TRUE ARTISTS TO BE             452B ANNO REYNOLDS   MARG
          PARTICULARLY
     THIS IS ADMIRABLY SAID WHY DOES HE NOT ALWAYS ALLOW AS MUCH   454D ANNO REYNOLDS   MARG
     BUT GENIUS (IS ALWAYS ABOVE THE AGE)  . . . . . . .          461A ANNO REYNOLDS  * MARG
     WHY DOES HE NOT ALWAYS ALLOW THIS  . . . . . . . .           461D ANNO REYNOLDS   MARG
     FINE & JUST NOTIONS WHY DOES HE NOT ALWAYS ALLOW AS MUCH      462C ANNO REYNOLDS   MARG
     APPEARS TO ME TO GIVE ALWAYS THE CHARACTERS OF VULGAR         464B ANNO REYNOLDS   MARG
          STUPIDITY
     THAT THE WORST PAINTERS ALWAYS CHOSE THE GRANDEST SUBJECTS    465C ANNO REYNOLDS   MARG
     THE GREAT STYLE IS ALWAYS NOVEL OR NEW IN ALL ITS            468A ANNO REYNOLDS   MARG
          OPERATIONS
     I ALWAYS THOUGHT THAT THE HUMAN MIND WAS THE MOST PROLIFIC    471A ANNO REYNOLDS   MARG
     INSPIRATION & VISION WAS THEN & NOW IS & I HOPE WILL ALWAYS   477A ANNO REYNOLDS   MARG
     BAD PICTURES ARE ALWAYS SR JOSHUA'S FRIENDS  . . . . .        478C ANNO REYNOLDS   MARG
     SHADE IS ALWAYS COLD &  . . . . . . . . . . . .             478D ANNO REYNOLDS   MARG
     THE MEMORY IS A STATE ALWAYS & THE REASON IS A STATE    .     522 MILTON 32         34
     FOR GOD HIMSELF ENTERS DEATH'S DOOR ALWAYS WITH THOSE THAT    522 MILTON 32         40
          ENTER
     TO CAST OFF THE IDIOT QUESTIONER WHO IS ALWAYS QUESTIONING    533 MILTON 41         12
     WHAT IS MOST GRAND IS ALWAYS MOST MINUTE   . . . . . .        547 PRETTY EPIGR/N     2
     AND WHEN THEY ARE DRUNK THEY ALWAYS PANT BEST  . . . .        549 ALL PICTURES/N *   4
     I ALWAYS TAKE MY JUDGMENT FROM A FOOL  . . . . . . .          549 CROMEK SPEAK/N     1
     BECAUSE [ I KNOW HE ALWAYS JUDGES] HIS JUDGMENT IS SO VERY    549 CROMEK SPEAK/N     2
          COOL
     WHEN YOU LOOK AT A PICTURE YOU ALWAYS CAN SEE  . . . . .      550 WHEN LOOK AT/N     1
     I ALWAYS THOUGHT THAT JESUS CHRIST WAS A SNUBBY   . . . .    555C ALWAYS THOT/N   PROSE
     AND IT IS ALWAYS WRONG IN TITIAN AND CORREGGIO   . . . .     564A DESC CAT       PROSE
     THAT UNAFFECTED SIMPLICITY WHEN IN HIGH RANK ALWAYS          568A DESC CAT 3     PROSE
          DISPLAYS
     ARE NO TRIFLES THEY ARE ALWAYS THOUGH UTTERED WITH AUDACITY   569D DESC CAT 3     PROSE
     ALWAYS SUBSTANTIALLY AND WEIGHTILY EXPRESSIVE OF  . . . .     569D DESC CAT 3     PROSE
     THE PARDONER THE AGE'S KNAVE WHO ALWAYS COMMANDS   . . .     570A DESC CAT 3     PROSE
     AS I WISH MEN OF LAW WOULD ALWAYS RIDE WITH THEM   . . .     570C DESC CAT 3     PROSE
     THERE ARE ALWAYS THESE TWO CLASSES OF LEARNED SAGES   . .    572C DESC CAT 3     PROSE
     LET THE PHILOSOPHER ALWAYS BE THE SERVANT AND   . . . .     572C DESC CAT 3     PROSE
     WHO HAVE ALWAYS RECOGNIZED HIM AND PATRONIZED HIM   . .      573A DESC CAT 3     PROSE
     BUT THE PAINTER'S THOUGHTS BEING ALWAYS UPON GOLD    . .     575B DESC CAT 3     PROSE
     SO AS IT ALWAYS HAPPENS AND NOT IN THAT DULL WAY THAT SOME    578D DESC CAT 5     PROSE
     WAS IMPOSSIBLE IF WE DID NOT SEE IT ALWAYS BEFORE OUR EYES    578D DESC CAT 5     PROSE
     THE DISPOSITION OF FORMS ALWAYS DIRECTS COLOURING    . .     580D DESC CAT 5     PROSE
     THOSE WHO KEEP MANUFACTORIES OF ART ALWAYS CHARGE   . . .    583B DESC CAT 9     PROSE
     ARE ALWAYS THE SUBTERFUGE OF THE BLOCKHEAD  . . . . . .      591C PUB ADDRESS/N   PROSE
     THEY ARE ALWAYS PAID FOR WHAT THEY PUT IN UPON THESE   .     592C PUB ADDRESS/N   PROSE
     YOUR ENEMY HE ALWAYS BEGINS WITH BEING YOUR FRIEND   . .     592C PUB ADDRESS/N   PROSE
     WONDER WHICH ALWAYS INTREATS HIM TO LEAVE MORTAL THINGS      611A V LAST JUDG/N   PROSE
     THERE WILL ALWAYS BE AS MANY HYPOCRITES BORN AS HONEST MEN    616A V LAST JUDG/N   PROSE
     & THEY WILL ALWAYS HAVE SUPERIOR POWER IN MORTAL THINGS      616A V LAST JUDG/N   PROSE
     THEY ARE NOT ALWAYS PRYING AFTER GOOD & EVIL IN ONE ANOTHER   616D V LAST JUDG/N   PROSE
     ALWAYS COMFORTING THE REMEMBRANCE THE FLOORS HUMILITY   .     632 JERUSALEM 12      36
     AND BUILDED BY THE DIVINE HAND THAT THE SINNER SHALL ALWAYS   657 JERUSALEM 31      31
          ESCAPE
     BUT THE POOR SPECTRES THAT THEY WORK FOR ALWAYS INCESSANTLY   691 JERUSALEM 59      38
     GIVE FORTH THY PITY & LOVE FEAR NOT LO I AM WITH              694 JERUSALEM 60      67
          THEE ALWAYS
     ONLY BELIEVE & TRUST IN ME LO I AM ALWAYS WITH THEE  . . .    696 JERUSALEM 62      29
     WHICH ALWAYS APPEAR TO THE IGNORANCE-LOVING HYPOCRITE AS     717C JERUSALEM 77    PROSE
          SINS
     SNEAKING SUBMISSION CAN ALWAYS LIVE  . . . . . . . .         752 EV GOSPEL(D)/N     34
     O THAT I WERE INSANE ALWAYS I WILL NEVER REST  . . . .      772C ANNO SPURZHEIM   MARG
     ALWAYS BEHOLD THE FACE OF THE ?HEAVENLY FATHER   . . . .    774A ANNO BERKELEY    MARG
     NATURAL OBJECTS ALWAYS DID & NOW DO WEAKEN DEADEN   . . .   783A ANNO WW POEMS    MARG
     & HER SICKNESS IS ALWAYS MY SORROW OF COURSE BUT WHAT YOU    811C LETTER 22       PROSE
     THIS HAS ALWAYS PURSUD ME  . . . . . . . . . .             812C LETTER 22       PROSE
```

83

		PAGE	TITLE	LINE

ALWAYS   (CONTINUED)
AND A DOUBLE VISION IS ALWAYS WITH ME . . . . 817 HAPPINESS/L   28
AND TWOFOLD ALWAYS MAY GOD US KEEP . . . . 818 HAPPINESS/L   87
ARE ALWAYS PERNICIOUS ESPECIALLY WHEN WE DOUBT OUR FRIENDS 822D LETTER 26   PROSE
AS YOU MY DEAR FRIEND HAVE ALWAYS LEFT ME . . . . 826A LETTER 27   PROSE
THE OFFENCE IS ALWAYS REPEATED THE LANDLORD OF THE INN & 827C LETTER 28   PROSE
ALWAYS BEEN FORWARD IN EXPRESSING THEIR KINDNESS FOR US 828A LETTER 28   PROSE
EXCEEDING JOY THAT IS ALWAYS POURED OUT ON MY SPIRIT . 830B LETTER 30   PROSE
MAY STILL BE REPLENISHD WITH THE SAME & BE AS YOU ALWAYS 830C LETTER 30   PROSE
    HAVE
& ALWAYS ANXIOUSLY REMEMBERD MISS POOLE . . . . . . 838C LETTER 37   PROSE
THE LAST TOUCHES WHICH ARE ALWAYS THE BEST I HAVE NOW I 840B LETTER 39   PROSE
    HOPE
ACROSS THE COUNTRY TO FELPHAM AS HE ALWAYS KEEPS A HORSE 843A LETTER 42   PROSE
TO SERVE THAT INTEREST AND OFTEN I THINK UNFAIRLY HE ALWAYS 846C LETTER 44   PROSE
YOU WILL I KNOW FEEL AS YOU ALWAYS DO ON SUCH OCCASIONS 861D LETTER 59   PROSE
HAMPSTEAD AIR AS IT ALWAYS DID SO I FEAR IT ALWAYS WILL DO 870D LETTER 72   PROSE
EVEN ISLINGTON & ALL PLACES NORTH OF LONDON ALWAYS LAID ME 871A LETTER 72   PROSE
AMAIN
FOR ENITHARMON SHRIEKD AMAIN CRYING O MY SWEET WORLD . . 298 FOUR ZOAS 4   50
AND THE SEA POURED IN AMAIN UPON THE GIANTS OF ALBION . . 663 JERUSALEM 36   40
AMALEK
UPON THE HEIGHTS OF AMALEK TAKING REFUGE IN HIS ARMS . 348 FOUR ZOAS 8   270
COLD DARK OPAKE THE ASSEMBLY MET TWELVEFOLD IN AMALEK . 348 FOUR ZOAS 8   275
THE DAUGHTERS OF AMALEK CANAAN & MOAB BINDING ON 348 FOUR ZOAS 8   * 295
    THE [STEMS] STONES
OVER THEIR VICTIMS HEAR YE THE SONG OF THE FEMALES 348 FOUR ZOAS 8   297
    OF AMALEK
SUCH ARE THE SONGS OF TIRZAH SUCH THE LOVES OF AMALEK . 349 FOUR ZOAS 8   322
UPON THE HEIGHTS OF [ENTUTHON THAT] AMALEK TAKING REFUGE 382 FOUR ZOAS AD 6   3
    IN HIS ARMS
COLD DARK OPAKE THE ASSEMBLY MET TWELVE FOLD IN AMALEK . 382 FOUR ZOAS AD 6   8
OF EDOM & ARAM & MOAB & MIDIAN & AMALEK . . . . . . 498 MILTON 17   20
RINTRAH THOU WELL REMEMBEREST WHEN AMALEK & CANAAN . . 508 MILTON 24   14
MOAB & AMMON & AMALEK & CANAAN & EGYPT & ARAM . . . 623 JERUSALEM 14   14
FROM HIS VALLEYS EASTWARD FROM AMALEK CANAAN & MOAB . 654 JERUSALEM 29   31
OF ALBION'S DAUGHTERS IN PHILISTEA BY THE SIDE OF AMALEK 715 JERUSALEM 74   46
AND FLAMES OF DUSKY FIRE TO AMALEK CANAAN AND MOAB . . 723 JERUSALEM 80   50
DIVIDE THEM INTO THREE NAME THEM AMALEK CANAAN & MOAB . 725 JERUSALEM 82   24
CREATE JERUSALEM & BABYLON & EGYPT & MOAB & AMALEK . . 725 JERUSALEM 82   27
I WOO TO AMALEK TO PROTECT MY FUGITIVES AMALEK TREMBLES 727 JERUSALEM 83   16
GUIDES THEM THERE I BEHOLD MOAB & AMMON & AMALEK . . . 731 JERUSALEM 86   28
AMALEK EDOM EGYPT MOAB AMMON ASHUR PHILISTEA AROUND 740 JERUSALEM 92   23
    JERUSALEM
AMALEKITE
OF EMBLEMATIC TEXTURE WAS SOLD TO THE AMALEKITE . . 508 MILTON 24   19
THE AMALEKITE THE CANAANITE THE MOABITE THE EGYPTIAN . 634 JERUSALEM 13   58
THE CANAANITE THE AMALEKITE THE MOABITE THE EGYPTIAN . 673 JERUSALEM 43   66
ME FROM MY CRADLE THE AMALEKITE STOLE ME AWAY UPON HIS 695 JERUSALEM 61   41
    CAMELS
FROM BASHAN TO TYRE & FROM TROY TO GAZA OF THE AMALEKITE 698 JERUSALEM 63   43
TO THE PLACE OF THE AMALEKITE I AM DRUNK WITH UNSATIATED 707 JERUSALEM 68   62
    LOVE
AMALEKITES
THE BEAUTIFUL AMALEKITES BEHOLD THE FIRES OF YOUTH . . . 501 MILTON 19   37
AMALGAMATING
WHAT DO I SEE THE BRITON SAXON ROMAN NORMAN AMALGAMATING 739 JERUSALEM 92   1
AMASS
AFTER HAVING BEEN A FOOL A STUDENT IS TO AMASS A STOCK . 455B ANNO REYNOLDS   MARG
AMATEUR
ATTENTION OF THE AMATEUR IN A LARGE [WORK] STROKE ENGRAVING 587D CHAUCER/N   *PROSE
AMATEURS   SEE AIM AT YOURS
THE MODERN CHALCOGRAPHIC CONNOISSEURS & AMATEURS . . . 596C PUB ADDRESS/N   PROSE
I DEMAND THEREFORE OF THE AMATEURS OF ART . . . . . 600C PUB ADDRESS/N   PROSE
THE TASTE OF ENGLISH AMATEURS HAS BEEN TOO MUCH FORMED . 864C LETTER 61   PROSE
AMAZD
AMAZD SHE FINDS HERSELF UPON HER FEET . . . . 4 FAIR ELENOR/PS   10
AMAZD HIS HEAVENS IMMENSE CRACKS . . . . 234 URIZEN 23   16
AMAZD STARTED URIZEN WHEN . . . . 252 AHANIA 3   68
AMAZD STARTED URIZEN WHEN HE FOUND HIMSELF COMPASSD ROUND 321 FOUR ZOAS 7   36
AMAZD & IN FEAR . . . . 804 TO BUTTS/L   18
AMAZED
ASTONISHD AMAZED . . . . 804 TO BUTTS/L   20
AMAZEMENT
OR AMAZEMENT OR DEVOUT WONDER AND UNRESISTING AWE . . 580C DESC CAT 5   PROSE
WITH TREMBLING & AMAZEMENT . . . . 621A JERUSALEM 3   PROSE
AMAZING
IN THEIR AMAZING [FRUCTIFYING] HARD SUBDUED COURSE IN THE 287 FOUR ZOAS 2   * 286
    VAST DEEP
AMAZONIA
PERU PATAGONIA AMAZONIA BRAZIL THIRTY-TWO NATIONS . . . 712 JERUSALEM 72   42
AMBASSADOR
LET THE NATION'S AMBASSADOR COME AMONG NOBLES . . . . . 143 FRENCH REVOLTN   197
THRO THE RANKS SILENT WALKD THE AMBASSADOR . . . . . . 145 FRENCH REVOLTN   256
AMBASSADORS
SO SPOKE THE AMBASSADORS FROM BEULAH & WITH SOLEMN MOURNING 277 FOUR ZOAS 1   481
AMBER
THEN BOSOMD IN AN AMBER CLOUD AROUND . . . . 15 IMIT SPENSER/PS   42
AMBIGUOUS
AMBIGUOUS WORDS BLASPHEMOUS FILLD WITH ENVY FIRM RESOLVD 302 FOUR ZOAS 4   205
AMBITION
AMBITION COME TAKE THE HELM MY CHANDOS . . . . 27 EDW THIRD/PS 3   238

```
                                                      PAGE      TITLE          LINE
AMBITION    (CONTINUED)
    AMBITION IS THE GROWTH OF EVRY CLIME . . . . . . .     28 EDW THIRD/PS 4       2
    AMBITION . . . . . . . . . . . . . . . . . . . .      28 EDW THIRD/PS 4      10
    AMBITION IS THE DESIRE OR PASSION THAT ONE MAN  . .    28 EDW THIRD/PS 4      14
    YES I HAVE I HAVE A GREAT AMBITION TO KNOW EVERY THING SIR  28D EDW THIRD/PS 4   PROSE
    THEN SIR I SHOULD BE GLAD TO KNOW IF IT WAS NOT AMBITION   28D EDW THIRD/PS 4   PROSE
    YET I WILL TELL YOU THAT IT WAS AMBITION . . . . .   28D EDW THIRD/PS 4   PROSE
    THEN IF AMBITION IS A SIN WE ARE ALL GUILTY  . . . .  28D EDW THIRD/PS 4   PROSE
    WHOSE MINDS ARE PROMPTED BY THAT SAME AMBITION . . . 29A EDW THIRD/PS 4   PROSE
    FORTH CAME AMBITION CRAWLING LIKE A TOAD  . . . . .   41A THEN SHE BORE    PROSE
    O URIZEN MY ENEMY I WEEP FOR THY STERN AMBITION . . . 283 FOUR ZOAS 2      109
    O WHY DID FOUL AMBITION SIEZE THEE [ L] URIZEN PRINCE OF  301 FOUR ZOAS 4  * 141
        LIGHT
AMBITIOUS
    TH AMBITIOUS TENDRILS IN THE PATHS OF WISDOM . . . .  26 EDW THIRD/PS 3      213
    LOS WITH AMBITIOUS FURY THAT HIS RACE SHALL ALL DEVOUR . . 323 FOUR ZOAS 7     134
    CHRIST & HIS PROPHETS & APOSTLES WERE NOT AMBITIOUS MIRACLE 392A ANNO WATSON   MARG
        MONGERS
    THE AMBITIOUS SPIDER IN HIS SULLEN WEB THE LUCKY GOLDEN   513 MILTON 27        15
        SPINNER
AMBUSH
    AND WHERE STRENGTH FAILED BLACK THOUGHTS IN AMBUSH LAY . . 37D SAMSON/PS   PROSE
    WHERE A THOUSAND FIGHTING MEN IN AMBUSH LIE  . . . .  130 BOOK OF THEL 6     14
AMELIORATE
    STRINGED OR FLUTED TO AMELIORATE THE SORROWS OF SLAVERY   509 MILTON 24       61
    SHEWD HER THE FIBRES OF HER BELOVED TO AMELIORATE  . . .  726 JERUSALEM 82     61
AMEN
    THE UNIVERSAL MAN TO WHOM BE GLORY EVERMORE AMEN  . . .   264 FOUR ZOAS 1      11
    TO WHOM BE GLORY & POWER & DOMINION EVERMORE AMEN . . .   495 MILTON 14         3
    YET THE DIVINE VISION REMAINS EVERY-WHERE FOR-EVER AMEN   505 MILTON 22         2
    TO WHOM BE GLORY & DOMINION EVERMORE AMEN  . . . . .  519 MILTON 30       16
    THE ETERNAL WHO IS BLESSED FOR EVER & EVER AMEN . . . .   519 MILTON 30        31
    BUT THEIR FORMS ETERNAL EXIST FOR-EVER AMEN HALLEUJAH . . 522 MILTON 32     * 38
    TO PUT OFF SELF & ALL I HAVE EVER & EVER AMEN . . . .  530 MILTON 38        49
    OF LOS THAT EVER BURNETH WITH FIRE EVER & EVER AMEN . . . 530 MILTON 39       12
    . . . THE DELIVERANCE OF INDIVIDUALS EVERMORE AMEN  . .   648 JERUSALEM 25     13
    AMEN HUZZA SELAH . . . . . . . . . . . . . . . . .    649B JERUSALEM 27   PROSE
    STATES TO DELIVER INDIVIDUALS EVERMORE AMEN  . . . .  662 JERUSALEM 35     16
    STEPS BEYOND AND REDEEMS MAN IN THE BODY OF JESUS AMEN    664 JERUSALEM 36    55
    MAY BE DELIVERD TIME AFTER TIME EVERMORE AMEN  . . .  680 JERUSALEM 49     71
    WHICH IS UNCHANGEABLE FOR EVER & EVER AMEN SO BE IT  .    728 JERUSALEM 83    48
    & NOT CAESAR'S OR SATAN'S AMEN . . . . . . . . . .   788B ANNO THORNTON  * MARG
    FOR GOD IS ONLY AN ALLEGORY OF KINGS & NOTHING ELSE AMEN  789A ANNO THORNTON  MARG
    BLESSING AMEN GOD BLESS YOU ALL O PEOPLE OF SUSSEX  . .   835B LETTER 34     PROSE
AMENDS
    THAT FOR THEIR FRIENDSHIP I MAY MAKE AMENDS . . . . .  541 HOMERS HERO/N      4
AMERICA
    UPON THEIR MOUNTAINS IN THEIR VALLEYS SIGHS TOWARD AMERICA  189 V DAU ALBION 1 *  2
    FOR THE SOFT SOUL OF AMERICA OOTHOON WANDERD IN WOE . . . 189 V DAU ALBION 1   3
    AMERICA A PROPHECY . . . . . . . . . . . . . . . .   195C AMERICA         TITLE
    WASHINGTON SPOKE FRIENDS OF AMERICA LOOK OVER THE ATLANTIC  197 AMERICA 3       6
        SEA
    BROTHERS & SONS OF AMERICA TILL OUR FACES PALE AND YELLOW  197 AMERICA 4        9
    ALBION IS SICK AMERICA FAINTS ENRAGD THE ZENITH GREW  .   197 AMERICA 4        4
    AMERICA IS DARKNED AND MY PUNISHING DEMONS TERRIFIED  .   199 AMERICA 9      *  3
    ON THOSE VAST SHADY HILLS BETWEEN AMERICA & ALBION'S SHORE  200 AMERICA 10      5
    DOWN ON THE LAND OF AMERICA INDIGNANT THEY DESCENDED  . . 200 AMERICA 12       4
    BEFORE THE DEMON RED WHO BURNT TOWARDS AMERICA  . . . .   201 AMERICA 12       9
    FALLING UPON AMERICA AS A STORM TO CUT THEM OFF  . . .    201 AMERICA 14       5
    FURY RAGE MADNESS IN A WIND SWEPT THROUGH AMERICA  . . .  201 AMERICA 14      10
    THEN HAD AMERICA BEEN LOST OERWHELMD BY THE ATLANTIC  . . 202 AMERICA 14      17
    WASHINGTON SPOKE FRIENDS OF AMERICA LOOK OVER THE ATLANTIC  204 AMERICA CANC A   6
        SEA
    BROTHERS & SONS OF AMERICA TILL OUR FACES PALE AND YELLOW  204 AMERICA CANC A   9
    SUCH WAS THE HOLLOW VOICE THAT OER [THE RED DEMON] AMERICA  205 AMERICA CANC C  31
        LAMENTED
    AMERICA A PROPHECY IN ILLUMINATED PRINTING FOLIO     207D PRSPECTUS 1793 PROSE
        WITH...DESIGNS PRICE
    ALBION CLOSD THE WESTERN GATE & SHUT AMERICA OUT BY THE   294 FOUR ZOAS 3      105
        . . .
    TO TARTARY & HINDOSTAN & CHINA & TO GREAT AMERICA  . . .  495 MILTON 14        7
    TOWARDS AMERICA INDIA ROSE UP FROM HIS GOLDEN BED  . . .  519 MILTON 31       14
    OF DEATH ACROSS THE ATLANTIC TO AMERICA NORTH & SOUTH  .  525 MILTON 35       17
    COLUMBUS DISCOVERD AMERICA BUT AMERICUS VESPUTIUS FINISHD & 598C PUB ADDRESS/N *PROSE
    THEY SAW AMERICA CLOSD OUT BY THE OAKS OF THE WESTERN SHORE 672 JERUSALEM 43     6
    I SEE AMERICA CLOSD APART & JERUSALEM DRIVEN IN TERROR  . 673 JERUSALEM 43      69
    THE SECRET COVERTS OF ALBION & THE HIDDEN PLACES OF AMERICA 679 JERUSALEM 49     1
    AMERICA NORTH & SOUTH ARE HIS BATHS OF LIVING WATERS  . . 690 JERUSALEM 58     43
    IS SABRINA JOIND WITH MEHETABEL SHE SHINES WEST OVER  710 JERUSALEM 71      45
        AMERICA
    EUROPE & ASIA & AFRICA & AMERICA IN FURY FOURFOLD  . . .  712 JERUSALEM 72     31
    AND THOU AMERICA I ONCE BEHELD THEE BUT NOW BEHOLD NO MORE  721 JERUSALEM 79    53
    BUT HIDE AMERICA FOR A CURSE AN ALTAR OF VICTIMS & A HOLY   725 JERUSALEM 82    29
        PLACE
    TO CUT HER OFF FROM AMERICA TO CLOSE UP HER SECRET ARK  .  725 JERUSALEM 82     34
    PLACE THE TRIBES OF LLEWELLYN IN AMERICA FOR A HIDING PLACE  728 JERUSALEM 83   59
    AMERICA ENABLE HIM TO CIRCULATE PUBLICATIONS TO AN IMMENSE  841C LETTER 41   PROSE
    AMERICA EUROPE VISIONS &C THEL SONGS OF INNOCENCE  . .    867B LETTER 66    PROSE
    AMERICA EUROPE VISIONS &C THEL . . . . . . . . . .   878D LETTER 88     PROSE
AMERICAN
    THIS THE NORTH AMERICAN TRIBES PRACTISE . . . . . . .  154B MARRIAGE HH 12  PROSE
    ALBION'S COAST IS SICK SILENT THE AMERICAN MEADOWS FAINT  159A SONG LIBERTY   PROSE
```

AMERICAN   (CONTINUED)
        THY SOFT AMERICAN PLAINS ARE MINE AND MINE THY NORTH &   190 V DAU ALBION 1   20
            SOUTH
        ON MY AMERICAN PLAINS I FEEL THE STRUGGLING AFFLICTIONS   196 AMERICA PREL 2   10
        THE ACCOUNTS OF NORTH AMERICAN SAVAGES AS THEY ARE CALLD   389C ANNO WATSON   MARG
        THE AMERICAN WAR BEGAN ALL ITS DARK HORRORS PASSED BEFORE   799 TO FLAXMAN/L   9
            MY FACE
        LIFE OF WASHINGTON I SUPPOSE AN AMERICAN WOULD TELL ME .   845B LETTER 44   PROSE
AMERICANS
        APPEAR TO THE AMERICANS UPON THE CLOUDY NIGHT . . . .   197 AMERICA 4   1
        AND BY THE FIERCE AMERICANS RUSHING TOGETHER IN THE NIGHT   202 AMERICA 15   12
        WEEPING IN DISMAL HOWLINGS BEFORE THE STERN AMERICANS   .   203 AMERICA 16   12
        SO THE AMERICANS WILL CONSIDER WASHINGTON AS THEIR GOD .   845B LETTER 44   PROSE
AMERICA'S
        SULLEN FIRES ACROSS THE ATLANTIC GLOW TO AMERICA'S SHORE   197 AMERICA 3   2
        I SEE THEE IN THICK CLOUDS AND DARKNESS ON AMERICA'S SHORE 199 AMERICA 9   16
        SULLEN FIRES ACROSS THE ATLANTIC GLOW TO AMERICA'S SHORE   203 AMERICA CANC A   2
        GLOW ON AMERICA'S SHORE ALBION TURNS UPON HIS COUCH . .   506 MILTON 23   7
        BUILD & PREPARE A WALL & CURTAIN FOR AMERICA'S SHORE   .   680 JERUSALEM 49   49
AMERICUS
        COLUMBUS DISCOVERD AMERICA BUT AMERICUS VESPUTIUS FINISHD & 598C PUB ADDRESS/N *PROSE
AMETHYST
        THE EMERALD ONYX SAPPHIRE JASPER BERYL AMETHYST . . . . 343 FOUR ZOAS 8   74
AMIABLE
        [BECAUSE WE KNOW] AMIABLE STATE HE CANNOT FEEL AT ALL   .   549 CROMEK SPEAK/N   4
        IS ONE OF THE MOST AMIABLE FEATURES OF THE CHRISTIAN CHURCH 590B CHAUCER 2   PROSE
        & GIVE OUR LOVES TO MRS BUTTS & YOUR AMIABLE FAMILY . .   823C LETTER 26   PROSE
        THE YOUNG & VERY AMIABLE MRS ENOCH WHO GAVE MY WIFE . .   833D LETTER 33   PROSE
        WERE TRULY AMIABLE AND FEELING LIKE HIMSELF . . . . . 844A LETTER 43   PROSE
        IT IS THEREFORE DOUBLY INTERESTING MR WALKER IS TRULY AN   845D LETTER 44   PROSE
            AMIABLE
AMIDST
        AMIDST THE LUSTFUL FIRES HE WALKS HIS FEET BECOME LIKE   199 AMERICA 8   16
            BRASS
        THE IMMORTAL STOOD FROZEN AMIDST . . . .   257 BOOK OF LOS 4   11
        . . . [AROUND] AMIDST THEM [STOOD] BEAMD   . . . . . 348 FOUR ZOAS 8   277
        INCOMPREHENSIBLE PERVADING ALL AMIDST & ROUND ABOUT . .   364 FOUR ZOAS 9   282
        THUS SATAN RAGD AMIDST THE ASSEMBLY AND HIS BOSOM GREW .   490 MILTON 9   30
        OF UNCONQUERABLE FEAR AMIDST DELIGHTS OF REVENGE   702 JERUSALEM 66   39
            EARTH-SHAKING
        WHO STRETCHD ON ALBION'S ROCKS REPOSES AMIDST HIS   730 JERUSALEM 85   25
            TWENTY-EIGHT
        DO I SLEEP AMIDST DANGER TO FRIENDS O MY CITIES & COUNTIES 744 JERUSALEM 96   33
        AMIDST THEM IN HIS GLORY BEAMS . . . .   758 EV GOSPEL (2)   15
AMISS
        TO CURE WHATEVER IS AMISS   . . . . 56 HAIL MATRIM/IM   20
AMITY
        WE FORM THE MUNDANE EGG THAT SPECTRES COMING BY FURY OR   511 MILTON 25   42
            AMITY
AMMON
        IN AMMON MOLECH LOUD HIS FURNACES RAGE AMONG THE WHEELS   528 MILTON 37   21
        MOAB & AMMON & AMALEK & CANAAN & EGYPT & ARAM . . . .   623 JERUSALEM 5   14
        GUIDES THEM THERE I BEHOLD MOAB & AMMON & AMALEK . . .   731 JERUSALEM 86   28
        HIS BOSOM WIDE REFLECTS MOAB & AMMON ON THE RIVER . . . 735 JERUSALEM 89   24
        AMALEK EDOM EGYPT MOAB AMMON ASHUR PHILISTEA AROUND   740 JERUSALEM 92   23
            JERUSALEM
AMMONITE
        NAAMAH THE AMMONITE ZIBEAH THE PHILISTINE & MARY . . .   696 JERUSALEM 62   12
AMONG
        . . . DISPLAYD GREEN FIELDS AMONG . . . .   274 FOUR ZOAS 1   367
        THE BREATH OF HEAVEN DWELT AMONG HIS LEAVES . . . . .   5 FAIR ELENOR/PS   51
        AND THY LOVELY LEAVES AMONG . . - . . . .   7 LOVE HARMNY/PS   15
        AND DOTH AMONG OUR BRANCHES PLAY . . . .   7 LOVE HARMNY/PS   20
        OFT WHEN THE SUMMER SLEEPS AMONG THE TREES . . . . .   10 WHEN EARLY/PS   11
        THE BREATH OF NIGHT SLEPT AMONG THE LEAVES OF THE FOREST   36C COUCH DEATH/PS PROSE
        HE SEEMED A MOUNTAIN HIS BROW AMONG THE CLOUDS . . .   38C SAMSON/PS   PROSE
        THAT YOU WOULD THINK YOU WAS AMONG YOUR FRIENDS . . .   44A ISLAND MOON 1   PROSE
        TAKING EXTRACTS FROM HERVEY'S MEDITATIONS AMONG THE TOMBS   52A ISLAND MOON 8   PROSE
        AMONG THE VIOLETS THAT SMELL SO SWEET . . . . . .   55 MAY MORNING/IM   4
        AMONG THE VIOLETS THAT SMELL SO SWEET . . . . . .   55 MAY MORNING/IM   7
        [OR LIKE HARMONIOUS THUNDERINGS THE SEATS OF HEAVN AMONG]   59 HOLY THURS/IM   11
        OR LIKE HARMONIOUS THUNDERINGS THE SEATS OF HEAVN AMONG   59 HOLY THURS/IM   16
        LOOK AT MY EYES BLIND AS THE ORBLESS [XXX] SCULL AMONG   99 TIRIEL 1   * 28
            THE STONES
        LET SNAKES RISE FROM THY BEDDED LOCKS & LAUGH AMONG THY   108 TIRIEL 6   43
            CURLS
        AMONG SHADOWS DEEP . . . .   114 LIT GRL FND/SI   10
        AMONG TYGERS WILD . . . . 115 LIT GRL FND/SI   48
        AMONG THE OLD FOLK . . . .   116 ECCHOING GR/SI   14
        OR LIKE HARMONIOUS THUNDERINGS THE SEATS OF HEAVEN AMONG   122 HOLY THURS/SI * 10
        AND WENT TO MIND HER NUMEROUS CHARGE AMONG THE VERDANT   128 BOOK OF THEL 2   18
            GRASS
        . . . AMONG THICK SHADES OF DISCONTENT . . . . .   137 FRENCH REVOLTN   64
        . . . WE ARE NOT NUMBERED AMONG THE LIVING LET US HIDE . 137 FRENCH REVOLTN   76
        IN STONES AMONG ROOTS OF TREES THE PRISONERS HAVE BURST   137 FRENCH REVOLTN   77
            THEIR DENS
        OF THE RULER WITHER AMONG BONES OF DEATH . . . . .   140 FRENCH REVOLTN   145
        LET THE NATION'S AMBASSADOR COME AMONG NOBLES . . . .   143 FRENCH REVOLTN   197
        SO FAYETTE STOOD SILENT AMONG THE ASSEMBLY . . . . .   146 FRENCH REVOLTN   268
        AS I WAS WALKING AMONG THE FIRES OF HELL . . . . . . 150C MARRIAGE HH 6 PROSE
        FORTH WENT THE HAND OF JEALOUSY AMONG THE FLAMING HAIR .   159C SONG LIBERTY PROSE
        CURLD VETERANS AMONG HELMS AND SHIELDS AND CHARIOTS . .   159D SONG LIBERTY PROSE

AMONG   (CONTINUED)
I HEARD AMONG THE RUSHES DANK . . . .   162 LAID ME DOWN/N   3
AND LAID ME DOWN AMONG THE SWINE . . . .   163 I SAW CHAPEL/N   17
WHY DOST THOU NOT FLY AMONG THE CORN FIELDS . . . . .   168 O LAPWING/N   3
THE GREEN LEAVES AMONG . . . .   175 WILD FLOWERS/N   2
A LITTLE BLACK THING AMONG THE SNOW . . . .   180 CHIMNEY SWP/N   1
AND SMILD AMONG THE [WINTER WIND] WINTER'S SNOW . . .   180 CHIMNEY SWP/N   *   6
OF ANY AGE OR COUNTRY AMONG WHICH ARE TWO LARGE . . . . 207C PRSPECTUS 1793   PROSE
THAT WALKD AMONG THE ANCIENT TREES . . . .   210 INTRODUCTN/SE   5
A LITTLE BLACK THING AMONG THE SNOW . . . .   212 CHIMNEY SWP/SE   1
AND SMILD AMONG THE WINTER'S SNOW . . . .   212 CHIMNEY SWP/SE   6
. . . SHE SAT AMONG THE ROCKS   266 FOUR ZOAS 1   70
SINGING HER LAMENTATION THARMAS GROAND AMONG HIS CLOUDS   266 FOUR ZOAS 1   71
[SO SAYING] IN TORMENT HE SUNK DOWN & FLOWD AMONG HER FILMY 266 FOUR ZOAS 1   77
  WOOF
SHE COUNTED EVERY VEIN & LACTEAL THREADING THEM AMONG . . 266 FOUR ZOAS 1   80
[AMONG THE CLOUDS TO TREMBLE IN THE WIND IN SOLITUDE] . . 268 FOUR ZOAS 1   138
[THAT WEPT AMONG THE CLOUDS & WHERE THE VOICE THAT SHALL   268 FOUR ZOAS 1   140
  REPLY]
. . . SITTING AMONG THE ROCKS] . . . .   268 FOUR ZOAS 1   143
[WHILE THE BRIGHT SPECTRE HID HIMSELF AMONG THE TRAILING   268 FOUR ZOAS 1   * 144
  CLOUDS]
[AMONG WILD BEASTS TO ROAM] . . . .   268 FOUR ZOAS 1   168
[THUS THEY CONTENDED ALL THE DAY AMONG THE CAVES   269 FOUR ZOAS 1   179
  OF THARMAS]
NINE TIMES THEY LIVD AMONG THE FORESTS FEEDING ON SWEET   270 FOUR ZOAS 1   233
  FRUITS
I HEARD HIS VOICE AMONG THE BRANCHES & AMONG SWEET FLOWERS 271 FOUR ZOAS 1   267
THRO THE CLEAR CHANGING ATMOSPHERE DISPLAYD GREEN FIELDS   274 FOUR ZOAS 1   367
  AMONG
AMONG THE DRUID TEMPLES ALBION GROAND ON TYBURN'S BROOK   281 FOUR ZOAS 2   40
WHILE THE PRINCE OF LIGHT ON SALISBURY PLAIN AMONG THE   281 FOUR ZOAS 2   65
  DRUID STONES
THE KING OF LIGHT BEHELD HER MOURNING AMONG THE BRICK KILNS 285 FOUR ZOAS 2   215
  COMPELLD
TO LABOUR NIGHT & DAY AMONG THE FIRES HER LAMENTING VOICE 285 FOUR ZOAS 2   216
AMONG THESE FLAMES INCESSANT LABOURING OUR HARD MASTERS   285 FOUR ZOAS 2   219
  LAUGH
DESCENDING SWEET UPON THE WIND AMONG SOFT HARPS & VOICES   287 FOUR ZOAS 2   288
WANDER AMONG THE VIRGINS OF THE SUMMER LOOK THEY CRY . . 288 FOUR ZOAS 2   306
HOWL THOU OVER THE BODY OF DEATH TIS THINE BUT IF AMONG   288 FOUR ZOAS 2   312
  THE VIRGINS
AMONG THE BEAUTIES OF THE WORLD COLD & REPINING LOS . . . 288 FOUR ZOAS 2   321
WHERE MEMORY WISHES TO REPOSE AMONG THE FLOCKS OF THARMAS 288 FOUR ZOAS 2   326
WHEN THE SHATTERD BONE HATH LAID HIM GROANING AMONG THE   291 FOUR ZOAS 2   416
  HAPPIER DEAD
AMONG THE FROZEN ARROWS THEY WILL TEAR THY TENDER FLESH   296 FOUR ZOAS 3   172
AGAINST THE MONSTROUS FORMS THAT BREED AMONG MY SILENT   301 FOUR ZOAS 4   145
  WAVES
PRINCE OF LIGHT BOUND IN CHAINS OF INTELLECT AMONG THE   305 FOUR ZOAS 5   16
  FURNACES
AND WALKED IN THE SILENT NIGHT AMONG SWEET SMELLING FLOWERS 310 FOUR ZOAS 5   203
FOR URIZEN BEHELD THE TERRORS OF THE ABYSS WANDRING AMONG 314 FOUR ZOAS 6   *   87
[NOT SO CLOSD UP THE PRINCE OF LIGHT NOW DARKEND WANDRING 314 FOUR ZOAS 6   *   100
  AMONG]
[FOR URIZEN BEHELD THE TERRORS OF THE ABYSS WANDRING AMONG] 314 FOUR ZOAS 6   *   102
THEN CAME HE AMONG FIERY CITIES & CASTLES BUILT OF BURNING 314 FOUR ZOAS 6   115
  STEEL
DESART AMONG THE STARS THEM WITHERING WITH ITS RIDGES COLD 319 FOUR ZOAS 6   306
FALLING WITH WHEEL IMPETUOUS DOWN AMONG URTHONA'S VALES   320 FOUR ZOAS 6   321
BENEATH THE TREE OF MYSTERY AMONG THE LEAVES & FRUIT . .   325 FOUR ZOAS 7   218
AMONG THE FLOWERS OF BEULAH WALKD THE ETERNAL MAN & SAW   326 FOUR ZOAS 7   239
ROUND BEULAH THERE HE REVELD IN DELIGHT AMONG THE FLOWERS 326 FOUR ZOAS 7   243
AMONG HIS FAMILY HIS FLOCKS & HERDS & TENTS & PASTURES . . 326 FOUR ZOAS 7   254
CONFERRING TIMES ON TIMES AMONG THE BRANCHES OF THAT TREE 327 FOUR ZOAS 7   314
THUS THEY CONFERRD AMONG THE INTOXICATING FUMES OF MYSTERY 328 FOUR ZOAS 7   315
ALL NIGHT AMONG THE SLAIN & MOCK THE WOUNDED THAT GROAN   334 FOUR ZOAS 7B   48
  IN THE FIELD
THARMAS LAUGHD FURIOUS AMONG THE BANNERS CLOTHD IN BLOOD   334 FOUR ZOAS 7B   49
AND WHAT I LOVED BEST WAS DIVIDED AMONG MY ENEMIES . . . 334 FOUR ZOAS 7B   59
I MUST HAVE DIED IN THE DARK DESART AMONG NOXIOUS WORMS   335 FOUR ZOAS 7B   86
NOW SMILE AMONG THY BITTER TEARS NOW PUT ON ALL THY BEAUTY 337 FOUR ZOAS 7B   188
WILT THOU NOW SMILE AMONG THE SLAIN . . . .   337 FOUR ZOAS 7B   190
THE FORM OF ORC WAS GONE HE REARD HIS SERPENT BULK AMONG   338 FOUR ZOAS 7B   215
WADING THRO FENS AMONG THE SLIMY WEEDS MAKING LAMENTATIONS 338 FOUR ZOAS 7B   225
AMONG THE APPLE TREES & ALL THE GARDENS OF DELIGHT . . . 339 FOUR ZOAS 7B   *   234
IN FURY A SERPENT WONDROUS AMONG THE CONSTELLATIONS OF   342 FOUR ZOAS 8   68
  URIZEN
. . . SUDDEN WAVD [HIS HURTLING HAND] AMONG THE STARS . . 343 FOUR ZOAS 8   87
[AMONG THE STARS] HIS HURTLING HAND GAVE THE DIRE SIGNAL   343 FOUR ZOAS 8   88
  . . .
THEY SEEM TO ONE ANOTHER LAUGHING TERRIBLE AMONG   344 FOUR ZOAS 8   122
  THE BANNERS
IN GOLGONOOZA'S FURNACES AMONG THE ANVILS OF TIME AND SPACE 345 FOUR ZOAS 8   186
AS IT IS WRITTEN HE WAS NUMBERD AMONG THE TRANSGRESSORS   348 FOUR ZOAS 8   274
SHE STOOD BEFORE LOS IN HER PRIDE [ABOVE] AMONG THE   350 FOUR ZOAS 8   *   345
  FURNACES
TO THE DELUSIVE FEMALE FORMS SHINING AMONG HIS FURNACES   350 FOUR ZOAS 8   350
AMONG THE STARS THE EARTH & ALL THE ABYSSES FEEL ?HIS FURY 352 FOUR ZOAS 8   *   448
SHE RISES AMONG FLOWERS & LOOKS TOWARD THE EASTERN   367 FOUR ZOAS 9   390
  CLEARNESS
I WALK AMONG HIS FLOCKS & HEAR THE BLEATING OF HIS LAMBS   368 FOUR ZOAS 9   425

	PAGE	TITLE	LINE
AMONG (CONTINUED)			
RUNNING AMONG MY GREEN PASTURES DELIGHTING AMONG MY TREES	368	FOUR ZOAS 9	442
HOW CLEAR THE SPRING OF THE ROCK RUNNING AMONG THE GOLDEN SAND	369	FOUR ZOAS 9	448
AMONG HER FLOCKS & SHE TURND HER EYES TOWARD HER PLEASANT HOUSE	370	FOUR ZOAS 9	506
SO SAYING THEY WENT DOWN INTO THE GARDEN AMONG THE FRUITS	371	FOUR ZOAS 9	535
AND ENION SANG AMONG THE FLOWERS THAT GREW AMONG THE TREES	371	FOUR ZOAS 9	536
THUS IN ETERNAL CHILDHOOD STRAYING AMONG VALA'S FLOCKS	371	FOUR ZOAS 9	553
AMONG THE FLOWERS OF BEULAH IN HIS SELFISH COLD REPOSE	374	FOUR ZOAS 9	628
AMONG THE WOOLY FLOCKS THE HAMMER OF URTHONA SOUNDS	379	FOUR ZOAS 9	840
AS IT IS WRITTEN HE WAS NUMBERD AMONG THE TRANSGRESSORS	382	FOUR ZOAS AD 6	7
TRAVELLER REPOSE & DREAM AMONG MY LEAVES WILL BLAKE	414	ILLUS GRAY	2
AMONG GREEN LEAVES & BLOSSOMS SWEET	423	THE BIRDS/N	20
AMONG THE LILLIES BY WATERS FAIR	427	LAND OF DREAMS	8
AMONG THE LAMBS CLOTHED IN WHITE	427	LAND OF DREAMS	9
CAME INTO THE BALL ROOM AMONG THE FAIR	428	MARY	2
AND MARY AROSE AMONG FRIENDS TO BE FREE	428	MARY	15
AMONG THEM IS A FIGURE CROWND WITH STARS	443D	LAST JUDGMNT/L	*PROSE
AMONG THESE DARK SATANIC MILLS	481	AND DID FEET/M	8
TERRIFIC AMONG THE SONS OF ALBION IN CHORUS SOLEMN & LOUD	482	MILTON 2	23
AMONG INDEFINITE DRUID ROCKS & SNOWS OF DOUBT & REASONING	482	MILTON 3	8
THUS THEY SING CREATING THE THREE CLASSES AMONG DRUID ROCKS	485	MILTON 5	38
AMONG THE DAUGHTERS OF ALBION AMONG THE ROCKS OF THE DRUIDS	485	MILTON 5	42
UPON THE MOUNTAINS OF ALBION AMONG THE CLIFFS OF THE DEAD	488	MILTON 8	26
AMONG ALBION'S DRUIDS & BARDS IN THE CAVES BENEATH ALBION'S	489	MILTON 9	2
TILL IT BECAME A PROVERB IN EDEN SATAN IS AMONG THE REPROBATE	489	MILTON 9	12
STANDING ON ALBION'S ROCKS AMONG HIGH-REARD DRUID TEMPLES	489	MILTON 9	14
AMONG THE ROCKS OF ALBION'S TEMPLES AND SATAN'S DRUID SONS	491	MILTON 11	7
DROVE THE FIERCE HARROW AMONG THE CONSTELLATIONS OF JEHOVAH	493	MILTON 12	25
FOR HE TOOK THE OUTSIDE COURSE AMONG THE GRAVES OF THE DEAD	496	MILTON 14	34
ONWARDS HIS SHADOW KEPT ITS COURSE AMONG THE SPECTRES CALLD	496	MILTON 15	17
IN THAT REGION CALLD MIDIAN AMONG THE ROCKS OF HOREB	498	MILTON 17	28
SILENT THEY MET AND SILENT STROVE AMONG THE STREAMS OF ARNON	500	MILTON 19	6
AND VALA LABOURS FOR HER BREAD & WATER AMONG THE FURNACES	501	MILTON 19	43
AND ALL PERFECTION IN HER CRUEL SPORTS AMONG THE VICTIMS	501	MILTON 19	45
OURSELVES TO DEATH IN ULRO AMONG THE TRANSGRESSORS	504	MILTON 21	46
GROANING WITH PITY HE AMONG THE WAILING SOULS LAMENTS	512	MILTON 26	22
WALKS AMONG ALL HIS AWFUL FAMILY SEEN IN EVERY FACE	519	MILTON 30	17
AND MEADOW-SWEET DOWNY & SOFT WAVING AMONG THE REEDS	520	MILTON 31	52
JERUSALEM'S CHILDREN CONSUME IN FLAMES AMONG THE STARS	527	MILTON 37	12
IN AMMON MOLECH LOUD HIS FURNACES RAGE AMONG THE WHEELS	528	MILTON 37	21
LABOUR WITH BLACKEND VISAGES AMONG ITS STUPENDOUS RUINS	529	MILTON 38	21
URIZEN FAINTS IN TERROR STRIVING AMONG THE BROOKS OF ARNON	531	MILTON 39	53
AMONG THE RIVERS OF PARADISE BEING ORIGINALS FROM WHICH	565C	DESC CAT 2	PROSE
CONVINCING PROOF AMONG MANY OTHERS THAT THESE ASSERTIONS	566C	DESC CAT 2	PROSE
PROPAGATED AMONG THE PUBLIC BY IGNORANT HIRELINGS	572C	DESC CAT 3	PROSE
HE HAS PUT AMONG HIS RABBLE AND INDEED HIS PROSPECTUS	573C	DESC CAT 3	PROSE
AMONG HONEST PEOPLE TO MAKE GAME OF AND LAUGH AT THEM	574D	DESC CAT 3	PROSE
ARMIES OF EDWARD ARE SEEN WINDING AMONG THE MOUNTAINS	577A	DESC CAT 4	PROSE
ARMED ROMANS STREW THE FIELD BENEATH AMONG THESE THE LAST OF	580C	DESC CAT 5	PROSE
IS SEEN FALLING OUTSTRETCHED AMONG THE DEAD AND THE DYING	580C	DESC CAT 5	PROSE
DISTANT AMONG THE MOUNTAINS ARE DRUID TEMPLES	580D	DESC CAT 5	PROSE
UNWORTHY MEN WHO GAIN FAME AMONG MEN	581D	DESC CAT 8	PROSE
THESE PICTURES AMONG NUMEROUS OTHERS PAINTED FOR	582B	DESC CAT 9	PROSE
AMONG OTHER WORKS BY THE SAME ARTIST	587B	CHAUCER 1	PROSE
[AMONG THE ANCIENTS IS EVIDENT FROM THE WORDS OF THE]	601A	PUB ADDRESS/N	*PROSE
PAINTING THE PRINCIPAL ART HAS NO PLACE [IN OUR] AMONG	601A	PUB ADDRESS/N	PROSE
JOSEPH OF ARIMATHEA AMONG THE ROCKS OF ALBION	604A	INSC ARIMATHEA	TITLE
COMING TO JUDGMENT AMONG HIS SAINTS & THROWING OFF	606A	V LAST JUDG/N	PROSE
INTO THE AIR AMONG THESE ARE THREE FEMALES	610A	V LAST JUDG/N	PROSE
NOT BEING AMONG THE CONDEMND	610B	V LAST JUDG/N	PROSE
AMONG THE WICKED WITH SCOURGES OF FIRE	611A	V LAST JUDG/N	PROSE
& YET WERE SAVED FROM AMONG THE ANTEDILUVIANS WHO PERISHED	611D	V LAST JUDG/N	PROSE
AMONG WHOSE BRANCHES TEMPLES & PINNACLES TENTS & PAVILIONS	613B	V LAST JUDG/N	PROSE
AMONG OTHER SPIRITS OF THE JUST MADE PERFECT [JUST]	614A	V LAST JUDG/N	PROSE
FOR THIS REASON AMONG MANY OTHERS THAT I HAVE PUT THE	614A	V LAST JUDG/N	PROSE
ARE DRIVEN AMONG THE STARRY WHEELS RENT AWAY AND DISSIPATED	623	JERUSALEM 5	4
TILL THE CLOUD REACHES AFAR OUTSTRETCHD AMONG THE STARRY WHEELS	624	JERUSALEM 5	52
AMONG THE DAUGHTERS OF ALBION AMONG THE STARRY WHEELS	624	JERUSALEM 5	64
A HORRIBLE SHADOW OF DEATH AMONG THE FURNACES BENEATH	625	JERUSALEM 7	4
IS HOWLING IN THE FURNACES IN FLAMES AMONG ALBION'S SPECTRES	626	JERUSALEM 7	39
THUS THEY CONTENDED AMONG THE FURNACES WITH GROANS & TEARS	628	JERUSALEM 9	32
SAKE WALKING UP AND DOWN AMONG THE SPACES OF ERIN	630	JERUSALEM 11	10
VALA IS BUT THY SHADOW O THOU LOVELIEST AMONG WOMEN	631	JERUSALEM 11	24
WITHOUT THE GATE OF LOS AMONG THE DARK SATANIC WHEELS	632	JERUSALEM 12	44
AMONG THE FURNACES OF LOS IN THE VALLEY OF THE SON OF HINNOM	636	JERUSALEM 15	34
AMONG THE SPIRITUAL FIRES LOUD THE CORN FIELDS THUNDER ALONG	636	JERUSALEM 16	5
LABOUR WITHIN THE FURNACES WALKING AMONG THE FIRES	637	JERUSALEM 16	20
TO MURDER THEIR OWN SOULS TO BUILD A KINGDOM AMONG THE DEAD	640	JERUSALEM 18	10
AND ALBION FLED INWARD AMONG THE CURRENTS OF HIS RIVERS	642	JERUSALEM 19	39
AMONG MY LAMBS & BROOKS OF WATER AMONG MY WARBLING BIRDS	642	JERUSALEM 20	8
AMONG THE SONS OF ALBION	649	SUCH VISIONS/J	4
THE LAMB OF GOD AMONG THEM SEEN	649	FIELDS FROM/J	6

```
                                                    PAGE    TITLE      LINE
AMONG    (CONTINUED)
     AMONG THE LITTLE MEADOWS GREEN  . . . . . . . . . .    649 FIELDS FROM/J    8
     AMONG HER GOLDEN PILLARS HIGH   . . . . . . . . . .    650 FIELDS FROM/J   10
     AMONG HER GOLDEN ARCHES WHICH   . . . . . . . . . .    650 FIELDS FROM/J   11
     FOLLOWING ALBION INTO HIS CENTRAL VOID AMONG HIS OAKS  .   656 JERUSALEM 30   20
     OF DESPAIR & DEATH TO SEARCH THE TEMPTERS OUT WALKING AMONG  656 JERUSALEM 31    5
     AMONG THE WINDING PLACES OF DEEP CONTEMPLATION INTRICATE     657 JERUSALEM 31   22
     AMONG THE RUINS OF THE TEMPLE AND VALA WHO IS HER SHADOW     657 JERUSALEM 31   41
     STOPS IT IN MIDST OF ITS PRIDE AMONG ITS HILLS & RIVERS     659 JERUSALEM 33   11
     THE RIVER OF LIFE TO FLOW AGAINST MY WALLS & AMONG MY TREES  660 JERUSALEM 33   38
     AND IN HER COURTS AMONG HER LITTLE CHILDREN OFFERING UP      660 JERUSALEM 33   42
     HIDDEN AMONG THE DEAD & MURED UP FROM THE PATHS OF LIFE      661 JERUSALEM 34   35
     UNKNOWN AMONG THE DEAD WHERE NEVER BEFORE EXISTENCE CAME     661 JERUSALEM 34   38
     HAVE YOU KNOWN THE JUDGMENT THAT IS ARISEN AMONG THE    .  . 663 JERUSALEM 36   44
     AMONG THE INFANT LOVES & AFFECTIONS AND THE DIVINE VISION    669 JERUSALEM 42    7
        WEPT
     THE CLOUDS OF EUROPE & ASIA AMONG THE SERPENT TEMPLES   . .  671 JERUSALEM 42   76
     THIS IS THE NET & VEIL OF VALA AMONG THE SOULS OF THE DEAD   671 JERUSALEM 42   81
     IN THE MIDST OF TEMPTATIONS & DESPAIR AMONG THE ROOTED OAKS  673 JERUSALEM 43   81
     AMONG REARED ROCKS OF ALBION'S SONS AT LENGTH THEY ROSE      673 JERUSALEM 43   82
     AMONG THE FURNACES OF LOS AMONG THE OAKS OF ALBION   . . .   674 JERUSALEM 44   37
     THE CAPTIVES REARD TO HEAVEN HOWL IN FLAMES AMONG THE STARS  677 JERUSALEM 47    8
     SHE SAT SHE WALKD AMONG THE ORNAMENTS SOLEMN MOURNING   . .  678 JERUSALEM 48   42
     JERUSALEM WEEPING OVER HER AMONG THE SPACES OF ERIN   . . .  678 JERUSALEM 48   51
     SHILOH THE MASCULINE EMANATION AMONG THE FLOWERS OF BEULAH   680 JERUSALEM 49   47
     THAT WALKS ABOUT AMONG THE STONES OF FIRE IN BLISS & WOE     680 JERUSALEM 49   73
     IN THE POTTER'S FURNACE AMONG THE FUNERAL URNS OF BEULAH     684 JERUSALEM 53   28
     AND JERUSALEM IS CALLED LIBERTY AMONG THE CHILDREN          684 JERUSALEM 54    5
        OF ALBION
     HE TOSSES LIKE A CLOUD OUTSTRETCHD AMONG JERUSALEM'S RUINS   685 JERUSALEM 54   13
     WHICH OVERSPREAD ALL THE EARTH HE GROANS AMONG HIS RUIND     685 JERUSALEM 54   14
        PORCHES
     AMONG THE FLOWERS OF BEULAH STILL RETAIN HIS AWFUL STRENGTH  686 JERUSALEM 55    2
     WALKETH AMONG US CALLING US HIS BROTHERS & HIS FRIENDS   . . 686 JERUSALEM 55  * 10
     WALKETH AMONG US GIVE DECISION BRING FORTH ALL YOUR FIRES    686 JERUSALEM 55   18
     AMONG THE FIRES OF THE DRUID & THE DEEP BLACK RETHUNDERING   689 JERUSALEM 57    3
        WATERS
     THE PLOW WENT OVER HIM & THE LIVING WAS PLOWED IN AMONG      689 JERUSALEM 57   14
        THE DEAD
     AMONG THE INHABITANTS OF ALBION THE PEOPLE FALL AROUND   . . 689 JERUSALEM 58    4
     ARE THE TEMPLES AMONG HIS PILLARS BRITAIN IS LOS'S FORGE     690 JERUSALEM 58   42
     REAR THEIR DARK ROCKS AMONG THE STARS OF GOD STUPENDOUS      690 JERUSALEM 58   49
     AROUND THE EARTH OF ALBION AMONG THE ROOTS OF HIS TREE   . . 691 JERUSALEM 59    4
     AND FLAMES AMONG THE DRUID TEMPLES & THE STARRY WHEELS   . . 692 JERUSALEM 60    7
     AMONG THE GODS OF ASIA AMONG THE FOUNTAINS OF PITCH &        693 JERUSALEM 60   24
        NITRE
     THAT HE HIMSELF MAY DWELL AMONG YOU FEAR NOT THEN TO TAKE    695 JERUSALEM 61   26
     UPON PISON & ARNON & JORDAN AND I HEARD THE VOICE AMONG      695 JERUSALEM 61   33
     BUT LOS BEHELD THE DIVINE VISION AMONG THE FLAMES OF THE     696 JERUSALEM 62   35
        FURNACES
     JEHOVAH STOOD AMONG THE DRUIDS IN THE VALLEY OF ANNANDALE    696 JERUSALEM 63    1
     TOOK VENGEANCE TWELVE-FOLD AMONG THE CHAOTIC ROCKS OF THE    697 JERUSALEM 63    8
        DRUIDS
     DANCE THE DANCE OF DEATH CONTENDING WITH JEHOVAH AMONG       697 JERUSALEM 63   10
        THE CHERUBIM
     IN VISIONS OF THE DREAMS OF BEULAH AMONG THE DAUGHTERS       698 JERUSALEM 63   37
        OF ALBION
     AND REUBEN FLED WITH HIS HEAD DOWNWARDS AMONG THE CAVERNS    698 JERUSALEM 63   44
     NOW SMILE AMONG THY BITTER TEARS NOW PUT ON ALL THY BEAUTY   700 JERUSALEM 65   30
     WILT THOU NOW SMILE AMONG THE SCYTHES . . . .  . . . . .     700 JERUSALEM 65   32
     YORK & LINCOLN HIDE AMONG THE FLOCKS BECAUSE OF THE GRIDING  703 JERUSALEM 66   65
        KNIFE
     IN THE HANDS OF ALBION'S DAUGHTERS AMONG THE DRUID TEMPLES   703 JERUSALEM 66   84
     WITH THE IRON SHUTTLE OF WAR AMONG THE ROOTED OAKS           711 JERUSALEM 71   61
        OF ALBION
     FOR ALBION IN ETERNITY HAS SIXTEEN GATES AMONG HIS PILLARS   711 JERUSALEM 72    5
     & IS PLANTED LIKE THE SEED OF A WILD FLOWER AMONG OUR WHEAT 716D JERUSALEM 77 PROSE
     O YE RELIGIOUS DISCOUNTENANCE EVERY ONE AMONG YOU   . . .  717B JERUSALEM 77 PROSE
     ANSWER THIS TO YOURSELVES & EXPEL FROM AMONG YOU . . . .   717B JERUSALEM 77 PROSE
     I STOOD AMONG MY VALLEYS OF THE SOUTH  . . . . . . . .       717 STOOD AMONG/J  1
     DISORGANIZD AN EVANESCENT SHADE SCARCE SEEN OR HEARD AMONG   719 JERUSALEM 78   28
     I MELT MY SOUL IN REASONINGS AMONG THE TOWERS OF HESHBON     719 JERUSALEM 79    3
     AMONG PRECIPICES OF DESPAIR IN GOSHEN I SEEK FOR LIGHT   . . 720 JERUSALEM 79   11
     THEY WATCH THEM IN THE NIGHT AND THE LAMB OF GOD APPEARS     720 JERUSALEM 79   32
        AMONG US
     THERE WE WALKED AS IN OUR SECRET CHAMBER AMONG OUR LITTLE    720 JERUSALEM 79   42
        ONES
     TOGETHER AMONG MY LITTLE-ONES BUT NOW MY ALTARS RUN WITH     721 JERUSALEM 79   55
        BLOOD
     FROM ALL MY MYRIADS ONCE THE FOUR-FOLD WORLD REJOICD AMONG   721 JERUSALEM 79   58
     ALONG THE VALLEY OF DESTRUCTION AMONG THESE DRUID TEMPLES    721 JERUSALEM 79   66
     TO DEVOUR THE HUMAN WHY DOST THOU WEEP UPON THE WIND AMONG   721 JERUSALEM 79   72
     WHERE SEXES WANDER IN DREAMS OF BLISS AMONG THE EMANATIONS   721 JERUSALEM 79   75
     LAMENTING AMONG THE TIMBRELS OF THE WARRIORS AMONG THE       721 JERUSALEM 80    7
        CAPTIVES
     AMONG THE FOUR FORESTS OF ALBION WHICH OVERSPREAD ALL THE    722 JERUSALEM 80   43
        EARTH
     AMONG THE TRIBES OF WARRIORS AMONG THE STONES OF POWER       722 JERUSALEM 80   45
     SHE HID THEM IN HIS LOINS RAVING HE RAN AMONG THE ROCKS      723 JERUSALEM 80   76
     ALONG THE ISLAND WHITE AMONG THE DRUID TEMPLES WHILE         725 JERUSALEM 82   15
        GWENDOLEN
     NAKED AMONG THE HUMAN CLUSTERS BRINGING WINE OF ANGUISH      726 JERUSALEM 82   65
```

```
                                                                  PAGE      TITLE        LINE
AMONG    (CONTINUED)
    O WHEN SHALL THE LAMB OF GOD DESCEND AMONG THE REPROBATE       727 JERUSALEM 83        15
    THEY LISTEN NOT TO MY CRY THEY (REJOICE) AMONG THEIR           727 JERUSALEM 83    *   18
       WARRIORS
    AMONG HIS FURNACES DIRECTING HIS LABORIOUS MYRIADS WATCHFUL    730 JERUSALEM 85        11
    AMONG THE GOLDEN LOOMS OF CATHEDRON SENDING FIBRES OF LOVE     731 JERUSALEM 86        40
    AMONG THE DARKNESS OF HIS FURNACES DIVIDING ASUNDER TILL       732 JERUSALEM 86        56
    CADENCES & PLAYING IN SWEET INTOXICATION AMONG THE             733 JERUSALEM 88        24
       GLISTENING
    MINUTE PARTICULARS IN SLAVERY I BEHOLD AMONG THE               735 JERUSALEM 89        17
       BRICK-KILNS
    WHERE HIDDEKEL PURSUES HIS COURSE AMONG THE ROCKS    . . .     735 JERUSALEM 89        35
    OF WARLIKE SONS AMONG THE SANDS OF MIDIAN & ARAM  .  .  .  .   735 JERUSALEM 89        57
    AND ON TYBURN'S BROOK AMONG THE HOWLING VICTIMS IN             737 JERUSALEM 90        48
       LOVELINESS
    FOR HIS WORDS ROLL IN THUNDERS & LIGHTNINGS AMONG              737 JERUSALEM 90        60
       THE TEMPLES
    BETWEEN THE STARS AMONG THE ARCHES OF ALBION'S TOMB SUBLIME    738 JERUSALEM 91        38
    MERLIN WAS LIKE THEE RINTRAH AMONG THE GIANTS OF ALBION        740 JERUSALEM 93        13
    OF HEAVEN FOURFOLD AMONG THE VISIONS OF GOD IN ETERNITY        744 JERUSALEM 96        43
    AWAKING IT TO LIFE AMONG THE FLOWERS OF BEULAH REJOICING       745 JERUSALEM 98        21
       IN UNITY
    . . . AMONG THE LIVING CREATURES   . . . . . . . .            746 JERUSALEM 98        56
    THAT HE HIMSELF MAY DWELL AMONG YOU   . . . . . . . .         757D EV GOSPEL         PROSE
    & HE CANNOT DWELL AMONG YOU [BY HIS]  . . . . . . . .         757D EV GOSPEL        *PROSE
    WHO WALKD AMONG THE STONES OF FIRE  . . . . . . . .           761 FOR SEXES/GP         4
    ABEL AMONG THE ELOHIM A HUMAN VICTIM I WANDER I AM THEIR       780 GHOST ABEL 1        10
       HOUSE
    WE HAVE ALL THINGS COMMON [ALL THINGS COMMON ] AMONG US        788B ANNO THORNTON  *  MARG
    UNFORTUNATELY OUR AUTHORS OF BOOKS ARE AMONG THIS CLASS HOW    795A LETTER 6         PROSE
    THAT SHE IS BUSIED AMONG MY FRIENDS WITH MINE & MY WIFE'S      796A LETTER 6         PROSE
    TO JOHN FLAXMAN I HAVE BEEN TOO LITTLE AMONG FRIENDS WHICH     798B LETTER 10        PROSE
       I
    THE ESTIMATION YOU ARE HELD IN AMONG ARTISTS & CONNOISSEURS    798B LETTER 10        PROSE
    TO PLEASE BECAUSE YOU AMONG ALL MEN HAVE ENABLED ME  .  .  .   815A LETTER 23        PROSE
    THE FURY OF MY COURSE AMONG THE STARS OF GOD  .  .  .  .  .    816A LETTER 23        PROSE
    HIS HYMN ON THE NATIVITY WHICH YOU WILL FIND AMONG HIS  .  .   823D LETTER 27        PROSE
    & MR PITT ARE BOTH AMONG THE SUBSCRIBERS WHICH ARE ALREADY     824D LETTER 27        PROSE
    AMONG THE OTHER NUMEROUS KINDNESSES I HAVE RECIEVD FROM YOU    826C LETTER 28        PROSE
    A PRINCE AMONG PRINCES & EVEN ON EARTH BELOVED BY THE GOOD     830A LETTER 30        PROSE
    BUT I WAS A SLAVE BOUND IN A MILL AMONG BEASTS AND DEVILS      852A LETTER 50        PROSE
    TO WELCOME THY ARRIVAL AMONG COWPER'S GLORIFIED BAND   .  .    854C LETTER 53        PROSE
    AS THEY ARE THE MOST EMINENT AMONG ANIMALS VIZ THE LION        859B LETTER 56        PROSE
    BEEN ASSIDUOUSLY SOWN AND PLANTED AMONG THE ENGLISH PUBLIC     864A LETTER 61        PROSE
    ITS BUSINESS AMONG HIS FRIENDS  .  .  .  .  .  .  .  .  .  .   875A LETTER 80        PROSE
    THE SHADE OF HENRY THE SIXTH IS SEEN AMONG THE TREES    .     SUPP ILLUS GRAY       *TITLE
    GRIEF AMONG THE ROOTS OF TREES  .  .  .  .  .  .  .  .  .     SUPP ILLUS GRAY       *TITLE
    CONTEMPLATION AMONG TOMBS   .  .  .  .  .  .  .  .  .  .      SUPP ILLUS GRAY       *TITLE
AMONGST    SEE MONGST
    WILL SO RECIEVE THE DIVINE IMAGE THAT AMONGST THE REPROBATE    272 FOUR ZOAS 1        297
    [REJOICING XXX ?SO ?AMONGST]  .  .  .  .  .  .  .  .  .       SUPP FOUR ZOAS 1       *
AMOROUS
    IF AN AMOROUS DELAY   .  .  .  .  .  .  .  .  .  .  .  .        178 THE FAIRY/N         5
    THE LUSTFUL JOY SHALL FORGET TO GENERATE & CREATE             194 V DAU ALBION 7       6
       AN AMOROUS IMAGE
    . . . & THESE THE SWEET DELIGHTS OF AMOROUS PLAY              377 FOUR ZOAS 9        769
    . . . & THESE THE SWEET DELIGHTS OF AMOROUS PLAY   .  .  .     514 MILTON 27           39
    SPINNING IT FROM THEIR BOWELS WITH SONGS OF AMOROUS DELIGHT    524 MILTON 34           28
    ELOQUENT AMOROUS WITTY AND SATYRICAL YOUNG HANDSOME AND        568D DESC CAT 3       PROSE
       RICH
    GOVERNING ALL BY THE SWEET DELIGHTS OF SECRET AMOROUS          638 JERUSALEM 16        59
       GLANCES
    AND THENCE IN BEULAH THEY ARE STOLEN BY SECRET AMOROUS         707 JERUSALEM 69        26
       THEFT
AMOUNT
    WILL AMOUNT TO ONLY ONE QUARTER OF WHAT HE PROPOSES TO YOU     841C LETTER 41        PROSE
    INTO ALL PARTS TO A VERY GREAT AMOUNT HE THEN SAID IF MR       856C LETTER 54        PROSE
    COST MY TIME THE AMOUNT OF TWENTY GUINEAS ONE I HAVE           878C LETTER 88        PROSE
       FINISHD
AMOUNTING
    NOW SEVEN AGES IS AMOUNTING TO TWO HUNDRED YEARS  .  .  .  .   516 MILTON 28           58
AMPLE
    AND ALL THY SONS & DAUGHTERS GATHERD ROUND MY AMPLE TABLE      360 FOUR ZOAS 9        127
    CONTAINING AMPLE ILLUSTRATIONS ON ART   .  .  .  .  .  .  .   560C EXHIBITION ADV   PROSE
AMSTERDAM
    IN ALL THE CITIES OF THE NATIONS PARIS MADRID AMSTERDAM        729 JERUSALEM 84        14
AMULET
    THE AMULET OF THOSE WHO PURIFY THE HEART OF MAN   .  .  .  .   88B ANNO LAVATER      MARG
AMUSE
    THAT SHALL AMUSE THE SPECTATORS IN THE SKY I THANK YOU   .    835A LETTER 34        PROSE
AMUSEMENT
    ONCE BORN FOR THE SPORT & AMUSEMENT OF MAN . . . . . .         272 FOUR ZOAS 1        278
    NOT BORN FOR THE SPORT AND AMUSEMENT OF MAN . . .  .  .  .     373 FOUR ZOAS 9        623
    SEEKING AMUSEMENT IN MAKING VERSES TO WHICH HE CONSTANTLY      830D LETTER 30        PROSE
    AMUSEMENT THAN HE COULD EVER BE IF EMPLOYD IN THE DRUDGERY     850B LETTER 49        PROSE
       OF
AN
    FOR FLIGHT AN PLEASE YOUR GRACE   .  .  .  .  .  .  .  .  .     24 EDW THIRD/PS 3     150
    I KNOW BETTER & PLEASE YOUR LORDSHIP   .  .  .  .  .  .  .    784C ANNO WW EXCUR     MARG
ANAK
    THE EMANATION & HER SONS THE SATAN & THE ANAK  .  .  .  .      278 FOUR ZOAS 1        507
    THERE CHAOS DWELLS & ANCIENT NIGHT & OG & ANAK OLD   .  .  .   502 MILTON 20           33
```

	PAGE	TITLE	LINE

ANAK   (CONTINUED)
WHICH FEW DARE UNBAR BECAUSE DREAD OG & ANAK GUARD THE   502 MILTON 20   35
    GATES
WITHIN AND OG & ANAK WATCH HERE HERE IS THE SEAT . . . .   502 MILTON 20   37
WILL UNCHAIN ORC & LET LOOSE SATAN OG SIHON & ANAK   . .   505 MILTON 22   33
ITS EVER DURING DOORS THAT OG & ANAK FIERCELY GUARD   . . . 520 MILTON 31   49
THE LOOMS & MILLS & PRISONS & WORK-HOUSES OF OG & ANAK   . . 634 JERUSALEM 13   57
HE HATH PLACED OG & ANAK THE GIANTS OF ALBION FOR THEIR   680 JERUSALEM 49   56
    GUARDS
PERUSING ALBION'S TOMB IN THE STARRY CHARACTERS OF OG &   713 JERUSALEM 73   16
    ANAK
ANAKIM
SIHON & OG THE ANAKIM & EMIM NEPHILIM & GIBBORIM . . . .   735 JERUSALEM 89   47
ANALOGY
OF DIVINE ANALOGY AND OG & SIHON IN THE TEARS OF BALAAM   680 JERUSALEM 49   58
HE CALLD IT DIVINE ANALOGY FOR IN BEULAH THE FEMININE   . . 730 JERUSALEM 85   7
ANALYSIS
AND AN ANALYSIS OF THE MORE SUBLIME BUT NO FURTHER   . . .   158A MARRIAGE HH 21 PROSE
HERE HE ALLOWS AN ANALYSIS OF CIRCUMSTANCES   . . . . .   462B ANNO REYNOLDS   MARG
ANALYTICS
WHICH IN THE MILL WAS ARISTOTLE'S ANALYTICS   . . . . .   157B MARRIAGE HH 17 PROSE
IS BUT LOST TIME TO CONVERSE WITH YOU WHOSE WORKS ARE ONLY   157B MARRIAGE HH 17 PROSE
    ANALYTICS
ANALYZING
YOU ACCUMULATE PARTICULARS & MURDER BY ANALYZING THAT YOU   738 JERUSALEM 91   27
ANANTON
THEOTORMON BROMION ANTAMON ANANTON OZOTH OHANA   . . . .   350 FOUR ZOAS 8   358
ANATOMY
HE UNDERSTANDS ANATOMY BETTER THAN ANY OF THE ANCIENTS . . 50A ISLAND MOON 6   PROSE
THE INFANT JOY IS BEAUTIFUL BUT ITS ANATOMY   . . . . .   265 FOUR ZOAS 1   49
THE INFANT JOY IS BEAUTIFUL BUT ITS ANATOMY   . . . . .   645 JERUSALEM 22   22
ANCESTOR
OUR ANCESTOR PATRIARCH OF THE ATLANTIC CONTINENT   . . . .   609C V LAST JUDG/N   PROSE
ANCESTORS
YOUR ANCESTORS CAME FROM THE FIRES OF TROY   . . . . .   32 EDW THIRD/PS 6   7
WHEN THE COLD CLAY BREATHED WITH LIFE AND OUR ANCESTORS   35C COUCH DEATH/PS   PROSE
WAS THE BEAUTY OF OUR ANCESTORS TILL AFTER ELIZABETH'S TIME 568B DESC CAT 3   PROSE
YOUR ANCESTORS DERIVED THEIR ORIGIN FROM   . . . . . .   649C JERUSALEM 27   PROSE
ANCESTRY
THE NERVES OF FIVE THOUSAND YEARS' ANCESTRY TREMBLE . . .   137 FRENCH REVOLTN   70
ANCHORS
THE MARINERS OF BOSTON DROP THEIR ANCHORS AND UNLADE   . .   201 AMERICA 14   14
ANCIENT   SEE ANTIENT
THE SEPULCHRE OF ANCIENT TROY FROM WHENCE   . . . . . .   32 EDW THIRD/PS 6   17
THE AGED SENATORS THEIR ANCIENT SWORDS ASSUME THE TREMBLING 34B KING JOHN/PS   PROSE
    SINEWS OF
BUT COMMON IN ANCIENT . . . .   94A ANNO SWED LOVE   MARG
THE VOICE OF THE ANCIENT BARD   . . . .   126A VOICE BARD/SI   TITLE
. . . RISE NECKER THE ANCIENT DAWN CALLS US   . . . .   134 FRENCH REVOLTN   7
LIKE OUR ANCIENT FATHERS IN REGIONS OF TWILIGHT . . . .   134 FRENCH REVOLTN   14
OF ANCIENT KINGS AND THE FROWN OF THE ETERNAL LION . . .   135 FRENCH REVOLTN   32
OF ANCIENT HORRORS COVERD FOR SNAKES AND SCORPIONS . . .   136 FRENCH REVOLTN   41
. . . AND TERRORS OF ANCIENT KINGS   . . . .   136 FRENCH REVOLTN   59
. . . BUT ANCIENT DARKNESS AND TREMBLING WANDER THRO THE   137 FRENCH REVOLTN   63
    PALACE
. . . THE SPIRITS OF ANCIENT KINGS   . . . .   137 FRENCH REVOLTN   72
. . . HIS NOBLES TOOK THEIR ANCIENT SEATS   . . . . .   137 FRENCH REVOLTN   82
AND THE ANCIENT FORESTS OF CHIVALRY HEWN . . . . . .   138 FRENCH REVOLTN   93
TO ROUZE UP THE ANCIENT FORESTS OF EUROPE . . . . . .   138 FRENCH REVOLTN   101
ANCIENT WONDERS FROWN OVER THE KINGDOM . . . .   139 FRENCH REVOLTN   118
BEFORE THE ANCIENT SEAT OF THE KINGDOM AND MOUNTAINS TO   143 FRENCH REVOLTN   205
    BE RENEWED
. . . BLOOD RAN DOWN THE ANCIENT PILLARS   . . . . .   145 FRENCH REVOLTN   246
LIKE PILLARS OF ANCIENT HALLS AND RUINS OF TIMES REMOTE   145 FRENCH REVOLTN   258
    THEY SAT
THE ANCIENT POETS ANIMATED ALL SENSIBLE OBJECTS WITH GODS   153A MARRIAGE HH 11 PROSE
THE ANCIENT TRADITION THAT THE WORLD WILL BE CONSUMED IN   154B MARRIAGE HH 14 PROSE
    FIRE
I HEAR THE [FATHER OF THE] ANCIENT [?FATHER OF] MEN   . . .   169 EARTHS ANSWR/N *   10
AN ANCIENT PROVERB . . . .   176B ANCNT PROVRB/N TITLE
[TWILL] YOULL QUITE REMOVE THE ANCIENT CURSE   . . . . .   176 ANCNT PROVRB/N 4
AN ANCIENT PROVERB . . . .   184D SEVRL QUESTN/N TITLE
YOULL QUITE REMOVE THE ANCIENT CURSE   . . . .   184 SEVRL QUESTN/N 18
TELL ME WHERE DWELL THE JOYS OF OLD & WHERE THE ANCIENT   192 V DAU ALBION 4 4
    LOVES
THOU KNOWEST THAT THE ANCIENT TREES SEEN BY THINE EYES   192 V DAU ALBION 4 13
    HAVE FRUIT
AH VISION FROM AFAR AH REBEL FORM THAT RENT THE ANCIENT   199 AMERICA 9   14
AN ANCIENT PALACE ARCHETYPE OF MIGHTY EMPERIES   . . . .   200 AMERICA 10   8
SICKNING LAY LONDON'S GUARDIAN AND THE ANCIENT MITERD YORK   202 AMERICA 15   9
WITH FIRES OF HELL DEFORM THEIR ANCIENT HEAVENS WITH SHAME   202 AMERICA 15   15
    & WOE
. . . ALL HIS ANGELS FRIGHT THEIR ANCIENT HEAVENS   . . .   202 AMERICA 15   18
THEY FEEL THE NERVES OF YOUTH RENEW AND DESIRES OF ANCIENT   202 AMERICA 15   25
    TIMES
IN TERROR VIEWD THE BANDS OF ALBION AND THE ANCIENT   203 AMERICA 16   17
    GUARDIANS
. . . TH [ETERNAL] (ANCIENT) PILLAR   . . . .   205 AMERICA CANC C *   11
GIANTS ANCIENT INHABITANTS OF ENGLAND THE LANDING   208C SUBJCTS HIST/N TITLE
    OF BRUTUS
THE ANCIENT BRITONS ACCORDING TO CAESAR [THE FRONTISPIECE]   208C SUBJCTS HIST/N TITLE
THAT WALKD AMONG THE ANCIENT TREES   . . . .   210 INTRODUCTN/SE   5

	PAGE	TITLE	LINE
ANCIENT (CONTINUED)			
I HEAR THE FATHER OF THE ANCIENT MEN	211	EARTHS ANSR/SE	10
HIS ANCIENT INFINITE MANSION	224	URIZEN 4	37
THE FIERY KING WHO SOUGHT HIS ANCIENT TEMPLE SERPENT-FORMD	241	EUROPE 10	2
NOW ARRIVD THE ANCIENT GUARDIAN AT THE SOUTHERN PORCH . .	241	EUROPE 10	24
THE GUARDIAN OF THE SECRET CODES FORSOOK HIS ANCIENT MANSION	242	EUROPE 12	15
FROM HIS ANCIENT WOVEN DEN	247	SONG OF LOS 6	4
AND STAYD IN HIS ANCIENT PLACE	248	SONG OF LOS 7	18
OF THE [ETERNAL] ANCIENT MAN	263B	FOUR ZOAS	*TITLE
THE DEATH AND JUDGEMENT OF ALBION THE ANCIENT MAN . . .	263C	FOUR ZOAS	TITLE
IN DARKNESS BUILDING THY STRONG THRONE & IN MY ANCIENT NIGHT	278	FOUR ZOAS 1	509
. . . THE FAINT HEART OF THE [ETERNAL] FALLEN [ANCIENT] MAN	283	FOUR ZOAS 2	* 143
. . . & THE [ETERNAL] ANCIENT MAN WAS SMITTEN	292	FOUR ZOAS 3	* 43
. . . THE [ETERNAL] ANCIENT MAN MIGHTY ALBION	293	FOUR ZOAS 3	* 79
WE HAVE DRUNK UP THE [(ANCIENT)] ETERNAL MAN BY OUR UNBOUNDED POWER	298	FOUR ZOAS 4	* 36
. . . IN FORGIVENESS OF [FORMER INJURIES] ANCIENT INJURIES	330	FOUR ZOAS 7	* 419
BEFORE MY FACE ASCENDING WITH DELIGHT AS IN ANCIENT TIMES	331	FOUR ZOAS 7	* 445
THE ANCIENT LEPROSY	354	FOUR ZOAS 8	498
LISTEN TO HER WHOSE MEMORY BEHOLDS YOUR ANCIENT DAYS .	354	FOUR ZOAS 8	504
AND ALL HIS SORROWS TILL HE REASSUMES HIS ANCIENT BLISS .	356	FOUR ZOAS 8	583
THE [ANCIENT MAN] REGENERATE MAN	366	FOUR ZOAS 9	360
AND THUS THEIR ANCIENT GOLDEN AGE RENEWD FOR LUVAH SPOKE	367	FOUR ZOAS 9	386
IN ALL THEIR ANCIENT INNOCENCE THE FLOODS DEPART THE CLOUDS	372	FOUR ZOAS 9	572
HOW IS IT THAT ALL THINGS ARE CHANGD EVEN AS IN ANCIENT TIMES	379	FOUR ZOAS 9	845
IN ALL HIS ANCIENT STRENGTH TO FORM THE GOLDEN ARMOUR OF SCIENCE	379	FOUR ZOAS 9	853
THE [ANCIENT] ETERNAL MAN BOWD HIS BRIGHT HEAD	380	FOUR ZOAS AD 1	2
LIKE TO THE ROOTS OF ANCIENT TREES	419	I SAW A MONK/N	18
LIKE TO THE ROOTS OF ANCIENT TREES	430	GREY MONK	8
THE MORE ANCIENT & CONSCIOUSLY & PROFESSEDLY INSPIRED MEN	480B	MILTON 1	PROSE
AND DID THOSE FEET IN ANCIENT TIME	480	AND DID FEET/M	1
ALL THINGS BEGIN & END IN ALBION'S ANCIENT DRUID ROCKY SHORE	486	MILTON 6	25
WERE LEAGUED TOGETHER AGAINST SATAN THRO ANCIENT ENMITY	487	MILTON 7	40
CHAOS & ANCIENT NIGHT FLED FROM BENEATH THE FIERY HARROW	493	MILTON 12	21
AND ANCIENT NIGHT & PURGATORY IT IS A CAVERNOUS EARTH .	498	MILTON 17	25
THERE CHAOS DWELLS & ANCIENT NIGHT & OG & ANAK OLD . . .	502	MILTON 20	33
ALL THE WISDOM WHICH WAS HIDDEN IN CAVES & DENS FROM ANCIENT	510	MILTON 25	20
THE ANCIENT MAN UPON THE ROCK OF ALBION AWAKES	510	MILTON 25	23
AWAKING OF ALBION OUR FRIEND AND ANCIENT COMPANION . .	511	MILTON 25	62
AND ANCIENT NIGHT SPREAD OVER ALL THE HEAVN HIS MANTLE OF LAWS	531	MILTON 39	30
LEANS ON THE ROCKS OF ERIN'S LAND IRELAND ANCIENT NATION	531	MILTON 39	45
THE ANCIENT BRITONS THREE ANCIENT BRITONS OVERTHROWING	560A	EXHIBITION ADV	PROSE
THE ANCIENT METHOD OF FRESCO PAINTING RESTORED AND DRAWINGS	563A	DESC CAT	TITLE
ARTIST HAVING BEEN TAKEN IN VISION INTO THE ANCIENT REPUBLICS	565C	DESC CAT 2	PROSE
AND ALL THE GRAND WORKS OF ANCIENT ART THEY WERE EXECUTED	565D	DESC CAT 2	PROSE
FOR ITS STAMINA CHAUCER HAS DIVIDED THE ANCIENT CHARACTER	571B	DESC CAT 3	PROSE
THE GRECIAN GODS WERE THE ANCIENT CHERUBIM OF PHOENICIA	571B	DESC CAT 3	PROSE
NUMBER V THE ANCIENT BRITONS	577B	DESC CAT 5	TITLE
THOSE OF OUR OWN COUNTRY THE ANCIENT BRITONS	577C	DESC CAT 5	PROSE
AND ITS ANCIENT GLORY WHEN IT WAS AS IT AGAIN SHALL BE .	577D	DESC CAT 5	PROSE
AND CONTAINS THE ANCIENT HISTORY OF BRITAIN	578B	DESC CAT 5	PROSE
BELIEVING WITH MILTON THE ANCIENT BRITISH HISTORY . .	578C	DESC CAT 5	PROSE
ANCIENT AUTHORS MUSIC AS IT EXISTS IN OLD TUNES OR MELODIES	579C	DESC CAT 5	PROSE
SPECIMENS OF ANCIENT SCULPTURE AND PAINTING AND ARCHITECTURE	579C	DESC CAT 5	PROSE
IN THAT ANCIENT HAPPY PERIOD WHICH HISTORY HAS RECORDED	580D	DESC CAT 5	PROSE
LYCON WILL PERCIEVE THAT THEY ARE NOT NOW IN ANCIENT GREECE	598B	PUB ADDRESS/N	PROSE
MORE ANCIENT WRITINGS	607A	V LAST JUDG/N	PROSE
MICH ANGELO & THE ANCIENT SCULPTORS IF WE DO	613C	V LAST JUDG/N	PROSE
WITH SOME OF THE ANCIENT GREEKS SAY	615D	V LAST JUDG/N	PROSE
THE BANKS OF THE THAMES ARE CLOUDED THE ANCIENT PORCHES OF ALBION ARE	623	JERUSALEM 5	1
MILD ZION'S HILL'S MOST ANCIENT PROMONTORY NEAR MOURNFUL	632	JERUSALEM 12	27
PITYING RENT IN ANCIENT TIMES I SEE IT WHOLE AND MORE . .	645	JERUSALEM 23	6
THE RELIGION OF JESUS THE MOST ANCIENT	649B	JERUSALEM 27	PROSE
ALL THINGS BEGIN & END IN ALBION'S ANCIENT DRUID ROCKY SHORE	649B	JERUSALEM 27	PROSE
MOST ANCIENT PROMONTORY AND IN THE SUN A HUMAN FORM APPEARD	653	JERUSALEM 29	4
UPON THE MOUNTAINS OF ALBION AS IN ANCIENT TIME BEHOLD . .	656	JERUSALEM 30	22
ALL THINGS BEGIN & END IN ALBION'S ANCIENT DRUID ROCKY SHORE	658	JERUSALEM 32	15
THE ANCIENT CITIES OF THE EARTH REMOVE AS A TRAVELLER . .	659	JERUSALEM 33	14
HEREFORD ANCIENT GUARDIAN OF WALES WHOSE HANDS	676	JERUSALEM 46	3
LIKE TO THE ROOTS OF ANCIENT TREES	683	I SAW A MONK/J	16
SUCH IS THE ANCIENT WORLD OF URIZEN IN THE SATANIC VOID	690	JERUSALEM 58	44
DRAVE THE SONS & DAUGHTERS OF ALBION FROM THEIR ANCIENT MOUNTAINS	714	JERUSALEM 74	21
AND CLOSE HER FROM THY ANCIENT WALLS	718	ENGLND AWAKE/J	4
A DRAGON FORM ON ZION HILL'S MOST ANCIENT PROMONTORY . .	722	JERUSALEM 80	36
LOS WALKS UPON HIS ANCIENT MOUNTAINS IN THE DEADLY DARKNESS	730	JERUSALEM 85	10
AWAKE AND OVERSPREAD ALL NATIONS AS IN ANCIENT TIME . .	744	JERUSALEM 97	2
THIS IS THE TRICK OF THE ANCIENT ELF	750	EV GOSPEL(C)/N	32
THIS IS THE TRICK OF THE ANCIENT ELF	752	EV GOSPEL(D)/N	66
THE ANCIENT HEAVENS IN SILENT AWE	754	EV GOSPEL(E)/N	12

```
                                                          PAGE      TITLE          LINE
ANCIENT     (CONTINUED)
     THAT HAVE FORGOT YOUR ANCIENT LOVE     . . . . . . . .  754 EV GOSPEL(E)/N    51
     THAT WHAT THEY SAY IS ANCIENT IS SO    . . . . . . . . .783C ANNO WW POEMS   MARG
     REMINISCENCE & BEHOLD OUR ANCIENT DAYS BEFORE THIS EARTH 802C LETTER 14      PROSE
     OF ANCIENT GREECE I SPEAK WITH PERFECT CONFIDENCE AND  . 852A LETTER 50      PROSE
     THE ANGEL THE SICK ROSE TO TIRZAH THE VOICE OF         SUPP LETTER 66A     *PROSE
        THE ANCIENT BARD
ANCIENTEST
     THEN THE ANCIENTEST PEER DUKE OF BURGUNDY . . . . . . .  138 FRENCH REVOLTN    83
ANCIENTLY
     NAMES ANCIENTLY REMEMBERD BUT NOW CONTEMND AS FICTIONS . . 624 JERUSALEM 5     38
     YOU HAVE A TRADITION THAT MAN ANCIENTLY CONTAIN  . . . .649C JERUSALEM 27    PROSE
ANCIENTS
     HE UNDERSTANDS ANATOMY BETTER THAN ANY OF THE ANCIENTS .  50A ISLAND MOON 6   PROSE
     WHICH BY THE ANCIENTS WAS CALLD AN ANGEL & SPIRIT & DEMON 98B ALL RELIGIONS   PROSE
     THE ANCIENTS KNEW BETTER . . . . . . . . . . .         394A ANNO WATSON      MARG
     BUT MORE NERVE IF BY ANCIENTS HE MEANS HEATHEN AUTHORS . 397D ANNO BACON      MARG
     FALSE THE ANCIENTS WERE CHIEFLY ATTENTIVE TO COMPLICATED 466B ANNO REYNOLDS   MARG
     THE ANCIENTS & THE WISEST OF THE MODERNS WERE  . . . . 473C ANNO REYNOLDS    MARG
     THE ANCIENTS DID NOT MEAN TO IMPOSE WHEN THEY AFFIRMD  . 473D ANNO REYNOLDS   MARG
     MR B(BLAKE) HAS DONE AS ALL THE ANCIENTS DID . . . . . 578C DESC CAT 5       PROSE
     BUT IN THIS I PLEAD THE AUTHORITY OF THE ANCIENTS WHO  . 583D DESC CAT 10     PROSE
     [AMONG THE ANCIENTS IS EVIDENT FROM THE WORDS OF THE] . 601A PUB ADDRESS/N   *PROSE
     ENDEAVOUR TO RESTORE WHAT THE ANCIENTS CALLD THE GOLDEN AGE 605D V LAST JUDG/N PROSE
     IT IS NOT BECAUSE I THINK THE ANCIENTS WRONG BUT THEY  . 608A V LAST JUDG/N   PROSE
     [IS REMINDED THAT THE ANCIENTS ENTRUSTED THEIR LOVE TO  621A JERUSALEM 3    *PROSE
        THEIR WRITING]
     TO WHOM THE ANCIENTS LOOKD AND SAW HIS DAY AFAR OFF   . 621A JERUSALEM 3     PROSE
     AS THE ANCIENTS SAW PLAINLY BY REVELATION  . . . . . . 682B JERUSALEM 52     PROSE
     THE ANCIENTS CALLD IT EATING OF THE TREE OF GOOD & EVIL 778C HOMERS POETRY   PROSE
     MY CARE THE WISEST OF THE ANCIENTS   . . . . . . . .   793B LETTER 5         PROSE
ANCLES     SEE ANKLES
     ALL AROUND HIS [ANCLES] BOSOM ROLLD  . . . . . . . .   177 DAY/N               4
ANECDOTE
     I DO NOT BELIEVE THIS ANECDOTE . . . . . . . . . . .   449D ANNO REYNOLDS    MARG
     I DO NOT BELIEVE THE TALES OF ANECDOTE WRITERS WHEN  . . 453B ANNO REYNOLDS   MARG
ANECDOTES
     PILGRIMS FROM CHAUCER CONTAINING ANECDOTES OF ARTISTS  591B PUB ADDRESS/N    PROSE
        PRICE...
ANEW
     OF URIZEN ENORMOUS WORK HE BUILDED THEM ANEW . . . . . 301 FOUR ZOAS 4       166
     THEY UNWEAVE THE SOFT THREADS THEN THEY WEAVE THEM ANEW 347 FOUR ZOAS 8       230
        IN THE FORMS
     TO THE DARK VALLEY WHENCE HE CAME TO BEGIN HIS LABOURS ANEW 355 FOUR ZOAS 8  *  575
     AND NATURAL RELIGION AS OF OLD SO NOW ANEW BEGAN . . . 357 FOUR ZOAS 8       619
     TURNING ANEW BEGAN HIS LABOURS THO IN TERRIBLE PAINS . 696 JERUSALEM 62       42
     ALL THAT HAS BEEN PRINTED AS LOST AND BEGIN ANEW UNLESS 858B LETTER 55       PROSE
ANGEL
     THINE ANGEL EYES UPON OUR WESTERN ISLE . . . . . . .     1 TO SPRING/PS        3
     THOU FAIR-HAIRD ANGEL OF THE EVENING . . . . . . . .     3 EVNING STAR/PS      1
     LIKE AS AN ANGEL GLITTERING IN THE SKY . . . . . . .     9 FRESH FROM/PS       9
     WEEP FROM THY GENTLE RIVERS THE ANGEL OF THE ISLAND WEEPS 34A KING JOHN/PS   PROSE
     TH ANGEL OF FATE TURNS THEM WITH MIGHTY HANDS  . . .    34 WAR SONG/PS         3
     AS THE VOICE OF THE ANGEL OF DEATH   . . . . . . . .   36B COUCH DEATH/PS    PROSE
     O WHITE-ROBED ANGEL GUIDE MY TIMOROUS HAND TO WRITE . . 37D SAMSON/PS         PROSE
     WHEN LO AN ANGEL FROM THE FIELDS OF LIGHT ENTERED THE HOUSE 39D SAMSON/PS    PROSE
     NOR KNEW HE WAS AN ANGEL MANOA LEFT HIS FIELDS . . . . 40A SAMSON/PS          PROSE
     AND LO AGAIN THE ANGEL CAME  . . . . . . . . . . . .   40B SAMSON/PS          PROSE
     THE ANGEL ANSWERED MY NAME IS WONDERFUL  . . . . . .   40C SAMSON/PS          PROSE
     THEN CHERISH PITY LEST YOU DRIVE AN ANGEL FROM YOUR DOOR 59 HOLY THURS/IM     18
     HIS LEADING VIRTUE & HIS GOOD ANGEL BUT  . . . . . .   88C ANNO LAVATER      MARG
     WHICH BY THE ANCIENTS WAS CALLD AN ANGEL & SPIRIT & DEMON 98B ALL RELIGIONS   PROSE
     AND BY CAME AN ANGEL WHO HAD A BRIGHT KEY  . . . . .   117 CHIMNEY SWP/SI      13
     AND THE ANGEL TOLD TOM IF HED BE A GOOD BOY  . . . .   118 CHIMNEY SWP/SI      19
     SWEET SLEEP ANGEL MILD   . . . . . . . . . . . . .    120 CRADLE SONG/SI       7
     THEN CHERISH PITY LEST YOU DRIVE AN ANGEL FROM YOUR DOOR 122 HOLY THURS/SI    12
     WHITE AS AN ANGEL IS THE ENGLISH CHILD   . . . . . .  125 LIT BLK BOY/SI       3
     SWEDENBORG IS THE ANGEL SITTING AT THE TOMB HIS WRITINGS 149A MARRIAGE HH 3   PROSE
     AN ANGEL CAME TO ME AND SAID O PITIABLE FOOLISH YOUNG MAN 155C MARRIAGE HH 17 PROSE
     FRIEND THE ANGEL CLIMBD UP FROM HIS STATION INTO THE MILL 156C MARRIAGE HH 17 PROSE
     BUT I AROSE AND SOUGHT FOR THE MILL & THERE I FOUND MY 156D MARRIAGE HH 17   PROSE
        ANGEL
     DRIVING THE ANGEL BEFORE ME SOON WE SAW SEVEN HOUSES OF 157A MARRIAGE HH 17  PROSE
        BRICK
     SO THE ANGEL SAID THY PHANTASY HAS IMPOSED UPON ME  . . 157B MARRIAGE HH 17  PROSE
     WHO AROSE BEFORE AN ANGEL THAT SAT ON A CLOUD  . . . . 158A MARRIAGE HH 22    PROSE
     THE ANGEL HEARING THIS BECAME ALMOST BLUE  . . . . .  158B MARRIAGE HH 22     PROSE
     WHEN HE HAD SO SPOKEN I BEHELD THE ANGEL   . . . . .  158D MARRIAGE HH 22     PROSE
     NOTE THIS ANGEL WHO IS NOW BECOME A DEVIL  . . . . .  158D MARRIAGE HH 22     PROSE
     AS SOON AS I WENT AN ANGEL CAME  . . . . . . . . . .  163 ASKED THIEF/N        5
     I HEARD AN ANGEL SINGING . . . . . . . . . . . . .    164 HEARD ANGEL/N        1
     THE ANGEL . . . . . . . . . . . . . . . . . . . .     182A THE ANGEL/N       TITLE
     GUARDED BY AN ANGEL MILD . . . . . . . . . . . . .    182 THE ANGEL/N          3
     SOON MY ANGEL CAME AGAIN . . . . . . . . . . . . .    182 THE ANGEL/N         13
     ALBION'S ANGEL STOOD BESIDE THE STONE OF NIGHT AND SAW . 197 AMERICA 5         1
     IN THUNDERS ENDS THE VOICE THEN ALBION'S ANGEL WRATHFUL 198 AMERICA 7         1
        BURNT
     THUS WEPT THE ANGEL VOICE & AS HE WEPT THE TERRIBLE BLASTS 200 AMERICA 10     1
     AND BOSTON'S ANGEL CRIED ALOUD AS THEY FLEW THRO THE DARK 200 AMERICA 11      3
        NIGHT
     THAT MOCK HIM WHO COMMANDED THIS WHAT GOD WHAT ANGEL  . . 200 AMERICA 11      7
     WHAT PITYING ANGEL LUSTS FOR TEARS AND FANS HIMSELF WITH 200 AMERICA 11       13
        SIGHS
```

```
                                                         PAGE      TITLE            LINE
ANGEL     (CONTINUED)
      OF ALBION'S ANGEL WHO ENRAGD HIS SECRET CLOUDS OPEND    .   .  201 AMERICA 13         10
      AND HEARD THE VOICE OF ALBION'S ANGEL GIVE THE THUNDEROUS     201 AMERICA 14          3
          COMMAND
      TO THE CLOSE HALL OF COUNSEL WHERE HIS ANGEL FORM RENEWS      204 AMERICA CANC B       2
      SHUT OUT FROM MORTAL SIGHT THE ANGEL CAME THE VALE WAS DARK   204 AMERICA CANC B      10
      [THEN ALBION'S ANGEL] ROSE RESOLVD TO THE COVE OF ARMOURY     205 AMERICA CANC C       1
      THE ANGEL  .  .  .  .  .  .  .  .  .  .  .  .  .  .  .  . 213D THE ANGEL/SE       TITLE
      GUARDED BY AN ANGEL MILD  .  .  .  .  .  .  .  .  .  .  .  213 THE ANGEL/SE         3
      SOON MY ANGEL CAME AGAIN  .  .  .  .  .  .  .  .  .  .  .  214 THE ANGEL/SE        13
      TILL ALBION'S ANGEL SMITTEN WITH HIS OWN PLAGUES FLED WITH    241 EUROPE 9           8
          HIS BANDS
      ROUND HIM ROLLD HIS CLOUDS OF WAR SILENT THE ANGEL WENT       241 EUROPE 10          4
      SHUT UP IN FINITE REVOLUTIONS AND MAN BECAME AN ANGEL         241 EUROPE 10         22
      ALBION'S ANGEL ROSE UPON THE STONE OF NIGHT  .  .  .  .  .    242 EUROPE 11          1
      INTO THE DEADLY NIGHT TO SEE THE FORM OF ALBION'S ANGEL       242 EUROPE 12          6
      THEY HEARD THE VOICE OF ALBION'S ANGEL HOWLING IN FLAMES      242 EUROPE 12         12
          OF ORC
      THE RED LIMBD ANGEL SIEZD IN HORROR AND TORMENT  .  .  .  .   243 EUROPE 13          1
      TILL MORNING OPED THE EASTERN GATE [AND THE ANGEL TRUMPET     244 EUROPE 14       *  35
          BLEW]
      AN ANGEL CAME  .  .  .  .  .  .  .  .  .  .  .  .  .  .  .    261 ASKED THIEF         6
      AND A SIGH IS THE SWORD OF AN ANGEL KING  .  .  .  .  .  .    420 I SAW A MONK/N      59
      AN ANGEL IS HERE FROM THE HEAVENLY CLIMES  .  .  .  .  .  .   428 MARY                5
      AND A SIGH IS THE SWORD OF AN ANGEL KING  .  .  .  .  .  .    430 GREY MONK          30
      AND AN ANGEL OF PROVIDENCE AT HIS FEET  .  .  .  .  .  .  .   435 WILLIAM BOND       13
      AND AN ANGEL OF PROVIDENCE AT HIS HEAD  .  .  .  .  .  .  .   435 WILLIAM BOND       14
      ACCOMPLISHD IN THIS WORLD OF SORROW MILTON'S ANGEL KNEW       504 MILTON 21          52
      BUT NOT THUS TO IMMORTALS THE LARK IS A MIGHTY ANGEL  .  .    527 MILTON 36          12
      THE ANGEL THAT PRESIDED OER MY BIRTH  .  .  .  .  .  .  .     541 ANGEL PRESID/N      1
      SO SPOKE AN ANGEL AT MY BIRTH  .  .  .  .  .  .  .  .  .  .   557 ART HAS LOST/N      3
      THAT ANGEL WHO PLEASED TO PERFORM THE ALMIGHTY'S ORDERS      565A DESC CAT 2       TITLE
      SOCIETY ARE PERHAPS EQUAL OF THE DEVIL AND OF THE ANGEL      570B DESC CAT 3       PROSE
      DRAGGED DOWN BY [AN ANGEL] A DEMON CROWND WITH LAUREL  .  . 606C V LAST JUDG/N     PROSE
      ANGEL OF THE DIVINE PRESENCE MENTIOND IN EXODUS XIV...      610A V LAST JUDG/N     PROSE
      & IN OTHER PLACES THIS ANGEL IS FREQUENTLY CALLD BY THE      610A V LAST JUDG/N     PROSE
      THE LARK IS AN ANGEL ON THE WING  .  .  .  .  .  .  .  .  . 618A ILLUS MILTON      PROSE
      OF THE WHOLE EARTH HE WAS THE ANGEL OF MY PRESENCE AND ALL    653 JERUSALEM 29        7
      AND A SIGH IS THE SWORD OF AN ANGEL KING  .  .  .  .  .  .    683 I SAW A MONK/J      26
      POLLUTED I HEARD HIS VOICE IN MY SLEEP & HIS ANGEL IN MY      694 JERUSALEM 61       16
          DREAM
      LUVAH SLEW THARMAS THE ANGEL OF THE TONGUE & ALBION BROUGHT   697 JERUSALEM 63        5
          HIM
      THOU ANGEL OF THE PRESENCE DIVINE  .  .  .  .  .  .  .  .  .  754 EV GOSPEL(E)/N      29
      HE SAYS ALSO THE SPIRITUAL BODY OR ANGEL AS LITTLE CHILDREN  774A ANNO BERKELEY     MARG
      THE ANGEL OF THE DIVINE PRESENCE (MALAKH YHWH)  .  .  .  .   775C INSC LAOCOON      TITLE
      OR ANGEL TO FOLLOW WHERE HE LED IF I WERE TO ACT OTHERWISE   791D LETTER 4         PROSE
      I SEND THE SHADOW OF THE DEPARTED ANGEL HOPE THE LIKENESS    797A LETTER 9         PROSE
      THE ANGEL OF THE DIVINE PRESENCE  .  .  .  .  .  .  .  .  .  824A LETTER 27        PROSE
      FROM THE ANGEL INN NEAR ST CLEMENTS CHURCH STRAND  .  .  .  871C LETTER 73        PROSE
      WIDOW FATHER BABE BAPTISM HERVEY ANGEL OF DEATH  .  .  .  .  SUPP INSC HERVEY      *TITLE
      VIRGIN WIFE INFANCY OLD AGE HUSBAND ANGEL OF                 SUPP INSC HERVEY      *TITLE
          PROVIDENCE
      GUARDIAN ANGEL CHILD ANGEL OF DEATH MOTHER  .  .  .  .  .    SUPP INSC HERVEY      *TITLE
      RECORDING ANGELS PROTECTING ANGEL NOAH ENOCH  .  .  .  .  .  SUPP INSC HERVEY      *TITLE
      PROTECTING ANGEL AARON ABRAHAM BELIEVED GOD  .  .  .  .  .   SUPP INSC HERVEY      *TITLE
      GOOD & EVIL ANGEL HOUSE OF DEATH GOD JUDGING ADAM LAMECH     SUPP LETTER 56A      *PROSE
      THE ANGEL THE SICK ROSE TO TIRZAH THE VOICE OF              SUPP LETTER 66A      *PROSE
          THE ANCIENT BARD
ANGEL-GUARDED
      OER MY ANGEL-GUARDED BED  .  .  .  .  .  .  .  .  .  .  .  .  111 A DREAM/SI          2
ANGELIC
      AND ITS ROOFS CRACK ACROSS DOWN FALLING ON TH ANGELIC SEATS  204 AMERICA CANC B      24
      BUT THO OBSCURD THIS IS THE FORM OF THE ANGELIC LAND  .  .    206 THIRALATHA          6
      YELLOW AS LEAVES OF AUTUMN THE MYRIADS OF ANGELIC HOSTS       243 EUROPE 13           6
      HIS EYES BEHOLD THE ANGELIC SPHERES ARISING NIGHT & DAY       379 FOUR ZOAS 9       828
ANGEL'S
      TO HEAR THE MUSIC OF AN ANGEL'S TONGUE  .  .  .  .  .  .  .     9 FRESH FROM/PS       12
      HAVE LABOURD HARD INDEED & HAVE BEEN BORNE ON ANGEL'S WINGS  826A LETTER 27        PROSE
ANGELS     SEE ARCH-ANGELS
      SWEET SYMPHONY TO FEATHERD ANGELS SITTING  .  .  .  .  .  .    28 EDW THIRD/PS 3     288
      ANGELS OF DEATH STAND IN THE LOWRING HEAVENS  .  .  .  .  .    35 WAR SONG/PS         17
      WHILE ON HIS MAJESTIC BROW THE VOICE OF ANGELS IS HEARD       36D COUCH DEATH/PS   PROSE
      HOVERING ANGELS ARE AROUND THEM  .  .  .  .  .  .  .  .  .     36D COUCH DEATH/PS   PROSE
      [LIKE ANGELS ON THE THRONE OF HEAVN RAISING THE VOICE OF       59 HOLY THURS/IM      13
          PRAISE]
      ("READY TO MOUNT LADDER ANGELS ASCEND AND DESCEND ")         73A ANNO LAVATER      MARG
          NOBLE
      IN DIFFERENT ?PERIODS OF TIME WISDOM OF ANGELS XXX  .  .  .   89B ANNO SWED LOVE   * MARG
      ("THOUGHTS OF ANGELS NOTHING FROM SPACE AND TIME")           92A ANNO SWED LOVE    MARG
          EXCELLENT
      SAID THE ANGELS COULD NOT EXPRESS THEMSELVES AT ALL TO HIM   94C ANNO SWED LOVE    MARG
      THE FEET OF ANGELS BRIGHT  .  .  .  .  .  .  .  .  .  .  .    119 NIGHT/SI           12
      THE ANGELS MOST HEEDFUL  .  .  .  .  .  .  .  .  .  .  .  .   119 NIGHT/SI           30
      ("PLACE FORESEEN ...TIME PROVIDED") DEVILS & ANGELS ARE     132B ANNO SWED PROV    MARG
          PREDESTINATED
      WHEN HE WROTE OF ANGELS & GOD  .  .  .  .  .  .  .  .  .  .  150B MARRIAGE HH 5     PROSE
      WHICH TO ANGELS LOOK LIKE TORMENT AND INSANITY  .  .  .  .  150C MARRIAGE HH 6     PROSE
      I HAVE ALWAYS FOUND THAT ANGELS HAVE THE VANITY TO SPEAK    157C MARRIAGE HH 21    PROSE
      AND NOW HEAR THE REASON HE CONVERSED WITH ANGELS WHO  .  .  157D MARRIAGE HH 21    PROSE
      WHY DOST THOU COME TO ANGELS EYES IN THIS TERRIFIC FORM       198 AMERICA 7           7
      SOUND SOUND MY LOUD WAR-TRUMPETS & ALARM MY THIRTEEN          199 AMERICA 9           1
          ANGELS
```

	PAGE	TITLE	LINE

ANGELS   (CONTINUED)
SOUND SOUND MY LOUD WAR-TRUMPETS & ALARM MY THIRTEEN   199 AMERICA 9   13
    ANGELS
SOUND SOUND MY LOUD WAR TRUMPETS & ALARM MY THIRTEEN   199 AMERICA 9   21
    ANGELS
SOUND SOUND MY LOUD WAR-TRUMPETS & ALARM MY THIRTEEN   199 AMERICA 9   26
    ANGELS
HERE ON THEIR MAGIC SEATS THE THIRTEEN ANGELS SAT PERTURBD 200 AMERICA 10   11
FIERY THE ANGELS ROSE & AS THEY ROSE DEEP THUNDER ROLLD   200 AMERICA 11   1
IN SIGHT OF ALBION'S GUARDIAN AND ALL THE THIRTEEN ANGELS   200 AMERICA 12   2
BENEATH HIM ROLLD HIS NUMROUS HOSTS ALL ALBION'S ANGELS   201 AMERICA 13   13
    CAMPD
ON ALBION'S ANGELS THEN THE PESTILENCE BEGAN IN STREAKS   202 AMERICA 15   1
    OF RED
. . . ALL HIS ANGELS FRIGHT THEIR ANCIENT HEAVENS   . . . 202 AMERICA 15   18
TILL ANGELS & WEAK MEN TWELVE YEARS SHOULD GOVERN OER THE   203 AMERICA 16   14
    STRONG
ANGELS OF CITIES AND OF PARISHES AND VILLAGES AND FAMILIES 205 AMERICA CANC C   18
OVER THE RUGGED OCEAN SO THE ANGELS OF ALBION HUNG   . . . 205 AMERICA CANC C   24
IN COUNCIL GATHER THE SMITTEN ANGELS OF ALBION   . . . .   241 EUROPE 9   11
ON THE HEADS OF ALBION'S ANGELS   . . . .   241 EUROPE 9   13
OF ASIA & ON THE DESARTS OF AFRICA ROUND THE FALLEN ANGELS 246 SONG OF LOS 4   20
WITH BEAUTIFUL ART THE STUDY OF ANGELS THE WORKMANSHIP   365 FOUR ZOAS 9   297
    OF DEMONS
BUT THE ANGELS OF PROVIDENCE DROVE THEM AWAY   . . . . .   434 WILLIAM BOND   7
AND THE ANGELS OF PROVIDENCE LEFT THE BED   . . . . . .   435 WILLIAM BOND   44
THE SAVIOUR WHILE THE EVIL ANGELS ARE DRIVEN GENTLY   441D INSC FALL MAN   PROSE
    CONDUCTS
OUR FIRST PARENTS OUT OF EDEN THROUGH A GUARD OF WEEPING   441D INSC FALL MAN   PROSE
    ANGELS
LIKE A SCROLL READY TO BE CONSUMED IN THE FIRES OF THE   443A LAST JUDGMNT/L PROSE
    ANGELS
& TEN HORNS CHAINED BY TWO ANGELS   . . . .   443A LAST JUDGMNT/L PROSE
IS THE HARLOT ALSO SIEZED & BOUND [CHAIND] BY TWO ANGELS   443A LAST JUDGMNT/L PROSE
BY TWO ANGELS & MANY GROUPES OF FIGURES ARE FALLING . .   443C LAST JUDGMNT/L PROSE
OPEND [BY TWO ANGELS ON CLOUDS] ON CLOUDS BY TWO ANGELS   443D LAST JUDGMNT/L *PROSE
FILLED WITH EYES ATTENDED BY SEVEN ANGELS   . . . . . .   444A LAST JUDGMNT/L PROSE
& ABOVE THESE [THERE ARE] SEVEN ANGELS WITH THE   . . .   444A LAST JUDGMNT/L PROSE
BY ANGELS FROM THE HANDS OF ANOTHER [AGED] APOSTLE   . .   444B LAST JUDGMNT/L PROSE
THE SEVEN ANGELS OF THE PRESENCE WEPT OVER MILTON'S SHADOW 496 MILTON 14   42
WITH HIM THE SPIRITS OF THE SEVEN ANGELS OF THE PRESENCE   496 MILTON 14   3
THO DARKEND AND THE SEVEN ANGELS OF THE PRESENCE ATTENDED   502 MILTON 20   14
    HIM
THE GUARD ARE ANGELS OF PROVIDENCE ON DUTY EVERMORE . .   516 MILTON 28   61
IN VISION & DREAM BEATIFIC WITH THE SEVEN ANGELS OF THE   521 MILTON 32   2
    PRESENCE
AND THUS THE SEVEN ANGELS INSTRUCTED HIM & THUS THEY   521 MILTON 32   9
    CONVERSE
WE WERE ANGELS OF THE DIVINE PRESENCE & WERE DRUIDS IN   521 MILTON 32   11
    ANNANDALE
TO THEIR RESPECTIVE EARTHS & THERE ALL NIGHT CONSULT WITH   526 MILTON 36   4
    ANGELS
ITS FURNACES OF AFFLICTION IN WHICH HIS ANGELS & EMANATIONS 529 MILTON 38   20
SEVEN ANGELS BEAR MY NAME & IN THOSE SEVEN I APPEAR   .   530 MILTON 38   55
NUMBER XIV THE ANGELS HOVERING OVER   . . . .   584B DESC CAT 14   TITLE
IN THIS CATARACT FOUR ANGELS DESCEND HEADLONG   . . . . .   609A V LAST JUDG/N   PROSE
TO THE SEVEN ANGELS THE SEVEN VIALS OF THE WRATH OF GOD   612A V LAST JUDG/N   PROSE
A GLORIFICATION OF ANGELS WITH HARPS SURROUND THE DOVE .   613B V LAST JUDG/N   PROSE
IT IS NOT BECAUSE ANGELS ARE HOLIER THAN MEN OR DEVILS .   616D V LAST JUDG/N   PROSE
THAT MAKES THEM ANGELS BUT BECAUSE THEY DO NOT   . . .   616D V LAST JUDG/N   PROSE
THE PLAYER IS A LIAR WHEN HE SAYS ANGELS ARE HAPPIER   .   616D V LAST JUDG/N   PROSE
ANGELS ARE HAPPIER THAN MEN & DEVILS BECAUSE   . . . . .   616D V LAST JUDG/N   PROSE
WHILE TWO ANGELS SOUND THEIR TRUMPETS   . . . .   618C ILLUS MILTON   PROSE
. . . & WHO CHARGETH HIS ANGELS WITH FOLLY   . . . . .   679 JERUSALEM 49   31
AND A LITTLE TENDER MOON & HOVERING ANGELS ON THE WING .   707 JERUSALEM 69   22
DENY A CONSCIENCE IN MAN & THE COMMUNION OF SAINTS & ANGELS 741 JERUSALEM 93   22
ALL GENIUS VARIES THUS DEVILS ARE VARIOUS ANGELS ARE ALL   773A NOTE NINE HEAD PROSE
    ALIKE
THEIR WORKS WERE DESTROYD BY THE SEVEN ANGELS   . . . . .   777B INSC LAOCOON   PROSE
ON EACH SIDE A CHORUS OF ANGELS ENTERING SING THE FOLLOWING 781A GHOST ABEL 2   PROSE
MAY JESUS AND HIS ANGELS ASSUAGE   . . . .   796C LETTER 8   PROSE
EVEN IN THIS WORLD BY IT I AM THE COMPANION OF ANGELS   .   797B LETTER 9   PROSE
ANGELS I KNOW YOU WILL BE PLEASED WITH THE INTENTION   .   799B LETTER 11   PROSE
ANGELS STAND ROUND MY SPIRIT IN HEAVEN   . . . .   799 TO FLAXMAN/L   2
AND MY ANGELS HAVE TOLD ME THAT SEEING SUCH VISIONS . . .   799 TO FLAXMAN/L   11
"THE ANGELS OF OUR JOURNEY HAVE INSPIRED A SONG TO YOU"   800B LETTER 12   PROSE
THE LADDER OF ANGELS DESCENDS THRO THE AIR   . . . . . .   800 MRS FLAXMAN/L   6
LEADER OF MY ANGELS MY DEAR & TOO CAREFUL & OVER JOYOUS   801B LETTER 13   PROSE
DEAR FRIEND OF MY ANGELS WE ARE SAFE ARRIVED AT OUR COTTAGE 803A LETTER 15   PROSE
BUT IF WE FEAR TO DO THE DICTATES OF OUR ANGELS & TREMBLE   813A LETTER 22   PROSE
WITH ANGELS PLANTED IN HAWTHORN BOWERS   . . . .   817 HAPPINESS/L   9
WITH SILVER ANGELS ACROSS MY WAY   . . . .   817 HAPPINESS/L   11
WITH A THOUSAND ANGELS UPON THE WIND   . . . .   817 HAPPINESS/L   21
THE TWO ANGELS WHO STAND AT HEAVEN'S GATE EVER OPEN . . . 834A LETTER 33   PROSE
ENGRAVED BY THE HANDS OF ANGELS & MUST NOT BY ANY MEANS   848C LETTER 45   PROSE
THE GOOD AND EVIL ANGELS   . . . .   SUPP COLOR PRT TATE *TITLE
THESE DIED FOR LOVE MINISTERING ANGELS   . . . .   SUPP INSC HERVEY   *TITLE
RECORDING ANGELS PROTECTING ANGEL NOAH ENOCH   . . . .   SUPP INSC HERVEY   *TITLE
ANGELS'
OH BLESS THOSE HOLY FEET LIKE ANGELS' FEET   . . . . . .   9 FRESH FROM/PS   7
YET DEATH IS TERRIBLE THO BORNE ON ANGELS' WINGS   . . . .   30 EDW THIRD/PS 5   17

95

		PAGE	TITLE	LINE

ANGER
```
    I WILL DIVIDE THEM IN MY ANGER & THOU O MY KING    . . . .    334 FOUR ZOAS 7B       69
    MY ANGER AGAINST THEE IS GREATER THAN AGAINST THIS LUVAH      361 FOUR ZOAS 9       151
    ANGER ME NOT THOU CANST NOT DRIVE THE HARROW IN PITY'S        483 MILTON 4           16
       PATHS
    OVER LONDON IN VOLUME TERRIFIC LOW BENDED IN ANGER   . . .    535 MILTON 42          35
    AT A FRIEND'S ERRORS ANGER SHEW   . . . . . . . . .          538 WAS I ANGRY/N       8
    ANGER & WRATH MY BOSOM RENDS                                  538 ANGER WRATH/N       1
    HE OPEND HIS FURNACES BEFORE VALA THEN ALBION FROWND IN       660 JERUSALEM 34       19
       ANGER
    DOST THOU NOT MURDER ME JOSEPH SPOKE IN ANGER & FURY SHOULD   694 JERUSALEM 61        5
       I
    . . . IN THE MIDST OF HIS ANGER IN FURNACE OF FIRE   . . .    694 JERUSALEM 61       13
    TO TELL HOW LOS IN GRIEF & ANGER WHIRLING ROUND HIS HAMMER    714 JERUSALEM 74       20
       ON HIGH
    IN ANGER THE WRATH OF GOD BREAKING BRIGHT FLAMING ON ALL      742 JERUSALEM 95        6
       SIDES AROUND
    SMILING ON OUR COTTAGE SAYS YOU LAY TOO LOW FOR MY ANGER TO  807B LETTER 17       PROSE
ANGLE     SEE OBTUSE ANGLE
    OPENING INTO BEULAH EVERY ANGLE IS A LOVELY HEAVEN   . . .    668 JERUSALEM 41       18
ANGLED    SEE RIGHT ANGLED
ANGLES
    NOR CAN HIS WATCH FIENDS FIND IT TIS TRANSLUCENT & HAS        668 JERUSALEM 41       16
       MANY ANGLES
ANGLESEA
    THE GATE OF ZEBULUN IN ANGLESEA & SODOR SO IS WALES DIVIDED   637 JERUSALEM 16       40
ANGLUS
    ANGLUS CAN NEVER SEE PERFECTION   . . . . . . . . .          548 GIVE PENSION/N      3
    CAN ANGLUS NEVER DISCERN PERFECTION BUT IN THE JOURNEYMAN'S  601D PUB ADDRESS/N   PROSE
       LABOUR
ANGRY
    AND YOU WAS VERY ANGRY WITH ME FOR NOT FLATTERING YOU   . .   30A EDW THIRD/PS 4  PROSE
    YOU MEAN THAT I WAS ANGRY WITH YOU   . . . . . . . .          30A EDW THIRD/PS 4  PROSE
    . . . A WHIRLWIND AND FIRE TORE FURIOUS FROM HIS ANGRY        143 FRENCH REVOLTN    200
       BOSOM
    I WAS ANGRY WITH MY FRIEND   . . . . . . . . . . . .          165 CHRISTN FORB/N      1
    I WAS ANGRY WITH MY FOE   . . . . . . . . . . . . .          165 CHRISTN FORB/N      3
    THE ANGRY SHORES AND THE FIERCE RUSHING OF TH INHABITANTS     201 AMERICA 14         12
       TOGETHER
    I WAS ANGRY WITH MY FRIEND   . . . . . . . . . . . .          218 POISON TREE/SE      1
    I WAS ANGRY WITH MY FOE   . . . . . . . . . . . . .          218 POISON TREE/SE      3
    SHADDAI WAS ANGRY PACHAD DESCENDED PACHAD WAS TERRIFIED       351 FOUR ZOAS 8       404
    HE TRIES THE SULLEN NORTH WIND RIDING ON ITS ANGRY FURROWS    355 FOUR ZOAS 8       564
    THE SULTRY SOUTH WHEN THE SUN RISES & THE ANGRY EAST   .      355 FOUR ZOAS 8       565
    CHOKD THE BRIGHT RIVERS BURDNING WITH MY SHIPS THE ANGRY      361 FOUR ZOAS 9       169
       DEEP
    IF YOU ACCOUNT IT WISDOM WHEN YOU ARE ANGRY TO BE SILENT      483 MILTON 4            6
       AND
    PALAMABRON FEARD TO BE ANGRY LEST SATAN SHOULD ACCUSE HIM     486 MILTON 7           13
       OF
    FLAMD ABOVE ALL THE PLOWED FURROWS ANGRY RED AND FURIOUS      488 MILTON 8           36
    SATAN WHO DRAVE THE TEAM BESIDE HIM STOOD ANGRY & RED   .     488 MILTON 8           38
    SHADDAI ANGRY PAHAD DESCENDED PAHAD TERRIFIED THEY SENT       494 MILTON 13          23
       JEHOVAH
    WAS I ANGRY WITH HAYLEY WHO USD ME SO ILL   . . . . . .       538 WAS I ANGRY/N       1
    OR CAN I BE ANGRY WITH FELPHAM'S OLD MILL   . . . . . .       538 WAS I ANGRY/N       2
    [ OR ANGRY WITH BOYDELL OR BOWYER OR BA ]   . . . . . .       538 WAS I ANGRY/N       3
    OR ANGRY WITH PLAXMAN OR CROMEK OR STOTHARD   . . . . .       538 WAS I ANGRY/N       4
    OR ANGRY WITH [ BOYDELL OR BOWYER OR BASIRE ]   . . . .       538 WAS I ANGRY/N *     6
    IN THE VOICE OF MY HUSBAND THO HE IS ANGRY FOR A MOMENT       694 JERUSALEM 61       10
       HE WILL NOT
    AND ANGRY FORCE ME TO OBEY   . . . . . . . . . . .          748 EV GOSPEL(B)/N      10
    AS TO HAVE MADE YOU ANGRY WITH MY METHOD OF STUDY   . . .    793A LETTER 5        PROSE
    THE ANGRY GOD OF THIS WORLD & HIS ?THRONE IN PURGATORY   .   SUPP ILLUS DANTE 3 *PROSE
ANGUISH
    THROBS OF ANGUISH BEAT ON BRAZEN WAR FOREHEADS   . . . . .    137 FRENCH REVOLTN     71
    TO QUENCH THEIR ANGUISH AT THE FEET OF WASHINGTON DOWN        201 AMERICA 13          4
       FALLN
    OF ANGUISH THREW THEIR SWORDS & MUSKETS TO THE EARTH & RAN    201 AMERICA 13          7
    THE MILLIONS SENT UP A HOWL OF ANGUISH . . . . . . . .        202 AMERICA 15          4
    IN FIERCE ANGUISH & QUENCHLESS FLAMES   . . . . . . .         225 URIZEN 5           19
    AND CURSING HIS LOT FOR IN ANGUISH   . . . . . . . .          226 URIZEN 6            3
    SHOOTING OUT IN ANGUISH DEEP   . . . . . . . . . . .          229 URIZEN 13          15
    IN ANGUISH DIVIDING & DIVIDING   . . . . . . . . . .          230 URIZEN 13          52
    AND ENITHARMON GROANS & CRIES IN ANGUISH AND DISMAY   . .     245 EUROPE 15           8
    AND HIS EYES PALE WITH ANGUISH HIS LIPS   . . . . . . .       250 AHANIA 3            2
    . . . THEIR BODIES JOIN IN BURNING ANGUISH ]                  269 FOUR ZOAS 1       181
    FILLD WITH THE WINE OF ANGUISH WAITED AT THE GOLDEN FEAST     273 FOUR ZOAS 1       348
    HIS LEFT ARM TO THE SOUTH SHOOTING OUT IN ANGUISH DEEP   .    303 FOUR ZOAS 4       244
    SITTING IN DARKNESS OVER HER LOS MOURND IN ANGUISH FIERCE     307 FOUR ZOAS 5        71
    VIBRATED IN SUCH ANGUISH THE EYELIDS QUIVERD   . . . . .      318 FOUR ZOAS 6       256
    STEEPING THY WOUNDS IN SALTS INFERNAL & IN BITTER ANGUISH     321 FOUR ZOAS 7        54
    THE CAUSE OF HER DIRE ANGUISH FOR SHE LAY THE IMAGE OF        328 FOUR ZOAS 7       320
       DEATH
    IN [ ANGUISH FOR ] RAGE AGAINST THE DARK DESPAIR THE HOWLING  340 FOUR ZOAS 7B *    287
       MELANCHOLY
    TREMBLING HE LAY SWELLD WITH THE DELUGE STIFLING IN THE       381 FOUR ZOAS AD 4      3
       ANGUISH
    . . . TOGETHER THEY JOIN IN BURNING ANGUISH   . . . .         381 FOUR ZOAS AD 5      1
    DRAWING JERUSALEM IN ANGUISH OF MATERNAL LOVE   . . . . .     624 JERUSALEM 5        47
    IN ANGUISH OF REGENERATION IN TERRORS OF SELF ANNIHILATION    626 JERUSALEM 7        61
    HER REVOLUTIONS TOWARD THE STARRY WHEELS IN MATERNAL          635 JERUSALEM 14       32
       ANGUISH
```

	PAGE	TITLE	LINE
ANGUISH (CONTINUED)			
IN CHILDHOOD WHAT WERT THOU UNUTTERABLE ANGUISH CONWENNA	644	JERUSALEM 21	23
VAST & SEVERE THE ANGUISH EER THEY KNEW THEIR FATHER WERE	713	JERUSALEM 73	8
NAKED AMONG THE HUMAN CLUSTERS BRINGING WINE OF ANGUISH	726	JERUSALEM 82	65
CHESHIRE & LANCASHIRE & WESTMORELAND GROAN IN ANGUISH	736	JERUSALEM 90	18
DESPERATE ATTACK OF THE ANGUISH (&) TREMBLING LAST NIGHT &	SUPP	LETTER 81A	*PROSE
ANGUISHD			
HEAVING DOLOROUS ANGUISHD UNBEARABLE	228	URIZEN 10	32
HE GROAND ANGUISHD & CALLED HER SIN	250	AHANIA 2	34
AS THE MOON ANGUISHD CIRCLES THE EARTH	250	AHANIA 2	40
ANGUISHD UNBEARABLE TILL A ROOF SHAGGY WILD INCLOSD	303	FOUR ZOAS 4	216
FOR GWENDOLEN SHE TOOK UP IN BITTER TEARS HIS ANGUISHD HEART	723	JERUSALEM 80	67
ANIMAL			
BEFORE HIS EYES LIKE THE ANIMAL UPON THE PYTHAGOREAN'S LAP	46A	ISLAND MOON 1	PROSE
CONVERSING WITH THE ANIMAL FORMS OF WISDOM NIGHT & DAY	379	FOUR ZOAS 9	836
MORE THAN ANIMAL FROM ANIMAL OF DIFFERENT SPECIES	470B	ANNO REYNOLDS	MARG
THE BELLOWS ARE THE ANIMAL LUNGS THE HAMMERS THE ANIMAL HEART	509	MILTON 24	58
TIME IS NOW SOUGHT OUT FROM ANIMAL & VEGETABLE & MINERAL	510	MILTON 25	21
OF AGE AND YOUTH AND BOY AND GIRL AND ANIMAL AND HERB	640	JERUSALEM 18	17
AND BOY & GIRL & ANIMAL & HERB & RIVER & MOUNTAIN	640	JERUSALEM 18	25
THE BELLOWS ARE THE ANIMAL LUNGS THE HAMMERS THE ANIMAL HEART	684	JERUSALEM 53	12
OF VIRGINS WAX I DONT KNOW WHAT ANIMAL PRODUCES IT	790C	LETTER 2	PROSE
ANIMALS			
THE MOST TERRIFIC SHAPES OF ANIMALS SPRUNG FROM CORRUPTION	156A	MARRIAGE HH 17	PROSE
RESOUNDED WITH PREPARATION OF ANIMALS WILD & TAME	484	MILTON 4	25
ALL ANIMALS UPON THE EARTH ARE PREPARD IN ALL THEIR STRENGTH	535	MILTON 42	39
THE SAME CHARACTERS REPEATED AGAIN AND AGAIN IN ANIMALS	567C	DESC CAT 3	PROSE
THE SAME CHARACTERS REPEATED AGAIN & AGAIN IN ANIMALS	589A	CHAUCER/N	PROSE
LET HIM BE OF WHAT CLASS OF ANIMALS HE WILL	616B	V LAST JUDG/N	PROSE
IF YOUR TRADITION THAT MAN CONTAINED IN HIS LIMBS ALL ANIMALS	652B	JERUSALEM 27	PROSE
AND THE BODIES IN WHICH ALL ANIMALS & VEGETATIONS THE EARTH & HEAVEN	679	JERUSALEM 49	13
EUPHRATES & TO FORESTS & FLOODS & ANIMALS WILD & TAME FROM	695	JERUSALEM 61	31
AS THEY ARE THE MOST EMINENT AMONG ANIMALS VIZ THE LION	859B	LETTER 56	PROSE
ANIMATE			
WONDRING SHE SAW HER WOOF BEGIN TO ANIMATE & NOT	266	FOUR ZOAS 1	83
THE BLOODY MASS BEGAN TO ANIMATE I BENDING OVER	300	FOUR ZOAS 4	96
THE ASHES OF MYSTERY BEGAN TO ANIMATE THEY CALLD IT DEISM	357	FOUR ZOAS 8	618
BENEATH THE DRAGON'S CAVERN A SKELETON BEGINS TO ANIMATE	609C	V LAST JUDG/N	PROSE
THE GOLDEN CORDS OF THE LOOMS ANIMATE BENEATH THEIR TOUCHES SOFT	725	JERUSALEM 82	14
ANIMATED			
TILL KNOWLEDGE ANIMATED IT TWAS CALLD SELFLOVE	42D	THEN SHE BORE	PROSE
THE ANCIENT POETS ANIMATED ALL SENSIBLE OBJECTS WITH GODS	153A	MARRIAGE HH 11	PROSE
AN ANIMATED PILLAR ROLLING ROUND & ROUND IN INCESSANT RAGE	353	FOUR ZOAS 8	470
A SHADOW ANIMATED BY THY TEARS O MOURNFUL JERUSALEM	631	JERUSALEM 11	25
BUT ANIMATED AND VEGETATED SHE IS A DEVOURING WORM	631	JERUSALEM 12	3
ANIMATING			
?WHO ANIMATING TIMES ON TIMES BY THE FORCE OF HER SWEET SONG	267	FOUR ZOAS 1	120
MUST WAR WITH SECRET MONSTERS OF THE ANIMATING WORLDS	325	FOUR ZOAS 7	201
ISSUD ON ALL SIDES GATHRING STRENGTH IN ANIMATING VOLUMES	358	FOUR ZOAS 9	* 35
ANIMATING THE DRAGON TEMPLES SOON TO BECOME THAT HOLY FIEND	677	JERUSALEM 47	6
ANIMATION			
THOUGH THE ORIGINAL CONCEPTION WAS ALL FIRE AND ANIMATION	583A	DESC CAT 9	PROSE
IN PREFERENCE TO THE INSPIRED MOMENTS OF GENIUS & ANIMATION	594B	PUB ADDRESS/N	PROSE
ANIMATIONS			
FIRST FLED MY SONS & THEN MY DAUGHTERS THEN MY WILD ANIMATIONS	643	JERUSALEM 21	7
ANKLE			
[WHAT THE [SHOULDER] ANKLE WHAT THE KNEE]	173	THE TYGER/N 1	* 27
ANKLES SEE ANCLES			
RAN TO THE DOOR WHEN TIRIEL FELT THE ANKLES OF AGED HAR	109	TIRIEL 8	6
CUT THEE IN GASHES THO THE BLOOD POURS DOWN AROUND THY ANKLES	322	FOUR ZOAS 7	84
BINDING HIS WRISTS & ANKLES WITH THE IRON ARMS OF LOVE	726	JERUSALEM 82	71
ANN			
TO MRS ANN FLAXMAN	414D	TO MRS FLAXMAN	TITLE
ANNA			
TO MY DEAR FRIEND MRS ANNA FLAXMAN	800B	MRS FLAXMAN/L	TITLE
ANNANDALE			
WE WERE ANGELS OF THE DIVINE PRESENCE & WERE DRUIDS IN ANNANDALE	521	MILTON 32	11
JEHOVAH STOOD AMONG THE DRUIDS IN THE VALLEY OF ANNANDALE	696	JERUSALEM 63	1
. . . & THE FLUTE OF SUMMER IN ANNANDALE	700	JERUSALEM 65	15
ANNEXD			
THE PRINT OF ROMEO & THE APOTHECARY ANNEXD TO YOUR COPY	855C	LETTER 53	PROSE
ANNEXED			
THE BEAUTY THAT IS ANNEXED AND APPENDED TO FOLLY IS A	579D	DESC CAT 5	PROSE
ANNEXED TO IMBECILITY AND DISEASE IS A SUBJECT FOR BURLESQUE	580A	DESC CAT 5	PROSE
THE ABOVE WAS WRITTEN & THE DRAWING ANNEXED BY THE DESIRE	781D	INSC UPCOTT	PROSE
ANNIHILABLE			
WHAT IS ETERNAL & WHAT CHANGEABLE & WHAT ANNIHILABLE	522	MILTON 32	31
ANNIHILATE			
FOR ME & THOU ANNIHILATE EVAPORATE & BE NO MORE	329	FOUR ZOAS 7	358
& SHALL IN THE END ANNIHILATE THEM	407D	ANNO BACON	MARG

```
                                                      PAGE      TITLE            LINE
ANNIHILATE    (CONTINUED)
    ANNIHILATE THEE ON THE ROCKS  . . . . . . . .  .  417 MY SPECTRE/N          64
    TO ANNIHILATE THE SELF-HOOD OF DECEIT & FALSE FORGIVENESS 497 MILTON 16       1
    SATAN MY SPECTRE I KNOW MY POWER THEE TO ANNIHILATE  . . .  529 MILTON 38     29
    ANNIHILATE HIMSELF FOR OTHERS GOOD AS I FOR THEE  . . .  530 MILTON 38        36
    ARE THOSE WHO CONTEMN RELIGION & SEEK TO ANNIHILATE IT  . .  532 MILTON 40     9
    ANNIHILATE THE SELFHOOD IN ME BE THOU ALL MY LIFE  . . .  623 JERUSALEM 5     22
    I CAME HERE WITH INTENTION TO ANNIHILATE THEE BUT   . . .  645 JERUSALEM 23    3
    IN SHAME & JEALOUSY TO ANNIHILATE JERUSALEM   . . . .  653 JERUSALEM 28      27
    EMBRACE WE SHALL PERISH ANNIHILATE DISCOVERD OUR DELUSIONS 725 JERUSALEM 82    4
    MY LOOMS WILL BE NO MORE & I ANNIHILATE VANISH FOR EVER  739 JERUSALEM 92     11
    THE DRUID SPECTRE WAS ANNIHILATE . . . . . . . .  745 JERUSALEM 98  .         6
ANNIHILATED
    ARE DRIVEN AWAY & ANNIHILATED WE NEVER CAN REPASS THE GATES 327 FOUR ZOAS 7  303
    CREATED TO BE ANNIHILATED & A NEW RATIO CREATED  . . . .  522 MILTON 32      35
    WHATEVER CAN BE CREATED CAN BE ANNIHILATED FORMS CANNOT   522 MILTON 32      36
    LEST THEY BE ANNIHILATED IN THY ANNIHILATION   . . . .  532 MILTON 40       16
    ALL THAT CAN BE ANN BE ANNIHILATED MUST BE ANNIHILATED .   532 MILTON 40   *  30
    SPIRIT A SELFHOOD WHICH MUST BE PUT OFF & ANNIHILATED ALWAY 533 MILTON 40    36
ANNIHILATES
    WHEN THE SIXFOLD FEMALE PERCIEVES THAT MILTON ANNIHILATES  522 MILTON 33     14
ANNIHILATING
    IN FEARLESS MAJESTY ANNIHILATING SELF LAUGHING TO SCORN   530 MILTON 38     41
ANNIHILATION    SEE SELF-ANNIHILATION,SELF ANNIHILATION
    CALLED ETERNAL ANNIHILATION THAT NONE BUT THE LIVING SHALL 522 MILTON 32     27
    BY DEATH & MISERY OF THOSE YOU LOVE & BY ANNIHILATION  . .  522 MILTON 33    13
    BUT THE DIVINE SAVIOUR CAN PASS IT WITHOUT ANNIHILATION   525 MILTON 35     21
    LEST THEY BE ANNIHILATED IN THY ANNIHILATION  . . . . .  532 MILTON 40       16
    REVENGEFUL O THAT DEATH & ANNIHILATION WERE THE SAME  . .  644 JERUSALEM 21   49
    LIKE ME THY VICTIM O THAT DEATH & ANNIHILATION WERE THE   646 JERUSALEM 23    40
        SAME
    FOURFOLD ANNIHILATION & AT THE CLANGOR OF THE ARROWS OF   745 JERUSALEM 98    7
        INTELLECT
ANNOUNCE
    IN THE HEAVENS TO ANNOUNCE THE SUNSHINE HOLIDAY  . . . .  618C ILLUS MILTON   PROSE
ANNOY
    HOW CAN A CHILD WHEN FEARS ANNOY  . . . . . . .  .   124 SCHOOL BOY/SI       18
    O LAMB (DIVINE) IT CANNOT THEE ANNOY O PITYING ONE  . . .  347 FOUR ZOAS 8  * 242
    THEY COME UP IN THE RIVERS & ANNOY THE NETHER PARTS   . .  354 FOUR ZOAS 8  * 512
ANNOYANCE
    LEADS ME VERY MUCH TO MY HURT & SOMETIMES TO THE ANNOYANCE 830D LETTER 30    PROSE
    THAT SPECTROUS FIEND TO HIS STATION WHOSE ANNOYANCE HAS   851D LETTER 50     PROSE
ANNOYD
    AS THE STENCH TERRIBLY ANNOYD US BOTH WE WENT INTO THE MILL 157B MARRIAGE HH 17 PROSE
    A FEARFUL JOURNEY ANNOYD . . . . . . . . . . .   234 URIZEN 20              49
    IN VAIN FOR HIDEOUS MONSTERS OF THE DEEPS ANNOYD HIM SORE  313 FOUR ZOAS 6    75
ANNOYING
    THE STINK OF YOUR DEAD CARCASES ANNOYING MAN & BEAST  . .  100 TIRIEL 1       46
ANOINT
    THEY ANOINT HIS FEET WITH OINTMENT . . . . . .   . . .  347 FOUR ZOAS 8     238
ANOINTED
    . . . SEAL THEM UP O ANOINTED IN EVERLASTING CHAINS  . . .  141 FRENCH REVOLTN 157
    ON BLACK CLOUDS HIS SORE WOUND ANOINTED  . . . .  . . .  251 AHANIA 3        48
    BUT DESTROY NOT THESE LITTLE ONES NOR MOCK THE LORD'S   670 JERUSALEM 42     41
        ANOINTED
    HE HATH CAST THEE OFF FOR EVER THE LITTLE ONES HE HATH   670 JERUSALEM 42     44
        ANOINTED
ANON
    BUT SOON I BUFFETTED THE TORRENT ANON LIKE TO A CLOUD  . .  105 TIRIEL 4      55
    THE RAGING FATHOMLESS ABYSS ANON A SERPENT FOLDING  . . .  196 AMERICA PREL 1  15
    WRITING THY BOOKS ANON A CLOUD FILLD WITH A WASTE OF SNOWS 322 FOUR ZOAS 7    81
ANOTHER    SEE ONE-ANOTHER
    IF I OBTAIN YOUR LEAVE I HAVE ANOTHER BOON  . . . . .  .   20 EDW THIRD/PS 2   43
    HE ANSWERD ME I HUNGER FOR ANOTHER BATTLE  . . . . . .    25 EDW THIRD/PS 3  156
    TO LIGHT ANOTHER PATTLE LAST NIGHT BENEATH  . . . . .     25 EDW THIRD/PS 3  160
    ANOTHER WEPT AND WISHD HEALTH TO HIS FATHER  . . . . .    25 EDW THIRD/PS 3  168
    HAS TO GET BEFORE ANOTHER IN ANY PURSUIT AFTER GLORY  . .   28 EDW THIRD/PS 4   15
    NO WILLIAM SAVE IT TILL ANOTHER TIME . . . . . . .      29B EDW THIRD/PS 4  PROSE
    AND HE IS TO WRITE ANOTHER ABOUT ALL US THAT ARE TO DIE  29C EDW THIRD/PS 4  PROSE
    ANOTHER MERRY MEETING AT THE HOUSE OF STEELYARD THE   59A ISLAND MOON 11     PROSE
        LAWGIVER
    THE HINDERING OF ACT IN ANOTHER THIS IS VICE  . . . . .   88D ANNO LAVATER    MARG
    TO HINDER ANOTHER IS NOT AN ACT IT IS THE CONTRARY  . . .   88D ANNO LAVATER    MARG
    HE WHO HINDERS ANOTHER OMITS HIS OWN DUTY AT THE SAME TIME  88D ANNO LAVATER    MARG
    MURDER IS HINDERING ANOTHER . . . . . . . . . .     88D ANNO LAVATER    MARG
    THEFT IS HINDERING ANOTHER BACKBITING UNDERMINING  . . .   88D ANNO LAVATER    MARG
    THE MOST SUBLIME ACT IS TO SET ANOTHER BEFORE YOU  . . .  151B MARRIAGE HH 7  PROSE
    SOME NATIONS HELD ONE PRINCIPLE FOR THE ORIGIN & SOME   153D MARRIAGE HH 12  PROSE
        ANOTHER
    AND SNATCHING AT ONE ANOTHER  . . . . . . . . .  157A MARRIAGE HH 17  PROSE
    BY PLUCKING OFF FIRST ONE LIMB AND THEN ANOTHER TILL THE  157B MARRIAGE HH 17  PROSE
        BODY
    I ANSWERD WE IMPOSE ON ONE ANOTHER & IT  . . . . . .  157B MARRIAGE HH 17  PROSE
    NOW HEAR ANOTHER HE HAS WRITTEN ALL THE OLD FALSHOODS  . .  157D MARRIAGE HH 21 *PROSE
    HAVE NOW ANOTHER PLAIN FACT ANY MAN OF MECHANICAL TALENTS  158A MARRIAGE HH 21  PROSE
    BUT FOR ANOTHER GIVES ITS EASE . . . . . . . .  .   162 CLOD PEBBLE/N    3
    TO BIND ANOTHER TO ITS DELIGHT . . . . . . . . .   162 CLOD PEBBLE/N   10
    NOUGHT LOVES ANOTHER AS ITSELF . . . . . . . . .   176 LIT BOY LST/N    1
    NOR VENERATES ANOTHER SO . . . . . . . . . .  .   176 LIT BOY LST/N    2
    ANOTHER FLOWER SHALL SPRING BECAUSE THE SOUL OF SWEET   189 V DAU ALBION 1   9
        DELIGHT
    OVER ANOTHER KIND OF SEAS AND IN ATMOSPHERES UNKNOWN   . .  192 V DAU ALBION 4   18
```

ANOTHER   (CONTINUED)

```
      HOW CAN ONE JOY ABSORB ANOTHER ARE NOT DIFFERENT JOYS  .  .   192 V DAU ALBION 5     5
      CAN THAT BE LOVE THAT DRINKS ANOTHER AS A SPONGE DRINKS        194 V DAU ALBION 7    17
         WATER
      AND EARTH HAD LOST ANOTHER PORTION OF THE INFINITE    .  .  .  202 AMERICA 14        18
      AND ANOTHER FROM THE HISTORY OF ENGLAND                      207C PRSPECTUS 1793  PROSE
      BUT FOR ANOTHER GIVES ITS EASE . . . . . . . . . .            211 CLOD PEBBLE/SE     3
      TO BIND ANOTHER TO ITS DELIGHT . . . . . . . . . .            211 CLOD PEBBLE/SE    10
      NOUGHT LOVES ANOTHER AS ITSELF . . . . . . . . . .            218 LIT BOY LST/SE     1
      NOR VENERATES ANOTHER SO . . . . . . . . . . . .             218 LIT BOY LST/SE     2
      BUT STILL ANOTHER GIRDLE . . . . . . . . .                    233 URIZEN 20         12
      ANOTHER GIRDLE SUCCEEDS                                       233 URIZEN 20         15
      AGAINST ONE ANOTHER SO LET THEM WAR ON SLAVES TO              245 SONG OF LOS 3     14
         THE ETERNAL ELEMENTS
      THE CITIES SEND TO ONE ANOTHER SAYING MY SONS ARE MAD  .  .   275 FOUR ZOAS 1      398
      IN WATERS & IN EARTH BENEATH THEY CRIED TO ONE ANOTHER  .     283 FOUR ZOAS 2      123
      WHAT ARE WE TERRORS TO ONE ANOTHER COME O BRETHREN            283 FOUR ZOAS 2      124
         WHEREFORE
      HE BURST IT BUT NEXT MORN ANOTHER GIRDLE SUCCEEDS    .  .  .  307 FOUR ZOAS 5       85
      FELT ALL THE SORROW PARENTS FEEL THEY WEPT TOWARD             309 FOUR ZOAS 5      144
         ONE ANOTHER
      AND IN ANOTHER RESURRECTION TO SORROW & WEARY TRAVEL   .  .   316 FOUR ZOAS 6      166
      THE WHOLE INTO ANOTHER WORLD BETTER SUITED TO OBEY    .  .    317 FOUR ZOAS 6      231
      THEN AS ANOTHER SELF ASTONISHD HUMANIZING & IN TEARS          328 FOUR ZOAS 7      340
      NOT AS ANOTHER BUT AS THY REAL SELF I AM THY SPECTRE   .  .   328 FOUR ZOAS 7      348
      IF [ONCE] WE UNITE IN ONE ANOTHER BETTER WORLD WILL BE   .    329 FOUR ZOAS 7      353
      BUT IF THOU DOST REFUSE ANOTHER BODY WILL BE PREPARED   .     329 FOUR ZOAS 7      357
      ALL THINGS SUBSIST ON ONE ANOTHER THENCEFORTH IN DESPAIR      330 FOUR ZOAS 7      391
      TROOP BY TROOP THE BEASTIAL DROVES REND ONE ANOTHER           344 FOUR ZOAS 8      116
         SOUNDING LOUD
      THEY SEEM TO ONE ANOTHER LAUGHING TERRIBLE AMONG              344 FOUR ZOAS 8      122
         THE BANNERS
      HIS MURDER ON ANOTHER SILENT I BOW WITH DREAD . . . .         345 FOUR ZOAS 8      166
      BUT FINDS THE POOLS FILLED WITH SERPENTS DEVOURING ONE        354 FOUR ZOAS 8      530
         ANOTHER
      TO BURN MYSTERY WITH FIRE & FORM ANOTHER FROM HER ASHES       357 FOUR ZOAS 8      616
      ONE PLANET [CRIES] CALLS TO ANOTHER & ONE STAR ENQUIRES       364 FOUR ZOAS 9   *  261
         OF ANOTHER
      TO ONE ANOTHER WHAT ARE WE & WHENCE IS OUR JOY & DELIGHT      373 FOUR ZOAS 9      609
      . . . THEY SAID TO ONE ANOTHER THIS IS SIN . . . . .          373 FOUR ZOAS 9      624
      THEY CATCH THE SHRIEKS IN CUPS OF GOLD THEY HAND THEM TO       377 FOUR ZOAS 9      768
         ONE ANOTHER
      WITH NEW WINE THAT THEY BEGAN TO TORMENT ONE ANOTHER . . .    378 FOUR ZOAS 9      787
      AWOKE THEY WEPT TO ONE ANOTHER & THEY REASCENDED   .  .  .    378 FOUR ZOAS 9      796
      REJOICE TO ONE ANOTHER LOUD THEIR VOICES SHAKE THE ABYSS      378 FOUR ZOAS 9      813
      OPINION IS (ONE) THING (PRINCIPLE) ANOTHER NO MAN            386B ANNO WATSON   *  MARG
         CAN CHANGE
      GOD NEVER MAKES ONE MAN MURDER ANOTHER NOR ONE NATION  .  .  388B ANNO WATSON      MARG
      & A DESTRUCTION FROM THE DESIGNS OF ANOTHER THE    .  .  .   388B ANNO WATSON      MARG
      TO EXTIRPATE A NATION BY MEANS OF ANOTHER NATION IS         388B ANNO WATSON   *  MARG
         AS WICKED
      AS TO DESTROY AN INDIVIDUAL BY MEANS OF ANOTHER    .  .  .   388B ANNO WATSON      MARG
      ANOTHER ARGUMENT IS THAT ALL THE COMMENTATORS . . . .       390C ANNO WATSON      MARG
      ANOTHER BUT IN THE SENTIMENTS & EXAMPLES WHICH     .  .  .   393B ANNO WATSON      MARG
      TRUTH THE RESULT OF REASONING IS ANOTHER THING    .  .  .   397C ANNO BACON       MARG
      MAN IS NOT IMPROVED BY THE HURT OF ANOTHER . . . . .        402C ANNO BACON       MARG
      WHAT IS SUSPITION IN ONE MAN IS CAUTION IN ANOTHER &  .     408D ANNO BACON       MARG
      TRUTH OR DISCERNMENT IN ANOTHER & IN SOME IT IS FOLLY  .    408D ANNO BACON       MARG
      AND ANOTHER FORM CREATE   . . . . . . . . .                  417 MY SPECTRE/N      65
      ANOTHER ENGLAND THERE I SAW . . . . . . . . . .              429 CRYSTL CABINET     9
      ANOTHER LONDON WITH ITS TOWER . . . . . . . . . .            429 CRYSTL CABINET    10
      ANOTHER THAMES & OTHER HILLS  . . . . . . . . . .            429 CRYSTL CABINET    11
      AND ANOTHER PLEASANT SURREY BOWER . . . . . . . .            429 CRYSTL CABINET    12
      ANOTHER MAIDEN LIKE HERSELF . . . . . . . . . .              429 CRYSTL CABINET    13
      O WILLIAM IF THOU DOST ANOTHER LOVE . . . . . . .            435 WILLIAM BOND      21
      DOST ANOTHER LOVE BETTER THAN POOR MARY . . . . . .          435 WILLIAM BOND      22
      YES MARY I DO ANOTHER LOVE  . . . . . . . . .                435 WILLIAM BOND      25
      ANOTHER I LOVE FAR BETTER THAN THEE . . . . . . .            435 WILLIAM BOND      26
      AND ANOTHER I WILL HAVE FOR MY WIFE . . . . . . .            435 WILLIAM BOND      27
      BY ANGELS FROM THE HANDS OF ANOTHER [AGED] APOSTLE   .  .   444B LAST JUDGMNT/L  PROSE
      IDLENESS IS ONE THING & DISSIPATION ANOTHER   .  .  .  .    454B ANNO REYNOLDS     MARG
      [HERES] HERE IS ANOTHER CONTRADICTION IF MICH ANGO  .  .    467D ANNO REYNOLDS  *  MARG
      LAID ON (INDISCRIMINATELY) & BROKEN ONE INTO ANOTHER   .    469A ANNO REYNOLDS  *  MARG
      ONE MAN STRIVING TO IMITATE ANOTHER MAN VARIES FROM MAN     470B ANNO REYNOLDS     MARG
      & COMES NOT AGAIN TILL ANOTHER IS BORN WITH IT   .  .  .    470D ANNO REYNOLDS     MARG
      THIS SENTENCE IS TO INTRODUCE ANOTHER IN CONDEMNATION  .    472B ANNO REYNOLDS     MARG
      IN ANOTHER DISCOURSE HE SAYS   . . . . . . . .              477B ANNO REYNOLDS     MARG
      & ONLY PROMOTES HARMONY OR BLENDING OF COLOURS ONE INTO     478C ANNO REYNOLDS     MARG
         ANOTHER
      [DORICK (OR) ?ONE ?COLUMN FROM ANOTHER]   . . . . .        SUPP ANNO REYNOLDS  *  MARG
      HOW SHOULD HE HE KNOW THE DUTIES OF ANOTHER O FOOLISH        487 MILTON 7          30
         FORBEARANCE
      AND ALL THE ELECT & ALL THE REDEEMD MOURND ONE TOWARD        488 MILTON 8          25
         ANOTHER
      AND ONE MUST DIE FOR ANOTHER THROUGHOUT ALL ETERNITY   .     491 MILTON 11         18
      THEY CATCH THE SHRIEKS IN CUPS OF GOLD THEY HAND THEM TO      514 MILTON 27         38
         ONE ANOTHER
      AT THAT BRIGHT GATE ANOTHER LARK MEETS HIM & BACK TO BACK     526 MILTON 36          2
      INSPIRED & AT THE DAWN OF DAY SEND OUT ANOTHER LARK   .       526 MILTON 36          6
      INTO ANOTHER HEAVEN TO CARRY NEWS UPON HIS WINGS . . . .      526 MILTON 36          7
      LOOK AT HIS PICTURES [TIS QUITE ANOTHER THING] ALL HAS        536 NO REAL STYL/N     4
         TAKEN WING
```

ANOTHER   (CONTINUED)
   ANOTHER   .   .   .   . 546A ANOTHER/N 1   TITLE
   ANOTHER   .   .   .   . 546A ANOTHER/N 2   TITLE
   "THAT RETURND AND THE MOST STRONG ANOTHER WITH THEM ALSO   560B EXHIBITION ADV   PROSE
      RETURND"
   IS TO BE ENQUIRED IN ANOTHER WORK ON PAINTING   .   .   .   .   .   565B DESC CAT 2   PROSE
   AS ONE AGE FALLS ANOTHER RISES DIFFERENT TO MORTAL SIGHT   567C DESC CAT 3   PROSE
   LIKE WALKING IN ANOTHER MAN'S STYLE OR SPEAKING   .   .   .   .   . 582D DESC CAT 9   PROSE
   OR LOOKING IN ANOTHER MAN'S STYLE AND MANNER   .   .   .   .   .   . 582D DESC CAT 9   PROSE
   AND OF ENDLESS REFLECTED LIGHTS THAT CONFUSE ONE ANOTHER   583B DESC CAT 9   PROSE
   DO WE DISTINGUISH ONE FACE OR COUNTENANCE FROM ANOTHER   .   585C DESC CAT 15   PROSE
   AS ONE AGE FALLS ANOTHER RISES DIFFERENT TO MORTAL SIGHT   589A CHAUCER/N   PROSE
   IS NOT LIKE A COAT MADE BY ANOTHER BUT IS AN EMANATION   593B PUB ADDRESS/N   PROSE
   INTEND IT SHOULD BE SO NONE BUT BLOCKHEADS COPY ONE ANOTHER   601D PUB ADDRESS/N   PROSE
   ANOTHER DEMON WITH A KEY HAS THE CHARGE OF SIN   .   .   .   .   606C V LAST JUDG/N   PROSE
   IN ETERNITY ONE THING NEVER CHANGES INTO ANOTHER THING   .   607A V LAST JUDG/N   PROSE
   BUT NOT CHANGED OR TRANSFORMED INTO ANOTHER IDENTITY   607A V LAST JUDG/N   PROSE
   ANOTHER THING CHANGING WATER INTO WINE BY JESUS   .   .   .   .   607B V LAST JUDG/N   PROSE
   & DESTROY ONE ANOTHER BY EVERY MEANS IN THEIR POWER   .   .   615A V LAST JUDG/N   PROSE
   EVEN THE DEVILS LOVE ONE ANOTHER IN THEIR WAY   .   .   .   .   . 616B V LAST JUDG/N   PROSE
   THEY TORMENT ONE ANOTHER FOR OTHER REASONS THAN HATE OR   616B V LAST JUDG/N   PROSE
      ENVY
   THE BIBLE NEVER TELLS US THAT DEVILS TORMENT ONE ANOTHER   616B V LAST JUDG/N   PROSE
      THRO ENVY
   BUT FOR WHAT DO THEY TORMENT ONE ANOTHER I ANSWER   .   .   .   . 616C V LAST JUDG/N   PROSE
   THEY DO NOT ENVY ONE ANOTHER THEY CONTEMN & DESPISE   .   .   616C V LAST JUDG/N   PROSE
   ONE ANOTHER FORGIVENESS OF SIN IS ONLY AT THE JUDGMENT SEAT   616D V LAST JUDG/N   PROSE
   EXPECT HOLINESS FROM ONE ANOTHER BUT FROM GOD ONLY   .   .   .   616D V LAST JUDG/N   PROSE
   THEY ARE NOT ALWAYS PRYING AFTER GOOD & EVIL IN ONE ANOTHER   616D V LAST JUDG/N   PROSE
   I MUST CREATE A SYSTEM OR BE ENSLAVD BY ANOTHER MAN'S   .   .   629 JERUSALEM 10   20
   VICTIMS TO ONE ANOTHER & DREADFULLY PLOTTING AGAINST EACH   671 JERUSALEM 43   4
      OTHER
   VERULAM LONDON YORK EDINBURGH MOURNING ONE TOWARDS ANOTHER   676 JERUSALEM 46   24
   HE WHO WOULD DO GOOD TO ANOTHER MUST DO IT IN MINUTE   687 JERUSALEM 55   60
      PARTICULARS
   AND ONE DAUGHTER OF LOS SAT AT THE FIERY REEL & ANOTHER   691 JERUSALEM 59   26
   AND ANOTHER DAUGHTER OF LOS SAT AT THE SPINNING WHEEL   .   691 JERUSALEM 59   29
   BABYLON COME UP TO JERUSALEM AND ANOTHER VOICE ANSWERD   695 JERUSALEM 61   35
      SAYING
   .   .   . PALE THEY LOOK ON ONE ANOTHER   .   .   .   .   .   .   701 JERUSALEM 65   76
   THEY LOOK ON ONE ANOTHER THE MOUNTAIN CALLS OUT TO THE   703 JERUSALEM 66   58
      MOUNTAIN
   IN ANOTHER CALLING IT PRIDE & SELFISHNESS & SIN   .   .   .   .   . 717C JERUSALEM 77   PROSE
   (DEFORMITY) SHE GAVE HER BEAUTY TO ANOTHER BEARING ABROAD   726 JERUSALEM 82   69
   THEN THOU WILT CREATE ANOTHER FEMALE ACCORDING TO THY WILL   739 JERUSALEM 92   12
   ONE FOR ANOTHER TO PUT OFF BY FORGIVENESS EVERY SIN   .   .   .   743 JERUSALEM 96   19
   OFFERING OF SELF FOR ANOTHER IS THIS FRIENDSHIP &   743 JERUSALEM 96   21
      BROTHERHOOD
   AS GOD IS LOVE EVERY KINDNESS TO ANOTHER IS A LITTLE DEATH   743 JERUSALEM 96   27
   WHICH IS THIS IF YOU FORGIVE ONE ANOTHER YOUR TRESPASSES   757D EV GOSPEL   PROSE
   CHARACTER ITS GOODNESS OR BADNESS IS ANOTHER CONSIDERATION   778B HOMERS POETRY   PROSE
   "RESULT" WAS WRIT BY ANOTHER HAND & MIND   .   .   .   .   .   .   783D ANNO WW POEMS   MARG
   & ONE ANOTHER LEAD US NOT TO READ THE BIBLE   .   .   .   .   .   788D ANNO THORNTON   MARG
   THAT EXECUTION IS THE POWER OF ONE & INVENTION OF ANOTHER   790C LETTER 2   PROSE
   BETTER THAN SLAVISHLY FOLLOWING THE TRACK OF ANOTHER   .   792A LETTER 4   PROSE
   IS NOT MERIT IN ONE A CAUSE OF ENVY IN ANOTHER   .   .   .   793B LETTER 5   PROSE
   TO ENGRAVE AFTER ANOTHER PAINTER IS INFINITELY MORE   794B LETTER 5   PROSE
      LABORIOUS
   I HAVE NO OBJECTION TO ENGRAVING AFTER ANOTHER ARTIST   .   794C LETTER 5   PROSE
   AFTER ANOTHER ARTIST BUT ABOVE ALL I FEEL MYSELF HAPPY &   795C LETTER 6   PROSE
   FROM ONE CHAISE TO ANOTHER FOR WE HAD SEVEN DIFFERENT   .   802B LETTER 14   PROSE
   A NEW LIFE BECAUSE ANOTHER COVERING OF EARTH IS SHAKEN OFF   802B LETTER 14   PROSE
   FROM ONE CHAISE TO ANOTHER WE HAD SEVEN DIFFERENT   .   .   803A LETTER 15   PROSE
   DETERMINED TO PAINT ANOTHER PORTRAIT OF YOU FROM LIFE IN MY   810B LETTER 20   PROSE
   HISTORICAL DESIGNING IS ONE THING & PORTRAIT PAINTING   810B LETTER 20   PROSE
      ANOTHER
   ABOUT YOUR HEALTH IN ANOTHER PART OF YOUR LETTER MAKES ME   811C LETTER 22   PROSE
   REMAIN ANOTHER WINTER HERE BUT TO RETURN TO LONDON   .   .   813C LETTER 22   PROSE
   ANOTHER SUN FEEDS OUR LIFE'S STREAMS   .   .   .   .   818 HAPPINESS/L   65
   THE SOLDIER SAID CONFIRMD BY ANOTHER PERSON IN THE COACH I   833C LETTER 33   PROSE
   FORWARDNESS & YOU SHALL HAVE PROOFS IN ANOTHER WEEK   .   .   837A LETTER 35   PROSE
   ANOTHER OF THE EXHIBITION WHICH I HAVE NOT YET SEEN   .   .   844C LETTER 43   PROSE
   IN LONDON EVERY CALUMNY AND FALSEHOOD UTTERD AGAINST   847B LETTER 44   PROSE
      ANOTHER
   THE PLEASURE OF SEEING ANOTHER POEM FROM YOUR HANDS HAS   851D LETTER 50   PROSE
   AND THE SHIPWRECK QUITE ANOTHER THING FROM WHAT YOU OR   .   852C LETTER 50   PROSE
   & AT THE VERY IDEA OF ANOTHER JOURNEY TO SWEET FELPHAM   .   857C LETTER 54   PROSE
   TO SEE ANOTHER COPY BY ANOTHER HAND   .   .   .   .   .   .   859C LETTER 56   PROSE
   IN TOGETHER & WITH ANOTHER PASSENGER ENTERD INTO   869C LETTER 70   PROSE
      CONVERSATION
   NO DISCIPLINE WILL TURN ONE MAN INTO ANOTHER EVEN IN   .   871A LETTER 72   PROSE
   I HAVE HAD ANOTHER DESPERATE SHIVERING FIT IT CAME ON   .   872B LETTER 75   PROSE
   SO THAT I CONCLUDE ANOTHER WEEK MUST PASS BEFORE I DARE   873A LETTER 76   PROSE
   CONGRATULATE YOU ON THE RECEIT OF ANOTHER FINE BOY   .   .   873B LETTER 77   PROSE
   THO NOT ITS EFFECTS WEAKNESS &C COMES ANOTHER TO HINDER MY   874D LETTER 80   PROSE
   NOT DARE TO LEAVE HIS ROOM BY ANY MEANS HE HAD ANOTHER   SUPP LETTER 81A   *PROSE
   ENGLISHMEN ARE ALL INTERMEASURABLE ONE BY ANOTHER   .   .   878B LETTER 88   PROSE
ANOTHER'S
   AND ONE MAN LAY IN ANOTHER'S WAY   .   .   .   .   17 BLIND-MANS/PS   69
   LEANING ON ONE ANOTHER'S NECKS ALTERNATELY   .   .   .   .   .   35D COUCH DEATH/PS   PROSE
   ("UNHAPPINESS AT ANOTHER'S ERRORS") EXCELLENT   .   .   .   .   . 73A ANNO LAVATER   MARG
   ON ANOTHER'S SORROW   .   .   .   . 122B ON ANOTHERS/SI   TITLE

                                                        PAGE   TITLE   LINE
ANOTHER'S   (CONTINUED)
    CAN I SEE ANOTHER'S WOE . . . .   122 ON ANOTHERS/SI   1
    CAN I SEE ANOTHER'S GRIEF . . . .   122 ON ANOTHERS/SI   3
    . . . ENTER INTO THE INFINITE LABYRINTH OF ANOTHER'S BRAIN   142 FRENCH REVOLTN   190
    OF ANOTHER'S HIGH FLAMING RICH BOSOM . . . .   142 FRENCH REVOLTN   192
    JOYS IN ANOTHER'S LOSS OF EASE . . . .   162 CLOD PEBBLE/N   11
    FOR THE STEPS OF ANOTHER'S DOOR . . . . . .   186 LET BROTHELS/N   47
    FOR THE [STEPS] STONE OF ANOTHER'S DOOR . . . . . .   186 LET BROTHELS/N   65
    JOYS IN ANOTHER'S LOSS OF EASE . . . .   211 CLOD PEBBLE/SE   11
    MUTUAL THERE WE DWELT IN ONE ANOTHER'S JOY REVOLVING   .   327 FOUR ZOAS 7   273
    WE FALL ON ONE ANOTHER'S NECKS MORE CLOSELY WE EMBRACE   .   374 FOUR ZOAS 9   639
    ONE MAN'S REVENGE OR LOVE IS NOT THE SAME AS ANOTHER'S   .   398D ANNO BACON   MARG
    AND THE BITTER GROAN [FOR ANOTHER'S] OF THE MARTYR'S WOE   420 I SAW A MONK/N   60
    A BEGGAR AT ANOTHER'S DOOR . . . .   426 MENTAL TRAVLER   52
    IN THE GENTLE RELIEF OF ANOTHER'S CARE . . . .   436 WILLIAM BOND   50
    THEY OUGHT NOT WHEN IT COMES TO ANOTHER'S TURN   . . .   556 IF MEN ACT/N   2
    MUTUAL IN ONE ANOTHER'S LOVE AND WRATH ALL RENEWING . . .   664 JERUSALEM 38   16
    A DREAM ON ANOTHER'S SORROW THE LITTLE BOY LOST . . . SUPP LETTER 66A   *PROSE
ANSWER
    O WHAT HAVE KINGS TO ANSWER FOR . . . .   13 GWIN KING/PS   97
    O WHO CAN ANSWER AT THE THRONE OF GOD . . . . . .   33 EDW FOURTH/PS   14
    ON EACH OTHER THEIR TONGUES WENT IN QUESTION & ANSWER .   44C ISLAND MOON 1   PROSE
    WAS PREPARED TO GIVE A FORMAL ANSWER TO THE COMPANY . .   45B ISLAND MOON 1   PROSE
    A QUERY & AN ANSWER ARE AS DIFFERENT . . . .   45D ISLAND MOON 1   PROSE
    ("ANSWER THIS...AND YOU WILL KNOW YOURSELF ") ALL GOLD   73C ANNO LAVATER   MARG
    ("YOU BEG AS YOU QUESTION YOU GIVE AS YOU ANSWER")   77D ANNO LAVATER   MARG
      EXCELLENT
    ANSWER ESSENCE IS NOT IDENTITY BUT FROM ESSENCE PROCEEDS   91A ANNO SWED LOVE   MARG
      IDENTITY
    AND NONE TO ANSWER NONE TO CHERISH THEE WITH MOTHER'S   129 BOOK OF THEL 4   6
      SMILES
    DEPART ANSWER NOT FOR THE TEMPEST MUST FALL . . .   .   139 FRENCH REVOLTN   120
    SOME WILL SAY IS NOT GOD ALONE THE PROLIFIC I ANSWER .   155B MARRIAGE HH 15   PROSE
    [THE] EARTH'S ANSWER . . . .   168D EARTHS ANSWR/N   TITLE
    AN ANSWER TO THE PARSON . . . .   181B ANSWR PARSON/N   TITLE
    NO TRUMPETS ANSWER NO REPLY OF CLARIONS OR OF FIFES   . .   200 AMERICA 10   3
    EARTH'S ANSWER . . . .   210D EARTHS ANSWR/SE   TITLE
    ANSWEREST THOU NOT SAID URIZEN THEN THOU MAIST ANSWER ME   312 FOUR ZOAS 6   12
    OR WILT THOU ANSWER YOUNGEST WOMAN CLAD IN SHINING GREEN   312 FOUR ZOAS 6   17
    HE CALLD THE DEEP BURIED HIS VOICE & ANSWER NONE RETURND   360 FOUR ZOAS 9   136
    O THOU CREATING VOICE THAT CALLEST & WHO SHALL ANSWER THEE   367 FOUR ZOAS 9   400
    YOU ANSWER NOT THEN AM I SET YOUR MISTRESS IN THIS GARDEN   368 FOUR ZOAS 9   429
    I WILL CALL & WHO SHALL ANSWER ME I WILL SING WHO SHALL   368 FOUR ZOAS 9   440
      REPLY
    SHE CALLD BUT NONE COULD ANSWER HER & THE ECCHO OF HER   370 FOUR ZOAS 9   499
      VOICE RETURND
    WHICH CALLS UPON HIS OPPONENT LOUDLY FOR AN ANSWER   . . .   390D ANNO WATSON   MARG
    THIS IS NOT A SATISFACTORY ANSWER TO PRODUCE AN EFFECT OF   463A ANNO REYNOLDS   MARG
    I ANSWER OF NONE AT ALL BUT THE CONTRARY AS YOU WELL KNOW   573A DESC CAT 3   PROSE
    BUT FOR WHAT DO THEY TORMENT ONE ANOTHER I ANSWER   . . .   616C V LAST JUDG/N   PROSE
    I HAVE TAUGHT MY CHILDREN SACRIFICES OF CRUELTY WHAT SHALL   646 JERUSALEM 23   17
      I ANSWER
    ANSWER THIS TO YOURSELVES & EXPEL FROM AMONG YOU . . .   717B JERUSALEM 77   PROSE
    WORLD ESPECIALLY IF I SHOULD HAVE TO ANSWER FOR IT I FEEL   793A LETTER 5   PROSE
      VERY
    YOU HAVE SAID IN IT CALLD UPON ME FOR AN IMMEDIATE ANSWER   811B LETTER 22   PROSE
    TIME TO YOU I ANSWER I HAVE BEEN VERY UNHAPPY & COULD NOT   815C LETTER 23   PROSE
    THE MINIATURE I PROMISSD TO MRS BUTTS I ANSWER I HAVE NOT   815C LETTER 23   PROSE
    HE MADE ME AN IMPERTINENT ANSWER I INSISTED ON HIS LEAVING   827A LETTER 28   PROSE
    YOUR ANSWER TO THE PROPOSAL YOU WILL IF YOU THINK   842A LETTER 41   PROSE
      FIT DIRECT
    & THEREFORE CANNOT TELL ME HOW HE UNDERSTOOD YOUR ANSWER   842C LETTER 42   *PROSE
    YOU FOR MORE MONEY BUT HOWEVER YOUR KIND ANSWER TO   . .   854D LETTER 53   PROSE
    COMMISSION ME TO ANSWER HIM WHATEVER YOU COMMAND . . .   857B LETTER 54   PROSE
    CANNOT ANSWER P'S (PHILLIPS) PROPOSAL TILL I HAVE YOUR .   858C LETTER 55   PROSE
    EARTH'S ANSWER NURSE'S SONG THE FLY THE TYGER   . . . SUPP LETTER 66A   *PROSE
    ON (ONE) PLATE O LAPWING &C AN ANSWER TO THE PARSON   . SUPP ON PLATE/N101   *PROSE
ANSWERABLE
    MY WIFE ALONE IS ANSWERABLE FOR THEIR HAVING EXISTED IN ANY   879C LETTER 89   PROSE
ANSWERD
    HE ANSWERD ME I HUNGER FOR ANOTHER BATTLE . . . . .   25 EDW THIRD/PS 3   156
    BURND OUT HE ANSWERD HE WAS PIG ENOUGH . . . . . .   25 EDW THIRD/PS 3   159
    THE CYNIC ANSWERD THEY ARE ONLY QUARRELING ABOUT VOLTAIRE   45C ISLAND MOON 1   PROSE
    OBTUSE ANGLE ANSWERD QUICKLY HE WAS THE GOD OF PHYSIC .   46D ISLAND MOON 3   PROSE
    OBTUSE ANGLE ANSWERD INDEED HE DID . . . .   47A ISLAND MOON 3   PROSE
    THAT WAS AS GREAT AS CHATTERTON [OBTUSE ANGLE ANSWERD]   47A ISLAND MOON 3   PROSE
    HAY HOW SHOULD I KNOW ANSWERD OBTUSE ANGLE WHO WAS   47A ISLAND MOON 3   PROSE
      IT ARADOBO
    OBTUSE ANGLE ANSWERD THE HEATHENS IN THE OLD AGES   .   47B ISLAND MOON 3   *PROSE
    TO THIS SCOPPRELL ANSWERD I THINK THE LADIES' DISCOURSES .   53C ISLAND MOON 8   PROSE
    VERY LIKE A GOAT'S FACE SHE ANSWERD . . . . . .   62D ISLAND MOON 11   PROSE
    THEN TIRIEL FROWND & ANSWERD DID I NOT COMMAND YOU SAYING   103 TIRIEL 3   36
    ANSWERD THE LOVELY MAID AND SAID I AM A WATRY WEED . . .   127 BOOK OF THEL 1   16
    THEL ANSWERD O THOU LITTLE VIRGIN OF THE PEACEFUL VALLEY   128 BOOK OF THEL 2   3
    QUEEN OF THE VALES THE LILLY ANSWERD ASK THE TENDER CLOUD   128 BOOK OF THEL 2   13
    THE CLOUD RECLIND UPON HIS AIRY THRONE AND ANSWERD THUS   129 BOOK OF THEL 3   24
    QUEEN OF THE VALES THE MATRON CLAY ANSWERD I HEARD THY   130 BOOK OF THEL 5   14
      SIGHS
    ISAIAH ANSWERD I SAW NO GOD NOR HEARD ANY . . . . .   153C MARRIAGE HH 12   PROSE
    MADE HIM GO NAKED AND BAREFOOT THREE YEARS HE ANSWERD   .   154A MARRIAGE HH 12   PROSE
    RIGHT & LEFT SIDE HE ANSWERD THE DESIRE OF RAISING OTHER   154B MARRIAGE HH 12   PROSE
      MEN

		PAGE	TITLE	LINE

ANSWERD   (CONTINUED)
```
    BUT HE ANSWERD DO NOT PRESUME O YOUNG-MAN  . . . . .  . 156A MARRIAGE HH 17    PROSE
    I ANSWERD ALL THAT WE SAW WAS OWING TO YOUR METAPHYSICS  156D MARRIAGE HH 17    PROSE
    I ANSWERD WE IMPOSE ON ONE ANOTHER & IT  .  . . . . .  . 157B MARRIAGE HH 17    PROSE
    THE DEVIL ANSWERD BRAY A FOOL IN A MORTER WITH WHEAT  .  158C MARRIAGE HH 22    PROSE
    THE QUESTION ANSWERD  .  . . . . . . . . . . . . . . .  . 180A QUESTN ANSRD/N   TITLE
    SEVERAL QUESTIONS ANSWERD  . . . . . . . . . . . . . .  184B SEVRL QUESTN/N  *TITLE
    THE TERROR ANSWERD I AM ORC WREATHD ROUND THE ACCURSED TREE  198 AMERICA 8          1
    SEEING HIMSELF IN MY POSSESSION THUS HE ANSWERD ME  . . .  237 EUROPE INTRO        11
    HE LAUGHING ANSWERD I WILL WRITE A BOOK ON LEAVES      237 EUROPE INTRO        14
       OF FLOWERS
    SHE TREMBLING ANSWERD WHEREFORE WAS I BORN AND WHAT AM I   268 FOUR ZOAS 1        158
    BUT ENITHARMON ANSWERD WITH A DROPPING TEAR & [?SMILING]   271 FOUR ZOAS 1    *   252
      . . .
    [LOS] HE ANSWERD DARKNING MORE WITH [FOUL] INDIGNATION     272 FOUR ZOAS 1        282
       HID IN SMILES
    LOS ANSWERD FURIOUS ART THOU ONE OF THOSE WHO WHEN MOST    273 FOUR ZOAS 1        331
       COMPLACENT
    ENITHARMON ANSWERD SECURE NOW FROM THE SMITINGS OF THY     288 FOUR ZOAS 2        309
       POWER . . .
    LOS ANSWERD THEREFORE FADE I THUS DISSOLVD IN RAPTURD      288 FOUR ZOAS 2        318
       TRANCE
    ENITHARMON ANSWERD WHEREFORE DIDST THOU THROW THINE ARMS   288 FOUR ZOAS 2        327
       AROUND
    FOR THOU HAST TOUCHD MY FIVE SENSES & THEY ANSWERD THEE    290 FOUR ZOAS 2        376
    LOS ANSWERD IN HIS FURIOUS PRIDE SPARKS ISSUING FROM HIS   298 FOUR ZOAS 4         34
       HAIR
    SHE ANSWERD NOT BUT FILLD HER URN & POURD IT FORTH ABROAD  312 FOUR ZOAS 6         11
    SHE ANSWERD NOT BUT STRETCHD HER ARMS & THREW HER LIMBS    312 FOUR ZOAS 6    *    16
       ABROAD
    SOOTHING OR FURIOUS NO ONE ANSWERD EVERY ONE WRAPD UP  .  . 315 FOUR ZOAS 6        127
    ORC ANSWERD CURSE THY HOARY BROWS WHAT DOST THOU IN THIS   322 FOUR ZOAS 7         69
       DEEP
    URIZEN ANSWERD READ MY BOOKS EXPLORE MY CONSTELLATIONS  .  322 FOUR ZOAS 7         90
    THEN ORC [ANSWERD] CRIED CURSE THY COLD HYPOCRISY . . .    323 FOUR ZOAS 7        135
    THE SHADOW OF ENITHARMON ANSWERD ART THOU TERRIBLE SHADE   326 FOUR ZOAS 7        231
    LOS FURIOUS ANSWERD SPECTRE HORRIBLE THY WORDS ASTOUND     329 FOUR ZOAS 7        361
       MY EAR
    LOS TREMBLING ANSWERD NOW I FEEL THE WEIGHT OF STERN       330 FOUR ZOAS 7        411
       REPENTANCE
    ENITHARMON ANSWERD I BEHOLD THE LAMB OF GOD DESCENDING     330 FOUR ZOAS 7        424
    [THE SHADOWY VOICE ANSWERD O URIZEN PRINCE OF LIGHT]  . .  333 FOUR ZOAS 7B   *    11
    HE ANSWERD HER WITH TENDERNESS & LOVE NOT UNINSPIRD  . .   350 FOUR ZOAS 8    *   347
    SHE ANSWERD THUS WHOSE VOICE IS THIS . . . . . . . .  · 367 FOUR ZOAS 9        393
    THEREFORE THE BISHOP HAS NOT ANSWERD PAINE . . . . . . 388B ANNO WATSON       MARG
    THE BISHOP HAS NOT ANSWERD ONE OF PAINE'S GRAND OBJECTIONS 396C ANNO WATSON       MARG
    ORC ANSWERD TAKE NOT THE HUMAN FORM O LOVELIEST TAKE NOT   499 MILTON 18          26
    THE VIRGIN ANSWERD KNOWEST THOU OF MILTON WHO DESCENDED    527 MILTON 37           1
    WHILE LOS ANSWERD UNTERRIFIED TO THE OPAKE BLACKENING FIEND 625 JERUSALEM 7         8
    LOS ANSWERD ALTHO I KNOW NOT THIS I KNOW FAR WORSE THAN    626 JERUSALEM 7         51
       THIS
    THE SPECTRE ANSWERD ART THOU NOT ASHAMD OF THOSE THY SINS  629 JERUSALEM 10       37
    JERUSALEM ANSWERD WITH SOFT TEARS OVER THE VALLEYS  . .   643 JERUSALEM 20       21
    THEN VALA ANSWERD SPREADING HER SCARLET VEIL OVER ALBION   644 JERUSALEM 21       50
    LOS ANSWERD TROUBLED AND HIS SOUL WAS RENT IN TWAIN  . . . 666 JERUSALEM 39   *   24
    LOS ANSWERD RIGHTEOUSNESS & JUSTICE I GIVE THEE IN RETURN  670 JERUSALEM 42       19
    MARRY A HARLOT & AN ADULTERESS MARY ANSWERD ART THOU MORE  694 JERUSALEM 61        6
       PURE
    BABYLON COME UP TO JERUSALEM AND ANOTHER VOICE ANSWERD     695 JERUSALEM 61       35
       SAYING
    ITS NAME HE ANSWERD IT IS THE WHEEL OF RELIGION  . . . .   718 STOOD AMONG/J  *   13
    HE ANSWERD JESUS DIED BECAUSE HE STROVE . . . . . . .      718 STOOD AMONG/J      16
    ENITHARMON ANSWERD NO I WILL SIEZE THY FIBRES & WEAVE  . . 732 JERUSALEM 87       12
    LOS ANSWERD SIGHING LIKE THE BELLOWS OF HIS FURNACES  .  . 733 JERUSALEM 88        1
    ENITHARMON ANSWERD THIS IS WOMAN'S WORLD NOR NEED SHE ANY  733 JERUSALEM 88       16
    SO LOS SPOKE ENITHARMON ANSWERD IN GREAT TERROR IN        739 JERUSALEM 92        7
       LAMBETH'S VALE
    LOS ANSWERD SWIFT AS THE SHUTTLE OF GOLD SEXES MUST VANISH 739 JERUSALEM 92       13
       & CEASE
    HAPPINESS IS NOT GOOD FOR MORTALS & THEY OUGHT TO         830C LETTER 30         PROSE
       BE ANSWERD
    WHICH IS THE SIZE OF A QUARTO PRINTED PAGE HE ANSWERD  . 848B LETTER 45         PROSE
    HOW A VALUE WAS SET ON ANY LITERARY WORK HE ANSWERD . . 860A LETTER 56         PROSE
ANSWERED
    I ANSWERED HEAVENLY GODDESS I AM WRAPPED IN MORTALITY  . .  37B CONTEMPLATN/PS  PROSE
    THE ANGEL ANSWERED MY NAME IS WONDERFUL . . . . . . .  .   40C SAMSON/PS        PROSE
    ANSWERED WITH A NINEFOLD YELL  . . . . . . . . . . . . . . 187 WHEN KLOPSTK/N    14
    THEN THEOTORMON BROKE HIS SILENCE AND HE ANSWERED  . .  .  191 V DAU ALBION 3     21
    BY ASKING IF HE KNEW WHO FURNISHD THE PAPER HE ANSWERED   846D LETTER 44         PROSE
ANSWEREST
    ANSWEREST THOU NOT SAID URIZEN THEN THOU MAIST ANSWER ME   312 FOUR ZOAS 6        12
ANSWERING
    TALKING WITH DEATH ANSWERING HIS HARD DEMANDS . . . . .     30 EDW THIRD/PS 5    10
    BUT NEVER CAPABLE OF ANSWERING WHO SITS WITH A SLY GRIN    533 MILTON 41          13
ANSWERS
    IM SURE THIS IS NOT RELIGION ANSWERS THE OTHER  . . . .     48C ISLAND MOON 4    PROSE
    THE SPECTRE OF URTHONA [ANSWERS] SEEING ENITHARMON WRITHD  299 FOUR ZOAS 4        76
    THE PRISONER ANSWERS YOU SCOURGD MY FATHER TO DEATH BEFORE 364 FOUR ZOAS 9       275
       MY FACE
ANTAGONIST
    THAT MY ANTAGONIST IS SILENCD COMPLETELY  . . . . . .  . 825D LETTER 27         PROSE
```

ANTAMON
    WHERE IS THE YOUTHFUL ANTAMON PRINCE OF THE PEARLY DEW . .   244 EUROPE 14   15
    O ANTAMON WHY WILT THOU LEAVE THY MOTHER ENITHARMON . .   244 EUROPE 14   16
    MY ANTAMON THE SEVEN CHURCHES OF LEUTHA SEEK THY LOVE   244 EUROPE 14   20
    SO ANTAMON CALLD UP LEUTHA FROM HER VALLEYS OF DELIGHT . .   246 SONG OF LOS 3   28
    THEOTORMON BROMION ANTAMON ANANTON OZOTH OHANA . . . .   350 FOUR ZOAS 8   358
    ANTAMON TAKES THEM INTO HIS BEAUTIFUL FLEXIBLE HANDS . .   515 MILTON 28   13
    THE SOFT HANDS OF ANTAMON DRAW THE INDELIBLE LINE . .   515 MILTON 28   16
    PUTS ON THE SWEET FORM THEN SMILES ANTAMON BRIGHT THRO   515 MILTON 28   18
      HIS WINDOWS
    WHERE HIDES MY CHILD IN OXFORD HIDEST THOU WITH ANTAMON   727 JERUSALEM 83   28
ANTEDILUVIANS
    ONE OF THE ANTEDILUVIANS WHO ARE OUR ENERGIES . . . .   155C MARRIAGE HH 15   PROSE
    & YET WERE SAVED FROM AMONG THE ANTEDILUVIANS WHO PERISHED   611D V LAST JUDG/N   PROSE
ANTHEM
    THIS EVENING [WE'D] WE'LL ALL GET DRUNK I SAY DASH AN ANTHEM 54B ISLAND MOON 9 *PROSE
    AN ANTHEM SAID SUCTION . . . .   54B ISLAND MOON 9   PROSE
ANTICHRIST
    BLASPHEMOUS DEMON ANTICHRIST HATER OF DIGNITIES . . .   198 AMERICA 7   5
    WATSON HAS DEFENDED ANTICHRIST . . . .   383D ANNO WATSON   MARG
    OF SELFHOOD BODY PUT OFF THE ANTICHRIST ACCURSED . . .   734 JERUSALEM 89   10
    THEY BECOME ONE WITH THE ANTICHRIST & ARE ABSORBD IN HIM   736 JERUSALEM 89   62
    IF HE HAD BEEN [THE] ANTICHRIST CREEPING JESUS . . .   750 EV GOSPEL(C)/N   25
    IF HE HAD BEEN [THE] ANTICHRIST CREEPING JESUS . . .   752 EV GOSPEL(D)/N   59
    FOR WHAT IS ANTICHRIST BUT THOSE . . . . . .   758 EV GOSPEL (1)   11
    THE OUTWARD CEREMONY IS ANTICHRIST . . . . .   776A INSC LAOCOON   PROSE
    OF THE SEVEN CHURCHES IN ASIA ANTICHRIST SCIENCE . . .   777B INSC LAOCOON   PROSE
    THIS IS THE MOST DAMNABLE FALSHOOD OF SATAN & HIS   785B ILLUS DANTE 7   PROSE
      ANTICHRIST
    THE GREEK & ROMAN CLASSICS IS THE ANTICHRIST I SAY IS . .   786C ANNO THORNTON   MARG
ANTIENT   SEE ANCIENT
    FROM ANTIENT MELODY HAVE CEASD . . . . . .   10 TO MUSES/PS   4
    HOW HAVE YOU LEFT THE ANTIENT LOVE . . . . .   11 TO MUSES/PS   13
ANTIQUARIAN
    IN COMES ETRUSCAN COLUMN THE ANTIQUARIAN & AFTER . . .   44B ISLAND MOON 1   PROSE
    WHILE THE ANTIQUARIAN SEEMD TO BE TALKING OF VIRTUOUS CATS   44B ISLAND MOON 1   PROSE
    SIR SAID THE ANTIQUARIAN I HAVE SEEN THESE WORKS . . .   44D ISLAND MOON 1   PROSE
    SIR SAID THE ANTIQUARIAN ACCORDING TO MY OPINION . . .   44D ISLAND MOON 1   PROSE
    REASON SIR SAID THE ANTIQUARIAN I'LL GIVE YOU AN . . .   45A ISLAND MOON 1   PROSE
    THE ANTIQUARIAN HERE GOT UP & HEMMING TWICE . . .   45D ISLAND MOON 1   PROSE
    HERE THE ANTIQUARIAN SHRUGGD UP HIS SHOULDERS . . .   46A ISLAND MOON 1   PROSE
    ARRANGED IS AN ENQUIRY WORTHY OF BOTH THE ANTIQUARIAN . .   578D DESC CAT 5   *PROSE
ANTIQUARIES
    SAME THING AS JACOB BRYANT AND ALL ANTIQUARIES HAVE PROVED   578D DESC CAT 5   PROSE
ANTIQUE
    HIS KIND EVERY ONE IS AN ANTIQUE STATUE . . . .   571A DESC CAT 3   PROSE
    AND THE ANTIQUE THOSE WHO SEPARATE PAINTING FROM DRAWING   573B DESC CAT 3   PROSE
    IS HYMEN AT A MARRIAGE & THE ANTIQUE PAGEANTRY ATTENDING IT 618D ILLUS MILTON   PROSE
    WHAT WE CALL ANTIQUE GEMS ARE THE GEMS OF AARON'S BREAST   777D INSC LAOCOON   PROSE
      PLATE
    NOW YOU WILL I HOPE SHEW ALL THE FAMILY OF ANTIQUE BORERS   790D LETTER 2   PROSE
    THEY ARE THOSE OF MICHAEL ANGELO RAFAEL & THE ANTIQUE & OF 793C LETTER 5   PROSE
    CORRECT & ENLARGED COPIES FROM ANTIQUE GEMS OF WHICH THE   836B LETTER 35   PROSE
ANTIQUES
    ANTIQUES SUPERIOR THEY CANNOT BE FOR HUMAN POWER CANNOT   579C DESC CAT 5   PROSE
    I STUDY YOUR OUTLINES AS USUAL JUST AS IF THEY WERE   795B LETTER 6   PROSE
      ANTIQUES
ANTIQUITIES
    THE BRITISH ANTIQUITIES ARE NOW IN THE ARTIST'S HANDS . .   577D DESC CAT 5   PROSE
    THE ANTIQUITIES OF EVERY NATION UNDER HEAVEN . . . .   578D DESC CAT 5   PROSE
    HOW OTHER ANTIQUITIES CAME TO BE NEGLECTED AND . . .   578D DESC CAT 5   PROSE
ANTIQUITY
    APOTHEOSES OF PERSIAN HINDOO AND EGYPTIAN ANTIQUITY . . .   565C DESC CAT 2   PROSE
    HIGHEST ANTIQUITY ADAM WAS A DRUID AND NOAH . . . .   578A DESC CAT 5   PROSE
    ANTIQUITY PREACHES THE GOSPEL OF JESUS THE REASONING . .   579A DESC CAT 5   PROSE
    HAD RESOLVED TO EMULATE THOSE PRECIOUS REMAINS OF ANTIQUITY 579C DESC CAT 5   PROSE
    OF ANTIQUITY AND IN THE WORKS OF MORE MODERN GENIUS . .   579C DESC CAT 5   PROSE
    THE ONLY LIGHT OF ANTIQUITY THAT REMAINS UNPERVERTED BY WAR 778D HOMERS POETRY   PROSE
ANTRIM
    DONNEGAL ANTRIM TYRONE FERMANAGH ARMAGH LONDONDERRY . . .   711 JERUSALEM 72   26
ANUS
    I'LL KICK YOUR ROMAN ANUS . . . .   54 LO THE BAT/IM   9
    AND KISS MY ROMAN ANUS . . . .   54 LO THE BAT/IM   13
ANVIL
    WHAT THE ANVIL WHAT [THE ARM] [ARM] [GRASP] [CLASP] DREAD   172 THE TYGER/N 1   20
      GRASP
    WHAT THE ANVIL WHAT DREAD GRASP . . . . . .   214 THE TYGER/SE   15
    FURNACES HE FORMED AN ANVIL . . . .   259 BOOK OF LOS 5   21
    LOS BEAT ON THE ANVIL TILL GLORIOUS . . . . .   260 BOOK OF LOS 5   33
    BESIDE HIS ANVIL STOOD URTHONA DARK A MASS OF IRON . .   278 FOUR ZOAS 1   519
    GLOWD FURIOUS ON THE ANVIL PREPARD FOR SPADES & COULTERS   278 FOUR ZOAS 1   520
      ALL
    SOME FIXD THE ANVIL SOME THE LOOM ERECTED SOME THE PLOW   281 FOUR ZOAS 2   27
    THE BELLOWS BEGAN TO BLOW & THE LIONS OF URIZEN STOOD ROUND 281 FOUR ZOAS 2   32
      THE ANVIL
    STOOD ROUND ME AT THE ANVIL WHERE NEW HEATED THE WEDGE . .   300 FOUR ZOAS 4   90
    BESIDE THE ANVIL COLD HE DANCD WITH THE HAMMER OF URTHONA   305 FOUR ZOAS 5   4
    A FEMALE BRIGHT I STOOD BESIDE MY ANVIL DARK A MASS . .   327 FOUR ZOAS 7   282
    LOS SIEZD HIS HAMMER & TONGS HE LABOURD AT HIS RESOLUTE   482 MILTON 3   7
      ANVIL
    HIS HAMMER OF GOLD HE SIEZD AND HIS ANVIL OF ADAMANT . .   628 JERUSALEM 9   3
    OF SORROW RED HOT I WORKD IT ON MY RESOLUTE ANVIL . .   628 JERUSALEM 9   20

	PAGE	TITLE	LINE

ANVIL   (CONTINUED)
HE STAMPS AROUND THE ANVIL BEATING BLOWS OF STERN DESPAIR   629 JERUSALEM 10   24
I SEE IN DEADLY FEAR IN LONDON LOS RAGING ROUND HIS ANVIL   636 JERUSALEM 15   21
BEFORE THE ANVIL WATCHES THE BELLOWING FLAMES THUNDERING   636 JERUSALEM 16   10
DEAD ON THE ANVIL WHERE THE RED HOT WEDGE GROANS IN PAIN   636 JERUSALEM 16   13
LOS STOOD AT HIS ANVIL HE HEARD THE CONTENTIONS OF VALA   660 JERUSALEM 34   17
THEN LOS UTTERED WITH HAMMER & ANVIL CHAUNT REVOICE   . . .   688 JERUSALEM 56   29
AND LOS FIXES THEM ON HIS ANVIL INCESSANT HIS BLOWS   . .   690 JERUSALEM 58   16
WHILE LOS STOOD AT HIS ANVIL IN WRATH THE VICTIM OF THEIR   734 JERUSALEM 88   46
    LOVE
WHEN THEY ARE MURDERERS AS FAR AS MY HAMMER & ANVIL PERMIT   738 JERUSALEM 91   7
SO LOS CRIED AT HIS ANVIL IN THE HORRIBLE DARKNESS WEEPING   738 JERUSALEM 91   32
SMITING THE SPECTRE ON HIS ANVIL & THE INTEGUMENTS OF HIS   738 JERUSALEM 91   45
    EYE
HIS ANVIL IN THE GREAT SPECTRE LOS UNWEARIED LABOURING   742 JERUSALEM 95   18
    & WEEPING
ANVILS
THE ETERNAL PROPHET BEAT ON HIS ANVILS . . . .   253 AHANIA 4   27
TEND THE DIRE ANVILS MOUNTAINS MOURN & RIVERS FAINT & FAIL   276 FOUR ZOAS 1   425
. . . THEY FORMD THE ANVILS OF GOLD BEATEN IN MILLS   . . .   281 FOUR ZOAS 2   30
AND LOS FORMD ANVILS OF IRON PETRIFIC FOR HIS BLOWS   . .   301 FOUR ZOAS 4   168
THE ANVILS OF URTHONA LINK BY LINK THE CHAINS OF SORROW   302 FOUR ZOAS 4   185
IN GOLGONOOZA'S FURNACES AMONG THE ANVILS OF TIME AND SPACE   345 FOUR ZOAS 8   186
IN GOLGONOOZA LOS'S ANVILS STAND & HIS FURNACES RAGE . .   346 FOUR ZOAS 8   202
AND ANVILS DANCE THE DANCE OF TEARS & PAIN LOUD LIGHTNINGS   484 MILTON 5   16
THE FURNACES LAMENTING AROUND THE ANVILS & THIS THEIR SONG   484 MILTON 5   18
IN BOWLAHOOLA LOS'S ANVILS STAND & HIS FURNACES RAGE .   509 MILTON 24   51
THESE HYPOCRITIC SELFHOODS ON THE ANVILS OF BITTER DEATH   627 JERUSALEM 8   16
INTO THE FURNACES & INTO THE VALLEYS OF THE ANVILS OF   629 JERUSALEM 10   1
    DEATH
AND INTO THE MOUNTAINS OF THE ANVILS & OF THE HEAVY HAMMERS   629 JERUSALEM 10   2
WITH GREAT LABOUR UPON HIS ANVILS & IN HIS LADLES THE ORE   630 JERUSALEM 11   3
IN ETERNAL LABOURS LOUD THE [FURNAES] FURNACES & LOUD   684 JERUSALEM 53   * 20
    THE ANVILS
WALKING & IN THE VALES IN HOWLINGS FIERCE THEN TO   696 JERUSALEM 62   41
    HIS ANVILS
WITH THE INNUMERABLE MULTITUDES OF GOLGONOOZA ROUND THE   713 JERUSALEM 73   6
    ANVILS
AND ON HIS ANVILS LEST THEY DESTROY THE FEMININE AFFECTIONS   719 JERUSALEM 78   8
ANVIL-STOCK,ANVIL STOCK
LOS SAT UPON HIS ANVIL STOCK THEY SAT BESIDE THE FORGE   350 FOUR ZOAS 8   348
HE SAT DOWN ON HIS ANVIL-STOCK AND LEAND UPON THE TROUGH   503 MILTON 20   54
ANXIETY
AND THE PRECIOUS STONES OF ANXIETY & CARE & DESPERATION   499 MILTON 18   23
    & DEATH
AND BLACK ANXIETY AND THE CITIES OF THE SALAMANDRINE MEN   634 JERUSALEM 13   * 43
ANXIOUS
AND SPEND MANY AN ANXIOUS HOUR . . . .   124 SCHOOL BOY/SI   12
ON THE ANXIOUS CITY . . . .   136 FRENCH REVOLTN   56
THEN HE LOOKD BACK WITH ANXIOUS DESIRE . . . .   230 URIZEN 13   45
HIS WEB IS LEFT ALL DESOLATE THAT HIS LITTLE ANXIOUS HEART   277 FOUR ZOAS 1   459
THE DEW OF ANXIOUS SOULS THE DEATH-SWEAT OF THE DYING . .   281 FOUR ZOAS 2   47
ANXIOUS ITS LITTLE SOUL LOOKS OUT INTO THE CLEAR EXPANSE   355 FOUR ZOAS 8   559
URIZEN WEPT IN THE DARK DEEP ANXIOUS HIS SCALY FORM . .   361 FOUR ZOAS 9   162
HOW VERY ANXIOUS . . . .   473D ANNO REYNOLDS   MARG
BUT THEOTORMON & SOTHA STAND IN THE GATE OF LUBAN ANXIOUS   515 MILTON 28   21
SO OLOLON UTTERD IN WORDS DISTINCT THE ANXIOUS THOUGHT .   527 MILTON 37   4
THE BEAUTIFUL MAN ACTS FROM DUTY AND ANXIOUS SOLICITUDE   580B DESC CAT 5   PROSE
AND TWEED & TYNE ANXIOUS GIVE UP THEIR SOULS FOR ALBION'S   636 JERUSALEM 16   17
    SAKE
LIFE IN BROODING CARES & ANXIOUS LABOURS THAT PROVE BUT   647 JERUSALEM 24   16
    CHAFF
THO HUNGRY THEY LABOUR THEY ROUZE THEMSELVES ANXIOUS .   691 JERUSALEM 59   31
HEAVENS A MOTH OF GOLD & SILVER MOCKING HIS ANXIOUS GRASP   739 JERUSALEM 91   50
& STUDY OF ARCHANGELS WHY THEN SHOULD I BE ANXIOUS ABOUT   802C LETTER 14   PROSE
    THE
BUT I THINK OF YOU & FEEL ANXIOUS FOR THE SIGHT OF THAT   826C LETTER 28   PROSE
    FRIEND
P S MY WIFE IS BETTER WE ARE VERY ANXIOUS ABOUT MISS   833A LETTER 32   PROSE
    POOLE'S
FELPHAM & ITS KIND INHABITANTS I FEEL ANXIOUS & THEREFORE   833D LETTER 33   PROSE
MY WIFE JOINS ME IN ANXIOUS WISHES FOR YOUR HEALTH &   .   862A LETTER 59   PROSE
ANXIOUSLY
& ALWAYS ANXIOUSLY REMEMBERD MISS POOLE . . . .   838C LETTER 37   PROSE
PLACE IN HIM I AM DEAR SIR YOUR ANXIOUSLY DEVOTED   . . .   842A LETTER 41   PROSE
ANY
ARE FINER THAN ANY WE HAVE IN ENGLAND . . . .   28 EDW THIRD/PS 4   6
HAS TO GET BEFORE ANOTHER IN ANY PURSUIT AFTER GLORY   . .   28 EDW THIRD/PS 4   15
BUT I DONT THINK YOU HAVE ANY OF IT . . . .   28 EDW THIRD/PS 4   16
I KNOW YOUR HONOUR DOES NOT THINK ANY THING OF YOURSELF   29D EDW THIRD/PS 4   PROSE
THAT I SHOULD DRINK NO WINE NOR EAT OF ANY UNCLEAN THING   39C SAMSON/PS   PROSE
NOW THEREFORE DRINK NO WINE AND EAT NOT ANY UNCLEAN THING   39D SAMSON/PS   PROSE
I DONT THINK THERES ANY HARM IN IT SAID TILLY LALLY . .   47C ISLAND MOON 3   PROSE
FOR YOU NEVER SAY ANY THING ABOUT THE SCRIPTURES . . . .   48A ISLAND MOON 4   PROSE
YOU WOULD YOU IGNORANT JADE I WISH I COULD SEE YOU HIT ANY   48C ISLAND MOON 4   PROSE
& THEY COULD NOT TALK ANY MORE TO THE PRESENT PURPOSE . .   49C ISLAND MOON 5   PROSE
WELL SAID SUCTION THAT IS NOT ANY PROOF . . . .   49D ISLAND MOON 6   PROSE
WHY SAID QUID I THINK THAT [A] ANY NATURAL FOOL   . . . .   50A ISLAND MOON 6   PROSE
HE UNDERSTANDS ANATOMY BETTER THAN ANY OF THE ANCIENTS .   50A ISLAND MOON 6   PROSE
I AM SURE I NEVER SEE ANY PLEASURE . . . .   52D ISLAND MOON 8   PROSE
NOT HAVE ANY THING TO SAY AND IF ANY BODY ASKD HIM   . . .   53B ISLAND MOON 8   PROSE
MR STEELYARD ARE SOME OF THEM MORE IMPROVING THAN ANY BOOK   53C ISLAND MOON 8   PROSE

104

```
                                                             PAGE     TITLE           LINE
ANY   (CONTINUED)
    OR ANY COMFORT FIND  . . . . . . . . . . . . . . . .  .  56  HAIL MATRIM/IM        12
    WITH FACE AS BROWN AS ANY NUT WITH DRINKING OF STRONG ALE  58  THIS CITY/IM         3
    HERE NOBODY COULD SING ANY LONGER  . . . . . . . . . .  60D ISLAND MOON 11     PROSE
    ANY MORE THAN [ ?ANY ?BIRD THE] A DOG OR A CAT  . . . . .  61  SAY YOU JOE/IM  *   13
    ANY WALK IN PATHLESS WAYS  . . . . . . . . . . . . .  .  61  LEAVE O/IM            6
    FOR MY ENEMY IS NOT MAN BUT BEAST AND DEVIL IF I HAVE ANY  72B ANNO LAVATER    * MARG
    & SUCH AN ONE CANNOT JUDGE OF ANY BUT IN LOVE & HIS  . . .  87A ANNO LAVATER      MARG
    THOSE WHO ARE OFFENDED WITH ANY THING IN THIS BOOK WOULD BE  87C ANNO LAVATER     MARG
    IF GOD IS ANY THING HE IS UNDERSTANDING  . . . . . . .  89A ANNO SWED LOVE      MARG
    MAN CAN HAVE NO IDEA OF ANY THING GREATER THAN MAN  . . .  90B ANNO SWED LOVE    MAPG
    & HAVE NO IDEA OF ANY BUT WORLDLY GAIN  . . . . . . .  94A ANNO SWED LOVE       MARG
    BY ANY THING BUT ORGANS OF SENSE MUST BE LIMITED TO OBJECTS  97B NAT RELIGION 1 PROSE
        OF SENSE
    IF ANY COULD DESIRE WHAT HE IS INCAPABLE OF POSSESSING  . .  97D NAT RELIGION 2 PROSE
    NO MATTER WHO I AM O MNETHA IF THOU HAST ANY FOOD  . . .  101 TIRIEL 2             21
    AND I REMAIN AN OUTCAST HAST THOU ANY THING TO DRINK  . .  102 TIRIEL 2            57
    IF THEY SEE ANY WEEPING  . . . . . . . . . . . . .  .  119 NIGHT/SI              21
    BETTER THAN ANY DESCRIPTION OF BUILDINGS OR GARMENTS  .  150C MARRIAGE HH 6    PROSE
    ISAIAH ANSWERD I SAW NO GOD NOR HEARD ANY  . . . . .  153C MARRIAGE HH 12      PROSE
    BUT MANY ARE NOT CAPABLE OF A FIRM PERSWASION OF ANY THING  153C MARRIAGE HH 12  PROSE
    HAVE NOW ANOTHER PLAIN FACT ANY MAN OF MECHANICAL TALENTS  158A MARRIAGE HH 21   PROSE   2
    NOR FOR ITSELF HATH ANY CARE  . . . . . . . . . . .  162 CLOD PEBBLE/N           2
    [[CANST] THOU CANST ANY SECRET KEEP]  . . . . . . . .  164 CRADLE SONG/N  *      4
    WAS NOT FOUND ON ANY TREE  . . . . . . . . . . . .  166 I FEARD FURY/N          6
    TO ANY TREE THAT GROWS ON GROUND  . . . . . . . . .  169 MIRTLE SHADE/N        10
    [TO ANY TREE THAT GROWS ON GROUND]  . . . . . . . .  176 TO MY MIRTLE/N         4
    [NOR] OR ANY OF MY BROTHERS MORE  . . . . . . . . .  177 LIT BOY LST/N          6
    IN A STYLE MORE ORNAMENTAL UNIFORM AND GRAND THAN ANY  . 207B PRSPECTUS 1793   PROSE
    OF ANY AGE OR COUNTRY AMONG WHICH ARE TWO LARGE  . . . 207C PRSPECTUS 1793     PROSE
    NOR FOR ITSELF HATH ANY CARE  . . . . . . . . . . .  211 CLOD PEBBLE/SE          2
    OR ANY OF MY BROTHERS MORE  . . . . . . . . . . . .  218 LIT BOY LST/SE          6
    DELUSION & I CANNOT CRAVE FOR ANY THING BUT THEE [& TILL]  327 FOUR ZOAS 7       307
    LEST ANY SHOULD IN FUTURITY DO AS WE HAVE DONE IN HEAVEN  331 FOUR ZOAS 7        430
    I PUT NOT ANY TRUST IN THEE NOR IN THY GLITTERING SCALES  335 FOUR ZOAS 7B   *   82
    WOULD BE AS GOOD AN INQUISITOR AS ANY OTHER PRIEST  . . 385C ANNO WATSON        MARG
    ANY MAN WHO WRITES [THAT] SO PRETEND THAT HE IS IN A GOOD  390B ANNO WATSON  * MARG
        HUMOUR
    WERE NEVER BELIEVD WILLINGLY BY ANY NATION &  . . . . 390C ANNO WATSON         MARG
    FOR HIS & SO HE WOULD DO BY ANY OTHER BOOK  . . . . . 393C ANNO WATSON         MARG
    AS IF REASONING WAS OF ANY CONSEQUENCE TO A QUESTION  . 394A ANNO WATSON        MARG
    THE BISHOP NEVER SAW THE EVERLASTING GOSPEL ANY MORE THAN  394D ANNO WATSON  * MARG
        TOM PAINE
    BACON HAS NO NOTION OF ANY THING BUT MAMMON  . . . . 402D ANNO BACON      * MARG
    FOR ANY THING IN ANY WAY  . . . . . . . . . . . .  403B ANNO BACON            MARG
    OR ANY USEFUL THING HIS BUSINESS & BOSOM WAS TO BE LORD  404D ANNO BACON        MARG
        CHANCELLOR
    SURELY THE MAN WHO WROTE THIS NEVER TALKD TO ANY  . . 408D ANNO BACON      * MARG
        BUT COXCOMBS
    BY HIS TRANSLATOR IF I HAVE ANY JUDGMENT IN SUCH THINGS  413A ANNO BOYD         MARG
    AND IF ANY GIRL'S LOVER FORSAKES HER FOR ME  . . . .  428 MARY                 31
    EITHER RELATING TO SEDITION OR ANY THING ELSE  . . . 437B BLAKES MEMORAN     PROSE
    THE WHOLE DISTANCE THAT WILLIAM COULD BE AT ANY TIME  . 437D BLAKES MEMORAN    PROSE
    AT THE STABLE DOOR THAT WE MAY NOT HAVE ANY WITNESSES  . 438B BLAKES MEMORAN   PROSE
    THERE WAS NOT ANY BODY IN GRINDER'S TAP-ROOM BUT  . . . 438C BLAKES MEMORAN    PROSE
    IF SUCH A PERJURY AS THIS CAN TAKE EFFECT ANY VILLAIN IN  438D BLAKES MEMORAN   PROSE
        FUTURE
    IS IT NOT IN THE POWER OF ANY THIEF WHO ENTERS  . . . 439A BLAKES MEMORAN     PROSE
    MICH ANG OR ANY OF THE ITALIANS  . . . . . . . . . 451D ANNO REYNOLDS        MARG
    TWENTY GUINEAS FOR THIS HORRIBLE DAWB & IF ANY ONE WOULD  451D ANNO REYNOLDS   MARG
        GIVE XXX
    ANY MORE THAN I BELIEVE THAT THE ROSE TEACHES THE LILLY  453B ANNO REYNOLDS     MARG
        HOW TO GROW
    ANY MORE THAN THE ENGRAVINGS OF STRANGE BARTOLLOZZI  . . 455A ANNO REYNOLDS     MARG
    THAN COLOURING WITHOUT ANY MEANING AT ALL  . . . . . 455D ANNO REYNOLDS       MARG
    [OR RAFAEL OR ANY THING]  . . . . . . . . . . . .  456B ANNO REYNOLDS    *  MARG
    CANNOT EVEN KNOW OR SEE MICH ANGO OR RAFAEL OR ANY THING  456B ANNO REYNOLDS    MARG
        ELSE
    THAT ANY MAN OF A PLAIN UNDERSTANDING MAY  . . . . . 457D ANNO REYNOLDS       MARG
    CAN ANY MAN WHO THINKS [ ?ARGUE] TALK SO  . . . . . 460C ANNO REYNOLDS    *  MARG
    & NOT TALK OF DARK AGES OR OF ANY AGE AGES ARE ALL EQUAL  461A ANNO REYNOLDS    MARG
    CAN ANY MAN BE SUCH A FOOL AS TO BELIEVE THAT RAFAEL &  . 467B ANNO REYNOLDS    MARG
    NEGLECTED ANY THING THAT TITIAN OR VERONESE DID  . . . 467D ANNO REYNOLDS      MARG
    LABOUR & TRICK AS TO IMAGINATION HE WAS TOTALLY WITHOUT ANY  468C ANNO REYNOLDS  MARG
    MORE THAN ANY OTHER MEN  . . . . . . . . . . . . . 468C ANNO REYNOLDS        MARG
    NOR MICH ANG COULD HAVE MADE HIM ANY BETTER  . . . . 472D ANNO REYNOLDS       MARG
    OF ANY THING ELSE  . . . . . . . . . . . . . . . 473B ANNO REYNOLDS        MARG
    CONTRARY OPINIONS CAN NEVER BY ANY LANGUAGE BE MADE ALIKE  474B ANNO REYNOLDS   MARG
    ANY FOOL MAY (CONCENTRATE) A LIGHT IN THE MIDDLE  . . . 477C ANNO REYNOLDS  * MARG
    [THE KNAVE CALLS ANY THING ?FOUND IN NATURE FIT FOR ART]  SUPP ANNO REYNOLDS  * MARG
    THAN ANY OTHER EARTHLY THINGS ARE MAN'S EARTHLY LINEAMENTS  503 MILTON 21       11
    NEITHER DID ANY LACK OR FALL INTO ERROR WITHOUT  . . . 519 MILTON 31            6
    MILD WAS THE VOICE BUT MORE DISTINCT THAN ANY EARTHLY  . 527 MILTON 37           5
    CAN THERE BE ANY THING MORE MEAN  . . . . . . . . . 539 CAN THERE BE/N          1
    GO LOVE WITHOUT THE HELP OF ANY [THING] ?KING ON EARTH  . 541 ANGEL PRESID/N *    3
    [TO [SAY] SPEAK MICHAEL ANGELO [ANY OTHER WORD] & [MEAN]  542 FLORENTINE/N   *   11
        ACT REMBRANT]
    NEVER CAN HAVE ANY TO SIR JEHOSHUAN  . . . . . . . . 542 FLORENTINE/N          34
    TO TELL YOU ANY THING THAT HE CAN'T PROVE  . . . . . 551 WILLM COWPER/N        10
    FOR ANY MAN TO PRETEND TO INSPIRATION  . . . . . . . 551 WILLM COWPER/N        12
    BUT NOBODY [AT ALL] SEES ANY HARM IN RHYMING  . . . . 555 BLAKES APL/N 1         9
    BUT NOBODY SEES ANY HARM IN RHYMING  . . . . . . . . 555 BLAKES APL/N 2         4
```

ANY   (CONTINUED)
    A WALL ON CANVAS OR WOOD OR ANY OTHER PORTABLE THING   . . 560D EXHIBITION ADV PROSE
    I COULD DIVIDE WESTMINSTER HALL OR THE WALLS OF ANY OTHER   560D EXHIBITION ADV PROSE
    POETS IN ANY AGE OR COUNTRY AND THESE IN A CORRUPT STATE   561C EXHIBITION ADV PROSE
    PLEASED WITH THE WORK ANY MORE THAN WITH THE LOOK   . . . 563D DESC CAT   PROSE
    WITH OIL OR WITH ANY CLOGGY VEHICLE . . . . 565A DESC CAT 2   PROSE
    OF HIS FINISHED PRODUCTIONS BY ANY CALUMNIES IN FUTURE   . 573A DESC CAT 3   PROSE
    ANY THING THAT A PROSPECTUS PLEASES BUT I KNOW THAT WHERE   575B DESC CAT 3   PROSE
    NOT WORTH ANY MAN'S RESPECT OR CARE . . . . 575B DESC CAT 3   PROSE
    DONE BY ANY OTHER POWER THAN THAT OF THE POETIC VISIONARY   576C DESC CAT 4   PROSE
    THAN ANY THING SEEN BY HIS MORTAL EYE . . . .   577A DESC CAT 4   PROSE
    COULD NOT BE REPRESENTED BY ANY HISTORICAL FACTS BUT   . . 577C DESC CAT 5   PROSE
    IS NOT WORTH ANY MAN'S READING HE WHO REJECTS A FACT   579B DESC CAT 5   PROSE
      BECAUSE
    AND HIS EXTREMITIES LARGE HIS EYES WITH SCARCE ANY WHITES   580A DESC CAT 5   PROSE
    FOR EXPERIMENT ON COLOURS WITHOUT ANY OILY VEHICLE IT MAY   582B DESC CAT 9   PROSE
    LOSES ALL ADMIRATION OF ANY OTHER ARTIST BUT RUBENS   . . 583A DESC CAT 9   PROSE
    CORREGGIO WAS NOT POOR HE WILL MAKE ANY THAT ARTIST SO . . 583B DESC CAT 9   PROSE
    OR THAN ANY OTHER METHOD OF PAINTING BUT HE MUST HAVE   . . 585B DESC CAT 15   PROSE
    TALK NO MORE THEN OF CORREGGIO OR REMBRANDT OR ANY OTHER   585C DESC CAT 15   PROSE
    TO THE AUTHOR AND HE THINKS WILL PROVE TO ANY DISCERNING   585D DESC CAT 16   PROSE
      EYE
    TO THE CONTRARY TO BE BETTER ABLE THAN ANY OTHER   . . . . 586D CHAUCER 1   PROSE
    AS PAINTING OUGHT TO BE DRAWING ON CANVAS OR ANY OTHER   . 591D PUB ADDRESS/N   PROSE
    DELINEATED BY ANY ENGRAVER WHO KNOWS HOW TO . . . . .   . 592B PUB ADDRESS/N   PROSE
    WITH CONTEMPT HE DID NOT CARE FOR THIS ANY MORE THAN WEST   593A PUB ADDRESS/N   PROSE
    OR A COPY OF ANY KIND CAN BE AS HONOURABLE TO A NATION . . 595C PUB ADDRESS/N PROSE
    ANY MORE THAN POPE'S METAPHYSICAL JARGON OF RHYMING   . . . 596B PUB ADDRESS/N PROSE
    WHOEVER LOOKS AT ANY OF THE GREAT & EXPENSIVE WORKS   . . . 596B PUB ADDRESS/N PROSE
    LET ANY MAN OF SENSE ASK HIMSELF ONE QUESTION IS THIS ART   597B PUB ADDRESS/N   PROSE
    A JOCKEY THAT IS ANY THING OF A JOCKEY WILL NEVER BUY   . . 597D PUB ADDRESS/N PROSE
    A HORSE BY THE COLOUR & A MAN WHO HAS GOT ANY BRAINS   . . 597D PUB ADDRESS/N   PROSE
    WHEN I TELL ANY TRUTH IT IS NOT . . . .   597D PUB ADDRESS/N   PROSE
    IT IS NO BETTER THAN ANY OTHER'S MANUAL LABOUR ANY BODY   598A PUB ADDRESS/N   *PROSE
      MAY
    THERE IS NOT BECAUSE THERE CANNOT BE ANY DIFFERENCE   . . . 598D PUB ADDRESS/N PROSE
    OR ANY OF THAT CLASS CHARACTER & EXPRESSION CAN   . . .   599B PUB ADDRESS/N   PROSE
    CAN ITS EXECUTION BE ANY OTHER THAN THE WORK OF A BLOCKHEAD 599C PUB ADDRESS/N   PROSE
    AS [IS] IT IS CAPABLE OF BEING PLACED IN ANY HEIGHTH &   601A PUB ADDRESS/N   *PROSE
      INDEED
    I DEFY ANY MAN TO CUT CLEANER STROKES THAN I DO OR   . .   602A PUB ADDRESS/N   PROSE
    WHENEVER ANY INDIVIDUAL REJECTS ERROR & EMBRACES TRUTH . . 613A V LAST JUDG/N PROSE
    [THEY] THEY MERELY APPEAR AS IN A CLOUD WHEN ANY THING . . 614C V LAST JUDG/N *PROSE
    & HE WHO PERFORMS WORKS OF MERCY IN ANY SHAPE WHATEVER . . 616C V LAST JUDG/N PROSE
    ANY MORE (THAN) I WOULD QUESTION A WINDOW CONCERNING A   617C V LAST JUDG/N   *PROSE
      SIGHT
    THAT WHENEVER ANY SPECTRE BEGAN TO DEVOUR THE DEAD   . . . 630 JERUSALEM 11   6
    THEE TO BE INVISIBLE TO ANY BUT WHOM I PLEASE & WHEN   . . 639 JERUSALEM 17   40
    AND IF ANY ENTER INTO THEE THOU SHALT BE AN UNQUENCHABLE   639 JERUSALEM 17   45
      FIRE
    AND FEET LEST ANY SHOULD ENTER HIS BOSOM & EMBRACE   . . . 664 JERUSALEM 38   2
    WILL ANY ONE SAY WHERE ARE THOSE WHO WORSHIP SATAN   . . . 682B JERUSALEM 52   PROSE
    THERE IS NO TIME FOR ANY THING BUT THE TORMENTS OF LOVE   707 JERUSALEM 68   68
      & DESIRE
    IS THE HOLY GHOST ANY OTHER THAN AN INTELLECTUAL FOUNTAIN   717A JERUSALEM 77   PROSE
    ARE THEY ANY OTHER THAN MENTAL STUDIES & PERFORMANCES   . . 717A JERUSALEM 77   PROSE
    NOR CAN ANY CONSUMMATE BLISS WITHOUT BEING GENERATED   . . 731 JERUSALEM 86   42
    CAN THERE BE ANY SECRET JOY ON EARTH GREATER THAN THIS . . 733 JERUSALEM 88   * 15
    ENITHARMON ANSWERD THIS IS WOMAN'S WORLD NOR NEED SHE ANY   733 JERUSALEM 88   16
    OR TO HIS EMANATION ANY OF THE UNIVERSAL CHARACTERISTICS   736 JERUSALEM 90   29
    GIVE ANY MARKS OF GENTILITY . . . .   748 EV GOSPEL(B)/N   2
    GIVE ANY PROOFS OF HUMILITY . . . .   750 EV GOSPEL(C)/N   2
    HE'D HAVE DONE ANY THING TO PLEASE US . . . .   750 EV GOSPEL(C)/N   26
    GIVE ANY PROOFS OF HUMILITY . . . .   751 EV GOSPEL(D)/N   2
    HE'D HAVE DONE ANY THING TO PLEASE US . . . .   752 EV GOSPEL(D)/N   60
    GIVE ANY LESSONS OF CHASTITY . . . . 753 EV GOSPEL(E)/N   2
    GIVE ANY LESSONS OF PHILOSOPHY . . . . 756 EV GOSPEL(H)/N   2
    YOU RETAIN HEALTH AND YET ARE AS MAD AS ANY OF US ALL   . . 772D ANNO SPURZHEIM MARG
    WHERE ANY VIEW OF MONEY EXISTS ART CANNOT BE CARRIED ON   776C INSC LAOCOON   PROSE
    & EQUAL TO ANY POET BUT NOT SUPERIOR . . . . 783A ANNO WW POEMS   MARG
    I CANNOT THINK THAT REAL POETS HAVE ANY COMPETITION   . . . 783A ANNO WW POEMS   MARG
    WITH ANY OTHER POET WHATEVER ROWLEY & CHATTERTON ALSO   . . 783C ANNO WW POEMS   MARG
    I CONGRATULATE YOU NOT ON ANY ATCHIEVEMENT . . . . .   . 790B LETTER 2   PROSE
    CAN EXECUTE THEM IN ANY MANNER . . . . 790B LETTER 2   PROSE
    WHICH WHEN COLD WILL RECIEVE ANY IMPRESSION MINUTELY   . . 790C LETTER 2   PROSE
    HOWEVER ADMIRABLE THAT TRACK MAY BE AT ANY RATE MY EXCUSE   792A LETTER 4   PROSE
    WHY IS THE BIBLE MORE ENTERTAINING & INSTRUCTIVE THAN ANY   794A LETTER 5   PROSE
      OTHER BOOK
    & SHOULD NEVER HAVE ATTEMPTED TO LIVE BY ANY THING ELSE   794C LETTER 5   PROSE
    DO NOT THROW ASIDE FOR ANY LONG TIME . . . . 795B LETTER 6   PROSE
    WITH ANY NEGLECT YET I AM LAID BY IN A CORNER . . . .   . 795C LETTER 6   PROSE
    MELANCHOLY WITHOUT ANY REAL REASON FOR IT A DISEASE WHICH   798A LETTER 10   PROSE
    AS MANY PRINTSHOPS AS OF ANY OTHER TRADE . . . . 798C LETTER 10   PROSE
    "FORGET YOUR SERVICES TO US OR ANY WAY NEGLECT TO LOVE &"   800A LETTER 12   PROSE
    MY NEST I HAVE NOT GOT ANY FORWARDER WITH THE THREE MARYS   804A LETTER 16   PROSE
      OR
    WITH ANY OTHER OF YOUR COMMISSIONS BUT HOPE NOW I HAVE . . 804A LETTER 16   PROSE
    SHE HAS NOT PRINTED ANY MORE SINCE YOU WENT TO LONDON BUT   807A LETTER 17   PROSE
      WE CAN
    ANY THING IN THE WALKS OF NATURAL PAINTING . . . . .   . 810B LETTER 20   PROSE
    & THEY ARE AS DISTINCT AS ANY TWO ARTS CAN BE . . . .   . 810B LETTER 20   PROSE
    & I FIND ON ALL HANDS GREAT OBJECTIONS TO MY DOING ANY   812C LETTER 22   PROSE
      THING

```
                                                          PAGE      TITLE         LINE
ANY   (CONTINUED)
      & WHENEVER ANY THING APPEARS TO AFFECT THAT INTEREST    . . 812D LETTER 22   PROSE
      ESPECIALLY IF I MYSELF OMIT ANY DUTY TO MY [SELF] STATION  812D LETTER 22   PROSE
      SUCH WORDS WOULD MAKE ANY STOUT MAN TREMBLE  . . . . . .813B LETTER 22   PROSE
      & SUPERIOR IN ONE TO ANY THING THAT HAS BEEN DONE   . . . 814B LETTER 23   PROSE
      THEM WAS TO BE ENCOURAGED TILL HE DID LIKE ANY OF         815B LETTER 23   PROSE
         THE OTHERS
      UNLIKE ANY OF THESE PAINTERS & I WOULD HAVE THEM TO BE SO  815B LETTER 23   PROSE
      I THINK THE MANNER I ADOPT MORE PERFECT THAN ANY OTHER  . 815B LETTER 23   PROSE
      THINK OF TROUBLING YOU ABOUT IT OR ANY OF MY REAL FRIENDS  815C LETTER 23   PROSE
      TILL NOW IN ANY DEGREE PLEASED MYSELF & NOW I MUST  . . 815C LETTER 23   PROSE
      SHE WILL FORGIVE ANY FAILURE IN CONSIDERATION OF          815D LETTER 23   PROSE
         THE ENDEAVOUR
      BEFORE NOW BUT COULD NOT GET ANY THING DONE FOR YOU  . . 819A LETTER 24   PROSE
      BE NOT THEN UNEASY ON ANY ACCOUNT & TELL MY SISTER NOT    819D LETTER 25   PROSE
         TO BE
      OR REMOVE TO ANY OTHER PLACE THAT I CHOOSE  . . . . . . 820A LETTER 25   PROSE
      THAT THINGS SHOULD BE AS THEY ARE THAN ANY OTHER WAY   . 821A LETTER 25   PROSE
      TOO MUCH EXPERIENCE TO BE ANY LONGER IMPOSED UPON   . . 821A LETTER 25   PROSE
      HONOURABLE AT ANY RATE THE PROJECT PLEASES LORD COWPER'S   821C LETTER 25   PROSE
      ANY OTHER THAN THE SECRETARY THE AUTHORS ARE IN ETERNITY   825A LETTER 27   PROSE
      NOT HIS AFFECTED CONTEMPT THAT CAN MOVE ME TO ANY THING BUT 825C LETTER 27   PROSE
      MY JUST RIGHT AS AN ARTIST & AS A MAN & IF ANY  . . . 825D LETTER 27   PROSE
      & WILL RELINQUISH ANY ENGAGEMENT OF DESIGNING AT ALL   . 826A LETTER 27   PROSE
      ABLE TO SEND ANY MORE BEFORE MY RETURN THO PERHAPS I MAY   826D LETTER 28   PROSE
      BURN WHAT I HAVE PEEVISHLY WRITTEN ABOUT ANY FRIEND  . . 828C LETTER 28   PROSE
      WHO HAS NOT LOST ANY OF HIS LIFE SINCE HE WAS FIVE YEARS   830A LETTER 30   PROSE
         OLD
      ANY ONE A BLIGHT NEVER DOES GOOD TO A TREE & IF A BLIGHT   830C LETTER 30   PROSE
      I HAVE SEEN MR SAUNDERS & ENQUIRD OF HIM WHETHER HE HAS ANY 832C LETTER 32   PROSE
      BUT I WILL NOT ADVISE ANY THING TILL FLAXMAN SEES THEM  . 839C LETTER 38   PROSE
      PICTURE & TWO DRAWINGS TO ANY PERSON WHOM YOU SHALL  . . 839D LETTER 38   PROSE
      IF YOU DO NOT WISH ANY MORE DONE BEFORE I DELIVER THEN PRAY 840C LETTER 39   PROSE
      TO ASSIST ANY HOW REMOTE SOEVER WILL CERTAINLY HEAR HER    842A LETTER 41   PROSE
         VOICE
      AND ADMIRED WITHOUT ANY PREFACE MY PRINT OF ROMNEY AND  . . 843C LETTER 43   PROSE
      MORE DISTINCTLY THAN IN ANY PRINCE OR HERO  . . . . . . 845C LETTER 44   PROSE
      TO COPY ANY OF HIS FATHER'S DESIGNS THAT MR FLAXMAN MAY    846A LETTER 44   PROSE
      READINESS TO SEND ANY OF THE CARTOONS TO LONDON YOU DESIRE 846A LETTER 44   PROSE
      TO EXECUTE ANY WORK I NEED ONLY REFER TO THE LITTLE JOB    847A LETTER 44   PROSE
      ENGRAVED BY THE HANDS OF ANGELS & MUST NOT BY ANY MEANS    848C LETTER 45   PROSE
      THE INFERIOR ONES CANNOT BE DONE AT ANY RATE UNDER        848C LETTER 45   PROSE
         (FIFTEEN)
      WILKES WAS NOT OUT WHEN I CALLD NOR ANY MORE OF WASHINGTON 853A LETTER 51  *PROSE
      FOR NOT BEING ABLE TO FURNISH ANY DESIGNS YOU WILL READILY 853A LETTER 51  *PROSE
      I THOUGHT AT ANY RATE IT WOULD NOT BE PREMATURE TO TELL HIM 853A LETTER 51 *PROSE
      I MUST SAY ARE FAR BEYOND ANY THING I HAVE EVER DONE  . . 853A LETTER 51  *PROSE
      HAS LEFT ME WITHOUT ANY RESOURCE BUT THAT OF APPLYING TO   853C LETTER 52   PROSE
         YOU
      ENGAGEMENT WITH ANY LONDON BOOKSELLER I MAY MYSELF   . . 856B LETTER 54   PROSE
      GREAT DEAL OF HONOUR IN LOSING THE FIRST PUBLICATION OF ANY 856C LETTER 54   PROSE
      PURCHASE IT & AT HIS OWN PRICE OR ANY OTHER OF HIS WORKS   856C LETTER 54   PROSE
      AS TO ANY THING LIKE A HINT OF A PROPOSAL RELATING TO  . 857A LETTER 54  *PROSE
      ACCORDINGLY I DID NOT SAY THAT I KNEW OF ANY POEM BUT  . 857A LETTER 54   PROSE
      TO ANY PERIODICAL MODE OF PUBLISHING ANY OF YOUR WORKS  . 858A LETTER 55   PROSE
      IN ANY WAY BE SEPARATED FROM THE GRAND BULK OF YOUR  . . 858C LETTER 55   PROSE
      CONSIDER MYSELF A ROBBER TO RETAIN MORE THAN YOU AT ANY    858C LETTER 55   PROSE
         TIME
      ASKD IF HE HAD ANY MESSAGE TO YOU AS I MEANT TO WRITE  . 860A LETTER 56   PROSE
      EMBARRASD AT THE IDEA OF SETTING A VALUE ON ANY WORK OF MR  860A LETTER 56   PROSE
      HOW A VALUE WAS SET ON ANY LITERARY WORK HE ANSWERD  . . 860A LETTER 56   PROSE
      IF ANY OF MY WRITINGS SHOULD HEREAFTER APPEAR BEFORE  . . 860D LETTER 57   PROSE
      I CANNOT GIVE YOU ANY ACCOUNT OF OUR BALLADS  . . . . . 862A LETTER 59   PROSE
      & IF ANY OTHERS ARE DISPLEASD IT IS ALSO AN ARGUMENT OF    862A LETTER 59   PROSE
         THEIR
      OWES SUCCESS TO SOMETHING BESIDE OR WITHOUT ITSELF IF IT   862A LETTER 59   PROSE
         HAS ANY
      I AM SURE THAT ANY PERSON CONSULTING HIS OWN EYES MUST  . 864D LETTER 61   PROSE
      PREFER WHAT IS SO SUPEREMINENT AND I AM AS SURE THAT ANY   864D LETTER 61   PROSE
      THAT PRECLUDE ALL POSSIBILITY OF PROMISING ANY THING I HAVE 865D LETTER 63   PROSE
      FROM BEGINNING TO END ANY REMARKS THAT YOU MAY BE PLEASED  866C LETTER 65   PROSE
         TO
      THESE LAST (TWELVE) PRINTS ARE UNACCOMPANIED BY ANY WRITING 867C LETTER 66   PROSE
      IT IS THEREFORE NECESSARY TO ME THAT ANY PERSON WISHING    867C LETTER 66   PROSE
         TO HAVE
      ANY OR ALL OF THEM SHOULD SEND ME THEIR ORDER TO PRINT THEM 867C LETTER 66   PROSE
      AT LEAST AS WELL AS ANY I HAVE YET PRODUCED  . . . . . 867C LETTER 66   PROSE
      (TWELVE) OCLOCK IT IS QUITE AS CONVENIENT TO ME AS ANY     868B LETTER 67   PROSE
         OTHER DAY
      IT APPEARS TO ME THAT NEITHER TIME NOR PLACE CAN MAKE ANY  868B LETTER 67   PROSE
      PROSPECT AT NORTH END MRS HURD'S I SHOULD LIKE AS WELL     873A LETTER 76   PROSE
         AS ANY
      IS CERTAIN THAT AT PRESENT ANY VENTURE TO GO OUT MUST BE   SUPP LETTER 81A *PROSE
      NOT DARE TO LEAVE HIS ROOM BY ANY MEANS HE HAD ANOTHER     SUPP LETTER 81A *PROSE
      ANY THING ELSE SUCH IS JOB BUT SINCE THE FRENCH REVOLUTION 878B LETTER 88   PROSE
      I HAVE LITTLE HOPE OF DOING ANY MORE OF SUCH THINGS  . . 878C LETTER 88   PROSE
      MY WIFE ALONE IS ANSWERABLE FOR THEIR HAVING EXISTED IN ANY 879C LETTER 89   PROSE
ANY BODY
      WHAT IS IT TO ANY BODY WHAT I DO I AM ALWAYS UNHAPPY TOO . 51C ISLAND MOON 6  PROSE
      NOT HAVE ANY THING TO SAY AND IF ANY BODY ASKD HIM  . . 53B ISLAND MOON 8  PROSE
      THERE WAS NOT ANY BODY IN GRINDER'S TAP-ROOM BUT  . . . 438C BLAKES MEMORAN PROSE
      OR THAT ANY BODY CAN THINK SO  . . . . . . . . . 462D ANNO REYNOLDS  MARG
```

```
                                                              PAGE      TITLE         LINE
ANY BODY      (CONTINUED)
       CAN IT BE WORTHY OF ADMIRATION TO ANY BODY OF UNDERSTANDING    597B PUB ADDRESS/N    PROSE
       IT IS NO BETTER THAN ANY OTHER'S MANUAL LABOUR ANY BODY MAY    598A PUB ADDRESS/N   *PROSE
       I KNOW MY EXECUTION IS NOT LIKE ANY BODY ELSE I DO NOT         601D PUB ADDRESS/N    PROSE
       MY WORK PRINTED I WILL SEND IT YOU FIRST OF ANY BODY    . .    866A LETTER 63        PROSE
ANYONE
       OF NO DOUBTFUL SIGNIFICATION TO ANYONE    . . . . . . . .      386B ANNO WATSON      MARG
       EXCEPT IS CHRIST YOU LIE EXCEPT DID ANYONE EVER DO THIS        400D ANNO BACON       MARG
       AS YOURS TO HIM HE WILL NOT EASILY MEET FROM ANYONE ELSE       858A LETTER 55        PROSE
ANY ONE
       BUT IF ANY ONE IS HURT BY HIS LYING WILL CONFESS HIS LIE        67B ANNO LAVATER     MARG
       NEITHER WILL ANY ONE BELIEVE THAT THE GREEK STATUES    . .     565D DESC CAT 2       PROSE
       WHICH CANNOT BE IMITATED BY ANY ONE WHO DOES NOT       . .     592B PUB ADDRESS/N    PROSE
       SUCH IMITATION WHICH ANY ONE MAY EASILY PERFORM        . .     597B PUB ADDRESS/N    PROSE
       FOR THEY LABOUR FOR LIFE & LOVE REGARDLESS OF ANY ONE          691 JERUSALEM 59        37
       I SHOULD NOT DARE TO SAY TO ANY ONE ELSE THAT I CAN ALONE      822C LETTER 26        PROSE
       NEITHER OUGHT ANY ONE TO ATTEMPT IT       . . . . . . . .      824C LETTER 27        PROSE
       WHO KNEW MOST CONCERNING HIM OF ANY ONE LAMENTED      . . .    846A LETTER 44        PROSE
ANY ONE'S
       READY TO KISS ANY ONE'S ARSE    . . . . . . . . . .           785C ILLUS DANTE 16    PROSE
ANYTHING
       SINCE THE OLD ANYTHING WAS CREATED     . . . . . . . . .       187 WHEN KLOPSTK/N      26
       OR WITH REMBRANDT'S OR ANYTHING VENETIAN OR FLEMISH  . .       573A DESC CAT 3        PROSE
       AND TO SAY THAT THE COUNTRY PRINTERS COULD NOT DO ANYTHING     846D LETTER 44        PROSE
       UNNECESSARY TO MENTION ANYTHING RELATING TO THE PURPOSED       858A LETTER 55        PROSE
       OF ANYTHING ELSE I HAVE PROVED THE SIX PLATES & REDUCED        879C LETTER 89        PROSE
ANY THING      (SEE ANY)
ANYTUS
       THE PAINTER HOPES THAT HIS FRIENDS ANYTUS [&] MELITUS &        598B PUB ADDRESS/N    PROSE
       ANYTUS MELITUS & LYCON THOUGHT SOCRATES A VERY PERNICIOUS      740B JERUSALEM 93    TITLE
         MAN
ANY WHERE
       WE DO NOT FIND ANY WHERE THAT SATAN IS ACCUSED OF SIN         615B V LAST JUDG/N    PROSE
APACE
       ALBION'S WESTERN GATE IS CLOSD HIS DEATH IS COMING APACE       675 JERUSALEM 45        17
       OUR RETURN TO LONDON DRAWS ON APACE OUR EXPECTATION OF  . .    826B LETTER 28        PROSE
APART
       HIDDEN SET APART IN MY STERN COUNSELS    . . . . . .           224 URIZEN 4             8
       ETERNITY ROLLD WIDE APART    . . . . . . . . . .               225 URIZEN 5             5
       FOR ETERNITY STOOD WIDE APART    . . . . . . . . .             226 URIZEN 5            41
       AS THE STARS ARE APART FROM THE EARTH    . . . . . .           226 URIZEN 6             1
       TILL THE WRENCHING APART WAS HEALED    . . . . . . . .         226 URIZEN 7             3
       DRIED LAID THEM APART TILL WINTER . . . . . . . .              251 AHANIA 3            22
       WHERE NOTHING WAS DASHD WIDE APART    . . . . . . .            256 BOOK OF LOS 3       38
       WIDE APART STOOD THE FIRES LOS REMAIND    . . . . . .          257 BOOK OF LOS 3       43
       THEY STOOD WIDE APART DRIVN BY HIS HANDS    . . . . . .        257 BOOK OF LOS 3       46
       HURLS APART STAMPING FURIOUS TO DUST    . . . . . .            257 BOOK OF LOS 4       20
       HURLD APART ON ALL SIDES AS A FALLING    . . . . . .           257 BOOK OF LOS 4       23
       APART FROM LOS BUT COVERD HER WITH SOFTEST BROODING CARE       299 FOUR ZOAS 4         57
       [ (URIZEN) ] THO WIDE APART . . .                              309 FOUR ZOAS 5    *  184
       THE LAMB OF GOD IT ROLLD APART REVEALING TO ALL IN HEAVEN      350 FOUR ZOAS 8        342
       BECAUSE AHANIA RENT APART INTO A DESOLATE NIGHT    . . .       501 MILTON 19           41
       LEST HE SHOULD FALL APART IN HIS ETERNAL DEATH TO IMITATE      531 MILTON 39           26
       THE CLOUD THAT OPENS ROLLING APART BEFORE THE THRONE   .      612A V LAST JUDG/N    PROSE
       THE CURTAINS ARE DRAWN APART CHRIST HAVING RENT THE VEIL      613B V LAST JUDG/N    PROSE
       THAT ALBION'S SONS MAY ROLL APART OVER THE NATIONS     . .     636 JERUSALEM 15        24
       I SEE AMERICA CLOSD APART & JERUSALEM DRIVEN IN TERROR         673 JERUSALEM 43        69
       WHY WILT THOU REND THYSELF APART JERUSALEM    . . . . .        692 JERUSALEM 60        22
       BECAUSE HIS CHILDREN WERE CLOSD FROM HIM APART & ENITHARMON    696 JERUSALEM 62        37
       THEREFORE THE MURDER WAS PUT APART IN THE LOOKING-GLASS        698 JERUSALEM 63        38
         OF ENITHARMON
       TILL CANAAN ROLLD APART FROM ALBION ACROSS THE RHINE ALONG     698 JERUSALEM 63        41
         THE DANUBE
       CUT THE FIBRES OF REUBEN HOW HE ROLLD APART & TOOK ROOT        715 JERUSALEM 74        42
       THEY HAVE DIVIDED SIMEON HE ALSO ROLLD APART IN BLOOD   .      715 JERUSALEM 74        44
       DAN NAPTHALI GAD ASHER ISSACHAR ZEBULUN ROLL APART    . . .    715 JERUSALEM 74    *   50
       WHENCE JOSEPH & BENJAMIN ROLLD APART AWAY FROM THE NATIONS     715 JERUSALEM 74        56
       IN VAIN THEY ROLLD APART THEY ARE FIXD INTO THE LAND OF        715 JERUSALEM 74        57
         CABUL
       TOUCHING ITS SUMMITS & SOMETIMES DIVIDED ROLL APART    . . .   728 JERUSALEM 83        44
       WHY WILT THOU REND THYSELF APART & BUILD AN EARTHLY KINGDOM    730 JERUSALEM 85        30
       OF EARTHQUAKES & CONSUMING FIRES THEY ROLL APART IN FEAR       733 JERUSALEM 88         9
       IN CRUEL PRIDE CUT REUBEN APART FROM THE HILLS OF SURREY       736 JERUSALEM 90        25
       AND THE BODY OF ALBION WAS CLOSED APART FROM ALL NATIONS       741 JERUSALEM 94        14
       . . . THEY ROLLED APART TREMBLING OVER THE    . . . . . .      781 GHOST ABEL 2        25
APE
       AT THE LABOUR THAT IS ABOVE PAYMENT AND WILT THOU TAKE         192 V DAU ALBION 5       8
         THE APE
APELLES
       WHEN HE MEANT TO MAKE HIMSELF KNOWN TO APELLES    . . . .     439C REMARKS MALKIN    PROSE
       IF THE FRESCOS OF APELLES OF PROTOGENES OF RAPHAEL    . .     560D EXHIBITION ADV    PROSE
       PROTOGENES AND APELLES KNEW EACH OTHER BY THIS LINE    . .    585B DESC CAT 15       PROSE
APELLES'
       GHIOTTO'S CIRCLE OR APELLES' LINE    . . . . . . . .          542 FLORENTINE/N          26
APHORISM
       FOR THE REASON OF THESE REMARKS SEE THE LAST APHORISM    .     65B ANNO LAVATER      MARG
       ("THE CENTRE") LET ME REFER HERE TO A REMARK ON APHORISM...    65C ANNO LAVATER      MARG
       THIS APHORISM CERTAINLY WAS AN OVERSIGHT    . . . . .          68D ANNO LAVATER      MARG
       THAT WHICH IS CAPABLE OF EVIL IS ALSO CAPABLE OF GOOD          80A ANNO LAVATER      MARG
         THIS APHORISM
       AND MAKES IT PHYSIOGNOMIC APHORISM...SPEAKS OF THE    . . .    81D ANNO LAVATER      MARG
       SEE N...THIS APHORISM SEEMS TO ME TO WANT DISCRIMINATION       82B ANNO LAVATER      MARG
```

```
                                                              PAGE    TITLE           LINE
APHORISM   (CONTINUED)
     ("ASK LESS THAN EXPECTED ") THIS WHOLE APHORISM IS AN      85A ANNO LAVATER      MARG
       OVERSIGHT
APHORISMS
     FALSE APHORISMS SHOULD BE UNIVERSALLY TRUE . . . . . .     67A ANNO LAVATER      MARG
     FEELINGS WILL BE ATTRACTIONS OR REPULSES SEE APHORISMS...  87A ANNO LAVATER      MARG
APIECE
     A HUNDRED POUNDS A PIECE THEY WOULD PRINT OFF TWO THOUSAND  62D ISLAND MOON 11   PROSE
APOLLO
     GOLDEN APOLLO THAT THRO HEAVEN WIDE  . . . . . . . .        14 IMIT SPEN/PS          1
     TO THE DETESTABLE GODS OF PRIAM TO APOLLO AND AT THE ASYLUM 511 MILTON 25           49
     VENUS OF MEDICIS APOLLO BELVIDERE . . . . . . . . .        565D DESC CAT 2       PROSE
     THE HOST IS THE SILENUS THE SQUIRE IS THE APOLLO . . . .   571A DESC CAT 3       PROSE
     THE MINERVA THE JUPITER THE APOLLO  . . . . . . . .        576C DESC CAT 4       PROSE
     IT HAS BEEN SAID TO THE ARTIST TAKE THE APOLLO FOR THE     579B DESC CAT 5       PROSE
       MODEL
APOLLYON
     IN THE TWO CORNERS OF THE PICTURE [WHERE XXX APOLLYON] . . 612B V LAST JUDG/N   *PROSE
     ON THE LEFT HAND APOLLYON IS FOILED BEFORE THE SWORD  . .  612B V LAST JUDG/N    PROSE
     WITH DEMONSTRATIVE SCIENCE PIERCING APOLLYON WITH HIS OWN  631 JERUSALEM 12         14
       BOW
APOLOGIZE
     FEAR THEY WILL NOT EXCUSE & I KNOW NOT HOW TO [XXX]        798B LETTER 10       *PROSE
       APOLOGIZE FOR
APOLOGY
     NOTES ON THE B(BISHOP) OF L'S(LANDAFF'S) APOLOGY   . . .  383A ANNO WATSON      *TITLE
     IS A SUFFICIENT APOLOGY FOR MY VIGOROUS INDIGNATION . . . 452B ANNO REYNOLDS     MARG
     BLAKE'S APOLOGY FOR HIS CATALOGUE . . . . . . . . .       554D BLAKES APL/N 1    TITLE
     THIS IS MY SWEET APOLOGY TO MY FRIENDS  . . . . . . .     556 BLAKES APL/N 2        21
     IS AN APOLOGY & CLOKE FOR HIS SIN & NOT A CONFESSION   . . 682D JERUSALEM 52     PROSE
APOSTLE
     APPROACH THE FIGURE OF AN AGED APOSTLE WHICH REPRESENTS   444B LAST JUDGMNT/L   PROSE
       BAPTISM
     BY ANGELS FROM THE HANDS OF ANOTHER [AGED] APOSTLE  . . . 444B LAST JUDGMNT/L   PROSE
     AN APOSTLE A REAL MESSENGER OF HEAVEN SENT IN EVERY AGE   570B DESC CAT 3       PROSE
     ON EACH SIDE OF THE OPENING HEAVEN APPEARS AN APOSTLE  .  612D V LAST JUDG/N    PROSE
APOSTLES
     CHRIST & HIS PROPHETS & APOSTLES WERE NOT AMBITIOUS MIRACLE 392A ANNO WATSON     MARG
       MONGERS
     BELIEVE CHRIST & HIS APOSTLES THAT THERE IS A CLASS OF MEN 480C MILTON 1        PROSE
     THE APOSTLES THE SAME . . . . . . . . . . . .            576D DESC CAT 4       PROSE
     THE APOSTLES KNEW OF NO OTHER GOSPEL  . . . . . . .      717A JERUSALEM 77     PROSE
     JESUS & HIS APOSTLES & DISCIPLES WERE ALL ARTISTS  . . . 777B INSC LAOCOON     PROSE
     (RE JOHNSON) CHRIST & HIS APOSTLES WERE ILLITERATE MEN   786D ANNO THORNTON     MARG
APOTHECARY
     THE PRINT OF ROMEO & THE APOTHECARY ANNEXD TO YOUR COPY   855C LETTER 53        PROSE
APOTHEOSES
     TWO PICTURES REPRESENTING GRAND APOTHEOSES . . . . . .    560C EXHIBITION ADV   PROSE
     APOTHEOSES OF PERSIAN HINDOO AND EGYPTIAN ANTIQUITY . . . 565C DESC CAT 2       PROSE
APPALL
     NOR POVERTY THE MIND APPALL . . . . . . . . . .          181 HOLY THURS/N          16
     NOR POVERTY THE MIND APPALL . . . . . . . . . .          212 HOLY THURS/SE         16
     INTO NON-ENTITY AND THEIR THUNDERS HOARSE APPALL THE DEAD 640 JERUSALEM 18          9
APPALLD
     HER MADDING BROWS HER SHRIEKS APPALLD THE SOUL OF TIRIEL  108 TIRIEL 6          *   45
     THE AGED SUN RISES APPALLD FROM DARK MOUNTAINS . . . . .  146 FRENCH REVOLTN      270
     LAY THE FAINT MAID AND SOON HER WOES APPALLD HIS THUNDERS  190 V DAU ALBION 1       17
       HOARSE
APPALLING
     AND APPALLING MIST HIS STRONG HAND OUTSTRETCHD . . .  . . 134 FRENCH REVOLTN        3
APPALLS
     EVERY BLACKNING CHURCH APPALLS . . . . . . . . . .       170 LONDON/N               11
     EVERY BLACKNING CHURCH APPALLS . . . . . . . . . .       216 LONDON/SE              11
     HIS CHILDREN'S CRY MY SOUL APPALLS . . . . . . . .       419 I SAW A MONK/N         33
     HIS CHILDREN'S CRY MY SOUL APPALLS  . . . . . . .        430 GREY MONK              18
APPAREL
     BUT KISS HIM & GIVE HIM BOTH [FOOD] DRINK & APPAREL . . . 180 LIT VAGABOND/N        18
     BUT KISS HIM & GIVE HIM BOTH DRINK AND APPAREL    . . .  216 LIT VAGABND/SE         16
     APPAREL ONLY MY BOOK OF DRAWINGS FROM DANTE & ONE PLATE   873A LETTER 76        PROSE
APPARENT    SEE EVER APPARENT
     MELTING APPARENT SURFACES AWAY AND  . . . . . . . .      154C MARRIAGE HH 14   PROSE
     THUS IS THE EARTH ONE INFINITE PLANE AND NOT AS APPARENT  497 MILTON 15            32
     BECOME APPARENT IN TIME & SPACE IN THE THREE PROFESSIONS  514 MILTON 27            59
     THE LAMB OF GOD THE SAVIOUR BECAME APPARENT ON EARTH   . 652B JERUSALEM 27     PROSE
     THAT APPARENT TO ALL IN ETERNITY GLOWS LIKE THE SUN IN    723 JERUSALEM 80        68
       THE BREAST
     GLOWING WITH LOVELINESS BEFORE HIM BECOMING APPARENT  .  723 JERUSALEM 80        71
     THAN WHEN THEY WERE APPARENT TO OUR MORTAL PART    . . . 797A LETTER 9         PROSE
     SHALL BE MADE FULLY APPARENT & PERFECT IN ETERNITY IN THE 822C LETTER 26        PROSE
APPARITION
     THE COUNCIL SAT ALL ROSE BEFORE THE AGED APPARITION . . . 204 AMERICA CANC B        15
     ON MOUNTAINS & CLIFFS OF SNOW THE AWFUL APPARITION HOVERD  205 AMERICA CANC C        28
     THE VISION OF ATOSSA FROM ESCHYLUS APPARITION OF DARIUS   848D LETTER 45        PROSE
APPEAL
     ADVERTISEMENT CALLING IT AN APPEAL TO CHARITY AND SAYS IT 861B LETTER 58        PROSE
APPEALD
     AND PALAMABRON APPEALD TO ALL EDEN AND RECIEVD   . . . . 489 MILTON 9              9
APPEALS
     MR B(BLAKE) APPEALS TO THE PUBLIC FROM THE JUDGMENT OF    563D DESC CAT         PROSE
       THOSE
APPEAR
     THY BUSKIND FEET APPEAR UPON OUR HILLS . . . . . . .       3 TO MORNING/PS         8
```

APPEAR   (CONTINUED)
    AND SWELLING SIGHS BURST FORTH HIS CHILDREN ALL IN ARMS   42B THEN SHE BORE   PROSE
        APPEAR
    NOW ALL THE GODS IN BLACKNING RANKS APPEAR . . . . .   .   42C THEN SHE BORE   PROSE
    BLACK BERRIES APPEAR THAT POISON ALL AROUND HIM SUCH [IS]   110 TIRIEL 8   *   34
        WAS TIRIEL
    OR THE SUMMER FRUITS APPEAR . . . .   124 SCHOOL BOY/SI   27
    WHEN THE BLASTS OF WINTER APPEAR . . . .   124 SCHOOL BOY/SI   30
    THE WHOLE CREATION WILL BE CONSUMED AND APPEAR INFINITE   154B MARRIAGE HH 14 PROSE
        AND HOLY
    EVERY THING WOULD APPEAR TO MAN AS IT IS INFINITE   . . 154C MARRIAGE HH 14 PROSE
    WHICH WILL SOON APPEAR WHEN THE DARKNESS PASSES AWAY   . 156A MARRIAGE HH 17 PROSE
    APPEAR TO THE AMERICANS UPON THE CLOUDY NIGHT   .   .   .   197 AMERICA 4   1
    AS A BLIGHT CUTS THE TENDER CORN WHEN IT BEGINS TO APPEAR   201 AMERICA 14   6
    HIS ETERNAL CREATIONS APPEAR . . . .   234 URIZEN 23   9
    THE BACK BONE OF URIZEN APPEAR . . . .   259 BOOK OF LOS 5   14
    WHEN I APPEAR BEFORE THEE . . . .   330 FOUR ZOAS 7   419
    APPEAR ABOVE THE (CRUMBLING) MOUNTAIN SILENCE WAITS AROUND   336 FOUR ZOAS 7B   *   130
        HIM
    THE FIERY DOGS ARISE THE SHOULDERS HUGE APPEAR   . . .   336 FOUR ZOAS 7B   132
    AND LIFE APPEAR & VANISH MOCKING ME WITH SHADOWS OF FALSE   339 FOUR ZOAS 7B   241
        HOPE
    THE PHARISEES APPEAR ON THE LEFT HAND PLEADING   . . . . 443C LAST JUDGMNT/L PROSE
    [THE] GREEN HILLS APPEAR BENEATH WITH THE GRAVES OF THE   443D LAST JUDGMNT/L PROSE
        BLESSED
    BEHIND THE SEAT & THRONE OF CHRIST APPEARS]APPEAR]   . . . 444B LAST JUDGMNT/L PROSE
    MANY INFANTS APPEAR IN THE GLORY REPRESENTING   . . . . 444C LAST JUDGMNT/L PROSE
    APPEAR AROUND IN THE EXTERNAL SPHERES OF VISIONARY LIFE   524 MILTON 34   51
    WITH POMP EVEN TILL MORNING BREAK & OSIRIS APPEAR IN THE   528 MILTON 37   29
        SKY
    SEVEN ANGELS BEAR MY NAME & IN THOSE SEVEN I APPEAR   . . 530 MILTON 38   55
    AND THE IMMORTAL FOUR IN WHOM THE TWENTY-FOUR APPEAR   534 MILTON 42   18
        FOUR-FOLD
    DELICATE HANDS & HEADS WILL NEVER APPEAR   . . . .   551 DELICATE/N   1
    CHARACTERS OF HUMAN LIFE APPEAR TO POETS IN ALL AGES   . 571B DESC CAT 3   PROSE
    APPEAR TO ME TO BE THE SAME PERSON BUT THIS IS ONLY AN   . 572A DESC CAT 3   PROSE
    THAT ALL HIS IMAGINATIONS APPEAR TO HIM . . . . . .   576D DESC CAT 4   PROSE
    INTO HEAVEN BY MEANS OF LEARNING APPEAR TO CHILDREN   . . 581D DESC CAT 8   PROSE
    OF HUMAN CHARACTERS AS THEY APPEAR AGE AFTER AGE   . . . 591A PUB ADDRESS/N   TITLE
    COMPELLD TO BE A TYRANNY PRINCES APPEAR TO ME TO BE FOOLS   600A PUB ADDRESS/N   PROSE
    HOUSES OF COMMONS & HOUSES OF LORDS APPEAR TO ME TO BE   600A PUB ADDRESS/N   PROSE
        FOOLS
    ADAM & EVE APPEAR FIRST BEFORE THE [THRONE]   . . . . . 606B V LAST JUDG/N   PROSE
    WHEN DISTANT THEY APPEAR AS ONE MAN . . . .   607C V LAST JUDG/N   PROSE
    BUT AS YOU APPROACH THEY APPEAR MULTITUDES OF NATIONS   . . 607C V LAST JUDG/N   PROSE
    ABRAHAM HOVERS ABOVE HIS POSTERITY WHICH APPEAR   . . . 607C V LAST JUDG/N   PROSE
    MULTITUDES OF MEN IN HARMONY APPEAR LIKE A SINGLE INFANT   607C V LAST JUDG/N   PROSE
    THEY APPEAR TO BE INNOCENTLY GAY & THOUGHTLESS   . . . 610B V LAST JUDG/N   PROSE
    THESE ARE CAUGHT UP BY THREE AGED MEN WHO APPEAR   . . 610D V LAST JUDG/N   PROSE
    WHEN SEEN REMOTE THEY APPEAR AS ONE MAN . . . . . .   611D V LAST JUDG/N   PROSE
    CANDLESTICK & THE TABLE OF SHEW BREAD APPEAR ON EACH SIDE   613B V LAST JUDG/N   PROSE
    [THEY] THEY MERELY APPEAR AS IN A CLOUD WHEN ANY THING   . 614C V LAST JUDG/N   *PROSE
    THE REASON THEY SO APPEAR IS   . . . .   614C V LAST JUDG/N   PROSE
    & THEN & NOT TILL THEN TRUTH OR ETERNITY WILL APPEAR   617B V LAST JUDG/N   PROSE
    MOUNTAINS CLOUDS RIVERS TREES APPEAR . . . .   618B ILLUS MILTON   PROSE
    ALL HIS AFFECTIONS NOW APPEAR WITHOUTSIDE ALL HIS SONS   641 JERUSALEM 19   17
    DOST THOU APPEAR BEFORE ME WHO LIEST DEAD IN LUVAH'S   648 JERUSALEM 24   57
        SEPULCHER
    O WHEN SHALL THE MORNING OF THE GRAVE APPEAR AND WHEN   .   671 JERUSALEM 42   71
    TILL JESUS SHALL APPEAR & THEY GAVE THEIR POWER TO LOS   . 674 JERUSALEM 44   30
    APPEAR IN STRONG DELUSIVE LIGHT OF TIME & SPACE DRAWN OUT   715 JERUSALEM 75   5
    WHICH ALWAYS APPEAR TO THE IGNORANCE-LOVING HYPOCRITE AS   717C JERUSALEM 77   PROSE
        SINS
    JESUS WILL APPEAR SO HE WHO WISHES TO SEE A VISION   738 JERUSALEM 91   21
        A PERFECT WHOLE
    APPEAR ONLY IN THE OUTWARD SPHERES OF VISIONARY SPACE AND   739 JERUSALEM 92   17
        TIME
    THO DEAD THEY APPEAR UPON MY PATH . . . .   817 HAPPINESS/L   17
    IF ANY OF MY WRITINGS SHOULD HEREAFTER APPEAR BEFORE   . . 860D LETTER 57   PROSE
    & HOPE THAT HE HAS A GOOD OPINION OF MY WILLINGNESS TO   868D LETTER 68   PROSE
        APPEAR
APPEARANCE
    I REMAIND ALONE & THEN THIS APPEARANCE WAS NO MORE   . . . 156C MARRIAGE HH 17 PROSE
    HIS SHADOWS WOULD DESTROY IT & DEFORM ITS APPEARANCE   . . 464A ANNO REYNOLDS   MARG
    UNITING IN ONE WITH OLOLON & THE APPEARANCE OF ONE MAN   505 MILTON 21   59
    AS TO THAT FALSE APPEARANCE WHICH APPEARS TO THE REASONER   516 MILTON 29   15
    HAVE BEEN CHRISTIANS IN OUTWARD APPEARANCE VOLTAIRE   . .   615B V LAST JUDG/N   PROSE
    AND THIS IS THE CAUSE OF THE APPEARANCE IN THE FROWNING   659 JERUSALEM 33   25
        CHAOS
    FOR THE DIVINE APPEARANCE IS BROTHERHOOD BUT I AM LOVE   . 660 JERUSALEM 33   52
    AND THE APPEARANCE OF A MAN WAS SEEN IN THE FURNACES   . . 662 JERUSALEM 35   5
    SUCH THE APPEARANCE IN CHEVIOT IN THE DIVISIONS OF REUBEN   697 JERUSALEM 63   23
    THEIR APPEARANCE WHEN COMBIND BUT OFTEN BY BIRTH PANGS   708 JERUSALEM 70   *   11
        & LOUD GROANS
    AND THE DIVINE APPEARANCE WAS THE LIKENESS & SIMILITUDE   743 JERUSALEM 96   7
        OF LOS
    & THAT THERE IS ALL THE APPEARANCE IN THE WORLD OF OUR   . 824C LETTER 27   PROSE
    AM BOUND IN...L FOR MY APPEARANCE AT THE QUARTER SESSIONS   >828A LETTER 28   PROSE
    APPEARANCE SHOULD NOT HAVE SUPPOSED HIM TO BE NEAR SIXTY   835C LETTER 35   PROSE
APPEARANCES
    IN CHASTE APPEARANCES FOR SWEET DECEITS OF LOVE & MODESTY   727 JERUSALEM 83   31
    MAY TURN OUT SO AGAIN NOTWITHSTANDING APPEARANCES   . . . 862C LETTER 60   PROSE

		PAGE	TITLE	LINE

APPEARANCES (CONTINUED)
    & NEVER MIND APPEARANCES . . . . 873A LETTER 76   PROSE
APPEARD
    APPEARD LIKE HIS FATHER IN WHITE . . . . 121 LIT BOY FND/SI   4
    AND THE PALACE APPEARD LIKE A CLOUD DRIVEN ABROAD . . . 145 FRENCH REVOLTN   246
    IT INDEED APPEARD TO REASON AS IF DESIRE WAS CAST OUT . . 150A MARRIAGE HH 5   PROSE
    TILL A VOID BOUNDLESS AS A NETHER SKY APPEARD BENEATH US 155D MARRIAGE HH 17   PROSE
    APPEARD AND SUNK AGAIN THE SCALY FOLD OF A MONSTROUS 156B MARRIAGE HH 17   PROSE
      SERPENT
    AT LAST TO THE EAST DISTANT ABOUT THREE DEGREES APPEARD 156C MARRIAGE HH 17   PROSE
    UNSEEN UNKNOWN CHANGES APPEARD . . . . 222 URIZEN 3   10
    IN LIVING CREATIONS APPEARD . . . . 225 URIZEN 5   1
    THE VAST WORLD OF URIZEN APPEARD . . . . 226 URIZEN 5   37
    OF THIRST & OF HUNGER APPEARD . . . . 229 URIZEN 13   9
    OF THE DARK SEPERATION APPEARD . . . . 231 URIZEN 15   8
    WEEPING WAILING FIRST THIRIEL APPEARD . . . . . . 234 URIZEN 23   11
    APPEARD TRANSPARENT AIR FOR THEIR EYES . . . . . . 236 URIZEN 25   35
    AND IN THE VINEYARDS OF RED FRANCE APPEARD THE LIGHT OF 245 EUROPE 15   2
      HIS FURY
    A FROWNING CONTINENT APPEARD WHERE ENION IN THE DESART . . 266 FOUR ZOAS 1   89
    ETERNITY APPEARD ABOVE THEM AS ONE MAN INFOLDED . . . . 274 FOUR ZOAS 1   363
    AND VALA LIKE A SHADOW OFT APPEARD TO URIZEN . . . . 285 FOUR ZOAS 2   214
    AND THE DIVINE VISION APPEARD IN LUVAH'S ROBES OF BLOOD . 286 FOUR ZOAS 2   247
    BUT FROM THE DOLOROUS GROAN ONE LIKE A SHADOW OF SMOKE 296 FOUR ZOAS 3   153
      APPEARD
    THE DOLOROUS SHADOW JOYD WEAK HOPE APPEARD AROUND HIS HEAD 300 FOUR ZOAS 4   127
    AND THIRST APPEARD AND A SIXTH AGE PASSED OF DISMAL WOE 303 FOUR ZOAS 4   * 242
    A SPECTRE VAST APPEARD WHOSE FEET & LEGS WITH IRON SCALED 319 FOUR ZOAS 6   298
    APPEARD OF MANY COLOURS & OF VARIOUS POISONOUS QUALITIES . 325 FOUR ZOAS 7   215
    OF THE NOW FALLEN MAN A DOUBLE FORM VALA APPEARD A MALE 326 FOUR ZOAS 7   246
    IN BEAUTIFUL SUBSTANTIAL FORMS APPEARD & SERVED HER . . . 340 FOUR ZOAS 7B   275
    AND THEY APPEARD A UNIVERSAL FEMALE FORM CREATED . . . 345 FOUR ZOAS 8   188
    WHICH TO THEIR PHANTOM EYES APPEARD STILL IN THE SEPULCHER 357 FOUR ZOAS 9   3
    SUCH AS GLOWS OUT FROM SLEEPING SPIRITS APPEARD IN THE 372 FOUR ZOAS 9   561
      DEEPS BENEATH
    THEN FIRST SHE SAW HIS GLORY & HER HARLOT FORM APPEARD . . 382 FOUR ZOAS AD 6   21
    HIS REAL AND IMMORTAL SELF WAS AS APPEARD TO THOSE . . . 496 MILTON 15   11
    AND ALL THIS VEGETABLE WORLD APPEARD ON MY LEFT FOOT . . 503 MILTON 21   12
    JESUS THE SAVIOUR APPEARD COMING IN THE CLOUDS OF OLOLON 505 MILTON 21   60
    APPEARD AS DOES THE FACE OF HEAVEN WHEN COVERD WITH THICK 507 MILTON 23   29
      STORMS
    SO SPAKE THE LOVELY EMANATIONS & THERE APPEARD A PLEASANT 519 MILTON 30   32
    APPEARD A VIRGIN OF TWELVE YEARS NOR TIME NOR SPACE WAS 527 MILTON 36   17
    AND HE APPEARD THE WICKER MAN OF SCANDINAVIA IN WHOM . 527 MILTON 37   11
    NO SOONER SHE HAD SPOKE BUT RAHAB BABYLON APPEARD . . . 532 MILTON 40   17
    APPEARD THE SEVEN KINGDOMS OF CANAAN & FIVE BAALIM . . . 532 MILTON 40   24
    TO HAVE APPEARD IN CHAUCER'S TIME INTERSPERSED . . . . 567A DESC CAT 3   PROSE
    TO HAVE APPEARD IN CHAUCER'S TIME INTERSPERSED . . . . 588D CHAUCER/N   PROSE
    TO HAVE APPEARD IN CHAUCER'S TIME INTERSPERSED . . . . 590B CHAUCER 2   PROSE
    THE HUMAN IMAGINATION WHO APPEARD TO ME AS . . . . . 606A V LAST JUDG/N   PROSE
    AND THEY APPEARD WITHIN & WITHOUT INCIRCLING ON BOTH SIDES 631 JERUSALEM 12   17
    APPEARD A ROCKY FORM AGAINST THE DIVINE HUMANITY . . . . 642 JERUSALEM 19   35
    SUCH VISIONS HAVE APPEARD TO ME . . . . 649 JERUSALEM 26   * 1
    THEN THE DIVINE VISION LIKE A SILENT SUN APPEARD ABOVE . . 653 JERUSALEM 29   1
    MOST ANCIENT PROMONTORY AND IN THE SUN A HUMAN FORM APPEARD 653 JERUSALEM 29   4
    INCLOSING LOS BUT THE DIVINE VISION APPEARD WITH LOS . . 656 JERUSALEM 30   19
    CHAOS BEFORE HIS FACE APPEARD AN UNFORMED MEMORY . . . . 659 JERUSALEM 33   2
    APPEARD NOW IN THE FROWNING CHAOS PROLIFIC UPON THE CHAOS 659 JERUSALEM 33   27
    THE FOUR APPEARD WITH THEIR EMANATIONS IN FIERY . . . . 666 JERUSALEM 40   4
    APPEARD AND THEY WERE ONE IN HIM A HUMAN VISION . . . . 667 JERUSALEM 40   46
    AND THESE THE FOUR IN WHOM THE TWENTY-FOUR APPEARD 676 JERUSALEM 46   23
      FOUR-FOLD
    OF STARS FOR ALL THE SONS OF ALBION APPEARD DISTANT STARS 681 JERUSALEM 50   20
    JERUSALEM & VALA APPEARD & ABOVE BETWEEN THE WINGS 685 JERUSALEM 54   31
      MAGNIFICENT
    THE DIVINE VISION DIMLY APPEARD IN CLOUDS OF BLOOD WEEPING 685 JERUSALEM 54   32
    IN FLAMING FIRE WITHIN THE FURNACES THE DIVINE VISION 692 JERUSALEM 60   5
      APPEARD
    A DOUBLE FEMALE NOW APPEARD WITHIN THE TABERNACLE . . . 735 JERUSALEM 89   52
    THE INNUMERABLE CHARIOTS OF THE ALMIGHTY APPEARD IN HEAVEN 745 JERUSALEM 98   8
    PARACELSUS & BEHMEN APPEARD TO ME . . . . 799 TO FLAXMAN/L   7
    . . . TERRORS APPEARD IN THE HEAVENS ABOVE . . . . . . 799 TO FLAXMAN/L   7
    APPEARD IN ITS VEGETATED MORTALITY TO MY MORTAL VEGETATED 802C LETTER 14   PROSE
      EYES
    APPEARD AS ONE MAN . . . . 805 TO BUTTS/L   51
    APPEARD ON THE SEA . . . . 806 TO BUTTS/L   78
    THEN LOS APPEARD IN ALL HIS POWER . . . . 818 HAPPINESS/L   55
    IN THE SUN HE APPEARD DESCENDING BEFORE . . . . 818 HAPPINESS/L   56
APPEARED
    AND JEHOVAH STOOD IN THE GATES OF THE VICTIM & HE APPEARED 697 JERUSALEM 63   16
    THEN JESUS APPEARED STANDING BY ALBION AS THE GOOD SHEPHERD 743 JERUSALEM 96   3
APPEAREST
    APPEAREST CLOTHD IN LUVAH'S GARMENTS THAT WE MAY BEHOLD 304 FOUR ZOAS 4   257
      THEE
    ALBION SPOKE WHO ART THOU THAT APPEAREST IN GLOOMY POMP 659 JERUSALEM 33   29
    THAT APPEAREST TO MY SPIRITUAL VISION EVE SEEST THOU ALSO 780 GHOST ABEL 1   22
APPEARING
    OFT ENITHARMON ENTERD WEEPING INTO THE SPACE THERE 490 MILTON 10   3
      APPEARING
    BEULAH IS EVERMORE CREATED AROUND ETERNITY APPEARING . . 518 MILTON 30   8
    AND HINDER ALL CORRECT DRAWING FROM APPEARING TO BE CORRECT 583C DESC CAT 9   PROSE
    GOD CREATING ADAM CHRIST APPEARING TOUCHG UP CHRIST SUPP LETTER 56A   *PROSE
      BAPTIZING

```
                                                         PAGE      TITLE          LINE
APPEARS
    GORDRED APPEARS HIS FROWNING BROW  . . . . . . .       12 GWIN KING/PS          63
    TILL THE MORNING APPEARS IN THE SKIES   . . . . . .    60 NURSES SONG/IM         8
    TILL THE MORNING APPEARS IN THE SKIES   . . . . . .   121 NURSES SONG/SI         8
    WHEREAS IT NOW APPEARS FINITE & CORRUPT   . . . . . . 154B MARRIAGE HH 14     PROSE
    OPEN TO JOY AND TO DELIGHT WHERE EVER BEAUTY APPEARS  . 194 V DAU ALBION 6       22
    OVER THEIR PALE LIMBS AS A VINE WHEN THE TENDER GRAPE   202 AMERICA 15           26
        APPEARS
    [BRIGHT] DARK AS A DEWY MORNING WHEN THE CRIMSON LIGHT  271 FOUR ZOAS 1      *  253
        APPEARS
    APPEARS UPON THE ROCKS & HILLS IN SILENT SHADES BUT SOON 355 FOUR ZOAS 8        539
    AND EVERY ONE OF THE DEAD APPEARS AS HE HAD LIVD BEFORE  363 FOUR ZOAS 9        245
    AND AFTER THE FLAMES APPEARS THE CLOUD OF THE SON OF MAN 364 FOUR ZOAS 9        272
    WHEN INFANT SPRING APPEARS IN SWELLING BUDS & OPENING    371 FOUR ZOAS 9        548
        FLOWERS
    IT APPEARS TO ME NOW   . . . . . . . . . . .          396B ANNO WATSON         MARG
    IT APPEARS TO ME THAT MEN ARE HIRED TO RUN DOWN MEN OF  413B ANNO BOYD          MARG
        GENIUS
    GOD APPEARS & GOD IS LIGHT  . . . . . . . . . .        434 AUGURIES            129
    BEHIND THE SEAT & THRONE OF CHRIST APPEARS ]APPEAR] . . 444B LAST JUDGMNT/L    PROSE
    APPEARS TO ME TO GIVE ALWAYS THE CHARACTERS OF VULGAR   464B ANNO REYNOLDS     MARG
        STUPIDITY
    AS TO THAT FALSE APPEARANCE WHICH APPEARS TO THE REASONER 516 MILTON 29          15
    BUT BEULAH TO ITS INHABITANTS APPEARS WITHIN EACH DISTRICT 518 MILTON 30         10
    APPEARS LISTENS SILENT THEN SPRINGING FROM THE WAVING    520 MILTON 31           30
        CORN-FIELD LOUD
    THEREFORE HE APPEARS ONLY A SMALL ROOT CREEPING IN GRASS 526 MILTON 35          56
    THUS IT APPEARS TO MORTAL EYES & THOSE OF THE ULRO HEAVENS 527 MILTON 36         11
    NO REAL STYLE OF COLOURING EVER APPEARS  . . . . . .   536 NO REAL STYL/N        1
    APPEARS DELIGHTED TO RIDE IN HIS COMPANY  . . . . . . 570C DESC CAT 3         PROSE
    APPEARS IN HER CHEEKS NOW HEAR WHAT CHAUCER HAS MADE HER 574B DESC CAT 3       PROSE
    BUT IT APPEARS IN ALL THE WRITINGS OF CHAUCER  . . . . 575A DESC CAT 3        PROSE
    TO DIFFERENT PEOPLE IT APPEARS DIFFERENTLY AS EVERYTHING 605A V LAST JUDG/N    PROSE
        ELSE
    BETWEEN THE FIGURES OF ADAM & EVE APPEARS A FIERY GULPH 609A V LAST JUDG/N     PROSE
    THIS STATE APPEARS LIKE A FEMALE CROWND WITH STARS  . . 610A V LAST JUDG/N     PROSE
    ON EACH SIDE OF THE OPENING HEAVEN APPEARS AN APOSTLE . 612D V LAST JUDG/N     PROSE
    FOR IT APPEARS SO AT THE LAST JUDGMENT FOR A PROTECTION 614B V LAST JUDG/N     PROSE
    I DIE & PASS THE LIMITS OF POSSIBILITY AS IT APPEARS .  696 JERUSALEM 62        19
    AND EARTH & ALL YOU BEHOLD THO IT APPEARS WITHOUT IT IS 709 JERUSALEM 71        18
        WITHIN
    NOR RAIN NO MORE THE SPRING OF THE ROCK APPEARS BUT COLD 719 JERUSALEM 79        5
    THEY WATCH THEM IN THE NIGHT AND THE LAMB OF GOD APPEARS 720 JERUSALEM 79       32
        AMONG US
    WHEREFORE IN DREADFUL MAJESTY & BEAUTY OUTSIDE APPEARS . 721 JERUSALEM 79       70
    (CORRUPTIBILITY) APPEARS UPON THY LIMBS AND NEVER MORE   727 JERUSALEM 83      *  1
    APPEARS UPON OUR HILLS AWAKE JERUSALEM AND COME AWAY  . 744 JERUSALEM 97        4
    IT APPEARS TO ME AS IF THE LAST PARAGRAPH BEGINNING WITH 783D ANNO WW POEMS  * MARG
    APPEARS TO BE LAW & GOSPEL TOO AT LEAST I HEAR SO FROM THE 798C LETTER 10      PROSE
    & WHENEVER ANY THING APPEARS TO AFFECT THAT INTEREST   . 812D LETTER 22        PROSE
    FEAR SO TOO BECAUSE THERE APPEARS SOME REASON WHY YOU MIGHT 814A LETTER 23     PROSE
    WHAT TO OTHERS A TRIFLE APPEARS  . . . . . . . . .     817 HAPPINESS/L         25
    BUT MY LETTER TO MR BUTTS APPEARS TO ME NOT TO BE      820B LETTER 25         PROSE
        SO EXPLICIT
    IT APPEARS TO ME THAT I AM NOW TOO OLD & HAVE HAD   . . 821A LETTER 25         PROSE
    MR H(HOARE) APPEARS TO ME TO CONSIDER IT AS A REJECTION OF 842C LETTER 42      PROSE
    IT APPEARS TO ME THAT NEITHER TIME NOR PLACE CAN MAKE ANY 868B LETTER 67       PROSE
    SAYING DO NOT VENTURE TILL SUMMER APPEARS AGAIN I ALSO  . 872D LETTER 76       PROSE
APPEASE
    NOR COULD CONCEAL AUGHT THAT MIGHT APPEASE HER THEN  . . .  39B SAMSON/PS      PROSE
APPENDED
    THE BEAUTY THAT IS ANNEXED AND APPENDED TO FOLLY IS A  . 579D DESC CAT 5       PROSE
APPENINES
    HIS VOICE IS HEARD FROM ALBION THE ALPS & APPENINES . . .  730 JERUSALEM 85     16
APPETITE
    CONCENTERD INTO LOVE OF PARENT STORGOUS APPETITE CRAVING  308 FOUR ZOAS 5      113
    BY GRATIFIED DESIRE BY STRONG DEVOURING APPETITE SHE FILLS 323 FOUR ZOAS 7     133
    THAT LIFE LIVES UPON DEATH & BY DEVOURING APPETITE  . . . 330 FOUR ZOAS 7      390
    FOR SUCH ALONE SLEEPERS REMAIN MEER PASSION & APPETITE .  512 MILTON 26         29
    NOR THAT THEIR EVERY THOUGHT WAS SIN & SECRET APPETITE .  644 JERUSALEM 21      27
    A WORLD OF SHAPES IN CRAVING LUST & DEVOURING APPETITE .  685 JERUSALEM 54      24
    AN EVER DEVOURING APPETITE  . . . . . . . . . . .      755 EV GOSPEL(E)/N      83
APPLAUDED
    PORTRAIT PAINTING APPLAUDED & REWARDED BY THE RICH & GREAT 445C ANNO REYNOLDS  MARG
    THINK HE IS TO BE APPLAUDED BUT I CONCIEVE THAT HE MAY BE A 850B LETTER 49     PROSE
APPLAUDS
    THE SOUL DRINKS MURDER & REVENGE & APPLAUDS ITS OWN     669 JERUSALEM 41        30
        HOLINESS
    TO LONDON AGAIN APPLAUDS IT AS THE ONLY COURSE FOR THE  . 822D LETTER 26       PROSE
APPLAUSE
    OR IS IT BECAUSE SECRESY GAINS [FEMININE] FEMALES' LOUD  171 TO NOBODADDY/N      9
        APPLAUSE
    PLATTED QUITE NEAT TO CATCH APPLAUSE WITH A SLIDING NOOSE 184 HER LIFE IS/N      2
        AT THE END
APPLE
    THE APPLE TREE NEVER ASKS THE BEECH HOW HE SHALL GROW  . 152B MARRIAGE HH 9   PROSE
    TILL IT BORE AN APPLE BRIGHT  . . . . . . . . . .      165 CHRISTN FORB/N      10
    TILL IT BORE AN APPLE BRIGHT  . . . . . . . . . .      218 POISON TREE/SE      10
    [THE PEAR TREE MILD THE FROWNING WALNUT THE SHARP CRAB   269 FOUR ZOAS 1       205
        & APPLE SWEET]
    AMONG THE APPLE TREES & ALL THE GARDENS OF DELIGHT  . . 339 FOUR ZOAS 7B   *  234
    SO SAYING SHE SAT DOWN & WEPT BENEATH THE APPLE TREES  . 368 FOUR ZOAS 9       413
```

```
                                                          PAGE    TITLE          LINE
APPLE    (CONTINUED)
    [OR THE APPLE TREE TEACHES THE PINE TREE TO BEAR]    . . . 453B ANNO REYNOLDS  * MARG
    OR THE APPLE TREE TEACHES THE PEAR TREE HOW TO BEAR FRUIT   453B ANNO REYNOLDS    MARG
    AN APPLE TREE A PEAR TREE A HORSE A LION ARE CHARACTERS     778B HOMERS POETRY    PROSE
    BUT A GOOD APPLE TREE OR A BAD IS AN APPLE TREE STILL       778B HOMERS POETRY    PROSE
APPLES
    THE CORN IS TURND TO THISTLES & THE APPLES INTO POISON  . . 360 FOUR ZOAS 9    * 109
    SHE [D] STOPD TO DRINK OF THE CLEAR SPRING & EAT THE GRAPES 369 FOUR ZOAS 9    * 476
      & APPLES
    THAT WHILE HE DID THAT WORK HE LIVED ON BREAD & APPLES  . . 446A ANNO REYNOLDS   MARG
    THE CORN IS TURND TO THISTLES & THE APPLES INTO POISON  . . 641 JERUSALEM 19      10
APPLICATION
    APPLICATION HE WHO SEES THE INFINITE IN ALL THINGS SEES     98A NAT RELIGION 2  PROSE
      GOD
    THE NECESSARY APPLICATION TO MY DUTY AS WELL AS TO MY OLD . . 808A LETTER 19     PROSE
    APPLICATION OF THE PROFITS AS HE ON READING YOUR LETTER     858A LETTER 55      PROSE
APPLIED
    WORD ELEGANCE OUGHT TO BE APPLIED TO FORMS NOT TO COLOURS   464C ANNO REYNOLDS   MARG
    THESE WORDS BE APPLIED TO SUCH A WRETCH AS SALVATOR ROSA    468B ANNO REYNOLDS   MARG
    APPLIED THEIR FOUR TRUMPETS & THEM SOUNDED TO THE FOUR      534 MILTON 42         23
      WINDS
    THE STORIES OF ARTHUR ARE THE ACTS OF ALBION APPLIED   . . 578C DESC CAT 5      PROSE
    THEIR COLOURING GRAVING & VERSE CAN NEVER BE APPLIED TO ART 602D PUB ADDR AD/N  PROSE
    BY THREE RHODIANS & APPLIED TO . . . . . . . . . .  775D INSC LAOCOON   TITLE
    OF CHARACTER WHICH FEW HAVE HE IS THE MAN WHO APPLIED TO    841C LETTER 41      PROSE
APPLY
    AND TO APPLY IT TO MODERN HEROES ON A SMALLER SCALE  . . . 565D DESC CAT 2      PROSE
    WE CAN APPLY SOME OF THE PLATES TO THE NEW EDITION          858B LETTER 55      PROSE
      I CONSIDER
APPLYING
    HAS LEFT ME WITHOUT ANY RESOURCE BUT THAT OF APPLYING TO    853C LETTER 52      PROSE
      YOU
APPOINTD
    MR JOHNSON'S FORGETFULNESS WHO APPOINTD TO CALL ON YOU BUT  809C LETTER 20     *PROSE
    BE APPOINTD BY HIM IN SO HONOURABLE A CONCERN AS THE   . . 856B LETTER 54     *PROSE
APPOINTED
    O CLOUD WELL APPOINTED . . . . . . . . . . .     134 FRENCH REVOLTN       2
    . . . AND EACH STAR APPOINTED FOR WATCHERS OF NIGHT . . .   143 FRENCH REVOLTN     212
    AS WHEN THE THUNDERBOLT DOWN FALLETH ON THE APPOINTED PLACE 295 FOUR ZOAS 3      140
    TO BE MY GREAT & AWFUL CURSES AT THE TIME APPOINTED  . . .  336 FOUR ZOAS 7B     120
    INTO THEIR OWN APPOINTED PLACES DRIVEN BACK BY THE WINDS    365 FOUR ZOAS 9      325
    IN HIS APPOINTED SEASON WHEN THE ENDS OF HEAVEN MEET   . . 517 MILTON 29         46
    THAT I SHALL SEE YOU ON SUNDAY AS WE HAVE APPOINTED  . . . 799A LETTER 11       PROSE
APPOINTS
    HIS PREY WHILE LOS APPOINTS & RINTRAH & PALAMABRON GUIDE    517 MILTON 29         44
APPREHENDED
    FORMS MUST BE APPREHENDED BY SENSE OR THE EYE OF           775A ANNO BERKELEY    MARG
      IMAGINATION
APPRENTICED
    ENGRAVING IS THE PROFESSION I WAS APPRENTICED TO  . . . . 794C LETTER 5         PROSE
APPROACH
    WHICH IN FULL CHOIR HAILS THY APPROACH O SPRING  . . . .    1 TO SPRING/PS        4
    WHO WOULD NOT SUFFER HIM TO APPROACH BUT DROVE HIM BACK     311 FOUR ZOAS 6        6
      WITH STORMS
    AND WATCHD HIS SWIFT APPROACH COLLECTED DARK THE SPECTRE    319 FOUR ZOAS 6      301
      STOOD
    COLD PALE IN SORROW AT MY APPROACH TREMBLING AT MY TERRIFIC 325 FOUR ZOAS 7      188
    APPROACH THE FIGURE OF AN AGED APOSTLE WHICH REPRESENTS    444B LAST JUDGMNT/L  PROSE
      BAPTISM
    I LOVED PALAMABRON & I SOUGHT TO APPROACH HIS TENT  . . .  492 MILTON 11         37
    BUT AS YOU APPROACH THEY APPEAR MULTITUDES OF NATIONS  . . 607C V LAST JUDG/N   PROSE
    O SPECTRE OF URTHONA REASON NOT AGAINST THEIR DEAR APPROACH 629 JERUSALEM 10      32
    DARE NOT APPROACH THE DAUGHTERS OPENLY LEST HE BE CONSUMED  638 JERUSALEM 17       7
    SO DREAD IS LOS'S FURY THAT NONE DARE HIM TO APPROACH  . . 732 JERUSALEM 86      48
    & ONLY NOW I APPROACH THE PROSPECT OF SENDING YOU SOME     809B LETTER 20       PROSE
      WHICH
    LIKE THE DISTANT APPROACH OF THINGS MIGHTY & MAGNIFICENT    835B LETTER 34       PROSE
APPROACHD
    TILL TO THE CAVES OF ZAZEL THEY APPROACHD AT EVEN TIDE  . . 108 TIRIEL 7          2
    APPROACHD URIZEN EVEN TO HIS KNEES  . . . . . . . .  250 AHANIA 3         15
    WHEN HE HAD PASSD THESE SOUTHERN TERRORS HE APPROACHD THE   315 FOUR ZOAS 6      147
      EAST
    THAT URIZEN APPROACHD NOT NEAR BUT TOOK HIS SEAT ON A ROCK  320 FOUR ZOAS 7       18
    ENLARGING AND ENLARGING TILL THEIR DISKS APPROACHD EACH     504 MILTON 21         39
      OTHER
    ARE PRACTISED IN BABEL & SHINAR & HAVE APPROACHD TO ZION'S  627 JERUSALEM 8       20
      HILL
APPROACHES
    OF ONE THAT FLED APPROACHES ELLEN STOOD  . . . . .    4 FAIR ELENOR/PS     19
    THE WRETCH APPROACHES CRYING THE DEED IS DONE  . . . . .    4 FAIR ELENOR/PS     21
    THOU WOULDST MY DEATH AND DEATH APPROACHES FAST  . . . .   38C SAMSON/PS        PROSE
    BEHOLD THE TIME APPROACHES FAST THAT THOU SHALT BE AS A     355 FOUR ZOAS 8      549
      THING
    SIX THOUSAND YEARS ARE PASSD AWAY THE END APPROACHES FAST   508 MILTON 23         55
    HE IS THE SIGNAL THAT THE LAST VINTAGE NOW APPROACHES  . . 509 MILTON 24         42
APPROACHING
    NOW DEAD I'LL GUARD THEE FROM APPROACHING ILL  . . . . .   43D WOE CRIED MUSE   PROSE
    HIS UGLY MAN ONE APPROACHING TO THE BEAST IN FEATURES  . . 580A DESC CAT 5      PROSE
    IN HIS IMAGINATION APPROACHING THEM  . . . . . . . .  611A V LAST JUDG/N   PROSE
APPROBATION
    IN CONDEMNATION OF MY WORK & APPROBATION OF  . . . . .  592B PUB ADDRESS/N   PROSE
    ARE NO PROOF OF POPULAR APPROBATION BUT OFTEN THE CONTRARY  593C PUB ADDRESS/N   PROSE
```

APPROBATION   (CONTINUED)
        I HAVE ENOUGH IN THE APPROBATION OF FELLOW LABOURERS   . . 600C PUB ADDRESS/N   PROSE
        YOUR APPROBATION OF MY PICTURES IS A MULTITUDE TO ME   . 811D LETTER 22   PROSE
        LONDON WITH THE FULL APPROBATION OF MR HAYLEY & WITH   . 822C LETTER 26   PROSE
        THE ASSISTANCE AND APPROBATION OF OUR GOOD FRIEND FLAXMAN   853B LETTER 52   PROSE
        CONNOISSEUR IN ENGRAVING HAS GIVEN HER WARM APPROBATION   853B LETTER 52   PROSE
        APPROBATION OF MY WORKS YOUR MOST OBEDIENT SERVANT   . . . 868A LETTER 66   PROSE
APPROPRIATE
        SHINING LIKE PRECIOUS STONES & ORNAMENTED WITH APPROPRIATE 516 MILTON 28   53
            SIGNS
        IMAGINATION ONLY CAN FURNISH US WITH COLOURING APPROPRIATE 580D DESC CAT 5   PROSE
        OF APPROPRIATE EXECUTION RESULTING FROM THE INVENTIONS . . 582D DESC CAT 9   PROSE
        WHERE EVERY HORSE IS APPROPRIATE TO HIS RIDER . . . . .   588A CHAUCER/N   PROSE
        IDEAS CANNOT BE GIVEN BUT IN THEIR MINUTELY APPROPRIATE   596A PUB ADDRESS/N   PROSE
        MADE WITHOUT ITS MINUTELY APPROPRIATE EXECUTION . . .   596A PUB ADDRESS/N   PROSE
        MICH ANG EVERY PICTURE OF THEIRS HAS A DIFFERENT   598D PUB ADDRESS/N   PROSE
            & APPROPRIATE EFFECT
        HAS INTIRELY PUT AN END TO ALL GENUINE & APPROPRIATE EFFECT 599B PUB ADDRESS/N   *PROSE
        LOS CRIES NO INDIVIDUAL OUGHT TO APPROPRIATE TO HIMSELF   736 JERUSALEM 90   28
        THOSE WHO DARE APPROPRIATE TO THEMSELVES UNIVERSAL   736 JERUSALEM 90   32
            ATTRIBUTES
        WHILE IN SELFHOOD HAND & HYLE & BOWEN & SKOFELD APPROPRIATE 737 JERUSALEM 90   40
        APPROPRIATE INDIVIDUALITY THEY BECOME AN ETERNAL DEATH . . 737 JERUSALEM 90   54
        WOULD BE AN APPROPRIATE ACCOMPANIMENT TO THE LIFE OF ROMNEY 832C LETTER 32   PROSE
        OF CERTAIN CONNOISSEURS THAT THEY CANNOT SEE APPROPRIATE   864C LETTER 61   PROSE
APPROPRIATED
        THE RIGHT HAND OF THE DESIGN IS APPROPRIATED TO   . . . .   443B LAST JUDGMNT/L   PROSE
        DESIGN IS APPROPRIATED TO THE RESURRECTION & FALL OF THE   443B LAST JUDGMNT/L   PROSE
            WICKED
        PROFITS OF THE WORK ARE INTENDED TO BE APPROPRIATED TO   824D LETTER 27   PROSE
            ERECT
APPROPRIATES
        FOR LOS SAID WHEN THE INDIVIDUAL APPROPRIATES UNIVERSALITY 737 JERUSALEM 90   52
APPROVAL
        TO ALLEDGE FOR OUR IMITATION & APPROVAL . . . .   406D ANNO BACON   MARG
        AT YOUR APPROVAL OF MY QUEEN CATHERINE BEG TO OBSERVE THAT 855C LETTER 53   PROSE
APPROVE
        IN A BOOK I LOVE SO MUCH & APPROVE SO GENERALLY . . . .   88A ANNO LAVATER   MARG
        THEREFORE [DEAR] READER [FORGIVE] WHAT YOU DO NOT APPROVE   621B JERUSALEM 3   PROSE
        IT ON EARTH & IF YOU APPROVE OF THIS . . . .   792B LETTER 4   PROSE
        IF YOU APPROVE OF MY MANNER & IT IS AGREEABLE TO YOU .   792C LETTER 4   PROSE
        I NOW SEND TWO PICTURES & HOPE YOU WILL APPROVE OF THEM   816A LETTER 23   PROSE
        HOPE THAT THE PUBLIC WILL APPROVE OF MY RATHER GIVING FEW   860C LETTER 56   PROSE
APPROVED
        APPROVED WITH AVIDITY POETRY CONSISTS IN THESE CONCEPTIONS 576B DESC CAT 4   PROSE
        THE DEATH OF DEMOSTHENES...HAS BEEN APPROVED BY MR FLAXMAN 796B LETTER 7   PROSE
        MR FLAXMAN HAS SEEN IT & APPROVED OF MY NOW SENDING IT .   796C LETTER 8   PROSE
        THEM APPROVED BY THE BEST THAT IS THE MOST SERIOUS PEOPLE   862A LETTER 59   PROSE
APPROVES
        WHICH HE ALMOST ALWAYS APPROVES & RECOMMENDS . . . . .   448C ANNO REYNOLDS   MARG
        APPROVES OF MY DESIGNS AS LITTLE AS HE DOES OF MY POEMS   825C LETTER 27   PROSE
            AND
        APPROVES OF IT WISHING ONLY THAT THE MONUMENT ITSELF MAY BE 832B LETTER 32   PROSE
        HE APPROVES MUCH I CANNOT HELP TELLING YOU SO MUCH   . . . 853B LETTER 52   PROSE
APRIL
        OUR DEAR FRIEND HAWKINS IS OUT OF TOWN & WILL NOT RETURN   855B LETTER 53   PROSE
            TILL APRIL
APT
        AM APT TO BELIEVE THAT WHAT IS DONE WITHOUT MEANING IS VERY 782A INSC UPCOTT   PROSE
        I AM NOT APT TO BELIEVE LITERALLY WHAT BOOKSELLERS SAY AND 846D LETTER 44   PROSE
APULEIUS'S
        APULEIUS'S GOLDEN ASS & OVID'S METAMORPHOSIS &   . . . .   607A V LAST JUDG/N   PROSE
AQUA FORTIS
        HIS EPITAPH [WITH] FOR MY TEARS [OF] ARE AQUA FORTIS   . . 537 AND HIS LEGS/N *   45
        I WILL POUR AQUA FORTIS ON THE NAME OF THE WICKED & TURN IT 598C PUB ADDRESS/N   PROSE
AQUA TINTA
        CHALK ENGRAVING IS AT LEAST SIX TIMES AS LABORIOUS AS   794C LETTER 5   PROSE
            AQUA TINTA
ARABIA
        MOUNT SINAI IN ARABIA . . . .   251 AHANIA 3   46
        ARABIA PALESTINE PERSIA HINDOSTAN CHINA TARTARY SIBERIA   712 JERUSALEM 72   39
ARADOBO
        TILLY LALLY THE SIPTIPPIDIST ARADOBO THE DEAN OF MOROCCO   46B ISLAND MOON 2   PROSE
        LIKE A CHERRY CLAPPER ARADOBO ASKD WHO WAS PHEBUS SIR .   46D ISLAND MOON 3   PROSE
        HERE ARADOBO LOOKD ASTONISHD & ASKD IF HE UNDERSTOOD   46D ISLAND MOON 3   PROSE
            ENGRAVING
        HAY HOW SHOULD I KNOW ANSWERD OBTUSE ANGLE WHO WAS   47A ISLAND MOON 3   PROSE
            IT ARADOBO
        AH THAT WAS THE GENTLEMAN SAID ARADOBO   47B ISLAND MOON 3   PROSE
        AH SAID ARADOBO I THOUGHT I HAD READ OF PHEBUS IN THE BIBLE 47B ISLAND MOON 3   PROSE
        ARADOBO YOU SHOULD ALWAYS THINK [OF WHAT YOU SP] BEFORE   47B ISLAND MOON 3   *PROSE
            YOU SPEAK
        HERE ARADOBO SUCKD HIS UNDER LIP . . . .   47D ISLAND MOON 3   PROSE
        OBTUSE ANGLE SCOPPRELL ARADOBO & TILLY LALLY ARE ALL   .   48C ISLAND MOON 5   PROSE
        PRAY SAID ARADOBO IS CHATTERTON A MATHEMATICIAN . . .   48D ISLAND MOON 5   PROSE
        OH I DID NOT THINK HE WAS I ONLY ASKD SAID ARADOBO   . .   48D ISLAND MOON 5   PROSE
        BUT I MEANT SAID ARADOBO I I I CAN'T THINK LAW SIR . .   49A ISLAND MOON 5   PROSE
        YOU MUST ALWAYS THINK FOR YOURSELF HOW SIR SAID ARADOBO   49B ISLAND MOON 5   PROSE
        & HANG THE MATHEMATICS COME ARADOBO SAY SOME THING   . .   49B ISLAND MOON 5   PROSE
        THEN ARADOBO BEGAN IN THE FIRST PLACE I THINK . . . . .   49C ISLAND MOON 5   PROSE
        I HATE YOUR SNEAKING RASCALS THERES ARADOBO   . . . .   49D ISLAND MOON 6   PROSE
        AH SAID THE PYTHAGOREAN ARADOBO WILL MAKE A VERY CLEVER   49D ISLAND MOON 6   PROSE
            FELLOW

```
                                                          PAGE    TITLE          LINE
ARADOBO   (CONTINUED)
     ARADOBO SAID THAT THE BOYS IN THE STREET SING SOMETHING     54D ISLAND MOON 9   PROSE
ARAM
     OF EDOM & ARAM & MOAB & MIDIAN & AMALEK  . . . . . .   498 MILTON 17          20
     THE HIGHLY CULTIVATED STATES OF EGYPT MOAB EDOM ARAM    .  565C DESC CAT 2    PROSE
     MOAB & AMMON & AMALEK & CANAAN & EGYPT & ARAM  . . . . .   623 JERUSALEM 5    14
     HAND HAS PEOPLED BABEL & NINEVEH HYLE ASHUR & ARAM   . .   625 JERUSALEM 7    18
     COBAN'S SON IS NIMROD HIS SON CUSH IS ADJOIND TO ARAM   .  625 JERUSALEM 7    19
     IN EGYPT & PHILISTEA IN MOAB & EDOM & ARAM  . . . . . .   680 JERUSALEM 49    43
     CONSTRICTING INTO DRUID ROCKS ROUND CANAAN AGAG & ARAM    685 JERUSALEM 54    26
       & PHAROH
     OF WARLIKE SONS AMONG THE SANDS OF MIDIAN & ARAM  . . .   735 JERUSALEM 89    57
ARARAT
     AND NOAH ON THE MOUNTAINS OF ARARAT  . . . . . . . .   245 SONG OF LOS 3      7
     ON THE MOUNTAINS OF ARARAT  . . . . . . . . . . .   248 SONG OF LOS 7        23
ARAUNAH
     HE IS ARAUNAH THE JEBUSITE MASTER OF THE THRESHING FLOOR   607D V LAST JUDG/N  PROSE
ARBITRARY
     CONSIDERED AS AN ARBITRARY COMMAND OF THE AGENT  . . . .  391C ANNO WATSON     MARG
     WHO CONSIDERS IT AS AN ARBITRARY ACT OF THE AGENT   . .  391D ANNO WATSON     MARG
     A PROPHET IS A SEER NOT AN ARBITRARY DICTATOR  . . . .  392B ANNO WATSON      MARG
     IF MEN WERE WISE THE MOST ARBITRARY PRINCES COULD NOT HURT  600A PUB ADDRESS/N  PROSE
ARCH
     [THE SWELLING TIDES THEY BENT OVER THE DEAD CORSE LIKE    341 FOUR ZOAS 8      13
       AN ARCH]
ARCHANGEL
     AND THE ORIGINAL ARCHANGEL  . . . . . . . . . . .   150A MARRIAGE HH 5       PROSE
     YOU O DEAR FLAXMAN ARE A SUBLIME ARCHANGEL MY FRIEND &  .  802C LETTER 14     PROSE
ARCHANGELS
     AND ARCHANGELS ROUND IT WEEP  . . . . . . . . . .   753 EV GOSPEL(D)/N        94
     & STUDY OF ARCHANGELS WHY THEN SHOULD I BE ANXIOUS ABOUT   802C LETTER 14     PROSE
       THE
ARCH-ANGELS
     . . . AND THE GRAVES OF ARCH-ANGELS UNSEALD   . . . . .  148 FRENCH REVOLTN    301
ARCHBISHOP
     IN DISMAL VOLUMES AS RISEN FROM BENEATH THE ARCHBISHOP    139 FRENCH REVOLTN   126
       OF PARIS AROSE
     . . . LOOKING ON THE ARCHBISHOP WHO CHANGED AS PALE AS    142 FRENCH REVOLTN   176
       LEAD
ARCHD
     AND SHINE GLORIOUS WITHIN HAND & KOBAN ARCHD OVER THE SUN  690 JERUSALEM 58    29
     ARCHD OVER THE MOON AT MIDNIGHT & LOS FIXD THEM THERE   .  690 JERUSALEM 58    31
ARCHED
     IN EVERY PILLARD HALL & ARCHED ROOF OF ALBION'S SKIES   .  281 FOUR ZOAS 2    48
ARCHES
     RUN FROM THEIR FETTERS REDDENING & IN LONG DRAWN ARCHES   202 AMERICA 15       24
       SITTING
     . . . IMMOVEABLE WITHIN ITS [ARCHES ALL] WALLS & CIELINGS  286 FOUR ZOAS 2    245
     AND BUILDING ARCHES HIGH & CITIES TURRETS & [HIGH] TOWERS  361 FOUR ZOAS 9    167
       & DOMES
     ALL ROUND THE HEAVENLY ARCHES & THE ODORS ROSE SINGING    376 FOUR ZOAS 9    727
       THIS SONG
     ARCHES & PYRAMIDS & PORCHES COLONADES & DOMES  . . . . .  529 MILTON 38       22
     AMONG HER GOLDEN ARCHES WHICH  . . . . . . . . .   650 FIELDS FROM/J         11
     HE HAS BUILDED THE ARCHES OF ALBION'S TOMB BINDING THE    680 JERUSALEM 49    54
       STARS
     ITS PILLARS EUPHRATES RAN UNDER ITS ARCHES WHITE SAILS   .  690 JERUSALEM 58   24
     IN LABYRINTHINE ARCHES MIGHTY THE ARCHITECT THRO          702 JERUSALEM 66     4
       WHICH
     BETWEEN THE STARS AMONG THE ARCHES OF ALBION'S TOMB SUBLIME  738 JERUSALEM 91  38
     TO REACH THE HEAVENLY ARCHES LOS BEHELD UNDAUNTED FURIOUS   738 JERUSALEM 91   42
ARCHETYPE
     AN ANCIENT PALACE ARCHETYPE OF MIGHTY EMPERIES   . . . .  200 AMERICA 10       8
ARCHIEREUS
     THE ARCHIEREUS THE IEREUS THE SADDUSAION DOUBLE  . . . .  734 JERUSALEM 89     7
ARCHING      SEE HIGH ARCHING
ARCHITECT
     THEN ROSE THE BUILDERS FIRST THE ARCHITECT DIVINE HIS PLAN  284 FOUR ZOAS 2   166
     BUILT BY THE ARCHITECT DIVINE WHOSE LOVE TO LOS &        298 FOUR ZOAS 4      51
       ENITHARMON
     WHAT SOVEREIGN ARCHITECT SAID THARMAS DARE MY WILL CONTROLL  299 FOUR ZOAS 4   53
     IN LABYRINTHINE ARCHES MIGHTY URIZEN THE ARCHITECT THRO    702 JERUSALEM 66     4
       WHICH
     A POET A PAINTER A MUSICIAN AN ARCHITECT THE   . . . . .  776A INSC LAOCOON    PROSE
ARCHITECTS
     CORPOREAL WAR PAINTERS ON YOU I CALL SCULPTORS ARCHITECTS   480C MILTON 1      PROSE
ARCHITECTURE
     AND ARCHITECTURE WHICH IS SCIENCE ARE THE FOUR FACES OF MAN  514 MILTON 27     56
     SPECIMENS OF ANCIENT SCULPTURE AND PAINTING             579C DESC CAT 5       PROSE
       AND ARCHITECTURE
ARCTURUS
     FOR THE CONSTELLATION ARCTURUS OR BOOTES THE KEEPER  . . .  577D DESC CAT 5    PROSE
ARDENT
     BIND ARDENT HOPE UPON YOUR FEET LIKE SHOES  . . . . . .   30 EDW THIRD/PS 5    33
     HER TEARS SHE ARDENT EMBRACD HER SORROWS OCCUPIED        678 JERUSALEM 48      40
       IN LABOURS
ARDENTLY
     FRIENDSHIP TO OUR DEAR MRS FLAXMAN WHOM WE ARDENTLY  . .  802D LETTER 14       PROSE
     VENTURE UPON WHAT I ARDENTLY DESIRE THE SEEING YOU WITH   873A LETTER 76       PROSE
     WHO PREPARES HIMSELF ARDENTLY FOR HIS RETURN TO LIFE   .  875A LETTER 80       PROSE
ARDOR
     . . . THAT THE ARDOR OF NOBLE SOULS QUENCHLESS   . . . .  142 FRENCH REVOLTN   173
```

```
                                                               PAGE      TITLE          LINE
ARDOR    (CONTINUED)
      THE LIMBS OF URIZEN SHONE WITH ARDOR [HE ROSE UP FROM THE     365 FOUR ZOAS 9       310
         ROCK]
      WITH ARDOR FIERCE & HANDS OF FLAME  . . . . . . . . . . .     429 CRYSTL CABINET     22
      MURMURING THE BOWSTRING BREATHES WITH ARDOR CLOUDS ROLL       742 JERUSALEM 95       14
         ROUND THE
      MURMURING THE BOW-STRING BREATHES WITH ARDOR . . . . . .      745 JERUSALEM 98        4
ARDOROUS
      THEN MILTON ROSE UP FROM THE HEAVENS OF ALBION ARDOROUS       495 MILTON 14          10
ARDORS
      LIKE A COUNCIL OF ARDORS SEATED IN CLOUDS . . . . . . .       146 FRENCH REVOLTN    264
      GOLD SILVER BRASS & IRON [ARDORS] CLANGORS CLAMORING REND     205 AMERICA CANC C     15
         THE SHORES
ARDOUR
      BLOW UP THE SLUGGISH INTO ARDOUR AND  . . . . . . . .          25 EDW THIRD/PS 3    180
      TILL FIRED WITH ARDOUR FRESH RECRUITED IN ITS HUMBLE          287 FOUR ZOAS 2      * 279
         [SPRING] SEASON
      MY BOWSTRING FIERCE WITH ARDOUR BREATHES  . . . . . . .       818 HAPPINESS/L        79
      DEAR CUMBERLAND I AM VERY MUCH OBLIGED BY YOUR KIND ARDOUR    865C LETTER 63        PROSE
ARDUOUS
      ON WHAT IS TO BE DONE IN OUR DESIRABLE & ARDUOUS TASK OF      849B LETTER 45        PROSE
ARGUE
      CAN ANY MAN WHO THINKS [?ARGUE] TALK SO  . . . . . . .        460C ANNO REYNOLDS   * MARG
ARGUMENT
      WHILE REASON RUNS AGROUND AS WE HAVE RUN OUR ARGUMENT  . .     29A EDW THIRD/PS 4   PROSE
      INFLAMMABLE GASS TO OVERTHROW THE ARGUMENT  . . . . . .        45B ISLAND MOON 1    PROSE
      THE ARGUMENT MAN HAS NO NOTION OF MORAL FITNESS BUT FROM       97A NAT RELIGION 1   PROSE
         EDUCATION
      THE ARGUMENT AS THE TRUE METHOD OF KNOWLEDGE IS EXPERIMENT     98B ALL RELIGIONS    PROSE
      THE ARGUMENT  . . . . . . . . . . . . . . . . . . . .         148C MARRIAGE HH 2    TITLE
      THE ARGUMENT  . . . . . . . . . . . . . . . . . . . .         189A ARGUMENT V DAU   TITLE
      ANOTHER ARGUMENT IS THAT ALL THE COMMENTATORS . . . . .       390C ANNO WATSON       MARG
      THE ARGUMENT IS BETTER FOR AFFLUENCE THAN POVERTY   . .       612C V LAST JUDG/N    PROSE
      & IF ANY OTHERS ARE DISPLEASD IT IS ALSO AN ARGUMENT OF       862A LETTER 59        PROSE
         THEIR
ARGUMENTS
      LETTERS ARE SUCH AS DO NOTHING AGAINST PAINE'S ARGUMENTS      390C ANNO WATSON       MARG
      INDIGNANT UNCONVINCD BY LOS'S ARGUMENTS & (THUNDERS)          509 MILTON 24          45
         ROLLING
      BY MEANS OF SUCH VILE ARGUMENTS & INSINUATIONS   . . . .      612D V LAST JUDG/N    PROSE
      TO LURE LOS BY TEARS BY ARGUMENTS OF SCIENCE & BY TERRORS     625 JERUSALEM 7         6
ARGYLL
      OF REUBEN KINCARD HADDNTN FORFAR SIMEON AYR ARGYLL BANFF      638 JERUSALEM 16        53
ARIDOLOGY
      FISSIC FOLLOGY PISTINOLOGY ARIDOLOGY AROGRAPHY                49C ISLAND MOON 5     PROSE
         TRANSMOGRAPHY
ARIGHT
      AND TO KNOW THAT LITTLE ARIGHT  . . . . . . . . . . .          28D EDW THIRD/PS 4   PROSE
ARIMATHEA
      I WILL TELL YOU WHAT JOSEPH OF ARIMATHEA  . . . . . . .       552 TELL YOU WHA/N      1
      COME LISTEN TO JOSEPH OF ARIMATHEA  . . . . . . . . . .       552 TELL YOU WHA/N      4
      JOSEPH OF ARIMATHEA AMONG THE ROCKS OF ALBION  . . . . .      604A INSC ARIMATHEA   TITLE
ARIOSTO
      ABSORBED BY THE POETS MILTON HOMER CAMOENS ERCILLA ARIOSTO    806D LETTER 17        PROSE
ARISE
      ARISE AND PULL THE TYRANT DOWN  . . . . . . . . . . .          11 GWIN KING/PS       11
      AND THE DEWS OF NIGHT ARISE  . . . . . . . . . . . . .         60 NURSES SONG/IM      6
      LIE STINKING ON THE EARTH THE BURIERS SHALL ARISE FROM        100 TIRIEL 1           49
         THE EAST
      SHALL ARISE AND SEEK  . . . . . . . . . . . . . . . .         112 LIT GRL LST/SI      5
      LET THY MOON ARISE  . . . . . . . . . . . . . . . . .         113 LIT GRL LST/SI     31
      THE SUN DOES ARISE  . . . . . . . . . . . . . . . . .         116 ECCHOING GR/SI      1
      AND THE DEWS OF NIGHT ARISE  . . . . . . . . . . . . .        121 NURSES SONG/SI      6
      HOW SHALL THE SUMMER ARISE IN JOY  . . . . . . . . . .        124 SCHOOL BOY/SI      26
      TILL WE ARISE LINKD IN A GOLDEN BAND AND NEVER PART  . . .    128 BOOK OF THEL 3     15
      AND THE DEWS OF NIGHT ARISE  . . . . . . . . . . . . .        171 NURSES SONG/N       6
      ARISE & COME BOTH FIFE & DRUM   . . . . . . . . . . .         185 LET BROTHELS/N      7
      I CRY ARISE O THEOTORMON FOR THE VILLAGE DOG  . . . . .       190 V DAU ALBION 2     23
      THE SUN THAT SLEEPS TOO LONG ARISE MY THEOTORMON I AM PURE    191 V DAU ALBION 2     28
      ARISE YOU LITTLE GLANCING WINGS AND SING YOUR INFANT JOY      195 V DAU ALBION 8      9
      ARISE AND DRINK YOUR BLISS FOR EVERY THING THAT LIVES IS      195 V DAU ALBION 8     10
         HOLY
      FOR NEVER FROM HER IRON TONGUE COULD VOICE OR SOUND ARISE     196 AMERICA PREL 1      9
      THEN AS ARMD CLOUDS ARISE TERRIFIC ROUND THE NORTHERN DRUM    204 AMERICA CANC B     18
      ARISE FROM OUT THE DEWY GRASS  . . . . . . . . . . . .        210 INTRODUCTN/SE      12
      AND THE DEWS OF NIGHT ARISE  . . . . . . . . . . . . .        212 NURSES SONG/SE      6
      ARISE FROM THEIR GRAVES AND ASPIRE  . . . . . . . . .         215 AH SUNFLOWR/SE      7
      ARISE O ORC FROM THY DEEP DEN  . . . . . . . . . . .          239 EUROPE 4           24
      ARISE O RINTRAH THEE I CALL & PALAMABRON THEE  . . . . .      240 EUROPE 5            4
      ARISE O RINTRAH ELDEST BORN SECOND TO NONE BUT ORC  . . .     240 EUROPE 8            1
      BUT AS THE STARS RISE FROM THE SALT LAKE THEY ARISE IN PAIN   240 EUROPE 8            8
      ARISE AROUND HIM IN THE CLOUDY HEAVENS OF ALBION FURIOUS      241 EUROPE 9           15
      ARISE ETHINTHUS THO THE EARTH-WORM CALL  . . . . . . .        243 EUROPE 12          35
      ARISE AND PLEASE THE HORRENT FIEND WITH YOUR MELODIOUS        243 EUROPE 13          16
         SONGS                                                      244 EUROPE 14          27
      ARISE O ORC AND GIVE OUR MOUNTAINS JOY OF THY RED LIGHT       244 EUROPE 14          31
      TO ARISE TO THE MOUNTAIN SPORT  . . . . . . . . . .          254 AHANIA 5            8
      ARISE IN ALL HIS VEINS HE THREW HIS ARMS AROUND HER LOINS     274 FOUR ZOAS 1       353
      IF I ARISE INTO THE ZENITH LEAVING THEE TO WATCH  . . . .     278 FOUR ZOAS 1       506
      SHE SHOULD ARISE AGAIN TO LIFE EMBALMD IN ENION'S BOSOM       278 FOUR ZOAS 1       527
      [ARISE O ENION ARISE & SMILE UPON MY HEAD]  . . . . .        SUPP FOUR ZOAS 1      *
```

116

ARISE   (CONTINUED)
```
[ARISE O ENION ARISE FOR LO I HAVE CALMD MY SEAS]   . . .  SUPP FOUR ZOAS 1       *
ARISE YOU LITTLE GLANCING WINGS & SING YOUR INFANT JOY   .  289 FOUR ZOAS 2       364
ARISE & DRINK YOUR BLISS   . . . . . . . . . . . .  289 FOUR ZOAS 2       365
I WILL ARISE EXPLORE THESE DENS & FIND THAT DEEP PULSATION  311 FOUR ZOAS 5       238
I WILL PRESERVE THO ENEMIES ARISE AROUND THEE NUMBERLESS    334 FOUR ZOAS 7B      53
THE FIERY DOGS ARISE THE SHOULDERS HUGE APPEAR   . . . .  336 FOUR ZOAS 7B      132
ARISE O VALA BRING THE BOW OF URIZEN BRING THE SWIFT        338 FOUR ZOAS 7B      200
    ARROWS OF LIGHT
WILL I ARISE TILL HIM I LOVE IS LOOSD FROM THIS DARK CHAIN  339 FOUR ZOAS 7B      255
SIT HOVRING OVER MY DARK THRESHOLD THO I ARISE LOOK OUT     360 FOUR ZOAS 9     * 118
ARISE TO ETERNAL BIRTHS SHAKE OFF THY COLD REPOSE   . . .  360 FOUR ZOAS 9       130
SCHOOLMASTER OF SOULS GREAT OPPOSER OF CHANGE ARISE   . .  360 FOUR ZOAS 9       131
ARISE O STONY FORM OF DEATH O DRAGON OF THE DEEPS   . . .  360 FOUR ZOAS 9       138
LIE DOWN BEFORE MY FEET O DRAGON LET URIZEN ARISE   . . .  360 FOUR ZOAS 9       139
BUT THOU SHALT STILL SURVIVE ARISE O DRY THY DEWY TEARS     368 FOUR ZOAS 9       421
AND SAID LET A PLEASANT HOUSE ARISE TO BE THE DWELLING      369 FOUR ZOAS 9       459
    PLACE
ARISE O ENION ARISE & SMILE UPON MY HEAD   . . . . . .  370 FOUR ZOAS 9       491
ARISE O ENION ARISE FOR LO I HAVE CALMD MY SEAS   . . .  370 FOUR ZOAS 9       494
ARISE SWEET BOY & LET US FOLLOW THE PATH OF ENION   . . .  371 FOUR ZOAS 9       534
THEN THE ETERNAL MAN SAID LUVAH THE VINTAGE IS RIPE ARISE   375 FOUR ZOAS 9       693
THE FALLING GRAPES THAT ODOROUS BURST UPON THE WINDS ARISE  376 FOUR ZOAS 9       698
ARISE BEFORE MY SIGHT   . . . . . . . . . . . . .  418 I SAW A MONK/N       2
MANY GROUPES ARISE [WITH] IN EXULTATION [IN JOY]   . . .  443D LAST JUDGMNT/L *PROSE
PARENTS & CHILDREN WIVES & HUSBANDS EMBRACE & ARISE         443D LAST JUDGMNT/L  PROSE
    TOGETHER
THEY ARISE UPON THE AIR REJOICING   . . . . . . . .  444A LAST JUDGMNT/L  PROSE
URGING HIM TO ARISE HE WEPT ENITHARMON SAW HIS TEARS   .  488 MILTON 8        40
I WILL ARISE AND LOOK FORTH FOR THE MORNING OF THE GRAVE    495 MILTON 14       20
ARISE INTO THE COVERING CHERUB WHO IS THE SPECTRE OF ALBION 508 MILTON 24       28
ARISE O SONS GIVE ALL YOUR STRENGTH AGAINST ETERNAL DEATH   509 MILTON 24       34
ARISE UPON THEIR THRONES TO JUDGE THE NATIONS OF THE EARTH  534 MILTON 42       17
ARISE AGAIN WITH TENFOLD SPLENDOR WHEN ARTHUR SHALL AWAKE   577B DESC CAT 5      TITLE
DESCENDING [AS A SCROLL] THE JUST ARISE   . . . . . .  606B V LAST JUDG/N  *PROSE
& TAKING ACCOUNT OF THE NUMBERS WHO ARISE IS THAT   . .  610A V LAST JUDG/N   PROSE
AS HE MUST KNOW THEN WOULD HE ARISE FROM HIS GRAVE   . .  611A V LAST JUDG/N   PROSE
ALL THESE ARISE TOWARD THE OPENING CLOUD BEFORE THE THRONE  611D V LAST JUDG/N   PROSE
THE CLOUDS ARISE FROM THE BOSOMS OF MOUNTAINS   . . . .  618C ILLUS MILTON    PROSE
THAT ENTHUSIASM AND LIFE MAY NOT CEASE ARISE SPECTRE ARISE  628 JERUSALEM 9       31
AND LOS PRAYED AND SAID O DIVINE SAVIOUR ARISE   . . . .  656 JERUSALEM 30      21
THE DEAD AWAKE TO GENERATION ARISE O LORD & REND THE VEIL   656 JERUSALEM 30      40
AND BE THOU FOR EVER ACCURSED THAT ALBION MAY ARISE AGAIN   662 JERUSALEM 35      14
ARISE AWAKE O FRIENDS OF THE GIANT ALBION   . . . . .  667 JERUSALEM 40      18
I SEE DISEASE ARISE UPON YOU YET SPEAK TO ME AND GIVE   .  673 JERUSALEM 43      76
BE LOST FOR EVER & EVER THEN THEY SHALL ARISE FROM SELF     680 JERUSALEM 49      45
ARISE SISTERS GO YE & MEET THE LORD WHILE I REMAIN   . .  681 JERUSALEM 50      12
ARISE BEFORE MY SIGHT   . . . . . . . . . . . . .  683 I SAW A MONK/J       2
SHALL ALBION ARISE I KNOW HE SHALL ARISE AT THE LAST DAY    696 JERUSALEM 62      15
ALL QUARRELS ARISE FROM REASONING THE SECRET MURDER AND     699 JERUSALEM 64      20
ARISE O VALA BRING THE BOW OF URIZEN BRING THE SWIFT        700 JERUSALEM 65      46
    ARROWS OF LIGHT
ARISE AS THE SMOKE OF THE FURNACE SHAKING THE ROCKS FROM    708 JERUSALEM 70      14
    SEA TO SEA
I SEE A FEMININE FORM ARISE FROM THE FOUR TERRIBLE ZOAS     715 JERUSALEM 74      52
WITHIN MY BOSOM LEST HE ARISE TO LIFE & SLAY MY LUVAH   .  722 JERUSALEM 80      29
CAN I ARISE AND LEAVE THY SIDE BUT LABOUR HERE INCESSANT    727 JERUSALEM 83       2
ARISE UPON THY WATCHES LET US SEE THY GLOBE OF FIRE   . .  729 JERUSALEM 84      27
BUT IF I DIE I SHALL ARISE AGAIN & THOU WITH ME   . . .  743 JERUSALEM 96      15
AWAKE ARISE TO SPIRITUAL STRIFE   . . . . . . . . .  753 EV GOSPEL (D)/N     78
BUT IF IT ALL ARISE FROM MY OWN FAULT I OUGHT TO BLAME      828D LETTER 28       PROSE
    MYSELF
OF VARIETY SHALL ENGAGE IN OTHER LITTLE WORKS AS THEY ARISE 831C LETTER 31       PROSE
OCCUPY MY THOUGHTS NEW PROFITS SEEM TO ARISE BEFORE ME SO   865C LETTER 63       PROSE
```
ARISEN
```
AND THE FALLN MAN WHO WAS ARISEN UPON THE ROCK OF AGES  .  364 FOUR ZOAS 9       285
BUT FOR YON NOURISHING SUN TIS THAT BY WHICH THOU          367 FOUR ZOAS 9       405
    ART ARISEN
URTHONA IS ARISEN IN HIS STRENGTH NO LONGER NOW   . . .  379 FOUR ZOAS 9       849
TILL ALBION IS ARISEN THEN PATIENT WAIT A LITTLE WHILE  .  508 MILTON 23       54
HAVE YOU KNOWN THE JUDGMENT THAT IS ARISEN AMONG THE   .  663 JERUSALEM 36      44
HAS ARISEN FROM DEISM WHICH IS NATURAL RELIGION   . . .  683A JERUSALEM 52     PROSE
& YOU DENY THAT HE IS ARISEN & ARE BLIND TO SPIRIT   . .  757D EV GOSPEL      PROSE
BECOME MY DUTY TO EXPLAIN MY UNHAPPINESS HAS ARISEN   . .  812B LETTER 22       PROSE
```
ARISES
```
THE [DAY] SUN ARISES IN THE EAST   . . . . . . . .  177 DAY/N             1
INSTEAD OF MORN ARISES A BRIGHT SHADOW LIKE AN EYE   . .  191 V DAU ALBION 2     35
AT THE FIRST SOUND THE GOLDEN SUN ARISES FROM THE DEEP  .  289 FOUR ZOAS 2       344
FOR IN MY BOSOM A NEW SONG ARISES TO MY LORD   . . . .  368 FOUR ZOAS 9       433
BUT IN THE MORNING SHE ARISES TO AVOID MY EYES   . . .  371 FOUR ZOAS 9       543
THE SUN ARISES FROM HIS DEWY BED & THE FRESH AIRS   . .  379 FOUR ZOAS 9       846
LO ORC ARISES ON THE ATLANTIC LO HIS BLOOD AND FIRE   . .  506 MILTON 23        6
THE DAWN WITH HER DAPPLED HORSES ARISES ABOVE THE EARTH     618A ILLUS MILTON    PROSE
TO BE WHEN ALBION ARISES FROM HIS DREAD REPOSE O LOVELY     739 JERUSALEM 92      14
    ENITHARMON
BECAUSE YOU MURDER HIM HE ARISES AGAIN   . . . . . .  757D EV GOSPEL       PROSE
ABEL SINKS DOWN INTO THE GRAVE FROM WHICH ARISES SATAN  .  780C GHOST ABEL 2    PROSE
INTO THE BOTTOMLESS ABYSS WHOSE TORMENT ARISES FOR EVER     781 GHOST ABEL 2      21
    & EVER
ARISES FROM MY HAVING TURNED HIM OUT OF MY GARDEN   . .  826D LETTER 28       PROSE
BUT AT CERTAIN PERIODS A BLAZE OF REPUTATION ARISES ROUND   830B LETTER 30       PROSE
    ME
```

	PAGE	TITLE	LINE

ARISEST
A DELUSION BUT I KNOW THEE O LORD WHEN THOU ARISEST UPON   693 JERUSALEM 60   58

ARISING
. . . THE VOICE OF THE PEOPLE ARISING FROM VALLEY AND HILL   143 FRENCH REVOLTN   206
LIKE THE MORNING STAR ARISING ABOVE THE BLACK WAVES . . .   145 FRENCH REVOLTN   255
ARISING IN HIS PRIDE ENLIGHTEN ALL THE GRIZLY DEEPS . . .   352 FOUR ZOAS 8   440
HIS SONS ARISING FROM THE FEAST WITH GOLDEN BASKETS FOLLOW   376 FOUR ZOAS 9   714
HIS EYES BEHOLD THE ANGELIC SPHERES ARISING NIGHT & DAY   379 FOUR ZOAS 9   828
AND I BECAME ONE MAN WITH HIM ARISING IN MY STRENGTH . .   505 MILTON 22   12
AROUND HIM ARE OTHER KINGDOMS ARISING TO JUDGMENT . . 608C V LAST JUDG/N   PROSE
LIKE A PALE CLOUD ARISING FROM THE ARMS OF BEULAH'S   635 JERUSALEM 14   33
     DAUGHTERS
THE PROFITS ARISING FROM PUBLICATIONS ARE IMMENSE & . . . 820A LETTER 25   PROSE

ARISTON
BY ARISTON THE KING OF BEAUTY FOR HIS STOLEN BRIDE . . .   200 AMERICA 10   10
URIZEN FADED ARISTON SHUDDERD . . . .   245 SONG OF LOS 3   4
AWAKEND VALA ARISTON RAN FORTH WITH BRIGHT ?ONANA . .   380 FOUR ZOAS AD 1 *   6

ARISTOTLE
OF HOMER SOCRATES PHIDIAS GLYCON ARISTOTLE ETC . . . 388D ANNO WATSON   MARG
("ARISTOTLE...HIS METAPHYSICS") GOD IS NOT A MATHEMATICAL 774D ANNO BERKELEY   MARG
     DIAGRAM
ARISTOTLE SAYS CHARACTERS ARE EITHER GOOD OR BAD . . . . 778B HOMERS POETRY   PROSE
HOMER ARISTOTLE . . . . SUPP ILLUS DANTE 99 *PROSE

ARISTOTLE'S
WHICH IN THE MILL WAS ARISTOTLE'S ANALYTICS . . . . . 157B MARRIAGE HH 17   PROSE

ARK
MAN IS THE ARK OF GOD . . . .   82A ANNO LAVATER   MARG
THE MERCY SEAT IS ABOVE UPON THE ARK CHERUBIMS . . .   82A ANNO LAVATER   MARG
MAN IS EITHER THE ARK OF GOD OR . . . .   82B ANNO LAVATER   MARG
IF THOU SEEKEST BY HUMAN POLICY TO GUIDE THIS ARK . . .   82B ANNO LAVATER   MARG
SINCE NOAH WAS SHUT IN THE ARK . . . .   187 WHEN KLOPSTK/N   23
YET HIDING THE SHADOWY FEMALE VALA AS IN AN ARK & CURTAINS   347 FOUR ZOAS 8   255
. . . THE BOSOM OF SATAN THE FALSE FEMALE AS IN AN ARK   348 FOUR ZOAS 8   292
     & VEIL
IN PLACE OF THE ARK [WITH] THE [TWO] CHERUBIM BOWING OVER 444B LAST JUDGMNT/L   PROSE
     IT
A MALE WITHIN A FEMALE HID AS IN AN ARK & CURTAINS . . .   528 MILTON 37   40
HIDING THE HUMAN LINEAMENTS AS WITH AN ARK & CURTAINS . .   533 MILTON 41   26
THEN AS A MOONY ARK OLOLON DESCENDED TO FELPHAM'S VALE . .   534 MILTON 42   7
IN WHICH ARE THE TWO CHERUBIM THAT BOWD OVER THE ARK . . 613B V LAST JUDG/N   PROSE
& THE ARK OF THE COVENANT IS AS A DOVE OF PEACE . . . . 613B V LAST JUDG/N   PROSE
WITH CUSH HIS SON & TOOK ME DOWN HE IN A GOLDEN ARK . . .   644 JERUSALEM 22   4
OF HER TABERNACLE & HER ARK & SECRET PLACE THE BEAUTIFUL   705 JERUSALEM 68   15
     DAUGHTER
AND THY ARK & HOLY PLACE AT THY FROWNS AT THY DIRE REVENGE   706 JERUSALEM 68   50
A MALE WITHIN A FEMALE HID AS IN AN ARK & CURTAINS . . .   716 JERUSALEM 75   15
TO CUT HER OFF FROM AMERICA TO CLOSE UP HER SECRET ARK . .   725 JERUSALEM 82   34

ARKS
CARRIED IN ARKS OF OAK BEFORE THE ARMIES IN THE SPRING . .   644 JERUSALEM 21   45
BURSTING THEIR ARKS THEY RISE AGAIN TO LIFE THEY   644 JERUSALEM 21   46
     PLAY BEFORE
BURST THE BOTTOMS OF THE GRAVES & FUNERAL ARKS OF BEULAH   736 JERUSALEM 89   60

ARM
BENEATH HIS ARM LIKE SHEEP THEY DIE . . . .   13 GWIN KING/PS   85
METHINKS I SEE THEM ARM MY GALLANT SOLDIERS . . . . .   26 EDW THIRD/PS 3   224
FOR TYRANNY HATH STRETCHD HIS PURPLE ARM AND BLOOD HE CRIES   34B KING JOHN/PS   PROSE
HIS MOTHER'S ARM WAS UNDER HIS HEAD . . . .   36C COUCH DEATH/PS   PROSE
AND LET THY MASTER DO THE DEED ONE BLOW OF THAT STRONG ARM   38C SAMSON/PS   PROSE
AND STRENGTHEN HER WEAK ARM [NOW DAY AROSE] . . . . .   40D THEN SHE BORE   PROSE
GIANTS OF MIGHTY ARM BEFORE THE FLOOD CAIN'S CITY . . .   41A THEN SHE BORE   PROSE
WHEN IJIM STRETCHD HIS MIGHTY ARM THE ARROW FROM HIS LIMBS   105 TIRIEL 4   71
ARM IN ARM SEVEN DAYS . . . .   113 LIT GRL FND/SI   7
WHAT THE ANVIL WHAT [THE ARM] [ARM] [GRASP] [CLASP] DREAD   172 THE TYGER/N 1   20
     GRASP
HE THREW HIS RIGHT ARM TO THE NORTH . . . .   229 URIZEN 13   13
HIS LEFT ARM TO THE SOUTH . . . .   229 URIZEN 13   14
BUT THE STRONG ARM THAT SENT IT REMEMBERD . . . . . .   249 AHANIA 2   26
DARING MY POWER WILT ARM MY SONS AGAINST ME IN THE [DEEP]   278 FOUR ZOAS 1   510
     ATLANTIC
ENRAGED & STIFLED WITH TORMENT HE THREW HIS RIGHT ARM TO   303 FOUR ZOAS 4   243
     THE NORTH
HIS LEFT ARM TO THE SOUTH SHOOTING OUT IN ANGUISH DEEP . .   303 FOUR ZOAS 4   244
BLACK SCALES OF IRON ARM THE DREAD VISAGE IRON SPIKES   319 FOUR ZOAS 6   307
     INSTEAD
HIS ARM IS WITHERD TO ITS ROOT . . . .   427 MENTAL TRAVLER   98
BY YOUR MILD POWER DESCENDING DOWN THE NERVES OF MY RIGHT   481 MILTON 2   6
     ARM
RIGHT ARM TO THE NORTH HIS LEFT ARM TO THE SOUTH & HIS   483 MILTON 3   25
     FEET
HIS ARM LEAND TREMBLINGLY OBSERVING ALL THESE THINGS . .   488 MILTON 8   15
OF MORTAL OR IMMORTAL ARM AND SOFTLY LILLING FLUTES . . .   509 MILTON 24   56
O THAT I COULD LIVE IN HIS SIGHT O THAT I COULD BIND HIM   726 JERUSALEM 82   44
     TO MY ARM

ARMAGH
DONNEGAL ANTRIM TYRONE FERMANAGH ARMAGH LONDONDERRY . . .   711 JERUSALEM 72   26

ARMD
ARMD WITH THE TERRORS OF ALMIGHTY JOVE . . . .   15 IMIT SPEN/PS   45
IF PHILIP CAME ARMD IN THE RIBS OF DEATH . . . . . .   25 EDW THIRD/PS 3   175
HER ARMD WITH SORROW SORE . . . .   114 LIT GRL FND/SI   22
A SPIRIT ARMD IN GOLD . . . .   114 LIT GRL FND/SI   36
I DRIED MY TEARS & ARMD MY FEARS . . . .   182 THE ANGEL/N   11
I WAS ARMD HE CAME IN VAIN . . . .   182 THE ANGEL/N   14

```
                                                          PAGE     TITLE        LINE
ARMD    (CONTINUED)
     ARMD WITH DISEASES OF THE EARTH TO CAST UPON THE ABYSS  . .  201 AMERICA 13       15
     THEN AS ARMD CLOUDS ARISE TERRIFIC ROUND THE NORTHERN DRUM  204 AMERICA CANC B    18
     I DRIED MY TEARS & ARMD MY FEARS  . . . . . . . . .  214 THE ANGEL/SE     11
     I WAS ARMD HE CAME IN VAIN  . . . . . . . . . . .  214 THE ANGEL/SE     14
     INTELLIGENT ORGANIZD ARMD  . . . . . . . . . .  256 BOOK OF LOS 3    29
     CALL TO THY DARK ARMD HOSTS FOR ALL THE SONS OF MEN MUSTER  275 FOUR ZOAS 1     406
        TOGETHER
     AND SCALED MONSTERS OR ARMD IN IRON SHELL OR SHELL OF    314 FOUR ZOAS 6     120
        BRASS
     THE EARWIG ARMD THE TENDER MAGGOT EMBLEM OF IMMORTALITY   377 FOUR ZOAS 9     759
     THE BROTHER HAS ARMD HIMSELF IN STEEL  . . . . . .  430 GREY MONK        23
     THE GAME COCK CLIPD & ARMD FOR FIGHT  . . . . . . .  431 AUGURIES         17
     THE SOLDIER ARMD WITH SWORD & GUN  . . . . . . . .  432 AUGURIES         77
     TO DO UNKIND THINGS IN KINDNESS WITH POWER ARMD TO SAY  .  493 MILTON 12        32
     THE EARWIG ARMD THE TENDER MAGGOT EMBLEM OF IMMORTALITY   513 MILTON 27        16
     AWKWARDNESS ARMD IN STEEL FOLLY IN A HELMET OF GOLD  . . .  628 JERUSALEM 9      12
     MY SELFHOOD SATAN ARMD IN GOLD  . . . . . . . . .  651 FIELDS FROM/J    76
ARMED
     USE MAKES THE ARMED FIELD AND NOISY WAR  . . . . . .   27 EDW THIRD/PS 3  247
     ARMED WITH SPEAR & SHIELD THEY DRINK & REJOICE OVER THE   308 FOUR ZOAS 5     141
        SLAIN
     FIRST TRADES & COMMERCE SHIPS & ARMED VESSELS HE BUILDED   333 FOUR ZOAS 7B     12
        LABORIOUS
     FROM THE STONE & THE ARMED FLY SPRINGS FROM THE ROCKY    373 FOUR ZOAS 9     607
        CREVICE
     AND BLACK HORSES & ARMED MEN & MISERABLE BOUND CAPTIVES   375 FOUR ZOAS 9     667
     THY BROTHER HAS ARMED HIMSELF IN STEEL  . . . . . .  419 I SAW A MONK/N   38
     THE ARMY OF ARMED ROMANS THE FIGURES FULL AS LARGE AS LIFE  560A EXHIBITION ADV  PROSE
     ARMED ROMANS STREW THE FIELD BENEATH AMONG THESE THE LAST  580C DESC CAT 5     PROSE
        OF
     ARMED IN GLITTERING SCALES WITH A CROWN & A SPEAR   . . .  780C GHOST ABEL 2    PROSE
ARMIES
     THE ARMIES STAND LIKE BALANCES  . . . . . . . . .   13 GWIN KING/PS     65
     AND NOW THE RAGING ARMIES RUSHD  . . . . . . . . .   13 GWIN KING/PS     69
     . . . FROM THE WINDOW HE SAW HIS VAST ARMIES SPREAD OVER  137 FRENCH REVOLTN   80
        THE HILLS
     . . . THEN LIFTED HIS HEAD AND LOOKD ON HIS ARMIES THAT  139 FRENCH REVOLTN  110
        SHONE
     AND OVER THE ARMIES OF STRIFE . . . . . . . . . .  146 FRENCH REVOLTN  265
     IN THE FLAMES STOOD & VIEWD THE ARMIES DRAWN OUT IN THE SKY  201 AMERICA 14       1
     LIKE WHITE CLOUDS RISING FROM THE DEEPS HIS FIFTY-TWO    205 AMERICA CANC C   16
        ARMIES
     ON URIZEN'S SELF-BEGOTTEN ARMIES  . . . . . . . .  225 URIZEN 5         16
     BUT URIZEN WITH DARKNESS OVERSPREADING ALL THE ARMIES  . .  279 FOUR ZOAS 1     535
     THEY PLAY BEFORE THE ARMIES BEFORE THE HOUNDS OF NIMROD   281 FOUR ZOAS 2      64
     LIKE WHITE CLOUDS RISING FROM THE VALES HIS FIFTY    319 FOUR ZOAS 6     312
        TWO ARMIES
     OVERTHROW ALL THE ARMIES OF EUROPE WITH A SMALL PAMPHLET  391C ANNO WATSON    MARG
     WITH THUNDER OF WAR & TRUMPETS SOUND WITH ARMIES OF DISEASE  489 MILTON 9        24
     THE FLEA LOUSE BUG THE TAPE-WORM ALL THE ARMIES OF DISEASE  513 MILTON 27        17
     WITH WORKS OF ART THEIR ARMIES MEET  . . . . . . .  557 ART HAS LOST/N    7
     AND [ARMIES] WAR SHALL SINK BENEATH THY FEET  . . . .  557 ART HAS LOST/N    8
     ARMIES OF EDWARD ARE SEEN WINDING AMONG THE MOUNTAINS  . .  577A DESC CAT 4     PROSE
     THE ARMIES ARE FLEEING UPON THE MOUNTAINS ON THE FOREGROUND  608B V LAST JUDG/N  PROSE
     CARRIED IN ARKS OF OAK BEFORE THE ARMIES IN THE SPRING  . .  644 JERUSALEM 21     45
     THE ARMIES I HEAR THEIR LOUD CYMBALS & THEIR DEADLY CRIES  644 JERUSALEM 21     47
     BEARS ME BEFORE HIS ARMIES THO MY SHADOW HOVERS HERE  . .  644 JERUSALEM 22      5
     THE ARMIES OF BALAAM WEEP NO WOMEN COME TO THE FIELD  . .  672 JERUSALEM 43     39
     HER HAND IS A COURT OF JUSTICE HER FEET TWO ARMIES    698 JERUSALEM 64      9
        IN BATTLE
     SURROUNDING THEM WITH ARMIES TO DESTROY THE LAMB OF GOD   719 JERUSALEM 78     14
ARMOUR
     BRING HITHER MY ARMOUR WILLIAM  . . . . . . . . .   28 EDW THIRD/PS 4    1
     EACH ONE BUCKLING ON HIS ARMOUR MORNING  . . . . . .   33 EDW THIRD/PS 6   50
     . . . THEY CLASPD THE ARMOUR OF TERRIBLE GOLD  . . . . .  205 AMERICA CANC C    6
     IN GLITTRING ARMOUR SWIFT AS WINDS INTELLIGENT AS [FLAMES]  205 AMERICA CANC C   13
        CLOUDS
     IN ARMOUR AS THE NERVES OF WISDOM EACH HIS STATION [FIRES]  205 AMERICA CANC C   19
        HOLDS
     IN BLUSHES LIKE THE MORNING AND HIS SCALY ARMOUR SOFTENING  269 FOUR ZOAS 1     186
     SPIRITS OF STRENGTH [REJOICE] IN PALACES REJOICE IN GOLDEN  308 FOUR ZOAS 5     140
        ARMOUR
     THE DRAGONS OF THE NORTH PUT ON THEIR ARMOUR  . . . .  336 FOUR ZOAS 7B    150
     THE SCALY ARMOUR SHOT OUT STUBBORN DOWN HIS BACK & BOSOM  343 FOUR ZOAS 8      73
     IN ALL HIS ANCIENT STRENGTH TO FORM THE GOLDEN ARMOUR OF  379 FOUR ZOAS 9     853
        SCIENCE
     . . . & HIS [SCALY ARMOUR] ROCKY FEATURES SOFTNING  . . .  381 FOUR ZOAS AD 5    6
     SCOFIELD IS BOUND IN IRON ARMOUR BEFORE REUBEN'S GATE  . .  501 MILTON 19        59
     RAGAN IS WHOLLY CRUEL SCOFIELD IS BOUND IN IRON ARMOUR  .  631 JERUSALEM 11     21
     SMITTEN AS UZZAH OF OLD HIS ARMOUR IS SOFTEND HIS SPEAR   706 JERUSALEM 68     51
     IN TERRIBLE ARMOUR RAGING AGAINST THE LAMB & AGAINST    719 JERUSALEM 78     13
        JERUSALEM
     AND TO INHABIT OUR LITTLE-ONES TO CLOTHE IN ARMOUR OF THE  729 JERUSALEM 84      9
        GOLD
ARMOUR'S
     LIKE TO THE ARMOUR'S IRON BRACE   . . . . . . . . .  433 AUGURIES        100
ARMOURS
     FURBISH OUR ARMOURS BRIGHT NEW PLUME OUR HELMS   . . . .   24 EDW THIRD/PS 3  147
ARMOURY
     [THEN ALBION'S ANGEL] ROSE RESOLVD TO THE COVE OF ARMOURY  205 AMERICA CANC C    1
```

119

		PAGE	TITLE	LINE
ARMS				
TAKE THIS HE CRYD AND THRUST INTO HER ARMS		4	FAIR ELENOR/PS	25
PAST HOWLING SHE RECEIVD INTO HER ARMS		4	FAIR ELENOR/PS	27
WHICH IN HER ARMS SHE BROUGHT AND NOW TENFOLD		5	FAIR ELENOR/PS	55
SHE TOOK THE GORY HEAD UP IN HER ARMS		6	FAIR ELENOR/PS	70
THE TRAMPLING HORSE AND CLANGING ARMS		11	GWIN KING/PS	23
THE BLIND-MAN'S ARMS EXTENDED WIDE		16	BLIND-MANS/PS	23
AND OFTEN HEARD THE DISMAL CLANG OF ARMS		31	EDW THIRD/PS 5	40
SHALL RISE CITIES AND THRONES AND ARMS AND AWFUL POWRS		32	EDW THIRD/PS 6	18
THE GLITTERING YOUTH OF COURTS MUST GLEAM IN ARMS		34B	KING JOHN/PS	PROSE
O YET MAY ALBION SMILE AGAIN AND STRETCH HER PEACEFUL ARMS		34C	KING JOHN/PS	PROSE
PREPARE YOUR ARMS FOR GLORIOUS VICTORY		34	WAR SONG/PS	8
THE BROOK STRETCHES ITS ARMS ALONG THE VELVET MEADOW		37B	CONTEMPLATN/PS	PROSE
WITH HER FAIR ARMS THOU LOVST ME NOT		38B	SAMSON/PS	PROSE
AND THOU HAST BEEN INCIRCLED IN HIS ARMS		38B	SAMSON/PS	PROSE
NERVOUS ARMS AND AFTER THAT WHEN I HAD FOUND THY FALSHOOD		38D	SAMSON/PS	*PROSE
AND SWELLING SIGHS BURST FORTH HIS CHILDREN ALL IN ARMS APPEAR		42B	THEN SHE BORE	PROSE
IN MY WEAK [AGED] ARMS I HERE HAVE BORNE YOUR DYING MOTHER		99	TIRIEL 1	9
THEY RAN WEEPING LIKE FRIGHTED INFANTS FOR REFUGE IN MNETHA'S ARMS		100	TIRIEL 2	* 12
THEN HEVA CAME & TOOK OLD TIRIEL IN HER MOTHER'S ARMS		101	TIRIEL 2	39
IN HIS ARMS HE BORE		114	LIT GRL FND/SI	21
BUT I BY FORCE SUDDENLY CAUGHT HIM IN MY ARMS		156D	MARRIAGE HH 17	PROSE
WHO STRETCHED OUT HIS ARMS EMBRACING THE FLAME OF FIRE		158D	MARRIAGE HH 22	PROSE
WHEN PESTILENCE IS SHOT FROM HEAVEN NO OTHER ARMS SHE NEED		196	AMERICA PREL 1	6
ENDURD BY ROOTS THAT WRITHE THEIR ARMS INTO THE NETHER DEEP		196	AMERICA PREL 2	11
[OVER THE] A FROWNING SHADOW LIKE [A] AN AGED KING IN ARMS OF GOLD		205	AMERICA CANC C	* 25
SHE FLED FROM HIS ARMS YET HE FOLLOWD		231	URIZEN 19	13
ARISE IN ALL HIS VEINS HE THREW HIS ARMS AROUND HER LOINS		274	FOUR ZOAS 1	353
FROM THE SUPPORTING ARMS OF THE ETERNAL SAVIOUR WHO DISPOSD		277	FOUR ZOAS 1	466
ENITHARMON ANSWERD WHEREFORE DIDST THOU THROW THINE ARMS AROUND		288	FOUR ZOAS 2	327
IN LOS'S ARMS HOWLINGS BEGAN OVER THE BODY OF DEATH		289	FOUR ZOAS 2	335
LOS HEARD REVIVING HE SIEZD HER IN HIS ARMS DELUSIVE HOPES		290	FOUR ZOAS 2	380
SHE ANSWERD NOT BUT STRETCHD HER ARMS & THREW HER LIMBS ABROAD		312	FOUR ZOAS 6	* 16
FOUR SONS OF URIZEN THE SQUADRONS OF URTHONA LED IN ARMS		319	FOUR ZOAS 6	314
SHOULD NEVER IN MY ARMS REPOSE NOW LISTEN I WILL TELL		326	FOUR ZOAS 7	236
[I HAVE THEE IN MY ARMS & AM AGAIN UNITED TO LOS]		327	FOUR ZOAS 7	308
COME THEN INTO MY BOSOM & IN THY SHADOWY ARMS BRING WITH THEE		329	FOUR ZOAS 7	367
THE REAPER IN BOTH ARMS EMBRACING THE FURIOUS RAGING FLAMES		332	FOUR ZOAS 7	463
IN YOUTH & BEAUTY IN THE ARMS OF ENITHARMON MILD REPOSING		332	FOUR ZOAS 7	475
AND CLOUDS ARE CLOSD AROUND MY TOWER MY ARMS LABOUR IN VAIN		335	FOUR ZOAS 7B	89
[NOW] CLOTHE YOURSELVES IN GOLDEN ARMS BROTHERS OF WAR		337	FOUR ZOAS 7B	163
WHEN THE SUN ROSE IN GLOWING MORN WITH ARMS OF MIGHTY HOSTS		338	FOUR ZOAS 7B	197
IN THE SAVIOUR'S ARMS IN THE ARMS OF TENDER MERCY & LOVING KINDNESS		341	FOUR ZOAS 8	19
UPON THE HEIGHTS OF AMALEK TAKING REFUGE IN HIS ARMS		348	FOUR ZOAS 8	270
HOW COOL THE BREEZES OF THE VALLY & THE ARMS OF THE BRANCHING TREES		369	FOUR ZOAS 9	* 449
UPON THE HEIGHTS OF [ENTUTHON THAT] AMALEK TAKING REFUGE IN HIS ARMS		382	FOUR ZOAS AD 6	3
HIS BODY BENT HIS ARMS & KNEES		419	I SAW A MONK/N	17
THE POOR MAN TAKES HER IN HIS ARMS		426	MENTAL TRAVLER	58
HIS BODY BENT HIS ARMS & KNEES		430	GREY MONK	7
HE TAKES IT IN HIS ARMS HE PASSES IT IN STRENGTH THRO HIS CURRENT		518	MILTON 29	61
WITH ARMS OF LOVE & PITY & SWEET COMPASSION BUT TO		518	MILTON 30	12
SHALT BRING JERUSALEM IN THINE ARMS IN THE NIGHT WATCHES AND		523	MILTON 33	21
SHALT GIVE HER INTO THE ARMS OF GOD YOUR LORD & HUSBAND		523	MILTON 33	23
FRANCE SHALL SUBDUE THE WORLD IN ARMS		557	ART HAS LOST/N	2
THEY WERE OVERWHELMED BY BRUTAL ARMS ALL BUT A SMALL		577C	DESC CAT 5	PROSE
IN ARTS AS WELL AS IN ARMS OR IN THE SENATE		584C	DESC CAT 14	PROSE
SOMETIMES IN THE ARMS OF A FEMALE [THEY] THIS REPRESENTED THE CHURCH		607C	V LAST JUDG/N	*PROSE
IN THE ARMS OF THEIR FATHER THESE ARE REPRESENTATIONS OF THE		610B	V LAST JUDG/N	PROSE
HOWLING IN PAIN REDOUNDING FROM THE ARMS OF BEULAH'S DAUGHTERS		624	JERUSALEM 5	49
LIKE A PALE CLOUD ARISING FROM THE ARMS OF BEULAH'S DAUGHTERS		635	JERUSALEM 14	33
IN THE ARMS OF VALA ASSIMILATING IN ONE WITH VALA		642	JERUSALEM 19	41
THE LAMB OF GOD RECIEVD ME IN HIS ARMS HE SMILD UPON US		643	JERUSALEM 20	39
I DIE I DIE IN THY ARMS THO HOPE IS BANISHD FROM ME		648	JERUSALEM 24	60
COME TO MY ARMS & NEVER MORE		651	FIELDS FROM/J	69
AND CURSES WITH HIS MIGHTY ARMS BRANDISHD AGAINST THE HEAVENS		667	JERUSALEM 40	37
OXFORD TREMBLED WHILE HE SPOKE THEN FAINTED IN THE ARMS		676	JERUSALEM 46	17
THESE WERE HIS LAST WORDS AND THE MERCIFUL SAVIOUR IN HIS ARMS		677	JERUSALEM 48	1
RECIEVD HIM IN THE ARMS OF TENDER MERCY AND REPOSD		677	JERUSALEM 48	2
WRITHING IN PAIN THE DAUGHTERS OF BEULAH IN KIND ARMS RECIEVD		678	JERUSALEM 48	50
HIS BODY BENT HIS ARMS & KNEES		683	I SAW A MONK/J	15
GATHERD JERUSALEM'S CHILDREN IN HIS ARMS & BORE THEM LIKE		692	JERUSALEM 60	8
HIS ARMS DOTH HE FORGIVE JERUSALEM & NOT EXACT PURITY FROM HER WHO IS		694	JERUSALEM 61	15
MANY STREAMS IN THE ARMS OF JOSEPH & GAVE FORTH HER TEARS OF JOY		695	JERUSALEM 61	29

```
                                                               PAGE      TITLE        LINE
ARMS    (CONTINUED)
     WHEN THE SUN ROSE IN GLOWING MORN WITH ARMS OF MIGHTY HOSTS   700 JERUSALEM 65      43
     HER STRUGGLING TORMENT IN HER IRON ARMS AND LIKE A CHAIN      726 JERUSALEM 82      70
     BINDING HIS WRISTS & ANKLES WITH THE IRON ARMS OF LOVE  .  .  726 JERUSALEM 82      71
     GWENDOLEN SAW THE INFANT IN HER (SISTER'S) ARMS SHE HOWLD     726 JERUSALEM 82   *  72
     AND IN HER FAIR ARMS  .  .  .  .  .  .  .  .  .  .  .         805 TO BUTTS/L        38
     THE CHILD IN HIS ARMS WHETHER BOY OR GIRL SIGNIFIES NOT      864B LETTER 61      PROSE
ARMY
     SCENE THE COAST OF FRANCE KING EDWARD AND NOBLES BEFORE       17D EDW THIRD/PS 1 PROSE
        IT THE ARMY
     SMILES ON OUR ARMY AND THE GALLANT SUN  .  .  .  .  .  .  .    21 EDW THIRD/PS 3     2
     AND SO WILL THE WHOLE ARMY TIS VERY CATCHING  .  .  .  .  .    22 EDW THIRD/PS 3    59
     OF A TRIUMPH SUCH AN ARMY OF HEROES  .  .  .  .  .  .  .  .    23 EDW THIRD/PS 3    75
     I SEE THEE HOVRING OER MY ARMY WITH  .  .  .  .  .  .  .  .    26 EDW THIRD/PS 3   205
     AN ARMY OF MIGHTY MEN ARE AS FLOCKS IN THE VALLIES WHAT      39A SAMSON/PS      PROSE
        CANST
     AWE SURROUNDED ALONE THRO THE ARMY  .  .  .  .  .  .  .  .    141 FRENCH REVOLTN *  162
     THIS ARMY OF SUPERSTITION AT LARGE  .  .  .  .  .  .  .  .    142 FRENCH REVOLTN    173
     THIS WAR-BREATHING ARMY  .  .  .  .  .  .  .  .  .  .  .  .    145 FRENCH REVOLTN    253
     THAT THIS ARMY OF TERRORS THAT PRISON OF HORRORS  .  .  .  .  145 FRENCH REVOLTN    254
     AND THE VOTE WAS THAT FAYETTE SHOULD ORDER THE ARMY  .  .  .  146 FRENCH REVOLTN    269
     ON FAYETTE BUT ON THE WHOLE ARMY A SHADOW  .  .  .  .  .  .   146 FRENCH REVOLTN    271
     .  .  .  AND ACROSS THE ARMY AND ACROSS THE LOUVRE  .  .  .   146 FRENCH REVOLTN    272
     THEY DASH LIKE FOAM AGAINST THE RIDGES OF THE ARMY  .  .  .   146 FRENCH REVOLTN    277
     .  .  .  AND OVER THE ARMY ROUSSEAU HIS WHITE CLOUD  .  .  .  147 FRENCH REVOLTN    282
     .  .  .  THAT THE ARMY REMOVE TEN MILES FROM PARIS  .  .  .   147 FRENCH REVOLTN    285
     AND FOLLOWD THE ARMY  .  .  .  .  .  .  .  .  .  .  .  .  .    148 FRENCH REVOLTN    306
     URIZEN'S ARMY OF HORRORS  .  .  .  .  .  .  .  .  .  .  .  .   253 AHANIA 4          35
     TO SEE IF HUNGRY WINDS ARE ABROAD WITH THEIR INVISIBLE ARMY   355 FOUR ZOAS 8      560
     THE ARMY OF ARMED ROMANS THE FIGURES FULL AS LARGE AS LIFE   560A EXHIBITION ADV PROSE
ARNON
     .  .  .  ON THE BANKS OF [THE MOON] ARNON  .  .  .  .  .  .   346 FOUR ZOAS 8    *  215
     AND MET HIM ON THE SHORES OF ARNON & BY THE STREAMS OF        500 MILTON 19         5
        THE BROOKS
     SILENT THEY MET AND SILENT STROVE AMONG THE STREAMS OF        500 MILTON 19         6
        ARNON
     THE RIVER STORGE WHICH IS ARNON INTO THE DEAD SEA            524 MILTON 34         30
     URIZEN FAINTS IN TERROR STRIVING AMONG THE BROOKS OF ARNON   531 MILTON 39         53
     I SEE THEE STRIVE UPON THE BROOKS OF ARNON THERE A DREAD     532 MILTON 40          4
     UPON PISON & ARNON & JORDAN AND I HEARD THE VOICE AMONG      695 JERUSALEM 61      33
     IN CRUEL HOLINESS AND HER LAMENTING SONGS WERE FROM ARNON    722 JERUSALEM 80       8
     PISON SINCE CALLD ARNON THERE IS HESHBON BEAUTIFUL  .  .  .  735 JERUSALEM 89      25
     THE ROCKS OF RABBATH ON THE ARNON & THE FISH-POOLS           735 JERUSALEM 89      26
        OF HESHBON
AROGRAPHY
     FISSIC FOLLOGY PISTINOLOGY ARIDOLOGY AROGRAPHY              49C ISLAND MOON 5   PROSE
        TRANSMOGRAPHY
AROSE
     AND STRENGTHEN HER WEAK ARM [ NOW DAY AROSE]  .  .  .  .  .   40D THEN SHE BORE  PROSE
     A SUN AROSE OUT OF THE SEA IT ROSE & SHED SWEET INFLUENCE    41B THEN SHE BORE  PROSE
     OF AGED TIRIEL AROSE THAT HIS SONS MIGHT HEAR IN THEIR        99 TIRIEL 1          6
        GATES
     THEN HAR AROSE & LAID HIS HAND UPON OLD TIRIEL'S HEAD  .  .  101 TIRIEL 2         34
     ALL NIGHT THEY WANDERD THRO THE WOOD & WHEN THE SUN AROSE    109 TIRIEL 7         18
     THE HELPLESS WORM AROSE AND SAT UPON THE LILLY'S LEAF  .  .  129 BOOK OF THEL 3   30
     IN DISMAL VOLUMES AS RISEN FROM BENEATH THE ARCHBISHOP       139 FRENCH REVOLTN   126
        OF PARIS AROSE
     .  .  .  AROSE AND UNFOLDED HIS ROBE AND PUT FORTH  .  .  .  142 FRENCH REVOLTN   175
     HE ENDED THE WIND OF CONTENTION AROSE  .  .  .  .  .  .  .    145 FRENCH REVOLTN   241
     BUT I AROSE AND SOUGHT FOR THE MILL & THERE I FOUND MY      156D MARRIAGE HH 17 PROSE
        ANGEL
     WHO AROSE BEFORE AN ANGEL THAT SAT ON A CLOUD  .  .  .  .   158B MARRIAGE HH 22 PROSE
     & HE WAS CONSUMED AND AROSE AS ELIJAH  .  .  .  .  .  .  .  158D MARRIAGE HH 22 PROSE
     BUT WHEN THE MORN AROSE HER LAMENTATION RENEWD  .  .  .  .  192 V DAU ALBION 5     1
     A DRAGON FORM CLASHING HIS SCALES AT MIDNIGHT HE AROSE  .   197 AMERICA 3         15
     A DRAGON FORM CLASHING HIS SCALES AT MIDNIGHT HE AROSE  .   204 AMERICA CANC A    15
     THE VAST WAVES & AROSE ON THE WATERS  .  .  .  .  .  .  .   224 URIZEN 4          22
     THENCE AROSE HIS CHANNELD THROAT  .  .  .  .  .  .  .  .  .  229 URIZEN 13          7
     AND THUS HER VOICE AROSE  .  .  .  .  .  .  .  .  .  .  .    238 EUROPE PREL 1      3
     THEN LOS AROSE HIS HEAD HE REARD IN SNAKY THUNDERS CLAD     245 EUROPE 15          9
     AROSE LIKE A PILLAR OF FIRE ABOVE THE ALPS  .  .  .  .  .   248 SONG OF LOS 7     27
     AROSE FOR HIS DIRE CONTEMPLATIONS  .  .  .  .  .  .  .  .    250 AHANIA 3           7
     HE AROSE BUT THE STEMS STOOD SO THICK  .  .  .  .  .  .  .   252 AHANIA 3          71
     AROSE IN THE PENDULOUS DEEP  .  .  .  .  .  .  .  .  .  .    253 AHANIA 4          42
     AND CONTEMPLATIVE THOUGHTS FIRST AROSE  .  .  .  .  .  .  .  258 BOOK OF LOS 4     40
     HE AROSE ON THE WATERS BUT SOON  .  .  .  .  .  .  .  .  .   259 BOOK OF LOS 4     63
     THE NUPTIAL SONG AROSE FROM ALL THE THOUSAND THOUSAND       274 FOUR ZOAS 1      375
        SPIRITS
     OTHERS AROSE & SCHOOLS ERECTED FORMING INSTRUMENTS  .  .  .  283 FOUR ZOAS 2      130
     [FOR] BUT INFINITELY BEAUTIFUL THE WONDROUS WORK AROSE  .   286 FOUR ZOAS 2      240
     IN BEAUTEOUS ORDER THENCE AROSE SOFT CLOUDS & EXHALATIONS   286 FOUR ZOAS 2      253
     .  .  .  [THE ETERNAL MAN] AROSE IN TERROR ALBION ROSE  .   293 FOUR ZOAS 3    *  69
     A CRAVING HUNGRY CAVERN THENCE AROSE HIS CHANNELD  .  .  .  303 FOUR ZOAS 4      240
     SO URIZEN AROSE & LEANING ON HIS SPEAR EXPLORD HIS DENS     311 FOUR ZOAS 6        1
     THEN URIZEN AROSE UPON THE WIND BACK MANY A MILE  .  .  .   319 FOUR ZOAS 6      316
     THEN URIZEN AROSE THE SPECTRE FLED & THARMAS FLED  .  .  .  320 FOUR ZOAS 7        1
     AND HIGH ROOFED OVER WITH TREES HE AROSE BUT THE STEMS  .   321 FOUR ZOAS 7       37
     AT DAWN & EER THE SUN AROSE THE RAVEN & VULTURE FOLLOWD     358 FOUR ZOAS 9       63
     SO URIZEN SPOKE HE SHOOK HIS SNOWS FROM OFF HIS SHOULDERS   362 FOUR ZOAS 9      188
        & AROSE
     BEHELD THE VISION OF GOD & HE AROSE UP FROM THE ROCK  .  .  364 FOUR ZOAS 9      286
     AND URIZEN AROSE UP WITH HIM WALKING THRO THE FLAMES  .  .  364 FOUR ZOAS 9      287
```

121

```
AROSE     (CONTINUED)
        SO SAYING SHE AROSE & WALKED ROUND HER BEAUTIFUL HOUSE  . .   369 FOUR ZOAS 9       471
        AND SHE AROSE OUT OF THE RIVER & GIRDED ON HER GOLDEN         370 FOUR ZOAS 9   *   504
          GIRDLE
        AND IN THE MORNING WHEN THE SUN AROSE IN THE CRYSTAL SKY      370 FOUR ZOAS 9       517
        CRIED TIMES ARE ENDED HE EXULTED HE AROSE IN JOY HE EXULTED   372 FOUR ZOAS 9       568
        THEN URIZEN AROSE & TOOK HIS SICKLE IN HIS HAND  . . . .      372 FOUR ZOAS 9       579
        THE ETERNAL MAN AROSE HE WELCOMD THEM TO THE FEAST   . . .    373 FOUR ZOAS 9       617
        THE SONG AROSE TO THE GOLDEN FEAST THE ETERNAL MAN REJOICD    375 FOUR ZOAS 9       692
        AS HE AROSE FROM THE BRIGHT FEAST DRUNK WITH THE WINE OF      376 FOUR ZOAS 9       710
          AGES
        THE BLOOD OF LIFE FLOWD PLENTIFUL ODORS OF LIFE AROSE  . .    376 FOUR ZOAS 9       726
        GIBBON AROSE WITH A LASH OF STEEL . . . . . . . . .           418 I SAW A MONK/N      5
        AROSE WITH WAR IN IRON & GOLD  . . . . . . . . .              418 I SAW A MONK/N      9
        AND MARY AROSE AMONG FRIENDS TO BE FREE . . . . . .           428 MARY               15
        WHICH NOW AROSE AND WALKD WITH THEM IN EDEN AS AN EIGHTH      496 MILTON 15           5
        HIS TERRORS NOW POSSESD ME WHOLE I AROSE IN FURY & STRENGTH   505 MILTON 22          14
        DIVIDE FOUR-FOLD INTO FOUR CHURCHES WHEN LAZARUS AROSE  .     508 MILTON 24          31
        HENCE AROSE ALL OUR TERRORS IN ETERNITY & NOW REMEMBRANCE     534 MILTON 41          34
        AROSE AROUND ALBION'S BODY JESUS WEPT & WALKED FORTH   . .    534 MILTON 42          19
        IN FURY THEN HE SAT DOWN AND WEPT TERRIFIED THEN AROSE  .     625 JERUSALEM 6        10
        AROSE UPON HIM PALE AND GHASTLY AND HE CALLD AROUND  . . .    666 JERUSALEM 40        2
        GIBBON AROSE WITH A LASH OF STEEL . . . . . . . . .           683 I SAW A MONK/J      5
        AROSE WITH WAR IN IRON & GOLD  . . . . . . . . .              683 I SAW A MONK/J      8
        DRINKING THEIR LIVES IN SWEET INTOXICATION HENCE AROSE        701 JERUSALEM 65       65
          FROM BATH
        PALACES RIVERS & MOUNTAINS AND BETWEEN HAND & HYLE AROSE      710 JERUSALEM 71       22
        SHE ADJOIND WITH GWANTOKE'S CHILDREN SOON LOVELY CORDELLA     710 JERUSALEM 71       28
          AROSE
        TURKEY & GRECIA SAW MY (INSTRUMENTS) OF MUSIC THEY AROSE      721 JERUSALEM 79       48
        WHILE LOS AROSE UPON HIS WATCH AND DOWN FROM GOLGONOOZA       728 JERUSALEM 83       75
        AND URIZEN & LUVAH & THARMAS & URTHONA AROSE INTO    . . .    744 JERUSALEM 96       41
AROUND    SEE ROUND
        AND AROUND OUR SOULS INTWINE  . . . . . . . .                   7 LOVE HARMNY/PS      2
        AND RISING GLORIES BEAM AROUND MY HEAD  . . . . . .             9 FRESH FROM/PS       4
        LIKE REARED STONES AROUND A GRAVE . . . . . . . .             12 GWIN KING/PS       41
        THEY STAND AROUND THE KING  . . . . . . . . . .              12 GWIN KING/PS       42
        LIKE CLOUDS AROUND HIM ROLLD  . . . . . . . .                 12 GWIN KING/PS       60
        THEN BOSOMD IN AN AMBER CLOUD AROUND  . . . . . .             15 IMIT SPEN/PS       42
        CONFUSION STARTLES ALL AROUND . . . . . . . . .              17 BLIND-MANS/PS      54
        HIS MIGHTY ROAR AND FAWNING PLAYD AROUND  . . . . .           21 EDW THIRD/PS 2     82
        AND A RAY OF LIGHT BEAMED AROUND HIS HEAD ALL WAS STILL      36C COUCH DEATH/PS   PROSE
        HOVERING ANGELS ARE AROUND THEM  . . . . . . . .             36D COUCH DEATH/PS   PROSE
        DELIGHTS BLOSSOM AROUND NUMBERLESS BEAUTIES BLOW THE  . .    37B CONTEMPLATN/PS   PROSE
        SCORN WAITS ON PRIDE BUT SLANDER FLIES AROUND THE WORLD      42D THEN SHE BORE    PROSE
        WHO MARRIED HONOUR THESE FOLLOW HER AROUND THE WORLD  . .    43A THEN SHE BORE    PROSE
        WHEN ALL AROUND SUMMER HATH SPRED HER PLUMES  . . . . .      43B WOE CRIED MUSE   PROSE
        & GOLDEN PLEASURES BEAM AROUND MY HEAD WHY GRIEF DOST THOU   43B WOE CRIED MUSE   PROSE
          ACCOST ME
        HONOUR TWINES AROUND HER BROWS  . . . . . . . .              63 SHEPHERD FIRST      7
        SERPENTS NOT SONS WREATHING AROUND THE BONES OF TIRIEL  .    99 TIRIEL 1           22
        AS THICK AS NORTHERN FOGS AROUND YOUR GATES TO CHOKE YOU    100 TIRIEL 1           44
          UP
        THEN HE WOULD CREEP LIKE A BRIGHT SERPENT TILL AROUND MY    105 TIRIEL 4           57
          NECK
        MEAN TIME THE OTHER SONS OF TIRIEL RAN AROUND THEIR FATHER  105 TIRIEL 4           68
        VISIT YOU BUT ETERNAL FOGS HOVER AROUND YOUR WALLS   . .    106 TIRIEL 5           23
        BUT WHEN TIRIEL TURND AROUND & RAISD HIS AWFUL VOICE  .  .  108 TIRIEL 7            6
        BLACK BERRIES APPEAR THAT POISON ALL AROUND HIM SUCH [IS]   110 TIRIEL 8       *   34
          WAS TIRIEL
        THEN HE STALKD AROUND  . . . . . . . . . . .                114 LIT GRL FND/SI     28
        SING LOUDER AROUND  . . . . . . . . . . . .                 116 ECCHOING GR/SI      7
        AND KISSES ME AND BINDS HIS NUPTIAL BANDS AROUND MY BREAST  129 BOOK OF THEL 5
        . . . DARKNESS OF OLD TIMES AROUND THEM  . . . . . .        135 FRENCH REVOLTN     17
        . . . AROUND HIM CROUD WEEPING IN HIS BURNING ROBE   . . .  138 FRENCH REVOLTN     87
        AND TEMPESTS OF DOUBT ROLL AROUND ME . . . . . . .         139 FRENCH REVOLTN    119
        . . . TROOPS OF WARRIORS DEPART NOR AROUND OUR PEACEABLE    145 FRENCH REVOLTN    239
          CITY
        . . . THAT MOATED AROUND KEEPS THIS CITY OF PARIS IN AWE    145 FRENCH REVOLTN    248
        A RUSHING OF WINGS AROUND HIM WAS HEARD AS HE BRIGHTEND     146 FRENCH REVOLTN    260
          . . .
        ON PESTILENT VAPOURS AROUND HIM FLOW . . . . . . . .  .     146 FRENCH REVOLTN    274
        AROUND WERE NUMBERS OF EAGLE LIKE MEN  . . . . . .          154D MARRIAGE HH 15   PROSE
        RAGING AROUND & MELTING THE METALS INTO LIVING FLUIDS  . .  155A MARRIAGE HH 15   PROSE
        O LAPWING THOU FLIEST AROUND THE HEATH  . . . . . .         168 O LAPWING/N         1
        THAT DOES [CLOSE] FREEZE MY BONES AROUND  . . . . .         169 EARTHS ANSWR/N     22
        [BLOSSOMS SHOWRING ALL AROUND]  . . . . . . . .            169 MIRTLE SHADE/N      2
        [WEAVES AROUND THE MARRIAGE HEARSE]  . . . . . .            170 LONDON/N           16
        BLOSSOMS SHOWRING ALL AROUND  . . . . . . . .               176 TO MY MIRTLE/N      6
        THAT PICKS UP CRUMBS AROUND THE DOOR . . . . . .           177 LIT BOY LST/N       8
        ALL AROUND HIS [ANCLES] BOSOM ROLLD  . . . . . .            177 DAY/N               4
        AND A GREAT MANY SUCKERS GROW ALL AROUND  . . . . .         185 LET BROTHELS/N     26
        AND GUARDED THEM AROUND  . . . . . . . . .                  185 LET BROTHELS/N     38
        [HIS CAPTAINS FALSE AROUND]  . . . . . . . . .              186 LET BROTHELS/N     44
        AND GUARDED THEM AROUND  . . . . . . . . .                  186 LET BROTHELS/N     63
        [THEY] [AND] AND HIS BOWELS TURNED [AROUND] ROUND THREE     187 WHEN KLOPSTK/N *   17
          TIMES THREE
        AND LET THE JEALOUS DOLPHINS SPORT AROUND THE LOVELY MAID   190 V DAU ALBION 1     19
        THEN STORMS RENT THEOTORMON'S LIMBS HE ROLLD HIS WAVES      190 V DAU ALBION 2      3
          AROUND
        TO SPIN A WEB OF AGE AROUND HIM GREY AND HOARY DARK  . . .  194 V DAU ALBION 7     19
        WITH LAMPLIKE EYES WATCHING AROUND THE FROZEN MARRIAGE BED  194 V DAU ALBION 7     22
```

		PAGE	TITLE	LINE
AROUND (CONTINUED)				
AROUND THE PILLARS OF URTHONA AND ROUND THY DARK LIMBS	. . .	196	AMERICA PREL 1	16
AROUND THEIR SHORES INDIGNANT BURNING WITH THE FIRES OF ORC		200	AMERICA 11	2
AND THE RED FLAMES OF ORC THAT FOLDED ROARING FIERCE AROUND		201	AMERICA 14	11
THAT PLAY AROUND THE GOLDEN ROOFS IN WREATHS OF FIERCE DESIRE		202	AMERICA 15	21
AROUND THE SMITTEN BANDS CLOTHED IN TEARS & TREMBLING SHUDDRING COLD		203	AMERICA 16	8
BETWEEN THE MOUNTAINS DISMAL VISIONS MOPE AROUND THE HOUSE		204	AMERICA CANC B	12
AROUND SAINT JAMES'S [GLOW THE FIRES]	. . . .	205	AMERICA CANC C	9
. . . [GLOWING] MUSTRING AROUND THEIR PRINCE	. . . . . .	205	AMERICA CANC C *	17
THAT DOES FREEZE MY BONES AROUND	. . . .	211	EARTHS ANSR/SE	22
THAT PICKS UP CRUMBS AROUND THE DOOR	. . . .	218	LIT BOY LST/SE	8
MUSTER AROUND THE BLEAK DESARTS	. . . .	223	URIZEN 4	1
MOUNTAINOUS ALL AROUND	. . . .	225	URIZEN 5	7
AND A ROOF VAST PETRIFIC AROUND	. . . .	225	URIZEN 5	28
LOS WEPT HOWLING AROUND THE DARK DEMON		226	URIZEN 6	2
SICK TORMENT AROUND HIM IN WHIRLWINDS	. . . .	227	URIZEN 10	6
AROUND HIS SOLID BONES	. . . .	228	URIZEN 11	7
ROLL LIKE A SEA AROUND HIM	. . . .	230	URIZEN 13	30
SPREAD A TENT WITH STRONG CURTAINS AROUND THEM	. . . .	231	URIZEN 19	2
AROUND HIS BOSOM IN SOBBINGS	. . . .	233	URIZEN 20	10
EXPLORD HIS DENS AROUND	. . . .	233	URIZEN 20	32
I WRAP MY TURBAN OF THICK CLOUDS AROUND MY LABRING HEAD		238	EUROPE PREL 1	12
THEN ENITHARMON SAW HER SONS & DAUGHTERS RISE AROUND	. .	239	EUROPE 4	5
AROUND THE LIMBS OF ALBION'S GUARDIAN HIS FLESH CONSUMING		243	EUROPE 12	33
ARISE AROUND HIM IN THE CLOUDY HEAVENS OF ALBION FURIOUS		243	EUROPE 12	35
MY DAUGHTER HOW DO I REJOICE FOR THY CHILDREN FLOCK AROUND		243	EUROPE 14	2
THE FURIOUS TERRORS FLEW AROUND	. . . .	245	EUROPE 15	4
ENROOTING ITSELF ALL AROUND	. . . .	252	AHANIA 4	3
AROUND THE IMMORTAL IN TORMENT	. . . .	253	AHANIA 4	23
PERCHING AROUND THE HURTLING BONES	. . . .	253	AHANIA 4	24
HE FORGD NETS OF IRON AROUND	. . . .	253	AHANIA 4	29
AND LOS THREW THEM AROUND THE BONES	. . . .	253	AHANIA 4	30
SHIVRING CLINGING AROUND LIKE A CLOUD	. . . .	258	BOOK OF LOS 4	56
AND A VAST WORLD OF WATERS AROUND HIM	. . . .	259	BOOK OF LOS 4	66
THEN HE SUNK & AROUND HIS SPENT LUNGS	. . . .	259	BOOK OF LOS 4	68
DOWN THE HEAVY SUNK CLEAVING AROUND	. . . .	259	BOOK OF LOS 5	6
FLOWD AROUND THE IMMENSE LOS BEHELD	. . . .	259	BOOK OF LOS 5	12
ETERNALLY CREATED BY THE LAMB OF GOD AROUND	. . . .	266	FOUR ZOAS 1	97
ARISE IN ALL HIS VEINS HE THREW HIS ARMS AROUND HER LOINS		274	FOUR ZOAS 1	353
LUVAH & URIZEN CONTEND IN WAR AROUND THE HOLY TENT	. . .	277	FOUR ZOAS 1	480
. . . & CLOSD THE MESSENGERS IN CLOUDS AROUND	. . . .	279	FOUR ZOAS 1	552
[?AT FIRST ?AROUND XXX THE SPECTRE]	. . . .	SUPP	FOUR ZOAS 1	*
[XXX ?MONSTERS HOWLD ?WITH ?URIZEN ?AROUND]	. . . .	SUPP	FOUR ZOAS 1	*
BUILD WE THE MUNDANE SHELL AROUND THE ROCK OF ALBION	. .	280	FOUR ZOAS 2	25
THE DAUGHTERS OF ALBION GIRDED AROUND THEIR GARMENTS OF NEEDLEWORK		281	FOUR ZOAS 2	57
DESCENDING SHE REPOSD BESIDE HIM FOLDING HIM AROUND	. . .	285	FOUR ZOAS 2	202
ENITHARMON ANSWERD WHEREFORE DIDST THOU THROW THINE ARMS AROUND		288	FOUR ZOAS 2	327
HE SPOKE MUSTERING HIS HEAVY CLOUDS AROUND HIM BLACK OPAKE		294	FOUR ZOAS 3	108
THEN THUNDERS ROLLD AROUND & LIGHTNINGS DARTED TO & FRO		294	FOUR ZOAS 3	109
AND THREW HER FROM THE STEPS OF ICE THAT FROZE AROUND HIS THRONE		294	FOUR ZOAS 3	112
THE DOLOROUS SHADOW JOYD WEAK HOPE APPEARD AROUND HIS HEAD		300	FOUR ZOAS 4	127
AROUND HIS SOLID BONES & A SECOND AGE PASSED OVER	. . .	303	FOUR ZOAS 4	226
HE STOOD TREMBLING & ENITHARMON CLUNG AROUND HIS KNEES	. .	305	FOUR ZOAS 5	18
HER PALE HANDS CLING AROUND HER HUSBAND & OVER HER WEAK HEAD		305	FOUR ZOAS 5	21
BEGAN A DISMAL DANCE THE WINDS AROUND ON POINTED ROCKS	. .	306	FOUR ZOAS 5	34
THE ENORMOUS DEMONS WOKE & HOWLD AROUND THE [YOUTHFUL] NEW BORN KING		306	FOUR ZOAS 5	41
OF ENITHARMON LOS AROUND HER BUILDED PILLARS OF IRON	. .	307	FOUR ZOAS 5	73
AROUND HIS BOSOM LIKE A BLOODY CORD IN SECRET SOBS	. . .	307	FOUR ZOAS 5	84
AROUND HIM EVERY DAY HE VIEWD THE FIERY YOUTH	. . .	307	FOUR ZOAS 5	86
HELD THE FIERCE BOY LOS NAILD HIM DOWN BINDING AROUND HIS LIMBS		307	FOUR ZOAS 5	101
OF LIFE [REJOICE] LAMENT AROUND THE DEMON GOING FORTH & RETURNING		308	FOUR ZOAS 5 *	117
THE SONS OF WISDOM STOOD AROUND THE HARPERS FOLLOWD WITH HARPS		310	FOUR ZOAS 5	199
I CALLD THE STARS AROUND MY FEET IN THE NIGHT OF COUNCILS DARK		311	FOUR ZOAS 5	223
[AROUND THE ABYSS (DEFIANTLY) ?SHOUTING ALL HIS DEMONS]		SUPP	FOUR ZOAS 5 *	
[OF HOPE & FEAR XXX SINGING THE ?SAME SONG AROUND THE ?GLOWING BED]		SUPP	FOUR ZOAS 5 *	
ALL THESE AROUND THE WORLD OF LOS CAST FORTH THEIR MONSTROUS BIRTHS		318	FOUR ZOAS 6	278
FROM THE FOUR CLIFFS OF URTHONA RISE GLOWING AROUND THE SPECTRE		319	FOUR ZOAS 6	313
AND RANGD HIS BOOKS AROUND HIM BROODING ENVIOUS OVER ORC		320	FOUR ZOAS 7	19
AGAIN HE TOOK HIS SEAT & RANGD HIS [BOOKS] BOOKS AROUND		321	FOUR ZOAS 7 *	40
AROUND THEE SOMETIMES LIKE A FLOOD & SOMETIMES LIKE A ROCK		321	FOUR ZOAS 7	49
BENEATH THEE & AROUND ABOVE A SHOWER OF FIRE NOW BEATS	. .	321	FOUR ZOAS 7	51
CUT THEE IN GASHES THO THE BLOOD POURS DOWN AROUND THY ANKLES		322	FOUR ZOAS 7	84
. . . LIGHTNINGS PLAYD AROUND THEE THUNDERS HOVERD	. .	325	FOUR ZOAS 7	227
THE DOUBLE ROOTED LABYRINTH SOON WAVD AROUND THEIR HEADS		328	FOUR ZOAS 7	335
I WILL PRESERVE THO ENEMIES ARISE AROUND THEE NUMBERLESS		334	FOUR ZOAS 7B	53
MY WATERS LIKE A FLOOD AROUND THEE FEAR NOT TRUST IN ME		334	FOUR ZOAS 7B	55

		PAGE	TITLE	LINE
AROUND	(CONTINUED)			
AND CLOUDS ARE CLOSD AROUND MY TOWER MY ARMS LABOUR IN VAIN		335	FOUR ZOAS 7B	89
APPEAR ABOVE THE (CRUMBLING) MOUNTAIN SILENCE WAITS AROUND HIM		336	FOUR ZOAS 7B	* 130
THEY HOWL AROUND THE FLAMING YOUTH RENDING THE NAMELESS SHADOW		336	FOUR ZOAS 7B	142
WHAT WORDS OF DREAD PIERCE MY FAINT EAR WHAT FALLING SNOWS AROUND		344	FOUR ZOAS 8	146
. . . [AROUND] AMIDST THEM [STOOD] BEAMD		348	FOUR ZOAS 8	277
PRESS IT AROUND THE LOINS OF THIS EXPANDING CRUELTY		349	FOUR ZOAS 8	313
WITH ENVY & IN VAIN HE SWAM AROUND HIS STONY FORM		352	FOUR ZOAS 8	437
HIS EYELIDS GIVE THEIR LIGHT AROUND HIS FOLDING TAIL ASPIRES		352	FOUR ZOAS 8	447
IN CLOUDS & FIRES AROUND THE ROCK & THE MYSTERIOUS TREE		355	FOUR ZOAS 8	557
[HER WEB OF RELIGION AROUND THE SEPULCHER . . .		356	FOUR ZOAS 8	588
AS SNOW THAT FALLS AROUND A LEAFLESS TREE UPON THE GREEN		358	FOUR ZOAS 9	49
AND DEEP DESPAIR RATTLING GO UP THE FLAMES AROUND THE SYNAGOGUE		359	FOUR ZOAS 9	68
AROUND THE DRAGON FORM OF URIZEN & ROUND HIS STONY FORM		359	FOUR ZOAS 9	81
WHILE LITTLE CHILDREN PLAY AROUND THY FEET IN GENTLE AWE		360	FOUR ZOAS 9	134
THE FURIOUS WIND STILL RENDS AROUND THEY FLEE IN SLUGGISH EFFORT		363	FOUR ZOAS 9	256
WAVE FRESHLY CLEAR WATERS FLOWING AROUND THE TENDER GRASS		368	FOUR ZOAS 9	436
FOR WEEDS OF DEATH HAVE WRAPD AROUND MY LIMBS IN THE HOARY DEEPS		370	FOUR ZOAS 9	488
THE CHILDREN CLUNG AROUND HER KNEES SHE EMBRACD THEM & WEPT OVER THEM		370	FOUR ZOAS 9	509
ABSTRACTED FROM THE ROOTS OF [NATURE] SCIENCE THEN INCLOSD AROUND		374	FOUR ZOAS 9	631
WHERE ARE YOUR CHAINS WHERE ARE YOUR TEARS WHY DO YOU LOOK AROUND		375	FOUR ZOAS 9	679
AND LO MY BRETHREN IN THEIR TENTS & THEIR LITTLE ONES AROUND THEM		375	FOUR ZOAS 9	691
INTO THE BARN WHILE CHILDREN GLEAN THE EARS AROUND THE DOOR		376	FOUR ZOAS 9	702
DROWND IN THE WINE IS MANY A YOUTH & MAIDEN THOSE AROUND		377	FOUR ZOAS 9	745
THEY DANCE AROUND THE DYING & THEY DRINK THE HOWL & GROAN		377	FOUR ZOAS 9	767
URTHONA CALLD HIS SONS AROUND HIM THARMAS CALLD HIS SONS		378	FOUR ZOAS 9	789
AROUND THE ETERNAL MAN'S BRIGHT TENT THE LITTLE CHILDREN PLAY		379	FOUR ZOAS 9	839
AROUND THE FURNACES & IN EVENING SPORT UPON THE PLAINS		379	FOUR ZOAS 9	842
SUCH SEEMD THE SYNAGOGUE TO DISTANT VIEW AROUND THEM STOOD		382	FOUR ZOAS AD 6	10
AROUND THE SPRINGS OF GRAY MY WILD ROOT WEAVES		414	ILLUS GRAY	1
MY SPECTRE AROUND ME NIGHT & DAY		415	MY SPECTRE/N	1
AROUND MY COUCH WITH TORCHES BRIGHT		416	MY SPECTRE/N	42
BIND AROUND MY AKING HEAD		417	MY SPECTR AD/N	12
MUSTER AROUND THE POLAR STAR		420	I SAW MNK AD/N	18
SHE BINDS IRON THORNS AROUND HIS HEAD		425	MENTAL TRAVLER	13
AND A DARK DESART ALL AROUND		426	MENTAL TRAVLER	68
THE YOUNG MEN & MAIDENS AROUND HER THRONG		428	MARY	3
DANCED AROUND HER SHINING HEAD		435	WILLIAM BOND	42
WITH THE OFFENCE AND REPEATED IT TO THOSE AROUND		437C	BLAKES MEMORAN	PROSE
AND RICH AND POOR AROUND IT WAIT		442	DEDICATN BLAIR	8
[THE HEAVENS IN CLOUDS ROLLING BEFORE HIM & AROUND HIM]		443A	LAST JUDGMNT/L	PROSE
BEFORE HIS FEET & AROUND HIM THE HEAVENS IN CLOUDS ARE ROLLING		443A	LAST JUDGMNT/L	*PROSE
& THE MOON BENEATH HER FEET WITH SIX INFANTS AROUND HER		443D	LAST JUDGMNT/L	PROSE
OPENED AROUND THE THRONE OF CHRIST		444A	LAST JUDGMNT/L	PROSE
AROUND THEIR LOINS POURD FORTH THEIR ARROWS & THEIR BOSOMS BEAM		484	MILTON 4	23
THE FURNACES LAMENTING AROUND THE ANVILS & THIS THEIR SONG		484	MILTON 5	18
OF FIRE ROUND THE WALLS COLUMNS OF FIRE GUARD AROUND		490	MILTON 9	44
AROUND THE FIERY FLAMING HARROW IN LABYRINTHINE FORMS		493	MILTON 12	18
AROUND THE LAMB A FEMALE TABERNACLE WOVEN IN CATHEDRON'S LOOMS		494	MILTON 13	26
TOLD OF THE ENORMOUS CONFLICT EARTHQUAKE BENEATH AROUND		500	MILTON 18	48
THEY ARE THE FOUR ZOAS THAT STOOD AROUND THE THRONE DIVINE		500	MILTON 19	18
AROUND THE MARROW AND THE ORBED SCULL AROUND THE BRAIN		501	MILTON 19	52
HE IS THE FOURTH ZOA THAT STOOD (AROUND) THE THRONE DIVINE		510	MILTON 24	76
WHILE LOS CALLD HIS SONS AROUND HIM TO THE HARVEST & THE VINTAGE		511	MILTON 25	65
AND IN THE CITY OF GOLGONOOZA & IN LUBAN & AROUND		512	MILTON 26	24
DROWND IN THE WINE IS MANY A YOUTH & MAIDEN THOSE AROUND		513	MILTON 27	5
AROUND THE WINE-PRESSES OF LUVAH NAKED & DRUNK WITH WINE		513	MILTON 27	24
THAT CREEP AROUND THE OBSCURE PLACES SHEW THEIR VARIOUS LIMBS		513	MILTON 27	28
THEY DANCE AROUND THE DYING & THEY DRINK THE HOWL & GROAN		514	MILTON 27	37
AROUND THE CITY OF GOLGONOOZA IN THE FORESTS OF ENTUTHON		514	MILTON 27	43
CREATING FORM & BEAUTY AROUND THE DARK REGIONS OF SORROW		514	MILTON 28	2
AND EVERY SPACE THAT A MAN VIEWS AROUND HIS DWELLING-PLACE		516	MILTON 29	5
BEULAH IS EVERMORE CREATED AROUND ETERNITY APPEARING		518	MILTON 30	8
TO THE INHABITANTS OF EDEN AROUND THEM ON ALL SIDES		518	MILTON 30	9
AROUND THIS POLYPUS LOS CONTINUAL BUILDS THE MUNDANE SHELL		524	MILTON 34	31
APPEAR AROUND IN THE EXTERNAL SPHERES OF VISIONARY LIFE		524	MILTON 34	51
SUDDENLY AROUND MILTON ON MY PATH THE STARRY SEVEN		530	MILTON 39	3
AROUND THE STARRY EIGHT WITH ONE ACCORD THE STARRY EIGHT BECAME		534	MILTON 42	10
AROSE AROUND ALBION'S BODY JESUS WEPT & WALKED FORTH		534	MILTON 42	19
A THING THATS TIED AROUND THE EXAMINER'S NECK		556	BLAKES APL/N 2	20
AWKWARD FRENCH PALACE ARE [ALL] THROWN TOGETHER AROUND		599C	PUB ADDRESS/N	*PROSE
AROUND HIM WERE SEEN THE IMAGES OF EXISTENCES		606A	V LAST JUDG/N	PROSE
THE HEAVENS OPENING AROUND HIM BY UNFOLDING THE CLOUDS		606B	V LAST JUDG/N	PROSE
AROUND HIS THRONE THE OLD (HEAVEN) & (OLD) EARTH ARE		606B	V LAST JUDG/N	PROSE

124

		PAGE	TITLE	LINE

AROUND   (CONTINUED)
```
    AROUND HIM ARE OTHER KINGDOMS ARISING TO JUDGMENT    . .   . 608C  V LAST JUDG/N   PROSE
    AROUND NOAH & BENEATH HIM ARE VARIOUS FIGURES RISEN  . .   . 610A  V LAST JUDG/N   PROSE
    [AROUND THE THRONE HEAVEN IS OPENED] ON THE CLOUD    . .   . 612B  V LAST JUDG/N   PROSE
    AROUND THE THRONE HEAVEN IS OPEND                    . .   . 612D  V LAST JUDG/N   PROSE
    AROUND HIM INFANTS EMANATING FROM HIM THESE REPRESENT  .   . 613D  V LAST JUDG/N   PROSE
    AROUND MILTON ARE SIX SPIRITS OR FAIRIES HOVERING ON THE    619C  ILLUS MILTON    PROSE
        AIR
    I SAW DISEASE FORMING A BODY OF DEATH AROUND THE LAMB   .  . 628  JERUSALEM 9          9
    HE STAMPS AROUND THE ANVIL BEATING BLOWS OF STERN DESPAIR   629  JERUSALEM 10        24
    AND THEY STOOD AROUND TERRIFIED WITH ADMIRATION AT ERIN'S   631  JERUSALEM 12        22
        SPACES
    AROUND GOLGONOOZA LIES THE LAND OF DEATH ETERNAL A LAND     633  JERUSALEM 13        30
    INFOLD AROUND MY LIMBS BRUISING MY MINUTE ARTICULATIONS     635  JERUSALEM 15        13
    WITH TRANSGRESSORS MEETING IN BROTHERHOOD AROUND THE TABLE  640  JERUSALEM 18        15
    SETTLED AROUND ALBION AND AROUND LUVAH IN HIS SECRET CLOUD  641  JERUSALEM 19        27
    WE REARED MIGHTY STONES WE DANCED NAKED AROUND THEM  . .  . 647  JERUSALEM 24         4
    COLD SNOWS DRIFTED AROUND HIM ICE COVERD HIS LOINS AROUND   652  JERUSALEM 28        13
    AND LUVAH HATH DRAWN THE CURTAINS AROUND ALBION IN VALA'S   656  JERUSALEM 30        39
        BOSOM
    REARING THEIR DRUID PATRIARCHAL ROCKY TEMPLES AROUND HIS    658  JERUSALEM 32        14
        LIMBS
    LET DOWN AT WILL AROUND AND CALLD THE UNIVERSAL TENT   .  . 665  JERUSALEM 38        50
    AROSE UPON HIM PALE AND GHASTLY AND HE CALLD AROUND  . . .  666  JERUSALEM 40         2
    THEY KNEELD AROUND THE COUCH OF DEATH IN DEEP HUMILIATION   668  JERUSALEM 41        24
    AND LOS DREW HIS SEVEN FURNACES AROUND ALBION'S ALTARS  .  . 671  JERUSALEM 42        77
    THEN LOS GREW FURIOUS RAGING WHY STAND WE HERE TREMBLING    672  JERUSALEM 43        12
        AROUND
    SO LOS SPOKE PALE THEY STOOD AROUND THE HOUSE OF DEATH  .  . 673  JERUSALEM 43        80
    THE FAMILY DIVINE HOVER AROUND THE DARKEND ALBION     . .   674  JERUSALEM 44        20
    THE SLUMBERS OF DEATH CAME OVER THEM AROUND THE COUCH OF    674  JERUSALEM 44        35
        DEATH
    AROUND ALBION BUT ALBION HEARD HIM NOT OBDURATE HARD   .  . 676  JERUSALEM 45        35
    JEHOVAH IS BEFORE BEHIND ABOVE BENEATH AROUND   . . . . .   680  JERUSALEM 49        53
    OF DEATH THUNDER INCESSANT AROUND THE FLAMING COUCHES OF    684  JERUSALEM 53        21
    LOOK BACK INTO THE CHURCH PAUL LOOK THREE WOMEN AROUND      688  JERUSALEM 56        42
    AMONG THE INHABITANTS OF ALBION THE PEOPLE FALL AROUND  .   689  JERUSALEM 58         4
    THE FOUR ZOAS RUSH AROUND ON ALL SIDES IN DIRE RUIN  . . .  690  JERUSALEM 58        47
    AROUND THE EARTH OF ALBION AMONG THE ROOTS OF HIS TREE  .  . 691  JERUSALEM 59         4
    THEY ARE THE FOUR ZOAS THAT STOOD AROUND THE THRONE DIVINE  691  JERUSALEM 59        13
    THE DRUID SONS OF ALBION & THE HEAVENS A VOID AROUND        697  JERUSALEM 63        19
        UNFATHOMABLE
    AROUND IN THE CLOUDS OF THE FEMALE ON ALBION'S CLIFFS OF    697  JERUSALEM 63        22
        THE DEAD
    DANCING AROUND IN HOWLING PAIN CLOTHED IN THE BLOODY VEIL   704  JERUSALEM 67        16
    IN VERULAM THE POLYPUS'S HEAD WINDING AROUND HIS BULK  .  . 704  JERUSALEM 67        35
    PRESS IT AROUND THE LOINS OF THIS EVER EXPANDING CRUELTY    705  JERUSALEM 67        60
    THE HEAVENS ARE CUT LIKE A MANTLE AROUND FROM THE CLIFFS    706  JERUSALEM 68        19
        OF ALBION
    THESE ARE CREATED BY RAHAB & TIRZAH IN ULRO BUT AROUND  .  . 713  JERUSALEM 73        39
    ON LONDON STONE & THE DAUGHTERS OF ALBION RAN AROUND        715  JERUSALEM 74        34
        ADMIRING
    BECAME A SPACE & AN ALLEGORY AROUND THE WINDING WORM  . .   730  JERUSALEM 85         1
    (AROUND) HIS HEAD THE THICK HAIL STONES STAND READY TO OBEY 731  JERUSALEM 86      * 36
    THE SMALL FIBRES AS THEY SHOOT AROUND ME DRAW OUT IN PITY   732  JERUSALEM 87         8
    IN MILD JERUSALEM AROUND THE LAMB OF GOD LOUD HOWL   . . .  734  JERUSALEM 88        53
    OF VEINS OF RED BLOOD GROWS AROUND THEM LIKE A SCARLET ROBE 736  JERUSALEM 90         5
    AMALEK EDOM EGYPT MOAB AMMON ASHUR PHILISTEA AROUND         740  JERUSALEM 92        23
        JERUSALEM
    OF ENRAGED THUNDERS AROUND THEM THE STARRY WHEELS OF THEIR  741  JERUSALEM 94        11
        GIANT SONS
    REVOLVE & OVER THEM THE FURNACES OF LOS & THE IMMORTAL      741  JERUSALEM 94        12
        TOMB AROUND
    OVER THEM THE FAMISHD EAGLE SCREAMS ON BONEY WINGS AND      741  JERUSALEM 94        15
        AROUND
    AROUND THE WORMY GARMENTS OF ALBION THEN PAUSING            741  JERUSALEM 94        17
        IN DEATHLIKE SILENCE
    IN ANGER THE WRATH OF GOD BREAKING BRIGHT FLAMING ON ALL    742  JERUSALEM 95         6
        SIDES AROUND
    DAZLING AROUND THY SKIRTS LIKE A SERPENT OF PRECIOUS STONES 743  JERUSALEM 96        12
        & GOLD
    SOON ALL AROUND REMOTE THE HEAVENS BURNT WITH FLAMING FIRES 744  JERUSALEM 96        40
    A SUN OF BLOOD RED WRATH SURROUNDING HEAVEN ON ALL SIDES    745  JERUSALEM 98        10
        AROUND
    AND THE DIM CHAOS BRIGHTEND BENEATH ABOVE AROUND EYED AS    745  JERUSALEM 98        14
        THE PEACOCK
    THUNDERS & LIGHTNINGS BROKE AROUND   . . . . . . . .   .   . 749  EV GOSPEL(B)/N     25
    PINND AROUND FROM STAR TO STAR . . . . . . . . . .   . .   . 757  EV GOSPEL(I)/N     24
    ON THE MOUNTAINS AROUND  . . . . . . . . . . . . .   . .   . 805  TO BUTTS/L         65
    AROUND YOUR HERMIT & BARD SO PRAYS THE EMULATOR OF BOTH    835B  LETTER 34        PROSE
AROUSE
    AROUSE THYSELF THE NATIONS BLACK  . . . . . . . . .   .     . 12  GWIN KING/PS       35
AROUZE
    I FEEL MY SPECTRE RISING UPON ME ALBION AROUZE THYSELF  .  . 664  JERUSALEM 37         2
ARPHAXAD
    NOAH SHEM ARPHAXAD CAINAN THE SECOND SALAH HEBER  . . . .   528  MILTON 37          38
    NOAH SHEM ARPHAXAD CAINAN THE SECOND SALAH HEBER  . . . .   716  JERUSALEM 75        13
ARRANGED    SEE DIS-ARRANGED
    AND TOOK THE FORMS OF BOOKS & WERE ARRANGED IN LIBRARIES   155A  MARRIAGE HH 15  PROSE
    ARRANGED IS AN ENQUIRY WORTHY OF BOTH THE ANTIQUARIAN   .  . 578D  DESC CAT 5      *PROSE
ARRAY
    MY SILKS AND FINE ARRAY  . . . . . . . . . . . . .   .     . 6  MY SILKS/PS          1
```

		PAGE	TITLE	LINE

ARRAY   (CONTINUED)
    FOLLOW IN WILD ARRAY . . . .   11 GWIN KING/PS   26
    THEY LANDED IN FIRM ARRAY UPON THE ROCKS   . . . . . .   32 EDW THIRD/PS 6   13
    OUR FATHERS MOVE IN FIRM ARRAY TO BATTLE   . . . . . .   32 EDW THIRD/PS 6   25
    CITIES SHALL SING AND VALES IN RICH ARRAY   . . . . . .   33 EDW THIRD/PS 6   47
    RANGD IN GLOOMD ARRAY STRETCH OUT ACROSS   . . . . . .   223 URIZEN 3   29
    I HOPE THINE ARE NOT HENCE IT CLOTHES ITSELF IN RICH ARRAY   502 MILTON 20   30
    BUT FIRST THEY SAID & THEIR WORDS STOOD IN CHARIOTS IN   686 JERUSALEM 55   34
        ARRAY
    AND THE ALL WONDROUS SERPENT CLOTHED IN GEMS & RICH ARRAY   746 JERUSALEM 98   44
        HUMANIZE
ARRAYD
    MY MIND IS NOT WITH THY LIGHT ARRAYD . . . .   818 HAPPINESS/L   69
ARRIVAL
    UNTILL THE ARRIVAL OF THAT HOUR   . . . .   421 EACH MAN/N   2
    UNTILL THE ARRIVAL OF THAT HOUR   . . . .   669 EACH MAN/J   2
    THE FIRST MORNING AFTER MY ARRIVAL & THE PLOWBOY SAID   . 803C LETTER 15   PROSE
    A MONTH AFTER MY ARRIVAL HERE I SHOULD HAVE DONE SO BUT   825D LETTER 27   PROSE
    WITH AN ACCOUNT OF HIS SAFE ARRIVAL WHICH WILL EXCUSE HIS   829C LETTER 30   PROSE
    I WRITE IMMEDIATELY ON MY ARRIVAL NOT MERELY TO INFORM . 833D LETTER 33   PROSE
    BUT MY ARRIVAL HAS DISPELLD THE FORMIDABLE MALADY & MY   833D LETTER 33   PROSE
        DEAR &
    BECAUSE I WOULD HASTEN ITS ARRIVAL BEFORE IT IS CONVENIENT   853D LETTER 52 PROSE
    TO WELCOME THY ARRIVAL AMONG COWPER'S GLORIFIED BAND . . 854C LETTER 53   PROSE
ARRIVD
    SHE FLED FROM FEAR TILL AT HER HOUSE ARRIVD   . . . . .   5 FAIR ELENOR/PS 36
    NOW ARRIVD THE ANCIENT GUARDIAN AT THE SOUTHERN PORCH . . 241 EUROPE 10   24
    WENT ALONG ALBION'S ROADS TILL THEY ARRIVD AT ALBION'S   667 JERUSALEM 40   24
        HOUSE
    IS ARRIVD WHEN MEN SHALL AGAIN CONVERSE IN HEAVEN & WALK   799B LETTER 11   PROSE
        WITH
    YOU THAT I AM SAFE ARRIVD BUT ALSO TO INFORM YOU THAT IN A 833B LETTER 33   PROSE
ARRIVE
    COMFORT THYSELF IN MY STRENGTH THE TIME WILL ARRIVE . . 626 JERUSALEM 7   54
    COULD NOT ARRIVE AT OUR COTTAGE BEFORE HALF PAST ELEVEN   802B LETTER 14   PROSE
    WILL ARRIVE AS SAFE AS WITH HER I SHALL HAVE AN   809C LETTER 20   PROSE
        OPPORTUNITY
ARRIVED
    DEAR SCULPTOR OF ETERNITY WE ARE SAFE ARRIVED AT   801D LETTER 14   PROSE
        OUR COTTAGE
    DEAR FRIEND OF MY ANGELS WE ARE SAFE ARRIVED AT OUR COTTAGE 803A LETTER 15   PROSE
    THE CXXXIX PSALM A LITTLE BEFORE YOUR LETTER ARRIVED I TAKE 823B LETTER 26   PROSE
    BE WORTH ARRIVED SAFE IN LONDON MY WIFE IN VERY POOR HEALTH 829D LETTER 30   PROSE
    I WRITE IN A VIOLENT HURRY YOUR LETTER HAS NEVER ARRIVED TO 832B LETTER 32   PROSE
    MR LINNELL WILL HAVE ARRIVED AT HIS JOURNEY'S END BEFORE   871C LETTER 73   PROSE
ARRIVES
    WHEN ON THE HIGHEST LIFT OF HIS LIGHT PINIONS HE ARRIVES   526 MILTON 36   1
ARRIVEST
    IF THOU ARRIVEST AT THE SANDY SHORE   . . . .   15 IMIT SPEN/PS   27
ARROGANCE
    [NO READER WILL THINK PRESUMPTUOUSNESS OR (ARROGANCE) WHEN 621A JERUSALEM 3   *PROSE
        HE]
ARROW
    WHEN IJIM STRETCHD HIS MIGHTY ARM THE ARROW FROM HIS LIMBS 105 TIRIEL 4   71
    SEES YOU SWIFT AS ARROW   . . . .   115 THE BLOSSOM/SI   4
    IS AN ARROW FROM THE ALMIGHTIE'S BOW . . . .   420 I SAW A MONK/N   61
    IS AN ARROW FROM THE ALMIGHTIE'S BOW . . . .   430 GREY MONK   32
    INTO THE SWORD OF WAR INTO THE BOW AND ARROW . . . . . 628 JERUSALEM 9   5
    IS AN ARROW FROM THE ALMIGHTIE'S BOW . . . .   683 I SAW A MONK/J   28
    THEN EACH AN ARROW FLAMING FROM HIS QUIVER FITTED CAREFULLY 744 JERUSALEM 98   1
    . . . LOUD SOUNDING FLEW THE FLAMING ARROW FOURFOLD . . 744 JERUSALEM 98   3
ARROWS
    THE PATHLESS PLAIN AS THE ARROWS THAT FLY   . . . . . .   5 FAIR ELENOR/PS   34
    THE ARROWS OF ALMIGHTY GOD ARE DRAWN . . . .   35 WAR SONG/PS   16
    SO THE ARROWS OF SIN STICK IN MY FLESH   . . . .   36B COUCH DEATH/PS PROSE
    AND CHOSE HER ARROWS THEN ADVANCD TO MEET THE TERRIBLE PAIR 109 TIRIEL 7   24
    WHY ARE EYELIDS STORD WITH ARROWS READY DRAWN   . . . . 130 BOOK OF THEL 6   13
    MY LITTLE ARROWS   . . . .   178 THE FAIRY/N   2
    ERE YET HIS EYELIDS CAN BEHOLD THE ARROWS OF THE DAY . . 193 V DAU ALBION 5   32
    FORTH FLEW THE ARROWS OF PESTILENCE   . . . .   252 AHANIA 4   9
    FORTY YEARS FLEW THE ARROWS OF PESTILENCE   . . . . . . 253 AHANIA 4   37
    AMONG THE FROZEN ARROWS THEY WILL TEAR THY TENDER FLESH   296 FOUR ZOAS 3   172
    AND TWANG THE BOWSTRING TO OUR HOWLINGS LET THINE ARROWS   306 FOUR ZOAS 5   51
        BLACK
    AND CUT THE WINDS LIKE ARROWS SHOT BY TROOPS OF DESTINY   325 FOUR ZOAS 7   208
    AND LET THE THUNDERING DRUM SPEED ON THE ARROWS BLACK . 337 FOUR ZOAS 7B   * 158
    THE ARROWS FLEW FROM CLOUDY BOW ALL DAY TILL BLOOD . . 337 FOUR ZOAS 7B   159
    ARISE O VALA BRING THE BOW OF URIZEN BRING THE SWIFT   338 FOUR ZOAS 7B   200
        ARROWS OF LIGHT
    HAVE SHOT THEIR ARROWS OR LONG BEAMED SPEARS IN WRATH &   358 FOUR ZOAS 9   41
        FURY
    BRING ME MY ARROWS OF DESIRE   . . . .   481 AND DID FEET/M   10
    AROUND THEIR LOINS POURD FORTH THEIR ARROWS & THEIR BOSOMS 484 MILTON 4   23
        BEAM
    WHEN SATAN FAINTED BENEATH THE ARROWS OF ELYNITTRIA . . 485 MILTON 5   43
    DARKENEST EVERY INTERNAL LIGHT WITH THE ARROWS OF   491 MILTON 10   17
        THY QUIVER
    BUT BEAUTIFUL ELYNITTRIA WITH HER SILVER ARROWS REPELLD ME 492 MILTON 11   38
    AND THREW ASIDE HER ARROWS AND LAID DOWN HER SOUNDING BOW   494 MILTON 13   37
    OF LIGHT AND LOVE THEIR LITTLE CHILDREN STAND WITH ARROWS   631 JERUSALEM 11   20
        OF GOLD
    WITH INTELLECTUAL SPEARS & LONG WINGED ARROWS OF THOUGHT   664 JERUSALEM 38   15

	PAGE	TITLE	LINE

ARROWS   (CONTINUED)
ARISE O VALA BRING THE BOW OF URIZEN BRING THE SWIFT   700 JERUSALEM 65   46
    ARROWS OF LIGHT
MINGLED OR SEPARATE FOR SWORDS ARROWS CANNONS MORTARS . .   713 JERUSALEM 73   11
THE ARROWS OF THE ALMIGHTY POUR UPON ME & MY CHILDREN . .   719 JERUSALEM 78   32
HE TAKES HIS BOW THEN CHOOSES OUT HIS ARROWS OF FLAMING   742 JERUSALEM 95   13
    GOLD
AND THE BOW IS A MALE & FEMALE & THE QUIVER OF THE ARROWS   744 JERUSALEM 97   12
    OF LOVE
AND HE CLOTHED HIMSELF IN BOW & ARROWS IN AWFUL STATE   744 JERUSALEM 97   16
    FOURFOLD
FOURFOLD ANNIHILATION & AT THE CLANGOR OF THE ARROWS OF   745 JERUSALEM 98   7
    INTELLECT
WITH THE BOWS OF MY MIND & THE ARROWS OF THOUGHT . . . . .   818 HAPPINESS/L   78
MY ARROWS GLOW IN THEIR GOLDEN SHEAVES . . . .   818 HAPPINESS/L   80
GENEROUS EXULTATION IN MY ESCAPE FROM THE ARROWS   833C LETTER 33   PROSE
    OF DARKNESS
ARROWY
MOULDED TO GLOBES & ARROWY WEDGES RENDING THY BLEEDING   321 FOUR ZOAS 7   52
    LIMBS
AND WOUNDED WITH ARROWY SMARTS . . . .   552 WHY CUPID/N   14
ARSE
CALL ME [ASS ARSE] ASS   . . . .   46B ISLAND MOON 2   PROSE
THE DEVIL'S ARSE A KING . . . .   400D ANNO BACON   MARG
READY TO KISS ANY ONE'S ARSE   . . . .   785C ILLUS DANTE 16   PROSE
ART   (NOUN)
O ROGER THOU UNSKILLD IN ART   . . . .   16 BLIND-MANS/PS   41
EVERY ART & SCIENCE ADORND HIM AS BEADS ROUND HIS NECK . .   46D ISLAND MOON 3   PROSE
("ART IS HIGHEST HUMAN NATURE") HUMAN NATURE IS THE   83A ANNO LAVATER   MARG
    IMAGE OF GOD
("THE INFINITELY LITTLE THE DIFFERENCE IN WORKS OF   84A ANNO LAVATER   MARG
    ART") UNEASY
AND WHAT SHOULDER & WHAT ART   . . . .   172 THE TYGER/N 1   9
AND WHAT SHOULDER & WHAT ART   . . . .   173 THE TYGER/N 2   9
AND WHAT SHOULDER & WHAT ART   . . . .   214 THE TYGER/SE   9
POISONOUS SOURCE PLACD WITH ART LIFTING DIFFICULT . . .   251 AHANIA 3   34
INTO INFINITUDE & ORNAMENTED IT WITH WONDROUS ART . . .   270 FOUR ZOAS 1   226
A GOLDEN ALTAR BURNT PERFUMES WITH ART CELESTIAL FORMD . . 285 FOUR ZOAS 2   190
WITH JEWELS & PRECIOUS ORNAMENT LABOURD WITH ART DIVINE   312 FOUR ZOAS 6   27
INTO THE BLUE EXPANSE & I INVENTED WITH LABORIOUS ART . .   312 FOUR ZOAS 6   31
REDUCE ALL TO OUR WILL AS SPANIELS ARE TAUGHT WITH ART . . 323 FOUR ZOAS 7   129
HE VANQUISHD WITH THE STRENGTH OF ART BENDING THEIR IRON   331 FOUR ZOAS 7   459
    POINTS
WITH BEAUTIFUL ART THE STUDY OF ANGELS THE WORKMANSHIP   365 FOUR ZOAS 9   297
    OF DEMONS
BACON'S BUSINESS IS NOT INTELLECT OR ART   . . . .   409D ANNO BACON   * MARG
IT WAS BYSSHE'S ART OF POETRY SHE OPEND THE   440D MEMORANDUM/N 5 PROSE
    FOLLOWING...BEHN
THIS MAN WAS HIRED TO DEPRESS ART . . . .   445A ANNO REYNOLDS   MARG
THE FOUNDATION OF EMPIRE IS ART & SCIENCE . . . .   445C ANNO REYNOLDS   MARG
EMPIRE FOLLOWS ART & NOT VICE VERSA AS ENGLISHMEN SUPPOSE   445D ANNO REYNOLDS   MARG
WHO WILL DARE TO SAY THAT [FINE] POLITE ART IS ENCOURAGED   446A ANNO REYNOLDS   * MARG
THE SOCIETY FOR THE ENCOURAGEMENT OF ART SUFFERD BARRY .   446A ANNO REYNOLDS   MARG
O SOCIETY FOR ENCOURAGEMENT OF ART   . . . .   446A ANNO REYNOLDS   MARG
TO LEARN THE LANGUAGE OF ART COPY FOR EVER IS MY RULE .   446B ANNO REYNOLDS   MARG
& PROPORTIONATE VALUE & A GENERAL DEMAND FOR ART   . . .   446D ANNO REYNOLDS   MARG
PRETEND THAT ART IS ENCOURAGED BY THAT NATION . . . . .   446D ANNO REYNOLDS   MARG
ART IS FIRST IN INTELLECTUALS & OUGHT TO BE FIRST   446D ANNO REYNOLDS   MARG
    IN NATIONS
WHOEVER IS SET TO UNDERMINE THE EXECUTION OF ART IS SET TO   447A ANNO REYNOLDS   MARG
DESTROY ART MICHAEL ANGELO'S ART DEPENDS   . . . .   447A ANNO REYNOLDS   MARG
FOR THAT IS THE ONLY SCHOOL TO THE LANGUAGE OF ART . .   448D ANNO REYNOLDS   MARG
THE INFERIOR PARTS OF ART AS REYNOLDS ARTFULLY CALLS THEM   449A ANNO REYNOLDS   MARG
OLD HARD STIFF & DRY UNFINISHD WORKS OF ART . . . . . .   449C ANNO REYNOLDS   MARG
DOES NOT KNOW THE BEGINNING NEVER CAN KNOW THE END OF ART   449C ANNO REYNOLDS   MARG
SUCH WAS BURKE'S PATRONAGE OF ART & SCIENCE . . . . . .   451D ANNO REYNOLDS   MARG
I ALWAYS CONSIDERD TRUE ART & TRUE ARTISTS TO BE   452B ANNO REYNOLDS   MARG
    PARTICULARLY
ARE AT ALL TIMES HIRED BY THE SATANS FOR THE DEPRESSION   452B ANNO REYNOLDS   MARG
    OF ART
A PRETENCE OF ART TO DESTROY ART XXX   . . . .   452B ANNO REYNOLDS   * MARG
IN A COUNTRY PRETENDING TO THE ENCOURAGEMENT OF ART . .   452B ANNO REYNOLDS   MARG
& OBEDIENT TO NOBLEMENS OPINIONS IN ART & SCIENCE . . .   453A ANNO REYNOLDS   MARG
A FACILITY IN COMPOSING IS THE GREATEST POWER OF ART . .   453D ANNO REYNOLDS   MARG
LEARND THE LANGUAGE OF ART BY MAKING MANY FINISHD COPIES   455D ANNO REYNOLDS   MARG
BOTH OF NATURE & ART   . . . .   455D ANNO REYNOLDS   MARG
IN ART & THAT EVERY THING IN ART IS DEFINITE & DETERMINATE   457B ANNO REYNOLDS   MARG
WHAT HAS REASONING TO DO WITH THE ART OF PAINTING . . .   458C ANNO REYNOLDS   MARG
THAT ART MUST BE PRODUCD WITHOUT SUCH METHOD   . . . . .   459D ANNO REYNOLDS   MARG
OF EXECUTION IN ART LET HIM WHO WILL FOLLOW SUCH ADVICE   461C ANNO REYNOLDS   MARG
IN A DISCOURSE ON ART SUCH IDIOTS ARE NOT ARTISTS . . .   464B ANNO REYNOLDS   MARG
& MINUTE DISCRIMINATION OF CHARACTER IT IS THE WHOLE OF ART 466B ANNO REYNOLDS   MARG
KNEW NOT THE SMALLER BEAUTIES OF THE ART   . . . .   467A ANNO REYNOLDS   MARG
KNEW NOTHING AT ALL ABOUT ART AS AN OBJECT OF IMITATION   467B ANNO REYNOLDS   MARG
MICHAEL ANGELO WERE INCAPABLE OF THE MEER LANGUAGE OF ART   467B ANNO REYNOLDS   MARG
IN THE LOWER PARTS OF ART . . . .   467D ANNO REYNOLDS   MARG
TO THE COLOURING OF REAL ART & SCIENCE   . . . .   469A ANNO REYNOLDS   MARG
RUBENS & THE VENETIANS ARE OPPOSITE IN EVERY THING TO TRUE   469A ANNO REYNOLDS   MARG
    ART
BACON'S (PHILOSOPHY) HAS DESTROYD (ALL) ART & SCIENCE . . 470A ANNO REYNOLDS   * MARG
IF ART WAS PROGRESSIVE WE SHOULD HAVE HAD MICH ANGELOS . . 470D ANNO REYNOLDS   MARG
THAT HE WANTS EITHER COLOURING OR ORNAMENTAL PARTS OF ART   472A ANNO REYNOLDS   MARG

ART   (CONTINUED)

OF ALL ART BECAUSE IT TAKES AWAY THE POSSIBILITY OF VARIETY	478C ANNO REYNOLDS	MARG
SUCH HARMONY OF COLOURING IS DESTRUCTIVE OF ART	478D ANNO REYNOLDS	MARG
ALL THIS IS DESTRUCTIVE OF ART	479A ANNO REYNOLDS	MARG
[FUNERAL GRANTED TO SIR JOSHUA FOR HAVING ?DESTROYD ART]	SUPP ANNO REYNOLDS	* MARG
[THE RASCALS WHO ?SEE PAINTING WANT TO DESTROY ART & LEARNING]	SUPP ANNO REYNOLDS	* MARG
[THE KNAVE CALLS ANY THING ?FOUND IN NATURE FIT FOR ART]	SUPP ANNO REYNOLDS	* MARG
BUT GOLGONOOZA IS NAMD ART & MANUFACTURE BY MORTAL MEN . .	509 MILTON 24	50
[CR(CROMEK)] HE LOVES THE ART BUT [THE] TIS THE ART TO CHEAT	540 CR LOVES ART/N *	2
AND WORSHIPPD THEM [TO] THAT THEY MIGHT MAKE INSPIRD ART ABHORRD	543 IF TRUE/N	10
NATURE & ART IN THIS TOGETHER SUIT	547 PRETTY EPIGR/N	1
ENGLISH ENCOURAGEMENT OF ART CROMEK'S OPINIONS PUT INTO RHYME	549C ENGL ENCOU/N 1	TITLE
WHO CRIES ALL ART IS A FRAUD & GENIUS A TRICK	555 BLAKES APL/N 1	20
[?WHEN] NOW ART HAS LOST ITS MENTAL CHARMS	557 ART HAS LOST/N *	1
WITH WORKS OF ART THEIR ARMIES MEET	557 ART HAS LOST/N	7
CONTAINING AMPLE ILLUSTRATIONS ON ART	560C EXHIBITION ADV	PROSE
THE ART HAS BEEN LOST I HAVE RECOVERED IT	561A EXHIBITION ADV	PROSE
THE WHOLE PROCESS IN A WORK ON ART NOW IN THE PRESS . . .	561A EXHIBITION ADV	PROSE
FROM DOING MY DUTY TO MY ART	561A EXHIBITION ADV	PROSE
IF MICHAEL ANGELO IS ITS SUPREME GLORY IF ART IS THE GLORY	561C EXHIBITION ADV	PROSE
THE GRAND STYLE OF ART RESTORED IN FRESCO OR	562B DESC CAT ADV	PROSE
PROTECTRESS OF BAD THAT IS BLOTTING AND BLURRING ART .	562B DESC CAT ADV	PROSE
IN THIS EXHIBITION WILL BE SEEN REAL ART	562B DESC CAT ADV	PROSE
OPINIONS AND DETERMINATIONS ON ART VERY NECESSARY TO BE KNOWN	562B DESC CAT ADV	PROSE
THESE ORIGINAL CONCEPTIONS ON ART BY AN ORIGINAL ARTIST	562C DESC CAT ADV	PROSE
AS THAT WHICH IS FABRICATED FOR THE PURPOSE TO DESTROY ART	563D DESC CAT	PROSE
NARROW BLINKING EYES THAT HAVE TOO LONG GOVERNED ART .	563D DESC CAT	PROSE
AND ALL THE GRAND WORKS OF ANCIENT ART THEY WERE EXECUTED	565D DESC CAT 2	PROSE
BUT THE ART OF FRESCO PAINTING BEING LOST	566C DESC CAT 2	PROSE
OIL BECAME A FETTER TO GENIUS AND A DUNGEON TO ART BUT ONE	566C DESC CAT 2	PROSE
ONE WHO STUDIED POETICAL ART SO MUCH SO THAT THE . . .	569A DESC CAT 3	PROSE
A MASTER OF ART AND LEARNING THOUGH AFFECTING TO DESPISE IT	569C DESC CAT 3	PROSE
DOCTOR IN HIS ART THUS THE READER WILL OBSERVE	570D DESC CAT 3	PROSE
THE SHIPMAN OR SAILOR IS A SIMILAR GENIUS OF ULYSSEAN ART	571D DESC CAT 3	PROSE
ENVIOUS IMPUTATION OF UNFITNESS FOR FINISHED AND SCIENTIFIC ART	572C DESC CAT 3	PROSE
THEIR ART IS TO LOSE FORM HIS ART IS TO FIND FORM . . .	573B DESC CAT 3	PROSE
WHOSE WHOLE ART AND SCIENCE IS FABRICATED FOR THE PURPOSE	573B DESC CAT 3	PROSE
OF DESTROYING ART WHO THESE ARE	573B DESC CAT 3	PROSE
TO SUPPOSE THAT ART CAN GO BEYOND	579D DESC CAT 5	PROSE
THE FINEST SPECIMENS OF ART THAT ARE NOW IN THE WORLD IS	579D DESC CAT 5	PROSE
NOT KNOWING WHAT ART IS IT IS BEING BLIND TO THE GIFTS OF THE SPIRIT	579D DESC CAT 5	PROSE
ART IS LINEAMENTS OR FORMS AND FEATURES THAT ARE CAPABLE OF	579D DESC CAT 5	PROSE
IN WORKS OF TRUE ART AS TO A MODERN MAN	581A DESC CAT 5	PROSE
THEY CAUSE THAT EVERY THING IN ART SHALL BECOME A MACHINE	582C DESC CAT 9	PROSE
THOSE WHO KEEP MANUFACTORIES OF ART ALWAYS CHARGE . . .	583B DESC CAT 9	PROSE
BY RESPECTABLE MEN OF OTHER COUNTRIES ON ACCOUNT OF ART	584B DESC CAT 14	PROSE
A PAINTING AND A DRAWING PROCEEDS FROM IGNORANCE OF ART	584D DESC CAT 15	PROSE
SUCH ART OF LOSING THE OUTLINES IS THE ART OF VENICE AND	585A DESC CAT 15	PROSE
THE GREAT AND GOLDEN RULE OF ART AS WELL AS OF LIFE IS THIS	585B DESC CAT 15	PROSE
THE MORE PERFECT THE WORK OF ART AND THE LESS KEEN AND SHARP	585B DESC CAT 15	PROSE
PRETEND TO ENCOURAGE ART HE WILL EMPLOY HIMSELF	586A DESC CAT 16	PROSE
NO WORK OF ART CAN TAKE LONGER THAN A YEAR	587A CHAUCER 1	PROSE
IF MEN OF WEAK CAPACITIES [IN ART] HAVE ALONE THE POWER	591B PUB ADDRESS/N	PROSE
OF EXECUTION IN ART MR B(BLAKE) HAS NOW PUT TO THE TEST	591B PUB ADDRESS/N	PROSE
ART & HIS STROKES ARE STILL TO BE CONDEMND BECAUSE THEY	591B PUB ADDRESS/N	PROSE
[BEEN THE VICTIM] IN A WORK OF ART IT IS NOT FINE TINTS	591C PUB ADDRESS/N	PROSE
[FROM AN] AS AN ART IS LOST IN ENGLAND OWING TO AN . . .	591D PUB ADDRESS/N	*PROSE
COMPARE THE MODERN ART WITH THE ART AS IT EXISTED . . .	592A PUB ADDRESS/N	PROSE
& ALL EXPRESSION WITHOUT WHICH THE ART IS LOST	592A PUB ADDRESS/N	PROSE
TROUBLE THEIR HEADS VERY LITTLE ABOUT ART & SCIENCE & THAT	592C PUB ADDRESS/N	PROSE
PRETENCES OF ENGLISHMEN TO IMPROVE [E] ART BEFORE THEY EVEN	593C PUB ADDRESS/N	*PROSE
KNOW THE FIRST [LINES] BEGINNINGS OF ART I HOPE THIS PRINT	593C PUB ADDRESS/N	PROSE
A MAN WHO PRETENDS TO IMPROVE FINE ART DOES NOT KNOW .	593C PUB ADDRESS/N	PROSE
WHAT FINE ART IS YE ENGLISH ENGRAVERS MUST COME DOWN .	593C PUB ADDRESS/N	PROSE
BUT LOVE TO MY ART & ZEAL FOR MY COUNTRY A MUCH GREATER	594D PUB ADDRESS/N	PROSE
THE SAME ART WITH THOSE OF MILTON & SHAKESPEARE . . .	595A PUB ADDRESS/N	PROSE
AS THE SAME ART WITH THOSE OF RAFAEL & ALBERT DURER . .	595B PUB ADDRESS/N	PROSE
THERE CAN BE NO ART IN A NATION BUT SUCH AS IS . . .	595B PUB ADDRESS/N	PROSE
[ART BY THE HANDS OF IGNORANT JOURNEYMEN]	595B PUB ADDRESS/N	PROSE
THESE PEOPLE KNOW ENOUGH OF ARTIFICE BUT NOTHING OF ART	596A PUB ADDRESS/N	PROSE
THE UNORGANIZED BLOTS & BLURS OF RUBENS & TITIAN ARE NOT ART	596A PUB ADDRESS/N	PROSE
MOST ENGLISHMEN HAVE A CONTEMPT FOR ART [WHICH WILL] .	596B PUB ADDRESS/N	PROSE
FOR SUCH NONSENSE & THINK IT FINE ART	596C PUB ADDRESS/N	PROSE
WHOM I HAVE CONTENDED IN ART HAVE STROVE NOT TO EXCELL BUT	596D PUB ADDRESS/N	PROSE
FOR THE ENCOURAGEMENT OF ART WHEN SUCH PICTURES AS THESE	596D PUB ADDRESS/N	PROSE
& FOLLOWS [WHEREVER ART LEADS] THE ARTS	597A PUB ADDRESS/N	*PROSE
OF THE OBJECTS OF NATURE IS THE ART OF PAINTING OR THAT	597B PUB ADDRESS/N	PROSE
IS WORTHY OF NOTICE MUCH LESS THAT SUCH AN ART SHOULD BE THE	597B PUB ADDRESS/N	PROSE
LET ANY MAN OF SENSE ASK HIMSELF ONE QUESTION IS THIS ART	597B PUB ADDRESS/N	PROSE
IS THIS ART OR IS IT GLORIOUS TO A NATION TO PRODUCE .	597C PUB ADDRESS/N	PROSE
IS THE ART OF PAINTING IF THE ART IS NO MORE THAN THIS	598A PUB ADDRESS/N	PROSE

ART   (CONTINUED)   PAGE   TITLE   LINE

A POINT OF LIGHT IS A WITTICISM MANY ARE DESTRUCTIVE OF   599A PUB ADDRESS/N   PROSE
    ALL ART
ACCOUNTED IGNORANT OF THAT EPIGRAMMATIC WIT IN ART   . .   599A PUB ADDRESS/N   PROSE
THAT VULGAR EPIGRAM IN ART REMBRANDT'S "HUNDRED GUELDERS"   599B PUB ADDRESS/N   PROSE
SINCE VENETIAN ART [IS] WAS THE FASHION . . . . 599B PUB ADDRESS/N   *PROSE
ART AS IT IS THIS DAY . . . . 600B PUB ADDRESS/N   PROSE
TO RECOVER ART [IS] HAS BEEN THE BUSINESS OF MY LIFE TO THE 600B PUB ADDRESS/N   *PROSE
OF ART SUCH AS MICHAEL ANGELO RAFAEL JUL R(ROMANO) ALB   600B PUB ADDRESS/N   PROSE
    DURER LEFT IT
[THE ART OF INVENTION NOT OF IMITATION] . . . . 600C PUB ADDRESS/N   PROSE
I DEMAND THEREFORE OF THE AMATEURS OF ART . . . . . . 600C PUB ADDRESS/N   PROSE
PAINTING THE PRINCIPAL ART HAS NO PLACE [IN OUR] AMONG . . 601A PUB ADDRESS/N   PROSE
OF ADVANCING FINE ART IN PROTESTANT COMMUNITIES . . . . 601B PUB ADDRESS/N   PROSE
AT AN IMMENSE PRICE & TOLD THAT SUCH IS THE ART OF PAINTING 601C PUB ADDRESS/N   PROSE
I SAY THE ENGLISH PUBLIC ARE TRUE ENCOURAGERS OF REAL ART   601C PUB ADDRESS/N   PROSE
WHILE THEY DISCOURAGE & LOOK WITH CONTEMPT ON FALSE ART   601C PUB ADDRESS/N   *PROSE
[AGAINST A CERTAIN IMPOSTOR WHO C] IN [OUR ART] THE ART   601C PUB ADDRESS/N   *PROSE
    OF
MADE TO OCCUPY THE ATTENTION TO THE NEGLECT OF ALL REAL ART 602A PUB ADDRESS/N   PROSE
THEIR COLOURING GRAVING & VERSE CAN NEVER BE APPLIED TO ART 602D PUB ADDRESS/N   PROSE
A MACHINE IS NOT A MAN NOR A WORK OF ART IT IS DESTRUCTIVE   603B PUB ADDR AD/N   PROSE
OF HUMANITY & OF ART THE WORD MACHINATION [?SEEMS] . . . 603B PUB ADDR AD/N   *PROSE
WHEN IMAGINATION ART & SCIENCE & ALL INTELLECTUAL GIFTS   604C V LAST JUDG/N   PROSE
OF TRUE ART CALLD GOTHIC IN ALL AGES BY THOSE . . . . . 610D V LAST JUDG/N   PROSE
BOTH IN ART & IN LIFE GENERAL MASSES ARE . . . . . .   611B V LAST JUDG/N   PROSE
AS MUCH ART AS A PASTEBOARD MAN IS HUMAN . . . . . .   611B V LAST JUDG/N   PROSE
& ON THIS DISCRIMINATION ALL ART IS FOUNDED I INTREAT THEN   611B V LAST JUDG/N   PROSE
WORKS OF ART CAN ONLY BE PRODUCD IN PERFECTION . . . .   612C V LAST JUDG/N   PROSE
THIS IS A LAST JUDGMENT WHEN MEN OF REAL ART GOVERN & . . 612C V LAST JUDG/N   PROSE
& THEIR INCAPABILITY OF ART THO ART IS ABOVE EITHER . . . 612C V LAST JUDG/N   PROSE
YET HE WOULD HAVE PRODUCD GREATER WORKS OF ART . . . .   612C V LAST JUDG/N   PROSE
NO MAN CAN EMBRACE TRUE ART TILL HE HAS EXPLORD & CAST OUT   613A V LAST JUDG/N   PROSE
FALSE ART SUCH IS THE NATURE OF MORTAL THINGS OR HE WILL BE 613A V LAST JUDG/N   PROSE
HIMSELF CAST OUT BY THOSE WHO HAVE ALREADY EMBRACED TRUE   613A V LAST JUDG/N   PROSE
    ART
THUS MY PICTURE IS A HISTORY OF ART & SCIENCE [& ITS] THE   613A V LAST JUDG/N   *PROSE
WHO WILL BE CAST OFF & LOST FROM ART . . . . 613C V LAST JUDG/N   PROSE
MANNERS MAKE THE MAN NOT HABITS IT IS THE SAME IN ART . . 615B V LAST JUDG/N   PROSE
THE LAST JUDGMENT IS AN OVERWHELMING OF BAD ART & SCIENCE   617A V LAST JUDG/N   PROSE
& THAT BAD ART WILL BE ADOPTED & MIXED WITH GOOD ART . .   617A V LAST JUDG/N   PROSE
TO MAN THE WONDROUS ART OF WRITING GAVE . . . . 621 READER LOVER/J   4
THE PRIMEVAL STATE OF MAN WAS WISDOM ART AND SCIENCE . .   621D JERUSALEM 3   PROSE
HE LIFTED POURING IT INTO THE CLAY GROUND PREPARD WITH ART   630 JERUSALEM 11   4
IN ALL THEIR VARIOUS COMBINATIONS WROUGHT WITH WONDROUS ART 638 JERUSALEM 16   66
THOU HADST WOVEN IT WITH ART THOU HADST CAUGHT ME IN THE   643 JERUSALEM 20   31
    BANDS
ART & SCIENCE CANNOT EXIST BUT BY NAKED BEAUTY DISPLAYD   663 JERUSALEM 36   49
A PRETENCE OF ART TO DESTROY ART A PRETENCE OF LIBERTY   672 JERUSALEM 43   35
GENERALIZING ART & SCIENCE TILL ART & SCIENCE IS LOST   673 JERUSALEM 43   54
FOR ART & SCIENCE CANNOT EXIST BUT IN MINUTELY ORGANIZED   687 JERUSALEM 55   62
    PARTICULARS
WITHIN IS ASIA & GREECE ORNAMENTED WITH EXQUISITE ART . . 690 JERUSALEM 58   37
WHO SHALL PRETEND TO DESPISE ART & SCIENCE . . . . . . 717B JERUSALEM 77   PROSE
WHAT IS THE LIFE OF MAN BUT ART & SCIENCE . . . . . . 717B JERUSALEM 77   PROSE
THOSE WHO PRETEND TO DESPISE THE LABOURS OF ART & SCIENCE   717B JERUSALEM 77   PROSE
IN HEAVEN THE ONLY ART OF LIVING . . . . 724 IN HEAVEN/J   1
HE SAYS WITH MOST CONSUMMATE ART . . . . 750 EV GOSPEL(C)/N   15
HE SAYS WITH MOST CONSUMMATE ART . . . . 751 EV GOSPEL(D)/N   17
ART DEGRADED IMAGINATION DENIED WAR GOVERNED THE NATIONS   775D INSC LAOCOON   PROSE
IS ART DELIVERD FROM NATURE & IMITATION . . . . 776A INSC LAOCOON   PROSE
IF THEY STAND IN THE WAY OF ART . . . .   776A INSC LAOCOON   PROSE
PRAYER IS THE STUDY OF ART . . . . 776A INSC LAOCOON   PROSE
PRAISE IS THE PRACTISE OF ART . . . . 776A INSC LAOCOON   PROSE
FASTING &C ALL RELATE TO ART . . . .   776A INSC LAOCOON   PROSE
IT MANIFESTS ITSELF IN HIS WORKS OF ART . . . . 776B INSC LAOCOON   PROSE
WHERE ANY VIEW OF MONEY EXISTS ART CANNOT BE CARRIED ON   776C INSC LAOCOON   PROSE
HEBREW ART IS CALLED SIN BY THE DEIST SCIENCE . . . . . 776C INSC LAOCOON   PROSE
ART CAN NEVER EXIST WITHOUT NAKED BEAUTY DISPLAYED . . . 776D INSC LAOCOON   PROSE
WHO FIRST SPOIL & THEN DESTROY IMAGINATIVE ART . . . .   777A INSC LAOCOON   PROSE
EMPIRE AGAINST ART SEE VIRGIL'S ENEID LIB VI... . . . . 777A INSC LAOCOON   PROSE
PRACTISE IS ART IF YOU LEAVE OFF YOU ARE LOST . . . . . 777B INSC LAOCOON   PROSE
THE OLD & NEW TESTAMENTS ARE THE GREAT CODE OF ART . . . 777C INSC LAOCOON   PROSE
ART IS THE TREE OF LIFE GOD IS JESUS . . . . 777C INSC LAOCOON   PROSE
NO SECRESY IN ART . . . . 777C INSC LAOCOON   PROSE
CHRISTIANITY IS ART & NOT MONEY MONEY IS ITS CURSE . . . 777D INSC LAOCOON   PROSE
& SCIENCES AS THEY PRETEND WERE DESTROYERS OF ALL ART . . 778C HOMERS POETRY   PROSE
VIRGIL IN THE ENEID BOOK VI LINE...SAYS "LET OTHERS STUDY   778D HOMERS POETRY   PROSE
    ART"
ROME & GREECE SWEPT ART INTO THEIR MAW & DESTROYD IT   . . 778D HOMERS POETRY   PROSE
A WARLIKE STATE NEVER CAN PRODUCE ART . . . .   778D HOMERS POETRY   PROSE
ARE IN SOME MEASURE WORKS OF ART & NOT OF NATURE OR CHANCE   782A INSC UPCOTT   PROSE
THAT PEACE & PLENTY & DOMESTIC HAPPINESS IS THE SOURCE   790D LETTER 2   PROSE
    OF SUBLIME ART
TO RENEW THE LOST ART OF THE GREEKS . . . . 792A LETTER 4   PROSE
HOPED YOUR PLAN COMPREHENDED ALL SPECIES OF THIS ART . .   793A LETTER 5   PROSE
WHAT IS IT SETS HOMER VIRGIL & MILTON IN SO HIGH A RANK   794A LETTER 5   PROSE
    OF ART
FOR AS TO ENGRAVING IN WHICH ART I CANNOT REPROACH MYSELF   795C LETTER 6   PROSE
TO US & TO HIS LABOURS OF ART & SCIENCE IN THIS WORLD . . 796D LETTER 8   PROSE
& I MYSELF REMEMBER WHEN I THOUGHT MY PURSUITS OF ART . . 798C LETTER 10   PROSE
NOW I HOPE TO SEE THE GREAT WORKS OF ART AS THEY ARE   . . 811A LETTER 21   PROSE

	PAGE	TITLE	LINE

ART   (CONTINUED)
        NAMELY I HAVE RECOLLECTED ALL MY SCATTERD THOUGHTS ON ART   812A LETTER 22   PROSE
        PARTS OF THE ART WHICH RELATE TO LIGHT & SHADE & COLOUR   814A LETTER 23   PROSE
        & AM
        WHICH I PAINTED FOR YOU ARE EQUAL IN EVERY PART OF THE ART 814A LETTER 23   PROSE
        IN ART CAN NEVER BE UNITED WITH THE MAJESTY OF COLOURING   814B LETTER 23   PROSE
        OF THE ART WHICH I NEGLECTED TO DISPLAY IN THOSE . . . .   814C LETTER 23   PROSE
        THERE IS NOTHING IN THE ART WHICH OUR PAINTERS DO   . . .   814C LETTER 23   PROSE
        A PICTURE TILL I HAD AGAIN RECONSIDERD MY NOTIONS OF ART   815A LETTER 23   PROSE
        OF WHAT WAS DOING IN LONDON IN WORKS OF ART BUT I DID . .   820C LETTER 25   PROSE
        IMPROVEMENTS IN WORKS OF ART GOING ON IN LONDON BUT . . .   823A LETTER 26   PROSE
        ART IN LONDON FLOURISHES ENGRAVERS IN PARTICULAR ARE WANTED 829D LETTER 30   PROSE
        STUDIOUS LOVER OF ART CAN SCARCELY BE IMAGIND YET SUCH IS   830A LETTER 30   PROSE
        EMINENT IN THE ART OF MASSING HIS LIGHTS AND SHADES . . .   844B LETTER 43   PROSE
        IN RETURN FOR THE SACRIFICE OF ART & GENIUS HE SAYS . . .   850B LETTER 49   PROSE
        HE NEVER WILL LEAVE TO PRACTISE THE ART BECAUSE HE LOVES IT 850C LETTER 49   PROSE
        YET OF TRUE ART WHICH IS ALL   . . . .   850C LETTER 49   PROSE
        IN THAT HIGHEST BRANCH OF ART I MUST NOW TELL MY WANTS .   851A LETTER 49   PROSE
        THE LIGHT OF ART O THE DISTRESS I HAVE UNDERGONE AND MY   852B LETTER 50   PROSE
        IT IS THE GREATEST OF CRIMES TO DEPRESS TRUE ART & SCIENCE 863A LETTER 60   PROSE
        DESPISED THE MEEKNESS OF TRUE ART AND SUCH I FIND HAVE BEEN 863B LETTER 60   PROSE
        THE MOCKER OF ART IS THE MOCKER OF JESUS   . . . . . .   863B LETTER 60   PROSE
        AGAINST TRUE ART SUCH AS IT EXISTED . . . .   864A LETTER 61   PROSE
        BEGUN TO PRINT AN ACCOUNT OF MY VARIOUS INVENTIONS IN ART   865D LETTER 63   PROSE
        PERCIEVE THAT I NOT ONLY DETEST FALSE ART BUT HAVE THE .   866B LETTER 64   PROSE
        TO OPPOSE FLORENTINE & VENETIAN ART CANNOT EXIST TOGETHER   866B LETTER 64   PROSE
        THAT REPUBLICAN ART IS INIMICAL TO THEIR ATOM . . . .   878A LETTER 88   PROSE
ART-BOUND
        OF LIFE BY MAGIC POWER CONDENSD INFERNAL FORMS ART-BOUND   204 AMERICA CANC B   14
ARTERY
        A MOMENT EQUALS A PULSATION OF THE ARTERY . . . . . .   516 MILTON 28   47
        EVERY TIME LESS THAN A PULSATION OF THE ARTERY   . . . .   516 MILTON 28   62
        WITHIN A MOMENT A PULSATION OF THE ARTERY . . . . . .   516 MILTON 29   3
ARTFUL
        NO ARTFUL FIEND BUT I WILL LEAD THEE DOST THOU WANT TO GO   104 TIRIEL 4   23
        DARK DISPUTES & ARTFUL TEAZING   . . . .   126 VOICE BARD/SI   5
        [I BEGAN TO SO] [SEEKING MANY AN ARTFUL WILE] . . . .   167 INFANT SORW/N   11
        THIS KNOWING ARTFUL SECRET FEARFUL CAUTIOUS TREMBLING   194 V DAU ALBION 6 17
            HYPOCRITE
        ARE ARTFUL OPINIONS & FALLACIOUS ALSO . . . .   474C ANNO REYNOLDS   MARG
        KNOWS IN ITS INTRICATE MAZES OF DELIGHT ARTFUL TO WEAVE   512 MILTON 26   4
        OR FINE WAX TO MOULD ARTFUL A MODEL FOR GOLDEN ORNAMENTS   515 MILTON 28   15
        I LOOK UPON THIS AS A MOST MALIGNANT & ARTFUL ATTACK . . 786C ANNO THORNTON   MARG
ARTFULLY
        THE INFERIOR PARTS OF ART AS REYNOLDS ARTFULLY CALLS THEM 449A ANNO REYNOLDS   MARG
        THIS IMPUTATION MOST ARTFULLY AND INDUSTRIOUSLY ENDEAVOURED 572C DESC CAT 3   PROSE
        NOTWITHSTANDING ARTFULLY DISSEMMINATED INSINUATIONS . . . 586D CHAUCER 1   *PROSE
        ARTFULLY PROPAGATED OPINION THAT DRAWING SPOILS AN ENGRAVER 591D PUB ADDRESS/N *PROSE
        UNDER THE ARTFULLY PROPAGATED PRETENCE THAT A TRANSLATION 595C PUB ADDRESS/N   PROSE
        SET ON FOOT TILL IN MY OUTSET INTO LIFE IT WAS ARTFULLY   602B PUB ADDRESS/N   PROSE
            PUBLISHD
ARTHUR
        "IN THE LAST BATTLE THAT ARTHUR FOUGHT THE MOST BEAUTIFUL 560B EXHIBITION ADV PROSE
            WAS ONE"
        IN THE LAST BATTLE OF KING ARTHUR ONLY THREE BRITONS   577B DESC CAT 5   TITLE
            ESCAPED
        ARISE AGAIN WITH TENFOLD SPLENDOR WHEN ARTHUR SHALL AWAKE 577B DESC CAT 5   TITLE
        THE SOURCE OF LEARNING AND INSPIRATION ARTHUR WAS A NAME   577D DESC CAT 5   PROSE
        OF THE NORTH POLE AND ALL THE FABLES OF ARTHUR AND HIS . 577D DESC CAT 5   PROSE
        THE STORIES OF ARTHUR ARE THE ACTS OF ALBION APPLIED . . 578C DESC CAT 5   PROSE
        SO SPOKE THE HARD COLD CONSTRICTIVE SPECTRE HE IS NAMED   685 JERUSALEM 54   25
            ARTHUR
        GO ASSUME PAPAL DIGNITY THOU SPECTRE THOU MALE HARLOT   698 JERUSALEM 64   15
            ARTHUR
        ARTHUR ALFRED THE NORMAN CONQUEROR RICHARD JOHN . . . .   713 JERUSALEM 73   36
        BATH STOOD UPON THE SEVERN WITH MERLIN & BLADUD & ARTHUR   715 JERUSALEM 75   2
        AND THE MASCULINE NAMES OF THE PLACES MERLIN & ARTHUR . . 733 JERUSALEM 88   18
ARTHUR'S
        OF ARTHUR'S CONQUEST OF THE WHOLE WORLD . . . .   577D DESC CAT 5   PROSE
ARTICLE
        SEND YOU FLAXMAN'S ADVICE UPON THIS ARTICLE WHEN I REPEATED 846B LETTER 44   PROSE
ARTICLES
        ALL THE ARTICLES OF PAINTING HE PUTS A MODEL BEFORE HIM   597B PUB ADDRESS/N   PROSE
        DEROGATE FROM HIM IN THE TRIFLES & SMALL ARTICLES OF THAT 673 JERUSALEM 43   57
            GOODNESS
        & OTHER ARTICLES COLLECTED FROM EVERY FOUNTAIN HE CAN VISIT 832D LETTER 32   PROSE
        HAVING A NUMBER OF ARTICLES RELATING TO ROMNEY EITHER . . 836A LETTER 35   PROSE
        TWO ARTICLES FOR YOU & FOR THE SAFETY OF WHICH BY THE COACH 850C LETTER 49   PROSE
ARTICULATE
        WORDS ARTICULATE BURSTING IN THUNDERS . . . .   223 URIZEN 4   4
        A MIGHTY SOUND ARTICULATE AWAKE YE DEAD & COME . . . .   357 FOUR ZOAS 9   12
        AND THUS THE SHADOWY FEMALE HOWLS IN ARTICULATE HOWLINGS   499 MILTON 18   4
        HUMAN WITH TRUMPETS INNUMERABLE SOUNDING ARTICULATE . . . 530 MILTON 39   7
        EXPRESSIONS OF ARTICULATE SPEECH IS A BOLD AND DARING . . 576B DESC CAT 4   PROSE
        WITH THE VOICES OF DEAD MEN LOW SCARCELY ARTICULATE . .   671 JERUSALEM 42   69
        THERE BELLS OF SILVER ROUND THY KNEES LIVING ARTICULATE   731 JERUSALEM 86   29
ARTICULATED
        AND MINUTELY ARTICULATED BEYOND ALL THAT THE MORTAL AND   576D DESC CAT 4   PROSE
        ORGANIZED & MINUTELY DELINEATED & ARTICULATED EITHER BY   595C PUB ADDRESS/N   PROSE
            GOD OR MAN
ARTICULATIONS
        INFOLD AROUND MY LIMBS BRUISING MY MINUTE ARTICULATIONS   635 JERUSALEM 15   13

```
                                                            PAGE     TITLE          LINE
ARTICULATIONS    (CONTINUED)
    THE ARTICULATIONS OF A MAN'S SOUL AND LAUGHING THROW IT   656 JERUSALEM 31        10
       DOWN
ARTIFICE
    I HAVE TAUGHT PALE ARTIFICE TO SPREAD HIS NETS UPON THE   290 FOUR ZOAS 2        394
       MORNING
    AN ARTIFICE . . . . . . . . . . . . . . . . . 403D ANNO BACON      MARG
    & ENTHUSIASTS FOR CUNNING & ARTIFICE . . . . . . . . 414B ANNO BOYD       MARG
    THE ARTIFICE OF THE EPICUREAN PHILOSOPHERS IS . . . . . 474A ANNO REYNOLDS   MARG
    ARE SET UP BY ARTIFICE AGAINST THE SUBLIME OF THE BIBLE   480B MILTON 1        PROSE
    ARTIFICE TURN OR TWIST ONE FACT OR DISARRANGE SELF EVIDENT  579A DESC CAT 5     PROSE
    THESE PEOPLE KNOW ENOUGH OF ARTIFICE BUT NOTHING OF ART     596A PUB ADDRESS/N  PROSE
    TENDER ARTIFICE TO LAUGH TO WEEP TO LEARN TO KNOW   . . .  688 JERUSALEM 56       24
ARTIFICER
    WITH MILTON'S SPIRIT AS THE PLOWMAN OR ARTIFICER          531 MILTON 39         54
       OR SHEPHERD
ARTIFICES
    HOWEVER HIDDEN BY ARTIFICES . . . . . . . . . . . . 573A DESC CAT 3     PROSE
ARTIFICIAL
    THEY GIVE DELIGHTS TO THE MAN UNKNOWN ARTIFICIAL RICHES   515 MILTON 28         31
    PITS OF BITUMEN EVER BURNING ARTIFICIAL RICHES OF         673 JERUSALEM 43       62
       THE CANAANITE
ARTIFICIALLY
    HE IS NOT NATURALLY GOOD NATURED BUT HE IS ARTIFICIALLY   798B LETTER 10       PROSE
ARTILLERY
    FROM BREATHING FIELDS SATAN FAINTED BENEATH THE ARTILLERY  484 MILTON 5         *   2
ARTIST
    THE LABOURS OF THE ARTIST THE POET THE MUSICIAN HAVE BEEN  207A PROSPECTUS 1793 PROSE
    SUFFERING AN ARTIST TO STARVE WHILE HE SUPPORTED REALLY    446A ANNO REYNOLDS   MARG
    TO SELL & NOT TO BUY PICTURES THE ARTIST WHO . . . . .  452C ANNO REYNOLDS   MARG
    WEAK MAN MAY BE VIRTUOUS ENOUGH BUT WILL NEVER BE AN ARTIST 454B ANNO REYNOLDS  MARG
    TO THE YOUNG ARTIST AS THE WORKS OF ORIGINAL CONCEPTION    455A ANNO REYNOLDS   MARG
    THE DIFFERENCE BETWEEN A BAD ARTIST & A GOOD ONE IS . . . 456A ANNO REYNOLDS   MARG
    THE BAD ARTIST SEEMS TO COPY A GREAT DEAL . . . . . . 456A ANNO REYNOLDS   MARG
    FINDS NOTHING OF INSPIRATION OUGHT NOT TO DARE TO BE AN    458B ANNO REYNOLDS   MARG
       ARTIST
    IS NO ARTIST ARTISTS WHO ARE ABOVE A PLAIN UNDERSTANDING   458C ANNO REYNOLDS   MARG
    HE IS A POOR ARTIST . . . . . . . . . . . . . 462B ANNO REYNOLDS   MARG
    IF THIS IS TRUE IT IS A DEVILISH FOOLISH THING TO BE AN    476D ANNO REYNOLDS   MARG
       ARTIST
    AS THE SOWER TAKES THE SEED OR AS THE ARTIST HIS CLAY . . 515 MILTON 28         14
    WHEN HE CALLD HIM THE ORNAMENTAL ARTIST . . . . . . . . 540 SIR JOSH RUB/N      4
    [FOR NO GOOD ARTIST WILL OR CAN SKETCH] . . . . . . . . 542 FLORENTINE/N         9
    MY TITLE AS AN [ARTIST] GENIUS THUS IS PROVD . . . . . . 546 MY TITLE AS/N       1
    THESE ORIGINAL CONCEPTIONS ON ART BY AN ORIGINAL ARTIST    562C DESC CAT ADV   PROSE
    ARTIST HAVING BEEN TAKEN IN VISION INTO THE ANCIENT        565C DESC CAT 2     PROSE
       REPUBLICS
    GRAND IN THE HIGHEST DEGREE THE ARTIST HAS ENDEAVOURED . 565D DESC CAT 2     PROSE
    WHERE MORE IS MEANT THAN MEETS THE EYE THE ARTIST . . . 566A DESC CAT 2     PROSE
    IN EDEN THE ARTIST IS AN INHABITANT OF THAT HAPPY COUNTRY   578A DESC CAT 5     PROSE
    AND PATHOS THE ARTIST HAS WRITTEN IT UNDER INSPIRATION . 578B DESC CAT 5     PROSE
    IT HAS BEEN SAID TO THE ARTIST TAKE THE APOLLO FOR THE     579B DESC CAT 5     PROSE
       MODEL
    UNNATURAL MIXTURE THE SUBLIME ARTIST CAN HAVE NOTHING TO DO 579D DESC CAT 5     PROSE
    AND NOT FOR HISTORICAL GRANDEUR THE ARTIST HAS IMAGINED    580A DESC CAT 5     PROSE
    THE ARTIST HAS CONSIDERED HIS STRONG MAN AS A RECEPTACLE   580B DESC CAT 5     PROSE
    OF THE ARTIST AND CONNOISSEUR FOR REASONS THAT FOLLOW . 581C DESC CAT 7     PROSE
    BY PLACING LEARNING ABOVE INSPIRATION O ARTIST   . . . 582A DESC CAT 8     PROSE
    WITH BROWN SHADOWS THEY PUT THE ORIGINAL ARTIST IN . . 582C DESC CAT 9     PROSE
    WHEN THE ARTIST TOOK HIS PENCIL TO EXECUTE HIS IDEAS   . 582D DESC CAT 9     PROSE
    TORMENTING THE TRUE ARTIST TILL HE LEAVES THE FLORENTINE   582D DESC CAT 9     PROSE
       AND
    LOSES ALL ADMIRATION OF ANY OTHER ARTIST BUT RUBENS . . 583A DESC CAT 9     PROSE
    CAUSES TO THE FLORENTINE AND ROMAN ARTIST FEAR TO EXECUTE  583A DESC CAT 9     PROSE
    CORREGGIO WAS NOT POOR HE WILL MAKE ANY TRUE ARTIST SO . 583B DESC CAT 9     PROSE
    I SAY AGAIN O ARTIST YOU MAY DISBELIEVE ALL THIS . . . 583C DESC CAT 9     PROSE
    THE ABOVE FOUR DRAWINGS THE ARTIST WISHES WERE IN FRESCO   584B DESC CAT 14    PROSE
    LAID TO OUR CHARGE THE ARTIST WHO HAS DONE THESE PICTURES  584B DESC CAT 14    PROSE
    THAT NO OTHER ARTIST CAN REACH THE ORIGINAL SPIRIT SO WELL  586D CHAUCER 1     PROSE
    BY (ONE) FOOT HIGH THE ARTIST ENGAGES TO DELIVER IT . . 587A CHAUCER 1     PROSE
    AMONG OTHER WORKS BY THE SAME ARTIST . . . . . . . . 587B CHAUCER 1     PROSE
    ARTIST HIMSELF EVEN TO THE STUFFS & EMBROIDERY   . . . . 588A CHAUCER/N   PROSE
    BY A PRECISION NOT TO BE SEEN BUT IN THE WORK OF          588A CHAUCER/N   PROSE
       AN ORIGINAL ARTIST
    [AN ARTIST WHO HAS CARRIED ON] . . . . . . . . . . 591C PUB ADDRESS/N  *PROSE
    THESE THIRTY YEARS BOTH AS AN ARTIST & A MAN MAY BE SEEN   592C PUB ADDRESS/N  PROSE
    BLASTING MY CHARACTER AS AN ARTIST TO MACKLIN MY EMPLOYER  592D PUB ADDRESS/N  PROSE
    THE ENGLISH ARTIST MAY BE ASSURED THAT HE IS DOING   . . 597C PUB ADDRESS/N  PROSE
    AS DESTRUCTIVE OF THE TRUE ARTIST AS IT IS FALSE BY ALL    601D PUB ADDRESS/N  PROSE
       EXPERIENCE
    & HE WHO DRAWS BEST MUST BE THE BEST ARTIST   . . . . . 602B PUB ADDRESS/N  PROSE
    & THO HE WOULD NOT HAVE BEEN A GREATER ARTIST . . . . . 612C V LAST JUDG/N  PROSE
    I DO NOT THINK AN ARTIST CAN WRITE AN AUTOGRAPH ESPECIALLY  781D INSC UPCOTT    PROSE
    I HAVE NO OBJECTION TO ENGRAVING AFTER ANOTHER ARTIST   . 794C LETTER 5      PROSE
    AFTER ANOTHER ARTIST BUT ABOVE ALL I FEEL MYSELF HAPPY &   795C LETTER 6      PROSE
    MY JUST RIGHT AS AN ARTIST & AS A MAN & IF ANY . . . . 825D LETTER 27     PROSE
    SUCH AN ARTIST AS FUSELI IS INVULNERABLE HE NEEDS NOT MY   864A LETTER 61     PROSE
    ME GREAT REPUTATION AS AN ARTIST WHICH WAS THE CHIEF THING  867C LETTER 66     PROSE
    RUINS ACTIVITY & ARE THE GREATEST HURT TO AN ARTIST SUCH   879C LETTER 89     PROSE
       AS I AM
ARTIST'S
    IS THE ARTIST'S JEALOUSY . . . . . . . . . . . . . 432 AUGURIES            50
```

```
                                                          PAGE     TITLE         LINE
ARTIST'S    (CONTINUED)
       WILL BE SOLD ONLY ON CONDITION OF ITS REMAINING IN THE     563B DESC CAT       PROSE
          ARTIST'S HANDS
       BY THE ARTIST'S VIOLENT TEMPER HE IS SURE  . . . . .  .    572D DESC CAT 3     PROSE
       THE BRITISH ANTIQUITIES ARE NOW IN THE ARTIST'S HANDS  .   577D DESC CAT 5     PROSE
       EVIDENCES THE [ IDEA OF WANT ] WANT OF IDEA IN THE ARTIST'S 585B DESC CAT 15    PROSE
       THE VALUE OF THIS ARTIST'S YEAR IS THE CRITERION OF SOCIETY 587A CHAUCER 1      PROSE
ARTISTS
       NOTHING OF ARTS OR ARTISTS OR LEARNED MEN OR OF AGRICULTURE 404D ANNO BACON   * MARG
       MEN WHO HAVE BEEN EDUCATED WITH WORKS OF VENETIAN ARTISTS   447B ANNO REYNOLDS   MARG
       [ TO GOOD ARTISTS ] THE STYLE THAT STRIKES THE EYE IS THE   448C ANNO REYNOLDS * MARG
          TRUE STYLE
       I ALWAYS CONSIDERD TRUE ART & TRUE ARTISTS TO BE           452B ANNO REYNOLDS   MARG
          PARTICULARLY
       REYNOLDS'S PAINTINGS & THAT SUCH ARTISTS AS REYNOLDS  . .  452B ANNO REYNOLDS   MARG
       OUGHT NOT THE [ ?ARTISTS ?& ?EMPLOYERS' ?IMBECILITY ] . .  452C ANNO REYNOLDS * MARG
       [ ARTISTS XXX ?FOOL THE XXX ] (THREE) FARTHINGS . . . .   453A ANNO REYNOLDS * MARG
       BELONGS TO NONE BUT THE GREATEST ARTISTS  . . . . . .     453D ANNO REYNOLDS   MARG
       IS NO ARTIST ARTISTS WHO ARE ABOVE A PLAIN UNDERSTANDING   458C ANNO REYNOLDS   MARG
       MAKES BOTH STATESMEN & ARTISTS FOOLS & KNAVES  . . . .    461C ANNO REYNOLDS   MARG
       FOR THE SETTING IGNORANT & VULGAR ARTISTS AS MODELS  . .  461C ANNO REYNOLDS   MARG
       IN A DISCOURSE ON ART SUCH IDIOTS ARE NOT ARTISTS  . . .  464B ANNO REYNOLDS   MARG
       TO REPRESENT VULGAR ARTISTS AS THE MODELS OF EXECUTIVE     465D ANNO REYNOLDS   MARG
          MERIT
       OBLIGATIONS REYNOLDS HAS LAID ON BAD ARTISTS OF ALL CLASSES 473A ANNO REYNOLDS   MARG
       [ ARE THERE ARTISTS WHO LIVE UPON ASSASINATIONS OF OTHER   SUPP ANNO REYNOLDS * MARG
          MEN ]
       [ THIS IS ENCOURAGEMENT FOR ARTISTS (?ONLY ?BY) ?DEFINITION ] SUPP ANNO REYNOLDS * MARG
       [ IS FASHION THE CONCERN OF ARTISTS ]  . . . . . . .    SUPP ANNO REYNOLDS * MARG
       [ YE ] COME ARTISTS KNOCK YOUR HEADS AGAINST THIS STONE  .  537 AND HIS LEGS/N     46
       CR (CROMEK) LOVES ARTISTS AS HE LOVES HIS MEAT  . . .     540 CR LOVES ART/N       1
       TO VENETIAN ARTISTS  . . . . . . . . . . . . .  . .    554B TO VENETIAN/N   TITLE
       BY ARTISTS AND CONNOISSEURS OF ALL RANKS  . . . . .      562B DESC CAT ADV    PROSE
       LET THE WORKS OF MODERN ARTISTS SINCE RUBENS' TIME  .     565B DESC CAT 2     PROSE
       AS THEY ARE CALLED WERE THE INVENTION OF GREEK ARTISTS .  565D DESC CAT 2     PROSE
       THE DESTRUCTION OF MEN SO THERE IS A CLASS OF ARTISTS  .  573B DESC CAT 3     PROSE
       THE CONNOISSEURS AND ARTISTS WHO HAVE MADE OBJECTIONS  .  576C DESC CAT 4     PROSE
       AND TO ALL ARTISTS WHO STUDY IN THE FLORENTINE AND  . .  582C DESC CAT 9     PROSE
       PILGRIMS FROM CHAUCER CONTAINING ANECDOTES OF ARTISTS     591B PUB ADDRESS/N  PROSE
          PRICE...
       ARE UNLIKE THOSE OF ARTISTS WHO  . . . . . . . . .      591B PUB ADDRESS/N  PROSE
       WE MAY BE CLEVER AS PUGILISTS BUT AS ARTISTS WE ARE  . .  594D PUB ADDRESS/N  PROSE
       ARTS & ARTISTS ARE SPIRITUAL & LAUGH AT MORTAL           597A PUB ADDRESS/N  PROSE
          CONTINGENCIES
       A FIRM & DETERMINATE CONDUCT ON THE PART OF ARTISTS  . .  600B PUB ADDRESS/N  PROSE
       HISTORICAL & POETICAL ARTISTS LIKE BARRY & MORTIMER  . .  601B PUB ADDRESS/N  PROSE
       I FORBEAR TO NAME [ A LI ] LIVING ARTISTS THO EQUALLY WORTHY 601B PUB ADDRESS/N *PROSE
       THIS IS ONE OF THE GOTHIC ARTISTS WHO BUILT THE CATHEDRALS 604A INSC ARIMATHEA PROSE
       PRETENDERS FALL SOME PEOPLE & NOT A FEW ARTISTS HAVE  .   612C V LAST JUDG/N  PROSE
       JESUS & HIS APOSTLES & DISCIPLES WERE ALL ARTISTS  . .    777B INSC LAOCOON   PROSE
       ALONE VALUED BY THE GREEKS & THE BEST MODERN ARTISTS  .   794A LETTER 5       PROSE
       GOD KEEP YOU FROM & ALL GOOD MEN OUR ARTISTS OF ALL RANKS  798A LETTER 10      PROSE
       THE ESTIMATION YOU ARE HELD IN AMONG ARTISTS & CONNOISSEURS 798B LETTER 10      PROSE
       IT IS CERTAINLY NECESSARY THAT THE BEST ARTISTS THAT CAN BE 849D LETTER 47      PROSE
ARTISTS'
       AND THEN I [ SAY TO MYSELF ] QUESTION THUS ARE ARTISTS' RULES 550 WHEN I SEE/N     3
ARTS
       SWEET PRINCE THE ARTS OF PEACE ARE GREAT  . . . . .       19 EDW THIRD/PS 2     18
       HOW HE WAS FOILED BY WOMAN'S ARTS  . . . . . . . .       37C SAMSON/PS       PROSE
       FOR DALILA'S FAIR ARTS HAVE LONG BEEN TRIED IN VAIN  . .  38A SAMSON/PS       PROSE
       CALL THINE ALLURING ARTS AND HONEST-SEEMING BROW  . . .   38A SAMSON/PS       PROSE
       EMBLEM OF PRIDE SHE SAW THE ARTS THEIR TREASURES BRING .  41B THEN SHE BORE   PROSE
       THE CRUELTIES USED BY KINGS & PRIESTS [ WHOSE ARTS ]  . . 209A SUBJCTS HIST/N *TITLE
       ONE MUST BE MASTER [ ?THY ] TRY THY ARTS I ALSO WILL TRY  273 FOUR ZOAS 1   *  333
          MINE
       COMPELL THE POOR TO LIVE UPON A CRUST OF BREAD BY SOFT    323 FOUR ZOAS 7      117
          MILD ARTS
       WITHOUT THESE ARTS IF YOU WOULD MAKE THE POOR LIVE WITH   323 FOUR ZOAS 7      122
          TEMPER
       KNOWING THE ARTS OF URIZEN WERE PITY & MEEK [ LOVE ]      336 FOUR ZOAS 7B     134
          AFFECTION
       AND THAT BY THESE ARTS THE SERPENT FORM EXUDED FROM HIS   336 FOUR ZOAS 7B     135
          LIMBS
       AND ALL THE ARTS OF LIFE THEY CHANGD INTO THE ARTS OF     337 FOUR ZOAS 7B     174
          DEATH
       BY DEVILISH ARTS ABOMINABLE UNLAWFUL UNUTTERABLE . . . .  348 FOUR ZOAS 8      288
       CRUSTED WITH SNOW IN A DIM VOID HERE BY THE ARTS OF URIZEN 350 FOUR ZOAS 8   *  373
       MUST HAVE GIVEN SATAN BY THESE MILD ARTS DOMINION OVER ALL 351 FOUR ZOAS 8      387
       BY SATAN'S-ARTS THEN THE ETERNALS SENT SHADDAI  . . . .   351 FOUR ZOAS 8      403
       CAPTIVE A WILLING CAPTIVE BY DELUSIVE ARTS IMPELLD  . . . 356 FOUR ZOAS 8      598
       NOTHING OF ARTS OR ARTISTS OR LEARNED MEN OR OF AGRICULTURE 404D ANNO BACON   * MARG
       BACON CALLS INTELLECTUAL ARTS UNMANLY POETRY PAINTING  .  407D ANNO BACON      MARG
       BY VARIOUS ARTS OF LOVE BEGUILD  . . . . . . . .         426 MENTAL TRAVLER     80
       BY VARIOUS ARTS OF LOVE & HATE  . . . . . . . . .        426 MENTAL TRAVLER     81
       TO PEACEFUL ARTS SHALL ENVY BOW  . . . . . . . .         433 AUGURIES         102
       DEGRADE FIRST THE ARTS IF YOUD MANKIND DEGRADE  . . .     445 ANNO REYNOLDS      1
       THE ARTS & SCIENCES ARE THE DESTRUCTION OF TYRANNIES  .   445C ANNO REYNOLDS   MARG
       OF THE ARTS & YOUR FALL WILL DEPEND ON [ YOUR ] THEIR NEGLECT 452C ANNO REYNOLDS   MARG
       LEO X WAS ADVISED NOT TO ENCOURAGE THE ARTS  . . . .     452C ANNO REYNOLDS   MARG
       WHEN NATIONS GROW OLD THE ARTS GROW COLD  . . . . .      452 ANNO REYNOLDS      1
       TO BE IN THE ARTS & IN ORDER TO THIS . . . . . .  . . .  458C ANNO REYNOLDS   MARG
       FOLLY OF WHAT CONSEQUENCE IS IT TO THE ARTS  . . . . .   465A ANNO REYNOLDS   MARG
```

		PAGE	TITLE	LINE

ARTS   (CONTINUED)

BUT IN ETERNITY THE FOUR ARTS POETRY PAINTING MUSIC . . . 514 MILTON 27   55
THESE ARE THE IDIOT'S CHIEFEST ARTS . . . .   547 LET BE TOLD/N   6
THEN GOD DEFEND US FROM THE ARTS I SAY . . . .   550 WHEN I SEE/N   5
RENEW THE ARTS ON BRITAIN'S SHORE . . . .   557 ART HAS LOST/N   5
BUT IF THY NATION ARTS REFUSE . . . .   557 ART HAS LOST/N   9
FRANCE SHALL THE ARTS OF PEACE RESTORE . . . .   557 ART HAS LOST/N   11
AS HE BLENDS LITERATURE AND THE ARTS WITH HIS WARLIKE   568A DESC CAT 3   PROSE
   STUDIES
AND TO KEEP IT HIS ARTS ARE OPPOSITE TO THEIRS IN   573B DESC CAT 3   PROSE
   ALL THINGS
IN ARTS AS WELL AS IN ARMS OR IN THE SENATE . . . . .   584C DESC CAT 14   PROSE
MR B(BLAKE) HAVING FROM EARLY YOUTH CULTIVATED THE TWO ARTS 587D CHAUCER/N   PROSE
COMMERCE IS SO FAR FROM BEING BENEFICIAL TO ARTS OR . . . 593D PUB ADDRESS/N   PROSE
STARVE ME OUT BY CALUMNY & THE ARTS OF TRADING COMBINATION 596D PUB ADDRESS/N PROSE
LET IT NO MORE BE SAID THAT EMPIRES ENCOURAGE ARTS . . . 597A PUB ADDRESS/N   PROSE
FOR IT IS ARTS THAT ENCOURAGE EMPIRES . . . .   597A PUB ADDRESS/N   PROSE
ARTS & ARTISTS ARE SPIRITUAL & LAUGH AT MORTAL   597A PUB ADDRESS/N   PROSE
   CONTINGENCIES
THAT IT IS NOT ARTS THAT FOLLOW & ATTEND UPON [EMPIRES]   597A PUB ADDRESS/N *PROSE
   EMPIRE
& FOLLOWS [WHEREVER ART LEADS] THE ARTS . . . .   597A PUB ADDRESS/N *PROSE
THE WRETCHED STATE OF THE ARTS IN THIS COUNTRY & IN EUROPE 600B PUB ADDRESS/N PROSE
TO RESIST THE CONTEMPTIBLE COUNTER ARTS [SET ON FOOT] . . 600B PUB ADDRESS/N PROSE
EXAMPLE OF THESE CONTRARY ARTS IS GIVEN US IN THE   600D PUB ADDRESS/N   PROSE
   CHARACTERS
TO THE SOCIETY FOR ENCOURAGEMENT OF ARTS I ADDRESS MYSELF 601A LETTER 6   PROSE
BY THE VARIOUS ARTS OF POVERTY & CRUELTY OF ALL KINDS . 615D V LAST JUDG/N   PROSE
THEY COMPELL THE POOR TO LIVE UPON A CRUST OF BREAD BY   656 JERUSALEM 30   30
   SOFT MILD ARTS
HE HATH LEAGUED HIMSELF WITH ROBBERS HE HATH STUDIED THE   667 JERUSALEM 40   13
   ARTS
I HAVE NO TIME FOR SEEMING AND LITTLE ARTS OF COMPLIMENT   670 JERUSALEM 42   27
AND ALL THE ARTS OF LIFE THEY CHANGD INTO THE ARTS OF DEATH 700 JERUSALEM 65   16
   IN ALBION
OF BODY & MIND TO EXERCISE THE DIVINE ARTS OF IMAGINATION 716D JERUSALEM 77   PROSE
THE WHOLE BUSINESS OF MAN IS THE ARTS & ALL THINGS COMMON 777C INSC LAOCOON   PROSE
AS BABYLON & EGYPT SO FAR FROM BEING PARENTS OF ARTS . 778C HOMERS POETRY   PROSE
WHO LOVE & ADMIRE YOUR WORKS BUT ABOVE ALL FOR THE SAKE   795B LETTER 6   PROSE
   OF THE ARTS
THAT FELPHAM IS PROPITIOUS TO THE ARTS GOD BLESS YOU   . 803C LETTER 15   PROSE
& THEY ARE AS DISTINCT AS ANY TWO ARTS CAN BE . . . . 810B LETTER 20   PROSE
THE REIGN OF LITERATURE & THE ARTS COMMENCES . . . . . 810D LETTER 21   PROSE
AS ONE COUNTRY AND THEIR ARTS ONE & THAT YOU WILL ERE LONG 811A LETTER 21   PROSE
TO IMPROVEMENT IN MY BELOVED ARTS ONE THING . . . . . 812A LETTER 22   PROSE
A MORE ASSIDUOUS PURSUIT OF BOTH ARTS INDEED BY MY LATE 825C LETTER 27   PROSE
MANY YEARS UNDER THE PRETENCE OF ADMIRATION OF THE ARTS 864A LETTER 61   PROSE

AS   (PARTIAL LISTING)

NOR ECHOES SWEET NOR WATERS CLEAR AS HEAVEN . . . . .   2 TO SUMMER/PS   18
OF DEATH ISSUE AS FROM A SEPULCHRE . . . .   '4 FAIR ELENOR/PS   7
AS THE DEER WOUNDED ELLEN FLEW OVER . . . .   5 FAIR ELENOR/PS   33
THE PATHLESS PLAIN AS THE ARROWS THAT FLY . . . . . .   5 FAIR ELENOR/PS   34
OF LUSTY MAY AH LIFE AS FRAIL AS FLOWER . . . . . .   5 FAIR ELENOR/PS   42
HIS FACE IS FAIR AS HEAVN . . . .   6 MY SILKS/PS   7
THEN DOWN I'LL LIE AS COLD AS CLAY . . . .   7 MY SILKS/PS   17
LIKE AS AN ANGEL GLITTRING IN THE SKY . . . .   9 FRESH FROM/PS   9
HOWLING LIKE GHOSTS FURIOUS AS WOLVES . . . .   11 GWIN KING/PS   27
GWIN LEADS HIS HOST AS BLACK AS NIGHT . . . .   12 GWIN KING/PS   55
AS THE WINGD EAGLE SCORNS THE TOWRY FENCE . . . . . .   15 IMIT SPEN/PS   37
STAND IN HIS STEAD AS LONG A-GONE . . . .   17 BLIND-MANS/PS   65
BUT AS DUST MAINTAIN THY SERVANT'S RIGHT . . . . . .   17 EDW THIRD/PS 1   2
BE ENGLAND'S TRADE OUR CARE AND WE AS TRADESMEN . . . . 19 EDW THIRD/PS 2   34
FROM YOUR TONGUE AS FROM A WORSHIPD OAK . . . . . .   20 EDW THIRD/PS 2   37
YOUR FATHER TIS WITH PRINCES AS TIS WITH THE SUN . . . . 20 EDW THIRD/PS 2   52
WORTHY THE BRAVE LORD PERCY AND AS WORTHY . . . . . .   21 EDW THIRD/PS 2   89
NOW MY HEART DANCES AND I AM AS LIGHT . . . .   24 EDW THIRD/PS 3   144
AS THE YOUNG BRIDEGROOM GOING TO BE MARRIED . . . . .   24 EDW THIRD/PS 3   145
FAIRER THAN SNOW AND RICH AS MIDSUMMER . . . .   25 EDW THIRD/PS 3   167
THAT PLAYS WITH DANGER AS THE INNOCENT CHILD . . . . .   27 EDW THIRD/PS 3   241
PASS OVER AS A SUMMER CLOUD UNREGARDED . . . .   27 EDW THIRD/PS 3   248
OR BUT EXPECTED AS A THING OF COURSE . . . .   27 EDW THIRD/PS 3   249
WHILE REASON RUNS AGROUND AS WE HAVE RUN OUR ARGUMENT . 29A EDW THIRD/PS 4   PROSE
BUT HERE COMES ONE WHO IS AS ENTERTAINING AS A GOOD STORY 29B EDW THIRD/PS 4 PROSE
THERES AS MUCH DIFFERENCE BETWEEN HIM AND ME . . . . . 29D EDW THIRD/PS 4   PROSE
AS BETWEEN GLITTERING SAND AND FRUITFUL MOLD . . . . . 29D EDW THIRD/PS 4   *PROSE
THO SUNSHINE LIGHT IT SEEMS TO ME AS PALE . . . . .   30 EDW THIRD/PS 5   22
AS THE PALE FAINTING MAN ON HIS DEATH-BED . . . . .   30 EDW THIRD/PS 5   23
THREATENING AS THE RED BROW OF STORMS AS FIRE . . . . 31 EDW THIRD/PS 6   5
THICK AS A FOREST READY FOR THE AXE . . . .   32 EDW THIRD/PS 6   24
LIKE AS A FOREST ROARS WITH CRACKLING FLAMES . . . . . 32 EDW THIRD/PS 6   27
HER SONS SHALL JOY AS IN THE MORNING . . . .   34C KING JOHN/PS   PROSE
HER DAUGHTERS SING AS TO THE RISING YEAR . . . . . . 34C KING JOHN/PS   PROSE
HIS VOICE WAS LOW AS THE WHISPERINGS OF THE WOODS . . 35D COUCH DEATH/PS   PROSE
IF I LIFT UP MY HEAD SIN COVERS ME AS A CLOAK . . . . 36A COUCH DEATH/PS   PROSE
AS THE VOICE OF AN OMEN HEARD IN THE SILENT VALLEY . . 36B COUCH DEATH/PS   PROSE
AS THE VOICE OF THE ANGEL OF DEATH . . . .   36B COUCH DEATH/PS   PROSE
AS THE DEER WOUNDED BY THE BROOKS OF WATER . . . . . . 36B COUCH DEATH/PS   PROSE
AND IN MY PLAY TILL HE BECAME TO ME AS MY BROTHER . . 37C CONTEMPLATN/PS   PROSE
AS ON A LOFTY ROCK WITH IRON PENS THE WORDS OF TRUTH . 37D SAMSON/PS   PROSE
AN ARMY OF MIGHTY MEN ARE AS FLOCKS IN THE VALLIES WHAT 39A SAMSON/PS   PROSE
   CANST

133

```
                                                         PAGE     TITLE          LINE
AS    (CONTINUED)
FOR HE SHALL BE A NAZARITE TO GOD THEN AS A NEIGHBOUR   .  .  39D SAMSON/PS         PROSE
CLAD AS A TRAVELLER FRESH RISEN ON HIS JOURNEY     .  .  .  .  40B SAMSON/PS         PROSE
& FILLD HIM WITH CONFUSION FEAR AS A TORRENT WILD    .  .   42B THEN SHE BORE      PROSE
BUT POLICY DOTH DRUDGE FOR HATE AS WELL AS SLANDER   .  .   42D THEN SHE BORE      PROSE
THE GODS ADMIRING LOADED HER WITH GIFTS AS ONCE PANDORA    42D THEN SHE BORE      PROSE
[WHILE ?LIVING CLAY COLD CORPSE CORSE] SWIFT AS THE   .  .  43D WOE CRIED MUSE    *PROSE
BUT VERY ODD AS IF SHE HOPED YOU HAD NOT AN ILL OPINION    44B ISLAND MOON 1      PROSE
   OF HER
A QUERY & AN ANSWER ARE AS DIFFERENT  .  .  .  .  .  .  .   45D ISLAND MOON 1      PROSE
AS A STRAIT LINE & A CROOKED ONE SECONDLY I I I   .  .  .   45D ISLAND MOON 1      PROSE
MRS GIMBLET LOOKD AS IF THEY MEANT HER TILLY LALLY LAUGHT   46D ISLAND MOON 3      PROSE
EVERY ART & SCIENCE ADORND HIM AS BEADS ROUND HIS NECK  .   46D ISLAND MOON 3      PROSE
WELL SAID THE OTHER HE WAS AS GREAT AS CHATTERTON    .  .   47A ISLAND MOON 3      PROSE
THAT WAS AS GREAT AS CHATTERTON [OBTUSE ANGLE ANSWERD]     47A ISLAND MOON 3      PROSE
NO SAID MRS NANNICANTIPOT I THINK A PERSON MAY BE AS GOOD   48A ISLAND MOON 4      PROSE
   AT HOME
A LITTLE BRAT NO HIGHER THAN A NETTLE & SHE HAD AS MUCH    53B ISLAND MOON 8      PROSE
TONGUE AS A CITY CLARK BUT A BOY WOULD BE SUCH A FOOL   .   53B ISLAND MOON 8      PROSE
I AM SURE I TAKE BUT LITTLE PLEASURE YOU HAVE AS MUCH   .   53C ISLAND MOON 8      PROSE
PLEASURE AS I HAVE THERE I STAND & BEAR EVERY FOOL'S INSULT 53C ISLAND MOON 8      PROSE
I CRY MY MATCHES AS FAR AS GUILD HALL   .  .  .  .  .  .    55 CRY MATCHES/IM         1
AS LOCKE OR DOCTOR SOUTH   .  .  .  .  .  .  .  .  .  .  .   57 TO BE OR/IM            28
WITH FACE AS BROWN AS ANY NUT WITH DRINKING OF STRONG ALE   58 THIS CITY/IM           3
WITH STOCKINGS ROLLD ABOVE THEIR KNEES & SHOES AS BLACK     58 THIS CITY/IM        *  6
   AS [GIT] JET
WERE FIT TO GIVE LAW TO THE CITY EACH EAT AS MUCH AS TEN    58 THIS CITY/IM          10
GREY HEADED BEADLES WALKD BEFORE WITH WANDS AS WHITE AS     59 HOLY THURS/IM          3
   SNOW
HIPOCRISY IS AS DISTANT FROM SUPERSTITION AS THE WOLF      75A ANNO LAVATER        MARG
   FROM THE LAMB
AS A CUP CANNOT CONTAIN MORE THAN ITS CAPACIOUSNESS   .  .  90B ANNO SWED LOVE     MARG
LOVE & WISDOM AS IT DOES BETWEEN BODY & SPIRIT    .  .  .   90D ANNO SWED LOVE     MARG
AS FROM ONE AFFECTION MAY PROCEED MANY THOUGHTS    .  .  .  91A ANNO SWED LOVE     MARG
IF THE ESSENCE WAS THE SAME AS THE IDENTITY     .  .  .  .  91B ANNO SWED LOVE     MARG
HE SPEAKS OF MEN AS MEER EARTHLY MEN NOT AS RECEPTACLES     92C ANNO SWED LOVE     MARG
   OF SPIRIT
MANY PERVERSELY UNDERSTAND HIM AS IF MAN WHILE    .  .  .   94A ANNO SWED LOVE     MARG
HOW ABSURD MUST MEN BE TO UNDERSTAND HIM AS IF HE   .  .    94C ANNO SWED LOVE     MARG
IF THE MANY BECOME THE SAME AS THE FEW WHEN POSSESSD   .    97D NAT RELIGION 2     PROSE
ARE CRUEL AS DEATH & AS OBDURATE AS THE DEVOURING PIT      99 TIRIEL 1              15
LOOK AT MY EYES BLIND AS THE ORBLESS [XXX] SCULL AMONG     99 TIRIEL 1           *  28
   THE STONES
THE SERPENTS SPRUNG FROM HER OWN BOWELS HAVE DRAIND HER   100 TIRIEL 1              32
   DRY AS THIS
AS THICK AS NORTHERN FOGS AROUND YOUR GATES TO CHOKE YOU  100 TIRIEL 1              44
   UP
THAT YOU MAY LIE AS NOW YOUR MOTHER LIES LIKE DOGS CAST OUT 100 TIRIEL 1             45
BUT THEY WERE AS THE SHADOW OF HAR & AS THE YEARS         100 TIRIEL 2               7
   FORGOTTEN
HE WAS AS CHEARFUL AS A PRINCE & GAVE ME ENTERTAINMENT    102 TIRIEL 3              10
HE KNEW TWAS VAIN FOR IJIM'S WORDS WERE AS THE VOICE OF    104 TIRIEL 4              27
   FATE
IT IS AS FALSE & [AS ] MATHA & AS DARK AS VACANT ORCUS    106 TIRIEL 4           *  87
AS TIRIEL'S & ALL EYES AS BLIND AS TIRIEL'S TO YOUR WOES  106 TIRIEL 5              21
   BY
AND THOU WILT BE AS FOOLISH AS THY FOOLISH BROTHER ZAZEL  109 TIRIEL 7              13
BUT HAR & HEVA SLEPT FEARLESS AS BABES ON LOVING BREASTS  109 TIRIEL 7              21
TILL I AM SUBTIL AS A SERPENT IN A PARADISE   .  .  .  .   110 TIRIEL 8              37
SEES YOU SWIFT AS ARROW   .  .  .  .  .  .  .  .  .  .  .   115 THE BLOSSOM/SI         4
GREY HEADED BEADLES WALKD BEFORE WITH WANDS AS WHITE AS    121 HOLY THURS/SI         3
   SNOW
WHITE AS AN ANGEL IS THE ENGLISH CHILD    .  .  .  .  .    125 LIT BLK BOY/SI         3
BUT I AM BLACK AS IF BEREAVD OF LIGHT   .  .  .  .  .  .    125 LIT BLK BOY/SI         4
.  .  .  HID FROM THE LIGHT AS IN A CLEFT ROCK    .  .     135 FRENCH REVOLTN        28
AND NARROW AS A GRAVE DUG FOR A CHILD .  .  .             136 FRENCH REVOLTN        40
AS IN DAY OF HAVOCK AND ROUTED BATTLE .  .  .  .  .  .     137 FRENCH REVOLTN        64
EACH STERN VISAGE LOCKD UP AS WITH STRONG BANDS OF IRON    137 FRENCH REVOLTN        66
   .  .  .
.  .  .  EACH STRONG LIMB BOUND DOWN AS WITH MARBLE   .  . 137 FRENCH REVOLTN        66
.  .  .  ROSE FROM THE MONARCH'S RIGHT HAND RED AS WINES  . 138 FRENCH REVOLTN        83
AND THE CHAMBER BECAME AS A CLOUDED SKY .  .  .  .  .  .   138 FRENCH REVOLTN        85
.  .  .  AS A RIPE VINEYARD STRETCHES OVER SHEAVES OF CORN 138 FRENCH REVOLTN        86
.  .  .  AS IN YEARS THAT ARE PASSED AWAY   .  .  .  .  .  139 FRENCH REVOLTN       120
AN AGED FORM WHITE AS SNOW HOVRING IN MIST  .  .  .  .  .  140 FRENCH REVOLTN       131
.  .  .  AND GOD SO LONG WORSHIPPD DEPARTS AS A LAMP    .  140 FRENCH REVOLTN       137
THEN ORLEANS GENEROUS AS MOUNTAINS   .  .  .  .  .  .  .   142 FRENCH REVOLTN       175
.  .  .  LOOKING ON THE ARCHBISHOP WHO CHANGED AS PALE AS  142 FRENCH REVOLTN       176
   LEAD
.  .  .  LEARN TO CONSIDER ALL MEN AS THY EQUALS  .  .  .  143 FRENCH REVOLTN       193
THY BRETHREN AND NOT AS THY FOOT OR THY HAND  .  .  .  .   143 FRENCH REVOLTN       194
.  .  .  AS A FATHER THAT BOWS TO HIS SON   .  .  .  .  .  143 FRENCH REVOLTN    *  203
SUDDEN AS THE BULLET WRAPPD IN HIS FIRE .  .  .  .  .  .   146 FRENCH REVOLTN       262
IT INDEED APPEARD TO REASON AS IF DESIRE WAS CAST OUT     150A MARRIAGE HH 5      PROSE
AS THE PLOW FOLLOWS WORDS SO GOD REWARDS PRAYERS   .  .  . 152A MARRIAGE HH 9      PROSE
AS THE CATTERPILLER CHOOSES THE FAIREST LEAVES TO LAY   .  152C MARRIAGE HH 9      PROSE
AS THE AIR TO A BIRD OR THE SEA TO A FISH   .  .  .  .  .  152D MARRIAGE HH 10     PROSE
THE DEVOURER AS A SEA RECIEVED THE EXCESS OF HIS DELIGHTS  155B MARRIAGE HH 15     PROSE
BUT TO SEPERATE THEM AS IN THE PARABLE OF SHEEP AND GOATS  155C MARRIAGE HH 15     PROSE
TILL A VOID BOUNDLESS AS A NETHER SKY APPEARD BENEATH US   155D MARRIAGE HH 17     PROSE
BY DEGREES WE BEHELD THE INFINITE ABYSS FIERY AS THE SMOKE 156A MARRIAGE HH 17     PROSE
SO THAT THE NETHER DEEP GREW BLACK AS A SEA   .  .  .  .   156B MARRIAGE HH 17     PROSE
```

```
                                                        PAGE      TITLE            LINE
AS   (CONTINUED)
  OF THEMSELVES AS THE ONLY WISE THIS THEY DO WITH  .  .  .  .  157C MARRIAGE HH 21   PROSE
  AND CONCIEVD HIMSELF AS MUCH WISER THAN SEVEN MEN  .  .  .  157D MARRIAGE HH 21   PROSE
  & HE WAS CONSUMED AND AROSE AS ELIJAH    .  .  .  .  .  .  .  158D MARRIAGE HH 22   PROSE
  SUCH A FLOWER AS MAY NEVER BORE    .  .  .  .  .  .  .  .  .  161 ROSE TREE/N          2
  AND STILL AS A MAID    .  .  .  .  .  .  .  .  .  .  .  .  .  163 ASKED THIEF/N        11
  SMILES AS OF THE MORNING [BROKE] STEAL  .  .  .  .  .  .  .  165 CRADLE SONG/N   *    11
  AS ROSY AS MORN    .  .  .  .  .  .  .  .  .  .  .  .  .  .  171 SLEPT DARK/N          6
  AND WE'D BE AS HAPPY AS BIRDS IN THE SPRING   .  .  .  .  .  179 LIT VAGABOND/N       11
  AS THE CLEAR SPRING MUDDED WITH FEET OF BEASTS GROWS PURE   190 V DAU ALBION 2       19
     & SMILES
  AND THEIR PURSUITS AS DIFFERENT AS THEIR FORMS AND AS      191 V DAU ALBION 3        6
     THEIR JOYS
  DOES THE WHALE WORSHIP AT THY FOOTSTEPS AS THE HUNGRY DOG   193 V DAU ALBION 5       33
  AS THE RAVEN'S EYE OR DOES HE MEASURE THE EXPANSE LIKE      193 V DAU ALBION 5       36
     THE VULTURE
  I CRY LOVE LOVE LOVE HAPPY HAPPY LOVE FREE AS              194 V DAU ALBION 7        16
     THE MOUNTAIN WIND
  CAN THAT BE LOVE THAT DRINKS ANOTHER AS A SPONGE DRINKS    194 V DAU ALBION 7        17
     WATER
  RED AS THE ROSY MORNING LUSTFUL AS THE FIRST BORN BEAM  .  . 195 V DAU ALBION 7      27
  THEIR AWFUL FOLDS IN THE DARK AIR SILENT SHE STOOD AS NIGHT 196 AMERICA PREL 1        8
  SILENT AS DESPAIRING LOVE AND STRONG AS JEALOUSY   .  .  .  196 AMERICA PREL 2        1
  AS WHEN A BLACK CLOUD SHEWS ITS LIGHTNINGS TO THE SILENT    196 AMERICA PREL 2        5
     DEEP
  AS HUMAN BLOOD SHOOTING ITS VEINS ALL ROUND THE ORBED      197 AMERICA 4             5
     HEAVEN
  INTENSE NAKED A HUMAN FIRE FIERCE GLOWING AS THE WEDGE  .  . 197 AMERICA 4            8
  TO THE FOUR WINDS AS A TORN BOOK & NONE SHALL GATHER THE    198 AMERICA 8             6
     LEAVES
  HEADLONG FROM OUT THEIR HEAVENLY HEIGHTS DESCENDING SWIFT   200 AMERICA 12            5
     AS FIRES
  IN FLAMES AS OF A FURNACE ON THE LAND FROM NORTH TO SOUTH   201 AMERICA 12           12
  FALLING UPON AMERICA AS A STORM TO CUT THEM OFF  .  .  .    201 AMERICA 14            5
  AS A BLIGHT CUTS THE TENDER CORN WHEN IT BEGINS TO APPEAR   201 AMERICA 14            6
  AND AS A PLAGUE WIND FILLD WITH INSECTS CUTS OFF MAN &      201 AMERICA 14            8
     BEAST
  AND AS A SEA OERWHELMS A LAND IN THE DAY OF AN EARTHQUAKE   201 AMERICA 14            9
  OVER THEIR PALE LIMBS AS A VINE WHEN THE TENDER GRAPE       202 AMERICA 15           26
     APPEARS
  REVEAL THE DRAGON THRO THE HUMAN COURSING SWIFT AS FIRE     204 AMERICA CANC B        1
  SO STILL TERRORS RENT THE HOUSE AS WHEN THE SOLEMN GLOBE    204 AMERICA CANC B       20
  IN GLITTRING ARMOUR SWIFT AS WINDS INTELLIGENT AS [FLAMES]  205 AMERICA CANC C       13
     CLOUDS
  IN ARMOUR AS THE NERVES OF WISDOM EACH HIS STATION [FIRES]  205 AMERICA CANC C       19
     HOLDS
  AS WHEN A DREAM OF THIRALATHA FLIES THE MIDNIGHT HOUR  .  . 206 THIRALATHA            1
  SUCH A FLOWER AS MAY NEVER BORE  .  .  .  .  .  .  .  .  .  215 ROSE TREE/SE          2
  AND WE'D BE AS HAPPY AS BIRDS IN THE SPRING   .  .  .  .  .  216 LIT VAGABND/SE       10
  AS OF SWELLING SEAS SOUND IN HIS CLOUDS  .  .  .  .  .  .  223 URIZEN 3              31
  AS THE STARS ARE APART FROM THE EARTH  .  .  .  .  .  .  .  226 URIZEN 6              1
  WHITE AS THE SNOW ON THE MOUNTAINS COLD  .  .  .  .  .  .  227 URIZEN 10             23
  AS GLASSES DISCOVER WORLDS  .  .  .  .  .  .  .  .  .  .  .  231 URIZEN 15             9
  PALE AS A CLOUD OF SNOW  .  .  .  .  .  .  .  .  .  .  .  .  231 URIZEN 18            11
  AND CAUGHT HIM IN MY HAT AS BOYS KNOCK DOWN A BUTTERFLY     237 EUROPE INTRO          9
  AND FOLD THE SHEETY WATERS AS A MANTLE ROUND MY LIMBS  .  . 238 EUROPE PREL 1        13
  AND LEAVE ME VOID AS DEATH  .  .  .  .  .  .  .  .  .  .  .  238 EUROPE PREL 2        11
  THICK AS THE SUMMER STARS  .  .  .  .  .  .  .  .  .  .  .  240 EUROPE 8             10
  YELLOW AS LEAVES OF AUTUMN THE MYRIADS OF ANGELIC HOSTS     243 EUROPE 13             6
  AS IF THEY HAD NOT BEEN  .  .  .  .  .  .  .  .  .  .  .  .  243 EUROPE 13            11
  ETHINTHUS THOU ART SWEET AS COMFORTS TO MY FAINTING SOUL    243 EUROPE 14             4
  AND NOAH AS WHITE AS SNOW  .  .  .  .  .  .  .  .  .  .  .  248 SONG OF LOS 7        22
  AS THE THUNDER-STONE IS MOULDED  .  .  .  .  .  .  .  .  .  249 AHANIA 2              8
  AS THE MOON ANGUISHD CIRCLES THE EARTH  .  .  .  .  .  .  .  250 AHANIA 2             40
  AS THE BONES OF MAN SOLID & DARK  .  .  .  .  .  .  .  .  .  253 AHANIA 4             21
  WITHOUT FLUCTUATION HARD AS ADAMANT  .  .  .  .  .  .  .  .  257 BOOK OF LOS 4         5
  BLACK AS MARBLE OF EGYPT IMPENETRABLE  .  .  .  .  .  .  .  257 BOOK OF LOS 4         6
  HURLD APART ON ALL SIDES AS A FALLING  .  .  .  .  .  .  .  257 BOOK OF LOS 4        23
  DIM & GLUTINOUS AS THE WHITE POLYPUS  .  .  .  .  .  .  .  .  258 BOOK OF LOS 4        57
  AND STILL AS A MAID  .  .  .  .  .  .  .  .  .  .  .  .  .  261 ASKED THIEF          11
  AS GARMENTS WOVEN SUBSERVIENT TO HER HANDS BUT HAVING A     266 FOUR ZOAS 1          84
     WILL
  THE DAZZLINGS AS OF GEMS SHONE CLEAR RAPTUROUS IN [JOY]     267 FOUR ZOAS 1         128
     FURY
  THE FIRST STATE WEEPING THEY BEGAN & HELPLESS AS A WAVE     269 FOUR ZOAS 1         193
  [AS ONE MAN HOVERING OVER GILEAD & HERMON]  .  .  .  .  .  269 FOUR ZOAS 1         199
  A MALE & FEMALE NAKED & RUDDY AS THE PRIDE OF SUMMER        270 FOUR ZOAS 1         236
  [BRIGHT] DARK AS A DEWY MORNING WHEN THE CRIMSON LIGHT      271 FOUR ZOAS 1    *    253
     APPEARS
  WHY DOST THOU WEEP [?O] AS VALA & WET THY VEIL WITH DEWY    271 FOUR ZOAS 1    *    271
     TEARS
  SLEPT AS A BIRD IN THE BLUE SHELL THAT SOON SHALL BURST     273 FOUR ZOAS 1         350
     AWAY
  ETERNITY APPEARD ABOVE THEM AS ONE MAN INFOLDED   .  .  .  274 FOUR ZOAS 1         363
  AS THE SUN SHINES DOWN ON THE MISTY EARTH SUCH WAS THE      274 FOUR ZOAS 1         365
     VISION
  AS ONE MAN FOR CONTRACTING THEIR EXALTED SENSES  .  .  .  277 FOUR ZOAS 1         470
  THEY BEHOLD MULTITUDE OR EXPANDING THEY BEHOLD AS ONE  .  . 277 FOUR ZOAS 1         471
  AS ONE MAN ALL THE UNIVERSAL FAMILY & THAT ONE MAN  .  .  . 277 FOUR ZOAS 1         472
  CONSULTING AS ONE MAN ABOVE [MOUNT GILEAD] .  .  .  .  .  .  277 FOUR ZOAS 1         475
  I CARRIED HER IN MY BOSOM AS A MAN CARRIES A LAMB  .  .  .  282 FOUR ZOAS 2          93
  INTO MILD CURRENTS AS THE WATER MINGLES WITH THE WINE  .  . 284 FOUR ZOAS 2         155
```

135

		PAGE	TITLE		LINE
AS	(CONTINUED)				
	TWO WILLS THEY HAD TWO INTELLECTS & NOT AS IN TIMES OF OLD	285	FOUR ZOAS	2	206
	I SEE NOT LUVAH AS OF OLD I ONLY SEE HIS FEET	286	FOUR ZOAS	2	229
	AT WILL TO MURMUR IN THE FLOWERS SMALL AS THE HONEY BEE	288	FOUR ZOAS	2	297
	I KNOW THEE NOT AS ONCE I KNEW THEE IN THOSE BLESSED FIELDS	288	FOUR ZOAS	2	325
	THEY HEARD THE VOICE & [THEY] FLED SWIFT AS THE WINTER'S SETTING SUN	294	FOUR ZOAS	3	* 93
	AND FROM HER BOSOM LUVAH FELL FAR AS THE EAST & WEST	294	FOUR ZOAS	3	100
	AS WHEN THE THUNDERBOLT DOWN FALLETH ON THE APPOINTED PLACE	295	FOUR ZOAS	3	140
	MAKE ME NOT LIKE THE THINGS FORGOTTEN AS THEY HAD NOT BEEN	297	FOUR ZOAS	3	192
	RED AS THE SUN IN THE HOT MORNING OF THE BLOODY DAY	297	FOUR ZOAS	4	5
	SETTLED A LAKE BRIGHT & SHINING CLEAR WHITE AS THE SNOW	303	FOUR ZOAS	4	210
	AND AS A DOUBLE FEMALE FORM LOVELINESS & PERFECTION OF BEAUTY	304	FOUR ZOAS	4	251
	BEAT ROUND THE ROCK IN MIGHTY WAVES & AS A POLYPUS	304	FOUR ZOAS	4	266
	INFECTED MAD HE DANCD ON HIS MOUNTAINS HIGH & DARK AS HEAVEN	305	FOUR ZOAS	5	1
	AS PLANTS WITHERD BY WINTER LEAVES & STEMS & ROOTS DECAYING	305	FOUR ZOAS	5	9
	AS FAR AS HIGHEST ZENITH FROM THE LOWEST (NADIR) SO FAR SHRUNK	305	FOUR ZOAS	5	* 14
	SING IN THE SKY AS ONCE THEY SANG UPON THE HILLS OF LIGHT	306	FOUR ZOAS	5	52
	AS THE STRONG BULL IN SUMMER TIME WHEN BEES SING ROUND THE HEATH	308	FOUR ZOAS	5	136
	. . . AS FURTHEST NORTH IS FROM THE FURTHEST SOUTH	309	FOUR ZOAS	5	184
	AS THE TREE KNOWS NOT WHAT IS OUTSIDE OF ITS LEAVES & BARK	314	FOUR ZOAS	6	95
	WERE NOW NOT VOCAL AS IN CLIMES OF HAPPY ETERNITY	315	FOUR ZOAS	6	135
	AS THE SEED FALLS FROM THE SOWER'S HAND SO URIZEN FELL & DEATH	316	FOUR ZOAS	6	160
	SHUT UP HIS POWERS IN OBLIVION THEN AS THE SEED SHOOTS FORTH	316	FOUR ZOAS	6	161
	OR SLEEP SUCH SLEEP AS SPIRITS ETERNAL WEARIED IN HIS DARK	316	FOUR ZOAS	6	181
	HAIR WHITE AS SNOW COVERED HIM IN FLAKY LOCKS TERRIFIC	318	FOUR ZOAS	6	240
	FOLLOWD BEHIND HIM AS THE WEB OF A SPIDER DUSKY & COLD	318	FOUR ZOAS	6	244
	THE EYELIDS EXPANSIVE AS MORNING & THE EARS	318	FOUR ZOAS	6	249
	AS A GOLDEN ASCENT WINDING ROUND TO THE HEAVENS OF HEAVENS	318	FOUR ZOAS	6	250
	FOR URIZEN FELL AS THE MIDDAY SUN FALLS DOWN INTO THE WEST	318	FOUR ZOAS	6	267
	AS WHEN THE THUNDER FOLDS HIMSELF IN THICKEST CLOUDS	320	FOUR ZOAS	7	23
	IN THAT TRANSPARENT ROCK AS IF IN JOY OF THY BRIGHT PRISON	322	FOUR ZOAS	7	76
	. . . THO FLOODS POUR THO WINDS BLACK AS THE SEA	322	FOUR ZOAS	7	83
	REDUCE ALL TO OUR WILL AS SPANIELS ARE TAUGHT WITH ART	323	FOUR ZOAS	7	129
	RECIEVING AS A POISOND CUP RECIEVES THE HEAVENLY WINE	324	FOUR ZOAS	7	154
	HER SHADOW WENT FORTH & RETURND NOW SHE WAS PALE AS SNOW	324	FOUR ZOAS	7	173
	BUT WHEN HER SPIRIT RETURND AS RUDDY AS A MORNING WHEN	324	FOUR ZOAS	7	175
	THE SPECTRES OF THE DEAD FOR I AM AS THE SPECTRE OF THE LIVING	327	FOUR ZOAS	7	310
	OF URTHONA LOS EMBRACD THE SPECTRE FIRST AS A BROTHER	328	FOUR ZOAS	7	339
	THEN AS ANOTHER SELF ASTONISHD HUMANIZING & IN TEARS	328	FOUR ZOAS	7	340
	NOT AS ANOTHER BUT AS THY REAL SELF I AM THY SPECTRE	328	FOUR ZOAS	7	348
	THREEFOLD AS IT WAS IN ETERNITY & THIS THE FOURTH UNIVERSE	329	FOUR ZOAS	7	355
	AS ON THE OUTSIDE OF EXISTENCE BUT LOOK BEHOLD TAKE COMFORT	330	FOUR ZOAS	7	414
	LEST ANY SHOULD IN FUTURITY DO AS WE HAVE DONE IN HEAVEN	331	FOUR ZOAS	7	430
	BEFORE MY FACE ASCENDING WITH DELIGHT AS IN ANCIENT TIMES	331	FOUR ZOAS	7	* 445
	SUCH AS THE PITEOUS SPECTRES MAY ASSIMILATE THEMSELVES INTO	331	FOUR ZOAS	7	454
	OR ORC BENDING DOWN AS THE BINDER OF THE SHEAVES FOLLOWS	332	FOUR ZOAS	7	462
	AS THE ELDEST BROTHER IS THE [SECOND] FATHER'S IMAGE SO ORC BECAME	332	FOUR ZOAS	7	* 479
	AS LOS A FATHER TO HIS BRETHREN & HE JOYD IN THE DARK LAKE	332	FOUR ZOAS	7	480
	MORTAL & NOT AS ENITHARMON WITHOUT A COVERING VEIL	332	FOUR ZOAS	7	489
	AS WHEN THE EARTHQUAKE ROUZES FROM HIS DEN HIS SHOULDERS HUGE	336	FOUR ZOAS	7B	129
	SILENT AS DESPAIRING LOVE & STRONG AS JEALOUSY	336	FOUR ZOAS	7B	136
	WAS AS THE WORKMANSHIP OF THE PLOWMAN & THE WATER WHEEL	337	FOUR ZOAS	7B	176
	GIRT AS A SOWER WITH HIS SEED TO SCATTER LIFE ABROAD	338	FOUR ZOAS	7B	199
	THEN SHE RETURNS SWIFT AS A BLIGHT UPON THE INFANT BUD	339	FOUR ZOAS	7B	261
	THAT ROSE FROM WATERS FOR THE WATERS WERE AS THE VOICE OF LUVAH	340	FOUR ZOAS	7B	272
	AS FOOD OR DRINK OR ORNAMENT OR IN DELIGHTFUL WORKS	340	FOUR ZOAS	7B	276
	AND WAS AJOIND TO BEULAH AS THE POLYPUS TO THE ROCK	340	FOUR ZOAS	7B	289
	[MET] AS ONE MAN EVEN JESUS UPON GILEAD & HERMON	341	FOUR ZOAS	8	2
	A CREST OF FIRE ROSE ON HIS FOREHEAD RED AS THE CARBUNCLE	342	FOUR ZOAS	8	69
	WITHIN AS IN A TABERNACLE ABOMINABLE DEADLY	343	FOUR ZOAS	8	106
	AS ONCE IN THOSE ETERNAL FIELDS IN BROTHERHOOD & LOVE	345	FOUR ZOAS	8	159
	UNITED WE SHOULD LIVE IN BLISS AS THOSE WHO SINNED NOT	345	FOUR ZOAS	8	160
	YET HIDING THE SHADOWY FEMALE VALA AS IN AN ARK & CURTAINS	347	FOUR ZOAS	8	255
	TO PUT OFF MYSTERY TIME AFTER TIME & AS A MAN	347	FOUR ZOAS	8	261
	TO JUDGE THE LAMB OF GOD TO DEATH AS A MURDERER & ROBBER	348	FOUR ZOAS	8	273
	TO MULTITUDE AS IT IS IN EDEN SO PERMITTED BECAUSE	348	FOUR ZOAS	8	284
	. . . THE BOSOM OF SATAN THE FALSE FEMALE AS IN AN ARK & VEIL	348	FOUR ZOAS	8	292
	SOMETIMES AS TWELVE DAUGHTERS LOVELY & SOMETIMES AS FIVE	349	FOUR ZOAS	8	328
	THEY STOOD IN BEAMING BEAUTY & SOMETIMES AS ONE EVEN RAHAB	349	FOUR ZOAS	8	329
	[HE] FELT THE FEMALE DEATH A DULL & NUMMING STUPOR SUCH AS NEER	352	FOUR ZOAS	8	416
	WHEN AS THE SNOW COVERS THE MOUNTAIN OFT PETRIFIC HARDNESS [COVERS]	352	FOUR ZOAS	8	* 449
	BEHOLD THE TIME APPROACHES FAST THAT THOU SHALT BE AS A THING	355	FOUR ZOAS	8	549
	AS THE SEED WAITS EAGERLY WATCHING FOR ITS FLOWER & FRUIT	355	FOUR ZOAS	8	* 558
	AS IN A STORE HOUSE IN HIS MEMORY HE REGULATES THE FORMS	355	FOUR ZOAS	8	568
	AND NATURAL RELIGION AS OF OLD SO NOW ANEW BEGAN	357	FOUR ZOAS	8	619
	TREMBLING & WEAK A FAINT EMBRACE A FIERCE DESIRE AS WHEN	358	FOUR ZOAS	9	27
	AS SNOW THAT FALLS AROUND A LEAFLESS TREE UPON THE GREEN	358	FOUR ZOAS	9	49

		PAGE	TITLE	LINE

AS   (CONTINUED)

	PAGE	TITLE	LINE
WHEN SHALL THE MAN OF FUTURE TIMES BECOME AS IN DAYS OF OLD	360	FOUR ZOAS 9	115
O PRINCE OF LIGHT WHERE ART THOU I BEHOLD THEE NOT AS ONCE	360	FOUR ZOAS 9	124
OF LIFE & PERSON FOR AS THE PERSON [IS] SO IS HIS LIFE PROPORTIOND	360	FOUR ZOAS 9 *	141
IF THOU REPENTEST NOT & LEAVE THEE AS A ROTTEN BRANCH TO BE BURND	361	FOUR ZOAS 9	156
REND DOWN THIS FABRIC AS A WALL RUIND & FAMILY EXTINCT . .	362	FOUR ZOAS 9	186
AS ON A PYRAMID OF MIST HIS WHITE ROBES SCATTERING . . .	362	FOUR ZOAS 9	189
EXULTING IN HER FLIGHT AS WHEN A BUBBLE RISES UP	362	FOUR ZOAS 9	195
AND RAVEN NUMEROUS AS THE LEAVES OF AUTUMN EVERY SPECIES	363	FOUR ZOAS 9	238
AND EVERY ONE OF THE DEAD APPEARS AS HE HAD LIVD BEFORE	363	FOUR ZOAS 9	245
AS OF A BATTLE IN THE HEAVENS HARK HEARD YOU NOT THE TRUMPET	364	FOUR ZOAS 9	263
AS OF FIERCE BATTLE	364	FOUR ZOAS 9	264
ABOVE UPON ITS VOLUMES IS BEHELD [AS] A THRONE & [AS] A PAVEMENT	364	FOUR ZOAS 9	279
IN THE IMMENSE AS WHEN THE SUN DANCES UPON THE MOUNTAINS	366	FOUR ZOAS 9	349
FROM SON TO SON AS IF THE STARS BEAMING INNUMERABLE . .	366	FOUR ZOAS 9	351
THEN O THOU FAIR ONE SIT THEE DOWN FOR THOU ART AS THE GRASS	367	FOUR ZOAS 9	408
ALAS AM I BUT AS A FLOWER THEN WILL I SIT ME DOWN . . .	368	FOUR ZOAS 9	410
HE SPOKE & PILLARS WERE BUILDED & WALLS AS WHITE AS IVORY	369	FOUR ZOAS 9	461
THE GRASS SHE SLEPT UPON WAS PAVD WITH PAVEMENT AS OF PEARL	369	FOUR ZOAS 9	462
SUCH AS GLOWS OUT FROM SLEEPING SPIRITS APPEARD IN THE DEEPS BENEATH	372	FOUR ZOAS 9	561
AS WHEN THE WIND SWEEPS OVER A CORN FIELD THE NOISE OF SOULS	372	FOUR ZOAS 9	562
HOW CAME I HERE METHINKS I AM AS I WAS IN MY YOUTH . . .	375	FOUR ZOAS 9	688
A FIERY TRAIN AS WHEN THE SUN SINGS IN THE RIPE VINEYARDS	376	FOUR ZOAS 9	715
HOW IS IT THAT ALL THINGS ARE CHANGD EVEN AS IN ANCIENT TIMES	379	FOUR ZOAS 9	845
AND HIS BRIGHT FEET FIRM AS A BRAZEN ALTAR BUT THE PARTS	380	FOUR ZOAS AD 1	12
FEMALE HER FORM BRIGHT AS THE SUMMER BUT THE PARTS OF LOVE	381	FOUR ZOAS AD 1	18
MALE & HER BROW RADIANT AS DAY DARTED A LOVELY SCORN . .	381	FOUR ZOAS AD 1	19
TO JUDGE THE LAMB OF GOD TO DEATH AS A MURDERER & ROBBER	382	FOUR ZOAS AD 6	6
SOMETIMES AS TWELVE DAUGHTERS LOVELY & SOMETIMES AS FIVE	382	FOUR ZOAS AD 6	16
THEY STOOD IN BEAMING BEAUTY & SOMETIMES AS ONE EVEN RAHAB	382	FOUR ZOAS AD 6	17
WOULD BE AS GOOD AN INQUISITOR AS ANY OTHER PRIEST . . .	385C	ANNO WATSON	MARG
MEN WHO GIVE THEMSELVES TO THEIR ENERGETIC GENIUS [AS] IN THE MANNER	386B	ANNO WATSON *	MARG
NEEDS NO ONE TO PROVE IT IT IS EVIDENT AS THE SUN & MOON	386C	ANNO WATSON	MARG
CHRIST DIED AS AN UNBELIEVER & IF THE BISHOPS HAD THEIR WILL	387C	ANNO WATSON	MARG
WITH CHRISTENDOM AS IN CHRIST HE STROVE WITH THE JEWS . .	387C	ANNO WATSON	MARG
TO EXTIRPATE A NATION BY MEANS OF ANOTHER NATION IS AS WICKED	388B	ANNO WATSON *	MARG
AS TO DESTROY AN INDIVIDUAL BY MEANS OF ANOTHER	388B	ANNO WATSON	MARG
INDIVIDUAL WHICH GOD CONSIDERS IN THE BIBLE AS MURDER . .	388B	ANNO WATSON	MARG
SUCH AS THE JEWS WERE & OF COURSE HE HOLDS THAT THE JEWS	389A	ANNO WATSON	MARG
LIVED BY SUCH YOU DO NOT SEE AS I DO	391D	ANNO WATSON	MARG
MILTON'S PARADISE LOST IS AS TRUE AS GENESIS OR EXODUS	392D	ANNO WATSON	MARG
AS IF HE KNEW THAT THERE WERE RECORDS	394A	ANNO WATSON	MARG
AS IF REASONING WAS OF ANY CONSEQUENCE TO A QUESTION . .	394A	ANNO WATSON	MARG
WORSHIPD IN THIS WORLD AS GOD & SET ABOVE ALL THAT IS CALLD GOD	394C	ANNO WATSON	MARG
CUNNING PLOTTERS WERE CONSIDERD AS WISE MACHIAVELS . . .	397B	ANNO BACON	MARG
THE INCREASE OF A STATE AS OF A MAN IS FROM INTERNAL IMPROVEMENT	402C	ANNO BACON	MARG
A LORD CHANCELLOR'S OPINIONS AS DIFFERENT FROM CHRIST . .	407A	ANNO BACON	MARG
AS THOSE OF CAIPHAS OR PILATE OR HEROD	407A	ANNO BACON	MARG
WHEN WILT THOU PITY [&] AS I FORGIVE	416	MY SPECTRE/N	50
AS BY DOWNY PINIONS SOFT	422	BENEATH/N	21
AS ON DOWNY PINIONS SOFT	424	THE GOLDEN NET	20
AS COLD EARTH WANDERERS NEVER KNEW	424	MENTAL TRAVLER	4
JUST AS WE REAP IN JOY THE FRUIT	424	MENTAL TRAVLER	7
JUST AS A MISER COUNTS HIS GOLD	425	MENTAL TRAVLER	18
JUST AS A HUSBANDMAN HIS MOULD	425	MENTAL TRAVLER	26
TO BE WEAK AS A LAMB & SMOOTH AS A DOVE	428	MARY	25
THO HE EAT & DRANK AS MUCH AS TEN MEN FOR HIS DINNER . .	434	LONG JOHN BRWN	12
BUT SHE IS RUDDY & BRIGHT AS DAY	435	WILLIAM BOND	31
STRUCK AT ONCE AS PROTOGENES STRUCK HIS LINE	439C	REMARKS MALKIN	PROSE
AS FAR AS GREATEST IS MORE THAN LEAST	450A	ANNO REYNOLDS	MARG
AS THE EYE SEES THE OBJECT	456B	ANNO REYNOLDS	MARG
KNOW THAT THE MAN'S EXECUTION IS AS HIS CONCEPTION & NO BETTER	461C	ANNO REYNOLDS	MARG
("ILLUSTRIOUS CHARACTERS") [GOD BLASTS THEM AS THOUGH]	SUPP	ANNO REYNOLDS *	MARG
AS THE CLOUD THAT BRINGS THE SNOW ALL THE WHILE FROM HIS BACK	483	MILTON 3	34
LOUD AS THE WIND OF BEULAH THAT UNROOTS THE ROCKS & HILLS	487	MILTON 7	33
AS NOW I REND THIS ACCURSED FAMILY FROM MY COVERING . . .	490	MILTON 9	29
FELL DOWN AS DEWS OF NIGHT & A LOUD SOLEMN UNIVERSAL GROAN	490	MILTON 9	37
CANAAN THEN SHE RETURND TO LOS WEARY FRIGHTED AS FROM DREAMS	490	MILTON 10 *	5
AS ELYNITTRIA USED TO DO BUT TOO WELL THOSE LIVING CREATURES	492	MILTON 12	12
BUT ME THE SERVANTS OF THE HARROW SAW NOT BUT AS A BOW . .	492	MILTON 12	14
DRAWING A THIRD PART IN THE FIRES AS STUBBLE NORTH & SOUTH	493	MILTON 12	26
HE DIED AS A REPROBATE HE WAS PUNISHD AS A TRANSGRESSOR	494	MILTON 13	27
I TOUCH THE HEAVENS AS AN INSTRUMENT TO GLORIFY THE LORD	494	MILTON 13	29
AS WHEN A MAN DREAMS HE REFLECTS NOT THAT HIS BODY SLEEPS	496	MILTON 15	1
WHICH NOW AROSE AND WALKD WITH THEM IN EDEN AS AN EIGHTH	496	MILTON 15	5

137

```
                                                    PAGE     TITLE      LINE
AS      (CONTINUED)
    IMAGE DIVINE THO DARKEND AND THO WALKING AS ONE WALKS   . .  496 MILTON 15      6
    LIKE AS A POLYPUS THAT VEGETATES BENEATH THE DEEP    . . .   496 MILTON 15      8
    WHO DWELL IN IMMORTALITY AS ONE SLEEPING ON A COUCH  . . .   496 MILTON 15     12
    SATAN BUT SWIFT AS LIGHTNING PASSING THEM STARTLED THE       496 MILTON 15     18
       SHADES
    OF HELL BEHELD HIM IN A TRAIL OF LIGHT AS OF A COMET    .    496 MILTON 15     19
    AS THE EYE OF MAN VIEWS BOTH THE EAST & WEST ENCOMPASSING    497 MILTON 15     28
    THUS IS THE EARTH ONE INFINITE PLANE AND NOT AS APPARENT     497 MILTON 15     32
    BUT AS A WINTRY GLOBE DESCENDS PRECIPITANT THRO BEULAH       497 MILTON 15     44
       BURSTING
    THEN FIRST I SAW HIM IN THE ZENITH AS A FALLING STAR   . .   497 MILTON 15     47
    DESCENDING PERPENDICULAR SWIFT AS THE SWALLOW OR SWIFT  .    497 MILTON 15     48
    THEY SAT RANGD ROUND HIM AS THE ROCKS OF HOREB ROUND THE     498 MILTON 17     12
       LAND
    AND GET BY ROTE AS A HARD TASK OF A LIFE OF SIXTY YEARS      499 MILTON 18     14
    AND I WILL PUT ON HOLINESS AS A BREASTPLATE & AS A HELMET    499 MILTON 18     21
    WHEN WILT THOU PUT ON THE FEMALE FORM AS IN TIMES OF OLD     499 MILTON 18     34
    AS WITH NEW CLAY A HUMAN FORM IN THE VALLEY OF BETH PEOR     500 MILTON 19     14
    SO SPOKE THEY AS IN ONE VOICE SILENT MILTON STOOD BEFORE     502 MILTON 20      7
    THE DARKEND URIZEN AS THE SCULPTOR SILENT STANDS BEFORE      502 MILTON 20      8
    EVEN AS REUBEN & AS GAD GAVE UP HIMSELF TO TEARS   . . .     503 MILTON 20     53
    AS A BRIGHT SANDAL FORMD IMMORTAL OF PRECIOUS STONES & GOLD  503 MILTON 21     13
    SEVEN MORNINGS LOS HEARD THEM AS THE POOR BIRD WITHIN THE    504 MILTON 21     28
       SHELL
    BUT ALL THE FAMILY DIVINE COLLECTED AS FOUR SUNS   . . . .   504 MILTON 21     37
    OVER OLOLON AND AS ONE MAN WHO WEEPS OVER HIS BROTHER   . .  504 MILTON 21     41
    SO SPAKE THE FAMILY DIVINE AS ONE MAN EVEN JESUS   . . . .   505 MILTON 21     58
    TO DESTROY JERUSALEM AS A HARLOT & HER SONS AS REPROBATES    506 MILTON 22     47
    HEAVEN AS A PUNISHER & HELL AS ONE UNDER PUNISHMENT   . .    506 MILTON 22     52
    ALBION'S DREAD SONS HAND HYLE & COBAN SURROUND HIM AS   . .  507 MILTON 23     15
    A GIRDLE GWENDOLEN & CONWENNA AS A GARMENT WOVEN   . . . .   507 MILTON 23     16
    APPEARD AS DOES THE FACE OF HEAVEN WHEN COVERD WITH THICK    507 MILTON 23     29
       STORMS
    BUT LOS DISPERSD THE CLOUDS EVEN AS THE STRONG WINDS OF      507 MILTON 23     31
       JEHOVAH
    O MY DEAR SONS LEAVE NOT YOUR FATHER AS YOUR BRETHREN LEFT   508 MILTON 23     61
       ME
    AS IT WAS SO IT REMAIND & NO HOPE OF AN END   . . . . .      509 MILTON 24     47
    TO THE WEAK AND PITY THE WEAK AS YOUR INFANT CARE BREAK      511 MILTON 25     57
       NOT
    BUT WE SEE ONLY AS IT WERE THE HEM OF THEIR GARMENTS   . .   512 MILTON 26     11
    AS COGS ARE FORMD IN A WHEEL TO TURN THE COGS OF            513 MILTON 27     10
       THE ADVERSE WHEEL
    AS THE SOWER TAKES THE SEED OR AS THE ARTIST HIS CLAY   . .  515 MILTON 28     14
    FORM IMMORTAL WITH GOLDEN PEN SUCH AS THE SPECTRE ADMIRING   515 MILTON 28     17
    AS TO THAT FALSE APPEARANCE WHICH APPEARS TO THE REASONER    516 MILTON 29     15
    AS OF A GLOBE ROLLING THRO VOIDNESS IT IS A DELUSION OF      516 MILTON 29     16
       ULRO
    AS THE BELOVED INFANT IN HIS MOTHER'S BOSOM ROUND INCIRCLED  518 MILTON 30     11
    AS THE BREATH OF THE ALMIGHTY SUCH ARE THE WORDS OF MAN      519 MILTON 30     18
       TO MAN
    TO US WE WILL OBEY YOUR WORDS AS YOU OBEY JESUS   . . . .    519 MILTON 30     30
    LIKE WOMEN & CHILDREN WERE TAKEN AWAY AS ON WINGS   . . .    519 MILTON 31      2
    AS ONE AWAKEND IN THE NIGHT THEY SAW THE LORD COMING   . .   519 MILTON 31     15
    NOT MENTAL AS THE WARS OF ETERNITY BUT A CORPOREAL STRIFE    520 MILTON 31     25
    (KERABIM) AS MULTITUDES VOX POPULI   . . . . . . . . .      521C MILTON 32   PROSE
    AND AS ONE FEMALE OLOLON AND ALL ITS MIGHTY HOSTS   . . .    527 MILTON 36     16
    TO THE PERCEPTION OF THE VIRGIN OLOLON BUT AS THE   . . .    527 MILTON 36     18
    THE VIRGIN OLOLON & ADDRESSD HER AS A DAUGHTER OF BEULAH     527 MILTON 36     27
    A MALE WITHIN A FEMALE HID AS IN AN ARK & CURTAINS   . . .   528 MILTON 37     40
    THY LAWS & TERRORS SHAKING DOWN THY SYNAGOGUES AS WEBS   .   530 MILTON 38     42
    BURND TERRIBLE MY PATH BECAME A SOLID FIRE AS BRIGHT   . .   530 MILTON 39      4
    AS THE CLEAR SUN & MILTON SILENT CAME DOWN ON MY PATH   .    530 MILTON 39      5
    THEN LOUD THE FURNACES OF LOS WERE HEARD & SEEN AS SEVEN     531 MILTON 39     14
       HEAVENS
    BUT HOWLS ROUND IT AS A LION ROUND HIS PREY CONTINUALLY      531 MILTON 39     21
    WITH MILTON'S SPIRIT AS THE PLOWMAN OR ARTIFICER            531 MILTON 39     54
       OR SHEPHERD
    GLORIOUS AS THE MIDDAY SUN IN SATAN'S BOSOM GLOWING   . .    532 MILTON 40     19
    HIDING THE HUMAN LINEAMENTS AS WITH AN ARK & CURTAINS   . .  533 MILTON 41     26
    OF MILTON'S SHADOW AS A DOVE UPON THE STORMY SEA   . . . .   534 MILTON 42      6
    THEN AS A MOONY ARK OLOLON DESCENDED TO FELPHAM'S VALE   .   534 MILTON 42      7
    THE CLOUDS OF OLOLON FOLDED AS A GARMENT DIPPED IN BLOOD     534 MILTON 42     12
    LIKE AS A PEDLAR BEARS HIS WEARY PACK   . . . . . . . .      536 AND HIS LEGS/N   7
    CR(CROMEK) LOVES ARTISTS AS HE LOVES HIS MEAT   . . . .      540 CR LOVES ART/N    1
    AS CROOKED LIMBS & LOUZY HEADS OF HAIR   . . . . . . .       540 SIR JOSH BUB/N    8
    [AND TIS ENGLISH POLITENESS AS FAIR AS [YOUR] MY AUNT]       542 FLORENTINE/N  *  10
    TO COMPELL US TO WORSHIP THEM AS GODS   . . . . . . . .      543 IF TRUE/N         8
    IF YOU THINK AS YOU SPEAK YOU ARE AN ASS   . . . . . .       544 F(LAXMAN)/N 2     3
    HE WALKS & STUMBLES AS IF HE CREP   . . . . . . . . .        548 CRIPPLE EVRY/N    8
    AS THE IGNORANT SAVAGE WILL SELL HIS OWN WIFE   . . . . .    548 ON GREAT ENC/N    1
    ARE PAINTED BY MADMEN AS SURE AS A GROAT   . . . . . .       548 ALL PICTURES/N    2
    I'LL WRITE IN RHYME AS SOFT AS [FEATHER PILLOWS]            555 BLAKES APL/N 1     7
       BARTOLLOZE
    I'LL WRITE IN VERSE AS SOFT AS BARTOLLOZE   . . . . . .      555 BLAKES APL/N 2    2
    SO [AS SURE] AS A CHURCH IS KNOWN BY ITS STEEPLE   . . . .   559 I ROSE UP AT/N *  23
    THE ARMY OF ARMED ROMANS THE FIGURES FULL AS LARGE AS LIFE  560A EXHIBITION ADV PROSE
    EVERY THING IN FRESCO IS AS HIGH FINISHED AS MINIATURE      561A EXHIBITION ADV PROSE
    IN HIGH FINISHED FRESCO WHERE THE COLOURS WOULD BE AS PURE  566A DESC CAT 2     PROSE
    AND AS PERMANENT AS PRECIOUS STONES   . . . . . . . . .     566A DESC CAT 2     PROSE
    ALL FRESCOES ARE AS HIGH FINISHED AS MINIATURES OR ENAMELS  566B DESC CAT 2     PROSE
```

AS   (CONTINUED)

	PAGE	TITLE	LINE
AS ONE AGE FALLS ANOTHER RISES DIFFERENT TO MORTAL SIGHT	567C	DESC CAT 3	PROSE
AS NEWTON NUMBERED THE STARS AND AS LINNEUS NUMBERED	567D	DESC CAT 3	PROSE
WHICH IN EVERY AGE STANDS AS THE GUARDIAN	568A	DESC CAT 3	PROSE
THIS HE DOES AS A MASTER AS A FATHER AND SUPERIOR WHO	569A	DESC CAT 3	PROSE
THEM AS WRETCHED OLD WOMEN AND NOT AS SHAKSPEARE INTENDED	569D	DESC CAT 3	PROSE
AS THE DOCTOR OF PHYSIC IS THE ESCULAPIUS	571A	DESC CAT 3	PROSE
IT IS USEFUL AS A SCARECROW THERE ARE	572B	DESC CAT 3	PROSE
THIS CHARACTER VARIES FROM THAT OF CHAUCER AS THE	572B	DESC CAT 3	PROSE
WHICH GAINED THAT PATRONAGE CRIED DOWN AS ECCENTRICITY	572D	DESC CAT 3	PROSE
AND MADNESS AS UNFINISHED AND NEGLECTED	572D	DESC CAT 3	PROSE
CHAUCER HIMSELF AS A KNAVE WHO THRUSTS HIMSELF	574D	DESC CAT 3	PROSE
HE HAS LAUGHED AT HIS KNAVES AND FOOLS AS I DO NOW	575A	DESC CAT 3	PROSE
PERISHING SUBSTANCES AND NOT BE AS POETRY AND MUSIC ARE	576B	DESC CAT 4	PROSE
AS REAL AND EXISTING MEN	576D	DESC CAT 4	PROSE
A SPIRIT AND A VISION ARE NOT AS THE MODERN PHILOSOPHY	576D	DESC CAT 4	PROSE
UNSUBDUED AS GODS AND THE SUN OF BRITAIN (SET) BUT SHALL	577B	DESC CAT 5	*TITLE
AND ITS ANCIENT GLORY WHEN IT WAS AS IT AGAIN SHALL BE	577D	DESC CAT 5	PROSE
AND IF EVERY THING GOES ON AS IT HAS BEGUN	578A	DESC CAT 5	PROSE
AS IT WAS IN THE BEGINNING	578A	DESC CAT 5	PROSE
MR B(BLAKE) HAS DONE AS ALL THE ANCIENTS DID	578C	DESC CAT 5	PROSE
AND AS ALL THE MODERNS WHO ARE WORTHY OF FAME	578C	DESC CAT 5	PROSE
SO AS IT ALWAYS HAPPENS AND NOT IN THAT DULL WAY THAT SOME	578D	DESC CAT 5	PROSE
THE ARTIST HAS CONSIDERED HIS STRONG MAN AS A RECEPTACLE	580B	DESC CAT 5	PROSE
IN WORKS OF TRUE ART AS TO A MODERN MAN	581A	DESC CAT 5	PROSE
IN ARTS AS WELL AS IN ARMS OR IN THE SENATE	584C	DESC CAT 14	PROSE
MERIT OF A PICTURE IS THE SAME AS THE MERIT OF A DRAWING	584D	DESC CAT 15	PROSE
AND AS IT IS VALUED SO DOES SOCIETY FLOURISH OR DECAY	587A	CHAUCER 1	PROSE
AS ONE AGE FALLS ANOTHER RISES DIFFERENT TO MORTAL SIGHT	589A	CHAUCER/N	PROSE
AS A PILGRIM TRAVELLING THROUGH THIS JOURNEY OF LIFE	590B	CHAUCER 2	PROSE
& BY WHICH HE GOT HIS REPUTATION AS A DRAUGHTSMAN	592B	PUB ADDRESS/N	PROSE
THESE THIRTY YEARS BOTH AS AN ARTIST & A MAN HE SPENT	592C	PUB ADDRESS/N	PROSE
BLASTING MY CHARACTER AS AN ARTIST TO MACKLIN MY EMPLOYER	592D	PUB ADDRESS/N	PROSE
HOW TO PUT SO MUCH LABOUR INTO A HEAD OR A FOOT AS BASIRE DID	593A	PUB ADDRESS/N	PROSE
AS THERE MAY BE A FOOL OR A KNAVE IN AN EMBROIDERD COAT	593B	PUB ADDRESS/N	PROSE
WE MAY BE CLEVER AS PUGILISTS BUT AS ARTISTS WE ARE	594D	PUB ADDRESS/N	PROSE
MEN THINK THEY CAN COPY NATURE AS CORRECTLY	594D	PUB ADDRESS/N	PROSE
AS I COPY IMAGINATION THIS THEY WILL FIND IMPOSSIBLE	594D	PUB ADDRESS/N	PROSE
JUST AS IT IS IN THEIR POWER TO MURDER A MAN BUT NOT TO MAKE A MAN	597A	PUB ADDRESS/N	PROSE
& HE COPIES THAT SO NEAT AS TO MAKE IT A DECEPTION NOW	597B	PUB ADDRESS/N	PROSE
LIKE [TO] AS A MONKEY PEEPING IN A MIRROR	597	PUBLC VOICE/PA	2
BECAUSE THEY AVOID IT AS A DESTRUCTIVE MACHINE AS IT IS	599A	PUB ADDRESS/N	PROSE
& HANG THEIR SOULS AS GUILTY OF MENTAL HIGH TREASON	599D	PUB ADDRESS/N	PROSE
THEIR CONSIDERATION OF MY PLAN AS A GREAT PUBLIC [DEED] MEANS	601B	PUB ADDRESS/N	*PROSE
ENGLISH ARE AS GOOD JUDGES [AS] OF PAINTING AS OF POETRY	601B	PUB ADDRESS/N	*PROSE
AS DESTRUCTIVE OF THE TRUE ARTIST AS IT IS FALSE BY ALL EXPERIENCE	601D	PUB ADDRESS/N	PROSE
YET THE OAK DIES AS WELL AS THE LETTUCE	605B	V LAST JUDG/N	PROSE
BUT RENEWS BY ITS SEED JUST [AS] SO THE IMAGINATIVE IMAGE	605B	V LAST JUDG/N	PROSE
THE GREEK MUSES WHICH ARE NOT INSPIRATION AS THE BIBLE IS	605C	V LAST JUDG/N	PROSE
DESCENDING [AS A SCROLL] THE JUST ARISE	606B	V LAST JUDG/N	*PROSE
FALLING INTO THE ABYSS SIN IS ALSO REPRESENTED AS A FEMALE	606C	V LAST JUDG/N	PROSE
WHEN DISTANT THEY APPEAR AS ONE MAN	607C	V LAST JUDG/N	PROSE
AS MULTITUDES OF CHILDREN ASCENDING FROM THE EARTH	607C	V LAST JUDG/N	PROSE
AS IT WAS SAID "AS THE STARS OF HEAVEN FOR MULTITUDE"	607C	V LAST JUDG/N	PROSE
REPRESENTED IN THIS PICTURE [AS IN THE PROPHETS] AS SINGLE	608C	V LAST JUDG/N	PROSE
REPRESENTED AS A STREAM OF [LIGHT] FIGURES	610B	V LAST JUDG/N	PROSE
& IN HIM SEES ALL REFLECTED AS IN A GLASS OF ETERNAL DIAMOND	610D	V LAST JUDG/N	PROSE
AS MUCH ART AS A PASTEBOARD MAN IS HUMAN	611B	V LAST JUDG/N	PROSE
WHEN SEEN REMOTE THEY APPEAR AS ONE MAN	611D	V LAST JUDG/N	PROSE
IT IS THE SAME WITH INDIVIDUALS AS NATIONS	612C	V LAST JUDG/N	PROSE
& THE ARK OF THE COVENANT IS AS A DOVE OF PEACE	613B	V LAST JUDG/N	PROSE
[THEY] THEY MERELY APPEAR AS IN A CLOUD WHEN ANY THING	614C	V LAST JUDG/N	*PROSE
THE GREEKS REPRESENT CHRONOS OR TIME AS A VERY AGED MAN THIS IS FABLE	614D	V LAST JUDG/N	PROSE
WAS ONE OF THIS NUMBER HE WAS AS INTOLERANT AS AN INQUISITOR	615B	V LAST JUDG/N	PROSE
THERE WILL ALWAYS BE AS MANY HYPOCRITES BORN AS HONEST MEN	616A	V LAST JUDG/N	PROSE
IT IS AS THE DIRT UPON MY FEET NO PART OF ME	617B	V LAST JUDG/N	PROSE
SEES THE MOON TERRIFIED AS ONE LED ASTRAY IN THE MIDST OF HER PATH	619A	ILLUS MILTON	PROSE
AS ATTENDING ON THE HEAVEN OF JUPITER THE GREAT BEAR	619B	ILLUS MILTON	PROSE
CONSOLIDATED & EXTENDED WORK WILL BE AS KINDLY RECIEVED	620D	JERUSALEM 3	PROSE
[TO THE FULL AS ENTHUSIASTICALLY AS I HAVE WHO ACKNOWLEDGE MINE]	621A	JERUSALEM 3	*PROSE
YET I PRETEND TO LOVE TO SEE TO CONVERSE WITH DAILY AS MAN WITH MAN	621A	JERUSALEM 3	PROSE
A BONDAGE AS RHYME ITSELF I THEREFORE HAVE PRODUCED A	621D	JERUSALEM 3	PROSE
NATIONS ARE DESTROYD OR FLOURISH IN PROPORTION AS THEIR	621D	JERUSALEM 3	PROSE
NAMES ANCIENTLY REMEMBERD BUT NOW CONTEMND AS FICTIONS	624	JERUSALEM 5	38
ETERNITY LOOKD UPON AS DEFORMITY & LOVELINESS AS A DRY TREE	628	JERUSALEM 9	8
EVERY EMANATIVE JOY FORBIDDEN AS A CRIME	628	JERUSALEM 9	14
HE MIGHT FEEL THE PAIN AS IF A MAN GNAWD HIS OWN TENDER NERVES	630	JERUSALEM 11	7
CLAY BAKD & ENAMELD ETERNAL GLOWING AS FOUR FURNACES	632	JERUSALEM 12	64
TAKING THEIR FORMS FROM THE WHEELS OF ALBION'S SONS AS COGS	633	JERUSALEM 13	13
IS CLOSD AS WITH A THREEFOLD CURTAIN OF IVORY & FINE LINEN & ERMINE	633	JERUSALEM 13	23

		PAGE	TITLE	LINE
AS	(CONTINUED)			
	BENEATH BEULAH AS A WATRY FLAME REVOLVING EVERY WAY . . .	634	JERUSALEM 14	7
	AND AS DARK ROOTS AND STEMS A FOREST OF AFFLICTION GROWING	634	JERUSALEM 14	8
	MOVING BY COMPULSION EACH OTHER NOT AS THOSE IN EDEN WHICH	636	JERUSALEM 15	19
	TO FOLLOW THE DAUGHTERS OF ALBION AS THE HOUND FOLLOWS	638	JERUSALEM 17	3
	THE SCENT			
	BUT AS A DISTORTED & REVERSED REFLEXION IN THE DARKNESS	639	JERUSALEM 17	42
	FIRST AS A RED GLOBE OF BLOOD TREMBLING BENEATH HIS BOSOM	639	JERUSALEM 17	51
	BECAME AS THREE IMMENSE WHEELS TURNING UPON ONE-ANOTHER	640	JERUSALEM 18	8
	STRINGING THEM ON THEIR REMEMBRANCE AS ON A THREAD	642	JERUSALEM 20	18
	OF SORROW			
	THEE WHOM I THOUGHT PURE AS THE HEAVENS IN INNOCENCE & FEAR	644	JERUSALEM 21	20
	YET THOU WAST LOVELY AS THE SUMMER CLOUD UPON MY HILLS . .	647	JERUSALEM 24	36
	OF BEULAH WERE MOVED AS THE TENDER BOWELS ARE MOVED &	648	JERUSALEM 25	2
	THEY SAID			
	AS THE SONS OF ALBION HAVE DONE TO LUVAH SO THEY HAVE IN	648	JERUSALEM 25	6
	HIM			
	AS THE DRUID TEMPLES WHICH ARE THE PATRIARCHAL PILLARS . .	649C	JERUSALEM 27	PROSE
	I HERE RECLAIM THEE AS MY OWN	651	FIELDS FROM/J	75
	AS THE PROPHETS HAD FORETOLD	652B	JERUSALEM 27	PROSE
	THEY HEARD THE VOICE AND FLED SWIFT AS THE WINTER'S SETTING	655	JERUSALEM 29	72
	SUN			
	AND FROM HER BOSOM LUVAH FELL FAR AS THE EAST AND WEST . .	655	JERUSALEM 29	79
	ATTENDS HER AS HER GUARD & LOS'S EMANATION IS NAMED . . .	655	JERUSALEM 30	3
	BACK SAFE TO THEIR HUMANITY AS DOVES TO THEIR WINDOWS . .	655	JERUSALEM 30	13
	UPON THE MOUNTAINS OF ALBION AS IN ANCIENT TIME BEHOLD . .	656	JERUSALEM 30	22
	THE KENNELS OF THE STREETS & LANES AS IF THEY WERE ABHORRD	657	JERUSALEM 31	18
	AND ALL THE TENDERNESSES OF THE SOUL CAST FORTH AS FILTH	657	JERUSALEM 31	21
	& MIRE			
	THE ANCIENT CITIES OF THE EARTH REMOVE AS A TRAVELLER . .	659	JERUSALEM 33	14
	SATAN WORSHIPD AS GOD BY THE MIGHTY ONES OF THE EARTH . .	659	JERUSALEM 33	18
	IS AS NOTHING BEFORE THEE FADED IS ALL LIFE AND JOY . . .	659	JERUSALEM 33	34
	THIS WOMAN HAS CLAIMD AS HER OWN & MAN IS NO MORE . . .	661	JERUSALEM 34	28
	THAT WE MAY PRY AFTER HIM AS AFTER A STOLEN TREASURE . .	661	JERUSALEM 34	34
	AND THE DIVINE VOICE CAME FROM THE FURNACES AS MULTITUDES	662	JERUSALEM 35	3
	WITHOUT			
	HAND STOOD BETWEEN REUBEN & MERLIN AS THE REASONING SPECTRE	663	JERUSALEM 36	23
	UTTERING NOT HIS JEALOUSY BUT HIDING IT AS WITH	664	JERUSALEM 38	4
	WE LIVE AS ONE MAN FOR CONTRACTING OUR INFINITE SENSES . .	664	JERUSALEM 38	17
	WE BEHOLD MULTITUDE OR EXPANDING WE BEHOLD AS ONE . . .	664	JERUSALEM 38	18
	AS ONE MAN ALL THE UNIVERSAL FAMILY AND THAT ONE MAN . .	664	JERUSALEM 38	19
	IN EVERY BOSOM A UNIVERSE EXPANDS AS WINGS	665	JERUSALEM 38	49
	WITH FORTITUDE AS WITH A GARMENT OF IMMORTAL TEXTURE . .	665	JERUSALEM 38	52
	AND THE DIVINE FAMILY WEPT OVER HIM AS ONE MAN	667	JERUSALEM 40	44
	ROUND MARYBONE TO TYBURN'S RIVER WEAVING BLACK MELANCHOLY	668	JERUSALEM 41	8
	AS A NET			
	AND DESPAIR AS MESHES CLOSELY WOVE OVER THE WEST OF LONDON	668	JERUSALEM 41	9
	DRINKING & EATING & PITYING & WEEPING AS AT A TRAJIC SCENE	669	JERUSALEM 41	29
	OF DEATH THEY CURB THEIR SPECTRES AS WITH IRON CURBS . .	671	JERUSALEM 42	67
	DEAD CORSES LAY BEFORE THEM & NOT AS IN WARS OF OLD . . .	672	JERUSALEM 43	40
	WITH ONE ACCORD IN LOVE SUBLIME & AS ON CHERUBS WINGS . .	674	JERUSALEM 44	1
	. . . FAINT AS THE VOICE OF THE DEAD IN THE HOUSE OF DEATH	675	JERUSALEM 44	44
	IN WHOSE SIGHT ALL ARE AS THE DUST	679	JERUSALEM 49	31
	TRUE HARMONIES & COMPREHENDING GREAT AS VERY SMALL . .	680	JERUSALEM 49	37
	LO SHILOH DWELLS OVER FRANCE AS JERUSALEM DWELLS OVER	680	JERUSALEM 49	48
	ALBION			
	OF SPIRITUAL HATE FROM WHICH SPRINGS SEXUAL LOVE AS IRON	685	JERUSALEM 54	12
	CHAINS			
	THE UNIVERSAL CONCAVE RAGED SUCH THUNDEROUS SOUNDS AS NEVER	686	JERUSALEM 55	20
	THEN AS THE MOSS UPON THE TREE OR DUST UPON THE PLOW . .	687	JERUSALEM 55	39
	OR AS THE SWEAT UPON THE LABOURING SHOULDER OR AS THE	687	JERUSALEM 55	40
	CHAFF			
	OF THE WHEAT-FLOOR OR AS THE DREGS OF THE SWEET WINE-PRESS	687	JERUSALEM 55	41
	LOS UTTERD SWIFT AS THE RATTLING THUNDER UPON THE MOUNTAINS	688	JERUSALEM 56	41
	AS A MIGHTY TEMPLE DELIVERING FORM OUT OF CONFUSION . . .	690	JERUSALEM 58	22
	THEY WERE AS ADAM BEFORE ME UNITED INTO ONE MAN	692	JERUSALEM 60	16
	AND PITY AM I BECOME LOVELY AS A VIRGIN IN HIS SIGHT WHO AM	692	JERUSALEM 60	21
	CALL HER PURE AS HE DID IN THE DAYS OF HER INFANCY WHEN SHE	695	JERUSALEM 61	37
	FOLLOWING THEE AS A SHEPHERD BY THE FOUR RIVERS OF EDEN	695	JERUSALEM 61	39
	GIRT AS A SOWER WITH HIS SEED TO SCATTER LIFE ABROAD OVER	700	JERUSALEM 65	45
	ALBION			
	THEIR EAR BENT OUTWARDS AS THEIR VICTIM SO ARE THEY IN	702	JERUSALEM 66	38
	THE PANGS			
	AS THE MISTLETOE GROWS ON THE OAK SO ALBION'S TREE	703	JERUSALEM 66	55
	ON ETERNITY LO			
	HE CHOKES UP THE PATHS OF THE SKY THE MOON IS LEPROUS AS	703	JERUSALEM 66	78
	SNOW			
	AS THE SENSES OF MEN SHRINK TOGETHER UNDER THE KNIFE OF	703	JERUSALEM 66	83
	FLINT			
	SMITTEN AS UZZAH OF OLD HIS ARMOUR IS SOFTEND HIS SPEAR	706	JERUSALEM 68	51
	THEREFORE REJECTING IDEAS AS NOTHING & HOLDING ALL WISDOM	708	JERUSALEM 70	7
	ARISE AS THE SMOKE OF THE FURNACE SHAKING THE ROCKS FROM	708	JERUSALEM 70	14
	SEA TO SEA			
	IN FIRES OF BEAUTY MELTING THEM AS GOLD & SILVER IN THE	709	JERUSALEM 70	28
	FURNACE			
	AS THE SUBSTANCE IS TO THE SHADOW AND ABOVE ALBION'S TWELVE	709	JERUSALEM 71	2
	SONS			
	OVER ALBION AS THE SOUL IS TO THE BODY SO JERUSALEM'S SONS	709	JERUSALEM 71	4
	IN HEAVENS & EARTHS AS IN YOUR OWN BOSOM YOU BEAR YOUR	709	JERUSALEM 71	17
	HEAVEN			
	WEPT ROUND HIM AS A FLOCK SILENT SEVEN DAYS OF ETERNITY	711	JERUSALEM 71	63
	RETURN JERUSALEM & DWELL TOGETHER AS OF OLD RETURN . . .	712	JERUSALEM 72	34

		PAGE	TITLE	LINE
AS	**(CONTINUED)**			
	AS IN THE TIMES OF OLD O ALBION AWAKE REUBEN WANDERS . .	712	JERUSALEM 72	36
	AS THE PILGRIM PASSES WHILE THE COUNTRY PERMANENT REMAINS	714	JERUSALEM 73	44
	FROM IMAGINATION AND CLOSING ITSELF AS IN STEEL IN A RATIO	714	JERUSALEM 74	11
	A MALE WITHIN A FEMALE HID AS IN AN ARK & CURTAINS . . .	716	JERUSALEM 75	15
	WHICH ALWAYS APPEAR TO THE IGNORANCE-LOVING HYPOCRITE AS	717C	JERUSALEM 77	PROSE
	SINS			
	AND SAW A FLAME OF FIRE EVEN AS A WHEEL	717	STOOD AMONG/J	2
	ON THE ROCKY SPECTRES AS THE POTTER BREAKS THE POTSHERDS	719	JERUSALEM 78	5
	AS IF I WAS NOT THEIR MOTHER THEY DESPISE ME & CAST ME OUT	720	JERUSALEM 79	21
	AS MY GARDEN & AS MY SECRET BATH SPAIN WAS MY HEAVENLY	720	JERUSALEM 79	40
	COUCH			
	THERE WE WALKED AS IN OUR SECRET CHAMBER AMONG OUR LITTLE	720	JERUSALEM 79	42
	ONES			
	THEY GO FORTH & RETURN SWIFT AS A FLASH OF LIGHTNING . .	722	JERUSALEM 80	44
	SHE WOVE TWO VESSELS OF SEED BEAUTIFUL AS SKIDDAW'S SNOW	723	JERUSALEM 80	74
	SEE SISTERS CANAAN IS PLEASANT EGYPT IS AS THE GARDEN OF	725	JERUSALEM 82	30
	EDEN			
	AS A BEAUTIFUL VEIL SO THESE FEMALES SHALL FOLD & UNFOLD	728	JERUSALEM 83	45
	WHERE THE OLD PARENT STILL RETAINS HIS YOUTH AS I ALAS . .	728	JERUSALEM 83	51
	WE BUILDED JERUSALEM AS A CITY & A TEMPLE FROM LAMBETH . .	729	JERUSALEM 84	3
	THENCE FEATHERD WITH SOFT CRIMSON OF THE RUBY BRIGHT AS	731	JERUSALEM 86	8
	FIRE			
	CLEAR AS THE RAINBOW AS THE CLOUD OF THE SUN'S TABERNACLE	731	JERUSALEM 86	21
	TWO WILLS THEY HAD TWO INTELLECTS & NOT AS IN TIMES OF OLD	732	JERUSALEM 86	61
	TO LIVE IN THY BOSOM'S TRANSLUCENCE AS IN AN ETERNAL	732	JERUSALEM 87	11
	MORNING			
	HOW THEN CAN I EVER AGAIN BE UNITED AS MAN WITH MAN . . .	733	JERUSALEM 88	12
	TWO WINGS SPRING FROM HIS RIBS OF BRASS STARRY BLACK AS	735	JERUSALEM 89	36
	NIGHT			
	BUT TRANSLUCENT THEIR BLACKNESS AS THE DAZLING OF GEMS . .	735	JERUSALEM 89	37
	INCLOSED BY EYELESS WINGS GLOWING WITH FIRE AS THE IRON	735	JERUSALEM 89	41
	HIDDEN WITHIN THE COVERING CHERUB AS IN A TABERNACLE . .	735	JERUSALEM 89	44
	SUCH AS THE FLOWERS OF BEULAH WEAVE TO BE THEIR FUNERAL	736	JERUSALEM 90	7
	MANTLES			
	THEY DRINK REUBEN & BENJAMIN AS THE IRON DRINKS THE FIRE	737	JERUSALEM 90	46
	MUST SEE IT IN ITS MINUTE PARTICULARS ORGANIZED & NOT AS	738	JERUSALEM 91	22
	THOU			
	LOS ANSWERD SWIFT AS THE SHUTTLE OF GOLD SEXES MUST VANISH	739	JERUSALEM 92	13
	& CEASE			
	AS REUBEN FOUND MANDRAKES IN THE FIELD & GAVE THEM TO HIS	740	JERUSALEM 93	8
	MOTHER			
	UPON THE WHITE ROCK ENGLAND A FEMALE SHADOW AS DEADLY DAMPS	741	JERUSALEM 94	7
	THEN JESUS APPEARED STANDING BY ALBION AS THE GOOD SHEPHERD	743	JERUSALEM 96	3
	A MAN & THEY CONVERSED AS MAN WITH MAN IN AGES	743	JERUSALEM 96	6
	OF ETERNITY			
	AWAKE AND OVERSPREAD ALL NATIONS AS IN ANCIENT TIME . . .	744	JERUSALEM 97	2
	AND THE DIM CHAOS BRIGHTEND BENEATH ABOVE AROUND EYED AS	745	JERUSALEM 98	14
	THE PEACOCK			
	WHICH VARY ACCORDING AS THE ORGANS OF PERCEPTION VARY	746	JERUSALEM 98	38
	& THEY WALKED			
	TO & PRO IN ETERNITY AS ONE MAN	746	JERUSALEM 98	39
	LOATHD AS A NATION'S BITTEREST CURSE	748	EV GOSPEL(A)/N	10
	LOUD AS SINAI'S TRUMPET SOUND	748	EV GOSPEL(B)/N	6
	BUT HUMBLE AS A LAMB OR AN ASS	750	EV GOSPEL(C)/N	29
	BUT HUMBLE AS A LAMB OR ASS	752	EV GOSPEL(D)/N	63
	JUST SUCH A ONE AS MAGDALEN	756	EV GOSPEL(I)/N	5
	YOU RETAIN HEALTH AND YET ARE AS MAD AS ANY OF US ALL . .	772D	ANNO SPURZHEIM	MARG
	OVER US ALL MAD AS A REFUGE FROM UNBELIEF	772D	ANNO SPURZHEIM	MARG
	("THE AEGYPTIANS") THEY ALSO CONSIDERD GOD AS ABSTRACTED	774A	ANNO BERKELEY	* MARG
	AS A MAN IN THE SPIRITUAL OR IMAGINATIVE VISION	774A	ANNO BERKELEY	MARG
	HE SAYS ALSO THE SPIRITUAL BODY OR ANGEL AS LITTLE CHILDREN	774A	ANNO BERKELEY	MARG
	PERMANENT IN THE IMAGINATION CONSIDERD AS NOTHING BY .	776D	INSC LAOCOON	PROSE
	BUT WHEN A WORK HAS UNITY IT IS AS MUCH IN A PART AS IN	778B	HOMERS POETRY	PROSE
	THE WHOLE			
	THE TORSO IS AS MUCH A UNITY AS THE LAOCOON	778B	HOMERS POETRY	PROSE
	IT IS THE SAME WITH THE MORAL OF A WHOLE POEM AS WITH . .	778B	HOMERS POETRY	PROSE
	AND THEN WHAT THEN BE AS POOR ABEL A THOUGHT OR AS . . .	780	GHOST ABEL 1	20
	ENTERD INTO ME AS INTO HIS HOUSE & I LOATHE THY	780	GHOST ABEL 2	6
	TABERNACLES			
	("WILL") SO YOU SEE THAT GOD IS JUST SUCH A TYRANT	788C	ANNO THORNTON	* MARG
	AS AUGUSTUS CAESAR			
	NATURE IS IMAGINATION ITSELF AS A MAN IS SO HE SEES . . .	793D	LETTER 5	PROSE
	AS THE EYE IS FORMED SUCH ARE ITS POWERS	793D	LETTER 5	PROSE
	CHALK ENGRAVING IS AT LEAST SIX TIMES AS LABORIOUS AS	794C	LETTER 5	PROSE
	AQUA TINTA			
	AS A PASSION WHICH IS FORBIDDEN BY LAW & RELIGION BUT NOW	798C	LETTER 10	PROSE
	APPEARD AS ONE MAN	805	TO BUTTS/L	51
	I REMAIND AS A CHILD	806	TO BUTTS/L	72
	& THEY ARE AS DISTINCT AS ANY TWO ARTS CAN BE	810B	LETTER 20	PROSE
	THEIR LAMPS BURNING & SUCH SHALL SHINE AS THE STARS . . .	810D	LETTER 21	PROSE
	AS ONE COUNTRY AND THEIR ARTS ONE & THAT YOU WILL ERE LONG	811A	LETTER 21	PROSE
	THINK AS HIGHLY OF OURSELVES AS IMMORTALS OUGHT TO THINK	811C	LETTER 22	PROSE
	AS A SOLDIER OF CHRIST IT GIVES ME THE GREATEST OF TORMENTS	812D	LETTER 22	PROSE
	UPON YOU AS THE CHIEF OF MY FRIENDS WHOM I WOULD ENDEAVOUR	815A	LETTER 23	PROSE
	& HAD PUT MYSELF BACK AS IF I WAS A LEARNER I HAVE PROVED	815A	LETTER 23	PROSE
	MUST FLAXMAN LOOK UPON ME AS WILD	818	HAPPINESS/L	47
	BECAME LEPROUS & WHITE AS SNOW	818	HAPPINESS/L	74
	THAT H(HAYLEY) IS JEALOUS AS STOTHARD WAS & WILL BE . . .	819C	LETTER 25	PROSE
	THE TRUTH IS AS A POET HE IS FRIGHTEND AT ME & AS	819C	LETTER 25	PROSE
	A PAINTER			
	& BEING UNDER MY OWN EYE THE PRINTS ARE AS FINE AS THE	821A	LETTER 25	PROSE

```
                                                         PAGE    TITLE        LINE
AS    (CONTINUED)
      I READ GREEK AS FLUENTLY AS AN OXFORD SCHOLAR &    . . . .  821D LETTER 25      PROSE
      IF THE HEBREW BIBLE IS AS WELL TRANSLATED WHICH I DO NOT    821D LETTER 25      PROSE
      I CONSIDER IT AS THE GRANDEST POEM THAT THIS WORLD CONTAINS 825A LETTER 27      PROSE
      SINCE HE IS AS MUCH AVERSE TO MY POETRY  . . . . . . .      825B LETTER 27      PROSE
      AS HE IS TO A CHAPTER IN THE BIBLE  . . . . . . . . .       825B LETTER 27      PROSE
      I REGARD FASHION IN POETRY AS LITTLE AS I DO IN PAINTING    825B LETTER 27      PROSE
      APPROVES OF MY DESIGNS AS LITTLE AS HE DOES OF MY POEMS     825C LETTER 27      PROSE
         AND
      MY JUST RIGHT AS AN ARTIST & AS A MAN & IF ANY  . . . .     825D LETTER 27      PROSE
      DESIRED HIM AS POLITELY AS WAS POSSIBLE TO GO OUT OF THE    827A LETTER 28      PROSE
         GARDEN
      WORK TO ME I AM CONTENT THAT IT SHALL BE SO AS LONG AS GOD  829D LETTER 30      PROSE
      O THAT I COULD LIVE AS OTHERS DO IN A REGULAR SUCCESSION    830B LETTER 30      PROSE
      SO LARGE AS TO OCCUPY THE WHOLE LENGTH OF HIS WORKSHOP  .   831B LETTER 31      PROSE
      AS THE TRAGIC MUSE HALF-LENGTH THAT IS THE HEAD & HANDS     836A LETTER 35      PROSE
      SO HONEST AS TO EXPOSE TO YOU HIS WHOLE ABSURD PREJUDICE    838C LETTER 37      PROSE
      BUT AS MUCH UNLIKE THE ORIGINAL AS POSSIBLE  . . . . .      839A LETTER 37      PROSE
      THE FIGURES AS LARGE AS LIFE HALF LENGTH MR W(WALKER)       843C LETTER 43      PROSE
      AS THE FRENCH NOW ADORE BUONAPARTE AND THE ENGLISH OUR      845B LETTER 44      PROSE
         POOR GEORGE
      SO THE AMERICANS WILL CONSIDER WASHINGTON AS THEIR GOD      845B LETTER 44      PROSE
      AS WOULD HAVE CALLED FOR THE SCEPTRE OF AGAMEMNON  . . .    847B LETTER 44      PROSE
      EMINENCE AS AN ENGRAVER MAKES HIS OPINION DESERVE NOTICE    848A LETTER 45      PROSE
      HAD TWENTY THANK GOD I WAS NOT ALTOGETHER A BEAST AS HE WAS 852A LETTER 50      PROSE
      EXACTLY TWENTY YEARS BEEN CLOSED FROM ME AS BY A DOOR  .    852B LETTER 50      PROSE
      SERVANT WHO DOMINEERED OVER ME HE IS EVEN AS A BROTHER  .   852C LETTER 50      PROSE
      WHENEVER I TAKE A PENCIL OR GRAVER INTO MY HAND EVEN AS I   852C LETTER 50      PROSE
      USED TO BE IN MY YOUTH AND AS I HAVE NOT BEEN FOR TWENTY    852C LETTER 50      PROSE
      SUDDENLY AS I WAS AT FIRST BY PRODUCING THE HEAD OF ROMNEY  852C LETTER 50      PROSE
      TO SAY THAT VENUSIA IS AS BEAUTIFUL AS SERENA IS ONLY  .    853A LETTER 51     *PROSE
      ALL THAT HAS BEEN PRINTED AS LOST AND BEGIN ANEW UNLESS     858B LETTER 55      PROSE
      OVER MY DOOR AS THE POOR BARBER DID MONEY FOR LIVE HERE     858C LETTER 55      PROSE
      WHICH I CONSIDER AS ONE OF MY BEST  . . . . . . . .         861B LETTER 58      PROSE
      RECIEVING A PROPHET AS A PROPHET IS A DUTY WHICH            863A LETTER 60      PROSE
         IF OMITTED
      AND YOUR MAGAZINE BEING AS EXTENSIVE IN ITS CIRCULATION     863D LETTER 61      PROSE
      AS THAT PAPER AND AS IT ALSO MUST FROM ITS NATURE BE MORE   863D LETTER 61      PROSE
      THE CHILD IS AS BEAUTIFULLY DRAWN AS IT IS COLOURED IN      864B LETTER 61      PROSE
         BOTH
      TASTE WILL SHORTEN THE HUNDRED YEARS INTO AS MANY HOURS FOR 864D LETTER 61      PROSE
      YOU AS SHERIFF ARE BOUND TO ATTEND TO IT  . . . . . .       865B LETTER 62      PROSE
      ME GREAT REPUTATION AS AN ARTIST WHICH WAS THE CHIEF THING  867C LETTER 66      PROSE
      OF THE STATE OF THE DEPARTED I CAN DRAW AS WELL A-BED AS    869A LETTER 68      PROSE
         UP
      I GO ON JUST AS IF PERFECTLY WELL WHICH INDEED I AM EXCEPT  873C LETTER 77      PROSE
      AS A CRIME IN WHICH I SHALL BE [A] THE PRINCIPAL  . . . .   874B LETTER 79      PROSE
      GOD SEND IT SO ON EARTH AS IT IS IN HEAVEN  . . . . .       879A LETTER 88      PROSE
      "THOU HAST SET THY HEART AS THE HEART OF GOD" EZEKIEL  .    SUPP LEGEND/N94     *
ASAPH
      LITCHFIELD SAINT DAVIDS LANDAFF ASAPH BANGOR SODOR  . . .   676 JERUSALEM 46      19
ASCEND
      . . . ASCEND ON THE HILLS AND BRIGHT INFANTRY RANK  . . .   147 FRENCH REVOLTN    291
      I SEE THY DARK CLOUDS ASCEND  . . . . . . . . . . . .       254 AHANIA 4           57
      THAT MILTON OF THE LAND OF ALBION SHOULD UP ASCEND  . .     503 MILTON 20          59
      SHOULD UP ASCEND FORWARD FROM FELPHAM'S VALE & BREAK THE    507 MILTON 23          37
         CHAIN
      UNIVERSAL THEOLOGY NO ...THE LEARNED WHO STRIVE TO ASCEND   581D DESC CAT 8      PROSE
      EMBRACE & ASCEND TO MEET ETERNITY  . . . . . . . . .        609D V LAST JUDG/N   PROSE
      THE PERSONS WHO ASCEND TO MEET THE LORD  . . . . . .        609D V LAST JUDG/N   PROSE
      THEY ASCEND FROM THE EARTH WHERE FIGURES KNEEL  . . . .     610B V LAST JUDG/N   PROSE
      DESCEND & ASCEND WITH THE BREAD & THE WINE  . . . . .       800 MRS FLAXMAN/L      12
ASCENDED
      OVER THE JOYFUL EARTH & SEA & ASCENDED INTO THE HEAVENS     274 FOUR ZOAS 1      376
      THEN MAN ASCENDED MOURNING INTO THE SPLENDORS OF HIS PALACE 293 FOUR ZOAS 3       49
      AS HE ASCENDED HOWLING LOUD THE WEB VIBRATED STRONG  . . .  319 FOUR ZOAS 6      318
      THEN ALBION ASCENDED MOURNING INTO THE PORCHES OF           654 JERUSALEM 29      36
         HIS PALACE
ASCENDING
      REVOLVE LIKE SWEET PERFUMES ASCENDING O LEUTHA SILKEN QUEEN 244 EUROPE 14         14
      ASCENDING INTO HER [CLOUDY] MISTY GARMENTS . . . . . .      285 FOUR ZOAS 2      192
      SLAIN ON THE ALTAR UP ASCENDING INTO HER CLOUDY BOSOM  .    285 FOUR ZOAS 2      196
      BUT FROM THE CAVES OF DEEPEST NIGHT ASCENDING IN CLOUDS     306 FOUR ZOAS 5       31
         OF MIST
      BORE ON THRO THE AFFRIGHTED VALES ASCENDING & DESCENDING    319 FOUR ZOAS 6      287
      BEFORE MY FACE ASCENDING WITH DELIGHT AS IN ANCIENT TIMES   331 FOUR ZOAS 7    * 445
      ROSE FROM THE FEAST IN JOY ASCENDING TO THEIR GOLDEN LOOMS  378 FOUR ZOAS 9      779
      AS MULTITUDES OF CHILDREN ASCENDING FROM THE EARTH  . . .   607C V LAST JUDG/N   PROSE
      MULTITUDES ARE SEEN ASCENDING FROM THE GREEN FIELDS  . . .  610C V LAST JUDG/N   PROSE
      AND ALBION'S SONS ASCENDING & DESCENDING IN THE HORRID VOID 674 JERUSALEM 44      17
      ASCENDING AND DESCENDING INTO ALBION'S SEA OF DEATH  . . .  681 JERUSALEM 50      21
ASCENDS
      THEIR CRY ASCENDS THE CLOUDS  . . . . . . . . . . .         11 GWIN KING/PS       22
      AND DUST ASCENDS THE SKIES  . . . . . . . . . . . .         13 GWIN KING/PS       72
      ASCENDS THE SKY . . . . . . . . . . . . . . . . .           421 MORNING/N         12
ASCENT
      AS A GOLDEN ASCENT WINDING ROUND TO THE HEAVENS OF HEAVENS  318 FOUR ZOAS 6      250
      LYBIA & THE LANDS UNKNOWN ARE THE ASCENT WITHOUT  . . . .   690 JERUSALEM 58      36
ASCENTS
      THE EVER-VARYING SPIRAL ASCENTS TO THE HEAVENS OF HEAVENS   241 EUROPE 10         13
ASH
      THE OAK FROWNS TERRIBLE THE BEECH & ASH & ELM ENROOT  . .   636 JERUSALEM 16       4
```

142

ASHAMD
    I AM ASHAMD OF YOU MAKING USE . . . .   47C ISLAND MOON 3   PROSE
    [THE STERN BARD CEASD ASHAMD OF HIS OWN SONG ENRAGD HE   196 AMERICA PREL 2   18
        SWUNG]
    THE SPECTRE ANSWERD ART THOU NOT ASHAMD OF THOSE THY SINS   629 JERUSALEM 10   37
    JEALOUS OF JERUSALEM'S CHILDREN ASHAMD OF HER LITTLE-ONES   640 JERUSALEM 18   6
    ENOUGH ASHAMD OF & HOPE TO MEND . . . .   875D LETTER 82   PROSE
ASHAMED
    DOTH IT NOT SEEM ASHAMED OF SUCH A PLACE . . . . . .   37A CONTEMPLATN/PS   PROSE
    & THOU OUGHTEST TO BE ASHAMED . . . .   157B MARRIAGE HH 17   PROSE
    ASHAMED OF THE LIGHT . . . .   172 ARE NOT JOYS/N   4
    AND I WAS NOT ASHAMED . . . .   189 ARGUMENT V DAU   2
    HE LISTENS TO THE SOUNDS OF WAR ASTONISHD & ASHAMED . . .   510 MILTON 25   24
    I HAVE ERRED I AM ASHAMED AND WILL NEVER RETURN MORE . .   646 JERUSALEM 23   16
    SHALL VALA BRING THEE FORTH SHALL THE CHASTE BE ASHAMED   696 JERUSALEM 62   7
        ALSO
    ASHAMED TO GIVE LOVE OPENLY TO THE PITEOUS & MERCIFUL MAN   704 JERUSALEM 67   19
    SO LOS SPOKE AND THE GIANTS OF ALBION TERRIFIED & ASHAMED   737 JERUSALEM 90   58
    I AM NOT ASHAMED AFRAID OR AVERSE TO TELL YOU WHAT OUGHT   812A LETTER 22   PROSE
    DEFENCE BUT I SHOULD BE ASHAMED NOT TO SET MY HAND AND . .   864A LETTER 61   PROSE
ASHER
    GAD ASHER ISSACHAR ZEBULUN JOSEPH BENJAMIN DAVID SOLOMON   350 FOUR ZOAS 8   361
    THEN DAN THEN NAPHTALI THEN GAD THEN ASHER THEN ISSACHAR   350 FOUR ZOAS 8   376
    THE GATE OF ASHER CARNARVONSHIRE THE GATE OF ISSACHAR   637 JERUSALEM 16   39
        BRECKNOKSHIRE
    GAD OXFORD BUCKS HARFORD ASHER SUSSEX HAMPSHIRE BERKSHIRE   637 JERUSALEM 16   47
    GAD PEEBLES PERTH RENFRU ASHER SUTHERLAN STERLING WIGTOUN   638 JERUSALEM 16   56
    AND THOSE UNDER DAN ASHER & NAPTHALI ARE THESE . . . .   711 JERUSALEM 72   25
    DAN NAPTHALI GAD ASHER ISSACHAR ZEBULUN ROLL APART . . .   715 JERUSALEM 74 * 50
ASHES
    AN EVANESCENT SHADOW LAST SHE FELL A HEAP OF ASHES . .   283 FOUR ZOAS 2   115
    IS PLACD IN BEDS OF MORTAR MINGLED WITH THE ASHES OF VALA   284 FOUR ZOAS 2   171
    THE SAND & ASHES & TO MIX THE CLAY WITH TEARS & REPENTANCE   286 FOUR ZOAS 2   222
    OUR BEAUTY IS COVERD OVER WITH CLAY & ASHES & OUR BACKS   286 FOUR ZOAS 2   225
    TO BURN MYSTERY WITH FIRE & FORM ANOTHER FROM HER ASHES   357 FOUR ZOAS 8   616
    THE ASHES OF MYSTERY BEGAN TO ANIMATE THEY CALLD IT DEISM   357 FOUR ZOAS 8   618
    DARK GLEAMS BEFORE THE FURNACE-MOUTH A HEAP OF BURNING   485 MILTON 6   17
        ASHES
    OUT FROM THE ASHES OF THE DEAD LOS LIFTS HIS IRON LADLES   486 MILTON 6   29
    THEN I REND THEE ASUNDER THEN I HOWL OVER THY CLAY & ASHES   499 MILTON 18   33
    "AND IN DEAD PARENTS BALEFUL ASHES BRED" (SPENSER) . . .   SUPP LEGEND/N19 *
ASHTAROTH
    IN TYRE & SIDON I SAW BAAL & ASHTAROTH IN MOAB CHEMOSH . .   528 MILTON 37   20
    WITH WAR WOVEN IN LOOMS OF TYRE & SIDON BY BEAUTIFUL   528 MILTON 37   24
        ASHTAROTH
ASHUR
    HAND HAS PEOPLED BABEL & NINEVEH HYLE ASHUR & ARAM . . .   625 JERUSALEM 7   18
    AMALEK EDOM EGYPT MOAB AMMON ASHUR PHILISTEA AROUND   740 JERUSALEM 92   23
        JERUSALEM
ASIA
    OF ASIA & ON THE DESARTS OF AFRICA ROUND THE FALLEN ANGELS   246 SONG OF LOS 4   20
    ASIA . . . .   247A SONG OF LOS 6   TITLE
    THE KINGS OF ASIA HEARD . . . .   247 SONG OF LOS 6   1
    FOR THE DARKNESS OF ASIA WAS STARTLED . . . . . .   247 SONG OF LOS 6   5
    AND THE KINGS OF ASIA STOOD . . . .   247 SONG OF LOS 6   7
    FELT THEIR SKULLS HARDEN THEN ASIA . . . .   253 AHANIA 4   41
    ACROSS EUROPE & ASIA TO CHINA & JAPAN LIKE LIGHTENINGS . .   281 FOUR ZOAS 2 * 59
    STRETCHD OVER EUROPE & ASIA COME O SONS COME COME AWAY   509 MILTON 24   33
    EASTWARD UPON THE PAVED WORK ACROSS EUROPE & ASIA . . .   532 MILTON 40   18
    MONARCHIES AND PATRIARCHES OF ASIA HAS SEEN THOSE . . .   565C DESC CAT 2   PROSE
    ACROSS ALL EUROPE & ASIA HE SAW THE TORTURES OF THE VICTIMS   627 JERUSALEM 8   24
    AND OVER ASIA STRETCHD HIS PRIDE . . . .   651 FIELDS FROM/J   48
    SO LOS SPOKE STANDING ON MAM-TOR LOOKING OVER EUROPE & ASIA   661 JERUSALEM 34   41
    THE CLOUDS OF EUROPE & ASIA AMONG THE SERPENT TEMPLES . .   671 JERUSALEM 42   76
    O POLYPUS OF DEATH O SPECTRE OVER EUROPE AND ASIA . . .   679 JERUSALEM 49   24
    TO THE TWELVE GODS OF ASIA THE SPECTRES OF THOSE WHO SLEEP   681 JERUSALEM 50   3
    WITHIN IS ASIA & GREECE ORNAMENTED WITH EXQUISITE ART . .   690 JERUSALEM 58   37
    SPREADING IN BLOODY VEINS IN TORMENTS OVER EUROPE & ASIA   692 JERUSALEM 60   3
    THEY STOOD IN INNOCENCE & THEIR SKIEY TENT REACHD OVER ASIA   692 JERUSALEM 60   17
    AMONG THE GODS OF ASIA AMONG THE FOUNTAINS OF PITCH &   693 JERUSALEM 60   24
        NITRE
    STRETCHING OVER EUROPE & ASIA FROM IRELAND TO JAPAN . . .   704 JERUSALEM 67   7
    LO THEY SHOOT FORTH IN TENDER NERVES ACROSS EUROPE & ASIA   706 JERUSALEM 68   26
    EUROPE & ASIA & AFRICA & AMERICA IN FURY FOURFOLD . . .   712 JERUSALEM 72   31
    THEY BECAME THE TWELVE GODS OF ASIA OPPOSING THE DIVINE   714 JERUSALEM 74   22
        VISION
    AND BRIGHT STRETCHD OVER EUROPE & ASIA GORGEOUS . . . .   734 JERUSALEM 89   12
    OF THE SEVEN CHURCHES IN ASIA ANTICHRIST SCIENCE . . . .   777B INSC LAOCOON   PROSE
ASIATIC
    FROM GREATER WORKS OF THE ASIATIC PATRIARCHS . . . . .   565D DESC CAT 2   PROSE
ASIDE
    ASIDE . . . .   20C EDW THIRD/PS 2   PROSE
    IT JOYD SHE PUT ASIDE HER CLOUDS & SMILED HER FIRST-BORN   196 AMERICA PREL 2   4
        SMILE
    AND THREW ASIDE HER ARROWS AND LAID DOWN HER SOUNDING BOW   494 MILTON 13   37
    TO CAST ASIDE FROM POETRY ALL THAT IS NOT INSPIRATION . .   533 MILTON 41   7
    STRIP THEM OFF FROM THEIR SHOULDERS AND BOSOMS THEY LAY   702 JERUSALEM 66   18
        ASIDE
    THEY PUT ASIDE HIS CURLS THEY DIVIDE HIS SEVEN LOCKS UPON   702 JERUSALEM 66   22
    SO SAYING SHE DREW ASIDE HER VEIL FROM MAM-TOR TO DOVEDALE   726 JERUSALEM 82   45
    DO NOT THROW ASIDE FOR ANY LONG TIME . . . .   795B LETTER 6   PROSE
    NOT STEPPED OUT AT THE GATE & PUTTING ASIDE HIS BLOWS . .   827A LETTER 28   PROSE

		PAGE	TITLE	LINE

ASK

	PAGE TITLE LINE
NOW BY THE QUEEN'S ADVICE I ASK YOUR LEAVE	20 EDW THIRD/PS 2 41
TO ASK WHICH IS THE FAVOUR OF YOUR COMPANY	20 EDW THIRD/PS 2 44
WHAT CAN SIR THOMAS DAGWORTH ASK THAT EDWARD	23 EDW THIRD/PS 3 96
HONOUR & GENIUS IS ALL I ASK	47 ASK GODS/IM 1 1
AND I ASK THE GODS NO MORE	47 ASK GODS/IM 1 2
HOW COULD YOU THINK HE WAS NOT & ASK IF HE WAS SAID OBTUSE ANGLE	48D ISLAND MOON 5 PROSE
HOW COULD YOU ASK & THINK THAT HE WAS NOT	49A ISLAND MOON 5 PROSE
I ASK THE GODS NO MORE	55 ASK GODS/IM 2 1
AND I ASK THE GODS NO MORE	55 ASK GODS/IM 3 1
AND I ASK THE GODS NO MORE	55 ASK GODS/IM 4 1
("ASK LESS THAN EXPECTED ") THIS WHOLE APHORISM IS AN OVERSIGHT	85A ANNO LAVATER MARG
ASK ME NO MORE I PRAY FOR GRIEF HATH SEALD MY PRECIOUS SIGHT	102 TIRIEL 2 53
NO VENERABLE MAN SAID TIRIEL ASK ME NOT SUCH THINGS . . .	103 TIRIEL 3 19
BUT WORSE O NEVER ASK ME MORE OR I MUST FLEE AWAY . . .	103 TIRIEL 3 21
OR WILT THOU GO ASK THE MOLE	127 THELS MOTTO/BT 2
QUEEN OF THE VALES THE LILLY ANSWERD ASK THE TENDER CLOUD	128 BOOK OF THEL 2 13
ASK THE WILD ASS WHY HE REFUSES BURDENS AND THE MEEK CAMEL	191 V DAU ALBION 3 7
ASK THE BLIND WORM THE SECRETS OF THE GRAVE AND WHY HER SPIRES	191 V DAU ALBION 3 10
LOVE TO CURL ROUND THE BONES OF DEATH AND ASK THE RAVNOUS SNAKE	191 V DAU ALBION 3 11
AND NOW WE KNOW THAT WHATSOEVER THOU WILT ASK OF GOD . .	304 FOUR ZOAS 4 254
AND IF YOULL ASK HER SHE WILL [TELL YOU] SO SWEAR IT SO	418 ON VIRGINITY/N * 2
LET ANY MAN OF SENSE ASK HIMSELF ONE QUESTION IS THIS ART	597B PUB ADDRESS/N PROSE
GO THOU TO SKOFIELD ASK HIM IF HE IS BATH OR IF HE IS CANTERBURY	640 JERUSALEM 17 59
ASK ME NOT OF MY GRIEFS THOU KNOWEST ALL MY GRIEFS . . .	642 JERUSALEM 20 20
ASK CAIAPHAS FOR HE CAN TELL	756 EV GOSPEL(I)/N 16
HALF WHAT I INTENDED TO SAY & IN PARTICULAR I WISH TO ASK	816C LETTER 24 PROSE
NOW I AM SHUT UP IN A CORNER THEREFORE AM FORCED TO ASK	878C LETTER 88 PROSE

ASKD

I KNOW NOT WHAT YOU COULD HAVE ASKD SIR THOMAS	23 EDW THIRD/PS 3 105
YOU ASKD ME IF HE DID NOT LOOK WELL WHEN HE FELL . . .	29D EDW THIRD/PS 4 PROSE
I ONLY ASKD YOU A CIVIL QUESTION--[HERE THE] I HAD A GREAT MIND	45A ISLAND MOON 1 *PROSE
LIKE A CHERRY CLAPPER ARADOBO ASKD WHO WAS PHEBUS SIR .	46D ISLAND MOON 3 PROSE
HERE ARADOBO LOOKD ASTONISHD & ASKD IF HE UNDERSTOOD ENGRAVING	46D ISLAND MOON 3 PROSE
TILLY LALLY TURND ROUND TO OBTUSE ANGLE & ASKD WHO IT WAS	47A ISLAND MOON 3 PROSE
OH I DID NOT THINK HE WAS I ONLY ASKD SAID ARADOBO . .	48D ISLAND MOON 5 PROSE
OH NO SIR I THOUGHT THAT HE WAS NOT BUT I ASKD TO KNOW .	49A ISLAND MOON 5 PROSE
THEN TILLY LALLY TOOK UP A QUADRANT & ASKD	49B ISLAND MOON 5 PROSE
THEY ALL WENT HOME & LEFT THE PHILOSOPHERS THEN SUCTION ASKD	49D ISLAND MOON 6 PROSE
NOT HAVE ANY THING TO SAY AND IF ANY BODY ASKD HIM . .	53B ISLAND MOON 8 PROSE
TRUE I WAS BORN THY [CHILD] SLAVE WHO ASKD THEE TO SAVE ME FROM DEATH	107 TIRIEL 6 14
AFTER DINNER I ASKD ISAIAH TO FAVOUR THE WORLD WITH . . .	154A MARRIAGE HH 12 PROSE
I ASKD A LITHE LADY TO LIE HER DOWN	163 ASKED THIEF/N 3
I ASKD THE SOFT SNOW WITH ME TO PLAY	176 SOFT SNOW/N 2
I ASKD A LITHE LADY TO LIE HER DOWN	261 ASKED THIEF 3
I ASKD MY DEAR FRIEND ORATOR PRIGG	553 ASKD PRIGG/N * 1
ASKD IF HE HAD ANY MESSAGE TO YOU AS I MEANT TO WRITE .	860A LETTER 56 PROSE

ASKED

THE PROPHETS ISAIAH AND EZEKIEL DINED WITH ME AND I ASKED	153B MARRIAGE HH 12 PROSE
THEN I ASKED DOES A FIRM PERSWASION THAT A THING IS SO MAKE IT SO	153C MARRIAGE HH 12 PROSE
EZEKIEL SAID THE SAME OF HIS I ALSO ASKED ISAIAH WHAT .	154A MARRIAGE HH 12 PROSE
I THEN ASKED EZEKIEL WHY HE EAT DUNG & LAY 3O LONG ON HIS	154A MARRIAGE HH 12 PROSE
I NOW ASKED MY COMPANION WHICH WAS MY ETERNAL LOT . .	156B MARRIAGE HH 17 PROSE
WHO SURPRISED ASKED ME HOW I ESCAPED	156D MARRIAGE HH 17 PROSE
I ASKED A THIEF [IF HE'D] TO STEAL ME A PEACH	163 ASKED THIEF/N * 1
IN HAND ARE ASKED FOR NONE ARE WANTED BUT THE AUTHOR .	208A PRSPECTUS 1793 PROSE
I ASKED A THIEF TO STEAL ME A PEACH	261 ASKED THIEF 1
AND I ASKED A WATCHER & A HOLY-ONE	718 STOOD AMONG/J 12
HAYLEY'S & FEAR THAT HE WILL WISH ME TO DO SO I ASKED HIM	860A LETTER 56 PROSE
I HAVE ASKED & INTREATED DIVINE HELP BUT FEAR CONTINUES	876B LETTER 83 PROSE

ASKING

PROSTRATE BEFORE THE STARRY EIGHT ASKING WITH TEARS FORGIVENESS	525 MILTON 35 32
ASKING PARDON OF HIS ENEMIES	752 EV GOSPEL(D)/N 32
BY ASKING IF HE KNEW WHO FURNISHD THE PAPER HE ANSWERED	846D LETTER 44 PROSE

ASKS

THE APPLE TREE NEVER ASKS THE BEECH HOW HE SHALL GROW .	152B MARRIAGE HH 9 PROSE
TREMBLE THE LION SHUDDERING ASKS THE LEOPARD FEELEST THOU	358 FOUR ZOAS 9 56

ASLEEP

WHEN THE WIND IS ASLEEP	35D COUCH DEATH/PS PROSE
VIEWD THE MAID ASLEEP	113 LIT GRL LST/SI 36
LYCA LIES ASLEEP	114 LIT GRL FND/SI 44
IN THY LITTLE HEART ASLEEP	165 CRADLE SONG/N 15
AND LULL [MY] THY OWN SINS FAST ASLEEP	417 MY SPECTR AD/N 4
YOU ARE ASLEEP I WON'T ATTEMPT TO WAKE YE	536 DONT BELIEVE/N 2

A SLEEPING

AS TOM WAS A SLEEPING HE HAD SUCH A SIGHT	117 CHIMNEY SWP/SI 10

ASPASIO

I AM READING THERON & ASPASIO SAID HE	52C ISLAND MOON 8 *PROSE

ASPECT

AND WITH A GRINNING ASPECT FIRST COUPLED WITH & THEN DEVOURD	157B MARRIAGE HH 17 PROSE

144

	PAGE	TITLE	LINE

ASPERITIES
    FATHER AND SON AND LIGHT AND LOVE ALL BOLD ASPERITIES . . 640 JERUSALEM 18   21
ASPERSION
    THAT IT NO LONGER SHALL DARE TO MOCK WITH THE ASPERSION   533 MILTON 41   8
        OF MADNESS
ASPERSIONS
    THE WORKS NOW EXHIBITED WILL GIVE THE LIE TO SUCH   572D DESC CAT 3   PROSE
        ASPERSIONS
ASPIRE
    ON WHAT WINGS DARE HE ASPIRE   . . . .   172 THE TYGER/N 1   7
    COULD HEART DESCEND OR WINGS ASPIRE   . . . .   173 THE TYGER/N 2   7
    ON WHAT WINGS DARE HE ASPIRE   . . . .   214 THE TYGER/SE   7
    ARISE FROM THEIR GRAVES AND ASPIRE   . . . .   215 AH SUNFLOWR/SE   7
    WE THEREFORE FOR WHOSE SAKE ALL THINGS ASPIRE TO BE & LIVE 272 FOUR ZOAS 1   296
    AND THERE TO ETERNITY ASPIRE   . . . .   421 EACH MAN/N   5
ASPIRES
    HIS EYELIDS GIVE THEIR LIGHT AROUND HIS FOLDING TAIL   352 FOUR ZOAS 8   447
        ASPIRES
ASPORTING
    MAIDENS DANCING LOVES ASPORTING   . . . .   53 PHEBE DREST/IM   5
ASS
    CALL ME [ASS ARSE] ASS   . . . .   46B ISLAND MOON 2   PROSE
    ASK THE WILD ASS WHY HE REFUSES BURDENS AND THE MEEK CAMEL 191 V DAU ALBION 3   7
    AND FROM THE OX & ASS COME MOPING TERRORS FROM THE EAGLE   363 FOUR ZOAS 9   237
    LAY THEM ON SKINS OF TYGERS OR THE SPOTTED LEOPARD OR WILD 377 FOUR ZOAS 9   746
        ASS
    & GENIUS BUT WHETHER HE IS PASSIVE & POLITE & A VIRTUOUS   453A ANNO REYNOLDS   MARG
        ASS
    LAY THEM ON SKINS OF TYGERS & OF THE SPOTTED LEOPARD &   513 MILTON 27   6
        THE WILD ASS
    IF YOU THINK AS YOU SPEAK YOU ARE AN ASS   544 F(LAXMAN)/N 2   3
    ID BE AN ASS A HOG A WORM A CHAIR A STOOL   . . . . .   550 WHEN I SEE/N   8
    APULEIUS'S GOLDEN ASS & OVID'S METAMORPHOSIS &   607A V LAST JUDG/N PROSE
    A MAN CAN NEVER BECOME ASS NOR HORSE   . . . . . .   607A V LAST JUDG/N PROSE
    BUT HUMBLE AS A LAMB OR AN ASS   . . . .   750 EV GOSPEL (C)/N   29
    BUT HUMBLE AS A LAMB OR ASS . . . .   752 EV GOSPEL (D)/N   63
ASSAILD
    DOUBT FIRST ASSAILD ME THEN SHAME TOOK POSSESSION OF ME   643 JERUSALEM 21   5
ASSASINATIONS
    AND SECRET ASSASINATIONS NOT WORSHIPD NOR ADORD BUT . .   528 MILTON 37   31
    [ARE THERE ARTISTS WHO LIVE UPON ASSASINATIONS OF OTHER   SUPP ANNO REYNOLDS * MARG
        MEN]
ASSASSIN
    ...ASSASSIN LAYING DEAD AT THE FEET OF (EDWARD) IST IN...   SUPP ILLUS HISTORY *TITLE
ASSASSINATIONS
    IN A CITY OF ASSASSINATIONS THIS MAKES YOUR LOT TRULY . . 847B LETTER 44   PROSE
ASSASSINETTI
    OR COULD FROM DEATH ASSASSINETTI WAKE   . . . . . .   537 AND HIS LEGS/N   33
ASSAULT
    ROYAL DRAGOONS FOR AN ASSAULT & SEDITIOUS WORDS   . . . . 826D LETTER 28   PROSE
ASSAULTED
    BEFORE ASSAULTED THE BRIGHT HUMAN FORM HE FELT HIS PORES   352 FOUR ZOAS 8   417
ASSAY
    FOR BRUTISH PAN IN VAIN MIGHT THEE ASSAY   . . . . . .   14 IMIT SPEN/PS   10
    . . . THE PRISONERS LOOK UP AND ASSAY TO SHOUT THEY LISTEN 136 FRENCH REVOLTN   52
ASSAYD
    BUT DUMB TILL THAT DREAD DAY WHEN ORC ASSAYD HIS FIERCE   196 AMERICA PREL 1   10
        EMBRACE
    THRICE HE ASSAYD PRESUMPTUOUS TO AWAKE THE DEAD TO JUDGMENT 243 EUROPE 13   3
    BUT WHEN UNSATIATED HIS THIRST HE ASSAYD TO GATHER MORE   311 FOUR ZOAS 6   4
    OF SWEET RESPONSE COULD HE OBTAIN THO OFT ASSAYD WITH TEARS 315 FOUR ZOAS 6   129
ASSAYS
    THE NIGHTINGALE AGAIN ASSAYS HIS SONG & THRO THE DAY . .   520 MILTON 31   42
ASSEMBLIES
    AGAINST THE DIVINE IMAGE CONGREGATED ASSEMBLIES OF WICKED   347 FOUR ZOAS 8   258
        MEN
ASSEMBLY
    AND LOWRING DARKNESS HOVERD OER TH ASSEMBLY   . . . . .   49B ISLAND MOON 5   *PROSE
    WE HAVE CALLD AN ASSEMBLY BUT NOT TO DESTROY . . . . .   139 FRENCH REVOLTN   115
    . . . TO SHUT UP THIS ASSEMBLY IN THEIR FINAL HOME   . .   141 FRENCH REVOLTN   154
    THE ABBE DE (SIEYES) FROM THE NATION'S ASSEMBLY . . . .   141 FRENCH REVOLTN * 163
    . . . BUT IF IT REFUSE LET THE NATION'S ASSEMBLY THENCE   145 FRENCH REVOLTN   253
        LEARN
    . . . BACK TO THE NATION'S ASSEMBLY AND TOLD   . . . .   145 FRENCH REVOLTN   256
    . . . THEN BOWING LIKE CLOUDS MAN TOWARD MAN THE ASSEMBLY   146 FRENCH REVOLTN   263
    SO FAYETTE STOOD SILENT AMONG THE ASSEMBLY . . . . . .   146 FRENCH REVOLTN   268
    THE NATION'S ASSEMBLY COMMAND   . . . .   147 FRENCH REVOLTN   285
    COLD DARK OPAKE THE ASSEMBLY MET TWELVEFOLD IN AMALEK .   348 FOUR ZOAS 8   275
    CALLD DOWN A GREAT SOLEMN ASSEMBLY RINTRAH IN FURY & FIRE   351 FOUR ZOAS 8   * 389
    COLD DARK OPAKE THE ASSEMBLY MET TWELVE FOLD IN AMALEK .   382 FOUR ZOAS AD 6   8
    BUT PALAMABRON CALLED DOWN A GREAT SOLEMN ASSEMBLY   . . . 489 MILTON 8   46
    AND IN THE MIDST OF THE GREAT ASSEMBLY PALAMABRON PRAYD   489 MILTON 9   4
    ACCUSD PALAMABRON BEFORE THE ASSEMBLY OF INGRATITUDE OF   489 MILTON 9   20
        MALICE
    THUS SATAN RAGD AMIDST THE ASSEMBLY AND HIS BOSOM GREW . . 490 MILTON 9   30
    OF THE ASSEMBLY IN SATAN'S BOSOM A VAST UNFATHOMABLE ABYSS 490 MILTON 9   35
    ASTONISHMENT HELD THE ASSEMBLY IN AN AWFUL SILENCE AND   490 MILTON 9   36
        TEARS
    AND IT WAS ENQUIRD WHY IN A GREAT SOLEMN ASSEMBLY   . . . 491 MILTON 11   15
    AND THEREFORE PALAMABRON DARED NOT TO CALL A SOLEMN   492 MILTON 11   24
        ASSEMBLY
    SHE DOWN DESCENDED INTO THE MIDST OF THE GREAT SOLEMN   492 MILTON 11   29
        ASSEMBLY

	PAGE	TITLE	LINE

ASSEMBLY   (CONTINUED)
    AND LOVELY & HER MOTH-LIKE ELEGANCE SHONE OVER THE ASSEMBLY   492 MILTON 11   33
    THUNDERD THE ASSEMBLY DARK & CLOUDED AND THEY RATIFYD   . .   494 MILTON 13   15
    THE WHOLE ASSEMBLY WEPT PROPHETIC SEEING IN MILTON'S FACE   495 MILTON 14   11
    HERE THE TWELVE SONS OF ALBION JOIND IN DARK ASSEMBLY . .   640 JERUSALEM 18   5
    TOGETHER INTO AN ASSEMBLY THEY SAID LET US GO DOWN . . .   686 JERUSALEM 55   4
ASSERT
    IS IT TO ASSERT THAT MAN IS BORN IN ONLY ONE DEGREE . . .   93A ANNO SWED LOVE   MARG
    THEY DARED SO ROUNDLY TO ASSERT THAT GOD SPAKE TO THEM   . .   153B MARRIAGE HH 12   *PROSE
    LIKE WHAT SR FRANCIS BACON [SHOULD DOWNRIGHT ASSERT] SAYS   599D PUB ADDRESS/N   PROSE
    MILTON'S PARADISE BE READ & I WILL ASSERT THAT EVERY BODY   600D PUB ADDRESS/N   PROSE
    ROUGHER WHEN I PLEASE & ASSERT THAT HE WHO THINKS HE CAN   602B PUB ADDRESS/N   *PROSE
    WHEN THEY ASSERT THAT JUPITER   605C V LAST JUDG/N   PROSE
    IT IS BURNT UP THE MOMENT MEN CEASE TO BEHOLD IT I ASSERT   617B V LAST JUDG/N   PROSE
    ON COMPARING COWPER WITH WASHINGTON MUST ASSERT . . . .   846D LETTER 44   PROSE
ASSERTED
    THE UNDERSTANDING AS WAS ASSERTED IN THE SOCIETY . . . .   96B ANNO SWED LOVE   MARG
    THE DEITIES OF SURROUNDING NATIONS AND ASSERTED THAT THEY   153D MARRIAGE HH 12   PROSE
    THESE MEN HAVE REPEATEDLY ASSERTED THIS ABSURDITY TO ME   592B PUB ADDRESS/N   PROSE
    AT WHICH TIME HE ASSERTED THAT WOOLETT'S PRINTS WERE . .   593A PUB ADDRESS/N   PROSE
    ASSERTED IN THE BIBLE THAT THE NAME OF THE WICKED SHALL ROT   598C PUB ADDRESS/N   PROSE
    ASSERTED THAT THE PAINTER OF THIS PICTURE WOULD NOT HAVE   612C V LAST JUDG/N   PROSE
ASSERTING
    ASSERTING THE SELF-RIGHTEOUSNESS AGAINST THE UNIVERSAL   506 MILTON 22   42
        SAVIOUR
    ASSERTING IN MY OWN DEFENCE THAT THIS PRINT IS THE FINEST   602A PUB ADDRESS/N   PROSE
ASSERTION
    THIS ASSERTION THAT THE SPIRITUAL SUN IS NOT LIFE   . . .   94B ANNO SWED LOVE   MARG
    THAT GAINSBOROUGH HAD IN MAKING THE ABOVE ASSERTION NAMELY   465D ANNO REYNOLDS   MARG
    THIS ABSURD ASSERTION HAS DONE ME & MAY STILL DO ME   . .   602A PUB ADDRESS/N   PROSE
    COMBAT HIS ASSERTION AS THE GARDENER REMAIND IN MY GARDEN   827D LETTER 28   PROSE
    SHORT TIME I SHALL MAKE MY ASSERTION GOOD THAT I AM BECOME   852C LETTER 50   PROSE
    I AM STARTLED AT SUCH AN ASSERTION I HOPE THE CONTEMPORARY   864D LETTER 61   PROSE
ASSERTIONS
    HIS ASSERTIONS IN ALL HIS DISCOURSES . . . .   476D ANNO REYNOLDS   MARG
    CONVINCING PROOF AMONG MANY OTHERS THAT THESE ASSERTIONS   566C DESC CAT 2   PROSE
ASSERTS
    THE MAN WHO ASSERTS THAT THERE IS NO SUCH THING AS SOFTNESS   457B ANNO REYNOLDS   MARG
    DOES NOT IMAGINE AT ALL THE PAINTER OF THIS WORK ASSERTS   576D DESC CAT 4   PROSE
ASSIDUOUS
    A MORE ASSIDUOUS PURSUIT OF BOTH ARTS INDEED BY MY LATE   825C LETTER 27   PROSE
    MAKE ME ASSIDUOUS & IT DOES SO THAT MR JOHN ROMNEY IS   .   838C LETTER 37   PROSE
ASSIDUOUSLY
    BEEN ASSIDUOUSLY SOWN AND PLANTED AMONG THE ENGLISH PUBLIC   864A LETTER 61   PROSE
ASSIGN
    ASTONISHED AT MY FAULTS AND COULD NOT ASSIGN A REASON   . .   852B LETTER 50   PROSE
ASSIMILATE
    SUCH AS THE PITEOUS SPECTRES MAY ASSIMILATE THEMSELVES INTO   331 FOUR ZOAS 7   454
    THEY ASSIMILATE WITH ALBION IN PITY & COMPASSION . . . .   674 JERUSALEM 44   33
    SEEING HIS SONS ASSIMILATE WITH LUVAH BOUND IN THE BONDS   685 JERUSALEM 54   11
    SOMETIMES IT SHALL ASSIMILATE WITH MIGHTY GOLGONOOZA   . .   728 JERUSALEM 83   43
ASSIMILATED
    WHOSE SPECTRE FIRST ASSIMILATED WITH LUVAH IN ALBION'S   668 JERUSALEM 41   3
        MOUNTAINS
    ASSIMILATED AND EMBRACD ETERNAL DEATH FOR ALBION'S SAKE   676 JERUSALEM 45   39
ASSIMILATING
    OF LOS ASSIMILATING TO THOSE FORMS EMBODIED & LOVELY   . .   332 FOUR ZOAS 7   474
    COMPOSITION BY ASSIMILATING IT WITH [THE] A PRETENCE TO &   453D ANNO REYNOLDS * MARG
    IN THE ARMS OF VALA ASSIMILATING IN ONE WITH VALA . . .   642 JERUSALEM 19   41
ASSIST
    O MERCURY ASSIST MY LABRING SENSE . . . .   15 IMIT SPEN/PS   35
    OF ENION & HIM ASSIST TO BIND THE FALLEN KING . . . . .   300 FOUR ZOAS 4   120
    ASSIST IN WEAVING THE DEADLY WOOF "...IN DREADFUL HARMONY"   576C DESC CAT 4   PROSE
    I WILL COMPELL THEE TO ASSIST ME IN MY TERRIBLE LABOURS   627 JERUSALEM 8   15
        TO BEAT
    SHUDDER NOT BUT WRITE & THE HAND OF GOD WILL ASSIST YOU   677 JERUSALEM 47   17
    TO ASSIST IN THEIR MOST GRIEVOUS WORK OF PITY & COMPASSION   692 JERUSALEM 59   47
    TO ASSIST IN THE WORK THE LAMB BLEATS THE SEA-FOWL CRIES   692 JERUSALEM 59   49
    TO ASSIST ANY HOW REMOTE SOEVER WILL CERTAINLY HEAR HER   842A LETTER 41   PROSE
        VOICE
ASSISTANCE
    YET WITH YOUR KIND ASSISTANCE LORDS I HOPE . . . . . .   19 EDW THIRD/PS 2   6
    THE ASSISTANCE & COUNTENANCE OF THOSE ALREADY IN THE TRUTH   614A V LAST JUDG/N   PROSE
    ASSISTANCE OF BRUNO'S FAIRIES BUT I INVOKE THE GOOD GENII   801B LETTER 13   PROSE
    YOUR KIND OFFER OF PECUNIARY ASSISTANCE I CAN ONLY THANK   811D LETTER 22   PROSE
    EVERY ASSISTANCE IN HIS POWER WITHOUT KNOWING MY INTENTION   820B LETTER 25   PROSE
    THIS POEM SHALL BY DIVINE ASSISTANCE BE PROGRESSIVELY   .   825A LETTER 27   PROSE
    HE PROPOSES TO COMMENCE WITH YOUR ASSISTANCE HE CAN AFFORD   841C LETTER 41   PROSE
    WHICH SHALL WITH YOUR GOOD ASSISTANCE . . . .   841D LETTER 41   PROSE
    SHE CALLS FOR YOUR ASSISTANCE YOU WHO NEVER REFUSE . .   842A LETTER 41   PROSE
    THE ASSISTANCE AND APPROBATION OF OUR GOOD FRIEND FLAXMAN   853B LETTER 52   PROSE
ASSISTANT
    INTO WHICH HE WAS INVITED AS AN ASSISTANT BY A GARDENER   827A LETTER 28   PROSE
        AT WORK
    HE MAY STILL PERFORM HIS BEST AS YOUR ASSISTANT IN IT I   845C LETTER 44   PROSE
        HAVE
ASSOCIATE
    THE PUBLICANS & SINNERS THAT CHRIST LOVED TO ASSOCIATE WITH   396A ANNO WATSON   MARG
    FEAR TO ASSOCIATE WITH BLAKE . . . .   545 COSWAY FRAZR/N   2
ASSOCIATES
    BENEATH THEM A MULTITUDE OF THEIR ASSOCIATES ARE SEEN   .   607D V LAST JUDG/N   PROSE

146

		PAGE	TITLE	LINE

ASSUAGE
    TO ASSUAGE HIS MISERY . . . . 542 PITIFUL CASE/N   3
    TO ASSUAGE HIS BITTER WOE . . . . 542 PITIFUL CASE/N   6
    MAY JESUS AND HIS ANGELS ASSUAGE . . . . 796C LETTER 8   PROSE
ASSUMD
    OF THE PRIMEVAL PRIEST'S ASSUMD POWER . . . . . . 222 URIZEN 2   1
    MY DEEP MY NIGHT WHICH THOU ASSUMING HAST ASSUMD MY CROWN 278 FOUR ZOAS 1   511
    ACCORDING TO THE WILL OF LUVAH WHO ASSUMD THE PLACE . . 326 FOUR ZOAS 7   263
    WHO ASSUMD LUVAH'S FORM & STOOD BEFORE HIM OPPOSITE . . 342 FOUR ZOAS 8   64
    HE WHO ASSUMD MY LUVAH'S THRONE IN TIMES OF EVERLASTING 345 FOUR ZOAS 8   * 154
    BUT WE MUST NOT BE TYRANTS ALSO HE HATH ASSUMD MY PLACE 487 MILTON 7   27
    TILL SATAN HAD ASSUMD RINTRAH'S WRATH IN THE DAY 492 MILTON 11   25
      OF MOURNING
    BUT WHEN LUVAH ASSUMD THE WORLD OF URIZEN TO THE SOUTH . . 500 MILTON 19   19
    TILL YOU HAVE ASSUMD THE PROVIDENCE OF GOD & SLAIN YOUR 648 JERUSALEM 24   56
      FATHER
ASSUME
    THE AGED SENATORS THEIR ANCIENT SWORDS ASSUME THE TREMBLING 34B KING JOHN/PS   PROSE
      SINEWS OF
    ASSUME THE DARK SATANIC BODY IN THE VIRGIN'S WOMB . . . 347 FOUR ZOAS 8   241
    TO ASSUME THE RIGHT TO PUT OTHER MEN'S IDEAS INTO 455B ANNO REYNOLDS   MARG
      HIS FOOLERY
    NOR SHALT THOU EVER ASSUME THE TRIPLE-FORM OF ALBION'S 627 JERUSALEM 8   34
      SPECTRE
    GO ASSUME PAPAL DIGNITY THOU SPECTRE THOU MALE HARLOT 698 JERUSALEM 64   15
      ARTHUR
ASSUMED
    THAT THE JEWS ASSUMED A RIGHT EXCLUSIVELY TO THE BENEFITS 389A ANNO WATSON   MARG
    BUT WHEN LUVAH ASSUMED THE WORLD OF URIZEN IN THE SOUTH 524 MILTON 34   38
    BUT WHEN LUVAH ASSUMED THE WORLD OF URIZEN SOUTHWARD . . 691 JERUSALEM 59   15
ASSUMES
    AND URIZEN ASSUMES THE EAST LUVAH ASSUMES THE SOUTH . . 663 JERUSALEM 36   29
ASSUMING
    MY DEEP MY NIGHT WHICH THOU ASSUMING HAST ASSUMD MY CROWN 278 FOUR ZOAS 1   511
    CEASING TO BE HIS EMANATIONS LIFE TO THEMSELVES ASSUMING 736 JERUSALEM 90   2
ASSURANCE
    AS IF GENIUS & ASSURANCE WERE THE SAME THING BUT . . . 825C LETTER 27   PROSE
    HE GIVES A VERY SPIRITED ASSURANCE OF MR JOHN ROMNEY'S . 835C LETTER 35   PROSE
ASSURD
    FROM THY EMBRACE ELSE BE ASSURD SO HORRIBLE A FORM . . . 326 FOUR ZOAS 7   235
    TO LIFE ETERNAL BE ASSURD I AM THY REAL SELF . . . . 328 FOUR ZOAS 7   345
    BE ASSURD MR DEVIL I WON'T PRAY TO YOU . . . . . . 559 I ROSE UP AT/N   20
ASSURE
    ASSURE HER THAT IT CANNOT BE LONG BEFORE I HAVE THE 815D LETTER 23   PROSE
      PLEASURE
    TO PLEASE MYSELF FOR I DO ASSURE YOU THAT I HAVE TRULY . 819A LETTER 24   PROSE
    & I DO ASSURE YOU THAT IF I COULD HAVE RETURND TO LONDON . 825D LETTER 27   PROSE
    AS I ASSURE MYSELF YOU WILL BE WITH HIS WORK . . . . 836D LETTER 35   PROSE
    I ASSURE YOU THAT I WILL NOT SPARE PAINS & AM . . . . 837A LETTER 35   PROSE
    A LINE FROM YOU DESIRES ME TO ASSURE YOU OF HIS WISH TO 845D LETTER 44   PROSE
      GIVE
    FOR I DO ASSURE YOU I FEEL IT A DUTY TO MY PROFESSION THAT 856C LETTER 54   PROSE
      I
    ASSURE YOU A PLEASING ONE TO ME IT WILL BE HIGHLY 859C LETTER 56   PROSE
      GRATIFYING
ASSURED
    THE ENGLISH ARTIST MAY BE ASSURED THAT HE IS DOING . . . 597C PUB ADDRESS/N   PROSE
    WITH LOVE BE THOU ASSURED I NEVER WILL BE THY SLAVE . . . 732 JERUSALEM 87   15
    CAN COMPREHEND IN A FORTNIGHT BE ASSURED MY DEAR FRIEND 814D LETTER 23   PROSE
      THAT
    KNEW IMMEDIATELY MY PORTRAIT OF ROMNEY & ASSURED ME . . . 836B LETTER 35   PROSE
    I ASSURED HIM THAT HE DID AND HERE HE LEFT OFF DESIRING ME 846D LETTER 44   PROSE
    FINISHD PROOF BE ASSURED THAT WITH OUR GOOD FLAXMAN'S . . 855B LETTER 53   PROSE
ASSUREDLY
    FOR ASSUREDLY HE IS VERY ILL . . . . 434 WILLIAM BOND   4
    UNDERSTAND & CAN ASSUREDLY AFFIRM THAT THE . . . . . 814D LETTER 23   PROSE
ASSURING
    AND NOW LET ME FINISH WITH ASSURING YOU THAT THO I HAVE 815D LETTER 23   PROSE
ASSYRIA
    THY SONS ARE LOVELIER THAN EGYPT OR ASSYRIA WHEREFORE . . 693 JERUSALEM 60   31
    UPON EGYPT'S IRON FLOORS & THE MARBLE PAVEMENTS OF ASSYRIA 719 JERUSALEM 79   2
    SANDALS OF GOLD & PEARL & EGYPT & ASSYRIA BEFORE ME . . . 731 JERUSALEM 86   31
ASSYRIAN
    HE [REPRESENTS THE ASSYRIAN] IS HAZAEL THE SYRIAN . . . 608B V LAST JUDG/N   PROSE
ASTERIAL
    OR WHERE THE COMETS OF THE NIGHT OR STARS OF [ETERNAL] 358 FOUR ZOAS 9   40
      ASTERIAL DAY
ASTONISH
    [ASTONISH LOOKD FROM HIS BRIGHT PORTALS CALLING THUS TO 380 FOUR ZOAS AD 1 *   3
      LUVAH]
    AS BOTH ASTONISH & COMFORT ME & MINE . . . . . . 391D ANNO WATSON   MARG
    FOR THE TRIAL OF MEN TO ASTONISH EVERY NEIGHBOURHOOD WITH 571D DESC CAT 3   PROSE
ASTONISHD
    THAT THE ASTONISHD WORLD WITH UP-TURND EYES . . . . . 18 EDW THIRD/PS 1   40
    STARTLED ASTONISHD AT THE CLAMBOUS COCK . . . . . . 24 EDW THIRD/PS 3   115
    HERE ARADOBO LOOKD ASTONISHD & ASKD IF HE UNDERSTOOD 46D ISLAND MOON 3   PROSE
      ENGRAVING
    DESOLATE LOATHED DUMB [CON] ASTONISHD WAITING FOR BLACK 107 TIRIEL 5   * 35
      DEATH
    ASTONISHD SILENT TILL THE MORNING BEAMS BEGAN TO SPRING 107 TIRIEL 6   2
    THEN THEL ASTONISHD VIEWD THE WORM UPON ITS DEWY BED . . 129 BOOK OF THEL 4   1
    ASTONISHD AT HIS OWN EXISTENCE . . . . 234 URIZEN 23   12

147

ASTONISHD   (CONTINUED)
```
  LOS ASTONISHD AND TERRIFIED BUILT  . . . . . . . .   259 BOOK OF LOS 5        20
  [ASTONISHD HE FOUND ENION HIDDEN IN THE DARKSOM CAVE]  . .  267 FOUR ZOAS 1       136
  ASTONISHD SAT HER SISTERS OF BEULAH TO SEE HER SOFT    270 FOUR ZOAS 1     *  227
    AFFECTIONS
  THE SONS OF WAR ASTONISHD AT THE GLITTRING MONSTER DROVE  279 FOUR ZOAS 1      533
  IN HER BRIGHT SKIRTS ASTONISHD & CONFOUNDED HE BEHELD  . .  285 FOUR ZOAS 2      203
  [I] WE HEARD ASTONISHD AT THE VISION & [MY] OUR . . . .  293 FOUR ZOAS 3       57
  ASTONISHD FILLD WITH TEARS THE SPIRIT OF ENITHARMON BEHELD  327 FOUR ZOAS 7      311
  THEN AS ANOTHER SELF ASTONISHD HUMANIZING & IN TEARS   .  328 FOUR ZOAS 7      340
  OF [ENITHARMON'S] THY POOR BROKEN HEART ASTONISHD . . .  341 FOUR ZOAS 8       21
  [ASTONISHD COMFORTED DELIGHTED THE DAUGHTERS OF BEULAH SAW]  342 FOUR ZOAS 8       45
  ASTONISHD COMFORTED DELIGHTED IN NOTES OF RAPTUROUS EXTACY  342 FOUR ZOAS 8       46
  ALL BEULAH STOOD ASTONISHD LOOKING DOWN TO ETERNAL DEATH  342 FOUR ZOAS 8       47
  TERRIFIED & ASTONISHD URIZEN BEHELD THE BATTLE TAKE A FORM  343 FOUR ZOAS 8      102
  WITH GIFTS & GOLD OF EDEN ASTONISHD STUPIFIED WITH DELIGHT  346 FOUR ZOAS 8     *  214
  ASTONISHD LOOKD FROM HIS BRIGHT PORTALS LUVAH KING OF LOVE  380 FOUR ZOAS AD 1       5
  TO LOVE DEVOTED FEMALE ALL ASTONISHD STOOD THE HOSTS   .  380 FOUR ZOAS AD 1      13
  I AM ASTONISHD HOW SUCH CONTEMPTIBLE KNAVERY & FOLLY  . 397A ANNO BACON       MARG
  IN THE EVENING RETURNING TERRIFIED OVERLABOURD & ASTONISHD  486 MILTON 7        16
  SATAN ASTONISHD AND WITH POWER ABOVE HIS OWN CONTROLL  .  492 MILTON 12       16
  ASTONISHD AT THE TRANSGRESSOR IN HIM BEHOLDING THE SAVIOUR  494 MILTON 13       31
  HE LISTENS TO THE SOUNDS OF WAR ASTONISHD AND CONFOUNDED  506 MILTON 23     *   8
  HE LISTENS TO THE SOUNDS OF WAR ASTONISHD & ASHAMED  . .  510 MILTON 25       24
  SO SPAKE OLOLON IN REMINISCENCE ASTONISHD BUT THEY   . .  525 MILTON 35       18
  TREMBLING I SIT DAY AND NIGHT MY FRIENDS ARE ASTONISHD   623 JERUSALEM 5       16
    AT ME
  ASTONISHD TERRIFIED THEY HOVERD OVER HIS GIANT LIMBS   .  642 JERUSALEM 20        2
  ASTONISHD AT HIS BEAUTY & PERFECTION THOU FORGAVEST HIS   643 JERUSALEM 20       37
    FURIOUS LOVE
  WE HEARD ASTONISHD AT THE VISION & OUR HEARTS TREMBLED    654 JERUSALEM 29       44
    WITHIN US
  FOR ALL TO AVOID THEE TO BE ASTONISHD AT THEE FOR THY SINS  658 JERUSALEM 31       62
  FROM LOS ASTONISHD HE BEHELD ONLY THE PETRIFIED SURFACES  658 JERUSALEM 32        5
  ASTONISHD LOVELY EMBRACING THE SUBLIME SHADE THE DAUGHTERS  678 JERUSALEM 48       29
    OF BEULAH
  ASTONISHD TERRIFIED & IN PAIN & TORMENT SUDDEN THEY BEHOLD  701 JERUSALEM 65       68
  ASTONISHD AMAZED  . . . . . . . . . . . . . .  804 TO BUTTS/L        20
  ASTONISHD AT MY PATIENCE & FORBEARANCE OF INJURIES UPON  825D LETTER 27       PROSE
    INJURIES
  THE FLAME SOON DIES AGAIN & I AM LEFT STUPIFIED AND   830B LETTER 30       PROSE
    ASTONISHD
  EDWARD & HIS QUEEN & NOBLES ASTONISHD AT THE BARD'S SONG  SUPP ILLUS GRAY    *TITLE
```
ASTONISHED
```
  ASTONISHED AT MY FAULTS AND COULD NOT ASSIGN A REASON  . 852B LETTER 50       PROSE
```
ASTONISHING
```
  THE TESTAMENT IS MY CHIEF MASTER ASTONISHING INDEED IS  . 821D LETTER 25       PROSE
```
ASTONISHMENT
```
  . . . BOUND IN ASTONISHMENT A QUARTER OF AN HOUR . . . .  137 FRENCH REVOLTN       67
  LOS SMITTEN WITH ASTONISHMENT   . . . . . . . . . .  226 URIZEN 8        1
  WONDER AWE FEAR ASTONISHMENT    . . . . . . . . . .  231 URIZEN 18       13
  ASTONISHMENT HELD THE ASSEMBLY IN AN AWFUL SILENCE AND   490 MILTON 9        36
    TEARS
  I BEHELD MILTON WITH ASTONISHMENT & IN HIM BEHELD   . .  528 MILTON 37       15
  HE TREMBLED WITH EXCEEDING GREAT TREMBLING & ASTONISHMENT  531 MILTON 39       17
  HE TREMBLED WITH EXCEEDING GREAT TREMBLING & ASTONISHMENT  531 MILTON 39       31
  SIR JOSHUA IN ASTONISHMENT CRIES OUT  . . . . . . . .  548 CRIPPLE EVRY/N        3
  LAMENTING & LOOKING UPON HER IN ASTONISHMENT & TERROR  . 609B V LAST JUDG/N    PROSE
  I NOW AM WHAT I AM A HORROR AND AN ASTONISHMENT  . . . .  627 JERUSALEM 8       18
  LOS WAS ALL ASTONISHMENT & TERROR HE TREMBLED SITTING ON  658 JERUSALEM 32        3
    THE STONE
  THE MOUNTAIN OF BLESSING IS ITSELF A CURSE  . . . . .  720 JERUSALEM 79        7
    & AN ASTONISHMENT
  ITALY SAW ME IN SUBLIME ASTONISHMENT FRANCE WAS WHOLLY MINE  720 JERUSALEM 79       39
```
ASTOUND
```
  LOS FURIOUS ANSWERD SPECTRE HORRIBLE THY WORDS ASTOUND   329 FOUR ZOAS 7      361
    MY EAR
```
ASTOUNDING
```
  A MOMENT THEN ASTOUNDING HORROR BELCHES FROM THE CENTER   336 FOUR ZOAS 7B      131
  BY LAND ASTOUNDING ERECTING PILLARS IN THE DEEPEST HELL   738 JERUSALEM 91       41
```
ASTRAY
```
  AH WEAK & WIDE ASTRAY AH SHUT IN NARROW DOLEFUL FORM   .  484 MILTON 5        19
  SEES THE MOON TERRIFIED AS ONE LED ASTRAY IN THE MIDST   619A ILLUS MILTON    PROSE
    OF HER PATH
  SHOULD I PITY IF I PITY NOT THE SINNER WHO IS GONE ASTRAY  657 JERUSALEM 31       35
  AH WEAK & WIDE ASTRAY AH SHUT IN NARROW DOLEFUL FORM   . .  679 JERUSALEM 49       32
```
ASTROLOGER
```
  PROPERTY OF AN ASTROLOGER & TO COMMIT HIM TO PRISON THE MAN 865A LETTER 62       PROSE
```
ASTROLOGY
```
  PHRASEOLOGY (THEOLOGY) MYTHOLOGY ASTROLOGY OSTEOLOGY   . .  46D ISLAND MOON 3    *PROSE
```
ASTRONOMICAL
```
  THY SUBSTANTIAL ASTRONOMICAL TELESCOPIC HEAVENS  . . . . 788D ANNO THORNTON      MARG
```
ASTRONOMY
```
  PAINTING PERSPECTIVE GEOMETRY GEOGRAPHY ASTRONOMY   . . .  46D ISLAND MOON 3    PROSE
```
ASUNDER
```
  WIDE ASUNDER ROLLING  . . . . . . . . . . . . .  225 URIZEN 5        6
  FELL ASUNDER AND HORRIBLE VACUUM  . . . . . . . . .  257 BOOK OF LOS 4        25
  O HOW LOS HOWLD AT THE RENDING ASUNDER ALL THE FIBRES RENT  299 FOUR ZOAS 4       59
  CRYING AS I WILL I REND THE NATIONS ALL ASUNDER RENDING   334 FOUR ZOAS 7B      50
  RENT THEM ASUNDER AND WRATH WAS LEFT TO WRATH & PITY TO   490 MILTON 9        47
    PITY
  THEN I REND THEE ASUNDER THEN I HOWL OVER THY CLAY & ASHES  499 MILTON 18       33
```

		PAGE	TITLE	LINE

ASUNDER   (CONTINUED)
    THE OBDURATE FORMS ARE CUT ASUNDER BY JEALOUSY & PITY   .   .   689 JERUSALEM 58   12
    BUT THEY CUT ASUNDER HIS INNER GARMENTS SEARCHING WITH   .   .   702 JERUSALEM 66   27
    ASUNDER & OPPOSED TO THOUGHT TO DRAW JERUSALEM'S SONS   .   .   715 JERUSALEM 74   29
    AMONG THE DARKNESS OF HIS FURNACES DIVIDING ASUNDER TILL   732 JERUSALEM 86   56
    ARE THE BLASPHEMOUS SELFHOODS & MUST BE BROKEN ASUNDER   .   .   736 JERUSALEM 90   33
    SO SAYING THE CLOUD OVERSHADOWING DIVIDED THEM ASUNDER   .   .   743 JERUSALEM 96   29
ASYLUM
    TO THE DETESTABLE GODS OF PRIAM TO APOLLO AND AT THE ASYLUM   511 MILTON 25   49
AT-ALL
    NEVER STRUCK ME AT ONCE NOR AT-ALL   .   .   .   . 448B ANNO REYNOLDS   MARG
ATCHIEVD
    BUT THIS IS NOT TO BE ATCHIEVD .   .   .   .   824B LETTER 27   PROSE
ATCHIEVEMENT
    MIGHTY ATCHIEVEMENT OF YOUR POWER BEWARE THE PUNISHMENT   272 FOUR ZOAS 1   289
    I CONGRATULATE YOU NOT ON ANY ATCHIEVEMENT   .   .   .   .   . 790B LETTER 2   PROSE
ATHEISM
    AN ATHEIST PRETENDING TO TALK AGAINST ATHEISM   .   .   .   . 404A ANNO BACON   MARG
    PRAISE OF ATHEISM   .   .   .   . 404B ANNO BACON   MARG
    ATHEISM IS THUS THE BEST OF ALL BACON FOOLS US   .   .   .   . 404B ANNO BACON   MARG
    SUCH IS THE END OF EPICUREAN OR NEWTONIAN PHILOSOPHY IT   475D ANNO REYNOLDS   MARG
      IS ATHEISM
ATHEIST
    BACON WAS A CONTEMPLATIVE ATHEIST EVIDENTLY AN EPICUREAN   403C ANNO BACON   MARG
    AN ATHEIST PRETENDING TO TALK AGAINST ATHEISM   .   .   .   . 404A ANNO BACON   MARG
ATHEISTICAL
    BY THE ATHEISTICAL EPICUREAN PHILOSOPHY OF ALBION'S TREE   704 JERUSALEM 67   13
ATHENS
    WAS SHEWN THE HOLY CITY THEN ATHENS LEARNING   .   .   .   .   41A THEN SHE BORE   PROSE
ATHLETIC
    MALE FORMD THE DEMON MILD ATHLETIC FORCE HIS SHOULDERS   380 FOUR ZOAS AD 1   11
      SPREAD
ATLANTEAN
    NOW BARRD OUT BY THE ATLANTIC SEA CALLD ATLANTEAN HILLS   200 AMERICA 10   6
ATLANTIC
    FROM THE ATLANTIC MOUNTAINS .   .   .   .   138 FRENCH REVOLTN   90
    NOW BARRD OUT BY THE ATLANTIC SEA   .   .   .   . 159B SONG LIBERTY   PROSE
    SULLEN FIRES ACROSS THE ATLANTIC GLOW TO AMERICA'S SHORE   197 AMERICA 3   2
    WASHINGTON SPOKE FRIENDS OF AMERICA LOOK OVER THE ATLANTIC   197 AMERICA 3   6
      SEA
    SOLEMN HEAVE THE ATLANTIC WAVES BETWEEN THE GLOOMY NATIONS   197 AMERICA 4   2
    RED ROSE THE CLOUDS FROM THE ATLANTIC IN VAST WHEELS OF   197 AMERICA 4   6
      BLOOD
    AND IN THE RED CLOUDS ROSE A WONDER OER THE ATLANTIC SEA   197 AMERICA 4   7
    OF TRUMPETS BLEW A LOUD ALARM ACROSS THE ATLANTIC DEEP   .   . 200 AMERICA 10   2
    NOW BARRD OUT BY THE ATLANTIC SEA CALLD ATLANTEAN HILLS   200 AMERICA 10   6
    FOR CLOUDS FROM THE ATLANTIC HOVER OER THE SOLEMN ROOF   .   . 200 AMERICA 10   12
    DARKEND THE ATLANTIC MOUNTAINS & THEIR TRUMPETS SHOOK THE   201 AMERICA 13   14
      VALLEYS
    THEN HAD AMERICA BEEN LOST OERWHELMD BY THE ATLANTIC   .   . 202 AMERICA 14   17
    HE OPEND ON THE DEEP AND ON THE ATLANTIC SEA WHITE   203 AMERICA 16   10
      SHIVRING
    SULLEN FIRES ACROSS THE ATLANTIC GLOW TO AMERICA'S SHORE   203 AMERICA CANC A   2
    WASHINGTON SPOKE FRIENDS OF AMERICA LOOK OVER THE ATLANTIC   204 AMERICA CANC A   6
      SEA
    WITH CLOUDS OF SMOKE FROM THE ATLANTIC THAT IN VOLUMES   204 AMERICA CANC B   11
      ROLLD
    HE SAW URIZEN ON THE ATLANTIC   .   .   .   .   242 EUROPE 11   2
    DARING MY POWER WILT ARM MY SONS AGAINST ME IN THE [DEEP]   278 FOUR ZOAS 1   510
      ATLANTIC
    ALBION GAVE HIS LOUD DEATH GROAN THE ATLANTIC MOUNTAINS   281 FOUR ZOAS 2   41
      TREMBLED
    .   .   .   ATLANTIC FOR A CURSE AND HIDDEN HORROR   .   .   . 294 FOUR ZOAS 3   105
    DEATH COUCH IN THE CAVERNS OF DEATH IN THE CORNER OF THE   489 MILTON 9   3
      ATLANTIC
    LO ORC ARISES ON THE ATLANTIC LO HIS BLOOD AND FIRE   .   . 506 MILTON 23   6
    HE WEEPS INTO THE ATLANTIC DEEP YET STILL IN DISMAL DREAMS   506 MILTON 23   9
    FROM THE ATLANTIC TO THE GREAT SOUTH SEA THE ERYTHREAN   .   . 518 MILTON 29   63
    ORC HOWLS ON THE ATLANTIC ENITHARMON TREMBLES ALL BEULAH   520 MILTON 31   27
      WEEPS
    OF DEATH ACROSS THE ATLANTIC TO AMERICA NORTH & SOUTH   .   . 525 MILTON 35   17
    ON THE GREAT ATLANTIC MOUNTAINS .   .   .   .   558 THE CAVERNS/N   18
    THE GIANT ALBION WAS PATRIARCH OF THE ATLANTIC   .   .   .   . 578C DESC CAT 5   PROSE
    OUR ANCESTOR PATRIARCH OF THE ATLANTIC CONTINENT   .   .   . 609C V LAST JUDG/N   PROSE
    IN ALL THE DARK ATLANTIC VALE DOWN FROM THE HILLS OF SURREY   622 JERUSALEM 4   9
    AND CAST IT INTO THE ATLANTIC DEEP TO CATCH THE SOULS OF   646 JERUSALEM 23   23
      THE DEAD
    JERUSALEM COVERD THE ATLANTIC MOUNTAINS & THE ERYTHREAN   648 JERUSALEM 24   46
    KNOT DAY BY DAY NIGHT BY NIGHT LOUD ROLL THE INDIGNANT   648 JERUSALEM 24   62
      ATLANTIC
    AND ALL THE ATLANTIC MOUNTAINS SHOOK   .   .   .   .   .   .   650 FIELDS FROM/J   36
    ALBION THE HIGH CLIFF OF THE ATLANTIC IS BECOME A BARREN   660 JERUSALEM 34   16
      LAND
    THE ATLANTIC CONTINENT SUNK ROUND ALBION'S CLIFFY SHORE   663 JERUSALEM 36   39
    THE NARROW SEA BETWEEN ALBION & THE ATLANTIC CONTINENT   .   . 674 JERUSALEM 44   14
    AND MANY SORROWS OBLIQUE ACROSS THE ATLANTIC VALE   .   .   . 678 JERUSALEM 48   32
    COME & MOURN OVER ALBION THE WHITE CLIFF OF THE ATLANTIC   679 JERUSALEM 49   6
    IN ONE NIGHT THE ATLANTIC CONTINENT WAS CAUGHT UP WITH   679 JERUSALEM 49   19
      THE MOON
    THE ATLANTIC MOUNTAINS WHERE GIANTS DWELT IN INTELLECT   .   . 681 JERUSALEM 50   1
    OF THE ATLANTIC WHICH POURED IN IMPETUOUS LOUD LOUD LOUDER   689 JERUSALEM 57   4
      & LOUDER

149

```
                                                          PAGE      TITLE       LINE
ATLANTIC    (CONTINUED)
        AND THE GREAT VOICE OF THE ATLANTIC HOWLED OVER THE DRUID   689 JERUSALEM 57     5
          ALTARS
        FOR THE VEIL OF VALA WHICH ALBION CAST INTO THE ATLANTIC    691 JERUSALEM 59     2
          DEEP
        JOIND WITH CORDELLA SHE SHINES SOUTHWARD OVER THE ATLANTIC  710 JERUSALEM 71    43
        FROM THE ATLANTIC SEA TO THE UNIVERSAL ERYTHREAN  . . . .   727 JERUSALEM 83    22
        ACROSS THE ATLANTIC TO FRANCE . . . . . . . . . . .         799 TO FLAXMAN/L    10
ATLAS
        ORC ON MOUNT ATLAS HOWLD CHAIND DOWN WITH THE CHAIN OF      246 SONG OF LOS 3    21
          JEALOUSY
        HE IS THE ATLAS OF THE GREEKS  . . . . . . . .             578C DESC CAT 5     PROSE
ATMOSPHERE
        [?WHILE] THRO THE CLEAR CHANGING ATMOSPHERE . . .           274 FOUR ZOAS 1   * 367
        A THREEFOLD ATMOSPHERE SUBLIME CONTINUOUS . . . . .         329 FOUR ZOAS 7     382
        THEREFORE THE NATURAL EARTH & ATMOSPHERE IS A PHANTASY .    94D ANNO SWED LOVE  MARG
        SURROUNDED HEAT BUT NOT LIGHT WENT THRO THE MURKY           197 AMERICA 4       11
          ATMOSPHERE
        TO EXHALE THE SPIRITS OF LUVAH & VALA THRO THE ATMOSPHERE   372 FOUR ZOAS 9     570
ATMOSPHERES
        OVER ANOTHER KIND OF SEAS AND IN ATMOSPHERES UNKNOWN   .    192 V DAU ALBION 4   18
        FIRST SPUN THEN WOVE THE ATMOSPHERES THERE THE SPIDER &     284 FOUR ZOAS 2     146
          WORM
        THE IMMORTAL ATMOSPHERES ARE THINE THERE THOU ART SEEN      291 FOUR ZOAS 3       8
          IN GLORY
        OF JEALOUSY AND THOUGHT IT A POETIC VISION OF THE           698 JERUSALEM 63     40
          ATMOSPHERES
ATOM
        IN DREADFUL DOLOR & PAIN & I AM LIKE AN ATOM  . . . . .     265 FOUR ZOAS 1      61
        SHE ALSO TOOK AN ATOM OF SPACE & OPEND ITS CENTER   . . .   270 FOUR ZOAS 1   * 225
        THE WHOLE EXTENT OF THE GLOBE IS EXPLORED EVERY SCATTERD    510 MILTON 25        18
          ATOM
        SHE ALSO TOOK AN ATOM OF SPACE WITH DIRE PAIN OPENING IT    678 JERUSALEM 48     38
          A CENTER
        BY NEWTON'S DOCTRINE OF THE FLUXIONS OF AN ATOM A THING    878A LETTER 88      PROSE
          THAT
        THAT REPUBLICAN ART IS INIMICAL TO THEIR ATOM  . . . . .   878A LETTER 88      PROSE
ATOMIC
        CALLING THE ROCKS ATOMIC ORIGINS OF EXISTENCE DENYING       704 JERUSALEM 67     12
          ETERNITY
ATOMS
        THE ATOMS OF DEMOCRITUS  . . . . . . . . . . . . .          418 MOCK ON/N         9
ATONE
        TO ATONE FOR YOU FOR SPIRITUAL DEATH MAN LIVES BY DEATHS    670 JERUSALEM 42     49
          OF MEN
ATONEMENT
        AND I HAVE MURDERD THEM WITH CRUELTY ABOVE ATONEMENT   . .  268 FOUR ZOAS 1   * 166
        BECAME ITS PREY A CURSE AN OFFERING AND AN ATONEMENT   . .  481 MILTON 2        13
        BY OFFERING & ATONEMENT IN THE (CRUELTIES) OF MORAL LAW     484 MILTON 5        12
        CHARLES CALLS ON MILTON FOR ATONEMENT CROMWELL IS READY     485 MILTON 5        39
        FOR ATONEMENT ALBION BEGAN TO ERECT TWELVE ALTARS   . . .   653 JERUSALEM 28    21
        MUST THE WISE DIE FOR AN ATONEMENT DOES MERCY ENDURE        666 JERUSALEM 39    25
          ATONEMENT
        OF GENERATION TO DESTROY BY SIN AND ATONEMENT HAPPY         676 JERUSALEM 46    27
          JERUSALEM
        JEHOVAH LO I HAVE GIVEN YOU A LAMB FOR AN ATONEMENT INSTEAD 780 GHOST ABEL 2    10
        AND NO ATONEMENT O JEHOVAH THE ELOHIM LIVE ON SACRIFICE     780 GHOST ABEL 2    14
ATONEMENTS
        ALL THE ATONEMENTS OF JEHOVAH SPURND . . . . . . .          543 IF TRUE/N        13
ATOSSA
        THE VISION OF ATOSSA FROM ESCHYLUS APPARITION OF DARIUS    848D LETTER 45      PROSE
ATROCIOUS
        FOR TIS [MOST WICKED] ATROCIOUS IN A FRIEND YOU LOVE   . .  551 WILLM COWPER/N    9
ATTACHD
        FINISHD STATE I AM TOO MUCH ATTACHD TO DANTE TO THINK MUCH 879C LETTER 89      PROSE
ATTACHING
        ATTACHING HIMSELF WHOLLY TO THE SALE OF FINE EDITIONS OF    831C LETTER 31     PROSE
ATTACK
        ELSE HE WOULD NEVER DARE TO ATTACK US NOW  . . . . .         24 EDW THIRD/PS 3   141
        ATTACK BUT IT IS NOT SO EASY FOR ONE WHO LOVES THE BIBLE    383B ANNO WATSON     MARG
        OUR EMANATIONS AND TO ATTACK OUR SECRET SUPREME DELIGHTS    664 JERUSALEM 37       9
        I LOOK UPON THIS AS A MOST MALIGNANT & ARTFUL ATTACK   . . 786C ANNO THORNTON   MARG
        SUNDAY AT HAMPSTEAD AS I FEAR THE ATTACK AGAIN  . . . .    872C LETTER 75      PROSE
        DESPERATE ATTACK OF THE ANGUISH (&) TREMBLING LAST NIGHT & SUPP LETTER 81A     *PROSE
ATTACKD
        TALK WITH THE HUSBANDMAN & SHEPHERD BUT THESE ATTACKD HIM   315 FOUR ZOAS 6     138
          SORE
        THE PERVERSIONS OF CHRIST'S WORDS & ACTS ARE ATTACKD   . . 383B ANNO WATSON     MARG
ATTACKED
        ("ALL CHRISTIAN STATES") PAINE HAS NOT ATTACKED            383D ANNO WATSON     MARG
          CHRISTIANITY
        SHIVERING FIT ATTACKED ME AGAIN & THE PAIN WITH ITS  . . . 872B LETTER 75      PROSE
ATTACKS
        SEIZES THE FRUITS OF TIME ATTACKS EXPERIENCE  . . . . .      27 EDW THIRD/PS 3   255
        TOMORROW MORNING THESE ATTACKS ARE TOO SERIOUS AT THE TIME 869B LETTER 69      PROSE
        VERY CONSIDERABLY WEAKEND BY THE LAST SEVERE ATTACKS  . .  873D LETTER 78      *PROSE
ATTAIN
        WITH MARROW SINEWS & FLESH EXALT THYSELF ATTAIN A VOICE     275 FOUR ZOAS 1     405
        CIRCLE OER CIRCLE NOR ON HIGH ATTAIN A VOID  . . . . .      316 FOUR ZOAS 6     197
ATTEMPT
        WHOSE SONG CALLD MILTON TO THE ATTEMPT AND LOS HEARD THESE  504 MILTON 21        34
          LAMENTS
```

```
                                                   PAGE    TITLE           LINE
ATTEMPT    (CONTINUED)
    YOU DONT BELIEVE I [WOUD] WON'T ATTEMPT TO MAKE YE  . . .  536 DONT BELIEVE/N *    1
    YOU ARE ASLEEP I WON'T ATTEMPT TO WAKE YE  . . . . .  536 DONT BELIEVE/N      2
    YOU ATTEMPT TO FINISH OR IMPROVE & WHEN YOU HAVE BEGUN  .  593D PUB ADDRESS/N  PROSE
    ATTEMPT TO EXPRESS YOUR & OUR MUCH BELOVED'S COUNTENANCE   796C LETTER 8       PROSE
    I TRANSMIT TO MRS BUTTS AN ATTEMPT [TO] AT YOUR LIKENESS   808D LETTER 20      *PROSE
    NEITHER OUGHT ANY ONE TO ATTEMPT IT  . . . . . . . .  824C LETTER 27      PROSE
    ATTEMPT SHOULD BE MADE TO REFUSE ME THIS I AM INFLEXIBLE   826A LETTER 27      PROSE
    SHOWED ME ROMNEY'S FIRST ATTEMPT AT OIL PAINTING  . . .  843C LETTER 43      PROSE
ATTEMPTED
    I ATTEMPTED EVERY MORNING FOR A FORTNIGHT TOGETHER        792A LETTER 4       PROSE
      TO FOLLOW
    & SHOULD NEVER HAVE ATTEMPTED TO LIVE BY ANY THING ELSE    794C LETTER 5       PROSE
    SHOULD THEY EVER BE ATTEMPTED WHAT HE CAN & I KNOW  . .  853A LETTER 51      *PROSE
ATTEMPTEST
    WHEN THOU ATTEMPTEST TO PUT ON THE HUMAN FORM MY WRATH  .  499 MILTON 18        31
ATTEMPTING
    ENSLAVD THE VULGAR BY ATTEMPTING TO REALIZE OR ABSTRACT THE  153A MARRIAGE HH 11  PROSE
    ATTEMPTING TO BE MORE THAN MAN WE BECOME LESS SAID LUVAH   376 FOUR ZOAS 9       709
ATTEMPTS
    HIS PRIMITIVE TYRANNICAL ATTEMPTS ON LOS WITH MOST        486 MILTON 7          7
      ENDEARING LOVE
    YOUR DICTATE BUT WHEN I FOUND MY ATTEMPTS WERE IN VAIN  .  792A LETTER 4       PROSE
    HIS IMBECILE ATTEMPTS TO DEPRESS ME ONLY DESERVE LAUGHTER  825C LETTER 27      PROSE
ATTEND
    I'LL WATCH YOU & ATTEND YOUR FOOTSTEPS YOU ARE NOT LIKE    368 FOUR ZOAS 9       430
      THE BIRDS
    AND SEVEN MORE LOVES ATTEND EACH NIGHT  . . . . . .  416 MY SPECTRE/N       41
    AND THREE PRIESTS HER GREYHOUNDS ATTEND HER  . . . . .  566D DESC CAT 3      PROSE
    & THREE PRIESTS HER GREYHOUNDS ATTEND HER  . . . . .  588B CHAUCER/N       PROSE
    AND THREE PRIESTS HER GREY-HOUNDS ATTEND HER  . . . . .  589D CHAUCER 2       PROSE
    THAT IT IS NOT ARTS THAT FOLLOW & ATTEND UPON [EMPIRES]    597A PUB ADDRESS/N  *PROSE
      EMPIRE
    THAT THE SPECTATOR WILL ATTEND TO THE HANDS & FEET  . .  611B V LAST JUDG/N   PROSE
    LABOUR WELL THE MINUTE PARTICULARS ATTEND TO THE         687 JERUSALEM 55      51
      LITTLE-ONES
    THIS I BEHOLD THE SHUDDERINGS OF DEATH ATTEND MY STEPS  .  714 JERUSALEM 74      18
    YOU AS SHERIFF ARE BOUND TO ATTEND TO IT  . . . . .  865B LETTER 62      PROSE
ATTENDANT
    ONE WHO IN WAR IS THE WORTHY ATTENDANT ON NOBLE HEROES  . .  568A DESC CAT 3      PROSE
    AND KENT AND THE OTHER ATTENDANT ARE ADMIRABLE  . . .  843D LETTER 43      PROSE
ATTENDANTS
    TO SUPPOSE THEM SUITABLE ATTENDANTS ON RANK AND FASHION    568C DESC CAT 3      PROSE
    COMMON RANK IN LIFE OR ATTENDANTS ON THOSE WHO WERE SO  .  568C DESC CAT 3      PROSE
ATTENDED
    SHE MONGST MEN WAS SENT AND WORSER ILLS ATTENDED HER BY FAR  43A THEN SHE BORE   PROSE
    PROVERBIALLY ATTENDED BY POVERTY AND OBSCURITY  . . . .  207A PRSPECTUS 1793  PROSE
    OF A BRIGHT UNIVERSE EMPERY ATTENDED DAY & NIGHT  . . .  264 FOUR ZOAS 1       15
    ATTENDED BY FAIRIES ONE TWO & THREE  . . . . . . .  434 WILLIAM BOND        6
    FILLED WITH EYES ATTENDED BY SEVEN ANGELS  . . . . .  444A LAST JUDGMNT/L  PROSE
    THO DARKEND AND THE SEVEN ANGELS OF THE PRESENCE ATTENDED  502 MILTON 20        14
      HIM
    FIRST RANK IN SOCIETY NOBLE RICH AND EXPENSIVELY ATTENDED  568C DESC CAT 3      PROSE
    THE REASON THEY HAVE NOT BEEN MORE ATTENDED TO IS  . .  581D DESC CAT 8      PROSE
    THE DAUGHTERS ATTENDED HER SHUDDERINGS WIPING THE DEATH    678 JERUSALEM 48      43
      SWEAT
ATTENDING
    ATTENDING HIS LOUD HARMONY WITH ADMIRATION & LOVE  . .  520 MILTON 31        44
    THE BARDS WHO WERE CAPABLE OF ATTENDING WARLIKE DEEDS  .  580C DESC CAT 5      PROSE
    IS HYMEN AT A MARRIAGE & THE ANTIQUE PAGEANTRY ATTENDING IT  618D ILLUS MILTON  PROSE
    AS ATTENDING ON THE HEAVEN OF JUPITER THE GREAT BEAR  .  619B ILLUS MILTON  PROSE
    SAT AT THE SHINING LOOM WITH HER SISTERS ATTENDING ROUND   691 JERUSALEM 59      27
ATTENDS
    BUT [EMPIRES] EMPIRE THAT ATTENDS UPON  . . . . . .  597A PUB ADDRESS/N  *PROSE
    ATTENDS HER AS HER GUARD & LOS'S EMANATION IS NAMED  .  655 JERUSALEM 30       3
ATTENTION
    TILL MUTE ATTENTION STRUCK MY [TREMBLING] LISTNING EAR  . .  43D WOE CRIED MUSE   PROSE
    SHE SEATED & [LISTEND] SEEMD TO LISTEN WITH GREAT ATTENTION  44B ISLAND MOON 1   PROSE
    AND THE POET IS A PHENOMENON WORTHY OF PUBLIC ATTENTION    207B PRSPECTUS 1793  PROSE
    THE ATTENTION OF MANY PERSONS OF EMINENCE AND FORTUNE  .  207C PRSPECTUS 1793  PROSE
    I HAVE READ THIS BOOK WITH ATTENTION & FIND THAT THE BISHOP  396B ANNO WATSON    MARG
    ACCOMODATION OF THOSE WHO GIVE IT THE HONOR OF ATTENTION   442D LAST JUDGMNT/L  PROSE
    [?THEIR VENETIAN ATTENTION IS TO A CONTEMPT & NEGLECT OF   463D ANNO REYNOLDS  * MARG
      FORM ITSELF
    THAT ABOUT IT WHICH MAY BE WORTHY THE ATTENTION  . . .  581C DESC CAT 7      PROSE
    THE WORKS OF THIS VISIONARY ARE WELL WORTHY THE ATTENTION   581D DESC CAT 8      PROSE
    BE WORTHY OF ATTENTION NOT ONLY ON ACCOUNT OF ITS        582B DESC CAT 9      PROSE
      COMPOSITION
    ATTENTION OF THE AMATEUR IN A LARGE [WORK] STROKE ENGRAVING  587D CHAUCER/N     *PROSE
    KNIGHT WHOSE SOLEMN GALLANTRY NO LESS FIXES ATTENTION  .  588C CHAUCER/N       PROSE
    MADE TO OCCUPY THE ATTENTION TO THE NEGLECT OF ALL REAL ART  602A PUB ADDRESS/N  PROSE
    ALL THE ATTENTION THAT A DAUGHTER COULD PAY TO A MOTHER    833D LETTER 33      PROSE
    ALL THE ENGRAVER'S NICEST ATTENTION INDEED IT IS         855A LETTER 53      PROSE
      MORE FINISHD
ATTENTIONS
    INCAPABLE OF MANY ATTENTIONS WHICH IT IS MY DUTY TO OBSERVE  816A LETTER 23      PROSE
ATTENTIVE
    ATTENTIVE ON THE MELANCHOLY SHORE  . . . . . . . .  32 EDW THIRD/PS 6      38
    THE LAWGIVER WAS VERY ATTENTIVE  . . . . . . . . .  57D ISLAND MOON 9   PROSE
    THOU IN THE SOUTH LISTEN ATTENTIVE IN SILENT OF THIS NIGHT  278 FOUR ZOAS 1       492
    FALSE THE ANCIENTS WERE CHIEFLY ATTENTIVE TO COMPLICATED   466B ANNO REYNOLDS  MARG
    A BARD BROKE FORTH ALL SAT ATTENTIVE TO THE AWFUL MAN  . .  482 MILTON 2         24
```

151

```
                                                            PAGE      TITLE            LINE
ATTENTIVE    (CONTINUED)
     BE ATTENTIVE BE OBEDIENT LO THE FURNACES ARE READY       627 JERUSALEM 8          9
       TO RECIEVE THEE
     THE TWELVE DAUGHTERS OF ALBION ATTENTIVE LISTEN IN SECRET 725 JERUSALEM 82        10
       SHADES
     THE NIGHT FALLS THICK I GO UPON MY WATCH BE ATTENTIVE  .  . 728 JERUSALEM 83       61
     HOLDING HIS IRON MACE THE SPECTRE REMAINS ATTENTIVE  .  .  729 JERUSALEM 83        78
     AS WAS SUPPOSED BY OUR KIND & ATTENTIVE FELLOW INHABITANT   833D LETTER 33       PROSE
ATTENTIVELY
     I HAVE READ THE BOOK THRO ATTENTIVELY AND WAS MUCH  .  .  . 845B LETTER 44       PROSE
ATTIRD
     SHE WENT OUT IN MORNING ATTIRD PLAIN & NEAT  .  .  .  .  .  428 MARY              33
ATTIRE
     NEGLECT THY HAIR TO SEEM MORE LOVELY IN THY LOOSE ATTIRE    38A SAMSON/PS       PROSE
     SHE WENT OUT IN MORNING IN PLAIN NEAT ATTIRE  .  .  .  .    428 MARY              35
ATTITUDES
     IN VARIOUS ATTITUDES OF DESPAIR & HORROR FALL THRO THE AIR  443C LAST JUDGMNT/L  PROSE
     & IN EXULTING ATTITUDES OF GREAT JOY TELL EACH OTHER   .    443D LAST JUDGMNT/L  PROSE
     BENEATH THEM ARE VARIOUS FIGURES IN ATTITUDES  .  .  .  .   608A V LAST JUDG/N   PROSE
ATTRACTED
     THE GOOD ARE ATTRACTED BY MEN'S PERCEPTIONS  .  .  .  .  .  183 MOTTO SONGS/N       1
     ATTRACTED BY THE REVOLUTIONS OF THOSE WHEELS THE CLOUD      624 JERUSALEM 5         61
       OF SMOKE
ATTRACTION
     . . . AND THE WORLD OF ATTRACTION IN HIS BOSOM  .  .  .  .  136 FRENCH REVOLTN      49
     WITHOUT CONTRARIES IS NO PROGRESSION ATTRACTION AND        149B MARRIAGE HH 3    PROSE
       REPULSION
     EARTH WAS NOT NOR GLOBES OF ATTRACTION  .  .  .  .  .  .    223 URIZEN 3            36
     DRAWS ALL INTO A FOUNTAIN AT THE ROCK OF THY ATTRACTION     312 FOUR ZOAS 6         14
     ("NO ATTRACTION UNLESS IT WARMS") OR FREEZES ("THE         411C ANNO BOYD        MARG
       HEART")
ATTRACTIONS
     FEELINGS WILL BE ATTRACTIONS OR REPULSES SEE APHORISMS...    87A ANNO LAVATER    MARG
ATTRACTIVE
     DOWNWARD TIS SUNK BENEATH TH ATTRACTIVE NORTH THAT ROUND    242 EUROPE 10          30
       THE FEET
     THOU TERRIBLE WOMAN CLAD IN BLUE WHOSE STRONG ATTRACTIVE    312 FOUR ZOAS 6         13
       POWER
     ART THOU THE COLD ATTRACTIVE POWER THAT HOLDS ME IN THIS    323 FOUR ZOAS 7        146
       CHAIN
     SOUND THE WAR TRUMPET TERRIFIC SOULS CLAD IN ATTRACTIVE     336 FOUR ZOAS 7B      147
       STEEL
     ATTRACTIVE OF HIS HAMMER'S BEATING & THE SILVER LOOMS  .  . 344 FOUR ZOAS 8       113
ATTRIBUTE
     TO WHAT DOES THE BISHOP ATTRIBUTE THE ENGLISH CRUSADE  .    385C ANNO WATSON     MARG
     WILL ATTRIBUTE IT TO ITS RIGHT CAUSE INTELLECTUAL          876B LETTER 83       PROSE
       PECULIARITY
ATTRIBUTED
     IS FALSE WHEN IT IS ATTRIBUTED TO A WRONG AUTHOR HES A FOOL 391B ANNO WATSON     MARG
     THUS IF I AM A PAINTER IT IS NOT TO BE ATTRIBUTED          794C LETTER 5        PROSE
       TO SEEKING AFTER
ATTRIBUTES
     THE ETERNAL ATTRIBUTES OR DIVINE NAMES WHICH  .  .  .  .    571C DESC CAT 3      PROSE
     THOSE WHO DARE APPROPRIATE TO THEMSELVES UNIVERSAL          736 JERUSALEM 90       32
       ATTRIBUTES
     GOD CAN ONLY BE KNOWN BY HIS ATTRIBUTES  .  .  .  .  .  .   752 EV GOSPEL(D)/N     44
AUDACITY
     ARE NO TRIFLES THEY ARE ALWAYS THOUGH UTTERED WITH AUDACITY 569D DESC CAT 3      PROSE
AUDIBLE
     AND THEN THE STORMS BECOME VISIBLE AUDIBLE & TERRIBLE  .  . 507 MILTON 23          25
AUDIENCE
     "FIT AUDIENCE FIND THO FEW" MILTON  .  .  .  .  .  .  .  .  560C EXHIBITION ADV   PROSE
AUDLEY
     SIR WALTER MANNY LORD AUDLEY LORD PERCY  .  .  .  .  .  .    17C EDW THIRD/PS     TITLE
     SCENE AT CRESSEY SIR THOMAS DAGWORTH AND LORD AUDLEY        21C EDW THIRD/PS 3 *PROSE
       MEETING
     WHY MY LORD AUDLEY I DONT KNOW  .  .  .  .  .  .  .  .  .    21 EDW THIRD/PS 3       6
     TO-MORROW WE SHALL KNOW I SAY LORD AUDLEY  .  .  .  .  .     22 EDW THIRD/PS 3      22
AUGHT    SEE OUGHT   (NOUN OR ADVERB)
     NOR COULD CONCEAL AUGHT THAT MIGHT APPEASE HER THEN  .  .   39B SAMSON/PS        PROSE
     LOOK KNOWST THOU AUGHT OF THIS GREY BEARD OR OF THESE      104 TIRIEL 4            44
       BLINDED EYES
     IS AUGHT BUT DEATH IN INDIVIDUAL WEAKNESS SORROW & PAIN     346 FOUR ZOAS 8       199
     MY DYING LIMBS THEREFORE O MANHOOD IF THOU ART AUGHT  .  .  646 JERUSALEM 23       36
AUGMENT
     OF HIS ETERNAL DAY & MEMORY STRIVES TO AUGMENT HIS         352 FOUR ZOAS 8       455
       RUTHFULNESS
     AND THAT HIS WISDOM SERVD BUT TO AUGMENT THE INDEFINITE     353 FOUR ZOAS 8       466
       LUST
     TO AUGMENT WITH SWEET SMILES ALL THE JOYS OF THE NIGHT  .   428 MARY              10
AUGMENTED
     SURROUNDED BY HIS DARK MACHINES FOR ORC AUGMENTED SWIFT     342 FOUR ZOAS 8        67
     A LONG SERPENT IN THE ABYSS OF THE SPECTRE WHICH AUGMENTED  685 JERUSALEM 54       29
AUGMENTING
     TO LISP OUT WORDS & SOON IN MASCULINE STRENGTH AUGMENTING   267 FOUR ZOAS 1       125
       HE
     BUT HE SAW ORC A SERPENT FORM AUGMENTING TIMES ON TIMES     342 FOUR ZOAS 8        65
AUGURIES
     AUGURIES OF INNOCENCE  .  .  .  .  .  .  .  .  .  .  .  .  . 431A AUGURIES        TITLE
AUGUST
     SOUTH MOLTON STREET SUNDAY AUGUST...  .  .  .  .  .  .  .  . 440D MEMORANDUM/N 5  PROSE
```

		PAGE	TITLE	LINE
AUGUSTUS				
	("WILL") SO YOU SEE THAT GOD IS JUST SUCH A TYRANT AS AUGUSTUS CAESAR	788C	ANNO THORNTON	* MARG
	OUR FATHER AUGUSTUS CAESAR WHO ART IN THESE	788D	ANNO THORNTON	* MARG
AUMONT				
	. . . WHEN AUMONT WHOSE CHAOS-BORN SOUL	141	FRENCH REVOLTN	159
	AUMONT WENT OUT AND STOOD IN THE HOLLOW PORCH	133	FRENCH REVOLTN	198
	THE PALE FIRES OF AUMONT INTO THE CHAMBER	143	FRENCH REVOLTN	203
AUNT				
	[AND TIS ENGLISH POLITENESS AS FAIR AS [YOUR] MY AUNT]	542	FLORENTINE/N	* 10
AURICULAR				
	IN EDEN IN THE AURICULAR NERVES OF HUMAN LIFE	264	FOUR ZOAS 1	17
	. . . GATE OF [AURICULAR POWER] THE TONGUE [NERVES] IN TREMBLING FEAR	267	FOUR ZOAS 1	* 108
AUSPICES				
	UNDER THE AUSPICES OF SHAKESPEARE & JOHNSON (JONSON) IN WHICH	618D	ILLUS MILTON	PROSE
AUTHENTIC				
	THE COSTUME IS CORRECT ACCORDING TO AUTHENTIC MONUMENTS	567D	DESC CAT 3	PROSE
	THE COSTUME IS CORRECT ACCORDING TO AUTHENTIC MONUMENTS	590D	CHAUCER 2	PROSE
AUTHOR				
	THE AUTHOR IS AN ERRANT BLOCKHEAD	44D	ISLAND MOON 1	PROSE
	THE AUTHOR & PRINTER W BLAKE	97A	NAT RELIGION 1	*TITLE
	SONGS OF INNOCENCE THE AUTHOR & PRINTER W BLAKE . . .	111A	SONGS OF INNOC	TITLE
	THE BOOK OF THEL THE AUTHOR & PRINTER WILLM BLAKE...	127A	BOOK OF THEL	TITLE
	THIS DIFFICULTY HAS BEEN OBVIATED BY THE AUTHOR OF THE .	207B	PRSPECTUS 1793	PROSE
	THE AUTHOR IS SURE OF HIS REWARD	207B	PRSPECTUS 1793	PROSE
	IN HAND ARE ASKED FOR NONE ARE WANTED BUT THE AUTHOR .	208A	PRSPECTUS 1793	PROSE
	SONGS OF EXPERIENCE THE AUTHOR & PRINTER W BLAKE . .	210B	SONGS OF EXPER	TITLE
	NOR KNEW THE SOURCE OF HIS OWN BUT THOUGHT HIMSELF THE SOLE AUTHOR	324	FOUR ZOAS 7	159
	THE FIRST AUTHOR OF THIS WAR & THE DISTRACTING OF HONEST MINDS	361	FOUR ZOAS 9	153
	IS FALSE WHEN IT IS ATTRIBUTED TO A WRONG AUTHOR HES A FOOL	391B	ANNO WATSON	MARG
	BUT HE SAYS THAT MOSES BEING PROVED NOT THE AUTHOR OF .	391B	ANNO WATSON	MARG
	MOSES IS NOT THE AUTHOR & THEN THE BISHOP LOSES HIS AUTHOR	391C	ANNO WATSON	MARG
	THE AUTHOR & PRINTER W BLAKE...	480A	MILTON	TITLE
	SHE SPAKE I AM THE AUTHOR OF THIS SIN BY MY SUGGESTION .	492	MILTON 11	35
	TO THE AUTHOR AND HE THINKS WILL PROVE TO ANY DISCERNING EYE	585D	DESC CAT 16	PROSE
	THE ENTHUSIASM OF THE FOLLOWING POEM THE AUTHOR HOPES .	620D	JERUSALEM 3	PROSE
	KNOWING HIMSELF THE AUTHOR OF THEIR DIVISIONS & SHRINKINGS GRATIFIED	733	JERUSALEM 88	35
	RESOLVD TO SHEW AN INDEPENDENCE WHICH I KNOW WILL PLEASE AN AUTHOR	792A	LETTER 4	PROSE
	REVD MR GILPIN AUTHOR OF A WORK ON PICTURESQUE SCENERY .	814B	LETTER 23	PROSE
	THEIR AUTHOR AND GRATEFUL TO YOU MY EMPLOYER & THAT I LOOK	814D	LETTER 23	PROSE
	SEAGRAVE TOGETHER WITH THE AUTHOR & PUBLISHER & ALSO THE	857A	LETTER 54	PROSE
	WHAT THEIR AUTHOR IS KINDLY PLEASED TO CALL TALENTS FOR	860C	LETTER 56	PROSE
	THE AUTHOR WRITING	SUPP	ILLUS GRAY	*TITLE
	BEGUN...& PUBLISHD MARCH...BY THE AUTHOR & J LINNELL .	SUPP	LETTER 67F	*PROSE
AUTHORITY				
	TAKES AWAY THE AUTHORITY ALTOGETHER IT CEASES TO BE HISTORY	390D	ANNO WATSON	MARG
	BUT IN THIS I PLEAD THE AUTHORITY OF THE ANCIENTS WHO .	583D	DESC CAT 10	PROSE
	HE SPOKE WITH AUTHORITY NOT LIKE A SCRIBE	750	EV GOSPEL(C)/N	12
	HE SPOKE WITH AUTHORITY NOT LIKE A SCRIBE	751	EV GOSPEL(D)/N	16
AUTHORIZE				
	AUTHORIZE TO RECIEVE THEM THEY ARE SOMEWHAT BATTERD . . .	839D	LETTER 38	PROSE
AUTHORS				
	MR PHILLIPS HAS SENT A SMALL POEM HE WOULD NOT TELL THE AUTHOR'S NAME	845C	LETTER 44	PROSE
AUTHORS				
	BUT MORE NERVE IF BY ANCIENTS HE MEANS HEATHEN AUTHORS . .	397D	ANNO BACON	MARG
	FRIENDS WERE QUITE HARD TO FIND OLD AUTHORS SAY	546	ANOTHER/N 2	3
	NOT AUTHORS OF SUCH SUBLIME CONCEPTIONS THOSE	566A	DESC CAT 2	PROSE
	ANCIENT AUTHORS MUSIC AS IT EXISTS IN OLD TUNES OR MELODIES	579C	DESC CAT 5	PROSE
	UNFORTUNATELY OUR AUTHORS OF BOOKS ARE AMONG THIS CLASS HOW	795A	LETTER 6	PROSE
	ANY OTHER THAN THE SECRETARY THE AUTHORS ARE IN ETERNITY	825A	LETTER 27	PROSE
	AUTHORS AND CURIOUS BOOKS IN GENERAL HE ADVISES THAT SOME	831C	LETTER 31	PROSE
AUTOGRAPH				
	OF MR LEIGH HOW FAR IT IS AN AUTOGRAPH IS A QUESTION . .	781D	INSC UPCOTT	PROSE
	I DO NOT THINK AN ARTIST CAN WRITE AN AUTOGRAPH ESPECIALLY	781D	INSC UPCOTT	PROSE
	BUT AN AUTOGRAPH AS I UNDERSTAND IT IS WRIT HELTER SKELTER	781D	INSC UPCOTT	PROSE
	I CONSIDER THE AUTOGRAPH OF MR CRUICKSHANK WHICH VERY . .	782A	INSC UPCOTT	PROSE
AUTUMN				
	TO AUTUMN	2B	TO AUTUMN/PS	TITLE
	O AUTUMN LADEN WITH FRUIT AND STAINED	2	TO AUTUMN/PS	1
	THUS SANG THE JOLLY AUTUMN AS HE SAT	2	TO AUTUMN/PS	16
	DOWN LIKE A FALLING STAR FROM AUTUMN SKY	15	IMIT SPEN/PS	25
	. . . HIS WORDS FALL LIKE PURPLE AUTUMN ON THE SHEAVES . .	138	FRENCH REVOLTN	88
	ARE HEARD LIKE THUNDERS OF AUTUMN	223	URIZEN 3	34
	YELLOW AS LEAVES OF AUTUMN THE MYRIADS OF ANGELIC HOSTS	243	EUROPE 13	6
	TURNS INTO AUTUMN SUCH THE PERIOD OF MANY WORLDS . . .	287	FOUR ZOAS 2	281
	AND RAVEN NUMEROUS AS THE LEAVES OF AUTUMN EVERY SPECIES	363	FOUR ZOAS 9	238
	CAN SUCH CLOSED NOSTRILS FEEL A JOY OR TELL OF AUTUMN FRUITS	485	MILTON 5	32
	THE TWO SEASONS OF SPRING & AUTUMN	611C	V LAST JUDG/N	PROSE
	INVOLVING THE DIVINE VISION IN COLOURS OF AUTUMN RIPENESS	659	JERUSALEM 33	30
AUTUMNAL				
	THRO ALL THE IMMENSE BORNE DOWN BY CLOUDS SWAGGING IN AUTUMNAL HEAT	372	FOUR ZOAS 9	563

153

```
                                                            PAGE      TITLE         LINE
AVAIL
        SHALL NOW AVAIL YOU NOUGHT SO SPEAKING HE DASHD HIM WITH      364 FOUR ZOAS 9      277
          HIS FOOT
        O WHAT AVAIL THE LOVES & TEARS OF BEULAH'S LOVELY DAUGHTERS   624 JERUSALEM 5       54
        THY HOLY WRATH & DEEP DECEIT CANNOT AVAIL AGAINST ME    .   . 627 JERUSALEM 8       33
        THIS -- CITY I SHALL NOT BE ABLE TO AVAIL MYSELF OF THE       801B LETTER 13      PROSE
AVARICE
        ("IF YOUR TURN BE PROFUSE AVOID AVARICE") EXCELLENT    .    . 78B ANNO LAVATER     MARG
        AVARICE & CHASTITY DID SHITE IT    .   .   .   .   .   .   .  187 HEBREW NATN/N      2
AVAUNT
        AVAUNT COLD HYPOCRITE I AM CHAIND OR THOU COULDST NOT USE     323 FOUR ZOAS 7      142
          ME THUS
AVENGD
        [SHE SAID I AM AVENGD FOR ALL MY SUFFERINGS OF OLD]   .   .   324 FOUR ZOAS 7      178
AVENGE
        TO AVENGE THE WRONGS THY CHILDREN FEEL   .   .   .   .   .   . 430 GREY MONK        24
        BUT IF YOU AVENGE YOU MURDER THE DIVINE IMAGE   .   .   .   . 757D EV GOSPEL      PROSE
AVENGED
        IS MORE SEVERELY AVENGED THAN EVERY SIN & WICKEDNESS BESIDE   863A LETTER 60     PROSE
AVENGER
        O CRUEL O DESTROYER O CONSUMER O AVENGER   .   .   .   .   .  107 TIRIEL 6         23
        THE BRIDE AND WIFE OF THE LAMB O GOD THOU ART NOT             676 JERUSALEM 46      28
          AN AVENGER
        SHE WILL BECOME AN ETERNAL DEATH AN AVENGER OF SIN   .   .   681 JERUSALEM 50      15
        IS THE RELIGION OF THE ENEMY & AVENGER AND   .   .   .   .   682B JERUSALEM 52   PROSE
        VAIN IS THY COVENANT O JEHOVAH I AM THE ACCUSER & AVENGER     780 GHOST ABEL 1     12
AVERSE
        I AM NOT ASHAMED AFRAID OR AVERSE TO TELL YOU WHAT OUGHT      812A LETTER 22     PROSE
        SINCE HE IS AS MUCH AVERSE TO MY POETRY   .   .   .   .   .   825B LETTER 27     PROSE
AVERSION
        KNOWING YOUR AVERSION TO REVIEWS & REVIEWING I CONSIDER       841D LETTER 41     PROSE
AVERT
        FOR THESE A MAN SHOULD NEVER AVERT HIS THOUGHTS FROM    .   . 81A ANNO LAVATER     MARG
        DESCEND THEY COULD NOT NOR FROM EACH OTHER AVERT THEIR EYES   274 FOUR ZOAS 1      362
        HE MIGHT AVERT HIS OWN DESPAIR IN WOE & FEAR HE SAW   .   .   282 FOUR ZOAS 2       76
        INTO THEIR OWN DESTRUCTION IF PERHAPS HE MIGHT [INVERT]       344 FOUR ZOAS 8   *  138
          AVERT
        HE MIGHT AVERT HIS OWN DESPAIR IN WOE & FEAR HE SAW   .   .   626 JERUSALEM 7       34
AVIDITY
        APPROVED WITH AVIDITY POETRY CONSISTS IN THESE CONCEPTIONS    576B DESC CAT 4    PROSE
AVOCATIONS
        NONE THERE IS NO COMPARISON BETWEEN OUR NECESSARY            873C LETTER 77     PROSE
          AVOCATIONS
AVOID
        ALWAYS BE READY TO SPEAK YOUR MIND AND A BASE MAN WILL        151D MARRIAGE HH 8 PROSE
          AVOID YOU
        BROODING SHUT IN THE DEEP ALL AVOID   .   .   .   .   .   .   223 URIZEN 3         25
        DOTH ENION AVOID THE SIGHT OF THY BLUE WATRY EYES    .   .   339 FOUR ZOAS 7B      230
        DOTH ENION AVOID THE SIGHT OF THY BLUE HEAVENLY EYES    .   . 371 FOUR ZOAS 9      531
        BUT IN THE MORNING SHE ARISES TO AVOID MY EYES   .   .   .   371 FOUR ZOAS 9      543
        BECAUSE THEY AVOID IT AS A DESTRUCTIVE MACHINE AS IT IS       599A PUB ADDRESS/N PROSE
        FOR ALL TO AVOID THEE TO BE ASTONISHD AT THEE FOR THY SINS    658 JERUSALEM 31      62
        AND IN THE VISION & IN THE PROPHECY THAT WE MAY FORESEE       739 JERUSALEM 92      19
          & AVOID
        AND IS NOT YET COMPLETED I COULD NOT AVOID SAYING THUS MUCH   847A LETTER 44     PROSE
AVOIDED
        INTO AN ORNAMENT & AN EXAMPLE TO BE AVOIDED BY SOME   .   .   598C PUB ADDRESS/N PROSE
        THAT (SHIVERING) FIT WHICH MUST BE AVOIDED TILL THE COLD      871D LETTER 74     *PROSE
          IS GONE
AWA
        ABOUT FREEDOM & JENNY SUCK AWA    .   .   .   .   .   .   .   550 WHEN LOOK AT/N     4
AWAIT
        HER MAIDS AWAIT HER ON HER BED SHE FALLS   .   .   .   .   .   5 FAIR ELENOR/PS     37
        AND TIME AWAIT TO GIVE HIM ALL THAT THE WORLD CAN GIVE   .   586A DESC CAT 16    PROSE
AWAITING
        LOS STOOD BEFORE HIS FURNACES AWAITING THE FURY OF THE DEAD   671 JERUSALEM 42      55
AWAITS
        THAT AN ETERNAL LIFE AWAITS THE WORMS OF SIXTY WINTERS   .   240 EUROPE 5          6
AWAKE
        AWAKE THE DAWN THAT SLEEPS IN HEAVEN LET LIGHT   .   .   .   . 3 TO MORNING/PS      3
        TO AWAKE FROM SLUMBERS OF FIVE THOUSAND YEARS   .   .   .   . 134 FRENCH REVOLTN     8
        . . . I AWAKE BUT MY SOUL IS IN DREAMS   .   .   .   .   .   134 FRENCH REVOLTN     8
        TO AWAKE THE [PESTILENCE] PHYSICIANS THRO THE CITY   .   .   185 LET BROTHELS/N     3
        [XXX] SHAKING THE DUST FROM HIS IMMORTAL PINIONS TO AWAKE     190 V DAU ALBION 2 *  27
        OR WERT THOU NOT AWAKE WHEN ALL THIS MYSTERY WAS DISCLOSD     193 V DAU ALBION 6     9
        AND BEGAN TO AWAKE FROM SLEEP   .   .   .   .   .   .   .   . 233 URIZEN 20        27
        AND BEGAN TO AWAKE TO LIFE   .   .   .   .   .   .   .   .   . 233 URIZEN 20        29
        AWAKE THE THUNDERS OF THE DEEP   .   .   .   .   .   .   .   . 239 EUROPE 4         14
        THRICE HE ASSAYD PRESUMPTUOUS TO AWAKE THE DEAD TO JUDGMENT   243 EUROPE 13         3
        TO AWAKE BRIGHT URIZEN MY KING   .   .   .   .   .   .   .   . 254 AHANIA 5          7
        TO AWAKE MY KING IN THE MORN   .   .   .   .   .   .   .   .  254 AHANIA 5         10
        . . . TO ZION AWAKE O BROTHER MOUNTAIN   .   .   .   .   .   274 FOUR ZOAS 1      386
        TO DESOLATE THEIR CITIES MAN SHALL BE NO MORE AWAKE O HOSTS   275 FOUR ZOAS 1      407
        WALKED IN ROBES OF BLOOD TILL HE WHO SLEPT SHOULD AWAKE       287 FOUR ZOAS 2      265
        LIFT UP LIFT UP O LOS AWAKE MY WATCHMAN FOR HE SLEEPETH       335 FOUR ZOAS 7B      95
        AWAKE I HEAR THE FLAPPINGS OF THE FOLDING BANNERS    .   .   336 FOUR ZOAS 7B   *  149
        OF DEATH O NORTHERN DRUM AWAKE O HAND OF IRON SOUND    .   .  336 FOUR ZOAS 7B     154
        HE STOOD IN FAIR JERUSALEM TO AWAKE UP INTO EDEN   .   .   . 348 FOUR ZOAS 8      264
        AWAKE THE BRIDEGROOM COMETH I AWOKE TO SLEEP NO MORE    .   . 355 FOUR ZOAS 8      541
        A MIGHTY SOUND ARTICULATE AWAKE YE DEAD & COME   .   .   .   357 FOUR ZOAS 9       12
        TO JUDGMENT FROM THE FOUR WINDS AWAKE & COME AWAY    .   .   357 FOUR ZOAS 9       13
        THE POOR SMITE THEIR OPRESSORS THEY AWAKE UP TO THE HARVEST   357 FOUR ZOAS 9   *  19
```

	PAGE	TITLE	LINE

AWAKE   (CONTINUED)
```
        AND ALL THE WHILE THE TRUMPET SOUNDS [AWAKE YE DEAD & COME]   358 FOUR ZOAS 9        42
        THEIR OPPRESSORS ARE FALLN THEY HAVE STRICKEN THEM THEY       358 FOUR ZOAS 9    *   50
            AWAKE TO LIFE
        ETERNAL & I THRO HIM AWAKE FROM DEATH'S DARK VALE    . . .    362 FOUR ZOAS 9       207
        SHALL REFLOURISH THEN BRIGHT AHANIA SHALL AWAKE FROM DEATH    362 FOUR ZOAS 9       210
        AWAKE O ENION AWAKE & LET THINE _ 'OCENT EYES    . . . .      371 FOUR ZOAS 9       519
        ENLIGHTEN ALL THE CRYSTAL HOUSE OF VALA AWAKE AWAKE   . . .   371 FOUR ZOAS 9       520
        AWAKE THARMAS AWAKE AWAKE THOU CHILD OF DEWY TEARS    . .     371 FOUR ZOAS 9       521
        SOUNDING HIS TRUMPET TO AWAKE THE DEAD ON HIGH HE SOARD       373 FOUR ZOAS 9       615
        [UNTILL] WHEN [THE] HIS HUMANITY AWAKE   . . . . . . .        421 EACH MAN/N          3
        AWAKE AWAKE MY LITTLE BOY    . . . . . . . . . .              427 LAND OF DREAMS      1
        AWAKE THY FATHER DOES THEE KEEP   . . . . . . . .             427 LAND OF DREAMS      4
        AND KEPT ONLY THE FEMININE AWAKE HENCE ROSE HIS SOFT    . .   492 MILTON 12           6
        WITHIN HER BOSOM ALBION LIES EMBALMD NEVER TO AWAKE   . . .   501 MILTON 19          57
        AWAKE THOU SLEEPER ON THE ROCK OF ETERNITY ALBION AWAKE       506 MILTON 23           3
        THE TRUMPET OF JUDGMENT HATH TWICE SOUNDED ALL NATIONS        506 MILTON 23           4
            ARE AWAKE
        BUT THOU ART STILL HEAVY AND DULL AWAKE ALBION AWAKE    . .   506 MILTON 23           5
        AWAKE THE SUN FROM HIS SWEET REVERIE UPON THE MOUNTAIN  . .   520 MILTON 31          41
        TILL THEY AWAKE & SEE JESUS & THE LINEN CLOTHES LYING   . .   522 MILTON 32          42
        AWAKE ALBION AWAKE RECLAIM THY REASONING SPECTRE SUBDUE       530 MILTON 39          10
        LET THE FOUR ZOAS AWAKE FROM SLUMBERS OF SIX THOUSAND YEARS   530 MILTON 39          13
        ARISE AGAIN WITH TENFOLD SPLENDOR WHEN ARTHUR SHALL AWAKE     577B DESC CAT 5     TITLE
        WITH FOUR TRUMPETS TO AWAKE THE DEAD   . . . . . . .        . 609A V LAST JUDG/N  PROSE
        ARE OPEND & THE DEAD AWAKE & OBEY THE CALL OF THE TRUMPET     609C V LAST JUDG/N  PROSE
        THOSE ON THE RIGHT HAND AWAKE IN JOY THOSE ON THE LEFT        609C V LAST JUDG/N  PROSE
            IN HORROR
        AWAKE AWAKE O SLEEPER OF THE LAND OF SHADOWS WAKE EXPAND      622 JERUSALEM 4        6
        THAT I MAY AWAKE ALBION FROM HIS LONG & COLD REPOSE    . .    635 JERUSALEM 15      10
        THE DEAD AWAKE TO GENERATION ARISE O LORD & REND THE VEIL     656 JERUSALEM 30      40
        CLOTHD IN BLACK MOURNING UPON MY RIVER'S CURRENTS VALA        657 JERUSALEM 31      47
            AWAKE
        MUST PASS THRO CONDEMNATION AND AWAKE BEYOND THE GRAVE  . .   662 JERUSALEM 35      10
        AWAKE ALBION AWAKE AND LET US AWAKE UP TOGETHER      . . .    665 JERUSALEM 38      32
        ARISE AWAKE O FRIENDS OF THE GIANT ALBION    . . . . .       667 JERUSALEM 40      18
        WHEN HIS HUMANITY AWAKE    . . . . . . . . .       .         669 EACH MAN/J          3
        WE CANNOT AWAKE AND OUR SPECTRES RAGE IN THE FORESTS    .     671 JERUSALEM 42      73
        HAVE PASSED OVER THE DEAD TO AWAKE THE DEAD TO JUDGMENT       676 JERUSALEM 46      15
        AND NOW THE SPECTRES OF THE DEAD AWAKE IN BEULAH ALL    . .   708 JERUSALEM 69      32
        AS IN THE TIMES OF OLD O ALBION AWAKE REUBEN WANDERS    .     712 JERUSALEM 72      36
        TO AWAKE THE PRISONERS OF DEATH TO BRING ALBION AGAIN   .     716 JERUSALEM 75      25
        ENGLAND AWAKE AWAKE AWAKE   . . . . . . . . . .              718 ENGLND AWAKE/J      1
        AWAY & MIGHTY HYLE & AFTER THEM JERUSALEM IS GONE AWAKE       729 JERUSALEM 83      87
        O PITIOUS SLEEP O PITIOUS DREAM O GOD O GOD AWAKE             742 JERUSALEM 94      22
            I HAVE SLAIN
        AWAKE AWAKE JERUSALEM O LOVELY EMANATION OF ALBION    . . .   744 JERUSALEM 97       1
        AWAKE AND OVERSPREAD ALL NATIONS AS IN ANCIENT TIME   . . .   744 JERUSALEM 97       2
        APPEARS UPON OUR HILLS AWAKE JERUSALEM AND COME AWAY    .     744 JERUSALEM 97       4
        AWAKE ARISE TO SPIRITUAL STRIFE    . . . . . . . .           753 EV GOSPEL(D)/N     78
AWAKED
        ON THE RIGHT A YOUTHFUL COUPLE ARE AWAKED BY THEIR CHILDREN   609C V LAST JUDG/N  PROSE
        AN AGED PATRIARCH IS AWAKED BY HIS AGED WIFE HE IS ALBION     609C V LAST JUDG/N  PROSE
        AS SOON AS I AWAKED & I AM NOW IN BED BETTER & AS I THINK     869B LETTER 69      PROSE
AWAKEN
        THAT PINES FOR MAN SHALL AWAKEN HER WOMB TO ENORMOUS JOYS     194 V DAU ALBION 7     4
        TO WATCH THE TIME PITYING & GENTLE TO AWAKEN URIZEN    . . .  524 MILTON 34         43
AWAKEND
        AWAKEND VALA ARISTON RAN FORTH WITH BRIGHT ?ONANA     . . .   380 FOUR ZOAS AD 1 *   6
        OTHERS NEWLY AWAKEND FROM THE GRAVE   . . . . . . .          444A LAST JUDGMNT/L  PROSE
        AS ONE AWAKEND IN THE NIGHT THEY SAW THE LORD COMING    .     519 MILTON 31         15
        HE IS JUST AWAKEND OUT OF HIS GRAVE    . . . . . . .         608C V LAST JUDG/N  PROSE
AWAKENER
        THAT IT WAS MILTON THE AWAKENER THEY HAD NOT HEARD THE BARD   504 MILTON 21         33
        THE AWAKENER IS COME OUTSTRETCHD OVER EUROPE . . . . . .      510 MILTON 25         22
AWAKENING
        REVIVING SHAKE INSPIRING MOVE BREATHING AWAKENING     . . .   198 AMERICA 6          4
AWAKES
        BECAUSE I LOVE FOR I [AM] WAS LOVE [&] BUT HATRED AWAKES      282 FOUR ZOAS 2    *  104
            IN ME
        HE AWAKES THE SLEEPERS IN ULRO THE DAUGHTERS OF BEULAH       347 FOUR ZOAS 8    *  237
            PRAISE HIM
        SATAN NOW AWAKES SIN DEATH & HELL TO CELEBRATE WITH HIM      441D INSC FALL MAN  PROSE
        THE SOUL AWAKES AND WONDRING SEES    . . . . . . . .         442 DEDICATN BLAIR     5
        THE ANCIENT MAN UPON THE ROCK OF ALBION AWAKES    . . . .    510 MILTON 25         23
        THE EARTH BENEATH AWAKES AT THE LARK'S VOICE    . . . . .    618B ILLUS MILTON   PROSE
        AWAKES ME AT SUN-RISE THEN I SEE THE SAVIOUR OVER ME    . .   622 JERUSALEM 4        4
        WHEN HE SAYS THAT THE MUSE VISITS HIS SLUMBERS & AWAKES      792C LETTER 4       PROSE
        A PICTURE OF LEAR AND CORDELIA WHEN HE AWAKES AND KNOWS HER   843D LETTER 43      PROSE
AWAKEST
        WHEN THOU AWAKEST WILT THOU DISSEMBLE ALL THY SECRET JOYS     193 V DAU ALBION 6     8
        AND ON THE BED OF SILENCE SLEEP TILL THOU AWAKEST ME    .     290 FOUR ZOAS 2      378
        WHO AWAKEST FROM SLEEP    . . . . . . . . . . .             805 TO BUTTS/L        63
AWAKING    SEE NEVER-AWAKING
        IN THE SPIRIT OF THE MORNING AWAKING THE SOUL FROM ITS       367 FOUR ZOAS 9      394
            GRASSY BED
        [AWAKING FROM HIS STONY SLUMBER]   . . . . . . . .          380 FOUR ZOAS AD 1     8
        AWAKING OF ALBION OUR FRIEND AND ANCIENT COMPANION     . .    511 MILTON 25         62
        THAT MAN MAY LIVE UPON EARTH TILL THE TIME OF HIS AWAKING     514 MILTON 27         61
        ETERNAL DEATH AND OF THE AWAKING TO ETERNAL LIFE    . . .    622 JERUSALEM 4        2
        OF REDEMPTION & OF AWAKING AGAIN INTO ETERNITY    . . . .    691 JERUSALEM 59       9
        TILL THY AWAKING YET ALAS I SHALL FORGET ETERNITY     . .    727 JERUSALEM 83       3
```

155

		PAGE	TITLE	LINE
AWAKING	(CONTINUED)			
IT MUST LIE IN CONFUSION TILL ALBION'S TIME OF AWAKING .	.	728	JERUSALEM 83	58
AWAKING IT TO LIFE AMONG THE FLOWERS OF BEULAH REJOICING		745	JERUSALEM 98	21
IN UNITY				
AND THEN AWAKING INTO HIS BOSOM IN THE LIFE OF IMMORTALITY		747	JERUSALEM 99	4
THE PURPLE YEAR AWAKING FROM THE ROOTS OF NATURE		SUPP	ILLUS GRAY	*TITLE
AWARE				
I AM AWARE OF YOU BECAUSE I KNOW THAT YOU ACT NOT FROM .		573A	DESC CAT 3	PROSE
FEEL MYSELF WEAKER THAN I WAS AWARE BEING NOT ABLE AS YET		872D	LETTER 76	PROSE
AWAY	SEE AWA			
BY LOVE ARE DRIVN AWAY	.	6	MY SILKS/PS	3
TRUE LOVE DOTH PASS AWAY	.	7	MY SILKS/PS	18
THERE HE SLEEPS THE NIGHT AWAY	.	7	LOVE HARMNY/PS	18
THEN TO MY BLACK EYD MAID I HASTE AWAY		10	WHEN EARLY/PS	2
AND GENTLY SIGHS AWAY THE SILENT HOUR		10	WHEN EARLY/PS	4
THE VILLAGE BELL ALARMS AWAY I GO		10	WHEN EARLY/PS	5
THAT EDWARD RUNS AWAY FROM PHILIP	.	22	EDW THIRD/PS 3	23
THE KING CAUGHT HERE IN FRANCE OF RUNNING AWAY . . .		22	EDW THIRD/PS 3	57
TOO OFTEN TAKES AWAY A SOLDIER'S COURAGE		23	EDW THIRD/PS 3	66
SHALL FLEE AWAY AND LEAVE [THEM] HIM ALL FORLORN . . .		28	EDW THIRD/PS 3	292
A VISIONARY HAND WIPED AWAY HIS TEARS		36C	COUCH DEATH/PS	PROSE
BUT WORN AWAY A BLOODLESS DAEMON		41D	THEN SHE BORE	PROSE
FOR KNOWLEDGE DROVE SWEET INNOCENCE AWAY		42B	THEN SHE BORE	PROSE
SING AWAY QUID THEN THE CYNIC SUNG	.	47C	ISLAND MOON 3	PROSE
OF THE PULPIT STAIRS & KNOCK HIM DOWN & RUN AWAY . . .		48B	ISLAND MOON 4	PROSE
CONSTABLE OR TAKING AWAY THE PARISH BUSINESS HAH . . .		52A	ISLAND MOON 8	PROSE
THEY CHIRP & HOP AWAY	.	56	HAIL MATRIM/IM	24
COME COME LEAVE OFF PLAY & LET US AWAY		60	NURSES SONG/IM	7
[THE FLOCKS ARE AT PLAY & WE CAN'T GO AWAY]		60	NURSES SONG/IM	11
WELL WELL GO & PLAY TILL THE LIGHT FADES AWAY		60	NURSES SONG/IM	14
AND AWAY THE VAPOUR FLEW	.	60	LIT BOY LST/IM	8
HERE I'LL SIT & FADE AWAY	.	61	LEAVE O/IM	2
PLAY AWAY PLAY AWAY	.	62	DR CLASH/IM	10
I CAST AWAY MY STAFF THE KIND COMPANION OF MY TRAVEL .	.	101	TIRIEL 2	30
BUT WORSE O NEVER ASK ME MORE OR I MUST FLEE AWAY . .	.	103	TIRIEL 3	21
[THEY] SOME FLED AWAY [& HID THEMSELVES] BUT [SOME] . . .		108	TIRIEL 7	7
THY CROWN IS BALD OLD MAN THE SUN WILL DRY THY BRAINS AWAY		109	TIRIEL 7	12
NEVER FADES AWAY	.	112	LIT GRL LST/SI	11
DOES LAUGH AWAY CARE	.	116	ECCHOING GR/SI	12
SEEKING TO DRIVE THEIR THIRST AWAY	.	119	NIGHT/SI	27
IS DRIVEN AWAY	.	119	NIGHT/SI	39
AND AWAY THE VAPOUR FLEW	.	121	LIT BOY LST/SI	8
COME COME LEAVE OFF PLAY AND LET US AWAY		121	NURSES SONG/SI	7
WELL WELL GO & PLAY TILL THE LIGHT FADES AWAY		121	NURSES SONG/SI	13
WIPING ALL OUR TEARS AWAY	.	122	ON ANOTHERS/SI	22
O IT DRIVES ALL JOY AWAY	.	124	SCHOOL BOY/SI	7
AND BLOSSOMS BLOWN AWAY	.	124	SCHOOL BOY/SI	22
AND GIVES HIS LIGHT AND GIVES HIS HEAT AWAY	.	125	LIT BLK BOY/SI	10
TO FADE AWAY LIKE MORNING BEAUTY FROM HER MORTAL DAY .	.	127	BOOK OF THEL 1	3
WHY THOU COMPLAINEST NOT WHEN IN ONE HOUR THOU FADE AWAY		128	BOOK OF THEL 3	2
I PASS AWAY YET I COMPLAIN AND NO ONE HEARS MY VOICE .	.	128	BOOK OF THEL 3	4
NOTHING REMAINS O MAID I TELL THEE WHEN I PASS AWAY .	.	128	BOOK OF THEL 3	10
BUT THEL DELIGHTS IN THESE NO MORE BECAUSE I FADE AWAY .	.	129	BOOK OF THEL 3	21
AND I HAVE GIVEN THEE A CROWN THAT NONE CAN TAKE AWAY .	.	129	BOOK OF THEL 5	4
AND I COMPLAIN IN THE MILD AIR BECAUSE I FADE AWAY . .	.	130	BOOK OF THEL 5	12
. . . THE OLD MOUNTAINS OF FRANCE LIKE AGED MEN FADING AWAY		134	FRENCH REVOLTN	9
OUR FLESH IS CORRUPTED AND WE (WEAR) AWAY		137	FRENCH REVOLTN *	76
. . . AS IN YEARS THAT ARE PASSED AWAY		139	FRENCH REVOLTN	120
. . . WHEN THE STORM IS PASSING AWAY		143	FRENCH REVOLTN	196
. . . THE THUNDERS SUBSIDED AWAY		146	FRENCH REVOLTN	259
MELTING APPARENT SURFACES AWAY AND	.	154C	MARRIAGE HH 14	PROSE
IN THE FIRST CHAMBER WAS A DRAGON-MAN CLEARING AWAY THE		154D	MARRIAGE HH 15	PROSE
WHICH WILL SOON APPEAR WHEN THE DARKNESS PASSES AWAY .	.	156A	MARRIAGE HH 17	PROSE
FROM WHICH THE SEA FLED AWAY IN CLOUDS OF SMOKE . . .		156C	MARRIAGE HH 17	PROSE
FOR WHEN YOU RAN AWAY I FOUND MYSELF ON A BANK BY MOONLIGHT		156D	MARRIAGE HH 17	PROSE
TURN AWAY THE LAW FROM THE WOMAN TAKEN IN ADULTERY . .		158C	MARRIAGE HH 22	PROSE
WAKD FROM HIS ETERNAL SLEEP THE HOARY ELEMENT ROARING FLED		159C	SONG LIBERTY	PROSE
AWAY				
[WAS FILLD] TURND AWAY WITH JEALOUSY		161	ROSE TREE/N	9
[I SPURND HIS WATERS AWAY FROM ME]	.	166	WHY CARE FOR/N *	7
REMOVE AWAY THAT BLACKNING CHURCH	.	176	ANCNT PROVRB/N	1
REMOVE AWAY THAT MARRIAGE HEARSE		176	ANCNT PROVRB/N	2
REMOVE AWAY THAT [PLACE] MAN OF BLOOD		176	ANCNT PROVRB/N	3
TO FLEE AWAY	.	178	THE FAIRY/N	14
AND HE WIPED MY TEARS AWAY	.	182	THE ANGEL/N	6
HATH BRUSHD AWAY	.	183	THE FLY/N	8
REMOVE AWAY THAT BLACKNING CHURCH	.	184	SEVRL QUESTN/N	15
REMOVE AWAY THAT MARRIAGE HEARSE		184	SEVRL QUESTN/N	16
REMOVE AWAY THAT -- OF BLOOD	.	184	SEVRL QUESTN/N	17
[THOU GAVEST THE TEARS OF PITY AWAY]		186	LET BROTHELS/N	58
CAN NEVER PASS AWAY SHE CEASD & CLOSD HER GOLDEN SHRINE		189	V DAU ALBION 1	10
REND AWAY THIS DEFILED BOSOM THAT I MAY REFLECT . . .		190	V DAU ALBION 2	15
I SEE A WHALE IN THE SOUTH-SEA DRINKING MY SOUL AWAY .	.	196	AMERICA PREL 2	14
[A RUIND PILLAR IN GLITTRING FRAGMENTS SILENT HE TURND		196	AMERICA PREL 2	20
AWAY]				
TURN AWAY NO MORE	.	210	INTRODUCTN/SE	16
WHY WILT THOU TURN AWAY	.	210	INTRODUCTN/SE	17
HAS BRUSHD AWAY	.	213	THE FLY/SE	4
AND HE WIPD MY TEARS AWAY	.	214	THE ANGEL/SE	6
BUT MY ROSE TURND AWAY WITH JEALOUSY		215	ROSE TREE/SE	7
WHERE THE YOUTH PINED AWAY WITH DESIRE	.	215	AH SUNFLOWR/SE	5
RENT AWAY WITH A TERRIBLE CRASH		225	URIZEN 5	4

	PAGE	TITLE	LINE
AWAY (CONTINUED)			
FOR WHEN URIZEN SHRUNK AWAY	252	AHANIA 3	55
ROCK THE INNUMERABLE FRAGMENTS AWAY	257	BOOK OF LOS 4	24
AWAY IN REDOUNDING SMOKE THE SUN	260	BOOK OF LOS 5	44
BUT NO LIGHT FOR THE DEEP FLED AWAY	260	BOOK OF LOS 5	48
AND THEN THEY WANDERD FAR AWAY SHE SOUGHT FOR THEM IN VAIN	270	FOUR ZOAS 1	214
REPELLING HER AWAY [FROM ?THEM] & AWAY BY A DREAD	270	FOUR ZOAS 1	* 218
REPULSIVE POWER			
SHE DRAVE THE FEMALES ALL AWAY FROM LOS	271	FOUR ZOAS 1	243
[?&] AND LOS DRAVE ALL THE MALES FROM HER AWAY . .	271	FOUR ZOAS 1	* 244
DRIVING THE FEMALE EMANATIONS ALL AWAY FROM LOS	271	FOUR ZOAS 1	273
[IF THOU DRIVST ALL THE [MALES] FEMALES AWAY	272	FOUR ZOAS 1	* 276
[THE MALES AWAY FROM THEE]	272	FOUR ZOAS 1	277
SLEPT AS A BIRD IN THE BLUE SHELL THAT SOON SHALL BURST	273	FOUR ZOAS 1	350
AWAY			
NOT LONG IN HARMONY THEY DWELL THEIR LIFE IS DRAWN AWAY	274	FOUR ZOAS 1	371
OF WAR THE MOUNTAINS FLED AWAY THEY SOUGHT A PLACE BENEATH	275	FOUR ZOAS 1	416
PRESENTLY COMES A FAMISHD BIRD & TAKES AWAY THE SPIDER . .	277	FOUR ZOAS 1	458
RAVISHD AWAY IN NIGHT MY STRONG COMMAND SHALL BE OBEYD .	278	FOUR ZOAS 1	501
HIS CHILDREN WANDERING OUTSIDE FROM HIS BOSOM FLEEING AWAY	279	FOUR ZOAS 1	559
[TILL THEY HAD ?DRAWN THE SPECTRE QUITE AWAY FROM ENION]	SUPP	FOUR ZOAS 1	*
[XXX BLOOD FROM TORRENT FLOODS MELTING [AWAY]]	SUPP	FOUR ZOAS 1	*
AND THEY HAVE TAKEN HER AWAY & HID HER FROM MY SIGHT . .	282	FOUR ZOAS 2	98
HE DRAVE THE MALE SPIRITS ALL AWAY FROM AHANIA	285	FOUR ZOAS 2	209
AND SHE DRAVE ALL THE FEMALES FROM HIM AWAY	285	FOUR ZOAS 2	210
FAREWELL THE GOD CALLS ME AWAY I DEPART IN MY SWEET BLISS	288	FOUR ZOAS 2	333
LISTEN TO HER WHO LOVES THEE LEST WE ALSO ARE DRIVEN AWAY	294	FOUR ZOAS 3	92
IN TERRORS SHE WITHERD AWAY TO ENTUTHON BENITHON	296	FOUR ZOAS 3	180
I BACK RETURN WEAKER & WEAKER CONSUME ME NOT AWAY . . .	296	FOUR ZOAS 3	190
MAKE NOT THE THING THAT LOVETH THEE A TEAR WIPED AWAY . .	297	FOUR ZOAS 3	193
FOR IF WE WHO ARE BUT FOR A TIME & WHO PASS AWAY IN WINTER	304	FOUR ZOAS 4	261
THE STARS THREW DOWN THEIR SPEARS & FLED NAKED AWAY . . .	311	FOUR ZOAS 5	224
AT THE TURNING WHEELS OF HEAVEN SHRUNK AWAY INWARD WITHRING	317	FOUR ZOAS 6	* 236
AWAY			
FLYING AWAY FROM URIZEN THAT HE MIGHT NOT GIVE HIM FOOD	318	FOUR ZOAS 6	274
THE FRUIT OF THIS DELIGHTFUL TREE I CANNOT FLEE AWAY . .	326	FOUR ZOAS 7	234
ARE DRIVEN AWAY & ANNIHILATED WE NEVER CAN REPASS THE GATES	327	FOUR ZOAS 7	303
OF WHICH THESE IN THE OUTWARD WORLD ARE SHADOWS WHICH PASS	329	FOUR ZOAS 7	366
AWAY			
FIRST HIS IMMORTAL SPIRIT DREW URIZEN [SPECTRE] SHADOW AWAY	332	FOUR ZOAS 7	* 490
LEAVING HIS SPECTROUS FORM WHICH COULD NOT BE DRAWN AWAY	332	FOUR ZOAS 7	492
I WAKEND ENION IN THE MORNING & SHE TURND AWAY	339	FOUR ZOAS 7B	233
DELUSIVE CRUELTY THEY DESCEND AWAY FROM THE DAUGHTERS OF	341	FOUR ZOAS 7	26
BEULAH			
BODIES OF VEGETATION SINGING LULLING CADENCES TO DRIVE AWAY	342	FOUR ZOAS 8	38
WHY DOST THOU WANDER AWAY FROM TIRZAH WHY ME COMPELL TO	348	FOUR ZOAS 8	299
BIND THEE			
IF THOU DOST GO AWAY FROM ME I SHALL CONSUME UPON THE ROCKS	348	FOUR ZOAS 8	300
[I HAVE] AWAY FROM ME I HAVE BOUND DOWN WITH A HOT IRON	349	FOUR ZOAS 8	* 302
OR MERCY & TRUTH ARE FLED AWAY FROM SHECHEM & MOUNT GILEAD	349	FOUR ZOAS 8	320
[SHE] JERUSALEM SAW THE BODY DEAD UPON THE CROSS SHE FLED	349	FOUR ZOAS 8	331
AWAY			
AWAY FROM [LOS] ME FIRST REUBEN FLED THEN SIMEON THEN LEVI	350	FOUR ZOAS 8	375
THEN JUDAH			
LOS DROPD A TEAR AT HER DEPARTURE BUT HE WIPD IT AWAY IN	351	FOUR ZOAS 8	411
HOPE			
THE SPECTRE QUITE AWAY FROM ENION THAT I DIE A DEATH . .	355	FOUR ZOAS 8	546
WHEN THE MAN GENTLY FADES AWAY IN HIS IMMORTALITY . .	355	FOUR ZOAS 8	551
WHEN THE MORTAL DISAPPEARS IN IMPROVED KNOWLEDGE CAST AWAY	355	FOUR ZOAS 8	552
THE FORMER THINGS SO SHALL THE MORTAL GENTLY FADE AWAY . .	355	FOUR ZOAS 8	553
THAT ENITHARMON HAD NUMBERD AWAY FROM THE HEAVENS . .	356	FOUR ZOAS 8	608
[THAT ENION HAD NUMBERD AWAY FROM HEAVEN]	SUPP	FOUR ZOAS 8	*
TO JUDGMENT FROM THE FOUR WINDS AWAKE & COME AWAY . .	357	FOUR ZOAS 9	13
A TERROR COMING FROM THE SOUTH THE EAGLE & HAWK FLED AWAY	358	FOUR ZOAS 9	62
I CAST [REMEMBRANCE] FUTURITY AWAY & TURN MY BACK UPON	361	FOUR ZOAS 9	182
THAT VOID			
THEY SING THEY SIEZE THE INSTRUMENTS OF HARMONY THEY THROW	365	FOUR ZOAS 9	302
AWAY			
HOPELESS IF I AM LIKE THE GRASS & SO SHALL PASS AWAY . .	368	FOUR ZOAS 9	417
THE FRUIT SHALL RIPEN & FALL DOWN & THE FLOWERS CONSUME	368	FOUR ZOAS 9	420
AWAY			
WHY DOST THOU TURN THYSELF AWAY FROM HIS SWEET WATRY EYES	371	FOUR ZOAS 9	526
FOR LO THE WINTER MELTED AWAY UPON THE DISTANT HILLS . .	373	FOUR ZOAS 9	600
AND ALL THY SONS O LUVAH BEAR AWAY THE FAMILIES OF EARTH	375	FOUR ZOAS 9	695
AND TOOK AWAY THE WINE OF AGES WITH SOLEMN SONGS & JOY . .	378	FOUR ZOAS 9	794
TAKES AWAY THE AUTHORITY ALTOGETHER IT CEASES TO BE HISTORY	390D	ANNO WATSON	MARG
[DRIVING ALL MY LOVES AWAY]	415	MY SPECTRE/N	22
[WHITHER YOUNG MAN WHITHER AWAY]	421	BENEATH/N	3
MELTED ALL MY SOUL AWAY	422	BENEATH/N	17
WHITHER YOUNG MAN WHITHER AWAY	424	THE GOLDEN NET	2
MELTED ALL MY SOUL AWAY	424	THE GOLDEN NET	16
HE WANDERS WEEPING FAR AWAY	426	MENTAL TRAVLER	53
THE STARS SUN MOON ALL SHRINK AWAY	426	MENTAL TRAVLER	65
LIKE THE WILD STAG SHE FLEES AWAY	426	MENTAL TRAVLER	77
AND FLEE AWAY ON EVERY SIDE	427	MENTAL TRAVLER	96
FOR JOHN EAT & DRANK TO DRIVE AWAY LOVE'S PAIN	434	LONG JOHN BRWN	10
BUT THE ANGELS OF PROVIDENCE DROVE THEM AWAY	434	WILLIAM BOND	7
TO DRIVE AWAY THE SICK MAN'S PAIN	435	WILLIAM BOND	20
OR IS ABLE & AFTERWARDS GO AND SWEAR OUR LIVES AWAY . . .	439A	BLAKES MEMORAN	PROSE
IN THE CLOUD WHICH ROLLS AWAY ARE THE FOUR LIVING CREATURES	444A	LAST JUDGMNT/L	PROSE
WHICH BY ITS ROLLING AWAY DISPLAYS THE OPENING SEATS OF	444A	LAST JUDGMNT/L	PROSE
SATAN TOOK AWAY ORNAMENT FIRST NEXT HE TOOK AWAY	446C	ANNO REYNOLDS	MARG
ACCOMODATIONS			

AWAY   (CONTINUED)

	PAGE	TITLE	LINE
OF ALL ART BECAUSE IT TAKES AWAY THE POSSIBILITY OF VARIETY	478C	ANNO REYNOLDS	MARG
[SO SATAN TOOK AWAY ORNAMENTS FIRST NECESSARIES LAST] .	446C	ANNO REYNOLDS	* MARG
THO DRIVEN AWAY WITH THE SEVEN STARRY ONES INTO THE ULRO	505	MILTON 22	1
SIX THOUSAND YEARS ARE PASSD AWAY THE END APPROACHES FAST	508	MILTON 23	55
TWELVE SONS SUCCESSIVE FLED AWAY IN THAT THOUSAND YEARS OF SORROW	508	MILTON 23	62
AND IF YOU ALSO FLEE AWAY AND LEAVE YOUR FATHER'S SIDE .	508	MILTON 24	22
STRETCHD OVER EUROPE & ASIA COME O SONS COME COME AWAY	509	MILTON 24	33
FOR IF WE WHO ARE BUT FOR A TIME & WHO PASS AWAY IN WINTER	519	MILTON 30	26
LIKE WOMEN & CHILDREN WERE TAKEN AWAY AS ON WINGS . .	519	MILTON 31	2
WHICH JESUS RENT & NOW SHALL WHOLLY PURGE AWAY WITH FIRE	533	MILTON 41	27
AWAY FROM OLOLON SHE DIVIDED & FLED INTO THE DEPTHS . .	534	MILTON 42	5
BUT MY SOUL ALSO WOULD HE BEAR AWAY	536	AND HIS LEGS/N	6
AND AWAY FLED EVERY JOY	552	WHY CUPID/N	20
GET THEE AWAY GET THEE AWAY	558	I ROSE UP AT/N	2
PRAYST THOU FOR RICHES AWAY AWAY	558	I ROSE UP AT/N	3
AND HE NEVER TURNS HIS FACE AWAY	558	I ROSE UP AT/N	14
THEM AS I PLEASE AWAY WITH YOUR REASONING AND YOUR RUBBISH	579A	DESC CAT 5	PROSE
EASY FOR HIM TO SNATCH AWAY THE VISION TIME AFTER TIME FOR	582C	DESC CAT 9	PROSE
THE LAST JUDGMENT WHEN ALL THOSE ARE CAST AWAY . . .	604C	V LAST JUDG/N	PROSE
PASSING AWAY & THE (NEW) (HEAVEN) & (NEW) EARTH . . .	606B	V LAST JUDG/N	PROSE
WHICH THE FLOOD DID NOT SWEEP AWAY ABOVE NOAH IS . .	609D	V LAST JUDG/N	PROSE
THAT CAN ENTER THE MIND AS IT TAKES AWAY ALL SUBLIMITY .	614B	V LAST JUDG/N	PROSE
AWAY FROM THE SUN'S FLARING BEAMS WHO	619B	ILLUS MILTON	*PROSE
BUT THE PERTURBED MAN AWAY TURNS DOWN THE VALLEYS DARK .	622	JERUSALEM 4	22
ARE DRIVEN AMONG THE STARRY WHEELS RENT AWAY AND DISSIPATED	623	JERUSALEM 5	4
WANDER AWAY INTO THE CHAOTIC VOID LAMENTING WITH HER SHADOW	624	JERUSALEM 5	63
TILL THY LIFE IS ALL TAKEN AWAY BY THIS DECEITFUL FRIENDSHIP	625	JERUSALEM 7	10
GO ON BUILDERS IN HOPE THO JERUSALEM WANDERS FAR AWAY .	632	JERUSALEM 12	43
ONE HAIR NOR PARTICLE OF DUST NOT ONE CAN PASS AWAY .	634	JERUSALEM 14	1
AWAY FROM THE CONFLICT OF LUVAH & URIZEN FIXING THE GATES	637	JERUSALEM 16	31
IN HER DARKNESS & WAS COMFORTED YET STILL SHE DIVIDED AWAY	639	JERUSALEM 17	49
THEN WAS A TIME OF LOVE O WHY IS IT PASSED AWAY . . .	643	JERUSALEM 20	41
MY SOUL IS MELTED AWAY INWOVEN WITHIN THE VEIL . .	645	JERUSALEM 23	4
HE RECOILD HE RUSHD OUTWARDS HE BORE THE VEIL WHOLE AWAY	646	JERUSALEM 23	20
THY SONS CAME TO JERUSALEM WITH GIFTS SHE SENT THEM AWAY	647	JERUSALEM 24	38
DESCEND O LAMB OF GOD & TAKE AWAY THE IMPUTATION OF SIN	648	JERUSALEM 25	12
ON HIS ROCK ERE YET THE STARRY HEAVENS WERE FLED AWAY .	660	JERUSALEM 34	20
BY THE DAUGHTERS OF BEULAH GENTLY SNATCHD AWAY AND HID IN BEULAH	668	JERUSALEM 41	14
AWAY FROM ALBION'S MOUNTAINS FAR AWAY FROM LONDON'S SPIRES	673	JERUSALEM 43	70
IN SELFHOOD WE ARE NOTHING BUT FADE AWAY IN MORNING'S BREATH	675	JERUSALEM 45	13
BUT ALBION TURND AWAY REFUSING COMFORT	676	JERUSALEM 46	16
AWAY FROM BEULAH'S HILLS & VALES BREAK FORTH THE SOULS OF THE DEAD	677	JERUSALEM 47	10
AWAY FROM THE STARRY WHEELS TO PREPARE JERUSALEM A PLACE	678	JERUSALEM 48	46
DRAW YE JERUSALEM AWAY FROM ALBION'S MOUNTAINS . . .	679	JERUSALEM 48	62
JERUSALEM JERUSALEM WHY WILT THOU TURN AWAY . . .	679	JERUSALEM 49	2
THE LUNGS THE HEART THE LIVER SHRUNK AWAY FAR DISTANT FROM MAN	679	JERUSALEM 49	17
AND LET WILD SEAS & ROCKS CLOSE UP JERUSALEM AWAY FROM .	680	JERUSALEM 49	77
COME O THOU LAMB OF GOD AND TAKE AWAY THE REMEMBRANCE OF SIN	681	JERUSALEM 50	24
COME THEN O LAMB OF GOD AND TAKE AWAY THE REMEMBRANCE OF SIN	681	JERUSALEM 50	30
AND WHO WEAVE IT A CRADLE OF THE GRASS THAT WITHERETH AWAY	688	JERUSALEM 56	7
HIS ESPOUSED WIFE AND MARY SAID IF THOU PUT ME AWAY FROM THEE	694	JERUSALEM 61	4
BUT HE DRIVETH ME AWAY FROM HIS PRESENCE YET I HEAR THE VOICE OF GOD	694	JERUSALEM 61	9
UTTERLY CAST ME AWAY IF I WERE PURE NEVER COULD I TASTE THE SWEETS	694	JERUSALEM 61	11
ME FROM MY CRADLE THE AMALEKITE STOLE ME AWAY UPON HIS CAMELS	695	JERUSALEM 61	41
AND WITHOUT THE BAPTISM OF REPENTANCE TO WASH AWAY CALUMNIES AND	697	JERUSALEM 63	28
WE WERE CARRIED AWAY IN THOUSANDS FROM LONDON & IN TENS	700	JERUSALEM 65	33
AND AS THEIR EYE & EAR SHRUNK THE HEAVENS SHRUNK AWAY . .	702	JERUSALEM 66	40
AFAR INTO THE UNKNOWN NIGHT THE MOUNTAINS FLED AWAY . .	702	JERUSALEM 66	44
AWAY INTO THE FAR REMOTE AND THE TREES & MOUNTAINS WITHERD	703	JERUSALEM 66	51
PLINLIMMON SHRUNK AWAY SNOWDON TREMBLED THE MOUNTAINS . .	703	JERUSALEM 66	59
WHY WILT THOU WANDER AWAY FROM TIRZAH WHY ME COMPEL TO BIND THEE	705	JERUSALEM 67	* 45
IF THOU DOST GO AWAY FROM ME I SHALL CONSUME UPON THESE ROCKS	705	JERUSALEM 67	46
AWAY FROM ME I HAVE BOUND DOWN WITH A HOT IRON . . .	705	JERUSALEM 67	48
OR MERCY & TRUTH ARE FLED AWAY FROM SHECHEM & MOUNT GILEAD	705	JERUSALEM 68	8
WHICH JESUS RENDS & THE WHOLE DRUID LAW REMOVES AWAY . .	708	JERUSALEM 69	39
AGE AFTER AGE DRAWING THEM AWAY TOWARDS BABYLON . . .	715	JERUSALEM 74	31
WHENCE JOSEPH & BENJAMIN ROLLD APART AWAY FROM THE NATIONS	715	JERUSALEM 74	56
AWAY FROM THE NATIONS OF THE EARTH & FROM THE CITIES OF THE NATIONS	720	JERUSALEM 79	9
RECIEVE THE FEET OF JERUSALEM THEY HAVE CAST ME QUITE AWAY	720	JERUSALEM 79	16
TO ENTICE HER SISTERS AWAY TO. BABYLON ON EUPHRATES . .	725	JERUSALEM 82	18
BEGAN TO GIVE THEIR SOULS AWAY IN THE (FURNACES) OF AFFLICTION	727	JERUSALEM 82	79
AWAY & MIGHTY HYLE & AFTER THEM JERUSALEM IS GONE AWAKE	729	JERUSALEM 83	87
STARTS FROM HIS LOFTY PLACES & CASTS DOWN HIS TENTS & FLEES AWAY	729	JERUSALEM 84	24

AWAY   (CONTINUED)
   JUDAH WAS LIKE PALAMABRON O SIMEON O LEVI YE FLED AWAY   740 JERUSALEM 93   14
   APPEARS UPON OUR HILLS AWAKE JERUSALEM AND COME AWAY   . . 744 JERUSALEM 97   4
   WHEN TWELVE YEARS OLD HE RAN AWAY . . . .   748 EV GOSPEL(B)/N   3
   COME SAID SATAN COME AWAY . . . .   749 EV GOSPEL(B)/N   15
   WHEN BUT A CHILD HE RAN AWAY   . . . .   750 EV GOSPEL(C)/N   3
   WHEN BUT A CHILD HE RAN AWAY   . . . .   751 EV GOSPEL(D)/N   5
   ALL AWAY BEGAN TO ROLL   . . . .   754 EV GOSPEL(E)/N   14
   AND DRIVEN AWAY MY TREMBLING DOVE . . . .   754 EV GOSPEL(E)/N   52
   THEN ROLLD THE SHADOWY MAN AWAY . . . .   755 EV GOSPEL(E)/N   81
   AND FROM THE ADULTERESS TURND AWAY . . . .   757 EV GOSPEL(I)/N   47
   THRO EVENING SHADES I HASTE AWAY . . . .   771 OF GATES/GP   41
   EVE COME AWAY & LET US NOT BELIEVE THESE VAIN DELUSIONS   780 GHOST ABEL 1   18
   BY TAKING AWAY MONEY OR A PRICE . . . .   788A ANNO THORNTON   MARG
   [?BY ?TAKING] ?OR ?TAKING ?IT & TAKE AWAY [XXX THING IN] 788A ANNO THORNTON   * MARG
   LONG AWAY & NOT CALLING TO KNOW OF YOUR WELFARE BUT HOPE   799A LETTER 11   PROSE
      NOW
   TO ENTICE HIM TO FELPHAM & FAR AWAY . . . .   800 MRS FLAXMAN/L   4
   AWAY TO SWEET FELPHAM FOR HEAVEN IS THERE . . . . .   800 MRS FLAXMAN/L   5
   I FEAR IT WILL BE THURSDAY BEFORE WE CAN GET AWAY FROM . 801B LETTER 13   PROSE
   AWAY FROM ALL CARE . . . .   804 TO BUTTS/L   10
   LIKE DROSS PURGD AWAY . . . .   805 TO BUTTS/L   55
   MUCH MILDER THAN IT WAS IN LONDON WHEN WE CAME AWAY . . 806B LETTER 16   PROSE
   I INTEND BECAUSE MY ABSTRACT FOLLY HURRIES ME OFTEN AWAY 809A LETTER 20   PROSE
   "I SEE A HAND YOU CANNOT SEE THAT BECKONS ME AWAY" . .   813C LETTER 22
   I OUGHT NOT TO BE AWAY FROM THE OPPORTUNITIES . . . .   823A LETTER 26   PROSE
   EVERY ENGRAVER TURNS AWAY WORK THAT HE CANNOT EXECUTE . 829C LETTER 30   PROSE
   AND CAN NEVER PASS AWAY MY WIFE CONTINUES WELL . . .   854A LETTER 52   PROSE
   CARES LITTLE FOR THIS WORLD WHICH PASSES AWAY WHOSE . . 862D LETTER 60   PROSE
   TAKES IT QUITE AWAY IT WAS NIGHT WHEN IT LEFT ME SO I DID 872B LETTER 75   PROSE
      NOT
   WHEN I AM AWAY FROM HOME I AM DR SIR YOURS SINCERELY .   872C LETTER 75   PROSE
   A GENIUS DRIVING AWAY "COMUS & HIS MIDNIGHT CREW" . .   SUPP ILLUS GRAY   *TITLE
AWE
   AWE SURROUNDED ALONE THRO THE ARMY . . . .   141 FRENCH REVOLTN *   162
   . . . KEPT IN AWE WITH THE WHIP . . . .   143 FRENCH REVOLTN   214
   . . . NOW BEAMING WITH KNOWLEDGE WITH GENTLE AWE ADORNED   144 FRENCH REVOLTN   230
   . . . THAT MOATED AROUND KEEPS THIS CITY OF PARIS IN AWE   145 FRENCH REVOLTN   248
   WONDER AWE FEAR ASTONISHMENT . . . .   231 URIZEN 18   13
   WONDRING WITH LOVE & [XXX] AWE THEY FELT THE DIVINE HAND   341 FOUR ZOAS 8   *   23
      UPON THEM
   WHILE LITTLE CHILDREN PLAY AROUND THY FEET IN GENTLE AWE   360 FOUR ZOAS 9   134
   IN PANGS OF AN ETERNAL BIRTH IN TORMENT & AWE & FEAR .   363 FOUR ZOAS 9   234
   AND LOS STOOD & CRIED TO THE LABOURERS OF THE VINTAGE IN   510 MILTON 25   16
      VOICE OF AWE
   WITH EYES OF SOFT HUMILITY & WONDER LOVE & AWE . . . .   520 MILTON 31   38
   OR AMAZEMENT OR DEVOUT WONDER AND UNRESISTING AWE . .   580C DESC CAT 5   PROSE
   THE ANCIENT HEAVENS IN SILENT AWE . . . .   754 EV GOSPEL(E)/N   12
   THEN WEPT THEN ROSE IN ZEAL & AWE . . . .   761 FOR SEXES/GP   7
AWE-STRUCK
   UNQUESTIONED UNHINDERED AWE-STRUCK ARE THE SOLDIERS . . . 141 FRENCH REVOLTN   164
AWFUL
   EACH LIKE AN AWFUL THUNDER CLOUD . . . .   12 GWIN KING/PS   39
   BEFORE THAT AWFUL THRONE . . . .   13 GWIN KING/PS   98
   HER SNOWY FEET AND OWND HIS AWFUL QUEEN . . . . .   21 EDW THIRD/PS 2   83
   SHALL RISE CITIES AND THRONES AND ARMS AND AWFUL POWRS .   32 EDW THIRD/PS 6   18
   SHE SPRED HER [SHADOWY] AWFUL WINGS & GAVE ME UP . . .   43C WOE CRIED MUSE   PROSE
   BUT WHEN TIRIEL TURND AROUND & RAISD HIS AWFUL VOICE .   108 TIRIEL 7   6
   HE CEAST OUTSTRETCHD AT HAR & HEVA'S FEET IN AWFUL DEATH   110 TIRIEL 8   42
   BENEATH IN THE AWFUL VOID . . . .   140 FRENCH REVOLTN   134
   UP ROSE AWFUL IN HIS MAJESTIC BEAMS BOURBON'S STRONG DUKE 141 FRENCH REVOLTN   168
      . . .
   . . . WHOSE AGED TREES UTTER AN AWFUL VOICE AND THEIR   145 FRENCH REVOLTN   242
      BRANCHES
   . . . OR CROAK ON THE AWFUL KNEE . . . .   147 FRENCH REVOLTN   298
   AWFUL UP ROSE THE KING . . . .   148 FRENCH REVOLTN   304
   THEIR AWFUL FOLDS IN THE DARK AIR SILENT SHE STOOD AS NIGHT 196 AMERICA PREL 1   8
   HIS VOICE HIS LOCKS HIS AWFUL SHOULDERS AND HIS GLOWING   197 AMERICA 3   17
      EYES
   THE EASTERN SKY SPREADING HIS AWFUL WINGS ACROSS   201 AMERICA 13   12
      THE HEAVENS
   HIS VOICE HIS LOCKS HIS AWFUL SHOULDERS & HIS GLOWING EYES 204 AMERICA CANC A   17
   INFINITE LONDON'S AWFUL SPIRES CAST A DREADFUL [GLEAM] COLD 205 AMERICA CANC C   7
   ON MOUNTAINS & CLIFFS OF SNOW THE AWFUL APPARITION HOVERD 205 AMERICA CANC C   28
   DEEP GROAND URIZEN STRETCHING HIS AWFUL HAND . . . . .   249 AHANIA 2   31
   THEY ARE THY SERVANTS IF THOU WILT OBEY MY AWFUL LAW .   273 FOUR ZOAS 1   328
   THUS URIZEN SPOKE COLLECTED IN HIMSELF IN AWFUL PRIDE .   273 FOUR ZOAS 1   342
   . . . THEN FIX THEM IN THEIR AWFUL STATIONS . . . .   283 FOUR ZOAS 2   144
   WITH EVER STREAMING FIRES BEAMING FROM HIS AWFUL LIMBS . 284 FOUR ZOAS 2   180
   AND SHAKES HIS AWFUL HAIR . . . .   289 FOUR ZOAS 2   345
   INDIGNANT ROSE THE [ETERNAL] [FALLEN] AWFUL MAN . . .   293 FOUR ZOAS 3   *   70
   IN PEACE BENEATH MY AWFUL FROWN MY WILL SHALL BE MY LAW   299 FOUR ZOAS 4   55
   ROUND HOWLING ORC WHOSE AWFUL LIMBS CAST FORTH RED SMOKE   320 FOUR ZOAS 7   17
      & FIRE
   HOWLING & RENDING HIS DARK CAVES THE AWFUL DEMON LAY .   320 FOUR ZOAS 7   20
   TREMBLE NOT SO MY ENITHARMON AT THE AWFUL GATES . . .   330 FOUR ZOAS 7   412
   TO BE MY GREAT & AWFUL CURSES AT THE TIME APPOINTED . .   336 FOUR ZOAS 7B   120
   EXUDED ROUND HIS AWFUL LIMBS STRETCHING TO SERPENT LENGTH 343 FOUR ZOAS 8   79
   INTOLERABLE AT LENGTH AN AWFUL WONDER BURST . . . .   347 FOUR ZOAS 8   250
   THEY SHAKE THEIR SLUMBERS OFF THEY WAVE IN AWFUL FEAR .   352 FOUR ZOAS 8   444
   THE ETERNAL MAN SAT ON THE ROCKS & CRIED WITH AWFUL VOICE 360 FOUR ZOAS 9   123
   A BARD BROKE FORTH ALL SAT ATTENTIVE TO THE AWFUL MAN .   482 MILTON 2   24

```
                                                               PAGE     TITLE        LINE
AWFUL    (CONTINUED)
         ASTONISHMENT HELD THE ASSEMBLY IN AN AWFUL SILENCE AND     490 MILTON 9          36
           TEARS
         TERMINATING IN HYDE PARK ON TYBURN'S AWFUL BROOK    .      491 MILTON 11          5
         FEELING THE ELECTRIC FLAME OF MILTON'S AWFUL PRECIPITATE   502 MILTON 20         26
           DESCENT
         SINCE ALBION'S DEATH & SATAN'S CUTTING-OFF FROM OUR AWFUL  510 MILTON 25         30
           FIELDS
         AND THE CALM OCEAN JOYS BENEATH & SMOOTHS HIS AWFUL WAVES  511 MILTON 25         71
         WALKS AMONG ALL HIS AWFUL FAMILY SEEN IN EVERY FACE   .  . 519 MILTON 30         17
         ALL NATURE LISTENS SILENT TO HIM & THE AWFUL SUN   .  .  . 520 MILTON 31         36
         AN AWFUL FORM EASTWARD FROM MIDST OF A BRIGHT PAVED-WORK   531 MILTON 39         24
         AND AWFUL MAN I SEE OERCOVERD WITH THE MANTLE OF YEARS  .  532 MILTON 40          5
         TERRIBLY THIS PORTION TREMBLES BEFORE THEE O AWFUL MAN  .  533 MILTON 41         31
         BECOME LEAD AGAIN THIS IS AN AWFUL THING TO SAY TO OIL    566B DESC CAT 2     PROSE
           PAINTERS
         WHO IN MYSTERIOUS SINAI'S AWFUL CAVE    .  .  .  .  .  .   621 READER LOVER/J    3
         FROM ALBION OVER THE WHOLE EARTH SUCH IS MY AWFUL VISION   635 JERUSALEM 15       5
         BEFORE HIS AWFUL FEET IN PRIDE OF VIRTUE FOR VICTORY    .  642 JERUSALEM 19      32
         INDIGNANT ROSE THE AWFUL MAN & TURND HIS BACK ON VALA   .  654 JERUSALEM 29      57
         FROM HIS AWFUL MEMBERS AND THUS LOS CRIED ALOUD    .  .  . 660 JERUSALEM 34      21
         I BEHOLD LONDON A HUMAN AWFUL WONDER OF GOD   .  .  .  .   665 JERUSALEM 38      29
         I SEE THEE AWFUL PARENT LAND IN LIGHT BEHOLD I SEE   .  .  665 JERUSALEM 38      44
         SWEARING THE OATH OF GOD WITH AWFUL VOICE OF THUNDERS ROUND 666 JERUSALEM 40      9
         THEIR AWFUL CHARGE BACK TO HIS NATIVE HOME BUT ALBION DARK 674 JERUSALEM 44       5
         OF NORWICH PETERBORO ROCHESTER CHESTER AWFUL WORCESTER  .  676 JERUSALEM 46      18
         BEHELD HER WITH WONDER WITH AWFUL HANDS SHE TOOK   .  .  . 678 JERUSALEM 48      30
         THE TWENTYFOUR FRIENDS OF ALBION AND ROUND THE AWFUL FOUR  684 JERUSALEM 53      22
         AMONG THE FLOWERS OF BEULAH STILL RETAIN HIS AWFUL STRENGTH 686 JERUSALEM 55      2
         URIZEN WRATHFUL STRODE ABOVE DIRECTING THE AWFUL BUILDING  690 JERUSALEM 58      21
         IN AWFUL POMP & GOLD IN ALL THE PRECIOUS UNHEWN STONES    701 JERUSALEM 66       1
           OF EDEN
         OF FIRE THEN AN AWFUL FIERY WHEEL SURROUNDING EARTH        702 JERUSALEM 66      42
           & HEAVEN
         BEAR THREE STRONG SINEWY NECKS & THREE AWFUL & TERRIBLE    708 JERUSALEM 70       4
           HEADS
         OBEYD HIS AWFUL VOICE IGNOGE IS HIS LOVELY EMANATION    .  710 JERUSALEM 71      27
         HIS AWFUL BEAUTY WITH MORAL VIRTUE THE FAIR DECIEVER       715 JERUSALEM 74      35
           OFFSPRING
         THESE AWFUL FORMS IN OUR SOFT BANDS DISTRACTED WITH        723 JERUSALEM 80      85
           TREMBLING
         UNLESS WE FIND A WAY TO BIND THESE AWFUL FORMS TO OUR   .  725 JERUSALEM 82       3
         LIKE A FAINT RAINBOW WAVED BEFORE HIM IN THE AWFUL GLOOM   728 JERUSALEM 83      67
         OUTWOVEN FROM THAMES & TWEED & SEVERN AWFUL STREAMS  .  .  735 JERUSALEM 89      20
         O RINTRAH O PALAMABRON WHAT ARE YOUR DIRE & AWFUL PURPOSES 740 JERUSALEM 93       2
         HIS AWFUL LIMBS INTO THE HEAVENS HE WALKED CLOTHED         742 JERUSALEM 95       7
           IN FLAMES
         SURROUNDING HIS AWFUL MEMBERS THOU SEEST THE SUN IN HEAVY  742 JERUSALEM 95      11
           CLOUDS
         AND HE CLOTHED HIMSELF IN BOW & ARROWS IN AWFUL STATE      744 JERUSALEM 97      16
           FOURFOLD
         AND IN HELL BENEATH & A MIGHTY & AWFUL CHANGE THREATENED   799 TO FLAXMAN/L      8
           THE EARTH
AWHILE
         LET THEM BUT SUFFER AWHILE AND YOU SHALL SEE   .  .  .  .   20 EDW THIRD/PS 2    75
A WHILE
         THIS DISMAL WORLD HE STOOD A WHILE & LOOKD BACK OER HIS    315 FOUR ZOAS 6     * 150
           FORMER
AWKWARD
         WERE THE AWKWARD IMITATORS AT THAT TIME IT IS THE   .  .  592B PUB ADDRESS/N   PROSE
         BLOATED [AWKWARD] GODS MERCURY JUNO VENUS & THE    .  .  . 599C PUB ADDRESS/N  *PROSE
         AWKWARD FRENCH PALACE ARE [ALL] THROWN TOGETHER AROUND  .  599C PUB ADDRESS/N  *PROSE
         SUCH MONOTONY WAS NOT ONLY AWKWARD BUT AS MUCH  .  .  .  . 621D JERUSALEM 3    PROSE
AWKWARDLY
         THAT I MUST GO A COURTING WHICH I SHALL DO AWKWARDLY IN    829D LETTER 30      PROSE
           THE MEAN TIME
AWKWARDNESS
         AWKWARDNESS ARMD IN STEEL FOLLY IN A HELMET OF GOLD  .  .  628 JERUSALEM 9       12
AWOKE
         [REFRESHING THE COLD EARTH WITH BEAMING JOY] BUT PRIDE      40D THEN SHE BORE  PROSE
           AWOKE
         MNETHA AWOKE SHE RAN & STOOD AT THE TENT DOOR [IN] & SAW   109 TIRIEL 7       *  22
         AND SO TOM AWOKE AND WE ROSE IN THE DARK   .  .  .  .  .   118 CHIMNEY SWP/SI    21
         .  .  . I AWOKE A COLD HAND PASSED OVER MY LIMBS AND BEHOLD 140 FRENCH REVOLTN  130
         THE KING AWOKE ON HIS COUCH OF GOLD    .  .  .  .  .  .    185 LET BROTHELS/N    5
         AWOKE & VAST CLOUDS OF BLOOD ROLLD    .  .  .  .  .  .  .  223 URIZEN 3          41
         LOS AWOKE HER O SORROW & PAIN   .  .  .  .  .  .  .  .  .  233 URIZEN 20          8
         THE MOISTURE AWOKE TO BIRTH   .  .  .  .  .  .  .  .  .  . 255 AHANIA 5          37
         .  .  . THE SHEEP AWOKE FROM THE MOULD]   .  .  .  .  .    270 FOUR ZOAS 1      208
         THE VOICE CAME & WENT LIKE A DREAM I AWOKE IN MY SWEET     272 FOUR ZOAS 1      280
           BLISS
         BUT URIZEN AWOKE & LUVAH WOKE & THUS CONFERRD    .  .  .   277 FOUR ZOAS 1    * 487
         AWAKE THE BRIDEGROOM COMETH I AWOKE TO SLEEP NO MORE   .  355 FOUR ZOAS 8      541
         VALA AWOKE WHEN IN THE PLEASANT GATES OF SLEEP I ENTERD    369 FOUR ZOAS 9      464
         VALA AWOKE & CALLD THE CHILDREN FROM THEIR GENTLE SLUMBERS 370 FOUR ZOAS 9      518
         AWOKE THEY WEPT TO ONE ANOTHER & THEY REASCENDED   .  .  . 378 FOUR ZOAS 9      796
         FROM THIS SWEET PLACE MATERNAL LOVE AWOKE JERUSALEM   .  . 677 JERUSALEM 48      18
         AND ENGLAND WHO IS BRITTANNIA AWOKE FROM DEATH ON ALBION'S 742 JERUSALEM 94      20
           BOSOM
         SHE AWOKE PALE & COLD SHE FAINTED SEVEN TIMES ON THE BODY  742 JERUSALEM 94      21
           OF ALBION
```

```
                                                      PAGE     TITLE          LINE
A WOOING
     THIS FROG HE WOULD A WOOING RIDE  . . . . . . . .   55 THIS FROG/IM       1
     THIS FROG HE WOULD A WOOING RIDE  . . . . . . . .   55 THIS FROG/IM       3
AX       SEE BATTLE-AX,BATTLE AX
     IN DENS OF DEATH TO FORGE THE SPADE THE MATTOCK & THE AX  365 FOUR ZOAS 9    306
     THE OAK IS CUT DOWN BY THE AX THE LAMB FALLS BY THE KNIFE  522 MILTON 32      37
     OF DEATH FORMING AN AX OF GOLD THE FOUR SONS OF LOS  . . .  636 JERUSALEM 15   22
AXE
     BRING ME AN AXE AND SPADE . . . . . . . . . . . .    7 MY SILKS/PS        13
     BRAVE LORDS WHO FELL BENEATH THE BLOODY AXE . . . . .   18 EDW THIRD/PS 1    44
     THICK AS A FOREST READY FOR THE AXE . . . . . . . .   32 EDW THIRD/PS 6    24
AXLE-TREES
     LONG TO TELL & OF THE IRON ROLLERS GOLDEN AXLE-TREES &  713 JERUSALEM 73     9
          YOKES
AY
     O AY COME I'LL SING YOU A SONG SAID THE CYNIC . . . . .   46C ISLAND MOON 3  PROSE
     O AY LOCK SAID SCOPPRELL [XXX ?ABOUT] . . . . . . . .   52D ISLAND MOON 8  *PROSE
     O AY SAID TILLY LALLY . . . . . . . . . . . . . .   55B ISLAND MOON 9  PROSE
     AY SAID SHE THAT WOULD BE EXCELLENT . . . . . . . .   62D ISLAND MOON 11 PROSE
     AY NOW THOU ART DISCOVERD I WILL USE THEE LIKE A SLAVE . .  104 TIRIEL 4       25
     AY & THE FINEST PICTURES I ALTOGETHER REJECT AS  . . . .  815B LETTER 23     PROSE
AYE
     AYE IT GROWS MOST IN LANDS MOST CULTIVATED  . . . . .   28 EDW THIRD/PS 4     4
     AYE BUT THE OAKS ARE NOT . . . . . . . . . . . .   28 EDW THIRD/PS 4     7
     O AYE I FORGOT TO TELL THAT HE HAS GOT THE SAME NAME  . .   29C EDW THIRD/PS 4 PROSE
     AYE SECONDLY VOLTAIRE S A FOOL SAYS THE EPICUREAN  . . .   45D ISLAND MOON 1  PROSE
     AYE NOW YOU FEEL THE CURSE YOU CRY BUT MAY ALL EARS BE DEAF  106 TIRIEL 5       20
     AYE THATS THE WAY TO MAKE ALL NATURE OUT  . . . . . .   536 DONT BELIEVE/N     8
AYR
     OF REUBEN KINCARD HADDNTN FORFAR SIMEON AYR ARGYLL BANFF  638 JERUSALEM 16    53
AZURE
     SIT SINGING IN THE AZURE CLOUDS AND STREW  . . . . .   30 EDW THIRD/PS 5    31
     AND EVERY MINUTE HAS AN AZURE TENT WITH SILKEN VEILS  .  516 MILTON 28       50
     REFLECTS ETERNITY BENEATH THY AZURE WINGS OF FEATHERY DOWN  730 JERUSALEM 86     5
     RIBBD DELICATE & CLOTHD WITH FEATHERD GOLD & AZURE & PURPLE  731 JERUSALEM 86     6
     SPREADING INTO THE AZURE WINGS WHICH LIKE A CANOPY  . . .  731 JERUSALEM 86     9
B
     BOUNCING B  . . . . . . . . . . . . . . . . . .   62 DR CLASH/IM         9
BA       SEE SA BA RA RA BA RARE RORO
     [OR ANGRY WITH BOYDELL OR BOWYER OR BA] . . . . . .   538 WAS I ANGRY/N       3
BAAL
     IN TYRE & SIDON I SAW BAAL & ASHTAROTH IN MOAB CHEMOSH . .  528 MILTON 37       20
BAALIM
     APPEARD THE SEVEN KINGDOMS OF CANAAN & FIVE BAALIM  . . .  532 MILTON 40       24
     THERE THE SEVEN KINGS OF CANAAN & FIVE BAALIM OF PHILISTEA  735 JERUSALEM 89    46
BAALZEBOLE
     . . . AND THE MILLS OF SATAN & [BAALZEBOLE] BEELZEBOUL   346 FOUR ZOAS 8   *  201
BABBLER
     FLATTERY IS DELICIOUS EVEN FROM THE LIPS OF A BABBLER    29D EDW THIRD/PS 4  PROSE
          EXIT PETER
BABE
     FROM THEM A CALLOW BABE DID SPRING  . . . . . . . .   50 WHEN CORRUP/IM *    5
     THE BABE WITH HIS OWN MILK . . . . . . . . . . .   50 WHEN CORRUP/IM     10
     SWEET BABE IN THY FACE . . . . . . . . . . . . .  120 CRADLE SONG/SI     21
     SWEET BABE ONCE LIKE THEE . . . . . . . . . . . .  120 CRADLE SONG/SI     23
     SWEET BABE IN THY FACE . . . . . . . . . . . . .  165 CRADLE SONG/N      18
     BABE CAN NEVER HUNGER THERE  . . . . . . . . . . .  181 HOLY THURS/N       15
     [WILL THE MOTHER EXCHANGE HER NEW BORN BABE]  . . . .  186 LET BROTHELS/N     52
     BABE CAN NEVER HUNGER THERE  . . . . . . . . . . .  212 HOLY THURS/SE      15
     FIRST IN WRATH THREW HIS LIMBS LIKE THE BABE  . . . .  258 BOOK OF LOS 4     38
     DESCENDS TO BE A WEEPING BABE  . . . . . . . . . .  289 FOUR ZOAS 2      367
     ON THE GOLDEN PALACE SONGS & JOY ON THE DESART THE COLD   363 FOUR ZOAS 9      251
          BABE
     FOR THERE THE BABE IS BORN IN JOY . . . . . . . . .  424 MENTAL TRAVLER      5
     AND IF THE BABE IS BORN A BOY . . . . . . . . . . .  425 MENTAL TRAVLER      9
     A LITTLE FEMALE BABE DOES SPRING  . . . . . . . . .  425 MENTAL TRAVLER     44
     TILL HE BECOMES A [XXX] WAYWARD BABE  . . . . . . .  426 MENTAL TRAVLER *   85
     BUT WHEN THEY FIND THE FROWNING BABE  . . . . . . .  427 MENTAL TRAVLER     93
     THEY CRY THE BABE THE BABE IS BORN  . . . . . . . .  427 MENTAL TRAVLER     95
     AND LIKE A WEEPING BABE BECAME  . . . . . . . . . .  429 CRYSTL CABINET     24
     A WEEPING BABE UPON THE WILD  . . . . . . . . . . .  430 CRYSTL CABINET     25
     THE BABE IS MORE THAN SWADLING BANDS  . . . . . . .  432 AUGURIES          63
     BECOMES A BABE IN ETERNITY  . . . . . . . . . . .  432 AUGURIES          68
     THE BABE THAT WEEPS THE ROD BENEATH  . . . . . . . .  432 AUGURIES          73
     WIDOW FATHER BABE BAPTISM HERVEY ANGEL OF DEATH  . . . SUPP INSC HERVEY  *TITLE
     "AH LUCKLESS BABE BORN UNDER CRUEL STAR" (SPENSER)  . . . SUPP LEGEND/N19   *
BABEL
     BUILT WITH MURDER THEN BABEL MIGHTY REARD HIM TO THE SKIES  41A THEN SHE BORE  PROSE
     BABEL WITH THOUSAND TONGUES CONFUSION IT WAS CALLD AND   41A THEN SHE BORE  *PROSE
          GIVN TO SHAME
     TO MEXICO & PERU WEST & EAST TO CHINA & JAPAN TILL BABEL  486 MILTON 6        23
     HAND HAS PEOPLED BABEL & NINEVEH HYLE ASHUR & ARAM  . . .  625 JERUSALEM 7     18
     BY THE DAUGHTER OF BABEL IN A WOVEN MANTLE OF PESTILENCE  625 JERUSALEM 7     20
          & WAR
     ARE PRACTISED IN BABEL & SHINAR & HAVE APPROACHD TO ZION'S  627 JERUSALEM 8     20
          HILL
     LOS OPEND THE FURNACES IN FEAR THE SPECTRE SAW TO BABEL   627 JERUSALEM 8     23
          & SHINAR
     IN THE WARS OF BABEL & SHINAR ALL THEIR EMANATIONS WERE   628 JERUSALEM 8     42
     BABEL MOCKS SAYING THERE IS NO GOD NOR SON OF GOD  . . .  693 JERUSALEM 60    56
     BABEL & SHINAR LOOK TOWARD THE WESTERN GATE THEY SIT DOWN  730 JERUSALEM 85    18
```

		PAGE	TITLE	LINE

BABES

THE CRIES OF WOMEN AND OF BABES		13	GWIN KING/PS	79
BUT HAR & HEVA SLEPT FEARLESS AS BABES ON LOVING BREASTS		109	TIRIEL 7	21
. . . AND CRIES OF WOMEN AND BABES ARE HEARD		139	FRENCH REVOLTN	118
BABES REDUCD TO MISERY		181	HOLY THURS/N *	3
BABES REDUCD TO MISERY		211	HOLY THURS/SE	3
WHEN I FOUND BABES OF BLISS ON MY BEDS		255	AHANIA 5	19
THARMAS THE MOON HAS CHAMBERS WHERE THE BABES OF LOVE LIE HID		339	FOUR ZOAS 7B	244

BABOONS

| ONE WE ENTERD IN IT WERE A NUMBER OF MONKEYS BABOONS . . | | 157A | MARRIAGE HH 17 | PROSE |

BABY

| DARES STRETCH TO TOUCH HER BABY FORM . . . . | | 425 | MENTAL TRAVLER | 47 |

BABYLON

THEN NINEVA & BABYLON AND COSTLY TYRE AND EVN JERUSALEM		41A	THEN SHE BORE	*PROSE
BINDING JERUSALEM'S CHILDREN IN THE DUNGEONS OF BABYLON		281	FOUR ZOAS 2	63
WHETHER THIS IS JERUSALEM OR BABYLON WE KNOW NOT . . .		294	FOUR ZOAS 3	102
WHO IS MYSTERY BABYLON THE GREAT THE MOTHER OF HARLOTS .		349	FOUR ZOAS 8	330
BABYLON AGAIN IN INFANCY CALLD NATURAL RELIGION . . .		357	FOUR ZOAS 8	620
WHO IS MYSTERY BABYLON THE GREAT MOTHER OF (HARLOTS) .		382	FOUR ZOAS AD 6 *	19
THEN BRINGS FORTH MORAL VIRTUE THE CRUEL VIRGIN BABYLON		484	MILTON 5	27
IN THE WHOLE PLACE OF THE COVERING CHERUB ROME BABYLON & TYRE		490	MILTON 9	51
OPENING INTERIORLY INTO JERUSALEM & BABYLON SHINING GLORIOUS		500	MILTON 18	41
BABYLON THE GREAT THE ABOMINATION OF DESOLATION		506	MILTON 22	49
SEEKING FOR PLEASURES IN MY PLEASURES O DAUGHTER OF BABYLON		522	MILTON 33	4
AS IT IS DONE IN BEULAH & THOU O VIRGIN BABYLON MOTHER OF WHOREDOMS		523	MILTON 33	20
IN WHICH DWELLS MYSTERY BABYLON HERE IS HER SECRET PLACE		529	MILTON 38	23
HERE IS JERUSALEM BOUND IN CHAINS IN THE DENS OF BABYLON		529	MILTON 38	27
HE VIEWS JERUSALEM & BABYLON HIS TEARS FLOW DOWN . . .		531	MILTON 39	48
NO SOONER SHE HAD SPOKE BUT RAHAB BABYLON APPEARD . . .		532	MILTON 40	17
BENEATH THE STEPS (IS) BABYLON REPRESENTED BY		608B	V LAST JUDG/N	PROSE
SUCH AS EGYPT & BABYLON IN WHICH WERE MULTITUDES . . .		610B	V LAST JUDG/N	PROSE
BABYLON THE CITY OF VALA THE GODDESS VIRGIN-MOTHER . . .		640	JERUSALEM 18	29
SLAY NOT MY LITTLE ONES BELOVED VIRGIN DAUGHTER OF BABYLON		643	JERUSALEM 20	27
HE DRIVES THEM THRO THE STREETS OF BABYLON BEFORE MY FACE		644	JERUSALEM 21	30
THERE BABYLON IS BUILDED IN THE WASTE FOUNDED IN HUMAN DESOLATION		647	JERUSALEM 24	25
O BABYLON THY WATCHMAN STANDS OVER THEE IN THE NIGHT .		647	JERUSALEM 24	26
THY SEVERE JUDGE ALL THE DAY LONG PROVES THEE O BABYLON		647	JERUSALEM 24	27
TO BUILD BABYLON BECAUSE THEY HAVE FORSAKEN JERUSALEM .		647	JERUSALEM 24	30
THE WALLS OF BABYLON ARE SOULS OF MEN HER GATES THE GROANS		647	JERUSALEM 24	31
LEST BABYLON WITH CRUEL OG		650	FIELDS FROM/J	22
ARE NOT THE STARS OF HEAVEN THY CHILDREN ART THOU NOT BABYLON		660	JERUSALEM 34	8
COME UP BUILD BABYLON RAHAB IS OURS & ALL HER MULTITUDES		671	JERUSALEM 42	63
TO PERPETUATE TYRANT PRIDE & THE LAWS OF THAT BABYLON .		682A	JERUSALEM 52	PROSE
AND BUILD THIS BABYLON & SACRIFICE IN SECRET GROVES . .		693	JERUSALEM 60	23
BUT JERUSALEM FAINTLY SAW HIM CLOSD IN THE DUNGEONS OF BABYLON		693	JERUSALEM 60	39
BABYLON COME UP TO JERUSALEM AND ANOTHER VOICE ANSWERD SAYING		695	JERUSALEM 61	35
I BEHOLD BABYLON IN THE OPENING STREETS OF LONDON I BEHOLD		714	JERUSALEM 74	16
AGE AFTER AGE DRAWING THEM AWAY TOWARDS BABYLON		715	JERUSALEM 74	31
BABYLON THE RATIONAL MORALITY DELUDING TO DEATH THE LITTLE ONES		715	JERUSALEM 74	32
AND RAHAB BABYLON THE GREAT HATH DESTROYED JERUSALEM . .		715	JERUSALEM 75	1
MYSTERY BABYLON THE GREAT THE ABOMINATION OF DESOLATION		716	JERUSALEM 75	19
TO ENTICE HER SISTERS AWAY TO BABYLON ON EUPHRATES . .		725	JERUSALEM 82	18
CREATE JERUSALEM & BABYLON & EGYPT & MOAB & AMALEK . .		725	JERUSALEM 82	27
BABYLON IS OUR CHIEF DESIRE MOAB OUR BATH IN SUMMER . .		725	JERUSALEM 82	31
SEE HOW THE FIRES OF OUR LOINS POINT EASTWARD TO BABYLON		725	JERUSALEM 82	36
BUT HERE WE BUILD BABYLON ON EUPHRATES COMPELLD TO BUILD		729	JERUSALEM 84	8
OF BABYLON LED BY A CHILD HIS TEARS RUN DOWN HIS BEARD .		729	JERUSALEM 84	12
O THOU THAT DWELLEST WITH BABYLON COME FORTH O LOVELY-ONE		730	JERUSALEM 85	32
HIS LOINS INCLOSE BABYLON ON EUPHRATES BEAUTIFUL . . .		735	JERUSALEM 89	38
FROM BABYLON TO ROME & THE WINGS SPREAD FROM JAPAN . .		735	JERUSALEM 89	48
MYSTERY BABYLON THE GREAT THE DRUID DRAGON & HIDDEN HARLOT		741	JERUSALEM 93	25
THESE ARE NOT THE WORKS OF EGYPT NOR BABYLON		777A	INSC LAOCOON	PROSE
AS BABYLON & EGYPT SO FAR FROM BEING PARENTS OF ARTS .		778C	HOMERS POETRY	PROSE

BACCHUS

| WHO IS THE GENIUS OF EATING AND DRINKING THE BACCHUS . | | 571A | DESC CAT 3 | PROSE |
| O CHEMOSH O BACCHUS O VENUS O DOUBLE GOD OF GENERATION | | 706 | JERUSALEM 68 | 18 |

BACK   SEE HORSE-BACK

I TURN MY BACK TO THE EAST		9	MAD SONG/PS	21
AND DOWN HIS BACK THEY STRAIT CONVEY		17	BLIND-MANS/PS	58
HIS BACK THEN I WILL SAY IT TO HIS FACE		21	EDW THIRD/PS 3	18
I CANNOT BEAR THE ENEMY AT MY BACK		22	EDW THIRD/PS 3	20
OF HAVING MY BACK LAID OPEN WE TURN		22	EDW THIRD/PS 3	37
HE FEARS TO TURN HIS FACE AND YOU TO TURN YOUR BACK . .		22	EDW THIRD/PS 3	41
BUT NOW A CLOUD OERCASTS AND BACK TO TH EAST		41B	THEN SHE BORE	PROSE
SO ONCE THE SUN HIS CHARIOT DREW BACK TO PROLONG A GOOD KING'S LIFE		41B	THEN SHE BORE	PROSE
ON THE BACK OF HIM CAME ALL THE OTHERS IN A HEAP . . .		59A	ISLAND MOON 10	PROSE
SO SAYING IJIM GLOOMY TURND HIS BACK & SILENT SOUGHT .		106	TIRIEL 4	89
TURNING BACK WAS VAIN		114	LIT GRL FND/SI	25
THAT CURLD LIKE A LAMB'S BACK WAS SHAVD SO I SAID . .		117	CHIMNEY SWP/SI	6
FLED BACK UNHINDERD TILL SHE CAME INTO THE VALES OF HAR		130	BOOK OF THEL 6	22
. . . DRIVEN BACK BY THE SANDY DESART		144	FRENCH REVOLTN	235

		PAGE	TITLE	LINE
BACK	(CONTINUED)			
. . . BACK TO THE NATION'S ASSEMBLY AND TOLD	. . . . .	145	FRENCH REVOLTN	256
IT SPUN BACK ?ON ?THE STILE	. . . .	187	WHEN KLOPSTK/N *	31
BOUND BACK TO BACK IN BROMION'S CAVES TERROR & MEEKNESS DWELL		190	V DAU ALBION 2	5
THE DAUGHTERS OF ALBION HEAR HER WOES & ECCHO BACK HER SIGHS		190	V DAU ALBION 2	20
THE DAUGHTERS OF ALBION HEAR HER WOES & ECCHO BACK HER SIGHS		192	V DAU ALBION 5	2
THE DAUGHTERS OF ALBION HEAR HER WOES & ECCHO BACK HER SIGHS		195	V DAU ALBION 8	13
THE RED FIRES RAGD THE PLAGUES RECOILD THEN ROLLD THEY BACK WITH FURY		202	AMERICA 14	20
AND A COWL OF FLESH GREW OER HIS HEAD & SCALES ON HIS BACK & RIBS		202	AMERICA 15	17
WHEN ETERNALS SPURND BACK HIS RELIGION	. . . .	222	URIZEN 2	2
THEN HE LOOKD BACK WITH ANXIOUS DESIRE	. . . .	230	URIZEN 13	45
BUT PALAMABRON SHOT HIS LIGHTNINGS TRENCHING DOWN HIS WIDE BACK		242	EUROPE 12	23
THE LISTNING STARS HEARD & THE FIRST BEAM OF THE MORNING STARTED BACK		275	FOUR ZOAS 1	410
AFAR OFF RUSHING BACK REDDNING WITH RAGE THE [ETERNAL] MIGHTY FATHER		275	FOUR ZOAS 1 *	413
BUT PERVERSE ROLLD THE WHEELS OF URIZEN & LUVAH BACK REVERSD		280	FOUR ZOAS 1	573
IN MISTS OVER HIS CARVED THRONE & WHEN HE TURND HIS BACK		285	FOUR ZOAS 2	184
ITS WASTED [(POWER)] STRENGTH IT BACK RETURNS UPON A NETHER COURSE		287	FOUR ZOAS 2 *	278
. . . & TURND HIS BACK ON VALA	. . . .	293	FOUR ZOAS 3	70
I BACK RETURN WEAKER & WEAKER CONSUME ME NOT AWAY	. . .	296	FOUR ZOAS 3	190
IN WRATH BUT PITYING BACK WITHDREW WITH MANY A SIGH	. . .	298	FOUR ZOAS 4	46
GO FORTH BEAR ENITHARMON BACK TO THE ETERNAL PROPHET	. .	299	FOUR ZOAS 4	70
FROM DEATH IN WRATH & FURY BUT NOW COME BEAR BACK	. . .	300	FOUR ZOAS 4	116
AND BACK RETURN WITH WINE & FOOD OR DIVE INTO THE DEEPS		308	FOUR ZOAS 5	119
WHEN SATIATED WITH GRIEF THEY RETURND BACK TO GOLGONOOZA		309	FOUR ZOAS 5	176
WERE KEPT BACK FROM MY LORD & FROM HIS CHARIOT OF MERCIES		310	FOUR ZOAS 5	209
WHO WOULD NOT SUFFER HIM TO APPROACH BUT DROVE HIM BACK WITH STORMS		311	FOUR ZOAS 6	6
THIS DISMAL WORLD HE STOOD A WHILE & LOOKD BACK OER HIS FORMER		315	FOUR ZOAS 6 *	150
NOR DOWN NOR UP REMAIND THEN IF HE TURND & LOOKD BACK	. .	316	FOUR ZOAS 6	191
THEN URIZEN AROSE UPON THE WIND BACK MANY A MILE	. . .	319	FOUR ZOAS 6	316
AND ROUND RED ORC RETURNING BACK TO URIZEN [GORD] GORGD WITH BLOOD		320	FOUR ZOAS 6 *	322
YET THROW THY LIMBS THESE FIRES ABROAD THAT BACK RETURN UPON THEE		321	FOUR ZOAS 7	60
THE VALES TO FIND HIS WAY BACK INTO HEAVEN BUT FOUND NONE		326	FOUR ZOAS 7	249
[THY] THAT MORTAL BODY & BY SELF ANNIHILATION BACK RETURNING		328	FOUR ZOAS 7	344
THE SCALY ARMOUR SHOT OUT STUBBORN DOWN HIS BACK & BOSOM		343	FOUR ZOAS 8	73
BUT WHEN RAHAB &C TURN BACK (THREE) LEAVES	. . . . .	349D	FOUR ZOAS 8	*PROSE
MY BACK DARKNING THE PRESENT CLOUDING WITH A CLOUD	. . .	361	FOUR ZOAS 9	166
I CAST [REMEMBRANCE] FUTURITY AWAY & TURN MY BACK UPON THAT VOID		361	FOUR ZOAS 9	182
INTO THEIR OWN APPOINTED PLACES DRIVEN BACK BY THE WINDS		365	FOUR ZOAS 9	325
IN MENTAL FLAMES THE FLAMES REFUSD THEY DROVE HIM BACK TO BEULAH		366	FOUR ZOAS 9	356
[THE] AND THE WIND BLOWS IT BACK AGAIN	. . . . . .	418	MOCK ON/N *	4
BLOWN BACK THEY [MO] BLIND THE [MOCKERS] MOCKING EYE	. .	418	MOCK ON/N *	7
AS THE CLOUD THAT BRINGS THE SNOW ALL THE WHILE FROM HIS BACK		483	MILTON 3	34
AND BACK RETURND TO LOS NOT FILLD WITH VENGEANCE BUT WITH TEARS		488	MILTON 8	6
I CAME FORTH FROM THE HEAD OF SATAN BACK THE GNOMES RECOILD		493	MILTON 12	38
BEHIND MY BACK I TURNED ROUND IN TERROR AND BEHOLD	. . .	505	MILTON 22	7
I HAVE TURNED MY BACK UPON THESE HEAVENS BUILDED ON CRUELTY		521	MILTON 32	3
EUROPE TO EUPHRATES & HINDU TO NILE & BACK IN CLOUDS	. .	525	MILTON 35	16
AT THAT BRIGHT GATE ANOTHER LARK MEETS HIM & BACK TO BACK		526	MILTON 36	2
WITH THE FINGER ON THE LIPS & THE BACK TURND TO THE LIGHT		528	MILTON 37	32
SO STEWHARD'S SOUL HE BUCKLD TO HIS BACK	. . . . . .	536	AND HIS LEGS/N	9
BUT NEITHER BACK NOR MOUTH THOSE EGGS COULD HOLD	. . . .	537	AND HIS LEGS/N	13
TURN BACK TURN BACK YOU TRAVEL ALL IN VAIN	. . . . .	541	MR CROMEK/N	3
IT WAS WITH DIFFICULTY BROUGHT BACK AGAIN TO A CERTAIN EFFECT		582B	DESC CAT 9	PROSE
ONLY BE FORCED TO BRING IT BACK TO WHAT IT WAS AND IT WILL		587A	CHAUCER 1	PROSE
THEIR PRODUCING FOR AGES BACK WHILE PAINTING IS EXCLUDED		601A	PUB ADDRESS/N	PROSE
BETWEEN SETH & THESE A FEMALE FIGURE [WITH THE BACK TURND]		611D	V LAST JUDG/N	PROSE
POVERTY IS THE FOOL'S ROD WHICH AT LAST IS TURND ON HIS OWN BACK		612C	V LAST JUDG/N	PROSE
OPAKE DIVIDED FROM HIS BACK HE LABOURS AND HE MOURNS	. .	624	JERUSALEM 6	2
AND THE SPECTROUS DARKNESS FROM HIS BACK DIVIDED IN TEMPTATIONS		639	JERUSALEM 17	57
YOU RECOIL BACK UPON ME . . .	. . . .	646	JERUSALEM 24	2
I HAVE TURNED MY BACK UPON THEE INTO THE WASTES OF MORAL LAW		647	JERUSALEM 24	24
INDIGNANT ROSE THE AWFUL MAN & TURND HIS BACK ON VALA	. .	654	JERUSALEM 29	57
BACK SAFE TO THEIR HUMANITY AS DOVES TO THEIR WINDOWS	. .	655	JERUSALEM 30	13
FEARING THAT ALBION SHOULD TURN HIS BACK AGAINST THE DIVINE VISION		656	JERUSALEM 31	2
TURNING HIS BACK TO THE DIVINE VISION HIS SPECTROUS	. . .	659	JERUSALEM 33	1
FROM THE BACK & LOINS WHERE DWELL THE SPECTROUS DEAD	. .	659	JERUSALEM 33	4
REFLECTING BACK TO ALBION IN SEXUAL REASONING HERMAPHRODITIC		659	JERUSALEM 33	28

		PAGE	TITLE	LINE

BACK   (CONTINUED)
```
      SEEING ALBION HAD TURND HIS BACK AGAINST THE DIVINE VISION    666 JERUSALEM 39      14
      GIVE ME MY EMANATIONS BACK FOOD FOR MY DYING SOUL   . . .     670 JERUSALEM 42      13
      THEY ALBION SURROUND WITH KINDEST VIOLENCE TO BEAR HIM BACK   674 JERUSALEM 44       2
      THEIR AWFUL CHARGE BACK TO HIS NATIVE HOME BUT ALBION DARK    674 JERUSALEM 44       5
      LAMENTATION IT FLEE BACK & HIDE IN NON-ENTITY'S DARK WILD     688 JERUSALEM 56      16
      LOOK BACK INTO THE CHURCH PAUL LOOK THREE WOMEN AROUND        688 JERUSALEM 56      42
      BUT HE SPOKE NOT TO ALBION FEARING LEST ALBION SHOULD         711 JERUSALEM 71      58
          TURN HIS BACK
      SHE HID IT IN HIS RIBS & BACK SHE HID HIS TONGUE WITH         723 JERUSALEM 80      69
          TEETH
      UPON HER BACK BEHIND HER LOINS & THUS UTTERD HER DECEIT       725 JERUSALEM 82      21
      PUTTING BACK THE BLOODY SHRINE . . . . . . . . .             754 EV GOSPEL(E)/N     18
      HIS BACK IS TURNED THEY WILL MURDER THE MOTHER & HER INFANT   792B LETTER 4       PROSE
      HE HAS SENT IT BACK WITH A LETTER FULL OF CRITICISMS   . .    794D LETTER 6      *PROSE
      OUR DWELLING PLACE I LOOK BACK INTO THE REGIONS OF   . . .    802C LETTER 14      PROSE
      & THIS FROM MR H(HAYLEY) WILL BRING ME BACK AGAIN   . . .     812C LETTER 22      PROSE
      & HAD PUT MYSELF BACK AS IF I WAS A LEARNER I HAVE PROVED     815A LETTER 23      PROSE
      IF THOU GOEST BACK THE THISTLE SAID . . . . . . . .          817 HAPPINESS/L       31
      TOOK HIM AGAIN BY THE ELBOWS & KEEPING HIS BACK TO ME   .     827B LETTER 28      PROSE
      ON THE BACK IS WRITTEN...HE SHEWD ME ALSO . . . . . .        843C LETTER 43      PROSE
      WHICH I HAVE HAD SOME TIME BUT KEPT THEM BACK TILL I COULD    850A LETTER 49      PROSE
      VENTURE OUT THE CHILL OF THE WEATHER SOON DRIVES ME BACK      871D LETTER 74      PROSE
          INTO
```
BACKBITING
```
      THEFT IS HINDERING ANOTHER BACKBITING UNDERMINING    . . .     88D ANNO LAVATER     MARG
      SNEAKING & [CALUMNY] BACKBITING & ODDS & ENDS . . . . .        541 MR STOTHARD/N      4
```
BACK BONE
```
      THE BACK BONE OF URIZEN APPEAR . . . . . . . . .              259 BOOK OF LOS 5      14
      AND IT STICKS IN THE DEEP BACK BONE   . . . . . . .           423 THE SMILE          10
```
BACKGROUND
```
      IN THE BACKGROUND A BUILDING WHICH MAY BE SUPPOSED   . .      824A LETTER 27      PROSE
```
BACK GROUND
```
      MORE MADE OUT & THE OTHER MONUMENT IN THE BACK GROUND    .    832B LETTER 32      PROSE
```
BACKS
```
      OUR BACKS TO THE FIRE TILL WE SHALL BURN OUR SKIRTS   . .      22 EDW THIRD/PS 3     38
      OUR BEAUTY IS COVERD OVER WITH CLAY & ASHES & OUR BACKS       286 FOUR ZOAS 2      225
      AND LET ME TOUCH YOUR WOOLY BACKS FOLLOW ME AS I SING   .     368 FOUR ZOAS 9    * 432
      MANY OF THE BACKS OF THE PAPER HAVE ON THEM IMPRESSIONS       877B LETTER 86      PROSE
```
BACKSIDES
```
      AND ALL THE [RIGHTEOUS] VIRTUOUS HAVE SHEWN THEIR BACKSIDES   545 COSWAY FRAZR/N      8
```
BACKWARD
```
      MY FEET ARE TURNED BACKWARD & MY FOOTSTEPS SLIDE IN CLAY      335 FOUR ZOAS 7B      88
      HAS PASSD THAT VORTEX HE PERCIEVES IT ROLL BACKWARD BEHIND    497 MILTON 15          23
      REPUGNANT ROLLD HIS WHEELS BACKWARD INTO NON-ENTITY . . .     674 JERUSALEM 44       6
      BECAUSE THOU BACKWARD DOST RETURN   . . . . . . . .           817 HAPPINESS/L        36
```
BACKWARDS
```
      HE WAS BACKWARDS AND FORWARDS IN THE GARDEN   . . . . .       437D BLAKES MEMORAN PROSE
      IT MAY BE WORKED BACKWARDS AND FORWARDS WITHOUT END . .       587A CHAUCER 1       PROSE
      SAYING THE LORD'S PRAYER BACKWARDS WHICH THEY SAY RAISES      788C ANNO THORNTON   MARG
          THE DEVIL
```
BACON
```
      THIS IS CERTAIN IF WHAT BACON SAYS IS TRUE WHAT CHRIST        396D ANNO BACON      MARG
          SAYS IS FALSE
      WHAT BACON CALLS LIES IS TRUTH ITSELF   . . . . . . .         397D ANNO BACON      MARG
      BACON PUT AN END TO FAITH   . . . . . . . . . . .             398B ANNO BACON      MARG
      BACON SUPPOSES ALL MEN ALIKE   . . . . . . . . . .            398C ANNO BACON      MARG
      A LIE EVERY BODY HATES A KING BACON WAS AFRAID TO SAY THAT    400B ANNO BACON      MARG
      A FLOGGING MAGISTRATE I HAVE SEEN MANY SUCH FLY BLOWS OF      400D ANNO BACON      MARG
          BACON
      WAS I MISTAKEN OR IS BACON A LIAR   . . . . . . . .           401C ANNO BACON      MARG
      BACON HAS NO NOTION OF ANY THING BUT MAMMON   . . . .         402D ANNO BACON    * MARG
      BACON WAS A CONTEMPTIBLE ATHEIST EVIDENTLY AN EPICUREAN       403C ANNO BACON      MARG
      HE DID NOT PERHAPS DISBELIEVE FOR ALL THAT BACON DID   .      403C ANNO BACON      MARG
      ATHEISM IS THUS THE BEST OF ALL BACON FOOLS US   . . .        404B ANNO BACON      MARG
      WHAT MUST OUR CLERGY BE WHO ALLOW BACON TO BE EITHER WISE     404B ANNO BACON      MARG
      BACON SUPPOSES THAT THE DRAGON BEAST & HARLOT ARE WORTHY OF   404D ANNO BACON      MARG
      WHAT A CONTEMPTIBLE FOOL IS THIS BACON   . . . . . .          406C ANNO BACON      MARG
      BACON KNOWS THE WISDOM OF WAR IF IT IS WISDOM   . . . .       407C ANNO BACON      MARG
      BACON CALLS INTELLECTUAL ARTS UNMANLY POETRY PAINTING   .     407D ANNO BACON      MARG
      BACON HATED TALENTS OF ALL KINDS ELOQUENCE IS DISCRETION      409A ANNO BACON      MARG
          OF SPEECH
      BACON WAS ALWAYS A POOR DEVIL IF HISTORY SAYS TRUE   . .      409A ANNO BACON    * MARG
      BACON WAS A USURER . . . . . . . . . . . . .                  409B ANNO BACON      MARG
      BACON IS IN HIS ELEMENT ON USURY IT IS HIMSELF &             409D ANNO BACON      MARG
          HIS PHILOSOPHY
      SUCH WAS BACON STUPID INDEED   . . . . . . . . . .            410A ANNO BACON      MARG
      BACON IS ONLY EPICURUS OVER AGAIN . . . . . . . .            456C ANNO REYNOLDS   MARG
      THE GREAT BACON HE IS CALLD I CALL HIM THE LITTLE BACON       459C ANNO REYNOLDS   MARG
      ("BACON MASTER THOUGHTS OTHERS") [THIS IS THE CHARACTER      SUPP ANNO REYNOLDS * MARG
          OF A KNAVE]
      TO CAST OFF BACON LOCKE & NEWTON FROM ALBION'S COVERING       533 MILTON 41         5
      NEWTON & BACON CRY BEING BADLY NURST . . . . . . .           548 CRIPPLE EVRY/N     6
      LIKE WHAT SR FRANCIS BACON [SHOULD DOWNRIGHT ASSERT] SAYS     599D PUB ADDRESS/N  PROSE
      FOR BACON & NEWTON SHEATHD IN DISMAL STEEL THEIR TERRORS      635 JERUSALEM 15      11
          HANG
      AM I NOT BACON & NEWTON & LOCKE WHO TEACH HUMILITY TO MAN     685 JERUSALEM 54      17
      FROZEN SONS OF THE FEMININE TABERNACLE OF BACON NEWTON        702 JERUSALEM 66      14
          & LOCKE
      AND THERE THEY COMBINE INTO THREE FORMS NAMED BACON           708 JERUSALEM 70      15
          & NEWTON & LOCKE
      TO OCCUPY THE VERY THRESHOLD OF ETERNAL LIFE IF BACON         741 JERUSALEM 93      21
          NEWTON LOCKE
```

BACON   (CONTINUED)
      AND BACON & NEWTON & LOCKE & MILTON & SHAKSPEAR & CHAUCER   745 JERUSALEM 98   9
      LIKE DR PRIESTLY & [SIR ISAAC] BACON & NEWTON   . . . 752 EV GOSPEL(D)/N   39
      THIS WAS SPOKEN BY MY SPECTRE TO VOLTAIRE BACON &C . . . 756B EV GOSPEL(H)/N *TITLE
      FROM BACON NEWTON AND LOCKE   . . . 772D ANNO SPURZHEIM   MARG
      CONSIDER WHAT LORD BACON SAYS "SENSE SENDS OVER TO" . . 794A LETTER 5   PROSE
      BACON & NEWTON WOULD PRESCRIBE WAYS OF MAKING THE WORLD   809A LETTER 20   PROSE
      FOR SOME TIME AFTER SR FRANCIS BACON WOULD SAY IT IS WANT 871A LETTER 72   PROSE
         OF
      DISCIPLINE IN MOUNTAINOUS PLACES SR FRANCIS BACON IS A LIAR 871A LETTER 72   PROSE
      GRAY THE POET FRIAR BACON . . . . SUPP PENC DRAW 2.37 *TITLE
BACONIAN
      THE ONLY THING FOR NEWTONIAN & BACONIAN PHILOSOPHERS   . . 787A ANNO THORNTON   MARG
BACON'S
      BACON'S (REFORMER) VILLAIN IS A KING OR WHO   . . . . 404C ANNO BACON   * MARG
      BACON'S BUSINESS IS NOT INTELLECT OR ART   . . . . .   409D ANNO BACON   * MARG
      KING JAMES WAS BACON'S PRIMUM MOBILE . . . .   410D ANNO BACON   MARG
      BACON'S PHILOSOPHY HAS RUIND ENGLAND . . . .   456C ANNO REYNOLDS   MARG
      [SIR JOSHUA PROVES THAT] BACON'S PHILOSOPHY   . . . . 461C ANNO REYNOLDS * MARG
      BACON'S (PHILOSOPHY) HAS DESTROYD (ALL) ART & SCIENCE   . 470A ANNO REYNOLDS * MARG
      UNDERSTANDING & BACON'S (ADVANCEMENT) OF LEARNING   . . 476D ANNO REYNOLDS * MARG
BAD
      ("AS THE GOOD LOVE THEE THE BAD WILL HATE THEE") UNEASY   72D ANNO LAVATER   MARG
      ("AVOID CHARACTERS WHOSE GOOD & BAD SIDES UNMIXED")   86D ANNO LAVATER   MARG
         MOST EXCELLENT
      MAN IS BAD OR GOOD AS HE UNITES HIMSELF WITH BAD OR GOOD   88A ANNO LAVATER   MARG
         SPIRITS
      WHO DOES THE BISHOP CALL BAD MEN ARE THEY   . . . . .   396A ANNO WATSON   MARG
      CELSUS WAS A BAD ADVISER . . . .   408D ANNO BACON   MARG
      A TRUTH THAT'S TOLD WITH BAD INTENT   . . . .   432 AUGURIES   53
      WITH SOME BAD INTENTION OR AT LEAST WITH A PREJUDICED MIND 438A BLAKES MEMORAN PROSE
      OR BAD GOVERNMENTS WHY SHOULD A GOOD GOVERNMENT ENDEAVOUR 445C ANNO REYNOLDS   MARG
      THE DIFFERENCE BETWEEN A BAD ARTIST & A GOOD ONE IS . . 456A ANNO REYNOLDS   MARG
      THE BAD ARTIST SEEMS TO COPY A GREAT DEAL   . . . . .   456A ANNO REYNOLDS   MARG
      OBLIGATIONS REYNOLDS HAS LAID ON BAD ARTISTS OF ALL CLASSES 473A ANNO REYNOLDS MARG
      BAD PICTURES ARE ALWAYS SR JOSHUA'S FRIENDS   . . . .   478C ANNO REYNOLDS   MARG
      [FOR BAD PICTURES] [AND NEVER A] . . . .   547A PRETTY EPIGR/N *TITLE
      PROTECTRESS OF BAD THAT IS BLOTTING AND BLURRING ART   . 562B DESC CAT ADV   PROSE
      WOOLETT ETCHD VERY BAD HIMSELF . . . .   594A PUB ADDRESS/N   PROSE
      AS THESE [VILLAINS] BAD MEN BOTH PRINT & PUBLISH   . . . 598B PUB ADDRESS/N   PROSE
      FOR THE PURPOSE OF MAKING BAD MEN BETTER BUT FOR   612D V LAST JUDG/N   PROSE
         THE PURPOSE
      THE LAST JUDGMENT IS AN OVERWHELMING OF BAD ART & SCIENCE 617A V LAST JUDG/N PROSE
      & THAT BAD ART WILL BE ADOPTED & MIXED WITH GOOD ART   . 617A V LAST JUDG/N   PROSE
      ARISTOTLE SAYS CHARACTERS ARE EITHER GOOD OR BAD   . . . 778B HOMERS POETRY   PROSE
      BUT A GOOD APPLE TREE OR A BAD IS AN APPLE TREE STILL   778B HOMERS POETRY   PROSE
      A HORSE IS NOT MORE A LION FOR BEING A BAD HORSE THAT   778B HOMERS POETRY   PROSE
         IS ITS
      TO SPEAK GOOD OR BAD . . . .   792C LETTER 4   PROSE
      A BAD OPINION OF THE RECEPTION HE HAS GIVEN TO ME   . . . 821A LETTER 25   PROSE
      BAD USE OF IT BUT IT IS A FACT TOO TRUE THAT IF I HAD ONLY 825D LETTER 27   PROSE
      FOR WHAT IS GOOD MUST SUCCEED FIRST OR LAST BUT WHAT IS BAD 862A LETTER 59   PROSE
      OF BAD PERHAPS OF FATAL CONSEQUENCE IS VERY SORRY INDEED   SUPP LETTER 81A   *PROSE
BADGER
      THE BADGER & FOX THEY WORSHIP BEFORE HIS FEET IN TREMBLING 515 MILTON 28   43
         FEAR
BADLY
      NEWTON & BACON CRY BEING BADLY NURST . . . .   548 CRIPPLE EVRY/N   6
      ABOUT CORREGGIO BEING POOR AND BUT BADLY PAID   . . . . 583B DESC CAT 9   PROSE
BADNESS
      NOW GOODNESS OR BADNESS HAS NOTHING TO DO WITH CHARACTER   778B HOMERS POETRY PROSE
      CHARACTER ITS GOODNESS OR BADNESS IS ANOTHER CONSIDERATION 778B HOMERS POETRY PROSE
BAG   SEE MONEY BAG
      A GUINEA IS MORE BEAUTIFUL THAN THE SUN & A BAG WORN WITH 793D LETTER 5   PROSE
BAGHAVAD-GITA   SEE GEETA
BAGS
      THEN NAKED & WHITE ALL THEIR BAGS LEFT BEHIND   . . . .   118 CHIMNEY SWP/SI   17
      AND GOT WITH OUR BAGS & OUR BRUSHES TO WORK   . . . .   118 CHIMNEY SWP/SI   22
      ARE TOADSTOOLS ON THE MISER'S BAGS   . . . .   432 AUGURIES   52
BAIL
      A FABRICATED PERJURY I HAVE BEEN FORCED TO FIND BAIL   . 827D LETTER 28   PROSE
BAILEY
      THE TABARD INNE BY HENRY BAILEY   . . . .   SUPP ILLUS CHAUCER   *TITLE
BAILLIE
      ARE AS FOLLOW "THE TABARDE INN BY HENRY BAILLIE THE"   . 567B DESC CAT 3   PROSE
      KNOWLEDGE AND EXPERIENCE HENRY BAILLIE THE KEEPER   . . 569D DESC CAT 3   PROSE
BAILLY
      OR BAILLY THE STRONG FOOT OF FRANCE . . . .   142 FRENCH REVOLTN   188
      "BY HENRY BAILLY THE LODGYNG HOUSE FOR PILGRIMS"   . . . 589C CHAUCER/N   PROSE
      "THE TABARDE INN BY HENRY BAILLY" . . . .   590C CHAUCER 2   PROSE
BAITS
      AND SPREADS HIS [NETS] BAITS WITH CARE   . . . . . .   174 HUMAN IMAGE/N   9
      AND SPREADS HIS BAITS WITH CARE   . . . .   217 HUMAN ABSTR/SE   8
BAKD
      CLAY BAKD & ENAMELD ETERNAL GLOWING AS FOUR FURNACES   . 632 JERUSALEM 12   64
      THAT TOWARD ULRO FOUR CLAY BAKD LABORIOUS WORKMANSHIP   . 633 JERUSALEM 13   4
      INTO THE FRAME THEN KNOCK IT OUT UPON THE PLANK & SOULS   657 JERUSALEM 31   11
         ARE BAKD
BALAAM
      THE ARMIES OF BALAAM WEEP NO WOMEN COME TO THE FIELD   . 672 JERUSALEM 43   39
      OF DIVINE ANALOGY AND OG & SIHON IN THE TEARS OF BALAAM   680 JERUSALEM 49   58

BALANCD   SEE SELF BALANCD,SELF-BALANCD
BALANCE
  THE GOLDEN COMPASSES THE QUADRANT & THE RULE & BALANCE . . 281 FOUR ZOAS 2   29
  A FOOL'S BALANCE IS NO CRITERION BECAUSE . . . . 476B ANNO REYNOLDS   MARG
  WITH MORAL LAW AN EQUAL BALANCE NOT GOING DOWN WITH   708 JERUSALEM 69   35
    DECISION
  BUT TO BALANCE ALL THIS I MUST IN DUTY TO MY FRIEND   846C LETTER 44   PROSE
    SEAGRAVE
  RECIEVD FROM YOU & THO I NEVER CAN BALANCE THE ACCOUNT . 854C LETTER 53   PROSE
  URIZEN HEAVEN &C & SONGS OF EXPERIENCE FOR BALANCE . . . SUPP LETTER 56A   *PROSE
  BALANCE DUE FROM ME PREVIOUS TO MY GOING TO FELPHAM . . . SUPP LETTER 56A   *PROSE
  THE BALANCE OF ACCOUNT OF MR UPTON'S PLATE . . . . . . SUPP LETTER 66F   *PROSE
BALANCES
  THE ARMIES STAND LIKE BALANCES . . . .   13 GWIN KING/PS   65
  I HOLD THE BALANCES OF RIGHT & JUST & MINE THE SWORD . 530 MILTON 38   54
  WITH THE SWORD & BALANCES HE IS OG KING OF BASHAN . . . 606C V LAST JUDG/N PROSE
  THIS I BELIEVE ABOUT BALANCES OUR ACCOUNT . . . . . . 826B LETTER 28   PROSE
BALD
  LOOK AT MY BALD HEAD HARK LISTEN YE SERPENTS [?ALL] LISTEN   99 TIRIEL 1   * 29
  GOD BLESS [XXX] THY POOR BALD PATE GOD BLESS THY HOLLOW   101 TIRIEL 2   * 35
    WINKING EYES
  THOU HAST NO TEETH OLD MAN & THUS I KISS THY SLEEK BALD   101 TIRIEL 2   37
    HEAD
  HEVA COME KISS HIS BALD HEAD FOR HE WILL NOT HURT US HEVA   101 TIRIEL 2   38
  BALD TYRANT WRINKLED CUNNING [WRETCH] LISTEN TO ZAZEL'S   108 TIRIEL 7   8
    CHAINS
  THY CROWN IS BALD OLD MAN THE SUN WILL DRY THY BRAINS AWAY 109 TIRIEL 7   12
  BUT THEY DEPICT HIM BALD & AGED WHO IS IN ETERNAL YOUTH   509 MILTON 24   69
BALDWIN
  COSWAY FRAZER & BALDWIN OF EGYPT'S LAKE . . . . 545 COSWAY FRAZR/N   1
BALEFUL
  "AND IN DEAD PARENTS BALEFUL ASHES BRED" (SPENSER) . . . SUPP LEGEND/N19   *
BALL
  THROW US THE BALL . . . .   60 SAY YOU JOE/IM   2
  TO BOWL THE BALL IN A [TURD] TANSEY . . . .   61 SAY YOU JOE/IM   6
  AND THE FLAT EARTH BECOMES A BALL . . . . 426 MENTAL TRAVLER   64
  I WILL KEEP FROM THE BALL & MY EYES SHALL NOT SHINE . . 428 MARY   30
  ONLY WIND IT INTO A BALL . . . . 551 GIVE YOU END/N   2
  THE TERRIBLE BALL THE WEDGE THE LOUD SOUNDING HAMMER OF   713 JERUSALEM 73   12
    DESTRUCTION
  ONLY WIND IT INTO A BALL . . . . 716 I GIVE YOU/J   2
  THIS PHARISAIC WORLDLY BALL . . . . 758 EV GOSPEL (2)   14
  LIGHTER THAN A BALL OF WOOL ROLLED BY THE WIND . . . . 809A LETTER 20   PROSE
BALLAD
  HAVE ENGRAVED ONE OF THE PLATES FOR THAT BALLAD OF THE   861A LETTER 58   PROSE
    HORSE
BALLAD'S
  SUFFERED HAD THE WORK BEEN COMPLETED WITHOUT THAT BALLAD'S 861A LETTER 58   PROSE
BALLADS
  I ALSO INCLOSE YOU SOME BALLADS BY MR HAYLEY WITH PRINTS   819A LETTER 24   PROSE
  OF WORK THAT I HAVE HAD NO TIME TO GO ON WITH THE BALLADS   820C LETTER 25   PROSE
  I SEND WITH THIS...COPIES OF...OF THE BALLADS FOR . . . 821B LETTER 25   PROSE
  FOR THEM THESE BALLADS ARE LIKELY TO BE PROFITABLE FOR WE   821B LETTER 25   PROSE
  THE REASON THE BALLADS HAVE BEEN SUSPENDED IS . . . . 822B LETTER 26   PROSE
  I CALLED ON MR EVANS WHO GIVES SMALL HOPES OF OUR BALLADS   831C LETTER 31   PROSE
    HE
  EDWD (FIRST) OR THE BALLADS HAVING COME FROM YOU . . . 857A LETTER 54   PROSE
  PRAY MIGHT I NOT SHEW PHILLIPS THE FOUR NUMBERS OF BALLADS 857B LETTER 54   PROSE
  PROPOSING THE BALLADS TO HIM ON MY ACCOUNT AND INFORM YOU   858B LETTER 55   PROSE
  OF THE BALLADS THE PRINTS (FIVE) IN NUMBER I HAVE ENGAGED   859A LETTER 56   PROSE
  TWO BALLADS ARE SO PREEMINENT & MY DESIGNS FOR THEM . . 859B LETTER 56   PROSE
  AT THE BEGINNING OF THE BALLADS HAS SET MY BRAINS TO WORK   860B LETTER 56   PROSE
  BALLADS WERE THE EFFUSIONS OF FRIENDSHIP TO COUNTENANCE   860C LETTER 56   PROSE
  I CANNOT GIVE YOU ANY ACCOUNT OF OUR BALLADS . . . . 862A LETTER 59   PROSE
  THE SITUATIONS OF OUR BEAUTIFUL AFFECTIONATE BALLADS I KNOW 863B LETTER 60   PROSE
  NOS OF HAYLEY'S BALLADS PRINTS NEBUCHADNEZZAR NEWTON   SUPP LETTER 56A   *PROSE
  HAYLEY'S BALLADS PER BROTHER DITTO MR BIRCH . . . . . SUPP LETTER 56A   *PROSE
BALLAST
  BUT IN VAIN THE FASTER I BIND THE BETTER IS THE BALLAST   809A LETTER 20   PROSE
BALLOON
  & HER FOOTMAN & HER MAIDS & STORMONTS & BALLOON HATS . .   52D ISLAND MOON 8 PROSE
BALL ROOM
  CAME INTO THE BALL ROOM AMONG THE FAIR . . . . 428 MARY   2
BALLS
  HOW TO BUILD A UNIVERSE WITH FARTHING BALLS . . . . . 598C PUB ADDRESS/N PROSE
BALM
  WILT THOU BRING COMFORTS ON THY WINGS AND DEWS AND HONEY   192 V DAU ALBION 4   10
    AND BALM
  THEN JESUS CHRIST COMES WITH A BALM TO HEAL IT . . . . 617A V LAST JUDG/N PROSE
  VIEWING LOS IN HIS SHUDDERINGS POURING BALM ON HIS SORROWS 732 JERUSALEM 86   47
BALMING
  ON A BROAD WAVE IN THE WARM WEST BALMING HER BLEEDING WOUND 299 FOUR ZOAS 4   58
BALMY
  UNSEEN DESCENDING WEIGH MY LIGHT WINGS UPON BALMY FLOWERS   128 BOOK OF THEL 3 12
  IN GOLDEN WREATHES THE SORROW OF MAN & THE BALMY DROPS   293 FOUR ZOAS 3   67
    FELL DOWN
  IN GOLDEN WREATHES THE SORROW OF MAN & THE BALMY DROPS   654 JERUSALEM 29   54
    FELL DOWN
BALTIMORE
  UPON THE LAKES OF IRELAND FROM RATHLIN TO BALTIMORE . . . 679 JERUSALEM 49   4
BAN
  IN EVERY VOICE IN EVERY BAN . . . . 170 LONDON/N   7

166

                                                            PAGE   TITLE   LINE
BAN   (CONTINUED)
    IN EVERY VOICE IN EVERY BAN   . . . .   216 LONDON/SE   7
BAND   SEE SWADDLING-BAND
    THEN DOWN CAME CONSCIENCE WITH HIS LOVELY BAND THE   . . .   42B THEN SHE BORE   PROSE
    TILL WE ARISE LINKD IN A GOLDEN BAND AND NEVER PART   . . . 128 BOOK OF THEL 3   15
    CHAIND HAND AND FOOT ROUND HIS NECK AN IRON BAND . . . . .   135 FRENCH REVOLTN   27
    . . . ROUND HIS MIDDLE A CHAIN AND A BAND   . . . .   136 FRENCH REVOLTN   44
    AND WHO SHALL BIND THE INFINITE WITH AN ETERNAL BAND   . .   239 EUROPE PREL 2   13
    TO WELCOME THY ARRIVAL AMONG COWPER'S GLORIFIED BAND   . .   854C LETTER 53   PROSE
BANDS
    BY BANDS OF ENEMIES STRETCH FORTH THY HAND AND SAVE   . .   40B SAMSON/PS   PROSE
    AND KISSES ME AND BINDS HIS NUPTIAL BANDS AROUND MY BREAST   129 BOOK OF THEL 5
    EACH STERN VISAGE LOCKD UP AS WITH STRONG BANDS OF IRON   137 FRENCH REVOLTN   66
    . . .
    . . . ARE THE BANDS OF THE MURMURING KINGDOM   . . . . .   145 FRENCH REVOLTN   254
    STRIVING AGAINST MY SWADDLING BANDS   . . . .   166 INFANT SORW/N   6
    AND THE LEPROSY LONDON'S SPIRIT SICKENING ALL THEIR BANDS   202 AMERICA 15   3
    AROUND THE SMITTEN BANDS CLOTHED IN TEARS & TREMBLING   203 AMERICA 16   9
        SHUDDRING COLD
    IN TERROR VIEWD THE BANDS OF ALBION AND THE ANCIENT   203 AMERICA 16   17
        GUARDIANS
    STRIVING AGAINST MY SWADLING BANDS   . . . .   217 INFANT SORW/SE   6
    TO COMPASS IT WITH SWADDLING BANDS AND WHO SHALL CHERISH IT 239 EUROPE PREL 2   14
    SHADOWS OF MEN IN FLEETING BANDS UPON THE WINDS   . . . .   241 EUROPE 9   6
    TILL ALBION'S ANGEL SMITTEN WITH HIS OWN PLAGUES FLED WITH   241 EUROPE 9   8
        HIS BANDS
    WITH BANDS OF IRON ROUND THEIR NECKS FASTEND INTO THE WALLS 243 EUROPE 12   29
    AND HEARD HIS WORD DIVIDE YE BANDS INFLUENCE BY INFLUENCE   280 FOUR ZOAS 2   23
    THE BANDS OF HEAVEN FLEW THRO THE AIR SINGING & SHOUTING   281 FOUR ZOAS 2   26
        TO URIZEN
    OF SAND IN BANDS OF HUNDREDS & OF FIFTIES & OF THOUSANDS   314 FOUR ZOAS 6   107
    . . .
    CLING ROUND THE MEN IN BANDS OF TWENTIES & OF FIFTIES PALE   358 FOUR ZOAS 9   48
    THE BABE IS MORE THAN SWADLING BANDS   . . . .   432 AUGURIES   63
    AND LET US BIND THEE IN THE BANDS OF WAR & BE THOU KING   501 MILTON 20   5
    THEY HOLD THE IMMORTAL FORM IN GENTLE BANDS & TENDER TEARS   624 JERUSALEM 5   55
    THOU HADST WOVEN IT WITH ART THOU HADST CAUGHT ME IN THE   643 JERUSALEM 20   31
        BANDS
    THESE AWFUL FORMS IN OUR SOFT BANDS DISTRACTED WITH   723 JERUSALEM 80   85
        TREMBLING
    OF RELIGION & HUMILITY THE TWO BANDS OF SOCIETY HAVING BEEN 804A LETTER 16   PROSE
BANDY
    WOULD NOT HAVE BANDY CHILDREN NOR FASTING NOR BIRCH   . . . 179 LIT VAGABOND/N   13
    WOULD NOT HAVE BANDY CHILDREN NOR FASTING NOR BIRCH   . . . 216 LIT VAGABND/SE   12
BANE
    [THOU MY] ETERNAL BANE   . . . .   169 EARTHS ANSWR/N   24
    ETERNAL BANE   . . . .   211 EARTHS ANSR/SE   24
    TIS THOU HAST DARKEND ALL MY WORLD O WOMAN LOVELY BANE   . . 269 FOUR ZOAS 1   178
    THE BANE OF ALL THAT ON EARTH I LOVE   . . . .   419 I SAW A MONK/A   31
    THE BANE OF ALL THAT ON EARTH I LOVD   . . . .   430 GREY MONK   16
    MUST MY WIFE LIVE IN MY SISTER'S BANE   . . . .   818 HAPPINESS/L   49
BANFF
    OF REUBEN KINCARD HADDNTN FORFAR SIMEON AYR ARGYLL BANFF   638 JERUSALEM 16   53
BANGOR
    LITCHFIELD SAINT DAVIDS LANDAFF ASAPH BANGOR SODOR   . . .   676 JERUSALEM 46   19
BANISH
    IN THEIR OWN SELFHOODS IN NATURAL SELFISH CHASTITY   679 JERUSALEM 49   28
        TO BANISH PITY
BANISHD
    I DIE I DIE IN THY ARMS THO HOPE IS BANISHD FROM ME   . .   648 JERUSALEM 24   60
    [WHEN ALBION UTTERD HIS LAST WORDS HOPE IS BANISHD FROM ME] 677 JERUSALEM 47   * 1
    THEREFORE I WRITE ALBION'S LAST WORDS HOPE IS BANISHD FROM   677 JERUSALEM 47   18
        ME
BANISHED
    I COME THAT I MAY FIND A WAY FOR MY BANISHED ONES TO RETURN 653 JERUSALEM 29   25
BANISHED-ONES
    BUT WILL PREPARE A WAY FOR MY BANISHED-ONES TO RETURN   . . 696 JERUSALEM 62   22
BANK
    SOME BANK BESIDE A RIVER CLEAR THROW THY   . . . . . .   2 TO SUMMER/PS   11
    THE BLUSHING BANK IS ALL MY CARE   . . . .   15 BLIND-MANS/PS   3
    BUT I FOUND MYSELF SITTING ON A PLEASANT BANK BESIDE A   156C MARRIAGE HH 17 PROSE
        RIVER
    FOR WHEN YOU RAN AWAY I FOUND MYSELF ON A BANK BY MOONLIGHT 156D MARRIAGE HH 17 PROSE
    I LAID ME DOWN UPON A BANK   . . . .   162 LAID ME DOWN/N   1
    SIT ON A BANK AND DRAW THE PLEASURES OF THIS FREE BORN JOY 194 V DAU ALBION 7   2
    I'LL LIE BESIDE THEE ON A BANK & VIEW THEIR WANTON PLAY   195 V DAU ALBION 7   25
    UPON THE ROSE OR LILLY PALE OR ON A BANK   288 FOUR ZOAS 2   * 314
        WHERE [SLEEPS] SLEEP
    THE YOUTHFUL POET SLEEPING ON A BANK   . . . .   618C ILLUS MILTON   PROSE
    MILTON SLEEPING ON A BANK SLEEP DESCENDING WITH A   . . . 619C ILLUS MILTON   PROSE
BANKS
    THO BORN ON THE CHEATING BANKS OF THAMES   . . . . . .   166 WHY CARE FOR/N   5
    COLD DEWS & HOARY FROST CREEPS THO I LIE ON BANKS OF SUMMER 288 FOUR ZOAS 2   * 320
    VALA SHRUNK IN LIKE THE DARK SEA THAT LEAVES ITS SLIMY   294 FOUR ZOAS 3   99
        BANKS
    . . . ON THE BANKS OF [THE MOON] ARNON   . . . .   346 FOUR ZOAS 8   * 215
    COMPELLD THE GNOMES TO CURB THE HORSES & TO THROW BANKS   493 MILTON 12   17
        OF SAND
    THE BANKS OF CAM COLD LEARNING'S STREAMS . . . . . .   501 MILTON 19   39
    NAMD OLOLON ON WHOSE MILD BANKS DWELT THOSE WHO MILTON   503 MILTON 21   16
        DROVE
    FOR SEVEN DAYS OF ETERNITY AND THE RIVER'S LIVING BANKS   503 MILTON 21   18

		PAGE	TITLE	LINE

BANKS   (CONTINUED)
THE RIVER RISES ABOVE HIS BANKS TO WASH THE WOOF . . . . 518 MILTON 29   60
ON WHOSE BANKS GROWS THE TREE OF LIFE   . . . . 613B V LAST JUDG/N   PROSE
AFTER MY THREE YEARS SLUMBER ON THE BANKS OF THE OCEAN . 620D JERUSALEM 3   PROSE
THE BANKS OF THE THAMES ARE CLOUDED THE ANCIENT PORCHES 623 JERUSALEM 5   1
    OF ALBION ARE
VALA SHRUNK IN LIKE THE DARK SEA THAT LEAVES ITS SLIMY   655 JERUSALEM 29   78
    BANKS
HERE ON THE BANKS OF THE THAMES LOS BUILDED GOLGONOOZA . . 684 JERUSALEM 53   15
RIVERS THUNDERD AGAINST THEIR BANKS LOUD WINDS FURIOUS   686 JERUSALEM 55   24
    FOUGHT
IN ERIN'S CONTINENT AND JERUSALEM WEPT UPON EUPHRATES'   719 JERUSALEM 78   27
    BANKS
THEY ARE RED HOT WITH CRUELTY RAVING ALONG THE BANKS OF 737 JERUSALEM 90   47
    THAMES
ON THE BANKS OF THE OCEAN UNLESS HE HAS SEEN THEM IN THE 823A LETTER 26   PROSE
    SPIRIT
BANKS THE SCULPTOR IS GONE TO HIS ETERNAL HOME   . . . . 859D LETTER 56   PROSE
BANKS'S
AT THE ROYAL ACADEMY ON THE OCCASION OF BANKS'S DEATH . . 859D LETTER 56   *PROSE
BANNER
[FAYETTE BESIDE HIS BANNER STOOD] . . . . 186 LET BROTHELS/N   43
TO WHERE THE CONTRARIES OF BEULAH WAR BENEATH NEGATION'S 524 MILTON 34   23
    BANNER
BANNERS
THE TROUBLD BANNERS WAVE . . . . 11 GWIN KING/PS   16
LET WAR STAIN THE BLUE HEAVENS WITH BLOODY BANNERS . . . 31 EDW THIRD/PS 5   63
AND BANNERS FLYING . . . . 62 CROWND KING/IM   4
HORSES ELEPHANTS BANNERS CASTLES SLINGS AND ROCKS . . . 159D SONG LIBERTY   PROSE
WITH MYRIADS OF CLOUDY TERRORS BANNERS DARK & TOWERS . . 197 AMERICA 4   10
THEY SPOTTED WITH PLAGUES FORSOOK THE FRONTIERS & THEIR 202 AMERICA 15   14
    BANNERS SEARD
THE WORLD IS SILENT AT THE FLAPPING OF THE FOLDING BANNERS 204 AMERICA CANC B   19
THARMAS LAUGHD FURIOUS AMONG THE BANNERS CLOTHD IN BLOOD 334 FOUR ZOAS 7B   49
AWAKE I HEAR THE FLAPPINGS OF THE FOLDING BANNERS   . . 336 FOUR ZOAS 7B * 149
THEY SEEM TO ONE ANOTHER LAUGHING TERRIBLE AMONG   344 FOUR ZOAS 8   122
    THE BANNERS
LO DARKNESS COVERS THE LONG POMP OF BANNERS ON THE WIND 375 FOUR ZOAS 9   666
BENEATH THE IRON WHIPS OF THEIR CAPTAINS & CONSECRATED   704 JERUSALEM 67   30
    BANNERS
BANQUETS
AND AT MY BANQUETS OF NEW WINE MY HEAD WAS CROWND WITH JOY 310 FOUR ZOAS 5   201
BANQUETTABLE
FLOWERS OF HEAVEN'S GROWTH OVER THE BANQUET-TABLE   . . . 30 EDW THIRD/PS 5   32
BAPTISM
ON THE RIGHT HAND OF THE THRONE OF CHRIST IS BAPTISM   . . 444B LAST JUDGMNT/L PROSE
APPROACH THE FIGURE OF AN AGED APOSTLE WHICH REPRESENTS 444B LAST JUDGMNT/L PROSE
    BAPTISM
[ONE] THAT ON THE RIGHT REPRESENTS BAPTISM . . . . . . 612D V LAST JUDG/N   PROSE
ON THE SIDE NEXT BAPTISM ARE SEEN THOSE CALLD IN THE BIBLE 613D V LAST JUDG/N PROSE
AND WITHOUT THE BAPTISM OF REPENTANCE TO WASH AWAY   697 JERUSALEM 63   28
    CALUMNIES AND
THEIR MARRIAGE & THEIR BAPTISM THEIR BURIAL & CONSECRATION 738 JERUSALEM 91   15
WIDOW FATHER BABE BAPTISM HERVEY ANGEL OF DEATH   . . SUPP INSC HERVEY   *TITLE
BAPTIST
THE HOLY FAMILY CONSISTING OF MARY JOSEPH JOHN THE BAPTIST 614A V LAST JUDG/N PROSE
BAPTIZING
CHRIST BAPTIZING SAMSON BREAKING BONDS SAMSON SUBDUD   SUPP LETTER 56A   *PROSE
GOD CREATING ADAM CHRIST APPEARING TOUCHG UP CHRIST   SUPP LETTER 56A   *PROSE
    BAPTIZING
BAR
O WINTER BAR THINE ADAMANTINE DOORS . . . .   2 TO WINTER/PS   1
THE ETERNAL GATES' TERRIFIC PORTER LIFTED THE NORTHERN BAR 130 BOOK OF THEL 6   1
MY GOLDEN LIPS NOR TOOK THE BAR FROM ENITHARMON'S BREAST 326 FOUR ZOAS 7   238
SHALL NEVER PASS THE POLAR BAR . . . . 432 AUGURIES   42
OF MORTAL LIFE TO CONDEMN THE ACCUSED WHO AT SATAN'S BAR 507 MILTON 23   42
AND TIMBERS CRAMPT WITH IRON CRAMPS BAR IN THE JOYS OF LIFE 515 MILTON 28   40
BROKE DOWN FROM EVERY CHAIN & BAR . . . . 749 EV GOSPEL(B)/N   41
BARBARITIES
THE SAVAGE BARBARITIES OF WAR   . . . . 580C DESC CAT 5   PROSE
BARBER
OVER MY DOOR AS THE POOR BARBER DID MONEY FOR LIVE HERE 858C LETTER 55   PROSE
BARD
THE VOICE OF THE ANCIENT BARD   . . . . 126A VOICE BARD/SI   TITLE
[THE STERN BARD CEASD ASHAMD OF HIS OWN SONG ENRAGD HE 196 AMERICA PREL 2   18
    SWUNG]
HID IN HIS CAVES THE BARD OF ALBION FELT THE ENORMOUS   202 AMERICA 15   16
    PLAGUES
HEAR THE VOICE OF THE BARD . . . . 210 INTRODUCTN/SE   1
A BARD BROKE FORTH ALL SAT ATTENTIVE TO THE AWFUL MAN . . 482 MILTON 2   24
THE BARD CEASD ALL CONSIDERD AND A LOUD RESOUNDING MURMUR 495 MILTON 13   45
LOUD VOICD BARD AND MANY CONDEMND THE HIGH TONED SONG . . 495 MILTON 13   47
LET THE BARD HIMSELF WITNESS WHERE HADST THOU THIS TERRIBLE 495 MILTON 13   50
    SONG
THE BARD REPLIED I AM INSPIRED I KNOW IT IS TRUTH FOR I 495 MILTON 13   51
    SING
THE LOUD VOICD BARD TERRIFYD TOOK REFUGE IN MILTON'S BOSOM 495 MILTON 14   9
THAT IT WAS MILTON THE AWAKENER THEY HAD NOT HEARD THE BARD 504 MILTON 21   33
NUMBER IV THE BARD FROM GRAY . . . . 576A DESC CAT 4   TITLE
THE BARD STANDS PROSTRATED BY THE TERRORS OF HIS HARP . . 577A DESC CAT 4   PROSE
A CORSE OF A SLAUGHTERED BARD AT THE FOOT OF THE ROCK . . 577A DESC CAT 4   PROSE
THEY ARE THERE NOW GRAY SAW THEM IN THE PERSON OF HIS BARD 578C DESC CAT 5   PROSE

```
                                                                PAGE     TITLE          LINE
BARD   (CONTINUED)
      DARE TOUCH OXFORD IMMORTAL BARD WITH ELOQUENCE      .   .   .  676 JERUSALEM 46         7
      MY MUCH ADMIRED & RESPECTED EDWARD THE BARD OF OXFORD    .  835A LETTER 34          PROSE
      AROUND YOUR HERMIT & BARD SO PRAYS THE EMULATOR OF BOTH     835B LETTER 34          PROSE
      THE BEGINNING OF POESY THE BLIND BEGGING BARD STUDY     .  SUPP ILLUS GRAY        *TITLE
      A WELCH BARD THE SLAUGHTERD BARDS TAKEN FROM THIS LINE     SUPP ILLUS GRAY        *TITLE
      THE BARD WEAVING EDWARD'S FATE   .   .   .   .   .   .   .  SUPP ILLUS GRAY        *TITLE
      A FESTAL BOARD THE BARD SINGING OWEN'S PRAISE             SUPP ILLUS GRAY        *TITLE
      INTRODUCTION HEAR THE VOICE OF THE BARD &C      .   .   .  SUPP LETTER 66A        *PROSE
      THE ANGEL THE SICK ROSE TO TIRZAH THE VOICE OF            SUPP LETTER 66A        *PROSE
          THE ANCIENT BARD
BARD'S
      A BARD'S PROPHETIC SONG FOR SITTING AT ETERNAL TABLES   .   .  482 MILTON 2           22
      EDWARD & HIS QUEEN & NOBLES ASTONISHD AT THE BARD'S SONG   SUPP ILLUS GRAY        *TITLE
BARDS
      OUR BARDS ARE FAMD WHO STRIKE THE SILVER WIRE   .   .   .   .    2 TO SUMMER/PS        14
      THAT BARDS OF OLD ENJOYD IN YOU   .   .   .   .   .   .   .   .   11 TO MUSES/PS         14
      AMONG ALBION'S DRUIDS & BARDS IN THE CAVES BENEATH ALBION'S    489 MILTON 9            2
      THE SPIRITS OF THE MURDERED BARDS   .   .   .   .   .   .   .  576C DESC CAT 4       PROSE
      THE BARDS WHO WERE CAPABLE OF ATTENDING WARLIKE DEEDS   .  580C DESC CAT 5       PROSE
      A WELCH BARD THE SLAUGHTERD BARDS TAKEN FROM THIS LINE     SUPP ILLUS GRAY        *TITLE
BARE
      HUSH TOM NEVER MIND IT FOR WHEN YOUR HEAD S BARE   .   .   .  117 CHIMNEY SWP/SI        7
      AND THEIR FIELDS ARE BLEAK & BARE   .   .   .   .   .   .   .  181 HOLY THURS/N         10
      AND THEIR FIELDS ARE BLEAK & BARE   .   .   .   .   .   .   .  212 HOLY THURS/SE        10
BAREFOOT
      MADE HIM GO NAKED AND BAREFOOT THREE YEARS HE ANSWERD   .  154A MARRIAGE HH 12  PROSE
BARGAIN
      SHAKE HANDS WITH DEATH AND STRIKE A BARGAIN FOR   .   .   .   22 EDW THIRD/PS 3        29
      FOR TWAS A KIND OF BARGAIN SCREWMUCH MADE   .   .   .   .   .  537 AND HIS LEGS/N       36
BARK
      FRAIL BARK CAN SEE NO SHORE OR BOUND FOR VAST   .   .   .   .   26 EDW THIRD/PS 3      237
      [THE ROUGH BARK OPENS TWITTERING PEEP FORTH LITTLE BEAKS    270 FOUR ZOAS 1        206
          & WINGS]
      AS THE TREE KNOWS NOT WHAT IS OUTSIDE OF ITS LEAVES & BARK    314 FOUR ZOAS 6         95
      THE BLEAT THE BARK BELLOW & ROAR   .   .   .   .   .   .   .  432 AUGURIES            71
BARKD
      . . . HIS SKIN BARKD OER WITH WRINKLES   .   .   .   .   .  318 FOUR ZOAS 6        262
BARKED
      [THE BARKED OAK THE LONG LIMBD BEECH THE CHESNUT TREE THE    269 FOUR ZOAS 1     *  204
          PINE]
BARKS
      BARKS AT THE BREAKING DAY THE NIGHTINGALE HAS DONE         190 V DAU ALBION 2        24
          LAMENTING
BARN
      WAILING RUNS ROUND THE VALLEYS FROM THE MILL & FROM THE    275 FOUR ZOAS 1        395
          BARN
      INTO THE BARN WHILE CHILDREN GLEAN THE EARS AROUND THE DOOR  376 FOUR ZOAS 9        702
BARNS
      THE BULBOUS ROOTS THROWN UP TOGETHER INTO BARNS & GARNERS    284 FOUR ZOAS 2        165
      THE WINTER THOU SHALT PLOW & LAY THY STORES INTO THY BARNS   362 FOUR ZOAS 9        214
      THEY TOOK THEM INTO THE WIDE BARNS WITH LOUD REJOICINGS      372 FOUR ZOAS 9        585
          & TRIUMPH
      I HEAR THE FLAIL OF URIZEN HIS BARNS ARE FULL NO (ROOM)      375 FOUR ZOAS 9     *  696
      THEIR WINE-PRESSES & BARNS STAND OPEN THE OVENS ARE PREPARD  535 MILTON 42          37
BAROCCIO
      ("TITIAN VERONESE TINTORET THE BASSANS CORREGGIO BAROCCIO")  457A ANNO REYNOLDS    MARG
BAROMETER
      A PIECE OF SEA WEED SERVES FOR A BAROMETER   .   .   .   .   .  816B LETTER 23       PROSE
BARON
      ELIZABETH "GIRT WITH MANY A BARON BOLD"   .   .   .   .   .  SUPP ILLUS GRAY        *TITLE
BARONS
      [CHARLEMAINE & HIS BARONS BOLD]   .   .   .   .   .   .   .   .  418 I SAW A MONK/N        7
      CHARLEMAINE & HIS BARONS BOLD   .   .   .   .   .   .   .   .  420 I SAW MNK AD/N        13
BARRATON
      LIKE THE TALL GHOST OF BARRATON   .   .   .   .   .   .   .   .   12 GWIN KING/PS        53
BARRD
      NOW BARRD OUT BY THE ATLANTIC SEA   .   .   .   .   .   .   .  159B SONG LIBERTY      PROSE
      NOW BARRD OUT BY THE ATLANTIC SEA CALLD ATLANTEAN HILLS      200 AMERICA 10           6
      TURND OUTWARD BARRD AND PETRIFYD AGAINST THE INFINITE   .  241 EUROPE 10           15
      REFUSD TO OPEN THE BRIGHT GATES SHE CLOSD AND BARRD THEM     279 FOUR ZOAS 1        565
          FAST
BARREL
      WOULD HAVE NO MORE QUARREL WITH THE DEVIL OR THE BARREL      180 LIT VAGABOND/N       16
      WOULD HAVE NO MORE QUARREL WITH THE DEVIL OR THE BARREL      216 LIT VAGABND/SE       15
BARREN
      AND ON THE BARREN HEATH   .   .   .   .   .   .   .   .   .   .  148 MARRIAGE HH 2        7
      THE JUST MAN INTO BARREN CLIMES   .   .   .   .   .   .   .   .  148 MARRIAGE HH 2       16
      WHERE MAN IS NOT NATURE IS BARREN   .   .   .   .   .   .   .  152D MARRIAGE HH 10  PROSE
      THE SWORD SUNG ON THE BARREN HEATH   .   .   .   .   .   .   .  178 SWORD SUNG/N         1
      BARREN A ROCK WHICH HIMSELF   .   .   .   .   .   .   .   .   .  252 AHANIA 3            57
      THARMAS ENDURD NOT HE FLED HOWLING THEN A BARREN WASTE       275 FOUR ZOAS 1        419
          SUNK DOWN
      IS GIVEN A CRAVING CRY THAT THEY MAY SIT AT NIGHT ON BARREN  325 FOUR ZOAS 7        205
          ROCKS
      AS THOU DOST SMILE UPON THE BARREN MOUNTAINS AND            370 FOUR ZOAS 9        492
          THEY REJOICE
      FROM THE CLIFFS OF MEMORY AND REASONING IT IS A BARREN ROCK  581B DESC CAT 6       TITLE
      IT IS ALSO CALLED THE BARREN WASTE OF LOCKE AND NEWTON  .  581B DESC CAT 6       TITLE
      EVERY UNIVERSAL FORM WAS BECOME BARREN MOUNTAINS OF MORAL    657 JERUSALEM 31         19
      ALBION THE HIGH CLIFF OF THE ATLANTIC IS BECOME A BARREN     660 JERUSALEM 34         16
          LAND
```

169

```
                                                           PAGE      TITLE          LINE
BARREN   (CONTINUED)
     THEREFORE THY MOUNTAINS ARE BECOME BARREN JERUSALEM  .  .   693 JERUSALEM 60       25
     [ AS THOU DOST SMILE UPON THE BARREN MOUNTAINS AND THEY     SUPP FOUR ZOAS 1     *
        REJOICE ]
BARRIERS
     GOLDEN SPAIN BURST THE BARRIERS OF OLD ROME   .  .  .  .  . 159A SONG LIBERTY     PROSE
     AND EVERY YEAR INVULNERABLE BARRIERS WITH HIGH TOWERS  .  . 516 MILTON 28          55
BARRY
     THE SOCIETY FOR THE ENCOURAGEMENT OF ART SUFFERD BARRY   .  446A ANNO REYNOLDS    MARG
     WERE ENDEAVOURING TO DEPRESS BARRY TOLD ME  .  .  .  .  .   446A ANNO REYNOLDS    MARG
     HOW MUCH DID BARRY GET   .  .  .  .  .  .  .  .  .  .  .  . 450B ANNO REYNOLDS    MARG
     BARRY PAINTED A PICTURE FOR BURKE EQUAL TO RAFAEL OR   .  . 451D ANNO REYNOLDS    MARG
     I THINK (THAT) BARRY OR FUSELI WROTE IT OR [ ?SAID ] DICTATED 463C ANNO REYNOLDS  * MARG
        IT
     TO COME IN BARRY A POEM  .  .  .  .  .  .  .  .  .  .  .  . 553D ASKD PRIGG/N     PROSE
     THEY COULD NOT WOUND EVEN MR BARRY SO  .  .  .  .  .  .  .  592D PUB ADDRESS/N    PROSE
     [ AND THE REALLY INDUSTRIOUS [ VIRTUOUS & INDEPENDENT ] BARRY ] 595B PUB ADDRESS/N  PROSE
     HISTORICAL & POETICAL ARTISTS LIKE BARRY & MORTIMER  .  .  601B PUB ADDRESS/N    PROSE
     [ BARRY WAS POOR & INDEPENDENT ?MORTIMER WAS DESPISED &     SUPP ANNO REYNOLDS   * MARG
        MOCKED ]
BARS
     MY FLESH IS A PRISON MY BONES THE BARS OF DEATH  .  .  .  .  37B CONTEMPLATN/PS  PROSE
     FOR THE BARS OF CHAOS ARE BURST HER MILLIONS PREPARE THEIR  140 FRENCH REVOLTN    141
        FIERY WAY
     SPRING LIKE REDEEMED CAPTIVES WHEN THEIR BONDS & BARS ARE   198 AMERICA 6           5
        BURST
     TILL COVET BROKE HIS LOCKS & BARS  .  .  .  .  .  .  .  .   256 BOOK OF LOS 3      20
     THE ROCKS SHOOK THE ETERNAL BARS TUGGD TO & FRO WERE RIFTED 310 FOUR ZOAS 5       186
     IN PERIODS OF PULSATIVE FUROR BEATING INTO [ BARS ] WEDGES  346 FOUR ZOAS 8     * 207
        & BARS
     FOR EVERY HUMAN HEART HAS GATES OF BRASS & BARS OF ADAMANT  502 MILTON 20          34
     AND THAT ONE HE CLOSES WITH IRON BARS  .  .  .  .  .  .  .  583A DESC CAT 9       PROSE
     FREEZE ROUND HIM TO BARS OF STEEL & TO IRON ROCKS BENEATH   626 JERUSALEM 7        72
     HE SIEZD THE BARS OF CONDENSD THOUGHTS TO FORGE THEM  .  .  628 JERUSALEM 9         4
     AND THE LOUD-RENDING BARS OF THE CREATION READY TO BURST    667 JERUSALEM 40       26
     WITH IRON BARS IN VIRTUOUS STATE  .  .  .  .  .  .  .  .    758 EV GOSPEL (1)      13
BARTOLLOZE
     I'LL WRITE IN RHYME AS SOFT AS [ FEATHER PILLOWS ]          555 BLAKES APL/N 1      7
        BARTOLLOZE
     I'LL WRITE IN VERSE AS SOFT AS BARTOLLOZE  .  .  .  .  .    555 BLAKES APL/N 2      2
BARTOLLOZZI
     ANY MORE THAN THE ENGRAVINGS OF STRANGE BARTOLLOZZI  .  .   455A ANNO REYNOLDS    MARG
     SUCH ARE BARTOLLOZZI WOOLETT & STRANGE  .  .  .  .  .  .    600D PUB ADDRESS/N   *PROSE
BARTOLOUZZI
     COMPARE THE PRINTS OF BARTOLOUZZI WOOLETT STRANGE &C   .    592A PUB ADDRESS/N   *PROSE
BARTOLOZZI
     TO ENGRAVE FINER THAN STRANGE WOOLETT HALL OR BARTOLOZZI    594C PUB ADDRESS/N    PROSE
     I DO NOT CONDEMN [ BARTOLOZZI ] STRANGE OR WOOLETT BECAUSE  602D PUB ADDR AD/N    PROSE
BASE
     WERE BASE WHO WERE NOT FIRD TO DEEDS  .  .  .  .  .  .  .    23 EDW THIRD/PS 3     79
     ALWAYS BE READY TO SPEAK YOUR MIND AND A BASE MAN WILL      151D MARRIAGE HH 8    PROSE
        AVOID YOU
     WHERE WINTER BEATS INCESSANT FIXING THEM FIRM ON THEIR BASE 281 FOUR ZOAS 2        31
     BE THEY AS VILE & BASE AS EER THEY CAN  .  .  .  .  .  .    544 SOME MEN/N          4
     OCCASION OF POETIC IMAGERY WHEN A BASE MAN MEANS TO BE  .   592C PUB ADDRESS/N    PROSE
     YOU WILL BE CALLD THE BASE JUDAS WHO BETRAYD HIS FRIEND     813B LETTER 22        PROSE
BASEMENT
     TILL RESTING EACH HIS [ CENTER ] [ BASEMENT ] FINDS  .  .  .  283 FOUR ZOAS 2      139
     I CALL THEM BY THEIR ENGLISH NAMES ENGLISH THE ROUGH        668 JERUSALEM 40       58
        BASEMENT
BASEMENTS
     LONDON IS BETWEEN HIS KNEES ITS BASEMENTS FOURFOLD  .  .    531 MILTON 39          39
BASEST
     THE BASEST & MOST OPPRESSIVE OF HUMAN CODES & BEING LIKE    393C ANNO WATSON      MARG
BASHAN
     ARE HOR & PEOR & BASHAN & ABARIM & LEBANON & HERMON  .  .   498 MILTON 17          16
     WITH THE SWORD & BALANCES HE IS OG KING OF BASHAN  .  .  .  606C V LAST JUDG/N    PROSE
     REPRESENTING OG KING OF BASHAN IS A FIGURE WITH A BASKET    607D V LAST JUDG/N    PROSE
     HAND ART THOU NOT REUBEN ENROOTING THYSELF INTO BASHAN   .  661 JERUSALEM 34       36
     REUBEN SLEPT IN BASHAN LIKE ONE DEAD IN THE VALLEY   .  .   661 JERUSALEM 34       43
     REUBEN RETURND TO BASHAN IN DESPAIR HE SLEPT ON THE STONE   661 JERUSALEM 34       51
     REMOVE EASTWARD TO BASHAN AND GILEAD AND LEAVE  .  .  .     679 JERUSALEM 48       64
     FROM BASHAN TO TYRE & FROM TROY TO GAZA OF THE AMALEKITE    698 JERUSALEM 63       43
     IN BASHAN TERROR-STRUCK ALBION'S SONS LOOK TOWARD BASHAN    715 JERUSALEM 74       43
BASILEIA
     I SWEAR THAT BASILEIA (BASILEIA ) IS NOT KINGDOM           789A ANNO THORNTON    MARG
        BUT KINGSHIP
BASIRE
     OR ANGRY WITH [ BOYDELL OR BOWYER OR BASIRE ] .  .  .   .  . 538 WAS I ANGRY/N    *  6
     HOW TO PUT SO MUCH LABOUR INTO A HEAD OR A FOOT AS BASIRE   593A PUB ADDRESS/N    PROSE
        DID
     I KNEW THE MEN INTIMATELY FROM THEIR INTIMACY WITH BASIRE   593B PUB ADDRESS/N    PROSE
     [ ALIAMET ] GRAVELOT ONCE SAID TO MY MASTER BASIRE [ YOU ]  594D PUB ADDRESS/N   *PROSE
        DE ENGLISH
     BY HIS INTIMACY WITH BASIRE & I KNEW HIM TO BE  .  .  .  .  603B PUB ADDR AD/N    PROSE
     TILL BASIRE WAS QUITE DASHD & OUT OF CONCEIT WITH WHAT  .   603C PUB ADDR AD/N    PROSE
BASIRE'S
     SUPERIOR TO BASIRE'S BECAUSE THEY HAD MORE LABOUR & CARE    593A PUB ADDRESS/N    PROSE
     AT BASIRE'S BY LAUGHING AT BASIRE'S KNIFE TOOLS &   .  .  . 603C PUB ADDR AD/N    PROSE
     RIDICULING THE FORMS OF BASIRE'S OTHER GRAVERS  .  .  .  .  603C PUB ADDR AD/N    PROSE
     ENGRAVED WHEN I WAS A BEGINNER AT BASIRE'S  .  .  .  .  .   SUPP INSC JOSEPH     *TITLE
```

```
                                                             PAGE      TITLE        LINE
BASKET
      TO CARRY THE HEAVY BASKET ON OUR SCORCHED SHOULDERS TO SIFT   286 FOUR ZOAS 2     221
      FURROWD WITH WHIPS & OUR FLESH BRUISED WITH THE HEAVY         286 FOUR ZOAS 2     226
         BASKET
      REPRESENTING OG KING OF BASHAN IS A FIGURE WITH A BASKET      607D V LAST JUDG/N  PROSE
      BENEATH THE MAN WITH THE BASKET ARE THREE FIERY FIENDS WITH   607D V LAST JUDG/N  PROSE
BASKETS
      HIS FOOD SHE BROUGHT IN IRON BASKETS HIS DRINK IN CUPS        195 AMERICA PREL 1    3
         OF IRON
      MEASURD HIS FOOD MORNING & EVENING IN CUPS & BASKETS OF       343 FOUR ZOAS 8      81
         IRON
      HIS SONS ARISING FROM THE FEAST WITH GOLDEN BASKETS FOLLOW    376 FOUR ZOAS 9     714
      IN GOLDEN & IN SILVER BASKETS IN HEAVENS OF PRECIOUS STONE    379 FOUR ZOAS 9     823
BASONS
      THAMES POURED HIS WATERS INTO MY BASONS AND BATHS    .   .  . 720 JERUSALEM 79     34
BASSANS
      ("TITIAN VERONESE TINTORET THE BASSANS CORREGGIO BAROCCIO")   457A ANNO REYNOLDS  MARG
BASSO RELIEVOS
      AND SOME CARVED AS BASSO RELIEVOS AND SOME AS GROUPES OF      566A DESC CAT 2     PROSE
BASTILE
      . . . HER GREY TOWERS GROAN AND THE BASTILE TREMBLES    .   . 135 FRENCH REVOLTN   18
      . . . LET THE BASTILE DEVOUR  . . . . . . . . . .    .   .  . 141 FRENCH REVOLTN  156
      . . . SAYING BASTILE DEPART AND TAKE THY SHADOWY COURSE       145 FRENCH REVOLTN  249
BAT
      AND THE OWL AND BAT FLEW ROUND THE DARKENING TREES     .   .  35C COUCH DEATH/PS  PROSE
      LO THE BAT WITH LEATHERN WING  . . . . . . . . . .    .   .  . 54 LO THE BAT/IM     1
      [TO HIT ME WITH THE BAT] . . . . . . . . . . .    .   .  .  .  61 SAY YOU JOE/IM *   9
      HE DOES NOT KNOW HOW TO HANDLE A BAT  . . . . .    .   .  .  . 61 SAY YOU JOE/IM    12
      THE BAT THE OWL THE GLOWING TYGER AND THE KING OF NIGHT       195 V DAU ALBION 8    5
      THE SPIDER THE BAT BURST FROM THE HARDEND SLIME CRYING    .   . 373 FOUR ZOAS 9    608
      THE BAT THAT FLITS AT CLOSE OF EVE  . . . . . . .    .   .  . 431 AUGURIES         25
      THE FOX THE OWL THE BEETLE & THE BAT . . . . . . .    .   .  . 545 ON S(TOTHRD)/N   3
BATH      SEE WIFE OF BATH
      HIS ROCKS LONDON & BATH & LEGIONS & EDINBURGH  . . . .    .  . 531 MILTON 39       35
      BATH OXFORD CAMBRIDGE NORWICH HIS RIGHT ELBOW  . . . .    .  . 531 MILTON 39       44
      THE WIFE OF BATH THE MILLER THE COOK THE OXFORD SCHOLAR      567A DESC CAT 3      PROSE
      AND THE WIFE OF BATH ARE BOTH TAKING THEIR MORNING'S         567A DESC CAT 3      PROSE
         DRAUGHT
      THE LADY PRIORESS AND THE WIFE OF BATH  . . . . .    .   .  . 572B DESC CAT 3     PROSE
      WIFE OF BATH IN WHOSE CHARACTER CHAUCER HAS BEEN EQUALLY     572B DESC CAT 3      PROSE
      THEY BOTH THINK THAT THE WIFE OF BATH IS A YOUNG  . . .    .  . 574B DESC CAT 3   PROSE
      THAT SHE IS THE FAIR WIFE OF BATH AND THAT THE SPRING    .   . 574B DESC CAT 3    PROSE
      THE WIFE OF BATH THE COOK THE OXFORD SCHOLAR   . . . .    .  . 588C CHAUCER/N     PROSE
      & WIFE OF BATH ARE BOTH TAKING THEIR MORNING'S DRAUGHT    .   . 588D CHAUCER/N    PROSE
      GO THOU TO SKOFIELD ASK HIM IF HE IS BATH OR IF HE           640 JERUSALEM 17     59
         IS CANTERBURY
      GLOUCESTER AND EXETER AND SALISBURY AND BRISTOL AND          668 JERUSALEM 40     61
         BENEVOLENT BATH
      BATH WHO IS LEGIONS HE IS THE SEVENTH THE PHYSICIAN AND      668 JERUSALEM 41      1
      BRISTOL & BATH LISTEN TO MY WORDS & YE SEVENTEEN GIVE EAR    673 JERUSALEM 43     55
      THE VOICE OF BATH . . . . . . . . . . . . . .    .   .  .  . 675 JERUSALEM 44     44
      BATH HEALING CITY WHOSE WISDOM IN MIDST OF POETIC    .   .  . 675 JERUSALEM 45      1
      AND THE SEVENTEEN (CONJOINING) WITH BATH THE SEVENTH    .   . 676 JERUSALEM 45 *   37
      BATH MILD PHYSICIAN OF ETERNITY MYSTERIOUS POWER  . . . .    . 676 JERUSALEM 46     1
      AND THE VOICES OF BATH & CANTERBURY & YORK & EDINBURGH CRY   689 JERUSALEM 57      1
      . . . & THEY NAILD HIM TO ALBION'S TREE IN BATH  . . . .    . 699 JERUSALEM 65      8
      DRINKING THEIR LIVES IN SWEET INTOXICATION HENCE AROSE       701 JERUSALEM 65     65
         FROM BATH
      COBAN DWELT IN BATH SOMERSET WILTSHIRE GLOUCESTERSHIRE   .   . 710 JERUSALEM 71    26
      BATH STOOD UPON THE SEVERN WITH MERLIN & BLADUD & ARTHUR     715 JERUSALEM 75      2
      AS MY GARDEN & AS MY SECRET BATH SPAIN WAS MY HEAVENLY       720 JERUSALEM 79     40
         COUCH
      BABYLON IS OUR CHIEF DESIRE MOAB OUR BATH IN SUMMER  . . .    . 725 JERUSALEM 82   31
      I HAVE NOT BEEN ABLE TO SEND A PROOF OF THE BATH THO    .   . 791A LETTER 2       PROSE
BATHD
      THUS IN FALSE TEARS SHE BATHD HIS FEET  . . . . . .    .   .   38C SAMSON/PS      PROSE
      SURE THOU ART BATHD IN RIVERS OF DELIGHT ON VERDANT FIELDS   321 FOUR ZOAS 7      63
      BATHD IN THE CLEAR SPRING OF THE ROCK THEN FROM HER          366 FOUR ZOAS 9  *  346
         DARKSOM CAVE
BATHE
      BROTHER IN BROTHER'S BLOOD MUST BATHE RIVERS OF DEATH    .   . 34A KING JOHN/PS   PROSE
      . . . THAT THREATEN TO BATHE THEIR FEET . . . . . .    .   . 141 FRENCH REVOLTN  155
      BY THE RED EARTH OF OUR IMMORTAL RIVER I BATHE MY WINGS      191 V DAU ALBION 3    19
      THE BROTHER & THE BROTHER BATHE IN BLOOD UPON THE SEVERN     281 FOUR ZOAS 2      49
      IF YOU ARE THIRSTY THERE IS THE RIVER GO BATHE YOUR PARCHED  375 FOUR ZOAS 9     680
         LIMBS
      TO BATHE IN THE WATERS OF LIFE TO WASH OFF THE NOT HUMAN     533 MILTON 41         1
      THE PONDS WHERE BOYS TO BATHE DELIGHT  . . . . . .    .   .  . 650 FIELDS FROM/J  14
BATHED
      THO HIS WATERS BATHED MY INFANT LIMBS  . . . . . .    .   .  . 166 WHY CARE FOR/N *  6
      HE BATHED HIM IN SPRINGS OF SORROW  . . . . . . . .    .   .  . 233 URIZEN 20       4
      BATHED IN BLOODY CLOUDS HIS LOINS IN FIRES OF WAR WHERE      334 FOUR ZOAS 7B     43
         SPEARS
BATHEST
      [XXX] WHERE ART THOU PESTILENCE THAT BATHEST IN FOGS &       106 TIRIEL 5     *    8
         STANDING LAKES
BATHING
      BATHING THEIR LIMBS IN THE BRIGHT VISIONS OF ETERNITY   .   . 358 FOUR ZOAS 9     45
      BATHING THEIR LIMBS IN THE BRIGHT VISIONS OF ETERNITY   .   . 359 FOUR ZOAS 9     90
BATHS
      AMERICA NORTH & SOUTH ARE HIS BATHS OF LIVING WATERS    .   . 690 JERUSALEM 58     43
      THAMES POURED HIS WATERS INTO MY BASONS AND BATHS    .   .  . 720 JERUSALEM 79     34
```

171

```
                                                              PAGE      TITLE          LINE
BATHSHEBA
    RUTH THE MOABITE & BATHSHEBA OF THE DAUGHTERS OF HETH   .  .  696 JERUSALEM 62        11
    URIAH THE HUSBAND OF BATHSHEBA BATHSHEBA  . . . . .   SUPP PENC DRAW 2.35 *TITLE
BATS
    SETTLED LIKE BATS INNUMERABLE READY TO FLY ABROAD      .  .  .  306 FOUR ZOAS 5       35
BATTERD
    AUTHORIZE TO RECIEVE THEM THEY ARE SOMEWHAT BATTERD    .  .  839D LETTER 38        PROSE
BATTERSEA
    BATTERSEA AND CHELSEA MOURN FOR CAMBEL & GWENDOLEN       .  .  644 JERUSALEM 21       32
    BATTERSEA & CHELSEA MOURN LONDON & CANTERBURY TREMBLE    .  .  659 JERUSALEM 33       12
BATTLE    SEE PATTLE
    THE BATTLE FAINTS AND BLOODY MEN  . . . . . . . .           13 GWIN KING/PS        87
    WHERE LIKE THE SEA THE WAVES OF BATTLE MOVE     . . . . .   15 IMIT SPEN/PS        50
    BLAZE IN EACH COUNTENANCE AND FIRE THE BATTLE   . . . . .   18 EDW THIRD/PS 1      12
    WE SPRING TO BATTLE OER THE FLOODS OF DEATH     . . . . .   18 EDW THIRD/PS 1      16
    INTO THE BATTLE SHAKING HIS GOLDEN LOCKS    . . . . . .     21 EDW THIRD/PS 3       4
    OF BATTLE LIKE THE YOUTH AT MORRICE PLAY   . . . . .        22 EDW THIRD/PS 3      31
    I HOPE YOULL STAY AND SEE US FIGHT THIS BATTLE    . . . .   24 EDW THIRD/PS 3     136
    HE ANSWERD ME I HUNGER FOR ANOTHER BATTLE   . . . . .       25 EDW THIRD/PS 3     156
    THESE ARE THE MINDS THAT GLORY IN THE BATTLE     . . . .    25 EDW THIRD/PS 3     170
    LEAD THEM ON TO BATTLE  . . . . . . . . . .                 26 EDW THIRD/PS 3     207
    METHINKS THE SHOUT BEGINS THE BATTLE BURNS    . . . . .     26 EDW THIRD/PS 3     228
    WE HAVE OUR BATTLE FOR OUR PAINS I KNOW   . . . . . .       27 EDW THIRD/PS 3     268
    OUR FATHERS MOVE IN FIRM ARRAY TO BATTLE   . . . . . .      32 EDW THIRD/PS 6      25
    WHEN SIN CLAPS HIS BROAD WINGS OVER THE BATTLE   . . . .    33 EDW FOURTH/PS        9
    THE ROARING VOICE OF WAR THE TRUMPET CALLS TO BATTLE     .  34A KING JOHN/PS     PROSE
    THE SUCKING INFANT LIVES TO DIE IN BATTLE    . . . . .      34B KING JOHN/PS     PROSE
    AND DREADFUL THUNDER OF THE BATTLE HEARD AFAR    . . . . .  34B KING JOHN/PS     PROSE
    AS IN DAY OF HAVOCK AND ROUTED BATTLE  . . .               137 FRENCH REVOLTN      64
    . . . WHERE THEIR CHILDREN ARE MARSHALLD TOGETHER TO BATTLE 146 FRENCH REVOLTN     265
    MARSHALLD IN ORDER FOR THE DAY OF INTELLECTUAL BATTLE    .  264 FOUR ZOAS 1         6
    AND CLAD IN STEEL & HIS HORSE PROUDLY NEIGHD HE SMELT THE   275 FOUR ZOAS 1       412
        BATTLE
    WHEN FLEEING FROM THE BATTLE THOU FLEETING LIKE THE RAVEN   299 FOUR ZOAS 4        86
    OF THOSE PITEOUS VICTIMS OF BATTLE . . . . . . . .          331 FOUR ZOAS 7       438
    RENDING THE HEAVENS & EARTHS & DRINKING BLOOD IN THE HOT    335 FOUR ZOAS 7B      103
        BATTLE
    WALKS THRO THE BATTLE DARK & FIERCE THE BULL HIS RAGE    .  .  335 FOUR ZOAS 7B      109
    THE TRUMPET FITTED TO THE BATTLE & THE FLUTE OF SUMMER   .  .  337 FOUR ZOAS 7B      173
    NOW NOW THE BATTLE RAGES ROUND THY TENDER LIMBS O VALA   .  .  337 FOUR ZOAS 7B      187
    MARCHING TO BATTLE WHO WAS WONT TO RISE WITH URIZEN'S HARPS   338 FOUR ZOAS 7B      198
    IN THE FIERCE BATTLE & HE SAW THE LAMB OF GOD & THE WORLD   342 FOUR ZOAS 8        66
        OF LOS
    TERRIFIED & ASTONISHD URIZEN BEHELD THE BATTLE TAKE A FORM  343 FOUR ZOAS 8       102
    THE BATTLE HOWLS THE TERRORS FIRD RAGE IN THE WORK OF DEATH 343 FOUR ZOAS 8       107
    LOS BUILDS THE WALLS OF GOLGONOOZA AGAINST THE STIRRING     343 FOUR ZOAS 8       109
        BATTLE
    THEY HUMANIZE IN THE FIERCE BATTLE WHERE IN DIREFUL PAIN    344 FOUR ZOAS 8       115
    THE DIRE CONFUSION TILL THE BATTLE FAINTS THOSE THAT REMAIN 344 FOUR ZOAS 8       118
    AS OF A BATTLE IN THE HEAVENS HARK HEARD YOU NOT            364 FOUR ZOAS 9       263
        THE TRUMPET
    AS OF FIERCE BATTLE . . . . . . . . . . .                  364 FOUR ZOAS 9       264
    THE (HORSES) NEIGH FROM THE BATTLE . . . . .               365 FOUR ZOAS 9       300
    SEND BATTLE MURDER SUDDEN DEATH [WE] O PRAY    . . . . .    550 WHEN I SEE/N        6
    "IN THE LAST BATTLE THAT ARTHUR FOUGHT THE MOST BEAUTIFUL   560B EXHIBITION ADV  PROSE
        WAS ONE"
    IN THE LAST BATTLE OF KING ARTHUR ONLY THREE BRITONS       577B DESC CAT 5      TITLE
        ESCAPED
    BLOODY WITH THE DAY OF BATTLE   . . . . . . . .          .  580D DESC CAT 5      PROSE
    OFFERING TO SUSTAIN THE GLORIOUS COMBAT & THE BATTLE & WAR  658 JERUSALEM 31       65
    HER HAND IS A COURT OF JUSTICE HER FEET TWO ARMIES         698 JERUSALEM 64        9
        IN BATTLE
    THE TRUMPET FITTED TO MORTAL BATTLE . . . . . . .          700 JERUSALEM 65       15
    NOW NOW THE BATTLE RAGES ROUND THY TENDER LIMBS O VALA   .  .  700 JERUSALEM 65       29
    MARCHING TO BATTLE WHO WAS WONT TO RISE WITH URIZEN'S HARPS   700 JERUSALEM 65       44
    THEY STRIP OFF JOSEPH'S COAT & DIP IT IN THE BLOOD         704 JERUSALEM 67       23
        OF BATTLE
    SHOUT IN THE NIGHT OF BATTLE & THEIR SPEARS GROW TO THEIR   704 JERUSALEM 67       32
        HANDS
    STATUARIES PRINTERS POETS WE ARE NOT IN A FIELD OF BATTLE   847B LETTER 44       PROSE
        BUT
    THE FATAL SISTERS RIDING THRO THE BATTLE THEY ARE   .  .  .  SUPP ILLUS GRAY     *TITLE
    A BATTLE . . . . . . . . . . . . . . .                  .  SUPP ILLUS GRAY     *TITLE
    A STANDARD BEARER FAINTING IN THE ROUTED BATTLE   .  .  .   SUPP ILLUS GRAY     *TITLE
    A BREACH IN A CITY THE MORNING AFTER THE BATTLE   .  .  .   SUPP ILLUS HISTORY  *TITLE
BATTLE-AX,BATTLE AX
    THEY FORGD THE SWORD THE CHARIOT OF WAR THE BATTLE AX    .  .  337 FOUR ZOAS 7B      172
    THEY FORGD THE SWORD ON CHEVIOT THE CHARIOT OF WAR & THE    699 JERUSALEM 65       14
        BATTLE-AX
BATTLES
    FOR HE STROVE IN BATTLES DIRE   . . . . . . . .            222 URIZEN 3            13
    AND SAID GO FORTH & GUIDE MY BATTLES LIKE THE JOINTED SPINE 336 FOUR ZOAS 7B      116
    AND WHEN THE REVOLUTION OF THEIR DAY OF BATTLES OVER    .  .  344 FOUR ZOAS 8       123
    MY MORN & EVENING FOOD WERE PREPARD IN BATTLES OF MEN       644 JERUSALEM 22        7
    TO MURDER ALBION THE KING OF MEN HE FOUGHT IN BATTLES       722 JERUSALEM 80       18
        FIERCE
    FOR IN OUR BATTLES WE THE SLAIN MEN VIEW WITH PITY AND LOVE 722 JERUSALEM 80       25
    TWO COPIES PERHAPS FROM BORGOGNONE OF BATTLES   . . . .     844A LETTER 43       PROSE
BAUBLE
    FOR A [ BUTTON A BAUBLE [ BUCKLE ] A BEAD OR A ] . . .  .  .  548 ON GREAT ENC/N      2
BAYS
    THE STAG TURNS HEAD AND BAYS THE CRYING HOUNDS     . . . .  24 EDW THIRD/PS 3     127
```

		PAGE	TITLE	LINE

BEACH
OPAKE AND LIKE THE BLACK PEBBLE ON THE ENRAGED BEACH . . 515 MILTON 28   35
BEAD
FOR A [BUTTON A BAUBLE [BUCKLE] A BEAD OR A] . . . . . 548 ON GREAT ENC/N   2
BEADLES
GREY HEADED BEADLES WALKD BEFORE WITH WANDS AS WHITE AS   59 HOLY THURS/IM   3
SNOW
GREY HEADED BEADLES WALKD BEFORE WITH WANDS AS WHITE AS   121 HOLY THURS/SI   3
SNOW
BEADS
EVERY ART & SCIENCE ADORND HIM AS BEADS ROUND HIS NECK . . 46D ISLAND MOON 3 PROSE
BEAK
FROM NIGHTLY PREY AND LIFTS HIS GOLDEN BEAK TO THE PURE   190 V DAU ALBION 2   26
EAST
WEAKNESS WITH HORNS & TALONS IGNORANCE WITH A RAVNING BEAK 628 JERUSALEM 9   13
BEAKS
[THE ROUGH BARK OPENS TWITTERING PEEP FORTH LITTLE BEAKS 270 FOUR ZOAS 1   206
& WINGS]
AND WHET THEIR BEAKS & SNUFF THE AIR & WATCH THE OPENING 325 FOUR ZOAS 7   206
DAWN
BEAM
AND RISING GLORIES BEAM AROUND MY HEAD . . . .   9 FRESH FROM/PS   4
SHALL BEAM A RADIANCE TO FIRE THE BREASTS . . . . . .   18 EDW THIRD/PS 1   24
THAT BEAM AND TWINKLE IN THE DEPTH OF NIGHT . . . . .   18 EDW THIRD/PS 1   33
AND BEAM FORTH LUSTRE ON A DARKLING WORLD . . . . . .   18 EDW THIRD/PS 1   36
THOU TOLDEST ME TO WEAVE THEE TO THE BEAM BY THY STRONG   39B SAMSON/PS   PROSE
HAIR
& GOLDEN PLEASURES BEAM AROUND MY HEAD WHY GRIEF DOST THOU 43B WOE CRIED MUSE PROSE
ACCOST ME
. . . AND GLEAMS A DUSKY BEAM . . . .   146 FRENCH REVOLTN 270
. . . AND THE SENATE IN PEACE SAT BENEATH MORNING'S BEAM 148 FRENCH REVOLTN 306
RED AS THE ROSY MORNING LUSTFUL AS THE FIRST BORN BEAM . 195 V DAU ALBION 7   27
ON HIS STONE THRESHOLD DOES HIS EYE BEHOLD THE BEAM THAT 195 V DAU ALBION 8   2
BRINGS
BESIDE THE OX TO THY HARD FURROW DOES NOT THAT MILD BEAM 195 V DAU ALBION 8   4
BLOT
LENGTHNING INTO A HUNGRY BEAM SWIFTLY . . . .   249 AHANIA 2   19
OPPOSD TO THE EXULTING FLAMD BEAM . . . .   249 AHANIA 2   20
THE SOUNDING BEAM LAUGHING IT TORE THROUGH . . . . . .   249 AHANIA 2   27
BUT THE FIERY BEAM OF FUZON . . . .   250 AHANIA 2   44
THE LISTNING STARS HEARD & THE FIRST BEAM OF THE MORNING 275 FOUR ZOAS 1   410
STARTED BACK
AROUND THEIR LOINS POURD FORTH THEIR ARROWS & THEIR BOSOMS 484 MILTON 4   23
BEAM
WHICH LOS WIPED OFF BUT COMFORT NONE COULD GIVE OR BEAM   630 JERUSALEM 10   61
OF HOPE
AS GWENDOLEN CAST THE SHUTTLE OF WAR AS CAMBEL RETURND   703 JERUSALEM 66   62
THE BEAM
THESE FIBRES OF THINE EYES THAT USED TO BEAM IN DISTANT   705 JERUSALEM 67   47
HEAVENS
BEAMD   SEE GOLD-BEAMD
HIS HEAD BEAMD LIGHT & IN HIS VIGOROUS VOICE WAS PROPHECY 270 FOUR ZOAS 1   239
. . . AMIDST THEM [STOOD] BEAMD . . . .   348 FOUR ZOAS 8   277
SHE CEASD & (LIGHT) BEAMD ROUND HER LIKE THE GLORY OF THE 370 FOUR ZOAS 9 * 503
MORNING
AND HER DELUSIVE LIGHT BEAMD FIERCE ABOVE THE MOUNTAIN . . 723 JERUSALEM 80   59
BEAMED   SEE LONG BEAMED
AND A RAY OF LIGHT BEAMED AROUND HIS HEAD ALL WAS STILL   36C COUCH DEATH/PS PROSE
BEAMING   SEE FAR BEAMING,OUT BEAMING
OH BLESS THOSE LIMBS BEAMING WITH HEAVNLY LIGHT . . . .   9 FRESH FROM/PS   8
[REFRESHING THE COLD EARTH WITH BEAMING JOY] BUT PRIDE   40D THEN SHE BORE   PROSE
AWOKE
SWEET ELFRID FAIRER THAN THE BEAMING SUN . . . . . .   43C WOE CRIED MUSE PROSE
. . . NOW BEAMING WITH KNOWLEDGE WITH GENTLE AWE ADORNED 144 FRENCH REVOLTN 230
WITH EVER STREAMING FIRES BEAMING FROM HIS AWFUL LIMBS . 284 FOUR ZOAS 3   180
WHERE THOU IN THRILLING JOY IN BEAMING SUMMER LOVELINESS 324 FOUR ZOAS 7   186
ENITHARMON SPREAD HER BEAMING LOCKS UPON THE WIND & SAID 331 FOUR ZOAS 7 * 446
OF FAIR JERUSALEM'S BOSOM IN A GENTLY BEAMING ?FIRE . . . 346 FOUR ZOAS 8   193
THEY STOOD IN BEAMING BEAUTY & SOMETIMES AS ONE EVEN RAHAB 349 FOUR ZOAS 8   329
FROM SON TO SON AS IF THE STARS BEAMING INNUMERABLE . .   366 FOUR ZOAS 9   351
THEY STOOD IN BEAMING BEAUTY & SOMETIMES AS ONE EVEN RAHAB 382 FOUR ZOAS AD 6 17
I SPRANG OUT OF THE BREAST OF SATAN OVER THE HARROW BEAMING 492 MILTON 12   10
BEAMING FORTH WITH HER DAUGHTERS INTO THE DIVINE BOSOM   622 JERUSALEM 4   15
[WHERE]
ON BOTH SIDES WITHIN & WITHOUT BEAMING GLORIOUSLY . . .   631 JERUSALEM 12   20
AND FROM THEM ALL THE LOVELY BEAMING DAUGHTERS OF ALBION 635 JERUSALEM 14   11
IS RAGAN SHE ADJOIND TO SLADE & PRODUCED GONORILL   710 JERUSALEM 71   33
FAR BEAMING
CAMBEL HIS BRIGHT BEAMING COUNTERPART DIVIDED FROM HIM . . 723 JERUSALEM 80   58
O SISTER CAMBEL SAID GWENDOLEN AS THEIR LONG BEAMING LIGHT 723 JERUSALEM 80   83
ON CAMBRIDGE AND OXFORD BEAMING SOFT UNITING WITH RAHAB'S 725 JERUSALEM 82   11
CLOUD
AND TOOK HIS BOW FOURFOLD THE VISION FOR BRIGHT BEAMING   744 JERUSALEM 97   7
URIZEN
HEAVENLY MEN BEAMING BRIGHT . . . .   805 TO BUTTS/L   50
BEAMS
WHO IN THE SUNNY BEAMS DID GLIDE . . . .   6 HOW SWEET/PS   4
SCATTERST THE RAYS OF LIGHT AND TRUTH'S BEAMS . . . . .   14 IMIT SPEN/PS   2
WHEN THE THIN BEAMS OF THE MOON GIVE A FAINT LIGHT . . . 36B COUCH DEATH/PS PROSE
O TRUTH THAT SHINEST WITH PROPITIOUS BEAMS . . . . .   37C SAMSON/PS   PROSE
ASTONISHD SILENT TILL THE MORNING BEAMS BEGAN TO SPRING 107 TIRIEL 6   2
BY HAPPY SILENT MOONY BEAMS . . . .   120 CRADLE SONG/SI   4

173

		PAGE	TITLE	LINE
BEAMS (CONTINUED)				
THAT WE MAY LEARN TO BEAR THE BEAMS OF LOVE	. . . .	125	LIT BLK BOY/SI	14
THROUGH HEAVEN TINGING MORNING WITH BEAMS OF BLOOD . . .		139	FRENCH REVOLTN	111
UP ROSE AWFUL IN HIS MAJESTIC BEAMS BOURBON'S STRONG DUKE . . .		141	FRENCH REVOLTN	168
TINGING THE BLACK DEEP WITH BEAMS OF BLOOD		156C	MARRIAGE HH 17	PROSE
WITH BEAMS OF BLOOD & THUS A VOICE CAME FORTH AND SHOOK THE TEMPLE		198	AMERICA 5	7
NAKED IN THE SUNNY BEAMS DELIGHT		219	LIT GRL LST/SE	9
BEAMS CONDUCTED BY FLUID SO PURE		259	BOOK OF LOS 5	11
WEEPING FOR LUVAH LOST IN THE BLOODY BEAMS OF		272	FOUR ZOAS 1 *	287
DRIVING THE STORMS BEFORE THEM OR DELIGHTING IN SUNNY BEAMS		288	FOUR ZOAS 2	300
URIZEN SAW THY SIN & HID HIS BEAMS IN DARKNING CLOUDS . .		288	FOUR ZOAS 2	329
I FAINT BENEATH THESE BEAMS OF THINE		290	FOUR ZOAS 2	375
IF THOU REFUSEST IN ETERNAL FLIGHT THY BEAMS IN VAIN . .		313	FOUR ZOAS 6	67
AND ENITHARMON TINCTURD IT WITH BEAMS OF BLUSHING LOVE .		332	FOUR ZOAS 7	468
TO LIGHT THE WAR BY DAY TO HIDE HIS SECRET BEAMS BY NIGHT		334	FOUR ZOAS 7B	36
LOOK HOW THE BEAMS FORESHEW THE RISING OF SOME GLORIOUS POWER		367	FOUR ZOAS 9	398
THE BIRDS ADORE THE SUN THE BEASTS RISE UP & PLAY IN HIS BEAMS		367	FOUR ZOAS 9	406
PLAY IN HIS SMILING BEAMS GIVING THE SEEDS OF LIFE TO GROW		379	FOUR ZOAS 9	847
AND THE FRESH EARTH BEAMS FORTH		379	FOUR ZOAS 9	848
REFLECTED IN THE BEAMS DIVINE		418	MOCK ON/N	6
IN BEAMS OF INFERNAL LIGHT		418	I SAW A MONK/N	4
WHEN THE SOUL SLEPT IN BEAMS OF LIGHT		434	AUGURIES	128
AND THE SUN BEAMS DAZZLE FROM HER EYNE		435	WILLIAM BOND	32
THE WINE-PRESS ON THE RHINE GROANS LOUD BUT ALL ITS CENTRAL BEAMS		510	MILTON 25	3
WITH COTTAGES AND VILLAGES THE FIRST BEAMS OF THE SUN .		567B	DESC CAT 3	PROSE
WITH COTTAGES & VILLAGES THE FIRST BEAMS OF THE SUN . . .		588D	CHAUCER/N	PROSE
WITH COTTAGES AND VILLAGES THE FIRST BEAMS OF THE SUN .		590C	CHAUCER 2	PROSE
THE ONE SHINES WITH BEAMS OF LIGHT		612B	V LAST JUDG/N	PROSE
ALL BEAMS FROM HIM [& [BECAUSE] AS HE HIMSELF HAS SAID]		612D	V LAST JUDG/N	PROSE
JESUS IS SURROUNDED BY BEAMS OF GLORY IN WHICH ARE SEEN ALL		613D	V LAST JUDG/N	PROSE
AWAY FROM THE SUN'S FLARING BEAMS WHO		619B	ILLUS MILTON	*PROSE
SPREADING HIS BEAMS OF LOVE & DICTATING THE WORDS OF THIS MILD SONG		622	JERUSALEM 4	5
LABOUR OF MERCIFUL HANDS THE BEAMS & RAFTERS ARE FORGIVENESS		632	JERUSALEM 12	32
WHERE THE HUMAN HARVEST WAVES ABUNDANT IN THE BEAMS OF EDEN		678	JERUSALEM 48	34
AND BECAME AN OPAKE GLOBE FAR DISTANT CLAD WITH MOONY BEAMS		679	JERUSALEM 49	20
IN BEAMS OF INFERNAL LIGHT		683	I SAW A MONK/J	4
AND FEEDS HER WITH THE FOOD OF EDEN HENCE ALL HER BEAUTY BEAMS		707	JERUSALEM 69	18
BEAMS MILD ALL LOVE AND ALL PERFECTION THAT WHEN THE LIPS		709	JERUSALEM 70	24
LIKE LOVELY BEAMS OF LIGHT		710	JERUSALEM 71	24
BEAUTIFUL SHE BEAMS TOWARDS THE EAST ALL KINDS OF PRECIOUS STONES		710	JERUSALEM 71	40
OVER THE NORTH WITH PEARLY BEAMS GORGEOUS & TERRIBLE . .		710	JERUSALEM 71	48
WHEN THE SOUL SLEPT IN THE BEAMS OF LIGHT		753	EV GOSPEL (D)/N	108
AMIDST THEM IN HIS GLORY BEAMS		758	EV GOSPEL (2)	15
HIS GLORIOUS BEAMS		804	TO BUTTS/L	5
OF HEAVEN'S BRIGHT BEAMS		805	TO BUTTS/L	34
IN HIS BEAMS OF BRIGHT GOLD		805	TO BUTTS/L	54
WE ARE NOT WARMED WITH THY BEAMS		818	HAPPINESS/L	66
AND ARE LAID ACROSS BEAMS AT THE TOP		831B	LETTER 31	PROSE
BEAMY				
GLANCING HIS BEAMY EYELIDS OVER THE DEEP IN DARK DISMAY		159D	SONG LIBERTY	PROSE
REPROACH THEE & THY BEAMY GARDENS SICKEN AT THY BEAUTY . .		288	FOUR ZOAS 2	303
THE BEAMY DAUGHTERS OF THE LIGHT STARTING THEY RISE THEY FLEE		288	FOUR ZOAS 2	315
SABRINA & IGNOGE BEGIN TO SHARPEN THEIR BEAMY SPEARS . .		631	JERUSALEM 11	19
BEAR				
THOU THE GOLDEN FRUIT DOST BEAR		7	LOVE HARMNY/PS	9
I CANNOT BEAR THE ENEMY AT MY BACK		22	EDW THIRD/PS 3	20
FOR LO THOU SHALT CONCEIVE AND BEAR A SON		39D	SAMSON/PS	PROSE
THEIR SAD COMPLAININGS BEAR FOR CONRADE LOST		43D	WOE CRIED MUSE	PROSE
THE THREE PHILOSOPHERS BEAR CHORUS		47D	ASK GODS/IM 1	PROSE
PLEASURE AS I HAVE THERE I STAND & BEAR EVERY FOOL'S INSULT		53C	ISLAND MOON 8	PROSE
TO BEAR ME FURTHER URGE ME NOT LEST I SHOULD DIE WITH TRAVEL		104	TIRIEL 4	33
DRINK OF THIS RUNNING BROOK & I WILL BEAR THEE ON MY SHOULDERS		104	TIRIEL 4	39
HEAR THE WOES THAT INFANTS BEAR		122	ON ANOTHERS/SI	16
THAT WE MAY LEARN TO BEAR THE BEAMS OF LOVE		125	LIT BLK BOY/SI	14
FOR WHEN OUR SOULS HAVE LEARND THE HEAT TO BEAR . . .		125	LIT BLK BOY/SI	17
I'LL SHADE HIM FROM THE HEAT TILL HE CAN BEAR		125	LIT BLK BOY/SI	25
STEAL THE LABOR OF OTHERS TO SUPPORT HIM BEAR		158C	MARRIAGE HH 22	PROSE
[THE VIRGINS OF YOUTH & MORNING BEAR]		169	EARTHS ANSWR/N	15
[O THAT I SUCH A FIEND SHOULD BEAR]		177	LIT BOY LST/N	12
THAT CANNOT BEAR THE MENTAL STORM		188	A FAIRY SKIPD	12
THE CLEAR HEAVEN OF HER ETERNAL SPRING TO BEAR THE WINTRY RAGE		193	V DAU ALBION 5	24
THE VIRGINS OF YOUTH AND MORNING BEAR		211	EARTHS ANSR/SE	15
TILL IMPATIENCE NO LONGER COULD BEAR		257	BOOK OF LOS 4	15
IT IS NOT LOVE I BEAR TO ENITHARMON IT IS PITY		265	FOUR ZOAS 1	31
THEY BEAR THE WOVEN DRAPERIES ON GOLDEN HOOKS THEY HANG ABROAD		284	FOUR ZOAS 2	152
GO FORTH BEAR ENITHARMON BACK TO THE ETERNAL PROPHET .		299	FOUR ZOAS 4	70
FROM DEATH IN WRATH & FURY BUT NOW COME BEAR BACK . . .		300	FOUR ZOAS 4	116
WHEN THOU DIDST BEAR THE GOLDEN CUP AT THE IMMORTAL TABLES		311	FOUR ZOAS 5	228

		PAGE	TITLE	LINE
BEAR	(CONTINUED)			
	TO BEAR THEE DOWN BENEATH THE WAVES IN STIFLING DESPAIR	321	FOUR ZOAS 7	56
	OR IS THY JOY FOUNDED ON TORMENT WHICH OTHERS BEAR FOR THEE	321	FOUR ZOAS 7	68
	TO BEAR THIS SELF CONVICTION TAKE THEN EAT THOU ALSO OF	330	FOUR ZOAS 7	393
	IN WAR SHALT THOU BEAR RULE IN BLOOD SHALT THOU TRIUMPH FOR ME	334	FOUR ZOAS 7B	57
	THE ELEPHANT THE WOLF THE BEAR THE LAMIA THE [SATUR] SATYR	352	FOUR ZOAS 8	* 446
	HARDENS THE LION & THE BEAR TREMBLING IN THE SOLID MOUNTAIN	352	FOUR ZOAS 8	451
	FLOW ON YE GENTLE AIRS & BEAR THE VOICE OF MY REJOICING	368	FOUR ZOAS 9	435
	AND ALL THY SONS O LUVAH BEAR AWAY THE FAMILIES OF EARTH	375	FOUR ZOAS 9	695
	AND EVENING WINDS MY SORROWS BEAR	423	THE BIRDS/N	8
	[OR THE APPLE TREE TEACHES THE PINE TREE TO BEAR] . . .	453B	ANNO REYNOLDS	* MARG
	OR THE APPLE TREE TEACHES THE PEAR TREE HOW TO BEAR FRUIT	453B	ANNO REYNOLDS	MARG
	REYNOLDS CANNOT BEAR EXPRESSION	466B	ANNO REYNOLDS	MARG
	REYNOLDS'S EYE COULD NOT BEAR CHARACTERISTIC COLOURING OR	475D	ANNO REYNOLDS	MARG
	SEVEN ANGELS BEAR MY NAME & IN THOSE SEVEN I APPEAR . .	530	MILTON 38	55
	BUT MY SOUL ALSO WOULD HE BEAR AWAY	536	AND HIS LEGS/N	6
	[HE WOULD BEAR MY SOUL]	536	AND HIS LEGS/N	8
	ON THE MARGIN OF THE RIVER CONWAY WHOSE WAVES BEAR UP .	577A	DESC CAT 4	PROSE
	THAT THEY CANNOT BEAR THE FIRMNESS OF A MASTER'S TOUCH .	603C	PUB ADDR AD/N	PROSE
	AS ATTENDING ON THE HEAVEN OF JUPITER THE GREAT BEAR .	619B	ILLUS MILTON	PROSE
	THEY ALBION SURROUND WITH KINDEST VIOLENCE TO BEAR HIM BACK	674	JERUSALEM 44	2
	THEIR WINGS WAVING OVER THE BOTTOMLESS IMMENSE TO BEAR . .	674	JERUSALEM 44	4
	BEAR THREE STRONG SINEWY NECKS & THREE AWFUL & TERRIBLE HEADS	708	JERUSALEM 70	4
	IN HEAVENS & EARTHS AS IN YOUR OWN BOSOM YOU BEAR YOUR HEAVEN	709	JERUSALEM 71	17
	TO CREATE THE LION & WOLF THE BEAR THE TYGER & OUNCE . .	713	JERUSALEM 73	17
	THO SHE NEVER COULD BEAR THE ORIGINAL PICTURE	820D	LETTER 25	PROSE
	I WAS COMMANDED BY MY SPIRITUAL FRIENDS TO BEAR ALL TO BE SILENT	825D	LETTER 27	PROSE
	KILL NOT A TREE BUT IT STILL BEAR FRUIT LET NONE SAY THAT	830C	LETTER 30	PROSE
	I FOUND I COULD BEAR WITH SAFETY & PERHAPS BENEFIT . . .	870D	LETTER 72	PROSE
BEARD				
	& OVERCAME DOWN HIS WHITE BEARD THE SILVER TORRENTS ROLL	42B	THEN SHE BORE	PROSE
	GOD BLESS THY SHRIVELD BEARD GOD BLESS THY MANY WRINKLED FOREHEAD	101	TIRIEL 2	* 36
	MY HAIR IS VERY LONG MY BEARD DOTH COVER ALL MY BREAST .	102	TIRIEL 3	4
	LOOK KNOWST THOU AUGHT OF THIS GREY BEARD OR OF THESE BLINDED EYES	104	TIRIEL 4	44
	. . . WHOSE WHITE BEARD COVERD THE STONE FLOOR LIKE WEEDS	135	FRENCH REVOLTN	38
	THE MOUTH OF WATER THE BEARD OF EARTH	152B	MARRIAGE HH 9	PROSE
	HIS SNOWY BEARD THAT STREAMS LIKE LAMBENT FLAMES DOWN HIS WIDE BREAST	204	AMERICA CANC B	16
	BY REBELS' HANDS WAS SLAIN HIS WHITE BEARD WAVD IN THE WILD WIND	205	AMERICA CANC C	27
	FLAMD FURIOUS SPARKLES HIS HAIR & BEARD	249	AHANIA 2	3
	HE STROKD THE WATER FROM HIS BEARD	369	FOUR ZOAS 9	485
	OF BABYLON LED BY A CHILD HIS TEARS RUN DOWN HIS BEARD . .	729	JERUSALEM 84	12
	SIGTRYG WITH THE SILKEN BEARD	SUPP	ILLUS GRAY	*TITLE
BEARDS				
	GREY BEARDS & SCOURGES OF FIRE THEY REPRESENT CRUEL LAWS	608A	V LAST JUDG/N	PROSE
BEARER	SEE STANDARD BEARER			
BEARING				
	BUT WALK UNITED BEARING FOOD TO ALL OUR TENDER FLOWERS . .	128	BOOK OF THEL 3	16
	IN (LUVAH'S) ROBES OF BLOOD & BEARING ALL HIS AFFLICTIONS	274	FOUR ZOAS 1	* 364
	BEARING HIS SORROWS & (?RECIEVING) ALL HIS CRUEL WOUNDS	349	FOUR ZOAS 8	* 324
	BEING NOT IRRITATED BY INSULT BEARING INSULTING BENEVOLENCES	655	JERUSALEM 30	9
	AND THE DIVINE HAND WAS UPON THEM BEARING THEM THRO DARKNESS	655	JERUSALEM 30	12
	BEARING THE IMAGES OF VARIOUS SPECIES OF CONTENTION . . .	707	JERUSALEM 69	12
	(DEFORMITY) SHE GAVE HER BEAUTY TO ANOTHER BEARING ABROAD	726	JERUSALEM 82	69
	PROTESTANT CONSIDERS NATURE AS INCAPABLE OF BEARING A CHILD	779A	ANNO CELLINI	MARG
BEARS				
	INSTEAD OF PEACEFUL PIPE THE SHEPHERD BEARS A SWORD . . .	40B	SAMSON/PS	PROSE
	PRIDE BEARS IT IN HER BOSOM AND THE GODS ALL BOW TO IT . .	41A	THEN SHE BORE	PROSE
	AND NOT LIKE CLUMSY BEARS	62	DR CLASH/IM	16
	SHE BEARS SHE GROANS NOT AT THE BIRTH OF HEUXOS OR YUVA	99	TIRIEL 1	25
	THE THANKFUL RECIEVER BEARS A PLENTIFUL HARVEST	152B	MARRIAGE HH 9	PROSE
	AND IT BEARS THE FRUIT OF DECEIT	174	HUMAN IMAGE/N	18
	AND IT BEARS THE FRUIT OF DECEIT	217	HUMAN ABSTR/SE	17
	THE CLOUD BEARS HARD ON ALBION'S SHORE	241	EUROPE 9	9
	THE CLOUD BEARS HARD UPON THE COUNCIL HOUSE DOWN RUSHING	241	EUROPE 9	12
	THE GOLDEN SUN BEARS ON MY SONG	289	FOUR ZOAS 2	347
	THE LOVERS' NIGHT BEARS ON MY SONG	289	FOUR ZOAS 2	352
	SICK COUCH BEARS THE DARK SHADES OF ETERNAL DEATH INFOLDING	493	MILTON 13	1
	LIKE AS A PEDLAR BEARS HIS WEARY PACK	536	AND HIS LEGS/N	7
	[BECAUSE IT BEARS THE [EVIDENT] EVIDENCE AT FIRST VIEW] TO BE	599C	PUB ADDRESS/N	*PROSE
	THE WORK OF A BLOCKHEAD IT BEARS THIS EVIDENCE IN ITS FACE	599C	PUB ADDRESS/N	PROSE
	BEARS ME BEFORE HIS ARMIES THO MY SHADOW HOVERS HERE . .	644	JERUSALEM 22	5
BEARST				
	OR BEARST THY EGIS OER THE BURNING FIELD	15	IMIT SPEN/PS	49
BEAST				
	O WHAT A WICKED BEAST	50	WHEN CORRUP/IM	4
	I THINK YOUR FACE SAID HE IS LIKE THAT NOBLE BEAST THE TYGER	62D	ISLAND MOON 11	PROSE
	FOR MY ENEMY IS NOT MAN BUT BEAST AND DEVIL IF I HAVE ANY	72B	ANNO LAVATER	* MARG
	I CAN LOVE HIM AS A BEAST & WISH TO BEAT HIM	72B	ANNO LAVATER	MARG
	THERE IS NO OTHER DEVIL HE WHO BITES WITHOUT PRAYING IS ONLY A BEAST	73D	ANNO LAVATER	MARG

	PAGE	TITLE	LINE

BEAST   (CONTINUED)
    THE STINK OF YOUR DEAD CARCASES ANNOYING MAN & BEAST   . .   100 TIRIEL 1   46
    THEY VISIT CAVES OF EVERY BEAST   . . . .   119 NIGHT/SI   19
    AND AS A PLAGUE WIND FILLD WITH INSECTS CUTS OFF MAN &   201 AMERICA 14   8
        BEAST
    OF BEAST BIRD FISH SERPENT & ELEMENT . . . .   222 URIZEN 3   16
    MANY FORMS OF FISH BIRD & BEAST . . . .   232 URIZEN 19   34
    NOR MAN NOR BEAST NOR CREEPING THING NOR SUN NOR CLOUD   319 FOUR ZOAS 6   285
        NOR STAR
    SO MAN LOOKS OUT IN TREE & HERB & FISH & BIRD & BEAST   . .   355 FOUR ZOAS 8   561
    HALF WOMAN & HALF [SERPENT] BEAST . . .   381 FOUR ZOAS AD 5 *   4
    THE BEAST & THE WHORE RULE WITHOUT CONTROL . . . . .   383B ANNO WATSON   MARG
    BACON SUPPOSES THAT THE DRAGON BEAST & HARLOT ARE WORTHY OF   404D ANNO BACON   MARG
    LIKE A WILD BEAST GUARDS MY WAY . . . .   415 MY SPECTRE/N   2
    AND IN EVERY SPECIES OF EARTH METAL TREE FISH BIRD & BEAST   511 MILTON 25   41
    HIS UGLY MAN ONE APPROACHING TO THE BEAST IN FEATURES   . . 580A DESC CAT 5   PROSE
    DRAWN OUT UPON IT BEFORE MAN OR BEAST CAN EXIST . . . . 585C DESC CAT 15   PROSE
    UPON THE WAYS OF MEN HIDING THE PATHS OF MAN AND BEAST   . .   642 JERUSALEM 20   13
    WHERE FISH & BIRD & BEAST & MAN & TREE & METAL & STONE   . .   681 JERUSALEM 50   6
    HAD TWENTY THANK GOD I WAS NOT ALTOGETHER A BEAST AS HE WAS   852A LETTER 50   PROSE
BEAST FORMD
    THY SELF DESTROYING BEAST FORMD SCIENCE SHALL BE   361 FOUR ZOAS 9   150
        THY ETERNAL LOT
BEASTIAL
    IN BEASTIAL FORMS OR MORE TERRIBLE MEN . . . .   144 FRENCH REVOLTN *   216
    HE ORDAIND & PRIESTESSES CLOTHD IN DISGUISES BEASTIAL   . .   333 FOUR ZOAS 7B   27
    TROOP BY TROOP THE BEASTIAL DROVES REND ONE ANOTHER   344 FOUR ZOAS 8   116
        SOUNDING LOUD
    RETURN IN PANGS & HORRIBLE CONVULSIONS TO THEIR BEASTIAL   344 FOUR ZOAS 8   119
        STATE
    FLATTEN ABOVE & BENEATH & STRETCH OUT INTO BEASTIAL LENGTH   344 FOUR ZOAS 8   128
BEASTLINESS
    THE POSSIBILITY OF HUMAN BEASTLINESS IN ALL ITS BRANCHES   387C ANNO WATSON   MARG
BEASTS
    [THEY] THE HOWLING MAIDEN LED HER FATHER WHERE WILD BEASTS   109 TIRIEL 7   16
        RESORT
    WHILE THE BEASTS OF PREY . . . .   113 LIT GRL LST/SI   34
    AND FLOWERS AND TREES AND BEASTS AND MEN RECIEVE . . . .   125 LIT BLK BOY/SI   11
    DESCENDING TO BEASTS . . . .   140 FRENCH REVOLTN   139
    THAT WALK IN BEASTS AND BIRDS OF NIGHT. . . . .   144 FRENCH REVOLTN   235
    AS THE CLEAR SPRING MUDDED WITH FEET OF BEASTS GROWS PURE   190 V DAU ALBION 2   19
        & SMILES
    TO GRATIFY SENSES UNKNOWN TREES BEASTS AND BIRDS UNKNOWN   192 V DAU ALBION 4   15
    AND TREES & BIRDS & BEASTS & MEN BEHOLD THEIR ETERNAL JOY   195 V DAU ALBION 8   8
    WHERE BONES OF BEASTS ARE STROWN . . . .   255 AHANIA 5   44
    [AMONG WILD BEASTS TO ROAM] . . . .   268 FOUR ZOAS 1   168
    AND THE LEOPARDS COVERD WITH SKINS OF BEASTS TENDED THE   281 FOUR ZOAS 2   33
        ROARING FIRES
    WAS THIS WIDE EARTH SPREAD ALL ABROAD NOT FOR WILD BEASTS   283 FOUR ZOAS 2   125
        TO ROAM
    ON THE EAST SIDE REVIVD HER SOUL WITH LIVES OF BEASTS &   285 FOUR ZOAS 2   195
        BIRDS
    THE BIRDS & BEASTS REJOICE & PLAY . . . .   289 FOUR ZOAS 2   357
    OF WILD BEASTS THERE THE LION GLARES THE TYGER & WOLF HOWL   308 FOUR ZOAS 5   128
        THERE
    ONCE HOW I SANG & CALLD THE BEASTS & BIRDS TO THEIR   325 FOUR ZOAS 7   *   199
        DELIGHTS
    OF THE HOARSE WHEELS & THE TERRIFIC HOWLINGS OF WILD BEASTS   333 FOUR ZOAS 7B   33
    EPHRAIM WAS A WILDERNESS OF JOY WHERE ALL MY WILD BEASTS   349 FOUR ZOAS 8   309
        RAN
    LOWING THEY KNEEL BEFORE THE HEAVENS THE WILD BEASTS OF   358 FOUR ZOAS 9   55
        THE FORESTS
    FLOAT THE DEAD CARCASES OF MEN & BEASTS DRIVEN TO & FRO   359 FOUR ZOAS 9   77
        ON WAVES
    IN FLOWERS IN FRUITS IN FISHES BIRDS & BEASTS & CLOUDS   367 FOUR ZOAS 9   378
        & WATERS
    THE BIRDS ADORE THE SUN THE BEASTS RISE UP & PLAY IN HIS   367 FOUR ZOAS 9   406
        BEAMS
    [WITH] BY BEASTS & WORMS & CREEPING THINGS & DARKNESS &   373 FOUR ZOAS 9   596
        DESPAIR
    HERDS THRONG UP THE VALLEY WILD BEASTS FILL THE FORESTS   373 FOUR ZOAS 9   612
    THEY BIT IN THEIR WILD FURY WHO ALSO MADDEND LIKE WILDEST   487 MILTON 7   49
        BEASTS
    HOW ARE THE BEASTS & BIRDS & FISHES & PLANTS & MINERALS   525 MILTON 34   53
    THEY RAGE LIKE WILD BEASTS IN THE FORESTS OF AFFLICTION   671 JERUSALEM 42   61
    EPHRAIM WAS A WILDERNESS OF JOY WHERE ALL MY WILD BEASTS   705 JERUSALEM 67   56
        RAN
    BUT I WAS A SLAVE BOUND IN A MILL AMONG BEASTS AND DEVILS   852A LETTER 50   PROSE
    THESE BEASTS AND THESE DEVILS ARE NOW TOGETHER WITH MYSELF   852A LETTER 50   PROSE
    [FLIES] SWARMS OF FLIES MURRAIN OF BEASTS BOILS & BLAINS   SUPP EXODUS/N   *PROSE
BEAT   SEE BROW-BEAT
    LET WINDS AND TEMPESTS BEAT . . . .   7 MY SILKS/PS   16
    LET US NOT FEAR TO BEAT ROUND NATURE'S WILDS . . . . .   27 EDW THIRD/PS 3   263
    BEAT SLOW AND TASTE AND TOUCH AND SIGHT AND SOUND AND SMELL   28 EDW THIRD/PS 3   290
    WELL LET THE TRUMPET SOUND AND THE DRUM BEAT . . . . .   31 EDW THIRD/PS 5   62
    I CAN LOVE HIM AS A BEAST & WISH TO BEAT HIM . . . . .   72B ANNO LAVATER   MARG
    THROBS OF ANGUISH BEAT ON BRAZEN WAR FOREHEADS . . .   137 FRENCH REVOLTN   71
    AND WHEN THY HEART BEGAN TO BEAT . . . .   172 THE TYGER/N 1   11
    AND WHEN THY HEART BEGAN TO BEAT . . . .   173 THE TYGER/N 2   11
    AND WHEN THY HEART BEGAN TO BEAT . . . .   214 THE TYGER/SE   11
    INCESSANT BEAT FORGING CHAINS NEW & NEW . . . .   227 URIZEN 10   17
    LOS BEAT ON HIS FETTERS OF IRON . . . .   228 URIZEN 10   28

```
                                                         PAGE      TITLE           LINE
BEAT    (CONTINUED)
        THEY BEAT DOWN THE STAKES THE CORDS  . . . . . . . .  232 URIZEN 19             48
        TILL LOS SIEZD IT AND BEAT IN A MASS  . . . . . . .   250 AHANIA 2             47
        THE ETERNAL PROPHET BEAT ON HIS ANVILS  . . . . . .   253 AHANIA 4             27
        OF ETERNITY BEAT ON HIS IRON LINKS  . . . . . . . .   259 BOOK OF LOS 5        26
        LOS BEAT ON THE ANVIL TILL GLORIOUS  . . . . . . .    260 BOOK OF LOS 5        33
        HE HEATED THE ROUND GLOBE THEN BEAT  . . . . . . .    260 BOOK OF LOS 5        38
        . . . BEAT THE HAMMERS MANY A [GLOBE] PYRAMID . . . . 283 FOUR ZOAS 2        136
        BUT ENITHARMON WRAPD IN CLOUDS WAILD LOUD FOR AS LOS BEAT 302 FOUR ZOAS 4      184
        THE PROPHET OF ETERNITY BEAT ON HIS IRON LINKS & LINKS 302 FOUR ZOAS 4        201
          OF BRASS
        AND AS HE BEAT ROUND THE HURTLING DEMON TERRIFIED AT THE 302 FOUR ZOAS 4      202
          SHAPES
        LOS BEAT ON HIS FETTERS & [POURD] HEATED HIS FURNACES . . 303 FOUR ZOAS 4     213
        BEAT ROUND THE ROCK IN MIGHTY WAVES & AS A POLYPUS  . . . 304 FOUR ZOAS 4     266
        PALE TERROR SIEZD THE EYES OF LOS AS HE BEAT ROUND  . . . 305 FOUR ZOAS 4   * 284
        VOID PATHLESS BEAT WITH [?ENION] SNOWS ETERNAL & IRON HAIL 318 FOUR ZOAS 6   * 271
          & RAIN
        PULSE AFTER PULSE BEAT ON HIS FETTERS PULSE AFTER PULSE 320 FOUR ZOAS 7        21
          HIS SPIRIT
        WHILE HIS SNOWS FELL & HIS STORMS BEAT TO COOL THE FLAMES 321 FOUR ZOAS 7      30
          OF ORC
        BEAT ROUND HER HEAD ALL NIGHT ALL DAY SHE RIOTS IN EXCESS 334 FOUR ZOAS 7B     74
        HIS STRONG BONES BEAT WITH SNOWS & HID WITHIN THE CAVES 354 FOUR ZOAS 8       517
          OF NIGHT
        EXCESS OF JOY IS WORSE THAN GRIEF HER HEART BEAT HIGH HER 362 FOUR ZOAS 9     197
          BLOOD
        THEY BEAT THE IRON ENGINES OF DESTRUCTION INTO WEDGES  . 365 FOUR ZOAS 9      304
        ARE WAVES THAT BEAT ON HEAVEN'S SHORE  . . . . . . .  432 AUGURIES             72
        & BEAT US IN THE GARDEN OR USE US AS HE PLEASE  . . . 439A BLAKES MEMORAN  PROSE
        THUNDERING THE HAMMERS BEAT & THE BELLOWS BLOW LOUD  . . . 509 MILTON 24       52
        HOW LONG SHALL I BE FORCED TO BEAT THIS INTO MEN'S EARS 602D PUB ADDR AD/N PROSE
        I WILL COMPELL THEE TO ASSIST ME IN MY TERRIBLE LABOURS 627 JERUSALEM 8        15
          TO BEAT
        TO BRISTOL & HIS HEART BEAT STRONG ON SALISBURY PLAIN  . . 704 JERUSALEM 67    37
        ALBION COLD LAYS ON HIS ROCK STORMS & SNOWS BEAT ROUND HIM 741 JERUSALEM 94     1
BEATEN
        AND FORGED HELM AND SHIELD OF SEVEN TIMES BEATEN BRASS  . .  17 EDW THIRD/PS 1   4
        YET SHALL NOT HIS FOLLY BE BEATEN OUT OF HIM  . . . . . 158C MARRIAGE HH 22 PROSE
        THAT BEATEN MASS KEEPING ITS DIRECTION  . . . . . . .  249 AHANIA 2             28
        BEATEN ALONG ITS SIGHTLESS WAY GROWING ENORMOUS IN ITS 269 FOUR ZOAS 1        194
          MOTION TO
        . . . THEY FORMD THE ANVILS OF GOLD BEATEN IN MILLS  . . . 281 FOUR ZOAS 2     30
        VOID PATHLESS BEATEN WITH [ETERNAL] IRON SLEET . . . . . 315 FOUR ZOAS 6     * 148
        MY LITTLE DAUGHTERS WERE MADE CAPTIVES & I SAW THEM BEATEN 334 FOUR ZOAS 7B    60
BEATIFIC
        IN VISION & DREAM BEATIFIC WITH THE SEVEN ANGELS OF THE 521 MILTON 32           2
          PRESENCE
BEATING
        DOWN RUSHD BEATING HIS WINGS IN VAIN THE JEALOUS KING  . 159C SONG LIBERTY  PROSE
        THE ETERNAL FIRES BEATING WITHOUT . . . . . . . .     226 URIZEN 5             32
        LIKE A HUMAN HEART STRUGLING & BEATING  . . . . . . . 226 URIZEN 5             36
        BEATING STILL ON HIS RIVETS OF IRON  . . . . . . . .  227 URIZEN 10             8
        HE SIEZD BEATING INCESSANT CONDENSING  . . . . . . .  260 BOOK OF LOS 5        29
        PETRIFY WITH INCESSANT BEATING MANY A ROCK MANY A PLANET 301 FOUR ZOAS 4      169
        DEADLY BETWEEN THE HAMMER'S BEATING GRATEFUL TO THE EARS 302 FOUR ZOAS 4      190
        ON HATE ETERNAL IN HIS VAST DISDAIN HE LABOURD BEATING  . 302 FOUR ZOAS 4     206
        ATTRACTIVE OF HIS HAMMER'S BEATING & THE SILVER LOOMS  . . 344 FOUR ZOAS 8    113
        IN PERIODS OF PULSATIVE FUROR BEATING INTO [BARS] WEDGES 346 FOUR ZOAS 8    * 207
          & BARS
        BEATING THE DESARTS & THE ROCKS THE DESARTS FEEL HIS POWER 352 FOUR ZOAS 8    443
        HE STAMPS AROUND THE ANVIL BEATING BLOWS OF STERN DESPAIR 629 JERUSALEM 10     24
BEATITUDE
        GLITTRING THE STREAMS REFLECT THE VISION OF BEATITUDE  . . 511 MILTON 25       70
BEATS
        THEN THE DRUM BEATS . . . . . . . . . . . . .        147 FRENCH REVOLTN       290
        BEATS INCESSANT TEN WINTERS THE DISK  . . . . . . .  249 AHANIA 2             24
        WHERE WINTER BEATS INCESSANT FIXING THEM FIRM ON THEIR BASE 281 FOUR ZOAS 2    31
        BENEATH THEE & AROUND ABOVE A SHOWER OF FIRE NOW BEATS  . 321 FOUR ZOAS 7      51
        AND NOW HE BEATS THE HEAVY AIR WITH HIS ENORMOUS WINGS  . . 354 FOUR ZOAS 8   526
        BEATS ALL THE LIES YOU CAN INVENT . . . . . . . . .  432 AUGURIES             54
        HE BEATS SEAS ROLL BENEATH HIS FEET TEMPESTS MUSTER  . . . 731 JERUSALEM 86    35
BEAU
        . . . BECAUSE THEY DID NOT SAY O WHAT A BEAU YE ARE  . . . 538 WAS I ANGRY/N    7
BEAUFORT
        IN BEAUFORT BUILDINGS WE ALL KNOW THAT EDITORS OF      592C PUB ADDRESS/N  PROSE
          NEWSPAPERS
BEAUTEOUS
        O LAND MOST HAPLESS O BEAUTEOUS ISLAND HOW FORSAKEN  . .  34A KING JOHN/PS  PROSE
        INWARD GRIEVD HE SAW AND LOVD THE BEAUTEOUS SUPPLIANT  . .  39B SAMSON/PS    PROSE
        IN BEAUTEOUS ORDER THENCE AROSE SOFT CLOUDS & EXHALATIONS 286 FOUR ZOAS 2    253
        AND TO HIS SONS IN THEIR DEGREES & TO HIS BEAUTEOUS    287 FOUR ZOAS 2       271
          DAUGHTERS
        IN CLOUDS OF SWEET OBSCURITY MY BEAUTEOUS FORM DISSOLVING 288 FOUR ZOAS 2    311
        I SIEZD THEE BEAUTEOUS LUVAH THOU ART FADED LIKE A FLOWER 311 FOUR ZOAS 5    226
        AND BEAUTEOUS FORMS THAT LOVE DOES WEAR . . . . . . .  447 ANNO REYNOLDS      2
BEAUTIE'S    SEE BEAUTY'S
        PHEBE DREST LIKE BEAUTIE'S QUEEN  . . . . . . . . .    53 PHEBE DREST/IM      1
BEAUTIES
        THE NARROW BUD OPENS HER BEAUTIES TO . . . . . . . . . .   2 TO AUTUMN/PS      7
        DELIGHTS BLOSSOM AROUND NUMBERLESS BEAUTIES BLOW THE  . . 37B CONTEMPLATN/PS PROSE
        AND LAID HER LILIED BEAUTIES ON THE GREEN . . . . . .  43C WOE CRIED MUSE PROSE
```

```
                                                                  PAGE     TITLE        LINE
BEAUTIES    (CONTINUED)
    [WHICH ARE BEAUTIES SWEETEST DRESS]  . . . . . . . . . . 182 WHICH ARE/N          1
    THESE ARE BEAUTIES SWEETEST DRESS  . . . . . . . . . . . 182 WHICH ARE/N          3
    AMONG THE BEAUTIES OF THE WORLD COLD & REPINING LOS  . . . 288 FOUR ZOAS 2        321
    ON WHOM I POURD THE BEAUTIES OF MY LIGHT ADORNING THEM  . 312 FOUR ZOAS 6         26
    KNEW NOT THE SMALLER BEAUTIES OF THE ART  . . . . . . . 467A ANNO REYNOLDS       MARG
    ALL THE BEAUTIES PICKD OUT [BUT] & BLURRD & BLOTTED  . . 595C PUB ADDRESS/N     *PROSE
    [SPOTS & BLEMISHES WHICH ARE BEAUTIES & NOT FAULTS]  . . 595D PUB ADDRESS/N      PROSE
    BEAUTIES NOW GENTLEMEN CRITICS HOW DO YOU LIKE THIS  . . 603B PUB ADDR AD/N      PROSE
    TORMENTED WITH SWEET DESIRE FOR THESE BEAUTIES OF ALBION  639 JERUSALEM 17        22
    COMPREHENDING THE BEAUTIES OF COLOURING OR THE PICTURES  814A LETTER 23          PROSE
    HIS CHIEF BEAUTIES BUT THERE ARE SOME WHICH MAY BE EXECUTED 848A LETTER 45       PROSE
BEAUTIFUL
    & A LILLY ARE VARIOUS & BOTH BEAUTIFUL BEAUTY IS EXUBERANT  81C ANNO LAVATER     MARG
    MOST SUPERLATIVELY BEAUTIFUL & MOST AFFECTIONATELY HOLY   82D ANNO LAVATER       MARG
    AND AGED TIRIEL STOOD BEFORE THE GATES OF HIS BEAUTIFUL    99 TIRIEL 1             1
        PALACE
    SHOUT BEAUTIFUL DAUGHTER OF TIRIEL THOU SINGEST A SWEET   109 TIRIEL 7            10
        SONG
    . . . LIKE SPIRITS OF FIRE IN THE BEAUTIFUL   . . . . . 136 FRENCH REVOLTN       54
    SAID THE BEAUTIFUL QUEEN OF FRANCE  . . . . . . . . . . 185 LET BROTHELS/N        4
    AND ON THE MOST BEAUTIFUL WOVE PAPER THAT COULD BE PROCURED 208A PRSPECTUS 1793  PROSE
    HIS BEAUTIFUL VISAGE HIS TRESSES  . . . . . . . . . . . 251 AHANIA 3             41
    THE INFANT JOY IS BEAUTIFUL BUT ITS ANATOMY  . . . . . 265 FOUR ZOAS 1           49
    THO THUS HEAVENLY BEAUTIFUL TO DRAW ME TO DESTRUCTION  . 265 FOUR ZOAS 1          58
    LEST LOS SHOULD ENTER INTO BEULAH THRO HER BEAUTIFUL GATES 279 FOUR ZOAS 1       566
    [FOR] BUT INFINITELY BEAUTIFUL THE WONDROUS WORK AROSE  . 286 FOUR ZOAS 2        240
    GOLDEN & BEAUTIFUL BUT O HOW UNLIKE THOSE SWEET FIELDS   292 FOUR ZOAS 3          39
        OF BLISS
    AND THE WING LIKE TENT OF THE UNIVERSE BEAUTIFUL         318 FOUR ZOAS 6         254
        SURROUNDING ALL
    IN BEAUTIFUL SUBSTANTIAL FORMS APPEARD & SERVED HER  . . 340 FOUR ZOAS 7B        275
    OF FEMALE FORMS BEAUTIFUL THRO POISONS HIDDEN IN SECRET   348 FOUR ZOAS 8         290
    LO ENITHARMON TERRIBLE & BEAUTIFUL IN ETERNAL YOUTH  . . 351 FOUR ZOAS 8         408
    O HOW COULDST THOU DEFORM THOSE BEAUTIFUL PROPORTIONS  . 360 FOUR ZOAS 9         140
    WITH BEAUTIFUL ART THE STUDY OF ANGELS THE WORKMANSHIP   365 FOUR ZOAS 9         297
        OF DEMONS
    SO SAYING SHE AROSE & WALKED ROUND HER BEAUTIFUL HOUSE  . 369 FOUR ZOAS 9        471
    BURKE'S TREATISE ON THE SUBLIME & BEAUTIFUL  . . . . . 476D ANNO REYNOLDS       MARG
    BUT BEAUTIFUL ELYNITTRIA WITH HER SILVER ARROWS REPELLD ME 492 MILTON 11          38
    THE BEAUTIFUL AMALEKITES BEHOLD THE FIRES OF YOUTH  . . 501 MILTON 19            37
    CREATING THE BEAUTIFUL HOUSE FOR THE PITEOUS SUFFERER  . 515 MILTON 28             7
    ANTAMON TAKES THEM INTO HIS BEAUTIFUL FLEXIBLE HANDS  . 515 MILTON 28            13
    HE SET ME DOWN IN FELPHAM'S VALE & PREPARD A BEAUTIFUL  . 527 MILTON 36           23
    WITH WAR WOVEN IN LOOMS OF TYRE & SIDON BY BEAUTIFUL     528 MILTON 37            24
        ASHTAROTH
    GORGEOUS & BEAUTIFUL LOUD ROLL HIS THUNDERS AGAINST MILTON 529 MILTON 38          12
    "IN THE LAST BATTLE THAT ARTHUR FOUGHT THE MOST BEAUTIFUL 560B EXHIBITION ADV    PROSE
        WAS ONE"
    "THE MOST BEAUTIFUL THE ROMAN WARRIORS TREMBLED"  . . . 560B EXHIBITION ADV      PROSE
    VOLUPTUOUSNESS AND FOLLY BEGAN TO BE ACCOUNTED BEAUTIFUL  568B DESC CAT 3         PROSE
    BEAUTIFUL BLOOMING DAMSEL AND H(HOPPNER) SAYS  . . . . 574B DESC CAT 3          *PROSE
    THE MOST BEAUTIFUL THE MOST STRONG AND THE MOST UGLY  . 577C DESC CAT 5          PROSE
    THE BEAUTIFUL MAN REPRESENTS THE HUMAN PATHETIC  . . . . 578A DESC CAT 5         PROSE
    OF YOUR BEAUTIFUL MAN AND THE HERCULES FOR YOUR STRONG MAN 579B DESC CAT 5       PROSE
    ACCORDINGLY THE PAINTER HAS GIVEN IN HIS BEAUTIFUL MAN  . 580A DESC CAT 5        PROSE
    THE BEAUTIFUL MAN ACTS FROM DUTY AND ANXIOUS SOLICITUDE   580B DESC CAT 5        PROSE
    GWINIVERRA & GWINEFRED & GONORILL & SABRINA BEAUTIFUL  . 624 JERUSALEM 5          43
    THEY ARE THE BEAUTIFUL EMANATIONS OF THE TWELVE SONS OF   624 JERUSALEM 5         45
        ALBION
    HAVE A BEAUTIFUL GOLDEN GATE WHICH OPENS INTO THE        635 JERUSALEM 14        20
        VEGETATIVE WORLD
    SLAY NOT MY INFANT LOVES & GRACES BEAUTIFUL DAUGHTER OF   643 JERUSALEM 20        28
        MOAB
    WHEN ALBION RENT THY BEAUTIFUL NET OF GOLD AND SILVER TWINE 643 JERUSALEM 20      30
    BEAUTIFUL THRO OUR LOVE'S COMELINESS BEAUTIFUL THRO PITY  643 JERUSALEM 20        33
    THE INFANT JOY IS BEAUTIFUL BUT ITS ANATOMY  . . . . . 645 JERUSALEM 22          22
    IN BEULAH THE FEMALE LETS DOWN HER BEAUTIFUL TABERNACLE   656 JERUSALEM 30        34
    REUBEN RETURND TO HIS PLACE IN VAIN HE SOUGHT BEAUTIFUL   662 JERUSALEM 36         1
        TIRZAH
    THUS IN PROCESS OF TIME IT BECAME THE BEAUTIFUL MUNDANE   691 JERUSALEM 59         7
        SHELL
    LOOK THE BEAUTIFUL DAUGHTER OF ALBION SITS NAKED UPON THE 705 JERUSALEM 68        11
        STONE
    OF HER TABERNACLE & HER ARK & SECRET PLACE THE BEAUTIFUL  705 JERUSALEM 68        15
        DAUGHTER
    MOLECH RUSHES INTO THE KINGS IN LOVE TO THE BEAUTIFUL    706 JERUSALEM 68        28
        DAUGHTERS
    TO THE BEAUTIFUL DAUGHTERS OF ALBION THEY SPORT BEFORE    706 JERUSALEM 68        32
        THE KINGS
    ON THE TWELVE STONES OF POWER & THE BEAUTIFUL DAUGHTERS   706 JERUSALEM 68        41
        OF ALBION
    O BEAUTIFUL DAUGHTER OF ALBION CRUELTY IS THY DELIGHT  . . 706 JERUSALEM 68       53
    . . . . A THREE-FOLD WONDER FEMININE MOST BEAUTIFUL      709 JERUSALEM 70        20
        THREE-FOLD
    OVER HER BEAUTIFUL FEMALE FEATURES SOFT FLOURISHING IN    709 JERUSALEM 70        23
        BEAUTY
    THE INHABITANTS OF THE WHOLE EARTH REJOICE IN THEIR       710 JERUSALEM 71        25
        BEAUTIFUL LIGHT
    LEICESTER & BERKSHIRE & HIS EMANATION IS GWINEFRED        710 JERUSALEM 71        37
        BEAUTIFUL
    BEAUTIFUL SHE BEAMS TOWARDS THE EAST ALL KINDS OF PRECIOUS 710 JERUSALEM 71       40
        STONES
```

178

BEAUTIFUL (CONTINUED)

	PAGE	TITLE	LINE
BEAUTIFUL BUT TERRIBLE STRUGGLING TO TAKE A FORM OF BEAUTY	715	JERUSALEM 74	53
HAND SLEPT ON SKIDDAW'S TOP DRAWN BY THE LOVE OF BEAUTIFUL	723	JERUSALEM 80	57
SHE WOVE TWO VESSELS OF SEED BEAUTIFUL AS SKIDDAW'S SNOW	723	JERUSALEM 80	74
I HAVE STRIPD OFF JOSEPH'S BEAUTIFUL INTEGUMENT FOR MY BELOVED	724	JERUSALEM 81	11
SHALL SURROUND HER IN BEAUTIFUL LABYRINTHS OOTHOON .	727	JERUSALEM 83	27
AS A BEAUTIFUL VEIL SO THESE FEMALES SHALL FOLD & UNFOLD	728	JERUSALEM 83	45
PISON SINCE CALLD ARNON THERE IS HESHBON BEAUTIFUL . .	735	JERUSALEM 89	25
HIS LOINS INCLOSE BABYLON ON EUPHRATES BEAUTIFUL . . .	735	JERUSALEM 89	38
THESE BEAUTIFUL WITCHCRAFTS OF ALBION ARE GRATIFYD BY CRUELTY	737	JERUSALEM 90	68
IN BEAUTIFUL PARADISES EXPAND THESE ARE THE FOUR RIVERS OF PARADISE	745	JERUSALEM 98	25
JUSTLY STANDS FIRST IN THE BOOK & THAT BEAUTIFUL SPECIMEN	782A	INSC UPCOTT	PROSE
HE IS GLAD TO EMBRACE THE OFFER OF ENGRAVING SUCH BEAUTIFUL THINGS	790A	LETTER 1	PROSE
[BEFORE] IMMEDIATELY ON THE RECEIT OF YOUR BEAUTIFUL BOOK	791A	LETTER 3	PROSE
A GUINEA IS MORE BEAUTIFUL THAN THE SUN & A BAG WORN WITH	793D	LETTER 5	PROSE
THE USE OF MONEY HAS MORE BEAUTIFUL PROPORTIONS THAN .	793D	LETTER 5	PROSE
WHICH IS MORE BEAUTIFUL THAN I THOUGHT IT & MORE CONVENIENT	801D	LETTER 14	PROSE
A MOST BEAUTIFUL COUNTRY ON A MOST GLORIOUS DAY OUR .	803A	LETTER 15	PROSE
COTTAGE IS MORE BEAUTIFUL THAN I THOUGHT IT & ALSO MORE CONVENIENT	803B	LETTER 15	PROSE
VERY BEAUTIFUL & ENCOURAGING VERSES WHICH I ACCOUNT . .	804A	LETTER 16	PROSE
BEAUTIFUL AND THO THE WEATHER IS WET THE AIR IS VERY MILD	806A	LETTER 16	PROSE
BUT WHAT WE HAVE SEEN IS MOST BEAUTIFUL & THE PEOPLE .	806B	LETTER 16	PROSE
AND "TWAS WHERE THE SEAS WERE ROARING" AND A BEAUTIFUL .	831A	LETTER 31	PROSE
SENSATION ON HIS RECEPTION OF YOUR VERY BEAUTIFUL VERSES	839B	LETTER 38	PROSE
DROWNING PEOPLE IS A BEAUTIFUL PERFORMANCE MR SAUNDERS .	839D	LETTER 38	PROSE
THANK YOU FOR YOUR VERY BEAUTIFUL LITTLE POEM ON THE KING'S RECOVERY	844D	LETTER 43	PROSE
ENVIABLE AND THE COUNTRY IS NOT ONLY MORE BEAUTIFUL ON .	847C	LETTER 44	PROSE
WISH THAT YOU MAY LONG ENJOY YOUR BEAUTIFUL RETIREMENT .	847C	LETTER 44	PROSE
MAKE A VERY BEAUTIFUL ENGRAVING DONE IN THE SAME MANNER AS	850D	LETTER 49	PROSE
TO SAY THAT VENUSIA IS AS BEAUTIFUL AS SERENA IS ONLY .	853A	LETTER 51	*PROSE
YOUR BEAUTIFUL AND ELEGANT DAUGHTER VENUSIA GROWS IN OUR	853D	LETTER 52	*PROSE
AND ROUND THE BEAUTIFUL TURRET I HAVE SAID SEEM BUT . .	854A	LETTER 52	PROSE
BEAUTIFUL POEM MUST NOW AFFORD YOU THEIR FULL REWARD .	854B	LETTER 53	PROSE
THAT YOUR LAST BEAUTIFUL POEM WAS NOT PUBLISHD IN THE .	856B	LETTER 54	PROSE
FOR YOUR BEAUTIFUL MUSE BUT MR PHILLIPS SAID MR HAYLEY .	857A	LETTER 54	PROSE
OF THIS BEAUTIFUL LITTLE ESTATE FOR THAT IT WILL BE HIGHLY	858C	LETTER 55	PROSE
WOULD NOT FOR THE WORLD INJURE THIS BEAUTIFUL WORK AND .	858C	LETTER 55	PROSE
THE SITUATIONS OF OUR BEAUTIFUL AFFECTIONATE BALLADS I KNOW	863B	LETTER 60	PROSE

BEAUTIFULLEST

	PAGE	TITLE	LINE
THESE WERE THE STRONGEST MAN THE BEAUTIFULLEST MAN AND	577B	DESC CAT 5	TITLE

BEAUTIFULLY

	PAGE	TITLE	LINE
TO ME THAT THE FIRST PAGE OF THE POEM WAS BEAUTIFULLY .	857B	LETTER 54	PROSE
THE CHILD IS AS BEAUTIFULLY DRAWN AS IT IS COLOURED IN BOTH	864B	LETTER 61	PROSE

BEAUTY

	PAGE	TITLE	LINE
& A LILLY ARE VARIOUS & BOTH BEAUTIFUL BEAUTY IS EXUBERANT	81C	ANNO LAVATER	MARG
BUT NOT OF UGLINESS BUT OF BEAUTY	81C	ANNO LAVATER	MARG
AND IF UGLINESS IS ADJOIND TO BEAUTY	81D	ANNO LAVATER	MARG
IT IS NOT THE EXUBERANCE OF BEAUTY SO IF RAFAEL IS HARD & DRY	81D	ANNO LAVATER	MARG
TO FADE AWAY LIKE MORNING BEAUTY FROM HER MORTAL DAY .	127	BOOK OF THEL 1	3
AND WHY IT SCATTERS ITS BRIGHT BEAUTY THRO THE HUMID AIR	128	BOOK OF THEL 2	15
O BEAUTY OF THE VALES OF HAR WE LIVE NOT FOR OURSELVES .	129	BOOK OF THEL 4	10
THE DAUGHTER OF BEAUTY WIPD HER PITYING TEARS WITH HER WHITE VEIL	130	BOOK OF THEL 5	7
. . . TO PLANT BEAUTY IN THE DESART CRAVING ABYSS THEY GLEAM	136	FRENCH REVOLTN	55
THE GENITALS BEAUTY THE HANDS & FEET PROPORTION	152C	MARRIAGE HH 10	PROSE
EXUBERANCE IS BEAUTY	152D	MARRIAGE HH 10	PROSE
SLEEP SLEEP BEAUTY BRIGHT	165	CRADLE SONG/N	5
NOR A THORN NOR A THREAT STAIN HER BEAUTY BRIGHT . . .	171	THE LILLY/N	6
AND [MAIDENS] BEAUTY FOR A BIT OF BREAD	174	HUMAN IMAGE/N	32
PLANTS FRUITS OF LIFE & BEAUTY THERE	178	ABSTINENCE/N	4
OPEN TO JOY AND TO DELIGHT WHERE EVER BEAUTY APPEARS . .	194	V DAU ALBION 6	22
TILL BEAUTY FADES FROM OFF MY SHOULDERS DARKEND AND CAST OUT	194	V DAU ALBION 7	14
BY ARISTON THE KING OF BEAUTY FOR HIS STOLEN BRIDE . . .	200	AMERICA 10	10
NOR A THORN NOR A THREAT STAIN HER BEAUTY BRIGHT . . .	215	THE LILLY/SE	4
IN SECRET OF SOFT WINGS IN MAZES OF DELUSIVE BEAUTY . . .	265	FOUR ZOAS 1	43
[SUCH WONDROUS BEAUTY REPINING IN THE MIDST OF ALL HIS GLORY]	267	FOUR ZOAS 1	132
. . . ALL THY SOFT DELUSIVE BEAUTY CANNOT	268	FOUR ZOAS 1	170
THAT I SHOULD HIDE THEE WITH MY POWER & DELIGHT THEE WITH MY BEAUTY	269	FOUR ZOAS 1	174
[BEAUTY ALL BLUSHING WITH DESIRE MOCKING HER FELL DESPAIR]	269	FOUR ZOAS 1	189
[IN BEAUTY LOVE & XXX SCORN [?THEY ?SULKD] THE BRIDE & BRIDEGROOM ?SULKD]	SUPP	FOUR ZOAS 1	*
SUBLIME DISTINCT THEIR LINEAMENTS DIVINE OF HUMAN BEAUTY	281	FOUR ZOAS 2	34
OUR BEAUTY IS COVERD OVER WITH CLAY & ASHES & OUR BACKS	286	FOUR ZOAS 2	225
REPROACH THEE & THE BEAMY GARDENS SICKEN AT THY BEAUTY . .	288	FOUR ZOAS 2	303
SCREAM & FALL OFF & LAUGH AT THARMAS LOVELY SUMMER BEAUTY	296	FOUR ZOAS 3	174
THARMAS I KNOW THEE HOW ARE WE ALTERD OUR BEAUTY DECAYD	299	FOUR ZOAS 4	79
AND AS A DOUBLE FEMALE FORM LOVELINESS & PERFECTION OF BEAUTY	304	FOUR ZOAS 4	251
YET MIGHTY BULK & MAJESTY & BEAUTY REMAIN BUT UNEXPANSIVE	305	FOUR ZOAS 5	13

		PAGE	TITLE	LINE

BEAUTY   (CONTINUED)

WHY CAN I NOT ENJOY THY BEAUTY LOVELY ENITHARMON	324 FOUR ZOAS 7	184
DELECTABLE REPOSEST RUDDY IN MY ABSENCE FLAMING WITH BEAUTY	325 FOUR ZOAS 7	187
ALL THINGS BESIDE THE WOFUL LOS ENJOY THE DELIGHTS OF BEAUTY	325 FOUR ZOAS 7	198
[TO HEW THE CAVERND ROCKS OF DRANTHON INTO FORMS OF BEAUTY]	331 FOUR ZOAS 7	457
IN YOUTH & BEAUTY IN THE ARMS OF ENITHARMON MILD REPOSING	332 FOUR ZOAS 7	475
NOW SMILE AMONG THY BITTER TEARS NOW PUT ON ALL THY BEAUTY	337 FOUR ZOAS 7B	188
THUS FORMING A VAST FAMILY WONDROUS IN BEAUTY & LOVE . .	345 FOUR ZOAS 8	187
A FALSE FEMININE COUNTERPART LOVELY OF DELUSIVE BEAUTY .	348 FOUR ZOAS 8	* 278
WHICH GIVE A TINCTURE TO FALSE BEAUTY	348 FOUR ZOAS 8	291
THEY STOOD IN BEAMING BEAUTY & SOMETIMES AS ONE EVEN RAHAB	349 FOUR ZOAS 8	329
SPOILD OF THEIR BEAUTY THEIR HAIR RENT & THEIR SKIN SHRIVELD UP	375 FOUR ZOAS 9	665
NAKED IN ALL THEIR BEAUTY DANCING ROUND THE WINE PRESSES	377 FOUR ZOAS 9	766
BEAUTY ALL BLUSHING WITH DESIRE A SELF ENJOYING WONDER . .	381 FOUR ZOAS AD 5	9
THAT I SHOULD HIDE THEE WITH MY POWER & [DELIGHT THEE WITH MY BEAUTY]	382 FOUR ZOAS AD 5	* 16
THEY STOOD IN BEAMING BEAUTY & SOMETIMES AS ONE EVEN RAHAB	382 FOUR ZOAS AD 6	17
[THAT LOVE & BEAUTY UNDERGO]	422 BENEATH/N	13
THAT LOVE & BEAUTY UNDERGO	424 THE GOLDEN NET	12
MARY MOVES IN SOFT BEAUTY & CONSCIOUS DELIGHT	428 MARY	9
THAT SWEET LOVE & BEAUTY ARE WORTHY OUR CARE	428 MARY	17
I WILL HUMBLE MY BEAUTY I WILL NOT DRESS FINE	428 MARY	29
("PERFECTION AND BEAUTY NOT TO BE SOUGHT IN HEAVENS ") A LIE	458D ANNO REYNOLDS	MARG
MINUTENESS IS THEIR WHOLE BEAUTY	459B ANNO REYNOLDS	MARG
KNOWLEDGE OF IDEAL BEAUTY IS NOT TO BE ACQUIRED	459B ANNO REYNOLDS	MARG
WHAT NONSENSE PASSION & EXPRESSION IS BEAUTY ITSELF . . .	466A ANNO REYNOLDS	MARG
OF VARIED BEAUTY TO DELIGHT THE WANDERER AND REPOSE . .	481 MILTON 2	4
DISPLAYING NAKED BEAUTY WITH FLUTE & HARP & SONG	484 MILTON 4	28
AND THIS IS THE MANNER OF THE DAUGHTERS OF ALBION IN THEIR BEAUTY	484 MILTON 5	5
PITYING HIS YOUTH AND BEAUTY TREMBLING AT ETERNAL DEATH	488 MILTON 8	31
FOR HER LIGHT IS TERRIBLE TO ME I FADE BEFORE HER IMMORTAL BEAUTY	492 MILTON 12	1
IN ALL MY BEAUTY THAT I MIGHT UNLOOSE THE FLAMING STEEDS	492 MILTON 12	11
LIKE FEMALES OF SWEET BEAUTY TO GUARD ROUND HIM & TO FEED	496 MILTON 15	14
A GIANT FORM OF PERFECT BEAUTY OUTSTRETCHD ON THE ROCK .	497 MILTON 15	38
OF FIRE IN INTERCHANGE OF BEAUTY & PERFECTION IN THE DARKNESS	500 MILTON 18	40
IN FEMALE BEAUTY SHINING IN THE UNFORMD VOID & ORC IN VAIN	500 MILTON 18	44
IN ALL THEIR BEAUTY TO ENTICE MILTON ACROSS THE RIVER . .	501 MILTON 19	31
BEFORE HIM IN THEIR BEAUTY & IN CRUELTIES OF HOLINESS . .	501 MILTON 19	34
THEREFORE BRIGHT TIRZAH TRIUMPHS PUTTING ON ALL BEAUTY .	501 MILTON 19	44
HENCE THOU ART CLOTHD WITH HUMAN BEAUTY O THOU MORTAL MAN	502 MILTON 20	* 31
NAKED IN ALL THEIR BEAUTY DANCING ROUND THE WINE-PRESSES	513 MILTON 27	29
CREATING FORM & BEAUTY AROUND THE DARK REGIONS OF SORROW	514 MILTON 28	2
THE DAUGHTERS OF BEAUTY LOOK UP FROM THEIR LOOM & PREPARE	515 MILTON 28	19
THE HONEYSUCKLE SLEEPING ON THE OAK THE FLAUNTING BEAUTY	520 MILTON 31	54
AND COMES FORTH IN THE MAJESTY OF BEAUTY EVERY FLOWER . .	520 MILTON 31	58
INTO A STRENGTH IMPREGNABLE OF MAJESTY & BEAUTY INFINITE	527 MILTON 37	7
WAS THE BEAUTY OF OUR ANCESTORS TILL AFTER ELIZABETH'S TIME	568B DESC CAT 3	PROSE
REMNANT STRENGTH BEAUTY AND UGLINESS ESCAPED THE WRECK .	577C DESC CAT 5	PROSE
AND OF THESE THREE WHO ESCAPED NAMELY BEAUTY STRENGTH .	578A DESC CAT 5	PROSE
IDEAS OF STRENGTH AND BEAUTY HAVE NOT BEEN GREATLY DIFFERENT	579C DESC CAT 5	PROSE
CONCERNING HIS IDEAS OF BEAUTY STRENGTH AND UGLINESS .	579D DESC CAT 5	PROSE
THE BEAUTY THAT IS ANNEXED AND APPENDED TO FOLLY IS A .	579D DESC CAT 5	PROSE
IT IS FIT FOR THE BURLESQUE THE BEAUTY PROPER FOR SUBLIME	579D DESC CAT 5	PROSE
HIS OWN IDEA OF INTELLECTUAL BEAUTY THE FACE AND . . .	580A DESC CAT 5	PROSE
IS THE FACE AND LIMBS OF GREATEST BEAUTY AND PERFECTION	580A DESC CAT 5	PROSE
THEIR [BEAUTY IS CONFESSD EVEN BY THE LIPS OF PASCH HIMSELF]	601A PUB ADDRESS/N	*PROSE
EVERY LINE IS THE LINE OF BEAUTY	603C PUB ADDR AD/N	PROSE
I SAW THE LIMBS FORMD FOR EXERCISE CONTEMND & THE BEAUTY OF	628 JERUSALEM 9	7
REUBEN IN HIS TWELVE-FOLD MAJESTY & BEAUTY SHALL TAKE REFUGE	636 JERUSALEM 15	27
IN THE FIRES OF THEIR BEAUTY & PERFECTION & BE VEGETATED BENEATH	638 JERUSALEM 17	8
IN THE FIERCE DESIRES OF BEAUTY & IN THE TORTURES OF REPULSE HE IS	638 JERUSALEM 17	12
OUTSTRETCHD HIS GIANT BEAUTY ON THE GROUND IN PAIN & TEARS	641 JERUSALEM 18	46
HIS GIANT BEAUTY AND PERFECTION FALLEN INTO DUST	641 JERUSALEM 19	8
THE HUMAN MAJESTY AND BEAUTY OF THE TWENTYFOUR	641 JERUSALEM 19	24
SIGHING TO MELT HIS GIANT BEAUTY ON THE MOONY RIVER . . .	642 JERUSALEM 19	47
OF LOVE THOU REFUSEDST TO LET ME GO ALBION BEHELD THY BEAUTY	643 JERUSALEM 20	32
ASTONISHD AT HIS BEAUTY & PERFECTION THOU FORGAVEST HIS FURIOUS LOVE	643 JERUSALEM 20	37
I BROUGHT LOVE INTO LIGHT OF DAY TO PRIDE IN CHASTE BEAUTY	645 JERUSALEM 22	17
PERFECT AND SHINING WITH BEAUTY BUT THOU O WRETCHED FATHER	645 JERUSALEM 23	7
I WAS A GARDEN PLANTED WITH BEAUTY I ALLURED ON HILL & VALLEY	659 JERUSALEM 33	37
KNOW ME NOW ALBION LOOK UPON ME I ALONE AM BEAUTY . . .	660 JERUSALEM 33	48
ART & SCIENCE CANNOT EXIST BUT BY NAKED BEAUTY DISPLAYD	663 JERUSALEM 36	49
FOR HUMAN BEAUTY KNOWS IT NOT NOR CAN MERCY FIND IT BUT	666 JERUSALEM 39	6
IN BEAUTY THE DAUGHTERS OF ALBION DIVIDE & UNITE AT WILL	689 JERUSALEM 58	1
WHY WILT THOU DEFACE THY BEAUTY & THE BEAUTY OF THY LITTLE-ONES	693 JERUSALEM 60	29
DOST THOU BLACKEN THEIR BEAUTY BY A SECLUDED PLACE OF REST	693 JERUSALEM 60	32
AND A PECULIAR TABERNACLE TO CUT THE INTEGUMENTS OF BEAUTY	693 JERUSALEM 60	33

```
                                                                PAGE      TITLE            LINE
BEAUTY    (CONTINUED)
    NOW SMILE AMONG THY BITTER TEARS NOW PUT ON ALL THY BEAUTY       700 JERUSALEM 65        30
    AND DISHES OF PAINTED CLAY GLOWING WITH BEAUTY & CRUELTY         702 JERUSALEM 66        33
    IN PRIDE OF BEAUTY IN CRUELTY OF HOLINESS IN THE BRIGHTNESS      705 JERUSALEM 68        14
    WHY TREMBLES THE WARRIOR'S LIMBS WHEN HE BEHOLDS THY BEAUTY      706 JERUSALEM 68        48
    SOMETIMES I CURSE & SOMETIMES BLESS THY FASCINATING BEAUTY       707 JERUSALEM 68        64
    IN BEAUTY ARE SHADOWS NOW NO MORE BUT ROCKS IN HOREB    .  .     707 JERUSALEM 68        70
    AND FEEDS HER WITH THE FOOD OF EDEN HENCE ALL HER BEAUTY         707 JERUSALEM 69        18
        BEAMS
    WITH SPACES OF SWEET GARDENS & A TENT OF ELEGANT BEAUTY          707 JERUSALEM 69        20
    OVER HER BEAUTIFUL FEMALE FEATURES SOFT FLOURISHING IN           709 JERUSALEM 70        23
        BEAUTY
    IN FIRES OF BEAUTY MELTING THEM AS GOLD & SILVER IN THE          709 JERUSALEM 70        28
        FURNACE
    IN STRONG TEMPTATIONS OF STOLEN BEAUTY I TELL HOW REUBEN         715 JERUSALEM 74        33
        SLEPT
    HIS AWFUL BEAUTY WITH MORAL VIRTUE THE FAIR DECIEVER             715 JERUSALEM 74        35
        OFFSPRING
    BEAUTIFUL BUT TERRIBLE STRUGGLING TO TAKE A FORM OF BEAUTY       715 JERUSALEM 74        53
    WHEREFORE IN DREADFUL MAJESTY & BEAUTY OUTSIDE APPEARS  .  .     721 JERUSALEM 79        70
    WHEREFORE THEN DO YOU REALIZE THESE NETS OF BEAUTY               721 JERUSALEM 79        78
        & DELUSION
    BESIDE HER VALA HOWLD UPON THE WINDS IN PRIDE OF BEAUTY          721 JERUSALEM 80         6
    TO THE STERN WARRIOR I AM BECOME PERFECT IN BEAUTY OVER          724 JERUSALEM 81         5
        MY WARRIOR
    DISCOVERING HER OWN PERFECT BEAUTY TO THE DAUGHTERS OF           726 JERUSALEM 82        46
        ALBION
    HYLE WAS A WINDING WORM AND HERSELF PERFECT IN BEAUTY   .  .     726 JERUSALEM 82        50
    [A REDNING SKELETON IN HOWLING WOE] INSTEAD OF BEAUTY   .  .     726 JERUSALEM 82    *   68
    (DEFORMITY) SHE GAVE HER BEAUTY TO ANOTHER BEARING ABROAD        726 JERUSALEM 82        69
    THE SEEDS OF BEAUTY IN THE SPACE LISTNING TO THEIR               730 JERUSALEM 85         9
        LAMENTATION
    IN HEAD & HEART & REINS THREE UNIVERSES OF LOVE & BEAUTY         730 JERUSALEM 86         3
    A SUBLIME ORNAMENT NOT OBSCURING THE OUTLINES OF BEAUTY          731 JERUSALEM 86        15
    TERRIBLE TO BEHOLD FOR THY EXTREME BEAUTY & PERFECTION  .  .     731 JERUSALEM 86        16
    TILL IT BECAME A SEPARATED CLOUD OF BEAUTY GRACE & LOVE          732 JERUSALEM 86        55
    LURED BY HER BEAUTY OUTSIDE OF HIMSELF IN SHADOWY GRIEF          732 JERUSALEM 86        60
    FROM ENION IN THE DESARTS TERRIFIED AT EACH OTHER'S BEAUTY       732 JERUSALEM 86        63
    OF BEAUTY & PERFECTION MY WILD FIBRES SHOOT IN VEINS    .  .     732 JERUSALEM 87         5
    ART CAN NEVER EXIST WITHOUT NAKED BEAUTY DISPLAYED      .  . 776D INSC LAOCOON         PROSE
    THE BEAUTY OF THE BIBLE IS THAT THE MOST IGNORANT &     .  . 786D ANNO THORNTON        MARG
    & SERENITY & HAPPINESS & BEAUTY A CAUSE OF MALEVOLENCE          793B LETTER 5          PROSE
    WHERE I OUGHT TO PLACE NAKED BEAUTY OR SIMPLE ORNAMENT  .  .    795A LETTER 6          PROSE
    THAT IT CAN BE IMPROVED EITHER IN BEAUTY OR USE   .  .  .  .    802A LETTER 14         PROSE
    NECESSARY TO HISTORICAL BEAUTY & IN A LETTER TO THE    .  .    814B LETTER 23         PROSE
    & IS SO UNTRACTABLE THO CAPABLE OF SUCH BEAUTY & PERFECTION    837D LETTER 36         PROSE
BEAUTY'S     SEE BEAUTIE'S
    THAT LIGHTLY TRIP ON BEAUTY'S TOE  .  .  .  .  .  .  .  .  .     56 HAIL MATRIM/IM       5
    OR SIT ON BEAUTY'S BUM  .  .  .  .  .  .  .  .  .  .  .  .       56 HAIL MATRIM/IM       6
    THESE ARE BEAUTY'S SWEETEST DRESS  .  .  .  .  .  .  .  .  .    184 SEVRL QUESTN/N      10
    [EGR(EGREMONT'S)] WHAT MIGHTY SOUL IN BEAUTY'S FORM    .  .    558 THE CAVERNS/N   *    5
BECAME
    AND IN MY PLAY TILL HE BECAME TO ME AS MY BROTHER      .  .   37C CONTEMPLATN/PS     PROSE
    HE BECAME A LITTLE CHILD  .  .  .  .  .  .  .  .  .  .  .  .    115 THE LAMB/SI         16
    WHO BECAME AN INFANT SMALL  .  .  .  .  .  .  .  .  .  .  .     120 CRADLE SONG/SI      30
    AND THE CHAMBER BECAME AS A CLOUDED SKY  .  .  .  .  .  .  .    138 FRENCH REVOLTN      85
    KNOW THAT AFTER CHRIST'S DEATH HE BECAME JEHOVAH   .  .  .  . 150B MARRIAGE HH 5      PROSE
    THE ANGEL HEARING THIS BECAME ALMOST BLUE  .  .  .  .  .  . 158B MARRIAGE HH 22     PROSE
    SHUT UP IN FINITE REVOLUTIONS AND MAN BECAME AN ANGEL          241 EUROPE 10           22
    BECAME ELEMENT PLIANT TO RISE  .  .  .  .  .  .  .  .  .  .     258 BOOK OF LOS 4       51
    THEY SULK UPON HER BREAST HER HAIR BECAME LIKE SNOW ON         270 FOUR ZOAS 1        211
        MOUNTAINS
    [TILL] [BUT] SHE BECAME A [DE] DRAGON WINGED BRIGHT            282 FOUR ZOAS 2    *    89
        & POISONOUS
    TILL SHE BECAME A LITTLE WEEPING INFANT A SPAN LONG   .  .  .  282 FOUR ZOAS 2         92
    SOME BECAME SEED OF EVERY PLANT THAT SHALL BE PLANTED SOME     284 FOUR ZOAS 2        164
    ENSLAVD HUMANITY PUT ON HE BECAME WHAT HE BEHELD  .  .  .  .   302 FOUR ZOAS 4        203
    ENSLAVD HUMANITY PUT ON HE BECAME WHAT HE BEHELD  .  .  .  .   305 FOUR ZOAS 4        286
    HE BECAME WHAT HE WAS DOING HE WAS HIMSELF TRANSFORMD    .  .  305 FOUR ZOAS 4        287
    OF ORC ENTERING WITH FIBRES BECAME ONE WITH HIM A LIVING      309 FOUR ZOAS 5    *   169
        CHAIN
    I WELL REMEMBER HOW I STOLE THY LIGHT & IT BECAME FIRE  .  .   323 FOUR ZOAS 7        147
    AS THE ELDEST BROTHER IS THE [SECOND] FATHER'S IMAGE SO        332 FOUR ZOAS 7    *   479
        ORC BECAME
    URIZEN BECAME RINTRAH THIRIEL BECAME PALAMABRON   .  .  .  .   332 FOUR ZOAS 7        494
    HERMAPHRODITIC IT AT LENGTH BECAME HIDING THE MALE   .  .  .   343 FOUR ZOAS 8        105
    AND THIS IS THE MANNER IN WHICH SATAN BECAME THE TEMPTER       351 FOUR ZOAS 8        378
    BUT WHEN LUVAH IN ORC BECAME A SERPENT HE (DESCENDED) INTO     351 FOUR ZOAS 8    *  382
    AND BECAME A TYRANT IN HIS STEAD   .  .  .  .  .  .  .  .  .    419 I SAW A MONK/N      48
    AND LIKE A WEEPING BABE BECAME  .  .  .  .  .  .  .  .  .  .    429 CRYSTL CABINET      24
    AND BECAME A TYRANT IN HIS STEAD   .  .  .  .  .  .  .  .  .    431 GREY MONK           36
    & THEN HE BECAME LORD & MASTER OF NECESSARIES    .  .  .  .  446C ANNO REYNOLDS        MARG
    [?UNTIL ?THEY (BECAME) THE LORDS ?OF ?DRAWING]    .  .  .  . SUPP ANNO REYNOLDS   *  MARG
    BECAME ITS PREY A CURSE AN OFFERING AND AN ATONEMENT   .  .    481 MILTON 2            13
    GREW DEADLY PALE HE BECAME WHAT HE BEHELD FOR A RED   .  .  .  483 MILTON 3            29
    TILL IT BECAME A PROVERB IN EDEN SATAN IS AMONG THE            489 MILTON 9            12
        REPROBATE
    BECAME CANAAN CLOSING LOS FROM ETERNITY IN ALBION'S CLIFFS     491 MILTON 10           10
    WILD WITH PROPHETIC FURY HIS FORMER LIFE BECAME LIKE A         493 MILTON 12           45
        DREAM
    AND I BECAME ONE MAN WITH HIM ARISING IN MY STRENGTH    .  .   505 MILTON 22           12
    THEY BECAME NATIONS IN OUR SIGHT BENEATH THE HANDS            508 MILTON 24           16
        OF TIRZAH
```

BECAME   (CONTINUED)
```
    IT BECAME OPAKE & INDEFINITE BUT THE DIVINE SAVIOUR  .  .  .   517 MILTON 29          37
    HIS JOY BECAME TERRIBLE TO THEM THEY TREMBLED & WEPT      .  .  519 MILTON 30          23
    BURND TERRIBLE MY PATH BECAME A SOLID FIRE AS BRIGHT       .  530 MILTON 39           4
    AROUND THE STARRY EIGHT WITH ONE ACCORD THE STARRY EIGHT     534 MILTON 42          10
        BECAME
    OIL BECAME A FETTER TO GENIUS AND A DUNGEON TO ART BUT ONE   566C DESC CAT 2      PROSE
    HOW HE BECAME DIVIDED IS A SUBJECT OF GREAT SUBLIMITY    .   578B DESC CAT 5      PROSE
    AND WHEN ONCE HE HAD RAISED THE DOUBT IT BECAME    .  .  .   582C DESC CAT 9      PROSE
    IT BECAME THE INTEREST OF CERTAIN ENVIOUS KNAVES  .  .  .   602C PUB ADDRESS/N   PROSE
    BECAME AS THREE IMMENSE WHEELS TURNING UPON ONE-ANOTHER      640 JERUSALEM 18          8
    TILL IT BECAME A MORTAL WORM  . . . . . . . . . .            651 FIELDS FROM/J         55
    THE LAMB OF GOD THE SAVIOUR BECAME APPARENT ON EARTH    .   652B JERUSALEM 27     PROSE
    A CIRCLE IN CONTINUAL GYRATIONS THIS BECAME A HEART    .  .  659 JERUSALEM 33          20
    AND DENS THEY LOOKED ON ONE-ANOTHER & BECAME WHAT THEY       661 JERUSALEM 34          50
        BEHELD
    OVER JORDAN ALL TERRIFIED FLED THEY BECAME WHAT THEY BEHELD  661 JERUSALEM 34          54
    FOR PAIN THEY BECAME WHAT THEY BEHELD IN REASONINGS REUBEN   662 JERUSALEM 36           9
        RETURNED
    THE SEVEN NATIONS FLED BEFORE HIM THEY BECAME WHAT THEY      662 JERUSALEM 36          14
        BEHELD
    HAND HYLE & COBAN FLED THEY BECAME WHAT THEY BEHELD  .  .  .  662 JERUSALEM 36          15
    KOTOPE & BOWEN BECAME WHAT THEY BEHELD FLEEING OVER THE      663 JERUSALEM 36          19
        EARTH
    BECAME FOUR ELEMENTS SEPARATING FROM THE LIMBS OF ALBION    663 JERUSALEM 36          32
    THAT EVERY LITTLE PARTICLE OF LIGHT & AIR BECAME OPAKE  .  .  674 JERUSALEM 44          10
    ITS WAVES OF PEARL BECAME A BOUNDLESS OCEAN BOTTOMLESS  .  .  674 JERUSALEM 44          15
    AND BECAME AN OPAKE GLOBE FAR DISTANT CLAD WITH MOONY BEAMS  679 JERUSALEM 49          20
    WHO FELL BENEATH HIS INSTRUMENTS OF HUSBANDRY & BECAME  .  .  688 JERUSALEM 56          35
    THUS IN PROCESS OF TIME IT BECAME THE BEAUTIFUL MUNDANE      691 JERUSALEM 59           7
        SHELL
    THE CITIES & VILLAGES OF ALBION BECAME ROCK & SAND          697 JERUSALEM 63          18
        UNHUMANIZED
    THEN ALL THE DAUGHTERS OF ALBION BECAME ONE BEFORE LOS      698 JERUSALEM 64           6
        EVEN VALA
    THE DIVINE VISION BECAME FIRST A BURNING FLAME THEN         702 JERUSALEM 66          41
        A COLUMN
    BECAME A RAVENING EATING CANCER GROWING IN THE FEMALE   .  .  707 JERUSALEM 69           2
    BECAME A LIMIT A ROCKY HARDNESS WITHOUT FORM & VOID   .  .  713 JERUSALEM 73          23
    THEY BECAME SPECTRES & THEIR HUMAN BODIES WERE REPOSED  .   714 JERUSALEM 74           8
    THEY BECAME THE TWELVE GODS OF ASIA OPPOSING THE DIVINE     714 JERUSALEM 74          22
        VISION
    HOW LOS DRAVE THEM FROM ALBION & THEY BECAME DAUGHTERS      715 JERUSALEM 74          38
        OF CANAAN
    BECAME A SPACE & AN ALLEGORY AROUND THE WINDING WORM    .   730 JERUSALEM 85           1
    TILL IT BECAME A SEPARATED CLOUD OF BEAUTY GRACE & LOVE     732 JERUSALEM 86          55
    ALL WAS A VISION ALL A DREAM THE FURNACES BECAME   .  .  .   744 JERUSALEM 96          36
    & BECAME A CHARIOT OF FIRE  . . . . . . . . . . .            749 EV GOSPEL(B)/N        34
    & BECAME A CONVERT TO THE HEATHEN MYTHOLOGY  .  .  .  .  .   784B ANNO WW EXCUR    MARG
    BECAME LEPROUS & WHITE AS SNOW  . . . . . . . . .            818 HAPPINESS/L           74
BECKET       SEE THOMAS A BECKET
BECKOND
    FOR THEY BECKOND TO ME    . . . . . . . . . . .             804 TO BUTTS/L            23
BECKONS
    STRETCH THE HAND THAT BECKONS THE EAGLES OF HEAVEN  .  .  .  138 FRENCH REVOLTN       103
    "I SEE A HAND YOU CANNOT SEE THAT BECKONS ME AWAY"  .  .   813C LETTER 22
BECOME
    FOR HE IS BECOME A WORM THAT HE MAY NOURISH THE WEAK    .  .  87A ANNO LAVATER     MARG
    WOULD SOON BECOME A MILL WITH COMPLICATED WHEELS   .  .  .   97D NAT RELIGION 2   PROSE
    IF THE MANY BECOME THE SAME AS THE FEW WHEN POSSESSD    .   97D NAT RELIGION 2   PROSE
    BECOME A GARDEN MILD   . . . . . . . . . . . .              112 LIT GRL LST/SI         8
    SHALL THIS MARBLE BUILT HEAVEN BECOME A CLAY COTTAGE  .  .  .  138 FRENCH REVOLTN        89
    THE MITRE BECOME BLACK  . . . . . . . . . . . .             140 FRENCH REVOLTN       144
    HE WHOSE FACE GIVES NO LIGHT SHALL NEVER BECOME A STAR  .  .  151A MARRIAGE HH 7   PROSE
    IF THE FOOL WOULD PERSIST IN HIS FOLLY HE WOULD BECOME WISE  151B MARRIAGE HH 7   PROSE
    NOTE THIS ANGEL WHO IS NOW BECOME A DEVIL   .  .  .  .  .   158D MARRIAGE HH 22  PROSE
    AMIDST THE LUSTFUL FIRES HE WALKS HIS FEET BECOME LIKE      199 AMERICA 8             16
        BRASS
    TILL PITY IS BECOME A TRADE AND GENEROSITY A SCIENCE    .  .  200 AMERICA 11            10
    [I AM] WE ARE BECOME A VICTIM TO THE LIVING [I] WE HIDE      264 FOUR ZOAS 1      *    26
        IN SECRET
    THAT I HAVE SINND & THAT MY EMANATIONS ARE BECOME HARLOTS   265 FOUR ZOAS 1            54
    THE MAN'S EXTERIORS ARE BECOME INDEFINITE OPEND TO PAIN     279 FOUR ZOAS 1           543
    JERUSALEM HIS EMANATION [WILL SOON] IS BECOME A RUIN    .   279 FOUR ZOAS 1           545
    THEY BECOME NATIONS FAR REMOTE IN A LITTLE & DARK LAND  .  .  281 FOUR ZOAS 2      *    56
    [?THAT] BUT VALA [?MAY] SHALL BECOME A WORM IN ENITHARMON'S  292 FOUR ZOAS 3      *    20
        WOMB
    ALAS FOR ME WHAT WILL BECOME OF ME AT THAT DREAD TIME   .  .  292 FOUR ZOAS 3            23
    SAYING ART THOU ALSO BECOME LIKE VALA THUS I CAST THEE OUT   295 FOUR ZOAS 3           113
    AND ART THOU ALSO BECOME LIKE VALA THUS I CAST THEE OUT     295 FOUR ZOAS 3           130
    BECOME A PREY TO ALL MY DEMONS OF DESPAIR & HOPE   .  .  .   299 FOUR ZOAS 4            75
    THOU ONCE THE MILDEST SON OF HEAVEN ART NOW BECOME A RAGE   299 FOUR ZOAS 4            81
    WHICH NOW OUR RIVERS WERE BECOME DELVING THRO CAVERNS HUGE   300 FOUR ZOAS 4           102
    THE HOUSES OF MY HARPERS ARE BECOME A HAUNT OF CROWS    .   310 FOUR ZOAS 5           195
    THE GARDENS OF WISDOM ARE BECOME A FIELD OF HORRID GRAVES   310 FOUR ZOAS 5           196
    WHICH NOW MY RIVERS WERE BECOME ROLLING IN [TUBLIKE]        327 FOUR ZOAS 7      *   285
        TUBELIKE FORMS
    JEALOUS THAT SHE WAS VALA NOW BECOME URIZEN'S HARLOT    .  .  336 FOUR ZOAS 7B          137
    AND SO BECOME INVISIBLE TO THOSE WHO STILL REMAIN   .  .  .  355 FOUR ZOAS 8           554
    THEY ARE BECOME LIKE WINTRY FLOCKS LIKE FORESTS STRIPD      357 FOUR ZOAS 9            22
        OF LEAVES
    WHEN SHALL THE MAN OF FUTURE TIMES BECOME AS IN DAYS OF OLD  360 FOUR ZOAS 9           115
```

```
                                                          PAGE     TITLE       LINE
BECOME    (CONTINUED)
     THEY ARE BECOME LIKE WINTRY FLOCKS LIKE FORESTS STRIPD    365 FOUR ZOAS 9      327
       OF LEAVES
     ATTEMPTING TO BE MORE THAN MAN WE BECOME LESS SAID LUVAH  376 FOUR ZOAS 9      709
     DID NOT JESUS DESCEND & BECOME A SERVANT THE  . . . . . 399C ANNO BACON      MARG
     BY THIEVING FROM OTHERS BECOME A MICH ANGELO   . . . .  457D ANNO REYNOLDS   MARG
     PRINCIPLES ACCORDING TO SR JOSHUA BECOME DEFECTS  . . . 477A ANNO REYNOLDS   MARG
     SHALL BECOME THE DAUGHTERS OF INSPIRATION  . . . . . . 480C MILTON 1        PROSE
     OF LIFE TILL THEY BECOME FINITE & ITSELF SEEMS INFINITE  490 MILTON 10      *   7
       [UNTIL]
     HAND IS BECOME A ROCK SINAI & HOREB IS HYLE & COBAN  . .  501 MILTON 19         58
     HE HATH ENTERD INTO THE COVERING CHERUB BECOME ONE WITH  507 MILTON 23         14
     AND THEN THE STORMS BECOME VISIBLE AUDIBLE & TERRIBLE  .  507 MILTON 23         25
     I HAVE EMBRACD THE FALLING DEATH HE IS BECOME ONE WITH ME 507 MILTON 23         33
     SURELY YOU ALSO SHALL BECOME POOR MORTAL VEGETATIONS  .   508 MILTON 24         24
     BECOME APPARENT IN TIME & SPACE IN THE THREE PROFESSIONS  514 MILTON 27         59
     ARE BECOME FOUNTAINS OF BITTER DEATH & OF CORRODING HELL  525 MILTON 35          3
     OR TILL YOU BECOME MORTAL & VEGETABLE IN SEXUALITY  . .   525 MILTON 35         24
     TILL ALL THINGS BECOME ONE GREAT SATAN IN HOLINESS   .    530 MILTON 39          1
     BECOME IN THEIR (FEMININE) PORTIONS THE CAUSES & PROMOTERS 532 MILTON 40         10
     TILL HES BECOME THE GOLDEN FOOL   . . . . . . . . . .     540 GOLDEN RULE/N      2
     TILL [HES] YOURE AT LAST BECOME THE [OLD] GOLDEN FOOL .   540 S(TOTHAR) D/N  *   2
     TILL HE IS BECOME A MAN  . . . . . . . . . . .           552 WHY CUPID/N        12
     BECOME NECESSARY THAT I SHOULD EXHIBIT TO THE PUBLIC IN  561C EXHIBITION ADV  PROSE
     BECOME LEAD AGAIN THIS IS AN AWFUL THING TO SAY TO OIL   566B DESC CAT 2     PROSE
       PAINTERS
     WHEN ERECTED INTO GODS BECOME DESTRUCTIVE TO HUMANITY  . 571C DESC CAT 3     PROSE
     BECOME A DUTY WHICH MR B(LAKE) OWES TO THE PUBLIC  . .   573A DESC CAT 3     PROSE
     THEY CAUSE THAT EVERY THING IN ART SHALL BECOME A MACHINE 582C DESC CAT 9    PROSE
     EMPIRES FLOURISH TILL THEY BECOME COMMERCIAL  . . . . .  594A PUB ADDRESS/N  PROSE
     A MAN CAN NEVER BECOME ASS NOR HORSE . . . . . . . .     607A V LAST JUDG/N  PROSE
     HIS SUBLIME & PATHOS BECOME TWO ROCKS FIXD IN THE EARTH   620 JERUSALEM 1        4
     OF JERUSALEM BECOME HER COVERING TILL THE TIME OF THE END 626 JERUSALEM 7       64
     AND MALICE & ENVY BUT MY EMANATION ALAS WILL BECOME  . . 639 JERUSALEM 17      38
     WAS BECOME AN ENVIED HORROR AND A REMEMBRANCE OF JEALOUSY 652 JERUSALEM 28       3
     MUST HAVE BECOME THE FIRST VICTIMS BEING THE FIRST      653 JERUSALEM 28      24
       TRANSGRESSORS
     HE HATH COMPELLD ALBION TO BECOME A PUNISHER & HATH     653 JERUSALEM 29      16
       POSSESSD
     EVERY UNIVERSAL FORM WAS BECOME BARREN MOUNTAINS OF MORAL 657 JERUSALEM 31      19
     ALBION THE HIGH CLIFF OF THE ATLANTIC IS BECOME A BARREN 660 JERUSALEM 34      16
       LAND
     GOD HATH FORSAKEN ME & MY FRIENDS ARE BECOME A BURDEN  . 666 JERUSALEM 39      22
     AND MAN HIMSELF BECOME A FIEND WRAPD IN AN ENDLESS CURSE 667 JERUSALEM 40      29
     BECOME A NET & A TRAP & EVERY ENERGY RENDERD CRUEL  . .  672 JERUSALEM 43      26
     ARE BECOME THE SOURCES OF DARK & BITTER DEATH & OF     672 JERUSALEM 43      32
       CORRODING HELL
     STRUCKEN WITH ALBION'S DISEASE THEY BECOME WHAT THEY BEHOLD 674 JERUSALEM 44    32
     FROM MISTRUST AND SUSPITION THE MAN IS HIMSELF BECOME  . 675 JERUSALEM 45       8
     ANIMATING THE DRAGON TEMPLES SOON TO BECOME THAT HOLY FIEND 677 JERUSALEM 47     6
     WHERE FRIENDS DIE FOR EACH OTHER WILL BECOME THE PLACE .  678 JERUSALEM 48      56
     THE MOUNTAIN OF GIANTS ALL THE GIANTS OF ALBION ARE BECOME 679 JERUSALEM 49     7
     ARE BECOME WEAK VISIONS OF TIME & SPACE FIXD INTO FURROWS 679 JERUSALEM 49     22
       OF DEATH
     AND DEAR MUTUAL FORGIVENESS & TO BECOME ONE GREAT SATAN   679 JERUSALEM 49     29
     OF ENVY ALBION IS BECOME AND HIS EMANATION CAST OUT  . . 681 JERUSALEM 50       9
     SHE WILL BECOME AN ETERNAL DEATH AN AVENGER OF SIN   . . 681 JERUSALEM 50      15
     IS BECOME A CLOD OF CLAY MERLIN IS A WORM OF THE VALLEY   688 JERUSALEM 56     28
     THEREFORE THY MOUNTAINS ARE BECOME BARREN JERUSALEM  . . 693 JERUSALEM 60     25
     AND PITY AM I BECOME LOVELY AS A VIRGIN IN HIS SIGHT WHO AM 695 JERUSALEM 61   37
     AND WILT THOU BECOME MY HUSBAND O MY LORD & SAVIOUR  . . 696 JERUSALEM 62       6
     BECOME THEIR EMANATION AND THEIR TEMPLE AND TABERNACLE .  701 JERUSALEM 65     70
     SUDDEN THEY BECOME LIKE WHAT THEY BEHOLD IN HOWLINGS &  701 JERUSALEM 65      75
       DEADLY PAIN
     THEY BECOME LIKE WHAT THEY BEHOLD YET IMMENSE IN STRENGTH 701 JERUSALEM 65     79
       & POWER
     ALL WHO SEE BECOME WHAT THEY BEHOLD THEIR EYES ARE COVERD 702 JERUSALEM 66     36
     THE JEALOUSIES BECOME MURDEROUS UNITING TOGETHER IN RAHAB 708 JERUSALEM 69     33
     WOMEN THE COMFORTERS OF MEN BECOME THE TORMENTERS      712D JERUSALEM 72    PROSE
       & PUNISHERS
     MOUNT ZION IS BECOME A CRUEL ROCK & NO MORE DEW  . . . . 719 JERUSALEM 79       4
     THEY ARE BECOME NARROW PLACES IN A LITTLE AND DARK LAND   720 JERUSALEM 79     14
     TO THE STERN WARRIOR I AM BECOME PERFECT IN BEAUTY OVER  724 JERUSALEM 81       5
       MY WARRIOR
     LET US LOOK LET US EXAMINE IS THE CRUEL BECOME AN INFANT  724 JERUSALEM 81      8
     I HAVE NAMED HIM JEHOVAH OF HOSTS HUMANITY IS BECOME  . . 724 JERUSALEM 81     13
     OF PAINTED CLAY THE MIGHTY HYLE IS BECOME A WEEPING INFANT 725 JERUSALEM 82     8
     LOOK HYLE IS BECOME AN INFANT LOVE LOOK BEHOLD SEE HIM LIE 725 JERUSALEM 82    37
     [HYLE WAS BECOME A WINDING WORM] & NOT A WEEPING INFANT   726 JERUSALEM 82     48
     BECOME A FOUNTAIN OF VEINY PIPES O ALBION MY BROTHER  .   727 JERUSALEM 82     84
     I SHALL BECOME AN INFANT HORROR ENION THARMAS FRIENDS  . 727 JERUSALEM 83       5
     TILL GOD HIMSELF BECOME A MALE SUBSERVIENT TO THE FEMALE  733 JERUSALEM 88     21
     THEY BECOME ONE WITH THE ANTICHRIST & ARE ABSORBD IN HIM  736 JERUSALEM 89     62
     MINGLING WITH LUVAH IN ONE THEY BECOME ONE GREAT SATAN    737 JERUSALEM 90     43
     APPROPRIATE INDIVIDUALITY THEY BECOME AN ETERNAL DEATH . . 737 JERUSALEM 90    54
     FEAR NOT MY SONS THIS WAKING DEATH HE IS BECOME ONE WITH ME 741 JERUSALEM 93   18
     ORDER OF LUXURIES SHOULD HAVE BECOME A CITY OF ELEGANCE  798C LETTER 10     PROSE
     MINIATURE (IS) BECOME A GODDESS IN MY EYES & MY FRIENDS  808B LETTER 19     *PROSE
     THIS WORLD ARE NOW BECOME THE KINGDOMS OF GOD & HIS CHRIST 810C LETTER 21    PROSE
     BECOME MY DUTY TO EXPLAIN MY UNHAPPINESS HAS ARISEN  . . 812B LETTER 22     PROSE
     FOR I AM BECOME A LIKENESS TAKER & SUCCEED ADMIRABLY WELL 824B LETTER 27     PROSE
     EVEN SNOW HILL IS BECOME ALMOST LEVEL  . . . . . . .     831D LETTER 31     PROSE
```

	PAGE	TITLE	LINE

BECOME (CONTINUED)
STRAND NEAR ST CLEMENTS IS WIDENED AND BECOME VERY ELEGANT — 831D LETTER 31 — PROSE
FOR MY DEMOSTHENES WHICH IS NOW BECOME A NOBLE SUBJECT . — 835A LETTER 34 — PROSE
HIS FATHER'S BEST FRIEND WILL I HOPE BECOME THE MOST — 838C LETTER 37 — PROSE
   RESPECTED
BECOME CHILDREN OF LIGHT AND LIBERTY AND MY FEET AND MY — 852A LETTER 50 — PROSE
CONFIDENCE THAT IT SHALL BE SO NO LONGER HE IS BECOME MY — 852C LETTER 50 — PROSE
SHORT TIME I SHALL MAKE MY ASSERTION GOOD THAT I AM BECOME — 852C LETTER 50 — PROSE
EXCEPT AT PRIVATE PRESSES I HOPE THIS WILL BECOME A SOURCE — 859C LETTER 56 — PROSE
JUST AS I HAD BECOME WELL THAT IS SUBDUED THE DISEASE . . — 874D LETTER 80 — PROSE

BECOMES
THEREFORE GOD BECOMES AS WE ARE THAT WE MAY BE AS HE IS — 98A NAT RELIGION 2 — PROSE
HE BECOMES AN INFANT SMALL . . . . — 122 ON ANOTHERS/SI — 26
HE BECOMES A MAN OF WOE . . . . — 122 ON ANOTHERS/SI — 27
AND BEING RESTRAIN IT BY DEGREES BECOMES PASSIVE . . . — 150A MARRIAGE HH 5 — PROSE
& BECOMES A POEM OF PROBABLE IMPOSSIBILITIES . . . . . — 390D ANNO WATSON — MARG
AND MY BED BECOMES THEIR GRAVE . . . . — 417 MY SPECTR AD/N — 8
AND EVERY SAND BECOMES A GEM . . . . — 418 MOCK ON/N — 5
TILL HE BECOMES A BLEEDING YOUTH . . . . — 425 MENTAL TRAVLER — 21
AND SHE BECOMES A VIRGIN BRIGHT . . . . — 425 MENTAL TRAVLER — 22
AND SHE BECOMES HIS DWELLING PLACE . . . . — 425 MENTAL TRAVLER — 27
AND THE FLAT EARTH BECOMES A BALL . . . . — 426 MENTAL TRAVLER — 64
TILL HE BECOMES A [XXX] WAYWARD BABE . . . . . . — 426 MENTAL TRAVLER * — 85
BECOMES A BABE IN ETERNITY . . . . — 432 AUGURIES — 68
SACRIFICE THE PARTS WHAT BECOMES OF THE WHOLE . . . . — 462A ANNO REYNOLDS — MARG
[THE SPACE ?BECOMES ?SERPENT-FORMD & THE WOMB ?ENGLOBES] — 490 MILTON 10 — * 7
AFFECTION OR LOVE BECOMES A STATE WHEN DIVIDED FROM — 522 MILTON 32 — 33
   IMAGINATION
AND SMITES ME AS I SMOTE THEE & BECOMES MY COVERING . . . — 529 MILTON 38 — 32
BECOMES A WOMB & IS THIS THE DEATH COUCH OF ALBION . . . — 534 MILTON 42 — 1
AND BECOMES THE ENEMY & BETRAYER OF HIS FRIENDS . . . . — 541 HOMERS HERO/N — 6
BECOMES A YELLOW MASK OVER ALL THAT IT TOUCHES . . . . — 565B DESC CAT 2 — PROSE
FROM (REMBRANDT) TO REYNOLDS PROVE THAT NATURE BECOMES — 595A PUB ADDRESS/N — *PROSE
   [TAME]
ENGLOBES ITSELF & BECOMES A WOMB SUCH WAS ALBION'S COUCH — 620 JERUSALEM 1 — 2
AND BECOMES ONE WITH HER MINGLING CONDENSING IN SELF-LOVE — 656 JERUSALEM 30 — 36
WHO BECOMES HIS FOOD SUCH IS THE WAY OF THE DEVOURING POWER — 659 JERUSALEM 33 — 24
BECOMES SEXUAL & IS CREATED AND VEGETATED AND BORN . . — 674 JERUSALEM 44 — 22
A VICTIM THEN HE BECOMES HER PRIEST & SHE HIS TABERNACLE — 701 JERUSALEM 65 — 60
BUT WHATEVER BECOMES OF MY LABOURS I WOULD RATHER . . . — 812B LETTER 22 — PROSE

BECOMING
HIS BOSOM INWARDS SHONE WITH FIRES BUT THE STONES BECOMING — 490 MILTON 9 — 32
   OPAKE
BECOMING OBEDIENT TO DEATH EVEN THE DEATH OF THE CROSS — 506 MILTON 22 — 58
THEY COULD NOT STEP INTO VEGETABLE WORLDS WITHOUT BECOMING — 527 MILTON 36 — 14
BECOMING A BUILDING OF PITY AND COMPASSION LO . . . . . — 632 JERUSALEM 12 — 29
AND THE PERCEPTIONS TO BE DISSIPATED INTO THE INDEFINITE — 703 JERUSALEM 66 — 47
   BECOMING
BECOMING A GENERATED MORTAL A VEGETATING DEATH . . . . — 708 JERUSALEM 69 — 31
GLOWING WITH LOVELINESS BEFORE HIM BECOMING APPARENT . . — 723 JERUSALEM 80 — 71
WITHOUT BECOMING HIS CHILDREN IN THE FURNACES OF AFFLICTION — 732 JERUSALEM 86 — 49

BED SEE A-BED,DEATH-BED,SICK BED
PUT ON AND SMILE UPON OUR EVENING BED . . . . — 3 EVNING STAR/PS — 4
HER MAIDS AWAIT HER ON HER BED SHE FALLS . . . . . . — 5 FAIR ELENOR/PS — 37
THAT BED OF JOY WHERE ERST HER LORD HATH PRESSD . . . — 5 FAIR ELENOR/PS — 38
THEY STOOD BY THE BED LIKE REEDS BENDING OVER A LAKE . — 35D COUCH DEATH/PS — PROSE
AN IGNORANT PACK OF WRETCHES SO THEY WENT TO BED . . . — 52A ISLAND MOON 7 — PROSE
AND THEN GO HOME TO BED . . . . — 60 NURSES SONG/IM — 15
OER MY ANGEL-GUARDED BED . . . . — 111 A DREAM/SI — 2
AND SIT DOWN BY THEIR BED . . . . — 119 NIGHT/SI — 24
AND THEN GO HOME TO BED . . . . — 121 NURSES SONG/SI — 14
THE WEAK WORM FROM ITS LOWLY BED AND THOU SHALT HEAR ITS — 129 BOOK OF THEL 3 — 28
   VOICE
THEN THEL ASTONISHD VIEWD THE WORM UPON ITS DEWY BED . — 129 BOOK OF THEL 4 — 1
AND LAY ME DOWN IN THY COLD BED AND LEAVE MY SHINING LOT — 130 BOOK OF THEL 5 — 13
WHY A LITTLE CURTAIN OF FLESH ON THE BED OF OUR DESIRE . — 130 BOOK OF THEL 6 — 20
TO A BED OF STRAW THE SEVEN DISEASES OF EARTH . . . . . — 135 FRENCH REVOLTN — 36
HATH FOUND OUT THY BED . . . . — 175 SICK ROSE/N — 5
NOW A NYMPH I DARE NOT PLUCK THEE FROM THY DEWY BED . . — 189 V DAU ALBION 1 — 7
THEN OOTHOON PLUCKD THE FLOWER SAYING I PLUCK THEE FROM — 189 V DAU ALBION 1 — 11
   THY BED
BROMION RENT HER WITH HIS THUNDERS ON HIS STORMY BED . — 190 V DAU ALBION 1 — 16
BROMION SPOKE BEHOLD THIS HARLOT HERE ON BROMION'S BED . — 190 V DAU ALBION 1 — 18
WITH LAMPLIKE EYES WATCHING AROUND THE FROZEN MARRIAGE BED — 194 V DAU ALBION 7 — 22
HAS FOUND OUT THY BED . . . . — 213 SICK ROSE/SE — 5
WHERE MY IVORY BED . . . . — 254 AHANIA 5 — 4
IN FIERCE TORMENTS ON HIS GLOWING BED . . . . . . — 260 BOOK OF LOS 5 — 51
AND ON THE BED OF SILENCE SLEEP TILL THOU AWAKEST ME . — 290 FOUR ZOAS 2 — 378
A DREAMFUL HORRIBLE STATE IN TOSSINGS ON HIS ICY BED . — 302 FOUR ZOAS 4 — 171
THE GOLDEN MOTH BUILDS THERE A HOUSE & SPREADS HER SILKEN — 308 FOUR ZOAS 5 — 134
   BED
NOR UNROOT THE INFERNAL FIBRES FROM THEIR ROCKY BED . . — 309 FOUR ZOAS 5 — 163
TILL ON MY SILVER BED I SLEPT & SWEET DREAMS ROUND — 310 FOUR ZOAS 5 — 204
   ME HOVERD
[OF HOPE & FEAR XXX SINGING THE ?SAME SONG AROUND THE — SUPP FOUR ZOAS 5 — *
   ?GLOWING BED]
IN PAIN & SORROW SO THE SLIMY BED HIS LIMBS RENEWD . . — 316 FOUR ZOAS 6 — 162
OF LIVING PANGS THY HORRIBLE BED GLOWING WITH CEASELESS — 321 FOUR ZOAS 7 — 50
   FIRES
SO ENITHARMON CRIED UPON HER TERRIBLE EARTHY BED . . . — 335 FOUR ZOAS 7B — 98
IN THE SPIRIT OF THE MORNING AWAKING THE SOUL FROM ITS — 367 FOUR ZOAS 9 — 394
   GRASSY BED

		PAGE	TITLE	LINE
BED	(CONTINUED)			
BENEATH HER ROSE A DOWNY BED & A CIELING COVERD ALL		369	FOUR ZOAS 9	463
O ENION MY WEARY HEAD IS IN THE BED OF DEATH		370	FOUR ZOAS 9	487
THE SUN ARISES FROM HIS DEWY BED & THE FRESH AIRS		379	FOUR ZOAS 9	846
AND SEVEN MORE LOVES IN MY BED		416	MY SPECTRE/N	43
AND MY BED BECOMES THEIR GRAVE		417	MY SPECTR AD/N	8
THE MONK SAT DOWN ON HER STONY BED		419	I SAW A MONK/N	22
HE TREMBLD & SHUDDERD UPON THE BED		419	I SAW A MONK/N	26
THE HAND OF VENGEANCE SOUGHT THE BED		419	I SAW A MONK/N *	44
[AND USURPD THE TYRANT'S THRONE & BED]		419	I SAW A MONK/N	47
THE MONK SAT DOWN ON THE STONY BED		430	GREY MONK	4
HE TREMBLED & SHUDDERD UPON THE BED		430	GREY MONK	11
THE HAND OF VENGEANCE FOUND THE BED		431	GREY MONK	33
AND TOOK TO HIS BED & THERE LAY DOWN		435	WILLIAM BOND	12
AND IN THE MIDST THE SICK MAN ON HIS BED		435	WILLIAM BOND	16
ON THE RIGHT HAND OF HIS LOVED BED		435	WILLIAM BOND	39
AND THE ANGELS OF PROVIDENCE LEFT THE BED		435	WILLIAM BOND	44
SHE SOOTHD HER WITH SOFT WORDS & BROUGHT HER TO PALAMABRON'S BED		494	MILTON 13	38
TOWARDS AMERICA INDIA ROSE UP FROM HIS GOLDEN BED		519	MILTON 31	14
THE LARK SITTING UPON HIS EARTHY BED JUST AS THE MORN		520	MILTON 31	29
NONE DARE TO WAKE HER SOON SHE BURSTS HER CRIMSON CURTAIN BED		520	MILTON 31	57
AND GETS INTO BED A REWARD FOR THE LABOURS OF THE DAY		586A	DESC CAT 16	PROSE
THRO THE COTTAGE WHERE "SHE" LAYS IN BED "PINCHD & PULLD"		618C	ILLUS MILTON	PROSE
BY FAIRIES AS THEY DANCE ON THE BED THE CIELING & THE FLOOR		618C	ILLUS MILTON	*PROSE
MARY WAS FOUND IN ADULTEROUS BED		753	EV GOSPEL(E)/N	4
IN SECRET BED OF MORTAL CLAY		754	EV GOSPEL(E)/N	16
WE HAVE ONE ROOM IN WHICH WE COULD MAKE A BED TO LODGE YOU		808B	LETTER 19	PROSE
I WISHD OWING TO A VIOLENT COLD WHICH CONFIND ME TO MY BED		834B	LETTER 34	PROSE
COUNCELLOR HE ALAS WAS ILL IN BED WHEN I CALLD YESTERDAY		836B	LETTER 35	*PROSE
OR WHATEVER IT IS I AM IN BED & AT WORK MY HEALTH I CANNOT		868B	LETTER 68	PROSE
AS SOON AS I AWAKED & I AM NOW IN BED BETTER & AS I THINK		869B	LETTER 69	PROSE
TO PERMIT ME TO BE OUT OF BED BUT THEY GO OFF BY REST WHICH		869B	LETTER 69	PROSE
THE BETTER FOR IT I CANNOT GET WELL & AM NOW IN BED BUT SEEM		870B	LETTER 71	PROSE
BRINGS ON THE SHIVERING FIT WHEN I AM FORCED TO GO TO BED		872B	LETTER 75	PROSE
& WAS WELL BUT SO MUCH WEAKEND THAT I AM STILL IN BED THIS		872B	LETTER 75	PROSE
BEDCHAMBER				
FORCIBLY THAT THE TOBIT & TOBIAS IN YOUR BEDCHAMBER WOULD		850D	LETTER 49	PROSE
BED CLOTHES				
& A GHOST PULLS THE BED CLOTHES AT HER FEET		618C	ILLUS MILTON	PROSE
BEDDED				
LET SNAKES RISE FROM THY BEDDED LOCKS & LAUGH AMONG THY CURLS		108	TIRIEL 6	43
BEDFORD				
ISSACHAR NORTHAMPTON RUTLAND NOTTGHAM ZEBULUN BEDFORD HUNTGN CAMB		637	JERUSALEM 16	48
HUTTN HAD WARWICK NORTHAMPTON BEDFORD BUCKINGHAM		710	JERUSALEM 71	36
BEDS				
AND THE RUSTLING [BEDS] BIRDS OF DAWN		9	MAD SONG/PS	7
WHEN MEN SLEEP IN THEIR BEDS WALKETH ABOUT		30	EDW THIRD/PS 5	7
TURNING THEMSELVES UPON THEIR BEDS		30	EDW THIRD/PS 5	9
THE CURTAINS OF THEIR BEDS DESTRUCTION IS		30	EDW THIRD/PS 5	12
THOU HAST REFUSD OUR CLOTHES OUR BEDS OUR HOUSES FOR THY DWELLING		100	TIRIEL 1	38
THE FOUR DAUGHTERS [& ALL THE CHILDREN IN THEIR SILENT BEDS]		107	TIRIEL 5	30
AND ALL THE CHILDREN IN THEIR BEDS WERE CUT OFF IN ONE NIGHT		107	TIRIEL 5	33
WHEN I FOUND BABES OF BLISS ON MY BEDS		255	AHANIA 5	19
REPOSD ON BEDS LET THEM SLEEP ON DO THOU ALONE DEPART		277	FOUR ZOAS 1	489
IS PLACD IN BEDS OF MORTAR MINGLED WITH THE ASHES OF VALA		284	FOUR ZOAS 2	171
. . . SOME LYING ON BEDS OF SULPHUR		314	FOUR ZOAS 6	105
TAKE THEIR REPOSE ON BEDS THEY DRINK THEY SING THEY VIEW THE FLAMES		366	FOUR ZOAS 9	341
SHE LAID THE CHILDREN ON THE BEDS WHICH SHE SAW PREPARD IN THE HOUSE		370	FOUR ZOAS 9	515
THEN URIZEN SITTING AT HIS REPOSE ON BEDS IN THE BRIGHT SOUTH		372	FOUR ZOAS 9	567
RESTLESS THEY TURN ON BEDS OF SORROW IN THEIR INMOST BRAIN		379	FOUR ZOAS 9	818
THE FOOTSTEPS AND INFIXING DEEP THE FEET IN MARBLE BEDS		500	MILTON 19	2
AND THE HERBS & FLOWERS & FURNITURE & BEDS & CHAMBERS		512	MILTON 26	34
THE UNFORGIVING PORCHES THE TABLES OF ENMITY AND BEDS		640	JERUSALEM 18	23
BOTH & IF THIS IS SUFFICIENT IT IS AT YOUR SERVICE BUT AS BEDS		808B	LETTER 19	PROSE
BED SIDE				
SHE TREMBLED & WEPT SITTING ON THE BED SIDE		429	MARY	37
BEE				
THE BUSY BEE HAS NO TIME FOR SORROW		151A	MARRIAGE HH 7	PROSE
WITH WHAT SENSE DOES THE BEE FORM CELLS HAVE NOT THE MOUSE & FROG		191	V DAU ALBION 3	4
AT WILL TO MURMUR IN THE FLOWERS SMALL AS THE HONEY BEE		288	FOUR ZOAS 2	297
THE POISON OF THE HONEY BEE		432	AUGURIES	49
THE CRUEL SCORPION IS THERE THE GNAT WASP HORNET & THE HONEY BEE		513	MILTON 27	21
BEECH				
THE APPLE TREE NEVER ASKS THE BEECH HOW HE SHALL GROW		152B	MARRIAGE HH 9	PROSE
[THE BARKED OAK THE LONG LIMBD BEECH THE CHESNUT TREE THE PINE]		269	FOUR ZOAS 1	* 204
THRO CAVES OF DEATH INTO EXISTENCE THE BEECH LONG LIMBD ADVANCD		335	FOUR ZOAS 7B	* 100

	PAGE	TITLE	LINE

BEECH (CONTINUED)
```
        HOW DO WE DISTINGUISH THE OAK FROM THE BEECH   . . . .   585C DESC CAT 15       PROSE
        THE OAK FROWNS TERRIBLE THE BEECH & ASH & ELM ENROOT  .   636 JERUSALEM 16        4
BEEF
        WITH EATING BEEF & DRINKING BEER O THEY WERE STOUT & HALE   58 THIS CITY/IM       7
        THE HUNGRY POOR ENTERD THE HALL TO EAT GOOD BEEF & ALE  .   58 THIS CITY/IM      11
BEELZEBOUL
        . . . AND THE MILLS OF SATAN & [BAALZEBOLE] BEELZEBOUL    346 FOUR ZOAS 8    *  201
        THE MILLS OF SATAN AND BEELZEBOUL STAND . . . . . . . .   346 FOUR ZOAS 8       227
BEELZEBUB
        NOR THY WILL DONE BUT [BEELZEBUB XXX ?UNJUST ?JEALOUS]  .   788A ANNO THORNTON  * MARG
BEER
        WITH EATING BEEF & DRINKING BEER O THEY WERE STOUT & HALE   58 THIS CITY/IM       7
BEES
        LIKE SUMMER BEES AND ALL THE GOLDEN CITIES  . . . . . .   19 EDW THIRD/PS 2      13
        SING THE HONEY BEES                                      148 MARRIAGE HH 2       8
        AS THE STRONG BULL IN SUMMER TIME WHEN BEES SING ROUND   308 FOUR ZOAS 5       136
          THE HEATH
        MY MILK OF COWS & HONEY OF BEES & FRUIT OF GOLDEN HARVEST 359 FOUR ZOAS 9       104
        HIS MILK OF COWS & HONEY OF BEES & FRUIT OF GOLDEN HARVEST 641 JERUSALEM 19       5
BEETLE
        WHILE THE BEETLE GOES HIS ROUND  . . . . . . . . . . .   112 A DREAM/SI         18
        THE EMMET & THE BEETLE HARK THEY LAUGH & MOCK AT LOS  . .   288 FOUR ZOAS 2     308
        THE SPORTIVE ROOT THE EARTHWORM THE SMALL BEETLE THE WISE  377 FOUR ZOAS 9     756
          EMMET
        THE SPORTIVE ROOT THE EARTH-WORM THE GOLD BEETLE THE WISE  513 MILTON 27        12
          EMMET
        THE SPECKLED NEWT THE SPIDER & BEETLE THE RAT & MOUSE   .   515 MILTON 28        42
        THE FOX THE OWL THE BEETLE & THE BAT . . . . . . . .      545 ON S(TOTHRD)/N     3
BEETLE'S
        FOLLOW NOW THE BEETLE'S HUM  . . . . . . . . . . . .      112 A DREAM/SI         19
BEFALL
        SWEET JOY BEFALL THEE  . . . . . . . . . . . . . . .      118 INFANT JOY/SI       6
        SWEET JOY BEFALL THEE  . . . . . . . . . . . . . . .      118 INFANT JOY/SI      12
BEFEL
        REMEMBER RECOLLECT WHAT DARK BEFEL IN WINTRY DAYS   . . .   688 JERUSALEM 56      25
BEFORE
        BEFORE THAT AWFUL THRONE  . . . . . . . . . . . .         13 GWIN KING/PS        98
        SCENE THE COAST OF FRANCE KING EDWARD AND NOBLES BEFORE   17D EDW THIRD/PS 1    PROSE
          IT THE ARMY
        IVE TOLD HIM BEFORE BUT HIS DISORDER . . . . . .          23 EDW THIRD/PS 3      69
        HAS TO GET ANOTHER IN ANY PURSUIT AFTER GLORY   . . .     28 EDW THIRD/PS 4      15
        YONDER S A MUSICIAN GOING TO PLAY BEFORE THE KING   . . .   29B EDW THIRD/PS 4   PROSE
        GIANTS OF MIGHTY ARM BEFORE THE FLOOD CAIN'S CITY   . .     41A THEN SHE BORE    PROSE
        BEFORE HIS EYES LIKE THE ANIMAL UPON THE PYTHAGOREAN'S LAP 46A ISLAND MOON 1    PROSE
        ARADOBO YOU SHOULD ALWAYS THINK [OF WHAT YOU SP] BEFORE   47B ISLAND MOON 3    *PROSE
          YOU SPEAK
        OH NO SIR I DID THINK HE WAS BEFORE YOU TOLD ME   . . .   48D ISLAND MOON 5     PROSE
        BEFORE TEN YEARS ARE AT AN END SAID QUID   . . . .        52A ISLAND MOON 7     PROSE
        GREY HEADED BEADLES WALKD BEFORE WITH WANDS AS WHITE AS   59 HOLY THURS/IM        3
          SNOW
        A MAN MUST FIRST DECIEVE HIMSELF BEFORE HE IS THUS   . .   75A ANNO LAVATER      MARG
        AND AGED TIRIEL STOOD BEFORE THE GATES OF HIS BEAUTIFUL   99 TIRIEL 1            1
          PALACE
        THEY STOOD BEFORE THEIR ONCE DELIGHTFUL PALACE & THUS THE  99 TIRIEL 1            5
          VOICE
        [THAT WE MAY TREMBLE & REPENT BEFORE THY MIGHTY KNEES]  . .   105 TIRIEL 4       76
        TILL BEFORE THEIR WAY  . . . . . . . . . . . . .          114 LIT GRL FND/SI     23
        GREY HEADED BEADLES WALKD BEFORE WITH WANDS AS WHITE AS   121 HOLY THURS/SI       3
          SNOW
        AND SITTING DOWN BEFORE THE HEAT OF DAY  . . . . . .      125 LIT BLK BOY/SI      6
        DESCEND O LITTLE CLOUD & HOVER BEFORE THE EYES OF THEL  . .   128 BOOK OF THEL 2  16
        HOVERING AND GLITTERING ON THE AIR BEFORE THE FACE OF THEL 128 BOOK OF THEL 3     6
        THE WEEPING VIRGIN TREMBLING KNEELS BEFORE THE RISEN SUN  128 BOOK OF THEL 3     14
        AND NOBLES AND CLERGY SHALL FAIL FROM BEFORE ME . . . .   140 FRENCH REVOLTN    143
        BEFORE THE RED COUNCIL HE STOOD . . . . . . . . .        141 FRENCH REVOLTN    161
        OF KING HENRY THE FOURTH WALKS BEFORE HIM IN FIRES . . .   141 FRENCH REVOLTN   165
        BEFORE THE ANCIENT SEAT OF THE KINGDOM AND MOUNTAINS TO   143 FRENCH REVOLTN    205
          BE RENEWED
        LIKE A FLAME OF FIRE HE STOOD BEFORE DARK RANKS . . . .   146 FRENCH REVOLTN    273
        . . . AND BEFORE EXPECTING CAPTAINS   . . . . . . . .     146 FRENCH REVOLTN    273
        THE MOST SUBLIME ACT IS TO SET ANOTHER BEFORE YOU   . . .   151B MARRIAGE HH 7  PROSE
        DRIVING THE ANGEL BEFORE ME SOON WE SAW SEVEN HOUSES OF   157A MARRIAGE HH 17   PROSE
          BRICK
        WHO AROSE BEFORE AN ANGEL THAT SAT ON A CLOUD  . . . .     158B MARRIAGE HH 22  PROSE
        FALSE WITNESS WHEN HE OMITTED MAKING A DEFENCE BEFORE     158C MARRIAGE HH 22   PROSE
          PILATE
        THE NEW BORN FIRE STOOD BEFORE THE STARRY KING   . . . .   159B SONG LIBERTY    PROSE
        AND I SAW BEFORE ME SHINE  . . . . . . . . . . . .        167 INFANT SORW/N      20
        PLUCK FRUITS BEFORE THE LIGHT  . . . . . . . . . .        172 ARE NOT JOYS/N      8
        WHERE MANY HAD BEEN BURND BEFORE   . . . . . . . .        177 LIT BOY LST/N      27
        BEFORE TWO VIRGINS CAN MEET TOGETHER  . . . . . . .       177 MERLNS PROPH/N      4
        IF YOU [CATCH] [TRAP ] TRAP THE MOMENT BEFORE ITS RIPE  . .   179 IF YOU TRAP/N *  1
        BEFORE MY FLOWER OF LOVE WAS LOST  . . . . . . . .        184 O I CANNOT/N        4
        HE NEER HAD SEEN SUCH A THING BEFORE  . . . . . . .       187 WHEN KLOPSTK/N     22
        TILL HIS EYES SICKEN AT THE FRUIT THAT HANGS BEFORE HIS   194 V DAU ALBION 7     20
          SIGHT
        THE SHADOWY DAUGHTER OF URTHONA STOOD BEFORE RED ORC  . .   195 AMERICA PREL 1    1
        CROUCH HOWLING BEFORE THEIR CAVERNS DEEP LIKE SKINS DRYD  199 AMERICA 9           4
          IN THE WIND
        BEFORE THE DEMON RED WHO BURNT TOWARDS AMERICA   . . .     201 AMERICA 12         9
        WEEPING IN DISMAL HOWLINGS BEFORE THE STERN AMERICANS  .   203 AMERICA 16        12
```

	PAGE	TITLE	LINE
BEFORE (CONTINUED)			
THE COUNCIL SAT ALL ROSE BEFORE THE AGED APPARITION . . .	204	AMERICA CANC B	15
IN THE RED AIR BEFORE THE DEMON [SEEN EVEN BY MORTAL MEN]	205	AMERICA CANC C	21
BEFORE DISCOVERED	207B	PRSPECTUS 1793	PROSE
BEFORE THE PUBLIC WORKS HE IS NOT AFRAID TO SAY	207C	PRSPECTUS 1793	PROSE
WHERE MANY HAD BEEN BURND BEFORE	219	LIT BOY LST/SE	22
BEFORE THE DEATH-IMAGE OF URIZEN	230	URIZEN 15	2
WAVES BEFORE HIS DEATHY FACE	231	URIZEN 18	8
WAVING BEFORE THE FACE OF LOS	231	URIZEN 18	12
WHERE WAS A WORM BEFORE	232	URIZEN 19	36
SHOT FROM THE HEIGHTS OF ENITHARMON [BEFORE THE TRUMPET BLEW]	245	EUROPE 15	1
BEFORE THEIR SHRUNKEN EYES	246	SONG OF LOS 4	12
BEFORE THEY SEE THE LIGHT	255	AHANIA 5	47
REST BEFORE LABOUR	263D	FOUR ZOAS	TITLE
SPREADING THEM OUT BEFORE THE SUN LIKE STALKS OF FLAX TO DRY	265	FOUR ZOAS 1	48
[SO WAILD SHE TREMBLING BEFORE HER OWN CREATED PHANTASM]	267	FOUR ZOAS 1	118
[THE SIXTEENTH MORN THE SPECTRE STOOD BEFORE HIM MANIFEST]	268	FOUR ZOAS 1	146
AND THOU THE DELUSIVE TEMPTER TO THESE DEEDS SITTST BEFORE ME	268	FOUR ZOAS 1	169
THEY WEPT BEFORE THE INNER GATES OF ENITHARMON'S BOSOM . .	279	FOUR ZOAS 1	561
THE EMANATION STOOD BEFORE THE GATES OF ENITHARMON . . .	280	FOUR ZOAS 1	567
THEY PLAY BEFORE THE ARMIES BEFORE THE HOUNDS OF NIMROD	281	FOUR ZOAS 2	64
BROUGHT HIM IN VARIOUS FORMS BEFORE HER STILL SHE KNEW HIM NOT	286	FOUR ZOAS 2	233
THAT HIS DREAD FANCY FORMD BEFORE HIM IN THE UNFORMD VOID	287	FOUR ZOAS 2	294
DRIVING THE STORMS BEFORE THEM OR DELIGHTING IN SUNNY BEAMS	288	FOUR ZOAS 2	300
AND BRIGHT AHANIA BOWD HERSELF BEFORE HIS SPLENDID FEET	291	FOUR ZOAS 3	2
AHANIA BOWD HER HEAD & WEPT SEVEN DAYS BEFORE THE KING . .	292	FOUR ZOAS 3	24
. . . ON THE STEPS OF FIRE BEFORE HIS HALLS	292	FOUR ZOAS 3	44
MAN FELL UPON HIS FACE PROSTRATE BEFORE THE WATRY SHADOW	293	FOUR ZOAS 3	54
PROPHETIC DREADS URGE ME TO SPEAK FUTURITY IS BEFORE ME	293	FOUR ZOAS 3	74
AND THE VAST FORM OF NATURE LIKE A SERPENT PLAYD BEFORE THEM	294	FOUR ZOAS 3	97
FLED FROM MY SIDE THEN PANGS SMOTE ME UNKNOWN BEFORE I SAW	300	FOUR ZOAS 4	93
BEFORE ME IN THE WIND ENGLOBING TREMBLING WITH STRONG VIBRATIONS	300	FOUR ZOAS 4	95
WITH WHOM I LIVD IN HAPPINESS BEFORE THAT DEADLY NIGHT . .	300	FOUR ZOAS 4	112
THY LOVED ENITHARMON FOR THOU HAST HER HERE BEFORE THINE EYES	300	FOUR ZOAS 4	117
GROANING THE TERROR ROSE & DRAVE HIS [SOLD] SOLID ROCKS BEFORE	300	FOUR ZOAS 4	* 124
THARMAS BEFORE LOS STOOD & THUS THE VOICE OF THARMAS ROLLD	300	FOUR ZOAS 4	128
BEFORE MY EYES & AN ETERNAL WEARY WORK TO STRIVE	301	FOUR ZOAS 4	144
DARKEND BEFORE HIM SILENT ON THE RIDGY WAVES HE TOOK . .	313	FOUR ZOAS 6	53
HIS GLOOMY WAY BEFORE HIM THARMAS FLED & FLYING FOUGHT . .	313	FOUR ZOAS 6	54
SCALED & FINND WITH IRON & BRASS THEY DEVOURD THE PATH BEFORE HIM	313	FOUR ZOAS 6	76
DARK GREW HIS GLOBE REDDNING WITH MISTS & FULL BEFORE HIS PATH	319	FOUR ZOAS 6	296
IN THEIR PROGRESSIONS & PREPARING URIZEN'S PATH BEFORE HIM	320	FOUR ZOAS 6	325
AND TO REVEAL MYSELF BEFORE THEE IN A FORM OF WISDOM . .	321	FOUR ZOAS 7	58
THEE SECRETS OF ETERNITY WHICH NEER BEFORE UNLOCKD . . .	326	FOUR ZOAS 7	237
IN ODOROUS STUPEFACTION STOOD BEFORE THE EYES OF MAN . .	327	FOUR ZOAS 7	281
THE SPECTRE OF URTHONA WEPT BEFORE LOS SAYING I AM THE CAUSE	330	FOUR ZOAS 7	403
WHEN I APPEAR BEFORE THEE	330	FOUR ZOAS 7	419
MAY LIVE BEFORE US IN OUR PALACES	331	FOUR ZOAS 7	441
BEFORE MY FACE ASCENDING WITH DELIGHT AS IN ANCIENT TIMES	331	FOUR ZOAS 7	* 445
THE NAMELESS SHADOWY VORTEX STOOD BEFORE THE FACE OF ORC	336	FOUR ZOAS 7B	125
SWAM LIKE A DREAM BEFORE MY EYES I WENT TO SEEK THE STEPS	339	FOUR ZOAS 7B	235
TREMBLING BEFORE ME LIKE A SHADOW LIKE A MIST LIKE AIR	339	FOUR ZOAS 7B	238
BEFORE MY EYES & FOR EVERY ONE OF THESE I AM CONDEMND . .	339	FOUR ZOAS 7B	252
WALKING BEFORE HER SHADOWY FACE & BOWING AT HER FEET . .	340	FOUR ZOAS 7B	279
WHO ASSUMD LUVAH'S FORM & STOOD BEFORE HIM OPPOSITE . . .	342	FOUR ZOAS 8	64
OR SECRET RELIGION IN THEIR TEMPLES BEFORE SECRET SHRINES	344	FOUR ZOAS 8	130
NAKED OF THEIR CLOTHING THE POOR SPECTRES BEFORE THE ACCUSING HEAVENS	346	FOUR ZOAS 8	219
THE LAMB OF GOD STOOD BEFORE SATAN OPPOSITE	348	FOUR ZOAS 8	268
SHE STOOD BEFORE LOS IN HER PRIDE [ABOVE] AMONG THE FURNACES	350	FOUR ZOAS 8	* 345
BUT SATAN ACCUSD PALAMABRON BEFORE [LOS] HIS BRETHREN ALSO HE MADDEND	350	FOUR ZOAS 8	368
BOW DOWN BEFORE HER YOU HER CHILDREN & SET JERUSALEM FREE	351	FOUR ZOAS 8	409
REVEALD BEFORE THE FACE OF HEAVEN HIS SECRET HOLINESS . .	351	FOUR ZOAS 8	413
BEFORE ASSAULTED THE BRIGHT HUMAN FORM HE FELT HIS PORES	352	FOUR ZOAS 8	417
AND SOMETIMES WEEPING BEFORE ORC IN HUMILITY & TREMBLING	357	FOUR ZOAS 8	613
TREMBLING BEFORE THE MULTITUDES OF SLAVES NOW SET AT LIBERTY	357	FOUR ZOAS 9	21
LOWING THEY KNEEL BEFORE THE HEAVENS THE WILD BEASTS OF THE FORESTS	358	FOUR ZOAS 9	55
THE DREAD I FEEL UNKNOWN BEFORE MY VOICE REFUSES TO ROAR	358	FOUR ZOAS 9	57
BEFORE THE MORNING'S DAWN THE EAGLE CALLD THE VULTURE . .	358	FOUR ZOAS 9	59
MY SONS EXILED FROM MY BREAST PASS TO & FRO BEFORE ME . .	359	FOUR ZOAS 9	100
WITH HARPS & SONGS WHERE BRIGHT AHANIA SANG BEFORE THY FACE	360	FOUR ZOAS 9	* 126
LIE DOWN BEFORE MY FEET O DRAGON LET URIZEN ARISE . . .	360	FOUR ZOAS 9	139
IS SEEN THO SLAIN BEFORE HER GATES HE SELF-RENEWD REMAINS	362	FOUR ZOAS 9	206
AND EVERY ONE OF THE DEAD APPEARS AS HE HAD LIVD BEFORE	363	FOUR ZOAS 9	245
AGAINST HER LITTLE ONES THE INNOCENT ACCUSED BEFORE THE JUDGES	364	FOUR ZOAS 9	267
THE PRISONER ANSWERS YOU SCOURGD MY FATHER TO DEATH BEFORE MY FACE	364	FOUR ZOAS 9	275

187

```
                                                              PAGE       TITLE         LINE
BEFORE    (CONTINUED)
     THE TREMBLING SOULS OF ALL THE DEAD STOOD BEFORE URIZEN       365 FOUR ZOAS 9       317
     SWIMS LIKE A DREAM BEFORE MY EYES BUT THE SWEET SMELLING      371 FOUR ZOAS 9       539
       FRUIT
     THE GOOD OF ALL THE LAND IS BEFORE YOU FOR MYSTERY IS NO      375 FOUR ZOAS 9       681
       MORE
     HIS GOLDEN FOOD AND IN THE EVENING SLEEP BEFORE THE DOOR      376 FOUR ZOAS 9       708
     THEN LUVAH STOOD BEFORE THE WINE PRESS ALL HIS FIERY SONS     376 FOUR ZOAS 9       716
     THE LAMB OF GOD STOOD BEFORE URIZEN OPPOSITE     . . . . .    382 FOUR ZOAS AD 6     1
     ARISE BEFORE MY SIGHT . . . . . . . . . . . . . .            418 I SAW A MONK/N      2
     BUT PITY STANDS BEFORE THE DOOR     . . . . . . . . . .      421 TERROR IN/N         2
     DAZZLING BRIGHT BEFORE MY EYES . . . . . . . . . . .         422 BENEATH/N           9
     [DAZZLING BRIGHT BEFORE MY EYES]    . . . . . . . . . .      422 BENEATH REWR/N      6
     DAZLING BRIGHT BEFORE MY EYES  . . . . . . . . . . .         424 THE GOLDEN NET      8
     THE COTTAGE FADES BEFORE HIS SIGHT     . . . . . . .         426 MENTAL TRAVLER     59
     DANCE BEFORE DEAD ENGLAND'S HEARSE . . . . . . . . .         433 AUGURIES          118
     THE SOLDIER'S COMRADE SWORE BEFORE THE MAGISTRATES   . .     437B BLAKES MEMORAN  PROSE
     WILLIAM'S TIMIDITY IN GIVING HIS EVIDENCE BEFORE THE  . .    438D BLAKES MEMORAN  PROSE
     BEFORE HER THRONE MY WINGS I WAVE . . . . . . . . .          442 DEDICATN BLAIR     16
     BOWING BEFORE MY SOVREIGN'S FEET    . . . . . . . .          442 DEDICATN BLAIR     17
     [THE HEAVENS IN CLOUDS ROLLING BEFORE HIM & AROUND HIM]      443A LAST JUDGMNT/L  PROSE
     [WHO DESCEND BEFORE HIS FEET WITH THEIR FOUR TRUMPETS]  .    443A LAST JUDGMNT/L  PROSE
     BEFORE HIS FEET & AROUND HIM THE HEAVENS IN CLOUDS ARE       443A LAST JUDGMNT/L *PROSE
       ROLLING
     IMMEDIATELY BEFORE THE THRONE OF CHRIST IS ADAM & EVE  .     443B LAST JUDGMNT/L  PROSE
     THEIR OWN RIGHTEOUSNESS BEFORE THE THRONE OF CHRIST    .     443C LAST JUDGMNT/L  PROSE
     & BEFORE THE BOOK OF DEATH WHICH IS OPEND ON CLOUDS   . .    443C LAST JUDGMNT/L  PROSE
     FROM BEFORE THE THRONE & FROM BEFORE THE SEA OF FIRE         443C LAST JUDGMNT/L *PROSE
       WHICH
     FLOWS BEFORE THE STEPS OF THE THRONE ON WHICH [ARE] IS SEEN  443C LAST JUDGMNT/L *PROSE
     THE SEVEN LAMPS OF THE ALMIGHTY BURNING BEFORE THE THRONE    443C LAST JUDGMNT/L  PROSE
     BEFORE THE THRONE OF CHRIST ON THE RIGHT HAND THE JUST IN    443D LAST JUDGMNT/L  PROSE
     & FAMILIES SOME OF WHOM ARE BOWING BEFORE THE BOOK OF LIFE   443D LAST JUDGMNT/L  PROSE
     UPON HIS KNEES BEFORE THE LIVING & THE DEAD  . . . . .       444C LAST JUDGMNT/L  PROSE
     FOR DEATH ETERNAL IN THE HEAVENS OF ALBION & BEFORE THE      481 MILTON 2          14
       GATES
     BEFORE LONDON TO HAMPSTEAD'S BREADTHS & HIGHGATE'S HEIGHTS   485 MILTON 6           9
       TO
     DARK GLEAMS BEFORE THE FURNACE-MOUTH A HEAP OF BURNING       485 MILTON 6          17
       ASHES
     THE FIRST THE ELECT FROM BEFORE THE FOUNDATION OF THE WORLD  486 MILTON 7           2
     PALAMABRON CALLD AND LOS & SATAN CAME BEFORE HIM . . . .     487 MILTON 7          34
     MEAN WHILE WEPT SATAN BEFORE LOS ACCUSING PALAMABRON   . .   487 MILTON 8           1
     HE DISPLACD CONTINENTS THE OCEANS FLED BEFORE HIS FACE  .    489 MILTON 9          16
     ACCUSD PALAMABRON BEFORE THE ASSEMBLY OF INGRATITUDE OF      489 MILTON 9          20
       MALICE
     FOR HER LIGHT IS TERRIBLE TO ME I FADE BEFORE HER IMMORTAL   492 MILTON 12          1
       BEAUTY
     I HUMBLY BOW IN ALL MY SIN BEFORE THE THRONE DIVINE  . . .   493 MILTON 13          3
     WHAT DO I HERE BEFORE THE JUDGMENT WITHOUT MY EMANATION      495 MILTON 14         28
     BEFORE HIM IN THEIR BEAUTY & IN CRUELTIES OF HOLINESS   .    501 MILTON 19         34
     SCOFIELD IS BOUND IN IRON ARMOUR BEFORE REUBEN'S GATE   .    501 MILTON 19         59
     SO SPOKE THEY AS IN ONE VOICE SILENT MILTON STOOD BEFORE     502 MILTON 20          7
     THE DARKEND URIZEN AS THE SCULPTOR SILENT STANDS BEFORE      502 MILTON 20          8
     THIS WORLD BENEATH UNSEEN BEFORE THIS REFUGE FROM THE WARS   504 MILTON 21         48
     AND THESE ARE THE CRIES OF THE CHURCHES BEFORE THE TWO       506 MILTON 22         56
       WITNESSES
     WHO DIED FROM EARTH & HE IS RETURND BEFORE THE JUDGMENT      508 MILTON 23         57
       THIS THING
     PAUL CONSTANTINE CHARLEMAINE LUTHER BEHOLD THEY STAND        509 MILTON 24         32
       BEFORE US
     BECAUSE OF SATAN BEFORE LUBAN IN THE CITY OF GOLGONOOZA      509 MILTON 24         49
     AND LEST THEY SHOULD DESCEND BEFORE THE NORTH & SOUTH GATES  512 MILTON 26         21
     BUT THE WINE-PRESS OF LOS IS EASTWARD OF GOLGONOOZA BEFORE   513 MILTON 27          1
       THE SEAT
     THE BADGER & FOX THEY WORSHIP BEFORE HIS FEET IN TREMBLING   515 MILTON 28         43
       FEAR
     THAT SATAN'S WATCH-FIENDS TOUCH THEM NOT BEFORE THEY         517 MILTON 29         50
       VEGETATE
     THEREFORE I SHEW MY JEALOUSY & SET BEFORE YOU DEATH  . . .   522 MILTON 33         10
     RETURND BUT OLOLON REMAIND BEFORE THE GATES OF THE DEAD      524 MILTON 34         48
     PROSTRATE BEFORE THE STARRY EIGHT ASKING WITH TEARS          525 MILTON 35         32
       FORGIVENESS
     BEFORE MY COTTAGE STOOD FOR THE SATANIC SPACE IS DELUSION    527 MILTON 36         20
     I COME TO DISCOVER BEFORE HEAVN & HELL THE                   530 MILTON 38         43
       SELF RIGHTEOUSNESS
     TREMBLING BEFORE HIM WITH EXCEEDING GREAT TREMBLING & FEAR   531 MILTON 39         47
     LABOURD IN CHASMS OF THE MUNDANE SHELL THO HERE BEFORE  . .  532 MILTON 39         57
     BEFORE OLOLON MILTON STOOD & PERCIEVD THE ETERNAL FORM  .    532 MILTON 40          1
     TERRIBLY THIS PORTION TREMBLES BEFORE THEE O AWFUL MAN  .    533 MILTON 41         31
     IF YOU PLAY A GAME OF CHANCE KNOW BEFORE YOU BEGIN  . . .    551 IF YOU PLAY/N      1
     HE HAD THEM BOTH BEFORE NOW HOW DO YE DO  . . . . . .        554 TO VENETIAN/N     14
     A GREAT DEAL BETTER THAN I WAS BEFORE  . . . . . . . .       554 TO VENETIAN/N     15
     "BEFORE AND WORSHIPPED THE MOST STRONG THEY MELTED"  . .     560B EXHIBITION ADV  PROSE
     "BEFORE HIM AND DISSOLVED IN HIS PRESENCE" . . . . . .       560B EXHIBITION ADV  PROSE
     OF THEM TO DO ME THE JUSTICE TO EXAMINE BEFORE THEY DECIDE   561B EXHIBITION ADV  PROSE
     TWO YEARS BEFORE MICHAEL ANGELO AND TITIAN BUT FOUR YEARS    563C DESC CAT        PROSE
       AFTER
     IN THE MEANTIME LET IT BE OBSERVED THAT BEFORE VANDYKE'S     565B DESC CAT 2      PROSE
       TIME
     THE TIME CHOSEN IS EARLY MORNING BEFORE SUNRISE  . . . . .   566C DESC CAT 3      PROSE
     WAS IMPOSSIBLE IF WE DID NOT SEE IT ALWAYS BEFORE OUR EYES   578D DESC CAT 5      PROSE
```

188

	PAGE	TITLE	LINE
BEFORE (CONTINUED)			
THE ROMAN SOLDIERS ROLLED TOGETHER IN A HEAP BEFORE THEM	580C	DESC CAT 5	PROSE
"LIKE THE ROLLING THING BEFORE THE WHIRLWIND"	580C	DESC CAT 5	PROSE
DRAWN OUT UPON IT BEFORE MAN OR BEAST CAN EXIST	585C	DESC CAT 15	PROSE
THE TIME CHOSEN IS EARLY MORNING BEFORE SUNRISE	588B	CHAUCER/N	PROSE
THE TIME CHOSEN IS EARLY MORNING BEFORE SUN-RISE	589C	CHAUCER 2	PROSE
PRETENCES OF ENGLISHMEN TO IMPROVE [E] ART BEFORE THEY EVEN	593C	PUB ADDRESS/N	*PROSE
MARC ANTONIO & ALBERT DURER YE MUST BEGIN BEFORE	593C	PUB ADDRESS/N	PROSE
ALL THE ARTICLES OF PAINTING HE PUTS A MODEL BEFORE HIM	597B	PUB ADDRESS/N	PROSE
TO LEAVE IT BEFORE HE HAS SPOILD IT HE WILL [PR] DO A BETTER THING	603A	PUB ADDR AD/N	*PROSE
I KNOW THIS HE HAS OFTEN PROVED HIS IGNORANCE BEFORE ME	603C	PUB ADDR AD/N	PROSE
A SEA OF FIRE ISSUES FROM BEFORE THE THRONE	606B	V LAST JUDG/N	PROSE
ADAM & EVE APPEAR FIRST BEFORE THE [THRONE]	606B	V LAST JUDG/N	PROSE
BEFORE THE FLOOD THAT THEY WERE FILLD WITH BLOOD & FIRE	606D	V LAST JUDG/N	PROSE
THEIR OWN RIGHTEOUSNESS BEFORE THE THRONE	607D	V LAST JUDG/N	PROSE
BEFORE CAIPHAS & PILATE ARE JUDAS & THOSE OF HIS CLASS	608D	V LAST JUDG/N	PROSE
DESCENDING FROM THE SEA OF FIRE BEFORE THE THRONE	609A	V LAST JUDG/N	PROSE
LYING ON THE ROCK OPEN BEFORE HIM HE IS BOUND IN CHAINS	609B	V LAST JUDG/N	PROSE
UNDER THE NAMES OF THE FATHERS BEFORE & AFTER THE FLOOD	609D	V LAST JUDG/N	PROSE
HE IS SEEN ON HIS FIERY CHARIOT BOWING BEFORE THE THRONE	611C	V LAST JUDG/N	PROSE
BEFORE THE FLOOD & THEIR GENERATIONS	611D	V LAST JUDG/N	PROSE
ALL THESE ARISE TOWARD THE OPENING CLOUD BEFORE THE THRONE	611D	V LAST JUDG/N	PROSE
THE CLOUD THAT OPENS ROLLING APART BEFORE THE THRONE	612A	V LAST JUDG/N	PROSE
& BEFORE THE NEW HEAVEN & THE NEW EARTH	612A	V LAST JUDG/N	PROSE
ON THE LEFT HAND APOLLYON IS FOILED BEFORE THE SWORD	612B	V LAST JUDG/N	PROSE
BEFORE THAT OF LIFE ON THE RIGHT SOME FIGURES [?BOW] BOW	612B	V LAST JUDG/N	*PROSE
IN HUMILIATION BEFORE THAT OF DEATH ON THE LEFT	612B	V LAST JUDG/N	PROSE
MANY SUPPOSE THAT BEFORE [ADAM] THE CREATION ALL	614B	V LAST JUDG/N	PROSE
THESE HEAVENS ARE VENUS JUPITER & MARS HERMES FLIES BEFORE	619B	ILLUS MILTON	PROSE
HE WHO WAITS TO BE RIGHTEOUS BEFORE HE ENTERS INTO THE	621A	JERUSALEM 3	PROSE
THY EMANATION THAT WAS WONT TO PLAY BEFORE THY FACE	622	JERUSALEM 4	14
HIS JEALOUSY BEFORE THE THRONE DIVINE DARKENING COLD	622	JERUSALEM 4	35
THE FURNACE OF LOS BEFORE THE EASTERN GATE BENDING THEIR FURY	623	JERUSALEM 5	28
INCESSANT BEFORE THE FURNACES AND HIS EMANATION DIVIDED IN PAIN	624	JERUSALEM 5	67
HAND SITS BEFORE HIS FURNACE SCORN OF OTHERS & FURIOUS PRIDE	626	JERUSALEM 7	71
WHILE LOS SPOKE THE TERRIBLE SPECTRE FELL SHUDDRING BEFORE HIM	627	JERUSALEM 8	21
HE SAW NOW FROM THE (OUTSIDE) WHAT HE BEFORE SAW & FELT FROM WITHIN	627	JERUSALEM 8	* 25
GROANING HE KNEELD BEFORE LOS'S IRON-SHOD FEET ON LONDON STONE	627	JERUSALEM 8	27
THOU ART REVEALD BEFORE ME IN ALL THY MAGNITUDE & POWER	627	JERUSALEM 8	31
HE IS LIKE A MANDRAKE IN THE EARTH BEFORE REUBEN'S GATE	631	JERUSALEM 11	22
TERRIFIED AT THE SUBLIME WONDER LOS STOOD BEFORE HIS FURNACES	631	JERUSALEM 12	21
HAS FOUR SCULPTURD BULLS TERRIBLE BEFORE THE GATE OF IRON	632	JERUSALEM 12	62
BEFORE ME O DIVINE SPIRIT SUSTAIN ME ON THY WINGS	635	JERUSALEM 15	9
BEFORE BROMION'S IRON TONGS & GLOWING POKER REDDENING FIERCE	636	JERUSALEM 16	2
BEFORE THE ANVIL WATCHES THE BELLOWING FLAMES THUNDERING	636	JERUSALEM 16	10
HUMBER & TRENT ROLL DREADFUL BEFORE THE SEVENTH FURNACE	636	JERUSALEM 16	16
AND OF HIS CHILDREN BEFORE SINFUL JERUSALEM TO BUILD	640	JERUSALEM 18	28
HIS CHILDREN EXILD FROM HIS BREAST PASS TO AND FRO BEFORE HIM	641	JERUSALEM 19	1
BEFORE HIS AWFUL FEET IN PRIDE OF VIRTUE FOR VICTORY	642	JERUSALEM 19	32
WHERE WE DELIGHT IN INNOCENCE BEFORE THE FACE OF THE LAMB	642	JERUSALEM 20	9
GOING IN AND OUT BEFORE HIM IN HIS LOVE AND SWEET AFFECTION	642	JERUSALEM 20	10
HE DRIVES THEM THRO THE STREETS OF BABYLON BEFORE MY FACE	644	JERUSALEM 21	30
CARRIED IN ARKS OF OAK BEFORE THE ARMIES IN THE SPRING	644	JERUSALEM 21	45
BURSTING THEIR ARKS THEY RISE AGAIN TO LIFE THEY PLAY BEFORE	644	JERUSALEM 21	46
BEARS ME BEFORE HIS ARMIES THO MY SHADOW HOVERS HERE	644	JERUSALEM 22	5
SPREADING THEM OUT BEFORE THE SUN LIKE STALKS OF FLAX TO DRY	645	JERUSALEM 22	21
THEY CAME UP TO JERUSALEM THEY WALKED BEFORE ALBION	647	JERUSALEM 24	41
DOST THOU APPEAR BEFORE ME WHO LIEST DEAD IN LUVAH'S SEPULCHER	648	JERUSALEM 24	57
OF ROUGH UNHEWN ROCKS BEFORE THE POTTER'S FURNACE	653	JERUSALEM 28	22
ALBION WALKD ON THE STEPS OF FIRE BEFORE HIS HALLS	654	JERUSALEM 29	33
ALBION FELL UPON HIS FACE PROSTRATE BEFORE THE WATRY SHADOW	654	JERUSALEM 29	41
AND THE VAST FORM OF NATURE LIKE A SERPENT PLAYD BEFORE THEM	655	JERUSALEM 29	76
SET YOUR SON BEFORE A MAN & HE SHALL TAKE YOU & YOUR SONS	658	JERUSALEM 31	52
FOR SLAVES BUT SET YOUR DAUGHTER BEFORE A MAN & SHE	658	JERUSALEM 31	53
CHAOS BEFORE HIS FACE APPEARD AN UNFORMED MEMORY	659	JERUSALEM 33	2
IS AS NOTHING BEFORE THEE FADED IS ALL LIFE AND JOY	659	JERUSALEM 33	34
HE OPEND HIS FURNACES BEFORE VALA THEN ALBION FROWND IN ANGER	660	JERUSALEM 34	19
UNKNOWN AMONG THE DEAD WHERE NEVER BEFORE EXISTENCE CAME	661	JERUSALEM 34	38
BEFORE THE FURNACES OF LOS IN A HORRIBLE DREAMFUL SLUMBER	662	JERUSALEM 36	11
THE SEVEN NATIONS FLED BEFORE HIM THEY BECAME WHAT THEY BEHELD	662	JERUSALEM 36	14
ALBION GROANS HE SEES THE ELEMENTS DIVIDE BEFORE HIS FACE	663	JERUSALEM 36	27
BEFORE THE GATE OF LOS URTHONA HERE IS NAMED LOS	666	JERUSALEM 39	9
BEFORE THE PORCH OF SIXTEEN PILLARS WEEPING EVERY ONE	666	JERUSALEM 40	7
BROODING ON EVIL BUT WHEN LOS OPEND THE FURNACES BEFORE HIM	669	JERUSALEM 42	2
MY DAUGHTERS ARE HARLOTS MY SONS ARE ACCURSED BEFORE ME	670	JERUSALEM 42	14
BRING HIM TO JUSTICE BEFORE HEAVEN HERE UPON LONDON STONE	670	JERUSALEM 42	50

189

BEFORE   (CONTINUED)

	PAGE	TITLE	LINE
LOS STOOD BEFORE HIS FURNACES AWAITING THE FURY OF THE DEAD	671	JERUSALEM 42	55
DEAD CORSES LAY BEFORE THEM & NOT AS IN WARS OF OLD . . .	672	JERUSALEM 43	40
BEFORE THE GATE OF LOS & IN THE DEPTHS OF NON ENTITY . .	674	JERUSALEM 44	36
HE WEPT BEFORE HIS WRATHFUL BRETHREN THANKFUL & CONSIDERATE	675	JERUSALEM 45	23
THE SUN SHALL GO BEFORE YOU IN DAY THE MOON SHALL GO . .	680	JERUSALEM 49	51
BEFORE YOU IN NIGHT COME ON COME ON COME ON THE LORD	680	JERUSALEM 49	52
JEHOVAH IS BEFORE BEHIND ABOVE BENEATH AROUND	680	JERUSALEM 49	53
STATE MUST BE PUT OFF BEFORE HE CAN BE THE FRIEND OF MAN	682A	JERUSALEM 52	PROSE
BUT CONFESSED HIS SINS BEFORE ALL THE WORLD	682D	JERUSALEM 52	PROSE
ARISE BEFORE MY SIGHT	683	I SAW A MONK/J	2
AS HE SAT BEFORE HIS FURNACES CLOTHED IN SACKCLOTH OF HAIR	684	JERUSALEM 53	5
THEY PLOWD IN TEARS THE TRUMPETS SOUNDED BEFORE THE GOLDEN PLOW	687	JERUSALEM 55	54
SAYING WHO WILL GO FORTH FOR US & WHO SHALL WE SEND BEFORE OUR FACE	687	JERUSALEM 55	69
THEY WERE AS ADAM BEFORE ME UNITED INTO ONE MAN	692	JERUSALEM 60	16
BEFORE I HAD EVER BEHELD WITH LOVE THE FACE OF JEHOVAH OR KNOWN	695	JERUSALEM 61	42
OF ALBION TREMBLE BEFORE THE SPECTRE	697	JERUSALEM 63	3
IRELAND TO JAPAN FURIOUS HER LIONS & TYGERS & WOLVES SPORT BEFORE	698	JERUSALEM 63	34
THEN ALL THE DAUGHTERS OF ALBION BECAME ONE BEFORE LOS EVEN VALA	698	JERUSALEM 64	6
AS REUBEN FLED BEFORE THE DAUGHTERS OF ALBION TAXING THE NATIONS	699	JERUSALEM 64	34
HEARTS OF THEIR WARRIORS GLOW HOT BEFORE THOR & FRIGA O MOLECH	706	JERUSALEM 68	17
TO THE BEAUTIFUL DAUGHTERS OF ALBION THEY SPORT BEFORE THE KINGS	706	JERUSALEM 68	32
BEFORE THE KINGS OF CANAAN TO CUT THE FLESH FROM THE VICTIM	706	JERUSALEM 68	57
BEFORE THE FACE OF ALBION A MIGHTY THREATNING FORM . . .	708	JERUSALEM 70	2
BUT HE RECEDED BEFORE ALBION & BEFORE VALA WEAVING THE VEIL	711	JERUSALEM 71	60
. . . THEIR EVENTS ARE PRESENT BEFORE ME	714	JERUSALEM 74	19
ENGAGE HIMSELF OPENLY & PUBLICLY BEFORE ALL THE WORLD . .	717C	JERUSALEM 77	PROSE
SITTING BEFORE HIS FURNACES CLOTHED IN SACKCLOTH OF HAIR	719	JERUSALEM 78	11
NAKED JERUSALEM LAY BEFORE THE GATES UPON MOUNT ZION .	719	JERUSALEM 78	21
OUTSIDE UNKNOWN BEFORE IN BEULAH & THE TWELVE GATES WERE FILLD	719	JERUSALEM 78	25
HE BURND BEFORE ME LUVAH FRAMD THE KNIFE & LUVAH GAVE .	722	JERUSALEM 80	22
BEFORE IN ALBION'S LAND	722	JERUSALEM 80	24
OF WAR THE CYMBALS PLAY LOUD BEFORE THE CAPTAINS	722	JERUSALEM 80	38
GLOWING WITH LOVELINESS BEFORE HIM BECOMING APPARENT . .	723	JERUSALEM 80	71
LET US LEAD THE STEMS OF THIS TREE LET US PLANT IT BEFORE JERUSALEM	725	JERUSALEM 82	32
BENEATH ALBION'S FATAL TREE BEFORE THE GATE OF LOS . . .	726	JERUSALEM 82	60
LISTEN TO YOUR WATCHMAN'S VOICE SLEEP NOT BEFORE THE FURNACES	728	JERUSALEM 83	64
LIKE A FAINT RAINBOW WAVED BEFORE HIM IN THE AWFUL GLOOM	728	JERUSALEM 83	67
BEFORE THE FURNACES LABOURING WHILE LOS ALL NIGHT WATCHES	729	JERUSALEM 83	80
SANDALS OF GOLD & PEARL & EGYPT & ASSYRIA BEFORE ME . . .	731	JERUSALEM 86	31
AND ENITHARMON LIKE A FAINT RAINBOW WAVED BEFORE HIM . . .	732	JERUSALEM 86	50
SHE SEPARATED STOOD BEFORE HIM A LOVELY FEMALE WEEPING . .	732	JERUSALEM 86	57
ENITHARMON'S NAME IS NOTHING BEFORE YOU YOU FORGET ALL MY LOVE	740	JERUSALEM 93	3
ALBION'S BOSOM THEN ALBION STOOD BEFORE JESUS IN THE CLOUDS	744	JERUSALEM 96	42
BEFORE HIS WRATH BEGAN TO BURN	752	EV GOSPEL(D)/N	56
CURSING THE RULERS BEFORE THE PEOPLE	752	EV GOSPEL(D)/N	69
YOU SHALL BOW BEFORE HER FEET	754	EV GOSPEL(E)/N	53
BUT PLATO & CICERO DID INCULCATE BEFORE HIM	757D	EV GOSPEL	PROSE
ADAM EVE THOU HAST SPOKEN TRULY LET US KNEEL BEFORE HIS FEET	780	GHOST ABEL 2	3
THEY KNEEL BEFORE JEHOVAH	780C	GHOST ABEL 2	PROSE
[BEFORE] IMMEDIATELY ON THE RECEIT OF YOUR BEAUTIFUL BOOK	791A	LETTER 3	PROSE
& IT WAS SOME TIME WHEN I FOUND THEM BEFORE I COULD . . .	791B	LETTER 3	PROSE
"IMAGINATION BEFORE REASON HAVE JUDGED & REASON "	794A	LETTER 5	PROSE
"SENDS OVER TO IMAGINATION BEFORE THE DECREE CAN BE ACTED"	794A	LETTER 5	PROSE
THAT IT WILL SOON BE BEFORE PARLIAMENT & THAT IT MUST BE	797D	LETTER 10	PROSE
THE AMERICAN WAR BEGAN ALL ITS DARK HORRORS PASSED BEFORE MY FACE	799	TO FLAXMAN/L	9
"NECESSARY TO BE FINISHD BEFORE OUR MIGRATION THE" . . .	800B	LETTER 12	PROSE
I FEAR IT WILL BE THURSDAY BEFORE WE CAN GET AWAY FROM . .	801B	LETTER 13	PROSE
COULD NOT ARRIVE AT OUR COTTAGE BEFORE HALF PAST ELEVEN	802B	LETTER 14	PROSE
OF ETERNITY BEFORE MY MORTAL LIFE & THOSE WORKS ARE THE DELIGHT	802C	LETTER 14	PROSE
REMINISCENCE & BEHOLD OUR ANCIENT DAYS BEFORE THIS EARTH	802C	LETTER 14	PROSE
& TWELVE OCLOCK AT NIGHT BEFORE WE COULD GET HOME . . .	803A	LETTER 15	PROSE
WITH GOD SPEED A ROLLER & TWO HARROWS LIE BEFORE MY WINDOW	803C	LETTER 15	PROSE
BEFORE ME BRIGHT SHONE	806	TO BUTTS/L	74
WITHOUT NATURE BEFORE THE PAINTER'S EYE HE CAN NEVER PRODUCE	810B	LETTER 20	PROSE
AT THE TASKS SET BEFORE US IF WE REFUSE TO DO SPIRITUAL ACTS	813A	LETTER 22	PROSE
DID NOT SEND & WHY I HAVE NOT BEFORE NOW FINISHD	815C	LETTER 23	PROSE
IF YOU HAVE NOT NATURE BEFORE YOU FOR EVERY TOUCH YOU CANNOT	815D	LETTER 23	PROSE
PAINT PORTRAIT & IF YOU HAVE NATURE BEFORE YOU AT ALL . .	815D	LETTER 23	PROSE
ASSURE HER THAT IT CANNOT BE LONG BEFORE I HAVE THE PLEASURE	815D	LETTER 23	PROSE
TO DRIVE THEM OFF & BEFORE MY WAY	817	HAPPINESS/L	23
IN THE SUN HE APPEARD DESCENDING BEFORE	818	HAPPINESS/L	56
MY BROTHERS & FATHER MARCH BEFORE	818	HAPPINESS/L	81

```
                                                    PAGE      TITLE        LINE
BEFORE    (CONTINUED)
      BEFORE NOW BUT COULD NOT GET ANY THING DONE FOR YOU  . . .  819A LETTER 24     PROSE
      & I MEAN TO TRY MANY BUT I AGAIN SAY AS I SAID BEFORE WE     820B LETTER 25     PROSE
        ARE
      THE CXXXIX PSALM A LITTLE BEFORE YOUR LETTER ARRIVED I TAKE  823B LETTER 26     PROSE
      WITHOUT THE ORIGINAL SITTING BEFORE YOU FOR EVERY TOUCH ALL  824B LETTER 27     PROSE
      ABLE TO SEND ANY MORE BEFORE MY RETURN THO PERHAPS I MAY     826D LETTER 28     PROSE
      I THEREFORE TOOK HIM BY THE ELBOWS & PUSHED HIM BEFORE ME    827A LETTER 28     PROSE
      SAW ME TURN HIM BEFORE ME DOWN THE ROAD & SAW & HEARD   .    827C LETTER 28     PROSE
      & I HAD NO WITNESS WITH ME BEFORE THE JUSTICES WHO COULD     827D LETTER 28     PROSE
      TO TAKE WITH ME I HAVE BEEN BEFORE A BENCH OF JUSTICES  . .  827D LETTER 28     PROSE
      TO SEE MY FRIENDS IN TOWN BEFORE THIS CONTEMPTIBLE BUSINESS  828A LETTER 28     PROSE
      LIKE THE SOUND OF HARPS WHICH I HEAR BEFORE THE SUN'S        835B LETTER 34     PROSE
        RISING
      THO I AM VERY SORRY THAT I CANNOT SEND BEFORE SATURDAY'S     837C LETTER 36     PROSE
        COACH
      IF YOU DO NOT WISH ANY MORE DONE BEFORE I DELIVER THEN PRAY  840C LETTER 39     PROSE
      THAT WASHINGTON DID ALL THAT WAS DONE BEFORE HE WAS BORN     845B LETTER 44     PROSE
      GREAT NEWPORT STREET BEFORE HE WENT TOOK THE HOUSE IN   .    847D LETTER 44     PROSE
      HAD BEFORE CONCLUDED UPON JUDGING AS HE DID THAT IF THE      848C LETTER 45     PROSE
      BEFORE NOW. PROOFS OF THE TWO PLATES THE HEAD OF R(ROMNEY)   851B LETTER 50     PROSE
      EXCUSE FOR TROUBLING YOU BEFORE IT CAN BE PROPERLY CALLED    853C LETTER 52     PROSE
      BECAUSE I WOULD HASTEN ITS ARRIVAL BEFORE IT IS CONVENIENT   853D LETTER 52     PROSE
      FAREWELL SWEET ROSE THOU HAST GOT BEFORE ME INTO THE    .    854C LETTER 53     PROSE
      ENGRAVER I CONSULTED MR PARKER ON THE SUBJECT BEFORE I  .    855A LETTER 53     PROSE
      IF ANY OF MY WRITINGS SHOULD HEREAFTER APPEAR BEFORE    .    860D LETTER 57     PROSE
      MY FEET IT WILL NOT BE LONG BEFORE I SHALL BE ABLE          862D LETTER 60     PROSE
        TO PRESENT
      HAVE ADDED UPON A PROOF BEFORE I PARTED WITH THE PICTURE     863C LETTER 60     PROSE
      OF RESENTMENT AGAINST MAN AND DEVIL AND OF HUMILIATION       864B LETTER 61     PROSE
        BEFORE GOD
      OCCUPY MY THOUGHTS NEW PROFITS SEEM TO ARISE BEFORE ME SO    865C LETTER 63     PROSE
      FIRST BEFORE I BEGIN ENGRAVING THEM AS IT WILL ENABLE ME     866C LETTER 65     PROSE
      BEFORE DINNER I MEAN IF YOU SET OFF BEFORE THAT & SECOND     870D LETTER 72     PROSE
      MR LINNELL WILL HAVE ARRIVED AT HIS JOURNEY'S END BEFORE     871C LETTER 73     PROSE
      THE TIME I NOW WRITE HE SET OFF LAST NIGHT BEFORE EIGHT      871C LETTER 73     PROSE
        OCLOCK
      BEFORE NOW I DO AS MR LINNELL DESIRED I WOULD DO BY THE      871C LETTER 73     PROSE
      COME TO YOU BEFORE TUESDAY BUT MUCH FEAR THAT MY PRESENT     872A LETTER 74     PROSE
      SO THAT I CONCLUDE ANOTHER WEEK MUST PASS BEFORE I DARE      873A LETTER 76     PROSE
      I DID NOT KNOW IT BEFORE YESTERDAY FROM MR FINCHAM    .  .   874C LETTER 79     PROSE
BEFORE HAND
      BECAUSE I AM GETTING BEFORE HAND IN MONEY MATTERS      . .   820A LETTER 25     PROSE
BEG
      THE MERCHANTS DO COMPLAIN AND BEG OUR AID  . . . . . .       20 EDW THIRD/PS 2     69
      THEREFORE I BEG I MAY RETURN TO ENGLAND . . . . . . .        23 EDW THIRD/PS 3    104
      THEREFORE I BEG I MAY RETURN TO ENGLAND . . . . . . .        24 EDW THIRD/PS 3    132
      ERE WHILE SO FAIR AND NOW THEY FALL & BEG THE SKIES WILL     43C WOE CRIED MUSE  PROSE
        WEEP
      O DEAR SIR HO HO HO I AM NO SINGER I MUST BEG       . . .    61D ISLAND MOON 11 *PROSE
      ("YOU BEG AS YOU QUESTION YOU GIVE AS YOU ANSWER")           77D ANNO LAVATER     MARG
        EXCELLENT
      A WANDERER I BEG FOR FOOD YOU SEE I CANNOT WEEP      . . .   101 TIRIEL 2            28
      AND I HAVE CAUSED THE EARTH WORM TO BEG FROM DOOR TO DOOR    290 FOUR ZOAS 2       392
      THEY BEG THEY INTREAT IN VAIN NOW THEY LISTEND NOT           363 FOUR ZOAS 9    *  257
        TO INTREATY
      BEG BREAD FROM HOUSE TO HOUSE LOVELY JERUSALEM    . . . .    693 JERUSALEM 60       28
      BE ON THIS I BEG TO SAY THAT THEY ARE WHAT I INTENDED THEM   815B LETTER 23      PROSE
      THEY BEG THEY INTREAT THEY DROP THEIR TEARS    . . . .  .    817 HAPPINESS/L        19
      TILL WE MEET I BEG OF GOD OUR SAVIOUR TO BE WITH YOU & ME    826A LETTER 27      PROSE
      TO BEG OF YOU TO CAUSE THE ENCLOSD LETTER TO BE DELIVERD     829B LETTER 28      PROSE
      THEREFORE AS IT IS MY DUTY BEG & INTREAT YOU NEVER TO MOUNT  833C LETTER 33      PROSE
      MR WALKER JUNR & BEG HIM TO SHEW ME THE PICTURES & MAKE      834C LETTER 34      PROSE
      BEG OF YOU TO SEND TO ME THAT I MAY ENGRAVE THEM            838A LETTER 37      PROSE
        IMMEDIATELY
      BEG PARDON FOR THE OMISSION OF MR BRAITHWAITE'S TWO PRINTS   839B LETTER 38      PROSE
      ENGRAVING IS OF SO SLOW PROCESS I MUST BEG OF YOU TO GIVE    842D LETTER 42      PROSE
        ME
      & BEG THE FAVOUR OF SOME MORE OF THE [XXX] NEEDFUL     .     851A LETTER 49     *PROSE
      I BEG YOUR REMARKS ALSO ON BOTH MY PERFORMANCES AS IN THEIR  853C LETTER 52      PROSE
      AT YOUR APPROVAL OF MY QUEEN CATHERINE BEG TO OBSERVE THAT   855C LETTER 53      PROSE
      COPYRIGHT IS FOR EVER YOURS I THEREFORE BEG THAT YOU WILL    858B LETTER 55      PROSE
      BUT MUST BEG YOU TO EXCUSE SUCH FOLLIES WHICH THO I AM  .    875D LETTER 82      PROSE
      I HAVE & BEG THE FAVOUR OF YOU TO SEND ME THE TWO PLATES     876A LETTER 83      PROSE
BEGAN
      AND LIBERTY BEGAN T INCREASE    . . . . . . . . . .          17 BLIND-MANS/PS       68
      [THE GOLDEN SUN HIS MIGHTY RACE BEGAN]                       40D THEN SHE BORE   PROSE
      & SHUTTING HIS EYES BEGAN TO SCRATCH HIS HEAD  . . . . .     45B ISLAND MOON 1   PROSE
      THEN ARADOBO BEGAN IN THE FIRST PLACE I THINK  . . . . .     49C ISLAND MOON 5   PROSE
      AND WHEN THE CHILD BEGAN TO SWELL       . . . . . . . .      51 WHEN CORRUP/IM     29
      HERE A LAUGH BEGAN AND MISS GITTIPIN SUNG      . . . . .     61B ISLAND MOON 11  PROSE
      SO SAYING HE BEGAN TO DIG A GRAVE WITH HIS AGED HANDS   .    100 TIRIEL 1           34
      ASTONISHD SILENT TILL THE MORNING BEAMS BEGAN TO SPRING      107 TIRIEL 6            2
      . . . [ZA ] ZAZEL STOOD STILL & THUS [?SCOFFING XXX ] ?BEGAN 108 TIRIEL 7        *    7
      BEGAN TO CRY BUT GOD EVER NIGH   . . . . . . . . . .         121 LIT BOY FND/SI      3
      AND POINTING TO THE EAST BEGAN TO SAY       . . . . . .      125 LIT BLK BOY/SI      8
      MENTAL DEITIES FROM THEIR OBJECTS THUS BEGAN PRIESTHOOD      153A MARRIAGE HH 11 PROSE
      [I BEGAN TO SO] [SEEKING MANY AN ARTFUL WILE]  . . . . .     167 INFANT SORW/N      11
      I BEGAN TO SOOTHE & SMILE   . . . . . . . . . . . .          167 INFANT SORW/N      13
      AND WHEN THY HEART BEGAN TO BEAT    . . . . . . . .  .       172 THE TYGER/N 1      11
      AND WHEN THY HEART BEGAN TO BEAT    . . . . . . . .  .       173 THE TYGER/N 2      11
      [ FROM MARY IT BEGAN ]   . . . . . . . . . . . . .           173 HOW CAME/N          2
```

191

```
                                                              PAGE      TITLE            LINE
BEGAN    (CONTINUED)
    AND ALL HIS BOWELS BEGAN TO [BURN] CHURN   . . . . . . .   187 WHEN KLOPSTK/N         16
    ON ALBION'S ANGELS THEN THE PESTILENCE BEGAN IN STREAKS     202 AMERICA 15             1
        OF RED
    AND WHEN THY HEART BEGAN TO BEAT   . . . . . . . . .        214 THE TYGER/SE          11
    THE ETERNAL MIND BOUNDED BEGAN TO ROLL   . . . . . . .      227 URIZEN 10             19
    THE PANGS OF HOPE BEGAN   . . . . . . . . . . .             229 URIZEN 11             19
    IN HIS CHAINS BOUND & PITY BEGAN   . . . . . . . .          230 URIZEN 13             51
    THEY BEGAN TO WEAVE CURTAINS OF DARKNESS   . . . . .        231 URIZEN 19              5
    BEGAN TO ERECT THE TENT   . . . . . . . . . . .             232 URIZEN 19             18
    WITH SHARP PANGS THE HISSINGS BEGAN   . . . . . . .         232 URIZEN 19             31
    AND BEGAN TO AWAKE FROM SLEEP   . . . . . . . . .           233 URIZEN 20             27
    AND BEGAN TO AWAKE TO LIFE   . . . . . . . . . .            233 URIZEN 20             29
    AND BEGAN TO EXPLORE THE ABYSS   . . . . . . . .            234 URIZEN 20             40
    AND HARDENING BONES BEGAN   . . . . . . . . . .             235 URIZEN 25             25
    AND THUS THE SONG BEGAN   . . . . . . . . . . .             245 SONG OF LOS 3          5
    THE HUMAN RACE BEGAN TO WITHER FOR THE HEALTHY BUILT   .    246 SONG OF LOS 3         25
    SLEEP BEGAN THE LUNGS HEAVE ON THE WAVE   . . . . . .       258 BOOK OF LOS 4         60
    IN FURIOUS TORRENTS BEGAN   . . . . . . . . . .             259 BOOK OF LOS 4         67
    BEGAN INTRICATE PIPES THAT DREW IN   . . . . . . .          259 BOOK OF LOS 4         69
    THEN LIGHT FIRST BEGAN FROM THE FIRES   . . . . . .         259 BOOK OF LOS 5         10
    A HAMMER OF ADAMANT THEN BEGAN   . . . . . . . .            259 BOOK OF LOS 5         22
    LISTNING TO HER SOFT LAMENTATIONS SOON HIS TONGUE BEGAN     267 FOUR ZOAS 1          124
    THE FIRST STATE WEEPING THEY BEGAN & HELPLESS AS A WAVE     269 FOUR ZOAS 1          193
    DISCORD BEGAN & YELLS & CRIES SHOOK THE WIDE FIRMAMENT  .   278 FOUR ZOAS 1          518
    THE BELLOWS BEGAN TO BLOW & THE LIONS OF URIZEN STOOD ROUND 281 FOUR ZOAS 2           32
        THE ANVIL
    EACH TOOK HIS STATION & HIS COURSE BEGAN . . .             287 FOUR ZOAS 2          268
    IN LOS'S ARMS HOWLINGS BEGAN OVER THE BODY OF DEATH  . . .  289 FOUR ZOAS 2          335
    THE BOUNDS OF DESTINY WERE BROKEN & HATRED NOW BEGAN  . .   296 FOUR ZOAS 3          177
    THE BLOODY MASS BEGAN TO ANIMATE I BENDING OVER   . . . .   300 FOUR ZOAS 4           96
    AND THUS BEGAN THE BINDING OF URIZEN DAY & NIGHT IN FEAR    302 FOUR ZOAS 4          199
    THE ETERNAL MIND BOUNDED BEGAN TO ROLL EDDIES OF WRATH      303 FOUR ZOAS 4          208
        CEASELESS
    THE PANGS OF HOPE BEGAN IN HEAVY PAIN STRIVING STRUGGLING   303 FOUR ZOAS 4          232
    BEGAN IN SOLEMN REVOLUTIONS EARTH CONVULSD WITH RENDING     306 FOUR ZOAS 5           28
        PANGS
    BEGAN A DISMAL DANCE THE WINDS AROUND ON POINTED ROCKS  .   306 FOUR ZOAS 5           34
    THEN DISCORD BEGAN [&] THEN YELLS & CRIES SHOOK THE WIDE    306 FOUR ZOAS 5    *      45
        (FIRMAMENT)
    CALLD IT THE CHAIN OF JEALOUSY NOW LOS BEGAN TO SPEAK   .   307 FOUR ZOAS 5           95
    WITHIN HER HEART [VALAN] VALA BEGAN TO REANIMATE   .  .     309 FOUR ZOAS 5    *     179
        IN BURSTING SOBS
    SO [SAYING] HE BEGAN TO [FORM] ?DIG OF GOLD SILVER          317 FOUR ZOAS 6    *     229
        & [BRASS] IRON
    AND THE SCIENCES WERE FIXD & THE VORTEXES BEGAN TO OPERATE  317 FOUR ZOAS 6          234
    WEAK & WEAKER THEIR EXPANSIVE ORBS BEGAN SHRINKING   .  .   318 FOUR ZOAS 6          257
    [SO SAYING] AND ORC HE BEGAN TO ORGANIZE A SERPENT BODY     324 FOUR ZOAS 7          152
    BEGAN TO BLOSSOM IN FIERCE PAIN SHOOTING ITS WRITHING BUDS  325 FOUR ZOAS 7          213
    THAT THIS DIRE STATE COMMENCES I BEGAN THE DREADFUL STATE   330 FOUR ZOAS 7          404
    SO ENITHARMON SPOKE & LOS HIS HANDS DIVINE INSPIRED BEGAN   331 FOUR ZOAS 7    *     456
    THE LIMIT OF CONTRACTION NOW WAS FIXD & MAN BEGAN   . .     341 FOUR ZOAS 8           16
    MISPLACING EVERY CENTER HUNGRY DESIRE & LUST BEGAN   .  .   345 FOUR ZOAS 8          178
    LOS WIPD THE SWEAT FROM HIS RED BROW & THUS BEGAN   . .     350 FOUR ZOAS 8          349
    FORGETFUL OF HIS OWN LAWS PITYING HE BEGAN TO EMBRACE   .   352 FOUR ZOAS 8          420
    THE ASHES OF MYSTERY BEGAN TO ANIMATE THEY CALLD IT DEISM   357 FOUR ZOAS 8          618
    AND NATURAL RELIGION AS OF OLD SO NOW ANEW BEGAN  . .       357 FOUR ZOAS 8          619
    OF ORC BEGAN TO CONSUME IN FIERCE RAVING FIRE HIS FIERCE    358 FOUR ZOAS 9           34
        FLAMES
    [BEGAN TO DRAW NEAR TO THE EARTH] . . . . . . .            359 FOUR ZOAS 9           83
    BEGAN TO ENTER THE HOLY CITY ENTRING THE DISMAL CLOUDS  .   359 FOUR ZOAS 9           84
    . . . THEY SIEZE THE OPRESSOR HOWLINGS BEGAN   . . . . .    363 FOUR ZOAS 9          250
    THEN HE BEGAN TO SOW THE SEED HE GIRDED ROUND HIS LOINS     365 FOUR ZOAS 9          321
    AND WENT FORTH & BEGAN TO REAP & ALL HIS JOYFUL SONS   .    372 FOUR ZOAS 9          583
    AND WHEN MORNING BEGAN TO DAWN UPON THE DISTANT HILLS   .   372 FOUR ZOAS 9          590
    WITH NEW WINE THAT THEY BEGAN TO TORMENT ONE ANOTHER . . .  378 FOUR ZOAS 9          787
    THAT HE DID NOT KNOW HOW THE QUARREL BEGAN   . . . . .     437A BLAKES MEMORAN   PROSE
    WHERE JERUSALEM'S FOUNDATIONS BEGAN WHERE THEY WERE LAID    485 MILTON 6             15
        IN RUINS
    NOW ALBION'S SLEEPING HUMANITY BEGAN TO TURN UPON HIS COUCH 502 MILTON 20            25
    OF EDEN HEARD THE LAMENTATION AND PROVIDENCE BEGAN   . . .  504 MILTON 21            24
    SINCE MEN BEGAN TO BE WOVE INTO NATIONS BY RAHAB & TIRZAH   510 MILTON 25            29
    VOLUPTUOUSNESS AND FOLLY BEGAN TO BE ACCOUNTED BEAUTIFUL    568B DESC CAT 3       PROSE
    WHICH BEGAN TO TURN ALLEGORIC AND MENTAL SIGNIFICATION  .  578A DESC CAT 5       PROSE
    & IN WHOSE SLEEP OR CHAOS CREATION BEGAN [HIS EMANATION    609C V LAST JUDG/N    PROSE
        OR WIFE IS]
    THAT WHENEVER ANY SPECTRE BEGAN TO DEVOUR THE DEAD   . . .  630 JERUSALEM 11          6
    ALBION'S CIRCUMFERENCE WAS CLOSD HIS CENTER BEGAN DARKNING  642 JERUSALEM 19         36
    FOR ATONEMENT ALBION BEGAN TO ERECT TWELVE ALTARS   . . .   653 JERUSALEM 28         21
    BEGAN TO RAGE THUNDERING LOUD THE STORMS BEGAN TO ROAR      676 JERUSALEM 46         21
    TO CATCH THE SOULS OF THE DEAD BEGAN TO VEGETATE & PETRIFY  691 JERUSALEM 59          3
    TURNING ANEW BEGAN HIS LABOURS THO IN TERRIBLE PAINS   .    696 JERUSALEM 62         42
    THE HUMAN FORM BEGAN TO BE ALTERD BY THE DAUGHTERS          703 JERUSALEM 66         46
        OF ALBION
    BEGAN HER DOLOROUS TASK OF LOVE IN THE WINE-PRESS OF LUVAH  726 JERUSALEM 82         75
    BEGAN TO GIVE THEIR SOULS AWAY IN THE (FURNACES)            727 JERUSALEM 82         79
        OF AFFLICTION
    WE BEGAN OUR FOUNDATIONS LOVELY LAMBETH O LOVELY HILLS      729 JERUSALEM 84          4
    DESARTS LOS FIRST BROKE SILENCE & BEGAN TO UTTER HIS LOVE   732 JERUSALEM 87          2
    TO THY OWN PURPOSES FOR WHEN SHE BEGAN TO WEAVE   . . . .   733 JERUSALEM 88         27
    WITH LOS'S THUNDEROUS WORDS BEGAN TO BUILD TREMBLING        737 JERUSALEM 90         59
        ROCKING STONES
```

192

BEGAN   (CONTINUED)
    BEFORE HIS WRATH BEGAN TO BURN . . . . 752 EV GOSPEL(D)/N   56
    ALL AWAY BEGAN TO ROLL . . . . 754 EV GOSPEL(E)/N   14
    THE AMERICAN WAR BEGAN ALL ITS DARK HORRORS PASSED BEFORE 799 TO FLAXMAN/L   9
       MY FACE
    WHO COMPLACENT BEGAN . . . . 805 TO BUTTS/L   52
    EXPERIENCED IT BEGAN BY A GNAWING PAIN IN THE STOMACH . . 872B LETTER 75   PROSE
    BEGAN PAIN OF MIND & THAT NOT A SMALL ONE IT IS ABOUT . 874B LETTER 79   PROSE
BEGAT
    AN IRON AGE & BEGAT ON MNEMOSYNE OR MEMORY . . . . . 605C V LAST JUDG/N   PROSE
BEGD
    & BEGD TO HAVE IT SUNG OVER AGAIN & AGAIN . . . . . 57D ISLAND MOON 9   PROSE
    AND SO FEELING HE BEGD HIM TO TURN AGAIN . . . . . . 187 WHEN KLOPSTK/N *   27
BEGETS
    IN HEAVEN LOVE BEGETS LOVE BUT FEAR IS THE PARENT 725 JERUSALEM 81   15
       OF EARTHLY LOVE
BEGETTING
    MAN BEGETTING HIS LIKENESS . . . . 232 URIZEN 19   15
    UTTERING MY LAMENTATIONS & BEGETTING LITTLE MONSTERS . . 296 FOUR ZOAS 3   165
BEGGAR
    TO BE A HYPOCRITE & STAND IN SHAPE OF A BLIND BEGGAR . 103 TIRIEL 4   9
    HE FEEDS THE BEGGAR & THE POOR . . . . 425 MENTAL TRAVLER   38
    A BEGGAR AT ANOTHER'S DOOR . . . . 426 MENTAL TRAVLER   52
BEGGARS
    THE PRINCE'S ROBES & BEGGAR'S RAGS . . . . 432 AUGURIES   51
    THE BEGGAR'S RAGS FLUTTERING IN AIR . . . . 432 AUGURIES   75
BEGGARS
    SHALL BE BEGGARS AT LOVE'S GATE . . . . 755 EV GOSPEL(E)/N   56
BEGGED
    I KNOW I BEGGED OF YOU TO GIVE ME YOUR IDEAS . . . . . 792A LETTER 4   PROSE
BEGGERS
    THE BEGGER'S DOG & WIDOW'S CAT . . . . 432 AUGURIES   43
BEGGING
    I SEE LONDON BLIND & AGE-BENT BEGGING THRO THE STREETS . 729 JERUSALEM 84   11
    BEGGING THE FAVOR OF A FEW LINES TO INFORM HIM HOW YOU . 829C LETTER 30   PROSE
    FOR YOUR CORRECTION OR CONDEMNATION BEGGING YOU TO SUPPLY 860B LETTER 56   PROSE
    THE BEGINNING OF POESY THE BLIND BEGGING BARD STUDY . SUPP ILLUS GRAY   *TITLE
BEGIN
    THEN LET THE CLARION OF WAR BEGIN . . . . 31 EDW THIRD/PS 5   50
    I'LL BEGIN AGAIN SAID THE CYNIC . . . . 46C ISLAND MOON 3   PROSE
    BEGIN WITH THARMAS PARENT POWER DARKNING IN THE WEST . 264 FOUR ZOAS 1   24
    WONDRING SHE SAW HER WOOF BEGIN TO ANIMATE & NOT . . . 266 FOUR ZOAS 1   83
    BEGIN THEIR WORK & MANY A NET IS NETTED MANY A NET . . . 284 FOUR ZOAS 2   158
    MY LOINS BEGIN TO BREAK FORTH INTO VEINY PIPES & WRITHE 300 FOUR ZOAS 4   94
    TIS UPWARD ALL WHICH WAY SOEVER I MY COURSE BEGIN . . . 317 FOUR ZOAS 6   203
    TO THE DARK VALLEY WHENCE HE CAME TO BEGIN HIS LABOURS ANEW 355 FOUR ZOAS 8 * 575
    WHERE THEIR VORTEXES BEGIN TO OPERATE THERE STANDS . . . 359 FOUR ZOAS 9 * 92
    THE HUMAN HARVEST TO BEGIN TOWARDS THE SOUTH FIRST SPRANG 366 FOUR ZOAS 9   338
    [WHEN MY LOVE DID FIRST BEGIN] . . . . 415 MY SPECTRE/N   19
    ALL THINGS BEGIN & END IN ALBION'S ANCIENT DRUID ROCKY 486 MILTON 6   25
       SHORE
    THOU HEAREST THE NIGHTINGALE BEGIN THE SONG OF SPRING . . 520 MILTON 31   28
    THEN LOUD FROM THEIR GREEN COVERT ALL THE BIRDS BEGIN THEIR 520 MILTON 31   39
       SONG
    SHE SHALL RELENT IN FEAR OF DEATH SHE SHALL BEGIN TO GIVE 522 MILTON 33   17
    WHEN MEN WILL DRAW OUTLINES BEGIN YOU TO JAW THEM . . . 549 ALL PICTURES/N   7
    IF YOU PLAY A GAME OF CHANCE KNOW BEFORE YOU BEGIN . . . 551 IF YOU PLAY/N   1
    MARC ANTONIO & ALBERT DURER YE MUST BEGIN BEFORE . . . . 593C PUB ADDRESS/N   PROSE
    SABRINA & IGNOGE BEGIN TO SHARPEN THEIR BEAMY SPEARS . . 631 JERUSALEM 11   19
    ALL THINGS BEGIN & END IN ALBION'S ANCIENT DRUID ROCKY 649B JERUSALEM 27   PROSE
       SHORE
    ALL THINGS BEGIN & END IN ALBION'S ANCIENT DRUID ROCKY 658 JERUSALEM 32   15
       SHORE
    FOR MORAL VIRTUES ALL BEGIN . . . . 759 EV GOSPEL (2)   34
    AND DEATH & HELL WHICH NOW BEGIN . . . . 759 EV GOSPEL (2)   42
    I BEGIN TO EMERGE FROM A DEEP PIT OF MELANCHOLY . . . . 798A LETTER 10   PROSE
    WE MEAN TO BEGIN PRINTING AGAIN TO-MORROW . . . . . . 807A LETTER 17   PROSE
    I DID NOT BEGIN TO LEARN LANGUAGES EARLY IN LIFE AS I FIND 821D LETTER 25   PROSE
       IT
    I BEGIN WITH THE LATTER END OF YOUR LETTER & GRIEVE MORE 837C LETTER 36   PROSE
       FOR
    ALL THAT HAS BEEN PRINTED AS LOST AND BEGIN ANEW UNLESS 858B LETTER 55   PROSE
    FIRST BEFORE I BEGIN ENGRAVING THEM AS IT WILL ENABLE ME 866C LETTER 65   PROSE
    I BEGIN TO AGAIN FEEL RETURNING STRENGTH ON THESE ACCOUNTS 874D LETTER 80   PROSE
BEGINING
    BEGINING AT JERUSALEM'S INNER COURT LAMBETH RUIND AND GIVEN 511 MILTON 25   48
BEGINNER
    ENGRAVED WHEN I WAS A BEGINNER AT BASIRE'S . . . . . . SUPP INSC JOSEPH   *TITLE
BEGINNEST
    IN SCALES THAT SHINE WITH GOLD & RUBIES THOU BEGINNEST 323 FOUR ZOAS 7   136
       TO WEAKEN
BEGINNETH
    [AND THUS BEGINNETH THE BOOK OF VALA WHICH WHOSOEVER READS] 264 FOUR ZOAS 1   3
    WHO NOW BEGINNETH TO PUT OFF THE DARK SATANIC BODY . . . 346 FOUR ZOAS 8   196
BEGINNING   SEE BEGINING
    BEGINNING OF THE [BOOK] SEVENTH NIGHT . . . . 333A FOUR ZOAS 7B   *TITLE
    STANDS NOW IN THE BEGINNING OF NIGHT THE SEVENTH . . . 336B FOUR ZOAS 7B   *PROSE
    BEGINNING AT THE TREE OF MYSTERY CIRCLING ITS ROOT . . . 345 FOUR ZOAS 8   173
    AND BEGINNING WITH THE SPOTS OF LIGHT ON EACH OBJECT . 440B MEMORANDUM/N 3   PROSE
    DOES NOT KNOW THE BEGINNING NEVER CAN KNOW THE END OF ART 449C ANNO REYNOLDS   MARG
    BEGINNING AT THE FEET OF URIZEN AND ON THE BONES . . . . 500 MILTON 19   12
    AS IT WAS IN THE BEGINNING . . . . 578A DESC CAT 5   PROSE

```
                                                            PAGE      TITLE          LINE
BEGINNING   (CONTINUED)
        SING SONG FROM BEGINNING TO END                . . 600D PUB ADDRESS/N    PROSE
        THEY ARE BEGINNING TO FORM HEAVENS & HELLS IN IMMENSE . . 680 JERUSALEM 49   61
        . . . WHICH WAS TOLD US IN THE BEGINNING  . . . . . . 741 JERUSALEM 93    26
        IT APPEARS TO ME AS IF THE LAST PARAGRAPH BEGINNING WITH 783D ANNO WW POEMS * MARG
        AT THE BEGINNING OF THE BALLADS HAS SET MY BRAINS TO WORK 860B LETTER 56   PROSE
        FROM BEGINNING TO END ANY REMARKS THAT YOU MAY BE PLEASED 866C LETTER 65   PROSE
          TO
        THE BEGINNING OF POESY THE BLIND BEGGING BARD STUDY  . . SUPP ILLUS GRAY  *TITLE
BEGINNINGS
        KNOW THE FIRST [LINES] BEGINNINGS OF ART I HOPE THIS PRINT 593C PUB ADDRESS/N PROSE
BEGINS
        TILL TIRD OF CHAT THE GAME BEGINS . . . . . . . .  16 BLIND-MANS/PS    11
        METHINKS THE SHOUT BEGINS THE BATTLE BURNS . . . .  26 EDW THIRD/PS 3  228
        AND THEN THE KNAVE BEGINS TO SNARL . . . . . . . . 183 MOTTO SONGS/N    5
        AS A BLIGHT CUTS THE TENDER CORN WHEN IT BEGINS TO APPEAR 201 AMERICA 14    6
        AND WEARINESS BEGINS ON ALL MY LIMBS THEN SLEEP REVIVES 317 FOUR ZOAS 6   205
        THIS NIGHT BEGINS AT LINE...THE FOLLOWING COMES IN AT THE 333A FOUR ZOAS 7B *TITLE
          END
        . . . TILL WAR BEGINS . . . . . . . . . . . . . 344 FOUR ZOAS 8    129
        LO THE LITTLE MOSS BEGINS TO SPRING & THE TENDER WEED . 373 FOUR ZOAS 9   610
        & ITS LAST NOW HE BEGINS TO DEGRADE [&] TO DENY [DESTROY] 458B ANNO REYNOLDS * MARG
          & TO MOCK
        AND THEN & THEN ALONE BEGINS THE HAPPY FEMALE JOY  . 522 MILTON 33    19
        YOUR ENEMY HE ALWAYS BEGINS WITH BEING YOUR FRIEND . . . 592C PUB ADDRESS/N PROSE
        THEN THE LAST JUDGMENT BEGINS & ITS VISION . . . . . . 604C V LAST JUDG/N PROSE
        BENEATH THE DRAGON'S CAVERN A SKELETON BEGINS TO ANIMATE 609C V LAST JUDG/N PROSE
        MORTALITY BEGINS TO ROLL THE BILLOWS OF ETERNAL DEATH . 666 JERUSALEM 39    8
        AND HERE BEGINS THE SYSTEM OF MORAL VIRTUE NAMED RAHAB . 666 JERUSALEM 39   10
        AND WHERE LUTHER ENDS ADAM BEGINS AGAIN IN ETERNAL CIRCLE 716 JERUSALEM 75   24
        HEAVY BOXES & PORTFOLIOS FULL OF PRINTS AND NOW BEGINS . 802B LETTER 14    PROSE
        & HE BEGINS TO THINK I HAVE SOME GENIUS . . . . . . 825C LETTER 27    PROSE
        GOOD WOMAN AGAIN BEGINS TO RESUME HER HEALTH & STRENGTH 833D LETTER 33    PROSE
        THEN BEGINS SONGS OF EXPERIENCE . . . . . . . . . SUPP LETTER 66A  *PROSE
BEGONE    SEE WOE-BEGONE
        "BEGONE & TROUBLE ME NO MORE"  . . . . . . . . . SUPP LEGEND/N101    *
BEGOT
        BEGOT A GIANT RACE . . . . . . . . . . . . . 256 BOOK OF LOS 3   26
        HIS MOTHER ON HIS FATHER HIM BEGOT  . . . . . . . 539 OF HS BIRTH/N    2
BEGOTTEN    SEE FIRST BEGOTTEN,SELF-BEGOTTEN
        FLAMD OUT FIRST BEGOTTEN LAST BORN . . . . . . . 234 URIZEN 23    18
        THAT WAS BEGOTTEN IN DIRE WOE  . . . . . . . . . 424 MENTAL TRAVLER   6
        BRING YOUR OFFERINGS YOUR FIRST BEGOTTEN PAMPERD WITH MILK 706 JERUSALEM 68   30
          & BLOOD
BEGS
        THE PAINTER BEGS PUBLIC PROTECTION & ALL WILL BE WELL . 598B PUB ADDRESS/N PROSE
BEGUILD
        AND THEY TOLD HOW THEY WERE BEGUILD . . . . . . . 162 LAID ME DOWN/N    7
        WITLESS WOE WAS NEER BEGUILD . . . . . . . . . 182 THE ANGEL/N      4
        WITLESS WOE WAS NEER BEGUILD . . . . . . . . . 213 THE ANGEL/SE     4
        BY VARIOUS ARTS OF LOVE BEGUILD . . . . . . . . 426 MENTAL TRAVLER  80
        AND ALL MY FRIENDS BE WITH DOUBTS BEGUILD . . . . . 818 HAPPINESS/L     48
BEGUILE
        WILL A MAN BEGUILE . . . . . . . . . . . . . 178 THE FAIRY/N      4
        THAT DID HEAVEN ITSELF BEGUILE . . . . . . . . 422 BENEATH/N       19
        THAT DID HEAVEN ITSELF BEGUILE . . . . . . . . 424 THE GOLDEN NET   18
        DOES HIM TO INFANCY BEGUILE . . . . . . . . . 426 MENTAL TRAVLER   72
BEGUILES
        ALL THE LIVELONG NIGHT BEGUILES . . . . . . . . 120 CRADLE SONG/SI   12
        ALL THE DOVELIKE MOANS BEGUILES . . . . . . . . 120 CRADLE SONG/SI   16
        HEAVEN & EARTH TO PEACE BEGUILES . . . . . . . . 120 CRADLE SONG/SI   32
        [ SUCH AS BURNING YOUTH BEGUILES] . . . . . . . . 165 CRADLE SONG/N    21
        HEAVEN & EARTH OF PEACE BEGUILES . . . . . . . . 165 CRADLE SONG/N    27
BEGUN
        THE DANCE WAS BROKE THE CIRCLE JUST BEGUN  . . . . . 43C WOE CRIED MUSE PROSE
        WHEN OLD CORRUPTION FIRST BEGUN  . . . . . . . .  50 WHEN CORRUP/IM    1
        AS A NEW HEAVEN IS BEGUN AND IT IS NOW THIRTY-THREE YEARS 149A MARRIAGE HH 3 PROSE
        BEGUN ALREADY IN ETERNITY COME THEN O LAMB OF GOD  . 347 FOUR ZOAS 8   244
        WHEN HIS MERIDIAN GLORIES WERE BEGUN . . . . . . 414 TO MRS FLAXMAN    4
        NOT EVEN BEGUN HOW CAN THEY THEN BE FINISHD THE MAN WHO 449C ANNO REYNOLDS MARG
        BEGUN BY THE WORDS "A FACILITY IN COMPOSING" I CANNOT TELL 453C ANNO REYNOLDS MARG
        THE SIN WAS BEGUN IN ETERNITY AND WILL NOT REST TO ETERNITY 494 MILTON 13   10
        AND IF EVERY THING GOES ON AS IT HAS BEGUN  . . . . 578A DESC CAT 5   PROSE
        YOU ATTEMPT TO FINISH OR IMPROVE & WHEN YOU HAVE BEGUN . 593D PUB ADDRESS/N PROSE
        I HAVE BEGUN TO WORK FELPHAM IS A SWEET PLACE FOR STUDY 802A LETTER 14    PROSE
        TO THE PLOWMAN "FATHER THE GATE IS OPEN" I HAVE BEGUN TO 803C LETTER 15    PROSE
          WORK
        REMEMBERD TO YOU HAD BEGUN A LETTER TO YOU A WEEK AGO  . 842D LETTER 42  *PROSE
        BEGUN TO PRINT AN ACCOUNT OF MY VARIOUS INVENTIONS IN ART 865D LETTER 63   PROSE
        BEGUN...& PUBLISHD MARCH...BY THE AUTHOR & J LINNELL  . SUPP LETTER 67F *PROSE
BEHALF
        & I DOUBT NOT THAT ALL YOUR KIND WISHES IN MY BEHALF  . 811D LETTER 22   PROSE
BEHAVE
        WHICH THE WORLD SHALL HAVE IF THEY BEHAVE WELL   . . . 158D MARRIAGE HH 22 PROSE
BEHAVES
        TO HELL TILL HE BEHAVES BETTER . . . . . . . . .  74B ANNO LAVATER   MARG
BEHEADED
        THE FIRE OF LONDON [CH(CHARLES) I BEHEADED]  . . . . 209A SUBJCTS HIST/N TITLE
BEHELD
        BENEATH OUR OAKS HAST SLEPT WHILE WE BEHELD  . . . . .   1 TO SUMMER/PS     5
        TILL I THE PRINCE OF LOVE BEHELD  . . . . . . . .   6 HOW SWEET/PS     3
        OR HAVE THY SOFT PITEOUS EYES BEHELD . . . . . . .  15 IMIT SPEN/PS    51
```

```
                                                              PAGE      TITLE        LINE
BEHELD    (CONTINUED)
  AND NOW WILL'S EYES BEHELD THE PLAY  . . . . . . .     16  BLIND-MANS/PS    27
  TIS NOW SEVEN YEARS SINCE IN MY PALACE I BEHELD THY FACE  104 TIRIEL 4       15
  BY DEGREES WE BEHELD THE INFINITE ABYSS FIERY AS THE SMOKE 156A MARRIAGE HH 17 PROSE
  WHEN HE HAD SO SPOKEN I BEHELD THE ANGEL   . . . . . .  158D MARRIAGE HH 22  PROSE
  AND MY FOE BEHELD IT SHINE   . . . . . . . . . . .    165  CHRISTN FORB/N    12
  [I BEHELD THE [PRIEST] PRIESTS BY NIGHT]   . . . . . .  167 INFANT SORW/N  *  31
  [I BEHELD THE [PRIEST] PRIESTS BY DAY]   . . . . . . .  167 INFANT SORW/N  *  33
  OFT [THE PRIEST BEHELD] MY FATHER SAW US SIGH   . . .   169  MIRTLE SHADE/N    13
  [FAYETTE BEHELD THE QUEEN TO SMILE]   . . . . . . .    185  LET BROTHELS/N    31
  FAYETTE BEHELD THE KING & QUEEN   . . . . . . . .      185  LET BROTHELS/N    35
  FAYETTE BEHELD THE KING & QUEEN   . . . . . . . .      186  LET BROTHELS/N    60
  AND MY FOE BEHELD IT SHINE   . . . . . . . . . . .    218  POISON TREE/SE    11
  BUT ETERNALS BEHELD HIS VAST FORESTS   . . . . . . .   223  URIZEN 3       23
  HIS EYES BEHELD THE DEEP  . . . . . . . . . . . .     228  URIZEN 11         16
  HIS FIRES BEHELD AND SICKENING   . . . . . . . . .     229  URIZEN 13         22
  BEHELD THE DARK VISIONS OF LOS   . . . . . . . . .     231  URIZEN 15         12
  NO MORE LOS BEHELD ETERNITY  . . . . . . . . . . .    233  URIZEN 20         2
  BEHELD THEIR BRETHREN SHRINK TOGETHER   . . . . . .    236  URIZEN 28         12
  BUT TERRIBLE ORC WHEN HE BEHELD THE MORNING IN THE EAST 244 EUROPE 14        37
  MOSES BEHELD UPON MOUNT SINAI FORMS OF DARK DELUSION   . 245 SONG OF LOS 3   17
  HE BEHELD HIMSELF COMPASSED ROUND   . . . . . . . .    252  AHANIA 3       69
  IN TREMBLING AND HORROR THEY BEHELD HIM   . . . . . .  257  BOOK OF LOS 3    45
  FLOWD AROUND THE IMMENSE LOS BEHELD   . . . . . . .    259  BOOK OF LOS 5    12
  TO ENION & HIS BODY FELL THARMAS BEHELD HIM FALL   . .  279  FOUR ZOAS 1      531
  THE DAUGHTERS OF BEULAH BEHELD THE EMANATION THEY PITIFD 279 FOUR ZOAS 1     560
  RISING UPON HIS COUCH OF DEATH ALBION BEHELD HIS SONS  . 280 FOUR ZOAS 2     1
  FIRST HE BEHELD THE BODY OF MAN PALE COLD THE HORRORS OF 280 FOUR ZOAS 2    11
    DEATH
  PALE HE BEHELD FUTURITY PALE HE BEHELD THE ABYSS   . .  280  FOUR ZOAS 2      15
  LUVAH & VALA TREMBLING & SHRINKING BEHELD THE GREAT WORK 280 FOUR ZOAS 2     22
    MASTER
  STERN URIZEN BEHELD URGD BY NECESSITY TO KEEP  . . . .  282  FOUR ZOAS 2      74
  TO MEASURE OUT THE COURSE OF HEAVEN STERN URIZEN BEHELD 283 FOUR ZOAS 2     131
  IN HER BRIGHT SKIRTS ASTONISHD & CONFOUNDED HE BEHELD  . 285 FOUR ZOAS 2     203
  THE KING OF LIGHT BEHELD HER MOURNING AMONG THE BRICK KILNS 285 FOUR ZOAS 2  215
    COMPELLD
  ON CLOUDS THE SONS OF URIZEN BEHELD  . . . . . . .     287  FOUR ZOAS 2      258
  THERE SHE BEHELD THE [TERRIBLE] SPECTROUS FORM OF ENION 291 FOUR ZOAS 2     423
    IN THE VOID
  THARMAS BEHELD THEM HIS BOWELS YEARND OVER THEM   . .   297  FOUR ZOAS 4      6
  I HOWLD IN SORROW I BEHELD THEE ROTTING UPON THE ROCKS  . 300 FOUR ZOAS 4    107
  TERRIFIED LOS BEHELD THE RUINS OF URIZEN BENEATH   . .  301  FOUR ZOAS 4      161
  ENSLAVD HUMANITY PUT ON HE BECAME WHAT HE BEHELD   . .  302  FOUR ZOAS 4      203
  HIDING CAREFULLY FROM THE WIND HIS EYES BEHELD THE DEEP 303 FOUR ZOAS 4     230
  AND LOS BEHELD THE HAND OF GOD OVER HIS FURNACES   . .  304  FOUR ZOAS 4      278
  ENSLAVD HUMANITY PUT ON HE BECAME WHAT HE BEHELD   . .  305  FOUR ZOAS 4      286
  THEIR SOLEMN HABITATION LOS BEHELD THE RUDDY BOY   . .  307  FOUR ZOAS 5      80
  EMBRACING HIS BRIGHT MOTHER & BEHELD MALIGNANT FIRES  . 307 FOUR ZOAS 5     81
  ENITHARMON BEHELD THE BLOODY CHAIN OF NIGHTS & DAYS   . 307 FOUR ZOAS 5     92
  AND WHEN THE GATE WAS OPEN SHE BEHELD THAT [DISMAL] DREARY 309 FOUR ZOAS 5 * 180
    DEEP
  SILENT IN RIDGES HE BEHELD THEM STAND ROUND URIZEN   .  313  FOUR ZOAS 6      50
  FOR URIZEN BEHELD THE TERRORS OF THE ABYSS WANDRING AMONG 314 FOUR ZOAS 6 *  87
  [FOR URIZEN BEHELD THE TERRORS OF THE ABYSS WANDRING AMONG] 314 FOUR ZOAS 6 * 102
  ON RACKS & WHEELS HE BEHELD WOMEN MARCHING OER BURNING  314 FOUR ZOAS 6     106
    WASTES
  THEN HE BEHELD THE FORMS OF TYGERS & OF LIONS DISHUMANIZD 314 FOUR ZOAS 6    116
    MEN
  TILL HE BEHELD THE WORLD OF LOS FROM THE PEAKED ROCK OF 319 FOUR ZOAS 6     290
    URTHONA
  ASTONISHD FILLD WITH TEARS THE SPIRIT OF ENITHARMON BEHELD 327 FOUR ZOAS 7   311
  WONDERING BEHELD THE CENTER OPEND BY DIVING MERCY INSPIRD 329 FOUR ZOAS 7    374
  FILLED WITH DOUBTS IN SELF ACCUSATION [GATHERD] BEHELD  329 FOUR ZOAS 7   *  385
    THE FRUIT
  URTHONA'S SPECTRE TERRIFIED BEHELD THE SPECTRES OF THE DEAD 330 FOUR ZOAS 7  401
  FOR HE BEHELD NEW FEMALE FORMS BORN FORTH UPON THE AIR  . 332 FOUR ZOAS 7    487
  HIS WHOLE SOUL LOVED HIM HE BEHELD HIM AN INFANT   . .  332  FOUR ZOAS 7      498
  THEN [FIRST] LOS [BEHELD] SAID . . .   . . . . . .    341  FOUR ZOAS 8    *  20
  WAS LUVAH BUT HE NOW BEHELD A NEW LUVAH OR ONE   . . .  342  FOUR ZOAS 8    *  63
  TERRIFIED & ASTONISHD URIZEN BEHELD THE BATTLE TAKE A FORM 343 FOUR ZOAS 8   102
  SHE WENT TO URIZEN IN PRIDE THE PRINCE OF LIGHT BEHELD  . . 351 FOUR ZOAS 8  412
  ABOVE UPON ITS VOLUMES IS BEHELD [AS] A THRONE & [AS ]  364 FOUR ZOAS 9     279
    A PAVEMENT
  BEHELD THE VISION OF GOD & HE AROSE UP FROM THE ROCK   . . 364 FOUR ZOAS 9   286
  [THE FALLEN MAN WONDRING BEHELD] HE LAID HIS [HAND] ON  365 FOUR ZOAS 9   *  311
    THE PLOW
  . . . BEHELD THESE VISIONS  . . . . . . . . . . .     372  FOUR ZOAS 9      557
  THARMAS WENT DOWN TO THE WINE PRESSES & BEHELD THE SONS 378 FOUR ZOAS 9     785
    & DAUGHTERS
  THARMAS BEHELD FROM HIS HIGH ROCKS &C   . . . . . .    381  FOUR ZOAS AD 1 *  20
  THE EYES BEHELD THE ABYSS LEST BONES OF SOLIDNESS FREEZE 482 MILTON 3       15
    OVER ALL
  GREW DEADLY PALE HE BECAME WHAT HE BEHELD FOR A RED   . . . 483 MILTON 3     29
  HIMSELF CONVINCD OF PALAMABRON'S TURPITUDE LOS BEHELD   . 488 MILTON 8      7
  BEHELD THE SIGNAL THEY IN SILENCE STOOD THO DRUNK WITH WINE 488 MILTON 8    13
  BUT WHEN LEUTHA A DAUGHTER OF BEULAH BEHELD SATAN'S    492  MILTON 11         28
    CONDEMNATION
  THEN ON THE VERGE OF BEULAH HE BEHELD HIS OWN SHADOW   . . 496 MILTON 14     36
  OF HELL BEHELD HIM IN A TRAIL OF LIGHT AS OF A COMET   . . 496 MILTON 15     19
  THEN MILTON KNEW THAT THE THREE HEAVENS OF BEULAH WERE  497 MILTON 15       51
    BEHELD
```

```
                                                              PAGE      TITLE          LINE
BEHELD    (CONTINUED)
   LOS THE VEHICULAR TERROR BEHELD HIM & DIVINE ENITHARMON      498 MILTON 17           31
   OF MILTON'S JOURNEY URIZEN BEHELD THE IMMORTAL MAN    . . .  498 MILTON 17           36
   THE MAN AND DEMON STROVE MANY PERIODS RAHAB BEHELD    . .    501 MILTON 19           27
   AND HE BEHELD THE CLOUD OF MILTON STRETCHING OVER EUROPE     504 MILTON 21           36
   WALKING IN MY COTTAGE GARDEN SUDDEN I BEHELD   . . . . .     527 MILTON 36           26
   I BEHELD MILTON WITH ASTONISHMENT & IN HIM BEHELD    . . .   528 MILTON 37           15
   THE SPECTRE OF SATAN STOOD UPON THE ROARING SEA & BEHELD     529 MILTON 38            9
   I ALSO STOOD IN SATAN'S BOSOM & BEHELD ITS DESOLATIONS  . .  529 MILTON 38           15
   AND I BEHELD THE TWENTY-FOUR CITIES OF ALBION  . . . . .     534 MILTON 42           16
   STERN URIZEN BEHELD URGD BY NECESSITY TO KEEP    . . . .     626 JERUSALEM 7         32
   AND NOT TREMBLE HOW CAN I BE BEHELD & NOT ABHORRD    . .     630 JERUSALEM 10        59
   AND THE FOUR POINTS ARE THUS BEHELD IN GREAT ETERNITY   .    632 JERUSALEM 12        54
   AND LOS BEHELD HIS SONS AND HE BEHELD HIS DAUGHTERS   . .    635 JERUSALEM 14        16
   AND LOS BEHELD THE MILD EMANATION JERUSALEM EASTWARD         635 JERUSALEM 14        31
      BENDING
   OF LOVE THOU REFUSEDST TO LET ME GO ALBION BEHELD            643 JERUSALEM 20        32
      THY BEAUTY
   AND THE MOUNT OF OLIVES WAS BEHELD OVER THE WHOLE EARTH      648 JERUSALEM 24        49
   AND HE BEHELD JERUSALEM IN WESTMINSTER & MARYBONE    . .     657 JERUSALEM 31        40
   FROM LOS ASTONISHD HE BEHELD ONLY THE PETRIFIED SURFACES     658 JERUSALEM 32         5
   I NEVER SAW THEE TILL THIS TIME NOR BEHELD LIFE ABSTRACTED   659 JERUSALEM 33        31
   AND DENS THEY LOOKED ON ONE-ANOTHER & BECAME WHAT THEY       661 JERUSALEM 34        50
      BEHELD
   OVER JORDAN ALL TERRIFIED FLED THEY BECAME WHAT THEY BEHELD  661 JERUSALEM 34        54
   ALL THAT BEHELD HIM FLED HOWLING AND GNAWED THEIR TONGUES    662 JERUSALEM 36         8
   FOR PAIN THEY BECAME WHAT THEY BEHELD IN REASONINGS REUBEN   662 JERUSALEM 36         9
      RETURNED
   THE SEVEN NATIONS FLED BEFORE HIM THEY BECAME WHAT THEY      662 JERUSALEM 36        14
      BEHELD
   HAND HYLE & COBAN FLED THEY BECAME WHAT THEY BEHELD  . . .   662 JERUSALEM 36        15
   KOTOPE & BOWEN BECAME WHAT THEY BEHELD FLEEING OVER THE      663 JERUSALEM 36        19
      EARTH
   ALSO LOS SICK & TERRIFIED BEHELD THE FURNACES OF DEATH  . .  669 JERUSALEM 42         5
   BEHELD HER WITH WONDER WITH AWFUL HANDS SHE TOOK    . . . .  678 JERUSALEM 48        30
   BEFORE I HAD EVER BEHELD WITH LOVE THE FACE OF JEHOVAH       695 JERUSALEM 61        42
      OR KNOWN
   BUT LOS BEHELD THE DIVINE VISION AMONG THE FLAMES OF THE     696 JERUSALEM 62        35
      FURNACES
   LOS BEHELD IN TERROR HE POURD HIS LOUD STORMS ON            702 JERUSALEM 66        16
      THE FURNACES
   OF WALES & SCOTLAND BEHELD THE DESCENDING WAR THE ROUTED     703 JERUSALEM 66        60
      FLYING
   FOR HELL IS OPEND TO HEAVEN THINE EYES BEHELD  . . . . .     718 STOOD AMONG/J       34
   THY GATES BEHELD SWEET ZION'S WAYS   . . . . . . . .         718 ENGLND AWAKE/J       7
   MY PILLARS REACHD FROM SEA TO SEA LONDON BEHELD ME COME      720 JERUSALEM 79        24
   THEY LOOKED UPON OUR LOVES WITH JOY THEY BEHELD OUR SECRET   720 JERUSALEM 79        43
      JOYS
   AND THOU AMERICA I ONCE BEHELD THEE BUT NOW BEHOLD NO MORE   721 JERUSALEM 79        53
   TO REACH THE HEAVENLY ARCHES LOS BEHELD UNDAUNTED FURIOUS    738 JERUSALEM 91        42
   AND LUVAH TO HIS LOOM URTHONA HE BEHELD MIGHTY LABOURING AT  742 JERUSALEM 95        17
   WHEN THEY THE GOSPEL LIGHT BEHELD  . . . . . . . . .         758 EV GOSPEL (2)       20
BEHEMOTH
   THE SPIRITUAL FORM OF PITT GUIDING BEHEMOTH HE IS    . . .  565A DESC CAT 2        TITLE
   AND BEHEMOTH THE WAR BY SEA ENORMOUS & THE WAR  . . .       738 JERUSALEM 91        40
BEHEST
   BUT IF THOU DAREST OBSTINATE REFUSE MY STERN BEHEST   . . .  360 FOUR ZOAS 9        144
BEHIND
   I LOOK BEHIND THERE IS NO RETURNING DEATH FOLLOWS AFTER ME  35D COUCH DEATH/PS    PROSE
   THEN NAKED & WHITE ALL THEIR BAGS LEFT BEHIND  . . . . .    118 CHIMNEY SWP/SI      17
   BEHIND RANK TO THE SOUL SHAKING DRUM AND SHRILL FIFE . . .  147 FRENCH REVOLTN     292
   THEY LOOK BEHIND AT EVERY STEP & BELIEVE IT IS A DREAM  .   198 AMERICA 6          12
   A COLD SHADOW FOLLOWD BEHIND HIM . . . . . . . . .          235 URIZEN 25           9
   FOLLOWD BEHIND HIM AS THE WEB OF A SPIDER DUSKY & COLD  .   318 FOUR ZOAS 6        244
   . . . SHE HEARD A VOICE BEHIND HER CALLING HER]  . . .      356 FOUR ZOAS 8        591
   BEHIND HER VEIL WITHDRAWS SO ENION TURND HER MODEST HEAD    371 FOUR ZOAS 9        549
   THEY LOOK BEHIND AT EVERY STEP & BELIEVE IT IS A DREAM  .   375 FOUR ZOAS 9        676
   BEHIND THE SEAT OF THE ETERNAL MAN & TOOK HIS WAY   . .     376 FOUR ZOAS 9        712
   [MY SPECTRE FOLLOWS THEE BEHIND]   . . . . . . . .          415 MY SPECTRE/N       12
   MY SPECTRE FOLLOWS THEE BEHIND . . . . . . . . .            415 MY SPECTRE/N       26
   BEHIND THE SEAT & THRONE OF CHRIST APPEARS ]APPEAR]  .     444B LAST JUDGMNT/L    PROSE
   HAS PASSD THAT VORTEX HE PERCIEVES IT ROLL BACKWARD BEHIND  497 MILTON 15          23
   GATES OPEN BEHIND SATAN'S SEAT TO THE CITY OF GOLGONOOZA    502 MILTON 20          39
   AND LOS BEHIND ME STOOD A TERRIBLE FLAMING SUN JUST CLOSE   505 MILTON 22           6
   BEHIND MY BACK I TURNED ROUND IN TERROR AND BEHOLD  . .     505 MILTON 22           7
   HE HAS NOT LEFT ONE ENEMY BEHIND . . . . . . . . .          546 ANOTHER/N 2         2
   MORTIMER AND GLOUCESTER LIE SPELL BOUND BEHIND THEIR KING  577B DESC CAT 4        PROSE
   SIMILAR TO STONE HENGE THE SUN SETS BEHIND THE MOUNTAINS   580D DESC CAT 5        PROSE
   THE FEMALES BEHIND THEM REPRESENT  . . . . . . . .         608D V LAST JUDG/N     PROSE
   ALBION'S DARK ROCKS SETTING BEHIND THE GARDENS OF           653 JERUSALEM 29         2
      KENSINGTON
   JEHOVAH IS BEFORE BEHIND ABOVE BENEATH AROUND  . . . . .    680 JERUSALEM 49        53
   FORGETTING THAT FALSHOOD IS PROPHETIC SHE HID HER HAND      725 JERUSALEM 82    *   20
      BEHIND HER
   UPON HER BACK BEHIND HER LOINS & THUS UTTERD HER DECEIT     725 JERUSALEM 82        21
   BEHIND THE SEA OF TIME & SPACE ROARS & FOLLOWS SWIFTLY  . 812A LETTER 22         PROSE
   AND MY BROTHER ROBERT JUST BEHIND  . . . . . . . .          817 HAPPINESS/L        14
   POURING DISCONSOLATE FROM BEHIND . . . . . . . . .          817 HAPPINESS/L        22
BEHMEN
   MAY FROM THE WRITINGS OF PARACELSUS OR JACOB BEHMEN   . .  158A MARRIAGE HH 21    PROSE
   PARACELSUS & BEHMEN APPEARD TO ME. . . . . . . . . . .      799 TO FLAXMAN/L        7
```

		PAGE	TITLE	LINE

BEHN

IT WAS BYSSHE'S ART OF POETRY SHE OPEND THE FOLLOWING...BEHN   440D MEMORANDUM/N 5   PROSE

BEHOLD

O ELENOR [I AM] BEHOLD THY HUSBAND'S HEAD . . . . .   5 FAIR ELENOR/PS   61
ACCURSED RACE OF TIRIEL BEHOLD YOUR [AGED] FATHER . . .   99 TIRIEL 1   7
AND WONDERING BEHOLD . . . .   114 LIT GRL FND/SI   35
. . . ALL CHILDREN NEW-BORN FIRST BEHOLD THEM TEARS ARE FLED   136 FRENCH REVOLTN   56
. . . I AWOKE A COLD HAND PASSED OVER MY LIMBS AND BEHOLD   140 FRENCH REVOLTN   130
BUT AS WE HERE REMAIN BEHOLD THY LOT . . . .   156A MARRIAGE HH 17   PROSE
TO BEHOLD MY HEAVY CHAIN   169 MIRTLE SHADE/N   12
BROMION SPOKE BEHOLD THIS HARLOT HERE ON BROMION'S BED .   190 V DAU ALBION 1   18
ERE YET HIS EYELIDS CAN BEHOLD THE ARROWS OF THE DAY .   193 V DAU ALBION 5   32
ON HIS STONE THRESHOLD DOES HIS EYE BEHOLD THE BEAM THAT BRINGS   195 V DAU ALBION 8   2
AND TREES & BIRDS & BEASTS & MEN BEHOLD THEIR ETERNAL JOY   195 V DAU ALBION 8   8
I HOWL MY JOY AND MY RED EYES SEEK TO BEHOLD THY FACE .   196 AMERICA PREL 1   19
THAT ETERNALS MAY NO MORE BEHOLD THEM . . . . . .   231 URIZEN 9   4
MANATHU-VORCYON I BEHOLD THEE FLAMING IN MY HALLS . .   244 EUROPE 14   * 6
[ALREADY ARE MY EYES REVERTED ALL THAT I BEHOLD] . . .   267 FOUR ZOAS 1   115
[AND ?COURTING THAT THE EARTH WOULD OPE HER EYELIDS & BEHOLD]   267 FOUR ZOAS 1   131
BEHOLD TWO [LITTLE INFANTS WEPT] [?FIGURES OF ?PAIN HOWLD] . . .   269 FOUR ZOAS 1   * 192
NOR SHALT THOU ME TORMENT FOR I BEHOLD THE [ETERNAL] FALLEN MAN   272 FOUR ZOAS 1   * 284
REFUSING TO BEHOLD THE DIVINE IMAGE WHICH ALL BEHOLD . .   272 FOUR ZOAS 1   290
THEY BEHOLD MULTITUDE OR EXPANDING THEY BEHOLD AS ONE . .   277 FOUR ZOAS 1   471
THOU LUVAH SAID THE PRINCE OF LIGHT BEHOLD OUR SONS & DAUGHTERS   277 FOUR ZOAS 1   488
[THE MAN] ALBION CALLD URIZEN & SAID BEHOLD THESE SICKNING SPHERES   280 FOUR ZOAS 2   * 3
THEIR EYES THEIR EARS NOSTRILS & TONGUES ROLL OUTWARD THEY BEHOLD   281 FOUR ZOAS 2   54
IF THOU DOST LAY THINE HAND UPON ME BEHOLD I AM SILENT . .   293 FOUR ZOAS 3   62
IF THOU WITHDRAW THY BREATH BEHOLD I AM OBLIVION . . . .   293 FOUR ZOAS 3   65
FOR HER BRIGHT EYES BEHOLD THE ABYSS SOMETIMES A LITTLE SLEEP   297 FOUR ZOAS 3   209
AND I WHAT CAN I NOW BEHOLD BUT AN ETERNAL DEATH . . .   301 FOUR ZOAS 4   143
APPEAREST CLOTHD IN LUVAH'S GARMENTS THAT WE MAY BEHOLD THEE   304 FOUR ZOAS 4   257
AND LIVE BEHOLD ETERNAL DEATH IS IN BEULAH BEHOLD . . .   304 FOUR ZOAS 4   258
BEHOLD THESE WONDERS OF ETERNITY WE SHALL CONSUME . . .   304 FOUR ZOAS 4   262
CONTRACTED THEY BEHOLD THE SECRETS OF THE INFINITE MOUNTAINS   308 FOUR ZOAS 5   122
EXPANDED THEY BEHOLD THE TERRORS OF THE SUN & MOON . .   308 FOUR ZOAS 5   125
IN ALL THIS CHASM I BEHOLD NO OTHER LIVING THING . . . .   321 FOUR ZOAS 7   46
FIRST BORN OF GENERATION THEN BEHOLD A WONDER TO THE EYES .   326 FOUR ZOAS 7   245
AS ON THE OUTSIDE OF EXISTENCE BUT lOOK BEHOLD TAKE COMFORT   330 FOUR ZOAS 7   414
TURN INWARDLY THINE EYES & THERE BEHOLD THE LAMB OF GOD .   330 FOUR ZOAS 7   415
ENITHARMON ANSWERD I BEHOLD THE LAMB OF GOD DESCENDING .   330 FOUR ZOAS 7   424
OF EXISTENCE TO BE A SIGN & TERROR TO ALL WHO BEHOLD . .   331 FOUR ZOAS 7   429
WHICH NOW OPEND WITHIN THE CENTER WE BEHOLD SPREAD ABROAD .   331 FOUR ZOAS 7   442
THAT WHOSOEVER ENTERD INTO THE TEMPLE MIGHT NOT BEHOLD .   333 FOUR ZOAS 7B   23
TO LABOUR & BEHOLD MY HEART SUNK DOWN BENEATH . . . .   334 FOUR ZOAS 7B   63
O MELANCHOLY MAGDALEN BEHOLD THE MORNING BREAKS . . . .   337 FOUR ZOAS 7B   192
. . . I BEHOLD THE DIVINE VISION THRO THE BROKEN GATES .   341 FOUR ZOAS 8   20
RESIDES THAT GOD OF MY DELIGHT O MIGHT MY EYES BEHOLD . .   345 FOUR ZOAS 8   156
NOW WE BEHOLD REDEMPTION NOW WE KNOW THAT LIFE ETERNAL .   346 FOUR ZOAS 8   197
. . . WE BEHOLD WITH WONDER ENITHARMON'S LOOMS & LOS'S FORGES   346 FOUR ZOAS 8   200
WE LOOK DOWN INTO ULRO WE BEHOLD THE WONDERS OF THE GRAVE   346 FOUR ZOAS 8   223
WE NOW BEHOLD THE ENDS OF BEULAH & WE NOW BEHOLD . . .   347 FOUR ZOAS 8   239
O RAHAB I BEHOLD THEE I WAS ONCE LIKE THEE A SON . . . .   350 FOUR ZOAS 8   354
UP BOUND THE WILD STAG & THE HORSE [BEHOLDS] BEHOLD THE KING OF PRIDE   352 FOUR ZOAS 8   * 453
LISTEN TO HER WHOSE EYES BEHOLD THE DARK BODY OF CORRUPTIBLE DEATH   354 FOUR ZOAS 8   505
BEHOLD THE TIME APPROACHES FAST THAT THOU SHALT BE AS A THING   355 FOUR ZOAS 8   549
[BUT AS SHE WOVE BEHOLD THE BOTTOM OF THE SEPULCHER] . .   356 FOUR ZOAS 8   589
O PRINCE OF LIGHT WHERE ART THOU I BEHOLD THEE NOT AS ONCE   360 FOUR ZOAS 9   124
BEHOLD JERUSALEM IN WHOSE BOSOM THE LAMB OF GOD [IS SEEN]   362 FOUR ZOAS 9   205
ALL NATIONS LOOK UP TO THE CLOUD & BEHOLD HIM WHO WAS CRUCIFIED   364 FOUR ZOAS 9   274
O THAT I COULD BEHOLD HIS FACE & FOLLOW HIS PURE FEET . .   368 FOUR ZOAS 9   426
FOR FROM MY PLEASANT HILLS BEHOLD THE LIVING LIVING SPRINGS   368 FOUR ZOAS 9   441
WONDERING TO BEHOLD THE EMMET THE GRASSHOPPER THE JOINTED WORM   373 FOUR ZOAS 9   603
EACH SHALL BEHOLD THE ETERNAL FATHER & LOVE & JOY ABOUND   374 FOUR ZOAS 9   642
O MYSTERY FIERCE THARMAS CRIES BEHOLD THY END IS COME . .   374 FOUR ZOAS 9   657
HIS EYES BEHOLD THE ANGELIC SPHERES ARISING NIGHT & DAY .   379 FOUR ZOAS 9   828
THAT MORTAL EYES CANNOT BEHOLD . . . .   442 DEDICATN BLAIR   2
BEHOLD THIS GATE OF PEARL AND GOLD . . . .   442 DEDICATN BLAIR   10
O READER BEHOLD THE PHILOSOPHER'S GRAVE . . . . . .   470 ANNO REYNOLDS   1
WHILE HE IS MURDERING THE JUST PROPHETIC I BEHOLD . . .   487 MILTON 7   25
AND THE ELECT SHALL SAY TO THE REDEEMD WE BEHOLD IT IS OF DIVINE   494 MILTON 13   32
TERROR UPON THEE BEHOLD HOW I AM & TREMBLE LEST THOU ALSO   499 MILTON 18   27
STANDING ON CARMEL RAHAB AND TIRZAH TREMBLED TO BEHOLD . .   501 MILTON 19   28

197

	PAGE	TITLE	LINE

BEHOLD   (CONTINUED)

SAYING COME THOU TO EPHRAIM BEHOLD THE KINGS OF CANAAN . .	501	MILTON 19	36
THE BEAUTIFUL AMALEKITES BEHOLD THE FIRES OF YOUTH	501	MILTON 19	37
BEHIND MY BACK I TURNED ROUND IN TERROR AND BEHOLD . . .	505	MILTON 22	7
UPON THE BODY OF ALBION FOR THIS HE IS COME BEHOLD	505	MILTON 22	34
IT WRITTEN			
PAUL CONSTANTINE CHARLEMAINE LUTHER BEHOLD THEY STAND	509	MILTON 24	32
BEFORE US			
BEHOLD THESE WONDERS OF ETERNITY WE SHALL CONSUME	519	MILTON 30	27
BEHOLD MILTON DESCENDED TO REDEEM THE FEMALE SHADE . . .	522	MILTON 33	11
COULD NOT BEHOLD GOLGONOOZA WITHOUT PASSING THE POLYPUS	525	MILTON 35	19
THEN YOU BEHOLD ITS MIGHTY SPIRES & DOMES OF IVORY & GOLD	525	MILTON 35	25
IS IT AGAIN TO PLUNGE INTO DEEPER AFFLICTION BEHOLD ME . .	527	MILTON 36	30
I BEHOLD LOS & URIZEN I BEHOLD ORC & THARMAS	532	MILTON 40	6
HE HAS DONE SO AND THE RESULT YOU BEHOLD HIS	579C	DESC CAT 5	PROSE
IT IS BURNT UP THE MOMENT MEN CEASE TO BEHOLD IT I ASSERT	617B	V LAST JUDG/N	PROSE
FOR MY SELF THAT I DO NOT BEHOLD THE OUTWARD CREATION .	617B	V LAST JUDG/N	PROSE
O [XXX ?BEHOLD ?PITYING] BEHOLD THE VISION OF ALBION . .	620	JERUSALEM 1	* 7
I BEHOLD THEM AND THEIR RUSHING FIRES OVERWHELM MY SOUL	623	JERUSALEM 5	35
SHUDDRING THE HEAVENS TO LOOK UPON ME BEHOLD WHAT CRUELTIES	627	JERUSALEM 8	19
I LABOUR DAY AND NIGHT I BEHOLD THE SOFT AFFECTIONS . . .	628	JERUSALEM 9	26
AND SEEING LIFE YET LIVING NOT HOW CAN I THEN BEHOLD . .	630	JERUSALEM 10	58
AND LOS SAID I BEHOLD THE FINGER OF GOD IN TERRORS . .	631	JERUSALEM 12	5
AND THERE BEHOLD THE LOOM OF LOCKE WHOSE WOOF RAGES DIRE	636	JERUSALEM 15	15
I DISCOVER THY SECRET PLACES CORDELLA I BEHOLD	644	JERUSALEM 21	19
FOR I SEE LUVAH WHOM I SLEW I BEHOLD HIM IN MY SPECTRE .	645	JERUSALEM 22	31
AS I BEHOLD JERUSALEM IN THEE O VALA DARK AND COLD . . .	645	JERUSALEM 22	32
WHICH WAY SOEVER I TURN I BEHOLD HUMANITY AND PITY . .	646	JERUSALEM 23	19
NO MORE SHALL I BEHOLD HIM HE IS CLOSD IN LUVAH'S SEPULCHER	648	JERUSALEM 24	51
THE REACTOR HATH HID HIMSELF THRO ENVY I BEHOLD HIM . .	653	JERUSALEM 29	9
BUT YOU CANNOT BEHOLD HIM TILL HE BE REVEALD IN HIS SYSTEM	653	JERUSALEM 29	10
IF THOU DOST LAY THINE HAND UPON ME BEHOLD I AM SILENT . .	654	JERUSALEM 29	49
IF THOU WITHDRAW THY BREATH BEHOLD I AM OBLIVION	654	JERUSALEM 29	52
UPON THE MOUNTAINS OF ALBION AS IN ANCIENT TIME BEHOLD .	656	JERUSALEM 30	22
AND IS THIS FAITH BEHOLD THE STRIFE OF ALBION & LUVAH .	658	JERUSALEM 31	55
IN CLOUD OF SECRET GLOOM WHICH BEHOLD INVOLVE ME ROUND	660	JERUSALEM 33	47
ABOUT			
WHICH IF MAN CEASES TO BEHOLD HE CEASES TO EXIST . . .	664	JERUSALEM 38	13
WE BEHOLD MULTITUDE OR EXPANDING WE BEHOLD AS ONE . . .	664	JERUSALEM 38	18
I BEHOLD LONDON A HUMAN AWFUL WONDER OF GOD	665	JERUSALEM 38	29
I SEE THEE AWFUL PARENT LAND IN LIGHT BEHOLD I SEE . . .	665	JERUSALEM 38	44
WHY SHOULD WE ENTER INTO OUR SPECTRES TO BEHOLD OUR OWN	672	JERUSALEM 43	10
CORRUPTIONS			
STRUCKEN WITH ALBION'S DISEASE THEY BECOME WHAT THEY BEHOLD	674	JERUSALEM 44	32
BEHOLD THE FOGGY MORNINGS OF THE DEAD ON ALBION'S CLIFFS	681	JERUSALEM 50	13
AND THEN BEHOLD WHAT ARE THESE ULRO VISIONS OF CHASTITY	686	JERUSALEM 55	38
AND WEPT AT OUR WINTRY DOOR LOOK LOOK BEHOLD GWENDOLEN	688	JERUSALEM 56	27
WONDER SIEZD ALL IN ETERNITY TO BEHOLD THE DIVINE VISION	689	JERUSALEM 57	17
OPEN			
FOR THOU ALSO SUFFEREST WITH ME ALTHO I BEHOLD THEE NOT	693	JERUSALEM 60	61
BEHOLD IN THE VISIONS OF ELOHIM JEHOVAH BEHOLD JOSEPH	694	JERUSALEM 61	1
& MARY			
. . . IF I WERE HOLY I NEVER COULD BEHOLD THE TEARS . . .	694	JERUSALEM 61	12
IN THE PERPETUAL MUTUAL SACRIFICE IN GREAT ETERNITY FOR	694	JERUSALEM 61	23
BEHOLD			
I SEE THE MATERNAL LINE I BEHOLD THE SEED OF THE WOMAN .	696	JERUSALEM 62	8
BUT I THY MAGDALEN BEHOLD THY SPIRITUAL RISEN BODY . . .	696	JERUSALEM 62	14
O MELANCHOLY MAGDALEN BEHOLD THE MORNING OVER MALDEN BREAK	700	JERUSALEM 65	38
ASTONISHD TERRIFIED & IN PAIN & TORMENT SUDDEN THEY BEHOLD	701	JERUSALEM 65	68
SUDDEN THEY BECOME LIKE WHAT THEY BEHOLD IN HOWLINGS &	701	JERUSALEM 65	75
DEADLY PAIN			
THEY BECOME LIKE WHAT THEY BEHOLD YET IMMENSE IN STRENGTH	701	JERUSALEM 65	79
& POWER			
THEY PUT INTO HIS HAND A REED THEY MOCK SAYING BEHOLD . .	702	JERUSALEM 66	24
ALL WHO SEE BECOME WHAT THEY BEHOLD THEIR EYES ARE COVERD	702	JERUSALEM 66	36
AND EARTH & ALL YOU BEHOLD THO IT APPEARS WITHOUT IT IS	709	JERUSALEM 71	18
WITHIN			
I BEHOLD BABYLON IN THE OPENING STREETS OF LONDON I BEHOLD	714	JERUSALEM 74	16
THIS I BEHOLD THE SHUDDERINGS OF DEATH ATTEND MY STEPS . .	714	JERUSALEM 74	18
AND THOU AMERICA I ONCE BEHELD THEE BUT NOW BEHOLD NO MORE	721	JERUSALEM 79	53
LOOK HYLE IS BECOME AN INFANT LOVE LOOK BEHOLD SEE HIM LIE	725	JERUSALEM 82	37
OF CAMBERWELL WE SHALL BEHOLD YOU NO MORE IN GLORY & PRIDE	729	JERUSALEM 84	5
TERRIBLE TO BEHOLD FOR THY EXTREME BEAUTY & PERFECTION . .	731	JERUSALEM 86	16
TWELVE-FOLD HERE ALL THE TRIBES OF ISRAEL I BEHOLD . . .	731	JERUSALEM 86	17
TWELVEFOLD I THEREFORE BEHOLD ISRAEL IN HER TENTS . . .	731	JERUSALEM 86	26
GUIDES THEM THERE I BEHOLD MOAB & AMMON & AMALEK	731	JERUSALEM 86	28
O LOVELY ENITHARMON I BEHOLD THY GRACEFUL FORMS	732	JERUSALEM 87	3
MINUTE PARTICULARS IN SLAVERY I BEHOLD AMONG THE	735	JERUSALEM 89	17
BRICK-KILNS			
IN MARTYRDOMS & SLAVERY I BEHOLD AH VISION OF SORROW .	735	JERUSALEM 89	40
TERRIFIED LOS SAT TO BEHOLD TREMBLING & WEEPING & HOWLING	739	JERUSALEM 91	54
BEHOLD HIM HERE WE SHALL NOT DIE WE SHALL BE UNITED IN	741	JERUSALEM 93	19
JESUS			
O ALL YE NATIONS OF THE EARTH BEHOLD YE THE JEALOUS WIFE	742	JERUSALEM 94	26
I BEHOLD THE VISIONS OF MY DEADLY SLEEP OF SIX THOUSAND	743	JERUSALEM 96	11
YEARS			
ALWAYS BEHOLD THE FACE OF THE ?HEAVENLY FATHER	774A	ANNO BERKELEY	MARG
"& WE NOT ONLY TALK BUT BEHOLD"	800B	LETTER 12	PROSE
REMINISCENCE & BEHOLD OUR ANCIENT DAYS BEFORE THIS EARTH	802C	LETTER 14	PROSE
OF HUMAN VEGETATION & BEHOLD	806	TO MRS BUTTS/L	4

BEHOLDEST

O BROTHER IJIM THOU BEHOLDEST WRETCHED TIRIEL	104	TIRIEL 4	21

	PAGE	TITLE	LINE
BEHOLDING			
WEPT BITTER TEARS INCESSANT STILL BEHOLDING HOW THE PITEOUS FORM	300	FOUR ZOAS 4	97
WITHIN LABOURING BEHOLDING WITHOUT FROM PARTICULARS TO GENERALS	483	MILTON 3	37
SCARCELY BEHOLDING THE GREAT LIGHT CONVERSING WITH THE VOID	484	MILTON 5	22
ASTONISHD AT THE TRANSGRESSOR IN HIM BEHOLDING THE SAVIOUR	494	MILTON 13	31
LOS SHUDDERD AT BEHOLDING ALBION FOR HIS DISEASE	666	JERUSALEM 40	1
CHARIOTS BLACK THEIR FIRES ROLL BEHOLDING ALBION'S HOUSE OF ETERNITY	666	JERUSALEM 40	5
WORSHIPPING MERCY & BEHOLDING THY FRIEND IN SUCH AFFLICTION	669	JERUSALEM 42	10
BEHOLDING ALBION UPON THE PRECIPICE READY TO FALL INTO NON-ENTITY	672	JERUSALEM 43	15
SCARCELY BEHOLDING THE GREAT LIGHT CONVERSING WITH THE (VOID)	680	JERUSALEM 49 *	35
WHILE LOS SAT TERRIFIED BEHOLDING ALBION'S SPECTRE WHO IS LUVAH	692	JERUSALEM 60	2
SO LOS TERRIFIED CRIES TREMBLING & WEEPING & HOWLING BEHOLDING	739	JERUSALEM 91	59
THE TERRORS OF CREATION & REDEMPTION & JUDGMENT BEHOLDING THEM	739	JERUSALEM 92	20
BEHOLDS			
RECIEVEST THE INTEGUMENTS WOVEN RAHAB BEHOLDS THE LAMB OF GOD	347	FOUR ZOAS 8	233
UP BOUND THE WILD STAG & THE HORSE [BEHOLDS] BEHOLD THE KING OF PRIDE	352	FOUR ZOAS 8 *	453
LISTEN TO HER WHOSE MEMORY BEHOLDS YOUR ANCIENT DAYS . .	354	FOUR ZOAS 8	504
THE STARS CONSUMD LIKE A LAMP BLOWN OUT & IN THEIR STEAD BEHOLDS	379	FOUR ZOAS 9 *	829
THE EXPANDING EYES OF MAN BEHOLDS THE DEPTHS OF WONDROUS WORLDS	379	FOUR ZOAS 9 *	830
WHY TREMBLES THE WARRIOR'S LIMBS WHEN HE BEHOLDS THY BEAUTY	706	JERUSALEM 68	48
DEPENDS ON THE ORGAN THAT BEHOLDS IT	760	FOR SEXES/GP	2
BEING (NOUN)			
MAN IS A TWOFOLD BEING ONE PART CAPABLE OF EVIL . . .	80A	ANNO LAVATER	MARG
NOW BOTH EVIL & GOOD CANNOT EXIST IN A SIMPLE BEING .	80A	ANNO LAVATER	MARG
THUS ONE PORTION OF BEING IS THE PROLIFIC THE OTHER THE DEVOURING	155B	MARRIAGE HH 15	PROSE
NO MORE BUT A DESIRE OF BEING A DISTRACTED RAVENING DESIRE	376	FOUR ZOAS 9	734
IS A VERY CRUEL BEING & BEING A WORSHIPPER OF CHRIST .	617A	V LAST JUDG/N	PROSE
FOR HE IS RIGHTEOUS HE IS NOT A BEING OF PITY & COMPASSION	630	JERUSALEM 10	44
BEING (VERB)			
BUT I MUST TELL YOU THAT GUILT BEING AN ACT OF THE MIND	29A	EDW THIRD/PS 4	PROSE
SECTS ARE NOT EVER MENTIOND THERE AS BEING QUITE OUT OF DATE	44B	ISLAND MOON 1	PROSE
BEING MET AT THE HOUSE OF INFLAMMABLE GASS THE WINDFINDER	58B	ISLAND MOON 10	PROSE
("ALL MORAL DEPENDENCE ON GUILTY") IS BEING HIM RATHER	68A	ANNO LAVATER	MARG
HELL IS THE BEING SHUT UP IN THE POSSESSION OF CORPOREAL DESIRES	74B	ANNO LAVATER	MARG
BY REASON OF ITS BEING UNITED WITH HYPOCRISY BUT LET THEM	85C	ANNO LAVATER	MARG
THINK OF A WHITE CLOUD AS BEING HOLY YOU CANNOT LOVE IT	90C	ANNO SWED LOVE	MARG
THE DESIRE OF MAN BEING INFINITE THE POSSESSION IS INFINITE	97D	NAT RELIGION 2	PROSE
THE TRUE MAN IS THE SOURCE HE BEING THE POETIC GENIUS . .	98D	ALL RELIGIONS	PROSE
AND BEING RESTRAIND IT BY DEGREES BECOMES PASSIVE . .	150A	MARRIAGE HH 5	PROSE
BEING NO OTHER THAN [THE DEVIL] HE WHO DWELLS IN FLAMING FIRE	150B	MARRIAGE HH 5	*PROSE
HIS WILL WHERE NONE SHOULD DARE OPPOSE HIS WILL HIMSELF BEING KING	317	FOUR ZOAS 6	232
ART NOTHING BEING CREATED CONTINUALLY BY MERCY & LOVE DIVINE	329	FOUR ZOAS 7	360
BEING A MEDIUM BETWEEN HIM & ENITHARMON BUT THIS UNION . .	330	FOUR ZOAS 7	398
BEING MULTITUDES OF TYRANT MEN IN UNION BLASPHEMOUS . . .	347	FOUR ZOAS 8	257
WHEREFORE [RINTRAH &] PALAMABRON BEING ACCUSD BY SATAN TO LOS	351	FOUR ZOAS 8 *	388
VALA NIGHT THE NINTH BEING THE LAST JUDGMENT	357B	FOUR ZOAS 9	TITLE
BUT HE SAYS THAT MOSES BEING PROVED NOT THE AUTHOR OF .	391B	ANNO WATSON	MARG
MANNER OF A MIRACLE BEING PERFORMED IS IN MODERN TIMES .	391C	ANNO WATSON	MARG
THE BASEST & MOST OPPRESSIVE OF HUMAN CODES & BEING LIKE	393C	ANNO WATSON	MARG
THESE BLOTS OF LIGHT AND DARK AS BEING THE RESULT OF LABOUR	439C	REMARKS MALKIN	PROSE
BEING AS CAREFUL AS POSSIBLE NOT TO HURT THE GROUND .	440C	MEMORANDUM/N 3	PROSE
BECAUSE IT BEING BLACK WILL SHEW PERFECTLY WHAT IS WANTED [XXX]	440C	MEMORANDUM/N 3	PROSE
PAINTERS ARE NOTED FOR BEING DISSIPATED & WILD . .	454B	ANNO REYNOLDS	MARG
WITHOUT FATIGUE EVERY THING BEING DEFINITE & DETERMINATE	457B	ANNO REYNOLDS	MARG
ONE CENTRAL FORM COMPOSED OF ALL OTHER FORMS BEING GRANTED	459C	ANNO REYNOLDS	MARG
SO FAR FROM BEING ALL OF A PIECE ARE THE MOST WRETCHED BUNGLES	468D	ANNO REYNOLDS	MARG
SEEMING A BROTHER BEING A TYRANT EVEN THINKING HIMSELF A BROTHER	487	MILTON 7	24
WAS SATAN'S ENEMY & THAT THE GNOMES BEING PALAMABRON'S FRIENDS	487	MILTON 7	39
BEING CALLD GOD SETTING HIMSELF ABOVE ALL THAT IS CALLED GOD	491	MILTON 11	12
BEING MOST IMPURE SELF-CONDEMND TO ETERNAL TEARS HE DROVE	493	MILTON 12	47
WHERE SOULS INCESSANT WAIL BEING PITEOUS PASSIONS & DESIRES	512	MILTON 26	26
BUT IN THE NERVES OF THE NOSTRILS ACCIDENT BEING FORMED	517	MILTON 29	35
SHALL WE FOR THE SAKE OF BEING POLITE	543	IF TRUE/N	3
NEWTON & BACON CRY BEING BADLY NURST	548	CRIPPLE EVRY/N	6
FOR THIS IS BEING A FRIEND JUST IN THE NICK	551	WILLM COWPER/N	1
UNTILL BY BEING SICK HIS WANTS ARE [PROVED] PROVD . . .	551	WILLM COWPER/N *	4
BEING ALL IN WATER-COLOURS THAT IS IN FRESCO	561B	EXHIBITION ADV	PROSE

BEING   (CONTINUED)
    FROM THE TOO JUST IMPUTATION OF BEING THE SEAT AND   . . .   562B DESC CAT ADV   PROSE
    INVENTIONS PAINTED BY WILLIAM BLAKE IN WATER COLOURS BEING   563A DESC CAT   TITLE
    BEING COPIES FROM SOME STUPENDOUS ORIGINALS   . . . . .   565C DESC CAT 2   PROSE
    AMONG THE RIVERS OF PARADISE BEING ORIGINALS FROM WHICH   565C DESC CAT 2   PROSE
    BEING WITH THEIR ACCOMPANIMENTS TERRIFIC AND   . . . . .   565D DESC CAT 2   PROSE
    AND THEY ARE KNOWN TO BE UNCHANGEABLE BUT OIL BEING A BODY   566B DESC CAT 2   PROSE
    BUT THE ART OF FRESCO PAINTING BEING LOST   . . . . . .   566C DESC CAT 2   PROSE
    NOT UNBECOMING IN HER BEING ACCOMPANIED WITH   . . . .   568B DESC CAT 3   PROSE
    CHARACTERS LIKELY TO RIDE IN COMPANY ALL BEING ABOVE THE   568C DESC CAT 3   PROSE
    BUT THE PAINTER'S THOUGHTS BEING ALWAYS UPON GOLD   . .   575B DESC CAT 3   PROSE
    I HAVE NO OBJECTION TO RUBENS AND REMBRANDT BEING EMPLOYED   575D DESC CAT 3   PROSE
    HISTORIANS PRETEND WHO BEING WEAKLY ORGANIZED THEMSELVES   578D DESC CAT 5   PROSE
    NOT KNOWING WHAT ART IS IT IS BEING BLIND TO THE GIFTS   579D DESC CAT 5   PROSE
       OF THE SPIRIT
    BEING THE RECEPTACLES OF INTELLECT   . . . .   580A DESC CAT 5   PROSE
    ABOUT CORREGGIO BEING POOR AND BUT BADLY PAID   . . . .   583B DESC CAT 9   PROSE
    CHAUCER'S CANTERBURY PILGRIMS BEING A COMPLETE INDEX   .   591A PUB ADDRESS/N   TITLE
    HEATH'S LAME IMITATION STOTHARD BEING SUCH A FOOL   . .   592B PUB ADDRESS/N   PROSE
    YOUR ENEMY HE ALWAYS BEGINS WITH BEING YOUR FRIEND   . .   592C PUB ADDRESS/N   PROSE
    COMMERCE IS SO FAR FROM BEING BENEFICIAL TO ARTS OR   . .   593D PUB ADDRESS/N   PROSE
    OF INDIVIDUAL MERIT BEING ITS GREAT HATRED   . . . . .   594A PUB ADDRESS/N   PROSE
    WITHOUT BEING A MASTER OF DRAWING IS AN IMPOSTOR   . . .   594D PUB ADDRESS/N   *PROSE
    AS [IS] IT IS CAPABLE OF BEING PLACED IN ANY HEIGHTH &   601A PUB ADDRESS/N   *PROSE
       INDEED
    ENGRAVE OR PAINT EITHER WITHOUT BEING A MASTER OF DRAWING   602B PUB ADDRESS/N   PROSE
       IS
    IN A SUBLIME DEGREE BEING DERIVED FROM REAL VISION IN   .   607A V LAST JUDG/N   PROSE
    LOT'S WIFE BEING CHANGED INTO (A) PILLAR OF SALT ALLUDES   607A V LAST JUDG/N   PROSE
    TO THE MORTAL BODY BEING RENDERD A PERMANENT STATUE   .   607A V LAST JUDG/N   PROSE
    SIGNIFIED BY THOSE NAMES THE INDIVIDUALS BEING   . . .   607B V LAST JUDG/N   PROSE
    NOT BEING AMONG THE CONDEMND   . . . .   610B V LAST JUDG/N   PROSE
    & WISDOM THAN NOAH BEING NEARER THE STATE OF INNOCENCE   .   611C V LAST JUDG/N   PROSE
    IS A VERY CRUEL BEING & BEING A WORSHIPPER OF CHRIST   .   617A V LAST JUDG/N   PROSE
    I SAID NOW IS MY GRIEF AT WORST INCAPABLE OF BEING   . . .   630 JERUSALEM 10   44
    MUST HAVE BECOME THE FIRST VICTIMS BEING THE FIRST   653 JERUSALEM 28   24
       TRANSGRESSORS
    BEING NOT IRRITATED BY INSULT BEARING INSULTING   655 JERUSALEM 30   9
       BENEVOLENCES
    WITH BEING THE CAUSES OF WAR   . . . .   683A JERUSALEM 52   PROSE
    FOR BEING DRIVEN FROM OUR FIELDS WHAT HAVE WE TO DO WITH   686 JERUSALEM 55   6
       THE DEAD
    NOR CAN ANY CONSUMMATE BLISS WITHOUT BEING GENERATED   .   731 JERUSALEM 86   42
    A HORSE IS NOT MORE A LION FOR BEING A BAD HORSE THAT   778B HOMERS POETRY   PROSE
       IS ITS
    AS BABYLON & EGYPT SO FAR FROM BEING PARENTS OF ARTS   .   778C HOMERS POETRY   PROSE
    WILLIAM BLAKE ONE WHO IS VERY MUCH DELIGHTED WITH BEING   781D INSC UPCOTT   PROSE
    I HAVE DONE THE CORRECTIONS MY PAPER NOT BEING IN ORDER   791A LETTER 2   PROSE
    BEING OF THE SAME OPINION WITH MILTON   . . . . . .   792B LETTER 4   PROSE
    & BEING ALSO IN THE PREDICAMENT OF THAT PROPHET WHO SAYS   792C LETTER 4   PROSE
    YOUR PLAN FOR A NATIONAL GALLERY BEING PUT INTO EXECUTION   797C LETTER 10   PROSE
    WHICH I HID MY FACE FOR NOT BEING ABLE TO ABANDON   . .   798C LETTER 10   PROSE
    "THINGS BEING NOW NEARLY COMPLETED FOR OUR SETTING FORTH   800B LETTER 12   PROSE
       ON"
    AND MY WIFE'S ILLNESS NOT BEING QUITE GONE OFF   . . . .   807A LETTER 17   PROSE
    FOR I SO FAR FROM BEING BOUND DOWN   . . . .   809A LETTER 20   PROSE
    SO NEAR TO FELPHAM PARIS BEING SCARCE FURTHER OFF THAN   811A LETTER 21   PROSE
       LONDON
    DISTANT WHEN WE SHALL DO SO BEING DETERMIND NOT TO   . . .   813C LETTER 22   PROSE
    WHAT CAME FROM MY HEAD & MY HEART IN UNISON THAT I AM PROUD   814D LETTER 23   PROSE
       OF BEING
    & BEING UNDER MY OWN EYE THE PRINTS ARE AS FINE AS THE   821A LETTER 25   PROSE
    I THINK THE GRAND REASON OF MY BEING BROUGHT DOWN HERE   .   823B LETTER 26   PROSE
    LIKENESSES FROM MEMORY BEING NECESSARILY VERY VERY   824B LETTER 27   PROSE
       DEFECTIVE
    BEING FULLY EMPLOYD IN ENGRAVING FOR HIS PROJECTED WORKS   824C LETTER 27   PROSE
    BEING OUT OF HIS LINE OF BUSINESS TO PUBLISH AND   . . .   831C LETTER 31   PROSE
    THE PRINTERS [BEING] HAVING BEEN THIS AFTERNOON UNABLE   .   833A LETTER 32   PROSE
    OR UNWILLING & MY PRESS NOT YET BEING PUT UP FAREWELL   .   833A LETTER 32   PROSE
    WHO IS NOT IN TOWN BEING AT BIRMINGHAM   . . . . . .   834B LETTER 34   PROSE
    I SENT OFF THE MORNING AFTER I RECIEVD IT FROM YOU BEING   834C LETTER 34   PROSE
    THE WRITING BEING EXACTLY COPIED FROM THE TRACING PAPER   838A LETTER 37   PROSE
    FOR THE PURPOSE OF BEING ENGRAVED FOR THE EUROPEAN MAGNE   838D LETTER 37   PROSE
    NOT BEING QUITE SURE THAT YOU HAD COPIES READY FOR THEM   840B LETTER 39   PROSE
    BEING DISPOSED OF BY MEANS OF A RAFFLE HE SUPPOSES IT IS   844C LETTER 43   PROSE
    THE WHOLE MIDDLE OF THE BOOK BEING PRINTED WITH A LARGER   847A LETTER 44   PROSE
    HOT-PRESSED I SAY THUS MUCH BEING URGED THERETO BY   . .   847A LETTER 44   PROSE
    FOR NOT BEING ABLE TO FURNISH ANY DESIGNS YOU WILL READILY   853A LETTER 51   *PROSE
    BEING AT FLAXMAN'S TAKING HIS ADVICE ABOUT OUR ENGRAVINGS   853A LETTER 51   *PROSE
    BEING SUCCESSFUL AS WELL AS RIGHT OF WHICH I HAVE NO DOUBT   862A LETTER 59   PROSE
    AND YOUR MAGAZINE BEING AS EXTENSIVE IN ITS CIRCULATION   863D LETTER 61   PROSE
    FEEL MYSELF WEAKER THAN I WAS AWARE BEING NOT ABLE AS YET   872D LETTER 76   PROSE
    IN THE STAGE & SHALL BE I FEAR FOR SOME TIME BEING ONLY   875B LETTER 81   PROSE
    THO I SEEM WELL BEING ENTIRELY FREE FROM BOTH PAIN &   .   875C LETTER 81   PROSE
    SEE TILL THE NEXT MORNING OWING TO ITS BEING WRIT ON THE   875D LETTER 82   PROSE
       OUTSIDE
BEINGS
    GOD ONLY ACTS & IS IN EXISTING BEINGS OR MEN   . . . . .   155B MARRIAGE HH 15   PROSE
    WHILE YET THOSE BEINGS WERE NOT BORN NOR KNEW OF GOOD OR   304 FOUR ZOAS 4   274
       EVIL
    ELEMENTAL BEINGS CALLED BY US BY THE GENERAL NAME   577D DESC CAT 5   PROSE
       OF FAIRIES

		PAGE	TITLE	LINE

BEINGS   (CONTINUED)
    IN THE REVELATIONS SHE IS [BOUND] SIEZED BY TWO BEINGS . . 609A V LAST JUDG/N   PROSE
    DISSIMULATIONS BUT TIME & SPACE ARE REAL BEINGS   . . . . 614D V LAST JUDG/N   PROSE
BELCH
    OF LUST THAT BELCH INCESSANT FROM THE SUMMITS OF THE EARTH   190 V DAU ALBION 2   10
    IS SILENT ON MY CLOUDED HILLS THAT BELCH FORTH STORMS &   359 FOUR ZOAS 9   * 103
      FIRES
    ARE SILENT ON HIS CLOUDED HILLS THAT BELCH FORTH STORMS   641 JERUSALEM 19   4
      & FIRE
BELCHD
    [FARTED & BELCHD & COUGHD] . . . .   185 LET BROTHELS/N   10
    FARTED & BELCHD & COUGHD   . . . .   186 WHEN KLOPSTK/N   4
    BELCHD FROM THE FURNACES WREATHD ROUND HER CHAIND   302 FOUR ZOAS 4   188
      IN CEASELESS FIRE
BELCHED
    THE EARTH TREMBLED [XXX] FIRES BELCHED FROM THE YAWNING   106 TIRIEL 5   *   16
      CLEFTS
BELCHES
    A MOMENT THEN ASTOUNDING HORROR BELCHES FROM THE CENTER   336 FOUR ZOAS 7B   131
BELCHING
    RISE FROM THE CENTER BELCHING FLAMES & ROARINGS DARK SMOKE 106 TIRIEL 5   7
    SWELLING BELCHING FROM ITS DEEPS RED CLOUDS & RAGING FIRES 197 AMERICA 4   3
    BY EARTHQUAKES RIVN BELCHING SULLEN FIRES . . . . .   227 URIZEN 10   4
BELIAL
    BUT BELIAL OF SODOM & GOMORRHA OBSCURE DEMON OF BRIBES . 528 MILTON 37   30
BELIEF
    FOLLY & IMPUDENCE DOES THE THOROUGH BELIEF OF POPERY   . 385C ANNO WATSON   MARG
    THEIR BELIEF IN VISION & REVELATION PLATO WAS IN EARNEST 473D ANNO REYNOLDS   MARG
    WHO TEACHES BELIEF TO THE NATIONS & AN UNKNOWN ETERNAL LIFE 685 JERUSALEM 54   20
BELIEVD
    EVERY THING POSSIBLE TO BE BELIEVD IS AN IMAGE OF TRUTH   151D MARRIAGE HH 8   PROSE
    TRUTH CAN NEVER BE TOLD SO AS TO BE UNDERSTOOD AND NOT   152D MARRIAGE HH 10   PROSE
      BE BELIEVD
    FORGOTTEN WHEN ONE SPEAKS OF THEE HE WILL NOT BE BELIEVD   355 FOUR ZOAS 8   550
    WERE NEVER BELIEVD WILLINGLY BY ANY NATION & . . . . 390C ANNO WATSON   MARG
    MILTON WAS IN EARNEST THEY BELIEVD THAT GOD DID VISIT MAN 473D ANNO REYNOLDS   MARG
    WHAT COULD LOS DO HOW COULD HE JUDGE WHEN SATAN'S SELF   487 MILTON 7   41
      BELIEVD
    HIMSELF EXCULPATING WITH MILDEST SPEECH FOR HIMSELF BELIEVD 487 MILTON 8   2
BELIEVE
    I BELIEVE THAT AS MUCH AS I BELIEVE . . . .   22 EDW THIRD/PS 3   35
    & I DO BELIEVE HE'LL GO IN PARTNERSHIP WITH HIS MASTER . 53A ISLAND MOON 8   PROSE
    SIX & TWENTY ROOMS IN HIS HOUSE AND I BELIEVE IT & HE IS   53A ISLAND MOON 8   PROSE
      NOT
    ("WHO PROVES HIMSELF INEXORABLE") UNEASY I DO   70D ANNO LAVATER   MARG
      NOT BELIEVE IT
    MARK THAT I DO NOT BELIEVE THERE IS SUCH A THING LITTERALLY 74B ANNO LAVATER   MARG
      BUT
    HE REPLIED ALL POETS BELIEVE THAT IT DOES & IN   . . . 153C MARRIAGE HH 12   PROSE
    FOR ALL NATIONS BELIEVE THE JEWS' CODE AND . . . . . 154A MARRIAGE HH 12   PROSE
    THEY LOOK BEHIND AT EVERY STEP & BELIEVE IT IS A DREAM . 198 AMERICA 6   12
    SAYING IF YE WILL BELIEVE YOUR BROTHER SHALL RISE AGAIN   304 FOUR ZOAS 4   270
    THESE WORDS IF YE WILL BELIEVE YOUR BROTHER SHALL RISE   340 FOUR ZOAS 7B   293
      AGAIN
    THEY LOOK BEHIND AT EVERY STEP & BELIEVE IT IS A DREAM . 375 FOUR ZOAS 9   676
    TO HAVE FOR PAINE I BELIEVE HIM TO BE A STATE TRICKSTER   384D ANNO WATSON   MARG
    ARE WE TO BELIEVE THAT BISHOPS DO NOT RAIL I . . . . 385C ANNO WATSON   MARG
    I BELIEVE THAT THE BISHOP LAUGHT AT THE BIBLE IN HIS SLIEVE 385D ANNO WATSON   MARG
    TO ME WHO BELIEVE THE BIBLE & PROFESS MYSELF A CHRISTIAN 387B ANNO WATSON   MARG
    THAT NONE BUT DESIGNING VILLAINS EVER PRETENDED TO BELIEVE 390C ANNO WATSON   MARG
    HOW CAN WATSON EVER BELIEVE THE ABOVE SENSE OF A MIRACLE 391D ANNO WATSON   MARG
    THOSE WHO BELIEVE WANT NOT TO BE CONFOUNDED BY MIRACLES   392A ANNO WATSON   MARG
    A LIE FEW BELIEVE IT IS A NEW BIRTH . . . . 403C ANNO BACON   MARG
    HAS LEFT THE BRAIN THAT WON'T BELIEVE . . . . 431 AUGURIES   26
    WILL NEER BELIEVE DO WHAT YOU PLEASE . . . . 433 AUGURIES   108
    WE ARE LED TO BELIEVE A LIE . . . . 433 AUGURIES   125
    I BELIEVE THE WHOLE CHARGE FALLS TO THE GROUND   . . . 437C BLAKES MEMORAN PROSE
    I DO NOT BELIEVE THIS ANECDOTE . . . . 449D ANNO REYNOLDS   MARG
    I DO NOT BELIEVE THAT RAFAEL TAUGHT MICH ANGELO   . . . 453B ANNO REYNOLDS   MARG
    ANY MORE THAN I BELIEVE THAT THE ROSE TEACHES THE LILLY   453B ANNO REYNOLDS   MARG
      HOW TO GROW
    I DO NOT BELIEVE THE TALES OF ANECDOTE WRITERS WHEN   . . 453B ANNO REYNOLDS   MARG
    I DO NOT BELIEVE THAT CARLO MARATTI THOUGHT SO . . . . 462D ANNO REYNOLDS   MARG
    CAN ANY MAN BE SUCH A FOOL AS TO BELIEVE THAT RAFAEL & . 467B ANNO REYNOLDS   MARG
    BELIEVE CHRIST & HIS APOSTLES THAT THERE IS A CLASS OF MEN 480C MILTON 1   PROSE
    INGRATITUDE & LOS BELIEVE THE ACCUSATION THRO SATAN'S   486 MILTON 7   14
      EXTREME
    SHALL BIND THEM SEPARATE THEY CANNOT BELIEVE IN ETERNAL   511 MILTON 25   33
      LIFE
    THE REPROBATE WHO NEVER CEASE TO BELIEVE AND THE REDEEMD   511 MILTON 25   35
    YOU DONT BELIEVE I [WOUD] WON'T ATTEMPT TO MAKE YE . . 536 DONT BELIEVE/N *   1
    DOUBT DOUBT & DONT BELIEVE WITHOUT EXPERIMENT   . . . . 536 DONT BELIEVE/N   9
    WHEN HE SAID [RICH] ONLY BELIEVE BELIEVE & TRY   . . . 536 DONT BELIEVE/N   11
    AND HES A FOOL WHO [SEEKS] TRIES TO MAKE SUCH A BLOCKHEAD 540 BLOCKHEAD/N   2
      BELIEVE
    DO YOU BELIEVE IT A CONFOUNDED LIE . . . . 551 WILLM COWPER/N   6
    NO MAN CAN BELIEVE THAT EITHER HOMER'S MYTHOLOGY . . . 565D DESC CAT 2   PROSE
    NEITHER WILL ANY ONE BELIEVE THAT THE GREEK STATUES . . 565D DESC CAT 2   PROSE
    [ALL] MOST OF THEM SUCH SILLY FELLOWS AS TO BELIEVE THIS   597B PUB ADDRESS/N   PROSE
    P S I DO NOT BELIEVE THAT THIS ABSURD OPINION EVER WAS . 602B PUB ADDRESS/N   PROSE
    VAIN FOOLISH MAN WILT THOU BELIEVE WITHOUT EXPERIMENT   . 685 JERUSALEM 54   22
    ONLY BELIEVE IN ME THAT I HAVE POWER TO RAISE FROM DEATH   694 JERUSALEM 60   68

```
                                                             PAGE    TITLE         LINE
BELIEVE    (CONTINUED)
      ONLY BELIEVE & TRUST IN ME LO I AM ALWAYS WITH THEE  . . .   696 JERUSALEM 62       29
      INTO THE INDEFINITE REFUSING TO BELIEVE WITHOUT            738 JERUSALEM 91       36
         DEMONSTRATION
      AND LEADS YOU TO BELIEVE A LIE . . . . . . . . .          753 EV GOSPEL (D)/N    105
      EVE COME AWAY & LET US NOT BELIEVE THESE VAIN DELUSIONS     780 GHOST ABEL 1       18
      ALIVE & NOT DEAD WERE IT NOT BETTER TO BELIEVE VISION  . .  780 GHOST ABEL 2        1
      AM APT TO BELIEVE THAT WHAT IS DONE WITHOUT MEANING IS VERY 782A INSC UPCOTT       PROSE
      I BELIEVE BOTH MACPHERSON & CHATTERTON  . . . . . . .      783C ANNO WW POEMS      MARG
      YOU SHALL NOT BRING ME DOWN TO BELIEVE SUCH FITTING        784C ANNO WW EXCUR      MARG
         & FITTED
      MY STUPID HEAD BELIEVE THAT IT WAS PROPER FOR ME TO TROUBLE 798A LETTER 10         PROSE
      BELIEVE AS MANY BOOKSELLERS AS THERE ARE BUTCHERS &   . .  798C LETTER 10         PROSE
      & BELIEVE ME TO BE FOR EVER YOURS . . . . . . . .         798D LETTER 10         PROSE
      "BELIEVE ME TO BE YOURS AFFECTIONATELY CATHERINE BLAKE"    801A LETTER 12         PROSE
      NOR SHALL I EVER BE PERSWADED I BELIEVE . . . . . .        802A LETTER 14         PROSE
      & BELIEVE ME FOR EVER YOUR GRATEFUL                        802D LETTER 14         PROSE
         & AFFECTIONATE
      ACCEPT THEM YOURSELF & BELIEVE ME FOR EVER . . . . .       803C LETTER 15         PROSE
      INJURE AS TO THE EAST AND NORTH I BELIEVE THEY CANNOT GET   807B LETTER 17         PROSE
      MR AND MRS FLAXMAN AND BELIEVE ME TO BE YOUR AFFECTIONATE   807B LETTER 17         PROSE
      ACCEPT MINE ALSO & BELIEVE ME TO REMAIN YOUR DEVOTED   .    808C LETTER 19         PROSE
      & BELIEVE ME TO BE EVER YOURS AFFECTIONATELY  . . . . .    823C LETTER 26         PROSE
      & FAMILY & BELIEVE ME TO REMAIN YOURS IN TRUTH & SINCERITY  826A LETTER 27         PROSE
      THIS I BELIEVE ABOUT BALANCES OUR ACCOUNT . . . . .        826B LETTER 28         PROSE
      YOURSELF & BELIEVE ME TO BE YOURS IN SINCERITY . . . .     834A LETTER 33         PROSE
      WHICH I BELIEVE IS NOW FOR EVER FALLEN INTO THE ABYSS  .   835A LETTER 34         PROSE
      COMPLIMENTS TO YOU HE IS SO BUSY THAT I BELIEVE I SHALL     836C LETTER 35         PROSE
      & BELIEVE ME TO REMAIN EVER YOURS . . . . . . . .         840A LETTER 38         PROSE
      I HOPE YOU WILL BELIEVE ME WHEN I SAY THAT MY SOLICITUDE    840B LETTER 39         PROSE
      WHICH I BELIEVE YOU THOUGHT FIT NOT TO PRINT  . . . .      841C LETTER 41         PROSE
      AND I BELIEVE TWO DAUGHTERS WITH MAPS INSTRUMENTS &C   .    843C LETTER 43         PROSE
      I AM NOT APT TO BELIEVE LITERALLY WHAT BOOKSELLERS SAY AND  846D LETTER 44         PROSE
      BELIEVE HE SAYS HIS ENGAGEMENTS ARE SO MULTIFORM THAT HE    853A LETTER 51        *PROSE
      PRAY ACCEPT MY & MY WIFE'S SINCEREST AFFECTION & BELIEVE    857C LETTER 54         PROSE
      IN THE MEAN TIME BELIEVE ME TO BE YOUR SINCERE FRIEND  .    866A LETTER 63         PROSE
      PERHAPS & I VERILY BELIEVE IT EVERY DEATH IS AN IMPROVEMENT 868D LETTER 68         PROSE
      I HAVE I BELIEVE DONE NEARLY ALL THAT WE AGREED ON &C  .    870B LETTER 71         PROSE
      I BELIEVE MY CONSTITUTION TO BE A GOOD ONE BUT IT HAS  .    870D LETTER 72         PROSE
      IN THOSE PAROXYSMS WHICH I NOW BELIEVE WILL NEVER MORE  .   873C LETTER 77         PROSE
      BELIEVE ME TO BE DR SIR YOURS SINCERELY . . . . . .        873C LETTER 77         PROSE
      & BELIEVE ME TO BE YOURS SINCERELY  . . . . . . .         874B LETTER 79         PROSE
BELIEVED
      AND MANY BELIEVED WHAT THEY SAW AND PROPHECIED OF JESUS     682B JERUSALEM 52      PROSE
      PROTECTING ANGEL AARON ABRAHAM BELIEVED GOD  . . . . .    SUPP INSC HERVEY       *TITLE
BELIEVES
      HIM OF MR ROSE MY BROTHER SAYS HE BELIEVES SR ALLAN IS  .  834D LETTER 34         PROSE
BELIEVING
      BELIEVING WITH MILTON THE ANCIENT BRITISH HISTORY   . . .  578C DESC CAT 5        PROSE
      OR CALL MEN WISE FOR NOT BELIEVING  . . . . . . . .       756 EV GOSPEL(H)/N      4
BELIN
      SATAN CAIN TUBAL NIMROD PHAROH PRIAM BLADUD BELIN   . . .  713 JERUSALEM 73       35
BELL
      THE BELL STRUCK ONE AND SHOOK THE SILENT TOWER   . . . .     4 FAIR ELENOR/PS      1
      THE VILLAGE BELL ALARMS AWAY I GO . . . . . . . . .        10 WHEN EARLY/PS       5
      AND THE SOUND OF THE BELL AND VOICE OF THE SABBATH . . .   140 FRENCH REVOLTN     146
      [THEY SHALL HAVE A PRIEST & A PASSING BELL]   . . . . .    185 LET BROTHELS/N      19
      LONG JOHN BROWN & LITTLE MARY BELL  . . . . . . . .      434A LONG JOHN BRWN     TITLE
      [PRETTY] LITTLE MARY BELL HAD A FAIRY IN A NUT  . . . .    434 LONG JOHN BRWN      1
      [YOUNG] LONG JOHN BROWN LOVD [PRETTY] LITTLE MARY BELL  .   434 LONG JOHN BRWN      3
      AND WOE & ALACK FOR PRETTY MARY BELL  . . . . . . .       434 LONG JOHN BRWN     18
      AND THERE GOES MISS BELL WITH HER RUSTY OLD NUT   . . .    434 LONG JOHN BRWN     20
      INDICATES THE SOUND OF THE CURFEW BELL  . . . . . .       619B ILLUS MILTON      PROSE
BELLEROPHON
      HE HAS TOLD THE STORY OF BELLEROPHON & OMITTED   . . . .   778A HOMERS POETRY     PROSE
BELLOW
      THE BULLS OF LUVAH BREATHING FIRE BELLOW ON BURNING        320 FOUR ZOAS 7        16
         PASTURES
      THE BLEAT THE BARK BELLOW & ROAR  . . . . . . . .        432 AUGURIES           71
BELLOWD
      THEN THE THUNDERS OF URIZEN BELLOWD ALOUD   . . . . .      248 SONG OF LOS 7      24
      SO THARMAS BELLOWD OER THE OCEAN THUNDRING SOBBING BURSTING 296 FOUR ZOAS 3       176
      HE FALLING ON THE ROCKS BELLOWD HIS DOLOR TILL THE BLOOD    299 FOUR ZOAS 4       61
      THE HORRID TRUMPETS OF THE DEEP BELLOWD WITH BITTER BLASTS  306 FOUR ZOAS 5       40
BELLOWING
      [THE BELLOWING ?FURNACES' BLARE BY THE LONG SOUNDING        346 FOUR ZOAS 8     * 204
         CLARION]
      THE BELLOWING FURNACES' BLARE BY THE LONG SOUNDING CLARION  509 MILTON 24         64
      BEFORE THE ANVIL WATCHES THE BELLOWING FLAMES THUNDERING    636 JERUSALEM 16      10
BELLOWS
      THE ETERNAL PROPHET HEAVD THE DARK BELLOWS  . . . . .      227 URIZEN 10          15
      THE BELLOWS & HAMMER ARE SILENT NOW . . . . . . . .       230 URIZEN 13          37
      MELT INTO FURROWS WINTER BLOWS HIS BELLOWS ICE & SNOW  . .  276 FOUR ZOAS 1      424
      THE BELLOWS BEGAN TO BLOW & THE LIONS OF URIZEN STOOD ROUND 281 FOUR ZOAS 2       32
         THE ANVIL
      HIS CLOUDY BELLOWS & THE SOUTH & EAST & DISMAL WEST  . .   282 FOUR ZOAS 2        69
      BUT ALL THE FURNACES WERE OUT & THE BELLOWS HAD CEAST TO    305 FOUR ZOAS 5        17
         BLOW
      MY SOUL IS SEVEN FURNACES INCESSANT ROARS THE BELLOWS  .   349 FOUR ZOAS 8     * 305
      LOUD SOUNDS THE HAMMER OF LOS & LOUD HIS BELLOWS IS HEARD   485 MILTON 6          8
      THUNDERING THE HAMMERS BEAT & THE BELLOWS BLOW LOUD  . .   509 MILTON 24         52
      THE BELLOWS ARE THE ANIMAL LUNGS THE HAMMERS THE ANIMAL     509 MILTON 24         58
         HEART
```

	PAGE	TITLE	LINE
BELLOWS (CONTINUED)			
TAKE THOU THIS HAMMER & IN PATIENCE HEAVE THE THUNDERING BELLOWS	627	JERUSALEM 8	39
GROANING THE SPECTRE HEAVD THE BELLOWS OBEYING LOS'S FROWNS	628	JERUSALEM 9 *	33
THE BELLOWS & THE HAMMERS MOVE COMPELLD BY LOS'S HAND . .	629	JERUSALEM 10	6
BENEATH THE STORMS OF THEOTORMON & THE THUNDRING BELLOWS	636	JERUSALEM 16	8
HE SIEZD HIS HAMMER & TONGS HIS IRON POKER & HIS BELLOWS	658	JERUSALEM 32	8
HE HEAVD HIS THUNDRING BELLOWS UPON THE VALLEYS OF MIDDLESEX	660	JERUSALEM 34	18
THE BELLOWS ARE THE ANIMAL LUNGS THE HAMMERS THE ANIMAL HEART	684	JERUSALEM 53	12
THEN LOS HEAVED HIS THUNDRING BELLOWS ON THE VALLEY OF MIDDLESEX	687	JERUSALEM 56	1
MY SOUL IS SEVEN FURNACES INCESSANT ROARS THE BELLOWS . .	705	JERUSALEM 67	52
INTO HIS THUNDERING BELLOWS HEAVING IT FOR A LOUD BLAST	726	JERUSALEM 82	58
REPENTANT AND SHE ALSO IN THE EDDYING WIND OF LOS'S BELLOWS	726	JERUSALEM 82	74
LOS ANSWERD SIGHING LIKE THE BELLOWS OF HIS FURNACES . .	733	JERUSALEM 88	1
BELL'S			
AND INCLOSE WITH THEM A CATALOGUE OF BELL'S GALLERY AND	844C	LETTER 43	PROSE
CRITICISM IN BELL'S WEEKLY MESSENGER...MAY ON THE PICTURE	863D	LETTER 61	PROSE
BELLS			
THE MERRY BELLS RING	116	ECCHOING GR/SI	3
EVERY FOOL SHOOK HIS BELLS THROUGHOUT THE LAND	554	BLAKES APL/N 1	2
EVERY FOOL SHOOK HIS BELLS THROUGHOUT THE LAND	555	BLAKES APL/N 2	6
EVERY FOOL SHOOK HIS BELLS THROUGHOUT THE LAND	595	BLAKES APOL/PA	2
THE CHURCH STEEPLE WITH ITS MERRY BELLS	618C	ILLUS MILTON	PROSE
THERE BELLS OF SILVER ROUND THY KNEES LIVING ARTICULATE	731	JERUSALEM 86	29
FOR I HEAR THE BELLS RING & THE TRUMPETS SOUND . . .	854C	LETTER 53	PROSE
BELLS'			
TO THE BELLS' CHEARFUL SOUND	116	ECCHOING GR/SI	8
BELL-WEATHER			
AND IF THE BELL-WEATHER IS TAINTED I WISH	22	EDW THIRD/PS 3	51
BELLY			
WITH HIS FAT BELLY & HIS ROUND CHIN	46	PHEBUS CAME/IM	2
COVERD & SCALES HIS HANDS & FEET UPON HIS BELLY FALLING	352	FOUR ZOAS 8	425
BESIDE HIM LIES THE LION DEAD & IN HIS BELLY WORMS . .	354	FOUR ZOAS 8	527
BELONG			
BY THE SLEEVE CRIES PRAY SIR WHO DO ALL THEY BELONG TO .	45A	ISLAND MOON 1	PROSE
THESE BELONG TO PLATO & SENECA & NERO	395D	ANNO WATSON	MARG
BELONG TO GOD ALONE AND ALL THY LITTLE ONES ARE HOLY . .	657	JERUSALEM 31	45
ALL BROAD & GENERAL PRINCIPLES BELONG TO BENEVOLENCE . .	672	JERUSALEM 43	22
CONSIDERATIONS & BELONG TO PHILOSOPHY & NOT TO POETRY . .	778C	HOMERS POETRY	PROSE
BELONGED			
IT BELONGED TO THE MONASTERY (OF) ST MARY OVERIES AND . .	590B	CHAUCER 2	*PROSE
BELONGING			
CHILDHOOD AND AGE ARE EQUALLY BELONGING TO EVERY CLASS . .	460B	ANNO REYNOLDS	MARG
THE FEMALES BELONGING TO SUCH STATES WHO ARE	608D	V LAST JUDG/N	PROSE
LEAR & CORDELIA BELONGING TO MR WALKER	849A	LETTER 45	PROSE
BELONGS			
BELONGS TO NONE BUT THE GREATEST ARTISTS	453D	ANNO REYNOLDS	MARG
BELOVD			
AND WOVE THEM BODIES CALLING THEM HER BELOVD SONS & DAUGHTERS	345	FOUR ZOAS 8	184
SHALL NEVER BE BELOVD BY MEN	431	AUGURIES	30
BELOVED SEE MUCH BELOVED			
AND PLENTY CROWNED HIS BOARD BELOVED REVERED OF MAN . . .	39C	SAMSON/PS	PROSE
& THIS IS BELOVED OF GOD AND MAN	75A	ANNO LAVATER	MARG
THE JOY OF WOMAN IS THE DEATH OF HER MOST BEST BELOVED . .	289	FOUR ZOAS 2	349
UNLESS MY BELOVED IS BOUND UPON THE STEMS OF VEGETATION	349	FOUR ZOAS 8	321
OF GOLGONOOZA HER WELL BELOVED KNOWING HE WAS ORC'S HUMAN REMAINS	351	FOUR ZOAS 8	384
TO DEFEND ME FROM THY TERRORS O ORC MY ONLY BELOVED . .	499	MILTON 18	25
COME TO MY IVORY PALACES O BELOVED OF THY MOTHER . . .	501	MILTON 20	4
THEY SAID O FATHER MOST BELOVED O MERCIFUL PARENT . . .	505	MILTON 22	29
MILTON WILL UTTERLY CONSUME US & THEE OUR BELOVED FATHER	507	MILTON 23	13
TO BOWLAHOOLA O FATHER MOST BELOVED O MILD PARENT . . .	507	MILTON 23	18
THO STRONG AND MIGHTY TO DESTROY O LOS OUR BELOVED FATHER	507	MILTON 23	20
AS THE BELOVED INFANT IN HIS MOTHER'S BOSOM ROUND INCIRCLED	518	MILTON 30	11
FOR ITS LIGHT AND ITS WARMTH THIS MAN IS BELOVED AND . .	570B	DESC CAT 3	PROSE
WHICH LOOKS FOR NO OTHER HEAVEN THAN THEIR BELOVED . . .	610D	V LAST JUDG/N	PROSE
SLAY NOT MY LITTLE ONES BELOVED VIRGIN DAUGHTER OF BABYLON	643	JERUSALEM 20	27
IN AN ETERNAL DEATH FOR ALBION'S SAKE OUR BEST BELOVED . .	646	JERUSALEM 23	10
ALL YOU MY FRIENDS & BROTHERS ALL YOU MY BELOVED COMPANIONS	673	JERUSALEM 43	74
THUNDER IN THE MIDST OF KINDNESS & LOVE THAT KILLS ITS BELOVED	677	JERUSALEM 48	16
THEY KNEW NOT THIS VALA WAS THEIR BELOVED MOTHER VALA ALBION'S WIFE	701	JERUSALEM 65	71
UNLESS MY BELOVED IS BOUND UPON THE STEMS OF VEGETATION	705	JERUSALEM 68	9
HE CONQUERD LUVAH MY BELOVED HE TOOK ME AND MY FATHER . .	722	JERUSALEM 80	19
I HAVE STRIPD OFF JOSEPH'S BEAUTIFUL INTEGUMENT FOR MY BELOVED	724	JERUSALEM 81	11
SHEWD HER THE FIBRES OF HER BELOVED TO AMELIORATE . . .	726	JERUSALEM 82	61
ALBION BELOVED LAND I SEE THY MOUNTAINS & THY HILLS . .	731	JERUSALEM 86	11
AH THEN I SAW MY BELOVED ONES FLEEING FROM MY TENT . . .	740	JERUSALEM 93	12
TO IMPROVEMENT IN MY BELOVED ARTS ONE THING	812A	LETTER 22	PROSE
A PRINCE AMONG PRINCES & EVEN ON EARTH BELOVED BY THE GOOD	830A	LETTER 30	PROSE
I WISH I COULD GIVE YOU A PLEASANT ACCOUNT OF OUR BELOVED	836B	LETTER 35	PROSE
AS WHEN SHE FIRST MOUNTED ME ON MY BELOVED BRUNO . . .	843A	LETTER 42	PROSE
OF SINCERE SORROW ON ACCOUNT OF THE BELOVED COUNCILLOR . .	851C	LETTER 50	PROSE
BELOVED-ONE			
COME THEN TO EPHRAIM & MANASSEH O BELOVED-ONE	501	MILTON 20	3

203

	PAGE	TITLE	LINE

BELOVED'S   SEE MUCH BELOVED'S
BELOVEDS
    AND HIS OWN BELOVEDS THEN HE TURND SICK HIS SOUL   669 JERUSALEM 42   4
        DIED WITHIN HIM
    IN NARROW VALES I WALK & COUNT THE BONES OF MY BELOVEDS   721 JERUSALEM 79   65
BELOVEDS'
    OR HOW UPON THE DISTANT HILLS SEE MY BELOVEDS' TENTS . . 740 JERUSALEM 93   16
BELOW
    WHO THE LEADERS OF THESE ARE WILL BE SHEWN BELOW . . . . 581D DESC CAT 8   PROSE
    A LITTLE BELOW SETH ON HIS RIGHT ARE TWO FIGURES . . . . 611D V LAST JUDG/N PROSE
    THE MOON THAT GLOWD REMOTE BELOW   818 HAPPINESS/L   73
BELVIDERE
    VENUS OF MEDICIS APOLLO BELVIDERE . . . . 565D DESC CAT 2   PROSE
BELYING
    AS AN ORIGINAL [BELYING] BE-LYING THE ENGLISH CHARACTER IN   595C PUB ADDRESS/N PROSE
BE-LYING
    AS AN ORIGINAL [BELYING] BE-LYING THE ENGLISH CHARACTER IN   595C PUB ADDRESS/N PROSE
BENCH
    TO TAKE WITH ME I HAVE BEEN BEFORE A BENCH OF JUSTICES . . 827D LETTER 28   PROSE
BEND
    NOR BEND THY PILLARS WITH THINE IRON CAR   2 TO WINTER/PS   4
    WILL BEND OR BREAK US MY BLOOD LIKE A SPRINGTIDE . . . 26 EDW THIRD/PS 3 234
    SHALL LAUGH WHOSE FRUITFUL LAPS BEND DOWN WITH FULNESS . 33 EDW THIRD/PS 6 48
    WHILE FAR INTO THE VAST UNKNOWN THE STRONG WINGD EAGLES 284 FOUR ZOAS 2   150
        BEND
    I WILL TURN THE VOLUTIONS OF YOUR EARS OUTWARD & BEND YOUR 294 FOUR ZOAS 3   86
        NOSTRILS
    TWINGE & HIS IRON SINEWS BEND LIKE LEAD & FOLD   . . . 305 FOUR ZOAS 4   294
    INWRAP THE PARENTS IN COLD CLOUDS AS THEY BEND HOWLING OVER 309 FOUR ZOAS 5   171
    WHEN I BEND DOWNWARD BENDING MY HEAD DOWNWARD INTO THE   317 FOUR ZOAS 6   202
        DEEP
    THE STARRY HEAVENS REACH NO FURTHER BUT HERE BEND AND SET   516 MILTON 29   10
    I WILL TURN THE VOLUTIONS OF YOUR EARS OUTWARD AND BEND   655 JERUSALEM 29   67
        YOUR NOSTRILS
    THEY TURN CONTORTED THEIR IRON NECKS BEND UNWILLING TOWARDS 701 JERUSALEM 65   77
    AND HE WHO WILL NOT BEND TO LOVE MUST BE SUBDUD BY FEAR   725 JERUSALEM 81   16
BENDED
    A BENDED BOW IS LIFTED IN HEAVEN & A HEAVY IRON CHAIN . . 197 AMERICA 3   7
    A BENDED BOW IN HEAVEN IS LIFTED & A HEAVY IRON CHAIN . . 204 AMERICA CANC A 7
    WERE BENDED DOWNWARD AND THE NOSTRILS GOLDEN GATES SHUT   241 EUROPE 10   14
    OVER LONDON IN VOLUME TERRIFIC LOW BENDED IN ANGER . . . 535 MILTON 42   35
    LOS BENDED HIS NOSTRILS DOWN TO THE EARTH THEN SENT HIM   661 JERUSALEM 34   47
        OVER
    ON MOUNT GILEAD LOOKING TOWARD GILGAL AND LOS BENDED . . 662 JERUSALEM 36   12
    AS LOS BENDED THE SENSES OF REUBEN REUBEN IS MERLIN . . 663 JERUSALEM 36   41
    BUT AS THE WILL MUST NOT BE BENDED BUT IN THE DAY OF DIVINE 674 JERUSALEM 44   18
BENDING
    THE SHINING SNAKE GLIDES OER THE BENDING GRASS   . . . . 24 EDW THIRD/PS 3 126
    THE HUSBANDMAN DOTH LEAVE HIS BENDING HARVEST . . . . 34B KING JOHN/PS PROSE
    THEY STOOD BY THE BED LIKE REEDS BENDING OVER A LAKE . . 35D COUCH DEATH/PS PROSE
    NOW LOWLY BENDING WHISPERS IN MINE EAR . . . . 36D CONTEMPLATN/PS PROSE
    SHALL WEEP BENDING TO EARTH EMBRACING THE VALLEYS . . . 144 FRENCH REVOLTN 224
    . . . BENDING OVER THE CITIES OF MEN . . . . 146 FRENCH REVOLTN 264
    RIBS LIKE A BENDING CAVERN . . . . 228 URIZEN 10   39
    TILL THE HORRID PLANT BENDING ITS BOUGHS . . . . . . 252 AHANIA 3   65
    WEEPING [AND] THEN BENDING FROM HIS CLOUDS . . . . . 266 FOUR ZOAS 1   72
    AFAR INTO THE ZENITH HIGH BENDING THY FURIOUS COURSE . . 278 FOUR ZOAS 1   495
    THE BLOODY MASS BEGAN TO ANIMATE I BENDING OVER . . . 300 FOUR ZOAS 4   96
    SHOOTING PAIND RIBBS LIKE A BENDING CAVERN . . . . . 303 FOUR ZOAS 4   220
    WHEN I BEND DOWNWARD BENDING MY HEAD DOWNWARD INTO THE   317 FOUR ZOAS 6   202
        DEEP
    BRANCHES INTO THE HEAVEN OF LOS THEY PIPE FORMD BENDING   321 FOUR ZOAS 7   33
        DOWN
    HE VANQUISHD WITH THE STRENGTH OF ART BENDING THEIR IRON   331 FOUR ZOAS 7   459
        POINTS
    OR ORC BENDING DOWN AS THE BINDER OF THE SHEAVES FOLLOWS   332 FOUR ZOAS 7   462
    . . . ON THE TOPS OF THE BENDING GRASS . . . . . . 367 FOUR ZOAS 9   391
    THE LION OF TERROR SHALL COME DOWN & BENDING HIS BRIGHT   376 FOUR ZOAS 9   706
        MANE
    THE FURNACE OF LOS BEFORE THE EASTERN GATE BENDING THEIR   623 JERUSALEM 5   28
        FURY
    AND LOS BEHELD THE MILD EMANATION JERUSALEM EASTWARD   635 JERUSALEM 14   31
        BENDING
    BENDING ACROSS THE ROAD OF OXFORD STREET IT FROM HYDE PARK 665 JERUSALEM 38   57
    IN MERCIFUL ORDER BENDING THE LAWS OF CRUELTY TO PEACE . . 680 JERUSALEM 49   55
    . . . BENDING THRO THE WIDE HEAVENS . . . . . . 744 JERUSALEM 98   2
BENDS
    FOR LOS AGAINST THE EAST HIS FORCE CONTINUALLY BENDS . . 512 MILTON 26   18
    HIS HEAD BENDS OVER LONDON HE SEES HIS EMBODIED SPECTRE   531 MILTON 39   46
    BUT LOS HIMSELF AGAINST ALBION'S SONS HIS FURY BENDS FOR HE 638 JERUSALEM 17   6
    GIVING THEM BENDS OF SELF INTEREST & SELFISH NATURAL VIRTUE 723 JERUSALEM 80   75
    BENDS OVER THY IMMORTAL HEAD IN WHICH ETERNITY DWELLS . . 731 JERUSALEM 86   10
BENEATH
    BENEATH OUR OAKS HAST SLEPT WHILE WE BEHELD . . . . . 1 TO SUMMER/PS   5
    BENEATH OUR THICKEST SHADES WE OFT HAVE HEARD . . . . 2 TO SUMMER/PS   7
    BENEATH MY SHADY ROOF THERE THOU MAYST REST . . . 2 TO AUTUMN/PS   3
    IS DRIVN YELLING TO HIS CAVES BENEATH MOUNT HECLA . . . 3 TO WINTER/PS   16
    LIKE GENTLE STREAMS BENEATH OUR FEET . . . . 7 LOVE HARMNY/PS   7
    BENEATH THE OAKEN TREE . . . . 8 LOVE JOCUND/PS   14
    CLOSES HER EYES IN SLEEP BENEATH NIGHT'S SHADE . . . . 10 FRESH FROM/PS   18
    WHEN EVENING SITS BENEATH HER DUSKY BOWR . . . . . 10 WHEN EARLY/PS   3
    DOTH DROP A TEAR BENEATH THE SILENT SHADE . . . . . 10 WHEN EARLY/PS   8

```
                                                           PAGE      TITLE        LINE
BENEATH    (CONTINUED)
    BENEATH THE BOSOM OF THE SEA    . . . . . . . .  .      11  TO MUSES/PS          10
    BENEATH THEM ROLLD LIKE TEMPESTS BLACK    . . . . .     11  GWIN KING/PS         17
    BENEATH HIS ARM LIKE SHEEP THEY DIE    . . . . . . .    13  GWIN KING/PS         85
    BRAVE LORDS WHO FELL BENEATH THE BLOODY AXE    . . . .  18  EDW THIRD/PS 1       44
    TO LIGHT ANOTHER PATTLE LAST NIGHT BENEATH    . . . .   25  EDW THIRD/PS 3      160
    THY WIDOWED VIRGINS WEEP BENEATH THY SHADES   . . . .  34B  KING JOHN/PS      PROSE
    BENEATH ME BURNS ETERNAL FIRE O FOR A HAND TO PLUCK ME 36B  COUCH DEATH/PS    PROSE
      FORTH
    SITTING ALL BENEATH A GROT    . . . . . . . .  .        53  PHEBE DREST/IM        3
    BENEATH THEM SIT THE REVREND MEN THE GUARDIANS OF THE POOR  59  HOLY THURS/IM    17
    AND HAR & HEVA LIKE TWO CHILDREN SAT BENEATH THE OAK   . .  100  TIRIEL 2          5
    ALL DAY THEY WALKD & ALL THE NIGHT BENEATH THE PLEASANT    104  TIRIEL 4         30
      MOON
    [WITH DAGGERS HID BENEATH THEIR LIPS & POISON IN THEIR    109  TIRIEL 8         14
      TONGUE ]
    AND WHY MEN BOUND BENEATH THE HEAVENS IN A REPTILE FORM   110  TIRIEL 8         23
    BENEATH THEM SIT THE AGED MEN WISE GUARDIANS OF THE POOR  122  HOLY THURS/SI    11
    IN DISMAL VOLUMES AS RISEN FROM BENEATH THE ARCHBISHOP    139  FRENCH REVOLTN  126
      OF PARIS AROSE
    BENEATH IN THE AWFUL VOID . . . . . . . . . .            140  FRENCH REVOLTN  134
    THEY MURMURING DIVIDE WHILE THE WIND SLEEPS BENEATH . . .  146  FRENCH REVOLTN  266
    . . . AND THE SENATE IN PEACE SAT BENEATH MORNING'S BEAM  148  FRENCH REVOLTN  306
    TILL A VOID BOUNDLESS AS A NETHER SKY APPEARD BENEATH US  155D  MARRIAGE HH 17 PROSE
    OF A BURNING CITY BENEATH US AT AN IMMENSE DISTANCE  . . 156A  MARRIAGE HH 17 PROSE
    FIRE BURST AND ROLLD THRO THE DEEP BLACKNING ALL BENEATH 156B  MARRIAGE HH 17 PROSE
    & ROLLED WITH A TERRIBLE NOISE BENEATH US WAS NOTHING NOW 156B MARRIAGE HH 17 PROSE
    ALL NIGHT BENEATH THE RUINS THEN   . . . . . . . .      159D  SONG LIBERTY    PROSE
    MY FOE OUTSTRETCHD BENEATH THE TREE                      166  CHRISTN FORB/N   17
    [[WHERE BENEATH MY]]                                     167  INFANT SORW/N    34
    NOR SEEST THE NET THAT IS SPREAD BENEATH                 168  O LAPWING/N       2
    AT LAMBETH BENEATH THE POPLAR TREES   . . . . . . .      187  WHEN KLOPSTK/N    8
    WITH SECRET TEARS BENEATH HIM SOUND LIKE WAVES ON A DESERT 190  V DAU ALBION 2   7
      SHORE
    THE VOICE OF SLAVES BENEATH THE SUN AND CHILDREN BOUGHT  190  V DAU ALBION 2    8
      WITH MONEY
    THAT SHIVER IN RELIGIOUS CAVES BENEATH THE BURNING FIRES 190  V DAU ALBION 2    9
    DOES NOT THE EAGLE SCORN THE EARTH & DESPISE THE TREASURES 193  V DAU ALBION 5  39
      BENEATH
    FOR CHAIND BENEATH I REND THESE CAVERNS WHEN THOU BRINGEST 196  AMERICA PREL 1  18
      FOOD
    AND FLAMD RED METEORS ROUND THE LAND OF ALBION BENEATH  . . 197  AMERICA 3      16
    THY MOTHER LAYS HER LENGTH OUTSTRETCHD UPON THE SHORE    199  AMERICA 9        25
      BENEATH
    BENEATH HIM ROLLD HIS NUMEROUS HOSTS ALL ALBION'S ANGELS 201  AMERICA 13       13
      CAMPD
    DARK IS THE HEAVEN ABOVE & COLD & HARD THE EARTH BENEATH 201  AMERICA 14        7
    AND FLAMD FIERCE METEORS ROUND THE LAND OF ALBION BENEATH 204  AMERICA CANC A * 16
    THEN BURST THE CENTER FROM ITS ORB AND FOUND A PLACE    204  AMERICA CANC B     6
      BENEATH
    THE VALLEY MOVD BENEATH ITS SHINING PILLARS SPLIT IN TWAIN 204  AMERICA CANC B  23
    EVEN [TO] ON RATIONAL THINGS BENEATH AND FROM THE PALACE  205  AMERICA CANC C    8
      WALLS
    THE BRITISH COLONIES BENEATH THE WOFUL PRINCES FADE . . . 206  THIRALATHA       4
    WHAT IS MAN I FOUND HIM BENEATH A TREE   . . . . . . . 209C  FOR CHILDRN/GP TITLE
    MY FOE OUTSTRETCHD BENEATH THE TREE   . . . . . . . .    218  POISON TREE/SE   16
    FROM BENEATH HIS ORBS OF VISION   . . . . . . . . .      229  URIZEN 11        22
    IN A WINTERLY NIGHT BENEATH . . . . . . . . . . .        230  URIZEN 15         4
    BENEATH URIZEN'S DEATHFUL SHADOW   . . . . . . . .       233  URIZEN 20        25
    TO DIVIDE THE ABYSS BENEATH . . . . . . . . . . .        233  URIZEN 20        34
    BENEATH THE DARK NET OF INFECTION   . . . . . . . .      236  URIZEN 25        30
    BENEATH THE NET OF URIZEN   . . . . . . . . . . .        236  URIZEN 28        13
    MY ROOTS ARE BRANDISHD IN THE HEAVENS MY FRUITS IN EARTH 238  EUROPE PREL 1     8
      BENEATH
    ONE HOUR THEY LAY BURIED BENEATH THE RUINS OF THAT HALL  241  EUROPE 9         14
    DOWNWARD TIS SUNK BENEATH TH ATTRACTIVE NORTH THAT ROUND 242  EUROPE 10        30
      THE FEET
    . . . BENEATH THE SOLEMN MOON   . . . . . . . . .        244  EUROPE 14        32
    NOAH SHRUNK BENEATH THE WATERS  . . . . . . . . . .      245  SONG OF LOS 3    15
    SITTING BENEATH THE ETERNAL OAK   . . . . . . . . .      256  BOOK OF LOS 3     4
    BENEATH HIM & ON ALL SIDES ROUND   . . . . . . .        257  BOOK OF LOS 4    26
    WEARY OVERWEIGHD SINKING BENEATH   . . . . . . . .       258  BOOK OF LOS 4    61
    SHOOTING OUT FROM THE SEED SHOT BENEATH   . . . . . .    259  BOOK OF LOS 4    65
    OFT HE QUENCHD IT BENEATH IN THE DEEPS   . . . . . .     260  BOOK OF LOS 5    35
    OF WAR THE MOUNTAINS FLED AWAY THEY SOUGHT A PLACE BENEATH 275  FOUR ZOAS 1    416
    DEEP HORRIBLE WITHOUT END SEPARATED FROM BEULAH FAR BENEATH 279  FOUR ZOAS 1   542
    [TWO FORMS OF HORROR HOWLD BENEATH IT]   . . . . . SUPP  FOUR ZOAS 1       *
    BENEATH HIS FEET SHOT THRO HIM AS HE STOOD IN THE HUMAN  280  FOUR ZOAS 2      12
      BRAIN
    NO MORE EXULTING FOR HE SAW ETERNAL DEATH BENEATH   . . . 280  FOUR ZOAS 2     14
    HE SAW THE INDEFINITE SPACE BENEATH & HIS SOUL SHRUNK WITH 280  FOUR ZOAS 2    20
      HORROR
    IN ULRO BEULAH WHERE THE DEAD WAIL NIGHT & DAY  . . 282  FOUR ZOAS 2           71
    BENEATH THE FURNACES A WOFUL HEAP IN LIVING DEATH  . . . 283  FOUR ZOAS 2     116
    IN WATERS & IN EARTH BENEATH THEY CRIED TO ONE ANOTHER . 283  FOUR ZOAS 2     123
    BENEATH THE CAVERNS ROLL THE WEIGHTS OF LEAD & SPINDLES  284  FOUR ZOAS 2     148
      OF IRON
    AND THE NINE SPHERES REJOICE BENEATH MY POWERFUL CONTROLL 289  FOUR ZOAS 2    353
    NOW MY LEFT HAND I STRETCH TO EARTH BENEATH   . . . . .  289  FOUR ZOAS 2     369
    I FAINT BENEATH THESE BEAMS OF THINE   . . . . . . .     290  FOUR ZOAS 2     375
    TO WEIGH ME DOWN BENEATH THE GRAVE INTO NON ENTITY  . .  295  FOUR ZOAS 3     127
    IN TORRENTS OF DESPAIR IN VAIN FOR IF I PLUNGE BENEATH . 298  FOUR ZOAS 4      13
```

205

		PAGE	TITLE	LINE

BENEATH   (CONTINUED)
. . . BENEATH THE BOTTOM OF THE RAGING OCEANS . . . .   298 FOUR ZOAS 4   *   16
GO FORTH REBUILD THIS UNIVERSE BENEATH MY INDIGNANT POWER   298 FOUR ZOAS 4   27
IN PEACE BENEATH MY AWFUL FROWN MY WILL SHALL BE MY LAW   299 FOUR ZOAS 4   55
SITTING BENEATH A TENT & VIEWING SHEEPFOLDS & SOFT PASTURES 301 FOUR ZOAS 4   148
TERRIFIED LOS BEHELD THE RUINS OF URIZEN BENEATH . . . .   301 FOUR ZOAS 4   161
AND FLUCTUATING ALL BENEATH IN EDDIES OF MOLTEN FLUID . .   301 FOUR ZOAS 4   164
FREEZING TO SOLID ALL BENEATH HIS GREY OBLIVIOUS FORM . .   302 FOUR ZOAS 4   172
THE LOVELY FEMALE HOWLD & URIZEN BENEATH DEEP GROAND . .   302 FOUR ZOAS 4   189
TWO EARS IN CLOSE VOLUTIONS FROM BENEATH HIS ORBS OF VISION   303 FOUR ZOAS 4   233
THAT VEGETATES BENEATH THE SEA THE LIMBS OF MAN VEGETATED   304 FOUR ZOAS 4   267
THEN WONDROUSLY THE [DEEP BENEATH] . . . .   304 FOUR ZOAS 4   275
BENEATH THE DEEPS IN DISMAL DARKNESS BENEATH IMMENSITY   304 FOUR ZOAS 4   279
AND ENITHARMON SHRUNK UP ALL THEIR FIBRES WITHRING BENEATH   305 FOUR ZOAS 5   8
GRIM FROST BENEATH & TERRIBLE SNOW LINKD IN A MARRIAGE   306 FOUR ZOAS 5   33
    CHAIN
INTO THE IRON ROCK & GREW A CHAIN BENEATH THE EARTH . . .   309 FOUR ZOAS 5   167
THEY SHRUNK INTO THEIR CHANNELS DRY THE ROCKY STRAND   312 FOUR ZOAS 6   22
    BENEATH HIS FEET
[CEASE] END & THE ETERNAL MAN NO MORE RENEW BENEATH OUR   313 FOUR ZOAS 6   66
    POWER
AN EARTH OF WINTRY WOE BENEATH THEIR FEET & ROUND THEIR   314 FOUR ZOAS 6   92
    LOINS
WHERE SELF SUSTAINING I MAY VIEW ALL THING BENEATH MY FEET   317 FOUR ZOAS 6   198
I THOUGHT PERHAPS TO FIND AN END A WORLD BENEATH   317 FOUR ZOAS 6   200
    OF VOIDNESS
AND LAUGHTER SAT BENEATH THE OAKS & INNOCENCE SPORTED ROUND   317 FOUR ZOAS 6   214
WHERE ARE THEY WHELMD BENEATH THESE RUINS . . . .   317 FOUR ZOAS 6   * 217
ABOVE BENEATH ON ALL SIDES ROUND IN THE VAST DEEP   318 FOUR ZOAS 6   275
    OF IMMENSITY
THE DARKNING SPECTRE OF URTHONA HID BENEATH A ROCK . . .   320 FOUR ZOAS 7   2
BENEATH THEE & AROUND ABOVE A SHOWER OF FIRE NOW BEATS .   321 FOUR ZOAS 7   51
TO BEAR THEE DOWN BENEATH THE WAVES IN STIFLING DESPAIR   321 FOUR ZOAS 7   56
TO BRING THE SHADOW OF ENITHARMON BENEATH OUR WONDROUS TREE   323 FOUR ZOAS 7   113
BENEATH THE TREE OF MYSTERY WHICH IN THE DISMAL ABYSS .   325 FOUR ZOAS 7   212
BENEATH THE TREE OF MYSTERY AMONG THE LEAVES & FRUIT   325 FOUR ZOAS 7   218
TILL ENITHARMON'S SHADOW PREGNANT IN THE DEEPS BENEATH .   328 FOUR ZOAS 7   316
BENEATH THE TREE OF MYSTERY FOR THE IMMORTAL SHADOW   328 FOUR ZOAS 7   326
    SHUDDERING
. . . BENEATH ENITHARMON'S COUCH   328 FOUR ZOAS 7   334
THO HORRIBLE & GHASTLY TO THINE EYES THO BURIED BENEATH   329 FOUR ZOAS 7   351
BUT ENITHARMON TREMBLING FLED & HID BENEATH URIZEN'S TREE   329 FOUR ZOAS 7   372
AND DOMES TERRIFIC IN THE NETHER HEAVENS FOR BENEATH .   329 FOUR ZOAS 7   379
WAS OPEND NEW HEAVENS & A NEW EARTH BENEATH & WITHIN .   329 FOUR ZOAS 7   380
WHEN IN THE DEEPS BENEATH I GATHERD OF THIS RUDDY FRUIT   329 FOUR ZOAS 7   387
. . . BENEATH THE [TREE] ROOTS OF MYSTERY IN DARKEST NIGHT   333 FOUR ZOAS 7B *   1
TO LABOUR & BEHOLD MY HEART SUNK DOWN BENEATH   334 FOUR ZOAS 7B   63
OR LIKE A CLOUD BENEATH & LIKE A FIRE FLAMING IN HIGH .   339 FOUR ZOAS 7B * 265
LIKE TO A RUSHING TORRENT BENEATH & A FLAMING ROCK ABOVE   340 FOUR ZOAS 7B   267
BENEATH DOWN TO HIS EYELIDS SCALES OF PEARL THEN GOLD &   342 FOUR ZOAS 8   70
    SILVER
FLATTEN ABOVE & BENEATH & STRETCH OUT INTO BEASTIAL LENGTH   344 FOUR ZOAS 8   128
I ALONE DARE THE LASH ABIDE TO SIT BENEATH THE BLAST . .   344 FOUR ZOAS 8   148
AND HE ROLLD DOWN BENEATH THE FIRES OF ORC A GLOBE IMMENSE   350 FOUR ZOAS 8   372
THEN JESUS CAME & DIED WILLING BENEATH TIRZAH & RAHAB .   351 FOUR ZOAS 8   406
LOS FELT THE STONY STUPOR & HIS HEAD ROLLD DOWN BENEATH   353 FOUR ZOAS 8   471
OF ALL BENEATH & ALL ABOVE & IN THE GENTLE WEST . . . .   355 FOUR ZOAS 8   569
OF FOAMING BLOOD BENEATH THE BLACK INCESSANT SKY TILL ALL   359 FOUR ZOAS 9   78
MY BIRDS ARE SILENT ON MY HILLS FLOCKS DIE BENEATH   359 FOUR ZOAS 9   101
    MY BRANCHES
FROM THE [BLACK] DARK JAWS OF DEATH BENEATH & DESOLATE   363 FOUR ZOAS 9   259
    SHORES REMOTE
HIDING HIS FACE IN THE DUST BENEATH [A] THE PRISONER'S   364 FOUR ZOAS 9   * 269
    FEET & SAYING
IN THE ETERNAL HEAVENS OF HUMAN [THOUGHT] IMAGINATION   366 FOUR ZOAS 9   368
    BURIED BENEATH
SO SAYING SHE SAT DOWN & WEPT BENEATH THE APPLE TREES . .   368 FOUR ZOAS 9   413
BENEATH HER ROSE A DOWNY BED & A CIELING COVERD ALL . . .   369 FOUR ZOAS 9   463
BUT HER FLOCKS WERE GONE UP FROM BENEATH THE TREES INTO   369 FOUR ZOAS 9   473
    THE HILLS
THEY FOLLOWD HER TO THE SILENT VALLY BENEATH THE SPREADING   369 FOUR ZOAS 9   * 479
    TREES
AND SAW IN THE DOOR WAY BENEATH THE TREES TWO LITTLE   370 FOUR ZOAS 9   507
    CHILDREN PLAYING
AND WHEN NIGHT CAME THE FLOCKS LAID ROUND THE HOUSE BENEATH   370 FOUR ZOAS 9   514
    THE TREES
DARKNESS WAS ALL BENEATH THE HEAVENS ONLY A LITTLE LIGHT   372 FOUR ZOAS 9   560
SUCH AS GLOWS OUT FROM SLEEPING SPIRITS APPEARD IN THE   372 FOUR ZOAS 9   561
    DEEPS BENEATH
BENEATH THICK CLOUDS DREADFUL LIGHTNINGS BURST & THUNDERS   372 FOUR ZOAS 9   565
    ROLL
ABOVE ON THE BRIGHT HEAVENS IN PEACE THE SPIRITS OF MEN   372 FOUR ZOAS 9   574
    BENEATH
BENEATH THEY SAW THEIR SONS & DAUGHTERS WONDERING   374 FOUR ZOAS 9   * 648
    INCONCEIVABLE
AT THE DARK MYRIADS IN SHADOWS IN THE WORLDS BENEATH .   374 FOUR ZOAS 9   649
SOUNDS ON THE FLOOR HEARD TERRIBLE BY ALL BENEATH   374 FOUR ZOAS 9   651
    THE HEAVENS
GO DOWN INTO THE DEPTHS GO DOWN & HIDE YOURSELVES BENEATH   374 FOUR ZOAS 9   660
REMAINS & IN THE VINEYARDS STAND THE ABOUNDING SHEAVES   375 FOUR ZOAS 9   697
    BENEATH
HEAVEN RANG WITH WINGED EXULTATION ALL BENEATH HOWLD LOUD   378 FOUR ZOAS 9   782

```
                                                              PAGE     TITLE           LINE
BENEATH   (CONTINUED)
  WITH TENFOLD ROUT & DESOLATION ROARD THE CHASMS BENEATH     378 FOUR ZOAS 9           783
  ONE EARTH ONE SEA BENEATH NOR ERRING GLOBES WANDER BUT      379 FOUR ZOAS 9           831
    STARS
  IN THE DEEP CAVES BENEATH HIS LIMBS RENEWD HIS LIONS ROAR   379 FOUR ZOAS 9           841
  BENEATH THE VEIL OF [?ENION] VALA ROSE THARMAS FROM DEWY    380 FOUR ZOAS AD 1 *        1
    TEARS
  THEY LIE IN TWISTING AGONIES BENEATH THE COVRING HEAVENS    381 FOUR ZOAS AD 2 *        5
  IN ALL ITS TURPITUDE BENEATH THE DIVINE LIGHT & OF LUVAH'S  382 FOUR ZOAS AD 6         22
    ROBES
  AND SUBMISSION TO DEATH BENEATH HIS FEET      . . . . . .   420 I SAW A MONK/N         54
  BENEATH THE WHITE THORN LOVELY MAY     . . . . . . . . .    421 BENEATH/N               1
  [BENEATH THE WHITE THORN LOVELY MAY]   . . . . . . . . .    422 BENEATH REWR/N          1
  THE BABE THAT WEEPS THE ROD BENEATH          . . . . . .    432 AUGURIES               73
  SOUNDING TO THE FOUR WINDS BENEATH [THE EARTH IS CONVULSD]  443A LAST JUDGMNT/L      PROSE
  HELL OPENS BENEATH THE HARLOT'S SEAT ON THE LEFT HAND    .  443B LAST JUDGMNT/L      PROSE
  ABRAHAM & MOSES KNEEL ON EACH SIDE BENEATH THEM    . . .    443B LAST JUDGMNT/L      PROSE
  FROM THE CLOUD ON WHICH EVE KNEELS [& BENEATH MOSES]    .   443B LAST JUDGMNT/L      PROSE
  THE ABYSS OF HELL WHICH OPENS [TO RECIEVE THEM] BENEATH     443C LAST JUDGMNT/L      PROSE
  & THE MOON BENEATH HER FEET WITH SIX INFANTS AROUND HER     443D LAST JUDGMNT/L      PROSE
  [THE] GREEN HILLS APPEAR BENEATH WITH THE GRAVES OF THE     443D LAST JUDGMNT/L      PROSE
    BLESSED
  BENEATH YOUR LAND OF SHADOWS OF ITS SACRIFICES AND    .     481 MILTON 2              11
  OF JERUSALEM HIS EMANATION IN THE HEAVENS BENEATH BEULAH    481 MILTON 2              15
  FROM BENEATH HIS ORBS OF VISION TWO EARS IN CLOSE VOLUTIONS 482 MILTON 3              17
  BENEATH THE PLOW OF RINTRAH & THE HARROW OF THE ALMIGHTY    483 MILTON 4               1
  ARE BUILT BENEATH THE EARTH & WATERS OF THE MUNDANE SHELL   483 MILTON 4               3
  FROM BREATHING FIELDS SATAN FAINTED BENEATH THE ARTILLERY   484 MILTON 5         *     2
  WHEN SATAN FAINTED BENEATH THE ARROWS OF ELYNITTRIA    . .  485 MILTON 5              43
  ON TYBURN'S BROOK LOUD GROANS THAMES BENEATH THE IRON FORGE 485 MILTON 6              11
  [BY ENITHARMON'S LOOMS & SPUN BENEATH THE SPINDLE          486 MILTON 7         *     1
    OF TIRZAH]
  AMONG ALBION'S DRUIDS & BARDS IN THE CAVES BENEATH ALBION'S 489 MILTON 9               2
  FOR SATAN FLAMING WITH RINTRAH'S FURY HIDDEN BENEATH HIS    489 MILTON 9              19
    OWN MILDNESS
  BENEATH THE COUCH OF ALBION ON THE SEVEN (MOUNTAINS) OF     490 MILTON 9              50
    ROME
  CHAOS & ANCIENT NIGHT FLED FROM BENEATH THE FIERY HARROW    493 MILTON 12             21
  LIKE A POLYPUS THAT VEGETATES BENEATH THE DEEP     . .  .   496 MILTON 15              8
  TO THE WEAK TRAVELLER CONFIND BENEATH THE MOONY SHADE    .  497 MILTON 15             33
  TOLD OF THE ENORMOUS CONFLICT EARTHQUAKE BENEATH AROUND     500 MILTON 18             48
  ARE OUR THREE HEAVENS BENEATH THE SHADES OF BEULAH LAND     501 MILTON 20              2
    OF REST
  IN ULRO BENEATH BEULAH THE VAST BREACH OF MILTON'S DESCENT  503 MILTON 21              7
  THIS WORLD BENEATH UNSEEN BEFORE THIS REFUGE FROM THE WARS  504 MILTON 21             48
  HOW LONG BENEATH THE COVERING CHERUB GIVE OUR EMANATIONS    507 MILTON 23             12
  THEY BECAME NATIONS IN OUR SIGHT BENEATH THE HANDS          508 MILTON 24             16
    OF TIRZAH
  BENEATH THE MOON OF ULRO PITY THEN YOUR FATHER'S TEARS  .   508 MILTON 24             25
  UPON HIS ROCK BENEATH HIS TOMB I SAW THE COVERING CHERUB    508 MILTON 24             30
  WHERE HUMAN THOUGHT IS CRUSHD BENEATH THE IRON HAND OF      510 MILTON 25              5
    POWER
  AND THE CALM OCEAN JOYS BENEATH & SMOOTHS HIS AWFUL WAVES   511 MILTON 25             71
  WHICH IS THE FALSE TONGUE BENEATH BEULAH IT IS THE SENSE    514 MILTON 27             46
    OF TOUCH
  MILD SHADOW ABOVE BENEATH & ON ALL SIDES ROUND    . . . .  519 MILTON 30             33
  TO WHERE THE CONTRARIES OF BEULAH WAR BENEATH NEGATION'S    524 MILTON 34             23
    BANNER
  AND THRO BEULAH TO EDEN BENEATH LOS'S WESTERN WALL  . . .   526 MILTON 35             51
  BENEATH SAT CHAOS SIN ON HIS RIGHT HAND DEATH ON HIS LEFT   531 MILTON 39             29
  IN MOONY BEULAH LOS HIS STRONG GUARD WALKS ROUND BENEATH    531 MILTON 39             52
    THE MOON
  AND ALL BENEATH THE NATIONS INNUMERABLE OF ULRO   . . . .  532 MILTON 40             23
  RINTRAH & PALAMABRON VIEW THE HUMAN HARVEST BENEATH . . .   535 MILTON 42             36
  AND [ARMIES] WAR SHALL SINK BENEATH THY FEET    . . . . .   557 ART HAS LOST/N         8
  ARMED ROMANS STREW THE FIELD BENEATH AMONG THESE THE LAST  580C DESC CAT 5           PROSE
    OF
  [IMAGINATION IS MY WORLD THIS WORLD OF DROSS IS BENEATH]   600C PUB ADDRESS/N        PROSE
  [MY NOTICE & BENEATH THE NOTICE OF THE PUBLIC]    . . .    600C PUB ADDRESS/N        PROSE
  ON THE RIGHT BENEATH THE CLOUD ON WHICH ABEL KNEELS . . .  606C V LAST JUDG/N        PROSE
  (BENEATH) ISHAMAEL IS MAHOMED & ON THE LEFT    . . . . .   607B V LAST JUDG/N       *PROSE
  BENEATH THE FALLING FIGURE OF CAIN   . . . . . . . . . .   607B V LAST JUDG/N        PROSE
  JACOB & [THEIR] HIS TWELVE SONS HOVER BENEATH THE   . . .  607C V LAST JUDG/N        PROSE
  BENEATH THE CLOUD ON WHICH MOSES KNEELS IS TWO FIGURES  .  607C V LAST JUDG/N        PROSE
  BENEATH THEM A MULTITUDE OF THEIR ASSOCIATES ARE SEEN   .  607D V LAST JUDG/N        PROSE
  BENEATH THE MAN WITH THE BASKET ARE THREE FIERY FIENDS WITH 607D V LAST JUDG/N       PROSE
  BENEATH THEM ARE VARIOUS FIGURES IN ATTITUDES   . . . .    608A V LAST JUDG/N        PROSE
  THE EARTH BENEATH THESE FALLING GROUPES OF FIGURES   . .   608A V LAST JUDG/N        PROSE
  BENEATH A ROCK [HOWLING & LAMENTING] WHERE   . . . . .     608B V LAST JUDG/N       *PROSE
  BENEATH THE STEPS (IS) BABYLON REPRESENTED BY    . . . .   608B V LAST JUDG/N        PROSE
  BENEATH THIS IS THE SEAT OF THE HARLOT NAMD MYSTERY  . .   609A V LAST JUDG/N        PROSE
  & HELL IS OPEND BENEATH HER SEAT ON THE LEFT HAND   . . .  609B V LAST JUDG/N        PROSE
  BENEATH HER FEET IS A FLAMING CAVERN IN WHICH IS SEEN   .  609B V LAST JUDG/N        PROSE
  THE SEVEN HEADED KINGDOMS THE GRAVES BENEATH    . . . .    609C V LAST JUDG/N        PROSE
  BENEATH THE DRAGON'S CAVERN A SKELETON BEGINS TO ANIMATE   609C V LAST JUDG/N        PROSE
  AROUND NOAH & BENEATH HIM ARE VARIOUS FIGURES RISEN    .   610A V LAST JUDG/N        PROSE
  BENEATH THE FEET OF SETH TWO FIGURES REPRESENT    . . .    611C V LAST JUDG/N        PROSE
  WHILE BENEATH THE FEET OF NOAH FOUR SEASONS    . . . . .   611C V LAST JUDG/N        PROSE
  WITH WHICH THEY HOVERING OVER THE DEEPS BENEATH   . . .    612A V LAST JUDG/N        PROSE
  BENEATH THESE A CLOUD OF WOMEN & CHILDREN ARE TAKEN UP  .  614A V LAST JUDG/N        PROSE
  THE EARTH BENEATH AWAKES AT THE LARK'S VOICE    . . . . .  618B ILLUS MILTON         PROSE
  VARIOUS OFFICES AT THE EASTERN GATE BENEATH IN SMALL       618B ILLUS MILTON         PROSE
    FIGURES
```

	PAGE	TITLE	LINE

BENEATH   (CONTINUED)

IS SEEN IN THE SKY BENEATH HERMES & THE SPIRITS OF FIRE	619B	ILLUS MILTON	PROSE
JERUSALEM HIS EMANATION IS A STONE LAYING BENEATH	620	JERUSALEM 1	6
A HORRIBLE SHADOW OF DEATH AMONG THE FURNACES BENEATH . .	625	JERUSALEM 7	4
FREEZE ROUND HIM TO BARS OF STEEL & TO IRON ROCKS BENEATH	626	JERUSALEM 7	72
CONDENSE BENEATH MY HAMMER INTO FORMS OF CRUELTY	628	JERUSALEM 9	27
HE SHOOTS BENEATH JERUSALEM'S WALLS TO UNDERMINE HER FOUNDATIONS	631	JERUSALEM 11	23
WITH THEIR INHABITANTS IN THE TWENTY-SEVEN HEAVENS BENEATH BEULAH	634	JERUSALEM 13	51
FORMING THE MUNDANE SHELL ABOVE BENEATH ON ALL SIDES SURROUNDING	634	JERUSALEM 13	54
BENEATH BEULAH AS A WATRY FLAME REVOLVING EVERY WAY . . .	634	JERUSALEM 14	7
IN ENTUTHON BENYTHON'S DEEP VALES BENEATH GOLGONOOZA . .	635	JERUSALEM 14	34
BENEATH THE STORMS OF THEOTORMON & THE THUNDRING BELLOWS	636	JERUSALEM 16	8
IN THE FIRES OF THEIR BEAUTY & PERFECTION & BE VEGETATED BENEATH	638	JERUSALEM 17	8
FIRST AS A RED GLOBE OF BLOOD TREMBLING BENEATH HIS BOSOM	639	JERUSALEM 17	51
BENEATH THE OAK & PALM BENEATH THE VINE AND FIG-TREE . .	640	JERUSALEM 18	19
HIS BIRDS ARE SILENT ON HIS HILLS FLOCKS DIE BENEATH HIS BRANCHES	641	JERUSALEM 19	2
REVOLVE UPON HIS MOUNTAINS GROANING IN PAIN BENEATH . .	641	JERUSALEM 19	21
CLOUDED WITH STORMS LOS HIS STRONG GUARD WALKD ROUND BENEATH THE MOON	642	JERUSALEM 19	38
I SEE THEM DIE BENEATH THE WHIPS OF THE CAPTAINS THEY ARE TAKEN	644	JERUSALEM 21	42
ALBION AGAIN UTTERD HIS VOICE BENEATH THE SILENT MOON . .	645	JERUSALEM 22	16
WHERE ALBION SLEPT BENEATH THE FATAL TREE	650	FIELDS FROM/J	29
BENEATH HIS VAST RANGES OF HILLS SURROUNDING JERUSALEM . .	654	JERUSALEM 29	32
BENEATH ITS WINDING LABYRINTHS TILL A STONE OF THE BROOK	659	JERUSALEM 33	10
FROM GROT & CAVE BENEATH THE MOON DIM REGION OF DEATH .	660	JERUSALEM 34	11
THE GRAVES THUNDER BENEATH HIS FEET FROM IRELAND TO JAPAN	661	JERUSALEM 34	42
GWANTOCK & PEACHY HID IN DAMASCUS BENEATH MOUNT LEBANON	662	JERUSALEM 36	16
HOVER WITHIN ME & BENEATH AND SPREADING THEMSELVES OUTSIDE	666	JERUSALEM 39	17
DAMP COUCH THE FLAMES BENEATH AND SILENT SICK STAND SHUDDERING	666	JERUSALEM 40	6
SHE FLED TO LAMBETH'S MILD VALE AND HID HERSELF BENEATH	668	JERUSALEM 41	11
THE SPECTRES OF THE DEAD CRY OUT FROM THE DEEPS BENEATH	671	JERUSALEM 42	57
FROM HYDE PARK SPREAD THEIR VEGETATING ROOTS BENEATH ALBION	674	JERUSALEM 44	23
UPON THE FURNACES AND LOUD THE FURNACES REBELLOW BENEATH	676	JERUSALEM 46	22
BENEATH THE BOTTOMS OF THE GRAVES WHICH IS EARTH'S CENTRAL JOINT	677	JERUSALEM 48	13
JEHOVAH IS BEFORE BEHIND ABOVE BENEATH AROUND	680	JERUSALEM 49	53
AND WE ALSO & ALL BEULAH CONSUME BENEATH ALBION'S CURSE	681	JERUSALEM 50	17
OUTSIDE OF THE GATES OF THE HUMAN HEART BENEATH BEULAH . .	684	JERUSALEM 53	16
WHO FELL BENEATH HIS INSTRUMENTS OF HUSBANDRY & BECAME . .	688	JERUSALEM 56	35
. . . ALBION FLED BENEATH THE PLOW	689	JERUSALEM 57	15
FEEL THEIR BRAIN CUT ROUND BENEATH THE TEMPLES SHRIEKING	689	JERUSALEM 58	7
JORDAN SPRANG BENEATH ITS THRESHOLD BUBBLING FROM BENEATH	690	JERUSALEM 58	23
OF WEEPING & THE PALM OF SUFFERING BENEATH ALBION'S TOMB	691	JERUSALEM 59	6
THE DEAD BENEATH BEULAH FROM TYBURN TO GOLGOTHA AND FROM	698	JERUSALEM 63	33
BENEATH THE IRON WHIPS OF THEIR CAPTAINS & CONSECRATED BANNERS	704	JERUSALEM 67	30
BENEATH & PIERCED IT THRO THE MIDST WITH A GOLDEN PIN . .	705	JERUSALEM 67	42
BLOOD HATH STAIND HER FAIR SIDE BENEATH HER BOSOM . . .	705	JERUSALEM 67	43
BENEATH THE MOUNTAINS OF LEBANON IN THE CITY OF REHOB IN HAMATH	706	JERUSALEM 68	55
OVER THE NATIONS TILL HE TOOK ROOT BENEATH THE SHINING LOOMS	715	JERUSALEM 74	45
THE GOLDEN CORDS OF THE LOOMS ANIMATE BENEATH THEIR TOUCHES SOFT	725	JERUSALEM 82	14
THAT GAVE ME SWEET DELIGHT BY HIS TORMENTS BENEATH MY VEIL	726	JERUSALEM 82	39
AND HYLE A WINDING WORM BENEATH [HER LOOM UPON THE SCALES]	726	JERUSALEM 82 *	47
BENEATH ALBION'S FATAL TREE BEFORE THE GATE OF LOS . . .	726	JERUSALEM 82	60
WHERE THE VICTIM NIGHTLY HOWLS BENEATH THE DRUID'S KNIFE	727	JERUSALEM 83	12
AND LULLING HARMONIES BENEATH THE LOOMS FROM CAITHNESS IN THE NORTH	728	JERUSALEM 83	70
REFLECTS ETERNITY BENEATH THY AZURE WINGS OF FEATHERY DOWN	730	JERUSALEM 86	5
HE BEATS SEAS ROLL BENEATH HIS FEET TEMPESTS MUSTER . . .	731	JERUSALEM 86	35
INTO A GLOBE OF BLOOD BENEATH HIS BOSOM TREMBLING IN DARKNESS	732	JERUSALEM 86	52
A ROUND WOMB BENEATH MY BOSOM LEST I ALSO BE OVERWOVEN . .	732	JERUSALEM 87	14
LOUD SCREAM THE DAUGHTERS OF ALBION BENEATH THE TONGS & HAMMER	737	JERUSALEM 90	44
BENEATH LOS'S HAMMER THAT LIFE MAY NOT BE BLOTTED OUT . .	737	JERUSALEM 90	51
BENEATH THE FURNACES & THE STARRY WHEELS & THE IMMORTAL TOMB	741	JERUSALEM 94	2
BENEATH THE FURNACES & STARRY WHEELS AND IN THE IMMORTAL TOMB	742	JERUSALEM 94	19
AND THE DIM CHAOS BRIGHTEND BENEATH ABOVE AROUND EYED AS THE PEACOCK	745	JERUSALEM 98	14
WHERE IS THE TREE OF GOOD & EVIL THAT ROOTED BENEATH THE CRUEL HEEL	746	JERUSALEM 98	47
FOR SIN IN WAR & IN THE DRUID TEMPLES OF THE ACCUSER OF SIN BENEATH	746	JERUSALEM 98	49
. . . THAT COVERD THE WHOLE EARTH BENEATH HIS SPECTRE . .	746	JERUSALEM 98	50
EARTH GROAND BENEATH & HEAVEN ABOVE	753	EV GOSPEL(E)/N	5
[HID IT BENEATH HIS MERCY SEAT]	761	FOR SEXES/GP	9
BURIED BENEATH HIS MERCY SEAT	761	FOR SEXES/GP	11
I FOUND HIM BENEATH A TREE	761D	FOR SEXES/GP	TITLE
AND SHE FOUND ME BENEATH A TREE	770	OF GATES/GP	3
AND IN HELL BENEATH & A MIGHTY & AWFUL CHANGE THREATENED THE EARTH	799	TO FLAXMAN/L	8

BENEATH   (CONTINUED)
     DESIRE TO ENTERTAIN BENEATH OUR THATCHED ROOF OF RUSTED   802D LETTER 14   PROSE
       GOLD
     BENEATH MY BRIGHT FEET . . . .   805 TO BUTTS/L   36
     THOSE DANGERS ARE NOW PASSED & I CAN SEE THEM BENEATH   . . 862D LETTER 60   PROSE
     I FOUND HIM BENEATH A TREE IN THE GARDEN . . . . . . SUPP LEGEND/N63   *TITLE
     HELL BENEATH IS MOVED FOR THEE &C FROM ISAIAH . . . . SUPP LETTER 56A   *PROSE
BENEDICTION
     THE PRECIOUS BENEDICTION FOR THEIR COLOURS OF LOVELINESS   312 FOUR ZOAS 6   36
BENEFACTOR
     TO ME THEIR BENEFACTOR CALLS ALOUD FOR VENGEANCE DEEP   . . 671 JERUSALEM 42   54
     A BENEFACTOR TO MANKIND . . . . 748 EV GOSPEL(A)/N   12
     ABOVE ALL YOU MY DEAR FRIEND & BENEFACTOR IN THE LORD   . . 834A LETTER 33   PROSE
BENEFACTORS
     [GOD BLESS MY BENEFACTORS FOR I CANNOT TARRY LONGER]   . . 103 TIRIEL 3   27
BENEFICIAL
     COMMERCE IS SO FAR FROM BEING BENEFICIAL TO ARTS OR   . . . 593D PUB ADDRESS/N   PROSE
     GONE AS THE FINE WEATHER IS VERY BENEFICIAL & COMFORTABLE   876A LETTER 83   PROSE
       TO ME
BENEFIT
     & PERHAPS A LITTLE PRACTISE IN THEM MAY TURN OUT TO BENEFIT 795D LETTER 6   PROSE
     I FOUND I COULD BEAR WITH SAFETY & PERHAPS BENEFIT   . . . 870D LETTER 72   PROSE
     AT FIRST & THOUGHT IT A THING OF BENEFIT & GOOD HOPE YOU   876B LETTER 83   PROSE
BENEFITS
     THAT THE JEWS ASSUMED A RIGHT EXCLUSIVELY TO THE BENEFITS   389A ANNO WATSON   MARG
     YEARS AGO & THIS IS ONE OF THE NUMEROUS BENEFITS I HAVE   820A LETTER 25   PROSE
BENEFITTED
     PUBLIC MAY BE MUTUALLY & EXTENSIVELY BENEFITTED HIS . . . 857A LETTER 54   PROSE
BENEVOLENCE
     WHEN UNDER PRETENCE TO BENEVOLENCE THE ELECT SUBDUD ALL   510 MILTON 25   31
     ENRAPTURD WITH AFFECTION SWEET AND MILD BENEVOLENCE . . . 518 MILTON 30   7
     HE SMILES WITH CONDESCENSION HE TALKS OF BENEVOLENCE &   533 MILTON 41   19
       VIRTUE
     AND THOSE WHO ACT WITH BENEVOLENCE & VIRTUE THEY MURDER   533 MILTON 41   20
       TIME ON TIME
     BENEVOLENCE IS THE PLOWMAN'S GREAT CHARACTERISTIC   . . . 571B DESC CAT 3   PROSE
     ALL BROAD & GENERAL PRINCIPLES BELONG TO BENEVOLENCE   . . 672 JERUSALEM 43   22
     AND THE SOFT SMILE OF FRIENDSHIP & THE OPEN DAWN   672 JERUSALEM 43   25
       OF BENEVOLENCE
     TILL THE EXISTENCE OF FRIENDSHIP & BENEVOLENCE IS DENIED   672 JERUSALEM 43   27
     DIVINE BENEVOLENCE & JOY FOR THE ETERNAL MAN . . . . .   686 JERUSALEM 55   9
     YOU SMILE WITH POMP & RIGOR YOU TALK OF BENEVOLENCE   738 JERUSALEM 91   25
       & VIRTUE
     I ACT WITH BENEVOLENCE & VIRTUE & GET MURDERD TIME AFTER   738 JERUSALEM 91   26
       TIME
     OPEN THE HIDDEN HEART IN WARS OF MUTUAL BENEVOLENCE WARS   744 JERUSALEM 97   14
       OF LOVE
     I HAVE NO DOUBT OF GIVING YOU BENEVOLENCE WITH EQUAL VIGOR 792B LETTER 4   PROSE
BENEVOLENCES
     BEING NOT IRRITATED BY INSULT BEARING INSULTING   655 JERUSALEM 30   9
       BENEVOLENCES
BENEVOLENT   SEE ALL BENEVOLENT
     THIS GOOD TO OTHERS OR BENEVOLENT UNDERSTANDING . . . . 89B ANNO SWED LOVE * MARG
     HIS BENEVOLENT HAND . . . .   142 FRENCH REVOLTN   176
     OR LIKE A HUMAN FORM A FRIEND WITH WITH WHOM HE LIVD   497 MILTON 15   27
       BENEVOLENT
     IF YOU ARE BENEVOLENT YOU WILL NEVER WIN . . . .   551 IF YOU PLAY/N   2
     GLOUCESTER AND EXETER AND SALISBURY AND BRISTOL AND   668 JERUSALEM 40   61
       BENEVOLENT BATH
     I MUCH ADMIRED HIS MILD AND GENTLE BENEVOLENT MANNERS   . 844A LETTER 43   PROSE
     BENEVOLENT MINDS MY WIFE JOINS WITH ME IN THE HEARTY   . 847C LETTER 44   PROSE
BENIGHTED
     DARK BENIGHTED TRAVEL-WORN . . . .   111 A DREAM/SI   6
BENJAMIN
     GAD ASHER ISSACHAR ZEBULUN JOSEPH BENJAMIN DAVID SOLOMON   350 FOUR ZOAS 8   361
     THEN ZEBULUN THEN JOSEPH THEN BENJAMIN TWELVE SONS OF LOS   350 FOUR ZOAS 8   377
     THE GATE OF JOSEPH DENBIGHSHIRE THE GATE OF BENJAMIN   637 JERUSALEM 16   41
       GLAMORGANSHIRE
     JOSEPH STAFFORD SHROPS HEREF BENJAMIN DERBY CHESHIRE   637 JERUSALEM 16   49
       MONMOUTH
     JOSEPH ELGIN LANERK KINROS BENJAMIN KROMARTY MURRA   638 JERUSALEM 16   58
       KIRKUBRIHT
     IN THE DIVIDING OF REUBEN & BENJAMIN BLEEDING FROM   697 JERUSALEM 63   12
       CHESTER'S RIVER
     REUBEN & BENJAMIN FLEE THEY HIDE IN THE VALLEY OF REPHAIM   706 JERUSALEM 68   47
     AND THOSE UNDER EPHRAIM MANASSEH & BENJAMIN ARE THESE   . 711 JERUSALEM 72   23
     WHENCE JOSEPH & BENJAMIN ROLLD APART AWAY FROM THE NATIONS 715 JERUSALEM 74   56
     OF BENJAMIN FROM CHESTER'S RIVER LOUD THE RIVER LOUD   736 JERUSALEM 90   15
       THE MERSEY
     OF REUBEN OR OF BENJAMIN OF JOSEPH OR JUDAH OR LEVI . . . 736 JERUSALEM 90   31
     THEY DRINK REUBEN & BENJAMIN AS THE IRON DRINKS THE FIRE   737 JERUSALEM 90   46
BENT   SEE AGE-BENT,AGE BENT
     WAS MISCHIEF BENT UPON A TRICK . . . .   16 BLIND-MANS/PS   46
     TWO NOSTRILS BENT DOWN TO THE DEEP . . . .   229 URIZEN 13   1
     WALK HEAVY SOFT AND BENT ARE THE BONES OF VILLAGERS   . . 243 EUROPE 12   31
     HE BENT THE ENORMOUS RIBS SLOWLY . . . .   251 AHANIA 3   31
     BENT BY ITS FALL FROM A HIGH TOWER THE DOLOROUS SHADOW ROSE 299 FOUR ZOAS 4   66
     TWO NOSTRILS BENT DOWN TO THE DEEPS . . . .   303 FOUR ZOAS 4   237
     THE SAVIOUR MILD & GENTLE BENT OVER THE CORSE OF DEATH   . 304 FOUR ZOAS 4   269
     INCESSANT WAS THE CONFLICT ON HE BENT HIS WEARY STEPS   . 313 FOUR ZOAS 6   77
     BY PROVIDENCE DIVINE CONDUCTED NOT BENT FROM HIS OWN WILL   319 FOUR ZOAS 6   282
     [THE SWELLING TIDES THEY BENT OVER THE DEAD CORSE LIKE   341 FOUR ZOAS 8   13
       AN ARCH]

		PAGE	TITLE	LINE

BENT   (CONTINUED)
    I HAVE BENT DOWNWARD WITH LEAD MOLTEN IN MY ROARING   349 FOUR ZOAS 8   304
        FURNACES
        HIS BODY BENT HIS ARMS & KNEES . . . .   419 I SAW A MONK/N   17
        MY BENT BODY MOCKS AT THEIR TORTURING PAIN . . . . .   419 I SAW A MONK/N   35
        THE TYRANT WHO FIRST THE BLACK BOW BENT . . . .   420 I SAW A MONK/N   50
        WHEN SATAN FIRST THE BLACK BOW BENT . . . .   420 I SAW MNK AD/N   1
        I BENT TO KISS THE LOVELY MAID . . . .   429 CRYSTL CABINET   19
        HIS BODY BENT HIS ARMS & KNEES . . . .   430 GREY MONK   7
        MY BENT BODY MOCKS THEIR TORTURING PAIN . . . . .   430 GREY MONK   20
        HANGING UPON THE WIND TWO NOSTRILS BENT DOWN INTO THE DEEP 482 MILTON 3   20
        HOVERING OVER THE COLD BOSOM IN ITS VORTEX MILTON BENT DOWN 497 MILTON 15   41
        THEY BENT DOWN THEY FELT THE EARTH AND AGAIN ENROOTING . . 653 JERUSALEM 28   18
        JERUSALEM'S SHADOW BENT NORTHWARD OVER THE ISLAND WHITE   657 JERUSALEM 31   42
        THE NOSTRILS BENT DOWN TO THE EARTH & CLOSD WITH SENSELESS 680 JERUSALEM 49   38
            FLESH
        HIS BODY BENT HIS ARMS & KNEES . . . .   683 I SAW A MONK/J   15
        WHEN SATAN FIRST THE BLACK BOW BENT . . . .   683 I SAW A MONK/J   17
        THEIR EAR BENT OUTWARDS AS THEIR VICTIM SO ARE THEY IN   702 JERUSALEM 66   38
            THE PANGS
        I HAVE BENT DOWNWARD WITH LEAD MELTED IN MY ROARING   705 JERUSALEM 67   50
            FURNACES
BEOR
    THE SON OF BEOR HAVE GIVEN THEIR POWER TO JOSHUA & CALEB   680 JERUSALEM 49   59
BEREAVD
    BUT I AM BLACK AS IF BEREAVD OF LIGHT . . . .   125 LIT BLK BOY/SI   4
BEREAVE
    HIRED A VILLAIN TO BEREAVE MY LIFE . . . .   6 FAIR ELENOR/PS   68
    HIRED A VILLAIN TO BEREAVE MY LIFE . . . .   544 HS FRENDSHIP/N   6
BEREAVED
    HAS BEREAVED OF THEIR LIFE . . . .   416 MY SPECTRE/N   36
BERKSHIRE
    GAD OXFORD BUCKS HARFORD ASHER SUSSEX HAMPSHIRE BERKSHIRE   637 JERUSALEM 16   47
    LEICESTER & BERKSHIRE & HIS EMANATION IS GWINEFRED   710 JERUSALEM 71   37
        BEAUTIFUL
BERNARD'S
    IN BERNARD'S HOUSE THE FLAMES COVERD THE LAND THEY ROUZE   201 AMERICA 13   2
        THEY CRY
BERNERS
    IN BERNERS STREET IT WAS IN THESE WORDS I SINCERELY THANK   826C LETTER 28   PROSE
BERRIES
    BLACK BERRIES APPEAR THAT POISON ALL AROUND HIM SUCH [IS]   110 TIRIEL 8   *   34
        WAS TIRIEL
    WITH PURPLE FLOWERS AND BERRIES RED IMAGE OF THAT SWEET   241 EUROPE 10   27
        SOUTH
BERWICK-STREET
    LONDON PRINTED BY D N SHURY...BERWICK-STREET SOHO   . . .   563B DESC CAT   PROSE
    D N SHURY PRINTER BERWICK-STREET SOHO LONDON . . . . .   586B DESC CAT 16   TITLE
BERWIK
    LEVI EDINBURH ROXBRO ROSS JUDAH ABRDEEN BERWIK DUMFRIES   638 JERUSALEM 16   *   54
BERYL
    THE EMERALD ONYX SAPPHIRE JASPER BERYL AMETHYST . . . .   343 FOUR ZOAS 8   74
BERYLL
    THE MALE IS A FURNACE OF BERYLL THE FEMALE IS A GOLDEN LOOM   623 JERUSALEM 5   34
    TRANSLUCENT THE FURNACES OF BERYLL & EMERALD IMMORTAL . .   684 JERUSALEM 53   9
    FOR THE MALE IS A FURNACE OF BERYLL THE FEMALE IS A GOLDEN   736 JERUSALEM 90   27
        LOOM
BESET
    BESET WITH GOLD GOLD WERE THE ORNAMENTS FORMD BY SONS   377 FOUR ZOAS 9   777
        OF URIZEN
BESIDE
    RODE OER THE DEEP OF HEAVEN BESIDE OUR SPRINGS   . . . .   2 TO SUMMER/PS   9
    SOME BANK BESIDE A RIVER CLEAR THROW THY . . . . . .   2 TO SUMMER/PS   11
    MORE HUMAN CREATURES ON THIS EARTH BESIDE THE SONS OF HAR   102 TIRIEL 2   55
    AND NOW BESIDE THEE BLEATING LAMB . . . .   119 NIGHT/SI   41
    AND NOT SIT BESIDE THE NEST . . . .   122 ON ANOTHERS/SI   17
    TILL SUMMER'S HEAT MELTS THEE BESIDE THE FOUNTAINS AND   127 BOOK OF THEL 1   24
        THE SPRINGS
    DOLOURS & LAMENTATIONS WAITING OFT BESIDE A DEWY GRAVE . .   130 BOOK OF THEL 6   7
    . . . THE HOLY BESIDE THE ACCURSED . . . .   141 FRENCH REVOLTN   149
    THE KING FROWNING IN PURPLE BESIDE THE GREY PLOWMAN . . .   141 FRENCH REVOLTN   150
    BUT I FOUND MYSELF SITTING ON A PLEASANT BANK BESIDE A   156C MARRIAGE HH 17   PROSE
        RIVER
    [FAYETTE BESIDE KING LEWIS STOOD] . . . .   185 LET BROTHELS/N   27
    [FAYETTE BESIDE HIS BANNER STOOD] . . . .   186 LET BROTHELS/N   43
    AH ARE THERE OTHER WARS BESIDE THE WARS OF SWORD AND FIRE   192 V DAU ALBION 4   19
    AND ARE THERE OTHER SORROWS BESIDE THE SORROWS OF POVERTY   192 V DAU ALBION 4   20
    AND ARE THERE OTHER JOYS BESIDE THE JOYS OF RICHES AND   192 V DAU ALBION 4   21
        EASE
    I'LL LIE BESIDE THEE ON A BANK & VIEW THEIR WANTON PLAY   195 V DAU ALBION 7   25
    BESIDE THE OX TO THY HARD FURROW DOES NOT THAT MILD BEAM   195 V DAU ALBION 8   4
        BLOT
    ALBION'S ANGEL STOOD BESIDE THE STONE OF NIGHT AND SAW .   197 AMERICA 5   1
    BESIDE THE STONE OF NIGHT AND LIKE THE ETERNAL LION'S HOWL   198 AMERICA 7   2
    SO SPOKE THE PRINCE OF LIGHT & SAT BESIDE THE SEAT OF LOS   273 FOUR ZOAS 1   329
    THEY POUR UPON THE GOLDEN SHORE BESIDE THE SILENT OCEAN   273 FOUR ZOAS 1   345
    THE ENORMOUS BRIDE & BRIDEGROOM SAT BESIDE THEM URIZEN . .   276 FOUR ZOAS 1   436
    BESIDE HIS ANVIL STOOD URTHONA DARK A MASS OF IRON . . .   278 FOUR ZOAS 1   519
    DESCENDING SHE REPOSD BESIDE HIM FOLDING HIM AROUND . . .   285 FOUR ZOAS 2   202
    BESIDE THE ANVIL COLD HE DANCD WITH THE HAMMER OF URTHONA   305 FOUR ZOAS 5   4
    FOR WHEN HE DIED THEY LAY BESIDE [HIM] HIS GRAVE & WHEN   316 FOUR ZOAS 6   *   168
        HE ROSE

210

	PAGE	TITLE	LINE
BESIDE (CONTINUED)			
BESIDE (HIM) THARMAS STAYD HIS FLIGHT & STOOD IN STERN DEFIANCE	319	FOUR ZOAS 6	302
ALL THINGS BESIDE THE WOFUL LOS ENJOY THE DELIGHTS OF BEAUTY	325	FOUR ZOAS 7	198
BESIDE LOS IN THE CAVERN DARK ENSLAVD TO VEGETATIVE FORMS	326	FOUR ZOAS 7	262
A FEMALE BRIGHT I STOOD BESIDE MY ANVIL DARK A MASS . . .	327	FOUR ZOAS 7	282
LOS SAT UPON HIS ANVIL STOCK THEY SAT BESIDE THE FORGE	350	FOUR ZOAS 8	348
BESIDE HIM LIES THE LION DEAD & IN HIS BELLY WORMS . . .	354	FOUR ZOAS 8	527
. . . TIMES AFTER TIMES BESIDE JERUSALEM'S GATE] . . .	356	FOUR ZOAS 8	588
BUT JESUS STOOD BESIDE THEM IN THE SPIRIT SEPARATING . .	357	FOUR ZOAS 9	4
OF A CURLD RAM WHO STRETCHD HIMSELF IN SLEEP BESIDE HIS MISTRESS	369	FOUR ZOAS 9	456
SHE SAW THARMAS SITTING UPON THE ROCKS BESIDE THE WAVY SEA	369	FOUR ZOAS 9	484
SATAN WHO DRAVE THE TEAM BESIDE HIM STOOD ANGRY & RED . .	488	MILTON 8	38
BESIDE THE FOUNT ABOVE THE LARK'S NEST IN GOLGONOOZA	526	MILTON 35	58
OLOLON SAT BESIDE THIS FOUNTAIN ON THE ROCK OF ODOURS . .	526	MILTON 35	60
"THE MOST UGLY AND NO OTHER BESIDE RETURND FROM THE BLOODY FIELD"	560B	EXHIBITION ADV	PROSE
[BY] BESIDE THEM A [SCALD] FIGURE IS SEEN	606C	V LAST JUDG/N	*PROSE
DOWN STONE STEPS & BESIDE A GATE	608B	V LAST JUDG/N	PROSE
DESTROYING ALL THE WORLD BESIDE	651	FIELDS PROM/J	80
BETWEEN SUCCOTH & ZARETAN BESIDE THE STONE OF BOHAN . . .	661	JERUSALEM 34	45
BUT THE DIVINE LAMB STOOD BESIDE JERUSALEM OFT SHE SAW .	693	JERUSALEM 60	50
HER PANTING VICTIM BESIDE HER HER HEART IS DRUNK WITH BLOOD	705	JERUSALEM 68	12
BESIDE HER VALA HOWLD UPON THE WINDS IN PRIDE OF BEAUTY	721	JERUSALEM 80	6
MOVING BESIDE ME TILL INTOXICATED WITH THE WOVEN LABYRINTH	732	JERUSALEM 87	4
OWES SUCCESS TO SOMETHING BESIDE OR WITHOUT ITSELF IF IT HAS ANY	862A	LETTER 59	PROSE
IS MORE SEVERELY AVENGED THAN EVERY SIN & WICKEDNESS BESIDE	863A	LETTER 60	PROSE
BESIDES			
BESIDES IN THE SKY THE LITTLE BIRDS FLY	60	NURSES SONG/IM	12
BESIDES IN THE SKY THE LITTLE BIRDS FLY	121	NURSES SONG/SI	11
BESIDES I CAN TELL [WHEN] WHERE I AM USD WELL	179	LIT VAGABOND/N *	3
BESIDES I CAN TELL WHERE I AM USED WELL	216	LIT VAGABND/SE	3
BESIDES LET THEM LOOK AT GOTHIC FIGURES & GOTHIC BUILDINGS	461A	ANNO REYNOLDS	MARG
FOR EVERY THING BESIDES I HAVE	558	I ROSE UP AT/N	7
& PAINTING ARE SOMEWHAT ELSE BESIDES DRAWING	594C	PUB ADDRESS/N	PROSE
THEY SEEM TO ME TO BE SOMETHING ELSE BESIDES HUMAN LIFE	600A	PUB ADDRESS/N	PROSE
I INTEND TO BRING WITH ME BESIDES OUR NECESSARY CHANGE OF	873A	LETTER 76	PROSE
BESPATTERD			
AND CAME HOME IN EVENING BESPATTERD WITH MIRE	428	MARY	36
BEST			
OUR BEST OF HOPES HOW SOON THEY FAIL	17	BLIND-MANS/PS	52
THESE ARE MY THOUGHTS YET IT WERE BEST TO GO	20	EDW THIRD/PS 2	49
A TRIFLE IVE GILT YOUR CAUSE WITH MY BEST BLOOD	23	EDW THIRD/PS 3	99
TIS THE BEST POLICY AND TIS OUR DUTY	26	EDW THIRD/PS 3	218
ALL BE WRONG OF COURSE TIS BEST TO KNOW A LITTLE	28D	EDW THIRD/PS 4	PROSE
CHILDLESS HE MOURNED BUT THOUGHT HIS GOD KNEW BEST . . .	39C	SAMSON/PS	PROSE
("KEEP DISTANT WHO HATES...LAUGH OF A CHILD") THE BEST IN THE BOOK	74B	ANNO LAVATER	MARG
[("HATES")] LOVES ("WISEST & BEST [HATES] ") LOVES ("FATHER OF MEN")	82D	ANNO LAVATER	MARG
THE BEST WINE IS THE OLDEST THE BEST WATER THE NEWEST .	152C	MARRIAGE HH 9	PROSE
EACH ACCORDING TO HIS GENIUS AND LOVING THE GREATEST MEN BEST	158B	MARRIAGE HH 22	PROSE
BOUND & WEARY I THOUGHT BEST	166	INFANT SORW/N	7
BOUND AND WEARY I THOUGHT BEST	217	INFANT SORW/SE	7
THE JOY OF WOMAN IS THE DEATH OF HER MOST BEST BELOVED .	289	FOUR ZOAS 2	349
O HORRIBLE O DREADFUL STATE THOSE WHOM I LOVED BEST . .	312	FOUR ZOAS 6	25
AND WHAT I LOVED BEST WAS DIVIDED AMONG MY ENEMIES . . .	334	FOUR ZOAS 7B	59
IT WAS THE BEST POSSIBLE IN THE STATE CALLD SATAN TO SAVE	348	FOUR ZOAS 8 *	285
ATHEISM IS THUS THE BEST OF ALL BACON FOOLS US	404B	ANNO BACON	MARG
THE CONTRARY IS THE BEST ADVICE	405A	ANNO BACON	MARG
GIVE HIGH PRICE FOR THE WORST LEAVE THE BEST IN DISGRACE	445	ANNO REYNOLDS	3
IF YOU ENDEAVOUR TO PLEASE THE WORST YOU WILL NEVER PLEASE THE BEST	478A	ANNO REYNOLDS	MARG
THIS IS ONE OF THE BEST COMPLIMENTS HE EVER HAD	538	TO H(UNT)/N	2
AND WHEN THEY ARE DRUNK THEY ALWAYS PANT BEST	549	ALL PICTURES/N *	4
FROM THOSE WHO BEST UNDERSTAND SUCH THINGS CALLS FOR . .	561C	EXHIBITION ADV	PROSE
WOOLETT'S BEST WORKS WERE ETCHD BY JACK BROWN	594A	PUB ADDRESS/N	PROSE
DO IT & THE FOOL OFTEN WILL DO IT BEST AS IT IS A WORK OF NO MIND	598A	PUB ADDRESS/N	PROSE
& HE WHO DRAWS BEST MUST BE THE BEST ARTIST	602B	PUB ADDRESS/N	PROSE
IN AN ETERNAL DEATH FOR ALBION'S SAKE OUR BEST BELOVED .	646	JERUSALEM 23	10
THE POISONER THE BEST AND WORST IN HEAVEN AND HELL . . .	668	JERUSALEM 41	2
IN OTHER MEN & LOVING THE GREATEST MEN BEST EACH ACCORDING	738	JERUSALEM 91	9
SIMPLE MINDS UNDERSTAND IT BEST	786D	ANNO THORNTON	MARG
THE BEST LIVING MODELS I PERCIEVE THAT YOUR EYE IS PERVERTED	793C	LETTER 5	PROSE
ALONE VALUED BY THE GREEKS & THE BEST MODERN ARTISTS .	794A	LETTER 5	PROSE
I HAVE MADE HIM A DRAWING IN MY BEST MANNER	794D	LETTER 6	PROSE
BEST COMPLIMENTS TO MRS CUMBERLAND I REMAIN YOURS SINCERELY	796A	LETTER 6	PROSE
FAREWELL MY BEST FRIEND REMEMBER ME & MY WIFE IN LOVE &	802D	LETTER 14	PROSE
IT WILL GIVE ME THE UTMOST DELIGHT TO DO MY BEST . . .	808C	LETTER 19	PROSE
WHICH I HOPE SHE WHO IS THE BEST JUDGE WILL THINK LIKE .	809A	LETTER 20	PROSE
OR RATHER CERTAINLY THE VERY BEST LETTERS THAT EVER WERE PUBLISHED	810A	LETTER 20	PROSE
BEST MANNER FOR MEMORY WILL NOT DO IN SUCH MINUTE OPERATIONS	810B	LETTER 20	PROSE
P S PLEASE TO REMEMBER OUR BEST RESPECTS TO MR BIRCH & TELL HIM THAT	810B	LETTER 20	PROSE

		PAGE	TITLE	LINE

BEST   (CONTINUED)
MY WAY TO MAKE THE BEST OF EVERYTHING I NEVER MAKE MYSELF   819B LETTER 25   PROSE
(FOUR) NUMBERS FOR MR BIRCH WITH BEST RESPECTS TO HIM   .   . 822B LETTER 26   PROSE
I SEND YOU THE RIPOSO WHICH I HOPE YOU WILL THINK MY BEST   823D LETTER 27   PROSE
TO PAY FOR ME MY BEST THANKS TO MISS POOLE TELL HER THAT   830C LETTER 30   PROSE
BEST PICTURES NOW ARE . . . . 832D LETTER 32   PROSE
EVERY ENQUIRY OF HIM IF YOU THINK BEST MR SANDERS HAS   .   834C LETTER 34   PROSE
& IN HIS BEST STYLE HE ALSO DESIRES ME TO EXPRESS TO YOU   836A LETTER 35   PROSE
   HIS
WHO WITH HER ADMIRABLE HUSBAND PRESENT THEIR BEST   .   .   . 836C LETTER 35   PROSE
HIS FATHER'S BEST FRIEND WILL I HOPE BECOME THE MOST   838C LETTER 37   PROSE
   RESPECTED
MY WIFE JOINS ME IN BEST AFFECTIONS TO YOU . . . . .   . 839A LETTER 37   PROSE
THE LAST TOUCHES WHICH ARE ALWAYS THE BEST I HAVE NOW I   840B LETTER 39   PROSE
   HOPE
THE BEST OF WHICH I HAVE I SEND ALSO THE FRENCH MONUMENTS   844C LETTER 43   PROSE
HE MAY STILL PERFORM HIS BEST AS YOUR ASSISTANT IN IT I   845C LETTER 44   PROSE
   HAVE
EXCEPT PAPER WHICH IS JOHNSON'S FAULT COWPER IS FAR THE   847A LETTER 44   PROSE
   BEST
I AM WITH BEST RESPECTS TO MISS POOLE FOR WHOSE HEALTH   .   . 847C LETTER 44   PROSE
MR FLAXMAN ADVISES THAT THE BEST ENGRAVERS SHOULD BE   .   . 848C LETTER 45   PROSE
IT IS CERTAINLY NECESSARY THAT THE BEST ARTISTS THAT CAN BE   849D LETTER 47   PROSE
BECAUSE I THOUGHT IT WOULD BE TO SAY THE BEST OF MYSELF   853A LETTER 51   *PROSE
IS A PUBLIC LOSS WHICH THOSE WHO KNEW HIM CAN BEST ESTIMATE   854B LETTER 53   PROSE
OF OBLIGATIONS WITH YOU I OUGHT TO DO MY BEST AT ALL TIMES   854C LETTER 53   PROSE
   &
AS NEAR AS I CAN RECOLLECT I THOUGHT IT BEST TO   856D LETTER 54   PROSE
   KEEP SILENT
OR WILL YOU WRITE TO HIM OR WILL YOU THINK IT BEST TO   .   . 857B LETTER 54   PROSE
HOW WE ADVANCE WITH ROMNEY HIS BEST WORKS ONLY   .   .   .   . 857C LETTER 54   PROSE
IMMEDIATELY HE SAID GIVE MY BEST RESPECTS & TELL MR HAYLEY   860A LETTER 56   PROSE
WHICH I CONSIDER AS ONE OF MY BEST . . . . 861D LETTER 58   PROSE
THEM APPROVED BY THE BEST THAT IS THE MOST SERIOUS PEOPLE   862A LETTER 59   PROSE
BEST THINGS FOR THEY WHEN PRINTED PERFECT ACCOMPANY . .   . 867A LETTER 66   PROSE
BEST USE AS ALSO FOR THE PROSPECT OF MR OTTLEY'S . . .   . 879C LETTER 89   PROSE
BESTIAL   SEE BEASTIAL
BESTIR
THEY WILL BESTIR THEMSELVES . . . . 20 EDW THIRD/PS 2   76
BESTOWED
BUT OF THE GREAT LABOUR WHICH HAS BEEN BESTOWED ON IT   .   . 582B DESC CAT 9   PROSE
BET
SUSAN JOHNNY BET & JOE . . . . 53 PHEBE DREST/IM   7
BETH
IN [BETH PEOR] CONWAY'S VALE . . . . 277 FOUR ZOAS 1   483
AS WITH NEW CLAY A HUMAN FORM IN THE VALLEY OF BETH PEOR   500 MILTON 19   14
OVER THE WHOLE EARTH LOUD THE WARRIORS RAGE IN BETH PEOR   704 JERUSALEM 67   29
I HAVE NAILD HIS HANDS ON BETH RABBIM & HIS (FEET)   726 JERUSALEM 82   * 43
   ON HESHBON'S WALL
VERY EASY AM NOW LEARNING MY HEBREW (ALEPH BETH GIMMEL)   821D LETTER 25   PROSE
BETHLEHEM
HIS SECLUDED COURT THENCE TO BETHLEHEM WHERE WAS BUILDED   657 JERUSALEM 31   25
BETIDE
SAM SLIPS BETWEEN O WOE BETIDE . . . . 16 BLIND-MANS/PS   24
BETRAY
THAT SWEET JOYS BETRAY . . . . 168 SILENT NIGHT/N   6
AND ME TO MORTAL LIFE BETRAY . . . . 220 TO TIRZAH/SE   14
HYPOCRITE WHO SMILES PARTICULARLY WHERE HE MEANS TO BETRAY   452A ANNO REYNOLDS   MARG
HE IS A PLATTERER WHO MEANS TO BETRAY . . . . 681D JERUSALEM 52   PROSE
BETRAYD
BY HIS BRETHREN & BETRAYD THEIR CAUSE TO THEIR ENEMIES   .   813B LETTER 22   PROSE
YOU WILL BE CALLD THE BASE JUDAS WHO BETRAYD HIS FRIEND   813B LETTER 22   PROSE
THOU ART TO ENDLESS WOE BETRAYD . . . . 817 HAPPINESS/L   32
BETRAYER
AND BECOMES THE ENEMY & BETRAYER OF HIS FRIENDS . . . . 541 HOMERS HERO/N   6
BETRAYS
("WHO ADHERES TO TRUTH NOR BETRAYS TRUST IS NEAR SUMMIT")   67B ANNO LAVATER   MARG
   EXCELLENT
HE WHO LOVES HIS ENEMIES [HATES] BETRAYS HIS FRIENDS   .   . 751 EV GOSPEL(D)/N   25
BETTER
BUT KITTY I BETTER LOVE THEE . . . . 8 LOVE JOCUND/PS   18
BETTER THAN FIGHT TO BE PLAIN I THINK RETREATING . . . . 23 EDW THIRD/PS 3   65
YOUR GRACE HAD BETTER MAKE . . . . 23 EDW THIRD/PS 3   90
CROWND WITH TRIPLE CROWN THEN PRIDE WAS BETTER PLEASD   .   41B THEN SHE BORE   PROSE
UNDERSTOOD BETTER WHEN HE SHUT HIS EYES [?SAID] . . .   . 45D ISLAND MOON 1   *PROSE
HANG NAMES SAID THE PYTHAGOREAN WHATS PHAROH BETTER THAN   47D ISLAND MOON 4   PROSE
   PHEBUS
IF PINDAR WAS NOT A BETTER POET THAN GHIOTTO WAS A PAINTER   49D ISLAND MOON 6   PROSE
HE UNDERSTANDS ANATOMY BETTER THAN ANY OF THE ANCIENTS   .   50A ISLAND MOON 6   PROSE
YOU HAD BETTER TAKE A WALK THAT WE MAY HAVE SOME PLEASURE   52D ISLAND MOON 8   PROSE
TO HELL TILL HE BEHAVES BETTER . . . . 74B ANNO LAVATER   MARG
NOBLE BUT MARK ACTIVE EVIL IS BETTER THAN PASSIVE GOOD   .   77B ANNO LAVATER   MARG
("HATE AS IF YOU COULD LOVE OR SHOULD BE") BETTER THAN   84D ANNO LAVATER   MARG
   EXCELLENT
BETTER THAN ANY DESCRIPTION OF BUILDINGS OR GARMENTS   .   150C MARRIAGE HH 6   PROSE
BETTER THAN HIS MASTER FOR HE ONLY HOLDS A CANDLE   158A MARRIAGE HH 21   PROSE
   IN SUNSHINE
FATTEND ON HUMAN BLOOD & DRUNK WITH WINE OF LIFE IS BETTER   274 FOUR ZOAS 1   389
   FAR
FOR DEATH TO ME IS BETTER FAR THAN LIFE DEATH MY DESIRE   313 FOUR ZOAS 6   58
THE WHOLE INTO ANOTHER WORLD BETTER SUITED TO OBEY   . .   . 317 FOUR ZOAS 6   231
YET MY FIERCE FIRES ARE BETTER THAN THY SNOWS SHUDDRING   322 FOUR ZOAS 7   72
   THOU SITTEST

		PAGE	TITLE	LINE

BETTER   (CONTINUED)

IF [ONCE] WE UNITE IN ONE ANOTHER BETTER WORLD WILL BE . . 329 FOUR ZOAS 7 353
. . . ARE BETTER THAN THE PANGS OF ETERNAL DEATH . . . 377 FOUR ZOAS 9 742
THE ANCIENTS KNEW BETTER . . . . 394A ANNO WATSON MARG
THAT TOM PAINE IS A BETTER CHRISTIAN THAN THE BISHOP . . 396B ANNO WATSON MARG
WHEN THE REVERENCE OF GOVERNMENT IS LOST IT IS BETTER THAN 401D ANNO BACON MARG
IS THIS TRUE IS IT BETTER . . . . 404A ANNO BACON MARG
BETTER CHOOSE FOOLS AT ONCE . . . . 405C ANNO BACON MARG
& MORAL SENTIMENTS HE WOULD BE NO BETTER THAN CLARISSA . . 411D ANNO BOYD MARG
THE LAND OF DREAMS IS BETTER FAR . . . . 427 LAND OF DREAMS 19
DOST ANOTHER LOVE BETTER THAN POOR MARY . . . . . . 435 WILLIAM BOND 22
ANOTHER I LOVE FAR BETTER THAN THEE . . . . 435 WILLIAM BOND 26
TRIFLING CONCEITS ARE BETTER . . . . 455D ANNO REYNOLDS MARG
KNOW THAT THE MAN'S EXECUTION IS AS HIS CONCEPTION & NO 461C ANNO REYNOLDS MARG
   BETTER
("THE GREAT STYLE") WHAT CAN BE BETTER SAID ON THIS 463C ANNO REYNOLDS MARG
   SUBJECT
NOR MICH ANG COULD HAVE MADE HIM ANY BETTER . . . . 472A ANNO REYNOLDS MARG
POUSSIN KNEW BETTER THAT(THAN) TO MAKE ALL HIS PICTURES 477C ANNO REYNOLDS MARG
HE KNEW BOTH LAW & GOSPEL BETTER THAN THEY . . . . . 537 AND HIS LEGS/N 31
A GREAT DEAL BETTER THAN I WAS BEFORE . . . . 554 TO VENETIAN/N 15
IN STRONGER AND BETTER LINEAMENTS AND IN STRONGER AND . 576B DESC CAT 4 PROSE
BETTER LIGHT THAN HIS PERISHING MORTAL EYE CAN SEE . . 576D DESC CAT 4 *PROSE
BETTER AND HIGHER AND THE POOR WRETCH WHO EXECUTED IT . 583C DESC CAT 9 PROSE
TO THE CONTRARY TO BE BETTER ABLE THAN ANY OTHER . . . 586D CHAUCER 1 PROSE
YOU WILL KNOW BETTER THAN TO THINK OF IMPROVING WHAT . 593D PUB ADDRESS/N PROSE
I DO NOT PRETEND TO PAINT BETTER THAN RAFAEL OR MCH ANGLO 594B PUB ADDRESS/N *PROSE
IT IS NO BETTER THAN ANY OTHER'S MANUAL LABOUR ANY BODY 598A PUB ADDRESS/N *PROSE
   MAY
SUPPOSED THAT A COPY COULD BE BETTER THAN AN ORIGINAL . 602C PUB ADDRESS/N PROSE
TO LEAVE IT BEFORE HE HAS SPOILD IT HE WILL [PR] DO A 603A PUB ADDR AD/N *PROSE
   BETTER THING
THE ARGUMENT IS BETTER FOR AFFLUENCE THAN POVERTY . . 612C V LAST JUDG/N PROSE
FOR THE PURPOSE OF MAKING BAD MEN BETTER BUT FOR 612D V LAST JUDG/N PROSE
   THE PURPOSE
THAN MEN BECAUSE THEY ARE BETTER . . . . 616D V LAST JUDG/N PROSE
SAYING IT IS BETTER TO PREVENT MISERY THAN TO RELEASE FROM 687 JERUSALEM 55 49
   MISERY
IT IS BETTER TO PREVENT ERROR THAN TO FORGIVE THE CRIMINAL 687 JERUSALEM 55 50
"ROME HAS SOMEWHAT BETTER TO DO NAMELY WAR & DOMINION" . . 778D HOMERS POETRY PROSE
ALIVE & NOT DEAD WERE IT NOT BETTER TO BELIEVE VISION . . 780 GHOST ABEL 2 1
I KNOW BETTER & PLEASE YOUR LORDSHIP . . . . 784C ANNO WW EXCUR MARG
BETTER THAN SLAVISHLY FOLLOWING THE TRACK OF ANOTHER . 792A LETTER 4 PROSE
THE MOST LOATHSOM MIRTH IS BETTER THAN FUN . . . . . 793C LETTER 5 PROSE
& HAPPINESS IS BETTER THAN MIRTH . . . . 793C LETTER 5 PROSE
SOON WE SHALL HAVE A CHANGE FOR THE BETTER I CANNOT 795A LETTER 6 PROSE
   PROPHECY
BETTER THINGS THAN I HAVE EVER SEEN MY WORK PLEASES MY . 795C LETTER 6 PROSE
GUINEA EACH WHICH IS SOMETHING BETTER THAN MERE COPYING 795C LETTER 6 PROSE
BUT IN VAIN THE FASTER I BIND THE BETTER IS THE BALLAST 809A LETTER 20 PROSE
& THAT I KNOW I NEVER SHALL DO BETTER FOR IF I WAS TO DO 815C LETTER 23 *PROSE
NOT MENTION ILLNESS BECAUSE I HOPED TO GET BETTER FOR I WAS 820C LETTER 25 PROSE
STILL I RESOLVE NOT TO LOSE HOPE OF SEEING BETTER DAYS . 829D LETTER 30 PROSE
THUS THE CASE STANDS AT PRESENT GOD SEND BETTER TIMES . 831D LETTER 31 PROSE
MY WIFE CONTINUES POORLY BUT FANCIES SHE IS BETTER 832A LETTER 31 PROSE
   IN HEALTH
P S MY WIFE IS BETTER WE ARE VERY ANXIOUS ABOUT MISS 833A LETTER 32 PROSE
   POOLE'S
MY WIFE GETS BETTER EVERY DAY HOPE EARNESTLY THAT YOU . 835A LETTER 34 PROSE
WE BOTH REJOICE THAT MISS POOLE IS BETTER . . . . . 840A LETTER 38 PROSE
IT IS NOW BETTER HE DESIRES TO BE MOST AFFECTIONATELY . 842D LETTER 42 PROSE
AND BETTER TYPE THAN THE TWO EXTREMITIES ALSO IT . 847A LETTER 44 PROSE
   IS CAREFULLY
CONTINUES TO GET BETTER & JOINS ME IN MY WARMEST LOVE & 849C LETTER 45 PROSE
MUCH BETTER PAINTER IF HE [PRACTICES] PRACTISES SECRETLY 850B LETTER 49 *PROSE
   & FOR
FOR FRIENDSHIP WITH SUCH A ONE IS BETTER THAN FAME . . . 853A LETTER 51 *PROSE
INFINITELY BETTER THE NEXT PROOF I FEEL VERY MUCH GRATIFIED 855C LETTER 53 PROSE
SAYS THAT WHEN MY PRINT IS LIKE THAT I NEED WISH IT NO 855D LETTER 53 PROSE
   BETTER
EXECUTED & COULD NOT BE BETTER DONE . . . . 857B LETTER 54 PROSE
THE SUBJECTS I CANNOT DO BETTER THAN THOSE ALREADY CHOSEN 859A LETTER 56 PROSE
WITH THEIR MASTERS & ARE LIKELY TO GET THE BETTER EACH 859B LETTER 56 PROSE
   PARTY
& NOT ONLY GRATIFYING BUT IMPROVING WHICH IS BETTER . . 859C LETTER 56 PROSE
& PERHAPS BETTER BUT I CANNOT ENGRAVE . . . . . . 869A LETTER 68 PROSE
AS SOON AS I AWAKED & I AM NOW IN BED BETTER & AS I THINK 869B LETTER 69 PROSE
THE BETTER FOR IT I CANNOT GET WELL & AM NOW IN BED BUT 870B LETTER 71 PROSE
   SEEM
AS IF I SHOULD BE BETTER TO-MORROW REST DOES ME GOOD . 870B LETTER 71 PROSE
& THE TROUBLE YOU WILL YET HAVE WITH ME BUT I GET BETTER 872D LETTER 76 PROSE
I AM GETTING BETTER EVERY HOUR MY PLAN IS DIET ONLY & . 873C LETTER 77 PROSE
I AM SO MUCH BETTER THAT I HAVE HOPES OF FULFILLING MY . 873D LETTER 78 PROSE
THO GETTING BETTER & STRONGER I AM STILL INCAPABLE 875B LETTER 81 PROSE
   OF RIDING
BETTER EVERY MORNING BUT SLOWLY AS I AM STILL FEEBLE & . 876A LETTER 83 PROSE
& AM GETTING BETTER OR I COULD NOT HAVE COME AT ALL YOURS 876D LETTER 84 PROSE
AIR YET I LOSE NOTHING BY IT DANTE GOES ON THE BETTER . 877D LETTER 88 PROSE
I AM GOING ON BETTER EVERY DAY AS I THINK BOTH . . . 879B LETTER 89 PROSE

BETWEEN

SAM SLIPS BETWEEN O WOE BETIDE . . . . 16 BLIND-MANS/PS 24
THERES AS MUCH DIFFERENCE BETWEEN HIM AND ME . . . . . 29D EDW THIRD/PS 4 PROSE

```
                                                            PAGE    TITLE        LINE
BETWEEN    (CONTINUED)
  AS BETWEEN GLITTERING SAND AND FRUITFUL MOLD  . . . . .   29D EDW THIRD/PS 4  *PROSE
  THROUGH THE VOID SPACE I WALK BETWEEN THE SINFUL WORLD    36A COUCH DEATH/PS   PROSE
     AND ETERNITY
  THOU SCARCE SHALL FIND BUT SELF LOVE STANDS BETWEEN  . .  43A THEN SHE BORE    PROSE
  BETWEEN NATURAL & SPIRITUAL AS SEEN BY MAN . . . . . .    90A ANNO SWED LOVE   MARG
  THOUGHT WITHOUT AFFECTION MAKES A DISTINCTION BETWEEN . . 90D ANNO SWED LOVE   MARG
  LOVE & WISDOM AS IT DOES BETWEEN BODY & SPIRIT . . . .    90D ANNO SWED LOVE   MARG
  HE SAID BETWEEN THE BLACK & WHITE SPIDERS . . . . . .    156B MARRIAGE HH 17   PROSE
  BUT NOW FROM BETWEEN THE BLACK & WHITE SPIDERS A CLOUD . 156B MARRIAGE HH 17   PROSE
  BETWEEN THE CLOUDS & THE WAVES WE SAW A CATARACT OF BLOOD 156B MARRIAGE HH 17  PROSE
  BETWEEN SATURN & THE FIXED STARS . . . . . . . . .      157A MARRIAGE HH 17    PROSE
  I SAW A SERPENT RISE BETWEEN  . . . . . . . . . .        163 I SAW CHAPEL/N      5
  SWEET FLOWER AND PUT THEE HERE TO GLOW BETWEEN MY BREASTS 189 V DAU ALBION 1    12
  SOLEMN HEAVE THE ATLANTIC WAVES BETWEEN THE GLOOMY NATIONS 197 AMERICA 4         2
  ON THOSE VAST SHADY HILLS BETWEEN AMERICA & ALBION'S SHORE 200 AMERICA 10        5
  BETWEEN THE MOUNTAINS DISMAL VISIONS MOPE AROUND THE HOUSE 204 AMERICA CANC B   12
  HANGING FROWNING CLIFFS & ALL BETWEEN  . . . . . . .     225 URIZEN 5           10
  BETWEEN THE CLOUDS OF URIZEN THE FLAMES OF ORC ROLL HEAVY 243 EUROPE 12         32
  BETWEEN TWO MOMENTS BLISS IS RIPE . . . . . . . .        244 EUROPE 14          23
  BETWEEN AHANIA AND THEE  . . . . . . . . . . .           254 AHANIA 4           55
  IN THE VOID BETWEEN FIRE AND FIRE . . . . . . . .        257 BOOK OF LOS 3      44
  AND THE VAST FORM OF NATURE LIKE A SERPENT ROLLD BETWEEN 294 FOUR ZOAS 3       101
  DEADLY BETWEEN THE HAMMER'S BEATING GRATEFUL TO THE EARS 302 FOUR ZOAS 4       190
  THE MIDST BETWEEN AN EQUILIBRIUM GREY OF AIR SERENE . .  316 FOUR ZOAS 6       194
  MAKING BETWEEN HORRIBLE CHASMS INTO THE VAST UNKNOWN . . 318 FOUR ZOAS 6       277
  BETWEEN THE ENORMOUS IRON WALLS BUILT BY THE SPECTRE DARK 319 FOUR ZOAS 6      295
  BEING A MEDIUM BETWEEN HIM & ENITHARMON BUT THIS UNION .  330 FOUR ZOAS 7      398
  THE DIFFERENCE BETWEEN STATES & INDIVIDUALS OF THOSE STATES 351 FOUR ZOAS 8    380
  THERE IS A VAST DIFFERENCE BETWEEN AN . . . . . .       388B ANNO WATSON        MARG
  MY BROTHER STARVD BETWEEN·TWO WALLS . . . . . . .        419 I SAW A MONK/N     32
  MY BROTHER STARVD BETWEEN TWO WALLS  . . . . . . .       430 GREY MONK          17
  OF THE CONVERSATION BETWEEN ME AND THE SOLDIER . . .    437D BLAKES MEMORAN     PROSE
  TUESDAY JANRY...BETWEEN TWO & SEVEN IN THE EVENING DESPAIR 440A MEMORANDUM/N 1  PROSE
  OTHER & DIVIDED ALL THE ENGLISH WORLD BETWEEN THEM  . . 445C ANNO REYNOLDS     MARG
  I KNEW IMMEDIATELY THE DIFFERENCE BETWEEN RAFAEL & RUBENS 447C ANNO REYNOLDS    MARG
  THE DIFFERENCE BETWEEN A BAD ARTIST & A GOOD ONE IS . . 456A ANNO REYNOLDS     MARG
  BETWEEN SOUTH MOLTON STREET & STRATFORD PLACE CALVARY'S   484 MILTON 4          21
     FOOT
  BETWEEN SATAN AND PALAMABRON IN THE TERRIBLE DARKNESS  . 490 MILTON 9          45
  AND BROOKS BETWEEN TO INTERSECT THE MEADOWS IN THEIR COURSE 493 MILTON 12      19
  A DISK OF BLOOD DISTANT & HEAVNS & EARTHS ROLL DARK BETWEEN 495 MILTON 14      27
  AND HE ALSO DARKEND HIS BROWS FREEZING DARK ROCKS BETWEEN 500 MILTON 19         1
  BETWEEN HIS PALMS AND FILLING UP THE FURROWS OF MANY YEARS 500 MILTON 19       11
  SOWD WAR AND STERN DIVISION BETWEEN PAPISTS & PROTESTANTS 507 MILTON 23        48
  AND BETWEEN EVERY TWO MOMENTS STANDS A DAUGHTER OF BEULAH 516 MILTON 28        48
  HOW WIDE THE GULF & UNPASSABLE BETWEEN SIMPLICITY       518B MILTON 30          TITLE
     & INSIPIDITY
  BY DIFFERENCES BETWEEN IDEAS THAT IDEAS THEMSELVES WHICH  525 MILTON 35          5
     ARE
  IN THE NEWTONIAN VOIDS BETWEEN THE SUBSTANCES OF CREATION 528 MILTON 37        46
  LONDON IS BETWEEN HIS KNEES ITS BASEMENTS FOURFOLD  . .  531 MILTON 39         39
  HE MAKES A WIDE DISTINCTION BETWEEN THE SHEEP & THE GOATS 556D JESUS NOT/N      PROSE
  AND BETWEEN HIM AND HIS BROTHER THE PLOWMAN . . . . .   570C DESC CAT 3        PROSE
  OF HERCULES BETWEEN HIS MILLER AND HIS PLOWMAN . . .    571B DESC CAT 3        PROSE
  BETWEEN HIS KNIGHT AND SQUIRE AS IF HE WAS . . . . .    574A DESC CAT 3        PROSE
  THE DISTINCTION THAT IS MADE IN MODERN TIMES BETWEEN  . 584D DESC CAT 15       PROSE
  IS NO DIFFERENCE BETWEEN RAFAEL'S CARTOONS AND HIS FRESCOS 584D DESC CAT 15    PROSE
  BETWEEN ALLEGORIC FABLE & SPIRITUAL MYSTERY LET IT HERE BE 605C V LAST JUDG/N  PROSE
  JESUS SEATED BETWEEN THE TWO PILLARS JACHIN & BOAZ . .  606B V LAST JUDG/N     PROSE
  BETWEEN THE FIGURES OF ADAM & EVE APPEARS A FIERY GULPH  609A V LAST JUDG/N    PROSE
  BETWEEN SETH & THESE A FEMALE FIGURE [WITH THE BACK TURND] 611D V LAST JUDG/N  PROSE
  & THE MORNING STARS SANG TOGETHER BETWEEN SETH & ELIJAH  611D V LAST JUDG/N   *PROSE
  O POINT OF MUTUAL FORGIVENESS BETWEEN ENEMIES . . . .    626 JERUSALEM 7        66
  AND THE ABSTRACT VOIDS BETWEEN THE STARS ARE THE SATANIC  633 JERUSALEM 13      37
     WHEELS
  IN SELF-DENIAL BUT WAR AND DEADLY CONTENTION BETWEEN  . . 640 JERUSALEM 18      20
  HE STOOD BETWEEN THE PALM TREE & THE OAK OF WEEPING  . . 646 JERUSALEM 23       24
  AND THE VAST FORM OF NATURE LIKE A SERPENT ROLLD BETWEEN  655 JERUSALEM 29      80
  WHICH THE MALE ENTERS MAGNIFICENT BETWEEN HER CHERUBIM .  656 JERUSALEM 30      35
  BETWEEN SUCCOTH & ZARETAN BESIDE THE STONE OF BOHAN  . . 661 JERUSALEM 34       45
  BETWEEN LIPS OF MIRE & CLAY THEN SENT HIM FORTH OVER JORDAN 662 JERUSALEM 36     6
  HAND STOOD BETWEEN REUBEN & MERLIN AS THE REASONING SPECTRE 663 JERUSALEM 36   23
  STANDS BETWEEN THE VEGETATIVE MAN & HIS IMMORTAL         663 JERUSALEM 36       24
     IMAGINATION
  BETWEEN BLACKHEATH & HOUNSLOW BETWEEN NORWOOD & FINCHLEY  670 JERUSALEM 42      51
  ALBION'S DREAD WHEELS STRETCHING OUT SPACES IMMENSE BETWEEN 674 JERUSALEM 44     9
  THE NARROW SEA BETWEEN ALBION & THE ATLANTIC CONTINENT . 674 JERUSALEM 44       14
  DISTINGUISH BETWEEN THE MAN & HIS PRESENT STATE  . . . 681D JERUSALEM 52       PROSE
  INTO HIS OWN CHAOS WHICH IS THE MEMORY BETWEEN MAN & MAN  685 JERUSALEM 54       8
  JERUSALEM & VALA APPEARD & ABOVE BETWEEN THE WINGS       685 JERUSALEM 54       31
     MAGNIFICENT
  FORBIDDING US THAT VEIL WHICH SATAN PUTS BETWEEN EVE & ADAM 686 JERUSALEM 55    11
  BETWEEN DWELLS A DAUGHTER OF BEULAH TO FEED THE HUMAN     688 JERUSALEM 56      10
     VEGETABLE
  THIS LOS FORMED INTO THE GATES & MIGHTY WALL BETWEEN THE  691 JERUSALEM 59       5
     OAK
  DEADLY HATE BETWEEN LEAH & RACHEL DAUGHTERS OF DECEIT &   707 JERUSALEM 69      11
     FRAUD
  PALACES RIVERS & MOUNTAINS AND BETWEEN HAND & HYLE AROSE  710 JERUSALEM 71      22
  THE PILLARS OF JERUSALEM BETWEEN MY WINGED CHERUBIM  . . 721 JERUSALEM 79       59
  BETWEEN THY WINGS OF GOLD & SILVER FEATHERD IMMORTAL  . . 731 JERUSALEM 86      20
```

		PAGE	TITLE	LINE

BETWEEN   (CONTINUED)
      BETWEEN THE STARS AMONG THE ARCHES OF ALBION'S TOMB SUBLIME   738 JERUSALEM 91   38
      AND THE HAND OF MAN GRASPS FIRM BETWEEN THE MALE & FEMALE   744 JERUSALEM 97   15
         LOVES
      BETWEEN THE FIFTH AND SIXTH CIRCLES . . . .   786A ILLS DANTE 101   PROSE
      FOR ALL IS DEBTS & TAXES BETWEEN [XXX] CAESAR & US . . . 788D ANNO THORNTON   * MARG
      DIFFERENCE BETWEEN THE DOCTRINES OF DR TRUSLER & THOSE   795A LETTER 6   PROSE
         OF CHRIST
      "HUNDRED FOR THE TERRIBLE DESART OF LONDON WAS BETWEEN"   800B LETTER 12   PROSE
      CHAISES & AS MANY DIFFERENT DRIVERS WE (SET) OUT BETWEEN   802B LETTER 14   *PROSE
      WITHOUT ACCIDENT OR HINDRANCE THO IT WAS BETWEEN ELEVEN   803A LETTER 15   PROSE
      BECAUSE OF PECUNIARY CONNEXIONS BETWEEN H(HAYLEY) & ME .   819D LETTER 25   PROSE
      THIS METHOD OF REVENGE WAS PLANND BETWEEN THEM   . . . . 827C LETTER 28   PROSE
      OVER HIS CHIMNEY PIECE BETWEEN TWO LITTLE PRETTY PICTURES 836A LETTER 35   PROSE
      INTIRE SECRET BETWEEN MR P(PHILLIPS) MR H(HOARE) & MYSELF 841B LETTER 41   PROSE
      THE LITTLE DIFFERENCE THAT SUBSISTED BETWEEN YOU SPEAKING 846A LETTER 44   PROSE
         OF
      I SHALL BE ABLE TO SETTLE WITH HIM SOON WHAT IS BETWEEN US 863B LETTER 60   PROSE
      BETWEEN YOU & ME YOU DEMAND OF ME TO MIX TWO THINGS . .   866A LETTER 64   PROSE
      NONE THERE IS NO COMPARISON BETWEEN OUR NECESSARY   873C LETTER 77   PROSE
         AVOCATIONS
      MEMORANDUM OF AGREEMENT BETWEEN WILLIAM BLAKE AND JOHN   SUPP LETTER 67D   *PROSE
         LINNELL
BETWIXT
      THAT BETWIXT THE CRADLE & GRAVE   . . . .   424 THE SMILE   13
BEULAH
      DAUGHTER OF BEULAH SING . . . .   264 FOUR ZOAS 1   20
      IN [BEULAH] EDEN FEMALES SLEEP THE WINTER IN SOFT SILKEN 266 FOUR ZOAS 1   64
         VEILS
      NAMD BEULAH A SOFT MOONY UNIVERSE FEMININE LOVELY   . . 266 FOUR ZOAS 1   95
      THE DAUGHTERS OF BEULAH FOLLOW SLEEPERS . . . .   267 FOUR ZOAS 1   99
      . . . A BRIGHT WONDER [THAT BEULAH] NATURE [SHUDDERD AT] 269 FOUR ZOAS 1   183
      THEN [?ONA] ENO A DAUGHTER OF BEULAH TOOK A MOMENT OF TIME 270 FOUR ZOAS 1   * 222
      ASTONISHD SAT HER SISTERS OF BEULAH TO SEE HER SOFT   270 FOUR ZOAS 1   * 227
         AFFECTIONS
      CONVERSING WITH THE VISIONS OF BEULAH IN DARK SLUMBEROUS 271 FOUR ZOAS 1   * 246
         BLISS
      [NINE YEARS THEY VIEW THE TURNING SPHERES OF ?BEULAH . . . 271 FOUR ZOAS 1   * 247
      . . . READING THE VISIONS OF BEULAH]   271 FOUR ZOAS 1   247
      WHICH STAND UPON THE EDGE OF BEULAH & HE SUNK DOWN   . . 277 FOUR ZOAS 1   465
      FOR MESSENGERS FROM BEULAH COME IN TEARS & DARKNING CLOUDS 277 FOUR ZOAS 1   476
      THE DAUGHTERS OF BEULAH TERRIFIED HAVE CLOSD THE GATE OF 277 FOUR ZOAS 1   479
         THE TONGUE
      SO SPOKE THE AMBASSADORS FROM BEULAH & WITH SOLEM MOURNING 277 FOUR ZOAS 1   481
      DEEP HORRIBLE WITHOUT END SEPARATED FROM BEULAH FAR BENEATH 279 FOUR ZOAS 1   542
      SO SPOKE THE MESSENGERS OF BEULAH SILENTLY REMOVING   . . 279 FOUR ZOAS 1   550
      THE DAUGHTERS OF BEULAH BEHELD THE EMANATION THEY PITIED 279 FOUR ZOAS 1   560
      THREE GATES WITHIN GLORIOUS & BRIGHT OPEN INTO [ETERNITY] 279 FOUR ZOAS 1   * 563
         BEULAH
      LEST LOS SHOULD ENTER INTO BEULAH THRO HER BEAUTIFUL GATES 279 FOUR ZOAS 1   566
      WEEPING THE DAUGHTERS OF BEULAH SILENT IN THE PORCHES   280 FOUR ZOAS 1   568
      IN ULRO BENEATH BEULAH WHERE THE DEAD WAIL NIGHT & DAY . 282 FOUR ZOAS 2   71
      DREWST ALL THE SONS OF BEULAH INTO THY [GREAT] DREAD VORTEX 299 FOUR ZOAS 4   88
         FOLLOWING
      THY EDDYING SPIRIT DOWN THE HILLS OF BEULAH ALL MY SONS   300 FOUR ZOAS 4   89
      THE DAUGHTERS OF BEULAH SAW THE DIVINE VISION THEY WERE   304 FOUR ZOAS 4   250
         COMFORTED
      AND LIVE BEHOLD ETERNAL DEATH IS IN BEULAH BEHOLD   . .   304 FOUR ZOAS 4   258
      SUCH WERE THE WORDS OF BEULAH OF THE FEMININE EMANATION   304 FOUR ZOAS 4   263
      AMONG THE FLOWERS OF BEULAH WALKD THE ETERNAL MAN & SAW   326 FOUR ZOAS 7   239
      ROUND BEULAH THERE HE REVELD IN DELIGHT AMONG THE FLOWERS 326 FOUR ZOAS 7   243
      URIZEN GREW UP IN THE PLAINS OF BEULAH MANY SONS . . .   326 FOUR ZOAS 7   251
      FROM ITS HINGES UTTERING ITS FINAL GROAN ALL BEULAH FELL 326 FOUR ZOAS 7   258
      AND WAS AJOIND TO BEULAH AS THE POLYPUS TO THE ROCK . . 340 FOUR ZOAS 7B   289
      MOURNING THE DAUGHTERS OF BEULAH SAW NOR COULD THEY HAVE 340 FOUR ZOAS 7B   290
         SUSTAIND
      AND ALL THE SONGS OF BEULAH SOUNDED COMFORTABLE NOTES   . 340 FOUR ZOAS 7B   296
      SUCH IS A VISION OF ALL BEULAH HOVRING OVER THE SLEEPER   341 FOUR ZOAS 8   15
      FOR NOTHING COULD RESTRAIN THE DEAD IN BEULAH FROM   341 FOUR ZOAS 8   24
         DESCENDING
      DELUSIVE CRUELTY THEY DESCEND AWAY FROM THE DAUGHTERS OF 341 FOUR ZOAS 8   26
         BEULAH
      IN GOLGONOOZA LOOKING DOWN THE DAUGHTERS OF BEULAH SAW . 342 FOUR ZOAS 8   42
      [ASTONISHD COMFORTED DELIGHTED THE DAUGHTERS OF BEULAH SAW] 342 FOUR ZOAS 8   45
      ALL BEULAH STOOD ASTONISHD LOOKING DOWN TO ETERNAL DEATH 342 FOUR ZOAS 8   47
      TO BEULAH & THE DEAD IN ULRO DESCENDED FROM THE WAR . . 342 FOUR ZOAS 8   56
      [DAUGHTERS OF BEULAH DESCRIBE] . . . .   346 FOUR ZOAS 8   * 200
      HE AWAKES THE SLEEPERS IN ULRO THE DAUGHTERS OF BEULAH   347 FOUR ZOAS 8   * 237
         PRAISE HIM
      WE NOW BEHOLD THE ENDS OF BEULAH & WE NOW BEHOLD . . . . 347 FOUR ZOAS 8   239
      SO SANG THEY IN ETERNITY LOOKING DOWN INTO BEULAH   . .   347 FOUR ZOAS 8   246
      AND ALL THE SONS OF ETERNITY DESCENDED INTO BEULAH   . . 359 FOUR ZOAS 9   66
      THE ETERNAL MAN ALSO SAT DOWN UPON THE COUCHES OF BEULAH 366 FOUR ZOAS 9   354
      IN MENTAL FLAMES THE FLAMES REFUSD THEY DROVE HIM BACK   366 FOUR ZOAS 9   356
         TO BEULAH
      AND THOSE UPON THE COUCHES VIEWD THEM IN THE DREAMS OF   367 FOUR ZOAS 9   383
         BEULAH
      THUS WERE THE SLEEPERS ENTERTAIND UPON THE COUCHES   372 FOUR ZOAS 9   558
         OF BEULAH
      AMONG THE FLOWERS OF BEULAH IN HIS SELFISH COLD REPOSE . 374 FOUR ZOAS 9   628
      CALLING THE MORNING INTO BEULAH THE ETERNAL MAN REJOICD   374 FOUR ZOAS 9   646
      TO BEULAH & THE DEAD IN BEULAH DESCENDED THRO THEIR GATES 382 FOUR ZOAS AD 6   26

215

	PAGE	TITLE	LINE
BEULAH (CONTINUED)			
DAUGHTERS OF BEULAH MUSES WHO INSPIRE THE POET'S SONG . .	481	MILTON 2	1
OF JERUSALEM HIS EMANATION IN THE HEAVENS BENEATH BEULAH	481	MILTON 2	15
HAS THREE GATES INTO THE THREE HEAVENS OF BEULAH WHICH SHINE	484	MILTON 5	7
LOUD AS THE WIND OF BEULAH THAT UNROOTS THE ROCKS & HILLS	487	MILTON 7	33
HE SUNK DOWN A DREADFUL DEATH UNLIKE THE SLUMBERS OF BEULAH	490	MILTON 9	48
WHERE BEULAH LOVELY TERMINATES IN ROCKY ALBION . . .	491	MILTON 11	4
BUT WHEN LEUTHA A DAUGHTER OF BEULAH BEHELD SATAN'S CONDEMNATION	492	MILTON 11	28
THE SLEEPERS OF BEULAH PITY THE REPENTANT LEUTHA MY . . .	493	MILTON 12	50
THEN ON THE VERGE OF BEULAH HE BEHELD HIS OWN SHADOW . .	496	MILTON 14	36
BUT AS A WINTRY GLOBE DESCENDS PRECIPITANT THRO BEULAH BURSTING	497	MILTON 15	44
THEN MILTON KNEW THAT THE THREE HEAVENS OF BEULAH WERE BEHELD	497	MILTON 15	51
ARE OUR THREE HEAVENS BENEATH THE SHADES OF BEULAH LAND OF REST	501	MILTON 20	2
LOOKING DOWN INTO BEULAH WRATHFUL FILLD WITH RAGE . .	502	MILTON 20	45
IN ULRO BENEATH BEULAH THE VAST BREACH OF MILTON'S DESCENT	503	MILTON 21	7
THEY PERVERTED SWEDENBORG'S VISIONS IN BEULAH & IN ULRO	506	MILTON 22	46
TO BE FORMED INTO THE CHURCHES OF BEULAH	511	MILTON 25	39
LEST THOSE THREE HEAVENS OF BEULAH SHOULD THE CREATION DESTROY	512	MILTON 26	20
THE TWENTY-SEVEN HEAVENS OF BEULAH IN ULRO SEAT OF SATAN	514	MILTON 27	45
WHICH IS THE FALSE TONGUE BENEATH BEULAH IT IS THE SENSE OF TOUCH	514	MILTON 27	46
AND BETWEEN EVERY TWO MOMENTS STANDS A DAUGHTER OF BEULAH	516	MILTON 28	48
THIS PLACE IS CALLED BEULAH IT IS A PLEASANT LOVELY SHADOW	518	MILTON 30	2
WEEPING FOR MILTON MUTE WONDER HELD THE DAUGHTERS OF BEULAH	518	MILTON 30	6
BEULAH IS EVERMORE CREATED AROUND ETERNITY APPEARING .	518	MILTON 30	8
BUT BEULAH TO ITS INHABITANTS APPEARS WITHIN EACH DISTRICT	518	MILTON 30	10
THE SONS OF EDEN THE MOONY HABITATIONS OF BEULAH . . .	518	MILTON 30	13
INTO THIS PLEASANT SHADOW BEULAH ALL OLOLON DESCENDED .	519	MILTON 31	8
AND WHEN THE DAUGHTERS OF BEULAH HEARD THE LAMENTATION .	519	MILTON 31	9
ALL BEULAH WEPT FOR THEY SAW THE LORD COMING IN THE CLOUDS	519	MILTON 31	10
AND THE SHADOWS OF BEULAH TERMINATE IN ROCKY ALBION . .	519	MILTON 31	11
ORC HOWLS ON THE ATLANTIC ENITHARMON TREMBLES ALL BEULAH WEEPS	520	MILTON 31	27
THIS IS A VISION OF THE LAMENTATION OF BEULAH OVER OLOLON	520	MILTON 31	45
SUCH IS A VISION OF THE LAMENTATION OF BEULAH OVER OLOLON	521	MILTON 31	63
AND THE DIVINE VOICE WAS HEARD IN THE SONGS OF BEULAH SAYING	522	MILTON 33	1
AS IT IS DONE IN BEULAH & THOU O VIRGIN BABYLON MOTHER OF WHOREDOMS	523	MILTON 33	20
SUCH ARE THE SONGS OF BEULAH IN THE LAMENTATIONS OF OLOLON	523	MILTON 33	24
AND ALL THE SONGS OF BEULAH SOUNDED COMFORTABLE NOTES .	523	MILTON 34	1
RENDING THE HEAVENS OF BEULAH WITH YOUR THUNDERS & LIGHTNINGS	523	MILTON 34	5
WERE SHEWED THEM FIRST OF BEULAH A MOST PLEASANT SLEEP . .	523	MILTON 34	9
ON COUCHES SOFT WITH MILD MUSIC TENDED BY FLOWERS OF BEULAH	523	MILTON 34	10
AND THE COUCHES OF THE MARTYRS & MANY DAUGHTERS OF BEULAH	524	MILTON 34	20
TO WHERE THE CONTRARIES OF BEULAH WAR BENEATH NEGATION'S BANNER	524	MILTON 34	23
AND MELTING CADENCES THAT LURE THE SLEEPERS OF BEULAH DOWN	524	MILTON 34	29
SEEING MILTON'S SHADOW SOME DAUGHTERS OF BEULAH TREMBLING	524	MILTON 34	47
BY OLOLON'S DESCENT THRO BEULAH TO LOS & ENITHARMON . .	525	MILTON 35	36
AND THROUGH BEULAH AND ALL SILENT FORBORE TO CONTEND .	526	MILTON 35	40
AND THRO BEULAH TO EDEN BENEATH LOS'S WESTERN WALL . .	526	MILTON 35	51
THE VIRGIN OLOLON & ADDRESSD HER AS A DAUGHTER OF BEULAH	527	MILTON 36	27
THE MONSTROUS CHURCHES OF BEULAH THE GODS OF ULRO DARK .	528	MILTON 37	16
THEN ALBION ROSE UP IN THE NIGHT OF BEULAH ON HIS COUCH	531	MILTON 39	32
IN MOONY BEULAH LOS HIS STRONG GUARD WALKS ROUND BENEATH THE MOON	531	MILTON 39	52
YE ARE MY MEMBERS O YE SLEEPERS OF BEULAH LAND OF SHADES	622	JERUSALEM 4	21
UPON THE THAMES AND MEDWAY RIVERS OF BEULAH DISSEMBLING	622	JERUSALEM 4	34
IN PULSATIONS OF TIME & EXTENSIONS OF SPACE LIKE URNS OF BEULAH	630	JERUSALEM 11	2
THEN ERIN CAME FORTH FROM THE FURNACES & ALL THE DAUGHTERS OF BEULAH	630	JERUSALEM 11	8
AND THAT TOWARD BEULAH AND THAT TOWARD ULRO	632	JERUSALEM 12	50
AND THAT TOWARD BEULAH FOUR GOLD SILVER BRASS & IRON . .	632	JERUSALEM 12	66
THAT TOWARDS GENERATION IRON THAT TOWARD BEULAH STONE .	633	JERUSALEM 13	9
OF FORMS OF DEATH AND THAT TOWARD BEULAH STONE . . .	633	JERUSALEM 13	16
WITH THEIR INHABITANTS IN THE TWENTY-SEVEN HEAVENS BENEATH BEULAH	634	JERUSALEM 13	51
BENEATH BEULAH AS A WATRY FLAME REVOLVING EVERY WAY . .	634	JERUSALEM 14	7
CRUEL HIPOCRISY UNLIKE THE LOVELY DELUSIONS OF BEULAH . .	639	JERUSALEM 17	27
BEYOND THE NIGHT OF BEULAH IN A DARK & UNKNOWN NIGHT . .	641	JERUSALEM 18	45
WHICH STAND UPON THE ENDS OF BEULAH AND WITHOUTSIDE ALL	642	JERUSALEM 19	34
INTO THE NIGHT OF BEULAH AND THE MOON OF BEULAH ROSE . .	642	JERUSALEM 19	37
WHICH STAND UPON THE EDGE OF BEULAH AND THERE ALBION SUNK	646	JERUSALEM 23	25
AND THERE WAS HEARD A GREAT LAMENTING IN BEULAH ALL THE REGIONS	648	JERUSALEM 25	1
OF BEULAH WERE MOVED AS THE TENDER BOWELS ARE MOVED & THEY SAID	648	JERUSALEM 25	2
THUS WEPT THEY IN BEULAH OVER THE FOUR REGIONS OF ALBION	648	JERUSALEM 25	14
HUMANITY KNOWS NOT OF SEX WHEREFORE ARE SEXES IN BEULAH	656	JERUSALEM 30	33
IN BEULAH THE FEMALE LETS DOWN HER BEAUTIFUL TABERNACLE	656	JERUSALEM 30	34
IN THE VISIONS OF THE DREAMS OF BEULAH ON THE EDGE OF NON-ENTITY	663	JERUSALEM 36	22
SHUT FROM MY NERVOUS FORM WHICH SLEEPS UPON THE VERGE OF BEULAH	665	JERUSALEM 38	35

216

		PAGE	TITLE		LINE

BEULAH   (CONTINUED)
    BY THE DAUGHTERS OF BEULAH GENTLY SNATCHD AWAY AND HID   668 JERUSALEM 41   14
        IN BEULAH
    OPENING INTO BEULAH EVERY ANGLE IS A LOVELY HEAVEN   . .   668 JERUSALEM 41   18
    BUT WHEN MAN SLEEPS IN BEULAH THE SAVIOUR IN MERCY TAKES   670 JERUSALEM 42   32
    ROSE IN THE NIGHT OF BEULAH AND BOUND DOWN THE SUN & MOON   675 JERUSALEM 45   20
    WEEPING WAS IN ALL BEULAH AND ALL THE DAUGHTERS OF BEULAH   678 JERUSALEM 48   21
    WHEN OUT OF BEULAH THE EMANATION OF THE SLEEPER DESCENDED   678 JERUSALEM 48   23
    ASTONISHD LOVELY EMBRACING THE SUBLIME SHADE THE DAUGHTERS   678 JERUSALEM 48   29
        OF BEULAH
    INTO BEULAH TREMBLING THE DAUGHTERS OF BEULAH DRIED   . . 678 JERUSALEM 48   39
    WRITHING IN PAIN THE DAUGHTERS OF BEULAH IN KIND   678 JERUSALEM 48   50
        ARMS RECIEVD
    IN THE ENDS OF BEULAH WHERE THE DEAD WAIL NIGHT & DAY   . . 678 JERUSALEM 48   52
    AND THUS ERIN SPOKE TO THE DAUGHTERS OF BEULAH IN SOFT   678 JERUSALEM 48   53
        TEARS
    TILL NOW IN BEULAH UNLESS A REFUGE CAN BE FOUND   . . . .   679 JERUSALEM 48   59
    COME YE O DAUGHTERS OF BEULAH LAMENT FOR OG & SIHON   .   679 JERUSALEM 49   3
    SHILOH THE MASCULINE EMANATION AMONG THE FLOWERS OF BEULAH   680 JERUSALEM 49   47
    AND WE ALSO & ALL BEULAH CONSUME BENEATH ALBION'S CURSE   681 JERUSALEM 50   17
    SO ERIN SPOKE TO THE DAUGHTERS OF BEULAH SHUDDERING   . . .   681 JERUSALEM 50   18
    EXPANDING ON WING THE DAUGHTERS OF BEULAH REPLIED IN SWEET   681 JERUSALEM 50   23
        RESPONSE
    FROM THE RIVERS OF BEULAH PLEASANT RIVER SOFT MILD PARENT   684 JERUSALEM 53   3
        STREAM
    OUTSIDE OF THE GATES OF THE HUMAN HEART BENEATH BEULAH   . . 684 JERUSALEM 53   16
    IN THE POTTER'S FURNACE AMONG THE FUNERAL URNS OF BEULAH   684 JERUSALEM 53   28
    AMONG THE FLOWERS OF BEULAH STILL RETAIN HIS AWFUL STRENGTH   686 JERUSALEM 55   2
    BETWEEN DWELLS A DAUGHTER OF BEULAH TO FEED THE HUMAN   688 JERUSALEM 56   10
        VEGETABLE
    AND FORMED INTO FOUR PRECIOUS STONES FOR ENTERANCE FROM   691 JERUSALEM 59   1
        BEULAH
    AND IN THE NORTH GATE IN THE WEST OF THE NORTH TOWARD   691 JERUSALEM 59   22
        BEULAH
    AH THAT IT COULD BE AS THE DAUGHTERS OF BEULAH WISH . . .   692 JERUSALEM 59   44
    THE DEAD BENEATH BEULAH FROM TYBURN TO GOLGOTHA AND FROM   698 JERUSALEM 63   33
    IN VISIONS OF THE DREAMS OF BEULAH AMONG THE DAUGHTERS   698 JERUSALEM 63   37
        OF ALBION
    TILL THEY REFUSE LIBERTY TO THE MALE & NOT LIKE BEULAH   . . 707 JERUSALEM 69   14
    AND THENCE IN BEULAH THEY ARE STOLEN BY SECRET AMOROUS   707 JERUSALEM 69   26
        THEFT
    FROM MALE & FEMALE LOVES IN BEULAH & THEIR JEALOUSIES   . . 708 JERUSALEM 69   29
    AND NOW THE SPECTRES OF THE DEAD AWAKE IN BEULAH ALL   . . 708 JERUSALEM 69   32
    AS SHE SLEPT IN BEULAH'S NIGHT HID BY THE DAUGHTERS OF   708 JERUSALEM 69   46
        BEULAH
    ALL WERE HIS FRIENDS & THEIR SONS & DAUGHTERS INTERMARRY   709 JERUSALEM 71   14
        IN BEULAH
    AND A SON OF EDEN WAS SET OVER EACH DAUGHTER OF BEULAH   712 JERUSALEM 72   48
        TO GUARD
    TOWARDS BEULAH IS TO THE SOUTH FENELON GUION TERESA . . .   712 JERUSALEM 72   50
    IN BEULAH BY THE DAUGHTERS OF BEULAH WITH TEARS   714 JERUSALEM 74   9
        & LAMENTATIONS
    OUTSIDE UNKNOWN BEFORE IN BEULAH & THE TWELVE GATES WERE   719 JERUSALEM 78   25
        FILLD
    SEXUAL ORGANIZATION & THE VISIONS OF THE NIGHT OF BEULAH   721 JERUSALEM 79   74
    SO LOS SPOKE TO THE DAUGHTERS OF BEULAH WHILE HIS EMANATION   728 JERUSALEM 83   66
    . . . & THE DAUGHTERS OF BEULAH   . . . .   729 JERUSALEM 83   85
    HE CALLD IT DIVINE ANALOGY FOR IN BEULAH THE FEMININE   . . 730 JERUSALEM 85   7
    CITIES WHERE BEULAH LOVELY TERMINATES . . . .   730 JERUSALEM 85   26
    OF BEULAH FOR JERUSALEM & SHILOH IN IMMORTAL GOLGONOOZA   731 JERUSALEM 86   44
    BURST THE BOTTOMS OF THE GRAVES & FUNERAL ARKS OF BEULAH   736 JERUSALEM 89   60
    SUCH AS THE FLOWERS OF BEULAH WEAVE TO BE THEIR FUNERAL   736 JERUSALEM 90   7
        MANTLES
    AWAKING IT TO LIFE AMONG THE FLOWERS OF BEULAH REJOICING   745 JERUSALEM 98   21
        IN UNITY
BEULAH'S
    DESCENDING OVER BEULAH'S MILD MOON COVERD REGIONS   . . .   304 FOUR ZOAS 4   249
    WITH SOLEMN MOURNING INTO BEULAH'S MOONY SHADES & HILLS   518 MILTON 30   5
    HOWLING IN PAIN REDOUNDING FROM THE ARMS OF BEULAH'S   624 JERUSALEM 5   49
        DAUGHTERS
    O WHAT AVAIL THE LOVES & TEARS OF BEULAH'S LOVELY DAUGHTERS   624 JERUSALEM 5   54
    LIKE A PALE CLOUD ARISING FROM THE ARMS OF BEULAH'S   635 JERUSALEM 14   33
        DAUGHTERS
    AND CRUEL FORMS UNLIKE THE MERCIFUL FORMS OF BEULAH'S   639 JERUSALEM 17   28
        NIGHT
    REPOSE IN BEULAH'S NIGHT TILL THE ERROR IS REMOVD   . .   676 JERUSALEM 46   12
    AWAY FROM BEULAH'S HILLS & VALES BREAK FORTH THE SOULS   677 JERUSALEM 47   10
        OF THE DEAD
    WITH PANGS SHE FORSOOK BEULAH'S PLEASANT LOVELY SHADOWY   678 JERUSALEM 48   19
        UNIVERSE
    WITH SOLEMN MOURNING OUT OF BEULAH'S MOONY SHADES AND HILLS   678 JERUSALEM 48   24
    HER FORM WAS HELD BY BEULAH'S DAUGHTERS BUT ALL WITHIN   693 JERUSALEM 60   40
        UNSEEN
    AS SHE SLEPT IN BEULAH'S NIGHT HID BY THE DAUGHTERS OF   708 JERUSALEM 69   46
        BEULAH
    BY THE TEARS & SMILES OF BEULAH'S DAUGHTERS . . . .   721 JERUSALEM 79   77
    AND THREEFOLD IN SOFT BEULAH'S NIGHT . . . .   818 HAPPINESS/L   86
BEWAIL
    TO BEWAIL THAT SAMSON LOVED ME NOT HE SAT AND . . . . .   39B SAMSON/PS   PROSE
    WHEREER HE GOES & ALL HIS NEIGHBOURHOOD BEWAIL HIS LOSS   516 MILTON 29   13
BEWARE
    O ELENOR BEWARE THE CURSED DUKE   . . . .   6 FAIR ELENOR/PS   65

BEWARE   (CONTINUED)
    BEWARE O PROUD THOU SHALT BE HUMBLED THY CRUEL BROW . . .   34B KING JOHN/PS   PROSE
    [TO SMITE ME WITH THY TONGUE BEWARE LEST I STING ALSO THEE] 268 FOUR ZOAS 1   148
    MIGHTY ATCHIEVEMENT OF YOUR POWER BEWARE THE PUNISHMENT   272 FOUR ZOAS 1   289
    BEWARE LEST WE ALSO DRINK UP THEE ROUGH DEMON OF THE WATERS 298 FOUR ZOAS 4   37
BEWILDERED   SEE WILDERD
BEYOND
    [AND BEYOND A MIRTLE TREE] . . . .   167 INFANT SORW/N   22
    BEYOND THE BOUNDS OF THEIR OWN SELF THEIR SENSES CANNOT   314 FOUR ZOAS 6   94
        PENETRATE
    HE SAW THEM CURSD BEYOND HIS CURSE HIS SOUL MELTED WITH   315 FOUR ZOAS 6   142
        FEAR
    THAT LIES BEYOND THE BOUNDS OF SCIENCE IN THE GREY OBSCURE   324 FOUR ZOAS 7   150
    BEYOND THE LIMIT OF TRANSLUCENCE ON THE LAKE OF UDAN ADAN   340 FOUR ZOAS 7B   300
    THEY SAW THE SAVIOUR BEYOND THE PIT OF DEATH & DESTRUCTION   342 FOUR ZOAS 8   48
    SURROUNDING THEM ON ALL SIDES BEYOND SIN & DEATH & HELL   342 FOUR ZOAS 8   51
    WEAKEND THEY STRETCH BEYOND THEIR POWER IN DIRE DROVES   344 FOUR ZOAS 8   129
    . . .
    [WITHOUT] BEYOND THIS UNIVERSAL CONFUSION BEYOND   359 FOUR ZOAS 9   91
        THE ?REMOTEST POLE
    SEEK NOT THY HEAVENLY FATHER THEN BEYOND THE SKIES . . .   502 MILTON 20   32
    BEYOND THE STARS IN CHAOS IN CAVERNS OF THE MUNDANE SHELL   502 MILTON 20   42
    LIKE THE BLACK STORM COMING OUT OF CHAOS BEYOND THE STARS   507 MILTON 23   21
    UNSEEN BEYOND THE MUNDANE SHELL SOUTHWARD IN MILTON'S TRACK 526 MILTON 35   47
    MEETING AGAIN IN GOLGONOOZA BEYOND SATAN'S SEAT . . .   526 MILTON 35   53
    BEYOND THE OUTLINE OF IDENTITY IN THE SELFHOOD DEADLY   527 MILTON 37   10
    WITH CAVERNS WHOSE REMOTEST BOTTOMS MEET AGAIN BEYOND   .   529 MILTON 37   55
    CITY & SANDY DESERT INTERMINGLED BEYOND MORTAL KEN . .   532 MILTON 40   27
    OF UNIVERSAL HUMAN LIFE BEYOND WHICH NATURE NEVER STEPS   567C DESC CAT 3   PROSE
    AND MINUTELY ARTICULATED BEYOND ALL THAT THE MORTAL AND   576D DESC CAT 4   PROSE
    GO BEYOND EITHER WHAT HE DOES OR WHAT THEY HAVE DONE   .   579C DESC CAT 5   PROSE
    THE HUMAN MIND CANNOT GO BEYOND THE GIFT OF GOD THE HOLY   579D DESC CAT 5   PROSE
        GHOST
    TO SUPPOSE THAT ART CAN GO BEYOND . . . .   579D DESC CAT 5   PROSE
    OF UNIVERSAL HUMAN LIFE BEYOND WHICH NATURE NEVER STEPS   590D CHAUCER 2   PROSE
    FLORENTINE ORIGINAL & IF POSSIBLE TO GO BEYOND THAT   600B PUB ADDRESS/N   PROSE
        ORIGINAL
    BEYOND THE OUTLINE OF IDENTITY BOTH WAYS WHICH MEET IN ONE   640 JERUSALEM 18   3
    BEYOND THE NIGHT OF BEULAH IN A DARK & UNKNOWN NIGHT   .   641 JERUSALEM 18   45
    MUST PASS THRO CONDEMNATION AND AWAKE BEYOND THE GRAVE .   662 JERUSALEM 35   10
    STEPS BEYOND AND REDEEMS MAN IN THE BODY OF JESUS AMEN .   664 JERUSALEM 36   55
    EVEN TO THE STARS EXALTING HER THRONE TO BUILD BEYOND THE   719 JERUSALEM 78   18
        THRONE
    WANDERING IN THAT UNKNOWN NIGHT BEYOND THE SILENT GRAVE   736 JERUSALEM 89   61
    I CANNOT GO BEYOND THE COMMAND OF THE LORD . . . . . .   792C LETTER 4   PROSE
    I MUST SAY ARE FAR BEYOND ANY THING I HAVE EVER DONE   .   853A LETTER 51   *PROSE
    IS A HUNDRED YEARS BEYOND THE PRESENT GENERATION THOUGH   864D LETTER 61   PROSE
    TOO MUCH TO DARE VENTURE BEYOND MY PRESENT PRECINCTS   .   872D LETTER 76   PROSE
BEZALEEL
    AND IF BEZALEEL & AHOLIAB DREW . . . .   543 IF TRUE/N   5
BIBBER   SEE WINE BIBBER
BIBLE
    YOU HAVE READ ABOUT THAT IN THE BIBLE . . . .   47B ISLAND MOON 3   PROSE
    AH SAID ARADOBO I THOUGHT I HAD READ OF PHEBUS IN THE BIBLE 47B ISLAND MOON 3   PROSE
    OF THE NAMES [OF] IN THE BIBLE SAID MRS [SISTAGATIST]   47C ISLAND MOON 3 *PROSE
        SIGTAGATIST
    THAT REASON MAY HAVE IDEAS TO BUILD ON THE JEHOVAH OF THE   150B MARRIAGE HH 5   PROSE
        BIBLE
    THE CHURCH & I TOOK HIM TO THE ALTAR AND OPEND THE BIBLE   157A MARRIAGE HH 17 PROSE
    READ THE BIBLE TOGETHER IN ITS INFERNAL OR DIABOLICAL SENSE 158D MARRIAGE HH 22 PROSE
    I HAVE ALSO THE BIBLE OF HELL WHICH THE WORLD SHALL HAVE   158D MARRIAGE HH 22 PROSE
    WHICH WILL COMMENCE A SERIES OF SUBJECTS FROM THE BIBLE   207C PROSPECTUS 1793 PROSE
    AND TO MAHOMET A LOOSE BIBLE GAVE . . . .   246 SONG OF LOS 3   29
    FOR THE BIBLE BY WILLIAM BLAKE . . . .   383A ANNO WATSON   TITLE
    TO DEFEND THE BIBLE IN THIS YEAR...WOULD COST A MAN HIS   383B ANNO WATSON   MARG
        LIFE
    ATTACK BUT IT IS NOT SO EASY FOR ONE WHO LOVES THE BIBLE   383B ANNO WATSON   MARG
    BY PAINE & ALSO THE PERVERSIONS OF THE BIBLE WHO DARE .   383B ANNO WATSON   MARG
    DEFEND EITHER THE ACTS OF CHRIST OR THE BIBLE UNPERVERTED   383B ANNO WATSON   MARG
    I BELIEVE THAT THE BISHOP LAUGHT AT THE BIBLE IN HIS SLIEVE 385D ANNO WATSON   MARG
    ("ON ALL OCCASIONS ACT RIGHT ") ALWAYS OR THE BIBLE   386B ANNO WATSON   MARG
        IS FALSE
    OR THE BIBLE IS FALSE . . . .   386B ANNO WATSON   MARG
    TO ME WHO BELIEVE THE BIBLE & PROFESS MYSELF A CHRISTIAN   387B ANNO WATSON   MARG
    THE BIBLE SAYS THAT GOD FORMED NATURE PERFECT BUT THAT MAN 388A ANNO WATSON   MARG
    INDIVIDUAL WHO GOD CONSIDERS IN THE BIBLE AS MURDER   .   388B ANNO WATSON   MARG
    THE BIBLE OR PECULIAR WORD OF GOD . . . .   389C ANNO WATSON   MARG
    THE BIBLE TELLS ME THAT THE PLAN OF PROVIDENCE WAS   390A ANNO WATSON   MARG
        SUBVERTED
    ONE FOR INSTANCE WHICH IS THAT THE BOOKS OF THE BIBLE .   390C ANNO WATSON   MARG
    THAT THE BIBLE IS ALL A STATE TRICK . . . .   390C ANNO WATSON   MARG
    ON THE BIBLE ARE DISHONEST DESIGNING KNAVES . . . .   390C ANNO WATSON   MARG
    I CANNOT CONCIEVE THE DIVINITY OF THE BOOKS IN THE BIBLE   393B ANNO WATSON   MARG
    CONSEQUENT GOOD THIS SENSE OF THE BIBLE IS EQUALLY TRUE   393B ANNO WATSON   MARG
    THE BIBLE SAYS THAT CULTIVATED LIFE EXISTED FIRST . .   446C ANNO REYNOLDS   MARG
    FOR IF IT IS A DECEIT THE WHOLE BIBLE IS MADNESS   452D ANNO REYNOLDS   MARG
        THIS OPINION
    ARE SET UP BY ARTIFICE AGAINST THE SUBLIME OF THE BIBLE   480B MILTON 3   PROSE
    ASSERTED IN THE BIBLE THAT THE NAME OF THE WICKED SHALL ROT 598C PUB ADDRESS/N   PROSE
    THE HEBREW BIBLE & THE GOSPEL OF JESUS ARE NOT ALLEGORY   604D V LAST JUDG/N PROSE
    WHILE THE BIBLE XXX IF VIRTUE & VICE XXX . . . . .   605C V LAST JUDG/N *PROSE
    THE GREEK MUSES WHICH ARE NOT INSPIRATION AS THE BIBLE IS   605C V LAST JUDG/N PROSE

	PAGE	TITLE	LINE

BIBLE   (CONTINUED)
```
    WHILE THE HEBREW BIBLE & THE GREEK GOSPEL ARE GENUINE   .  .   605C V LAST JUDG/N    PROSE
    AS THEY ARE WRITTEN IN THE BIBLE  . . . . . . . . . . .      607B V LAST JUDG/N    PROSE
    ARE REPRESENTATIONS OF THOSE STATES DESCRIBED IN THE BIBLE   609D V LAST JUDG/N    PROSE
    ON THE SIDE NEXT BAPTISM ARE SEEN THOSE CALLD IN THE BIBLE   613D V LAST JUDG/N    PROSE
    FROM THE BIBLE & LIMITS ALL EXISTENCE TO CREATION & TO       614B V LAST JUDG/N    PROSE
        CHAOS
    THE BIBLE NEVER TELLS US THAT DEVILS TORMENT ONE ANOTHER     616B V LAST JUDG/N    PROSE
        THRO ENVY
    BOTH READ THE BIBLE DAY & NIGHT  . . . . . . . . .           748 EV GOSPEL(A)/N       13
    THE WHOLE BIBLE IS FILLD WITH IMAGINATION & VISIONS   . . .  774D ANNO BERKELEY     MARG
    IS NOT EVERY VICE POSSIBLE TO MAN DESCRIBED IN THE BIBLE     777D INSC LAOCOON      PROSE
        OPENLY
    STOLEN & PERVERTED FROM THE BIBLE NOT BY CHANCE   . . . .    785B ILLUS DANTE 7    PROSE
    THE HELL OF THE BIBLE NEITHER IN THE WAY OUR PARSONS         785C ILLS DANTE 101   PROSE
        EXPLAIN IT
    THE BEAUTY OF THE BIBLE IS THAT THE MOST IGNORANT &  . . .   786D ANNO THORNTON      MARG
    & ONE ANOTHER LEAD US NOT TO READ THE BIBLE   . . . . .      788D ANNO THORNTON      MARG
    BUT LET OUR BIBLE BE VIRGIL & SHAKSPEARE   . . . . . .       789A ANNO THORNTON      MARG
    WHY IS THE BIBLE MORE ENTERTAINING & INSTRUCTIVE THAN ANY    794A LETTER 5         PROSE
        OTHER BOOK
    LIVE BY MIRACLE I AM PAINTING SMALL PICTURES FROM THE BIBLE  795C LETTER 6         PROSE
    IF THE HEBREW BIBLE IS AS WELL TRANSLATED WHICH I DO NOT     821D LETTER 25        PROSE
    AS HE IS TO A CHAPTER IN THE BIBLE   . . . . . . . . .       825B LETTER 27        PROSE
    READING IN THE BIBLE OF THE EYES OF THE ALMIGHTY   . . . .   860D LETTER 57        PROSE
    CHAIND ROUND BIBLE CHAIND ROUND   . . . . . . . .           SUPP ILLUS DANTE 99  *PROSE
    THE BIBLE OF HELL IN NOCTURNAL VISIONS COLLECTED VOL I      SUPP INSCRIPTION     *TITLE
        LAMBETH
BIBLES
    ALL BIBLES OR SACRED CODES HAVE BEEN THE CAUSES   . . . .    149C MARRIAGE HH 4    PROSE
BID
    GAVE THEE LIFE & BID THEE FEED  . . . . . . . . .            115 THE LAMB/SI          3
    AND WHEN HE BID THEM SHAKE OFF THE DUST OF THEIR FEET   . .  158C MARRIAGE HH 22   PROSE
BIDDING
    SO THEY NEED NOT BIDDING GO  . . . . . . . . . .             59A ISLAND MOON 10    PROSE
BIDS
    PROJECTED WORK IT BIDS FAIR TO SET ME ABOVE                  862C LETTER 60        PROSE
        THE DIFFICULTIES
BIER
    THAT SHALL NEVER BE QUIET TILL LAID ON ITS BIER   . . .      429 MARY                48
    SHALL BRING THY WIFE UPON A BIER  . . . . . . . .            817 HAPPINESS/L          38
BIG      SEE PIG
BIGGER
    TO HAVE THRASHD THE FELLOW ONLY HE WAS BIGGER THAN I   . .   45A ISLAND MOON 1     PROSE
BILL
    TO HEAVE THE BLOODY BILL  . . . . . . . . . .                12 GWIN KING/PS          52
    THAT BILL S A FOOLISH FELLOW  . . . . . . . . . .            61 SAY YOU JOE/IM         9
BILLINGSGATE
    AND WITH THE BLAST OF HIS FURNACE UPON FISHY BILLINGSGATE    726 JERUSALEM 82         59
BILLOWS
    HIS BILLOWS ROLL WHERE MONSTERS WANDER IN THE FOAMY PATHS    286 FOUR ZOAS 2        257
    PLUNGD INTO THE COLD BILLOWS LIVING [&] A LIFE IN MIDST      296 FOUR ZOAS 3      *  179
        OF WATERS
    I ROLL MY FLOODS OVER HIS BODY MY BILLOWS & WAVES PASS       301 FOUR ZOAS 4        133
        OVER HIM
    THE EAST WAS VOID BUT THARMAS ROLLD HIS BILLOWS IN           318 FOUR ZOAS 6        270
        CEASELESS EDDIES
    MORTALITY BEGINS TO ROLL THE BILLOWS OF ETERNAL DEATH   . .  666 JERUSALEM 39          8
BILLOWY
    [WHEN THARMAS SHOOK HIS BILLOWY HAIR]   . . . . . .         SUPP FOUR ZOAS 1       *
BILLY
    AND FELPHAM BILLY RODE OUT EVERY MORN   . . . . . .          537 AND HIS LEGS/N       22
BILLY'S
    THE EARS OF BILLY'S LAWYER & DRAGOON   . . . . . . . .       537 AND HIS LEGS/N       25
BIND
    BIND ARDENT HOPE UPON YOUR FEET LIKE SHOES   . . . . . .     30 EDW THIRD/PS 5        33
    DIDST THOU NOT TELL ME WITH GREEN WITHS(WITHES) TO BIND THY  38D SAMSON/PS         PROSE
    WITH NEW ROPES TO BIND THEE FAST  . . . . . . . . . .        39A SAMSON/PS         PROSE
    LIKE FABLED HECATE SHE DOTH BIND THEM TO HER LAW   . . .     41D THEN SHE BORE     PROSE
    NOW THEY SURROUND THE GOD AND BIND HIM FAST  . . . . .       42C THEN SHE BORE     PROSE
    REPLY NOT LEST I BIND THEE WITH THE GREEN FLAGS OF THE       104 TIRIEL 4            24
        BROOK
    TO BIND ANOTHER TO ITS DELIGHT  . . . . . . . . . .          162 CLOD PEBBLE/N        10
    TO BIND THE PHANTOMS OF EXISTENCE FROM ETERNAL LIFE   . .    192 V DAU ALBION 4       24
    EXPANSION TO THE EYE OF PITY OR WILL HE BIND HIMSELF   . .   195 V DAU ALBION 8        3
    DESCENDS LINK BY LINK FROM ALBION'S CLIFFS ACROSS THE        197 AMERICA 3             8
        SEA TO BIND
    DESCENDS LINK BY LINK FROM ALBION'S CLIFFS ACROSS THE        204 AMERICA CANC A        8
        SEA TO BIND
    TO BIND ANOTHER TO ITS DELIGHT  . . . . . . . . . .          211 CLOD PEBBLE/SE       10
    DIDST BIND MY NOSTRILS EYES & EARS   . . . . . . .           220 TO TIRZAH/SE         12
    LET CORDS & STAKES BIND IN THE VOID  . . . . . . . .         231 URIZEN 19             3
    AND WHO SHALL BIND THE INFINITE WITH AN ETERNAL BAND   .  .  239 EUROPE PREL 2        13
    SIEZE ALL THE SPIRITS OF LIFE AND BIND  . . . . . . .        239 EUROPE 4             17
    BIND ALL THE NOURISHING SWEETS OF EARTH  . . . . . . .       239 EUROPE 4             19
    STILL ALL YOUR THUNDERS GOLDEN HOOFD & BIND YOUR HORSES      244 EUROPE 14            28
        BLACK
    BIND THEM [TOGETHER] CONDENSING THE STRONG ENERGIES . . .    284 FOUR ZOAS 2      *  163
    TO BIND THE BODY OF MAN TO HEAVEN FROM FALLING INTO THE      287 FOUR ZOAS 2         267
        ABYSS
    OF ENION & HIM ASSIST TO BIND THE FALLEN KING  . . . .       300 FOUR ZOAS 4         120
    BIND HIM TAKE ENITHARMON FOR THY SWEET REWARD WHILE I  . .   300 FOUR ZOAS 4         122
```

		PAGE	TITLE	LINE

BIND   (CONTINUED)
       FROM WRATH NOW WHEN I RAGE MY FETTERS BIND ME MORE   . . .   323 FOUR ZOAS 7   138
       TO BIND THE FATHER & ENSLAVE THE BRETHREN NOUGHT HE KNEW   326 FOUR ZOAS 7   256
       AND BIND THEM TO THEE THAT MY CRYSTAL FORM MAY COME TO ME   334 FOUR ZOAS 7B   71
       TO PERPLEX YOUTH IN THEIR OUTGOINGS & TO BIND TO LABOURS   337 FOUR ZOAS 7B   180
       WHY DOST THOU WANDER AWAY FROM TIRZAH WHY ME COMPELL TO   348 FOUR ZOAS 8   299
           BIND THEE
       BIND HIM DOWN SISTERS BIND HIM DOWN ON EBAL MOUNT OF   349 FOUR ZOAS 8   315
           CURSING
       BIND AROUND MY AKING HEAD   . . . .   417 MY SPECTR AD/N   12
       RISE WAR & BIND HIM IN HIS CELL   . . . .   419 I SAW A MONK/N   14
       AND LET US BIND THEE IN THE BANDS OF WAR & BE THOU KING   501 MILTON 20   5
       THEREFORE YOU MUST BIND THE SHEAVES NOT BY NATIONS   510 MILTON 25   26
           OR FAMILIES
       YOU SHALL BIND THEM IN THREE CLASSES ACCORDING TO THEIR   510 MILTON 25   27
           CLASSES
       SO SHALL YOU BIND THEM SEPARATING WHAT HAS BEEN MIXED   . .   510 MILTON 25   28
       SHALL BIND THEM SEPARATE THEY CANNOT BELIEVE IN ETERNAL   511 MILTON 25   33
           LIFE
       THESE YOU SHALL BIND IN A TWIN-BUNDLE FOR THE CONSUMMATION   511 MILTON 25   37
       FOR THY RIGHTEOUSNESS BUT I ADD MERCY ALSO AND BIND   . . .   670 JERUSALEM 42   20
       RISE WAR & BIND HIM IN HIS CELL   . . . .   683 I SAW A MONK/J   12
       TO PERPLEX YOUTH IN THEIR OUTGOINGS & TO BIND TO LABOURS   700 JERUSALEM 65   22
           IN ALBION
       HIS FOREHEAD THEY BIND HIS FOREHEAD WITH THORNS OF IRON   702 JERUSALEM 66   23
       WHY WILT THOU WANDER AWAY FROM TIRZAH WHY ME COMPEL TO   705 JERUSALEM 67 *   45
           BIND THEE
       BIND HIM DOWN SISTERS BIND HIM DOWN ON EBAL MOUNT OF   705 JERUSALEM 68   3
           CURSING
       I HAVE DESTROYD WANDRING REUBEN WHO STROVE TO BIND MY WILL   724 JERUSALEM 81   10
       UNLESS WE FIND A WAY TO BIND THESE AWFUL FORMS TO OUR   .   725 JERUSALEM 82   3
       O THAT I COULD LIVE IN HIS SIGHT O THAT I COULD BIND HIM   726 JERUSALEM 82   44
           TO MY ARM
       AND IN HIS BODY TIGHT DOES BIND   . . . .   749 EV GOSPEL(B)/N   50
       ALL MENTAL POWERS BY DISEASES WE BIND   . . . . . .   755 EV GOSPEL(E)/N   87
       BUT IN VAIN THE FASTER I BIND THE BETTER IS THE BALLAST   809A LETTER 20   PROSE
BINDER
       OR ORC BENDING DOWN AS THE BINDER OF THE SHEAVES FOLLOWS   332 FOUR ZOAS 7   462
BINDEST
       THE STARS OF ALBION CRUEL RISE THOU BINDEST TO SWEET   693 JERUSALEM 60   60
           INFLUENCES
BINDING
       AND BINDING WITH BRIARS MY JOYS & DESIRES   . . . . .   163 GARDEN LOVE/N   12
       AND BINDING WITH BRIARS MY JOYS & DESIRES   . . . . .   215 GARDEN LOVE/SE   12
       LAWS & RELIGIONS TO THE SONS OF HAR BINDING THEM MORE   . .   246 SONG OF LOS 4   14
       THE BINDING OF URIZEN DAY AND NIGHT   . . . .   259 BOOK OF LOS 5   23
       BINDING JERUSALEM'S CHILDREN IN THE DUNGEONS OF BABYLON   281 FOUR ZOAS 2   63
       AND THUS BEGAN THE BINDING OF URIZEN DAY & NIGHT IN FEAR   302 FOUR ZOAS 4   199
       HELD THE FIERCE BOY LOS NAILD HIM DOWN BINDING AROUND HIS   307 FOUR ZOAS 5   101
           LIMBS
       THE DAUGHTERS OF AMALEK CANAAN & MOAB BINDING ON   348 FOUR ZOAS 8 *   295
           THE [STEMS] STONES
       THE DAUGHTERS OF CANAAN & MOAB BINDING ON THE STONES   .   382 FOUR ZOAS AD 6   11
       HE HAS BUILDED THE ARCHES OF ALBION'S TOMB BINDING THE   680 JERUSALEM 49   54
           STARS
       BINDING HIS WRISTS & ANKLES WITH THE IRON ARMS OF LOVE   .   726 JERUSALEM 82   71
BINDS
       THE MERCHANT BINDS HIS BROWS IN STEEL   . . . . . .   12 GWIN KING/PS   47
       AND KISSES ME AND BINDS HIS NUPTIAL BANDS AROUND MY BREAST   129 BOOK OF THEL 5
       HE WHO BINDS [HIMSELF TO] TO HIMSELF A JOY   . . . . .   179 ETERNITY/N   *   1
       HE WHO BINDS TO HIMSELF A JOY   . . . .   184 SEVRL QUESTN/N *   11
       TO RISE ON HIGH YET LOVE HERE BINDS ME DOWN & NEVER NEVER   339 FOUR ZOAS 7B   254
       SHE BINDS IRON THORNS AROUND HIS HEAD   . . . . . .   425 MENTAL TRAVLER   13
       AND BINDS HER DOWN FOR HIS DELIGHT   . . . .   425 MENTAL TRAVLER   24
       AND OCALYTHRON BINDS THE SUN INTO A JEALOUS GLOBE   . . .   491 MILTON 10   19
       SEEKING TO KEEP MY SOUL A VICTIM TO THY LOVE WHICH BINDS   622 JERUSALEM 4   25
BIQUADRATE
       IN INTRICATE WAYS BIQUADRATE TRAPEZIUMS RHOMBS RHOMBOIDS   287 FOUR ZOAS 2   284
BIRCH
       WOULD NOT HAVE BANDY CHILDREN NOR FASTING NOR BIRCH   . .   179 LIT VAGABOND/N   13
       WOULD NOT HAVE BANDY CHILDREN NOR FASTING NOR BIRCH   . .   216 LIT VAGABND/SE   12
       P S PLEASE TO REMEMBER OUR BEST RESPECTS TO MR BIRCH &   810B LETTER 20   PROSE
           TELL HIM THAT
       (FOUR) NUMBERS FOR MR BIRCH WITH BEST RESPECTS TO HIM   .   822B LETTER 26   PROSE
       HAYLEY'S BALLADS PER BROTHER DITTO MR BIRCH   . . . .   SUPP LETTER 56A   *PROSE
BIRCH'S
       THANKS TO MR BIRCH'S ELECTRICAL MAGIC   . . . . . .   854A LETTER 52   PROSE
BIRD
       ANY MORE THAN [?ANY ?BIRD THE] A DOG OR A CAT   . . . .   61 SAY YOU JOE/IM *   13
       HOW CAN THE BIRD THAT IS BORN FOR JOY   . . . . .   124 SCHOOL BOY/SI   16
       HOW DO YOU KNOW BUT EVRY BIRD THAT CUTS THE AIRY WAY   .   150D MARRIAGE HH 6   PROSE
       NO BIRD SOARS TOO HIGH IF HE SOARS WITH HIS OWN WINGS   .   151B MARRIAGE HH 7   PROSE
       THE BIRD A NEST THE SPIDER A WEB MAN FRIENDSHIP   . . .   151D MARRIAGE HH 8   PROSE
       AS THE AIR TO A BIRD OR THE SEA TO A FISH   . . . . .   152D MARRIAGE HH 10   PROSE
       I LOVE [MYSELF SO DOES THE BIRD] YOU LIKE THE LITTLE BIRD   177 LIT BOY LST/N   7
       I LOVE YOU LIKE THE LITTLE BIRD   . . . .   218 LIT BOY LST/SE   7
       OF BEAST BIRD FISH SERPENT & ELEMENT   . . . . . .   222 URIZEN 3   16
       MANY FORMS OF FISH BIRD & BEAST   . . . .   232 URIZEN 19   34
       WHERE IS MY LUREING BIRD OF EDEN LEUTHA SILENT LOVE   . .   244 EUROPE 14   9
       SLEPT AS A BIRD IN THE BLUE SHELL THAT SOON SHALL BURST   273 FOUR ZOAS 1   350
           AWAY
       PRESENTLY COMES A FAMISHD BIRD & TAKES AWAY THE SPIDER   . .   277 FOUR ZOAS 1   458

220

	PAGE	TITLE	LINE

BIRD   (CONTINUED)

SO MAN LOOKS OUT IN TREE & HERB & FISH & BIRD & BEAST   .   . 355 FOUR ZOAS 8   561
SEVEN MORNINGS LOS HEARD THEM AS THE POOR BIRD WITHIN THE   504 MILTON 21   28
    SHELL
HEARS ITS IMPATIENT PARENT BIRD AND ENITHARMON HEARD THEM   504 MILTON 21   29
AND IN EVERY SPECIES OF EARTH METAL TREE FISH BIRD & BEAST   511 MILTON 25   41
STANDS STILL UPON THE MOUNTAIN LOOKING ON THIS LITTLE BIRD   520 MILTON 31   37
AND THRO THE NIGHT WARBLES LUXURIANT EVERY BIRD OF SONG   520 MILTON 31   43
WHERE FISH & BIRD & BEAST & MAN & TREE & METAL & STONE   . . 681 JERUSALEM 50   6
WE REMEMBER WHEN A PRINT SHOP WAS A RARE BIRD IN LONDON   798C LETTER 10   PROSE
FAME A BIRD SINGING   .   .   .   . SUPP ILLUS GRAY   *TITLE

BIRD'S

HEAR THE SMALL BIRD'S GRIEF & CARE   .   .   .   .   .   . 122 ON ANOTHERS/SI   15

BIRDS

AND THE RUSTLING [BEDS] BIRDS OF DAWN   .   .   .   .   .   .   9 MAD SONG/PS   7
THE BIRDS OF DAY WERE HEARD IN THEIR NESTS   .   .   .   .   . 35C COUCH DEATH/PS PROSE
LIKE BIRDS JUST CURED OF THE PIP   .   .   .   . 56 HAIL MATRIM/IM   23
BESIDES IN THE SKY THE LITTLE BIRDS FLY   .   .   .   .   .   60 NURSES SONG/IM   12
WHEN THE PAINTED BIRDS LAUGH IN THE SHADE   .   .   .   .   . 63 SHEPHERD YOUNG   9
PLAYING WITH FLOWERS & RUNNING AFTER BIRDS THEY SPENT THE   100 TIRIEL 2   8
    DAY
AND THOU SHALT HELP US TO CATCH BIRDS & GATHER THEM RIPE   102 TIRIEL 3   15
    CHERRIES
THOU SHALT NOT GO SAID HEVA TILL THOU HAST SEEN OUR SINGING 103 TIRIEL 3   22
    BIRDS
BLIND TO THE PLEASURES OF THE SIGHT & DEAF TO WARBLING   104 TIRIEL 4   29
    BIRDS
FOR BIRDS TO EAT BUT I HAVE SCARCE DEPARTED FROM THE PLACE   105 TIRIEL 4   * 52
CONSUMING ALL BOTH FLOWERS & FRUITS INSECTS & WARBLING   110 TIRIEL 8   38
    BIRDS
THE BIRDS OF THE BUSH   .   .   .   . 116 ECCHOING GR/SI   6
LIKE BIRDS IN THEIR NEST   .   .   .   . 116 ECCHOING GR/SI   27
THE BIRDS ARE SILENT IN THEIR NEST   .   .   .   . 118 NIGHT/SI   3
WHERE BIRDS ARE COVERD WARM   .   .   .   . 119 NIGHT/SI   18
BESIDES IN THE SKY THE LITTLE BIRDS FLY   .   .   .   .   . . 121 NURSES SONG/SI 11
BIRDS DELIGHT   .   .   .   . 123 SPRING/SI   3
WHEN THE BIRDS SING ON EVERY TREE   .   .   .   . 124 SCHOOL BOY/SI   2
WHEN THE PAINTED BIRDS LAUGH IN THE SHADE   .   .   .   .   . 125 LAUGHING/SI   9
BUT I FEED NOT THE LITTLE FLOWERS I HEAR THE WARBLING BIRDS 129 BOOK OF THEL 3 19
BUT I FEED NOT THE WARBLING BIRDS THEY FLY AND SEEK THEIR   129 BOOK OF THEL 3 20
    FOOD
.   .   . LIKE BIRDS OF PREY STOOD ON THE COUCH   .   .   . . 135 FRENCH REVOLTN 36
THAT WALK IN BEASTS AND BIRDS OF NIGHT. . .   .   . 144 FRENCH REVOLTN 235
AND WE'D BE AS HAPPY AS BIRDS IN THE SPRING   .   .   .   . . 179 LIT VAGABOND/N 11
TO GRATIFY SENSES UNKNOWN TREES BEASTS AND BIRDS UNKNOWN   192 V DAU ALBION 4 15
AND TREES & BIRDS & BEASTS & MEN BEHOLD THEIR ETERNAL JOY   195 V DAU ALBION 8   8
AND WE'D BE AS HAPPY AS BIRDS IN THE SPRING   .   .   .   . . 216 LIT VAGABND/SE 10
ON THE EAST SIDE REVIVD HER SOUL WITH LIVES OF BEASTS &   285 FOUR ZOAS 2   195
    BIRDS
THE BIRDS & BEASTS REJOICE & PLAY   .   .   .   . 289 FOUR ZOAS 2   357
ONCE HOW I SANG & CALLD THE BEASTS & BIRDS TO THEIR   325 FOUR ZOAS 7   * 199
    DELIGHTS
SHE HEARD SWEET VOICES IN THE WINDS & IN THE VOICES OF   340 FOUR ZOAS 7B   271
    BIRDS
DROOPING & THE BIRDS HIDE IN THEIR SILENT NESTS   .   .   . . 355 FOUR ZOAS 8   567
SCREAMING IN BIRDS OVER THE DEEP & HOWLING IN THE WOLF   . . 355 FOUR ZOAS 8   * 577
MY BIRDS ARE SILENT ON MY HILLS FLOCKS DIE BENEATH   359 FOUR ZOAS 9   101
    MY BRANCHES
THE BIRDS OF SONG TO MURDEROUS CROWS MY JOYS TO BITTER   360 FOUR ZOAS 9   110
    GROANS
IN FLOWERS IN FRUITS IN FISHES BIRDS & BEASTS & CLOUDS   367 FOUR ZOAS 9   378
    & WATERS
THE BIRDS ADORE THE SUN THE BEASTS RISE UP & PLAY IN HIS   367 FOUR ZOAS 9   406
    BEAMS
I'LL WATCH YOU & ATTEND YOUR FOOTSTEPS YOU ARE NOT LIKE   368 FOUR ZOAS 9   430
    THE BIRDS
AND YOU BIRDS THAT SING & ADORN THE SKY YOU ARE MY SISTERS   368 FOUR ZOAS 9   444
THE BIRDS   .   .   .   . 422D THE BIRDS/N   TITLE
THEN LOUD FROM THEIR GREEN COVERT ALL THE BIRDS BEGIN THEIR 520 MILTON 31   39
    SONG
HOW ARE THE BEASTS & BIRDS & FISHES & PLANTS & MINERALS   525 MILTON 34   53
HIS BIRDS ARE SILENT ON HIS HILLS FLOCKS DIE BENEATH HIS   641 JERUSALEM 19   2
    BRANCHES
THE BIRDS OF SONG TO MURDEROUS CROWS HIS JOYS TO BITTER   641 JERUSALEM 19   11
    GROANS
AMONG MY LAMBS & BROOKS OF WATER AMONG MY WARBLING BIRDS   642 JERUSALEM 20   8
THE VOICES OF WINDS TREES & BIRDS & THE ODOURS OF THE HAPPY 803B LETTER 15   PROSE
    GROUND

BIRDS'

HEARING WILD BIRDS' SONG   .   .   .   . 112 LIT GRL LST/SI   16

BIRMINGHAM

WHO IS NOT IN TOWN BEING AT BIRMINGHAM   .   .   .   .   .   . 834B LETTER 34   PROSE

BIRTH

WHERE THE MELODIOUS WINDS HAVE BIRTH   .   .   .   . 10 TO MUSES/PS   8
OR EVN THE LEAST BY BIRTH SHALL GAIN THE BRIGHTEST FAME   18 EDW THIRD/PS 1 30
TO ENGLAND WHEN AT THE BIRTH OF NATURE   .   .   .   .   .   . 21 EDW THIRD/PS 2 80
PITY FORSOOK THEE AT THY BIRTH O DAGON FURIOUS   .   .   . . 38C SAMSON/PS   PROSE
THOUGH I SHOULD TELL THIS SECRET OF MY BIRTH THE UTMOST MAY 38D SAMSON/PS   PROSE
TWICE WAS MY BIRTH FORETOLD FROM HEAVEN AND   .   .   .   . . 39B SAMSON/PS   PROSE
SHE BEARS SHE GROANS NOT AT THE BIRTH OF HEUXOS OR YUVA   99 TIRIEL 1   25
TO THE ABHORRED BIRTH OF CHERUBS IN THE HUMAN FORM   .   . . 193 V DAU ALBION 5 28
AND THE IMPURE SCOURGE FORCE HIS SEED INTO ITS UNRIPE BIRTH 193 V DAU ALBION 5 31

221

	PAGE	TITLE	LINE

BIRTH   (CONTINUED)

	PAGE	TITLE	LINE
WRITHING IN PANGS OF ABHORRED BIRTH RED FLAMES THE CREST REBELLIOUS	199	AMERICA 9	17
AH TERRIBLE BIRTH A YOUNG ONE BURSTING WHERE IS THE WEEPING MOUTH	199	AMERICA 9	22
WHATEER IS BORN OF MORTAL BIRTH	220	TO TIRZAH/SE	1
AT THE BIRTH OF THE HUMAN SHADOW	232	URIZEN 19	43
THE MOISTURE AWOKE TO BIRTH	255	AHANIA 5	37
WHERE BONES FROM THE BIRTH ARE BURIED	255	AHANIA 5	46
IN THROES OF BIRTH & NOW THE BLOSSOMS FALLING SHINING FRUIT	325	FOUR ZOAS 7	214
AND ITS BIRTH IN FAINTING & SLEEP & [WOE] SWEET DELUSIONS OF VALA	326	FOUR ZOAS 7	* 230
AND IN THE CRIES OF BIRTH & IN THE GROANS OF DEATH HIS VOICE	356	FOUR ZOAS 8	580
BY A NEW SPIRITUAL BIRTH REGENERATED FROM DEATH	363	FOUR ZOAS 9	224
IN PANGS OF AN ETERNAL BIRTH IN TORMENT & AWE & FEAR	363	FOUR ZOAS 9	234
. . . THAN PAINS OF ETERNAL [DEATH] BIRTH	377	FOUR ZOAS 9	739
THE PANGS OF ETERNAL BIRTH	377	FOUR ZOAS 9	742
PAINE SAYS THAT KINGS & PRIESTS HAVE DONE HIM HARM FROM HIS BIRTH	393A	ANNO WATSON	MARG
A LIE FEW BELIEVE IT IS A NEW BIRTH	403C	ANNO BACON	MARG
THE BIRTH OF WAR & MISERY WHILE THE LION SEIZES THE BULL THE	441D	INSC FALL MAN	PROSE
EXCEPT BY MIRACLE & A NEW BIRTH THE OTHER TWO CLASSES	511	MILTON 25	34
OF H'S(HAYLEY'S) BIRTH THIS WAS THE HAPPY LOT	539	OF HS BIRTH/N	1
THE ANGEL THAT PRESIDED OER MY BIRTH	541	ANGEL PRESID/N	1
SO SPOKE AN ANGEL AT MY BIRTH	557	ART HAS LOST/N	3
AND IN A DARK LAND GAVE HER BIRTH	651	FIELDS FROM/J	52
ENTERING THRO THE GATES OF BIRTH	651	FIELDS FROM/J	63
A WEEPING INFANT IN THE GATES OF BIRTH IN THE MIDST OF HEAVEN	697	JERUSALEM 63	17
BLASPHEMY BY HIS MATERNAL BIRTH HE IS THAT EVIL-ONE	736	JERUSALEM 90	35
FALLEN FIENDS OF HEAVNLY BIRTH	754	EV GOSPEL(E)/N	50
LIKE A WEAK MORTAL BIRTH	805	TO BUTTS/L	44

BIRTH PANGS

	PAGE	TITLE	LINE
THEIR APPEARANCE WHEN COMBIND BUT OFTEN BY BIRTH PANGS & LOUD GROANS	708	JERUSALEM 70	* 11

BIRTHPLACE

	PAGE	TITLE	LINE
BIRTHPLACE OF THE LAMB OF GOD INCOMPREHENSIBLE	626	JERUSALEM 7	67

BIRTH PLACE

	PAGE	TITLE	LINE
THE BIRTH PLACE OF MICHAEL ANGELO	541	FLORENTINE/N	2

BIRTHS

	PAGE	TITLE	LINE
O ETERNAL BIRTHS SUNG ROUND AHANIA	255	AHANIA 5	22
ALL THESE AROUND THE WORLD OF LOS CAST FORTH THEIR MONSTROUS BIRTHS	318	FOUR ZOAS 6	278
PERPETUALLY VEGETATING IN DETESTABLE BIRTHS	348	FOUR ZOAS 8	289
ARISE TO ETERNAL BIRTHS SHAKE OFF THY COLD REPOSE	360	FOUR ZOAS 9	130
WHICH ARE SEEN BURSTING WITH THEIR BIRTHS OF IMMORTALITY	443D	LAST JUDGMNT/L	PROSE
THE ETERNAL BIRTHS OF INTELLECT FROM THE DIVINE HUMANITY	613D	V LAST JUDG/N	PROSE

BISHOP

	PAGE	TITLE	LINE
BISHOP WILLIAM DAGWORTH'S MAN PETER BLUNT A COMMON SOLDIER	17C	EDW THIRD/PS	TITLE
QUEEN PHILIPPA LORDS BISHOP ETC	19A	EDW THIRD/PS 2	PROSE
MY LORD BISHOP YOU WOULD RECOMMEND US AGRICULTURE	19	EDW THIRD/PS 2	17
LORD BISHOP WHAT WAS RASH IN ME IS WISE	21	EDW THIRD/PS 2	91
NOTES ON THE B(BISHOP) OF L'S(LANDAFF'S) APOLOGY	383A	ANNO WATSON	*TITLE
IT IS AN EASY MATTER FOR A BISHOP TO TRIUMPH OVER PAINE'S	383B	ANNO WATSON	MARG
I HAVE NOT THE CHARITY FOR THE BISHOP THAT HE PRETENDS	384D	ANNO WATSON	MARG
TO WHAT DOES THE BISHOP ATTRIBUTE THE ENGLISH CRUSADE	385C	ANNO WATSON	MARG
BE IN THE GOOD HUMOUR THE BISHOP PRETENDS TO BE	385C	ANNO WATSON	MARG
I BELIEVE THAT THE BISHOP LAUGHT AT THE BIBLE IN HIS SLIEVE	385D	ANNO WATSON	MARG
LET THE BISHOP PROVE THAT HE HAS	387C	ANNO WATSON	MARG
THE BISHOP IS AN INQUISITOR	388B	ANNO WATSON	MARG
THEREFORE THE BISHOP HAS NOT ANSWERD PAINE	388B	ANNO WATSON	MARG
TO IMPROVEMENT & THE BISHOP HAS NOT SHEWN THE CONTRARY	388D	ANNO WATSON	MARG
HAS NOT THE BISHOP GIVEN HIMSELF THE LIE	390A	ANNO WATSON	MARG
THE TRIFLES WHICH THE BISHOP HAS COMBATED IN THE FOLLOWING	390C	ANNO WATSON	MARG
NONE OF WHICH THE BISHOP HAS DARED TO CONSIDER	390C	ANNO WATSON	MARG
MOSES IS NOT THE AUTHOR & THEN THE BISHOP LOSES HIS AUTHOR	391C	ANNO WATSON	MARG
PIETY & VIRTUE IS SENECA CLASSICAL O FINE BISHOP	394D	ANNO WATSON	MARG
THE BISHOP NEVER SAW THE EVERLASTING GOSPEL ANY MORE THAN TOM PAINE	394D	ANNO WATSON	* MARG
WHO DOES THE BISHOP CALL BAD MEN ARE THEY	396A	ANNO WATSON	MARG
THAT TOM PAINE IS A BETTER CHRISTIAN THAN THE BISHOP	396B	ANNO WATSON	MARG
I HAVE READ THIS BOOK WITH ATTENTION & FIND THAT THE BISHOP	396B	ANNO WATSON	MARG
THE BISHOP HAS NOT ANSWERD ONE OF PAINE'S GRAND OBJECTIONS	396C	ANNO WATSON	MARG

BISHOP'S

	PAGE	TITLE	LINE
THERSITES' SLY INSINUATION SUCH IS THE BISHOP'S	384D	ANNO WATSON	MARG
HE WAS CERTAINLY A SAVAGE IN THE BISHOP'S SENSE	389C	ANNO WATSON	MARG
HE KNEW NOTHING OF GOD IN THE BISHOP'S SENSE OF THE WORD	389C	ANNO WATSON	MARG
IS NOT THIS THE BISHOP'S CLOVEN FOOT	390B	ANNO WATSON	MARG

BISHOPS

	PAGE	TITLE	LINE
ARE WE TO BELIEVE THAT BISHOPS DO NOT RAIL I	385C	ANNO WATSON	MARG
CHRIST DIED AS AN UNBELIEVER & IF THE BISHOPS HAD THEIR WILL	387C	ANNO WATSON	MARG

BISHOPSGATE

	PAGE	TITLE	LINE
MR CUMBERLAND BISHOPSGATE WINDSOR GREAT PARK	SUPP	ADDRESSES/L	*TITLE
G CUMBERLAND ESQ BISHOPSGATE NEAR EGHAM SURREY	SUPP	ADDRESS/L 2	*TITLE

BIT

	PAGE	TITLE	LINE
YES SAID THE EPICUREAN & HAVING A BIT OF FUN WITH HIM	45C	ISLAND MOON 1	PROSE
AND [MAIDENS] BEAUTY FOR A BIT OF BREAD	174	HUMAN IMAGE/N	32
[SO] EVERY BIT AS WELL AS WAR & SLAUGHTERING	185	LET BROTHELS/N	* 12

222

	PAGE	TITLE	LINE

BIT   (CONTINUED)
        AND THE STRONG LION DEIGND IN HIS MOUTH TO WEAR THE GOLDEN   340 FOUR ZOAS 7B   282
        BIT
        THEY BIT IN THEIR WILD FURY WHO ALSO MADDEND LIKE WILDEST   487 MILTON 7   49
        BEASTS
BITE
        THE SNAKE DOTH TURN AND BITE THE PADDING FOOT . . . . .   24 EDW THIRD/PS 3   129
        INSTEAD OF ETCHING THE BLACKS ETCH THE WHITES & BITE IT IN   440C MEMORANDUM/N 4   PROSE
BITES
        THERE IS NO OTHER DEVIL HE WHO BITES WITHOUT PRAYING IS   73D ANNO LAVATER   MARG
        ONLY A BEAST
BITS
        CURBING THEIR TYGERS WITH GOLDEN BITS & BRIDLES OF SILVER   686 JERUSALEM 55   35
        & IVORY
BITTER
        I CURSE MY STARS IN BITTER GRIEF AND WOE   . . . . . .   10 WHEN EARLY/PS   15
        IS READY FOR YOUR BITTER TAUNTS [XXX] COME FORTH SONS OF   105 TIRIEL 4   * 67
        THE CURSE
        AND CAUGHT HIM BY THE GARMENTS WEEPING WITH CRIES OF BITTER   106 TIRIEL 5   19
        WOE
        THEN TIRIEL STOOD SAYING WHAT SOFT VOICE THREATENS SUCH   109 TIRIEL 8   3
        BITTER THINGS
        BLUE & CHANGING IN TEARS AND BITTER . . . .   250 AHANIA 3   3
        TURND ROUND THE CIRCLE OF DESTINY WITH TEARS & BITTER SIGHS   266 FOUR ZOAS 1   74
        THEY WILL WITHOLD SWEET LOVE WHOSE FOOD IS THORNS & BITTER   271 FOUR ZOAS 1   257
        ROOTS
        WEPT BITTER TEARS INCESSANT STILL BEHOLDING HOW THE PITEOUS   300 FOUR ZOAS 4   97
        FORM
        THE HORRID TRUMPETS OF THE DEEP BELLOWD WITH BITTER BLASTS   306 FOUR ZOAS 5   40
        IN VAIN THEY STROVE NOW TO UNCHAIN IN VAIN WITH BITTER   309 FOUR ZOAS 5   160
        TEARS
        WRITING IN BITTER TEARS & GROANS IN BOOKS OF IRON & BRASS   314 FOUR ZOAS 6   85
        STEEPING THY WOUNDS IN SALTS INFERNAL & IN BITTER ANGUISH   321 FOUR ZOAS 7   54
        . . . AND [MANY TEARS] OF BITTER CONTRITION   . . . . .   330 FOUR ZOAS 7   400
        NOW SMILE AMONG THY BITTER TEARS NOW PUT ON ALL THY BEAUTY   337 FOUR ZOAS 7B   188
        MANTLES OF DESPAIR GIRDLES OF BITTER COMPUNCTION SHOES   346 FOUR ZOAS 8   221
        OF INDOLENCE
        O THE PANGS THE BITTER PANGS OF LOVE FORSAKEN   . . . .   349 FOUR ZOAS 8   308
        OF BITTER HOPE ALTHO I CONSUME IN THESE RAGING WATERS   . .   355 FOUR ZOAS 8   * 547
        THE BIRDS OF SONG TO MURDEROUS CROWS MY JOYS TO BITTER   360 FOUR ZOAS 9   110
        GROANS
        HER DELICATE WOMEN & CHILDREN SHRIEK UPON THE BITTER WIND   375 FOUR ZOAS 9   664
        FEELING THE CRUSHING WHEELS THEY RISE THEY WRITE THE BITTER   379 FOUR ZOAS 9   819
        WORDS
        AND THE BITTER GROAN [FOR ANOTHER'S] OF THE MARTYR'S WOE   420 I SAW A MONK/N   60
        WHICH WE IN BITTER TEARS DID SOW . . . .   424 MENTAL TRAVLER   8
        AND THE BITTER GROAN OF THE MARTYR'S WOE . . . . . .   430 GREY MONK   31
        WITH BITTER WAILING THESE IN THE AGGREGATE ARE NAMED SATAN   519 MILTON 31   18
        ARE BECOME FOUNTAINS OF BITTER DEATH & OF CORRODING HELL   525 MILTON 35   3
        TO ASSUAGE HIS BITTER WOE . . . .   542 PITIFUL CASE/N   6
        THESE HYPOCRITIC SELFHOODS ON THE ANVILS OF BITTER DEATH   627 JERUSALEM 8   16
        I SAW TERRIFIED I TOOK THE SIGHS & TEARS & BITTER GROANS   628 JERUSALEM 9   17
        THE BIRDS OF SONG TO MURDEROUS CROWS HIS JOYS TO BITTER   641 JERUSALEM 19   11
        GROANS
        ARE BECOME THE SOURCES OF DARK & BITTER DEATH & OF   672 JERUSALEM 43   32
        CORRODING HELL
        AND THE BITTER GROAN OF A MARTYR'S WOE . . . .   683 I SAW A MONK/J   27
        ENDLESS THEIR LABOUR WITH BITTER FOOD VOID OF SLEEP . . .   691 JERUSALEM 59   30
        MADDENS IN THE FURY OF THEIR HANDS WEAVING IN BITTER TEARS   692 JERUSALEM 59   54
        TO SEE JERUSALEM DEFACE HER LINEAMENTS WITH BITTER BLOWS   693 JERUSALEM 60   46
        NOW SMILE AMONG THY BITTER TEARS NOW PUT ON ALL THY BEAUTY   700 JERUSALEM 65   30
        WHILE THEY REJOICE OVER LUVAH IN MOCKERY & BITTER SCORN   701 JERUSALEM 65   74
        O PAIN O THE PANGS THE BITTER PANGS OF LOVE FORSAKEN   . .   705 JERUSALEM 67   55
        FOR GWENDOLEN SHE TOOK UP IN BITTER TEARS HIS ANGUISHD   723 JERUSALEM 80   67
        HEART
        OVER THE FORESTS WITH BITTER TEARS AND OVER THE WINDING   726 JERUSALEM 82   73
        WORM
        OF ALBION'S CLOUDS HE FED IT WITH HIS TEARS & BITTER GROANS   732 JERUSALEM 86   53
BITTEREST
        IN BITTEREST CONTRITION SOMETIMES SELF CONDEMNING REPENTANT   356 FOUR ZOAS 8   610
        THOU HAST GIVN ME POWER TO PROTECT MYSELF FROM MY BITTEREST   489 MILTON 9   6
        ENEMIES
        HALF FRIENDSHIP IS THE BITTEREST ENMITY SAID LOS . . . .   620 JERUSALEM 1   8
        LOATHD AS A NATION'S BITTEREST CURSE . . . .   748 EV GOSPEL(A)/N   10
BITTERLY
        AND HEARD THE SPECTRE BITTERLY SHE WEPT EMBRACING FERVENT   327 FOUR ZOAS 7   312
        THE GNOMES IN ALL THAT DAY SPARD NOT THEY CURSD SATAN   493 MILTON 12   31
        BITTERLY
        CURSING THE TERRIBLE LOS BITTERLY CURSING HIM FOR HIS   624 JERUSALEM 6   6
        FRIENDSHIP
BITTERNESS
        AND CRIED IN BITTERNESS OF SOUL . . . .   247 SONG OF LOS 6   8
        THE INDIGNANT THISTLE WHOSE BITTERNESS IS BRED IN HIS MILK   377 FOUR ZOAS 9   763
        THE INDIGNANT THISTLE WHOSE BITTERNESS IS BRED IN HIS MILK   513 MILTON 27   26
BITUMEN
        THE FOREST AND THE MARSH AND THE PITS OF BITUMEN DEADLY   634 JERUSALEM 13   39
        PITS OF BITUMEN EVER BURNING ARTIFICIAL RICHES OF   673 JERUSALEM 43   62
        THE CANAANITE
        OF THE VALLEYS OF DESTRUCTION INTO A DARK LAND OF PITCH   721 JERUSALEM 79   61
        & BITUMEN
BLAB
        ("THE VULGAR...BLAB THEIR WISHES") UNEASY SEE... . . . . .   66D ANNO LAVATER   * MARG

	PAGE	TITLE	LINE
BLACK			
CURSE MY BLACK STARS AND BLESS MY PLEASING WOE	10	WHEN EARLY/PS	10
BENEATH THEM ROLLD LIKE TEMPESTS BLACK	11	GWIN KING/PS	17
AROUSE THYSELF THE NATIONS BLACK	12	GWIN KING/PS	35
GWIN LEADS HIS HOST AS BLACK AS NIGHT	12	GWIN KING/PS	55
AND BLEAR-EYD WILL THE BLACK LOT HOLDS	16	BLIND-MANS/PS	20
WHILE THE BLACK GORE DROPS FROM HIS HORRID JAWS	31	EDW THIRD/PS 5	46
AND RATTLING GUNS AND BLACK AND DREARY WAR	31	EDW THIRD/PS 5	60
IN NAVIES BLACK BROKEN WITH WIND AND TIDE	32	EDW THIRD/PS 6	12
AND WHERE STRENGTH FAILED BLACK THOUGHTS IN AMBUSH LAY	37D	SAMSON/PS	PROSE
FROM WHENCE A RIVER SPRINGS MOST BLACK & LOATHSOM	41C	THEN SHE BORE	PROSE
TO TEAR HIM FROM HIS THRONE BLACK WAS THE DEED	42B	THEN SHE BORE	PROSE
MOST BLACK SHAME IN A MIST SAT ROUND HIS TROUBLED HEAD	42B	THEN SHE BORE	PROSE
& THEY HAVE BLACK SERVANTS LODGE AT THEIR HOUSE	53A	ISLAND MOON 8	PROSE
WITH STOCKINGS ROLLD ABOVE THEIR KNEES & SHOES AS BLACK AS [GIT] JET	58	THIS CITY/IM	* 6
HE HAS GIVEN ME A BLACK EYE	61	SAY YOU JOE/IM	11
DESOLATE LOATHED DUMB [CON] ASTONISHD WAITING FOR BLACK DEATH	107	TIRIEL 5	* 35
BLACK BERRIES APPEAR THAT POISON ALL AROUND HIM SUCH [IS] WAS TIRIEL	110	TIRIEL 8	* 34
WERE ALL OF THEM LOCKD UP IN COFFINS OF BLACK	117	CHIMNEY SWP/SI	12
THE LITTLE BLACK BOY	125B	LIT BLK BOY/SI	TITLE
AND I AM BLACK BUT O MY SOUL IS WHITE	125	LIT BLK BOY/SI	2
BUT I AM BLACK AS IF BEREAVD OF LIGHT	125	LIT BLK BOY/SI	4
AND THESE BLACK BODIES AND THIS SUN-BURNT FACE	125	LIT BLK BOY/SI	15
WHEN I FROM BLACK AND HE FROM WHITE CLOUD FREE	125	LIT BLK BOY/SI	23
SUDDEN SEIZD WITH HOWLINGS DESPAIR AND BLACK NIGHT	135	FRENCH REVOLTN	21
THE MITRE BECOME BLACK	140	FRENCH REVOLTN	144
TO WANDER INSLAVD BLACK DEPREST IN DARK IGNORANCE	143	FRENCH REVOLTN	* 214
. . . BUT NOW I WILL BLESS THEE NO MORE IN DEADLY BLACK	144	FRENCH REVOLTN	225
AND THOU BLACK SOUTHERN PRISON	145	FRENCH REVOLTN	251
LIKE THE MORNING STAR ARISING ABOVE THE BLACK WAVES	145	FRENCH REVOLTN	255
I SAW A MIGHTY DEVIL FOLDED IN BLACK CLOUDS	150C	MARRIAGE HH 6	PROSE
THE CROW WISHD EVERY THING WAS BLACK	152D	MARRIAGE HH 10	PROSE
WAS THE SUN BLACK BUT SHINING ROUND IT WERE FIERY TRACKS	156A	MARRIAGE HH 17	PROSE
HE SAID BETWEEN THE BLACK & WHITE SPIDERS	156B	MARRIAGE HH 17	PROSE
BUT NOW FROM BETWEEN THE BLACK & WHITE SPIDERS A CLOUD	156B	MARRIAGE HH 17	PROSE
SO THAT THE NETHER DEEP GREW BLACK AS A SEA	156B	MARRIAGE HH 17	PROSE
TO BE SEEN BUT A BLACK TEMPEST TILL LOOKING EAST	156B	MARRIAGE HH 17	PROSE
TINGING THE BLACK DEEP WITH BEAMS OF BLOOD	156C	MARRIAGE HH 17	PROSE
O AFRICAN BLACK AFRICAN GO WINGED THOUGHT WIDEN HIS FOREHEAD	159C	SONG LIBERTY	PROSE
LET THE PRIESTS OF THE RAVEN OF DAWN NO LONGER IN DEADLY BLACK	160A	SONG LIBERTY	PROSE
AND PRIESTS IN BLACK GOUNDS WERE WALKING THEIR ROUNDS	163	GARDEN LOVE/N	11
A LITTLE BLACK THING AMONG THE SNOW	180	CHIMNEY SWP/N	1
AND FOLDED HIS BLACK JEALOUS WATERS ROUND THE ADULTERATE PAIR	190	V DAU ALBION 2	4
BECAUSE THE NIGHT IS GONE THAT CLOSD ME IN ITS DEADLY BLACK	191	V DAU ALBION 2	29
AS WHEN A BLACK CLOUD SHEWS ITS LIGHTNINGS TO THE SILENT DEEP	196	AMERICA PREL 2	5
IN BLACK SMOKE THUNDERS AND LOUD WINDS REJOICING IN ITS TERROR	201	AMERICA 12	10
AND ROUGH WITH BLACK SCALES	202	AMERICA 15	18
A LITTLE BLACK THING AMONG THE SNOW	212	CHIMNEY SWP/SE	1
AND PRIESTS IN BLACK GOWNS WERE WALKING THEIR ROUNDS	215	GARDEN LOVE/SE	11
BY THE BLACK WINDS OF PERTURBATION	222	URIZEN 3	12
FROM ETERNALS & LIKE A BLACK GLOBE	226	URIZEN 5	33
HE SAW URIZEN DEADLY BLACK	230	URIZEN 13	50
O LION RINTRAH RAISE THY FURY FROM THY FORESTS BLACK	240	EUROPE 8	2
STILL ALL YOUR THUNDERS GOLDEN HOOFD & BIND YOUR HORSES BLACK	244	EUROPE 14	28
ADAM SHUDDERD NOAH FADED BLACK GREW THE SUNNY AFRICAN	245	SONG OF LOS 3	10
THEN A BOW BLACK PREPARD ON THIS BOW	251	AHANIA 3	23
THE BLACK CLOUDS ON THE BOSOM OF FUZON	251	AHANIA 3	29
ON BLACK CLOUDS HIS SORE WOUND ANOINTED	251	AHANIA 3	48
I SEE THY BLACK FORESTS AND FLOODS	254	AHANIA 4	58
BLACK AS MARBLE OF EGYPT IMPENETRABLE	257	BOOK OF LOS 4	6
THE BLACK MARBLE ON HIGH INTO FRAGMENTS	257	BOOK OF LOS 4	22
IN A STIFLING BLACK FLUID HE WOKE	258	BOOK OF LOS 4	62
AND I COMMANDED SPRINGS TO RISE FOR HER IN THE BLACK DESART	282	FOUR ZOAS 2	88
. . . THE BLACK HAIL STORM [?LEAPING]	294	FOUR ZOAS 3	* 104
HE SPOKE MUSTERING HIS HEAVY CLOUDS AROUND HIM BLACK OPAKE	294	FOUR ZOAS 3	108
THE WINTER SPREAD HIS WIDE BLACK WINGS ACROSS FROM POLE TO POLE	306	FOUR ZOAS 5	32
. . . FROM THE DEPTHS OF HELL THY BLACK BOW DRAW	306	FOUR ZOAS 5	50
AND TWANG THE BOWSTRING TO OUR HOWLINGS LET THINE ARROWS BLACK	306	FOUR ZOAS 5	51
TORN BY BLACK STORMS & CEASELESS TORRENTS OF CONSUMING FIRE	306	FOUR ZOAS 5	56
I WENT NOT FORTH I HID MYSELF IN BLACK CLOUDS OF MY WRATH	311	FOUR ZOAS 5	222
. . . NOUGHT FINDING BUT THE BLACK SEA WEED & SICKNING SLIME	318	FOUR ZOAS 6	273
BLACK SCALES OF IRON ARM THE DREAD VISAGE IRON SPIKES INSTEAD	319	FOUR ZOAS 6	307
HIS SWIFT WINGD DAUGHTERS SWEEP ACROSS THE VAST BLACK OCEAN	320	FOUR ZOAS 7	26
. . . THO FLOODS POUR THO WINDS BLACK AS THE SEA	322	FOUR ZOAS 7	83
THE MOON HIS FURIOUS FOREHEAD CIRCLED WITH BLACK BURSTING THUNDERS	334	FOUR ZOAS 7B	41
RED RAGE THE FURIES OF FIERCE ORC BLACK THUNDERS ROLL ROUND LOS	335	FOUR ZOAS 7B	78
RED RAGE REDOUNDS HE ROUZD HIS LIONS FROM HIS FORESTS BLACK	336	FOUR ZOAS 7B	* 141

224

BLACK   (CONTINUED)
WITH DARTS OF WINTRY HAIL AGAIN THE BLACK BOW DRAW . . .   337 FOUR ZOAS 7B   156
AND LET THE THUNDRING DRUM SPEED ON THE ARROWS BLACK   . .   337 FOUR ZOAS 7B   * 158
THE SUN WAS BLACK & THE MOON ROLLD A USELESS GLOBE THRO   337 FOUR ZOAS 7B   169
    HEAVEN
HOWLING IN DISCONTENT BLACK & HEAVY UTTERING BRUTE SOUNDS   338 FOUR ZOAS 7B   224
WHICH HE INTENDED NOT A SHADOWY [MALE] HERMAPHRODITE BLACK   343 FOUR ZOAS 8   103
    & OPAKE
PERTURBD BLACK & DEADLY IN [THE] . . . .   346 FOUR ZOAS 8   * 226
THE RAVEN CALLD THE HAWK I HEARD THEM FROM MY FORESTS BLACK   358 FOUR ZOAS 9   60
THE TORRENTS BLACK UPON THE EARTH THE BLOOD POURS DOWN   359 FOUR ZOAS 9   73
    INCESSANT
ROLL DOWN THE MOUNTAINS IN BLACK TORRENTS CITIES VILLAGES   359 FOUR ZOAS 9   75
HIGH SPIRES & CASTLES DROWND IN THE BLACK DELUGE SHOAL   359 FOUR ZOAS 9   76
    ON SHOAL
OF FOAMING BLOOD BENEATH THE BLACK INCESSANT SKY TILL ALL   359 FOUR ZOAS 9   78
FROM THE [BLACK] DARK JAWS OF DEATH BENEATH & DESOLATE   363 FOUR ZOAS 9   259
    SHORES REMOTE
THE SEED IS HARROWD IN WHILE FLAMES HEAT THE BLACK MOULD   366 FOUR ZOAS 9   337
    & CAUSE
AND ALL THE BLACK MOULD SINGS SHE SPEAKS TO HER INFANT   373 FOUR ZOAS 9   601
    RACE HER MILK
AND BLACK HORSES & ARMED MEN & MISERABLE BOUND CAPTIVES   375 FOUR ZOAS 9   667
COMPOSED BY AN AFRICAN BLACK FROM THE LITTLE EARTH OF SOTHA   375 FOUR ZOAS 9   686
("BOUNDS...TO LIBERTY") IF IT IS THUS THE EXTREME OF BLACK   414B ANNO BOYD   MARG
    IS WHITE
THE TYRANT WHO FIRST THE BLACK BOW BENT . . . .   420 I SAW A MONK/N   50
WHEN SATAN FIRST THE BLACK BOW BENT . . . .   420 I SAW MNK AD/N   1
BUT HE CAME HOME IN A BLACK BLACK CLOUD   . . . . . .   435 WILLIAM BOND   11
AND IN THE MIDST A BLACK BLACK CLOUD   . . . .   435 WILLIAM BOND   15
AND THEIR TEARS FELL THRO THE BLACK BLACK CLOUD . . . .   435 WILLIAM BOND   19
CORRECTLY WITH BLACK LEAD PENCIL LET NOTHING BE TO SEEK   440B MEMORANDUM/N 2 PROSE
BECAUSE IT BEING BLACK WILL SHEW PERFECTLY WHAT IS WANTED   440C MEMORANDUM/N 3 PROSE
    [XXX]
BUT FROM MY LEFT FOOT A BLACK CLOUD REDOUNDING SPREAD OVER   497 MILTON 15   50
    EUROPE
LOOKING INTO THE BLACK WATER MINGLING IT WITH TEARS . . .   503 MILTON 20   55
HARNESSD WITH STARRY HARNESS BLACK & SHINING KEPT BY BLACK   503 MILTON 21   21
    SLAVES
UPON HIS FIBROUS LEFT FOOT BLACK MOST DISMAL TO OUR EYES   506 MILTON 22   35
LIKE THE BLACK STORM COMING OUT OF CHAOS BEYOND THE STARS   507 MILTON 23   21
OPAKE AND LIKE THE BLACK PEBBLE ON THE ENRAGED BEACH   515 MILTON 28   35
WEAVE THE BLACK WOOF OF DEATH UPON ENTUTHON BENYTHON   . .   517 MILTON 29   56
GARDEN CLOTHED IN BLACK SEVERE & SILENT HE DESCENDED   529 MILTON 38   8
AND THE DEVIL IS A BLACK OUTLINE ALL OF US KNOW . . . .   554 TO VENETIAN/N   2
A BLACK WATER ACCUMULATES RETURN ALBION RETURN   . . . .   622 JERUSALEM 4   10
EASTWARD TOWARD THE STARRY WHEELS BUT WESTWARD A BLACK   624 JERUSALEM 5   68
    HORROR
HIS SPECTRE DRIVN BY THE STARRY WHEELS OF ALBION'S SONS   624 JERUSALEM 6   1
    BLACK AND
AND BLACK ANXIETY AND THE CITIES OF THE SALAMANDRINE MEN   634 JERUSALEM 13   43
WASHD BY THE WATER-WHEELS OF NEWTON BLACK THE CLOTH . . .   636 JERUSALEM 15   16
HE QUENCHES IT IN THE BLACK TROUGH OF HIS FORGE LONDON'S   636 JERUSALEM 16   14
    RIVER
CLOTHD IN BLACK MOURNING UPON MY RIVER'S CURRENTS VALA   657 JERUSALEM 31   47
    AWAKE
BOUND THESE BLACK SHOES OF DEATH & ON MY HANDS DEATH'S   666 JERUSALEM 39   21
    IRON GLOVES
CHARIOTS BLACK THEIR FIRES ROLL BEHOLDING ALBION'S HOUSE   666 JERUSALEM 40   5
    OF ETERNITY
TORN WITH BLACK STORMS & CEASELESS TORRENTS OF HIS OWN   667 JERUSALEM 40   39
    CONSUMING FIRE
ROUND MARYBONE TO TYBURN'S RIVER WEAVING BLACK MELANCHOLY   668 JERUSALEM 41   8
    AS A NET
BLACK & IMMENSE A ROCK OF DIFFICULTY & A CLIFF   . . . .   674 JERUSALEM 44   11
OF BLACK DESPAIR THAT THE IMMORTAL WINGS LABOURD AGAINST   674 JERUSALEM 44   12
WHEN SATAN FIRST THE BLACK BOW BENT . . . .   683 I SAW A MONK/J   17
AMONG THE FIRES OF THE DRUID & THE DEEP BLACK RETHUNDERING   689 JERUSALEM 57   3
    WATERS
THE SUN WAS BLACK & THE MOON ROLLD A USELESS GLOBE THRO   699 JERUSALEM 65   11
    BRITAIN
HIS VOICE IN THE BLACK CLOUD HIS SONS LABOUR IN THUNDERS   731 JERUSALEM 86   37
ABOVE HIS HEAD HIGH ARCHING WINGS BLACK FILLD WITH EYES   735 JERUSALEM 89   28
TWO WINGS SPRING FROM HIS RIBS OF BRASS STARRY BLACK AS   735 JERUSALEM 89   36
    NIGHT
THEM HOWLS THE WOLF OF FAMINE DEEP HEAVES THE OCEAN BLACK   741 JERUSALEM 94   16
    THUNDERING
BUT THOU READST BLACK WHERE I READ WHITE . . . . . .   748 EV GOSPEL(A)/N   14
MUSTER A FEW IN COLOURS AND SOME IN BLACK WHICH I HOPE WILL 807A LETTER 17   PROSE
THE DAWBED BLACK & YELLOW SHADOWS THAT ARE FOUND IN MOST   815B LETTER 23   PROSE
    FINE
IN A BLACK CLOUD MAKING HIS MONE . . . .   817 HAPPINESS/L   16
A DARK BLACK ROCK & A GLOOMY CAVE . . . .   817 HAPPINESS/L   40
ON ACCOUNT OF THAT VERY COLOURING WHICH OUR CRITIC CALLS   864C LETTER 61   PROSE
    BLACK
LITTLE BLACK BOY DITTO LAUGHING SONG SPRING DITTO   .   SUPP LETTER 66A   *PROSE
THE CHIMNEY SWEEPER A LITTLE BLACK THING &C THE HUMAN   SUPP LETTER 66A   *PROSE
    ABSTRACT
BLACKAMOORS
[[IF] HOW MANY BLACKAMOORS] . . . .   61 DR CLASH/IM   *   6
BLACK-BROWD
AND LION HEART AND BLACK-BROWD EDWARD WITH . . . . . .   35 WAR SONG/PS   28

225

	PAGE	TITLE	LINE

BLACKEN
DOST THOU BLACKEN THEIR BEAUTY BY A SECLUDED PLACE OF REST · 693 JERUSALEM 60 · 32
BLACKEND
LABOUR WITH BLACKEND VISAGES AMONG ITS STUPENDOUS RUINS · 529 MILTON 38 · 21
BLACKENING
WHILE LOS ANSWERD UNTERRIFIED TO THE OPAKE BLACKENING FIEND · 625 JERUSALEM 7 · 8
BLACKENS
[BLACKENS OER THE CHURCHES WALLS] . . . . · 170 LONDON/N · 10
BLACKEST
THAT PLANTED THICK WITH TREES OF BLACKEST LEAF & IN A VALE · 241 EUROPE 10 · 25
BLACK-EYD,BLACK EYD
BUT THAT SWEET VILLAGE WHERE MY BLACK-EYD MAID · . . . . · 10 FRESH FROM/PS · 17
THEN TO MY BLACK EYD MAID I HASTE AWAY · . . . . · 10 WHEN EARLY/PS · 2
TO THAT SWEET VILLAGE WHERE MY BLACK EYD MAID · . . . . . · 10 WHEN EARLY/PS · 7
BLACK EYD SUSAN A FIGURE ON THE SEA SHORE EMBRACING A CORSE · 848D LETTER 45 · PROSE
BLACKFRIARS
FROM ST PAULS TO A NOBLE HOUSE IN BRIDGE STREET BLACKFRIARS · 856A LETTER 54 · PROSE
RICHARD PHILLIPS ESQR...BRIDGE STREET BLACK FRIARS · . . · SUPP ADDRESS/L 62 · *TITLE
BLACKHEATH
FROM LONDON STONE TO BLACKHEATH EAST TO HOUNSLOW WEST · . . · 485 MILTON 6 · 4
ALONG THE VALLEYS OF MIDDLESEX FROM HOUNSLOW TO BLACKHEATH · 512 MILTON 26 · 19
MALAH'S ON BLACKHEATH RAHAB & NOAH DWELL ON WINDSOR'S HEIGHTS · 525 MILTON 35 · 9
TO SHOOTERS HILL AND THENCE TO BLACKHEATH THE DARK WOOF LOUD · 525 MILTON 35 · 13
BETWEEN BLACKHEATH & HOUNSLOW BETWEEN NORWOOD & FINCHLEY · 670 JERUSALEM 42 · 51
TILL NORWOOD & FINCHLEY & BLACKHEATH & HOUNSLOW . . . . · 671 JERUSALEM 42 · 80
BLACKNESS
SINGING THE SUN HAS LEFT HIS BLACKNESS & HAS FOUND A FRESHER MORNING · 198 AMERICA 6 · 13
I WILL GIVE BLACKNESS FOR JEWELS HOARY FROST FOR ORNAMENT DEFORMITY · 312 FOUR ZOAS 6 · 37
THE SUN HAS LEFT HIS BLACKNESS & HAS FOUND A FRESHER MORNING · 379 FOUR ZOAS 9 · 825
HID HIM FROM SIGHT IN AN EXTREME BLACKNESS AND DARKNESS · 490 MILTON 9 · 33
COVERING THE EAST WITH SOLID BLACKNESS ROUND HIS HIDDEN HEART · 490 MILTON 9 · 40
TO A SUPERABUNDANT BLACKNESS IT HAS HOWEVER . . . . . · 581C DESC CAT 7 · PROSE
BUT TRANSLUCENT THEIR BLACKNESS AS THE DAZLING OF GEMS · . . · 735 JERUSALEM 89 · 37
BLACKNING
NOW ALL THE GODS IN BLACKNING RANKS APPEAR . . . . . · 42C THEN SHE BORE · PROSE
FIRE BURST AND ROLLED THRO THE DEEP BLACKNING ALL BENEATH · 156B MARRIAGE HH 17 · PROSE
EVERY BLACKNING CHURCH APPALLS . . . . · 170 LONDON/N · 11
REMOVE AWAY THAT BLACKNING CHURCH . . . . · 176 ANCNT PROVRB/N · 1
REMOVE AWAY THAT BLACKNING CHURCH . . . . · 184 SEVRL QUESTN/N · 15
EVERY BLACKNING CHURCH APPALLS . . . . · 216 LONDON/SE · 10
HOWLING IN PAIN A BLACKNING SHADOW BLACKNING DARK & OPAKE · 624 JERUSALEM 6 · 5
PERSONS KING EDWARD THE BLACK PRINCE QUEEN PHILIPPA · . . · 17C EDW THIRD/PS · TITLE
ENTER KING EDWARD AND BLACK PRINCE . . . . · 23A EDW THIRD/PS 3 · TITLE
EDWARD THE BLACK PRINCE BRINGS HIS CAPTIVES TO HIS FATHER · 209A SUBJCTS HIST/N · TITLE
BLACKS
INSTEAD OF ETCHING THE BLACKS ETCH THE WHITES & BITE IT IN · 440C MEMORANDUM/N 4 · PROSE
PICKING OUT OF WHITES & BLACKS IN WHAT IS CALLD TINTS · . . · 596C PUB ADDRESS/N · PROSE
BLADDER
THE POOR PARSONS WITH WIND LIKE A BLOWN BLADDER SWELL · . . · 179 LIT VAGABOND/N · 5
BLADE
THE BLADE BONE OF A TITTLEBACK NO NO HERES A BOTTLE OF WIND · 58C ISLAND MOON 10 · PROSE
WHICH THOU DOST SCATTER ON EVERY LITTLE BLADE OF GRASS THAT SPRINGS · 128 BOOK OF THEL 2 · 9
SO PAINTING ADMITS NOT A GRAIN OF SAND OR A BLADE OF GRASS · 611B V LAST JUDG/N · PROSE
BLADUD
SATAN CAIN TUBAL NIMROD PHAROH PRIAM BLADUD BELIN · . . · 713 JERUSALEM 73 · 35
BATH STOOD UPON THE SEVERN WITH MERLIN & BLADUD & ARTHUR · 715 JERUSALEM 75 · 2
BLAINS
[FLIES] SWARMS OF FLIES MURRAIN OF BEASTS BOILS & BLAINS · SUPP EXODUS/N · *PROSE
BLAIR
HIM ILLUSTRATIONS OF THE GRAVE A POEM BY ROBERT BLAIR · . · 861C LETTER 59 · PROSE
A MR BLAIR A SURGEON HAS WITH THE COLD FURY OF ROBESPIERRE · 865A LETTER 62 · PROSE
BLAIR'S
DESIGNS FOR BLAIR'S GRAVE HAVE LEFT HIM TO SHIFT FOR HIMSELF · 572D DESC CAT 3 · PROSE
BLAKE
WILLIAM BLAKE NUMERATION BLAKE LAMB · . . . . . . · 63A ISLAND MOON 11 · *PROSE
THE AUTHOR & PRINTER W BLAKE · . . . . · 97A NAT RELIGION 1 · *TITLE
SONGS OF INNOCENCE THE AUTHOR & PRINTER W BLAKE · . . . · 111A SONGS OF INNOC · TITLE
THE BOOK OF THEL THE AUTHOR & PRINTER WILLM BLAKE... · . · 127A BOOK OF THEL · TITLE
UPROSE TERRIBLE BLAKE IN HIS PRIDE · . . . . · 186 WHEN KLOPSTK/N * · 2
AND CALLD ALOUD TO ENGLISH BLAKE · . . . . · 187 WHEN KLOPSTK/N · 6
BLAKE WAS GIVING HIS BODY EASE · . . . . · 187 WHEN KLOPSTK/N · 7
IF BLAKE COULD DO THIS WHEN HE [SAT DOWN TO] ROSE UP FROM SHITE · 187 WHEN KLOPSTK/N · 33
PRINTED BY WILLM BLAKE... · . . . . · 189A V DAU ALBION · TITLE
LAMBETH PRINTED BY WILLIAM BLAKE IN THE YEAR... · . . . · 195D AMERICA · TITLE
PUBLISHED BY W BLAKE...HERCULES BUILDINGS · . . . . . · 209B FOR CHILDRN/GP · *TITLE
SONGS OF EXPERIENCE THE AUTHOR & PRINTER W BLAKE · . . . · 210B SONGS OF EXPER · TITLE
THE [FIRST] BOOK OF URIZEN LAMBETH PRINTED BY WILL BLAKE... · 222A URIZEN 1 · TITLE
EUROPE A PROPHECY LAMBETH PRINTED BY WILL BLAKE ... · . . · 237B EUROPE · TITLE
THE SONG OF LOS LAMBETH PRINTED BY W BLAKE... · . . . · 245B SONG OF LOS · TITLE
THE BOOK OF AHANIA LAMBETH PRINTED BY W BLAKE... · . . · 249A AHANIA · TITLE
THE BOOK OF LOS LAMBETH PRINTED BY W BLAKE... · . . . · 255D BOOK OF LOS · TITLE

226

```
                                                        PAGE      TITLE          LINE
BLAKE     (CONTINUED)
  W BLAKE LAMBETH...  . . . . .  . . . .   . . . . . .   261C ASKED THIEF       TITLE
  A DREAM OF NINE NIGHTS BY WILLIAM BLAKE... . . . . .   263B FOUR ZOAS         TITLE
  B BLAKE CATHERINE BLAKE   . . .  . . . .   . . . . .   380A FOUR ZOAS NOTE   *PROSE
  FOR THE BIBLE BY WILLIAM BLAKE  . . . . . .  . . . .   383A ANNO WATSON       TITLE
  PER WILLIAM BLAKE  . . . . . . . . . . .  . . . . . .  397A ANNO BACON        MARG
  TRAVELLER REPOSE & DREAM AMONG MY LEAVES WILL BLAKE  .  414 ILLUS GRAY         2
  TIS YOUR OWN FAULT IF YOU DONT FLOURISH NOW WILLIAM BLAKE  414 TO MRS FLAXMAN  10
  JANUARY...[FEBRUARY]...WILLIAM BLAKE  . . . .  . . .   444C LAST JUDGMNT/L     PROSE
  THIS IS THE OPINION OF WILL BLAKE  . . . . . . . .  .  445A ANNO REYNOLDS      MARG
  THE AUTHOR & PRINTER W BLAKE...  . . . . . .  . . . .  480A MILTON             TITLE
  HE BORE THE WRETCHED SOUL OF WILLIAM BLAKE  . . . . .  536 AND HIS LEGS/N      11
  O THAT I NEER HAS (HAD) SEEN THAT WILLIAM BLAKE  . . . 537 AND HIS LEGS/N      32
  THAT BLAKE WOULD ETCH FOR HIM & DRAW FOR ME  . . . .  537 AND HIS LEGS/N       35
  FEAR TO ASSOCIATE WITH BLAKE  . . . . . .  . . . . .  545 COSWAY FRAZR/N        2
  THEY NEVER CAN RAFAEL IT FUSELI IT NOR BLAKE IT  . .  549 ALL PICTURES/N        5
  AND BLAKE IS AN UNFORTUNATE LUNATIC  . . . . . . . .  555 BLAKES APL/N 1        21
  BY WM BLAKE  . . . . . . . . . . . . . . .  . . . .  560A EXHIBITION ADV       TITLE
  MAY...WILLIAM BLAKE  . . . . . . . . .  . . . . . .  561C EXHIBITION ADV       PROSE
  RUBENS AND REMBRANDT TITIAN AND CORREGGIO BY WILLIAM BLAKE  562B DESC CAT ADV  PROSE
  INVENTIONS PAINTED BY WILLIAM BLAKE IN WATER COLOURS BEING  563A DESC CAT      TITLE
  FOR J BLAKE...BROAD-STREET GOLDEN-SQUARE  . . . . .  563B DESC CAT            PROSE
  MR B(BLAKE) APPEALS TO THE PUBLIC FROM THE JUDGMENT OF  563D DESC CAT          PROSE
    THOSE
  BECOME A DUTY WHICH MR B(BLAKE) OWES TO THE PUBLIC  . . 573A DESC CAT 3        PROSE
  MR B(BLAKE) REQUIRES THE SAME LATITUDE AND ALL IS WELL . 576D DESC CAT 4       PROSE
  AND UGLINESS MR B(BLAKE) HAS IN HIS HANDS POEMS OF THE . 578A DESC CAT 5       PROSE
  MR B(BLAKE) HAS DONE AS ALL THE ANCIENTS DID  . . . . 578C DESC CAT 5          PROSE
  THE FIRST MR B(BLAKE) EVER DID IN FRESCO FORTUNATELY OR 581B DESC CAT 6        PROSE
  ADOPTS THE VENETIAN PRACTICE OR DOES AS MR B(BLAKE) HAS 582D DESC CAT 9        PROSE
    DONE
  MORE FINISHED WHEN MR B(BLAKE) FORMERLY PAINTED IN OIL  . 584D DESC CAT 15     PROSE
  MR B(BLAKE) THOUGHT THIS THE GREATEST OF COMPLIMENTS  . 585A DESC CAT 15       PROSE
  MR B(BLAKE) WILL NEVER BE SO FOOLISH AS TO DO ONE  . . 585A DESC CAT 15        PROSE
  REPRESENTING CHAUCER'S CHARACTERS PAINTED BY WILLIAM BLAKE  586C CHAUCER 1     TITLE
  AS THE PAINTER HIMSELF ESPECIALLY AS MR B(BLAKE) IS  . 586D CHAUCER 1          PROSE
  BLAKE'S CHAUCER AN ORIGINAL ENGRAVING BY WILLIAM BLAKE  . 587D CHAUCER/N       TITLE
  MR B(BLAKE) HAVING FROM EARLY YOUTH CULTIVATED THE TWO ARTS  587D CHAUCER/N    PROSE
  OF EXECUTION IN ART MR B(BLAKE) HAS NOW PUT TO THE TEST  591B PUB ADDRESS/N    PROSE
  IN THIS PLATE MR B(BLAKE) HAS RESUMED THE STYLE  . . . 592A PUB ADDRESS/N      PROSE
  MR B(BLAKE) SUBMITS TO A MORE SEVERE TRIBUNAL HE  . . . 596C PUB ADDRESS/N     PROSE
  MR B(BLAKE) REPEATS THAT THERE IS NOT ONE CHARACTER  . . 599B PUB ADDRESS/N    PROSE
  I WILLIAM BLAKE A MENTAL PRINCE SHOULD DECOLLATE  . . . 599D PUB ADDRESS/N     PROSE
  [OLLLLEE W HYYYISS WELL SAIITHL BLAKE JOHN THOMAS F]  . 601A PUB ADDRESS/N    *PROSE
  [MR B(BLAKE) THINKS IT HIS DUTY TO CAUTION THE PUBLIC]  . 601C PUB ADDRESS/N   PROSE
  [&] TO THIS I SUBSCRIBE MY NAME AS A PUBLIC DUTY WILLIAM  602B PUB ADDRESS/N  *PROSE
    BLAKE
  ENGRAVED BY W BLAKE...FROM AN OLD ITALIAN DRAWING  . .  604A INSC ARIMATHEA    TITLE
  [IN XXVIII CHAPTERS]...PRINTED BY W BLAKE STH MOLTON ST  620A JERUSALEM       *TITLE
  DRAWN & ENGRAVED BY WILLIAM BLAKE  . . . . . . . . .  775C INSC LAOCOON       *TITLE
  A REVELATION IN THE VISIONS OF JEHOVAH SEEN BY WILLIAM  779B GHOST ABEL 1      TITLE
    BLAKE
  WILLIAM BLAKE ONE WHO IS VERY MUCH DELIGHTED WITH BEING  781D INSC UPCOTT      PROSE
  "BELIEVE ME TO BE YOURS AFFECTIONATELY CATHERINE BLAKE"  801A LETTER 12        PROSE
  DIRECT TO MR BLAKE FELPHAM NEAR CHICHESTER SUSSEX  . .  803D LETTER 15        *PROSE
  I REMAIN YOURS SINCERELY WILLM BLAKE  . . . . . . .  843A LETTER 42           *PROSE
  YOUR SINCERE & OBLIGED WILL BLAKE STH MOLTON ST  . . .  853A LETTER 51        *PROSE
  YOUR AFFECTIONATE WILL BLAKE & HIS WIFE CATHERINE BLAKE  863C LETTER 60        PROSE
  MEMORANDUM OF AGREEMENT BETWEEN WILLIAM BLAKE AND JOHN  SUPP LETTER 67D       *PROSE
    LINNELL
  THE HISTORY OF JOB DESIGNED & ENGRAVED BY WILLIAM BLAKE  SUPP LETTER 67F       PROSE
  CATHERINE BLAKE  . . . . . . . . . . .  . . . . . . .  SUPP PENC DRAW 2.10    *TITLE
  BY WILLIAM BLAKE ?THO NOW SURROUNDED BY CALUMNY & ENVY  .  SUPP PILGRIMS/N    *PROSE
  CHAINING OF ORC TYPE BY W BLAKE...  . . . . . . . .  SUPP INSCR CHAINING      *TITLE
BLAKE'S
  MR BLAKE'S POWERS OF INVENTION VERY EARLY ENGAGED  . .  207C PRSPECTUS 1793    PROSE
  PUBLISHED AND ON SALE AT MR BLAKE'S  . . . . . . . .  207C PRSPECTUS 1793      PROSE
  BLAKE'S MEMORANDUM IN REFUTATION OF THE INFORMATION  .  437A BLAKES MEMORAN    TITLE
  BLAKE'S COTTAGE AT FELPHAM  . . . . . . .  . . . . .  527C MILTON 36           TITLE
  THAT BLAKE'S DESIGNS SHOULD BE BY US DISPLAYED  . . .  537 AND HIS LEGS/N  *   37
  THEN SCREWMUCH AT BLAKE'S SOUL TOOK A LONG LEAP  . . .  537 AND HIS LEGS/N     39
  BLAKE'S APOLOGY FOR HIS CATALOGUE  . . . . . . . .  . 554D BLAKES APL/N 1      TITLE
  A DESCRIPTIVE CATALOGUE OF BLAKE'S EXHIBITION  . . . .  562A DESC CAT ADV      TITLE
  THE DESCRIPTIVE CATALOGUE PRICE...CONTAINING  . . . .  562B DESC CAT ADV       PROSE
    MR B'S(BLAKE'S)
  AS THEY ARE IN ALL THE OLD PICTURES AND IN MR B'S(BLAKE'S)  566C DESC CAT 2    PROSE
    FRESCOS
  BROKEN MASSES AND BROKEN COLOURS MR B'S(BLAKE'S) PRACTICE  573B DESC CAT 3     PROSE
    IS
  IN IMMORTAL THOUGHTS IF MR B'S(BLAKE'S) CANTERBURY PILGRIMS  576B DESC CAT 4   PROSE
  TO MR B'S(BLAKE'S) MODE OF REPRESENTING SPIRITS  . . .  576C DESC CAT 4        PROSE
  WILL NOT ADMIT OF GRAND COLOURING IN MR B'S(BLAKE'S)  .  581A DESC CAT 5       PROSE
    BRITONS
  BLAKE'S CHAUCER THE CANTERBURY PILGRIMS THE FRESCO PICTURE  586C CHAUCER 1     TITLE
  BLAKE'S CHAUCER AN ORIGINAL ENGRAVING BY WILLIAM BLAKE  . . 587D CHAUCER/N     TITLE
  PECULIAR TO MR B'S(BLAKE'S) PRINTS WILL BE HERE FOUND  588A CHAUCER/N          PROSE
    ACCOMPANIED
  BLAKE'S CHAUCER AN ORIGINAL ENGRAVING BY HIM  . . . . .  589C CHAUCER 2        TITLE
  THIS DAY IS PUBLISHD ADVERTIZEMENTS TO BLAKE'S CANTERBURY  591B PUB ADDRESS/N  PROSE
  IS NOW TO BE DECIDED BY THE PUBLIC MR B'S(BLAKE'S)  . . 591B PUB ADDRESS/N     PROSE
    INVENTIVE
  FOR THE YEAR...ADDITIONS TO BLAKE'S CATALOGUE OF PICTURES  604B V LAST JUDG/N  TITLE
    &C
```

```
                                                    PAGE      TITLE          LINE
BLAKE'S   (CONTINUED)
   ...W BLAKE'S ORIGINAL STEREOTYPE WAS...  . . . . .  . . . .  781C GHOST ABEL 2    *TITLE
   MR BLAKE'S COMPTS TO MR REVELEY THO FULL OF WORK  . . .  790A LETTER 1        PROSE
   MR BLAKE'S RESPECTFUL COMPLIMENTS TO MRS (ADERS) IS SORRY TO SUPP LETTER 81A  *PROSE
   MR BLAKE'S RESPECTFUL COMPLIMENTS TO MISS DENMAN  . . . .  877B LETTER 86     PROSE
BLAKIFIED
   CRY BLAKIFIED DRAWING SPOILS PAINTER & ENGRAVER  . . . .  555 BLAKES APL/N 1    15
   CRY BLAKIFIED DRAWING SPOILS PAINTER & ENGRAVER  . . . .  556 BLAKES APL/N 2    14
BLAMABLE
   LOS GAVE TO HIM THE HARROW OF THE ALMIGHTY ALAS BLAMABLE   486 MILTON 7         12
BLAME
   WHETHER TIS GOOD OR EVIL NONE S TO BLAME  . . . . . .  418 ON VIRGINITY/N       3
   BUT IF YOU RAISE ENVY YOUR MERIT S TO BLAME  . . . . .  428 MARY              27
   BUT IF IT ALL ARISE FROM MY OWN FAULT I OUGHT TO BLAME   828D LETTER 28       PROSE
      MYSELF
BLAMED
   HE IS NOT IN THE LEAST TO BE BLAMED FOR THE PRESENT SCRAPE  830D LETTER 30    PROSE
BLAMELESS
   YET THEY ARE BLAMELESS & INIQUITY MUST BE IMPUTED ONLY  . .  680 JERUSALEM 49    65
BLAMES
   HE BLAMES RAFAEL FOR THE ONLY QUALITIES WHICH RAFAEL   452A ANNO REYNOLDS     MARG
      VALUED
BLANCHETAQUE
   DID YOU (EER) SEE HIM FEAR AT BLANCHETAQUE  . . . . . .   21 EDW THIRD/PS 3 *   10
BLANDISHMENTS
   WE MEET IT WITH OUR SONGS & LOVING BLANDISHMENTS & GIVE   267 FOUR ZOAS 1      105
   HIMSELF HAD WROUGHT LOS TREMBLED SATAN'S BLANDISHMENTS   487 MILTON 7          37
      ALMOST
   BUT WHEN THE GNOMES REFUSD TO LABOUR MORE WITH   493 MILTON 12                 37
      BLANDISHMENTS
   AND THE SCREWS & IRON BRACES ARE WELL WROUGHT BLANDISHMENTS   632 JERUSALEM 12   34
BLANK
   MUST BE A BLANK IN NATURE FOLLOW WITH ME AND TOMORROW AGAIN   488 MILTON 8      21
   EXPRESSION OF FEAR OR REVENGE OR ENVY OR BLANK HORROR  . .  580C DESC CAT 5    PROSE
   & SHAKSPEARE & ALL WRITERS OF ENGLISH BLANK VERSE  . . .  621C JERUSALEM 3    PROSE
BLARE
   [THE BELLOWING ?FURNACES' BLARE BY THE LONG SOUNDING   346 FOUR ZOAS 8      *  204
      CLARION]
   THE BELLOWING FURNACES' BLARE BY THE LONG SOUNDING CLARION   509 MILTON 24     64
BLASPHEME
   AND ALTHO I SIN & BLASPHEME THY HOLY NAME THOU PITIEST ME   693 JERUSALEM 60    62
BLASPHEMIES
   NOT SHAKESPEARE'S YOU MIGHT AS WELL QUOTE SATAN'S   SUPP ANNO SWED HELL * MARG
      BLASPHEMIES
BLASPHEMING
   OF WARLIKE SELFHOOD CONTRADICTING AND BLASPHEMING  . . .  495 MILTON 14        16
   BLASPHEMING LOVE BLASPHEMING THEE  . . . . . . . .  755 EV GOSPEL(E)/N        72
BLASPHEMOUS
   BLASPHEMOUS DEMON ANTICHRIST HATER OF DIGNITIES  . . . .  198 AMERICA 7         5
   AMBIGUOUS WORDS BLASPHEMOUS FILLD WITH ENVY FIRM RESOLVD   302 FOUR ZOAS 4     205
   BEING MULTITUDES OF TYRANT MEN IN UNION BLASPHEMOUS  . .  347 FOUR ZOAS 8      257
   THIS MUST BE A MOST WICKED & BLASPHEMOUS BOOK  . . . . .  384A ANNO WATSON     MARG
   FROM GOD IS ALTOGETHER ABOMINABLE & BLASPHEMOUS  . . . .  387B ANNO WATSON     MARG
   BLASPHEMOUS SONS OF FEMININE DELUSION GOD IN THE DREARY   646 JERUSALEM 23     29
      VOID
   ARE THE BLASPHEMOUS SELFHOODS & MUST BE BROKEN ASUNDER  .  736 JERUSALEM 90    33
BLASPHEMY
   BLASPHEMY  . . . . . . . . . . . . . . .  401B ANNO BACON        MARG
   IN WHICH MAN LIVETH ETERNALLY MADNESS & BLASPHEMY AGAINST   521 MILTON 32      20
   BLASPHEMY BY HIS MATERNAL BIRTH HE IS THAT EVIL-ONE  . .  736 JERUSALEM 90     35
   CANST THOU FORGIVE MY BLASPHEMY  . . . . . . . .  755 EV GOSPEL(E)/N          76
BLAST
   NIGHTLY BLAST THAT BLIGHTS THE INFANT BUD THE WINDS  . .   43D WOE CRIED MUSE *PROSE
   . . . SMOTE THE PALACE WALLS WITH A BLAST  . . . . . .  147 FRENCH REVOLTN    293
   THE SEA FOWL TAKES THE WINTRY BLAST FOR A COVRING TO HER   195 V DAU ALBION 8    6
      LIMBS
   THE STRONG VOICE CEASD FOR A TERRIBLE BLAST . . . .  . .  197 AMERICA 3        13
   THE STRONG VOICE CEASD FOR A TERRIBLE BLAST . . . .  . .  204 AMERICA CANC A   13
   COMBUSTION BLAST VAPOUR AND CLOUD  . . . . . . . .  222 URIZEN 3              17
   NAMD NEWTON HE SIEZD THE TRUMP & BLOWD THE ENORMOUS BLAST   243 EUROPE 13       5
   TO SEE A GOD ON EVERY WIND & A BLESSING ON EVERY BLAST   291 FOUR ZOAS 2      410
   I ALONE DARE THE LASH ABIDE TO SIT BENEATH THE BLAST  .  344 FOUR ZOAS 8      148
   . . . WILL YOU TAKE THE WINTRY BLAST  . . . . . .  353 FOUR ZOAS 8           493
   INTO HIS THUNDERING BELLOWS HEAVING IT FOR A LOUD BLAST   726 JERUSALEM 82     58
   AND WITH THE BLAST OF HIS FURNACE UPON FISHY BILLINGSGATE   726 JERUSALEM 82    59
BLASTED    SEE LAW BLASTED
   HOVERS WITH BLASTED WINGS ALOFT WATCHING WITH EAGER EYE   354 FOUR ZOAS 8      523
   THE MANNER IN WHICH MY CHARACTER HAS BEEN BLASTED  . . .  592C PUB ADDRESS/N   PROSE
BLASTING
   . . . AND BLASTING OF TRUMPETS CONSUME  . . . . . .  143 FRENCH REVOLTN       209
   FILLED WITH BLASTING FANCIES AND WITH MILDEWS OF DESPAIR   203 AMERICA 16       20
   NOT LONG THUNDERS LIGHTNINGS SWIFT RENDINGS & BLASTING   381 FOUR ZOAS AD 2     3
      WINDS
   BLASTING MY CHARACTER AS AN ARTIST TO MACKLIN MY EMPLOYER   592D PUB ADDRESS/N  PROSE
BLASTS
   WHEN THE BLASTS OF WINTER APPEAR  . . . . . . . .  124 SCHOOL BOY/SI          30
   OR SHRINK AT THE LITTLE BLASTS OF FEAR  . . . . . .  166 WHY CARE FOR/N        3
   [AND BLASTS THE NEW BORN INFANT'S TEAR]  . . . . . .  170 LONDON/N            17
   BLASTS THE NEW BORN INFANT'S TEAR  . . . . . . . .  170 LONDON/N             20
   THUS WEPT THE ANGEL VOICE & AS HE WEPT THE TERRIBLE BLASTS   200 AMERICA 10      1
   FOUR WINGED HERALDS MOUNT THE FURIOUS BLASTS & BLOW THEIR   205 AMERICA CANC C   14
      TRUMPS
```

```
                                                                PAGE      TITLE           LINE
BLASTS    (CONTINUED)
     BLASTS THE NEW-BORN INFANT'S TEAR  . . . . . . . .        216 LONDON/SE             15
     THE HORRID TRUMPETS OF THE DEEP BELLOW WITH BITTER BLASTS  306 FOUR ZOAS 5          40
     FOUR WINGED HERALDS MOUNT THE FURIOUS BLASTS & BLOW THEIR  319 FOUR ZOAS 6         310
          TRUMPS
     ("ILLUSTRIOUS CHARACTERS") [GOD BLASTS THEM AS THOUGH]  . . SUPP ANNO REYNOLDS  * MARG
BLAZD
     OVER THE MOUNTAINS & THE FIRES BLAZD ON DRUID ALTARS   .  696 JERUSALEM 62          33
BLAZE
     BLAZE IN EACH COUNTENANCE AND FIRE THE BATTLE  . . . . .    18 EDW THIRD/PS 1       12
     BUT AT CERTAIN PERIODS A BLAZE OF REPUTATION ARISES ROUND  830B LETTER 30        PROSE
          ME
BLAZED
     LIGHTNINGS WHICH BLAZED AFTER THEM UPON THEIR SHOULDERS    314 FOUR ZOAS 6         108
          . . .
BLAZES
     WHEN THE CLOUD BLAZES OVER THE HARVESTS  . . . . . . .     223 URIZEN 3             35
BLAZING
     LIKE BLAZING COMETS SCATTERING DEATH  . . . . . . . .       13 GWIN KING/PS         83
     LIKE BLAZING COMETS IN THE SKY  . . . . . . . . . . .       14 GWIN KING/PS        101
     [SLEEP LIKE THE DEAD] BUT LIKE A CONSTELLATION RISN AND    205 AMERICA CANC C       23
          BLAZING
BLEACHD
     TILL YOUR WHITE BONES ARE BLEACHD WITH AGE FOR A MEMORIAL  100 TIRIEL 1             47
     LAY BLEACHD ON THE GARDEN OF EDEN  . . . . . . . . .       248 SONG OF LOS 7        21
BLEACHED
     SHIVERING OVER THEIR BLEACHED BONES . . . . . . . . .      137 FRENCH REVOLTN       73
     AND ON THE BLEACHED BONES   . . . . . . . . . . .          148 MARRIAGE HH 2        12
BLEAK
     THEN ROSE GIRDED HIMSELF AND OER THE BLEAK  . . . . .  .     2 TO AUTUMN/PS         17
     IN THE BLEAK WINTRY DAY  . . . . . . . . . . . . . .        11 GWIN KING/PS         28
     AND THEIR FIELDS ARE BLEAK & BARE  . . . . . . . . .       181 HOLY THURS/N         10
     AND THEIR FIELDS ARE BLEAK & BARE  . . . . . . . . .       212 HOLY THURS/SE        10
     MUSTER AROUND THE BLEAK DESARTS    . . . . . . . . .       223 URIZEN 4              1
     BLEAK DARK ABRUPT IT STANDS & OVERSHADOWS LONDON CITY  .   242 EUROPE 12             9
     ON THE BLEAK AND SNOWY MOUNTAINS  . . . . . . . . .        255 AHANIA 5             45
BLEAR-EYD
     AND BLEAR-EYD WILL THE BLACK LOT HOLDS  . . . . . .         16 BLIND-MANS/PS        20
BLEAT
     THE BLEAT THE BARK BELLOW & ROAR  . . . . . . . . .        432 AUGURIES             71
     HER LAMBS BLEAT TO THE SEA-FOWLS CRY LAMENTING STILL FOR   667 JERUSALEM 40         51
          ALBION
BLEATING
     AND NOW BESIDE THEE BLEATING LAMB  . . . . . . . . .       119 NIGHT/SI             41
     I WALK AMONG HIS FLOCKS & HEAR THE BLEATING OF HIS LAMBS   368 FOUR ZOAS 9         425
     AND THEN FROM HER WHITE DOOR SHE LOOKD TO SEE HER BLEATING 369 FOUR ZOAS 9         472
          LAMBS
BLEATS
     TO ASSIST IN THE WORK THE LAMB BLEATS THE SEA-FOWL CRIES   692 JERUSALEM 59         49
BLED
     THAT MILTON LABOURD WITH HIS JOURNEY & HIS FEET BLED SORE  500 MILTON 19             3
     JOHN FOR DISOBEDIENCE BLED  . . . . . . . . . . .          749 EV GOSPEL(B)/N       17
BLEED
     ERE LONG TO BLEED & DIE A SACRIFICE DONE BY A PRIESTLY HAND  41B THEN SHE BORE    PROSE
     FOR THOU DOST MAKE MY HEART TO BLEED MY SONS WERE NOT LIKE 103 TIRIEL 3             20
          THINE
BLEEDING
     THE EAGLES AT HER CALL DESCEND & REND THEIR BLEEDING PREY  190 V DAU ALBION 2       17
     FEET BLEEDING ON THE SULTRY SANDS AND THE FURROWS OF THE   197 AMERICA 3            11
          WHIP
     FEET BLEEDING ON THE SULTRY SANDS & THE FURROWS OF THE WHIP  204 AMERICA CANC A     11
     ON A BROAD WAVE IN THE WARM WEST BALMING HER BLEEDING WOUND  299 FOUR ZOAS 4        58
     MOULDED TO GLOBES & ARROWY WEDGES RENDING THY BLEEDING     321 FOUR ZOAS 7          52
          LIMBS
     TILL HE BECOMES A BLEEDING YOUTH  . . . . . . . . . .      425 MENTAL TRAVLER       21
     TWO BLEEDING CONTRARIES EQUALLY TRUE ARE HIS WITNESSES     646 JERUSALEM 24          3
          AGAINST ME
     IN THE DIVIDING OF REUBEN & BENJAMIN BLEEDING FROM         697 JERUSALEM 63         12
          CHESTER'S RIVER
     BLEEDING IN TORRENTS FROM MOUNTAIN TO MOUNTAIN A LOVELY    697 JERUSALEM 63         15
          VICTIM
BLEEDS
     HE BLEEDS IN TORRENTS OF BLOOD AS HE ROLLS THRO HEAVEN     703 JERUSALEM 66         77
          ABOVE
BLEMISHES
     [SPOTS & BLEMISHES WHICH ARE BEAUTIES & NOT FAULTS]  . . . 595D PUB ADDRESS/N     PROSE
BLEND
     TO BLEND & NOT DEFINE THE PARTS   . . . . . . . . .        547 LET BE TOLD/N         7
BLENDING
     & ONLY PROMOTES HARMONY OR BLENDING OF COLOURS ONE INTO    478C ANNO REYNOLDS      MARG
          ANOTHER
BLENDS
     AS HE BLENDS LITERATURE AND THE ARTS WITH HIS WARLIKE      568A DESC CAT 3        PROSE
          STUDIES
BLERON'S
     DOWN BLERON'S HILLS THEY DREADFUL RUSH  . . . . . . .       11 GWIN KING/PS         21
BLESS
     OH BLESS THOSE HOLY FEET LIKE ANGELS' FEET . . . . . .       9 FRESH FROM/PS         7
     OH BLESS THOSE LIMBS BEAMING WITH HEAVNLY LIGHT   . . .      9 FRESH FROM/PS         8
     CURSE MY BLACK STARS AND BLESS MY PLEASING WOE   . . . .    10 WHEN EARLY/PS        10
     GOD BLESS THE DUKE & HIS ALDERMEN ALL   . . . . . . .       55 CRY MATCHES/IM  *     2
     GOD BLESS [ XXX ] THY POOR BALD PATE GOD BLESS THY HOLLOW  101 TIRIEL 2        *    35
          WINKING EYES
```

		PAGE	TITLE	LINE

BLESS   (CONTINUED)

GOD BLESS THY SHRIVELD BEARD GOD BLESS THY MANY WRINKLED FOREHEAD — 101 TIRIEL 2 * 36

BLESS THY POOR EYES OLD MAN & BLESS THE OLD FATHER OF TIRIEL — 101 TIRIEL 2 40

HOW DIDST THOU LOSE THY EYES OLD TIRIEL BLESS THY WRINKLED FACE — 101 TIRIEL 2 43

GOD BLESS THY PITEOUS FACE TO COUNT THE WRINKLES IN THY FACE — 102 TIRIEL 3 5

WOULD PUZZLE [HAR] MNETHA BLESS THY FACE FOR THOU ART TIRIEL — 102 TIRIEL 3 6

THEN TIRIEL ROSE UP FROM THE SEAT & SAID GOD BLESS THESE TENTS — 103 TIRIEL 3 26

[GOD BLESS MY BENEFACTORS FOR I CANNOT TARRY LONGER] . . — 103 TIRIEL 3 27

LITTLE LAMB GOD BLESS THEE . . . . — 115 THE LAMB/SI 19

LITTLE LAMB GOD BLESS THEE . . . . — 115 THE LAMB/SI 20

OR BLESS THE MELLOWING YEAR . . . . — 124 SCHOOL BOY/SI 29

. . . BUT NOW I WILL BLESS THEE NO MORE IN DEADLY BLACK — 144 FRENCH REVOLTN 225

DAMN BRACES BLESS RELAXES . . . . — 152C MARRIAGE HH 9 PROSE

AND SHE SAID THARMAS I AM VALA BLESS THY INNOCENT FACE . — 339 FOUR ZOAS 7B 229

O BLESS THE LOVELY EYES OF THARMAS & THE EYES OF ENION — 371 FOUR ZOAS 9 528

SOMETIMES I CURSE & SOMETIMES BLESS THY FASCINATING BEAUTY — 707 JERUSALEM 68 64

I BLESS THEE O FATHER OF HEAVEN & EARTH . . . . — 799 TO FLAXMAN/L 1

THAT FELPHAM IS PROPITIOUS TO THE ARTS GOD BLESS YOU . — 803C LETTER 15 PROSE

WILL NEXT SUMMER JOKE US FACE TO FACE GOD BLESS YOU ALL — 810C LETTER 20 PROSE

OF THE TIME I HAVE SPENT UPON THEM GOD BLESS YOU YOURS . — 819A LETTER 24 PROSE

GOD BLESS YOU & PRESERVE YOU & REWARD YOUR KINDNESS TO ME — 833A LETTER 32 PROSE

GOD BLESS & PRESERVE YOU AND OUR GOOD LADY PAULINA . . — 835A LETTER 34 PROSE

BLESSING AMEN GOD BLESS YOU ALL O PEOPLE OF SUSSEX . . — 835B LETTER 34 PROSE

I CURSE & BLESS ENGRAVING ALTERNATELY BECAUSE IT TAKES SO MUCH TIME — 837D LETTER 36 PROSE

GOD BLESS HER FOR SHE IS A PEERLESS JEWEL FOR A PRINCE . — 853A LETTER 51 *PROSE

BLESSD

AND THEY BLESSD THE SEVENTH DAY IN SICK HOPE . . . . . — 236 URIZEN 25 41

AND AT HIS OWN DOOR THE BLESSD HERMIT DOES STAND . . . . — 800 MRS FLAXMAN/L 15

BLESSED

THOU VISITEST OUR DARKLING WORLD WITH BLESSED FEET . . — 37D SAMSON/PS PROSE

SHE SAW THE MAIDENS PLAY AND BLESSED THEIR INNOCENT MIRTH — 39C SAMSON/PS PROSE

SHE BLESSED EACH NEW-JOINED PAIR . . . . — 39D SAMSON/PS PROSE

THE LAMB OF GOD BLESSED FOR EVER & HE FOLLOWD THE MAN . — 279 FOUR ZOAS 1 556

I KNOW THEE NOT AS ONCE I KNEW THEE IN THOSE BLESSED FIELDS — 288 FOUR ZOAS 2 325

BUT [ALL] THOU O UNIVERSAL HUMANITY WHO IS ONE MAN BLESSED FOR EVER — 347 FOUR ZOAS 8 232

TIMES UPON TIMES THINKING TO DESTROY THE LAMB BLESSED FOR EVER — 347 FOUR ZOAS 8 235

[THE] GREEN HILLS APPEAR BENEATH WITH THE GRAVES OF THE BLESSED — 443D LAST JUDGMNT/L PROSE

THE BLESSED ON THE RIGHT & THE LEFT OF WHICH ARE SEEN THE — 444A LAST JUDGMNT/L PROSE

WHICH IS THE DIVINE BODY OF THE LORD JESUS BLESSED FOR EVER — 482 MILTON 5 4

THE ETERNAL WHO IS BLESSED FOR EVER & EVER AMEN . . . — 519 MILTON 30 31

THOSE WHO ARE BLESSED WITH IMAGINATIVE VISION SEE . . — 609B V LAST JUDG/N PROSE

THE BLESSED WHO IN VARIOUS JOYFUL COMPANIES . . . . — 609D V LAST JUDG/N PROSE

OF THE BLESSED IN WHICH A GOTHIC CHURCH IS REPRESENTATIVE — 610C V LAST JUDG/N PROSE

IS TO BE [BLESSED] I CANNOT DOUBT THAT THIS MORE . . — 620D JERUSALEM 3 PROSE

WHICH IS THE DIVINE BODY OF THE LORD JESUS BLESSED FOR EVER — 624 JERUSALEM 5 59

HUMAN DIVINE JESUS THE SAVIOUR BLESSED FOR EVER AND EVER — 667 JERUSALEM 40 47

EVERY ONE KNOWS WE ARE ONE FAMILY ONE MAN BLESSED FOR EVER — 687 JERUSALEM 55 46

FROM MY EAST & FROM MY WEST HE BLESSED ME AND GAVE . . — 720 JERUSALEM 79 25

. . . THE BLESSED OF HEAVEN ARE MY FRIENDS UPON EARTH . — 799 TO FLAXMAN/L 2

BLESSED ARE THOSE WHO ARE FOUND STUDIOUS OF LITERATURE & — 810C LETTER 21 PROSE

FAR BEAMING TURRET LIKE THE VILLA OF LAVANT BLESSED & . — 835B LETTER 34 PROSE

BLESSES

WORK IN ABUNDANCE & IF GOD BLESSES ME WITH HEALTH . . — 835A LETTER 34 PROSE

BLESSING

WHEN HIS EVENING TALE IS TOLD DEPARTS HIS BLESSING LEAVING — 40A SAMSON/PS PROSE

HIS BLESSING WAS A CRUEL CURSE HIS CURSE MAY BE A BLESSING — 99 TIRIEL 1 18

UNSEEN THEY POUR BLESSING . . . . — 119 NIGHT/SI 13

HOW GREAT THY USE HOW GREAT THY BLESSING EVERY THING THAT LIVES — 129 BOOK OF THEL 3 26

TO SEE A GOD ON EVERY WIND & A BLESSING ON EVERY BLAST — 291 FOUR ZOAS 2 410

THY CLOUDS OF BLESSING THY CHERUBIMS OF TENDER-MERCY . — 647 JERUSALEM 24 21

THE MOUNTAIN OF BLESSING IS ITSELF A CURSE & AN ASTONISHMENT — 720 JERUSALEM 79 7

HAND UPON MY HEAD & GIVES A BLESSING TO ALL MY WORKS . — 823B LETTER 26 PROSE

WHICH IS A BLESSING I CAN NEVER BE TOO THANKFUL FOR . . — 824B LETTER 27 PROSE

BLESSING AMEN GOD BLESS YOU ALL O PEOPLE OF SUSSEX . . — 835B LETTER 34 PROSE

BLESSINGS

THAT GREATEST OF ALL BLESSINGS A STRONG IMAGINATION . . — 439D REMARKS MALKIN PROSE

WITH BLESSINGS ON THEIR HANDS & ON THEIR FEET BLESSINGS OF GOLD — 647 JERUSALEM 24 39

BLEST

[BUT CRYD O THIS IS THE BLEST TIME] . . . . — 41B THEN SHE BORE *PROSE

AND GAVE TO HIM HIS STAFF & BLEST HIM HE WENT ON HIS WAY — 103 TIRIEL 3 40

FOR THE GREATER THE FOOL IN THE PENCIL MORE BLEST . . . — 548 ALL PICTURES/N 3

BLEW

[BUT] AND MY WIND IT NEVER BLEW . . . . — 166 I FEARD FURY/N 4

OF TRUMPETS BLEW A LOUD ALARM ACROSS THE ATLANTIC DEEP . — 200 AMERICA 10 2

TILL MORNING OPED THE EASTERN GATE [AND THE ANGEL TRUMPET BLEW] — 244 EUROPE 14 * 35

SHOT FROM THE HEIGHTS OF ENITHARMON [BEFORE THE TRUMPET BLEW] — 245 EUROPE 15 1

230

	PAGE	TITLE	LINE
BLEW (CONTINUED)			
FOR ELEMENTAL GODS THEIR THUNDEROUS ORGANS BLEW CREATING	274	FOUR ZOAS 1	377
THUS SANG THE DEMONS OF THE DEEP THE CLARIONS OF WAR BLEW LOUD	276	FOUR ZOAS 1	434
THE FURNACES A TIME & TIMES ALL THE WHILE BLEW THE NORTH	282	FOUR ZOAS 2	68
THE NIGHT BLEW COLD AND ENITHARMON SHRIEKD ON THE DISMAL WIND	305	FOUR ZOAS 5	20
SO SUNG THE DEMONS OF THE DEEP THE CLARIONS OF WAR BLEW LOUD	338	FOUR ZOAS 7B	210
BLIGHT			
. . . A FEAR AND A WITHRING BLIGHT BLOWN BY THE NORTH . .	141	FRENCH REVOLTN	162
WOULD BLIGHT ALL BLOSSOMS FAIR & TRUE	166	I FEARD FURY/N	2
AS A BLIGHT CUTS THE TENDER CORN WHEN IT BEGINS TO APPEAR	201	AMERICA 14	6
TO REJOICE IN THE BLIGHT THAT COVERS HIS FIELD	291	FOUR ZOAS 2	412
THEN SHE RETURNS SWIFT AS A BLIGHT UPON THE INFANT BUD .	339	FOUR ZOAS 7B	261
A BLIGHT FOR A TRIAL OF MEN TO DIVIDE THE CLASSES OF MEN	570A	DESC CAT 3	PROSE
MINUTE AND EXACT BECAUSE SHE IS ALSO A SCOURGE AND A BLIGHT	572B	DESC CAT 3	PROSE
GO FORTH OUT OF THY MOUTH TO BLIGHT THEIR PEACE	718	STOOD AMONG/J	33
LOS SAW THE ENVIOUS BLIGHT ABOVE HIS SEVENTH FURNACE . .	726	JERUSALEM 82	56
ANY ONE A BLIGHT NEVER DOES GOOD TO A TREE & IF A BLIGHT	830C	LETTER 30	PROSE
THE FRUIT WAS IN CONSEQUENCE OF THE BLIGHT WHEN THIS .	830C	LETTER 30	PROSE
BLIGHTED			
LOS FELT THE ENVY IN HIS LIMBS LIKE TO A BLIGHTED TREE . .	321	FOUR ZOAS 7	27
AND THE STRONG EAGLE NOW WITH NUMMING COLD BLIGHTED OF FEATHERS	354	FOUR ZOAS 8	521
HER LILLIES & ROSES ARE BLIGHTED & SHED	428	MARY	20
BLIGHTING			
IN SCORN STOOD LOS RED SPARKS OF BLIGHTING FROM HIS FURIOUS HEAD	298	FOUR ZOAS 4	48
FROM HIS MOUTH CURSES & FROM HIS EYES SPARKS OF BLIGHTING	305	FOUR ZOAS 5	3
BLIGHTINGS			
COME IN THE HEAVEN OF GENEROUS LOVE NOR SELFISH BLIGHTINGS BRING	195	V DAU ALBION 7	29
DISMAY & SHARP BLIGHTINGS THE PROPHET	259	BOOK OF LOS 5	25
CIRCLING ROUND THE DARK DEMON WITH HOWLINGS DISMAY & SHARP BLIGHTINGS	302	FOUR ZOAS 4	200
BLIGHTS			
NIGHTLY BLAST THAT BLIGHTS THE INFANT BUD THE WINDS . . .	43D	WOE CRIED MUSE	*PROSE
FOR THE HUSBANDMAN WEEPS AT BLIGHTS OF THE PIPE	143	FRENCH REVOLTN	209
AND BLIGHTS WITH PLAGUES THE MARRIAGE HEARSE	216	LONDON/SE	16
IN BLIGHTS OF THE EAST THE HEAVY ROLLER FOLLOWS IN HOWLINGS OF WOE.	514	MILTON 27	48
BLIND			
SAW A TREACLE JAR SO HE GOES OF HIS BLIND SIDE	55B	ISLAND MOON 9	PROSE
FOR IF A DAMSEL S BLIND OR LAME	56	HAIL MATRIM/IM	13
STUDY SCIENCES TILL YOU ARE BLIND	93A	ANNO SWED LOVE	MARG
LOOK AT MY EYES BLIND AS THE ORBLESS [XXX] SCULL AMONG THE STONES	99	TIRIEL 1	* 28
OER MOUNTAINS & THRO VALES OF WOE THE BLIND & AGED MAN . .	100	TIRIEL 2	3
SOON AS THE BLIND WANDERER ENTERD THE PLEASANT GARDENS OF HAR	100	TIRIEL 2	10
THE BLIND MAN FELT HIS WAY & CRIED PEACE TO THESE OPEN DOORS	101	TIRIEL 2	13
LET NO ONE FEAR FOR POOR BLIND TIRIEL HURTS NONE BUT HIMSELF	101	TIRIEL 2	14
WHO ART THOU POOR BLIND MAN THAT TAKEST THE NAME OF TIRIEL ON THEE	101	TIRIEL 2	17
MADNESS & DEEP DISMAY (POSSESS) THE HEART OF THE BLIND MAN	103	TIRIEL 3	* 37
OVER THE WEARY HILLS THE BLIND MAN TOOK HIS LONELY WAY . .	103	TIRIEL 4	1
TO BE A HYPOCRITE & STAND IN SHAPE OF A BLIND BEGGAR . .	103	TIRIEL 4	9
THE BLIND MAN HEARD HIS BROTHER'S VOICE & KNEELD DOWN ON HIS KNEE	104	TIRIEL 4	10
BLIND TO THE PLEASURES OF THE SIGHT & DEAF TO WARBLING BIRDS	104	TIRIEL 4	29
AT LAST I CAUGHT HIM IN THE FORM OF TIRIEL BLIND & OLD . .	105	TIRIEL 4	61
FOR POOR BLIND TIRIEL IS RETURND & THIS MUCH INJURD HEAD	105	TIRIEL 4	66
AS TIRIEL'S & ALL EYES AS BLIND AS TIRIEL'S TO YOUR WOES	106	TIRIEL 5	21
WHEREFORE FROM MY BLIND ORBS ART THOU NOT SIEZD WITH POISNOUS STINGS	108	TIRIEL 6	31
THEIR TYRANT PRINCE BLIND & HIS DAUGHTER HOWLING & LEADING HIM	108	TIRIEL 7	4
THE BLIND MAN HEARD & SMOTE HIS BREAST & TREMBLING PASSED ON	109	TIRIEL 7	14
LOVE TO FAULTS IS ALWAYS BLIND	175	HOW TO KNOW/N	1
[NEVER IS TO] TO EVERY THING BUT INTEREST BLIND	175	HOW TO KNOW/N	8
TILL SOME BLIND HAND	183	THE FLY/N	19
ASK THE BLIND WORM THE SECRETS OF THE GRAVE AND WHY HER SPIRES	191	V DAU ALBION 3	10
TILL SOME BLIND HAND	213	THE FLY/SE	11
[AND] ENION BLIND & AGE-BENT WEPT UPON THE DESOLATE WIND	276	FOUR ZOAS 1	* 444
WHERE ENION BLIND & AGE BENT WEPT IN DIREFUL HUNGER CRAVING	280	FOUR ZOAS 2	16
INSTEAD OF LOVE TO ENION ENION BLIND & AGE BENT	296	FOUR ZOAS 3	178
WHERE ENION BLIND & AGE BENT WANDERD AHANIA WANDERS NOW	297	FOUR ZOAS 3	207
AND CALL IT DEMONSTRATION BLIND TO ALL THE SIMPLE RULES OF LIFE	337	FOUR ZOAS 7B	186
BLOWN BACK THEY [MO] BLIND THE [MOCKERS] MOCKING EYE . .	418	MOCK ON/N	* 7
OFT BLIND & AGE-BENT SORE DISTREST	426	MENTAL TRAVLER	55
AND PUTTING IN LIKE THE PROGRESS OF A BLIND MAN	439C	REMARKS MALKIN	PROSE
BUT THEN HE STRIVES TO BLIND THOSE WHO CAN SEE	463	ANNO REYNOLDS	2
I FOUND [THEE] THEM BLIND I TAUGHT [THEE] THEM HOW TO SEE	543	ON F AND S/N	1
RATHER THAN [LET] BE SUCH A BLIND HUMAN FOOL	550	WHEN I SEE/N	7
I FOUND THEM BLIND I TAUGHT THEM HOW TO SEE	575	DESC CAT 3	3

231

		PAGE	TITLE	LINE

BLIND   (CONTINUED)
NOT KNOWING WHAT ART IS IT IS BEING BLIND TO THE GIFTS   579D DESC CAT 5   PROSE
OF THE SPIRIT
AND CALL IT DEMONSTRATION BLIND TO ALL THE SIMPLE RULES   700 JERUSALEM 65   28
OF LIFE
I SEE LONDON BLIND & AGE-BENT BEGGING THRO THE STREETS . .   729 JERUSALEM 84   11
REPELLING WEEPING ENION BLIND & AGE-BENT INTO THE FOURFOLD   732 JERUSALEM 87   1
MINE SPEAKS IN PARABLES TO THE BLIND . . . .   748 EV GOSPEL(A)/N   6
BUT HE HEALS THE DEAF & THE DUMB & THE BLIND . . . . .   755 EV GOSPEL(E)/N   88
& YOU DENY THAT HE IS ARISEN & ARE BLIND TO SPIRIT . . .   757D EV GOSPEL   PROSE
BLIND IN FIRE WITH SHIELD & SPEAR . . . .   770 OF GATES/GP   10
BLIND STUPID IGNORANT AND INCAPABLE IN TWO YEARS' STUDY   814D LETTER 23   PROSE
COLOURING AND ARE BLIND TO THE GLOOM OF A REAL TERROR   .   864C LETTER 61   PROSE
THE BEGINNING OF POESY THE BLIND BEGGING BARD STUDY   .   SUPP ILLUS GRAY   *TITLE
BLINDED
WHO ON THE BLINDED MAN IMPOSE . . . .   17 BLIND-MANS/PS   64
LOOK KNOWST THOU AUGHT OF THIS GREY BEARD OR OF THESE   104 TIRIEL 4   44
BLINDED EYES
HIS FEET AND HANDS CUT OFF AND HIS EYES BLINDED . . . .   136 FRENCH REVOLTN   44
BLIND-MAN'S
BLIND-MAN'S BUFF . . . .   15D BLIND-MANS/PS   TITLE
BUT NOW FOR BLIND-MAN'S BUFF THEY CALL . . . .   16 BLIND-MANS/PS   17
THE BLIND-MAN'S ARMS EXTENDED WIDE . . . .   16 BLIND-MANS/PS   23
DIRECTLY IN THE BLIND-MAN'S WAY . . . .   16 BLIND-MANS/PS   48
BLINDNESS
IN WEEPING BLINDNESS STUMBLING SHE FOLLOWD THEM OER ROCKS   270 FOUR ZOAS 1   215
& MOUNTAINS
AH HAPPY BLINDNESS [SHE] ENION SEES NOT THE TERRORS OF   290 FOUR ZOAS 2   * 385
THE UNCERTAIN
[IN WEEPING BLINDNESS STUMBLING . . . .   SUPP FOUR ZOAS 1   *
BLINDS
WHICH BLINDS THE EYE OF IMAGINATION THE REAL MAN . . . . 775B ANNO BERKELEY   MARG
BLINKING
WINKING & BLINKING . . . .   54 LO THE BAT/IM   2
WINKING & BLINKING . . . .   54 LO THE BAT/IM   3
WINKING & BLINKING . . . .   54 LO THE BAT/IM   4
NARROW BLINKING EYES THAT HAVE TOO LONG GOVERNED ART .   563D DESC CAT   PROSE
BLISS
. . . AND MEN WALK WITH THEIR FATHERS IN BLISS . . .   145 FRENCH REVOLTN   237
OVER HIS PORCH THESE WORDS ARE WRITTEN TAKE THY BLISS O MAN   193 V DAU ALBION 6   2
THE VIGOROUS JOYS OF MORNING LIGHT OPEN TO VIRGIN BLISS   193 V DAU ALBION 6   6
IN LOVELY COPULATION BLISS ON BLISS WITH THEOTORMON   .   195 V DAU ALBION 7   26
ARISE AND DRINK YOUR BLISS FOR EVERY THING THAT LIVES IS   195 V DAU ALBION 8   10
HOLY
WHEN HOLY ZEAL SCENTS THE SWEET VALLEYS OF RIPE VIRGIN   205 AMERICA CANC C   30
BLISS
TO GIVE US BLISS THAT WE MAY DRINK THE SPARKLING WINE OF   239 EUROPE 4   20
LOS
AND I MAY SEE THEE IN THE HOUR OF BLISS MY ELDEST BORN .   239 EUROPE 4   28
MY WEARY EYELIDS DRAW TOWARDS THE EVENING MY BLISS IS YET   240 EUROPE 5   10
BUT NEW
BETWEEN TWO MOMENTS BLISS IS RIPE . . . .   244 EUROPE 14   23
TO THE BLISS OF ETERNAL VALLEYS . . . .   254 AHANIA 5   9
WHEN I FOUND BABES OF BLISS ON MY BEDS . . . . . .   255 AHANIA 5   19
MY MOTHERS-JOYS SLEEPING IN BLISS . . . .   255 AHANIA 5   38
SAT IN A [SWEET] DREAD INTOXICATION OF [FALSE WOVEN BLISS]   266 FOUR ZOAS 1   91
. . .
CONVERSING WITH THE VISIONS OF BEULAH IN DARK SLUMBEROUS   271 FOUR ZOAS 1   * 246
BLISS
THE VOICE CAME & WENT LIKE A DREAM I AWOKE IN MY SWEET   272 FOUR ZOAS 1   280
BLISS
CRAVING THE MORE THE MORE ENJOYING DRAWING OUT SWEET BLISS   276 FOUR ZOAS 1   440
WITH WHOM SHE WALKD IN BLISS IN TIMES OF INNOCENCE & YOUTH   282 FOUR ZOAS 2   79
FAREWELL THE GOD CALLS ME AWAY I DEPART IN MY SWEET BLISS   288 FOUR ZOAS 2   333
NIGHT PASSD & ENITHARMON EER THE DAWN RETURND IN BLISS .   289 FOUR ZOAS 2   * 341
ARISE & DRINK YOUR BLISS . . . .   289 FOUR ZOAS 2   365
GOLDEN & BEAUTIFUL BUT O HOW UNLIKE THOSE SWEET FIELDS   292 FOUR ZOAS 3   39
OF BLISS
SHALL THE FEMININE INDOLENT BLISS THE INDULGENT SELF OF   295 FOUR ZOAS 3   114
WEARINESS
HAVE QUITE FORSAKEN O FOOL FOOL TO LOSE MY SWEETEST BLISS   296 FOUR ZOAS 3   168
O WHAT A WORLD IS HERE UNLIKE THOSE CLIMES OF BLISS . .   317 FOUR ZOAS 6   208
WITH VISIONS OF SWEET BLISS FAR OTHER THAN THIS BURNING   321 FOUR ZOAS 7   62
CLIME
FROM THY SWEET LOINS OF BLISS RED FLOWD THY BLOOD . . .   325 FOUR ZOAS 7   226
UPON HER BOSOM IN SWEET BLISS HE FAINTED WONDER SIEZD .   326 FOUR ZOAS 7   241
THAT BODY I CREATED THEN SHALL WE UNITE AGAIN IN BLISS .   327 FOUR ZOAS 7   301
THARMAS REPLIED VALA THY SINS HAVE LOST US HEAVEN & BLISS   339 FOUR ZOAS 7B   256
UNITED WE SHOULD LIVE IN BLISS AS THOSE WHO SINNED NOT .   345 FOUR ZOAS 8   160
AND ALL HIS SORROWS TILL HE REASSUMES HIS ANCIENT BLISS   356 FOUR ZOAS 8   583
COOPERATING IN THE BLISS OF MAN OBEYING HIS WILL . . .   366 FOUR ZOAS 9   373
FROM THE SEATS OF BLISS THESE REPRESENT THOSE WHO   .   614A V LAST JUDG/N   PROSE
WITH WHOM SHE LIVD IN BLISS IN TIMES OF INNOCENCE & YOUTH   626 JERUSALEM 7   37
THAT WALKS ABOUT AMONG THE STONES OF FIRE IN BLISS & WOE   680 JERUSALEM 49   73
DRINKING HIS EMANATION IN INTOXICATING BLISS REJOICING   701 JERUSALEM 65   58
IN GIANT DANCE
BUT NO ONE CAN CONSUMMATE FEMALE BLISS IN LOS'S WORLD   708 JERUSALEM 69   30
WITHOUT
WHERE SEXES WANDER IN DREAMS OF BLISS AMONG THE EMANATIONS   721 JERUSALEM 79   75
AND THAT I CAN AT WILL EXPATIATE IN THE GARDENS OF BLISS   727 JERUSALEM 82   82
NOR CAN ANY CONSUMMATE BLISS WITHOUT BEING GENERATED   .   731 JERUSALEM 86   42
. . . EAST IN RIVERS OF BLISS THE NERVES OF THE . . .   745 JERUSALEM 98   16

BLITHE
   [WITH FORTUNE SPORTING MERRY BLITHE & GAY] . . . . . .   540 GOLDEN RULE/N   *   3
   I SPORT WITH FORTUNE MERRY BLITHE & GAY . . . .   540 S(TOTHAR)D/N   3
BLOATED
   WITHIN HIS RIBS BLOATED ROUND . . . .   229 URIZEN 13   5
   IN GHASTLY TORMENT SICK WITHIN HIS RIBS BLOATED ROUND . .   303 FOUR ZOAS 4   239
   BLOATED [AWKWARD] GODS MERCURY JUNO VENUS & THE . . . .   599C PUB ADDRESS/N *PROSE
   SWELLD & BLOATED GENERAL FORMS REPUGNANT TO THE . . . .   672 JERUSALEM 43   19
   AND YOU CALL THAT SWELLD & BLOATED FORM A MINUTE PARTICULAR   738 JERUSALEM 91   29
BLOCKED
   THEY CAUSE THAT THE EXECUTION SHALL BE ALL BLOCKED UP .   582C DESC CAT 9   PROSE
BLOCKHEAD
   THE AUTHOR IS AN ERRANT BLOCKHEAD . . . .   44D ISLAND MOON 1   PROSE
   TO CALL A MAN A BLOCKHEAD THAT YOU KNOW NOTHING OF . . .   44D ISLAND MOON 1   PROSE
   THOU CALLST ME MADMAN BUT I CALL THEE BLOCKHEAD . . . .   539 F(LAXMAN)/N 1   2
   HES A BLOCKHEAD WHO WANTS A PROOF OF WHAT HE CAN'T PERCIEVE   540 BLOCKHEAD/N   1
   AND HES A FOOL WHO [SEEKS] TRIES TO MAKE SUCH A BLOCKHEAD   540 BLOCKHEAD/N   2
     BELIEVE
   ARE ALWAYS THE SUBTERFUGE OF THE BLOCKHEAD . . . . . .   591C PUB ADDRESS/N   PROSE
   [ENCOURAGE A BLOCKHEAD & HE IS COUNTED THE GREATEST GENIUS]   595B PUB ADDRESS/N   PROSE
   THE WORK OF A BLOCKHEAD IT BEARS THIS EVIDENCE IN ITS FACE   599C PUB ADDRESS/N   PROSE
   CAN ITS EXECUTION BE ANY OTHER THAN THE WORK OF A BLOCKHEAD   599C PUB ADDRESS/N   PROSE
BLOCKHEADS
   AND YET THEY ARE BLOCKHEADS YOU ALL AGREE . . . . .   550 SAY PICTURES/N   2
   & CHARLES THE FIRST WERE TO PATRONIZE SUCH BLOCKHEADS . .   599D PUB ADDRESS/N   PROSE
   INTEND IT SHOULD BE SO NONE BUT BLOCKHEADS COPY ONE ANOTHER   601D PUB ADDRESS/N   PROSE
BLOCK HEADS
   INTERESTING TO BLOCK HEADS AS IT ENDEAVOURS TO PROVE .   457D ANNO REYNOLDS   MARG
BLOCKS
   AND BLOCKS UP ALL ITS GATES OF LIGHT EXCEPT ONE . . .   583A DESC CAT 9   PROSE
BLOOD   SEE LIFE BLOOD
   WITH THE BLOOD OF THE GRAPE PASS NOT BUT SIT . . . .   2 TO AUTUMN/PS   2
   HES DEAD AND HOWLING AFTER ME FOR BLOOD . . . . . .   4 FAIR ELENOR/PS   24
   WITH GORY BLOOD IT GROAND AND THUS IT SPAKE . . . . .   5 FAIR ELENOR/PS   60
   THE NUMROUS SONS OF BLOOD . . . .   11 GWIN KING/PS   18
   EARTH SMOKES WITH BLOOD AND GROANS AND SHAKES . . . .   13 GWIN KING/PS   73
   A SEA OF BLOOD NOR CAN THE EYE . . . .   13 GWIN KING/PS   75
   THE GOD OF WAR IS DRUNK WITH BLOOD . . . .   13 GWIN KING/PS   93
   THE STENCH OF BLOOD MAKES SICK THE HEAVNS . . . . .   13 GWIN KING/PS   95
   THE RIVER DORMAN ROLLD THEIR BLOOD . . . .   14 GWIN KING/PS   113
   THE COLD RELIEF THE BLOOD IS STAYD . . . .   17 BLIND-MANS/PS   59
   WHEN THE CRIES OF BLOOD TEAR HORROR FROM HEAVN . . . .   18 EDW THIRD/PS 1   7
   A TRIFLE IVE GILT YOUR CAUSE WITH MY BEST BLOOD . . . .   23 EDW THIRD/PS 3   99
   WILL BEND OR BREAK US MY BLOOD LIKE A SPRINGTIDE . . .   26 EDW THIRD/PS 3   234
   FOR ALL OUR BLOOD AND BONES ARE IN FRANCE AND A . . .   29C EDW THIRD/PS 4   PROSE
   AND BLOOD SHALL FLOW LIKE STREAMS ACROSS THE MEADOWS . .   31 EDW THIRD/PS 5   54
   HEATED WITH WAR FILLD WITH THE BLOOD OF GREEKS . . . .   32 EDW THIRD/PS 6   10
   THE MIGHTY DEAD GIANT BODIES STREAMING BLOOD . . . .   32 EDW THIRD/PS 6   35
   BROTHER IN BROTHER'S BLOOD MUST BATHE RIVERS OF DEATH . .   34A KING JOHN/PS   PROSE
   BLOOD CRIES AFAR THE LAND DOTH SOW ITSELF . . . . .   34B KING JOHN/PS   PROSE
   FOR TYRANNY HATH STRETCHD HIS PURPLE ARM AND BLOOD HE CRIES   34B KING JOHN/PS   PROSE
   OUR COUNTRY IS PLOWED WITH SWORDS AND REAPED IN BLOOD . .   40A SAMSON/PS   PROSE
   GO SEE THE NATURAL TIE OF FLESH & BLOOD . . . . .   43A THEN SHE BORE   PROSE
   MY NERVES WITH TREMBLING CURDLE ALL MY BLOOD . . . .   43C WOE CRIED MUSE   PROSE
   [SOME NOSTRILD WIDE BREATHING OUT BLOOD SOME CLOSE SHUT   109 TIRIEL 8   12
     UP]
   THROUGH HEAVEN TINGING MORNING WITH BEAMS OF BLOOD . . .   139 FRENCH REVOLTN   111
   IN THE BLOOD OF NOBILITY TRAMPLING THE HEART AND THE HEAD   141 FRENCH REVOLTN   156
   . . .
   . . . BRED FROM THE BLOOD OF REVENGE AND BREATH OF DESIRE   144 FRENCH REVOLTN   215
   . . . BLOOD RAN DOWN THE ANCIENT PILLARS . . . . .   145 FRENCH REVOLTN   246
   . . . THE FROZEN BLOOD REFLOWD . . . .   148 FRENCH REVOLTN   303
   BETWEEN THE CLOUDS & THE WAVES WE SAW A CATARACT OF BLOOD   156B MARRIAGE HH 17 PROSE
   TINGING THE BLACK DEEP WITH BEAMS OF BLOOD . . . . .   156C MARRIAGE HH 17 PROSE
   RUNS IN BLOOD DOWN PALACE WALLS . . . .   170 LONDON/N   13
   REMOVE AWAY THAT [PLACE] MAN OF BLOOD . . . . . .   176 ANCNT PROVRB/N   3
   CLOTHD IN ROBES OF BLOOD & GOLD . . . .   177 DAY/N   2
   REMOVE AWAY THAT -- OF BLOOD . . . .   184 SEVRL QUESTN/N   17
   [[THE BLOOD OF TEN THOUSAND BY FIGHTING OR SWINGING]] .   185 LET BROTHELS/N   15
   [WHO WILL EXCHANGE HIS OWN HEART'S BLOOD] . . . . .   186 LET BROTHELS/N   50
   MEET ON THE COAST GLOWING WITH BLOOD FROM ALBION'S FIERY   197 AMERICA 3   5
     PRINCE
   AS HUMAN BLOOD SHOOTING ITS VEINS ALL ROUND THE ORBED   197 AMERICA 4   5
     HEAVEN
   RED ROSE THE CLOUDS FROM THE ATLANTIC IN VAST WHEELS OF   197 AMERICA 4   6
     BLOOD
   WITH BEAMS OF BLOOD & THUS A VOICE CAME FORTH AND SHOOK   198 AMERICA 5   7
     THE TEMPLE
   MEET ON THE COAST GLOWING WITH BLOOD FROM ALBION'S FIERY   203 AMERICA CANC A   5
     PRINCE
   RUNS IN BLOOD DOWN PALACE WALLS . . . .   216 LONDON/SE   12
   AWOKE & VAST CLOUDS OF BLOOD ROLLD . . . .   223 URIZEN 3   41
   IN CATARACTS OF FIRE BLOOD & GALL . . . .   225 URIZEN 4   46
   IN WHIRLWINDS & CATARACTS OF BLOOD . . . .   225 URIZEN 5   13
   OF BLOOD POUR DOWN THE MOUNTAINS TO COOL . . . . . .   225 URIZEN 5   31
   AND LEFT A ROUND GLOBE OF BLOOD . . . .   230 URIZEN 13   58
   FIBRES OF BLOOD MILK AND TEARS . . . .   231 URIZEN 18   4
   DREAD TERRORS DELIGHTING IN BLOOD . . . .   234 URIZEN 23   7
   ON GOLDEN CHARIOTS RAGING WITH RED WHEELS DROPPING WITH   245 EUROPE 15   5
     BLOOD
   CALLD ALL HIS SONS TO THE STRIFE OF BLOOD . . . . .   245 EUROPE 15   11
   AND MILK & BLOOD & GLANDOUS WINE . . . .   248 SONG OF LOS 7   38

BLOOD   (CONTINUED)

	PAGE	TITLE		LINE
FIRST HE POISOND THE ROCKS WITH HIS BLOOD	251	AHANIA 3		20
MIXD WITH BLOOD HERE THE SNAKE GETS HER POISON	251	AHANIA 3		50
WINGED SCREAMING IN BLOOD & TORMENT	253	AHANIA 4		26
I SEE THE SHOWER OF BLOOD I SEE THE SWORDS & SPEARS OF FUTURITY	272	FOUR ZOAS 1		301
. . . BUT WAR & PRINCEDOM & VICTORY & BLOOD	272	FOUR ZOAS 1		311
OF LUVAH & VALA SHUDDERD IN THEIR ORB AN ORB OF BLOOD . .	273	FOUR ZOAS 1		314
REJOICING IN THE VICTORY & THE HEAVENS WERE FILLD WITH BLOOD	273	FOUR ZOAS 1		346
THEY STOOD ABOVE THE HEAVENS FORSAKEN DESOLATE SUSPENDED IN BLOOD	274	FOUR ZOAS 1		361
IN (LUVAH'S) ROBES OF BLOOD & BEARING ALL HIS AFFLICTIONS	274	FOUR ZOAS 1	*	364
FATTEND ON HUMAN BLOOD & DRUNK WITH WINE OF LIFE IS BETTER FAR	274	FOUR ZOAS 1		389
RED WITH THE BLOOD OF MEN SWELLS LUSTFUL ROUND MY ROCKY KNEES	275	FOUR ZOAS 1		391
WITH MILK BUT WHEREFORE NOW ARE CHILDREN FED WITH BLOOD	275	FOUR ZOAS 1		401
LAUGHS AT THE HUMAN FORM THE LION MOCKS & THIRSTS FOR BLOOD	275	FOUR ZOAS 1		403
I WILL REMAIN AS WELL AS THOU & HERE WITH HANDS OF BLOOD	278	FOUR ZOAS 1		512
[XXX BLOOD FROM TORRENT FLOODS MELTING [AWAY]]	SUPP	FOUR ZOAS 1	*	
ALOFT THE MOON FLED WITH A CRY THE SUN WITH STREAMS OF BLOOD	281	FOUR ZOAS 2		42
THE BROTHER & THE BROTHER BATHE IN BLOOD UPON THE SEVERN	281	FOUR ZOAS 2		49
AND THE DIVINE VISION APPEARD IN LUVAH'S ROBES OF BLOOD	286	FOUR ZOAS 2		247
FOR WHEN LUVAH SUNK DOWN HIMSELF PUT ON THE ROBES OF BLOOD	287	FOUR ZOAS 2		263
WALKED IN ROBES OF BLOOD TILL HE WHO SLEPT SHOULD AWAKE	287	FOUR ZOAS 2		265
WHEN THE RED BLOOD IS FILLD WITH WINE & WITH THE MARROW OF LAMBS	290	FOUR ZOAS 2		407
THEY CALL THY LIONS TO THE FIELDS OF BLOOD THEY ROWZE THY TYGERS	292	FOUR ZOAS 3	*	37
AND NOW THE HUMAN BLOOD FOAMD HIGH I SAW THAT LUVAH & VALA	294	FOUR ZOAS 3		94
HE FALLING ON THE ROCKS BELLOWD HIS DOLOR TILL THE BLOOD	299	FOUR ZOAS 4		61
OF GOARY BLOOD STRUGGLING TO BE DELIVERD FROM OUR BONDS	300	FOUR ZOAS 4		103
OF MAN CLOTHD IN LUVAH'S ROBES OF BLOOD SAW & WEPT . . .	304	FOUR ZOAS 4		248
BRING IN HERE THE GLOBE OF BLOOD AS IN THE (BOOK) OF URIZEN	305A	FOUR ZOAS 4		PROSE
IN THUNDER SMOKE & SULLEN FLAMES & HOWLINGS & FURY & BLOOD	306	FOUR ZOAS 5		38
AND BREATHING TERRIBLE BLOOD & VENGEANCE GNASHING HIS TEETH WITH PAIN	306	FOUR ZOAS 5		58
SWEAT & BLOOD STOOD ON THE LIMBS OF LOS IN GLOBES HIS FIERY EYELIDS	307	FOUR ZOAS 5		67
REORGANIZE ME SHOOTING FORTH IN BONES & FLESH & BLOOD . .	317	FOUR ZOAS 6		224
AND ROUND RED ORC RETURNING BACK TO URIZEN [GORD] GORGD WITH BLOOD	320	FOUR ZOAS 6	*	322
OF GOARY BLOOD THE IMMORTAL SEED IS NOURISHD FOR THE SLAUGHTER	320	FOUR ZOAS 7		15
CUT THEE IN GASHES THO THE BLOOD POURS DOWN AROUND THY ANKLES	322	FOUR ZOAS 7		84
THE LITTLE HEART THE LIVER & THE RED BLOOD IN ITS LABYRINTHS	323	FOUR ZOAS 7		132
AND SHRIEK TILL AT THE SMELLS OF BLOOD THEY STRETCH THEIR BONEY WINGS	325	FOUR ZOAS 7		207
FROM THY SWEET LOINS OF BLISS RED FLOWD THY BLOOD . . .	325	FOUR ZOAS 7		226
OF SWEET ETERNITY THE BLOOD FLOWD ROUND THE HOLY TENT & RIVN	326	FOUR ZOAS 7		257
LISTEN O VISION OF DELIGHT ONE DREAD MORN OF GOARY BLOOD	327	FOUR ZOAS 7	*	278
I SUNK WITH CRIES OF BLOOD ISSUING DOWNWARD IN THE VEINS	327	FOUR ZOAS 7		284
CLOTHED IN LUVAH'S ROBES OF BLOOD DESCENDING TO REDEEM . .	330	FOUR ZOAS 7		416
PAMPERD IN PALACES [OF] FOR OUR FOOD THE BLOOD OF CAPTAINS NURTURD	334	FOUR ZOAS 7B	*	46
THARMAS LAUGHD FURIOUS AMONG THE BANNERS CLOTHD IN BLOOD	334	FOUR ZOAS 7B		49
IN WAR SHALT THOU BEAR RULE IN BLOOD SHALT THOU TRIUMPH FOR ME	334	FOUR ZOAS 7B		57
FOLLOWD HER DAUGHTERS TO THE FIELDS OF BLOOD THEY LEFT ME NAKED	334	FOUR ZOAS 7B		66
RENDING THE HEAVENS & EARTHS & DRINKING BLOOD IN THE HOT BATTLE	335	FOUR ZOAS 7B		103
THE ARROWS FLEW FROM CLOUDY BOW ALL DAY TILL BLOOD . . .	337	FOUR ZOAS 7B		159
THEY GIVE THE OATH OF BLOOD THEY CAST THE LOTS INTO THE HELMET	337	FOUR ZOAS 7B		165
SCATTER THE BLOOD FROM THY GOLDEN BROW	338	FOUR ZOAS 7B		194
BUT BLOOD & WOUNDS & DISMAL CRIES & CLARIONS OF WAR . . .	338	FOUR ZOAS 7B		205
WE HEAR THY SIGHS IN TRUMPETS SHRILL WHEN MORN SHALL BLOOD RENEW	338	FOUR ZOAS 7B		209
OF DAY IN JEALOUSY & BLOOD MY CHILDREN ARE LED TO URIZEN'S WAR	339	FOUR ZOAS 7B		251
A TEAR OF BLOOD DROPPED FROM EITHER EYE AGAIN HE REPOSD	341	FOUR ZOAS 8		18
I SEE THE MURDERER OF MY LUVAH CLOTHD IN ROBES OF BLOOD	345	FOUR ZOAS 8		153
HE PUTS OFF THE CLOTHING OF BLOOD	347	FOUR ZOAS 8		236
AND ON HER FOREHEAD WAS HER NAME WRITTEN IN BLOOD MYSTERY	348	FOUR ZOAS 8		282
INTO THE ABYSSES OF HIS BOSOM THE VESSELS OF HIS BLOOD . .	353	FOUR ZOAS 8		472
BLOOD ISSUD OUT IN MIGHTY VOLUMES POURING IN WHIRLPOOLS FIERCE	359	FOUR ZOAS 9	*	71
THE TORRENTS BLACK UPON THE EARTH THE BLOOD POURS DOWN INCESSANT	359	FOUR ZOAS 9		73
OF FOAMING BLOOD BENEATH THE BLACK INCESSANT SKY TILL ALL	359	FOUR ZOAS 9		78
WHENCE IS THIS SOUND OF RAGE OF MEN DRINKING EACH OTHER'S BLOOD	360	FOUR ZOAS 9		121
BUT SIN EVEN RAHAB IS REDEEMD IN BLOOD & FURY & JEALOUSY	361	FOUR ZOAS 9		159
THAT LINE OF BLOOD THAT STRETCHD ACROSS THE WINDOWS OF THE MORNING	361	FOUR ZOAS 9		160
EXCESS OF JOY IS WORSE THAN GRIEF HER HEART BEAT HIGH HER BLOOD	362	FOUR ZOAS 9		197

234

		PAGE	TITLE	LINE

BLOOD   (CONTINUED)

	PAGE	TITLE	LINE
THE CLOUD IS BLOOD DAZLING UPON THE HEAVENS & IN THE CLOUD	364	FOUR ZOAS 9	278
THE BLOOD OF LIFE FLOWD PLENTIFUL ODORS OF LIFE AROSE · ·	376	FOUR ZOAS 9	726
THE BLOOD RED RAN FROM THE GREY MONK'S SIDE · · · · ·	419	I SAW A MONK/N	15
AND SPILLD THE BLOOD OF MERCY'S LORD · · · · · · ·	420	I SAW MNK AD/N	4
THE BLOOD RED RAN FROM THE GREY MONK'S SIDE · · · ·	430	GREY MONK	5
CALLS TO HEAVEN FOR HUMAN BLOOD · · · · · · · ·	431	AUGURIES	12
A DISK OF BLOOD DISTANT & HEAVNS & EARTHS ROLL DARK BETWEEN	495	MILTON 14	27
IN CONFLICT WITH THOSE FEMALE FORMS WHICH IN BLOOD & JEALOUSY	498	MILTON 17	7
GLOWD BUT IN TERRORS FOLDED ROUND HIS CLOUDS OF BLOOD · ·	502	MILTON 20	24
IN ALBION & TO DENY THE VALUE OF THE SAVIOUR'S BLOOD · ·	506	MILTON 22	54
LO ORC ARISES ON THE ATLANTIC LO HIS BLOOD AND FIRE · ·	506	MILTON 23	6
FOR EVERY SPACE LARGER THAN A RED GLOBULE OF MAN'S BLOOD ·	516	MILTON 29	19
AND EVERY SPACE SMALLER THAN A GLOBULE OF MAN'S BLOOD OPENS	516	MILTON 29	21
WHILE THOSE COMBIN'D BY SATAN'S TYRANNY FIRST IN THE BLOOD OF WAR	521	MILTON 32	16
IN CLOUDS OF BLOOD IN STREAMS OF GORE WITH DREADFUL THUNDERINGS	534	MILTON 42	8
THE CLOUDS OF OLOLON FOLDED AS A GARMENT DIPPED IN BLOOD ·	534	MILTON 42	12
FROM FELPHAM'S VALE CLOTHED IN CLOUDS OF BLOOD TO ENTER INTO	534	MILTON 42	20
THE BLOOD IS SEEN TO CIRCULATE IN THEIR LIMBS · · · · ·	581A	DESC CAT 5	PROSE
BEFORE THE FLOOD THAT THEY WERE FILLD WITH BLOOD & FIRE	606D	V LAST JUDG/N	PROSE
& INTO BLOOD BY MOSES RELATES TO VEGETABLE NATURE ALSO ·	607B	V LAST JUDG/N	PROSE
ALBION'S MOUNTAINS RUN WITH BLOOD THE CRIES OF WAR & OF TUMULT	623	JERUSALEM 5	6
FIRST AS A RED GLOBE OF BLOOD TREMBLING BENEATH HIS BOSOM	639	JERUSALEM 17	51
BUT COME O VALA WITH KNIFE & CUP DRAIN MY BLOOD · · · ·	645	JERUSALEM 22	29
· · · IN THE BLOOD OF THE LAMB SLAIN IN HIS CHILDREN ·	646	JERUSALEM 24	2
THE RHINE WAS RED WITH HUMAN BLOOD · · · · · · · ·	651	FIELDS FROM/J	45
IN CLOUDS OF BLOOD & RUIN ROLLD · · · · · · · · ·	651	FIELDS FROM/J	74
ON TYBURN'S RIVER IN CLOUDS OF BLOOD WHERE WAS MILD ZION HILL'S	653	JERUSALEM 29	3
AND NOW THE HUMAN BLOOD FOAMD HIGH THE SPIRITS LUVAH & VALA	655	JERUSALEM 29	73
IS GREAT IN THE EAST THEIR SPEARS OF BLOOD RAGE IN THE EASTERN HEAVEN	658	JERUSALEM 31	56
IN DREAMS OF DARKNESS WHILE MY VEGETATING BLOOD IN VEINY PIPES	665	JERUSALEM 38	36
BREATHING CRUELTY BLOOD & VENGEANCE GNASHING HIS TEETH WITH PAIN	667	JERUSALEM 40	38
AND LAY ITS HEAVENS & THEIR INHABITANTS IN BLOOD OF PUNISHMENT	668	JERUSALEM 41	20
WE SMELL THE BLOOD OF THE ENGLISH · · · · · · · · ·	673	JERUSALEM 43	48
· · · WE DELIGHT IN THEIR BLOOD ON OUR ALTARS · · · ·	673	JERUSALEM 43	48
OF BLOOD OVER EUROPE A VEGETATING ROOT IN GRINDING PAIN	677	JERUSALEM 47	5
ALBION IS NOW POSSESSD BY THE WAR OF BLOOD THE SACRIFICE	681	JERUSALEM 50	8
A BROODER OF AN EVIL DAY AND A SUN RISING IN BLOOD · ·	681	JERUSALEM 50	29
THE BLOOD RED RAN FROM THE GREY MONK'S SIDE · · · · ·	683	I SAW A MONK/J	13
AND SPILLD THE BLOOD OF MERCY'S LORD · · · · · · ·	683	I SAW A MONK/J	20
THE DIVINE VISION DIMLY APPEARD IN CLOUDS OF BLOOD WEEPING	685	JERUSALEM 54	32
NAKED & DRUNK WITH BLOOD GWENDOLEN DANCING TO THE TIMBREL	689	JERUSALEM 58	2
TWO CONTRARIES WAR AGAINST EACH OTHER IN FURY & BLOOD · ·	690	JERUSALEM 58	15
BURST FORTH IN STREAMS OF BLOOD UPON THE HEAVENS & DARK NIGHT	696	JERUSALEM 62	31
GLITTERING WITH PRECIOUS STONES & GOLD WITH GARMENTS OF BLOOD & FIRE	699	JERUSALEM 64	26
· · · THEY GIVE THE OATH OF BLOOD IN LAMBETH · · · · ·	699	JERUSALEM 65	7
SCATTER THE BLOOD FROM THY GOLDEN BROW · · · · · · ·	700	JERUSALEM 65	40
BUT BLOOD AND WOUNDS AND DISMAL CRIES AND SHADOWS OF THE OAK	701	JERUSALEM 65	51
WE HEAR THY SIGHS IN TRUMPETS SHRILL WHEN MORN SHALL BLOOD RENEW	701	JERUSALEM 65	55
THE KNIFE OF FLINT PASSES OVER THE HOWLING VICTIM HIS BLOOD	702	JERUSALEM 66	20
AND THEN A GLOBE OF BLOOD WANDERING DISTANT IN AN UNKNOWN NIGHT	702	JERUSALEM 66	43
RED RUN THE STREAMS OF ALBION THAMES IS DRUNK WITH BLOOD	703	JERUSALEM 66	61
THE HUMBER & THE SEVERN ARE DRUNK WITH THE BLOOD OF THE SLAIN	703	JERUSALEM 66	63
HE BLEEDS IN TORRENTS OF BLOOD AS HE ROLLS THRO HEAVEN ABOVE	703	JERUSALEM 66	77
BY THOSE WHO DRINK THEIR BLOOD & THE BLOOD OF THEIR COVENANT	704	JERUSALEM 67	1
THEY ADORE & HIS REVENGE CHERISH WITH THE BLOOD OF THE INNOCENT	704	JERUSALEM 67	21
THEY STRIP OFF JOSEPH'S COAT & DIP IT IN THE BLOOD OF BATTLE	704	JERUSALEM 67	23
WITH BLOOD WEAVING THE DEATHS OF THE MIGHTY INTO A TABERNACLE	704	JERUSALEM 67	33
BLOOD HATH STAIND HER FAIR SIDE BENEATH HER BOSOM · · ·	705	JERUSALEM 67	43
HER PANTING VICTIM BESIDE HER HER HEART IS DRUNK WITH BLOOD	705	JERUSALEM 68	12
A SHEET & VEIL & CURTAIN OF BLOOD IS LET DOWN FROM HEAVEN	706	JERUSALEM 68	21
BRING YOUR OFFERINGS YOUR FIRST BEGOTTEN PAMPERD WITH MILK & BLOOD	706	JERUSALEM 68	30
CLOTHED IN THE SKIN OF THE VICTIM BLOOD HUMAN BLOOD IS THE LIFE	706	JERUSALEM 68	33
WITH PLEASURE WITHOUT PAIN FOR THEIR FOOD IS BLOOD OF THE CAPTIVE	706	JERUSALEM 68	37
SPOTTED WITH VICTIMS' BLOOD BY THE FIRES OF THY SECRET TABERNACLE	706	JERUSALEM 68	49
THEY HAVE DIVIDED SIMEON HE ALSO ROLLD APART IN BLOOD · ·	715	JERUSALEM 74	44
WITH BLOOD FROM JAPAN EASTWARD TO THE GIANTS CAUSWAY WEST	719	JERUSALEM 78	26

	PAGE	TITLE	LINE

BLOOD (CONTINUED)
HER CHILDREN'S DRUID TEMPLES DROPPING WITH BLOOD WANDERD   719 JERUSALEM 78   29
  WEEPING
TOGETHER AMONG MY LITTLE-ONES BUT NOW MY ALTARS RUN WITH   721 JERUSALEM 79   55
  BLOOD
DROP WITH THE GORE OF THE SLAIN WHY EUPHRATES IS RED WITH   721 JERUSALEM 79   69
  BLOOD
THE SPINDLE TURND IN BLOOD & FIRE LOUD SOUND THE TRUMPETS   722 JERUSALEM 80   37
ALBION MUST BE A ROCK OF BLOOD MARK YE THE POINTS . . .   728 JERUSALEM 83   56
INTO A GLOBE OF BLOOD BENEATH HIS BOSOM TREMBLING   732 JERUSALEM 86   52
  IN DARKNESS
OF BLOOD THRO ALL MY NERVOUS LIMBS SOON OVERGROWN IN ROOTS   732 JERUSALEM 87   6
OF VEINS OF RED BLOOD GROWS AROUND THEM LIKE A SCARLET ROBE   736 JERUSALEM 90   5
MONEY THE LIFE'S BLOOD OF POOR FAMILIES . . . .   776B INSC LAOCOON   PROSE
VOICE O EARTH COVER NOT THOU MY BLOOD COVER NOT THOU MY   780 GHOST ABEL 1   8
  BLOOD
OF BLOOD O EARTH COVER NOT THOU THE BLOOD OF ABEL . . .   780 GHOST ABEL 1   13
AND HE DOTH RULE OVER ME THEREFORE MY SOUL IN FUMES OF   780 GHOST ABEL 2   8
  BLOOD
CRIES FOR VENGEANCE SACRIFICE ON SACRIPICE BLOOD ON BLOOD   780 GHOST ABEL 2   9
ABEL COMPELLED I CRY O EARTH COVER NOT THE BLOOD OF ABEL   780 GHOST ABEL 2   12
SATAN I WILL HAVE HUMAN BLOOD & NOT THE BLOOD OF BULLS   780 GHOST ABEL 2   13
  OR GOATS
CAIN'S CITY BUILT WITH HUMAN BLOOD NOT BLOOD OF BULLS   781 GHOST ABEL 2   17
  & GOATS
THE VOICE OF ABEL'S BLOOD . . . .   781B GHOST ABEL 2   *PROSE
BLOODED
BUT IN COOL BLOODED DESIGN & INTENTION . . . .   615D V LAST JUDG/N   PROSE
BLOODLESS
BUT WORN AWAY A BLOODLESS DAEMON . . . .   41D THEN SHE BORE   PROSE
MARROWLESS BLOODLESS FALLING INTO DUST DRIVEN BY THE WINDS   354 FOUR ZOAS 8   518
BLOOD RED
A SUN OF BLOOD RED WRATH SURROUNDING HEAVEN ON ALL SIDES   745 JERUSALEM 98   10
  AROUND
BLOODTHIRSTY
[BUT THE BLOODTHIRSTY PEOPLE ACROSS THE WATER] . . . .   185 LET BROTHELS/N   22
BLOOD-VESSELS
THE CHILDREN OF MY THOUGHTS WALKING WITHIN MY BLOOD-VESSELS   665 JERUSALEM 38   34
BLOODY
AND SAW THE BLOODY NAPKIN BY HER SIDE . . . .   5 FAIR ELENOR/PS   54
HER EYES WERE FIXD THE BLOODY CLOTH UNFOLDS . . . . .   5 FAIR ELENOR/PS   57
TO HEAVE THE BLOODY BILL . . . .   12 GWIN KING/PS   52
THE BATTLE FAINTS AND BLOODY MEN . . . .   13 GWIN KING/PS   87
BRAVE LORDS WHO FELL BENEATH THE BLOODY AXE . . . . .   18 EDW THIRD/PS 1   44
LET WAR STAIN THE BLUE HEAVENS WITH BLOODY BANNERS . . .   31 EDW THIRD/PS 5   63
AND RAN ABOUT WITH BLOODY HANDS . . . .   50 WHEN CORRUP/IM   15
IN THE TOWER NAMED BLOODY . . . .   135 FRENCH REVOLTN   33
WEEPING FOR LUVAH LOST IN THE BLOODY BEAMS OF . . . .   272 FOUR ZOAS 1   * 287
THEY EAT THE [XXX] FLESHLY BREAD THEY DRANK THE NERVOUS   274 FOUR ZOAS 1   * 355
  [BLOODY] WINE
[THE ?SHADES ?OF] BUT LUVAH & VALA STANDING IN THE BLOODY   274 FOUR ZOAS 1   * 359
  SKY
TRIUMPHANT IN THE BLOODY SKY & THE HUMAN FORM IS NO MORE   275 FOUR ZOAS 1   409
[XXX BLOODY XXX] . . . .   SUPP FOUR ZOAS 2   *
RED AS THE SUN IN THE HOT MORNING OF THE BLOODY DAY . . .   297 FOUR ZOAS 4   5
THE BLOODY MASS BEGAN TO ANIMATE I BENDING OVER . . . .   300 FOUR ZOAS 4   96
SOFT TEARS & SIGHS WHERE ARE YOU COME FORTH SHOUT ON BLOODY   306 FOUR ZOAS 5   48
  FIELDS
AROUND HIS BOSOM LIKE A BLOODY CORD IN SECRET SOBS . . .   307 FOUR ZOAS 5   84
ENITHARMON BEHELD THE BLOODY CHAIN OF NIGHTS & DAYS . .   307 FOUR ZOAS 5   92
BATHED IN BLOODY CLOUDS HIS LOINS IN FIRES OF WAR WHERE   334 FOUR ZOAS 7B   43
  SPEARS
UPON THE BLOODY ALTAR JOHN SAW THESE THINGS REVEALD IN   356 FOUR ZOAS 8   600
  HEAVEN
THE BLOODY DELUGE LIVING FLAMES WINGED WITH INTELLECT . .   359 FOUR ZOAS 9   86
SLAUGHTER SHALL HEAP THE BLOODY PLAIN . . . .   420 I SAW A MONK/N   51
SHE TIES THE KNOT OF BLOODY VEINS INTO A RED HOT HEART . .   501 MILTON 19   56
"THE MOST UGLY AND NO OTHER BESIDE RETURND FROM THE BLOODY   560B EXHIBITION ADV   PROSE
  FIELD"
BLOODY WITH THE DAY OF BATTLE . . . .   580D DESC CAT 5   PROSE
ABEL KNEELS ON A BLOODY CLOUD &C . . . .   606D V LAST JUDG/N   PROSE
ABEL KNEELS ON A BLOODY CLOUD DESCRIPTIVE OF THOSE CHURCHES   606D V LAST JUDG/N   PROSE
PILATE HAS BLOODY HANDS THAT NEVER CAN BE CLEANSED . . .   608D V LAST JUDG/N   PROSE
AND ON THE COUCH REPOSD HIS LIMBS TREMBLING FROM THE BLOODY   658 JERUSALEM 32   13
  FIELD
SPREADING IN BLOODY VEINS IN TORMENTS OVER EUROPE & ASIA   692 JERUSALEM 60   3
DANCING AROUND IN HOWLING PAIN CLOTHED IN THE BLOODY VEIL   704 JERUSALEM 67   16
LIKE THE RED SUN UPON THE MOUNTAINS IN THE BLOODY DAY . .   734 JERUSALEM 88   57
IF HEROD YOU WITH BLOODY PREY . . . .   749 EV GOSPEL(B)/N   22
HE HAD SOON BEEN BLOODY CAESAR'S ELF . . . .   752 EV GOSPEL(D)/N   41
PUTTING BACK THE BLOODY SHRINE . . . .   754 EV GOSPEL(E)/N   18
TIS THE BLOODY SHRINE OF WAR . . . .   757 EV GOSPEL(I)/N   23
BLOOM
BLOOM ON EVERY MAIDEN'S CHEEK . . . .   63 SHEPHERD FIRST   6
BLOOMING
I HEARD A BLOOMING YOUTH SINGING A SONG . . . . . .   25 EDW THIRD/PS 3   163
BEAUTIFUL BLOOMING DAMSEL AND H(OPPNER) SAYS . . . .   574B DESC CAT 3   *PROSE
BLOSSOM
DELIGHTS BLOSSOM AROUND NUMBERLESS BEAUTIES BLOW THE . .   37B CONTEMPLATN/PS   PROSE
THE BLOSSOM . . . .   115D THE BLOSSOM/SI   TITLE
A HAPPY BLOSSOM . . . .   115 THE BLOSSOM/SI   3
A HAPPY BLOSSOM . . . .   116 THE BLOSSOM/SI   9

	PAGE	TITLE	LINE

BLOSSOM   (CONTINUED)
```
    ON EACH BUD AND BLOSSOM  . . . . . . . . . . . .   119 NIGHT/SI              15
    BUT A BLOSSOM FAIR OR TRUE  . . . . . . . . . .    166 I FEARD FURY/N         5
    WHEN BUDS & BLOSSOM GROW  . . . . . . . . . . .    169 EARTHS ANSWR/N        17
    TO MAKE THE DESARTS BLOSSOM & THE DEEPS SHRINK TO THEIR    199 AMERICA 8       8
        FOUNTAINS
    BEGAN TO BLOSSOM IN FIERCE PAIN SHOOTING ITS WRITHING BUDS    325 FOUR ZOAS 7    213
    TO THE BLOSSOM OF HOPE FOR A SWEET DECOY  . . . . . .   800 MRS FLAXMAN/L       2
    THE BLOSSOM THE CHIMNEY SWEEPER THE DIVINE IMAGE NIGHT   SUPP LETTER 66A    *PROSE
BLOSSOMING
    BRIGHT SOULS [?ELEMENTS] OF VEGETATIVE LIFE BUDDING AND    274 FOUR ZOAS 1    *  379
        BLOSSOMING
BLOSSOMS
    BLOSSOMS HANG ROUND THE BROWS OF MORNING AND  . . . . .     2 TO AUTUMN/PS        9
    AND BLOSSOMS BLOWN AWAY  . . . . . . . . . . . .   124 SCHOOL BOY/SI         22
    WOULD BLIGHT ALL BLOSSOMS FAIR & TRUE  . . . . . . .   166 I FEARD FURY/N        2
    FOR ALL BLOSSOMS GREW & GREW  . . . . . . . . .    166 I FEARD FURY/N         7
    STRETCHD [ITS] THEIR BLOSSOMS OUT TO ME  . . . . .    167 INFANT SORW/N        24
    [WHO THE FRUIT OR BLOSSOMS SHED]  . . . . . . . .   167 INFANT SORW/N        29
    [[HE] THEY EMBRACD [MY MIRTLE] THE BLOSSOMS BRIGHT]  .    167 INFANT SORW/N    *   32
    [[HE] THEY EMBRACD MY [MIRTLE] BLOSSOMS BRIGHT]  . . .    167 INFANT SORW/N    *   37
    [BLOSSOMS SHOWRING ALL AROUND]  . . . . . . . . .   169 MIRTLE SHADE/N        2
    BLOSSOMS SHOWRING ALL AROUND  . . . . . . . . .    176 TO MY MIRTLE/N         6
    WHEN BUDS AND BLOSSOMS GROW  . . . . . . . . . .   211 EARTHS ANSR/SE        17
    THAT SHAKES THE BLOSSOMS OF MY HOARY HAIR  . . . . .   219 LTT GRL LST/SE       34
    IN THROES OF BIRTH & NOW THE BLOSSOMS FALLING SHINING FRUIT    325 FOUR ZOAS 7    214
    AMONG GREEN LEAVES & BLOSSOMS SWEET  . . . . . . .   423 THE BIRDS/N          20
    THE GRAVE PRODUCD THESE BLOSSOMS SWEET  . . . . . .    442 DEDICATN BLAIR       18
    THE BLOSSOMS OF ETERNAL LIFE  . . . . . . . . .    442 DEDICATN BLAIR       20
BLOT
    . . . AND DARK MISTS ROLL ROUND ME AND BLOT THE WRITING    139 FRENCH REVOLTN   113
        OF GOD
    BESIDE THE OX TO THY HARD FURROW DOES NOT THAT MILD BEAM    195 V DAU ALBION 8    4
        BLOT
    AND DOES THE SUN & MOON BLOT OUT  . . . . . . . .    753 EV GOSPEL(D)/N      100
BLOTS
    WE SHOULD HAVE SEEN BLOTS CALLED MASSES  . . . . . .  439C REMARKS MALKIN    PROSE
    BLOTS WITHOUT FORM AND THEREFORE WITHOUT MEANING   . . .  439C REMARKS MALKIN    PROSE
    THESE BLOTS OF LIGHT AND DARK AS BEING THE RESULT OF LABOUR  439C REMARKS MALKIN   PROSE
    CAST ON THE INSPIRED BY THE TAME HIGH FINISHER OF PALTRY    533 MILTON 41          9
        BLOTS
    TO ITS VICTIM NOTHING BUT BLOTS & BLURS  . . . . . .  595A PUB ADDRESS/N     PROSE
    THE UNORGANIZED BLOTS & BLURS OF RUBENS & TITIAN ARE NOT   596A PUB ADDRESS/N    PROSE
        ART
BLOTTED
    [A LIFE IS BLOTTED OUT & I ALONE REMAIN POSSESSD    267 FOUR ZOAS 1        112
        WITH FEARS]
    THE HAND OF URIZEN IS UPON ME BECAUSE I BLOTTED OUT  . . .   282 FOUR ZOAS 2    106
    I HAVE BLOTTED OUT FROM LIGHT & LIVING THE DOVE &    290 FOUR ZOAS 2        391
        NIGHTINGALE
    OF MAN I MADE THEE WHEN I BLOTTED MAN FROM LIFE & LIGHT    336 FOUR ZOAS 7B    117
    O BE THOU BLOTTED OUT THOU SUN THAT RAISEDST ME TO TROUBLE    368 FOUR ZOAS 9    414
    REYNOLDS & GAINSBOROUGH BLOTTED & BLURRED ONE AGAINST THE    445C ANNO REYNOLDS   MARG
    ALL THE BEAUTIES PICKD OUT [BUT] & BLURRD & BLOTTED  . . .   595C PUB ADDRESS/N  *PROSE
    BENEATH LOS'S HAMMER THAT LIFE MAY NOT BE BLOTTED OUT  . .   737 JERUSALEM 90     51
BLOTTING
    PROTECTRESS OF BAD THAT IS BLOTTING AND BLURRING ART  .  562B DESC CAT ADV    PROSE
    ALTHOUGH MOLESTED CONTINUALLY BY BLOTTING AND BLURRING  . .   581B DESC CAT 6    PROSE
BLOW
    AND THE FIRST BLOW DECIDES  . . . . . . . . . .    14 GWIN KING/PS        106
    BLOW UP THE SLUGGISH INTO ARDOUR AND  . . . . . . .    25 EDW THIRD/PS 3      180
    I SEE THEE BLOW THY GOLDEN TRUMPET WHILE  . . . . . .    26 EDW THIRD/PS 3      208
    TILL ENGLAND BLOW THE TRUMP OF VICTORY  . . . . . .    31 EDW THIRD/PS 5       65
    DELIGHTS BLOSSOM AROUND NUMBERLESS BEAUTIES BLOW THE  .   37B CONTEMPLATN/PS   PROSE
    AND LET THY MASTER DO THE DEED ONE BLOW OF THAT STRONG ARM   38C SAMSON/PS      PROSE
    BLOW BOISTEROUS WIND STERN WINTER FROWN  . . . . . .    64 SHEPHERD OLD          9
    FOUR WINGED HERALDS MOUNT THE FURIOUS BLASTS & BLOW THEIR    205 AMERICA CANC C    14
        TRUMPS
    THE TRUMP OF THE LAST DOOM BUT HE COULD NOT BLOW THE IRON    243 EUROPE 13         2
        TUBE
    LOS SAW THE WOUND OF HIS BLOW HE SAW HE PITID HE WEPT  . .   274 FOUR ZOAS 1   *  351
    THE BELLOWS BEGAN TO BLOW & THE LIONS OF URIZEN STOOD ROUND    281 FOUR ZOAS 2     32
        THE ANVIL
    BUT ALL THE FURNACES WERE OUT & THE BELLOWS HAD CEAST TO    305 FOUR ZOAS 5       17
        BLOW
    FOUR WINGED HERALDS MOUNT THE FURIOUS BLASTS & BLOW THEIR    319 FOUR ZOAS 6      310
        TRUMPS
    . . . THUNDEROUS CLARIONS BLOW  . . . . . . . . .    343 FOUR ZOAS 8         88
    THUNDERING THE HAMMERS BEAT & THE BELLOWS BLOW LOUD  . . .   509 MILTON 24         52
    ROUND FROM HEAVEN TO EARTH DOWN FALLING WITH HEAVY BLOW    636 JERUSALEM 16       12
    THE BLOW OF HIS HAMMER IS JUSTICE THE SWING OF HIS HAMMER    734 JERUSALEM 88      49
        MERCY
    HIS HEAVD HAMMER HE SWUNG IT ROUND & AT ONE BLOW  . . . .   738 JERUSALEM 91      43
    HEALTH & HOW YOU HAVE ESCAPED THE DOUBLE BLOW BOTH  . . .   833D LETTER 33      PROSE
BLOWD
    BLOWD IN THE MORN IN EVENING DIED  . . . . . . . .   220 TO TIRZAH/SE          6
    NAMD NEWTON HE SIEZD THE TRUMP & BLOWD THE ENORMOUS BLAST    243 EUROPE 13          5
BLOWN    SEE FULL-BLOWN
    THE FLOWERS OF IMMORTALITY ARE BLOWN  . . . . . . .    31 EDW THIRD/PS 5       36
    THE FLOWER WAS PLUCKD & YET IT WAS NOT BLOWN  . . . . .   43C WOE CRIED MUSE   PROSE
    AND BLOSSOMS BLOWN AWAY  . . . . . . . . . . . .   124 SCHOOL BOY/SI         22
    . . . A FEAR AND A WITHRING BLIGHT BLOWN BY THE NORTH  . .   141 FRENCH REVOLTN   162
```

```
                                                              PAGE    TITLE        LINE
BLOWN    (CONTINUED)
     THE POOR PARSONS WITH WIND LIKE A BLOWN BLADDER SWELL   .  .  179 LIT VAGABOND/N     5
     THE STARS CONS"MD LIKE A LAMP BLOWN OUT & IN THEIR STEAD     379 FOUR ZOAS 9    *  829
       BEHOLDS
     BLOWN BACK THEY [MO] BLIND THE [MOCKERS] MOCKING EYE   .  .  418 MOCK ON/N      *   7
     THE WEEDS OF DEATH INWRAP HIS HANDS & FEET BLOWN INCESSANT   741 JERUSALEM 94       5
BLOWS     SEE FLY BLOWS
     THAT THE HIRELING BLOWS INTO MY EAR   .  .  .  .  .  .  .  . 166 WHY CARE FOR/N     4
     MELT INTO FURROWS WINTER BLOWS HIS BELLOWS ICE & SNOW   .  . 276 FOUR ZOAS 1      424
     AND LOS FORMD ANVILS OF IRON PETRIFIC FOR HIS BLOWS   .  .  . 301 FOUR ZOAS 4      168
     [THE] AND THE WIND BLOWS IT BACK AGAIN   .  .  .  .  .  .  . 418 MOCK ON/N      *   4
     THE WIND BLOWS HEAVY LOUD THEY THUNDER THRO THE DARKSOM SKY  512 MILTON 26          8
     HE STAMPS AROUND THE ANVIL BEATING BLOWS OF STERN DESPAIR    629 JERUSALEM 10      24
     TO PROTECT FROM THE GIANT BLOWS IN THE SPORTS OF INTELLECT   677 JERUSALEM 48      15
     AND LOS FIXES THEM ON HIS ANVIL INCESSANT HIS BLOWS   .  .   690 JERUSALEM 58      16
     HE FIXES THEM WITH STRONG BLOWS PLACING THE STONES   .  .    690 JERUSALEM 58      17
       & TIMBERS
     TO SEE JERUSALEM DEFACE HER LINEAMENTS WITH BITTER BLOWS     693 JERUSALEM 60      46
     I AM DEFACED WITH BLOWS & WITH THE DIRT OF THE PRISON    .   695 JERUSALEM 62       5
     WALKS ROUND LOUD HIS THREATS LOUD HIS BLOWS FALL    .  .  .  719 JERUSALEM 78       4
     THESE ARE THE DEMONSTRATIONS OF LOS & THE BLOWS OF          737 JERUSALEM 90      57
       MY MIGHTY HAMMER
     AND EAR UNBINDING IN DIRE PAIN WITH MANY BLOWS    .  .  .  . 738 JERUSALEM 91      46
     NOT STEPPED OUT AT THE GATE & PUTTING ASIDE HIS BLOWS   .  . 827A LETTER 28      PROSE
BLUBBERS
     ("OR THE PIETIST WHO CRAWLS GROANS BLUBBERS") I HATE        67D ANNO LAVATER     MARG
       CRAWLERS
BLUE
     BLUE CURTAINS OF THE SKY SCATTER THY SILVER DEW   .  .  .  .   3 EVNING STAR/PS     6
     OR THE BLUE REGIONS OF THE AIR   .  .  .  .  .  .  .  .  .  .  10 TO MUSES/PS       7
     LET WAR STAIN THE BLUE HEAVENS WITH BLOODY BANNERS    .  .    31 EDW THIRD/PS 5    63
     CASTING HER BLUE EYES OVER THE GREEN OCEAN   .  .  .  .  .  .  33 EDW THIRD/PS 6    56
     THE CHILDREN WALKING TWO & TWO IN GREY & BLUE & GREEN    .    59 HOLY THURS/IM      2
     THE CHILDREN WALKING TWO & TWO IN RED & BLUE & GREEN    .  . 121 HOLY THURS/SI      2
     THE ANGEL HEARING THIS BECAME ALMOST BLUE   .  .  .  .  .  . 158B MARRIAGE HH 22  PROSE
     BLUE & CHANGING IN TEARS AND BITTER   .  .  .  .  .  .  .  . 250 AHANIA 3           3
     A WHITE LAKE ON THE DARK BLUE AIR   .  .  .  .  .  .  .  .  . 252 AHANIA 4          14
     SLEPT AS A BIRD IN THE BLUE SHELL THAT SOON SHALL BURST     273 FOUR ZOAS 1      350
       AWAY
     .  .  . THE BLUE SMOKE ROLLD TO REVIVE   .  .  .  .  .  .  . 285 FOUR ZOAS 2      192
     .  .  . BLUE (SULPHUREOUS) FIRE FROM THE FLAME   .  .  .  .  295 FOUR ZOAS 3    * 146
     A SHADOW BLUE OBSCURE & DISMAL LIKE A STATUE OF LEAD    .  . 299 FOUR ZOAS 4       65
     A SHADOW BLUE OBSCURE & DISMAL FROM THE BREATHING NOSTRILS   300 FOUR ZOAS 4      105
     THOU TERRIBLE WOMAN CLAD IN BLUE WHOSE STRONG ATTRACTIVE     312 FOUR ZOAS 6       13
       POWER
     INTO THE BLUE EXPANSE & I INVENTED WITH LABORIOUS ART   .  . 312 FOUR ZOAS 6       31
     HIS NAKED LIMBS GLITTRING UPON THE DARK BLUE SKY HIS KNEES   334 FOUR ZOAS 7B   *  42
     LIFT UP THY BLUE EYES VALA & PUT ON THY SAPPHIRE SHOES   .  . 337 FOUR ZOAS 7B     191
     DOTH ENION AVOID THE SIGHT OF THY BLUE WATRY EYES    .  .  . 339 FOUR ZOAS 7B     230
     [SILVERY WHITE SHINING UPON THE DARK BLUE SKY IN SILENCE]    341 FOUR ZOAS 8    *  11
     HE LIFTS THE BLUE LAMPS OF HIS EYES & CRIES WITH HEAVENLY    359 FOUR ZOAS 9       97
       VOICE
     FROM THE BLUE WALLS OF HEAVEN STARRY JINGLING ORNAMENTED     365 FOUR ZOAS 9      296
     OPEN THE ORBS OF THY BLUE EYES & SMILE UPON MY GARDENS       371 FOUR ZOAS 9      522
     DOTH ENION AVOID THE SIGHT OF THY BLUE HEAVENLY EYES    .  . 371 FOUR ZOAS 9      531
     A BLUE FLUID EXUDED IN SINEWS HARDENING IN THE ABYSS    .  . 483 MILTON 3          35
     BUT SAW THEM NOT FOR THE BLUE MUNDANE SHELL INCLOSD THEM IN  504 MILTON 21         30
     REECHOING AGAINST THE LOVELY BLUE & SHINING HEAVENLY SHELL   520 MILTON 31         33
     & JUSTICE CAIPHAS HAS A BLUE FLAME LIKE A MITER ON HIS HEAD  608D V LAST JUDG/N  PROSE
     AS SUDDENLY EMERGING FROM THE BLUE SKY FOR THEIR HELP   .  . 610D V LAST JUDG/N  PROSE
     LIKE A DOVE IS SURROUNDED BY A BLUE HEAVEN   .  .  .  .  .  . 613B V LAST JUDG/N  PROSE
     FROM THE BLUE MUNDANE SHELL REACHING TO THE VEGETATIVE       633 JERUSALEM 13      33
       EARTH
     FROM THE BLUE MUNDANE SHELL EVEN TO THE EARTH OF VEGETATION  637 JERUSALEM 16      25
     WITH A BLUE SKY SPREAD OVER WITH WINGS AND A MILD MOON   .  . 642 JERUSALEM 19      44
     .  .  . ON ONE-ANOTHER FOR ABHORRENCE THE BLUE   .  .  .  .  647 JERUSALEM 24       7
     SO LOS SPOKE BUT WHEN HE SAW [PALE] BLUE DEATH IN ALBION'S   664 JERUSALEM 37      10
       FEET
     THEY STAIND HIM WITH POISONOUS BLUE THEY INWOVE HIM IN       699 JERUSALEM 65       9
       CRUEL ROOTS
     LIFT UP THY BLUE EYES VALA & PUT ON THY SAPPHIRE SHOES   .  . 700 JERUSALEM 65      37
     WITH A BLUE SKY SPREAD OVER WITH WINGS   .  .  .  .  .  .  . 816 HAPPINESS/L        3
BLUNDERED
     BLUNDERED OVER NOVELS AND CATCHPENNY TRIFLES OF BOOKSELLERS  574A DESC CAT 3      PROSE
BLUNDERER'S
     ("BLUNDERER'S FRIENDSHIP THAN CALUMNIATOR'S ENMITY") I      69C ANNO LAVATER     MARG
       DOUBT THIS
BLUNDERING
     EXCEPT BY BLUNDERING IGNORANCE TILL AFTER VANDYKE'S TIME     566C DESC CAT 2      PROSE
     DIS-ARRANGED IMITATIONS AND BLUNDERING MISAPPLIED COPIES     585D DESC CAT 15     PROSE
     AS TO SUPPOSE THAT HIS BLUNDERING BLURS CAN BE MADE OUT &    592B PUB ADDRESS/N   PROSE
BLUNT
     BISHOP WILLIAM DAGWORTH'S MAN PETER BLUNT A COMMON           17C EDW THIRD/PS    TITLE
       SOLDIER
     ENTER PETER BLUNT   .  .  .  .  .  .  .  .  .  .  .  .  .  .  29B EDW THIRD/PS 4   PROSE
     THE GLITTERING DISSIMULATION ACHILLES' WRATH IS BLUNT ABUSE  384D ANNO WATSON     MARG
BLUR
     INSIGNIFICANT MUCH LESS AN INSIGNIFICANT BLUR OR MARK   .  . 611C V LAST JUDG/N  PROSE
BLURRD
     ALL THE BEAUTIES PICKD OUT [BUT] & BLURRD & BLOTTED    .  .  . 595C PUB ADDRESS/N *PROSE
BLURRED
     REYNOLDS & GAINSBOROUGH BLOTTED & BLURRED ONE AGAINST THE    445C ANNO REYNOLDS   MARG
```

238

                                              PAGE   TITLE   LINE
BLURRER
     AS THEY WERE THE WORKS OF A CORRECT MIND & NO BLURRER   . . 553B BELLS WEEKLY/N   MARG
BLURRING
     PROTECTRESS OF BAD THAT IS BLOTTING AND BLURRING ART   . . 562B DESC CAT ADV   PROSE
     ALTHOUGH MOLESTED CONTINUALLY BY BLOTTING AND BLURRING . . 581B DESC CAT 6   PROSE
BLURS
     AS TO SUPPOSE THAT HIS BLUNDERING BLURS CAN BE MADE OUT &   592B PUB ADDRESS/N   PROSE
     TO ITS VICTIM NOTHING BUT BLOTS & BLURS . . . . 595A PUB ADDRESS/N   PROSE
     THE UNORGANIZED BLOTS & BLURS OF RUBENS & TITIAN ARE NOT   596A PUB ADDRESS/N   PROSE
          ART
BLUSH
     AGAINST FRANCE IS IT NOT TO STATE RELIGION BLUSH FOR SHAME   385C ANNO WATSON   MARG
     AND WHAT IS THE SECOND WITH MOST MODEST BLUSH . . . . . 553 ASKD PRIGG/N   9
     SOME BLUSH AT WHAT OTHERS CAN SEE NO CRIME IN . . . . . 555 BLAKES APL/N 1   8
     SOME BLUSH AT WHAT OTHERS CAN SEE NO CRIME IN . . . . . 555 BLAKES APL/N 2   3
     SOME BLUSH AT WHAT OTHERS CAN SEE NO CRIME IN . . . . . 595 BLAKES APOL/PA   5
BLUSHD
     SHE BLUSHD SO RED WITH SIDE-LONG GLANCE . . . . 16 BLIND-MANS/PS   15
     THEN THE MORN BLUSHD ROSY RED . . . . 182 THE ANGEL/N   10
     THE MOON AT THAT SIGHT BLUSHD SCARLET RED . . . . . . 187 WHEN KLOPSTK/N   11
     THEN THE MORN BLUSHD ROSY RED . . . . 214 THE ANGEL/SE   10
     THE MORNING BLUSHD FIERY RED   . . . . 753 EV GOSPEL(E)/N   3
BLUSHES
     IN BLUSHES LIKE THE MORNING AND HIS SCALY ARMOUR SOFTENING   269 FOUR ZOAS 1   186
     THE RIPE FRUIT BLUSHES INTO JOY IN HEAVEN'S ETERNAL HALLS   324 FOUR ZOAS 7   176
     IN BLUSHES LIKE THE MORNING . . . . 381 FOUR ZOAS AD 5   6
     NOR ONCE BLUSHES TO OWN TO THE REST OF THE FAIR . . . . 428 MARY   11
     A DAMP COLD CAME OER HER HER BLUSHES ALL FLED . . . . . 428 MARY   19
BLUSHING
     AND BLUSHING ROSES FOR MY BROW . . . .   6 HOW SWEET/PS   6
     THE BLUSHING BANK IS ALL MY CARE . . . .   15 BLIND-MANS/PS   3
     THRICE [AGAIN] BLUSHING HE REDEND ROUND . . . . 187 WHEN KLOPSTK/N *   29
     SWEET SMILING PESTILENCE I SEE THY BLUSHING LIGHT . . .   244 EUROPE 14   12
     [BEAUTY ALL BLUSHING WITH DESIRE MOCKING HER FELL DESPAIR]   269 FOUR ZOAS 1   189
     AND ENITHARMON TINCTURD IT WITH BEAMS OF BLUSHING LOVE . . 332 FOUR ZOAS 7   468
     BEAUTY ALL BLUSHING WITH DESIRE A SELF ENJOYING WONDER . . 381 FOUR ZOAS AD 5   9
     [AND] YORKSHIRE JACK HEMP & GENTLE BLUSHING DAW . . . . 537 AND HIS LEGS/N   20
BOADICEA
     BOADICEA INSPIRING THE BRITONS AGAINST THE ROMANS . . . 208D SUBJCTS HIST/N   TITLE
     BOADICEA CONWENNA ESTRILD GWINEFRID IGNOGE CAMBEL . . . 281 FOUR ZOAS 2   62
     GWENDOLEN & CAMBEL WHO IS BOADICEA THEY GO ABROAD & RETURN   710 JERUSALEM 71   23
     TO BROCKLEY HILLS ACROSS THE THAMES HE WITH DOUBLE BOADICEA 736 JERUSALEM 90   24
BOAR
     WHERE ROAMS THE LION WOLF & BOAR . . . . 426 MENTAL TRAVLER *   84
BOARD
     AND PLENTY CROWNED HIS BOARD BELOVED REVERED OF MAN . . . 39C SAMSON/PS   PROSE
     AND SOME GOATS ON BOARD THE MISSIONARY SHIP STRIPPED   . . 581C DESC CAT 7   PROSE
     HAS CONTINUED A BOARD OVER THE GATEWAY   . . . . 590A CHAUCER 2   PROSE
     A FESTAL BOARD THE BARD SINGING OWEN'S PRAISE . . . . . SUPP ILLUS GRAY   *TITLE
BOARDING SCHOOL
     TO UNDERSTAND THOSE THINGS WHICH A BOARDING SCHOOL MISS   814D LETTER 23   PROSE
BOARS
     LIONS BOARS WOLVES ALL HOWLING FLEE . . . . 427 MENTAL TRAVLER   99
BOAST
     WITH CERTAIN VICTORY AND TIS MY BOAST . . . .   23 EDW THIRD/PS 3   87
     CAN SUCH A TONGUE BOAST OF THE LIVING WATERS OR TAKE IN   485 MILTON 5   34
     & THEY BOAST THAT IT IS ITS FOUNDATION   . . . . 617B V LAST JUDG/N   PROSE
     BOAST OF HIGH THINGS WITH HUMBLE TONE . . . .   751 EV GOSPEL(D)/N   3
     OR OF CHRIST & HIS FATHER ITS ALL A BOAST . . . . . . 752 EV GOSPEL(D)/N   46
BOASTED
     TO BE BOASTED OF & THEREFORE I CANNOT FEEL DEPRESSD . . . 821C LETTER 25   PROSE
BOASTFUL
     TO TRAMPLE THE CORN FIELDS IN BOASTFUL NEIGHINGS . . . . 338 FOUR ZOAS 7B   203
     TO TRAMPLE THE CORN FIELDS IN BOASTFUL NEIGHINGS . . . . 700 JERUSALEM 65   49
BOASTING
     A CERTAIN PORTRAIT PAINTER SAID TO ME IN A BOASTING WAY   592D PUB ADDRESS/N   PROSE
BOASTS
     THUS SWEDENBORG BOASTS THAT WHAT HE WRITES IS NEW THO . . 157C MARRIAGE HH 21   PROSE
     EXPENSIVE ADVERTIZING BOASTS THAT THEY MAKE OF SUCH WORKS   480C MILTON 1   PROSE
BOAT
     AS EVERY MASTER OF A BOAT IS BUT THIS DOES NOT MAKE HIM A   575C DESC CAT 3   PROSE
BOAZ
     JESUS SEATED BETWEEN THE TWO PILLARS JACHIN & BOAZ . . . 606B V LAST JUDG/N   PROSE
BOB
     FOR SORROW THAT [YOUR] OUR FRIEND BOB SCREWMUCH S GONE . . 537 AND HIS LEGS/N   47
BOBBINS
     BONES & SINEWS ALL STRINGS & BOBBINS LIKE A WEAVER'S LOOM   875B LETTER 81   PROSE
BODIES
     THE MIGHTY DEAD GIANT BODIES STREAMING BLOOD   . . . . . 32 EDW THIRD/PS 6   35
     YOUR SOULS FOR FLIGHT YOUR BODIES FOR THE EARTH . . . .   34 WAR SONG/PS   7
     ENDEAVORING TO INCORPORATE THEIR SOULS WITH THEIR BODIES   45C ISLAND MOON 1   PROSE
     AND THESE BLACK BODIES AND THIS SUN-BURNT FACE   . . . . 125 LIT BLK BOY/SI   15
     . . . THEIR BODIES JOIN IN BURNING ANGUISH]   . . . . 269 FOUR ZOAS 1   181
     [THEY HAD WHICH CLOTHD THEIR BODIES LIKE A GARMENT OF SOFT   341 FOUR ZOAS 8   10
          DOWN]
     BODIES OF VEGETATION SINGING LULLING CADENCES TO DRIVE AWAY 342 FOUR ZOAS 8   38
     ALSO THE VEGETATED BODIES WHICH ENITHARMON WOVE . . . . 342 FOUR ZOAS 8   54
     AND WOVE THEM BODIES CALLING THEM HER BELOVD SONS   345 FOUR ZOAS 8   184
          & DAUGHTERS
     RECIEVD HER IN THE DARKNING SOUTH THEIR BODIES LOST THEY   358 FOUR ZOAS 9   *   26
          STOOD
     THEIR BODIES BURIED IN THE RUINS OF THE UNIVERSE . . . . 358 FOUR ZOAS 9   30

BODIES   (CONTINUED)
OPENING HIS RIFTED ROCKS MINGLING [THEIR BODIES] . . . .   . 381 FOUR ZOAS AD 5 *   1
ALSO THE VEGETATED BODIES WHICH ENITHARMON WOVE IN HER   382 FOUR ZOAS AD 6   24
    LOOMS
THOSE THAT PUT THEIR BODIES TO ENDURE ARE FOOLS   . . 408C ANNO BACON   MARG
IN THEIR ETERNAL SPHERES NOW HUMAN THO THEIR BODIES REMAIN   498 MILTON 17   4
    CLOSD
TREMBLE IN SPECTROUS BODIES CONTINUALLY DAY AND NIGHT   . . 507 MILTON 23   43
BUT NOW THEY STAND IN EVERY BODIES WAY   . . . . 546 ANOTHER/N 2   4
WITH REAL BODIES WOULD DO WELL TO CONSIDER THAT THE VENUS   576C DESC CAT 4   PROSE
AND IN THEIR SPIRITUAL BODIES OPPOSE THE SPIRITS OF THOSE   582A DESC CAT 8   PROSE
AND CONCUPISCENCE THEY POSSESS THEMSELVES OF THE BODIES   582A DESC CAT 8   PROSE
FOR VALA PRODUCD THE BODIES JERUSALEM GAVE THE SOULS   . . 640 JERUSALEM 18   7
AND THE MURDERD BODIES OF HER LITTLE ONES ARE SCOTLAND   653 JERUSALEM 29   21
    AND WALES
WHILE THE DAUGHTERS OF ALBION DIVIDED LUVAH INTO THREE   661 JERUSALEM 34   46
    BODIES
AND THE BODIES IN WHICH ALL ANIMALS & VEGETATIONS THE EARTH 679 JERUSALEM 49   13
    & HEAVEN
THEY BECAME SPECTRES & THEIR HUMAN BODIES WERE REPOSED   . . 714 JERUSALEM 74   8
& IN WHICH WE SHALL LIVE IN OUR ETERNAL OR IMAGINATIVE   717A JERUSALEM 77   PROSE
    BODIES
WHEN THESE VEGETABLE MORTAL BODIES ARE NO MORE   . . . . 717A JERUSALEM 77   PROSE
IN GENERAL FOUND GREAT BODIES TO BE THEY WERE MUCH PLEASED   850C LETTER 49   PROSE
BODILY
DEMONSTRATION IS ONLY BY BODILY SENSES   . . . . 91C ANNO SWED LOVE   MARG
THROUGH HIS NATURAL OR BODILY ORGANS . . . . 97A NAT RELIGION 1   PROSE
IS NECESSARY FROM THE CONFINED NATURE OF BODILY SENSATION   98D ALL RELIGIONS   PROSE
INTO THIS BODILY HOUSE TO TEND MY FLOCKS IN MY PLEASANT   369 FOUR ZOAS 9   470
    GARDEN
IVE ALL BUT RICHES BODILY   . . . .   558 I ROSE UP AT/N   12
WHAT ARE THE PAINS OF HELL BUT IGNORANCE BODILY LUST   . . 717B JERUSALEM 77   PROSE
I WISHD TO TAKE WITH ME A BODILY PARDON   . . . . 753 EV GOSPEL(D)/N   90
BODY   SEE ANY BODY   (FOR EVERY BODY SEE EVERY)
LOVE & WISDOM AS IT DOES BETWEEN BODY & SPIRIT   . . . . 90D ANNO SWED LOVE   MARG
WHILE IN THE BODY   . . . .   91B ANNO SWED LOVE   MARG
("INFLUX FROM ABOVE ") THIS IS WHILE IN THE BODY   . . . 94A ANNO SWED LOVE   MARG
IN THE BODY WAS ONLY CONVERSANT WITH NATURAL SUBSTANCES   94A ANNO SWED LOVE   MARG
AND THAT THE BODY OR OUTWARD FORM . . . .   98B ALL RELIGIONS   PROSE
THERE TAKE THE BODY CURSED SONS & MAY THE HEAVENS RAIN   100 TIRIEL 1   43
    WRATH
AND FED ON THE BODY SHE REFUSD TO BE WHORE TO THE MINISTER   135 FRENCH REVOLTN   37
    . . .
IS THE BODY DISEASD WHEN THE MEMBERS ARE HEALTHFUL . . .   142 FRENCH REVOLTN   182
OR EXTERNAL OF HEAVEN & IS OF THE BODY OF THE LORD   . . SUPP ANNO SWED HELL * MARG
THAT MAN HAS TWO REAL EXISTING PRINCIPLES VIZ A BODY &   149C MARRIAGE HH 4   PROSE
    A SOUL
THAT ENERGY CALLD EVIL IS ALONE FROM THE BODY   . . . . 149C MARRIAGE HH 4   PROSE
MAN HAS NO BODY DISTINCT FROM HIS SOUL   . . . . 149D MARRIAGE HH 4   PROSE
FOR THAT CALLD BODY IS A PORTION OF SOUL DISCERND BY   . . 149D MARRIAGE HH 4   PROSE
ENERGY IS THE ONLY LIFE AND IS FROM THE BODY AND   . . . 149D MARRIAGE HH 4   PROSE
A DEAD BODY REVENGES NOT INJURIES   . . . . 151B MARRIAGE HH 7   PROSE
FIRST THE NOTION THAT MAN HAS A BODY DISTINCT FROM HIS SOUL 154C MARRIAGE HH 14   PROSE
THEN I FLUNG MYSELF WITH HIM DIRECTLY INTO THE BODY OF   156D MARRIAGE HH 17   PROSE
    THE SUN
BY PLUCKING OFF FIRST ONE LIMB AND THEN ANOTHER TILL THE   157B MARRIAGE HH 17   PROSE
    BODY
& I IN MY HAND BROUGHT THE SKELETON OF A BODY   . . . . 157B MARRIAGE HH 17   PROSE
BLAKE WAS GIVING HIS BODY EASE   . . . .   187 WHEN KLOPSTK/N   7
THAT FROM HIS BODY IT NEER COULD BE PARTED   . . . . . 187 WHEN KLOPSTK/N   19
IT IS RAISED A SPIRITUAL BODY   . . . . 220C TO TIRZAH/SE   TITLE
THEN LEFT A NOISOM BODY   . . . .   236 URIZEN 28   2
WITH THE BODY OF THE SUN   . . . .   250 AHANIA 2   48
WITHOUT THE BODY OF MAN AN EXUDATION FROM HIS SICKNING   277 FOUR ZOAS 1   463
    LIMBS
TO ENION & HIS BODY FELL THARMAS BEHELD HIM FALL   . . . . 279 FOUR ZOAS 1   531
FIRST HE BEHELD THE BODY OF MAN PALE COLD THE HORRORS OF   280 FOUR ZOAS 2   11
    DEATH
THE MAIDEN'S FATHER & HER MOTHER FAINTING OVER THE BODY   281 FOUR ZOAS 2   51
TO BIND THE BODY OF MAN TO HEAVEN FROM FALLING INTO THE   287 FOUR ZOAS 2   267
    ABYSS
HOWL THOU OVER THE BODY OF DEATH TIS THINE BUT IF AMONG   288 FOUR ZOAS 2   312
    THE VIRGINS
IN LOS'S ARMS HOWLINGS BEGAN OVER THE BODY OF DEATH   . . 289 FOUR ZOAS 2   335
THEY STROVE TOGETHER ABOVE THE BODY WHERE VALA WAS INCLOSD   294 FOUR ZOAS 3   80
AND THE DARK BODY OF [MAN] ALBION LEFT PROSTRATE . . . . .   294 FOUR ZOAS 3   81
I ROLL MY FLOODS OVER HIS BODY MY BILLOWS & WAVES PASS   301 FOUR ZOAS 4   133
    OVER HIM
THE COUNCIL OF GOD ON HIGH WATCHING OVER THE BODY   . . 304 FOUR ZOAS 4   247
THAT DREW THE BODY OF MAN FROM HEAVEN INTO THIS DARK ABYSS   306 FOUR ZOAS 5   47
THE BODY OF MAN IS GIVEN TO ME I SEEK IN VAIN TO DESTROY   313 FOUR ZOAS 6   60
[SO SAYING] AND ORC HE BEGAN TO ORGANIZE A SERPENT BODY   324 FOUR ZOAS 7   152
MY MASCULINE SPIRIT SCORNING THE FRAIL BODY ISSUD FORTH   327 FOUR ZOAS 7   * 290
THAT BODY I CREATED THEN SHALL WE UNITE AGAIN IN BLISS   . . 327 FOUR ZOAS 7   301
[TO BE ONE BODY & ONE SPIRIT WITH HIM] NOT SO   . . . . 327 FOUR ZOAS 7   309
[THY] THAT MORTAL BODY & BY SELF ANNIHILATION BACK   328 FOUR ZOAS 7   344
    RETURNING
BUT IF THOU DOST REFUSE ANOTHER BODY WILL BE PREPARED   . . 329 FOUR ZOAS 7   357
THAT BODY HE CREATED BUT IN VAIN FOR LOS PERFORMD   . . 329 FOUR ZOAS 7   376
FOR WITHOUT A CREATED BODY THE SPECTRE IS ETERNAL DEATH   330 FOUR ZOAS 7   410
WHO NOW BEGINNETH TO PUT OFF THE DARK SATANIC BODY   . . 346 FOUR ZOAS 8   196
ASSUME THE DARK SATANIC BODY IN THE VIRGIN'S WOMB   . . 347 FOUR ZOAS 8   241

		PAGE	TITLE	LINE

BODY   (CONTINUED)

. . . TO [?REND THE VEIL OF MYSTERY] GIVE HIS VEGETATED BODY	348	FOUR ZOAS 8	* 265
TO BE CUT OFF & SEPARATED THAT THE SPIRITUAL BODY MAY BE REVEALD	348	FOUR ZOAS 8	267
VALA DRAWN DOWN INTO A VEGETATED BODY NOW TRIUMPHANT . .	348	FOUR ZOAS 8	280
[SHE] JERUSALEM SAW THE BODY DEAD UPON THE CROSS SHE FLED AWAY	349	FOUR ZOAS 8	331
LOS TOOK THE BODY FROM THE CROSS JERUSALEM WEEPING OVER	349	FOUR ZOAS 8	338
LISTEN TO HER WHOSE EYES BEHOLD THE DARK BODY OF CORRUPTIBLE DEATH	354	FOUR ZOAS 8	505
NOR SILENT MOON NOR ALL THE HOSTS OF HEAVEN MOVE IN HIS BODY	354	FOUR ZOAS 8	508
TILL MAN SHALL LEAVE A CORRUPTIBLE BODY HE FAMISHD HEARS HIM GROAN	354	FOUR ZOAS 8	524
COLLECTING UP THE SCATTERD PORTIONS OF HIS IMMORTAL BODY	355	FOUR ZOAS 8	562
[AND PLACING IN THE SEPULCHER THE BODY WHICH SHE HAD TAKEN]	356	FOUR ZOAS 8	586
AND LOS & ENITHARMON TOOK THE BODY OF THE LAMB	356	FOUR ZOAS 8	593
OVER THE SEPULCHER & OVER THE CRUCIFIED BODY	357	FOUR ZOAS 9	2
THEIR SPIRIT FROM THEIR BODY TERRIFIED AT NON EXISTENCE	357	FOUR ZOAS 9	5
FOR SUCH THEY DEEMD THE DEATH OF THE BODY LOS HIS VEGETABLE HANDS	357	FOUR ZOAS 9	6
SORROWFUL THAT HE COULD NOT PUT OFF HIS NEW RISEN BODY . .	366	FOUR ZOAS 9	355
HIS BODY WAS REDEEMD TO BE PERMANENT THRO THE MERCY DIVINE	366	FOUR ZOAS 9	* 357
HIS BODY BENT HIS ARMS & KNEES	419	I SAW A MONK/N	17
MY BENT BODY MOCKS AT THEIR TORTURING PAIN	419	I SAW A MONK/N	35
[ROUND THEIR BODY WHEN THEY CHOSE]	422	BENEATH AD/N	2
HIS BODY BENT HIS ARMS & KNEES	430	GREY MONK	7
MY BENT BODY MOCKS THEIR TORTURING PAIN	430	GREY MONK	20
WHICH IS THE DIVINE BODY OF THE LORD JESUS BLESSED FOR EVER	482	MILTON 3	4
GLORYING TO INVOLVE ALBION'S BODY IN FIRES OF ETERNAL WAR	493	MILTON 13	6
FOR THEN THE BODY OF DEATH WAS PERFECTED IN HYPOCRITIC HOLINESS	494	MILTON 13	25
WHEN WILL THE RESURRECTION COME TO DELIVER THE SLEEPING BODY	495	MILTON 14	17
IN ONE WONDERFUL BODY AND HE ENTERD INTO IT	496	MILTON 14	38
AS WHEN A MAN DREAMS HE REFLECTS NOT THAT HIS BODY SLEEPS	496	MILTON 15	1
ENTERING THEY GAVE HIM STILL PERCEPTIONS OF HIS SLEEPING BODY	496	MILTON 15	4
HIS DICTATE AND HIS BODY WAS THE ROCK SINAI THAT BODY .	498	MILTON 17	14
FOR THAT PORTION NAMD THE ELECT THE SPECTROUS BODY OF MILTON	502	MILTON 20	20
BROODED OVER HIS BODY IN HOREB AGAINST THE RESURRECTION	502	MILTON 20	22
UPON THE BODY OF ALBION FOR THIS HE IS COME BEHOLD IT WRITTEN	505	MILTON 22	34
LAZARUS WHO IS THE VEHICULAR BODY OF ALBION THE REDEEMD	508	MILTON 24	27
BY MARTYRDOMS TO SUFFER TO WATCH OVER THE SLEEPING BODY	508	MILTON 24	29
THE SOULS DESCENDING TO THE BODY WAIL ON THE RIGHT HAND	512	MILTON 26	16
OF LOS & THOSE DELIVERD FROM THE BODY ON THE LEFT HAND . .	512	MILTON 26	17
AND EVERY GENERATED BODY IN ITS INWARD FORM	512	MILTON 26	31
AND HE WHOSE GATES ARE OPEND IN THOSE REGIONS OF HIS BODY	524	MILTON 34	17
SATAN HEARD TREMBLING ROUND HIS BODY HE INCIRCLED IT .	531	MILTON 39	16
HOWLING IN HIS SPECTRE ROUND HIS BODY HUNGRING TO DEVOUR	531	MILTON 39	18
THIS IS A FALSE BODY AN INCRUSTATION OVER MY IMMORTAL .	533	MILTON 40	35
AROSE AROUND ALBION'S BODY JESUS WEPT & WALKED FORTH .	534	MILTON 42	19
TO RESURRECTION & JUDGMENT IN THE VEGETABLE BODY . . .	534	MILTON 42	27
AND THEY ARE KNOWN TO BE UNCHANGEABLE BUT OIL BEING A BODY	566B	DESC CAT 2	PROSE
NUMBER XI THE BODY OF ABEL FOUND BY ADAM AND EVE . . .	584A	DESC CAT 11	TITLE
THE BODY OF JESUS IN THE SEPULCHRE A DRAWING	584B	DESC CAT 14	TITLE
AFTER THE DEATH OF THE VEGETATED BODY	605D	V LAST JUDG/N	PROSE
IN THE DIVINE BODY OF THE SAVIOUR THE TRUE VINE OF ETERNITY	606A	V LAST JUDG/N	PROSE
TO THE MORTAL BODY BEING RENDERD A PERMANENT STATUE . .	607A	V LAST JUDG/N	PROSE
YOU MAY DO SO IN SPIRIT BUT NOT IN THE MORTAL BODY . . .	616A	V LAST JUDG/N	PROSE
FOR IN PARADISE THEY HAVE NO CORPOREAL & MORTAL BODY .	616A	V LAST JUDG/N	PROSE
SAVIOUR'S KINGDOM THE DIVINE BODY WILL NEVER ENTER THERE	621A	JERUSALEM 3	PROSE
WHICH IS THE DIVINE BODY OF THE LORD JESUS BLESSED FOR EVER	624	JERUSALEM 5	59
I SAW DISEASE FORMING A BODY OF DEATH AROUND THE LAMB .	628	JERUSALEM 9	9
OF GOD TO DESTROY JERUSALEM & TO DEVOUR THE BODY OF ALBION	628	JERUSALEM 9	10
A MURDERER OF ITS OWN BODY BUT ALSO A MURDERER	629	JERUSALEM 10	12
WHY WILT THOU GIVE TO HER A BODY WHOSE LIFE IS BUT A SHADE	631	JERUSALEM 12	1
GIVING A BODY TO FALSHOOD THAT IT MAY BE CAST OFF FOR EVER	631	JERUSALEM 12	* 13
EVERY BOIL UPON MY BODY IS A SEPARATE & DEADLY SIN . .	643	JERUSALEM 21	4
BODY OVER AN UNCHASTE MIND VALA O THAT THOU WERT PURE .	643	JERUSALEM 21	12
O HUMAN IMAGINATION O DIVINE BODY I HAVE CRUCIFIED . .	647	JERUSALEM 24	23
THEY STROVE TOGETHER ABOVE THE BODY WHERE VALA WAS INCLOSD	655	JERUSALEM 29	62
AND THE DARK BODY OF ALBION LEFT PROSTRATE UPON THE CRYSTAL PAVEMENT	655	JERUSALEM 29	63
STEPS BEYOND AND REDEEMS MAN IN THE BODY OF JESUS AMEN . .	664	JERUSALEM 36	55
AGAIN HE JOIND THE DIVINE BODY FOLLOWING MERCIFUL . .	664	JERUSALEM 37	11
FOR HAD THE BODY OF ALBION FALLN DOWN AND FROM ITS DREADFUL RUINS	667	JERUSALEM 40	31
BUILDING THE BODY OF MOSES IN THE VALLEY OF PEOR THE BODY	680	JERUSALEM 49	57
HIS BODY BENT HIS ARMS & KNEES	683	I SAW A MONK/J	15
THAT THOU O HUMAN IMAGINATION O DIVINE BODY ART ALL . .	693	JERUSALEM 60	57
THESE ARE THE DAUGHTERS OF VALA MOTHER OF THE BODY OF DEATH	696	JERUSALEM 62	13
BUT I THY MAGDALEN BEHOLD THY SPIRITUAL RISEN BODY . . .	696	JERUSALEM 62	14
PLOTTING TO DEVOUR ALBION'S BODY OF HUMANITY & LOVE . .	708	JERUSALEM 70	9
OVER ALBION AS THE SOUL IS TO THE BODY SO JERUSALEM'S SONS	709	JERUSALEM 71	4
TO DEVOUR THE BODY OF ALBION HUNGRING & THIRSTING & RAVNING	714	JERUSALEM 73	48
TO DESTROY IMAGINATION THE DIVINE BODY BY MARTYRDOMS & WARS	714	JERUSALEM 74	13
OF BODY & MIND TO EXERCISE THE DIVINE ARTS OF IMAGINATION	716D	JERUSALEM 77	PROSE
IS IT MEAT & DRINK IS NOT THE BODY MORE THAN RAIMENT . .	717B	JERUSALEM 77	PROSE

		PAGE	TITLE	LINE

BODY   (CONTINUED)
```
            WHAT IS MORTALITY BUT THE THINGS RELATING TO THE BODY WHICH   717B JERUSALEM 77    PROSE
               DIES
            OVER THE TOMB & OVER THE BODY RAVNING TO DEVOUR   . . . .   718 JERUSALEM 78       2
            BUT I VALA LUVAH'S DAUGHTER KEEP HIS BODY EMBALMD IN MORAL    722 JERUSALEM 80      27
               LAWS
            TO WEAVE JERUSALEM A BODY ACCORDING TO HER WILL   . . . .   722 JERUSALEM 80       35
            TO WEAVE JERUSALEM A BODY REPUGNANT TO THE LAMB   . . . .   723 JERUSALEM 80       65
            OF SELFHOOD BODY PUT OFF THE ANTICHRIST ACCURSED   . . . .   734 JERUSALEM 89      10
            COME LORD JESUS TAKE ON THEE THE SATANIC BODY OF HOLINESS    737 JERUSALEM 90      38
            WILL YOU SUFFER THIS SATAN THIS BODY OF DOUBT THAT SEEMS     741 JERUSALEM 93      20
               BUT IS NOT
            AND THE BODY OF ALBION WAS CLOSED APART FROM ALL NATIONS     741 JERUSALEM 94      14
            SHE AWOKE PALE & COLD SHE FAINTED SEVEN TIMES ON THE BODY    742 JERUSALEM 94      21
               OF ALBION
            DRIVING OUTWARD THE BODY OF DEATH IN AN ETERNAL DEATH        745 JERUSALEM 98      20
               & RESURRECTION
            AND IN HIS BODY TIGHT DOES BIND   . . . . . . .   749 EV GOSPEL(B)/N     50
            THAT DIDST CREATE THIS BODY OF MINE   . . . . . .   754 EV GOSPEL(E)/N     30
            AND STILL HE DEVOURS THE BODY OF CLAY   . . . . . .   755 EV GOSPEL(E)/N     94
            A BODY SUBJECT TO BE TEMPTED   . . . . . . . .   756 EV GOSPEL(I)/N     11
            OR SUCH A BODY AS MIGHT NOT FEEL   . . . . . . .   756 EV GOSPEL(I)/N     13
            IMAGINATION OR THE HUMAN ETERNAL BODY IN EVERY MAN   . . .   773C ANNO BERKELEY   MARG
            IMAGINATION OR THE DIVINE BODY IN EVERY MAN   . . . . .   773D ANNO BERKELEY  * MARG
            HE SAYS ALSO THE SPIRITUAL BODY OR ANGEL AS LITTLE CHILDREN  774A ANNO BERKELEY   MARG
            NATURAL BODY IS AN OBSTRUCTION TO THE SOUL OR SPIRITUAL      775A ANNO BERKELEY   MARG
               BODY
            THE ETERNAL BODY OF MAN IS THE IMAGINATION THAT IS   . .   776B INSC LAOCOON    PROSE
            GOD HIMSELF THE DIVINE BODY (YESHUA) JESUS WE ARE           776B INSC LAOCOON    PROSE
               HIS MEMBERS
            EVE FAINTED OVER THE DEAD BODY OF ABEL WHICH LAYS NEAR       779C GHOST ABEL 1    PROSE
               A GRAVE
            BUT TO WHAT NOT TO MIND BUT TO THE VILE BODY ONLY   . . .   784D ANNO WW EXCUR    MARG
            HER BROTHER A GIANT IN BODY MILD & POLITE IN SOUL AS I HAVE  850C LETTER 49       PROSE
            IT IS NOW PASSED AS I HOPE BUT THE MOMENT I GOT EASE OF      874B LETTER 79       PROSE
               BODY
            ARE A MOST SORE PLAGUE & ON A WEAK BODY TRULY AFFLICTIVE     874D LETTER 80       PROSE
            BODY DECAYS I THANK YOU FOR THE PAINS YOU HAVE TAKEN   . .   878A LETTER 88       PROSE
BOG HOUSE
            THAT I TOOK UP IN THE BOG HOUSE O DEAR   . . . . . . .   58C ISLAND MOON 10  *PROSE
BOGNOR
            HE MOVD HIS RIGHT FOOT TO CORNWALL HIS LEFT TO THE ROCKS     531 MILTON 39        49
               OF BOGNOR
            BOGNOR A PLEASANT RELIEF FROM BUSINESS IN THE SUMMER   . .   808C LETTER 19       PROSE
            WILLIAM HAYLEY ESQRE FELPHAM NEAR BOGNOR SUSSEX   . . . .   SUPP ADDRESSES/L    *TITLE
BOHAN
            BETWEEN SUCCOTH & ZARETAN BESIDE THE STONE OF BOHAN   . . .   661 JERUSALEM 34      45
BOIL
            EVERY BOIL UPON MY BODY IS A SEPARATE & DEADLY SIN   . . .   643 JERUSALEM 21       4
BOILS
            COVERD WITH BOILS FROM HEAD TO FOOT THE TERRIBLE SMITINGS    294 FOUR ZOAS 3       82
               OF LUVAH
            COVERD WITH BOILS FROM HEAD TO FOOT THE TERRIBLE SMITINGS    655 JERUSALEM 29      64
               OF LUVAH
            [FLIES] SWARMS OF FLIES MURRAIN OF BEASTS BOILS & BLAINS     SUPP EXODUS/N       *PROSE
BOISTEROUS
            BLOW BOISTEROUS WIND STERN WINTER FROWN   . . . . . . .   64 SHEPHERD OLD        9
BOLD
            AND ALL HIS SPEARMEN BOLD   . . . . . . . .   12 GWIN KING/PS       58
            [CHARLEMAINE & HIS BARONS BOLD]   . . . . . . . .   418 I SAW A MONK/N      7
            CHARLEMAINE & HIS BARONS BOLD   . . . . . . . .   420 I SAW MNK AD/N     13
            EXPRESSIONS OF ARTICULATE SPEECH IS A BOLD AND DARING   . .   576B DESC CAT 4      PROSE
            FATHER AND SON AND LIGHT AND LOVE ALL BOLD ASPERITIES   . .   640 JERUSALEM 18      21
            ELIZABETH "GIRT WITH MANY A BARON BOLD"   . . . . . .   SUPP ILLUS GRAY     *TITLE
BOLDER
            OUR YOUTH ARE BOLDER THAN THE SOUTHERN SWAINS   . . . . .   2 TO SUMMER/PS    *  15
BOLDLY
            THE TIMES REQUIRE THAT EVERY ONE SHOULD SPEAK OUT BOLDLY    584C DESC CAT 14      PROSE
BOLINGBROKE
            THIS VOLTAIRE & ROUSSEAU THIS HUME & GIBBON & BOLINGBROKE    532 MILTON 40        12
BOLOGNIAN
            BOLOGNIAN SCHOOLS MAY BE INSINUATED NOT TO BE ORNAMENTAL     476B ANNO REYNOLDS    MARG
BOLT
            A [KNAVE] FOOL TO A BOLT A [FOOL ] KNAVE TO A GLASS OF GIN    544 ON F AND S/N      4
BOLTS
            BUT THE FIVE GATES WERE CONSUMD & THEIR BOLTS AND HINGES     203 AMERICA 16       22
               MELTED
BOMBAST
            THEN SAID QUID I THINK THAT HOMER IS BOMBAST &   . . . .   51D ISLAND MOON 7    PROSE
BOND
            WILLIAM BOND   . . . . . . . . . . . . . . . .   434D WILLIAM BOND    TITLE
            AND I WONDER IF WILLIAM BOND WILL DIE   . . . . . . .   434 WILLIAM BOND        3
            THAT WILLIAM BOND & HIS SISTER JANE   . . . . . . .   435 WILLIAM BOND       35
            AND SAW HER WILLIAM BOND SO NEAR   . . . . . . . .   435 WILLIAM BOND       40
            THE FAIRIES THAT FLED FROM WILLIAM BOND   . . . . . .   435 WILLIAM BOND       41
            CALLD ALL HER DAUGHTERS SAYING SURELY TO UNLOOSE MY BOND     498 MILTON 17        32
            AND BOND OF SOCIETY THE DISTINCTION MY WORKS HAVE OBTAINED   561C EXHIBITION ADV   PROSE
BONDAGE
            [HAST MY] THAT FREE LOVE WITH BONDAGE BOUND   . . . . .   169 EARTHS ANSWR/N     25
            THAT FREE LOVE WITH BONDAGE BOUND   . . . . . . .   211 EARTHS ANSB/SE     25
            THE HARD BONDAGE RENT RENT THE VAST SOLID   . . . . .   257 BOOK OF LOS 4      16
            FROM BONDAGE OF THE HUMAN FORM O FIRST BORN SON OF LIGHT     283 FOUR ZOAS 2      108
```

		PAGE	TITLE	LINE
BONDAGE	(CONTINUED)			
. . . SPIRITS MOURND THEIR BONDAGE NIGHT & DAY	. . . .	286	FOUR ZOAS 2	246
FROM BONDAGE OF [THE HUMAN FORM] THESE TERRORS	.	345	FOUR ZOAS 8	158
DERIVED FROM THE MODERN BONDAGE OF RHYMING	.	621D	JERUSALEM 3	PROSE
A BONDAGE AS RHYME ITSELF I THEREFORE HAVE PRODUCED A	.	621D	JERUSALEM 3	PROSE
DRAWING THE FREE LOVES OF JERUSALEM INTO INFERNAL BONDAGE		707	JERUSALEM 69	9
THERE ISRAEL IN BONDAGE TO HIS GENERALIZING GODS		735	JERUSALEM 89	30
BONDS				
. . . OUR BONDS AND OUR PRISNERS SHOUT IN THE OPEN FIELD		137	FRENCH REVOLTN	74
SPRING LIKE REDEEMED CAPTIVES WHEN THEIR BONDS & BARS ARE		198	AMERICA 6	5
BURST				
FOR THE FEMALE SPIRITS OF THE DEAD PINING IN BONDS		202	AMERICA 15	23
OF RELIGION				
BROKE FROM MY BONDS I SCORN MY PRISON I SCORN & YET I LOVE		268	FOUR ZOAS 1	150
YET THOU IN INDOLENCE REPOSEST HOLDING ME IN BONDS . . .		271	FOUR ZOAS 1	259
TRIGONS & CUBES DIVIDE THE ELEMENTS IN FINITE BONDS . . .		284	FOUR ZOAS 2	169
BURST FROM ITS BONDS IN WHIRLPOOLS FIERCE ROARING WITH		295	FOUR ZOAS 3	137
HUMAN VOICE				
OF GOARY BLOOD STRUGGLING TO BE DELIVERD FROM OUR BONDS		300	FOUR ZOAS 4	103
. . . HE REDEEMS THE SPECTRES FROM THEIR BONDS		347	FOUR ZOAS 8	236
WHERE ARE YOUR BONDS & TASK MASTERS ARE THESE THE PRISONERS		375	FOUR ZOAS 9	678
THEREFORE I BREAK THY BONDS OF RIGHTEOUSNESS I CRUSH THY		670	JERUSALEM 42	37
MESSENGERS				
SEEING HIS SONS ASSIMILATE WITH LUVAH BOUND IN THE BONDS		685	JERUSALEM 54	11
CHRIST BAPTIZING SAMSON BREAKING BONDS SAMSON SUBDUD		SUPP	LETTER 56A	*PROSE
BONE	SEE BACK BONE			
THE BLADE BONE OF A TITTLEBACK NO NO HERES A BOTTLE OF		58C	ISLAND MOON 10	PROSE
WIND				
AND NOT A BONE OF ALL THE SONS OF TIRIEL REMAIN		100	TIRIEL 1	50
. . . FROM HIS SHOULDER DOWN THE BONE		134	FRENCH REVOLTN	3
WHEN THE SHATTERD BONE HATH LAID HIM GROANING AMONG THE		291	FOUR ZOAS 2	416
HAPPIER DEAD				
IS NOT THE WOUND OF THE SWORD SWEET & THE BROKEN		337	FOUR ZOAS 7B	189
BONE DELIGHTFUL				
AND HILLS OUT FROM THE OPTIC NERVE & HARDENING IT INTO		515	MILTON 28	34
A BONE				
A BONE WHICH HE HAD STOLEN HE HAD IN HIS MOUTH		554	TO VENETIAN/N	6
AS HE SWAM HE SAW THE REFLECTION OF THE BONE		554	TO VENETIAN/N	8
IS NOT THE WOUND OF THE SWORD SWEET & THE BROKEN		700	JERUSALEM 65	31
BONE DELIGHTFUL				
THE FLEMINGS THEY CALL IT BURNT BONE HAS POSSESSED THE EYE		864C	LETTER 61	PROSE
& STRONGER EVERY DAY THO WEAKER IN MUSCLE & BONE THAN .		872D	LETTER 76	PROSE
BONES	SEE KEY-BONES			
TO HIS STRONG BONES STRIDES OER THE GROANING ROCKS . . .		3	TO WINTER/PS	10
FANCY RETURNS AND NOW SHE THINKS OF BONES		4	FAIR ELENOR/PS	13
FOR ALL OUR BLOOD AND BONES ARE IN FRANCE AND A		29C	EDW THIRD/PS 4	PROSE
MY FLESH IS A PRISON MY BONES THE BARS OF DEATH		37B	CONTEMPLATN/PS	PROSE
NONE CAN HURT THEE THY BONES ARE BRASS THY SINEWS ARE IRON		39A	SAMSON/PS	PROSE
THEM THAT HE'LL SCRAPE THEIR BONES IF THEY DONT LAY STILL &		50A	ISLAND MOON 6	PROSE
SERPENTS NOT SONS WREATHING AROUND THE BONES OF TIRIEL .		99	TIRIEL 1	22
TILL YOUR WHITE BONES ARE BLEACHD WITH AGE FOR A MEMORIAL		100	TIRIEL 1	47
FOR HE IS THE KING OF ROTTEN WOOD & OF THE BONES OF DEATH		101	TIRIEL 2	24
THAT THOU SHALT FEEL WORMS IN THY MARROW CREEPING THRO		107	TIRIEL 6	21
THY BONES				
BUT THAT I FEEL THEY WILL CURSE THEE & HANG UPON THY BONES		108	TIRIEL 6	37
THEY STUMBLE ALL NIGHT OVER BONES OF THE DEAD		126	VOICE BARD/SI	9
. . . HIS STRONG BONES SCARCE COVERD WITH SINEWS THE IRON		135	FRENCH REVOLTN	30
RINGS				
SHIVERING OVER THEIR BLEACHED BONES		137	FRENCH REVOLTN	73
HIDE IN THE NETHER EARTH HIDE IN THE BONES		137	FRENCH REVOLTN	75
OF THE RULER WITHER AMONG BONES OF DEATH		140	FRENCH REVOLTN	145
AND ON THE BLEACHED BONES		148	MARRIAGE HH 2	12
DRIVE YOUR CART AND YOUR PLOW OVER THE BONES OF THE DEAD		150D	MARRIAGE HH 7	PROSE
THAT DOES [CLOSE] FREEZE MY BONES AROUND		169	EARTHS ANSWR/N	22
LOVE TO CURL ROUND THE BONES OF DEATH AND ASK THE RAVNOUS		191	V DAU ALBION 3	11
SNAKE				
THE BONES OF DEATH THE COVRING CLAY THE SINEWS SHRUNK &		198	AMERICA 6	3
DRYD				
THAT DOES FREEZE MY BONES AROUND		211	EARTHS ANSR/SE	22
FRIGHTEND AT THE HURTLING BONES		226	URIZEN 8	2
AND BONES OF SOLIDNESS FROZE		228	URIZEN 10	40
AROUND HIS SOLID BONES		228	URIZEN 11	7
AND HARDENING BONES BEGAN		235	URIZEN 25	25
WALK HEAVY SOFT AND BENT ARE THE BONES OF VILLAGERS . .		243	EUROPE 12	31
RATTLING THEIR HOLLOW BONES IN HOWLING AND LAMENTATION .		243	EUROPE 13	8
FORTH FROM THE DEAD DUST RATTLING BONES TO BONES		248	SONG OF LOS 7	31
AS THE BONES OF MAN SOLID & DARK		253	AHANIA 4	21
PERCHING AROUND THE HURTLING BONES		253	AHANIA 4	24
AND LOS THREW THEM AROUND THE BONES		253	AHANIA 4	30
WHERE BONES OF BEASTS ARE STROWN		255	AHANIA 5	44
WHERE BONES FROM THE BIRTH ARE BURIED		255	AHANIA 5	46
THEY CRY O SPIDER SPREAD THY WEB ENLARGE THY BONES & FILLD		275	FOUR ZOAS 1	404
THEY MELT THE BONES OF VALA & THE BONES OF LUVAH INTO		276	FOUR ZOAS 1	422
WEDGES				
AND HUMAN BONES RATTLING TOGETHER IN THE SMOKE & STAMPING		296	FOUR ZOAS 3	154
CRYING FURY IN MY LIMBS DESTRUCTION IN MY BONES & MARROW		296	FOUR ZOAS 3	162
SO SHALL THE SPUNGY MARROW ISSUING FROM THY SPLINTERD BONES		299	FOUR ZOAS 4	68
BUT WHEN HE POURD IT ROUND THE BONES OF URIZEN HE LAUGHD		302	FOUR ZOAS 4	196
AND BONES OF SOLIDNESS FROZE OVER ALL HIS NERVES OF JOY		303	FOUR ZOAS 4	221
AROUND HIS SOLID BONES & A SECOND AGE PASSED OVER . .		303	FOUR ZOAS 4	226
THE BONES OF URIZEN HURTLE ON THE WIND THE BONES OF LOS		305	FOUR ZOAS 4	293
AND ON THE BONES I DROP MY TEARS & WATER THEM IN VAIN .		310	FOUR ZOAS 5	197

243

BONES   (CONTINUED)

REORGANIZE ME SHOOTING FORTH IN BONES & FLESH & BLOOD   .   .   317 FOUR ZOAS 6   224
OF ENITHARMON HOW IT BUDS WITH LIFE & FORMS THE BONES   .   .   323 FOUR ZOAS 7   131
AND SHRUNK UP TO THE BONES ALAS THAT MAN SHOULD COME TO   354 FOUR ZOAS 8   516
   THIS
HIS STRONG BONES BEAT WITH SNOWS & HID WITHIN THE CAVES   354 FOUR ZOAS 8   517
   OF NIGHT
ALL THINGS REVERSD FLEW FROM THEIR CENTERS RATTLING BONES   363 FOUR ZOAS 9   231
   [TO BONES]
TO BONES JOIN SHAKING CONVULSD THE SHIVERING CLAY BREATHES   363 FOUR ZOAS 9   232
IN LINEAMENTS TOO EXTENDED & IN BONES TOO STRAIT & LONG   363 FOUR ZOAS 9   249
AND IN THE SHRIEK A RATTLING OF BONES & IN THE RATTLING   373 FOUR ZOAS 9   592
   OF BONES
THE WINTER COMES HE FOLDS HIS SLENDER BONES WITHOUT   377 FOUR ZOAS 9   761
   A MURMUR
THE EYES BEHELD THE ABYSS LEST BONES OF SOLIDNESS FREEZE   482 MILTON 3   15
   OVER ALL
BEGINNING AT THE FEET OF URIZEN AND ON THE BONES   .   .   .   .   500 MILTON 19   12
HER SHADOWY SISTERS FORM THE BONES EVEN THE BONES OF HOREB   501 MILTON 19   51
WINTER COMES HE FOLDS HIS SLENDER BONES WITHOUT A MURMUR   513 MILTON 27   20
MY BONES TREMBLED I FELL OUTSTRETCHD UPON THE PATH   .   .   .   534 MILTON 42   25
MINE IS THE FLESH THE BONES MAY BE [HIS] [THY] YOUR SHARE   540 S(TOTHAR)D/N   *   6
FEED THEM WITH THE JUICE OF OUR MARROW BONES   .   .   .   .   .   543 IF TRUE/N   4
IN NARROW VALES I WALK & COUNT THE BONES OF MY BELOVEDS   721 JERUSALEM 79   65
IRON OF HIS FORGE & FIXES THEM INTO BONES OF CHALK & ROCK   736 JERUSALEM 90   20
FIBRES OF LIFE OUT FROM THE BONES INTO HER GOLDEN LOOM   .   736 JERUSALEM 90   22
ON MY BONES & SINEWS MUSCLE I HAVE NONE BUT A FEW DAYS   .   875A LETTER 80   PROSE
BONES & SINEWS ALL STRINGS & BOBBINS LIKE A WEAVER'S LOOM   875B LETTER 81   PROSE

BONEY

THEY SAW HIS BONEY FEET ON THE ROCK THE FLESH CONSUMD IN   242 EUROPE 12   10
   FLAMES
AND SHRIEK TILL AT THE SMELLS OF BLOOD THEY STRETCH THEIR   325 FOUR ZOAS 7   207
   BONEY WINGS
OVER THEM THE FAMISHD EAGLE SCREAMS ON BONEY WINGS AND   741 JERUSALEM 94   15
   AROUND

BONIFIED

INORBD AND BONIFIED WITH LOCKS OF SHADOWING MODESTY SHINING   709 JERUSALEM 70   22

BONIFY

BONIFY & THOU SHALT HAVE REST WHEN THIS THY LABOUR IS DONE   299 FOUR ZOAS 4   69
AND WHILE THE SONS OF ALBION BY SEVERE WAR & JUDGMENT   689 JERUSALEM 58   10
   BONIFY

BONIFYING

BONIFYING INTO A SCULL THE MARROW EXUDING IN DISMAL PAIN   689 JERUSALEM 58   8
THEY FLEE OVER THE ROCKS BONIFYING HORSES OXEN FEEL THE   689 JERUSALEM 58   9
   KNIFE

BOOK

SO ALL THE PEOPLE IN THE BOOK ENTERD INTO THE ROOM   .   .   .   49C ISLAND MOON 5   PROSE
OBTUSE ANGLE TOOK UP THE BOOK   .   .   .   .   52C ISLAND MOON 8   PROSE
SCOPPRELL TOOK UP A BOOK & READ THE FOLLOWING PASSAGE   .   .   52D ISLAND MOON 8   PROSE
MR STEELYARD ARE SOME OF THEM MORE IMPROVING THAN ANY BOOK   53C ISLAND MOON 8   PROSE
("KEEP DISTANT WHO HATES...LAUGH OF A CHILD") THE BEST   74B ANNO LAVATER   MARG
   IN THE BOOK
THOSE WHO ARE OFFENDED WITH ANY THING IN THIS BOOK WOULD BE   87C ANNO LAVATER   MARG
IN A BOOK I LOVE SO MUCH & APPROVE SO GENERALLY   .   .   .   .   88A ANNO LAVATER   MARG
THAT THIS BOOK IS WRITTEN BY CONSULTATION WITH GOOD SPIRITS   88B ANNO LAVATER   MARG
IN A BOOK THAT ALL MAY READ   .   .   .   .   111 INTRODUCTN/SI   14
NOR IN MY BOOK CAN I TAKE DELIGHT   .   .   .   .   124 SCHOOL BOY/SI   13
THE BOOK OF THEL THE AUTHOR & PRINTER WILLM BLAKE...   .   127A BOOK OF THEL   TITLE
THE FRENCH REVOLUTION A POEM IN SEVEN BOOKS BOOK THE FIRST   134A FRENCH REVOLTN   TITLE
BOOK THE FIRST   .   .   .   .   134A FRENCH REVOLTN   TITLE
END OF THE FIRST BOOK   .   .   .   .   148B FRENCH REVOLTN   TITLE
BUT IN THE BOOK OF JOB MILTON'S MESSIAH IS CALLD SATAN   .   150A MARRIAGE HH 5   PROSE
IN [HIS HAND] [THEIR] HANDS A HOLY BOOK   .   .   .   .   .   .   167 INFANT SORW/N   *   27
TO THE FOUR WINDS AS A TORN BOOK & NONE SHALL GATHER THE   198 AMERICA 8   6
   LEAVES
THE BOOK OF THEL A POEM IN ILLUMINATED PRINTING QUARTO   .   .   207D PRSPECTUS 1793   PROSE
THE HISTORY OF ENGLAND A SMALL BOOK OF ENGRAVINGS PRICE...   208A PRSPECTUS 1793   PROSE
THE GATES OF PARADISE A SMALL BOOK OF ENGRAVINGS PRICE...   208A PRSPECTUS 1793   PROSE
LIKE THE HOLY BOOK   .   .   .   .   219 LIT GRL LST/SE   28
THE [FIRST] BOOK OF URIZEN LAMBETH PRINTED BY WILL   222A URIZEN 1   TITLE
   BLAKE...
PRELUDIUM TO THE [FIRST] BOOK OF URIZEN   .   .   .   .   .   .   222A URIZEN 2   TITLE
THIS ROCK PLACE WITH STRONG HAND THE BOOK   .   .   .   .   .   224 URIZEN 4   32
THE BOOK OF BRASS RAGE SIEZD THE STRONG   .   .   .   .   .   .   224 URIZEN 4   44
THE END OF THE [FIRST] BOOK OF URIZEN   .   .   .   .   .   .   237A URIZEN 28   TITLE
HE LAUGHING ANSWERD I WILL WRITE A BOOK ON LEAVES   237 EUROPE INTRO   14
   OF FLOWERS
AND HIS BRAZEN BOOK   .   .   .   .   242 EUROPE 11   3
FOR URIZEN UNCLASPD HIS BOOK FEEDING HIS SOUL WITH PITY   242 EUROPE 12   4
THE BOOK OF AHANIA LAMBETH PRINTED BY W BLAKE...   .   .   249A AHANIA   TITLE
IN SILENCE HIS BOOK OF IRON   .   .   .   .   252 AHANIA 3   64
BROUGHT HIS BOOKS ALL BUT THE BOOK   .   .   .   .   252 AHANIA 3   73
THE BOOK OF LOS LAMBETH PRINTED BY W BLAKE...   .   .   .   .   255D BOOK OF LOS   TITLE
THE END OF THE BOOK OF LOS   .   .   .   .   260D BOOK OF LOS 5   TITLE
THE BOOK OF MY REMEMBRANCE   .   .   .   .   262B SMALL BK DSGNS   TITLE
[AND THUS BEGINNETH THE BOOK OF VALA WHICH WHOSOEVER READS]   264 FOUR ZOAS 1   3
BRING IN HERE THE GLOBE OF BLOOD AS IN THE (BOOK) OF URIZEN   305A FOUR ZOAS 4   PROSE
END OF THE FOURTH [BOOK] NIGHT   .   .   .   .   305B FOUR ZOAS 4   *TITLE
VALA [BOOK] NIGHT THE FIFTH   .   .   .   .   305B FOUR ZOAS 5   *TITLE
END OF THE FIFTH [BOOK] NIGHT   .   .   .   .   311C FOUR ZOAS 5   *TITLE
HIS BOOK OF IRON ON HIS KNEES HE TRACD THE DREADFUL LETTERS   321 FOUR ZOAS 7   29
HIS BOOKS OUT OF THE DISMAL SHADE ALL BUT THE BOOK OF IRON   321 FOUR ZOAS 7   39

		PAGE	TITLE	LINE

BOOK   (CONTINUED)

```
        IN THE DIM AIR THEY TOOK THE BOOK OF IRON & PLACD ABOVE      322 FOUR ZOAS 7        97
        SINGING AT THEIR DIRE WORK THE WORDS OF URIZEN'S BOOK OF     322 FOUR ZOAS 7       104
          IRON
        AND URIZEN READ IN HIS BOOK OF BRASS IN SOUNDING TONES  . .  322 FOUR ZOAS 7       109
        BEGINNING OF THE [BOOK] SEVENTH NIGHT  . . . . . . . . .    333A FOUR ZOAS 7B    *TITLE
        READ PATIENTLY TAKE NOT UP THIS BOOK IN AN IDLE HOUR  . .   383C ANNO WATSON      MARG
        THIS MUST BE A MOST WICKED & BLASPHEMOUS BOOK  . . . . .    384A ANNO WATSON      MARG
        THE IMPRESSION WHICH HE RECIEVES FROM A BOOK OF EXAMPLES    393B ANNO WATSON      MARG
        FOR HIS & SO HE WOULD DO BY ANY OTHER BOOK  . . . . . .     393C ANNO WATSON      MARG
        I HAVE READ THIS BOOK WITH ATTENTION & FIND THAT THE BISHOP 396B ANNO WATSON      MARG
        AS THIS BOOK CONTAINS CAN EVER HAVE BEEN CALLD WISDOM       397A ANNO BACON       MARG
        & ALL MEN OF SENSE HAVE DESPISED THE BOOK AS MUCH AS I DO   397A ANNO BACON       MARG
        OPENING BY CHANCE A BOOK WHICH SHE HAD IN HER HAND  . . .   440D MEMORANDUM/N 5   PROSE
        & BEFORE THE BOOK OF DEATH WHICH IS OPEND ON CLOUDS  . . .  443C LAST JUDGMNT/L   PROSE
        & FAMILIES SOME OF WHOM ARE BOWING BEFORE THE BOOK OF LIFE  443D LAST JUDGMNT/L   PROSE
        THIS WHOLE BOOK WAS WRITTEN TO SERVE POLITICAL PURPOSES     451C ANNO REYNOLDS    MARG
        A NOBLE SENTENCE HERE IS A SENTENCE WHICH OVERTHROWS ALL    461B ANNO REYNOLDS    MARG
          HIS BOOK
        OVER FIND THAT MY NOTES ON REYNOLDS IN THIS BOOK           477A ANNO REYNOLDS    MARG
          ARE EXACTLY
        MILTON BOOK THE FIRST  . . . . . . . . . . . . . . .       481B MILTON 1         TITLE
        NO FAITH IS IN ALL THE EARTH THE BOOK OF GOD IS TRODDEN     506 MILTON 22          60
          UNDER FOOT
        END OF THE FIRST BOOK  . . . . . . . . . . . . . . . .     518A MILTON 29        TITLE
        MILTON BOOK THE SECOND  . . . . . . . . . . . . . . .      518B MILTON 30        TITLE
        WHILE TITIAN'S &C AS IN THE BOOK OF MOONLIGHT P (FIVE)  .   551A DELICATE/N       PROSE
        IN THE BOOK OF RUTH WHERE NAOMI HAVING TAKEN LEAVE OF HER   584C DESC CAT 15      PROSE
        WITH A BOOK IN HIS HAND WHICH IS SHUT HE REPRESENTS  . .   607V V LAST JUDG/N     PROSE
        [WHO] HE HAS SATAN'S BOOK OF ACCUSATIONS  . . . . . . .    609B V LAST JUDG/N     PROSE
        SAMUEL A DOUBLE BOOK & KINGS A DOUBLE BOOK THE PSALMS       677 JERUSALEM 48       10
          & PROPHETS
        THE BOOK WRITTEN BY ROUSSEAU CALLD HIS CONFESSIONS  . . .   682D JERUSALEM 52     PROSE
        VIRGIL IN THE ENEID BOOK VI LINE...SAYS "LET OTHERS STUDY   778D HOMERS POETRY    PROSE
          ART"
        JUSTLY STANDS FIRST IN THE BOOK & THAT BEAUTIFUL SPECIMEN   782A INSC UPCOTT      PROSE
        WHATEVER BOOK IS FOR VENGEANCE FOR SIN & WHATEVER  . . .    785D ILLS DANTE 101   PROSE
        BOOK IS AGAINST THE FORGIVENESS OF SINS IS NOT OF          785D ILLS DANTE 101   PROSE
          THE FATHER
        IN A BOOK WHERE ALL MAY READ &  . . . . . . . . . . .      787A ANNO THORNTON    MARG
        IN A BOOK WHICH ALL MAY READ  . . . . . . . . . . . .      787A ANNO THORNTON    MARG
        IN A BOOK THAT ALL MAY READ ARE EQUALLY RIGHT  . . . .     787A ANNO THORNTON    MARG
        [BEFORE] IMMEDIATELY ON THE RECEIT OF YOUR BEAUTIFUL BOOK   791A LETTER 3         PROSE
        WHY IS THE BIBLE MORE ENTERTAINING & INSTRUCTIVE THAN ANY   794A LETTER 5         PROSE
          OTHER BOOK
        A BOOK PRICE HALF A GUINEA MAY BE GOT OUT AT THE EXPENSE OF 820A LETTER 25        PROSE
        THAT ARE OUT & THE BOOK OF ITALIAN LETTERS FROM MRS FLAXMAN 836C LETTER 35        PROSE
        I HAVE READ THE BOOK THRO ATTENTIVELY AND WAS MUCH  . . .   845B LETTER 44        PROSE
        THE WHOLE MIDDLE OF THE BOOK BEING PRINTED WITH A LARGER    847A LETTER 44        PROSE
        MEN & ACCORDINGLY HAVE GIVEN A LOOK OVER MY ACCOUNT BOOK    854C LETTER 53        PROSE
        APPAREL ONLY MY BOOK OF DRAWINGS FROM DANTE & ONE PLATE     873A LETTER 76        PROSE
        SHUT UP IN THE BOOK ALL WILL GO VERY WELL IN THE COACH      873A LETTER 76        PROSE
          WHICH
        SUBSCRIBERS & PURCHASERS OF THE BOOK OF ILLUSTRATIONS OF    SUPP LETTER 67F     *PROSE
BOOKS
        OBTUSE ANGLE TOOK UP THE BOOKS ONE BY ONE  . . . . . .       52C ISLAND MOON 8    PROSE
        IN MY LIFE YOU ARE ALWAYS TALKING OF YOUR BOOKS  . . .       52D ISLAND MOON 8    PROSE
        THE FRENCH REVOLUTION A POEM IN SEVEN BOOKS BOOK THE FIRST  134A FRENCH REVOLTN   TITLE
        ADVERTISEMENT THE REMAINING BOOKS OF THIS POEM ARE FINISHED 134A FRENCH REVOLTN   TITLE
        AND TOOK THE FORMS OF BOOKS & WERE ARRANGED IN LIBRARIES    155A MARRIAGE HH 15   PROSE
        IT IS ONLY THE CONTENTS OR INDEX OF ALREADY PUBLISHD BOOKS  157C MARRIAGE HH 21   PROSE
        THE CITIZENS OF NEW-YORK CLOSE THEIR BOOKS & LOCK THEIR     201 AMERICA 14         13
          CHESTS
        THE ILLUMINATED BOOKS ARE PRINTED IN COLOURS  . . . . .    208A PRSPECTUS 1793   PROSE
        HERE ALONE I IN BOOKS FORMD OF METALS  . . . . . . . .      224 URIZEN 4          24
        AND HIS BOOKS OF BRASS IRON & GOLD  . . . . . . . . .       248 SONG OF LOS 7     14
        BROUGHT HIS BOOKS ALL BUT THE BOOK  . . . . . . . . .       252 AHANIA 3          73
        HIDING THEIR BOOKS & PICTURES UNDERNEATH THE DENS OF EARTH  275 FOUR ZOAS 1      397
        WRITING IN BITTER TEARS & GROANS IN BOOKS OF IRON & BRASS   314 FOUR ZOAS 6       85
        BUT STILL HIS BOOKS HE BORE IN HIS STRONG HANDS & HIS IRON  316 FOUR ZOAS 6      167
          PEN
        WERE ROTTED BY THE WINDS THE BOOKS REMAIN STILL UNCONSUMD   316 FOUR ZOAS 6      171
        OFT WOULD HE SIT IN A DARK RIFT & REGULATE HIS BOOKS  . .   316 FOUR ZOAS 6      180
        AND BOOKS & INSTRUMENTS OF SONG & PICTURES OF DELIGHT  .    317 FOUR ZOAS 6      216
        AND RANGD HIS BOOKS AROUND HIM BROODING ENVIOUS OVER ORC    320 FOUR ZOAS 7       19
        HIS BOOKS OUT OF THE DISMAL SHADE ALL BUT THE BOOK OF IRON  321 FOUR ZOAS 7       39
        AGAIN HE TOOK HIS SEAT & RANGD HIS [BOOKS] BOOKS AROUND     321 FOUR ZOAS 7   *   40
        WRITING THY BOOKS ANON A CLOUD FILLD WITH A WASTE OF SNOWS  322 FOUR ZOAS 7       81
        URIZEN ANSWERD READ MY BOOKS EXPLORE MY CONSTELLATIONS  .   322 FOUR ZOAS 7       90
        THUS IN THE TEMPLE OF THE SUN HIS BOOKS OF IRON & BRASS     344 FOUR ZOAS 8      140
        ABOMINABLE TO THE EYES OF MORTALS WHO EXPLORE HIS BOOKS     352 FOUR ZOAS 8      430
        THE BOOKS OF URIZEN UNROLL WITH DREADFUL NOISE THE FOLDING  358 FOUR ZOAS 9       33
          SERPENT
        ONE FOR INSTANCE WHICH IS THAT THE BOOKS OF THE BIBLE  .    390C ANNO WATSON      MARG
        I CANNOT CONCIEVE THE DIVINITY OF THE BOOKS IN THE BIBLE    393B ANNO WATSON      MARG
        WHO GAVE THEM THE NAME OF BOOKS OF SAMUEL  . . . . . .      394C ANNO WATSON    * MARG
        ON THESE BOOKS NOTHING BUT INDIGNATION & RESENTMENT  . .    445B ANNO REYNOLDS    MARG
        ON EVERY ONE OF THESE BOOKS I WROTE MY OPINIONS &          476D ANNO REYNOLDS    MARG
          ON LOOKING THEM
        MILTON A POEM IN...BOOKS  . . . . . . . . . . . . . .      480A MILTON           TITLE
        AND GRACES LEST THEY WRITE THEM IN THEIR BOOKS & IN THE     507 MILTON 23         41
          SCROLL
```

```
                                                          PAGE      TITLE        LINE
BOOKS    (CONTINUED)
     ARE OPEND THE BOOKS OF REMEMBRANCE OF LIFE & OF DEATH   .  612B V LAST JUDG/N   PROSE
     READER [LOVER] OF BOOKS [LOVER ] OF HEAVEN  . . . . .    621 READER LOVER/J     1
     AND OF THAT GOD FROM WHOM [ALL BOOKS ARE GIVEN]  . . . . 621 READER LOVER/J *   2
     THE FIVE BOOKS OF THE DECALOGUE THE BOOKS OF JOSHUA &    677 JERUSALEM 48       9
        JUDGES
     UNFORTUNATELY OUR AUTHORS OF BOOKS ARE AMONG THIS CLASS HOW 795A LETTER 6       PROSE
     BOOKS & PICTURES OF OLD WHICH I WROTE & PAINTED IN AGES   802B LETTER 14       PROSE
     AUTHORS AND CURIOUS BOOKS IN GENERAL HE ADVISES THAT SOME 831C LETTER 31       PROSE
     TO MR PHILLIPS YOUR INTENTION OF TAKING THE BOOKS YOU WANT 846B LETTER 44      PROSE
     I HOPE YOU WILL EXCUSE MY DELAY IN SENDING THE BOOKS   .  850A LETTER 49       PROSE
     I AT LENGTH SEND THE BOOKS WHICH I HAVE IN VAIN CALLD FOR 856A LETTER 54       PROSE
     ARE A SELECTION FROM THE DIFFERENT BOOKS OF SUCH AS COULD 867A LETTER 66       PROSE
        BE
BOOKSELLER
     TILL SOME BOOKSELLER & THE PUBLIC FAME  . . . . . . .    551 WILLM COWPER/N     7
     EVANS THE BOOKSELLER IN PALLMALL SAYS THEY GO OFF VERY WELL 821B LETTER 25      PROSE
     MR JOHNSON THE BOOKSELLER TELLS ME THAT THERE IS NO WANT  831B LETTER 31       PROSE
        OF WORK
     I INTEND TO SEE MRS LAMBERT & MR JOHNSON BOOKSELLER THIS  833C LETTER 33       PROSE
     ENGAGEMENT WITH ANY LONDON BOOKSELLER I MAY MYSELF  .  .  856B LETTER 54       PROSE
BOOKSELLERS
     BLUNDERED OVER NOVELS AND CATCHPENNY TRIFLES OF BOOKSELLERS 574A DESC CAT 3     PROSE
     INTO WHICH BOOKSELLERS & TRADING DEALERS HAVE THROWN YOU  595B PUB ADDRESS/N    PROSE
     BELIEVE AS MANY BOOKSELLERS AS THERE ARE BUTCHERS &   .   798C LETTER 10       PROSE
     THAT I PERCEIVE A DETERMINATION IN THE LONDON BOOKSELLERS  846C LETTER 44      PROSE
     I AM NOT APT TO BELIEVE LITERALLY WHAT BOOKSELLERS SAY AND 846D LETTER 44      PROSE
     AND AS TO THE TIME THE BOOKSELLERS WOULD TAKE  .  .  .  . 847A LETTER 44       PROSE
     HONOUR OF LONDON BOOKSELLERS & CONSIDER THEM AS LOSING A   856C LETTER 54      PROSE
     FROM OTHER PLATES FOR BOOKSELLERS WHICH HE WAS EMPLOYD  .  877B LETTER 86      PROSE
BOON
     IF I OBTAIN YOUR LEAVE I HAVE ANOTHER BOON . . . . . .    20 EDW THIRD/PS 2    43
BOOR
     JAN STEEN WAS A BOOR & NEITHER RAFAEL   . . . . . . .    472D ANNO REYNOLDS    MARG
     IT IS A COPY FROM A DUTCH PICTURE DUTCH BOOR SMOKING  .   843C LETTER 43       PROSE
BOOTES
     FOR THE CONSTELLATION ARCTURUS OR BOOTES THE KEEPER  .  . 577D DESC CAT 5       PROSE
BORD
     AND BRASS & MOLTEN METALS CAST IN HOLLOW GLOBES & BORD  . 343 FOUR ZOAS 8      93
BORDER
     THE MISERY OF UNHAPPY FAMILIES SHALL BE DRAWN OUT INTO    499 MILTON 18         7
        ITS BORDER
BORDERD
     AND PALE HIS PRIESTESSES INFOLDED IN VEILS OF PESTILENCE  528 MILTON 37        23
        BORDERD
BORE
     HIS CRUEL SCEPTRE BORE   . . . . . . . . . . . .         11 GWIN KING/PS        4
     THEN SHE BORE PALE DESIRE FATHER OF CURIOSITY  .  .  .   40D THEN SHE BORE     PROSE
     SHE BROUGHT FORTH RAGE [THEN] AND SHAME BORE HONOUR &  .  42C THEN SHE BORE    *PROSE
     WAS BORN ENVY IN DIREFUL PAINS HIM BORE THEN ENVY BROUGHT 42C THEN SHE BORE    PROSE
        FORTH CARE
     GREW PREGNANT & [BROUGHT FORTH] BORE SCORN & SLANDER  .   42D THEN SHE BORE    PROSE
     SHE WAS A GODDESS POWERFUL & BORE [CONCEIT & EMULATION]   43A THEN SHE BORE    *PROSE
     [BY SHAME SHE HAD A SON CALLD HONOUR WHO BORE REVENGE]  . 43A THEN SHE BORE    PROSE
     THEN [SELF LOVE] BORE A DAUGHTER CALLED EMULATION  . . .  43A THEN SHE BORE    PROSE
     EVERY PROVOKING SPEECH THAT EVER SHE COULD & HE BORE IT   53B ISLAND MOON 8    PROSE
     COME FORTH & LOOK ON HER THAT BORE YOU COME YOU ACCURSED  99 TIRIEL 1          8
        SONS
     HE DRANK & IJIM RAISD HIM UP & BORE HIM ON HIS SHOULDERS  104 TIRIEL 4        40
     ALL DAY HE BORE HIM & WHEN EVENING DREW HER SOLEMN CURTAIN 104 TIRIEL 4       41
     IN HIS ARMS HE BORE  .  . . . . . . . . . . . .          114 LIT GRL FND/SI   21
     BORE THEM TO THE GROUND  . . . . . . . . . . . .         114 LIT GRL FND/SI   27
     OR THINK ON HIM WHO BORE THY NAME . . . . . . . . .      119 NIGHT/SI         43
     MY MOTHER BORE ME IN THE SOUTHERN WILD  . . . . . . .    125 LIT BLK BOY/SI    1
     SUCH A FLOWER AS MAY NEVER BORE   . . . . . . . . .      161 ROSE TREE/N       2
     THAT SO MANY SWEET FLOWERS BORE   . . . . . . . . .      162 GARDEN LOVE/N     8
     TILL IT BORE AN APPLE BRIGHT  . . . . . . . . . .        165 CHRISTN FORB/N   10
     STAIND THE ROOTS MY MIRTLE BORE   . . . . . . . . .      167 INFANT SORW/N    41
     STAIND THE ROOTS MY MIRTLE BORE   . . . . . . . . .      169 MIRTLE SHADE/N   16
     SUCH A FLOWER AS MAY NEVER BORE   . . . . . . . . .      215 ROSE TREE/SE      2
     THAT SO MANY SWEET FLOWERS BORE   . . . . . . . . .      215 GARDEN LOVE/SE    8
     TILL IT BORE AN APPLE BRIGHT  . . . . . . . . . .        218 POISON TREE/SE   10
     AND SHE BORE AN ENORMOUS RACE  . . . . . . . . . .       234 URIZEN 20        45
     ON HIS SHOULDERS HE BORE IT TO WHERE   . . . . . . .     251 AHANIA 3         53
     TILL IN PROCESS FROM FALLING HE BORE  . . . . . . .      258 BOOK OF LOS 4    46
     INEXTRICABLE LABYRINTHS SHE BORE ME SONS & DAUGHTERS  .  282 FOUR ZOAS 2      97
     ROUND LOS AFAR HIS WATERS BORE ON ALL SIDES ROUND WITH   301 FOUR ZOAS 4      159
        NOISE
     BUT STILL HIS BOOKS HE BORE IN HIS STRONG HANDS & HIS IRON 316 FOUR ZOAS 6    167
        PEN
     BORE ON THRO THE AFFRIGHTED VALES ASCENDING & DESCENDING  319 FOUR ZOAS 6     287
     OF ENITHARMON BORE URTHONA'S SPECTRE ON ITS WINGS  .  .  328 FOUR ZOAS 7      337
     INSPIRING SECRECY & LAMPS THEY BORE INTOXICATING FUMES .  . 333 FOUR ZOAS 7B   28
     AND THE STRONG PINIOND EAGLE BORE THE FIRE OF HEAVEN . .  340 FOUR ZOAS 7B    285
     THEY BORE IT TO THE SEPULCHER WHICH LOS HAD HEWN IN THE   349 FOUR ZOAS 8     339
        ROCK
     THAT NOT OF HIS OWN POWER HE BORE THE HUMAN FORM ERECT  .  353 FOUR ZOAS 8    458
     SHE BORE THE FRUITS IN HER LAP SHE GATHERD FLOWERS FOR    369 FOUR ZOAS 9     477
        HER BOSOM
     THEY BORE A NET OF GOLDEN TWINE   . . . . . . . . .      422 BENEATH/N        10
     BORE THE GOLDEN NET ALOFT . . . . . . . . . . . .        422 BENEATH/N        20
     THEY BORE A NET OF GOLDEN TWINE   . . . . . . . . .      424 THE GOLDEN NET    9
```

BORE   (CONTINUED)

BORE THE GOLDEN NET ALOFT	424	THE GOLDEN NET	19
IN DREAMS SHE BORE THE SHADOWY SPECTRE OF SLEEP & NAMD HIM DEATH	494	MILTON 13	40
IN DREAMS SHE BORE RAHAB THE MOTHER OF TIRZAH & HER SISTERS	494	MILTON 13	41
HE BORE THE WRETCHED SOUL OF WILLIAM BLAKE	536	AND HIS LEGS/N	11
THE FLORENTINES SAID TIS A DUTCH ENGLISH BORE	542	FLORENTINE/N	13
HE RECOILD HE RUSHD OUTWARDS HE BORE THE VEIL WHOLE AWAY	646	JERUSALEM 23	20
BOWEN ALBION'S SONS THEY BORE HIM A GOLDEN COUCH INTO THE PORCH	658	JERUSALEM 32	12
GATHERD JERUSALEM'S CHILDREN IN HIS ARMS & BORE THEM LIKE	692	JERUSALEM 60	8
. . . & BORE A SILVER BOW BRIGHT SHINING	744	JERUSALEM 97	9
BUT I WILL BORE YOU MORE WITH SOME VERSES WHICH MY WIFE	816D	LETTER 24	PROSE
BORED   SEE BORD
OR AS IT IS POLITELY CALLD BORED YOU TOO MUCH ALREADY .	816C	LETTER 24	PROSE
BORERS
NOW YOU WILL I HOPE SHEW ALL THE FAMILY OF ANTIQUE BORERS	790D	LETTER 2	PROSE
BORGOGNE
. . . THE DUKE OF BRETAGNE AND THE EARL OF BORGOGNE . . .	141	FRENCH REVOLTN	169
BORGOGNONE
TWO COPIES PERHAPS FROM BORGOGNONE OF BATTLES	844A	LETTER 43	PROSE
BORING
THRO RANKS OF WAR SPONTANEOUS & THAT HOOKS & BORING SCREWS	344	FOUR ZOAS 8	133
BORN   SEE CHAOS-BORN,EARTH-BORN,FIRST-BORN,FIRST BORN,FREE BORN,NATURAL BORN
NEW-BORN,NEW/BORN,WOMAN-BORN,YOUNGEST/BORN
BY NIGHT I AM DECEIVED WHO SAYS THAT THOU WAST BORN OF MORTAL KIND	38B	SAMSON/PS	PROSE
FOR SORROW IS THE LOT OF ALL OF WOMAN BORN	39B	SAMSON/PS	PROSE
NOR KNEW THAT JOY WAS BORN AND TAKING POISNOUS SEED . . .	40D	THEN SHE BORE	PROSE
WAS BORN ENVY IN DIREFUL PAINS HIM BORE THEN ENVY BROUGHT FORTH CARE	42C	THEN SHE BORE	PROSE
IS IT TO ASSERT THAT MAN IS BORN IN ONLY ONE DEGREE . . .	93A	ANNO SWED LOVE	MARG
HEAVEN & HELL ARE BORN TOGETHER	96D	ANNO SWED LOVE	MARG
TRUE I WAS BORN THY [CHILD] SLAVE WHO ASKD THEE TO SAVE ME FROM DEATH	107	TIRIEL 6	14
HOW CAN THE BIRD THAT IS BORN FOR JOY	124	SCHOOL BOY/SI	16
IMAGE OF TRUTH NEW BORN	126	VOICE BARD/SI	3
WHY FADE THESE CHILDREN OF THE SPRING BORN BUT TO SMILE & FALL	127	BOOK OF THEL 1	7
BURGUNDY THOU WAST BORN A LION MY SOUL IS OERGROWN WITH DISTRESS	139	FRENCH REVOLTN	112
THO BORN ON THE CHEATING BANKS OF THAMES	166	WHY CARE FOR/N	5
I WAS BORN A SLAVE BUT I [LONG] GO TO BE FREE	166	WHY CARE FOR/N *	9
WHATEER IS BORN OF MORTAL BIRTH	220	TO TIRZAH/SE	1
LIKE A MAN FROM A CLOUD BORN & UTHA	234	URIZEN 23	13
FLAMD OUT FIRST BEGOTTEN LAST BORN	234	URIZEN 23	18
SURGE FOAM AND LABOUR INTO LIFE FIRST BORN & FIRST CONSUMD	238	EUROPE PREL 1	9
FIRST BORN OF ENITHARMON RISE	239	EUROPE 4	25
AND I MAY SEE THEE IN THE HOUR OF BLISS MY ELDEST BORN . .	239	EUROPE 4	28
ARISE O RINTRAH ELDEST BORN SECOND TO NONE BUT ORC . .	240	EUROPE 8	1
NEW BORN INTO OUR WORLD WRATH SUBSIDED	258	BOOK OF LOS 4	39
SHE TREMBLING ANSWERD WHEREFORE WAS I BORN AND WHAT AM I	268	FOUR ZOAS 1	158
ONCE BORN FOR THE SPORT & AMUSEMENT OF MAN	272	FOUR ZOAS 1	278
. . . NOW BORN TO DRINK UP ALL HIS POWERS	272	FOUR ZOAS 1	278
AND THAT HE MUST BE BORN IS CERTAIN FOR ONE MUST BE ALL	272	FOUR ZOAS 1	294
CONGLOBING IN THE DARK CONFUSION MEAN TIME LOS WAS BORN	275	FOUR ZOAS 1	420
O BRIGHT [AHANIA] [SHADOW] A BOY IS BORN OF THE DARK OCEAN	292	FOUR ZOAS 3 *	14
WHILE YET THOSE BEINGS WERE NOT BORN NOR KNEW OF GOOD OR EVIL	304	FOUR ZOAS 4	274
BORN EVEN FROM TOO MANY & OUR EARTH WILL BE OVERRUN . .	323	FOUR ZOAS 7	121
IS IT IN STRONG DECEIT THAT MAN IS BORN IN STRONG DECEIT	323	FOUR ZOAS 7	140
FIRST BORN OF GENERATION THEN BEHOLD A WONDER TO THE EYES	326	FOUR ZOAS 7	245
IN DARK CONFUSION MEAN TIME LOS WAS BORN & ENITHARMON .	326	FOUR ZOAS 7	259
THOU & THAT DEMON LOS [WERE] WERT BORN AH JEALOUSY & WOE	327	FOUR ZOAS 7 *	295
FOR HE BEHELD NEW FEMALE FORMS BORN FORTH UPON THE AIR . .	332	FOUR ZOAS 7	487
IS BORN ON EARTH SO WAS HE BORN OF FAIR JERUSALEM . . .	347	FOUR ZOAS 8	262
MOTHER OF MYRIADS REDEEMD & BORN IN HER SPIRITUAL PALACES	363	FOUR ZOAS 9	223
NOT BORN FOR THE SPORT AND AMUSEMENT OF MAN	373	FOUR ZOAS 9	623
. . . BUT BORN TO DRINK UP ALL HIS POWERS	373	FOUR ZOAS 9	623
IN FAMILIES WE SEE OUR SHADOWS BORN & THENCE WE KNOW . .	374	FOUR ZOAS 9	637
AND THUS HER VOICE GLORY DELIGHT & SWEET ENJOYMENT BORN	381	FOUR ZOAS AD 5	11
FOR THERE THE BABE IS BORN IN JOY	424	MENTAL TRAVLER	5
AND IF THE BABE IS BORN A BOY	425	MENTAL TRAVLER	9
THEY CRY THE BABE THE BABE IS BORN	427	MENTAL TRAVLER	95
O WHY WAS I BORN WITH A DIFFERENT FACE	428	MARY	21
WHY WAS I NOT BORN LIKE THIS ENVIOUS RACE	428	MARY	22
TOOLS WERE MADE & BORN WERE HANDS	432	AUGURIES	65
SOME TO MISERY ARE BORN	433	AUGURIES	120
SOME ARE BORN TO SWEET DELIGHT	433	AUGURIES	122
SOME ARE BORN TO SWEET DELIGHT	433	AUGURIES	123
SOME ARE BORN TO ENDLESS NIGHT	433	AUGURIES	124
WHICH WAS BORN IN A NIGHT TO PERISH IN A NIGHT	434	AUGURIES	127
UNLESS THEY ARE BORN WITH DETERMINATE ORGANS	447C	ANNO REYNOLDS	MARG
FOR ALL ARE BORN POOR AGED SIXTY THREE	452	ANNO REYNOLDS	4
IT IS BORN WITH US INNATE IDEAS ARE IN EVERY MAN . . .	459B	ANNO REYNOLDS	MARG
BORN WITH HIM THEY ARE TRULY HIMSELF	459B	ANNO REYNOLDS	MARG
THE MAN WHO SAYS THAT THE GENIUS IS NOT BORN (BUT) TAUGHT IS A KNAVE	470A	ANNO REYNOLDS *	MARG
HE WAS BORN QUITE A FOOL BUT HE DIED QUITE A KNAVE . . .	470	ANNO REYNOLDS	2
& COMES NOT AGAIN TILL ANOTHER IS BORN WITH IT	470D	ANNO REYNOLDS	MARG
MAN IS BORN LIKE A GARDEN READY PLANTED & SOWN	471A	ANNO REYNOLDS	MARG
CORREGGIO BORN...MICH ANGELO BORN	471C	ANNO REYNOLDS	MARG

	PAGE	TITLE	LINE

BORN   (CONTINUED)

THAT THE STUPID ARE BORN WITH FACULTIES EQUAL TO OTHER MEN   473A ANNO REYNOLDS   MARG
BUT ARE BORN WITH US REYNOLDS SAYS THE CONTRARY   .   .   .   .   474B ANNO REYNOLDS   MARG
[?HOWEVER ?DISCOURAGING TO THOSE WHO ARE BORN FOR IT]   .   SUPP ANNO REYNOLDS   * MARG
FIRST ORC WAS BORN THEN THE SHADOWY FEMALE THEN ALL LOS'S   483 MILTON 3   40
    FAMILY
WHICH WAS ON EARTH BORN TO CORRUPTION & THE SIX FEMALES   498 MILTON 17   15
THAT EVERY INFANT THAT IS BORN UPON THE EARTH SHALL READ   499 MILTON 18   13
HIS IMAGES ARE BORN FOR WAR FOR SACRIFICE TO TIRZAH   .   .   .   501 MILTON 19   53
FOR IN EVERY NATION & EVERY FAMILY THE THREE CLASSES ARE   511 MILTON 25   40
    BORN
SO THEY ARE BORN ON EARTH & EVERY CLASS IS DETERMINATE   .   .   512 MILTON 26   39
OF KINDNESS & COMPASSION & IS BORN A WEEPING TERROR   .   .   .   515 MILTON 28   26
WITHIN THE VEGETATED MORTAL NERVES FOR EVERY MAN BORN IS   517 MILTON 29   30
    JOINED
OR CORREGGIO THEY OUGHT TO KNOW THAT CORREGGIO WAS BORN   563C DESC CAT   PROSE
WHO IN EVERY AGE IS BORN TO RECORD AND ETERNIZE ITS ACTS   569A DESC CAT 3   PROSE
NOR CAN A CHILD BE BORN WHO IS NOT ONE OF THESE CHARACTERS   570D DESC CAT 3   PROSE
OF SUCH CHARACTERS BORN TOO MANY FOR THE PEACE OF THE WORLD   572B DESC CAT 3   PROSE
THE OTHER NEVER CAN BE ACQUIRED BUT MUST BE BORN   .   .   .   .   602D PUB ADDR AD/N   PROSE
SOME ARE BORN WITH SHAPES OF MEN WHO MAY BE BORN   .   .   .   .   607A V LAST JUDG/N   PROSE
THERE WILL ALWAYS BE AS MANY HYPOCRITES BORN AS HONEST MEN   616A V LAST JUDG/N   PROSE
OR ARE YOU BORN TO FEED THE HUNGRY RAVENINGS OF DESTRUCTION   647 JERUSALEM 24   14
CHILDREN OF WHOREDOMS BORN FOR SACRIFICE FOR THE MEAT &   658 JERUSALEM 31   64
    DRINK
BORN OF THE WOMAN TO OBEY THE WOMAN O ALBION THE MIGHTY   660 JERUSALEM 33   51
SUBMITTING TO BE CALLD ENITHARMON'S DAUGHTERS AND BE BORN   668 JERUSALEM 40   55
HIMSELF MAY IN PROCESS OF TIME BE BORN MAN TO REDEEM   .   .   670 JERUSALEM 42   34
BECOMES SEXUAL & IS CREATED AND VEGETATED AND BORN   .   .   .   674 JERUSALEM 44   22
& OF UNIVERSAL NATURE MAN IS BORN A SPECTRE OR SATAN &   .   682A JERUSALEM 52   PROSE
INTO EGYPT FOR NEGATION A VEIL THE SAVIOUR BORN & DYING   686 JERUSALEM 55   16
    RENDS
THAT THEY MIGHT BE BORN IN CONTENTIONS OF CHASTITY & IN   707 JERUSALEM 69   10
HE WROTE YE MUST BE BORN AGAIN . . . .   750 EV GOSPEL(C)/N   14
HE WROTE YE MUST BE BORN AGAIN . . . .   751 EV GOSPEL(D)/N   14
CAN THAT WHICH WAS OF WOMAN BORN . . . .   753 EV GOSPEL(D)/N   91
THAT WAS BORN IN A NIGHT TO PERISH IN A NIGHT . . . . .   753 EV GOSPEL(D)/N   107
WAS JESUS BORN OF A VIRGIN PURE . . . .   756 EV GOSPEL(I)/N   1
BORN... (NOVEMBER)...IN LONDON & HAS DIED SEVERAL TIMES   781D INSC UPCOTT   PROSE
    SINCE
O WHY WAS I BORN WITH A DIFFERENT FACE . . . .   828 O WHY BORN/L   1
WHY WAS I NOT BORN LIKE THE REST OF MY RACE . . . . .   828 O WHY BORN/L   2
THAT WASHINGTON DID ALL THAT WAS DONE BEFORE HE WAS BORN   845B LETTER 44   PROSE
THAN HIMSELF CONSEQUENTLY WAS BORN . . . .   847D LETTER 44   PROSE
"AH LUCKLESS BABE BORN UNDER CRUEL STAR" (SPENSER) . . .   SUPP LEGEND/N 19   *
BORNE   SEE DOWNWARD-BORNE
YET DEATH IS TERRIBLE THO BORNE ON ANGELS' WINGS . . . .   30 EDW THIRD/PS 5   17
WHEN THE RED LIGHTNING BORNE BY FURIOUS STORMS . . . .   32 EDW THIRD/PS 6   28
IN MY WEAK [AGED] ARMS I HERE HAVE BORNE YOUR DYING MOTHER   99 TIRIEL 1   9
AND SAW THEIR AGED FATHER BORNE UPON HIS MIGHTY SHOULDERS   105 TIRIEL 4   46
AND RUNNING THEIR IMMORTAL COURSE THRO SOLID DARKNESS BORNE   336 FOUR ZOAS 7B   143
THRO ALL THE IMMENSE BORNE DOWN BY CLOUDS SWAGGING . . .   372 FOUR ZOAS 9   563
    IN AUTUMNAL HEAT
WHAT I HAVE BORNE ON SOLEMN WING . . . .   442 DEDICATN BLAIR   14
BORNE BY THE LIVING CREATURES OF THE THIRD PROCESSION . .   667 JERUSALEM 40   22
HAVE LABOURD HARD INDEED & HAVE BEEN BORNE ON ANGEL'S WINGS   826A LETTER 27   PROSE
BOSOM
THY SOFT KISSES ON HER BOSOM AND PUT . . . .   1 TO SPRING/PS   14
BENEATH THE BOSOM OF THE SEA . . . .   11 TO MUSES/PS   10
OR DOES TH AFFLICTED MAN THY HEAVNLY BOSOM MOVE . . . .   15 IMIT SPEN/PS   53
LIKE LILIES DROPPING TEARS IN EACH OTHER'S BOSOM . . . .   35D COUCH DEATH/PS   PROSE
THE BOSOM OF THE LOFTY HILL DRANK IN THE SILENT DEW . . .   36C COUCH DEATH/PS   PROSE
USING DECEIT TO THE WIFE OF HIS BOSOM . . . .   38D SAMSON/PS   PROSE
LEANING ON HER BOSOM THUS HE SPOKE HEAR O DALILA . . . .   39B SAMSON/PS   PROSE
PRIDE BEARS IT IN HER BOSOM AND THE GODS ALL BOW TO IT .   41A THEN SHE BORE   PROSE
("CAN HE LOVE TRUTH WHO CAN TAKE A KNAVE TO HIS BOSOM")   68A ANNO LAVATER   MARG
    NO
EARTH THUS I STAMP THY BOSOM ROUSE THE EARTHQUAKE FROM   106 TIRIEL 5   4
    HIS DEN
THE YOUNG BOSOM IS COLD FOR LACK OF MOTHER'S NOURISHMENT   110 TIRIEL 8   27
    & MILK
AND HER BOSOM LICK . . . .   113 LIT GRL LST/SI   45
NEAR MY BOSOM . . . .   115 THE BLOSSOM/SI   6
NEAR MY BOSOM . . . .   116 THE BLOSSOM/SI   12
AND EACH SLEEPING BOSOM . . . .   119 NIGHT/SI   16
MY BOSOM OF ITSELF IS COLD AND OF ITSELF IS DARK . . . .   129 BOOK OF THEL 4   12
. . . AND THE WORLD OF ATTRACTION IN HIS BOSOM . . .   136 FRENCH REVOLTN   49
. . . THEN HIS BOSOM . . . .   137 FRENCH REVOLTN   81
WRITTEN IN MY BOSOM NECKER RISE . . . .   139 FRENCH REVOLTN   114
HANDS HEAD BOSOM AND PARTS OF LOVE FOLLOW THEIR HIGH   142 FRENCH REVOLTN   185
    BREATHING JOY
OF ANOTHER'S HIGH FLAMING RICH BOSOM . . . .   142 FRENCH REVOLTN   192
. . . A WHIRLWIND AND FIRE TORE FURIOUS FROM HIS ANGRY   143 FRENCH REVOLTN   200
    BOSOM
ALL AROUND HIS [ANCLES] BOSOM ROLLD . . . .   177 DAY/N   4
REND AWAY THIS DEFILED BOSOM THAT I MAY REFLECT . . . .   190 V DAU ALBION 2   15
HIS BOSOM EARTHQUAKD WITH SIGHS . . . .   230 URIZEN 13   49
WANDRING WIDE ON THE BOSOM OF NIGHT . . . .   230 URIZEN 13   57
ALL DAY THE WORM LAY ON HER BOSOM . . . .   232 URIZEN 19   24
AROUND HIS BOSOM IN SOBBINGS . . . .   233 URIZEN 20   10
OPRESSD HIS BOSOM IN SOBBINGS . . . .   233 URIZEN 20   * 13
I TOOK HIM HOME IN MY WARM BOSOM AS WE WENT ALONG . . .   238 EUROPE INTRO   19

248

	PAGE	TITLE	LINE
BOSOM (CONTINUED)			
I BRING FORTH FROM MY TEEMING BOSOM MYRIADS OF FLAMES . .	238	EUROPE PREL 2	9
THE BOSOM OF THE GROUND	246	SONG OF LOS 4	10
HER BOSOM SWELLS WITH WILD DESIRE	248	SONG OF LOS 7	37
SHOT DOWN HIS WIDE BOSOM AND SHOULDERS	249	AHANIA 2	4
THE BLACK CLOUDS ON THE BOSOM OF FUZON	251	AHANIA 3	29
ON FUZON FLEW ENTERD HIS BOSOM	251	AHANIA 3	40
ON THE BREDTH OF HIS OPEN BOSOM	254	AHANIA 5	12
CAST OUT FROM THY LOVELY BOSOM	255	AHANIA 5	40
SHE HATH TAKEN REFUGE IN MY BOSOM & I CANNOT CAST HER OUT	265	FOUR ZOAS 1	32
SO SAYING FROM HER BOSOM WEAVING SOFT IN SINEWY THREADS	266	FOUR ZOAS 1	69
HE DROPD HIS HAMMER DIVIDING FROM HIS AKING BOSOM FLED .	278	FOUR ZOAS 1	523
MURDERD HER & HID HER IN HER BOSOM EMBALMING HER FOR FEAR	278	FOUR ZOAS 1	526
SHE SHOULD ARISE AGAIN TO LIFE EMBALMD IN ENION'S BOSOM	278	FOUR ZOAS 1	527
HIS CHILDREN WANDERING OUTSIDE FROM HIS BOSOM FLEEING AWAY	279	FOUR ZOAS 1	559
THEY WEPT BEFORE THE INNER GATES OF ENITHARMON'S BOSOM . .	279	FOUR ZOAS 1	561
I CARRIED HER IN MY BOSOM AS A MAN CARRIES A LAMB . .	282	FOUR ZOAS 2	93
SLAIN ON THE ALTAR UP ASCENDING INTO HER CLOUDY BOSOM .	285	FOUR ZOAS 2	196
AND FROM HER BOSOM LUVAH FELL FAR AS THE EAST & WEST .	294	FOUR ZOAS 3	100
AND THREW AHANIA FROM HIS BOSOM OBDURATE SHE FELL LIKE LIGHTNING	295	FOUR ZOAS 3	132
RAGE RAGE SHALL NEVER FROM MY BOSOM WINDS & WATERS OF WOE	297	FOUR ZOAS 3	203
AT NOON & LAID HER HEAD UPON MY WEARIED BOSOM AT NIGHT .	301	FOUR ZOAS 4	139
IN ALBION'S BOSOM FOR IN EVERY HUMAN BOSOM THESE LIMITS STAND	304	FOUR ZOAS 4	272
AROUND HIS BOSOM LIKE A BLOODY CORD IN SECRET SOBS . . .	307	FOUR ZOAS 5	84
AROUND HIS BOSOM EVERY DAY HE VIEWD THE FIERY YOUTH . . .	307	FOUR ZOAS 5	86
DEPENDING FROM THE BOSOM OF LOS & HOW WITH [DISMAL] GRIDING PAIN	307	FOUR ZOAS 5	93
FELL FROM HIS BOSOM ON THE MOUNTAIN THE SPECTRE DARK .	307	FOUR ZOAS 5	100
HIS BOSOM IS LIKE STARRY HEAVEN EXPANDED ALL THE STARS .	308	FOUR ZOAS 5	130
AND IN THE DARK VACUITY CREATED A BOSOM OF [SLIME] CLAY	316	FOUR ZOAS 6	158
WHEN WEARIED DEAD HE FELL HIS LIMBS REPOSD IN THE BOSOM OF SLIME	316	FOUR ZOAS 6	159
AND IF ETERNAL FALLING I REPOSE ON THE DARK BOSOM . .	317	FOUR ZOAS 6	218
UPON HER BOSOM IN SWEET BLISS HE FAINTED WONDER SIEZD .	326	FOUR ZOAS 7	241
BUT THEN THE SPECTRE ENTERD LOS'S BOSOM EVERY SIGH & GROAN	328	FOUR ZOAS 7	336
COME THEN INTO MY BOSOM & IN THY SHADOWY ARMS BRING WITH THEE	329	FOUR ZOAS 7	367
THY BOSOM TRANSLUCENT IS A SOFT REPOSE FOR THE WEEPING SOULS	331	FOUR ZOAS 7	437
THAT VANISH AGAIN INTO MY BOSOM BUT IF THOU MY LOS . .	331	FOUR ZOAS 7	452
IN INFANT INNOCENCE REPOSD ON ENITHARMON'S BOSOM . . .	332	FOUR ZOAS 7	477
IN TWAIN & LO MY CRYSTAL FORM THAT LIVED IN MY BOSOM .	334	FOUR ZOAS 7B	65
FOR LOS COULD ENTER INTO ENITHARMON'S BOSOM & EXPLORE .	342	FOUR ZOAS 8	32
THE SCALY ARMOUR SHOT OUT STUBBORN DOWN HIS BACK & BOSOM	343	FOUR ZOAS 8	73
OF FAIR JERUSALEM'S BOSOM IN A GENTLY BEAMING ?FIRE . .	346	FOUR ZOAS 8	193
FROM THE HERMAPHRODITIC BOSOM SATAN HE WAS NAMD . . .	347	FOUR ZOAS 8	251
. . . THE BOSOM OF SATAN THE FALSE FEMALE AS IN AN ARK & VEIL	348	FOUR ZOAS 8	292
FELL FROM MY STATION IN THE ETERNAL BOSOM I DIVIDED . .	350	FOUR ZOAS 8	352
INTO THE DEEP TO SIEZE THE SHADOW SCALES HIS NECK & BOSOM	352	FOUR ZOAS 8	424
INTO THE ABYSSES OF HIS BOSOM THE VESSELS OF HIS BLOOD .	353	FOUR ZOAS 8	472
I AM THE NOURISHER THOU THE DESTROYER IN MY BOSOM IS MILK & WINE	354	FOUR ZOAS 8	500
I FOUND HIM IN MY BOSOM & I SAID THE TIME OF LOVE . .	355	FOUR ZOAS 8	538
BEHOLD JERUSALEM IN WHOSE BOSOM THE LAMB OF GOD [IS SEEN]	362	FOUR ZOAS 9	205
FOR IN MY BOSOM A NEW SONG ARISES TO MY LORD	368	FOUR ZOAS 9	433
SHE BORE THE FRUITS IN HER LAP SHE GATHERD FLOWERS FOR HER BOSOM	369	FOUR ZOAS 9	477
AND NOW HER FEET STEP ON THE GRASSY BOSOM OF THE GROUND	370	FOUR ZOAS 9	505
SHE PRESD THEM TO HER BOSOM & HER PEARLY TEARS DROPD DOWN	371	FOUR ZOAS 9	524
THARMAS HENCEFORTH IN VALA'S BOSOM THOU SHALT FIND SWEET PEACE	371	FOUR ZOAS 9	527
OR ANY USEFUL THING HIS BUSINESS & BOSOM WAS TO BE LORD CHANCELLOR	404D	ANNO BACON	MARG
ROUND GLOBE SUNK DOWN FROM HIS BOSOM INTO THE DEEP IN PANGS	483	MILTON 3	30
CREEPING IN REPTILE FLESH UPON THE BOSOM OF THE GROUND .	484	MILTON 5	20
THUS SATAN RAGD AMIDST THE ASSEMBLY AND HIS BOSOM GREW . .	490	MILTON 9	30
HIS BOSOM INWARDS SHONE WITH FIRES BUT THE STONES BECOMING OPAKE	490	MILTON 9	32
OF THE ASSEMBLY IN SATAN'S BOSOM A VAST UNFATHOMABLE ABYSS	490	MILTON 9	35
THE LOUD VOICD BARD TERRIFYD TOOK REFUGE IN MILTON'S BOSOM	495	MILTON 14	9
HOVERING OVER THE COLD BOSOM IN ITS VORTEX MILTON BENT DOWN	497	MILTON 15	41
TO THE BOSOM OF DEATH WHAT WAS UNDERNEATH SOON SEEMD ABOVE	497	MILTON 15	42
IN THE SHADOWY FEMALE'S BOSOM JEALOUS HER DARKNESS GREW	500	MILTON 18	42
WITHIN HER BOSOM ALBION LIES EMBALMD NEVER TO AWAKE . . .	501	MILTON 19	57
FELL FROM MY STATION IN THE ETERNAL BOSOM SIX THOUSAND YEARS	505	MILTON 22	16
AS THE BELOVED INFANT IN HIS MOTHER'S BOSOM ROUND INCIRCLED	518	MILTON 30	11
THE BOSOM OF THE FATHER IN ETERNITY ON ETERNITY	519	MILTON 31	5
I ALSO STOOD IN SATAN'S BOSOM & BEHELD ITS DESOLATIONS .	529	MILTON 39	15
HIS LEFT SCOTLAND HIS BOSOM GIRT WITH GOLD INVOLVES . .	531	MILTON 39	42
GLORIOUS AS THE MIDDAY SUN IN SATAN'S BOSOM GLOWING . .	532	MILTON 40	19
ALBION'S BOSOM THE BOSOM OF DEATH & THE FOUR SURROUNDED HIM	534	MILTON 42	21
ANGER & WRATH MY BOSOM RENDS	538	ANGER WRATH/N	1
THEY TOO LARGE AND UNWIELDY FOR HIS BRAIN AND BOSOM . .	580B	DESC CAT 5	PROSE
IT IS THE DIVINE BOSOM INTO WHICH WE SHALL ALL GO . . .	605D	V LAST JUDG/N	PROSE
IF HE COULD ENTER INTO NOAH'S RAINBOW OR INTO HIS BOSOM	611A	V LAST JUDG/N	PROSE
BEAMING FORTH WITH HER DAUGHTERS INTO THE DIVINE BOSOM [WHERE]	622	JERUSALEM 4	15

249

		PAGE	TITLE	LINE

BOSOM   (CONTINUED)

	PAGE	TITLE	LINE
EVER EXPANDING IN THE BOSOM OF GOD THE HUMAN IMAGINATION	623	JERUSALEM 5	20
ALTHOUGH IN EVERY BOSOM THEY CONTROLL OUR VEGETATIVE POWERS	624	JERUSALEM 5	39
IN GNAWING PAIN FROM LOS'S BOSOM IN THE DEADLY NIGHT .	639	JERUSALEM 17	50
FIRST AS A RED GLOBE OF BLOOD TREMBLING BENEATH HIS BOSOM	639	JERUSALEM 17	51
OUT FROM HIS BOSOM A MIGHTY POLYPUS VEGETATING IN DARKNESS	641	JERUSALEM 18	40
IN WAR FORTH FROM HIS BOSOM THEY WENT AND RETURND . . .	641	JERUSALEM 18	42
JERUSALEM HIS EMANATION SHUT WITHIN HIS BOSOM	641	JERUSALEM 19	29
I REDOUNDED FROM ALBION'S BOSOM IN MY VIRGIN LOVELINESS	643	JERUSALEM 20	38
JERUSALEM DISSEMBLER JERUSALEM I LOOK INTO THY BOSOM .	643	JERUSALEM 21	18
I SEE THEM DISTANT FROM MY BOSOM SCOURGD ALONG THE ROADS	644	JERUSALEM 21	40
FATHER ONCE PITEOUS IS PITY A SIN EMBALMD IN VALA'S BOSOM	646	JERUSALEM 23	9
AND THEREFORE GOD TAKES VENGENCE ON ME FROM MY CLAY-COLD BOSOM	646	JERUSALEM 23	33
MUTUAL EACH WITHIN OTHER'S BOSOM IN VISIONS OF REGENERATION	648	JERUSALEM 24	45
BUT VENGEANCE IS THE DESTROYER OF GRACE & REPENTANCE IN THE BOSOM	648	JERUSALEM 25	10
AND FROM HER BOSOM LUVAH FELL FAR AS THE EAST AND WEST . .	655	JERUSALEM 29	79
INTO HIS BOSOM FROM WHICH ALBION SHRUNK IN DISMAL PAIN .	656	JERUSALEM 30	17
AND LUVAH HATH DRAWN THE CURTAINS AROUND ALBION IN VALA'S BOSOM	656	JERUSALEM 30	39
BOSOM IN ALL THE TERRORS OF FRIENDSHIP ENTERING THE CAVES	656	JERUSALEM 31	4
IN STERN DEFIANCE CAME FROM ALBION'S BOSOM HAND HYLE KOBAN	658	JERUSALEM 32	10
IN ALBION'S BOSOM FOR IN EVERY HUMAN BOSOM THOSE LIMITS STAND	662	JERUSALEM 35	2
HIS FACE AND BOSOM WITH PETRIFIC HARDNESS AND HIS HANDS	664	JERUSALEM 38	1
AND FEET LEST ANY SHOULD ENTER HIS BOSOM & EMBRACE . . .	664	JERUSALEM 38	2
IN EVERY BOSOM A UNIVERSE EXPANDS AS WINGS	665	JERUSALEM 38	49
THOSE WHO DEVOUR HIS SOUL ARE TAKEN INTO HIS BOSOM . .	667	JERUSALEM 40	16
IN THE BOSOM OF MAN FOR EVER FROM ETERNITY TO ETERNITY .	670	JERUSALEM 42	36
THAT THE SPEAR THAT LIGHTS IT FORTH MAY SHATTER THE RIBS & BOSOM	672	JERUSALEM 43	34
BURST FROM HIS BOSOM IN THE TOMB LIKE A PALE SNOWY CLOUD	678	JERUSALEM 48	43
UPON HIS SONS & DAUGHTERS SELF-EXILED FROM HIS BOSOM .	679	JERUSALEM 48	61
CREEPING IN REPTILE FLESH UPON THE BOSOM OF THE GROUND .	680	JERUSALEM 49	33
THEN ALBION DREW ENGLAND INTO HIS BOSOM IN GROANS & TEARS	685	JERUSALEM 54	27
THEN THE SPECTRE DREW VALA INTO HIS BOSOM MAGNIFICENT TERRIFIC	699	JERUSALEM 64	25
FOR IN THE DEPTHS OF ALBION'S BOSOM IN THE EASTERN HEAVEN	699	JERUSALEM 65	5
BLOOD HATH STAIND HER FAIR SIDE BENEATH HER BOSOM . .	705	JERUSALEM 67	43
HIS BOSOM WIDE & SHOULDERS HUGE OVERSPREADING WONDROUS .	708	JERUSALEM 70	3
HER BRAIN ENLABYRINTHS THE WHOLE HEAVEN OF HER BOSOM & LOINS	709	JERUSALEM 70	29
IN HEAVENS & EARTHS AS IN YOUR OWN BOSOM YOU BEAR YOUR HEAVEN	709	JERUSALEM 71	17
HE SLEW THEM I REVIVED THEM TO LIFE IN MY WARM BOSOM . .	722	JERUSALEM 80	20
HE SAW THEM ISSUE FROM MY BOSOM DARK IN JEALOUSY . . .	722	JERUSALEM 80	21
WITHIN MY BOSOM LEST HE ARISE TO LIFE & SLAY MY LUVAH .	722	JERUSALEM 80	29
UPON MY BOSOM LOOK HERE IS THE LOVELY WAYWARD FORM . . .	726	JERUSALEM 82	38
UPON HIS PARENT BOSOM LAY THY LITTLE ONES O LAND . . .	727	JERUSALEM 83	24
THE SEEDS OF CITIES & OF VILLAGES IN THE HUMAN BOSOM .	728	JERUSALEM 83	55
THE SEEDS O SISTERS IN THE BOSOM OF TIME & SPACE'S WOMB	730	JERUSALEM 85	28
IN THE OPACOUS BOSOM OF THE SLEEPER LOVELY THREE-FOLD .	730	JERUSALEM 86	2
THY BOSOM WHITE TRANSLUCENT COVERD WITH IMMORTAL GEMS .	731	JERUSALEM 86	14
INTO A GLOBE OF BLOOD BENEATH HIS BOSOM TREMBLING IN DARKNESS	732	JERUSALEM 86	52
AND LET THEM RUN ON THE WINDS OF THY BOSOM I WILL FIX THEM	732	JERUSALEM 87	9
A ROUND WOMB BENEATH MY BOSOM LEST I ALSO BE OVERWOVEN . .	732	JERUSALEM 87	14
INTO EACH OTHER'S BOSOM WHICH ARE UNIVERSES OF DELIGHT .	733	JERUSALEM 88	4
SHOOTING OUT IN SWEET PLEASURE HER BOSOM IN MILKY LOVE .	733	JERUSALEM 88	28
HIS BOSOM WIDE REFLECTS MOAB & AMMON ON THE RIVER . .	735	JERUSALEM 89	24
OF THE MINES OF CORNWALL & DERBYSHIRE LAYS UPON HIS BOSOM HEAVY	741	JERUSALEM 94	8
HIS LOINS & BOSOM UNREMOVABLE BY SWELLING STORMS & LOUD RENDING	741	JERUSALEM 94	10
AND ENGLAND WHO IS BRITTANNIA AWOKE FROM DEATH ON ALBION'S BOSOM	742	JERUSALEM 94	20
ENGLAND WHO IS BRITTANNIA ENTERD ALBION'S BOSOM REJOICING	743	JERUSALEM 95	22
ENGLAND WHO IS BRITTANNIA ENTERED ALBION'S BOSOM REJOICING	743	JERUSALEM 96	2
ALBION'S BOSOM THEN ALBION STOOD BEFORE JESUS IN THE CLOUDS	744	JERUSALEM 96	42
AND THEN AWAKING INTO HIS BOSOM IN THE LIFE OF IMMORTALITY	747	JERUSALEM 99	4
AND IN MY BURNING BOSOM DWELL	755	EV GOSPEL(E)/N	78
O THAT IN THE BOSOM OF GOD I WAS HID	772C	ANNO SPURZHEIM	MARG
COMPANION FROM ETERNITY IN THE DIVINE BOSOM IN	802C	LETTER 14	PROSE
IN HIS BOSOM SUN BRIGHT	805	TO BUTTS/L	58

BOSOMD

	PAGE	TITLE	LINE
THEN BOSOMD IN AN AMBER CLOUD AROUND	15	IMIT SPEN/PS	42
FLOTING UPON THE BOSOMD AIR	244	EUROPE 14	* 18

BOSOM'S

	PAGE	TITLE	LINE
TO LIVE IN THY BOSOM'S TRANSLUCENCE AS IN AN ETERNAL MORNING	732	JERUSALEM 87	11

BOSOMS

	PAGE	TITLE	LINE
AND THEY NESTLE IN EARTH-BREATHING BOSOMS	136	FRENCH REVOLTN	57
WHICH THE BOSOMS OF ALL INHABIT	224	URIZEN 4	29
AND BOSOMS OF MILK IN MY CHAMBERS	255	AHANIA 5	20
WITH MONSTERS GIRDING ROUND THEIR BOSOMS	314	FOUR ZOAS 6	105
. . . IN THEIR DREADFUL [BOWELS] BOSOMS	317	FOUR ZOAS 6	* 228
("TO MEN'S BUSINESS AND BOSOMS") ERRATUM TO MEN'S POCKETS	397B	ANNO BACON	MARG
AROUND THEIR LOINS POURD FORTH THEIR ARROWS & THEIR BOSOMS BEAM	484	MILTON 4	23
TRANSLUCENT IN THEIR FOREHEADS & THEIR BOSOMS & THEIR LOINS	484	MILTON 5	8
FIRST EER THE MORNING BREAKS JOY OPENS IN THE FLOWERY BOSOMS	520	MILTON 31	50

250

```
                                                         PAGE     TITLE          LINE
BOSOMS    (CONTINUED)
     THE CLOUDS ARISE FROM THE BOSOMS OF MOUNTAINS  . . . . .  618C ILLUS MILTON     PROSE
     WITHIN YOUR BOSOMS I RESIDE AND YOU RESIDE IN ME    . . .  622 JERUSALEM 4         19
     REASON NOT ON BOTH SIDES REPOSE UPON OUR BOSOMS    . . . .  676 JERUSALEM 46        13
     STRIP THEM OFF FROM THEIR SHOULDERS AND BOSOMS THEY LAY     702 JERUSALEM 66        18
        ASIDE
     THE SPIES FROM EGYPT TO RAISE JEALOUSY IN THE BOSOMS OF     707 JERUSALEM 68        60
        THE TWELVE
     ALL ARE HUMAN & WHEN YOU ENTER INTO THEIR BOSOMS YOU WALK   709 JERUSALEM 71        16
     GENTLY UPON THEIR BOSOMS MOVE  . . . . . . . . . .          718 ENGLND AWAKE/J       6
BOSTON
     THE MARINERS OF BOSTON DROP THEIR ANCHORS AND UNLADE   . .  201 AMERICA 14          14
BOSTON'S
     AND BOSTON'S ANGEL CRIED ALOUD AS THEY FLEW THRO THE DARK   200 AMERICA 11           3
        NIGHT
BOTH
     I CHID THEM BOTH BUT GAVE THEM NOBLE HOPES  . . . . . .      25 EDW THIRD/PS 3      169
     ETRUSCAN COLUMN THEN (STARTING) UP & CLENCHING BOTH HIS     45B ISLAND MOON 1     PROSE
        FISTS
     OR PHEBUS THAN PHAROH HANG THEM BOTH SAID THE CYNIC  . . .   47D ISLAND MOON 4    PROSE
     NOW BOTH EVIL & GOOD CANNOT EXIST IN A SIMPLE BEING  . .     80A ANNO LAVATER      MARG
     & A LILLY ARE VARIOUS & BOTH BEAUTIFUL BEAUTY IS EXUBERANT   81C ANNO LAVATER      MARG
     IT IS A RESTRAINT ON ACTION BOTH IN OURSELVES &  . . . .     88D ANNO LAVATER      MARG
     GOOD & EVIL ARE HERE BOTH GOOD & THE TWO CONTRARIES         91D ANNO SWED LOVE     MARG
        MARRIED
     HE WANDERD DAY & NIGHT TO HIM BOTH DAY & NIGHT WERE DARK    100 TIRIEL 2            1
     BOTH SPEAR & SHIELD WERE USELESS & THE COAT OF IRON MAIL    105 TIRIEL 4           70
     CONSUMING ALL BOTH FLOWERS & FRUITS INSECTS & WARBLING      110 TIRIEL 8           38
        BIRDS
     AND NOT SIT BOTH NIGHT & DAY  . . . . . . . .               122 ON ANOTHERS/SI     21
     FOR THIS HISTORY HAS BEEN ADOPTED BY BOTH PARTIES   . . .   150A MARRIAGE HH 5    PROSE
     SHALL BE BOTH THOUGHT WISE THAT THEY MAY BE A ROD   . . .   151D MARRIAGE HH 8    PROSE
     AS THE STENCH TERRIBLY ANNOYD US BOTH WE WENT INTO THE MILL 157B MARRIAGE HH 17   PROSE
     BUT KISS HIM & GIVE HIM BOTH [FOOD] DRINK & APPAREL  . .    180 LIT VAGABOND/N      18
     THEY ARE BOTH GONE UP TO CHURCH TO PRAY  . . . . . .        180 CHIMNEY SWP/N        4
     AND I WEPT BOTH NIGHT & DAY  . . . . . . . . .              182 THE ANGEL/N          5
     AND I WEPT BOTH DAY & NIGHT  . . . . . . . . . .            182 THE ANGEL/N          7
     ARISE & COME BOTH FIFE & DRUM  . . . . . . . . .            185 LET BROTHELS/N       7
     AND THE [FAMINE] SHALL EAT BOTH CRUST & CRUMB  . . . .      185 LET BROTHELS/N       8
     ARE BOTH ALIKE A NIGHT OF SIGHS A MORNING OF FRESH TEARS    191 V DAU ALBION 2      38
     AND IS THERE NOT ONE LAW FOR BOTH THE LION AND THE OX   .   192 V DAU ALBION 4      22
     INVENTED A METHOD OF PRINTING BOTH LETTER-PRESS AND        207B PRSPECTUS 1793    PROSE
        ENGRAVING
     THEY ARE BOTH GONE UP TO THE CHURCH TO PRAY  . . . . .      212 CHIMNEY SWP/SE       4
     AND I WEPT BOTH NIGHT AND DAY  . . . . . . . . .            214 THE ANGEL/SE         5
     AND I WEPT BOTH DAY AND NIGHT  . . . . . . . . . .          214 THE ANGEL/SE         7
     BUT KISS HIM & GIVE HIM BOTH DRINK AND APPAREL  . . . .     216 LIT VAGABND/SE      16
     AND IT GREW BOTH DAY AND NIGHT  . . . . . . . . .           218 POISON TREE/SE       9
     BOTH SONS & DAUGHTERS FOR HE SAW  . . . . . . . . .         235 URIZEN 23           24
     AND COMPREHEND WITHIN HIMSELF ALL THINGS BOTH SMALL & GREAT 272 FOUR ZOAS 1      *  295
     WHAT HAVE I DONE BOTH RAGE & MERCY ARE ALIKE TO ME  . .     297 FOUR ZOAS 3        196
     THE REAPER IN BOTH ARMS EMBRACING THE FURIOUS RAGING FLAMES 332 FOUR ZOAS 7        463
     GO ON THY COURSE REJOICING & LET US BOTH REJOICE TOGETHER   368 FOUR ZOAS 9        424
     AND THAT HE WILL BE EQUALLY PROFITABLE BOTH WAYS  . . . .  380B FOUR ZOAS NOTE    PROSE
     FIND THAT YOU HAVE BOTH DONE SUCH MIRACLES &  . . . . .    391D ANNO WATSON        MARG
     AS BOTH ASTONISH & COMFORT ME & MINE  . . . . . . .        391D ANNO WATSON        MARG
     BOTH OF PRIVATE & PUBLIC MATTERS  . . . . . . . . .        392B ANNO WATSON        MARG
     MURDER THE LAWS OF THE JEWS WERE BOTH CEREMONIAL & REAL    393C ANNO WATSON        MARG
     IF CAESAR IS RIGHT CHRIST IS WRONG BOTH IN POLITICS       396D ANNO BACON         MARG
        & RELIGION
     SHE PIERCES BOTH HIS HANDS & FEET  . . . . . . . .         425 MENTAL TRAVLER      14
     TO MAKE IT FEEL BOTH COLD & HEAT  . . . . . . . . .        425 MENTAL TRAVLER      16
     AND ON THE DESART WILD THEY BOTH  . . . . . . . . .        426 MENTAL TRAVLER      75
     [?THEY EXCELL BOTH IN MINUTE & DISCRIMINATING             453D ANNO REYNOLDS    * MARG
        DETERMINATION]
     BOTH OF NATURE & ART  . . . . . . . . . . . .             455D ANNO REYNOLDS      MARG
     MAKES BOTH STATESMEN & ARTISTS FOOLS & KNAVES  . . . . .   461C ANNO REYNOLDS      MARG
     BOTH IN POETRY & PAINTING  . . . . . . . . . .            461D ANNO REYNOLDS      MARG
     IN THE HIGHEST DEGREE FOR HE HAS EVERY [PERQUISITE] THING 472A ANNO REYNOLDS    * MARG
        OF BOTH
     HE STATES ABSURDITIES IN COMPANY WITH TRUTHS & CALLS BOTH 474A ANNO REYNOLDS      MARG
        ABSURD
     SHAKSPEARE & MILTON WERE BOTH CURBD BY THE GENERAL MALADY 480C MILTON 1          *PROSE
     AS THE EYE OF MAN VIEWS BOTH THE EAST & WEST ENCOMPASSING  497 MILTON 15           28
     ARE FINISHD I RETURN BOTH TIME & SPACE OBEY MY WILL  . .   505 MILTON 22           17
     BOTH WENT TO LAW WITH DEATH TO KEEP OUR EARS ON  . . . .   537 AND HIS LEGS/N      27
     HE KNEW BOTH LAW & GOSPEL BETTER THAN THEY  . . . . .      537 AND HIS LEGS/N      31
     [HE MIXD THEM BOTH & SO HE LEARND TO PAINT]  . . . . .     546 RUBENS HAD/N         3
     MAY I GOVERN ALL BOTH GREAT & SMALL  . . . . . . .         547 IF I GROW/N          3
     SET TO WORK BOTH IGNORANCE & SKILL  . . . . . . . .        549 ENGL ENCOU/N 1       2
     MENNY WOUVER BOTH BUNGLISHNESS & SKILL  . . . . . . .      549 ENGL ENCOU/N 2       2
     WAS FUSELI HE WAS BOTH TURK & JEW  . . . . . . . . .       551 ONLY MAN/N           3
     AND THEY BOTH ARE MERRY & GLAD  . . . . . . . . .          552 WHY CUPID/N          7
     HE HAD THEM BOTH BEFORE NOW HOW DO YE DO  . . . . . .      554 TO VENETIAN/N       14
     BOTH RAFAEL AND MICHAEL ANGELO KNEW THE VENETIAN AND   . 563C DESC CAT           PROSE
     WHETHER RUBENS OR VANDYKE OR BOTH WERE GUILTY OF         565B DESC CAT 2         *PROSE
        THIS VILLANY
     AND THE WIFE OF BATH ARE BOTH TAKING THEIR MORNING'S      567A DESC CAT 3         PROSE
        DRAUGHT
     AND IS PRAISED BY HIS EQUALS FOR IT FOR BOTH HIMSELF   .  574B DESC CAT 3         PROSE
     THEY BOTH THINK THAT THE WIFE OF BATH IS A YOUNG  . .  .  574B DESC CAT 3         PROSE
     ARRANGED IS AN ENQUIRY WORTHY OF BOTH THE ANTIQUARIAN  .  578D DESC CAT 5         *PROSE
```

251

	PAGE	TITLE	LINE

BOTH   (CONTINUED)

SAME MASTER SUPPOSING BOTH TO BE DONE WITH EQUAL CARE . .	585B	DESC CAT 15	PROSE
& WIFE OF BATH ARE BOTH TAKING THEIR MORNING'S DRAUGHT . .	588D	CHAUCER/N	PROSE
AND THE WIFE OF BATH ARE BOTH TAKING THEIR MORNING'S DRAUGHT	590A	CHAUCER 2	PROSE
THESE THIRTY YEARS BOTH AS AN ARTIST & A MAN MAY BE SEEN	592C	PUB ADDRESS/N	PROSE
MY MASTER & KNEW THEM BOTH TO BE	593B	PUB ADDRESS/N	PROSE
BOTH OF US CANNOT BE IN OUR RIGHT SENSES	593D	PUB ADDRESS/N	PROSE
TO EMPIRE THAT IT IS DESTRUCTIVE OF BOTH AS ALL . . .	593D	PUB ADDRESS/N	*PROSE
AS THESE [VILLAINS] BAD MEN BOTH PRINT & PUBLISH . . .	598B	PUB ADDRESS/N	PROSE
ALL BOTH MORNING & NIGHT IS NOW A DARK CAVERN XXX WHEN YOU VIEW	599B	PUB ADDRESS/N	*PROSE
BOTH IN GENIUS & FORTUNE HAVE SUBSCRIBED THEIR NAMES .	601D	PUB ADDRESS/N	PROSE
BOTH IN WHISPERS & IN PRINT BY CERTAIN PERSONS . . .	602B	PUB ADDRESS/N	PROSE
SOME ARE BORN WITH SHAPES OF MEN WHO MAY BE BOTH . . .	607A	V LAST JUDG/N	PROSE
BOTH IN ART & IN LIFE GENERAL MASSES ARE	611B	V LAST JUDG/N	PROSE
BOTH OF DECEIT & OF OPEN VIOLENCE THE DEIST & THE CHRISTIAN	615A	V LAST JUDG/N	PROSE
BUT THEY MAY BOTH OF THEM ENVY THE SUCCESS OF SATAN . .	616B	V LAST JUDG/N	PROSE
VARIETY IN EVERY LINE BOTH OF CADENCES & NUMBER OF SYLLABLES	621D	JERUSALEM 3	PROSE
AND THEY APPEARD WITHIN & WITHOUT INCIRCLING ON BOTH SIDES	631	JERUSALEM 12	17
ON BOTH SIDES WITHIN & WITHOUT BEAMING GLORIOUSLY . . .	631	JERUSALEM 12	20
AND THERE IT MEETS ETERNITY AGAIN BOTH WITHIN AND WITHOUT	633	JERUSALEM 13	36
BEYOND THE OUTLINE OF IDENTITY BOTH WAYS WHICH MEET IN ONE	640	JERUSALEM 18	3
BOTH HEART IN HEART & HAND IN HAND	652	FIELDS FROM/J	88
I WRITE IN SOUTH MOLTON STREET WHAT I BOTH SEE AND HEAR	665	JERUSALEM 38	42
REASON NOT ON BOTH SIDES REPOSE UPON OUR BOSOMS	676	JERUSALEM 46	13
BOTH OF THE HEAD & HEART & LOINS CLOSD UP IN MORAL PRIDE	693	JERUSALEM 60	49
YOU ONE TO WEAVE YOU BOTH IN THE SAME MANTLE OF SKIN .	705	JERUSALEM 68	2
NO OTHER CHRISTIANITY AND OF NO OTHER GOSPEL THAN THE LIBERTY BOTH	716D	JERUSALEM 77	PROSE
WHICH STAND BOTH MALE & FEMALE AT THE GATES OF EACH HUMANITY	733	JERUSALEM 88	11
THE FEMININE SEPARATES FROM THE MASCULINE & BOTH FROM MAN	736	JERUSALEM 90	1
BOTH READ THE BIBLE DAY & NIGHT	748	EV GOSPEL(A)/N	13
I BELIEVE BOTH MACPHERSON & CHATTERTON	783C	ANNO WW POEMS	MARG
OR PERHAPS IT OCCUPIES BOTH CIRCLES WITH ITS ENVIRONS .	786A	ILLS DANTE 101	PROSE
BOTH FOR THE ENGRAVER AND THE SCULPTOR	796B	LETTER 7	PROSE
EXTENDED & ENLARGED TO TAKE IN ORIGINALS BOTH OF PAINTING &	797D	LETTER 10	PROSE
OF GRATITUDE OR FRIENDSHIP BUT PERHAPS AN EXCESS OF BOTH	798D	LETTER 10	PROSE
WIFE & SISTER ARE BOTH WELL COURTING NEPTUNE FOR AN EMBRACE	802A	LETTER 14	PROSE
MY WIFE & SISTER ARE BOTH VERY WELL & COURTING NEPTUNE FOR AN EMBRACE	803B	LETTER 15	PROSE
TO YOU PLEASE TO REMEMBER US BOTH IN LOVE TO	807B	LETTER 17	PROSE
BOTH & IF THIS IS SUFFICIENT IT IS AT YOUR SERVICE BUT AS BEDS	808B	LETTER 19	PROSE
INTREAT YOU TO TAKE DUE CARE OF BOTH IT IS A PART OF OUR DUTY	811C	LETTER 22	PROSE
THAT BOTH HE & I WISH THAT IS TO LIFT ME OUT OF DIFFICULTY	811D	LETTER 22	PROSE
& RESUMED MY PRIMITIVE & ORIGINAL WAYS OF EXECUTION IN BOTH	812B	LETTER 22	PROSE
PRAY REMEMBER US BOTH TO MR HALL WHEN YOU SEE HIM . . .	821B	LETTER 25	PROSE
MY WIFE JOINS ME IN LOVE TO YOU BOTH I AM SINCERELY YOURS	822A	LETTER 25	PROSE
BOTH TO GOD & MAN WE LOOK FORWARD EVERY DAY WITH PLEASURE	824B	LETTER 27	PROSE
& MR PITT ARE BOTH AMONG THE SUBSCRIBERS WHICH ARE ALREADY	824D	LETTER 27	PROSE
SO IF BOTH POETS & PAINTERS SHOULD ALTERNATELY DISLIKE .	825B	LETTER 27	PROSE
I HAVE BEEN FORCED TO INSIST ON HIS LEAVING ME IN BOTH TO	825C	LETTER 27	PROSE
I KNOW MYSELF BOTH POET & PAINTER & IT IS	825C	LETTER 27	PROSE
A MORE ASSIDUOUS PURSUIT OF BOTH ARTS INDEED BY MY LATE	825C	LETTER 27	PROSE
DEPENDED ON MORTAL THINGS BOTH MYSELF & MY WIFE MUST .	825D	LETTER 27	PROSE
HERE THAN BY THE SEASIDE WE BOTH SINCERELY PRAY FOR . .	832A	LETTER 31	PROSE
HEALTH & HOW YOU HAVE ESCAPED THE DOUBLE BLOW BOTH . .	833D	LETTER 33	PROSE
OUT BOTH TIMES I WILL REPEAT MY CALL ON HIM TOMORROW MORNING	834D	LETTER 34	PROSE
WITH THE GOOD THINGS BOTH OF THIS LIFE & OF ETERNITY & WITH	835A	LETTER 34	PROSE
AROUND YOUR HERMIT & BARD SO PRAYS THE EMULATOR OF BOTH	835B	LETTER 34	PROSE
THE PLATES OF COWPER'S MONUMENT ARE BOTH IN GREAT . .	837A	LETTER 35	PROSE
& WE BOTH REMAIN YOUR AFFECTIONATE	837D	LETTER 36	PROSE
OTHER BOTH HELD ABOVE HER HEAD & A FIGURE KNEELING AT HER FEET	839C	LETTER 38	PROSE
WE BOTH REJOICE THAT MISS POOLE IS BETTER	840A	LETTER 38	PROSE
REMEMBER US BOTH AFFECTIONATELY & GRATEFULLY TO MISS POOLE	840A	LETTER 38	PROSE
INTERESTING TOPIC IN BOTH YOUR LAST LETTERS GOD BE WITH YOU	841A	LETTER 40	PROSE
YOU BOTH WITH GREAT AFFECTION MR FLAXMAN HAS ALSO PROMISED	846A	LETTER 44	PROSE
BOTH AS TO TYPE AND PRINTING PRAY LOOK AT WASHINGTON AS FAR AS	847A	LETTER 44	PROSE
OPINION BUT THAT OF MR FLAXMAN & MR PARKER BOTH OF . .	848A	LETTER 45	PROSE
WE BOTH REJOICE IN THE GENEROUS PAULINA'S RETURN . . .	849B	LETTER 45	PROSE
TO WEAR & THAT WE ARE BOTH HIGHLY DELIGHTED	853A	LETTER 51	*PROSE
WITH ALL THE WARMTH OF FRIENDSHIP BOTH TO YOU AND ME .	853B	LETTER 52	PROSE
I BEG YOUR REMARKS ALSO ON BOTH MY PERFORMANCES AS IN THEIR	853C	LETTER 52	PROSE
THE VIOLENCE ON BOTH SIDES PRINTING IS SUSPENDED IN LONDON	859B	LETTER 56	PROSE
THE CHILD IS AS BEAUTIFULLY DRAWN AS IT IS COLOURED IN BOTH	864B	LETTER 61	PROSE
OF THE WAY ON HIS JOURNEY IN THE COACH FOR WE BOTH GOT .	869C	LETTER 70	PROSE
THO I SEEM WELL BEING ENTIRELY FREE FROM BOTH PAIN & .	875C	LETTER 81	PROSE
PROOFS HE HAS REMAINING [ALL] ARE ALL PRINTED ON BOTH SIDES OF	877B	LETTER 86	*PROSE
I AM GOING ON BETTER EVERY DAY AS I THINK BOTH . . .	879B	LETTER 89	PROSE

BOTHERATION

I WRITE IN GREAT HASTE & WITH A HEAD FULL OF BOTHERATION	821B	LETTER 25	PROSE

BOTHERD

OR POOR SCHIAVONETTI WHOM THEY TO DEATH BOTHERD	538	WAS I ANGRY/N	5

	PAGE	TITLE	LINE
BOTTLE			
I HAVE GOT A BOTTLE OF AIR THAT WOULD SPREAD A PLAGUE . .	46A	ISLAND MOON 1	PROSE
THE BLADE BONE OF A TITTLEBACK NO NO HERES A BOTTLE OF WIND	58C	ISLAND MOON 10	PROSE
HE SAW THE PESTILENCE FLY OUT OF THE BOTTLE & CRIED OUT	58D	ISLAND MOON 10	PROSE
BOTTLES			
& GLASSES & PICTURES & BROKE THE BOTTLES OF WIND	58D	ISLAND MOON 10	PROSE
BOTTOM			
AH MR HUFFCAP WOULD KICK THE BOTTOM OF THE PULPIT OUT . .	48B	ISLAND MOON 4	PROSE
A PASSIONATE WRETCH IF I WAS A MAN ID WAIT AT THE BOTTOM	48B	ISLAND MOON 4	PROSE
. . . BENEATH THE BOTTOM OF THE RAGING OCEANS	298	FOUR ZOAS 4	* 16
[BUT AS SHE WOVE BEHOLD THE BOTTOM OF THE SEPULCHER] . .	356	FOUR ZOAS 8	589
[RENT & A DOOR WAS OPEND THRO THE BOTTOM OF THE SEPULCHER]	356	FOUR ZOAS 8	590
BOTTOMLESS			
BUT THEY SHALL ROT ON DESART SANDS & CONSUME IN BOTTOMLESS DEEPS	199	AMERICA 8	7
IN THE HORRID VACUITY BOTTOMLESS	258	BOOK OF LOS 4	36
IN THE HORRID BOTTOMLESS VACUITY FALLING FALLING FALLING	315	FOUR ZOAS 6	155
THEIR WINGS WAVING OVER THE BOTTOMLESS IMMENSE TO BEAR . .	674	JERUSALEM 44	4
ITS WAVES OF PEARL BECAME A BOUNDLESS OCEAN BOTTOMLESS . .	674	JERUSALEM 44	15
INTO THE BOTTOMLESS ABYSS WHOSE TORMENT ARISES FOR EVER & EVER	781	GHOST ABEL 2	21
BOTTOMS			
AND THE BOTTOMS OF THE WORLD WERE OPEND	148	FRENCH REVOLTN	301
THRO THE BOTTOMS OF IMMENSITY RAGING	259	BOOK OF LOS 5	2
TILL MANY OF THE DEAD BURST FORTH FROM THE BOTTOMS OF THEIR TOMBS	328	FOUR ZOAS 7	328
THEN MYRIADS OF THE DEAD BURST THRO THE BOTTOMS OF THEIR TOMBS	340	FOUR ZOAS 7B	* 298
WITH CAVERNS WHOSE REMOTEST BOTTOMS MEET AGAIN BEYOND . .	529	MILTON 37	55
IN THE REMOTEST BOTTOMS OF THE CAVES THAT NONE CAN PASS	529	MILTON 37	57
WAVES & THE ERYTHREAN TURNING UP THE BOTTOMS OF THE DEEPS	648	JERUSALEM 24	63
BENEATH THE BOTTOMS OF THE GRAVES WHICH IS EARTH'S CENTRAL JOINT	677	JERUSALEM 48	13
BURST THE BOTTOMS OF THE GRAVES & FUNERAL ARKS OF BEULAH	736	JERUSALEM 89	60
BOUGH			
WHERE JOY DOTH SIT ON EVERY BOUGH	63	SHEPHERD FIRST	2
BOUGHS			
THY SWEET BOUGHS PERFUME THE AIR	7	LOVE HARMNY/PS	11
TILL THE HORRID PLANT BENDING ITS BOUGHS	252	AHANIA 3	65
ITS TOPMOST [BRANCHES] BOUGHS SHOOTING A [STEM] FIBRE . . .	328	FOUR ZOAS 7	334
BOUGHT SEE MONEY BOUGHT			
THERE SOULS OF MEN ARE BOUGHT & SOLD	174	HUMAN IMAGE/N	29
[FAYETTE FAYETTE THOURT BOUGHT & SOLD]	186	LET BROTHELS/N	39
[THOURT BOUGHT & SOLD]	186	LET BROTHELS/N	45
[FAYETTE FAYETTE THOURT BOUGHT & SOLD]	186	LET BROTHELS/N	56
THE VOICE OF SLAVES BENEATH THE SUN AND CHILDREN BOUGHT WITH MONEY	190	V DAU ALBION 2	8
IS BOUGHT & SOLD & IN DIM NIGHT MY WORD SHALL BE THEIR LAW	278	FOUR ZOAS 1	503
OR WISDOM FOR A DANCE IN THE STREET NO IT IS BOUGHT WITH THE PRICE	290	FOUR ZOAS 2	398
LAWFUL BREAD BOUGHT WITH LAWFUL MONEY	787D	ANNO THORNTON	MARG
AN INCOMPARABLE PRODUCTION WHICH MR W(WALKER) BOUGHT FOR	843D	LETTER 43	PROSE
BOULSTERD			
THAN BOULSTERD PLASTERS ON A CROOKED WHORE	464	ANNO REYNOLDS	2
BOUNCING			
BOUNCING B	62	DR CLASH/IM	9
BOUND SEE ART-BOUND,ROOT BOUND,SCALE BOUND,SPELL BOUND			
WHOSE MODEST TRESSES WERE BOUND UP FOR THEE	1	TO SPRING/PS	16
MUST SURER BOUND GO THRO THY PART	16	BLIND-MANS/PS	42
WHOM I AM DOUBLY BOUND TO OBEY MY PARENT	19	EDW THIRD/PS 2	2
BY HIM WHOM I AM BOUND TO OBEY MY HANDS	23	EDW THIRD/PS 3	101
FRAIL BARK CAN SEE NO SHORE OR BOUND FOR VAST	26	EDW THIRD/PS 3	237
I BOUND THEE WITH THEM TO TRY THY TRUTH I CRIED . . .	39A	SAMSON/PS	PROSE
PRIDE BOUND HIM THEN USURPD OER ALL THE GODS	42C	THEN SHE BORE	PROSE
IN THE CIRCUMFERENCE THEY CAST A BOUND ABOUT THE INFINITE	92A	ANNO SWED LOVE	MARG
AND WHY MEN BOUND BENEATH THE HEAVENS IN A REPTILE FORM	110	TIRIEL 8	23
. . . BOUND TO THE IMPREGNABLE WALL	135	FRENCH REVOLTN	27
. . . A LOATHSOME SICK WOMAN BOUND DOWN	135	FRENCH REVOLTN	35
. . . EACH STRONG LIMB BOUND DOWN AS WITH MARBLE . .	137	FRENCH REVOLTN	66
. . . BOUND IN ASTONISHMENT A QUARTER OF AN HOUR . .	137	FRENCH REVOLTN	67
. . . AND THE KINGDOMS OF EARTH BOUND IN SHEAVES . . .	138	FRENCH REVOLTN	92
. . . THE CAPTAINS LIKE MEN BOUND IN CHAINS	141	FRENCH REVOLTN	165
. . . CAN THE MAN BE BOUND IN SORROW	142	FRENCH REVOLTN	182
AND CAN NOBLES BE BOUND WHEN THE PEOPLE ARE FREE	142	FRENCH REVOLTN	186
. . . WERE BOUND IN THE RUINS OF SULPHUR HEAVEN . . .	143	FRENCH REVOLTN	213
. . . HONESTY BOUND IN THE DENS OF SUPERSTITION . . .	144	FRENCH REVOLTN	228
REASON IS THE BOUND OR OUTWARD CIRCUMFERENCE OF ENERGY . .	149D	MARRIAGE HH 4	PROSE
LAY THE BOUND OR BUILD THE ROOF NOR PALE RELIGIOUS LETCHERY	160B	SONG LIBERTY	PROSE
BOUND & WEARY I THOUGHT BEST	166	INFANT SORW/N	7
AND BOUND ME IN A MIRTLE SHADE	167	INFANT SORW/N	30
[HAST MY] THAT FREE LOVE WITH BONDAGE BOUND	169	EARTHS ANSWR/N	25
[TO A LOVELY MIRTLE BOUND]	169	MIRTLE SHADE/N	1
UNDERNEATH MY MIRTLE BOUND	169	MIRTLE SHADE/N	6
WHY SHOULD I BE BOUND TO THEE	169	MIRTLE SHADE/N	7
LOVE FREE LOVE CANNOT BE BOUND	169	MIRTLE SHADE/N	9
WHY SHOULD I BE BOUND TO THEE	176	TO MY MIRTLE/N	1
[LOVE FREE LOVE CANNOT BE BOUND]	176	TO MY MIRTLE/N	3
TO A LOVELY MIRTLE BOUND	176	TO MY MIRTLE/N	5
[UNDERNEATH MY MIRTLE BOUND]	176	TO MY MIRTLE/N	8
[THEY BOUND HIS LITTLE IVORY LIMBS]	177	LIT BOY LST/N	22
& BOUND HIM IN AN IRON CHAIN	177	LIT BOY LST/N	25

253

		PAGE	TITLE	LINE

BOUND   (CONTINUED)

Entry	PAGE	TITLE	LINE
IN TEARS & IRON BOUND	185	LET BROTHELS/N	36
IN [TEARS] CURSES & IRON BOUND	186	LET BROTHELS/N	61
BOUND BACK TO BACK IN BROMION'S CAVES TERROR & MEEKNESS DWELL	190	V DAU ALBION 2	5
TILL SHE WHO BURNS WITH YOUTH AND KNOWS NO FIXED LOT IS BOUND	193	V DAU ALBION 5	21
OF A HARSH TERROR DRIVN TO MADNESS BOUND TO HOLD A ROD . .	193	V DAU ALBION 5	25
HIS SHIELD THAT BOUND TWELVE DEMONS & THEIR CITIES IN ITS ORB	205	AMERICA CANC C	2
THAT FREE LOVE WITH BONDAGE BOUND	211	EARTHS ANSR/SE	25
BOUND AND WEARY I THOUGHT BEST	217	INFANT SORW/SE	7
AND BOUND HIM IN AN IRON CHAIN	218	LIT BOY LST/SE	20
BOUND BUT CONDENSING IN TORRENTS	224	URIZEN 4	20
THE DARK CHANGES & BOUND EVERY CHANGE	227	URIZEN 8	10
THO BOUND IN A DEADLY SLEEP	229	URIZEN 13	27
IN HIS CHAINS BOUND & PITY BEGAN	230	URIZEN 13	51
IN THE INFINITE VOID BUT BOUND DOWN	236	URIZEN 25	46
FOR NOW THOU ART BOUND	239	EUROPE 4	27
EVERY HOUSE A DEN EVERY MAN BOUND THE SHADOWS ARE FILLD	243	EUROPE 12	26
THE ETERNAL PROPHET BOUND IN A CHAIN	256	BOOK OF LOS 3	31
DARKNESS ROUND LOS HEAT WAS NOT FOR BOUND UP	257	BOOK OF LOS 4	1
BOUND IN THE FIERCE RAGING IMMORTAL	257	BOOK OF LOS 4	7
BOUND IN HIS EXPANDING CLEAR SENSES	257	BOOK OF LOS 4	10
AND BOUND DOWN TO THE GLOWING ILLUSION	260	BOOK OF LOS 5	47
THE IMMORTAL ENDURD THO BOUND IN A DEADLY SLEEP	304	FOUR ZOAS 4	283
PRINCE OF LIGHT BOUND IN CHAINS OF INTELLECT AMONG THE FURNACES	305	FOUR ZOAS 5	16
OVER HER SON OBDURATE LOS BOUND DOWN HER LOVED JOY . . .	308	FOUR ZOAS 5	103
HIS LIMBS BOUND DOWN MOCK AT HIS CHAINS FOR OVER THEM A FLAME	308	FOUR ZOAS 5	114
BUT NOW THOU ART BOUND DOWN WITH HIM EVEN TO THE GATES OF HELL	311	FOUR ZOAS 5	* 233
OF ALL & ALL FUTURITY BE·BOUND IN HIS VAST CHAIN . . .	317	FOUR ZOAS 6	233
HERE BOUND TO FIERY MANGERS FURIOUS DASH THEY GOLDEN HOOFS	320	FOUR ZOAS 7	7
DARE THY MOST TERRIBLE WRATH ABIDE BOUND HERE TO WASTE IN PAIN	321	FOUR ZOAS 7	47
THE MAN SHALL RAGE BOUND WITH THIS CHAIN THE WORM IN SILENCE CREEP	323	FOUR ZOAS 7	143
THO BOUND WITH CHAINS OF JEALOUSY & IN SCALES OF IRON & BRASS	332	FOUR ZOAS 7	481
TO DIE A DEATH OF SIX THOUSAND YEARS BOUND ROUND WITH DESOLATION	337	FOUR ZOAS 7B	168
HOW RAGD THE GOLDEN HORSES OF URIZEN BOUND TO THE CHARIOT OF LOVE	338	FOUR ZOAS 7B	201
[I HAVE] AWAY FROM ME I HAVE BOUND DOWN WITH A HOT IRON	349	FOUR ZOAS 8	* 302
UNLESS MY BELOVED IS BOUND UPON THE STEMS OF VEGETATION	349	FOUR ZOAS 8	321
UP BOUND THE WILD STAG & THE HORSE [BEHOLDS] BEHOLD THE KING OF PRIDE	352	FOUR ZOAS 8	* 453
THUS IN A LIVING DEATH THE NAMELESS SHADOW ALL THINGS BOUND	353	FOUR ZOAS 8	481
WHILE I STOOD BOUND WITH CORDS & HEAVY CHAINS YOUR HIPOCRISY	364	FOUR ZOAS 9	276
REAPD THE WIDE UNIVERSE & BOUND IN SHEAVES A WONDROUS HARVEST	372	FOUR ZOAS 9	584
AND BLACK HORSES & ARMED MEN & MISERABLE BOUND CAPTIVES	375	FOUR ZOAS 9	667
AND MEN ARE BOUND TO SULLEN CONTEMPLATIONS IN THE NIGHT	379	FOUR ZOAS 9	* 817
A DESERT VAST WITHOUT A BOUND	426	MENTAL TRAVLER	66
IS THE HARLOT ALSO SIEZED & BOUND [CHAIND] BY TWO ANGELS	443A	LAST JUDGMNT/L	PROSE
MANY FIGURES [CHAIND] CHAINED & BOUND TOGETHER &	443C	LAST JUDGMNT/L	*PROSE
HE WHO CAN BE BOUND DOWN IS NO GENIUS	472D	ANNO REYNOLDS	MARG
GENIUS CANNOT BE BOUND	472D	ANNO REYNOLDS	MARG
BOUND UP IN THE HORNS OF JEALOUSY TO A DEADLY FADING MOON	491	MILTON 10	18
BOUND WITH THE CHAIN OF JEALOUSY BY LOS & ENITHARMON	501	MILTON 19	38
SCOFIELD IS BOUND IN IRON ARMOUR BEFORE REUBEN'S GATE . .	501	MILTON 19	59
I STOOPED DOWN & BOUND IT ON TO WALK FORWARD THRO ETERNITY	503	MILTON 21	14
WHILE LOS HEARD INDISTINCT IN FEAR WHAT TIME I BOUND MY SANDALS	505	MILTON 22	4
AND BOUND MY SANDALS ON IN UDAN-ADAN TREMBLING I STOOD .	505	MILTON 22	9
HERE IS JERUSALEM BOUND IN CHAINS IN THE DENS OF BABYLON	529	MILTON 38	27
BOUND IN ONE OF THE SERPENT'S FOLDS SURROUNDED BY HER FIENDS	606C	V LAST JUDG/N	PROSE
IN THE REVELATIONS SHE IS [BOUND] SIEZED BY TWO BEINGS .	609A	V LAST JUDG/N	PROSE
LYING ON THE ROCK OPEN BEFORE HIM HE IS BOUND IN CHAINS	609B	V LAST JUDG/N	PROSE
WHO WERE BOUND UNDER THE KNAVE NOT TO DELIVER THE KNAVE	615B	V LAST JUDG/N	PROSE
AND IRON BOUND IT OVER ME FOR EVER LIFE LIVES ON MY . .	630	JERUSALEM 10	55
RAGAN IS WHOLLY CRUEL SCOFIELD IS BOUND IN IRON ARMOUR .	631	JERUSALEM 11	21
BOUND THESE BLACK SHOES OF DEATH & ON MY HANDS DEATH'S IRON GLOVES	666	JERUSALEM 39	21
ROSE IN THE NIGHT OF BEULAH AND BOUND DOWN THE SUN & MOON	675	JERUSALEM 45	20
TO HIM WHOM HE HAS MURDERD BOUND IN VENGEANCE & ENMITY .	677	JERUSALEM 47	16
SEEING HIS SONS ASSIMILATE WITH LUVAH BOUND IN THE BONDS	685	JERUSALEM 54	11
AND THOU HAST BOUND ME DOWN UPON THE STEMS OF VEGETATION	692	JERUSALEM 60	11
TO DIE A DEATH OF SIX THOUSAND YEARS BOUND ROUND WITH VEGETATION	699	JERUSALEM 65	10
THE HEAVENS MIGHT REVOLVE & ETERNITY BE BOUND IN THEIR CHAIN	702	JERUSALEM 66	5
AWAY FROM ME I HAVE BOUND DOWN WITH A HOT IRON	705	JERUSALEM 67	48
UNLESS MY BELOVED IS BOUND UPON THE STEMS OF VEGETATION	705	JERUSALEM 68	9
HE BOUND OLD SATAN IN HIS CHAIN	749	EV GOSPEL(B)/N	32
DIVINE WHENCE THEY CAME OR WHITHER THEY WERE BOUND . . .	791B	LETTER 3	PROSE
FOR I SO FAR FROM BEING BOUND DOWN	809A	LETTER 20	PROSE
AM BOUND IN...L FOR MY APPEARANCE AT THE QUARTER SESSIONS	828A	LETTER 28	PROSE

	PAGE	TITLE	LINE

BOUND   (CONTINUED)
```
    BUT I WAS A SLAVE BOUND IN A MILL AMONG BEASTS AND DEVILS    852A LETTER 50        PROSE
    YOU AS SHERIFF ARE BOUND TO ATTEND TO IT  . . . . .       865B LETTER 62        PROSE
BOUNDARIES
    THE STARS WHICH ARE THE BOUNDARIES OF KINGDOMS PROVINCES     528 MILTON 37          48
    HE INFUSES A LOVE OF SOFT AND EVEN TINTS WITHOUT BOUNDARIES  583B DESC CAT 9       PROSE
BOUNDED
    MAN'S PERCEPTIONS ARE NOT BOUNDED BY ORGANS OF PERCEPTION    97C NAT RELIGION 2    PROSE
    THE BOUNDED IS LOATHED BY ITS POSSESSOR  . . . . . . .       97D NAT RELIGION 2    PROSE
    THE ETERNAL MIND BOUNDED BEGAN TO ROLL  . . . . . .         227 URIZEN 10           19
    THE ETERNAL MIND BOUNDED BEGAN TO ROLL EDDIES OF WRATH      303 FOUR ZOAS 4        208
        CEASELESS
BOUNDING
    HE TOOK HIGH BOUNDING OVER HILLS & DESARTS FLOODS           313 FOUR ZOAS 6         73
        & HORRIBLE CHASMS
    THAT THE MORE DISTINCT SHARP AND WIREY THE BOUNDING LINE    585B DESC CAT 15      PROSE
    THIS ALONE THE WANT OF THIS DETERMINATE AND BOUNDING FORM   585B DESC CAT 15      PROSE
    THE HORSE FROM THE OX BUT BY THE BOUNDING OUTLINE HOW  . .  585C DESC CAT 15      PROSE
    THE BOUNDING LINE AND ITS INFINITE INFLEXIONS AND MOVEMENTS 585C DESC CAT 15      PROSE
BOUNDLESS
    TILL A VOID BOUNDLESS AS A NETHER SKY APPEARD BENEATH US    155D MARRIAGE HH 17   PROSE
    [ A FATHOMLESS & BOUNDLESS DEEP ]  . . . . . . . . .        415 MY SPECTRE/N        17
    A FATHOMLESS & BOUNDLESS DEEP  . . . . . . . . . . . .      415 MY SPECTRE/N        23
    ITS WAVES OF PEARL BECAME A BOUNDLESS OCEAN BOTTOMLESS  . . 674 JERUSALEM 44        15
BOUNDS
    DOES RISE SO HIGH TO OVERFLOW ALL BOUNDS  . . . . . .        26 EDW THIRD/PS 3     235
    ROAMS ROUND VAST NATURE'S FOREST WHERE NO BOUNDS  . . . .    27 EDW THIRD/PS 3     256
    TRUTH HAS BOUNDS ERROR NONE FALLING FALLING  . . . . .      258 BOOK OF LOS 4       30
    A CRASH RAN THRO THE IMMENSE THE BOUNDS OF DESTINY WERE     295 FOUR ZOAS 3        135
        BROKEN
    THE BOUNDS OF DESTINY CRASHD DIREFUL & THE SWELLING SEA     295 FOUR ZOAS 3        136
    THE BOUNDS OF DESTINY WERE BROKEN & HATRED NOW BEGAN  . .   296 FOUR ZOAS 3        177
    BEYOND THE BOUNDS OF THEIR OWN SELF THEIR SENSES CANNOT     314 FOUR ZOAS 6         94
        PENETRATE
    THAT LIES BEYOND THE BOUNDS OF SCIENCE IN THE GREY OBSCURE  324 FOUR ZOAS 7        150
    ("BOUNDS...TO LIBERTY") IF IT IS THUS THE EXTREME OF BLACK  414B ANNO BOYD        MARG
        IS WHITE
    DELIGHTFUL WITH BOUNDS TO THE INFINITE PUTTING OFF THE      515 MILTON 28            4
        INDEFINITE
    AT A DISTANCE THE SOUTH BOUNDS ON HIGH OVER OUR THATCH AND  807B LETTER 17        PROSE
BOUNTEOUS
    AND LUXURY HIS BOUNTEOUS TABLE SPREAD  . . . . . . .         41B THEN SHE BORE     PROSE
BOUNTIFUL
    WHY DID HEAVEN ADORN ME WITH BOUNTIFUL HAND  . . . . .      428 MARY                23
BOUNTY
    LET YOUR BOUNTY DESCEND TO OUR FAIR EARS  . . . . . .        55C ISLAND MOON 9     PROSE
    THE LUST OF THE GOAT IS THE BOUNTY OF GOD  . . . . .        151C MARRIAGE HH 8     PROSE
BOURBON
    . . . SAID BOURBON AND REND THE FLAMES  . . . . . . .       142 FRENCH REVOLTN     171
BOURBON'S
    UP ROSE AWFUL IN HIS MAJESTIC BEAMS BOURBON'S STRONG DUKE   141 FRENCH REVOLTN     168
        . . .
BOW
    EACH SHINING HELM AND STRING EACH STUBBORN BOW  . . . .      26 EDW THIRD/PS 3     226
    PRIDE BEARS IT IN HER BOSOM AND THE GODS ALL BOW TO IT  . .  41A THEN SHE BORE     PROSE
    HAVING MADE A GENTLE BOW PROCEEDED TO EMPTY HIS POCKETS      45B ISLAND MOON 1     PROSE
    THE AGED WANDERER LED TOWARDS THE TENTS SHE TOOK HER BOW    109 TIRIEL 7            23
    STAND STILL OR FROM MY BOW RECIEVE A SHARP & WINGED DEATH   109 TIRIEL 7             2
    AH THEL IS LIKE A WATRY BOW AND LIKE A PARTING CLOUD  . .   127 BOOK OF THEL 1       8
    THE STRONG SOLDIERS TREMBLE THE HORSES THEIR MANES BOW      141 FRENCH REVOLTN     167
        . . .
    AND WEEP [ AND BOW THY REVEREND LOCKS ]  . . . . . . .      159B SONG LIBERTY     PROSE
    A QUIVER WITH ITS BURNING STORES A BOW LIKE THAT OF NIGHT   196 AMERICA PREL 1       5
    A BENDED BOW IS LIFTED IN HEAVEN & A HEAVY IRON CHAIN  . .  197 AMERICA 3            7
    A BENDED BOW IN HEAVEN IS LIFTED & A HEAVY IRON CHAIN  . .  204 AMERICA CANC A       7
    LEUTHA THE MANY COLOURED BOW DELIGHTS UPON THY WINGS  . . . 244 EUROPE 14           10
    CONTRITION HE PREPARD HIS BOW  . . . . . . . . . . .        250 AHANIA 3             4
    THEN A BOW BLACK PREPARD ON THIS BOW  . . . . . . . .       251 AHANIA 3            23
    HE UTTERD THESE WORDS TO THE BOW  . . . . . . . . .         251 AHANIA 3            25
    O BOW OF THE CLOUDS OF SECRESY  . . . . . . . . . .         251 AHANIA 3            26
    HIS VOICE & BOW NOR SEE HIS EYES  . . . . . . . . .         254 AHANIA 4            67
    BUT MOST THE POLISHD PALACES [?WEAK] DARK SILENT BOW WITH   275 FOUR ZOAS 1    *   396
        DREAD
    DO THEY NOT BOW THEIR BRIGHT HEADS AT THY VOICE AT THY      291 FOUR ZOAS 3          6
        COMMAND
    SHEW THY SOUL VALA SHEW THY BOW & QUIVER OF SECRET FIRES    306 FOUR ZOAS 5         49
    DRAW THY BOW [VALAN] VALA . . .                            306 FOUR ZOAS 5    *    50
    . . . FROM THE DEPTHS OF HELL THY BLACK BOW DRAW  . . . .   306 FOUR ZOAS 5         50
    THE HEAVENS BOW WITH TERROR UNDERNEATH THEIR IRON HANDS     322 FOUR ZOAS 7        103
    AND ALL THE SONS OF ?EVERLASTING SHALL BOW DOWN AT MY FEET  333 FOUR ZOAS 7B        10
    WITH DARTS OF WINTRY HAIL AGAIN THE BLACK BOW DRAW  . . .   337 FOUR ZOAS 7B       156
    THE ARROWS FLEW FROM CLOUDY BOW ALL DAY TILL BLOOD  . . .   337 FOUR ZOAS 7B       159
    ARISE O VALA BRING THE BOW OF URIZEN BRING THE SWIFT        338 FOUR ZOAS 7B       200
        ARROWS OF LIGHT
    HIS MURDER ON ANOTHER SILENT I BOW WITH DREAD  . . . . .    345 FOUR ZOAS 8        166
    BOW DOWN BEFORE HER YOU HER CHILDREN & SET JERUSALEM FREE   351 FOUR ZOAS 8        409
    THE SPEAR THE BOW THE GUN THE [MORTAL] MORTAR . . . . . .   365 FOUR ZOAS 9    *   303
    SINGING & SHOUTING TO THE MAN THEY BOW THEIR HOARY HEADS    378 FOUR ZOAS 9        804
    BUT VAIN THE SWORD & VAIN THE BOW  . . . . . . . .          419 I SAW A MONK/N      40
    THE TYRANT WHO FIRST THE BLACK BOW BENT  . . . . . . .      420 I SAW A MONK/N      50
    IS AN ARROW FROM THE ALMIGHTIE'S BOW  . . . . . . . .       420 I SAW A MONK/N      61
    WHEN SATAN FIRST THE BLACK BOW BENT  . . . . . . . .        420 I SAW MNK AD/N       1
```

		PAGE	TITLE	LINE

BOW   (CONTINUED)
```
    BUT VAIN THE SWORD & VAIN THE BOW          . . . . . . . .   430 GREY MONK        25
    IS AN ARROW FROM THE ALMIGHTIE'S BOW   . . . . . . .        430 GREY MONK        32
    TO PEACEFUL ARTS SHALL ENVY BOW            . . . . . . . .  433 AUGURIES        102
    BRING ME MY BOW OF BURNING GOLD        . . . . . . . . .    481 AND DID FEET/M     9
    STRATFORD & OLD BOW & ACROSS TO THE GARDENS OF KENSINGTON   485 MILTON 6         10
    FROM HYDE PARK TO THE ALMS-HOUSES OF MILE-END & OLD BOW     486 MILTON 6         31
    BUT ME THE SERVANTS OF THE HARROW SAW NOT BUT AS A BOW  .   492 MILTON 12        14
    I HUMBLY BOW IN ALL MY SIN BEFORE THE THRONE DIVINE  . .    493 MILTON 13         3
    AND THREW ASIDE HER ARROWS AND LAID DOWN HER SOUNDING BOW   494 MILTON 13        37
    AND ON ITS VERGE THE SUN RISES & SETS THE CLOUDS BOW   .    516 MILTON 29         8
    DICTATE TO MY ETERNAL WILL & TO MY DICTATE BOW     . . . .  530 MILTON 38        53
    OF ALL THAT LIVE DARE UTTER THIS OTHERS TREMBLE & BOW   .   530 MILTON 38        57
    FOR HE SHOOTS WITH HIS BOW    . . . . . . . . . .           552 WHY CUPID/N        5
    AND WHAT IS THE THIRD HE'LL BOW LIKE A RUSH    . . . . .    553 ASKD PRIGG/N      11
    READ CHAUCER'S DESCRIPTION OF THE GOOD PARSON AND BOW   .   570C DESC CAT 3   PROSE
    BEFORE THAT OF LIFE ON THE RIGHT SOME FIGURES [?BOW] BOW    612B V LAST JUDG/N  *PROSE
    INTO THE SWORD OF WAR INTO THE BOW AND ARROW      . . . .   628 JERUSALEM 9        5
    WITH DEMONSTRATIVE SCIENCE PIERCING APOLLYON WITH HIS OWN   631 JERUSALEM 12      14
        BOW
    DOWN THRO POPLAR & OLD BOW    . . . . . . . . . .           650 FIELDS FROM/J     42
    TO CAST JERUSALEM FORTH UPON THE WILDS TO POPLAR & BOW  .   668 JERUSALEM 41       5
    AND ERIN'S LOVELY BOW ENCLOSD THE WHEELS OF ALBION'S SONS   681 JERUSALEM 50      22
    WHEN SATAN FIRST THE BLACK BOW BENT   . . . . . . .         683 I SAW A MONK/J    17
    IS AN ARROW FROM THE ALMIGHTIE'S BOW   . . . . . . . .      683 I SAW A MONK/J    28
    ARISE O VALA BRING THE BOW OF URIZEN BRING THE SWIFT        700 JERUSALEM 65      46
        ARROWS OF LIGHT
    HIGHGATE'S HEIGHTS & HAMPSTEAD'S TO POPLAR HACKNEY & BOW    729 JERUSALEM 84       1
    LISTEN HERMON & LEBANON BOW THEIR CROWNED HEADS   . . .     730 JERUSALEM 85      17
    HE TAKES HIS BOW THEN CHOOSES OUT HIS ARROWS OF FLAMING     742 JERUSALEM 95      13
        GOLD
    HORNS OF THE WIDE BOW LOUD SOUNDING WINDS SPORT ON THE      742 JERUSALEM 95      15
        MOUNTAIN BROWS
    AND TOOK HIS BOW FOURFOLD THE VISION FOR BRIGHT BEAMING     744 JERUSALEM 97       7
        URIZEN
    LAYD HIS HAND ON THE SOUTH & TOOK A BREATHING BOW OF CARVED 744 JERUSALEM 97       8
        GOLD
    . . . & BORE A SILVER BOW BRIGHT SHINING    . . . . . . .   744 JERUSALEM 97       9
    THARMAS WESTWARD A BOW OF BRASS PURE FLAMING RICHLY WROUGHT 744 JERUSALEM 97      10
    URTHONA NORTHWARD IN THICK STORMS A BOW OF IRON TERRIBLE    744 JERUSALEM 97      11
        THUNDERING
    AND THE BOW IS A MALE & FEMALE & THE QUIVER OF THE ARROWS   744 JERUSALEM 97      12
        OF LOVE
    ARE THE CHILDREN OF THIS BOW A BOW OF MERCY                 744 JERUSALEM 97      13
        & LOVING-KINDNESS LAYING
    AND HE CLOTHED HIMSELF IN BOW & ARROWS IN AWFUL STATE       744 JERUSALEM 97      16
        FOURFOLD
    IN THE MIDST OF HIS TWENTY-EIGHT CITIES EACH WITH HIS BOW   744 JERUSALEM 97      17
        BREATHING
    THE HORNED BOW FOURFOLD . . . . . . . . . . . . . .         744 JERUSALEM 98       3
    OF THE WIDE BOW LOUD SOUNDING WINDS SPORT ON THE MOUNTAINS  745 JERUSALEM 98       5
        BROWS
    YOU SHALL BOW BEFORE HER FEET    . . . . . . . . . .        754 EV GOSPEL(E)/N    53
BOWD
    THEY KNEW TWAS VAIN TO STRIVE WITH IJIM THEY BOWD & SILENT  105 TIRIEL 4         48
        STOOD
    BOWD HIS MANE OF GOLD . . . . . . . . . . . . . .           113 LIT GRL LST/SI   44
    THE CLOUD DESCENDED AND THE LILLY BOWD HER MODEST HEAD  .   128 BOOK OF THEL 2   17
    SHE BOWD OVER THE WEEPING INFANT AND HER LIFE EXHALD   .    129 BOOK OF THEL 4    8
    THE WANDERING MAN BOWD HIS FAINT HEAD AND URIZEN DESCENDED  273 FOUR ZOAS 1     316
    AND BRIGHT AHANIA BOWD HERSELF BEFORE HIS SPLENDID FEET     291 FOUR ZOAS 3       2
    AHANIA BOWD HER HEAD & WEPT SEVEN DAYS BEFORE THE KING  .   292 FOUR ZOAS 3      24
    THEY BOWD THE HEAD & WORSHIPPD & WITH MILD VOICE SPOKE      304 FOUR ZOAS 4     252
        THESE WORDS
    FOR HER DELIGHT THE HORSE HIS PROUD NECK BOWD & HIS WHITE   340 FOUR ZOAS 7B    281
        MANE
    THE [ANCIENT] ETERNAL MAN BOWD HIS BRIGHT HEAD . . .       380 FOUR ZOAS AD 1    2
    IN WHICH ARE THE TWO CHERUBIM THAT BOWD OVER THE ARK   .    613B V LAST JUDG/N PROSE
BOWED     SEE SILVER BOWED
    . . . SO THE VOICE OF THE PEOPLE BOWED    . . . . . . .     143 FRENCH REVOLTN   204
BOWELS
    FROM HER OWN BOWELS IN THE MONSTER SHAME INFUSD    . . .    40D THEN SHE BORE   PROSE
    THE SERPENTS SPRUNG FROM HER OWN BOWELS HAVE DRAIND HER     100 TIRIEL 1         32
        DRY AS THIS
    AND ALL HIS BOWELS BEGAN TO [BURN] CHURN    . . . . . .     187 WHEN KLOPSTK/N   16
    [THEY] [AND] AND HIS BOWELS TURNED [AROUND] ROUND THREE     187 WHEN KLOPSTK/N *  17
        TIMES THREE
    AND OF HER FINE WROUGHT BRAIN & OF HER BOWELS WITHIN HER    279 FOUR ZOAS 1     562
        LOINS
    IN STRENGTH & BRIGHTNESS FROM THE ABYSS HIS BOWELS YEARND   297 FOUR ZOAS 4       3
        OVER THEM
    THARMAS BEHELD THEM HIS BOWELS YEARND OVER THEM    . . . .  297 FOUR ZOAS 4       6
    . . . IN THEIR DREADFUL [BOWELS] BOSOMS . . . . . . .       317 FOUR ZOAS 6    *  228
    AND BOWELS HIDDEN [IN DARKNESS] IN HAMMERD STEEL [ARE]      338 FOUR ZOAS 7B   *  207
        . . .
    OR LIKE AN EARTHQUAKE RUMBLING IN THE BOWELS OF THE EARTH   339 FOUR ZOAS 7B    264
    IN SOFT SILK DRAWN FROM THEIR OWN BOWELS IN LASCIVIOUS      346 FOUR ZOAS 8     211
        DELIGHT
    SPINNING IT FROM THEIR BOWELS WITH SONGS OF AMOROUS DELIGHT 524 MILTON 34        28
    AND FALSE BOWELS ALTOGETHER COMPOSING THE FALSE TONGUE      634 JERUSALEM 14      6
    OF BEULAH WERE MOVED AS THE TENDER BOWELS ARE MOVED &       648 JERUSALEM 25      2
        THEY SAID
```

	PAGE	TITLE	LINE

BOWELS   (CONTINUED)
    AND OF THE CRADLED INFANCY IN HIS BOWELS OF COMPASSION . .   688 JERUSALEM 56   34
    AND BOWELS HID IN HAMMERD STEEL RIPD QUIVERING ON   701 JERUSALEM 65   53
        THE GROUND
BOWEN
    SCOFIELD KOX KOTOPE AND BOWEN REVOLVE MOST MIGHTILY UPON   623 JERUSALEM 5   27
    AND KOX KOTOPE & BOWEN ONE IN HIM A FOURFOLD WONDER . . .   626 JERUSALEM 7   48
    SCOFELD KOX KOTOPE & BOWEN HIS TWELVE SONS SATANIC MILL   641 JERUSALEM 19   19
    BOWEN ALBION'S SONS THEY BORE HIM A GOLDEN COUCH INTO THE   658 JERUSALEM 32   12
        PORCH
    KOTOPE & BOWEN BECAME WHAT THEY BEHELD FLEEING OVER THE   663 JERUSALEM 36   19
        EARTH
    BOWEN HAD ALL SCOTLAND THE ISLES NORTHUMBERLAND &   710 JERUSALEM 71   46
        CUMBERLAND
    JERUSALEM & VALA REJOICE IN BOWEN & CONWENNA . . . . .   710 JERUSALEM 71   49
    BOWEN & CONWENNA STOOD ON SKIDDAW CUTTING THE FIBRES . .   736 JERUSALEM 90   14
    WHILE IN SELFHOOD HAND & HYLE & BOWEN & SKOFELD APPROPRIATE 737 JERUSALEM 90   40
BOWER   SEE BOWR
    IN HEAVEN'S HIGH BOWER   . . . .   118 NIGHT/SI   6
    NOR SIT IN LEARNING'S BOWER . . . .   124 SCHOOL BOY/SI   14
    BUILD WE A BOWER FOR HEAVEN'S DARLING IN THE GRIZLY DEEP   280 FOUR ZOAS 2   24
    BUILD HER A BOWER IN THE MIDST OF ALL MY DASHING WAVES .   299 FOUR ZOAS 4   71
    TO WHERE MY BOWER HANGS ON HIGH   . . . .   423 THE BIRDS/N   18
    AND ANOTHER PLEASANT SURREY BOWER . . . .   429 CRYSTL CABINET   12
    WEAVES A BOWER IN ENDLESS NIGHT   . . . .   431 AUGURIES   36
    ROUND THE ROCKY PEAK OF DERBYSHIRE LONDON STONE & ROSAMONDS 689 JERUSALEM 57   7
        BOWER
    "IN PREPARING YOU A SUMMER BOWER AT FELPHAM" . . . . .   800B LETTER 12   PROSE
    AND HERE IS ENITHARMON'S BOWER . . . .   817 HAPPINESS/L   34
BOWERS
    . . . IN THEIR SILENT SECRET BOWERS . . . .   271 FOUR ZOAS 1   251
    I HID HER IN SOFT GARDENS & IN SECRET BOWERS OF SUMMER .   282 FOUR ZOAS 2   95
    TO BUILD HER BOWERS FOR THE ELEMENTS BROUGHT FORTH   340 FOUR ZOAS 7B   277
        ABUNDANTLY
    IN ENGLAND'S GREEN & PLEASANT BOWERS . . . .   718 ENGLND AWAKE/J   12
    WEAVING BOWERS OF DELIGHT ON THE CURRENT OF INFANT THAMES   728 JERUSALEM 83   50
    WITH ANGELS PLANTED IN HAWTHORN BOWERS . . . . .   817 HAPPINESS/L   9
BOWING
    . . . THEN BOWING LIKE CLOUDS MAN TOWARD MAN THE ASSEMBLY   146 FRENCH REVOLTN   263
    WALKING BEFORE HER SHADOWY FACE & BOWING AT HER FEET .   340 FOUR ZOAS 7B   279
    BOWING HIS HEAD OVER THE CONSUMING UNIVERSE HE CRIED .   359 FOUR ZOAS 9   98
    BOWING BEFORE MY SOVREIGN'S FEET . . . .   442 DEDICATN BLAIR   17
    & FAMILIES SOME OF WHOM ARE BOWING BEFORE THE BOOK OF LIFE   443D LAST JUDGMNT/L   PROSE
    IN PLACE OF THE ARK [WITH] THE [TWO] CHERUBIM BOWING OVER   444B LAST JUDGMNT/L   PROSE
        IT
    AND BOWING PROFOUNDLY HE SAID A GREAT WIG . . . . .   573 ASKD PRIGG/N   4
    HE IS SEEN ON HIS FIERY CHARIOT BOWING BEFORE THE THRONE   611C V LAST JUDG/N   PROSE
    BOWING THEIR HEADS DEVOTED AND THE FURNACES OF LOS . .   676 JERUSALEM 46   20
BOWL
    TO BOWL THE BALL IN A [TURD] TANSEY . . . .   61 SAY YOU JOE/IM   6
    [CAN WISDOM BE PUT IN A SILVER ROD OR LOVE IN A GOLDEN   110 TIRIEL 8   18
        BOWL]
    OR LOVE IN A GOLDEN BOWL . . . .   127 THELS MOTTO/BT   4
    HIS LABORIOUS TASK DROPPING HIS FLAIL & CREAM BOWL . .   618C ILLUS MILTON   PROSE
BOWLAHOOLA
    TO BOWLAHOOLA O FATHER MOST BELOVED O MILD PARENT   . .   507 MILTON 23   18
    A WEB OF DEATH & WERE IT NOT FOR BOWLAHOOLA & ALLAMANDA   509 MILTON 24   36
    THROW ALL THE VEGETATED MORTALS INTO BOWLAHOOLA . .   509 MILTON 24   40
    SO LOS SPOKE FURIOUS THEY DESCENDED TO BOWLAHOOLA   509 MILTON 24   44
        & ALLAMANDA
    BOWLAHOOLA IS NAMD LAW BY MORTALS THARMAS FOUNDED IT   .   509 MILTON 24   48
    IN BOWLAHOOLA LOS'S ANVILS STAND & HIS FURNACES RAGE .   509 MILTON 24   51
    BOWLAHOOLA THRO ALL ITS PORCHES FEELS THO TOO FAST FOUNDED   509 MILTON 24   54
    BOWLAHOOLA IS THE STOMACH IN EVERY INDIVIDUAL MAN   . .   509 MILTON 24   67
    BUILT BY THE SONS OF LOS IN BOWLAHOOLA & ALLAMANDA . .   512 MILTON 26   33
    IN BOWLAHOOLA & AS THE SPECTRES CHOOSE THEIR AFFINITIES   512 MILTON 26   38
    AND SCIENCE IS DIVIDED INTO BOWLAHOOLA & ALLAMANDA . .   514 MILTON 27   63
    BOWLAHOOLA & ALLAMANDA ARE PLACED ON EACH SIDE . . . .   517 MILTON 29   25
    TO BOWLAHOOLA & ALLAMANDA & TO ENTUTHON BENYTHON . . .   529 MILTON 37   59
    IN BOWLAHOOLA & ALLAMANDA WHERE THE DEAD WAIL NIGHT & DAY   668 JERUSALEM 40   57
    SONS & DAUGHTERS OF LOS IN BOWLAHOOLA & IN CATHEDRON .   714 JERUSALEM 73   52
    OF SPACE HE MAKES PERMANENT IN BOWLAHOOLA & CATHEDRON .   716 JERUSALEM 75   9
BOWLER
    I NEVER SAW SAW SUCH A BOWLER . . . .   61 SAY YOU JOE/IM *   5
BOWR
    I LOVE THE INNOCENT BOWR . . . .   8 LOVE JOCUND/PS   10
    WHEN EVENING SITS BENEATH HER DUSKY BOWR . . . . .   10 WHEN EARLY/PS   3
BOWS
    . . . AS A FATHER THAT BOWS TO HIS SON . . . . . .   143 FRENCH REVOLTN *   203
    WITH THE BOWS OF MY MIND & THE ARROWS OF THOUGHT . . .   818 HAPPINESS/L   78
BOWSTRING
    AND TWANG THE BOWSTRING TO OUR HOWLINGS LET THINE ARROWS   306 FOUR ZOAS 5   51
        BLACK
    MURMURING THE BOWSTRING BREATHES WITH ARDOR CLOUDS ROLL   742 JERUSALEM 95   14
        ROUND THE
    MY BOWSTRING FIERCE WITH ARDOUR BREATHES . . . . . .   818 HAPPINESS/L   79
BOW-STRING
    THE BOW STRING SANG UPON THE HILLS LUVAH & VALA RIDE .   275 FOUR ZOAS 1   408
    MURMURING THE BOW-STRING BREATHES WITH ARDOR . . . . .   745 JERUSALEM 98   4
BOWYER
    [OR ANGRY WITH BOYDELL OR BOWYER OR BA] . . . .   538 WAS I ANGRY/N   3
    OR ANGRY WITH [BOYDELL OR BOWYER OR BASIRE] . . . . .   538 WAS I ANGRY/N *   6

```
                                                     PAGE      TITLE        LINE
BOWYER    (CONTINUED)
    . . . MACKLIN OR BOYDEL OR BOWYER . . . . . . . . .  538 WAS I ANGRY/N      6
BOWYER'S
    BOWYER'S & OTHER GREAT WORKS I WAS KNOWN BY THEM & WAS  862C LETTER 60     PROSE
       LOOKD
BOX
    HIS MONEY IN A BOX . . . . . . . . . . . . . . .    57 TO BE OR/IM        14
BOXED
    OF THE MINISTERS YOU DESERVE TO HAVE YOUR EARS BOXED YOU DO  48C ISLAND MOON 4  PROSE
BOXES
    HEAVY BOXES & PORTFOLIOS FULL OF PRINTS AND NOW BEGINS  . . 802B LETTER 14    PROSE
    OWING TO THE NECESSARY SHIFTING OF OUR BOXES & PORTFOLIOS  803A LETTER 15    PROSE
BOY       SEE SCHOOL BOY
    A GIRL HAS ALWAYS MORE TONGUE THAN A BOY I HAVE SEEN  . . 53B ISLAND MOON 8   PROSE
    TONGUE AS A CITY CLARK BUT A BOY WOULD BE SUCH A FOOL  . . 53B ISLAND MOON 8   PROSE
    OH SPEAK FATHER SPEAK TO YOUR LITTLE BOY . . . . . .   60 LIT BOY LST/IM     3
    AND THE ANGEL TOLD TOM IF HED BE A GOOD BOY . . . . .  118 CHIMNEY SWP/SI    19
    THE LITTLE BOY LOST . . . . . . . . . . . . . .      120D LIT BOY LST/SI  TITLE
    SPEAK FATHER SPEAK TO YOUR LITTLE BOY . . . . . . .   120 LIT BOY LST/SI     3
    THE LITTLE BOY FOUND . . . . . . . . . . . . .       121A LIT BOY FND/SI  TITLE
    THE LITTLE BOY LOST IN THE LONELY FEN . . . . . . .   121 LIT BOY FND/SI     1
    HER LITTLE BOY WEEPING SOUGHT . . . . . . . . . .     121 LIT BOY FND/SI     8
    LITTLE BOY . . . . . . . . . . . . . . . . . .       123 SPRING/SI         10
    THE LITTLE BLACK BOY . . . . . . . . . . . . . .     125B LIT BLK BOY/SI  TITLE
    AND THUS I SAY TO LITTLE ENGLISH BOY . . . . . . .    125 LIT BLK BOY/SI    22
    WHY A TENDER CURB UPON THE YOUTHFUL BURNING BOY . . . .  130 BOOK OF THEL 6    19
    COME HITHER MY BOY TELL ME WHAT THOU SEEST THERE . . . .  180 LACEDEMONIAN/N     1
    SOON AS SHE SAW THE TERRIBLE BOY THEN BURST THE VIRGIN CRY  196 AMERICA PREL 2    6
    A LITTLE BOY LOST . . . . . . . . . . . . . . .     218B LIT BOY LST/SE  TITLE
    RAISD THE [BRIGHT] FIERCE BOY & GIRL . . . . . . .    269 FOUR ZOAS 1      196
    THY NAME IS ENITHARMON SAID THE [BRIGHT] FIERCE PROPHETIC  271 FOUR ZOAS 1      249
       BOY
    O BRIGHT [AHANIA][SHADOW] A BOY IS BORN OF THE DARK OCEAN  292 FOUR ZOAS 3    *  14
    ALL THIS IS MINE YET I MUST SERVE & THAT PROPHETIC BOY . .  292 FOUR ZOAS 3       18
    COVERD WITH GLOOM THE FIERY BOY GREW FED BY THE MILK  . .  307 FOUR ZOAS 5       72
    THEIR SOLEMN HABITATION LOS BEHELD THE RUDDY BOY . . . .  307 FOUR ZOAS 5       80
    HIS UNCOUTH PLAGUE HE SIEZD THE BOY IN HIS IMMORTAL HANDS  307 FOUR ZOAS 5       97
    HELD THE FIERCE BOY LOS NAILD HIM DOWN BINDING AROUND HIS  307 FOUR ZOAS 5      101
       LIMBS
    AND OVER THE IMMORTAL LIMBS OF THE TERRIBLE FIERY BOY  . .  309 FOUR ZOAS 5      159
    THE TERRIBLE BOY TILL FAINTING BY HIS SIDE THE PARENTS FELL  309 FOUR ZOAS 5      172
    SET OVER THIS SWEET BOY OF MINE TO GUARD HIM LEST HE REND  326 FOUR ZOAS 7      232
    TO BRING HER DOWN SUBJECTED TO THE RAGE OF MY FIERCE BOY  326 FOUR ZOAS 7      266
    [TO SEE THE BOY SPRING INTO HEAVEN SOUNDING FROM MY SIGHT]  349 FOUR ZOAS 8      311
    THOU LITTLE BOY ART THARMAS & THOU BRIGHT GIRL ENION  . .  370 FOUR ZOAS 9      510
    ARISE SWEET BOY & LET US FOLLOW THE PATH OF ENION  . . .  371 FOUR ZOAS 9      534
    CHEAR UP THY COUNTENANCE BRIGHT BOY & GO TO ENION  . . .  371 FOUR ZOAS 9      545
    AND IF THE BABE IS BORN A BOY . . . . . . . . . .     425 MENTAL TRAVLER      9
    AWAKE AWAKE MY LITTLE BOY . . . . . . . . . . . .     427 LAND OF DREAMS      1
    THE WANTON BOY THAT KILLS THE FLY . . . . . . . . .   431 AUGURIES           33
    DETERMINATE ALL HIS EFFORTS PROVE THIS LITTLE BOY TO HAVE  439C REMARKS MALKIN  PROSE
       HAD
    WHY WAS CUPID A BOY . . . . . . . . . . . . . .      552 WHY CUPID/N         1
    AND WHY A BOY WAS HE . . . . . . . . . . . . . .     552 WHY CUPID/N         2
    [THEN] AND TO MAKE CUPID A BOY . . . . . . . . . .    552 WHY CUPID/N         9
    FOR A BOY [NEVER LEARNS SO MUCH] CAN'T INTERPRET THE THING  552 WHY CUPID/N        11
    TURND LOVE INTO A BOY . . . . . . . . . . . . .      552 WHY CUPID/N        18
    OF AGE AND YOUTH AND BOY AND GIRL AND ANIMAL AND HERB  . .  640 JERUSALEM 18      17
    AND BOY & GIRL & ANIMAL & HERB & RIVER & MOUNTAIN  . . .  640 JERUSALEM 18      25
    TO SEE THE BOY SPRING INTO HEAVENS SOUNDING FROM MY SIGHT  705 JERUSALEM 67      58
    A ONE WITH ORDINARY COMMON SENSE CAN BE INFERIOR TO A BOY  830A LETTER 30    PROSE
    THE COMPASS OF A BOY OF (FOURTEEN) & . . . . . . .    859C LETTER 56      PROSE
    THE CHILD IN HIS ARMS WHETHER BOY OR GIRL SIGNIFIES NOT  864B LETTER 61    PROSE
    AND WHO DOES NOT KNOW A BOY FROM A GIRL I SAY . . . . .  864B LETTER 61    PROSE
    CONGRATULATE YOU ON THE RECEIT OF ANOTHER FINE BOY . . .  873B LETTER 77    PROSE
    WINDSOR TERRACE A BOY CONTEMPLATING A DISTANT VIEW OF ETON  SUPP ILLUS GRAY   *TITLE
       COLLEGE
    A BOY FLYING A KITE . . . . . . . . . . . . . .     SUPP ILLUS GRAY    *TITLE
    LITTLE BLACK BOY DITTO LAUGHING SONG SPRING DITTO  . . .  SUPP LETTER 66A   *PROSE
    A DREAM ON ANOTHER'S SORROW THE LITTLE BOY LOST  . . .  SUPP LETTER 66A   *PROSE
    THE LITTLE BOY FOUND END OF SONGS OF INNOCENCE . . . .  SUPP LETTER 66A   *PROSE
    MY PRETTY ROSE TREE THE GARDEN OF LOVE A LITTLE BOY LOST  SUPP LETTER 66A   *PROSE
BOYDEL
    . . . MACKLIN OR BOYDEL OR BOWYER . . . . . . . .    538 WAS I ANGRY/N      6
    I HAVE ALSO SEEN ALDERMAN BOYDEL WHO HAS PROMISED  . . .  844A LETTER 43    PROSE
BOYDELL
    [OR ANGRY WITH BOYDELL OR BOWYER OR BA] . . . . . . .  538 WAS I ANGRY/N      3
    OR ANGRY WITH [BOYDELL OR BOWYER OR BASIRE] . . .  . . .  538 WAS I ANGRY/N  *   6
BOYDELL'S
    SAME TALENTS I NOW HAVE ALL THE TIME OF BOYDELL'S MACKLIN'S  862C LETTER 60     PROSE
BOY'S
    AND COUCHING AT THEIR SIDE SHALL EAT FROM THE CURLD BOY'S  376 FOUR ZOAS 9    *  707
       WHITE LAP
    AS TO REAL ACTING IT IS LIKE HISTORICAL PAINTING NO BOY'S  859C LETTER 56    PROSE
       WORK
BOYS
    ARADOBO SAID THAT THE BOYS IN THE STREET SING SOMETHING  54D ISLAND MOON 9   PROSE
    THOUSANDS OF LITTLE GIRLS & BOYS RAISING THEIR INNOCENT   59 HOLY THURS/IM      9
       HANDS
    WHEN WE ALL GIRLS & BOYS . . . . . . . . . . . .   116 ECCHOING GR/SI     18
    THOUSANDS OF LITTLE BOYS & GIRLS RAISING THEIR INNOCENT  122 HOLY THURS/SI      8
       HANDS
```

```
                                                                   PAGE     TITLE         LINE
BOYS    (CONTINUED)
    AND CAUGHT HIM IN MY HAT AS BOYS KNOCK DOWN A BUTTERFLY        237 EUROPE INTRO        9
    THE PONDS WHERE BOYS TO BATHE DELIGHT  . . . . . . . . . .     650 FIELDS FROM/J      14
    TO SAY TIS A GIRL PROMISING BOYS HEREAFTER & TO SAY  . . .   853A LETTER 51         *PROSE
    TWO BOYS WANDERING IN THE WOODS BY ETON COLLEGE   . . . .    SUPP ILLUS GRAY        *TITLE
    BOYS PLAYING AT TOP  . . . . . . . . . . . . . . . . .       SUPP ILLUS GRAY        *TITLE
BRACE
    LIKE TO THE ARMOUR'S IRON BRACE   . . . . . . . . . .          433 AUGURIES          100
BRACELETS
    BRACELETS & STAYS & POWDERD HAIR  . . . . . . . . . .          447 ANNO REYNOLDS       4
BRACES
    DAMN BRACES BLESS RELAXES  . . . . . . . . . . . .            152C MARRIAGE HH 9     PROSE
    AND THE SCREWS & IRON BRACES ARE WELL WROUGHT BLANDISHMENTS    632 JERUSALEM 12       34
    OF BRASS IRON CHAINS & BRACES & THE GOLD SILVER & BRASS        713 JERUSALEM 73       10
BRADLEY
    JOE BRADLEY & I WAS GOING ALONG ONE DAY IN THE SUGAR HOUSE    55B ISLAND MOON 9     PROSE
    JOE BRADLEY SAW FOR HE HAD BUT ONE EYE [?COME]   . . . .      55B ISLAND MOON 9    *PROSE
BRAIN
    FOR LIGHT DOTH SEIZE MY BRAIN  . . . . . . . . . . . .           9 MAD SONG/PS        23
    LET RAYS OF TRUTH ENLIGHT HIS SLEEPING BRAIN  . . . . .         14 IMIT SPEN/PS        9
    . . . CAN THE SOUL WHOSE BRAIN AND HEART  . . . . . . .        142 FRENCH REVOLTN     183
    . . . ENTER INTO THE INFINITE LABYRINTH OF ANOTHER'S BRAIN    142 FRENCH REVOLTN     190
    IN WHAT FURNACE WAS THY BRAIN  . . . . . . . . . . . .         172 THE TYGER/N 1      19
    [TILL THEY SOUGHT IN THE HUMAN BRAIN]  . . . . . . . .         174 HUMAN IMAGE/N      25
    THERE GROWS ONE IN THE HUMAN BRAIN   . . . . . . . . .         174 HUMAN IMAGE/N      26
    AND THEY INCLOSD MY INFINITE BRAIN INTO A NARROW CIRCLE        191 V DAU ALBION 2     32
    PALE QUIVRING TOWARD THE BRAIN HIS GLIMMERING EYES TEETH       202 AMERICA 15          7
        CHATTERING
    IN WHAT FURNACE WAS THY BRAIN  . . . . . . . . . . . .         214 THE TYGER/SE       14
    THERE GROWS ONE IN THE HUMAN BRAIN   . . . . . . . . .         217 HUMAN ABSTR/SE     24
    HIS NERVOUS BRAIN SHOT BRANCHES   . . . . . . . . . .          228 URIZEN 11          11
    THE MESHES TWISTED LIKE TO THE HUMAN BRAIN  . . . . . .        235 URIZEN 25          21
    TILL HIS BRAIN IN A ROCK & HIS HEART  . . . . . . . . .        260 BOOK OF LOS 5      52
    INTO THE BRAIN FROM THENCE UPON THE PILLOW VALA SLUMBERD       271 FOUR ZOAS 1       263
    THO IN THE BRAIN OF MAN WE LIVE & IN HIS CIRCLING NERVES       272 FOUR ZOAS 1       302
    THO THIS BRIGHT WORLD OF ALL OUR JOY IS IN THE HUMAN BRAIN     272 FOUR ZOAS 1       303
    OF THARMAS & URTHONA I REMAINING IN PORCHES OF THE BRAIN       278 FOUR ZOAS 1       497
    AND OF HER FINE WROUGHT BRAIN & OF HER BOWELS WITHIN HER       279 FOUR ZOAS 1       562
        LOINS
    BENEATH HIS FEET SHOT THRO HIM AS HE STOOD IN THE HUMAN        280 FOUR ZOAS 2        12
        BRAIN
    IN HARROWING FEAR ROLLING HIS NERVOUS [BRAINS] BRAIN SHOT      303 FOUR ZOAS 4    *  227
        BRANCHES
    A UNIVERSE OF FIERY CONSTELLATIONS IN THEIR BRAIN   . . .      314 FOUR ZOAS 6        91
    PANGS SMOTE THRO THE BRAIN & A UNIVERSAL SHRIEK   . . . .      318 FOUR ZOAS 6       258
    LO HOW THE HEART & BRAIN ARE FORMED IN THE BREEDING WOMB       323 FOUR ZOAS 7       130
    FROM ENION'S BRAIN IN THIS DEFORMED FORM LEAVING THEE THERE    327 FOUR ZOAS 7       291
    OPEND WITHIN YOUR HEART & LOINS & WONDROUS BRAIN   . . . .     329 FOUR ZOAS 7       354
    THREEFOLD WITHIN THE BRAIN WITHIN THE HEART WITHIN THE         329 FOUR ZOAS 7       381
        LOINS
    OPEND WITHIN THEIR HEARTS & IN THEIR LOINS & IN THEIR BRAIN    342 FOUR ZOAS 8        55
    HEAVENS OF MY BRAIN NOR WILL I LOOK UPON [REMEMBRANCE]         361 FOUR ZOAS 9       181
        FUTURITY MORE
    WILD FURIES FROM THE TYGER'S BRAIN & FROM THE LION'S EYES      363 FOUR ZOAS 9       236
    INTO YOUR PLACE THE PLACE OF SEED NOT IN THE BRAIN OR          366 FOUR ZOAS 9       365
        HEART
    RESTLESS THEY TURN ON BEDS OF SORROW IN THEIR INMOST BRAIN     379 FOUR ZOAS 9       818
    OPEND WITHIN THE HEART & IN THE LOINS & IN THE BRAIN   . .     382 FOUR ZOAS AD 6     25
    LIKE FOUL FIENDS INHABITING MARY'S MILD BRAIN  . . . . .       429 MARY              42
    A FIBRE FROM THE BRAIN DOES TEAR  . . . . . . . . . .          431 AUGURIES          14
    HAS LEFT THE BRAIN THAT WON'T BELIEVE  . . . . . . . .         431 AUGURIES          26
    FROM OUT THE PORTALS OF MY BRAIN WHERE BY YOUR MINISTRY        481 MILTON 2           7
    THIS TO PREVENT ENTERING THE DOORS OF SATAN'S BRAIN NIGHT      492 MILTON 12          4
        AFTER NIGHT
    THE GNOMES LABOURD I WEEPING HID IN SATAN'S INMOST BRAIN       493 MILTON 12         36
    IN SATAN'S INMOST PALACE OF HIS NERVOUS FINE WROUGHT BRAIN     493 MILTON 12         41
    ME FROM HIS INMOST BRAIN & THE DOORS CLOSD WITH THUNDERS       493 MILTON 12         48
        SOUND
    TO MILTON'S BRAIN THE ICY FLUID FROM HIS BROAD COLD PALM       500 MILTON 19          9
    AROUND THE MARROW AND THE ORBED SCULL AROUND THE BRAIN         501 MILTON 19         52
    SHE TIES THE KNOT OF NERVOUS FIBRES INTO A WHITE BRAIN  . .    501 MILTON 19         55
    IT HAS A HEART LIKE THEE A BRAIN OPEN TO HEAVEN & HELL  . .    502 MILTON 20         28
    TERRIFIC AND EACH MORTAL BRAIN IS WALLD AND MOATED ROUND       502 MILTON 20         36
    OF SATAN IN ITS WEBS FOR IN BRAIN AND HEART AND LOINS   . .    502 MILTON 20         38
    OF LOS AND HERE HE LAYS HIS WORDS IN ORDER ABOVE THE MORTAL    513 MILTON 27          9
        BRAIN
    THEY TOO LARGE AND UNWIELDY FOR HIS BRAIN AND BOSOM   . . .   580B DESC CAT 5       PROSE
    PHANTOM OF THE OVER HEATED BRAIN SHADOW OF IMMORTALITY  . .    622 JERUSALEM 4        24
    A THREEFOLD REGION A FALSE BRAIN A FALSE HEART   . . . .       634 JERUSALEM 14        5
    FEEL THEIR BRAIN CUT BOUND BENEATH THE TEMPLES SHRIEKING       689 JERUSALEM 58        7
    THEY POUR COLD WATER ON HIS BRAIN IN FRONT TO CAUSE   . . .    702 JERUSALEM 66       30
    LONDON FEELS HIS BRAIN CUT ROUND EDINBURGH'S HEART            703 JERUSALEM 66       64
        IS CIRCUMSCRIBED
    THE TWELVE DAUGHTERS IN RAHAB & TIRZAH HAVE CIRCUMSCRIBD       705 JERUSALEM 67       41
        THE BRAIN
    THO HER BRAIN IS NOT DRUNK WITH WINE SHE GOES FORTH FROM       705 JERUSALEM 68       13
        ALBION
    HER BRAIN ENLABYRINTHS THE WHOLE HEAVEN OF HER BOSOM &         709 JERUSALEM 70       29
        LOINS
    HIS HEAD DARK DEADLY IN ITS BRAIN INCLOSES A REFLEXION  . .    734 JERUSALEM 89       14
    AND WHILE THEY CIRCUMSCRIBE HIS BRAIN & WHILE THEY             736 JERUSALEM 90        3
        CIRCUMSCRIBE
```

BRAIN   (CONTINUED)
    CONCIEVE IN MY BRAIN ARE STUDIES & CHAMBERS FILLD WITH . . 802B LETTER 14   PROSE
BRAIN PAN
    AND WEAK IS THEIR BRAIN PAN . . . . 538 SUSSEX MEN/N   2
BRAINS
    THY CROWN IS BALD OLD MAN THE SUN WILL DRY THY BRAINS AWAY 109 TIRIEL 7   12
    IN HARROWING FEAR ROLLING HIS NERVOUS [BRAINS] BRAIN SHOT 303 FOUR ZOAS 4   * 227
        BRANCHES
    A HORSE BY THE COLOUR & A MAN WHO HAS GOT ANY BRAINS   . 597D PUB ADDRESS/N   PROSE
    THREE BRAINS IN CONTRADICTORY COUNCIL BROODING INCESSANTLY 708 JERUSALEM 70   5
    AT THE BEGINNING OF THE BALLADS HAS SET MY BRAINS TO WORK 860B LETTER 56   PROSE
BRAITHWAITE
    I CALLD YESTERDAY ON MR BRAITHWAITE AS YOU DESIRED   . . 835C LETTER 35   PROSE
    MR B(BRAITHWAITE) DESIRES I WILL PRESENT HIS COMPLIMENTS 836A LETTER 35   PROSE
        TO YOU
    BUT I HASTEND TO WRITE TO YOU ABOUT MR BRAITHWAITE HOPE 837A LETTER 35   PROSE
    MR BRAITHWAITE CALLD ON ME & BROUGHT TWO PRINTS WHICH HE 838D LETTER 37   PROSE
    YET BEEN ABLE TO MEET MR BRAITHWAITE AT HOME BUT INTEND 849B LETTER 45   PROSE
BRAITHWAITE'S
    IN MR BRAITHWAITE'S POSSESSION . . . . 839A LETTER 37   PROSE
    BEG PARDON FOR THE OMISSION OF MR BRAITHWAITE'S TWO PRINTS 839B LETTER 38   PROSE
BRAKE
    KNEW THAT I WAS NOT ELYNITTRIA AND THEY BRAKE THE TRACES 492 MILTON 12   13
BRAKES
    RUSTLING IN BRAKES AND THICKETS   . . . . 35C COUCH DEATH/PS PROSE
BRAMA
    WHEN RINTRAH GAVE ABSTRACT PHILOSOPHY TO BRAMA IN THE EAST 245 SONG OF LOS 3   11
BRAMINS
    NUMBER X THE BRAMINS A DRAWING   . . . . 583D DESC CAT 10   TITLE
BRANCH
    IF THOU REPENTEST NOT & LEAVE THEE AS A ROTTEN BRANCH TO 361 FOUR ZOAS 9   156
        BE BURND
    IN THAT HIGHEST BRANCH OF ART I MUST NOW TELL MY WANTS . 851A LETTER 49   PROSE
BRANCHD
    . . . WHERE BRANCHD THE MYSTERIOUS TREE . . . . . . 331 FOUR ZOAS 7   * 434
BRANCHES
    WHILE THY BRANCHES MIX WITH MINE . . . .   7 LOVE HARMNY/PS   3
    JOYS UPON OUR BRANCHES SIT   . . . .   7 LOVE HARMNY/PS   5
    AND DOTH AMONG OUR BRANCHES PLAY . . . .   7 LOVE HARMNY/PS   20
    IN SOLEMN GLOOM OF BRANCHES INTERWOVE . . . . . . 15 IMIT SPEN/PS   48
    RAIN FRESHNING DEW UPON HIS BRANCHES AND . . . . . 26 EDW THIRD/PS 3   215
    . . . WHOSE AGED TREES UTTER AN AWFUL VOICE AND THEIR 145 FRENCH REVOLTN   242
        BRANCHES
    THEIR UNMOVD BRANCHES STOOD THE HALL BUILT WHEN THE MOON 204 AMERICA CANC B   4
        SHOT FORTH
    SHOOTING OUT TEN THOUSAND BRANCHES . . . . 228 URIZEN 11   6
    HIS NERVOUS BRAIN SHOT BRANCHES . . . . 228 URIZEN 11   11
    ROUND THE BRANCHES OF HIS HEART . . . . 228 URIZEN 11   12
    I HEARD HIS VOICE AMONG THE BRANCHES & AMONG SWEET FLOWERS 271 FOUR ZOAS 1   267
    PANTING CONGLOBING TREMBLING SHOOTING OUT TEN THOUSAND 303 FOUR ZOAS 4   225
        BRANCHES
    IN HARROWING FEAR ROLLING HIS NERVOUS [BRAINS] BRAIN SHOT 303 FOUR ZOAS 4   * 227
        BRANCHES
    [ROUND THE BRANCHES OF HIS HEART] . . . . 303 FOUR ZOAS 4   228
    BRANCHES INTO THE HEAVEN OF LOS THEY PIPE FORMD BENDING 321 FOUR ZOAS 7   33
        DOWN
    SICKLY LOOK FORTH & SCARCELY STRETCH THEIR BRANCHES TO 325 FOUR ZOAS 7   193
        THE PLAIN
    CONFERRING TIMES ON TIMES AMONG THE BRANCHES OF THAT TREE 327 FOUR ZOAS 7   314
    ITS TOPMOST [BRANCHES] BOUGHS SHOOTING A [STEM] FIBRE . . . 328 FOUR ZOAS 7   334
    SHE SPREAD HERSELF THRO ALL THE BRANCHES IN THE POWER OF 343 FOUR ZOAS 8   85
        ORC
    SHE SPREAD HERSELF THRO ALL THE BRANCHES IN THE POWER OF 345 FOUR ZOAS 8   174
        ORC
    MY BIRDS ARE SILENT ON MY HILLS FLOCKS DIE BENEATH 359 FOUR ZOAS 9   101
        MY BRANCHES
    THE POSSIBILITY OF HUMAN BEASTLINESS IN ALL ITS BRANCHES 387C ANNO WATSON   MARG
    TO HANG UPON THE BRANCHES FINE . . . . 422 BENEATH/N   11
    TO HANG UPON THE BRANCHES FINE . . . . 424 THE GOLDEN NET   10
    MIND AND THE PRETENCE OF THE PLAGIARY IN ALL ITS BRANCHES 585C DESC CAT 15   PROSE
    THE [EXPRESSION] CHARACTERS IN ALL THEIR BRANCHES   . . 611B V LAST JUDG/N   PROSE
    AMONG WHOSE BRANCHES TEMPLES & PINNACLES TENTS & PAVILIONS 613B V LAST JUDG/N PROSE
    HIS BIRDS ARE SILENT ON HIS HILLS FLOCKS DIE BENEATH HIS 641 JERUSALEM 19   2
        BRANCHES
    HAVING A WHITE DOT CALLD A CENTER FROM WHICH BRANCHES OUT 659 JERUSALEM 33   19
    FROM WHICH SPRANG NUMEROUS BRANCHES VARYING THEIR MOTIONS 659 JERUSALEM 33   21
BRANCHING
    BRANCHING OUT INTO ROOTS . . . . 231 URIZEN 18   2
    TAKE ROOT AGAIN WHEREEVER THEY TOUCH AGAIN BRANCHING FORTH 321 FOUR ZOAS 7   34
    OUTSTRETCHD HIS RIGHT HAND BRANCHING OUT IN FIBROUS 357 FOUR ZOAS 9   7
        STRENGTH
    HOW COOL THE BREEZES OF THE VALLY & THE ARMS OF THE 369 FOUR ZOAS 9   * 449
        BRANCHING TREES
BRANCHY
    BRANCHY FORMS ORGANIZING THE HUMAN . . . . 258 BOOK OF LOS 4   44
BRAND
    AND BRAND IT WITH THE NAME OF WHORE & SELL IT IN THE NIGHT 194 V DAU ALBION 6   12
BRANDISHD
    MY ROOTS ARE BRANDISHD IN THE HEAVENS MY FRUITS IN EARTH 238 EUROPE PREL 1   8
        BENEATH
    AND CURSES WITH HIS MIGHTY ARMS BRANDISHD AGAINST 667 JERUSALEM 40   37
        THE HEAVENS

		PAGE	TITLE	LINE
BRANDISHING				
	HER SNAKY HAIR BRANDISHING IN THE WINDS OF ENITHARMON . .	238	EUROPE PREL 1	2
BRANDS				
	[OR EYED WITH LITTLE SPARKS OF HELL OR WITH INFERNAL BRANDS]	109	TIRIEL 8	15
BRASS				
	AND FORGED HELM AND SHIELD OF SEVEN TIMES BEATEN BRASS . .	17	EDW THIRD/PS 1	4
	NONE CAN HURT THEE THY BONES ARE BRASS THY SINEWS ARE IRON	39A	SAMSON/PS	PROSE
	& BRASS TUBES & MAGIC PICTURES	58C	ISLAND MOON 10	PROSE
	AMIDST THE LUSTFUL FIRES HE WALKS HIS FEET BECOME LIKE BRASS	199	AMERICA 8	16
	GOLD SILVER BRASS & IRON [ARDORS] CLANGORS CLAMORING REND THE SHORES	205	AMERICA CANC C	15
	OF ETERNAL BRASS WRITTEN IN MY SOLITUDE	224	URIZEN 4	33
	THE BOOK OF BRASS RAGE SIEZD THE STRONG	224	URIZEN 4	44
	WITH RIVETS OF IRON & BRASS	227	URIZEN 8	11
	IRON SODOR AND SODOR OF BRASS	228	URIZEN 10	30
	AND HIS BOOKS OF BRASS IRON & GOLD	248	SONG OF LOS 7	14
	THEY HAVE SURROUNDED ME WITH WALLS OF IRON & BRASS [I ?DIE] O LAMB	282	FOUR ZOAS 2	* 99
	WITH LIVES OF VICTIMS SACRIFICED UPON AN ALTAR OF BRASS	285	FOUR ZOAS 2	194
	MY HEAVENS ARE BRASS MY EARTH IS IRON MY MOON A CLOD OF CLAY	290	FOUR ZOAS 2	395
	TO FORGE THE CURBS OF IRON & BRASS TO BUILD THE IRON MANGERS	292	FOUR ZOAS 3	34
	THE PROPHET OF ETERNITY BEAT ON HIS IRON LINKS & LINKS OF BRASS	302	FOUR ZOAS 4	201
	AND POURD IRON SODOR & SODOR OF BRASS	303	FOUR ZOAS 4	214
	AND BRASS & SILVER & GOLD FOURFOLD IN DARK PROPHETIC FEAR	307	FOUR ZOAS 5	74
	THE HAMMER OF URTHONA SMOTE THE RIVETS IN TERROR OF BRASS	308	FOUR ZOAS 5	104
	SCALED & FINND WITH IRON & BRASS THEY DEVOURD THE PATH BEFORE HIM	313	FOUR ZOAS 6	76
	WRITING IN BITTER TEARS & GROANS IN BOOKS OF IRON & BRASS	314	FOUR ZOAS 6	85
	AND SCALED MONSTERS OR ARMD IN IRON SHELL OR SHELL OF BRASS	314	FOUR ZOAS 6	120
	STILL TO BE WRITTEN & INTERLEAVD WITH BRASS & IRON & GOLD	316	FOUR ZOAS 6	172
	HERE MOUNTAINS OF BRASS PROMISE MUCH RICHES	317	FOUR ZOAS 6	228
	SO [SAYING] HE BEGAN TO [FORM] ?DIG OF GOLD SILVER & [BRASS] IRON	317	FOUR ZOAS 6	* 229
	AND BRASS VAST INSTRUMENTS TO MEASURE OUT THE IMMENSE & FIX	317	FOUR ZOAS 6	230
	GOLD SILVER BRASS & IRON CLANGORS CLAMORING REND THE [DEEPS] SHORES	319	FOUR ZOAS 6	311
	OF GOLD & SILVER BRASS & IRON HE KNEW HIS MIGHTY SONS . .	319	FOUR ZOAS 6	315
	AND URIZEN READ IN HIS BOOK OF BRASS IN SOUNDING TONES . .	322	FOUR ZOAS 7	109
	THO BOUND WITH CHAINS OF JEALOUSY & IN SCALES OF IRON & BRASS	332	FOUR ZOAS 7	481
	AND POLISH BRASS & IRON HOUR AFTER HOUR LABORIOUS WORKMANSHIP	337	FOUR ZOAS 7B	182
	AND BRASS & MOLTEN METALS CAST IN HOLLOW GLOBES & BORD .	343	FOUR ZOAS 8	93
	THUS IN THE TEMPLE OF THE SUN HIS BOOKS OF IRON & BRASS	344	FOUR ZOAS 8	140
	GO NOAH FETCH THE GIRDLE OF STRONG BRASS [PRE] HEAT IT RED HOT	349	FOUR ZOAS 8	312
	FOR EVERY HUMAN HEART HAS GATES OF BRASS & BARS OF ADAMANT	502	MILTON 20	34
	AND EVERY DAY & NIGHT HAS WALLS OF BRASS & GATES OF ADAMANT	516	MILTON 28	52
	[HIS] WHOSE HEART IS IRON HIS HEAD WOOD & HIS FACE BRASS	545	ON S(TOTHRD)/N	2
	WITH IRON & BRASS BUILDING GOLGONOOZA IN GREAT CONTENDINGS	630	JERUSALEM 10	63
	AND THAT TOWARD BEULAH FOUR GOLD SILVER BRASS & IRON . .	632	JERUSALEM 12	66
	AND THAT TOWARD EDEN FOUR FORMD OF GOLD SILVER BRASS & IRON	633	JERUSALEM 13	1
	THAT TOWARD EDEN FOUR IMMORTAL GOLD SILVER BRASS & IRON	633	JERUSALEM 13	5
	AND POLISH BRASS & IRON HOUR AFTER HOUR LABORIOUS TASK	700	JERUSALEM 65	24
	GO NOAH FETCH THE GIRDLE OF STRONG BRASS HEAT IT RED-HOT	705	JERUSALEM 67	59
	OF BRASS IRON CHAINS & BRACES & THE GOLD SILVER & BRASS	713	JERUSALEM 73	10
	TWO WINGS SPRING FROM HIS RIBS OF BRASS STARRY BLACK AS NIGHT	735	JERUSALEM 89	36
	THARMAS WESTWARD A BOW OF BRASS PURE FLAMING RICHLY WROUGHT	744	JERUSALEM 97	10
	HOPE SOON TO HEAR THAT YOU HAVE GOT A LIVING ONE OF BRASS	843A	LETTER 42	*PROSE
BRAT				
	A LITTLE BRAT NO HIGHER THAN A NETTLE & SHE HAD AS MUCH	53B	ISLAND MOON 8	PROSE
BRAVD				
	FRAUGHT WITH THE SWORDS OF LIGHTNING BUT I BRAVD THE VENGEANCE TOO	105	TIRIEL 4	* 56
BRAVE				
	BRAVE LORDS WHO FELL BENEATH THE BLOODY AXE	18	EDW THIRD/PS 1	44
	WORTHY THE BRAVE LORD PERCY AND AS WORTHY	21	EDW THIRD/PS 2	89
	THANKS BRAVE LORD PERCY YOU HAVE THE THANKS	21	EDW THIRD/PS 2	98
	GOOD MORROW BRAVE SIR THOMAS THE BRIGHT MORN	21	EDW THIRD/PS 3	1
	FOR WHEN THE COWARD RUNS THE BRAVE MAN TOTTERS	22	EDW THIRD/PS 3	60
	BY THESE BRAVE TROOPS	23	EDW THIRD/PS 3	89
	YOU ARE A MAN MY PRINCE AND A BRAVE MAN	27	EDW THIRD/PS 3	244
	WHY BRAVE SIR WALTER YOU OR I MAY FALL	30	EDW THIRD/PS 5	3
	STOP BRAVE SIR WALTER LET ME DROP A TEAR	31	EDW THIRD/PS 5	49
	AND GROW IMMODERATE TO BRAVE IT OUT	37A	CONTEMPLATN/PS	PROSE
	FORTUNE FAVOURS THE BRAVE OLD PROVERBS SAY	541	MR CROMEK/N	1
BRAVELY				
	THE NORTHERN DRUM NOW GIVE THE CHARGE BRAVELY OBSCURD . .	337	FOUR ZOAS 7B	155
BRAVEST				
	MY ENGLISHMEN THE BRAVEST PEOPLE ON	25	EDW THIRD/PS 3	192
BRAVO				
	("A STILL RABIES IS MORE DANGEROUS THAN PAROXISMS OF FEVER") BRAVO	68A	ANNO LAVATER	MARG
	("AFFECTATION OF SANCTITY IS A BLOTCH ON FACE OF PIETY") BRAVO	71B	ANNO LAVATER	MARG

		PAGE	TITLE	LINE

BRAVO   (CONTINUED)
  ("NOT HONEST PUBLICLY CHRISTIAN PRIVATELY DEIST") BRAVO   72C ANNO LAVATER   MARG
BRAWLS
  CLAMOUR BRAWLS ALONG THE STREETS . . . . 37A CONTEMPLATN/PS PROSE
BRAY
  THE DEVIL ANSWERD BRAY A FOOL IN A MORTER WITH WHEAT . . 158C MARRIAGE HH 22 PROSE
BRAZEN
  THROBS OF ANGUISH BEAT ON BRAZEN WAR FOREHEADS . . . . 137 FRENCH REVOLTN 71
  . . . WHEN BRAZEN CANNONS RAGE IN THE FIELD . . . . . 146 FRENCH REVOLTN 262
  HE FORMED A BRAZEN QUADRANT . . . . 234 URIZEN 20 38
  AND HIS BRAZEN BOOK . . . . 242 EUROPE 11 3
  STRIKING FIERCE SPARKLES FROM THEIR BRAZEN FETTERS FIERCE 320 FOUR ZOAS 7 8
    HIS LIONS
  THERE IS A BRAZEN SICKLE & A SCYTHE OF IRON HID . . . 372 FOUR ZOAS 9 580
  AND HIS BRIGHT FEET FIRM AS A BRAZEN ALTAR BUT THE PARTS 380 FOUR ZOAS AD 1 12
  O SHAME O STRONG & MIGHTY SHAME I BREAK THY BRAZEN 629 JERUSALEM 10 34
    FETTERS
  AND HATE DIVIDING THE SPACE OF LOVE WITH BRAZEN COMPASSES 734 JERUSALEM 88 47
BRAZIL
  PERU PATAGONIA AMAZONIA BRAZIL THIRTY-TWO NATIONS . . . 712 JERUSALEM 72 42
BREACH
  IN ULRO BENEATH BEULAH THE VAST BREACH OF MILTON'S DESCENT 503 MILTON 21 7
  SOUTHWARD & BY THE EAST WITHIN THE BREACH OF MILTON'S 524 MILTON 34 42
    DESCENT
  A BREACH IN A CITY THE MORNING AFTER THE BATTLE . . . . SUPP ILLUS HISTORY *TITLE
BREAD   SEE SHEW BREAD
  AND CHILDREN CRY FOR BREAD . . . . 11 GWIN KING/PS 10
  HOW TO EMPLOY THE HAND THAT LACKETH BREAD . . . . . . 19 EDW THIRD/PS 2 23
  "PRIDE FULLNESS OF BREAD & ABUNDANCE OF IDLENESS" WAS THE 79D ANNO LAVATER MARG
    SIN
  ON THE BREAD & ON THE WINE . . . . 163 I SAW CHAPEL/N 15
  AND [MAIDENS] BEAUTY FOR A BIT OF BREAD . . . . 174 HUMAN IMAGE/N 32
  FOR STOLEN JOYS ARE SWEET & BREAD EATEN IN SECRET PLEASANT 237 EUROPE INTRO 6
  TO CUT OFF THE BREAD FROM THE CITY . . . . 247 SONG OF LOS 7 1
  THEY EAT THE [XXX] FLESHLY BREAD THEY DRANK THE NERVOUS 274 FOUR ZOAS 1 * 355
    [BLOODY] WINE
  AND IN THE WITHERD FIELD WHERE THE FARMER PLOWS FOR BREAD 290 FOUR ZOAS 2 401
    IN VAIN
  KNEAD BREAD OF SORROW BY MY STERN COMMAND FOR I AM GOD . 322 FOUR ZOAS 7 93
  ON CLOUDS OF DEATH & SANG THEIR SONGS KNEADING THE BREAD 322 FOUR ZOAS 7 98
    OF ORC
  OF ELETH & THE ICY HANDS OF UVETH KNEADED THE BREAD . . 322 FOUR ZOAS 7 102
  THE BREAD IS KNEADED LET US REST O CRUEL FATHER OF CHILDREN 322 FOUR ZOAS 7 107
  COMPELL THE POOR TO LIVE UPON A CRUST OF BREAD BY SOFT 323 FOUR ZOAS 7 117
    MILD ARTS
  WITH POMP GIVE EVERY CRUST OF BREAD YOU GIVE WITH GRACIOUS 323 FOUR ZOAS 7 123
    CUNNING
  IN STRONG DRINK THO YOU KNOW THAT BREAD & WATER ARE ALL 323 FOUR ZOAS 7 127
  IN SORROWFUL DRUDGERY TO OBTAIN A SCANTY PITTANCE OF BREAD 337 FOUR ZOAS 7B 184
  SAYING O THAT I HAD NEVER DRANK THE WINE NOR EAT THE BREAD 361 FOUR ZOAS 9 * 164
  IMMENSE UPON THE HEAVENS WITH BREAD & DELICATE REPASTS . . 366 FOUR ZOAS 9 334
  . . . & KNEAD THE BREAD OF KNOWLEDGE WITH TEARS & GROANS 379 FOUR ZOAS 9 820
  URTHONA MADE THE BREAD OF AGES & HE PLACED IT . . . . 379 FOUR ZOAS 9 822
  THIS THE WINE & THIS THE BREAD . . . . 417 MY SPECTRE/N 74
  MY CHILDREN WILL DIE FOR LACK OF BREAD . . . . 419 I SAW A MONK/N 20
  THE BREAD & WINE OF HER SWEET SMILE . . . . 426 MENTAL TRAVLER 70
  MY CHILDREN DIE FOR LACK OF BREAD . . . . 430 GREY MONK 2
  THE TABLE WITH THE SHEW BREAD ON THE LEFT . . . . . 444B LAST JUDGMNT/L *PROSE
  WITHOUT EMPLOYMENT & AS MUCH AS COULD POSSIBLY BE WITHOUT 445B ANNO REYNOLDS MARG
    BREAD
  THAT WHILE HE DID THAT WORK HE LIVED ON BREAD & APPLES . 446A ANNO REYNOLDS MARG
  AND VALA LABOURS FOR HER BREAD & WATER AMONG THE FURNACES 501 MILTON 19 43
  GIVEN TO HERCULES WHO LABOUR IN TIRZAH'S LOOMS FOR BREAD 511 MILTON 25 50
  [ALL DWELLS IN HIM] HE IS THE BREAD & THE WINE . . . 612D V LAST JUDG/N PROSE
  ZACHARIAS & ELIZABETH RECIEVING THE BREAD & WINE . . . . 614A V LAST JUDG/N PROSE
  THEY COMPELL THE POOR TO LIVE UPON A CRUST OF BREAD BY 656 JERUSALEM 30 30
    SOFT MILD ARTS
  DENS OF DESPAIR IN THE HOUSE OF BREAD ENQUIRING IN VAIN 657 JERUSALEM 31 26
  FOR BREAD OF THE SONS OF ALBION OF THE GIANTS HAND 673 JERUSALEM 43 50
    & SCOFIELD
  COME HITHER INTO THE DESART & TURN THESE STONES TO BREAD 685 JERUSALEM 54 21
  BEG BREAD FROM HOUSE TO HOUSE LOVELY JERUSALEM . . . . 693 JERUSALEM 60 28
  IN SORROWFUL DRUDGERY TO OBTAIN A SCANTY PITTANCE OF BREAD 700 JERUSALEM 65 26
  THEIR BREAD THEIR ALTAR-TABLE THEIR INCENSE & THEIR OATH 738 JERUSALEM 91 14
  BUT YOU CAN TURN THE STONES TO BREAD . . . . 749 EV GOSPEL(B)/N 18
  TWAS DARK DECEIT TO EARN MY BREAD . . . . 755 EV GOSPEL(E)/N 60
  LAWFUL BREAD BOUGHT WITH LAWFUL MONEY . . . . 787D ANNO THORNTON MARG
  GIVE US THE BREAD THAT IS OUR DUE & RIGHT . . . . . 788A ANNO THORNTON MARG
  GIVE [XXX] US THIS ETERNAL DAY [XXX] OUR [GHOSTLY] OWN 788A ANNO THORNTON * MARG
    RIGHT BREAD
  SUBSTANTIAL MONEY BOUGHT BREAD [& TAKE XXX TAKE] . . . 788D ANNO THORNTON * MARG
  DESCEND & ASCEND WITH THE BREAD & THE WINE . . . . . 800 MRS FLAXMAN/L 12
  THE BREAD OF SWEET THOUGHT & THE WINE OF DELIGHT . . . 800 MRS FLAXMAN/L 13
  SHOULD WANT NATURAL BREAD SORROW & DESPERATION PURSUES . 813B LETTER 22 PROSE
  BREAD ALONE I SHALL LIVE ALTHO I SHOULD WANT BREAD NOTHING 830B LETTER 30 PROSE
BREADTH   SEE BREDTH
  SOMETIMES IN [BREADTH] LENGTH SOMETIMES ENGLOBING . . . 315 FOUR ZOAS 6 123
  HE KNEW THAT WEAKNESS STRETCHES OUT IN BREADTH & LENGTH 324 FOUR ZOAS 7 161
    HE KNEW
  INVISIBLE OR VISIBLE DRAWN OUT IN LENGTH OR STRETCHD IN 338 FOUR ZOAS 7B * 222
    BREADTH
  INCREASING INWARDS INTO LENGTH AND BREADTH AND HEIGHTH . . 635 JERUSALEM 14 18

```
                                                          PAGE    TITLE            LINE
BREADTH    (CONTINUED)
       AND THE NORTH IS BREADTH THE SOUTH IS HEIGHTH & DEPTH   .   .   635 JERUSALEM 14       29
       INVISIBLE OR VISIBLE STRETCHD OUT IN LENGTH OR SPREAD IN     723 JERUSALEM 80       54
         BREADTH
BREADTHS    SEE BREDTHS
       BEFORE LONDON TO HAMPSTEAD'S BREADTHS & HIGHGATE'S HEIGHTS   485 MILTON 6          9
         TO
BREAK     SEE DAY-BREAK
       WILL BEND OR BREAK US MY BLOOD LIKE A SPRINGTIDE  .  .  .  .   26 EDW THIRD/PS 3     234
       THEN THE DREADFUL LIGHTNINGS BREAK  .  .  .  .  .  .  .  .   165 CRADLE SONG/N       17
       BREAK THIS HEAVY CHAIN  .  .  .  .  .  .  .  .  .  .  .  .   169 EARTHS ANSWR/N      21
       THE TIMES ARE ENDED SHADOWS PASS THE MORNING GINS TO BREAK   198 AMERICA 8            2
       IS GIVN THEE TILL THE BREAK OF DAY  .  .  .  .  .  .  .  .   210 INTRODUCTN/SE       20
       BREAK THIS HEAVY CHAIN  .  .  .  .  .  .  .  .  .  .  .  .   211 EARTHS ANSR/SE      21
       NONE COULD BREAK THE WEB NO WINGS OF FIRE  .  .  .  .  .  .   235 URIZEN 25           19
       MY LOINS BEGIN TO BREAK FORTH INTO VEINY PIPES & WRITHE      300 FOUR ZOAS 4         94
       PITY FOR THEE MOVD ME TO BREAK MY DARK & LONG REPOSE   .  .   321 FOUR ZOAS 7         57
       IN FURROWD LIGHTNINGS BREAK THEIR WAY  .  .  .  .  .  .  .   359 FOUR ZOAS 9         85
       THE HEAVY ROLLER TO BREAK THE CLODS TO PASS OVER            365 FOUR ZOAS 9        307
         THE NATIONS
       I SEE THE BREAK OF DAY  .  .  .  .  .  .  .  .  .  .  .  .   421 MORNING/N            6
       [THREE VIRGINS AT THE BREAK OF DAY]  .  .  .  .  .  .  .  .   421 BENEATH/N            2
       [THREE VIRGINS AT THE BREAK OF DAY]  .  .  .  .  .  .  .  .   422 BENEATH REWR/N       2
       THREE VIRGINS AT THE BREAK OF DAY  .  .  .  .  .  .  .  .    424 THE GOLDEN NET       1
       SHOULD UP ASCEND FORWARD FROM FELPHAM'S VALE & BREAK THE     507 MILTON 23           37
         CHAIN
       TO THE WEAK AND PITY THE WEAK AS YOUR INFANT CARE BREAK      511 MILTON 25           57
         NOT
       WITH POMP EVEN TILL MORNING BREAK & OSIRIS APPEAR IN THE     528 MILTON 37           29
         SKY
       IF YOU BREAK NOT YOUR NECK TIS NOT HIS FAULT  .  .  .  .  .   544 HS FRENDSHIP/N       3
       I WILL BREAK THEE INTO SHIVERS & MELT THEE IN THE FURNACES   627 JERUSALEM 8         10
         OF DEATH
       O SHAME O STRONG & MIGHTY SHAME I BREAK THY BRAZEN          629 JERUSALEM 10        34
         FETTERS
       THEREFORE I BREAK THY BONDS OF RIGHTEOUSNESS I CRUSH THY     670 JERUSALEM 42        37
         MESSENGERS
       AWAY FROM BEULAH'S HILLS & VALES BREAK FORTH THE SOULS       677 JERUSALEM 47        10
         OF THE DEAD
       O MELANCHOLY MAGDALEN BEHOLD THE MORNING OVER MALDEN BREAK   700 JERUSALEM 65        38
BREAKING    SEE HEART-BREAKING
       TILL DAWN TILL MORNING TILL THE BREAKING OF CLOUDS  .  .  .   144 FRENCH REVOLTN     217
       NO VIRTUE CAN EXIST WITHOUT BREAKING THESE TEN COMMANDMENTS  158C MARRIAGE HH 22  PROSE
       BARKS AT THE BREAKING DAY THE NIGHTINGALE HAS DONE           190 V DAU ALBION 2      24
         LAMENTING
       BREAKING IN SMOKY WREATHS FROM THE WILD DEEP & GATHRING      201 AMERICA 12          11
         THICK
       SOMETIMES I THINK THOU ART FRUIT BREAKING FROM ITS BUD  .    265 FOUR ZOAS 1          60
       [LAUGHING & MOCKING LUVAH [?BURSTING] ?BREAKING IN THE WOES  SUPP FOUR ZOAS 2       *
         OF VALA]
       SHE STROVE IN VAIN NOT SO URTHONA STROVE FOR BREAKING        300 FOUR ZOAS 4        104
         FORTH
       WITH A CRASH BREAKING ACROSS THE HORRIBLE MASS COMES DOWN    322 FOUR ZOAS 7         78
       BUT JESUS BREAKING THRO THE CENTRAL ZONES OF DEATH & HELL    716 JERUSALEM 75        21
       IN ANGER THE WRATH OF GOD BREAKING BRIGHT FLAMING ON ALL     742 JERUSALEM 95         6
         SIDES AROUND
       CHRIST BAPTIZING SAMSON BREAKING BONDS SAMSON SUBDUD         SUPP LETTER 56A    *PROSE
BREAKS
       TILL CLUSTRING SUMMER BREAKS FORTH INTO SINGING  .  .  .  .     2 TO AUTUMN/PS        11
       AND BREAKS ALL CHAINS FROM EVERY MIND  .  .  .  .  .  .  .   175 HOW TO KNOW/N        4
       AT LENGTH FOR HATCHING RIPE HE BREAKS THE SHELL  .  .  .  .   209C FOR CHILDRN/GP  TITLE
       O MELANCHOLY MAGDALEN BEHOLD THE MORNING BREAKS  .  .  .  .   337 FOUR ZOAS 7B       192
       I WILL GO DOWN TO THE SEPULCHER TO SEE IF MORNING BREAKS     495 MILTON 14           21
       FIRST EER THE MORNING BREAKS JOY OPENS IN THE FLOWERY        520 MILTON 31           50
         BOSOMS
       ON THE ROCKY SPECTRES AS THE POTTER BREAKS THE POTSHERDS     719 JERUSALEM 78         5
       AT LENGTH FOR HATCHING RIPE HE BREAKS THE SHELL  .  .  .  .   765B FOR SEXES/GP   TITLE
       "AT LENGTH FOR HATCHING RIPE HE BREAKS THE SHELL" DRYDEN     SUPP LEGEND/N68     *
BREAST    SEE RED BREAST
       SHE HUGGD IT TO HER BREAST AND GROAND HER LAST  .  .  .  .     6 FAIR ELENOR/PS      72
       HIS BREAST IS LOVE'S ALL WORSHIPD TOMB  .  .  .  .  .  .  .     6 MY SILKS/PS         11
       DOWN FROM THE BROW UNTO THE BREAST  .  .  .  .  .  .  .  .    14 GWIN KING/PS       107
       AND BRINGS GOOD COUNSEL FROM THE BREAST OF LAUGHTER  .  .  .   24 EDW THIRD/PS 3     135
       IN THAT ENLARGED BREAST OF HIS THAT ALL  .  .  .  .  .  .  .   25 EDW THIRD/PS 3     187
       TILL GLORY FIRES HIS BREAST TO ENLARGE HIS CASTLE  .  .  .  .   26 EDW THIRD/PS 3     201
       IT IS A ROOT THAT GROWS IN EVERY BREAST  .  .  .  .  .  .  .   28 EDW THIRD/PS 4      13
       OF TIME COME ROLLING OER MY BREAST HE SAID  .  .  .  .  .  .   32 EDW THIRD/PS 6      40
       JUSTICE HATH HEAVED A SWORD TO PLUNGE IN ALBION'S BREAST      34A KING JOHN/PS    PROSE
       TYRANNY HATH STAIND FAIR ALBION'S BREAST WITH HER            34A KING JOHN/PS    PROSE
         OWN CHILDREN'S GORE
       O VOICE THAT DWELLEST IN MY BREAST  .  .  .  .  .  .  .  .    36B COUCH DEATH/PS  PROSE
       DOUBT NO MORE OF SAMSON'S LOVE FOR THAT FAIR BREAST WAS       39B SAMSON/PS       PROSE
         MADE
       IT IS THE CURSED THORN WOUNDING MY BREAST THAT MAKES ME       41D THEN SHE BORE   PROSE
         SING
       MY HEART IS AT REST WITHIN MY BREAST  .  .  .  .  .  .  .  .   60 NURSES SONG/IM      3
       MY HAIR IS VERY LONG MY BEARD DOTH COVER ALL MY BREAST  .  .   102 TIRIEL 3            4
       THE BLIND MAN HEARD & SMOTE HIS BREAST & TREMBLING PASSED     109 TIRIEL 7           14
         ON
       MY HEART IS AT REST WITHIN MY BREAST  .  .  .  .  .  .  .  .   121 NURSES SONG/SI      3
       POURING PITY IN THEIR BREAST  .  .  .  .  .  .  .  .  .  .    122 ON ANOTHERS/SI      18
       AND KISSES ME AND BINDS HIS NUPTIAL BANDS AROUND MY BREAST    129 BOOK OF THEL 5
```

263

```
                                                              PAGE      TITLE             LINE
BREAST    (CONTINUED)
    THUS MEN FORGOT THAT ALL DEITIES RESIDE IN THE HUMAN BREAST  153B MARRIAGE HH 11   PROSE
    WHILE THE MORNING PLUMES HER GOLDEN BREAST  . . . . . .   160A SONG LIBERTY     PROSE
    OER THY CHEEK & OER THY BREAST      . . . . . . . . .     165 CRADLE SONG/N        12
    TO SULK UPON MY MOTHER'S BREAST     . . . . . . . . .     166 INFANT SORW/N         8
    THE IMAGE OF THEOTORMON ON MY PURE TRANSPARENT BREAST   .  190 V DAU ALBION 2      16
    AND I AM WHITE AND PURE TO HOVER ROUND THEOTORMON'S BREAST  191 V DAU ALBION 3      20
    HIS KNEES AND THIGHS LIKE SILVER & HIS BREAST AND HEAD     199 AMERICA 8           17
      LIKE GOLD
    HIS SNOWY BEARD THAT STREAMS LIKE LAMBENT FLAMES DOWN HIS  204 AMERICA CANC B      16
      WIDE BREAST
    TO SULK UPON MY MOTHER'S BREAST     . . . . . . . .       217 INFANT SORW/SE        8
    THE NAMELESS SHADOWY FEMALE ROSE FROM OUT THE BREAST OF ORC 238 EUROPE PREL 1       1
    THEY SULK UPON HER BREAST HER HAIR BECAME LIKE SNOW ON     270 FOUR ZOAS 1        211
      MOUNTAINS
    ALTERNATE LOVE & HATE HIS BREAST HERS SCORN & JEALOUSY  . .  270 FOUR ZOAS 1      237
    I CAN INFUSE MY DEAR REVENGE INTO HIS GLOWING BREAST   .  .  289 FOUR ZOAS 2      337
    WHENCE IS THIS POWER GIVEN TO THEE ONCE THOU WAST IN MY    295 FOUR ZOAS 3        120
      BREAST
    WITHIN HIS BREAST HIS FIERY SONS CHAIND DOWN & FILLD WITH  306 FOUR ZOAS 5         57
      CURSINGS
    MY GOLDEN LIPS NOR TOOK THE BAR FROM ENITHARMON'S BREAST    326 FOUR ZOAS 7       238
    MY SONS EXILED FROM MY BREAST PASS TO & FRO BEFORE ME  . .  359 FOUR ZOAS 9       100
    FOR FROM WITHIN MY [NARROW] WITHERD BREAST GROWN NARROW    360 FOUR ZOAS 9        108
      WITH MY WOES
    THOU SHALT NEVER HAVE PEACE WITHIN THY BREAST  . . . . .   380 FOUR ZOAS NOTE       2
    I SPRANG OUT OF THE BREAST OF SATAN OVER THE HARROW BEAMING 492 MILTON 12          10
    ON THROAT & BREAST & WINGS VIBRATES WITH THE EFFLUENCE     520 MILTON 31          35
      DIVINE
    TO CHLOE'S BREAST YOUNG CUPID SLILY STOLE  . . . . . .     557 TO CHLOES/N          1
    HIS CHILDREN EXILD FROM HIS BREAST PASS TO AND FRO BEFORE  641 JERUSALEM 19         1
      HIM
    TILL FROM WITHIN HIS WITHERD BREAST GROWN NARROW WITH HIS  641 JERUSALEM 19         9
      WOES
    WITHIN HIS BREAST HIS MIGHTY SONS CHAIND DOWN & FILLD WITH 667 JERUSALEM 40        40
      CURSINGS
    THAT APPARENT TO ALL IN ETERNITY GLOWS LIKE THE SUN IN     723 JERUSALEM 80        68
      THE BREAST
    MOLECH & CHEMOSH & IN HIS LEFT BREAST IS PHILISTEA   . . .  735 JERUSALEM 89       31
    SHALL PLANT THEIR GLORIES IN YOUR BREAST  . . . . . .     749 EV GOSPEL(B)/N      20
BREASTPLATE
    AND I WILL PUT ON HOLINESS AS A BREASTPLATE & AS A HELMET  499 MILTON 18           21
BREAST PLATE
    WHAT WE CALL ANTIQUE GEMS ARE THE GEMS OF AARON'S BREAST   777D INSC LAOCOON     PROSE
      PLATE
BREASTS
    SHALL BEAM A RADIANCE TO FIRE THE BREASTS  . . . . . .    18 EDW THIRD/PS 1        24
    BUT HAR & HEVA SLEPT FEARLESS AS BABES ON LOVING BREASTS    109 TIRIEL 7           21
    SWEET FLOWER AND PUT THEE HERE TO GLOW BETWEEN MY BREASTS   189 V DAU ALBION 1     12
    I GAVE SWEET LILLIES TO THEIR BREASTS & ROSES TO THEIR HAIR 312 FOUR ZOAS 6        29
    AGAIN THE ELEMENTAL STRINGS TO YOUR RIGHT BREASTS DRAW  .  337 FOUR ZOAS 7B       157
    AND A FOUNTAIN FROM MY BREASTS TO ME COME ALL MULTITUDES    354 FOUR ZOAS 8       501
    HIS CHILDREN TO MY BREASTS HIS SONS & DAUGHTERS TO MY KNEES 720 JERUSALEM 79       26
BREATH
    THY MORN AND EVENING BREATH SCATTER THY PEARLS   . . . .   1 TO SPRING/PS          11
    THE BREATH OF HEAVEN DWELT AMONG HIS LEAVES  . . . . .     5 FAIR ELENOR/PS        51
    MY BREATH IS LOATHSOME HOW SHOULD HE NOT BE OFFENDED  .    36A COUCH DEATH/PS    PROSE
    O MY CHILD MY CHILD IS THY BREATH INFECTED SO IS MINE  .   36B COUCH DEATH/PS    PROSE
    THE BREATH OF NIGHT SLEPT AMONG THE LEAVES OF THE FOREST   36C COUCH DEATH/PS    PROSE
    HISSING WITH HUNDRED TONGUES HER POISNOUS BREATH  . . .    41C THEN SHE BORE     PROSE
    & QUITE OUT OF BREATH WHILE TILLY LALLY & SCOPPRELL  . . . 58D ISLAND MOON 10    PROSE
    THY BREATH DOTH NOURISH THE INNOCENT LAMB . . . . . . .    128 BOOK OF THEL 2       5
    HIS SORROWFUL BREATH . . . . . . . . . . . . . . .        136 FRENCH REVOLTN      42
    . . . BRED FROM THE BLOOD OF REVENGE AND BREATH OF DESIRE  144 FRENCH REVOLTN     215
    [AND STRENGTH & BREATH]  . . . . . . . . . . . . .        183 THE FLY/N           26
    AND STRENGTH & BREATH    . . . . . . . . . . . . .        183 THE FLY/N           30
    AND STRENGTH & BREATH    . . . . . . . . . . . . .        213 THE FLY/SE          14
    IF THOU WITHDRAW THY BREATH I DIE & VANISH INTO HADES  .   293 FOUR ZOAS 3         61
    IF THOU WITHDRAW THY BREATH BEHOLD I AM OBLIVION  . . .    293 FOUR ZOAS 3         65
    TO MY BREATH THEY OBEY THEY WORSHIP ME I AM A GODDESS &    354 FOUR ZOAS 8        502
      QUEEN
    WITH VOICE MILD FROM HIS GOLDEN CLOUD UPON THE BREATH OF   367 FOUR ZOAS 9        387
      MORNING
    I DRINK NEW LIFE & FEEL THE BREATH OF SLEEPING ENION   .   371 FOUR ZOAS 9        542
    SCATTER THE PERFUME OF HIS BREATH WHILE FROM HIS MOUNTAINS 376 FOUR ZOAS 9        705
      HIGH
    AS THE BREATH OF THE ALMIGHTY SUCH ARE THE WORDS OF MAN    519 MILTON 30          18
      TO MAN
    THE HUMAN HANDS & FEET & BREATH   . . . . . . . . .       651 FIELDS FROM/J       62
    IF THOU WITHDRAW THY BREATH I DIE & VANISH INTO HADES  .   654 JERUSALEM 29        48
    IF THOU WITHDRAW THY BREATH BEHOLD I AM OBLIVION  . . .    654 JERUSALEM 29        52
    IN SELFHOOD WE ARE NOTHING BUT FADE AWAY IN MORNING'S      675 JERUSALEM 45        13
      BREATH
    TIME WAS FINISHED THE BREATH DIVINE BREATHED OVER ALBION   742 JERUSALEM 94        18
    THE BREATH DIVINE WENT FORTH UPON THE MORNING HILLS ALBION 742 JERUSALEM 95         2
      MOVD
    THE BREATH DIVINE WENT FORTH OVER THE MORNING HILLS ALBION 742 JERUSALEM 95         5
      ROSE
    WHAT WAS THE [WORDS] SOUND OF JESUS' BREATH   . . . . .   754 EV GOSPEL(E)/N      10
    AND SHE HEARD THE BREATH OF GOD   . . . . . . . . . .     754 EV GOSPEL(E)/N      19
    STILL THE BREATH DIVINE DOES MOVE  . . . . . . . . . .    754 EV GOSPEL(E)/N      41
    AND THE BREATH DIVINE IS LOVE  . . . . . . . . . . .      754 EV GOSPEL(E)/N      42
```

```
                                                          PAGE      TITLE         LINE
BREATH     (CONTINUED)
    PRAISES YOU & DISPRAISES WITH THE SAME BREATH  . . . . . 798B LETTER 10        PROSE
BREATHD
    HE BREATHD ON THEM AND SAID . . . . . . . . . .         142 FRENCH REVOLTN      179
    SWEET ENITHARMON MILD ENTRANCD BREATHD FORTH UPON THE WIND 332 FOUR ZOAS 7       472
    LOVELY BREATHD FROM ENITHARMON HE TREMBLED WITHIN HIMSELF 332 FOUR ZOAS 7        499
    THAT STATE CALLD SATAN ENITHARMON BREATHD FORTH ON THE   351 FOUR ZOAS 8         383
        WINDS
BREATHE
    AND BREATHE MY HOPES INTO THE BURNING AIR  . . . . . .    26 EDW THIRD/PS 3      221
    . . . ARE HIS COMPANIONS HARMLESS THEY BREATHE  . . . . 136 FRENCH REVOLTN        41
    BREATHE FIRES BUT TEN MILES FROM PARIS LET ALL BE PEACE  145 FRENCH REVOLTN       240
        . . .
    HIS NOSTRILS BREATHE [WITH] A FIERY FLAME . . . . . . .  308 FOUR ZOAS 5          127
    HID IN A LITTLE SILKEN VEIL SCARCE BREATHE & FAINTLY SHINE 325 FOUR ZOAS 7        195
    I BREATHE HIM FORTH INTO THE HEAVEN FROM MY SECRET CAVE  660 JERUSALEM 33          50
    THAT RAHAB & TIRZAH MAY EXIST & LIVE & BREATHE & LOVE  .  692 JERUSALEM 59          43
BREATHED
    WHEN THE COLD CLAY BREATHED WITH LIFE AND OUR ANCESTORS   35C COUCH DEATH/PS    PROSE
    AND HEARD THIS VOICE OF SORROW BREATHED FROM THE HOLLOW PIT 130 BOOK OF THEL 6    10
    THEREFORE HE LIVED & BREATHED IN HOPE BUT HIS TEARS FELL  696 JERUSALEM 62          36
        INCESSANT
    TIME WAS FINISHED THE BREATH DIVINE BREATHED OVER ALBION  742 JERUSALEM 94          18
BREATHES
    AND THE DROPS OF RAIN GLISTEN THE YELLOW HARVEST BREATHES  36C COUCH DEATH/PS   PROSE
    AND THE YOUTH BREATHES OUT HIS SOUL WITH JOY INTO ETERNITY 36D COUCH DEATH/PS   PROSE
    FIVE WINDOWS LIGHT THE CAVERND MAN THRO ONE HE BREATHES   237 EUROPE INTRO          1
        THE AIR
    THE WORLD WHERE EVERY PARTICLE OF DUST BREATHES FORTH ITS 237 EUROPE INTRO         18
        JOY
    JOIN SHAKING CONVULSD THE SHIVRING CLAY BREATHES  . . .  248 SONG OF LOS 7         32
    WHATEVER GROWS FROM ITS PURE BUD OR BREATHES A FRAGRANT   308 FOUR ZOAS 5          124
        SOUL
    HIS OWN DESPAIR EVEN AT THE COST OF EVERY THING THAT      344 FOUR ZOAS 8          139
        BREATHES
    TO BONES JOIN SHAKING CONVULSD THE SHIVERING CLAY BREATHES 363 FOUR ZOAS 9         232
    MURMURING THE BOWSTRING BREATHES WITH ARDOR CLOUDS ROLL   742 JERUSALEM 95          14
        ROUND THE
    MURMURING THE BOW-STRING BREATHES WITH ARDOR . . . . . . 745 JERUSALEM 98           4
    MY BOWSTRING FIERCE WITH ARDOUR BREATHES  . . . . . . .  818 HAPPINESS/L           79
BREATHING      SEE EARTH-BREATHING,FIRE-BREATHING,HIGH BREATHING,LOUD BREATHING,
        SOFTLY-BREATHING,WAR-BREATHING
    I KNOW THIS BREATHING FLESH MUST LIE AND ROT  . . . . .   30 EDW THIRD/PS 5         4
    ON DUSKY WING BREATHING FORTH CLAMOUR & DESTRUCTION  . . . 42D THEN SHE BORE    PROSE
    [SOME NOSTRILD WIDE BREATHING OUT BLOOD SOME CLOSE SHUT   109 TIRIEL 8              12
        UP]
    THE LILLY OF THE VALLEY BREATHING IN THE HUMBLE GRASS  .  127 BOOK OF THEL 1        15
    . . . BREATHING RED CLOUDS OF POWER AND DOMINION  . . .  135 FRENCH REVOLTN         20
    BREATHING RED FIRES FROM MAN TO MAN AND FROM HORSE TO     137 FRENCH REVOLTN         81
        HORSE . . .
    OR BREATHING NOSTRILS NO FOR THESE THE WOLF AND TYGER HAVE 191 V DAU ALBION 3         9
    REVIVING SHAKE INSPIRING MOVE BREATHING AWAKENING   . . . 198 AMERICA 6              4
    . . . XXX AND XXX AND LXXX SILENT STOOD THE KING BREATHING 205 AMERICA CANC C *      5
        . . .
    A SHADOW BLUE OBSCURE & DISMAL FROM THE BREATHING NOSTRILS 300 FOUR ZOAS 4         105
    AND BREATHING TERRIBLE BLOOD & VENGEANCE GNASHING HIS TEETH 306 FOUR ZOAS 5        58
        WITH PAIN
    THE BULLS OF LUVAH BREATHING FIRE BELLOW ON BURNING       320 FOUR ZOAS 7          16
        PASTURES
    . . . THEN HIS BREATHING NOSTRILS DRAWN FORTH . . . . .   352 FOUR ZOAS 8         422
    FROM BREATHING FIELDS SATAN FAINTED BENEATH THE ARTILLERY 484 MILTON 5          *   2
    THE CORN-FIELDS & THE BREATHING GARDENS OUTSIDE SEPARATED 643 JERUSALEM 21          9
    THE IMAGINATIVE HUMAN FORM IS BUT A BREATHING OF VALA  .  660 JERUSALEM 33          49
    BREATHING CRUELTY BLOOD & VENGEANCE GNASHING HIS TEETH    667 JERUSALEM 40          38
        WITH PAIN
    LIKE EVENING DEW ON EVERY HERB UPON THE BREATHING GROUND  669 JERUSALEM 42           8
    LAYD HIS HAND ON THE SOUTH & TOOK A BREATHING BOW OF CARVED 744 JERUSALEM 97         8
        GOLD
    IN THE MIDST OF HIS TWENTY-EIGHT CITIES EACH WITH HIS BOW 744 JERUSALEM 97          17
        BREATHING
BRECKNOKSHIRE
    THE GATE OF ASHER CARNARVONSHIRE THE GATE OF ISSACHAR     637 JERUSALEM 16          39
        BRECKNOKSHIRE
BRED      SEE SIN-BRED
    . . . BRED FROM THE BLOOD OF REVENGE AND BREATH OF DESIRE 144 FRENCH REVOLTN        215
    BRED FROM HIS FORSAKEN WILDERNESS . . . . . . . . . . .   222 URIZEN 3              15
    THE INDIGNANT THISTLE WHOSE BITTERNESS IS BRED IN HIS MILK 377 FOUR ZOAS 9         763
    THE INDIGNANT THISTLE WHOSE BITTERNESS IS BRED IN HIS MILK 513 MILTON 27            26
    "AND IN DEAD PARENTS BALEFUL ASHES BRED" (SPENSER)  . . . SUPP LEGEND/N19      *
BREDTH     SEE BREADTH
    ON THE BREDTH OF HIS OPEN BOSOM . . . . . . . . . . .    254 AHANIA 5              12
    MOCKING DRUIDICAL MATHEMATICAL PROPORTION OF LENGTH BREDTH 484 MILTON 4            27
        HIGHTH
    RETAINING ONLY SATAN'S MATHEMATIC HOLINESS LENGTH BREDTH  521 MILTON 32            18
        & HIGHTH
    AND ACCIDENT & CHANCE WERE FOUND HIDDEN IN LENGTH BREDTH  663 JERUSALEM 36          35
        & HIGHTH
    AND LENGTH BREDTH HIGHTH AGAIN OBEY THE DIVINE VISION     664 JERUSALEM 36          56
        HALLELUJAH
    AND FRAMED THE MUNDANE SHELL CAVERNOUS IN LENGTH BREDTH   740 JERUSALEM 92          27
        & HIGHTH
```

	PAGE	TITLE	LINE

BREDTHS
IN SOLEMN POMP INTO CHALDEA ACROSS THE BREDTHS OF EUROPE   644 JERUSALEM 21   43
BREED
WITHOUT YOU WE SHOUD NEVER BREED . . . . 56 HAIL MATRIM/IM   11
AGAINST THE MONSTROUS FORMS THAT BREED AMONG MY SILENT   301 FOUR ZOAS 4   145
    WAVES
MY FOUNTAINS ONCE THE HAUNT OF SWANS NOW BREED THE SCALY   310 FOUR ZOAS 5   194
    TORTOISE
BREEDER
THYSELF FEMALE A MALE A BREEDER OF SEED A SON & HUSBAND   698 JERUSALEM 64   13
    & LO
BREEDING
BREEDING DARK PLOTS . . . . 38A SAMSON/PS   PROSE
SET STATIONS ON THIS BREEDING EARTH & LET US BUY & SELL   283 FOUR ZOAS 2   129
LO HOW THE HEART & BRAIN ARE FORMED IN THE BREEDING WOMB   323 FOUR ZOAS 7   130
BREEDING WOMEN WALKING IN PRIDE & BRINGING FORTH UNDER   706 JERUSALEM 68   36
    GREEN TREES
BREEDS
BREEDS SATIRE FOUL CONTAGION FROM WHICH NONE ARE FREE . . 41C THEN SHE BORE   PROSE
HE WHO DESIRES BUT ACTS NOT BREEDS PESTILENCE . . . . . 151A MARRIAGE HH 7   PROSE
IS LIKE STANDING WATER & BREEDS REPTILES OF THE MIND . . 156D MARRIAGE HH 17   PROSE
THE LAMB MISUSD BREEDS PUBLIC STRIFE . . . . 431 AUGURIES   23
THIS EARTH BREEDS NOT OUR HAPPINESS . . . . 818 HAPPINESS/L   9
BREEZE
WHISPRING FAINT MURMURS TO THE SCANTY BREEZE . . . . . 10 WHEN EARLY/PS   12
HEAR MY VOICE UPON THE BREEZE . . . . 61 LEAVE O/IM   8
THE WEAK BREEZE IN EFFORTS OERWEARIED . . . . 258 BOOK OF LOS 4   48
BREEZES
HOW COOL THE BREEZES OF THE VALLY & THE ARMS OF THE   369 FOUR ZOAS 9   *   449
    BRANCHING TREES
IF THOU REFUSE THY PRESENT TORMENTS WILL SEEM SOUTHERN   629 JERUSALEM 10   35
    BREEZES
BRERETON
OF HAND & HYLE & COBAN OF KWANTOK PEACHEY BRERETON SLAYD   623 JERUSALEM 5   25
    & HUTTON
HAND HYLE & COBAN GUANTOK PEACHEY BRERETON SLAYD & HUTTON   641 JERUSALEM 19   18
BRERETON & SLADE IN EGYPT HUTTON & SKOFELD & KOX . . . . 662 JERUSALEM 36   17
BRERTUN
GWANTOK PEACHY BRERTUN SLAID HUTTN SKOFELD KOCK KOTOPE . . 658 JERUSALEM 32   11
BRERTUN HAD YORKSHIRE DURHAM WESTMORELAND & HIS EMANATION   710 JERUSALEM 71   32
BRETAGNE
. . . THE DUKE OF BRETAGNE AND THE EARL OF BORGOGNE . . . 141 FRENCH REVOLTN   169
BRETHREN
THY BRETHREN AND NOT AS THY FOOT OR THY HAND . . . . . . 143 FRENCH REVOLTN   194
NOR HIS ACCEPTED BRETHREN WHOM TYRANT HE CALLS FREE . . . 160A SONG LIBERTY   PROSE
BEHELD THEIR BRETHREN SHRINK TOGETHER . . . . 236 URIZEN 28   12
THEIR BRETHREN OF OTHER CITIES . . . . 236 URIZEN 28   18
ARISE MY SON BRING ALL THY BRETHREN O THOU KING OF FIRE   240 EUROPE 8   8
BECAUSE THEIR BRETHREN & SISTERS LIVD IN WAR & LUST . . . 246 SONG OF LOS 4   6
WHAT ARE WE TERRORS TO ONE ANOTHER COME O BRETHREN   283 FOUR ZOAS 2   124
    WHEREFORE
IN WOE HIS BRETHREN & HIS SONS IN DARKNING WOE LAMENTING   283 FOUR ZOAS 2   132
TO BIND THE FATHER & ENSLAVE THE BRETHREN NOUGHT HE KNEW   326 FOUR ZOAS 7   256
AS LOS A FATHER TO HIS BRETHREN & HE JOYD IN THE DARK LAKE   332 FOUR ZOAS 7   480
BUT SATAN ACCUSD PALAMABRON BEFORE [LOS] HIS BRETHREN ALSO   350 FOUR ZOAS 8   368
    HE MADDEND
SHE TENDERLY LOVD HIM ABOVE ALL HIS BRETHREN HE GREW UP   351 FOUR ZOAS 8   385
I AM NOT HERE ALONE MY FLOCKS YOU ARE MY BRETHREN . . . 368 FOUR ZOAS 9   443
AND LO MY BRETHREN IN THEIR TENTS & THEIR LITTLE   375 FOUR ZOAS 9   691
    ONES AROUND THEM
O MY DEAR SONS LEAVE NOT YOUR FATHER AS YOUR BRETHREN LEFT   508 MILTON 23   61
    ME
THY BRETHREN CALL THEE AND THY FATHERS AND THY SONS . . . 622 JERUSALEM 4   11
OF ALBION'S SONS & THE FATHER OF ALL HIS BRETHREN IN THE   626 JERUSALEM 7   43
    SHADOWY
CONDENSD HAND HAS ABSORBD ALL HIS BRETHREN IN HIS MIGHT   628 JERUSALEM 8   43
WHILE REUBEN ENROOTS HIS BRETHREN IN THE NARROW CANAANITE   636 JERUSALEM 15   25
I GIVE MYSELF AND THESE MY BRETHREN GIVE THEMSELVES FOR   665 JERUSALEM 38   39
    ALBION
HE WEPT BEFORE HIS WRATHFUL BRETHREN THANKFUL & CONSIDERATE   675 JERUSALEM 45   23
O GOD DESCEND GATHER OUR BRETHREN DELIVER JERUSALEM . . . 675 JERUSALEM 45   28
HOW ALL YOUR BRETHREN SAY THE SOUND OF HIS HARP . . . . 791B LETTER 3   PROSE
BY HIS BRETHREN & BETRAYD THEIR CAUSE TO THEIR ENEMIES . . 813B LETTER 22   PROSE
BREWER'S
AND NOT A BREWER'S SERVANT MY GOOD SIR . . . . 546 ENGLISH CONN/N   6
BRIARS
AND BINDING WITH BRIARS MY JOYS & DESIRES . . . . . . 163 GARDEN LOVE/N   12
AND BINDING WITH BRIARS MY JOYS & DESIRES . . . . . . 215 GARDEN LOVE/SE   12
FEAR NOT O POOR FORSAKEN ONE O LAND OF BRIARS & THORNS   354 FOUR ZOAS 8   534
BRIBE
HE WAS TOO PROUD TO TAKE A BRIBE . . . . 750 EV GOSPEL(C)/N   11
HE WAS TOO PROUD TO TAKE A BRIBE . . . . 751 EV GOSPEL(D)/N   15
BRIBES
BUT BELIAL OF SODOM & GOMORRHA OBSCURE DEMON OF BRIBES . . 528 MILTON 37   30
BRICK
WITH WALLS OF BRICK & STONE . . . . 57 TO BE OR/IM   9
DRIVING THE ANGEL BEFORE ME SOON WE SAW SEVEN HOUSES OF   157A MARRIAGE HH 17   PROSE
    BRICK
BRICK-KILNS,BRICK KILNS
THE KING OF LIGHT BEHELD HER MOURNING AMONG THE BRICK KILNS   285 FOUR ZOAS 2   215
    COMPELLD
MINUTE PARTICULARS IN SLAVERY I BEHOLD AMONG THE   735 JERUSALEM 89   17
    BRICK-KILNS

BRICKLAYER
    TO GREEN THE BRICKLAYER . . . . 57 TO BE OR/IM   16
BRICKS
    PRISONS ARE BUILT WITH STONES OF LAW BROTHELS WITH BRICKS   151B MARRIAGE HH 8   PROSE
      OF RELIGION
    THE STONES ARE PITY AND THE BRICKS WELL WROUGHT AFFECTIONS   632 JERUSALEM 12   30
    IN BRICKS TO BUILD THE PYRAMIDS OF HEBER & TERAH BUT LOS   657 JERUSALEM 31   12
BRIDE
    THAT [PANTED] PANTETH FOR A BRIDE . . . .   56 HAIL MATRIM/IM *   18
    BY ARISTON THE KING OF BEAUTY FOR HIS STOLEN BRIDE . . . 200 AMERICA 10   10
    RINTRAH WHERE HAST THOU HID THY BRIDE   . . . . 240 EUROPE 8   5
    THE ENORMOUS BRIDE & BRIDEGROOM SAT BESIDE THEM URIZEN . . 276 FOUR ZOAS 1   436
    AND OF AHANIA HIS PURE BRIDE BUT SHE WAS DISTANT FAR . . 276 FOUR ZOAS 1   438
    [IN BEAUTY LOVE & XXX SCORN [?THEY ?SULKD] THE BRIDE &   SUPP FOUR ZOAS 1   *
      BRIDEGROOM ?SULKD]
    BECAUSE THE LAMB OF GOD CREATES HIMSELF A BRIDE & WIFE . . 362 FOUR ZOAS 9   220
    AND DARK URTHONA ROUZD HIS SHADY BRIDE FROM HER DEEP DEN   380 FOUR ZOAS AD 1   7
    [ONCE THOU WAST A VIRGIN BRIDE] . . . . 415 MY SPECTRE/N   10
    VEGETATION THE SUPPER OF THE LAMB & HIS BRIDE AND THE . . 511 MILTON 25   61
    [JERUSALEM WHO IS ABOUT TO BE RECIEVD LIKE THE BRIDE   609C V LAST JUDG/N *PROSE
      OF THE]
    IS WROUGHT LAMBETH THE BRIDE THE LAMB'S WIFE LOVETH THEE   632 JERUSALEM 12   41
    HE MADE ME HIS BRIDE & WIFE HE GAVE THEE TO ALBION . . . 643 JERUSALEM 20   40
    AND FAIR JERUSALEM HIS BRIDE . . . . 649 FIELDS FROM/J   7
    CHILDREN OF JESUS & HIS BRIDE . . . . 650 FIELDS FROM/J   20
    AND IS JERUSALEM THY BRIDE . . . . 651 FIELDS FROM/J   68
    VALA WAS ALBION'S BRIDE & WIFE IN GREAT ETERNITY . . . . 660 JERUSALEM 33   39
    THE BRIDE AND WIFE OF THE LAMB O GOD THOU ART NOT   676 JERUSALEM 46   28
      AN AVENGER
    THE NATIONS WAIT FOR JERUSALEM THEY LOOK UP FOR THE BRIDE   712 JERUSALEM 72   37
BRIDEGROOM
    AS THE YOUNG BRIDEGROOM GOING TO BE MARRIED . . . . .   24 EDW THIRD/PS 3   145
    THE ENORMOUS BRIDE & BRIDEGROOM SAT BESIDE THEM URIZEN . . 276 FOUR ZOAS 1   436
    [IN BEAUTY LOVE & XXX SCORN [?THEY ?SULKD] THE BRIDE &   SUPP FOUR ZOAS 1   *
      BRIDEGROOM ?SULKD]
    AWAKE THE BRIDEGROOM COMETH I AWOKE TO SLEEP NO MORE . . 355 FOUR ZOAS 8   541
BRIDGE
    STIFLING IN MUD FAIR ELLEN PASSD THE BRIDGE . . . . .   4 FAIR ELENOR/PS   31
    FROM ST PAULS TO A NOBLE HOUSE IN BRIDGE STREET BLACKFRIARS   856A LETTER 54   PROSE
    RICHARD PHILLIPS ESQR...BRIDGE STREET BLACK FRIARS . . SUPP ADDRESS/L 62   *TITLE
BRIDGES
    AND EVERY AGE IS MOATED DEEP WITH BRIDGES OF SILVER & GOLD   516 MILTON 28   56
BRIDGEWATER
    PRINTED BY WATTS & BRIDGEWATER SOUTHMOLTON-STREET . . . 562C DESC CAT ADV   PROSE
    PRINTED BY WATTS & BRIDGEWATER SOUTHMOULTON-STREET . . . 587B CHAUCER 1   PROSE
BRIDLES
    CURBING THEIR TYGERS WITH GOLDEN BITS & BRIDLES OF SILVER   686 JERUSALEM 55   35
      & IVORY
BRIGHT   SEE ALL BRIGHT
    [TO] INFOLDING THE BRIGHT WOMAN [FROM THE DESOLATING WINDS   381 FOUR ZOAS AD 5 *   15
    . . .
    UP TO THY BRIGHT PAVILLIONS ISSUE FORTH . . . .   1 TO SPRING/PS   7
    FLOURISH DOWN THE BRIGHT CHEEK OF MODEST EVE . . . . .   2 TO AUTUMN/PS   10
    THY BRIGHT TORCH OF LOVE THY RADIANT CROWN . . . . . .   3 EVNING STAR/PS   3
    ID CURSE BRIGHT FORTUNE FOR MY MIXED LOT . . . . . .   10 WHEN EARLY/PS   19
    REGARDLESS OF THE MOON AND THOSE THAT ONCE WERE BRIGHT . .   18 EDW THIRD/PS 1   41
    GOOD MORROW BRAVE SIR THOMAS THE BRIGHT MORN . . . . .   21 EDW THIRD/PS 3   1
    IN THE BRIGHT SUNSHINE OF THIS FATAL DAY . . . . . .   24 EDW THIRD/PS 3   143
    FURBISH OUR ARMOURS BRIGHT NEW PLUME OUR HELMS . . . .   24 EDW THIRD/PS 3   147
    THE SWORD WAS BRIGHT WHILE THE PLOW-SHARE RUSTED . . . . 40A SAMSON/PS   PROSE
    THE SUN HE FELT BUT THE BRIGHT MOON WAS NOW A USELESS GLOBE   100 TIRIEL 2   2
    THEN HE WOULD CREEP LIKE A BRIGHT SERPENT TILL AROUND MY   105 TIRIEL 4   57
      NECK
    OER THIS DESART BRIGHT . . . . 113 LIT GRL LST/SI   30
    SOFTEST CLOTHING WOOLY BRIGHT . . . . 115 THE LAMB/SI   6
    AND BY CAME AN ANGEL WHO HAD A BRIGHT KEY . . . . . . 117 CHIMNEY SWP/SI   13
    THE FEET OF ANGELS BRIGHT . . . . 119 NIGHT/SI   12
    MY BRIGHT MANE FOR EVER . . . . 119 NIGHT/SI   46
    AND WHY IT SCATTERS ITS BRIGHT BEAUTY THRO THE HUMID AIR   128 BOOK OF THEL 2   15
    THE CLOUD THEN SHEWD HIS GOLDEN HEAD & HIS BRIGHT FORM   128 BOOK OF THEL 3   5
      EMERGD
    AND THE BRIGHT CLOUD SAILD ON TO FIND HIS PARTNER IN THE   129 BOOK OF THEL 3   31
      VALE
    A BRIGHT CLOUD OF INFANT SOULS . . . . 138 FRENCH REVOLTN   88
    AND BRIGHT CHILDREN LOOK AFTER HIM INTO THE GRAVE . . . 139 FRENCH REVOLTN   108
    . . . ASCEND ON THE HILLS AND BRIGHT INFANTRY RANK . . . 147 FRENCH REVOLTN   291
    SET WITH PEARLS & RUBIES BRIGHT . . . . 163 I SAW CHAPEL/N   11
    SLEEP SLEEP BEAUTY BRIGHT . . . . 165 CRADLE SONG/N   5
    TILL IT BORE AN APPLE BRIGHT . . . . 165 CHRISTN FORB/N   10
    [[HB] THEY EMBRACD [MY MIRTLE] THE BLOSSOMS BRIGHT] . . . 167 INFANT SORW/N *   32
    [[HB] THEY EMBRACD MY [MIRTLE] BLOSSOMS BRIGHT] . . . 167 INFANT SORW/N *   37
    OF THY TORCHES BRIGHT . . . . 168 SILENT NIGHT/N   3
    NOR A THORN NOR A THREAT STAIN HER BEAUTY BRIGHT . . . . 171 THE LILLY/N   6
    TYGER TYGER BURNING BRIGHT . . . . 172 THE TYGER/N 1   1
    TYGER TYGER BURNING BRIGHT . . . . 173 THE TYGER/N 1   22
    TYGER TYGER BURNING BRIGHT . . . . 173 THE TYGER/N 2   1
    TYGER TYGER BURNING BRIGHT . . . . 173 THE TYGER/N 2   17
    AND THUS SHE SPOKE TO THE BRIGHT MARYGOLD OF LEUTHA'S VALE   189 V DAU ALBION 1   5
    INSTEAD OF MORN ARISES A BRIGHT SHADOW LIKE AN EYE . . . 191 V DAU ALBION 2   35
    THE NEW WASHD LAMB TINGD WITH THE VILLAGE SMOKE &   191 V DAU ALBION 3   18
      THE BRIGHT SWAN
    WHERE THE COLD MISER SPREADS HIS GOLD OR DOES THE BRIGHT   195 V DAU ALBION 8   1
      CLOUD DROP

```
                                                        PAGE     TITLE          LINE
BRIGHT    (CONTINUED)
    LET HIM LOOK UP INTO THE HEAVENS & LAUGH IN THE BRIGHT AIR    198 AMERICA 6         7
    BECAUSE FROM THEIR BRIGHT SUMMITS YOU MAY PASS TO             200 AMERICA 10        7
        THE GOLDEN WORLD
    TYGER TYGER BURNING BRIGHT    . . . . . . . . . .             214 THE TYGER/SE      1
    TYGER TYGER BURNING BRIGHT    . . . . . . . . . .             214 THE TYGER/SE     21
    NOR A THORN NOR A THREAT STAIN HER BEAUTY BRIGHT  . . . .     215 THE LILLY/SE      4
    TILL IT BORE AN APPLE BRIGHT    . . . . . . . . .             218 POISON TREE/SE   10
    YOUTH AND MAIDEN BRIGHT    . . . . . . . . . . .              219 LIT GRL LST/SE    7
    MET IN GARDEN BRIGHT    . . . . . . . . . . . .               219 LIT GRL LST/SE   12
    CAME THE MAIDEN BRIGHT    . . . . . . . . . . .               219 LIT GRL LST/SE   26
    SETTLED A LAKE BRIGHT & SHINING CLEAR    . . . . . .          227 URIZEN 10        22
    THUS SPEAKING WHILE HIS NUMROUS SONS SHOOK THEIR BRIGHT       239 EUROPE 4          8
        FIERY WINGS
    IN THOUGHTS PERTURBD THEY ROSE FROM THE BRIGHT RUINS SILENT   241 EUROPE 10         1
        FOLLOWING
    TO CAST ME FROM THY BRIGHT PRESENCE    . . . . . . .          254 AHANIA 4     *   63
    WHEREON HIS BRIGHT FEET HAD TROD    . . . . . . . .           254 AHANIA 4         71
    TO AWAKE BRIGHT URIZEN MY KING  . . . . . . . .               254 AHANIA 5          7
    ROARING INDIGNANT THE BRIGHT SPARKS    . . . . . .            260 BOOK OF LOS 5    31
    OF A BRIGHT UNIVERSE EMPERY ATTENDED DAY & NIGHT  . . . .     264 FOUR ZOAS 1      15
    BUT ON THE TENTH [?BRIGHT] TREMBLING MORN .    . . . . .      266 FOUR ZOAS 1  *   87
    [BUT STANDING ON THE ROCKS HER WOVEN SHADOW GLOWING BRIGHT]   267 FOUR ZOAS 1     119
    [WHILE THE BRIGHT SPECTRE HID HIMSELF AMONG THE TRAILING      268 FOUR ZOAS 1  *  144
        CLOUDS]
    . . . A BRIGHT WONDER [THAT BEULAH] NATURE [SHUDDERD AT]      269 FOUR ZOAS 1     183
    RAISD THE [BRIGHT] FIERCE BOY & GIRL . . . . . . . . .        269 FOUR ZOAS 1     196
    [INFOLDING THE BRIGHT INFANTS FROM THE DESOLATING WINDS]      270 FOUR ZOAS 1     210
    FADED & HER BRIGHT EYES DECAYD MELTED WITH PITY & LOVE  .     270 FOUR ZOAS 1     213
    AND NINE BRIGHT SPACES WANDERD WEAVING MAZES OF DELIGHT       270 FOUR ZOAS 1     234
    THY NAME IS ENITHARMON SAID THE [BRIGHT] FIERCE PROPHETIC     271 FOUR ZOAS 1     249
        BOY
    [BRIGHT] DARK AS A DEWY MORNING WHEN THE CRIMSON LIGHT        271 FOUR ZOAS 1  *  253
        APPEARS
    THO THIS BRIGHT WORLD OF ALL OUR JOY IS IN THE HUMAN BRAIN    272 FOUR ZOAS 1     303
    BUT THE BRIGHT SUN WAS NOT AS YET HE FILLING ALL             273 FOUR ZOAS 1     349
        THE EXPANSE
    BRIGHT SOULS [?ELEMENTS] OF VEGETATIVE LIFE BUDDING AND       274 FOUR ZOAS 1  *  379
        BLOSSOMING
    SIEZD HIS BRIGHT SHEEPHOOK STUDDED WITH GEMS & GOLD HE        275 FOUR ZOAS 1     414
        SWUNG IT ROUND
    THREE GATES WITHIN GLORIOUS & BRIGHT OPEN INTO [ETERNITY]     279 FOUR ZOAS 1  *  563
        BEULAH
    FROM ENITHARMON'S INWARD PARTS BUT THE BRIGHT FEMALE TERROR   279 FOUR ZOAS 1     564
    REFUSD TO OPEN THE BRIGHT GATES SHE CLOSD AND BARRD THEM      279 FOUR ZOAS 1     565
        FAST
    URIZEN ROSE FROM THE BRIGHT FEAST LIKE A STAR THRO THE        280 FOUR ZOAS 2       9
        EVENING SKY
    [TILL] [BUT] SHE BECAME A [DE] DRAGON WINGED BRIGHT           282 FOUR ZOAS 2  *   89
        & POISONOUS
    ROAR THE BRIGHT MASSES THUNDRING . . . . . . . . .            283 FOUR ZOAS 2     136
    OF HIS THREE DAUGHTERS WERE ENCOMPASSD BY THE TWELVE BRIGHT   284 FOUR ZOAS 2     175
        HALLS
    EVERY HALL SURROUNDED BY BRIGHT PARADISES OF DELIGHT    . .   284 FOUR ZOAS 2     176
    THE GOLDEN HALL OF URIZEN WHOSE WESTERN SIDE GLOWD BRIGHT     284 FOUR ZOAS 2     179
    HIS SHADOWY FEMININE SEMBLANCE HERE REPOSD ON A [BRIGHT]      284 FOUR ZOAS 2  *  181
        WHITE COUCH
    LIKE A BRIGHT CLOUD IN HARVEST BUT WHEN URIZEN FROWND SHE     284 FOUR ZOAS 2     183
        WEPT
    IN HER BRIGHT SKIRTS ASTONISHD & CONFOUNDED HE BEHELD  .  .   285 FOUR ZOAS 2     203
    [THERE] REPINING HE CONTEMPLATED THE PAST IN HIS BRIGHT       287 FOUR ZOAS 2  *  292
        SPHERE
    IN THE BRIGHT SANDS OF LOS EVADING MY EMBRACE THEN I ALONE    288 FOUR ZOAS 2     305
    FROM THY FIERCE LOVE FOR THO I AM DISSOLVD IN THE BRIGHT      288 FOUR ZOAS 2     316
        GOD
    AND NINE BRIGHT SPHERES OF HARMONY RISE ROUND THE FIERY       289 FOUR ZOAS 2     348
        KING
    UPON THE IMMENSE LIKE A BRIGHT RAINBOW WEEPING & SMILING      290 FOUR ZOAS 2     382
        & FADING
    ONTO THE MARGIN OF NON ENTITY THE BRIGHT FEMALE CAME    .  .  291 FOUR ZOAS 2  *  422
    AND BRIGHT AHANIA BOWD HERSELF BEFORE HIS SPLENDID FEET       291 FOUR ZOAS 3       2
    . . . [WETS] WET [HER] MY BRIGHT HAIR WITH [HER] MY TEARS     291 FOUR ZOAS 3       4
    DO THEY NOT BOW THEIR BRIGHT HEADS AT THY VOICE AT THY        291 FOUR ZOAS 3       6
        COMMAND
    O BRIGHT [AHANIA] [SHADOW] A BOY IS BORN OF THE DARK OCEAN    292 FOUR ZOAS 3  *   14
    SHE RAISD HER BRIGHT HEAD SWEET PERFUMD & THUS WITH           292 FOUR ZOAS 3      26
        HEAVENLY VOICE
    TRIUMPHING EVEN TO THE STARS AT BRIGHT AHANIA'S FALL    .  .  295 FOUR ZOAS 3     138
    FOR HER BRIGHT EYES BEHOLD THE ABYSS SOMETIMES A LITTLE       297 FOUR ZOAS 3     209
        SLEEP
    SO SAYING IN A WAVE HE RAPD BRIGHT ENITHARMON FAR    .  .  .  299 FOUR ZOAS 4      56
    SETTLED A LAKE BRIGHT & SHINING CLEAR WHITE AS THE SNOW       303 FOUR ZOAS 4     210
    EMBRACING HIS BRIGHT MOTHER & BEHELD MALIGNANT FIRES    .  .  307 FOUR ZOAS 5      81
    THE [DISMAL] ACCURSED CHAIN O HOW BRIGHT ENITHARMON HOWLD     308 FOUR ZOAS 5     102
        & CRIED
    OF HER BRIGHT HEART    . . . . . . . . . . . .               309 FOUR ZOAS 5     178
    WHERE BRIGHT AHANIA WEPT SHE ALSO SAW THE INFERNAL ROOTS      309 FOUR ZOAS 5     181
    O FOOL COULD I FORGET THE LIGHT THAT FILLED MY BRIGHT         310 FOUR ZOAS 5     216
        SPHERES
    LO THREE TERRIFIC WOMEN AT THE VERGE OF THE BRIGHT FLOOD      311 FOUR ZOAS 6       5
    TILL HIS BRIGHT HAIR SCATTERD IN SNOWS . . . . . .  .  .      318 FOUR ZOAS 6     262
    WALKING IN JOY IN BRIGHT EXPANSES SLEEPING ON BRIGHT          321 FOUR ZOAS 7      64
        CLOUDS
```

	PAGE	TITLE	LINE
BRIGHT (CONTINUED)			
IN THAT TRANSPARENT ROCK AS IF IN JOY OF THY BRIGHT PRISON	322	FOUR ZOAS 7	76
A FEMALE BRIGHT I STOOD BESIDE MY ANVIL DARK A MASS . . .	327	FOUR ZOAS 7	282
OF IRON GLOWD BRIGHT PREPARD FOR SPADES & PLOWSHARES SUDDEN DOWN	327	FOUR ZOAS 7 *	283
FLAMING HIS HEAD LIKE THE BRIGHT SUN SEEN THRO A MIST THAT MAGNIFIES	335	FOUR ZOAS 7B	79
HE SAID ART THOU BRIGHT ENION IS THE SHADOW OF HOPE RETURND	339	FOUR ZOAS 7B	228
WITH JOY THE BRIGHT LIGHT & IN IT A HUMAN FORM	342	FOUR ZOAS 8	43
TO UNDERMINE THE WORLD OF LOS & TEAR BRIGHT ENITHARMON . .	343	FOUR ZOAS 8	98
BEFORE ASSAULTED THE BRIGHT HUMAN FORM HE FELT HIS PORES	352	FOUR ZOAS 8	417
HE DROOPS HIS HEAD & TREMBLING STANDS & HIS BRIGHT EYES DECAY	354	FOUR ZOAS 8	531
BATHING THEIR LIMBS IN THE BRIGHT VISIONS OF ETERNITY . .	358	FOUR ZOAS 9	45
BATHING THEIR LIMBS IN THE BRIGHT VISIONS OF ETERNITY . .	359	FOUR ZOAS 9	90
MY ROBE IS TURNED TO CONFUSION & MY BRIGHT GOLD TO STONES	360	FOUR ZOAS 9 *	106
WITH HARPS & SONGS WHERE BRIGHT AHANIA SANG BEFORE THY FACE	360	FOUR ZOAS 9 *	126
CHOKD THE BRIGHT RIVERS BURDNING WITH MY SHIPS THE ANGRY DEEP	361	FOUR ZOAS 9	169
INTO THE FIRES THEN GLORIOUS BRIGHT EXULTING IN HIS JOY	362	FOUR ZOAS 9	191
BURST ITS BRIGHT VESSELS SHE FELL DOWN DEAD AT THE FEET OF URIZEN	362	FOUR ZOAS 9	198
SHALL REFLOURISH THEN BRIGHT AHANIA SHALL AWAKE FROM DEATH	362	FOUR ZOAS 9	210
WITH A BRIGHT GIRDLE & HIS SKIRT FILLD WITH IMMORTAL SOULS	365	FOUR ZOAS 9	322
AND BRIGHT AHANIA TOOK HER SEAT BY URIZEN IN SONGS & JOY	366	FOUR ZOAS 9	353
INVISIBLE LUVAH IN BRIGHT CLOUDS HOVERD OVER VALA'S HEAD	367	FOUR ZOAS 9	385
THAT SING & FLY IN THE BRIGHT AIR BUT YOU DO LICK MY FEET	368	FOUR ZOAS 9	431
I SAW MY LUVAH LIKE A SPIRIT STAND IN THE BRIGHT AIR . .	369	FOUR ZOAS 9	465
ROUND HIM STOOD SPIRITS LIKE ME WHO REARD ME A BRIGHT HOUSE	369	FOUR ZOAS 9	466
AND HER BRIGHT HAIR WAS WET WITH THE WATERS	369	FOUR ZOAS 9	482
THOU LITTLE BOY ART THARMAS & THOU BRIGHT GIRL ENION . .	370	FOUR ZOAS 9	510
AND THEN SHE ENTERD HER BRIGHT HOUSE LEADING HER MIGHTY CHILDREN	370	FOUR ZOAS 9	513
WHY WEEPEST THOU THARMAS CHILD OF TEARS IN THE BRIGHT HOUSE OF JOY	371	FOUR ZOAS 9 *	530
WITH THY BRIGHT TEARS BECAUSE THE STEPS OF ENION ARE IN THE GARDENS	371	FOUR ZOAS 9	533
CHEAR UP THY COUNTENANCE BRIGHT BOY & GO TO ENION . . .	371	FOUR ZOAS 9	545
THEN URIZEN SITTING AT HIS REPOSE ON BEDS IN THE BRIGHT SOUTH	372	FOUR ZOAS 9	567
ABOVE ON THE BRIGHT HEAVENS IN PEACE THE SPIRITS OF MEN BENEATH	372	FOUR ZOAS 9	574
THE FEAST WAS SPREAD IN THE BRIGHT SOUTH & THE REGENERATE MAN	372	FOUR ZOAS 9	587
THE FEAST WAS SPREAD IN THE BRIGHT SOUTH & THE ETERNAL MAN	373	FOUR ZOAS 9	618
LET HIM LOOK UP INTO THE HEAVENS & LAUGH IN THE BRIGHT AIR	375	FOUR ZOAS 9	671
THE LION OF TERROR SHALL COME DOWN & BENDING HIS BRIGHT MANE	376	FOUR ZOAS 9	706
AS HE AROSE FROM THE BRIGHT FEAST DRUNK WITH THE WINE OF AGES	376	FOUR ZOAS 9	710
SOUNDING THE SONG OF LOS DESCENDING TO THE VINEYARDS BRIGHT	376	FOUR ZOAS 9	713
AROUND THE ETERNAL MAN'S BRIGHT TENT THE LITTLE CHILDREN PLAY	379	FOUR ZOAS 9	839
THE [ANCIENT] ETERNAL MAN BOWD HIS BRIGHT HEAD	380	FOUR ZOAS AD 1	2
[ASTONISHD LOOKD FROM HIS BRIGHT PORTALS CALLING THUS TO LUVAH]	380	FOUR ZOAS AD 1 *	3
ASTONISHD LOOKD FROM HIS BRIGHT PORTALS LUVAH KING OF LOVE	380	FOUR ZOAS AD 1	5
AWAKEND VALA ARISTON RAN FORTH WITH BRIGHT ?ONANA . . .	380	FOUR ZOAS AD 1 *	6
AND HIS BRIGHT FEET FIRM AS A BRAZEN ALTAR BUT THE PARTS	380	FOUR ZOAS AD 1	12
FEMALE HER FORM BRIGHT AS THE SUMMER BUT THE PARTS OF LOVE	381	FOUR ZOAS AD 1	18
SHRIEKING ABOVE THE OCEAN A BRIGHT WONDER THAT NATURE SHUDDERD AT	381	FOUR ZOAS AD 5	3
[TO] INFOLDING THE BRIGHT WOMAN [FROM THE DESOLVING WINDS . . .	381	FOUR ZOAS AD 5 *	15
AROUND MY COUCH WITH TORCHES BRIGHT	416	MY SPECTRE/N	42
WHERE ISRAEL'S TENTS DO SHINE SO BRIGHT	418	MOCK ON/N	12
DAZZLING BRIGHT BEFORE MY EYES	422	BENEATH/N	9
[DAZZLING BRIGHT BEFORE MY EYES]	422	BENEATH REWR/N	6
DAZLING BRIGHT BEFORE MY EYES	424	THE GOLDEN NET	8
AND SHE BECOMES A VIRGIN BRIGHT	425	MENTAL TRAVLER	22
AND PEARL & CRYSTAL SHINING BRIGHT	429	CRYSTL CABINET	6
THIS IS CAUGHT BY FEMALES BRIGHT	432	AUGURIES	69
BUT SHE IS RUDDY & BRIGHT AS DAY	435	WILLIAM BOND	31
BY HIM ON EARTH IN HIS BRIGHT PILGRIMAGE OF SIXTY YEARS	497	MILTON 15	52
THEREFORE BRIGHT TIRZAH TRIUMPHS PUTTING ON ALL BEAUTY . .	501	MILTON 19	44
THUS MILTON STOOD FORMING BRIGHT URIZEN WHILE HIS MORTAL PART	502	MILTON 20	10
AS A BRIGHT SANDAL FORMD IMMORTAL OF PRECIOUS STONES & GOLD	503	MILTON 21	13
IN BRIGHT CATHEDRON'S GOLDEN DOME WITH CARE & LOVE & TEARS	512	MILTON 26	36
PUTS ON THE SWEET FORM THEN SMILES ANTAMON BRIGHT THRO HIS WINDOWS	515	MILTON 28	18
AND IN HIS HALLOWD CENTER HOLDS THE HEAVENS OF BRIGHT ETERNITY	515	MILTON 28	38
AND EVERY HOUR HAS A BRIGHT GOLDEN GATE CARVED WITH SKILL	516	MILTON 28	51
COVERING OVER THE ROCK OF ODOURS HIS BRIGHT PURPLE MANTLE	526	MILTON 35	57
AT THAT BRIGHT GATE ANOTHER LARK MEETS HIM & BACK TO BACK	526	MILTON 36	2
IN THE EAST GATE OF GOLGONOOZA & THE TWENTY-EIGHTH BRIGHT	527	MILTON 36	9
BURND TERRIBLE MY PATH BECAME A SOLID FIRE AS BRIGHT . .	530	MILTON 39	4
AN AWFUL FORM EASTWARD FROM MIDST OF A BRIGHT PAVED-WORK	531	MILTON 39	24
NAMD MORAL VIRTUE CRUEL TWO-FOLD MONSTER SHINING BRIGHT	532	MILTON 40	21
THE MORE BRIGHT SUN OF SUN OF IMAGINATION	618D	ILLUS MILTON	*PROSE
EMBRACE HIM TENFOLD BRIGHT RISING FROM HIS TOMB IN IMMORTALITY	626	JERUSALEM 7	56

		PAGE	TITLE	LINE

BRIGHT   (CONTINUED)
STARRY & GLORIOUS AND THEY EVERY ONE IN THEIR BRIGHT LOINS   635 JERUSALEM 14   19
ALL THINGS ACTED ON EARTH ARE SEEN IN THE BRIGHT SCULPTURES   638 JERUSALEM 16   61
    OF
FROM BRIGHT JAPAN & CHINA TO HESPERIA FRANCE & ENGLAND   . .   648 JERUSALEM 24   47
IS BRIGHT CATHEDRON'S GOLDEN HALL ITS COURTS TOWERS   691 JERUSALEM 59   25
    & PINNACLES
BUT JESUS IS THE BRIGHT PREACHER OF LIFE   . . . . . .   718 STOOD AMONG/J   21
CAMBEL HIS BRIGHT BEAMING COUNTERPART DIVIDED FROM HIM . .   723 JERUSALEM 80   58
JOYD IN THE MANY WEAVING THREADS IN BRIGHT CATHEDRON'S DOME   728 JERUSALEM 83   72
THY FOREHEAD BRIGHT HOLINESS TO THE LORD WITH GATES OF   730 JERUSALEM 86   4
    PEARL
THENCE FEATHERD WITH SOFT CRIMSON OF THE RUBY BRIGHT AS   731 JERUSALEM 86   8
    FIRE
AND BRIGHT STRETCHD OVER EUROPE & ASIA GORGEOUS   . . . .   734 JERUSALEM 89   12
IN ANGER THE WRATH OF GOD BREAKING BRIGHT FLAMING ON ALL   742 JERUSALEM 95   6
    SIDES AROUND
AND TOOK HIS BOW FOURFOLD THE VISION FOR BRIGHT BEAMING   744 JERUSALEM 97   7
    URIZEN
    . . . & BORE A SILVER BOW BRIGHT SHINING   . . . . .   744 JERUSALEM 97   9
AND THEY CONVERSED TOGETHER IN VISIONARY FORMS DRAMATIC   746 JERUSALEM 98   28
    WHICH BRIGHT
AND IN HIS HAND THE SCOURGE SHONE BRIGHT   . . . . . .   749 EV GOSPEL(B)/N   47
THO THOU WAST SO PURE & BRIGHT . . . .   754 EV GOSPEL(E)/N   35
GLITTERING WITH FESTERING VENOMS BRIGHT . . . .   755 EV GOSPEL(E)/N   84
IN PARTICLES BRIGHT   . . . .   804 TO BUTTS/L   15
OF HEAVEN'S BRIGHT BEAMS . . . .   805 TO BUTTS/L   34
BENEATH MY BRIGHT FEET   . . . .   805 TO BUTTS/L   36
HEAVENLY MEN BEAMING BRIGHT . . . .   805 TO BUTTS/L   50
IN HIS BEAMS OF BRIGHT GOLD . . . .   805 TO BUTTS/L   54
IN HIS BOSOM SUN BRIGHT   . . . .   805 TO BUTTS/L   58
BEFORE ME BRIGHT SHONE ` . . . .   806 TO BUTTS/L   74
BRIGHTEN
CREEPS ROUND OUR SECRET NEST FLOCKS BRIGHTEN THE MOUNTAINS   373 FOUR ZOAS 9   611
BRIGHTEND
A RUSHING OF WINGS AROUND HIM WAS HEARD AS HE BRIGHTEND   146 FRENCH REVOLTN   260
    . . .
SMILE BROKE FROM URIZEN FOR ENITHARMON BRIGHTEND MORE &   273 FOUR ZOAS 1   322
    MORE
OR HOVERD OER HIS STARRY HEAD & WHEN HE SMILD SHE BRIGHTEND   284 FOUR ZOAS 2   * 182
AND THE DIM CHAOS BRIGHTEND BENEATH ABOVE AROUND EYED AS   745 JERUSALEM 98   14
    THE PEACOCK
BRIGHTEST
OR EVN THE LEAST BY BIRTH SHALL GAIN THE BRIGHTEST FAME   18 EDW THIRD/PS 1   30
THE ENORMOUS WONDERS OF THE ABYSSES ONCE HIS BRIGHTEST JOY   314 FOUR ZOAS 6   86
BRIGHTNESS
MINGLING HIS HORRIBLE [TERRIBLE] BRIGHTNESS   . . . . .   269 FOUR ZOAS 1   * 182
IN STRENGTH & BRIGHTNESS FROM THE ABYSS HIS BOWELS YEARND   297 FOUR ZOAS 4   3
    OVER THEM
BUT THOU MY SON GLORIOUS IN BRIGHTNESS COMFORTER OF THARMAS   298 FOUR ZOAS 4   26
AT THEIR EXCEEDING BRIGHTNESS & THE SONS OF ETERNITY SENT   312 FOUR ZOAS 6   34
    THEM GIFTS
THEY MUST RENEW THEIR BRIGHTNESS & THEIR DISORGANIZD   366 FOUR ZOAS 9   371
    FUNCTIONS
THE SUN IS THINE [WHEN] HE GOETH FORTH IN HIS MAJESTIC   367 FOUR ZOAS 9   399
    BRIGHTNESS
TO YONDER BRIGHTNESS THERE I HASTE FOR SURE I CAME FROM   367 FOUR ZOAS 9   402
    THENCE
FOLLOW THE STEPS OF THARMAS O THOU BRIGHTNESS OF   371 FOUR ZOAS 9   551
    THE GARDENS
MINGLING HIS HORRIBLE [BRIGHTNESS] DARKNESS . . . . . .   381 FOUR ZOAS AD 5   2
THE VEIL SHONE WITH THY BRIGHTNESS IN THE EYES OF ALBION   643 JERUSALEM 20   34
IN PRIDE OF BEAUTY IN CRUELTY OF HOLINESS IN THE BRIGHTNESS   705 JERUSALEM 68   14
BRIGHTNING
    . . . AND BRIGHTNING OF SWORDS AND VISAGES REDDNING WITH   139 FRENCH REVOLTN   116
    WAR
SHE FOLDED THEM UP IN CARE IN SILENCE & HER BRIGHTNING   366 FOUR ZOAS 9   345
    LIMBS
BRIGHTON
AT BRIGHTON WHERE HE HAS A RESIDENCE FROM WHENCE HE SENT IT   842C LETTER 42   PROSE
AT BRIGHTON MY WIFE JOINS ME IN LOVE TO YOU   . . . . .   843A LETTER 42   PROSE
BRILLIANT
HER EYES OUTSHINE EVERY BRILLIANT RAY . . . .   428 MARY   7
    . . . [WHAT A BRILLIANT TONE] ONE GENERALIZING TONE . .   554 TO VENETIAN/N   9
THIRTY FIGURES ON HORSE-BACK IN A BRILLIANT MORNING SCENE   560B EXHIBITION ADV PROSE
BRING
RISE FROM THE CHAMBERS OF THE EAST AND BRING   . . . . .   3 TO MORNING/PS   4
BRING ME AN AXE AND SPADE   . . . .   7 MY SILKS/PS   13
BRING ME A WINDING SHEET . . . .   7 MY SILKS/PS   14
IS CULTIVATED AND WILL BRING FORTH FRUIT   . . . . .   19 EDW THIRD/PS 2   26
BUT WE WILL BRING THESE GALLIC ROVERS UNDER   . . . .   21 EDW THIRD/PS 2   97
BRING HITHER MY ARMOUR WILLIAM . . . .   28 EDW THIRD/PS 4   1
CRAVE OR BE HEARD FOR PLENTY SHALL BRING FORTH   . . . .   33 EDW THIRD/PS 6   46
BRING FORTH THE LOTS CAST IN THE SPACIOUS ORB   . . . .   34 WAR SONG/PS   2
OR IF THEY LIST TOGETHER MINGLING BRING FORTH MIGHTY POWRS   40D THEN SHE BORE   PROSE
EMBLEM OF PRIDE SHE SAW THE ARTS THEIR TREASURES BRING . .   41B THEN SHE BORE   PROSE
BRING THE PUPPETS . . . .   58C ISLAND MOON 10 PROSE
AND I WILL BRING THEE FOOD OLD MAN TILL DEATH SHALL CALL   103 TIRIEL 3   35
    THEE HENCE
[HIS LITTLE HANDS INTO THE DEPTHS OF THE SEA TO BRING   110 TIRIEL 8   21
    FORTH]
    . . . I ROSE TO BRING MY PRINCE HEAVEN UTTERD COUNSEL . . 141 FRENCH REVOLTN   152

	PAGE	TITLE	LINE

BRING   (CONTINUED)

BRING OUT NUMBER WEIGHT & MEASURE IN A YEAR OF DEARTH   . . 151B MARRIAGE HH 7   PROSE
JOYS IMPREGNATE SORROWS BRING FORTH   . . . .   151C MARRIAGE HH 8   PROSE
THE [IDLE MAN] INDOLENT NEVER CAN BRING TO THE MART   . . .   181 RICHES/N   3
[[UNLESS THEY WILL BRING IN]]   . . . .   185 LET BROTHELS/N   14
THAT I MIGHT TRAVERSE TIMES & SPACES FAR REMOTE AND BRING   192 V DAU ALBION 4   6
WILT THOU BRING COMFORTS ON THY WINGS AND DEWS AND HONEY   192 V DAU ALBION 4   10
   AND BALM
COME IN THE HEAVEN OF GENEROUS LOVE NOR SELFISH BLIGHTINGS   195 V DAU ALBION 7   29
   BRING
THEY CANNOT BRING THE STUBBED OAK TO OVERGROW THE HILLS   199 AMERICA 9   8
BY WHOSE MEANS HE HAS BEEN REGULARLY ENABLED TO BRING   . . 207C PRSPECTUS 1793   PROSE
O MOTHER ENITHARMON WILT THOU BRING FORTH OTHER SONS   .   238 EUROPE PREL 1   4
THEN WHY SHOULDST THOU ACCURSED MOTHER BRING ME INTO LIFE   238 EUROPE PREL 1   11
AND BRING FORTH HOWLING TERRORS ALL DEVOURING FIERY KINGS   238 EUROPE PREL 2   4
I BRING FORTH FROM MY TEEMING BOSOM MYRIADS OF FLAMES   . .   238 EUROPE PREL 2   9
BRING PALAMABRON HORNED PRIEST SKIPPING UPON THE MOUNTAINS   240 EUROPE 8   3
ALAS MY RINTRAH BRING THE LOVELY JEALOUS OCALYTHRON   . . .   240 EUROPE 8   7
ARISE MY SON BRING ALL THY BRETHREN O THOU KING OF FIRE   240 EUROPE 8   8
UPON THEM MORE DESPAIR WILL BRING SELF MURDER ON MY SOUL   265 FOUR ZOAS 1   56
AND UNPOLLUTED & WILL BRING TO RIGID STRICT ACCOUNT   . . .   268 FOUR ZOAS 1   152
. . . & OUR CHILDREN BRING FRUITS & FLOWERS   . . . .   291 FOUR ZOAS 2   413
BRING IN HERE THE GLOBE OF BLOOD AS IN THE (BOOK) OF URIZEN   305A FOUR ZOAS 4   PROSE
OF CIRCLING FIRE UNCEASING PLAYS TO FEED THEM WITH LIFE   308 FOUR ZOAS 5   115
   & BRING
TO BRING THE THRILLING JOYS OF SENSE TO QUELL HIS CEASELESS   308 FOUR ZOAS 5   120
   RAGE
TO BRING THE SHADOW OF ENITHARMON BENEATH OUR WONDROUS TREE   323 FOUR ZOAS 7   113
TO BRING HER DOWN SUBJECTED TO THE RAGE OF MY FIERCE BOY   326 FOUR ZOAS 7   266
I VIEW FUTURITY IN THEE I WILL BRING DOWN SOFT VALA   . . .   327 FOUR ZOAS 7   299
COME THEN INTO MY BOSOM & IN THY SHADOWY ARMS BRING WITH   329 FOUR ZOAS 7   367
   THEE
ARISE O VALA BRING THE BOW OF URIZEN BRING THE SWIFT   338 FOUR ZOAS 7B   200
   ARROWS OF LIGHT
THOU ART OUR CURSE [IN] AND TILL I CAN BRING LOVE INTO   339 FOUR ZOAS 7B   * 257
   THE LIGHT
TO BRING HER FRUITS OF SWEET DELIGHT FROM TREES OF RICHEST   340 FOUR ZOAS 7B   284
   WONDERS
THE TREES BRING FORTH SWEET EXTACY   . . . .   427 MENTAL TRAVLER   89
AND BY HER KIND PERMISSION BRING   . . . .   442 DEDICATN BLAIR   13
BUT BRING TWO PEOPLE & THE HEARING IS STOPPED . . . . .   450D ANNO REYNOLDS   MARG
BRING ME MY BOW OF BURNING GOLD   . . . .   481 AND DID FEET/M   9
BRING ME MY ARROWS OF DESIRE   . . . .   481 AND DID FEET/M   10
BRING ME MY SPEAR O CLOUDS UNFOLD   . . . .   481 AND DID FEET/M   11
BRING ME MY CHARIOT OF FIRE . . . .   481 AND DID FEET/M   12
COME BRING WITH THEE JERUSALEM WITH SONGS ON THE GRECIAN   501 MILTON 19   46
   LYRE
OF WAR & RELIGION LET US DESCEND & BRING HIM CHAINED   . .   507 MILTON 23   17
SHALT BRING JERUSALEM IN THINE ARMS IN THE NIGHT WATCHES   523 MILTON 33   21
   AND
FOR FORTUNE'S FAVOURS YOU YOUR RICHES BRING   . . . . .   541 MR STOTHARD/N   1
BUT YOU MUST NOT BRING IN YOUR HAND A LIE   . . . . .   542 FLORENTINE/N   22
ONLY BE FORCED TO BRING IT BACK TO WHAT IT WAS AND IT WILL   587A CHAUCER 1   PROSE
TILL HE SHOULD BRING THE SONS & DAUGHTERS OF JERUSALEM   629 JERUSALEM 10   3
   TO BE
THINKING TO BRING LOVE INTO LIGHT OF DAY TO JERUSALEM'S   647 JERUSALEM 24   5
   SHAME
BRING HIM TO JUSTICE BEFORE HEAVEN HERE UPON LONDON STONE   670 JERUSALEM 42   50
WALKETH AMONG US GIVE DECISION BRING FORTH ALL YOUR FIRES   686 JERUSALEM 55   18
SHALL VALA BRING THEE FORTH SHALL THE CHASTE BE ASHAMED   696 JERUSALEM 62   7
   ALSO
ARISE O VALA BRING THE BOW OF URIZEN BRING THE SWIFT   700 JERUSALEM 65   46
   ARROWS OF LIGHT
BRING YOUR OFFERINGS YOUR FIRST BEGOTTEN PAMPERD WITH MILK   706 JERUSALEM 68   30
   & BLOOD
IN CRUELTIES OF HOLINESS TO REFUSE THE JOYS OF LOVE TO   707 JERUSALEM 68   59
   BRING
TO AWAKE THE PRISONERS OF DEATH TO BRING ALBION AGAIN   . .   716 JERUSALEM 75   25
ARE BUT THE SINNER TO JUDGMENT TO BRING   . . . . . .   751 EV GOSPEL(C)/N   46
IS BUT THE SINNER TO JUDGMENT TO BRING   . . . . . .   753 EV GOSPEL(D)/N   82
THAT HE MIGHT BRING SALVATION   . . . .   756 EV GOSPEL(I)/N   10
PLATO DID NOT BRING LIFE & IMMORTALITY TO LIGHT   . . . .   774C ANNO BERKELEY   MARG
YOU SHALL NOT BRING ME DOWN TO BELIEVE SUCH FITTING   784C ANNO WW EXCUR   MARG
   & FITTED
MY SISTER WILL BE IN TOWN IN A WEEK & BRING WITH HER YOUR   803D LETTER 15   PROSE
& THIS FROM MR H(HAYLEY) WILL BRING ME BACK AGAIN   . . .   812C LETTER 22   PROSE
SHALL BRING THY WIFE UPON A BIER   . . . .   817 HAPPINESS/L   38
BRING SOME WITH ME FINISHD I AM AT PRESENT IN A BUSTLE   .   826D LETTER 28   PROSE
TO BRING THEM TO PERFECTION HAS CAUSED THIS DELAY AS ALSO   840B LETTER 39   PROSE
O THAT I COULD BUT BRING PELPHAM TO ME OR GO TO HER   . . .   857C LETTER 54   PROSE
I HOPE A FEW MORE DAYS WILL BRING US TO A CONCLUSION   .   870B LETTER 71   PROSE
I INTEND TO BRING WITH ME BESIDES OUR NECESSARY CHANGE OF   873A LETTER 76   PROSE

BRINGER

WHEN WILT THOU SMILE ON THARMAS O THOU BRINGER OF GOLDEN   370 FOUR ZOAS 9   493
   DAY
[WHEN WILT THOU SMILE ON THARMAS O THOU BRINGER OF GOLDEN   SUPP FOUR ZOAS 1   *
   DAY]

BRINGEST

FOR CHAIND BENEATH I REND THESE CAVERNS WHEN THOU BRINGEST   196 AMERICA PREL 1   18
   FOOD

BRINGING

BRINGING GOOD NEWS OF SIN AND DEATH DESTROYED   . . . . .   37D SAMSON/PS   PROSE

271

	PAGE	TITLE	LINE

BRINGING   (CONTINUED)
IN MILD PERSWASION BRINGING LEAVES OF THE TREE OF LIFE . . 676 JERUSALEM 46   9
BREEDING WOMEN WALKING IN PRIDE & BRINGING FORTH UNDER   706 JERUSALEM 68   36
   GREEN TREES
NAKED AMONG THE HUMAN CLUSTERS BRINGING WINE OF ANGUISH   726 JERUSALEM 82   65
BRINGS
BRINGS ME YEW TO DECK MY GRAVE . . . .   6 MY SILKS/PS   5
AND BRINGS GOOD COUNSEL FROM THE BREAST OF LAUGHTER . . .   24 EDW THIRD/PS 3   135
BRINGS FORTH FRUIT TO THE MIND'S TREASURE-HOUSE . . . .   27 EDW THIRD/PS 3   251
BRINGS TRUE JOY ONCE FLED & CONTEMPLATION IS HER DAUGHTER 42A THEN SHE BORE PROSE
SHE BRINGS HUMILITY TO MAN TAKE HER SHE SAYS . . . . . 42A THEN SHE BORE PROSE
AND MUTUAL FEAR BRINGS PEACE . . . .   174 HUMAN IMAGE/N   6
ON HIS STONE THRESHOLD DOES HIS EYE BEHOLD THE BEAM THAT   195 V DAU ALBION 8   2
   BRINGS
EDWARD THE BLACK PRINCE BRINGS HIS CAPTIVES TO HIS FATHER   209A SUBJCTS HIST/N TITLE
AND MUTUAL FEAR BRINGS PEACE . . . . 217 HUMAN ABSTR/SE   5
FOR ALL MY SECRET FAULTS WHICH HE BRINGS FORTH UPON THE   339 FOUR ZOAS 7B   250
   LIGHT
MAN BRINGS ALL THAT HE HAS OR CAN HAVE INTO THE WORLD WITH 471A ANNO REYNOLDS   MARG
   HIM
AS THE CLOUD THAT BRINGS THE SNOW ALL THE WHILE FROM HIS   483 MILTON 3   34
   BACK
THEN BRINGS FORTH MORAL VIRTUE THE CRUEL VIRGIN BABYLON   484 MILTON 5   27
HE BRINGS TO ME THE IMAGES OF HIS LOVE & I REJECT   724 JERUSALEM 81   3
   IN CHASTITY
FROM HIS SUPERABUNDANT EMPLOYMENT YET NO ONE BRINGS . . . 829D LETTER 30   PROSE
BRINGS ON THE SHIVERING FIT WHEN I AM FORCED TO GO TO BED 872B LETTER 75   PROSE
BRINGS ON THE SYMPTOMS OF THE ORIGINAL COMPLAINT HE DOES   SUPP LETTER 81A   *PROSE
BRINK
[WHILE OTHERS RISE FROM THEIR GRAVES ON THE BRINK OF THE   443B LAST JUDGMNT/L PROSE
   PIT]
FIGHTING WITH EACH OTHER ON THE [VERY] BRINK OF PERDITION   443D LAST JUDGMNT/L PROSE
CONTEND WITH EACH OTHER ON THE BRINK OF PERDITION . . . 609C V LAST JUDG/N PROSE
LINCOLN & NORWICH STAND TREMBLING ON THE BRINK OF UDAN-ADAN 623 JERUSALEM 5   10
BRISKLY
GOES ON BRISKLY THIS WORK IS TO BE A VERY ELEGANT ONE . . 824C LETTER 27   PROSE
GOING ON BRISKLY WITH THE PLATES FIND EVERY THING PROMISING 835A LETTER 34   PROSE
BRISTLED
NOR BRISTLED WRATH . . . . 256 BOOK OF LOS 3   12
BRISTOL
A PARCEL OF FOOLS GOING TO BRISTOL IF I WAS TO GO   . . . 51D ISLAND MOON 7 PROSE
GLOUCESTER AND EXETER AND SALISBURY AND BRISTOL AND   668 JERUSALEM 40   61
   BENEVOLENT BATH
BRISTOL & BATH LISTEN TO MY WORDS & YE SEVENTEEN GIVE EAR   673 JERUSALEM 43   55
TO BRISTOL & HIS HEART BEAT STRONG ON SALISBURY PLAIN . . 704 JERUSALEM 67   37
FOR HIS BRISTOL FRIENDS AS THEY THINK I SAW MR TATHAM SENR 877A LETTER 85   PROSE
GEORGE CUMBERLAND ESQRE CULVER STREET BRISTOL . . . . . SUPP ADDRESS/L 88 *TITLE
BRISTOL'S
. . . THE SPOTTED PLAGUE SMOTE BRISTOL'S . . . . 202 AMERICA 15   2
BRISTOW
LANDLORD ROBERT BRISTOW ESQ OF BROXMORE NEAR RUMSEY . . . 590A CHAUCER 2   PROSE
BRITAIN
UNSUBDUED AS GODS AND THE SUN OF BRITAIN (SET) BUT SHALL   577B DESC CAT 5   *TITLE
OF THE GIANTS OF IRELAND AND BRITAIN OF THE . . . . . 577D DESC CAT 5   PROSE
AND CONTAINS THE ANCIENT HISTORY OF BRITAIN . . . . . 578B DESC CAT 5   PROSE
WAS BRITAIN THE PRIMITIVE SEAT OF THE PATRIARCHAL RELIGION 649B JERUSALEM 27   PROSE
WITH CYMBAL TRUMPET CLARION & THE SCYTHED CHARIOTS   677 JERUSALEM 47   11
   OF BRITAIN
THE SUN SHALL BE A SCYTHED CHARIOT OF BRITAIN THE MOON   688 JERUSALEM 56   18
   A SHIP
ARE THE TEMPLES AMONG HIS PILLARS BRITAIN IS LOS'S FORGE   690 JERUSALEM 58   42
THE SUN WAS BLACK & THE MOON ROLLD A USELESS GLOBE THRO   699 JERUSALEM 65   11
   BRITAIN
BRITAIN'S
RENEW THE ARTS ON BRITAIN'S SHORE . . . . 557 ART HAS LOST/N   5
AND SAVE [THY WORKS] THEE FROM [BRITAIN'S] THE UNGRATEFUL   557 ART HAS LOST/N   12
   SHORE
BRITANNIA   SEE BRITTANNIA
THREE PLATES FOR THE STATUE OF BRITANNIA &...FOR COPPER   SUPP LETTER 6A   *PROSE
BRITISH
. . .IN DAY OF THE BRITISH FLAG WHEN HEAVY CANNONS . . . 147 FRENCH REVOLTN 280
THE BRITISH SOLDIERS THRO THE THIRTEEN STATES SENT UP A   201 AMERICA 13   6
   HOWL
THE BRITISH COLONIES BENEATH THE WOFUL PRINCES FADE . . . 206 THIRALATHA   4
BRITISH WOMEN WERE NOT JEALOUS WHEN GREEK & ROMAN WERE   491 MILTON 10   15
   JEALOUS
THE BRITISH INSTITUTION HAS THIS YEAR FOLLOWED ITS EXAMPLE 561B EXHIBITION ADV PROSE
THE BRITISH ANTIQUITIES ARE NOW IN THE ARTIST'S HANDS . . 577D DESC CAT 5   PROSE
WHICH SUPPOSES THAT IN THE REIGN OF THAT BRITISH PRINCE   578B DESC CAT 5   PROSE
BELIEVING WITH MILTON THE ANCIENT BRITISH HISTORY . . . 578C DESC CAT 5   PROSE
[CLLLLLNNN AOOJLMN ALL ALLS HANDS BRITISH ALLS WWWNDJ   601A PUB ADDRESS/N *PROSE
   BLUUUU]
IN THE BRITISH OCEAN CREATED BY LOS'S HAMMER MEASURED OUT   688 JERUSALEM 56   19
LAWFUL SPIRIT [REAL] NO SMUGGLING REAL BRITISH SPIRIT   787D ANNO THORNTON   MARG
   & TRUTH
BRITON   SEE TRUE BRITON
WHAT DO I SEE THE BRITON SAXON ROMAN NORMAN AMALGAMATING   739 JERUSALEM 92   1
BRITONS
THE SUN FLED FROM THE BRITON'S FOREHEAD . . . . 647 JERUSALEM 24   10
BRITONS
THE ANCIENT BRITONS ACCORDING TO CAESAR [THE FRONTISPIECE] 208C SUBJCTS HIST/N TITLE
BOADICEA INSPIRING THE BRITONS AGAINST THE ROMANS . . . 208D SUBJCTS HIST/N TITLE

```
                                                         PAGE     TITLE        LINE
BRITONS    (CONTINUED)
    THE ANCIENT BRITONS THREE ANCIENT BRITONS OVERTHROWING     560A EXHIBITION ADV   PROSE
    NUMBER V THE ANCIENT BRITONS  . . . . . . . . .  . . 577B DESC CAT 5       TITLE
    IN THE LAST BATTLE OF KING ARTHUR ONLY THREE BRITONS   577B DESC CAT 5      TITLE
        ESCAPED
    THOSE OF OUR OWN COUNTRY THE ANCIENT BRITONS  . . . . . 577C DESC CAT 5      PROSE
    WITHOUT VIOLATING COSTUME THE BRITONS SAY HISTORIANS   . 577C DESC CAT 5     PROSE
    ROUND TABLE OF THE WARLIKE NAKED BRITONS OF MERLIN  . . 577D DESC CAT 5      PROSE
    THE DEAD AND THE DYING BRITONS NAKED MINGLED WITH   . . 580C DESC CAT 5      PROSE
    WILL NOT ADMIT OF GRAND COLOURING IN MR B'S(BLAKE'S)  581A DESC CAT 5       PROSE
        BRITONS
BRITONS
    THE BRITONS' DISTRESS & DEPOPULATION . . . . . . . . 208D SUBJCTS HIST/N    TITLE
BRITTANNIA    SEE BRITANNIA
    AND ENGLAND WHO IS BRITTANNIA DIVIDED INTO JERUSALEM & VALA  663 JERUSALEM 36   28
    AND ENGLAND WHO IS BRITTANNIA AWOKE FROM DEATH ON ALBION'S   742 JERUSALEM 94   20
        BOSOM
    ENGLAND WHO IS BRITTANNIA ENTERD ALBION'S BOSOM REJOICING   743 JERUSALEM 95   22
    ENGLAND WHO IS BRITTANNIA ENTERED ALBION'S BOSOM REJOICING  743 JERUSALEM 96    2
BRITTANNIA'S
    SPIRIT WHO LOVST BRITTANNIA'S [SHORE] ISLE . . . . . . 557 ART HAS LOST/N    13
BRITTANNICA
    THEIR HEAD THE AGED WOMAN IS BRITTANNICA THE WIFE OF ALBION 609C V LAST JUDG/N PROSE
BRITTANY
    BY YOUR ADVICE WE LANDED HERE IN BRITTANY . . . . . .  18 EDW THIRD/PS 1     46
BROAD
    WHEN SIN CLAPS HIS BROAD WINGS OVER THE BATTLE  . . . . 33 EDW FOURTH/PS      9
    WITH SCARLET GOWNS & BROAD GOLD LACE WOULD MAKE A YEOMAN   58 THIS CITY/IM     5
        SWEAT
    THE BROAD DISK OF URIZEN UPHEAVD . . . . . . . . . 249 AHANIA 3            21
    ON BROAD PAVILIONS ON PILLARD ROOFS & PORCHES &    286 FOUR ZOAS 2         252
        HIGH TOWERS
    ON A BROAD WAVE IN THE WARM WEST BALMING HER BLEEDING WOUND  299 FOUR ZOAS 4    58
    WHILE THE BROAD OAK WREATHD HIS ROOTS ROUND HER FORCING  335 FOUR ZOAS 7B     99
        HIS DARK WAY
    AND HEARTS LAID OPEN TO THE LIGHT BY THE BROAD GRIZLY SWORD  338 FOUR ZOAS 7B  206
    THEY CRY OUT IN JOYS OF EXISTENCE THE BROAD STEMS  . . 373 FOUR ZOAS 9        605
    TO MILTON'S BRAIN THE ICY FLUID FROM HIS BROAD COLD PALM  500 MILTON 19        9
    ALL BROAD & GENERAL PRINCIPLES BELONG TO BENEVOLENCE  . . 672 JERUSALEM 43    22
    AND HEARTS LAID OPEN TO THE LIGHT BY THE BROAD GRIZLY SWORD  701 JERUSALEM 65  52
    IN THE DEEP DARKNESS BROAD LIGHTNINGS GLARE LONG THUNDERS  741 JERUSALEM 94     4
        ROLL
    LOUD THUNDRING WITH BROAD FLASHES OF FLAMING LIGHTNING  742 JERUSALEM 95       8
        & PILLARS
BROAD-STREET,BROAD STREET
    AT NO...CORNER OF BROAD STREET GOLDEN-SQUARE  . . . . . 560C EXHIBITION ADV   PROSE
    AT NO...CORNER OF BROAD-STREET GOLDEN-SQUARE  . . . . . 562A DESC CAT ADV     TITLE
    ARE SOLD ONLY AT THE CORNER OF BROAD STREET  . . . . . 562C DESC CAT ADV      PROSE
    AT N...CORNER OF BROAD STREET GOLDEN SQUARE  . . . . . 563A DESC CAT        *TITLE
    FOR J BLAKE...BROAD-STREET GOLDEN-SQUARE  . . . . . . 563B DESC CAT           PROSE
    SUBSCRIPTIONS RECEIVED AT NO...CORNER OF BROAD-STREET  . 587A CHAUCER 1       PROSE
    SUBSCRIPTIONS RECEIVED AT NO...CORNER OF BROAD STREET   590D CHAUCER 2        PROSE
        GOLDEN SQUARE
    THE CORNER OF BROAD STREET WEEPS POLAND STREET LANGUISHES  729 JERUSALEM 84   15
BROCKLEY
    TO BROCKLEY HILLS ACROSS THE THAMES HE WITH DOUBLE BOADICEA  736 JERUSALEM 90  24
BROKE    SEE AGE-BROKE,HEART-BROKE
    THE DANCE WAS BROKE THE CIRCLE JUST BEGUN  . . . . . . 43C WOE CRIED MUSE     PROSE
    YES SAID SCOPPRELL BUT ITS BROKE . . . . . . . . . 49B ISLAND MOON 5        PROSE
    HERE THEY GAVE A SHOUT & THE COMPANY BROKE UP  . . . . 58B ISLAND MOON 9      PROSE
    & GLASSES & PICTURES & BROKE THE BOTTLES OF WIND . . . 58D ISLAND MOON 10     PROSE
    AND BROKE THE STUMPS . . . . . . . . . . . . .  61 SAY YOU JOE/IM       15
    REBOUNDED & THE PIERCING SWORD BROKE ON HIS NAKED [LIMBS]  105 TIRIEL 4        72
        FLESH
    & HIMSELF BROKE THE SINGLE ONE ON EARTH THAT EVER BROKE A NET  157D MARRIAGE HH 21  PROSE
    [TILL HE BROKE THE PEARLY DOOR]  . . . . . . . . . 163 I SAW CHAPEL/N        8
    SMILES AS OF THE MORNING [BROKE] STEAL  . . . . . . . 165 CRADLE SONG/N  *   11
    THEN THEOTORMON BROKE HIS SILENCE AND HE ANSWERED  . . . 191 V DAU ALBION 3    21
    AND THUS HER SPEECH BROKE FORTH  . . . . . . . . . 256 BOOK OF LOS 3         6
    TILL COVET BROKE HIS LOCKS & BARS  . . . . . . . . . 256 BOOK OF LOS 3        20
    BROKE FROM MY BONDS I SCORN MY PRISON I SCORN & YET I LOVE  268 FOUR ZOAS 1   150
    SMILE BROKE FROM URIZEN FOR ENITHARMON BRIGHTEND MORE &  273 FOUR ZOAS 1      322
        MORE
    SITTING UPON [HIS] AN IRON CRAG AT LENGTH HIS WORDS BROKE  321 FOUR ZOAS 7    43
        FORTH
    AND THE GATES [BURST] BROKE IN SUNDER & THEIR ORNAMENTS  328 FOUR ZOAS 7  *  325
        DEFACD
    A BARD BROKE FORTH ALL SAT ATTENTIVE TO THE AWFUL MAN  . . 482 MILTON 2       24
    SO LOS SPOKE BUT LIGHTNINGS OF DISCONTENT BROKE ON ALL  511 MILTON 25         63
        SIDES ROUND
    THEN ALBION BROKE SILENCE AND WITH GROANS REPLYD . . . . 643 JERUSALEM 20     42
    DESARTS LOS FIRST BROKE SILENCE & BEGAN TO UTTER HIS LOVE  732 JERUSALEM 87    2
    A SULLEN SMILE BROKE FROM THE SPECTRE IN MOCKERY & SCORN  733 JERUSALEM 88    34
    THUNDERS & LIGHTNINGS BROKE AROUND  . . . . . . . . 749 EV GOSPEL(B)/N       25
    BROKE DOWN FROM EVERY CHAIN & BAR . . . . . . . . . 749 EV GOSPEL(B)/N      41
    AND BROKE HIM UP FROM HIS DELVING ROOT . . . . . . . 817 HAPPINESS/L          42
BROKEN    SEE HEART BROKEN
    IN NAVIES BLACK BROKEN WITH WIND AND TIDE  . . . . . . 32 EDW THIRD/PS 6      12
    LIKE THE SOUND OF A BROKEN PIPE  . . . . . . . . . 35D COUCH DEATH/PS       PROSE
    TWICE WAS IT TOLD THAT IT MIGHT NOT BE BROKEN . . . . . 39C SAMSON/PS        PROSE
    I LAID MY HEAD IN THE HOT NOON AFTER THE BROKEN CLODS  . 295 FOUR ZOAS 3     123
    A CRASH RAN THRO THE IMMENSE THE BOUNDS OF DESTINY WERE  295 FOUR ZOAS 3     135
        BROKEN
```

BROKEN   (CONTINUED)
   THE BOUNDS OF DESTINY WERE BROKEN & HATRED NOW BEGAN   . .   296 FOUR ZOAS 3   177
   WHIRLING UP BROKEN ROCKS ON HIGH INTO THE DISMAL AIR   . .   301 FOUR ZOAS 4   163
   NOR COULD THEY EVER BE CLOSD AGAIN THE GOLDEN HINGES WERE   328 FOUR ZOAS 7   324
     BROKEN
   OF THY POOR BROKEN HEART I SEE THEE LIKE A SHADOW WITHERING   330 FOUR ZOAS 7   413
   THAT RAISES WATER INTO CISTERNS BROKEN & BURND IN FIRE   . .   337 FOUR ZOAS 7B   177
   IS NOT THE WOUND OF THE SWORD SWEET & THE BROKEN   337 FOUR ZOAS 7B   189
     BONE DELIGHTFUL
   LIKE CLOUDS UPON THE WINTER SKY BROKEN WITH WINDS   338 FOUR ZOAS 7B   *   218
     & THUNDERS
   . . . I BEHOLD THE DIVINE VISION THRO THE BROKEN GATES   . .   341 FOUR ZOAS 8   20
   OF [ENITHARMON'S] THY POOR BROKEN HEART ASTONISHD . . .   341 FOUR ZOAS 8   21
   GATES BROKEN DOWN THEY DESCEND THRO THE GATE OF PITY   . .   341 FOUR ZOAS 8   28
   THE BROKEN HEART GATE OF ENITHARMON [WHICH JOINS   341 FOUR ZOAS 8   *   29
     TO URIZEN'S TEMPLE]
   ITS INTRICATE LABYRINTHS NOW THE OBDURATE HEART WAS BROKEN   342 FOUR ZOAS 8   33
   HAS ONLY HURT PAINE'S HEEL WHILE PAINE HAS BROKEN HIS HEAD   396C ANNO WATSON   MARG
   BROKEN COLOURS & BROKEN LINES & BROKEN MASSES   . . . .   464C ANNO REYNOLDS   MARG
   LAID ON (INDISCRIMINATELY) & BROKEN ONE INTO ANOTHER   .   469A ANNO REYNOLDS * MARG
   AND ALL MY ORNAMENTS SHALL BE OF THE GOLD OF BROKEN HEARTS   499 MILTON 18   22
   THE VENETIAN AND FLEMISH PRACTICE IS BROKEN LINES   .   573A DESC CAT 3   PROSE
   BROKEN MASSES AND BROKEN COLOURS MR B'S(BLAKE'S) PRACTICE   573B DESC CAT 3   PROSE
     IS
   CONCERNING MY CHIEF DELIGHT BUT THOU HAST BROKEN SILENCE   630 JERUSALEM 10   41
   ART THOU BROKEN AH ME SABRINA RUNNING BY MY SIDE   . . . .   644 JERUSALEM 21   22
   THEY LABOUR & WHEN THEIR WHEELS ARE BROKEN BY SCORN   692 JERUSALEM 59   40
     & MALICE
   THAT RAISES WATER INTO CISTERNS BROKEN & BURND WITH FIRE   700 JERUSALEM 65   19
   IS NOT THE WOUND OF THE SWORD SWEET & THE BROKEN   700 JERUSALEM 65   31
     BONE DELIGHTFUL
   THEY ARE BROKEN LOUD HOWL THE SPECTRES IN HIS IRON FURNACE   719 JERUSALEM 78   9
   ARE THE BLASPHEMOUS SELPHOODS & MUST BE BROKEN ASUNDER   .   736 JERUSALEM 90   33
   ABEL ARE THESE THE SACRIFICES OF ETERNITY O JEHOVAH   780 GHOST ABEL 1   4
     A BROKEN SPIRIT
BROKER'S
   FIVE SHILLINGS AT A BROKER'S SHOP IT IS ABOUT FIVE FEET   843D LETTER 43   PROSE
     BY FOUR
BROMION
   BROMION RENT HER WITH HIS THUNDERS ON HIS STORMY BED   . .   190 V DAU ALBION 1   16
   BROMION SPOKE BEHOLD THIS HARLOT HERE ON BROMION'S BED   . .   190 V DAU ALBION 1   18
   AND NONE BUT BROMION CAN HEAR MY LAMENTATIONS . . . . .   191 V DAU ALBION 3   1
   THEN BROMION SAID AND SHOOK THE CAVERN WITH HIS LAMENTATION   192 V DAU ALBION 4   12
   THEOTORMON BROMION ANTAMON ANANTON OZOTH OHANA   . . . .   350 FOUR ZOAS 8   358
   OF [RINTRAH] & PALAMABRON OF THEOTORM & BROMION . . . . . .   485 MILTON 6   12
   THEOTORMON & BROMION CONTENDED ON THE SIDE OF SATAN   . . .   488 MILTON 8   30
   THEOTORMON FILLD WITH CARE BROMION LOVING SCIENCE   . .   508 MILTON 24   12
   ARE RINTRAH AND PALAMABRON AND THEOTORMON AND BROMION THEY   710 JERUSALEM 71   51
   ARE RINTRAH & PALAMABRON & THEOTORMON & BROMION   . . . .   711 JERUSALEM 72   11
   RINTRAH & PALAMABRON THEOTORMON & BROMION LOUD LABRING   .   713 JERUSALEM 73   5
   WITH RINTRAH AND PALAMABRON AND THEOTORMON AND BROMION   .   714 JERUSALEM 74   2
BROMION'S
   BROMION SPOKE BEHOLD THIS HARLOT HERE ON BROMION'S BED   . .   190 V DAU ALBION 1   18
   NOW THOU MAIST MARRY BROMION'S HARLOT AND PROTECT THE CHILD   190 V DAU ALBION 2   1
   OF BROMION'S RAGE THAT OOTHOON SHALL PUT FORTH IN NINE   190 V DAU ALBION 2   2
     MOONS' TIME
   BOUND BACK TO BACK IN BROMION'S CAVES TERROR & MEEKNESS   190 V DAU ALBION 2   5
     DWELL
   BEFORE BROMION'S IRON TONGS & GLOWING POKER REDDENING   636 JERUSALEM 16   2
     FIERCE
BROOD   SEE GIANT-BROOD
   THE DEAD BROOD OVER EUROPE . . . .   134 FRENCH REVOLTN   1
   FOR HE OUGHT TO BE RECKOND OF THE GIANT BROOD . . . . . .   824A LETTER 27   PROSE
BROODED
   AND NAMD THE SPACE ULRO & BROODED OVER IT IN CARE & LOVE   267 FOUR ZOAS 1   102
   ENION BROODED OER THE ROCKS . . . .   269 FOUR ZOAS 1   202
   OF LIGHT SILENT THE PRINCE OF LIGHT VIEWD LOS AT LENGTH   273 FOUR ZOAS 1   321
     A BROODED
   THIS URIZEN PERCIEVD & SILENT BROODED IN DARKNING CLOUDS   285 FOUR ZOAS 2   207
   LOS BROODED ON THE DARKNESS NOR SAW URIZEN WITH A GLOBE   314 FOUR ZOAS 6   83
     OF FIRE
   WHERE URIZEN SAT ON HIS ROCK THE SHADOW BROODED [DISMAL]   333 FOUR ZOAS 7B   *   2
   FOR ENION BROODED GROANING LOUD THE ROUGH SEAS VEGETATE   381 FOUR ZOAS AD 5   10
   . . . ENION BROODED GROANING THE GOLDEN ROCKS VEGETATE   381 FOUR ZOAS AD 5 *   14
     THE (?VORTEX)]
   BROODED OVER HIS BODY IN HOREB AGAINST THE RESURRECTION   502 MILTON 20   22
BROODER
   A BROODER OF AN EVIL DAY AND A SUN RISING IN BLOOD   . .   681 JERUSALEM 50   29
   AND SNOWY CLOUD BROODER OF TEMPESTS & DESTRUCTIVE WAR   .   738 JERUSALEM 91   24
BROODING   SEE EVER BROODING
   AND STRIFE BROUGHT FORTH REVENGE HATE BROODING IN   42C THEN SHE BORE   PROSE
     HER DISMAL DEN
   FROWNING AND LOOKING UP FROM BROODING VILLAGES . . . . .   139 FRENCH REVOLTN   117
   BROODING SECRET THE DARK POWER HID . . . .   222 URIZEN 3   7
   BROODING SHUT IN THE DEEP ALL AVOID . . . .   223 URIZEN 3   25
   BUT DEATH DESPAIR & EVERLASTING BROODING MELANCHOLY   . .   265 FOUR ZOAS 1   51
   [WITHIN MY SOUL HAS LOST ITS SPLENDOR & A BROODING FEAR]   267 FOUR ZOAS 1   116
   URIZEN CAST DEEP DARKNESS ROUND HIM SILENT BROODING DEATH   278 FOUR ZOAS 1   515
   APART FROM LOS BUT COVERD HER WITH SOFTEST BROODING CARE   299 FOUR ZOAS 4   57
   IN BROODING CONTEMPLATION STRETCHING OUT FROM NORTH TO   302 FOUR ZOAS 4   174
     SOUTH

```
                                                         PAGE      TITLE           LINE
BROODING   (CONTINUED)
     . . . OR BROODING LIGHTNINGS & PESTILENTIAL PLAGUES . . .   314 FOUR ZOAS 6      93
     I DWELL IN DIM OBLIVION BROODING OVER ME THE ENORMOUS       317 FOUR ZOAS 6     223
       WORLDS
     AND RANGD HIS BOOKS AROUND HIM BROODING ENVIOUS OVER ORC    320 FOUR ZOAS 7      19
     FOR URIZEN FIXD IN ENVY SAT BROODING & COVERD WITH SNOW     321 FOUR ZOAS 7      28
     RENDS THY WHITE HAIR YET THOU DOST FIXD OBDURATE BROODING   322 FOUR ZOAS 7      80
       SIT
     URIZEN ENVIOUS BROODING SAT & SAW THE SECRET TERROR . . .   324 FOUR ZOAS 7     157,
     HIS HUMAN BULK WHILE THE DARK SHADOWY FEMALE [ BROODS ]     343 FOUR ZOAS 8    *  80
       BROODING OVER
     THE DICTATE WATCH OVER THIS WORLD AND WITH YOUR BROODING    504 MILTON 21       55
       WINGS
     CLOUDED WITH DISCONTENT & BROODING IN THEIR MINDS TERRIBLE  505 MILTON 22       28
       THINGS
     BUT DARK DESPAIR & EVERLASTING BROODING MELANCHOLY  . . .   645 JERUSALEM 22    24
     LIFE IN BROODING CARES & ANXIOUS LABOURS THAT PROVE BUT     647 JERUSALEM 24    16
       CHAFF
     IRON AND STEEL DARK AND OPAKE WITH CLOUDS & TEMPESTS        664 JERUSALEM 38     5
       BROODING
     BROODING ON EVIL BUT WHEN LOS OPEND THE FURNACES BEFORE HIM 669 JERUSALEM 42     2
     BROODING IN HOLY HYPOCRITIC LUST DRINKING THE CRIES OF PAIN 672 JERUSALEM 43    17
     THREE BRAINS IN CONTRADICTORY COUNCIL BROODING INCESSANTLY  708 JERUSALEM 70     5
     BROODING ABSTRACT PHILOSOPHY TO DESTROY . . . . . . . .     709 JERUSALEM 70    19
BROODINGS
     HIS BROODINGS RUSH DOWN TO HIS FEET PRODUCING EGGS THAT     324 FOUR ZOAS 7     167
       HATCHING
     THE SILENT BROODINGS OF DEADLY REVENGE SPRINGING FROM THE   685 JERUSALEM 54     9
BROODS
     HIS HUMAN BULK WHILE THE DARK SHADOWY FEMALE [ BROODS ]     343 FOUR ZOAS 8    *  80
       BROODING OVER
BROOK
     LIKE THE BUBBLING WATERS OF THE BROOK IN THE DEAD OF NIGHT  36B COUCH DEATH/PS PROSE
     THE BROOK STRETCHES ITS ARMS ALONG THE VELVET MEADOW  .     37B CONTEMPLATN/PS PROSE
     MISERY BUILDS OVER OUR COTTAGE ROOFS AND DISCONTENT RUNS    37B CONTEMPLATN/PS PROSE
       LIKE A BROOK
     REPLY NOT LEST I BIND THEE WITH THE GREEN FLAGS OF THE      104 TIRIEL 4        24
       BROOK
     A LITTLE REST I CRAVE A LITTLE WATER FROM A BROOK   . . .   104 TIRIEL 4        34
     DRINK OF THIS RUNNING BROOK & I WILL BEAR THEE ON           104 TIRIEL 4        39
       MY SHOULDERS
     BUT A PEBBLE OF THE BROOK   . . . . . . . . . .             162 CLOD PEBBLE/N     7
     BUT A PEBBLE OF THE BROOK   . . . . . . . . . .             211 CLOD PEBBLE/SE    7
     GROANS RAN ALONG TYBURN'S BROOK AND ALONG THE RIVER OF      281 FOUR ZOAS 2      39
       OXFORD
     AMONG THE DRUID TEMPLES ALBION GROAND ON TYBURN'S BROOK     281 FOUR ZOAS 2      40
     THIS IS NO WARBLING BROOK NOR SHADOW OF A MYRTLE TREE  .    338 FOUR ZOAS 7B    204
     ON TYBURN'S BROOK LOUD GROANS THAMES BENEATH THE IRON FORGE 485 MILTON 6        11
     TERMINATING IN HYDE PARK ON TYBURN'S AWFUL BROOK  . . .     491 MILTON 11        5
     THUS THEY WEEP UPON THE FATAL BROOK OF ALBION'S RIVER  .    494 MILTON 13       35
     NETS & WEBS UNFOLDED BY SPIRITS IN THE AIR & IN THE BROOK   619C ILLUS MILTON  PROSE
     ROSE UP AGAINST ME THUNDERING FROM THE BROOK OF ALBION'S    627 JERUSALEM 8      1
       RIVER
     THEY GROAND ALOUD ON TYBURN'S BROOK  . . . . . . . .        650 FIELDS FROM/J   34
     HE SAT BY TYBURN'S BROOK AND UNDERNEATH HIS HEEL SHOT UP    652 JERUSALEM 28    14
     BENEATH ITS WINDING LABYRINTHS TILL A STONE OF THE BROOK    659 JERUSALEM 33    10
     AND THE SUN SET IN TYBURN'S BROOK WHERE VICTIMS HOWL & CRY  696 JERUSALEM 62    34
     THIS IS NO WARBLING BROOK NOR SHADOW OF A MIRTLE TREE  .    701 JERUSALEM 65    50
     TO ISLINGTON & PADDINGTON & THE BROOK OF ALBION'S RIVER     729 JERUSALEM 84     2
     AND ON TYBURN'S BROOK AMONG THE HOWLING VICTIMS IN          737 JERUSALEM 90    48
       LOVELINESS
BROOKS
     AS THE DEER WOUNDED BY THE BROOKS OF WATER . . . . . .      36B COUCH DEATH/PS PROSE
     THOU GENTLE MAID OF SILENT VALLEYS AND OF MODEST BROOKS     127 BOOK OF THEL 1  22
     AND BROOKS BETWEEN TO INTERSECT THE MEADOWS IN THEIR COURSE 493 MILTON 12       19
     AND MET HIM ON THE SHORES OF ARNON & BY THE STREAMS OF      500 MILTON 19        5
       THE BROOKS
     UPON THE SUNNY BROOKS & MEADOWS EVERY ONE THE DANCE . . .   512 MILTON 26        3
     URIZEN FAINTS IN TERROR STRIVING AMONG THE BROOKS OF ARNON  531 MILTON 39       53
     I SEE THEE STRIVE UPON THE BROOKS OF ARNON THERE A DREAD    532 MILTON 40        4
     AMONG MY LAMBS & BROOKS OF WATER AMONG MY WARBLING BIRDS    642 JERUSALEM 20     8
BROTH
     AND THE DEVIL ENTERD INTO THE YOUNG MAN'S BROTH  . . . .    434 LONG JOHN BRWN   8
BROTHELS
     PRISONS ARE BUILT WITH STONES OF LAW BROTHELS WITH BRICKS   151B MARRIAGE HH 8 PROSE
       OF RELIGION
     LET THE BROTHELS OF PARIS BE OPENED  . . . . . . . .        185 LET BROTHELS/N   1
BROTHER
     BROTHER IN BROTHER'S BLOOD MUST BATHE RIVERS OF DEATH   .   34A KING JOHN/PS   PROSE
     AND IN MY PLAY TILL HE BECAME TO ME AS MY BROTHER   . . .   37C CONTEMPLATN/PS PROSE
     FOR OUR GOD HIMSELF SAYS "YOU ARE MY BROTHER"   . . . .     87A ANNO LAVATER    MARG
     O BROTHER IJIM IF IT IS THY VOICE THAT SPEAKS TO ME . . .   104 TIRIEL 4        11
     SMITE NOT THY BROTHER TIRIEL THO WEARY OF HIS LIFE  . . .   104 TIRIEL 4        12
     O BROTHER IJIM THOU BEHOLDEST WRETCHED TIRIEL . . . . .     104 TIRIEL 4        21
     KISS ME MY BROTHER & THEN LEAVE ME TO WANDER DESOLATE  . .  104 TIRIEL 4        22
     TWAS THOU THAT CHAIND THY BROTHER ZAZEL WHERE ARE NOW THINE 108 TIRIEL 7         9
       EYES
     AND THOU WILT BE AS FOOLISH AS THY FOOLISH BROTHER ZAZEL .  109 TIRIEL 7        13
     . . . TO ZION AWAKE O BROTHER MOUNTAIN . . . . . . . .      274 FOUR ZOAS 1     386
     SAYING SHILOH IS IN RUINS OUR BROTHER IS SICK [SHILOH ]     277 FOUR ZOAS 1    * 477
       ALBION HE
     THE ETERNAL MAN WEPT IN THE HOLY TENT OUR BROTHER          277 FOUR ZOAS 1     484
       IN ETERNITY
```

		PAGE	TITLE	LINE

BROTHER   (CONTINUED)

THY BROTHER LUVAH HATH SMITTEN ME BUT PITY THOU HIS YOUTH — 280 FOUR ZOAS 2 — 7
THE BROTHER & THE BROTHER BATHE IN BLOOD UPON THE SEVERN — 281 FOUR ZOAS 2 — 49
LORD SAVIOUR IF THOU HADST BEEN HERE OUR BROTHER HAD NOT DIED — 304 FOUR ZOAS 4 — 253
SAYING IF YE WILL BELIEVE YOUR BROTHER SHALL RISE AGAIN — 304 FOUR ZOAS 4 — 270
OF URTHONA LOS EMBRACD THE SPECTRE FIRST AS A BROTHER . . 328 FOUR ZOAS 7 — 339
AS THE ELDEST BROTHER IS THE [SECOND] FATHER'S IMAGE SO ORC BECAME — 332 FOUR ZOAS 7 * 479
THESE WORDS IF YE WILL BELIEVE YOUR BROTHER SHALL RISE AGAIN — 340 FOUR ZOAS 7B — 293
BROTHER OF JESUS WHAT HAVE I DONE INTREAT THY LORD FOR ME — 364 FOUR ZOAS 9 — 270
CALLING HIM BROTHER IMAGE OF THE ETERNAL FATHER THEY SAT DOWN — 374 FOUR ZOAS 9 — 644
MY BROTHER STARVD BETWEEN TWO WALLS . . . . 419 I SAW A MONK/N — 32
THY BROTHER HAS ARMED HIMSELF IN STEEL . . . . 419 I SAW A MONK/N — 38
MY BROTHER STARVD BETWEEN TWO WALLS . . . . 430 GREY MONK — 17
THE BROTHER HAS ARMD HIMSELF IN STEEL . . . . 430 GREY MONK — 23
SEEMING A BROTHER BEING A TYRANT EVEN THINKING HIMSELF A BROTHER — 487 MILTON 7 — 24
OVER OLOLON AND AS ONE MAN WHO WEEPS OVER HIS BROTHER . 504 MILTON 21 — 41
AND BETWEEN HIM AND HIS BROTHER THE PLOWMAN . . . . . 570C DESC CAT 3 — PROSE
HIS BROTHER FALLING WITH THE HEAD DOWNWARD . . . . . 606B V LAST JUDG/N — PROSE
I AM NOT A GOD AFAR OFF I AM A BROTHER AND FRIEND . . 622 JERUSALEM 4 — 18
THOU ART MY FATHER & MY BROTHER WHY HAST THOU HIDDEN ME — 646 JERUSALEM 23 — 11
AND EVERY RIVER OUR BROTHER ALBION IS SICK TO DEATH . . . 667 JERUSALEM 40 — 12
FOR THE SOLDIER WHO FIGHTS FOR TRUTH CALLS HIS ENEMY HIS BROTHER — 672 JERUSALEM 43 — 41
IF THOU HADST BEEN HERE OUR BROTHER ALBION HAD NOT DIED — 681 JERUSALEM 50 — 11
THY BROTHER WHO SLEEPETH IN ALBION FEAR NOT TREMBLING SHADE — 694 JERUSALEM 60 — 69
MY BROTHER & MY FATHER ARE NO MORE GOD HATH FORSAKEN ME — 719 JERUSALEM 78 — 31
BECOME A FOUNTAIN OF VEINY PIPES O ALBION MY BROTHER . 727 JERUSALEM 82 — 84
ABSORB ME NOT IN SUCH DIRE GRIEF O ALBION MY BROTHER . 727 JERUSALEM 83 — 6
O WHEN SHALL THE SAXON RETURN WITH THE ENGLISH HIS REDEEMED BROTHER — 727 JERUSALEM 83 — 14
THIRTEEN YEARS AGO I LOST A BROTHER & WITH HIS SPIRIT I — 797A LETTER 9 — PROSE
AND MY BROTHER IS THERE & MY FRIEND & THINE . . . . . 800 MRS FLAXMAN/L — 11
MY BROTHER TELLS ME THAT HE FEARS YOU ARE OFFENDED WITH ME I — 814A LETTER 23 — PROSE
AND MY BROTHER ROBERT JUST BEHIND . . . . 817 HAPPINESS/L — 14
AND MY BROTHER JOHN THE EVIL ONE . . . . 817 HAPPINESS/L — 15
TO MY BROTHER WHICH YOU WILL BE SO KIND AS TO SEND . . 819A LETTER 24 — PROSE
DEAR BROTHER YOUR LETTER MENTIONING MR BUTTS'S ACCOUNT OF MY AGUE — 819B LETTER 25 — *PROSE
MY BROTHER I INTENDED TO HAVE SENT THE PICTURE OF . . 822B LETTER 26 — PROSE
YOU HAVE FAITH IN THE ENDEAVOURS OF ME YOUR WEAK BROTHER — 822B LETTER 26 — PROSE
TO MY BROTHER & REMAIN SINCERELY & AFFECTIONATELY YOURS — 829B LETTER 28 — PROSE
HIM OF MR ROSE MY BROTHER SAYS HE BELIEVES SR ALLAN IS . 834D LETTER 34 — PROSE
ACKNOWLEDGMENTS TO YOU AS DO MY BROTHER & SISTER . . . 849C LETTER 45 — PROSE
HER BROTHER A GIANT IN BODY MILD & POLITE IN SOUL AS I HAVE — 850C LETTER 49 — PROSE
SERVANT WHO DOMINEERED OVER ME HE IS EVEN AS A BROTHER . 852C LETTER 50 — PROSE
HAYLEY'S BALLADS PER BROTHER DITTO MR BIRCH . . . . . SUPP LETTER 56A — *PROSE

BROTHERHOOD

CANNOT EXIST BUT FROM THE UNIVERSAL BROTHERHOOD OF EDEN — 264 FOUR ZOAS 1 — 10
RENT FROM ETERNAL BROTHERHOOD WE DIE & ARE NO MORE . . 293 FOUR ZOAS 3 — 76
AS ONCE IN THOSE ETERNAL FIELDS IN BROTHERHOOD & LOVE . 345 FOUR ZOAS 8 — 159
FORSAKING BROTHERHOOD & UNIVERSAL LOVE IN SELFISH CLAY . 374 FOUR ZOAS 9 — 629
THAT MAN SUBSISTS BY BROTHERHOOD & UNIVERSAL LOVE . . 374 FOUR ZOAS 9 — 638
KEEP NOR IN PITY FALSE NOR IN OFFICIOUS BROTHERHOOD WHERE — 487 MILTON 7 — 44
WE WERE PLACD HERE BY THE UNIVERSAL BROTHERHOOD & MERCY — 507 MILTON 23 — 50
BECAUSE WE WERE COMBIND IN FREEDOM & HOLY BROTHERHOOD . 521 MILTON 32 — 15
TILL BROTHERHOOD IS CHANGD INTO A CURSE & A FLATTERY . 525 MILTON 35 — 4
WITH TRANSGRESSORS MEETING IN BROTHERHOOD AROUND THE TABLE — 640 JERUSALEM 18 — 15
RENDING THE FIBRES OF BROTHERHOOD & IN FEMININE ALLEGORIES — 656 JERUSALEM 30 * 18
FOR THE DIVINE APPEARANCE IS BROTHERHOOD BUT I AM LOVE . 660 JERUSALEM 33 — 52
ELEVATE INTO THE REGION OF BROTHERHOOD WITH MY RED FIRES — 660 JERUSALEM 34 — 1
ARE NOT RELIGION & POLITICS THE SAME THING BROTHERHOOD IS RELIGION — 689 JERUSALEM 57 — 10
WHEN SOULS MINGLE & JOIN THRO ALL THE FIBRES OF BROTHERHOOD — 733 JERUSALEM 88 — 14
THIS IS FRIENDSHIP & BROTHERHOOD WITHOUT IT MAN IS NOT . . 743 JERUSALEM 96 — 16
OFFERING OF SELF FOR ANOTHER IS THIS FRIENDSHIP & BROTHERHOOD — 743 JERUSALEM 96 — 21
IN THE DIVINE IMAGE NOR CAN MAN EXIST BUT BY BROTHERHOOD — 743 JERUSALEM 96 — 28
. . . DEATH O HOLY IS THIS BROTHERHOOD . . . . 781 GHOST ABEL 2 — 24
. . . FIXT IN THE FIRMAMENT BY PEACE BROTHERHOOD AND LOVE — 781 GHOST ABEL 2 — 26

BROTHERLY

MR HAYLEY RECIEVD US WITH HIS USUAL BROTHERLY AFFECTION — 802A LETTER 14 — PROSE
MR HAYLEY RECIEVD ME WITH HIS USUAL BROTHERLY AFFECTION — 803B LETTER 15 — PROSE

BROTHER'S

BROTHER IN BROTHER'S BLOOD MUST BATHE RIVERS OF DEATH . 34A KING JOHN/PS — PROSE
THE BLIND MAN HEARD HIS BROTHER'S VOICE & KNEELD DOWN ON HIS KNEE — 104 TIRIEL 4 — 10
MAN LIVETH NOT BY SELF ALONE BUT IN HIS BROTHER'S FACE . 374 FOUR ZOAS 9 — 641
DOST THOU O PRIEST WISH THY BROTHER'S DEATH . . . . 384D ANNO WATSON — MARG
EMBRACD SOFT WITH A BROTHER'S TEARS PALAMABRON WHO ALSO WEPT — 486 MILTON 7 — 17
THE PARENT'S FEAR THE BROTHER'S JEALOUSY THE SISTER'S CURSE — 636 JERUSALEM 16 — 7
& FEELING HEARTILY YOUR GRIEF WITH A BROTHER'S SYMPATHY — 797B LETTER 9 — PROSE

BROTHERS

MANY SISTERS AND BROTHERS . . . . 116 ECCHOING GR/SI — 26
[NOR] OR ANY OF MY BROTHERS MORE . . . . 177 LIT BOY LST/N — 6
BROTHERS & SONS OF AMERICA TILL OUR FACES PALE AND YELLOW — 197 AMERICA 3 — 9

```
                                                        PAGE      TITLE           LINE
BROTHERS   (CONTINUED)
  BROTHERS & SONS OF AMERICA TILL OUR FACES PALE AND YELLOW    204 AMERICA CANC A    9
  OR ANY OF MY BROTHERS MORE . . . . . . . . .               218 LIT BOY LST/SE    6
  . . . OF [LIFE & LOVE] SACRIFICE OF BROTHERS & SONS        331 FOUR ZOAS 7      443
    & DAUGHTERS
  [NOW] CLOTHE YOURSELVES IN GOLDEN ARMS BROTHERS OF WAR . .  337 FOUR ZOAS 7B    163
  BUT YOU O OUR FATHERS & BROTHERS REMAIN IN ETERNITY . . .   519 MILTON 30        28
  IN LOVES AND TEARS OF BROTHERS SISTERS SONS FATHERS AND     664 JERUSALEM 38     12
    FRIENDS
  ALL YOU MY FRIENDS & BROTHERS ALL YOU MY BELOVED            673 JERUSALEM 43     74
    COMPANIONS
  BROTHERS OF ETERNITY THIS MAN WHOSE GREAT EXAMPLE    . . .  675 JERUSALEM 45      4
  WALKETH AMONG US CALLING US HIS BROTHERS & HIS FRIENDS . .  686 JERUSALEM 55   *  10
  . . . FROM THE MINGLED AFFECTIONS OF THE BROTHERS    . . .  710 JERUSALEM 71     24
  MY BROTHERS & FATHER MARCH BEFORE . . . . . . . .          818 HAPPINESS/L      81
BROUGHT
  WHICH IN HER ARMS SHE BROUGHT AND NOW TENFOLD . . . . .      5 FAIR ELENOR/PS    55
  THAT BROUGHT OVER OUR KING TO FRANCE TO FIGHT FOR HIS RIGHT 28D EDW THIRD/PS 4 PROSE
  BY A FALSE WIFE BROUGHT TO THE GATES OF DEATH . . . . .    37C SAMSON/PS       PROSE
  FOR CARE WAS I BROUGHT FORTH AND LABOUR IS MY LOT   . . .  39B SAMSON/PS       PROSE
  FROM WHOM CAME IGNORANCE WHO BROUGHT FORTH WONDER   . . .  40D THEN SHE BORE   PROSE
  TWAS CONSCIENCE WHO BROUGHT MELANCHOLY DOWN   . . . . .    42B THEN SHE BORE   PROSE
  SHE BROUGHT FORTH RAGE [THEN] AND SHAME BORE HONOUR &  . . 42C THEN SHE BORE  *PROSE
  WAS BORN ENVY IN DIREFUL PAINS HIM BORE THEN ENVY BROUGHT  42C THEN SHE BORE   PROSE
    FORTH CARE
  CARE BROUGHT FORTH COVET EYELESS & PRONE TO TH EARTH    .. 42C THEN SHE BORE   PROSE
  AND STRIFE BROUGHT FORTH REVENGE HATE BROODING IN         42C THEN SHE BORE   PROSE
    HER DISMAL DEN
  GREW PREGNANT & [BROUGHT FORTH] BORE SCORN & SLANDER   .. 42D THEN SHE BORE   PROSE
  POLICY BROUGHT FORTH GUILE & FRAUD   . . . . . . .        42D THEN SHE BORE   PROSE
  HE SLEPT VERY LITTLE WHICH HE BROUGHT INTO A CONSUMSION   49C ISLAND MOON 5   PROSE
  WOULD MAKE A CLEVER FELLOW IF HE WAS PROPERLY BROUGHT UP  50A ISLAND MOON 6   PROSE
  SHE SOON GREW PREGNANT & BROUGHT FORTH . . . . . . .       51 WHEN CORRUP/IM    21
  THIS CITY & THIS COUNTRY HAS BROUGHT FORTH MANY MAYORS . .  58 THIS CITY/IM      1
  FOR HOW CAN SCIENCE BE BROUGHT TO DEMONSTRATE INTELLECT   93B ANNO SWED LOVE   MARG
  MNETHA NOW AGED WAITED ON THEM & BROUGHT THEM FOOD        100 TIRIEL 2          6
    & CLOTHING
  HEUXOS COME FORTH I HERE HAVE BROUGHT THE FIEND THAT      104 TIRIEL 4         43
    TROUBLES IJIM
  [O NOBLE IJIM THOU HAST BROUGHT OUR FATHER TO [THE GATES] 105 TIRIEL 4         75
    OUR EYES]
  AND TO HIS MOTHER BROUGHT   . . . . . . . . . . .         121 LIT BOY FND/SI    6
  RED CLAY BROUGHT FORTH . . . . . . . . . . . . .          148 MARRIAGE HH 2    13
  & I IN MY HAND BROUGHT THE SKELETON OF A BODY . . . . .  157B MARRIAGE HH 17  PROSE
  OR DOES THE FLY REJOICE BECAUSE THE HARVEST IS BROUGHT IN 193 V DAU ALBION 5   38
  HIS FOOD SHE BROUGHT IN IRON BASKETS HIS DRINK IN CUPS    195 AMERICA PREL 1    3
    OF IRON
  HIS HELM WAS BROUGHT BY LONDON'S GUARDIAN & HIS THIRSTY   205 AMERICA CANC C    4
    SPEAR
  BROUGHT FORTH AN INFANT FORM . . . . . . . . . .          232 URIZEN 19        35
  BROUGHT TOGETHER BY NARROWING PERCEPTIONS  . . . . . .    236 URIZEN 25        34
  THEIR PARENTS BROUGHT THEM FORTH & AGED IGNORANCE PREACHES 242 EUROPE 12        7
    CANTING
  BROUGHT HIS BOOKS ALL BUT THE BOOK   . . . . . . .        252 AHANIA 3         73
  TILL WITH FIERCE PAIN SHE BROUGHT FORTH ON THE ROCKS HER  269 FOUR ZOAS 1     191
    SORROW & WOE
  I BROUGHT HER THRO THE WILDERNESS A DRY & THIRSTY LAND . . 282 FOUR ZOAS 2     87
  BROUGHT HIM IN VARIOUS FORMS BEFORE HER STILL SHE KNEW    286 FOUR ZOAS 2     233
    HIM NOT
  . . . IT HAS BROUGHT FORTH A POISON TREE   . . . . .      290 FOUR ZOAS 2     388
  STOOD SO THICK HE WITH DIFFICULTY & GREAT PAIN BROUGHT  .. 321 FOUR ZOAS 7      38
  [VALAN] VALA WAS PREGNANT & BROUGHT FORTH URIZEN PRINCE   326 FOUR ZOAS 7   *  244
    OF LIGHT
  BROUGHT FORTH A WONDER HORRIBLE WHILE ENITHARMON SHRIEKD  328 FOUR ZOAS 7     317
  BROUGHT FORTH THIS WONDER HORRIBLE A CLOUD SHE GREW & GREW 328 FOUR ZOAS 7     327
  AND WHENCE THEY NEVER CAN BE BROUGHT IN ALL ETERNITY   .. 339 FOUR ZOAS 7B    245
  TO BUILD HER BOWERS FOR THE ELEMENTS BROUGHT FORTH        340 FOUR ZOAS 7B    277
    ABUNDANTLY
  THEN URIZEN COMMANDED & THEY BROUGHT THE SEED OF MEN   .. 365 FOUR ZOAS 9     316
  HOW ARE YE THUS RENEWD & BROUGHT INTO THE GARDENS OF VALA 370 FOUR ZOAS 9     511
  BROUGHT UP THE LOADED WAGGONS WITH SHOUTINGS RAMPING TYGERS 376 FOUR ZOAS 9    717
    PLAY
  FOR THARMAS BROUGHT HIS FLOCKS UPON THE HILLS & IN THE    379 FOUR ZOAS 9     838
    VALES
  ACCIDENT BROUGHT ON BY A MAN'S OWN CARELESSNESS  . . . .  388B ANNO WATSON    MARG
  BROUGHT AGAINST US THAT WERE NOT THERE  . . . . . . .    438B BLAKES MEMORAN PROSE
  AT LAST ENITHARMON BROUGHT FORTH SATAN REFUSING FORM IN   483 MILTON 3        41
    VAIN
  I HAVE BROUGHT THEM FROM THE UPPERMOST INNERMOST RECESSES 490 MILTON 9        27
  SHE SOOTHD HER WITH SOFT WORDS & BROUGHT HER             494 MILTON 13        38
    TO PALAMABRON'S BED
  BROUGHT OIL PAINTING INTO GENERAL OPINION AND PRACTICE  . 565B DESC CAT 2     PROSE
  IT WAS WITH DIFFICULTY BROUGHT BACK AGAIN TO A CERTAIN   582B DESC CAT 9      PROSE
    EFFECT
  OF ALL THE RUBBISH OF THE CONTINENT BROUGHT HERE BY .  .. 601C PUB ADDRESS/N  PROSE
  USURPED THE THRONE OF HIS FATHER SATURN & BROUGHT ON  .. 605C V LAST JUDG/N   PROSE
  THESE PERSONIFICATIONS ARE ALL BROUGHT TOGETHER IN THE   618A ILLUS MILTON   PROSE
    FIRST DESIGN
  THESE PERSONIFICATIONS ARE ALL BROUGHT TOGETHER  . . . . 619A ILLUS MILTON   PROSE
  I BROUGHT LOVE INTO LIGHT OF DAY TO PRIDE IN CHASTE BEAUTY 645 JERUSALEM 22    17
  I BROUGHT LOVE INTO LIGHT & FANCIED INNOCENCE IS NO MORE  645 JERUSALEM 22    18
  HAD BROUGHT HUMANITY INTO A FEMININE TABERNACLE  . . . . 652B JERUSALEM 27   PROSE
```

                                277

BROUGHT   (CONTINUED)
    LUVAH SLEW THARMAS THE ANGEL OF THE TONGUE & ALBION BROUGHT   697 JERUSALEM 63   5
        HIM
    LOS SMILD WITH JOY THINKING ON ENITHARMON & HE BROUGHT . .   730 JERUSALEM 85   3
    THEY BROUGHT THE TREMBLING WOMAN THERE . . . .   753 EV GOSPEL(E)/N   8
    BROUGHT TO LIGHT BY JESUS EVEN THE COVENANT OF JEHOVAH . . 757D EV GOSPEL   PROSE
    WHAT WAS [IT] IT THAT HE BROUGHT TO LIGHT . . . . .   758 EV GOSPEL (2)   *   3
    BROUGHT INTO ENGLAND OR CAN BE PURCHASD ABROAD AS ITS . . 797D LETTER 10   *PROSE
    MAY YET SHINE & THEN THEY WILL BE BROUGHT INTO OPEN AIR   812B LETTER 22   PROSE
    THIS FROM JOHNSON & FUSELI BROUGHT ME DOWN HERE . . . . 812C LETTER 22   PROSE
    CANVAS WHICH I BROUGHT DOWN WITH ME FOR THERE WERE THREE   816C LETTER 24   PROSE
    I THINK THE GRAND REASON OF MY BEING BROUGHT DOWN HERE . . 823B LETTER 26   PROSE
    FIRMNESS I HAVE BROUGHT DOWN HIS AFFECTED LOFTINESS . . 825C LETTER 27   PROSE
    MR BRAITHWAITE CALLD ON ME & BROUGHT TWO PRINTS WHICH HE   838D LETTER 37   PROSE
    THREE YEARS THAT HAS BROUGHT ME INTO MY PRESENT STATE &   862D LETTER 60   PROSE
    I CALLD THIS MORNING FOR A WALK & BROUGHT MY PLATES WITH ME 876C LETTER 84   PROSE
    BROUGHT ON A RELAPSE WHICH IS LASTED TILL NOW I FIND I AM   880A LETTER 90   PROSE
BROW
    AND BLUSHING ROSES FOR MY BROW . . . .   6 HOW SWEET/PS   6
    WHETHER ON IDA'S SHADY BROW . . . .   10 TO MUSES/PS   1
    GORDRED APPEARS HIS FROWNING BROW . . . .   12 GWIN KING/PS   63
    DOWN FROM THE BROW UNTO THE BREAST . . . .   14 GWIN KING/PS   107
    AND THOU MERCURIUS THAT WITH WINGED BROW . . . . .   15 IMIT SPEN/PS   19
    THAT DEATH CAN NEVER RAVISH FROM THY BROW . . . . .   18 EDW THIRD/PS 1   22
    THREATENING AS THE RED BROW OF STORMS AS FIRE . . . .   31 EDW THIRD/PS 6   5
    BEWARE O PROUD THOU SHALT BE HUMBLED THY CRUEL BROW . .   34B KING JOHN/PS   PROSE
    WHILE ON HIS MAJESTIC BROW THE VOICE OF ANGELS IS HEARD   36D COUCH DEATH/PS   PROSE
    CALL THINE ALLURING ARTS AND HONEST-SEEMING BROW . . . .   38A SAMSON/PS   PROSE
    HE SEEMED A MOUNTAIN HIS BROW AMONG THE CLOUDS . . . .   38C SAMSON/PS   PROSE
    HIS SPACIOUS BROW SHOT TERRORS THROUGH THE EVENING SHADE   39D SAMSON/PS   PROSE
    CARE SITTETH IN THE WRINKLED BROW . . . .   42C THEN SHE BORE   PROSE
    GRIEF PERCHT UPON MY BROW AND THOUGHT EMBRACD HER . . .   43B WOE CRIED MUSE   PROSE
    WITH FROWNING BROW THOU SITTEST MISTRESS OF THESE MIGHTY   312 FOUR ZOAS 6   15
        WATERS
    SCATTER THE BLOOD FROM THY GOLDEN BROW . . . .   338 FOUR ZOAS 7B   194
    LOS WIPD THE SWEAT FROM HIS RED BROW & THUS BEGAN . . .   350 FOUR ZOAS 8   349
    THE CLOUDS FALL OFF FROM MY WET BROW THE DUST FROM MY   373 FOUR ZOAS 9   597
        COLD LIMBS
    MALE & HER BROW RADIANT AS DAY DARTED A LOVELY SCORN . .   381 FOUR ZOAS AD 1   19
    THEN PLANTING IT UPON A MOUNTAIN'S BROW . . . . . .   414 TO MRS FLAXMAN   9
    SCATTER FROM THY GOLDEN BROW . . . .   700 JERUSALEM 65   40
    "WHOSE CHANGELESS BROW NEER SMILES NOR FROWNS" DONNE . . SUPP LEGEND/N85   *
BROWBEAT
    CONSEQUENTLY OUR COUNTRYMEN ARE EASILY BROW-BEAT ON THE   864C LETTER 61   PROSE
BROWD   SEE BLACK-BROWD,GREY-BROWD,GREY BROWD,HEAVY BROWD
BROWN   SEE NUT-BROWN
    WHERE WHITE AND BROWN IS OUR LOT . . . .   8 LOVE JOCUND/PS   11
    WITH FACE AS BROWN AS ANY NUT WITH DRINKING OF STRONG ALE   58 THIS CITY/IM   3
    HOW CAME THINE HAIR TO LEAVE THY FOREHEAD HOW CAME THY   102 TIRIEL 3   3
        FACE SO BROWN
    AND HAYCOCKS LOOKED BROWN . . . .   164 HEARD ANGEL/N   8
    LONG JOHN BROWN & LITTLE MARY BELL . . . .   434A LONG JOHN BRWN   TITLE
    [YOUNG] LONG JOHN BROWN HAD THE DEVIL IN HIS GUT . .   434 LONG JOHN BRWN   2
    [YOUNG] LONG JOHN BROWN LOVD [PRETTY] LITTLE MARY BELL .   434 LONG JOHN BRWN   3
    AND HE LAUGHD AT THE DEVIL TILL POOR JOHN BROWN DIED .   434 LONG JOHN BRWN   16
    HIS SHADOWS ARE OF A FILTHY BROWN SOMEWHAT OF THE COLOUR   469A ANNO REYNOLDS   MARG
        OF EXCREMENT
    NEVER AS IN RUBENS & THE COLOURISTS HOT & YELLOWY BROWN   478D ANNO REYNOLDS   MARG
    VERY LITTLE TIME AND OF THE AIR IT GROWS YELLOW AND AT   561A EXHIBITION ADV   PROSE
        LENGTH BROWN
    AND CHANGING YELLOW AND AT LENGTH BROWN DESTROYS EVERY . . 566B DESC CAT 2   PROSE
    IT TURNS EVERY PERMANENT WHITE TO A YELLOW AND BROWN PUTTY   566B DESC CAT 2   PROSE
    HOW SPOTS OF BROWN AND YELLOW SMEARED ABOUT AT RANDOM . . 575A DESC CAT 3   PROSE
    WITH BROWN SHADOWS THEY PUT THE ORIGINAL ARTIST IN . . . 582C DESC CAT 9   PROSE
    WOOLETT'S BEST WORKS WERE ETCHD BY JACK BROWN . . . . 594A PUB ADDRESS/N   PROSE
    ADMIRES ALL HIS COLOURS BROWN & WARM . . . . . .   597 PUBLC VOICE/PA   3
BROWNE
    BY JACK BROWNE & IN WOOLETT'S WORKS THE ETCHING IS ALL . . 594A PUB ADDRESS/N   PROSE
BROWNNESS
    HE LOADS IT WITH HELLISH BROWNNESS . . . . 583A DESC CAT 9   PROSE
BROWS
    BLOSSOMS HANG ROUND THE BROWS OF MORNING AND . . . . .   2 TO AUTUMN/PS   9
    MY LORD WAS LIKE A FLOWER UPON THE BROWS . . . . .   5 FAIR ELENOR/PS   41
    ROUND MY YOUNG BROWS THE LAUREL WREATHES A SHADE . . .   9 FRESH FROM/PS   3
    THE MERCHANT BINDS HIS BROWS IN STEEL . . . . . .   12 GWIN KING/PS   47
    AND WING THEIR BROWS WITH HOPE AND EXPECTATION . . . .   25 EDW THIRD/PS 3   182
    HONOUR TWINES AROUND HER BROWS . . . .   63 SHEPHERD FIRST   7
    HER MADDING BROWS HER SHRIEKS APPALLD THE SOUL OF TIRIEL   108 TIRIEL 6   * 45
    WEAVE THY BROWS AN INFANT CROWN . . . .   120 CRADLE SONG/SI   6
    . . . HIS BROWS FOLDED HEAVY HIS FOREHEAD WAS IN AFFLICTION 137 FRENCH REVOLTN   79
    SAT ROUND HIS BROWS FADED IN FAINT DEATH . . . . . .   147 FRENCH REVOLTN   296
    FROM STONY BROWS . . . .   147 FRENCH REVOLTN   300
    GRIEF ROSE UPON HIS RUDDY BROWS A TIGHTENING GIRDLE GREW   307 FOUR ZOAS 5   83
    DARKEND HIS BROWS WITH HIS COLD HELMET & HIS GLOOMY SPEAR   313 FOUR ZOAS 6   52
    ORC ANSWERD CURSE THY HOARY BROWS WHAT DOST THOU IN THIS   322 FOUR ZOAS 7   69
        DEEP
    AND HE ALSO DARKEND HIS BROWS FREEZING DARK ROCKS BETWEEN   500 MILTON 19   1
    ALL POWERFUL AND HIS LOCKS FLOURISH LIKE THE BROWS   509 MILTON 24   70
        OF MORNING
    HORNS OF THE WIDE BOW LOUD SOUNDING WINDS SPORT ON THE   742 JERUSALEM 95   15
        MOUNTAIN BROWS
    OF THE WIDE BOW LOUD SOUNDING WINDS SPORT ON THE MOUNTAINS   745 JERUSALEM 98   5
        BROWS

```
                                                           PAGE      TITLE       LINE
BROWZE
     MY FLOCKS & HERDS TRAMPLE THE CORN MY CATTLE BROWZE UPON   376 FOUR ZOAS 9       699
BROXMORE
     LANDLORD ROBERT BRISTOW ESQ OF BROXMORE NEAR RUMSEY  . . . 590A CHAUCER 2       PROSE
BRUGES
     ABOUT JOHN OF BRUGES INVENTING OIL COLOURS . . . . . . 565B DESC CAT 2          PROSE
BRUISD    SEE WORK-BRUISD
     THAT WILFUL BRUISD ITS HELPLESS FORM BUT THAT HE CHERISHD  130 BOOK OF THEL 5     10
       IT
BRUISE
     . . . NOR IN CRUELTY BRUISE THE MILD FLOURISHING MOUNTAINS 134 FRENCH REVOLTN      5
     SHOULD BRUISE THE SERPENT'S HEAD IS THIS THE SERPENT AH    779 GHOST ABEL 1        4
BRUISED      SEE WORK BRUISED
     AND SEEKS TO HIDE HER BRUISED HEAD UNDER THE MISTS OF NIGHT 37D SAMSON/PS        PROSE
     FURROWD WITH WHIPS & OUR FLESH BRUISED WITH THE HEAVY      286 FOUR ZOAS 2        226
       BASKET
BRUISES
     NO ONE BRUISES OR STARVES HIMSELF TO MAKE HIMSELF FIT      639 JERUSALEM 17        21
       FOR LABOUR
BRUISING
     INFOLD AROUND MY LIMBS BRUISING MY MINUTE ARTICULATIONS    635 JERUSALEM 15        13
BRUIZED
     NOTE THESE EXPERIMENT PICTURES HAVE BEEN BRUIZED . . . . 583D DESC CAT 9         PROSE
BRUNO
     AS WHEN SHE FIRST MOUNTED ME ON MY BELOVED BRUNO . . . . 843A LETTER 42          PROSE
BRUNO'S
     ASSISTANCE OF BRUNO'S FAIRIES BUT I INVOKE THE GOOD GENII  801B LETTER 13        PROSE
BRUSH
     SHALL BRUSH MY WING  . . . . . . . . . . .            183 THE FLY/N         20
     SHALL BRUSH MY WING  . . . . . . . . . . .            213 THE FLY/SE        12
     WHATS THE FIRST PART OF PAINTING HE'LL SAY A PAINT BRUSH   553 ASKD PRIGG/N         8
     . . . SMILE LIKE A CHERUB & SAY A PAINT BRUSH  . . . . 553 ASKD PRIGG/N        10
     WITH A LEAR IN HIS EYE HE'LL REPLY A PAINT BRUSH  . . . 553 ASKD PRIGG/N        12
     HAVE ENTIRELY ESCAPED THE BRUSH OF MY EVIL STAR  . . . 835A LETTER 34          PROSE
BRUSHD
     [BRUSHD ACROSS THY SUMMER JOY] . . . . . . .          182 THE FLY/N          2
     HATH BRUSHD AWAY  . . . . . . . . . . .               183 THE FLY/N          8
     HAS BRUSHD AWAY . . . . . . . . . . . .               213 THE FLY/SE         4
BRUSHES
     AND GOT WITH OUR BAGS & OUR BRUSHES TO WORK  . . . . . 118 CHIMNEY SWP/SI       22
BRUTAL
     BRUTAL STRENGTH AND COURAGE . . . . . . . . .        571D DESC CAT 3         PROSE
     THEY WERE OVERWHELMED BY BRUTAL ARMS ALL BUT A SMALL  . 577C DESC CAT 5         PROSE
     AFTER MRS LINNELL'S FATHER IT WILL BE BRUTAL NOT TO SAY   874B LETTER 79        PROSE
BRUTE
     HOWLING IN DISCONTENT BLACK & HEAVY UTTERING BRUTE SOUNDS  338 FOUR ZOAS 7B       224
BRUTISH
     FOR BRUTISH PAN IN VAIN MIGHT THEE ASSAY  . . . . . .  14 IMIT SPEN/PS        10
     THOU KNOWEST THAT THE SPECTRE IS IN EVERY MAN INSANE      327 FOUR ZOAS 7        304
       BRUTISH
     DEFORMD [(BRUTISH)] . . .                             327 FOUR ZOAS 7    *  305
BRUTUS
     O SONS OF TROJAN BRUTUS CLOATHD IN WAR  . . . . . .   31 EDW THIRD/PS 6       1
     THEN BRUTUS SPOKE INSPIRD OUR FATHERS SIT  . . . . .  32 EDW THIRD/PS 6      37
     HEAR YE THE VOICE OF BRUTUS THE FLOWING WAVES . . . . . 32 EDW THIRD/PS 6      39
     GIANTS ANCIENT INHABITANTS OF ENGLAND THE LANDING        208C SUBJCTS HIST/N   TITLE
       OF BRUTUS
BRYANT
     SAME THING AS JACOB BRYANT AND ALL ANTIQUARIES HAVE PROVED 578D DESC CAT 5     PROSE
BUBBLE
     EXULTING IN HER FLIGHT AS WHEN A BUBBLE RISES UP . . . . 362 FOUR ZOAS 9        195
BUBBLING
     LIKE THE BUBBLING WATERS OF THE BROOK IN THE DEAD OF NIGHT 36B COUCH DEATH/PS  PROSE
     AND WAKE THE BUBBLING SPRINGS OF LIFE IN REGIONS OF DARK  289 FOUR ZOAS 2        373
       DEATH
     FLOATING UPON THE TIDE WANDER BUBBLING & BUBBLING   . . 296 FOUR ZOAS 3        164
     JORDAN SPRANG BENEATH ITS THRESHOLD BUBBLING FROM BENEATH 690 JERUSALEM 58       23
BUCKINGHAM
     HUTTN HAD WARWICK NORTHAMPTON BEDFORD BUCKINGHAM . . . . 710 JERUSALEM 71       36
     MR HOARE'S ADDRESS IS TO PRINCE HOARE ESQRE BUCKINGHAM    842B LETTER 41        PROSE
       STREET STRAND
     MR PLAXMAN SCULPTOR BUCKINGHAM STREET FITZROY SQUARE LONDON SUPP ADDRESSES/L  *TITLE
     TO MISS DENMAN BUCKINGHAM STREET FITZROY SQUARE . . . . SUPP ADDRESS/L 86   *TITLE
BUCKLD
     SO STEWHARD'S SOUL HE BUCKLD TO HIS BACK  . . . . . . 536 AND HIS LEGS/N        9
BUCKLE
     FOR A [BUTTON A BAUBLE [BUCKLE] A BEAD OR A] . . . . . 548 ON GREAT ENC/N        2
BUCKLES
     THE FAMINE SHALL CLASP IT TOGETHER WITH BUCKLES & CLASPS  499 MILTON 18          16
BUCKLING
     EACH ONE BUCKLING ON HIS ARMOUR MORNING . . . . . . . 33 EDW THIRD/PS 6      50
BUCKS
     GAD OXFORD BUCKS HARFORD ASHER SUSSEX HAMPSHIRE BERKSHIRE 637 JERUSALEM 16       47
BUD
     THE NARROW BUD OPENS HER BEAUTIES TO . . . . . . . .  2 TO AUTUMN/PS         7
     NIGHTLY BLAST THAT BLIGHTS THE INFANT BUD THE WINDS  . . 43D WOE CRIED MUSE *PROSE
     ("FORWARDNESS NIPS AFFECTION IN THE BUD") THE MORE IS THE 85A ANNO LAVATER   MARG
       PITY
     ON EACH BUD AND BLOSSOM  . . . . . . . . . . .       119 NIGHT/SI           15
     SOMETIMES I THINK THOU ART FRUIT BREAKING FROM ITS BUD . . 265 FOUR ZOAS 1       60
     WHATEVER GROWS FROM ITS PURE BUD OR BREATHES A FRAGRANT   308 FOUR ZOAS 5        124
       SOUL
```

		PAGE	TITLE	LINE

BUD   (CONTINUED)
SHUT UP IN LITTLE PURPLE COVERING FAINTLY BUD & DIE . . . 325 FOUR ZOAS 7   191
THEN SHE RETURNS SWIFT AS A BLIGHT UPON THE INFANT BUD   . . 339 FOUR ZOAS 7B   261
"PLUCKD IN THE BUD & FADED IN THE SPRING" SHAKESPEARE . . SUPP LEGEND/N83   *

BUDDING
BRIGHT SOULS [?ELEMENTS] OF VEGETATIVE LIFE BUDDING AND   274 FOUR ZOAS 1   *   379
    BLOSSOMING
HIS FURIOUS NECK (WRITHING) CONTORTIVE IN DIRE BUDDING   343 FOUR ZOAS 8   *   72
    PAINS

BUDS
WHEN SPRINGING BUDS UNFOLD . . . .   6 MY SILKS/PS   8
O FATHER & MOTHER IF BUDS ARE NIPD . . . . 124 SCHOOL BOY/SI   21
WHEN BUDS & BLOSSOM GROW . . . . 169 EARTHS ANSWR/N   17
WHEN BUDS AND BLOSSOMS GROW . . . . 211 EARTHS ANSR/SE   17
OF ENITHARMON HOW IT BUDS WITH LIFE & FORMS THE BONES   . . 323 FOUR ZOAS 7   131
BEGAN TO BLOSSOM IN FIERCE PAIN SHOOTING ITS WRITHING BUDS   325 FOUR ZOAS 7   213
OR A LEAF BUDS THE ETERNAL MAN IS SEEN IS HEARD IS FELT   . 356 FOUR ZOAS 8   582
WHEN INFANT SPRING APPEARS IN SWELLING BUDS & OPENING   371 FOUR ZOAS 9   548
    FLOWERS

BUFF
BLIND-MAN'S BUFF . . . . 15D BLIND-MANS/PS   TITLE
BUT NOW FOR BLIND-MAN'S BUFF THEY CALL . . . . 16 BLIND-MANS/PS   17

BUFFETTED
BUT SOON I BUFFETTED THE TORRENT ANON LIKE TO A CLOUD . . 105 TIRIEL 4   55

BUFFOON
FOR A BUFFOON OR BURLESQUE CHARACTER KNOW LITTLE OF CHAUCER 569C DESC CAT 3   PROSE

BUG
THE FLEA LOUSE BUG THE TAPE-WORM ALL THE ARMIES OF DISEASE 513 MILTON 27   17

BUGBEAR
[("SUPERSTITION")] HYPOCRISY SUPERSTITION HAS BEEN LONG   85C ANNO LAVATER   MARG
    A BUGBEAR

BUILD
OFF SLOTH AND BUILD HIMSELF A HUT AND HEDGE . . . . .   26 EDW THIRD/PS 3   197
HERE BUILD THY NEST HERE FIX THY STAFF . . . . 37B CONTEMPLATN/PS PROSE
FOR HE DID BUILD A HOUSE . . . . 57 TO BE OR/IM   7
THAT REASON MAY HAVE IDEAS TO BUILD ON THE JEHOVAH OF THE   150B MARRIAGE HH 5   PROSE
    BIBLE
LAY THE BOUND OR BUILD THE ROOF NOR PALE RELIGIOUS LETCHERY 160B SONG LIBERTY   PROSE
TO BUILD HIM CASTLES AND HIGH SPIRES WHERE KINGS & PRIESTS 193 V DAU ALBION 5   20
    MAY DWELL
I WILL BUILD THEE A LABYRINTH . . . . 265 FOUR ZOAS 1   28
BUILD WE A BOWER FOR HEAVEN'S DARLING IN THE GRIZLY DEEP   280 FOUR ZOAS 2   24
BUILD WE THE MUNDANE SHELL AROUND THE ROCK OF ALBION   . . 280 FOUR ZOAS 2   25
TO FORGE THE CURBS OF IRON & BRASS TO BUILD THE IRON   292 FOUR ZOAS 3   34
    MANGERS
BUILD HER A BOWER IN THE MIDST OF ALL MY DASHING WAVES . . 299 FOUR ZOAS 4   71
AND SILENCE BUILD THEIR DAY IN SHADOW OF SOFT CLOUDS & DEWS 331 FOUR ZOAS 7   450
TO BUILD HER BOWERS FOR THE ELEMENTS BROUGHT FORTH   340 FOUR ZOAS 7B   277
    ABUNDANTLY
BUILD MILLS OF RESISTLESS WHEELS TO UNWIND THE SOFT THREADS 346 FOUR ZOAS 8   218
    & REVEAL
PITY ME LOS PITY ME URIZEN & [BUILD] LET US BUILD . . . 349 FOUR ZOAS 8   333
HERE WILL I BUILD MYSELF A HOUSE & HERE I'LL CALL ON HIS   369 FOUR ZOAS 9   453
    NAME
THEY BUILD THE OVENS OF URTHONA NATURE IN DARKNESS GROANS   379 FOUR ZOAS 9   816
WHERE THOU THY CHARMING NEST DOST BUILD . . . . 422 THE BIRDS/N   3
LICENCD BUILD THAT NATION'S FATE . . . . 433 AUGURIES   114
BUT OTHERS OF THE SONS OF LOS BUILD MOMENTS & MINUTES &   516 MILTON 28   44
    HOURS
TO BUILD THE UNIVERSE STUPENDOUS MENTAL FORMS CREATING . . 519 MILTON 30   20
HOW TO BUILD A UNIVERSE WITH FARTHING BALLS . . . . . . 598C PUB ADDRESS/N PROSE
ARE MINE HERE WILL I BUILD MY LAWS OF MORAL VIRTUE . . . 622 JERUSALEM 4   31
TO MURDER THEIR OWN SOULS TO BUILD A KINGDOM AMONG THE DEAD 640 JERUSALEM 18   10
AND OF HIS CHILDREN BEFORE SINFUL JERUSALEM TO BUILD   . . 640 JERUSALEM 18   28
TO BUILD BABYLON BECAUSE THEY HAVE FORSAKEN JERUSALEM   . . 647 JERUSALEM 24   30
MUTUAL SHALL BUILD JERUSALEM . . . . 652 FIELDS FROM/J   87
IN BRICKS TO BUILD THE PYRAMIDS OF HEBER & TERAH BUT LOS   657 JERUSALEM 31   12
LIKE ROCKY CLOUDS BUILD ME A GLOOMY MONUMENT OF WOE . . . 666 JERUSALEM 39   18
COME UP BUILD BABYLON RAHAB IS OURS & ALL HER MULTITUDES   671 JERUSALEM 42   63
BUILD & PREPARE A WALL & CURTAIN FOR AMERICA'S SHORE   . . 680 JERUSALEM 49   49
AND BUILD A WORLD OF PHANTASY UPON MY GREAT ABYSS . . . 685 JERUSALEM 54   23
AND BUILD THIS BABYLON & SACRIFICE IN SECRET GROVES . . . 693 JERUSALEM 60   23
THEY BUILD A STUPENDOUS BUILDING ON THE PLAIN OF SALISBURY 701 JERUSALEM 66   2
    . . .
THEY RETURN NOT BUT BUILD A HABITATION SEPARATE FROM MAN   703 JERUSALEM 66   73
THAT TO LABOUR IN KNOWLEDGE IS TO BUILD UP JERUSALEM AND   717C JERUSALEM 77   PROSE
EVEN TO THE STARS EXALTING HER THRONE TO BUILD BEYOND THE   719 JERUSALEM 78   18
    THRONE
WHERE I WILL BUILD HER A COUCH OF REPOSE & MY PILLARS . . 727 JERUSALEM 83   26
BUT HERE WE BUILD BABYLON ON EUPHRATES COMPELLD TO BUILD   729 JERUSALEM 84   8
WHY WILT THOU REND THYSELF APART & BUILD AN EARTHLY KINGDOM 730 JERUSALEM 85   30
IN HOWLING TORMENT TO BUILD STONE WALLS OF SEPARATION   736 JERUSALEM 90   12
    COMPELLING
WITH LOS'S THUNDEROUS WORDS BEGAN TO BUILD TREMBLING   737 JERUSALEM 90   59
    ROCKING STONES
& PROMISED TO BUILD ON THEM . . . . 792A LETTER 4   PROSE
EVER BUILD A PALACE IT WOULD BE ONLY MY COTTAGE ENLARGED   803B LETTER 15   PROSE

BUILDED
THUS WAS THE MUNDANE SHELL BUILDED BY URIZEN'S STRONG POWER 286 FOUR ZOAS 2   248
OF URIZEN ENORMOUS WORK HE BUILDED THEM ANEW . . . . . 301 FOUR ZOAS 4   166
OF ENITHARMON LOS AROUND HER BUILDED PILLARS OF IRON   . . 307 FOUR ZOAS 5   73
HE BUILDED GOLGONOOZA ON THE LAKE OF UDAN ADAN . . . . 307 FOUR ZOAS 5   76

```
                                                          PAGE      TITLE         LINE
BUILDED    (CONTINUED)
     UPON THE LIMIT OF TRANSLUCENCE THEN HE BUILDED LUBAN    .  .   307 FOUR ZOAS 5          77
     THEY BUILDED GOLGONOOZA LOS LABOURING [ INSPIRD] BUILDED       329 FOUR ZOAS 7     *  378
        PILLARS HIGH
     FIRST TRADES & COMMERCE SHIPS & ARMED VESSELS HE BUILDED       333 FOUR ZOAS 7B        12
        LABORIOUS
     BUILDED A TEMPLE IN THE IMAGE OF THE HUMAN HEART  .  .  .  .   333 FOUR ZOAS 7B        20
     AND LOS & ENITHARMON BUILDED JERUSALEM WEEPING   .  .  .  .   357 FOUR ZOAS 9          1
     HE SPOKE & PILLARS WERE BUILDED & WALLS AS WHITE AS IVORY     369 FOUR ZOAS 9        461
     AND WAS JERUSALEM BUILDED HERE  .  .  .  .  .  .  .  .  .     481 AND DID FEET/M        7
     SUBDUING HIS SPECTRE THEY BUILDED THE LOOMS OF GENERATION     483 MILTON 3             38
     THEY BUILDED GREAT GOLGONOOZA TIMES ON TIMES AGES ON AGES     483 MILTON 3             39
     AND EVERY MONTH A SILVER PAVED TERRACE BUILDED HIGH  .  .  .  516 MILTON 28            54
     I HAVE TURNED MY BACK UPON THESE HEAVENS BUILDED ON CRUELTY   521 MILTON 32             3
     AND THEY BUILDED GOLGONOOZA TERRIBLE ETERNAL LABOUR  .  .  .  631 JERUSALEM 12         24
     HAVING A WALL BUILDED AGAINST IT AND THEREBY THE GATES  .  .  635 JERUSALEM 14         27
     IN ENITHARMON'S HALLS BUILDED BY LOS & HIS MIGHTY CHILDREN    638 JERUSALEM 16         60
     WHICH HARDEND AGAINST THEM MORE AND MORE AS HE BUILDED        641 JERUSALEM 19         30
        ONWARDS
     THERE BABYLON IS BUILDED IN THE WASTE FOUNDED IN HUMAN        647 JERUSALEM 24         25
        DESOLATION
     WERE BUILDED OVER WITH PILLARS OF GOLD  .  .  .  .  .  .  .   649 FIELDS FROM/J         3
     A BUILDING OF LUVAH BUILDED IN JERUSALEM'S EASTERN GATE       657 JERUSALEM 31         24
        TO BE
     HIS SECLUDED COURT THENCE TO BETHLEHEM WHERE WAS BUILDED      657 JERUSALEM 31         25
     AND BUILDED BY THE DIVINE HAND THAT THE SINNER SHALL ALWAYS   657 JERUSALEM 31         31
        ESCAPE
     SHADOW IS VALA BUILDED BY THE REASONING POWER IN MAN    .  .  675 JERUSALEM 44         40
     BUILDED THE MOUNTAIN PALACES OF EDEN STUPENDOUS WORKS   .  .  676 JERUSALEM 46          4
     IN SILENCE THE DIVINE LORD BUILDED WITH IMMORTAL LABOUR       677 JERUSALEM 48          5
     HE HAS BUILDED THE ARCHES OF ALBION'S TOMB BINDING THE        680 JERUSALEM 49         54
        STARS
     HERE ON THE BANKS OF THE THAMES LOS BUILDED GOLGONOOZA  .  .  684 JERUSALEM 53         15
     HE BUILDED IT IN RAGE & IN FURY IT IS THE SPIRITUAL          684 JERUSALEM 53         18
        FOURFOLD
     CATHEDRON'S LOOMS ARE BUILDED AND LOS'S FURNACES IN THE       691 JERUSALEM 59         23
        SOUTH
     WE BUILDED JERUSALEM AS A CITY & A TEMPLE FROM LAMBETH  .  .  729 JERUSALEM 84          3
     FOR JERUSALEM LIES IN RUINS & THE FURNACES OF LOS            729 JERUSALEM 84          6
        ARE BUILDED THERE
     TO IRELAND'S FARTHEST ROCKS WHERE GIANTS BUILDED THEIR        735 JERUSALEM 89         50
        CAUSEWAY
     THE SPECTRE BUILDED STUPENDOUS WORKS TAKING THE STARRY        738 JERUSALEM 91         33
        HEAVENS
BUILDER
     THE BUILDER OF VIRGINIA THROWS HIS HAMMER DOWN IN FEAR  .  .  201 AMERICA 14      *   16
BUILDERS
     THEN ROSE THE BUILDERS FIRST THE ARCHITECT DIVINE HIS PLAN    284 FOUR ZOAS 2        166
     WHAT ARE THOSE GOLDEN BUILDERS DOING WHERE WAS THE            632 JERUSALEM 12         25
        BURYING-PLACE
     GO ON BUILDERS IN HOPE THO JERUSALEM WANDERS FAR AWAY   .  .  632 JERUSALEM 12         43
     BUT ALBION IS CAST FORTH TO THE POTTER HIS CHILDREN TO        647 JERUSALEM 24         29
        THE BUILDERS
     WHAT ARE THOSE GOLDEN BUILDERS DOING  .  .  .  .  .  .  .     650 FIELDS FROM/J        25
     TO DESPISE KNOWLEDGE IS TO DESPISE JERUSALEM & HER          717C JERUSALEM 77      PROSE
        BUILDERS
BUILDETH
     AND THE TURTLE BUILDETH THERE  .  .  .  .  .  .  .  .  .  .     7 LOVE HARMNY/PS       12
BUILDGS
     HERCULES BUILDGS LAMBETH  .  .  .  .  .  .  .  .  .  .  .  . SUPP ADDRESSES/L     *TITLE
BUILDING
     THE [GOLDEN] WONDROUS BUILDING & [?HALLS OF] .  .  .  .  .    284 FOUR ZOAS 2     *  174
     IN DARKNESS BUILDING THY STRONG THRONE & IN MY ANCIENT        278 FOUR ZOAS 1        509
        NIGHT
     QUADRANGULAR THE BUILDING ROSE THE HEAVENS SQUARED BY A       284 FOUR ZOAS 2        168
        LINE
     A WONDROUS GOLDEN BUILDING MANY A WINDOW MANY A DOOR    .  .  286 FOUR ZOAS 2        243
     AND BUILDING ARCHES HIGH & CITIES TURRETS & [HIGH ] TOWERS    361 FOUR ZOAS 9        167
        & DOMES
     IN IMMENSE LABOURS & SORROWS EVER BUILDING EVER FALLING       485 MILTON 6            2
     RETURN RETURN TO LAMBETH'S VALE O BUILDING OF HUMAN SOULS     485 MILTON 6           19
     CREATING NEW FLESH ON THE DEMON COLD AND BUILDING HIM   .  .  500 MILTON 19          13
     IS A GARDEN OF DELIGHT & A BUILDING OF MAGNIFICENCE  .  .  .  512 MILTON 26          32
     A RUIND MAN A RUIND BUILDING OF GOD NOT MADE WITH HANDS       529 MILTON 38          16
     GREAT BUILDING INTO COMPARTMENTS AND ORNAMENT THEM   .  .  . 560D EXHIBITION ADV   PROSE
     THE INN IS A GOTHIC BUILDING WHICH THYNNE IN HIS GLOSSARY    567B DESC CAT 3       PROSE
     THE INN IS A GOTHIC BUILDING WHICH THYNNE IN HIS GLOSSARY    588D CHAUCER/N        PROSE
     THE INN IS A GOTHIC BUILDING WHICH THYNNE IN HIS GLOSSARY    590C CHAUCER 2        PROSE
     WHILE I WRITE OF THE BUILDING OF GOLGONOOZA .  .  .  .  .     623 JERUSALEM 5         24
     THEREFORE LOS STANDS IN LONDON BUILDING GOLGONOOZA   .  .  .  629 JERUSALEM 10        17
     WITH IRON & BRASS BUILDING GOLGONOOZA IN GREAT CONTENDINGS    630 JERUSALEM 10        63
     BECOMING A BUILDING OF PITY AND COMPASSION LO  .  .  .  .  .  632 JERUSALEM 12        29
     YET IT IS PERFECT IN ITS BUILDING ORNAMENTS & PERFECTION     632 JERUSALEM 12        53
     IN THOSE CHURCHES EVER CONSUMING & EVER BUILDING BY THE       634 JERUSALEM 13        62
        SPECTRES
     BUILDING CASTLES IN DESOLATED PLACES AND STRONG              641 JERUSALEM 18        38
        FORTIFICATIONS
     BUT THEY FLED TO THE MOUNTAINS TO SEEK RANSOM BUILDING        653 JERUSALEM 28        25
        A STRONG
     A BUILDING OF LUVAH BUILDED IN JERUSALEM'S EASTERN GATE       657 JERUSALEM 31        24
        TO BE
     BUILDING THE MOON OF ULRO PLANK BY PLANK & RIB BY RIB   .  .  662 JERUSALEM 36         4
```

```
                                                               PAGE     TITLE          LINE
BUILDING   (CONTINUED)
    FROM HOWLING VICTIMS OF LAW BUILDING HEAVENS               672 JERUSALEM 43         18
      TWENTY-SEVEN-FOLD
    BUILDING THE BODY OF MOSES IN THE VALLEY OF PEOR THE BODY   680 JERUSALEM 49        57
    LONDON CONTINUALLY BUILDING & CONTINUALLY DECAYING          684 JERUSALEM 53        19
      DESOLATE
    URIZEN WRATHFUL STRODE ABOVE DIRECTING THE AWFUL BUILDING   690 JERUSALEM 58        21
    A WONDROUS GOLDEN BUILDING IMMENSE WITH ORNAMENTS SUBLIME   691 JERUSALEM 59        24
    THEY BUILD A STUPENDOUS BUILDING ON THE PLAIN OF SALISBURY  701 JERUSALEM 66         2
      . . .
    THE BUILDING IS NATURAL RELIGION & ITS ALTARS NATURAL       702 JERUSALEM 66         8
      MORALITY
    A BUILDING OF ETERNAL DEATH WHOSE PROPORTIONS ARE ETERNAL   702 JERUSALEM 66         9
      DESPAIR
    CONTINUALLY BUILDING CONTINUALLY DECAYING BECAUSE OF LOVE   712A JERUSALEM 72      PROSE
      & JEALOUSY
    IN SOME MENTAL PURSUIT FOR THE BUILDING UP OF JERUSALEM     717C JERUSALEM 77      PROSE
    CONTINUALLY BUILDING CONTINUALLY DESTROYING IN FAMILY       734 JERUSALEM 88        40
      FEUDS
    IN THE BACKGROUND A BUILDING WHICH MAY BE SUPPOSED  . . .   824A LETTER 27         PROSE
BUILDINGS
    BETTER THAN ANY DESCRIPTION OF BUILDINGS OR GARMENTS  . .   150C MARRIAGE HH 6     PROSE
    NO...HERCULES BUILDINGS LAMBETH  . . . . . . . . .          207C PRSPECTUS 1793    PROSE
    PUBLISHED BY W BLAKE...HERCULES BUILDINGS  . . . . .        209B FOR CHILDRN/GP   *TITLE
    BESIDES LET THEM LOOK AT GOTHIC FIGURES & GOTHIC BUILDINGS  461A ANNO REYNOLDS     MARG
    AND DAYS & MONTHS & YEARS & AGES & PERIODS WONDROUS         516 MILTON 28          45
      BUILDINGS
    ARE SEEN ABOVE THE HORIZON SOME BUILDINGS AND SPIRES  .     567B DESC CAT 3       PROSE
    ARE SEEN ABOVE THE HORIZON SOME BUILDINGS & SPIRES  . .     588D CHAUCER/N        PROSE
    ARE SEEN ABOVE THE HORRIZON SOME BUILDINGS AND SPIRES  .    590C CHAUCER 2       *PROSE
    IN BEAUFORT BUILDINGS WE ALL KNOW THAT EDITORS OF           592C PUB ADDRESS/N    PROSE
      NEWSPAPERS
    SUCH ARE THE BUILDINGS OF LOS & SUCH ARE THE WOOFS OF       635 JERUSALEM 14        15
      ENITHARMON
BUILDS
    MISERY BUILDS OVER OUR COTTAGE ROOFS AND DISCONTENT RUNS    37B CONTEMPLATN/PS    PROSE
      LIKE A BROOK
    . . . IN FOLDS OF THE ROBE THE CROWND ADDER BUILDS AND      147 FRENCH REVOLTN     299
      HISSES
    AND BUILDS A HEAVEN IN HELL'S DESPAIR  . . . . . . .        162 CLOD PEBBLE/N        4
    AND BUILDS A HELL IN HEAVEN'S DESPITE  . . . . . . .        162 CLOD PEBBLE/N       12
    AND BUILDS A HEAVEN IN HELL'S DESPAIR  . . . . . . .        211 CLOD PEBBLE/SE       4
    AND BUILDS A HELL IN HEAVEN'S DESPITE  . . . . . . .        211 CLOD PEBBLE/SE      12
    THE GOLDEN MOTH BUILDS THERE A HOUSE & SPREADS HER SILKEN   308 FOUR ZOAS 5        134
      BED
    LOS BUILDS THE WALLS OF GOLGONOOZA AGAINST THE STIRRING     343 FOUR ZOAS 8        109
      BATTLE
    OZOTH HERE BUILDS WALLS OF ROCKS AGAINST THE SURGING SEA    515 MILTON 28          39
    AROUND THIS POLYPUS LOS CONTINUAL BUILDS THE MUNDANE SHELL  524 MILTON 34          31
    WHAT IS IT THAT BUILDS A HOUSE AND PLANTS A GARDEN  . .     585C DESC CAT 15      PROSE
    THE RUINS OF TIME BUILDS MANSIONS IN ETERNITY  . . . . .    797B LETTER 9         PROSE
BUILT      SEE LAW-BUILT,MARBLE BUILT
    THE NORTH IS THINE THERE HAST THOU BUILT THY DARK  . . .    2 TO WINTER/PS          2
    THEIR TOWERS SHALL BE BUILT UPON THE ROCKS  . . . . .       33 EDW THIRD/PS 6      53
    BUILT WITH MURDER THEN BABEL MIGHTY REARD HIM TO THE SKIES  41A THEN SHE BORE      PROSE
    PRISONS ARE BUILT WITH STONES OF LAW BROTHELS WITH BRICKS   151B MARRIAGE HH 8     PROSE
      OF RELIGION
    WHO BUILT PALACES IN THE IMMENSE CLIFFS  . . . . . . .      154D MARRIAGE HH 15    PROSE
    A CHAPEL WAS BUILT IN THE MIDST  . . . . . . . . . .        162 GARDEN LOVE/N        3
    REARS ITS IMMORTAL PINNACLES BUILT IN THE FOREST OF GOD     200 AMERICA 10          9
    THEIR UNMOVD BRANCHES STOOD THE HALL BUILT WHEN THE MOON    204 AMERICA CANC B      4
      SHOT FORTH
    A CHAPEL WAS BUILT IN THE MIDST  . . . . . . . . . .        215 GARDEN LOVE/SE       3
    AND THEIR CHILDREN WEPT & BUILT  . . . . . . . . . .        236 URIZEN 28            4
    THE HUMAN RACE BEGAN TO WITHER FOR THE HEALTHY BUILT  .     246 SONG OF LOS 3       25
    LOS ASTONISHD AND TERRIFIED BUILT  . . . . . . . .          259 BOOK OF LOS 5       20
    BUILT BY THE ARCHITECT DIVINE WHOSE LOVE TO LOS &           298 FOUR ZOAS 4         51
      ENITHARMON
    THEN CAME HE AMONG FIERY CITIES & CASTLES BUILT OF BURNING  314 FOUR ZOAS 6        115
      STEEL
    BETWEEN THE ENORMOUS IRON WALLS BUILT BY THE SPECTRE DARK   319 FOUR ZOAS 6        295
    ALL HEAVEN THEY SAW HIM DARK THEY BUILT A GOLDEN WALL  .    326 FOUR ZOAS 7        242
    AND IF THAT LOS HAD NOT BUILT ME A TOWER UPON A ROCK  .     335 FOUR ZOAS 7B   *   85
    [BUT RAHAB [BUILT] HEWD A SEPULCHER IN THE ROCK OF          356 FOUR ZOAS 8    *  585
      ETERNITY]
    THEIR MARBLE [TOMB] TOMBS I BUILT WITH TEARS  . . . . .     416 MY SPECTRE/N   *   37
    TILL MANY A CITY THERE IS BUILT  . . . . . . . . .          427 MENTAL TRAVLER      91
    TILL WE HAVE BUILT JERUSALEM  . . . . . . . . . .           481 AND DID FEET/M      15
    ARE BUILT BENEATH THE EARTH & WATERS OF THE MUNDANE SHELL   483 MILTON 4            3
    IS BUILT ETERNALLY THE UNIVERSE OF LOS AND ENITHARMON  .    500 MILTON 19          25
    BUILT BY THE SONS OF LOS IN BOWLAHOOLA & ALLAMANDA  . .     512 MILTON 26          33
    THE SKY IS AN IMMORTAL TENT BUILT BY THE SONS OF LOS  .     516 MILTON 29           9
    BUILT IN JERUSALEM'S WALL  . . . . . . . . . .              551 GIVE YOU END/N       4
    THIS IS ONE OF THE GOTHIC ARTISTS WHO BUILT THE CATHEDRALS  604A INSC ARIMATHEA   PROSE
    WAS BUILT IN FROM ETERNITY IN THE CLIFFS OF ALBION  . .     631 JERUSALEM 11        15
    HER STREETS ARE PAVED WITH DESTRUCTION HER HOUSES BUILT     647 JERUSALEM 24        33
      WITH DEATH
    I WAS A CITY & A TEMPLE BUILT BY ALBION'S CHILDREN  . .     659 JERUSALEM 33        36
    LOS BUILT THE STUBBORN STRUCTURE OF THE LANGUAGE ACTING     668 JERUSALEM 40        59
      AGAINST
    AND AS ALBION BUILT HIS FROZEN ALTARS LOS BUILT            671 JERUSALEM 42        78
      THE MUNDANE SHELL
```

282

	PAGE	TITLE	LINE

BUILT   (CONTINUED)
    LIKE LAKES OF LIQUID LEAD INSTEAD OF HEAVENLY CHAPELS BUILT   673 JERUSALEM 43   63
    IS BUILT ETERNALLY THE SUBLIME UNIVERSE OF LOS & ENITHARMON   691 JERUSALEM 59   21
    IS A HOUSE OF (PLEASANTNESS) & A GARDEN OF DELIGHT BUILT   714 JERUSALEM 73   51
      BY THE
    BUILT IN JERUSALEM'S WALL . . . .   716 I GIVE YOU/J   4
    ON THEIR ENORMOUS ALTARS BUILT IN THE TERRIBLE NORTH . .   727 JERUSALEM 83   20
    THEY NAMD IT CANAAN & BUILT FOR IT A TENDER MOON . . . .   730 JERUSALEM 85   2
    THO THY COVENANT BUILT HELL'S JAIL . . . .   754 EV GOSPEL(E)/N   38
    CAIN'S CITY BUILT WITH HUMAN BLOOD NOT BLOOD OF BULLS   781 GHOST ABEL 2   17
      & GOATS
    HE COULD NEVER HAVE BUILT DANTE'S HELL NOR . . . . .   785C ILLS DANTE 101   PROSE
    ON ONE OF THE STRONGEST & HANDSOMEST BUILT STAGES I E̶ ̶ ̶ ̶ ̶   871C LETTER 73   PROSE
      SAW
BULBOUS
    THE BULBOUS ROOTS THROWN UP TOGETHER INTO BARNS & GARNERS   284 FOUR ZOAS 2   165
BULK
    ENVY HATH A SERPENT'S HEAD OF FEARFUL BULK . . . . . .   41C THEN SHE BORE   PROSE
    ITS WEIGHTY BULK SILENT THE ROCK LAY . . . .   251 AHANIA 3   35
    NOW FIXD INTO ONE STEDFAST BULK HIS FEATURES STONIFY . .   305 FOUR ZOAS 5   2
    YET MIGHTY BULK & MAJESTY & BEAUTY REMAIND BUT UNEXPANSIVE   305 FOUR ZOAS 5   13
    THEIR SENSES UNEXPANSIVE IN ONE STEDFAST BULK REMAIN . .   305 FOUR ZOAS 5   19
    THE FORM OF ORC WAS GONE HE REARD HIS SERPENT BULK AMONG   338 FOUR ZOAS 7B   215
    HIS HUMAN BULK WHILE THE DARK SHADOWY FEMALE [BROODS]   343 FOUR ZOAS 8   * 80
      BROODING OVER
    HERE FIXD INTO A FROZEN BULK SUBJECT TO DECAY & DEATH .   525 MILTON 34   54
    SUBORDINATION STRENGTH IS COMPACTNESS NOT EXTENT NOR BULK   580B DESC CAT 5   PROSE
    WHOSE BULK NAILD TO THE CROSS ROUND WHICH HE WREATHES .   606C V LAST JUDG/N   PROSE
    IN VERULAM THE POLYPUS'S HEAD WINDING AROUND HIS BULK .   704 JERUSALEM 67   35
    THE SERPENT BULK OF NATURE'S DROSS . . . .   749 EV GOSPEL(B)/N   53
    IN ANY WAY BE SEPARATED FROM THE GRAND BULK OF YOUR . .   858C LETTER 55   PROSE
BULL
    AS THE STRONG BULL IN SUMMER TIME WHEN BEES SING ROUND   308 FOUR ZOAS 5   136
      THE HEATH
    WALKS THRO THE BATTLE DARK & FIERCE THE BULL HIS RAGE .   335 FOUR ZOAS 7B   109
    THE BIRTH OF WAR & MISERY WHILE THE LION SEIZES THE BULL   441D INSC FALL MAN   PROSE
      THE
    THOSE OF A BULL EVERY THING HAS ITS OWN HARMONY &   774B ANNO BERKELEY   MARG
      PROPORTION
BULLET
    SUDDEN AS THE BULLET WRAPPD IN HIS FIRE . . . .   146 FRENCH REVOLTN   262
BULLS
    IN MANY A VALLEY FOR THE BULLS OF LUVAH DRAGD THE PLOW . .   283 FOUR ZOAS 2   120
    NOR ALL URTHONA'S STRENGTH NOR ALL THE POWER OF LUVAH'S   309 FOUR ZOAS 5   164
      BULLS
    THE BULLS OF LUVAH BREATHING FIRE BELLOW ON BURNING   320 FOUR ZOAS 7   16
      PASTURES
    . . . THE WILD BULLS FROM THE SULTRY WASTE . . . . . .   365 FOUR ZOAS 9   300
    LET THE BULLS OF LUVAH TREAD THE CORN & DRAW THE LOADED   376 FOUR ZOAS 9   701
      WAGGON
    WHEN LUVAH'S BULLS EACH MORNING DRAG THE SULPHUR SUN OUT   503 MILTON 21   20
      OF THE DEEP
    HE MAKES THY SONS THE TRAMPLING OF HIS BULLS THEY ARE PLOWD   625 JERUSALEM 7   13
    HAS FOUR SCULPTURD BULLS TERRIBLE BEFORE THE GATE OF IRON   632 JERUSALEM 12   62
    AND IRON THE BULLS AND THAT WHICH LOOKS TOWARD ULRO . . .   632 JERUSALEM 12   63
    SATAN I WILL HAVE HUMAN BLOOD & NOT THE BLOOD OF BULLS   780 GHOST ABEL 2   13
      OR GOATS
    CAIN'S CITY BUILT WITH HUMAN BLOOD NOT BLOOD OF BULLS   781 GHOST ABEL 2   17
      & GOATS
BULWARK
    THE PRESS & A BULWARK FOR GENIUS . . . .   841D LETTER 41   PROSE
BUM
    OR SIT ON BEAUTY'S BUM . . . .   56 HAIL MATRIM/IM   6
BUNDLE   SEE TWIN-BUNDLE
BUNGLE
    IT IS ONLY FUMBLE & BUNGLE WHICH CANNOT DRAW A LINE . . .   603C PUB ADDR AD/N   PROSE
BUNGLERY
    FOR A GREAT CONQUEST ARE BUNGLERY . . . .   549 ENGL ENCOU/N 2 *   3
BUNGLES
    SO FAR FROM BEING ALL OF A PIECE ARE THE MOST WRETCHED   468D ANNO REYNOLDS   MARG
      BUNGLES
BUNGLING
    AND BUNGLING GREAT INVENTORS IN ALL AGES KNEW THIS . . .   585B DESC CAT 15   PROSE
    ENGLISHMEN HAVE BEEN SO USED TO JOURNEYMEN'S UNDECIDED   603C PUB ADDR AD/N   PROSE
      BUNGLING
BUNGLISHNESS
    MENNY WOUVER BOTH BUNGLISHNESS & SKILL . . . .   549 ENGL ENCOU/N 2   2
BUNYAN
    LIKE PUTTING JOHN MILTON WITH JOHN BUNYAN . . . . . .   853A LETTER 51   *PROSE
BUONAPARTE
    LET US TEACH BUONAPARTE & WHOMSOEVER ELSE IT MAY CONCERN   597A PUB ADDRESS/N   PROSE
    AS THE FRENCH NOW ADORE BUONAPARTE AND THE ENGLISH OUR   845B LETTER 44   PROSE
      POOR GEORGE
BURDEN
    MY TASK IS GREAT MY BURDEN HEAVIER THAN . . . .   19 EDW THIRD/PS 2   4
    AND STILL THE BURDEN OF THEIR SONG IN TEARS WAS POURED   322 FOUR ZOAS 7   * 106
      FORTH
    AND SLAVES IN MYRIADS IN SHIP LOADS BURDEN THE HOARSE   333 FOUR ZOAS 7B   16
      SOUNDING DEEP
    TO MAKE LEARNING A BURDEN & THE WORK OF THE HOLY SPIRIT   511 MILTON 25   52
      STRIFE
    GOD HATH FORSAKEN ME & MY FRIENDS ARE BECOME A BURDEN . .   666 JERUSALEM 39   22

```
                                                                    PAGE       TITLE          LINE
BURDEND
     OUR BURDEND VESSELS SPOILING OUR NAVAL FLOCKS  . . . . .        20 EDW THIRD/PS 2         68
     RINTRAH ROARS & SHAKES HIS FIRES IN THE BURDEND AIR  . . .     148 MARRIAGE HH 2           1
     RINTRAH ROARS & SHAKES HIS FIRES IN THE BURDEND AIR  . . .     149 MARRIAGE HH 2          21
     BURDEND WITH CLOUDS HOWL ROUND THE COUCH SULLEN THE WOOLY      335 FOUR ZOAS 7B          108
     SHEEP
BURDENED
     BUT GOD HATH OTHER JOYS IN STORE IS BURDENED ISRAEL HIS       39C SAMSON/PS            PROSE
     GRIEF
BURDENS
     ASK THE WILD ASS WHY HE REFUSES BURDENS AND THE MEEK CAMEL     191 V DAU ALBION 3          7
BURDNING
     CHOKD THE BRIGHT RIVERS BURDNING WITH MY SHIPS THE ANGRY       361 FOUR ZOAS 9          169
     DEEP
BURGUNDY
     THEN THE ANCIENTEST PEER DUKE OF BURGUNDY . . . . . . .        138 FRENCH REVOLTN         83
     . . . THEN TURNING TO BURGUNDY TROUBLED  . . . . . . .         139 FRENCH REVOLTN        111
     BURGUNDY THOU WAST BORN A LION MY SOUL IS OERGROWN WITH        139 FRENCH REVOLTN        112
     DISTRESS
     LIKE A VOICE IN THE VINEYARDS OF BURGUNDY . . . . . . .        145 FRENCH REVOLTN        244
     . . . THE DUKE OF BURGUNDY DELIVERS THE KING'S COMMAND  .      145 FRENCH REVOLTN        247
BURIAL
     . . . AND LIKE THUNDER ON THE JUST MAN'S BURIAL DAY HE         139 FRENCH REVOLTN        106
     PAUSD
     THEIR MARRIAGE & THEIR BAPTISM THEIR BURIAL & CONSECRATION     738 JERUSALEM 91          15
BURIED
     FALLING RUSHING RUINING BURIED IN THE RUINS ON URTHONA'S      159D SONG LIBERTY        PROSE
     DENS
     ONE HOUR THEY LAY BURIED BENEATH THE RUINS OF THAT HALL        241 EUROPE 9              14
     WHERE BONES FROM THE BIRTH ARE BURIED  . . . . . . .           255 AHANIA 5              46
     THO HORRIBLE & GHASTLY TO THINE EYES THO BURIED BENEATH        329 FOUR ZOAS 7          351
     THEIR BODIES BURIED IN THE RUINS OF THE UNIVERSE . . .         358 FOUR ZOAS 9           30
     HE CALLD THE DEEP BURIED HIS VOICE & ANSWER NONE RETURND       360 FOUR ZOAS 9          136
     OUTSTRETCHD A SMILING CORSE THEY BURIED HER IN A SILENT        362 FOUR ZOAS 9          199
     CAVE
     IN THE ETERNAL HEAVENS OF HUMAN [THOUGHT] IMAGINATION          366 FOUR ZOAS 9          368
     BURIED BENEATH
     LOS SECRET BURIED THULLOH WEEPING DISCONSOLATE OVER THE        489 MILTON 8             45
     MOONY SPACE
     AND I'LL BE BURIED NEAR A DIKE . . . . . . . . . .             537 AND HIS LEGS/N        50
     I WAS BURIED NEAR THIS DIKE  . . . . . . . . . . .             546 ANOTHER/N 1            1
     NOW LOST OR PERHAPS BURIED TILL SOME HAPPIER AGE THE  .       565C DESC CAT 2          PROSE
     AND THE EMANATIONS BURIED ALIVE IN THE EARTH WITH POMP         628 JERUSALEM 9           15
     OF RELIGION
     THE BURIED SOUL & ALL ITS GEMS . . . . . . . . . .            753 EV GOSPEL(D)/N       102
     BURIED BENEATH HIS MERCY SEAT  . . . . . . . . . .            761 FOR SEXES/GP          11
     THE EGYPTIAN TASKMASTER WHO WAS KILLED AND BURIED BY MOSES    SUPP DRAWING WGR       *TITLE
BURIERS
     LIE STINKING ON THE EARTH THE BURIERS SHALL ARISE FROM        100 TIRIEL 1              49
     THE EAST
BURKE
     BARRY PAINTED A PICTURE FOR BURKE EQUAL TO RAFAEL OR  .      451D ANNO REYNOLDS        MARG
     BURKE USED TO SHEW THIS PICTURE TO HIS FRIENDS & TO SAY      451D ANNO REYNOLDS        MARG
     I GAVE
     ("REYNOLDS JOHNSON BURKE") [?OLIVER GOLDSMITH ?NEVER         SUPP ANNO REYNOLDS       * MARG
     ?SHOULD ?HAVE]
BURKE'S
     SUCH WAS BURKE'S PATRONAGE OF ART & SCIENCE  . . . .         451D ANNO REYNOLDS        MARG
     BURKE'S TREATISE ON THE SUBLIME & BEAUTIFUL  . . . .         476D ANNO REYNOLDS        MARG
     I READ BURKE'S TREATISE WHEN VERY YOUNG . . . . . .          476D ANNO REYNOLDS        MARG
BURLESQUE
     FOR A BUFFOON OR BURLESQUE CHARACTER KNOW LITTLE OF CHAUCER  569C DESC CAT 3          PROSE
     BECAUSE THEY WERE A BURLESQUE SET OF SCARE-CROWS  . . .      575B DESC CAT 3          PROSE
     IT IS FIT FOR THE BURLESQUE THE BEAUTY PROPER FOR SUBLIME    579C DESC CAT 5          PROSE
     ANNEXED TO IMBECILITY AND DISEASE IS A SUBJECT FOR          580A DESC CAT 5          PROSE
     BURLESQUE
BURN
     OUR BACKS TO THE FIRE TILL WE SHALL BURN OUR SKIRTS . . .     22 EDW THIRD/PS 3        38
     MAY YET BURN IN FRANCE . . . . . . . . . . . . . .           142 FRENCH REVOLTN       174
     BUT THOSE WHO BURN WITH VIGROUS YOUTH  . . . . . . .         172 ARE NOT JOYS/N         7
     AND ALL HIS BOWELS BEGAN TO [BURN] CHURN  . . . . .          187 WHEN KLOPSTK/N        16
     HARROW BURN ALL THESE CORN FIELDS THROW DOWN ALL THESE       274 FOUR ZOAS 1          388
     FENCES
     BURN LIKE TWO FURNACES HE CALLD WITH VOICE OF THUNDER  .     319 FOUR ZOAS 6          309
     IF MILD THEY BURN IN JUST PROPORTION & IN SECRET NIGHT  .    331 FOUR ZOAS 7          449
     TO BURN MYSTERY WITH FIRE & FORM ANOTHER FROM HER ASHES      357 FOUR ZOAS 8          616
     STILL FOR VICTORY I BURN  . . . . . . . . . . . .            416 MY SPECTRE/N          52
     THEY STRIP HER NAKED & BURN HER WITH FIRE IT REPRESENTS     609A V LAST JUDG/N       PROSE
     BEFORE HIS WRATH BEGAN TO BURN . . . . . . . . . .           752 EV GOSPEL(D)/N        56
     YOU TO KEEP IT A SECRET & TO BURN THIS LETTER BECAUSE IT    819D LETTER 25           PROSE
     SPEAKS
     BURN WHAT I HAVE PEEVISHLY WRITTEN ABOUT ANY FRIEND  . .    828C LETTER 28           PROSE
     IN HEALTH BUT HAS HAD SUCH A BURN ON HIS HAND AS YOU HAD    842D LETTER 42           PROSE
BURND
     BURND OUT HE ANSWERD HE WAS PIG ENOUGH  . . . . . .           25 EDW THIRD/PS 3       159
     HE CEASD AND BURND SILENT RED CLOUDS ROLL ROUND NECKER       139 FRENCH REVOLTN       105

     BUT THE NOBLES BURND WRATHFUL AT NECKER'S DEPARTURE . . .    139 FRENCH REVOLTN       125
     [THEY] AND BURND HIM IN A HOLY [FIRE] PLACE  . . . . .       177 LIT BOY LST/N         26
     WHERE MANY HAD BEEN BURND BEFORE  . . . . . . . . .          177 LIT BOY LST/N         27
     AND BURND HIM IN A HOLY PLACE . . . . . . . . . . .          219 LIT BOY LST/SE        21
     WHERE MANY HAD BEEN BURND BEFORE  . . . . . . . . .          219 LIT BOY LST/SE        22
```

284

BURND   (CONTINUED)

	PAGE	TITLE	LINE
THAT RAISES WATER INTO CISTERNS BROKEN & BURND IN FIRE .	337	FOUR ZOAS 7B	177
IF THOU REPENTEST NOT & LEAVE THEE AS A ROTTEN BRANCH TO	361	FOUR ZOAS 9	156
BE BURND			
FILLD ME THAT LIKE A FLAME I BURND	429	CRYSTL CABINET	18
BURND TERRIBLE MY PATH BECAME A SOLID FIRE AS BRIGHT .	530	MILTON 39	4
THAT RAISES WATER INTO CISTERNS BROKEN & BURND WITH FIRE	700	JERUSALEM 65	19
HE BURND BEFORE ME LUVAH FRAMD THE KNIFE & LUVAH GAVE . .	722	JERUSALEM 80	22
I HAVE WRITTEN MANY LETTERS TO YOU WHICH I BURND & . .	815C	LETTER 23	PROSE

BURNED

THE SPEARY HAND BURNED ALOFT UNBUCKLED WAS THE SHIELD .	159B	SONG LIBERTY	PROSE
ERROR OR CREATION WILL BE BURNED UP	617B	V LAST JUDG/N	PROSE
THE VEGETATING CITIES ARE BURNED & CONSUMED FROM THE EARTH	679	JERUSALEM 49	12

BURNETH

OF LOS THAT EVER BURNETH WITH FIRE EVER & EVER AMEN . .	530	MILTON 39	12

BURNING

AND THROW ALL PITY ON THE BURNING AIR	10	WHEN EARLY/PS	18
THRO THE FIERCE BURNING NIGHT	14	GWIN KING/PS	104
OR BEARST THY EGIS OER THE BURNING FIELD	15	IMIT SPEN/PS	49
AND BREATHE MY HOPES INTO THE BURNING AIR	26	EDW THIRD/PS 3	221
IVE OFTEN SEEN THE BURNING FIELD OF WAR	31	EDW THIRD/PS 5	39
BURNING UP NATIONS IN YOUR WRATH AND FURY	31	EDW THIRD/PS 6	6
[DISPLAY THY] TO RAISE HIS DARK & BURNING VISAGE	106	TIRIEL 5	5
WHY A TENDER CURB UPON THE YOUTHFUL BURNING BOY . . .	130	BOOK OF THEL 6	19
IN FLAMES OF RED WRATH BURNING	137	FRENCH REVOLTN	67
. . . AROUND HIM CROUD WEEPING IN HIS BURNING ROBE . .	138	FRENCH REVOLTN	87
O HORRIBLE O DREADFUL STATE CONSIDER THE HOT BURNING . .	155C	MARRIAGE HH 17	PROSE
OF A BURNING CITY BENEATH US AT AN IMMENSE DISTANCE . . .	156A	MARRIAGE HH 17	PROSE
[SUCH AS BURNING YOUTH BEGUILES]	165	CRADLE SONG/N	21
TYGER TYGER BURNING BRIGHT	172	THE TYGER/N 1	1
TYGER TYGER BURNING BRIGHT	173	THE TYGER/N 1	22
TYGER TYGER BURNING BRIGHT	173	THE TYGER/N 2	1
TYGER TYGER BURNING BRIGHT	173	THE TYGER/N 2	17
THAT SHIVER IN RELIGIOUS CAVES BENEATH THE BURNING FIRES .	190	V DAU ALBION 2	9
AND SUNK MY HEART INTO THE ABYSS A RED ROUND GLOBE HOT	191	V DAU ALBION 2	33
BURNING			
A QUIVER WITH ITS BURNING STORES A BOW LIKE THAT OF NIGHT	196	AMERICA PREL 1	5
AROUND THEIR SHORES INDIGNANT BURNING WITH THE FIRES OF ORC	200	AMERICA 11	2
THE PLAGUES CREEP ON THE BURNING WINDS DRIVEN BY FLAMES	202	AMERICA 15	11
OF ORC			
TYGER TYGER BURNING BRIGHT	214	THE TYGER/SE	1
TYGER TYGER BURNING BRIGHT	214	THE TYGER/SE	21
LONG PERIODS IN BURNING FIRES LABOURING	225	URIZEN 5	25
ROUND GLOBE HOT BURNING DEEP	228	URIZEN 11	3
I SIEZE THEIR BURNING POWER	238	EUROPE PREL 2	3
THE HOWLING GLOBE BURNING IT FLEW	249	AHANIA 2	18
. . . THEIR BODIES JOIN IN BURNING ANGUISH]	269	FOUR ZOAS 1	181
MY SUN A PESTILENCE BURNING AT NOON & A VAPOUR OF DEATH	290	FOUR ZOAS 2	396
IN NIGHT			
A RED ROUND GLOBE HOT BURNING DEEP DEEP DOWN INTO THE	303	FOUR ZOAS 4	224
ABYSS			
SOON AS HIS BURNING EYES WERE OPEND ON THE ABYSS . . .	306	FOUR ZOAS 5	39
THE HORRID SHAPES & SIGHTS OF TORMENT IN BURNING DUNGEONS	314	FOUR ZOAS 6	103
& IN			
ON RACKS & WHEELS HE BEHELD WOMEN MARCHING OER BURNING	314	FOUR ZOAS 6	106
WASTES			
OVER THE BURNING DESARTS THEN THE DESARTS PASSD INVOLVD	314	FOUR ZOAS 6	110
IN CLOUDS			
THEN CAME HE AMONG FIERY CITIES & CASTLES BUILT OF BURNING	314	FOUR ZOAS 6	115
STEEL			
HOWL IN THE BURNING DENS HIS TYGERS ROAM IN THE REDOUNDING	320	FOUR ZOAS 7	9
SMOKE			
THE BULLS OF LUVAH BREATHING FIRE BELLOW ON BURNING	320	FOUR ZOAS 7	16
PASTURES			
AND NOW A WHIRLING PILLAR OF BURNING SANDS TO OVERWHELM	321	FOUR ZOAS 7	53
THEE			
WITH VISIONS OF SWEET BLISS FAR OTHER THAN THIS BURNING	321	FOUR ZOAS 7	62
CLIME			
. . . MY FEET & HANDS ARE NAILD TO THE BURNING ROCK . . .	322	FOUR ZOAS 7	71
RAHAB BURNING WITH PRIDE & REVENGE DEPARTED FROM LOS . .	351	FOUR ZOAS 8	410
. . . TOGETHER THEY JOIN IN BURNING ANGUISH	381	FOUR ZOAS AD 5	1
[TO BE CONSUMD IN BURNING FIRES]	422	BENEATH/N	14
TO BE CONSUMD IN BURNING FIRES	424	THE GOLDEN NET	13
NOW INTREATING BURNING FIRE	424	THE GOLDEN NET	23
THE SEVEN LAMPS OF THE ALMIGHTY BURNING BEFORE THE THRONE	443C	LAST JUDGMNT/L	PROSE
BRING ME MY BOW OF BURNING GOLD	481	AND DID FEET/M	9
HIS BURNING THIRST & FREEZING HUNGER COME INTO MY HAND . .	481	MILTON 2	5
DOWN SUNK WITH FRIGHT A RED ROUND GLOBE HOT BURNING DEEP	482	MILTON 3	11
DARK GLEAMS BEFORE THE FURNACE-MOUTH A HEAP OF BURNING	485	MILTON 6	17
ASHES			
THEY GAVE SATAN THEIR WINE INDIGNANT AT THE BURNING WRATH	493	MILTON 12	44
AND IN THE SOUTH REMAINS A BURNING FIRE IN THE EAST A VOID	500	MILTON 19	22
DRUNK WITH THE SPIRIT BURNING ROUND THE COUCH OF DEATH	502	MILTON 20	44
THEY STOOD			
WHERE ORC INCESSANT HOWLS BURNING IN FIRES OF ETERNAL YOUTH	517	MILTON 29	29
ITS PLAINS OF BURNING SAND ITS MOUNTAINS OF MARBLE TERRIBLE	529	MILTON 38	17
SUCH A BURNING AND A SHINING LIGHT SEARCH O YE RICH AND	570C	DESC CAT 3	PROSE
IS ROCKY & BURNING AND SEEMS AS IF CONVULSD	608B	V LAST JUDG/N	PROSE
SO LOS IN FURY & STRENGTH IN INDIGNATION & BURNING WRATH	629	JERUSALEM 10	22
OF BURNING SAND THE RIVERS CATARACT & LAKES OF FIRE . . .	634	JERUSALEM 13	41
IN HIDDEN DECEIT THEY ARE VEGETABLE ONLY FIT FOR BURNING	663	JERUSALEM 36	48
PITS OF BITUMEN EVER BURNING ARTIFICIAL RICHES OF	673	JERUSALEM 43	62
THE CANAANITE			

```
                                                        PAGE      TITLE         LINE

BURNING    (CONTINUED)
     IN ERIN'S LAND TOWARD THE NORTH JOINT AFTER JOINT        674 JERUSALEM 44     26
       & BURNING
     LIKE SEVEN BURNING HEAVENS RANGD FROM SOUTH TO NORTH   .  . 684 JERUSALEM 53   14
     IN THE SOUTH REMAINS A BURNING FIRE IN THE EAST A VOID .  . 691 JERUSALEM 59   18
     THY VALLEYS PLAINS OF BURNING SAND THY RIVERS WATERS OF    693 JERUSALEM 60     26
       DEATH
     THE DIVINE VISION BECAME FIRST A BURNING FLAME THEN        702 JERUSALEM 66     41
       A COLUMN
     IN AN ETERNAL CONDEMNATION IN FIERCE BURNING FLAMES   .  . . 722 JERUSALEM 80   13
     DOLOROUS ARE THEIR LAMENTATIONS IN THE BURNING FORGE   .  . 737 JERUSALEM 90   45
     BY SEVERE CONTENTIONS OF FRIENDSHIP & THE BURNING FIRE     738 JERUSALEM 91     18
       OF THOUGHT
     STRUGGLING TO RISE ABOVE THE MOUNTAINS IN HIS BURNING HAND  742 JERUSALEM 95    12
     AND IN MY BURNING BOSOM DWELL   .  .  .  .  .  .  .  .  . 755 EV GOSPEL(E)/N    78
     THEIR LAMPS BURNING & SUCH SHALL SHINE AS THE STARS   .  . . 810D LETTER 21   PROSE
BURNINGS
     WHY LIVE IN UNQUENCHABLE BURNINGS  .  .  .  .  .  .  .  . 224 URIZEN 4          13
     SON OF URIZEN'S SILENT BURNINGS     .  .  .  .  .  .  .  . 249 AHANIA 2          9
BURNS
     BURNS IN MY SOUL AND DOES MY SONG INSPIRE    .  .  .  .  .  10 FRESH FROM/PS    20
     METHINKS THE SHOUT BEGINS THE BATTLE BURNS    .  .  .  .  .  26 EDW THIRD/PS 3  228
     BENEATH ME BURNS ETERNAL FIRE O FOR A HAND TO PLUCK ME     36B COUCH DEATH/PS PROSE
       FORTH
     TILL SHE WHO BURNS WITH YOUTH AND KNOWS NO FIXED LOT IS    193 V DAU ALBION 5   21
       BOUND
     THE GUARDIAN PRINCE OF ALBION BURNS IN HIS NIGHTLY TENT    197 AMERICA 3          1
     THE GUARDIAN PRINCE OF ALBION BURNS IN HIS NIGHTLY TENT    203 AMERICA CANC A    1
     THE GUARDIAN PRINCE OF ALBION BURNS IN HIS NIGHTLY TENT    246 SONG OF LOS 4    21
     AND HIS RIGHT HAND BURNS RED IN ITS CLOUD    .  .  .  .  . 249 AHANIA 2          6
     BURNS TO THE TOP OF HEAVEN AGAINST THEE IN JEALOUSY & FEAR 499 MILTON 18        32
     IN FLAMING FIRE UNCEASING BURNS FROM ETERNITY TO ETERNITY  731 JERUSALEM 86     25
BURNT    SEE SUN-BURNT
     .  .  . AND THE JOYS OF THE COMBAT BURNT FOR FUEL    .  .  . 138 FRENCH REVOLTN  93
     [IN WHAT] [BURNT IN] DISTANT DEEPS OR SKIES    .  .  .  .  . 172 THE TYGER/N 1    5
     [BURNT THE] [THE CRUEL] FIRE OF THINE EYES   .  .  .  .  . 172 THE TYGER/N 1     6
     BURNT IN DISTANT DEEPS OR SKIES  .  .  .  .  .  .  .  .  . 173 THE TYGER/N 2     5
     IN THUNDERS ENDS THE VOICE THEN ALBION'S ANGEL WRATHFUL    198 AMERICA 7          1
       BURNT
     BEFORE THE DEMON RED WHO BURNT TOWARDS AMERICA    .  .  . . 201 AMERICA 12       9
     FROM NORTH TO SOUTH AND BURNT OUTSTRETCHD ON WINGS OF WRATH 201 AMERICA 13      11
       COVRING
     AND THE FIERCE FLAMES BURNT ROUND THE HEAVENS .  .  .  .  . 203 AMERICA 16      23
     BURNT THE FIRE OF THINE EYES   .  .  .  .  .  .  .  .  .  . 214 THE TYGER/SE     6
     A GOLDEN ALTAR BURNT PERFUMES WITH ART CELESTIAL FORMD  . . 285 FOUR ZOAS 2    190
     IT IS BURNT UP THE MOMENT MEN CEASE TO BEHOLD IT I ASSERT  617B V LAST JUDG/N PROSE
     SOON ALL AROUND REMOTE THE HEAVENS BURNT WITH FLAMING FIRES 744 JERUSALEM 96    40
     THE FLEMINGS THEY CALL IT BURNT BONE HAS POSSESSED THE EYE 864C LETTER 61     PROSE
BURST
     AND SWELLING SIGHS BURST FORTH HIS CHILDREN ALL IN ARMS     42B THEN SHE BORE  PROSE
       APPEAR
     .  .  . AND UTTERD A WITHRING HEAT AND THESE WORDS BURST    137 FRENCH REVOLTN  69
       FORTH
     IN STONES AMONG ROOTS OF TREES THE PRISONERS HAVE BURST    137 FRENCH REVOLTN  77
       THEIR DENS
     FOR THE BARS OF CHAOS ARE BURST HER MILLIONS PREPARE THEIR 140 FRENCH REVOLTN 141
       FIERY WAY
     .  .  . LIKE THUNDER-CLOUDS READY TO BURST    .  .  .  .  . 141 FRENCH REVOLTN 170
     FIRE BURST AND ROLLED THRO THE DEEP BLACKNING ALL BENEATH  156B MARRIAGE HH 17 PROSE
     GOLDEN SPAIN BURST THE BARRIERS OF OLD ROME   .  .  .  .  .159A SONG LIBERTY   PROSE
     SOON AS SHE SAW THE TERRIBLE BOY THEN BURST THE VIRGIN CRY 196 AMERICA PREL 2   6
     THE GRAVE IS BURST THE SPICES SHED THE LINEN WRAPPED UP    198 AMERICA 6          2
     SPRING LIKE REDEEMED CAPTIVES WHEN THEIR BONDS & BARS ARE  198 AMERICA 6          5
       BURST
     AND TO RENEW THE FIERY JOY AND BURST THE STONY ROOF   .  . 199 AMERICA 8          9
     THEN BURST THE CENTER FROM ITS ORB AND FOUND A PLACE       204 AMERICA CANC B    6
       BENEATH
     HE BURST THE GIRDLE IN TWAIN     .  .  .  .  .  .  .  .  . 233 URIZEN 20        11
     AGAIN HE BURST IT AGAIN   .  .  .  .  .  .  .  .  .  .  .  . 233 URIZEN 20        14
     BY NIGHT WAS BURST IN TWAIN   .  .  .  .  .  .  .  .  .  . 233 URIZEN 20        17
     SLEPT AS A BIRD IN THE BLUE SHELL THAT SOON SHALL BURST    273 FOUR ZOAS 1     350
       AWAY
     INFOLDED IN THICK CLOUDS FROM WHENCE HIS MIGHTY VOICE BURST 292 FOUR ZOAS 3     13
       FORTH
     SHE ENDED FOR HIS WRATHFUL THRONE BURST FORTH .  .  .  .  . 294 FOUR ZOAS 3    104
     BURST FROM ITS BONDS IN WHIRLPOOLS FIERCE ROARING WITH     295 FOUR ZOAS 3    137
       HUMAN VOICE
     HE BURST IT BUT NEXT MORN ANOTHER GIRDLE SUCCEEDS   .  .  . 307 FOUR ZOAS 5     85
     THE GIRDLE WAS FORMD BY DAY BY NIGHT WAS BURST IN TWAIN    307 FOUR ZOAS 5     90
     .  .  . BURST OPEN & AGAIN CLOSE WITH A [?DISMAL] DEADLY PAIN 309 FOUR ZOAS 5  * 178
     OF PROPHECY & LUVAH HATH BURST HIS WAY FROM ENITHARMON  . . 311 FOUR ZOAS 5   240
     BURST FORTH UPON THE WINDS ABOVE THE TREE OF MYSTERY  .  . 324 FOUR ZOAS 7    168
     HOW ART THOU SHRUNK THY GRAPES THAT BURST IN SUMMER'S VAST 325 FOUR ZOAS 7    190
       EXCESS
     SHE BURST THE GATES OF ENITHARMON'S HEART WITH DIREFUL     328 FOUR ZOAS 7    323
       CRASH
     AND THE GATES [BURST] BROKE IN SUNDER & THEIR ORNAMENTS    328 FOUR ZOAS 7   * 325
       DEFACD
     TILL MANY OF THE DEAD BURST FORTH FROM THE BOTTOMS OF THEIR 328 FOUR ZOAS 7   328
       TOMBS
     THEN MYRIADS OF THE DEAD BURST THRO THE BOTTOMS OF THEIR   340 FOUR ZOAS 7B  * 298
       TOMBS
```

286

		PAGE	TITLE	LINE
BURST	**(CONTINUED)**			
	INTOLERABLE AT LENGTH AN AWFUL WONDER BURST	347	FOUR ZOAS 8	250
	FROM OUT THE FLOOD GATES OF THE SKY THE GATES ARE BURST DOWN POUR	359	FOUR ZOAS 9	72
	THEN WRATH BURST ROUND THE ETERNAL MAN WAS WRATH AGAIN HE CRIED	360	FOUR ZOAS 9	137
	BURST ITS BRIGHT VESSELS SHE FELL DOWN DEAD AT THE FEET OF URIZEN	362	FOUR ZOAS 9	198
	BENEATH THICK CLOUDS DREADFUL LIGHTNINGS BURST & THUNDERS ROLL	372	FOUR ZOAS 9	565
	THE SPIDER THE BAT BURST FROM THE HARDEND SLIME CRYING . .	373	FOUR ZOAS 9	608
	THE FALLING GRAPES THAT ODOROUS BURST UPON THE WINDS ARISE	376	FOUR ZOAS 9	698
	BUT BURST THE CRYSTAL CABINET	429	CRYSTL CABINET	23
	WHEN GRAPES & FIGS BURST THEIR COVERING TO THE JOYFUL AIR	485	MILTON 5	33
	AND THE LOUD-RENDING BARS OF THE CREATION READY TO BURST	667	JERUSALEM 40	26
	BURST FROM HIS BOSOM IN THE TOMB LIKE A PALE SNOWY CLOUD	678	JERUSALEM 48	48
	THEN MARY BURST FORTH INTO A SONG SHE FLOWED LIKE A RIVER OF	695	JERUSALEM 61	28
	BURST FORTH IN STREAMS OF BLOOD UPON THE HEAVENS & DARK NIGHT	696	JERUSALEM 62	31
	THE DUNGEONS BURST & THE PRISONERS SET FREE	718	STOOD AMONG/J	35
	THE FOUR ZOAS IN ALL THEIR FADED MAJESTY BURST OUT IN FURY	734	JERUSALEM 88	55
	BURST THE BOTTOMS OF THE GRAVES & FUNERAL ARKS OF BEULAH	736	JERUSALEM 89	60
BURSTING				
	AH TERRIBLE BIRTH A YOUNG ONE BURSTING WHERE IS THE WEEPING MOUTH	199	AMERICA 9	22
	WORDS ARTICULATE BURSTING IN THUNDERS	223	URIZEN 4	4
	BURSTING ON WINDS MY ODORS	255	AHANIA 5	25
	AND CRUMBLING WITH BURSTING SOBS HEAVES	257	BOOK OF LOS 4	21
	BURSTING FORTH FROM THE LOINS OF ENITHARMON THOU FIERCE TERROR	276	FOUR ZOAS 1	430
	[LAUGHING & MOCKING LUVAH [?BURSTING] ?BREAKING IN THE WOES OF VALA]	SUPP	FOUR ZOAS 2	*
	THICK SHORT INCESSANT BURSTING SOBBING	296	FOUR ZOAS 3	156
	SO THARMAS BELLOWD OER THE OCEAN THUNDRING SOBBING BURSTING	296	FOUR ZOAS 3	176
	FORMING A GIRDLE IN THE DAY & BURSTING IT AT NIGHT . . .	307	FOUR ZOAS 5	89
	WITHIN HER HEART [VALAN] VALA BEGAN TO REANIMATE IN BURSTING SOBS	309	FOUR ZOAS 5	* 179
	THEN BURSTING FROM HIS TROUBLED HEAD	320	FOUR ZOAS 7	25
	THE MOON HIS FURIOUS FOREHEAD CIRCLED WITH BLACK BURSTING THUNDERS	334	FOUR ZOAS 7B	41
	HE CEASD FOR RIVN LINK FROM LINK THE BURSTING UNIVERSE EXPLODES	363	FOUR ZOAS 9	230
	THE ROOTS SHOOT THICK THRO THE SOLID ROCKS BURSTING THEIR WAY	373	FOUR ZOAS 9	604
	WHICH ARE SEEN BURSTING WITH THEIR BIRTHS OF IMMORTALITY	443D	LAST JUDGMNT/L	PROSE
	BUT AS A WINTRY GLOBE DESCENDS PRECIPITANT THRO BEULAH BURSTING	497	MILTON 15	44
	BURSTING THEIR ARKS THEY RISE AGAIN TO LIFE THEY PLAY BEFORE	644	JERUSALEM 21	46
	AND BURSTING FORTH [WITH] HIS FURIOUS IRE	749	EV GOSPEL(B)/N	33
BURSTINGS				
	. . . SHUDDERINGS SOBBINGS BURSTINGS	313	FOUR ZOAS 6	81
	AND UTTERING SUCH WOES SUCH [BURSTINGS] BURSTS SUCH THUNDERINGS	318	FOUR ZOAS 6	* 248
BURSTS				
	AND UTTERING SUCH WOES SUCH [BURSTINGS] BURSTS SUCH THUNDERINGS	318	FOUR ZOAS 6	* 248
	NONE DARE TO WAKE HER SOON SHE BURSTS HER CRIMSON CURTAIND BED	520	MILTON 31	57
	BURSTS FORTH INTO A RAPTUROUS PROPHETIC STRAIN	619C	ILLUS MILTON	PROSE
BURY				
	CURSE ON YOUR [XXX] RUTHLESS HEADS FOR I WILL BURY HER EVEN HERE	100	TIRIEL 1	* 33
	AND NOW YOU FEEL IT DIG A GRAVE & LET US BURY OUR MOTHER	100	TIRIEL 1	42
	BURY YOUR MOTHER BUT YOU CANNOT BURY THE CURSE OF TIRIEL	100	TIRIEL 1	51
	TILL THEY REVIVE OR BURY THEM IN COOL GROTS MAKING LAMENTATION	377	FOUR ZOAS 9	747
	TILL THEY REVIVE OR BURY THEM IN COOL GROTS MAKING LAMENTATION	513	MILTON 27	7
	CAIN WHO WAS ABOUT TO BURY IT	584A	DESC CAT 11	TITLE
	REFUSE & BURY YOUR TALENT IN THE EARTH EVEN THO YOU . .	813A	LETTER 22	PROSE
	MEAN TIME I MUST NOT BURY THE TALENTS IN THE EARTH BUT DO MY	822C	LETTER 26	PROSE
	ALL MY TALENTS I BURY AND DEAD IS MY FAME	829	O WHY BORN/L	8
	& THE USE OF THAT TALENT WHICH IT IS DEATH TO BURY . .	863B	LETTER 60	PROSE
BURYING-PLACE				
	WHAT ARE THOSE GOLDEN BUILDERS DOING WHERE WAS THE BURYING-PLACE	632	JERUSALEM 12	25
BUSH				
	THE BIRDS OF THE BUSH	116	ECCHOING GR/SI	6
	FAINT SHIVERING THEY SIT ON LEAFLESS BUSH OR FROZEN STONE	276	FOUR ZOAS 1	447
BUSIED				
	AND WE WILL SING LIKE THE YOUNG HOUSEWIVES BUSIED . . .	24	EDW THIRD/PS 3	148
	BUT MANY STOOD SILENT & BUSIED IN THEIR FAMILIES	283	FOUR ZOAS 2	126
	THAT SHE IS BUSIED AMONG MY FRIENDS WITH MINE & MY WIFE'S	796A	LETTER 6	PROSE
BUSINESS				
	FIE FIE LORD CLARENCE YOU PROCEED NOT TO BUSINESS . . .	20	EDW THIRD/PS 2	62
	CONSTABLE OR TAKING AWAY THE PARISH BUSINESS HAH	52A	ISLAND MOON 8	PROSE
	BUT THESE CONSIDERATIONS (ARE THE) BUSINESS OF ETERNITY	383C	ANNO WATSON	MARG
	("TO MEN'S BUSINESS AND BOSOMS") ERRATUM TO MEN'S POCKETS	397B	ANNO BACON	MARG
	CHRISTIANITY IS CIVIL BUSINESS ONLY	398B	ANNO BACON	MARG

287

```
                                                         PAGE     TITLE          LINE
BUSINESS    (CONTINUED)
      OR ANY USEFUL THING HIS BUSINESS & BOSOM WAS TO BE LORD   404D ANNO BACON     MARG
         CHANCELLOR
      BACON'S BUSINESS IS NOT INTELLECT OR ART   .   .   .   .   . 409D ANNO BACON   * MARG
      THAT THE WHOLE BUSINESS OF HIS LIFE  .   .   .   .   .   . . 552 WHY CUPID/N     15
      TO RECOVER ART [IS] HAS BEEN THE BUSINESS OF MY LIFE TO THE  600B PUB ADDRESS/N *PROSE
      I WILL NOT REASON & COMPARE MY BUSINESS IS TO CREATE   .  . 629 JERUSALEM 10     21
      MY HEAVENLY FATHER'S BUSINESS   .   .   .   .   .   .   .  . 748 EV GOSPEL (B)/N   8
      I AM DOING MY FATHER'S BUSINESS   .   .   .   .   .   .   . . 750 EV GOSPEL (C)/N   8
      I AM DOING MY FATHER'S BUSINESS   .   .   .   .   .   .   . . 751 EV GOSPEL (D)/N  10
      ABOUT HIS FATHER'S BUSINESS  .   .   .   .   .   .   .   .  . 752 EV GOSPEL (D)/N  54
      I AM DOING MY FATHER'S BUSINESS   .   .   .   .   .   .   . . 757 EV GOSPEL (I)/N  34
      THAT IS THE ?BUSINESS OF PLATO & THE GREEKS &   .   .   .  . 774D ANNO BERKELEY  * MARG
      THE WHOLE BUSINESS OF MAN IS THE ARTS & ALL THINGS COMMON    777C INSC LAOCOON   PROSE
      BUSINESS & THO I LAUGH AT FORTUNE I AM PERSWADED THAT SHE    795D LETTER 6       PROSE
      SO FULL OF THE BUSINESS OF SETTLING THE STICKS & FEATHERS    804A LETTER 16      PROSE
         OF
      BOGNOR A PLEASANT RELIEF FROM BUSINESS IN THE SUMMER   .  . 808C LETTER 19      PROSE
      BUT THE MEER DRUDGERY OF BUSINESS & INTIMATIONS   .   .   . . 812C LETTER 22      PROSE
      PRESSURE OF OTHER BUSINESS BUT THEY WILL GO ON AGAIN SOON    822B LETTER 26      PROSE
      TO SEE MY FRIENDS IN TOWN BEFORE THIS CONTEMPTIBLE BUSINESS  828A LETTER 28      PROSE
      THE PLAYHOUSES WHO EATS & DRINKS FOR BUSINESS NOT FOR NEED   830A LETTER 30      PROSE
      BEING OUT OF HIS LINE OF BUSINESS TO PUBLISH AND   .   .   . 831C LETTER 31      PROSE
      BUSINESS COMES IN & I SHALL BE AT EASE   .   .   .   .   .  . 832C LETTER 32      PROSE
      IF THIS INFERNAL BUSINESS OF THE SOLDIER CAN BE GOT OVER     832C LETTER 32      PROSE
      TO WRITE IMMEDIATELY THO I HAVE NOT DONE HALF THE BUSINESS   834B LETTER 34      PROSE
      BUT WILL NOW IMMEDIATELY PROCEED IN THAT BUSINESS   .   .  . 838B LETTER 37      PROSE
      OF THE ORDINARY BUSINESS OF A REVIEW   .   .   .   .   .   . 842D LETTER 42      PROSE
      THAT HIS MULTIPLICITY OF BUSINESS MAY VERY WELL ACCOUNT FOR  842D LETTER 42      PROSE
      A HISTORY OF THE REVIEWING BUSINESS AS FAR AS I             845C LETTER 44      PROSE
         AM ACQUAINTED
      HEARTILY DEVOTE HIMSELF TO THE BUSINESS IN ALL ITS          845C LETTER 44      PROSE
         LABORIOUS
      THIS BUSINESS ARE NOT WHOLLY AT AN END BUT THAT ON HIS      845C LETTER 44      PROSE
         RETURN
      BECAUSE NO TIME SHOULD BE LOST IN THIS TRULY INTERESTING     849A LETTER 45      PROSE
         BUSINESS
      ITS BUSINESS AMONG HIS FRIENDS   .   .   .   .   .   .   .  . 875A LETTER 80      PROSE
BUSKIND
      THY BUSKIND FEET APPEAR UPON OUR HILLS   .   .   .   .   .  . 3 TO MORNING/PS      8
BUSTLE
      BRING SOME WITH ME FINISHD I AM AT PRESENT IN A BUSTLE   .  . 826D LETTER 28      PROSE
      "BUSY BUSY BUSY I BUSTLE ALONG "   .   .   .   .   .   .   . 837A LETTER 35
BUSY
      WHEN BUSY DAY WAS FADING AND CALM EVENING   .   .   .   .  . 39D SAMSON/PS        PROSE
      THE BUSY BEE HAS NO TIME FOR SORROW   .   .   .   .   .   . . 151A MARRIAGE HH 7   PROSE
      "WE HAVE BEEN INCESSANTLY BUSY IN OUR GREAT REMOVAL"   .  . 800A LETTER 12       PROSE
      COMPLIMENTS TO YOU HE IS SO BUSY THAT I BELIEVE I SHALL      836C LETTER 35      PROSE
      "BUSY BUSY BUSY I BUSTLE ALONG "   .   .   .   .   .   .   . 837A LETTER 35
BUTCHER'S
      AND YET FORGIVES THE BUTCHER'S KNIFE   .   .   .   .   .   . . 431 AUGURIES        24
BUTCHERS
      BELIEVE AS MANY BOOKSELLERS AS THERE ARE BUTCHERS &   .  . 798C LETTER 10       PROSE
BUTE
      DAN BUTE CAITNES CLAKMANAN NAPTHALI NAIRN INVERNES          638 JERUSALEM 16      55
         LINLITHGO
BUTTER
      KNOWING & FEELING THAT WE ALL HAVE NEED OF BUTTER   .   .  . 556 IF MEN ACT/N      4
BUTTERFLY
      A FLEA OR A BUTTERFLY OR A COCK CHAFER   .   .   .   .   . . 58C ISLAND MOON 10  PROSE
      SO WEAK THE GILDED BUTTERFLY SCARCE PERCHES ON MY HEAD   . . 127 BOOK OF THEL 1   18
      HES MY BUTTERFLY   .   .   .   .   .   .   .   .   .   .   . . 178 THE FAIRY/N      18
      AND CAUGHT HIM IN MY HAT AS BOYS KNOCK DOWN A BUTTERFLY      237 EUROPE INTRO      9
      KILL NOT THE MOTH NOR BUTTERFLY   .   .   .   .   .   .   . . 432 AUGURIES        39
BUTTON
      FOR A [ BUTTON A BAUBLE [BUCKLE] A BEAD OR A]   .   .   . . 548 ON GREAT ENC/N    2
      POOR SPIRITUAL KNOWLEDGE IS NOT WORTH A BUTTON   .   .   . . 752 EV GOSPEL(D)/N   40
BUTTS
      PLEASE TO TELL MRS BUTTS THAT WE HAVE DEDICATED A CHAMBER    803B LETTER 15      PROSE
      MY & MY WIFE & SISTER'S LOVE & RESPECTS TO MRS BUTTS   .  . 803C LETTER 15      PROSE
      TO MY FRIEND BUTTS I WRITE   .   .   .   .   .   .   .   .  . 804 TO BUTTS/L       1
      MRS BUTTS WILL I HOPE EXCUSE MY NOT HAVING FINISHD THE       806A LETTER 16      PROSE
         PORTRAIT I
      MRS BUTTS WILL EXCUSE THE FOLLOWING LINES   .   .   .   .  . 806B LETTER 16      PROSE
      TO MRS BUTTS   .   .   .   .   .   .   .   .   .   .   .   . . 806B TO MRS BUTTS/L TITLE
      ACCOMODATION IN MY POWER TO RECIEVE YOU & MRS BUTTS   .   . . 808B LETTER 19      PROSE
      AS IS MOST AGREEABLE TO YOU IF YOU & MRS BUTTS SHOULD THINK  808C LETTER 19      PROSE
      WIFE WHO DESIRES HER KINDEST LOVE TO MRS BUTTS & YOURSELF    808C LETTER 19      PROSE
      I TRANSMIT TO MRS BUTTS AN ATTEMPT [TO] AT YOUR LIKENESS     808D LETTER 20     *PROSE
      MY WIFE JOINS WITH ME IN LOVE TO YOU & MRS BUTTS   .   .  . 810A LETTER 20      PROSE
      MY WIFE DESIRES HER KINDEST LOVE TO MRS BUTTS & I HAVE  . . 813B LETTER 22      PROSE
      PRAY GIVE MY LOVE TO MRS BUTTS & YOUR FAMILY I AM YOURS      913C LETTER 22      PROSE
         SINCERELY
      THE MINIATURE I PROMISSD TO MRS BUTTS I ANSWER I HAVE NOT    815C LETTER 23      PROSE
      & IS MINE PRAY GIVE MY WIFE'S LOVE WITH MINE TO MRS BUTTS    815D LETTER 23      PROSE
      AND BUTTS SHALL GIVE WHAT FUSELI GAVE   .   .   .   .   . . 817 HAPPINESS/L       39
      MUST MY DEAR BUTTS FEEL COLD NEGLECT   .   .   .   .   .   . . 817 HAPPINESS/L      45
      NOT MENTION OUR SICKNESS TO YOU & SHOULD NOT TO MR BUTTS     819C LETTER 25      PROSE
      I SPOKE OF TO MR BUTTS BUT I DID NOT TELL HIM SO PLAIN       819D LETTER 25      PROSE
         & WISH
      SO PLAIN I TOLD MR BUTTS THAT I DID NOT WISH TO EXPLORE      819D LETTER 25      PROSE
      BUT MY LETTER TO MR BUTTS APPEARS TO ME NOT TO BE            820B LETTER 25      PROSE
         SO EXPLICIT
```

		PAGE	TITLE	LINE

BUTTS (CONTINUED)
& GIVE OUR LOVES TO MRS BUTTS & YOUR AMIABLE FAMILY . . . . 823C LETTER 26   PROSE
DELIGHTFUL THEN I AM DETERMIND THAT MRS BUTTS SHALL HAVE   824B LETTER 27   PROSE
& YOURS & MINE PRAY GIVE MY & MY WIFE'S LOVE TO MRS BUTTS   826A LETTER 27   PROSE
YOU & MRS BUTTS & ALL YOUR FAMILY I AGAIN TAKE THE LIBERTY   829A LETTER 28   PROSE
MR BUTTS IS TO HAVE A PROOF COPY FOR THREE GUINEAS . . .   877D LETTER 88   PROSE
MR BUTTS GREAT MARLBOROUGH STREET OXFORD STREET LONDON . . SUPP ADDRESSES/L *TITLE
BUTTS'S
DEAR BROTHER YOUR LETTER MENTIONING MR BUTTS'S ACCOUNT OF   819B LETTER 25   *PROSE
MY AGUE
BUXOM
AND TUNES HER [?CHAUNTANT] NOTES WHEN BUXOM JOY DOTH FAN   43B WOE CRIED MUSE *PROSE
HIS WINGS
BUY
SET STATIONS ON THIS BREEDING EARTH & LET US BUY & SELL   283 FOUR ZOAS 2   129
WHAT IS THE PRICE OF EXPERIENCE DO MEN BUY IT FOR A SONG   290 FOUR ZOAS 2   397
WISDOM IS SOLD IN THE DESOLATE MARKET WHERE NONE COME TO   290 FOUR ZOAS 2   400
BUY
SHALL BUY & SELL THE MISER'S LANDS . . . .   433 AUGURIES   82
DOES THAT WHOLE NATION SELL & BUY . . . .   433 AUGURIES   84
TO SELL & NOT TO BUY PICTURES THE ARTIST WHO . . . . .   452C ANNO REYNOLDS   MARG
IF YOU MEAN THAT THE FLORENTINES [TO] SHOULD BUY . . . .   542 FLORENTINE/N   *   23
A JOCKEY THAT IS ANY THING OF A JOCKEY WILL NEVER BUY .   597C PUB ADDRESS/N   PROSE
WILL NEVER BUY A PICTURE BY THE COLOUR . . . .   597C PUB ADDRESS/N   PROSE
THEY BUY HIS DAUGHTERS THAT THEY MAY HAVE POWER TO SELL   656 JERUSALEM 30   29
HIS SONS
& TRANSLATE & COPY & BUY & SELL & CRITICISE BUT NOT MAKE   778D HOMERS POETRY PROSE
BUYER
TWELVE MONTHS WHEN IT WILL BE DELIVERED TO THE BUYER . . 563B DESC CAT   PROSE
EXPENSIVE TO THE BUYER THOSE I PRINTED FOR MR HUMPHRY . . 867A LETTER 66   PROSE
BUYS
WHO BUYS WHOLE CORN FIELDS INTO WASTES AND SINGS UPON THE   193 V DAU ALBION 5   15
HEATH
BUZZ
LIKE SHOULDRING FIRE OR IN THE BUZZ OF CITIES FLIES ABROAD   42C THEN SHE BORE PROSE
BUZZING
AND CORDED SHIPS HER MERCHANTS BUZZING ROUND . . . . .   19 EDW THIRD/PS 2   12
BY AND BY
GREAT DEAL MORE THAT WE SHALL ALL HEAR BY AND BY AND I CAME   29C EDW THIRD/PS 4 PROSE
BYRON
TO LORD BYRON IN THE WILDERNESS . . . .   779C GHOST ABEL 1   PROSE
(RE BYRON) IF MORALITY WAS CHRISTIANITY SOCRATES WAS THE   786D ANNO THORNTON   MARG
SAVIOUR
BYSSHE'S
IT WAS BYSSHE'S ART OF POETRY SHE OPEND THE   440D MEMORANDUM/N 5 PROSE
FOLLOWING...BEHN
CABINET
THE CRYSTAL CABINET . . . .   429B CRYSTL CABINET TITLE
SHE PUT ME INTO HER CABINET . . . .   429 CRYSTL CABINET   3
THIS CABINET IS FORMD OF GOLD . . . .   429 CRYSTL CABINET   5
BUT BURST THE CRYSTAL CABINET . . . .   429 CRYSTL CABINET   23
THE CANTERBURY PILGRIMS FROM CHAUCER A CABINET PICTURE   560B EXHIBITION ADV PROSE
IN FRESCO
OF NELSON AND PITT WITH VARIETY OF CABINET PICTURES . . . 560C EXHIBITION ADV PROSE
ALL THE LITTLE OLD PICTURES CALLED CABINET PICTURES . . . 561A EXHIBITION ADV PROSE
ALL THE GENUINE OLD LITTLE PICTURES CALLED CABINET PICTURES 566B DESC CAT 2   PROSE
NOTE I MEAN FRESCO EASEL OR CABINET PICTURES . . . . . 598A PUB ADDRESS/N   PROSE
BY THIS MEANS YOU WILL HAVE A NUMBER OF CABINET PICTURES   792C LETTER 4   PROSE
CABINETS
OTHERS CABINETS RICHLY FABRICATE OF GOLD & IVORY . . . . 515 MILTON 28   8
CABRIOLET
THURSDAY MORNING OUR CARRIAGE WILL BE A CABRIOLET FOR . 875B LETTER 81   PROSE
CABUL
IN VAIN THEY ROLLD APART THEY ARE FIXD INTO THE LAND OF   715 JERUSALEM 74   57
CABUL
SHRUNK TO A NARROW DOLEFUL FORM IN THE DARK LAND OF CABUL   721 JERUSALEM 79   63
CADENCE
WITH SONGS OF SWEETEST CADENCE TO THE TURNING SPINDLE &   346 FOUR ZOAS 8   212
REEL
A MONOTONOUS CADENCE LIKE THAT USED BY MILTON . . . . . 621C JERUSALEM 3   PROSE
CADENCES
BODIES OF VEGETATION SINGING LULLING CADENCES TO DRIVE AWAY 342 FOUR ZOAS 8   38
OF ENITHARMON SINGING LULLING CADENCES ON THE WIND . . . 344 FOUR ZOAS 8   114
OF ENITHARMON'S LOOM PLAY LULLING CADENCES ON THE WINDS   485 MILTON 6   6
OF ALBION
AND MELTING CADENCES THAT LURE THE SLEEPERS OF BEULAH DOWN   524 MILTON 34   29
VARIETY IN EVERY LINE BOTH OF CADENCES & NUMBER OF   621D JERUSALEM 3   PROSE
SYLLABLES
CADENCES & PLAYING IN SWEET INTOXICATION AMONG THE   733 JERUSALEM 88   24
GLISTENING
ENITHARMON WHO AT HER SHINING LOOMS SINGS LULLING CADENCES   734 JERUSALEM 88   45
CONWENNA SAT ABOVE WITH SOLEMN CADENCES SHE DREW . . . . 736 JERUSALEM 90   21
CAESAR
THE ANCIENT BRITONS ACCORDING TO CAESAR [THE FRONTISPIECE]   208C SUBJCTS HIST/N TITLE
THE DRUIDS THE LANDING OF JULIUS CAESAR . . . . 208D SUBJCTS HIST/N TITLE
IF CAESAR IS RIGHT CHRIST IS WRONG BOTH IN POLITICS   396D ANNO BACON   MARG
& RELIGION
CAESAR SEEMS TO ME A VERY SMALL MATTER & SO HE SEEMD TO   410D ANNO BACON   MARG
JESUS
BUT DANTE GIVES TOO MUCH ?CAESAR HE IS NOT A REPUBLICAN   413B ANNO BOYD   MARG
[IN ROME (?WAS NOT) CAESAR (A) DUTCH PAINTER] . . . . . SUPP ANNO REYNOLDS * MARG
AND AT LAST HE WOULD HAVE BEEN CAESAR HIMSELF . . . . . 752 EV GOSPEL(D)/N   42

289

```
                                                            PAGE     TITLE          LINE
CAESAR    (CONTINUED)
      THAT IS ON CAESAR OR EMPIRE OR NATURAL RELIGION  . . . .  776B INSC LAOCOON     PROSE
      ("WILL") SO YOU SEE THAT GOD IS JUST SUCH A TYRANT        788C ANNO THORNTON    * MARG
         AS AUGUSTUS CAESAR
      OUR FATHER AUGUSTUS CAESAR WHO ART IN THESE  . . . . .    788D ANNO THORNTON    * MARG
      FOR ALL IS DEBTS & TAXES BETWEEN [XXX] CAESAR & US  . . . 788D ANNO THORNTON    * MARG
      IS HERESY & REBELLION AGAINST CAESAR VIRGIL'S ONLY GOD .  789B ANNO THORNTON    * MARG
      THE THUNDER OF EGYPT CAESAR  . . . . . . . . . .          SUPP ILLUS DANTE 3    *PROSE
      [CAESAR SAID HE'D RATHER BE THE (FIRST IN) A VILLAGE (THAN) SUPP ANNO REYNOLDS  * MARG
         SECOND]
CAESAR'S
      THOUGHT IS ACT CHRIST'S ACTS WERE NOTHING TO CAESAR'S IF  400C ANNO BACON       MARG
         THIS IS NOT
      DANTE WAS AN EMPEROR'S A CAESAR'S MAN  . . . . . . .      413B ANNO BOYD        MARG
      CAME FROM CAESAR'S LAUREL CROWN  . . . . . . . . .        433 AUGURIES          98
      HE HAD SOON BEEN BLOODY CAESAR'S ELF  . . . . . . . .     752 EV GOSPEL(D)/N    41
      MOCKD BY CAESAR'S SOLDIERS WILLINGLY & [I HOPE THEY WILL] 787A ANNO THORNTON    MARG
      & NOT CAESAR'S OR SATAN'S AMEN  . . . . . . . . . .       788B ANNO THORNTON    * MARG
CAESARS
      WHILE YOU ACQUIT & FLATTER THE ALEXANDERS & CAESARS  . .  683A JERUSALEM 52     PROSE
CAFFRARIA
      EGYPT LYBIA ETHIOPIA GUINEA CAFFRARIA NEGROLAND MOROCCO   712 JERUSALEM 72      40
CAGE
      AND SHUT ME IN HIS GOLDEN CAGE  . . . . . . . . . .       6 HOW SWEET/PS        12
      IN MATRIMONY'S GOLDEN CAGE  . . . . . . . . . . .         56 HAIL MATRIM/IM     27
      AND AFTER DINNER WE WILL WALK INTO THE CAGE OF HAR  . . . 102 TIRIEL 3          14
      AND [HE] HEARD HAR SING IN THE GREAT CAGE & SLEPT UPON    103 TIRIEL 3          *  23
         OUR FLEECES
      SIT IN A CAGE AND SING  . . . . . . . . . . . .          124 SCHOOL BOY/SI     17
      AND TO CAGE THE FAIRIES & ELVES  . . . . . . . . .        183 MOTTO SONGS/N     4
      A ROBIN RED BREAST IN A CAGE  . . . . . . . . . .         431 AUGURIES          5
CAIAPHAS    SEE CAIPHAS
      [FRIEND CAIAPHAS IS ONE DO WHAT HE CAN]  . . . . . .      544 SOME MEN/N        3
      IS CAIAPHAS THE DARK PREACHER OF DEATH  . . . . . . .     718 STOOD AMONG/J     18
      IF CAIAPHAS YOU WILL OBEY  . . . . . . . . . . .          749 EV GOSPEL(B)/N    21
      OBEY HIMSELF TO CAIAPHAS  . . . . . . . . . . . .         750 EV GOSPEL(C)/N    30
      OBEYD HIMSELF TO CAIAPHAS  . . . . . . . . . . .          752 EV GOSPEL(D)/N    64
      ASK CAIAPHAS FOR HE CAN TELL  . . . . . . . . . .         756 EV GOSPEL(I)/N    16
CAIAPHAS'
      THAT QUITE UNNERVD [THE ?GUILTY] CAIAPHAS' HAND  . . . .  752 EV GOSPEL(D)/N *  58
CAIN
      CAIN WHO WAS ABOUT TO BURY IT  . . . . . . . . . .        584A DESC CAT 11      TITLE
      & CAIN WITH THE FLINT IN HIS HAND WITH WHICH HE SLEW  .   606B V LAST JUDG/N    PROSE
      BENEATH THE FALLING FIGURE OF CAIN  . . . . . . . .       607B V LAST JUDG/N    PROSE
      SATAN CAIN TUBAL NIMROD PHAROH PRIAM BLADUD BELIN  . .    713 JERUSALEM 73      35
      ABEL IS DEAD & CAIN SLEW HIM WE SHALL ALSO DIE A DEATH .  780 GHOST ABEL 1      19
      AS THOU HAST SAID SO IS IT COME TO PASS MY DESIRE IS UNTO 780 GHOST ABEL 2      7
         CAIN
      CAIN SERPENT ABEL EVE ADAM  . . . . . . . . . .          SUPP INSC HERVEY      *TITLE
CAINA
      ADAH ZILLAH CAINA NAAMAH TAMAR RAHAB TIRZAH MARY  . . .   350 FOUR ZOAS 8       365
CAINAH
      CAINAH & ADA & ZILLAH & NAAMAH WIFE OF NOAH  . . . . .    696 JERUSALEM 62      9
CAINAN
      ADAM SETH ENOS CAINAN MAHALALEEL JARED ENOCH  . . . . .   528 MILTON 37         36
      NOAH SHEM ARPHAXAD CAINAN THE SECOND SALAH HEBER  . . .   528 MILTON 37         38
      ADAM SETH ENOS CAINAN MAHALALEEL JARED ENOCH  . . . . .   716 JERUSALEM 75      11
      NOAH SHEM ARPHAXAD CAINAN THE SECOND SALAH HEBER  . . .   716 JERUSALEM 75      13
CAIN'S
      GIANTS OF MIGHTY ARM BEFORE THE FLOOD CAIN'S CITY  . . .  41A THEN SHE BORE     PROSE
      JEHOVAH HE WHO SHALL TAKE CAIN'S LIFE MUST ALSO DIE O ABEL 780 GHOST ABEL 1     15
      CAIN'S CITY BUILT WITH HUMAN BLOOD NOT BLOOD OF BULLS     781 GHOST ABEL 2      17
         & GOATS
CAIPHAS    SEE CAIAPHAS
      AS THOSE OF CAIPHAS OR PILATE OR HEROD  . . . . . . .     407A ANNO BACON       MARG
      THESE ARE CAIPHAS & PILATE TWO STATES WHERE ALL THOSE  .  608D V LAST JUDG/N    PROSE
      & JUSTICE CAIPHAS HAS A BLUE FLAME LIKE A MITER ON HIS HEAD 608D V LAST JUDG/N  PROSE
      BEFORE CAIPHAS & PILATE ARE JUDAS & THOSE OF HIS CLASS    608D V LAST JUDG/N    PROSE
      SO CAIPHAS THOUGHT JESUS  . . . . . . . . . . .          740B JERUSALEM 93     TITLE
      AND CAIPHAS WAS IN HIS OWN MIND  . . . . . . . . .        748 EV GOSPEL(A)/N    11
      IF HE HAD CAIPHAS WOULD FORGIVE  . . . . . . . . .        752 EV GOSPEL(D)/N    33
      AND CAIPHAS & PILATE MEN  . . . . . . . . . . .          758 EV GOSPEL (1)     3
      LOUD PILATE HOWLD LOUD CAIPHAS YELLD  . . . . . . .       758 EV GOSPEL (2)     19
      CAIPHAS PILATE & HEROD WERE LEARNED  . . . . . . .        786D ANNO THORNTON    MARG
CAITHNESS
      FROM CAITHNESS IN THE NORTH TO LIZARD-POINT & DOVER IN    485 MILTON 6          7
         THE SOUTH
      CAITHNESS & ROCKY DURNESS PENTLAND & JOHN GROATS HOUSE .  512 MILTON 26         15
      AND LULLING HARMONIES BENEATH THE LOOMS FROM CAITHNESS    728 JERUSALEM 83      70
         IN THE NORTH
CAITNES
      DAN BUTE CAITNES CLAKMANAN NAPTHALI NAIRN INVERNES        638 JERUSALEM 16      55
         LINLITHGO
CAKE
      AS TO LAYING ON THE WAX IT IS AS FOLLOWS TAKE A CAKE  .   790C LETTER 2         PROSE
CALAIS
      A FAMINE OCCASIOND BY THE POPISH INTERDICT EDWARD         208D SUBJCTS HIST/N   TITLE
         AT CALAIS
      THE KEYS OF CALAIS  . . . . . . . . . . . . .           SUPP ILLUS HISTORY    *TITLE
CALCULATED
      TWO FOLLOWING DISCOURSES ARE PARTICULARLY CALCULATED  . . 461C ANNO REYNOLDS    MARG
```

		PAGE	TITLE	LINE

CALCULATION
NOR OF SIR ISAAC NEWTON'S CALCULATION . . . . 542 FLORENTINE/N 29

CALD
[HE] URIZEN CALD TOGETHER . . . . 382 FOUR ZOAS AD 6 * 5
PARTICULARLY IN A SUNDAY PAPER CALD THE EXAMINER PUBLISHD 592C PUB ADDRESS/N PROSE

CALEB
OSHEA AND CALEB FIGHT THEY CONTEND IN THE VALLEYS OF OF 672 JERUSALEM 43 37
PEOR
THE SON OF BEOR HAVE GIVEN THEIR POWER TO JOSHUA & CALEB 680 JERUSALEM 49 59

CALENDAR
SHALL BE MARKED ON MY CALENDAR WITH A STAR OF THE FIRST 801B LETTER 13 PROSE
MAGNITUDE

CALIBAN
PROSPERO HAD ONE CALIBAN & I HAVE TWO . . . . 538 OLD ACQUAINT/N 2

CALL
BUT NOW FOR BLIND-MAN'S BUFF THEY CALL . . . . . . 16 BLIND-MANS/PS 17
AND THIS SIR THOMAS YOU CALL FEAR YOUR FEAR . . . . . 22 EDW THIRD/PS 3 39
THERE SIR THOMAS DO YOU CALL THAT FEAR . . . . . . 22 EDW THIRD/PS 3 47
MY VOICE HATH USED DECEIT HOW SHOULD I CALL ON HIM WHO 36A COUCH DEATH/PS PROSE
IS TRUTH
CALL THINE ALLURING ARTS AND HONEST-SEEMING BROW . . . . 38A SAMSON/PS PROSE
I CALL THEM BY THE NAMES OF THOSE SECTS THO THE . . . 44A ISLAND MOON 1 PROSE
TO CALL A MAN A BLOCKHEAD THAT YOU KNOW NOTHING OF . . . 44D ISLAND MOON 1 PROSE
FOOL SAID HE WHO DO YOU CALL FOOL . . . . 45A ISLAND MOON 1 PROSE
CALL ME [ASS ARSE] ASS . . . . 46B ISLAND MOON 2 PROSE
THEY CALL WOMEN THE WEAKEST VESSEL . . . . 53B ISLAND MOON 8 PROSE
I HOPE NO ONE WILL CALL WHAT I HAVE WRITTEN CAVILLING . . 88A ANNO LAVATER MARG
WE WHO ARE PHILOSOPHERS OUGHT NOT TO CALL . . . . . . 88C ANNO LAVATER MARG
WE CALL THE OMISSIONS OF INTELLECT SPRINGING FROM POVERTY 88C ANNO LAVATER MARG
AND I WILL BRING THEE FOOD OLD MAN TILL DEATH SHALL CALL 103 TIRIEL 3 35
THEE HENCE
WHAT HEUXOS CALL THY FATHER FOR I [?MUST] MEAN TO SPORT 105 TIRIEL 4 49
TO NIGHT
WHAT SHALL I CALL THEE . . . . 118 INFANT JOY/SI 3
SWEET JOY I CALL THEE . . . . 118 INFANT JOY/SI 9
FOR HE HEARS THE LAMB'S INNOCENT CALL . . . . 118 SHEPHERD/SI 5
LIVES NOT ALONE NOR FOR ITSELF FEAR NOT AND I WILL CALL 129 BOOK OF THEL 3 27
FROM THESE CONTRARIES SPRING WHAT THE RELIGIOUS CALL GOOD 149B MARRIAGE HH 3 PROSE
& EVIL
WE OF ISRAEL TAUGHT THAT THE POETIC GENIUS AS YOU NOW CALL 153D MARRIAGE HH 12 PROSE
IT
CALL THAT VIRGINITY THAT WISHES BUT ACTS NOT . . . . . 160B SONG LIBERTY PROSE
I CALL WITH HOLY VOICE KINGS OF THE SOUNDING AIR . . . . 190 V DAU ALBION 2 14
THE EAGLES AT HER CALL DESCEND & REND THEIR BLEEDING PREY 190 V DAU ALBION 2 17
TELL ME WHERE DWELL THE THOUGHTS FORGOTTEN TILL THOU CALL 192 V DAU ALBION 4 3
THEM FORTH
[WHO CALL IT FANCY [&] OR SHUT THE GATES OF SENSE . . . 205 AMERICA CANC C 22
ETERNALS I HEAR YOUR CALL GLADLY . . . . 222 URIZEN 2 5
WHO SHALL I CALL WHO SHALL I SEND . . . . 240 EUROPE 5 2
ARISE O RINTRAH THEE I CALL & PALAMABRON THEE . . . . . 240 EUROPE 5 4
ARISE ETHINTHUS THO THE EARTH-WORM CALL . . . . 243 EUROPE 13 16
LET HIM CALL IN VAIN . . . . 243 EUROPE 13 17
SHALL NOT THE KING CALL FOR FAMINE FROM THE HEATH . . . 247 SONG OF LOS 6 9
CALL FOR FIRES IN THE CITY . . . . 247 SONG OF LOS 6 20
CALL TO THY DARK ARMD HOSTS FOR ALL THE SONS OF MEN MUSTER 275 FOUR ZOAS 1 406
TOGETHER
THEY CALL JESUS THE CHRIST & THEY IN HIM & HE IN THEM . . 277 FOUR ZOAS 1 473
LOS SPOKE THY GOD IN VAIN SHALL CALL THEE IF BY MY STRONG 289 FOUR ZOAS 2 336
POWER
THEY CALL THY LIONS TO THE FIELDS OF BLOOD THEY ROWZE THY 292 FOUR ZOAS 3 * 37
TYGERS
CALL [VALAN] VALA FROM HER CLOSE RECESS IN ALL HER DARK 307 FOUR ZOAS 5 * 64
DECEIT
AT HIS ENORMOUS CALL THEY FLEE INTO THE HEAVENS OF HEAVENS 308 FOUR ZOAS 5 118
I WILL COMMAND MY WINDS & THEY SHALL SCATTER THEM OR CALL 334 FOUR ZOAS 7B 54
AND CALL IT DEMONSTRATION BLIND TO ALL THE SIMPLE RULES 337 FOUR ZOAS 7B 186
OF LIFE
CALL FORTH THY SMILES OF SOFT DECEIT CALL FORTH 338 FOUR ZOAS 7B 208
THY CLOUDY TEARS
[AND THEN CALL URIZEN & LUVAH & THARMAS & URTHONA] . . . 348 FOUR ZOAS 8 266
MINGLED WITH THE CONFUSION WHO SHALL CALL THEM FROM THE 358 FOUR ZOAS 9 31
GRAVE
HARNESSD THEY CALLD TO URIZEN THE HEAVENS MOVED AT THEIR 365 FOUR ZOAS 9 309
CALL
I WILL CALL & WHO SHALL ANSWER ME I WILL SING WHO SHALL 368 FOUR ZOAS 9 440
REPLY
HERE WILL I BUILD MYSELF A HOUSE & HERE I'LL CALL ON HIS 369 FOUR ZOAS 9 453
NAME
THEN VALA LIFTED UP HER HANDS TO HEAVEN TO CALL ON ENION 370 FOUR ZOAS 9 498
O HOW VIRTUOUS CHRIST CAME NOT TO CALL THE VIRTUOUS . . 395D ANNO WATSON MARG
WHO DOES THE BISHOP CALL BAD MEN ARE THEY . . . . . . 396A ANNO WATSON MARG
WHAT SUCH MEN CALL GREAT IS INDEED DETESTABLE . . . . 407A ANNO BACON MARG
[THOU DIDST CALL THAT LOVE A SIN] . . . . 415 MY SPECTRE/N 20
I SAID TO MOSER THESE THINGS THAT YOU CALL FINISHD ARE . 449C ANNO REYNOLDS MARG
THE GREAT BACON HE IS CALLD I CALL HIM THE LITTLE BACON 459C ANNO REYNOLDS MARG
TO CALL ALL OTHER OPINIONS UNSOLID . . . . 474A ANNO REYNOLDS MARG
[IF THE ?INSPIRATION ?IS GREAT ?WHY CALL IT MADNESS] . SUPP ANNO REYNOLDS * MARG
CORPOREAL WAR PAINTERS ON YOU I CALL SCULPTORS ARCHITECTS 480C MILTON 1 PROSE
ALL MAY BE WELL SILENT REMAIN WHILE I CALL LOS AND SATAN 487 MILTON 7 32
YOUR LABOURS CALL YOU PALAMABRON IS ALSO IN SAD DILEMMA 488 MILTON 8 17
AND THEREFORE PALAMABRON DARED NOT TO CALL A SOLEMN 492 MILTON 11 24
ASSEMBLY

	PAGE	TITLE	LINE

CALL   (CONTINUED)

HE HEARD THEM CALL IN PRAYER ALL THE DIVINE FAMILY . . .	504	MILTON 21	35
MADMAN I HAVE BEEN CALLD FOOL THEY CALL THEE	538	MADMAN CALLD/N	1
THOU CALLST ME MADMAN BUT I CALL THEE BLOCKHEAD	539	F(LAXMAN)/N 1	2
THE FLORENTINES CALL IT AN ENGLISH FETCH	542	FLORENTINE/N	15
YOU CALL ME MAD TIS FOLLY TO DO SO	544	F(LAXMAN)/N 2	1
AND I CALL UPON COLONEL WARDLE	548	ON GREAT ENC/N	5
THEY MAY CALL IT MADNESS BUT IT IS TRUE	566B	DESC CAT 2	PROSE
AND WHAT CONNOISSEURS CALL TOUCH I KNOW BY EXPERIENCE .	575B	DESC CAT 3	PROSE
CALL EXPRESSION BUT THIS IS A FALSE NOTION OF EXPRESSION	585A	DESC CAT 15	PROSE
CALL THAT THE PUBLIC VOICE WHICH IS THEIR ERROR	597	PUBLC VOICE/PA	1
THE GREATEST MISCHIEF I CALL FOR PUBLIC PROTECTION . . .	602A	PUB ADDRESS/N	PROSE
IN WHAT WE CALL THE DARK AGES	604A	INSC ARIMATHEA	PROSE
BUT WHAT CRITICS CALL THE FABLE IS VISION ITSELF . . .	604D	V LAST JUDG/N	PROSE
ARE OPEND & THE DEAD AWAKE & OBEY THE CALL OF THE TRUMPET	609C	V LAST JUDG/N	PROSE
WHAT YOU CALL MORAL VIRTUE & YOU CANNOT HAVE	616A	V LAST JUDG/N	PROSE
OF THE HUMAN RACE WHO HATE WHAT YOU CALL MORAL VIRTUE .	616A	V LAST JUDG/N	PROSE
THY BRETHREN CALL THEE AND THY FATHERS AND THY SONS . .	622	JERUSALEM 4	11
YOU CALL DIVINE IS BUT A WORM SEVENTY INCHES LONG . . .	659	JERUSALEM 33	6
HIS OWN WIFE FOR THE TERRORS OF CHASTITY THAT THEY CALL	663	JERUSALEM 36	46
WE CALL JESUS THE CHRIST AND HE IN US AND WE IN HIM . .	665	JERUSALEM 38	20
I CALL THEM BY THEIR ENGLISH NAMES ENGLISH THE ROUGH BASEMENT	668	JERUSALEM 40	58
BUT SHOULD THE WATCH FIENDS FIND IT THEY WOULD CALL IT SIN	668	JERUSALEM 41	19
OF WHAT YOU CALL NATURAL RELIGION AND NATURAL PHILOSOPHY	682C	JERUSALEM 52	PROSE
DOES THE VOICE OF MY LORD CALL ME AGAIN AM I PURE THRO HIS MERCY	695	JERUSALEM 61	36
CALL HER PURE AS HE DID IN THE DAYS OF HER INFANCY WHEN SHE	695	JERUSALEM 61	39
AND CALL IT DEMONSTRATION BLIND TO ALL THE SIMPLE RULES OF LIFE	700	JERUSALEM 65	28
CALL FORTH THY SMILES OF SOFT DECEIT CALL FORTH THY CLOUDY TEARS	701	JERUSALEM 65	54
THEY CALL THE ROCKS PARENTS OF MEN & ADORE THE FROWNING CHAOS	704	JERUSALEM 67	15
I CALL UPON YOU IN THE NAME OF JESUS	717B	JERUSALEM 77	PROSE
I CALL TO CANAAN & MOAB IN MY NIGHT WATCHES THEY MOURN .	727	JERUSALEM 83	17
MAY TAKE THE AGGREGATE & YOU CALL THE AGGREGATE MORAL LAW	738	JERUSALEM 91	28
AND YOU CALL THAT SWELLD & BLOATED FORM A MINUTE PARTICULAR	738	JERUSALEM 91	29
THAT THEY MAY CALL A [CRIME] SHAME & SIN	755	EV GOSPEL(E)/N	63
OR CALL MEN WISE FOR NOT BELIEVING	756	EV GOSPEL(H)/N	4
WHAT WE CALL ANTIQUE GEMS ARE THE GEMS OF AARON'S BREAST PLATE	777D	INSC LAOCOON	PROSE
THIS O WHAT SHALL I CALL THEE FORM DIVINE FATHER OF MERCIES	780	GHOST ABEL 1	21
DELIVER FROM THE HOLY GHOST SO WE CALL NATURE	788D	ANNO THORNTON	* MARG
AND THO I CALL THEM MINE I KNOW THAT THEY ARE NOT MINE .	792B	LETTER 4	PROSE
AS TO CALL THEM COPIES FROM LIFE & MANNERS	795A	LETTER 6	PROSE
SHE WILL CALL ON ME TILL THEN I WAIT WITH PATIENCE IN HOPES	796A	LETTER 6	PROSE
SUNDAY AFTERNOON TO CALL ON MRS FLAXMAN AT HAMPSTEAD I SEND	799A	LETTER 11	PROSE
"PROPER DUTY TO YOU & MR FLAXMAN WE INTEND TO CALL" . .	800A	LETTER 12	PROSE
"SWALLOWS CALL US FLEETING PAST OUR WINDOW AT THIS MOMENT"	800B	LETTER 12	PROSE
MR JOHNSON'S FORGETFULNESS WHO APPOINTD TO CALL ON YOU BUT	809C	LETTER 20	*PROSE
DID ME THE FAVOR TO CALL ON ME I HAVE PROMISD HIM TO SEND	810D	LETTER 21	PROSE
NOT AS YOU MISTAKENLY CALL IT DUNG HILL	812B	LETTER 22	PROSE
AS TO GIVE TO MRS CHETWYND IF SHE SHOULD CALL OR SEND .	821B	LETTER 25	PROSE
HIS SON WAS LIKEWISE NOT AT HOME BUT I WILL AGAIN CALL ON	834B	LETTER 34	PROSE
OUT BOTH TIMES I WILL REPEAT MY CALL ON HIM TOMORROW MORNING	834D	LETTER 34	PROSE
BUT I WILL CALL AGAIN IN A DAY OR TWO NEITHER MR FLAXMAN NOR	836B	LETTER 35	PROSE
NEVER SEE HIM AGAIN BUT WHEN I CALL ON HIM FOR HE HAS .	836C	LETTER 35	PROSE
TO CALL ON ME MRS FLAXMAN & HER SISTERS GAVE ALSO THEIR	836C	LETTER 35	PROSE
VERY SOON TO CALL AGAIN & AS YOU WISH TO WRITE ALL I CAN	849B	LETTER 45	PROSE
I HAD THE PLEASURE OF A CALL FROM MRS CHETWYND & . . .	850C	LETTER 49	PROSE
BUT THE HECATE IS A FINISHD PRODUCTION WHICH WILL CALL FOR	855A	LETTER 53	PROSE
MIGHT AGAIN CALL I HAVE HOWEVER SEEN HIM THIS MORNING .	856A	LETTER 54	PROSE
WHAT THEIR AUTHOR IS KINDLY PLEASED TO CALL TALENTS FOR	860C	LETTER 56	PROSE
THE FLEMINGS THEY CALL IT BURNT BONE HAS POSSESSED THE EYE	864C	LETTER 61	PROSE
THE LEAST PARTICLE & SUCH DISCIPLINE I CALL PRESUMPTION & FOLLY	871A	LETTER 72	PROSE
THOUGH I HOPE IN A MORNING OR TWO TO CALL ON YOU IN . .	871B	LETTER 72	PROSE
EVERY THING WHICH IS IN HARMONY WITH ME I CALL . . .	SUPP	IN HARMONY/N	*PROSE

CALLD   SEE CALD,CALLED

AND MY SOVEREIGN CALLD YOU TOGETHER	19	EDW THIRD/PS 2	3
BABEL WITH THOUSAND TONGUES CONFUSION IT WAS CALLD AND GIVN TO SHAME	41A	THEN SHE BORE	*PROSE
TILL KNOWLEDGE ANIMATED IT TWAS CALLD SELFLOVE . . .	42D	THEN SHE BORE	PROSE
[BY SHAME SHE HAD A SON CALLD HONOUR WHO BORE REVENGE] .	43A	THEN SHE BORE	PROSE
HE CALLD HIM SURGERY & FED	50	WHEN CORRUP/IM	9
THEN QUID CALLD UPON OBTUSE ANGLE FOR A SONG & HE . . .	57A	ISLAND MOON 9	PROSE
THIS IS HUMAN POLICY AS IT IS CALLD	85A	ANNO LAVATER	MARG
SIGNIFY WHAT THE LAWS OF KINGS & PRIESTS HAVE CALLD VICE	88C	ANNO LAVATER	MARG
EVERY MAN'S LEADING PROPENSITY OUGHT TO BE CALLD . . .	88C	ANNO LAVATER	MARG
WHICH BY THE ANCIENTS WAS CALLD AN ANGEL & SPIRIT & DEMON	98B	ALL RELIGIONS	PROSE
WHICH IS EVERY WHERE CALLD THE SPIRIT OF PROPHECY . . .	98C	ALL RELIGIONS	PROSE
OLD MAN UNWORTHY TO BE CALLD THE FATHER OF TIRIEL'S RACE	99	TIRIEL 1	13
BUT HEUXOS CALLD A SON OF ZAZEL TO [XXX] DIG THEIR MOTHER A GRAVE	100	TIRIEL 1	* 35
ENTERD THE GATES OF TIRIEL'S PALACE & STOOD & CALLD ALOUD	104	TIRIEL 4	42
AND ALL THY MOANS FLEW OER MY ROOF BUT I HAVE CALLD THEM DOWN	130	BOOK OF THEL 5	15
WE HAVE CALLD AN ASSEMBLY BUT NOT TO DESTROY	139	FRENCH REVOLTN	115
THAT ENERGY CALLD EVIL IS ALONE FROM THE BODY	149C	MARRIAGE HH 4	PROSE

CALLD   (CONTINUED)
        & THAT REASON CALLD GOOD IS ALONE FROM THE SOUL   . . .   149C MARRIAGE HH 4   PROSE
        FOR THAT CALLD BODY IS A PORTION OF SOUL DISCERND BY   . . 149D MARRIAGE HH 4   PROSE
        & THE GOVERNOR OR REASON IS CALLD MESSIAH . . . . .   150A MARRIAGE HH 5   PROSE
        OR POSSESSOR OF THE COMMAND OF THE HEAVENLY HOST IS CALLD 150A MARRIAGE HH 5   PROSE
          THE DEVIL
        OR SATAN AND HIS CHILDREN ARE CALLD SIN & DEATH   . . .   150A MARRIAGE HH 5   PROSE
        BUT IN THE BOOK OF JOB MILTON'S MESSIAH IS CALLD SATAN . 150A MARRIAGE HH 5   PROSE
        IF SPACE IT MAY BE CALLD SOON WE SAW THE STABLE AND   . . 157A MARRIAGE HH 17   PROSE
        AND THE WINTER CALLD IT A DREADFUL CRIME . . . . . .   176 SOFT SNOW/N   5
        AND CALLD ALOUD TO ENGLISH BLAKE . . . .   187 WHEN KLOPSTK/N   6
        NOW BARRD OUT BY THE ATLANTIC SEA CALLD ATLANTEAN HILLS   200 AMERICA 10   6
        IN THAT DREAD NIGHT WHEN URIZEN CALLD THE STARS ROUND HIS 204 AMERICA CANC B   5
          FEET
        THEY CALLD HER PITY AND FLED . . . .   231 URIZEN 19   1
        AND ALL CALLD IT THE NET OF RELIGION . . . .   235 URIZEN 25   22
        AND FORMD LAWS OF PRUDENCE AND CALLD THEM   . . . . .   236 URIZEN 28   6
        SURROUNDED BY SALT FLOODS NOW CALLD   . . . .   236 URIZEN 28   9
        SO FUZON CALLD ALL TOGETHER   . . . .   237 URIZEN 28   19
        SHE CALLD HER SONS & DAUGHTERS . . . .   243 EUROPE 13   12
        CALLD ALL HIS SONS TO THE STRIFE OF BLOOD   . . . . .   245 EUROPE 15   11
        SO ANTAMON CALLD UP LEUTHA FROM HER VALLEYS OF DELIGHT . 246 SONG OF LOS 3   28
        [THE MOUNTAIN] EPHRAIM CALLD OUT [TO THE MOUNTAIN] . . . 274 FOUR ZOAS 1   386
        [THE MAN] ALBION CALLD URIZEN & SAID BEHOLD THESE SICKNING 280 FOUR ZOAS 2   *   3
          SPHERES
        [EXULTING] [INDIGNANT] EXULTING AT THE VOICE THAT CALLD   280 FOUR ZOAS 2   *   10
          HIM . . .
        WHEN I CALLD FORTH THE EARTH-WORM FROM THE COLD & DARK   282 FOUR ZOAS 2   83
          OBSCURE
        LEST THE STATE CALLD LUVAH SHOULD CEASE & THE DIVINE VISION 287 FOUR ZOAS 2   264
        AND THARMAS CALLD TO THE DARK SPECTRE WHO UPON THE SHORES 299 FOUR ZOAS 4   63
        MY COUNTER PART & CALLD IT LOVE I NAMD HER ENITHARMON   . 300 FOUR ZOAS 4   100
        CALLD IT THE CHAIN OF JEALOUSY NOW LOS BEGAN TO SPEAK   . . 307 FOUR ZOAS 5   95
        WAS A REFLECTION OF HIS FACE WHO CALLD ME FROM THE DEEP   310 FOUR ZOAS 5   217
        I CALLD THE STARS AROUND MY FEET IN THE NIGHT OF COUNCILS 311 FOUR ZOAS 5   223
          DARK
        BURN LIKE TWO FURNACES HE CALLD WITH VOICE OF THUNDER   . . 319 FOUR ZOAS 6   309
        ONCE HOW I SANG & CALLD THE BEASTS & BIRDS TO THEIR   325 FOUR ZOAS 7   * 199
          DELIGHTS
        FROM THE ENORMITY & CALLD THEM LUVAH & VALA TURNING DOWN   326 FOUR ZOAS 7   248
        AND CALLD THE LOOMS CATHEDRON IN THESE LOOMS SHE WOVE   342 FOUR ZOAS 8   37
          THE SPECTRES
        URIZEN CALLD TOGETHER THE SYNAGOGUE OF SATAN IN DIRE   348 FOUR ZOAS 8   272
          SANHEDRIM
        IT WAS THE BEST POSSIBLE IN THE STATE CALLD SATAN TO SAVE 348 FOUR ZOAS 8   * 285
        . . . [THEREFORE THEY WERE CALLD] THERE WAS HIDDEN WITHIN 348 FOUR ZOAS 8   * 291
        WHICH CHRIST MUST REND & HER REVEAL HER DAUGHTERS ARE CALLD 348 FOUR ZOAS 8   293
        TIRZAH SHE IS [CALLD] NAMD RAHAB THEY HER VARIOUS DIVISIONS 348 FOUR ZOAS 8   * 294
          ARE CALLD
        THAT STATE CALLD SATAN ENITHARMON BREATHD FORTH ON THE   351 FOUR ZOAS 8   383
          WINDS
        CALLD DOWN A GREAT SOLEMN ASSEMBLY RINTRAH IN FURY & FIRE 351 FOUR ZOAS 8   * 389
        THE ASHES OF MYSTERY BEGAN TO ANIMATE THEY CALLD IT DEISM 357 FOUR ZOAS 8   618
        BABYLON AGAIN IN INFANCY CALLD NATURAL RELIGION . . .   357 FOUR ZOAS 8   620
        BEFORE THE MORNING'S DAWN THE EAGLE CALLD THE VULTURE   . 358 FOUR ZOAS 9   59
        THE RAVEN CALLD THE HAWK I HEARD THEM FROM MY FORESTS BLACK 358 FOUR ZOAS 9   60
        HE CALLD THE DEEP BURIED HIS VOICE & ANSWER NONE RETURND   360 FOUR ZOAS 9   136
        HARNESSD THEY CALLD TO URIZEN THE HEAVENS MOVED AT THEIR   365 FOUR ZOAS 9   309
          CALL
        SHE CALLD BUT NONE COULD ANSWER HER & THE ECCHO OF HER   370 FOUR ZOAS 9   499
          VOICE RETURND
        WHERE IS THE VOICE OF GOD THAT CALLD ME FROM THE SILENT DEW 370 FOUR ZOAS 9   500
        VALA AWOKE & CALLD THE CHILDREN FROM THEIR GENTLE SLUMBERS 370 FOUR ZOAS 9   518
        URTHONA CALLD HIS SONS AROUND HIM THARMAS CALLD HIS SONS   378 FOUR ZOAS 9   789
        WHICH THEY CALLD GOD & SO WERE LIARS AS CHRIST SAYS . . . 389A ANNO WATSON   MARG
        THE ACCOUNTS OF NORTH AMERICAN SAVAGES AS THEY ARE CALLD   389C ANNO WATSON   MARG
        WORSHIPD IN THIS WORLD AS GOD & SET ABOVE ALL THAT IS CALLD 394C ANNO WATSON   MARG
          GOD
        AS THIS BOOK CONTAINS CAN EVER HAVE BEEN CALLD WISDOM   . . 397A ANNO BACON   MARG
        SOME SAID SHE WAS PROUD SOME CALLD HER A WHORE   . . . .   428 MARY   17
        AND NOT TO RAISE ENVY IS CALLD CHRISTIAN LOVE . . . . .   428 MARY   26
        MORTIMER WAS CALLD A MADMAN & ONLY   . . . .   445C ANNO REYNOLDS   MARG
        THE GREAT BACON HE IS CALLD I CALL HIM THE LITTLE BACON   459C ANNO REYNOLDS   MARG
        THE VENETIAN OUGHT NOT TO BE CALLD THE ORNAMENTAL STYLE   463A ANNO REYNOLDS   MARG
        HOW CAN THAT BE CALLD THE ORNAMENTAL STYLE . . . . . .   464D ANNO REYNOLDS   MARG
        HE MUST EXPECT TO BE CALLD A FOOL BY MEN OF UNDERSTANDING 469D ANNO REYNOLDS   MARG
        HERE IT IS CALLD ORNAMENTAL THAT THE ROMAN &   . . . . .   476B ANNO REYNOLDS   MARG
        CALLD HARMONY IT IS LIKE THE SMILE OF A FOOL   . . . . .   478D ANNO REYNOLDS   MARG
        PALAMABRON CALLD AND LOS & SATAN CAME BEFORE HIM   . . . . 487 MILTON 7   34
        BEING CALLD GOD SETTING HIMSELF ABOVE ALL THAT IS CALLED   491 MILTON 11   12
          GOD
        AND THEREFORE THE CLASS OF SATAN SHALL BE CALLD THE ELECT 492 MILTON 11   21
          & THOSE
        THE HORSES OF PALAMABRON CALLD FOR REST AND PLEASANT DEATH 492 MILTON 12   9
        AND CALLD ME SIN AND FOR A SIGN PORTENTOUS HELD ME SOON   493 MILTON 12   *   39
        AND JEHOVAH WAS LEPROUS LOUD HE CALLD STRETCHING HIS HAND 494 MILTON 13   24
          TO ETERNITY
        ONWARDS HIS SHADOW KEPT ITS COURSE AMONG THE SPECTRES CALLD 496 MILTON 15   17
        IN THAT REGION CALLD MIDIAN AMONG THE ROCKS OF HOREB   . . 498 MILTON 17   28
        CALLD ALL HER DAUGHTERS SAYING SURELY TO UNLOOSE MY BOND   498 MILTON 17   32
        WHOSE SONG CALLD MILTON TO THE ATTEMPT AND LOS HEARD THESE 504 MILTON 21   34
          LAMENTS

		PAGE	TITLE	LINE
CALLD	**(CONTINUED)**			
WE CALLD HIM MENASSHEH BECAUSE OF THE GENERATIONS OF TIRZAH		508	MILTON 24	6
WHILE LOS CALLD HIS SONS AROUND HIM TO THE HARVEST & THE VINTAGE		511	MILTON 25	65
THIS WINE-PRESS IS CALLD WAR ON EARTH IT IS THE PRINTING-PRESS		513	MILTON 27	8
BUT ALLAMANDA CALLD ON EARTH COMMERCE IS THE CULTIVATED LAND		514	MILTON 27	42
OF PHILISTEA INTO TWELVE DIVIDED CALLD AFTER THE NAMES	. .	532	MILTON 40	25
CALLD DEATH A MADMAN [DEADLY THE AFFRONT] TREMBLING FOR THE AFFRONT		537	AND HIS LEGS/N	17
MADMAN I HAVE BEEN CALLD FOOL THEY CALL THEE	. . . . .	538	MADMAN CALLD/N	1
WHEN HE CALLD HIM THE ORNAMENTAL ARTIST	. . . . . .	540	SIR JOSH RUB/N	4
THE WOOD & STONE WERE CALLD THE HOLY THINGS	. . . . .	543	IF TRUE/N	11
WHAT IS CALLD THE ENGLISH STYLE OF ENGRAVING	.	593B	PUB ADDRESS/N	PROSE
& IN SHORT ALL THAT ARE CALLD WOOLETT'S WERE ETCHD	. .	594A	PUB ADDRESS/N	PROSE
[OBEDIENCE TO THE WILL OF THE MONOPOLIST IS CALLD VIRTUE]		595B	PUB ADDRESS/N	PROSE
PICKING OUT OF WHITES & BLACKS IN WHAT IS CALLD TINTS	.	596C	PUB ADDRESS/N	PROSE
THE GREATEST PART OF WHAT ARE CALLD IN ENGLAND OLD PICTURES		598C	PUB ADDRESS/N	PROSE
THE CONTEMPTIBLE IDIOTS WHO HAVE BEEN CALLD GREAT MEN	.	598C	PUB ADDRESS/N	PROSE
WHO IN THE AGGREGATE ARE CALLD JERUSALEM FABLE IS ALLEGORY		604D	V LAST JUDG/N	PROSE
AS TWO DISTINCT THINGS & SO CALLD FOR THE SAKE OF ETERNAL LIFE		605A	V LAST JUDG/N	PROSE
IF THEY DO NOT PRAY IS AN INFERIOR KIND TO BE CALLD KNOWING		605A	V LAST JUDG/N	PROSE
REMEMBERD & CALLD REALITY SUCH IS THE MIGHTY DIFFERENCE		605C	V LAST JUDG/N	PROSE
ENDEAVOUR TO RESTORE WHAT THE ANCIENTS CALLD THE GOLDEN AGE		605D	V LAST JUDG/N	PROSE
& IN OTHER PLACES THIS ANGEL IS FREQUENTLY CALLD BY THE		610A	V LAST JUDG/N	PROSE
OF TRUE ART CALLD GOTHIC IN ALL AGES BY THOSE	. . . .	610D	V LAST JUDG/N	PROSE
WHO FOLLOW THE FASHION AS THAT IS CALLD WHICH IS	. . .	610D	V LAST JUDG/N	*PROSE
A WOMAN WITH CHILDREN REPRESENTS THE STATE CALLD LABAN THE		610D	V LAST JUDG/N	PROSE
REPRESENTATIVE OF THAT LOVE CALLD FRIENDSHIP	. . . .	610D	V LAST JUDG/N	PROSE
ABOVE THE HEAD OF NOAH IS SETH THIS STATE CALLD	. . .	611C	V LAST JUDG/N	PROSE
ON THE SIDE NEXT BAPTISM ARE SEEN THOSE CALLD IN THE BIBLE		613D	V LAST JUDG/N	PROSE
THAT ORIGINATED WITH THE FALL & WAS CALLD DEATH	. . .	616A	V LAST JUDG/N	PROSE
WHAT IS CALLD CORPOREAL NOBODY KNOWS OF ITS DWELLING PLACE		617A	V LAST JUDG/N	PROSE
A PLEASANT SHADOW OF REPOSE CALLD ALBION'S LOVELY LAND	. .	620	JERUSALEM 1	3
THEY TAKE THE TWO CONTRARIES WHICH ARE CALLD QUALITIES WITH WHICH		629	JERUSALEM 10	8
HAVING A WHITE DOT CALLD A CENTER FROM WHICH BRANCHES OUT		659	JERUSALEM 33	19
LET DOWN AT WILL AROUND AND CALLD THE UNIVERSAL TENT	. .	665	JERUSALEM 38	50
AROSE UPON HIM PALE AND GHASTLY AND HE CALLD AROUND	. .	666	JERUSALEM 40	2
SUBMITTING TO BE CALLD THE SON OF LOS THE TERRIBLE VISION		668	JERUSALEM 40	52
SUBMITTING TO BE CALLD ENITHARMON'S DAUGHTERS AND BE BORN		668	JERUSALEM 40	55
HE OUGHT NOT TO BE CALLD A HYPOCRITE THIS TITLE IS	. .	682C	JERUSALEM 52	PROSE
THE BOOK WRITTEN BY ROUSSEAU CALLD HIS CONFESSIONS	. .	682D	JERUSALEM 52	PROSE
AND THEY ELECTED SEVEN CALLD THE SEVEN EYES OF GOD	. .	686	JERUSALEM 55	31
A HARLOT I AM CALLD I AM SOLD FROM STREET TO STREET	. .	695	JERUSALEM 62	4
HENCE ALBION WAS CALLD THE CANAANITE & ALL HIS GIANT SONS		715	JERUSALEM 74	39
HE CALLD IT DIVINE ANALOGY FOR IN BEULAH THE FEMININE	. .	730	JERUSALEM 85	7
PISON SINCE CALLD ARNON THERE IS HESHBON BEAUTIFUL	. .	735	JERUSALEM 89	25
WHAT I CALLD HUMILITY THEY CALLD PRIDE	. . . . . .	751	EV GOSPEL(D)/N	24
THE ANCIENTS CALLD IT EATING OF THE TREE OF GOOD & EVIL		778C	HOMERS POETRY	PROSE
& OUGHT NOT TO BE CALLD BY THE SAME NAME	. . . . .	782A	INSC UPCOTT	PROSE
JESUS OUR FATHER WHO ART IN THY HEAVNS CALLD BY THY NAME		788A	ANNO THORNTON	* MARG
"CALLD ON YOU SINCE MY HUSBAND'S FIRST RETURN FROM FELPHAM"		800A	LETTER 12	PROSE
YOU HAVE SAID IN IT CALLD UPON ME FOR AN IMMEDIATE ANSWER		811B	LETTER 22	PROSE
YOU WILL BE CALLD THE BASE JUDAS WHO BETRAYD HIS FRIEND		813B	LETTER 22	PROSE
OR AS IT IS POLITELY CALLD BORED YOU TOO MUCH ALREADY	.	816C	LETTER 24	PROSE
A MASTER IN CHANCERY THO I HAVE CALLD ON MR EDWARDS TWICE		834D	LETTER 34	PROSE
I CALLD YESTERDAY ON MR BRAITHWAITE AS YOU DESIRED	. .	835C	LETTER 35	PROSE
COUNCELLOR HE ALAS WAS ILL IN BED WHEN I CALLD YESTERDAY		836B	LETTER 35	*PROSE
ROMNEY WHICH ARE AT SAUNDERS' I CALLD ONCE OF(ON) MR F(FLAXMAN)		838B	LETTER 37	PROSE
I CALLD ON MR HOARE WITH YOUR ELEGANT & HEART LIFTING	. .	838C	LETTER 37	PROSE
MR BRAITHWAITE CALLD ON ME & BROUGHT TWO PRINTS WHICH HE		838D	LETTER 37	PROSE
IT MAY BE CALLD A DEFENCE OF LITERATURE AGAINST THOSE PESTS OF		841D	LETTER 41	PROSE
CALLD ON HIM EVERY DAY & NOT FINDING HIM I NOW UNDERSTAND		842B	LETTER 42	*PROSE
THINK THAT IT WAS A FIGURE WITH CHILDREN WHICH HE CALLD A CHARITY		849A	LETTER 45	PROSE
WILKES WAS NOT OUT WHEN I CALLD NOR ANY MORE OF WASHINGTON		853A	LETTER 51	*PROSE
I AT LENGTH SEND THE BOOKS WHICH I HAVE IN VAIN CALLD FOR		856A	LETTER 54	PROSE
REGARDLESS OF THAT FAINT SHADOW CALLD NATURAL LIFE	. .	863A	LETTER 60	PROSE
PROGRESS CALLD THE PILES WHICH WHEN TO THE DEGREE I HAVE HAD		874D	LETTER 80	PROSE
I CALLD THIS MORNING FOR A WALK & BROUGHT MY PLATES WITH ME		876C	LETTER 84	PROSE
CALLD IN SOME NORTHERN POEMS "CHOOSERS OF THE SLAIN"	. .	SUPP	ILLUS GRAY	*TITLE
CALLED	**SEE CALD,CALLD**			
AND HE SHALL BE CALLED ISRAEL'S DELIVERER	. . . . . .	39D	SAMSON/PS	PROSE
SHE RAN AND CALLED HER HUSBAND WHO CAME AND TALKED WITH HIM		40B	SAMSON/PS	PROSE
BUT AT THE LAST IT SETTLES IN A LAKE CALLED OBLIVION	. .	41C	THEN SHE BORE	PROSE
[SHE HAD A SON CALLED SUSPITION] CONCEIT & & POLICY DOTH		43A	THEN SHE BORE	*PROSE
THEN [SELF LOVE] BORE A DAUGHTER CALLED EMULATION	. . .	43A	THEN SHE BORE	PROSE
HE IS CALLED BY THY NAME	. . . .	115	THE LAMB/SI	13
WE ARE CALLED BY HIS NAME	. . . .	115	THE LAMB/SI	18
THESE ARE DEVILS AND ARE CALLED POWERS OF THE AIR	. . .	156B	MARRIAGE HH 17	PROSE
A WOOF WOVE AND CALLED IT SCIENCE	. . . .	231	URIZEN 19	9
AND HE WEPT & HE CALLED IT PITY	. . . .	235	URIZEN 25	3
THEY CALLED IT EGYPT & LEFT IT	. . . .	237	URIZEN 28	22
HE GROAND ANGUISHD & CALLED HER SIN	. . . .	250	AHANIA 2	34
TILL THE TIME OF THE END THEN THEY ELECTED SEVEN CALLED THE SEVEN		279	FOUR ZOAS 1	553

	PAGE	TITLE	LINE

CALLED   (CONTINUED)

THE TYGERS OF WRATH CALLED . . . . 281 FOUR ZOAS 2   35
THEN ALL IN GREAT ETERNITY [WHICH IS CALLED] . . . . . . 341 FOUR ZOAS 8   1
SHE CALLED TO HER FLOCKS SAYING FOLLOW ME O MY FLOCKS . 369 FOUR ZOAS 9   478
HE CALLED ME A MILITARY PAINTER I SUPPOSE [HE] MISTAKING   438A BLAKES MEMORAN PROSE
   THE
WORDS MINIATURE PAINTER WHICH HE MIGHT HAVE HEARD ME CALLED 438A BLAKES MEMORAN PROSE
WE SHOULD HAVE SEEN BLOTS CALLED MASSES . . . . . . 439C REMARKS MALKIN PROSE
BUT PALAMABRON CALLED DOWN A GREAT SOLEMN ASSEMBLY . . 489 MILTON 8   46
BEING CALLD GOD SETTING HIMSELF ABOVE ALL THAT IS CALLED   491 MILTON 11   12
   GOD
SUCH ARE THE SPACES CALLED EARTH & SUCH ITS DIMENSION   . . 516 MILTON 29   14
THIS PLACE IS CALLED BEULAH IT IS A PLEASANT LOVELY SHADOW   518 MILTON 30   2
CALLED ETERNAL ANNIHILATION THAT NONE BUT THE LIVING SHALL   522 MILTON 32   27
[HE'LL] THEYLL STILL BE CALLED THE WORLD'S HONEST MAN   . . 544 SOME MEN/N   5
ALL THE LITTLE OLD PICTURES CALLED CABINET PICTURES . . 561A EXHIBITION ADV PROSE
WONDERFUL ORIGINALS CALLED IN THE SACRED SCRIPTURES . . 565C DESC CAT 2   PROSE
AS THEY ARE CALLED WERE THE INVENTION OF GREEK ARTISTS   . . 565C DESC CAT 2   PROSE
ALL THE GENUINE OLD LITTLE PICTURES CALLED CABINET PICTURES   566B DESC CAT 2   PROSE
HIS FRIEND H(HOPPNER) WHO HAS CALLED HIS "A COMMON SCENE"   574D DESC CAT 3   *PROSE
CHAUCER HAS NO WHERE CALLED THE PLOWMAN OLD . . . . 575A DESC CAT 3   PROSE
A TRADING MASTER OF A VESSEL CALLED BY COURTESY CAPTAIN   575C DESC CAT 3   PROSE
ELEMENTAL BEINGS CALLED BY US BY THE GENERAL NAME . . 577D DESC CAT 5   PROSE
   OF FAIRIES
ALSO ABRAHAM WAS CALLED TO SUCCEED THE DRUIDICAL AGE   . . 578A DESC CAT 5   PROSE
ONE OF THOSE THE GREEKS CALLED TITANS   . . . . . . 578C DESC CAT 5   PROSE
IT IS ALSO CALLED THE BARREN WASTE OF LOCKE AND NEWTON   . 581B DESC CAT 6   TITLE
THAT INFERNAL MACHINE CALLED CHIARO OSCURO IN THE HANDS OF   532C DESC CAT 9   PROSE
PRAYER IS VAIN I CALLED FOR COMPASSION COMPASSION MOCKD   630 JERUSALEM 10   53
AND JERUSALEM IS CALLED LIBERTY AMONG THE CHILDREN   684 JERUSALEM 54   5
   OF ALBION
BY LOS FOR JERUSALEM'S SAKE & CALLED THE GATES OF JERUSALEM   711 JERUSALEM 72   8
INTO THE VORTEX OF HIS WHEELS THEREFORE HYLE IS CALLED GOG   715 JERUSALEM 74   30
HEBREW ART IS CALLED SIN BY THE DEIST SCIENCE . . . . 776C INSC LAOCOON   PROSE
INTO THE ABSTRACT VOID IT IS CALLED THE DIVINE MERCY   . 784B ANNO WW EXCUR   MARG
I CALLED ON MR EVANS WHO GIVES SMALL HOPES OF OUR BALLADS   831C LETTER 31   PROSE
   HE
MR CARR CALLED ON ME AND I AS YOU DESIRED GAVE HIM   . . 845C LETTER 44   PROSE
AS WOULD HAVE CALLED FOR THE SCEPTRE OF AGAMEMNON   . . 847B LETTER 44   PROSE
EXCUSE FOR TROUBLING YOU BEFORE IT CAN BE PROPERLY CALLED   853C LETTER 52   PROSE
& OF THAT SPIRIT TO WHICH WE ARE CALLED . . . . . . 863B LETTER 60   PROSE
HE CALLED ON ME THIS WEEK YOURS SINCERELY . . . . . 877D LETTER 88   PROSE

CALLEST   SEE CALLST

O THOU CREATING VOICE THAT CALLEST & WHO SHALL ANSWER THEE   367 FOUR ZOAS 9   400
THAT THOU CALLEST THY CHILDREN LO THE LAW OF GOD COMMANDS   629 JERUSALEM 10   38

CALLING

ALAS MY LORD WHAT AM I CALLING THEE THOU ART MY GOD . . . 38B SAMSON/PS   PROSE
OR GENIUSES CALLING THEM BY THE NAMES AND ADORNING THEM   153A MARRIAGE HH 11 PROSE
AND CALLING THEOTORMON'S EAGLES TO PREY UPON HER FLESH . 190 V DAU ALBION 2   13
CALLING THE LAPSED SOUL . . . . 210 INTRODUCTN/SE   6
STILL SHE DESPISD HIM CALLING ON HIS NAME & KNOWING HIM NOT   286 FOUR ZOAS 2   234
SHRINKING & SHRINKING FROM HER LORD & CALLING HIM THE   295 FOUR ZOAS 3   129
   TEMPTER
AND WOVE THEM BODIES CALLING THEM HER BELOVD SONS   345 FOUR ZOAS 8   184
   & DAUGHTERS
AND THEN MOCKING & THEN WORSHIPPING CALLING HIM LORD & KING   349 FOUR ZOAS 8   327
CALLING THE LION & THE TYGER THE HORSE & THE WILD STAG . . 352 FOUR ZOAS 8   445
. . . SHE HEARD A VOICE BEHIND HER CALLING HER]   356 FOUR ZOAS 8   591
CALLING UPON THEIR FATHER'S NAME UPON THEIR RIVERS DARK   362 FOUR ZOAS 9   203
CALLING HIM BROTHER IMAGE OF THE ETERNAL FATHER THEY SAT   374 FOUR ZOAS 9   644
   DOWN
CALLING THE MORNING INTO BEULAH THE ETERNAL MAN REJOICD   374 FOUR ZOAS 9   646
CALLING THE PLOWMAN TO HIS LABOUR & THE SHEPHERD TO HIS   379 FOUR ZOAS 9   834
   REST
[ASTONISH LOOKD FROM HIS BRIGHT PORTALS CALLING THUS TO   380 FOUR ZOAS AD 1 *   3
   LUVAH]
AND MOCKING & THEN WORSHIPING CALLING HIM LORD & KING . . 382 FOUR ZOAS AD 6   15
ORIGINATES IN THE GREEKS' CALLING THE MUSES DAUGHTERS OF   452D ANNO REYNOLDS   MARG
   MEMORY
AND ALL THE SPECTRES OF THE DEAD CALLING THEMSELVES SONS   491 MILTON 11   13
   OF GOD
LAMBETH MOURNS CALLING JERUSALEM SHE WEEPS & LOOKS ABROAD   511 MILTON 25   54
CALLING THE HUMAN IMAGINATION WHICH IS THE DIVINE VISION   521 MILTON 32   19
   & FRUITION
WHILE IN THE LABOURS OF HIS CALLING SENDS HIS THOUGHT   531 MILTON 39   55
   ABROAD
BY CALLING HIS THE ORNAMENTAL STYLE . . . . 540 SIR JOSH RUB/N   2
NUMBER IX SATAN CALLING UP HIS LEGIONS FROM MILTON'S . . 582A DESC CAT 9   TITLE
CALLING THAT HOLY LOVE WHICH IS ENVY REVENGE & CRUELTY   . 639 JERUSALEM 17   30
CALLING ON GOD FOR HELP AND NOT OURSELVES IN WHOM GOD   672 JERUSALEM 43   13
   DWELLS
IN LOVE & JEALOUSY IMMINGLED & CALLING IT RELIGION . . 674 JERUSALEM 44   27
NAMING HIM THE SPIRIT OF PROPHECY CALLING HIM ELIJAH   . . 674 JERUSALEM 44   31
CALLING THE PRINCE OF THIS WORLD GOD AND DESTROYING ALL   682B JERUSALEM 52   PROSE
FOOTE IN CALLING WHITEFIELD HYPOCRITE WAS HIMSELF ONE . . 682D JERUSALEM 52   PROSE
WALKETH AMONG US CALLING US HIS BROTHERS & HIS FRIENDS   . . 686 JERUSALEM 55   *   10
CALLING THE ROCKS ATOMIC ORIGINS OF EXISTENCE DENYING   704 JERUSALEM 67   12
   ETERNITY
IN ANOTHER CALLING IT PRIDE & SELFISHNESS & SIN . . . . 717C JERUSALEM 77   PROSE
CALLING THE DEFINITE SIN DEFACING EVERY DEFINITE FORM . . 723 JERUSALEM 80   53
COLLUSION CALLING THEMSELVES DEISTS WORSHIPPING THE   737 JERUSALEM 90   65
   MATERNAL

```
                                                            PAGE     TITLE          LINE
CALLING    (CONTINUED)
    HUMANITY CALLING IT NATURE AND NATURAL RELIGION  . . . .   737 JERUSALEM 90        66
    LONG AWAY & NOT CALLING TO KNOW OF YOUR WELFARE BUT HOPE   799A LETTER 11       PROSE
        NOW
    AND OFTEN WE THINK WE HEAR YOUR VOICE CALLING AT THE GATE  854A LETTER 52       PROSE
    & MORE CEREMONY ALSO IN SO SERIOUS AN AFFAIR AS THE CALLING 854D LETTER 53      PROSE
        ON
    ADVERTISEMENT CALLING IT AN APPEAL TO CHARITY AND SAYS IT  861B LETTER 58       PROSE
CALLOW
    FROM THEM A CALLOW BABE DID SPRING  . . . . . . . .     50 WHEN CORRUP/IM *       5
CALLS
    THE ROARING VOICE OF WAR THE TRUMPET CALLS TO BATTLE  . .   34A KING JOHN/PS    PROSE
    TIS DALILA THAT CALLS THY MASTER'S WIFE NO STAY  . . . .    38B SAMSON/PS       PROSE
    HA HA HA SHE CALLS THE EXPERIMENTS PUPPETS  . . . . .    58C ISLAND MOON 10    PROSE
    THY FATHER CALLS THY FATHER LIFTS HIS HAND UNTO THE [AIR]  108 TIRIEL 6           41
        HEAVENS
    CALLS THE WATCHMAN OF THE NIGHT  . . . . . . . . .    112 A DREAM/SI           16
    FOR HE CALLS HIMSELF A LAMB  . . . . . . . . . .    115 THE LAMB/SI          14
    . . . RISE NECKER THE ANCIENT DAWN CALLS US  . . . .    134 FRENCH REVOLTN       7
    NOR HIS ACCEPTED BRETHREN WHOM TYRANT HE CALLS FREE  . .  160A SONG LIBERTY    PROSE
    FAREWELL THE GOD CALLS ME AWAY I DEPART IN MY SWEET BLISS  288 FOUR ZOAS 2        333
    THE VOICE INCESSANT CALLS ON ALL THE CHILDREN OF MEN  .   353 FOUR ZOAS 8        489
    ONE PLANET [CRIES] CALLS TO ANOTHER & ONE STAR ENQUIRES   364 FOUR ZOAS 9    *   261
        OF ANOTHER
    WHO DISGUISES HIS PRINCIPLES & CALLS THAT CHANGE  . . .  386B ANNO WATSON      MARG
    WHICH CALLS UPON HIS OPPONENT LOUDLY FOR AN ANSWER  . .  390D ANNO WATSON      MARG
    WHAT BACON CALLS LIES IS TRUTH ITSELF  . . . . . .  397D ANNO BACON       MARG
    BACON CALLS INTELLECTUAL ARTS UNMANLY POETRY PAINTING .  407D ANNO BACON       MARG
    CALLS TO HEAVEN FOR HUMAN BLOOD  . . . . . . . .  431 AUGURIES            12
    THE OWL [TAHT] THAT CALLS UPON THE NIGHT  . . . . .  431 AUGURIES        *   27
    THE INFERIOR PARTS OF ART AS REYNOLDS ARTFULLY CALLS THEM 449A ANNO REYNOLDS   MARG
    HE CALLS ALL OTHERS VAGUE ENTHUSIASTS OR MADMEN  . . .  458C ANNO REYNOLDS    MARG
    HE STATES ABSURDITIES IN COMPANY WITH TRUTHS & CALLS BOTH 474A ANNO REYNOLDS   MARG
        ABSURD
    HE CALLS THE ABOVE PROCEEDING WITH METHOD  . . . . .  475B ANNO REYNOLDS    MARG
    [THE KNAVE CALLS ANY THING ?FOUND IN NATURE FIT FOR ART]  SUPP ANNO REYNOLDS * MARG
    CHARLES CALLS ON MILTON FOR ATONEMENT CROMWELL IS READY   485 MILTON 5           39
    JAMES CALLS FOR FIRES IN GOLGONOOZA FOR HEAPS OF SMOKING   485 MILTON 5           40
        RUINS
    WHO CALLS THE INDIVIDUAL LAW HOLY AND DESPISES THE SAVIOUR 493 MILTON 13           5
    WHO PUBLISHES DOUBT & CALLS IT KNOWLEDGE WHOSE SCIENCE     533 MILTON 41          15
        IS DESPAIR
    HE CALLS YOU TO HIS HELP BE YOU NOT [MOVED] MOVD  . . .   551 WILLM COWPER/N *    3
    FROM THOSE WHO BEST UNDERSTAND SUCH THINGS CALLS FOR  .  561C EXHIBITION ADV   PROSE
    CALLS THE SQUIRE THE FOP OF CHAUCER'S AGE NOW HEAR CHAUCER 573C DESC CAT 3      PROSE
    THIS THEME CALLS ME IN SLEEP NIGHT AFTER NIGHT & EVRY MORN 622 JERUSALEM 4         3
    TO ME THEIR BENEFACTOR CALLS ALOUD FOR VENGEANCE DEEP  .   671 JERUSALEM 42       54
    FOR THE SOLDIER WHO FIGHTS FOR TRUTH CALLS HIS ENEMY HIS   672 JERUSALEM 43       41
        BROTHER
    THAN THY MAKER WHO FORGIVETH SINS & CALLS AGAIN HER THAT   694 JERUSALEM 61        7
        IS LOST
    THO SHE HATES HE CALLS HER AGAIN IN LOVE I LOVE MY DEAR    694 JERUSALEM 61        8
        JOSEPH
    IN THE END OF HIS SLEEP WHEN JESUS CALLS HIM FROM HIM HIS  701 JERUSALEM 65   *   62
        GRAVE
    THEY LOOK ON ONE ANOTHER THE MOUNTAIN CALLS OUT TO THE     703 JERUSALEM 66       58
        MOUNTAIN
    JERUSALEM THY SISTER CALLS  . . . . . . . . . .   718 ENGLND AWAKE/J       2
    HE COMFORTS & HEALS & CALLS THEM FRIENDS  . . . . .   755 EV GOSPEL(E)/N      90
    ALL IS NOT SIN THAT SATAN CALLS SO  . . . . . . .  777D INSC LAOCOON     PROSE
    DANTE CALLS THEM CERCHIETTI  . . . . . . . . .  786A ILLS DANTE 101   PROSE
    PICTURES LIKEWISE CALLS FOR MY THANKS I WILL FINISH THE   813D LETTER 22       PROSE
        OTHER
    SHE CALLS FOR YOUR ASSISTANCE YOU WHO NEVER REFUSE  . .  842A LETTER 41       PROSE
    ON ACCOUNT OF THAT VERY COLOURING WHICH OUR CRITIC CALLS  864C LETTER 61       PROSE
        BLACK
CALLST
    THOU CALLST ME MADMAN BUT I CALL THEE BLOCKHEAD  . . . .   539 F(LAXMAN)/N 1       2
CALM
    EACH FIELD SEEMS EDEN AND EACH CALM RETREAT  . . . . .     9 FRESH FROM/PS       15
    WHERE PEACE AND JOY AND LOVE AND CALM CONTENT  . . . . .    30 EDW THIRD/PS 5      30
    WHEN BUSY DAY WAS FADING AND CALM EVENING  . . . . .    39D SAMSON/PS        PROSE
    AND THE SWEET SOUND OF SILVER VOICES CALM THE WEARY COUCH  306 FOUR ZOAS 5        24
    STILL THE FAINT HARPS & SILVER VOICES CALM THE WEARY COUCH 306 FOUR ZOAS 5        30
    NOR COULD HE CALM THE ELEMENTS BECAUSE HIMSELF WAS SUBJECT 315 FOUR ZOAS 6       145
    THE OCEAN CALM THE CLOUDS FOLD ROUND & FIERY FLAMES OF LOVE 381 FOUR ZOAS AD 2      1
    COME & MAKE THY CALM RETREAT  . . . . . . . . .   423 THE BIRDS/N         19
    BUT THO CALM & WARM THE WATERS WIDE  . . . . . .   427 LAND OF DREAMS      15
    AND THE CALM OCEAN JOYS BENEATH & SMOOTHS HIS AWFUL WAVES  511 MILTON 25          71
    POWER SILENT CALM & MOTIONLESS IN THE MID-AIR SUBLIME  .   674 JERUSALEM 44       19
CALMD
    ARISE O ENION ARISE FOR LO I HAVE CALMD MY SEAS  . . .   370 FOUR ZOAS 9        494
    [ARISE O ENION ARISE FOR LO I HAVE CALMD MY SEAS]  . .  SUPP FOUR ZOAS 1       *
CALUMNIATE
    THOSE WHO ENVY OR CALUMNIATE GREAT MEN HATE GOD  . . .  158B MARRIAGE HH 22   PROSE
    RESIDE WHO CALUMNIATE & MURDER UNDER PRETENCE OF HOLINESS  608D V LAST JUDG/N  PROSE
CALUMNIATES
    HE WHO ENVIES OR CALUMNIATES WHICH IS MURDER & CRUELTY .   738 JERUSALEM 91       12
CALUMNIATOR'S
    ("BLUNDERER'S FRIENDSHIP THAN CALUMNIATOR'S ENMITY") I     69C ANNO LAVATER    MARG
        DOUBT THIS
```

296

		PAGE	TITLE	LINE

CALUMNIES
   OF HIS FINISHED PRODUCTIONS BY ANY CALUMNIES IN FUTURE . 573A DESC CAT 3   PROSE
   AND WITHOUT THE BAPTISM OF REPENTANCE TO WASH AWAY   697 JERUSALEM 63   28
      CALUMNIES AND
CALUMNY
   AND FROM LAUGHTER PROCEEDS TO MURDER BY UNDERVALUING   521 MILTON 32   7
      CALUMNY
   SNEAKING & [CALUMNY] BACKBITING & ODDS & ENDS . . . . . 541 MR STOTHARD/N   4
   WHICH I WILL SOON PUBLISH SECRET CALUMNY & . . . . . . 592C PUB ADDRESS/N   PROSE
   STARVE ME OUT BY CALUMNY & THE ARTS OF TRADING COMBINATION 596D PUB ADDRESS/N   PROSE
   & THO THEY CAN USE THE POISON OF CALUMNY   . . . . 598B PUB ADDRESS/N   PROSE
   IN LONDON EVERY CALUMNY AND FALSEHOOD UTTERD AGAINST   847B LETTER 44   PROSE
      ANOTHER
   BY WILLIAM BLAKE ?THO NOW SURROUNDED BY CALUMNY & ENVY . SUPP PILGRIMS/N   *PROSE
CALVARY
   EVER WEEPING PADDINGTON IS THAT CALVARY AND GOLGOTHA   632 JERUSALEM 12   28
   AND SUCH THE HOLY GOSPEL OF MOUNT OLIVET & CALVARY . . . 638 JERUSALEM 16   69
   THOU SHALT THYSELF BE SACRIFICED TO ME THY GOD ON CALVARY   781 GHOST ABEL 2   18
CALVARY'S
   BETWEEN SOUTH MOLTON STREET & STRATFORD PLACE CALVARY'S   484 MILTON 4   21
      FOOT
CALVIN
   WHAT COULD CALVIN SAY MORE THAN IS SAID IN THIS NUMBER . . 132A ANNO SWED PROV   MARG
   REMEMBER HOW CALVIN AND LUTHER IN FURY PREMATURE . . . . 507 MILTON 23   47
CALVIN'S
   PREDESTINATION AFTER THIS LIFE IS MORE ABOMINABLE THAN   133A ANNO SWED PROV   MARG
      CALVIN'S
CAM
   THE BANKS OF CAM COLD LEARNING'S STREAMS . . . . . . 501 MILTON 19   39
   CAM IS A LITTLE STREAM ELY IS ALMOST SWALLOWD UP . . . . 623 JERUSALEM 5   9
CAMB
   ISSACHAR NORTHAMPTON RUTLAND NOTTGHAM ZEBULUN BEDFORD   637 JERUSALEM 16   48
      HUNTGN CAMB
CAMBEL
   BOADICEA CONWENNA ESTRILD GWINEFRID IGNOGE CAMBEL   . . . 281 FOUR ZOAS 2   62
   CAMBEL & GWENDOLEN & CONWENNA & CORDELLA & IGNOGE   . . . 624 JERUSALEM 5   41
   GENERATION CAMBEL & GWENDOLEN WOVE WEBS OF WAR & OF . . . 626 JERUSALEM 7   44
   NINE TIMES GWENDOLEN & CAMBEL & GWINEVERRA . . . . 628 JERUSALEM 9   22
   BATTERSEA AND CHELSEA MOURN FOR CAMBEL & GWENDOLEN   . . 644 JERUSALEM 21   32
   AS GWENDOLEN CAST THE SHUTTLE OF WAR AS CAMBEL RETURND   703 JERUSALEM 66   62
      THE BEAM
   GWENDOLEN & CAMBEL WHO IS BOADICEA THEY GO ABROAD & RETURN 710 JERUSALEM 71   23
   WITH CAMBEL & GWENDOLEN IN DANCE AND SOLEMN SONG . . . . 722 JERUSALEM 80   39
   CAMBEL HIS BRIGHT BEAMING COUNTERPART DIVIDED FROM HIM . 723 JERUSALEM 80   58
   O SISTER CAMBEL SAID GWENDOLEN AS THEIR LONG BEAMING LIGHT 723 JERUSALEM 80   83
   WHILE GWENDOLEN SPOKE TO CAMBEL TURNING SOFT THE SPINNING   725 JERUSALEM 82   12
      REEL
   CAMBEL TREMBLED WITH JEALOUSY SHE TREMBLED SHE ENVIED . 726 JERUSALEM 82   52
   ON LONDON'S TOWER ON THE THAMES HE DREW CAMBEL IN WRATH   726 JERUSALEM 82   57
   LET CAMBEL AND HER SISTERS SIT WITHIN THE MUNDANE SHELL   727 JERUSALEM 83   33
CAMBERWELL
   TO WEAVE THE WOOF OF DEATH ON CAMBERWELL TIRZAH'S COURTS   525 MILTON 35   8
   FROM CAMBERWELL TO HIGHGATE WHERE THE MIGHTY THAMES   677 JERUSALEM 47   2
      SHUDDERS ALONG
   FROM THE HILLS OF CAMBERWELL & WIMBLEDON FROM THE VALLEYS   706 JERUSALEM 68   43
   OF CAMBERWELL WE SHALL BEHOLD YOU NO MORE IN GLORY & PRIDE 729 JERUSALEM 84   5
   OF THE DRUID ALONG THE VALLEY OF REPHAIM FROM CAMBERWELL   740 JERUSALEM 92   26
      TO GOLGOTHA
CAMBRIDGE
   IN LAMBETH'S VALES IN CAMBRIDGE & IN OXFORD PLACES   494 MILTON 13   42
      OF THOUGHT
   BATH OXFORD CAMBRIDGE NORWICH HIS RIGHT ELBOW . . . . . 531 MILTON 39   44
   MILTON IN HIS CHARACTER OF A STUDENT AT CAMBRIDGE . . . 619A ILLUS MILTON   PROSE
   THE VOID IN (INCOHERENT) DESPAIR CAMBRIDGE & OXFORD   623 JERUSALEM 5   3
      & LONDON
   WORCESTER & HEREFORD OXFORD & CAMBRIDGE REEL & STAGGER . . 703 JERUSALEM 66   66
   SKOFELD HAD ELY RUTLAND CAMBRIDGE HUNTINGDON NORFOLK . . 710 JERUSALEM 71   38
   . . . & IN OXFORD & CAMBRIDGE & WINCHESTER . . . . . 710 JERUSALEM 71   53
   ON CAMBRIDGE AND OXFORD BEAMING SOFT UNITING WITH RAHAB'S   725 JERUSALEM 82   11
      CLOUD
CAMBRIDGESHIRE
   LOS WAS THE FRIEND OF ALBION WHO MOST LOVD HIM IN   666 JERUSALEM 39   12
      CAMBRIDGESHIRE
CAME
   BUT DOWN HE CAME ALAS HOW FRAIL . . . . 17 BLIND-MANS/PS   51
   IF PHILIP CAME ARMD IN THE RIBS OF DEATH . . . . . 25 EDW THIRD/PS 3   175
   GREAT DEAL MORE THAT WE SHALL ALL HEAR BY AND BY AND I CAME 29C EDW THIRD/PS 4   PROSE
   YOUR ANCESTORS CAME FROM THE FIRES OF TROY . . . . . 32 EDW THIRD/PS 6   7
   TILL VENERABLE AGE CAME ON HIS FLOCKS INCREASED . . . 39C SAMSON/PS   PROSE
   AND LO AGAIN THE ANGEL CAME . . . . 40B SAMSON/PS   PROSE
   SHE RAN AND CALLED HER HUSBAND WHO CAME AND TALKED WITH HIM 40B SAMSON/PS   PROSE
   FROM WHOM CAME IGNORANCE WHO BROUGHT FORTH WONDER . . 40D THEN SHE BORE   PROSE
   THESE ARE THE GODS WHICH CAME FROM FEAR FOR . . . 40D THEN SHE BORE   PROSE
   FORTH CAME AMBITION CRAWLING LIKE A TOAD . . . . . 41A THEN SHE BORE   PROSE
   SO ENVY CAME & HATE TWIN PROGENY . . . . 41C THEN SHE BORE   PROSE
   IS IN THE HEAVENLY MIND FOR SHE FROM HEAVEN CAME . . . 42A THEN SHE BORE   PROSE
   I'LL SHEW HOW CONSCIENCE CAME FROM HEAVEN . . . . 42A THEN SHE BORE   PROSE
   THEN DOWN CAME CONSCIENCE WITH HIS LOVELY BAND THE . . 42B THEN SHE BORE   PROSE
   THE MUSE THEN STRUCK HER DEEPEST [NOTE] STRING & SYMPATHY 43C WOE CRIED MUSE   PROSE
      CAME FORTH
   WERE EMPLOYD WHEN MRS GIMBLET CAME IN [?HOPING] . . . . 44B ISLAND MOON 1   *PROSE
   LITTLE PHEBUS CAME STRUTTING IN . . . . 46 PHEBUS CAME/IM   1

```
                                                    PAGE     TITLE           LINE
CAME    (CONTINUED)
    WHY SAID HE IT CAME INTO MY HEAD THAT HE WAS NOT  . . . .  49A ISLAND MOON 5    PROSE
    ON THE BACK OF HIM CAME ALL THE OTHERS IN A HEAP  . . . .  59A ISLAND MOON 10   PROSE
    AT THIS INSTANT OBTUSE ANGLE CAME IN . . . . . . . .  63A ISLAND MOON 11   PROSE
    THEN HEVA CAME & TOOK OLD TIRIEL IN HER MOTHER'S ARMS . . 101 TIRIEL 2        39
    HOW CAME THINE HAIR TO LEAVE THY FOREHEAD HOW CAME THY   102 TIRIEL 3         3
        FACE SO BROWN
    HOW CAME THINE HAIR TO LEAVE THY FOREHEAD HOW CAME THY   102 TIRIEL 3         3
        FACE SO BROWN
    RUBY TEARS THERE CAME . . . . . . . . . . . . . 113 LIT GRL LST/SI   48
    AND BY CAME AN ANGEL WHO HAD A BRIGHT KEY . . . . . . 117 CHIMNEY SWP/SI   13
    TILL TO HER OWN GRAVE PLOT SHE CAME & THERE SHE SAT DOWN 130 BOOK OF THEL 6   9
    FLED BACK UNHINDERD TILL SHE CAME INTO THE VALES OF HAR  130 BOOK OF THEL 6  22
    WHEN I CAME HOME ON THE ABYSS OF THE FIVE SENSES . . . 150C MARRIAGE HH 6   PROSE
    CAME TO THINK THAT ALL NATIONS WOULD AT LAST BE SUBJECT  154A MARRIAGE HH 12 PROSE
        TO THE JEWS
    & HE SAYS I CAME NOT TO SEND PEACE BUT A SWORD . . . . 155C MARRIAGE HH 15 PROSE
    AN ANGEL CAME TO ME AND SAID O PITIABLE FOOLISH YOUNG MAN 155C MARRIAGE HH 17 PROSE
    THRO THE MILL WE WENT AND CAME TO A CAVE . . . . . 155D MARRIAGE HH 17 PROSE
    AND PASSED ALL THE PLANETS TILL WE CAME TO SATURN . . 157A MARRIAGE HH 17 PROSE
    A TRAVELLER CAME BY . . . . . . . . . 161 NEVER PAIN/N    10
    AS SOON AS I WENT AN ANGEL CAME . . . . . . . . 163 ASKED THIEF/N    5
    [HOW CAME PRIDE IN MAN] . . . . . . . . . . . 173 HOW CAME/N       1
    SOON MY ANGEL CAME AGAIN . . . . . . . . . . . 182 THE ANGEL/N     13
    I WAS ARMD HE CAME IN VAIN . . . . . . . . . . 182 THE ANGEL/N     14
    WITH BEAMS OF BLOOD & THUS A VOICE CAME FORTH AND SHOOK  198 AMERICA 5        7
        THE TEMPLE
    SHUT OUT FROM MORTAL SIGHT THE ANGEL CAME THE VALE WAS DARK 204 AMERICA CANC B  10
    TILL TO THAT VOID IT CAME & FELL SO THE DARK HOUSE WAS RENT 204 AMERICA CANC B  22
    SOON MY ANGEL CAME AGAIN . . . . . . . . . . . 214 THE ANGEL/SE    13
    I WAS ARMD HE CAME IN VAIN . . . . . . . . . . 214 THE ANGEL/SE    14
    STRANGERS CAME NOT NEAR . . . . . . . . . . . 219 LIT GRL LST/SE  18
    CAME THE MAIDEN BRIGHT . . . . . . . . . . . 219 LIT GRL LST/SE  26
    THEY HOVERD ROUND ME LIKE A CLOUD OF INCENSE WHEN I CAME 238 EUROPE INTRO    22
    THE DEEP OF WINTER CAME . . . . . . . . . . . 239 EUROPE 4         1
    AN ANGEL CAME . . . . . . . . . . . . . 261 ASKED THIEF      6
    THE VOICE CAME & WENT LIKE A DREAM I AWOKE IN MY SWEET   272 FOUR ZOAS 1    280
        BLISS
    JERUSALEM CAME DOWN IN A DIRE RUIN OVER ALL THE EARTH . . 281 FOUR ZOAS 2     45
    ONTO THE MARGIN OF NON ENTITY THE BRIGHT FEMALE CAME  . . 291 FOUR ZOAS 2   * 422
    . . . HIS STRONG RIGHT [HAD] HAND CAME FORTH . . . . 294 FOUR ZOAS 3   * 110
    WHERE NEVER YET EXISTENCE CAME THERE LOSING ALL MY LIFE  296 FOUR ZOAS 3    189
    BUT WHEN THEY CAME TO THE DARK ROCK & TO THE SPECTROUS CAVE 309 FOUR ZOAS 5    155
    AND HE CAME RIDING IN HIS FURY FROZE TO SOLID WERE HIS   313 FOUR ZOAS 6     49
        WAVES
    THEN CAME HE AMONG FIERY CITIES & CASTLES BUILT OF BURNING 314 FOUR ZOAS 6    115
        STEEL
    FOR WHEN HE CAME TO WHERE A VORTEX CEASD TO OPERATE . . 316 FOUR ZOAS 6    190
    FROM WHENCE HE CAME TWAS UPWARD ALL & IF HE TURND AND VIEWD 316 FOUR ZOAS 6    192
    AND NOW HE CAME INTO THE ABHORRED WORLD OF DARK URTHONA  319 FOUR ZOAS 6    281
    THE LIVING SOUL IN GLORIOUS FORMS & EVERY ONE CAME FORTH 340 FOUR ZOAS 7B   278
    THEN JESUS CAME & DIED WILLING BENEATH TIRZAH & RAHAB  . . 351 FOUR ZOAS 8    406
    CRIED TO THE CHURCHYARDS & THE EARTHWORM CAME IN DISMAL  355 FOUR ZOAS 8    537
        STATE
    A VOICE CAME IN THE NIGHT A MIDNIGHT CRY UPON THE MOUNTAINS 355 FOUR ZOAS 8    540
    TO THE DARK VALLEY WHENCE HE CAME TO BEGIN HIS LABOURS ANEW 355 FOUR ZOAS 8  * 575
    WHEN VOCAL MAY COMES DANCING FROM THE EAST AHANIA CAME . . 362 FOUR ZOAS 9    194
    TO YONDER BRIGHTNESS THERE I HASTE FOR SURE I CAME FROM  367 FOUR ZOAS 9    402
        THENCE
    HAH SHALL I STILL SURVIVE WHENCE CAME THAT SWEET        368 FOUR ZOAS 9    422
        & COMFORTING VOICE
    AND WHEN HE LAID HIS HAND UPON ME FROM THE GATES OF SLEEP 369 FOUR ZOAS 9    469
        I CAME
    AND WHEN NIGHT CAME THE FLOCKS LAID ROUND THE HOUSE BENEATH 370 FOUR ZOAS 9    514
        THE TREES
    AHA AHA HOW CAME I HERE SO SOON IN MY SWEET NATIVE LAND  375 FOUR ZOAS 9    687
    HOW CAME I HERE METHINKS I AM AS I WAS IN MY YOUTH . . . 375 FOUR ZOAS 9    688
    O HOW VIRTUOUS CHRIST CAME NOT TO CALL THE VIRTUOUS . . . 395D ANNO WATSON   MARG
    CAME INTO THE BALL ROOM AMONG THE FAIR . . . . . . 428 MARY             2
    A DAMP COLD CAME OER HER HER BLUSHES ALL FLED . . . . 428 MARY            19
    AND CAME HOME IN EVENING BESPATTERD WITH MIRE . . . . 428 MARY            36
    CAME FROM CAESAR'S LAUREL CROWN . . . . . . . . 433 AUGURIES        98
    BUT HE CAME HOME IN A BLACK BLACK CLOUD . . . . . . 435 WILLIAM BOND    11
    THE SOLDIER AFTER HE AND HIS COMRADE CAME TOGETHER INTO THE 438C BLAKES MEMORAN PROSE
    MR HAYLEY'S GARDENER CAME PAST AT THE TIME OF THE . . . 438D BLAKES MEMORAN PROSE
    MOSER CAME TO ME & SAID YOU SHOULD NOT STUDY THESE . . . 449C ANNO REYNOLDS  MARG
    PALAMABRON CALLD AND LOS & SATAN CAME BEFORE HIM . . . 487 MILTON 7        34
    LOS WEPT BUT RINTRAH ALSO CAME AND ENITHARMON ON . . . 488 MILTON 8        14
    I CAME FORTH FROM THE HEAD OF SATAN BACK THE GNOMES RECOILD 493 MILTON 12       38
    TRIPLE ELOHIM CAME ELOHIM WEARIED FAINTED THEY ELECTED   494 MILTON 13       22
        SHADDAI
    AND WHEN NIGHT CAME ALL WAS SILENT IN OLOLON & ALL REFUSD 504 MILTON 21       26
        TO LAMENT
    AS THE CLEAR SUN & MILTON SILENT CAME DOWN ON MY PATH  . . 530 MILTON 39        5
    SO REYNOLDS WHEN HE CAME TO DIE . . . . . . . . 542 PITIFUL CASE/N   5
    HOW OTHER ANTIQUITIES CAME TO BE NEGLECTED AND . . . 578D DESC CAT 5     PROSE
    CHRIST COMES AS HE CAME AT FIRST TO DELIVER THOSE . . . 615B V LAST JUDG/N  PROSE
    TILL HIS SONS & DAUGHTERS CAME FORTH FROM THE FURNACES . . 630 JERUSALEM 10    64
    THEN ERIN CAME FORTH FROM THE FURNACES & ALL THE DAUGHTERS 630 JERUSALEM 11     8
        OF BEULAH
    CAME FROM THE FURNACES BY LOS'S MIGHTY POWER FOR        630 JERUSALEM 11     9
        JERUSALEM'S
```

CAME   (CONTINUED)
AND THE SONS AND DAUGHTERS OF LOS CAME FORTH IN PERFECTION   630 JERUSALEM 11   11
    LOVELY
TILL SKOFIELD'S NIMROD THE MIGHTY HUNTSMAN JEHOVAH CAME   644 JERUSALEM 22   3
I CAME HERE WITH INTENTION TO ANNIHILATE THEE BUT   . . .   645 JERUSALEM 23   3
THY SONS CAME TO JERUSALEM WITH GIFTS SHE SENT THEM AWAY   647 JERUSALEM 24   38
THEY CAME UP TO JERUSALEM THEY WALKED BEFORE ALBION . . .   647 JERUSALEM 24   41
FORTHWITH FROM ALBION'S DARKNING LOCKS CAME TWO IMMORTAL   654 JERUSALEM 29   28
    FORMS
HE CAME DOWN FROM HIGHGATE THRO HACKNEY & HOLLOWAY TOWARDS   657 JERUSALEM 31   14
    LONDON
TILL HE CAME TO OLD STRATFORD & THENCE TO STEPNEY & THE   657 JERUSALEM 31   15
    ISLE
IN STERN DEFIANCE CAME FROM ALBION'S BOSOM HAND HYLE KOBAN   658 JERUSALEM 32   10
UNKNOWN AMONG THE DEAD WHERE NEVER BEFORE EXISTENCE CAME   661 JERUSALEM 34   38
AND THE DIVINE VOICE CAME FROM THE FURNACES AS MULTITUDES   662 JERUSALEM 35   3
    WITHOUT
THE TWENTY-FOUR HEARD THEY CAME TREMBLING ON WATRY CHARIOTS   667 JERUSALEM 40   21
THE SLUMBERS OF DEATH CAME OVER THEM AROUND THE COUCH OF   674 JERUSALEM 44   35
    DEATH
THEY NAMD THE EIGHTH HE CAME NOT HE HID IN ALBION'S FORESTS   686 JERUSALEM 55   33
KNOWETH THE INFANT SORROW WHENCE IT CAME AND WHERE IT GOETH   688 JERUSALEM 56   6
O IT WAS LOST FOR EVER AND WE FOUND IT NOT IT CAME   . . .   688 JERUSALEM 56   26
THEN THE RESPONSE CAME WARBLING FROM TRILLING LOOMS IN   688 JERUSALEM 56   38
    ALBION
TILL HE CAME TO THE ROCK OF AGES & HE TOOK HIS SEAT UPON   689 JERUSALEM 57   16
    THE ROCK
OF DEATH BUT HOW THEY CAME FORTH FROM THE FURNACES & HOW   713 JERUSALEM 73   7
    LONG
CAME TO CONSULT HIM SECRETLY   . . . .   750 EV GOSPEL(C)/N   10
CAME TO CONSULT HIM SECRETLY   . . . .   751 EV GOSPEL(D)/N   12
METHODISM ETC P...COWPER CAME TO ME AND SAID   . . .   772B ANNO SPURZHEIM   MARG
JESUS CAME TO REMOVE WAS THE HEATHEN OR PLATONIC PHILOSOPHY   775B ANNO BERKELEY   MARG
IN THE WILDERNESS LO WHAT ARE THESE WHENCE CAME THEY   . .   776D INSC LAOCOON   PROSE
DIVINE WHENCE THEY CAME OR WHITHER THEY WERE BOUND   . .   791B LETTER 3   PROSE
EZRA CAME WITH ISAIAH THE PROPHET . . . .   799 TO FLAXMAN/L   6
MUCH MILDER THAN IT WAS IN LONDON WHEN WE CAME AWAY   . .   806B LETTER 16   PROSE
WHEN I CAME DOWN HERE I WAS MORE SANGUINE THAN I AM   . .   811C LETTER 22   PROSE
NAKED WE CAME HERE NAKED OF NATURAL THINGS & NAKED   . .   813C LETTER 22   PROSE
WHAT CAME FROM MY HEAD & MY HEART IN UNISON THAT I AM PROUD 814D LETTER 23   PROSE
    OF BEING
CONVERSATION WITH AN OLD SOLDIER WHO CAME IN THE COACH WITH 833B LETTER 33   PROSE
WHEN HIS DAUGHTER CAME IN HE GAVE THE PRINT INTO HER HAND   843C LETTER 43   PROSE
MR CROMEK THE ENGRAVER CAME TO ME DESIRING TO HAVE SOME   861C LETTER 59   PROSE
A RETURN OF THE OLD SHIVERING FIT CAME ON THIS MORNING   . . 869B LETTER 69   PROSE
I HAVE HAD ANOTHER DESPERATE SHIVERING FIT IT CAME ON   . . 872B LETTER 75   PROSE
CAMEL
    ASK THE WILD ASS WHY HE REFUSES BURDENS AND THE MEEK CAMEL   191 V DAU ALBION 3   7
CAMELS
    ME FROM MY CRADLE THE AMALEKITE STOLE ME AWAY UPON HIS   695 JERUSALEM 61   41
    CAMELS
CAMERA OBSCURA
    NO SAID INFLAMMABLE GASS I HAVE GOT A CAMERA OBSCURA AT   47C ISLAND MOON 3 PROSE
    HOME
CAMEST
    WHENCE CAMEST THOU WHO ART THOU O LOVELIEST THE DIVINE   659 JERUSALEM 33   33
    VISION
CAMOENS
    ABSORBED BY THE POETS MILTON HOMER CAMOENS ERCILLA ARIOSTO   806D LETTER 17   PROSE
CAMP
    THROUGHOUT THE CAMP ENFLAME THE TIMOROUS   . . . . .   25 EDW THIRD/PS 3   179
    SCENE IN THE CAMP SEVERAL OF THE WARRIORS MET AT . . . .   31D EDW THIRD/PS 6 PROSE
    WE HAVE HIRELINGS IN THE CAMP THE COURT & THE UNIVERSITY   480C MILTON 1   PROSE
    FOR THE SANCTUARY OF EDEN IS IN THE CAMP IN THE OUTLINE   708 JERUSALEM 69   41
CAMPD
    BENEATH HIM ROLLD HIS NUMROUS HOSTS ALL ALBION'S ANGELS   201 AMERICA 13   13
    CAMPD
CAMPS
    ARE THUS DIVIDED THE FOUR COUNTIES ARE IN THE FOUR CAMPS   711 JERUSALEM 72   2
CAN (NOUN)
    THE MERRY CAN OF NUT-BROWN ALE   . . . .   16 BLIND-MANS/PS   9
CANAAN
    THE DAUGHTERS OF AMALEK CANAAN & MOAB BINDING ON   348 FOUR ZOAS 8   * 295
    THE [STEMS] STONES
    THE DAUGHTERS OF CANAAN & MOAB BINDING ON THE STONES   . . 382 FOUR ZOAS AD 6   11
    CANAAN THEN SHE RETURND TO LOS WEARY FRIGHTED AS   490 MILTON 10   *   5
    FROM DREAMS
    BECAME CANAAN CLOSING LOS FROM ETERNITY IN ALBION'S CLIFFS   491 MILTON 10   10
    OF CANAAN AND THEY WROTE IN THUNDER SMOKE AND FIRE   498 MILTON 17   13
    SAYING COME THOU TO EPHRAIM BEHOLD THE KINGS OF CANAAN   . 501 MILTON 19   36
    OF CANAAN AND REIGN IN HAZOR WHERE THE TWELVE TRIBES MEET   501 MILTON 20   6
    RINTRAH THOU WELL REMEMBEREST WHEN AMALEK & CANAAN   . . . 508 MILTON 24   14
    APPEARD THE SEVEN KINGDOMS OF CANAAN & FIVE BAALIM   . . . 532 MILTON 40   24
    MOAB & AMMON & AMALEK & CANAAN & EGYPT & ARAM   . . . . .   623 JERUSALEM 5   14
    FROM HIS VALLEYS EASTWARD FROM AMALEK CANAAN & MOAB   . .   654 JERUSALEM 29   31
    CONSTRICTING INTO DRUID ROCKS ROUND CANAAN AGAG & ARAM   685 JERUSALEM 54   26
    & PHAROH
    CANAAN IS HIS PORTICO JORDAN IS A FOUNTAIN IN HIS PORCH   690 JERUSALEM 58   33
    TO NIMROD'S TOWER TO HAM & CANAAN WALKING WITH MIZRAIM   . 692 JERUSALEM 60   18
    INSTEAD OF HUMAN VICTIMS BY THE DAUGHTERS OF ALBION   697 JERUSALEM 63   31
    & CANAAN
    TILL CANAAN ROLLD APART FROM ALBION ACROSS THE RHINE ALONG 698 JERUSALEM 63   41
    THE DANUBE

```
                                                             PAGE     TITLE            LINE
CANAAN    (CONTINUED)
    AND ALL THE LAND OF CANAAN SUSPENDED OVER THE VALLEY OF      698 JERUSALEM 63        42
      CHEVIOT
    OF THE MUNDANE SHELL WHICH FROZE ON ALL SIDES ROUND CANAAN   698 JERUSALEM 64         1
      ON
    THAT DROP WITH CRIMSON GORE WITH THE LOVES OF ALBION &       699 JERUSALEM 64        37
      CANAAN
    THE KING OF CANAAN WHOSE ARE SEVEN HUNDRED CHARIOTS OF IRON  702 JERUSALEM 66        25
    BEFORE THE KINGS OF CANAAN TO CUT THE FLESH FROM THE VICTIM  706 JERUSALEM 68        57
    KINGS OF CANAAN THEN TO LET THE SPIES DEPART TO MERIBAH      707 JERUSALEM 68        61
      KADESH
    GOING FORTH & RETURNING FROM ALBION'S ROCKS TO CANAAN    . . 707 JERUSALEM 69         4
    AND ABOVE ALBION'S LAND WAS SEEN THE HEAVENLY CANAAN     . . 709 JERUSALEM 71         1
    HOW LOS DRAVE THEM FROM ALBION & THEY BECAME DAUGHTERS       715 JERUSALEM 74        38
      OF CANAAN
    OVER THE LAND OF CANAAN THEY HAVE DIVIDED JUDAH   . . . .    715 JERUSALEM 74        48
    AND FLAMES OF DUSKY FIRE TO AMALEK CANAAN AND MOAB   . . .   723 JERUSALEM 80        50
    DIVIDE THEM INTO THREE NAME THEM AMALEK CANAAN & MOAB    . . 725 JERUSALEM 82        24
    SEE SISTERS CANAAN IS PLEASANT EGYPT IS AS THE GARDEN OF     725 JERUSALEM 82        30
      EDEN
    I CALL TO CANAAN & MOAB IN MY NIGHT WATCHES THEY MOURN   . . 727 JERUSALEM 83        17
    THEY NAMD IT CANAAN & BUILT FOR IT A TENDER MOON    . . . .  730 JERUSALEM 85         2
    THERE THE SEVEN KINGS OF CANAAN & FIVE BAALIM OF PHILISTEA   735 JERUSALEM 89        46
    DISPLAYD IN THE EMANATIVE VISIONS OF CANAAN IN JERUSALEM     739 JERUSALEM 92        21
      & IN SHILOH
CANAANITE
    THE AMALEKITE THE CANAANITE THE MOABITE THE EGYPTIAN     .   634 JERUSALEM 13        58
    WHILE REUBEN ENROOTS HIS BRETHREN IN THE NARROW CANAANITE    636 JERUSALEM 15        25
    PITS OF BITUMEN EVER BURNING ARTIFICIAL RICHES OF           673 JERUSALEM 43        62
      THE CANAANITE
    THE CANAANITE THE AMALEKITE THE MOABITE THE EGYPTIAN     . . 673 JERUSALEM 43        66
    HENCE ALBION WAS CALLD THE CANAANITE & ALL HIS GIANT SONS    715 JERUSALEM 74        39
    IN THE LOINS OF ALBION THE CANAANITE UNITED WITH            739 JERUSALEM 92         3
      THE FUGITIVE
    HE SCOURGD THE MERCHANT CANAANITE . . . . . . . . .          749 EV GOSPEL(B)/N     48
CANAANITES
    BUT THE DESTRUCTION OF THE CANAANITES BY JOSHUA    . . . .388B ANNO WATSON      * MARG
    SHUAH'S DAUGHTER & TAMAR & RAHAB THE CANAANITES    . . . .   696 JERUSALEM 62        10
CANADA
    I SEE A SERPENT IN CANADA WHO COURTS ME TO HIS LOVE   . . .  196 AMERICA PREL 2      12
    CONGO ZAARA CANADA GREENLAND CAROLINA MEXICO     . . . . .   712 JERUSALEM 72        41
CANADIAN
    ON THE CANADIAN WILDS I FOLD FEEBLE MY SPIRIT FOLDS   . . .  196 AMERICA PREL 1      17
CANCER
    HAVING HER CANCER CUT & SHE SHRIEKD SO THAT I WAS QUITE      51C ISLAND MOON 6    PROSE
      SICK
    BECAME A RAVENING EATING CANCER GROWING IN THE FEMALE    . . 707 JERUSALEM 69         2
CANDLE
    I TOLD HIM HE LOOKD LIKE A CANDLE HALF   . . . . . . .        25 EDW THIRD/PS 3      158
    THE EPICUREAN SEEMING [NOT] STUDYING THE FLAME OF            44C ISLAND MOON 1    PROSE
      THE CANDLE
    BETTER THAN HIS MASTER FOR HE ONLY HOLDS A CANDLE          158A MARRIAGE HH 21   PROSE
      IN SUNSHINE
    AS SOON AS HE PUTS IT OFF AND PUTS OUT THE CANDLE    . . .  586A DESC CAT 16     PROSE
CANDLESTICK
    [&] THE CANDLESTICK ON THE RIGHT   . . . . . . . .          444B LAST JUDGMNT/L  PROSE
    CANDLESTICK & THE TABLE OF SHEW BREAD APPEAR ON EACH SIDE   613B V LAST JUDG/N   PROSE
CANDOUR
    HIS SOFTNESS & CANDOUR THE HIDDEN TRAP & THE POISONED FEAST 452A ANNO REYNOLDS    MARG
    UNDER PRETENCE OF FAIR CRITICISM AND CANDOUR   . . . . .    864A LETTER 61       PROSE
CANNON
    INTO THE THUNDERING CANNON AND INTO THE MURDERING GUN    . . 628 JERUSALEM 9          6
CANNONS
    . . . WHEN BRAZEN CANNONS RAGE IN THE FIELD    . . . . .     146 FRENCH REVOLTN     262
    . . . IN DAY OF THE BRITISH FLAG WHEN HEAVY CANNONS   . . .  147 FRENCH REVOLTN     280
    MINGLED OR SEPARATE FOR SWORDS ARROWS CANNONS MORTARS    .   713 JERUSALEM 73        11
CANON
    "HIS CANON GAINST SELF SLAUGHTER" SHAKESPEARE   . . . . .   SUPP LEGEND/N95      *
CANOPIED
    ON CHAIRS OF IRON CANOPIED WITH MYSTIC ORNAMENTS    . . . .  204 AMERICA CANC B      13
    NOAH IS SEEN IN THE MIDST OF THESE CANOPIED BY A RAINBOW    609D V LAST JUDG/N   PROSE
    WITH SIXTEEN PILLARS CANOPIED WITH EMBLEMS & WRITTEN VERSE   677 JERUSALEM 48         7
CANOPY
    SPREADING INTO THE AZURE WINGS WHICH LIKE A CANOPY    . . .  731 JERUSALEM 86         9
CANST
    AN ARMY OF MIGHTY MEN ARE AS FLOCKS IN THE VALLIES WHAT      39A SAMSON/PS       PROSE
      CANST
    WHAT CANST THOU GIVE WHEN SUCH A TRIFLE IS DENIED ME BUT     39A SAMSON/PS       PROSE
    THINK NOT THOU CANST SIGH A SIGH   . . . . . . . . .         123 ON ANOTHERS/SI     29
    THINK NOT THOU CANST WEEP A TEAR   . . . . . . . . .         123 ON ANOTHERS/SI     31
    AH WEEP NOT LITTLE VOICE THOU CANST NOT SPEAK BUT THOU       129 BOOK OF THEL 4      4
      CANST WEEP
    IF THOU CANST NOT DO THIS DOUBT THY THEORIES . . . . . .    143 FRENCH REVOLTN     193
    [[CANST] THOU CANST ANY SECRET KEEP] . . . . . . . . .      164 CRADLE SONG/N  *     4
    THOU CANST REPOSE ON CLOUDS OF SECRECY WHILE OER MY LIMBS    288 FOUR ZOAS 2       319
    THOU NEVER CANST EMBRACE SWEET ENITHARMON TERRIBLE DEMON     328 FOUR ZOAS 7       342
      TILL
    ANGER ME NOT THOU CANST NOT DRIVE THE HARROW IN PITY'S       483 MILTON 4          16
      PATHS
    TROUBLE ME NO MORE THOU CANST NOT HAVE ETERNAL LIFE . . .    483 MILTON 4          18
    THREE THOU HAST SLAIN I AM THE FOURTH THOU CANST            670 JERUSALEM 42        24
      NOT DESTROY ME
```

	PAGE	TITLE	LINE

CANST (CONTINUED)

JESUS REPLIED FEAR NOT ALBION UNLESS I DIE THOU CANST NOT   743 JERUSALEM 96   14
    LIVE
CANST THOU FORGIVE MY BLASPHEMY   . . . . 755 EV GOSPEL(E)/N   76
CANST THOU RETURN TO THIS DARK HELL   . . . . 755 EV GOSPEL(E)/N   77
AND CANST THOU DIE THAT I MAY LIVE   . . . . 755 EV GOSPEL(E)/N   79
AND CANST THOU PITY & FORGIVE   . . . . 755 EV GOSPEL(E)/N   80
NOR CANST THOU EVER CHANGE KATE INTO NAN   . . . . 771 EPILOGUE/GP   4

CAN'T

AND GIVEN HIM I DONT KNOW WHAT AND I CAN'T TELL   . . 29C EDW THIRD/PS 4   PROSE
BUT I MEANT SAID ARADOBO I I I CAN'T THINK LAW SIR   . . . 49A ISLAND MOON 5   PROSE
[THE FLOCKS ARE AT PLAY & WE CAN'T GO AWAY]   . . . . 60 NURSES SONG/IM   11
HES A BLOCKHEAD WHO WANTS A PROOF OF WHAT HE CAN'T PERCIEVE   540 BLOCKHEAD/N   1
IF THEY CAN'T SEE AN OUTLINE PRAY HOW CAN THEY MAKE IT   . . 549 ALL PICTURES/N   6
TO TELL YOU ANY THING THAT HE CAN'T PROVE   . . . . . 551 WILLM COWPER/N   10
FOR A BOY [NEVER LEARNS SO MUCH] CAN'T INTERPRET THE THING   552 WHY CUPID/N   11

CANT

[IS THIS POLITENESS OR IS IT CANT]   . . . . 542 FLORENTINE/N   *   19
TIS THE TRADING ENGLISH VENETIAN CANT   . . . . . . 542 FLORENTINE/N   20

CANTERBURY

THE CANTERBURY PILGRIMS FROM CHAUCER A CABINET PICTURE   560B EXHIBITION ADV   PROSE
    IN FRESCO
PICTURE OF THE CANTERBURY PILGRIMS WHICH IS TO BE ENGRAVED   563B DESC CAT   PROSE
THE CANTERBURY PILGRIMS FROM CHAUCER   . . . . . . 564B DESC CAT   TITLE
PILGRIMS ON THEIR JOURNEY TO CANTERBURY   . . . . . 566C DESC CAT 3   TITLE
OF CHAUCER'S CHARACTERS AS DESCRIBED IN HIS CANTERBURY   567C DESC CAT 3   PROSE
    TALES
EVERY AGE IS A CANTERBURY PILGRIMAGE WE   . . . . 570D DESC CAT 3   PROSE
AND PARTICULARLY IN HIS CANTERBURY TALES THAT HE WAS VERY   575A DESC CAT 3   PROSE
WHICH WAS NOT THE WAY TO CANTERBURY BUT PERHAPS   . . . . 575B DESC CAT 3   PROSE
IN IMMORTAL THOUGHTS IF MR B'S(BLAKE'S) CANTERBURY PILGRIMS   576B DESC CAT 4   PROSE
BLAKE'S CHAUCER THE CANTERBURY PILGRIMS THE FRESCO PICTURE   586C CHAUCER 1   TITLE
FROM HIS FRESCO PAINTING OF CHAUCER'S CANTERBURY PILGRIMS   587D CHAUCER/N   TITLE
ON THEIR JOURNEY TO CANTERBURY   . . . . 588B CHAUCER/N   TITLE
"WHO JOURNEY TO SAINT THOMAS'S SHRINE AT CANTERBURY"   . 589A CHAUCER/N   PROSE
FROM SOUTHWARK ON THEIR JOURNEY TO CANTERBURY   . . . . 589C CHAUCER 2   TITLE
"SIR JEFFREY CHAUCER AND HIS PILGRIMS SET OUT FOR   590B CHAUCER 2   PROSE
    CANTERBURY"
"WHO JOURNEY TO ST THOMAS'S SHRINE AT CANTERBURY"   . . . 590C CHAUCER 2   PROSE
OF CHAUCER'S CHARACTERS AS DESCRIBED IN HIS CANTERBURY   590C CHAUCER 2   PROSE
    TALES
CHAUCER'S CANTERBURY PILGRIMS BEING A COMPLETE INDEX   . 591A PUB ADDRESS/N   TITLE
THIS DAY IS PUBLISHD ADVERTIZEMENTS TO BLAKE'S CANTERBURY   591B PUB ADDRESS/N   PROSE
GO THOU TO SKOFIELD ASK HIM IF HE IS BATH OR IF HE   640 JERUSALEM 17   59
    IS CANTERBURY
BATTERSEA & CHELSEA MOURN LONDON & CANTERBURY TREMBLE   . . 659 JERUSALEM 33   12
VERULAM CANTERBURY VENERABLE PARENT OF MEN   . . . . . 665 JERUSALEM 38   45
TO MALDEN & CANTERBURY IN THE DELIGHTS OF CRUELTY   . . . 668 JERUSALEM 41   6
AND THE VOICES OF BATH & CANTERBURY & YORK & EDINBURGH CRY   689 JERUSALEM 57   1
LOS ON THE THAMES & MEDWAY LONDON & CANTERBURY GROAN IN   698 JERUSALEM 63   35
    PAIN
GIRD ON THY FLAMING ZONE DESCEND INTO THE SEPULCHER OF   700 JERUSALEM 65   39
    CANTERBURY
ABILITIES AS ALSO FOR THE D(DEAN) OF C(CANTERBURY) BUT   . . 868D LETTER 68   PROSE
TO SAINT THOMAS'S SHRINE AT CANTERBURY   . . . . . . SUPP ILLUS CHAUCER   *TITLE

CANTERBURY'S

ON CANTERBURY'S RUINS HIS RIGHT HAND COVERS LOFTY WALES   531 MILTON 39   41

CANTING

THEIR PARENTS BROUGHT THEM FORTH & AGED IGNORANCE PREACHES   242 EUROPE 12   7
    CANTING

CANTO

LESSER CIRCLE POINT OF THE UNIVERSE CANTO ELEVENTH LINE...   786A ILLS DANTE 101   PROSE
CENTAURS MOST LIKELY DANTE DESCRIBES THE...CIRCLES IN CANTO   786A ILLS DANTE 101   PROSE
    XI...

CANTOS

METAL RULES AT THE ENDS OF THE CANTOS BUT HE CONFESSD   . 857B LETTER 54   PROSE

CANUTE

CANUTE DARK HAIR & EYES   . . . . SUPP ILLUS HISTORY   *TITLE

CANVAS

A WALL ON CANVAS OR WOOD OR ANY OTHER PORTABLE THING   . 560D EXHIBITION ADV   PROSE
AS PAINTING OUGHT TO BE DRAWING ON CANVAS OR ANY OTHER   . 591D PUB ADDRESS/N   PROSE
PAINTING IS DRAWING ON CANVAS   . . . . 594C PUB ADDRESS/N   PROSE
ON CANVAS & WOOD & COPPER &C   . . . . 598A PUB ADDRESS/N   PROSE
A POOL [?& HE] PAINTING IS DRAWING ON CANVAS   . . . . 602B PUB ADDRESS/N   *PROSE
CANVAS WHICH I BROUGHT DOWN WITH ME FOR THERE WERE THREE   816C LETTER 24   PROSE
ON A CANVAS ABOUT TWO FEET BY ONE AND A HALF   . . . . 843D LETTER 43   PROSE

CANVASS

DRAWINGS ON CANVASS BUT NOT PICTURES   . . . . . . 585A DESC CAT 15   PROSE

CAP

IF YOU SHOULD PUT ON YOUR CONSIDERING CAP JUST AS YOU DID   870B LETTER 71   PROSE

CAPABLE

MAN IS A TWOFOLD BEING ONE PART CAPABLE OF EVIL   . . . . 80A ANNO LAVATER   MARG
& THE OTHER CAPABLE OF GOOD   . . . . 80A ANNO LAVATER   MARG
THAT WHICH IS CAPABLE OF GOOD IS NOT ALSO CAPABLE OF EVIL   80A ANNO LAVATER   MARG
    BUT
THAT WHICH IS CAPABLE OF EVIL IS ALSO CAPABLE OF GOOD   80A ANNO LAVATER   MARG
    THIS APHORISM
SEEMS TO CONSIDER MAN AS SIMPLE & YET CAPABLE OF EVIL   . . 80A ANNO LAVATER   MARG
BUT MANY ARE NOT CAPABLE OF A FIRM PERSWASION OF ANY THING   153C MARRIAGE HH 12   PROSE
BUT NEVER CAPABLE OF ANSWERING WHO SITS WITH A SLY GRIN   533 MILTON 41   13
ART IS LINEAMENTS OR FORMS AND FEATURES THAT ARE CAPABLE OF   579D DESC CAT 5   PROSE
THE BARDS WHO WERE CAPABLE OF ATTENDING WARLIKE DEEDS   . . 580C DESC CAT 5   PROSE

```
                                                           PAGE     TITLE           LINE
CAPABLE    (CONTINUED)
    AS [IS] IT IS CAPABLE OF BEING PLACED IN ANY HEIGHT &   601A PUB ADDRESS/N    *PROSE
        INDEED
    & IS SO UNTRACTABLE THO CAPABLE OF SUCH BEAUTY & PERFECTION 837D LETTER 36       PROSE
    PRESENT STATE THEY WILL BE CAPABLE OF VERY MUCH IMPROVEMENT 853C LETTER 52       PROSE
    IF THE MACHINE IS CAPABLE OF IT SHALL MAKE AN OLD MAN YET  873C LETTER 77        PROSE
CAPACIOUSNESS
    AS A CUP CANNOT CONTAIN MORE THAN ITS CAPACIOUSNESS . . .    90B ANNO SWED LOVE  MARG
CAPACITIES
    IF MEN OF WEAK CAPACITIES [IN ART] HAVE ALONE THE POWER     591B PUB ADDRESS/N   PROSE
CAPACITY
    OF GREAT CAPACITY  . . . . . . . . . . . . .                 57 TO BE OR/IM        2
    OR EVEN OF COMMON CAPACITY I CANNOT  . . . . . . .          404B ANNO BACON      MARG
    ONE HOUR OF THE LABOUR OF ORDINARY CAPACITY   . . . . .     593A PUB ADDRESS/N   PROSE
CAPANIUS
    VERY SATAN CAPANIUS OTHELLO A MURDERER PROMETHEUS JUPITER   412B ANNO BOYD       MARG
CAPER
    ON WHICH HE USD TO DANCE & SPORT & CAPER    . . . . . .     537 AND HIS LEGS/N     19
CAPTAIN     SEE CAPTN,SEA CAPTAIN
    DEPART AND THE STERN CAPTAIN STROKES HIS PROUD STEED . . .  147 FRENCH REVOLTN    288
    A TRADING MASTER OF A VESSEL CALLED BY COURTESY CAPTAIN    575C DESC CAT 3       PROSE
CAPTAINS
    . . . THE CAPTAINS LIKE MEN BOUND IN CHAINS  . . . . .      141 FRENCH REVOLTN    165
    . . . AND BEFORE EXPECTING CAPTAINS   . . . . . . . .       146 FRENCH REVOLTN    273
    . . . CAPTAINS OF FOOT STAND EACH BY HIS CLOUDY DRUM   . .  147 FRENCH REVOLTN    289
    [HIS CAPTAINS FALSE AROUND]  . . . . . . . . . .            186 LET BROTHELS/N     44
    PAMPERD IN PALACES [OF] FOR OUR FOOD THE BLOOD OF CAPTAINS  334 FOUR ZOAS 7B   *  46
        NURTURD
    I SEE THEM DIE BENEATH THE WHIPS OF THE CAPTAINS THEY ARE   644 JERUSALEM 21      42
        TAKEN
    OF OUR CAPTAINS FEARING OUR OFFICERS MORE THAN THE ENEMY    700 JERUSALEM 65      36
    BENEATH THE IRON WHIPS OF THEIR CAPTAINS & CONSECRATED      704 JERUSALEM 67      30
        BANNERS
    OF WAR THE CYMBALS PLAY LOUD BEFORE THE CAPTAINS  . . . .   722 JERUSALEM 80      38
CAPTIVE
    AND SHE HERSELF (LED) CAPTIVE & . . . . . . . . . .         279 FOUR ZOAS 1      547
    AND THE CAPTIVE IN CHAINS & THE POOR IN THE PRISON . . .    291 FOUR ZOAS 2      415
    CAPTIVE A WILLING CAPTIVE BY DELUSIVE ARTS IMPELLD   . . .  356 FOUR ZOAS 8      598
    THE CAPTIVE IN THE MILL OF THE STRANGER SOLD FOR SCANTY     642 JERUSALEM 20      16
        HIRE
    WITH PLEASURE WITHOUT PAIN FOR THEIR FOOD IS BLOOD OF THE   706 JERUSALEM 68      37
        CAPTIVE
CAPTIVES
    SPRING LIKE REDEEMED CAPTIVES WHEN THEIR BONDS & BARS ARE   198 AMERICA 6          5
        BURST
    EDWARD THE BLACK PRINCE BRINGS HIS CAPTIVES TO HIS FATHER  209A SUBJCTS HIST/N  TITLE
    MY LITTLE DAUGHTERS WERE MADE CAPTIVES & I SAW THEM BEATEN  334 FOUR ZOAS 7B      60
    THEY SOUND THE CLARIONS STRONG THEY CHAIN THE HOWLING       337 FOUR ZOAS 7B     164
        CAPTIVES
    PRIESTS & CHAIND CAPTIVES MET TOGETHER IN A HORRIBLE FEAR   363 FOUR ZOAS 9      244
    AND BLACK HORSES & ARMED MEN & MISERABLE BOUND CAPTIVES     375 FOUR ZOAS 9      667
    AND WHO SHALL MOURN FOR MYSTERY WHO NEVER LOOSD HER         375 FOUR ZOAS 9      669
        CAPTIVES
    THE CAPTIVES REARD TO HEAVEN HOWL IN FLAMES AMONG THE STARS 677 JERUSALEM 47       8
    THEY SOUND THE CLARIONS STRONG THEY CHAIN THE HOWLING       699 JERUSALEM 65       6
        CAPTIVES
    LAMENTING AMONG THE TIMBRELS OF THE WARRIORS AMONG THE      721 JERUSALEM 80       7
        CAPTIVES
    BY CONTENTIONS OF THE MIGHTY FOR SACRIFICE OF CAPTIVES  . . 726 JERUSALEM 82      41
    YOUR SLAVES & CAPTIVES YOU COMPELL TO WORSHIP A GOD OF      737 JERUSALEM 90      56
        MERCY
CAPTIVITY
    PARENTS MUST BE CARRIED INTO CAPTIVITY TO REDEEM HER SOUL   640 JERUSALEM 18      34
    HER TWELVE GATES THROWN DOWN HER CHILDREN CARRIED INTO      719 JERUSALEM 78      23
        CAPTIVITY
    HER CHILDREN IN CAPTIVITY LISTENING TO VALA'S LAMENTATION   722 JERUSALEM 80      10
    TO ENGRAVE...PLATES FROM HIS OWN DESIGNS OF JOB'S CAPTIVITY SUPP LETTER 67D    *PROSE
CAPTN
    AGAINST ME BY A PRIVATE IN CAPTN LEATHES'S TROOP OF (FIRST) 826D LETTER 28       PROSE
        OR
CAR
    THY VOICE WHEN NOON UPON HIS FERVID CAR . . . . . . . .       2 TO SUMMER/PS       8
    NOR BEND THY PILLARS WITH THINE IRON CAR  . . . . . . .       2 TO WINTER/PS       4
    SMILES ON MY HEAD AND MOUNTS HIS FLAMING CAR  . . . . .       9 FRESH FROM/PS      2
CARACCHE     SEE CARRACHE
    FAULTS CARACCHE CORREGIO'S & RAFAEL'S HAVE FAULTS    . . . 815A LETTER 23       *PROSE
CARACTACUS
    CARACTACUS  . . . . . . . . . . . . . . . . . . . . . . . SUPP ILLUS HISTORY  *TITLE
CARBUNCLE
    A CREST OF FIRE ROSE ON HIS FOREHEAD RED AS THE CARBUNCLE   342 FOUR ZOAS 8      69
CARCASES
    AND SEEM TO SCENT THE ROTTEN CARCASES  . . . . . . . .       31 EDW THIRD/PS 5    44
    THE STINK OF YOUR DEAD CARCASES ANNOYING MAN & BEAST   . .  100 TIRIEL 1          46
    NO YOUR REMEMBRANCE SHALL PERISH FOR WHEN YOUR CARCASES     100 TIRIEL 1          48
    FLOAT THE DEAD CARCASES OF MEN & BEASTS DRIVEN TO & FRO     359 FOUR ZOAS 9      77
        ON WAVES
CARD
    THE LITTLE CARD I WILL DO AS SOON AS POSSIBLE BUT WHEN YOU  879A LETTER 88       PROSE
CARDIGANSHIRE
    CARDIGANSHIRE & THE GATE OF LEVI IN MONTGOMERYSHIRE  . . .  637 JERUSALEM 16      36
CARDINAL
    AND THE FOUR FACES OF HUMANITY FRONTING THE FOUR CARDINAL   745 JERUSALEM 98      26
        POINTS
```

	PAGE	TITLE	LINE

CARDINAL'S

O ENGLISHMEN WHY ARE YOU STILL OF THIS FOOLISH CARDINAL'S — 445D ANNO REYNOLDS — MARG
OPINION

CARE

THE BLUSHING BANK IS ALL MY CARE . . . . 15 BLIND-MANS/PS 3
GLORY MAY NOT BE DIMMD WITH CLOUDS OF CARE . . . . . 19 EDW THIRD/PS 2 15
BE ENGLAND'S TRADE OUR CARE AND WE AS TRADESMEN . . . . 19 EDW THIRD/PS 2 34
THY CARE PRUNE ALL EXTRAVAGANT SHOOTS AND GUIDE . . 26 EDW THIRD/PS 3 212
FOR CARE WAS I BROUGHT FORTH AND LABOUR IS MY LOT . . . 39B SAMSON/PS PROSE
WAS BORN ENVY IN DIREFUL PAINS HIM BORE THEN ENVY BROUGHT 42C THEN SHE BORE PROSE
FORTH CARE
CARE SITTETH IN THE WRINKLED BROW . . . . 42C THEN SHE BORE PROSE
CARE BROUGHT FORTH COVET EYELESS & PRONE TO TH EARTH . 42C THEN SHE BORE PROSE
IF I HAD ONLY MYSELF TO CARE FOR . . . . 52B ISLAND MOON 8 PROSE
IF I HAD ONLY MYSELF TO CARE FOR ID WRING OFF THEIR NOSES 53C ISLAND MOON 8 PROSE
WHY SHOULD THY SONS CARE FOR THY CURSES THOU ACCURSED MAN 99 TIRIEL 1 16
GONE WAS ALL THEIR CARE . . . . 114 LIT GRL FND/SI 40
DOES LAUGH AWAY CARE . . . . 116 ECCHOING GR/SI 12
IS MAN HIS CHILD AND CARE . . . . 117 DIVNE IMAGE/SI 8
HEAR THE SMALL BIRD'S GRIEF & CARE . . . . 122 ON ANOTHERS/SI 15
SAYING COME OUT FROM THE GROVE MY LOVE & CARE . . . . . 125 LIT BLK BOY/SI 19
AND FEEL THEY KNOW NOT WHAT BUT CARE . . . . 126 VOICE BARD/SI 10
NOR FOR ITSELF HATH ANY CARE . . . . 162 CLOD PEBBLE/N 2
WHY SHOULD I CARE FOR THE MEN OF THAMES . . . . 166 WHY CARE FOR/N 1
AND SPREADS HIS [NETS] BAITS WITH CARE . . . . 174 HUMAN IMAGE/N 9
[TO SHOW HIS ZEALOUS PRIESTLY CARE] . . . . 177 LIT BOY LST/N 14
AND ALL ADMIRD HIS PRIESTLY CARE . . . . 177 LIT BOY LST/N 15
NOR FOR ITSELF HATH ANY CARE . . . . 211 CLOD PEBBLE/SE 2
AND SPREADS HIS BAITS WITH CARE . . . . 217 HUMAN ABSTR/SE 8
AND ALL ADMIRD THE PRIESTLY CARE . . . . 218 LIT BOY LST/SE 12
FILLD WITH SOFTEST CARE . . . . 219 LIT GRL LST/SE 11
O THE DISMAL CARE . . . . 219 LIT GRL LST/SE 33
DESPISING TOIL AND CARE . . . . 239 EUROPE 4 22
AND NAMD THE SPACE ULRO & BROODED OVER IT IN CARE & LOVE 267 FOUR ZOAS 1 102
. . . WITH MUCH CARE & AFFLICTION 270 FOUR ZOAS 1 223
UPON THE ROCK OF AGES WATCHING OVER HIM WITH LOVE & CARE 277 FOUR ZOAS 1 468
COMMANDING ALL THE WORK WITH CARE & POWER & SEVERITY . 283 FOUR ZOAS 2 134
IN [SONGS & JOY] SORROW & CARE A GOLDEN WORLD . . . . . 286 FOUR ZOAS 2 * 241
. . . WITH [SONGS & JOY] SORROW & CARE [?ETERNAL FEAR] . 287 FOUR ZOAS 2 * 268
APART FROM LOS BUT COVERD HER WITH SOFTEST BROODING CARE 299 FOUR ZOAS 4 57
AT MIDNIGHT HASTING TO THEIR MUCH BELOVED CARE . . . . 309 FOUR ZOAS 5 148
AND WHEREFORE DOST THOU POUR THIS WATER FORTH IN SIGHS 312 FOUR ZOAS 6 10
& CARE
WITH LABOUR & CARE THOU DOST DIVIDE THE [RIVER] CURRENT 312 FOUR ZOAS 6 18
INTO FOUR
FOR LABOURD FATHERLY CARE & SWEET INSTRUCTION I WILL GIVE 312 FOUR ZOAS 6 40
BUT WHEN A VORTEX FORMD ON HIGH BY LABOUR & SORROW & CARE 317 FOUR ZOAS 6 204
THE OFFSPRING OF THEIR CARE & PITY URTHONA'S SPECTRE WAS 332 FOUR ZOAS 7 485
COMFORTED
TO MULTITUDE & MY MULTITUDES ARE CHILDREN OF CARE & LABOUR 350 FOUR ZOAS 8 353
AND ON THE FLEECES OF MILD FLOCKS WHO NEITHER CARE NOR 361 FOUR ZOAS 9 173
LABOUR
SHE FOLDED THEM UP IN CARE IN SILENCE & HER BRIGHTNING 366 FOUR ZOAS 9 345
LIMBS
THAT SWEET LOVE & BEAUTY ARE WORTHY OUR CARE . . . . . 428 MARY 12
AND THINE IS A FACE OF MILD SORROW & CARE . . . . . . 429 MARY 46
KEEPS THE HUMAN SOUL FROM CARE . . . . 431 AUGURIES 22
IN THE GENTLE RELIEF OF ANOTHER'S CARE . . . . 436 WILLIAM BOND 50
AND THE PRECIOUS STONES OF ANXIETY & CARE & DESPERATION 499 MILTON 18 23
& DEATH
BUT MILTON TOOK OF THE RED CLAY OF SUCCOTH MOULDING IT 500 MILTON 19 10
WITH CARE
THEOTORMON FILLD WITH CARE BROMION LOVING SCIENCE . . . 508 MILTON 24 12
TO THE WEAK AND PITY THE WEAK AS YOUR INFANT CARE BREAK 511 MILTON 25 57
NOT
IN BRIGHT CATHEDRON'S GOLDEN DOME WITH CARE & LOVE & TEARS 512 MILTON 26 36
THEY GIVE TO SCORN & THEIR POSESSORS TO TROUBLE & SORROW 515 MILTON 28 * 32
& CARE
TO FEED THE SLEEPERS ON THEIR COUCHES WITH MATERNAL CARE 516 MILTON 28 49
AND THEN HES SO PIERCD WITH CARE . . . . 552 WHY CUPID/N * 13
NOT WORTH ANY MAN'S RESPECT OR CARE . . . . 575B DESC CAT 3 PROSE
THE PROSPECTUS DOES NOT EXPLAIN BUT IT TAKES CARE . . 575C DESC CAT 3 PROSE
AND DRAWINGS WILL TAKE CARE OF THAT . . . . 584C DESC CAT 14 PROSE
LET THOSE WHO GOVERN THE NATION TAKE CARE OF THE OTHER . 584C DESC CAT 14 PROSE
SAME MASTER SUPPOSING BOTH TO BE DONE WITH EQUAL CARE . 585B DESC CAT 15 PROSE
WITH CONTEMPT HE DID NOT CARE FOR THIS ANY MORE THAN WEST 593A PUB ADDRESS/N PROSE
SUPERIOR TO BASIRE'S BECAUSE THEY HAD MORE LABOUR & CARE 593A PUB ADDRESS/N PROSE
SHOULD HE BE ABLE TO MAKE USE OF EITHER LABOUR OR CARE . 593A PUB ADDRESS/N PROSE
UNLESS THE LABOUR & CARE OF IMBECILLITY . . . . 593A PUB ADDRESS/N PROSE
WHERE THE MAN IS EITHER IN AFFLUENCE OR IS ABOVE THE CARE 612C V LAST JUDG/N PROSE
OF IT
WHAT YOU HAVE ENWOVEN WITH SO MUCH TEARS & CARE SO MUCH 688 JERUSALEM 56 23
JERUSALEM DIVIDES THY CARE WHILE THOU CAREST FOR JERUSALEM 732 JERUSALEM 87 21
I CARE NOT THE SWING OF MY HAMMER SHALL MEASURE THE STARRY 733 JERUSALEM 88 2
ROUND
I CARE NOT WHETHER A MAN IS GOOD OR EVIL ALL THAT I CARE 739 JERUSALEM 91 55
AND SOME A MALE WOVEN WITH CARE . . . . 771 OF GATES/GP 22
MY CARE THE WISEST OF THE ANCIENTS . . . . 793B LETTER 5 PROSE
AWAY FROM ALL CARE . . . . 804 TO BUTTS/L 10
INTREAT YOU TO TAKE DUE CARE OF BOTH IT IS A PART OF OUR 811C LETTER 22 PROSE
DUTY
TO GOD & MAN TO TAKE DUE CARE OF HIS GIFTS & . . . . . 811C LETTER 22 PROSE

303

```
                                                           PAGE       TITLE        LINE
CARE     (CONTINUED)
         IS NOT AS SOME SUPPOSE WITHOUT TROUBLE OR CARE    . . . . 812A LETTER 22    PROSE
         BUT OF THIS WORK I TAKE CARE TO SAY LITTLE TO MR H(HAYLEY) 825A LETTER 27    PROSE
         & LEFT IT WITH CHARGE TO THE SERVANT OF GREAT CARE  . . . 834C LETTER 34     PROSE
         WITH ALL THE FIDELITY I COULD & WILL FINISH WITH EQUAL CARE 838A LETTER 37   PROSE
         HAS TAKEN CARE WHEN I HAVE SEEN HIM TO RAIL AGAINST       846C LETTER 44     PROSE
           SEAGRAVE
         MR PHILLIPS TOOK CARE TO REPEAT JOHNSON'S RAILING TO ME   846D LETTER 44     PROSE
         ON THE ABOVE TERMS & I WILL TAKE CARE THAT THEY SHALL BE  867C LETTER 66     PROSE
           DONE
         PILGRIMS UNDER YOUR CARE WITH THE TWO FIRST PLATES OF JOB 869B LETTER 69     PROSE
         PRAY TAKE CARE OF YOUR HEALTH THIS WET WEATHER & THO I    870B LETTER 71     PROSE
           WRITE
         MY HEARTIEST THANKS FOR YOUR CARE IN MY ACCOMODATION  . . 872D LETTER 76     PROSE
         WHICH IS ALL I CARE ABOUT  . . . . . . . . . . . .  . . . 877D LETTER 88     PROSE
CARED
         I CARED NOT FOR CONSEQUENCES BUT WROTE   . . . . . . .  . 153C MARRIAGE HH 12 PROSE
         HE CARED NOT WHETHER THE WIND WAS NORTH OR SOUTH . . . .  554  TO VENETIAN/N     7
CAREER
         TO WHICH THOU ART GOING IN SUCH CAREER   . . . . . . . .  155D MARRIAGE HH 17 PROSE
CAREFUL
         PERPLEXD VIBRATE ROUND EACH CAREFUL COUNTENANCE . . . .   135  FRENCH REVOLTN    17
         SO CAREFUL WOVE & SPREAD IT OUT WITH SIGHS AND WEARINESS  277  FOUR ZOAS 1      460
         BEING AS CAREFUL AS POSSIBLE NOT TO HURT THE GROUND  .  . 440C MEMORANDUM/N 3  PROSE
         LEADER OF MY ANGELS MY DEAR & TOO CAREFUL & OVER JOYOUS   801B LETTER 13      PROSE
CAREFULLY
         HIDING CAREFULLY FROM THE WIND . . . . . . . . . . .  .   228  URIZEN 11         15
         HIDING CAREFULLY FROM THE WIND HIS EYES BEHELD THE DEEP   303  FOUR ZOAS 4      230
         THEN EACH AN ARROW FLAMING FROM HIS QUIVER FITTED CAREFULLY 744 JERUSALEM 98      1
         AND BETTER TYPE THAN THE TWO EXTREMITIES ALSO IT         847A LETTER 44      PROSE
           IS CAREFULLY
CAREFULNESS
         . . . & THE EVENING BY CAREFULNESS  . . . . . . .  . .   363  FOUR ZOAS 9    *  227
CARELESS
         BE DONE IN A CARELESS OR TOO HASTY MANNER THE PRICE  . . 848C LETTER 45       PROSE
CARELESSNESS
         ACCIDENT BROUGHT ON BY A MAN'S OWN CARELESSNESS  . . . . 388B ANNO WATSON     MARG
CARE'S
         BY SORROW AND CARE'S DISMAY . . . . . . . . . . .  . .   124  SCHOOL BOY/SI     25
CARES
         MIDAS THE PRAISE HATH GAIND OF LENGTHEND [CARES] EARS  . 14   IMIT SPEN/PS      15
         WERE WE NOT SLAVES TILL WE REBELD WHO CARES FOR TIRIEL'S 99   TIRIEL 1          17
           CURSE
         NOURISHD WITH MILK YE SERPENTS NOURISHD WITH MOTHER'S TEARS 99 TIRIEL 1         27
           & CARES
         WAS NOT TO BE EFFECTED WITHOUT CARES & SORROWS & TROUBLES 330  FOUR ZOAS 7      399
         BUT SUCH A HIRED KNAVE CARES NOT FOR THE FEW  . . . . . 469D ANNO REYNOLDS    MARG
         LIFE IN BROODING CARES & ANXIOUS LABOURS THAT PROVE BUT  647  JERUSALEM 24      16
           CHAFF
         AIR ON CLOUDY DOUBTS & REASONING CARES  . . . . . . .   763C FOR SEXES/GP     TITLE
         CARES LITTLE FOR THIS WORLD WHICH PASSES AWAY WHOSE  . . 862D LETTER 60       PROSE
CARESSES
         TILL HER CARESSES & HER TEARS REVIVD HIM TO LIFE & JOY  . 285 FOUR ZOAS 2      205
CAREST
         JERUSALEM DIVIDES THY CARE WHILE THOU CAREST FOR JERUSALEM 732 JERUSALEM 87     21
CARICATURE
         BY CARICATURE PRINTS WHICH OUGHT NOT TO ABOUND SO MUCH . . 793C LETTER 5      PROSE
CARICATURES
         SHOULD BE SO ENAMOURD OF ROWLANDSON'S CARICATURES  . . . 795B LETTER 6        PROSE
CARING
         [TWAS] SOME TRIFLE NOT WORTH CARING FOR . . . . . . . . 755  EV GOSPEL(E)/N     62
CARLISLE
         YORK EDINBURGH DURHAM & CARLISLE & ON THE FRONT  . . .  531  MILTON 39         43
         LINCOLN DURHAM & CARLISLE COUNCELLORS OF LOS  . . . . . 676  JERUSALEM 46       5
CARLO
         I DO NOT BELIEVE THAT CARLO MARATTI THOUGHT SO   . . .  462D ANNO REYNOLDS    MARG
CARMARTHENSHIRE
         THE GATE OF REUBEN IN CARMARTHENSHIRE THE GATE OF SIMEON 637  JERUSALEM 16      35
           IN
CARMEL
         STANDING ON CARMEL RAHAB AND TIRZAH TREMBLED TO BEHOLD  . 501 MILTON 19         28
CARNAGE
         NOW COMES THE NIGHT OF CARNAGE NOW THE FLESH OF KINGS &  334  FOUR ZOAS 7B      45
           PRINCES
         LOUD SPORT THE DANCERS IN THE DANCE OF DEATH REJOICING   509  MILTON 24         62
           IN CARNAGE
         UGLY MAN ACTS FROM LOVE OF CARNAGE AND DELIGHT IN   . . 580C DESC CAT 5       PROSE
CARNARVONSHIRE
         THE GATE OF ASHER CARNARVONSHIRE THE GATE OF ISSACHAR    637  JERUSALEM 16      39
           BRECKNOKSHIRE
CARNATION
         THE PINK THE JESSAMINE THE WALL-FLOWER THE CARNATION  . 520  MILTON 31         59
CAROLINA
         CONGO ZAARA CANADA GREENLAND CAROLINA MEXICO  . . . . . 712  JERUSALEM 72      41
CAROLINE
         AN ENGRAVING OF COWPER BY THE HAND OF CAROLINE WATSON IS I 859C LETTER 56      PROSE
CARPENTER
         AND TO THE CARPENTER  . . . . . . . . . . . . . . . .   57   TO BE OR/IM       17
         OF POOR FISHERMEN & A JOURNEYMAN CARPENTER . . . . . .  465D ANNO REYNOLDS    MARG
         I UNDERSTOOD CHRIST WAS A CARPENTER  . . . . . . . . .  546  ENGLISH CONN/N     5
         SHE LOOKED & SAW JOSEPH THE CARPENTER IN NAZARETH & MARY 694  JERUSALEM 61       3
```

		PAGE	TITLE	LINE
CARR				
	MR CARR CALLED ON ME AND I AS YOU DESIRED GAVE HIM . . .	845C	LETTER 44	PROSE
CARRACHE	SEE CARACCHE			
	WORKS I HAVE DONE FOR YOU ARE EQUAL TO CARRACHE OR RAFAEL	814D	LETTER 23	PROSE
	I SAY THEY ARE EQUAL TO CARRACHE OR RAFAEL OR ELSE I AM	814D	LETTER 23	PROSE
CARRACHE'S				
	LET ME ALSO NOTICE THAT CARRACHE'S PICTURES ARE NOT LIKE	815B	LETTER 23	PROSE
CARRIAGE				
	BECAUSE I SHALL BE TOO LATE FOR THE CARRIAGE	832D	LETTER 32	PROSE
	THURSDAY MORNING OUR CARRIAGE WILL BE A CABRIOLET FOR .	875B	LETTER 81	PROSE
CARRIED				
	A MAN CARRIED A MONKEY ABOUT FOR A SHEW &	157C	MARRIAGE HH 21	PROSE
	I CARRIED HER IN MY BOSOM AS A MAN CARRIES A LAMB . . .	282	FOUR ZOAS 2	93
	WHO CARRIED HIM DOWN INTO EGYPT WHERE EPHRAIM & MENASSHEH	508	MILTON 24	20
	AND HIS LEGS CARRIED IT LIKE A LONG FORK	536	AND HIS LEGS/N	1
	[AN ARTIST WHO HAS CARRIED ON]	591C	PUB ADDRESS/N	*PROSE
	PARENTS MUST BE CARRIED INTO CAPTIVITY TO REDEEM HER SOUL	640	JERUSALEM 18	34
	CARRIED IN ARKS OF OAK BEFORE THE ARMIES IN THE SPRING .	644	JERUSALEM 21	45
	THAT IN THE INTERIOR WORLDS IS CARRIED ON IN FEAR	692	JERUSALEM 59	51
	& TREMBLING			
	WE WERE CARRIED AWAY IN THOUSANDS FROM LONDON & IN TENS	700	JERUSALEM 65	33
	HER TWELVE GATES THROWN DOWN HER CHILDREN CARRIED INTO	719	JERUSALEM 78	23
	CAPTIVITY			
	WHERE ANY VIEW OF MONEY EXISTS ART CANNOT BE CARRIED ON	776C	INSC LAOCOON	PROSE
	CARRIED INTO EXECUTION AS IT MUST BE IF ENGLAND CONTINUES	797C	LETTER 10	PROSE
CARRIES				
	THAN TO THE GAPING WORLD HE CARRIES WINDOWS	25	EDW THIRD/PS 3	186
	I CARRIED HER IN MY BOSOM AS A MAN CARRIES A LAMB . . .	282	FOUR ZOAS 2	93
	THAT FIEND WHO CARRIES THE KEY [& DRAGS] IN ONE HAND & .	608B	V LAST JUDG/N	PROSE
CARRY				
	I SELDOM CARRY MONEY IN MY POCKETS	86B	ANNO LAVATER	MARG
	TO CARRY THE HEAVY BASKET ON OUR SCORCHED SHOULDERS TO SIFT	286	FOUR ZOAS 2	221
	INTO ANOTHER HEAVEN TO CARRY NEWS UPON HIS WINGS . . .	526	MILTON 36	7
	CARRY ON MY VISIONARY STUDIES IN LONDON UNANNOYD	822C	LETTER 26	PROSE
	THE FAVOR OF TEN POUNDS MORE WILL CARRY ME THRO THIS PLATE	851A	LETTER 49	PROSE
CARRYING				
	WHILE I AM AT WORK CARRYING ME OVER MOUNTAINS & VALLEYS	809A	LETTER 20	PROSE
CART				
	DRIVE YOUR CART AND YOUR PLOW OVER THE BONES OF THE DEAD	150D	MARRIAGE HH 7	PROSE
CARTOON				
	THESE ARE NOT SO EVEN THE COPY FROM RAPHAEL'S CARTOON .	439C	REMARKS MALKIN	PROSE
CARTOONS				
	IS NO DIFFERENCE BETWEEN RAFAEL'S CARTOONS AND HIS FRESCOS	584D	DESC CAT 15	PROSE
	ONE OR TWO LARGE CARTOONS THE SUBJECTS HE DOES NOT KNOW	834C	LETTER 34	PROSE
	READINESS TO SEND ANY OF THE CARTOONS TO LONDON YOU DESIRE	846A	LETTER 44	PROSE
	THE TWO CARTOONS WHICH I HAVE OF HECATE & PLINY ARE . . .	855A	LETTER 53	PROSE
CARVD				
	THAT TOWARD GENERATION FOUR OF IRON CARVD WONDROUS . . .	633	JERUSALEM 13	3
CARVED				
	IN MISTS OVER HIS CARVED THRONE & WHEN HE TURND HIS BACK	285	FOUR ZOAS 2	184
	AND EVERY HOUR HAS A BRIGHT GOLDEN GATE CARVED WITH SKILL	516	MILTON 28	51
	AND SOME CARVED AS BASSO RELIEVOS AND SOME AS GROUPES OF	566A	DESC CAT 2	PROSE
	THE SEVEN DISEASES OF THE EARTH ARE CARVED TERRIBLE . . .	633	JERUSALEM 13	17
	WAYWARD LOVE & EVERY SORROW & DISTRESS IS CARVED HERE . .	638	JERUSALEM 16	64
	LAYD HIS HAND ON THE SOUTH & TOOK A BREATHING BOW OF CARVED	744	JERUSALEM 97	8
	GOLD			
CARY				
	[THIS FROG] SING COCK I CARY KITTY ALONE	55	THIS FROG/IM	* 5
	COCK I CARY KITTY ALONE	55	THIS FROG/IM	7
CASE				
	BY MEN OF SENSE BUT PERHAPS THIS NEVER WAS THE CASE . . .	397A	ANNO BACON	MARG
	NEVER IS THE CASE EXCEPT IN THE ROMAN & FLORENTINE SCHOOLS	479B	ANNO REYNOLDS	MARG
	A [PITIABLE] PITIFUL CASE	542D	PITIFUL CASE/N	*TITLE
	THUS THE CASE STANDS AT PRESENT GOD SEND BETTER TIMES .	831D	LETTER 31	PROSE
	MAY DO & HAVE DONE MIRACLES IN THE CASE OF A CONVALESCENT	875A	LETTER 80	PROSE
CASH				
	O THEY SWEEP [INTO] IN THE CASH	61	DR CLASH/IM	* 3
	HAVE HAD THE CASH FROM HIM I SHOULD HAVE RETURNED MY THANKS	851B	LETTER 50	PROSE
	CASH ON ACCT OF PLATES IN THE FOREGOING AGREEMENT . . .	SUPP	LETTER 67D	*PROSE
CAST				
	TO THIS MOST GLORIOUS VOYAGE ON WHICH CAST	21	EDW THIRD/PS 2	95
	BRING FORTH THE LOTS CAST IN THE SPACIOUS ORB	34	WAR SONG/PS 2	2
	IN THE CIRCUMFERENCE THEY CAST A BOUND ABOUT THE INFINITE	92A	ANNO SWED LOVE	MARG
	THAT YOU MAY LIE AS NOW YOUR MOTHER LIES LIKE DOGS CAST OUT	100	TIRIEL 1	45
	I CAST AWAY MY STAFF THE KIND COMPANION OF MY TRAVEL . .	101	TIRIEL 2	30
	CAST THEIR RIVERS IN EQUAL TIDES THRO THE GREAT PARADISE	142	FRENCH REVOLTN	184
	. . . AND THE CLOUDS CAST THEIR SHADOWS THE PRINCES . . .	145	FRENCH REVOLTN	241
	IT INDEED APPEARD TO REASON AS IF DESIRE WAS CAST OUT . .	150A	MARRIAGE HH 5	PROSE
	WHICH CAST THE METALS INTO THE EXPANSE	155A	MARRIAGE HH 15	PROSE
	CAST THY KEYS O ROME INTO THE DEEP DOWN FALLING	159B	SONG LIBERTY	PROSE
	WHY DOST THOU NOT CAST THY SEED	168	HAST LAP/N	3
	[OFT IVE] SHALL I CAST IT ON THE SAND	168	HAST LAP/N	5
	TILL BEAUTY FADES FROM OFF MY SHOULDERS DARKEND AND CAST	194	V DAU ALBION 7	14
	OUT			
	ARMD WITH DISEASES OF THE EARTH TO CAST UPON THE ABYSS .	201	AMERICA 13	15
	AND CAST THEIR SWORDS & SPEARS TO EARTH & STOOD A NAKED	202	AMERICA 15	5
	MULTITUDE			
	WETTING WITH TEARS & HIS WHITE GARMENTS CAST A WINTRY LIGHT	204	AMERICA CANC B	17
	INFINITE LONDON'S AWFUL SPIRES CAST A DREADFUL [GLEAM] COLD	205	AMERICA CANC C	7
	TO CAST ME FROM THY BRIGHT PRESENCE	254	AHANIA 4	* 63
	ON THE HUMAN SOUL TO CAST	255	AHANIA 5	33

305

```
                                                         PAGE      TITLE          LINE
CAST    (CONTINUED)
     CAST OUT FROM THY LOVELY BOSOM . . . . . . . . .    255  AHANIA 5             40
     SHE HATH TAKEN REFUGE IN MY BOSOM & I CANNOT CAST HER OUT  265  FOUR ZOAS 1   32
     AND CAST THEIR YOUNG OUT TO THE HUNGRY WILDS & SANDY       276  FOUR ZOAS 1  453
        DESARTS
     URIZEN CAST DEEP DARKNESS ROUND HIM SILENT BROODING DEATH  278  FOUR ZOAS 1  515
     LUVAH WAS CAST INTO THE FURNACES OF AFFLICTION & SEALED    282  FOUR ZOAS 2   72
     TO CAST AHANIA TO THE EARTH HE SIEZD HER BY THE HAIR  . .  294  FOUR ZOAS 3  111
     SAYING ART THOU ALSO BECOME LIKE VALA THUS I CAST THEE OUT 295  FOUR ZOAS 3  113
     AND ART THOU ALSO BECOME LIKE VALA THUS I CAST THEE OUT    295  FOUR ZOAS 3  130
     [WHEN] URIZEN CAST DEEP DARKNESS ROUND HIM RAGING LUVAH    306  FOUR ZOAS 5  *  43
        POURD
     ALL THESE AROUND THE WORLD OF LOS CAST FORTH THEIR         318  FOUR ZOAS 6  278
        MONSTROUS BIRTHS
     ROUND HOWLING ORC WHOSE AWFUL LIMBS CAST FORTH RED SMOKE   320  FOUR ZOAS 7   17
        & FIRE
     THEY GIVE THE OATH OF BLOOD THEY CAST THE LOTS INTO THE    337  FOUR ZOAS 7B 165
        HELMET
     AND BRASS & MOLTEN METALS CAST IN HOLLOW GLOBES & BORD . . 343  FOUR ZOAS 8   93
     WHEN THE MORTAL DISAPPEARS IN IMPROVED KNOWLEDGE CAST AWAY 355  FOUR ZOAS 8  552
     IN STERN SEVERITY & CAST THEE OUT INTO THE INDEFINITE  . . 360  FOUR ZOAS 9  146
     IS A DECEIT SO DETESTABLE THAT I WILL CAST THEE OUT  . . . 361  FOUR ZOAS 9  *  155
     OF DARK MORTALITY NOR CAST MY VIEW INTO THE [PAST] FUTURITY 361  FOUR ZOAS 9  *  165
        NOR TURND
     . . . I WILL CAST THEE FORTH FROM THESE  . . . . . . . .   361  FOUR ZOAS 9  180
     I CAST [REMEMBRANCE] FUTURITY AWAY & TURN MY BACK UPON     361  FOUR ZOAS 9  182
        THAT VOID
     AND LO LIKE THE HARVEST MOON AHANIA CAST OFF HER DEATH     366  FOUR ZOAS 9  344
        CLOTHES
     I SHALL CAST OFF MY DEATH CLOTHES & EMBRACE THARMAS AGAIN  373  FOUR ZOAS 9  599
     IN WALLS OF GOLD WE CAST HIM LIKE A SEED INTO THE EARTH    374  FOUR ZOAS 9  632
     THEY PLUNGE INTO THE ELEMENTS THE ELEMENTS CAST THEM FORTH 376  FOUR ZOAS 9  736
     TO THE ETERNAL MAN IN WOE HE CAST THEM WAILING INTO  . . . 378  FOUR ZOAS 9  797
     OR DOES HE NOT CAST THEM OFF  . . . . . . . . . . .      396A  ANNO WATSON   MARG
     AND CAST [THE] HIS OWN SPECTRE INTO THE LAKE  . . . . . .  421  EACH MAN/N     4
     UNLESS IT WAS TO CAST [AN EYE] A STIGMA UPON REAL FACILITY 453D  ANNO REYNOLDS *  MARG
        IN
     THE HARROW CAST THICK FLAMES JEHOVAH THUNDERD ABOVE  . . . 493  MILTON 12     20
     THE HARROW CAST THICK FLAMES & ORBD US ROUND IN CONCAVE    493  MILTON 12     22
        FIRES
     HIM TO THE DIVINE MERCY CAST HIM DOWN INTO THE LAKE  . . . 530  MILTON 39     11
     TO CAST OFF RATIONAL DEMONSTRATION BY FAITH IN THE SAVIOUR 533  MILTON 41      3
     TO CAST OFF THE ROTTEN RAGS OF MEMORY BY INSPIRATION  . .  533  MILTON 41      4
     TO CAST OFF BACON LOCKE & NEWTON FROM ALBION'S COVERING    533  MILTON 41      5
     TO CAST ASIDE FROM POETRY ALL THAT IS NOT INSPIRATION  .   533  MILTON 41      7
     CAST ON THE INSPIRED BY THE TAME HIGH FINISHER OF PALTRY   533  MILTON 41      9
        BLOTS
     TO CAST OFF THE IDIOT QUESTIONER WHO IS ALWAYS QUESTIONING 533  MILTON 41     12
     ARE COMPOSITIONS OF A MYTHOLOGICAL CAST SIMILAR TO THOSE   565C  DESC CAT 2    PROSE
     THE LAST JUDGMENT WHEN ALL THOSE ARE CAST AWAY  . . . .   604C  V LAST JUDG/N PROSE
     TO BE AN ERROR & TO BE CAST OUT IS A PART OF GOD'S DESIGN  613A  V LAST JUDG/N PROSE
     NO MAN CAN EMBRACE TRUE ART TILL HE HAS EXPLORD & CAST OUT 613A  V LAST JUDG/N PROSE
     HIMSELF CAST OUT BY THOSE WHO HAVE ALREADY EMBRACED TRUE   613A  V LAST JUDG/N PROSE
        ART
     WE MUST CAST OFF IF WE WOULD BE PAINTERS SUCH AS (RAFAEL)  613C  V LAST JUDG/N *PROSE
     NOT CAST OFF THIS WORLD WE SHALL BE ONLY VENETIAN PAINTERS 613C  V LAST JUDG/N PROSE
     WHO WILL BE CAST OFF & LOST FROM ART . . . . . . .        613C  V LAST JUDG/N PROSE
     THOSE WHO ARE CAST OUT ARE ALL THOSE WHO  . . . . . . .   615D  V LAST JUDG/N PROSE
     OF JESUS THE SAVIOUR WHERE THE ACCUSER IS CAST OUT NOT  .  616D  V LAST JUDG/N PROSE
     LUVAH WAS CAST INTO THE FURNACES OF AFFLICTION AND SEALED  625  JERUSALEM 7    30
     THE DEAD DESPISE & SCORN THEE & CAST THEE OUT AS ACCURSED  626  JERUSALEM 7    68
     I WILL CAST THEE INTO FORMS OF ABHORRENCE & TORMENT IF THOU 627  JERUSALEM 8   11
     IF THOU WAST CAST FORTH FROM MY LIFE IF I WAS DEAD UPON    627  JERUSALEM 8    36
        THE MOUNTAINS
     GIVING A BODY TO FALSHOOD THAT IT MAY BE CAST OFF FOR EVER 631  JERUSALEM 12  *  13
     CAST CAST YE JERUSALEM FORTH THE SHADOW OF DELUSIONS  .    640  JERUSALEM 18   11
     WITH SIN AND SHAME CAST HER INTO THE POTTER'S FIELD        640  JERUSALEM 18   32
     AND CAST IT INTO THE ATLANTIC DEEP TO CATCH THE SOULS OF   646  JERUSALEM 23   23
        THE DEAD
     BUT ALBION IS CAST FORTH TO THE POTTER HIS CHILDREN TO     647  JERUSALEM 24   29
        THE BUILDERS
     AND ALL THE TENDERNESSES OF THE SOUL CAST FORTH AS FILTH   657  JERUSALEM 31   21
        & MIRE
     SO SAYING SHE HER DARK THREADS CAST OVER THE TREMBLING     658  JERUSALEM 31   67
        RIVER
     TO CAST JERUSALEM FORTH UPON THE WILDS TO POPLAR & BOW  .  668  JERUSALEM 41    5
     AND CAST HIS SPECTRE INTO THE LAKE . . . . . . . .        669  EACH MAN/J      4
     HE HATH CAST THEE OFF FOR EVER THE LITTLE ONES HE HATH     670  JERUSALEM 42   44
        ANOINTED
     WEAK WITHERD DARKEND & JERUSALEM IS CAST FORTH FROM ALBION 679  JERUSALEM 49    8
     OF ENVY ALBION IS BECOME AND HIS EMANATION CAST OUT  . . . 681  JERUSALEM 50    9
     FOR THE VEIL OF VALA WHICH ALBION CAST INTO THE ATLANTIC   691  JERUSALEM 59    2
        DEEP
     UTTERLY CAST ME AWAY IF I WERE PURE NEVER COULD I TASTE    694  JERUSALEM 61   11
        THE SWEETS
     WAS CAST OUT TO THE LOATHING OF HER PERSON THE CHALDEAN    695  JERUSALEM 61   40
        TOOK
     TO CAST LUVAH INTO THE WRATH AND ALBION INTO THE PITY  .   699  JERUSALEM 65    3
     THEY CAST THE LOTS INTO THE HELMET . . . . . . . . .      699  JERUSALEM 65    7
     AS GWENDOLEN CAST THE SHUTTLE OF WAR AS CAMBEL RETURND     703  JERUSALEM 66   62
        THE BEAM
     GO THEREFORE CAST OUT DEVILS IN CHRIST'S NAME . . . . .   718  STOOD AMONG/J  24
```

```
                                                                 PAGE      TITLE          LINE
CAST     (CONTINUED)
     RECIEVE THE FEET OF JERUSALEM THEY HAVE CAST ME QUITE AWAY   720 JERUSALEM 79          16
     AS IF I WAS NOT THEIR MOTHER THEY DESPISE ME & CAST ME OUT   720 JERUSALEM 79          21
     CAST THOU IN JERUSALEM'S SHADOWS THY LOVES SILK OF LIQUID    732 JERUSALEM 87          19
     NOR MAY THE SINNER CAST ONE STONE  . . . . . . . . .  .      754 EV GOSPEL (E)/N       26
CASTING
     CASTING HER BLUE EYES OVER THE GREEN OCEAN  . . . . . .       33 EDW THIRD/PS 6        56
     BY CASTING OUT THE EVIL BY THE GOOD SEE MATTHEW XII... . .    80A ANNO LAVATER       MARG
     THE SERPENT GREW CASTING ITS SCALES  . . . . . . . .  .      232 URIZEN 19             30
     WHEN LOS HEATED THE GLOWING MASS CASTING  . . . . . .        260 BOOK OF LOS 5         42
     CASTING THEIR SPARKLES DIRE ABROAD INTO THE DISMAL DEEP      283 FOUR ZOAS 2          140
     AND CASTING ROUND THICK GLOOMS THUS UTTERD HIS FIERCE PANGS  299 FOUR ZOAS 4           78
        OF HEART
     NUMBER XII THE SOLDIERS CASTING LOTS FOR CHRIST'S GARMENT    584A DESC CAT 12        TITLE
        A DRAWING
     IS MOSES CASTING HIS TABLES OF STONE INTO THE DEEPS  . . .   607B V LAST JUDG/N      PROSE
CASTLE
     WALKD BY THE CASTLE GATE AND LOOKED IN  . . . . . . .          4 FAIR ELENOR/PS        3
     TILL GLORY FIRES HIS BREAST TO ENLARGE HIS CASTLE   . . .     26 EDW THIRD/PS 3       201
     SEEST THOU YONDER DARK CASTLE . . . . . . . . . . . .  .     145 FRENCH REVOLTN       248
     THEY CANNOT WALL THE CITY NOR MOAT ROUND THE CASTLE OF       199 AMERICA 9             7
        PRINCES
CASTLES
     HORSES ELEPHANTS BANNERS CASTLES SLINGS AND ROCKS   . . .   159D SONG LIBERTY       PROSE
     TO BUILD HIM CASTLES AND HIGH SPIRES WHERE KINGS & PRIESTS   193 V DAU ALBION 5        20
        MAY DWELL
     FROM THEIR ENCAMPMENTS AND DARK CASTLES SEEKING WHERE TO     201 AMERICA 13            8
        HIDE
     THESE WERE THE CHURCHES HOSPITALS CASTLES PALACES   . . .    246 SONG OF LOS 4         1
     THEN CAME HE AMONG FIERY CITIES & CASTLES BUILT OF BURNING   314 FOUR ZOAS 6          115
        STEEL
     HIGH SPIRES & CASTLES DROWND IN THE BLACK DELUGE SHOAL       359 FOUR ZOAS 9           76
        ON SHOAL
     BUILDING CASTLES IN DESOLATED PLACES AND STRONG             641 JERUSALEM 18          38
        FORTIFICATIONS
CASTS
     AND CASTS THEM OUT UPON THE DARKEND EARTH  . . . . . .        34 WAR SONG/PS           4
     THE SCRIBE OF PENSYLVANIA CASTS HIS PEN UPON THE EARTH . .   201 AMERICA 14           15
     THEY HEAL THE SICK HE CASTS OUT DEVILS  . . . . . . .        545 COSWAY FRAZR/N        4
     STARTS FROM HIS LOFTY PLACES & CASTS DOWN HIS TENTS & FLEES  729 JERUSALEM 84          24
        AWAY
CAT
     & THE PYTHAGOREAN PLAYING WITH THE CAT  . . . . . . .        44D ISLAND MOON 1       PROSE
     ANY MORE THAN [?ANY ?BIRD THE] A DOG OR A CAT  . . . . .      61 SAY YOU JOE/IM  *     13
     THE BEGGER'S DOG & WIDOW'S CAT  . . . . . . . . . .  .       432 AUGURIES              43
     A DOG WILL ENVY A CAT WHO IS PAMPERD AT [HIS] THE   . . .    616B V LAST JUDG/N      PROSE
CATALANI
     CATALANI DU CROWE & DILBURY DOODLE   . . . . . . . .         548B ON GREAT ENC/N     TITLE
CATALOGUE
     BLAKE'S APOLOGY FOR HIS CATALOGUE  . . . . . . . . .         554D BLAKES APL/N        TITLE
     ADMITTANCE...EACH PERSON A DISCRIPTIVE CATALOGUE INCLUDED    560C EXHIBITION ADV     PROSE
     A DESCRIPTIVE CATALOGUE OF BLAKE'S EXHIBITION  . . . . .     562A DESC CAT ADV       TITLE
     THE DESCRIPTIVE CATALOGUE PRICE...CONTAINING                562B DESC CAT ADV       PROSE
        MR B'S (BLAKE'S)
     EVERY PURCHASER OF A CATALOGUE WILL BE ENTITLED   . . . .    562B DESC CAT ADV       PROSE
     AN INDEX TO THE CATALOGUE GRATIS   . . . . . . . . .         562C DESC CAT ADV       PROSE
     A DESCRIPTIVE CATALOGUE OF PICTURES POETICAL AND HISTORICAL  563A DESC CAT           TITLE
     INDEX TO THE CATALOGUE  . . . . . . . . . . . . .  .         564A DESC CAT           TITLE
     FOR THE YEAR...ADDITIONS TO BLAKE'S CATALOGUE OF PICTURES    604B V LAST JUDG/N      TITLE
        &C
     YOUR USE AS ALSO THE CATALOGUE OF HAMPSTEAD SALE  . . . .    836A LETTER 35          PROSE
     YOU DESIRED HE HAS SENT A CATALOGUE OF ALL HIS COLLECTION    844A LETTER 43          PROSE
     AND INCLOSE WITH THEM A CATALOGUE OF BELL'S GALLERY AND      844C LETTER 43          PROSE
CATARACT
     BETWEEN THE CLOUDS & THE WAVES WE SAW A CATARACT OF BLOOD   156B MARRIAGE HH 17      PROSE
     IN THIS CATARACT FOUR ANGELS DESCEND HEADLONG  . . . . .    609A V LAST JUDG/N      PROSE
     OF BURNING SAND THE RIVERS CATARACT & LAKES OF FIRE  . . .   634 JERUSALEM 13          41
CATARACTS
     IN CATARACTS OF FIRE BLOOD & GALL  . . . . . . . . .         225 URIZEN 5             46
     IN WHIRLWINDS & CATARACTS OF BLOOD  . . . . . . . . .        225 URIZEN 5             13
     LIFE IN CATARACTS POURD DOWN HIS CLIFFS  . . . . . . .       230 URIZEN 13            55
CATCH
     THE PRINCE MAY NOT CATCH THE DISTEMPER TOO  . . . . . .       22 EDW THIRD/PS 3       52
     AND THOU SHALT HELP US TO CATCH BIRDS & GATHER THEM RIPE     102 TIRIEL 3             15
        CHERRIES
     IF YOU [CATCH] [TRAP ] TRAP THE MOMENT BEFORE ITS RIPE  . .  179 IF YOU TRAP/N   *     1
     TILL EXPERIENCE TEACHES THEM TO CATCH   . . . . . . .        183 MOTTO SONGS/N         3
     PLATTED QUITE NEAT TO CATCH APPLAUSE WITH A SLIDING NOOSE    184 HER LIFE IS/N         2
        AT THE END
     WITH NETS FOUND UNDER THY NIGHT PILLOW TO CATCH VIRGIN JOY   194 V DAU ALBION 6       11
     AND CATCH FOR THEE GIRLS OF MILD SILVER OR OF FURIOUS GOLD   194 V DAU ALBION 7       24
     LIKE NETS & GINS & TRAPS TO CATCH THE JOYS OF ETERNITY  . .  246 SONG OF LOS 4         2
     THEY CATCH THE SHRIEKS IN CUPS OF GOLD THEY HAND THEM TO     377 FOUR ZOAS 9         768
        ONE ANOTHER
     THEY CATCH THE SHRIEKS IN CUPS OF GOLD THEY HAND THEM TO     514 MILTON 27            39
        ONE ANOTHER
     AND CAST IT INTO THE ATLANTIC DEEP TO CATCH THE SOULS OF     646 JERUSALEM 23         23
        THE DEAD
     TO CATCH THE SOULS OF THE DEAD BEGAN TO VEGETATE & PETRIFY   691 JERUSALEM 59          3
CATCHES
     SHE CATCHES HIM THEN ROGER TIES  . . . . . . . . . .  .       16 BLIND-MANS/PS        31
     CATCHES HIS SHRIEKS IN CUPS OF GOLD  . . . . . . . .  .      425 MENTAL TRAVLER       12
```

```
                                                            PAGE        TITLE          LINE
CATCHING
    AND SO WILL THE WHOLE ARMY TIS VERY CATCHING  . . . . .    22 EDW THIRD/PS 3       59
CATCHPENNY
    BLUNDERED OVER NOVELS AND CATCHPENNY TRIFLES OF BOOKSELLERS 574A DESC CAT 3       PROSE
CATHEDRALS
    MONUMENTS IN WESTMINSTER ST PAULS & OTHER CATHEDRALS  . . 601A PUB ADDRESS/N      PROSE
    THIS IS ONE OF THE GOTHIC ARTISTS WHO BUILT THE CATHEDRALS 604A INSC ARIMATHEA    PROSE
    THEIR VILLAGES TOWNS CITIES SEA-PORTS TEMPLES SUBLIME      709 JERUSALEM 71         13
        CATHEDRALS
CATHEDRON
    AND CALLD THE LOOMS CATHEDRON IN THESE LOOMS SHE WOVE      342 FOUR ZOAS 8          37
        THE SPECTRES
    OF SPECTROUS DEAD THENCE TO THE LOOMS OF CATHEDRON CONVEYD 346 FOUR ZOAS 8         209
    SURROUNDS LUBAN LOS'S PALACE & THE GOLDEN LOOMS OF         633 JERUSALEM 13         25
        CATHEDRON
    SONS & DAUGHTERS OF LOS IN BOWLAHOOLA & IN CATHEDRON  . . 714 JERUSALEM 73         52
    OF SPACE HE MAKES PERMANENT IN BOWLAHOOLA & CATHEDRON  . . 716 JERUSALEM 75          9
    MOUNTAINOUS WALES INTO THE LOOM OF CATHEDRON FIBRE BY FIBRE 723 JERUSALEM 80         63
    AMONG THE GOLDEN LOOMS OF CATHEDRON SENDING FIBRES OF LOVE 731 JERUSALEM 86         40
CATHEDRON'S
    AROUND THE LAMB A FEMALE TABERNACLE WOVEN IN CATHEDRON'S   494 MILTON 13            26
        LOOMS
    LEST WE ARE VEGETATED FOR CATHEDRON'S LOOMS WEAVE ONLY     509 MILTON 24            35
        DEATH
    IN BRIGHT CATHEDRON'S GOLDEN DOME WITH CARE & LOVE & TEARS 512 MILTON 26            36
    CATHEDRON'S LOOMS ARE BUILDED AND LOS'S FURNACES IN THE    691 JERUSALEM 59         23
        SOUTH
    IS BRIGHT CATHEDRON'S GOLDEN HALL ITS COURTS TOWERS        691 JERUSALEM 59         25
        & PINNACLES
    SUCH ARE CATHEDRON'S GOLDEN HALLS IN THE CITY OF GOLGONOOZA 713 JERUSALEM 73          1
    HIM OVER EUROPE IN STREAMS OF GORE OUT OF CATHEDRON'S LOOMS 715 JERUSALEM 74         37
    THE ENVY RAN THRO CATHEDRON'S LOOMS INTO THE HEART  . .    726 JERUSALEM 82         53
    JOYD IN THE MANY WEAVING THREADS IN BRIGHT CATHEDRON'S DOME 728 JERUSALEM 83         72
CATHERINE
    B BLAKE CATHERINE BLAKE  . . . . . . . . . . . . . .      380A FOUR ZOAS NOTE *PROSE
    "BELIEVE ME TO BE YOURS AFFECTIONATELY CATHERINE BLAKE"   801A LETTER 12           PROSE
    AT YOUR APPROVAL OF MY QUEEN CATHERINE BEG TO OBSERVE THAT 855C LETTER 53           PROSE
    YOUR AFFECTIONATE WILL BLAKE & HIS WIFE CATHERINE BLAKE    863C LETTER 60           PROSE
    CATHERINE BLAKE  . . . . . . . . . . . . . . . . . .     SUPP PENC DRAW 2.10 *TITLE
CATHERLOH
    QUEENS COUNTY WICKLOW CATHERLOH WEXFORD KILKENNY  . . . .  711 JERUSALEM 72         20
CATHNES
    FROM STONE-HENGE AND FROM LONDON STONE FROM CORNWALL       690 JERUSALEM 58         46
        TO CATHNES
CATO
    CATO  . . . . . . . . . . . . . . . . . . . . . . . .    SUPP ILLUS DANTE 72 *PROSE
CATS
    WHILE THE ANTIQUARIAN SEEMD TO BE TALKING OF VIRTUOUS CATS  44B ISLAND MOON 1       PROSE
CATTERPILLER
    AS THE CATTERPILLER CHOOSES THE FAIREST LEAVES TO LAY  . . 152C MARRIAGE HH 9       PROSE
    AND THE CATTERPILLER & FLY  . . . . . . . . . . . .       174 HUMAN IMAGE/N         16
    AND THE CATTERPILLER AND FLY  . . . . . . . . . . .       217 HUMAN ABSTR/SE        15
    THE CATTERPILLER ON THE LEAF  . . . . . . . . . .         432 AUGURIES              37
    WHO CREEPS INTO STATE GOVERNMENT LIKE A CATTERPILLER TO    533 MILTON 41            11
        DESTROY
    CREATE THE SILK-WORM & THE SPIDER & THE CATTERPILLER  . .  692 JERUSALEM 59         46
    THE CATTERPILLER ON THE LEAF  . . . . . . . . . .         770 THE KEYS/GP           1
CATTLE
    HIS DAUGHTERS FROM GREEN HERBS & CATTLE  . . . . . . .     234 URIZEN 23            20
    WHEN THE SUN SETS WHEN THE CLODS HARDEN & THE CATTLE STAND 355 FOUR ZOAS 8         566
    OVER THE SLAIN & MOANING IN THE CATTLE & IN THE WINDS  . . 355 FOUR ZOAS 8         578
    THEIR RIVERS CRY WITH A DISMAL CRY THE CATTLE GATHER       358 FOUR ZOAS 9          54
        TOGETHER
    MY FLOCKS & HERDS TRAMPLE THE CORN MY CATTLE BROWZE UPON   376 FOUR ZOAS 9         699
    MY CATTLE NEXT LAST EVN THE DOG OF MY GATE THE FORESTS FLED 643 JERUSALEM 21          8
    SUBSERVIENT TO THE CLODS OF THE FURROW THE CATTLE AND EVEN 688 JERUSALEM 56         36
CATTLES
    TRODDEN WITH THE CATTLE'S FEET  . . . . . . . . . . .     162 CLOD PEBBLE/N          6
    TRODDEN WITH THE CATTLE'S FEET  . . . . . . . . . . .     211 CLOD PEBBLE/SE         6
CAUGHT
    HE CAUGHT ME IN HIS SILKEN NET  . . . . . . . . . .         6 HOW SWEET/PS          11
    THE KING CAUGHT HERE IN FRANCE OF RUNNING AWAY  . . . .    22 EDW THIRD/PS 3        57
    SIR THOMAS YOU SAY YOU HAVE CAUGHT IT TOO  . . . . . .     22 EDW THIRD/PS 3        58
    AT LAST I CAUGHT HIM IN THE FORM OF TIRIEL BLIND & OLD . . 105 TIRIEL 4             61
    AND CAUGHT HIM BY THE GARMENTS WEEPING WITH CRIES OF BITTER 106 TIRIEL 5            19
        WOE
    ALL WHOLSOM FOOD IS CAUGHT WITHOUT A NET OR A TRAP  . . . 151A MARRIAGE HH 7   *PROSE
    BUT I BY FORCE SUDDENLY CAUGHT HIM IN MY ARMS  . . . . . 156D MARRIAGE HH 17   PROSE
    AND THEN THE WEAK WERE CAUGHT BY THE STRONG  . . . . . . 157B MARRIAGE HH 17   PROSE
    [AND] BUT IN MY HAT CAUGHT  . . . . . . . . . . .         178 THE FAIRY/N      *  15
    AND CAUGHT HIM IN MY HAT AS BOYS KNOCK DOWN A BUTTERFLY    237 EUROPE INTRO        9
    SPREAD & MANY A SPIRIT CAUGHT INNUMERABLE THE NETS  . . . 284 FOUR ZOAS 2        159
    THE MAIDEN CAUGHT ME IN THE WILD  . . . . . . . . .       429 CRYSTL CABINET       1
    THIS IS CAUGHT BY FEMALES BRIGHT  . . . . . . . . .       432 AUGURIES            69
    DEFEND A LIE THAT HE MAY BE SNARED & CAUGHT & TAKEN  . .   489 MILTON 8            48
    THESE ARE CAUGHT UP BY THREE AGED MEN WHO APPEAR  . . . . 610D V LAST JUDG/N    PROSE
    A LIE THAT HE MAY BE SNARED AND CAUGHT AND SNARED AND     628 JERUSALEM 9         30
        TAKEN
    THOU HADST WOVEN IT WITH ART THOU HADST CAUGHT ME IN THE   643 JERUSALEM 20         31
        BANDS
    HAVE YOU ALSO CAUGHT THE INFECTION OF SIN & STERN         673 JERUSALEM 43         75
        REPENTANCE
```

CAUGHT   (CONTINUED)
    WAS CAUGHT UP WITH THE SUN IN ONE DAY OF FURY AND WAR   . .   679 JERUSALEM 49   16
    IN ONE NIGHT THE ATLANTIC CONTINENT WAS CAUGHT UP WITH   679 JERUSALEM 49   19
        THE MOON
    WERE CAUGHT INTO THE FLAX OF HER DISTAFF & IN HER CLOUD   722 JERUSALEM 80   34
    FOR MEN ARE CAUGHT BY LOVE WOMAN IS CAUGHT BY PRIDE   . .   724 JERUSALEM 81   6
CAULDRONS
    THY WORK IS ETERNAL DEATH WITH MILLS & OVENS & CAULDRONS   483 MILTON 4   17
CAUSD
    AND IN IT CAUSD THE SPECTRES OF THE DEAD TO TAKE SWEET   481 MILTON 2   9
        FORMS
'CAUSE
    WHERE 'CAUSE HIS GARMENTS ARE SWOLN WITH WIND . . . . .   37A CONTEMPLATN/PS   PROSE
CAUSE
    AND CAUSE IN SWEET SOCIETY TO DWELL   . . . .   15 IMIT SPEN/PS   33
    VENTRING THEIR LIVES IN MY MOST RIGHTEOUS CAUSE   . . . .   18 EDW THIRD/PS 1   18
    PERHAPS THE AIR OF THE COUNTRY IS THE CAUSE   . . . . .   22 EDW THIRD/PS 3   61
    A TRIFLE IVE GILT YOUR CAUSE WITH MY BEST BLOOD   . . .   23 EDW THIRD/PS 3   99
    I'LL FIGHT AND WEEP TIS IN MY COUNTRY'S CAUSE   . . . . .   31 EDW THIRD/PS 5   51
    HAD I THREE LIVES ID DIE IN SUCH A CAUSE   . . . . . .   35 WAR SONG/PS   13
    SOLDIERS PREPARE OUR CAUSE IS HEAVEN'S CAUSE   . . . . .   35 WAR SONG/PS   21
    SOLDIERS PREPARE BE WORTHY OF OUR CAUSE   . . . . . .   35 WAR SONG/PS   22
    WELL GENTLEMEN SAID HE WHAT IS THE CAUSE OF STRIFE   . . . 45C ISLAND MOON 1   PROSE
    AS IT HAS ALL HIS COTEMPORARIES EACH THING IS ITS OWN CAUSE 88C ANNO LAVATER   MARG
    WORLDLY WISDOM OR DEMONSTRATION BY THE SENSES IS THE CAUSE   90D ANNO SWED LOVE   MARG
        OF THIS
    WE SEE HERE THAT THE CAUSE OF AN ULTIMATE   . . . . .   94D ANNO SWED LOVE   MARG
    LAUGH FOR THY FATHER TIRIEL SHALL GIVE (THEE) CAUSE TO   108 TIRIEL 6   33
        LAUGH
    WOULD BE MISUNDERSTOOD & SO BE THE CAUSE OF IMPOSITION   . 153B MARRIAGE HH 12   PROSE
    WAS THE CAUSE OF OUR DESPISING THE PRIESTS & PHILOSOPHERS 153D MARRIAGE HH 12   PROSE
    TO CAUSE MY NAME TO VANISH THAT MY PLACE MAY NOT BE FOUND   238 EUROPE PREL 1   5
    THE CAUSE OF HER DIRE ANGUISH FOR SHE LAY THE IMAGE OF   328 FOUR ZOAS 7   320
        DEATH
    THE SPECTRE OF URTHONA WEPT BEFORE LOS SAYING I AM THE   330 FOUR ZOAS 7   403
        CAUSE
    THE SEED IS HARROWD IN WHILE FLAMES HEAT THE BLACK MOULD   366 FOUR ZOAS 9   337
        & CAUSE
    I WILL CAUSE MY VOICE TO BE HEARD . . . .   368 FOUR ZOAS 9   439
    A TYRANT IS THE WORST DISEASE & THE CAUSE OF ALL OTHERS   402B ANNO BACON   MARG
    THERE IS NO SUCH THING AS A SECOND CAUSE NOR AS A NATURAL 403B ANNO BACON   MARG
        CAUSE
    THE WORD CAUSE IS A FOOLISH WORD   . . . .   403C ANNO BACON   MARG
    HAVE BEEN THE CAUSE OF MY PRODUCING   . . . .   444C LAST JUDGMNT/L   PROSE
    IDENTITIES OR THINGS ARE NEITHER CAUSE NOR EFFECT THEY   470D ANNO REYNOLDS   MARG
        ARE ETERNAL
    WHAT CAUSE AT LENGTH MOVD MILTON TO THIS UNEXAMPLED DEED   482 MILTON 2   *   21
    MILTON'S RELIGION IS THE CAUSE THERE IS NO END TO   506 MILTON 22   39
        DESTRUCTION
    AND EVERY NATURAL EFFECT HAS A SPIRITUAL CAUSE AND NOT   . 513 MILTON 26   44
    A NATURAL FOR A NATURAL CAUSE ONLY SEEMS IT IS A DELUSION   513 MILTON 26   45
    IS OLOLON THE CAUSE OF THIS O WHERE SHALL I HIDE MY FACE   532 MILTON 40   14
    THEY CAUSE THAT EVERY THING IN ART SHALL BECOME A MACHINE 582C DESC CAT 9   PROSE
    THEY CAUSE THAT THE EXECUTION SHALL BE ALL BLOCKED UP   . 582C DESC CAT 9   PROSE
    MOST CRUEL DEMON WHOSE WHOLE DELIGHT IS TO CAUSE   . . .   583A DESC CAT 9   PROSE
    [BUT FOR NO OTHER CAUSE] & MONOTONOUS SING SONG   . . .   600D PUB ADDRESS/N   PROSE
    HAST JUST CAUSE TO BE IRRITATED BUT LOOK STEDFASTLY UPON ME 626 JERUSALEM 7   53
    THIS CAUSE OF THESE SHAKINGS OF MY TOWERS ON EUPHRATES   . 658 JERUSALEM 31   59
    AND THIS IS THE CAUSE OF THE APPEARANCE IN THE FROWNING   659 JERUSALEM 33   25
        CHAOS
    CAN NEVER BE THE CAUSE OF A WAR NOR OF A SINGLE MARTYRDOM 683A JERUSALEM 52   PROSE
    THOSE WHO MARTYR OTHERS OR WHO CAUSE WAR ARE DEISTS   . . 683A JERUSALEM 52   PROSE
    THEY POUR COLD WATER ON HIS BRAIN IN FRONT TO CAUSE   .   702 JERUSALEM 66   30
    AND THIS IS THE CAUSE THAT JESUS DIED   . . . . . .   751 EV GOSPEL(D)/N   30
    CRYING [IVE FOUND HI] CRUCIFY THIS CAUSE OF DISTRESS   .   755 EV GOSPEL(E)/N *   85
    THE MORAL CHRISTIAN IS THE CAUSE   . . . .   758 EV GOSPEL (1)   7
    WHICH IS THAT I HAVE SUPPOSED MALEVOLENCE WITHOUT A CAUSE 793B LETTER 5   PROSE
    IS NOT MERIT IN ONE A CAUSE OF ENVY IN ANOTHER   . . .   793B LETTER 5   PROSE
    & SERENITY & HAPPINESS & BEAUTY A CAUSE OF MALEVOLENCE . 793B LETTER 5   PROSE
    BE ALLEDGED AS THE CAUSE OF HIS THIEVERY FOR   . . . .   793B LETTER 5   *PROSE
    WE MUST THEREFORE SEEK THE CAUSE ELSEWHERE THAN IN   . . 793C LETTER 5   PROSE
    THE ACTUAL CAUSE OF MY UNEASINESS INTO WHICH YOU ARE SO   813A LETTER 22   PROSE
        KIND
    BY HIS BRETHREN & BETRAYD THEIR CAUSE TO THEIR ENEMIES . 813B LETTER 22   PROSE
    TOO MUCH THE CAUSE OF OUR DETERMINATION TO LEAVE FELPHAM   819D LETTER 25   PROSE
    TO BEG OF YOU TO CAUSE THE ENCLOSD LETTER TO BE DELIVERD   829B LETTER 28   PROSE
    ELECTRICITY IS THE WONDERFUL CAUSE THE SWELLING OF HER LEGS 851C LETTER 50   PROSE
    IN MY CAUSE & SHOULD IMMEDIATELY ENGAGE IN REVIVING   . . 865C LETTER 63   *PROSE
    YOU WILL SEE IN THIS LITTLE WORK THE CAUSE OF DIFFERENCE   866A LETTER 64   PROSE
    WILL ATTRIBUTE IT TO ITS RIGHT CAUSE INTELLECTUAL   876B LETTER 83   PROSE
        PECULIARITY
CAUSED
    O WHO CAN STAND O WHO HATH CAUSED THIS   . . . . . .   33 EDW FOURTH/PS   13
    OF AIR HE CAUSED THE INSIDE OF THE CAVE TO BE INFINITE . 154D MARRIAGE HH 15   PROSE
    AND I HAVE CAUSED THE EARTH WORM TO BEG FROM DOOR TO DOOR   290 FOUR ZOAS 2   392
    TO BRING THEM TO PERFECTION HAS CAUSED THIS DELAY AS ALSO   840B LETTER 39   PROSE
    CAUSED THE POLICE TO SIEZE UPON THE PERSON & GOODS OR   .   865A LETTER 62   PROSE
CAUSELESS
    THE WOLF IS HUNTED DOWN BY CAUSELESS FEAR   . . . . .   24 EDW THIRD/PS 3   113
CAUSES
    GOD IS IN THE LOWEST EFFECTS AS WELL AS IN THE HIGHEST   87A ANNO LAVATER   MARG
        CAUSES

	PAGE	TITLE	LINE

CAUSES   (CONTINUED)
```
      THE PHILOSOPHY OF CAUSES & CONSEQUENCES MISLED LAVATER . .   88C ANNO LAVATER      MARG
      ALL BIBLES OR SACRED CODES HAVE BEEN THE CAUSES    . . .    149C MARRIAGE HH 4     PROSE
      SEEM TO LIVE IN IT IN CHAINS ARE IN TRUTH THE CAUSES OF     155A MARRIAGE HH 15    PROSE
        ITS LIFE
      HE WHO SAYS THERE ARE SECOND CAUSES HAS ALREADY DENIED      403B ANNO BACON        MARG
        A FIRST
      BECOME IN THEIR (FEMININE) PORTIONS THE CAUSES & PROMOTERS   532 MILTON 40           10
      HISTORIAN TURNER AND TWISTER OF CAUSES AND CONSEQUENCES     579A DESC CAT 5        PROSE
      CAUSES TO THE FLORENTINE AND ROMAN ARTIST FEAR TO EXECUTE   583A DESC CAT 9        PROSE
      WITH BEING THE CAUSES OF WAR   . . . . . . . . . . . . .    683A JERUSALEM 52      PROSE
      THE LEWISS & FREDERICKS WHO ALONE ARE ITS CAUSES &   . .  . 683A JERUSALEM 52     *PROSE
CAUSEWAY
      TO IRELAND'S FARTHEST ROCKS WHERE GIANTS BUILDED THEIR      735 JERUSALEM 89         50
        CAUSEWAY
CAUSWAY
      WITH BLOOD FROM JAPAN EASTWARD TO THE GIANTS CAUSWAY WEST   719 JERUSALEM 78         26
CAUTION
      WHAT IS SUSPITION IN ONE MAN IS CAUTION IN ANOTHER &   .  . 408D ANNO BACON        MARG
      [MR B(BLAKE) THINKS IT HIS DUTY TO CAUTION THE PUBLIC] .  . 601C PUB ADDRESS/N     PROSE
CAUTIOUS
      LAWFUL CAUTIOUS [XXX] & REFIND . . . . . . . . .            175 HOW TO KNOW/N         7
      THIS KNOWING ARTFUL SECRET FEARFUL CAUTIOUS TREMBLING       194 V DAU ALBION 6       17
        HYPOCRITE
CAVALCADE
      "OUR HOST" WHO OCCUPIES THE CENTER OF THE CAVALCADE . .  .  566D DESC CAT 3         PROSE
      OF THE CAVALCADE IS A FIRST RATE CHARACTER AND HIS JOKES    569D DESC CAT 3         PROSE
      "OUR HOST" WHO OCCUPIES THE CENTER OF THE CAVALCADE . .  .  588B CHAUCER/N          PROSE
      "OUR HOST" WHO OCCUPIES THE CENTER OF THE CAVALCADE . .  .  589D CHAUCER 2          PROSE
CAVALRY
      DARK CAVALRY LIKE CLOUDS FRAUGHT WITH THUNDER . . . . . .   147 FRENCH REVOLTN       291
CAVAN
      DOWN MONAGHAN CAVAN THESE ARE THE LAND OF ERIN    . . . .   711 JERUSALEM 72    *    27
CAVE
      FROM SLEEPING IN HIS CAVE    . . . . . . . .   .            11 GWIN KING/PS           14
      FAR IN A DIREFUL CAVE SHE LIVES UNSEEN  . . . . . . .       41D THEN SHE BORE          2
      WITHIN A NUMBER OF DRAGONS WERE HOLLOWING THE CAVE   . .    154D MARRIAGE HH 15    PROSE
      FOLDING ROUND THE ROCK & THE CAVE   . . . . . . . . . .     154D MARRIAGE HH 15    PROSE
      OF AIR HE CAUSED THE INSIDE OF THE CAVE TO BE INFINITE  .   154D MARRIAGE HH 15    PROSE
      THRO THE MILL WE WENT AND CAME TO A CAVE    . . . . . . .   155D MARRIAGE HH 17    PROSE
      [ASTONISHD HE FOUND ENION HIDDEN IN THE DARKSOM CAVE]  . .  267 FOUR ZOAS 1          136
      BUT WHEN THEY CAME TO THE DARK ROCK & TO THE SPECTROUS CAVE 309 FOUR ZOAS 5          155
      IN A SWIFT-VEGETATION ROUND THE ROCK & ROUND THE CAVE  .    309 FOUR ZOAS 5          158
      THE CAVE OF ORC STOOD TO THE SOUTH A FURNACE OF DIRE FLAMES 318 FOUR ZOAS 6          265
      QUENCHLESS UNCEASING IN THE WEST THE CAVE OF URIZEN . . .   318 FOUR ZOAS 6          266
      OUTSTRETCHD A SMILING CORSE THEY BURIED HER IN A SILENT     362 FOUR ZOAS 9          199
        CAVE
      BATHD IN THE CLEAR SPRING OF THE ROCK THEN FROM HER         366 FOUR ZOAS 9    *     346
        DARKSOM CAVE
      SILENT PLOTTING WHEN TO QUESTION LIKE A THIEF IN A CAVE     533 MILTON 41             14
      WHO IN MYSTERIOUS SINAI'S AWFUL CAVE  . . . . . . . . .     621 READER LOVER/J         3
      THERE IS THE CAVE THE ROCK THE TREE THE LAKE OF UDAN ADAN   634 JERUSALEM 13          38
      I BREATHE HIM FORTH INTO THE HEAVEN FROM MY SECRET CAVE     660 JERUSALEM 33          50
      FROM GROT & CAVE BENEATH THE MOON DIM REGION OF DEATH  .    660 JERUSALEM 34          11
      REUBEN SLEPT IN THE CAVE OF ADAM AND LOS FOLDED HIS TONGUE  662 JERUSALEM 36           5
      I SEE A CAVE A ROCK A TREE DEADLY AND POISONOUS             673 JERUSALEM 43          60
        UNIMAGINATIVE
      THE VIOLENT MAN-SLAUGHTER THESE ARE THE SPECTRE'S DOUBLE    699 JERUSALEM 64          21
        CAVE
      WHEN WEARY MAN ENTERS HIS CAVE . . . . . . . . . .   .      771 OF GATES/GP           19
      A DARK BLACK ROCK & A GLOOMY CAVE   . . . . . . . . . .     817 HAPPINESS/L           40
CAVENDISH
      CAVENDISH SQUARE IMMEDIATELY ON HIS RETURN BUT AS    . .    847D LETTER 44          PROSE
      OR LEFT THE CAVENDISH SQUARE HOUSE  . . . . . . . . .       847D LETTER 44          PROSE
CAVERN
      THRO NARROW CHINKS OF HIS CAVERN    . . . . . . . . . .     154C MARRIAGE HH 14    PROSE
      DOWN THE WINDING CAVERN WE GROPED OUR TEDIOUS WAY    . . .  155D MARRIAGE HH 17    PROSE
      THEN BROMION SAID AND SHOOK THE CAVERN WITH HIS LAMENTATION 192 V DAU ALBION 4       12
      HE TOOK DOWN FROM ITS TREMBLING PILLAR FROM ITS CAVERN      205 AMERICA CANC C         3
        DEEP
      RIBS LIKE A BENDING CAVERN  . . . . . . . . . . . .         228 URIZEN 10             39
      A CRAVING HUNGRY CAVERN . . . . . . . . . . . . . .         229 URIZEN 13              6
      A CAVERN SHAGGD WITH HORRID SHADES DARK COOL & DEADLY WHERE 295 FOUR ZOAS 3          122
      SHOOTING PAIND RIBBS LIKE A BENDING CAVERN  . . . . . .     303 FOUR ZOAS 4          220
      A CRAVING HUNGRY CAVERN THENCE AROSE HIS CHANNELD   . . .   303 FOUR ZOAS 4          240
      BESIDE LOS IN THE CAVERN DARK ENSLAVD TO VEGETATIVE FORMS   326 FOUR ZOAS 7          262
      & ABOVE HIS [CAVERNS] CAVERN ON THE EARTH'S SURFACE   . .   443A LAST JUDGMNT/L     PROSE
      ALL BOTH MORNING & NIGHT IS NOW A DARK CAVERN XXX WHEN      599D PUB ADDRESS/N     *PROSE
        YOU VIEW
      BENEATH HER FEET IS A FLAMING CAVERN IN WHICH IS SEEN  .    609B V LAST JUDG/N      PROSE
      BENEATH THE DRAGON'S CAVERN A SKELETON BEGINS TO ANIMATE    609C V LAST JUDG/N      PROSE
      DRAGON'S CAVERN REPRESENTS THE LATTER STATE OF THE CHURCH   610C V LAST JUDG/N      PROSE
      WINCHESTER IN HIS DEN & CAVERN THEY LAMENT AGAINST  . . .   671 JERUSALEM 42          59
CAVERND
      FIVE WINDOWS LIGHT THE CAVERND MAN THRO ONE HE BREATHES     237 EUROPE INTRO           1
        THE AIR
      HIM FAR INTO THE WORLD OF THARMAS INTO A CAVERND ROCK  .    279 FOUR ZOAS 1          534
      REVOLVING ROUND IN WHIRLPOOLS FIERCE ALL ROUND THE CAVERND  320 FOUR ZOAS 7            4
        WORLDS
      A CAVERND UNIVERSE OF FLAMING FIRE THE HORSES OF URIZEN     320 FOUR ZOAS 7            6
      THE HOLY OIL RAGES THRO ALL THE CAVERND ROCKS FIERCE FLAMES 320 FOUR ZOAS 7           12
      [TO HEW THE CAVERND ROCKS OF DRANTHON INTO FORMS OF BEAUTY] 331 FOUR ZOAS 7          457
```

	PAGE	TITLE	LINE
CAVERNOUS			
CAVERNOUS DWELLERS FILLD THE ENORMOUS REVELRY RESPONSING	274	FOUR ZOAS 1	383
AND ANCIENT NIGHT & PURGATORY IT IS A CAVERNOUS EARTH .	498	MILTON 17	25
AND FRAMED THE MUNDANE SHELL CAVERNOUS IN LENGTH BREDTH & HIGHTH	740	JERUSALEM 92	27
CAVERNS			
COME FROM CAVERNS DEEP	113	LIT GRL LST/SI	35
FOR CHAIND BENEATH I REND THESE CAVERNS WHEN THOU BRINGEST FOOD	196	AMERICA PREL 1	18
CROUCH HOWLING BEFORE THEIR CAVERNS DEEP LIKE SKINS DRYD IN THE WIND	199	AMERICA 9	4
FROM THE CAVERNS OF HIS JOINTED SPINE	228	URIZEN 11	1
DOES THE SOUL LABOUR THUS IN CAVERNS OF THE GRAVE .	262A	SMALL BK DSGNS	TITLE
WHILE THY MILD VOICE FILLS ALL THESE CAVERNS WITH SWEET HARMONY	271	FOUR ZOAS 1	250
[?HE ?FELL XXX HID IN ?HORRIBLE ?CAVERNS OF MOUNTAINS]	SUPP	FOUR ZOAS 1	*
AND ALL THE TIME IN CAVERNS SHUT THE GOLDEN LOOMS ERECTED	284	FOUR ZOAS 2	145
BENEATH THE CAVERNS ROLL THE WEIGHTS OF LEAD & SPINDLES OF IRON	284	FOUR ZOAS 2	148
INTO THE CAVERNS OF THE GRAVE & PLACES OF HUMAN SEED . .	295	FOUR ZOAS 3	142
WHICH NOW OUR RIVERS WERE BECOME DELVING THRO CAVERNS HUGE	300	FOUR ZOAS 4	102
FROM THE CAVERNS OF HIS JOINTED SPINE DOWN SUNK WITH FRIGHT	303	FOUR ZOAS 4	223
RENDING THE CAVERNS LIKE A MIGHTY WIND PENT IN THE EARTH	309	FOUR ZOAS 5	183
THAT SHAKES MY CAVERNS WITH STRONG SHUDDERS PERHAPS THIS IS THE NIGHT	311	FOUR ZOAS 5	* 239
FOUR CAVERNS ROOTING DOWNWARDS THEIR FOUNDATIONS THRUSTING FORTH	318	FOUR ZOAS 6	263
ALL THRO THE CAVERNS OF FIRE & AIR & EARTH SEEKING . . .	318	FOUR ZOAS 6	272
THEN FOLLOWS THUS IN THE CAVERNS OF THE GRAVE &C AS IT . .	336B	FOUR ZOAS 7B	*PROSE
NOW IN THE CAVERNS OF THE GRAVE & PLACES OF HUMAN SEED . .	336	FOUR ZOAS 7B	124
AND THUS AHANIA CRIES ALOUD TO THE CAVERNS OF THE GRAVE	353	FOUR ZOAS 8	492
THUS CRIES AHANIA ENION REPLIES FROM THE CAVERNS OF THE GRAVE	354	FOUR ZOAS 8	533
LISTEN I WILL TELL THEE WHAT IS DONE IN THE CAVERNS OF THE GRAVE	355	FOUR ZOAS 8	555
AND HEARD ENION'S VOICE SOUND FROM THE CAVERNS OF THE GRAVE	356	FOUR ZOAS 8	605
OVER THE GRAVES & CAVERNS OF THE DEAD OVER THE PLANETS	365	FOUR ZOAS 9	314
O TERRIBLE WINE PRESSES OF LUVAH O CAVERNS OF THE GRAVE	376	FOUR ZOAS 9	728
IN THE CAVERNS OF THE EARTH IS THE DRAGON WITH SEVEN HEADS	443A	LAST JUDGMNT/L	PROSE
& ABOVE HIS [CAVERNS] CAVERN ON THE EARTH'S SURFACE . . .	443A	LAST JUDGMNT/L	PROSE
DEATH COUCH IN THE CAVERNS OF DEATH IN THE CORNER OF THE ATLANTIC	489	MILTON 9	3
BEYOND THE STARS IN CHAOS IN CAVERNS OF THE MUNDANE SHELL	502	MILTON 20	42
THESE ARE THE STARRY VOIDS OF NIGHT & THE DEPTHS & CAVERNS OF EARTH	514	MILTON 27	51
SURROUNDING THE MUNDANE SHELL OUTSIDE IN ITS CAVERNS . .	526	MILTON 35	39
WITH CAVERNS WHOSE REMOTEST BOTTOMS MEET AGAIN BEYOND . .	529	MILTON 37	55
THE [VISIONS] CAVERNS OF THE GRAVE IVE SEEN	558	THE CAVERNS/N	1
OF WATLING-STREET OF LONDON STONE OF THE CAVERNS IN . . .	577D	DESC CAT 5	PROSE
WITHIN THE UNFATHOMD CAVERNS OF MY EAR	621	READER LOVER/J	8
HOARSE FROM HIS ROCKS FROM CAVERNS OF DERBYSHIRE & WALES	646	JERUSALEM 23	27
AND REUBEN FLED WITH HIS HEAD DOWNWARDS AMONG THE CAVERNS	698	JERUSALEM 63	44
LIDS TO GROW OVER HIS EYES IN VEILS OF TEARS AND CAVERNS	702	JERUSALEM 66	31
CAVE'S SEE LE CAVE'S			
RUBBISH FROM A CAVE'S MOUTH	154D	MARRIAGE HH 15	PROSE
CAVES			
IS DRIVN YELLING TO HIS CAVES BENEATH MOUNT HECLA . . .	3	TO WINTER/PS	16
OF OCEAN RUN FROM ROCKS AND CAVES WILD MEN	32	EDW THIRD/PS 6	21
TILL TO THE CAVES OF ZAZEL THEY APPROACHD AT EVEN TIDE . .	108	TIRIEL 7	2
FORTH FROM THEIR CAVES [THE SONS OF ZAZEL]	108	TIRIEL 7	3
TO CAVES THE SLEEPING MAID	113	LIT GRL LST/SI	52
THEY VISIT CAVES OF EVERY BEAST	119	NIGHT/SI	19
TILL MAN RAISE HIS DARKEND LIMBS OUT OF THE CAVES OF NIGHT . . .	144	FRENCH REVOLTN	218
BOUND BACK TO BACK IN BROMION'S CAVES TERROR & MEEKNESS DWELL	190	V DAU ALBION 2	5
THAT SHIVER IN RELIGIOUS CAVES BENEATH THE BURNING FIRES	190	V DAU ALBION 2	9
HID IN HIS CAVES THE BARD OF ALBION FELT THE ENORMOUS PLAGUES	202	AMERICA 15	16
AND FIXED IN TWO LITTLE CAVES	228	URIZEN 11	14
SOTHA & THIRALATHA SECRET DWELLERS OF DREAMFUL CAVES . .	244	EUROPE 14	26
[THUS THEY CONTENDED ALL THE DAY AMONG THE CAVES OF THARMAS]	269	FOUR ZOAS 1	179
ON HIGH INTO TWO LITTLE ORBS HIDING IN TWO LITTLE CAVES	303	FOUR ZOAS 4	229
BUT FROM THE CAVES OF DEEPEST NIGHT ASCENDING IN CLOUDS OF MIST	306	FOUR ZOAS 5	31
URIZEN SHUDDRING HEARD HIS TREMBLING LIMBS SHOOK THE STRONG CAVES	310	FOUR ZOAS 5	188
WHEN THOUGHT IS CLOSD IN CAVES	311	FOUR ZOAS 5	241
SIEZING UPON HIS FEET & RENDING THE SINEWS THAT IN CAVES	315	FOUR ZOAS 6	139
BUT URIZEN SILENT DESCENDED TO THE CAVES OF ORC & SAW .	320	FOUR ZOAS 7	5
HOWLING & RENDING HIS DARK CAVES THE AWFUL DEMON LAY . .	320	FOUR ZOAS 7	20
THRO CAVES OF DEATH INTO EXISTENCE THE BEECH LONG LIMBD ADVANCD	335	FOUR ZOAS 7B	* 100
HIS STRONG BONES BEAT WITH SNOWS & HID WITHIN THE CAVES OF NIGHT	354	FOUR ZOAS 8	517
HIS FAINT GROANS SHAKE THE CAVES & ISSUE THRO THE DESOLATE ROCKS	354	FOUR ZOAS 8	520
MAN IS A WORM WEARIED WITH JOY HE SEEKS THE CAVES OF SLEEP	374	FOUR ZOAS 9	627
LO HOW THE POMP OF MYSTERY GOES DOWN INTO THE CAVES . . .	375	FOUR ZOAS 9	662
IN THE DEEP CAVES BENEATH HIS LIMBS RENEWD HIS LIONS ROAR	379	FOUR ZOAS 9	841
ROLLING ROUND INTO TWO LITTLE ORBS & CLOSED IN TWO LITTLE CAVES	482	MILTON 3	14

CAVES   (CONTINUED)
 AMONG ALBION'S DRUIDS & BARDS IN THE CAVES BENEATH ALBION'S   489 MILTON 9   2
IT ISSUES THRO THE DARK & INTRICATE CAVES OF THE MUNDANE   507 MILTON 23   22
  SHELL
ALL THE WISDOM WHICH WAS HIDDEN IN CAVES & DENS FROM   510 MILTON 25   20
  ANCIENT
(?TO) THOR & CRUEL ODIN WHO FIRST REARD THE POLAR CAVES   511 MILTON 25   * 53
IN THE REMOTEST BOTTOMS OF THE CAVES THAT NONE CAN PASS   529 MILTON 37   57
[SHE'D] BUT NOW THE CAVES OF HELL I VIEW . . . . .   558 THE CAVERNS/N * 3
BOSOM IN ALL THE TERRORS OF FRIENDSHIP ENTERING THE CAVES   656 JERUSALEM 31   4
ALBION'S ROCKS & PRECIPICES CAVES OF SOLITUDE & DARK   656 JERUSALEM 31   6
  DESPAIR
FLED THEY FLED AT HIS HORRIBLE FORM THEY HID IN CAVES . .   661 JERUSALEM 34   49
THE TWENTY-EIGHT TREMBLED IN DEATH'S DARK CAVES IN COLD   668 JERUSALEM 41   23
  DESPAIR
. . . WEAVING OVER THE CAVES OF MACHPELAH . . . . . .   699 JERUSALEM 64   38
CAVILLING
I HOPE NO ONE WILL CALL WHAT I HAVE WRITTEN CAVILLING . .   88A ANNO LAVATER   MARG
CAWDLE
TO GIVE THESE RASCALS A DOSE OF CAWDLE . . . .   548 ON GREAT ENC/N   6
CEASD
FROM ANTIENT MELODY HAVE CEASD . . . .   10 TO MUSES/PS   4
SHE WAS SEATED IN THE DEEP THE OCEAN CEASD . . . . .   21 EDW THIRD/PS 2   81
SHE CEASD & SMILD IN TEARS THEN SAT DOWN IN HER SILVER   128 BOOK OF THEL 2   2
  SHRINE
THE VOICE CEASD THE NATION SAT . . . .   137 FRENCH REVOLTN   62
THE VOICE CEASD THE NATION SAT . . . .   137 FRENCH REVOLTN   63
HE CEASD SILENT PONDRING . . . .   137 FRENCH REVOLTN   79
HE CEASD AND BURND SILENT RED CLOUDS ROLL ROUND NECKER   139 FRENCH REVOLTN 105
  . . .
THE VOICE CEASD A GROAN SHOOK MY CHAMBER . . . .   141 FRENCH REVOLTN 151
SHOOK THE CHAMBER HE CEASD ABASHD THEN ORLEANS SPOKE ALL   142 FRENCH REVOLTN 178
  WAS SILENT
CAN NEVER PASS AWAY SHE CEASD & CLOSD HER GOLDEN SHRINE   189 V DAU ALBION 1   10
[THE STERN BARD CEASD ASHAMD OF HIS OWN SONG ENRAGD HE   196 AMERICA PREL 2   18
  SWUNG]
THE STRONG VOICE CEASD FOR A TERRIBLE BLAST . . . . . .   197 AMERICA 3   13
THE STRONG VOICE CEASD FOR A TERRIBLE BLAST . . . . . .   204 AMERICA CANC A   13
THINKING NONE SAW HIM WHEN HE CEASD I STARTED FROM THE   237 EUROPE INTRO   8
  TREES
WAR CEASD & ALL THE TROOPS LIKE SHADOWS FLED TO THEIR   239 EUROPE 4   4
  ABODES
SHE CEASD [AND] FOR ALL [WENT] WERE FORTH [TO] AT SPORT   244 EUROPE 14   * 32
  . . .
SHE CEASD THE PRINCE HIS LIGHT OBSCURD & THE SPLENDORS   292 FOUR ZOAS 3   12
  OF HIS CROWN
HE CEASD THE SHADOWY VOICE WAS SILENT . . . .   293 FOUR ZOAS 3   66
FOR WHEN HE CAME TO WHERE A VORTEX CEASD TO OPERATE . . .   316 FOUR ZOAS 6   190
THE PRESTER SERPENT CEASD THE WAR SONG SOUNDED LOUD   336 FOUR ZOAS 7B   121
  & STRONG
HE CEASD FOR RIVN LINK FROM LINK THE BURSTING UNIVERSE   363 FOUR ZOAS 9   230
  EXPLODES
SHE CEASD & (LIGHT) BEAMD ROUND HER LIKE THE GLORY OF THE   370 FOUR ZOAS 9   * 503
  MORNING
NOW LEUTHA CEASD TEARS FLOWD BUT THE DIVINE PITY SUPPORTED   493 MILTON 13   7
  HER
THE BARD CEASD ALL CONSIDERD AND A LOUD RESOUNDING MURMUR   495 MILTON 13   45
YET CEASD HE NOT FROM LABOURING AT THE ROARINGS OF HIS   630 JERUSALEM 10   62
  FORGE
HE CEASD THE SHADOWY VOICE WAS SILENT . . . .   654 JERUSALEM 29   53
CEASE
. . . AND PLAGUE AND WRATH AND TEMPEST SHALL CEASE   137 FRENCH REVOLTN   78
BUT THE PROLIFIC WOULD CEASE TO BE PROLIFIC UNLESS . . .   155B MARRIAGE HH 15 PROSE
EMPIRE IS NO MORE AND NOW THE LION & WOLF SHALL CEASE . .   160A SONG LIBERTY   PROSE
THEY SAID THIS MYSTERY NEVER SHALL CEASE . . . .   174 HUMAN IMAGE/N   27
FOR EMPIRE IS NO MORE AND NOW THE LION & WOLF SHALL CEASE   198 AMERICA 6   15
LEST THE STATE CALLD LUVAH SHOULD CEASE & THE DIVINE VISION   287 FOUR ZOAS 2   264
HITHERTO SHALT THOU COME NO FURTHER HERE THY PROUD WAVES   298 FOUR ZOAS 4   35
  CEASE
FROM THEE THY FOOD SO SHALL WE CEASE TO BE & ALL   313 FOUR ZOAS 6   65
  OUR SORROWS
[CEASE] END & THE ETERNAL MAN NO MORE RENEW BENEATH OUR   313 FOUR ZOAS 6   66
  POWER
THOU WILT NOT CEASE FROM RAGE GREY DEMON SILENCE ALL THY   323 FOUR ZOAS 7   144
  STORMS
COULDST THOU BUT CEASE FROM TERROR & TREMBLING & AFFRIGHT   330 FOUR ZOAS 7   418
CAN THAT WHICH HAS EXISTED CEASE OR CAN LOVE & LIFE EXPIRE   345 FOUR ZOAS 8   170
A CHERUBIM DOES CEASE TO SING . . . .   431 AUGURIES   16
I WILL NOT CEASE FROM MENTAL FIGHT . . . .   481 AND DID FEET/M   13
THE REPROBATE WHO NEVER CEASE TO BELIEVE AND THE REDEEMD   511 MILTON 25   35
STATES CHANGE BUT INDIVIDUAL IDENTITIES NEVER CHANGE NOR   521 MILTON 32   23
  CEASE
IT IS BURNT UP THE MOMENT MEN CEASE TO BEHOLD IT I ASSERT   617B V LAST JUDG/N PROSE
WHEN ALL ALBION'S INJURIES SHALL CEASE AND WHEN WE SHALL   626 JERUSALEM 7   55
THAT ENTHUSIASM AND LIFE MAY NOT CEASE ARISE SPECTRE ARISE 628 JERUSALEM 9   31
O THAT I COULD CEASE TO BE DESPAIR I AM DESPAIR . . . .   630 JERUSALEM 10   51
THE STARS STAND STILL TO HEAR JERUSALEM & VALA CEASE TO   730 JERUSALEM 85   15
  MOURN
LOS ANSWERD SWIFT AS THE SHUTTLE OF GOLD SEXES MUST VANISH 739 JERUSALEM 92   13
  & CEASE
SINAI'S TRUMPETS CEASE TO ROAR . . . .   754 EV GOSPEL(E)/N   22
CEASE FINGER OF GOD TO WRITE . . . .   754 EV GOSPEL(E)/N   23

		PAGE	TITLE	LINE

CEASE   (CONTINUED)
    FOR WHICH I SHALL NEVER CEASE TO HONOUR & RESPECT YOU   . . 826A LETTER 27   PROSE
CEASED   SEE CEASD,CEAST
    CEASED PUTS IT OUT OF HIS OWN POWER TO EVER WITNESS ONE   391C ANNO WATSON   MARG
CEASELESS
    EDDIES OF WRATH CEASELESS ROUND & ROUND . . . .   227 URIZEN 10   20
    LOOKD OUT INTO THE WORLD OF THARMAS WHERE IN CEASELESS   286 FOUR ZOAS 2   256
      TORRENTS
    BELCHD FROM THE FURNACES WREATHD ROUND HER CHAIND   302 FOUR ZOAS 4   188
      IN CEASELESS FIRE
    THE ETERNAL MIND BOUNDED BEGAN TO ROLL EDDIES OF WRATH   303 FOUR ZOAS 4   208
      CEASELESS
    TORN BY BLACK STORMS & CEASELESS TORRENTS OF CONSUMING FIRE 306 FOUR ZOAS 5   56
    TO BRING THE THRILLING JOYS OF SENSE TO QUELL HIS CEASELESS 308 FOUR ZOAS 5   120
      RAGE
    THE EAST WAS VOID BUT THARMAS ROLLD HIS BILLOWS IN   318 FOUR ZOAS 6   270
      CEASELESS EDDIES
    OF LIVING PANGS THY HORRIBLE BED GLOWING WITH CEASELESS   321 FOUR ZOAS 7   50
      FIRES
    IN CHAINS OF IRON & IN DUNGEONS CIRCLED WITH CEASELESS   377 FOUR ZOAS 9   750
      FIRES
    IN CHAINS OF IRON & IN DUNGEONS CIRCLED WITH CEASELESS   514 MILTON 27   32
      FIRES
    TORN WITH BLACK STORMS & CEASELESS TORRENTS OF HIS OWN   667 JERUSALEM 40   39
      CONSUMING FIRE
    AND LOS SHOUTED WITH CEASELESS SHOUTINGS & HIS TEARS POURED 711 JERUSALEM 71   56
      DOWN
CEASES
    TAKES AWAY THE AUTHORITY ALTOGETHER IT CEASES TO BE HISTORY 390D ANNO WATSON   MARG
    WHICH IF MAN CEASES TO BEHOLD HE CEASES TO EXIST   . . .   664 JERUSALEM 38   13
CEASING
    AND JOY WITHOUT CEASING . . . .   119 NIGHT/SI   14
    FEEDING IT WITH HIS GROANS & TEARS DAY & NIGHT WITHOUT   639 JERUSALEM 17   56
      CEASING
    CEASING TO BE HIS EMANATIONS LIFE TO THEMSELVES ASSUMING   736 JERUSALEM 90   2
CEAST
    HE CEAST THE AGED MAN [XXX] RAISD UP HIS RIGHT HAND TO   99 TIRIEL 1   *   19
      THE HEAVENS
    HE CEAST & DARKLING OER THE MOUNTAINS SOUGHT HIS PATHLESS   100 TIRIEL 1   52
      WAY
    HE CEAST THE HEAVY CLOUDS CONFUSD ROLLD ROUND THE LOFTY   106 TIRIEL 5   14
      TOWERS
    AND WHEN THE SHAKING CEAST A FOG POSSEST THE ACCURSED CLIME 106 TIRIEL 5   17
    HE CEAST & [?HILI] HELA LED HER FATHER FROM THE NOISOM   107 TIRIEL 5   *   26
      PLACE
    HE CEAST HER DARK HAIR UPRIGHT STOOD WHILE SNAKES INFOLDED   108 TIRIEL 6   44
      ROUND
    HE CEAST OUTSTRETCHD AT HAR & HEVA'S FEET IN AWFUL DEATH   110 TIRIEL 8   42
    SHE CEAST & ROLLD HER SHADY CLOUDS . . . .   239 EUROPE PREL 2   17
    A GROAN WAS HEARD ON HIGH THE WARLIKE CLARIONS CEAST THE   273 FOUR ZOAS 1   313
      SPIRITS
    BUT ALL THE FURNACES WERE OUT & THE BELLOWS HAD CEAST TO   305 FOUR ZOAS 5   17
      BLOW
    THEN LOS AGAIN TOOK UP HIS SPEECH AS ENITHARMON CEAST   . . 741 JERUSALEM 93   17
CEDAR
    WHERE ONCE THE OLIVE FLOURISHD & THE CEDAR SPREAD HIS WINGS 354 FOUR ZOAS 8   * 535
CEDARS
CEILING   SEE CIELING
CELEBRATE
    SATAN NOW AWAKES SIN DEATH & HELL TO CELEBRATE WITH HIM   441D INSC FALL MAN   PROSE
CELESTIAL
    A GOLDEN ALTAR BURNT PERFUMES WITH ART CELESTIAL FORMD . . 285 FOUR ZOAS 2   190
    LIKE DEAD HORSES WHEN REPELLED BY THE CELESTIAL SPHERES   581D DESC CAT 8   PROSE
    VOICES OF CELESTIAL INHABITANTS ARE MORE DISTINCTLY HEARD   802A LETTER 14   PROSE
    CELESTIAL CITY I ALSO HAVE BUT A FEW MORE MOUNTAINS TO PASS 854C LETTER 53   PROSE
    CELESTIAL GLOBE TERESTRIAL GLOBE . . . .   SUPP ILLUS DANTE 16 *PROSE
CELL
    VILE SAVAGE MINDS THAT LURK IN LONELY CELL . . . . . .   15 IMIT SPEN/PS   34
    AND IN THY CELL THOU SHALL EVER DWELL   . . . .   419 I SAW A MONK/N   13
    RISE WAR & BIND HIM IN HIS CELL   . . . .   419 I SAW A MONK/N   14
    MILTON IN HIS OLD AGE SITTING IN HIS MOSSY CELL . .   619C ILLUS MILTON   PROSE
    AND IN YOUR CELL YOU SHALL EVER DWELL . . . .   683 I SAW A MONK/J   11
    RISE WAR & BIND HIM IN HIS CELL . . . .   683 I SAW A MONK/J   12
CELLAR
    AND THE CELLAR GOES DOWN WITH A STEP . . . .   54 LO THE BAT/IM   14
CELLS
    WITH WHAT SENSE DOES THE BEE FORM CELLS HAVE NOT THE MOUSE   191 V DAU ALBION 3   4
      & FROG
CELSUS
    CELSUS WAS A BAD ADVISER . . . .   408D ANNO BACON   MARG
CEMENT
    THE MORTAR & CEMENT OF THE WORK TEARS OF HONESTY THE NAILS   632 JERUSALEM 12   33
CENSERS
    IN WHITE ROBES STREWN IN AIR CENSERS AND HARPS . . .   . .   140 FRENCH REVOLTN   133
CENTAURS
    CENTAURS MOST LIKELY DANTE DESCRIBES THE...CIRCLES IN CANTO 786A ILLS DANTE 101   PROSE
      XI...
CENTER   SEE CENTRE
    RISE FROM THE CENTER BELCHING FLAMES & ROARINGS DARK SMOKE   106 TIRIEL 5   7
    THEN MARS THOU WAST OUR CENTER & THE PLANETS THREE FLEW   197 AMERICA 5   4
      ROUND
    THEN BURST THE CENTER FROM ITS ORB AND FOUND A PLACE   204 AMERICA CANC B   6
      BENEATH

	PAGE	TITLE	LINE

CENTER   (CONTINUED)
```
       SHE ALSO TOOK AN ATOM OF SPACE & OPEND ITS CENTER    . . .   . 270 FOUR ZOAS 1   * 225
       TILL RESTING EACH HIS [CENTER][BASEMENT] FINDS . . . . .   . 283 FOUR ZOAS 2     139
       EVEN TO THE CENTER WRAPPING ROUND THE CENTER & THE LIMBS     309 FOUR ZOAS 5     168
       WONDERING BEHELD THE CENTER OPEND BY DIVING MERCY INSPIRD     329 FOUR ZOAS 7     374
       WHICH NOW OPEND WITHIN THE CENTER WE BEHOLD SPREAD ABROAD     331 FOUR ZOAS 7     442
       AND HE COMMANDED HIS SONS FOUND A CENTER IN THE DEEP   .   . 333 FOUR ZOAS 7B     18
       A MOMENT THEN ASTOUNDING HORROR BELCHES FROM THE CENTER       336 FOUR ZOAS 7B    131
       MISPLACING EVERY CENTER HUNGRY DESIRE & LUST BEGAN   . . .   . 345 FOUR ZOAS 8     178
       HE TOUCHES THE REMOTEST POLE & IN THE CENTER WEEPS   .   . . 355 FOUR ZOAS 8     573
       EACH SPECK OF DUST TO THE EARTH'S CENTER NESTLES ROUND       363 FOUR ZOAS 9     233
          & ROUND
       [THEN] A WHIRLWIND ROSE UP IN THE CENTER & IN THE WHIRLWIND   372 FOUR ZOAS 9     591
          A SHRIEK
       ALL FELL TOWARDS THE CENTER IN DIRE RUIN SINKING DOWN   .  . 500 MILTON 19        21
       AND IN HIS HALLOWD CENTER HOLDS THE HEAVENS OF BRIGHT         515 MILTON 28        38
          ETERNITY
       AND NONE CAN TELL HOW FROM SO SMALL A CENTER COMES SUCH       520 MILTON 31        47
          SWEETS
       FORGETTING THAT WITHIN THAT CENTER ETERNITY EXPANDS   . . . . 520 MILTON 31        48
       ALL FELL TOWARDS THE CENTER SINKING DOWNWARD IN DIRE RUIN     524 MILTON 34        39
       . . . LOOKING UP FROM [CIRCUMFERENCE] SKUMFERENCE TO CENTER   555 BLAKES APL/N 1   18
       CRY LOOKING QUITE FROM SKUMFERENCE TO CENTER     . . . . .   . 556 BLAKES APL/N 2   17
       "OUR HOST" WHO OCCUPIES THE CENTER OF THE CAVALCADE   . . . 566D DESC CAT 3      PROSE
       FOR THE HOST WHO FOLLOWS THIS GROUP AND HOLDS THE CENTER     569D DESC CAT 3      PROSE
       "OUR HOST" WHO OCCUPIES THE CENTER OF THE CAVALCADE   . . . 588B CHAUCER/N       PROSE
       "OUR HOST" WHO OCCUPIES THE CENTER OF THE CAVALCADE   . . . 589D CHAUCER 2       PROSE
       CRY TOM COOKE PROVES FROM CIRCUMFERENCE TO CENTER    . . .   . 596 BLAKES APOL/PA  11
       THE NADIR EAST THE CENTER UNAPPROACHABLE FOR EVER    . . . 632 JERUSALEM 12      56
       THE VEGETATIVE UNIVERSE OPENS LIKE A FLOWER FROM             633 JERUSALEM 13      34
          THE EARTH'S CENTER
       ALBION'S CIRCUMFERENCE WAS CLOSD HIS CENTER BEGAN DARKNING   642 JERUSALEM 19      36
       HAVING A WHITE DOT CALLD A CENTER FROM WHICH BRANCHES OUT    659 JERUSALEM 33      19
       SHE ALSO TOOK AN ATOM OF SPACE WITH DIRE PAIN OPENING IT     678 JERUSALEM 48      38
          A CENTER
       THE CENTER INTO AN EXPANSE & THE CENTER ROLLED OUT INTO      689 JERUSALEM 57      18
          AN EXPANSE
       ALL FELL TOWARDS THE CENTER SINKING DOWNWARDS IN DIRE RUIN   691 JERUSALEM 59      17
       FROM THE INNER SANCTUARY A FALSE HOLINESS HID WITHIN THE     708 JERUSALEM 69      40
          CENTER
       THE CIRCUMFERENCE IS WITHIN WITHOUT IS FORMED THE SELFISH    709 JERUSALEM 71       7
          CENTER
       AND THE CENTER HAS ETERNAL STATES THESE STATES WE NOW        709 JERUSALEM 71       9
          EXPLORE
       ALL THESE CENTER IN LONDON & IN GOLGONOOZA FROM WHENCE   . . 712 JERUSALEM 72      28
       STAND IN THE CENTER & SOMETIMES STRETCH FLAT IN THE EXPANSE  728 JERUSALEM 83      41
       EASTWARD INTO HER OWN CENTER CREATING THE FEMALE WOMB   . . 734 JERUSALEM 88      52
       SO THAT HOMER IS THE CENTER OF ALL I MEAN THE POETRY OF     785B ILLUS DANTE 7    PROSE
          THE HEATHEN
       AFTER THEY HAVE PASSED THE CENTER . . . . . . . . . . .     785D ILLS DANTE 101  PROSE
       CENTER ORNAMENT IS WORTHY HE SAYS THAT IT IS BY FAR IN HIS  836B LETTER 35       PROSE
CENTERD
       CENTERD AND THE RUSHING OF CHAOS OVERWHELMD HIS DARK SOUL    136 FRENCH REVOLTN    50
          . . .
CENTERS
       ALL THINGS REVERSD FLEW FROM THEIR CENTERS RATTLING BONES    363 FOUR ZOAS 9     231
          [TO BONES ]
CENTINELS
       FOR I HAVE PLACD MY CENTINELS IN STATIONS EACH TENTH MAN     278 FOUR ZOAS 1     502
CENTIPEDE
       DANCE ROUND THE WINE PRESSES OF LUVAH THE CENTIPEDE IS       377 FOUR ZOAS 9     757
          THERE
       DANCE ROUND THE WINE-PRESSES OF LUVAH THE CENTIPEDE IS       513 MILTON 27        13
          THERE
CENTRAL
       . . . THREE CENTRAL DOMES AFTER THE NAMES  . . . . . .       284 FOUR ZOAS 2     174
       LIKE THE CENTRAL FIRE . . . . . . . . . . . .                137 FRENCH REVOLTN   80
       ONE CENTRAL FORM COMPOSED OF ALL OTHER FORMS BEING GRANTED  459C ANNO REYNOLDS    MARG
       HERE HE LOSES SIGHT OF A CENTRAL FORM & . . . . . . . .     460A ANNO REYNOLDS    MARG
       GETS INTO MANY CENTRAL FORMS  . . . . . . . . . . .         460A ANNO REYNOLDS    MARG
       HERE HE COMES AGAIN TO HIS CENTRAL FORM . . .. . . . .      460B ANNO REYNOLDS    MARG
       THE WINE-PRESS ON THE RHINE GROANS LOUD BUT ALL ITS CENTRAL  510 MILTON 25         3
          BEAMS
       ACT MORE TERRIFIC IN THE CENTRAL CITIES OF THE NATIONS  .   . 510 MILTON 25         4
       FOLLOWING ALBION INTO HIS CENTRAL VOID AMONG HIS OAKS   .   . 656 JERUSALEM 30      20
       BENEATH THE BOTTOMS OF THE GRAVES WHICH IS EARTH'S CENTRAL   677 JERUSALEM 48      13
          JOINT
       BUT JESUS BREAKING THRO THE CENTRAL ZONES OF DEATH & HELL    716 JERUSALEM 75      21
CENTRE    SEE CENTER
       ("THE CENTRE") LET ME REFER HERE TO A REMARK ON APHORISM...  65C ANNO LAVATER     MARG
       ("MAN'S INTEREST...HIS GOD...VORTEX...CENTRE") PURE GOLD      66A ANNO LAVATER     MARG
CENTURY
       WAS WRITTEN WITHIN THE FIRST CENTURY SEE P...&...   . . .   . 394C ANNO WATSON      MARG
       WHO LIVED IN THE FIFTH CENTURY THERE WERE REMAINS   . .   . 578B DESC CAT 5       PROSE
       TO A PRINCE OF THE FIFTH CENTURY WHO CONQUERED EUROPE   .   . 578C DESC CAT 5       PROSE
CERBERUS
       CERBERUS  . . . . . . . . . . . . . . . . .                786A ILLS DANTE 101   PROSE
CERCHIETTI
       DANTE CALLS THEM CERCHIETTI . . . . . . . . . . . . .       786A ILLS DANTE 101   PROSE
CEREMONIAL
       MURDER THE LAWS OF THE JEWS WERE BOTH CEREMONIAL & REAL      393C ANNO WATSON      MARG
```

		PAGE	TITLE	LINE
CEREMONIES
& NOT IN CEREMONIES AT ALL . . . . 92D ANNO SWED LOVE MARG
IS THAT ABOMINATION WHICH LIKE THE JEWISH CEREMONIES . 389C ANNO WATSON MARG
CEREMONY
THEY REDUCE THE MAN TO WANT THEN GIVE WITH POMP & CEREMONY 656 JERUSALEM 30 31
THE OUTWARD CEREMONY IS ANTICHRIST . . . . 776A INSC LAOCOON PROSE
& MORE CEREMONY ALSO IN SO SERIOUS AN AFFAIR AS THE CALLING 854D LETTER 53 PROSE
ON
CERTAIN
WITH CERTAIN VICTORY AND TIS MY BOAST . . . . 23 EDW THIRD/PS 3 87
IN THE MOON IS A CERTAIN ISLAND NEAR BY A MIGHTY CONTINENT 44A ISLAND MOON 1 PROSE
AND THAT HE MUST BE BORN IS CERTAIN FOR ONE MUST BE ALL 272 FOUR ZOAS 1 294
TERRIFIED URIZEN HEARD ORC NOW CERTAIN THAT HE WAS LUVAH 324 FOUR ZOAS 7 151
THIS IS NO CERTAIN FACT PRESUMPTION IS NO PROOF . . . . 395B ANNO WATSON MARG
THIS IS CERTAIN IF WHAT BACON SAYS IS TRUE WHAT CHRIST 396D ANNO BACON MARG
SAYS IS FALSE
& IS TO ME AN HOST OF STRENGTH I AM CERTAIN THAT IF I HAD 438D BLAKES MEMORAN PROSE
NOT
THIS WILL PRODUCE CERTAIN & DETERMIND FORMS ON THE PLATE 440B MEMORANDUM/N 2 PROSE
SHE HAS CERTAIN PECULIARITIES AND LITTLE DELICATE 568B DESC CAT 3 PROSE
AFFECTATIONS
WITH CERTAIN HUMOUROUS ACCOMPANIMENTS IN HIS CHARACTER . 568D DESC CAT 3 *PROSE
THAT I MAY SET CERTAIN MISTAKEN CRITICS RIGHT IN THEIR . 569A DESC CAT 3 PROSE
AS IT ONLY EXISTS IN CERTAIN PERIODS IT IS THE SOLDIER 575C DESC CAT 3 PROSE
BY SEA
IT WAS WITH DIFFICULTY BROUGHT BACK AGAIN TO A CERTAIN 582B DESC CAT 9 PROSE
EFFECT
COLOURS HIS PICTURES WERE SHEWN TO CERTAIN PAINTERS AND 584D DESC CAT 15 PROSE
A CERTAIN PORTRAIT PAINTER SAID TO ME IN A BOASTING WAY 592D PUB ADDRESS/N PROSE
[AGAINST A CERTAIN IMPOSTOR WHO C] IN [OUR ART] THE ART 601C PUB ADDRESS/N *PROSE
OF
BOTH IN WHISPERS & IN PRINT BY CERTAIN PERSONS . . . . 602B PUB ADDRESS/N PROSE
IT BECAME THE INTEREST OF CERTAIN ENVIOUS KNAVES . . . 602C PUB ADDRESS/N PROSE
ACCORDING TO [THEIR AGGREGATE IMAGINATIONS] A CERTAIN ORDER 606A V LAST JUDG/N *PROSE
MANY ARE DEISTS WHO WOULD IN CERTAIN CIRCUMSTANCES . . . 615A V LAST JUDG/N PROSE
OF DEXTERITY IN CERTAIN POINTS EMBOLDENS ME [TH] TO HOPE 808A LETTER 19 *PROSE
THAT
IN HEAVEN IS CERTAIN & DETERMINED & TO THIS I HAVE LONG 812C LETTER 22 PROSE
NAMELY TO LEAVE THIS PLACE BECAUSE I AM NOW CERTAIN . . 819C LETTER 25 PROSE
H(HAYLEY) LIKE S(STOTHARD) ENVIOUS & THAT HE IS I AM NOW 819C LETTER 25 PROSE
CERTAIN
TEN POUNDS & ITS ALMOST CERTAIN PROFITS ARE...G I AM . 820A LETTER 25 PROSE
& THE CERTAIN PROFITS OF THAT WORK ARE . . . . 820B LETTER 25 PROSE
& MY PROSPECTS OF MORE & MORE WORK CONTINUALLY ARE CERTAIN 820C LETTER 25 PROSE
KNOW THAT YOU SEE CERTAIN MERITS IN ME WHICH BY GOD'S GRACE 822B LETTER 26 PROSE
IT IS CERTAIN THAT A TOO PASSIVE MANNER INCONSISTENT . 828C LETTER 28 PROSE
BUT AT CERTAIN PERIODS A BLAZE OF REPUTATION ARISES ROUND 830B LETTER 30 PROSE
ME
GOING ON WOULD BE A CERTAIN LOSS OF ALMOST ALL THE EXPENSES 831C LETTER 31 PROSE
UNDERTAKING IT IS CERTAIN THAT THE PICTURES DESERVE TO BE 848C LETTER 45 PROSE
OF CERTAIN CONNOISSEURS THAT THEY CANNOT SEE APPROPRIATE 864C LETTER 61 PROSE
IS CERTAIN THAT AT PRESENT ANY VENTURE TO GO OUT MUST BE SUPP LETTER 81A *PROSE
CERTAINLY
THIS APHORISM CERTAINLY WAS AN OVERSIGHT . . . . . . 68D ANNO LAVATER MARG
THIS IS CERTAINLY NOT TO BE UNDERSTOOD ACCORDING TO THE 92D ANNO SWED LOVE MARG
LETTER
THE TEARS OF REPENTANCE YOULL CERTAINLY WIPE . . . . . 179 IF YOU TRAP/N 2
HE WAS CERTAINLY A SAVAGE IN THE BISHOP'S SENSE . . . . 389C ANNO WATSON MARG
HE HEARD NOTHING BUT SAYS WE CERTAINLY WERE NOT QUARRELLING 437D BLAKES MEMORAN PROSE
HE CERTAINLY WOULD HAVE BEEN MORE LIKE A FOOL THAN A WISE 450D ANNO REYNOLDS MARG
MAN
I CERTAINLY DO THANK GOD THAT I AM NOT LIKE REYNOLDS . 471A ANNO REYNOLDS MARG
I WILL CERTAINLY CREATE AN ETERNAL HELL FOR THEE LISTEN 627 JERUSALEM 8 8
THOU WILT CERTAINLY PROVOKE MY SPECTRE AGAINST THINE IN 664 JERUSALEM 37 5
FURY
CERTAINLY WAS NOT WHAT CHRIST MEANT . . . . 752 EV GOSPEL(D)/N 50
YOU CERTAINLY MISTAKE WHEN YOU SAY . . . . 793D LETTER 5 PROSE
SUSSEX IS CERTAINLY A HAPPY PLACE & FELPHAM IN PARTICULAR 808C LETTER 19 PROSE
IS
OR RATHER CERTAINLY THE VERY BEST LETTERS THAT EVER WERE 810A LETTER 20 PROSE
PUBLISHED
AFTER ALL & CERTAINLY DOES NOT LEAD ME INTO SCRAPES . . 830D LETTER 30 PROSE
TO ASSIST ANY HOW REMOTE SOEVER WILL CERTAINLY HEAR HER 842A LETTER 41 PROSE
VOICE
IT IS CERTAINLY NECESSARY THAT THE BEST ARTISTS THAT CAN BE 849D LETTER 47 PROSE
FOR I CERTAINLY AM THAT DREAMER BUT THO I DREAM OVER MY 854C LETTER 53 PROSE
MR ROBINSON CERTAINLY DID SUBSCRIBE FOR PRINTS ONLY & . 872A LETTER 74 PROSE
THE NAME OF THE CHILD WHICH CERTAINLY OUGHT TO BE THOMAS 874B LETTER 79 PROSE
CERTAINLY A HAPPY STATE OF AGREEMENT TO WHICH I FOR ONE DO 878B LETTER 88 PROSE
CERTAINTIES
("CERTAINTIES") NONSENSE . . . . 406D ANNO BACON MARG
CERTAINTY
AND URIZEN WHO WAS FAITH & CERTAINTY IS CHANGD TO DOUBT 282 FOUR ZOAS 2 105
THAT THOU DREAD FORM OF CERTAINTY MAIST SIT IN TOWN 360 FOUR ZOAS 9 133
& VILLAGE
THE TRUTH & CERTAINTY OF VIRTUE & HONESTY I E INSPIRATION 386C ANNO WATSON MARG
LINE OF RECTITUDE AND CERTAINTY IN THE ACTIONS AND 585C DESC CAT 15 PROSE
INTENTIONS
A FOUNDATION AND CERTAINTY AND DEMONSTRATIVE TRUTH . . 652 JERUSALEM 28 11
& THEN WE SHALL JUDGE OF THE MATTER WITH CERTAINTY . . 813D LETTER 22 PROSE
CERTAINTY OF THE FACT WHICH HAS PASSED UPON ME . . . . 852A LETTER 50 PROSE

315

```
                                                         PAGE      TITLE          LINE
CERTIFIED
    ON ALL HANDS ACKNOWLEDGD IT ONLY REMAINS TO BE CERTIFIED   591C PUB ADDRESS/N   PROSE
CHACE
    ROUZD LIKE A HUNTSMAN TO THE CHACE AND WITH     . . . . .     3 TO MORNING/PS      7
    BUT ROGER STILL PURSUES THE CHACE . . . . . . . . .        16 BLIND-MANS/PS      39
    THE YOUTHFUL SUN JOYS LIKE A HUNTER ROUZED TO THE CHACE    37B CONTEMPLATN/PS   PROSE
CHAFER     SEE COCK CHAFER
CHAFER'S
    HE WHO TORMENTS THE CHAFER'S SPRITE  . . . . . . .        431 AUGURIES           35
CHAFF
    TOSSED THE NATIONS LIKE CHAFF INTO THE SEAS OF THARMAS  . 374 FOUR ZOAS 9       656
    LIFE IN BROODING CARES & ANXIOUS LABOURS THAT PROVE BUT   647 JERUSALEM 24       16
        CHAFF
    OR AS THE SWEAT UPON THE LABOURING SHOULDER OR AS THE     687 JERUSALEM 55       40
        CHAFF
CHAIN
    . . . ROUND HIS MIDDLE A CHAIN AND A BAND    . . . . .    136 FRENCH REVOLTN     44
    BREAK THIS HEAVY CHAIN   . . . . . . . . . . .           169 EARTHS ANSWR/N     21
    TO BEHOLD MY HEAVY CHAIN   . . . . . . . . . . .         169 MIRTLE SHADE/N     12
    [WHAT] WHERE THE HAMMER [WHAT] WHERE THE CHAIN   . . . .  172 THE TYGER/N 1      18
    [IN A CRUEL IRON CHAIN]   . . . . . . . . . . .          177 LIT BOY LST/N      23
    & BOUND HIM IN AN IRON CHAIN   . . . . . . . . .         177 LIT BOY LST/N      25
    IN SPELLS OF LAW TO ONE SHE LOATHES AND MUST SHE DRAG THE 193 V DAU ALBION 5     22
        CHAIN
    A BENDED BOW IS LIFTED IN HEAVEN & A HEAVY IRON CHAIN  .  197 AMERICA 3           7
    A BENDED BOW IN HEAVEN IS LIFTED & A HEAVY IRON CHAIN  .  204 AMERICA CANC A      7
    BREAK THIS HEAVY CHAIN   . . . . . . . . . . .           211 EARTHS ANSR/SE     21
    WHAT THE HAMMER WHAT THE CHAIN  . . . . . . . . .        214 THE TYGER/SE       13
    AND BOUND HIM IN AN IRON CHAIN  . . . . . . . . .        218 LIT BOY LST/SE     20
    LIKE THE LINKED INFERNAL CHAIN  . . . . . . . . .        228 URIZEN 10          36
    INTO AN IRON CHAIN  . . . . . . . . . . . . .            233 URIZEN 20          19
    WITH THE CHAIN OF JEALOUSY  . . . . . . . . . .          233 URIZEN 20          24
    ORC ON MOUNT ATLAS HOWLD CHAIND DOWN WITH THE CHAIN OF    246 SONG OF LOS 3      21
        JEALOUSY
    THE ETERNAL PROPHET BOUND IN A CHAIN  . . . . . .        256 BOOK OF LOS 3      31
    LIKE A SERPENT LIKE AN IRON CHAIN  . . . . . . . .       259 BOOK OF LOS 5      16
    THUS WERE THE STARS OF HEAVEN CREATED LIKE A GOLDEN CHAIN 287 FOUR ZOAS 2       266
    THE LINKS OF FATE LINK AFTER LINK AN ENDLESS CHAIN OF    302 FOUR ZOAS 4       207
        SORROWS
    IN A HORRIBLE DREAMFUL SLUMBER LIKE THE LINKED CHAIN   .  303 FOUR ZOAS 4       218
    GRIM FROST BENEATH & TERRIBLE SNOW LINKD IN A MARRIAGE    306 FOUR ZOAS 5        33
        CHAIN
    FALLING DOWN ON THE ROCK AN IRON CHAIN LINK BY LINK LOCKD 307 FOUR ZOAS 5        91
    ENITHARMON BEHELD THE BLOODY CHAIN OF NIGHTS & DAYS . . . 307 FOUR ZOAS 5        92
    CALLD IT THE CHAIN OF JEALOUSY NOW LOS BEGAN TO SPEAK  .  307 FOUR ZOAS 5        95
    UP TO THE IRON MOUNTAIN'S TOP & THERE THE JEALOUS CHAIN   307 FOUR ZOAS 5        99
    THE [DISMAL] ACCURSED CHAIN O HOW BRIGHT ENITHARMON HOWLD 308 FOUR ZOAS 5       102
        & CRIED
    THO TERRIBLE HIS DREAD OF THAT INFERNAL CHAIN THEY ROSE   309 FOUR ZOAS 5       147
    FIBRES HAD FROM THE CHAIN OF JEALOUSY INWOVE THEMSELVES   309 FOUR ZOAS 5       157
    TO MELT THE CHAIN OF JEALOUSY NOT ENITHARMON'S DEATH  .   309 FOUR ZOAS 5       161
    NOR THE CONSUMMATION OF LOS COULD EVER MELT THE CHAIN  .  309 FOUR ZOAS 5       162
    COULD UPROOT THE INFERNAL CHAIN FOR [ITS] IT HAD TAKEN ROOT 309 FOUR ZOAS 5   *  166
    INTO THE IRON ROCK & GREW A CHAIN BENEATH THE EARTH  . .  309 FOUR ZOAS 5       167
    OF ORC ENTERING WITH FIBRES BECAME ONE WITH HIM A LIVING  309 FOUR ZOAS 5   *  169
        CHAIN
    OF THE CHAIN OF JEALOUSY & FELT THE RENDINGS OF FIERCE    309 FOUR ZOAS 5       182
        HOWLING ORC
    OF ALL & ALL FUTURITY BE BOUND IN HIS VAST CHAIN   . . .  317 FOUR ZOAS 6       233
    TENFOLD WITH FIERCE DESIRE TO REND THY CHAIN & HOWL IN FURY 321 FOUR ZOAS 7      66
    THE MAN SHALL RAGE BOUND WITH THIS CHAIN THE WORM        323 FOUR ZOAS 7       143
        IN SILENCE CREEP
    ART THOU THE COLD ATTRACTIVE POWER THAT HOLDS ME IN THIS  323 FOUR ZOAS 7       146
        CHAIN
    THEY SOUND THE CLARIONS STRONG THEY CHAIN THE HOWLING     337 FOUR ZOAS 7B      164
        CAPTIVES
    WILL I ARISE TILL HIM I LOVE IS LOOSD FROM THIS DARK CHAIN 339 FOUR ZOAS 7B     255
    WHAT CHAIN ENCOMPASSES IN WHAT LOCK IS THE RIVER OF LIGHT 363 FOUR ZOAS 9       226
        CONFIND
    [BUT] I MOCKD AT THE WRACK & GRIDING CHAIN  . . . . . .   419 I SAW A MONK/N     34
    I MOCKD AT THE WRACK & GRIDING CHAIN . . . . . . . .      430 GREY MONK          19
    BOUND WITH THE CHAIN OF JEALOUSY BY LOS & ENITHARMON  .   501 MILTON 19          38
    ORC FROM HIS CHAIN OF JEALOUSY HE STARTED AT THE THOUGHT  503 MILTON 20          61
    SHOULD UP ASCEND FORWARD FROM FELPHAM'S VALE & BREAK THE  507 MILTON 23          37
        CHAIN
    THEY SOUND THE CLARIONS STRONG THEY CHAIN THE HOWLING     699 JERUSALEM 65        6
        CAPTIVES
    THE HEAVENS MIGHT REVOLVE & ETERNITY BE BOUND IN THEIR    702 JERUSALEM 66        5
        CHAIN
    HER STRUGGLING TORMENT IN HER IRON ARMS AND LIKE A CHAIN  726 JERUSALEM 82       70
    HE BOUND OLD SATAN IN HIS CHAIN  . . . . . . . . .       749 EV GOSPEL(B)/N     32
    BROKE DOWN FROM EVERY CHAIN & BAR . . . . . . . .        749 EV GOSPEL(B)/N     41
    WHOLE MIGHT CHAIN MY FEET TO THE WORLD OF DUTY & REALITY  809A LETTER 20        PROSE
CHAIND
    CHAIND IN THICK DARKNESS UTTERD CRIES OF MOURNING ALL THE 107 TIRIEL 5          28
        NIGHT
    TWAS THOU THAT CHAIND THY BROTHER ZAZEL WHERE ARE NOW THINE 108 TIRIEL 7         9
        EYES
    CHAIND HAND AND FOOT ROUND HIS NECK AN IRON BAND . . . .  135 FRENCH REVOLTN     27
    & ALL OF THAT SPECIES CHAIND BY THE MIDDLE GRINNING  . . . 157A MARRIAGE HH 17  PROSE
    [CLOSD] CHAIND IN NIGHT  . . . . . . . . . . . .         169 EARTHS ANSWR/N     14
    FOR CHAIND BENEATH I REND THESE CAVERNS WHEN THOU BRINGEST 196 AMERICA PREL 1    18
        FOOD
```

316

		PAGE	TITLE	LINE

CHAIND   (CONTINUED)

CHAIND IN NIGHT . . . . 211 EARTHS ANSR/SE 14
THEY CHAIND HIS YOUNG LIMBS TO THE ROCK . . . . . . 233 URIZEN 20 23
ORC ON MOUNT ATLAS HOWLD CHAIND DOWN WITH THE CHAIN OF 246 SONG OF LOS 3 21
  JEALOUSY
THE CHAIND ORB IN THEIR INFINITE WOMBS . . . . . . 260 BOOK OF LOS 5 40
BELCHD FROM THE FURNACES WREATHD ROUND HER CHAIND 302 FOUR ZOAS 4 188
  IN CEASELESS FIRE
WITHIN HIS BREAST HIS FIERY SONS CHAIND DOWN & FILLD WITH 306 FOUR ZOAS 5 57
  CURSINGS
AND LOS REPENTED THAT HE HAD CHAIND ORC UPON THE MOUNTAIN- 309 FOUR ZOAS 5 145
THOU ART NOT CHAIND . . . . 322 FOUR ZOAS 7 73
AVAUNT COLD HYPOCRITE I AM CHAIND OR THOU COULDST NOT USE 323 FOUR ZOAS 7 142
  ME THUS
PRIESTS & CHAIND CAPTIVES MET TOGETHER IN A HORRIBLE FEAR 363 FOUR ZOAS 9 244
IS THE HARLOT ALSO SIEZED & BOUND [CHAIND] BY TWO ANGELS 443A LAST JUDGMNT/L PROSE
MANY FIGURES [CHAIND] CHAINED & BOUND TOGETHER & . . . . 443C LAST JUDGMNT/L *PROSE
DEATH IS CHAIND TO THE CROSS & TIME FALLS TOGETHER WITH 606C V LAST JUDG/N PROSE
  DEATH
A MALE & FEMALE CHAIND [TO] TOGETHER BY THE FEET . . . 607D V LAST JUDG/N *PROSE
THERE TO ETERNITY CHAIND DOWN AND ISSUING IN RED FLAMES 667 JERUSALEM 40 36
WITHIN HIS BREAST HIS MIGHTY SONS CHAIND DOWN & FILLD WITH 667 JERUSALEM 40 40
  CURSINGS
CHAIND HAND & FOOT COMPELLD TO FIGHT UNDER THE IRON WHIPS 700 JERUSALEM 65 35
CHAIND ROUND BIBLE CHAIND ROUND   . . . . SUPP ILLUS DANTE 99 *PROSE

CHAINED

& TEN HORNS CHAINED BY TWO ANGELS . . . . 443A LAST JUDGMNT/L PROSE
MANY FIGURES [CHAIND] CHAINED & BOUND TOGETHER & . . . 443C LAST JUDGMNT/L *PROSE
OF WAR & RELIGION LET US DESCEND & BRING HIM CHAINED . 507 MILTON 23 17

CHAINING

CHAINING OF ORC TYPE BY W BLAKE... . . . . SUPP INSCR CHAINING *TITLE

CHAINS

THE ENEMY FIGHT IN CHAINS INVISIBLE CHAINS BUT HEAVY . . 18 EDW THIRD/PS 1 13
BALD TYRANT WRINKLED CUNNING [WRETCH] LISTEN TO ZAZEL'S 108 TIRIEL 7 8
  CHAINS
. . . A SKELETON YELLOW REMAINED IN ITS CHAINS ON ITS COUCH 135 FRENCH REVOLTN 33
MAD WITH CHAINS LOOSE WHICH HE DRAGGD UP AND DOWN . . . 136 FRENCH REVOLTN 48
. . . SEAL THEM UP O ANOINTED IN EVERLASTING CHAINS . . . 141 FRENCH REVOLTN 157
. . . THE CAPTAINS LIKE MEN BOUND IN CHAINS . . . . . 141 FRENCH REVOLTN 165
SEEM TO LIVE IN IT IN CHAINS ARE IN TRUTH THE CAUSES OF 155A MARRIAGE HH 15 PROSE
  ITS LIFE
& THE SOURCES OF ALL ACTIVITY BUT THE CHAINS ARE 155A MARRIAGE HH 15 PROSE
  THE CUNNING OF
TO THE DEVOURER IT SEEMS AS IF THE PRODUCER WAS IN HIS 155B MARRIAGE HH 15 PROSE
  CHAINS
BUT WITHELD BY THE SHORTNESS OF THEIR CHAINS . . . . . 157A MARRIAGE HH 17 *PROSE
AND BREAKS ALL CHAINS FROM EVERY MIND . . . . 175 HOW TO KNOW/N 4
[AND CHAINS & FETTERS EVERY MIND] . . . . 175 HOW TO KNOW/N * 9
AND IS THERE NOT ETERNAL FIRE AND ETERNAL CHAINS . . . 192 V DAU ALBION 4 23
RIVETS MY TENFOLD CHAINS WHILE STILL ON HIGH MY SPIRIT 196 AMERICA PREL 1 12
  SOARS
RISE AND LOOK OUT HIS CHAINS ARE LOOSE HIS DUNGEON DOORS 198 AMERICA 6 10
  ARE OPEN
SHAKING THEIR MENTAL CHAINS THEY RUSH IN FURY TO THE SEA 201 AMERICA 13 3
INCESSANT BEAT FORGING CHAINS NEW & NEW . . . . 227 URIZEN 10 17
IN CHAINS OF THE MIND LOCKED UP   . . . . 228 URIZEN 10 25
THE IMMORTAL ENDURD HIS CHAINS . . . . 229 URIZEN 13 26
IN HIS CHAINS BOUND & PITY BEGAN . . . . 230 URIZEN 13 51
AND URIZEN UNLOOSD FROM CHAINS . . . . 239 EUROPE 4 11
RENEW IN THESE CHAINS OF DARKNESS . . . . 255 AHANIA 5 43
ROUND THE FLAMES ROLL AS LOS HURLS HIS CHAINS . . . . 256 BOOK OF LOS 3 34
RATTLING THE ADAMANTINE CHAINS & HOOKS HEAVE UP THE ORE 282 FOUR ZOAS 2 66
AND THE CAPTIVE IN CHAINS & THE POOR IN THE PRISON . . . 291 FOUR ZOAS 2 415
THE DAYS & YEARS IN CHAINS OF IRON ROUND THE LIMBS 302 FOUR ZOAS 4 180
  OF URIZEN
THE ANVILS OF URTHONA LINK BY LINK THE CHAINS OF SORROW 302 FOUR ZOAS 4 185
FORGETFULNESS DUMBNESS NECESSITY IN CHAINS OF THE MIND 303 FOUR ZOAS 4 211
  LOCKD UP
PRINCE OF LIGHT BOUND IN CHAINS OF INTELLECT AMONG THE 305 FOUR ZOAS 5 16
  FURNACES
HIS LIMBS BOUND DOWN MOCK AT HIS CHAINS FOR OVER THEM A 308 FOUR ZOAS 5 114
  FLAME
CHAINS OF DARK IGNORANCE & CORDS OF TWISTED SELF CONCEIT 312 FOUR ZOAS 6 41
THO BOUND WITH CHAINS OF JEALOUSY & IN SCALES OF IRON & 332 FOUR ZOAS 7 481
  BRASS
RATTLING WITH CLANKING CHAINS THE UNIVERSAL EMPIRE GROANS 333 FOUR ZOAS 7B 17
COMPELLD THE SUN REDDNING LIKE A FIERCE LION IN HIS CHAINS 333 FOUR ZOAS 7B 31
AND CHAINS & PULLIES FABRICATED ALL ROUND THE HEAVENS OF 343 FOUR ZOAS 8 95
  LOS
TO ALL HIS ENGINES OF DECEIT THAT LINKED CHAINS MIGHT RUN 344 FOUR ZOAS 8 132
WHILE I STOOD BOUND WITH CORDS & HEAVY CHAINS YOUR 364 FOUR ZOAS 9 276
  HIPOCRISY
RISE & LOOK OUT HIS CHAINS ARE LOOSE HIS DUNGEON DOORS 375 FOUR ZOAS 9 674
  ARE OPEN
WHERE ARE YOUR CHAINS WHERE ARE YOUR TEARS WHY DO YOU LOOK 375 FOUR ZOAS 9 679
  AROUND
IN CHAINS OF IRON & IN DUNGEONS CIRCLED WITH CEASELESS 377 FOUR ZOAS 9 750
  FIRES
WITH CHAINS WHILE HER PALACES ARE FALLING INTO [IN] RUINS 443A LAST JUDGMNT/L PROSE
URIZEN LAY IN DARKNESS & SOLITUDE IN CHAINS OF THE MIND 482 MILTON 3 6
  LOCKD UP
WITH MOLTEN ORE HE HEAVES THE IRON CLIFFS IN HIS RATTLING 486 MILTON 6 30
  CHAINS

317

		PAGE	TITLE	LINE
CHAINS (CONTINUED)				
IN CHAINS OF IRON & IN DUNGEONS CIRCLED WITH CEASELESS FIRES		514	MILTON 27	32
AND SACRIFICE & NEXT IN CHAINS OF IMPRISONMENT ARE SHAPELESS ROCKS		521	MILTON 32	17
HERE IS JERUSALEM BOUND IN CHAINS IN THE DENS OF BABYLON		529	MILTON 38	27
LYING ON THE ROCK OPEN BEFORE HIM HE IS BOUND IN CHAINS		609B	V LAST JUDG/N	PROSE
TO LABOURS MIGHTY WITH VAST STRENGTH WITH HIS MIGHTY CHAINS		630	JERUSALEM 11	1
HIS FRIENDS CUT HIS STRONG CHAINS & OVERWHELMD HIS DARK		675	JERUSALEM 45	21
OF SPIRITUAL HATE FROM WHICH SPRINGS SEXUAL LOVE AS IRON CHAINS		685	JERUSALEM 54	12
. . WITH CHAINS		701	JERUSALEM 66	2
OF BRASS IRON CHAINS & BRACES & THE GOLD SILVER & BRASS		713	JERUSALEM 73	10
HERSELF IN CHAINS THIS FROM WITHIN WAS SEEN IN A DISMAL NIGHT		719	JERUSALEM 78	24
CHAIR				
AS GUARDIANS ROUND YOUR CHAIR THEN SHALL THE PULSE . . .		28	EDW THIRD/PS 3	289
INFLAMMABLE GASS TURNING ROUND HASTILY IN HIS CHAIR SAID		45C	ISLAND MOON 1	PROSE
[I'LL DASH YOU THROUGH YOUR CHAIR SAYS THE CYNIC] . . .		57A	ISLAND MOON 9	PROSE
MORE WONDROUS STILL THE TABLE STOOL & CHAIR		545	IMIT POPE/N	3
ID BE AN ASS A HOG A WORM A CHAIR A STOOL		550	WHEN I SEE/N	8
AIR WATER & EARTH SURROUND MILTON'S CHAIR		619B	ILLUS MILTON	PROSE
JESUS WAS SITTING IN MOSES' CHAIR		753	EV GOSPEL(E)/N	7
CHAIRS				
TO SIT IN STATE & GIVE FORTH LAWS OUT OF THEIR OLD OAK CHAIRS		58	THIS CITY/IM	2
ON CHAIRS OF IRON CANOPIED WITH MYSTIC ORNAMENTS		204	AMERICA CANC B	13
RUBENS THINKS TABLES CHAIRS & STOOLS ARE GRAND		547	PRETTY EPIGR/N	3
CHAISE				
FROM ONE CHAISE TO ANOTHER FOR WE HAD SEVEN DIFFERENT . .		802B	LETTER 14	PROSE
FROM ONE CHAISE TO ANOTHER WE HAD SEVEN DIFFERENT . . .		803A	LETTER 15	PROSE
CHAISES				
CHAISES & AS MANY DIFFERENT DRIVERS WE (SET) OUT BETWEEN		802B	LETTER 14	*PROSE
CHAISES & AS MANY DIFFERENT DRIVERS ALL UPON THE ROAD WAS		803A	LETTER 15	PROSE
CHALCOGRAPHIC				
TO THE CHALCOGRAPHIC SOCIETY & TO EXPRESS TO THEM MY OPINION		591D	PUB ADDRESS/N	PROSE
THE MODERN CHALCOGRAPHIC CONNOISSEURS & AMATEURS		596C	PUB ADDRESS/N	PROSE
CHALDEA				
ABRAM FLED IN FIRES FROM CHALDEA		245	SONG OF LOS 3	16
AS ABRAHAM FLEES FROM CHALDEA SHAKING HIS GOARY LOCKS .		636	JERUSALEM 15	28
IN SOLEMN POMP INTO CHALDEA ACROSS THE BREDTHS OF EUROPE		644	JERUSALEM 21	43
FLED OVER CHALDEA IN TERROR IN PAINS IN EVERY NERVE . . .		663	JERUSALEM 36	18
AND SWEET HESPERIA EVEN TO GREAT CHALDEA & TESSHINA . .		692	JERUSALEM 60	20
CHALDEAN				
WAS CAST OUT TO THE LOATHING OF HER PERSON THE CHALDEAN TOOK		695	JERUSALEM 61	40
CHALK				
LIKE LEATHER AND CHALK THEIR MEN ARE LIKE LEATHER AND		581A	DESC CAT 5	PROSE
THEIR WOMEN LIKE CHALK FOR THE DISPOSITION OF THEIR FORMS		581A	DESC CAT 5	PROSE
IRON OF HIS FORGE & FIXES THEM INTO BONES OF CHALK & ROCK		736	JERUSALEM 90	20
CHALK ENGRAVING IS AT LEAST SIX TIMES AS LABORIOUS AS AQUA TINTA		794C	LETTER 5	PROSE
[XXX CHALK WHITE ROCKS]		SUPP	FOUR ZOAS 1	*
CHALLENGE				
I IN MY OWN DEFENCE CHALLENGE A COMPETITION		602A	PUB ADDRESS/N	PROSE
CHAMBER				
. . . TO HIS CHAMBER OF COUNCIL SHADY MOUNTAINS		134	FRENCH REVOLTN	10
AND THE CHAMBER BECAME A CLOUDED SKY		138	FRENCH REVOLTN	85
THE VOICE CEASD A GROAN SHOOK MY CHAMBER . . .		141	FRENCH REVOLTN	151
. . . PALE ENTERD THE CHAMBER		141	FRENCH REVOLTN	160
ROSE INFLAMD TO AND FRO IN THE CHAMBER		141	FRENCH REVOLTN	170
SHOOK THE CHAMBER HE CEASD ABASHD THEN ORLEANS SPOKE ALL WAS SILENT		142	FRENCH REVOLTN	178
THE PALE FIRES OF AUMONT INTO THE CHAMBER		143	FRENCH REVOLTN	203
IN THE FIRST CHAMBER WAS A DRAGON-MAN CLEARING AWAY THE		154D	MARRIAGE HH 15	PROSE
IN THE SECOND CHAMBER WAS A VIPER		154D	MARRIAGE HH 15	PROSE
IN THE THIRD CHAMBER WAS AN EAGLE WITH WINGS AND FEATHERS		154D	MARRIAGE HH 15	PROSE
IN THE FOURTH CHAMBER WERE LIONS OF FLAMING FIRE		155A	MARRIAGE HH 15	PROSE
IN THE FIFTH CHAMBER WERE UNNAMD FORMS		155A	MARRIAGE HH 15	PROSE
THEY WERE RECIEVD BY MEN WHO OCCUPIED THE SIXTH CHAMBER		155A	MARRIAGE HH 15	PROSE
IN THE SECRET SHADOWS OF HER CHAMBER THE YOUTH SHUT UP FROM		194	V DAU ALBION 7	5
FOR COMFORT THERE THE SECRET FURNITURE OF JERUSALEM'S CHAMBER		632	JERUSALEM 12	40
THERE WE WALKED AS IN OUR SECRET CHAMBER AMONG OUR LITTLE ONES		720	JERUSALEM 79	42
THE FURNITURE OF THEIR HOUSES WAS THE FURNITURE OF MY CHAMBER		720	JERUSALEM 79	47
FORSAKEN SURREY AND SUSSEX ARE ENITHARMON'S CHAMBER . . .		727	JERUSALEM 83	25
PLEASE TO TELL MRS BUTTS THAT WE HAVE DEDICATED A CHAMBER		803B	LETTER 15	PROSE
(THREE) DAYS & TO MY CHAMBER A WEEK I AM NOW SO WELL THANK		834B	LETTER 34	PROSE
CHAMBERS				
RISE FROM THE CHAMBERS OF THE EAST AND BRING		3	TO MORNING/PS	4
OR IN THE CHAMBERS OF THE EAST		10	TO MUSES/PS	2
THE CHAMBERS OF THE SUN THAT NOW		10	TO MUSES/PS	3
. . . [&] OR IN THEIR CHAMBERS]		205	AMERICA CANC C	22
INTO MY CHAMBERS OF LOVE		254	AHANIA 5	18
AND BOSOMS OF MILK IN MY CHAMBERS		255	AHANIA 5	20
OF SECRET LUST WHEN HID IN CHAMBERS DARK THE NIGHTLY HARLOT		333	FOUR ZOAS 7B	25
THE SUBTLEST THOUGHTS SHUT UP FROM LIGHT IN CHAMBERS OF THE MOON		339	FOUR ZOAS 7B	243

		PAGE	TITLE	LINE

CHAMBERS   (CONTINUED)
THARMAS THE MOON HAS CHAMBERS WHERE THE BABES OF LOVE LIE   339 FOUR ZOAS 7B   244
    HID
AND THE HERBS & FLOWERS & FURNITURE & BEDS & CHAMBERS . .   512 MILTON 26   34
AND CHAMBERS OF TREMBLING & SUSPITION HATREDS OF AGE &   640 JERUSALEM 18   24
    YOUTH
WHY HAVE THOU ELEVATE INWARD O DWELLER OF OUTWARD CHAMBERS   660 JERUSALEM 34   10
POLAND & RUSSIA & SWEDEN HIS SOFT RETIRED CHAMBERS . . .   690 JERUSALEM 58   40
SAYING LO JERUSALEM IS HERE SHE SITTETH IN OUR SECRET   720 JERUSALEM 79   29
    CHAMBERS
CONCIEVE IN MY BRAIN ARE STUDIES & CHAMBERS FILLD WITH . .   802B LETTER 14   PROSE
CHAMBRE
WITH SR ALLAN CHAMBRE RECOMMENDS ME TO ENQUIRE CONCERNING   834D LETTER 34   PROSE
CHAMPION
URIZEN IS THE CHAMPION OF ALBION THEY WILL SLAY MY LUVAH   658 JERUSALEM 31   57
& DARKNESS NOT UNLIKE A CHAMPION I HAVE CONQUERD . . . .   816A LETTER 23   PROSE
CHANCE
AT HOB-NAIL DICK WHO GRIEVD THE CHANCE . . . .   16 BLIND-MANS/PS   16
NOW KITTY NOW WHAT CHANCE HAST THOU . . . .   16 BLIND-MANS/PS   29
WITH HOOD-WINKD CHANCE SURE OF HIS MAN . . . .   17 BLIND-MANS/PS   50
THEN IF CHANCE ALONG THIS FOREST . . . .   61 LEAVE O/IM   5
OPENING BY CHANCE A BOOK WHICH SHE HAD IN HER HAND . . .   440D MEMORANDUM/N 5   PROSE
IF YOU PLAY A GAME OF CHANCE KNOW BEFORE YOU BEGIN . . .   551 IF YOU PLAY/N   1
BY CHANCE OR PERHAPS HIS FORTUNE MONEY MONEY . . . . .   574A DESC CAT 3   PROSE
AND ACCIDENT & CHANCE WERE FOUND HIDDEN IN LENGTH BREDTH   663 JERUSALEM 36   35
    & HIGHTH
ARE IN SOME MEASURE WORKS OF ART & NOT OF NATURE OR CHANCE   782A INSC UPCOTT   PROSE
STOLEN & PERVERTED FROM THE BIBLE NOT BY CHANCE . . . .   785B ILLUS DANTE 7   PROSE
A KIND OF CRIMINAL DISSIPATION & NEGLECT OF THE MAIN CHANCE   798C LETTER 10   PROSE
TO PLEASE LADY H(HESKETH) WAS A DOUBTFUL CHANCE . . . .   820C LETTER 25   PROSE
PUBLICATION NO CHANCE IS LEFT TO ONE OUT OF THE TRADE .   831D LETTER 31   PROSE
FOR A LINE OR LINEAMENT IS NOT FORMED BY CHANCE . . . .   878B LETTER 88   PROSE
CHANCELLOR
PRINCE OF DARKNESS IS A GENTLEMAN & NOT A MAN HE IS A LORD   399C ANNO BACON   MARG
    CHANCELLOR
OR ANY USEFUL THING HIS BUSINESS & BOSOM WAS TO BE LORD   404D ANNO BACON   MARG
    CHANCELLOR
CHANCELLOR'S
A LORD CHANCELLOR'S OPINIONS AS DIFFERENT FROM CHRIST . .   407A ANNO BACON   MARG
CHANCERY
A MASTER IN CHANCERY THO I HAVE CALLD ON MR EDWARDS TWICE   834D LETTER 34   PROSE
CHANDOS
DUKE OF CLARENCE SIR JOHN CHANDOS SIR THOMAS DAGWORTH   17C EDW THIRD/PS   TITLE
ENTER SIR JOHN CHANDOS . . . .   22C EDW THIRD/PS 3   PROSE
WHY NOBLE CHANDOS LOOK YOU HERE . . . .   22 EDW THIRD/PS 3   49
WHY CHANDOS YOU ARE A WISE MAN . . . .   22 EDW THIRD/PS 3   55
HE IS A GENUINE ENGLISHMAN MY CHANDOS . . . .   25 EDW THIRD/PS 3   189
O NOBLE CHANDOS THINK THYSELF A GARDENER . . . . . .   26 EDW THIRD/PS 3   210
AND MAY OUR DUTY CHANDOS BE OUR PLEASURE . . . . . .   26 EDW THIRD/PS 3   219
CHANDOS THOU SEEST MY WEAKNESS STRONG NATURE . . . . .   26 EDW THIRD/PS 3   233
AMBITION COME TAKE THE HELM MY CHANDOS . . . .   27 EDW THIRD/PS 3   238
I AM A COWARD IN MY REASON CHANDOS . . . .   27 EDW THIRD/PS 3   243
YOU CAN FIND FRIENDLY EXCUSES FOR ME CHANDOS . . . . .   27 EDW THIRD/PS 3   277
AS SIR JOHN CHANDOS THAT THE PRINCE IS ALWAYS WITH . . .   29C EDW THIRD/PS 4   PROSE
FITTED TO THE FINGER OF AN EMPEROR SUCH IS THAT WORTHY   29D EDW THIRD/PS 4   PROSE
    CHANDOS
CHANGABLE
LIKE A DARK WASTE STRETCHING CHANGABLE . . . .   227 URIZEN 10   3
CHANGD
BUT MERCY CHANGD DEATH INTO SLEEP . . . .   220 TO TIRZAH/SE   7
THOUGHT CHANGD THE INFINITE TO A SERPENT THAT WHICH PITIETH   241 EUROPE 10   16
AND HIS DOWNWARD-BORNE FALL CHANGD OBLIQUE . . . . . .   258 BOOK OF LOS 4   42
. . . [?ALONE ?POSSESSD BY DEADLY FEARS] LOVE IS CHANGD   267 FOUR ZOAS 1 * 111
    TO DEADLY HATE
AND URIZEN WHO WAS FAITH & CERTAINTY IS CHANGD TO DOUBT   282 FOUR ZOAS 2   105
HIS VISAGE CHANGD TO DARKNESS & . . . .   294 FOUR ZOAS 3   110
AND ALL THE ARTS OF LIFE THEY CHANGD INTO THE ARTS OF   337 FOUR ZOAS 7B   174
    DEATH
HOW IS IT THAT ALL THINGS ARE CHANGD EVEN AS IN ANCIENT   379 FOUR ZOAS 9   845
    TIMES
UPON THE CLAY NOW CHANGD TO MARBLE ALSO URIZEN ROSE . .   500 MILTON 19   4
IS TERROR CHANGD TO PITY O WONDER OF ETERNITY . . . . .   523 MILTON 34   7
TILL BROTHERHOOD IS CHANGD INTO A CURSE & A FLATTERY . .   525 MILTON 35   4
AND ALL THE ARTS OF LIFE THEY CHANGD INTO THE ARTS OF DEATH   700 JERUSALEM 65   16
    IN ALBION
HUMANITY THE GREAT DELUSION IS CHANGD TO WAR & SACRIFICE   726 JERUSALEM 82   42
CHANGE
("CHANGE IN CONSEQUENCE OF BEING OBSERVED BY OTHERS ")   71A ANNO LAVATER   MARG
    RATHER UNEASY
THE DARK CHANGES & BOUND EVERY CHANGE . . . .   227 URIZEN 8   10
TO CHANGE TO A GRATING CRY . . . .   232 URIZEN 19   32
FELT THEIR NERVES CHANGE INTO MARROW . . . .   235 URIZEN 25   24
SAYING O LORD WHENCE IS THIS CHANGE THOU KNOWEST   293 FOUR ZOAS 3   55
    I AM NOTHING
SCHOOLMASTER OF SOULS GREAT OPPOSER OF CHANGE ARISE . . .   360 FOUR ZOAS 9   131
OPINION IS (ONE) THING (PRINCIPLE) ANOTHER NO MAN   386B ANNO WATSON * MARG
    CAN CHANGE
WHO DISGUISES HIS PRINCIPLES & CALLS THAT CHANGE . . . .   386B ANNO WATSON   MARG
I DO NOT THINK THAT THE CHANGE IS SO MUCH IN THE PICTURES   450B ANNO REYNOLDS   MARG
TO TOUCH EACH OTHER & RECEDE TO CROSS & CHANGE & RETURN   512 MILTON 26   6
STATES CHANGE BUT INDIVIDUAL IDENTITIES NEVER CHANGE NOR   521 MILTON 32   23
    CEASE

```
                                                         PAGE     TITLE        LINE
CHANGE    (CONTINUED)
    SUBSTANCE CAN NEVER SUFFER CHANGE NOR DECAY   . . . . .  567C DESC CAT 3    PROSE
    SUBSTANCE CAN NEVER SUFFER CHANGE NOR DECAY   . . . . .  589A CHAUCER/N     PROSE
    SAYING O LORD WHENCE IS THIS CHANGE THOU KNOWEST         654 JERUSALEM 29      42
      I AM NOTHING
    THEY CHANGE THEIR SITUATIONS IN THE UNIVERSAL MAN   . . .  663 JERUSALEM 36     26
    NOR CANST THOU EVER CHANGE KATE INTO NAN                 771 EPILOGUE/GP       4
    SOON WE SHALL HAVE A CHANGE FOR THE BETTER I CANNOT      795A LETTER 6      PROSE
      PROPHECY
    AND IN HELL BENEATH & A MIGHTY & AWFUL CHANGE THREATENED  799 TO FLAXMAN/L     8
      THE EARTH
    I INTEND TO BRING WITH ME BESIDES OUR NECESSARY CHANGE OF  873A LETTER 76  PROSE
CHANGEABLE    SEE CHANGABLE
    FOR IN CHANGEABLE CLOUDS AND DARKNESS  . . . . . . .  230 URIZEN 15          3
    HE WHO THINKS THAT HONESTY IS CHANGEABLE KNOWS NOTHING   386B ANNO WATSON   MARG
      ABOUT IT
    WHAT IS ETERNAL & WHAT CHANGEABLE & WHAT ANNIHILABLE   . . 522 MILTON 32       31
CHANGED
    . . . LOOKING ON THE ARCHBISHOP WHO CHANGED AS PALE AS    142 FRENCH REVOLTN  176
      LEAD
    SUPPOSES THAT HIS PRINCIPLES ARE TO BE CHANGED IS       386B ANNO WATSON   MARG
      A DISSEMBLER
    LOT'S WIFE BEING CHANGED INTO (A) PILLAR OF SALT ALLUDES  607A V LAST JUDG/N PROSE
    BUT NOT CHANGED OR TRANSFORMED INTO ANOTHER IDENTITY    . 607A V LAST JUDG/N PROSE
    THE CHANGED STATE MADE BY THE FLOOD  . . . . . . .  611C V LAST JUDG/N PROSE
    & MUST CONTINUALLY BE CHANGED INTO HIS DIRECT CONTRARY . . 682A JERUSALEM 52 PROSE
CHANGELESS
    "WHOSE CHANGELESS BROW NEER SMILES NOR FROWNS" DONNE   . . SUPP LEGEND/N85     *
CHANGES
    UNSEEN UNKNOWN CHANGES APPEARD . . . . . . . . .  222 URIZEN 3           10
    RIFTED WITH DIREFUL CHANGES  . . . . . . . . . .  226 URIZEN 7            6
    THE DARK CHANGES & BOUND EVERY CHANGE    . . . . . .  227 URIZEN 8           10
    AND THESE WERE THE CHANGES OF URIZEN . . . . . . .  227 URIZEN 8           12
    HIS PRINCIPLES EVERY MAN CHANGES HIS OPINIONS HE WHO   . . 386B ANNO WATSON    MARG
    IN ETERNITY ONE THING NEVER CHANGES INTO ANOTHER THING . . 607A V LAST JUDG/N PROSE
    REPRESENT [OUR PRESENT CHANGES OF EXTREMES]   . . . .  611C V LAST JUDG/N PROSE
    AND SEE THESE CHANGES OTHERS SAID IF YOU DO SO PREPARE . . 686 JERUSALEM 55     5
    . . . CHANGES HIS SEXUAL [GARENTS] GARMENTS AT WILL   . . 695 JERUSALEM 61   * 51
    ACCORDING TO HIS CHANGES SHE ROLLD HIS KIDNEYS ROUND   . 723 JERUSALEM 80     72
CHANGING    SEE EVER CHANGING,MANY CHANGING
    [?WHILE] THRO THE CLEAR CHANGING ATMOSPHERE . . . . . .  274 FOUR ZOAS 1    * 367
    WITH THE CHANGING SAMENESS OLD VARIETY  . . . . . .  27 EDW THIRD/PS 3      259
    ERE ONCE AGAIN THE CHANGING MOON HER CIRCUIT HATH PERFORMED  38A SAMSON/PS   PROSE
    BLUE & CHANGING IN TEARS AND BITTER  . . . . . . .  250 AHANIA 3            3
    . . . ALL HIS LOVELY CHANGING COLOURS MIX     . . . .  269 FOUR ZOAS 1      184
    . . . ALL HIS [LOVELY CHANGING] DARKLY WAVING COLOURS MIX   381 FOUR ZOAS AD 5   4
    AND CHANGING YELLOW AND AT LENGTH BROWN DESTROYS EVERY . . 566B DESC CAT 2  PROSE
    ANOTHER THING CHANGING WATER INTO WINE BY JESUS   . . . 607B V LAST JUDG/N PROSE
CHANNEL
    SO LONG BEEN TURNED OUT OF THE OLD CHANNEL INTO A NEW ONE  865C LETTER 63   PROSE
CHANNELD
    THENCE AROSE HIS CHANNELD THROAT   . . . . . . . .  229 URIZEN 13           7
    A CRAVING HUNGRY CAVERN THENCE AROSE HIS CHANNELD   . . . 303 FOUR ZOAS 4     240
CHANNELS
    THAT MURMUR DOWN THEIR PEBBLY CHANNELS AND    . . . . .  31 EDW THIRD/PS 5     55
    ROARING LET OUT THE FLUID THE MOLTEN METAL RAN IN CHANNELS  283 FOUR ZOAS 2   118
    THEY DUG THE CHANNELS FOR THE RIVERS & THEY POURD ABROAD  286 FOUR ZOAS 2     250
    THEY SHRUNK INTO THEIR CHANNELS DRY THE ROCKY STRAND    312 FOUR ZOAS 6      22
      BENEATH HIS FEET
    IN CHANNELS THRO MY FIERY LIMBS O LOVE O PITY O PAIN   . 349 FOUR ZOAS 8     307
    AND MURMURING IN THEIR CHANNELS FLOW & CIRCLE ROUND HIS  378 FOUR ZOAS 9     805
      FEET
    IN CHANNELS THRO MY FIERY LIMBS O LOVE O PITY O FEAR   . . 705 JERUSALEM 67    54
CHANT    SEE CHAUNT
CHANTER'S
    [AND ALL IN ORDER SIT WAITING THE CHIEF CHANTER'S COMMANDS]  59 HOLY THURS/IM   8
CHANTRY
    I WISH TO HAVE A COPY OF JOB TO SHEW TO MR CHANTRY   . . . 870D LETTER 72    PROSE
CHAOS
    FROM AN OAK ITS HEIGHTH FROM A DAISY ITS LOWNESS & [CHAOS]  81C ANNO LAVATER  * MARG
    & THEN WE SHALL RETURN TO CHAOS & GOD WILL BE COMPELLD  . . 81C ANNO LAVATER  MARG
    CENTERD AND THE RUSHING OF CHAOS OVERWHELMD HIS DARK SOUL   136 FRENCH REVOLTN  50
      . . .
    FOR THE BARS OF CHAOS ARE BURST HER MILLIONS PREPARE THEIR  140 FRENCH REVOLTN 141
      FIERY WAY
    THE PETRIFIC ABOMINABLE CHAOS  . . . . . . . . .  223 URIZEN 3           26
    IN CHAOS AND CIRCLING DARK URIZEN  . . . . . . . .  250 AHANIA 2           39
    TO OUR PRIMEVAL CHAOS IN FORTUITOUS CONCOURSE OF INCOHERENT  282 FOUR ZOAS 2   102
    A HORRIBLE CHAOS TO HIS EYES A FORMLESS UNMEASURABLE DEATH  301 FOUR ZOAS 4   162
    SWIFT SWIFT FROM CHAOS TO CHAOS FROM VOID TO VOID A    316 FOUR ZOAS 6      189
      ROAD IMMENSE
    THRO CHAOS SEEKING FOR DELIGHT & IN SPACES REMOTE   . . . 361 FOUR ZOAS 9     170
    CHAOS & ANCIENT NIGHT FLED FROM BENEATH THE FIERY HARROW   493 MILTON 12      21
    THAT TRAVELS INTO CHAOS SO MILTON WENT GUARDED WITHIN   . 496 MILTON 15       20
    IN TWENTY-SEVEN HEAVENS AND ALL THEIR HELLS WITH CHAOS  . 498 MILTON 17       24
    THERE CHAOS DWELLS & ANCIENT NIGHT & OG & ANAK OLD   . . 502 MILTON 20        33
    BEYOND THE STARS IN CHAOS IN CAVERNS OF THE MUNDANE SHELL   502 MILTON 20      42
    LIKE THE BLACK STORM COMING OUT OF CHAOS BEYOND THE STARS   507 MILTON 23      21
    THE SUN ROLLS INTO CHAOS & THE STARS INTO THE DESARTS  . 507 MILTON 23        24
    A LONG JOURNEY & DARK THRO CHAOS IN THE TRACK OF MILTON'S  524 MILTON 34       22
      COURSE
    IN MIDST STRETCHING FROM ZENITH TO NADIR IN MIDST OF CHAOS  524 MILTON 34      34
```

320

```
                                                         PAGE     TITLE            LINE
CHAOS    (CONTINUED)
    AND EMPIRES OF CHAOS INVISIBLE TO THE VEGETABLE MAN  . . .  528 MILTON 37            49
    BENEATH SAT CHAOS SIN ON HIS RIGHT HAND DEATH ON HIS LEFT   531 MILTON 39            29
    ALL IS CHAOS AGAIN AND THE LINE OF THE ALMIGHTY MUST BE     585C DESC CAT 15       PROSE
    & IN WHOSE SLEEP OR CHAOS CREATION BEGAN [HIS EMANATION     609C V LAST JUDG/N     PROSE
        OR WIFE IS]
    WAS SOLITUDE & CHAOS THIS IS THE MOST PERNICIOUS IDEA   .   614B V LAST JUDG/N     PROSE
    FROM THE BIBLE & LIMITS ALL EXISTENCE TO CREATION & TO      614B V LAST JUDG/N     PROSE
        CHAOS
    AND THENCE I SEE THE CHAOS OF SATAN & THE WORLD OF ADAM     636 JERUSALEM 15        31
    OF GOD WHO DWELLS IN CHAOS HIDDEN FROM THE HUMAN SIGHT  . . 652 JERUSALEM 28        16
    CHAOS BEFORE HIS FACE APPEARD AN UNFORMED MEMORY  . . . .   659 JERUSALEM 33         2
    THEN SPOKE THE SPECTROUS CHAOS TO ALBION DARKNING COLD  . . 659 JERUSALEM 33         3
    AND THIS IS THE CAUSE OF THE APPEARANCE IN THE FROWNING     659 JERUSALEM 33        25
        CHAOS
    APPEARD NOW IN THE FROWNING CHAOS PROLIFIC UPON THE CHAOS   659 JERUSALEM 33        27
    INTO HIS OWN CHAOS WHICH IS THE MEMORY BETWEEN MAN & MAN    685 JERUSALEM 54         8
    THEY CALL THE ROCKS PARENTS OF MEN & ADORE THE FROWNING     704 JERUSALEM 67        15
        CHAOS
    AND IN THE SHADOWS OF REMEMBRANCE & IN THE CHAOS OF THE     740 JERUSALEM 92        22
        SPECTRE
    AND THE DIM CHAOS BRIGHTEND BENEATH ABOVE AROUND EYED AS    745 JERUSALEM 98        14
        THE PEACOCK
    [THOU] THO THOU DIDST ALL TO CHAOS ROLL . . . . . . .       754 EV GOSPEL(E)/N *    39
CHAOS-BORN
    . . . WHEN AUMONT WHOSE CHAOS-BORN SOUL . . . . . . .       141 FRENCH REVOLTN     159
CHAOSES
    HERE IN THESE CHAOSES THE SONS OF OLOLON TOOK THEIR ABODE   524 MILTON 34           40
CHAOTIC
    FOUR UNIVERSES ROUND THE MUNDANE EGG REMAIN CHAOTIC  . . .  500 MILTON 19           15
    FOUR UNIVERSES ROUND THE UNIVERSE OF LOS REMAIN CHAOTIC     524 MILTON 34           32
    FOR THE CHAOTIC VOIDS OUTSIDE OF THE STARS ARE MEASURED BY  528 MILTON 37           47
    WANDER AWAY INTO THE CHAOTIC VOID LAMENTING WITH HER SHADOW 624 JERUSALEM 5         63
    & IN HIS CHAOTIC STATE OF SLEEP . . . . . . . .           649D JERUSALEM 27       PROSE
    FOR FOUR UNIVERSES ROUND THE MUNDANE EGG REMAIN CHAOTIC     691 JERUSALEM 59        10
    TOOK VENGEANCE TWELVE-FOLD AMONG THE CHAOTIC ROCKS OF THE   697 JERUSALEM 63         8
        DRUIDS
CHAPEL
    A CHAPEL WAS BUILT IN THE MIDST . . . . . . . .            162 GARDEN LOVE/N         3
    AND THE [GATE] GATES OF THE CHAPEL [WAS] WERE SHUT  . . .   162 GARDEN LOVE/N *      5
    I SAW A CHAPEL ALL OF GOLD . . . . . . . . . .             163 I SAW CHAPEL/N        1
    A CHAPEL WAS BUILT IN THE MIDST . . . . . . . .            215 GARDEN LOVE/SE        3
    AND THE GATES OF THIS CHAPEL WERE SHUT . . . . . . .       215 GARDEN LOVE/SE        5
    ST EDMUNDS CHAPEL EAST DEREHAM MAY BE UNDERSTOOD TO . . .   838B LETTER 37         PROSE
    MEAN A CHAPEL IN EAST DEREHAM TOWN & NOT TO EXPRESS  . .    838B LETTER 37         PROSE
CHAPELS
    IF IT WAS NOT FOR CHURCHES & CHAPELS . . . . . . . .        48B ISLAND MOON 4      PROSE
    LIKE LAKES OF LIQUID LEAD INSTEAD OF HEAVENLY CHAPELS BUILT 673 JERUSALEM 43        63
CHAPLAIN
    THE PRIORESS FOLLOWS THESE WITH HER FEMALE CHAPLAIN  . . .  568B DESC CAT 3        PROSE
CHAPTER
    HEAVEN & HELL ?CHAPTER... . . . . . . . . . .              89B ANNO SWED LOVE * MARG
    JERUSALEM C(CHAPTER) (FOUR) . . . . . . . . . .            718D JERUSALEM 78        TITLE
    AS HE IS TO A CHAPTER IN THE BIBLE . . . . . . . .         825B LETTER 27         PROSE
    GENESIS CHAPTER I THE CREATION OF THE NATURAL MAN  . .      SUPP ILLUS GENESIS    *TITLE
    CHAPTER II THE NATURAL MAN DIVIDED INTO MALE & FEMALE &     SUPP ILLUS GENESIS    *TITLE
    CHAPTER III OF THE SEXUAL NATURE & ITS FALL INTO            SUPP ILLUS GENESIS    *TITLE
        GENERATION & DEATH
    CHAPTER IV HOW GENERATION & DEATH TOOK POSSESSION OF THE    SUPP ILLUS GENESIS    *TITLE
        NATURAL MAN
CHAPTERS
    [IN XXVIII CHAPTERS] ...PRINTED BY W BLAKE STH MOLTON ST    620A JERUSALEM        *TITLE
CHARACTER
    IF I HAVE NOT PRESENTED YOU WITH EVERY CHARACTER IN THE     46B ISLAND MOON 2      PROSE
        PIECE
    OR PROPHETIC CHARACTER THE PHILOSOPHIC & EXPERIMENTAL   . . 97B NAT RELIGION 1    PROSE
    AS THE SAYINGS USED IN A NATION MARK ITS CHARACTER  . . .  150C MARRIAGE HH 6     PROSE
    EVERY BODY NATURALLY HATES A PERFECT CHARACTER BECAUSE  . . 412A ANNO BOYD         MARG
    THE MAP OF ALLESTONE HAS THE SAME CHARACTER OF THE FIRM AND 439C REMARKS MALKIN   PROSE
    THEY MILITATE AGAINST INDIVIDUAL CHARACTER . . . . . .     453B ANNO REYNOLDS      MARG
    REYNOLDS THOUGHT CHARACTER ITSELF EXTRAVAGANCE & DEFORMITY  460C ANNO REYNOLDS      MARG
    IF REYNOLDS COULD NOT SEE VARIETY OF CHARACTER IN RAFAEL    466B ANNO REYNOLDS      MARG
        OTHERS CAN
    & MINUTE DISCRIMINATION OF CHARACTER IT IS THE WHOLE OF ART 466B ANNO REYNOLDS      MARG
    ("BACON MASTER THOUGHTS OTHERS") [THIS IS THE CHARACTER     SUPP ANNO REYNOLDS    * MARG
        OF A KNAVE]
    HAS EVER BEEN A CONQUEROR AND IS THAT SPECIES OF CHARACTER  567D DESC CAT 3       PROSE
    THE SQUIRE'S YEOMAN IS ALSO A GREAT CHARACTER . . . . .    568A DESC CAT 3       PROSE
    WITH CERTAIN HUMOUROUS ACCOMPANIMENTS IN HIS CHARACTER  . . 568D DESC CAT 3      *PROSE
    THE FRIAR IS A CHARACTER ALSO OF A MIXED KIND . . . . .    568D DESC CAT 3       PROSE
    IT IS NECESSARY HERE TO SPEAK OF CHAUCER'S OWN CHARACTER    569A DESC CAT 3       PROSE
    FOR A BUFFOON OR BURLESQUE CHARACTER KNOW LITTLE OF CHAUCER 569C DESC CAT 3       PROSE
    OF THE CAVALCADE IS A FIRST RATE CHARACTER AND HIS JOKES    569D DESC CAT 3       PROSE
    BUT I HAVE OMITTED TO SPEAK OF A VERY PROMINENT CHARACTER   570A DESC CAT 3       PROSE
    CHAUCER'S LAWYER IS A CHARACTER OF GREAT VENERABLENESS  .   570D DESC CAT 3       PROSE
    FOR ITS STAMINA CHAUCER HAS DIVIDED THE ANCIENT CHARACTER   571B DESC CAT 3       PROSE
    AS HIS DRESS IS DIFFERENT AND HIS CHARACTER IS MORE MARKED  572A DESC CAT 3       PROSE
    WIFE OF BATH IN WHOSE CHARACTER CHAUCER HAS BEEN EQUALLY    572B DESC CAT 3       PROSE
    THIS CHARACTER VARIES FROM THAT OF CHAUCER AS THE   . . .  572B DESC CAT 3       PROSE
    A KNAVISH CHARACTER WILL OFTEN SAY OF WHAT INTEREST IS      572D DESC CAT 3       PROSE
        IT TO ME
    THE CHARACTER AND EXPRESSION IN THIS PICTURE COULD NEVER    573A DESC CAT 3       PROSE
```

321

	PAGE	TITLE	LINE

CHARACTER   (CONTINUED)
NO VULGAR CHARACTER AS HE HAS ENDEAVOURED TO MAKE HIM   . . 574A DESC CAT 3   PROSE
THERE ARE NO LINEAMENTS THERE CAN BE NO CHARACTER   . . 575B DESC CAT 3   PROSE
MUST BE THE DESTRUCTION OF ALL CHARACTER AND EXPRESSION   575B DESC CAT 3   PROSE
HE HAS INTRODUCED A CHARACTER THAT CHAUCER HAS NOT   . . 575B DESC CAT 3   PROSE
EACH SHEW A DIFFERENT CHARACTER AND A DIFFERENT   . . . 580C DESC CAT 5   PROSE
UNAPPROPRIATE AND REPUGNANT TO YOUR OWN INDIVIDUAL   582D DESC CAT 9   PROSE
    CHARACTER
FLANDERS IT LOSES ALL CHARACTER AND LEAVES WHAT SOME PEOPLE 585A DESC CAT 15   PROSE
EXPRESSION CANNOT EXIST WITHOUT CHARACTER AS ITS STAMINA   585A DESC CAT 15   PROSE
AND NEITHER CHARACTER NOR EXPRESSION CAN EXIST   . . . 585A DESC CAT 15   PROSE
AND DESIGNING WHOSE METHOD ALONE CAN DELINEATE CHARACTER   586D CHAUCER 1   PROSE
ON HORSEBACK OF CHAUCER'S CHARACTERS WHERE EVERY CHARACTER   587D CHAUCER/N   PROSE
    &
ENGRAVING BY LOSING DRAWING HAS LOST ALL CHARACTER   . . . 592A PUB ADDRESS/N   *PROSE
THE MANNER IN WHICH MY CHARACTER HAS BEEN BLASTED   . . 592C PUB ADDRESS/N   PROSE
BLASTING MY CHARACTER AS AN ARTIST TO MACKLIN MY EMPLOYER   592D PUB ADDRESS/N   PROSE
CAN NEVER PRODUCE CHARACTER & EXPRESSION   . . . . . 593B PUB ADDRESS/N   PROSE
AS AN ORIGINAL [BELYING] BE-LYING THE ENGLISH CHARACTER IN   595C PUB ADDRESS/N   PROSE
MR B(BLAKE) REPEATS THAT THERE IS NOT ONE CHARACTER   . . 599B PUB ADDRESS/N   PROSE
OR ANY OF THAT CLASS CHARACTER & EXPRESSION CAN   . . 599B PUB ADDRESS/N   PROSE
ALL DESCRIPTIVE OF CHARACTER & NOT A LINE IS DRAWN   . . . 611B V LAST JUDG/N   PROSE
MILTON IN HIS CHARACTER OF A STUDENT AT CAMBRIDGE   619A ILLUS MILTON   PROSE
ACCORDING TO THE SUBJECT OF DISCOURSE & EVERY WORD & EVERY   746 JERUSALEM 98   35
    CHARACTER
NOW GOODNESS OR BADNESS HAS NOTHING TO DO WITH CHARACTER   778B HOMERS POETRY   PROSE
CHARACTER ITS GOODNESS OR BADNESS IS ANOTHER CONSIDERATION 778B HOMERS POETRY   PROSE
OF CHARACTER WHICH FEW HAVE HE IS THE MAN WHO APPLIED TO   841C LETTER 41   PROSE
GREAT LEADING CHARACTER IN LITERATURE & HIS TERMS TO OTHERS 841C LETTER 41   PROSE
THIS IS HIS OWN DECISION QUITE IN CHARACTER   . . . . . 877D LETTER 88   PROSE
CHARACTERISTIC
IF SUCH IS THE CHARACTERISTIC OF A MODERN POLITE GENTLEMAN   384D ANNO WATSON   MARG
REYNOLDS'S EYE COULD NOT BEAR CHARACTERISTIC COLOURING OR   475D ANNO REYNOLDS   MARG
BENEVOLENCE IS THE PLOWMAN'S GREAT CHARACTERISTIC   . . . 571B DESC CAT 3   PROSE
CHARACTERISTICAL
ORIGINAL & (CHARACTERISTICAL) ARE . . . . 468B ANNO REYNOLDS   * MARG
CHARACTERISTICS
OR TO HIS EMANATION ANY OF THE UNIVERSAL CHARACTERISTICS   736 JERUSALEM 90   29
CHARACTERS
("THE GREATEST OF CHARACTERS...") THIS WAS CHRIST   . . . 66B ANNO LAVATER   MARG
("AVOID CHARACTERS WHOSE GOOD & BAD SIDES UNMIXED")   86D ANNO LAVATER   MARG
    MOST EXCELLENT
THE GRANDEST POETRY IS IMMORAL THE GRANDEST CHARACTERS   412B ANNO BOYD   MARG
    WICKED
APPEARS TO ME TO GIVE ALWAYS THE CHARACTERS OF VULGAR   464B ANNO REYNOLDS   MARG
    STUPIDITY
("ILLUSTRIOUS CHARACTERS") [GOD BLASTS THEM AS THOUGH]   SUPP ANNO REYNOLDS   * MARG
THE CHARACTERS OF CHAUCER'S PILGRIMS ARE THE CHARACTERS   567B DESC CAT 3   PROSE
THE SAME CHARACTERS REPEATED AGAIN AND AGAIN IN ANIMALS   567C DESC CAT 3   PROSE
OF CHAUCER'S CHARACTERS AS DESCRIBED IN HIS CANTERBURY   567C DESC CAT 3   PROSE
    TALES
BUT THE CHARACTERS THEMSELVES FOR EVER REMAIN UNALTERED   567C DESC CAT 3   PROSE
CHARACTERS LIKELY TO RIDE IN COMPANY ALL BEING ABOVE THE   568C DESC CAT 3   PROSE
CHAUCER'S CHARACTERS LIVE AGE AFTER AGE . . . . 570D DESC CAT 3   PROSE
ALL PASS ON EACH SUSTAINING ONE OR OTHER OF THESE   570D DESC CAT 3   PROSE
    CHARACTERS
NOR CAN A CHILD BE BORN WHO IS NOT ONE OF THESE CHARACTERS   570D DESC CAT 3   PROSE
THAT CHAUCER MAKES EVERY ONE OF HIS CHARACTERS PERFECT IN   570D DESC CAT 3   PROSE
THE MILLER IS THE HERCULES &C CHAUCER'S CHARACTERS ARE . 571A DESC CAT 3   PROSE
CHARACTERS OF HUMAN LIFE APPEAR TO POETS IN ALL AGES   . . 571B DESC CAT 3   PROSE
THE REEVE AND THE MANCIPLE ARE TWO CHARACTERS OF THE MOST   571D DESC CAT 3   PROSE
THE CHARACTERS OF WOMEN CHAUCER HAS DIVIDED INTO   572B DESC CAT 3   PROSE
    TWO CLASSES
OF SUCH CHARACTERS BORN TOO MANY FOR THE PEACE OF THE WORLD 572B DESC CAT 3   PROSE
SUCH ARE THE CHARACTERS THAT COMPOSE THIS PICTURE   . . . 572C DESC CAT 3   PROSE
TWO FIRST CHARACTERS IN CHAUCER THE KNIGHT AND THE SQUIRE   573C DESC CAT 3   PROSE
IT IS THE SAME WITH ALL HIS CHARACTERS HE HAS DONE ALL . 574A DESC CAT 3   PROSE
REPRESENTING CHAUCER'S CHARACTERS PAINTED BY WILLIAM BLAKE   586C CHAUCER 1   TITLE
TO KEEP HIS OWN CHARACTERS AND EXPRESSIONS HAVING HAD . . 586D CHAUCER 1   PROSE
ON HORSEBACK OF CHAUCER'S CHARACTERS WHERE EVERY CHARACTER   587D CHAUCER/N   PROSE
    &
THE CHARACTERS OF CHAUCER'S PILGRIMS ARE THE CHARACTERS   589A CHAUCER/N   PROSE
THE SAME CHARACTERS REPEATED AGAIN & AGAIN IN ANIMALS   . 589A CHAUCER/N   PROSE
OF CHAUCER'S CHARACTERS AS DESCRIBED IN HIS CANTERBURY   590C CHAUCER 2   PROSE
    TALES
BUT THE CHARACTERS THEMSELVES FOR EVER REMAIN UNALTERED   590D CHAUCER 2   PROSE
OF HUMAN CHARACTERS AS THEY APPEAR AGE AFTER AGE   . . . . 591A PUB ADDRESS/N   TITLE
EXAMPLE OF THESE CONTRARY ARTS IS GIVEN US IN THE   600D PUB ADDRESS/N   PROSE
    CHARACTERS
THE [EXPRESSION] CHARACTERS IN ALL THEIR BRANCHES   . . . 611B V LAST JUDG/N   PROSE
HE COMPREHENDS ALL THE PROPHETIC CHARACTERS   . . . . . 611C V LAST JUDG/N   PROSE
PERUSING ALBION'S TOMB IN THE STARRY CHARACTERS OF OG &   713 JERUSALEM 73   16
    ANAK
ARISTOTLE SAYS CHARACTERS ARE EITHER GOOD OR BAD   . . . . 778B HOMERS POETRY   PROSE
AN APPLE TREE A PEAR TREE A HORSE A LION ARE CHARACTERS   778B HOMERS POETRY   PROSE
CHARGE
AND WENT TO MIND HER NUMEROUS CHARGE AMONG THE VERDANT   128 BOOK OF THEL 2   18
    GRASS
O LITTLE CLOUD THE VIRGIN SAID I CHARGE THEE TELL TO ME   128 BOOK OF THEL 3   1
GIVING THE SPECTRE STERNEST CHARGE OVER THE HOWLING FIEND   308 FOUR ZOAS 5   112
THE SPECTRE [SMILD] TERRIFIED & GAVE HER CHARGE OVER THE   328 FOUR ZOAS 7   * 332
    HOWLING ORC

	PAGE	TITLE	LINE

CHARGE   (CONTINUED)

THE NORTHERN DRUM NOW GIVE THE CHARGE BRAVELY OBSCURD   .   . 337 FOUR ZOAS 7B   155
LUCIFER REFUSD TO DIE FOR SATAN & IN PRIDE HE FORSOOK HIS   351 FOUR ZOAS 8   399
    CHARGE
AND THAT NOT ONE WORD OF CHARGE AGAINST ME WAS UTTERED   . 437B BLAKES MEMORAN   PROSE
CHARGE MUST HAVE BEEN FABRICATED IN THE STABLE AFTERWARDS 437C BLAKES MEMORAN   PROSE
I BELIEVE THE WHOLE CHARGE FALLS TO THE GROUND   .   .   . 437C BLAKES MEMORAN   PROSE
BUT LUCIFER REFUSD TO DIE & IN PRIDE HE FORSOOK HIS CHARGE   494 MILTON 13   18
BUT ENITHARMON AND HER DAUGHTERS TAKE THE PLEASANT CHARGE   517 MILTON 29   51
SUCH IS THEIR LOVELY CHARGE BUT RAHAB & TIRZAH PERVERT   . 517 MILTON 29   53
THOSE WHO KEEP MANUFACTORIES OF ART ALWAYS CHARGE   .   . 583B DESC CAT 9   PROSE
LAID TO OUR CHARGE THE ARTIST WHO HAS DONE THESE PICTURES 584B DESC CAT 14   PROSE
ANOTHER DEMON WITH A KEY HAS THE CHARGE OF SIN   .   .   . 606C V LAST JUDG/N   PROSE
THEIR AWFUL CHARGE BACK TO HIS NATIVE HOME BUT ALBION DARK   674 JERUSALEM 44   5
CHARGE THE SPIRITUALLY RELIGIOUS WITH HYPOCRISY   .   .   . 682C JERUSALEM 52   PROSE
VOLTAIRE ROUSSEAU YOU CANNOT ESCAPE MY CHARGE THAT   .   . 682D JERUSALEM 52   PROSE
BUT YOU ALSO CHARGE THE POOR MONKS & RELIGIOUS   .   .   . 683A JERUSALEM 52   PROSE
CHARGE VISIONARIES WITH DECIEVING   .   .   .   .   .   . 756 EV GOSPEL(H)/N   3
& LEFT IT WITH CHARGE TO THE SERVANT OF GREAT CARE   .   . 834C LETTER 34   PROSE

CHARGED

HEARD PEOPLE QUARREL BUT THEY ALWAYS CHARGED EACH OTHER   437B BLAKES MEMORAN   PROSE
THEREFORE AS THE SOLDIER CHARGED NOT ME WITH SEDITIOUS   . 437C BLAKES MEMORAN   PROSE

CHARGETH

.   .   . & WHO CHARGETH HIS ANGELS WITH FOLLY   .   .   .   .   . 679 JERUSALEM 49   31

CHARIOT

SO ONCE THE SUN HIS CHARIOT DREW BACK TO PROLONG A GOOD   41B THEN SHE BORE   PROSE
    KING'S LIFE
FUZON ON A CHARIOT IRON-WINGD   .   .   .   . 249 AHANIA 2   1
ON CLOUDS OF SMOKE RAGES HIS CHARIOT   .   .   .   .   . 249 AHANIA 2   5
WHO THE CHARIOT OF LEUTHA GUIDES   .   .   .   .   .   . 255 BOOK OF LOS 3   2
AND LUVAH SIEZD THE HORSES OF LIGHT & ROSE INTO THE CHARIOT   271 FOUR ZOAS 1   264
    OF DAY
UPON THE SANDY SHORE RESTED HIS CHARIOT OF FIRE   .   .   . 273 FOUR ZOAS 1   330
[XXX ?CHARIOT XXX]   .   .   .   . SUPP FOUR ZOAS 1   *
WERE KEPT BACK FROM MY LORD & FROM HIS CHARIOT OF MERCIES   310 FOUR ZOAS 5   209
.   .   . THAT THEY MIGHT RUN IN THY GOLDEN CHARIOT OF PRIDE   311 FOUR ZOAS 5   235
[THEN DEMONS ?HOWLD ROUND HIS CHARIOT ?RAGING ?LUVAH   SUPP FOUR ZOAS 5   *
    (EMPTIED)]
THAT DRAGD THE WHEELS OF THE SUN'S CHARIOT & THEY PUT THE   333 FOUR ZOAS 7B   34
    SUN
THEY FORGD THE SWORD THE CHARIOT OF WAR THE BATTLE AX   . 337 FOUR ZOAS 7B   172
HOW RAGD THE GOLDEN HORSES OF URIZEN BOUND TO THE CHARIOT   338 FOUR ZOAS 7B   201
    OF LOVE
EXECUTION IS THE CHARIOT OF GENIUS   .   .   .   .   .   . 454A ANNO REYNOLDS   MARG
BRING ME MY CHARIOT OF FIRE   .   .   .   . 481 AND DID FEET/M   12
ON THE FIERY CHARIOT OF HIS CONTEMPLATIVE THOUGHT   .   . 611A V LAST JUDG/N   PROSE
HE IS SEEN ON HIS FIERY CHARIOT BOWING BEFORE THE THRONE   611C V LAST JUDG/N   PROSE
THE NATIONS ARE HER DUST GROUND BY THE CHARIOT WHEELS   . 653 JERUSALEM 29   23
THE SUN SHALL BE A SCYTHED CHARIOT OF BRITAIN THE MOON   688 JERUSALEM 56   18
    A SHIP
THE CHARIOT WHEELS FILLED WITH EYES RAGE ALONG THE HOWLING   697 JERUSALEM 63   11
    VALLEY
THEY FORGD THE SWORD ON CHEVIOT THE CHARIOT OF WAR & THE   699 JERUSALEM 65   14
    BATTLE-AX
HOW RAGD THE GOLDEN HORSES OF URIZEN COMPELLD TO   700 JERUSALEM 65   47
    THE CHARIOT OF LOVE
.   .   . & EACH CHARIOT WAS SEXUAL [TWOFOLD] THREEFOLD   .   .   . 745 JERUSALEM 98   * 11
BECAME A CHARIOT OF FIRE   .   .   .   . 749 EV GOSPEL(B)/N   34
WHERE EER HIS CHARIOT TOOK ITS WAY   .   .   .   .   .   . 749 EV GOSPEL(B)/N   39
DRAGD AT HIS CHARIOT WHEELS LOUD HOWLD   .   .   .   .   . 749 EV GOSPEL(B)/N   43
THE CHARIOT [WHELD] [WHEEL &] WHEELS & LOUDER STILL   .   . 749 EV GOSPEL(B)/N   45

CHARIOTS

WITH HORSES AND WITH CHARIOTS   .   .   .   . 12 GWIN KING/PS   57
THE CHARIOTS AND THE HORSES THE NOISE OF SHOUT   .   .   . 34B KING JOHN/PS   PROSE
CURLD VETERANS AMONG HELMS AND SHIELDS AND CHARIOTS   .   . 159D SONG LIBERTY   PROSE
ON GOLDEN CHARIOTS RAGING WITH RED WHEELS DROPPING WITH   245 EUROPE 15   5
    BLOOD
DESCEND O URIZEN DESCEND WITH HORSE & CHARIOTS   .   .   . 272 FOUR ZOAS 1   * 308
TEN THOUSAND THOUSAND GLITTERING CHARIOTS SHINING IN THE   273 FOUR ZOAS 1   344
    SKY
FROM ALL THE TURNING WHEELS OF HEAVEN & THE CHARIOTS OF   276 FOUR ZOAS 1   441
    THE SLAIN
SIEZING THE CHARIOTS OF THE MORNING GO OUTFLEETING RIDE   278 FOUR ZOAS 1   494
THE LANCES OF URIZEN FROM CHARIOTS ROUND THE HOLY TENT   . 278 FOUR ZOAS 1   517
SO SAYING THARMAS ON HIS FURIOUS CHARIOTS OF THE DEEP   . 301 FOUR ZOAS 4   157
THE SPEARS OF URIZEN FROM CHARIOTS ROUND THE ETERNAL TENT   306 FOUR ZOAS 5   44
GO DOWN WITH HORSE & CHARIOTS & TRUMPETS OF HOARSE WAR   . 374 FOUR ZOAS 9   661
CHARIOTS BLACK THEIR FIRES ROLL BEHOLDING ALBION'S HOUSE   666 JERUSALEM 40   5
    OF ETERNITY
THE TWENTY-FOUR HEARD THEY CAME TREMBLING ON WATRY CHARIOTS   667 JERUSALEM 40   21
WITH CYMBAL TRUMPET CLARION & THE SCYTHED CHARIOTS   677 JERUSALEM 47   11
    OF BRITAIN
BUT FIRST THEY SAID & THEIR WORDS STOOD IN CHARIOTS IN   686 JERUSALEM 55   34
    ARRAY
UPON THE CHARIOTS OF THE MORNING CONTRACTING OR EXPANDING   687 JERUSALEM 55   45
    TIME
THE KING OF CANAAN WHOSE ARE SEVEN HUNDRED CHARIOTS OF IRON   702 JERUSALEM 66   25
THE INNUMERABLE CHARIOTS OF THE ALMIGHTY APPEARD IN HEAVEN   745 JERUSALEM 98   8
.   .   . CHARIOTS OF HUMANITY DIVINE INCOMPREHENSIBLE   . 745 JERUSALEM 98   24
ON CHARIOTS OF GOLD & JEWELS WITH LIVING CREATURES STARRY   . 746 JERUSALEM 98   42
    & FLAMING
TO CLIP THE WINGS AND TO TAKE OFF THE WHEELS OF OUR   807A LETTER 17   PROSE
    CHARIOTS

```
                                                        PAGE      TITLE            LINE
CHARITABLE
   CONSEQUENTLY HE IS NOT CHARITABLE . . . . . . . .  556D JESUS NOT/N       PROSE
CHARITY
   ("NO GIFTS CAN EXHAUST GENIUS IMPOVERISH CHARITY") MOST   84B ANNO LAVATER    MARG
      EXCELLENT
   THOU HAST REFUSD OUR CHARITY THOU HAST REFUSD OUR FOOD    100 TIRIEL 1        37
   I HAVE NOT THE CHARITY FOR THE BISHOP THAT HE PRETENDS .  384D ANNO WATSON     MARG
   [TILL AT LENGTH CHRISTIAN CHARITY IS HELD OUT AS A MOTIVE 595B PUB ADDRESS/N   PROSE
      TO]
   AND GIVE WITH CHARITY A STONE . . . . . . . . .    751 EV GOSPEL(D)/N     4
   THE TRUE CHRISTIAN CHARITY NOT DEPENDENT ON . . .  776B INSC LAOCOON      PROSE
   THINK THAT IT WAS A FIGURE WITH CHILDREN WHICH HE CALLD   849A LETTER 45       PROSE
      A CHARITY
   ADVERTISEMENT CALLING IT AN APPEAL TO CHARITY AND SAYS IT 861B LETTER 58       PROSE
CHARLEMAINE
   PAUL CONSTANTINE CHARLEMAINE LUTHER MILTON . . .   350 FOUR ZOAS 8       362
   I SAW A MONK OF [CONSTANTINE] CHARLEMAINE . . . . .   418 I SAW A MONK/N    1
   [CHARLEMAINE & HIS BARONS BOLD] . . . . . . . .    418 I SAW A MONK/N     7
   [SEDITIOUS] THOU LAZY MONK [SAID CHARLEMAINE] THEY SOUND  419 I SAW A MONK/N    10
      AFAR
   [O CHARLEMAINE O CHARLEMAINE ] . . . . . . . .     420 I SAW MNK AD/N     5
   TITUS CONSTANTINE CHARLEMAINE . . . . . . . . .    420 I SAW MNK AD/N     6
   CHARLEMAINE & HIS BARONS BOLD . . . . . . . . .    420 I SAW MNK AD/N    13
   CHARLEMAINE & HIS CLOUDS OF WAR . . . . . . . .    420 I SAW MNK AD/N    17
   PAUL CONSTANTINE CHARLEMAINE LUTHER BEHOLD THEY STAND    509 MILTON 24        32
      BEFORE US
   ABRAHAM MOSES SOLOMON PAUL CONSTANTINE CHARLEMAINE . .   528 MILTON 37        41
   I SAW A MONK OF CHARLEMAINE . . . . . . . . . .    683 I SAW A MONK/J     1
   TITUS CONSTANTINE CHARLEMAINE . . . . . . . . .    683 I SAW A MONK/J    21
   ABRAHAM MOSES SOLOMON PAUL CONSTANTINE CHARLEMAINE . .   716 JERUSALEM 75     16
CHARLES
   THE FIRE OF LONDON [CH(CHARLES) I BEHEADED] . . .  209A SUBJCTS HIST/N    TITLE
   CHARLES CALLS ON MILTON FOR ATONEMENT CROMWELL IS READY   485 MILTON 5        39
   & CHARLES THE FIRST WERE TO PATRONIZE SUCH BLOCKHEADS .  599D PUB ADDRESS/N   PROSE
   [EDWARD HENRY ELIZABETH JAMES CHARLES WILLIAM GEORGE] .  713 JERUSALEM 73  *  37
CHARM
   CAN CHARM TO HARMONY WITH POTENT SPELL . . . . . .    15 IMIT SPEN/PS     30
CHARMD
   THE PORTRAITS & CHARMD BY THE GREAT HEAD IN PARTICULAR . 820D LETTER 25       PROSE
CHARMING
   THERE HIS CHARMING NEST DOTH LAY . . . . . . . .     7 LOVE HARMNY/PS    17
   A CHARMING SONG INDEED MISS SAID SCOPPRELL . . . . .   54A ISLAND MOON 8    PROSE
   CHARMING TRULY ELEGANT SAID SCOPPRELL . . . . . .    55D ISLAND MOON 9    PROSE
   WHERE THOU THY CHARMING NEST DOST BUILD . . . . .    422 THE BIRDS/N       3
   IN PALAMABRON'S TENT AND OOTHOON WAS HER CHARMING GUARD   494 MILTON 13        44
   BUT AH MORE WONDROUS STILL THE CHARMING FAIR . . . .   545 IMIT POPE/N       4
CHARMS
   THE GARDEN & ITS LOVELY CHARMS . . . . . . . . .    426 MENTAL TRAVLER    60
   [?WHEN] NOW ART HAS LOST ITS MENTAL CHARMS . . . .   557 ART HAS LOST/N *   1
   IN SOFT FEMALE CHARMS . . . . . . . . . . . .      805 TO BUTTS/L        37
CHARNEL-HOUSE,CHARNEL HOUSE
   I SEEM TO BE IN ONE GREAT CHARNEL-HOUSE . . . . .    31 EDW THIRD/PS 5    43
   IN THE EASTERN CLOUD INSTEAD OF NIGHT A SICKLY CHARNEL   191 V DAU ALBION 2    36
      HOUSE
CHARON
   LIMBO CHARON . . . . . . . . . . . . . . .        785D ILLS DANTE 101   PROSE
CHARTA
   KING JOHN & MAG(MAGNA) CHARTA . . . . . . . . .   208D SUBJCTS HIST/N    TITLE
CHARTERD
   LET LIBERTY THE CHARTERD RIGHT OF ENGLISHMEN . . . .    18 EDW THIRD/PS 1     9
   OR THE CHEATING WAVES OF CHARTERD STREAMS . . . . .   166 WHY CARE FOR/N     2
   I WANDER THRO EACH CHARTERD STREET . . . . . . .    216 LONDON/SE         1
   NEAR WHERE THE CHARTERD THAMES DOES FLOW . . . . .   216 LONDON/SE         2
CHASE     SEE CHACE
   CHASE NOT SLUMBER FROM THY EYES . . . . . . . .    120 CRADLE SONG/SI    14
CHASM
   [THEN SLEEP FELL ON HER EYELIDS IN A CHASM OF THE VALLEY]  268 FOUR ZOAS 1      145
   IN ALL THIS CHASM I BEHOLD NO OTHER LIVING THING . . .   321 FOUR ZOAS 7       46
   DERBY PEAK YAWND A HORRID CHASM AT THE CRIES OF GWENDOLEN  699 JERUSALEM 64     35
      & AT
CHASMAL
   A CONCAVE EARTH WONDROUS CHASMAL ABYSSAL INCOHERENT . .   634 JERUSALEM 13     53
CHASMS
   HE TOOK HIGH BOUNDING OVER HILLS & DESARTS FLOODS . .   313 FOUR ZOAS 6       73
      & HORRIBLE CHASMS
   MAKING BETWEEN HORRIBLE CHASMS INTO THE VAST UNKNOWN .   318 FOUR ZOAS 6      277
   WITH TENFOLD ROUT & DESOLATION ROARD THE CHASMS BENEATH   378 FOUR ZOAS 9      783
   IN CHASMS OF THE MUNDANE SHELL WHICH OPEN ON ALL SIDES   524 MILTON 34        41
      ROUND
   LABOURD IN CHASMS OF THE MUNDANE SHELL THO HERE BEFORE .  532 MILTON 39        57
   IN CHASMS & ABYSSES OF SORROW ENLARGD WITHOUT DIMENSION   623 JERUSALEM 5       5
      TERRIBLE
CHASTE
   DRIVEN OUT & COMPELD TO BE CHASTE . . . . . . .    162 LAID ME DOWN/N     8
   ALL IS ETERNAL DEATH UNLESS YOU CAN WEAVE A CHASTE . .   643 JERUSALEM 21     11
   I BROUGHT LOVE INTO LIGHT OF DAY TO PRIDE IN CHASTE BEAUTY  645 JERUSALEM 22     17
   SHALL VALA BRING THEE FORTH SHALL THE CHASTE BE ASHAMED   696 JERUSALEM 62      7
      ALSO
   HOW CAN THE FEMALE BE CHASTE O THOU STUPID DRUID CRIED LOS  697 JERUSALEM 63     26
   IN CHASTE APPEARANCES FOR SWEET DECEITS OF LOVE & MODESTY  727 JERUSALEM 83     31
   WAS JESUS CHASTE OR DID HE &C . . . . . . . . .    753 EV GOSPEL(D)/N   109
   WAS JESUS CHASTE OR DID HE . . . . . . . . . .    753 EV GOSPEL(E)/N     1
```

```
                                               PAGE    TITLE           LINE
CHASTISE
    MY PERSON DEGRADE & MY TEMPER CHASTISE  . . . . . . .   829 O WHY BORN/L       6
CHASTITIES
    TO PLEASE THY IDOLS IN THE PRETENDED CHASTITIES OF      693 JERUSALEM 60       30
        UNCIRCUMCISION
CHASTITY
    AVARICE & CHASTITY DID SHITE IT  . . . . . . . . .  .   187 HEBREW NATN/N       2
    THY UNCIRCUMCISED PRETENCES TO CHASTITY MUST BE CUT IN  627 JERUSALEM 8        32
        SUNDER
    SHUDDRING THEY FLEE THEY HIDE IN THE DRUID TEMPLES IN COLD  638 JERUSALEM 17   14
        CHASTITY
    HIS OWN WIFE FOR THE TERRORS OF CHASTITY THAT THEY CALL 663 JERUSALEM 36       46
    BY LAWS OF CHASTITY & ABHORRENCE I AM WITHERD UP  . . . 679 JERUSALEM 49       26
    IN THEIR OWN SELFHOODS IN NATURAL SELFISH CHASTITY      679 JERUSALEM 49       28
        TO BANISH PITY
    IN CRUEL HOLINESS IN THEIR HEAVENS OF CHASTITY &        680 JERUSALEM 49       64
        UNCIRCUMCISION
    AND THEN BEHOLD WHAT ARE THESE ULRO VISIONS OF CHASTITY 686 JERUSALEM 55       38
    IN A RELIGION OF CHASTITY & UNCIRCUMCISED SELFISHNESS . 693 JERUSALEM 60       48
    WHEN THE DRUIDS DEMANDED CHASTITY FROM WOMAN & ALL WAS LOST 697 JERUSALEM 63   25
    THAT THEY MIGHT BE BORN IN CONTENTIONS OF CHASTITY & IN 707 JERUSALEM 69       10
    A RELIGION OF CHASTITY FORMING A COMMERCE TO SELL LOVES 708 JERUSALEM 69       34
    HE BRINGS TO ME THE IMAGES OF HIS LOVE & I REJECT       724 JERUSALEM 81        3
        IN CHASTITY
    IN DREAMS OF (CHASTITY) & MORAL LAW I HAVE MURDERED ALBION 742 JERUSALEM 94    23
        AH
    GIVE ANY LESSONS OF CHASTITY  . . . . . . . . . . . .   753 EV GOSPEL(E)/N      2
    IN DARK PRETENCE TO CHASTITY  . . . . . . . . . . .  .  755 EV GOSPEL(E)/N     71
    IMPOSSIBILITIES CHASTITY & ABSTINENCE GODS OF THE HEATHEN 776C INSC LAOCOON  PROSE
CHAT
    TILL TIRD OF CHAT THE GAME BEGINS . . . . . . . . .  .   16 BLIND-MANS/PS      11
CHATTERING
    PALE QUIVRING TOWARD THE BRAIN HIS GLIMMERING EYES TEETH 202 AMERICA 15         7
        CHATTERING
CHATTERTON
    WELL SAID THE OTHER HE WAS AS GREAT AS CHATTERTON  . . .  47A ISLAND MOON 3   PROSE
    THAT WAS AS GREAT AS CHATTERTON [OBTUSE ANGLE ANSWERD]    47A ISLAND MOON 3   PROSE
    PRAY SAID ARADOBO IS CHATTERTON A MATHEMATICIAN  . . .    48D ISLAND MOON 5   PROSE
    I THINK IN THE FIRST PLACE THAT CHATTERTON WAS CLEVER AT  49C ISLAND MOON 5   PROSE
    BE EASILY OUTDONE CHATTERTON NEVER WRIT THOSE POEMS  . .  51D ISLAND MOON 7   PROSE
    I BELIEVE BOTH MACPHERSON & CHATTERTON  . . . . . . .  .783C ANNO WW POEMS    MARG
    WITH ANY OTHER POET WHATEVER ROWLEY & CHATTERTON ALSO  . .783C ANNO WW POEMS  MARG
CHAUCER
    THE CANTERBURY PILGRIMS FROM CHAUCER A CABINET PICTURE   560B EXHIBITION ADV  PROSE
        IN FRESCO
    THE CANTERBURY PILGRIMS FROM CHAUCER . . . . . . . .  . 564B DESC CAT         TITLE
    NUMBER III SIR JEFFERY CHAUCER AND THE NINE AND TWENTY   566C DESC CAT 3      TITLE
    CHAUCER HIMSELF AND THE REEVE COMES AS CHAUCER HAS       567A DESC CAT 3      PROSE
        DESCRIBED
    THE PLANTS SO CHAUCER NUMBERED THE CLASSES OF MEN  . . . 567D DESC CAT 3      PROSE
    AS CHAUCER HAS ALSO PLACED THEM FIRST IN HIS PROLOGUE  . 567D DESC CAT 3      PROSE
    HIS WHOLE LENGTH PORTRAIT ON HORSEBACK AS WRITTEN        567D DESC CAT 3      PROSE
        BY CHAUCER
    CHAUCER DESCRIBES HERE A MIGHTY MAN  . . . . . . . .  . 568A DESC CAT 3       PROSE
    CHAUCER HAS DESCRIBED WITH MINUTENESS IT IS VERY ELEGANT 568B DESC CAT 3      PROSE
    FOR THE MONK IS DESCRIBED BY CHAUCER AS A MAN OF THE  .  568C DESC CAT 3      PROSE
    CHAUCER IS HIMSELF THE GREAT POETICAL OBSERVER OF MEN  . 569A DESC CAT 3      PROSE
    ACCORDINGLY CHAUCER HAS MADE HIS MONK A GREAT TRAGEDIAN  569A DESC CAT 3      PROSE
    FOR A BUFFOON OR BURLESQUE CHARACTER KNOW LITTLE OF CHAUCER 569C DESC CAT 3   PROSE
    THE GODDESSES OF DESTINY THIS SHEWS HOW CHAUCER HAS BEEN 569D DESC CAT 3      PROSE
    OF CHAUCER THE DOCTOR OF PHYSIC IS DESCRIBED AS THE FIRST 570D DESC CAT 3     PROSE
        OF
    THAT CHAUCER MAKES EVERY ONE OF HIS CHARACTERS PERFECT IN 570D DESC CAT 3     PROSE
    FOR ITS STAMINA CHAUCER HAS DIVIDED THE ANCIENT CHARACTER 571B DESC CAT 3     PROSE
    THE PLOWMAN OF CHAUCER IS HERCULES IN HIS SUPREME ETERNAL 571C DESC CAT 3     PROSE
    CHAUCER HAS BEEN SOMEHOW MADE TO NUMBER FOUR CITIZENS  . 571D DESC CAT 3      PROSE
    LESS BUT I DARE SAY THAT CHAUCER  . . . . . . . . .  . 572A DESC CAT 3        PROSE
    WHEREAS CHAUCER SAYS OF HIS RICH CITIZENS  . . . . . .  572A DESC CAT 3       PROSE
    THE CHARACTERS OF WOMEN CHAUCER HAS DIVIDED INTO        572B DESC CAT 3       PROSE
        TWO CLASSES
    WIFE OF BATH IN WHOSE CHARACTER CHAUCER HAS BEEN EQUALLY 572B DESC CAT 3      PROSE
    SAY NO MORE OF HER NOR EXPOSE WHAT CHAUCER HAS LEFT HIDDEN 572B DESC CAT 3    PROSE
    THIS CHARACTER VARIES FROM THAT OF CHAUCER AS THE  . .  572B DESC CAT 3       PROSE
    TWO FIRST CHARACTERS IN CHAUCER THE KNIGHT AND THE SQUIRE 573C DESC CAT 3     PROSE
    CALLS THE SQUIRE THE POP OF CHAUCER'S AGE NOW HEAR CHAUCER 573C DESC CAT 3    PROSE
    CANNOT FIND IN CHAUCER WHO HAS ONLY ONE MONK AND THAT  . 574A DESC CAT 3      PROSE
    TO BE SURE CHAUCER IS A LITTLE DIFFICULT TO HIM WHO HAS  574A DESC CAT 3      PROSE
        ONLY
    RESOLVED TO GO CONTRARY IN EVERYTHING TO CHAUCER WHO SAYS 574A DESC CAT 3     PROSE
    APPEARS IN HER CHEEKS NOW HEAR WHAT CHAUCER HAS MADE HER 574B DESC CAT 3      PROSE
    CHAUCER HIMSELF AS A KNAVE WHO THRUSTS HIMSELF  . . . . 574D DESC CAT 3       PROSE
    BUT IT APPEARS IN ALL THE WRITINGS OF CHAUCER  . . . .  575A DESC CAT 3       PROSE
    CHAUCER HAS NO WHERE CALLED THE PLOWMAN OLD  . . . . .  575A DESC CAT 3       PROSE
    HE HAS INTRODUCED A CHARACTER THAT CHAUCER HAS NOT  . . 575B DESC CAT 3       PROSE
    A SEA CAPTAIN CHAUCER HAS A SHIP-MAN A SAILOR  . . . .  575C DESC CAT 3       PROSE
    SEA CAPTAIN CHAUCER HAS PURPOSELY OMITTED SUCH A PERSONAGE 575C DESC CAT 3    PROSE
    BLAKE'S CHAUCER THE CANTERBURY PILGRIMS THE FRESCO PICTURE 586C CHAUCER 1     TITLE
    BLAKE'S CHAUCER AN ORIGINAL ENGRAVING BY WILLIAM BLAKE . 587D CHAUCER/N       TITLE
    SIR JEFFERY CHAUCER & THE NINE & TWENTY PILGRIMS  . .   588B CHAUCER/N        TITLE
    CHAUCER HIMSELF & THE REEVE COMES AS CHAUCER HAS DESCRIBED 588C CHAUCER/N     PROSE
    BLAKE'S CHAUCER AN ORIGINAL ENGRAVING BY HIM  . . . .  589C CHAUCER 2         TITLE
    FROM HIS FRESCO PAINTING OF SIR JEFFREY CHAUCER AND  . . 589C CHAUCER 2       TITLE
```

	PAGE	TITLE	LINE
CHAUCER (CONTINUED)			
CHAUCER HIMSELF AND THE REEVE COMES AS CHAUCER HAS DESCRIBED	590A	CHAUCER 2	PROSE
"SIR JEFFREY CHAUCER AND HIS PILGRIMS SET OUT FOR CANTERBURY"	590B	CHAUCER 2	PROSE
PILGRIMS FROM CHAUCER CONTAINING ANECDOTES OF ARTISTS PRICE...	591B	PUB ADDRESS/N	PROSE
AND BACON & NEWTON & LOCKE & MILTON & SHAKSPEAR & CHAUCER	745	JERUSALEM 98	9
CHAUCER'S			
TO HAVE APPEARD IN CHAUCER'S TIME INTERSPERSED	567A	DESC CAT 3	PROSE
THE CHARACTERS OF CHAUCER'S PILGRIMS ARE THE CHARACTERS	567B	DESC CAT 3	PROSE
OF CHAUCER'S CHARACTERS AS DESCRIBED IN HIS CANTERBURY TALES	567C	DESC CAT 3	PROSE
PERFECTLY DELINEATED IN THOSE PARTS OF CHAUCER'S WORK .	568C	DESC CAT 3	PROSE
IT IS NECESSARY HERE TO SPEAK OF CHAUCER'S OWN CHARACTER	569A	DESC CAT 3	PROSE
AND NOBLE HOUSEKEEPER CHAUCER'S MONK IS INTENDED . . .	569C	DESC CAT 3	PROSE
AND SO ARE CHAUCER'S LET THEM BE SO CONSIDERED	570A	DESC CAT 3	PROSE
READ CHAUCER'S DESCRIPTION OF THE GOOD PARSON AND BOW .	570C	DESC CAT 3	PROSE
CHAUCER'S LAWYER IS A CHARACTER OF GREAT VENERABLENESS .	570D	DESC CAT 3	PROSE
CHAUCER'S CHARACTERS LIVE AGE AFTER AGE	570D	DESC CAT 3	PROSE
THE MILLER IS THE HERCULES &C CHAUCER'S CHARACTERS ARE .	571A	DESC CAT 3	PROSE
CALLS THE SQUIRE THE FOP OF CHAUCER'S AGE NOW HEAR CHAUCER	573C	DESC CAT 3	PROSE
AND HIS FRIEND ARE EQUALLY MASTERS OF CHAUCER'S LANGUAGE	574B	DESC CAT 3	PROSE
REPRESENTING CHAUCER'S CHARACTERS PAINTED BY WILLIAM BLAKE	586C	CHAUCER 1	TITLE
FROM HIS FRESCO PAINTING OF CHAUCER'S CANTERBURY PILGRIMS	587D	CHAUCER/N	TITLE
ON HORSEBACK OF CHAUCER'S CHARACTERS WHERE EVERY CHARACTER &	587D	CHAUCER/N	PROSE
TO HAVE APPEARD IN CHAUCER'S TIME INTERSPERSED	588D	CHAUCER/N	PROSE
THE CHARACTERS OF CHAUCER'S PILGRIMS ARE THE CHARACTERS	589A	CHAUCER/N	PROSE
TO HAVE APPEARD IN CHAUCER'S TIME INTERSPERSED . . .	590B	CHAUCER 2	PROSE
OF CHAUCER'S CHARACTERS AS DESCRIBED IN HIS CANTERBURY TALES	590C	CHAUCER 2	PROSE
CHAUCER'S CANTERBURY PILGRIMS BEING A COMPLETE INDEX . .	591A	PUB ADDRESS/N	TITLE
CHAUNT			
THEN LOS UTTERED WITH HAMMER & ANVIL CHAUNT REVOICE . . .	688	JERUSALEM 56	29
CHAUNTANT			
AND TUNES HER [?CHAUNTANT] NOTES WHEN BUXOM JOY DOTH FAN HIS WINGS	43B	WOE CRIED MUSE	*PROSE
CHAUNTED			
AND CHAUNTED HIS SONG LABOURING WITH THE TONGS AND HAMMER	625	JERUSALEM 6	* 11
THE PRAISE OF JEHOVAH IS CHAUNTED FROM LIPS OF HUNGER & THIRST	656	JERUSALEM 30	32
AND THUS HE CHAUNTED HIS SONG THE DAUGHTERS OF ALBION REPLY	687	JERUSALEM 56	2
CHEAP			
BECAUSE HE MAKES DESIGNS SO VERY CHEAP	537	AND HIS LEGS/N	38
CHEAPER			
MODEST MEAT IS CHEAPER THAN IN LONDON BUT THE SWEET AIR &	803B	LETTER 15	PROSE
CHEAR			
SO I PIPED WITH MERRY CHEAR	111	INTRODUCTN/SI	6
SING THY SONGS OF HAPPY CHEAR	111	INTRODUCTN/SI	10
CHEAR UP THY COUNTENANCE BRIGHT BOY & GO TO ENION . . .	371	FOUR ZOAS 9	545
CHEARFUL			
HE WAS AS CHEARFUL AS A PRINCE & GAVE ME ENTERTAINMENT	102	TIRIEL 3	10
TO THE BELLS' CHEARFUL SOUND	116	ECCHOING GR/SI	8
. . . THE CLOUD AND VISION DESCENDS OVER CHEARFUL FRANCE	134	FRENCH REVOLTN	1
& FOUND HIM QUITE AS CHEARFUL AS YOU DESCRIBE HIM & BY HIS	835C	LETTER 35	PROSE
CHEARFULNESS			
ALL WAS CHEARFULNESS & GOOD HUMOUR ON THE ROAD & YET WE	802B	LETTER 14	PROSE
CHEARFULNESS & WELCOME THO OUR LUGGAGE WAS VERY HEAVY .	803A	LETTER 15	PROSE
CHEARING			
WHEN IN MY FATHER'S HOUSE I SAT & HEARD HIS CHEARING VOICE	375	FOUR ZOAS 9	689
CHEARS			
& HIS FLUTE HEARD FROM HIS SECRET FORESTS CHEARS US TO . .	791C	LETTER 3	PROSE
CHEAT			
[CR (CROMEK)] HE LOVES THE ART BUT [THE] TIS THE ART TO CHEAT	540	CR LOVES ART/N	* 2
CHEATED			
PERSUADED TO PRINT IN LONDON YOU WILL BE CHEATED EVERY WAY	847B	LETTER 44	PROSE
CHEATING			
WHERE CHEATING IS THERES MISCHIEF THERE	16	BLIND-MANS/PS	38
OR THE CHEATING WAVES OF CHARTERD STREAMS	166	WHY CARE FOR/N	2
THO BORN ON THE CHEATING BANKS OF THAMES	166	WHY CARE FOR/N	5
CHEATS			
WATCHMAN THE NIGHT IS THICK & DARKNESS CHEATS MY RAYIE SIGHT	335	FOUR ZOAS 7B	94
CHEBAR'S			
IN EVERY MAN EZEKIEL SAW THEM BY CHEBAR'S FLOOD	632	JERUSALEM 12	58
CHECKING			
THEY WONDERD CHECKING THEIR WILD FLAMES & MANY GATHERING	686	JERUSALEM 55	3
CHEEK			
FLOURISH DOWN THE BRIGHT CHEEK OF MODEST EVE	2	TO AUTUMN/PS	10
ON THE COLD STONE HER PALE [CHEEKS] CHEEK SICKLY SMELLS	4	FAIR ELENOR/PS	6
SEEST THOU WHERE MIRTH SITS ON THE PAINTED CHEEK . . .	37A	CONTEMPLATN/PS	PROSE
BLOOM ON EVERY MAIDEN'S CHEEK	63	SHEPHERD FIRST	6
OER THY CHEEK & OER THY BREAST	165	CRADLE SONG/N	12
FROM THY CHEEK & FROM THY EYE	165	CRADLE SONG/N	24
OF SUMMER I HAVE SEEN THEE SLEEP & TURN THY CHEEK DELIGHTED	288	FOUR ZOAS 2	313
O MY SWEET CHILDREN ENION LET THARMAS KISS THY CHEEK . .	371	FOUR ZOAS 9	525
CHEEKS			
ON THE COLD STONE HER PALE [CHEEKS] CHEEK SICKLY SMELLS	4	FAIR ELENOR/PS	6
. . . TEARS FELL DOWN THE SHADY CHEEKS AT HIS FEET MANY CLOTHD	140	FRENCH REVOLTN	132

	PAGE	TITLE	LINE
CHEEKS (CONTINUED)			
WITH HER FAIR CRYSTAL CLEARNESS IN HER LIPS & CHEEKS HIS POISONS ROSE	269	FOUR ZOAS 1	185
WITH SILENT FEAR & HIS IMMORTAL CHEEKS GREW DEADLY PALE	307	FOUR ZOAS 5	87
. . . IN HER LIPS & CHEEKS HIS [POISONS] METALS ROSE .	381	FOUR ZOAS AD 5	5
. . . PUFFING HIS CHEEKS HE REPLIED A GREAT WIG	553	ASKD PRIGG/N	6
APPEARS IN HER CHEEKS NOW HEAR WHAT CHAUCER HAS MADE HER	574B	DESC CAT 3	PROSE
AND WITH TEARS COLD ON THEIR CHEEKS THEY WEARY REPOSE .	671	JERUSALEM 42	70
HIS IMMORTAL CHEEKS REARING HIS HANDS TO HEAVEN FOR AID DIVINE	711	JERUSALEM 71	57
CHEER SEE CHEAR			
CHEERFULLY			
EVERY BODY COMPLAINS YET ALL GO ON CHEERFULLY AND WITH SPIRIT	831D	LETTER 31	PROSE
CHELSEA			
FROM RANELAGH & STRUMBOLO FROM CROMWELLS GARDENS & CHELSEA	627	JERUSALEM 8	2
BATTERSEA AND CHELSEA MOURN FOR CANBEL & GWENDOLEN . . .	644	JERUSALEM 21	32
BATTERSEA & CHELSEA MOURN LONDON & CANTERBURY TREMBLE . .	659	JERUSALEM 33	12
CHELTENHAM			
& TAKE A MUTTON CHOP WITH US THE DAY YOU GO TO CHELTENHAM	870C	LETTER 72	PROSE
CHEMOSH			
IN TYRE & SIDON I SAW BAAL & ASHTAROTH IN MOAB CHEMOSH . .	528	MILTON 37	20
O CHEMOSH O BACCHUS O VENUS O DOUBLE GOD OF GENERATION	706	JERUSALEM 68	18
HE COMBINES INTO A MIGHTY-ONE THE DOUBLE MOLECH & CHEMOSH	729	JERUSALEM 84	21
MOLECH & CHEMOSH & IN HIS LEFT BREAST IS PHILISTEA . . .	735	JERUSALEM 89	31
CHERISH			
THEN CHERISH PITY LEST YOU DRIVE AN ANGEL FROM YOUR DOOR	59	HOLY THURS/IM	18
THEN CHERISH PITY LEST YOU DRIVE AN ANGEL FROM YOUR DOOR	122	HOLY THURS/SI	12
AND NONE TO ANSWER NONE TO CHERISH THEE WITH MOTHER'S SMILES	129	BOOK OF THEL 4	6
TO COMPASS IT WITH SWADDLING BANDS AND WHO SHALL CHERISH IT	239	EUROPE PREL 2	14
THEY ADORE & HIS REVENGE CHERISH WITH THE BLOOD OF THE INNOCENT	704	JERUSALEM 67	21
CHERISHD			
THAT WILFUL BRUISD ITS HELPLESS FORM BUT THAT HE CHERISHD IT	130	BOOK OF THEL 5	10
THE NETHER ABYSS IN TREMBLINGS HE WEPT OVER IT HE CHERISHD IT	483	MILTON 3	32
CHERRIES			
WHERE OUR TABLE WITH CHERRIES AND NUTS IS SPREAD	63	SHEPHERD YOUNG	10
AND THOU SHALT HELP US TO CATCH BIRDS & GATHER THEM RIPE CHERRIES	102	TIRIEL 3	15
WHERE OUR TABLE WITH CHERRIES AND NUTS IS SPREAD	125	LAUGHING/SI	10
CHERRY			
LIKE A CHERRY CLAPPER ARADOBO ASKD WHO WAS PHEBUS SIR . .	46D	ISLAND MOON 3	PROSE
CHERUB			
FOR THE CHERUB WITH HIS FLAMING SWORD IS HEREBY COMMANDED	154B	MARRIAGE HH 14	PROSE
IN THE WHOLE PLACE OF THE COVERING CHERUB ROME BABYLON & TYRE	490	MILTON 9	51
JERUSALEM IS HIS GARMENT & NOT THY COVERING CHERUB O LOVELY	499	MILTON 18	37
PREPARING IT FOR THE GREAT CONSUMMATION RED THE CHERUB ON SINAI	502	MILTON 20	23
UNWAKEND AND THE COVERING CHERUB ADVANCES FROM THE EAST	506	MILTON 23	10
HOW LONG BENEATH THE COVERING CHERUB GIVE OUR EMANATIONS	507	MILTON 23	12
HE HATH ENTERD INTO THE COVERING CHERUB BECOME ONE WITH	507	MILTON 23	14
ARISE INTO THE COVERING CHERUB WHO IS THE SPECTRE OF ALBION	508	MILTON 24	28
UPON HIS ROCK BENEATH HIS TOMB I SAW THE COVERING CHERUB	508	MILTON 24	30
I SAW HE WAS THE COVERING CHERUB & WITHIN HIM SATAN . . .	527	MILTON 37	8
ALL THESE ARE SEEN IN MILTON'S SHADOW WHO IS THE COVERING CHERUB	528	MILTON 37	44
THE HEAVENS ARE THE CHERUB THE TWELVE GODS ARE SATAN . .	529	MILTON 37	60
AND [SMILD LIKE A CHERUB & SAID]	553	ASKD PRIGG/N *	6
. . . SMILE LIKE A CHERUB & SAY A PAINT BRUSH	553	ASKD PRIGG/N	10
AND THESE UNITED INTO RAHAB IN THE COVERING CHERUB ON EUPHRATES	624	JERUSALEM 5	42
HE VIEWS THE CHERUB AT THE TREE OF LIFE ALSO THE SERPENT	634	JERUSALEM 14	2
NOR IN HAVILAH WHERE THE CHERUB ROLLD HIS REDOUNDING FLAME	686	JERUSALEM 55	22
THUS WAS THE COVERING CHERUB REVEALD MAJESTIC IMAGE . .	734	JERUSALEM 89	9
HIDDEN WITHIN THE COVERING CHERUB AS IN A TABERNACLE . .	735	JERUSALEM 89	44
SO JESUS SPOKE THE COVERING CHERUB COMING ON IN DARKNESS	743	JERUSALEM 96	17
CHERUBIM			
[LET CHERUBIM & SERAPHIM NOW RAISE THEIR VOICES HIGH] . .	59	HOLY THURS/IM	14
A CHERUBIM DOES CEASE TO SING	431	AUGURIES	16
IN PLACE OF THE ARK [WITH] THE [TWO] CHERUBIM BOWING OVER IT	444B	LAST JUDGMNT/L	PROSE
WHERE THE VICTIMS WERE PREPARING FOR SACRIFICE THEIR CHERUBIM	484	MILTON 4	22
OF PRECIOUS STONES BY CHERUBIM SURROUNDED SO PERMITTED . .	531	MILTON 39	25
HIS CHERUBIM & SERAPHIM IN EVER HAPPY ETERNITY	531	MILTON 39	28
THE CHERUBIM WHICH WERE SCULPTURED AND PAINTED	565C	DESC CAT 2	PROSE
THE GRECIAN GODS WERE THE ANCIENT CHERUBIM OF PHOENICIA	571B	DESC CAT 3	PROSE
IN WHICH ARE THE TWO CHERUBIM THAT BOWD OVER THE ARK .	613B	V LAST JUDG/N	PROSE
THE WESTERN GATE FOURFOLD IS CLOSD HAVING FOUR CHERUBIM	633	JERUSALEM 13	6
THY TABERNACLE TAKEN DOWN THY SECRET CHERUBIM DISCLOSED	644	JERUSALEM 21	21
WHEN FORGIVENESS MIGHT IT WEAVE WITH WINGS OF CHERUBIM .	645	JERUSALEM 22	35
WHICH THE MALE ENTERS MAGNIFICENT BETWEEN HER CHERUBIM .	656	JERUSALEM 30	35
WHEN THE FOUR ZOAS OF ALBION THE FOUR LIVING CREATURES THE CHERUBIM	696	JERUSALEM 63	2
DANCE THE DANCE OF DEATH CONTENDING WITH JEHOVAH AMONG THE CHERUBIM	697	JERUSALEM 63	10
THOR & FRIGA & THE FAIRIES LEAD THE MOON ALONG THE VALLEY OF CHERUBIM	697	JERUSALEM 63	14

	PAGE	TITLE	LINE

CHERUBIM   (CONTINUED)
WHEN THE CHERUBIM HID THEIR HEADS UNDER THEIR WINGS IN   697 JERUSALEM 63   24
    DEEP SLUMBERS
OF AGES & GENERATIONS FOLDING & UNFOLDING IT LIKE A VEIL   698 JERUSALEM 64   3
    OF CHERUBIM
THY GOLDEN MOUNTAINS WHERE MY CHERUBIM & SERAPHIM REJOICD   721 JERUSALEM 79   54
THE PILLARS OF JERUSALEM BETWEEN MY WINGED CHERUBIM   . .   721 JERUSALEM 79   59
WERE COPIED FROM THE CHERUBIM OF SOLOMON'S TEMPLE   . . . 775D INSC LAOCOON   TITLE
THE GODS OF PRIAM ARE THE CHERUBIM OF MOSES & SOLOMON   . . 777B INSC LAOCOON   PROSE
CHERUBIMS
THE MERCY SEAT IS ABOVE UPON THE ARK CHERUBIMS   . . . .   82A ANNO LAVATER   MARG
THY CLOUDS OF BLESSING THY CHERUBIMS OF TENDER-MERCY   . . 647 JERUSALEM 24   21
OF JERUSALEM'S CHERUBIMS & TO FORGE THEM SWORDS OF HER   729 JERUSALEM 84   10
    ALTARS
CHERUBS
TO THE ABHORRED BIRTH OF CHERUBS IN THE HUMAN FORM   . . . 193 V DAU ALBION 5   28
WHERE ONCE THE CHERUBS OF JERUSALEM SPREAD TO LAMBETH'S   525 MILTON 35   10
    VALE
WITH ONE ACCORD IN LOVE SUBLIME & AS ON CHERUBS WINGS   . . 674 JERUSALEM 44   1
HER TWO COVERING CHERUBS AFTERWARDS NAMED VOLTAIRE   702 JERUSALEM 66   12
    & ROUSSEAU
CHESELDEN
UPON THE CHESELDEN HILLS THINKING TO SLEEP ON THE SEVERN   703 JERUSALEM 66   75
CHESHIRE
JOSEPH STAFFORD SHROPS HEREF BENJAMIN DERBY CHESHIRE   637 JERUSALEM 16   49
    MONMOUTH
PEACHEY HAD NORTH WALES SHROPSHIRE CHESHIRE & THE ISLE   710 JERUSALEM 71   30
    OF MAN
CHESHIRE & LANCASHIRE & WESTMORELAND GROAN IN ANGUISH   . . 736 JERUSALEM 90   18
CHESNUT
[THE BARKED OAK THE LONG LIMBD BEECH THE CHESNUT TREE THE   269 FOUR ZOAS 1   * 204
    PINE]
CHEST
HIS NOSE HIGH ON THE RIDGE AND NARROW HIS CHEST AND THE   580A DESC CAT 5   PROSE
THEY DIVIDE TO TWELVE THE KEY-BONES & THE CHEST DIVIDING   708 JERUSALEM 70   12
    IN PAIN
CHESTER
OF NORWICH PETERBORO ROCHESTER CHESTER AWFUL WORCESTER   . . 676 JERUSALEM 46   18
CHESTER'S
IN THE DIVIDING OF REUBEN & BENJAMIN BLEEDING FROM   697 JERUSALEM 63   12
    CHESTER'S RIVER
OF BENJAMIN FROM CHESTER'S RIVER LOUD THE RIVER LOUD   736 JERUSALEM 90   15
    THE MERSEY
CHESTS
THE CITIZENS OF NEW-YORK CLOSE THEIR BOOKS & LOCK THEIR   201 AMERICA 14   13
    CHESTS
CHETWYND
AS TO GIVE TO MRS CHETWYND IF SHE SHOULD CALL OR SEND   . . 821B LETTER 25   PROSE
I HAD THE PLEASURE OF A CALL FROM MRS CHETWYND &   . . . . 850C LETTER 49   PROSE
WITH ROMNEY'S DESIGNS MRS C(CHETWYND) SENT TO ME THE   . . 850C LETTER 49   PROSE
CHEVIOT
THE MALVERN AND THE CHEVIOT THE WOLDS PLINLIMMON & SNOWDON   622 JERUSALEM 4   30
BECAUSE THE PEAK MALVERN & CHEVIOT REASON IN CRUELTY   . . 644 JERUSALEM 21   34
SUCH THE APPEARANCE IN CHEVIOT IN THE DIVISIONS OF REUBEN   697 JERUSALEM 63   23
AND ALL THE LAND OF CANAAN SUSPENDED OVER THE VALLEY OF   698 JERUSALEM 63   42
    CHEVIOT
THEY FORGD THE SWORD ON CHEVIOT THE CHARIOT OF WAR & THE   699 JERUSALEM 65   14
    BATTLE-AX
UPON EAST MOOR IN DERBYSHIRE & ALONG THE VALLEYS OF CHEVIOT 740 JERUSALEM 93   6
CHIARO SCURO,CHIARO OSCURO
ALL IS CHIARO SCURO POCO PEN [&] ITS ALL COLORING   . . . 554 TO VENETIAN/N   * 11
THAT INFERNAL MACHINE CALLED CHIARO OSCURO IN THE HANDS OF   582C DESC CAT 9   PROSE
CHICHESTER
BECAUSE W(WILLIAM) REFUSED TO GO WITH HIM TO CHICHESTER   438C BLAKES MEMORAN PROSE
REACHD ALL THE WAY FROM CHICHESTER TO YORK   . . . . .   536 AND HIS LEGS/N   2
THE FLOOD AND WAS NAMD CHICHESTER LOVELY MILD & GENTLE LO   667 JERUSALEM 40   50
THRO ROCHESTER AND CHICHESTER & EXETER & SALISBURY   . . . 704 JERUSALEM 67   36
DIRECT TO MR BLAKE FELPHAM NEAR CHICHESTER SUSSEX   . . . 803D LETTER 15   *PROSE
CHICHESTER IS A VERY HANDSOM CITY SEVEN MILES FROM US   . . 806B LETTER 16   PROSE
FROM A JUSTICE OF PEACE IN CHICHESTER WHICH WAS TAKEN OUT   826D LETTER 28   PROSE
AT CHICHESTER THIS MORNING BUT THEY AS THE LAWYER WHO   . . 827D LETTER 28   PROSE
& MR SEAGRAVE PRINTER AT CHICHESTER   . . . . 828A LETTER 28   PROSE
YET RECEIVED THE HISTORY OF CHICHESTER I MENTION THIS NOT   853D LETTER 52   PROSE
WITH THE PRINTING OF OUR FRIEND THE CHICHESTER PRINTER HERE 856B LETTER 54   PROSE
(SECOND) FOR THE HONOUR OF CHICHESTER MR P(PHILLIPS)   . . 856B LETTER 54   PROSE
WILLIAM HAYLEY ESQRE FELPHAM NEAR CHICHESTER SUSSEX   . . . SUPP ADDRESSES/L   *TITLE
WILLIAM HAYLEY ESQR EARTHAM NEAR CHICHESTER SUSSEX   . . . SUPP ADDRESSES/L   *TITLE
WILLIAM HAYLEY ESQRE AT MISS POOLE'S LAVANT NEAR CHICHESTER SUPP ADDRESS/L 13   *TITLE
    SUSSEX
CHICKEN
WITH WHAT SENSE IS IT THAT THE CHICKEN SHUNS THE RAVENOUS   191 V DAU ALBION 3   2
    HAWK
CHID
I CHID THEM BOTH BUT GAVE THEM NOBLE HOPES   . . . . . . 25 EDW THIRD/PS 3   169
CHIDE
AND CHIDE MY MAKER THEE O SUN THAT RAISEDST ME TO FALL   . . 368 FOUR ZOAS 9   412
CHIEF
[AND ALL IN ORDER SIT WAITING THE CHIEF CHANTER'S COMMANDS]   59 HOLY THURS/IM   8
THE FIVE SENSES THE CHIEF INLETS OF SOUL IN THIS AGE   . . 149D MARRIAGE HH 4   PROSE
AND WAS ERECTED AT THE CHIEF ENTRANCE OF URIZEN'S HALL   . . 285 FOUR ZOAS 2   200
TO DEPRESS WHAT IS ITS CHIEF & ONLY SUPPORT   . . . . . 445C ANNO REYNOLDS   MARG
CLEARNESS AND PRECISION HAVE BEEN THE CHIEF OBJECTS   . . . 564D DESC CAT 1   PROSE

	PAGE	TITLE	LINE
CHIEF (CONTINUED)			
THESE I SUPPOSE TO HAVE THE CHIEF AGENCY IN	612A	V LAST JUDG/N	PROSE
TO WHOM I MAKE THEE INVISIBLE BUT CHIEF TO MY OWN CHILDREN	629	JERUSALEM 10	31
CONCERNING MY CHIEF DELIGHT BUT THOU HAST BROKEN SILENCE	630	JERUSALEM 10	41
BABYLON IS OUR CHIEF DESIRE MOAB OUR BATH IN SUMMER . . .	725	JERUSALEM 82	31
AGAINST THE ACCUSER'S CHIEF DESIRE	761	FOR SEXES/GP	3
UPON YOU AS THE CHIEF OF MY FRIENDS WHOM I WOULD ENDEAVOUR	815A	LETTER 23	PROSE
THE TESTAMENT IS MY CHIEF MASTER ASTONISHING INDEED IS . .	821D	LETTER 25	PROSE
HIS CHIEF BEAUTIES BUT THERE ARE SOME WHICH MAY BE EXECUTED	848A	LETTER 45	PROSE
FOR OUR GOOD SEAGRAVE & SAID I KNEW YOUR CHIEF INTENTIONS IN	856B	LETTER 54	PROSE
P'S(PHILLIPS') CHIEF OBJECTION TO THE MANNER IN WHICH . .	857B	LETTER 54	PROSE
ME GREAT REPUTATION AS AN ARTIST WHICH WAS THE CHIEF THING	867C	LETTER 66	PROSE
CHIEFEST			
THESE ARE THE IDIOT'S CHIEFEST ARTS	547	LET BE TOLD/N	6
CHIEFLY			
FALSE THE ANCIENTS WERE CHIEFLY ATTENTIVE TO COMPLICATED	466B	ANNO REYNOLDS	MARG
BY THIS DISPLAY OF PRETENDED VIRTUE CHIEFLY DESIGN TO EXPOSE	682D	JERUSALEM 52	PROSE
WHICH HAVE SINCE OCCURRED & CHIEFLY THE UNHEALTHINESS OF THE	811C	LETTER 22	PROSE
CHIEFS			
HIS CHIEFS COME RUSHING ROUND	12	GWIN KING/PS	38
CHILD SEE MAN CHILD			
FOR COMMERCE THO THE CHILD OF AGRICULTURE	19	EDW THIRD/PS 2	31
THAT PLAYS WITH DANGER AS THE INNOCENT CHILD	27	EDW THIRD/PS 3	241
O MY CHILD MY CHILD IS THY BREATH INFECTED SO IS MINE . .	36B	COUCH DEATH/PS	PROSE
FOR NOW HE HAD A CHILD	50	WHEN CORRUP/IM	8
AND WHEN THE CHILD BEGAN TO SWELL	51	WHEN CORRUP/IM	29
AND THE CHILD WAS WET WITH DEW	60	LIT BOY LST/IM	6
THE MIRE WAS DEEP & THE CHILD DID WEEP	60	LIT BOY LST/IM	7
("KEEP DISTANT WHO HATES...LAUGH OF A CHILD") THE BEST IN THE BOOK	74B	ANNO LAVATER	MARG
OFFENDED WITH THE INNOCENCE OF A CHILD & FOR THE SAME REASON	87C	ANNO LAVATER	MARG
TRUE I WAS BORN THY [CHILD] SLAVE WHO ASKD THEE TO SAVE ME FROM DEATH	107	TIRIEL 6	14
UNLESS THOU LEAD ME TO THE TENT OF HAR CHILD OF THE CURSE	108	TIRIEL 6	34
THE CHILD SPRINGS FROM THE WOMB THE FATHER READY STANDS TO FORM	110	TIRIEL 8	25
ON A CLOUD I SAW A CHILD	111	INTRODUCTN/SI	3
EVERY CHILD MAY JOY TO HEAR	111	INTRODUCTN/SI	20
IS YOUR LITTLE CHILD	112	LIT GRL LST/SI	22
AND DREAM THEY SEE THEIR CHILD	114	LIT GRL FND/SI	11
AND SAW THEIR SLEEPING CHILD	115	LIT GRL FND/SI	47
HE BECAME A LITTLE CHILD	115	THE LAMB/SI	16
I A CHILD & THOU A LAMB	115	THE LAMB/SI	17
IS MAN HIS CHILD AND CARE	117	DIVINE IMAGE/SI	8
HOVER OER MY HAPPY CHILD	120	CRADLE SONG/SI	8
SLEEP SLEEP HAPPY CHILD	120	CRADLE SONG/SI	17
THE CHILD WAS WET WITH DEW	121	LIT BOY LST/SI	6
THE MIRE WAS DEEP & THE CHILD DID WEEP	121	LIT BOY LST/SI	7
HE KISSED THE CHILD & BY THE HAND LED	121	LIT BOY FND/SI	5
CAN A FATHER SEE HIS CHILD	122	ON ANOTHERS/SI	7
HOW CAN A CHILD WHEN FEARS ANNOY	124	SCHOOL BOY/SI	18
WHITE AS AN ANGEL IS THE ENGLISH CHILD	125	LIT BLK BOY/SI	3
AND NARROW AS A GRAVE DUG FOR A CHILD	136	FRENCH REVOLTN	40
. . . THE PALE MOTHER NOURISHES HER CHILD TO THE DEADLY SLAUGHTER	143	FRENCH REVOLTN	210
IN [EVERY VOICE OF EVERY CHILD] EVERY INFANT'S CRY OF FEAR	170	LONDON/N	6
THE PRIEST SAT BY AND HEARD THE CHILD	177	LIT BOY LST/N	9
THE WEEPING CHILD COULD NOT BE HEARD	177	LIT BOY LST/N	20
OR WHO WILL EXCHANGE HIS NEW BORN CHILD	186	LET BROTHELS/N	70
NOW THOU MAIST MARRY BROMION'S HARLOT AND PROTECT THE CHILD	190	V DAU ALBION 2	1
TILL THE CHILD DWELL WITH ONE HE HATES AND DO THE DEED HE LOATHS	193	V DAU ALBION 5	30
WHO TAUGHT THEE MODESTY SUBTIL MODESTY CHILD OF NIGHT & SLEEP	193	V DAU ALBION 6	7
THE PRIEST SAT BY AND HEARD THE CHILD	218	LIT BOY LST/SE	9
THE WEEPING CHILD COULD NOT BE HEARD	218	LIT BOY LST/SE	17
HOWLING THE CHILD WITH FIERCE FLAMES	232	URIZEN 19	45
THEY NAMED THE CHILD ORC HE GREW	233	URIZEN 20	6
THE DEAD HEARD THE VOICE OF THE CHILD	233	URIZEN 20	26
ALL THINGS HEARD THE VOICE OF THE CHILD	233	URIZEN 20	28
WHAT TIME THE SECRET CHILD	239	EUROPE 4	2
WHY WILT THOU GIVE UP WOMAN'S SECRECY MY MELANCHOLY CHILD	244	EUROPE 14	22
TO RESTRAIN THE CHILD FROM THE WOMB	247	SONG OF LOS 6	24
CHILDREN ARE NOURISHD FOR THE SLAUGHTER ONCE THE CHILD WAS FED	275	FOUR ZOAS 1	400
TILL FROM HER HEART RENDING HIS WAY A TERRIBLE CHILD SPRANG FORTH	306	FOUR ZOAS 5	37
ENITHARMON NURSD HER FIERY CHILD IN THE DARK DEEPS . . .	307	FOUR ZOAS 5	70
O THOU POOR HUMAN FORM O THOU POOR CHILD OF WOE . . .	348	FOUR ZOAS 8	298
AWAKE THARMAS AWAKE AWAKE THOU CHILD OF DEWY TEARS . .	371	FOUR ZOAS 9	521
WHY WEEPEST THOU THARMAS CHILD OF TEARS IN THE BRIGHT HOUSE OF JOY	371	FOUR ZOAS 9	* 530
DEAR CHILD I ALSO BY PLEASANT STREAMS	427	LAND OF DREAMS	13
PROUD MARY S GONE MAD SAID THE CHILD IN THE STREET . . .	428	MARY	34
HE WHO SHALL TEACH THE CHILD TO DOUBT	433	AUGURIES	87
NOR CAN A CHILD BE BORN WHO IS NOT ONE OF THESE CHARACTERS	570D	DESC CAT 3	PROSE
THAT A HEALTHY CHILD SHOULD BE TAUGHT & COMPELLD TO WALK	599D	PUB ADDRESS/N	PROSE

329

```
                                                          PAGE      TITLE          LINE
CHILD    (CONTINUED)
   AND EVERY ENGLISH CHILD IS SEEN      . . . . . . . .    650  FIELDS FROM/J       19
   TO THEE MARY THY WIFE FOR SHE IS WITH CHILD BY THE HOLY  695  JERUSALEM 61        27
      GHOST
   O THOU POOR HUMAN FORM SAID SHE O THOU POOR CHILD OF WOE  705  JERUSALEM 67       44
   WHERE HIDES MY CHILD IN OXFORD HIDEST THOU WITH ANTAMON   727  JERUSALEM 83       28
   OF BABYLON LED BY A CHILD HIS TEARS RUN DOWN HIS BEARD . .  729  JERUSALEM 84     12
   WHEN BUT A CHILD HE RAN AWAY     . . . . . . . . . .     750  EV GOSPEL(C)/N       3
   WHEN BUT A CHILD HE RAN AWAY     . . . . . . . . . .     751  EV GOSPEL(D)/N       5
   JESUS SUPPOSES EVERY THING TO BE EVIDENT TO THE CHILD  . .  774D  ANNO BERKELEY    MARG
   PROTESTANT CONSIDERS NATURE AS INCAPABLE OF BEARING A CHILD  779A  ANNO CELLINI    MARG
   A FATHER TAKING LEAVE OF HIS WIFE & CHILD IS WATCHD  . . .  792B  LETTER 4         PROSE
   I REMAIND AS A CHILD    . . . . . . . . . . . .          806  TO BUTTS/L          72
   ON THE SCORE OF PARENTAL DUTY LITERATURE IS YOUR CHILD  .  842A  LETTER 41        PROSE
   THE CHILD IN HIS ARMS WHETHER BOY OR GIRL SIGNIFIES NOT   864B  LETTER 61        PROSE
   THE CHILD IS AS BEAUTIFULLY DRAWN AS IT IS COLOURED IN    864B  LETTER 61        PROSE
      BOTH
   THE NAME OF THE CHILD WHICH CERTAINLY OUGHT TO BE THOMAS   874B  LETTER 79        PROSE
   GUARDIAN ANGEL CHILD ANGEL OF DEATH MOTHER       . . . .  SUPP  INSC HERVEY      *TITLE
   WHERE IS YOUR FATHER THE LOST CHILD ORPHANS     . . . .   SUPP  INSC HERVEY      *TITLE
   FRONTISPIECE OF CHILD ON THE SHEPHERD'S HEAD    . . . .   SUPP  LETTER 66A       *PROSE
CHILDBED
   SOPHRONIA DIED IN CHILDBED SHE DIED ON THE WEDDING DAY    SUPP  INSC HERVEY      *TITLE
CHILDBIRTH
   I HEAR THE SCREECH OF CHILDBIRTH LOUD PEALING & THE GROANS  661  JERUSALEM 34     23
CHILDHOOD
   EVEN IN CHILDHOOD SORROW SLEPT WITH ME IN MY CRADLE . . .  37B  CONTEMPLATN/PS   PROSE
   FORBID ALL JOY & FROM HER CHILDHOOD SHALL THE LITTLE FEMALE  240  EUROPE 5          8
   THUS IN ETERNAL CHILDHOOD STRAYING AMONG VALA'S FLOCKS . .  371  FOUR ZOAS 9       553
   FROM MY EARLIEST CHILDHOOD HIDDEN FROM ME I SAW &  . . .  447C  ANNO REYNOLDS     MARG
   & OF WHATEVER COMES IN HIS WAY FROM EARLIEST CHILDHOOD  .  455D  ANNO REYNOLDS     MARG
   CHILDHOOD AND AGE ARE EQUALLY BELONGING TO EVERY CLASS  . .  460B  ANNO REYNOLDS   MARG
   S (?STOTHARD) IN CHILDHOOD ON THE NURSERY FLOOR  . . . .  539  IN CHILDHOOD/N      1
   AND EVERY ONE HAS THE THREE REGIONS CHILDHOOD MANHOOD & AGE  635  JERUSALEM 14     25
   IN CHILDHOOD WHAT WERT THOU UNUTTERABLE ANGUISH CONWENNA   644  JERUSALEM 21       23
   THE FLESH OF MULTITUDES FED & NOURISD ME IN MY CHILDHOOD   644  JERUSALEM 22        6
   OF CHILDHOOD MANHOOD & OLD AGE . . . . . . . . . .        746  JERUSALEM 98       33
   NEITHER YOUTH NOR CHILDHOOD IS FOLLY OR INCAPACITY  . .   794B  LETTER 5         PROSE
   . . . MILTON LOVD ME IN CHILDHOOD & SHEWD ME HIS FACE  .  799  TO FLAXMAN/L        5
   GO ON WITH THE VIGOR I WAS IN MY CHILDHOOD FAMOUS FOR  .  815A  LETTER 23        *PROSE
CHILDLESS
   CHILDLESS HE MOURNED BUT THOUGHT HIS GOD KNEW BEST  . . .  39C  SAMSON/PS        PROSE
CHILDREN
   AND CHILDREN CRY FOR BREAD     . . . . . . . . . .        11  GWIN KING/PS        10
   THEIR WIVES AND CHILDREN WEEPING LOUD    . . . . . .      11  GWIN KING/PS        25
   SAMSON THE STRONGEST OF THE CHILDREN OF MEN I SING  . . .  37C  SAMSON/PS         PROSE
   AND SWELLING SIGHS BURST FORTH HIS CHILDREN ALL IN ARMS   42B  THEN SHE BORE     PROSE
      APPEAR
   THE CHILDREN WALKING TWO & TWO IN GREY & BLUE & GREEN  . .  59  HOLY THURS/IM      2
   WHEN THE TONGUES OF CHILDREN ARE HEARD ON THE GREEN . . .  60  NURSES SONG/IM     1
   THEN COME HOME MY CHILDREN THE SUN IS GONE DOWN  . . . .  60  NURSES SONG/IM      5
   ("FATHER OF MEN SEEN IN MOST PERFECT CHILDREN") THIS IS   82D  ANNO LAVATER      MARG
      TRUE WORSHIP
   AND HAR & HEVA LIKE TWO CHILDREN SAT BENEATH THE OAK  . .  100  TIRIEL 2           5
   THE FOUR DAUGHTERS [& ALL THE CHILDREN IN THEIR SILENT    107  TIRIEL 5          30
      BEDS]
   AND ALL THE CHILDREN IN THEIR BEDS WERE CUT OFF IN ONE    107  TIRIEL 5          33
      NIGHT
   FORGETTING THE OFFENCES OF THEIR MOST REBELLIOUS CHILDREN  108  TIRIEL 6          27
   OR ELSE THOU WOULDEST NOT HAVE LIVD TO CURSE THY HELPLESS  108  TIRIEL 6          28
      CHILDREN
   SILENCE THY EVIL TONGUE THOU MURDERER OF THY HELPLESS     108  TIRIEL 6          35
      CHILDREN
   O MY CHILDREN DO THEY CRY     . . . . . . . . . .        112  A DREAM/SI         9
   WHEN THE VOICES OF CHILDREN ARE HEARD ON THE GREEN  . . .  121  NURSES SONG/SI     1
   THEN COME HOME MY CHILDREN THE SUN IS GONE DOWN  . . . .  121  NURSES SONG/SI     5
   THE CHILDREN WALKING TWO & TWO IN RED & BLUE & GREEN  . .  121  HOLY THURS/SI     2
   WHY FADE THESE CHILDREN OF THE SPRING BORN BUT TO SMILE   127  BOOK OF THEL 1     7
      & FALL
   AND SAYS THOU MOTHER OF MY CHILDREN I HAVE LOVED THEE  . .  129  BOOK OF THEL 5    3
   . . . ALL CHILDREN NEW-BORN FIRST BEHOLD THEM TEARS ARE   136  FRENCH REVOLTN    56
      FLED
   . . . SO THE CITY OF PARIS THEIR WIVES AND CHILDREN . . .  136  FRENCH REVOLTN    57
   AND BRIGHT CHILDREN LOOK AFTER HIM INTO THE GRAVE . . .   139  FRENCH REVOLTN   108
   . . . AND THE WOMEN AND CHILDREN OF THE CITY   . . . . .  139  FRENCH REVOLTN   122
   . . . OR GOD WEEP WHEN HIS CHILDREN ARE HAPPY   . . . . .  142  FRENCH REVOLTN   186
   . . . WHERE THEIR CHILDREN ARE MARSHALLD TOGETHER TO BATTLE  146  FRENCH REVOLTN 265
   OR SATAN AND HIS CHILDREN ARE CALLD SIN & DEATH  . . . .  150A  MARRIAGE HH 5    PROSE
   WHEN THE VOICES OF CHILDREN ARE HEARD ON THE GREEN  . . .  171  NURSES SONG/N     1
   THEN COME HOME MY CHILDREN THE SUN IS GONE DOWN  . . . .  171  NURSES SONG/N     5
   WOULD NOT HAVE BANDY CHILDREN NOR FASTING NOR BIRCH  . .  179  LIT VAGABOND/N    11
   HIS CHILDREN AS PLEASANT & HAPPY AS HE   . . . . . . .    180  LIT VAGABOND/N    15
   STAMPT WITH MY SIGNET ARE THE SWARTHY CHILDREN OF THE SUN  190  V DAU ALBION 1    21
   THE VOICE OF SLAVES BENEATH THE SUN AND CHILDREN BOUGHT   190  V DAU ALBION 2     8
      WITH MONEY
   FOR THY COUNCELLOR OR THE DOG FOR A SCHOOLMASTER TO THY   192  V DAU ALBION 5     9
      CHILDREN
   AND LET HIS WIFE AND CHILDREN RETURN FROM THE OPRESSOR'S  198  AMERICA 6       *  11
      SCOURGE
   STANDS AT THE GATE OF ENITHARMON TO DEVOUR HER CHILDREN   198  AMERICA 7          4
   CHILDREN TAKE SHELTER FROM THE LIGHTNINGS THERE STANDS    199  AMERICA 9         10
      WASHINGTON
```

330

	PAGE	TITLE	LINE

CHILDREN   (CONTINUED)

	PAGE	TITLE	LINE
FOR CHILDREN THE GATES OF PARADISE	209B FOR CHILDRN/GP	TITLE
AND SO MANY CHILDREN POOR	212 HOLY THURS/SE	7
WHEN THE VOICES OF CHILDREN ARE HEARD ON THE GREEN . . .	212 NURSES SONG/SE	1
THEN COME HOME MY CHILDREN THE SUN IS GONE DOWN . . .	212 NURSES SONG/SE	5
WOULD NOT HAVE BANDY CHILDREN NOR FASTING NOR BIRCH . . .	216 LIT VAGABND/SE	12
HIS CHILDREN AS PLEASANT AND HAPPY AS HE	216 LIT VAGABND/SE	14
CHILDREN OF THE FUTURE AGE	219 LIT GRL LST/SE	1
AND THEIR CHILDREN WEPT & BUILT	236 URIZEN 28	4
THE REMAINING CHILDREN OF URIZEN	237 URIZEN 28	20
AND THUS HER VOICE ROSE TO HER CHILDREN THE DISTANT HEAVENS REPLY	240 EUROPE 4	32
MY DAUGHTER HOW DO I REJOICE FOR THY CHILDREN FLOCK AROUND	243 EUROPE 14	2
ORC SMILE UPON MY CHILDREN	244 EUROPE 14	29
BY THE HANDS OF THE CHILDREN OF LOS	245 SONG OF LOS 3	9
TO ENION & HER CHILDREN & THEY PONDERD THESE THINGS WONDRING	270 FOUR ZOAS 1	228
WHERE DWELL THE CHILDREN OF THE ELEMENTAL WORLDS IN HARMONY	274 FOUR ZOAS 1	370
CHILDREN ARE NOURISHD FOR THE SLAUGHTER ONCE THE CHILD WAS FED	275 FOUR ZOAS 1	400
WITH MILK BUT WHEREFORE NOW ARE CHILDREN FED WITH BLOOD	275 FOUR ZOAS 1	401
HIS CHILDREN WANDERING OUTSIDE FROM HIS BOSOM FLEEING AWAY	279 FOUR ZOAS 1	559
BINDING JERUSALEM'S CHILDREN IN THE DUNGEONS OF BABYLON	281 FOUR ZOAS 2	63
WITH TREMBLING HORROR PALE AGHAST THE CHILDREN OF MAN . .	283 FOUR ZOAS 2	121
FOR A SCHOOLMASTER TO MY CHILDREN	290 FOUR ZOAS 2	390
OF ALL THAT A MAN HATH HIS HOUSE HIS WIFE HIS CHILDREN . .	290 FOUR ZOAS 2	* 399
. . . & THE SICKNESS THAT CUTS OFF HIS CHILDREN	291 FOUR ZOAS 2	412
. . . & OUR CHILDREN BRING FRUITS & FLOWERS	291 FOUR ZOAS 2	413
THY CHILDREN SMOTE THEIR FIERY WINGS CROWND WITH THE GOLD OF HEAVEN	311 FOUR ZOAS 5	229
THE RUIND SPIRITS ONCE HIS CHILDREN & THE CHILDREN OF LUVAH	314 FOUR ZOAS 6	88
[THE RUIND SPIRITS ONCE HIS CHILDREN & THE CHILDREN OF LUVAH]	314 FOUR ZOAS 6	101
HE KNEW THEY WERE HIS CHILDREN RUIND IN HIS RUIND WORLD	315 FOUR ZOAS 6	130
THE BREAD IS KNEADED LET US REST O CRUEL FATHER OF CHILDREN	322 FOUR ZOAS 7	107
AND WHEN HIS CHILDREN SICKEN LET THEM DIE THERE ARE ENOUGH	323 FOUR ZOAS 7	120
HE CAN AFFORD FLATTER HIS WIFE PITY HIS CHILDREN TILL WE CAN	323 FOUR ZOAS 7	128
TO SWIM THE DEEP & ON THE LAND CHILDREN ARE SOLD TO TRADES	333 FOUR ZOAS 7B	13
OF DAY IN JEALOUSY & BLOOD MY CHILDREN ARE LED TO URIZEN'S WAR	339 FOUR ZOAS 7B	251
TO MULTITUDE & MY MULTITUDES ARE CHILDREN OF CARE & LABOUR	350 FOUR ZOAS 8	353
BOW DOWN BEFORE HER YOU HER CHILDREN & SET JERUSALEM FREE	351 FOUR ZOAS 8	409
THE VOICE INCESSANT CALLS ON ALL THE CHILDREN OF MEN . .	353 FOUR ZOAS 8	489
TO WORSHIP URIZEN'S DRAGON FORM TO OFFER HER OWN CHILDREN	356 FOUR ZOAS 8	599
OF WOMEN & CHILDREN THROUGHOUT EVERY NATION UNDER HEAVEN	358 FOUR ZOAS 9	47
THE VOICES OF CHILDREN IN MY TENTS TO CRIES OF HELPLESS INFANTS	360 FOUR ZOAS 9	111
WHILE LITTLE CHILDREN PLAY AROUND THY FEET IN GENTLE AWE	360 FOUR ZOAS 9	134
THAT WE HIS CHILDREN EVERMORE MAY LIVE IN JERUSALEM . . .	362 FOUR ZOAS 9	221
STANDS IN THE FURIOUS AIR HE CRIES THE CHILDREN OF SIX THOUSAND YEARS	363 FOUR ZOAS 9	252
AND SAW IN THE DOOR WAY BENEATH THE TREES TWO LITTLE CHILDREN PLAYING	370 FOUR ZOAS 9	507
THE CHILDREN CLUNG AROUND HER KNEES SHE EMBRACD THEM & WEPT OVER THEM	370 FOUR ZOAS 9	509
AND THEN SHE ENTERD HER BRIGHT HOUSE LEADING HER MIGHTY CHILDREN	370 FOUR ZOAS 9	513
SHE LAID THE CHILDREN ON THE BEDS WHICH SHE SAW PREPARD IN THE HOUSE	370 FOUR ZOAS 9	515
VALA AWOKE & CALLD THE CHILDREN FROM THEIR GENTLE SLUMBERS	370 FOUR ZOAS 9	518
THE CHILDREN WOKE & SMILD ON VALA SHE KNEELD BY THE GOLDEN COUCH	371 FOUR ZOAS 9	523
O MY SWEET CHILDREN ENION LET THARMAS KISS THY CHEEK . .	371 FOUR ZOAS 9	525
HER DELICATE WOMEN & CHILDREN SHRIEK UPON THE BITTER WIND	375 FOUR ZOAS 9	664
AND LET HIS WIFE & CHILDREN RETURN FROM THE OPRESSOR'S SCOURGE	375 FOUR ZOAS 9	675
INTO THE BARN WHILE CHILDREN GLEAN THE EARS AROUND THE DOOR	376 FOUR ZOAS 9	702
AROUND THE ETERNAL MAN'S BRIGHT TENT THE LITTLE CHILDREN PLAY	379 FOUR ZOAS 9	839
MY CHILDREN WILL DIE FOR LACK OF BREAD	419 I SAW A MONK/N	20
TO REVENGE THE WRONGS THY CHILDREN FEEL	419 I SAW A MONK/N	39
MY CHILDREN DIE FOR LACK OF BREAD	430 GREY MONK	2
TO AVENGE THE WRONGS THY CHILDREN FEEL	430 GREY MONK	24
CHILDREN TO GO & SWEAR AS THIS MAN HAS SWORN . . .	439A BLAKES MEMORAN	PROSE
HUMILIATION & IN EXULTATION RISE THRO THE AIR WITH THEIR CHILDREN	443D LAST JUDGMNT/L	PROSE
PARENTS & CHILDREN WIVES & HUSBANDS EMBRACE & ARISE TOGETHER	443D LAST JUDGMNT/L	PROSE
HIS GARMENTS ARE LONG SUFFERINGS FOR THE CHILDREN OF MEN	499 MILTON 18	36
HE SEES HIS CHILDREN MOCK AT FAITH AND DENY PROVIDENCE . .	510 MILTON 25	25
THESE ARE THE CHILDREN OF LOS THOU SEEST THE TREES ON MOUNTAINS	512 MILTON 26	7
LIKE WOMEN & CHILDREN WERE TAKEN AWAY AS ON WINGS . . .	519 MILTON 31	2
JERUSALEM'S CHILDREN CONSUME IN FLAMES AMONG THE STARS . .	527 MILTON 37	12
THESE TEARS FALL FOR THE LITTLE-ONES THE CHILDREN OF JERUSALEM	532 MILTON 40	15
THAT THE CHILDREN OF JERUSALEM MAY BE SAVED FROM SLAVERY	532 MILTON 40	31
GO SEND YOUR CHILDREN TO THE SLOBBERING SCHOOL	547 RAFAEL SUBLI/N	7
AND ARE COMPOSED OF AN OLD MAN A WOMAN AND CHILDREN . . .	567A DESC CAT 3	PROSE
INTO HEAVEN BY MEANS OF LEARNING APPEAR TO CHILDREN . . .	581D DESC CAT 8	PROSE

CHILDREN   (CONTINUED)

	PAGE	TITLE	LINE
& ARE COMPOSED OF AN OLD MAN A WOMAN & CHILDREN . . .	588D	CHAUCER/N	PROSE
AND ARE COMPOSED OF AN OLD MAN A WOMAN AND CHILDREN . . .	590A	CHAUCER 2	PROSE
AS MULTITUDES OF CHILDREN ASCENDING FROM THE EARTH . . .	607C	V LAST JUDG/N	PROSE
FEET OF ABRAHAM & RECIEVE THEIR CHILDREN FROM THE EARTH	607C	V LAST JUDG/N	PROSE
ON THE RIGHT A YOUTHFUL COUPLE ARE AWAKED BY THEIR CHILDREN	609C	V LAST JUDG/N	PROSE
THE CHILDREN OF ABRAHAM OR HEBREW CHURCH ARE	610B	V LAST JUDG/N	PROSE
A WOMAN WITH CHILDREN REPRESENTS THE STATE CALLD LABAN THE	610D	V LAST JUDG/N	PROSE
A MALE & FEMALE WITH NUMEROUS CHILDREN THESE	611D	V LAST JUDG/N	PROSE
BENEATH THESE A CLOUD OF WOMEN & CHILDREN ARE TAKEN UP	614A	V LAST JUDG/N	PROSE
LAMENTING FOR HER CHILDREN FOR THE SONS & DAUGHTERS OF ALBION	624	JERUSALEM 5	65
I AM CLOSD UP FROM MY CHILDREN MY EMANATION IS DIVIDING	627	JERUSALEM 8	13
TO WHOM I MAKE THEE INVISIBLE BUT CHIEF TO MY OWN CHILDREN	629	JERUSALEM 10	31
THAT THOU CALLEST THY CHILDREN LO THE LAW OF GOD COMMANDS	629	JERUSALEM 10	38
OF LIGHT AND LOVE THEIR LITTLE CHILDREN STAND WITH ARROWS OF GOLD	631	JERUSALEM 11	20
GIVES TO THE CHILDREN OF ALBION & TO THE CHILDREN OF JERUSALEM	637	JERUSALEM 16	24
IN ENITHARMON'S HALLS BUILDED BY LOS & HIS MIGHTY CHILDREN	638	JERUSALEM 16	60
TO MAKE A WAY FOR THE CHILDREN OF LOS TO COME FROM THE FURNACES	638	JERUSALEM 17	5
I WILL COMPELL MY SPECTRE TO OBEY I WILL RESTORE TO THEE THY CHILDREN	639	JERUSALEM 17	20
JEALOUS OF JERUSALEM'S CHILDREN ASHAMD OF HER LITTLE-ONES	640	JERUSALEM 18	6
AND OF HIS CHILDREN BEFORE SINFUL JERUSALEM TO BUILD .	640	JERUSALEM 18	28
RETURND WITH CHILDREN OF POLLUTION TO DEFILE OUR HOUSE .	640	JERUSALEM 18	31
HIS CHILDREN EXILD FROM HIS BREAST PASS TO AND FRO BEFORE HIM	641	JERUSALEM 19	1
THE VOICES OF CHILDREN IN HIS TENTS TO CRIES OF HELPLESS INFANTS	641	JERUSALEM 19	12
AND ALL MY CHILDREN FOLLOWD HIS LOUD HOWLINGS INTO THE DEEP	643	JERUSALEM 21	17
I HAVE TAUGHT MY CHILDREN SACRIFICES OF CRUELTY WHAT SHALL I ANSWER	646	JERUSALEM 23	17
I WILL HIDE IT FROM ETERNALS I WILL GIVE MYSELF FOR MY CHILDREN	646	JERUSALEM 23	18
MY CHILDREN WANDER TREMBLING VICTIMS OF HIS MORAL JUSTICE	646	JERUSALEM 23	34
. . . IN THE BLOOD OF THE LAMB SLAIN IN HIS CHILDREN .	646	JERUSALEM 24	2
ARE YOU MY CHILDREN NATIVES IN THE GRAVE TO WHERE I GO .	647	JERUSALEM 24	13
BUT ALBION IS CAST FORTH TO THE POTTER HIS CHILDREN TO THE BUILDERS	647	JERUSALEM 24	29
THOU ART A DELUSION AND JERUSALEM IS MY SIN O MY CHILDREN	648	JERUSALEM 24	54
CHILDREN OF JESUS & HIS BRIDE	650	FIELDS FROM/J	20
NOT WHERE TO FLEE THEY HAD BEEN ON A VISIT TO ALBION'S CHILDREN	655	JERUSALEM 30	5
OF ALBION'S CHILDREN FLEEING THRO ALBION'S VALES IN STREAMS OF GORE	655	JERUSALEM 30	8
THEY MOCK AT THE LABOURER'S LIMBS THEY MOCK AT HIS STARVD CHILDREN	656	JERUSALEM 30	28
BECAUSE THOU ART THE IMPURITY & THE HARLOT & THY CHILDREN	658	JERUSALEM 31	63
CHILDREN OF WHOREDOMS BORN FOR SACRIFICE FOR THE MEAT & DRINK	658	JERUSALEM 31	64
I WAS A CITY & A TEMPLE BUILT BY ALBION'S CHILDREN . . .	659	JERUSALEM 33	36
AND IN HER COURTS AMONG HER LITTLE CHILDREN OFFERING UP	660	JERUSALEM 33	42
ARE NOT THE STARS OF HEAVEN THY CHILDREN ART THOU NOT BABYLON	660	JERUSALEM 34	8
JERUSALEM TREMBLED SEEING HER CHILDREN DRIVN BY LOS'S HAMMER	663	JERUSALEM 36	21
THE CHILDREN OF MY THOUGHTS WALKING WITHIN MY BLOOD-VESSELS	665	JERUSALEM 38	34
JERUSALEM'S CHILDREN HARK HEAR THE GIANTS OF ALBION CRY AT NIGHT	673	JERUSALEM 43	47
I SEE A WICKER IDOL WOVEN ROUND JERUSALEM'S CHILDREN I SEE	673	JERUSALEM 43	65
THE CHILDREN MUST BE SACRIFICD A HORROR NEVER KNOWN . . .	678	JERUSALEM 48	58
INCLOSING ALL THE CHILDREN OF LOS TIME AFTER TIME . .	684	JERUSALEM 53	7
AND JERUSALEM IS CALLED LIBERTY AMONG THE CHILDREN OF ALBION	684	JERUSALEM 54	5
WEEPING OVER HIS CHILDREN IN STONE-HENGE IN MALDEN & COLCHESTER	689	JERUSALEM 57	6
GATHERD JERUSALEM'S CHILDREN IN HIS ARMS & BORE THEM LIKE	692	JERUSALEM 60	8
BECAUSE HIS CHILDREN WERE CLOSD FROM HIM APART & ENITHARMON	696	JERUSALEM 62	37
SHE ADJOIND WITH GWANTOKE'S CHILDREN SOON LOVELY CORDELLA AROSE	710	JERUSALEM 71	28
WEEPING & SHOUTING TO THE LORD DAY & NIGHT AND HIS CHILDREN	711	JERUSALEM 71	62
HER TWELVE GATES THROWN DOWN HER CHILDREN CARRIED INTO CAPTIVITY	719	JERUSALEM 78	23
THE ARROWS OF THE ALMIGHTY POUR UPON ME & MY CHILDREN .	719	JERUSALEM 78	32
MY TENTS ARE FALLN MY PILLARS ARE IN RUINS MY CHILDREN DASHD	719	JERUSALEM 79	1
HIS CHILDREN TO MY BREASTS HIS SONS & DAUGHTERS TO MY KNEES	720	JERUSALEM 79	26
I WALK WEEPING IN PANGS OF A MOTHER'S TORMENT FOR HER CHILDREN	721	JERUSALEM 80	2
HER CHILDREN IN CAPTIVITY LISTENING TO VALA'S LAMENTATION	722	JERUSALEM 80	10
THE CHILDREN OF JERUSALEM THE SOULS OF THOSE WHO SLEEP . .	722	JERUSALEM 80	33
JERUSALEM HUNGERS IN THE DESART AFFECTION TO HER CHILDREN	727	JERUSALEM 83	7
WITHOUT BECOMING HIS CHILDREN IN THE FURNACES OF AFFLICTION	732	JERUSALEM 86	49
SURROUNDED BY THEIR CHILDREN IF THEY EMBRACE & COMINGLE	733	JERUSALEM 88	6
THRO ALL THE WORLD OF ERIN & OF LOS & ALL THEIR CHILDREN	733	JERUSALEM 88	33
HE WHO WOULD SEE THE DIVINITY MUST SEE HIM IN HIS CHILDREN	738	JERUSALEM 91	19
ARE THE CHILDREN OF THIS BOW A BOW OF MERCY & LOVING-KINDNESS LAYING	744	JERUSALEM 97	13
HE SAYS ALSO THE SPIRITUAL BODY OR ANGEL AS LITTLE CHILDREN	774A	ANNO BERKELEY	MARG
THE ETERNAL PARENTS DEMAND FROM THEIR CHILDREN	791B	LETTER 3	PROSE

	PAGE	TITLE	LINE

CHILDREN   (CONTINUED)
    ELUCIDATED BY CHILDREN WHO HAVE TAKEN A GREATER DELIGHT   794A LETTER 5   PROSE
    SOME CHILDREN ARE FOOLS & SO ARE SOME OLD MEN BUT THERE   794B LETTER 5   PROSE
        IS A
    THINK THAT IT WAS A FIGURE WITH CHILDREN WHICH HE CALLD   849A LETTER 45   PROSE
        A CHARITY
    BECOME CHILDREN OF LIGHT AND LIBERTY AND MY FEET AND MY   852A LETTER 50   PROSE
    PROVIDENCE O WHAT WONDERS ARE THE CHILDREN OF MEN . . . 863A LETTER 60   PROSE
    A WIDOWER & CHILDREN   . . . SUPP ILLUS GRAY   *TITLE
CHILDREN'S
    TO DRINK HER CHILDREN'S GORE   . . . .   13 GWIN KING/PS   74
    OUR CHILDREN'S MOTHER AND THOU SHALT BE OUR GRAVE   . . . 32 EDW THIRD/PS 6   16
    TYRANNY HATH STAIND FAIR ALBION'S BREAST WITH HER   34A KING JOHN/PS   PROSE
        OWN CHILDREN'S GORE
    . . . WERE MY CHILDREN'S SOULS . . . .   268 FOUR ZOAS 1   165
    HIS CHILDREN'S CRY MY SOUL APPALLS   . . . .   419 I SAW A MONK/N   33
    HIS CHILDREN'S CRY MY SOUL APPALLS   . . . .   430 GREY MONK   18
    MALDEN & COLCHESTER DEMONSTRATE I HEAR MY CHILDREN'S VOICES 644 JERUSALEM 21   37
    HER CHILDREN'S DRUID TEMPLES DROPPING WITH BLOOD WANDERD   719 JERUSALEM 78   29
        WEEPING
CHILD'S
    [[IS A FOOLISH THING] IS A CHILD'S PLAY THING]   . . . . 178 THE FAIRY/N   *   21
    THE CHILD'S TOYS & THE OLD MAN'S REASONS   . . . . . .   433 AUGURIES   91
CHILL
    CHILL DEATH WITHDRAWS HIS HAND AND SHE REVIVES   . . .   4 FAIR ELENOR/PS   9
    . . . A DARKNESS CREPT OVER HIS EYE-LIDS AND CHILL COLD   147 FRENCH REVOLTN   295
        SWEAT
    . . . [?TILL ?BY THE] ?FROZEN CHILL & HEAVY EVEN TO THE   205 AMERICA CANC C *   9
        CITY GATE
    VENTURE OUT THE CHILL OF THE WEATHER SOON DRIVES ME BACK   871D LETTER 74   PROSE
        INTO
CHILLD
    THE ETERNAL VOICE HE STOOD THE SWEAT CHILLD ON HIS MIGHTY 278 FOUR ZOAS 1   522
        LIMBS
    MARY TREMBLED & MARY CHILLD   . . . .   435 WILLIAM BOND   33
CHILLING
    OF LIFE IN WEARY LUST MUST CHILLING MURDEROUS THOUGHTS   193 V DAU ALBION 5   23
        OBSCURE
CHIMNEY PIECE
    OVER HIS CHIMNEY PIECE BETWEEN TWO LITTLE PRETTY PICTURES 836A LETTER 35   PROSE
CHIMNEYS
    THE [WINDOWS] CHIMNEYS WERE THREE SCORE   . . . . . .   57 TO BE OR/IM   *   19
    SO YOUR CHIMNEYS I SWEEP & IN SOOT I SLEEP   . . . . .   117 CHIMNEY SWP/SI   4
    OVER THE DOORS THOU SHALT NOT & OVER THE CHIMNEYS FEAR   243 EUROPE 12   28
        IS WRITTEN
CHIMNEY SWEEPER
    THE CHIMNEY SWEEPER   . . . .   117C CHIMNEY SWP/SI   TITLE
    THE CHIMNEY SWEEPER   . . . .   180B CHIMNEY SWP/N   TITLE
    THE CHIMNEY SWEEPER   . . . .   212B CHIMNEY SWP/SE   TITLE
    THE BLOSSOM THE CHIMNEY SWEEPER THE DIVINE IMAGE NIGHT   SUPP LETTER 66A   *PROSE
    THE CHIMNEY SWEEPER A LITTLE BLACK THING &C THE HUMAN   SUPP LETTER 66A   *PROSE
        ABSTRACT
CHIMNEY-SWEEPER'S,CHIMNEY SWEEPER'S
    [BUT MOST] HOW THE CHIMNEY SWEEPER'S CRY   . . . . . .   170 LONDON/N   9
    HOW THE CHIMNEY-SWEEPER'S CRY   . . . .   216 LONDON/SE   9
CHIN
    WITH HIS FAT BELLY & HIS ROUND CHIN   . . . .   46 PHEBUS CAME/IM   2
    PUT HIS CHIN IN HIS HAND & SAID WHENEVER YOU THINK   . .   49B ISLAND MOON 5   PROSE
CHINA
    ACROSS EUROPE & ASIA TO CHINA & JAPAN LIKE LIGHTENINGS . .281 FOUR ZOAS 2   *   59
    TO MEXICO & PERU WEST & EAST TO CHINA & JAPAN TILL BABEL   486 MILTON 6   23
    TO TARTARY & HINDOSTAN & CHINA & TO GREAT AMERICA   . . . 495 MILTON 14   7
    FROM BRIGHT JAPAN & CHINA TO HESPERIA FRANCE & ENGLAND . .648 JERUSALEM 24   47
    CHINA & INDIA & SIBERIA ARE HIS TEMPLES FOR ENTERTAINMENT 690 JERUSALEM 58   39
    TO SODOM & GOMORRHA THENCE TO INDIA CHINA & JAPAN   . . . 704 JERUSALEM 67   40
    ARABIA PALESTINE PERSIA HINDOSTAN CHINA TARTARY SIBERIA   712 JERUSALEM 72   39
    AND HELLE & HESPERIA & HINDOSTAN & CHINA & JAPAN   . . . 725 JERUSALEM 82   28
CHINKS
    THRO NARROW CHINKS OF HIS CAVERN   . . . .   154C MARRIAGE HH 14   PROSE
CHIRP
    THEY CHIRP & HOP AWAY   . . . .   56 HAIL MATRIM/IM   24
CHIRPING
    CHIRPING LOUD AND SINGING SWEET   . . . .   7 LOVE HARMNY/PS   6
CHISEL
    AND THE SAW AND THE HAMMER THE CHISEL   . . .   144 FRENCH REVOLTN   231
    THE HAMMER & THE CHISEL & THE RULE & COMPASSES   . . . . 337 FOUR ZOAS 7B   171
    AND WITH THE CHISEL & THE MALLET I WHOSE LABOURS VAST   . .361 FOUR ZOAS 9   176
    THE HAMMER & THE CHISEL & THE RULE & COMPASSES FROM LONDON 699 JERUSALEM 65   13
        FLEEING
CHIVALRY
    AND THE ANCIENT FORESTS OF CHIVALRY HEWN . . .   138 FRENCH REVOLTN   93
CHLOE'S
    TO CHLOE'S BREAST YOUNG CUPID SLILY STOLE   . . . . .   557 TO CHLOES/N   1
CHOICE
    THE LOST DRAWING YOU SHALL HAVE CHOICE OF EITHER OF THE   839C LETTER 38   PROSE
CHOIR
    WHICH IN FULL CHOIR HAILS THY APPROACH O SPRING   . . . . 1 TO SPRING/PS   4
    . . . AND SINGING OF THE HOLY CHOIR   . . . . . .   140 FRENCH REVOLTN   146
    HE LEADS THE CHOIR OF DAY TRILL TRILL TRILL TRILL   . . . 520 MILTON 31   31
CHOKD
    CHOKD THE BRIGHT RIVERS BURDNING WITH MY SHIPS THE ANGRY   361 FOUR ZOAS 9   169
        DEEP

CHOKE
    AS THICK AS NORTHERN FOGS AROUND YOUR GATES TO CHOKE YOU   100 TIREL 1   44
      UP
CHOKES
    HE CHOKES UP THE PATHS OF THE SKY THE MOON IS LEPROUS AS   703 JERUSALEM 66   78
      SNOW
CHOOSE   SEE CHUSE
    DEATH CHOOSE OR LIFE THOU STRUGGLEST IN MY WATERS   301 FOUR ZOAS 4   152
      NOW CHOOSE LIFE
    BETTER CHOOSE FOOLS AT ONCE . . . . 405C ANNO BACON   MARG
    IN BOWLAHOOLA & AS THE SPECTRES CHOOSE THEIR AFFINITIES   512 MILTON 26   38
    CHOOSE TO PURCHASE THE LIFE'S LABOUR OF IGNORANCE   594B PUB ADDRESS/N   PROSE
      & IMBECILLITY
    YOU WHAT SUBJECT YOU CHOOSE TO BE PAINTED ON THE REMAINING 816C LETTER 24   PROSE
    OR REMOVE TO ANY OTHER PLACE THAT I CHOOSE . . . . . . 820A LETTER 25   PROSE
    THAT ONE THOUSAND COPIES SHOULD BE THE FIRST EDITION AND   858B LETTER 55   PROSE
      IF WE CHOOSE
CHOOSERS
    CALLD IN SOME NORTHERN POEMS "CHOOSERS OF THE SLAIN"   . SUPP ILLUS GRAY   *TITLE
CHOOSES
    AS THE CATTERPILLER CHOOSES THE FAIREST LEAVES TO LAY   . 152C MARRIAGE HH 9   PROSE
    & HE WILL PRODUCE A PICTURE OR PAINTING BUT IF HE CHOOSES 603A PUB ADDR AD/N   PROSE
    HE TAKES HIS BOW THEN CHOOSES OUT HIS ARROWS OF FLAMING   742 JERUSALEM 95   13
      GOLD
CHOOSING   SEE CHUSING
    CHOOSING FORMS OF WORSHIP FROM POETIC TALES AND AT LENGTH 153B MARRIAGE HH 11 PROSE
    I SPOKE TO MR FLAXMAN ABOUT CHOOSING OUT PROPER SUBJECTS   846A LETTER 44   PROSE
CHOP
    & TAKE A MUTTON CHOP WITH US THE DAY YOU GO TO CHELTENHAM   870C LETTER 72   PROSE
CHORUS
    THE THREE PHILOSOPHERS BEAR CHORUS . . . .   47D ASK GODS/IM 1   PROSE
    GRAND CHORUS . . . .   54C LO THE BAT/IM   TITLE
    TO SING THE SWEET CHORUS OF HA HA HE . . . .   63 SHEPHERD YOUNG   12
    TO SING THE SWEET CHORUS OF HA HA HE . . . .   125 LAUGHING/SI   12
    CHORUS . . . .   160A SONG LIBERTY   TITLE
    TERRIFIC AMONG THE SONS OF ALBION IN CHORUS SOLEMN & LOUD   482 MILTON 2   23
    ENTUNE DAUGHTERS OF ALBION YOUR HYMNING CHORUS MILDLY . . 688 JERUSALEM 56   11
    ON EACH SIDE A CHORUS OF ANGELS ENTERING SING THE FOLLOWING 781A GHOST ABEL 2   PROSE
CHOSE
    AND CHOSE HER ARROWS THEN ADVANCD TO MEET THE TERRIBLE PAIR 109 TIRIEL 7   24
    SINCE EVE FIRST CHOSE HER HELL FIRE SPARK . . . . . . 187 WHEN KLOPSTK/N 24
    THEY RATHER CHOSE TO MEET ETERNAL DEATH THAN TO DESTROY   332 FOUR ZOAS 7   484
    [WINGS THEY HAD [& WHEN THEY CHOSE] THAT SOFT INCLOSE] . 422 BENEATH AD/N   1
    [ROUND THEIR BODY WHEN THEY CHOSE] . . . .   422 BENEATH AD/N   2
    THAT THE WORST PAINTERS ALWAYS CHOSE THE GRANDEST SUBJECTS 465C ANNO REYNOLDS MARG
CHOSEN
    I HAVE CHOSEN THE SERPENT FOR A COUNCELLOR & THE DOG   . . 290 FOUR ZOAS 2   389
    THE TIME CHOSEN IS EARLY MORNING BEFORE SUNRISE . . . . 566C DESC CAT 3   PROSE
    THE TIME CHOSEN IS EARLY MORNING BEFORE SUNRISE . . . 588B CHAUCER/N   PROSE
    THE TIME CHOSEN IS EARLY MORNING BEFORE SUN-RISE . . . . 589C CHAUCER 2   PROSE
    AND HYLE & COBAN WERE HIS TWO CHOSEN ONES FOR EMISSARIES 641 JERUSALEM 18   41
    DESTROY NOT BY MORAL VIRTUE THE LITTLE ONES WHOM HE HATH   670 JERUSALEM 42   42
      CHOSEN
    THE LITTLE ONES WHOM HE HATH CHOSEN IN PREFERENCE TO THEE 670 JERUSALEM 42   43
    WHICH SHALL BE CHOSEN INSTEAD OF THE WITCH IF THAT CANNOT 840D LETTER 40   PROSE
    THE SUBJECTS I CANNOT DO BETTER THAN THOSE ALREADY CHOSEN 859A LETTER 56   PROSE
    PLEASE ME SO WELL THAT I HAVE CHOSEN THAT DESIGN IN OUR   859B LETTER 56   PROSE
      LAST
CHRIST
    ("THE GREATEST OF CHARACTERS...") THIS WAS CHRIST   . . . 66B ANNO LAVATER   MARG
    NOTE JESUS CHRIST DID NOT WISH TO UNITE . . . . 155C MARRIAGE HH 15 PROSE
    IN JESUS CHRIST AND HAS NOT JESUS CHRIST . . . . 158B MARRIAGE HH 22 PROSE
    IF JESUS CHRIST IS THE GREATEST MAN YOU OUGHT TO LOVE HIM 158C MARRIAGE HH 22 PROSE
    THEY CALL JESUS THE CHRIST & THEY IN HIM & HE IN THEM   . . 277 FOUR ZOAS 1   473
    WHICH CHRIST MUST REND & HER REVEAL HER DAUGHTERS ARE CALLD 348 FOUR ZOAS 8   293
    DEFEND EITHER THE ACTS OF CHRIST OR THE BIBLE UNPERVERTED 383B ANNO WATSON   MARG
    WHEREFORE DID CHRIST COME WAS IT NOT TO ABOLISH THE JEWISH 387B ANNO WATSON   * MARG
      IMPOSTURE
    WAS NOT CHRIST MURDERD BECAUSE HE TAUGHT THAT GOD LOVED   387B ANNO WATSON   * MARG
    CHRIST DIED AS AN UNBELIEVER & IF THE BISHOPS HAD THEIR   387C ANNO WATSON   MARG
      WILL
    WITH CHRISTENDOM AS IN CHRIST HE STROVE WITH THE JEWS   . . 387C ANNO WATSON   MARG
    WHICH THEY CALLD GOD & SO WERE LIARS AS CHRIST SAYS . . . 389A ANNO WATSON   MARG
    IT WAS NOT RESTORED TILL [WE ?IN] CHRIST [XXX] . . . . 390A ANNO WATSON   * MARG
    AS NEITHER COULD CHRIST BUT I CAN & DO WORK SUCH . . . . 391D ANNO WATSON   MARG
    THAT CHRIST COULD NOT DO A MIRACLE BECAUSE OF UNBELIEF . . 391D ANNO WATSON   MARG
    IF CHRIST COULD NOT DO MIRACLES BECAUSE OF UNBELIEF . . . 391D ANNO WATSON   MARG
    CHRIST & HIS PROPHETS & APOSTLES WERE NOT AMBITIOUS MIRACLE 392A ANNO WATSON   MARG
      MONGERS
    CHRIST PRONOUNCD THEM THE ABOMINATION THAT MAKETH DESOLATE 393D ANNO WATSON   * MARG
    O HOW VIRTUOUS CHRIST CAME NOT TO CALL THE VIRTUOUS . . . 395D ANNO WATSON   MARG
    THE PUBLICANS & SINNERS THAT CHRIST LOVED TO ASSOCIATE WITH 396A ANNO WATSON   MARG
    THIS IS CERTAIN IF WHAT BACON SAYS IS TRUE WHAT CHRIST   396D ANNO BACON   MARG
      SAYS IS FALSE
    IF CAESAR IS RIGHT CHRIST IS WRONG BOTH IN POLITICS   396D ANNO BACON   MARG
      & RELIGION
    RATIONAL TRUTH IS NOT THE TRUTH OF CHRIST BUT OF PILATE   397C ANNO BACON   MARG
    EXCEPT IS CHRIST YOU LIE EXCEPT DID ANYONE EVER DO THIS   400D ANNO BACON   MARG
    & NOT FOLLOW CHRIST WHO DOES BY NATURE . . . . 400D ANNO BACON   MARG
    SUCH AS CHRIST DESCRIBES BY RAVENING WOLVES . . . . . 401D ANNO BACON   MARG
    A LORD CHANCELLOR'S OPINIONS AS DIFFERENT FROM CHRIST . . 407A ANNO BACON   MARG
    VILLAIN DID CHRIST SEEK THE PRAISE OF THE RULERS . . . . 410D ANNO BACON   MARG

	PAGE	TITLE	LINE

CHRIST (CONTINUED)
```
CHRIST SEATED ON THE THRONE OF JUDGMENT  . . . . . . . 443A LAST JUDGMNT/L  PROSE
IMMEDIATELY BEFORE THE THRONE OF CHRIST IS ADAM & EVE  . 443B LAST JUDGMNT/L  PROSE
THEIR OWN RIGHTEOUSNESS BEFORE THE THRONE OF CHRIST  . . 443C LAST JUDGMNT/L  PROSE
BEFORE THE THRONE OF CHRIST ON THE RIGHT HAND THE JUST IN  443D LAST JUDGMNT/L  PROSE
OPENED AROUND THE THRONE OF CHRIST  . . . . . . . . 444A LAST JUDGMNT/L  PROSE
BEHIND THE SEAT & THRONE OF CHRIST APPEARS ]APPEAR]  . . 444B LAST JUDGMNT/L  PROSE
ON THE RIGHT HAND OF THE THRONE OF CHRIST IS BAPTISM  . 444B LAST JUDGMNT/L  PROSE
ONE OF RAFAEL'S GRANDEST SUBJECTS NAMELY CHRIST DELIVERING  465C ANNO REYNOLDS  MARG
BELIEVE CHRIST & HIS APOSTLES THAT THERE IS A CLASS OF MEN  480C MILTON 1  PROSE
CHRIST TOOK ON SIN IN THE VIRGIN'S WOMB & PUT IT OFF ON  484 MILTON 5  3
  THE CROSS
CHRIST USD THE PHARISEES IN A ROUGHER WAY  . . . . . 539 SIR JOSH MIC/N  7
I UNDERSTOOD CHRIST WAS A CARPENTER  . . . . . . . . 546 ENGLISH CONN/N  5
I ALWAYS THOUGHT THAT JESUS CHRIST WAS A SNUBBY  . . . . 555C ALWAYS THOT/N  PROSE
HE WHO COULD REPRESENT CHRIST UNIFORMLY LIKE A DRAYMAN  . 596C PUB ADDRESS/N  PROSE
THE CURTAINS ARE DRAWN APART CHRIST HAVING RENT THE VEIL  613B V LAST JUDG/N  PROSE
CHRIST COMES AS HE CAME AT FIRST TO DELIVER THOSE  . . 615B V LAST JUDG/N  PROSE
THE MODERN CHURCH CRUCIFIES CHRIST WITH THE HEAD DOWNWARDS  615D V LAST JUDG/N  PROSE
IS A VERY CRUEL BEING & BEING A WORSHIPPER OF CHRIST  . 617A V LAST JUDG/N  PROSE
THEN JESUS COMES WITH A BALM TO HEAL IT  . . . . . . 617A V LAST JUDG/N  PROSE
WE CALL JESUS THE CHRIST AND HE IN US AND WE IN HIM  . . 665 JERUSALEM 38  20
A VEGETATED CHRIST & A VIRGIN EVE ARE THE HERMAPHRODITIC  736 JERUSALEM 90  34
THE VISION OF CHRIST THAT THOU DOST SEE  . . . . . . 748 EV GOSPEL(A)/N  1
OR OF CHRIST & HIS FATHER ITS ALL A BOAST  . . . . . 752 EV GOSPEL(D)/N  46
CERTAINLY WAS NOT WHAT CHRIST MEANT  . . . . . . . . 752 EV GOSPEL(D)/N  50
SEEING THIS FALSE CHRIST IN FURY & PASSION  . . . . . 756 EV GOSPEL(G)/N  1
WHAT THEN DID CHRIST INCULCATE FORGIVENESS OF SINS  . . 757D EV GOSPEL  PROSE
CHRIST ADDRESSES HIMSELF TO THE MAN NOT TO HIS REASON  . 774C ANNO BERKELEY  MARG
(RE JOHNSON) CHRIST & HIS APOSTLES WERE ILLITERATE MEN  786D ANNO THORNTON  MARG
DIFFERENCE BETWEEN THE DOCTRINES OF DR TRUSLER & THOSE  795A LETTER 6  PROSE
  OF CHRIST
THIS WORLD ARE NOW BECOME THE KINGDOMS OF GOD & HIS CHRIST  810C LETTER 21  PROSE
AS A SOLDIER OF CHRIST IT GIVES ME THE GREATEST OF TORMENTS  812D LETTER 22  PROSE
CHRIST IS VERY DECIDED ON THIS POINT "HE WHO IS NOT WITH"  822D LETTER 26  PROSE
THE PICTURE OF "CHRIST IN THE DESERT" HE SUPPOSES TO BE  831B LETTER 31  PROSE
GOD OUT OF CHRIST IS A CONSUMING FIRE MERCY WRATH  . . SUPP INSC HERVEY  *TITLE
CHRIST GIRDING HIMSELF WITH STRENGTH FOUR & TWENTY ELDERS  SUPP LETTER 56A  *PROSE
CHRIST BAPTIZING SAMSON BREAKING BONDS SAMSON SUBDUD  SUPP LETTER 56A  *PROSE
GOD CREATING ADAM CHRIST APPEARING TOUCHG UP CHRIST  SUPP LETTER 56A  *PROSE
  BAPTIZING
```

CHRISTENDOM
```
WITH CHRISTENDOM AS IN CHRIST HE STROVE WITH THE JEWS  . 387C ANNO WATSON  MARG
```

CHRISTIAN
```
THIS IS TRUE CHRISTIAN PHILOSOPHY FAR ABOVE ALL ABSTRACTION  65C ANNO LAVATER  MARG
("NOT HONEST PUBLICLY CHRISTIAN PRIVATELY DEIST") BRAVO  72C ANNO LAVATER  MARG
("THE MOST REFINED EPICURISM") TRUE CHRISTIAN PHILOSOPHY  75D ANNO LAVATER  MARG
THE JEWISH & CHRISTIAN TESTAMENTS  . . . . . . . . 98D ALL RELIGIONS  PROSE
CHRISTIAN FORBEARANCE  . . . . . . . . . . . . 165C CHRISTN FORB/N  TITLE
THE CHRISTIAN RELIGION TEACHES THAT NO MAN IS INDIFFERENT  380B FOUR ZOAS NOTE  PROSE
("ALL CHRISTIAN STATES") PAINE HAS NOT ATTACKED  383D ANNO WATSON  MARG
  CHRISTIANITY
TO ME WHO BELIEVE THE BIBLE & PROFESS MYSELF A CHRISTIAN  387B ANNO WATSON  MARG
THAT TOM PAINE IS A BETTER CHRISTIAN THAN THE BISHOP  . 396B ANNO WATSON  MARG
& YET EVERY BODY SAYS THAT IT IS CHRISTIAN PHILOSOPHY  . 397B ANNO BACON  MARG
IS THIS GREAT IS THIS CHRISTIAN NO  . . . . . . . 407D ANNO BACON  MARG
AND NOT TO RAISE ENVY IS CALLD CHRISTIAN LOVE  . . . . 428 MARY  26
SHE REPRESENTS THE CHRISTIAN CHURCH  . . . . . . . 443D LAST JUDGMNT/L  PROSE
TIS CHRISTIAN MILDNESS WHEN [FOOLS] KNAVES PRAISE A FOE  539 SIR JOSH MIC/N  4
[IT WOULD BE CHRISTIAN MILDNESS TO MAINTAIN]  . . . . 539 SIR JOSH MIC/N *  5
AND TIS MOST WICKED IN A CHRISTIAN NATION  . . . . . 551 WILLM COWPER/N  11
AND SO [SWEET] DEAR [CHRISTIANS] CHRISTIAN FRIENDS HOW  551 ONLY MAN/N  *  4
  DO YOU DO
IS ONE OF THE MOST AMIABLE FEATURES OF THE CHRISTIAN CHURCH  590B CHAUCER 2  PROSE
[TILL AT LENGTH CHRISTIAN CHARITY IS HELD OUT AS A MOTIVE  595B PUB ADDRESS/N  PROSE
  TO]
OR CIVILIZED LIFE SUCH AS IT IS IN THE CHRISTIAN CHURCH  610C V LAST JUDG/N  PROSE
BOTH OF DECEIT & OF OPEN VIOLENCE THE DEIST & THE CHRISTIAN  615A V LAST JUDG/N  PROSE
ALL THE DESTRUCTION THEREFORE IN CHRISTIAN EUROPE  . . 683A JERUSALEM 52  PROSE
LET EVERY CHRISTIAN AS MUCH AS IN HIM LIES  . . . . . 717C JERUSALEM 77  PROSE
HE DID NOT DIE WITH CHRISTIAN EASE  . . . . . . . . 751 EV GOSPEL(D)/N  31
AND THE DEVIL WAS GOD LIKE A CHRISTIAN CIVIL  . . . . 752 EV GOSPEL(D)/N  36
MILD CHRISTIAN REGRETS TO THE DEVIL CONFESS  . . . . 752 EV GOSPEL(D)/N  37
THE MORAL CHRISTIAN IS THE CAUSE  . . . . . . . . 758 EV GOSPEL (1)  7
THE CHRISTIAN TRUMPETS LOUD PROCLAIM  . . . . . . . 758 EV GOSPEL (2)  24
MAN OR WOMAN WHO IS NOT ONE OF THESE IS NOT A CHRISTIAN  776A INSC LAOCOON  PROSE
THE TRUE CHRISTIAN CHARITY NOT DEPENDENT ON  . . . . 776B INSC LAOCOON  PROSE
THE UNPRODUCTIVE MAN IS NOT A CHRISTIAN MUCH LESS  777D INSC LAOCOON  PROSE
  THE DESTROYER
```

CHRISTIANITY
```
("ALL CHRISTIAN STATES") PAINE HAS NOT ATTACKED  383D ANNO WATSON  MARG
  CHRISTIANITY
[THE DEISTS SAY] PAINE SAYS THAT CHRISTIANITY PUT A STOP  388D ANNO WATSON  * MARG
CHRISTIANITY IS CIVIL BUSINESS ONLY  . . . . . . . 398B ANNO BACON  MARG
CIVIL IS CHRISTIANITY OR RELIGION OR WHATEVER IS HUMANE  398B ANNO BACON  MARG
& NEVER CAN BE EXCEPT FACTIOUS IS CHRISTIANITY  . . . 403A ANNO BACON  MARG
THE KNAVE WHO IS CONVERTED TO [CHRISTIANITY] DEISM  . . 615B V LAST JUDG/N  PROSE
& THE KNAVE WHO IS CONVERTED TO CHRISTIANITY IS STILL A  615B V LAST JUDG/N  PROSE
  KNAVE
IF HUMILITY IS CHRISTIANITY YOU O JEWS ARE THE TRUE  652A JERUSALEM 27  PROSE
  CHRISTIANS
YOU O DEISTS PROFESS YOURSELVES THE ENEMIES OF CHRISTIANITY  682A JERUSALEM 52  PROSE
```

	PAGE	TITLE	LINE

CHRISTIANITY   (CONTINUED)
      THE GLORY OF CHRISTIANITY IS TO CONQUER BY FORGIVENESS . . 683A JERUSALEM 52   PROSE
      NO OTHER CHRISTIANITY AND OF NO OTHER GOSPEL THAN THE   716D JERUSALEM 77   PROSE
        LIBERTY BOTH
      IF MORAL VIRTUE WAS CHRISTIANITY . . . . 758 EV GOSPEL (1)   1
      IF MORALITY WAS CHRISTIANITY SOCRATES WAS THE SAVIOUR . . 775D INSC LAOCOON   PROSE
      CHRISTIANITY IS ART & NOT MONEY MONEY IS ITS CURSE . . . 777D INSC LAOCOON   PROSE
      (RE BYRON) IF MORALITY WAS CHRISTIANITY SOCRATES WAS THE   786D ANNO THORNTON   MARG
        SAVIOUR
      CHRISTIANITY AND ADORE HIM WHO IS THE EXPRESS IMAGE OF GOD 815D LETTER 23   PROSE
CHRISTIANS
      & THE SAME WILL IT BE AGAINST [OF] CHRISTIANS . . . . . 389B ANNO WATSON   MARG
      AND SO [SWEET] DEAR [CHRISTIANS] CHRISTIAN FRIENDS HOW   551 ONLY MAN/N   *   4
        DO YOU DO
      WORLD WAS NOT WORTHY SUCH WERE THE CHRISTIANS IN ALL AGES 604A INSC ARIMATHEA   PROSE
      STAND TWO A MAN & WOMAN THESE ARE THE PRIMITIVE CHRISTIANS 610C V LAST JUDG/N   PROSE
      HAVE BEEN CHRISTIANS IN OUTWARD APPEARANCE VOLTAIRE . . . 615B V LAST JUDG/N   PROSE
      IF HUMILITY IS CHRISTIANITY YOU O JEWS ARE THE TRUE   652A JERUSALEM 27   PROSE
        CHRISTIANS
      TO THE CHRISTIANS . . . . 716C JERUSALEM 77   TITLE
      O CHRISTIANS CHRISTIANS TELL ME WHY . . . . 761 FOR SEXES/GP   12
CHRISTMAS
      YOURS IN HEAD & HEART...A MERRY CHRISTMAS . . . . . . 791C LETTER 3   PROSE
      MERRY WITH MY FRIENDS TILL CHRISTMAS FOR AS MAN LIVETH   830B LETTER 30   PROSE
        NOT BY
      WITH DESIRE AND CURIOSITY BUT HOWEVER CHRISTMAS IS A-COMING 851D LETTER 50   PROSE
      WISHING YOU A MERRY CHRISTMAS REMEMBERING OUR . . . . . 853D LETTER 52   PROSE
      HAPPY CHRISTMAS AT LOVELY FELPHAM OUR SPIRITS SEEM STILL   853D LETTER 52   PROSE
      A HAPPY CHRISTMAS I REMAIN EVER . . . . 863C LETTER 60   PROSE
CHRIST'S
      KNOW THAT AFTER CHRIST'S DEATH HE BECAME JEHOVAH . . . . 150B MARRIAGE HH 5   PROSE
      CHRIST'S CRUCIFIX SHALL BE MADE AN EXCUSE FOR EXECUTING   380A FOUR ZOAS NOTE   PROSE
        CRIMINALS
      THE PERVERSIONS OF CHRIST'S WORDS & ACTS ARE ATTACKD . . 383B ANNO WATSON   MARG
      WE MAY HOPE TO SEE CHRIST'S DISCOURSES EXPUNGD . . . . 384D ANNO WATSON   MARG
      EVER DOUBT CHRIST'S IN THE ABOVE SENSE OF THE WORD MIRACLE 391D ANNO WATSON   MARG
      THOUGHT IS ACT CHRIST'S ACTS WERE NOTHING TO CAESAR'S IF   400C ANNO BACON   MARG
        THIS IS NOT
      IF TO THE MIDDLE CLASS IT IS THE DIRECT CONTRARY   406D ANNO BACON   MARG
        TO CHRIST'S ADVICE
      AND IS SERVED BY NONE HE IS ACCORDING TO CHRIST'S   570B DESC CAT 3   PROSE
        DEFINITION
      NUMBER XII THE SOLDIERS CASTING LOTS FOR CHRIST'S GARMENT 584A DESC CAT 12   TITLE
        A DRAWING
      GO THEREFORE CAST OUT DEVILS IN CHRIST'S NAME . . . . . 718 STOOD AMONG/J   24
      CHRIST'S PRETENSIONS WERE ALL VANITY . . . . 758 EV GOSPEL (1)   2
CHRONOS
      THE GREEKS REPRESENT CHRONOS OR TIME AS A VERY AGED MAN   614D V LAST JUDG/N   PROSE
        THIS IS FABLE
CHRYSTAL   SEE CRYSTAL
      WHETHER ON CHRYSTAL ROCKS YE ROVE . . . . 11 TO MUSES/PS   9
CHURCH
      & YOU HINDER YOUR HUSBAND FROM GOING TO CHURCH . . . . 48A ISLAND MOON 4   PROSE
      HA HA SAID INFLAMMABLE GASS WHAT DONT YOU LIKE TO GO TO   48A ISLAND MOON 4   PROSE
        CHURCH
      IF I HAD NOT A PLACE OF PROFIT THAT FORCES ME TO GO TO   48A ISLAND MOON 4   PROSE
        CHURCH
      THE WHOLE OF THE NEW CHURCH IS IN THE ACTIVE LIFE . . . 92D ANNO SWED LOVE   MARG
      SO HE TOOK ME THRO A STABLE & THRO A CHURCH & DOWN . . . 155D MARRIAGE HH 17   PROSE
      INTO THE CHURCH VAULT AT THE END OF WHICH WAS A MILL . . 155D MARRIAGE HH 17   PROSE
      THE CHURCH & I TOOK HIM TO THE ALTAR AND OPEND THE BIBLE   157A MARRIAGE HH 17   PROSE
      EVERY BLACKNING CHURCH APPALLS . . . . 170 LONDON/N   11
      REMOVE AWAY THAT BLACKNING CHURCH . . . . 176 ANCNT PROVRB/N   1
      [O] DEAR MOTHER DEAR MOTHER THE CHURCH IS COLD . . . . 179 LIT VAGABOND/N *   1
      BUT IF AT THE CHURCH THEY WOULD GIVE US SOME ALE . . . . 179 LIT VAGABOND/N   6
      NOR EVER ONCE WISH FROM THE CHURCH TO STRAY . . . . . 179 LIT VAGABOND/N   9
      AND MODEST DAME LURCH WHO IS ALWAYS AT CHURCH . . . . . 179 LIT VAGABOND/N   12
      THEY ARE BOTH GONE UP TO CHURCH TO PRAY . . . . 180 CHIMNEY SWP/N   4
      REMOVE AWAY THAT BLACKNING CHURCH . . . . 184 SEVRL QUESTN/N   15
      THEY ARE BOTH GONE UP TO THE CHURCH TO PRAY . . . . . 212 CHIMNEY SWP/SE   4
      DEAR MOTHER DEAR MOTHER THE CHURCH IS COLD . . . . . . 216 LIT VAGABND/SE   1
      BUT IF AT THE CHURCH THEY WOULD GIVE US SOME ALE . . . . 216 LIT VAGABND/SE   5
      NOR EVER ONCE WISH FROM THE CHURCH TO STRAY . . . . . 216 LIT VAGABND/SE   8
      AND MODEST DAME LURCH WHO IS ALWAYS AT CHURCH . . . . . 216 LIT VAGABND/SE   11
      EVERY BLACKNING CHURCH APPALLS . . . . 216 LONDON/SE   10
      HE WENT TO CHURCH IN A MAY MORNING . . . . 434 WILLIAM BOND   5
      SHE REPRESENTS THE CHRISTIAN CHURCH . . . . 443B LAST JUDGMNT/L   PROSE
      SO [AS SURE] AS A CHURCH IS KNOWN BY ITS STEEPLE . . . . 559 I ROSE UP AT/N *   23
      NUMBER XVI THE PENANCE OF JANE SHORE IN ST PAULS CHURCH   585D DESC CAT 16   TITLE
        A DRAWING
      IS ONE OF THE MOST AMIABLE FEATURES OF THE CHRISTIAN CHURCH 590B CHAUCER 2   PROSE
      SOMETIMES IN THE ARMS OF A FEMALE [THEY] THIS REPRESENTED 607C V LAST JUDG/N   *PROSE
        THE CHURCH
      THE MAN STRANGLING TWO WOMEN REPRESENTS A CRUEL CHURCH . . 608C V LAST JUDG/N   PROSE
      THE CHURCH UNIVERSAL REPRESENTED BY A WOMAN . . . . . 609D V LAST JUDG/N   PROSE
      THE CHILDREN OF ABRAHAM OR HEBREW CHURCH ARE . . . . . 610B V LAST JUDG/N   PROSE
      OR CIVILIZED LIFE SUCH AS IT IS IN THE CHRISTIAN CHURCH   610C V LAST JUDG/N   PROSE
      DRAGON'S CAVERN REPRESENTS THE LATTER STATE OF THE CHURCH 610C V LAST JUDG/N   PROSE
      OF THE BLESSED IN WHICH A GOTHIC CHURCH IS REPRESENTATIVE 610C V LAST JUDG/N   PROSE
      REPRESENT THOSE WHO WERE NOT IN THE LINE OF THE CHURCH . . 611D V LAST JUDG/N   PROSE
      HE WHO IS OUT OF THE CHURCH & OPPOSES IT . . . . . . 613A V LAST JUDG/N   PROSE
      THE COURTS OF JUSTICE MORE MERCIFUL THAN THE CHURCH . . . 615D V LAST JUDG/N   PROSE

```
                                                              PAGE     TITLE          LINE
CHURCH    (CONTINUED)
         THE MODERN CHURCH CRUCIFIES CHRIST WITH THE HEAD DOWNWARDS   615D V LAST JUDG/N    PROSE
         THE CHURCH STEEPLE WITH ITS MERRY BELLS  . . . . . .  . 618C ILLUS MILTON       PROSE
         LOOK BACK INTO THE CHURCH PAUL LOOK THREE WOMEN AROUND     688 JERUSALEM 56        42
         WHAT IS A WIFE & WHAT IS A HARLOT WHAT IS A CHURCH & WHAT   689 JERUSALEM 57         8
         TO BE WORSHIPD BY THE CHURCH OF ROME  . . . . . . . .  . 749 EV GOSPEL(B)/N       59
         SUFFICIENTLY THAT THE MONUMENT IS IN EAST DEREHAM CHURCH   838B LETTER 37        PROSE
         FROM THE ANGEL INN NEAR ST CLEMENTS CHURCH STRAND  . .  . 871C LETTER 73        PROSE
CHURCHES
         IF IT WAS NOT FOR CHURCHES & CHAPELS  . . . . . . . .   48B ISLAND MOON 4      PROSE
         IT IS SO WITH SWEDENBORG HE SHEWS THE FOLLY OF CHURCHES    157D MARRIAGE HH 21   PROSE
         [ BLACKENS OER THE CHURCHES WALLS]  . . . . . . . .  .   170 LONDON/N            10
         ROLLING VOLUMES OF GREY MIST INVOLVE CHURCHES PALACES     242 EUROPE 12           3
             TOWERS
         MY ANTAMON THE SEVEN CHURCHES OF LEUTHA SEEK THY LOVE   . . 244 EUROPE 14          20
         THESE WERE THE CHURCHES HOSPITALS CASTLES PALACES    . . 246 SONG OF LOS 4         1
         I WILL NOT WORSHIP IN THEIR CHURCHES NOR KING IN THEIR     491 MILTON 10          13
             THEATRES
         SEEING THE CHURCHES AT THEIR PERIOD IN TERROR & DESPAIR    506 MILTON 22          40
         O SWEDENBORG STRONGEST OF MEN THE SAMSON SHORN BY          506 MILTON 22          50
             THE CHURCHES
         AND THESE ARE THE CRIES OF THE CHURCHES BEFORE THE TWO     506 MILTON 22          56
             WITNESSES
         DIVIDE FOUR-FOLD INTO FOUR CHURCHES WHEN LAZARUS AROSE  . . 508 MILTON 24          31
         TO BE FORMED INTO THE CHURCHES OF BEULAH . . . . . .      511 MILTON 25          39
         SATAN & ADAM ARE STATES CREATED INTO TWENTY-SEVEN CHURCHES 521 MILTON 32          25
         THE OTHER FLOWS THRO THE AERIAL VOID & ALL THE CHURCHES    526 MILTON 35          52
         THE LARK IS LOS'S MESSENGER THRO THE TWENTY-SEVEN CHURCHES 526 MILTON 35          63
         THE MONSTROUS CHURCHES OF BEULAH THE GODS OF ULRO DARK  . . 528 MILTON 37          16
         AND THESE THE NAMES OF THE TWENTY-SEVEN HEAVENS & THEIR    528 MILTON 37          35
             CHURCHES
         FROM HENCE SHE COMES FORTH ON THE CHURCHES IN DELIGHT   . . 529 MILTON 38          24
         THY PURPOSE & THE PURPOSE OF THY PRIESTS & OF THY CHURCHES 530 MILTON 38          37
         THO SEEN IN FALLACY OUTSIDE A FALLACY OF SATAN'S CHURCHES  532 MILTON 39          61
         ON AN ENLARGED SCALE TO ORNAMENT THE ALTARS OF CHURCHES    584B DESC CAT 14     PROSE
         CHURCHES & THE INN IN SOUTHWARK IS MINUTELY LABOURD  . .  . 588A CHAUCER/N      PROSE
         OUR CHURCHES & ABBEYS ARE TREASURES OF [ SPIRITUAL RICHES] 601A PUB ADDRESS/N  *PROSE
         ABEL KNEELS ON A BLOODY CLOUD DESCRIPTIVE OF THOSE CHURCHES 606D V LAST JUDG/N  PROSE
         IN THOSE CHURCHES EVER CONSUMING & EVER BUILDING BY THE     634 JERUSALEM 13      62
             SPECTRES
         AND THESE THE NAMES OF THE TWENTY-SEVEN HEAVENS & THEIR     716 JERUSALEM 75      10
             CHURCHES
         OF THE SEVEN CHURCHES IN ASIA ANTICHRIST SCIENCE  . . . . 777B INSC LAOCOON    PROSE
CHURCHILL
         AS POOR CHURCHILL SAID "NATURE THOU [ XXX] ART MY GODDESS"  785A ILLUS DANTE 7  *PROSE
CHURCH YARD
         DOES NOT THE WORM ERECT A PILLAR IN THE MOULDERING CHURCH   193 V DAU ALBION 5      41
             YARD
         LAMBETH AND J JOHNSON ST PAULS CHURCH YARD  . . . . .  . 209B FOR CHILDRN/GP  *TITLE
         WILL YOU ERECT A LASTING HABITATION IN THE MOULDERING      353 FOUR ZOAS 8        495
             CHURCH YARD
         FROM MR PHILLIPS OF ST PAULS CHURCH YARD IT IS AS YET AN   841B LETTER 41      PROSE
         MIRTH THE THREE TABERNACLES THE CHURCH YARD DEATH HOPE    SUPP PENC DRAW 2.19 *TITLE
CHURCHYARDS
         CRIED TO THE CHURCHYARDS & THE EARTHWORM CAME IN DISMAL     355 FOUR ZOAS 8        537
             STATE
CHURCH-YARDS
         I WALKED THROUGH DREARY PLACES WITH HIM AND IN CHURCH-YARDS  37C CONTEMPLATN/PS  PROSE
CHURN
         AND ALL HIS BOWELS BEGAN TO [ BURN] CHURN  . . . . . .    187 WHEN KLOPSTK/N      16
         IF MEN WILL ACT LIKE A MAID SMILING OVER A CHURN  . . . . 556 IF MEN ACT/N         1
CHUSE     SEE CHOOSE
         & WE THINK YOU ARE RASCALS I DO AS I CHUSE  . . . . . .   51C ISLAND MOON 6     PROSE
         LET EACH CHUSE ONE HABITATION  . . . . . . . . . .  .   224 URIZEN 4            36
         IF THOU CHUSE TO ELECT A WORM IT SHALL REMOVE THE MOUNTAINS 502 MILTON 20          19
CHUSING
         CHUSING TO WANDER LIKE A SON OF ZAZEL IN THE ROCKS   . . . 100 TIRIEL 1            39
CHYMISTRY
         COOKERY CHYMISTRY [ ?CONJUNCTIVES] MECHANICS TACTICS        46D ISLAND MOON 3  *PROSE
             PATHOLOGY
CICERO
         OF PLATO & CICERO WHICH ALL MEN OUGHT TO CONTEMN  . . . . 480B MILTON 1        PROSE
         BUT PLATO & CICERO DID INCULCATE BEFORE HIM     . . . . . 757D EV GOSPEL       PROSE
         THAT PLATO & CICERO DID NOT WRITE  . . . . . . . . .  . 758 EV GOSPEL (2)        4
CIELING
         WIPING HIS FACE & LOOKING ON THE CORNER OF THE CIELING SANG  57A ISLAND MOON 9  *PROSE
         BENEATH HER ROSE A DOWNY BED & A CIELING COVERD ALL  . . . 369 FOUR ZOAS 9       463
         BY FAIRIES AS THEY DANCE ON THE BED THE CIELING & THE FLOOR 618C ILLUS MILTON   *PROSE
CIELINGS
         . . . IMMOVEABLE WITHIN ITS [ ARCHES ALL] WALLS & CIELINGS  286 FOUR ZOAS 2       245
         THE CIELINGS DEVOTION THE HEARTHS THANKSGIVING   . . . . 632 JERUSALEM 12        37
CIRCLE
         THAT ROUND THE CIRCLE OF THE WORLD WOUD FLY  . . . . .    15 IMIT SPEN/PS        36
         THE DANCE WAS BROKE THE CIRCLE JUST BEGUN  . . . . . .   43C WOE CRIED MUSE   PROSE
         ERE THOU MEASURE THE CIRCLE THAT HE SHALL RUN  . . . . . 142 FRENCH REVOLTN     191
         AND THEY INCLOSD MY INFINITE BRAIN INTO A NARROW CIRCLE    191 V DAU ALBION 2      32
         HEAVEN A MIGHTY CIRCLE TURNING GOD A TYRANT CROWND   . . . 241 EUROPE 10          23
         A CIRCLE OF DARKNESS THEN FIXED  . . . . . . . . .  .   251 AHANIA 3            32
         TURND ROUND THE CIRCLE OF DESTINY WITH TEARS & BITTER SIGHS 266 FOUR ZOAS 1        74
         . . . THE CIRCLE OF DESTINY COMPLETE  . . . . . . . .    266 FOUR ZOAS 1          87
         THE CIRCLE OF DESTINY COMPLETE THEY GAVE TO IT A SPACE  . . 267 FOUR ZOAS 1        101
         [ ?TURND ?ROUND THE CIRCLE OF ?DESTINY XXX SIGHS]   . . . SUPP FOUR ZOAS 1        *
```

	PAGE	TITLE	LINE

CIRCLE   (CONTINUED)

YOUR WITHRING LIPS & TONGUE SHRINK UP INTO A NARROW CIRCLE   294 FOUR ZOAS 3   88
CIRCLE OER CIRCLE NOR ON HIGH ATTAIN A VOID . . . . .   316 FOUR ZOAS 6   197
INTO THE HEAVENS OF ENITHARMON IN A MIGHTY CIRCLE . . .   332 FOUR ZOAS 7   466
AND MURMURING IN THEIR CHANNELS FLOW & CIRCLE ROUND HIS   378 FOUR ZOAS 9   805
   FEET

THEY REND THE HEAVENS ROUND THE WATCHERS IN A FIERY CIRCLE   502 MILTON 20   46
ARE YOU THE FIERY CIRCLE THAT LATE DROVE IN FURY & FIRE   523 MILTON 34   3
GHIOTTO'S CIRCLE OR APELLES' LINE . . . .   542 FLORENTINE/N   26
IF YOU HAVE FORMD A CIRCLE TO GO INTO   . . . .   557 TO GOD/N   1
YOUR WITHRING LIPS AND TONGUE SHRINK UP INTO A NARROW   655 JERUSALEM 29   69
   CIRCLE
A CIRCLE IN CONTINUAL GYRATIONS THIS BECAME A HEART . . .   659 JERUSALEM 33   20
HIS EAR IN A SPIRAL CIRCLE OUTWARD THEN SENT HIM   662 JERUSALEM 36   13
   OVER JORDAN
TAUGHT TO TOUCH THE HARP TO DANCE IN THE CIRCLE OF WARRIORS   706 JERUSALEM 68   56
AND WHERE LUTHER ENDS ADAM BEGINS AGAIN IN ETERNAL CIRCLE   716 JERUSALEM 75   24
RESTING IN A CIRCLE IN MALDEN OR IN STRATHNESS OR DURA . .   737 JERUSALEM 90   62
OF SIN & THE TREE OF GOOD & EVIL SPRANG FROM THE ROCKY   740 JERUSALEM 92   25
   CIRCLE & SNAKE
LESSER CIRCLE POINT OF THE UNIVERSE CANTO ELEVENTH LINE...   786A ILLS DANTE 101   PROSE
PURGATORY FIRST CIRCLE . . . .   SUPP ILLUS DANTE 7   *PROSE

CIRCLED

[CIRCLED] [?CUBED] IN [INFINITE ORB] [?WINDOW SQUARE] . . .   286 FOUR ZOAS 2   * 245
THE MOON HIS FURIOUS FOREHEAD CIRCLED WITH BLACK BURSTING   334 FOUR ZOAS 7B   41
   THUNDERS
IN CHAINS OF IRON & IN DUNGEONS CIRCLED WITH CEASELESS   377 FOUR ZOAS 9   750
   FIRES
IN CHAINS OF IRON & IN DUNGEONS CIRCLED WITH CEASELESS   514 MILTON 27   32
   FIRES

CIRCLES

HEAVES IN ENORMOUS CIRCLES NOW THE TIMES ARE RETURND UPON   199 AMERICA 9   19
   THEE
WHIRLING ABOUT IN FURIOUS CIRCLES ROUND THE IMMORTAL FIEND   240 EUROPE 4   30
INTO EARTHS ROLLING IN CIRCLES OF SPACE THAT LIKE AN OCEAN   241 EUROPE 10   19
   RUSHD
AS THE MOON ANGUISHD CIRCLES THE EARTH . . . . . .   250 AHANIA 2   40
NINE AGES COMPLETED THEIR CIRCLES . . . .   260 BOOK OF LOS 5   41
THE THREE DESTINIES SIT ON THE CIRCLES OF PLATO'S HEAVENS   619B ILLUS MILTON   PROSE
LOS ROLLED HIS EYES INTO TWO NARROW CIRCLES THEN SENT HIM   661 JERUSALEM 34   53
CIRCLES THE HELLS FOR FOOD TO THE HEAVENS FOOD OF TORMENT   680 JERUSALEM 49   62
WHERE THE DRUIDS REARD THEIR ROCKY CIRCLES . . . . . .   740 JERUSALEM 92   24
BETWEEN THE FIFTH AND SIXTH CIRCLES . . . .   786A ILLS DANTE 101   PROSE
OR PERHAPS IT OCCUPIES BOTH CIRCLES WITH ITS ENVIRONS .   786A ILLS DANTE 101   PROSE
CENTAURS MOST LIKELY DANTE DESCRIBES THE...CIRCLES IN CANTO   786A ILLS DANTE 101   PROSE
   XI...

CIRCLING

THE WELL-WASHD STOOLS A CIRCLING ROW . . . .   16 BLIND-MANS/PS   7
IN CHAOS AND CIRCLING DARK URIZEN . . . .   250 AHANIA 2   39
CIRCLING ROUND THE DARK DEMON WITH HOWLINGS . . . . .   259 BOOK OF LOS 5   24
THO IN THE BRAIN OF MAN WE LIVE & IN HIS CIRCLING NERVES   272 FOUR ZOAS 1   302
THE FEAST REDOUNDS & CROWND WITH ROSES & THE CIRCLING VINE   276 FOUR ZOAS 1   435
CIRCLING ROUND THE DARK DEMON WITH HOWLINGS DISMAY & SHARP   302 FOUR ZOAS 4   200
   BLIGHTINGS
OF CIRCLING FIRE UNCEASING PLAYS TO FEED THEM WITH LIFE   308 FOUR ZOAS 5   115
   & BRING
GATHRING THE FRUIT OF THAT MYSTERIOUS TREE CIRCLING ITS   343 FOUR ZOAS 8   * 84
   ROOT
BEGINNING AT THE TREE OF MYSTERY CIRCLING ITS ROOT . . .   345 FOUR ZOAS 8   173
TO THE GOLDEN WHEELS CIRCLING UPON THE PAVEMENT OF HEAVEN   376 FOUR ZOAS 9   719
   & ALL
CIRCLING ALBION'S CLIFFS IN WHICH THE FOUR-FOLD WORLD   532 MILTON 39   60
   RESIDES

CIRCUIT

ERE ONCE AGAIN THE CHANGING MOON HER CIRCUIT HATH PERFORMED   38A SAMSON/PS   PROSE

CIRCULAR

A CIRCULAR DANCE . . . .   SUPP ILLUS GRAY   *TITLE

CIRCULATE

THE BLOOD IS SEEN TO CIRCULATE IN THEIR LIMBS . . . . .   581A DESC CAT 5   PROSE
AMERICA ENABLE HIM TO CIRCULATE PUBLICATIONS TO AN IMMENSE   841C LETTER 41   PROSE

CIRCULATION

AND YOUR MAGAZINE BEING AS EXTENSIVE IN ITS CIRCULATION   863D LETTER 61   PROSE

CIRCUMCISING

. . . CIRCUMSCRIBING & CIRCUMCISING THE EXCREMENTITIOUS   745 JERUSALEM 98   18

CIRCUMCISION

ON CIRCUMCISION NOT ON VIRGINITY O REASONERS OF ALBION   687 JERUSALEM 55   66

CIRCUMFERENCE   SEE SKUMFERENCE

IN THE CIRCUMFERENCE THEY CAST A BOUND ABOUT THE INFINITE   92A ANNO SWED LOVE   MARG
REASON IS THE BOUND OR OUTWARD CIRCUMFERENCE OF ENERGY .   149D MARRIAGE HH 4   PROSE
. . . LOOKING UP FROM [CIRCUMFERENCE] SKUMFERENCE TO CENTER   555 BLAKES APL/N 1   18
CRY TOM COOKE PROVES FROM CIRCUMFERENCE TO CENTER . . .   596 BLAKES APOL/PA   11
WEST THE CIRCUMFERENCE SOUTH THE ZENITH NORTH . . . . .   632 JERUSALEM 12   55
ALBION'S CIRCUMFERENCE WAS CLOSD HIS CENTER BEGAN DARKNING   642 JERUSALEM 19   36
AND SCOTLAND UTTERD FROM THE CIRCUMFERENCE INTO ETERNITY   646 JERUSALEM 23   28
IN THE CIRCUMFERENCE & EVERY MINUTE PARTICULAR IS HOLY .   708 JERUSALEM 69   42
THE CIRCUMFERENCE IS WITHIN WITHOUT IS FORMED THE SELFISH   709 JERUSALEM 71   7
   CENTER
AND THE CIRCUMFERENCE STILL EXPANDS GOING FORWARD   709 JERUSALEM 71   8
   TO ETERNITY
IN THE FOUR SENSES IN THE OUTLINE THE CIRCUMFERENCE & FORM   745 JERUSALEM 98   22
   FOR EVER

```
                                                            PAGE      TITLE        LINE
CIRCUMSCRIBD
     THE TWELVE DAUGHTERS IN RAHAB & TIRZAH HAVE CIRCUMSCRIBD    705 JERUSALEM 67      41
       THE BRAIN
CIRCUMSCRIBE
     COME CIRCUMSCRIBE THIS TONGUE OF SWEETS & WITH A SCREW      349 FOUR ZOAS 8      317
       OF IRON
     WITH POWERS FITTED TO CIRCUMSCRIBE THIS DARK SATANIC DEATH  507 MILTON 23        51
     COME CIRCUMSCRIBE THIS TONGUE OF SWEETS & WITH A SCREW      705 JERUSALEM 68       5
       OF IRON
     AND WHILE THEY CIRCUMSCRIBE HIS BRAIN & WHILE THEY          736 JERUSALEM 90       3
       CIRCUMSCRIBE
     HIS HEART & WHILE THEY CIRCUMSCRIBE HIS LOINS A VEIL & NET  736 JERUSALEM 90       4
CIRCUMSCRIBED
     LONDON FEELS HIS BRAIN CUT ROUND EDINBURGH'S HEART          703 JERUSALEM 66      64
       IS CIRCUMSCRIBED
CIRCUMSCRIBING
     . . . CIRCUMSCRIBING & CIRCUMCISING THE EXCREMENTITIOUS     745 JERUSALEM 98      18
CIRCUMSPECT
     REMEMBRANCE I FEEL IT IS NECESSARY TO BE VERY CIRCUMSPECT  857C LETTER 54       PROSE
CIRCUMSTANCE
     IS TAKEN OF THIS CIRCUMSTANCE TO DESCRIBE THE SUBJECT    .  567B DESC CAT 3      PROSE
     IS TAKEN OF THIS CIRCUMSTANCE TO DESCRIBE THE SUBJECT    .  588D CHAUCER/N      PROSE
     IS TAKEN OF THIS CIRCUMSTANCE TO DESCRIBE THE SUBJECT    .  590C CHAUCER 2      PROSE
     A CIRCUMSTANCE HAS OCCURRED WHICH HAS AGAIN RAISED         865A LETTER 62       PROSE
       MY INDIGNATION
CIRCUMSTANCES
     HERE HE ALLOWS AN ANALYSIS OF CIRCUMSTANCES     .    .    .  462B ANNO REYNOLDS   MARG
     MANY ARE DEISTS WHO WOULD IN CERTAIN CIRCUMSTANCES   .    .  615A V LAST JUDG/N  PROSE
     MIGHT HURT MY PECUNIARY CIRCUMSTANCES    .    .    .    .    812B LETTER 22      PROSE
     NO FURTHER MY FRIEND THAN HE IS COMPELLD BY CIRCUMSTANCES   819C LETTER 25      PROSE
     IN ALL CIRCUMSTANCES I FIND THAT YOU WAS RIGHT IN SUPPOSING 854C LETTER 53      PROSE
CIRCUMVENTING
     CIRCUMVENTING & WHATEVER IS NEGATIVE IS VICE   .    .    .    88D ANNO LAVATER    MARG
CIRENCESTER
     CIRENCESTER PLACE I FEARED YOU MIGHT BE GONE OR I MIGHT    871B LETTER 72       PROSE
     JOHN LINNELL ESQRE CIRENCESTER PLACE FITZROY SQUARE    .    .   SUPP ADDRESSES/L  *TITLE
CISTERN
     THE CISTERN CONTAINS THE FOUNTAIN OVERFLOWS    .    .    .    151D MARRIAGE HH 8  PROSE
CISTERNS
     THAT RAISES WATER INTO CISTERNS BROKEN & BURND IN FIRE   .  337 FOUR ZOAS 7B     177
     THE PLATES & SCREWS & WRACKS & SAWS & CORDS & FIRES         514 MILTON 27        34
       & CISTERNS
     THAT RAISES WATER INTO CISTERNS BROKEN & BURND WITH FIRE    700 JERUSALEM 65      19
CITIES
     LIKE SUMMER BEES AND ALL THE GOLDEN CITIES    .    .    .    .   19 EDW THIRD/PS 2     13
     HOW MANY IN WALLED CITIES LIE AND GROAN    .    .    .    .     30 EDW THIRD/PS 5      8
     SHALL RISE CITIES AND THRONES AND ARMS AND AWFUL POWRS   .    32 EDW THIRD/PS 6     18
     CITIES SHALL SING AND VALES IN RICH ARRAY    .    .    .    .    33 EDW THIRD/PS 6     47
     LIKE SMOULDRING FIRE OR IN THE BUZZ OF CITIES FLIES ABROAD  42C THEN SHE BORE    PROSE
     THESE GODS LAST NAMD LIVE IN THE SMOKE OF CITIES    .    .    42D THEN SHE BORE    PROSE
     ALAS IN CITIES WHERES THE MAN WHOSE FACE IS NOT A MASK      42D THEN SHE BORE    PROSE
       UNTO HIS HEART
     . . .HEAR THE VOICE OF VALLIES THE VOICE OF MEEK CITIES     143 FRENCH REVOLTN    207
     LIKE PESTILENT FOGS ROUND CITIES OF MEN . . . . . . . .    144 FRENCH REVOLTN    236
     . . . BENDING OVER THE CITIES OF MEN    .    .    .    .    .    146 FRENCH REVOLTN    264
     WITH THE PROPERTIES OF WOODS RIVERS MOUNTAINS LAKES CITIES  153A MARRIAGE HH 11  PROSE
       NATIONS
     OVER THE HILLS THE VALES THE CITIES RAGE THE RED FLAMES     202 AMERICA 16         1
       FIERCE
     HIS SHIELD THAT BOUND TWELVE DEMONS & THEIR CITIES IN ITS   205 AMERICA CANC C     2
       ORB
     ANGELS OF CITIES AND OF PARISHES AND VILLAGES AND FAMILIES  205 AMERICA CANC C    18
     COLD HE WANDERD ON HIGH OVER THEIR CITIES    .    .    .    .    235 URIZEN 25          5
     WALKD OVER THE CITIES IN SORROW    .    .    .    .    .    .    235 URIZEN 25      *   14
     THEN THE INHABITANTS OF THOSE CITIES    .    .    .    .    .    235 URIZEN 25         23
     AND THEIR THIRTY CITIES DIVIDED    .    .    .    .    .    .    236 URIZEN 25         43
     AND THE THIRTY CITIES REMAIND    .    .    .    .    .    .    .    236 URIZEN 28          8
     THEIR BRETHREN OF OTHER CITIES    .    .    .    .    .    .    236 URIZEN 28         18
     THE CITIES SEND TO ONE ANOTHER SAYING MY SONS ARE MAD   .  275 FOUR ZOAS 1       398
     TO DESOLATE THEIR CITIES MAN SHALL BE NO MORE AWAKE O HOSTS 275 FOUR ZOAS 1       407
     IN WHICH [ARE] WERE TOWNS & CITIES NATIONS SEAS MOUNTAINS   284 FOUR ZOAS 2      *  177
       & RIVERS
     THEN CAME HE AMONG FIERY CITIES & CASTLES BUILT OF BURNING  314 FOUR ZOAS 6       115
       STEEL
     ROLL DOWN THE MOUNTAINS IN BLACK TORRENTS CITIES VILLAGES   359 FOUR ZOAS 9        75
     AND BUILDING ARCHES HIGH & CITIES TURRETS & [HIGH ] TOWERS  361 FOUR ZOAS 9       167
       & DOMES
     THRO DISMAL DARKNESS DRAVE THE PLOW OF AGES OVER CITIES     365 FOUR ZOAS 9       312
     ACT MORE TERRIFIC IN THE CENTRAL CITIES OF THE NATIONS   .  510 MILTON 25         4
     AND THE FORTY-EIGHT STARRY REGIONS ARE CITIES OF           529 MILTON 38         1
       THE LEVITES
     OF PITCH & NITRE ITS RUIND PALACES & CITIES & MIGHTY WORKS  529 MILTON 38        19
     AND I BEHELD THE TWENTY-FOUR CITIES OF ALBION    .    .    .    534 MILTON 42        16
     AND THE PLOWMAN TO PLOW UP THE CITIES AND TOWERS    .    .  565A DESC CAT 2      TITLE
     ON WALLS OF TEMPLES TOWERS CITIES PALACES AND ERECTED IN   565C DESC CAT 2      PROSE
     CITIES & NATIONS FAMILIES & PEOPLES TONGUES & LAWS    .    .  629 JERUSALEM 10      27
     AND BLACK ANXIETY AND THE CITIES OF THE SALAMANDRINE MEN    634 JERUSALEM 13      43
     HE VIEWS THE CITY OF GOLGONOOZA & ITS SMALLER CITIES    .    634 JERUSALEM 13      56
     THE CITIES OF THE NATIONS ARE THE SMOKE OF HER CONSUMMATION 653 JERUSALEM 29      22
     THE CITIES OF ALBION SEEK THY FACE LONDON GROANS IN PAIN    656 JERUSALEM 30      23
     THE TWENTY-EIGHT CITIES OF ALBION STRETCH THEIR HANDS TO    656 JERUSALEM 30      26
       THEE
```

339

CITIES   (CONTINUED)
THE ANCIENT CITIES OF THE EARTH REMOVE AS A TRAVELLER   . .   659 JERUSALEM 33   14
AND SHALL ALBION'S CITIES REMAIN WHEN I PASS OVER THEM   . .   659 JERUSALEM 33   15
GENEROUS IMMORTAL GUARDIAN GOLDEN CLAD FOR CITIES   . .   665 JERUSALEM 38   46
OUR PALACES AND CITIES AND HOWEVER FRUITFUL ARE OUR FIELDS   675 JERUSALEM 45   12
THE VEGETATING CITIES ARE BURNED & CONSUMED FROM THE EARTH   679 JERUSALEM 49   12
CITIES & NATIONS CONTENDED IN FIRES & CLOUDS & TEMPESTS   686 JERUSALEM 55   25
THY VILLAGES DIE OF THE FAMINE AND THY CITIES . . . . .   693 JERUSALEM 60   27
COME NOW WITH ME INTO THE VILLAGES WALK THRO ALL THE CITIES   696 JERUSALEM 62   23
THE CITIES & VILLAGES OF ALBION BECAME ROCK & SAND   697 JERUSALEM 63   18
    UNHUMANIZED
AND FIRE & THE RUIN OF CITIES & NATIONS & FAMILIES   698 JERUSALEM 64   11
    & TONGUES
THEIR VILLAGES TOWNS CITIES SEA-PORTS TEMPLES SUBLIME   709 JERUSALEM 71   13
    CATHEDRALS
FOR ALL ARE MEN IN ETERNITY RIVERS MOUNTAINS CITIES   709 JERUSALEM 71   15
    VILLAGES
THEIR VILLAGES CITIES SEA PORTS THEIR CORN FIELDS & GARDENS   710 JERUSALEM 71   21
    SPACIOUS
IN THE TERRIBLE FAMILY FEUDS OF ALBION'S CITIES & VILLAGES   714 JERUSALEM 73   47
AWAY FROM THE NATIONS OF THE EARTH & FROM THE CITIES OF   720 JERUSALEM 79   9
    THE NATIONS
AND ALL THE NATIONS OF THE EARTH WERE SEEN IN THE CITIES   720 JERUSALEM 79   23
    OF ALBION
THE SEEDS OF CITIES & OF VILLAGES IN THE HUMAN BOSOM   . .   728 JERUSALEM 83   55
WHERE CITIES SHALL REMAIN & WHERE VILLAGES FOR THE REST   728 JERUSALEM 83   57
IN ALL THE CITIES OF THE NATIONS PARIS MADRID AMSTERDAM   729 JERUSALEM 84   14
CITIES WHERE BEULAH LOVELY TERMINATES . . . .   730 JERUSALEM 85   26
CITIES NOT YET EMBODIED IN TIME AND SPACE PLANT YE   . .   730 JERUSALEM 85   27
AND VALLEYS & THY PLEASANT CITIES HOLINESS TO THE LORD   . .   731 JERUSALEM 86   12
DO I SLEEP AMIDST DANGER TO FRIENDS O MY CITIES & COUNTIES   744 JERUSALEM 96   33
AND ALL THE CITIES OF ALBION ROSE FROM THEIR SLUMBERS AND   744 JERUSALEM 96   38
    ALL
IN THE MIDST OF HIS TWENTY-EIGHT CITIES EACH WITH HIS BOW   744 JERUSALEM 97   17
    BREATHING
CITIE'S
DEATH WONS IN CITIES' SMOKE AND IN STILL NIGHT   . . . .   30 EDW THIRD/PS 5   6
CITIZEN
LOOK UP LOOK UP O CITIZEN OF LONDON ENLARGE THY   159C SONG LIBERTY   PROSE
    COUNTENANCE
HOW THE INDUSTRIOUS CITIZEN THE PAINS OF THE HUSBANDMAN   193 V DAU ALBION 5   13
CITIZENS
HER CITIZENS SHALL THRONG ABOUT HER GATES . . . . . .   34C KING JOHN/PS   PROSE
THE CITIZENS OF NEW-YORK CLOSE THEIR BOOKS & LOCK THEIR   201 AMERICA 14   13
    CHESTS
THE CITIZENS IN LEADEN GYVES THE INHABITANTS OF SUBURBS   243 EUROPE 12   30
HAS HERE ALSO INTRODUCED ONE OF THE RICH CITIZENS OF LONDON   568C DESC CAT 3   PROSE
PHYSICIAN AND ON HIS OTHER HAND WITH TWO CITIZENS OF LONDON   570D DESC CAT 3   PROSE
THE CITIZENS AND THEIR COOK ARE EACH LEADERS OF A CLASS   571D DESC CAT 3   PROSE
CHAUCER HAS BEEN SOMEHOW MADE TO NUMBER FOUR CITIZENS   . .   571D DESC CAT 3   PROSE
THE MERCHANT CANNOT BE ONE OF THE THREE CITIZENS . . .   572A DESC CAT 3   PROSE
WHEREAS CHAUCER SAYS OF HIS RICH CITIZENS . . . . . .   572A DESC CAT 3   PROSE
CITY
GIANTS OF MIGHTY ARM BEFORE THE FLOOD CAIN'S CITY   . . .   41A THEN SHE BORE   PROSE
WAS SHEWN THE HOLY CITY THEN ATHENS LEARNING   . . . .   41A THEN SHE BORE   PROSE
TO CONSTANTINE'S GREAT CITY EMPIRE FLED   . . . . . .   41B THEN SHE BORE   PROSE
OER THE EARTH PRIDE FEARED FOR HER CITY BUT NOT LONG   . .   41B THEN SHE BORE   PROSE
GO SEE THE CITY FRIENDS JOIND HAND IN HAND . . . . . .   43A THEN SHE BORE   PROSE
TONGUE AS A CITY CLARK BUT A BOY WOULD BE SUCH A FOOL   .   53B ISLAND MOON 8   PROSE
THIS CITY & THIS COUNTRY HAS BROUGHT FORTH MANY MAYORS   .   58 THIS CITY/IM   1
WERE FIT TO GIVE LAW TO THE CITY EACH EAT AS MUCH AS TEN   58 THIS CITY/IM   *   10
. . . . HE BY CONSCIENCE URGD IN THE CITY OF PARIS RAISD   136 FRENCH REVOLTN   42
    A PULPIT
ON THE ANXIOUS CITY . . . .   136 FRENCH REVOLTN   56
. . . SO THE CITY OF PARIS THEIR WIVES AND CHILDREN   . .   136 FRENCH REVOLTN   57
THY NOBLES HAVE GATHERD THY STARRY HOSTS ROUND THIS   138 FRENCH REVOLTN   100
    REBELLIOUS CITY
. . . AND EVERY DARKNING CITY . . . .   139 FRENCH REVOLTN   117
. . . AND THE WOMEN AND CHILDREN OF THE CITY . . . . .   139 FRENCH REVOLTN   122
THEN FLED AND THE WHOLE CITY KNEW HE WAS FLED TO GENEVA   139 FRENCH REVOLTN   124
    . . .
LET THY SOLDIERS POSSESS THIS CITY OF REBELS . . . . .   141 FRENCH REVOLTN   155
. . . TROOPS OF WARRIORS DEPART NOR AROUND OUR PEACEABLE   145 FRENCH REVOLTN   239
    CITY
. . . THAT MOATED AROUND KEEPS THIS CITY OF PARIS IN AWE   145 FRENCH REVOLTN   248
HOVERD AND STRETCHD ACROSS THE CITY . . . .   146 FRENCH REVOLTN   272
AND PARTICULARLY THEY STUDIED THE GENIUS OF EACH CITY &   153A MARRIAGE HH 11   PROSE
OF A BURNING CITY BENEATH US AT AN IMMENSE DISTANCE   . .   156A MARRIAGE HH 17   PROSE
TO AWAKE THE [PESTILENCE] PHYSICIANS THRO THE CITY   . .   185 LET BROTHELS/N   3
THEY CANNOT WALL THE CITY NOR MOAT ROUND THE CASTLE OF   199 AMERICA 9   7
    PRINCES
. . . [?TILL ?BY THE] ?FROZEN CHILL & HEAVY EVEN TO THE   205 AMERICA CANC C *   9
    CITY GATE
BLEAK DARK ABRUPT IT STANDS & OVERSHADOWS LONDON CITY   .   242 EUROPE 12   9
CALL FOR FIRES IN THE CITY . . . .   247 SONG OF LOS 6   20
TO CUT OFF THE BREAD FROM THE CITY . . . .   247 SONG OF LOS 7   1
WITH WINE OF CRUELTY LET US [LIGHT] PLAT A SCOURGE O SISTER   275 FOUR ZOAS 1   * 399
    CITY
THERE IS NO CITY NOR CORN FIELD NOR ORCHARD ALL IS ROCK   276 FOUR ZOAS 1   426
    & SAND
BEGAN TO ENTER THE HOLY CITY ENTRING THE DISMAL CLOUDS   . . 359 FOUR ZOAS 9   84
WHICH NOW DESCENDETH OUT OF HEAVEN A CITY YET A WOMAN   . . 362 FOUR ZOAS 9   222

```
                                                          PAGE     TITLE           LINE
CITY    (CONTINUED)
    TILL MANY A CITY THERE IS BUILT     . . . . . . . .   427 MENTAL TRAVLER          91
    GATES OPEN BEHIND SATAN'S SEAT TO THE CITY OF GOLGONOOZA  502 MILTON 20           39
    THE WITNESSES LIE DEAD IN THE STREET OF THE GREAT CITY . .  506 MILTON 22         59
    HOW LONG SHALL WE LAY DEAD IN THE STREET OF THE GREAT CITY  507 MILTON 23         11
    BECAUSE OF SATAN BEFORE LUBAN IN THE CITY OF GOLGONOOZA   509 MILTON 24           49
    AND IN THE CITY OF GOLGONOOZA & IN LUBAN & AROUND    . .   512 MILTON 26          24
    AROUND THE CITY OF GOLGONOOZA IN THE FORESTS OF ENTUTHON   514 MILTON 27          43
    CITY & SANDY DESART INTERMINGLED BEYOND MORTAL KEN   . . .  532 MILTON 40         27
    NOR OF THE CITY CLARK'S MERRY HEARTED FASHION        . . .  542 FLORENTINE/N  *   28
    NOR OF THE CITY CLARK'S IDLE FACILITIES . . . . . . .  542 FLORENTINE/N           30
    INDICATE THE SITUATION OF THE GREAT CITY     . . . . .   567B DESC CAT 3       PROSE
    OF THE GREATEST INN OF THE GREATEST CITY     . . . . .   569D DESC CAT 3       PROSE
    INDICATE THE SITUATION OF THE GREAT CITY     . . . . .   588D CHAUCER/N        PROSE
    INDICATE THE SITUATION OF THE GREAT CITY     . . . . .   590C CHAUCER 2        PROSE
    BY EARTHQUAKES A GREAT CITY ON FIRE IS SEEN IN THE DISTANCE  608B V LAST JUDG/N PROSE
    OF MOUNTAIN & RIVER & CITY ARE SMALL & WITHERD & DARKEND   623 JERUSALEM 5           8
    THE GREAT CITY OF GOLGONOOZA FOURFOLD TOWARD THE NORTH . .  632 JERUSALEM 12         46
    AND EVERY PART OF THE CITY IS FOURFOLD & EVERY INHABITANT   633 JERUSALEM 13         20
        FOURFOLD
    AND LUBAN STANDS IN MIDDLE OF THE CITY A MOAT OF FIRE      633 JERUSALEM 13         24
    HE VIEWS THE CITY OF GOLGONOOZA & ITS SMALLER CITIES   . .  634 JERUSALEM 13         56
    AND RIVER AND MOUNTAIN AND CITY & VILLAGE AND HOUSE        640 JERUSALEM 18         18
        & FAMILY
    AND CITY & VILLAGE AND HOUSE & FAMILY THAT THE PERFECT  . .  640 JERUSALEM 18         26
    BABYLON THE CITY OF VALA THE GODDESS VIRGIN-MOTHER    . .   640 JERUSALEM 18         29
    HE FOUND JERUSALEM UPON THE RIVER OF HIS CITY SOFT REPOSD   642 JERUSALEM 19         40
    THE CITY OF THE WOODS IN THE FOREST OF EPHRATAH IS TAKEN    653 JERUSALEM 29         18
    BECAUSE OF THE OPRESSORS OF ALBION IN EVERY CITY & VILLAGE  656 JERUSALEM 30         27
    AND THUS HE SPOKE LOOKING ON ALBION'S CITY WITH MANY TEARS  657 JERUSALEM 31         28
    I WAS A CITY & A TEMPLE BUILT BY ALBION'S CHILDREN         659 JERUSALEM 33         36
    BATH HEALING CITY WHOSE WISDOM IN MIDST OF POETIC    . .    675 JERUSALEM 45          1
    I GAVE THEE PRIAM'S CITY AND THE ISLES OF GRECIA LOVELY     692 JERUSALEM 60         13
    TO JUSTICE IN HIS OWN CITY OF PARIS DENYING                697 JERUSALEM 63          6
        THE RESURRECTION
    BENEATH THE MOUNTAINS OF LEBANON IN THE CITY OF REHOB IN    706 JERUSALEM 68         55
        HAMATH
    SUCH ARE CATHEDRON'S GOLDEN HALLS IN THE CITY OF GOLGONOOZA  713 JERUSALEM 73          1
    HIS AGED PARENTS SOUGHT ME OUT IN EVERY CITY & VILLAGE  . .  720 JERUSALEM 79         27
    FOUND YE LONDON ENORMOUS CITY WEEPS THY RIVER    . . . .   727 JERUSALEM 83         23
    OF LONDON CITY ON THE THAMES FROM SURREY HILLS TO HIGHGATE  728 JERUSALEM 83         68
    WE BUILDED JERUSALEM AS A CITY & A TEMPLE FROM LAMBETH  . .  729 JERUSALEM 84          3
    AND FROM THE GREAT CITY OF GOLGONOOZA IN THE SHADOWY        746 JERUSALEM 98         55
        GENERATION
    CAIN'S CITY BUILT WITH HUMAN BLOOD NOT BLOOD OF BULLS       781 GHOST ABEL 2         17
        & GOATS
    CITY OF DIS QUEEN OF ENDLESS WOE [XXX] FURIES &  . . . .   786A ILLS DANTE 101 *PROSE
    MINOTAUR THE CITY OF DIS SEEMS TO OCCUPY THE SPACE   . . .  786A ILLS DANTE 101 PROSE
    EXTRAORDINARY THAT LONDON IN SO FEW YEARS FROM A CITY OF    798B LETTER 10       PROSE
    ORDER OF LUXURIES SHOULD HAVE BECOME A CITY OF ELEGANCE     798C LETTER 10       PROSE
    THIS -- CITY I SHALL NOT BE ABLE TO AVAIL MYSELF OF THE     801B LETTER 13       PROSE
    CHICHESTER IS A VERY HANDSOM CITY SEVEN MILES FROM US   . .  806B LETTER 16       PROSE
    IN A CITY OF ASSASSINATIONS THIS MAKES YOUR LOT TRULY  . .  847B LETTER 44       PROSE
    CELESTIAL CITY I ALSO HAVE BUT A FEW MORE MOUNTAINS TO PASS  854C LETTER 53       PROSE
    A BREACH IN A CITY THE MORNING AFTER THE BATTLE  . . . .   SUPP ILLUS HISTORY  *TITLE
CITY'S    SEE CITIE'S
    AND DESTRUCTION HOVERS IN THE CITY'S SMOAK BUT   . . . .    37A CONTEMPLATN/PS  PROSE
CIVIL
    I ONLY ASKD YOU A CIVIL QUESTION--[HERE THE] I HAD A GREAT   45A ISLAND MOON 1  *PROSE
        MIND
    CHRISTIANITY IS CIVIL BUSINESS ONLY     . . . . . . .   398B ANNO BACON         MARG
    CIVIL IS CHRISTIANITY OR RELIGION OR WHATEVER IS HUMANE     398B ANNO BACON         MARG
    AND THE DEVIL WAS GOD LIKE A CHRISTIAN CIVIL     . . . .   752 EV GOSPEL(D)/N       36
CIVILITY
    HE MUST MEAN THE MEER LOVE OF CIVILITY   . . . . . . .   750 EV GOSPEL(C)/N        21
CIVILIZATION
    SYRIAN IT IS THE REMAINS OF CIVILIZATION IN THE STATE   . .  610D V LAST JUDG/N  PROSE
CIVILIZED
    WERE NAKED CIVILIZED MEN LEARNED STUDIOUS       . . . .   577C DESC CAT 5       PROSE
    A CIVILIZED MAN WHO HAS BEEN ACCUSTOMED TO GO NAKED   . .   580D DESC CAT 5       PROSE
    IT IS COMPOSED OF THE INNOCENT CIVILIZED HEATHEN &   . . .  610A V LAST JUDG/N  PROSE
    OR CIVILIZED LIFE SUCH AS IT IS IN THE CHRISTIAN CHURCH     610C V LAST JUDG/N  PROSE
CLAD    SEE COARSE-CLAD
    O HOLY VIRGIN CLAD IN PUREST WHITE  . . . . . . . . .     3 TO MORNING/PS          1
    I AM CLAD IN FLOWERS FAIR     . . . . . . . . . . .     7 LOVE HARMNY/PS         10
    EACH CLAD IN GLORY ACCORDING TO HIS SPHERE       . . . .    18 EDW THIRD/PS 1        34
    CLAD AS A TRAVELLER FRESH RISEN ON HIS JOURNEY    . . .    40B SAMSON/PS        PROSE
    SO CLAD WE'LL ABIDE LIFE'S PELTING STORM     . . . . .    64 SHEPHERD OLD         11
    THEN LOS AROSE HIS HEAD HE REARD IN SNAKY THUNDERS CLAD    245 EUROPE 15            9
    AND CLAD IN STEEL & HIS HORSE PROUDLY NEIGHD HE SMELT THE   275 FOUR ZOAS 1        412
        BATTLE
    THOU TERRIBLE WOMAN CLAD IN BLUE WHOSE STRONG ATTRACTIVE    312 FOUR ZOAS 6         13
        POWER
    OR WILT THOU ANSWER YOUNGEST WOMAN CLAD IN SHINING GREEN    312 FOUR ZOAS 6         17
    SOUND THE WAR TRUMPET TERRIFIC SOULS CLAD IN ATTRACTIVE     336 FOUR ZOAS 7B       147
        STEEL
    GENEROUS IMMORTAL GUARDIAN GOLDEN CLAD FOR CITIES    . . .  665 JERUSALEM 38         46
    AND BECAME AN OPAKE GLOBE FAR DISTANT CLAD WITH MOONY BEAMS  679 JERUSALEM 49         20
CLAIM
    WITH WHAT SENSE DOES THE PARSON CLAIM THE LABOUR OF THE     193 V DAU ALBION 5       17
        FARMER
    FOR I PERCIEVE THOU HAST ABUNDANCE WHICH I CLAIM AS MINE    273 FOUR ZOAS 1        334
```

```
                                                            PAGE      TITLE            LINE
CLAIM   (CONTINUED)
      TO CLAIM THE HELLS MY FURNACES I GO TO ETERNAL DEATH    . .   496 MILTON 14          32
      PROVES THERE IS TRUTH IN HIS EXTRAVAGANT CLAIM    . . . .     551 WILLM COWPER/N       8
CLAIMD
      THIS WOMAN HAS CLAIMD AS HER OWN & MAN IS NO MORE    . . .    661 JERUSALEM 34         28
CLAIMING
      MOCKING THE CONFESSORS & MARTYRS CLAIMING                     506 MILTON 22           43
        SELF-RIGHTEOUSNESS
CLAKMANAN
      DAN BUTE CAITNES CLAKMANAN NAPTHALI MAIRN INVERNES            638 JERUSALEM 16         55
        LINLITHGO
CLAMORING
      GOLD SILVER BRASS & IRON [ARDORS] CLANGORS CLAMORING REND     205 AMERICA CANC C       15
        THE SHORES
      GOLD SILVER BRASS & IRON CLANGORS CLAMORING REND             319 FOUR ZOAS 6         311
        THE [DEEPS] SHORES
CLAMOUR
      CLAMOUR BRAWLS ALONG THE STREETS    . . . . . . . .    .  37A CONTEMPLATN/PS   PROSE
      ON DUSKY WING BREATHING FORTH CLAMOUR & DESTRUCTION   . . .  42D THEN SHE BORE     PROSE
CLAMROUS
      STARTLED ASTONISHD AT THE CLAMROUS COCK  . . . . . .   .      24 EDW THIRD/PS 3      115
CLANG
      AND OFTEN HEARD THE DISMAL CLANG OF ARMS    . . . . . .       31 EDW THIRD/PS 5       40
CLANGING
      THE TRAMPLING HORSE AND CLANGING ARMS   . . . . . . .         11 GWIN KING/PS         23
CLANGOR
      FOURFOLD ANNIHILATION & AT THE CLANGOR OF THE ARROWS OF       745 JERUSALEM 98         7
        INTELLECT
CLANGORS
      GOLD SILVER BRASS & IRON [ARDORS] CLANGORS CLAMORING REND     205 AMERICA CANC C       15
        THE SHORES
      GOLD SILVER BRASS & IRON CLANGORS CLAMORING REND             319 FOUR ZOAS 6         311
        THE [DEEPS] SHORES
CLANKING
      RATTLING WITH CLANKING CHAINS THE UNIVERSAL EMPIRE GROANS     333 FOUR ZOAS 7B         17
CLAP
      CLAP CLAP CLAP  . . . . . . .    . . . . . .   .   .  .        62 DR CLASH/IM          21
      & CLAP THE PICTURE INTO A DARK CORNER   . . . . . .  .       599A PUB ADDRESS/N     PROSE
CLAPD    SEE CLAPT
      CLAPD DEATH INTO THE CORNER OF THEIR JAW    . . . . .  .      537 AND HIS LEGS/N       21
CLAPPER
      LIKE A CHERRY CLAPPER ARADOBO ASKD WHO WAS PHEBUS SIR    . .  46D ISLAND MOON 3     PROSE
CLAPPING
      ON WINGS OF TENFOLD JOY CLAPPING HIS HANDS HIS FEET HIS       366 FOUR ZOAS 9        348
        RADIANT WINGS
CLAPS
      WHEN SIN CLAPS HIS BROAD WINGS OVER THE BATTLE     . . . .     33 EDW FOURTH/PS         9
CLAPT
      & CLAPT IT ON HIS HEAD SAID THE PYTHAGOREAN    . . . . .      46C ISLAND MOON 3     PROSE
CLARE
      WATERFORD TIPPERARY CORK LIMERICK KERRY CLARE   . . . . .     711 JERUSALEM 72         22
CLARENCE
      DUKE OF CLARENCE SIR JOHN CHANDOS SIR THOMAS DAGWORTH         17C EDW THIRD/PS     TITLE
      SCENE ENGLISH COURT LIONEL DUKE OF CLARENCE    . . . .  .    19A EDW THIRD/PS 2    PROSE
      FIE FIE LORD CLARENCE YOU PROCEED NOT TO BUSINESS    . . .     20 EDW THIRD/PS 2       62
CLARION
      THEN LET THE CLARION OF WAR BEGIN    . . . . . . . .   .       31 EDW THIRD/PS 5       50
      [THE BELLOWING ?FURNACES' BLARE BY THE LONG SOUNDING         346 FOUR ZOAS 8      *  204
        CLARION]
      OF FLUTE & HARP & DRUM & TRUMPET HORN & CLARION   . . . .    372 FOUR ZOAS 9        586
      THE BELLOWING FURNACES' BLARE BY THE LONG SOUNDING CLARION   509 MILTON 24           64
      WITH FLUTE & CLARION WITH CUPS & MEASURES FILLD WITH         511 MILTON 25           69
        FOAMING WINE
      WITH CYMBAL TRUMPET CLARION & THE SCYTHED CHARIOTS           677 JERUSALEM 47         11
        OF BRITAIN
CLARIONS
      . . . WITH CLARIONS OF ?LOUD BREATHING WAR   . . . . .       138 FRENCH REVOLTN *    101
      NO TRUMPETS ANSWER NO REPLY OF CLARIONS OR OF FIFES    . .   200 AMERICA 10            3
      WE HEAR THE WARLIKE CLARIONS WE VIEW THE TURNING SPHERES     271 FOUR ZOAS 1        258
      A GROAN WAS HEARD ON HIGH THE WARLIKE CLARIONS CEAST THE     273 FOUR ZOAS 1        313
        SPIRITS
      THUS SANG THE DEMONS OF THE DEEP THE CLARIONS OF WAR BLEW    276 FOUR ZOAS 1        434
        LOUD
      OF WHEELS & HORSES' HOOFS & TRUMPETS HORNS & CLARIONS   . .  301 FOUR ZOAS 4        160
      NOW HOLDS THEE SOON TO ISSUE FORTH SOUND CLARIONS OF WAR     307 FOUR ZOAS 5         63
      NOW SOUND THE CLARIONS OF VICTORY NOW STRIP THE SLAIN   . .  337 FOUR ZOAS 7B       162
      THEY SOUND THE CLARIONS STRONG THEY CHAIN THE HOWLING        337 FOUR ZOAS 7B       164
        CAPTIVES
      BUT BLOOD & WOUNDS & DISMAL CRIES & CLARIONS OF WAR   . . .  338 FOUR ZOAS 7B       205
      SO SUNG THE DEMONS OF THE DEEP THE CLARIONS OF WAR BLEW      338 FOUR ZOAS 7B       210
        LOUD
      THEY GO OUT TO WAR WITH STRONG SHOUTS & LOUD CLARIONS O      338 FOUR ZOAS 7B    *  220
        PITY
      . . . THUNDEROUS CLARIONS BLOW  . . . . . . .    . .         343 FOUR ZOAS 8          88
      BUT WHEN THE CLARIONS OF DAY SOUNDED THEY DROWND             504 MILTON 21           25
        THE LAMENTATIONS
      THEY SOUND THE CLARIONS STRONG THEY CHAIN THE HOWLING        699 JERUSALEM 65          6
        CAPTIVES
CLARISSA
      & MORAL SENTIMENTS HE WOULD BE NO BETTER THAN CLARISSA    . 411D ANNO BOYD          MARG
CLARK    SEE CLERK
      TONGUE AS A CITY CLARK BUT A BOY WOULD BE SUCH A FOOL    .   53B ISLAND MOON 8     PROSE
```

	PAGE	TITLE	LINE

CLARK'S
NOR OF THE CITY CLARK'S MERRY HEARTED FASHION . . . . 542 FLORENTINE/N * 28
NOR OF THE CITY CLARK'S IDLE FACILITIES . . . . 542 FLORENTINE/N 30
CLASH
THERES DOCTOR CLASH . . . . 61 DR CLASH/IM * 1
CLASHING
AND CLASHING STEEL DOES RING . . . . 12 GWIN KING/PS 44
A DRAGON FORM CLASHING HIS SCALES AT MIDNIGHT HE AROSE . 197 AMERICA 3 15
A DRAGON FORM CLASHING HIS SCALES AT MIDNIGHT HE AROSE . 204 AMERICA CANC A 15
CLASHINGS
WITH HURTLINGS & CLASHINGS & GROANS . . . . 229 URIZEN 13 25
FOR [IN] WITH NOISES RUINOUS HURTLINGS & CLASHINGS & GROANS 304 FOUR ZOAS 4 282
CLASP
WHAT THE ANVIL WHAT [THE ARM] [ARM] [GRASP] [CLASP] DREAD 172 THE TYGER/N 1 20
GRASP
[COULD] DARE ITS DEADLY TERRORS [CLASP] [GRASP] CLASP . 172 THE TYGER/N 1 21
DARE ITS DEADLY TERRORS CLASP . . . . 214 THE TYGER/SE 16
THE FAMINE SHALL CLASP IT TOGETHER WITH BUCKLES & CLASPS . 499 MILTON 18 16
CLASPD
. . . THEY CLASPD THE ARMOUR OF TERRIBLE GOLD . . . . . 205 AMERICA CANC C 6
CLASPS
HER HOLLOW WOMB & CLASPS THE SOLID STEM . . . . 248 SONG OF LOS 7 36
THE FAMINE SHALL CLASP IT TOGETHER WITH BUCKLES & CLASPS . 499 MILTON 18 16
CLASS
IF TO THE MIDDLE CLASS IT IS THE DIRECT CONTRARY 406D ANNO BACON MARG
TO CHRIST'S ADVICE
EVERY CLASS IS INDIVIDUAL . . . . 460A ANNO REYNOLDS MARG
CHILDHOOD AND AGE ARE EQUALLY BELONGING TO EVERY CLASS . 460B ANNO REYNOLDS MARG
OF EACH CLASS SO ARE LEANNESS & FATNESS . . . . . . 460C ANNO REYNOLDS MARG
BELIEVE CHRIST & HIS APOSTLES THAT THERE IS A CLASS OF MEN 480C MILTON 1 PROSE
OF THE FIRST CLASS WAS SATAN WITH INCOMPARABLE MILDNESS 486 MILTON 7 6
AND THEREFORE THE CLASS OF SATAN SHALL BE CALLD THE ELECT 492 MILTON 11 21
& THOSE
FROM THE FOUNDATION OF THE WORLD THE ELECT IS ONE CLASS YOU 511 MILTON 25 32
SO THEY ARE BORN ON EARTH & EVERY CLASS IS DETERMINATE . . 512 MILTON 26 39
THE IMAGE OF A CLASS AND NOT OF AN IMPERFECT INDIVIDUAL 571A DESC CAT 3 PROSE
THE CITIZENS AND THEIR COOK ARE EACH LEADERS OF A CLASS 571D DESC CAT 3 PROSE
AS THERE IS A CLASS OF MEN WHOSE WHOLE DELIGHT IS . 573B DESC CAT 3 PROSE
THE DESTRUCTION OF MEN SO THERE IS A CLASS OF ARTISTS . 573B DESC CAT 3 PROSE
BUT TO SHEW THE STUPIDITY OF THIS CLASS OF MEN . . 573C DESC CAT 3 PROSE
HENCE RUBENS TITIAN CORREGGIO AND ALL OF THAT CLASS ARE . 581A DESC CAT 5 PROSE
UPON AS [IN THE SAME CLASS OF] . . . . 595A PUB ADDRESS/N PROSE
OR ANY OF THAT CLASS CHARACTER & EXPRESSION CAN . . 599B PUB ADDRESS/N PROSE
BEFORE CAIPHAS & PILATE ARE JUDAS & THOSE OF HIS CLASS . 608D V LAST JUDG/N PROSE
THE VIRGIN MARY WAS OF THIS CLASS . . . . 610B V LAST JUDG/N PROSE
LET HIM BE OF WHAT CLASS OF ANIMALS HE WILL . . . . 616B V LAST JUDG/N PROSE
I DESPAIR OF EVER PLEASING ONE CLASS OF MEN . . . 795A LETTER 6 PROSE
UNFORTUNATELY OUR AUTHORS OF BOOKS ARE AMONG THIS CLASS HOW 795A LETTER 6 PROSE
CLASSD
AND ALL ARE CLASSD BY SPIRITUAL & NOT BY NATURAL POWER . . 513 MILTON 26 43
CLASSES
THESE TWO CLASSES OF MEN ARE ALWAYS UPON EARTH . . . . 155B MARRIAGE HH 15 PROSE
AGE & YOUTH ARE NOT CLASSES BUT [ACCIDENTS] [SITUATIONS] 460C ANNO REYNOLDS * MARG
PROPERTIES
OBLIGATIONS REYNOLDS HAS LAID ON BAD ARTISTS OF ALL CLASSES 473A ANNO REYNOLDS MARG
THREE CLASSES ARE CREATED BY THE HAMMER OF LOS & WOVEN . . 482 MILTON 2 26
HERE THE THREE CLASSES OF MEN TAKE THEIR SEXUAL TEXTURE 483 MILTON 4 4
WOVEN
HENCE THE THREE CLASSES OF MEN TAKE THEIR FIXD DESTINATIONS 484 MILTON 5 13
THUS THEY SING CREATING THE THREE CLASSES AMONG DRUID ROCKS 485 MILTON 5 38
HERE THE THREE CLASSES OF MORTAL MEN TAKE THEIR FIXD 486 MILTON 6 32
DESTINATIONS
AND THE THREE CLASSES OF MEN . . . . 486 MILTON 6 35
YOU SHALL BIND THEM IN THREE CLASSES ACCORDING TO THEIR 510 MILTON 25 27
CLASSES
EXCEPT BY MIRACLE & A NEW BIRTH THE OTHER TWO CLASSES . . 511 MILTON 25 34
FOR IN EVERY NATION & EVERY FAMILY THE THREE CLASSES ARE 511 MILTON 25 40
BORN
FOR THE VARIOUS CLASSES OF MEN ARE ALL MARKD OUT 512 MILTON 26 37
DETERMINATE
THE PLANTS SO CHAUCER NUMBERED THE CLASSES OF MEN . . 567D DESC CAT 3 PROSE
A BLIGHT FOR A TRIAL OF MEN TO DIVIDE THE CLASSES OF MEN 570A DESC CAT 3 PROSE
THE CHARACTERS OF WOMEN CHAUCER HAS DIVIDED INTO 572B DESC CAT 3 PROSE
TWO CLASSES
THERE ARE ALWAYS THESE TWO CLASSES OF LEARNED SAGES . . 572C DESC CAT 3 PROSE
THE THREE GENERAL CLASSES OF MEN WHO ARE REPRESENTED BY 577C DESC CAT 5 PROSE
AND UNDER THESE THIRTY-TWO CLASSES OF ISLANDS IN THE OCEAN 712 JERUSALEM 72 43
CLASSICAL
PIETY & VIRTUE IS SENECA CLASSICAL O FINE BISHOP . . . 394D ANNO WATSON MARG
UPON THE KINGDOM OF JESUS BY THE CLASSICAL LEARNED . . 786C ANNO THORNTON MARG
& IS NOT THIS GOOD & LEARNED & WISE & CLASSICAL THIS IS 788C ANNO THORNTON MARG
ITS DISGUISE IN THE CLASSICAL & SCOTCH LANGUAGE . . . 788D ANNO THORNTON * MARG
CLASSICS
THE CLASSICS IT IS THE CLASSICS & NOT GOTHS NOR MONKS . 778C HOMERS POETRY PROSE
THE GREEK & ROMAN CLASSICS IS THE ANTICHRIST I SAY IS . 786C ANNO THORNTON MARG
CLAY
THEN DOWN I'LL LIE AS COLD AS CLAY . . . . 7 MY SILKS/PS 17
WHEN THE COLD CLAY BREATHED WITH LIFE AND OUR ANCESTORS 35C COUCH DEATH/PS PROSE
AND I LOSE THIS FORM OF CLAY . . . . 61 LEAVE O/IM 4
THE CLOD OF CLAY HEARD THE WORM'S VOICE & RAISD HER PITYING 129 BOOK OF THEL 4 7
HEAD
QUEEN OF THE VALES THE MATRON CLAY ANSWERD I HEARD THY 130 BOOK OF THEL 5 14
SIGHS

```
                                                            PAGE     TITLE          LINE
CLAY    (CONTINUED)
      SHALL THIS MARBLE BUILT HEAVEN BECOME A CLAY COTTAGE . . .   138 FRENCH REVOLTN     89
      . . . AND WATER HIS CLAY WITH LOVE  . . . . . . . .          139 FRENCH REVOLTN    108
      RED CLAY BROUGHT FORTH   . . . . . . . . . . .               148 MARRIAGE HH 2      13
      SO SUNG A LITTLE CLOD OF CLAY  . . . . . . . . .             162 CLOD PEBBLE/N       5
      [IN WHAT CLAY & IN WHAT MOULD] . . . . . . . . .             172 THE TYGER/N 1      16
      THE BONES OF DEATH THE COVRING CLAY THE SINEWS SHRUNK &      198 AMERICA 6           3
          DRYD
      SO [SUNG] SANG A LITTLE CLOD OF CLAY . . . . . . .           211 CLOD PEBBLE/SE *    5
      DIDST CLOSE MY TONGUE IN SENSELESS CLAY . . . . . . .        220 TO TIRZAH/SE       13
      URIZEN IS A CLOD OF CLAY  . . . . . . . . . .                226 URIZEN 6           12
      COLD FEATURELESS FLESH OR CLAY  . . . . . . . . .            226 URIZEN 7            5
      JOIN SHAKING CONVULSD THE SHIVRING CLAY BREATHES  . . . .    248 SONG OF LOS 7      32
      THE SAND & ASHES & TO MIX THE CLAY WITH TEARS & REPENTANCE   286 FOUR ZOAS 2       222
      OUR BEAUTY IS COVERD OVER WITH CLAY & ASHES & OUR BACKS      286 FOUR ZOAS 2       225
      MY HEAVENS ARE BRASS MY EARTH IS IRON MY MOON A CLOD OF      290 FOUR ZOAS 2       395
          CLAY
      WE HAVE NO OTHER GOD BUT HE THOU FATHER OF WORMS & CLAY      298 FOUR ZOAS 4        39
      AND LOS REMAINS GOD OVER ALL WEAK FATHER OF WORMS & CLAY     298 FOUR ZOAS 4        41
      AND IN THE DARK VACUITY CREATED A BOSOM OF [SLIME] CLAY      316 FOUR ZOAS 6       158
      MY FEET ARE TURNED BACKWARD & MY FOOTSTEPS SLIDE IN CLAY     335 FOUR ZOAS 7B       88
      TO BONES JOIN SHAKING CONVULSD THE SHIVERING CLAY BREATHES   363 FOUR ZOAS 9       232
      FORSAKING BROTHERHOOD & UNIVERSAL LOVE IN SELFISH CLAY  . .  374 FOUR ZOAS 9       629
      THEN I REND THEE ASUNDER THEN I HOWL OVER THY CLAY & ASHES   499 MILTON 18          33
      UPON THE CLAY NOW CHANGD TO MARBLE ALSO URIZEN ROSE  . . .   500 MILTON 19           4
      BUT MILTON TOOK OF THE RED CLAY OF SUCCOTH MOULDING IT       500 MILTON 19          10
          WITH CARE
      AS WITH NEW CLAY A HUMAN FORM IN THE VALLEY OF BETH PEOR     500 MILTON 19          14
      THUS FORMD THE CLAY OF URIZEN BUT WITHIN THAT PORTION  . .   502 MILTON 20          12
      OR HOW CAN I WITH MY COLD HAND OF CLAY BUT THOU O LORD  . .  502 MILTON 20          17
      AS THE SOWER TAKES THE SEED OR AS THE ARTIST HIS CLAY  . .   515 MILTON 28          14
      HE LIFTED POURING IT INTO THE CLAY GROUND PREPARD WITH ART   630 JERUSALEM 11        4
      CLAY BAKD & ENAMELD ETERNAL GLOWING AS FOUR FURNACES  . .    632 JERUSALEM 12       64
      THAT TOWARD ULRO FOUR CLAY BAKD LABORIOUS WORKMANSHIP  . .   633 JERUSALEM 13        4
      THAT TOWARD ULRO CLAY THAT TOWARD EDEN METALS  . . . . .     633 JERUSALEM 13       10
      WEEPING IN WEAK & MORTAL CLAY . . . . . . . . .             651 FIELDS FROM/J      59
      BETWEEN LIPS OF MIRE & CLAY THEN SENT HIM FORTH OVER JORDAN  662 JERUSALEM 36        6
      IS BECOME A CLOD OF CLAY MERLIN IS A WORM OF THE VALLEY      688 JERUSALEM 56       28
      AND DISHES OF PAINTED CLAY GLOWING WITH BEAUTY & CRUELTY     702 JERUSALEM 66       33
      OF PAINTED CLAY THE MIGHTY HYLE IS BECOME A WEEPING INFANT   725 JERUSALEM 82        8
      IN SECRET BED OF MORTAL CLAY  . . . . . . . . .             754 EV GOSPEL(E)/N     16
      AND STILL HE DEVOURS THE BODY OF CLAY  . . . . . . .         755 EV GOSPEL(E)/N     94
      FOR DUST & CLAY IS THE SERPENT'S MEAT  . . . . . . .         755 EV GOSPEL(E)/N     95
      ALL MY MIRE & MY CLAY . . . . . . . . . . .                 805 TO BUTTS/L         56
      SLIDE IN CLAY HOW CAN WE DO OTHERWISE THAN FEAR & TREMBLE   813A LETTER 22        PROSE
CLAY-COLD,CLAY COLD
      [WHILE ?LIVING CLAY COLD CORPSE CORSE] SWIFT AS THE   . .    43D WOE CRIED MUSE   PROSE
      AND THEREFORE GOD TAKES VENGEANCE ON ME FROM MY CLAY-COLD    646 JERUSALEM 23       33
          BOSOM
      HER VOICE PIERCD ALBION'S CLAY COLD EAR HE MOVED UPON THE    742 JERUSALEM 95        1
          ROCK
CLEAN
      UPON A HOLY THURSDAY THEIR INNOCENT FACES CLEAN  . . . .      59 HOLY THURS/IM       1
      AND TO CLEAN IT WITH MY HANDKERCHER  . . . . . . .            61 SAY YOU JOE/IM      7
      NOW THAT THE CURSE SHALL CLEAN DEVOUR ALL THOSE GUILTY SONS  107 TIRIEL 6            4
      TWAS ON A HOLY THURSDAY THEIR INNOCENT FACES CLEAN  . . .    121 HOLY THURS/SI       1
      TOM COOKE CUT HOGARTH DOWN WITH HIS CLEAN GRAVING  . . .     554 BLAKES APL/N 1      3
      TOM COOKE CUT HOGARTH DOWN WITH HIS CLEAN GRAVING  . . .     555 BLAKES APL/N 2      7
      ALL HIS STUDY WAS CLEAN STROKES & MOSSY TINTS HOW THEN  .   593A PUB ADDRESS/N    PROSE
      TOM COOKE CUT HOGARTH DOWN WITH HIS CLEAN GRAVING  . . .     595 BLAKES APOL/PA      3
      ABSURD NONSENSE ABOUT DOTS & LOZENGES & CLEAN STROKES  .    602A PUB ADDRESS/N    PROSE
      THE HEAVENS ARE NOT CLEAN IN THY SIGHT  . . . . . .         754 EV GOSPEL(E)/N     24
      THE SHOPS IN LONDON IMPROVE EVERY THING IS ELEGANT CLEAN    831D LETTER 31        PROSE
CLEANER
      I DEFY ANY MAN TO CUT CLEANER STROKES THAN I DO OR  . . .   602A PUB ADDRESS/N    PROSE
CLEANSE
      TO CLEANSE THE FACE OF MY SPIRIT BY SELF-EXAMINATION  . .    533 MILTON 40          37
CLEANSED
      IF THE DOORS OF PERCEPTION WERE CLEANSED  . . . . . .      154C MARRIAGE HH 14    PROSE
      PILATE HAS BLOODY HANDS THAT NEVER CAN BE CLEANSED  . . .   608D V LAST JUDG/N    PROSE
CLEAR
      THRO THE CLEAR WINDOWS OF THE MORNING TURN  . . . . .         1 TO SPRING/PS        2
      SOME BANK BESIDE A RIVER CLEAR THROW THY  . . . . . .         2 TO SUMMER/PS       11
      NOR ECHOES SWEET NOR WATERS CLEAR AS HEAVEN  . . . . .        2 TO SUMMER/PS       18
      I'LL DRINK OF THE CLEAR STREAM  . . . . . . . . .             8 MEMORY COME/PS      9
      AND WASH MY EARTHY MIND IN THY CLEAR STREAMS  . . . . .      14 IMIT SPEN/PS        4
      OF EACH INCUMBRANCE CLEAR THE HALL  . . . . . . .            16 BLIND-MANS/PS      18
      AND I STAIND THE WATER CLEAR  . . . . . . . . .             111 INTRODUCTN/SI      18
      AS THE CLEAR SPRING MUDDED WITH FEET OF BEASTS GROWS PURE    190 V DAU ALBION 2     19
          & SMILES
      THE CLEAR HEAVEN OF HER ETERNAL SPRING TO BEAR THE WINTRY    193 V DAU ALBION 5     24
          RAGE
      AND THE FAIR MOON REJOICES IN THE CLEAR & CLOUDLESS NIGHT    198 AMERICA 6          14
      SETTLED A LAKE BRIGHT & SHINING CLEAR  . . . . . . .         227 URIZEN 10          22
      BOUND IN HIS EXPANDING CLEAR SENSES  . . . . . . . .         257 BOOK OF LOS 4      10
      THE DAZZLINGS AS OF GEMS SHONE CLEAR RAPTUROUS IN [JOY]      267 FOUR ZOAS 1       128
          FURY
      [?WHILE] THRO THE CLEAR CHANGING ATMOSPHERE . . .   . .      274 FOUR ZOAS 1    *  367
      SETTLED A LAKE BRIGHT & SHINING CLEAR WHITE AS THE SNOW      303 FOUR ZOAS 4       210
      AND HIS DARK WIFE THAT ONCE FAIR CRYSTAL FORM DIVINELY       306 FOUR ZOAS 5        60
          CLEAR
      ANXIOUS ITS LITTLE SOUL LOOKS OUT INTO THE CLEAR EXPANSE     355 FOUR ZOAS 8       559
```

```
                                                          PAGE     TITLE        LINE
CLEAR    (CONTINUED)
    BATHD IN THE CLEAR SPRING OF THE ROCK THEN FROM HER      366 FOUR ZOAS 9   *  346
        DARKSOM CAVE
    WAVE FRESHLY CLEAR WATERS FLOWING AROUND THE TENDER GRASS 368 FOUR ZOAS 9      436
    HOW CLEAR THE SPRING OF THE ROCK RUNNING AMONG THE GOLDEN 369 FOUR ZOAS 9      448
        SAND
    SHE [D] STOPD TO DRINK OF THE CLEAR SPRING & EAT THE GRAPES 369 FOUR ZOAS 9 *  476
        & APPLES
    SO LOUD SO CLEAR IN THE WIDE HEAVENS . . . . . . . . .   375 FOUR ZOAS 9      685
    [THEN] AND THE MILD MOON REJOICES IN THE CLEAR & CLOUDLESS 379 FOUR ZOAS 9  *  826
        NIGHT
    TRANSLUCENT LOVELY SHINING CLEAR  . . . . . . . . .      429 CRYSTL CABINET    14
    A CLEAR IDEA AND A DETERMINATE VISION OF THINGS IN HIS  439D REMARKS MALKIN PROSE
        OWN MIND
    THE SOULS CLEAR FROM THE ROCK OF DEATH THAT DEATH HIMSELF 517 MILTON 29        45
        MAY WAKE
    AS THE CLEAR SUN & MILTON SILENT CAME DOWN ON MY PATH . . 530 MILTON 39         5
    OF REASON YOU MAY DRINK OF LIFE'S CLEAR STREAMS    . .   536 DONT BELIEVE/N     4
    IN PAINTING THESE PICTURES CLEAR COLOURS UNMUDDED BY OIL 564D DESC CAT 1     PROSE
    AND HIS DARK EON THAT ONCE FAIR CRYSTAL FORM DIVINELY CLEAR 667 JERUSALEM 40   41
    CLEAR AS THE RAINBOW AS THE CLOUD OF THE SUN'S TABERNACLE 731 JERUSALEM 86     21
    DISTINCT SHONE & CLEAR  . . . . . . . . . . .           804 TO BUTTS/L        17
    DEAR SIR THIS PERHAPS WAS SUFFERD TO CLEAR UP SOME DOUBTS 828C LETTER 28     PROSE
    TO CLEAR THEMSELVES OF ALL IMPUTATION IF A MAN OFFENDS ME 828C LETTER 28     PROSE
    HIM MAD IF HE HAD NOT FOR SUCH CLEAR AND GENEROUS PROPOSALS 857D LETTER 55   PROSE
CLEARED
    NOW CLEARED THE WAY TO ROMNEY IN WHOSE SERVICE I NOW  . 841A LETTER 40       PROSE
CLEARER
    THE CLEARER THE ORGAN THE MORE DISTINCT THE OBJECT  . . . 576D DESC CAT 4    PROSE
CLEARING
    IN THE FIRST CHAMBER WAS A DRAGON-MAN CLEARING AWAY THE  154D MARRIAGE HH 15 PROSE
CLEARLY
    . . . REFLECTING EACH IN EACH & CLEARLY SEEN  . . . . .  746 JERUSALEM 98      39
CLEARNESS
    WITH HER FAIR CRYSTAL CLEARNESS IN HER LIPS & CHEEKS HIS 269 FOUR ZOAS 1      185
        POISONS ROSE
    SHE RISES AMONG FLOWERS & LOOKS TOWARD THE EASTERN      367 FOUR ZOAS 9      390
        CLEARNESS
    WITH HER FAIR CRYSTAL CLEARNESS . . . . . . . . . . .   381 FOUR ZOAS AD 5     5
    CLEARNESS AND PRECISION HAVE BEEN THE CHIEF OBJECTS . . . 564D DESC CAT 1     PROSE
CLEAVETH
    O HOW CAN I WITH MY GROSS TONGUE THAT CLEAVETH TO THE DUST 502 MILTON 20       15
CLEAVING
    . . . THRO THE CLEAVING [?WORLD] GROUND . . . . . . . .  106 TIRIEL 5           5
    DOWN THE HEAVY SUNK CLEAVING AROUND  . . . . . . . . .   259 BOOK OF LOS 5      6
CLEFT
    . . . HID FROM THE LIGHT AS IN A CLEFT ROCK  . . . . .   135 FRENCH REVOLTN    28
CLEFTS
    THE EARTH TREMBLED [XXX] FIRES BELCHED FROM THE YAWNING  106 TIRIEL 5      *   16
        CLEFTS
    WHERE IS THE LORD OF VALA DOST THOU HIDE IN CLEFTS OF THE 370 FOUR ZOAS 9     501
        ROCK
CLEMENTS
    STRAND NEAR ST CLEMENTS IS WIDENED AND BECOME VERY ELEGANT 831D LETTER 31    PROSE
    FROM THE ANGEL INN NEAR ST CLEMENTS CHURCH STRAND  . . . 871C LETTER 73       PROSE
CLENCHING
    ETRUSCAN COLUMN THEN (STARTING) UP & CLENCHING BOTH HIS   45B ISLAND MOON 1   PROSE
        FISTS
CLERGY
    AND NOBLES AND CLERGY SHALL FAIL FROM BEFORE ME . . . . . 140 FRENCH REVOLTN  143
    WHAT MUST OUR CLERGY BE WHO ALLOW BACON TO BE EITHER WISE 404B ANNO BACON      MARG
CLERGYMAN
    OR FIT THINGS FOR A CLERGYMAN TO WRITE UPON  . . . . .   795B LETTER 6        PROSE
CLERGYMEN
    THE SPECTATOR MAY SUPPOSE THEM CLERGYMEN IN THE PULPIT . 608A V LAST JUDG/N   PROSE
CLERK     SEE CLARK
    THE NORMAN WILLIAM AND THE LEARNED CLERK  . . . . . . .   35 WAR SONG/PS        27
    I COME AT LENGTH TO THE CLERK OF OXENFORD . . . . . . . 572B DESC CAT 3       PROSE
    CLERK HAD PUT HIMSELF UNDER THE TUITION OF THE MATURE POET 572C DESC CAT 3    PROSE
CLERMONT
    . . . OR CLERMONT THE TERRIBLE VOICE AND YOUR ROBES . . . 142 FRENCH REVOLTN  188
CLEVER
    I THINK IN THE FIRST PLACE THAT CHATTERTON WAS CLEVER AT  49C ISLAND MOON 5   PROSE
    AH SAID THE PYTHAGOREAN ARADOBO WILL MAKE A VERY CLEVER   49D ISLAND MOON 6   PROSE
        FELLOW
    WOULD MAKE A CLEVER FELLOW IF HE WAS PROPERLY BROUGHT UP  50A ISLAND MOON 6   PROSE
    THIS IS A VERY CLEVER SENTENCE WHO WROTE (IT) GOD KNOWS  471C ANNO REYNOLDS * MARG
    WE MAY BE CLEVER AS PUGILISTS BUT AS ARTISTS WE ARE  . . 594D PUB ADDRESS/N   PROSE
    MAY BE VERY CLEVER IN [YOUR] DEIR OWN OPINIONS  . . . . 594D PUB ADDRESS/N    PROSE
    VERY CLEVER & INDEED A SUBLIME BUT VERY UNFINISHD SKETCH 839D LETTER 38       PROSE
CLIFF
    ON EVERY CLIFF AND TOMB . . . . . . . . . . . . .       148 MARRIAGE HH 2      11
    [THE GOAT LEAPD FROM THE CRAGGY [?ROCK] CLIFF . . . . . 270 FOUR ZOAS 1    *  208
    SHRUNK INTO FIXED SPACE STOOD TREMBLING ON A ROCKY CLIFF 305 FOUR ZOAS 5       12
    FROM DOVER CLIFF TO LIZARD POINT THE OTHER TOWARD THE NORTH 512 MILTON 26      14
    ALBION THE HIGH CLIFF OF THE ATLANTIC IS BECOME A BARREN 660 JERUSALEM 34      16
        LAND
    BLACK & IMMENSE A ROCK OF DIFFICULTY & A CLIFF  . . . .  674 JERUSALEM 44      11
    CLIFF AFTER CLIFF & OVER VALLEYS OF DESPAIR & DEATH  . . 674 JERUSALEM 44      13
    COME & MOURN OVER ALBION THE WHITE CLIFF OF THE ATLANTIC 679 JERUSALEM 49       6
CLIFFS
    HE TAKES HIS SEAT UPON THE CLIFFS THE MARINER . . . . .    3 TO WINTER/PS      13
```

		PAGE	TITLE	LINE

CLIFFS   (CONTINUED)

LIBERTY SHALL STAND UPON THE CLIFFS OF ALBION . . . . .   33 EDW THIRD/PS 6   55
. . . AND LOOK OVER THE ROCKY CLIFFS . . . . 148 FRENCH REVOLTN   302
WHO BUILT PALACES IN THE IMMENSE CLIFFS . . . . 154D MARRIAGE HH 15 PROSE
DOES THE STILL SPIDER VIEW THE CLIFFS WHERE EAGLES HIDE 193 V DAU ALBION 5   37
   THEIR YOUNG
DESCENDS LINK BY LINK FROM ALBION'S CLIFFS ACROSS THE   197 AMERICA 3   8
   SEA TO BIND
THE EASTERN CLOUD RENT ON HIS CLIFFS STOOD ALBION'S   197 AMERICA 3   14
   WRATHFUL PRINCE
DESCENDS LINK BY LINK FROM ALBION'S CLIFFS ACROSS THE   204 AMERICA CANC A   8
   SEA TO BIND
THE EASTERN CLOUD RENT ON HIS CLIFFS STOOD ALBION'S FIERY 204 AMERICA CANC A   14
   PRINCE
FROM THE FOUR CLIFFS OF ALBION RISE . . . . 205 AMERICA CANC C   17
ON MOUNTAINS & CLIFFS OF SNOW THE AWFUL APPARITION HOVERD 205 AMERICA CANC C 28
HANGING FROWNING CLIFFS & ALL BETWEEN . . . . 225 URIZEN 5   10
LIFE IN CATARACTS POURD DOWN HIS CLIFFS . . . . 230 URIZEN 13   55
ROUND ALBION'S CLIFFS & LONDON'S WALLS STILL ENITHARMON 242 EUROPE 12   2
   SLEPT
AND THERE THE EAGLE HIDES HER YOUNG IN CLIFFS & PRECIPICES 308 FOUR ZOAS 5   129
FROM THE FOUR CLIFFS OF URTHONA RISE GLOWING AROUND THE 319 FOUR ZOAS 6   313
   SPECTRE
WITH MOLTEN ORE HE HEAVES THE IRON CLIFFS IN HIS RATTLING 486 MILTON 6   30
   CHAINS
UPON THE MOUNTAINS OF ALBION AMONG THE CLIFFS OF THE DEAD 488 MILTON 8   26
BECAME CANAAN CLOSING LOS FROM ETERNITY IN ALBION'S CLIFFS 491 MILTON 10   10
HIS RIGHT FOOT STRETCHES TO THE SEA ON DOVER CLIFFS HIS 531 MILTON 39   40
   HEEL
CIRCLING ALBION'S CLIFFS IN WHICH THE FOUR-FOLD WORLD 532 MILTON 39   60
   RESIDES
FROM THE CLIFFS OF MEMORY AND REASONING IT IS A BARREN ROCK 581B DESC CAT 6 TITLE
AND HIS INFANT THOUGHTS & DESIRES INTO COLD DARK CLIFFS 628 JERUSALEM 9   2
   OF DEATH
WAS BUILT IN FROM ETERNITY IN THE CLIFFS OF ALBION . . . 631 JERUSALEM 11   15
AND LOS WAS ROOFD IN FROM ETERNITY IN ALBION'S CLIFFS . . 642 JERUSALEM 19   33
BEHOLD THE FOGGY MORNINGS OF THE DEAD ON ALBION'S CLIFFS 681 JERUSALEM 50   13
AROUND IN THE CLOUDS OF THE FEMALE ON ALBION'S CLIFFS OF 697 JERUSALEM 63   22
   THE DEAD
OF HOREB STILL EYEING ALBION'S CLIFFS EAGERLY SIEZING & 704 JERUSALEM 67   27
   TWISTING
THE HEAVENS ARE CUT LIKE A MANTLE AROUND FROM THE CLIFFS 706 JERUSALEM 68   19
   OF ALBION
AND THIS THE FORM OF MIGHTY HAND SITTING ON ALBION'S CLIFFS 708 JERUSALEM 70   1
HOW HYLE ROOFD LOS IN ALBION'S CLIFFS BY THE AFFECTIONS 715 JERUSALEM 74   28
   RENT
CLIFFS DIVIDING THEM INTO MALE & FEMALE FORMS IN   719 JERUSALEM 78   7
   HIS FURNACES

CLIFFY

THE ATLANTIC CONTINENT SUNK ROUND ALBION'S CLIPPY SHORE 663 JERUSALEM 36   39
DRIVN FORTH BY LOS TIME AFTER TIME FROM ALBION'S CLIPPY 707 JERUSALEM 69   8
   SHORE

CLIMB

HE SUFFERD HIM TO CLIMB THAT HE MIGHT DRAW ALL HUMAN FORMS 324 FOUR ZOAS 7   164

CLIMBD

FRIEND THE ANGEL CLIMBD UP FROM HIS STATION INTO THE MILL 156C MARRIAGE HH 17 PROSE
OR DOWN DARK PRECIPICES OR CLIMBD WITH PAIN & LABOUR HUGE 319 FOUR ZOAS 6   * 289

CLIMBING

CLIMBING THRO NIGHT'S HIGHEST NOON . . . . 771 OF GATES/GP   32

CLIME

AND LET THY HOLY FEET VISIT OUR CLIME . . . .   1 TO SPRING/PS   8
AMBITION IS THE GROWTH OF EVRY CLIME . . . .   28 EDW THIRD/PS 4   2
AND WHEN THE SHAKING CEAST A FOG POSSEST THE ACCURSED CLIME 106 TIRIEL 5   17
IN THE SOUTHERN CLIME . . . . 112 LIT GRL LST/SI   9
THEN EVERY MAN OF EVERY CLIME . . . .   117 DIVNE IMAGE/SI   13
SUNK FROM THE GLORIOUS CLIME . . . . 157A MARRIAGE HH 17   PROSE
SEEKING AFTER THAT SWEET GOLDEN CLIME . . . . 215 AH SUNFLOWR/SE   3
WITH VISIONS OF SWEET BLISS FAR OTHER THAN THIS BURNING 321 FOUR ZOAS 7   62
   CLIME

CLIMES

THE JUST MAN INTO BARREN CLIMES . . . .   148 MARRIAGE HH 2   16
WERE NOW NOT VOCAL AS IN CLIMES OF HAPPY ETERNITY . . . 315 FOUR ZOAS 6   135
O WHAT A WORLD IS HERE UNLIKE THOSE CLIMES OF BLISS . . . 317 FOUR ZOAS 6 208
AN ANGEL IS HERE FROM THE HEAVENLY CLIMES . . . . . . 428 MARY   5

CLIMING

HERE LADIES & GENTLEMEN SAID HE I'LL SHEW YOU A LOUSE   58C ISLAND MOON 10 *PROSE
   [?CLIMING] OR

CLING

WHEN THE FEW INHABITANTS CLING TREMBLING TOGETHER . . . 36B COUCH DEATH/PS PROSE
HER PALE HANDS CLING AROUND HER HUSBAND & OVER HER WEAK 305 FOUR ZOAS 5   21
   HEAD
CLING ROUND THE MEN IN BANDS OF TWENTIES & OF FIFTIES PALE 358 FOUR ZOAS 9   48

CLINGING

SHIVRING CLINGING AROUND LIKE A CLOUD . . . .   258 BOOK OF LOS 4   56

CLINGS

LO NOW THE DIREFUL MONSTER WHOSE SKIN CLINGS . . . . .   3 TO WINTER/PS   9

CLINKERS

THE SURREY HILLS GLOW LIKE THE CLINKERS OF THE FURNACE 485 MILTON 6   14
   LAMBETH'S VALE

CLIP

TO CLIP THE WINGS AND TO TAKE OFF THE WHEELS OF OUR   807A LETTER 17   PROSE
   CHARIOTS

		PAGE	TITLE	LINE

CLIPD
    THE GAME COCK CLIPD & ARMD FOR FIGHT . . . . 431 AUGURIES   17
    HOLY & COLD I CLIPD THE WINGS . . . . 771 OF GATES/GP   35
CLITHYMA
    [THEN IJIM SAID LOTHO CLITHYMA MAKUTH FETCH YOUR FATHER] 105 TIRIEL 4   73
CLOAK   SEE CLOKE
    IF I LIFT UP MY HEAD SIN COVERS ME AS A CLOAK . . . . . 36A COUCH DEATH/PS   PROSE
CLOATHD
    O SONS OF TROJAN BRUTUS CLOATHD IN WAR . . . . 31 EDW THIRD/PS 6   1
CLOATHED   SEE CLOTHED,CLOTHD
    O WEAK WOMAN IT IS DEATH CLOATHED IN FLESH THOU LOVEST . . 38B SAMSON/PS   PROSE
CLOATHING
    STRIPPED FROM HIS LOAD OF CLOATHING HE IS LIKE A   581A DESC CAT 5   PROSE
    DEAD CORPSE
CLOATHS   SEE CLOTHES
    WHEN SILVER SNOW DECKS SUSAN'S CLOATHS . . . . 15 BLIND-MANS/PS   1
CLOCK   SEE O CLOCK
    HEAVEN WOULD UPON THIS PLAN BE BUT A CLOCK . . . . . . 91B ANNO SWED LOVE   MARG
    THE HOURS OF FOLLY ARE MEASURD BY THE CLOCK . . . . . 151A MARRIAGE HH 7   PROSE
    BUT OF WISDOM NO CLOCK CAN MEASURE . . . . 151A MARRIAGE HH 7   PROSE
CLOD
    THE CLOD OF CLAY HEARD THE WORM'S VOICE & RAISD HER PITYING 129 BOOK OF THEL 4   7
    HEAD
    SO SUNG A LITTLE CLOD OF CLAY . . . . 162 CLOD PEBBLE/N   5
    THE CLOD & THE PEBBLE . . . . 211C CLOD PEBBLE/SE   TITLE
    SO [SUNG] SANG A LITTLE CLOD OF CLAY . . . . 211 CLOD PEBBLE/SE *   5
    URIZEN IS A CLOD OF CLAY . . . . 226 URIZEN 6   12
    MY HEAVENS ARE BRASS MY EARTH IS IRON MY MOON A CLOD OF 290 FOUR ZOAS 2   395
    CLAY
    AND TOOK THE FLOWER UP IN ITS NATIVE CLOD . . . . . . 414 TO MRS FLAXMAN   8
    IS BECOME A CLOD OF CLAY MERLIN IS A WORM OF THE VALLEY 688 JERUSALEM 56   28
    LITTLE GIRL LOST DITTO DITTO THE CLOD & PEBBLE . . . SUPP LETTER 66A   *PROSE
CLODS
    I LAID MY HEAD IN THE HOT NOON AFTER THE BROKEN CLODS . 295 FOUR ZOAS 3   123
    WHEN THE SUN SETS WHEN THE CLODS HARDEN & THE CATTLE STAND 355 FOUR ZOAS 8   566
    THE HEAVY ROLLER TO BREAK THE CLODS TO PASS OVER   365 FOUR ZOAS 9   307
    THE NATIONS
    THE PLOWED FURROW LISTNING TO THE WEEPING CLODS TILL WE 687 JERUSALEM 55   43
    SUBSERVIENT TO THE CLODS OF THE FURROW THE CATTLE AND EVEN 688 JERUSALEM 56   36
CLOGGY
    WITH OIL OR WITH ANY CLOGGY VEHICLE . . . . 565A DESC CAT 2   PROSE
CLOKE   SEE CLOAK
    FOLLY IS THE CLOKE OF KNAVERY . . . . 151B MARRIAGE HH 7   PROSE
    SHAME IS PRIDE'S CLOKE . . . . 151B MARRIAGE HH 7   PROSE
    IN THAT DARK VALLEY I HAVE GIRDED ROUND MY CLOKE AND ON 666 JERUSALEM 39   20
    MY FEET
    IS AN APOLOGY & CLOKE FOR HIS SIN & NOT A CONFESSION . 682D JERUSALEM 52   PROSE
    AS UNITY IS THE CLOKE OF FOLLY . . . . 778B HOMERS POETRY   PROSE
    SO GOODNESS IS THE CLOKE OF KNAVERY . . . . 778B HOMERS POETRY   PROSE
CLOSD   SEE SELF-CLOSD
    CLOSD FROM THE EYE OF DAY TO THE HARD ROCK TRANSFIXT BY 41D THEN SHE BORE   PROSE
    FATE
    TWAS THE RUDE THUNDER STROKE THAT CLOSD HER EYES . . 43C WOE CRIED MUSE   PROSE
    . . . AND THE TERRIBLE SUN CLOSD IN AN ORB AND THE MOON 143 FRENCH REVOLTN   211
    IS AN IMMENSE WORLD OF DELIGHT CLOSD BY YOUR SENSES FIVE 150D MARRIAGE HH 6   PROSE
    [CLOSD] CHAIND IN NIGHT . . . . 169 EARTHS ANSWR/N   14
    CAN NEVER PASS AWAY SHE CEASD & CLOSD HER GOLDEN SHRINE 189 V DAU ALBION 1   10
    BECAUSE THE NIGHT IS GONE THAT CLOSD ME IN ITS DEADLY BLACK 191 V DAU ALBION 2   29
    AGE ON AGES HE LAY CLOSD UNKNOWN . . . . 223 URIZEN 3   24
    THE ETERNAL PROPHET & URIZEN CLOSD . . . . 230 URIZEN 13   40
    HE IN DARKNESS CLOSD VIEWD ALL HIS RACE . . . . . . 235 URIZEN 23   22
    ON A VAST ROCK PERCIEVD BY THOSE SENSES THAT ARE CLOSD 242 EUROPE 12   8
    FROM THOUGHT
    MAY BE DULLD AND THE NOSTRILS CLOSD UP . . . . . . 247 SONG OF LOS 7   6
    SO SPOKE THEY & CLOSD THE . . . . 267 FOUR ZOAS 1   108
    THE INNUMERABLE SONS & DAUGHTERS OF LUVAH CLOSD IN FURNACES 276 FOUR ZOAS 1   423
    THE DAUGHTERS OF BEULAH TERRIFIED HAVE CLOSD THE GATE OF 277 FOUR ZOAS 1   479
    THE TONGUE
    . . . & CLOSD THE MESSENGERS IN CLOUDS AROUND . . 279 FOUR ZOAS 1   552
    REFUSD TO OPEN THE BRIGHT GATES SHE CLOSD AND BARRD THEM 279 FOUR ZOAS 1   565
    FAST
    VALA INCIRCLE ROUND THE FURNACES WHERE LUVAH WAS CLOSD . 282 FOUR ZOAS 2   77
    THE HEAVENS WERE CLOSD [&] AND . . . . 286 FOUR ZOAS 2   246
    ALBION CLOSD THE WESTERN GATE & SHUT AMERICA OUT BY THE 294 FOUR ZOAS 3   105
    . . .
    WHEN THOUGHT IS CLOSD IN CAVES . . . . 311 FOUR ZOAS 5   241
    [NOT SO CLOSD UP THE PRINCE OF LIGHT NOW DARKEND WANDRING 314 FOUR ZOAS 6   * 100
    AMONG]
    SWEEPS OVER THEE FREEZING TO SOLID STILL THOU SITST CLOSD 322 FOUR ZOAS 7   75
    UP
    NOR COULD THEY EVER BE CLOSD AGAIN THE GOLDEN HINGES WERE 328 FOUR ZOAS 7   324
    BROKEN
    AND CLOUDS ARE CLOSD AROUND MY TOWER MY ARMS LABOUR IN VAIN 335 FOUR ZOAS 7B   89
    AND CLOSD ME IN A WATRY WORLD OF WOE WHERE ENION STOOD . . 339 FOUR ZOAS 7B   * 237
    WEPT OVER HIM CREATED HIM A SPACE CLOSD WITH A TENDER MOON 350 FOUR ZOAS 8   371
    FOR IN THEIR ORBED SENSES WITHIN CLOSD UP THEY WANDERD 367 FOUR ZOAS 9   382
    AT WILL
    I SIT IN THE PLACE OF SHELLS & MOURN & THOU ART CLOSD IN 370 FOUR ZOAS 9   489
    CLOUDS
    THEN LAST HERSELF LAID DOWN & CLOSD HER EYELIDS IN SOFT 370 FOUR ZOAS 9   516
    SLUMBERS
    WHEN LUVAH & VALA WERE CLOSD UP IN THEIR WORLD OF SHADOWY 372 FOUR ZOAS 9   559
    FORMS

347

		PAGE	TITLE	LINE

CLOSD   (CONTINUED)

THREEFOLD EACH IN THE OTHER CLOSD	429 CRYSTL CABINET	15
BUT WHEN THE MORTAL EYES ARE CLOSD	442 DEDICATN BLAIR	3
THE EYE OF MAN A LITTLE NARROW ORB CLOSD UP & DARK . . .	484 MILTON 5	21
TREMBLING SHE WEPT OVER THE SPACE & CLOSD IT WITH A TENDER MOON	489 MILTON 8	44
BUT HE CLOSD UP ENITHARMON FROM THE SIGHT OF ALL THESE THINGS	489 MILTON 9	18
ME FROM HIS INMOST BRAIN & THE DOORS CLOSD WITH THUNDERS SOUND	493 MILTON 12	48
IN THEIR ETERNAL SPHERES NOW HUMAN THO THEIR BODIES REMAIN CLOSD	498 MILTON 17	4
WITHINSIDE WONDROUS & EXPANSIVE ITS GATES ARE NOT CLOSD	502 MILTON 20	29
VALA INCIRCLE ROUND THE FURNACES WHERE LUVAH WAS CLOSD . .	626 JERUSALEM 7	35
I AM CLOSD UP FROM MY CHILDREN MY EMANATION IS DIVIDING	627 JERUSALEM 8	13
THE WESTERN GATE FOURFOLD IS CLOSD HAVING FOUR CHERUBIM	633 JERUSALEM 13	6
BUT ALL CLOSD UP TILL THE LAST DAY	633 JERUSALEM 13	11
IS CLOSD AS WITH A THREEFOLD CURTAIN OF IVORY & FINE LINEN & ERMINE	633 JERUSALEM 13	23
BUT THE GATE OF THE TONGUE THE WESTERN GATE IN THEM IS CLOSD	635 JERUSALEM 14	26
ALBION'S CIRCUMFERENCE WAS CLOSD HIS CENTER BEGAN DARKNING	642 JERUSALEM 19	36
AND CLOSD UP THE SWEET REGIONS OF YOUTH AND VIRGIN INNOCENCE	642 JERUSALEM 20	6
THAT THE DEEP WOUND OF SIN MIGHT BE CLOSD UP WITH THE NEEDLE	643 JERUSALEM 21	13
NO MORE SHALL I BEHOLD HIM HE IS CLOSD IN LUVAH'S SEPULCHER	648 JERUSALEM 24	51
SEARCHD IN VAIN CLOSD FROM THE MINUTIA HE WALKD DIFFICULT	657 JERUSALEM 31	13
THEY SAW AMERICA CLOSD OUT BY THE OAKS OF THE WESTERN SHORE	672 JERUSALEM 43	6
. . . IS CLOSD IN BY DEADLY TEETH	672 JERUSALEM 43	24
I SEE AMERICA CLOSD APART & JERUSALEM DRIVEN IN TERROR . .	673 JERUSALEM 43	69
O ALBION MILDEST SON OF EDEN CLOSD IS THY WESTERN GATE . .	675 JERUSALEM 45	3
ALBION'S WESTERN GATE IS CLOSD HIS DEATH IS COMING APACE	675 JERUSALEM 45	17
THE EYE OF MAN A LITTLE NARROW ORB CLOSD UP & DARK . . .	680 JERUSALEM 49	34
THE NOSTRILS BENT DOWN TO THE EARTH & CLOSD WITH SENSELESS FLESH	680 JERUSALEM 49	38
BUT JERUSALEM FAINTLY SAW HIM CLOSD IN THE DUNGEONS OF BABYLON	693 JERUSALEM 60	39
BOTH OF THE HEAD & HEART & LOINS CLOSD UP IN MORAL PRIDE	693 JERUSALEM 60	49
BECAUSE HIS CHILDREN WERE CLOSD FROM HIM APART & ENITHARMON	696 JERUSALEM 62	37
DIVIDING IN FIERCE PAIN ALSO THE VISION OF GOD WAS CLOSD IN CLOUDS	696 JERUSALEM 62	38
OF THOUSANDS FROM WESTMINSTER & MARYBONE IN SHIPS CLOSD UP	700 JERUSALEM 65	34
BUT NOW I AM CLOSD OUT FROM THEM IN THE NARROW PASSAGES	721 JERUSALEM 79	60
THERE IS REUBEN & GAD & JOSEPH & JUDAH & LEVI CLOSD UP . .	721 JERUSALEM 79	64

CLOSE

OR CLOSE UP OR THEY WILL DESCEND IF HE CLOSES UP THE TWO	93A ANNO SWED LOVE	MARG
[SOME NOSTRILD WIDE BREATHING OUT BLOOD SOME CLOSE SHUT UP]	109 TIRIEL 8	12
WHILE I CLOSE MY EYES	113 LIT GRL LST/SI	32
THAT DOES [CLOSE] FREEZE MY BONES AROUND	169 EARTHS ANSWR/N	22
THE CITIZENS OF NEW-YORK CLOSE THEIR BOOKS & LOCK THEIR CHESTS	201 AMERICA 14	13
TO THE CLOSE HALL OF COUNSEL WHERE HIS ANGEL FORM RENEWS	204 AMERICA CANC B	2
DIDST CLOSE MY TONGUE IN SENSELESS CLAY	220 TO TIRZAH/SE	13
TWO EARS IN CLOSE VOLUTIONS	229 URIZEN 11	21
SWEET LAUGHTER SIEZD ME IN MY SLEEP SILENT & CLOSE I LAUGHD	271 FOUR ZOAS 1	265
TWO EARS IN CLOSE VOLUTIONS FROM BENEATH HIS ORBS OF VISION	303 FOUR ZOAS 4	233
CALL [VALAN] VALA FROM HER CLOSE RECESS IN ALL HER DARK DECEIT	307 FOUR ZOAS 5 *	64
. . . BURST OPEN & AGAIN CLOSE WITH A [?DISMAL] DEADLY PAIN	309 FOUR ZOAS 5 *	178
O DID I CLOSE MY TREASURIES WITH ROOFS OF SOLID STONE . .	310 FOUR ZOAS 5	212
BUT LUVAH CLOSE CONFERRD WITH URIZEN IN DARKSOM NIGHT . .	326 FOUR ZOAS 7	255
THAT FAR WITHIN THE CLOSE RECESSES OF THEIR SECRET PALACES	335 FOUR ZOAS 7B	105
THE BAT THAT FLITS AT CLOSE OF EVE	431 AUGURIES	25
FROM BENEATH HIS ORBS OF VISION TWO EARS IN CLOSE VOLUTIONS	482 MILTON 3	17
AND ROUND THE SHADOWY EIGHTH THE EIGHT CLOSE UP THE COUCH	502 MILTON 20	47
AND LOS BEHIND ME STOOD A TERRIBLE FLAMING SUN JUST CLOSE	505 MILTON 22	6
TILL ITS CLOSE WHICH WILL BE THE...OF SEPTEMBER... . .	563B DESC CAT	*PROSE
IF THE PERCEPTIVE ORGANS CLOSE THEIR OBJECTS SEEM TO CLOSE ALSO	661 JERUSALEM 34	56
AND LET WILD SEAS & ROCKS CLOSE UP JERUSALEM AWAY FROM . .	680 JERUSALEM 49	77
AND CLOSE HER FROM THY ANCIENT WALLS	718 ENGLND AWAKE/J	4
TO CUT HER OFF FROM AMERICA TO CLOSE UP HER SECRET ARK . .	725 JERUSALEM 82	34
WHO AGAINST SINNERS HEAVEN CLOSE	758 EV GOSPEL (1)	12
AGED IGNORANCE PERCEPTIVE ORGANS CLOSED THEIR OBJECTS CLOSE	767D FOR SEXES/GP	TITLE
TO CLOSE THE LABOURS OF MY DAY	771 OF GATES/GP	42

CLOSED

WHY CANNOT THE EAR BE CLOSED TO ITS OWN DESTRUCTION . . .	130 BOOK OF THEL 6	11
FOR MAN HAS CLOSED HIMSELF UP TILL HE SEES ALL THINGS . .	154C MARRIAGE HH 14	PROSE
THE ETERNALS CLOSED THE TENT	232 URIZEN 19	47
WERE HEAVY & DULL & THEIR EYES & NOSTRILS CLOSED UP . . .	315 FOUR ZOAS 6	125
ROLLING ROUND INTO TWO LITTLE ORBS & CLOSED IN TWO LITTLE CAVES	482 MILTON 3	14
CAN SUCH CLOSED NOSTRILS FEEL A JOY OR TELL OF AUTUMN FRUITS	485 MILTON 5	32
AND WHEN THEY TOUCHD CLOSED TOGETHER SOUTHWARD IN ONE SUN	504 MILTON 21	40
AND IN THE NERVES OF THE EAR FOR THE NERVES OF THE TONGUE ARE CLOSED	517 MILTON 29	40
SIN & DEATH ARE TO BE CLOSED ETERNALLY BY	608B V LAST JUDG/N	*PROSE
AND IN ITS HOLINESS IS CLOSED THE ABOMINATION OF DESOLATION	629 JERUSALEM 10	16

```
                                                              PAGE      TITLE         LINE
CLOSED    (CONTINUED)
     WITHIN THE HUMAN HEART WHOSE GATES CLOSED WITH SOLEMN SOUND   678  JERUSALEM 48       25
     CLOSED IN BY A SANDY DESART & A NIGHT OF STARS SHINING  .  .  707  JERUSALEM 69       21
     AND THUS SHE CLOSED HER LEFT HAND AND UTTERD HER FALSHOOD     725  JERUSALEM 82   *   19
     EVEN ENITHARMON SEPARATED OUTSIDE & HIS LOINS CLOSED    .     732  JERUSALEM 86       58
     I SHALL BE CLOSED FROM THY SIGHT SIEZE THEREFORE IN THY       732  JERUSALEM 87        7
        HAND
     AND THE BODY OF ALBION WAS CLOSED APART FROM ALL NATIONS      741  JERUSALEM 94       14
     AGED IGNORANCE PERCEPTIVE ORGANS CLOSED THEIR OBJECTS         767D FOR SEXES/GP    TITLE
        CLOSE
     CLOSED THE FATHER & THE SONS   . . . . . . . . . .  .  .  .   771  OF GATES/GP        38
     EXACTLY TWENTY YEARS BEEN CLOSED FROM ME AS BY A DOOR   .     852B LETTER 50       PROSE
CLOSELY
     WE FALL ON ONE ANOTHER'S NECKS MORE CLOSELY WE EMBRACE    .   374  FOUR ZOAS 9       639
     AND DESPAIR AS MESHES CLOSELY WOVE OVER THE WEST OF LONDON    668  JERUSALEM 41        9
     AH MY MARY SAID JOSEPH WEEPING OVER & EMBRACING HER CLOSELY   694  JERUSALEM 61       14
        IN
CLOSER
     WILL BE IMPOSED ON BY THE CLOSER SORT   . . . . . . .  .       20  EDW THIRD/PS 2     58
CLOSES
     CLOSES HER EYES IN SLEEP BENEATH NIGHT'S SHADE    . . .  .     10  FRESH FROM/PS      18
     OR CLOSE UP OR THEY WILL DESCEND IF HE CLOSES UP THE TWO      93A  ANNO SWED LOVE   MARG
     AND THAT ONE HE CLOSES WITH IRON BARS   . . . . . .  .  .  .  583A DESC CAT 9       PROSE
CLOSET
     THAT MAN S A HERO IN HIS CLOSET AND MORE    . . . . .  .       25  EDW THIRD/PS 3    184
CLOSING
     AND MORE TO EARTH CLOSING AND RESTRAINING   . . . . .  .  .   246  SONG OF LOS 4      15
     HIS INWARD EYES CLOSING FROM THE DIVINE VISION & ALL   .  .   279  FOUR ZOAS 1       558
     BECAME CANAAN CLOSING LOS FROM ETERNITY IN ALBION'S CLIFFS    491  MILTON 10          10
     HIDING ALBION'S SONS WITHIN THE VEIL CLOSING JERUSALEM'S      704  JERUSALEM 67       17
     FROM IMAGINATION AND CLOSING ITSELF AS IN STEEL IN A RATIO    714  JERUSALEM 74       11
CLOTH
     HER EYES WERE FIXD THE BLOODY CLOTH UNFOLDS     . . . .  .      5  FAIR ELENOR/PS     57
     FOR THRO THE SLENDER CLOTH HE SEES    . . . . . . .  .  .      16  BLIND-MANS/PS      33
     WROTE "A WEBBE DYER" THAT IS A CLOTH DYER     . . . . .  .    572A DESC CAT 3       PROSE
     WASHD BY THE WATER-WHEELS OF NEWTON BLACK THE CLOTH    .  .   636  JERUSALEM 15       16
CLOTHD     SEE CLOATHD,CLOATHED,CLOTHED
     CLOTHD IN FLAMES OF CRIMSON . . . . . . . . . . . .  .  .  .  138  FRENCH REVOLTN     86
     . . . TEARS FELL DOWN THE SHADY CHEEKS AT HIS FEET MANY       140  FRENCH REVOLTN    132
        CLOTHD
     CLOTHD IN ROBES OF BLOOD & GOLD   . . . . . . . . .  .  .  .  177  DAY/N               2
     OF MAN CLOTHD IN LUVAH'S ROBES OF BLOOD SAW & WEPT   .  .     304  FOUR ZOAS 4       248
     APPEAREST CLOTHD IN LUVAH'S GARMENTS THAT WE MAY BEHOLD       304  FOUR ZOAS 4       257
        THEE
     NINE VIRGINS CLOTHD IN LIGHT . . . . . . . . . . . .  .  .    310  FOUR ZOAS 5       200
     HE ORDAIND & PRIESTESSES CLOTHD IN DISGUISES BEASTIAL    .    333  FOUR ZOAS 7B       27
     THARMAS LAUGHD FURIOUS AMONG THE BANNERS CLOTHD IN BLOOD      334  FOUR ZOAS 7B       49
     [THEY HAD WHICH CLOTHD THEIR BODIES LIKE A GARMENT OF SOFT    341  FOUR ZOAS 8        10
        DOWN]
     I SEE THE MURDERER OF MY LUVAH CLOTHD IN ROBES OF BLOOD       345  FOUR ZOAS 8       153
     THE ONE WAS CLOTHD IN FLAMES OF FIRE   . . . . . . .  .  .    421  BENEATH/N           6
     THE OTHER [IN] CLOTHD IN [SWEET DESIRE] IRON WIRE    . . .    421  BENEATH/N      *    7
     THE OTHER CLOTHD IN [SIGHS] & TEARS & SIGHS   . . . . .  .    422  BENEATH/N           8
     AND IN TEARS CLOTHD NIGHT & DAY   . . . . . . . . .  .  .  .  422  BENEATH/N          16
     [THE ONE WAS CLOTHD IN FLAMES OF FIRE]  . . . . . . .  .  .   422  BENEATH REWR/N      3
     [THE OTHER CLOTHD IN [SWEET DESIRE] IRON WIRE]   . . . .  .   422  BENEATH REWR/N      4
     [THE OTHER CLOTHD IN TEARS & SIGHS]   . . . . . . . .  .  .   422  BENEATH REWR/N      5
     THE ONE WAS CLOTHD IN FLAMES OF FIRE  . . . . . . . .  .  .   424  THE GOLDEN NET      5
     THE OTHER CLOTHD IN IRON WIRE   . . . . . . . . . .  .  .  .  424  THE GOLDEN NET      6
     THE OTHER CLOTHD IN TEARS & SIGHS   . . . . . . . .  .  .  .  424  THE GOLDEN NET      7
     AND IN TEARS CLOTHD NIGHT & DAY   . . . . . . . . .  .  .  .  424  THE GOLDEN NET     15
     CLOTHD IN THE SERPENT'S FOLDS IN SELFISH HOLINESS DEMANDING   493  MILTON 12          46
        PURITY
     HENCE THOU ART CLOTHD WITH HUMAN BEAUTY O THOU MORTAL MAN     502  MILTON 20      *   31
     THE TOAD & VENOMOUS NEWT THE SERPENT CLOTHD IN GEMS & GOLD    513  MILTON 27          22
     WHILE THE POOR INDIGENT IS LIKE THE DIAMOND WHICH            515  MILTON 28          36
        THO CLOTHD
     CLOTHD IN BLACK MOURNING UPON MY RIVER'S CURRENTS VALA        657  JERUSALEM 31       47
        AWAKE
     YORK CROWND WITH LOVING KINDNESS EDINBURGH CLOTHD    . . .    665  JERUSALEM 38       51
     RIBBD DELICATE & CLOTHD WITH FEATHERD GOLD & AZURE & PURPLE   731  JERUSALEM 86        6
     WE SHALL RETURN BUT WHILE CLOTHD WITH THE DIVINE MERCY   .    813C LETTER 22       PROSE
     WE ARE RICHLY CLOTHD IN SPIRITUAL & SUFFER ALL THE REST       813C LETTER 22       PROSE
        GLADLY
CLOTHE
     [NOW] CLOTHE YOURSELVES IN GOLDEN ARMS BROTHERS OF WAR    .   337  FOUR ZOAS 7B      163
     THE SONS OF LOS CLOTHE THEM & FEED & PROVIDE HOUSES           512  MILTON 26          30
        & FIELDS
     TO TAKE OFF HIS FILTHY GARMENTS & CLOTHE HIM WITH            533  MILTON 41           6
        IMAGINATION
     THE SONS OF LOS CLOTHE THEM & FEED & PROVIDE HOUSES           714  JERUSALEM 73       49
        & GARDENS
     THE CRUEL-ONE OF ALBION TO CLOTHE HIM IN GEMS OF MY ZONE      724  JERUSALEM 81       12
     AND TO INHABIT OUR LITTLE-ONES TO CLOTHE IN ARMOUR OF THE     729  JERUSALEM 84        9
        GOLD
CLOTHED
     FOR THOU SHALT BE CLOTHED IN LIGHT AND FED WITH MORNING       127  BOOK OF THEL 1     23
        MANNA
     HERE I CLOTHED MYSELF IN WHITE  . . . . . . . . . .  .  .  .  156D MARRIAGE HH 17  PROSE
     THEY CLOTHED ME IN THE CLOTHES OF DEATH   . . . . .  .  .  .  180  CHIMNEY SWP/N       7
     AROUND THE SMITTEN BANDS CLOTHED IN TEARS & TREMBLING         203  AMERICA 16          8
        SHUDDRING COLD
```

349

	PAGE	TITLE	LINE

CLOTHED   (CONTINUED)
THEY CLOTHED ME IN THE CLOTHES OF DEATH . . . . 212 CHIMNEY SWP/SE 7
OF GOD CLOTHED IN LUVAH'S GARMENTS LITTLE KNOWEST THOU . . 282 FOUR ZOAS 2 100
CLOTHED IN AGED VENERABLENESS OBSTINATELY RESOLVD . . . 318 FOUR ZOAS 6 242
CLOTHED IN LUVAH'S ROBES OF BLOOD DESCENDING TO REDEEM . . 330 FOUR ZOAS 7 416
WHEN URIZEN SAW THE LAMB OF GOD CLOTHED IN LUVAH'S ROBES . 342 FOUR ZOAS 8 61
THE SYNAGOGUE OF SATAN CLOTHED HER WITH SCARLET ROBES & 348 FOUR ZOAS 8 281
    GEMS
THE GROUND SPIDER WITH MANY EYES THE MOLE CLOTHED IN VELVET 377 FOUR ZOAS 9 758
AMONG THE LAMBS CLOTHED IN WHITE . . . . 427 LAND OF DREAMS 9
THOU SEEST THE GORGEOUS CLOTHED FLIES THAT DANCE & SPORT 512 MILTON 26 2
    IN SUMMER
THE GROUND SPIDER WITH MANY EYES THE MOLE CLOTHED IN VELVET 513 MILTON 27 14
GARDEN CLOTHED IN BLACK SEVERE & SILENT HE DESCENDED . . 529 MILTON 38 8
FROM FELPHAM'S VALE CLOTHED IN CLOUDS OF BLOOD TO ENTER 534 MILTON 42 20
    INTO
THE GREAT SUN IS REPRESENTED CLOTHED IN FLAMES . . . . 618B ILLUS MILTON PROSE
EVERY SUBSTANCE IS CLOTHED THEY NAME THEM GOOD & EVIL . . 629 JERUSALEM 10 9
DELIGHTING IN CRIES & TEARS & CLOTHED IN HOLINESS 630 JERUSALEM 10 49
    & SOLITUDE
AS HE SAT BEFORE HIS FURNACES CLOTHED IN SACKCLOTH OF HAIR 684 JERUSALEM 53 5
THE DAUGHTERS OF ALBION CLOTHED IN GARMENTS OF NEEDLE WORK 702 JERUSALEM 66 17
DANCING AROUND IN HOWLING PAIN CLOTHED IN THE BLOODY VEIL 704 JERUSALEM 67 16
CLOTHED IN THE SKIN OF THE VICTIM BLOOD HUMAN BLOOD IS 706 JERUSALEM 68 33
    THE LIFE
SITTING BEFORE HIS FURNACES CLOTHED IN SACKCLOTH OF HAIR 719 JERUSALEM 78 11
HIS AWFUL LIMBS INTO THE HEAVENS HE WALKED CLOTHED 742 JERUSALEM 95 7
    IN FLAMES
AND HE CLOTHED HIMSELF IN BOW & ARROWS IN AWFUL STATE 744 JERUSALEM 97 16
    FOURFOLD
AND THE ALL WONDROUS SERPENT CLOTHED IN GEMS & RICH ARRAY 746 JERUSALEM 98 44
    HUMANIZE
. . . IN THE MIDST OF THE DARKNESS OF THE OATH ALL CLOTHED 781 GHOST ABEL 2 23
CLOTHES   SEE CLOATHS,BED CLOTHES,DEATH CLOTHES
WHEN SILVER SNOW DECKS SYLVIO'S CLOTHES . . . . 64 SHEPHERD OLD 1
THOU HAST REFUSD OUR CLOTHES OUR BEDS OUR HOUSES FOR THY 100 TIRIEL 1 38
    DWELLING
ARE THE LINEN CLOTHES FOLDED UP NOW IS THE DOMINION OF EDOM 149B MARRIAGE HH 3 PROSE
THEY CLOTHED ME IN THE CLOTHES OF DEATH . . . . . . 180 CHIMNEY SWP/N 7
WHAT GOD IS HE WRITES LAWS OF PEACE & CLOTHES HIM IN A 200 AMERICA 11 12
    TEMPEST
THEY CLOTHED ME IN THE CLOTHES OF DEATH . . . . . . 212 CHIMNEY SWP/SE 7
. . . FOR WRAPD IN HIS DEATH CLOTHES . . . . 316 FOUR ZOAS 6 169
HE HID THEM WHEN HE SLEPT IN DEATH WHEN HE REVIVD 316 FOUR ZOAS 6 170
    THE CLOTHES
I HOPE THINE ARE NOT HENCE IT CLOTHES ITSELF IN RICH ARRAY 502 MILTON 20 30
TILL THEY AWAKE & SEE JESUS & THE LINEN CLOTHES LYING . 522 MILTON 32 42
MALE GENIUS WHO IN RETURN CLOTHES HER IN GEMS & GOLD . 707 JERUSALEM 69 17
CLOTHING   SEE CLOATHING
MNETHA NOW AGED WAITED ON THEM & BROUGHT THEM FOOD 100 TIRIEL 2 6
    & CLOTHING
GAVE THEE CLOTHING OF DELIGHT . . . . 115 THE LAMB/SI 5
SOFTEST CLOTHING WOOLY BRIGHT . . . . 115 THE LAMB/SI 6
LULLING THE WEEPING SPECTRES OF THE DEAD CLOTHING THEIR 346 FOUR ZOAS 8 213
    LIMBS
THE TERRORS PUT ON THEIR SWEET CLOTHING . . . . . . 346 FOUR ZOAS 8 215
NAKED OF THEIR CLOTHING THE POOR SPECTRES BEFORE 346 FOUR ZOAS 8 219
    THE ACCUSING HEAVENS
HE PUTS OFF THE CLOTHING OF BLOOD . . . . 347 FOUR ZOAS 8 236
A CLOTHING FOR THE SOUL DIVINE . . . . 432 AUGURIES 60
EVEN PITY & HUMANITY BUT MY CLOTHING SHALL BE CRUELTY . 499 MILTON 18 20
THE INTEGUMENT SOFT FOR ITS CLOTHING WITH JOY & DELIGHT 515 MILTON 28 20
CLOTHING ADAM & EVE WITH COATS OF SKINS . . . . . 824A LETTER 27 PROSE
CLOTHINGS
A TENT & TABERNACLE OF MUTUAL FORGIVENESS MALE & FEMALE 684 JERUSALEM 54 4
    CLOTHINGS
CLOTTED
OF HER DEAR LORD ALL GHASTLY PALE CLOTTED . . . . . . 5 FAIR ELENOR/PS 59
[TO JUDGMENT] FROM THE CLOTTED GORE & FROM THE HOLLOW DEN 358 FOUR ZOAS 9 43
FROM THE CLOTTED GORE & FROM THE HOLLOW DEN . . . . 359 FOUR ZOAS 9 88
CLOUD   SEE THUNDER CLOUD
LIKE A FIEND IN A CLOUD . . . . 9 MAD SONG/PS 17
THEN BOSOMD IN AN AMBER CLOUD AROUND . . . . 15 IMIT SPEN/PS 42
PASS OVER AS A SUMMER CLOUD UNREGARDED . . . . . . 27 EDW THIRD/PS 3 248
HE WAS LIKE A CLOUD TOSSED BY THE WINDS TILL THE SUN SHINE 36C COUCH DEATH/PS PROSE
BUT NOW A CLOUD OERCASTS AND BACK TO THE EAST . . . 41B THEN SHE BORE PROSE
THE CLOUD OER PAST & ROME NOW SHONE AGAIN MITERD AND . 41B THEN SHE BORE PROSE
LIKE A TEMPESTUOUS THUNDER CLOUD PRIDE LEADS THEM ON . 42C THEN SHE BORE PROSE
THINK OF A WHITE CLOUD AS BEING HOLY YOU CANNOT LOVE IT 90C ANNO SWED LOVE MARG
BUT THINK OF A HOLY MAN WITHIN THE CLOUD LOVE SPRINGS UP 90C ANNO SWED LOVE MARG
BUT SOON I BUFFETTED THE TORRENT ANON LIKE TO A CLOUD . 105 TIRIEL 4 55
ON A CLOUD I SAW A CHILD . . . . 111 INTRODUCTN/SI 3
IS BUT A CLOUD AND LIKE A SHADY GROVE . . . . . . 125 LIT BLK BOY/SI 16
THE CLOUD WILL VANISH WE SHALL HEAR HIS VOICE . . . 125 LIT BLK BOY/SI 18
WHEN I FROM BLACK AND HE FROM WHITE CLOUD FREE . . . 125 LIT BLK BOY/SI 23
AH THEL IS LIKE A WATRY BOW AND LIKE A PARTING CLOUD . 127 BOOK OF THEL 1 8
BUT THEL IS LIKE A FAINT CLOUD KINDLED AT THE RISING SUN 128 BOOK OF THEL 2 11
QUEEN OF THE VALES THE LILLY ANSWERD ASK THE TENDER CLOUD 128 BOOK OF THEL 2 13
DESCEND O LITTLE CLOUD & HOVER BEFORE THE EYES OF THEL . 128 BOOK OF THEL 2 16
THE CLOUD DESCENDED AND THE LILLY BOWD HER MODEST HEAD . 128 BOOK OF THEL 2 17
O LITTLE CLOUD THE VIRGIN SAID I CHARGE THEE TELL TO ME 128 BOOK OF THEL 3 1
THE CLOUD THEN SHEWD HIS GOLDEN HEAD & HIS BRIGHT FORM 128 BOOK OF THEL 3 5
    EMERGD

		PAGE	TITLE	LINE
CLOUD	(CONTINUED)			
DOST THOU O LITTLE CLOUD I FEAR THAT I AM NOT LIKE THEE		129	BOOK OF THEL 3	17
THE CLOUD RECLIND UPON HIS AIRY THRONE AND ANSWERD THUS		129	BOOK OF THEL 3	24
AND THE BRIGHT CLOUD SAILD ON TO FIND HIS PARTNER IN THE VALE		129	BOOK OF THEL 3	31
. . . THE CLOUD AND VISION DESCENDS OVER CHEARFUL FRANCE		134	FRENCH REVOLTN	1
O CLOUD WELL APPOINTED		134	FRENCH REVOLTN	2
PALE IS THE MORNING CLOUD IN HIS VISAGE		134	FRENCH REVOLTN	7
A BRIGHT CLOUD OF INFANT SOULS		138	FRENCH REVOLTN	88
. . . WITH CLARIONS OF ?CLOUD BREATHING WAR		138	FRENCH REVOLTN *	101
LIKE A DARK CLOUD NECKER PAUSD		139	FRENCH REVOLTN	106
WAVD ITS SOLEMN CLOUD OVER MY HEAD		140	FRENCH REVOLTN	130
. . . AND MY CLOUD AND VISION BE NO MORE		140	FRENCH REVOLTN	143
. . .I SLEPT FOR THE CLOUD OF REPOSE RETURNED		141	FRENCH REVOLTN	151
. . . THEN THE PRIEST IN HIS THUNDROUS CLOUD		144	FRENCH REVOLTN	223
DEVOUR THY LABOUR NOR LIFT UP A CLOUD IN THY HEAVENS . . .		144	FRENCH REVOLTN	226
AND THE PALACE APPEARD LIKE A CLOUD DRIVEN ABROAD . . .		145	FRENCH REVOLTN	246
THRO THE CLOUD A DEEP THUNDER		145	FRENCH REVOLTN	247
. . . FOR A CLOUD ON THE EASTERN HILLS		146	FRENCH REVOLTN	271
DRIVEN OUT BY THE FIERY CLOUD OF VOLTAIRE		146	FRENCH REVOLTN	276
. . . AND OVER THE ARMY ROUSSEAU HIS WHITE CLOUD . . .		147	FRENCH REVOLTN	282
BUT NOW FROM BETWEEN THE BLACK & WHITE SPIDERS A CLOUD		156B	MARRIAGE HH 17	PROSE
WHO AROSE BEFORE AN ANGEL THAT SAT ON A CLOUD		158B	MARRIAGE HH 22	PROSE
WHERE THE SON OF FIRE IN HIS EASTERN CLOUD		160A	SONG LIBERTY	PROSE
LIKE A FIEND HID IN A CLOUD		166	INFANT SORW/N	4
IN THE EASTERN CLOUD INSTEAD OF NIGHT A SICKLY CHARNEL HOUSE		191	V DAU ALBION 2	36
DRAW IN THE OCEAN DOES HIS EYE DISCERN THE FLYING CLOUD		193	V DAU ALBION 5	35
OOTHOON SHALL VIEW HIS DEAR DELIGHT NOR EER WITH JEALOUS CLOUD		195	V DAU ALBION 7	28
WHERE THE COLD MISER SPREADS HIS GOLD OR DOES THE BRIGHT CLOUD DROP		195	V DAU ALBION 8	1
AS WHEN A BLACK CLOUD SHEWS ITS LIGHTNINGS TO THE SILENT DEEP		196	AMERICA PREL 2	5
THE EASTERN CLOUD RENT ON HIS CLIFFS STOOD ALBION'S WRATHFUL PRINCE		197	AMERICA 3	14
THE EASTERN CLOUD RENT ON HIS CLIFFS STOOD ALBION'S FIERY PRINCE		204	AMERICA CANC A	14
IN OPPOSITION DIRE A WARLIKE CLOUD THE MYRIADS STOOD . .		205	AMERICA CANC C	20
A PROSPECT OF LIBERTY A CLOUD		209A	SUBJCTS HIST/N	TITLE
LIKE A FIEND HID IN A CLOUD		217	INFANT SORW/SE	4
COMBUSTION BLAST VAPOUR AND CLOUD		222	URIZEN 3	17
WHEN THE CLOUD BLAZES OVER THE HARVESTS		223	URIZEN 3	35
PALE AS A CLOUD OF SNOW		231	URIZEN 18	11
LIKE A MAN FROM A CLOUD BORN & UTHA		234	URIZEN 23	13
THEY HOVERED ROUND ME LIKE A CLOUD OF INCENSE WHEN I CAME		238	EUROPE INTRO	22
LIKE THE DARK CLOUD DISBURDEND IN THE DAY OF DISMAL THUNDER		238	EUROPE PREL 1	7
THE CLOUD BEARS HARD ON ALBION'S SHORE		241	EUROPE 9	9
THE CLOUD BEARS HARD UPON THE COUNCIL HOUSE DOWN RUSHING		241	EUROPE 9	12
NIGHT SPOKE TO THE CLOUD		245	SONG OF LOS 3	12
AND HIS RIGHT HAND BURNS RED IN ITS CLOUD		249	AHANIA 2	6
FROM MY SOFT CLOUD OF DEW TO FALL		254	AHANIA 5	13
SHIVRING CLINGING AROUND LIKE A CLOUD		258	BOOK OF LOS 4	56
. . . A [CLOUD] TERROR & HER SMILE A WHIRLWIND		271	FOUR ZOAS 1	269
[XXX ?CLOUD]		SUPP	FOUR ZOAS 1	*
[ORBITS HIGH] [DEMONS BY THE THOUSANDS OUT OF A GOLDEN CLOUD XXX]		SUPP	FOUR ZOAS 1	*
LIKE A BRIGHT CLOUD IN HARVEST BUT WHEN URIZEN FROWND SHE WEPT		284	FOUR ZOAS 2	183
AND ENITHARMON JOYD PLOTTING TO REND THE SECRET CLOUD . .		286	FOUR ZOAS 2	238
[[OF] IN A SOFT CLOUD OUTSTRETCHD ACROSS & LUVAH DWELT IN THE CLOUD]		292	FOUR ZOAS 3	48
. . . BUT THE CLOUD HOVERD OVER THEIR HEADS		293	FOUR ZOAS 3	66
LUVAH DESCENDED FROM THE CLOUD		293	FOUR ZOAS 3	69
DRIVEN BY THY RAGE I WANDER LIKE A CLOUD INTO THE DEEP		296	FOUR ZOAS 3	188
WHY DOES THY PITEOUS FACE EVANISH LIKE A RAINY CLOUD . .		297	FOUR ZOAS 3	199
SOFT CLOUD OF SNOW A FEMALE PALE & WEAK I SOFT EMBRACD		300	FOUR ZOAS 4	99
LOS FOLDED ENITHARMON IN A COLD WHITE CLOUD IN FEAR . . .		308	FOUR ZOAS 5	110
OF URIZEN IN VAIN THE ELOQUENT TONGUE A ROCK A CLOUD A MOUNTAIN		315	FOUR ZOAS 6	134
GIVING THEM SWEET INSTRUCTIONS WHERE THE CLOUD THE RIVER & THE FIELD		315	FOUR ZOAS 6	137
NOR MAN NOR BEAST NOR CREEPING THING NOR SUN NOR CLOUD NOR STAR		319	FOUR ZOAS 6	285
WRITING THY BOOKS ANON A CLOUD FILLD WITH A WASTE OF SNOWS		322	FOUR ZOAS 7	81
BROUGHT FORTH THIS WONDER HORRIBLE A CLOUD SHE GREW & GREW		328	FOUR ZOAS 7	327
OR LIKE A CLOUD BENEATH & LIKE A FIRE FLAMING IN HIGH . .		339	FOUR ZOAS 7B *	265
A SHAPELESS & INDEFINITE CLOUD IN TEARS OF SORROW INCESSANT		345	FOUR ZOAS 8	175
MY BACK DARKNING THE PRESENT CLOUDING WITH A CLOUD . . .		361	FOUR ZOAS 9	166
AND AFTER THE FLAMES APPEARS THE CLOUD OF THE SON OF MAN		364	FOUR ZOAS 9	272
ALL NATIONS LOOK UP TO THE CLOUD & BEHOLD HIM WHO WAS CRUCIFIED		364	FOUR ZOAS 9	274
THE CLOUD IS BLOOD DAZLING UPON THE HEAVENS & IN THE CLOUD		364	FOUR ZOAS 9	278
WITH VOICE MILD FROM HIS GOLDEN CLOUD UPON THE BREATH OF MORNING		367	FOUR ZOAS 9	387
BUT HE CAME HOME IN A BLACK BLACK CLOUD		435	WILLIAM BOND	11
AND IN THE MIDST A BLACK BLACK CLOUD		435	WILLIAM BOND	15
AND THEIR TEARS FELL THRO THE BLACK BLACK CLOUD . . .		435	WILLIAM BOND	19
FROM THE CLOUD ON WHICH EVE KNEELS [& BENEATH MOSES] . .		443B	LAST JUDGMNT/L	PROSE
IN THE CLOUD WHICH ROLLS AWAY ARE THE FOUR LIVING CREATURES		444A	LAST JUDGMNT/L	PROSE
SEVEN TRUMPETS THESE COMPOSE [COMPOSING] THE CLOUD . . .		444A	LAST JUDGMNT/L	*PROSE
AS THE CLOUD THAT BRINGS THE SNOW ALL THE WHILE FROM HIS BACK		483	MILTON 3	34

```
                                                           PAGE     TITLE      LINE
CLOUD     (CONTINUED)
    BUT FROM MY LEFT FOOT A BLACK CLOUD REDOUNDING SPREAD OVER   497 MILTON 15      50
      EUROPE
    AND HE BEHELD THE CLOUD OF MILTON STRETCHING OVER EUROPE     504 MILTON 21      36
    REACHING FROM HEAVEN TO EARTH A CLOUD & HUMAN FORM    . . .  528 MILTON 37      14
    SATAN HEARD COMING IN A CLOUD WITH TRUMPETS & FLAMING FIRE   530 MILTON 38      50
    COMING IN A CLOUD WITH TRUMPETS & WITH FIERY FLAME    . . .  531 MILTON 39      23
    LOS LISTENS TO THE CRY OF THE POOR MAN HIS CLOUD     . . . . 535 MILTON 42      34
    NUMBER VI A SPIRIT VAULTING FROM A CLOUD TO TURN AND WIND   581A DESC CAT 6   TITLE
      A
    FROM THE CLOUD ON WHICH EVE STANDS SATAN IS SEEN     . . . .606B V LAST JUDG/N  PROSE
    ON THE RIGHT BENEATH THE CLOUD ON WHICH ABEL KNEELS   . . .606C V LAST JUDG/N  PROSE
    ABEL KNEELS ON A BLOODY CLOUD &C   . . . . . . . . . .606D V LAST JUDG/N  PROSE
    ABEL KNEELS ON A BLOODY CLOUD DESCRIPTIVE OF THOSE CHURCHES 606D V LAST JUDG/N  PROSE
    BENEATH THE CLOUD ON WHICH MOSES KNEELS IS TWO FIGURES  . .607C V LAST JUDG/N  PROSE
    ABOVE HIM ARE TWO FIGURES ELEVATED ON A CLOUD     . . . .607D V LAST JUDG/N  PROSE
    ALL THESE ARISE TOWARD THE OPENING CLOUD BEFORE THE THRONE 611D V LAST JUDG/N  PROSE
    THE CLOUD THAT OPENS APART BEFORE THE THRONE     . . .612A V LAST JUDG/N  PROSE
    [AROUND THE THRONE HEAVEN IS OPENED] ON THE CLOUD    . .612B V LAST JUDG/N  PROSE
    BENEATH THESE A CLOUD OF WOMEN & CHILDREN ARE TAKEN UP  . .614A V LAST JUDG/N  PROSE
    FLEEING FROM THE ROLLING CLOUD WHICH SEPARATES THE WICKED  614A V LAST JUDG/N  PROSE
    IN A CLOUD WITHIN THE RAINBOW THAT SURROUNDS THE THRONE    614C V LAST JUDG/N  PROSE
    [THEY] THEY MERELY APPEAR AS IN A CLOUD WHEN ANY THING  . .614C V LAST JUDG/N *PROSE
    DULL NIGHT STARTS FROM HIS WATCH TOWER ON A CLOUD    . .618A ILLUS MILTON   PROSE
    JERUSALEM IS SCATTERD ABROAD LIKE A CLOUD OF SMOKE THRO     623 JERUSALEM 5     13
      NON-ENTITY
    EASTWARD A PILLAR OF A CLOUD WITH VALA UPON THE MOUNTAINS   624 JERUSALEM 5     48
    TILL THE CLOUD REACHES AFAR OUTSTRETCHD AMONG THE STARRY    624 JERUSALEM 5     52
      WHEELS
    ATTRACTED BY THE REVOLUTIONS OF THOSE WHEELS THE CLOUD      624 JERUSALEM 5     61
      OF SMOKE
    IMMENSE AND JERUSALEM & VALA WEEPING IN THE CLOUD    . .    624 JERUSALEM 5     62
    VALA COMES FROM THE FURNACE IN A CLOUD BUT WRETCHED LUVAH   626 JERUSALEM 7     38
    WITH A TENDER CLOUD AS THOU ART NOW SUCH WAS HE O SPECTRE   627 JERUSALEM 8      6
    LIKE A PALE CLOUD ARISING FROM THE ARMS OF BEULAH'S        635 JERUSALEM 14     33
      DAUGHTERS
    SETTLED AROUND ALBION AND AROUND LUVAH IN HIS SECRET CLOUD  641 JERUSALEM 19     27
    YET THOU WAST LOVELY AS THE SUMMER CLOUD UPON MY HILLS  . . 647 JERUSALEM 24     36
    . . . BUT THE CLOUD HOVERD OVER THEIR HEADS     . . . . .   654 JERUSALEM 29     53
    LUVAH DESCENDED FROM THE CLOUD IN TERROR ALBION ROSE  . .   654 JERUSALEM 29     56
    IN CLOUD OF SECRET GLOOM WHICH BEHOLD INVOLVE ME ROUND      660 JERUSALEM 33     47
      ABOUT
    UPON THE ROCK OF AGES THEN SURROUNDED WITH A CLOUD   . .    677 JERUSALEM 48      4
    BURST FROM HIS BOSOM IN THE TOMB LIKE A PALE SNOWY CLOUD    678 JERUSALEM 48     48
    HE TOSSES LIKE A CLOUD OUTSTRETCHD AMONG JERUSALEM'S RUINS  685 JERUSALEM 54     13
    WERE SOUNDED FROM A MORTAL CLOUD NOR ON MOUNT SINAI OLD     686 JERUSALEM 55     21
    AND I WILL LEAD THEE THRO THE WILDERNESS IN SHADOW OF MY    693 JERUSALEM 60     36
      CLOUD
    I WILL COMMAND THE CLOUD TO GIVE THEE FOOD & THE HARD ROCK  696 JERUSALEM 62     25
    THO VALA'S CLOUD HIDE THEE & LUVAH'S FIRES FOLLOW THEE  . . 696 JERUSALEM 62     28
    SO SPOKE THE LAMB OF GOD WHILE LUVAH'S CLOUD REDDENING      696 JERUSALEM 62     30
      ABOVE
    OF SEVEN DISEASES ONCE A CONTINUAL CLOUD OF SALVATION ROSE  721 JERUSALEM 79     57
    IN THE THICK CLOUD & DARKNESS & THE VOICE WENT FORTH FROM   722 JERUSALEM 80     11
    THE CLOUD O RENT IN SUNDER FROM JERUSALEM THE HARLOT        722 JERUSALEM 80     12
      DAUGHTER
    WERE CAUGHT INTO THE FLAX OF HER DISTAFF & IN HER CLOUD     722 JERUSALEM 80     34
    THE CLOUD OF RAHAB VIBRATING WITH THE DAUGHTERS OF ALBION   722 JERUSALEM 80     40
    AND RAHAB LIKE A DISMAL AND INDEFINITE HOVERING CLOUD  . .  723 JERUSALEM 80     51
    A WEEPING INFANT IN RUIND LOVELY JERUSALEM'S FOLDING CLOUD  724 JERUSALEM 81     14
    ON CAMBRIDGE AND OXFORD BEAMING SOFT UNITING WITH RAHAB'S   725 JERUSALEM 82     11
      CLOUD
    CLEAR AS THE RAINBOW AS THE CLOUD OF THE SUN'S TABERNACLE   731 JERUSALEM 86     21
    A PILLAR OF A CLOUD BY DAY A PILLAR OF FIRE BY NIGHT   . .  731 JERUSALEM 86     27
    HIS VOICE IN THE BLACK CLOUD HIS SONS LABOUR IN THUNDERS    731 JERUSALEM 86     37
    TILL IT BECAME A SEPARATED CLOUD OF BEAUTY GRACE & LOVE     732 JERUSALEM 86     55
    AND SNOWY CLOUD BROODER OF TEMPESTS & DESTRUCTIVE WAR  . .  738 JERUSALEM 91     24
    MOVED BY THE WIND IN VOLUMES OF THICK CLOUD RETURNING       741 JERUSALEM 94      9
      FOLDING ROUND
    SO SAYING THE CLOUD OVERSHADOWING DIVIDED THEM ASUNDER  . . 743 JERUSALEM 96     29
    CLOUD METEOR & STAR    . . . . . . . . . . . . . . . .      805 TO BUTTS/L     31
    IN A CLOUD THAT DEWY SWEETNESS DISTILLS   . . . . . . . .   816 HAPPINESS/L     2
    IN A BLACK CLOUD MAKING HIS MONE   . . . . . . . . . . .    817 HAPPINESS/L    16
CLOUDED    SEE OER-CLOUDED
    CLOUDED FALLN LIKE THE STATELY TREE CUT DOWN     . . . . .    5 FAIR ELENOR/PS  50
    AND THE CHAMBER BECAME AS A CLOUDED SKY . . . . . . . .     138 FRENCH REVOLTN  85
    TILL THE SHRUNKEN EYES CLOUDED OVER    . . . . . . . . .    236 URIZEN 25      31
    IS SILENT ON MY CLOUDED HILLS THAT BELCH FORTH STORMS &     359 FOUR ZOAS 9  * 103
      FIRES
    SHINE FORTH UPON OUR CLOUDED HILLS    . . . . . . . .       481 AND DID FEET/M   6
    THUNDERD THE ASSEMBLY DARK & CLOUDED AND THEY RATIFYD  . .  494 MILTON 13      15
    CLOUDED WITH DISCONTENT & BROODING IN THEIR MINDS TERRIBLE  505 MILTON 22      28
      THINGS
    & REAL VISION AND REAL VISIONS WHICH ARE LOST & CLOUDED    605C V LAST JUDG/N *PROSE
    THE BANKS OF THE THAMES ARE CLOUDED THE ANCIENT PORCHES     623 JERUSALEM 5      1
      OF ALBION ARE
    ARE SILENT ON HIS CLOUDED HILLS THAT BELCH FORTH STORMS     641 JERUSALEM 19     4
      & FIRE
    CLOUDED WITH STORMS LOS HIS STRONG GUARD WALKD ROUND        642 JERUSALEM 19     38
      BENEATH THE MOON
    BECAUSE THEY TAUGHT LUVAH TO RISE INTO MY CLOUDED HEAVENS   644 JERUSALEM 21     31
    AND WANDERD DISTANT IN A DISMAL NIGHT CLOUDED & DARK   . .  647 JERUSALEM 24     9
```

352

	PAGE	TITLE	LINE

CLOUDED   (CONTINUED)

	PAGE	TITLE	LINE
AND THE FOUR ZOAS CLOUDED RAGE EAST & WEST & NORTH & SOUTH	663	JERUSALEM 36	25
THE FOUR ZOAS IN TERRIBLE COMBUSTION CLOUDED RAGE . . .	668	JERUSALEM 41	26
AND ALL THE GATE OF LOS CLOUDED WITH CLOUDS REDOUNDING FROM	674	JERUSALEM 44	8
THE FOUR ZOAS CLOUDED RAGE URIZEN STOOD BY ALBION . . .	714	JERUSALEM 74	1

CLOUDING

	PAGE	TITLE	LINE
MY BACK DARKNING THE PRESENT CLOUDING WITH A CLOUD . . .	361	FOUR ZOAS 9	166

CLOUDLESS

	PAGE	TITLE	LINE
AND THE FAIR MOON REJOICES IN THE CLEAR & CLOUDLESS NIGHT	198	AMERICA 6	14
[THEN] AND THE MILD MOON REJOICES IN THE CLEAR & CLOUDLESS NIGHT	379	FOUR ZOAS 9	* 826

CLOUDS   SEE THUNDER-CLOUDS,THUNDER CLOUDS

	PAGE	TITLE	LINE
AND FEATHERD CLOUDS STREW FLOWERS ROUND HER HEAD	2	TO AUTUMN/PS	12
HE SHOOK THE HILLS AND IN THE CLOUDS	11	GWIN KING/PS	15
THEIR CRY ASCENDS THE CLOUDS	11	GWIN KING/PS	22
LIKE CLOUDS COME ROLLING OER	12	GWIN KING/PS	36
LIKE CLOUDS AROUND HIM ROLLD	12	GWIN KING/PS	60
SPORTS IN THE CLOUDS TO HEAR THE THUNDER'S SOUND	15	IMIT SPEN/PS	40
GLORY MAY NOT BE DIMMD WITH CLOUDS OF CARE	19	EDW THIRD/PS 2	15
UPON THE CLOUDS OF HEAVEN TO DIE NO MORE	30	EDW THIRD/PS 5	16
SIT SINGING IN THE AZURE CLOUDS AND STREW	30	EDW THIRD/PS 5	31
ROLLING DARK CLOUDS OER FRANCE MUFFLING THE SUN . . .	31	EDW THIRD/PS 6	3
AND WALK TOGETHER ON THE CLOUDS OF HEAVEN	35	WAR SONG/PS	19
HE SEEMED A MOUNTAIN HIS BROW AMONG THE CLOUDS	38C	SAMSON/PS	PROSE
THRO THE CLOUDS OF SMOKE HE MAKES HIS WAY	62	CROWND KING/IM	5
DROP FROM THY GARMENTS AS THOU WALKEST WRAPT IN YELLOW CLOUDS	106	TIRIEL 5	10
HE CEAST THE HEAVY CLOUDS CONFUSD ROLLD ROUND THE LOFTY TOWERS	106	TIRIEL 5	14
THEY RISE UPON CLOUDS AND SPORT IN THE WIND	118	CHIMNEY SWP/SI	18
DOUBT IS FLED & CLOUDS OF REASON	126	VOICE BARD/SI	4
SHE WANDERD IN THE LAND OF CLOUDS THRO VALLEYS DARK LISTNING	130	BOOK OF THEL 6	6
CLOUDS OF WISDOM PROPHETIC REPLY AND ROLL OVER THE PALACE ROOF HEAVY	134	FRENCH REVOLTN	12
. . . THE MORNING PROPHECIES TO ITS CLOUDS	134	FRENCH REVOLTN	15
. . . BREATHING RED CLOUDS OF POWER AND DOMINION . . .	135	FRENCH REVOLTN	20
. . . LIKE THE SUN OF OLD TIME QUENCHD IN CLOUDS . . .	137	FRENCH REVOLTN	68
I SEE THRO DARKNESS THRO CLOUDS ROLLING ROUND ME	137	FRENCH REVOLTN	72
HE CEASD AND BURND SILENT RED CLOUDS ROLL ROUND NECKER . . .	139	FRENCH REVOLTN	105
. . . SO NECKER PAUSD AND HIS VISAGE WAS COVERD WITH CLOUDS	139	FRENCH REVOLTN	109
. . . AND WREATHD THEIR CLOUDS AND WATERS	139	FRENCH REVOLTN	125
THE NOBLES SAT ROUND LIKE CLOUDS ON THE MOUNTAINS . . .	143	FRENCH REVOLTN	196
TILL DAWN TILL MORNING TILL THE BREAKING OF CLOUDS . . .	144	FRENCH REVOLTN	217
AND SHEPHERD DELIVERD FROM CLOUDS OF WAR	144	FRENCH REVOLTN	233
. . . DEPART O CLOUDS OF NIGHT AND NO MORE	145	FRENCH REVOLTN	238
. . . AND THE CLOUDS CAST THEIR SHADOWS THE PRINCES . .	145	FRENCH REVOLTN	241
. . . THEN BOWING LIKE CLOUDS MAN TOWARD MAN THE ASSEMBLY	146	FRENCH REVOLTN	263
LIKE A COUNCIL OF ARDORS SEATED IN CLOUDS	146	FRENCH REVOLTN	264
DARK CAVALRY LIKE CLOUDS FRAUGHT WITH THUNDER	147	FRENCH REVOLTN	291
HUNGRY CLOUDS SWAG ON THE DEEP	148	MARRIAGE HH 2	2
HUNGRY CLOUDS SWAG ON THE DEEP	149	MARRIAGE HH 2	22
I SAW A MIGHTY DEVIL FOLDED IN BLACK CLOUDS	150C	MARRIAGE HH 6	PROSE
BETWEEN THE CLOUDS & THE WAVES WE SAW A CATARACT OF BLOOD	156B	MARRIAGE HH 17	PROSE
FROM WHICH THE SEA FLED AWAY IN CLOUDS OF SMOKE . . .	156C	MARRIAGE HH 17	PROSE
SPURNING THE CLOUDS WRITTEN WITH CURSES	160A	SONG LIBERTY	PROSE
WHY DOST THOU HIDE THYSELF IN CLOUDS	171	TO NOBODADDY/N	3
CLOUDS A SUNSHINY DAY	178	THE FAIRY/N	6
THAT CLOUDS WITH JEALOUSY HIS NIGHTS WITH WEEPINGS ALL THE DAY	194	V DAU ALBION 7	18
INVULNERABLE THO NAKED SAVE WHERE CLOUDS ROLL ROUND HER LOINS	196	AMERICA PREL 1	7
IN VAIN THESE CLOUDS ROLL TO & FRO & HIDE THEE FROM MY SIGHT	196	AMERICA PREL 1	20
IT JOYD SHE PUT ASIDE HER CLOUDS & SMILED HER FIRST-BORN SMILE	196	AMERICA PREL 2	4
SWELLING BELCHING FROM ITS DEEPS RED CLOUDS & RAGING FIRES	197	AMERICA 4	3
RED ROSE THE CLOUDS FROM THE ATLANTIC IN VAST WHEELS OF BLOOD	197	AMERICA 4	6
AND IN THE RED CLOUDS ROSE A WONDER OER THE ATLANTIC SEA	197	AMERICA 4	7
BUT CLOUDS OBSCURE MY AGED SIGHT A VISION FROM AFAR . . .	199	AMERICA 9	12
HEAVENS ETERNAL VIPER SELF-RENEWD ROLLING IN CLOUDS . . .	199	AMERICA 9	15
I SEE THEE IN THICK CLOUDS AND DARKNESS ON AMERICA'S SHORE	199	AMERICA 9	16
AND PARCHED LIPS DROP WITH FRESH GORE NOW ROLL THOU IN THE CLOUDS	199	AMERICA 9	24
FOR CLOUDS FROM THE ATLANTIC HOVER OER THE SOLEMN ROOF . .	200	AMERICA 10	12
OF ALBION'S ANGEL WHO ENRAGD HIS SECRET CLOUDS OPEND . .	201	AMERICA 13	10
HIS PLAGUES OBEDIENT TO HIS VOICE FLEW FORTH OUT OF THEIR CLOUDS	201	AMERICA 14	4
HIDING THE DEMON RED WITH CLOUDS & COLD MISTS FROM THE EARTH	203	AMERICA 16	13
WITH CLOUDS OF SMOKE FROM THE ATLANTIC THAT IN VOLUMES ROLLD	204	AMERICA CANC B	11
THEN AS ARMD CLOUDS ARISE TERRIFIC ROUND THE NORTHERN DRUM	204	AMERICA CANC B	18
IN GLITTRING ARMOUR SWIFT AS WINDS INTELLIGENT AS [FLAMES] CLOUDS	205	AMERICA CANC C	13
LIKE WHITE CLOUDS RISING FROM THE DEEPS HIS FIFTY-TWO ARMIES	205	AMERICA CANC C	16
AS OF SWELLING SEAS SOUND IN HIS CLOUDS	223	URIZEN 3	31
AWOKE & VAST CLOUDS OF BLOOD ROLLD	223	URIZEN 3	41
NOW FILLD WITH CLOUDS DARKNESS & WATERS	223	URIZEN 4	2

		PAGE	TITLE	LINE

CLOUDS   (CONTINUED)

```
  FOR IN CHANGEABLE CLOUDS AND DARKNESS     . . . . . . .  230 URIZEN 15        3
  I WRAP MY TURBAN OF THICK CLOUDS AROUND MY LABRING HEAD   238 EUROPE PREL 1   12
  SHE CEAST & ROLLD HER SHADY CLOUDS    . . . . . . . . .  239 EUROPE PREL 2   17
  LIKE PEARLY CLOUDS THEY MEET TOGETHER IN THE CRYSTAL HOUSE 239 EUROPE 4        6
  ROUND HIM ROLLD HIS CLOUDS OF WAR SILENT THE ANGEL WENT   241 EUROPE 10        4
  AND THE CLOUDS & FIRES PALE ROLLD ROUND IN THE NIGHT OF   242 EUROPE 12        1
    ENITHARMON
  BETWEEN THE CLOUDS OF URIZEN THE FLAMES OF ORC ROLL HEAVY 243 EUROPE 12       32
  CLOUDS ROLL HEAVY UPON THE ALPS ROUND ROUSSEAU & VOLTAIRE 246 SONG OF LOS 4   18
  DRAWING CLOUDS OF DESPAIR THRO THE HEAVENS  . . . . . .  248 SONG OF LOS 7   12
  AND STRETCHD HIS CLOUDS OVER JERUSALEM    . . . . . . .  248 SONG OF LOS 7   19
  ON CLOUDS OF SMOKE RAGES HIS CHARIOT  . . . . . . . .    249 AHANIA 2         5
  O BOW OF THE CLOUDS OF SECRESY  . . . . . . . . . . .    251 AHANIA 3        26
  THE BLACK CLOUDS ON THE BOSOM OF FUZON    . . . . . .    251 AHANIA 3        29
  ON BLACK CLOUDS HIS SORE WOUND ANOINTED   . . . . . .    251 AHANIA 3        48
  IN NOXIOUS CLOUDS THESE HOVERD THICK  . . . . . . . .    253 AHANIA 4        18
  THE CLOUDS OF DISEASE HOVERD WIDE . . . . . . . . . .    253 AHANIA 4        22
  HAD SHE BUT HER TEARS FROM CLOUDS . . . . . . . . . .    253 AHANIA 4        50
  I SEE THY DARK CLOUDS ASCEND  . . . . . . . . . . . .    254 AHANIA 4        57
  WALKED FORTH FROM THE CLOUDS OF MORNING   . . . . . .    255 AHANIA 5        31
  IN DARKNESS AND DEEP CLOUDS INVOLVD   . . . . . . . .    260 BOOK OF LOS 5   57
  TREMBLING & PALE SAT THARMAS WEEPING IN HIS CLOUDS  . .  265 FOUR ZOAS 1     46
  SINGING HER LAMENTATION THARMAS GROAND AMONG HIS CLOUDS   266 FOUR ZOAS 1     71
  WEEPING [AND] THEN BENDING FROM HIS CLOUDS  . . . . .    266 FOUR ZOAS 1     72
  AND SAID RETURN O WANDERER WHEN THE DAY OF CLOUDS IS OER  266 FOUR ZOAS 1     75
  [HE SPURND ENION WITH HIS FOOT HE SPRANG ALOFT IN CLOUDS] 266 FOUR ZOAS 1     92
  [AMONG THE CLOUDS TO TREMBLE IN THE WIND IN SOLITUDE]  .  268 FOUR ZOAS 1    138
  [THAT WEPT AMONG THE CLOUDS & WHERE THE VOICE THAT SHALL  268 FOUR ZOAS 1    140
    REPLY]
  [WHILE THE BRIGHT SPECTRE HID HIMSELF AMONG THE TRAILING  268 FOUR ZOAS 1  * 144
    CLOUDS]
  THE VARYING CLOUDS LIKE PARADISES STRETCHD IN THE EXPANSE 274 FOUR ZOAS 1    368
  MY CLOUDS ARE NOT THE CLOUDS OF VERDANT FIELDS & GROVES   275 FOUR ZOAS 1    392
    OF FRUIT
  BUT CLOUDS OF HUMAN SOULS MY NOSTRILS DRINK THE LIVES OF  275 FOUR ZOAS 1    393
    MEN
  FOR MESSENGERS FROM BEULAH COME IN TEARS & DARKNING CLOUDS 277 FOUR ZOAS 1   476
  I WILL INFOLD THE ETERNAL TENT IN CLOUDS OPAKE WHILE THOU 278 FOUR ZOAS 1    493
  SOUTHWARD WITH HALF THE TENTS OF MEN INCLOSD IN CLOUDS .  278 FOUR ZOAS 1    496
  MUSTRING TOGETHER IN THICK CLOUDS LEAVING THE RAGE OF LUVAH 279 FOUR ZOAS 1  539
  . . . & CLOSD THE MESSENGERS IN CLOUDS AROUND  . . . .   279 FOUR ZOAS 1    552
  [AND SAID RETURN O WANDERER WHEN THE DAY OF CLOUDS IS OER] SUPP FOUR ZOAS 1  *
  UPON THE WINDS IN CLOUDS INVOLVD UTTERING HIS VOICE IN    283 FOUR ZOAS 2    133
    THUNDERS
  THIS URIZEN PERCIEVD & SILENT BROODED IN DARKNING CLOUDS  285 FOUR ZOAS 2    207
  IN BEAUTEOUS ORDER THENCE AROSE SOFT CLOUDS & EXHALATIONS 286 FOUR ZOAS 2    253
  ON CLOUDS THE SONS OF URIZEN BEHELD . . . . . . . . .    287 FOUR ZOAS 2    258
  IN CLOUDS OF SWEET OBSCURITY MY BEAUTEOUS FORM DISSOLVING 288 FOUR ZOAS 2    311
  THOU CANST REPOSE ON CLOUDS OF SECRECY WHILE OER MY LIMBS 288 FOUR ZOAS 2    319
  URIZEN SAW THY SIN & HID HIS BEAMS IN DARKNING CLOUDS  .  288 FOUR ZOAS 2    329
  INFOLDED IN THICK CLOUDS FROM WHENCE HIS MIGHTY VOICE BURST 292 FOUR ZOAS 3   13
    FORTH
  AND ON THE EIGHTH DAY WHEN HIS CLOUDS UNFOLDED FROM HIS   292 FOUR ZOAS 3     25
    THRONE
  [AND COMFORTS SHALL DESCEND FROM HEAVEN INTO THY DARKNING 292 FOUR ZOAS 3     29
    CLOUDS]
  WHY ROLL THY CLOUDS IN SICKNING MISTS I CAN NO LONGER HIDE 293 FOUR ZOAS 3    72
  HE SPOKE MUSTERING HIS HEAVY CLOUDS AROUND HIM BLACK OPAKE 294 FOUR ZOAS 3   108
  DOWN FROM THE DISMAL NORTH THE PRINCE IN THUNDERS & THICK 295 FOUR ZOAS 3    139
    CLOUDS
  BUT ENITHARMON WRAPD IN CLOUDS WAILD LOUD FOR AS LOS BEAT 302 FOUR ZOAS 4    184
  BUT FROM THE CAVES OF DEEPEST NIGHT ASCENDING IN CLOUDS   306 FOUR ZOAS 5     31
    OF MIST
  INWRAP THE PARENTS IN COLD CLOUDS AS THEY BEND HOWLING OVER 309 FOUR ZOAS 5  171
  I WENT NOT FORTH I HID MYSELF IN BLACK CLOUDS OF MY WRATH 311 FOUR ZOAS 5    222
  WHO ART THOU ELDEST WOMAN SITTING IN THY CLOUDS  . . . . 312 FOUR ZOAS 6      8
  WATERS OR WINDS OR CLOUDS . . . . . . . . . . . . . .    314 FOUR ZOAS 6     93
  OVER THE BURNING DESARTS THEN THE DESARTS PASSD INVOLVD   314 FOUR ZOAS 6    110
    IN CLOUDS
  AND THE WEB OF URIZEN (STRETCHD) DIREFUL SHIVRING IN CLOUDS 318 FOUR ZOAS 6 * 247
  LIKE WHITE CLOUDS RISING FROM THE VALES HIS FIFTY         319 FOUR ZOAS 6    312
    TWO ARMIES
  AS WHEN THE THUNDER FOLDS HIMSELF IN THICKEST CLOUDS  . . 320 FOUR ZOAS 7     23
  WALKING IN JOY IN BRIGHT EXPANSES SLEEPING ON BRIGHT      321 FOUR ZOAS 7     64
    CLOUDS
  ON CLOUDS OF DEATH & SANG THEIR SONGS KNEADING THE BREAD  322 FOUR ZOAS 7     98
    OF ORC
  WHEN I RETURN FROM CLOUDS OF GRIEF IN THE WANDRING ELEMENTS 324 FOUR ZOAS 7  185
  CLOUDS WOULD HAVE FOLDED ROUND IN EXTACY & LOVE UNITING   329 FOUR ZOAS 7    371
  AND SILENCE BUILD THEIR DAY IN SHADOW OF SOFT CLOUDS & DEWS 331 FOUR ZOAS 7  450
  BATHED IN BLOODY CLOUDS HIS LOINS IN FIRES OF WAR WHERE   334 FOUR ZOAS 7B    43
    SPEARS
  SO CRIED THE DEMON OF THE WATERS IN THE CLOUDS OF LOS  . . 334 FOUR ZOAS 7B   72
  OUTSTRETCHD UPON THE HILLS LAY ENITHARMON CLOUDS & TEMPESTS 334 FOUR ZOAS 7B  73
  AND CLOUDS ARE CLOSD AROUND MY TOWER MY ARMS LABOUR IN VAIN 335 FOUR ZOAS 7B  89
  BURDEND WITH CLOUDS HOWL ROUND THE COUCH SULLEN THE WOOLY 335 FOUR ZOAS 7B   108
    SHEEP
  SO ORC ROLLD ROUND HIS CLOUDS UPON THE DEEPS OF DARK      336 FOUR ZOAS 7B   133
    URTHONA
  . . . SPUR SPUR YOUR [STEEDS] CLOUDS    . . . . . . . .  336 FOUR ZOAS 7B   153
  LIKE CLOUDS UPON THE WINTER SKY BROKEN WITH WINDS         338 FOUR ZOAS 7B  * 218
    & THUNDERS
```

354

CLOUDS   (CONTINUED)

	PAGE	TITLE		LINE
NOT SUFFRING DOUBT TO RISE UP FROM THE CLOUDS OF THE SHADOWY FEMALE	340	FOUR ZOAS 7B	*	297
DESCENDING ON THE SHADOWY FEMALE'S CLOUDS IN SPECTROUS TERROR	340	FOUR ZOAS 7B		299
OF URIZEN & THARMAS & FROM THE SHADOWY FEMALE'S CLOUDS . .	342	FOUR ZOAS 8		57
IN CLOUDS & FIRES AROUND THE ROCK & THE MYSTERIOUS TREE	355	FOUR ZOAS 8		557
AND WEEPING OVER ORC & URIZEN IN CLOUDS & [DISMAL] FLAMING FIRES	355	FOUR ZOAS 8		579
BEGAN TO ENTER THE HOLY CITY ENTRING THE DISMAL CLOUDS . .	359	FOUR ZOAS 9		84
IN THOSE ETERNAL FIELDS IN CLOUDS OF MORNING STEPPING FORTH	360	FOUR ZOAS 9		125
MANY A WOFUL COMPANY & MANY ON CLOUDS & WATERS	363	FOUR ZOAS 9		242
IN FLOWERS IN FRUITS IN FISHES BIRDS & BEASTS & CLOUDS & WATERS	367	FOUR ZOAS 9		378
INVISIBLE LUVAH IN BRIGHT CLOUDS HOVERD OVER VALA'S HEAD	367	FOUR ZOAS 9		385
. . . ON THE CLOUDS THAT GLITTER IN THE SUN	368	FOUR ZOAS 9		439
I SIT IN THE PLACE OF SHELLS & MOURN & THOU ART CLOSD IN CLOUDS	370	FOUR ZOAS 9		489
WHEN WILL THE TIME OF CLOUDS BE PAST & THE DISMAL NIGHT OF THARMAS	370	FOUR ZOAS 9		490
THRO ALL THE IMMENSE BORNE DOWN BY CLOUDS SWAGGING IN AUTUMNAL HEAT	372	FOUR ZOAS 9		563
BENEATH THICK CLOUDS DREADFUL LIGHTNINGS BURST & THUNDERS ROLL	372	FOUR ZOAS 9		565
IN ALL THEIR ANCIENT INNOCENCE THE FLOODS DEPART THE CLOUDS	372	FOUR ZOAS 9		572
THE CLOUDS FALL OFF FROM MY WET BROW THE DUST FROM MY COLD LIMBS	373	FOUR ZOAS 9		597
THE OCEAN CALM THE CLOUDS FOLD ROUND & FIERY FLAMES OF LOVE	381	FOUR ZOAS AD 2		1
THE SCHOOLS IN CLOUDS OF LEARNING ROLLD	418	I SAW A MONK/N		8
CHARLEMAINE & HIS CLOUDS OF WAR	420	I SAW MNK AD/N		17
[THE HEAVENS IN CLOUDS ROLLING BEFORE HIM & AROUND HIM]	443A	LAST JUDGMNT/L		PROSE
BEFORE HIS FEET & AROUND HIM THE HEAVENS IN CLOUDS ARE ROLLING	443A	LAST JUDGMNT/L		*PROSE
& BEFORE THE BOOK OF DEATH WHICH IS OPEND IN ON CLOUDS . .	443C	LAST JUDGMNT/L		PROSE
OPEND [BY TWO ANGELS ON CLOUDS] ON CLOUDS BY TWO ANGELS	443D	LAST JUDGMNT/L		*PROSE
WHO COMETH IN THE CLOUDS WITH POWER & GREAT GLORY . . .	444A	LAST JUDGMNT/L		PROSE
BRING ME MY SPEAR O CLOUDS UNFOLD	481	AND DID FEET/M		11
OF MORAL LAWS AND CRUEL PUNISHMENTS UPON THE CLOUDS OF JEHOVAH	489	MILTON 9		22
OVER THE SEPULCHERS IN CLOUDS OF JEHOVAH & WINDS OF ELOHIM	495	MILTON 14		26
GLOWD BUT IN TERRORS FOLDED ROUND HIS CLOUDS OF BLOOD . .	502	MILTON 20		24
JESUS THE SAVIOUR APPEARD COMING IN THE CLOUDS OF OLOLON	505	MILTON 21		60
BUT LOS DISPERSD THE CLOUDS EVEN AS THE STRONG WINDS OF JEHOVAH	507	MILTON 23		31
WITH NEITHER LINEAMENT NOR FORM BUT LIKE TO WATRY CLOUDS	512	MILTON 26		27
THESE HILLS ARE OCEANS CLOUDS & WATERS UNGOVERNABLE IN THEIR FURY	514	MILTON 27		52
SHUTTING THE SUN & MOON & STARS & TREES & CLOUDS & WATERS	515	MILTON 28		33
AND ON ITS VERGE THE SUN RISES & SETS THE CLOUDS BOW . .	516	MILTON 29		8
ALL BEULAH WEPT FOR THEY SAW THE LORD COMING IN THE CLOUDS	519	MILTON 31		10
IN THE CLOUDS OF OLOLON WITH POWER & GREAT GLORY . . .	519	MILTON 31		16
EUROPE TO EUPHRATES & HINDU TO NILE & BACK IN CLOUDS .	525	MILTON 35		16
WITH OLOLON FOR THEY SAW THE LORD IN THE CLOUDS OF OLOLON	526	MILTON 35		41
THEN TREMBLED THE VIRGIN OLOLON & REPLYD IN CLOUDS OF DESPAIR	533	MILTON 41		29
IN CLOUDS OF BLOOD IN STREAMS OF GORE WITH DREADFUL THUNDERINGS	534	MILTON 42		8
THE CLOUDS OF OLOLON FOLDED AS A GARMENT DIPPED IN BLOOD	534	MILTON 42		12
FROM FELPHAM'S VALE CLOTHED IN CLOUDS OF BLOOD TO ENTER INTO	534	MILTON 42		20
THEIR CLOUDS ROLL OVER LONDON WITH A SOUTH WIND SOFT OOTHOON	535	MILTON 42		32
THE HEAVENS OPENING AROUND HIM BY UNFOLDING THE CLOUDS . .	606B	V LAST JUDG/N		PROSE
COMING IN THE CLOUDS WITH POWER & GREAT GLORY	609D	V LAST JUDG/N		PROSE
WHO SHALL MEET THE LORD COMING IN THE CLOUDS	610B	V LAST JUDG/N		PROSE
SURROUNDED BY THE CLOUDS IN THEIR LIVERIES IN THEIR . . .	618B	ILLUS MILTON		PROSE
MOUNTAINS CLOUDS RIVERS TREES APPEAR	618B	ILLUS MILTON		PROSE
THE CLOUDS ARISE FROM THE BOSOMS OF MOUNTAINS	618C	ILLUS MILTON		PROSE
THE VOIDS THE SOLIDS & THE LAND OF CLOUDS & REGIONS OF WATERS	634	JERUSALEM 13		50
THEN LOST IN CLOUDS I HEAR THEIR TENDER VOICES CLOUDS DIVIDE	644	JERUSALEM 21		41
THY CLOUDS OF BLESSING THY CHERUBIMS OF TENDER-MERCY . .	647	JERUSALEM 24		21
IN CLOUDS OF BLOOD & RUIN ROLLD	651	FIELDS FROM/J		74
ON TYBURN'S RIVER IN CLOUDS OF BLOOD WHERE WAS MILD ZION HILL'S	653	JERUSALEM 29		3
HIS WESTERN HEAVEN WITH ROCKY CLOUDS OF DEATH & DESPAIR	656	JERUSALEM 31		1
VALA REPLIED IN CLOUDS OF TEARS ALBION'S GARMENT EMBRACING	659	JERUSALEM 33		35
OF DEATH IN ALBION'S CLOUDS DREADFUL UTTERD OVER ALL THE EARTH	661	JERUSALEM 34		24
IRON AND STEEL DARK AND OPAKE WITH CLOUDS & TEMPESTS BROODING	664	JERUSALEM 38		5
FIRES AND CLOUDS OF ROLLING SMOKE BUT MILD THE SAVIOUR FOLLOWD HIM	664	JERUSALEM 38		10
LIKE ROCKY CLOUDS BUILD ME A GLOOMY MONUMENT OF WOE . .	666	JERUSALEM 39		18
THE CLOUDS OF EUROPE & ASIA AMONG THE SERPENT TEMPLES . .	671	JERUSALEM 42		76
AND ALL THE GATE OF LOS CLOUDED WITH CLOUDS REDOUNDING FROM	674	JERUSALEM 44		8
OF GREY OBSCURITY FILLD WITH CLOUDS & ROCKS & WHIRLING WATERS	674	JERUSALEM 44		16
THE SCHOOLS IN CLOUDS OF LEARNING ROLLD	683	I SAW A MONK/J		7
THE DIVINE VISION DIMLY APPEARD IN CLOUDS OF BLOOD WEEPING	685	JERUSALEM 54		32
CITIES & NATIONS CONTENDED IN FIRES & CLOUDS & TEMPESTS	686	JERUSALEM 55		25

```
                                                             PAGE      TITLE            LINE
CLOUDS   (CONTINUED)
. . . WERE HEARD IN THE CLOUDS OF HEAVEN     . . . . . .    687 JERUSALEM 55            55
AND THE GREAT VOICE OF ETERNITY ROLLED ABOVE TERRIBLE IN    687 JERUSALEM 55            68
      CLOUDS
THE CLOUDS OF ALBION'S DRUID TEMPLES RAGE IN THE EASTERN    692 JERUSALEM 60             1
      HEAVEN
ON ALBION'S HILLS OFTEN WALKING FROM THE FURNACES IN CLOUDS 692 JERUSALEM 60             6
DIVIDING IN FIERCE PAIN ALSO THE VISION OF GOD WAS CLOSD    696 JERUSALEM 62            38
      IN CLOUDS
AROUND IN THE CLOUDS OF THE FEMALE ON ALBION'S CLIFFS OF    697 JERUSALEM 63            22
      THE DEAD
WITHOUT THE FORGIVENESS OF SINS IN THE MERCIFUL CLOUDS      697 JERUSALEM 63            27
      OF JEHOVAH
OF ALBION'S CLOUDS HE FED IT WITH HIS TEARS & BITTER GROANS 732 JERUSALEM 86            53
SURROUNDING HIS AWFUL MEMBERS THOU SEEST THE SUN IN HEAVY   742 JERUSALEM 95            11
      CLOUDS
MURMURING THE BOWSTRING BREATHES WITH ARDOR CLOUDS ROLL     742 JERUSALEM 95            14
      ROUND THE
THE SONS & DAUGHTERS OF ALBION ON SOFT CLOUDS WAKING FROM   744 JERUSALEM 96            39
      SLEEP
ALBION'S BOSOM THEN ALBION STOOD BEFORE JESUS IN THE CLOUDS 744 JERUSALEM 96            42
. . . CLOUDS ROLL ROUND THE HORNS    . . . . . . . . .      745 JERUSALEM 98             4
. . . THEN THE FRENCH REVOLUTION COMMENCD IN THICK CLOUDS   799 TO FLAXMAN/L           10
CLOUDY
RETURN BE WITHDRAWN CLOUDY WAR . . . . . . . . . . .        145 FRENCH REVOLTN        239
. . . CAPTAINS OF FOOT STAND EACH BY HIS CLOUDY DRUM   . .  147 FRENCH REVOLTN        289
APPEAR TO THE AMERICANS UPON THE CLOUDY NIGHT  . . . . .    197 AMERICA 4               1
WITH MYRIADS OF CLOUDY TERRORS BANNERS DARK & TOWERS   . .  197 AMERICA 4              10
ON THE VAST STONE WHOSE NAME IS TRUTH HE STOOD HIS CLOUDY   205 AMERICA CANC C         10
      SHIELD
ARISE AROUND HIM IN THE CLOUDY HEAVENS OF ALBION FURIOUS    243 EUROPE 12              35
THIS CLOUDY GOD SEATED ON WATERS  . . . . . . . . .         249 AHANIA 2               12
HIS CLOUDY BELLOWS & THE SOUTH & EAST & DISMAL WEST  . . .  282 FOUR ZOAS 2            69
ASCENDING INTO HER [CLOUDY] MISTY GARMENTS . . . . . .      285 FOUR ZOAS 2           192
SLAIN ON THE ALTAR UP ASCENDING INTO HER CLOUDY BOSOM   . . 285 FOUR ZOAS 2           196
HIS CLOUDY FORM IN JEALOUS FEAR & MUTTERING THUNDERS HOARSE 299 FOUR ZOAS 4            77
THE ARROWS FLEW FROM CLOUDY BOW ALL DAY TILL BLOOD   . . .  337 FOUR ZOAS 7B          159
CALL FORTH THY SMILES OF SOFT DECEIT CALL FORTH             338 FOUR ZOAS 7B          208
      THY CLOUDY TEARS
A CLOUDY HEAVEN MINGLED WITH STORMY SEAS IN LOUDEST RUIN    497 MILTON 15              43
SUPPOSES A CLOUDY VAPOUR OR A NOTHING THEY ARE ORGANIZED    576D DESC CAT 4         PROSE
THEY PUT FORTH THEIR SPECTROUS CLOUDY SAILS WHICH DRIVE     625 JERUSALEM 7            21
      THEIR IMMENSE
UPON THE HILLS & VALLEYS AND THE CLOUDY OATH ROLLD FAR      666 JERUSALEM 40           10
      AND WIDE
CALL FORTH THY SMILES OF SOFT DECEIT CALL FORTH             701 JERUSALEM 65           54
      THY CLOUDY TEARS
INTO INDEFINITE CLOUDY SHADOWS IN DARKNESS & SEPARATION     703 JERUSALEM 66           52
MY FIRES ARE CORRUPT MY INCENSE IS A CLOUDY PESTILENCE  . . 721 JERUSALEM 79           56
AIR ON CLOUDY DOUBTS & REASONING CARES  . . . . . . .       763C FOR SEXES/GP       TITLE
CLOVEN
IS NOT THIS THE BISHOP'S CLOVEN FOOT  . . . . . . . .       390B ANNO WATSON         MARG
TWO HORND REASONING CLOVEN FICTION   . . . . . . . .        770 OF GATES/GP           11
CLOYS
THE TONGUE A LITTLE MOISTURE FILLS A LITTLE FOOD IT CLOYS   484 MILTON 5              25
THE TONGUE A LITTLE MOISTURE FILLS A LITTLE FOOD IT CLOYS   680 JERUSALEM 49           40
CLUB
IN HIS HAND A KNOTTED CLUB WHOSE KNOTS LIKE MOUNTAINS       319 FOUR ZOAS 6           305
      FROWND
CLUBS
AND WIELDING KNOTTY CLUBS LIKE OAKS ENTANGLED  . . . . .    32 EDW THIRD/PS 6          23
CLUMSY
THEE CLUMSY WILL BUT TITTHING KATE   . . . . . . . .        16 BLIND-MANS/PS           25
HIS CLUMSY HOLD AND DODGING ROUND  . . . . . . . . .        16 BLIND-MANS/PS           35
AND NOT LIKE CLUMSY BEARS   . . . . . . . . . . . .         62 DR CLASH/IM             16
ARE ALWAYS CLUMSY AND INDEFINITE THE EFFECT OF RUBBING OUT  439C REMARKS MALKIN      PROSE
CLUMSY & RICKETTY PRINCES & PRINCESSES HIGGLEDY PIGGLEDY    599C PUB ADDRESS/N       PROSE
CLUNG
HE STOOD TREMBLING & ENITHARMON CLUNG AROUND HIS KNEES  . . 305 FOUR ZOAS 5            18
THE CHILDREN CLUNG AROUND HER KNEES SHE EMBRACD THEM &      370 FOUR ZOAS 9           509
      WEPT OVER THEM
CLUSTER
TEARS OF THE GRAPE THE DEATH SWEAT OF THE CLUSTER THE LAST  377 FOUR ZOAS 9           770
      SIGH
TEARS OF THE GRAPE THE DEATH SWEAT OF THE CLUSTER THE LAST  514 MILTON 27             40
      SIGH
CLUSTERS
CLUSTERS OF THE WANDRING VINE   . . . . . . . . .          167 INFANT SORW/N           21
THE RIPE CLUSTERS THE SHEPHERDS SHOUT FOR LUVAH PRINCE      376 FOUR ZOAS 9           700
      OF LOVE
INTO THE WINE PRESSES OF LUVAH HOWLING FELL THE CLUSTERS    376 FOUR ZOAS 9           724
NAKED AMONG THE HUMAN CLUSTERS BRINGING WINE OF ANGUISH     726 JERUSALEM 82           65
CLUSTRING
TILL CLUSTRING SUMMER BREAKS FORTH INTO SINGING  . . . .    2 TO AUTUMN/PS            11
COACH
TO VAUXHALL & RANELAGH AND I HARDLY KNOW WHAT A COACH IS    53A ISLAND MOON 8        PROSE
AS THE COACH GOES THREE TIMES A WEEK TO LONDON &            809B LETTER 20          *PROSE
      THEY [SHALL]
CONVERSATION WITH AN OLD SOLDIER WHO CAME IN THE COACH WITH 833B LETTER 33          PROSE
THE SOLDIER SAID CONFIRMD BY ANOTHER PERSON IN THE COACH I  833C LETTER 33          PROSE
THO I AM VERY SORRY THAT I CANNOT SEND BEFORE SATURDAY'S    837C LETTER 36          PROSE
      COACH
```

COACH (CONTINUED)
    NOT HAVE GOT THEM PRINTED TO SEND BY TUESDAY'S COACH . 840B LETTER 39   PROSE
    BY TUESDAY'S COACH THAT YOU WILL RECIEVE (TWELVE) OF EACH 840C LETTER 39   PROSE
    TWO ARTICLES FOR YOU & FOR THE SAFETY OF WHICH BY THE COACH 850C LETTER 49   PROSE
    A VERY COMFORTABLE COACH & I MAY SAY I ACCOMPANIED HIM PART 869C LETTER 70   PROSE
    OF THE WAY ON HIS JOURNEY IN THE COACH FOR WE BOTH GOT . 869C LETTER 70   PROSE
    & I WILL GO WITH YOU TO THE COACH ALSO I WILL GO . . 870D LETTER 72   PROSE
    SHUT UP IN THE BOOK ALL WILL GO VERY WELL IN THE COACH 873A LETTER 76   PROSE
        WHICH
COACHES
    & THERES MISS FILLIGREE WORK SHE GOES OUT IN HER COACHES 52D ISLAND MOON 8 PROSE
COACHMAN
    COACHMAN UNDERSTAND THAT ONE OF HIS PASSENGERS WAS 869D LETTER 70   PROSE
        UNWILLING
COAL   SEE SEA-COAL
COARSE-CLAD
    MAY FIND IT IN A HARLOT AND IN COARSE-CLAD HONESTY . . . 199 AMERICA 8   11
COARSER
    I SHALL EAT COARSER FOOD & GO WORSE SHOD . . . . . 559 I ROSE UP AT/N   26
COAST
    SCENE THE COAST OF FRANCE KING EDWARD AND NOBLES BEFORE 17D EDW THIRD/PS 1 PROSE
        IT THE ARMY
    ALBION'S COAST IS SICK SILENT THE AMERICAN MEADOWS FAINT 159A SONG LIBERTY   PROSE
    MEET ON THE COAST GLOWING WITH BLOOD FROM ALBION'S FIERY 197 AMERICA 3   5
        PRINCE
    MEET ON THE COAST GLOWING WITH BLOOD FROM ALBION'S FIERY 203 AMERICA CANC A   5
        PRINCE
COASTS   SEE SEA COASTS
    AFFRIGHT THE COASTS . . . . 147 FRENCH REVOLTN   281
    THRO ALL THE COASTS TILL WEAKEND . . . . . . 236 URIZEN 25   28
COAT
    BOTH SPEAR & SHIELD WERE USELESS & THE COAT OF IRON MAIL 105 TIRIEL 4   70
    [THEN] HE LED HIM BY HIS LITTLE COAT . . . . . . 177 LIT BOY LST/N   13
    HE LED HIM BY HIS LITTLE COAT . . . . 218 LIT BOY LST/SE   11
    AS THERE MAY BE A FOOL OR A KNAVE IN AN EMBROIDERD COAT 593B PUB ADDRESS/N PROSE
    IS NOT LIKE A COAT MADE BY ANOTHER BUT IS AN EMANATION . 593B PUB ADDRESS/N PROSE
    THEY STRIP OFF JOSEPH'S COAT & DIP IT IN THE BLOOD 704 JERUSALEM 67   23
        OF BATTLE
COATS
    CLOTHING ADAM & EVE WITH COATS OF SKINS . . . . . . 824A LETTER 27   PROSE
COBAN   SEE KOBAN
    HAND IS BECOME A ROCK SINAI & HOREB IS HYLE & COBAN . . 501 MILTON 19   58
    ALBION'S DREAD SONS HAND HYLE & COBAN SURROUND HIM AS . 507 MILTON 23   15
    OF HAND & HYLE & COBAN OF KWANTOK PEACHEY BRERETON SLAYD 623 JERUSALEM 5   25
        & HUTTON
    I HEATED IT IN THE FLAMES OF HAND & HYLE & COBAN . . 628 JERUSALEM 9   21
    AND HYLE & COBAN WERE HIS TWO CHOSEN ONES FOR EMISSARIES 641 JERUSALEM 18   41
    HAND HYLE & COBAN GUANTOK PEACHEY BRERETON SLAYD & HUTTON 641 JERUSALEM 19   18
    HAND HYLE & COBAN FLED THEY BECAME WHAT THEY BEHELD . . 662 JERUSALEM 36   15
    COBAN DWELT IN BATH SOMERSET WILTSHIRE GLOUCESTERSHIRE . 710 JERUSALEM 71   26
COBAN'S
    COBAN'S SON IS NIMROD HIS SON CUSH IS ADJOIND TO ARAM . 625 JERUSALEM 7   19
COCK
    STARTLED ASTONISHD AT THE CLAMROUS COCK . . . . . . 24 EDW THIRD/PS 3   115
    [THIS FROG] SING COCK I CARY KITTY ALONE . . . . 55 THIS FROG/IM *   5
    COCK I CARY KITTY ALONE . . . . 55 THIS FROG/IM   7
    COCK DOES CROW . . . . 123 SPRING/SI   14
    THE GAME COCK CLIPD & ARMD FOR FIGHT . . '. . . . 431 AUGURIES   17
    THE SPECTRE REFUSES HE SEEKS CRUELTY THEY CREATE 515 MILTON 28   24
        THE CRESTED COCK
    HE IS A COCK [WONT] WOULD . . . . 540 COCK WOULD/N *   1
    AND WOULD BE A [CROW] COCK IF HE COULD . . . . . 540 COCK WOULD/N *   2
    MORE WONDROUS WONDROUS STILL THE COCK & HEN . . . 545 IMIT POPE/N   2
COCK CHAFER
    A FLEA OR A BUTTERFLY OR A COCK CHAFER . . . . . 58C ISLAND MOON 10 PROSE
CODE
    FOR ALL NATIONS BELIEVE THE JEWS' CODE AND . . . . . 154A MARRIAGE HH 12 PROSE
    BUT IN THE NORTH TO ODIN SOTHA GAVE A CODE OF WAR . . 246 SONG OF LOS 3   30
    THE OLD & NEW TESTAMENTS ARE THE GREAT CODE OF ART . . 777C INSC LAOCOON   PROSE
CODES
    ALL BIBLES OR SACRED CODES HAVE BEEN THE CAUSES . . . 149C MARRIAGE HH 4   PROSE
    THE GUARDIAN OF THE SECRET CODES FORSOOK HIS ANCIENT 242 EUROPE 12   15
        MANSION
    THE BASEST & MOST OPPRESSIVE OF HUMAN CODES & BEING LIKE 393C ANNO WATSON   MARG
    ALL OTHER CODES GIVEN UNDER PRETENCE OF DIVINE COMMAND . 393C ANNO WATSON   MARG
COERCIVE
    FOR THE COERCIVE LAWS OF HELL MORAL HYPOCRISY . . . . 616C V LAST JUDG/N PROSE
COFFEE
    & OUR GOOD LADY PAULINA OVER A DISH OF COFFEE I LONG TO 862A LETTER 59   PROSE
        HEAR
COFFINS
    WERE ALL OF THEM LOCKD UP IN COFFINS OF BLACK . . . . 117 CHIMNEY SWP/SI   12
    AND HE OPEND THE COFFINS & SET THEM ALL FREE . . . . 117 CHIMNEY SWP/SI   14
COGS
    AS COGS ARE FORMD IN A WHEEL TO TURN THE COGS OF 513 MILTON 27   10
        THE ADVERSE WHEEL
    TAKING THEIR FORMS FROM THE WHEELS OF ALBION'S SONS AS COGS 633 JERUSALEM 13   13
    ARE FORMD IN A WHEEL TO FIT THE COGS OF THE ADVERSE WHEEL 633 JERUSALEM 13   14
    OF MANY WHEELS I VIEW WHEEL WITHOUT WHEEL WITH COGS 636 JERUSALEM 15   18
        TYRANNIC
COILD
    IN HIS SOUL WAS THE SERPENT COILD ROUND IN HIS HEART . . . 135 FRENCH REVOLTN   28

```
                                                              PAGE       TITLE          LINE
COILD     (CONTINUED)
     COILD WITHIN ENITHARMON'S WOMB  . . . . . . . . .        232 URIZEN 19            29
     ORC THE FIRST BORN COILD IN THE SOUTH THE DRAGON URIZEN  634 JERUSALEM 14          3
COINED
     OR AN EYE OF GIFTS & GRACES SHOWRING FRUITS & COINED GOLD 130 BOOK OF THEL 6       15
COL
     I HAVE SENT TO HIM BY A PARCEL FROM COL SIBTHORPE'S  . . . 855B LETTER 53       PROSE
COLCHESTER
     MALDEN & COLCHESTER DEMONSTRATE I HEAR MY CHILDREN'S VOICES 644 JERUSALEM 21      37
     WEEPING OVER HIS CHILDREN IN STONE-HENGE IN MALDEN        689 JERUSALEM 57         6
       & COLCHESTER
COLD      SEE A-COLD,CLAY-COLD,CLAY COLD
     ON THE COLD STONE HER PALE [CHEEKS] CHEEK SICKLY SMELLS     4 FAIR ELENOR/PS       6
     WALKING FEELING THE COLD WALLS WITH HER HANDS  . . . .      4 FAIR ELENOR/PS      12
     SHE SAT WITH DEAD COLD LIMBS STIFFEND TO STONE  . . . .     6 FAIR ELENOR/PS      69
     WHOSE HEART IS WINTRY COLD  . . . . . . . . . .             6 MY SILKS/PS         10
     THEN DOWN I'LL LIE AS COLD AS CLAY  . . . . . . .           7 MY SILKS/PS         17
     THE COLD RELIEF THE BLOOD IS STAYD  . . . . . .            17 BLIND-MANS/PS       59
     PREPARE YOUR HEARTS FOR DEATH'S COLD HAND PREPARE  . . .   34 WAR SONG/PS          6
     WHEN THE COLD CLAY BREATHED WITH LIFE AND OUR ANCESTORS   35C COUCH DEATH/PS    PROSE
     [REFRESHING THE COLD EARTH WITH BEAMING JOY] BUT PRIDE    40D THEN SHE BORE     PROSE
       AWOKE
     ("COLD AND VEHEMENT AT THE SAME TIME A FANATIC") I E      73C ANNO LAVATER       MARG
       HYPOCRITE
     STUDY INTELLECTUALS TILL YOU ARE COLD  . . . . . . .      93A ANNO SWED LOVE     MARG
     THE YOUNG BOSOM IS COLD FOR LACK OF MOTHER'S NOURISHMENT  110 TIRIEL 8           27
       & MILK
     THO THE MORNING WAS COLD TOM WAS HAPPY & WARM  . . . . .  118 CHIMNEY SWP/SI     23
     MY BOSOM OF ITSELF IS COLD AND OF ITSELF IS DARK  . . .   129 BOOK OF THEL 4     12
     AND LAY ME DOWN IN THY COLD BED AND LEAVE MY SHINING LOT  130 BOOK OF THEL 5     13
     RUNS ACHING COLD INTO THE SCEPTER TOO HEAVY FOR MORTAL    134 FRENCH REVOLTN      4
       GRASP NO MORE
     . . . AND COLD OF NIGHT HIS DEN WAS SHORT  . . . . . .    136 FRENCH REVOLTN     39
     . . . COLD WAVING THE NOBLES FOLD ROUND THE KING  . . .   137 FRENCH REVOLTN     65
     . . . I AWOKE A COLD HAND PASSED OVER MY LIMBS AND BEHOLD 140 FRENCH REVOLTN    130
     HE SAT DOWN A DAMP COLD PERVADED THE NOBLES . . .         141 FRENCH REVOLTN    158
     . . . GO THOU COLD RECLUSE INTO THE FIRES  . . . . .      142 FRENCH REVOLTN    191
     A COLD ORB OF DISDAIN REVOLVD ROUND HIM . . . . . .       143 FRENCH REVOLTN    199
     . . . FROM COLD FROM SLANDER DISCONTENT AND SLOTH  . .    144 FRENCH REVOLTN    234
     PALE AND COLD SAT THE KING IN MIDST OF HIS PEERS . . . .  147 FRENCH REVOLTN    294
     . . . A DARKNESS CREPT OVER HIS EYE-LIDS AND CHILL COLD   147 FRENCH REVOLTN    295
       SWEAT
     . . . GROANING SHAKING FORESTS AND FLOODS THE COLD NEWT   147 FRENCH REVOLTN    297
     A FAINT HEAT FROM THEIR FIRES REVIVD THE COLD LOUVRE . .  148 FRENCH REVOLTN    303
     TREMBLING COLD IN GHASTLY FEARS  . . . . . . . . .        161 NEVER PAIN/N        7
     COLD & HOAR  . . . . . . . . . . . . . .                  169 EARTHS ANSWR/N      8
     [O] DEAR MOTHER DEAR MOTHER THE CHURCH IS COLD  . . .     179 LIT VAGABOND/N *    1
     FED WITH COLD & USUROUS HAND  . . . . . . . . .           181 HOLY THURS/N        4
     DRUNKEN WITH WOE FORGOTTEN AND SHUT UP FROM COLD DESPAIR  192 V DAU ALBION 4      2
     WITH COLD FLOODS OF ABSTRACTION AND WITH FORESTS          193 V DAU ALBION 5     19
       OF SOLITUDE
     WHERE THE COLD MISER SPREADS HIS GOLD OR DOES THE BRIGHT  195 V DAU ALBION 8      1
       CLOUD DROP
     DARK IS THE HEAVEN ABOVE & COLD & HARD THE EARTH BENEATH  201 AMERICA 14          7
     AROUND THE SMITTEN BANDS CLOTHED IN TEARS & TREMBLING     203 AMERICA 16          8
       SHUDDRING COLD
     HIDING THE DEMON RED WITH CLOUDS & COLD MISTS FROM THE    203 AMERICA 16         13
       EARTH
     INFINITE LONDON'S AWFUL SPIRES CAST A DREADFUL [GLEAM] COLD 205 AMERICA CANC C    7
     COLD AND HOAR  . . . . . . . . . . . . . .  . .          211 EARTHS ANSR/SE      8
     FED WITH COLD AND USUROUS HAND . . . . . . . . .         211 HOLY THURS/SE       4
     DEAR MOTHER DEAR MOTHER THE CHURCH IS COLD  . . . .      216 LIT VAGABND/SE      1
     FREE FROM WINTER'S COLD  . . . . . . . . . .            219 LIT GRL LST/SE       6
     HIS COLD HORRORS SILENT DARK URIZEN  . . . . . .        223 URIZEN 3            27
     COLD FEATURELESS FLESH OR CLAY . . . . . . .            226 URIZEN 7             5
     WHITE AS THE SNOW ON THE MOUNTAINS COLD  . . . . .      227 URIZEN 10           23
     SIEZD A COLD SOLITUDE & DARK VOID  . . . . . . .        230 URIZEN 13           39
     COLD HE WANDERD ON HIGH OVER THEIR CITIES  . . . .      235 URIZEN 25            5
     A COLD SHADOW FOLLOWD BEHIND HIM  . . . . . . .         235 URIZEN 25            9
     LIKE A SPIDER'S WEB MOIST COLD & DIM . . . . . . .      235 URIZEN 25           10
     TILL A WEB DARK & COLD THROUGHOUT ALL  . . . . . .      235 URIZEN 25           15
     WERE WITHERD & DEAFEND & COLD  . . . . . . . .          236 URIZEN 28           16
     LIKE THE GAY FISHES ON THE WAVE WHEN THE COLD MOON DRINKS 243 EUROPE 14           3
       THE DEW
     UNREMITTING ENDURD THE COLD HAMMER  . . . . . . .       249 AHANIA 2            25
     THE COLD LOINS OF URIZEN DIVIDING  . . . . . . .        249 AHANIA 2            29
     IN COLD POISONS BUT URIZEN SMOTE HIM  . . . . . .       250 AHANIA 3            19
     THOU NEER SHALT LEAVE THIS COLD EXPANSE WHERE WATRY THARMAS 272 FOUR ZOAS 1     305
       MOURNS
     HEART COLD AND THE LITTLE TONGUE CONSUMD THAT ONCE      276 FOUR ZOAS 1        449
       IN THOUGHTLESS JOY
     FIRST HE BEHELD THE BODY OF MAN PALE COLD THE HORRORS OF 280 FOUR ZOAS 2        11
       DEATH
     SHE FELL COLD FROM LAMBETH'S VALES IN GROANS & DEWY DEATH 281 FOUR ZOAS 2       46
     WHEN I CALLD FORTH THE EARTH-WORM FROM THE COLD & DARK   282 FOUR ZOAS 2        83
       OBSCURE
     THE FIRES OF VALA FADED LIKE A SHADOW COLD & PALE  . . .  283 FOUR ZOAS 2      114
     OF HIS WIDE HEAVEN TREMBLING COLD IN PALING FEARS SHE SAT 285 FOUR ZOAS 2      186
     HER COLD LIMBS IN THE ABSENCE OF HER LORD ALSO HER SONS   285 FOUR ZOAS 2      193
     COLD DEWS & HOARY FROST CREEPS THO I LIE ON BANKS OF SUMMER 288 FOUR ZOAS 2 *  320
     AMONG THE BEAUTIES OF THE WORLD COLD & REPINING LOS  . . . 288 FOUR ZOAS 2     321
     SHE FLED VANISHING ON THE WIND AND LEFT A DEAD COLD CORSE  289 FOUR ZOAS 2     334
```

		PAGE	TITLE	LINE

COLD   (CONTINUED)
PLUNGD INTO THE COLD BILLOWS LIVING [&] A LIFE IN MIDST   296 FOUR ZOAS 3   * 179
  OF WATERS
THESE ARE THE WORDS OF ENION HEARD FROM THE COLD WAVES   296 FOUR ZOAS 3   182
  OF DESPAIR
FROM DEATH'S COLD SLEEP [UPON] . . . .   298 FOUR ZOAS 4   16
DREAMER OF FURIOUS OCEANS COLD SLEEPER OF WEEDS & SHELLS   301 FOUR ZOAS 4   135
FRIGHTEND WITH COLD INFECTIOUS MADNESS IN HIS HAND THE   302 FOUR ZOAS 4   178
  THUNDERING
BESIDE THE ANVIL COLD HE DANCD WITH THE HAMMER OF URTHONA   305 FOUR ZOAS 5   4
LOS FROM THE FURNACES A SPACE IMMENSE & LEFT THE COLD   . .   305 FOUR ZOAS 5   15
THE NIGHT BLEW COLD AND ENITHARMON SHRIEKD ON THE DISMAL   305 FOUR ZOAS 5   20
  WIND
LOS FOLDED ENITHARMON IN A COLD WHITE CLOUD IN FEAR . . .   308 FOUR ZOAS 5   110
INWRAP THE PARENTS IN COLD CLOUDS AS THEY BEND HOWLING OVER   309 FOUR ZOAS 5   171
DARKEND HIS BROWS WITH HIS COLD HELMET & HIS GLOOMY SPEAR   313 FOUR ZOAS 6   52
CRYING WHAT & WHO ART THOU COLD DEMON ART THOU URIZEN   . .   313 FOUR ZOAS 6   55
TILL A WHITE WOOF COVERD HIS COLD LIMBS FROM HEAD TO [FOOT]   318 FOUR ZOAS 6   * 239
  FEET
FOLLOWD BEHIND HIM AS THE WEB OF A SPIDER DUSKY & COLD . .   318 FOUR ZOAS 6   244
DESART AMONG THE STARS THEM WITHERING WITH ITS RIDGES COLD   319 FOUR ZOAS 6   306
. . . WHY SHOULDST THOU SIT COLD GROVELLING DEMON OF WOE   322 FOUR ZOAS 7   73
ORC LISTEND TO THE SONG COMPELLD HUNGRING ON THE COLD WIND   322 FOUR ZOAS 7   99
THEN ORC [ANSWERD] CRIED CURSE THY COLD HYPOCRISY . . .   323 FOUR ZOAS 7   135
AVAUNT COLD HYPOCRITE I AM CHAIND OR THOU COULDST NOT USE   323 FOUR ZOAS 7   142
  ME THUS
ART THOU THE COLD ATTRACTIVE POWER THAT HOLDS ME IN THIS   323 FOUR ZOAS 7   146
  CHAIN
LOS SAT IN SHOWERS OF URIZEN'S [COLD] WATCHING COLD   324 FOUR ZOAS 7   * 166
  ENITHARMON
LIKE A COLD NIGHT THAT NIPS THE [ROOTS] ROOT . . . . .   324 FOUR ZOAS 7   * 180
HE SPOKE NOT HE WAS SILENT TILL HE FELT THE COLD DISEASE   324 FOUR ZOAS 7   182
COLD PALE IN SORROW AT MY APPROACH TREMBLING AT MY TERRIFIC   325 FOUR ZOAS 7   188
VEILS OF IGNORANCE COVERING FROM HEAD TO FEET WITH A COLD   346 FOUR ZOAS 8   222
  WEB
COLD DARK OPAKE THE ASSEMBLY MET TWELVEFOLD IN AMALEK   . .   348 FOUR ZOAS 8   275
SCALES COVERD OVER A COLD FOREHEAD & A NECK OUTSTRETCHD   352 FOUR ZOAS 8   423
AND ENITHARMON PALE & COLD IN MILKY JUICES FLOWD . . . .   353 FOUR ZOAS 8   474
AND THE STRONG EAGLE NOW WITH NUMMING COLD BLIGHTED OF   354 FOUR ZOAS 8   521
  FEATHERS
ONCE LIKE THE PRIDE OF THE SUN NOW FLAGGING IN COLD NIGHT   354 FOUR ZOAS 8   * 522
ENWRAPPED ROUND WITH WEEDS OF DEATH PALE COLD IN SORROW   359 FOUR ZOAS 9   96
  & WOE
COME FORTH FROM SLUMBERS OF THY COLD ABSTRACTION COME   360 FOUR ZOAS 9   129
  FORTH
ARISE TO ETERNAL BIRTHS SHAKE OFF THY COLD REPOSE   . .   360 FOUR ZOAS 9   130
ON THE GOLDEN PALACE SONGS & JOY ON THE DESART THE COLD   363 FOUR ZOAS 9   251
  BABE
THE CLOUDS FALL OFF FROM MY WET BROW THE DUST FROM MY   373 FOUR ZOAS 9   597
  COLD LIMBS
AMONG THE FLOWERS OF BEULAH IN HIS SELFISH COLD REPOSE . .   374 FOUR ZOAS 9   628
COLD DARK OPAKE THE ASSEMBLY MET TWELVE FOLD IN AMALEK . .   382 FOUR ZOAS AD 6   8
WILL [ALWAYS BE FOUND TO BE NEITHER COLD NOR HOT & WILL]   386C ANNO WATSON   MARG
[A DEEP WINTER [NIGHT] DARK & COLD] . . . .   415 MY SPECTRE/N   13
[[[TO] IN A DARK COLD WINTER NIGHT]] . . . .   415 MY SPECTRE/N   *   14
AND WITH COLD & SHUDDERING FEARS . . . .   416 MY SPECTRE/N   38
AS COLD EARTH WANDERERS NEVER KNEW . . . .   424 MENTAL TRAVLER   4
TO MAKE IT FEEL BOTH COLD & HEAT . . . .   425 MENTAL TRAVLER   16
A DAMP COLD CAME OER HER HER BLUSHES ALL FLED . . . .   428 MARY   19
AND ON THY HEAD IS THE COLD MOON'S SHINE . . . . . .   435 WILLIAM BOND   30
AND COLD AND PALE THE LIMBS REPOSD . . . .   442 DEDICATN BLAIR   4
HIRE IDIOTS TO PAINT WITH COLD LIGHT & HOT SHADE . . .   445 ANNO REYNOLDS   2
WHEN NATIONS GROW OLD THE ARTS GROW COLD . . . . . .   452 ANNO REYNOLDS   1
SHADE IS ALWAYS COLD & . . . .   478D ANNO REYNOLDS   MARG
HIS LIPS WITH FOOD OF EDEN IN HIS COLD AND DIM REPOSE   . .   496 MILTON 15   15
DEADLY PALE OUTSTRETCHD AND SNOWY COLD STORM COVERD   . .   497 MILTON 15   37
HOVERING OVER THE COLD BOSOM IN ITS VORTEX MILTON BENT DOWN   497 MILTON 15   41
EVEN TO MAHANAIM WHEN WITH COLD HAND URIZEN STOOPD DOWN   500 MILTON 19   7
TO MILTON'S BRAIN THE ICY FLUID FROM HIS BROAD COLD PALM   500 MILTON 19   9
CREATING NEW FLESH ON THE DEMON COLD AND BUILDING HIM   . .   500 MILTON 19   13
THE BANKS OF CAM COLD LEARNING'S STREAMS . . . . . .   501 MILTON 19   39
OR HOW CAN I WITH MY COLD HAND OF CLAY BUT THOU O LORD . .   502 MILTON 20   17
LOS SAW THEM AND A COLD PALE HORROR COVERD OER HIS LIMBS   503 MILTON 20   51
WHERE LIE IN EVIL DEATH THE FOUR IMMORTALS PALE AND COLD   524 MILTON 34   45
HIS JEALOUSY BEFORE THE THRONE DIVINE DARKENING COLD   . .   622 JERUSALEM 4   35
WHIRLD ROUND FROM HEAVEN TO EARTH TREMBLING HE SAT HIS COLD   627 JERUSALEM 8   4
AND HIS INFANT THOUGHTS & DESIRES INTO COLD DARK CLIFFS   628 JERUSALEM 9   2
  OF DEATH
THAT I MAY AWAKE ALBION FROM HIS LONG & COLD REPOSE . . .   635 JERUSALEM 15   10
SHUDDRING THEY FLEE THEY HIDE IN THE DRUID TEMPLES IN COLD   638 JERUSALEM 17   14
  CHASTITY
HIS EON WEEPING IN THE COLD AND DESOLATED EARTH . . . .   641 JERUSALEM 19   16
AS I BEHOLD JERUSALEM IN THEE O VALA DARK AND COLD   . . .   645 JERUSALEM 22   32
COLD SNOWS DRIFTED AROUND HIM ICE COVERD HIS LOINS AROUND   652 JERUSALEM 28   13
THE TREE SPREAD OVER HIM ITS COLD SHADOWS ALBION GROAND   653 JERUSALEM 28   17
THEN SPOKE THE SPECTROUS CHAOS TO ALBION DARKNING COLD . .   659 JERUSALEM 33   3
HIS COLD AGAINST THE WARMTH OF EDEN RAGD WITH LOUD   . .   664 JERUSALEM 38   8
THE TWENTY-EIGHT TREMBLED IN DEATH'S DARK CAVES IN COLD   668 JERUSALEM 41   23
  DESPAIR
AND WITH TEARS COLD ON THEIR CHEEKS THEY WEARY REPOSE   . .   671 JERUSALEM 42   70
URIZEN COLD & SCIENTIFIC LUVAH PITYING & WEEPING . . . .   671 JERUSALEM 43   2
SO SPOKE THE HARD COLD CONSTRICTIVE SPECTRE HE IS NAMED   685 JERUSALEM 54   25
  ARTHUR

359

COLD   (CONTINUED)
    THEY POUR COLD WATER ON HIS BRAIN IN FRONT TO CAUSE . . .   702 JERUSALEM 66   30
    NOR RAIN NO MORE THE SPRING OF THE ROCK APPEARS BUT COLD   719 JERUSALEM 79   5
    HEATED IN THE SMITH'S FORGE BUT COLD THE WIND OF THEIR   735 JERUSALEM 89   42
        DREAD FURY
    ALBION COLD LAYS ON HIS ROCK STORMS & SNOWS BEAT ROUND HIM   741 JERUSALEM 94   1
    SHE AWOKE PALE & COLD SHE FAINTED SEVEN TIMES ON THE BODY   742 JERUSALEM 94   21
        OF ALBION
    A COLD LEPER THOU SHALT BE . . . .   754 EV GOSPEL(E)/N   34
    HOLY & COLD I CLIPD THE WINGS   771 OF GATES/GP   35
    WHICH WHEN COLD WILL RECIEVE ANY IMPRESSION MINUTELY   .   790C LETTER 2   PROSE
    THAN IN THE COLD GALLERY OF FASHION THE SUN   . . . .   812B LETTER 22   PROSE
    MUST MY DEAR BUTTS FEEL COLD NEGLECT . . . .   817 HAPPINESS/L   45
    SURPRIZED ME BECAUSE I HAVE NO AGUE BUT HAVE HAD A COLD   819B LETTER 25   PROSE
    I WISHD OWING TO A VIOLENT COLD WHICH CONFIND ME TO MY BED 834B LETTER 34   PROSE
    A MR BLAIR A SURGEON HAS WITH THE COLD FURY OF ROBESPIERRE 865A LETTER 62   PROSE
    SPEAK OF FOR IF IT WAS NOT FOR THE COLD WEATHER I THINK I   868D LETTER 68   PROSE
    FOR I AM AGAIN LAID UP BY A COLD IN MY STOMACH THE   . . . 870D LETTER 72   PROSE
    THAT (SHIVERING) FIT WHICH MUST BE AVOIDED TILL THE COLD   871D LETTER 74   *PROSE
        IS GONE
    MY DEAREST FRIEND THIS SUDDEN COLD WEATHER HAS CUT UP   .   872D LETTER 76   PROSE
    TO SIT UP LONGER THAN SIX HOURS AT A TIME & ALSO FEEL THE   872D LETTER 76   PROSE
        COLD
    I AM STILL FAR FROM RECOVERED & DARE NOT GET OUT IN THE   877D LETTER 87   PROSE
        COLD
COLD HEARTED
    INSANITY AND FURY AND WHATEVER PALTRY COLD HEARTED CRITICS 864B LETTER 61   PROSE
COLDNESS
    COLDNESS DARKNESS OBSTRUCTION A SOLID   . . . .   257 BOOK OF LOS 4   4
    IN TORTURES OF DIRE COLDNESS NOW A LAKE OF WATERS DEEP . . 322 FOUR ZOAS 7   74
    AND SUCH IS THE COLDNESS WITH WHICH REYNOLDS SPEAKS . .   458A ANNO REYNOLDS   MARG
COLLECT
    AND MR WALKER PROMISES TO COLLECT ALL HE CAN OF INFORMATION 844A LETTER 43   PROSE
    HE PROMISES TO COLLECT NUMEROUS PARTICULARS CONCERNING .   845D LETTER 44   PROSE
    TO WRITE ALL HE KNOWS OR CAN COLLECT CONCERNING ROMNEY .   846A LETTER 44   PROSE
    EXPECT A FULL ACCOUNT OF ALL HE CAN COLLECT MR SANDERS .   847D LETTER 44   PROSE
    COLLECT FROM HIM BE SO GOOD AS TO GIVE ME YOUR EARLIEST   849B LETTER 45   PROSE
COLLECTED
    I COLLECTED SOME OF THEIR PROVERBS THINKING THAT . . . .   150C MARRIAGE HH 6   PROSE
    THUS URIZEN SPOKE COLLECTED IN HIMSELF IN AWFUL PRIDE .   273 FOUR ZOAS 1   342
    AND WATCHD HIS SWIFT APPROACH COLLECTED DARK THE SPECTRE   319 FOUR ZOAS 6   301
        STOOD
    BUT ALL THE FAMILY DIVINE COLLECTED AS FOUR SUNS . . . .   504 MILTON 21   37
    DISBELIEVED WHILE THOSE OF THE JEWS ARE COLLECTED AND . . 578D DESC CAT 5   PROSE
    & OTHER ARTICLES COLLECTED FROM EVERY FOUNTAIN HE CAN VISIT 832D LETTER 32   PROSE
    THE BIBLE OF HELL IN NOCTURNAL VISIONS COLLECTED VOL I   SUPP INSCRIPTION   *TITLE
        LAMBETH
COLLECTING
    COLLECTING UP THE SCATTERD PORTIONS OF HIS IMMORTAL BODY   355 FOUR ZOAS 8   562
    AND MILTON COLLECTING ALL HIS FIBRES INTO IMPREGNABLE   529 MILTON 38   5
        STRENGTH
COLLECTION
    A COLLECTION OF PICTURES PAINTED . . . .   599B PUB ADDRESS/N   PROSE
    YOU DESIRED HE HAS SENT A CATALOGUE OF ALL HIS COLLECTION   844A LETTER 43   PROSE
COLLECTIONS
    & THEY PROVE IT IN THEIR CONTEMPT FOR GREAT COLLECTIONS   601C PUB ADDRESS/N   PROSE
COLLEGE
    WINDSOR TERRACE A BOY CONTEMPLATING A DISTANT VIEW OF ETON SUPP ILLUS GRAY   *TITLE
        COLLEGE
    TWO BOYS WANDERING IN THE WOODS BY ETON COLLEGE . . . .   SUPP ILLUS GRAY   *TITLE
COLLINS'S
    MRS LINNELL COLLINS'S FARM NORTH END HAMPSTEAD . . . .   SUPP ADDRESS/L 70   *TITLE
COLLUSION
    COLLUSION CALLING THEMSELVES DEISTS WORSHIPPING THE   737 JERUSALEM 90   65
        MATERNAL
COLONADES
    ARCHES & PYRAMIDS & PORCHES COLONADES & DOMES . . . . .   529 MILTON 38   22
COLONEL   SEE COL
    AND I CALL UPON COLONEL WARDLE . . . .   548 ON GREAT ENC/N   5
COLONIES
    SILENT THE COLONIES REMAIN AND REFUSE THE LOUD ALARM   . . 200 AMERICA 10   4
    THE BRITISH COLONIES BENEATH THE WOFUL PRINCES FADE . . . 206 THIRALATHA   4
COLORING
    ALL IS CHIARO SCURO POCO PEN [&] ITS ALL COLORING . . .   554 TO VENETIAN/N *   11
COLOUR   SEE WATER-COLOUR
    & ROBINSONS & THE QUEEN OF FRANCE'S PUSS COLOUR . . . .   53A ISLAND MOON 8   PROSE
    HIS SHADOWS ARE OF A FILTHY BROWN SOMEWHAT OF THE COLOUR   469A ANNO REYNOLDS   MARG
        OF EXCREMENT
    THESE ARE EXCELLENT REMARKS ON (PROPORTIONAL) COLOUR   .   479B ANNO REYNOLDS   * MARG
    OIL WILL NOT DRINK OR ABSORB COLOUR ENOUGH TO STAND THE   561A EXHIBITION ADV   PROSE
        TEST
    KNOW HOW TO COLOUR IT . . . .   563D DESC CAT   PROSE
    OIL WILL NOT DRINK OR ABSORB COLOUR ENOUGH TO STAND THE   565A DESC CAT 2   PROSE
        TEST
    OF VERY LITTLE TIME AND OF THE AIR IT DEADENS EVERY COLOUR 565A DESC CAT 2   PROSE
    ITSELF WILL DRINK OR ABSORB VERY LITTLE COLOUR . . . .   566B DESC CAT 2   PROSE
    COLOUR IT IS MIXED WITH ESPECIALLY EVERY DELICATE COLOUR   566B DESC CAT 2   PROSE
    AND HAS COMPELLED THE USE OF THAT DESTROYER OF COLOUR   .   566B DESC CAT 2   PROSE
    COLOUR BUT HE COULD[NT] NOT [& HOGARTH WITH ALL HIS MERIT 594B PUB ADDRESS/N   *PROSE
        NEVER G]
    A HORSE BY THE COLOUR & A MAN WHO HAS GOT ANY BRAINS   .   597D PUB ADDRESS/N   PROSE
    WILL NEVER BUY A PICTURE BY THE COLOUR . . . . . .   597D PUB ADDRESS/N   PROSE

```
                                                          PAGE      TITLE         LINE
COLOUR    (CONTINUED)
        ARE OIL COLOUR COPIES FROM FRESCO ORIGINALS   . . . . .  598A PUB ADDRESS/N   PROSE
        FROM THE COMPARISON IN EITHER RELIEF OR STRENGTH OF COLOUR  598D PUB ADDRESS/N  PROSE
        WITH EVERY COLOUR LION TYGER HORSE ELEPHANT EAGLE DOVE   746 JERUSALEM 98     43
           FLY WORM
        PARTS OF THE ART WHICH RELATE TO LIGHT & SHADE & COLOUR   814A LETTER 23      PROSE
           & AM
        AND HEAVY THE GERMAN FLUTE COLOUR WHICH WAS USED BY  . . .  864C LETTER 61    PROSE
        TO MAKE SOME SHEW OF COLOUR & STRENGTH  . . . . . .  876B LETTER 83           PROSE
COLOURD    SEE MANY COLOURD
COLOURED
        CRY OUT THAT IT CANNOT BE WELL COLOURED THOSE ARE THE MEN   573B DESC CAT 3    PROSE
        THE CHILD IS AS BEAUTIFULLY DRAWN AS IT IS COLOURED IN   864B LETTER 61       PROSE
           BOTH
COLOURING    SEE COLORING
        [WHENEVER ?REYNOLDS ?TALKS OF COLOURING A GREATER   450B ANNO REYNOLDS  * MARG
           ?COLOURIST]
        THAN COLOURING WITHOUT ANY MEANING AT ALL  . . . . . .  455D ANNO REYNOLDS   MARG
        VENETIAN ALL THY COLOURING IS NO MORE  . . . . . .  464 ANNO REYNOLDS         1
        TO MY EYE RUBENS'S COLOURING IS MOST CONTEMPTIBLE   . .  469A ANNO REYNOLDS   MARG
        ALTOGETHER HIS COLOURING (IS) CONTRARY  . . . . . .  469A ANNO REYNOLDS  * MARG
        TO THE COLOURING OF REAL ART & SCIENCE  . . . . . .  469A ANNO REYNOLDS       MARG
        OPPOSED TO RUBENS'S COLOURING SR [JOSHUA'S] JOSHUA HAS   469A ANNO REYNOLDS  * MARG
           PLACD POUSSIN
        THAT HE WANTS EITHER COLOURING OR ORNAMENTAL PARTS OF ART   472A ANNO REYNOLDS  MARG
        REYNOLDS'S EYE COULD NOT BEAR CHARACTERISTIC COLOURING OR   475D ANNO REYNOLDS  MARG
        COLOURING FORMED UPON THESE PRINCIPLES IS DESTRUCTIVE  .  478C ANNO REYNOLDS   MARG
        SUCH HARMONY OF COLOURING IS DESTRUCTIVE OF ART  . . .  478D ANNO REYNOLDS     MARG
        NO REAL STYLE OF COLOURING EVER APPEARS  . . . . . .  536 NO REAL STYL/N       1
        LOOK THERE YOULL SEE SR JOSHUA'S COLOURING  . . . . .  536 NO REAL STYL/N      3
        THAT GOD IS COLOURING NEWTON DOES SHEW  . . . . . . .  554 TO VENETIAN/N       1
        THOSE WHO TASTE COLOURING LOVE IT MORE & MORE  . . . .  554 TO VENETIAN/N      17
        THE EYE THAT CAN PREFER THE COLOURING OF TITIAN AND RUBENS   563C DESC CAT     PROSE
        AND MICHAEL ANGELO HAD NEVER SEEN THE COLOURING OF TITIAN   563C DESC CAT      PROSE
        BUT BECAUSE HE DOES NOT UNDERSTAND COLOURING HOW SHOULD HE   563D DESC CAT     PROSE
        COLOURING DOES NOT DEPEND ON WHERE THE COLOURS ARE PUT   .  563D DESC CAT      PROSE
        WHERE THAT IS WRONG THE COLOURING NEVER CAN BE RIGHT   . .  563D DESC CAT      PROSE
        IMAGINATION ONLY CAN FURNISH US WITH COLOURING APPROPRIATE   580D DESC CAT 5   PROSE
        THE DISPOSITION OF FORMS ALWAYS DIRECTS COLOURING  . . .  580D DESC CAT 5      PROSE
        WILL NOT ADMIT OF GRAND COLOURING IN MR B'S(BLAKE'S)   581A DESC CAT 5         PROSE
           BRITONS
        HE DEFIES COMPETITION IN COLOURING  . . . . . . . .  581A DESC CAT 5           PROSE
        THE GREAT STRENGTH OF COLOURING & DEPTH OF WORK  . . . .  588A CHAUCER/N       PROSE
        BUT BECAUSE THEY DID NOT UNDERSTAND COLOURING  . . . . .  602D PUB ADDR AD/N   PROSE
        BUT BECAUSE THEY DID NOT UNDERSTAND [ (COLOURING) ] GRAVING   602D PUB ADDR AD/N  *PROSE
        THEIR COLOURING GRAVING & VERSE CAN NEVER BE APPLIED TO ART   602D PUB ADDR AD/N  PROSE
        THAT IS NOT EITHER COLOURING GRAVING OR VERSE WHICH IS  .  603A PUB ADDR AD/N  PROSE
        HE WHO MAKES A DESIGN MUST KNOW THE EFFECT & COLOURING  .  603A PUB ADDR AD/N  PROSE
        COMPREHENDING THE BEAUTIES OF COLOURING OR THE PICTURES   814A LETTER 23       PROSE
        IN ART CAN NEVER BE UNITED WITH THE MAJESTY OF COLOURING   814B LETTER 23      PROSE
        ON ACCOUNT OF THAT VERY COLOURING WHICH OUR CRITIC CALLS   864C LETTER 61      PROSE
           BLACK
        COLOURING AND ARE BLIND TO THE GLOOM OF A REAL TERROR  .  864C LETTER 61       PROSE
COLOURIST
        A GREAT COLOURIST & YET INFERIOR TO THE VENETIANS   . . .  450B ANNO REYNOLDS  MARG
        [WHENEVER ?REYNOLDS ?TALKS OF COLOURING A GREATER   450B ANNO REYNOLDS  * MARG
           ?COLOURIST]
COLOURISTS
        NEVER AS IN RUBENS & THE COLOURISTS HOT & YELLOW BROWN   478D ANNO REYNOLDS    MARG
COLOURS    SEE WATER-COLOURS,WATER COLOURS
        . . . ALL HIS LOVELY CHANGING COLOURS MIX  . . . . . .  269 FOUR ZOAS 1        184
        THE ILLUMINATED BOOKS ARE PRINTED IN COLOURS  . . . . .  208A PRSPECTUS 1793  PROSE
        OF COLOURS TWELVE FEW KNOWN ON EARTH GIVE LIGHT IN THE   241 EUROPE 10         9
           OPAKE
        . . . ALL HIS LOVELY CHANGING COLOURS MIX  . . . . . .  269 FOUR ZOAS 1        184
        VESTS OF THE RADIANT COLOURS OF HEAVEN & CROWNS OF GOLDEN   312 FOUR ZOAS 6    28
           FIRE
        THE PRECIOUS BENEDICTION FOR THEIR COLOURS OF LOVELINESS   312 FOUR ZOAS 6     36
        APPEARD OF MANY COLOURS & OF VARIOUS POISONOUS QUALITIES   325 FOUR ZOAS 7     215
        . . . ALL HIS [LOVELY CHANGING] DARKLY WAVING COLOURS MIX   381 FOUR ZOAS AD 5  4
        ITS FORM WAS LOVELY BUT ITS COLOURS PALE  . . . . . .  414 TO MRS FLAXMAN      2
        OIL COLOURS WILL NOT DO WHY ARE WE TOLD THAT REYNOLDS IS   450B ANNO REYNOLDS  MARG
        WORD ELEGANCE OUGHT TO BE APPLIED TO FORMS NOT TO COLOURS   464C ANNO REYNOLDS  MARG
        BROKEN COLOURS & BROKEN LINES & BROKEN MASSES   . . . .  464C ANNO REYNOLDS    MARG
        HIS LIGHTS ARE ALL THE COLOURS OF THE RAINBOW  . . . .  469A ANNO REYNOLDS     MARG
        & ONLY PROMOTES HARMONY OR BLENDING OF COLOURS ONE INTO   478C ANNO REYNOLDS   MARG
           ANOTHER
        WITH ALL COLOURS OF PRECIOUS STONES & THEIR INMOST PALACES   484 MILTON 4      24
        AND LEUTHA STOOD GLOWING WITH VARYING COLOURS IMMORTAL   492 MILTON 11         32
           HEART-PIERCING
        OF VARYING COLOURS ON THE HILLS TERRIBLY RAGD THE HORSES   492 MILTON 12       15
        COLOURING DOES NOT DEPEND ON WHERE THE COLOURS ARE PUT  .  563D DESC CAT       PROSE
        IN PAINTING THESE PICTURES CLEAR COLOURS UNMUDDED BY OIL   564D DESC CAT 1     PROSE
        THIS PICTURE ALSO IS A PROOF OF THE POWER OF COLOURS   565A DESC CAT 2         PROSE
           UNSULLIED
        OIL HAS FALSELY BEEN SUPPOSED TO GIVE STRENGTH TO COLOURS   565A DESC CAT 2    PROSE
           BUT
        ABOUT JOHN OF BRUGES INVENTING OIL COLOURS  . . . . .  565B DESC CAT 2         PROSE
        IN HIGH FINISHED FRESCO WHERE THE COLOURS WOULD BE AS PURE   566A DESC CAT 2   PROSE
        BROKEN MASSES AND BROKEN COLOURS MR B'S(BLAKE'S) PRACTICE   573B DESC CAT 3    PROSE
           IS
        UNBROKEN LINES UNBROKEN MASSES AND UNBROKEN COLOURS   .  573B DESC CAT 3       PROSE
```

	PAGE	TITLE	LINE

COLOURS   (CONTINUED)
    FOR EXPERIMENT WITH THE COLOURS AND IS LABOURED   . . . .   581C DESC CAT 7   PROSE
    FOR EXPERIMENT ON COLOURS WITHOUT ANY OILY VEHICLE IT MAY   582B DESC CAT 9   PROSE
    COLOURS HIS PICTURES WERE SHEWN TO CERTAIN PAINTERS AND   584D DESC CAT 15   PROSE
    A MAN SETS HIMSELF DOWN WITH COLOURS & WITH   . . . . .   597B PUB ADDRESS/N   PROSE
    ADMIRES ALL HIS COLOURS BROWN & WARM   . . . .   597 PUBLC VOICE/PA   3
    SEES ONLY THE COLOURS OF THINGS & NOT THE FORMS OF THINGS   597D PUB ADDRESS/N   PROSE
    INVOLVING THE DIVINE VISION IN COLOURS OF AUTUMN RIPENESS   659 JERUSALEM 33   30
    MY WIFE IS LIKE A FLAME OF MANY COLOURS OF PRECIOUS JEWELS   801B LETTER 13   PROSE
    MUSTER A FEW IN COLOURS AND SOME IN BLACK WHICH I HOPE WILL 807A LETTER 17   PROSE
    HISTORICAL & POETICAL PRINTED IN COLOURS EACH   . . . . .   867B LETTER 66   PROSE
    "WHO IN THE COLOURS OF THE RAINBOW LIVE" MILTON   . . . .   SUPP LEGEND/N30   *
COLUMBUS
    COLUMBUS DISCOVERD AMERICA BUT AMERICUS VESPUTIUS FINISHD & 598C PUB ADDRESS/N   *PROSE
COLUMN   SEE ETRUSCAN COLUMN
    AS THE SEVEN SPAKE AND THEY STOOD IN A MIGHTY COLUMN OF   530 MILTON 39   8
      FIRE
    IN THE COLUMN OF FIRE IN FELPHAM'S VALE THEN TO THEIR   534 MILTON 42   22
      MOUTHS THE FOUR
    THE DIVINE VISION BECAME FIRST A BURNING FLAME THEN   702 JERUSALEM 66   41
      A COLUMN
    [DORICK (OR) ?ONE ?COLUMN FROM ANOTHER]   . . . .   SUPP ANNO REYNOLDS * MARG
COLUMNS
    SOME [?AS] COLUMNS OF FIRE [&] OR OF WATER . . . .   315 FOUR ZOAS 6   * 122
    OF FIRE ROUND THE WALLS COLUMNS OF FIRE GUARD AROUND   . . 490 MILTON 9   44
COMBAT
    . . . AND THE JOYS OF THE COMBAT BURNT FOR FUEL   . . . .   138 FRENCH REVOLTN   93
    AND OFTEN MALIGNANT THEY COMBAT HEART-BREAKING SORROWFUL   515 MILTON 28   12
      & PITEOUS
    OFFERING TO SUSTAIN THE GLORIOUS COMBAT & THE BATTLE & WAR   658 JERUSALEM 31   65
    COMBAT HIS ASSERTION AS THE GARDENER REMAIND IN MY GARDEN   827D LETTER 28   PROSE
COMBATED
    THE TRIFLES WHICH THE BISHOP HAS COMBATED IN THE FOLLOWING   390C ANNO WATSON   MARG
    WHICH SHE HAS COMBATED IN VAIN EVER SINCE WE HAVE BEEN HERE 811C LETTER 22   PROSE
COMBATS
    FOR THE FATES OF THOSE FOR WHOM HE COMBATS THE   . . . .   580C DESC CAT 5   PROSE
    DIRECTING THE COMBATS IN THE UPPER ELEMENTS   . . . . .   612A V LAST JUDG/N   PROSE
    THE COMBATS OF GOOD & EVIL [& OF TRUTH & ERROR WHICH]   .   615A V LAST JUDG/N   PROSE
    THE COMBATS OF TRUTH & ERROR IS EATING OF THE TREE OF LIFE   615A V LAST JUDG/N   PROSE
COMBINATION
    STARVE ME OUT BY CALUMNY & THE ARTS OF TRADING COMBINATION   596D PUB ADDRESS/N   PROSE
COMBINATIONS
    THE PEOPLE VAIN THEIR COMBINATIONS I WILL SCATTER THEM . . 334 FOUR ZOAS 7B   51
    IF HOMER'S MERIT WAS ONLY IN THESE HISTORICAL COMBINATIONS   411D ANNO BOYD   MARG
    WE ARE NOT INDIVIDUALS BUT STATES COMBINATIONS OF   521 MILTON 32   10
      INDIVIDUALS
    IN ALL THEIR VARIOUS COMBINATIONS WROUGHT WITH WONDROUS ART 638 JERUSALEM 16   66
COMBIND
    SOME COMBIND INTO MUSCLES & GLANDS   . . . .   253 AHANIA 4   32
    SHALL SEE HIM ENITHARMON & AHANIA COMBIND WITH ENION   . . 339 FOUR ZOAS 7B   248
    BECAUSE WE WERE COMBIND IN FREEDOM & HOLY BROTHERHOOD   .   521 MILTON 32   15
    WHILE THOSE COMBIND BY SATAN'S TYRANNY FIRST IN THE BLOOD   521 MILTON 32   16
      OF WAR
    THEIR APPEARANCE WHEN COMBIND BUT OFTEN BY BIRTH PANGS   708 JERUSALEM 70   * 11
      & LOUD GROANS
COMBINE
    LOVE AND HARMONY COMBINE . . . .   7 LOVE HARMNY/PS   1
    IF GODS COMBINE AGAINST MAN SETTING THEIR DOMINION ABOVE   366 FOUR ZOAS 9   366
    COMPELLD TO COMBINE INTO FORM BY SATAN THE SPECTRE   521 MILTON 32   12
      OF ALBION
    AND THERE THEY COMBINE INTO THREE FORMS NAMED BACON   708 JERUSALEM 70   15
      & NEWTON & LOCKE
COMBINED
    THEN ALL THE MALES [CONJOINED] COMBINED INTO ONE MALE &   707 JERUSALEM 69   *   1
      EVERY ONE
COMBINES
    IF A METHOD OF PRINTING WHICH COMBINES THE PAINTER   . . . 207B PRSPECTUS 1793 PROSE
    HE COMBINES INTO A MIGHTY-ONE THE DOUBLE MOLECH & CHEMOSH   729 JERUSALEM 84   21
COMBINING
    TO HIDE BUT [THEY] HE COULD NOT COMBINING   . . . . . .   225 URIZEN 5   * 21
    AND THESE THE NAMES OF THE EIGHTEEN COMBINING WITH THOSE   676 JERUSALEM 45   40
      TEN
COMBS
    WHERE THE DEVIL COMBS HIS LICE . . . .   757 EV GOSPEL(I)/N   26
COMBUSTIBLES
    TUBES IN PETRIFIC STEEL & RAMMD COMBUSTIBLES & WHEELS   .   343 FOUR ZOAS 8   94
COMBUSTION
    COMBUSTION BLAST VAPOUR AND CLOUD . . . .   222 URIZEN 3   17
    THE FOUR ZOAS IN TERRIBLE COMBUSTION CLOUDED RAGE   . .   668 JERUSALEM 41   26
COMBUSTIONS
    FOR INFINITE THE DISTANCE & OBSCURD BY COMBUSTIONS DIRE   316 FOUR ZOAS 6   177
COME
    COME OER THE EASTERN HILLS AND LET OUR WINDS   . . . . .   1 TO SPRING/PS   9
    WHERE ALL LOVE'S PILGRIMS COME . . . .   6 MY SILKS/PS   12
    MEMORY HITHER COME . . . .   8 MEMORY COME/PS   1
    COME HITHER SLEEP . . . .   8 MAD SONG/PS   3
    COME KINGS AND LISTEN TO MY SONG . . . .   11 GWIN KING/PS   1
    LIKE CLOUDS COME ROLLING OER   . . . .   12 GWIN KING/PS   36
    HIS CHIEFS COME RUSHING ROUND . . . .   12 GWIN KING/PS   38
    HEAP THE SEA-COAL COME HEAP IT HIGHER . . . . . .   16 BLIND-MANS/PS   5
    AMBITION COME TAKE THE HELM MY CHANDOS . . . . . .   27 EDW THIRD/PS 3   238
    NOW THERES A STORY COME INTO MY HEAD . . . .   29B EDW THIRD/PS 4   PROSE

362

```
                                                            PAGE    TITLE        LINE
COME    (CONTINUED)
        OF TIME COME ROLLING OER MY BREAST HE SAID . . . . . .   32 EDW THIRD/PS 6      40
        STRETCH FORTH YOUR HANDS THAT MY HELPER MAY COME . . . .  36A COUCH DEATH/PS   PROSE
        COME HITHER DEATH ART THOU NOT SAMSON'S SERVANT . . . .   38B SAMSON/PS       PROSE
        THE OX GOAD IS TURNED INTO A SPEAR O WHEN SHALL OUR       40B SAMSON/PS       PROSE
            DELIVERER COME
        THAT WHEN THY SAYINGS COME TO PASS WE MAY HONOUR THEE  . .  40B SAMSON/PS       PROSE
        IT SPOKE I COME MY FRIEND TO TAKE MY LAST FAREWELL . . .  43D WOE CRIED MUSE   PROSE
        O AY COME I'LL SING YOU A SONG SAID THE CYNIC . . . . .   46C ISLAND MOON 3    PROSE
        COME SAID THE EPICUREAN LET'S HAVE SOME RUM & WATER . . . 49B ISLAND MOON 5    PROSE
        & HANG THE MATHEMATICS COME ARADOBO SAY SOME THING . . .  49B ISLAND MOON 5    PROSE
        THEN SAID SUCTION COME MR LAWGIVER YOUR SONG AND          55A ISLAND MOON 9    PROSE
            THE LAWGIVER SUNG
        JOE BRADLEY SAW FOR HE HAD BUT ONE EYE [?COME] . . . . .  55B ISLAND MOON 9   *PROSE
        ON PURPOSE TO BE YOKD DO COME . . . . . . . . . . .       56 HAIL MATRIM/IM       3
        TIS YOU THAT COME IN TIME OF NEED . . . . . . . . .       56 HAIL MATRIM/IM      10
        THEN COME YE MAIDENS COME YE SWAINS . . . . . . . .       56 HAIL MATRIM/IM      25
        COME & BE EASED OF ALL YOUR PAINS . . . . . . . . .       56 HAIL MATRIM/IM      26
        COME FLAMMABLE SAID GIBBLE GABBLE & LET'S ENJOY OURSELVES 58C ISLAND MOON 10   PROSE
        WHILE HE RAN OUT OF THE ROOM [BE] COME OUT . . . . .      58D ISLAND MOON 10  *PROSE
        COME OUT [GIVE ME] WE ARE PUTRIFIED WE ARE CORRUPTED  .   58D ISLAND MOON 10  *PROSE
        THEN COME HOME MY CHILDREN THE SUN IS GONE DOWN . . . .   60 NURSES SONG/IM       5
        COME COME LEAVE OFF PLAY & LET US AWAY . . . . . .        60 NURSES SONG/IM       7
        OH I AM GLAD YOU ARE COME SAID QUID . . . . . . . .       63A ISLAND MOON 11   PROSE
        COME LIVE AND BE MERRY AND JOIN WITH ME . . . . . .       63 SHEPHERD YOUNG      11
        FORGIVENESS OF ENEMIES CAN ONLY COME UPON THEIR REPENTANCE 77A ANNO LAVATER     MARG
        IS NOT INFINITE THEY SHALL COME TO AN END WHICH GOD FORBID 91A ANNO SWED LOVE   MARG
        COME FORTH & LOOK ON HER THAT BORE YOU COME YOU ACCURSED  99 TIRIEL 1            8
            SONS
        COME FORTH SONS OF THE CURSE COME FORTH SEE THE DEATH     99 TIRIEL 1           10
            OF MYRATANA
        WHY DOST THOU CURSE IS NOT THE CURSE NOW COME UPON YOUR  100 TIRIEL 1           40
            HEAD
        HE KNEELED DOWN & MNETHA SAID COME HAR & HEVA RISE . . . 101 TIRIEL 2           32
        HEVA COME KISS HIS BALD HEAD FOR HE WILL NOT HURT US HEVA 101 TIRIEL 2           38
        MNETHA SAID COME IN AGED WANDERER TELL US OF THY NAME  .  101 TIRIEL 2           46
        BUT FAR HE HAD NOT GONE WHEN IJIM FROM HIS WOODS COME DOWN 103 TIRIEL 4      *    3
        COME THOU DARK FIEND I DARE THY CUNNING KNOW THAT IJIM   104 TIRIEL 4           17
            SCORNS
        COME I WILL LEAD THEE ON THY WAY & USE THEE AS A SCOFF .  . 104 TIRIEL 4         20
        HEUXOS COME FORTH I HERE HAVE BROUGHT THE FIEND THAT     104 TIRIEL 4           43
            TROUBLES IJIM
        BUT LIKE A TYGER HE WOULD COME & SO I [REND] RENT HIM TOO 105 TIRIEL 4      *   53
        IS READY FOR YOUR BITTER TAUNTS [XXX] COME FORTH SONS OF 105 TIRIEL 4      *   67
            THE CURSE
        WHERE ARE YOU GOING COME & EAT SOME ROOTS & DRINK SOME   109 TIRIEL 7           11
            WATER
        SWEET SLEEP COME TO ME . . . . . . . . . . . . .        112 LIT GRL LST/SI     17
        COME FROM CAVERNS DEEP . . . . . . . . . . . . .        113 LIT GRL LST/SI     35
        THEN COME HOME MY CHILDREN THE SUN IS GONE DOWN . . .    121 NURSES SONG/SI      5
        COME COME LEAVE OFF PLAY AND LET US AWAY . . . . .       121 NURSES SONG/SI      7
        COME AND LICK . . . . . . . . . . . . . . . . .        123 SPRING/SI          21
        COME LIVE & BE MERRY AND JOIN WITH ME . . . . . .        125 LAUGHING/SI        11
        SAYING COME OUT FROM THE GROVE MY LOVE & CARE . . . . .  125 LIT BLK BOY/SI     19
        YOUTH OF DELIGHT COME HITHER . . . . . . . . . .        126 VOICE BARD/SI       1
        COME FORTH WORM OF THE SILENT VALLEY TO THY PENSIVE QUEEN 129 BOOK OF THEL 3    29
        . . . HE IS COME TO THE LOUVRE O KING WITH A MESSAGE . . 141 FRENCH REVOLTN    166
        LET THE NATION'S AMBASSADOR COME AMONG NOBLES . . . .    143 FRENCH REVOLTN    197
        THIS SAID HE LIKE ALL FIRM PERSWASIONS IS COME TO PASS . 154A MARRIAGE HH 12   PROSE
        THIS WILL COME TO PASS BY AN IMPROVEMENT OF SENSUAL      154C MARRIAGE HH 14   PROSE
            ENJOYMENT
        THEN COME HOME MY CHILDREN THE SUN IS GONE DOWN . . . .  171 NURSES SONG/N       5
        COME HITHER MY SPARROWS . . . . . . . . . . . .        178 THE FAIRY/N         1
        COME HITHER MY BOY TELL ME WHAT THOU SEEST THERE . . .   180 LACEDEMONIAN/N      1
        ARISE & COME BOTH FIFE & DRUM . . . . . . . . .        185 LET BROTHELS/N      7
        COME IN THE HEAVEN OF GENEROUS LOVE NOR SELFISH BLIGHTINGS 195 V DAU ALBION 7   29
            BRING
        WHY DOST THOU COME TO ANGELS EYES IN THIS TERRIFIC FORM  198 AMERICA 7           7
        AND THEN THEIR END SHOULD COME WHEN FRANCE RECIEVD THE   203 AMERICA 16         15
            DEMON'S LIGHT
        THEN COME HOME MY CHILDREN THE SUN IS GONE DOWN . . . .  212 NURSES SONG/SE      5
        AGAIN THE NIGHT IS COME . . . . . . . . . . . .        239 EUROPE 4            9
        IN AN ALLEGORICAL ABODE WHERE EXISTENCE HATH NEVER COME  240 EUROPE 5            7
        LOST LOST LOST ARE MY EMANATIONS ENION [COME FORTH] O    264 FOUR ZOAS 1        25
            ENION
        THIS LINE TO COME IN . . . . . . . . . . . . .        268D FOUR ZOAS 1       PROSE
        NOW MAN WAS COME TO THE PALM TREE & TO THE OAK OF WEEPING 277 FOUR ZOAS 1       464
        FOR MESSENGERS FROM BEULAH COME IN TEARS & DARKNING CLOUDS 277 FOUR ZOAS 1      476
        WHAT ARE WE TERRORS TO ONE ANOTHER COME O BRETHREN       283 FOUR ZOAS 2       124
            WHEREFORE
        TO COME IN . . . . . . . . . . . . . . . . .         286B FOUR ZOAS 2      PROSE
        WISDOM IS SOLD IN THE DESOLATE MARKET WHERE NONE COME TO 290 FOUR ZOAS 2       400
            BUY
        FALL OFF AFAR FROM THARMAS COME NOT TOO NEAR MY STRONG FURY 296 FOUR ZOAS 3    173
        HITHERTO SHALT THOU COME NO FURTHER HERE THY PROUD WAVES 298 FOUR ZOAS 4        35
            CEASE
        FROM DEATH IN WRATH & FURY BUT NOW COME BEAR BACK . . .  300 FOUR ZOAS 4       116
        SOFT TEARS & SIGHS WHERE ARE YOU COME FORTH SHOUT ON BLOODY 306 FOUR ZOAS 5     48
            FIELDS
        COME THEN INTO MY BOSOM & IN THY SHADOWY ARMS BRING WITH  329 FOUR ZOAS 7      367
            THEE
        COME HITHER BE PATIENT LET US CONVERSE TOGETHER BECAUSE   330 FOUR ZOAS 7      422
```

```
                                                             PAGE      TITLE          LINE
COME    (CONTINUED)
     AND BIND THEM TO THEE THAT MY CRYSTAL FORM MAY COME TO ME       334 FOUR ZOAS 7B      71
     TAKE THOU THE SEVEN DISEASES OF MAN STORE THEM FOR TIMES        336 FOUR ZOAS 7B     118
        TO COME
     BEGUN ALREADY IN ETERNITY COME THEN O LAMB OF GOD     .   .     347 FOUR ZOAS 8      244
     COME LORD JESUS COME QUICKLY  .  .  .  .  .  .  .  .            347 FOUR ZOAS 8      245
     MALAH COME FORTH FROM LEBANON & HOGLAH FROM MOUNT SINAI         349 FOUR ZOAS 8      316
     COME CIRCUMSCRIBE THIS TONGUE OF SWEETS & WITH A SCREW          349 FOUR ZOAS 8      317
        OF IRON
     AND A FOUNTAIN FROM MY BREASTS TO ME COME ALL MULTITUDES        354 FOUR ZOAS 8      501
     THEY COME UP IN THE RIVERS & ANNOY THE NETHER PARTS      .  .   354 FOUR ZOAS 8    * 512
     AND SHRUNK UP TO THE BONES ALAS THAT MAN SHOULD COME TO         354 FOUR ZOAS 8      516
        THIS
     A MIGHTY SOUND ARTICULATE AWAKE YE DEAD & COME   .  .  .  .     357 FOUR ZOAS 9       12
     TO JUDGMENT FROM THE FOUR WINDS AWAKE & COME AWAY    .  .  .    357 FOUR ZOAS 9       13
     AND ALL THE WHILE THE TRUMPET SOUNDS [AWAKE YE DEAD & COME]     358 FOUR ZOAS 9       42
     COME FORTH FROM SLUMBERS OF THY COLD ABSTRACTION COME           360 FOUR ZOAS 9      129
        FORTH
     ALL SPIRITS DECEASD LET LOOSE FROM REPTILE PRISONS COME         363 FOUR ZOAS 9      235
        IN SHOALS
     AND FROM THE OX & ASS COME MOPING TERRORS FROM THE EAGLE        363 FOUR ZOAS 9      237
     .  .  .  WHILE THEY SPOKE THE FLAMES COME ON INTENSE ROARING    364 FOUR ZOAS 9      264
     COME FORTH O VALA FROM THE GRASS & FROM THE SILENT DEW          367 FOUR ZOAS 9      388
     I WALK BY THE FOOTSTEPS OF HIS FLOCKS COME HITHER TENDER        368 FOUR ZOAS 9      427
        FLOCKS
     COVER US FROM THE SUN COME & LET US SIT IN THE SHADE            369 FOUR ZOAS 9      450
     O MYSTERY FIERCE THARMAS CRIES BEHOLD THY END IS COME    .  .   374 FOUR ZOAS 9      657
     THE LION OF TERROR SHALL COME DOWN & BENDING HIS BRIGHT         376 FOUR ZOAS 9      706
        MANE
     WHEREFORE DID CHRIST COME WAS IT NOT TO ABOLISH THE JEWISH      387B ANNO WATSON   * MARG
        IMPOSTURE
     ILL SHAPEN BECAUSE THEY ARE NOT YET COME TO THEIR MATURITY      406C ANNO BACON     MARG
     TO COME IN  .  .  .  .  .  .  .  .  .  .  .  .  .  .  .  .       416A MY SPECTRE/N  *PROSE
     HE COME ON WINGS OF JOY WE'LL FLY   .  .  .  .  .  .  .         423 THE BIRDS/N       17
     COME & MAKE THY CALM RETREAT   .  .  .  .  .  .  .  .           423 THE BIRDS/N       19
     I THINK THAT THIS PROVES HIS HAVING COME INTO THE GARDEN        438A BLAKES MEMORAN PROSE
     COME OUT HE IS THE SAME MAN WHO LATELY HURT HIS HAND     .  .   438C BLAKES MEMORAN PROSE
     MAY COME & DRAG ME AND MY WIFE OUT OF OUR HOUSE      .  .  .    439A BLAKES MEMORAN PROSE
     HIS BURNING THIRST & FREEZING HUNGER COME INTO MY HAND   .  .   481 MILTON 2           5
     WHEN WILL THE RESURRECTION COME TO DELIVER THE SLEEPING         495 MILTON 14         17
        BODY
     FROM CORRUPTIBILITY O WHEN LORD JESUS WILT THOU COME    .  .    495 MILTON 14         18
     LEST THE LAST JUDGMENT COME & FIND ME UNANNIHILATE   .  .  .    495 MILTON 14         23
     IS THIS MAN COME SATAN SHALL BE UNLOOSD UPON ALBION   .  .  .   498 MILTON 17         33
     TO DIVIDE INTO RAHAB & TIRZAH THAT MILTON MAY COME TO OUR       499 MILTON 18         18
        TENTS
     SAYING COME THOU TO EPHRAIM BEHOLD THE KINGS OF CANAAN   .  .   501 MILTON 19         36
     COME BRING WITH THEE JERUSALEM WITH SONGS ON THE GRECIAN        501 MILTON 19         46
        LYRE
     COME THEN TO EPHRAIM & MANASSEH O BELOVED-ONE   .  .  .  .  .   501 MILTON 20          3
     COME TO MY IVORY PALACES O BELOVED OF THY MOTHER   .  .  .      501 MILTON 20          4
     UPON THE BODY OF ALBION FOR THIS HE IS COME BEHOLD              505 MILTON 22         34
        IT WRITTEN
     THIS MIGHTY ONE IS COME FROM EDEN HE IS OF THE ELECT     .  .   508 MILTON 23         56
     STRETCHD OVER EUROPE & ASIA COME O SONS COME COME AWAY          509 MILTON 24         33
     THE AWAKENER IS COME OUTSTRETCHD OVER EUROPE  .  .  .  .  .     510 MILTON 25         22
     WHERE NO DISPUTE CAN COME BECAUSE OF THOSE WHO SLEEP     .  .   518 MILTON 30          3
     IN GREAT ETERNITY WHICH THOU KNOWEST I COME HIM TO SEEK         527 MILTON 37          3
     ARE NOT SUCH KNOW THOU I COME TO SELF ANNIHILATION    .  .  .   530 MILTON 38         34
     I COME TO DISCOVER BEFORE HEAVN & HELL THE                      530 MILTON 38         43
        SELF RIGHTEOUSNESS
     I COME IN SELF-ANNIHILATION & THE GRANDEUR OF INSPIRATION       533 MILTON 41          2
     [YE] COME ARTISTS KNOCK YOUR HEADS AGAINST THIS STONE    .  .   537 AND HIS LEGS/N    46
     SOME MEN CREATED FOR DESTRUCTION COME   .  .  .  .  .  .  .     544 SOME MEN/N         1
     COME KNOCK YOUR HEADS AGAINST THIS STONE  .  .  .  .  .  .      545 AN EPITAPH/N       1
     AND SAYS COME LEARN TO WALK OF ME GOOD NEIGHBOURS    .  .  .    548 CRIPPLE EVRY/N     2
     COME LISTEN TO JOSEPH OF ARIMATHEA   .  .  .  .  .  .  .  .     552 TELL YOU WHA/N     4
     TO COME IN BARRY A POEM  .  .  .  .  .  .  .  .  .  .  .         553D ASKD PRIGG/N   PROSE
     I COME AT LENGTH TO THE CLERK OF OXENFORD   .  .  .  .  .  .    572B DESC CAT 3     PROSE
     WHAT FINE ART IS YE ENGLISH ENGRAVERS MUST COME DOWN     .  .   593C PUB ADDRESS/N  PROSE
     TO COME IN HERE AS TWO LEAVES FORWARD   .  .  .  .  .  .  .     606D V LAST JUDG/N  PROSE
     TO MAKE A WAY FOR THE CHILDREN OF LOS TO COME FROM THE          638 JERUSALEM 17       5
        FURNACES
     BUT COME O VALA WITH KNIFE & CUP DRAIN MY BLOOD   .  .  .  .    645 JERUSALEM 22      29
     COME TO MY ARMS & NEVER MORE  .  .  .  .  .  .  .  .  .  .       651 FIELDS FROM/J     69
     I COME THAT I MAY FIND A WAY FOR MY BANISHED ONES TO RETURN     653 JERUSALEM 29      25
     FEAR NOT O LITTLE FLOCK I COME ALBION SHALL RISE AGAIN   .  .   653 JERUSALEM 29      26
     COME UP BUILD BABYLON RAHAB IS OURS & ALL HER MULTITUDES        671 JERUSALEM 42      63
     SHALL OUR SALVATION COME WE SLEEP UPON OUR WATCH    .  .  .     671 JERUSALEM 42      72
     THE ARMIES OF BALAAM WEEP NO WOMEN COME TO THE FIELD     .  .   672 JERUSALEM 43      39
     NOR DAUGHTER NOR SISTER NOR MOTHER COME FORTH TO EMBOSOM        673 JERUSALEM 43      44
        THE SLAIN
     ALAS THE TIME WILL COME WHEN A MAN'S WORST ENEMIES    .  .  .   676 JERUSALEM 46      25
     WHERE NO DISPUTE CAN COME CREATED FOR THOSE WHO SLEEP    .  .   678 JERUSALEM 48      20
     COME YE O DAUGHTERS OF BEULAH LAMENT FOR OG & SIHON   .  .      679 JERUSALEM 49       3
     COME & MOURN OVER ALBION THE WHITE CLIFF OF THE ATLANTIC        679 JERUSALEM 49       6
     BEFORE YOU IN NIGHT COME ON COME ON COME ON THE LORD            680 JERUSALEM 49      52
     COME LORD JESUS LAMB OF GOD DESCEND FOR IF O LORD    .  .  .    681 JERUSALEM 50      10
     COME O THOU LAMB OF GOD AND TAKE AWAY THE REMEMBRANCE OF        681 JERUSALEM 50      24
        SIN
     COME THEN O LAMB OF GOD AND TAKE AWAY THE REMEMBRANCE OF        681 JERUSALEM 50      30
        SIN
```

COME (CONTINUED)

COME HITHER INTO THE DESERT & TURN THESE STONES TO BREAD   685 JERUSALEM 54   21
THEY HAVE PERSWADED THEE TO THIS THEREFORE THEIR END SHALL   693 JERUSALEM 60   35
  COME
BABYLON COME UP TO JERUSALEM AND ANOTHER VOICE ANSWERD   695 JERUSALEM 61   35
  SAYING
COME NOW WITH ME INTO THE VILLAGES WALK THRO ALL THE CITIES   696 JERUSALEM 62   23
MALAH COME FORTH FROM LEBANON & HOGLAH FROM MOUNT SINAI   705 JERUSALEM 68   4
COME CIRCUMSCRIBE THIS TONGUE OF SWEETS & WITH A SCREW   705 JERUSALEM 68   5
  OF IRON
O COME YE NATIONS COME YE PEOPLE COME UP TO JERUSALEM   712 JERUSALEM 72   33
MY PILLARS REACHD FROM SEA TO SEA LONDON BEHELD ME COME   720 JERUSALEM 79   24
COME INTO LUVAH'S TENTS AND SEEK NOT TO REVIVE THE DEAD   722 JERUSALEM 80   31
BUT WE WOO HIM ALL THE NIGHT IN SONGS O LOS COME FORTH   729 JERUSALEM 84   25
  O LOS
O THOU THAT DWELLEST WITH BABYLON COME FORTH O LOVELY-ONE   730 JERUSALEM 85   32
COME LORD JESUS TAKE ON THEE THE SATANIC BODY OF HOLINESS   737 JERUSALEM 90   38
APPEARS UPON OUR HILLS AWAKE JERUSALEM AND COME AWAY   . .   744 JERUSALEM 97   4
COME SAID SATAN COME AWAY   . . . .   749 EV GOSPEL(B)/N   15
I COME YOUR KING & GOD TO SIEZE   . . . .   749 EV GOSPEL(B)/N   29
WHO SHALL ACCUSE THEE COME YE FORTH   . . . .   754 EV GOSPEL(E)/N   49
THIS TO COME FIRST   . . . .   758A EV GOSPEL   PROSE
FROM GENERATED ORGANS GONE AS SOON AS COME   . . . . .   776D INSC LAOCOON   PROSE
COME OUT WITH A MORAL LIKE A STING IN THE TAIL   . . .   778B HOMERS POETRY   PROSE
EVE COME AWAY & LET US NOT BELIEVE THESE VAIN DELUSIONS   780 GHOST ABEL 1   18
AS THOU HAST SAID SO IS IT COME TO PASS MY DESIRE IS UNTO   780 GHOST ABEL 2   7
  CAIN
THY KINGSHIP COME UPON EARTH FIRST & THENCE IN HEAVEN   . .   788D ANNO THORNTON   * MARG
IF ORDERS HAD NOT COME IN FOR MY DESIGNS & PAINTINGS   . .   794C LETTER 5   PROSE
CONTENTED LET WHAT WILL COME HAVING PASSED NOW   . . .   795C LETTER 6   PROSE
TO TAKE BUT WHETHER I COME ON WEDNESDAY OR THURSDAY THAT   801B LETTER 13   PROSE
  DAY
THESE (TWO) LINES WERE OMITTED IN TRANSCRIBING & OUGHT   817D HAPPINESS/L   PROSE
  TO COME IN
AS THAT TO YOU FOR I TOLD YOU THAT I SHOULD COME TO LONDON   820B LETTER 25   PROSE
DID NOT COME INTO MY THOUGHTS YET IT IS VERY SIMILAR TO   823D LETTER 27   PROSE
TO COME & TO SPEAK TO FUTURE GENERATIONS BY A SUBLIME   825A LETTER 27   PROSE
  ALLEGORY
MR HAYLEY WAS KIND ENOUGH TO COME FORWARDS   . . . . .   828A LETTER 28   PROSE
ALL IS COME FROM THE SPIRITUAL WORLD FOR GOOD & NOT FOR   828C LETTER 28   PROSE
  EVIL
ENTERTAIND AND INSTRUCTED BUT HAVE NOT YET COME TO THE   . .   845B LETTER 44   PROSE
EDWD (FIRST) OR THE BALLADS HAVING COME FROM YOU   . . .   857A LETTER 54   PROSE
THAT MY PLATE MAY COME INTO THE WORK AS ITS OMISSION   . .   861A LETTER 58   PROSE
FOR MANY VERY MANY YEARS BUT NOW I SAY NOW ITS END IS COME   866A LETTER 61   PROSE
I AM FORCED TO WRITE BECAUSE I CANNOT COME TO YOU & THIS   870C LETTER 72   PROSE
ON TWO ACCOUNTS FIRST I OMITTED TO DESIRE YOU WOULD COME   870C LETTER 72   PROSE
I SHOULD HAVE WRITTEN LAST NIGHT BUT AS IT WOULD NOT COME   871C LETTER 73   PROSE
COME TO YOU BEFORE TUESDAY BUT MUCH FEAR THAT MY PRESENT   872A LETTER 74   PROSE
PLEASE TO LET ME KNOW BUT FINDING MYSELF WELL ENOUGH TO   875B LETTER 81   PROSE
  COME
& AM GETTING BETTER OR I COULD NOT HAVE COME AT ALL YOURS   876D LETTER 84   PROSE
OUR END IS COME   . . . .   SUPP INSC OUR END   *TITLE

COMEDIA
EVERY THING IN DANTE'S COMEDIA SHEWS THAT   . . . . . .   785A ILLUS DANTE 7   PROSE

COMELINESS
BEAUTIFUL THRO OUR LOVE'S COMELINESS BEAUTIFUL THRO PITY   643 JERUSALEM 20   33

COMELY
NOR IS THE HIDE A COMELY VESTMENT SO   . . . .   27 EDW THIRD/PS 3   267

COMES
AND WHEN NIGHT COMES I'LL GO   . . . .   8 MEMORY COME/PS   13
SO WHEN WE WALK NOTHING IMPURE COMES NEAR   . . . . . .   9 FRESH FROM/PS   14
HERE COMES THE KING HIMSELF TELL HIM YOUR THOUGHTS   . . .   23 EDW THIRD/PS 3   67
BUT HERE COMES ONE WHO IS AS ENTERTAINING AS A GOOD STORY   29B EDW THIRD/PS 4   PROSE
WHEN THE WHIRLWIND OF FURY COMES FROM THE   . . . . . .   33 EDW FOURTH/PS   6
IN COMES ETRUSCAN COLUMN THE ANTIQUARIAN & AFTER   . . . .   44B ISLAND MOON 1   PROSE
FALSE TAKE IT SO OR THE CONTRARY IT COMES TO THE SAME   . .   91C ANNO SWED LOVE   MARG
THE MORNING COMES THE NIGHT DECAYS THE WATCHMEN LEAVE THEIR   198 AMERICA 6   1
  STATIONS
NOW COMES THE NIGHT OF ENITHARMON'S JOY   . . . .   240 EUROPE 5   1
PRESENTLY COMES A FAMISHD BIRD & TAKES AWAY THE SPIDER   . .   277 FOUR ZOAS 1   458
CAN DIE WHEN DARK DESPAIR COMES OVER CAN I NOT   . . . .   298 FOUR ZOAS 4   22
NOW ALL COMES INTO THE POWER OF THARMAS URIZEN IS FALLN   301 FOUR ZOAS 4   129
WITH A CRASH BREAKING ACROSS THE HORRIBLE MASS COMES DOWN   322 FOUR ZOAS 7   78
THIS NIGHT BEGINS AT LINE...THE FOLLOWING COMES IN AT THE   333A FOUR ZOAS 7B   *TITLE
  END
NOW COMES THE NIGHT OF CARNAGE NOW THE FLESH OF KINGS &   334 FOUR ZOAS 7B   45
  PRINCES
BUT URIZEN HIS MIGHTY RAGE COMES IN HERE TO QUENCHLESS RAGE   343B FOUR ZOAS 9   *PROSE
WHEN VOCAL MAY COMES DANCING FROM THE EAST AHANIA CAME   . .   362 FOUR ZOAS 9   194
THE WINTER COMES HE FOLDS HIS SLENDER BONES WITHOUT   377 FOUR ZOAS 9   761
  A MURMUR
[TILL SHE FORGIVES & COMES TO ME]   . . . .   415 MY SPECTRE/N   8
BUT SHE COMES TO THE MAN SHE LOVES   . . . .   426 MENTAL TRAVLER   49
UNCULTIVATED LIFE COMES AFTERWARDS FROM SATAN'S HIRELINGS   446C ANNO REYNOLDS   MARG
& OF WHATEVER COMES IN HIS WAY FROM EARLIEST CHILDHOOD   . .   455D ANNO REYNOLDS   MARG
HERE HE COMES AGAIN TO HIS CENTRAL FORM   . . . .   460B ANNO REYNOLDS   MARG
& COMES NOT AGAIN TILL ANOTHER IS BORN WITH IT   . . . .   470D ANNO REYNOLDS   MARG
WINTER COMES HE FOLDS HIS SLENDER BONES WITHOUT A MURMUR   513 MILTON 27   20
AND NONE CAN TELL HOW FROM SO SMALL A CENTER COMES SUCH   520 MILTON 31   47
  SWEETS
AND COMES FORTH IN THE MAJESTY OF BEAUTY EVERY FLOWER   . .   520 MILTON 31   58

```
                                                           PAGE      TITLE          LINE
COMES    (CONTINUED)
      FROM HENCE SHE COMES FORTH ON THE CHURCHES IN DELIGHT   . .  529 MILTON 38           24
      A COVERING FOR THEE TO DO THY WILL TILL ONE GREATER COMES   529 MILTON 38           31
      THEY OUGHT NOT WHEN IT COMES TO ANOTHER'S TURN    . . .  .  556 IF MEN ACT/N          2
      CHAUCER HIMSELF AND THE REEVE COMES AS CHAUCER HAS        567A DESC CAT 3         PROSE
         DESCRIBED
      THE DANCING FAWN FOR YOUR UGLY MAN NOW HE COMES TO HIS    579B DESC CAT 5         PROSE
         TRIAL
      CHAUCER HIMSELF & THE REEVE COMES AS CHAUCER HAS DESCRIBED   588C CHAUCER/N        PROSE
      CHAUCER HIMSELF AND THE REEVE COMES AS CHAUCER HAS        590A CHAUCER 2          PROSE
         DESCRIBED
      CHRIST COMES AS HE CAME AT FIRST TO DELIVER THOSE  . . .  615B V LAST JUDG/N      PROSE
      HE COMES TO DELIVER MAN THE [ FORGIVEN] ACCUSED     . . .  615B V LAST JUDG/N    *PROSE
      FIRST GOD ALMIGHTY COMES WITH A THUMP ON THE HEAD      . .  617A V LAST JUDG/N     PROSE
      THEN JESUS CHRIST COMES WITH A BALM TO HEAL IT   . . . .  617A V LAST JUDG/N      PROSE
      VALA COMES FROM THE FURNACE IN A CLOUD BUT WRETCHED LUVAH  626 JERUSALEM 7           38
      THE NIGHT FALLS THICK HAND COMES FROM ALBION IN HIS      729 JERUSALEM 84          20
         STRENGTH
      AND EASE COMES NEVER IN MY SIGHT  . . . . . . . . .  . .  818 HAPPINESS/L          60
      EXCEPT WHAT COMES TO HER FROM HEAVEN  . . . . . . . . .  . 818 HAPPINESS/L          62
      BUT IF SICKNESS COMES ALL IS UNPLEASANT  . . . . . . . .  820B LETTER 25         PROSE
      COMES ON I SAY CONTEMPTIBLE FOR IT MUST BE MANIFEST  . . .  828A LETTER 28        PROSE
      BUSINESS COMES IN & I SHALL BE AT EASE  . . . . . . . .  832C LETTER 32          PROSE
      & EMBRACE IT COMES THRO MR HOARE  . . . . . . . . .  . .  841B LETTER 41         PROSE
      THO NOT ITS EFFECTS WEAKNESS &C COMES ANOTHER TO HINDER MY  874D LETTER 80        PROSE
      MUST SUBMIT TO THE NECESSITY & BE PATIENT TILL WARM WEATHER  SUPP LETTER 81A      *PROSE
         COMES
COMEST    SEE COMST
      O MAN OF GOD SAID HE THOU COMEST FROM FAR   . . . . . .  403 SAMSON/PS           PROSE
      I EVERMORE WILL HOLD THEE WHEN THOU GOEST OUT OR COMEST IN  269 FOUR ZOAS 1         177
COMET
      ETERNALLY WANDRING A COMET AND SWIFT-FALLING FIRE . . .  141 FRENCH REVOLTN        160
      THE TERROR LIKE A COMET OR MORE LIKE THE PLANET RED    . .  197 AMERICA 5            2
      OF HELL BEHELD HIM IN A TRAIL OF LIGHT AS OF A COMET   . .  496 MILTON 15           19
COMETH
      THE HONIED DEW THAT COMETH ON WAKING DAY    . . . . . .    3 TO MORNING/PS          5
      BUT SPARE MY LIFE BUT HE KNOWS NOT THAT [THE] WINTER COMETH  276 FOUR ZOAS 1        456
         FAST
      AWAKE THE BRIDEGROOM COMETH I AWOKE TO SLEEP NO MORE  . .  355 FOUR ZOAS 8         541
      WHO COMETH IN THE CLOUDS WITH POWER & GREAT GLORY   . . .  444A LAST JUDGMNT/L     PROSE
      BUT THE TIME OF YOUR REFRESHING COMETH ONLY A LITTLE MOMENT  511 MILTON 25          45
COMETS
      LIKE BLAZING COMETS SCATTERING DEATH . . . . . . . .  .   13 GWIN KING/PS          83
      LIKE BLAZING COMETS IN THE SKY . . . . . . . . . .  . .   14 GWIN KING/PS         101
      THAT ONCE INCLOSD THE TERRIBLE WANDERING COMETS IN ITS   197 AMERICA 5         *    3
         SPHERE
      COMPULSIVE ROLLD THE COMETS AT HIS DREAD COMMAND THE DREARY  320 FOUR ZOAS 6       320
         WAY
      OR WHERE THE COMETS OF THE NIGHT OR STARS OF [ETERNAL]    358 FOUR ZOAS 9          40
         ASTERIAL DAY
COMFIELD
      OF WRITING BY MR COMFIELD & MY OWN    . . . . . . .  .  782A INSC UPCOTT          PROSE
COMFORT
      VOICES OF COMFORT ARE HEARD OVER THE COUCH OF DEATH  . . .  36D COUCH DEATH/PS    PROSE
      OR ANY COMFORT FIND   . . . . . . . . . . . . .  . .  .   56 HAIL MATRIM/IM        12
      COMFORT IN MORNING JOY IN THE NOON DAY   . . . . . .  .  125 LIT BLK BOY/SI        12
      ALONG THE VALES OF LEUTHA SEEKING FLOWERS TO COMFORT HER  189 V DAU ALBION 1        4
      SEEKING TO COMFORT VALA SHE WILL NOT BE COMFORTED   . . .  272 FOUR ZOAS 1         285
      [ TO ?LIGHT ?THE] BY NIGHT NOR DAY TO COMFORT HER  . . .  275 FOUR ZOAS 1     *   418
      THEY WEIGHD & ORDERD ALL & URIZEN [ ?IN ?COMFORT SAW]     287 FOUR ZOAS 2     *   259
         COMFORTED SAW
      THAT IN ETERNAL FIELDS IN COMFORT WANDERD WITH MY FLOCKS   301 FOUR ZOAS 4         130
      AS ON THE OUTSIDE OF EXISTENCE BUT LOOK BEHOLD TAKE COMFORT  330 FOUR ZOAS 7       414
      O SPECTRE OF URTHONA TAKE COMFORT O ENITHARMON    . . . .  330 FOUR ZOAS 7         417
      TO COMFORT ORC IN HIS DIRE SUFFERINGS LOOK MY FIRES ENLUME  331 FOUR ZOAS 7        444
         AFRESH
      AND PITYING COMFORT AS SHE SIGHD FORTH ON THE WIND THE    342 FOUR ZOAS 8          53
         SPECTRES
      AND PITYING COMFORT AS SHE SIGHD FORTH ON THE WIND THE    345 FOUR ZOAS 8         183
         SPECTRES
      AS BOTH ASTONISH & COMFORT ME & MINE . . . . . . . .  .  391D ANNO WATSON          MARG
      THEIR LIFE'S WHOLE COMFORT TO INTIRE SCORN & INJURY & DEATH  506 MILTON 23           2
      TO COMFORT OLOLON'S LAMENTATION FOR THEY SAID  . . . . .  523 MILTON 34            2
      ENTER MY COTTAGE COMFORT HER FOR SHE IS SICK WITH FATIGUE  527 MILTON 36           32
      OF COMFORT SPECTATORS STAND AT THE GATEWAY OF THE INN   . 567A DESC CAT 3         PROSE
      OF COMFORT SPECTATORS STAND AT THE GATEWAY OF THE INN   . 588D CHAUCER/N          PROSE
      OF COMFORT SPECTATORS STAND AT THE GATEWAY OF THE INN   . 590A CHAUCER 2          PROSE
      EXPENSE OF HIS COMFORT AS I HAVE OFTEN SEEN   . . . . .  616B V LAST JUDG/N       PROSE
      COMFORT THYSELF IN MY STRENGTH THE TIME WILL ARRIVE  . . .  626 JERUSALEM 7         54
      WHICH LOS WIPED OFF BUT COMFORT NONE COULD GIVE OR BEAM   630 JERUSALEM 10         61
         OF HOPE
      FOR COMFORT THERE THE SECRET FURNITURE OF JERUSALEM'S    632 JERUSALEM 12          40
         CHAMBER
      ME SOME COMFORT WHY DO YOU ALL STAND SILENT I ALONE  . . .  673 JERUSALEM 43        77
      BUT ALBION TURND AWAY REFUSING COMFORT  . . . . . .  . .  676 JERUSALEM 46         16
      I KNOW MY COTTAGE IS TOO NARROW FOR YOUR EASE & COMFORT   808B LETTER 19          PROSE
COMFORTABLE
      AND ALL THE SONGS OF BEULAH SOUNDED COMFORTABLE NOTES    . .  340 FOUR ZOAS 7B      296
      AND ALL THE SONGS OF BEULAH SOUNDED COMFORTABLE NOTES    . .  523 MILTON 34          1
      THAT SEEMS TO MAKE LIFE COMFORTABLE WITHOUT    . . . . .  812D LETTER 22          PROSE
      A VERY COMFORTABLE COACH & I MAY SAY I ACCOMPANIED HIM PART  869C LETTER 70        PROSE
      GONE AS THE FINE WEATHER IS VERY BENEFICIAL & COMFORTABLE  876A LETTER 83         PROSE
         TO ME
```

```
                                                      PAGE     TITLE          LINE
COMFORTED
   SEEKING TO COMFORT VALA SHE WILL NOT BE COMFORTED    . . .   272 FOUR ZOAS 1       285
   SEEKING TO COMFORT VALA SHE WILL NOT BE COMFORTED    . . .   272 FOUR ZOAS 1       285
   THEY WEIGHD & ORDERD ALL & URIZEN [?IN ?COMFORT SAW]          287 FOUR ZOAS 2    *  259
      COMFORTED SAW
   THE DAUGHTERS OF BEULAH SAW THE DIVINE VISION THEY WERE       304 FOUR ZOAS 4       250
      COMFORTED
   URTHONA'S SPECTRE IN PART MINGLING WITH HIM COMFORTED HIM     330 FOUR ZOAS 7       397
   ORC WAS COMFORTED IN THE DEEPS HIS SOUL REVIVD IN THEM  . .   332 FOUR ZOAS 7       478
   THE OFFSPRING OF THEIR CARE & PITY URTHONA'S SPECTRE WAS      332 FOUR ZOAS 7       485
      COMFORTED
   [ASTONISHD COMFORTED DELIGHTED THE DAUGHTERS OF BEULAH SAW]   342 FOUR ZOAS 8        45
   ASTONISHD COMFORTED DELIGHTED IN NOTES OF RAPTUROUS EXTACY    342 FOUR ZOAS 8        46
   IN SLEEP AND THE SEVEN COMFORTED AND SUPPORTED HIM  . . .     496 MILTON 15          7
   IN HER DARKNESS & WAS COMFORTED YET STILL SHE DIVIDED AWAY    639 JERUSALEM 17      49
   AND BE COMFORTED O JERUSALEM IN THE VISIONS OF JEHOVAH        694 JERUSALEM 61       2
      ELOHIM
   LOS SAW & WAS COMFORTED AT HIS FURNACES UTTERING THUS HIS     727 JERUSALEM 82      80
      VOICE
COMFORTER
   TO SEND THE COMFORTER OR DESIRE    . . . . . . . .   150B MARRIAGE HH 5    PROSE
   BUT THOU MY SON GLORIOUS IN BRIGHTNESS COMFORTER OF THARMAS   298 FOUR ZOAS 4       26
   BUT SWEET LOVE IS THE COMFORTER OF NIGHT   . . . . .   436 WILLIAM BOND        48
   IN VAIN AND IN GILEAD FOR A PHYSICIAN AND A COMFORTER  . .   720 JERUSALEM 79      12
COMFORTERS
   WOMEN THE COMFORTERS OF MEN BECOME THE TORMENTERS            712D JERUSALEM 72    PROSE
      & PUNISHERS
COMFORTING
   HAH SHALL I STILL SURVIVE WHENCE CAME THAT SWEET             368 FOUR ZOAS 9      422
      & COMFORTING VOICE
   ALWAYS COMFORTING THE REMEMBRANCE THE FLOORS HUMILITY  . .   632 JERUSALEM 12      36
   COMFORTING SOUNDS OF LOVE & HARMONY & ON THY FEET   . . .   731 JERUSALEM 86      30
COMFORTLESS
   ALONE AND COMFORTLESS . . . . . . . . . . .    35D COUCH DEATH/PS   PROSE
COMFORTS
   FROM WHENCE COMFORTS HAVE INCREASD    . . . . . .      9 MAD SONG/PS        22
   COMFORTS INTO A PRESENT SORROW AND A NIGHT OF PAIN   . . .   192 V DAU ALBION 4     7
   WILT THOU BRING COMFORTS ON THY WINGS AND DEWS AND HONEY     192 V DAU ALBION 4    10
      AND BALM
   ETHINTHUS THOU ART SWEET AS COMFORTS TO MY FAINTING SOUL     243 EUROPE 14          4
   [AND COMFORTS SHALL DESCEND FROM HEAVEN INTO THY DARKNING    292 FOUR ZOAS 3       29
      CLOUDS]
   HE COMFORTS & HEALS & CALLS THEM FRIENDS   . . . . .   755 EV GOSPEL(E)/N     90
COMING   SEE A-COMING
   I FEEL IT COMING UPON ME SO I STRIVE AGAINST IT   . . . .    22 EDW THIRD/PS 3     62
   IN COMING WITH HIM AND IN FIGHTING FOR HIM  . . . . .    28D EDW THIRD/PS 4   PROSE
   WHEN STEELYARD THE LAWGIVER COMING IN STALKING WITH  . . .    46A ISLAND MOON 1   PROSE
   [& THE THREE PHILOSOPHERS (COMING) QUID THE CYNIC SIPSOP]     46B ISLAND MOON 2  *PROSE
   THEN SCOPPRELL & MISS GITTIPIN COMING IN   . . . . .    52D ISLAND MOON 8   PROSE
   A TERROR COMING FROM THE SOUTH THE EAGLE & HAWK FLED AWAY    358 FOUR ZOAS 9       62
   THE TIMES REVOLVE THE TIME IS COMING WHEN ALL THESE         362 FOUR ZOAS 9      208
      DELIGHTS
   WHAT FLAMES ARE THESE COMING FROM THE SOUTH . . .   . . .   364 FOUR ZOAS 9      262
   TO MEET THE LORD COMING TO JUDGMENT BUT THE FLAMES REPELLD   364 FOUR ZOAS 9      288
      THEM
   WHERE IS THE LAMB OF GOD WHERE IS THE PROMISE OF HIS COMING   501 MILTON 19        50
   JESUS THE SAVIOUR APPEARD COMING IN THE CLOUDS OF OLOLON     505 MILTON 21        60
   LIKE THE BLACK STORM COMING OUT OF CHAOS BEYOND THE STARS    507 MILTON 23        21
   WE FORM THE MUNDANE EGG THAT SPECTRES COMING BY FURY OR      511 MILTON 25        42
      AMITY
   FOR THE LORD'S COMING THAT JERUSALEM MAY OVERSPREAD ALL      511 MILTON 25        55
      NATIONS
   ALL BEULAH WEPT FOR THEY SAW THE LORD COMING IN THE CLOUDS   519 MILTON 31        10
   AS ONE AWAKEND IN THE NIGHT THEY SAW THE LORD COMING   . .   519 MILTON 31        15
   SATAN HEARD COMING IN A CLOUD WITH TRUMPETS & FLAMING FIRE   530 MILTON 38        50
   COMING IN A CLOUD WITH TRUMPETS & WITH FIERY FLAME   . . .   531 MILTON 39        23
   COMING TO JUDGMENT AMONG HIS SAINTS & THROWING OFF   . . .  606A V LAST JUDG/N   PROSE
   COMING IN THE CLOUDS WITH POWER & GREAT GLORY . . . . .   609D V LAST JUDG/N   PROSE
   WHO SHALL MEET THE LORD COMING IN THE CLOUDS   . . . . .  610B V LAST JUDG/N   PROSE
   ALBION'S WESTERN GATE IS CLOSD HIS DEATH IS COMING APACE    675 JERUSALEM 45      17
   SO JESUS SPOKE THE COVERING CHERUB COMING ON IN DARKNESS    743 JERUSALEM 96      17
   A VOICE IS HEARD COMING ON  . . . . . . . . .  780A GHOST ABEL 1    PROSE
   THE IMMENSE FLOOD OF GRECIAN LIGHT & GLORY WHICH IS COMING   797C LETTER 10      PROSE
   PLACE YET I DO NOT REPENT OF COMING ON A THOUSAND ACCOUNTS   811C LETTER 22      PROSE
   OF REAL CONSEQUENCE I HAVE ACCOMPLISHD BY COMING   . . .   812A LETTER 22      PROSE
   OBTAIND BY COMING HERE FOR I SHOULD NEVER HAVE KNOWN  . .   820A LETTER 25      PROSE
   TO PREVENT THE TROUBLE OF YOUR COMING THRO CURIOSITY TO SEE  876C LETTER 84      PROSE
COMINGLE
   HE WHO WILL NOT COMINGLE IN LOVE MUST BE ADJOIND BY HATE     703 JERUSALEM 66      56
   SURROUNDED BY THEIR CHILDREN IF THEY EMBRACE & COMINGLE      733 JERUSALEM 88       6
COMINGLING
   IN MIGHTY & MYSTERIOUS COMINGLING ENEMY WITH ENEMY   . . .   529 MILTON 38         3
   TREMBLING THEN IN ONE COMINGLING IN ETERNAL TEARS   . . .   642 JERUSALEM 19      46
   DIVIDING THE MASCULINE & FEMININE FOR THE COMINGLING  . .   690 JERUSALEM 58      19
   COMINGLING WITH LUVAH & WITH THE SEPULCHER OF LUVAH  . . .   736 JERUSALEM 90      26
COMINGLINGS
   EMBRACES ARE COMINGLINGS FROM THE HEAD EVEN TO THE FEET      708 JERUSALEM 69      43
COMMAND
   AND GIVE COMMAND AND LIGHTNING HAS FLASHED  . . . . . .    22 EDW THIRD/PS 3     27
   MOST HAPPY HAVING SUCH COMMAND THE MAN  . . . . . . .    23 EDW THIRD/PS 3     78
   WORTHY THE HIGH COMMAND THAT HEAVEN AND YOU   . . . . .    23 EDW THIRD/PS 3     83
   THEN TIRIEL FROWND & ANSWERD DID I NOT COMMAND YOU SAYING   103 TIRIEL 3          36
```

```
                                                            PAGE    TITLE        LINE
COMMAND    (CONTINUED)
      YET THOU SHALT LEAD ME LEAD ME I COMMAND TO HAR & HEVA      107 TIRIEL 6           22
      HOWLING AND GIVING THE DARK COMMAND . . . . . . . .   .   135 FRENCH REVOLTN      24
      . . . THE COMMAND OF HEAVEN IS UPON THEE    . . . . . . . 141 FRENCH REVOLTN     153
      THEN DO THOU COMMAND O KING . . . . . . . . . . . . .   . 141 FRENCH REVOLTN     154
      . . . RISE MONARCH OF FRANCE COMMAND ME AND I WILL LEAD   142 FRENCH REVOLTN     172
      . . . THE DUKE OF BURGUNDY DELIVERS THE KING'S COMMAND  . . 145 FRENCH REVOLTN    247
      GO COMMAND YONDER TOWER . . . . .  . . . . . . . . .   . 145 FRENCH REVOLTN     249
      THE NATION'S ASSEMBLY COMMAND . . . . . . . . . . .   . . 147 FRENCH REVOLTN     285
      . . . TILL THE NATION COMMAND RETURN . . . . . . . . .   . 147 FRENCH REVOLTN    286
      OR POSSESSOR OF THE COMMAND OF THE HEAVENLY HOST IS CALLD  150A MARRIAGE HH 5   PROSE
            THE DEVIL
      AND HEARD THE VOICE OF ALBION'S ANGEL GIVE THE THUNDEROUS  201 AMERICA 14          3
            COMMAND
      ONE COMMAND ONE JOY ONE DESIRE . . . . . . . . . . .   . 224 URIZEN 4           38
      MY MASTER I AM YOURS COMMAND ME FOR I MUST OBEY . . . .   237 EUROPE INTRO       12
      RAVISHD AWAY IN NIGHT MY STRONG COMMAND SHALL BE OBEYD  . . 278 FOUR ZOAS 1      501
      DO THEY NOT BOW THEIR BRIGHT HEADS AT THY VOICE AT THY    291 FOUR ZOAS 3          6
            COMMAND
      MUST GROW UP TO COMMAND HIS PRINCE . . . . . . .  . .   . 292 FOUR ZOAS 3        19
      COMPULSIVE ROLLD THE COMETS AT HIS DREAD COMMAND THE DREARY 320 FOUR ZOAS 6      320
            WAY
      SLOW ROLL THE MASSY GLOBES AT HIS COMMAND & SLOW OERWHEEL  320 FOUR ZOAS 6       323
      KNEAD BREAD OF SORROW BY MY STERN COMMAND FOR I AM GOD  . . 322 FOUR ZOAS 7       93
      OF ALL THIS DREADFUL RUIN RISE O DAUGHTERS AT MY STERN    322 FOUR ZOAS 7         94
            COMMAND
      I WILL COMMAND MY WINDS & THEY SHALL SCATTER THEM OR CALL  334 FOUR ZOAS 7B        54
      UPON THE WHEELS THE STORMY SEAS HOWL AT HIS DREAD COMMAND  378 FOUR ZOAS 9       810
      SO MANY THOUSANDS UNDER PRETENCE OF A COMMAND . . . . .   387B ANNO WATSON      MARG
      CONSIDERED AS AN ARBITRARY COMMAND OF THE AGENT  . . . .  391C ANNO WATSON      MARG
      ALL OTHER CODES GIVEN UNDER PRETENCE OF DIVINE COMMAND  .  393C ANNO WATSON      MARG
      INTO CORPOREAL COMMAND WHEREBY HUMAN SACRIFICE . . . .   578A DESC CAT 5        PROSE
      DESIST NOT FROM THINE OWN WILL & OBEY NOT MY STERN COMMAND 627 JERUSALEM 8        12
      I WILL COMMAND THE CLOUD TO GIVE THEE FOOD & THE HARD ROCK 696 JERUSALEM 62       25
      THE RIVER SEVERN STAYD HIS COURSE AT MY COMMAND . . . .   720 JERUSALEM 79       33
      MY FATHER GAVE TO ME COMMAND TO MURDER ALBION . . . . .   722 JERUSALEM 80       16
      I CANNOT GO BEYOND THE COMMAND OF THE LORD . . . . . .   792C LETTER 4         PROSE
      COMMISSION ME TO ANSWER HIM WHATEVER YOU COMMAND . . .  . 857B LETTER 54       PROSE
COMMANDED
      YOU SEE THE PARENTS CURSE NOW LEAD ME WHERE I HAVE       107 TIRIEL 6           12
            COMMANDED
      FOR THE CHERUB WITH HIS FLAMING SWORD IS HEREBY COMMANDED 154B MARRIAGE HH 14   PROSE
      THAT MOCK HIM WHO COMMANDED THIS WHAT GOD WHAT ANGEL   . . 200 AMERICA 11          7
      AND I COMMANDED SPRINGS TO RISE FOR HER IN THE BLACK DESART 282 FOUR ZOAS 2       88
      AND I COMMANDED THE GREAT DEEP TO HIDE HER IN HIS HAND  .  282 FOUR ZOAS 2        91
      I AM SET HERE A KING OF TROUBLE COMMANDED HERE TO SERVE   292 FOUR ZOAS 3         16
      AND HE COMMANDED HIS SONS FOUND A CENTER IN THE DEEP   .  333 FOUR ZOAS 7B        18
      THEN URIZEN COMMANDED & THEY BROUGHT THE SEED OF MEN   .  365 FOUR ZOAS 9        316
      I HAVE BEEN COMMANDED FROM HELL NOT TO PRINT THIS   . .   383C ANNO WATSON      MARG
      WHEN GOD COMMANDED THIS HAND TO WRITE  . . . . . . . .   419 I SAW A MONK/N     28
      WHEN GOD COMMANDED THIS HAND TO WRITE   . . . . . . .    430 GREY MONK          13
      I WAS COMMANDED BY MY SPIRITUAL FRIENDS TO BEAR ALL TO   825D LETTER 27       PROSE
            BE SILENT
COMMANDING
      SENT ROUND HIS HERALDS SECRETLY COMMANDING TO DEPART   . . 279 FOUR ZOAS 1      536
      COMMANDING ALL THE WORK WITH CARE & POWER & SEVERITY  . . 283 FOUR ZOAS 2       134
      THE HEAVENS COMMANDING  . . . . . . . . . . . . .   . . . 805 TO BUTTS/L        48
COMMANDMENTS
      GIVEN HIS SANCTION TO THE LAW OF TEN COMMANDMENTS   . . . 158B MARRIAGE HH 22   PROSE
      HIS SANCTION TO THE LAW OF TEN COMMANDMENTS  . . . . .   158C MARRIAGE HH 22   PROSE
      NO VIRTUE CAN EXIST WITHOUT BREAKING THESE TEN COMMANDMENTS 158C MARRIAGE HH 22 PROSE
COMMANDS
      [AND ALL IN ORDER SIT WAITING THE CHIEF CHANTER'S COMMANDS] 59 HOLY THURS/IM      8
      THRO THE WASTE WILDERNESS HE PROMULGATES HIS TEN COMMANDS 159D SONG LIBERTY     PROSE
      THE FIERY JOY THAT URIZEN PERVERTED TO TEN COMMANDS   . . 198 AMERICA 8           3
      & COMMANDS THAT IT SHALL NOT BE DONE  . . . . . . . .   . 388B ANNO WATSON      MARG
      THE PARDONER THE AGE'S KNAVE WHO ALWAYS COMMANDS . . .  . 570A DESC CAT 3       PROSE
      THAT THOU CALLEST THY CHILDREN LO THE LAW OF GOD COMMANDS  629 JERUSALEM 10       38
      MOSES COMMANDS SHE BE STONED TO DEATH  . . . . . . .    . 754 EV GOSPEL(E)/N      9
      DIRECTIONS AND COMMANDS CONCERNING IT FOR HE WISHES TO SET 858C LETTER 55       PROSE
COMMENCD
      . . . THEN THE FRENCH REVOLUTION COMMENCD IN THICK CLOUDS  799 TO FLAXMAN/L       10
COMMENCE
      WHICH WILL COMMENCE A SERIES OF SUBJECTS FROM THE BIBLE   207C PRSPECTUS 1793   PROSE
      TO COMMENCE THEIR TASK OF EACH TELLING A TALE IN THEIR   566D DESC CAT 3        PROSE
            ORDER
      TO COMMENCE THEIR TASK OF EACH TELLING A TALE IN THEIR   589D CHAUCER 2         PROSE
            ORDER
      I NOW HAVE IT IN MY POWER TO COMMENCE PUBLICATION WITH  . 820A LETTER 25        PROSE
      IN THE SPRING TO COMMENCE PUBLISHER & HE HAS OFFERD ME  . 820B LETTER 25        PROSE
      HE PROPOSES TO COMMENCE WITH YOUR ASSISTANCE HE CAN AFFORD 841C LETTER 41       PROSE
      ON ACCOUNT OF TEACHING YOUR SON AT...TO COMMENCE THIS DAY  SUPP LETTER 56A     *PROSE
COMMENCED
      COMMENCED A NEW LIFE OF INDUSTRY TO DO CREDIT TO  . . .   804B LETTER 16        PROSE
COMMENCES
      THAT THIS DIRE STATE COMMENCES I BEGAN THE DREADFUL STATE  330 FOUR ZOAS 7       404
      THE REIGN OF LITERATURE & THE ARTS COMMENCES . . . . .   810D LETTER 21        PROSE
COMMENDATION
      IN YOUR COMMENDATION & MORE AND MORE OF A GRECIAN   . . . 798A LETTER 10        PROSE
COMMENDATIONS
      WHILE YOU EXALT ME BY SUCH DISTINGUISHING COMMENDATIONS I  822B LETTER 26       PROSE
```

```
                                                    PAGE    TITLE        LINE
COMMENDS
     IN VERY GREAT FORWARDNESS PARKER COMMENDS IT HIGHLY  . . . 849A LETTER 45      PROSE
COMMENSE
     TO COMMENSE THEIR TASK OF EACH TELLING A TALE IN THEIR    588C CHAUCER/N      PROSE
         ORDER
COMMENT
     TO CONSIDER THIS TO ALL ETERNITY WILL BE COMMENT ENOUGH   787A ANNO THORNTON  MARG
COMMENTATORS
     ANOTHER ARGUMENT IS THAT ALL THE COMMENTATORS . . . . . . 390C ANNO WATSON    MARG
COMMERCE
     HIS NATIVE SHORE AND SEES COMMERCE FLY ROUND  . . . . .    19 EDW THIRD/PS 2     9
     SAY LORDS SHOULD NOT OUR THOUGHTS BE FIRST TO COMMERCE . .  19 EDW THIRD/PS 2    16
     AND ENGLAND IS THE LAND FAVOURD BY COMMERCE   . . . . . .  19 EDW THIRD/PS 2    30
     FOR COMMERCE THO THE CHILD OF AGRICULTURE  . . . . . . .   19 EDW THIRD/PS 2    31
     FIRST TRADES & COMMERCE SHIPS & ARMED VESSELS HE BUILDED  333 FOUR ZOAS 7B      12
         LABORIOUS
     AND COMMERCE SETTLES ON EVERY TREE  . . . . . . . . . . . 452 ANNO REYNOLDS      2
     BUT ALLAMANDA CALLD ON EARTH COMMERCE IS THE CULTIVATED   514 MILTON 27         42
         LAND
     ROUND WHICH THE FIENDS OF COMMERCE [ROAR] SMILE  . . . .  557 ART HAS LOST/N    14
     SUITED TO THE PURPOSES OF COMMERCE NO DOUBT   . . . . .  593D PUB ADDRESS/N   PROSE
     FOR COMMERCE CANNOT ENDURE INDIVIDUAL MERIT   . . . . .  593D PUB ADDRESS/N   PROSE
     COMMERCE IS SO FAR FROM BEING BENEFICIAL TO ARTS OR  . . 593D PUB ADDRESS/N   PROSE
     A RELIGION OF CHASTITY FORMING A COMMERCE TO SELL LOVES  708 JERUSALEM 69       34
     MEER NECESSARIES OR AT (LEAST) A COMMERCE OF THE LOWEST  798C LETTER 10       PROSE
     INTO THE VERY EARTH BY THE FOOTSTEPS OF THE FIENDS       849D LETTER 47       PROSE
         OF COMMERCE
COMMERCIAL
     A SEA CAPTAIN IN COMMERCIAL NATIONS  . . . . . . . . .   575D DESC CAT 3      PROSE
     EMPIRES FLOURISH TILL THEY BECOME COMMERCIAL  . . . . .  594A PUB ADDRESS/N   PROSE
     IN A COMMERCIAL NATION IMPOSTORS ARE ABROAD   . . . . .  601C PUB ADDRESS/N   PROSE
COMMISSION
     THEN HE SHOULD NOT DOUBT OF HAVING A NATIONAL COMMISSION  566A DESC CAT 2      PROSE
     COMMISSION TO (EXECUTE) FOR YOU BUT SHALL NOT BE . . . . 826D LETTER 28      *PROSE
     COMMISSION ME TO ANSWER HIM WHATEVER YOU COMMAND  . . .  857B LETTER 54       PROSE
COMMISSIOND
     COMMISSIOND TO THIS FATAL FIELD OF CRESSY  . . . . . .    26 EDW THIRD/PS 3   223
COMMISSIONS
     WITH ANY OTHER OF YOUR COMMISSIONS BUT HOPE NOW I HAVE  . . 804A LETTER 16      PROSE
COMMIT
     MY SON A VINE WHICH I COMMIT UNTO  . . . . . . . . . .    26 EDW THIRD/PS 3   211
     I SAID IF YOU PLEASE WE WILL COMMIT OURSELVES TO THIS VOID 155D MARRIAGE HH 17 PROSE
     WHAT TRANSGRESSIONS I COMMIT  . . . . . . . . . . . .    417 MY SPECTR AD/N     5
     TILL THEY HAVE HAD PUNISHMENT ENOUGH TO MAKE THEM COMMIT  707 JERUSALEM 69      27
         CRIMES
     PROPERTY OF AN ASTROLOGER & TO COMMIT HIM TO PRISON THE MAN 865A LETTER 62     PROSE
COMMITTED
     HE COMMITTED ON FLESH A WHOREDOM  . . . . . . . . . . .    50 WHEN CORRUP/IM    3
     MY PARENT POWER SATAN HAS COMMITTED THIS TRANSGRESSION  . . 492 MILTON 11       36
     WITHOUT WHICH PERJURY I COULD NOT HAVE BEEN COMMITTED  . 827D LETTER 28       PROSE
     IS THE ORIGIN OF ALL OFFENCES COMMITTED AGAINST ME IF I  828C LETTER 28       PROSE
         HAVE
COMMITTING
     BUT ONCE ALAS COMMITTING A MISTAKE   . . . . . . . . .   536 AND HIS LEGS/N    10
COMMODITIES
     COMMODITIES OF USURY CAN IT BE . . . . . . . . . . . .   409C ANNO BACON      MARG
COMMODITY
     [WHO CAN SELL A GOOD FOR NOTHING COMMODITY FOR A GREAT    595B PUB ADDRESS/N   PROSE
         PRICE]
COMMON
     BISHOP WILLIAM DAGWORTH'S MAN PETER BLUNT A COMMON        17C EDW THIRD/PS    TITLE
         SOLDIER
     A DEED WHICH IS NOT COMMON  . . . . . . . . . . . . . .    50 WHEN CORRUP/IM   20
     BUT COMMON IN ANCIENT . . . . . . . . . . . . . . . .     94A ANNO SWED LOVE  MARG
     IT WAS A COMMON OPINION IN THE COURT OF QUEEN ELIZABETH  397B ANNO BACON      MARG
     OR EVEN OF COMMON CAPACITY I CANNOT  . . . . . . . . .   404B ANNO BACON      MARG
     TO MAKE [EITHER SENSE OR] MEER COMMON HONESTY  . . . .   543 TO ROYL ACAD/N     9
     COMMON RANK IN LIFE OR ATTENDANTS ON THOSE WHO WERE SO  . 568C DESC CAT 3     PROSE
     HIS FRIEND H(HOPPNER) WHO HAS CALLED HIS "A COMMON SCENE" 574D DESC CAT 3    *PROSE
     OPEN PROFESSIONS OF FRIENDSHIP ARE COMMON ENOUGH  . . . . 592C PUB ADDRESS/N  PROSE
     [THAT PAINTED AS WELL AS SCULPTURED MONUMENTS WERE COMMON] 601A PUB ADDRESS/N *PROSE
     TO THE COMMON OPINION AS I MYSELF AM ALSO INFECTED WITH IT 614D V LAST JUDG/N PROSE
     THE WHOLE BUSINESS OF MAN IS THE ARTS & ALL THINGS COMMON 777C INSC LAOCOON   PROSE
     OR TAX UPON WHAT IS COMMON TO ALL IN THY KINGDOM  . . . . 788A ANNO THORNTON  MARG
     WE HAVE ALL THINGS COMMON [ALL THINGS COMMON ] AMONG US  788B ANNO THORNTON  * MARG
     A ONE WITH ORDINARY COMMON SENSE CAN BE INFERIOR TO A BOY 830A LETTER 30      PROSE
     SUBJECT OF PAINTING AND HENCE IT IS SO COMMON TO HEAR  . 864C LETTER 61       PROSE
COMMONS
     FOR THE COMMONS CONVENE IN THE HALL OF THE NATION . . .  134 FRENCH REVOLTN    16
     FOR THE COMMONS CONVENE IN THE HALL OF THE NATION . . .  136 FRENCH REVOLTN    54
     WHERE GEORGE THE THIRD HOLDS COUNCIL & HIS LORDS & COMMONS 204 AMERICA CANC B    9
         MEET
     HOUSES OF COMMONS & HOUSES OF LORDS APPEAR TO ME TO BE   600A PUB ADDRESS/N   PROSE
         FOOLS
COMMUND
     SHE COMMUND WITH ORC IN SECRET SHE HID HIM WITH THE FLAX  356 FOUR ZOAS 8      607
COMMUNED
     SO LOS IN SECRET WITH HIMSELF COMMUNED & ENITHARMON HEARD 639 JERUSALEM 17     48
COMMUNICATION
     EXCUSE THIS COMMUNICATION OF SENTIMENTS WHICH I FELT  . . 798C LETTER 10      PROSE
COMMUNING
     COMMUNING WITH THE SPECTRE WHO REJOICD ALONG THE VALE  . . 319 FOUR ZOAS 6    303
```

```
                                                           PAGE      TITLE            LINE
COMMUNING    (CONTINUED)
    COMMUNING WITH THE SERPENT OF ORC IN DARK DISSIMULATION   343 FOUR ZOAS 8          96
COMMUNION
    DENY A CONSCIENCE IN MAN & THE COMMUNION OF SAINTS & ANGELS  741 JERUSALEM 93       22
    DIVINE UNION DERIDING AND DENYING IMMEDIATE COMMUNION  . . 776D INSC LAOCOON      PROSE
    ARE ORGANIZED BY DIVINE PROVIDENCE FOR SPIRITUAL COMMUNION  813A LETTER 22       *PROSE
COMMUNITIES
    OF ADVANCING FINE ART IN PROTESTANT COMMUNITIES   . . . . 601B PUB ADDRESS/N     PROSE
COMPACTNESS
    SUBORDINATION STRENGTH IS COMPACTNESS NOT EXTENT NOR BULK  580B DESC CAT 5        PROSE
COMPANIED
    O DREAMS OF DEATH THE HUMAN FORM DISSOLVING COMPANIED   . . 373 FOUR ZOAS 9        595
COMPANIES
    SEATED IN COMPANIES THEY SIT WITH RADIANCE ALL THEIR OWN    59 HOLY THURS/IM        6
    SEATED IN COMPANIES THEY SIT WITH RADIANCE ALL THEIR OWN   122 HOLY THURS/SI        6
    THE BLESSED WHO IN VARIOUS JOYFUL COMPANIES   . . . . . 609D V LAST JUDG/N       PROSE
COMPANION
    IT IS THE GOD IN ALL THAT IS OUR COMPANION & FRIEND  . . .  87A ANNO LAVATER       MARG
    I CAST AWAY MY STAFF THE KIND COMPANION OF MY TRAVEL  . .  101 TIRIEL 2            30
    I NOW ASKED MY COMPANION WHICH WAS MY ETERNAL LOT  . . . 156B MARRIAGE HH 17     PROSE
    THARMAS REPLIED ART THOU URTHONA MY FRIEND MY OLD COMPANION  300 FOUR ZOAS 4       111
    AWAKING OF ALBION OUR FRIEND AND ANCIENT COMPANION   . . . 511 MILTON 25           62
    NUMBER II ITS COMPANION  . . . . . . . . . . . . . . 565A DESC CAT 2            TITLE
    HER COMPANION AND HER THREE PRIESTS WERE NO DOUBT ALL   . 568C DESC CAT 3         PROSE
    HIS COMPANION THE SOMPNOUR IS ALSO A DEVIL  . . . . . . 570A DESC CAT 3          PROSE
    OR COULD MAKE A FRIEND & COMPANION OF ONE OF THESE IMAGES  611A V LAST JUDG/N     PROSE
      OF
    EVEN IN THIS WORLD BY IT I AM THE COMPANION OF ANGELS  . . 797B LETTER 9          PROSE
    COMPANION FROM ETERNITY IN THE DIVINE BOSOM IN   . . . . 802C LETTER 14          PROSE
    COMPANION TO MY DRAWING OF THE HEAD OF COWPER YOU  . . . 855D LETTER 53          PROSE
COMPANIONS
    . . . ARE HIS COMPANIONS HARMLESS THEY BREATHE   . . . . 136 FRENCH REVOLTN        41
    THE SEA ENCOMPASSES HIM & MONSTERS OF THE DEEP ARE HIS    301 FOUR ZOAS 4         134
      COMPANIONS
    TO KNOW SWEET SCIENCE & TO DO WITH SIMPLE COMPANIONS   . . 301 FOUR ZOAS 4         147
    ENITHARMON'S MOONY SPACE & IN IT SATAN & HIS COMPANIONS    351 FOUR ZOAS 8         395
    HIS HORSES ARE MAD HIS HARROW CONFOUNDED HIS COMPANIONS    488 MILTON 8            18
      ENRAGD
    ALL YOU MY FRIENDS & BROTHERS ALL YOU MY BELOVED          673 JERUSALEM 43         74
      COMPANIONS
COMPANY
    TO ASK WHICH IS THE FAVOUR OF YOUR COMPANY  . . . . . .  20 EDW THIRD/PS 2        44
    THIS WAS THE SITUATION OF THIS IMPROVING COMPANY WHEN  . . 44C ISLAND MOON 1      PROSE
    WAS PREPARED TO GIVE A FORMAL ANSWER TO THE COMPANY  . .  45B ISLAND MOON 1      PROSE
    SO ENGROSSED HIS MIND THAT HE DID NOT SALUTE THE COMPANY   46A ISLAND MOON 1      PROSE
    NOW HERE SAID MISS GITTIPIN I NEVER SAW SUCH COMPANY  . .  52D ISLAND MOON 8      PROSE
    HE ADDRESSD THE COMPANY IN THESE WORDS  . . . . . . . .  53B ISLAND MOON 8      PROSE
    [ALWAYS SPOILS GOOD COMPANY IN THIS MANNER & ITS A SHAME]   57A ISLAND MOON 9      PROSE
    TILL THE COMPANY WERE TIRED & INSISTED ON THE LAWGIVER  .  57D ISLAND MOON 9      PROSE
    HERE THEY GAVE A SHOUT & THE COMPANY BROKE UP  . . . . .  58B ISLAND MOON 9      PROSE
    O WHAT SWEET COMPANY  . . . . . . . . . . . . . . . . 124 SCHOOL BOY/SI         5
    MANY A WOFUL COMPANY & MANY ON CLOUDS & WATERS   . . . . 363 FOUR ZOAS 9         242
    HE STATES ABSURDITIES IN COMPANY WITH TRUTHS & CALLS BOTH  474A ANNO REYNOLDS     MARG
      ABSURD
    WHEN THE JOLLY COMPANY ARE JUST QUITTING THE TABARDE INN   566C DESC CAT 3        PROSE
    CHARACTERS LIKELY TO RIDE IN COMPANY ALL BEING ABOVE THE   568C DESC CAT 3        PROSE
    APPEARS DELIGHTED TO RIDE IN HIS COMPANY   . . . . . . 570C DESC CAT 3          PROSE
    MAKE HIS WHOLE COMPANY HIMSELF INCLUDED THIRTY-ONE   . . 571D DESC CAT 3         PROSE
    BUT HE SAYS THERE WAS BUT NINE AND TWENTY IN HIS COMPANY   571D DESC CAT 3        PROSE
    OF HIS COMPANY AND ARE NOT THROWN TOGETHER IN THE RANDOM   575A DESC CAT 3        PROSE
    WHEN THE JOLLY COMPANY ARE JUST QUITTING THE TABARDE INN   588B CHAUCER/N         PROSE
    WHEN THE JOLLY COMPANY ARE JUST QUITTING THE TABARDE INN   589C CHAUCER 2         PROSE
    FROM OUR COMPANY CONTINUALLY & RECIEVING TRUTH OR WISE MEN  613A V LAST JUDG/N    PROSE
    INTO OUR COMPANY CONTINUALLY  . . . . . . . . . . . . 613A V LAST JUDG/N       PROSE
    O NO NO I SEE AN INNUMERABLE COMPANY OF THE HEAVENLY HOST   617B V LAST JUDG/N    PROSE
    SELECTED FOR HIS COMPANY  . . . . . . . . . . . . . . 757 EV GOSPEL(I)/N        46
    IN GOOD COMPANY  . . . . . . . . . . . . . . . . . . 781D INSC UPCOTT         PROSE
    IF I AM WRONG I AM WRONG IN GOOD COMPANY I HAD   . . . . 793A LETTER 5           PROSE
COMPARATIVE
    SOFTNESS IS PRODUCED ALONE BY COMPARATIVE STRENGTH &   . 457B ANNO REYNOLDS      MARG
COMPARATIVELY
    STAMINA OF HIS MAKE COMPARATIVELY LITTLE AND HIS JOINTS    580A DESC CAT 5        PROSE
COMPARD
    IN HAPPINESS COMPARD WITH YE   . . . . . . . . . . .  54 PHEBE DREST/IM        10
COMPARE
    MAN BY HIS REASONING POWER CAN ONLY COMPARE & JUDGE  . . .  97A NAT RELIGION 1   PROSE
    COMPARE THE PRINTS OF BARTOLOUZZI WOOLETT STRANGE &C   . 592A PUB ADDRESS/N     *PROSE
    COMPARE THE MODERN ART WITH THE ART AS IT EXISTED  . . . 592A PUB ADDRESS/N      PROSE
    I WILL NOT REASON & COMPARE MY BUSINESS IS TO CREATE   . . 629 JERUSALEM 10       21
COMPARED
    [SAVANTS WHO COMPARED [THE PLAIN UNPAINTED]]  . . . . . 601A PUB ADDRESS/N     *PROSE
COMPARING
    ON COMPARING COWPER WITH WASHINGTON MUST ASSERT   . . . . 846D LETTER 44         PROSE
    I NOW SEND IS TWENTY-FIVE GUINEAS EACH ON COMPARING THEM   853D LETTER 52        PROSE
    [?WHY SHOUD ?COMPARING GREAT MASTERS ?BE ?DONE PAINFULLY]  SUPP ANNO REYNOLDS   * MARG
COMPARISON
    THE PAINTER COURTS COMPARISON WITH HIS COMPETITORS   . . 572C DESC CAT 3         PROSE
    & I AM SURE [OF THE] RESULT OF [THE] THIS COMPARISON WILL  592A PUB ADDRESS/N    *PROSE
      BE
    THE COMPARISON IS EASILY MADE & THE COPY DETECTED   . . 598A PUB ADDRESS/N      PROSE
    FROM THE COMPARISON IN EITHER RELIEF OR STRENGTH OF COLOUR 598D PUB ADDRESS/N    PROSE
    I COURT THE COMPARISON & FEAR NOT THE RESULT BUT NOT IN   598D PUB ADDRESS/N     PROSE
      A DARK CORNER
```

		PAGE	TITLE	LINE

COMPARISON   (CONTINUED)
    TO MAKE THE COMPARISON HONESTLY . . . . 602A PUB ADDRESS/N   PROSE
    NONE THERE IS NO COMPARISON BETWEEN OUR NECESSARY   873C LETTER 77   PROSE
      AVOCATIONS
COMPARTMENTS
    GREAT BUILDING INTO COMPARTMENTS AND ORNAMENT THEM . . . 560D EXHIBITION ADV PROSE
    (THREE) COMPARTMENTS . . . . 786A ILLS DANTE 101   PROSE
COMPASS
    TO COMPASS IT WITH SWADDLING BANDS AND WHO SHALL CHERISH IT 239 EUROPE PREL 2   14
    . . . INTO LITTLE COMPASS . . . .   284 FOUR ZOAS 2   163
    PRINCE OF THE AIR & OUR DIMENSIONS COMPASS ZENITH & NADIR   780 GHOST ABEL 1   11
    THE COMPASS OF A BOY OF (FOURTEEN) & . . . . 859C LETTER 56   PROSE
COMPASSD
    AMAZD STARTED URIZEN WHEN HE FOUND HIMSELF COMPASSD ROUND   321 FOUR ZOAS 7   36
    OF ENION IN THE GARDENS & THE SHADOWS COMPASSD ME   . . . 339 FOUR ZOAS 7B   236
COMPASSED
    HE BEHELD HIMSELF COMPASSED ROUND . . . .   252 AHANIA 3   69
COMPASSES
    HE FORMED GOLDEN COMPASSES . . . .   234 URIZEN 20   39
    THE GOLDEN COMPASSES THE QUADRANT & THE RULE & BALANCE . . 281 FOUR ZOAS 2   29
    WITH COMPASSES DIVIDE THE DEEP THEY THE STRONG SCALES ERECT 283 FOUR ZOAS 2   142
    THE HAMMER & THE CHISEL & THE RULE & COMPASSES . . . .   337 FOUR ZOAS 7B   171
    THE HAMMER & THE CHISEL & THE RULE & COMPASSES FROM LONDON   699 JERUSALEM 65   13
      FLEEING
    AND HATE DIVIDING THE SPACE OF LOVE WITH BRAZEN COMPASSES   734 JERUSALEM 88   47
COMPASSION
    OF PITY COMPASSION FORGIVENESS . . . .   224 URIZEN 4   35
    . . . MELTED INTO COMPASSION & LOVE . . . .   341 FOUR ZOAS 8   21
    OF MOST MERCIFUL PITY & COMPASSION TO THE SPECTROUS DEAD   342 FOUR ZOAS 8   60
    OF MOST MOURNFUL PITY & COMPASSION TO THE SPECTROUS DEAD   382 FOUR ZOAS AD 6 *   29
    WITH A GARMENT OF PITY & COMPASSION LIKE THE GARMENT OF   499 MILTON 18   35
      GOD
    OF KINDNESS & COMPASSION & IS BORN A WEEPING TERROR . . . 515 MILTON 28   26
    WITH ARMS OF LOVE & PITY & SWEET COMPASSION BUT TO   . . . 518 MILTON 30   12
    FOR HE IS RIGHTEOUS HE IS NOT A BEING OF PITY & COMPASSION   630 JERUSALEM 10   47
    PRAYER IS VAIN I CALLED FOR COMPASSION COMPASSION MOCKD   630 JERUSALEM 10   53
    BECOMING A BUILDING OF PITY AND COMPASSION LO . . . . . 632 JERUSALEM 12   29
    THEY ASSIMILATE WITH ALBION IN PITY & COMPASSION . . . . 674 JERUSALEM 44   33
    AND OF THE CRADLED INFANCY IN HIS BOWELS OF COMPASSION . . 688 JERUSALEM 56   34
    TO ASSIST IN THEIR MOST GRIEVOUS WORK OF PITY & COMPASSION   692 JERUSALEM 59   47
    O FORGIVENESS & PITY & COMPASSION IF I WERE PURE I SHOULD   695 JERUSALEM 61   44
      NEVER
COMPASSIONATE
    OR THEY CREATE THE LION & TYGER IN COMPASSIONATE   515 MILTON 28   27
      THUNDERINGS
    GENEROUS KNIGHT IS IN THE COMPASSIONATE DICTATES OF HIS   569A DESC CAT 3   PROSE
      SOUL
COMPEER
    SO IN THE REGIONS OF THE GRAVE NONE KNOWS HIS DARK COMPEER   314 FOUR ZOAS 6   97
COMPEL
    WHY WILT THOU WANDER AWAY FROM TIRZAH WHY ME COMPEL TO   705 JERUSALEM 67   *   45
      BIND THEE
COMPELD
    DRIVEN OUT & COMPELD TO BE CHASTE . . . .   162 LAID ME DOWN/N   8
COMPELL
    WHY SHOULD THE DIVINE VISION COMPELL THE SONS OF EDEN . . 273 FOUR ZOAS 1   339
    I WILL COMPELL THEE TO REBUILD BY THESE MY FURIOUS WAVES   301 FOUR ZOAS 4   151
    COMPELL THE POOR TO LIVE UPON A CRUST OF BREAD BY SOFT   323 FOUR ZOAS 7   117
      MILD ARTS
    WHY DOST THOU WANDER AWAY FROM TIRZAH WHY ME COMPELL TO   348 FOUR ZOAS 8   299
      BIND THEE
    TO COMPELL US TO WORSHIP THEM AS GODS . . . .   543 IF TRUE/N   8
    I WILL COMPELL THEE TO ASSIST ME IN MY TERRIBLE LABOURS   627 JERUSALEM 8   15
      TO BEAT
    I MUST COMPELL HIM TO OBEY ME WHOLLY THAT ENITHARMON MAY   638 JERUSALEM 17   17
      NOT
    I WILL COMPELL MY SPECTRE TO OBEY I WILL RESTORE TO THEE   639 JERUSALEM 17   20
      THY CHILDREN
    MY CONTRARY O THOU NEGATION I WILL CONTINUALLY COMPELL . 639 JERUSALEM 17   39
    THEY COMPELL THE POOR TO LIVE UPON A CRUST OF BREAD BY   656 JERUSALEM 30   30
      SOFT MILD ARTS
    CRYING COMPELL THE REASONER TO DEMONSTRATE WITH UNHEWN   687 JERUSALEM 55   56
      DEMONSTRATIONS
    YOUR SLAVES & CAPTIVES YOU COMPELL TO WORSHIP A GOD OF   737 JERUSALEM 90   56
      MERCY
COMPELLD
    & THEN WE SHALL RETURN TO CHAOS & GOD WILL BE COMPELLD . . 81C ANNO LAVATER   MARG
    THEN WALKS THE WEAK INFANT IN SORROW COMPELLD TO NUMBER   110 TIRIEL 8   32
      FOOTSTEPS
    COMPELLD TO PRAY REPUGNANT & TO HUMBLE THE IMMORTAL SPIRIT   110 TIRIEL 8   36
    THE YOUTH OF ENGLAND HID IN GLOOM CURSE THE PAIND HEAVENS   242 EUROPE 12   5
      COMPELLD
    COMPELLD TO WATCH URIZEN'S SHADOW . . . .   256 BOOK OF LOS 3   32
    THE KING OF LIGHT BEHELD HER MOURNING AMONG THE BRICK KILNS 285 FOUR ZOAS 2   215
      COMPELLD
    THUS SHE LAMENTED DAY & NIGHT COMPELLD TO LABOUR & SORROW   286 FOUR ZOAS 2   231
    NO LONGER NOW OBEDIENT TO THY WILL THOU ART COMPELLD   .   292 FOUR ZOAS 3   33
    THE VOICE OF LOS COMPELLD HE LABOURD ROUND THE FURNACES   302 FOUR ZOAS 4   198
    ORC LISTEND TO THE SONG COMPELLD HUNGRING ON THE COLD WIND   322 FOUR ZOAS 7   99
    O TORMENT O TORMENT A WORM COMPELLD AM I A WORM   . . .   323 FOUR ZOAS 7   139
    IN SERPENT FORM COMPELLD STRETCH OUT & UP THE MYSTERIOUS   324 FOUR ZOAS 7   163
      TREE

371

	PAGE	TITLE	LINE

COMPELLD   (CONTINUED)

COMPELLD THE SUN REDDNING LIKE A FIERCE LION IN HIS CHAINS   333 FOUR ZOAS 7B   31
CRYING IN SECRET TENTS AT NIGHT & IN THE MORN COMPELLD   . .   334 FOUR ZOAS 7B   62
COMPELLD TO LEAVE THE PLOW TO THE OX . . . .   338 FOUR ZOAS 7B   202
COMPELLD BY THE IRON HEARTED SISTERS DAUGHTERS OF URIZEN   343 FOUR ZOAS 8   83
TO DIE FOR SATAN ADAM REFUSD BUT WAS COMPELLD TO DIE   .   .   351 FOUR ZOAS 8   402
COMPELLD OTHERS TO SERVE HIM IN MORAL GRATITUDE &   491 MILTON 11   11
    SUBMISSION
COMPELLD THE GNOMES TO CURB THE HORSES & TO THROW BANKS   493 MILTON 12   17
    OF SAND
COMPELLD TO COMBINE INTO FORM BY SATAN THE SPECTRE   521 MILTON 32   12
    OF ALBION
O DREADFUL LOOM OF DEATH O PITEOUS FEMALE FORMS COMPELLD   525 MILTON 35   7
THAT A HEALTHY CHILD SHOULD BE TAUGHT & COMPELLD TO WALK   599D PUB ADDRESS/N   PROSE
COMPELLD TO BE A TYRANNY PRINCES APPEAR TO ME TO BE FOOLS   600A PUB ADDRESS/N   PROSE
BEEN COMPELLD TO SUBDUE THEIR MASTER EZEKIEL XXXVIII...   609B V LAST JUDG/N   PROSE
ARE COMPELLD TO ALLOW IS NOT DONE IN PASSION . . . . .   615D V LAST JUDG/N   PROSE
THAT HE WHO WILL NOT DEFEND TRUTH MAY BE COMPELLD TO DEFEND   628 JERUSALEM 9   29
THE BELLOWS & THE HAMMERS MOVE COMPELLD BY LOS'S HAND   .   .   629 JERUSALEM 10   6
AT THE SUBLIME LABOURS FOR LOS COMPELLD THE INVISIBLE   630 JERUSALEM 10   65
    SPECTRE
HE HATH COMPELLD ALBION TO BECOME A PUNISHER & HATH   653 JERUSALEM 29   16
    POSSESSD
CHAIND HAND & FOOT COMPELLD TO FIGHT UNDER THE IRON WHIPS   700 JERUSALEM 65   35
HOW RAGD THE GOLDEN HORSES OF URIZEN COMPELLD TO   700 JERUSALEM 65   47
    THE CHARIOT OF LOVE
COMPELLD TO LEAVE THE PLOW TO THE OX . . . .   700 JERUSALEM 65   48
COMPELLD INTO A SHAPE OF MORAL VIRTUE AGAINST THE LAMB   .   723 JERUSALEM 80   77
BUT HERE WE BUILD BABYLON ON EUPHRATES COMPELLD TO BUILD   729 JERUSALEM 84   8
& IN THIS WHICH I SEND YOU HAVE BEEN COMPELLD BY MY GENIUS   791D LETTER 4   PROSE
NO FURTHER MY FRIEND THAN HE IS COMPELLD BY CIRCUMSTANCES   819C LETTER 25   PROSE
& I HAVE COMPELLD WHAT SHOULD HAVE BEEN OF FREEDOM   .   .   .   825D LETTER 27   PROSE
MY LANDLORD COMPELLD THE SOLDIERS TO GO IN DOORS   .   .   .   827B LETTER 28   PROSE
WROTE DOWN THE ACCUSATION TOLD ME IN PRIVATE ARE COMPELLD   827D LETTER 28   PROSE

COMPELLED

THAT HE WHO WILL NOT DEFEND TRUTH MAY BE COMPELLED TO   .   .   489 MILTON 8   47
AND HAS COMPELLED THE USE OF THAT DESTROYER OF COLOUR   .   566B DESC CAT 2   PROSE
COMPELLED TO CRY OUT   . . . .   569A DESC CAT 3   PROSE
AND NOT MAN COMPELLED TO SACRIFICE TO THEM   . . . . .   571C DESC CAT 3   PROSE
DEMONS BUT HE WAS ALSO COMPELLED TO LEAVE IT UNFINISHED   581B DESC CAT 6   PROSE
DRUDGE AND A MISERABLE MAN COMPELLED TO SOFTNESS BY POVERTY   583C DESC CAT 9   PROSE
ABEL COMPELLED I CRY O EARTH COVER NOT THE BLOOD OF ABEL   780 GHOST ABEL 2   12

COMPELLING

OF AFFLICTION AND LOS DREW THEM FORTH COMPELLING THE HARSH   628 JERUSALEM 9   35
    SPECTRE
COMPELLING HIS SPECTRE TO LABOURS MIGHTY TREMBLING IN FEAR   629 JERUSALEM 10   18
IN HOWLING TORMENT TO BUILD STONE WALLS OF SEPARATION   736 JERUSALEM 90   12
    COMPELLING
COMPELLING URIZEN TO HIS FURROW & THARMAS TO HIS SHEEPFOLD   742 JERUSALEM 95   16

COMPELLS

HIS SPECTRE DIVIDES & LOS IN FURY COMPELLS TO DIVIDE   638 JERUSALEM 17   1
YOUR EAGER EXPECTATION OF HEARING FROM ME COMPELLS ME   .   834B LETTER 34   PROSE

COMPENSATE

HER SON IN TENFOLD JOY & TO COMPENSATE FOR HER TEARS   .   309 FOUR ZOAS 5   153

COMPETITION

HE DEFIES COMPETITION IN COLOURING   . . . .   581A DESC CAT 5   PROSE
I IN MY OWN DEFENCE CHALLENGE A COMPETITION   . . . .   602A PUB ADDRESS/N   PROSE
I CANNOT THINK THAT REAL POETS HAVE ANY COMPETITION   .   .   783A ANNO WW POEMS   MARG
("COMPETITION BY PAINTING") [WHAT BUT A PUPPY WILL DARE   SUPP ANNO REYNOLDS   * MARG
    TO DO THIS]

COMPETITOR

I CONCIEVE FLAXMAN STANDS WITHOUT A COMPETITOR IN SCULPTURE   860A LETTER 56   PROSE

COMPETITORS

THE PAINTER COURTS COMPARISON WITH HIS COMPETITORS   .   .   .   572C DESC CAT 3   PROSE

COMPLACENCIES

NOR SONS NOR HATEFUL PEACE & LOVE NOR SOFT COMPLACENCIES   640 JERUSALEM 18   14

COMPLACENCY

INWARD COMPLACENCY OF SOUL A SELF-ANNIHILATION   . . . .   646 JERUSALEM 23   15

COMPLACENT

LOS ANSWERD FURIOUS ART THOU ONE OF THOSE WHO WHEN MOST   273 FOUR ZOAS 1   331
    COMPLACENT
OF DEATH WAS SEEN IN (REGENERATIONS) TERRIFIC OR COMPLACENT   746 JERUSALEM 98   *   34
    VARYING
WHO COMPLACENT BEGAN   . . . .   805 TO BUTTS/L   52

COMPLAIN

THE MERCHANTS DO COMPLAIN AND BEG OUR AID   . . . . .   .   20 EDW THIRD/PS 2   69
TO FLOURISH IN ETERNAL VALES THEN WHY SHOULD THEL COMPLAIN   127 BOOK OF THEL 1   25
I PASS AWAY YET I COMPLAIN AND NO ONE HEARS MY VOICE   .   .   128 BOOK OF THEL 3   4
THEN WILL I WEEP THEN I'LL COMPLAIN & SIGH FOR IMMORTALITY   368 FOUR ZOAS 9   411

COMPLAIND

AND I COMPLAIND IN THE MILD AIR BECAUSE I FADE AWAY   .   .   .   130 BOOK OF THEL 5   12

COMPLAINEST

WHY THOU COMPLAINEST NOT WHEN IN ONE HOUR THOU FADE AWAY   128 BOOK OF THEL 3   2

COMPLAININGS

THEIR SAD COMPLAININGS BEAR FOR CONRADE LOST   . . . . .   43D WOE CRIED MUSE   PROSE

COMPLAINS

EVERY BODY COMPLAINS YET ALL GO ON CHEERFULLY AND WITH   831D LETTER 31   PROSE
    SPIRIT

COMPLAINT

AND COMPLAINT OF JOHN SCHOLFIELD A PRIVATE SOLDIER &C   .   .   437A BLAKES MEMORAN   TITLE
WITH PRECISELY THE SAME COMPLAINT & THE SAME TORMENT OF   871A LETTER 72   PROSE
    THE STOMACH

PAGE TITLE LINE

COMPLAINT   (CONTINUED)
     BRINGS ON THE SYMPTOMS OF THE ORIGINAL COMPLAINT HE DOES   SUPP LETTER 81A   *PROSE
     TOTTERING THO ALL THE SYMPTOMS OF MY COMPLAINT SEEM ALMOST   876A LETTER 83   PROSE
COMPLAINTS
     AND MY COMPLAINTS ARE SWEETER THAN THEIR JOYS . . . . .   41D THEN SHE BORE   PROSE
COMPLEAT
     SEES YOUR HAPPINESS COMPLEAT   . . . .   54 PHEBE DREST/IM   12
COMPLETE
     TILL A PHILOSOPHY OF FIVE SENSES WAS COMPLETE . . . . .   246 SONG OF LOS 4   16
     . . . THE CIRCLE OF DESTINY COMPLETE . . . .   266 FOUR ZOAS 1   87
     THE CIRCLE OF DESTINY COMPLETE THEY GAVE TO IT A SPACE . .   267 FOUR ZOAS 1   101
     HE IS A COMPLETE ROGUE WITH CONSTITUTIONAL GAIETY ENOUGH   568D DESC CAT 3   PROSE
     CHAUCER'S CANTERBURY PILGRIMS BEING A COMPLETE INDEX . .   591A PUB ADDRESS/N   TITLE
     MR HAYLEY ACTS LIKE A PRINCE I AM AT COMPLETE EASE BUT . .   808A LETTER 19   PROSE
     I LOSE NO MOMENT TO COMPLETE ROMNEY TO SATISFACTION . .   829D LETTER 30   PROSE
     SUFFERING TILL THE TIME OF COMPLETE DELIVERANCE IN THE . .   863A LETTER 60   PROSE
COMPLETED
     NINE AGES COMPLETED THEIR CIRCLES . . . .   260 BOOK OF LOS 5   41
     WAS COMPLETED A HUMAN ILLUSION . . . .   260 BOOK OF LOS 5   56
     THE DESIGN OF THE LAST JUDGMENT WHICH I HAVE COMPLETED . .   442D LAST JUDGMNT/L   PROSE
     EVERY THING IS NEARLY COMPLETED FOR OUR REMOVAL TO FELPHAM   799A LETTER 11   PROSE
     "THINGS BEING NOW NEARLY COMPLETED FOR OUR SETTING FORTH   800B LETTER 12   PROSE
       ON"
     WHICH I HAVE NEARLY COMPLETED IN THE MEAN TIME BY   808D LETTER 20   PROSE
       MY SISTER'S HANDS
     OF INCLOSING SEVERAL TOGETHER WHICH ARE NOT YET COMPLETED   809C LETTER 20   PROSE
     WHICH IS NOW PERFECTLY COMPLETED INTO A GRAND POEM . . .   825A LETTER 27   PROSE
     AND IS NOT YET COMPLETED I COULD NOT AVOID SAYING THUS MUCH   847A LETTER 44   PROSE
     SUFFERED HAD THE WORK BEEN COMPLETED WITHOUT THAT BALLAD'S   861A LETTER 58   PROSE
COMPLETELY
     HIS PROFESSION PERFECT LEARNED COMPLETELY MASTER AND . .   570D DESC CAT 3   PROSE
     TILL HE HAD COMPLETELY DIVIDED HIM INTO A SEPARATE SPACE   739 JERUSALEM 91   53
     THAT MY ANTAGONIST IS SILENCD COMPLETELY . . . . .   825D LETTER 27   PROSE
COMPLEXIONS
     TO PREVENT ALBION WALKING ABOUT IN THE FOUR COMPLEXIONS   671 JERUSALEM 43   5
COMPLICATED
     WOULD SOON BECOME A MILL WITH COMPLICATED WHEELS . . .   97D NAT RELIGION 2   PROSE
     FALSE THE ANCIENTS WERE CHIEFLY ATTENTIVE TO COMPLICATED   466B ANNO REYNOLDS   MARG
COMPLIED
     SINGING A SONG HIMSELF WHICH HE READILY COMPLIED WITH . .   57D ISLAND MOON 9   PROSE
COMPLIMENT
     BUT NOT FOR YOUR COMPLIMENT WHICH IS NOT TRUE . . . .   29C EDW THIRD/PS 4   PROSE
     IMITATION OF POPE A COMPLIMENT TO THE LADIES . . . . .   545B IMIT POPE/N   TITLE
     I HAVE NO TIME FOR SEEING AND LITTLE ARTS OF COMPLIMENT   670 JERUSALEM 42   27
     YOU WITH A LETTER OF MEER COMPLIMENT & EXPRESSION OF THANKS   798A LETTER 10   PROSE
     COMPLIMENT HE WAS NOT AT HOME I LEFT IT WITH A SHORT NOTE   838C LETTER 37   PROSE
COMPLIMENTS   SEE COMPTS
     THIS IS ONE OF THE BEST COMPLIMENTS HE EVER HAD . . . .   538 TO H(UNT)/N   2
     WITH THANKS & COMPLIMENTS ARE QUITE DRAWN DRY . . . .   549 H PICK THANK/N   2
     MR B(BLAKE) THOUGHT THIS THE GREATEST OF COMPLIMENTS . .   585A DESC CAT 15   PROSE
     COMPLIMENTS TO MRS CUMBERLAND & FAMILY . . . . . .   791C LETTER 3   PROSE
     BEST COMPLIMENTS TO MRS CUMBERLAND I REMAIN YOURS SINCERELY   796A LETTER 6   PROSE
     RESPECTFUL COMPLIMENTS TO MRS CUMBERLAND & FAMILY . . .   798D LETTER 10   PROSE
     MR B(BRAITHWAITE) DESIRES I WILL PRESENT HIS COMPLIMENTS   836A LETTER 35   PROSE
       TO YOU
     COMPLIMENTS TO YOU HE IS SO BUSY THAT I BELIEVE I SHALL   836C LETTER 35   PROSE
     DESIRES MAY BE SENT TO YOU WITH HIS COMPLIMENTS WHICH . .   838D LETTER 37   PROSE
     RESPECTFUL COMPLIMENTS TO YOU SPEAKS OF TAKING A RIDE . .   843A LETTER 42   PROSE
     SCHEME OF HIS LOTTERY DESIRES HIS COMPLIMENTS TO YOU . .   844A LETTER 43   PROSE
     MY AFFECTIONATE COMPLIMENTS TO HIM . . . .   850C LETTER 49   PROSE
     AND AFFECTIONATE COMPLIMENTS TO HIM ALSO TO OUR KIND FRIEND   852D LETTER 50   PROSE
     MR BLAKE'S RESPECTFUL COMPLIMENTS TO MRS (ADERS) IS SORRY TO   SUPP LETTER 81A   *PROSE
     MR BLAKE'S RESPECTFUL COMPLIMENTS TO MISS DENMAN . . . .   877B LETTER 86   PROSE
COMPOSD
     HE HAD COMPOSD AND AT EACH PAUSE HE WIPD . . . . . .   25 EDW THIRD/PS 3   164
     TWELVE HALLS AFTER THE NAMES OF HIS TWELVE SONS COMPOSD   284 FOUR ZOAS 2   173
     . . . COMPOSD THE SONG TO THEIR IMMORTAL VOICES . . . .   310 FOUR ZOAS 5   200
COMPOSE
     SEVEN TRUMPETS THESE COMPOSE [COMPOSING] THE CLOUD . . .   444A LAST JUDGMNT/L   *PROSE
     STRETCHD OUT COMPOSE THE MUNDANE SHELL A MIGHTY   528 MILTON 37   53
       INCRUSTATION
     WHICH COMPOSE ALL AGES AND NATIONS . . . .   567B DESC CAT 3   PROSE
     SUCH ARE THE CHARACTERS THAT COMPOSE THIS PICTURE . . .   572C DESC CAT 3   PROSE
     THAT COMPOSE ALL AGES & NATIONS . . . .   589A CHAUCER/N   PROSE
COMPOSED
     & THE AIR WAS FULL OF THEM & SEEMD COMPOSED OF THEM . . .   156B MARRIAGE HH 17   PROSE
     COMPOSED BY AN AFRICAN BLACK FROM THE LITTLE EARTH OF SOTHA   375 FOUR ZOAS 9   686
     TO GIVE THEM HIS LABOUR FOR NOTHING A SOCIETY COMPOSED .   446A ANNO REYNOLDS   MARG
     ONE CENTRAL FORM COMPOSED OF ALL OTHER FORMS BEING GRANTED   459C ANNO REYNOLDS   MARG
     AND ARE COMPOSED OF AN OLD MAN A WOMAN AND CHILDREN . .   567A DESC CAT 3   PROSE
     & ARE COMPOSED OF AN OLD MAN A WOMAN & CHILDREN . . .   588D CHAUCER/N   PROSE
     AND ARE COMPOSED OF AN OLD MAN A WOMAN AND CHILDREN . .   590A CHAUCER 2   PROSE
     IT IS COMPOSED OF THE INNOCENT CIVILIZED HEATHEN & . . .   610A V LAST JUDG/N   PROSE
     IS COMPOSED OF VARIOUS GROUPES OF FIGURES . . . . . .   612A V LAST JUDG/N   PROSE
     AND THE VEIL OF VALA IS COMPOSED OF THE SPECTRES OF THE   677 JERUSALEM 47   12
       DEAD
     & RESPECT THEY WERE COMPOSED ABOVE A TWELVE-MONTH AGO . .   816D LETTER 24   PROSE
     FOR I HAVE IN THESE THREE YEARS COMPOSED . . . . .   823A LETTER 26   PROSE
COMPOSES
     ("POET COMPOSES...INSPIRATION...FOR ALL MEN ") MOST   80C ANNO LAVATER   MARG
       EXCELLENT

COMPOSING
    SEVEN TRUMPETS THESE COMPOSE [COMPOSING] THE CLOUD . . 444A LAST JUDGMNT/L *PROSE
    BEGUN BY THE WORDS "A FACILITY IN COMPOSING" I CANNOT TELL 453C ANNO REYNOLDS MARG
    HIM TO MEAN THAT FACILITY IN COMPOSING IS A FRIVOLOUS 453D ANNO REYNOLDS MARG
        PURSUIT
    A FACILITY IN COMPOSING IS THE GREATEST POWER OF ART . 453D ANNO REYNOLDS MARG
    AND FALSE BOWELS ALTOGETHER COMPOSING THE FALSE TONGUE 634 JERUSALEM 14 6
COMPOSITE
    THERE IS NO SUCH A THING AS A COMPOSITE STYLE . . . . 465B ANNO REYNOLDS * MARG
COMPOSITION
    COMPOSITION BY ASSIMILATING IT WITH [THE] A PRETENCE TO & 453D ANNO REYNOLDS * MARG
    PARADISE LOST A COMPOSITION FOR A MORE PERFECT PICTURE . 582A DESC CAT 9 TITLE
    BE WORTHY OF ATTENTION NOT ONLY ON ACCOUNT OF ITS 582B DESC CAT 9 PROSE
        COMPOSITION
    NOT ONLY ON ACCOUNT OF MR HAYLEY'S COMPOSITION BUT ALSO 810A LETTER 20 PROSE
COMPOSITIONS
    ARE COMPOSITIONS OF A MYTHOLOGICAL CAST SIMILAR TO THOSE 565C DESC CAT 2 PROSE
COMPOUNDED
    BUT THESE ARE NOT ABSTRACTED NOR COMPOUNDED FROM NATURE 459C ANNO REYNOLDS MARG
COMPREHEND
    MAN MAY COMPREHEND BUT NOT THE NATURAL OR EXTERNAL MAN . . 90A ANNO SWED LOVE MARG
    [IF WITH HIS INTELLECT HE COMPREHEND THE TERRIBLE SENTENCE] 264 FOUR ZOAS 1 * 4
    AND COMPREHEND WITHIN HIMSELF ALL THINGS BOTH SMALL & GREAT 272 FOUR ZOAS 1 * 295
    COMPREHEND WONDEROUS THINGS OUT OF THE DIVINE LAW . . . 714 JERUSALEM 74 15
    CAN COMPREHEND IN A FORTNIGHT BE ASSURED MY DEAR FRIEND 814D LETTER 23 PROSE
        THAT
COMPREHENDED
    ALL THINGS ARE COMPREHENDED IN THEIR ETERNAL FORMS . . 605D V LAST JUDG/N PROSE
    HOPED YOUR PLAN COMPREHENDED ALL SPECIES OF THIS ART . . 793A LETTER 5 PROSE
COMPREHENDING
    ALL MELODIES & COMPREHENDING ONLY DISCORD AND HARMONY . 484 MILTON 5 24
    TRUE HARMONIES & COMPREHENDING GREAT AS VERY SMALL . . 680 JERUSALEM 49 37
    HYLE DWELT IN WINCHESTER COMPREHENDING HANTS DORSET DEVON 710 JERUSALEM 71 20
        CORNWALL
    COMPREHENDING THE BEAUTIES OF COLOURING OR THE PICTURES 814A LETTER 23 PROSE
COMPREHENDS
    HE COMPREHENDS ALL THE PROPHETIC CHARACTERS . . . . 611C V LAST JUDG/N PROSE
    THE FIGURES OF SETH & HIS WIFE COMPREHENDS THE FATHERS . 611C V LAST JUDG/N PROSE
COMPTS
    MR BLAKE'S COMPTS TO MR REVELEY THO FULL OF WORK . . . 790A LETTER 1 PROSE
COMPULSION
    MOVING BY COMPULSION EACH OTHER NOT AS THOSE IN EDEN WHICH 636 JERUSALEM 15 19
COMPULSIVE
    COMPULSIVE ROLLD THE COMETS AT HIS DREAD COMMAND THE DREARY 320 FOUR ZOAS 6 320
        WAY
COMPULSORY
    AND WHEN COMPULSORY CRUEL SACRIFICES . . . . 652B JERUSALEM 27 PROSE
COMPUNCTION
    MANTLES OF DESPAIR GIRDLES OF BITTER COMPUNCTION SHOES 346 FOUR ZOAS 8 221
        OF INDOLENCE
COMRADE
    THE SOLDIER'S COMRADE SWORE BEFORE THE MAGISTRATES . . . 437B BLAKES MEMORAN PROSE
    WORDS AT THAT TIME NEITHER DID HIS COMRADE THE WHOLE . . 437C BLAKES MEMORAN PROSE
    IF WE PROVE THE COMRADE PERJURED . . . . 437C BLAKES MEMORAN PROSE
    THE SOLDIER AFTER HE AND HIS COMRADE CAME TOGETHER INTO THE 438C BLAKES MEMORAN PROSE
    CONTENTION AT THE STABLE DOOR & GOING TO THE COMRADE . 438D BLAKES MEMORAN PROSE
    SAID TO HIM IS YOUR COMRADE DRUNK A PROOF THAT HE . . 438D BLAKES MEMORAN PROSE
    THE WRETCHED MAN HAS TERRIBLY PERJURD HIMSELF AS HAS HIS 826D LETTER 28 PROSE
        COMRADE
    & THE MAN'S COMRADE & SEVERAL OTHER PEOPLE . . . . . 827B LETTER 28 PROSE
    PROVE THE COMRADE PERJURD WHO SWORE THAT HE HEARD ME WHILE 827D LETTER 28 PROSE
COMST
    THEN COMST THOU FORTH A MODEST VIRGIN KNOWING TO DISSEMBLE 194 V DAU ALBION 6 10
COMUS
    MY DESIGNS FOR COMUS WHEN I HAVE DONE THEM DIRECTED TO YOU 810D LETTER 21 PROSE
    A GENIUS DRIVING AWAY "COMUS & HIS MIDNIGHT CREW" . . . SUPP ILLUS GRAY *TITLE
CONCAVE
    WITH PRINTLESS FEET SCORNING THE CONCAVE OF THE JOYFUL SKY 381 FOUR ZOAS AD 1 17
    THE HARROW CAST THICK FLAMES & ORBD US ROUND IN CONCAVE 493 MILTON 12 22
        FIRES
    THE MUNDANE SHELL IS A VAST CONCAVE EARTH AN IMMENSE . . 498 MILTON 17 21
    A CONCAVE EARTH WONDROUS CHASMAL ABYSSAL INCOHERENT . . . 634 JERUSALEM 13 53
    THE UNIVERSAL CONCAVE RAGED SUCH THUNDEROUS SOUNDS AS NEVER 686 JERUSALEM 55 20
    THE CONCAVE EARTH ROUND GOLGONOOZA IN ENTUTHON BENYTHON 719 JERUSALEM 78 17
CONCEAL
    NOR COULD CONCEAL AUGHT THAT MIGHT APPEASE HER THEN . . . 39B SAMSON/PS PROSE
    WERE EACH [ENDEAVOURED] ENDEAVOURING TO CONCEAL . . . 44C ISLAND MOON 1 *PROSE
    WHY SHOULDEST THOU CONCEAL THYSELF FROM THOSE OF THINE 101 TIRIEL 2 47
        OWN FLESH
CONCEIT   SEE SELF CONCEIT
    SHE WAS A GODDESS POWERFUL & BORE [CONCEIT & EMULATION] 43A THEN SHE BORE *PROSE
    [SHE HAD A SON CALLED SUSPITION] CONCEIT & & POLICY DOTH 43A THEN SHE BORE *PROSE
    TILL BASIRE WAS QUITE DASHD & OUT OF CONCEIT WITH WHAT . . 603C PUB ADDR AD/N PROSE
    IT PLOWS THE EARTH IN ITS OWN CONCEIT IT OVERWHELMS THE 659 JERUSALEM 33 9
        HILLS
CONCEITED
    FOR HE WAS INCAPABLE THRO HIS CONCEITED NOTIONS . . . 157D MARRIAGE HH 21 PROSE
CONCEITS
    TRIFLING CONCEITS ARE BETTER . . . . 455D ANNO REYNOLDS MARG
CONCEIVE   SEE CONCIEVE
    FOR LO THOU SHALT CONCEIVE AND BEAR A SON . . . . . 39D SAMSON/PS PROSE
    ("A MANNER OF FORGIVING SO DIVINE THAT") THIS I CANNOT 76D ANNO LAVATER MARG
        CONCEIVE

```
                                                              PAGE     TITLE        LINE
CONCEIVE    (CONTINUED)
    WHICH I CONCEIVE WERE URGED UPON HIM BY JOHNSON   . . . . 847A LETTER 44        PROSE
CONCENTER
    CONCENTER IN ONE FEMALE FORM AN AGED PENSIVE WOMAN   . . . 678 JERUSALEM 48       28
CONCENTERD
    CONCENTERD INTO LOVE OF PARENT STORGOUS APPETITE CRAVING   308 FOUR ZOAS 5       113
CONCENTERING
    EACH MALE FORMD WITHOUT A COUNTERPART WITHOUT A          330 FOUR ZOAS 7        402
        CONCENTERING VISION
    CONCENTERING IN THE MAJESTIC FORM OF ERIN IN ETERNAL TEARS 731 JERUSALEM 86      45
CONCENTRATE
    ANY FOOL MAY (CONCENTRATE) A LIGHT IN THE MIDDLE  . . . . 477C ANNO REYNOLDS  * MARG
CONCENTRATING
    INTO TWO STATIONARY ORBS CONCENTRATING ALL THINGS   . . . 241 EUROPE 10          12
CONCEPTION
    TO THE YOUNG ARTIST AS THE WORKS OF ORIGINAL CONCEPTION   455A ANNO REYNOLDS    MARG
    KNOW THAT THE MAN'S EXECUTION IS AS HIS CONCEPTION & NO   461C ANNO REYNOLDS    MARG
        BETTER
    OF LEARNING HOW TO PRODUCE ORIGINAL CONCEPTION   . . . . 469D ANNO REYNOLDS    MARG
    CONCEPTION OF THE HUMOUR AND FUN THAT OCCURS ON THE JOURNEY 569A DESC CAT 3     PROSE
    MOST MASTERLY CONCEPTION THAT THE PUBLIC HAVE EMBRACED  . 576B DESC CAT 4       PROSE
    AND VISIONARY CONCEPTION NO IT SHALL NOT BE SO   . . . . 576B DESC CAT 4        PROSE
    FEAR AND DOUBT OF HIS OWN ORIGINAL CONCEPTION THE   . . . 582C DESC CAT 9       PROSE
    THOUGH THE ORIGINAL CONCEPTION WAS ALL FIRE AND ANIMATION 583A DESC CAT 9       PROSE
    MY CONCEPTION & INVENTION ARE ON ALL HANDS ALLOWD   . . . 601D PUB ADDRESS/N    PROSE
CONCEPTIONS
    THESE ORIGINAL CONCEPTIONS ON ART BY AN ORIGINAL ARTIST   562C DESC CAT ADV     PROSE
    NOT AUTHORS OF SUCH SUBLIME CONCEPTIONS THOSE   . . . . . 566A DESC CAT 2       PROSE
    APPROVED WITH AVIDITY POETRY CONSISTS IN THESE CONCEPTIONS 576B DESC CAT 4      PROSE
    MUST HAVE QUEER CONCEPTIONS   . . . . . . . . . . . . . . 596C PUB ADDRESS/N    PROSE
    CONCEPTIONS OF THE VISIONARY FANCY BY THEIR VARIOUS   . . 605B V LAST JUDG/N    PROSE
CONCERN
    LET US TEACH BUONAPARTE & WHOMSOEVER ELSE IT MAY CONCERN  597A PUB ADDRESS/N    PROSE
    BE APPOINTD BY HIM IN SO HONOURABLE A CONCERN AS THE   . 856B LETTER 54        *PROSE
    [IS FASHION THE CONCERN OF ARTISTS]  . . . . . . . . .    SUPP ANNO REYNOLDS  * MARG
CONCERND
    THO I KNOW THAT AS FAR AS DESIGNING & POETRY ARE CONCERND 821C LETTER 25        PROSE
    INTEREST OF ALL CONCERND IN MY WORKS OBSERVING THAT   . . 822D LETTER 26        PROSE
CONCERNED
    IS CONCERNED BUT I MUST SAY THAT HE LEAVES NO STONE UNTURND 846C LETTER 44      PROSE
CONCERNING
    WITH OPINIONS CONCERNING HISTORICAL FACT   . . . . . . . 384D ANNO WATSON       MARG
    CONCERNING GENERATION & THE VEGETATIVE POWER & CONCERNING 495 MILTON 14           5
    IT CONFIRMS THE SUSPITION I ENTERTAIN CONCERNING THOSE    553B BELLS WEEKLY/N    MARG
    ACTION AND REALITY REASONS AND OPINIONS CONCERNING ACTS   579A DESC CAT 5       PROSE
    CONCERNING HIS IDEAS OF BEAUTY STRENGTH AND UGLINESS   . 579D DESC CAT 5        PROSE
    CONCERNING THE POSSIBILITY OF EXECUTING WITHOUT A MODEL   582C DESC CAT 9       PROSE
    CONCERNING MY THREE YEARS' HERCULEAN LABOURS AT FELPHAM   592C PUB ADDRESS/N    PROSE
    WHO TROUBLE RELIGION WITH QUESTIONS CONCERNING GOOD & EVIL 604C V LAST JUDG/N   PROSE
    WALKING UP & DOWN IN CONVERSATIONS CONCERNING   . . . . . 613C V LAST JUDG/N    PROSE
    THO THEIR WHOLE CONTEMPLATION IS CONCERNING THESE THINGS  614C V LAST JUDG/N    PROSE
    WE WILL NOT CONVERSE CONCERNING GOOD & EVIL   . . . . .   615D V LAST JUDG/N    PROSE
    ANY MORE (THAN) I WOULD QUESTION A WINDOW CONCERNING A    617C V LAST JUDG/N   *PROSE
        SIGHT
    CONCERNING MY CHIEF DELIGHT BUT THOU HAST BROKEN SILENCE  630 JERUSALEM 10       41
    CONVERSE CONCERNING WEIGHT & DISTANCE IN THE WILDS        661 JERUSALEM 34       40
        OF NEWTON & LOCKE
    AND SO HE MUST MEAN CONCERNING HUMILITY   . . . . . . .   750 EV GOSPEL(C)/N     22
    PRAY MY DEAR SIR FAVOUR ME WITH A LINE CONCERNING YOUR  . 833D LETTER 33        PROSE
    WITH SR ALLAN CHAMBRE RECOMMENDS ME TO ENQUIRE CONCERNING 834D LETTER 34        PROSE
    & WRITE YOU THAT HE HAS SPOKEN WITH MR READ CONCERNING  . 836A LETTER 35        PROSE
    HE PROMISES TO COLLECT NUMEROUS PARTICULARS CONCERNING  . 845D LETTER 44        PROSE
    WHO KNEW MOST CONCERNING HIM OF ANY ONE LAMENTED   . . .  846A LETTER 44        PROSE
    TO WRITE ALL HE KNOWS OR CAN COLLECT CONCERNING ROMNEY  . 846A LETTER 44        PROSE
    OF MR JOHNSON'S INTEGRITY WHILE WE WERE TALKING CONCERNING 846C LETTER 44       PROSE
    CONCERNING HER HEALTH SHE IS SURPRISINGLY RECOVERED   . . 851C LETTER 50        PROSE
    THE PROPOSAL CONCERNING THE THREE DRAMAS I FOUND IT   . . 858A LETTER 55        PROSE
    OF HIS ADVICE CONCERNING THEM AND HE THINKS THAT THEY   . 858B LETTER 55        PROSE
    DIRECTIONS AND COMMANDS CONCERNING IT FOR HE WISHES TO SET 858C LETTER 55       PROSE
    WILL GIVE HIM MY PROPOSAL CONCERNING IT IN WRITING   . .  858D LETTER 55        PROSE
    SOLICITUDE CONCERNING ME AT REST YOU HAVE A FAMILY I HAVE 873C LETTER 77        PROSE
CONCESSION
    ALL THIS CONCESSION IS TO PROVE THAT GENIUS IS ACQUIRED   448A ANNO REYNOLDS    MARG
CONCESSIONS
    HE MAKES LITTLE CONCESSIONS THAT HE MAY TAKE GREAT        463C ANNO REYNOLDS    MARG
        ADVANTAGES
    CONCESSIONS TO TRUTH FOR THE SAKE OF OVERSETTING TRUTH  . 465D ANNO REYNOLDS    MARG
CONCIEVD
    AND CONCIEVD HIMSELF AS MUCH WISER THAN SEVEN MEN   . . . 157D MARRIAGE HH 21   PROSE
    EVENTS OF TIME START FORTH & ARE CONCIEVD IN SUCH A PERIOD 516 MILTON 29          2
CONCIEVE    SEE CONCEIVE
    I CANNOT CONCIEVE BUT THE SUBSTANCE GIVES TINCTURE TO   .  81D ANNO LAVATER   * MARG
        THE ACCIDENT
    I CANNOT CONCIEVE THE DIVINITY OF THE BOOKS IN THE BIBLE  393B ANNO WATSON      MARG
    THIS HE CAN CONCIEVE BUT HE CANNOT EXECUTE   . . . . . . 602A PUB ADDRESS/N    PROSE
    I CANNOT CONCIEVE WE ARE MEN OF LIKE PASSIONS   . . . . . 682C JERUSALEM 52     PROSE
    CONCIEVE IN MY BRAIN ARE STUDIES & CHAMBERS FILLD WITH  . 802B LETTER 14        PROSE
    PARTAKERS OF THE JOY THAT THE WORLD CANNOT CONCIEVE THAT  830C LETTER 30        PROSE
        YOU
    THINK HE IS TO BE APPLAUDED BUT I CONCIEVE THAT HE MAY BE A 850B LETTER 49      PROSE
    I CONCIEVE FLAXMAN STANDS WITHOUT A COMPETITOR IN SCULPTURE 860A LETTER 56      PROSE
```

		PAGE	TITLE	LINE

CONCLUDE
HENCE WE MUST CONCLUDE THAT THE MAN WHO HOLDS MIRACLES . . 391C ANNO WATSON MARG
IN THE MEAN WHILE I CONCLUDE THIS HASTY SCRAWL WITH . . 853A LETTER 51 *PROSE
SO THAT I CONCLUDE ANOTHER WEEK MUST PASS BEFORE I DARE 873A LETTER 76 PROSE
CONCLUDED
PICKD UP BUT WHAT I HAVE CONCLUDED FROM YOUR LESSONS . . 20 EDW THIRD/PS 2 40
HAD BEFORE CONCLUDED UPON JUDGING AS HE DID THAT IF THE 848C LETTER 45 PROSE
CONCLUDING
OF FUSELI'S SHAKESPEARE THE CONCLUDING NUMBERS OF WHICH 853C LETTER 52 PROSE
CONCLUSION
CONCLUSION IF IT WERE NOT FOR THE POETIC . . . . . . 97B NAT RELIGION 1 PROSE
I HOPE A FEW MORE DAYS WILL BRING US TO A CONCLUSION . 870B LETTER 71 PROSE
CONCORDS
I TELL HOW ALBION'S SONS BY HARMONIES OF CONCORDS 715 JERUSALEM 74 24
& DISCORDS
CONCOURSE
TO OUR PRIMEVAL CHAOS IN FORTUITOUS CONCOURSE OF INCOHERENT 282 FOUR ZOAS 2 102
IN FORTUITOUS CONCOURSE OF MEMORYS ACCUMULATED & LOST . . 659 JERUSALEM 33 8
CONCUPISCENCE
AND CONCUPISCENCE THEY POSSESS THEMSELVES OF THE BODIES 582A DESC CAT 8 PROSE
CONCUR
INTENDED FLIGHT INTO YOUR DELIGHTFUL COUNTRY CONCUR IN . . 872D LETTER 76 PROSE
CONCUSSIONS
THRO LIGHTNINGS THUNDERS EARTHQUAKES & CONCUSSIONS FIRES 316 FOUR ZOAS 6 185
& FLOODS
CONDEMN
IN THE WILD TEMPEST CONDEMN MY VENTROUS YOUTH . . . . . 27 EDW THIRD/PS 3 240
CONDEMN PAINE'S HATRED OF PRIESTS IF YOU DARE . . . . 384A ANNO WATSON MARG
OF MORTAL LIFE TO CONDEMN THE ACCUSED WHO AT SATAN'S BAR 507 MILTON 23 42
I DO NOT CONDEMN RUBENS REMBRANT OR TITIAN BECAUSE THEY 602D PUB ADDR AD/N *PROSE
I DO NOT CONDEMN [BARTOLOZZI] STRANGE OR WOOLETT BECAUSE 602D PUB ADDR AD/N PROSE
I DO NOT CONDEMN POPE OR DRYDEN BECAUSE THEY DID NOT . 602D PUB ADDR AD/N PROSE
CONDEMNATION   SEE SELF-CONDEMNATION
THIS SENTENCE IS TO INTRODUCE ANOTHER IN CONDEMNATION . 472B ANNO REYNOLDS MARG
BUT WHEN LEUTHA A DAUGHTER OF BEULAH BEHELD SATAN'S 492 MILTON 11 28
CONDEMNATION
IN CONDEMNATION OF MY WORK & APPROBATION OF . . . . . 592B PUB ADDRESS/N PROSE
THE ROCKY LAW OF CONDEMNATION & DOUBLE GENERATION & DEATH 656 JERUSALEM 30 37
MUST PASS THRO CONDEMNATION AND AWAKE BEYOND THE GRAVE . 662 JERUSALEM 35 10
IN AN ETERNAL CONDEMNATION IN FIERCE BURNING FLAMES . 722 JERUSALEM 80 13
FOR YOUR CORRECTION OR CONDEMNATION BEGGING YOU TO SUPPLY 860B LETTER 56 PROSE
CONDEMND   SEE SELF-CONDEMND
BEFORE MY EYES & FOR EVERY ONE OF THESE I AM CONDEMND . 339 FOUR ZOAS 7B 252
THUS WAS THE LAMB OF GOD CONDEMND TO DEATH . . . . . 349 FOUR ZOAS 8 325
WAS SOON CONDEMND & WRATH WAS LEFT TO WRATH & PITY TO PITY 351 FOUR ZOAS 8 393
OVER THEIR VICTIMS THUS WAS THE LAMB OF GOD CONDEMND TO 382 FOUR ZOAS AD 6 13
DEATH
THE INNOCENT SHOULD BE CONDEMND FOR THE GUILTY THEN AN 491 MILTON 11 16
ETERNAL ROSE
SAYING IF THE GUILTY SHOULD BE CONDEMND HE MUST BE 491 MILTON 11 17
AN ETERNAL DEATH
LOUD VOICD BARD AND MANY CONDEMND THE HIGH TONED SONG . 495 MILTON 13 47
ART & HIS STROKES ARE STILL TO BE CONDEMND BECAUSE THEY 591B PUB ADDRESS/N PROSE
NOT BEING AMONG THE CONDEMND . . . . 610B V LAST JUDG/N PROSE
THAT THEY MAY BE CONDEMND BY LAW & THE LAMB OF GOD BE SLAIN 672 JERUSALEM 43 30
FOOD OF DESPAIR THEY DRINK THE CONDEMND SOUL & REJOICE . . 680 JERUSALEM 49 63
CONDEMNED
HAS NO MAN CONDEMNED THEE . . . . 754 EV GOSPEL(E)/N 47
CONDEMNEST
TO WRATH WHICH THOU CONDEMNEST TILL THOU OBEY MY VOICE . . 739 JERUSALEM 91 58
CONDEMNING   SEE SELF CONDEMNING
IN VAIN CONDEMNING GLORIOUS WAR . . . . 419 I SAW A MONK/N 12
IN VAIN CONDEMNING GLORIOUS WAR . . . . 683 I SAW A MONK/J 10
CONDEMNS
THE FOX CONDEMNS THE TRAP NOT HIMSELF . . . . 151C MARRIAGE HH 8 PROSE
("GENERAL COPYING...DELUSIVE") HERE HE CONDEMNS 448C ANNO REYNOLDS MARG
GENERALIZING
OF THE OPINION THAT REYNOLDS CONDEMNS & LAUGHS AT . . . 473C ANNO REYNOLDS MARG
MAKES THEM DO WHAT HE CONDEMNS AS SIN . . . . . . 616D V LAST JUDG/N PROSE
CONDEMNST
[THE GLORY OF WAR THOU CONDEMNST IN VAIN] . . . . . . 419 I SAW A MONK/N 11
CONDENSATIONS
THE HERMAPHRODITIC CONDENSATIONS ARE DIVIDED BY THE KNIFE 689 JERUSALEM 58 11
OF VEGETATIVE NATURE BY THEIR HARD RESTRICTING 713 JERUSALEM 73 21
CONDENSATIONS
CONDENSD
OF LIFE BY MAGIC POWER CONDENSD INFERNAL FORMS ART-BOUND 204 AMERICA CANC B 14
MOUNTING UP FROM HIS FURY CONDENSD . . . . 256 BOOK OF LOS 3 35
CONDENSD HAND HAS ABSORBD ALL HIS BRETHREN IN HIS MIGHT 628 JERUSALEM 8 43
CONDENSD HIS EMANATIONS INTO HARD OPAKE SUBSTANCES . . 628 JERUSALEM 9 1
HE SIEZD THE BARS OF CONDENSD THOUGHTS TO FORGE THEM . . 628 JERUSALEM 9 4
CONDENSE
CONDENSE BENEATH MY HAMMER INTO FORMS OF CRUELTY . . . 628 JERUSALEM 9 27
I THEREFORE CONDENSE THEM INTO SOLID ROCKS STEDFAST . . 652 JERUSALEM 28 10
WHILE HAND & HYLE CONDENSE THE LITTLE-ONES & ERECT THEM 737 JERUSALEM 90 49
INTO
CONDENSING
BOUND BUT CONDENSING IN TORRENTS . . . . 224 URIZEN 4 20
HE SIEZD BEATING INCESSANT CONDENSING . . . . 260 BOOK OF LOS 5 29
BIND THEM [TOGETHER] CONDENSING THE STRONG ENERGIES . . . 284 FOUR ZOAS 2 * 163
THAT MILTON'S SHADOW HEARD & CONDENSING ALL HIS FIBRES . 527 MILTON 37 6
CONDENSING THEM INTO SOLID ROCKS WITH CRUELTY AND 641 JERUSALEM 19 25
ABHORRENCE

376

	PAGE	TITLE	LINE

CONDENSING   (CONTINUED)
AND BECOMES ONE WITH HER MINGLING CONDENSING IN SELF-LOVE   656 JERUSALEM 30   36
THEIR GIANT FORMS CONDENSING INTO NATIONS & PEOPLES   684 JERUSALEM 53   8
     & TONGUES
THEMSELVES CONDENSING TO ROCKS & INTO THE RIBS OF A MAN   706 JERUSALEM 68   25
CONDESCEND
FROM YOUR HIGH FLIGHTS YE MUST CONDESCEND TO STUDY   .   .   . 593C PUB ADDRESS/N   PROSE
CONDESCENSION
HE SMILES WITH CONDESCENSION HE TALKS OF BENEVOLENCE &   533 MILTON 41   19
     VIRTUE
CONDITION
WILL BE SOLD ONLY ON CONDITION OF ITS REMAINING IN THE   563B DESC CAT   PROSE
     ARTIST'S HANDS
SAYING DOTH JEHOVAH FORGIVE A DEBT ONLY ON CONDITION THAT   694 JERUSALEM 61   17
     IT SHALL
CONDITIONS
CONDITIONS OF SALE ONE THIRD OF THE PRICE TO BE PAID   .   . 563B DESC CAT   PROSE
BE PAYED DOTH HE FORGIVE POLLUTION ONLY ON CONDITIONS OF   694 JERUSALEM 61   18
     PURITY
CONDUCED
SPIRITUAL AID HAS NOT A LITTLE CONDUCED TO MY RESTORATION   852B LETTER 50   PROSE
     TO
CONDUCT
TO CONDUCT THE VOICE OF ENION TO AHANIA'S MIDNIGHT PILLOW   287 FOUR ZOAS 2   290
A SCHEME OF HUMAN CONDUCT INVISIBLE & INCOMPREHENSIBLE   .   . 483 MILTON 4   13
A FIRM & DETERMINATE CONDUCT ON THE PART OF ARTISTS   .   . 600B PUB ADDRESS/N   PROSE
TO THE FOUR POINTS CONDUCT TO ENGLAND & SCOTLAND & IRELAND   637 JERUSALEM 16   33
AGAINST FORMER CONDUCT & TO DEMAND JUSTICE & TRUTH   .   .   . 825D LETTER 27   PROSE
WHEN WE MEET I WILL PERFECTLY DESCRIBE TO YOU MY CONDUCT &   826A LETTER 27   PROSE
THE CONDUCT OF OTHERS TOWARD ME & YOU WILL SEE THAT I   .   826A LETTER 27   PROSE
WHICH WAS TO LEAVE THE WHOLE CONDUCT OF THE AFFAIR TO YOU   842C LETTER 42   PROSE
CONDUCTED
BEAMS CONDUCTED BY FLUID SO PURE   .   .   .   .   259 BOOK OF LOS 5   11
BY PROVIDENCE DIVINE CONDUCTED NOT BENT FROM HIS OWN WILL   319 FOUR ZOAS 6   282
EVERY THING IS CONDUCTED BY SPIRITS NO LESS THAN DIGESTION   621C JERUSALEM 3   PROSE
     OR SLEEP
GRATITUDE HAVING CONDUCTED ME THRO THREE THAT WOULD   .   .   . 862C LETTER 60   PROSE
A SPIRIT CONDUCTED TO PARADISE   .   .   .   .   SUPP ILLUS GRAY   *TITLE
CONDUCTS
THE SAVIOUR WHILE THE EVIL ANGELS ARE DRIVEN GENTLY   441D INSC FALL MAN   PROSE
     CONDUCTS
THEN LOS CONDUCTS THE SPIRITS TO BE VEGETATED INTO   .   .   . 517 MILTON 29   47
CONFERRD
BUT URIZEN AWOKE & LUVAH WOKE & THUS CONFERRD   .   .   .   .   277 FOUR ZOAS 1   * 487
BUT LUVAH CLOSE CONFERRD WITH URIZEN IN DARKSOM NIGHT   .   . 326 FOUR ZOAS 7   255
THUS THEY CONFERRD AMONG THE INTOXICATING FUMES OF MYSTERY   328 FOUR ZOAS 7   315
CONFERRING
CONFERRING TIMES ON TIMES AMONG THE BRANCHES OF THAT TREE   327 FOUR ZOAS 7   314
CONFESS
BUT IF ANY ONE IS HURT BY HIS LYING WILL CONFESS HIS LIE   67B ANNO LAVATER   MARG
     SEE...
I HEARD THIS WITH SOME WONDER & MUST CONFESS MY OWN   154A MARRIAGE HH 12   PROSE
     CONVICTION
NO EARTHLY PARENTS I CONFESS   .   .   .   .   748 EV GOSPEL(B)/N   7
NO EARTHLY PARENTS I CONFESS   .   .   .   .   750 EV GOSPEL(C)/N   7
NO EARTHLY PARENTS I CONFESS   .   .   .   .   751 EV GOSPEL(D)/N   9
MILD CHRISTIAN REGRETS TO THE DEVIL CONFESS   .   .   .   .   . 752 EV GOSPEL(D)/N   37
NO EARTHLY PARENTS I CONFESS   .   .   .   .   757 EV GOSPEL(I)/N   33
THAT I CAN CONFESS MYSELF IGNORANT OF I ALSO KNOW &   .   .   . 814D LETTER 23   PROSE
CONFESSD
RUBENS'S LUXEMBOURG GALLERY IS CONFESSD ON ALL HANDS   .   . 599C PUB ADDRESS/N   *PROSE
THEIR [BEAUTY IS CONFESSD EVEN BY THE LIPS OF PASCH   601A PUB ADDRESS/N   *PROSE
     HIMSELF]
METAL RULES AT THE ENDS OF THE CANTOS BUT HE CONFESSD   .   . 857B LETTER 54   PROSE
THAT REYNOLDS HAS CONFESSD CANNOT BE MIXED YOU WILL   .   .   . 866B LETTER 64   PROSE
CONFESSED
BUT CONFESSED HIS SINS BEFORE ALL THE WORLD   .   .   .   .   . 682D JERUSALEM 52   PROSE
CONFESSEDLY
CONFESSEDLY THE FIRST POET OF ENGLAND OUGHT TO BE GIVEN   856B LETTER 54   PROSE
CONFESSING
CONFESSING THEIR CRIME WITH HUMILIATION AND SORROW   .   .   . 525 MILTON 35   33
CONFESSION
A CONFESSION   .   .   .   .   472B ANNO REYNOLDS   MARG
HERE IS A PLAIN CONFESSION THAT HE THINKS MIND &   .   .   .   475D ANNO REYNOLDS   MARG
THE TEAR AND THE CONFESSION OF HONESTY OPEN & UNDISGUISD   675 JERUSALEM 45   7
IS AN APOLOGY & CLOKE FOR HIS SIN & NOT A CONFESSION   .   . 682D JERUSALEM 52   PROSE
CONFESSIONS
THE BOOK WRITTEN BY ROUSSEAU CALLD HIS CONFESSIONS   .   .   . 682D JERUSALEM 52   PROSE
CONFESSORS
MOCKING THE CONFESSORS & MARTYRS CLAIMING   506 MILTON 22   43
     SELF-RIGHTEOUSNESS
CONFIDENCE
("LET THE DEGREE OF EGOTISM BE THE MEASURE OF   66D ANNO LAVATER   MARG
     CONFIDENCE") UNEASY
SUBMITS WITH CONFIDENCE TO PUBLIC PATRONAGE & REQUESTS   .   . 587D CHAUCER/N   PROSE
TO MR HOARE WHO IS WORTHY OF EVERY CONFIDENCE YOU CAN   .   . 842A LETTER 41   PROSE
THE GREATEST CONFIDENCE IN HER PERFECT RECOVERY   .   .   .   . 851C LETTER 50   PROSE
OF ANCIENT GRECE I SPEAK WITH PERFECT CONFIDENCE AND   .   . 852A LETTER 50   PROSE
AND BY WINDOW-SHUTTERS CONSEQUENTLY I CAN WITH CONFIDENCE   852B LETTER 50   PROSE
CONFIDENCE THAT IT SHALL BE SO NO LONGER HE IS BECOME MY   852C LETTER 50   PROSE
I SEND WITH SOME CONFIDENCE PROOFS OF MY TWO PLATES   .   .   . 853B LETTER 52   PROSE
SO HIGH FINISHED A STATE I AM SURE MARK MY CONFIDENCE   .   . 853B LETTER 52   PROSE

PAGE TITLE LINE

CONFIDENCE   (CONTINUED)
    CONFIDENCE IN MY DISCRETION SUCH WAS OUR CONVERSATION   . . 856D LETTER 54   PROSE
CONFIDENT
    A CONFIDENT INSOLENCE SPROUTING FROM SYSTEMATIC REASONING   157C MARRIAGE HH 21 PROSE
CONFIND
    AND THE MAN WAS CONFIND FOR A WRITING PROPHETIC . . . . . . 135 FRENCH REVOLTN   29
    . . . HE WAS CONFIND . . . . 136 FRENCH REVOLTN   50
    DECEIT TO SECRESY [INCLIND] CONFIND   . . . . 175 HOW TO KNOW/N   5
    [MODEST PRUDISH & CONFIND] . . . . 175 HOW TO KNOW/N   6
    WHAT CHAIN ENCOMPASSES IN WHAT LOCK IS THE RIVER OF LIGHT   363 FOUR ZOAS 9   226
        CONFIND
    TO THE WEAK TRAVELLER CONFIND BENEATH THE MOONY SHADE   . . 497 MILTON 15   33
    I WISHD OWING TO A VIOLENT COLD WHICH CONFIND ME TO MY BED 834B LETTER 34   PROSE
CONFINE
    KEPT WATCH FOR ETERNALS TO CONFINE   . . . . 226 URIZEN 5   39
    THAT IF I DO NOT CONFINE MYSELF TO THIS I SHALL NOT LIVE   812C LETTER 22   PROSE
CONFINED
    IS NECESSARY FROM THE CONFINED NATURE OF BODILY SENSATION   98D ALL RELIGIONS   PROSE
    THAT TRUTH SHOULD BE CONFINED TO MATHEMATICAL DEMONSTRATION 474D ANNO REYNOLDS   MARG
    AND SHALL PAINTING BE CONFINED TO THE SORDID DRUDGERY   . . 576B DESC CAT 4   PROSE
CONFIRM
    CONFIRM THE STRONG WITH STRENGTH THE WEAK INSPIRE   . . . 25 EDW THIRD/PS 3   181
    HOMER VIRGIL & OVID CONFIRM THIS OPINION   . . . . 778D HOMERS POETRY   PROSE
CONFIRMD
    AND AS I WAS THEN PERSWADED & REMAIN CONFIRMD   . . . . 153C MARRIAGE HH 12   PROSE
    SO SPAKE THE ETERNAL AND CONFIRMD IT WITH A THUNDEROUS OATH 492 MILTON 11   27
    WHAT IT WAS ONLY ENLARGED AND CONFIRMD   . . . . 816A LETTER 23   PROSE
    THE SOLDIER SAID CONFIRMD BY ANOTHER PERSON IN THE COACH I 833C LETTER 33   PROSE
CONFIRMS
    IT CONFIRMS THE SUSPITION I ENTERTAIN CONCERNING THOSE   553B BELLS WEEKLY/N   MARG
CONFLICT
    GREAT THE CONFLICT & GREAT THE JEALOUSY   . . . . 250 AHANIA 3   18
    HIS SONS FLED FROM HIS SIDE TO JOIN THE CONFLICT PALE HE   278 FOUR ZOAS 1   521
        HEARD
    RETREAT FROM THE FIERCE CONFLICT ALL THE SONS OF URIZEN   279 FOUR ZOAS 1   538
        AT ONCE
    INCESSANT WAS THE CONFLICT ON HE BENT HIS WEARY STEPS   . . 313 FOUR ZOAS 6   77
    SHE JOYD IN ALL THE CONFLICT . . . . 338 FOUR ZOAS 7B   213
    IN CONFLICT WITH THOSE FEMALE FORMS WHICH IN BLOOD   498 MILTON 17   7
        & JEALOUSY
    TOLD OF THE ENORMOUS CONFLICT EARTHQUAKE BENEATH AROUND   500 MILTON 18   48
    AWAY FROM THE CONFLICT OF LUVAH & URIZEN FIXING THE GATES   637 JERUSALEM 16   31
    LOUD THE SUN & MOON RAGE IN THE CONFLICT LOUD THE STARS   704 JERUSALEM 67   31
CONFLICTIONS
    IN UNSEEN CONFLICTIONS WITH SHAPES   . . . . 222 URIZEN 3   14
CONFLICTS
    BY FIGHTINGS AND CONFLICTS DIRE   . . . . 224 URIZEN 4   27
CONFOUND
    THE RUSHING OF THY SCALES CONFOUND ME THY HOARSE RUSHING   335 FOUR ZOAS 7B   84
        SCALES
    [HERE LIES THE MAN XXX CONFOUND]   . . . . 551 WILLM COWPER/N *   1
CONFOUNDED
    THEY STOOD CONFOUNDED AND THUS TIRIEL RAISD HIS SILVER   105 TIRIEL 4   63
        VOICE
    CONFOUNDED AT THE TERRIBLE STRENGTH OF IJIM THEY KNEW TWAS 105 TIRIEL 4   69
        VAIN
    [WHY DO YOU STAND CONFOUNDED THUS HEUXOS WHY ART   105 TIRIEL 4   74
        THOU SILENT]
    IN HER BRIGHT SKIRTS ASTONISHD & CONFOUNDED HE BEHELD   . . 285 FOUR ZOAS 2   203
    THOSE WHO BELIEVE WANT NOT TO BE CONFOUNDED BY MIRACLES   392A ANNO WATSON   MARG
    HIS HORSES ARE MAD HIS HARROW CONFOUNDED HIS COMPANIONS   488 MILTON 8   18
        ENRAGD
    HE LISTENS TO THE SOUNDS OF WAR ASTONISHD AND CONFOUNDED   506 MILTON 23   * 8
    DO YOU BELIEVE IT A CONFOUNDED LIE   . . . . 551 WILLM COWPER/N   6
CONFUSD
    HE CEAST THE HEAVY CLOUDS CONFUSD ROLLD ROUND THE LOFTY   106 TIRIEL 5   14
        TOWERS
CONFUSE
    AND OF ENDLESS REFLECTED LIGHTS THAT CONFUSE ONE ANOTHER   583B DESC CAT 9   PROSE
CONFUSED
    INTO CONFUSED PERTURBATION & STRIFE & HONOUR & PRIDE   . . 361 FOUR ZOAS 9   154
CONFUSION
    CONFUSION STARTLES ALL AROUND   . . . . 17 BLIND-MANS/PS   54
    WHEN CONFUSION RAGES WHEN THE FIELD IS IN A FLAME   . . . 18 EDW THIRD/PS 1   6
    THINKING OF THIS MY SPIRIT IS TURNED WITHIN ME INTO   36B COUCH DEATH/PS PROSE
        CONFUSION
    BABEL WITH THOUSAND TONGUES CONFUSION IT WAS CALLD AND   41A THEN SHE BORE *PROSE
        GIVN TO SHAME
    & FILLD HIM WITH CONFUSION FEAR AS A TORRENT WILD   . . . 42B THEN SHE BORE   PROSE
    HERE WAS GREAT CONFUSION & DISORDER   . . . . 54D ISLAND MOON 9   PROSE
    CONGLOBING IN THE DARK CONFUSION MEAN TIME LOS WAS BORN   275 FOUR ZOAS 1   420
    ALL IS CONFUSION ALL IS TUMULT & WE ALONE ARE ESCAPED   . . 294 FOUR ZOAS 3   103
    A DOLOROUS GROAN THAT STRUCK WITH DUMBNESS ALL CONFUSION   295 FOUR ZOAS 3   147
    THRO THE CONFUSION LIKE A CRACK ACROSS FROM IMMENSE TO   295 FOUR ZOAS 3   149
        IMMENSE
    WHENCE I MIGHT TRAVEL ROUND THE OUTSIDE OF THIS DARK   317 FOUR ZOAS 6   201
        CONFUSION
    . . . IN HORRIBLE [CONFUSION] DESTRUCTION   . . . . . 317 FOUR ZOAS 6   217
    IN DARK CONFUSION MEAN TIME LOS WAS BORN & ENITHARMON   . . 326 FOUR ZOAS 7   259
    THE DIRE CONFUSION TILL THE BATTLE FAINTS THOSE THAT REMAIN 344 FOUR ZOAS 8   118
    WAILD SHRILL IN THE CONFUSION & THE SPECTRE OF URTHONA   . . 358 FOUR ZOAS 9   25
    MINGLED WITH THE CONFUSION WHO SHALL CALL THEM FROM THE   358 FOUR ZOAS 9   31
        GRAVE

378

```
                                                          PAGE    TITLE        LINE
CONFUSION    (CONTINUED)
   [WITHOUT] BEYOND THIS UNIVERSAL CONFUSION BEYOND        359 FOUR ZOAS 9        91
      THE ?REMOTEST POLE
   MY ROBE IS TURNED TO CONFUSION & MY BRIGHT GOLD TO STONES  360 FOUR ZOAS 9   *  106
   SEE YOU NOT ALL THIS WRACKING FURIOUS CONFUSION   . . .  360 FOUR ZOAS 9       128
   RISING FROM THE CONFUSION IN TEARS & HOWLINGS & DESPAIR  362 FOUR ZOAS 9       202
   THEY SAW NO MORE THE TERRIBLE CONFUSION OF THE WRACKING  367 FOUR ZOAS 9       380
      UNIVERSE
   THEY HEARD NOT SAW NOT FELT NOT ALL THE TERRIBLE CONFUSION  367 FOUR ZOAS 9   381
   SING A NEW SONG DROWNING CONFUSION IN ITS HAPPY NOTES  . .  375 FOUR ZOAS 9   683
   THEN FELL THE LEGIONS OF MYSTERY IN MADDNING CONFUSION  . .  376 FOUR ZOAS 9  722
   THE MILLS OF SATAN AS THE EASIER TASK FOUND ALL CONFUSION  488 MILTON 8         5
   WITH ECCHOING CONFUSION THO THE SUN WAS RISEN ON HIGH  . .  488 MILTON 8       10
   OF WOOL HE HID HER FROM THE SPECTRE IN SHAME & CONFUSION OF  639 JERUSALEM 17  53
   ALL IS CONFUSION ALL IS TUMULT & WE ALONE ARE ESCAPED  . .  655 JERUSALEM 29  82
   AS A MIGHTY TEMPLE DELIVERING FORM OUT OF CONFUSION  . . .  690 JERUSALEM 58  22
   IT MUST LIE IN CONFUSION TILL ALBION'S TIME OF AWAKING  . .  728 JERUSALEM 83 58
   PAINTING & ENGRAVING WHICH IN THE CONFUSION OF LONDON  . . 8128 LETTER 22    PROSE
   YOU THRO LIFE & AFTER DEATH SHAME & CONFUSION OF FACE  . .  813B LETTER 22   PROSE
   I HAVE LOST MY CONFUSION OF THOUGHT WHILE AT WORK  . . .  853A LETTER 51    *PROSE
CONFUTE
   IT IS FOLLY TO CONFUTE HIM SO SERIOUSLY IN THEM  . . . .  392D ANNO WATSON    MARG
CONFUTES
   PLATO CONFUTES HIMSELF  . . . . . . . . . . . . .  605A V LAST JUDG/N    PROSE
   [AS] FOR THUS THE GOSPEL SIR ISAAC CONFUTES  . . . . .  752 EV GOSPEL(D)/N     43
CONGENERATED
   WHETHER OF JERUSALEM'S OR VALA'S RUINS CONGENERATED WE  655 JERUSALEM 29       81
      KNOW NOT
CONGENIAL
   SPONTANEOUS EFFUSION OF HUMANITY CONGENIAL TO THE WANTS  802A LETTER 14      PROSE
CONGLOBD
   AND EARTH CONGLOBD IN NARROW ROOM ROLLD ROUND ITS SULPHUR  204 AMERICA CANC B   7
      SUN
CONGLOBINC
   PANTING CONGLOBING TREMBLING  . . . . . . . . .  228 URIZEN 11              5
   NOW STRETCHING OUT NOW SWIFT CONGLOBING  . . . . . .  252 AHANIA 4            16
   CONGLOBING IN THE DARK CONFUSION MEAN TIME LOS WAS BORN  275 FOUR ZOAS 1      420
   PANTING CONGLOBING TREMBLING SHOOTING OUT TEN THOUSAND  303 FOUR ZOAS 4       225
      BRANCHES
   DEEP DOWN INTO THE ABYSS PANTING CONGLOBING TREMBLING  . .  482 MILTON 3       12
   SEEING THESE HEAVENS & HELLS CONGLOBING IN THE VOID . . .  672 JERUSALEM 43    16
CONGLOMERATING
   SELF-RIGHTEOUSNESSES CONGLOMERATING AGAINST THE DIVINE  634 JERUSALEM 13    *  52
      VISION
CONGO
   CONGO ZAARA CANADA GREENLAND CAROLINA MEXICO  . . . . .  712 JERUSALEM 72      41
CONGRATULATE
   I CONGRATULATE YOU NOT ON ANY ATCHIEVEMENT  . . . . . .  790B LETTER 2      PROSE
   DEAR CUMBERLAND I HAVE TO CONGRATULATE YOU ON  . . . . .  797C LETTER 10    PROSE
   AND NOW MY DEAR SIR CONGRATULATE ME ON MY RETURN TO  . .  822C LETTER 26    PROSE
   CONGRATULATE YOU ON THE RECEIT OF ANOTHER FINE BOY  . .  873B LETTER 77     PROSE
CONGREGATED
   AGAINST THE DIVINE IMAGE CONGREGATED ASSEMBLIES OF WICKED  347 FOUR ZOAS 8   258
      MEN
CONJECTURE
   THE RUIN OF A PART OF NIMROD'S TOWER WHICH I CONJECTURE  824A LETTER 27     PROSE
CONJOINED
   THEN ALL THE MALES [CONJOINED] COMBINED INTO ONE MALE &  707 JERUSALEM 69   *   1
      EVERY ONE
CONJOINING
   AND THE SEVENTEEN (CONJOINING) WITH BATH THE SEVENTH  . .  676 JERUSALEM 45 *  37
CONJUGAL
   OF MY LIFE HE IS THE ENEMY OF CONJUGAL LOVE AND IS THE  . .  852A LETTER 50  PROSE
CONJUNCTION
   CONJUNCTION WITH THOSE WHO KNOW GOD & HEAVENLY THINGS  . .  88B ANNO LAVATER  MARG
   IS IN CONJUNCTION WITH SUCH MEN AS MY FRIEND CUMBERLAND  792A LETTER 4      PROSE
   BUT BY MY CONJUNCTION WITH FLAXMAN WHO KNOWS TO FORGIVE  799 TO FLAXMAN/L     12
      NERVOUS FEAR
   IT DRAWS THE SOUL TOWARDS ETERNAL LIFE & CONJUNCTION WITH  834A LETTER 33   PROSE
CONJUNCTIVES
   COOKERY CHYMISTRY [?CONJUNCTIVES] MECHANICS TACTICS  46D ISLAND MOON 3     *PROSE
      PATHOLOGY
CONJURING
   CONJURING HIM BY THE HIGHEST THAT HE SHOULD WATCH OVER THEM  674 JERUSALEM 44  29
CONNAUT
   MUNSTER SOUTH IN REUBEN'S GATE CONNAUT WEST IN JOSEPH'S  711 JERUSALEM 72      3
      GATE
CONNECTED
   THE [LOVE] AND [FRIENDSHIP] OF THOSE WITH WHOM TO  620D JERUSALEM 3        PROSE
      BE CONNECTED
CONNECTIONS
   HIS CONNECTIONS THROUGHOUT ENGLAND & INDEED EUROPE &  . .  841C LETTER 41   PROSE
CONNEXIONS
   BECAUSE OF PECUNIARY CONNEXIONS BETWEEN H(HAYLEY) & ME  . .  819D LETTER 25 PROSE
   HIS CONNEXIONS & HIS METHOD OF MANAGING IT NOW WOULD BE  820A LETTER 25     PROSE
   CONNEXIONS ARE UNIVERSAL HIS PRESENT HOUSE IS ON THE MOST  857A LETTER 54   PROSE
CONNOISSEUR
   OF THE ARTIST AND CONNOISSEUR FOR REASONS THAT FOLLOW  . .  581C DESC CAT 7  PROSE
   CONNOISSEUR IN ENGRAVING HAS GIVEN HER WARM APPROBATION  853B LETTER 52     PROSE
CONNOISSEURED
   EVERY MAN IS SO WHO HAS NOT BEEN CONNOISSEURED OUT OF HIS  864C LETTER 61   PROSE
      SENSES
```

```
                                                               PAGE    TITLE          LINE
CONNOISSEURS    SEE CUNNING SURES
     TO ENGLISH CONNOISSEURS  . . . . . . . . . . . . . . .  546C  ENGLISH CONN/N   TITLE
     THOUSANDS OF CONNOISSEURS WITH JOY RAN RAVING  . . . . .  555  BLAKES APL/N 1      5
     THOUSANDS OF CONNOISSEURS WITH JOY RAN RAVING  . . . . .  556  BLAKES APL/N 2      8
     BY ARTISTS AND CONNOISSEURS OF ALL RANKS  . . . . . . .  562B  DESC CAT ADV     PROSE
     AND TO DOUBT ITS OWN POWERS CONNOISSEURS TALK AS IF RAFAEL 563C  DESC CAT        PROSE
     AND WHAT CONNOISSEURS CALL TOUCH I KNOW BY EXPERIENCE  .  575B  DESC CAT 3       PROSE
     THE CONNOISSEURS AND ARTISTS WHO HAVE MADE OBJECTIONS  .  576C  DESC CAT 4       PROSE
     CONNOISSEURS WHO SAID THAT THEY WERE VERY ADMIRABLE  . .  585A  DESC CAT 15      PROSE
     HOW MANY THOUSAND CONNOISSEURS RAN RAVING  . . . . . . .  595  BLAKES APOL/PA *    4
     THE MODERN CHALCOGRAPHIC CONNOISSEURS & AMATEURS  . . .  596C  PUB ADDRESS/N    PROSE
     THE ITALIANS LAUGH AT ENGLISH CONNOISSEURS WHO ARE  . .  597B  PUB ADDRESS/N    PROSE
     PRONOUNCD BY ENGLISH CONNOISSEURS & REYNOLDS THEIR DOLL   599D  PUB ADDRESS/N    PROSE
     THE ESTIMATION YOU ARE HELD IN AMONG ARTISTS & CONNOISSEURS 798B  LETTER 10      PROSE
     RUINOUS TO EFFECT THO CONNOISSEURS MAY THINK OTHERWISE  .  815B  LETTER 23       PROSE
     OF CERTAIN CONNOISSEURS THAT THEY CANNOT SEE APPROPRIATE   864C  LETTER 61       PROSE
     MUCH SURPRISED AT THE DISLIKE THAT SOME CONNOISSEURS SHEW  864D  LETTER 61       PROSE
CONQR
     TO RESIST W(WILLIAM) THE CONQR  . . . . . . . . . .  208D  SUBJCTS HIST/N   TITLE
     W(WILLIAM) THE CONQR CROWNED  . . . . . . . . . .  208D  SUBJCTS HIST/N   TITLE
CONQUER
     THOU SHALT OVERCOME AND CONQUER HIM  . . . . . . . .  38A  SAMSON/PS        PROSE
     THE GLORY OF CHRISTIANITY IS TO CONQUER BY FORGIVENESS  .  683A  JERUSALEM 52    PROSE
CONQUERD
     HE CONQUERD LUVAH MY BELOVED HE TOOK ME AND MY FATHER  .  722  JERUSALEM 80       19
     & DARKNESS NOT UNLIKE A CHAMPION I HAVE CONQUERD  . . .  816A  LETTER 23        PROSE
CONQUERED
     TO A PRINCE OF THE FIFTH CENTURY WHO CONQUERED EUROPE  .  578C  DESC CAT 5       PROSE
CONQUERING
     AND SHALL STILL GO ON CONQUERING NOTHING CAN WITHSTAND  .  816A  LETTER 23       PROSE
CONQUEROR
     ("MAGNANIMOUSLY A CONQUEROR") THIS WAS OLD GEORGE  . .  82B  ANNO LAVATER     MARG
          THE SECOND
     A GOD & NOT A MAN A CONQUEROR IN TRIUMPHANT GLORY  . . .  333  FOUR ZOAS 7B       9
     HAS EVER BEEN A CONQUEROR AND IS THAT SPECIES OF CHARACTER  567D  DESC CAT 3      PROSE
     ARTHUR ALFRED THE NORMAN CONQUEROR RICHARD JOHN  . . . .  713  JERUSALEM 73       36
CONQUERORS
     BUT WE ARE CONQUERORS EVERY WHERE NOTHING  . . . . . .  23  EDW THIRD/PS 3      73
     OF HER LORDLY CONQUERORS HER PALACES LEVELLD WITH THE DUST  653  JERUSALEM 29     24
CONQUERS
     SAYING BY THIS HE CONQUERS ENEMIES & GOVERNS KINGDOMS  .  153D  MARRIAGE HH 12  PROSE
     TILL HE ULTIMATELY CONQUERS  . . . . . . . . . . . .  582D  DESC CAT 9       PROSE
CONQUEST
     FOR A GREAT CONQUEST ARE BUNGLERY  . . . . . . . . .  549  ENGL ENCOU/N 2 *    3
     OF ARTHUR'S CONQUEST OF THE WHOLE WORLD  . . . . . . .  577D  DESC CAT 5       PROSE
CONRADE
     THEIR SAD COMPLAININGS BEAR FOR CONRADE LOST  . . . . .  43D  WOE CRIED MUSE  PROSE
     UNTIMELY LOST THY CONRADE ONCE WHEN LIVING THEE I LOVD    43D  WOE CRIED MUSE  PROSE
          EVN UNTO DEATH
CONSANGUINITIES
     OF LOVES OF UNNATURAL CONSANGUINITIES AND FRIENDSHIPS  .  652  JERUSALEM 28       7
CONSCIENCE
     WITH TREMBLING AGE THE VOICE OF CONSCIENCE THEN  . . . .  28  EDW THIRD/PS 3     285
     YET NOT FORLORN IF CONSCIENCE IS HIS FRIEND  . . . . .  28  EDW THIRD/PS 3     293
     I'LL SHEW HOW CONSCIENCE CAME FROM HEAVEN  . . . . . .  42A  THEN SHE BORE    PROSE
     TWAS CONSCIENCE WHO BROUGHT MELANCHOLY DOWN  . . . . .  42B  THEN SHE BORE    PROSE
     CONSCIENCE WAS SENT A GUARD TO REASON  . . . . . . . .  42B  THEN SHE BORE    PROSE
     THEN DOWN CAME CONSCIENCE WITH HIS LOVELY BAND THE  . .  42B  THEN SHE BORE    PROSE
     . . . HE BY CONSCIENCE URGD IN THE CITY OF PARIS RAISD    136  FRENCH REVOLTN    42
          A PULPIT
     & IS HE HONEST WHO RESISTS HIS GENIUS OR CONSCIENCE  . .  154B  MARRIAGE HH 12  PROSE
     CONSCIENCE IN THOSE THAT HAVE IT IS UNEQUIVOCAL IT  . .  385C  ANNO WATSON      MARG
     IF CONSCIENCE IS NOT A CRITERION OF MORAL RECTITUDE WHAT   386B  ANNO WATSON     MARG
          IS IT
     ("CRIMINALS FOLLOW DICTATES OF CONSCIENCE") CONTEMPTIBLE  386B  ANNO WATSON      MARG
     VIRTUE & HONESTY OR THE DICTATES OF CONSCIENCE ARE  . .  386B  ANNO WATSON      MARG
     EXCLUSIVE OF CONSCIENCE OR THE WORD OF GOD UNIVERSAL  .  389C  ANNO WATSON      MARG
     DENY A CONSCIENCE IN MAN & THE COMMUNION OF SAINTS & ANGELS  741  JERUSALEM 93    22
     I HAVE LATELY HAD SOME PRICKS OF CONSCIENCE  . . . . .  791A  LETTER 3         PROSE
CON-SCIENCE
     THE STUDY OF NATURE WITHOUT CON- OR INNATE SCIENCE  . .  457C  ANNO REYNOLDS  * MARG
          (CON-SCIENCE)
     A FOOL & KNAVE HAVING NO CON-SCIENCE OR INNATE SCIENCE  .  459B  ANNO REYNOLDS   MARG
CONSCIOUS
     MARY MOVES IN SOFT BEAUTY & CONSCIOUS DELIGHT  . . . . .  428  MARY               9
     THE STRONG MAN ACTS FROM CONSCIOUS SUPERIORITY  . . . .  580B  DESC CAT 5       PROSE
     COURAGE OF CONSCIOUS INDUSTRY WORTHY OF HIS FORMER KINDNESS 851D  LETTER 50      PROSE
CONSCIOUSLY
     THE MORE ANCIENT & CONSCIOUSLY & PROFESSEDLY INSPIRED MEN  480B  MILTON 1        PROSE
CONSECRATED
     AND SILVER & GOLD HE CONSECRATED READING INCESSANTLY  .  344  FOUR ZOAS 8       141
     BENEATH THE IRON WHIPS OF THEIR CAPTAINS & CONSECRATED    704  JERUSALEM 67       30
          BANNERS
CONSECRATION
     THEIR MARRIAGE & THEIR BAPTISM THEIR BURIAL & CONSECRATION  738  JERUSALEM 91     15
CONSEQUENCE
     BECAUSE HE MAY THINK MY REMARKS OF SMALL CONSEQUENCE  . .  88A  ANNO LAVATER     MARG
     IN CONSEQUENCE ALL THE LOVES & GRACES WITH THEM ARE SIN    88D  ANNO LAVATER   * MARG
     OF EQUAL MAGNITUDE AND CONSEQUENCE WITH THE PRODUCTIONS   207C  PRSPECTUS 1793  PROSE
     CONSEQUENCE IS IT WHETHER MOSES WROTE THE PENTATEUCH  . .  392D  ANNO WATSON     MARG
     AS IF REASONING WAS OF ANY CONSEQUENCE TO A QUESTION  . .  394A  ANNO WATSON     MARG
     IT IS NOT OF CONSEQUENCE  . . . . . . . . . . . . .  394C  ANNO WATSON      MARG
```

```
                                                                   PAGE      TITLE          LINE
CONSEQUENCE    (CONTINUED)
      FOLLY OF WHAT CONSEQUENCE IS IT TO THE ARTS    . . . . .    465A ANNO REYNOLDS       MARG
      AN OPINION OF FATAL & ACCURSED CONSEQUENCE TO MAN     .     682A JERUSALEM 52        PROSE
      OF REAL CONSEQUENCE I HAVE ACCOMPLISHD BY COMING   . . .    812A LETTER 22           PROSE
      VERY LIKELY BE OF GREAT CONSEQUENCE IT IS COWPER'S MILTON   821C LETTER 25           PROSE
      THE FRUIT WAS IN CONSEQUENCE OF THE BLIGHT WHEN THIS    .   830C LETTER 30           PROSE
      & THE MERIT OF THE DESIGNS AN OBJECT OF CONSEQUENCE  . .    832D LETTER 32           PROSE
      OF CONSEQUENCE LUCKILY HE FOUND FAULT WITH THE PAPER   .    846D LETTER 44           PROSE
      OF NO CONSEQUENCE BUT I COULD NOT OMIT TELLING IT YOU  .    860B LETTER 56           PROSE
      IN CONSEQUENCE OF THIS I PRODUCED ABOUT TWENTY DESIGNS  .   861C LETTER 59           PROSE
      OF BAD PERHAPS OF FATAL CONSEQUENCE IS VERY SORRY INDEED   SUPP LETTER 81A          *PROSE
CONSEQUENCES
      THE PHILOSOPHY OF CAUSES & CONSEQUENCES MISLED LAVATER  .    88C ANNO LAVATER        MARG
      I CARED NOT FOR CONSEQUENCES BUT WROTE    .   .   .   .     153C MARRIAGE HH 12      PROSE
      HISTORIAN TURNER AND TWISTER OF CAUSES AND CONSEQUENCES     579A DESC CAT 5          PROSE
      CONSEQUENCES TO THOSE TO WHOM IT SEEMS TO BE EVEN OF   .    663 JERUSALEM 36          53
CONSEQUENT
      & ITS CONSEQUENT EVIL & THE HONESTY OF OTHERS & ITS  . .   393B ANNO WATSON          MARG
      CONSEQUENT GOOD THIS SENSE OF THE BIBLE IS EQUALLY TRUE    393B ANNO WATSON          MARG
CONSEQUENTLY
      CONSEQUENTLY HE IS NOT CHARITABLE . . . . . . . . .        556D JESUS NOT/N          PROSE
      AND CONSEQUENTLY THEY ARE THE PHYSIOGNOMIES OR LINEAMENTS   567C DESC CAT 3          PROSE
      THE PAINTER HAS CONSEQUENTLY VARIED THE HEADS AND FORMS     567C DESC CAT 3          PROSE
      CORREGGIO IS A SOFT AND EFFEMINATE AND CONSEQUENTLY A  .   583A DESC CAT 9           PROSE
      (AND) CONSEQUENTLY THEY ARE THE PHYSIOGNOMIES OR           590D CHAUCER 2           *PROSE
         (LINEAMENTS)
      THE PAINTER HAS CONSEQUENTLY VARIED THE HEADS AND FORMS     590D CHAUCER 2           PROSE
      CONSEQUENTLY HIS (EXECUTION) MUST HAVE BEEN AS QUEER  .    596C PUB ADDRESS/N       *PROSE
      EACH IDENTITY [&] IS ETERNAL CONSEQUENTLY   .   .   .   .  607A V LAST JUDG/N       *PROSE
      GIVEN THEM & WE DIRECTLY GO TO PRINTING CONSEQUENTLY IT    840C LETTER 39            PROSE
      THAN HIMSELF CONSEQUENTLY WAS BORN . . . . . . . .         847D LETTER 44            PROSE
      AND BY WINDOW-SHUTTERS CONSEQUENTLY I CAN WITH CONFIDENCE   852B LETTER 50           PROSE
      CONSEQUENTLY OUR COUNTRYMEN ARE EASILY BROW-BEAT ON THE    864C LETTER 61            PROSE
CONSIDER
      WOULD TO GOD THAT EVERY ONE WOULD CONSIDER THIS   . . .     73C ANNO LAVATER         MARG
      AND CONSIDER THAT LOVE IS LIFE . . . . . . . . .            76A ANNO LAVATER         MARG
      SEEMS TO CONSIDER MAN AS SIMPLE & YET CAPABLE OF EVIL  .    80A ANNO LAVATER         MARG
      & PURE WOULD TO GOD THAT ALL MEN WOULD CONSIDER IT   . .    82D ANNO LAVATER         MARG
      . . . LEARN TO CONSIDER ALL MEN AS THY EQUALS  . . .       143 FRENCH REVOLTN        193
      O HORRIBLE O DREADFUL STATE CONSIDER THE HOT BURNING  .    155C MARRIAGE HH 17      PROSE
      NONE OF WHICH THE BISHOP HAS DARED TO CONSIDER    . . .    390C ANNO WATSON          MARG
      IS THE DEVIL GREAT CONSIDER . . . . . . . . . .            410D ANNO BACON           MARG
      I CONSIDER REYNOLDS'S DISCOURSES TO THE ROYAL ACADEMY  .   452A ANNO REYNOLDS        MARG
      I CONSIDER THE FOLLOWING SENTENCE IS SUPREMELY INSOLENT     453C ANNO REYNOLDS       MARG
      MACBETH THOSE WHO DRESS THEM FOR THE STAGE CONSIDER   . .  569D DESC CAT 3           PROSE
      WITH REAL BODIES WOULD DO WELL TO CONSIDER THAT THE VENUS   576C DESC CAT 4          PROSE
      SHOULD CONSIDER THE FOLLOWING . . . . . . . . .           599C PUB ADDRESS/N        PROSE
      THAT I DO NOT CONSIDER EITHER THE JUST OR THE WICKED   .   614C V LAST JUDG/N        PROSE
      CONSIDER THIS O MORTAL MAN O WORM OF SIXTY WINTERS SAID    661 JERUSALEM 34           57
         LOS
      CONSIDER SEXUAL ORGANIZATION & HIDE THEE IN THE DUST  .    661 JERUSALEM 34           58
      CONSIDER ME AS THINE ENEMY ON ME TURN ALL THY FURY  . .    670 JERUSALEM 42           40
      AS SUCH [?A ?MAN] AN ONE WILL CONSIDER WHAT HE IS DOING    781D INSC UPCOTT         *PROSE
      I CONSIDER THE AUTOGRAPH OF MR CRUICKSHANK WHICH VERY  .   782A INSC UPCOTT          PROSE
      TO CONSIDER IS THIS WHETHER JESUS DID NOT SUFFER HIMSELF   787A ANNO THORNTON        MARG
         TO BE
      TO CONSIDER THIS TO ALL ETERNITY WILL BE COMMENT ENOUGH    787A ANNO THORNTON        MARG
      CONSIDER WHAT LORD BACON SAYS "SENSE SENDS OVER TO"  . .   794A LETTER 5             PROSE
      I CONSIDER IT AS THE GRANDEST POEM THAT THIS WORLD CONTAINS 825A LETTER 27           PROSE
      IGNORANTLY & NOT DESIGNEDLY SURELY I OUGHT TO CONSIDER HIM  828C LETTER 28           PROSE
      KNOWING YOUR AVERSION TO REVIEWS & REVIEWING I CONSIDER    841D LETTER 41            PROSE
      MR H(HOARE) APPEARS TO ME TO CONSIDER IT AS A REJECTION OF  842C LETTER 42           PROSE
      I COULD NOT CONSIDER IT SO BUT THAT AS I UNDERSTAND OUR    842C LETTER 42            PROSE
      SO THE AMERICANS WILL CONSIDER WASHINGTON AS THEIR GOD  .  845B LETTER 44            PROSE
      THEREFORE HECATE MUST BE A FINISHD PLATE I CONSIDER   . .  855B LETTER 53            PROSE
      HONOUR OF LONDON BOOKSELLERS & CONSIDER THEM AS LOSING A   856C LETTER 54            PROSE
      AND THAT SEAGRAVE IS TO BE THE PRINTER THAT WE MUST        858B LETTER 55            PROSE
         CONSIDER
      WE CAN APPLY SOME OF THE PLATES TO THE NEW EDITION         858B LETTER 55            PROSE
         I CONSIDER
      CONSIDER MYSELF A ROBBER TO RETAIN MORE THAN YOU AT ANY    858C LETTER 55            PROSE
         TIME
      WHICH I CONSIDER AS ONE OF MY BEST    .   .   .   .   .    861B LETTER 58            PROSE
      WOULD TO GOD THAT THEY WOULD CONSIDER IT   .   .   .   .   863A LETTER 60            PROSE
      THAT THEY WOULD CONSIDER THEIR SPIRITUAL LIFE  .   .   .   863A LETTER 60            PROSE
      CONSIDER THAT I HAVE BEEN REDUCED TO A SKELETON FROM   .   879A LETTER 88            PROSE
CONSIDERABLY
      THE PRICE WILL BE CONSIDERABLY RAISED TO NON-SUBSCRIBERS   587B CHAUCER 1            PROSE
         MAY...
      VERY CONSIDERABLY WEAKEND BY THE LAST SEVERE ATTACKS   .   873D LETTER 78           *PROSE
CONSIDERATE
      CONSIDERATE AGE MY LORD VIEWS MOTIVES   . . . . . .         27 EDW THIRD/PS 3         282
      HE WEPT BEFORE HIS WRATHFUL BRETHREN THANKFUL & CONSIDERATE 675 JERUSALEM 45          23
CONSIDERATION
      DUTY TO HIS COUNTRY IS THE FIRST CONSIDERATION & SAFETY    383C ANNO WATSON          MARG
         THE LAST
      THE CONSIDERATION OF THESE THINGS IS THE WHOLE DUTY OF MAN  383C ANNO WATSON         MARG
      IS WORTHY THE CONSIDERATION OF THE RICH   .   .   .   .    560D EXHIBITION ADV       PROSE
      A LITTLE CONSIDERATION MUST SHEW THE FALLACY OF THIS       565A DESC CAT 2           PROSE
         OPINION
      THEIR CONSIDERATION OF MY PLAN AS A GREAT PUBLIC [DEED]    601B PUB ADDRESS/N       *PROSE
         MEANS
```

```
                                                              PAGE      TITLE            LINE
CONSIDERATION    (CONTINUED)
        CHARACTER ITS GOODNESS OR BADNESS IS ANOTHER CONSIDERATION   778B HOMERS POETRY      PROSE
        SHE WILL FORGIVE ANY FAILURE IN CONSIDERATION OF             815D LETTER 23         PROSE
          THE ENDEAVOUR
        IF I HAD CONSIDERD I SHOULD HAVE USED MORE CONSIDERATION     854D LETTER 53         PROSE
CONSIDERATIONS
        BUT THESE CONSIDERATIONS (ARE THE) BUSINESS OF ETERNITY      383C ANNO WATSON        MARG
        CONSIDERATIONS & BELONG TO PHILOSOPHY & NOT TO POETRY    .   778C HOMERS POETRY      PROSE
CONSIDERD
        BUT IF MAN IS CONSIDERD AS ONLY EVIL & GOD ONLY GOOD     .   80A ANNO LAVATER        MARG
        CUNNING PLOTTERS WERE CONSIDERD AS WISE MACHIAVELS   . . .   397B ANNO BACON         MARG
        I ALWAYS CONSIDERD TRUE ART & TRUE ARTISTS TO BE            452B ANNO REYNOLDS       MARG
          PARTICULARLY
        ARE TO BE CONSIDERD AS WEAK HEADED FANATICS    . . . . .    473A ANNO REYNOLDS       MARG
        THE BARD CEASD ALL CONSIDERD AND A LOUD RESOUNDING MURMUR    495 MILTON 13             45
        OF ITS EVER EXISTENT IMAGES IS CONSIDERD AS LESS PERMANENT  605B V LAST JUDG/N       PROSE
        WHEN THIS VERSE WAS FIRST DICTATED TO ME I CONSIDERD    .   621C JERUSALEM 3         PROSE
        ("THE AEGYPTIANS") THEY ALSO CONSIDERD GOD AS ABSTRACTED   774A ANNO BERKELEY      * MARG
        BUT JESUS AS ALSO ABRAHAM & DAVID CONSIDERD GOD    . . . .  774A ANNO BERKELEY       MARG
        JESUS CONSIDERD IMAGINATION TO BE THE REAL MAN & SAYS   .   774A ANNO BERKELEY     * MARG
        PERMANENT IN THE IMAGINATION CONSIDERD AS NOTHING BY    .   776D INSC LAOCOON       PROSE
        CONSIDERD WHAT IS NOT TOO EXPLICIT AS THE FITTEST          793B LETTER 5           PROSE
          FOR INSTRUCTION
        CONSIDERD AS ONE DISTINGUISHD BY SOME MENTAL PERFECTION    830B LETTER 30          PROSE
        IF I HAD CONSIDERD I SHOULD HAVE USED MORE CONSIDERATION   854D LETTER 53          PROSE
        I CONSIDERD IT MY DUTY TO INTERFERE I EXPRESSD MY         856B LETTER 54          PROSE
          OWN RESPECT
CONSIDERED
        CONSIDERED AS AN ARBITRARY COMMAND OF THE AGENT    . . . .  391C ANNO WATSON         MARG
        AND SO ARE CHAUCER'S LET THEM BE SO CONSIDERED   . . . .   570A DESC CAT 3          PROSE
        THE ARTIST HAS CONSIDERED HIS STRONG MAN AS A RECEPTACLE   580B DESC CAT 5          PROSE
        WHO WANTS THE SUCCOUR OF IT IS CONSIDERED    . . . . . .   590B CHAUCER 2           PROSE
        [ ?WHY SHOULD LAELIUS BE ?CONSIDERED SIR JOSHUA'S          SUPP ANNO REYNOLDS     * MARG
          ?COUNTERPART ]
CONSIDERING
        OR A MAN WHO WALKS WITHOUT CONSIDERING    . . . . . . .    782A INSC UPCOTT         PROSE
        SCULPTURE BY CONSIDERING EVERY VALUABLE ORIGINAL THAT IS   797D LETTER 10           PROSE
        TOLERABLY CONSIDERING THE TERRIBLE STORM HE HAS BEEN THRO  844D LETTER 43           PROSE
        IF YOU SHOULD PUT ON YOUR CONSIDERING CAP JUST AS YOU DID  870B LETTER 71           PROSE
CONSIDERS
        INDIVIDUAL WHICH GOD CONSIDERS IN THE BIBLE AS MURDER   .  388B ANNO WATSON         MARG
        WHO CONSIDERS IT AS AN ARBITRARY ACT OF THE AGENT    . .   391D ANNO WATSON         MARG
        NOBODY CONSIDERS THESE THINGS WHEN THEY READ HOMER OR  .   411B ANNO BOYD           MARG
        PROTESTANT CONSIDERS NATURE AS INCAPABLE OF BEARING A CHILD 779A ANNO CELLINI        MARG
        TO EXPEND (TWO THOUSAND) A YEAR MR PHILLIPS CONSIDERS YOU  841C LETTER 41           PROSE
          AS
        CONSIDERS AS IMPOLITIC AND THAT A HANDSOME GENERAL EDITION 858A LETTER 55           PROSE
CONSIST
        TO CONSIST EITHER IN WHO THEY WERE WRITTEN BY . . . . .    393B ANNO WATSON         MARG
        TO CONSIST IN THE AGREEMENTS & (DISAGREEMENTS) OF IDEAS    708 JERUSALEM 70             8
        & TO CONSIST OF ALL MILTON'S POEMS WITH COWPER'S NOTES AND 824C LETTER 27           PROSE
CONSISTENT
        & IF IT IS CONSISTENT WITH HIS DIVINE PROVIDENCE RESTORE   796C LETTER 8            PROSE
          HIM
        UNDER SIX MONTHS CONSISTENT WITH MY OTHER WORK SO THAT  .  878C LETTER 88           PROSE
CONSISTING
        THE HOLY FAMILY CONSISTING OF MARY JOSEPH JOHN THE BAPTIST 614A V LAST JUDG/N       PROSE
CONSISTS
        APPROVED WITH AVIDITY POETRY CONSISTS IN THESE CONCEPTIONS 576B DESC CAT 4          PROSE
        STRENGTH CONSISTS IN ACCUMULATION OF POWER TO THE    . .   580B DESC CAT 5          PROSE
        IT IS IN PARTICULARS THAT WISDOM CONSISTS & HAPPINESS TOO  611B V LAST JUDG/N       PROSE
        ALL LIFE CONSISTS OF THESE TWO THROWING OFF ERROR & KNAVES 612D V LAST JUDG/N       PROSE
CONSOLATION
        INTO THE COUNTRY WHICH IS TO ME CONSOLATION ENOUGH    . .  812A LETTER 22           PROSE
CONSOLATIONS
        OUR SORROW IS SWALLOWD UP IN HOPE SUCH CONSOLATIONS   . .  854B LETTER 53           PROSE
CONSOLIDATED
        CONSOLIDATED & EXTENDED WORK WILL BE AS KINDLY RECIEVED    620D JERUSALEM 3         PROSE
CONSTABLE
        CONSTABLE OR TAKING AWAY THE PARISH BUSINESS HAH    . . .  52A ISLAND MOON 8        PROSE
CONSTANT
        AGUE & RHEUMATISM HAVE BEEN ALMOST HER CONSTANT ENEMIES    811B LETTER 22           PROSE
CONSTANTINE
        PAUL CONSTANTINE CHARLEMAINE LUTHER MILTON    . . . . .    350 FOUR ZOAS 8           362
        I SAW A MONK OF [CONSTANTINE] CHARLEMAINE   . . . . . .    418 I SAW A MONK/N          1
        TITUS CONSTANTINE CHARLEMAINE . . . . . . . . . . .        420 I SAW MNK AD/N          6
        PAUL CONSTANTINE CHARLEMAINE LUTHER BEHOLD THEY STAND      509 MILTON 24             32
          BEFORE US
        ABRAHAM MOSES SOLOMON PAUL CONSTANTINE CHARLEMAINE    . .  528 MILTON 37             41
        TITUS CONSTANTINE CHARLEMAINE  . . . . . . . . . . .       683 I SAW A MONK/J         21
        ABRAHAM MOSES SOLOMON PAUL CONSTANTINE CHARLEMAINE    . .  716 JERUSALEM 75           16
CONSTANTINE'S
        TO CONSTANTINE'S GREAT CITY EMPIRE FLED . . . . . . .      41B THEN SHE BORE       PROSE
CONSTANTLY
        YOU ARE PHARISEES & HYPOCRITES FOR YOU ARE CONSTANTLY   .  682D JERUSALEM 52        PROSE
        SEEKING AMUSEMENT IN MAKING VERSES TO WHICH HE CONSTANTLY  830D LETTER 30           PROSE
        WE CONSTANTLY SEND WISHES TO OUR SPIRITUAL FRIENDS YOURS   847C LETTER 44           PROSE
          SINCERELY
CONSTELLATION
        [SLEEP LIKE THE DEAD] BUT LIKE A CONSTELLATION RISN AND    205 AMERICA CANC C         23
          BLAZING
        AND OVER THE VOID SPACES OVER SUN & MOON & STAR           365 FOUR ZOAS 9           315
          & CONSTELLATION
```

```
                                                            PAGE      TITLE           LINE
CONSTELLATION    (CONTINUED)
    FOR THE CONSTELLATION ARCTURUS OR BOOTES THE KEEPER  . . .  577D DESC CAT 5      PROSE
CONSTELLATIONS
    A UNIVERSE OF FIERY CONSTELLATIONS IN THEIR BRAIN      . . .  314 FOUR ZOAS 6        91
    URIZEN ANSWERD READ MY BOOKS EXPLORE MY CONSTELLATIONS  . .  322 FOUR ZOAS 7        90
    IN FURY A SERPENT WONDROUS AMONG THE CONSTELLATIONS OF       342 FOUR ZOAS 8        68
        URIZEN
    DROVE THE FIERCE HARROW AMONG THE CONSTELLATIONS OF JEHOVAH  493 MILTON 12          25
    THOU SEEST THE CONSTELLATIONS IN THE DEEP & WONDROUS NIGHT   511 MILTON 25          66
    CONTEMPLATING THE CONSTELLATIONS   . . . . . . . . .  619C ILLUS MILTON     PROSE
    CONSTELLATIONS OVER THE DEADLY DEEPS OF INDEFINITE          625 JERUSALEM 7        22
        UDAN-ADAN
CONSTERNATION
    WITHOUT SOME ADVENTURE IT HAS STRUCK A CONSTERNATION THRO    828A LETTER 28       PROSE
CONSTITUTES
    IF LOSING AND OBLITERATING THE OUTLINE CONSTITUTES         585A DESC CAT 15      PROSE
        A PICTURE
CONSTITUTION
    I BELIEVE MY CONSTITUTION TO BE A GOOD ONE BUT IT HAS  . .  870D LETTER 72       PROSE
CONSTITUTIONAL
    HE IS A COMPLETE ROGUE WITH CONSTITUTIONAL GAIETY ENOUGH    568D DESC CAT 3      PROSE
CONSTRICTING
    CONSTRICTING INTO DRUID ROCKS ROUND CANAAN AGAG & ARAM      685 JERUSALEM 54       26
        & PHAROH
CONSTRICTION
    TREMBLING & FEAR TERROR CONSTRICTION ABJECT SELFISHNESS     530 MILTON 38          39
CONSTRICTIVE
    SO SPOKE THE HARD COLD CONSTRICTIVE SPECTRE HE IS NAMED     685 JERUSALEM 54       25
        ARTHUR
CONSTRUCTED
    I COULD NOT DARE TO TAKE VENGEANCE FOR ALL THINGS ARE SO    657 JERUSALEM 31       30
        CONSTRUCTED
CONSULT
    GENERAL PRINCIPLE AGAIN UNLESS YOU CONSULT PARTICULARS  . . 456B ANNO REYNOLDS  * MARG
    TO THEIR RESPECTIVE EARTHS & THERE ALL NIGHT CONSULT WITH   526 MILTON 36           4
        ANGELS
    CAME TO CONSULT HIM SECRETLY     . . . . . . . . .  750 EV GOSPEL(C)/N       10
    CAME TO CONSULT HIM SECRETLY     . . . . . . . . .  751 EV GOSPEL(D)/N       12
    BEEN ABLE TO CONSULT MR FLAXMAN ABOUT THE DESIGNS OF MR     838B LETTER 37       PROSE
    MEET TO CONSULT AGAINST THE OTHER NOTHING CAN BE GREATER    859B LETTER 56       PROSE
        THAN
CONSULTATION
    THAT THIS BOOK IS WRITTEN BY CONSULTATION WITH GOOD SPIRITS  88B ANNO LAVATER      MARG
CONSULTED
    WHOM I HAVE CONSULTED THAT TO GIVE A TRUE IDEA OF  . . . 848A LETTER 45       PROSE
    ENGRAVER I CONSULTED MR PARKER ON THE SUBJECT BEFORE I  . . 855A LETTER 53       PROSE
CONSULTING
    CONSULTING AS ONE MAN ABOVE [MOUNT GILEAD] . . . . . . . 277 FOUR ZOAS 1        475
    YET HAD AN OPPORTUNITY OF CONSULTING ABOUT IT BUT SOON WILL  836C LETTER 35       PROSE
    HAS PREVENTED OUR CONSULTING YOU IN OUR PROGRESS  . . .  861D LETTER 59       PROSE
    I AM SURE THAT ANY PERSON CONSULTING HIS OWN EYES MUST  .  864D LETTER 61       PROSE
    PERSON CONSULTING HIS OWN REPUTATION OR THE REPUTATION OF   864D LETTER 61       PROSE
CONSUMD
    FIRES INWRAP THE EARTHLY GLOBE YET MAN IS NOT CONSUMD  .  199 AMERICA 8          15
    BUT THE FIVE GATES WERE CONSUMD & THEIR BOLTS AND HINGES    203 AMERICA 16         22
        MELTED
    FIRST I FOUGHT WITH THE FIRE CONSUMD . . . . . . . .  224 URIZEN 4            14
    SURGE FOAM AND LABOUR INTO LIFE FIRST BORN & FIRST CONSUMD   238 EUROPE PREL 1       9
    THEY SAW HIS BONEY FEET ON THE ROCK THE FLESH CONSUMD IN    242 EUROPE 12          10
        FLAMES
    HEART COLD AND THE LITTLE TONGUE CONSUMD THAT ONCE         276 FOUR ZOAS 1       449
        IN THOUGHTLESS JOY
    CONSUMING WHAT MUST BE CONSUMD THEN IN POWER & MAJESTY  . . 333 FOUR ZOAS 7B        7
    ORC RENT HER & HIS HUMAN FORM CONSUMD IN HIS OWN FIRES  . . 338 FOUR ZOAS 7B      211
    STRENGTH FROM THE EARTHS CONSUMD & HEAVENS & ALL HIDDEN     358 FOUR ZOAS 9    *   38
        ABYSSES
    AND NOW FIERCE ORC HAD QUITE CONSUMD HIMSELF IN MENTAL      366 FOUR ZOAS 9       358
        FLAMES
    AND MAN WALKS FORTH FROM MIDST OF THE FIRES THE EVIL IS     379 FOUR ZOAS 9       827
        ALL CONSUMD
    THE STARS CONSUMD LIKE A LAMP BLOWN OUT & IN THEIR STEAD    379 FOUR ZOAS 9    *  829
        BEHOLDS
    HOW IS IT WE HAVE WALKD THRO FIRES & YET ARE NOT CONSUMD    379 FOUR ZOAS 9       844
    [ TO BE CONSUMD IN BURNING FIRES ] . . . . . . . . .  422 BENEATH/N           14
    TO BE CONSUMD IN BURNING FIRES  . . . . . . . . . .  424 THE GOLDEN NET       13
    CONSUMING AND CONSUMD FOR-EVER IN FLAMES OF MORAL JUSTICE   667 JERUSALEM 40       30
    THE RAGING FLAMES THO SHE RETURND [ CONSUMD DAY AFTER DAY ] 726 JERUSALEM 82       67
    BE FORGIVENESS THAT HE MAY BE (CONSUMD) IN HIS OWN SHAME    788A ANNO THORNTON  * MARG
    THAT HE MAY BE CONSUMD IN HIS OWN SHAME . . . . . . . 788A ANNO THORNTON  * MARG
    SOFT CONSUMD IN DELIGHT    . . . . . . . . . . . .  805 TO BUTTS/L          57
CONSUME
    . . . THEY SHALL CONSUME FROM THE THISTLY FIELD       140 FRENCH REVOLTN     145
    . . . AND BLASTING OF TRUMPETS CONSUME   . . . . . .  143 FRENCH REVOLTN     209
    BUT THEY SHALL ROT ON DESART SANDS & CONSUME IN BOTTOMLESS  199 AMERICA 8           7
        DEEPS
    I BACK RETURN WEAKER & WEAKER CONSUME ME NOT AWAY  . .  296 FOUR ZOAS 3       190
    BEHOLD THESE WONDERS OF ETERNITY WE SHALL CONSUME  . . .  304 FOUR ZOAS 4       262
    IF THOU DOST GO AWAY FROM ME I SHALL CONSUME UPON THE ROCKS  348 FOUR ZOAS 8       300
    OF BITTER HOPE ALTHO I CONSUME IN THESE RAGING WATERS  . . 355 FOUR ZOAS 8    *  547
    SHE GATHERD IT TOGETHER TO CONSUME HER HARLOT ROBES  . .  356 FOUR ZOAS 8       609
    OF ORC BEGAN TO CONSUME IN FIERCE RAVING FIRE HIS FIERCE    358 FOUR ZOAS 9        34
        FLAMES
```

```
                                                           PAGE     TITLE           LINE
CONSUME   (CONTINUED)
        LET ORC CONSUME LET THARMAS RAGE LET DARK URTHONA GIVE    362 FOUR ZOAS 9       184
        SHALL BE RENEWD & ALL THESE ELEMENTS THAT NOW CONSUME  .  . 362 FOUR ZOAS 9     209
        THE FRUIT SHALL RIPEN & FALL DOWN & THE FLOWERS CONSUME    368 FOUR ZOAS 9       420
            AWAY
        OR ELSE CONSUME THEIR SHADOWY SEMBLANCE YET THEY OBSTINATE 376 FOUR ZOAS 9       737
        ETERNAL DEATH WHO CAN ENDURE LET US CONSUME IN FIRES   .  . 377 FOUR ZOAS 9     740
        CONSUME IN MY CONSUMMATION BUT THOU MAIST TAKE A FORM  .  . 499 MILTON 18        28
        FEMALE & LOVELY THAT CANNOT CONSUME IN MAN'S CONSUMMATION  499 MILTON 18         29
        MILTON WILL UTTERLY CONSUME US & THEE OUR BELOVED FATHER   507 MILTON 23         13
        BEHOLD THESE WONDERS OF ETERNITY WE SHALL CONSUME  .  .  . 519 MILTON 30         27
        JERUSALEM'S CHILDREN CONSUME IN FLAMES AMONG THE STARS .  . 527 MILTON 37        12
        AND WE ALSO & ALL BEULAH CONSUME BENEATH ALBION'S CURSE    681 JERUSALEM 50      17
        IF THOU DOST GO AWAY FROM ME I SHALL CONSUME UPON THESE    705 JERUSALEM 67      46
            ROCKS
        WODEN AND THOR AND FRIGA WHOLLY CONSUME MY SAXONS  .  .  . 727 JERUSALEM 83      19
CONSUMED
        THE ANCIENT TRADITION THAT THE WORLD WILL BE CONSUMED IN   154B MARRIAGE HH 14  PROSE
            FIRE
        THE WHOLE CREATION WILL BE CONSUMED AND APPEAR INFINITE    154B MARRIAGE HH 14  PROSE
            AND HOLY
        & HE WAS CONSUMED AND AROSE AS ELIJAH  .  .  .  .  .  .  . 158D MARRIAGE HH 22  PROSE
        MUST BE CONSUMED WITH THE EARTH  .  .  .  .  .  .  .  .  . 220 TO TIRZAH/SE       2
        CONSUMED AND CONSUMING  .  .  .  .  .  .  .  .  .  .  .  . 238 EUROPE PREL 1      10
        LIKE A SCROLL READY TO BE CONSUMED IN THE FIRES OF THE     443A LAST JUDGMNT/L  PROSE
            ANGELS
        WAIT TILL THE JUDGEMENT IS PAST TILL THE CREATION         511 MILTON 25         59
            IS CONSUMED
        DARE NOT APPROACH THE DAUGHTERS OPENLY LEST HE BE CONSUMED 638 JERUSALEM 17       7
        THE WICKER MAN OF SCANDINAVIA IN WHICH CRUELLY CONSUMED    677 JERUSALEM 47       7
        FILLD WITH THE LITTLE-ONES ARE CONSUMED IN THE FIRES OF    679 JERUSALEM 49      11
            THEIR ALTARS
        THE VEGETATING CITIES ARE BURNED & CONSUMED FROM THE EARTH 679 JERUSALEM 49      12
CONSUMER
        O CRUEL O DESTROYER O CONSUMER O AVENGER  .  .  .  .  .  . 107 TIRIEL 6          23
        MORE HAPPY IS THE DARK CONSUMER HOPE DROWNS ALL MY TORMENT 355 FOUR ZOAS 8      544
CONSUMES
        HER OWN POISON WHICH CONSUMES HER NETHER PARTS  .  .  .  . 41C THEN SHE BORE    PROSE
CONSUMING   SEE SELF CONSUMING
        CONSUMING ALL BOTH FLOWERS & FRUITS INSECTS & WARBLING    110 TIRIEL 8          38
            BIRDS
        .  .  . O PRINCES OF FIRE WHOSE FLAMES ARE FOR GROWTH NOT  142 FRENCH REVOLTN  179
            CONSUMING
        CONSUMED AND CONSUMING  .  .  .  .  .  .  .  .  .  .  .  . 238 EUROPE PREL 1      10
        AROUND THE LIMBS OF ALBION'S GUARDIAN HIS FLESH CONSUMING  243 EUROPE 12         33
        DOWNWARDS & OUTWARDS [TENDING] CONSUMING IN THE WARS OF    280 FOUR ZOAS 1    * 574
            ETERNAL DEATH
        CONSUMING ALL TO THE END CONSUMING LOVE AND [JOY] HOPE     297 FOUR ZOAS 3      204
            ARE ENDED
        TORN BY BLACK STORMS & CEASELESS TORRENTS OF CONSUMING FIRE 306 FOUR ZOAS 5     56
        CONSUMING IN THE RAGING LAMPS OF MERCY POURD IN RIVERS  .  . 320 FOUR ZOAS 7    11
        CONSUMING THOU KNOWST ME NOW O URIZEN PRINCE OF LIGHT  .  . 324 FOUR ZOAS 7     148
        CONSUMING WHAT MUST BE CONSUMD THEN IN POWER & MAJESTY  .  . 333 FOUR ZOAS 7B     7
        IN THE FIERCE FLAMES THE LIMBS OF MYSTERY LAY CONSUMING    359 FOUR ZOAS 9       67
            WITH HOWLING
        BOWING HIS HEAD OVER THE CONSUMING UNIVERSE HE CRIED  .  . 359 FOUR ZOAS 9       98
        THEY HOWL & WRITHE IN SHOALS OF TORMENT IN FIERCE FLAMES   377 FOUR ZOAS 9      749
            CONSUMING
        THEY HOWL & WRITHE IN SHOALS OF TORMENT IN FIERCE FLAMES   513 MILTON 27         31
            CONSUMING
        WHICH HINDER THE VISION OF GOD TURNING ALL INTO A CONSUMING 604C V LAST JUDG/N  PROSE
            FIRE
        CONSUMING & THE ALMIGHTY HATH MADE ME HIS CONTRARY  .  .  . 630 JERUSALEM 10     56
        IN THOSE CHURCHES EVER CONSUMING & EVER BUILDING BY THE    634 JERUSALEM 13      62
            SPECTRES
        CONSUMING AND CONSUMD FOR-EVER IN FLAMES OF MORAL JUSTICE  667 JERUSALEM 40      30
        TORN WITH BLACK STORMS & CEASELESS TORRENTS OF HIS OWN     667 JERUSALEM 40      39
            CONSUMING FIRE
        THREE-FOLD EMBRACE RETURNS CONSUMING LIVES OF GODS & MEN   709 JERUSALEM 70      27
        OF EARTHQUAKES & CONSUMING FIRES THEY ROLL APART IN FEAR   733 JERUSALEM 88       9
        GOD OUT OF CHRIST IS A CONSUMING FIRE MERCY WRATH  .  .  . SUPP INSC HERVEY    *TITLE
CONSUMMATE
        CONSUMMATE WORLDLY WISDOM  .  .  .  .  .  .  .  .  .  .  . 571D DESC CAT 3       PROSE
        BUT NO ONE CAN CONSUMMATE FEMALE BLISS IN LOS'S WORLD      708 JERUSALEM 69      30
            WITHOUT
        NOR CAN ANY CONSUMMATE BLISS WITHOUT BEING GENERATED  .  . 731 JERUSALEM 86      42
        HE SAYS WITH MOST CONSUMMATE ART  .  .  .  .  .  .  .  .  . 750 EV GOSPEL(C)/N   15
        HE SAYS WITH MOST CONSUMMATE ART  .  .  .  .  .  .  .  .  . 751 EV GOSPEL(D)/N   17
CONSUMMATED
        WILL BE RENEWD BY THE THREE & CONSUMMATED IN MENTAL FIRES  329 FOUR ZOAS 7      356
CONSUMMATING
        .  .  . CONSUMMATING BY PAINS & LABOURS  .  .  .  .  .  .  . 328 FOUR ZOAS 7     343
CONSUMMATION
        NOR THE CONSUMMATION OF LOS COULD EVER MELT THE CHAIN  .  . 309 FOUR ZOAS 5     162
        BUT AN ETERNAL CONSUMMATION IS DARK ENION  .  .  .  .  .  . 355 FOUR ZOAS 8     542
        .  .  . THEY GIVE UP THEMSELVES TO CONSUMMATION  .  .  .  . 358 FOUR ZOAS 9      32
        I HEAR MYSTERY HOWLING IN THESE FLAMES OF CONSUMMATION  .  . 360 FOUR ZOAS 9    114
        LET LUVAH RAGE IN THE DARK DEEP EVEN TO CONSUMMATION  .  . 360 FOUR ZOAS 9      142
        STILL TO THE ROCK IN VAIN THEY STROVE TO ENTER THE        364 FOUR ZOAS 9      289
            CONSUMMATION
        .  .  . COULD NOT ENTER THE CONSUMMATION  .  .  .  .  .  . 364 FOUR ZOAS 9      290
        CONSUME IN MY CONSUMMATION BUT THOU MAIST TAKE A FORM  .  . 499 MILTON 18        28
```

	PAGE	TITLE	LINE

CONSUMMATION   (CONTINUED)
FEMALE & LOVELY THAT CANNOT CONSUME IN MAN'S CONSUMMATION   499 MILTON 18   29
PREPARING IT FOR THE GREAT CONSUMMATION RED THE CHERUB   502 MILTON 20   23
  ON SINAI
THESE YOU SHALL BIND IN A TWIN-BUNDLE FOR THE CONSUMMATION   511 MILTON 25   37
THE ETERNAL CONSUMMATION OF VEGETABLE LIFE & DEATH   . . . 609A V LAST JUDG/N   PROSE
VEGETATION IT IS AN ETERNAL CONSUMMATION   . . . . . . 609A V LAST JUDG/N   PROSE
THE CITIES OF THE NATIONS ARE THE SMOKE OF HER CONSUMMATION 653 JERUSALEM 29   22
CONSUMSION
HE SLEPT VERY LITTLE WHICH HE BROUGHT INTO A CONSUMSION   49C ISLAND MOON 5   PROSE
CONTAGION
BREEDS SATIRE FOUL CONTAGION FROM WHICH NONE ARE FREE   . . 41C THEN SHE BORE   PROSE
ESCAPED THE CONTAGION OF THE COURT OF JUSTICE I FEAR THAT   829C LETTER 30   PROSE
CONTAGIOUS
WIPING HIS MILD AND MEEKIN MOUTH FROM ALL CONTAGIOUS TAINTS 128 BOOK OF THEL 2   7
CONTAIN
AS A CUP CANNOT CONTAIN MORE THAN ITS CAPACIOUSNESS   . . . 90B ANNO SWED LOVE MARG
OTHERS OF THE LIKE KIND ARE FABLE YET THEY CONTAIN VISION   607A V LAST JUDG/N   PROSE
AS IT WILL CONTAIN LETTERS OF COWPER TO HIS FRIENDS PERHAPS 810A LETTER 20   PROSE
CONTAIND
HAD REPRESENTED AND CONTAIND THAT THEY MIGHT BE RESUMD . . 498 MILTON 17   2
DO BY NATURE THE THINGS CONTAIND IN THE LAW   . . . . . 610A V LAST JUDG/N   PROSE
YOU HAVE A TRADITION THAT MAN ANCIENTLY CONTAIND   . . . 649C JERUSALEM 27   PROSE
WERE CONTAIND IN THE ALL GLORIOUS IMAGINATION ARE WITHERD   679 JERUSALEM 49   14
  & DARKEND
CONTAINED
IF YOUR TRADITION THAT MAN CONTAINED IN HIS LIMBS   652B JERUSALEM 27   PROSE
  ALL ANIMALS
CONTAINING
CONTAINING AMPLE ILLUSTRATIONS ON ART   . . . . 560C EXHIBITION ADV   PROSE
THE DESCRIPTIVE CATALOGUE PRICE...CONTAINING   562B DESC CAT ADV   PROSE
  MR B'S(BLAKE'S)
STATUES ALL CONTAINING MYTHOLOGICAL AND RECONDITE MEANING   566A DESC CAT 2   PROSE
(THREE) FEET (ONE) INCH LONG BY ONE FOOT HIGH CONTAINING   587D CHAUCER/N   PROSE
PILGRIMS FROM CHAUCER CONTAINING ANECDOTES OF ARTISTS   591B PUB ADDRESS/N   PROSE
  PRICE...
GERYON MALEBOLGE CONTAINING (TEN) GULPHS   . . . . . . 786A ILLS DANTE 101 *PROSE
LUCIFER CONTAINING (NINE) ROUNDS   . . . . 786B ILLS DANTE 101 PROSE
CONTAINS
THE CISTERN CONTAINS THE FOUNTAIN OVERFLOWS   . . . . . 151D MARRIAGE HH 8   PROSE
AS THIS BOOK CONTAINS CAN EVER HAVE BEEN CALLD WISDOM   . . 397A ANNO BACON   MARG
AND CONTAINS THE ANCIENT HISTORY OF BRITAIN   . . . . . 578B DESC CAT 5   PROSE
I CONSIDER IT AS THE GRANDEST POEM THAT THIS WORLD CONTAINS 825A LETTER 27   PROSE
CONTAINS (A HUNDRED) PLATES BUT IT IS NOT LIKELY THAT I   878C LETTER 88   PROSE
  SHALL GET
CONTEMN
THY PITY I CONTEMN SCATTER THY SNOWS ELSEWHERE   . . . . 322 FOUR ZOAS 7   70
REYNOLDS IS TO DISPROVE & CONTEMN SPIRITUAL PERCEPTION . . 473D ANNO REYNOLDS   MARG
OF PLATO & CICERO WHICH ALL MEN OUGHT TO CONTEMN   . . . 480B MILTON 1   PROSE
ARE THOSE WHO CONTEMN RELIGION & SEEK TO ANNIHILATE IT   . 532 MILTON 40   9
THEY DO NOT ENVY ONE ANOTHER THEY CONTEMN & DESPISE   . . 616C V LAST JUDG/N   PROSE
CONTEMND
HOW MUCH BY US CONTEMND ABHORRD   . . . . 188 A FAIRY SKIPD   10
THE HOUR GLASS CONTEMND BECAUSE ITS SIMPLE WORKMANSHIP . . 337 FOUR ZOAS 7B   175
OUGHT TO BE CONTEMND & I ACCORDINGLY HOLD REYNOLDS   . . . 467A ANNO REYNOLDS   MARG
THEN HEAR IT CONTEMND WITHOUT RETURNING SCORN FOR SCORN   477A ANNO REYNOLDS * MARG
WHERE DRAWING ITS FOUNDATION IS CONTEMND AND   . . . . . 602A PUB ADDRESS/N   PROSE
NAMES ANCIENTLY REMEMBERD BUT NOW CONTEMND AS FICTIONS . . 624 JERUSALEM 5   38
I SAW THE LIMBS FORMD FOR EXERCISE CONTEMND & THE BEAUTY OF 628 JERUSALEM 9   7
THE HOUR-GLASS CONTEMND BECAUSE ITS SIMPLE WORKMANSHIP . . 700 JERUSALEM 65   17
THE SCORND AND CONTEMND YOUTHFUL GIRL WHERE SHALL SHE FLY   727 JERUSALEM 83   8
CONTEMNED
CONTEMNED AND REJECTED ALL HE DID WITH THE UTMOST DISDAIN   563C DESC CAT   PROSE
CONTEMNING
CONTEMNING THE DIVINE VISION & FRUITION WORSHIPING THE DEUS 741 JERUSALEM 93   23
CONTEMNS
DOES HE WHO CONTEMNS POVERTY AND HE WHO TURNS WITH   192 V DAU ALBION 5   10
  ABHORRENCE
CONTEMPLATE
& WE WILL CONTEMPLATE TOGETHER UPON IT   . . . . 155D MARRIAGE HH 17 PROSE
THEN THOSE IN GREAT ETERNITY WHO CONTEMPLATE ON DEATH   . . 663 JERUSALEM 36   50
CONTEMPLATED
[THERE] REPINING HE CONTEMPLATED THE PAST IN HIS BRIGHT   287 FOUR ZOAS 2   * 292
  SPHERE
ENORMOUS WORKS LOS CONTEMPLATED INSPIRD BY THE HOLY SPIRIT   343 FOUR ZOAS 8   108
CONTEMPLATING   SEE SELF-CONTEMPLATING
CONTEMPLATING THE CONSTELLATIONS   . . . . 619C ILLUS MILTON   PROSE
IN CONTEMPLATING MY PICTURES THAN I EVEN HOPED   . . . . 794B LETTER 5   PROSE
WINDSOR TERRACE A BOY CONTEMPLATING A DISTANT VIEW OF ETON SUPP ILLUS GRAY   *TITLE
  COLLEGE
CONTEMPLATION
CONTEMPLATION   . . . . 36D CONTEMPLATN/PS TITLE
TIS CONTEMPLATION DAUGHTER OF THE GREY MORNING   . . . . 36D CONTEMPLATN/PS PROSE
TIME FOR CONTEMPLATION ROSE FROM THE FORSAKEN EAST   . . . 39D SAMSON/PS   PROSE
BRINGS TRUE JOY ONCE FLED & CONTEMPLATION IS HER DAUGHTER   42A THEN SHE BORE   PROSE
SWEET CONTEMPLATION [SHE TEACHETH KNOWLEDGE HOW TO KNOW]   42A THEN SHE BORE   PROSE
TIS CONTEMPLATION TEACHETH KNOWLEDGE TRULY HOW TO KNOW   .   42A THEN SHE BORE *PROSE
THE SECRETS OF DARK CONTEMPLATION   . . . . 224 URIZEN 4   26
IN BROODING CONTEMPLATION STRETCHING OUT FROM NORTH TO   302 FOUR ZOAS 4   174
  SOUTH
ABSTRUSE IN THOUGHT AND CONTEMPLATION NAKED SIMPLE   . . . 577C DESC CAT 5   PROSE
ARE THE SUBJECTS OF CONTEMPLATION   . . . . 614C V LAST JUDG/N PROSE

```
                                                           PAGE      TITLE           LINE
CONTEMPLATION    (CONTINUED)
    THO THEIR WHOLE CONTEMPLATION IS CONCERNING THESE THINGS    614C  V LAST JUDG/N    PROSE
    THE SPIRIT OF PLATO UNFOLDS HIS WORLDS TO MILTON            619B  ILLUS MILTON     PROSE
        IN CONTEMPLATION
    AMONG THE WINDING PLACES OF DEEP CONTEMPLATION INTRICATE     657  JERUSALEM 31        22
    DIVINE & SELF WAS LOST IN THE CONTEMPLATION OF FAITH   .  .  743  JERUSALEM 96        31
    OF JEHOVAH AS A VERY INFERIOR OBJECT OF MAN'S CONTEMPLATION  784B  ANNO WW EXCUR     MARG
    CONTEMPLATION AMONG TOMBS  .  .  .  .  .  .  .  .  .  .  .  SUPP  ILLUS GRAY      *TITLE
CONTEMPLATIONS
    AROSE FOR HIS DIRE CONTEMPLATIONS  .  .  .  .  .  .  .  .  .  250  AHANIA 3             7
    AND MEN ARE BOUND TO SULLEN CONTEMPLATIONS IN THE NIGHT      379  FOUR ZOAS 9     *  817
    ALL HIS VISIONARY CONTEMPLATIONS RELATING TO HIS           577D  DESC CAT 5       PROSE
        OWN COUNTRY
CONTEMPLATIVE
    AGE IS CONTEMPLATIVE EACH ROLLING YEAR  .  .  .  .  .  .     27  EDW THIRD/PS 3     250
    AND CONTEMPLATIVE THOUGHTS FIRST AROSE  .  .  .  .  .  .     258  BOOK OF LOS 4       40
    THE CONTEMPLATIVE TERROR FRIGHTEND IN HIS SCORNFUL SPHERE    302  FOUR ZOAS 4        177
    BACON WAS A CONTEMPLATIVE ATHEIST EVIDENTLY AN EPICUREAN    403C  ANNO BACON        MARG
    CONTEMPLATIVE PHILOSOPHER VARIES FROM THE POETICAL GENIUS   572B  DESC CAT 3       PROSE
    RETURNS [ACCORDING TO] BY THE SEED OF CONTEMPLATIVE THOUGHT 605B  V LAST JUDG/N    PROSE
    ON THE FIERY CHARIOT OF HIS CONTEMPLATIVE THOUGHT  .  .  .  611A  V LAST JUDG/N    PROSE
CONTEMPLATOR
    INNUMERABLE AT WILL OF THE UNFORTUNATE CONTEMPLATOR  .  .  .  659  JERUSALEM 33        23
    WHICH WILL PRESENT THEMSELVES TO THE CONTEMPLATOR  .  .  .  792B  LETTER 4         PROSE
CONTEMPORARY
    I AM STARTLED AT SUCH AN ASSERTION I HOPE THE CONTEMPORARY  864D  LETTER 61        PROSE
CONTEMPT
    I TURND MYSELF ABOUT WITH GREAT CONTEMPT SAID I GO ALONG     45A  ISLAND MOON 1    PROSE
        YOU FOOL
    .  .  . THE SHOES OF CONTEMPT AND UNBUCKLE  .  .  .  .  .  .  144  FRENCH REVOLTN     222
    SO IS CONTEMPT TO THE CONTEMPTIBLE  .  .  .  .  .  .  .  .  152D  MARRIAGE HH 10   PROSE
    [HOW CONTEMPT & SCORN]  .  .  .  .  .  .  .  .  .  .  .      173  HOW CAME/N          3
    AND WHO LIVES ON THE CONTEMPT OF HIS NEIGHBOUR .  .  .  .    377  FOUR ZOAS 9        764
    CONTEMPT IS THE ELEMENT OF THE CONTEMPTIBLE  .  .  .  .  .  410B  ANNO BACON        MARG
    DOES NOT THROW HIS CONTEMPT ON SUCH TRADING EXHIBITIONS     452C  ANNO REYNOLDS     MARG
    [ ?THEIR VENETIAN ATTENTION IS TO A CONTEMPT & NEGLECT OF   463D  ANNO REYNOLDS   * MARG
        FORM ITSELF
    IN CONTEMPT (FOR THIS) SENTENCE IN PARTICULAR  .  .  .  .  467A  ANNO REYNOLDS   * MARG
    & CONTEMPT OF ALB DURER  .  .  .  .  .  .  .  .  .  .  .     472B  ANNO REYNOLDS     MARG
    SIMILAR I FELT THE SAME CONTEMPT & ABHORRENCE THEN THAT     477A  ANNO REYNOLDS     MARG
        I DO
    WHO FEEDS ON CONTEMPT OF HIS NEIGHBOUR THERE ALL THE IDLE    513  MILTON 27           27
        WEEDS
    LIVING IN A COTTAGE AND IN CONTEMPT AND DERISION  .  .  .  575D  DESC CAT 3       PROSE
    WITH CONTEMPT HE DID NOT CARE FOR THIS ANY MORE THAN WEST   593A  PUB ADDRESS/N    PROSE
    & HAVE LONG BEEN THE CONTEMPT OF THE CONTINENT  .  .  .  .  594D  PUB ADDRESS/N    PROSE
    MOST ENGLISHMEN HAVE A CONTEMPT FOR ART [WHICH WILL]        596B  PUB ADDRESS/N    PROSE
    WITH TOO GREAT CONTEMPT OF SUCH CONTEMPTIBLE FELLOWS  .  .  599D  PUB ADDRESS/N    PROSE
    & THEIRS IS THE CONTEMPT OF POSTERITY  .  .  .  .  .  .  .  600C  PUB ADDRESS/N    PROSE
    & THEY PROVE IT IN THEIR CONTEMPT FOR GREAT COLLECTIONS     601C  PUB ADDRESS/N    PROSE
    WHILE THEY DISCOURAGE & LOOK WITH CONTEMPT ON FALSE ART     601C  PUB ADDRESS/N   *PROSE
    SUFFICIENT CONTEMPT TO INHANCE MY OPINION OF IT BUT I DO    825B  LETTER 27        PROSE
        NOT
    NOT HIS AFFECTED CONTEMPT THAT CAN MOVE ME TO ANY THING BUT 825C  LETTER 27        PROSE
    CONTEMPT FOR MY PERSON IT AFFRONTED MY FOOLISH PRIDE  .  .  827A  LETTER 28        PROSE
CONTEMPTIBLE
    SO IS CONTEMPT TO THE CONTEMPTIBLE  .  .  .  .  .  .  .  .  152D  MARRIAGE HH 10   PROSE
    ("LAMENT TALENTS NOT MORE USEFUL") CONTEMPTIBLE FALSHOOD    384D  ANNO WATSON     * MARG
        & DETRACTION
    ("CRIMINALS FOLLOW DICTATES OF CONSCIENCE") CONTEMPTIBLE    386B  ANNO WATSON       MARG
    CONTEMPTIBLE THAN TO SUPPOSE PUBLIC RECORDS TO BE TRUE  .  392C  ANNO WATSON       MARG
    I AM ASTONISHD HOW SUCH CONTEMPTIBLE KNAVERY & FOLLY  .  .  397A  ANNO BACON        MARG
    POLITIC FOOLERY & MOST CONTEMPTIBLE VILLAINY & MURDER  .  400A  ANNO BACON      * MARG
    ("A KING IS A MORTAL GOD") O CONTEMPTIBLE & ABJECT SLAVE    401A  ANNO BACON        MARG
    CONTEMPTIBLE KNAVE LET THE PEOPLE LOOK TO THIS  .  .  .  .  403A  ANNO BACON        MARG
    WHAT A CONTEMPTIBLE FOOL IS THIS BACON  .  .  .  .  .  .  406C  ANNO BACON        MARG
    FALSE CONTEMPTIBLE  .  .  .  .  .  .  .  .  .  .  .  .  .  410A  ANNO BACON        MARG
    IS NOT THIS VERY VERY CONTEMPTIBLE  .  .  .  .  .  .  .  .  410B  ANNO BACON        MARG
    CONTEMPT IS THE ELEMENT OF THE CONTEMPTIBLE  .  .  .  .  .  410B  ANNO BACON        MARG
    CONTEMPTIBLE MOCKS  .  .  .  .  .  .  .  .  .  .  .  .  .  455C  ANNO REYNOLDS     MARG
    CONTEMPTIBLE SERVILE COPYING IS THE GREAT MERIT OF COPYING  456A  ANNO REYNOLDS     MARG
    TO MY EYE RUBENS'S COLOURING IS MOST CONTEMPTIBLE  .  .  .  469A  ANNO REYNOLDS     MARG
    TO GIVE FOR CONTEMPTIBLE WORKS OR THE  .  .  .  .  .  .  .  480C  MILTON 1         PROSE
    AND THEIR WORKS PROVE THEMSELVES CONTEMPTIBLE  .  .  .  .  585D  DESC CAT 15      PROSE
    TO ALL THE CONTINENT WHO LAUGH AT THE CONTEMPTIBLE  .  .  593D  PUB ADDRESS/N    PROSE
    SUCH CONTEMPTIBLE COPIES COUNTRYMEN COUNTRYMEN  .  .  .  .  597C  PUB ADDRESS/N    PROSE
    THE CONTEMPTIBLE IDIOTS WHO HAVE BEEN CALLD GREAT MEN  .  598C  PUB ADDRESS/N    PROSE
    WITH TOO GREAT CONTEMPT OF SUCH CONTEMPTIBLE FELLOWS  .  .  599D  PUB ADDRESS/N    PROSE
    TO RESIST THE CONTEMPTIBLE COUNTER ARTS [SET ON FOOT]  .  600B  PUB ADDRESS/N    PROSE
    ESTABLISHD BY SUCH CONTEMPTIBLE POLITICIANS AS LOUIS XIV &  600B  PUB ADDRESS/N    PROSE
    TO SEE MY FRIENDS IN TOWN BEFORE THIS CONTEMPTIBLE BUSINESS 828A  LETTER 28        PROSE
    COMES ON I SAY CONTEMPTIBLE FOR IT MUST BE MANIFEST  .  .  828A  LETTER 28        PROSE
CONTEND
    LUVAH & URIZEN CONTEND IN WAR AROUND THE HOLY TENT  .  .    277  FOUR ZOAS 1        480
    TIGER THE HORSE THE VULTURE AND THE EAGLE CONTEND FOR THE   441D  INSC FALL MAN    PROSE
        LAMB
    THEY CONTEND WITH THE WEAK SPECTRES THEY FABRICATE SOOTHING  515  MILTON 28          23
        FORMS
    AND THROUGH BEULAH AND ALL SILENT FORBORE TO CONTEND  .    526  MILTON 35           40
    CONTEND WITH EACH OTHER ON THE BRINK OF PERDITION  .  .  .  609C  V LAST JUDG/N    PROSE
    OSHEA AND CALEB FIGHT THEY CONTEND IN THE VALLEYS OF OF     672  JERUSALEM 43        37
        PEOR
```

```
                                                        PAGE      TITLE            LINE
CONTEND    (CONTINUED)
   THEY FIGHT & CONTEND FOR LIFE & NOT FOR ETERNAL DEATH    . .  672 JERUSALEM 43       42
CONTENDED
   [THUS THEY CONTENDED ALL THE DAY AMONG THE CAVES         269 FOUR ZOAS 1         179
     OF THARMAS]
   THEOTORMON & BROMION CONTENDED ON THE SIDE OF SATAN  . . .  488 MILTON 8          30
   MICHAEL CONTENDED AGAINST SATAN IN THE ROLLING THUNDER   . .  488 MILTON 8          32
   WHOM I HAVE CONTENDED IN ART HAVE STROVE NOT TO EXCELL BUT  596D PUB ADDRESS/N    PROSE
   THUS THEY CONTENDED AMONG THE FURNACES WITH GROANS & TEARS  628 JERUSALEM 9        32
   CITIES & NATIONS CONTENDED IN FIRES & CLOUDS & TEMPESTS   686 JERUSALEM 55        25
CONTENDING
   DRAGGING EACH OTHER INTO HELL & [OF] IN CONTENDING IN    . .  443D LAST JUDGMNT/L *PROSE
   THICK FIRES CONTENDING WITH THE RAIN THUNDERD ABOVE ROLLING  488 MILTON 8          28
   REPRESENTS THE INQUISITION AS DO THOSE CONTENDING    . . .  608C V LAST JUDG/N   PROSE
   CONTENDING FOR ALBION & FOR JERUSALEM HIS EMANATION   . . .  686 JERUSALEM 55        28
   DANCE THE DANCE OF DEATH CONTENDING WITH JEHOVAH AMONG   697 JERUSALEM 63        10
     THE CHERUBIM
   FLOWD INTO THE ACHING FIBRES OF LOS YET CONTENDING AGAINST  733 JERUSALEM 88        29
     HIM
CONTENDINGS
   WITH IRON & BRASS BUILDING GOLGONOOZA IN GREAT CONTENDINGS  630 JERUSALEM 10        63
CONTENT
   WHERE PEACE AND JOY AND LOVE AND CALM CONTENT  . . . . .   30 EDW THIRD/PS 5      30
   MUST BE TRIED IN PUBLIC WELL I AM CONTENT I MURMUR NOT &  828B LETTER 28         PROSE
   WORK TO ME I AM CONTENT THAT IT SHALL BE SO AS LONG AS GOD  829D LETTER 30         PROSE
CONTENTED
   BUT I AM CONTENTED WHETHER I LIVE BY PAINTING OR ENGRAVING  794C LETTER 5          PROSE
   CONTENTED LET WHAT WILL COME HAVING PASSED NOW   . . .   795C LETTER 6          PROSE
   AS A GOOD MAN THIS I SHOULD BE PERFECTLY CONTENTED WITH   830A LETTER 30         PROSE
CONTENTION
   HE ENDED THE WIND OF CONTENTION AROSE . . . . .  . . .  145 FRENCH REVOLTN      241
   ALL MEN & WAS THEIR FATHER & FORBAD ALL CONTENTION   . .  387B ANNO WATSON      MARG
   CONTENTION AT THE STABLE DOOR & GOING TO THE COMRADE    .  438D BLAKES MEMORAN   PROSE
   SUCH THING AS GENEROUS CONTENTION I KNOW THAT ALL THOSE   596D PUB ADDRESS/N    PROSE
     WITH
   AS OF NO USE & ONLY CONTENTION REMAINS TO MAN  . . . .  604C V LAST JUDG/N    PROSE
   OF CONTENTION REPRESENTING VARIOUS STATES OF MISERY  . .  608A V LAST JUDG/N    PROSE
   IN SELF-DENIAL BUT WAR AND DEADLY CONTENTION BETWEEN    .  640 JERUSALEM 18        20
   BEARING THE IMAGES OF VARIOUS SPECIES OF CONTENTION  . .  707 JERUSALEM 69        12
CONTENTIONS
   ALTHO OUR HUMAN POWER CAN SUSTAIN THE SEVERE CONTENTIONS   533 MILTON 41          32
   LOS STOOD AT HIS ANVIL HE HEARD THE CONTENTIONS OF VALA   660 JERUSALEM 34        17
   IN THE TERRIBLE FAMILY CONTENTIONS OF THOSE WHO LOVE EACH   672 JERUSALEM 43        38
     OTHER
   THAT THEY MIGHT BE BORN IN CONTENTIONS OF CHASTITY & IN   707 JERUSALEM 69        10
   BY CONTENTIONS OF THE MIGHTY FOR SACRIFICE OF CAPTIVES   .  726 JERUSALEM 82        41
   AT THEIR CONTENTIONS HE WIPED HIS TEARS HE WASHD HIS VISAGE  733 JERUSALEM 88        36
   BY SEVERE CONTENTIONS OF FRIENDSHIP & THE BURNING FIRE   738 JERUSALEM 91        18
     OF THOUGHT
CONTENTMENTS
   WHILE OTHERS IN CONTENTMENT'S DOWNY NEST DO SLEEP    . . .  41D THEN SHE BORE    PROSE
CONTENTS
   IT IS ONLY THE CONTENTS OR INDEX OF ALREADY PUBLISHD BOOKS  157C MARRIAGE HH 21  PROSE
   ON WHICH HES WRITTEN RECIEVD THE CONTENTS  . . . . . .  537 AND HIS LEGS/N      43
CONTINENCE
   ARE NOT THESE THE PLACES OF RELIGION THE REWARDS         194 V DAU ALBION 7       8
     OF CONTINENCE
CONTINENT
   IN THE MOON IS A CERTAIN ISLAND NEAR BY A MIGHTY CONTINENT   44A ISLAND MOON 1   PROSE
   A FROWNING CONTINENT APPEARD WHERE ENION IN THE DESERT  . .  266 FOUR ZOAS 1         89
   TO ALL THE CONTINENT WHO LAUGH AT THE CONTEMPTIBLE   . . .  593C PUB ADDRESS/N    PROSE
   & HAVE LONG BEEN THE CONTEMPT OF THE CONTINENT    . . .  594D PUB ADDRESS/N    PROSE
   OF ALL THE RUBBISH OF THE CONTINENT BROUGHT HERE BY  . . .  601C PUB ADDRESS/N    PROSE
   OUR ANCESTOR PATRIARCH OF THE ATLANTIC CONTINENT  . . . .  609C V LAST JUDG/N    PROSE
   THE ATLANTIC CONTINENT SUNK ROUND ALBION'S CLIFFY SHORE   663 JERUSALEM 36        39
   THE NARROW SEA BETWEEN ALBION & THE ATLANTIC CONTINENT   .  674 JERUSALEM 44        14
   IN ONE NIGHT THE ATLANTIC CONTINENT WAS CAUGHT UP WITH   679 JERUSALEM 49        19
     THE MOON
   IN ERIN'S CONTINENT AND JERUSALEM WEPT UPON EUPHRATES'   719 JERUSALEM 78        27
     BANKS
CONTINENTS
   HE DISPLACD CONTINENTS THE OCEANS FLED BEFORE HIS FACE  . .  489 MILTON 9          16
CONTINGENCIES
   ARTS & ARTISTS ARE SPIRITUAL & LAUGH AT MORTAL          597A PUB ADDRESS/N    PROSE
     CONTINGENCIES
CONTINUAL
   IN LOS'S HALLS CONTINUAL LABOURING IN THE FURNACES       520 MILTON 31          26
     OF GOLGONOOZA
   AROUND THIS POLYPUS LOS CONTINUAL BUILDS THE MUNDANE SHELL   524 MILTON 34          31
   WHILE THE SCULPTORS HAVE CONTINUAL & SUPERABUNDANT       601A PUB ADDRESS/N    PROSE
     EMPLOYMENT
   THE SPIRIT OF JESUS IS CONTINUAL FORGIVENESS OF SIN  . . .  621A JERUSALEM 3      PROSE
   A CIRCLE IN CONTINUAL GYRATIONS THIS BECAME A HEART  . . .  659 JERUSALEM 33        20
   . . . IN THE CONTINUAL FORGIVENESS OF SINS  . . . . . .  694 JERUSALEM 61        22
   OF SEVEN DISEASES ONCE A CONTINUAL CLOUD OF SALVATION ROSE  721 JERUSALEM 79        57
   ALL WARRIORS THE MORAL VIRTUES ARE CONTINUAL ACCUSERS   . . 774D ANNO BERKELEY   MARG
CONTINUALLY
   . . . THAT I AM THUS A RAVENING DEVOURING LUST CONTINUALLY  327 FOUR ZOAS 7        305
   ART NOTHING BEING CREATED CONTINUALLY BY MERCY &         329 FOUR ZOAS 7        360
     LOVE DIVINE
   TEN THOUSAND DEMONS LABOUR AT THE FORGES CREATING        346 FOUR ZOAS 8        205
     CONTINUALLY
```

CONTINUALLY   (CONTINUED)
    BUT REYNOLDS CONTRADICTS WHAT HE SAYS CONTINUALLY   . . . 463C ANNO REYNOLDS   MARG
    FOR THE ELECT CANNOT BE REDEEMD BUT CREATED CONTINUALLY   484 MILTON 5   11
    BUT MUST BE NEW CREATED CONTINUALLY MOMENT BY MOMENT   . . 492 MILTON 11   20
    TREMBLE IN SPECTROUS BODIES CONTINUALLY DAY AND NIGHT   507 MILTON 23   43
    BECAUSE OF SATAN & THE SEVEN EYES OF GOD CONTINUALLY   . . 508 MILTON 24   7
    FOR LOS AGAINST THE EAST HIS FORCE CONTINUALLY BENDS   . 512 MILTON 26   18
    CONTINUALLY WOVEN IN THE LOOMS OF ENITHARMON'S DAUGHTERS   512 MILTON 26   35
    THE NATURAL POWER CONTINUALLY SEEKS & TENDS TO DESTRUCTION 513 MILTON 26   41
    FROM DEATH ETERNAL SUCH YOUR LOT TO BE CONTINUALLY REDEEMD 522 MILTON 33   12
    BUT HOWLS ROUND IT AS A LION ROUND HIS PREY CONTINUALLY   531 MILTON 39   21
    ALTHOUGH MOLESTED CONTINUALLY BY BLOTTING AND BLURRING . .581B DESC CAT 6   PROSE
    FROM OUR COMPANY CONTINUALLY & RECIEVING TRUTH OR WISE MEN 613A V LAST JUDG/N   PROSE
    INTO OUR COMPANY CONTINUALLY   . . . . 613A V LAST JUDG/N   PROSE
    THEY WOOE LOS CONTINUALLY TO SUBDUE HIS STRENGTH   638 JERUSALEM 17   10
        HE CONTINUALLY
    MY CONTRARY O THOU NEGATION I WILL CONTINUALLY COMPELL . . 639 JERUSALEM 17   39
    LIVE BY DEVOURING GOING INTO ETERNAL DEATH CONTINUALLY . 681 JERUSALEM 50   7
    IS ALTOGETHER AN EVIL & REQUIRES A NEW SELFHOOD CONTINUALLY 682A JERUSALEM 52   PROSE
    & MUST CONTINUALLY BE CHANGED INTO HIS DIRECT CONTRARY . 682A JERUSALEM 52   PROSE
    OF SINS CONTINUALLY   . . . . 682D JERUSALEM 52   PROSE
    LONDON CONTINUALLY BUILDING & CONTINUALLY DECAYING   684 JERUSALEM 53   19
        DESOLATE
    ESTABLISHMENT OF TRUTH DEPENDS ON DESTRUCTION OF FALSHOOD 687 JERUSALEM 55   *   65
        CONTINUALLY
    WORKS A WORLD OF GENERATION CONTINUALLY CREATING OUT OF   690 JERUSALEM 58   50
    THEY ARE CREATED CONTINUALLY EAST & WEST & NORTH & SOUTH 712 JERUSALEM 72   29
    CONTINUALLY BUILDING CONTINUALLY DECAYING BECAUSE OF LOVE 712A JERUSALEM 72   PROSE
        & JEALOUSY
    FOR LOS IN SIX THOUSAND YEARS WALKS UP & DOWN CONTINUALLY 716 JERUSALEM 75   7
    CONTINUALLY BUILDING CONTINUALLY DESTROYING IN FAMILY   734 JERUSALEM 88   40
        FEUDS
    RISING UP AGAINST THE SPIRITUAL MAN CONTINUALLY . . . . 782D ANNO WW POEMS   MARG
    & MY PROSPECTS OF MORE & MORE WORK CONTINUALLY ARE CERTAIN 820C LETTER 25   PROSE
CONTINUD
    SHE CONTINUED FALLING LOUD THE CRASH CONTINUD LOUD   295 FOUR ZOAS 3   145
        & HOARSE
    CONTINUD ROUND THE HALLS AND MUCH THEY QUESTIOND   495 MILTON 13   46
        THE IMMORTAL
    BUT MILTON'S HUMAN SHADOW CONTINUD JOURNEYING ABOVE . . . 498 MILTON 17   18
CONTINUE
    THEY RISE IN ORDER AND CONTINUE THEIR IMMORTAL COURSES . . 511 MILTON 25   67
    YOU WILL CONTINUE TO FOLLOW   . . . . 570C DESC CAT 3   PROSE
    CONTINUE TO GOVERN MANKIND AFTER DEATH   . . . . . 581D DESC CAT 8   PROSE
    IF THEY CONTINUE TO REFUSE THEIRS IS THE LOSS NOT MINE . 600C PUB ADDRESS/N   PROSE
    MAY YOU CONTINUE TO BE SO MORE & MORE & TO BE   . . . 797B LETTER 9   PROSE
    MUST BE THE PLAN IF ENGLAND WISHES TO CONTINUE AT ALL WORTH 798A LETTER 10   PROSE
    CONTINUE EXPANDING   . . . . 805 TO BUTTS/L   47
    I HOPE YOU WILL CONTINUE TO EXCUSE MY WANT OF STEADY   . 808D LETTER 20   PROSE
    I CONTINUE PAINTING MINIATURES & IMPROVE MORE & MORE   . 809C LETTER 20   PROSE
    I IMPROVE VERY MUCH & SHALL CONTINUE TO DO SO WHILE I LIVE 824B LETTER 27   PROSE
CONTINUED
    SHE CONTINUED FALLING LOUD THE CRASH CONTINUD LOUD   295 FOUR ZOAS 3   145
        & HOARSE
    HAS CONTINUED A BOARD OVER THE GATEWAY   . . . . . . 590A CHAUCER 2   PROSE
    TO ME THIS WORLD IS ALL ONE CONTINUED VISION OF FANCY OR 793D LETTER 5   PROSE
    FORGIVENESS TO BE CONTINUED TO ME A LITTLE LONGER WHEN . 808A LETTER 19   PROSE
    I WISH HER A CONTINUED EXCESS OF HAPPINESS SOME SAY THAT 830C LETTER 30   PROSE
    CONTINUED RECOVERY MY WIFE DESIRES WITH ME HER RESPECTS   851A LETTER 49   PROSE
        TO YOU
    LADY OF LAVANT'S CONTINUED RECOVERY BUT WITH A MIXTURE . 851C LETTER 50   PROSE
    CONTINUED HEALTH I AM DEAR SIR YOURS SINCERELY   . . . 855C LETTER 53   PROSE
CONTINUES
    SUCH A ONE I CAN NEVER FORGIVE WHILE HE CONTINUES SUCH   72C ANNO LAVATER   MARG
        A ONE
    IT CONTINUES ACCUMULATING TO ETERNITY THE JOYS OF   630 JERUSALEM 10   46
        GOD ADVANCE
    CARRIED INTO EXECUTION AS IT MUST BE IF ENGLAND CONTINUES 797C LETTER 10   PROSE
    MY WIFE CONTINUES POORLY BUT FANCIES SHE IS BETTER   832A LETTER 31   PROSE
        IN HEALTH
    CONTINUES TO GET BETTER & JOINS ME IN MY WARMEST LOVE &   849C LETTER 45   PROSE
    AND CAN NEVER PASS AWAY MY WIFE CONTINUES WELL   . . . 854A LETTER 52   PROSE
    MY WIFE CONTINUES IN HEALTH & DESIRES TO JOIN ME IN EVERY 860B LETTER 56   PROSE
    I HAVE ASKED & INTREATED DIVINE HELP BUT FEAR CONTINUES   876B LETTER 83   PROSE
CONTINUOUS
    A THREEFOLD ATMOSPHERE SUBLIME CONTINUOUS . . . . . 329 FOUR ZOAS 7   382
    DISCRETE & NOT CONTINUOUS SO AS TO EXPLAIN EACH OTHER   93A ANNO SWED LOVE   MARG
        EXCEPT
    WITHOUT MAKING THEM CONTINUOUS & NOT DISCRETE   . . . . 93B ANNO SWED LOVE   MARG
CONTORTED
    THEY TURN CONTORTED THEIR IRON NECKS BEND UNWILLING TOWARDS 701 JERUSALEM 65   77
CONTORTION
    "THE MOST UGLY THEY FLED WITH OUTCRIES AND CONTORTION OF 560B EXHIBITION ADV   PROSE
        THEIR LIMBS"
CONTORTIVE
    HIS FURIOUS NECK (WRITHING) CONTORTIVE IN DIRE BUDDING   343 FOUR ZOAS 8   *   72
        PAINS
CONTRACT
    HIS EYES THE LIGHTS OF HIS LARGE SOUL CONTRACT OR ELSE   308 FOUR ZOAS 5   121
        EXPAND
    FOR PUBLIC INSPECTION AND FOR SALE BY PRIVATE CONTRACT . 560C EXHIBITION ADV   PROSE
    FOR PUBLIC INSPECTION AND FOR SALE BY PRIVATE CONTRACT . 563A DESC CAT   TITLE

```
                                                                PAGE    TITLE           LINE
CONTRACT    (CONTINUED)
    CONTRACT OR EXPAND SPACE AT WILL OR IF WE RAISE OURSELVES    687 JERUSALEM 55       44
CONTRACTED
    OR CONTRACTED HIS ALL FLEXIBLE SENSES   . . . . .  .  . .    223 URIZEN 3           38
    CONTRACTED THEY BEHOLD THE SECRETS OF THE INFINITE           308 FOUR ZOAS 5        122
        MOUNTAINS
CONTRACTING
    AS ONE MAN FOR CONTRACTING THEIR EXALTED SENSES    . . . .   277 FOUR ZOAS 1        470
    CONTRACTING OR EXPANDING THEIR ALL FLEXIBLE SENSES   . . .   288 FOUR ZOAS 2        296
    WE LIVE AS ONE MAN FOR CONTRACTING OUR INFINITE SENSES  . .  664 JERUSALEM 38       17
    AT WILL CONTRACTING INTO WORMS OR EXPANDING INTO GODS   . .  686 JERUSALEM 55       37
    UPON THE CHARIOTS OF THE MORNING CONTRACTING OR EXPANDING    687 JERUSALEM 55       45
        TIME
CONTRACTION
    AND NEXT HE FOUND THE LIMIT OF CONTRACTION & NAMD IT ADAM    304 FOUR ZOAS 4        273
    UPON THE LIMIT OF CONTRACTION TO CREATE THE FALLEN MAN  .    341 FOUR ZOAS 8        3
    THE LIMIT OF CONTRACTION NOW WAS FIXD & MAN BEGAN       .    341 FOUR ZOAS 8        16
    . . . FIRST OF OPACITY THEN OF CONTRACTION       . . . . .   494 MILTON 13          20
    OPACITY WAS NAMED SATAN CONTRACTION WAS NAMED ADAM          494 MILTON 13          21
    THERE IS A LIMIT OF OPAKENESS AND A LIMIT OF CONTRACTION     670 JERUSALEM 42       29
    IS NAMED SATAN AND THE LIMIT OF CONTRACTION IS NAMED ADAM    670 JERUSALEM 42       31
    NAMING THE LIMIT OF OPAKENESS SATAN & THE LIMIT             713 JERUSALEM 73       27
        OF CONTRACTION
    WAS HUMAN ACCORDING TO THE EXPANSION OR CONTRACTION . . .    746 JERUSALEM 98       36
CONTRACTIONS
    CONTRACTION'S LIMIT AND OF THE LIMIT HE FORMS WOMAN THAT     670 JERUSALEM 42       33
CONTRADICTING      SEE SELF-CONTRADICTING
    OF WARLIKE SELFHOOD CONTRADICTING AND BLASPHEMING    . .  .  495 MILTON 14          16
CONTRADICTION      SEE SELF-CONTRADICTION,SELF CONTRADICTION
    [ HERES] HERE IS ANOTHER CONTRADICTION IF MICH ANGO    . .  .467D ANNO REYNOLDS   * MARG
    AND IS MADE [ UPO ] UP OF CONTRADICTION    . . .  .  .  .    751 EV GOSPEL (C)/N  *  51
    [ AND IS MADE UP OF CONTRADICTION] . . . .  . .  .  . .      753 EV GOSPEL(D)/N      86
CONTRADICTIONS
    THE CONTRADICTIONS IN REYNOLDS'S DISCOURSES ARE STRONG  .   .449B ANNO REYNOLDS     MARG
    ALL HE KNOWS FROM OTHERS MUST BE FULL OF CONTRADICTIONS     .449B ANNO REYNOLDS     MARG
CONTRADICTORY      SEE SELF-CONTRADICTORY
    THREE BRAINS IN CONTRADICTORY COUNCIL BROODING INCESSANTLY   708 JERUSALEM 70       5
CONTRADICTS
    OR ELSE HE CONTRADICTS N...    . . . . . . .  .  .  .  . .    92C ANNO SWED LOVE    MARG
    READ N...& THERE SEE HOW SWEDENBORG CONTRADICTS HIMSELF     133D ANNO SWED PROV  * MARG
        & [ XXX] N...
    THIS SECTION CONTRADICTS THE PRECEDING     . . . . . .  .   .401D ANNO BACON       MARG
    BUT REYNOLDS CONTRADICTS WHAT HE SAYS CONTINUALLY    . .    .463C ANNO REYNOLDS     MARG
CONTRARIES
    FOR THUS (TWO) CONTRARIES WOULD SPRING FROM ONE ESSENCE      80A ANNO LAVATER      MARG
    GOOD & EVIL ARE HERE BOTH GOOD & THE TWO CONTRARIES          91D ANNO SWED LOVE    MARG
        MARRIED
    WITHOUT CONTRARIES IS NO PROGRESSION ATTRACTION AND        149B MARRIAGE HH 3      PROSE
        REPULSION
    FROM THESE CONTRARIES SPRING WHAT THE RELIGIOUS CALL GOOD   149B MARRIAGE HH 3      PROSE
        & EVIL
    BUT THE FOLLOWING CONTRARIES TO THESE ARE TRUE    . . .     149D MARRIAGE HH 4      PROSE
    THEY ARE THE TWO CONTRARIES & THE REASONING NEGATIVE    .    484 MILTON 5           14
    CONTRARIES ARE POSITIVES A NEGATION IS NOT A CONTRARY   .    518B MILTON 30         TITLE
    TO WHERE THE CONTRARIES OF BEULAH WAR BENEATH NEGATION'S     524 MILTON 34          23
        BANNER
    THE NEGATION MUST BE DESTROYD TO REDEEM THE CONTRARIES  .    533 MILTON 40          33
    RETURNS UPON US ARE WE CONTRARIES O MILTON THOU & I  . .     534 MILTON 41          35
    THEY TAKE THE TWO CONTRARIES WHICH ARE CALLD QUALITIES       629 JERUSALEM 10       8
        WITH WHICH
    NEGATIONS ARE NOT CONTRARIES CONTRARIES MUTUALLY EXIST       639 JERUSALEM 17       33
    TWO BLEEDING CONTRARIES EQUALLY TRUE ARE HIS WITNESSES       646 JERUSALEM 24       3
        AGAINST ME
    OF ACTION FOR OBEDIENCE TO DESTROY THE CONTRARIES OF MAN     653 JERUSALEM 29       15
    TO MAKE ONE FAMILY OF CONTRARIES THAT JOSEPH MAY BE SOLD     686 JERUSALEM 55       15
    TWO CONTRARIES WAR AGAINST EACH OTHER IN FURY & BLOOD   .    690 JERUSALEM 58       15
    IN THE TWO CONTRARIES OF HUMANITY & IN THE FOUR REGIONS      699 JERUSALEM 65       4
CONTRARIETIES
    THERE IS A PLACE WHERE CONTRARIETIES ARE EQUALLY TRUE   .    518 MILTON 30          1
    THERE IS A PLACE WHERE CONTRARIETIES ARE EQUALLY TRUE   .    677 JERUSALEM 48       14
CONTRARIOUS
    THESE ARE THE GODS OF THE KINGDOMS OF THE EARTH IN          520 MILTON 31          23
        CONTRARIOUS
    THE REALMS OF DARK DEATH O PERVERSE TO THYSELF CONTRARIOUS   733 JERUSALEM 88       26
CONTRARY
    ("WHO HAS A DARING EYE TELLS ...") CONTRARY TO...BUT MOST    70B ANNO LAVATER      MARG
        TRUE
    CONTRARY TO...BUT MOST TRUE . . . . . . . . .  .  .  . .     70B ANNO LAVATER      MARG
    LIE IS THE CONTRARY TO PASSION     . . . . . . .  .  . .     74C ANNO LAVATER      MARG
    TO HINDER ANOTHER IS NOT AN ACT IT IS THE CONTRARY    . .    88D ANNO LAVATER      MARG
    FALSE TAKE IT SO OR THE CONTRARY IT COMES TO THE SAME   .    91C ANNO SWED LOVE    MARG
    SHEWING THE TWO CONTRARY STATES OF THE HUMAN SOUL    . .     210A SONGS OF EXPER    TITLE
    TO IMPROVEMENT & THE BISHOP HAS NOT SHEWN THE CONTRARY  .    388D ANNO WATSON      MARG
    OF SUN MOON OR STARS IS STRANGE ON A CONTRARY ACCOUNT   .    390A ANNO WATSON      MARG
    THE CONTRARY IS THE BEST ADVICE    . . . . . . .  .  . .     405A ANNO BACON       MARG
    IF TO THE MIDDLE CLASS IT IS THE DIRECT CONTRARY            406D ANNO BACON       MARG
        TO CHRIST'S ADVICE
    HIRELING WRITER WHOSE PRAISE IS CONTRARY TO WHAT HE KNOWS    413D ANNO BOYD        MARG
    ALTOGETHER HIS COLOURING (IS) CONTRARY     . . . . . .  .    469A ANNO REYNOLDS  * MARG
    I SAY ON THE CONTRARY THAT     . . . . . . . .  .  . . .     471A ANNO REYNOLDS     MARG
    CONTRARY OPINIONS CAN NEVER BY ANY LANGUAGE BE MADE ALIKE    474B ANNO REYNOLDS     MARG
    BUT ARE BORN WITH US REYNOLDS SAYS THE CONTRARY    . . .     474B ANNO REYNOLDS     MARG
```

CONTRARY   (CONTINUED)
```
     EXCELLENT & CONTRARY TO HIS USUAL OPINIONS  .  .  .  .  .    . . 479C ANNO REYNOLDS    MARG
     CONTRARIES ARE POSITIVES A NEGATION IS NOT A CONTRARY   .  . 518B MILTON 30         TITLE
     THERE IS A NEGATION & THERE IS A CONTRARY   .  .  .  .  .    . . 533 MILTON 40           32
     RESOLVD TO BE A VERY CONTRARY FELLOW  .  .  .  .  .  .  .    . . 555 BLAKES APL/N 1        17
     RESOLVD TO BE A VERY CONTRARY FELLOW  .  .  .  .  .  .  .  . . . 556 BLAKES APL/N 2        16
     LIKE MOST OTHER THINGS THE CONTRARY OF WHAT IT PRETENDS       561A EXHIBITION ADV    PROSE
          TO BE
     I ANSWER OF NONE AT ALL BUT THE CONTRARY AS YOU WELL KNOW     573A DESC CAT 3        PROSE
     RESOLVED TO GO CONTRARY IN EVERYTHING TO CHAUCER WHO SAYS     574A DESC CAT 3        PROSE
     TO THE CONTRARY TO BE BETTER ABLE THAN ANY OTHER  .  .  .    586D CHAUCER 1         PROSE
     NOW THIS IS CONTRARY TO THE TRUTH WOOLETT DID NOT KNOW   .    593A PUB ADDRESS/N     PROSE
     ARE NO PROOF OF POPULAR APPROBATION BUT OFTEN THE CONTRARY    593C PUB ADDRESS/N     PROSE
     RESOLVD TO BE A VERY CONTRARY FELLOW  .  .  .  .  .  .  .     596 BLAKES APOL/PA         10
     WITH EITHER REMBRANDT OR RUBENS ON THE CONTRARY   .  .  .    598D PUB ADDRESS/N     PROSE
     ON THE CONTRARY JULIO (ROMANO'S) PALACE OF T AT MANTUA   .    599C PUB ADDRESS/N     PROSE
     EXAMPLE OF THESE CONTRARY ARTS IS GIVEN US IN THE            600D PUB ADDRESS/N     PROSE
          CHARACTERS
     HE HIMSELF KNEW BUT HIS IMPUDENCE HAD A CONTRARY EFFECT       603C PUB ADDR AD/N     PROSE
          ON ME
     CONSUMING & THE ALMIGHTY HATH MADE ME HIS CONTRARY   .  .    630 JERUSALEM 10         56
     MY CONTRARY O THOU NEGATION I WILL CONTINUALLY COMPELL   .    639 JERUSALEM 17         39
     & MUST CONTINUALLY BE CHANGED INTO HIS DIRECT CONTRARY   .    682A JERUSALEM 52     PROSE
     MISCHIEVOUS & DIRECT CONTRARY TO WORDSWORTH'S OWN PRACTISE    783B ANNO WW POEMS     MARG
     CONTRARY TO DESIGNING & HISTORICAL PAINTING IN EVERY         815D LETTER 23        PROSE
          RESPECT
```
CONTRASTED
```
     THE VOLUPTUOUS COUNTRY GENTLEMAN CONTRASTED WITH  .  .  .  . 570D DESC CAT 3        PROSE
```
CONTRITE
```
     AND A CONTRITE HEART O I CANNOT FORGIVE THE ACCUSER HATH      780 GHOST ABEL 2          5
```
CONTRITION
```
     CONTRITION HE PREPARD HIS BOW  .  .  .  .  .  .  .  .  .     250 AHANIA 3              4
     .  .  .[ENITHARMON] JERUSALEM IN SILENT CONTRITION O PITY ME  264 FOUR ZOAS 1      *  27
     .  .  .[SELF WOVEN SORROW] REPENTANCE & CONTRITION   .  .  .  266 FOUR ZOAS 1         91
     .  .  .AND [MANY TEARS] OF BITTER CONTRITION   .  .  .  .     330 FOUR ZOAS 7        400
     IN BITTEREST CONTRITION SOMETIMES SELF CONDEMNING REPENTANT   356 FOUR ZOAS 8        610
```
CONTRIVE
```
     INSERTION I WRITE TO ENTREAT THAT YOU WOULD CONTRIVE SO AS    861A LETTER 58        PROSE
     WHERE I CONTRIVE TO GET INTO A LITTLE PERSPIRATION WHICH      872B LETTER 75        PROSE
```
CONTRIVED   SEE WELL CONTRIVED
```
     THO ADMIRABLY CONTRIVED FOR AN EFFECT EQUAL TO REMBRANDT      855A LETTER 53        PROSE
```
CONTROL
```
     THE BEAST & THE WHORE RULE WITHOUT CONTROL  .  .  .  .  .    383B ANNO WATSON       MARG
```
CONTROLL
```
     THAT MIGHT CONTROLL  .  .  .  .  .  .  .  .  .  .  .  .     210 INTRODUCTN/SE         8
     HE COULD CONTROLL THE TIMES & SEASONS & THE DAYS & YEARS      270 FOUR ZOAS 1        240
     SHE COULD CONTROLL THE SPACES REGIONS DESART FLOOD & FOREST   271 FOUR ZOAS 1        241
     AND THE NINE SPHERES REJOICE BENEATH MY POWERFUL CONTROLL     289 FOUR ZOAS 2        353
     WHAT SOVEREIGN ARCHITECT SAID THARMAS DARE MY WILL CONTROLL   299 FOUR ZOAS 4         53
     SATAN ASTONISHD AND WITH POWER ABOVE HIS OWN CONTROLL   .     492 MILTON 12          16
     EGREMONT'S COUNTESS [DARE] CAN CONTROLL  .  .  .  .  .  .     558 THE CAVERNS/N        7
     ALTHOUGH IN EVERY BOSOM THEY CONTROLL OUR VEGETATIVE POWERS   624 JERUSALEM 5         39
     THAT HE MIGHT LIVE ABOVE CONTROLL  .  .  .  .  .  .  .  .     757 EV GOSPEL(I)/N      44
```
CONTROLLABLE
```
     WHO WHEN CONVINCD CAN STILL PERSIST THO FURIOUS              329 FOUR ZOAS 7        363
          CONTROLLABLE
```
CONTROLLS
```
     NOW ENVY SHE CONTROLLS WITH NUMMING TRANCE  .  .  .  .  .    41D THEN SHE BORE     PROSE
     INDEED HATE CONTROLLS ALL THE GODS AT WILL  .  .  .  .  .    42D THEN SHE BORE     PROSE
```
CONTROVERTED
```
     IS IN THESE PRELIMINARY ESSAYS CONTROVERTED & PROVED         413A ANNO BOYD        MARG
          FOOLISH
     IT IS TRUE AND CANNOT BE CONTROVERTED   .  .  .  .  .  .     649B JERUSALEM 27     PROSE
```
CONVALESCENT
```
     MAY DO & HAVE DONE MIRACLES IN THE CASE OF A CONVALESCENT     875A LETTER 80        PROSE
```
CONVENE
```
     FOR THE COMMONS CONVENE IN THE HALL OF THE NATION  .  .  .    134 FRENCH REVOLTN      16
     FOR THE COMMONS CONVENE IN THE HALL OF THE NATION  .  .  .    136 FRENCH REVOLTN      54
     WHAT TIME THE THIRTEEN GOVERNORS THAT ENGLAND SENT CONVENE    201 AMERICA 13           1
```
CONVENIENCE
```
     AND FOR CONVENIENCE  .  .  .  .  .  .  .  .  .  .  .  .     57 TO BE OR/IM          21
     REMOVED WITH THE SAME CONVENIENCE AS SO MANY EASEL PICTURES   560D EXHIBITION ADV   PROSE
     SAKE OF CONVENIENCE I ALSO OUGHT TO INFORM YOU THAT I READ    820D LETTER 25        PROSE
     RETURN PRAY LET YOUR OWN HEALTH & CONVENIENCE PUT ALL   .     873C LETTER 77        PROSE
     IF THIS NOTICE SHOULD BE TOO SHORT FOR YOUR CONVENIENCE       875B LETTER 81        PROSE
```
CONVENIENCES
```
     HE WILL STILL MOVE ONWARD TO PLAN CONVENIENCES   .  .  .  .   26 EDW THIRD/PS 3     200
     WE CAN GET MOST CONVENIENCES THERE THE COUNTRY IS   .  .     806B LETTER 16        PROSE
```
CONVENIENT
```
     WHICH IS MORE BEAUTIFUL THAN I THOUGHT IT & MORE             801D LETTER 14        PROSE
          CONVENIENT
     COTTAGE IS MORE BEAUTIFUL THAN I THOUGHT IT & ALSO MORE       803B LETTER 15        PROSE
          CONVENIENT
     CONVENIENT TO DO SO IT WILL BE GRATEFULLY REMEMBERD BY ME     826C LETTER 28        PROSE
     BECAUSE I WOULD HASTEN ITS ARRIVAL BEFORE IT IS CONVENIENT    853D LETTER 52        PROSE
     IT WILL BE MORE CONVENIENT TO ME TO MAKE ALL THE DRAWINGS     866C LETTER 65        PROSE
     (TWELVE) OCLOCK IT IS QUITE AS CONVENIENT TO ME AS ANY        868B LETTER 67        PROSE
          OTHER DAY
     & IF IT IS MORE CONVENIENT TO MR HEAPHY FOR US TO MEET   .    868B LETTER 67        PROSE
```
CONVENT
```
     "HE" IS SEEN FOLLOWING THE FRIAR'S LANTERN TOWARDS THE       618C ILLUS MILTON    PROSE
          CONVENT
```

CONVERSANT
    IN THE BODY WAS ONLY CONVERSANT WITH NATURAL SUBSTANCES   94A ANNO SWED LOVE   MARG
CONVERSATION
    OF THE CONVERSATION BETWEEN ME AND THE SOLDIER   . . . . .437D BLAKES MEMORAN   PROSE
    SUPPOSING SUCH CONVERSATION TO HAVE EXISTED   . . . . . .437D BLAKES MEMORAN   PROSE
    CONVERSATION WITH AN OLD SOLDIER WHO CAME IN THE COACH WITH 833B LETTER 33   PROSE
    CONFIDENCE IN MY DISCRETION SUCH WAS OUR CONVERSATION   . .856D LETTER 54   PROSE
    COURSE OF OUR CONVERSATION HIS WORDS WERE I FEEL SOMEWHAT   860A LETTER 56   PROSE
    IN TOGETHER & WITH ANOTHER PASSENGER ENTERD INTO   869C LETTER 70   PROSE
        CONVERSATION
CONVERSATIONS
    WALKING UP & DOWN IN CONVERSATIONS CONCERNING . . . . .613C V LAST JUDG/N   PROSE
CONVERSE
    O THAT MEN WOULD CONVERSE WITH GOD   . . . . 80C ANNO LAVATER   MARG
    THEREFORE ALL WHO CONVERSE IN THE SPIRIT CONVERSE WITH   88B ANNO LAVATER   MARG
        SPIRITS
    [& THEY CONVERSE WITH THE SPIRIT OF GOD] FOR THESE REASONS   88B ANNO LAVATER   * MARG
        I SAY
    IS BUT LOST TIME TO CONVERSE WITH YOU WHOSE WORKS ARE ONLY   157B MARRIAGE HH 17 PROSE
        ANALYTICS
    COME HITHER BE PATIENT LET US CONVERSE TOGETHER BECAUSE   330 FOUR ZOAS 7   422
    CAN YOU CONVERSE WITH A PURE SOUL THAT SEEKETH FOR HER   368 FOUR ZOAS 9   428
        MAKER
    THAT GOD DOES & ALWAYS DID CONVERSE WITH HONEST MEN   . . .389A ANNO WATSON   MARG
    CONVERSE WITH GOD & BE A KING & PRIEST IN HIS OWN HOUSE   389C ANNO WATSON   MARG
    AND THUS THE SEVEN ANGELS INSTRUCTED HIM & THUS THEY   521 MILTON 32   9
        CONVERSE
    THUS THEY CONVERSE WITH THE DEAD WATCHING ROUND THE COUCH   522 MILTON 32   39
        OF DEATH
    HAPPY IS HE WHO CAN SEE AND CONVERSE WITH THEM   . . . .578C DESC CAT 5   PROSE
    WE WILL NOT CONVERSE CONCERNING GOOD & EVIL   . . . . .615D V LAST JUDG/N   PROSE
    YET I PRETEND TO LOVE TO SEE TO CONVERSE WITH DAILY AS   621A JERUSALEM 3   PROSE
        MAN WITH MAN
    CONVERSE CONCERNING WEIGHT & DISTANCE IN THE WILDS   661 JERUSALEM 34   40
        OF NEWTON & LOCKE
    THUS THEY CONVERSE UPON MAM-TOR THE GRAVES THUNDER UNDER   741 JERUSALEM 93   27
        THEIR FEET
    CONVERSE DAILY & HOURLY IN THE SPIRIT & . . . . . . .797A LETTER 9   PROSE
    IS ARRIVD WHEN MEN SHALL AGAIN CONVERSE IN HEAVEN & WALK   799B LETTER 11   PROSE
        WITH
    & THAT I MAY CONVERSE WITH MY FRIENDS IN ETERNITY   . . .822C LETTER 26   PROSE
CONVERSED
    AND NOW HEAR THE REASON HE CONVERSED WITH ANGELS WHO   . .157D MARRIAGE HH 21 PROSE
    ARE ALL RELIGIOUS & CONVERSED NOT WITH DEVILS WHO ALL   157D MARRIAGE HH 21 PROSE
        HATE RELIGION
    THAT GOD CONVERSED WITH MURDERERS & REVENGERS   . . . . .389A ANNO WATSON   MARG
    CONVERSED WITH THEIR OWN [SELF WILL] STATE RELIGION   . . .389A ANNO WATSON   MARG
    AND MILTON OFT SAT UP ON THE COUCH OF DEATH & OFT CONVERSED 521 MILTON 32   * 1
    AND MANY CONVERSED ON THESE THINGS AS THEY LABOURD AT THE   687 JERUSALEM 55   48
        FURROW
    A MAN & THEY CONVERSED AS MAN WITH MAN IN AGES   743 JERUSALEM 96   6
        OF ETERNITY
    AND THEY CONVERSED TOGETHER IN VISIONARY FORMS DRAMATIC   746 JERUSALEM 98   28
        WHICH BRIGHT
CONVERSES
    WHEN IN ETERNITY MAN CONVERSES WITH MAN THEY ENTER   . . .733 JERUSALEM 88   3
CONVERSING
    FORTY MEN EACH CONVERSING WITH WOES . . . . .134 FRENCH REVOLTN   13
    UPON THE MARGIND OCEAN CONVERSING WITH SHADOWS DIRE   . . .195 V DAU ALBION 8   12
    CONVERSING WITH THE VISIONS OF BEULAH IN DARK SLUMBEROUS   271 FOUR ZOAS 1   * 246
        BLISS
    CONVERSING WITH THE ANIMAL FORMS OF WISDOM NIGHT & DAY . . .379 FOUR ZOAS 9   836
    THEY RAISE THEIR FACES FROM THE EARTH CONVERSING WITH THE   379 FOUR ZOAS 9   843
        MAN
    SCARCELY BEHOLDING THE GREAT LIGHT CONVERSING WITH THE VOID 484 MILTON 5   22
    THE THREE POWERS IN MAN OF CONVERSING WITH PARADISE   . . .609D V LAST JUDG/N   PROSE
    BUT ARE CONVERSING WITH   . . . . .613C V LAST JUDG/N   PROSE
    SCARCELY BEHOLDING THE GREAT LIGHT CONVERSING WITH THE   680 JERUSALEM 49   * 35
        (VOID)
CONVERT
    & BECAME A CONVERT TO THE HEATHEN MYTHOLOGY   . . . . .784B ANNO WW EXCUR   MARG
CONVERTED
    THE KNAVE WHO IS CONVERTED TO [CHRISTIANITY] DEISM   . . .615B V LAST JUDG/N   PROSE
    & THE KNAVE WHO IS CONVERTED TO CHRISTIANITY IS STILL A   615B V LAST JUDG/N   PROSE
        KNAVE
CONVEY
    AND DOWN HIS BACK THEY STRAIT CONVEY . . . . 17 BLIND-MANS/PS   58
    [MIRTH S ALL YOUR SUFFERINGS CONVEY SIR] . . . . .538 WAS I ANGRY/N   * 7
    TO CONVEY THEM SAFE HE IS NOW I SUPPOSE ENJOYING THE   . .850C LETTER 49   PROSE
CONVEYD
    AND NAKED THEY CONVEYD . . . . .113 LIT GRL LST/SI   51
    OF SPECTROUS DEAD THENCE TO THE LOOMS OF CATHEDRON CONVEYD   346 FOUR ZOAS 8   209
CONVICTION   SEE SELF CONVICTION
    I HEARD THIS WITH SOME WONDER & MUST CONFESS MY OWN   154A MARRIAGE HH 12 PROSE
        CONVICTION
    WITH IRRESISTIBLE CONVICTION I FEEL I AM NOT ONE OF THOSE   329 FOUR ZOAS 7   362
    I MUST NOW EXPRESS TO YOU MY CONVICTION THAT   . . . . .828C LETTER 28   PROSE
CONVINCD
    WHO WHEN CONVINCD CAN STILL PERSIST THO FURIOUS   329 FOUR ZOAS 7   363
        CONTROLLABLE
    HIMSELF CONVINCD OF PALAMABRON'S TURPITUDE LOS BEHELD   . .488 MILTON 8   7
    THE ENGLISH PUBLIC WILL BE CONVINCD THAT SUCH A   . . . .598B PUB ADDRESS/N   PROSE

```
                                                        PAGE      TITLE          LINE
CONVINCD   (CONTINUED)
    CONVINCD THAT EITHER MY UNDERSTANDING IS INCAPABLE OF   . . 814A LETTER 23        PROSE
CONVINCE
    OFTEN ENOUGH TO CONVINCE THY JEALOUSY & FEAR & TERROR   . . 330 FOUR ZOAS 7       421
CONVINCED
    BE CONVINCED THAT THE LABOUR I HAVE USED ON THE TWO PLATES  853C LETTER 52        PROSE
CONVINCING
    CONVINCING PROOF AMONG MANY OTHERS THAT THESE ASSERTIONS    566C DESC CAT 2       PROSE
    FOR THE SAKE OF CONVINCING THOSE WHO DO NOT KNOW IT . . . 597D PUB ADDRESS/N      PROSE
CONVULSD
    HOWLING & SHUDDERING HIS LEGS QUIVERING CONVULSD           202 AMERICA 15          8
        EACH MUSCLE & SINEW
    JOIN SHAKING CONVULSD THE SHIVRING CLAY BREATHES . . . . . 248 SONG OF LOS 7      32
    BEGAN IN SOLEMN REVOLUTIONS EARTH CONVULSD WITH RENDING    306 FOUR ZOAS 5        28
        PANGS
    TO BONES JOIN SHAKING CONVULSD THE SHIVERING CLAY BREATHES  363 FOUR ZOAS 9       232
    SOUNDING TO THE FOUR WINDS BENEATH [THE EARTH IS CONVULSD] 443A LAST JUDGMNT/L    PROSE
    IS ROCKY & BURNING AND SEEMS AS IF CONVULSD  . . . . . 608B V LAST JUDG/N        PROSE
CONVULSED
    EARTH IS CONVULSED WITH THE LABOURS OF THE RESURRECTION    443A LAST JUDGMNT/L   *PROSE
CONVULSION
    THE THROB THE DOLOR THE CONVULSION IN SOUL SICKENING WOES  314 FOUR ZOAS 6        99
CONVULSIONS
    RETURN IN PANGS & HORRIBLE CONVULSIONS TO THEIR BEASTIAL   344 FOUR ZOAS 8        119
        STATE
    IN TERRIBLE CONVULSIONS PITYING & GRATIFIED DRUNK WITH PITY 723 JERUSALEM 80      70
CONVULSIVE
    [HEAVING XXX] HEAVD LIKE AN EARTHQUAKE LABRING WITH        347 FOUR ZOAS 8    *  249
        CONVULSIVE GROANS
CONWAY
    ON THE MARGIN OF THE RIVER CONWAY WHOSE WAVES BEAR UP  . . 577A DESC CAT 4        PROSE
CONWAYS
    IN [BETH PEOR] CONWAY'S VALE . . .   . . . . . . . .       277 FOUR ZOAS 1        483
CONWENNA
    BOADICEA CONWENNA ESTRILD GWINEFRID IGNOGE CAMBEL    . . . 281 FOUR ZOAS 2        62
    A GIRDLE GWENDOLEN & CONWENNA AS A GARMENT WOVEN . . . .   507 MILTON 23          16
    CAMBEL & GWENDOLEN & CONWENNA & CORDELLA & IGNOGE . . .    624 JERUSALEM 5        41
    IN CHILDHOOD WHAT WERT THOU UNUTTERABLE ANGUISH CONWENNA   644 JERUSALEM 21       23
    HIS EMANATION IS CONWENNA SHE SHINES A TRIPLE FORM  . . .  710 JERUSALEM 71       47
    JERUSALEM & VALA REJOICE IN BOWEN & CONWENNA  . . . . .    710 JERUSALEM 71       49
    BOWEN & CONWENNA STOOD ON SKIDDAW CUTTING THE FIBRES  . .  736 JERUSALEM 90       14
    CONWENNA SAT ABOVE WITH SOLEMN CADENCES SHE DREW . . . .   736 JERUSALEM 90       21
COOK
    THE WIFE OF BATH THE COOK THE MILLER THE OXFORD SCHOLAR    567A DESC CAT 3        PROSE
    THESE LAST ARE ISSUING FROM THE GATEWAY OF THE INN THE COOK 567A DESC CAT 3       PROSE
    THE CITIZENS AND THEIR COOK ARE EACH LEADERS OF A CLASS    571D DESC CAT 3        PROSE
    THE WIFE OF BATH THE COOK THE OXFORD SCHOLAR . . . . .     588C CHAUCER/N         PROSE
    THESE LAST ARE ISSUING FROM THE GATEWAY OF THE INN THE COOK 588D CHAUCER/N        PROSE
    THE WIFE OF BATH THE COOK THE OXFORD SCHOLAR . . . . .     590A CHAUCER 2         PROSE
    THESE LAST ARE ISSUING FROM THE GATEWAY OF THE INN THE COOK 590A CHAUCER 2        PROSE
COOKE
    TOM COOKE CUT HOGARTH DOWN WITH HIS CLEAN GRAVING   . . .  554 BLAKES APL/N 1      3
    CRY [TOM COOKE PROVES] . . . . . . . . . . . .             555 BLAKES APL/N 1     18
    TOM COOKE CUT HOGARTH DOWN WITH HIS CLEAN GRAVING   . . .  555 BLAKES APL/N 2      7
    I ALSO KNEW SOMETHING OF TOM COOKE WHO ENGRAVED  . . .    594B PUB ADDRESS/N      PROSE
    AFTER HOGARTH [COGAR] COOKE WISHED TO GIVE TO HOGARTH  . .594B PUB ADDRESS/N     *PROSE
    TOM COOKE CUT HOGARTH DOWN WITH HIS CLEAN GRAVING   . . .  595 BLAKES APOL/PA      3
    CRY TOM COOKE PROVES FROM CIRCUMFERENCE TO CENTER  . . .   596 BLAKES APOL/PA     11
COOKERY
    COOKERY CHYMISTRY [?CONJUNCTIVES] MECHANICS TACTICS        46D ISLAND MOON 3     *PROSE
        PATHOLOGY
COOL
    OF BLOOD POUR DOWN THE MOUNTAINS TO COOL  . . . . . .      225 URIZEN 5           31
    A CAVERN SHAGGD WITH HORRID SHADES DARK COOL & DEADLY WHERE 295 FOUR ZOAS 3       122
    WHILE HIS SNOWS FELL & HIS STORMS BEAT TO COOL THE FLAMES  321 FOUR ZOAS 7        30
        OF ORC
    HOW COOL THE BREEZES OF THE VALLY & THE ARMS OF THE        369 FOUR ZOAS 9    *  449
        BRANCHING TREES
    AND GIVEN ME FRUITS & PLEASANT WATERS & WARM HILLS & COOL  369 FOUR ZOAS 9        452
        VALLEYS
    TILL THEY REVIVE OR BURY THEM IN COOL GROTS MAKING         377 FOUR ZOAS 9        747
        LAMENTATION
    TILL THEY REVIVE OR BURY THEM IN COOL GROTS MAKING         513 MILTON 27           7
        LAMENTATION
    BECAUSE [I KNOW HE ALWAYS JUDGES] HIS JUDGMENT IS SO VERY  549 CROMEK SPEAK/N      2
        COOL
    FOR ITS SURE TO KEEP YOUR JUDGMENT COOL . . . . . . .      556 SOME PEOPLE/N       2
COOL BLOODED
    BUT IN COOL BLOODED DESIGN & INTENTION  . . . . . . . .   615D V LAST JUDG/N      PROSE
COOLING
    DESIRE STILL PINES BUT FOR ONE COOLING DROP AND TIS DENYD  41C THEN SHE BORE      PROSE
COOPERATING
    COOPERATING IN THE BLISS OF MAN OBEYING HIS WILL . . . .   366 FOUR ZOAS 9        373
COPIED
    THAT KINGS & PRIESTS HAD COPIED ON EARTH  . . . . . .      242 EUROPE 11           4
    THE GREEKS AND HETRURIANS COPIED HERCULES FARNESE  . . .  565C DESC CAT 2         PROSE
    EVEN HOGARTH'S EXECUTION CANNOT BE COPIED OR IMPROVED  . . 599C PUB ADDRESS/N     PROSE
    EVEN HOGARTH CANNOT BE EITHER COPIED OR IMPROVED   . . .  601D PUB ADDRESS/N      PROSE
    WERE COPIED FROM THE CHERUBIM OF SOLOMON'S TEMPLE  . . .  775D INSC LAOCOON       TITLE
    THE WRITING BEING EXACTLY COPIED FROM THE TRACING PAPER    838A LETTER 37         PROSE
COPIER
    WHERE WILL THE COPIER OF NATURE AS IT NOW IS FIND  . . .  580D DESC CAT 5         PROSE
```

                                                                   PAGE   TITLE   LINE

COPIERS
   & ALL THE COPIES OR PRETENDED COPIERS OF NATURE   . . . . 594D PUB ADDRESS/N PROSE
   WHY ARE COPIERS OF NATURE INCORRECT WHILE . . . . . . 595A PUB ADDRESS/N PROSE
   COPIERS OF IMAGINATION ARE CORRECT THIS IS MANIFEST TO ALL 595A PUB ADDRESS/N PROSE
COPIES
   LEARND THE LANGUAGE OF ART BY MAKING MANY FINISHD COPIES 455D ANNO REYNOLDS MARG
   BECAUSE VISION IS DETERMINATE & PERFECT & HE COPIES THAT 457B ANNO REYNOLDS MARG
   BEING COPIES FROM SOME STUPENDOUS ORIGINALS . . . . . 565C DESC CAT 2   PROSE
   IN A VERY SUPERIOR STYLE TO THOSE JUSTLY ADMIRED COPIES 565D DESC CAT 2   PROSE
   ALL THE REST ARE EVIDENTLY COPIES THOUGH FINE ONES . . 565D DESC CAT 2   PROSE
   DIS-ARRANGED IMITATIONS AND BLUNDERING MISAPPLIED COPIES 585D DESC CAT 15   PROSE
   & ALL THE COPIES OR PRETENDED COPIERS OF NATURE . . . . 594D PUB ADDRESS/N PROSE
   AFFECTATION & FOPPERY HE WHO COPIES DOES NOT EXECUTE . 596B PUB ADDRESS/N PROSE
   & HE COPIES THAT SO NEAT AS TO MAKE IT A DECEPTION NOW . 597B PUB ADDRESS/N PROSE
   SUCH CONTEMPTIBLE COPIES COUNTRYMEN COUNTRYMEN . . . . 597C PUB ADDRESS/N PROSE
   ARE OIL COLOUR COPIES FROM FRESCO ORIGINALS . . . . . 598A PUB ADDRESS/N PROSE
   AS TO CALL THEM COPIES FROM LIFE & MANNERS . . . . . . 795B LETTER 6   PROSE
   I SEND WITH THIS...COPIES OF...OF THE BALLADS FOR . . 821B LETTER 25   PROSE
   I SEND THE FIVE COPIES OF COWPER'S PLATES WHICH YOU WILL 832D LETTER 32   PROSE
   CORRECT & ENLARGED COPIES FROM ANTIQUE GEMS OF WHICH THE 836B LETTER 35   PROSE
   NOT BEING QUITE SURE THAT YOU HAD COPIES READY FOR THEM 840B LETTER 39   PROSE
   I COULD NOT THINK OF DELIVERING THE (TWELVE) COPIES WITHOUT 840B LETTER 39   PROSE
      GIVING
   TWO COPIES PERHAPS FROM BORGOGNONE OF BATTLES . . . . 844A LETTER 43   PROSE
   DELIVERD A DOZEN COPIES AT STATIONER'S HALL . . . . . 846D LETTER 44   PROSE
   BY THE METHODS WHICH THEY USE TO PUBLISH & DISPERSE COPIES 856C LETTER 54   PROSE
   THAT ONE THOUSAND COPIES SHOULD BE THE FIRST EDITION AND 858B LETTER 55   PROSE
      IF WE CHOOSE
   TO PAY ME THREE GUINEAS FOR EACH OF THE COPIES . . . 872A LETTER 74   PROSE
COPIOUSNESS
   ("THE DEGREE OF GENIUS IS DETERMINED BY") COPIOUSNESS   69C ANNO LAVATER   MARG
      OF GLANCE
COPPER
   MEMORANDUM TO WOODCUT ON COPPER . . . . 440C MEMORANDUM/N 4 PROSE
   COPPER PLATES OF ALBERT DURER LUCAS HISBEN ALDEGRAVE AND 586D CHAUCER 1   PROSE
      THE
   NEVER SUSPENDED HIS LABOURS ON COPPER FOR A SINGLE DAY . 587D CHAUCER/N   PROSE
   & INDEED THE SUPERSTRUCTURE IT IS DRAWING ON COPPER . . 591D PUB ADDRESS/N PROSE
   & ENGRAVING IS DRAWING ON COPPER & NOTHING ELSE . . . 594C PUB ADDRESS/N PROSE
   ON CANVAS & WOOD & COPPER &C . . . . 598A PUB ADDRESS/N PROSE
   & ENGRAVING IS DRAWING ON COPPER & NOTHING ELSE . . . 602B PUB ADDRESS/N PROSE
   THE FIGHTING DEVILS READY FOR THE COPPER I COUNT MYSELF 879C LETTER 89   PROSE
   THREE PLATES FOR THE STATUE OF BRITANNIA &...FOR COPPER SUPP LETTER 6A   *PROSE
COPULATION
   IN HAPPY COPULATION IF IN EVENING MILD WEARIED WITH WORK 194 V DAU ALBION 7   1
   IN LOVELY COPULATION BLISS ON BLISS WITH THEOTORMON . 195 V DAU ALBION 7   26
   SWEEP OER THE STRUGGLING COPULATION IN FELL WRITHING PANGS 381 FOUR ZOAS AD 2   4
COPY
   THESE ARE NOT SO EVEN THE COPY FROM RAPHAEL'S CARTOON . 439C REMARKS MALKIN PROSE
   TO LEARN THE LANGUAGE OF ART COPY FOR EVER IS MY RULE . 446B ANNO REYNOLDS MARG
   THE BAD ARTIST SEEMS TO COPY A GREAT DEAL . . . . . . 456B ANNO REYNOLDS MARG
   THE GOOD ONE REALLY DOES COPY A GREAT DEAL . . . . . 456A ANNO REYNOLDS MARG
   MEN THINK THEY CAN COPY NATURE AS CORRECTLY . . . . . 594D PUB ADDRESS/N PROSE
   AS I COPY IMAGINATION THIS THEY WILL FIND IMPOSSIBLE . 594D PUB ADDRESS/N PROSE
   OR A COPY OF ANY KIND CAN BE AS HONOURABLE TO A NATION . 595C PUB ADDRESS/N PROSE
   ENGLAND WILL NEVER RIVAL ITALY WHILE WE SERVILELY COPY . 597C PUB ADDRESS/N PROSE
   THE COMPARISON IS EASILY MADE & THE COPY DETECTED . . 598A PUB ADDRESS/N PROSE
   INTEND IT SHOULD BE SO NONE BUT BLOCKHEADS COPY ONE ANOTHER 601D PUB ADDRESS/N PROSE
   SUPPOSED THAT A COPY COULD BE BETTER THAN AN ORIGINAL . 602C PUB ADDRESS/N PROSE
   & TRANSLATE & COPY & BUY & SELL & CRITICISE BUT NOT MAKE 778D HOMERS POETRY PROSE
   COPY THESE WELL BUT PATIENCE IF GREAT THINGS DO NOT TURN 812A LETTER 22   PROSE
      OUT
   DESIRES ME TO COPY OUT & SEND YOU WITH HER KIND LOVE . 816D LETTER 24   PROSE
   VERY UNACCOUNTABLY TO COPY OUT IN MY LAST LETTER   826C LETTER 28   PROSE
      THAT PASSAGE
   WRITTEN OR PRINTED WHICH HE PROMISES TO COPY OUT FOR . 836A LETTER 35   PROSE
   I DID BUT EXPRESS TO HIM MY DESIRE OF SENDING YOU A COPY OF 836D LETTER 35   PROSE
   COPY OF COWPER'S LETTERS OUGHT TO BE PRINTED IN . . 837D LETTER 36   PROSE
   YOU WILL FIND INCLOSED ONE IS A COPY FROM THAT MINIATURE 838D LETTER 37   PROSE
   IT IS A COPY FROM A DUTCH PICTURE DUTCH BOOR SMOKING . 843C LETTER 43   PROSE
   LEAR AND CORDELIA TO COPY IF YOU DESIRE' IT SHOULD BE DONE 845D LETTER 44   PROSE
   TO COPY ANY OF HIS FATHER'S DESIGNS THAT MR FLAXMAN MAY 846A LETTER 44   PROSE
   THE PRINT OF ROMEO & THE APOTHECARY ANNEXD TO YOUR COPY 855C LETTER 53   PROSE
   TO SEE ANOTHER COPY BY ANOTHER HAND . . . . 859C LETTER 56   PROSE
   I WISH TO HAVE A COPY OF JOB TO SHEW TO MR CHANTRY . . 870D LETTER 72   PROSE
   IN WHICH HE SAYS HE WILL TAKE ONE COPY OF JOB FOR HIMSELF 876D LETTER 85   PROSE
   MR BUTTS IS TO HAVE A PROOF COPY FOR THREE GUINEAS . . 877D LETTER 88   PROSE
   OF MR LINNELL FOR SONGS OF INNOCENCE & EXPERIENCE ONE COPY SUPP LETTER 66G   *PROSE
COPYING
   ("GENERAL COPYING...DELUSIVE") HERE HE CONDEMNS   448C ANNO REYNOLDS MARG
      GENERALIZING
   IF HE MEANS THAT COPYING CORRECTLY IS A HINDRANCE HE IS 448D ANNO REYNOLDS MARG
      A LIAR
   WHAT IS LAYING UP MATERIALS BUT COPYING . . . . . . 455B ANNO REYNOLDS MARG
   CONTEMPTIBLE SERVILE COPYING IS THE GREAT MERIT OF COPYING 456A ANNO REYNOLDS MARG
   HOW CAN I HELP THY HUSBAND'S COPYING ME . . . . . . 539 TO NANCY F/N   1
   NO MAN OF SENSE EVER SUPPOSES THAT COPYING FROM NATURE . 598A PUB ADDRESS/N PROSE
   GUINEA EACH WHICH IS SOMETHING BETTER THAN MERE COPYING 795C LETTER 6   PROSE
COPYRIGHT
   COPYRIGHT AND AS FAR AS I CAN JUDGE OF THE NATURE OF . 831C LETTER 31   PROSE
   COPYRIGHT IS FOR EVER YOURS I THEREFORE BEG THAT YOU WILL 858B LETTER 55   PROSE

393

		PAGE	TITLE	LINE

COPY-RIGHT,COPY RIGHT
    THAT WOULD LEAD TO A VALUATION OF THE COPY RIGHT . . . . 860B LETTER 56   PROSE
    THE PLATES & COPY-RIGHT OF JOB & THE SAME IS HIS   874A LETTER 78   PROSE
        SOLE PROPERTY
CORAL
    WANDRING IN MANY A CORAL GROVE . . . .   11 TO MUSES/PS   11
CORD
    AROUND HIS BOSOM LIKE A BLOODY CORD IN SECRET SOBS . . . 307 FOUR ZOAS 5   84
    ACHITOPHEL IS ALSO HERE WITH THE CORD IN HIS HAND . . . 608D V LAST JUDG/N   PROSE
    CORD OF AFFECTION THRILLING EXTATIC ON THE IRON REEL .   688 JERUSALEM 56   12
CORDED
    AND CORDED SHIPS HER MERCHANTS BUZZING ROUND . . . . .   19 EDW THIRD/PS 2   12
    IS FORMD & MANY A CORDED LYRE OUTSPREAD OVER THE IMMENSE 284 FOUR ZOAS 2   161
    MILTON STRUCK THE CORDED SHELL . . . .   SUPP ILLUS GRAY   *TITLE
CORDELIA
    A PICTURE OF LEAR AND CORDELIA WHEN HE AWAKES AND KNOWS HER 843D LETTER 43   PROSE
    THE HEADS OF LEAR AND CORDELIA CAN NEVER BE SURPASSED . 843D LETTER 43   PROSE
    LEAR AND CORDELIA TO COPY IF YOU DESIRE IT SHOULD BE DONE 845D LETTER 44   PROSE
    LEAR & CORDELIA BELONGING TO MR WALKER . . . .   849A LETTER 45   PROSE
CORDELLA
    GWENDOLEN RAGAN SABRINA GONORILL MEHETABEL CORDELLA . . . 281 FOUR ZOAS 2   61
    CAMBEL & GWENDOLEN & CONWENNA & CORDELLA & IGNOGE . . . 624 JERUSALEM 5   41
    I DISCOVER THY SECRET PLACES CORDELLA I BEHOLD . . . .   644 JERUSALEM 21   19
    SHE ADJOIND WITH GWANTOKE'S CHILDREN SOON LOVELY CORDELLA 710 JERUSALEM 71   28
        AROSE
    JOIND WITH CORDELLA SHE SHINES SOUTHWARD OVER THE ATLANTIC 710 JERUSALEM 71   43
CORDS
    . . . & CORDS & FIRES & FLOODS . . . .   377 FOUR ZOAS 9   752
    LET CORDS & STAKES BIND IN THE VOID . . . .   231 URIZEN 19   3
    THEY BEAT DOWN THE STAKES THE CORDS . . . .   232 URIZEN 19   48
    SO TWISTED THE CORDS & SO KNOTTED . . . .   235 URIZEN 25   20
    THE THREADS ARE SPUN & THE CORDS TWISTED & DRAWN OUT THEN 284 FOUR ZOAS 2   157
        THE WEAK
    CHAINS OF DARK IGNORANCE & CORDS OF TWISTED SELF CONCEIT 312 FOUR ZOAS 6   41
    HORRIBLE HOOKS & NETS HE FORMD TWISTING THE CORDS OF IRON 343 FOUR ZOAS 8   92
    WHILE I STOOD BOUND WITH CORDS & HEAVY CHAINS YOUR   364 FOUR ZOAS 9   276
        HIPOCRISY
    THE PLATES THE SCREWS [THE NETS] AND RACKS & SAWS & CORDS 377 FOUR ZOAS 9   * 752
        . . .
    THE PLATES & SCREWS & WRACKS & SAWS & CORDS & FIRES   514 MILTON 27   34
        & CISTERNS
    OR THROWING THE WINGD SHUTTLE OR DRAWING THE CORDS WITH   725 JERUSALEM 82   13
        SOFTEST SONGS
    THE GOLDEN CORDS OF THE LOOMS ANIMATE BENEATH THEIR TOUCHES 725 JERUSALEM 82   14
        SOFT
    & ITS GOLDEN CORDS & PINS . . . .   757 EV GOSPEL(I)/N   22
CORE
    FOR IT STICKS IN THE HEART'S DEEP CORE . . . . . .   423 THE SMILE   9
COREGGIO   SEE CORREGGIO,COREGIO
    WITH THE EXECUTION OF TITIAN RUBENS COREGGIO REMBRANT . 599B PUB ADDRESS/N   *PROSE
CORINEUS
    CORINEUS THROWS GOGMAGOG THE GIANT INTO THE SEA KING LEAR 208C SUBJCTS HIST/N   TITLE
CORINNA
    CORINNA THE RIVAL OF PINDAR CORINNA THE GRAECIAN POETESS SUPP PENC DRAW 1.45 *TITLE
CORINTHIAN
    A PEGASUS OF CORINTHIAN METAL . . . .   843A LETTER 42   PROSE
    [?HE ?COULD ?NOT (TELL) IONICK (FROM) THE (CORINTHIAN) OR] SUPP ANNO REYNOLDS   * MARG
CORK
    WATERFORD TIPPERARY CORK LIMERICK KERRY CLARE . . . . . 711 JERUSALEM 72   22
CORN   SEE CORN FIELD,CORN FIELDS
    "MY CROP OF CORN IS BUT A FIELD OF TARES" . . . . . .   52B ISLAND MOON 8
    . . . AS A RIPE VINEYARD STRETCHES OVER SHEAVES OF CORN   138 FRENCH REVOLTN   86
    THE LARK DOES RUSTLE IN THE RIPE CORN AND THE EAGLE RETURNS 190 V DAU ALBION 2   25
    AS A BLIGHT CUTS THE TENDER CORN WHEN IT BEGINS TO APPEAR 201 AMERICA 14   6
    [UPON ITS GREEN STALK ROSE THE CORN WAVING INNUMERABLE]   270 FOUR ZOAS 1   209
    AND IN THE VINTAGE & TO SING ON THE WAGGON LOADED WITH CORN 290 FOUR ZOAS 2   403
    THE CORN IS TURND TO THISTLES & THE APPLES INTO POISON . 360 FOUR ZOAS 9   * 109
    MY FLOCKS & HERDS TRAMPLE THE CORN MY CATTLE BROWZE UPON 376 FOUR ZOAS 9   699
    LET THE BULLS OF LUVAH TREAD THE CORN & DRAW THE LOADED   376 FOUR ZOAS 9   701
        WAGGON
    THEN DARK URTHONA TOOK THE CORN OUT OF THE STORES OF URIZEN 378 FOUR ZOAS 9   806
    SUCH ARE THE WORKS OF DARK URTHONA THARMAS SIFTED THE CORN 379 FOUR ZOAS 9   821
    HORSEBACK WITH DEATH OVER THE FIELDS OF CORN . . . . .   537 AND HIS LEGS/N   23
    THE CORN IS TURND TO THISTLES & THE APPLES INTO POISON . 641 JERUSALEM 19   10
CORNER
    IS PEND UP IN THE CORNER STRAIT . . . .   16 BLIND-MANS/PS   26
    WIPING HIS FACE & LOOKING ON THE CORNER OF THE CIELING SANG 57A ISLAND MOON 9   *PROSE
    HE TURND THE HORSES LOOSE & LAID HIS PLOW IN THE NORTHERN 365 FOUR ZOAS 9   319
        CORNER
    SOME MEN CANNOT SEE A PICTURE EXCEPT IN A DARK CORNER . 476A ANNO REYNOLDS   MARG
    DEATH COUCH IN THE CAVERNS OF DEATH IN THE CORNER OF THE 489 MILTON 9   3
        ATLANTIC
    CLAPD DEATH INTO THE CORNER OF THEIR JAW . . . . . .   537 AND HIS LEGS/N   21
    AT NO...CORNER OF BROAD STREET GOLDEN-SQUARE . . . . .   560C EXHIBITION ADV   PROSE
    AT NO...CORNER OF BROAD-STREET GOLDEN-SQUARE . . . . .   562A DESC CAT ADV   TITLE
    ARE SOLD ONLY AT THE CORNER OF BROAD STREET . . . . .   562C DESC CAT ADV   PROSE
    AT N...CORNER OF BROAD STREET GOLDEN SQUARE . . . . .   563A DESC CAT   *TITLE
    IN A DARK CORNER THE EYES OF STUPID CUNNING NEVER WILL BE 563D DESC CAT   PROSE
    SUBSCRIPTIONS RECEIVED AT NO...CORNER OF BROAD-STREET . 587A CHAUCER 1   PROSE
    SUBSCRIPTIONS RECEIVED AT NO...CORNER OF BROAD STREET   590D CHAUCER 2   PROSE
        GOLDEN SQUARE
    I COURT THE COMPARISON & FEAR NOT THE RESULT BUT NOT IN   598D PUB ADDRESS/N   PROSE
        A DARK CORNER

CORNER   (CONTINUED)
    & CLAP THE PICTURE INTO A DARK CORNER   . . . . 599A PUB ADDRESS/N   PROSE
    THAT I SHOULD BE [LEFT] HID IN A CORNER IT NEVER WAS   . . 602C PUB ADDRESS/N   PROSE
    THE CORNER OF BROAD STREET WEEPS POLAND STREET LANGUISHES   729 JERUSALEM 84   15
    WITH ANY NEGLECT YET I AM LAID BY IN A CORNER   . . . . 795C LETTER 6   PROSE
    NOW I AM SHUT UP IN A CORNER THEREFORE AM FORCED TO ASK   878C LETTER 88   PROSE
CORNERS
    OR THE GREEN CORNERS OF THE EARTH . . . . 10 TO MUSES/PS   6
    AND SEARCHES THRO THE CORNERS OF THE SKY   . . . . . . 15 IMIT SPEN/PS   39
    THE CORNERS OF HER MOUTH SEEMD I DONT KNOW HOW   . . 44B ISLAND MOON 1   PROSE
    ONE GRINS [ONE] T OTHER SPITS & IN CORNERS HIDES   . . 545 COSWAY FRAZR/N   7
    IN THE TWO CORNERS OF THE PICTURE [WHERE XXX APOLLYON] . 612B V LAST JUDG/N   *PROSE
    AT THE REMOTEST CORNERS OF HEAVEN FROM EACH OTHER   . . 802D LETTER 14   PROSE
CORN-FIELD,CORN FIELD
    THERE IS NO CITY NOR CORN FIELD NOR ORCHARD ALL IS ROCK   276 FOUR ZOAS 1   426
      & SAND
    THE WATRY GRAVE O THOU CORN FIELD O THOU VEGETATER HAPPY   355 FOUR ZOAS 8   543
    AS WHEN THE WIND SWEEPS OVER A CORN FIELD THE NOISE OF   372 FOUR ZOAS 9   562
      SOULS
    APPEARS LISTENS SILENT THEN SPRINGING FROM THE WAVING   520 MILTON 31   30
      CORN-FIELD LOUD
CORN-FIELDS,CORN FIELDS
    WHY DOST THOU NOT FLY AMONG THE CORN FIELDS   . . . . . 168 O LAPWING/N   3
    WHO BUYS WHOLE CORN FIELDS INTO WASTES AND SINGS UPON THE   193 V DAU ALBION 5   15
      HEATH
    HARROW BURN ALL THESE CORN FIELDS THROW DOWN ALL THESE   274 FOUR ZOAS 1   388
      FENCES
    GAVE SONGS OF GRATITUDE TO [THE] WAVING CORN FIELDS ROUND   276 FOUR ZOAS 1   * 450
      THEIR NEST
    TO TRAMPLE THE CORN FIELDS IN BOASTFUL NEIGHINGS . . . .   338 FOUR ZOAS 7B   203
    HIS CORN-FIELDS AND HIS VALLEYS OF FIVE HUNDRED ACRES   497 MILTON 15   31
      SQUARE
    AMONG THE SPIRITUAL FIRES LOUD THE CORN FIELDS THUNDER   636 JERUSALEM 16   5
      ALONG
    THE CORN-FIELDS & THE BREATHING GARDENS OUTSIDE SEPARATED   643 JERUSALEM 21   9
    GIHON TO HIDDEKEL & TO CORN FIELDS & VILLAGES & INHABITANTS 695 JERUSALEM 61   32
    TO TRAMPLE THE CORN FIELDS IN BOASTFUL NEIGHINGS . . . . . 700 JERUSALEM 65   49
    THEIR VILLAGES CITIES SEA PORTS THEIR CORN FIELDS & GARDENS 710 JERUSALEM 71   21
      SPACIOUS
CORNWAL
    DAN CORNWAL DEVON DORSET NAPTHALI WARWICK LEICESTER   637 JERUSALEM 16   46
      WORCESTER
CORNWALL
    HE MOVD HIS RIGHT FOOT TO CORNWALL HIS LEFT TO THE ROCKS   531 MILTON 39   49
      OF BOGNOR
    CORNWALL WALES DERBYSHIRE AND SCOTLAND . . . .   577D DESC CAT 5   PROSE
    OF ULRO ROLLD ROUND HIS SKIRTS FROM DOVER TO CORNWALL   . . 670 JERUSALEM 42   18
    FROM STONE-HENGE AND FROM LONDON STONE FROM CORNWALL   690 JERUSALEM 58   46
      TO CATHNES
    HYLE DWELT IN WINCHESTER COMPREHENDING HANTS DORSET DEVON   710 JERUSALEM 71   20
      CORNWALL
    OF THE MINES OF CORNWALL & DERBYSHIRE LAYS UPON HIS BOSOM   741 JERUSALEM 94   8
      HEAVY
CORPOREAL
    HELL IS THE BEING SHUT UP IN THE POSSESSION OF CORPOREAL   74B ANNO LAVATER   MARG
      DESIRES
    CORPOREAL WAR PAINTERS ON YOU I CALL SCULPTORS ARCHITECTS 480C MILTON 1   PROSE
    MARK WELL MY WORDS CORPOREAL FRIENDS ARE SPIRITUAL ENEMIES 484 MILTON 4   26
    NOT MENTAL AS THE WARS OF ETERNITY BUT A CORPOREAL STRIFE   520 MILTON 31   25
    INTO CORPOREAL COMMAND WHEREBY HUMAN SACRIFICE   . . . . 578A DESC CAT 5   PROSE
    BECAUSE CORPOREAL DEMONS HAVE GAINED A PREDOMINANCE   . . 581D DESC CAT 8   PROSE
    BUT ETERNAL IDENTITY IS ONE THING & CORPOREAL VEGETATION IS 607A V LAST JUDG/N   PROSE
    TO THE TIME & SPACE FIXED BY THE CORPOREAL VEGETATIVE EYE 614B V LAST JUDG/N   PROSE
    FOR IN PARADISE THEY HAVE NO CORPOREAL & MORTAL BODY   . 616A V LAST JUDG/N   PROSE
    WHAT IS CALLD CORPOREAL NOBODY KNOWS OF ITS DWELLING PLACE 617A V LAST JUDG/N   PROSE
    I QUESTION NOT MY CORPOREAL OR VEGETATIVE EYE . . . .   617B V LAST JUDG/N   PROSE
    THEY PERCIEVED THAT CORPOREAL FRIENDS ARE SPIRITUAL ENEMIES 655 JERUSALEM 30   10
    IN A CORPOREAL & EVER DYING VEGETATION & CORRUPTION   . . 737 JERUSALEM 90   42
    I HAVE TRIED TO MAKE FRIENDS BY CORPOREAL GIFTS BUT HAVE   738 JERUSALEM 91   16
      ONLY
    [[ALL] THIS CORPOREAL LIFE S A] [ALL LIFE S A FICTION]   753 EV GOSPEL(D)/N * 85
    CORPOREAL DISEASE TO WHICH I READILY AGREE . . . . . .   772B ANNO SPURZHEIM   MARG
    HEAVEN IS A MERCY A FIG FOR ALL CORPOREAL SUCH DISTRESS IS 809B LETTER 20   PROSE
    PRETENDS TO BE THE FRIEND OF MY CORPOREAL HE IS A REAL   822D LETTER 26   PROSE
      ENEMY
    WHILE HE SEEMS THE ENEMY OF MY CORPOREAL BUT NOT VICE VERSA 822D LETTER 26   PROSE
    ALTOGETHER HIDDEN FROM THE CORPOREAL UNDERSTANDING   . . . 825A LETTER 27   PROSE
CORPSE   SEE CORSE
    [WHILE ?LIVING CLAY COLD CORPSE CORSE] SWIFT AS THE   . . . 43D WOE CRIED MUSE *PROSE
    STRIPPED FROM HIS LOAD OF CLOATHING HE IS LIKE A   581A DESC CAT 5   PROSE
      DEAD CORPSE
    AND THE DEAD CORPSE FROM SINAI'S HEAT   . . . . 761 FOR SEXES/GP   10
CORRECT
    NIGGLING WITHOUT THE CORRECT & DEFINITE OUTLINE   . . . . 448D ANNO REYNOLDS   MARG
    AS THEY WERE THE WORKS OF A CORRECT MIND & NO BLURRER   . . 553B BELLS WEEKLY/N   MARG
    THE COSTUME IS CORRECT ACCORDING TO AUTHENTIC MONUMENTS   567D DESC CAT 3   PROSE
    AND HINDER ALL CORRECT DRAWING FROM APPEARING TO BE CORRECT 583C DESC CAT 9   PROSE
    THE DESIGNER PROPOSES TO ENGRAVE IN A CORRECT AND FINISHED 586C CHAUCER 1   PROSE
    THE COSTUME IS CORRECT ACCORDING TO AUTHENTIC MONUMENTS   590D CHAUCER 2   PROSE
    THO EVEN IN THESE A SINGLE LEAF OF A TREE IS NEVER CORRECT 594A PUB ADDRESS/N   PROSE
    COPIERS OF IMAGINATION ARE CORRECT THIS IS MANIFEST TO ALL 595A PUB ADDRESS/N   PROSE
    & NOT ARE AS MOST EXPRESSIVE & CORRECT TOO . . . . . .   786C ANNO THORNTON   MARG

```
                                                                  PAGE     TITLE        LINE
CORRECT    (CONTINUED)
     CORRECT & ENLARGED COPIES FROM ANTIQUE GEMS OF WHICH THE     836B LETTER 35        PROSE
CORRECTED
     SHOULD BE CORRECTED BY THE YOUNG GENTLEMEN . . . . . .  .    543 TO ROYL ACAD/N       3
CORRECTION
     FOR YOUR CORRECTION OR CONDEMNATION BEGGING YOU TO SUPPLY    860B LETTER 56        PROSE
CORRECTIONS
     I HAVE DONE THE CORRECTIONS MY PAPER NOT BEING IN ORDER      791A LETTER 2         PROSE
CORRECTLY
     CORRECTLY WITH BLACK LEAD PENCIL LET NOTHING BE TO SEEK      440B MEMORANDUM/N 2   PROSE
     HUDSON DREW CORRECTLY . . . . . . . . . . . . .  .  .       447B ANNO REYNOLDS    MARG
     IF HE MEANS THAT COPYING CORRECTLY IS A HINDRANCE HE IS      448D ANNO REYNOLDS    MARG
         A LIAR
     MEN THINK THEY CAN COPY NATURE AS CORRECTLY     . . . . .    594D PUB ADDRESS/N    PROSE
CORREGGIO     SEE COREGGIO,COREGGIO
     THE LABOURD WORKS OF JOURNEYMEN EMPLOYD BY CORREGGIO    . .  455A ANNO REYNOLDS    MARG
     ("TITIAN VERONESE TINTORET THE BASSANS CORREGGIO BAROCCIO")  457A ANNO REYNOLDS    MARG
     & THAT SUCH IDIOTS AS RUBENS CORREGGIO & TITIAN KNEW    .    467B ANNO REYNOLDS    MARG
     IF SO THEY KNEW ALL THAT TITIAN & CORREGGIO KNEW . . . .     471C ANNO REYNOLDS    MARG
     CORREGGIO WAS TWO YEARS OLDER THAN MICH ANGELO   . . . .     471C ANNO REYNOLDS    MARG
     CORREGGIO BORN...MICH ANGELO BORN ...                        471C ANNO REYNOLDS    MARG
     GENTRY TO CORREGGIO RUBENS REMBRANT REYNOLDS GAINSBOROUGH    548B ON GREAT ENC/N  *TITLE
     WHEN I SEE A RUBENS REMBRANT [OR] CORREGGIO      . . . .     550 WHEN I SEE/N     *   1
     RUBENS AND REMBRANDT TITIAN AND CORREGGIO BY WILLIAM BLAKE   562B DESC CAT ADV     PROSE
     OR CORREGGIO THEY OUGHT TO KNOW THAT CORREGGIO WAS BORN      563C DESC CAT         PROSE
     AND IT IS ALWAYS WRONG IN TITIAN AND CORREGGIO   . . .  .    564A DESC CAT         PROSE
     CORREGGIO RUBENS AND REMBRANDT WE NEVER SHALL EQUAL . . .    564A DESC CAT         PROSE
     HENCE RUBENS TITIAN CORREGGIO AND ALL OF THAT CLASS ARE      581A DESC CAT 5       PROSE
     CORREGGIO IS A SOFT AND EFFEMINATE AND CONSEQUENTLY A    .   583A DESC CAT 9       PROSE
     ABOUT CORREGGIO BEING POOR AND BUT BADLY PAID . . . . .  .   583B DESC CAT 9       PROSE
     THE MANUAL LABOUR IN THESE PICTURES OF CORREGGIO IS IMMENSE  583B DESC CAT 9       PROSE
     CORREGGIO WAS NOT POOR HE WILL MAKE ANY TRUE ARTIST SO  .    583B DESC CAT 9       PROSE
     WOULD BE THE CORREGGIO THAT THE LIFE WRITERS HAVE WRITTEN    583C DESC CAT 9       PROSE
         OF
     TALK NO MORE THEN OF CORREGGIO OR REMBRANDT OR ANY OTHER     585C DESC CAT 15      PROSE
     WORKS ARE LIKE THOSE OF TITIAN & CORREGGIO . . . . .  .  .   593D PUB ADDRESS/N    PROSE
     CORREGGIO OR TITIAN I DO NOT PRETEND TO ENGRAVE FINER   .    594C PUB ADDRESS/N    PROSE
     WHO THAT HAS EYES CANNOT SEE THAT RUBENS & CORREGGIO    .    599D PUB ADDRESS/N   *PROSE
CORREGGIO'S
     CORREGGIO'S REFLECTIONS AND REFRACTIONS TO BE ADDED TO IT    583C DESC CAT 9       PROSE
     CORREGGIO'S NOR CORREGGIO'S LIKE RAFAEL'S & IF NEITHER OF    815B LETTER 23        PROSE
COREGGIO
     SMOOTHD IT OVER LIKE AN ENGLISH ENGRAVER OR COREGGIO &       598C PUB ADDRESS/N    PROSE
         TITIAN
COREGGIO'S
     FAULTS CARACCHE COREGGIO'S & RAFAEL'S HAVE FAULTS     . . .  815A LETTER 23       *PROSE
CORRESPOND
     USES AND SUBSTANCES ARE SO DIFFERENT AS NOT TO CORRESPOND    95B ANNO SWED LOVE    MARG
     THE VENETIAN WILL NOT CORRESPOND WITH THE GREAT STYLE   .    463B ANNO REYNOLDS    MARG
     STYLE WILL ILL CORRESPOND WITH THE GREAT STYLE     . . .     468A ANNO REYNOLDS    MARG
CORRESPONDENCE
     BY CORRESPONDENCE WHICH HAS NOTHING TO DO WITH              93B ANNO SWED LOVE    MARG
         DEMONSTRATION
     I INCLOSE LIKEWISE THE ACADEMICAL CORRESPONDENCE OF . . .    836D LETTER 35        PROSE
CORRODING
     WITH CORRODING FIRES HE WROTE THE FOLLOWING SENTENCE NOW     150D MARRIAGE HH 6    PROSE
     IN WATERS STIFLING OR IN AIR CORRODING OR IN EARTH SHUT UP   377 FOUR ZOAS 9        741
     THEY STOOD IN A DARK LAND OF DEATH OF FIERY CORRODING        524 MILTON 34          44
         WATERS
     ARE BECOME FOUNTAINS OF BITTER DEATH & OF CORRODING HELL     525 MILTON 35           3
     ARE BECOME THE SOURCES OF DARK & BITTER DEATH & OF           672 JERUSALEM 43       32
         CORRODING HELL
CORROSIVES
     BY CORROSIVES WHICH IN HELL ARE SALUTARY AND MEDICINAL  . .  154C MARRIAGE HH 14   PROSE
CORRUPT
     WHEREAS IT NOW APPEARS FINITE & CORRUPT      . . . . .  .    154B MARRIAGE HH 14   PROSE
     POETS IN ANY AGE OR COUNTRY AND THESE IN A CORRUPT STATE     561C EXHIBITION ADV   PROSE
     MY FIRES ARE CORRUPT MY INCENSE IS A CLOUDY PESTILENCE  .    721 JERUSALEM 79       56
CORRUPTED
     COME OUT [GIVE ME] WE ARE PUTRIFIED WE ARE CORRUPTED    .    58D ISLAND MOON 10   *PROSE
     OUR FLESH IS CORRUPTED AND WE (WEAR) AWAY . . . . . .  .     137 FRENCH REVOLTN   *  76
     BECAUSE IGNORANT OF CRIME IN THE MIDST OF A CORRUPTED AGE    610B V LAST JUDG/N    PROSE
CORRUPTIBILITY
     FOR CROWNS WREATHD SERPENTS FOR SWEET ODORS STINKING         312 FOUR ZOAS 6        38
         CORRUPTIBILITY
     FROM CORRUPTIBILITY O WHEN LORD JESUS WILT THOU COME    .    495 MILTON 14          18
     (CORRUPTIBILITY) APPEARS UPON THY LIMBS AND NEVER MORE       727 JERUSALEM 83     *  1
CORRUPTIBLE
     AND GRINNING SKULLS AND CORRUPTIBLE DEATH    . . . . . .  .  4 FAIR ELENOR/PS       14
     LISTEN TO HER WHOSE EYES BEHOLD THE DARK BODY OF             354 FOUR ZOAS 8        505
         CORRUPTIBLE DEATH
     TILL MAN SHALL LEAVE A CORRUPTIBLE BODY HE FAMISHD HEARS     354 FOUR ZOAS 8        524
         HIM GROAN
     TO HAVE POWER OVER MAN FROM CRADLE TO CORRUPTIBLE GRAVE      661 JERUSALEM 34       26
     TO HAVE POWER OVER MAN FROM CRADLE TO CORRUPTIBLE GRAVE      688 JERUSALEM 56        4
CORRUPTING
     FOLD WITHOUT FOLD ENCOMPASSES HIM AND HIS CORRUPTING         354 FOUR ZOAS 8        510
         MEMBERS
CORRUPTION
     WHEN OLD CORRUPTION FIRST BEGUN     . . . . . . . .  .  .    50 WHEN CORRUP/IM       1
     AND OLD CORRUPTION SMILD . . . . . . . . . . . .  .  .       50 WHEN CORRUP/IM       6
     THE MOST TERRIFIC SHAPES OF ANIMALS SPRUNG FROM CORRUPTION   156A MARRIAGE HH 17   PROSE
```

```
                                                        PAGE      TITLE           LINE
CORRUPTION    (CONTINUED)
     TO WASTE IN ENDLESS CORRUPTION RENEW THOU I WILL DESTROY      298 FOUR ZOAS 4      *   31
     WHICH WAS ON EARTH BORN TO CORRUPTION & THE SIX FEMALES       498 MILTON 17           15
     IN A CORPOREAL & EVER DYING VEGETATION & CORRUPTION  .  .  .  737 JERUSALEM 90        42
     "I HAVE SAID TO CORRUPTION THOU ART MY FATHER" (JOB)   .  . SUPP LEGEND/N45       *
CORRUPTIONS
     WHY SHOULD WE ENTER INTO OUR SPECTRES TO BEHOLD OUR OWN       672 JERUSALEM 43        10
          CORRUPTIONS
CORSE
     [WHILE ?LIVING CLAY COLD CORPSE CORSE] SWIFT AS THE  .  .  .   43D WOE CRIED MUSE *PROSE
     LIFTED ON HIGH THE DEAD CORSE  .  .  .  .  .  .  .  .  .  .   251 AHANIA 3            52
     THE CORSE OF HIS FIRST BEGOTTEN  .  .  .  .  .  .  .  .  .    252 AHANIA 4             5
     URIZEN NAILD FUZON'S CORSE  .  .  .  .  .  .  .  .  .  .  .   252 AHANIA 4             8
     ROUND THE PALE LIVING CORSE ON THE TREE  .  .  .  .  .  .  .  252 AHANIA 4            10
     ROUND THE PALE LIVING CORSE ON THE TREE  .  .  .  .  .  .  .  253 AHANIA 4            36
     SO SAYING HE SUNK DOWN INTO THE SEA A PALE WHITE CORSE  .  .  266 FOUR ZOAS 1         76
     ENITHARMON REMAINS A CORSE SUCH THING WAS NEVER KNOWN   .     278 FOUR ZOAS 1        528
     STILL DIES FOR ENITHARMON NOR A SPIRIT SPRINGS FROM MY        288 FOUR ZOAS 2        322
          DEAD CORSE
     SHE FLED VANISHING ON THE WIND AND LEFT A DEAD COLD CORSE     289 FOUR ZOAS 2        334
     I PITYING HOVERD OVER THEE I PROTECTED THY GHASTLY CORSE      300 FOUR ZOAS 4        108
     THE CORSE OF [MAN] ALBION LAY ON THE ROCK THE SEA OF TIME     304 FOUR ZOAS 4        265
          & SPACE
     THE SAVIOUR MILD & GENTLE BENT OVER THE CORSE OF DEATH  .     304 FOUR ZOAS 4        269
     THE [ETERNAL] FALLEN MAN STRETCHD LIKE A CORSE UPON THE       341 FOUR ZOAS 8          4
          OOZY ROCK
     [THE SWELLING TIDES THEY BENT OVER THE DEAD CORSE LIKE        341 FOUR ZOAS 8         13
          AN ARCH]
     OUTSTRETCHD A SMILING CORSE THEY BURIED HER IN A SILENT       362 FOUR ZOAS 9        199
          CAVE
     A CORSE OF A SLAUGHTERED BARD AT THE FOOT OF THE ROCK  .    577A DESC CAT 4       PROSE
     BUT HERE THE SOLDIER STRIKES & A DEAD CORSE FALLS AT HIS      672 JERUSALEM 43        43
          FEET
     IN THREE NIGHTS HE DEVOURD THE REJECTED CORSE OF DEATH  .     734 JERUSALEM 89        13
     BLACK EYD SUSAN A FIGURE ON THE SEA SHORE EMBRACING A CORSE  848D LETTER 45       PROSE
CORSES
     DEAD CORSES LAY BEFORE THEM & NOT AS IN WARS OF OLD  .  .  .  672 JERUSALEM 43        40
COSENS
     MR COSENS OWNER OF THE MILL AT FELPHAM WAS PASSING BY   .  . 437D BLAKES MEMORAN  PROSE
COST
     HIS OWN DESPAIR EVEN AT THE COST OF EVERY THING THAT          344 FOUR ZOAS 8        139
          BREATHES
     TO DEFEND THE BIBLE IN THIS YEAR...WOULD COST A MAN HIS      383B ANNO WATSON     MARG
          LIFE
     AS I HAVE FOUND TO MY COST THESE FORTY YEARS  .  .  .  .  .  593D PUB ADDRESS/N   P-OSE
     I KNOW IT HAS COST ME IMMENSE LABOUR  .  .  .  .  .  .  .  . 861B LETTER 58       PROSE
     COST MY TIME THE AMOUNT OF TWENTY GUINEAS ONE I HAVE         878C LETTER 88       PROSE
          FINISHD
COSTLY
     THEN NINEVA & BABYLON AND COSTLY TYRE AND EVN JERUSALEM       41A THEN SHE BORE   *PROSE
     THE GOLD & SILVER & COSTLY STONES HIS HOLY WORKMANSHIP  .  .  310 FOUR ZOAS 5        215
     AND WITH THE LOOM TO COVER GWENDOLEN & RAGAN WITH COSTLY      643 JERUSALEM 21        14
          ROBES
COSTUME
     THE COSTUME IS CORRECT ACCORDING TO AUTHENTIC MONUMENTS      567D DESC CAT 3      PROSE
     WITHOUT VIOLATING COSTUME THE BRITONS SAY HISTORIANS  .  .  577C DESC CAT 5      PROSE
     I UNDERSTAND THAT MY COSTUME IS INCORRECT  .  .  .  .  .  .  583D DESC CAT 10     PROSE
     EVERY PARTICULAR OF DRESS OR COSTUME  .  .  .  .  .  .  .  . 588A CHAUCER/N       PROSE
     THE COSTUME IS CORRECT ACCORDING TO AUTHENTIC MONUMENTS      590D CHAUCER 2       PROSE
COSWAY
     COSWAY FRAZER & BALDWIN OF EGYPT'S LAKE  .  .  .  .  .  .  .  545 COSWAY FRAZR/N     1
COT
     I LOVE THE PLEASANT COT  .  .  .  .  .  .  .  .  .  .  .  .     8 LOVE JOCUND/PS      9
     WANDRING ROUND AN EARTHLY COT  .  .  .  .  .  .  .  .  .  .   425 MENTAL TRAVLER      30
     THRO THE VILLAGE THEN WINDS AT MY COT IT DOES END  .  .  .   800 MRS FLAXMAN/L       8
COTEMPORARIES
     AS IT HAS ALL HIS COTEMPORARIES EACH THING IS ITS OWN CAUSE  88C ANNO LAVATER     MARG
     & HIS COTEMPORARIES IS THEY SUPPOSE THAT WOMAN'S LOVE IS     88D ANNO LAVATER     MARG
          SIN
COTTAGE
     MISERY BUILDS OVER OUR COTTAGE ROOFS AND DISCONTENT RUNS     37B CONTEMPLATN/PS  PROSE
          LIKE A BROOK
     SHALL THIS MARBLE BUILT HEAVEN BECOME A CLAY COTTAGE  .  .  .  138 FRENCH REVOLTN     89
     THE COTTAGE FADES BEFORE HIS SIGHT  .  .  .  .  .  .  .  .   426 MENTAL TRAVLER      59
     BEFORE MY/COTTAGE STOOD FOR THE SATANIC SPACE IS DELUSION    527 MILTON 36          20
     COTTAGE FOR ME THAT IN THREE YEARS I MIGHT WRITE ALL THESE   527 MILTON 36          24
          VISIONS
     WALKING IN MY COTTAGE GARDEN SUDDEN I BEHELD  .  .  .  .  .  527 MILTON 36          26
     VIRGIN OF PROVIDENCE FEAR NOT TO ENTER INTO MY COTTAGE  .    527 MILTON 36          28
     ENTER MY COTTAGE COMFORT HER FOR SHE IS SICK WITH FATIGUE    527 MILTON 36          32
     BLAKE'S COTTAGE AT FELPHAM  .  .  .  .  .  .  .  .  .  .  . 527C MILTON 36         TITLE
     OUT FROM THE EASTERN SKY DESCENDING DOWN INTO MY COTTAGE     529 MILTON 38           7
     MY COTTAGE MIDST THE STARRY SEVEN WHERE THE VIRGIN OLOLON    532 MILTON 39          58
     LIVING IN A COTTAGE AND IN CONTEMPT AND DERISION  .  .  .  . 575D DESC CAT 3      PROSE
     THRO THE COTTAGE WHERE "SHE" LAYS IN BED "PINCHD & PULLD"   618C ILLUS MILTON    PROSE
     DEAR SCULPTOR OF ETERNITY WE ARE SAFE ARRIVED AT           801D LETTER 14       PROSE
          OUR COTTAGE
     & MY COTTAGE IS ALSO A SHADOW OF THEIR HOUSES MY  .  .  . 802A LETTER 14       PROSE
     COULD NOT ARRIVE AT OUR COTTAGE BEFORE HALF PAST ELEVEN    802B LETTER 14       PROSE
     DEAR FRIEND OF MY ANGELS WE ARE SAFE ARRIVED AT OUR COTTAGE 803A LETTER 15       PROSE
     COTTAGE IS MORE BEAUTIFUL THAN I THOUGHT IT & ALSO MORE    803B LETTER 15       PROSE
          CONVENIENT
```

COTTAGE   (CONTINUED)
        EVER BUILD A PALACE IT WOULD BE ONLY MY COTTAGE ENLARGED   803B LETTER 15   PROSE
        WAIT FOR LESS HURRIED MOMENTS OUR COTTAGE LOOKS MORE & MORE   806A LETTER 16   PROSE
        FRIENDS OUR COTTAGE IS SURROUNDED BY THE SAME GUARDIANS YOU   807B LETTER 17   PROSE
        SMILING ON OUR COTTAGE SAYS YOU LAY TOO LOW FOR MY ANGER TO   807B LETTER 17   PROSE
        I KNOW MY COTTAGE IS TOO NARROW FOR YOUR EASE & COMFORT   808B LETTER 19   PROSE
        EITHER IN MY COTTAGE OR IN A (LODGING) IN THE VILLAGE   . . 808C LETTER 19   PROSE
        FELPHAM COTTAGE OF COTTAGES THE PRETTIEST   . . . . 810A LETTER 20   PROSE
        BUT OUR TIME IS ALMOST OUT THAT WE TOOK THE COTTAGE FOR   819C LETTER 25   PROSE
            I DID
        VERY HAPPY SITTING AT TEA BY A WOOD FIRE IN OUR COTTAGE THE   820B LETTER 25   PROSE
        PROPRIETOR OF MY COTTAGE & HIS WIFE & DAUGHTER   . . . .   827B LETTER 28   PROSE
        TO HOVER ROUND OUR SWEET COTTAGE   . . . . 854A LETTER 52   PROSE
        WE ARE OFTEN SITTING BY OUR COTTAGE FIRE   . . . . . . 854A LETTER 52   PROSE
COTTAGERS
        "THE COTTAGERS" & "JOCUND PEASANTS"   . . . . 594A PUB ADDRESS/N PROSE
COTTAGES
        WITH COTTAGES AND VILLAGES THE FIRST BEAMS OF THE SUN   . . 567B DESC CAT 3   PROSE
        & THE SCENE OR LANDSCAPE WITH ITS VILLAGES COTTAGES   . . . 588A CHAUCER/N   PROSE
        WITH COTTAGES & VILLAGES THE FIRST BEAMS OF THE SUN   . . . 588D CHAUCER/N   PROSE
        WITH COTTAGES AND VILLAGES THE FIRST BEAMS OF THE SUN   . . 590C CHAUCER 2   PROSE
        IT IS A PERFECT MODEL FOR COTTAGES & I THINK FOR PALACES   801D LETTER 14   PROSE
        FELPHAM COTTAGE OF COTTAGES THE PRETTIEST   . . . . . . 810A LETTER 20   PROSE
COUCH   SEE DEATH COUCH
        THE COUCH OF DEATH . . . . 35C COUCH DEATH/PS TITLE
        VOICES OF COMFORT ARE HEARD OVER THE COUCH OF DEATH   . . . 36D COUCH DEATH/PS PROSE
        NOW UPON HER SUMPTUOUS COUCH RECLINED IN GORGEOUS PRIDE   38A SAMSON/PS   PROSE
        THE INFANT HEAD WHILE THE MOTHER IDLE PLAYS WITH HER DOG   110 TIRIEL 8   26
            ON HER COUCH
        . . . SICK SICK THE PRINCE ON HIS COUCH WREATHD IN DIM   134 FRENCH REVOLTN   2
        . . . A SKELETON YELLOW REMAINED IN ITS CHAINS ON ITS COUCH 135 FRENCH REVOLTN   33
        . . . LIKE BIRDS OF PREY STOOD ON THE COUCH   . . . . . 135 FRENCH REVOLTN   36
        THE KING AWOKE ON HIS COUCH OF GOLD   . . . . 185 LET BROTHELS/N   5
        THE TIGERS COUCH UPON THE PREY & SUCK THE RUDDY TIDE   . . 245 EUROPE 15   7
        SPREAD HER A COUCH UNKNOWN TO ENITHARMON HERE REPOSD   . .   280 FOUR ZOAS 1   569
        RISING UPON HIS COUCH OF DEATH ALBION BEHELD HIS SONS   . . 280 FOUR ZOAS 2   1
        THEY GO FORTH & RETURN TO ALBION ON HIS ROCKY COUCH   . .   281 FOUR ZOAS 2   60
        HIS SHADOWY FEMININE SEMBLANCE HERE REPOSD ON A [BRIGHT]   284 FOUR ZOAS 2   * 181
            WHITE COUCH
        WHEN URIZEN SLEPT ON HIS COUCH DRAWN THRO UNBOUNDED SPACE   291 FOUR ZOAS 2   421
        INVOLUNTARY TO THE COUCH WHERE ENITHARMON LAY   . . . .   305 FOUR ZOAS 4   292
        AND THE SWEET SOUND OF SILVER VOICES CALM THE WEARY COUCH   306 FOUR ZOAS 5   24
        STILL THE FAINT HARPS & SILVER VOICES CALM THE WEARY COUCH   306 FOUR ZOAS 5   30
        THE WATRY NATIONS COUCH & HIDE IN THE PROFOUNDEST DEEPS   320 FOUR ZOAS 7   24
        . . . BENEATH ENITHARMON'S COUCH   . . . .   328 FOUR ZOAS 7   334
        BURDEND WITH CLOUDS HOWL ROUND THE COUCH SULLEN THE WOOLY   335 FOUR ZOAS 7B   108
            SHEEP
        REMEMBER ALL THY FEIGNED TERRORS ON THE SECRET COUCH   . . 338 FOUR ZOAS 7B   196
        TO WAKE UPON THE COUCH OF DEATH HE SNEEZED SEVEN TIMES   . . 341 FOUR ZOAS 8   17
        THE THREE DAUGHTERS OF URIZEN GUARD AHANIA'S DEATH COUCH   362 FOUR ZOAS 9   201
        ISSUD IN MAJESTY DIVINE URIZEN ROSE UP FROM HIS COUCH   . . 366 FOUR ZOAS 9   347
        THE CHILDREN WOKE & SMILD ON VALA SHE KNEELD BY THE GOLDEN   371 FOUR ZOAS 9   523
            COUCH
        IN THE SUN'S HEAT TILL IN THE NIGHT ON THE COUCH OF ENION   371 FOUR ZOAS 9   541
        AROUND MY COUCH WITH TORCHES BRIGHT   . . . . 416 MY SPECTRE/N   42
        THE SEPARATION WAS TERRIBLE THE DEAD WAS REPOSD ON HIS   490 MILTON 9   49
            COUCH
        BENEATH THE COUCH OF ALBION ON THE SEVEN (MOUNTAINS) OF   490 MILTON 9   50
            ROME
        SICK COUCH BEARS THE DARK SHADES OF ETERNAL DEATH INFOLDING   493 MILTON 13   1
        THEY SAW HIS SHADOW VEGETATED UNDERNEATH THE COUCH   . . . 496 MILTON 15   9
        WHO DWELL IN IMMORTALITY AS ONE SLEEPING ON A COUCH   . .   496 MILTON 15   12
        SO SPOKE ORC WHEN OOTHOON & LEUTHA HOVERD OVER HIS COUCH   500 MILTON 18   39
        GLOWD ON HIS ROCKY COUCH AGAINST THE DARKNESS LOUD THUNDERS   500 MILTON 18   47
        NOW ALBION'S SLEEPING HUMANITY BEGAN TO TURN UPON HIS COUCH   502 MILTON 20   25
        DRUNK WITH THE SPIRIT BURNING ROUND THE COUCH OF DEATH   502 MILTON 20   44
            THEY STOOD
        AND ROUND THE SHADOWY EIGHTH THE EIGHT CLOSE UP THE COUCH   502 MILTON 20   47
        AND SATAN SAT SLEEPING UPON HIS COUCH IN UDAN-ADAN   . . . 503 MILTON 21   2
        GLOW ON AMERICA'S SHORE ALBION TURNS UPON HIS COUCH   . .   506 MILTON 23   7
        AND EVERY MOMENT HAS A COUCH OF GOLD FOR SOFT REPOSE   . . 516 MILTON 28   46
        AND MILTON OFT SAT UP ON THE COUCH OF DEATH & OFT CONVERSED   521 MILTON 32   *   1
        THEN HILLEL WHO IS LUCIFER REPLIED OVER THE COUCH OF DEATH   521 MILTON 32   8
        THUS THEY CONVERSE WITH THE DEAD WATCHING ROUND THE COUCH   522 MILTON 32   39
            OF DEATH
        IN MIDST OF THESE WAS MILTON'S COUCH & WHEN THEY SAW EIGHT   525 MILTON 35   29
        IMMORTAL STARRY-ONES GUARDING THE COUCH IN FLAMING FIRES   525 MILTON 35   30
        THEN ALBION ROSE UP IN THE NIGHT OF BEULAH ON HIS COUCH   531 MILTON 39   32
        FORBAD & DOWN WITH DREADFUL GROANS HE SUNK UPON HIS COUCH   531 MILTON 39   51
        ENGLOBES ITSELF & BECOMES A WOMB SUCH WAS ALBION'S COUCH   620 JERUSALEM 1   2
        BOWEN ALBION'S SONS THEY BORE HIM A GOLDEN COUCH INTO THE   658 JERUSALEM 32   12
            PORCH
        AND ON THE COUCH REPOSD HIS LIMBS TREMBLING FROM THE BLOODY   658 JERUSALEM 32   13
            FIELD
        DAMP COUCH THE FLAMES BENEATH AND SILENT SICK STAND   666 JERUSALEM 40   6
            SHUDDERING
        THEY KNEELD AROUND THE COUCH OF DEATH IN DEEP HUMILIATION   668 JERUSALEM 41   24
        THE SLUMBERS OF DEATH CAME OVER THEM AROUND THE COUCH OF   674 JERUSALEM 44   35
            DEATH
        OF GOLD & JEWELS A SUBLIME ORNAMENT A COUCH OF REPOSE   . . 677 JERUSALEM 48   6
        . . . ON THE SECRET COUCH OF LAMBETH'S VALE   . . . . .700 JERUSALEM 65   42
        AS MY GARDEN & AS MY SECRET BATH SPAIN WAS MY HEAVENLY   720 JERUSALEM 79   40
            COUCH

	PAGE	TITLE	LINE
COUCH (CONTINUED)			
WHERE I WILL BUILD HER A COUCH OF REPOSE & MY PILLARS . .	727	JERUSALEM 83	26
COUCHES			
SHE SAW THE COUCHES OF THE DEAD & WHERE THE FIBROUS ROOTS	130	BOOK OF THEL 6	3
THE ETERNAL MAN ALSO SAT DOWN UPON THE COUCHES OF BEULAH	366	FOUR ZOAS 9	354
AND THOSE UPON THE COUCHES VIEWD THEM IN THE DREAMS OF BEULAH	367	FOUR ZOAS 9	383
THUS WERE THE SLEEPERS ENTERTAIND UPON THE COUCHES OF BEULAH	372	FOUR ZOAS 9	558
TO FEED THE SLEEPERS ON THEIR COUCHES WITH MATERNAL CARE	516	MILTON 28	49
ON COUCHES SOFT WITH MILD MUSIC TENDED BY FLOWERS OF BEULAH	523	MILTON 34	10
AND THE COUCHES OF THE MARTYRS & MANY DAUGHTERS OF BEULAH	524	MILTON 34	20
AND OLOLON EXAMINED ALL THE COUCHES OF THE DEAD	525	MILTON 35	26
THEIR HUMAN MAJESTIC FORMS SIT UP UPON THEIR COUCHES .	671	JERUSALEM 42	66
OF DEATH THUNDER INCESSANT AROUND THE FLAMING COUCHES OF	684	JERUSALEM 53	21
COUCHING			
A COUCHING LION LAY	114	LIT GRL FND/SI	24
AND COUCHING AT THEIR SIDE SHALL EAT FROM THE CURLD BOY'S WHITE LAP	376	FOUR ZOAS 9	* 707
COUD			
[COUD SING WITH THEIR THICK LIPS]	61	DR CLASH/IM	* 7
COUGHD			
[FARTED & BELCHD & COUGHD]	185	LET BROTHELS/N	10
FARTED & BELCHD & COUGHD	186	WHEN KLOPSTK/N	4
COULDST			
AVAUNT COLD HYPOCRITE I AM CHAIND OR THOU COULDST NOT USE ME THUS	323	FOUR ZOAS 7	142
COULDST THOU BUT CEASE FROM TERROR & TREMBLING & AFFRIGHT	330	FOUR ZOAS 7	418
O HOW COULDST THOU DEFORM THOSE BEAUTIFUL PROPORTIONS .	360	FOUR ZOAS 9	140
COULTERS			
GLOWD FURIOUS ON THE ANVIL PREPARD FOR SPADES & COULTERS ALL	278	FOUR ZOAS 1	520
COUNCELLOR			
FOR THY COUNCELLOR OR THE DOG FOR A SCHOOLMASTER TO THY CHILDREN	192	V DAU ALBION 5	9
SHALL NOT THE COUNCELLOR THROW HIS CURB	247	SONG OF LOS 6	15
I HAVE CHOSEN THE SERPENT FOR A COUNCELLOR & THE DOG .	290	FOUR ZOAS 2	389
COUNCELLOR HE ALAS WAS ILL IN BED WHEN I CALLD YESTERDAY	836B	LETTER 35	*PROSE
COUNCELLORS SEE COUNSELLORS			
HIS GREY BROWD COUNCELLORS THUNDEROUS WARRIORS	159D	SONG LIBERTY	PROSE
GO DOWN YE KINGS & COUNCELLORS & GIANT WARRIORS .	374	FOUR ZOAS 9	659
& HER COUNCELLORS & WARRIORS	443A	LAST JUDGMNT/L	PROSE
I WILL HAVE KINGS INWOVEN UPON IT & COUNCELLORS & MIGHTY MEN	499	MILTON 18	15
HER KINGS & COUNCELLORS & WARRIORS DESCEND IN FLAMES .	609B	V LAST JUDG/N	PROSE
LINCOLN DURHAM & CARLISLE COUNCELLORS OF LOS	676	JERUSALEM 46	5
COUNCIL			
TO SIT IN COUNCIL WITH HIS MODERN PEERS	14	IMIT SPEN/PS	17
BUT AS I SIT IN COUNCIL WITH MY PRINCE	19	EDW THIRD/PS 2	28
THEN TO OUR TENT RETURN AND MEET TO COUNCIL	25	EDW THIRD/PS 3	183
WHILE IN DARK COUNCIL SAT PHILISTA'S LORDS	37D	SAMSON/PS	PROSE
. . . TO HIS CHAMBER OF COUNCIL SHADY MOUNTAINS . . .	134	FRENCH REVOLTN	10
. . . OER THE COUNCIL HE STRETCHD HIS RED LIMBS . . .	138	FRENCH REVOLTN	85
THE FIERCE DUKE HUNG OVER THE COUNCIL	138	FRENCH REVOLTN	87
BEFORE THE RED COUNCIL HE STOOD	141	FRENCH REVOLTN	161
LIKE A COUNCIL OF ARDORS SEATED IN CLOUDS	146	FRENCH REVOLTN	264
WHERE GEORGE THE THIRD HOLDS COUNCIL & HIS LORDS & COMMONS MEET	204	AMERICA CANC B	9
THE COUNCIL SAT ALL ROSE BEFORE THE AGED APPARITION . . .	204	AMERICA CANC B	15
IN COUNCIL GATHER THE SMITTEN ANGELS OF ALBION	241	EUROPE 9	11
[BUT THOSE IN GREAT ETERNITY MET IN THE COUNCIL OF GOD]	269	FOUR ZOAS 1	198
THEN THOSE IN GREAT ETERNITY MET IN THE COUNCIL OF GOD .	277	FOUR ZOAS 1	469
THE COUNCIL OF GOD ON HIGH WATCHING OVER THE BODY . . .	304	FOUR ZOAS 4	247
. . . MET IN THE COUNCIL OF GOD	341	FOUR ZOAS 8	1
DID HE MEAN TO RIDICULE A KING & HIS COUNCIL	405C	ANNO BACON	MARG
THREE BRAINS IN CONTRADICTORY COUNCIL BROODING INCESSANTLY	708	JERUSALEM 70	5
COUNCIL HOUSE			
THE CLOUD BEARS HARD UPON THE COUNCIL HOUSE DOWN RUSHING	241	EUROPE 9	12
COUNCILLOR			
OF SINCERE SORROW ON ACCOUNT OF THE BELOVED COUNCILLOR .	851C	LETTER 50	PROSE
COUNCILS			
I CALLD THE STARS AROUND MY FEET IN THE NIGHT OF COUNCILS DARK	311	FOUR ZOAS 5	223
NEITHER DARING TO PUT IN ACT ITS COUNCILS FEARING EACH-OTHER	708	JERUSALEM 70	6
COUNSEL			
JOVE WEIGHS THE COUNSEL OF FUTURITY	15	IMIT SPEN/PS	23
AND BRINGS GOOD COUNSEL FROM THE BREAST OF LAUGHTER . . .	24	EDW THIRD/PS 3	135
. . . AND LET THY SOUL DRINK OF MY COUNSEL	140	FRENCH REVOLTN	128
. . . I ROSE TO BRING MY PRINCE HEAVEN UTTERD COUNSEL .	141	FRENCH REVOLTN	152
HEAR MY COUNSEL O KING AND SEND FORTH THY GENERALS . . .	141	FRENCH REVOLTN	153
TO THE CLOSE HALL OF COUNSEL WHERE HIS ANGEL FORM RENEWS	204	AMERICA CANC B	2
POWERFUL FOR THESE MEN AND OBEY THEIR COUNSEL THEN . . .	570C	DESC CAT 3	PROSE
THEY ALSO ARE "FULL SOLEMN MEN" AND THEIR COUNSEL . . .	570C	DESC CAT 3	PROSE
AND TAKE THEIR COUNSEL ESPECIALLY IN ALL DIFFICULT POINTS	570D	DESC CAT 3	PROSE
COUNSELLORS			
. . . ROUND THEM THEIR COUNSELLORS LOOK UP FROM THE DUST	137	FRENCH REVOLTN	73
COUNSELS			
HIDDEN SET APART IN MY STERN COUNSELS	224	URIZEN 4	8
AND KEEPING THEM FROM SIN BY THE MILD COUNSELS OF HIS LOVE	662	JERUSALEM 35	8
COUNT			
GOD BLESS THY PITEOUS FACE TO COUNT THE WRINKLES IN THY FACE	102	TIRIEL 3	5

```
                                                              PAGE      TITLE         LINE
COUNT    (CONTINUED)
    THE [ WE ] [ ?COUNT ] [ (WEALTH) ] COUNTLESS GOLD OF A MERRY    181 RICHES/N          *    1
        HEART
    UNWILLING I LOOK UP TO HEAVEN UNWILLING COUNT THE STARS         238 EUROPE PREL 2         1
    IN NARROW VALES I WALK & COUNT THE BONES OF MY BELOVEDS         721 JERUSALEM 79        65
    COUNT UGOLINO BY MR FUSELI IN THE ROYAL ACADEMY EXHIBITION      863D LETTER 61       PROSE
    FUSELI'S COUNT UGOLINO IS THE FATHER OF SONS OF FEELING AND     864A LETTER 61       PROSE
    FUSELI'S COUNT UGOLINO IS A MAN OF WONDER AND ADMIRATION        864B LETTER 61       PROSE
    ADVANTAGEOUS ACQUAINTANCE I GO ON WITHOUT DARING TO COUNT       879C LETTER 89       PROSE
    THE FIGHTING DEVILS READY FOR THE COPPER I COUNT MYSELF         879C LETTER 89       PROSE
COUNTED
    . . . AND THE NUMBERS ARE COUNTED IN SILENCE   . . . .  .      146 FRENCH REVOLTN     266
    SHE COUNTED EVERY VEIN & LACTEAL THREADING THEM AMONG  . .     266 FOUR ZOAS 1          80
    [ ENCOURAGE A BLOCKHEAD & HE IS COUNTED THE GREATEST GENIUS ]  595B PUB ADDRESS/N    PROSE
    HERE I COUNTED WITHOUT MY HOST I NOW FIND MY MISTAKE   . .     792A LETTER 4         PROSE
COUNTENANCE
    BLAZE IN EACH COUNTENANCE AND FIRE THE BATTLE  . . . . .  .     18 EDW THIRD/PS 1       12
    REQUIRES OUR COUNTENANCE AND HELP  . . . . . . . . .  .         20 EDW THIRD/PS 2       73
    AND IN EACH COUNTENANCE THE SOUL OF WAR  . . . . . . .  .       23 EDW THIRD/PS 3       85
    THRONE OF GOD WHEN THE FROWNS OF HIS COUNTENANCE   . . . .      33 EDW FOURTH/PS         7
    PERPLEXD VIBRATE ROUND EACH CAREFUL COUNTENANCE . . . . .      135 FRENCH REVOLTN      17
    LOOK UP LOOK UP O CITIZEN OF LONDON ENLARGE THY               159C SONG LIBERTY     PROSE
        COUNTENANCE
    AND UPON ENITHARMON & THE DIVINE COUNTENANCE SHONE   . . .     342 FOUR ZOAS 8         41
    CHEAR UP THY COUNTENANCE BRIGHT BOY & GO TO ENION   . . .      371 FOUR ZOAS 9        545
    AND DID THE COUNTENANCE DIVINE . . . . . . . . .  .            481 AND DID FEET/M        5
    DO WE DISTINGUISH ONE FACE OR COUNTENANCE FROM ANOTHER  .      585C DESC CAT 15      PROSE
    THE ASSISTANCE & COUNTENANCE OF THOSE ALREADY IN THE TRUTH     614A V LAST JUDG/N    PROSE
    . . . FROM THY DREAD [ COUTENANCE ] COUNTENANCE & SEARCHING     645 JERUSALEM 22     *   13
        EYES
    WE ALL ADMIRD & LOVD WHOSE ALL BENEVOLENT COUNTENANCE SEEN     675 JERUSALEM 45          5
    THEY DISCERND MY COUNTENANCE WITH JOY THEY SHEWD ME TO         720 JERUSALEM 79         28
        THEIR SONS
    ATTEMPT TO EXPRESS YOUR & OUR MUCH BELOVED'S COUNTENANCE       796C LETTER 8        PROSE
    THAT THE KING SHEWS IT A GREAT COUNTENANCE & ENCOURAGEMENT     797D LETTER 10       PROSE
    THE DIVINE COUNTENANCE IN SUCH MEN AS COWPER AND MILTON        845C LETTER 44       PROSE
    BALLADS WERE THE EFFUSIONS OF FRIENDSHIP TO COUNTENANCE        860C LETTER 56       PROSE
COUNTENANCES
    TO THE LINEAMENTS OF THE COUNTENANCES THEY ARE   . . . .      611B V LAST JUDG/N    PROSE
COUNTER
    TO RESIST THE CONTEMPTIBLE COUNTER ARTS [ SET ON FOOT ]   .   600B PUB ADDRESS/N    PROSE
COUNTERACT
    & NOT ENDEAVOUR TO COUNTERACT BY TRICKS  . . . . . .  .       597A PUB ADDRESS/N    PROSE
    TO COUNTERACT THE WIDELY DIFFUSED MALICE WHICH HAS FOR  .     863D LETTER 61       PROSE
COUNTERPART
    THOU LITTLE DIMINUTIVE PORTION THAT DARST BE A COUNTERPART     295 FOUR ZOAS 3        117
    AND FORMD A MALE TO BE A COUNTERPART TO THEE O LOVE  . .       327 FOUR ZOAS 7        293
    EACH MALE FORMD WITHOUT A COUNTERPART WITHOUT A                330 FOUR ZOAS 7        402
        CONCENTERING VISION
    BUT I HAVE THEE MY [ COUNTERPART ] [ VEGETATING ] MIRACULOUS   330 FOUR ZOAS 7      *  407
    A MALE WITHOUT A FEMALE COUNTERPART A HOWLING FIEND  . .       347 FOUR ZOAS 8        253
    A FALSE FEMININE COUNTERPART LOVELY OF DELUSIVE BEAUTY  .      348 FOUR ZOAS 8      *  278
    CAMBEL HIS BRIGHT BEAMING COUNTERPART DIVIDED FROM HIM  .      723 JERUSALEM 80         58
    [ ?WHY SHOULD LAELIUS BE ?CONSIDERED SIR JOSHUA'S            SUPP ANNO REYNOLDS * MARG
        ?COUNTERPART ]
COUNTER PART
    MY COUNTER PART & CALLD IT LOVE I NAMD HER ENITHARMON    . .   300 FOUR ZOAS 4        100
COUNTERPARTS
    IN MALE FORMS WITHOUT FEMALE COUNTERPARTS OR EMANATIONS        328 FOUR ZOAS 7        329
    THESE SPECTRES HAVE NO [ (COUNTERPARTS) ] THEREFORE THEY       330 FOUR ZOAS 7      *  408
        RAVIN
    WITHOUT THE FOOD OF LIFE LET US CREATE THEM (COUNTERPARTS)     330 FOUR ZOAS 7        409
    THEY DIVIDED INTO MANY LOVELY DAUGHTERS TO BE COUNTERPARTS     704 JERUSALEM 67          8
COUNTESS
    FOR THE COUNTESS OF EGREMONT [ BY A HAPPY ACCIDENT ]   . . .  442D LAST JUDGMNT/L   PROSE
    EGREMONT'S COUNTESS [ DARE ] CAN CONTROLL  . . . . . .  .     558 THE CAVERNS/N        7
COUNTEST
    WHO COUNTEST THE STEPS OF THE SUN  . . . . . . . .  .         215 AH SUNFLOWR/SE        2
COUNTIES
    HERE LOS FIXD DOWN THE FIFTY-TWO COUNTIES OF ENGLAND &         637 JERUSALEM 16         28
        WALES
    IN THE TWELVE COUNTIES OF WALES & THENCE GATES LOOKING         637 JERUSALEM 16         32
        EVERY WAY
    AND THE FORTY COUNTIES OF ENGLAND ARE THUS DIVIDED IN THE      637 JERUSALEM 16         43
        GATES
    AND THE THIRTY-SIX COUNTIES OF SCOTLAND DIVIDED IN THE         638 JERUSALEM 16         52
        GATES
    I GAVE THEE HAND & SCOFIELD & THE COUNTIES OF ALBION    . .    692 JERUSALEM 60         14
    AND THE THIRTY-TWO COUNTIES OF THE FOUR PROVINCES              711 JERUSALEM 72          1
        OF IRELAND
    ARE THUS DIVIDED THE FOUR COUNTIES ARE IN THE FOUR CAMPS       711 JERUSALEM 72          2
    WHOSE FOUNDATIONS REMAIN IN THE THIRTY-TWO COUNTIES OF         711 JERUSALEM 72         14
        IRELAND
    AND IN TWELVE COUNTIES OF WALES & IN THE FORTY COUNTIES        711 JERUSALEM 72         15
    OF ENGLAND & IN THE THIRTY-SIX COUNTIES OF SCOTLAND  . . .     711 JERUSALEM 72         16
    AND THE NAMES OF THE THIRTY-TWO COUNTIES OF IRELAND ARE        711 JERUSALEM 72         17
        THESE
    THE FIFTY-TWO COUNTIES OF ENGLAND ARE HARDEND AGAINST ME       720 JERUSALEM 79         20
    DO I SLEEP AMIDST DANGER TO FRIENDS O MY CITIES & COUNTIES     744 JERUSALEM 96         33
COUNTING
    O JEW LEAVE COUNTING GOLD RETURN TO THY OIL AND WINE    .     159C SONG LIBERTY     PROSE
    HE FROWND ON ALL HIS FRIENDS COUNTING THEM ENEMIES IN HIS      676 JERUSALEM 45         36
        SORROW
```

```
                                                            PAGE      TITLE           LINE
COUNTING    (CONTINUED)
    COUNTING HIM AN IMBECILE MOCKERY BUT THE WARRIOR  . . . .  704  JERUSALEM 67       20
COUNTLESS
    THE [WE] [?COUNT] [(WEALTH)] COUNTLESS GOLD OF A MERRY     181  RICHES/N         *  1
        HEART
    THE COUNTLESS GOLD OF THE AKEING HEART  . . . . . . .      425  MENTAL TRAVLER     35
COUNTRIES
    OF OTHER COUNTRIES AND PROPHECYING THAT ALL GODS WOULD  .  . 153D  MARRIAGE HH 12  PROSE
    BY RESPECTABLE MEN OF OTHER COUNTRIES ON ACCOUNT OF ART    584B  DESC CAT 14      PROSE
    TO HAVE SPREAD OVER MANY COUNTRIES  . . . . . . . . . .    824A  LETTER 27        PROSE
    HEAVEN HAVILAH EDEN & ALL THE COUNTRIES WHERE JEWELS ABOUND  837D  LETTER 36      PROSE
COUNTRY
    THE PLEASANT SOUTH COUNTRY  . . . . . . . . . . . . . .     14  GWIN KING/PS      116
    A COUNTRY NOT YET SOWN WITH DESTRUCTION  . . . . . . .      18  EDW THIRD/PS 1     47
    PERHAPS THE AIR OF THE COUNTRY IS THE CAUSE  . . . . .      22  EDW THIRD/PS 3     61
    SPEND THEIR SWEET LIVES TO DO THEIR COUNTRY SERVICE  .      31  EDW THIRD/PS 5     56
    EYES THE DISTANT COUNTRY WITH JOY . . . . . . . . . .      36C  COUCH DEATH/PS   PROSE
    OUR COUNTRY IS PLOWED WITH SWORDS AND REAPED IN BLOOD  .   40A  SAMSON/PS        PROSE
    ALL THE COUNTRY FOLKS ACOURTING  . . . . . . . . . .       53  PHEBE DREST/IM      6
    THIS CITY & THIS COUNTRY HAS BROUGHT FORTH MANY MAYORS  .  . 58  THIS CITY/IM       1
    . . . AND GET THEE UP INTO THE COUNTRY TEN MILES  . . . .  145  FRENCH REVOLTN    250
    COUNTRY PLACING IT UNDER ITS MENTAL DEITY  . . . . . .     153A  MARRIAGE HH 11   PROSE
    AND THIS IS A FINE COUNTRY  . . . . . . . . . . . . .      168  HAST LAP/N         2
    OF ANY AGE OR COUNTRY AMONG WHICH ARE TWO LARGE  . . .     207C  PRSPECTUS 1793   PROSE
    DUTY TO HIS COUNTRY IS THE FIRST CONSIDERATION & SAFETY    383C  ANNO WATSON       MARG
        THE LAST
    YET SIMPLE COUNTRY HINDS ARE MORAL ENTHUSIASTS  . . . .    414A  ANNO BOYD         MARG
    WHILE OTHER COUNTRY HINDS ARE AS INDIGNANT AGAINST HONESTY  414A  ANNO BOYD        MARG
    TO HAVE MY HOUSE SEARCHED AS I MIGHT HAVE PLANS OF THE     438A  BLAKES MEMORAN   PROSE
        COUNTRY
    IN A COUNTRY PRETENDING TO THE ENCOURAGEMENT OF ART  . .   452B  ANNO REYNOLDS     MARG
    DELUGE ALL THE COUNTRY ROUND SUCH IS A VISION OF LOS  .    507  MILTON 23          27
    POETS IN ANY AGE OR COUNTRY AND THESE IN A CORRUPT STATE   561C  EXHIBITION ADV   PROSE
    MY EXHIBITION AS THE GREATEST OF DUTIES TO MY COUNTRY  .   561C  EXHIBITION ADV   PROSE
    THE LANDSCAPE IS AN EASTWARD VIEW OF THE COUNTRY  . . .    567A  DESC CAT 3       PROSE
    THE VOLUPTUOUS COUNTRY GENTLEMAN CONTRASTED WITH  . . .    570D  DESC CAT 3       PROSE
    THOSE OF OUR OWN COUNTRY THE ANCIENT BRITONS  . . . .     577C  DESC CAT 5       PROSE
    ALL HIS VISIONARY CONTEMPLATIONS RELATING TO HIS          577D  DESC CAT 5       PROSE
        OWN COUNTRY
    IN EDEN THE ARTIST IS AN INHABITANT OF THAT HAPPY COUNTRY  578A  DESC CAT 5       PROSE
    DAUGHTERS IN LAW WITH INTENT TO RETURN TO HER OWN COUNTRY  584C  DESC CAT 15      PROSE
    THE LANDSCAPE IS AN EASTWARD VIEW OF THE COUNTRY  . . .    588D  CHAUCER/N        PROSE
    THE LANDSCAPE IS AN EASTWARD VIEW OF THE COUNTRY  . . .    590B  CHAUCER 2        PROSE
    INTO THIS COUNTRY SINCE WHICH ENGLISH ENGRAVING IS LOST    592A  PUB ADDRESS/N    PROSE
    WILL REDEEM MY COUNTRY FROM THIS COXCOMB SITUATION &       593C  PUB ADDRESS/N    PROSE
    BUT LOVE TO MY ART & ZEAL FOR MY COUNTRY A MUCH GREATER    594D  PUB ADDRESS/N    PROSE
    AN INJURY & INJUSTICE TO HIS COUNTRY WHILE HE STUDIES  .   597C  PUB ADDRESS/N    PROSE
    THE WRETCHED STATE OF THE ARTS IN THIS COUNTRY & IN EUROPE  600B  PUB ADDRESS/N   PROSE
    AS THE PILGRIM PASSES WHILE THE COUNTRY PERMANENT REMAINS  714  JERUSALEM 73       44
    SCENE A ROCKY COUNTRY . . . . . . . . . . . . . . .      779C  GHOST ABEL 1     PROSE
    A MOST BEAUTIFUL COUNTRY ON A MOST GLORIOUS DAY OUR  .     803A  LETTER 15        PROSE
    WE CAN GET MOST CONVENIENCES THERE THE COUNTRY IS  . .     806B  LETTER 16        PROSE
    WE HAVE HAD BUT LITTLE TIME FOR VIEWING THE COUNTRY  . .   806B  LETTER 16        PROSE
    AS ONE COUNTRY AND THEIR ARTS ONE & THAT YOU WILL ERE LONG  811A  LETTER 21       PROSE
    INTO THE COUNTRY WHICH IS TO ME CONSOLATION ENOUGH  . .    812A  LETTER 22        PROSE
    HAVE BEEN LOST I SHALL LEAVE EVERY ONE IN THIS COUNTRY .   825D  LETTER 27        PROSE
    ACROSS THE COUNTRY TO FELPHAM AS HE ALWAYS KEEPS A HORSE   843A  LETTER 42        PROSE
    AND TO SAY THAT THE COUNTRY PRINTERS COULD NOT DO ANYTHING  846D  LETTER 44       PROSE
    ENVIABLE AND THE COUNTRY IS NOT ONLY MORE BEAUTIFUL ON  .  847C  LETTER 44        PROSE
    HIS COUNTRY WILL REFRAIN FROM DISGRACING EITHER BY SUCH    864D  LETTER 61        PROSE
    INTENDED FLIGHT INTO YOUR DELIGHTFUL COUNTRY CONCUR IN  .  872D  LETTER 76        PROSE
COUNTRYMAN'S
    ALFRED IN THE COUNTRYMAN'S HOUSE  . . . . . . . . .       208D  SUBJCTS HIST/N   TITLE
COUNTRYMEN
    SUCH CONTEMPTIBLE COPIES COUNTRYMEN COUNTRYMEN  . . .      597C  PUB ADDRESS/N    PROSE
    I HOPE MY COUNTRYMEN WILL EXCUSE ME IF I TELL THEM         599A  PUB ADDRESS/N    PROSE
        A WHOLESOME TRUTH
    SORRY TO SEE MY COUNTRYMEN TROUBLE THEMSELVES ABOUT        600A  PUB ADDRESS/N    PROSE
        POLITICS
    CONSEQUENTLY OUR COUNTRYMEN ARE EASILY BROW-BEAT ON THE    864C  LETTER 61        PROSE
COUNTRY'S
    I'LL FIGHT AND WEEP TIS IN MY COUNTRY'S CAUSE  . . . .      31  EDW THIRD/PS 5     51
    PUT ON THY COUNTRY'S PRIDE DECEIT AND EYES OF LOVE  . . .  38A  SAMSON/PS        PROSE
COUNTS
    JUST AS A MISER COUNTS HIS GOLD  . . . . . . . . .        425  MENTAL TRAVLER     18
    [AND COUNTS IT COURAGE THUS TO PRAISE HIS FOE]  . . . .    539  SIR JOSH MIC/N     2
COUNTY
    EASTMEATH WESTMEATH DUBLIN KILDARE KINGS COUNTY  . . . .   711  JERUSALEM 72       19
    QUEENS COUNTY WICKLOW CATHERLOH WEXFORD KILKENNY  . . . .  711  JERUSALEM 72       20
COUPLE
    ON THE RIGHT A YOUTHFUL COUPLE ARE AWAKED BY THEIR CHILDREN  609C  V LAST JUDG/N  PROSE
COUPLED
    AND WITH A GRINNING ASPECT FIRST COUPLED WITH & THEN      157B  MARRIAGE HH 17   PROSE
        DEVOURD
COURAGE
    TOO OFTEN TAKES AWAY A SOLDIER'S COURAGE  . . . . . .       23  EDW THIRD/PS 3     66
    GOOD MORROW GENERALS WHEN ENGLISH COURAGE FAILS  . . . .    23  EDW THIRD/PS 3     71
    ARE TIED UP MY COURAGE SHRUNK AND WITHERD  . . . . . .      23  EDW THIRD/PS 3    102
    COURAGE MY LORD PROCEEDS FROM SELF-DEPENDENCE  . . . .      25  EDW THIRD/PS 3    194
    ("WANT OF FRIENDS ARGUES WANT OF HUMILITY OR COURAGE")     74A  ANNO LAVATER      MARG
        UNEASY
    THE WEAK IN COURAGE IS STRONG IN CUNNING  . . . . . . .   152B  MARRIAGE HH 9    PROSE
```

```
                                                               PAGE      TITLE          LINE
COURAGE    (CONTINUED)
         ACCORDING TO THE PROVERB THE WEAK IN COURAGE IS STRONG      155A MARRIAGE HH 15  PROSE
           IN CUNNING
         THE UNDAUNTED COURAGE OF A VIRGIN MIND . . . . . . .        184 O I CANNOT/N        2
         [AND COUNTS IT COURAGE THUS TO PRAISE HIS FOE]  . . . .     539 SIR JOSH MIC/N      2
         BRUTAL STRENGTH AND COURAGE . . . . . . . . . . . .         571D DESC CAT 3      PROSE
         BUT WITH THE HIGHEST COURAGE SUPERADDED . . . . . . .       571D DESC CAT 3      PROSE
         HAS THE COURAGE TO SUFFER POVERTY AND DISGRACE  . . . .     582D DESC CAT 9      PROSE
         COURAGE OF CONSCIOUS INDUSTRY WORTHY OF HIS FORMER KINDNESS 851D LETTER 50       PROSE
         COURAGE TO SAY SO PUBLICKLY & TO DARE ALL THE POWER ON      866B LETTER 64       PROSE
           EARTH
COURAGEOUSLY
         I COURAGEOUSLY PURSUED MY COURSE THROUGH DARKNESS   . . . 852C LETTER 50        PROSE
COURSE
         OR BUT EXPECTED AS A THING OF COURSE . . . . . . . . .       27 EDW THIRD/PS 3     249
         ALL BE WRONG OF COURSE TIS BEST TO KNOW A LITTLE . . . .     28D EDW THIRD/PS 4   PROSE
         . . . AND THE HAPPY EARTH SING IN ITS COURSE  . . . . .     144 FRENCH REVOLTN    236
         . . . SAYING BASTILE DEPART AND TAKE THY SHADOWY COURSE     145 FRENCH REVOLTN    249
         THE JUST MAN KEPT HIS COURSE ALONG . . . . . . . . . .      148 MARRIAGE HH 2       4
         AND OVER THEOTORMON'S REIGN TOOK HER IMPETUOUS COURSE  . .  189 V DAU ALBION 1     15
         AFAR INTO THE ZENITH HIGH BENDING THY FURIOUS COURSE  . .   278 FOUR ZOAS 1       495
         MEASURE THE COURSE OF THAT SULPHUR ORB . . . . . . . .      283 FOUR ZOAS 2       128
         TO MEASURE OUT THE COURSE OF HEAVEN STERN URIZEN BEHELD     283 FOUR ZOAS 2       131
         EACH TOOK HIS STATION & HIS COURSE BEGAN . . . . . . .      287 FOUR ZOAS 2       268
         ITS WASTED [(POWER)] STRENGTH IT BACK RETURNS UPON A NETHER 287 FOUR ZOAS 2     *  278
           COURSE
         IT RISES UP ON HIGH ALL SUMMER TILL ITS WEARIED COURSE  . . 287 FOUR ZOAS 2       280
         OTHERS TRIANGULAR [THEIR] RIGHT ANGLED COURSE MAINTAIN      287 FOUR ZOAS 2       282
           OTHERS OBTUSE
         IN THEIR AMAZING [FRUCTIFYING] HARD SUBDUED COURSE IN THE   287 FOUR ZOAS 2     *  286
           VAST DEEP
         BY THE FIERCE MANE STAYING [THEIR] HIS HOWLING COURSE . . . 315 FOUR ZOAS 6     *  133
         TIS UPWARD ALL WHICH WAY SOEVER I MY COURSE BEGIN   . . .   317 FOUR ZOAS 6       203
         AND RUNNING THEIR IMMORTAL COURSE THRO SOLID DARKNESS BORNE 336 FOUR ZOAS 7B      143
         UPON THE EASTERN SEA DIRECT THEY TAKE THEIR COURSE  . . .   336 FOUR ZOAS 7B      151
         GO ON THY COURSE REJOICING & LET US BOTH REJOICE TOGETHER   368 FOUR ZOAS 9       424
         SUCH AS THE JEWS WERE & OF COURSE HE HOLDS THAT THE JEWS    389A ANNO WATSON      MARG
         HIS FUTURE COURSE THRO DARKNESS AND DESPAIR TO ETERNAL      487 MILTON 7           26
           DEATH
         AND BROOKS BETWEEN TO INTERSECT THE MEADOWS IN THEIR COURSE 493 MILTON 12          19
         FOR HE TOOK THE OUTSIDE COURSE AMONG THE GRAVES OF THE DEAD 496 MILTON 14          34
         ONWARDS HIS SHADOW KEPT ITS COURSE AMONG THE SPECTRES CALLD 496 MILTON 15          17
         A LONG JOURNEY & DARK THRO CHAOS IN THE TRACK OF MILTON'S   524 MILTON 34          22
           COURSE
         I GO ON & NOTHING CAN HINDER MY COURSE  . . . . . . .      600C PUB ADDRESS/N    PROSE
         WHICH DOUBTS & HESITATES IN THE MIDST OF ITS COURSE . . . 603C PUB ADDR AD/N     PROSE
         THE SUN FORGETS HIS COURSE LIKE A DRUNKEN MAN HE HESITATES  703 JERUSALEM 66       74
         FURY & THUNDERING COURSE ROUND HEAVEN & EARTH . . . . .     717 STOOD AMONG/J       6
         THE RIVER SEVERN STAYD HIS COURSE AT MY COMMAND . . . .     720 JERUSALEM 79       33
         MARCHING THRO EGYPT IN HIS FURY THE EAST IS PALE AT HIS     729 JERUSALEM 84       22
           COURSE
         WHERE HIDDEKEL PURSUES HIS COURSE AMONG THE ROCKS   . . .   735 JERUSALEM 89       35
         THROUGHOUT THE LAND HE TOOK HIS COURSE  . . . . . . .      749 EV GOSPEL(B)/N     35
         & HER SICKNESS IS ALWAYS MY SORROW OF COURSE BUT WHAT YOU  811C LETTER 22        PROSE
         SEEMS THAT OTHER THINGS WILL FOLLOW IN COURSE IF I DO BUT  812A LETTER 22        PROSE
         THE FURY OF MY COURSE AMONG THE STARS OF GOD  . . . . .   816A LETTER 23        PROSE
         TO LONDON AGAIN APPLAUDS IT AS THE ONLY COURSE FOR THE  .  822D LETTER 26        PROSE
         OF COURSE THAT SHALL BE DISTINGUISHD  . . . . . . . .     832B LETTER 32        PROSE
         I DID NOT RECIEVE YOUR LETTER TILL MONDAY OF COURSE COULD  840B LETTER 39        PROSE
         I COURAGEOUSLY PURSUED MY COURSE THROUGH DARKNESS         852C LETTER 50        PROSE
         HE WILL OF COURSE INFORM YOU WHAT HIS SENTIMENTS ARE OF    858A LETTER 55        PROSE
         COURSE OF OUR CONVERSATION HIS WORDS WERE I FEEL SOMEWHAT  860A LETTER 56        PROSE
         MY PRESENT COURSE NEW VANITIES OR RATHER NEW PLEASURES     865C LETTER 63        PROSE
COURSERS
         HE RUSHES UP THE SKY AND LAYS HOLD ON THE IMMORTAL COURSERS 37B CONTEMPLATN/PS  PROSE
           OF DAY
COURSES
         THEY RISE IN ORDER AND CONTINUE THEIR IMMORTAL COURSES  . . 511 MILTON 25          67
         THE STARS IN THEIR COURSES FOUGHT THE SUN MOON HEAVEN EARTH 686 JERUSALEM 55       27
COURSING
         REVEAL THE DRAGON THRO THE HUMAN COURSING SWIFT AS FIRE     204 AMERICA CANC B      1
COURT
         SCENE ENGLISH COURT LIONEL DUKE OF CLARENCE   . . . . .     19A EDW THIRD/PS 2   PROSE
         ONLY GOOD HEARTS CAN OR DARE COURT . . . . . . . . .        85B ANNO LAVATER     MARG
         HERE TAKE THY SEAT IN THIS WIDE COURT LET IT BE STROWN      106 TIRIEL 5          11
           WITH DEAD
         AND COURT THE FAIR EYED DEW TO TAKE ME TO HER SHINING TENT  128 BOOK OF THEL 3    13
         . . . FROM COURT TO COURT RESTLESS HE DRAGGD . . . . .      135 FRENCH REVOLTN    22
         . . . FROM COURT TO COURT CURSD THE FIERCE TORMENT          135 FRENCH REVOLTN    23
           UNQUELLD
         ALL PENAL LAWS COURT TRANSGRESSION & THEREFORE ARE CRUELTY  393C ANNO WATSON     MARG
           &
         IT WAS A COMMON OPINION IN THE COURT OF QUEEN ELIZABETH     397B ANNO BACON      MARG
         WE HAVE HIRELINGS IN THE CAMP THE COURT & THE UNIVERSITY    480C MILTON 1        PROSE
         BEGINING AT JERUSALEM'S INNER COURT LAMBETH RUIND AND GIVEN 511 MILTON 25          48
         I COURT THE COMPARISON & FEAR NOT THE RESULT BUT NOT IN    598D PUB ADDRESS/N    PROSE
           A DARK CORNER
         HIS SECLUDED COURT THENCE TO BETHLEHEM WHERE WAS BUILDED    657 JERUSALEM 31       25
         HER HAND IS A COURT OF JUSTICE HER FEET TWO ARMIES          698 JERUSALEM 64        9
           IN BATTLE
         DISORGANIZD & THERE IS PHAROH IN HIS IRON COURT  . . . .    735 JERUSALEM 89       18
         ESCAPED THE CONTAGION OF THE COURT OF JUSTICE I FEAR THAT  829C LETTER 30        PROSE
```

402

```
                                                    PAGE    TITLE          LINE
COURT    (CONTINUED)
      FOUNTAIN COURT STRAND . . . . . . . . . . .  SUPP ADDRESSES/L    *TITLE
COURTED
      PRUDENCE IS A RICH UGLY OLD MAID COURTED BY INCAPACITY  .  . 151A MARRIAGE HH 7  PROSE
      IN WANT OF HANDS OTHER ENGRAVERS ARE COURTED I SUPPOSE  .  . 829D LETTER 30    PROSE
COURTESY
      A TRADING MASTER OF A VESSEL CALLED BY COURTESY CAPTAIN   575C DESC CAT 3    PROSE
COURTING     SEE A COURTING
      [AND ?COURTING THAT THE EARTH WOULD OPE HER EYELIDS     267 FOUR ZOAS 1       131
        & BEHOLD]
      WIFE & SISTER ARE BOTH WELL COURTING NEPTUNE FOR AN EMBRACE 802A LETTER 14   PROSE
      MY WIFE & SISTER ARE BOTH VERY WELL & COURTING NEPTUNE   803B LETTER 15   PROSE
        FOR AN EMBRACE
COURTS
      THE GLITTERING YOUTH OF COURTS MUST GLEAM IN ARMS   . . . 34B KING JOHN/PS    PROSE
      . . . HIM THE PEERS FOLLOWD THEY SAW THE COURTS OF THE   148 FRENCH REVOLTN    304
        PALACE
      I SEE A SERPENT IN CANADA WHO COURTS ME TO HIS LOVE  . . . 196 AMERICA PREL 2    12
      OF KINGS & COURTS WHO MAKE THEMSELVES EVERY BODY  . . . . 397B ANNO BACON     MARG
      TO WEAVE THE WOOF OF DEATH ON CAMBERWELL TIRZAH'S COURTS  525 MILTON 35          8
      THE SWALLOW SINGS IN COURTS OF KINGS  . . . . . . . . . 547 LET BE TOLD/N       2
      THE PAINTER COURTS COMPARISON WITH HIS COMPETITORS  . . . 572C DESC CAT 3    PROSE
      THE COURTS OF JUSTICE MORE MERCIFUL THAN THE CHURCH  . . . 615D V LAST JUDG/N  PROSE
      O JERUSALEM JERUSALEM I HAVE FORSAKEN THY COURTS  . . . . 647 JERUSALEM 24     17
      AND PEARL & DIAMOND THY DAUGHTERS SANG IN HER COURTS  . . 647 JERUSALEM 24     40
      AND IN HER COURTS AMONG HER LITTLE CHILDREN OFFERING UP   660 JERUSALEM 33     42
      BY SELF ANNIHILATION INTO JERUSALEM'S COURTS & INTO SHILOH 680 JERUSALEM 49    46
      IS BRIGHT CATHEDRON'S GOLDEN HALL ITS COURTS TOWERS      691 JERUSALEM 59     25
        & PINNACLES
      THEY SOUNDED THANKSGIVINGS IN MY COURTS EGYPT & LYBIA HEARD 721 JERUSALEM 79   50
COUSIN
      & MY COUSIN GIBBLE GABBLE SAYS THAT I AM LIKE NOBODY ELSE   53A ISLAND MOON 8  PROSE
      WHO ALMOST ADORD HER COUSIN THE POET & THOUGHT HIM  . . . 820D LETTER 25   PROSE
COUSIN'S
      THIS EXCEPT IT BE THE MORNING AIR & THAT IN MY COUSIN'S   870D LETTER 72   PROSE
        TIME
COVE
      [THEN ALBION'S ANGEL] ROSE RESOLVD TO THE COVE OF ARMOURY  205 AMERICA CANC C    1
      TWO FROWNING ROCKS ON EACH SIDE OF THE COVE & STONE OF   702 JERUSALEM 66     13
        TORTURE
      THEY LOOK FORTH FROM STONE-HENGE FROM THE COVE ROUND     703 JERUSALEM 66     57
        LONDON STONE
      OF WALTON & ESHER FROM STONE-HENGE & FROM MALDEN'S COVE   706 JERUSALEM 68     44
COVENANT
      & THE ARK OF THE COVENANT IS AS A DOVE OF PEACE  . . . . 613B V LAST JUDG/N  PROSE
      THERE IS NONE THAT LIVETH & SINNETH NOT AND THIS IS THE   694 JERUSALEM 61     24
        COVENANT
      BY THOSE WHO DRINK THEIR BLOOD & THE BLOOD OF THEIR      704 JERUSALEM 67      1
        COVENANT
      . . . IT IS THE COVENANT OF JEHOVAH  . . . . . . . .   745 JERUSALEM 98      23
      . . . & SAW THE WORDS OF THE MUTUAL COVENANT DIVINE  . . . 746 JERUSALEM 98   41
      . . . ACCORDING TO [THY] THE COVENANT [OF] JEHOVAH THEY CRY 746 JERUSALEM 98  *  45
      WHERE IS THE COVENANT OF PRIAM THE MORAL VIRTUES OF THE   746 JERUSALEM 98     46
        HEATHEN
      THO THY COVENANT BUILT HELL'S JAIL  . . . . . . . . . 754 EV GOSPEL(E)/N     38
      BROUGHT TO LIGHT BY JESUS EVEN THE COVENANT OF JEHOVAH  . . 757D EV GOSPEL   PROSE
      VAIN IS THY COVENANT O JEHOVAH I AM THE ACCUSER & AVENGER  780 GHOST ABEL 1    12
      IN THY COVENANT OF THE FORGIVENESS OF SINS . . . . . .   781 GHOST ABEL 2     24
COVER
      MY HAIR IS VERY LONG MY BEARD DOTH COVER ALL MY BREAST  . . 102 TIRIEL 3       4
      THE NUMROUS FLOCKS COVER THE MOUNTAIN & SHINE ALONG THE   308 FOUR ZOAS 5   *  138
        VALLEY
      COVER US FROM THE SUN COME & LET US SIT IN THE SHADE  . . 369 FOUR ZOAS 9      450
      WITH WINDOWS FROM THE INCLEMENT SKY WE COVER HIM & WITH   374 FOUR ZOAS 9      635
        WALLS
      AND WITH THE LOOM TO COVER GWENDOLEN & RAGAN WITH COSTLY   643 JERUSALEM 21     14
        ROBES
      HIS SNOWS FALL ON ME AND COVER ME WHILE IN THE VEIL I FOLD 646 JERUSALEM 23    35
      HOWLING WINDS COVER HIM ROARING SEAS DASH FURIOUS AGAINST  741 JERUSALEM 94     3
        HIM
      VOICE O EARTH COVER NOT THOU MY BLOOD COVER NOT THOU MY   780 GHOST ABEL 1      8
        BLOOD
      OF BLOOD O EARTH COVER NOT THOU THE BLOOD OF ABEL  . . . 780 GHOST ABEL 1     13
      ABEL COMPELLD I CRY O EARTH COVER NOT THE BLOOD OF ABEL   780 GHOST ABEL 2     12
COVERD     SEE MOON COVERD,STORM COVERD
      THE FLEECES OF OUR FLOCKS ARE COVERD WITH  . . . . . .    3 EVNING STAR/PS    13
      COVERD WITH SILENCE AND FORGETFULNESS  . . . . . . . .   30 EDW THIRD/PS 5     5
      IN EARTH COVERD WITH STONES AND DEATHY DUST  . . . . .   30 EDW THIRD/PS 5    14
      AND THE MEADOWS ARE COVERD WITH SHEEP  . . . . . . . .   60 NURSES SONG/IM    13
      WHERE BIRDS ARE COVERD WARM . . . . . . . . . . . . .  119 NIGHT/SI          18
      AND THE HILLS ARE ALL COVERD WITH SHEEP  . . . . . . .  121 NURSES SONG/SI    12
      . . . HIS STRONG BONES SCARCE COVERD WITH SINEWS THE IRON 135 FRENCH REVOLTN   30
        RINGS
      . . . WHOSE WHITE BEARD COVERD THE STONE FLOOR LIKE WEEDS 135 FRENCH REVOLTN   38
      OF ANCIENT HORRORS COVERD FOR SNAKES AND SCORPIONS . . .  136 FRENCH REVOLTN   41
      . . . SO NECKER PAUSD AND HIS VISAGE WAS COVERD WITH CLOUDS 139 FRENCH REVOLTN  109
      COVERD WITH DEWS OF NIGHT . . . . . . . . . . . . . .  147 FRENCH REVOLTN   297
      AND HER LOCKS COVERD WITH GREY DESPAIR  . . . . . . . .  168 EARTHS ANSWR/N    5
      AND NOW IM COVERD OER & OER . . . . . . . . . . . . .  184 O I CANNOT/N       7
      IN BERNARD'S HOUSE THE FLAMES COVERD THE LAND THEY ROUZE  201 AMERICA 13        2
        THEY CRY
      AND HER LOCKS COVERD WITH GREY DESPAIR  . . . . . . . .  210 EARTHS ANSR/SE    5
```

		PAGE	TITLE	LINE
COVERD	(CONTINUED)			
NOW OVERGROWN WITH HAIR AND COVERD WITH A STONY ROOF	. .	242	EUROPE 10	29
AND THE LEOPARDS COVERD WITH SKINS OF BEASTS TENDED THE ROARING FIRES		281	FOUR ZOAS 2	33
OUR BEAUTY IS COVERD OVER WITH CLAY & ASHES & OUR BACKS		286	FOUR ZOAS 2	225
AND VALA TREMBLED & COVERD HER FACE	.	293	FOUR ZOAS 3	56
COVERD WITH BOILS FROM HEAD TO FOOT THE TERRIBLE SMITINGS OF LUVAH		294	FOUR ZOAS 3	82
APART FROM LOS BUT COVERD HER WITH SOFTEST BROODING CARE		299	FOUR ZOAS 4	57
COVERD WITH GLOOM THE FIERY BOY GREW FED BY THE MILK	. .	307	FOUR ZOAS 5	72
TILL A WHITE WOOF COVERD HIS COLD LIMBS FROM HEAD TO [FOOT] FEET		318	FOUR ZOAS 6	* 239
HAIR WHITE AS SNOW COVERD HIM IN FLAKY LOCKS TERRIFIC	. .	318	FOUR ZOAS 6	240
FOR URIZEN FIXD IN ENVY SAT BROODING & COVERD WITH SNOW		321	FOUR ZOAS 7	28
WHEN THE MOUNTAINS & HILLS ARE COVERD OVER & THE PATHS OF MEN SHUT UP		324	FOUR ZOAS 7	174
DARKNESS & SORROW COVERD ALL FLESH ETERNITY WAS DARKEND		351	FOUR ZOAS 8	414
SCALES COVERD OVER A COLD FOREHEAD & A NECK OUTSTRETCHD		352	FOUR ZOAS 8	423
COVERD & SCALES HIS HANDS & FEET UPON HIS BELLY FALLING		352	FOUR ZOAS 8	425
HIS EYES SINK HOLLOW IN HIS HEAD HIS FLESH COVERD WITH SLIME		354	FOUR ZOAS 8	515
SIEZD THE SUN HIS LEFT HAND LIKE DARK ROOTS COVERD THE MOON		357	FOUR ZOAS 9	8
BENEATH HER ROSE A DOWNY BED & A CIELING COVERD ALL	. .	369	FOUR ZOAS 9	463
AND DARKNESS COVERD ALL THE DEEP THE LIGHT OF ENION FADED		370	FOUR ZOAS 9	496
COVERD THE HILLS HE SAID O THARMAS RISE & O URTHONA	. .	377	FOUR ZOAS 9	773
DARKNESS & SORROW COVERD ALL FLESH ETERNITY WAS DARKEND		382	FOUR ZOAS AD 6	30
THEN RUB IT OFF ON THE PLATE COVERD WITH WHITE WAX	. .	440B	MEMORANDUM/N 2	PROSE
LOS SAW THEM AND A COLD PALE HORROR COVERD OER HIS LIMBS		503	MILTON 20	51
APPEARD AS DOES THE FACE OF HEAVEN WHEN COVERD WITH THICK STORMS		507	MILTON 23	29
. . . ARE COVERD WITH HUMAN GORE		517	MILTON 29	58
POISONS ROSE UP & HIS SWEET DECEITS COVERD THEM ALL OVER		627	JERUSALEM 8	5
ALBION COVERD THE WHOLE EARTH ENGLAND ENCOMPASSD THE NATIONS		648	JERUSALEM 24	44
JERUSALEM COVERD THE ATLANTIC MOUNTAINS & THE ERYTHREAN		648	JERUSALEM 24	46
COLD SNOWS DRIFTED AROUND HIM ICE COVERD HIS LOINS AROUND		652	JERUSALEM 28	13
AND VALA TREMBLED & COVERD HER FACE		654	JERUSALEM 29	43
COVERD WITH BOILS FROM HEAD TO FOOT THE TERRIBLE SMITINGS OF LUVAH		655	JERUSALEM 29	64
SO LOS IN LAMENTATIONS FOLLOWD ALBION ALBION COVERD	. .	656	JERUSALEM 30	41
. . . COVERD THE WHOLE EARTH		671	JERUSALEM 42	80
THE NIGHT WITH DRAGON WINGS COVERD WITH STARS & IN THE WINGS		685	JERUSALEM 54	30
ALL WHO SEE BECOME WHAT THEY BEHOLD THEIR EYES ARE COVERD		702	JERUSALEM 66	36
LONDON COVERD THE WHOLE EARTH ENGLAND ENCOMPASSD THE NATIONS		720	JERUSALEM 79	22
THY BOSOM WHITE TRANSLUCENT COVERD WITH IMMORTAL GEMS	. .	731	JERUSALEM 86	14
THY REINS COVERD WITH WINGS TRANSLUCENT SOMETIMES COVERING		731	JERUSALEM 86	22
COVERD WITH PRECIOUS STONES A HUMAN DRAGON TERRIBLE	. .	734	JERUSALEM 89	11
AND ALBION'S FORESTS OF OAKS COVERD THE EARTH FROM POLE TO POLE		735	JERUSALEM 89	23
. . . THAT COVERD THE WHOLE EARTH BENEATH HIS SPECTRE	. .	746	JERUSALEM 98	50
COVERED				
WITH HELMETS HEWN AND SHIELDS COVERED WITH GORE	. . .	32	EDW THIRD/PS 6	11
THEY COVERED THEIR FACES AND WEPT THE YOUTH LAY SILENT	. .	36C	COUCH DEATH/PS	PROSE
MY DAYS ARE COVERED WITH SORROW SHUT UP DARKENED	. . . .	38B	SAMSON/PS	PROSE
. . . AND COVERED HIS SOUL WITH SNOWS ETERNAL		143	FRENCH REVOLTN	199
. . . TILL THE GREAT POLYPUS OF GENERATION COVERED THE EARTH		704	JERUSALEM 67	34
COVERETH				
WHILE WITH HER EAGLE WINGS SHE COVERETH		33	EDW THIRD/PS 6	59
COVERING	SEE COVRING				
[I THOUGHT TO WEAVE A COVERING [FROM] FOR MY SINS . . .		268	FOUR ZOAS 1	160
BUT HAD NO POWER TO WEAVE A VEIL OF COVERING FOR HER SINS		271	FOUR ZOAS 1	* 242
SHUT UP IN LITTLE PURPLE COVERING FAINTLY BUD & DIE	. . .	325	FOUR ZOAS 7	191
WHO WOVE SOFT SILKEN VEILS OF COVERING IN SWEET RAPTURD TRANCE		332	FOUR ZOAS 7	488
MORTAL & NOT AS ENITHARMON WITHOUT A COVERING VEIL	. .	332	FOUR ZOAS 7	489
VEILS OF IGNORANCE COVERING FROM HEAD TO FEET WITH A COLD WEB		346	FOUR ZOAS 8	222
FOR A COVERING TO YOUR LIMBS	.	353	FOUR ZOAS 8	494
THESE COVERING VAULTS OF HEAVEN & THESE TREMBLING GLOBES OF EARTH		364	FOUR ZOAS 9	260
WE VISIT HIM COVERING WITH A VEIL THE IMMORTAL SEED	. .	374	FOUR ZOAS 9	634
[IN WHICH IS TIRZAH ?UNTRANSLUCENT AN OPAKE COVERING]	.	382	FOUR ZOAS AD 6	* 18
WHEN GRAPES & FIGS BURST THEIR COVERING TO THE JOYFUL AIR		485	MILTON 5	33
AS NOW I REND THIS ACCURSED FAMILY FROM MY COVERING	. .	490	MILTON 9	29
COVERING THE EAST WITH SOLID BLACKNESS ROUND HIS HIDDEN HEART		490	MILTON 9	40
IN THE WHOLE PLACE OF THE COVERING CHERUB ROME BABYLON & TYRE		490	MILTON 9	51
WHEREFORE DOST THOU CREATE & WEAVE THIS SATAN FOR A COVERING		499	MILTON 18	30
JERUSALEM IS HIS GARMENT & NOT THY COVERING CHERUB O LOVELY		499	MILTON 18	37
UNWAKEND AND THE COVERING CHERUB ADVANCES FROM THE EAST		506	MILTON 23	10
HOW LONG BENEATH THE COVERING CHERUB GIVE OUR EMANATIONS		507	MILTON 23	12
HE HATH ENTERD INTO THE COVERING CHERUB BECOME ONE WITH		507	MILTON 23	14
COVERING THE LIGHT OF DAY & ROLLING DOWN UPON THE MOUNTAINS		507	MILTON 23	26
ARISE INTO THE COVERING CHERUB WHO IS THE SPECTRE OF ALBION		508	MILTON 24	28
UPON HIS ROCK BENEATH HIS TOMB I SAW THE COVERING CHERUB		508	MILTON 24	30
IN RUGGED COVERING IN THE MINE IS OPEN ALL WITHIN	. . .	515	MILTON 28	37
COVERING OVER THE ROCK OF ODOURS HIS BRIGHT PURPLE MANTLE		526	MILTON 35	57

	PAGE	TITLE	LINE
COVERING (CONTINUED)			
I SAW HE WAS THE COVERING CHERUB & WITHIN HIM SATAN . . .	527	MILTON 37	8
ALL THESE ARE SEEN IN MILTON'S SHADOW WHO IS THE COVERING CHERUB	528	MILTON 37	44
A COVERING FOR THEE TO DO THY WILL TILL ONE GREATER COMES	529	MILTON 38	31
AND SMITES ME AS I SMOTE THEE & BECOMES MY COVERING . . .	529	MILTON 38	32
TO CAST OFF BACON LOCKE & NEWTON FROM ALBION'S COVERING	533	MILTON 41	5
AND THESE UNITED INTO RAHAB IN THE COVERING CHERUB ON EUPHRATES	624	JERUSALEM 5	42
OF JERUSALEM BECOME HER COVERING TILL THE TIME OF THE END	626	JERUSALEM 7	64
WHILE ALBION FLED MORE INDIGNANT REVENGEFUL COVERING . .	664	JERUSALEM 37	12
HER TWO COVERING CHERUBS AFTERWARDS NAMED VOLTAIRE & ROUSSEAU	702	JERUSALEM 66	12
THE ROCKS ARE OPAKE HARDNESSES COVERING ALL VEGETATED THINGS	704	JERUSALEM 67	5
THY REINS COVERD WITH WINGS TRANSLUCENT SOMETIMES COVERING	731	JERUSALEM 86	22
EACH WITHOUTSIDE OF THE OTHER COVERING EASTERN HEAVEN . .	734	JERUSALEM 89	8
THUS WAS THE COVERING CHERUB REVEALD MAJESTIC IMAGE . . .	734	JERUSALEM 89	9
HIDDEN WITHIN THE COVERING CHERUB AS IN A TABERNACLE . .	735	JERUSALEM 89	44
COVERING THEM FROM THE SIGHT OF MAN LIKE THE WOVEN VEIL OF SLEEP	736	JERUSALEM 90	6
SO JESUS SPOKE THE COVERING CHERUB COMING ON IN DARKNESS	743	JERUSALEM 96	17
HUSK & COVERING INTO VACUUM EVAPORATING . . .	745	JERUSALEM 98	19
NOTE THE DANGER IS IN NOT COVERING THE PLATE ALL OVER . .	790C	LETTER 2	PROSE
A NEW LIFE BECAUSE ANOTHER COVERING OF EARTH IS SHAKEN OFF	802B	LETTER 14	PROSE
COVERS			
IF I LIFT UP MY HEAD SIN COVERS ME AS A CLOAK	36A	COUCH DEATH/PS	PROSE
TO REJOICE IN THE BLIGHT THAT COVERS HIS FIELD	291	FOUR ZOAS 2	412
COVERS THEE STILL OBDURATE STILL RESOLVD & WRITING STILL	322	FOUR ZOAS 7	82
WHEN AS THE SNOW COVERS THE MOUNTAIN OFT PETRIFIC HARDNESS [COVERS]	352	FOUR ZOAS 8	* 449
COVERS THE DEEPS AT HIS VAST FURY (MOANING) IN HIS ROCK	352	FOUR ZOAS 8	* 450
LO DARKNESS COVERS THE LONG PCMP OF BANNERS ON THE WIND	375	FOUR ZOAS 9	666
COVERS THE SHADES OF TYBURN HIS INSTEP FROM WINDSOR . . .	531	MILTON 39	37
ON CANTERBURY'S RUINS HIS RIGHT HAND COVERS LOFTY WALES	531	MILTON 39	41
HIS REASON HIS SPECTROUS POWER COVERS THEM ABOVE	620	JERUSALEM 1	5
THE DISEASE OF SHAME COVERS ME FROM HEAD TO FEET I HAVE NO HOPE	643	JERUSALEM 21	3
A DEWY GARMENT COVERS ME ALL OVER ALL MANHOOD IS GONE . .	660	JERUSALEM 34	4
WHICH LIKE A ROBE COVERS & LIKE A VEIL OF SERAPHIM . .	731	JERUSALEM 86	24
COVERT			
THEY THREW DIRT AFTER THEM TILL TO THE COVERT OF A WOOD	109	TIRIEL 7	15
THEN LOUD FROM THEIR GREEN COVERT ALL THE BIRDS BEGIN THEIR SONG	520	MILTON 31	39
TO HIDE THE MOST EVIDENT GOD IN A HIDDEN COVERT EVEN . .	661	JERUSALEM 34	32
COVERTS			
RUSH INTO REPTILE COVERTS HIDING FROM THE FIRES OF ORC . .	202	AMERICA 15	20
THE SECRET COVERTS OF ALBION & THE HIDDEN PLACES OF AMERICA	679	JERUSALEM 49	1
COVET			
CARE BROUGHT FORTH COVET EYELESS & PRONE TO TH EARTH . .	42C	THEN SHE BORE	PROSE
COVET WHEN HE PRAYD FOR HIS DISCIPLES	158C	MARRIAGE HH 22	PROSE
NOT EYELESS COVET	256	BOOK OF LOS 3	10
BUT COVET WAS POURED FULL	256	BOOK OF LOS 3	14
TILL COVET BROKE HIS LOCKS & BARS	256	BOOK OF LOS 3	20
TWAS COVET OR TWAS CUSTOM OR	755	EV GOSPEL(E)/N	61
AND THENCE DID COVET ALSO RISE	755	EV GOSPEL(E)/N	74
COVEY			
TILL PHILIP SPRINGS THE TIMROUS COVEY AGAIN	24	EDW THIRD/PS 3	112
COVRING			
THE SEA FOWL TAKES THE WINTRY BLAST FOR A COVRING TO HER LIMBS	195	V DAU ALBION 8	6
THE BONES OF DEATH THE COVRING CLAY THE SINEWS SHRUNK & DRYD	198	AMERICA 6	3
FROM NORTH TO SOUTH AND BURNT OUTSTRETCHD ON WINGS OF WRATH COVRING	201	AMERICA 13	11
THEY LIE IN TWISTING AGONIES BENEATH THE COVRING HEAVENS	381	FOUR ZOAS AD 2	* 5
COW			
REVIVES THE MILKED COW & TAMES THE FIRE-BREATHING STEED	128	BOOK OF THEL 2	10
COWARD			
HE SEEKS THY LOVE WHO COWARD IN THE NIGHT	6	FAIR ELENOR/PS	67
FOR WHEN THE COWARD RUNS THE BRAVE MAN TOTTERS	22	EDW THIRD/PS 3	60
I AM A COWARD IN MY REASON CHANDOS	27	EDW THIRD/PS 3	243
THE [COWARD] HUMBLE SHEEP A THREATNING HORN	171	THE LILLY/N	2
COWL			
AND A COWL OF FLESH GREW OER HIS HEAD & SCALES ON HIS BACK & RIBS	202	AMERICA 15	17
THIS COWL UPON MY HEAD HE PLACD IN TIMES OF EVERLASTING	336	FOUR ZOAS 7B	115
COWPER			
[EPITAPH FOR] WILLIAM COWPER ESQRE	551C	WILLM COWPER/N	*TITLE
METHODISM ETC P...COWPER CAME TO ME AND SAID	772B	ANNO SPURZHEIM	MARG
HE IS NEPHEW TO THE LATE MR COWPER THE POET YOU WOULD LIKE HIM MUCH	809C	LETTER 20	PROSE
AS IT WILL CONTAIN LETTERS OF COWPER TO HIS FRIENDS PERHAPS	810A	LETTER 20	PROSE
MY HEADS OF COWPER FOR MR H'S(HAYLEY'S) LIFE OF COWPER HAVE	820C	LETTER 25	PROSE
& IN PARTICULAR LADY HESKETH & LORD COWPER	820C	LETTER 25	PROSE
TRANSLATIONS BY COWPER FROM MILTON'S LATIN & ITALIAN POEMS	824C	LETTER 27	PROSE
A MONUMENT TO THE MEMORY OF COWPER IN ST PAUL'S OR . . .	824D	LETTER 27	PROSE
COWPER FOR THAT SONNET IN FAVOR OF A PRISONER AT LEICESTER	841C	LETTER 41	PROSE
THE DIVINE COUNTENANCE IN SUCH MEN AS COWPER AND MILTON	845C	LETTER 44	PROSE
ON COMPARING COWPER WITH WASHINGTON MUST ASSERT	846D	LETTER 44	PROSE
EXCEPT PAPER WHICH IS JOHNSON'S FAULT COWPER IS FAR THE BEST	847A	LETTER 44	PROSE

```
                                                            PAGE     TITLE            LINE
COWPER    (CONTINUED)
      THE HEAD OF COWPER AFTER LAWRENCE THE HEADS TO BE FINISHD    850D LETTER 49      PROSE
      COMPANION TO MY DRAWING OF THE HEAD OF COWPER YOU    .   .   855D LETTER 53      PROSE
      AN ENGRAVING OF COWPER BY THE HAND OF CAROLINE WATSON IS I   859C LETTER 56      PROSE
      PORTRAITS WHICH ACCOMPANY THE LIFE OF COWPER   .   .   .   . 860C LETTER 56      PROSE
COWPER'S
      AT THIS TIME IS ENGRAVING PLATES FOR COWPER'S LIFE   .   .   . 809D LETTER 20     PROSE
      OF THE PLATES FOR COWPER'S WORK WHICH SHE DOES TO            821A LETTER 25      PROSE
         ADMIRATION
      PROPOSED TO THE PUBLIC AT THE END OF COWPER'S LIFE WHICH     821C LETTER 25      PROSE
      VERY LIKELY BE OF GREAT CONSEQUENCE IT IS COWPER'S MILTON    821C LETTER 25      PROSE
      HONOURABLE AT ANY RATE THE PROJECT PLEASES LORD COWPER'S     821C LETTER 25      PROSE
      PARTICULARLY COWPER'S MILTON A WORK NOW ON FOOT    .   .   . 824C LETTER 27      PROSE
      & TO CONSIST OF ALL MILTON'S POEMS WITH COWPER'S NOTES AND   824C LETTER 27      PROSE
      BY COWPER'S MONUMENT HE TELLS ME IS MRS UNWIN'S   .   .   .  832B LETTER 32      PROSE
      I SEND THE FIVE COPIES OF COWPER'S PLATES WHICH YOU WILL     832D LETTER 32      PROSE
      THE PLATES OF COWPER'S MONUMENT ARE BOTH IN GREAT    .   .   837A LETTER 35      PROSE
      COPY OF COWPER'S LETTERS OUGHT TO BE PRINTED IN   .   .   .  837D LETTER 36      PROSE
      ACCEPT ALSO OF MY THANKS FOR COWPER'S THIRD VOLUME    .   .  844C LETTER 43      PROSE
      WHICH COWPER'S LIFE IS PRINTED ON NOT KNOWING THAT IT WAS    846D LETTER 44      PROSE
      TO WELCOME THY ARRIVAL AMONG COWPER'S GLORIFIED BAND     .   854C LETTER 53      PROSE
COWS
      MY MILK OF COWS & HONEY OF BEES & FRUIT OF GOLDEN HARVEST    359 FOUR ZOAS 9      104
      HIS MILK OF COWS & HONEY OF BEES & FRUIT OF GOLDEN HARVEST   641 JERUSALEM 19      5
      THE FIELDS OF COWS BY WILLANS FARM   .   .   .   .   .   .   650 FIELDS FROM/J     15
COXCOMB
      WILL REDEEM MY COUNTRY FROM THIS COXCOMB SITUATION &    .    593C PUB ADDRESS/N   PROSE
COXCOMBS
      SURELY THE MAN WHO WROTE THIS NEVER TALKD TO ANY            408D ANNO BACON     * MARG
         BUT COXCOMBS
COY
      FOR A HARLOT COY    .   .   .   .   .   .   .   .   .   .   . 168 SILENT NIGHT/N    12
COYPEL
      ("THOUGH COYPEL WANTED A SIMPLICITY") [O YES COYPEL         SUPP ANNO REYNOLDS  * MARG
         ?INDEED]
CRAB
      [THE PEAR TREE MILD THE FROWNING WALNUT THE SHARP CRAB       269 FOUR ZOAS 1      205
         & APPLE SWEET]
CRACK
      AND ITS ROOFS CRACK ACROSS DOWN FALLING ON TH ANGELIC SEATS  204 AMERICA CANC B    24
      THRO THE CONFUSION LIKE A CRACK ACROSS FROM IMMENSE TO       295 FOUR ZOAS 3      149
         IMMENSE
CRACKD
      CRACKD ACROSS INTO NUMBERLESS FRAGMENTS   .   .   .   .   .  257 BOOK OF LOS 4     18
CRACKING
      .   .   . CRACKING THE HEAVENS ACROSS FROM IMMENSE TO IMMENSE  357 FOUR ZOAS 9      9
CRACKLING
      LIKE AS A FOREST ROARS WITH CRACKLING FLAMES   .   .   .   .  32 EDW THIRD/PS 6    27
      CRACKLING THE FLAMES WENT UP WITH FURY FROM THE IMMORTAL     308 FOUR ZOAS 5      108
         DEMON
CRACKS
      AMAZD HIS HEAVENS IMMENSE CRACKS   .   .   .   .   .   .   .  234 URIZEN 23        16
CRADLE
      EVEN IN CHILDHOOD SORROW SLEPT WITH ME IN MY CRADLE   .   .   37B CONTEMPLATN/PS  PROSE
      SEEK YOUR CRADLE NARROW   .   .   .   .   .   .   .   .   .   115 THE BLOSSOM/SI    5
      A CRADLE SONG   .   .   .   .   .   .   .   .   .   .   .   . 120A CRADLE SONG/SI  TITLE
      AND NOT SIT THE CRADLE NEAR   .   .   .   .   .   .   .   .   122 ON ANOTHERS/SI   19
      SOONER MURDER AN INFANT IN ITS CRADLE THAN NURSE UNACTED     152D MARRIAGE HH 10  PROSE
         DESIRES
      A CRADLE SONG   .   .   .   .   .   .   .   .   .   .   .   . 164D CRADLE SONG/N   TITLE
      THE UNDEFILD THO RAVISHD IN HER CRADLE NIGHT AND MORN   .    199 AMERICA 8         12
      THAT BETWIXT THE CRADLE & GRAVE   .   .   .   .   .   .   .   424 THE SMILE        13
      STOLEN FROM HIS NURSE'S CRADLE WRAPD IN NEEDLE-WORK   .   .  508 MILTON 24         18
      TO HAVE POWER OVER MAN FROM CRADLE TO CORRUPTIBLE GRAVE      661 JERUSALEM 34      26
      TO HAVE POWER OVER MAN FROM CRADLE TO CORRUPTIBLE GRAVE      688 JERUSALEM 56       4
      HE WHO IS AN INFANT AND WHOSE CRADLE IS A MANGER   .   .   . 688 JERUSALEM 56       5
      AND WHO WEAVE IT A CRADLE OF THE GRASS THAT WITHERETH AWAY   688 JERUSALEM 56       7
      THIS WORLD IS ALL A CRADLE FOR THE ERRED WANDERING PHANTOM   688 JERUSALEM 56       8
      A GARMENT AND CRADLE WEAVING FOR THE INFANTINE TERROR   .    688 JERUSALEM 56      14
      ROCK THE CRADLE AND IN MILD MELODIES TELL ME WHERE FOUND     688 JERUSALEM 56      22
      AND ROCK THE CRADLE WHILE AH ME OF THAT ETERNAL MAN   .   .  688 JERUSALEM 56      33
      ME FROM MY CRADLE THE AMALEKITE STOLE ME AWAY UPON HIS       695 JERUSALEM 61      41
         CAMELS
      CRADLE SONG DITTO NURSE'S SONG HOLY THURSDAY     .   .   .   SUPP LETTER 66A     *PROSE
CRADLED
      [THERE] AND [CRADLED] MILK FED INFANCY [IS SOLD] FOR GOLD    174 HUMAN IMAGE/N   *  30
      THY CRADLED INFANCY IS MOST PITEOUS O HIDE O HIDE   .   .    644 JERUSALEM 21      24
      AND OF THE CRADLED INFANCY IN HIS BOWELS OF COMPASSION   .   688 JERUSALEM 56      34
CRAFTY
      AND OOTHOON IS THE CRAFTY SLAVE OF SELFISH HOLINESS   .   .  194 V DAU ALBION 6    20
CRAG
      SITTING UPON [HIS] AN IRON CRAG AT LENGTH HIS WORDS BROKE    321 FOUR ZOAS 7      43
         FORTH
      UPON THE IRON CRAG OF URIZEN THENCE SPRINGING UP ALOFT   .   332 FOUR ZOAS 7      465
CRAGGY
      [THE GOAT LEAPD FROM THE CRAGGY [?ROCK] CLIFF . . .     .    270 FOUR ZOAS 1    * 208
CRAM
      I AM ENVIED IN MANY QUARTERS BUT I WILL CRAM THE DOGS   .    821C LETTER 25      PROSE
CRAMPD
      LUVAH THEIR LIPS TREMBLE THEIR MUSCULAR FIBRES ARE CRAMPD    701 JERUSALEM 65      78
         & SMITTEN
```

406

		PAGE	TITLE	LINE

CRAMPS
    AND TIMBERS CRAMPT WITH IRON CRAMPS BAR IN THE JOYS OF LIFE   515 MILTON 28   40
CRAMPT
    AND TIMBERS CRAMPT WITH IRON CRAMPS BAR IN THE JOYS OF LIFE   515 MILTON 28   40
CRANE
    THE FEARFUL CRANE SPRINGS FROM THE SPLASHY FEN . . . . 24 EDW THIRD/PS 3   125
    THE CRANE OERTAKEN FIGHTETH WITH THE HAWK . . . . . . 24 EDW THIRD/PS 3   128
    YOU ARE MORE LIKE A LION THAN A CRANE . . . . 24 EDW THIRD/PS 3   131
CRASH
    RENT AWAY WITH A TERRIBLE CRASH . . . . 225 URIZEN 5   4
    WITH A CRASH FROM IMMENSE TO IMMENSE . . . . 257 BOOK OF LOS 4   17
    A CRASH RAN THRO THE IMMENSE THE BOUNDS OF DESTINY WERE 295 FOUR ZOAS 3   135
      BROKEN
    SHE CONTINUED FALLING LOUD THE CRASH CONTINUD LOUD 295 FOUR ZOAS 3   145
      & HOARSE
    FROM THE CRASH [REARED] ROARED A FLAME OF . . . . 295 FOUR ZOAS 3 * 146
    WITH A CRASH BREAKING ACROSS THE HORRIBLE MASS COMES DOWN 322 FOUR ZOAS 7   78
    SHE BURST THE GATES OF ENITHARMON'S HEART WITH DIREFUL 328 FOUR ZOAS 7   323
      CRASH
CRASHD
    THE BOUNDS OF DESTINY CRASHD DIREFUL & THE SWELLING SEA 295 FOUR ZOAS 3   136
CRATELOS
    FROM CRATELOS . . . . 555C FRM CRATELOS/N TITLE
CRAVD
    AND THE UNFORMED PART CRAVD REPOSE . . . . 258 BOOK OF LOS 4   59
CRAVE
    WHILE VACANT YOUTH DOTH CRAVE AND SEEK ABOUT . . . . . 27 EDW THIRD/PS 3   252
    CRAVE OR BE HEARD FOR PLENTY SHALL BRING FORTH . . . . 33 EDW THIRD/PS 6   46
    A LITTLE REST I CRAVE A LITTLE WATER FROM A BROOK . . . 104 TIRIEL 4   34
    GIVING TO THOSE THAT CANNOT CRAVE THE VOICELESS THE 128 BOOK OF THEL 2   4
      OERTIRED
    SHALL PURSUE THARMAS & IN VAIN SHALT CRAVE FOR FOOD I WILL 313 FOUR ZOAS 6   68
    DELUSION & I CANNOT CRAVE FOR ANY THING BUT THEE [& TILL] 327 FOUR ZOAS 7   307
    THAT GAVEST ME A HEART TO CRAVE & RAISEDST ME THY PHANTOM 368 FOUR ZOAS 9   415
    CRAVE NOT FOR THE MORTAL & PERISHING DELIGHTS BUT LEAVE 511 MILTON 25   56
      THEM
    IT IS ONLY FOR RICHES THAT I CAN CRAVE . . . . 558 I ROSE UP AT/N   8
CRAVES
    TO ENRICH THE LEAN EARTH THAT CRAVES . . . . 138 FRENCH REVOLTN   99
    WHERE ENION CRAVES SUCCESSIVE DRAWN INTO THE GOLDEN FEAST 274 FOUR ZOAS 1   373
CRAVING
    . . . TO PLANT BEAUTY IN THE DESART CRAVING ABYSS THEY 136 FRENCH REVOLTN   55
      GLEAM
    A CRAVING HUNGRY CAVERN . . . . 229 URIZEN 13   6
    AND URIZEN CRAVING WITH HUNGER . . . . 233 URIZEN 20   30
    SOME ORGANS FOR CRAVING AND LUST . . . . 253 AHANIA 4   33
    CRAVING THE MORE THE MORE ENJOYING DRAWING OUT SWEET BLISS 276 FOUR ZOAS 1   440
    AT DISTANCE FAR IN NIGHT REPELLD IN DIREFUL HUNGER CRAVING 276 FOUR ZOAS 1   442
    WHERE ENION BLIND & AGE BENT WEPT IN DIREFUL HUNGER CRAVING 280 FOUR ZOAS 2   16
    A CRAVING HUNGRY CAVERN THENCE AROSE HIS CHANNELD . . . 303 FOUR ZOAS 4   240
    CONCENTERD INTO LOVE OF PARENT STORGOUS APPETITE CRAVING 308 FOUR ZOAS 5   113
    IS GIVEN A CRAVING CRY THAT THEY MAY SIT AT NIGHT ON BARREN 325 FOUR ZOAS 7   205
      ROCKS
    CRAVING & DEVOURING BUT MY EYES ARE ALWAYS UPON THEE O 327 FOUR ZOAS 7   306
      LOVELY
    ON THE HUNGRY CRAVING WIND . . . . 415 MY SPECTRE/N   25
    A WORLD OF SHAPES IN CRAVING LUST & DEVOURING APPETITE . . 685 JERUSALEM 54   24
CRAWL
    AND SNAKE AND DAMP TOAD ON THE KINGLY FOOT CRAWL . . . . . 147 FRENCH REVOLTN   298
CRAWLERS
    ("OR THE PIETIST WHO CRAWLS GROANS BLUBBERS") I HATE 67D ANNO LAVATER   MARG
      CRAWLERS
    FOR WHAT ARE ALL CRAWLERS BUT MIMICKERS OF HUMILITY & LOVE 68D ANNO LAVATER   MARG
CRAWLING
    FORTH CAME AMBITION CRAWLING LIKE A TOAD . . . . . . 41A THEN SHE BORE   PROSE
    SAYS JEROME HAPPINESS IS NOT FOR US POOR CRAWLING REPTILES 52B ISLAND MOON 8   PROSE
    UPON THE SAND &C AND WHEN THE [FOOLISH ?CRAWLING] DRONE 110 TIRIEL 8 * 33
      . . .
    . . . HAS REACHD HIS CRAWLING LENGTH . . . . 110 TIRIEL 8   33
    CRAWLING AFTER THEIR PREY . . . . 156A MARRIAGE HH 17 PROSE
    WHAT CRAWLING VILLAIN PREACHES ABSTINENCE & WRAPS HIMSELF 200 AMERICA 11   14
CRAY
    THE "VIEWS IN KEW GARDENS" "FOOTS CRAY" & "DIANA" 594A PUB ADDRESS/N PROSE
      & "ACTEON"
CREAM
    HIS LABORIOUS TASK DROPPING HIS FLAIL & CREAM BOWL . . . 618C ILLUS MILTON PROSE
CREATE   SEE NEW CREATE
    HOW COULD LIFE CREATE DEATH . . . . 92B ANNO SWED LOVE MARG
    TO CREATE A LITTLE FLOWER IS THE LABOUR OF AGES . . . . 152C MARRIAGE HH 9 PROSE
    THE LUSTFUL JOY SHALL FORGET TO GENERATE & CREATE 194 V DAU ALBION 7   6
      AN AMOROUS IMAGE
    [TO CREATE MAN MORNING BY MORNING TO GIVE GIFTS AT NOON 269 FOUR ZOAS 1   201
      DAY]
    MINGLE TOGETHER TO CREATE A WORLD FOR LOS IN CRUEL DELIGHT 313 FOUR ZOAS 6   82
    WITHOUT THE FOOD OF LIFE LET US CREATE THEM (COUNTERPARTS) 330 FOUR ZOAS 7   409
    UPON THE LIMIT OF CONTRACTION TO CREATE THE FALLEN MAN . . 341 FOUR ZOAS 8   3
    [TO CREATE MAN MORNING BY MORNING TO GIVE GIFTS AT NOON SUPP FOUR ZOAS 8 *
      DAY]
    AND ANOTHER FORM CREATE . . . . 417 MY SPECTRE/N   65
    O DIVINE VISION WHO DIDST CREATE THE FEMALE TO REPOSE . . 493 MILTON 12   49
    WHEREFORE DOST THOU CREATE & WEAVE THIS SATAN FOR 499 MILTON 18   30
      A COVERING

407

		PAGE	TITLE	LINE
CREATE	(CONTINUED)			
WHO SET PLEASURE AGAINST DUTY WHO CREATE OLYMPIC CROWNS		511	MILTON 25	51
THE SPECTRE REFUSES HE SEEKS CRUELTY THEY CREATE THE CRESTED COCK		515	MILTON 28	24
OR THEY CREATE THE LION & TYGER IN COMPASSIONATE THUNDERINGS		515	MILTON 28	27
I WILL CERTAINLY CREATE AN ETERNAL HELL FOR THEE LISTEN		627	JERUSALEM 8	8
THOU ABSTAIN RAVENING I WILL CREATE AN ETERNAL HELL FOR THEE		627	JERUSALEM 8	38
I MUST CREATE A SYSTEM OR BE ENSLAVD BY ANOTHER MAN'S	.	629	JERUSALEM 10	20
I WILL NOT REASON & COMPARE MY BUSINESS IS TO CREATE	. .	629	JERUSALEM 10	21
CREATE MY SPIRIT TO THY LOVE	. . .	651	FIELDS FROM/J	71
WHEREFORE DID I LOVING CREATE LOVE WHICH NEVER YET	. . .	660	JERUSALEM 33	45
O ALBION WHY WILT THOU CREATE A FEMALE WILL	. .	661	JERUSALEM 34	31
AND BE THOU CREATED INTO A STATE I GO FORTH TO CREATE	. .	662	JERUSALEM 35	15
STRIVING TO CREATE A HEAVEN IN WHICH ALL SHALL BE PURE & HOLY		679	JERUSALEM 49	27
THE CROSS O ALBION WHY DIDST THOU A FEMALE WILL CREATE	. .	688	JERUSALEM 56	43
TO CREATE A WORLD OF GENERATION FROM THE WORLD OF DEATH	. .	690	JERUSALEM 58	18
CREATE THE SILK-WORM & THE SPIDER & THE CATTERPILLER	. .	692	JERUSALEM 59	46
AND OTHERS CREATE THE WOOLY LAMB & THE DOWNY FOWL	. . .	692	JERUSALEM 59	48
TO CREATE THE LION & WOLF THE BEAR THE TYGER & OUNCE	. .	713	JERUSALEM 73	17
TO CREATE THE WOOLY LAMB & DOWNY FOWL & SCALY SERPENT	. .	713	JERUSALEM 73	18
CREATE JERUSALEM & BABYLON & EGYPT & MOAB & AMALEK	. . .	725	JERUSALEM 82	27
EMANATIONS CREATE SPACE THE MASCULINE CREATE TIME & PLANT		730	JERUSALEM 85	8
THEM NOT AS THOU WILT BUT AS I WILL FOR I WILL CREATE	. .	732	JERUSALEM 87	13
SPECTRE TO DEFEND HER FROM MAN I WILL CREATE SECRET PLACES		733	JERUSALEM 88	17
THEN THOU WILT CREATE ANOTHER FEMALE ACCORDING TO THY WILL		739	JERUSALEM 92	12
THAT DIDST CREATE THIS BODY OF MINE	. . . .	754	EV GOSPEL(E)/N	30
ITS DEFICIENCY OR TO NEW CREATE IT ACCORDING TO YOUR WISH		860C	LETTER 56	PROSE
CREATED	SEE NEW-CREATED			
("LOVE") THEREFORE IT WAS NOT CREATED IMPURE & IS NOT NATURALLY SO		96C	ANNO SWED LOVE	MARG
SINCE THE OLD ANYTHING WAS CREATED	. . . .	187	WHEN KLOPSTK/N	26
ETERNALLY CREATED BY THE LAMB OF GOD AROUND	. .	266	FOUR ZOAS 1	97
[SO WAILD SHE TREMBLING BEFORE HER OWN CREATED PHANTASM]		267	FOUR ZOAS 1	118
THUS WERE THE STARS OF HEAVEN CREATED LIKE A GOLDEN CHAIN		287	FOUR ZOAS 2	266
CREATED FOR MY WILL MY SLAVE THO STRONG THO I AM WEAK	. .	288	FOUR ZOAS 2	332
AND IN THE DARK VACUITY CREATED A BOSOM OF [SLIME] CLAY		316	FOUR ZOAS 6	158
THE DERPS OF LOS THE SLAVE OF THAT CREATION I CREATED	. .	327	FOUR ZOAS 7	297
THAT BODY I CREATED THEN SHALL WE UNITE AGAIN IN BLISS	. .	327	FOUR ZOAS 7	301
ART NOTHING BEING CREATED CONTINUALLY BY MERCY & LOVE DIVINE		329	FOUR ZOAS 7	360
THAT BODY HE CREATED BUT IN VAIN FOR LOS PERFORMD	. . .	329	FOUR ZOAS 7	376
FOR WITHOUT A CREATED BODY THE SPECTRE IS ETERNAL DEATH		330	FOUR ZOAS 7	410
AND THEY APPEARD A UNIVERSAL FEMALE FORM CREATED	. . . .	345	FOUR ZOAS 8	188
THE SYNAGOGUE CREATED HER FROM FRUIT OF URIZEN'S TREE	. .	348	FOUR ZOAS 8	287
WEPT OVER HIM CREATED HIM A SPACE CLOSD WITH A TENDER MOON		350	FOUR ZOAS 8	371
MOLECH IMPATIENT THEY SENT ELOHIM WHO CREATED ADAM	. . .	351	FOUR ZOAS 8	401
THREE CLASSES ARE CREATED BY THE HAMMER OF LOS & WOVEN	. .	482	MILTON 2	26
FOR THE ELECT CANNOT BE REDEEMD BUT CREATED CONTINUALLY		484	MILTON 5	11
IN THE NIGHT OF PROSPERITY AND WANTONNESS WHICH HE HIMSELF CREATED		485	MILTON 5	41
THE WEB OF LIFE IS WOVEN & THE TENDER SINEWS OF LIFE CREATED		486	MILTON 6	34
HE CREATED SEVEN DEADLY SINS DRAWING OUT HIS INFERNAL SCROLL		489	MILTON 9	21
BUT MUST BE NEW CREATED CONTINUALLY MOMENT BY MOMENT	. .	492	MILTON 11	20
CREATED A NEW SPACE TO PROTECT SATAN FROM PUNISHMENT	. .	494	MILTON 13	13
IN MOMENTS NEW CREATED FOR DELUSION INTERWOVEN ROUND ABOUT		494	MILTON 13	39
RAHAB CREATED VOLTAIRE TIRZAH CREATED ROUSSEAU	. . . .	506	MILTON 22	41
HERE ARE THE STARS CREATED & THE SEEDS OF ALL THINGS PLANTED		514	MILTON 27	53
IS VISIONARY AND IS CREATED BY THE HAMMER OF LOS	. . . .	516	MILTON 29	20
THE RED GLOBULE IS THE UNWEARIED SUN BY LOS CREATED	. . .	517	MILTON 29	23
BEULAH IS EVERMORE CREATED AROUND ETERNITY APPEARING	. .	518	MILTON 30	8
AND IT IS THUS CREATED LO THE ETERNAL GREAT HUMANITY	. .	519	MILTON 30	15
BUT MUST BE CREATED FOR THEY KNOW ONLY OF GENERATION	. .	520	MILTON 31	22
SATAN & ADAM ARE STATES CREATED INTO TWENTY-SEVEN CHURCHES		521	MILTON 32	25
AND THOU O MILTON ART A STATE ABOUT TO BE CREATED	. . .	521	MILTON 32	26
CREATED TO BE ANNIHILATED & A NEW RATIO CREATED	. . . .	522	MILTON 32	35
WHATEVER CAN BE CREATED CAN BE ANNIHILATED FORMS CANNOT		522	MILTON 32	36
SOME MEN CREATED FOR DESTRUCTION COME	. . . .	544	SOME MEN/N	1
ERROR IS CREATED TRUTH IS ETERNAL	. . . . . .	617B	V LAST JUDG/N	PROSE
CREATED TO BE THE GREAT EXAMPLE OF HORROR & AGONY ALSO MY		630	JERUSALEM 10	52
OF ALL THE INHABITANTS OF EARTH WAILING TO BE CREATED	.	634	JERUSALEM 13	63
IN A SWEET MOONY NIGHT & SILENCE THAT THEY HAD CREATED	.	642	JERUSALEM 19	43
SATAN & ADAM & THE WHOLE WORLD WAS CREATED BY THE ELOHIM		649D	JERUSALEM 27	PROSE
AND BE THOU CREATED INTO A STATE I GO FORTH TO CREATE	. .	662	JERUSALEM 35	15
IN VEGETABLE MOULD CREATED BY THE HAMMER AND LOOM	. . .	668	JERUSALEM 40	56
BECOMES SEXUAL & IS CREATED AND VEGETATED AND BORN	. . .	674	JERUSALEM 44	22
WHERE NO DISPUTE CAN COME CREATED FOR THOSE WHO SLEEP	. .	678	JERUSALEM 48	20
BECAUSE THE EVIL IS CREATED INTO A STATE THAT MEN	. . .	680	JERUSALEM 49	70
IN THE BRITISH OCEAN CREATED BY LOS'S HAMMER MEASURED OUT		688	JERUSALEM 56	19
CREATED FROM THE VALLEY OF MIDDLESEX BY LONDON'S RIVER	.	690	JERUSALEM 58	45
TO INDIVIDUAL PERCEPTION LUVAH MUST BE CREATED	. . . .	696	JERUSALEM 62	20
THEY ARE CREATED CONTINUALLY EAST & WEST & NORTH & SOUTH		712	JERUSALEM 72	29
AND FROM THEM ARE CREATED ALL THE NATIONS OF THE EARTH	. .	712	JERUSALEM 72	30
THESE ARE CREATED BY RAHAB & TIRZAH IN ULRO BUT AROUND	. .	713	JERUSALEM 73	39
IN SHADOWY POMP BY THE ETERNAL PROPHET CREATED EVERMORE		716	JERUSALEM 75	6
THIS SINFUL NATION CREATED IN OUR FURNACES & LOOMS IS ALBION		739	JERUSALEM 92	6

```
                                                              PAGE     TITLE          LINE
CREATED    (CONTINUED)
    AND CREATED HELL'S DARK JAWS  .  .  .  .  .  .  .  .      754  EV GOSPEL(E)/N       32
    WHAT CAN BE CREATED CAN BE DESTROYED  .  .  .  .  .  .   776C  INSC LAOCOON      PROSE
    [?FIRST ?WERE CREATED WINE & (HAPPINESS) ?GOOD ?LOOKS &  SUPP  ANNO REYNOLDS    * MARG
       ?FORTUNE XXX]
CREATES
    TO BE EXCENTRIC IF HE CREATES O HAPPY PHILOSOPHER  .  .    81C  ANNO LAVATER     * MARG
    BECAUSE THE LAMB OF GOD CREATES HIMSELF A BRIDE & WIFE  .  362  FOUR ZOAS 9        220
    FROM FELL DESTRUCTION IN THE SPECTROUS CUNNING OR RAGE     515  MILTON 28           41
       HE CREATES
    AND WHEN UNWEARIED IN THE EVENING HE CREATES THE MOON   .  517  MILTON 29           42
    SHE CREATES AT HER WILL A LITTLE MOONY NIGHT & SILENCE  .  707  JERUSALEM 69        19
    THESE TO PRESERVE THEM FROM ETERNAL DEATH LOS CREATES   .  714  JERUSALEM 73        40
    & THAT GOD CREATES NOTHING BUT WHAT CAN BE TOUCHD &  .  . 789B  ANNO THORNTON      MARG
CREATING      SEE THOUGHT-CREATING
    CREATING SPACES LEST THEY FALL INTO ETERNAL DEATH  .  .    267  FOUR ZOAS 1        100
    FOR ELEMENTAL GODS THEIR THUNDEROUS ORGANS BLEW CREATING   274  FOUR ZOAS 1        377
    CREATING MANY A VORTEX FIXING MANY A SCIENCE IN THE DEEP   316  FOUR ZOAS 6        187
    TEN THOUSAND DEMONS LABOUR AT THE FORGES CREATING         346  FOUR ZOAS 8        205
       CONTINUALLY
    O THOU CREATING VOICE THAT CALLEST & WHO SHALL ANSWER THEE 367  FOUR ZOAS 9        400
    THUS THEY SING CREATING THE THREE CLASSES AMONG DRUID ROCKS 485 MILTON 5            38
    CREATING NEW FLESH ON THE DEMON COLD AND BUILDING HIM   .  500  MILTON 19           13
    CREATING FORM & BEAUTY AROUND THE DARK REGIONS OF SORROW   514  MILTON 28            2
    CREATING THE BEAUTIFUL HOUSE FOR THE PITEOUS SUFFERER   .  515  MILTON 28            7
    ON ALBION'S ROCK LOS STANDS CREATING THE GLORIOUS SUN EACH 517  MILTON 29           41
       MORNING
    TO BUILD THE UNIVERSE STUPENDOUS MENTAL FORMS CREATING  .  519  MILTON 30           20
    WORKS A WORLD OF GENERATION CONTINUALLY CREATING OUT OF    690  JERUSALEM 58        50
    PERMANENTLY CREATING TO BE IN TIME REVEALD & DEMOLISHD  .  713  JERUSALEM 73        34
    CREATING NATURE FROM THIS FIERY LAW  .  .  .  .  .  .  .   718  STOOD AMONG/J       22
    EASTWARD INTO HER OWN CENTER CREATING THE FEMALE WOMB   .  734  JERUSALEM 88        52
    IN NEW EXPANSES CREATING EXEMPLARS OF MEMORY AND         746  JERUSALEM 98         30
       OF INTELLECT
    CREATING SPACE CREATING TIME ACCORDING TO THE WONDERS     746  JERUSALEM 98         31
       DIVINE
    ELOHIM CREATING ADAM  .  .  .  .  .  .  .  .  .  .  .  .  SUPP  COLOR PRT TATE   *TITLE
    SPENSER CREATING HIS FAIRIES  .  .  .  .  .  .  .  .  .  SUPP  ILLUS GRAY       *TITLE
    GOD CREATING ADAM CHRIST APPEARING TOUCHG UP CHRIST      SUPP  LETTER 56A       *PROSE
       BAPTIZING
CREATION
    FOR LET IT BE REMEMBERD THAT CREATION IS  .  .  .  .  .    87B  ANNO LAVATER       MARG
    ("IMAGE OF CREATION") A GOING FORTH & RETURNING  .  .  .   95A  ANNO SWED LOVE     MARG
    ALL CREATION SLEPT AND SMILD  .  .  .  .  .  .  .  .  .    120  CRADLE SONG/SI      18
    THE WHOLE CREATION WILL BE CONSUMED AND APPEAR INFINITE   154B  MARRIAGE HH 14    PROSE
       AND HOLY
    TERRIFIED IN HER OWN CREATION VIEWING HER WOVEN SHADOW  .  266  FOUR ZOAS 1         90
    THE DEEPS OF LOS THE SLAVE OF THAT CREATION I CREATED   .  327  FOUR ZOAS 7        297
    THE ETERNAL CREATION FLOWING FROM THE DIVINE HUMANITY   .  444C  LAST JUDGMNT/L   PROSE
    WAIT TILL THE JUDGEMENT IS PAST TILL THE CREATION         511  MILTON 25           59
       IS CONSUMED
    LEST THOSE THREE HEAVENS OF BEULAH SHOULD THE CREATION    512  MILTON 26           20
       DESTROY
    IN THE NEWTONIAN VOIDS BETWEEN THE SUBSTANCES OF CREATION  528  MILTON 37           46
    DOLOROUS THAT RAN THRO ALL CREATION A DOUBLE SIX-FOLD     534  MILTON 42            4
       WONDER
    & IN WHOSE SLEEP OR CHAOS CREATION BEGAN [HIS EMANATION   609C  V LAST JUDG/N    PROSE
       OR WIFE IS]
    MANY SUPPOSE THAT BEFORE [ADAM] THE CREATION ALL  .  .  . 614B  V LAST JUDG/N    PROSE
    FROM THE BIBLE & LIMITS ALL EXISTENCE TO CREATION & TO   614B  V LAST JUDG/N    PROSE
       CHAOS
    ETERNITY INDEPENDENT OF CREATION WHICH WAS AN ACT OF MERCY 614B  V LAST JUDG/N   PROSE
    OF CREATION REDEMPTION OR JUDGMENT  .  .  .  .  .  .  .  . 614C  V LAST JUDG/N    PROSE
    THE WHOLE CREATION GROANS TO BE DELIVERD  .  .  .  .  .  . 616A  V LAST JUDG/N    PROSE
    ERROR OR CREATION WILL BE BURNED UP  .  .  .  .  .  .  . 617B  V LAST JUDG/N    PROSE
    FOR MY SELF THAT I DO NOT BEHOLD THE OUTWARD CREATION  . 617B  V LAST JUDG/N    PROSE
    IS A CREATION OF MERCY & LOVE FROM THE SATANIC VOID  .  . 634  JERUSALEM 13        45
    THROUGHOUT THE WHOLE CREATION WHICH GROANS TO BE DELIVERD  637  JERUSALEM 16        26
    BY THE CREATION OF STATES &  .  .  .  .  .  .  .  .  .  .  648  JERUSALEM 25        13
    EXPLORING THE THREE STATES OF ULRO CREATION REDEMPTION    663  JERUSALEM 36        42
       & JUDGMENT
    AND THE LOUD-RENDING BARS OF THE CREATION READY TO BURST   667  JERUSALEM 40        26
    A MURDEROUS PROVIDENCE A CREATION THAT GROANS LIVING ON    681  JERUSALEM 50         5
       DEATH
    IN ALBION'S TOMB THE WONDROUS CREATION & THE FOUR-FOLD GATE 712  JERUSALEM 72       49
    CREATION AND DEVOURD ALL THINGS IN ITS LOUD  .  .  .  .    717  STOOD AMONG/J        5
    THE TERRORS OF CREATION & REDEMPTION & JUDGMENT BEHOLDING   739  JERUSALEM 92       20
       THEM
    GENESIS CHAPTER I THE CREATION OF THE NATURAL MAN  .  .  . SUPP  ILLUS GENESIS   *TITLE
CREATIONS
    WHY AN EAR A WHIRLPOOL FIERCE TO DRAW CREATIONS IN  .  .   130  BOOK OF THEL 6      17
    IN LIVING CREATIONS APPEARD  .  .  .  .  .  .  .  .  .  .  225  URIZEN 5             1
    HIS ETERNAL CREATIONS APPEAR  .  .  .  .  .  .  .  .  .  .  234  URIZEN 23            9
CREATIVE      SEE ALL CREATIVE
CREATOR
    BUT BECAUSE HE IS THE CREATOR OF MAN  .  .  .  .  .  .  .   90B  ANNO SWED LOVE     MARG
    O URIZEN CREATOR OF MEN MISTAKEN DEMON OF HEAVEN  .  .  .   192  V DAU ALBION 5       3
    THINKING AS I DO THAT THE CREATOR OF THIS WORLD  .  .  .  617A  V LAST JUDG/N    PROSE
    I KNOW IT IS MY SELF O MY DIVINE CREATOR & REDEEMER  .  .  743  JERUSALEM 96        13
CREATURE
    SAID LITTLE CREATURE [THOU ART] FORMD [FOR] OF JOY & MIRTH  541  ANGEL PRESID/N       2
    THAT LIVING CREATURE ON THE LEFT OF THE THRONE GIVES  .  . 612A  V LAST JUDG/N    PROSE
```

```
                                                              PAGE      TITLE          LINE
CREATURES
    TO BE SURE WE ARE ALL POOR CREATURES WELL  . . . . .  . 44B ISLAND MOON 1     PROSE
    HAIL FINGERFOOTED LOVELY CREATURES  . . . . . . . .  .  56 HAIL MATRIM/IM        7
    MORE HUMAN CREATURES ON THIS EARTH BESIDE THE SONS OF HAR  102 TIRIEL 2         55
    WHAT ARE THE NATURES OF THOSE LIVING CREATURES . . .  . 264 FOUR ZOAS 1        12
    THE LIVING CREATURES OF THE WHEELS IN THE WARS OF ETERNAL  280 FOUR ZOAS 1      572
        LIFE
    IN THE CLOUD WHICH ROLLS AWAY ARE THE FOUR LIVING CREATURES  444A LAST JUDGMNT/L PROSE
    CURBING HIS LIVING CREATURES MANY OF THE STRONGEST GNOMES  487 MILTON 7         48
    AS ELYNITTRIA USED TO DO BUT TOO WELL THOSE LIVING    492 MILTON 12             12
        CREATURES
    THEY IN RETURN RETALIATED AND THE LIVING CREATURES MADDEND  493 MILTON 12       35
    AND ALL THE LIVING CREATURES OF THE FOUR ELEMENTS WAILD  519 MILTON 31          17
    PARTICULARLY THE FOUR LIVING CREATURES  . . . . . .  . 612A V LAST JUDG/N     PROSE
    THE OTHER LIVING CREATURES ARE DESCENDING WITH A SHOUT  . 612A V LAST JUDG/N   PROSE
    BORNE BY THE LIVING CREATURES OF THE THIRD PROCESSION  . 667 JERUSALEM 40       22
    OF HUMAN MAJESTY THE LIVING CREATURES WEPT ALOUD AS THEY  667 JERUSALEM 40      23
    AND THE VOICES OF THE LIVING CREATURES . . . . . .  . 687 JERUSALEM 55          55
    THE LIVING CREATURES MADDEN AND ALBION FELL INTO     689 JERUSALEM 57           13
        THE FURROW AND
    WHEN THE FOUR ZOAS OF ALBION THE FOUR LIVING CREATURES  696 JERUSALEM 63         2
        THE CHERUBIM
    THE FOUR LIVING CREATURES . . . . . . . . . . .  . 745 JERUSALEM 98            24
    ON CHARIOTS OF GOLD & JEWELS WITH LIVING CREATURES STARRY  746 JERUSALEM 98     42
        & FLAMING
    . . . FROM THE LIVING CREATURES OF THE EARTH  . . .  . 746 JERUSALEM 98         54
    . . . AMONG THE LIVING CREATURES  . . . . . . .  . 746 JERUSALEM 98             56
    "A FAIRY VISION OF SOME GAY CREATURES OF THE ELEMENT"  SUPP LEGEND/N30         *
        (MILTON)
CREDIT
    COMMENCED A NEW LIFE OF INDUSTRY TO DO CREDIT TO  . . . . 804B LETTER 16       PROSE
    THAT YOU THINK MY PRINTS WILL DO ME CREDIT  . . . . . 857C LETTER 54           PROSE
CREDITABLE
    THIS & OTHER WORKS EQUALLY CREDITABLE THESE ARE WORKS  . 821C LETTER 25        PROSE
CREDIT-ER
    & YOU SO MUCH MY CREDIT-ER BUT SUCH AS I CAN BE I WILL  . 808D LETTER 20        PROSE
CREEP
    WHEN WESTERN WINDS CREEP SOFTLY OER THE FLOWERS  . . . .   5 FAIR ELENOR/PS     48
    THEN HE WOULD CREEP LIKE A BRIGHT SERPENT TILL AROUND MY  105 TIRIEL 4          57
        NECK
    O THE CUNNING WILES THAT CREEP  . . . . . . . .  . 165 CRADLE SONG/N          14
    [O THE CUNNING WILES THAT CREEP]  . . . . . . . .  . 165 CRADLE SONG/N       * 23
    THE PLAGUES CREEP ON THE BURNING WINDS DRIVEN BY FLAMES  202 AMERICA 15         11
        OF ORC
    TILL INTO NARROW FORMS YOU CREEP GO TAKE YOUR FIERY WAY  294 FOUR ZOAS 3        89
    THE MAN SHALL RAGE BOUND WITH THIS CHAIN THE WORM    323 FOUR ZOAS 7          143
        IN SILENCE CREEP
    THAT CREEP ABOUT THE OBSCURE PLACES SHEW THEIR VARIOUS  377 FOUR ZOAS 9        765
        LIMBS
    THAT CREEP AROUND THE OBSCURE PLACES SHEW THEIR VARIOUS  513 MILTON 27          28
        LIMBS
    JERUSALEM IS THEIR DAUGHTER LITTLE INFANTS CREEP OUT OF THE  609B V LAST JUDG/N PROSE
    WHERE THE INFANTS CREEP OUT OF THE GROUND  . . . . .  . 610C V LAST JUDG/N     PROSE
    TILL INTO NARROW FORMS YOU CREEP GO TAKE YOUR FIERY WAY  655 JERUSALEM 29       70
CREEPING
    IS IT A LITTLE CREEPING ROOT THAT GROWS IN DITCHES  . .  . 28 EDW THIRD/PS 4    11
    THAT THOU SHALT FEEL WORMS IN THY MARROW CREEPING THRO  107 TIRIEL 6           21
        THY BONES
    A WORM OF SIXTY WINTERS CREEPING ON THE DUSKY GROUND  . 110 TIRIEL 8           24
    SUCH IS SELF-LOVE THAT ENVIES ALL A CREEPING SKELETON  . 194 V DAU ALBION 7     21
    CREEPING IN REPTILE FLESH UPON . . . . . . . .  . 246 SONG OF LOS 4            9
    NOR MAN NOR BEAST NOR CREEPING THING NOR SUN NOR CLOUD  319 FOUR ZOAS 6        285
        NOR STAR
    [WITH] BY BEASTS & WORMS & CREEPING THINGS & DARKNESS &  373 FOUR ZOAS 9       596
        DESPAIR
    CREEPING IN REPTILE FLESH UPON THE BOSOM OF THE GROUND  . 484 MILTON 5          20
    THEREFORE HE APPEARS ONLY A SMALL ROOT CREEPING IN GRASS  526 MILTON 35         56
    CREEPING IN REPTILE FLESH UPON THE BOSOM OF THE GROUND  . 680 JERUSALEM 49      33
    IF HE HAD BEEN [THE] ANTICHRIST CREEPING JESUS  . . .  . 750 EV GOSPEL(C)/N     25
    IF HE HAD BEEN [THE] ANTICHRIST CREEPING JESUS  . . .  . 752 EV GOSPEL(D)/N     59
    BY THE ROCK & OAK OF THE DRUID CREEPING MISTLETOE & THORN  781 GHOST ABEL 2     16
    THE YEA NAY CREEPING JESUS FROM SUPPOSING UP & DOWN  . . . 878B LETTER 88      PROSE
CREEPS
    COLD DEWS & HOARY FROST CREEPS THO I LIE ON BANKS OF SUMMER  288 FOUR ZOAS 2  * 320
    REAR ON THE MOUNTAINS STEM AFTER STEM THE SCALY     373 FOUR ZOAS 9            606
        NEWT CREEPS
    CREEPS ROUND OUR SECRET NEST FLOCKS BRIGHTEN THE MOUNTAINS  373 FOUR ZOAS 9    611
    WHO CREEPS INTO STATE GOVERNMENT LIKE A CATTERPILLER TO  533 MILTON 41          11
        DESTROY
    THAT CREEPS FORTH IN A NIGHT & IS DRIED IN THE MORNING SUN  659 JERUSALEM 33     7
CREP
    HE WALKS & STUMBLES AS IF HE CREP  . . . . . . . .  . 548 CRIPPLE EVRY/N        8
CREPT
    CREPT IN THE SKELETON IN THE DEN NAMD RELIGION . . .  . 135 FRENCH REVOLTN     35
    . . . A DARKNESS CREPT OVER HIS EYE-LIDS AND CHILL COLD  147 FRENCH REVOLTN    295
        SWEAT
    FOR THE DEVIL CREPT IN WHEN THE FAIRY SKIPD OUT  . . . . 434 LONG JOHN BRWN    19
    BUT HE CREPT IN AT MYRA'S POCKET HOLE  . . . . . .  . 557 TO CHLOES/N           2
CRESSEY
    SCENE AT CRESSEY SIR THOMAS DAGWORTH AND LORD AUDLEY  21C EDW THIRD/PS 3 *PROSE
        MEETING
```

		PAGE	TITLE	LINE

CRESSY
```
    NOW HERE WE ARE AT CRESSY WHERE TO-MORROW  . . . . . .     22 EDW THIRD/PS 3      21
    WELCOME TO THE FIELDS OF CRESSY HERE WE STOP  . . . . .     22 EDW THIRD/PS 3      44
    HERE ON THE FIELDS OF CRESSY WE ARE SETTLED  . . . . .      24 EDW THIRD/PS 3     111
    AND REAP RICH HARVEST IN THE FIELDS OF CRESSY  . . . . .    24 EDW THIRD/PS 3     137
    COMMISSIOND TO THIS FATAL FIELD OF CRESSY  . . . . . . .    26 EDW THIRD/PS 3     223
    BUT NEVER TILL THIS FATAL DAY OF CRESSY . . . . . . . .     31 EDW THIRD/PS 5      41
```
CREST
```
    A FIERY CREST ABOVE THE WAVES SLOWLY IT REARED LIKE A RIDGE 156C MARRIAGE HH 17   PROSE
    WRITHING IN PANGS OF ABHORRED BIRTH RED FLAMES THE CREST   199 AMERICA 9           17
      REBELLIOUS
    THY EYELIDS ARE A TERROR TO ME & THE FLAMING OF THY CREST  335 FOUR ZOAS 7B        83
    A CREST OF FIRE ROSE ON HIS FOREHEAD RED AS THE CARBUNCLE  342 FOUR ZOAS 8         69
```
CRESTED
```
    THE SPECTRE REFUSES HE SEEKS CRUELTY THEY CREATE          515 MILTON 28           24
      THE CRESTED COCK
```
CRESTS
```
    METHINKS I SEE THEM PERCH ON ENGLISH CRESTS  . . . . .     26 EDW THIRD/PS 3     229
```
CREVICE
```
    THE NEGRO IN THE CREVICE OF THE ROCK  . . . . . . . .      24 EDW THIRD/PS 3     120
    FROM THE STONE & THE ARMED FLY SPRINGS FROM THE ROCKY     373 FOUR ZOAS 9        607
      CREVICE
```
CREW
```
    SATAN & ALL HIS HELLISH CREW  . . . . . . . . . . .       749 EV GOSPEL(B)/N      51
    A GENIUS DRIVING AWAY "COMUS & HIS MIDNIGHT CREW"  . . .  SUPP ILLUS GRAY       *TITLE
```
CRICKETS
```
    A RIDDLE OR THE CRICKET'S CRY  . . . . . . . . . . .      433 AUGURIES           103
```
CRIED   SEE CRYD
```
    I BOUND THEE WITH THEM TO TRY THY TRUTH I CRIED  . . . .   39A SAMSON/PS         PROSE
    I DID EVEN THAT TO TRY THY TRUTH BUT WHEN I CRIED  . . .   39B SAMSON/PS         PROSE
    GRANT ME A SON KIND HEAVEN MANOA CRIED BUT HEAVEN REFUSED  39C SAMSON/PS         PROSE
    WOE CRIED THE MUSE TEARS STARTED AT THE SOUND . . . . .    43B WOE CRIED MUSE    PROSE
    WHAT DOES THIS MEAN I CRIED  . . . . . . . . . . . .       43B WOE CRIED MUSE    PROSE
    HE SAW THE PESTILENCE FLY OUT OF THE BOTTLE & CRIED OUT    58D ISLAND MOON 10    PROSE
    THE BLIND MAN FELT HIS WAY & CRIED PEACE TO THESE OPEN    101 TIRIEL 2            13
      DOORS
    THERES LITTLE TOM DACRE WHO CRIED WHEN HIS HEAD  . . . .  117 CHIMNEY SWP/SI       5
    . . . AND CRIED OUT ALOUD  . . . . . . . . . . . .       146 FRENCH REVOLTN      260
    AND BOSTON'S ANGEL CRIED ALOUD AS THEY FLEW THRO THE DARK 200 AMERICA 11           3
      NIGHT
    HE CRIED WHY TREMBLES HONESTY AND LIKE A MURDERER  . . .  200 AMERICA 11           4
    SO CRIED HE RENDING OFF HIS ROBE & THROWING DOWN  . . .   200 AMERICA 12           1
      HIS SCEPTER
    AND CRIED IN BITTERNESS OF SOUL  . . . . . . . . .        247 SONG OF LOS 6        8
    AND THE VOICE CRIED AH URIZEN LOVE  . . . . . . . .       254 AHANIA 4            52
    URIZEN STARTLED STOOD BUT NOT LONG SOON HE CRIED  . . .   273 FOUR ZOAS 1        335
    HE CRIED OUT TO HIS FATHER DEPART DEPART BUT SUDDEN SIEZD 275 FOUR ZOAS 1        411
    IN WATERS & IN EARTH BENEATH THEY CRIED TO ONE ANOTHER .  283 FOUR ZOAS 2        123
    ROCKD TO & FRO & [&] CRIED SORE AT THE GROANS OF ENITHARMON 306 FOUR ZOAS 5   *   29
    THE [DISMAL] ACCURSED CHAIN O HOW BRIGHT ENITHARMON HOWLD 308 FOUR ZOAS 5        102
      & CRIED
    THEN ORC [ANSWERD] CRIED CURSE THY COLD HYPOCRISY  . . .  323 FOUR ZOAS 7        135
    URIZEN SAW & TRIUMPHD & HE CRIED TO [THE SHADOWY FEMALE]  333 FOUR ZOAS 7B         3
      HIS WARRIORS
    SO CRIED THE DEMON OF THE WATERS IN THE CLOUDS OF LOS  . . 334 FOUR ZOAS 7B       72
    SO ENITHARMON CRIED UPON HER TERRIBLE EARTHY BED  . . . . 335 FOUR ZOAS 7B       98
    CRIED TO THE CHURCHYARDS & THE EARTHWORM CAME IN DISMAL   355 FOUR ZOAS 9        537
      STATE
    BOWING HIS HEAD OVER THE CONSUMING UNIVERSE HE CRIED  . . 359 FOUR ZOAS 9         98
    THE ETERNAL MAN SAT ON THE ROCKS & CRIED WITH AWFUL VOICE 360 FOUR ZOAS 9        123
    THEN WRATH BURST ROUND THE ETERNAL MAN WAS WRATH AGAIN    360 FOUR ZOAS 9        137
      HE CRIED
    CRIED TIMES ARE ENDED HE EXULTED HE AROSE IN JOY HE EXULTED 372 FOUR ZOAS 9      568
    CRIED OUT TO BE DELIVERD & THE SPIRIT OF LUVAH WEPT  . . . 372 FOUR ZOAS 9       575
    SHE FORGOT IT WAS NIGHT & SHE TREMBLED & CRIED  . . . .   429 MARY                38
    AND LOS STOOD & CRIED TO THE LABOURERS OF THE VINTAGE IN  510 MILTON 25           16
      VOICE OF AWE
    WHICH GAINED THAT PATRONAGE CRIED DOWN AS ECCENTRICITY  . 572D DESC CAT 3        PROSE
    FROM HIS AWFUL MEMBERS AND THUS LOS CRIED ALOUD  . . . .  660 JERUSALEM 34        21
    SO CRIED THEY AT THE PLOW ALBION'S ROCK FROWNED ABOVE  . . 687 JERUSALEM 55       67
    HOW CAN THE FEMALE BE CHASTE O THOU STUPID DRUID CRIED LOS 697 JERUSALEM 63       26
    SO LOS CRIED IN THE VALLEYS OF MIDDLESEX IN THE SPIRIT    737 JERUSALEM 90        39
      OF PROPHECY
    SO LOS CRIED AT HIS ANVIL IN THE HORRIBLE DARKNESS WEEPING 738 JERUSALEM 91       32
    JOHN FROM THE WILDERNESS LOUD CRIED  . . . . . . . .      748 EV GOSPEL(B)/N      13
    CRIED OUT CRUCIFY CRUCIFY  . . . . . . . . . . . .        759 EV GOSPEL (2)       31
```
CRIES
```
    CRIES IN VAIN POOR LITTLE WRETCH THAT DEALST  . . . . .     3 TO WINTER/PS        14
    PREPARE FOR WAR HE CRIES . . . . . . . . . . . . .        12 GWIN KING/PS        62
    THE CRIES OF WOMEN AND OF BABES  . . . . . . . . . .      13 GWIN KING/PS        79
    HE SEES HE SEES CRIES SOFTLY GRACE  . . . . . . . .       16 BLIND-MANS/PS       40
    THEN CRIES OUT HEM HODGE HEARD AND RAN  . . . . . . .     16 BLIND-MANS/PS       49
    WHEN THE CRIES OF BLOOD TEAR HORROR FROM HEAVN  . . . .   18 EDW THIRD/PS 1        7
    BLOOD CRIES AFAR THE LAND DOTH SOW ITSELF  . . . . . .    34B KING JOHN/PS       PROSE
    FOR TYRANNY HATH STRETCHD HIS PURPLE ARM AND BLOOD HE CRIES 34B KING JOHN/PS     PROSE
    BY THE SLEEVE CRIES PRAY SIR WHO DO ALL THEY BELONG TO  . 45A ISLAND MOON 1      PROSE
    [THIS QUID CRIES OUT MISS GITTIPIN]  . . . . . . . .      57A ISLAND MOON 9      PROSE
    AND CAUGHT HIM BY THE GARMENTS WEEPING WITH CRIES OF BITTER 106 TIRIEL 5          19
      WOE
    CHAIND IN THICK DARKNESS UTTERD CRIES OF MOURNING ALL THE 107 TIRIEL 5           28
      NIGHT
    HOPING TO END HER [LIFE] WOES BUT FROM HER CRIES THE TYGERS 109 TIRIEL 7         17
      FLED
```

411

```
                                                              PAGE      TITLE            LINE
CRIES    (CONTINUED)
    WERE FRIGHTED BY THE DISMAL CRIES OF HELA ON THE MOUNTAINS   109 TIRIEL 7            20
    AND PITYING THE TENDER CRIES  . . . . . . . . . .         119 NIGHT/SI             35
    AGAIN THE LOUD VOICE OF FRANCE CRIES TO THE MORNING . . .    134 FRENCH REVOLTN       15
    . . . URGD BY CRIES IN DAY AND PROPHETIC DREAMS HOVERING     138 FRENCH REVOLTN       98
        IN NIGHT
    . . . AND CRIES OF WOMEN AND BABES ARE HEARD  . . . . .    139 FRENCH REVOLTN      118
    . . . AND CRIES OF THE VIRGIN IN NIGHT  . . . . . . .      140 FRENCH REVOLTN      147
    [AND] HOLY & MEEK SHE CRIES  . . . . . . . . . . .       163 ASKED THIEF/N         4
    AT LENGTH IN TEARS & CRIES IMBODIED  . . . . . . . .      231 URIZEN 18             6
    AND ENITHARMON GROANS & CRIES IN ANGUISH AND DISMAY  . . .   245 EUROPE 15             8
    HOLY & MEEK SHE CRIES  . . . . . . . . . . . . .         261 ASKED THIEF           4
    NOR PITY THOU THE CRIES OF LUVAH LO THESE STARRY HOSTS  . .   273 FOUR ZOAS 1         327
    DISCORD BEGAN & YELLS & CRIES SHOOK THE WIDE FIRMAMENT  . .   278 FOUR ZOAS 1         518
    OF LOS ABSORBD IN DIRE REVENGE HE DRANK WITH JOY THE CRIES    302 FOUR ZOAS 4         191
    THEN DISCORD BEGAN [&] THEN YELLS & CRIES SHOOK THE WIDE      306 FOUR ZOAS 5       *  45
        (FIRMAMENT)
    MY SONGS ARE TURNED [INTO] TO CRIES OF LAMENTATION  . . .    310 FOUR ZOAS 5       * 206
    I SUNK WITH CRIES OF BLOOD ISSUING DOWNWARD IN THE VEINS      327 FOUR ZOAS 7         284
    BUT BLOOD & WOUNDS & DISMAL CRIES & CLARIONS OF WAR . . .    338 FOUR ZOAS 7B        205
    AND THUS AHANIA CRIES ALOUD TO THE CAVERNS OF THE GRAVE       353 FOUR ZOAS 8         492
    THUS CRIES AHANIA ENION REPLIES FROM THE CAVERNS OF THE       354 FOUR ZOAS 8         533
        GRAVE
    AND IN THE CRIES OF BIRTH & IN THE GROANS OF DEATH HIS        356 FOUR ZOAS 8         580
        VOICE
    HE LIFTS THE BLUE LAMPS OF HIS EYES & CRIES WITH HEAVENLY     359 FOUR ZOAS 9          97
        VOICE
    THE VOICES OF CHILDREN IN MY TENTS TO CRIES OF HELPLESS       360 FOUR ZOAS 9         111
        INFANTS
    STANDS IN THE FURIOUS AIR HE CRIES THE CHILDREN OF SIX        363 FOUR ZOAS 9         252
        THOUSAND YEARS
    ONE PLANET [CRIES] CALLS TO ANOTHER & ONE STAR ENQUIRES       364 FOUR ZOAS 9       * 261
        OF ANOTHER
    O MYSTERY FIERCE THARMAS CRIES BEHOLD THY END IS COME  . .   374 FOUR ZOAS 9         657
    SHE LIVES UPON HIS SHRIEKS & CRIES  . . . . . . . .      425 MENTAL TRAVLER       19
    A LITTLE SOUND IT UTTERS & ITS CRIES ARE FAINTLY HEARD  .     484 MILTON 5             26
    INTO A TABERNACLE AND FLEE WITH CRIES DOWN TO THE DEEPS       503 MILTON 20            48
    AND THESE ARE THE CRIES OF THE CHURCHES BEFORE THE TWO        506 MILTON 22            56
        WITNESSES
    THE DOUBLE DRUM DROWNS HOWLS & GROANS THE SHRILL             509 MILTON 24            65
        FIFE SHRIEKS & CRIES
    OF OG & PEALING LOUD THE CRIES OF THE VICTIMS OF FIRE  . .   528 MILTON 37            22
    SIR JOSHUA IN ASTONISHMENT CRIES OUT  . . . . . . .      548 CRIPPLE EVRY/N        3
    DRYDEN IN RHYME CRIES MILTON ONLY PLANND  . . . . . .     554 BLAKES APL/N 1        1
    WHO CRIES ALL ART IS A FRAUD & GENIUS A TRICK . . . . .    555 BLAKES APL/N 1       20
    DRYDEN IN RHYME CRIES MILTON ONLY PLANND  . . . . . .     555 BLAKES APL/N 2        5
    CRIES HOMER IS VERY MUCH IMPROVD BY POPE  . . . . . .     556 BLAKES APL/N 2       10
    DRYDEN IN RHYME CRIES MILTON ONLY PLANND  . . . . . .     595 BLAKES APOL/PA *      1
    ALBION'S MOUNTAINS RUN WITH BLOOD THE CRIES OF WAR & OF       623 JERUSALEM 5           6
        TUMULT
    LOS CRIES OBEY MY VOICE & NEVER DEVIATE FROM MY WILL  . .    629 JERUSALEM 10         29
    DELIGHTING IN CRIES & TEARS & CLOTHED IN HOLINESS           630 JERUSALEM 10         49
        & SOLITUDE
    THE VOICES OF CHILDREN IN HIS TENTS TO CRIES OF HELPLESS      641 JERUSALEM 19         12
        INFANTS
    THE ARMIES I HEAR THEIR LOUD CYMBALS & THEIR DEADLY CRIES     644 JERUSALEM 21         47
    BROODING IN HOLY HYPOCRITIC LUST DRINKING THE CRIES OF PAIN   672 JERUSALEM 43         17
    LOUD THE CRIES OF WAR ON THE RHINE & DANUBE WITH ALBION'S     677 JERUSALEM 47          9
        SONS
    HARK THE MINGLING CRIES OF LUVAH WITH THE SONS OF ALBION      677 JERUSALEM 47         13
    A LITTLE SOUND IT UTTERS & ITS CRIES ARE FAINTLY HEARD  . .   680 JERUSALEM 49         41
    TO ASSIST IN THE WORK THE LAMB BLEATS THE SEA-FOWL CRIES      692 JERUSALEM 59         49
    SHE CRIES THE HUMAN IS BUT A WORM & THOU O MALE THOU ART      698 JERUSALEM 64         12
    DERBY PEAK YAWND A HORRID CHASM AT THE CRIES OF GWENDOLEN     699 JERUSALEM 64         35
        & AT
    BUT BLOOD AND WOUNDS AND DISMAL CRIES AND SHADOWS OF THE      701 JERUSALEM 65         51
        OAK
    THE DAUGHTERS WEAVE THEIR WORK IN LOUD CRIES OVER THE ROCK    704 JERUSALEM 67         26
    RESOUND WITH CRIES OF VICTIMS SHOUTS & SONGS & DYING GROANS   723 JERUSALEM 80         49
    FILLING CUPS OF SILVER & CRYSTAL WITH SHRIEKS & CRIES WITH    723 JERUSALEM 80         81
        GROANS
    I HAVE HEARD JERUSALEM'S GROANS FROM VALA'S CRIES           725 JERUSALEM 82          1
        & LAMENTATIONS
    LOS CRIES NO INDIVIDUAL OUGHT TO APPROPRIATE TO HIMSELF       736 JERUSALEM 90         28
    SO LOS TERRIFIED CRIES TREMBLING & WEEPING & HOWLING         739 JERUSALEM 91         59
        BEHOLDING
    CRIES FOR VENGEANCE SACRIFICE ON SACRIFICE BLOOD ON BLOOD     780 GHOST ABEL 2          9
CRIME
    [AH THAT SWEET LOVE SHOULD BE THOUGHT A CRIME]  . . . .    176 SOFT SNOW/N           4
    AND THE WINTER CALLD IT A DREADFUL CRIME  . . . . . .     176 SOFT SNOW/N           5
    LOVE SWEET LOVE WAS THOUGHT A CRIME  . . . . . . .       219 LIT GRL LST/SE        4
    CONFESSING THEIR CRIME WITH HUMILIATION AND SORROW  . . .    525 MILTON 35            33
    SOME BLUSH AT WHAT OTHERS CAN SEE NO CRIME IN . . . . .    555 BLAKES APL/N 1        8
    SOME BLUSH AT WHAT OTHERS CAN SEE NO CRIME IN . . . . .    555 BLAKES APL/N 2        3
    SOME BLUSH AT WHAT OTHERS CAN SEE NO CRIME IN . . . . .    595 BLAKES APOL/PA        5
    BECAUSE IGNORANT OF CRIME IN THE MIDST OF A CORRUPTED AGE    610B V LAST JUDG/N     PROSE
    EVERY EMANATIVE JOY FORBIDDEN AS A CRIME  . . . . . .     628 JERUSALEM 9           14
    AND EVERY ACT A CRIME AND ALBION THE PUNISHER & JUDGE  . .   652 JERUSALEM 28          4
    THAT THEY MAY CALL A [CRIME] SHAME & SIN  . . . . . .     755 EV GOSPEL(E)/N       63
    THAT WE ARE NOT ALL SUBJECT TO CRIME  . . . . . . .      865B LETTER 62           PROSE
    AS A CRIME IN WHICH I SHALL BE [A] THE PRINCIPAL . . . .    874B LETTER 79          PROSE
```

412

| | PAGE | TITLE | LINE |
| CRIMES |
| HINDER CRIMES OR CAN THE MAN WHO WRITES THE LATTER | 385C ANNO WATSON | MARG |
| SENTIMENT |
IF WE ARE TO EXPECT CRIMES FROM PAINE & HIS FOLLOWERS . .	385C ANNO WATSON	MARG
AND MILDLY CURSING PALAMABRON HIM ACCUSD OF CRIMES . . .	487 MILTON 7	36
ALL THESE ORNAMENTS ARE CRIMES THEY ARE MADE BY THE LABOURS	652 JERUSALEM 28	6
TILL THEY HAVE HAD PUNISHMENT ENOUGH TO MAKE THEM COMMIT	707 JERUSALEM 69	27
CRIMES
WHEN ALL THEIR CRIMES THEIR PUNISHMENTS THEIR ACCUSATIONS	739 JERUSALEM 92	15
OF SIN
IT IS THE GREATEST OF CRIMES TO DEPRESS TRUE ART & SCIENCE	863A LETTER 60	PROSE
CRIMINAL
AND HE WHO TAKES VENGEANCE ALONE IS THE CRIMINAL	657 JERUSALEM 31	32
OF PROVIDENCE
IT IS BETTER TO PREVENT ERROR THAN TO FORGIVE THE CRIMINAL	687 JERUSALEM 55	50
EVERY HARLOT WAS ONCE A VIRGIN EVERY CRIMINAL AN INFANT	695 JERUSALEM 61	52
LOVE
A KIND OF CRIMINAL DISSIPATION & NEGLECT OF THE MAIN CHANCE	798C LETTER 10	PROSE
CRIMINALS
CHRIST'S CRUCIFIX SHALL BE MADE AN EXCUSE FOR EXECUTING	380A FOUR ZOAS NOTE	PROSE
CRIMINALS
AND CRIMINALS TO SACRIFICES TURND	543 IF TRUE/N	15
DOES FORGIVE SIN IS CRUCIFIED AS AN ABETTOR OF CRIMINALS	616C V LAST JUDG/N	PROSE
WHAT SHALL I DO WHAT COULD I DO IF I COULD FIND THESE	657 JERUSALEM 31	29
CRIMINALS
CRIMSON
WITH CRIMSON DROPS HE STAINS THE GROUND	17 BLIND-MANS/PS	53
FOR ALBION'S SINS ARE CRIMSON DYD	344 KING JOHN/PS	PROSE
CLOTHD IN FLAMES OF CRIMSON	138 FRENCH REVOLTN	86
TILL OUR PURPLE AND CRIMSON IS FADED TO RUSSET	138 FRENCH REVOLTN	92
STILL RETAIN THEIR OWN CRIMSON	142 FRENCH REVOLTN	189
GOLDEN ROCKS TILL WE DISCOVERD TWO GLOBES OF CRIMSON FIRE	156C MARRIAGE HH 17	PROSE
OF CRIMSON JOY	175 SICK ROSE/N	6
THY CRIMSON DISK SO EER THE SUN WAS RENT FROM THY	198 AMERICA 5	5
RED SPHERE
OF CRIMSON JOY	213 SICK ROSE/SE	6
[BRIGHT] DARK AS A DEWY MORNING WHEN THE CRIMSON LIGHT	271 FOUR ZOAS 1	* 253
APPEARS
[THE] BUT PURPLE NIGHT [THE] AND CRIMSON MORNING . . .	274 FOUR ZOAS 1	* 366
NONE DARE TO WAKE HER SOON SHE BURSTS HER CRIMSON CURTAIND	520 MILTON 31	57
BED
CRIMSON WITH WRATH & GREEN WITH JEALOUSY DAZLING WITH LOVE	699 JERUSALEM 64	28
THAT DROP WITH CRIMSON GORE WITH THE LOVES OF ALBION &	699 JERUSALEM 64	37
CANAAN
THENCE FEATHERD WITH SOFT CRIMSON OF THE RUBY BRIGHT AS	731 JERUSALEM 86	8
FIRE
CRIPPLE
THE CRIPPLE EVERY STEP DRUDGES & LABOURS	548 CRIPPLE EVRY/N	1
LIKE A CRIPPLE WHILE THE CRIPPLE MUST BE TAUGHT TO WALK	600A PUB ADDRESS/N	PROSE
CRIPPLED
I THINK OF THE CRIPPLED HARRY & SLOBBERING JOE	550 WHEN I SEE/N	2
CRISPED
I WILL GO MAD AND TEAR MY CRISPED HAIR I'LL RUN ABOUT . .	38C SAMSON/PS	PROSE
CRITERION
IF CONSCIENCE IS NOT A CRITERION OF MORAL RECTITUDE WHAT	386A ANNO WATSON	MARG
IS IT
WITHOUT A MORAL CRITERION OTHER THAN NATIVE HONESTY	414A ANNO BOYD	MARG
UNTAUGHT
BUT A FOOL'S EYE IS NOT TO BE A CRITERION	448C ANNO REYNOLDS	MARG
A FOOL'S BALANCE IS NO CRITERION BECAUSE	476B ANNO REYNOLDS	MARG
THE VALUE OF THIS ARTIST'S YEAR IS THE CRITERION OF SOCIETY	587A CHAUCER 1	PROSE
CRITIC
BUT THE CRITIC MUST BE A FOOL WHO HAS NOT READ DANTE . .	864B LETTER 61	PROSE
ON ACCOUNT OF THAT VERY COLOURING WHICH OUR CRITIC CALLS	864C LETTER 61	PROSE
BLACK
CRITICAL
WITH THE FINEST ENGRAVINGS & DEFY THE MOST CRITICAL JUDGE	602A PUB ADDRESS/N	PROSE
CRITICISE
& TRANSLATE & COPY & BUY & SELL & CRITICISE BUT NOT MAKE	778D HOMERS POETRY	PROSE
CRITICISM
IMITATION IS CRITICISM	453C ANNO REYNOLDS	MARG
CRITICISM IN BELL'S WEEKLY MESSENGER...MAY ON THE PICTURE	863D LETTER 61	PROSE
UNDER PRETENCE OF FAIR CRITICISM AND CANDOUR	864A LETTER 61	PROSE
UNDER PRETENCE OF CRITICISM USE THE DAGGER AND THE POISON	864A LETTER 61	PROSE
MY CRITICISM ON THIS PICTURE IS AS FOLLOWS MR	864A LETTER 61	PROSE
CRITICISMS
HE HAS SENT IT BACK WITH A LETTER FULL OF CRITICISMS . .	794D LETTER 6	*PROSE
ILL-JUDGED CRITICISMS IN FUTURE YOURS	864D LETTER 61	PROSE
CRITICS
THAT I MAY SET CERTAIN MISTAKEN CRITICS RIGHT IN THEIR . .	569A DESC CAT 3	PROSE
BEAUTIES NOW GENTLEMEN CRITICS HOW DO YOU LIKE THIS . . .	603B PUB ADDR AD/N	PROSE
BUT WHAT CRITICS CALL THE FABLE IS VISION ITSELF . . .	604D V LAST JUDG/N	PROSE
INSANITY AND FURY AND WHATEVER PALTRY COLD HEARTED CRITICS	864B LETTER 61	PROSE
CROAK
. . . OR CROAK ON THE AWFUL KNEE	147 FRENCH REVOLTN	298
CROAKINGS
FOR VOICES OF DELIGHT HOARSE CROAKINGS INARTICULATE THRO	312 FOUR ZOAS 6	39
FROST
CROCODILE
NUMBER OF THE DOG & CROCODILE & THAT OF THE DOG DEFENDING	859B LETTER 56	PROSE
CROMEK
OR ANGRY WITH FLAXMAN OR CROMEK OR STOTHARD	538 WAS I ANGRY/N	4

```
                                                             PAGE     TITLE        LINE
CROMEK    (CONTINUED)
    CR(CROMEK) LOVES ARTISTS AS HE LOVES HIS MEAT . . . . .  540 CR LOVES ART/N       1
    [CR(CROMEK)] HE LOVES THE ART BUT [THE] TIS THE ART TO   540 CR LOVES ART/N *     2
      CHEAT
    O MR CR(CROMEK) HOW DO YE DO . . . . . . . . . . . . .   540 PETTY SNEAK/N        2
    [MR CROMEK TO] MR STOTHARD TO MR CROMEK . . . . . . .  541A MR STOTHARD/N     TITLE
    MR CROMEK TO MR STOTHARD . . . . . . . . . . . . . .   541B MR CROMEK/N       TITLE
    CROMEK SPEAKS . . . . . . . . . . . . . . . . . . . . 549B CROMEK SPEAK/N     TITLE
    THUS POOR SCHIAVONETTI DIED OF THE CROMEK . . . . . . .  555 BLAKES APL/N 1      10
    THUS POOR SCHIAVONETTI DIED OF THE CROMEK . . . . . . .  556 BLAKES APL/N 2      19
    MR CROMEK THE ENGRAVER CAME TO ME DESIRING TO HAVE SOME 861C LETTER 59        PROSE
    TO PROMOTE THE SPIRITED EXERTIONS OF MY FRIEND CROMEK . 861D LETTER 59        PROSE
CROMEK'S
    ENGLISH ENCOURAGEMENT OF ART CROMEK'S OPINIONS PUT INTO 549C ENGL ENCOU/N 1   TITLE
      RHYME
CROMWELL
    CHARLES CALLS ON MILTON FOR ATONEMENT CROMWELL IS READY  485 MILTON 5           39
CROMWELL'S
    FROM RANELAGH & STRUMBOLO FROM CROMWELLS GARDENS & CHELSEA 627 JERUSALEM 8        2
CROOK
    THE PILGRIM WITH HIS CROOK & HAT . . . . . . . . . . .    54 PHEBE DREST/IM      11
    IN HIS RIGHT HAND HIS HAMMER THARMAS HELD HIS SHEPHERD'S 377 FOUR ZOAS 9        776
      CROOK
CROOKD
    . . . STRETCH OUT HIS CROOKD SICKLE OER FERTILE FRANCE . 138 FRENCH REVOLTN      91
    ME TIME HAS CROOKD NO GOOD WORKMAN . . . . . . . . . .   555 FRM CRATELOS/N       1
CROOKED
    AS A STRAIT LINE & A CROOKED ONE SECONDLY I I I . . . . 45D ISLAND MOON 1      PROSE
    AND FORMD A CROOKED KNIFE . . . . . . . . . . . . . .    50 WHEN CORRUP/IM      14
    OR NATURE'S HAND HAS CROOKED HER FRAME . . . . . . . .    56 HAIL MATRIM/IM      14
    BUT THE CROOKED ROADS WITHOUT IMPROVEMENT ARE ROADS OF 152D MARRIAGE HH 10    PROSE
      GENIUS
    OF CROOKED HUMPY WOMAN . . . . . . . . . . . . . . .    464 ANNO REYNOLDS        2
    THAN BOULSTERD PLASTERS ON A CROOKED WHORE . . . . . .  464 ANNO REYNOLDS        2
    THE CROOKED HORN MELLOWS THE HOARSE RAVING SERPENT . . . 509 MILTON 24          66
    [A CROOKED STICK & LOUZY HEAD OF HAIR] . . . . . . . .  540 SIR JOSH RUB/N       7
    AS CROOKED LIMBS & LOUZY HEADS OF HAIR . . . . . . . .  540 SIR JOSH RUB/N       8
    STRAIT OR CROOKED IT IS ITSELF & NOT INTERMEASURABLE WITH 878B LETTER 88       PROSE
      OR
CROP
    "MY CROP OF CORN IS BUT A FIELD OF TARES" . . . . . .   52B ISLAND MOON 8
    THE GOBLIN CROP FULL FLINGS OUT OF DOORS FROM . . . . . 618C ILLUS MILTON      PROSE
CROPS
    HE CROPS THY FLOWERS WHILE THOU SITTEST SMILING IN HIS FACE 128 BOOK OF THEL 2     6
CROSS
    [SHE] JERUSALEM SAW THE BODY DEAD UPON THE CROSS SHE FLED 349 FOUR ZOAS 8        331
      AWAY
    LOS TOOK THE BODY FROM THE CROSS JERUSALEM WEEPING OVER  349 FOUR ZOAS 8        338
    DOWN FROM THE CROSS & PLACD IT IN A SEPULCHER WHICH LOS  356 FOUR ZOAS 8        594
      HAD HEWN
    [&] IN [THE] MIDST IS THE CROSS . . . . . . . . . . . 444B LAST JUDGMNT/L *PROSE
    CHRIST TOOK ON SIN IN THE VIRGIN'S WOMB & PUT IT OFF ON  484 MILTON 5            3
      THE CROSS
    BECOMING OBEDIENT TO DEATH EVEN THE DEATH OF THE CROSS   506 MILTON 22          58
    TO TOUCH EACH OTHER & RECEDE TO CROSS & CHANGE & RETURN  512 MILTON 26           6
    NAIL HIS NECK TO THE CROSS NAIL IT WITH A NAIL . . . .   557 NAIL NECK/N         1
    NAIL HIS NECK TO THE CROSS YE ALL HAVE POWER OVER HIS TAIL 557 NAIL NECK/N        2
    WHOSE BULK NAILD TO THE CROSS ROUND WHICH HE WREATHES . 606C V LAST JUDG/N    PROSE
    DEATH IS CHAIND TO THE CROSS & TIME FALLS TOGETHER WITH 606C V LAST JUDG/N    PROSE
      DEATH
    TAKE UP THE CROSS O ISRAEL & FOLLOW JESUS . . . . . . 652B JERUSALEM 27       PROSE
    THE CROSS O ALBION WHY DIDST THOU A FEMALE WILL CREATE .  688 JERUSALEM 56      43
    JERUSALEM FAINTED OVER THE CROSS & SEPULCHER SHE HEARD   695 JERUSALEM 61      49
      THE VOICE
    THO DIVIDED BY THE CROSS & NAILS & THORNS & SPEAR . . .  734 JERUSALEM 89       1
    TILL HE HAD NAILD IT TO THE CROSS . . . . . . . . . .   749 EV GOSPEL(B)/N     54
    [AND ON THE CROSS HE SEALD ITS DOOM] . . . . . . . . .  749 EV GOSPEL(B)/N     56
    AND PUT IT OFF ON THE CROSS & TOMB . . . . . . . . . .  749 EV GOSPEL(B)/N *   58
    THOU ON THE CROSS FOR THEM SHALT PRAY . . . . . . . .   751 EV GOSPEL(C)/N     47
    THOU ON THE CROSS FOR THEM SHALT PRAY . . . . . . . .   753 EV GOSPEL(D)/N     83
    FORMED THE CROSS & NAILS & SPEAR . . . . . . . . . . .  759 EV GOSPEL (2)      29
    MUST THE DUTIES OF LIFE EACH OTHER CROSS . . . . . . .  817 HAPPINESS/L        43
    LET US GO ON DEAR SIR FOLLOWING HIS CROSS LET US TAKE  863B LETTER 60        PROSE
      IT UP
CROST
    FOR [SOON] EARLY I IN LOVE WAS CROST . . . . . . . .    184 O I CANNOT/N   *    3
CROUCH
    CROUCH HOWLING BEFORE THEIR CAVERNS DEEP LIKE SKINS DRYD 199 AMERICA 9          4
      IN THE WIND
CROUD
    AFTER NIGHT I DO CROUD . . . . . . . . . . . . . . .      9 MAD SONG/PS        19
    . . . AROUND HIM CROUD WEEPING IN HIS BURNING ROBE . .   138 FRENCH REVOLTN     87
CROW
    COCK DOES CROW . . . . . . . . . . . . . . . . . . .    123 SPRING/SI          14
    TO LEARN OF THE CROW . . . . . . . . . . . . . . . . 151D MARRIAGE HH 8      PROSE
    THE CROW WISHD EVERY THING WAS BLACK . . . . . . . .  152D MARRIAGE HH 10    PROSE
    AND WOULD BE A [CROW] COCK IF HE COULD . . . . . . . .  540 COCK WOULD/N   *    2
CROWD
    AND MYRIADS SHALL TO HER TEMPLES CROWD . . . . . . .   34C KING JOHN/PS      PROSE
CROWE
    CATALANI DU CROWE & DILBURY DOODLE . . . . . . . . . 548B ON GREAT ENC/N     TITLE
```

```
                                                            PAGE    TITLE            LINE
CROWN
    THY GOLDEN CROWN UPON HER LANGUISHD HEAD    . . . . . .    1 TO SPRING/PS          15
    THY BRIGHT TORCH OF LOVE THY RADIANT CROWN  . . . . . .    3 EVNING STAR/PS         3
    AND THOU MY SON BE STRONG THOU FIGHTEST FOR A CROWN  . . . 18 EDW THIRD/PS 1       21
    A CROWN OF GLORY BUT FROM THY VERY DUST  . . . . . . .    18 EDW THIRD/PS 1       23
    CROWND WITH TRIPLE CROWN THEN PRIDE WAS BETTER PLEASD  .  41B THEN SHE BORE     PROSE
    THY CROWN IS BALD OLD MAN THE SUN WILL DRY THY BRAINS AWAY 109 TIRIEL 7           12
    ON HIS HEAD A CROWN  . . . . . . . . . . . .            114 LIT GRL FND/SI      37
    WEAVE THY BROWS AN INFANT CROWN  . . . . . . . . .      120 CRADLE SONG/SI       6
    AND I HAVE GIVEN THEE A CROWN THAT NONE CAN TAKE AWAY  . . 129 BOOK OF THEL 5      4
    . . . THE CROWN VANISH AND THE SCEPTER AND IVORY STAFF  . . 140 FRENCH REVOLTN    144
    THE RED ROBE OF TERROR THE CROWN OF OPPRESSION . . . . . 144 FRENCH REVOLTN     222
    AND WE WILL CROWN THY HEAD WITH GARLANDS OF THE RUDDY VINE 239 EUROPE 4           26
    MY DEEP MY NIGHT WHICH THOU ASSUMING HAST ASSUMD MY CROWN 278 FOUR ZOAS 1        511
    SHE CEASD THE PRINCE HIS LIGHT OBSCURD & THE SPLENDORS  292 FOUR ZOAS 3          12
        OF HIS CROWN
    HE GAVE TO ME A SILVER SCEPTER & CROWND ME WITH A GOLDEN 310 FOUR ZOAS 5         220
        CROWN
    THY CROWN & SCEPTER I WILL SIEZE & REGULATE ALL MY MEMBERS 360 FOUR ZOAS 9       145
    AND ALL THE MARKS REMAIN OF THE SLAVE'S SCOURGE & TYRANT'S 363 FOUR ZOAS 9       246
        CROWN
    HIS CROWN OF THORNS FELL FROM HIS HEAD HE HUNG HIS LIVING 376 FOUR ZOAS 9        711
        LYRE
    [PITY] CROWN WITH WINE MY MOURNFUL HEAD . . . . . . .   416 MY SPECTRE/N     *   44
    CAME FROM CAESAR'S LAUREL CROWN  . . . . . . . . .      433 AUGURIES            98
    ARMED IN GLITTERING SCALES WITH A CROWN & A SPEAR  . . . 780C GHOST ABEL 2      PROSE
    A CROWN OF LAURELS & I ALSO THANK YOU FOR YOUR REPREHENSION 804A LETTER 16      PROSE
CROWND
    CROWND WITH TRIPLE CROWN THEN PRIDE WAS BETTER PLEASD  .  41B THEN SHE BORE     PROSE
    . . . IN FOLDS OF THE ROBE THE CROWND ADDER BUILDS AND  147 FRENCH REVOLTN     299
        HISSES
    CROWND WITH WARLIKE FIRES & RAGING DESIRES  . . . . .   177 DAY/N                5
    CROWND WITH A HELMET & DARK HAIR THE NAMELESS FEMALE STOOD 195 AMERICA PREL 1     4
    HEAVEN A MIGHTY CIRCLE TURNING GOD A TYRANT CROWND  . . . 241 EUROPE 10          23
    THE FEAST REDOUNDS & CROWND WITH ROSES & THE CIRCLING VINE 276 FOUR ZOAS 1       435
    AND AT MY BANQUETS OF NEW WINE MY HEAD WAS CROWND WITH JOY 310 FOUR ZOAS 5       201
    HE GAVE TO ME A SILVER SCEPTER & CROWND ME WITH A GOLDEN 310 FOUR ZOAS 5         220
        CROWN
    THY CHILDREN SMOTE THEIR FIERY WINGS CROWND WITH THE GOLD 311 FOUR ZOAS 5        229
        OF HEAVEN
    AMONG THEM IS A FIGURE CROWND WITH STARS  . . . . . .   443D LAST JUDGMNT/L *PROSE
    DRAGGED DOWN BY [AN ANGEL] A DEMON CROWND WITH LAUREL  . 606C V LAST JUDG/N    PROSE
    HE DRAGS SATAN DOWN HEADLONG HE IS CROWND WITH OAK  . . 607D V LAST JUDG/N     PROSE
    THIS STATE APPEARS LIKE A FEMALE CROWND WITH STARS  . . 610A V LAST JUDG/N     PROSE
    THREE FEMALE FIGURES CROWND WITH GARLANDS REPRESENT  . . 611D V LAST JUDG/N    PROSE
    YORK CROWND WITH LOVING KINDNESS EDINBURGH CLOTHD  . . . 665 JERUSALEM 38        51
    THEY TOOK THEIR MOTHER VALA AND THEY CROWND HER WITH GOLD 719 JERUSALEM 78       15
    AT THE MAN WHO WAS CROWND WITH GLORY & HONOUR  . . . . 813B LETTER 22          PROSE
CROWNED
    AND PLENTY CROWNED HIS BOARD BELOVED REVERED OF MAN  . . . 39C SAMSON/PS       PROSE
    A CROWNED KING  . . . . . . . . . . . . .               62 CROWND KING/IM        1
    W(WILLIAM) THE CONQR CROWNED  . . . . . . . . . .      208D SUBJCTS HIST/N    TITLE
    BUT THOU O SON WHOM I HAVE CROWNED AND INTHROND THEE STRONG 334 FOUR ZOAS 78  *  52
    A KING CROWNED GRASPING HIS SWORD & HIS SCEPTRE  . . . 608B V LAST JUDG/N     PROSE
    LISTEN HERMON & LEBANON BOW THEIR CROWNED HEADS  . . . . 730 JERUSALEM 85        17
CROWNS
    VESTS OF THE RADIANT COLOURS OF HEAVEN & CROWNS OF GOLDEN 312 FOUR ZOAS 6        28
        FIRE
    FOR CROWNS WREATHD SERPENTS FOR SWEET ODORS STINKING   312 FOUR ZOAS 6          38
        CORRUPTIBILITY
    FETTERS OF RED HOT IRON SOME WITH CROWNS OF SERPENTS & SOME 314 FOUR ZOAS 6     104
    THE THRONES OF KINGS ARE SHAKEN THEY HAVE LOST THEIR ROBES 357 FOUR ZOAS 9      18
        & CROWNS
    WHO SET PLEASURE AGAINST DUTY WHO CREATE OLYMPIC CROWNS 511 MILTON 25           51
    NURSING FATHERS & NURSING MOTHERS [THEY HAVE CROWNS]  . 613D V LAST JUDG/N     PROSE
CROWS      SEE SCARE-CROWS
    THE HOUSES OF MY HARPERS ARE BECOME A HAUNT OF CROWS  . . 310 FOUR ZOAS 5      195
    THE BIRDS OF SONG TO MURDEROUS CROWS MY JOYS TO BITTER  360 FOUR ZOAS 9        110
        GROANS
    THE BIRDS OF SONG TO MURDEROUS CROWS HIS JOYS TO BITTER 641 JERUSALEM 19        11
        GROANS
CRUCIFIED
    OVER THE SEPULCHER & OVER THE CRUCIFIED BODY  . . . . . 357 FOUR ZOAS 9          2
    ALL NATIONS LOOK UP TO THE CLOUD & BEHOLD HIM WHO  . . . 364 FOUR ZOAS 9        274
        WAS CRUCIFIED
    DOES FORGIVE SIN IS CRUCIFIED AS AN ABETTOR OF CRIMINALS 616C V LAST JUDG/N    PROSE
    O HUMAN IMAGINATION O DIVINE BODY I HAVE CRUCIFIED  . . . 647 JERUSALEM 24      23
    BUT WHEN JESUS WAS CRUCIFIED  . . . . . . . . .        755 EV GOSPEL(E)/N       91
CRUCIFIES
    THE MODERN CHURCH CRUCIFIES CHRIST WITH THE HEAD DOWNWARDS 615D V LAST JUDG/N  PROSE
CRUCIFIX
    CHRIST'S CRUCIFIX SHALL BE MADE AN EXCUSE FOR EXECUTING 380A FOUR ZOAS NOTE    PROSE
        CRIMINALS
CRUCIFY
    SHOULD CRUCIFY IN SATAN'S SYNAGOGUE  . . . . . . . .   650 FIELDS FROM/J        24
    CRYING [IVE FOUND HI] CRUCIFY THIS CAUSE OF DISTRESS  . . 755 EV GOSPEL(E)/N *  85
    CRIED OUT CRUCIFY CRUCIFY  . . . . . . . . . .         759 EV GOSPEL (2)        31
CRUCIFYING
    I HAVE EDUCATED YOU IN THE CRUCIFYING CRUELTIES OF  . . 648 JERUSALEM 24         55
        DEMONSTRATION
    CRUCIFYING & ENCOMPASSING SEA & LAND  . . . . . . .    718 STOOD AMONG/J         29
```

415

```
                                                        PAGE      TITLE          LINE
CRUEL
  O GHASTLY DEATH WITHDRAW THY CRUEL HAND . . . . . . .    5 FAIR ELENOR/PS       43
  HIS CRUEL SCEPTRE BORE  . . . . . . . . . . . . . .     11 GWIN KING/PS          4
  BEWARE O PROUD THOU SHALT BE HUMBLED THY CRUEL BROW  . . 34B KING JOHN/PS     PROSE
  ARE CRUEL AS DEATH & AS OBDURATE AS THE DEVOURING PIT    99 TIRIEL 1           15
  HIS BLESSING WAS A CRUEL CURSE HIS CURSE MAY BE A BLESSING  99 TIRIEL 1        18
  MY SONS HAVE LEFT ME DID THINE LEAVE THEE O TWAS VERY CRUEL 102 TIRIEL 3       18
  [O WE ARE BUT THE SLAVES OF FORTUNE & THAT MOST CRUEL MAN]  105 TIRIEL 4       77
  TWAS FOR THY SELF THOU CRUEL MAN BECAUSE THOU WANTEST EYES  107 TIRIEL 6       15
  TRUE [?HILI] HELA THIS IS THE DESERT OF ALL THOSE CRUEL   107 TIRIEL 6     *   16
    ONES
  IS TIRIEL CRUEL LOOK HIS DAUGHTER & HIS YOUNGEST DAUGHTER  107 TIRIEL 6       17
  O CRUEL O DESTROYER O CONSUMER O AVENGER    . . . . .    107 TIRIEL 6         23
  UNDER A CRUEL EYE OUTWORN . . . . . . . . . . . . .      124 SCHOOL BOY/SI      8
  [[CRUEL] SELFISH FATHER OF MEN] . . . . . . . . . . .    169 EARTHS ANSWR/N    11
  [CRUEL JEALOUS [WINTRY] SELFISH FEAR] . . . . . . . .    169 EARTHS ANSWR/N *  12
  [BURNT THE] [THE CRUEL] FIRE OF THINE EYES . . . . . .   172 THE TYGER/N 1      6
  THE CRUEL FIRE OF THINE EYES . . . . . . . . . . .       173 THE TYGER/N 2  *   6
  [IN A CRUEL IRON CHAIN] . . . . . . . . . . . . .        177 LIT BOY LST/N     23
  CRUEL JEALOUS SELFISH FEAR . . . . . . . . . . . .       211 EARTHS ANSR/SE    12
  IN PERVERSE AND CRUEL DELIGHT . . . . . . . . . . .      231 URIZEN 19
  BY CRUEL ENORMITIES FORMS . . . . . . . . . . . . .      234 URIZEN 20         50
  CRUEL JEALOUSY SELFISH FEAR . . . . . . . . . . .        255 AHANIA 5          41
  AND VALA FED IN CRUEL DELIGHT THE FURNACES WITH FIRE  .  282 FOUR ZOAS 2       73
  IN CRUEL DELIGHT THEY TRAP THE LISTENERS & IN CRUEL      284 FOUR ZOAS 2      162
    DELIGHT
  O CRUEL PITY O DARK DECEIT CAN LOVE SEEK FOR DOMINION .  . 293 FOUR ZOAS 3     78
  MINGLE TOGETHER TO CREATE A WORLD FOR LOS IN CRUEL DELIGHT 313 FOUR ZOAS 6     82
  THE BREAD IS KNEADED LET US REST O CRUEL FATHER OF CHILDREN 322 FOUR ZOAS 7   107
  CRUEL AND RAVENING WITH ENMITY & HATRED & WAR . . . . .  328 FOUR ZOAS 7      330
  WHEN I WAS A RAVNING HUNGRING & THIRSTING CRUEL LUST &   329 FOUR ZOAS 7    * 350
    MURDER
  BEARING HIS SORROWS & (?RECIEVING) ALL HIS CRUEL WOUNDS  349 FOUR ZOAS 8    * 324
  THE CRUEL JOY OF LUVAH'S DAUGHTERS LACERATING WITH KNIVES  377 FOUR ZOAS 9    753
  THE TENDER MERCIES OF SOME MEN ARE CRUEL  . . . . . .    398D ANNO BACON      MARG
  IT IS NOT TRUE WHAT A CRUEL MAN SAYS . . . . . . . .     409D ANNO BACON      MARG
  [?I] AND TO END THY CRUEL MOCKS . . . . . . . . . .      417 MY SPECTRE/N   *  63
  THEN BRINGS FORTH MORAL VIRTUE THE CRUEL VIRGIN BABYLON  484 MILTON 5          27
  OF MORAL LAWS AND CRUEL PUNISHMENTS UPON THE CLOUDS OF   489 MILTON 9          22
    JEHOVAH
  OUR VIRTUES & CRUEL GOODNESSES HAVE DESERVD ETERNAL DEATH  494 MILTON 13       34
  AND ALL PERFECTION IN HER CRUEL SPORTS AMONG THE VICTIMS  501 MILTON 19        45
  WITH CRUEL VIRTUE MAKING WAR UPON THE LAMB'S REDEEMED  .  506 MILTON 22        44
  CRUEL IN THY MILDNESS PITYING AND PERMITTING EVIL  . .   507 MILTON 23         19
  (?TO) THOR & CRUEL ODIN WHO FIRST REARD THE POLAR CAVES  511 MILTON 25      *  53
  THE CRUEL SCORPION IS THERE THE GNAT WASP HORNET & THE   513 MILTON 27         21
    HONEY BEE
  THE CRUEL JOYS OF LUVAH'S DAUGHTERS LACERATING WITH KNIVES  514 MILTON 27      35
  THE PLOW GOES FORTH IN TEMPESTS & LIGHTNINGS & THE HARROW  514 MILTON 27       47
    CRUEL
  AND CRUEL OPPOSITION ELEMENT AGAINST ELEMENT OPPOSED IN  520 MILTON 31         24
    WAR
  TO DISPLAY NATURE'S CRUEL HOLINESS THE DECEITS OF NATURAL  527 MILTON 36       25
    RELIGION
  NAMD MORAL VIRTUE CRUEL TWO-FOLD MONSTER SHINING BRIGHT  532 MILTON 40         21
  MOST CRUEL DEMON WHOSE WHOLE DELIGHT IS TO CAUSE . . .   583A DESC CAT 9     PROSE
  GREY BEARDS & SCOURGES OF FIRE THEY REPRESENT CRUEL LAWS  608A V LAST JUDG/N PROSE
  THE MAN STRANGLING TWO WOMEN REPRESENTS A CRUEL CHURCH . 608C V LAST JUDG/N  PROSE
  IS A VERY CRUEL BEING & BEING A WORSHIPPER OF CHRIST  .  617A V LAST JUDG/N  PROSE
  AND VALA FED IN CRUEL DELIGHT THE FURNACES WITH FIRE  .  625 JERUSALEM 7       31
  RAGAN IS WHOLLY CRUEL SCOFIELD IS BOUND IN IRON ARMOUR   631 JERUSALEM 11      21
  AND ITS FALLEN EMANATION THE SPECTRE & ITS CRUEL SHADOW  635 JERUSALEM 15       7
  IN HEAVY WREATHES FOLDS OVER EVERY NATION CRUEL WORKS  . 636 JERUSALEM 15      17
  CRUEL HIPOCRISY UNLIKE THE LOVELY DELUSIONS OF BEULAH    639 JERUSALEM 17      27
  AND CRUEL FORMS UNLIKE THE MERCIFUL FORMS OF BEULAH'S    639 JERUSALEM 17      28
    NIGHT
  REASONING & DEROGATION FROM ME AN OBJECTING & CRUEL SPITE  639 JERUSALEM 17    37
  IN JEALOUS FEAR IN STERN ACCUSATION WITH CRUEL STRIPES . . 644 JERUSALEM 21    29
  I SEE THEIR PITEOUS FACES GLEAM OUT UPON THE CRUEL WINDS  644 JERUSALEM 21      38
  ARE THE DEAD CRUEL ARE THOSE WHO ARE INFOLDED IN MORAL LAW  644 JERUSALEM 21   48
  HE DREW THE VEIL OF MORAL VIRTUE WOVEN FOR CRUEL LAWS  . 646 JERUSALEM 23      22
  OF EVER-HARDENING DESPAIR SQUARD & POLISHD WITH CRUEL SKILL  647 JERUSALEM 24  35
  LEST BABYLON WITH CRUEL OG . . . . . . . . . . .         650 FIELDS FROM/J     22
  THY CRUEL PATRIARCHAL PRIDE . . . . . . . . . . . .      651 FIELDS FROM/J     78
  IS TRUE & THEY WERE SEPARATED FROM HIM BY CRUEL SACRIFICES  652B JERUSALEM 27 PROSE
  AND WHEN COMPULSORY CRUEL SACRIFICES . . . . . . . .     652B JERUSALEM 27   PROSE
  O CRUEL PITY O DARK DECEIT CAN LOVE SEEK FOR DOMINION  . 654 JERUSALEM 29      60
  AND FILLD WITH CRUEL TORTURES BUT NO MORTAL MAN CAN FIND  666 JERUSALEM 39      4
    THE MILL
  MERCIFUL TO THEE AND CRUEL TO ALL THAT THOU HATEST  . .  670 JERUSALEM 42      22
  BECOME A NET & A TRAP & EVERY ENERGY RENDERD CRUEL  . .  672 JERUSALEM 43      26
  BY DEMONSTRATIONS THE CRUEL SONS OF QUALITY & NEGATION . 673 JERUSALEM 43      67
  IN CRUEL HOLINESS IN THEIR HEAVENS OF CHASTITY &        680 JERUSALEM 49      64
    UNCIRCUMCISION
  TO SIN IN THE OPEN FACE OF DAY IS CRUEL & PITILESS BUT . . 681 JERUSALEM 50    26
  FOR FEAR AT ENTERING THE GATE INTO OUR WORLD OF CRUEL  . 688 JERUSALEM 56      15
  THE STARS OF ALBION CRUEL RISE THOU BINDEST TO SWEET    693 JERUSALEM 60      60
    INFLUENCES
  THEY STAIND HIM WITH POISONOUS BLUE THEY INWOVE HIM IN   699 JERUSALEM 65       9
    CRUEL ROOTS
  OVER ALBION'S MOUNTAINS A FEMININE INDEFINITE CRUEL      701 JERUSALEM 65      67
    DELUSION
```

416

	PAGE	TITLE	LINE

CRUEL   (CONTINUED)

LABOUR UNPARALLELLD A WONDROUS ROCKY WORLD OF CRUEL DESTINY	702	JERUSALEM 66	6
THEIR CRUEL FINGERS FOR HIS HEART & THERE THEY ENTER IN POMP	702	JERUSALEM 66	23
THY SHRIEKS BECAUSE HAND & HYLE ARE CRUEL & OBDURATE TO ME	705	JERUSALEM 67	62
O SKOFIELD WHY ART THOU CRUEL LO JOSEPH IS THINE TO MAKE	705	JERUSALEM 68	1
THEREFORE THE MALE SEVERE & CRUEL FILLD WITH STERN REVENGE	708	JERUSALEM 69	36
VOLTAIRE INSINUATES THAT THESE LIMITS ARE THE CRUEL WORK OF GOD	713	JERUSALEM 73	29
BY CRUEL LAWS DIVIDED SIXTEEN INTO TWELVE DIVISIONS . . .	715	JERUSALEM 74	27
BUT THAT WHICH IS A SIN IN THE SIGHT OF CRUEL MAN IS NOT SO	717C	JERUSALEM 77	PROSE
MOUNT ZION IS BECOME A CRUEL ROCK & NO MORE DEW	719	JERUSALEM 79	4
WHICH OVERSPREAD ALL THE EARTH IN PATRIARCHAL POMP & CRUEL PRIDE	721	JERUSALEM 79	67
THESE CRUEL DRUID TEMPLES O VALA HUMANITY IS FAR ABOVE . .	721	JERUSALEM 79	73
IN CRUEL HOLINESS AND HER LAMENTING SONGS WERE FROM ARNON	722	JERUSALEM 80	8
THE CRUEL WARRIOR I HAVE REFUSED TO GIVE LOVE TO MERLIN THE PITEOUS	723	JERUSALEM 81	2
LET US LOOK LET US EXAMINE IS THE CRUEL BECOME AN INFANT	724	JERUSALEM 81	8
OR IS HE STILL A CRUEL WARRIOR LOOK SISTERS LOOK O PITEOUS	724	JERUSALEM 81	9
IN CRUEL PRIDE CUT REUBEN APART FROM THE HILLS OF SURREY	736	JERUSALEM 90	25
ALBION SAID O LORD WHAT CAN I DO MY SELFHOOD CRUEL . . .	743	JERUSALEM 96	8
WHERE IS THE TREE OF GOOD & EVIL THAT ROOTED BENEATH THE CRUEL HEEL	746	JERUSALEM 98	47
THEN DESCENDED THE CRUEL ROD	750	EV GOSPEL(C)/N	36
THEN DESCENDED THE CRUEL ROD	752	EV GOSPEL(D)/N	72
AND HIM THEIR CRUEL MURDERER TELL	757	EV GOSPEL(I)/N	40
"AH LUCKLESS BABE BORN UNDER CRUEL STAR" (SPENSER) . . .	SUPP	LEGEND/N19	*

CRUELLY

IN JEALOUSY & UNLOVELY IN MY SIGHT BECAUSE THOU HAST CRUELLY	522	MILTON 33	6
OF THE INJURER IN WHICH THE DIVINE LAMB IS CRUELLY SLAIN	648	JERUSALEM 25	11
THE WICKER MAN OF SCANDINAVIA IN WHICH CRUELLY CONSUMED	677	JERUSALEM 47	7

CRUEL—ONE

THE CRUEL—ONE OF ALBION TO CLOTHE HIM IN GEMS OF MY ZONE	724	JERUSALEM 81	12

CRUELTIES

THE CRUELTIES USED BY KINGS & PRIESTS [WHOSE ARTS] . . .	209A	SUBJCTS HIST/N	*TITLE
DIVIDING & UNITING AT WILL IN THE CRUELTIES OF HOLINESS	348	FOUR ZOAS 8	279
BY OFFERING & ATONEMENT IN THE (CRUELTIES) OF MORAL LAW	484	MILTON 5	12
HE SAW THE CRUELTIES OF ULRO AND HE WROTE THEM DOWN . . .	498	MILTON 17	9
BEFORE HIM IN THEIR BEAUTY & IN CRUELTIES OF HOLINESS .	501	MILTON 19	34
INTO SUBSTANCE & PRINCIPLE BY THE CRUELTIES OF DEMONSTRATION	517	MILTON 29	36
SHUDDRING THE HEAVENS TO LOOK UPON ME BEHOLD WHAT CRUELTIES	627	JERUSALEM 8	19
I HAVE EDUCATED YOU IN THE CRUCIFYING CRUELTIES OF DEMONSTRATION	648	JERUSALEM 24	55
IN CRUELTIES OF HOLINESS TO REFUSE THE JOYS OF LOVE TO BRING	707	JERUSALEM 68	59
IN CRUELTIES OF RAHAB & TIRZAH PERMANENT ENDURE	734	JERUSALEM 89	2

CRUELTY

OLD CRUELTY DESIST & LET US DIG A GRAVE FOR THEE . . .	100	TIRIEL 1	36
. . . NOR IN CRUELTY BRUISE THE MILD FLOURISHING MOUNTAINS	134	FRENCH REVOLTN	5
THEN CRUELTY KNITS A SNARE	174	HUMAN IMAGE/N	8
THEN CRUELTY KNITS A SNARE	217	HUMAN ABSTR/SE	7
WITH CRUELTY DIDST MOULD MY HEART	220	TO TIRZAH/SE	10
CRUELTY HAS A HUMAN HEART	221	DIVNE IMAGE/SE	1
AND I HAVE MURDERD THEM WITH CRUELTY ABOVE ATONEMENT .	268	FOUR ZOAS 1	* 166
THOSE THAT REMAIN HAVE FLED FROM MY CRUELTY INTO THE DESARTS	268	FOUR ZOAS 1	167
WITH WINE OF CRUELTY LET US [LIGHT] PLAT A SCOURGE O SISTER CITY	275	FOUR ZOAS 1	* 399
AND FOR HIS PITY SECRET FEEDING ON THOUGHTS OF CRUELTY .	302	FOUR ZOAS 4	193
PEACE TO THE SOUL OF DARK REVENGE & REPENTANCE TO CRUELTY	329	FOUR ZOAS 7	369
DELUSIVE CRUELTY THEY DESCEND AWAY FROM THE DAUGHTERS OF BEULAH	341	FOUR ZOAS 8	26
MIGHT ACT ACCORDING TO THEIR FORMS BY INNATE CRUELTY .	344	FOUR ZOAS 8	134
PRESS IT AROUND THE LOINS OF THIS EXPANDING CRUELTY . . .	349	FOUR ZOAS 8	313
ALL PENAL LAWS COURT TRANSGRESSION & THEREFORE ARE CRUELTY &	393C	ANNO WATSON	MARG
I E STATE RELIGION WHICH IS THE SOURCE OF ALL CRUELTY .	393D	ANNO WATSON	MARG
EVEN PITY & HUMANITY BUT MY CLOTHING SHALL BE CRUELTY .	499	MILTON 18	20
THE SPECTRE REFUSES HE SEEKS CRUELTY THEY CREATE THE CRESTED COCK	515	MILTON 28	24
I HAVE TURNED MY BACK UPON THESE HEAVENS BUILDED ON CRUELTY	521	MILTON 32	3
BY THE VARIOUS ARTS OF POVERTY & CRUELTY OF ALL KINDS . .	615D	V LAST JUDG/N	PROSE
RECIEVE HER LITTLE-ONES FOR SACRIFICES AND THE DELIGHTS OF CRUELTY	623	JERUSALEM 5	15
CONDENSE BENEATH MY HAMMER INTO FORMS OF CRUELTY	628	JERUSALEM 9	27
THAT THEY BE OFFERED UPON HIS ALTAR O CRUELTY & TORMENT	629	JERUSALEM 10	39
TO PROTECT THE EMANATIONS OF ALBION'S MIGHTY ONES FROM CRUELTY	631	JERUSALEM 11	18
CALLING THAT HOLY LOVE WHICH IS ENVY REVENGE & CRUELTY .	639	JERUSALEM 17	30
CONDENSING THEM INTO SOLID ROCKS WITH CRUELTY AND ABHORRENCE	641	JERUSALEM 19	25
BECAUSE THE PEAK MALVERN & CHEVIOT REASON IN CRUELTY .	644	JERUSALEM 21	34
I HAVE TAUGHT MY CHILDREN SACRIFICES OF CRUELTY WHAT SHALL I ANSWER	646	JERUSALEM 23	17
BREATHING CRUELTY BLOOD & VENGEANCE GNASHING HIS TEETH WITH PAIN	667	JERUSALEM 40	38
TO MALDEN & CANTERBURY IN THE DELIGHTS OF CRUELTY . . .	668	JERUSALEM 41	6
IN MERCIFUL ORDER BENDING THE LAWS OF CRUELTY TO PEACE .	680	JERUSALEM 49	55
O DEMONSTRATIONS OF REASON DIVIDING FAMILIES IN CRUELTY & PRIDE	689	JERUSALEM 57	11

		PAGE	TITLE	LINE

CRUELTY   (CONTINUED)
          THE DAUGHTERS OF ALBION DIVIDE & UNITE IN JEALOUSY   689 JERUSALEM 58   5
               & CRUELTY
          HEATHEN WHOSE TENDER MERCIES ARE CRUELTY BUT JEHOVAH'S   694 JERUSALEM 61   21
               SALVATION
          AND DISHES OF PAINTED CLAY GLOWING WITH BEAUTY & CRUELTY   702 JERUSALEM 66   33
          PRESS IT AROUND THE LOINS OF THIS EVER EXPANDING CRUELTY   705 JERUSALEM 67   60
          IN PRIDE OF BEAUTY IN CRUELTY OF HOLINESS IN THE BRIGHTNESS 705 JERUSALEM 68   14
          BUT THEY FROWN & DELIGHT IN CRUELTY REFUSING ALL OTHER JOY   706 JERUSALEM 68   29
          O BEAUTIFUL DAUGHTER OF ALBION CRUELTY IS THY DELIGHT   . . 706 JERUSALEM 68   53
          I HAVE MOCKD THOSE WHO REFUSED CRUELTY & I HAVE ADMIRED   723 JERUSALEM 81   1
          AGAINST THE PATRIARCHAL POMP AND CRUELTY LABOURING   727 JERUSALEM 83   4
               INCESSANT
          THEY ARE RED HOT WITH CRUELTY RAVING ALONG THE BANKS OF   737 JERUSALEM 90   47
               THAMES
          HERMAPHRODITIC WORSHIPPERS OF A GOD OF CRUELTY & LAW   . . 737 JERUSALEM 90   55
          THESE BEAUTIFUL WITCHCRAFTS OF ALBION ARE GRATIFYD   737 JERUSALEM 90   68
               BY CRUELTY
          HE WHO ENVIES OR CALUMNIATES WHICH IS MURDER & CRUELTY . . 738 JERUSALEM 91   12
          ALL THEIR JEALOUSIES REVENGES MURDERS HIDINGS OF CRUELTY   739 JERUSALEM 92   16
               IN DECEIT
CRUICKSHANK
          I CONSIDER THE AUTOGRAPH OF MR CRUICKSHANK WHICH VERY   . . 782A INSC UPCOTT   PROSE
CRUMB
          AND THE [FAMINE] SHALL EAT BOTH CRUST & CRUMB . . . . .   185 LET BROTHELS/N   8
CRUMBLING
          AND CRUMBLING WITH BURSTING SOBS HEAVES . . . .   257 BOOK OF LOS 4   21
          APPEAR ABOVE THE (CRUMBLING) MOUNTAIN SILENCE WAITS AROUND   336 FOUR ZOAS 7B   * 130
               HIM
CRUMBS
          THAT PICKS UP CRUMBS AROUND THE DOOR . . . .   177 LIT BOY LST/N   8
          THAT PICKS UP CRUMBS AROUND THE DOOR . . . .   218 LIT BOY LST/SE   8
CRUSADE
          TO WHAT DOES THE BISHOP ATTRIBUTE THE ENGLISH CRUSADE .   385C ANNO WATSON   MARG
CRUSH
          THE WRECK OF MATTER & THE CRUSH OF WORLDS AS YOUNGE SAYS   52C ISLAND MOON 8   *PROSE
          THEREFORE I BREAK THY BONDS OF RIGHTEOUSNESS I CRUSH THY   670 JERUSALEM 42   37
               MESSENGERS
          THAT THEY MAY NOT CRUSH ME AND MINE DO THOU BE RIGHTEOUS   670 JERUSALEM 42   38
CRUSHD
          THE IRON HAND [CRUSD] CRUSHD THE TYRANT'S HEAD   . . . .   419 I SAW A MONK/N * 46
          THE IRON HAND CRUSHD THE TYRANT'S HEAD . . . .   431 GREY MONK   35
          WHERE HUMAN THOUGHT IS CRUSHD BENEATH THE IRON HAND OF   510 MILTON 25   5
               POWER
CRUSHING
          FEELING THE CRUSHING WHEELS THEY RISE THEY WRITE THE BITTER 379 FOUR ZOAS 9   819
               WORDS
CRUST
          AND THE [FAMINE] SHALL EAT BOTH CRUST & CRUMB . . . .   185 LET BROTHELS/N   8
          COMPELL THE POOR TO LIVE UPON A CRUST OF BREAD BY SOFT   323 FOUR ZOAS 7   117
               MILD ARTS
          WITH POMP GIVE EVERY CRUST OF BREAD YOU GIVE WITH GRACIOUS   323 FOUR ZOAS 7   123
               CUNNING
          THEY COMPELL THE POOR TO LIVE UPON A CRUST OF BREAD BY   656 JERUSALEM 30   30
               SOFT MILD ARTS
CRUSTED
          CRUSTED WITH SNOW IN A DIM VOID HERE BY THE ARTS OF URIZEN   350 FOUR ZOAS 8   * 373
          THEY ROLLD DOWN A DIM WORLD CRUSTED WITH SNOW DEADLY & DARK 351 FOUR ZOAS 8   * 396
          BY OUR DEAR LORD I SEE WORLDS CRUSTED WITH SNOWS & ICE . . 673 JERUSALEM 43   64
CRY
          AND HEARD A GLOOMY VOICE CRY IS IT DONE . . . .   4 FAIR ELENOR/PS   32
          AND CHILDREN CRY FOR BREAD . . . .   11 GWIN KING/PS   10
          THEIR CRY ASCENDS THE CLOUDS . . . .   11 GWIN KING/PS   22
          THEY CRY AND LET TEN THOUSAND LIVES . . . .   12 GWIN KING/PS   31
          FROM TOWR TO TOWR THE WATCHMEN CRY   . . . .   12 GWIN KING/PS   33
          FAMINE AND DEATH DOTH CRY . . . .   13 GWIN KING/PS   78
          WHEN THOUSAND DEATHS FOR VENGEANCE CRY . . . . . .   13 GWIN KING/PS   99
          THE AGED WOMAN RAISED HER CRY AND SAID . . . . . .   36B COUCH DEATH/PS   PROSE
          CAN I NOT CRY AND LIFT MY EYES TO HEAVEN . . . . . .   36B COUCH DEATH/PS   PROSE
          & EVRY PIECE OF FLESH DOTH CRY OUT WOE . . . .   43C WOE CRIED MUSE   PROSE
          & SET HIS WIG ON FIRE & THROW IT AT THE PEOPLE HED CRY . . 48B ISLAND MOON 4   PROSE
          HE DOES NOT MIND THEIR CRYING THO THEY CRY EVER SO   . . .   50A ISLAND MOON 6   PROSE
          I CRY MY MATCHES AS FAR AS GUILD HALL . . . .   55 CRY MATCHES/IM   1
          MORE MORE IS THE CRY OF A MISTAKEN SOUL . . . . . .   97D NAT RELIGION 2   PROSE
          THE CRY WAS GREAT IN TIRIEL'S PALACE HIS FIVE DAUGHTERS RAN 106 TIRIEL 5   18
          AYE NOW YOU FEEL THE CURSE YOU CRY BUT MAY ALL EARS BE DEAF 106 TIRIEL 5   20
          OR WHEREFORE DOST THOU CRY AH WRETCH TO CURSE THY AGED   108 TIRIEL 6   47
               FATHER
          . . . OR DOES HE CRY WITH A VOICE] . . . .   110 TIRIEL 8   19
          O MY CHILDREN DO THEY CRY   . . . .   112 A DREAM/SI   9
          COULD SCARCELY CRY 'WEEP 'WEEP 'WEEP 'WEEP   . . . . .   117 CHIMNEY SWP/SI   3
          BEGAN TO CRY BUT GOD EVER NIGH . . . .   121 LIT BOY FND/SI   3
          . . . THEY CRY OVER PARIS AND WAIT . . . .   138 FRENCH REVOLTN 103
          THEN THE VALLEYS OF FRANCE SHALL CRY TO THE SOLDIER . . .   144 FRENCH REVOLTN 220
          . . . UTTERING A FAINT FEEBLE CRY . . . .   146 FRENCH REVOLTN 277
          IN EVERY CRY OF EVERY MAN . . . .   170 LONDON/N   5
          IN [EVERY VOICE OF EVERY CHILD] EVERY INFANT'S CRY OF   170 LONDON/N   6
               FEAR
          [BUT MOST] HOW THE CHIMNEY SWEEPER'S CRY   . . . . .   170 LONDON/N   9
          LET HIM LAUGH LET HIM CRY . . . .   178 THE FAIRY/N   17
          IS THAT TREMBLING CRY A SONG . . . .   181 HOLY THURS/N   5
          I CRY ARISE O THEOTORMON FOR THE VILLAGE DOG . . . . .   190 V DAU ALBION 2 23

		PAGE	TITLE	LINE
CRY	(CONTINUED)			
	I CRY LOVE LOVE LOVE HAPPY HAPPY LOVE FREE AS THE MOUNTAIN WIND	194	V DAU ALBION 7	16
	SOON AS SHE SAW THE TERRIBLE BOY THEN BURST THE VIRGIN CRY	196	AMERICA PREL 2	6
	IN BERNARD'S HOUSE THE FLAMES COVERD THE LAND THEY ROUZE THEY CRY	201	AMERICA 13	2
	IS THAT TREMBLING CRY A SONG	212	HOLY THURS/SE	5
	IN EVERY CRY OF EVERY MAN	216	LONDON/SE	5
	IN EVERY INFANT'S CRY OF FEAR	216	LONDON/SE	6
	HOW THE CHIMNEY-SWEEPER'S CRY	216	LONDON/SE	9
	TO CHANGE TO A GRATING CRY	232	URIZEN 19	32
	AND WITH A CRY THAT SHOOK ALL NATURE TO THE UTMOST POLE	245	EUROPE 15	10
	URIZEN HEARD THEM CRY	248	SONG OF LOS 7	9
	THEY CRY O SPIDER SPREAD THY WEB ENLARGE THY BONES & FILLD	275	FOUR ZOAS 1	404
	WHY DOES THE RAVEN CRY ALOUD AND NO EYE PITIES HER	276	FOUR ZOAS 1	445
	ALOFT THE MOON FLED WITH A CRY THE SUN WITH STREAMS OF BLOOD	281	FOUR ZOAS 2	42
	WANDER AMONG THE VIRGINS OF THE SUMMER LOOK THEY CRY	288	FOUR ZOAS 2	306
	AND LOST IN INFINITE HUMING WINGS VANISHES WITH A CRY	289	FOUR ZOAS 2	361
	THE FADING CRY IS EVER DYING	289	FOUR ZOAS 2	362
	TO LISTEN TO THE HUNGRY RAVENS CRY IN WINTRY SEASON	290	FOUR ZOAS 2	406
	IS GIVEN A CRAVING CRY THAT THEY MAY SIT AT NIGHT ON BARREN ROCKS	325	FOUR ZOAS 7	205
	AND SWORDS RAGE WHERE THE EAGLES CRY & THE VULTURES LAUGH SAYING	334	FOUR ZOAS 7B	44
	I CRY THE WATCHMAN HEARETH NOT I POUR MY VOICE IN ROARINGS	335	FOUR ZOAS 7B	93
	A VOICE CAME IN THE NIGHT A MIDNIGHT CRY UPON THE MOUNTAINS	355	FOUR ZOAS 8	540
	ON PATMOS ISLE & HEARD THE SOULS CRY OUT TO BE DELIVERD	356	FOUR ZOAS 8	601
	THEIR RIVERS CRY WITH A DISMAL CRY THE CATTLE GATHER TOGETHER	358	FOUR ZOAS 9	54
	THE KINGS & PRINCES OF THE EARTH CRY WITH A FEEBLE CRY	365	FOUR ZOAS 9	328
	THEY CRY OUT IN JOYS OF EXISTENCE THE BROAD STEMS	373	FOUR ZOAS 9	605
	THO PAINED TO DISTRACTION CRY O LET US EXIST FOR	376	FOUR ZOAS 9	738
	AT LENGTH WITH A FEEBLE CRY HE SAID	419	I SAW A MONK/N	27
	HIS CHILDREN'S CRY MY SOUL APPALLS	419	I SAW A MONK/N	33
	THEY CRY & TEARS FOR EVER FLOW	421	BENEATH/N	5
	THEY CRY & TEARS FOR EVER FLOW	424	THE GOLDEN NET	4
	THEY CRY THE BABE THE BABE IS BORN	427	MENTAL TRAVLER	95
	AT LENGTH WITH A FEEBLE CRY HE SAID	430	GREY MONK	12
	HIS CHILDREN'S CRY MY SOUL APPALLS	430	GREY MONK	18
	A RIDDLE OR THE CRICKET'S CRY	433	AUGURIES	103
	THE HARLOT'S CRY FROM STREET TO STREET	433	AUGURIES	115
	LOS LISTENS TO THE CRY OF THE POOR MAN HIS CLOUD	535	MILTON 42	34
	IN VIRTUE'S PRAISE DOES CRY	542	PITIFUL CASE/N	4
	THUS ALOUD [WAS HEARD TO] DID HOWL & CRY	542	PITIFUL CASE/N *	7
	NEWTON & BACON CRY BEING BADLY NURST	548	CRIPPLE EVRY/N	6
	AND LAUGH WHEN WE DO CRY	552	WHY CUPID/N	8
	CRY BLAKIFIED DRAWING SPOILS PAINTER & ENGRAVER	555	BLAKES APL/N 1	15
	CRY [TOM COOKE PROVES]	555	BLAKES APL/N 1	18
	CRY BLAKIFIED DRAWING SPOILS PAINTER & ENGRAVER	556	BLAKES APL/N 2	14
	CRY LOOKING QUITE FROM SKUMFERENCE TO CENTER	556	BLAKES APL/N 2	17
	COMPELLED TO CRY OUT	569A	DESC CAT 3	PROSE
	CRY OUT THAT IT CANNOT BE WELL COLOURED THOSE ARE THE MEN	573B	DESC CAT 3	PROSE
	CRY TOM COOKE PROVES FROM CIRCUMFERENCE TO CENTER	596	BLAKES APOL/PA	11
	WILL SIT ME DOWN & CRY I I	600	MELODIOUS/PA	2
	OF UNDERSTANDING [& (SENSE) WILL] MUST CRY OUT SHAME ON SUCH	600D	PUB ADDRESS/N	*PROSE
	SO CRY HAND & HYLE THE ELDEST OF THE FATHERS OF ALBION'S	641	JERUSALEM 18	36
	GREAT IS THE CRY OF THE HOUNDS OF NIMROD ALONG THE VALLEY	644	JERUSALEM 22	8
	HER LAMBS BLEAT TO THE SEA-FOWLS CRY LAMENTING STILL FOR ALBION	667	JERUSALEM 40	51
	THE SPECTRES OF THE DEAD CRY OUT FROM THE DEEPS BENEATH	671	JERUSALEM 42	57
	JERUSALEM'S CHILDREN HARK HEAR THE GIANTS OF ALBION CRY AT NIGHT	673	JERUSALEM 43	47
	AND THE VOICES OF BATH & CANTERBURY & YORK & EDINBURGH CRY	689	JERUSALEM 57	1
	AND THE SUN SET IN TYBURN'S BROOK WHERE VICTIMS HOWL & CRY	696	JERUSALEM 62	34
	AND THUS THE WARRIORS CRY IN THE HOT DAY OF VICTORY IN SONGS	705	JERUSALEM 68	10
	THEY LISTEN NOT TO MY CRY THEY [REJOICE] AMONG THEIR WARRIORS	727	JERUSALEM 83 *	18
	BUT STILL THE THUNDER OF LOS PEALS LOUD & THUS THE THUNDER'S CRY	737	JERUSALEM 90 *	67
	. . . ACCORDING TO [THY] THE COVENANT [OF] JEHOVAH THEY CRY	746	JERUSALEM 98 *	45
	SUCH IS THE CRY FROM ALL THE EARTH	746	JERUSALEM 98	54
	ABEL COMPELLED I CRY O EARTH COVER NOT THE BLOOD OF ABEL	780	GHOST ABEL 2	12
	OR IF YOU WOULD RATHER CRY OUT ENOUGH OFF OFF	816C	LETTER 24	PROSE
	WHY SHOULD I BE TROUBLED WHY SHOULD MY HEART & FLESH CRY OUT	823C	LETTER 26	PROSE
CRYD	SEE CRIED			
	TAKE THIS HE CRYD AND THRUST INTO HER ARMS	4	FAIR ELENOR/PS	25
	AH WOMAN'S FEAR SHE CRYD AH CURSED DUKE	5	FAIR ELENOR/PS	39
	[BUT CRYD O THIS IS THE BLEST TIME]	41B	THEN SHE BORE	*PROSE
CRYING				
	THE WRETCH APPROACHES CRYING THE DEED IS DONE	4	FAIR ELENOR/PS	21
	THE STAG TURNS HEAD AND BAYS THE CRYING HOUNDS	24	EDW THIRD/PS 3	127
	HE DOES NOT MIND THEIR CRYING THO THEY CRY EVER SO	50A	ISLAND MOON 6	PROSE
	THE VOICE OF ONE CRYING IN THE WILDERNESS	98B	ALL RELIGIONS	TITLE
	CRYING HIDE FROM THE LIVING	137	FRENCH REVOLTN	74
	LOOSING THE ETERNAL HORSES FROM THE DENS OF NIGHT CRYING	160A	SONG LIBERTY	PROSE
	CRYING 'WEEP 'WEEP IN NOTES OF WOE	180	CHIMNEY SWP/N	2
	CRYING 'WEEP 'WEEP IN NOTES OF WOE	212	CHIMNEY SWP/SE	2
	WHENCE IS THIS VOICE CRYING ENION THAT SOUNDETH IN MY EARS	293	FOUR ZOAS 3	77

```
                                                             PAGE     TITLE          LINE
CRYING    (CONTINUED)
     CRYING FURY IN MY LIMBS DESTRUCTION IN MY BONES & MARROW    296  FOUR ZOAS 3       162
     FOR ENITHARMON SHRIEKD AMAIN CRYING O MY SWEET WORLD   .  . 298  FOUR ZOAS 4        50
     CRYING LUVAH KING OF LOVE THOU ART THE KING OF RAGE &       306  FOUR ZOAS 5        42
       DEATH
     CRYING WHAT & WHO ART THOU COLD DEMON ART THOU URIZEN   .  . 313  FOUR ZOAS 6        55
     CRYING AS I WILL I REND THE NATIONS ALL ASUNDER RENDING     334  FOUR ZOAS 7B       50
     CRYING IN SECRET TENTS AT NIGHT & IN THE MORN COMPELLD  .  . 334  FOUR ZOAS 7B       62
     ALONG THE RANKS CRYING LISTEN TO THE PRIEST OF GOD         336  FOUR ZOAS 7B      114
       YE WARRIORS
     THEY VIEW THE LIGHT & WONDER CRYING OUT IN TERRIBLE        352  FOUR ZOAS 8       452
       EXISTENCE
     FLOCK TO THE TRUMPET MUTTRING OVER THE SIDES OF THE GRAVE  363  FOUR ZOAS 9       239
       & CRYING
     THE SPIDER THE BAT BURST FROM THE HARDEND SLIME CRYING  .  . 373  FOUR ZOAS 9       608
     CRYING O GOD DELIVER US TO THE HEAVENS OR TO THE EARTHS    510  MILTON 25          13
     CRYING WITH ONE VOICE GIVE US A HABITATION & A PLACE   .  . 519  MILTON 30          24
     CRYING HOLY HOLY HOLY IS THE [G ] LORD GOD ALMIGHTY    .  . 617B V LAST JUDG/N    *PROSE
     WHENCE IS THIS VOICE CRYING ENION THAT SOUNDETH IN MY EARS  654  JERUSALEM 29       59
     CRYING COMPELL THE REASONER TO DEMONSTRATE WITH UNHEWN     687  JERUSALEM 55       56
       DEMONSTRATIONS
     CRYING [IVE FOUND HI] CRUCIFY THIS CAUSE OF DISTRESS   .  . 755  EV GOSPEL (E)/N *   85
CRYSOLITE
     THE CRYSOLITE THE TOPAZ THE JACINTH & EVERY PRECIOUS STONE  628  JERUSALEM 9        24
CRYSOLITES
     RUBIES JACINTHS CRYSOLITES ISSUING FROM THY FURNACES WHILE  732  JERUSALEM 87       20
CRYSTAL      SEE CHRYSTAL
     LIKE PEARLY CLOUDS THEY MEET TOGETHER IN THE CRYSTAL HOUSE  239  EUROPE 4            6
     WITHIN HER CRYSTAL HOUSE . . . . . . . . . . . .           243  EUROPE 13          14
     ALONE I SEE THEE CRYSTAL FORM   . . . . . . . . .          244  EUROPE 14          17
     DOWN THE STEPS OF MY CRYSTAL HOUSE  . . . . . . . .        244  EUROPE 14          25
     WITH HER FAIR CRYSTAL CLEARNESS IN HER LIPS & CHEEKS HIS   269  FOUR ZOAS 1       185
       POISONS ROSE
     [HIS WOE FOUND XXX THE CRYSTAL SKY] . . . . . . . .        SUPP FOUR ZOAS 1   *
     . . . UPON THE CRYSTAL PAVEMENT  . . . . . . . . .         294  FOUR ZOAS 3        81
     AND HIS DARK WIFE THAT ONCE FAIR CRYSTAL FORM DIVINELY     306  FOUR ZOAS 5        60
       CLEAR
     THEN RAGE ON RAGE SHALL FIERCE REDOUND OUT OF HER CRYSTAL  307  FOUR ZOAS 5        65
       QUIVER
     IN TWAIN & LO MY CRYSTAL FORM THAT LIVED IN MY BOSOM   .   334  FOUR ZOAS 7B       65
     AND BIND THEM TO THEE THAT MY CRYSTAL FORM MAY COME TO ME  334  FOUR ZOAS 7B       71
     AND IN THE MORNING WHEN THE SUN AROSE IN THE CRYSTAL SKY   370  FOUR ZOAS 9       517
     ENLIGHTEN ALL THE CRYSTAL HOUSE OF VALA AWAKE AWAKE   .  . 371  FOUR ZOAS 9       520
     WITH HER FAIR CRYSTAL CLEARNESS . . . . . . . . .         381  FOUR ZOAS AD 5      5
     THE CRYSTAL CABINET  . . . . . . . . . . . . .            429B CRYSTL CABINET    TITLE
     AND PEARL & CRYSTAL SHINING BRIGHT  . . . . . . . .       429  CRYSTL CABINET      6
     BUT BURST THE CRYSTAL CABINET  . . . . . . . . .          429  CRYSTL CABINET     23
     OF CRYSTAL FLOWING INTO TWO STREAMS ONE FLOWS THRO        526  MILTON 35          50
       GOLGONOOZA
     JUST AT THE PLACE TO WHERE THE LARK MOUNTS IS A CRYSTAL   526  MILTON 35          61
       GATE
     AND THE DARK BODY OF ALBION LEFT PROSTRATE UPON THE CRYSTAL 655 JERUSALEM 29       63
       PAVEMENT
     AND HIS DARK EON THAT ONCE FAIR CRYSTAL FORM DIVINELY CLEAR 667 JERUSALEM 40       41
     FILLING CUPS OF SILVER & CRYSTAL WITH SHRIEKS & CRIES WITH  723 JERUSALEM 80       81
       GROANS
CUBE
     IN FIERY PYRAMID OR CUBE OR [ORNAMENTED] UNORNAMENTED     287  FOUR ZOAS 2    *  275
       PILLAR [SQUARE]
CUBED
     [CIRCLED] [?CUBED] IN [INFINITE ORB] [?WINDOW SQUARE] . . . 286 FOUR ZOAS 2    *  245
CUBES
     AND WEIGH THE MASSY [GLOBES] CUBES . . .  . . . . .       283  FOUR ZOAS 2       144
     TRIGONS & CUBES DIVIDE THE ELEMENTS IN FINITE BONDS  . .  284  FOUR ZOAS 2       169
     WANDERING EVEN TO THE SUNNY [ORBS] CUBES OF LIGHT & HEAT   286  FOUR ZOAS 2       254
CUBITS
     OF TWENTY-FIVE CUBITS IN HEIGHT SUCH SPACE IS HIS UNIVERSE 516  MILTON 29          7
CUFFD
     [AND] WHO WITH IRON HAND CUFFD IN THE AFTERNOON  . . . .  537  AND HIS LEGS/N     24
CULTIVATED
     IS CULTIVATED AND WILL BRING FORTH FRUIT  . . . . . .      19  EDW THIRD/PS 2     26
     AYE IT GROWS MOST IN LANDS MOST CULTIVATED  . . . . .      28  EDW THIRD/PS 4      4
     THE BIBLE SAYS THAT CULTIVATED LIFE EXISTED FIRST  . . .  446C ANNO REYNOLDS    MARG
     ONLY THEY HAVE NOT CULTIVATED THEM BECAUSE  . . . . .     473A ANNO REYNOLDS    MARG
     BUT ALLAMANDA CALLD ON EARTH COMMERCE IS THE CULTIVATED   514  MILTON 27          42
       LAND
     THE HIGHLY CULTIVATED STATES OF EGYPT MOAB EDOM ARAM  . . 565C DESC CAT 2       PROSE
     MR B(BLAKE) HAVING FROM EARLY YOUTH CULTIVATED THE TWO ARTS 587D CHAUCER/N      PROSE
     BUT BECAUSE THEY HAVE CULTIVATED THEIR UNDERSTANDINGS  . . 615C V LAST JUDG/N   PROSE
CULVER
     GEORGE CUMBERLAND ESQRE CULVER STREET BRISTOL . . . . .   SUPP ADDRESS/L 88    *TITLE
CUMBERLAND
     AND CUMBERLAND NORTHUMBERLAND WESTMORELAND & DURHAM ARE    637  JERUSALEM 16       50
     BOWEN HAD ALL SCOTLAND THE ISLES NORTHUMBERLAND &         710  JERUSALEM 71       46
       CUMBERLAND
     YOURS SINCERELY...HEALTH TO MRS CUMBERLAND & FAMILY . . . 790D LETTER 2        PROSE
     COMPLIMENTS TO MRS CUMBERLAND & FAMILY  . . . . . .       791C LETTER 3        PROSE
     IS IN CONJUNCTION WITH SUCH MEN AS MY FRIEND CUMBERLAND   792A LETTER 4        PROSE
     BEST COMPLIMENTS TO MRS CUMBERLAND I REMAIN YOURS SINCERELY 796A LETTER 6      PROSE
     DEAR CUMBERLAND I HAVE TO CONGRATULATE YOU ON . . . .     797C LETTER 10       PROSE
     RESPECTFUL COMPLIMENTS TO MRS CUMBERLAND & FAMILY   . . . 798D LETTER 10       PROSE
     P S MR WALKER SAYS THAT MR CUMBERLAND IS RIGHT IN        847C LETTER 44       PROSE
       HIS RECKONING
```

                                                    PAGE   TITLE   LINE
CUMBERLAND   (CONTINUED)
    DEAR CUMBERLAND I AM VERY MUCH OBLIGED BY YOUR KIND ARDOUR   865C LETTER 63   PROSE
    ON ACCOUNT I HAVE RECIEVD A LETTER FROM MR CUMBERLAND . . 876D LETTER 85   PROSE
    DEAR CUMBERLAND I HAVE BEEN VERY NEAR THE GATES OF DEATH   878A LETTER 88   PROSE
    MR CUMBERLAND BISHOPSGATE WINDSOR GREAT PARK . . . . . SUPP ADDRESSES/L   *TITLE
    G CUMBERLAND ESQ BISHOPSGATE NEAR EGHAM SURREY . . . . SUPP ADDRESS/L 2   *TITLE
    GEORGE CUMBERLAND ESQRE CULVER STREET BRISTOL . . . . . SUPP ADDRESS/L 88   *TITLE
CUMBEROUS
    OERWEARIED OR IN CUMBEROUS FLIGHT HE VENTURD OER DARK RIFTS 319 FOUR ZOAS 6   * 288
CUMBROUS
    BUT URIZEN SAID CAN I NOT LEAVE THIS WORLD OF CUMBROUS   316 FOUR ZOAS 6   196
        WHEELS
CUNNING
    COME THOU DARK FIEND I DARE THY CUNNING KNOW THAT IJIM   104 TIRIEL 4   17
        SCORNS
    BALD TYRANT WRINKLED CUNNING [WRETCH] LISTEN TO ZAZEL'S   108 TIRIEL 7   8
        CHAINS
    [THE DEADLY CUNNING OF THE [SCALY TRIBE] FLATTERER . . .   110 TIRIEL 8   * 22
    THE WEAK IN COURAGE IS STRONG IN CUNNING . . . . . . 152B MARRIAGE HH 9   PROSE
    IF THE LION WAS ADVISED BY THE FOX HE WOULD BE CUNNING . . 152D MARRIAGE HH 10   PROSE
    & THE SOURCES OF ALL ACTIVITY BUT THE CHAINS ARE   155A MARRIAGE HH 15   PROSE
        THE CUNNING OF
    ACCORDING TO THE PROVERB THE WEAK IN COURAGE IS STRONG   155A MARRIAGE HH 15   PROSE
        IN CUNNING
    O THE CUNNING WILES THAT CREEP . . . . 165 CRADLE SONG/N   14
    [O THE CUNNING WILES THAT CREEP] . . . . 165 CRADLE SONG/N   * 23
    NOR THE [CUNNING] SECRET HOARD UP IN HIS TREASURY . . . 181 RICHES/N   4
    WHERE ART THOU ENION AH TOO NEAR TO CUNNING TOO FAR OFF   296 FOUR ZOAS 3   169
    WITH POMP GIVE EVERY CRUST OF BREAD YOU GIVE WITH GRACIOUS   323 FOUR ZOAS 7   123
        CUNNING
    CUNNING PLOTTERS WERE CONSIDERD AS WISE MACHIAVELS . . . 397B ANNO BACON   MARG
    CUNNING & MORALITY ARE NOT POETRY BUT PHILOSOPHY . . . 412C ANNO BOYD   MARG
    & ENTHUSIASTS FOR CUNNING & ARTIFICE . . . . 414B ANNO BOYD   MARG
    OPRESSION OF SR JOSHUA & HIS GANG OF CUNNING HIRED KNAVES   445B ANNO REYNOLDS   MARG
    FOOL & A CUNNING KNAVE SUITED TO THE PURPOSES OF   458B ANNO REYNOLDS   MARG
        EVIL DEMONS
    BUT A CUNNING FOOL . . . . 460D ANNO REYNOLDS   MARG
    FROM FELL DESTRUCTION IN THE SPECTROUS CUNNING OR RAGE   515 MILTON 28   41
        HE CREATES
    IN A DARK CORNER THE EYES OF STUPID CUNNING NEVER WILL BE   563D DESC CAT   PROSE
    NARROW AND CUNNING AND EVERY THING TENDING . . . . . 580B DESC CAT 5   PROSE
    HEAVY LUMPS OF CUNNING & IGNORANCE AS THEIR WORKS SHEW . . 593C PUB ADDRESS/N   PROSE
    AND DEADLY CUNNING & MEAN ABJECTNESS ONLY SHALL ENJOY THEM   734 JERUSALEM 88   38
CUNNING SURES (CONNOISSEURS)
    THE CUNNING SURES & THE AIM AT YOURS . . . . 548 CUNNING SURE/N   1
CUP   SEE DEATH-CUP
    TIS AT THIS RIVER'S FOUNT WHERE EVRY MORTAL'S CUP IS MIXT   41C THEN SHE BORE   PROSE
    MY CUP IS FILLD WITH ENVY'S RANKEST DRAUGHT [AND DEATH]   41C THEN SHE BORE   PROSE
    AS A CUP CANNOT CONTAIN MORE THAN ITS CAPACIOUSNESS . . 90B ANNO SWED LOVE   MARG
    A CUP OF SPARKLING POETIC FANCIES SO WHEN I AM TIPSIE . . 237 EUROPE INTRO   16
    THE EARTH SPREAD FORTH HER TABLE WIDE THE NIGHT A SILVER   273 FOUR ZOAS 1   347
        CUP
    WHEN THOU DIDST BEAR THE GOLDEN CUP AT THE IMMORTAL TABLES   311 FOUR ZOAS 5   228
    RECIEVING AS A POISOND CUP RECIEVES THE HEAVENLY WINE . . 324 FOUR ZOAS 7   154
    HE SAW THE HARLOT OF THE KINGS OF EARTH & SAW HER CUP . . 356 FOUR ZOAS 8   602
    ART THOU SHE THAT MADE THE NATIONS DRUNK WITH THE CUP OF   374 FOUR ZOAS 9   658
        RELIGION
    HERE IS HER CUP FILLD WITH ITS POISONS IN THESE HORRID   529 MILTON 38   25
        VALES
    BUT COME O VALA WITH KNIFE & CUP DRAIN MY BLOOD . . . . 645 JERUSALEM 22   29
    HE SAW IN VALA'S HAND THE DRUID KNIFE OF REVENGE & THE   698 JERUSALEM 63   39
        POISON CUP
    THE CUP OF RAHAB IN HIS HAND HER POISONS TWENTY-SEVEN-FOLD   715 JERUSALEM 75   3
    TO REIGN IN PRIDE & TO OPRESS & TO MIX THE CUP OF DELUSION   730 JERUSALEM 85   31
    AND FIRE JERUSALEM TOOK THE CUP WHICH FOAMD IN VALA'S HAND   734 JERUSALEM 88   56
    MURDERS THE HOLY-ONE GO TELL THEM THIS & OVERTHROW THEIR   738 JERUSALEM 91   13
        CUP
CUPID
    WHY WAS CUPID A BOY . . . . 552 WHY CUPID/N   1
    [THEN] AND TO MAKE CUPID A BOY . . . . 552 WHY CUPID/N   9
    WAS [SURELY A WOMAN'S] THE CUPID GIRL'S MOCKING PLAN . . 552 WHY CUPID/N   10
    TO CHLOE'S BREAST YOUNG CUPID SLILY STOLE . . . . . . 557 TO CHLOES/N   1
CUPIDITY
    CUPIDITY UNCONQUERABLE MY FAULT WHEN AT NOON OF DAY . . . 492 MILTON 12   8
CUPS
    THE STARS THREW DOWN THEIR CUPS & FLED . . . . 187 WHEN KLOPSTK/N   12
    HIS FOOD SHE BROUGHT IN IRON BASKETS HIS DRINK IN CUPS   195 AMERICA PREL 1   3
        OF IRON
    MEASURD HIS FOOD MORNING & EVENING IN CUPS & BASKETS OF   343 FOUR ZOAS 8   81
        IRON
    THE DAUGHTERS OF URIZEN STAND WITH CUPS & MEASURES   365 FOUR ZOAS 9   333
        OF FOAMING WINE
    THEY CATCH THE SHRIEKS IN CUPS OF GOLD THEY HAND THEM TO   377 FOUR ZOAS 9   768
        ONE ANOTHER
    CATCHES HIS SHRIEKS IN CUPS OF GOLD . . . . 425 MENTAL TRAVLER   12
    WITH FLUTE & CLARION WITH CUPS & MEASURES FILLD WITH   511 MILTON 25   69
        FOAMING WINE
    THEY CATCH THE SHRIEKS IN CUPS OF GOLD THEY HAND THEM TO   514 MILTON 27   38
        ONE ANOTHER
    TO FREEZE OVER HIS NOSTRILS WHILE THEY FEED HIS TONGUE   702 JERUSALEM 66   32
        FROM CUPS
    FILLING CUPS OF SILVER & CRYSTAL WITH SHRIEKS & CRIES WITH   723 JERUSALEM 80   81
        GROANS

421

CUPS   (CONTINUED)
    OF LAMBS AND DOVES MINGLED TOGETHER IN CUPS AND DISHES . . 725 JERUSALEM 82   7
CUR
    AND CUR MY LAWYER & DADY [MY] JACK HEMP'S PARSON   . . . 537 AND HIS LEGS/N * 26
CURB
    THY STRENGTH CURB THY FIERCE STEEDS ALLAY THE HEAT   . . .   1 TO SUMMER/PS   2
    WHY A TENDER CURB UPON THE YOUTHFUL BURNING BOY   . . . . 130 BOOK OF THEL 6   19
    SHALL NOT THE COUNCELLOR THROW HIS CURB . . . . . .   247 SONG OF LOS 6   15
    COMPELLD THE GNOMES TO CURB THE HORSES & TO THROW BANKS   493 MILTON 12   17
        OF SAND
    TO GET RICH AND POWERFUL TO CURB THE PRIDE OF MAN   . . . 571D DESC CAT 3   PROSE
    OF DEATH THEY CURB THEIR SPECTRES AS WITH IRON CURBS   . . 671 JERUSALEM 42   67
CURBD
    CURBD BY THE MANLIEST REASON I HAVE BEEN WINGD   . . . .   23 EDW THIRD/PS 3   86
    SHAKSPEARE & MILTON WERE BOTH CURBD BY THE GENERAL MALADY 480C MILTON 1   *PROSE
CURBED
    HAVE CURBED & GOVERND THEIR PASSIONS OR HAVE NO PASSIONS   615C V LAST JUDG/N PROSE
CURBING
    CURBING HIS LIVING CREATURES MANY OF THE STRONGEST GNOMES 487 MILTON 7   48
    HAVE SPENT THEIR LIVES IN CURBING & GOVERNING OTHER   615D V LAST JUDG/N PROSE
        PEOPLE'S
    CURBING THEIR TYGERS WITH GOLDEN BITS & BRIDLES OF SILVER 686 JERUSALEM 55   35
        & IVORY
CURBS
    TO FORGE THE CURBS OF IRON & BRASS TO BUILD THE IRON   292 FOUR ZOAS 3   34
        MANGERS
    RAGE ORC RAGE THARMAS URIZEN NO LONGER CURBS YOUR RAGE   362 FOUR ZOAS 9   187
    OF DEATH THEY CURB THEIR SPECTRES AS WITH IRON CURBS   . . 671 JERUSALEM 42   67
CURDLE
    MY NERVES WITH TREMBLING CURDLE ALL MY BLOOD . . . . .   43C WOE CRIED MUSE PROSE
CURE
    AND FAIN WOULD CURE THE HURT HE MADE . . . .   17 BLIND-MANS/PS   56
    TO CURE WHATEVER IS AMISS . . . .   56 HAIL MATRIM/IM   20
CURED
    LIKE BIRDS JUST CURED OF THE PIP . . . .   56 HAIL MATRIM/IM   23
CURFEW
    INDICATES THE SOUND OF THE CURFEW BELL . . . .   619B ILLUS MILTON   PROSE
CURIOSITY
    THEN SHE BORE PALE DESIRE FATHER OF CURIOSITY . . . . .   40D THEN SHE BORE PROSE
    WITH DESIRE AND CURIOSITY BUT HOWEVER CHRISTMAS IS A-COMING 851D LETTER 50   PROSE
    I HAVE NO CURIOSITY TO SEE HIM AS I WELL KNOW WHAT   859C LETTER 56   PROSE
        IS WITHIN
    TO PREVENT THE TROUBLE OF YOUR COMING THRO CURIOSITY TO SEE 876C LETTER 84   PROSE
CURIOUS
    AUTHORS AND CURIOUS BOOKS IN GENERAL HE ADVISES THAT SOME 831C LETTER 31   PROSE
CURL
    LOVE TO CURL ROUND THE BONES OF DEATH AND ASK THE RAVNOUS 191 V DAU ALBION 3   11
        SNAKE
CURLD
    THAT CURLD LIKE A LAMB'S BACK WAS SHAVD SO I SAID   . . . 117 CHIMNEY SWP/SI   6
    CURLD VETERANS AMONG HELMS AND SHIELDS AND CHARIOTS . .   159D SONG LIBERTY PROSE
    OF A CURLD RAM WHO STRETCHD HIMSELF IN SLEEP BESIDE HIS   369 FOUR ZOAS 9   456
        MISTRESS
    AND COUCHING AT THEIR SIDE SHALL EAT FROM THE CURLD BOY'S 376 FOUR ZOAS 9   * 707
        WHITE LAP
CURLED
    NOR CURLED WANTONNESS . . . .   256 BOOK OF LOS 3   13
CURLS
    LET SNAKES RISE FROM THY BEDDED LOCKS & LAUGH AMONG THY   108 TIRIEL 6   43
        CURLS
    THEY PUT ASIDE HIS CURLS THEY DIVIDE HIS SEVEN LOCKS UPON 702 JERUSALEM 66   22
CURRENT
    A SLUGGISH CURRENT OF DIM WATERS ON WHOSE VERDANT MARGIN   295 FOUR ZOAS 3   121
    WITH LABOUR & CARE THOU DOST DIVIDE THE [RIVER] CURRENT   312 FOUR ZOAS 6   18
        INTO FOUR
    HE TAKES IT IN HIS ARMS HE PASSES IT IN STRENGTH THRO HIS 518 MILTON 29   61
        CURRENT
    FROM WEST TO EAST AGAINST THE CURRENT OF . . . . . .   717 STOOD AMONG/J   4
    AGAINST THE CURRENT OF THIS WHEEL ITS NAME . . . . .   718 STOOD AMONG/J   17
    WEAVING BOWERS OF DELIGHT ON THE CURRENT OF INFANT THAMES 728 JERUSALEM 83   50
CURRENTS
    INTO MILD CURRENTS AS THE WATER MINGLES WITH THE WINE . . 284 FOUR ZOAS 2   155
    AND ALBION FLED INWARD AMONG THE CURRENTS OF HIS RIVERS   642 JERUSALEM 19   39
    CLOTHD IN BLACK MOURNING UPON MY RIVER'S CURRENTS VALA   657 JERUSALEM 31   47
        AWAKE
    WEPT VEHEMENTLY OVER ALBION WHERE THAMES' CURRENTS SPRING 684 JERUSALEM 53   2
    WHOSE CURRENTS FLOW INTO THE DEAD SEA BY SODOM & GOMORRA   735 JERUSALEM 89   27
CURSD   SEE SELF CURSD
    WAS IT NOT YOU ENSLAVD THE SONS OF ZAZEL & THEY HAVE CURSD 100 TIRIEL 1   41
    . . . FROM COURT TO COURT CURSD THE FIERCE TORMENT   135 FRENCH REVOLTN   23
        UNQUELLD
    AND HIS SOUL SICKEND HE CURSD . . . .   235 URIZEN 23   23
    HE SAW THEM CURSD BEYOND HIS CURSE HIS SOUL MELTED WITH   315 FOUR ZOAS 6   142
        FEAR
    LOS IN HIS WRATH CURSD HEAVEN & EARTH HE RENT UP NATIONS   489 MILTON 9   13
    THE GNOMES IN ALL THAT DAY SPARD NOT THEY CURSD SATAN   493 MILTON 12   31
        BITTERLY
    HE CURSD THE SCRIBE & PHARISEE . . . .   749 EV GOSPEL(B)/N   37
CURSE
    CURSE MY BLACK STARS AND BLESS MY PLEASING WOE   . . . . 10 WHEN EARLY/PS   10
    I CURSE MY STARS IN BITTER GRIEF AND WOE . . . . . .   10 WHEN EARLY/PS   15
    ID CURSE BRIGHT FORTUNE FOR MY MIXED LOT . . . . . .   10 WHEN EARLY/PS   19

```
                                                       PAGE     TITLE        LINE
CURSE    (CONTINUED)
     AND LOVE OF FOLLY NEEDS NONE [OTHERS] OTHER CURSE  .  .    14 IMIT SPEN/PS     14
     COME FORTH SONS OF THE CURSE COME FORTH SEE THE DEATH      99 TIRIEL 1        10
        OF MYRATANA
     WERE WE NOT SLAVES TILL WE REBELD WHO CARES FOR TIRIEL'S   99 TIRIEL 1        17
        CURSE
     HIS BLESSING WAS A CRUEL CURSE HIS CURSE MAY BE A BLESSING 99 TIRIEL 1        18
     CURSE ON YOUR [XXX] RUTHLESS HEADS FOR I WILL BURY HER    100 TIRIEL 1     *  33
        EVEN HERE
     WHY DOST THOU CURSE IS NOT THE CURSE NOW COME UPON YOUR   100 TIRIEL 1        40
        HEAD
     BURY YOUR MOTHER BUT YOU CANNOT BURY THE CURSE OF TIRIEL  100 TIRIEL 1        51
     THE CURSE THAT ROLLS OVER THEIR HEADS WILL REST ITSELF    104 TIRIEL 4        14
        ON THINE
     [SEVEN YEARS OF SORROW THEN THE CURSE OF ZAZEL]  .  .  .  .  104 TIRIEL 4     16
     IS READY FOR YOUR BITTER TAUNTS [XXX] COME FORTH SONS OF  105 TIRIEL 4     *  67
        THE CURSE
     THUNDER & FIRE & PESTILENCE (HEAR) YOU NOT TIRIEL'S CURSE 106 TIRIEL 5        13
     DISCHARGING THEIR ENORMOUS VOICES AT THE FATHER'S CURSE   106 TIRIEL 5        15
     AYE NOW YOU FEEL THE CURSE YOU CRY BUT MAY ALL EARS BE DEAF 106 TIRIEL 5      20
     AND LET THE CURSE FALL ON THE REST & WRAP THEM UP TOGETHER 106 TIRIEL 5       25
     NOW THAT THE CURSE SHALL CLEAN DEVOUR ALL THOSE GUILTY SONS 107 TIRIEL 6       4
     THEN BE OBEDIENT TO THY FATHER FOR THE CURSE IS TAKEN OFF 107 TIRIEL 6         7
        THEE
     YOU SEE THE PARENTS CURSE NOW LEAD ME WHERE I HAVE        107 TIRIEL 6        12
        COMMANDED
     OR I WILL WRAP (THEE) UP IN SUCH A TERRIBLE FATHER'S CURSE 107 TIRIEL 6       20
     TO HAR & HEVA I WILL LEAD THEE THEN WOULD THAT THEY WOULD 107 TIRIEL 6        24
        CURSE
     THEN WOULD THEY CURSE AS THOU HAST CURSED BUT THEY ARE    107 TIRIEL 6        25
        NOT LIKE THEE
     OR ELSE THOU WOULDEST NOT HAVE LIVD TO CURSE THY HELPLESS 108 TIRIEL 6        28
        CHILDREN
     UNLESS THOU LEAD ME TO THE TENT OF HAR CHILD OF THE CURSE 108 TIRIEL 6        34
     I LEAD THEE TO THE TENT OF HAR NOT THAT I MIND THY CURSE  108 TIRIEL 6        36
     BUT THAT I FEEL THEY WILL CURSE THEE & HANG UPON THY BONES 108 TIRIEL 6       37
     WHAT HAVE I DONE HELA MY DAUGHTER FEARST THOU NOW THE CURSE 108 TIRIEL 6      46
     OR WHEREFORE DOST THOU CRY AH WRETCH TO CURSE THY AGED    108 TIRIEL 6        47
        FATHER
     LEAD ME TO HAR & HEVA & THE CURSE OF TIRIEL   .  .  .  .  .  108 TIRIEL 6     48
     THY LAWS O HAR & TIRIEL'S WISDOM END TOGETHER IN A CURSE  109 TIRIEL 8         8
     RETURNS MY THIRSTY HISSINGS IN A CURSE ON THEE O HAR   .  110 TIRIEL 8        40
     .  .  .  FOR A CURSE IS HEARD HOARSE THRO THE LAND FROM A 140 FRENCH REVOLTN 138
        GODLESS RACE
     SHALL SAY NO MORE I CURSE THEE .  .  .  .  .  .  .  .  .  .  144 FRENCH REVOLTN 225
     HER EGGS ON SO THE PRIEST LAYS HIS CURSE ON THE FAIREST  152C MARRIAGE HH 9  PROSE
        JOYS
     WITH HOARSE NOTE CURSE THE SONS OF JOY  .  .  .  .  .  .  160A SONG LIBERTY  PROSE
     I HEARD A DEVIL CURSE  .  .  .  .  .  .  .  .  .  .  .  .  164 HEARD ANGEL/N    9
     AT HIS CURSE THE SUN WENT DOWN  .  .  .  .  .  .  .  .  .  164 HEARD ANGEL/N   16
     [BUT MOST THE MIDNIGHT HARLOT'S CURSE]  .  .  .  .  .  .  170 LONDON/N        14
     HOW THE MIDNIGHT HARLOT'S CURSE   .  .  .  .  .  .  .  .  170 LONDON/N        19
     [TWILL] YOULL QUITE REMOVE THE ANCIENT CURSE  .  .  .  .  176 ANCNT PROVRB/N   4
     YOULL QUITE REMOVE THE ANCIENT CURSE  .  .  .  .  .  .  .  184 SEVRL QUESTN/N  18
     HOW THE YOUTHFUL HARLOT'S CURSE   .  .  .  .  .  .  .  .  216 LONDON/SE       14
     ONE CURSE ONE WEIGHT ONE MEASURE   .  .  .  .  .  .  .  .  224 URIZEN 4       39
     THE YOUTH OF ENGLAND HID IN GLOOM CURSE THE PAIND HEAVENS 242 EUROPE 12        5
        COMPELLD
     CURSE THEE THOU PLAGUE OF WOFUL LOS & SEEK REVENGE ON THEE 289 FOUR ZOAS 2   339
     .  .  .  ATLANTIC FOR A CURSE AND HIDDEN HORROR .  .  .  .  294 FOUR ZOAS 3   105
     THE ALL POWERFUL CURSE OF AN HONEST MAN BE UPON URIZEN    298 FOUR ZOAS 4     25
        & LUVAH
     THAT THEY MAY CURSE THARMAS THEIR GOD & LOS HIS ADOPTED SON 313 FOUR ZOAS 6   43
     THAT THEY MAY CURSE & WORSHIP THE OBSCURE DEMON OF        313 FOUR ZOAS 6     44
        DESTRUCTION
     GO FORTH SONS OF MY CURSE GO FORTH DAUGHTERS OF          313 FOUR ZOAS 6     46
        MY ABHORRENCE
     HERE HE HAD TIME ENOUGH TO REPENT OF HIS RASHLY THREATEND 315 FOUR ZOAS 6    141
        CURSE
     HE SAW THEM CURSD BEYOND HIS CURSE HIS SOUL MELTED WITH   315 FOUR ZOAS 6    142
        FEAR
     ORC ANSWERD CURSE THY HOARY BROWS WHAT DOST THOU IN THIS  322 FOUR ZOAS 7     69
        DEEP
     THEN ORC [ANSWERD] CRIED CURSE THY COLD HYPOCRISY .  .  . 323 FOUR ZOAS 7    135
     OF SEPARATION & ON MY DARK HEAD THE CURSE & PUNISHMENT  . 330 FOUR ZOAS 7    405
     THOU ART OUR CURSE [IN] AND TILL I CAN BRING LOVE INTO    339 FOUR ZOAS 7B  * 257
        THE LIGHT
     THE WINNER'S SHOUT THE LOSER'S CURSE  .  .  .  .  .  .  .  433 AUGURIES      117
     BECAME ITS PREY A CURSE AN OFFERING AND AN ATONEMENT  .  . 481 MILTON 2       13
     TILL BROTHERHOOD IS CHANGD INTO A CURSE & A FLATTERY   .  . 525 MILTON 35      4
     WHICH IS THE GREATEST CURSE THAT CAN FALL UPON A NATION   596B PUB ADDRESS/N PROSE
     THE PARENT'S FEAR THE BROTHER'S JEALOUSY THE SISTER'S CURSE 636 JERUSALEM 16   7
     TO BE FOR A SHAME & A CURSE AND TO BE OUR SLAVES FOR EVER 640 JERUSALEM 18    35
     DAUGHTER OF MY PHANTASY UNLAWFUL PLEASURE ALBION'S CURSE  645 JERUSALEM 23     2
     LO HERE IS VALA'S VEIL WHOLE FOR A LAW A TERROR & A CURSE 646 JERUSALEM 23    32
     BUT A MEER PHANTASY HEAR DYING ALBION'S CURSE  .  .  .  . 646 JERUSALEM 23    37
     AND HE WHO MAKES HIS LAW A CURSE  .  .  .  .  .  .  .  .  652 FIELDS FROM/J   83
     AND MAN HIMSELF BECOME A FIEND WRAPD IN AN ENDLESS CURSE  667 JERUSALEM 40    29
     ENITHARMON IS MY DAUGHTER ACCURSED WITH A FATHER'S CURSE  670 JERUSALEM 42    15
     ALBION THEY CURSE THEIR HUMAN KINDNESS & AFFECTION  .  .  670 JERUSALEM 42    60
     AND WE ALSO & ALL BEULAH CONSUME BENEATH ALBION'S CURSE   681 JERUSALEM 50    17
     SOMETIMES I CURSE & SOMETIMES BLESS THY FASCINATING BEAUTY 707 JERUSALEM 68   64
```

```
                                                                 PAGE     TITLE        LINE
CURSE    (CONTINUED)
    WHAT IS THAT TALENT WHICH IT IS A CURSE TO HIDE   . . . . 717A JERUSALEM 77      PROSE
    TEACH THEM TRUE HAPPINESS BUT LET NO CURSE  . . . . . .   718 STOOD AMONG/J        32
    THE MOUNTAIN OF BLESSING IS ITSELF A CURSE               720 JERUSALEM 79          7
        & AN ASTONISHMENT
    BUT HIDE AMERICA FOR A CURSE AN ALTAR OF VICTIMS & A HOLY 725 JERUSALEM 82         29
        PLACE
    LOATHD AS A NATION'S BITTEREST CURSE . . . . . . . . .    748 EV GOSPEL(A)/N       10
    CHRISTIANITY IS ART & NOT MONEY MONEY IS ITS CURSE   . .  777D INSC LAOCOON      PROSE
    I CURSE & BLESS ENGRAVING ALTERNATELY BECAUSE IT TAKES    837D LETTER 36         PROSE
        SO MUCH TIME
CURSED    SEE CURST
    AH WOMAN'S FEAR SHE CRYD AH CURSED DUKE   . . . . . .       5 FAIR ELENOR/PS       39
    O ELENOR BEWARE THE CURSED DUKE  . . . . . . . . .          6 FAIR ELENOR/PS       65
    IT IS THE CURSED THORN WOUNDING MY BREAST THAT MAKES ME   41D THEN SHE BORE      PROSE
        SING
    THERE TAKE THE BODY CURSED SONS & MAY THE HEAVENS RAIN    100 TIRIEL 1            43
        WRATH
    AND SIT & SMILE UPON THESE CURSED SONS OF TIRIEL  . . .   106 TIRIEL 5            12
    THEN WOULD THEY CURSE AS THOU HAST CURSED BUT THEY ARE    107 TIRIEL 6            25
        NOT LIKE THEE
    WITNESS THIS NUMBER & MANY OTHERS...CURSED FOLLY  . . . . 133A ANNO SWED PROV     MARG
    AND WE SO LOVED OUR GOD THAT WE CURSED IN HIS NAME ALL  . 153D MARRIAGE HH 12    PROSE
    WHAT A CURSED FOOL IS THIS ILL SHAPEN ARE INFANTS OR SMALL 406C ANNO BACON        MARG
        PLANTS
    ONE SPECIES OF GENERAL HUE OVER ALL IS THE CURSED THING   478D ANNO REYNOLDS      MARG
CURSES
    WHY SHOULD THY SONS CARE FOR THY CURSES THOU ACCURSED MAN  99 TIRIEL 1            16
    PLANT WORMS OF DEATH TO FEAST UPON THE TONGUE OF TERRIBLE 108 TIRIEL 6            39
        CURSES
    SPURNING THE CLOUDS WRITTEN WITH CURSES . . . . . . . . 160A SONG LIBERTY        PROSE
    PRONOUNCD CURSES ON [HIS] MY HEAD . . . . . . . . . . .   167 INFANT SORW/N        28
    IN [TEARS] CURSES & IRON BOUND  . . . . . . . . . . .     186 LET BROTHELS/N       61
    WITH SPECTRES AND THE WINDOWS WOVE OVER WITH CURSES OF IRON 243 EUROPE 12          27
    RAGD WITH CURSES & SPARKLES OF FURY  . . . . . . .        256 BOOK OF LOS 3        33
    FROM HIS MOUTH CURSES & FROM HIS EYES SPARKS OF BLIGHTING 305 FOUR ZOAS 5          3
    TO BE MY GREAT & AWFUL CURSES AT THE TIME APPOINTED  . .  336 FOUR ZOAS 7B        120
    HE CURSES HEAVEN & EARTH DAY & NIGHT & SUN & MOON   . .   629 JERUSALEM 10         25
    HE CURSES FOREST SPRING & RIVER DESART & SANDY WASTE  .   629 JERUSALEM 10         26
    AND CURSES WITH HIS MIGHTY ARMS BRANDISHD AGAINST         667 JERUSALEM 40         37
        THE HEAVENS
    WRIT WITH CURSES FROM POLE TO POLE  . . . . . . . .       754 EV GOSPEL(E)/N       13
    THE CURSES OF LOS THE TERRIBLE SHADE  . . . . . . . .     818 HAPPINESS/L          51
CURSING
    AND CURSING HIS LOT FOR IN ANGUISH   . . . . . . . . .    226 URIZEN 6             3
    CURSING THE VOICE THAT MOCKD HIM WITH FALSE HOPE IN FURIOUS 339 FOUR ZOAS 7B      260
        MOOD
    BIND HIM DOWN SISTERS BIND HIM DOWN ON EBAL MOUNT OF      349 FOUR ZOAS 8         315
        CURSING
    AND MILDLY CURSING PALAMABRON HIM ACCUSD OF CRIMES  . .   487 MILTON 7             36
    CURSING THE TERRIBLE LOS BITTERLY CURSING HIM FOR HIS     624 JERUSALEM 6          6
        FRIENDSHIP
    BIND HIM DOWN SISTERS BIND HIM DOWN ON EBAL MOUNT OF      705 JERUSALEM 68         3
        CURSING
    CURSING THE RULERS BEFORE THE PEOPLE  . . . . . . . .     752 EV GOSPEL(D)/N       69
    & RAGING & CURSING WHICH DREW OUT SEVERAL NEIGHBOURS  . 827B LETTER 28           PROSE
CURSINGS
    WITHIN HIS BREAST HIS FIERY SONS CHAIND DOWN & FILLD WITH 306 FOUR ZOAS 5         57
        CURSINGS
    WITHIN HIS BREAST HIS MIGHTY SONS CHAIND DOWN & FILLD WITH 667 JERUSALEM 40       40
        CURSINGS
CURST
    FOR THOU HAST LAUGHED AT MY TEARS & CURST THY AGED FATHER 108 TIRIEL 6            42
    THAN URIZEN & ALL HIS HOSTS IN CURST DESPAIR DOWN RUSHING 296 FOUR ZOAS 3        152
    OR WERE JEW VIRGINS STILL MORE CURST . . . . . . . .     756 EV GOSPEL(I)/N       7
CURTAIN
    ALL DAY HE BORE HIM & WHEN EVENING DREW HER SOLEMN CURTAIN 104 TIRIEL 4           41
    WHY A LITTLE CURTAIN OF FLESH ON THE BED OF OUR DESIRE  . 130 BOOK OF THEL 6      20
    IS CLOSD AS WITH A THREEFOLD CURTAIN OF IVORY & FINE LINEN 633 JERUSALEM 13       23
        & ERMINE
    BUILD & PREPARE A WALL & CURTAIN FOR AMERICA'S SHORE  . . 680 JERUSALEM 49        49
    THE DIVINE VISION WITH CURTAIN & VEIL & FLESHLY TABERNACLE 688 JERUSALEM 56    *  40
    A SHEET & VEIL & CURTAIN OF BLOOD IS LET DOWN FROM HEAVEN 706 JERUSALEM 68        21
    LIKE TO A CURTAIN & FOLDING THEM ACCORDING TO HIS WILL  . 738 JERUSALEM 91        34
    THE CURTAIN FALLS . . . . . . . . . . . . . . . . .      781B GHOST ABEL 2      PROSE
CURTAIND
    NONE DARE TO WAKE HER SOON SHE BURSTS HER CRIMSON CURTAIND 520 MILTON 31          57
        BED
    THAMMUZ IN LEBANON & RIMMON IN DAMASCUS CURTAIND  . . . . 528 MILTON 37           26
CURTAINS
    BLUE CURTAINS OF THE SKY SCATTER THY SILVER DEW  . . . .    3 EVNING STAR/PS       6
    THE CURTAINS OF THEIR BEDS DESTRUCTION IS  . . . . . .     30 EDW THIRD/PS 5      12
    TILL THE CURTAINS OF DARKNESS WERE DRAWN  . . . . . .     35D COUCH DEATH/PS     PROSE
    AND DREW THE CURTAINS OF HEAVEN  . . . . . . . . .        39D SAMSON/PS          PROSE
    IN THE SHADOWS OF HIS CURTAINS AND IN THE FOLDS OF HIS   194 V DAU ALBION 7        7
        SILENT PILLOW
    HAD JUST REMOVD THE CURTAINS OF THE NIGHT  . . . . . .    219 LIT GRL LST/Sଫ      14
    SPREAD A TENT WITH STRONG CURTAINS AROUND THEM   . . .    231 URIZEN 19            2
    THEY BEGAN TO WEAVE CURTAINS OF DARKNESS  . . . . . .     231 URIZEN 19            5
    STRIPPING JERUSALEM'S CURTAINS FROM MILD DEMONS OF THE    281 FOUR ZOAS 2         58
        HILLS
    THE UNIVERSAL CURTAINS & SPREAD OUT FROM SUN TO SUN  . .  284 FOUR ZOAS 2        153
```

CURTAINS (CONTINUED)
YET HIDING THE SHADOWY FEMALE VALA AS IN AN ARK & CURTAINS   347 FOUR ZOAS 8   255
A MALE WITHIN A FEMALE HID AS IN AN ARK & CURTAINS . . .   528 MILTON 37   40
HIDING THE HUMAN LINEAMENTS AS WITH AN ARK & CURTAINS .   533 MILTON 41   26
THE CURTAINS ARE DRAWN APART CHRIST HAVING RENT THE VEIL   613B V LAST JUDG/N   PROSE
THE CURTAINS WOVEN TEARS & SIGHS WROUGHT INTO LOVELY FORMS   632 JERUSALEM 12   39
THY PILLARS OF IVORY & GOLD THY CURTAINS OF SILK & FINE   647 JERUSALEM 24   18
AND LUVAH HATH DRAWN THE CURTAINS AROUND ALBION IN VALA'S   656 JERUSALEM 30   39
    BOSOM
INSTEAD OF ALBION'S LOVELY MOUNTAINS & THE CURTAINS OF   673 JERUSALEM 43   59
    JERUSALEM
A MALE WITHIN A FEMALE HID AS IN AN ARK & CURTAINS . . .   716 JERUSALEM 75   15
MY GATES IN ALL THEIR MOUNTAINS & MY CURTAINS IN ALL THEIR   720 JERUSALEM 79   46
    VALES
THE PATHOS TO WEAVE CURTAINS OF HIDING SECRESY FROM THE   736 JERUSALEM 90   13
    TORMENT
CUSH
COBAN'S SON IS NIMROD HIS SON CUSH IS ADJOIND TO ARAM .   625 JERUSALEM 7   19
WITH CUSH HIS SON & TOOK ME DOWN HE IN A GOLDEN ARK . . .   644 JERUSALEM 22   4
CUSHION
OTHER DAUGHTERS WEAVE ON THE CUSHION & PILLOW NETWORK FINE   692 JERUSALEM 59   42
CUSTOM
TWAS COVET OR TWAS CUSTOM OR . . . .   755 EV GOSPEL(E)/N   61
CUSTOMER
BUT CANNOT AS YET FIND A CUSTOMER FOR ONE . . . . . .   876D LETTER 85   PROSE
CUSTOMER FOR IT AS YOU WISH ME TO SEND YOU A LIST WITH .   878D LETTER 88   PROSE
CUT
CLOUDED FALLN LIKE THE STATELY TREE CUT DOWN . . . . .   5 FAIR ELENOR/PS   50
LITTLE SPORT AND CUT A PATH INTO THE HEAVEN OF GLORY . .   27 EDW THIRD/PS 3   274
O SOON CUT OFF I TH MORNING OF HER DAYS . . . . . .   43C WOE CRIED MUSE   PROSE
AND CUT OUT ALL ITS SPOTS . . . .   51 WHEN CORRUP/IM   34
HAVING HER CANCER CUT & SHE SHRIEKD SO THAT I WAS QUITE   51C ISLAND MOON 6   PROSE
    SICK
AND ALL THE CHILDREN IN THEIR BEDS WERE CUT OFF IN ONE   107 TIRIEL 5   33
    NIGHT
IS CUT OFF FROM THE WEEPING MOUTH WITH DIFFICULTY & PAIN   110 TIRIEL 8   28
HIS FEET AND HANDS CUT OFF AND HIS EYES BLINDED . . . .   136 FRENCH REVOLTN   44
THE CUT WORM FORGIVES THE PLOW . . . .   151A MARRIAGE HH 7   PROSE
[THE CUT WORM] . . . .   183 THE FLY/N   9
FALLING UPON AMERICA AS A STORM TO CUT THEM OFF . . . .   201 AMERICA 14   5
CUT OFF FROM LIFE & LIGHT FROZEN . . . .   230 URIZEN 13   42
TO CUT OFF THE BREAD FROM THE CITY . . . .   247 SONG OF LOS 7   1
AND ALL THE WHILE THE PLOW OF IRON CUT THE DREADFUL FURROWS   282 FOUR ZOAS 2   70
CUT BY THE PLOW OF AGES HELD IN URIZEN'S STRONG HAND . .   283 FOUR ZOAS 2   119
CUT THEE IN GASHES THO THE BLOOD POURS DOWN AROUND THY   322 FOUR ZOAS 7   84
    ANKLES
AND CUT THE WINDS LIKE ARROWS SHOT BY TROOPS OF DESTINY   325 FOUR ZOAS 7   208
TO BE CUT OFF & SEPARATED THAT THE SPIRITUAL BODY MAY BE   348 FOUR ZOAS 8   267
    REVEALD
[AND] BUT WHEN RAHAB HAD CUT OFF THE MANTLE OF LUVAH FROM   350 FOUR ZOAS 8   341
CUT HIM OFF FROM GOLGONOOZA BUT ENITHARMON IN TEARS . .   350 FOUR ZOAS 8   370
RINTRAH & PALAMABRON CUT SHEER OFF FROM GOLGONOOZA . . .   351 FOUR ZOAS 8   394
MYSTERY'S TYRANTS ARE CUT OFF & NOT ONE LEFT ON EARTH .   359 FOUR ZOAS 9   79
AND WHEN ALL TYRANNY WAS CUT OFF FROM THE FACE OF EARTH   359 FOUR ZOAS 9   * 80
FELL AND WAS CUT OFF ALL THINGS VANISH & ARE SEEN NO MORE   505 MILTON 22   22
THE OAK IS CUT DOWN BY THE AX THE LAMB FALLS BY THE KNIFE   522 MILTON 32   37
CUT OFF MY LOVES IN FURY TILL I HAVE NO LOVE LEFT FOR THEE   522 MILTON 33   7
DEPEND THY PLEASURES WHICH THOU HAST CUT OFF BY JEALOUSY   522 MILTON 33   9
HIMSELF THAT SEEING ALL HIS LOVES BY HER CUT OFF HE LEAVES   522 MILTON 33   15
TOM COOKE CUT HOGARTH DOWN WITH HIS CLEAN GRAVING . . .   554 BLAKES APL/N 1   3
TOM COOKE CUT HOGARTH DOWN WITH HIS CLEAN GRAVING . . .   555 BLAKES APL/N 2   7
CUT DOTS & LOZENGES EQUALLY WELL WITH THOSE LITTLE PRINTS   592B PUB ADDRESS/N   PROSE
TOM COOKE CUT HOGARTH DOWN WITH HIS CLEAN GRAVING . . .   595 BLAKES APOL/PA   3
I DEFY ANY MAN TO CUT CLEANER STROKES THAN I DO OR . . .   602A PUB ADDRESS/N   PROSE
THY UNCIRCUMCISED PRETENCES TO CHASTITY MUST BE CUT IN   627 JERUSALEM 8   32
    SUNDER
CUT OFF FROM ALBION'S MOUNTAINS & FROM ALL THE EARTH'S   661 JERUSALEM 34   44
    SUMMITS
HIS FRIENDS CUT HIS STRONG CHAINS & OVERWHELMD HIS DARK   675 JERUSALEM 45   21
FEEL THEIR BRAIN CUT ROUND BENEATH THE TEMPLES SHRIEKING   689 JERUSALEM 58   7
THE OBDURATE FORMS ARE CUT ASUNDER BY JEALOUSY & PITY .   689 JERUSALEM 58   12
AND A PECULIAR TABERNACLE TO CUT THE INTEGUMENTS OF BEAUTY   693 JERUSALEM 60   33
CUT WITH THE FLINTS HER TEARS RUN DOWN HER REASON GROWS   693 JERUSALEM 60   42
    LIKE
BUT THEY CUT ASUNDER HIS INNER GARMENTS SEARCHING WITH .   702 JERUSALEM 66   27
LONDON FEELS HIS BRAIN CUT ROUND EDINBURGH'S HEART   703 JERUSALEM 66   64
    IS CIRCUMSCRIBED
AND AS THEY WOVE & CUT FROM THE LOOMS IN VARIOUS DIVISIONS   704 JERUSALEM 67   6
THEY CUT THE FIBRES FROM THE ROCKS GROANING IN PAIN THEY   704 JERUSALEM 67   11
    WEAVE
THE HEAVENS ARE CUT LIKE A MANTLE AROUND FROM THE CLIFFS   706 JERUSALEM 68   19
    OF ALBION
BEFORE THE KINGS OF CANAAN TO CUT THE FLESH FROM THE VICTIM   706 JERUSALEM 68   57
CUT THE FIBRES OF REUBEN HOW HE ROLLD APART & TOOK ROOT   715 JERUSALEM 74   42
TO CUT HER OFF FROM AMERICA TO CLOSE UP HER SECRET ARK . .   725 JERUSALEM 82   34
AS THEY CUT THE FIBRES FROM THE RIVERS HE SEARS THEM WITH   736 JERUSALEM 90   19
    HOT
IN CRUEL PRIDE CUT REUBEN APART FROM THE HILLS OF SURREY   736 JERUSALEM 90   25
SCANDALOUS AND UNFIT FOR SUCH A WORK HERE I CUT HIM SHORT   846D LETTER 44   PROSE
WOULD CUT OFF TEN GUINEAS FROM MY NEXT DEMAND ON PHILLIPS   861B LETTER 58   PROSE
MY DEAREST FRIEND THIS SUDDEN COLD WEATHER HAS CUT UP .   872D LETTER 76   PROSE

```
                                                    PAGE     TITLE           LINE
CUTLASS
    . . . SWORD OR A CUTLASS A DAGGER OR KNIFE  . . . . . .  548 ON GREAT ENC/N     2
CUTS
    HOW DO YOU KNOW BUT EVRY BIRD THAT CUTS THE AIRY WAY  .  150D MARRIAGE HH 6  PROSE
    AS A BLIGHT CUTS THE TENDER CORN WHEN IT BEGINS TO APPEAR 201 AMERICA 14        6
    AND AS A PLAGUE WIND FILLD WITH INSECTS CUTS OFF MAN &   201 AMERICA 14         8
      BEAST
    . . . & THE SICKNESS THAT CUTS OFF HIS CHILDREN  . . . . 291 FOUR ZOAS 2     412
    SHE CUTS HIS HEART OUT AT HIS SIDE  . . . . . . . .      425 MENTAL TRAVLER    15
CUTTING
    WISH JACK [HUNTER] TEARGUTS HAD HAD THE CUTTING OF PLUTARCH 50A ISLAND MOON 6 PROSE
    STAND ROUND HIM CUTTING THE FIBRES FROM ALBION'S HILLS . . 636 JERUSALEM 15    23
    BOWEN & CONWENNA STOOD ON SKIDDAW CUTTING THE FIBRES  . . 736 JERUSALEM 90     14
CUTTING-OFF
    SINCE ALBION'S DEATH & SATAN'S CUTTING-OFF FROM OUR AWFUL  510 MILTON 25       30
      FIELDS
CYMBAL
    BUT THE SOFT PIPE THE FLUTE THE VIOL ORGAN HARP & CYMBAL   306 FOUR ZOAS 5     23
    REPLY TO VIOLINS & TABORS TO THE PIPE FLUTE LYRE & CYMBAL  376 FOUR ZOAS 9    721
    WITH CYMBAL TRUMPET CLARION & THE SCYTHED CHARIOTS         677 JERUSALEM 47    11
      OF BRITAIN
CYMBALS
    THE ARMIES I HEAR THEIR LOUD CYMBALS & THEIR DEADLY CRIES  644 JERUSALEM 21    47
    OF WAR THE CYMBALS PLAY LOUD BEFORE THE CAPTAINS  . . . . 722 JERUSALEM 80    38
CYNIC
    SUCTION THE EPICUREAN QUID THE CYNIC & SIPSOP THE          44A ISLAND MOON 1 PROSE
      PYTHAGOREAN
    THE (THREE) PHILOSOPHERS [THE ?OLDER] THE CYNIC SMILING    44C ISLAND MOON 1 *PROSE
    THE CYNIC ANSWERD THEY ARE ONLY QUARRELING ABOUT VOLTAIRE  45C ISLAND MOON 1  PROSE
    [& THE THREE PHILOSOPHERS (COMING) QUID THE CYNIC SIPSOP]  46B ISLAND MOON 2 *PROSE
    O AY COME I'LL SING YOU A SONG SAID THE CYNIC  . . . . .  46C ISLAND MOON 3  PROSE
    I'LL BEGIN AGAIN SAID THE CYNIC  . . . . . . . .          46C ISLAND MOON 3  PROSE
    SING AWAY QUID THEN THE CYNIC SUNG  . . . . . . .         47C ISLAND MOON 3  PROSE
    OR PHEBUS THAN PHAROH HANG THEM BOTH SAID THE CYNIC  . .  47D ISLAND MOON 4  PROSE
    THEN [SIPSOP ?SANG] THE CYNIC ?SANG  . . . . . . .        50B ISLAND MOON 6 *PROSE
    [I'LL DASH YOU THROUGH YOUR CHAIR SAYS THE CYNIC]  . .    57A ISLAND MOON 9  PROSE
DACRE
    THERES LITTLE TOM DACRE WHO CRIED WHEN HIS HEAD  . . . .  117 CHIMNEY SWP/SI    5
DADY
    AND CUR MY LAWYER & DADY [MY] JACK HEMP'S PARSON  . . .   537 AND HIS LEGS/N *  26
DAEMON
    BUT WORN AWAY A BLOODLESS DAEMON  . . . . . . . .         41D THEN SHE BORE  PROSE
DAGGER
    . . . SWORD OR A CUTLASS A DAGGER OR KNIFE  . . . . . .   548 ON GREAT ENC/N     2
    UNDER PRETENCE OF CRITICISM USE THE DAGGER AND THE POISON  864A LETTER 61    PROSE
DAGGERS
    [WITH DAGGERS HID BENEATH THEIR LIPS & POISON IN THEIR     109 TIRIEL 8        14
      TONGUE]
    NEVER READ ONE THAT IS TO ME IT IS ALL DAGGERS & POISON    384C ANNO WATSON    MARG
DAGON
    PITY FORSOOK THEE AT THY BIRTH O DAGON FURIOUS  . . . .    38C SAMSON/PS     PROSE
    IN PALESTINE DAGON SEA MONSTER WORSHIPD OER THE SEA  . .   528 MILTON 37        25
DAGWORTH
    DUKE OF CLARENCE SIR JOHN CHANDOS SIR THOMAS DAGWORTH      17C EDW THIRD/PS   TITLE
    SCENE AT CRESSEY SIR THOMAS DAGWORTH AND LORD AUDLEY       21C EDW THIRD/PS 3 *PROSE
      MEETING
    SIR THOMAS DAGWORTH YOU MUST HAVE YOUR JOKE  . . . . .     23 EDW THIRD/PS 3    92
    WHAT CAN SIR THOMAS DAGWORTH ASK THAT EDWARD  . . . . .    23 EDW THIRD/PS 3    96
    SIR THOMAS DAGWORTH BE THOU NEAR OUR PERSON  . . . . .     25 EDW THIRD/PS 3   172
    EXIT DAGWORTH  . . . . . . . . . . . . . . .              25C EDW THIRD/PS 3 PROSE
    SCENE IN SIR THOMAS DAGWORTH'S TENT DAGWORTH AND WILLIAM   28B EDW THIRD/PS 4 PROSE
      HIS MAN
    SIR THOMAS DAGWORTH TO HIM ENTER SIR WALTER MANNY  . .     30A EDW THIRD/PS 5 PROSE
    SIR THOMAS DAGWORTH I HAVE BEEN WEEPING  . . . . . .       30 EDW THIRD/PS 5     1
    O DAGWORTH FRANCE IS SICK THE VERY SKY  . . . . . . .      30 EDW THIRD/PS 5    21
DAGWORTH'S
    BISHOP WILLIAM DAGWORTH'S MAN PETER BLUNT A COMMON         17C EDW THIRD/PS   TITLE
      SOLDIER
    SCENE IN SIR THOMAS DAGWORTH'S TENT DAGWORTH AND WILLIAM   28B EDW THIRD/PS 4 PROSE
      HIS MAN
    SCENE SIR THOMAS DAGWORTH'S TENT  . . . . . . . . .        30A EDW THIRD/PS 5 PROSE
DAILY
    YET I PRETEND TO LOVE TO SEE TO CONVERSE WITH DAILY AS     621A JERUSALEM 3   PROSE
      MAN WITH MAN
    CONVERSE DAILY & HOURLY IN THE SPIRIT &  . . . . . . .     797A LETTER 9      PROSE
    FROM HEAVEN DAILY & NIGHTLY BUT THE NATURE OF SUCH THINGS  812A LETTER 22     PROSE
    DAILY PERSISTING IN SPIRITUAL LABOURS  . . . . . .         863B LETTER 60     PROSE
DAINTY
    . . . THE NETTLE FOR A NOURISHING DAINTY  . . . . . .      290 FOUR ZOAS 2     387
DAIRY
    IN THE DAIRY MY FEET ARE WINGD BUT NOT  . . . . . .        24 EDW THIRD/PS 3   149
DAISY
    FROM AN OAK ITS HEIGHTH FROM A DAISY ITS LOWNESS & [CHAOS]  81C ANNO LAVATER  * MARG
DALE
    WHO IN SORROW PALE THRO THE LONELY DALE  . . . . . .       121 LIT BOY FND/SI    7
    IN THE DALE  . . . . . . . . . . . . . . . .              123 SPRING/SI          6
    AND WHISPRINGS ARE IN THE DALE  . . . . . . . . .         171 NURSES SONG/N     2
    AND WHISPRINGS ARE IN THE DALE  . . . . . . . . .         212 NURSES SONG/SE    2
    ON MOUNTAIN DALE AND PLAIN  . . . . . . . . . .           248 SONG OF LOS 7    40
    & THE SHEPHERD & HIS LASS UNDER A HAWTHORN IN THE DALE  .  618B ILLUS MILTON  PROSE
DALES
    AND THEY WENT ON TOGETHER OVER HILLS THRO WOODY DALES  . . 104 TIRIEL 4        28
```

	PAGE	TITLE	LINE

DALES   (CONTINUED)
    WALKING IN PLEASURE OF THE HILLS OR MURMURING IN THE DALES   340 FOUR ZOAS 7B   266
DALILA
    THOURT WAR THOU ART NOT LOVE O FOOLISH DALILA . . . . .   38B SAMSON/PS   PROSE
    TIS DALILA THAT CALLS THY MASTER'S WIFE NO STAY   . . . .   38B SAMSON/PS   PROSE
    LEANING ON HER BOSOM THUS HE SPOKE HEAR O DALILA   . . .   39B SAMSON/PS   PROSE
DALILAS
    FOR DALILA'S FAIR ARTS HAVE LONG BEEN TRIED IN VAIN   . . .   38A SAMSON/PS   PROSE
DALLINGTON
    HIS ADDRESS IS THIS TO JOHN HAWKINS ESQR DALLINGTON . . .   855B LETTER 53   PROSE
DALLY
    MR DALLY TO WHOM I ENCLOSED...IN A LETTER A FORTNIGHT   .   841A LETTER 40   PROSE
    WHICH MR JOHNSON WAS TO GET DONE FOR OUR FRIEND DALLY .   847A LETTER 44   PROSE
DAMASCUS
    THAMMUZ IN LEBANON & RIMMON IN DAMASCUS CURTAIND   . . . .   528 MILTON 37   26
    GWANTOCK & PEACHY HID IN DAMASCUS BENEATH MOUNT LEBANON   662 JERUSALEM 36   16
    FROM GAZA TO DAMASCUS TYRE & SIDON & THE GODS . . . . .   735 JERUSALEM 89   33
DAME
    AND [HE] SMILD AT THE DAME   163 ASKED THIEF/N   7
    [HE] ENJOYD THE [(DAME)] LADY . . . .   163 ASKED THIEF/N * 12
    AND MODEST DAME LURCH WHO IS ALWAYS AT CHURCH . . . . .   179 LIT VAGABOND/N   12
    AND MODEST DAME LURCH WHO IS ALWAYS AT CHURCH . . . . .   216 LIT VAGABND/SE   11
    AND SMILD AT THE DAME . . . .   261 ASKED THIEF   8
DAMN
    ("SNEER IS OFTEN SIGN OF HEARTLESS MALIGNITY") DAMN   67D ANNO LAVATER   MARG
        SNEERERS
    ("HE WHO NIBBLES IN A LOW VOICE ...NIBBLING") DAMN SUCH   73D ANNO LAVATER   MARG
    ("TO AVERT SUSPICION ACCUSES THE INNOCENT") DAMN HIM . .   78A ANNO LAVATER   MARG
    DAMN BRACES BLESS RELAXES . . . .   152C MARRIAGE HH 9   PROSE
    [[DAMN PRAYING & SINGING]] . . . .   185 LET BROTHELS/N   13
    (DAMN) THE (KING) NOW I HAVE ALL THE PERSONS WHO WERE .   437C BLAKES MEMORAN   PROSE
    WHO SWORE THAT HE HEARD ME (DAMN) THE (KING)   . . . .   437C BLAKES MEMORAN   PROSE
    [DAMN THE FOOL] MEER ENTHUSIASM IS THE ALL IN ALL   . .   456C ANNO REYNOLDS * MARG
    AT THE GATE UTTER SEDITIOUS WORDS & (DAMN) THE (KING) .   827D LETTER 28   PROSE
DAMNABLE
    THIS IS THE MOST DAMNABLE FALSHOOD OF SATAN & HIS   785B ILLUS DANTE 7   PROSE
        ANTICHRIST
DAMND
    A PLACE IN THE NEW JERUSALEM EXCZLLENT TRAVELLER GO ON   404D ANNO BACON * MARG
        & BE DAMND
    ("NEVER ATTEMPTED THOSE LESSER ELEGANCIES") DAMND FOOL   467C ANNO REYNOLDS * MARG
    ("IF GENIUS IS NOT TAKEN FOR INSPIRATION") DAMND FOOL   470C ANNO REYNOLDS * MARG
DAMNED
    THAT ALL WHO PASS MAY READ NOW NIGHT NOON-TIDE OF DAMNED   37D SAMSON/PS   PROSE
        SPIRITS
DAMP
    HE SAT DOWN A DAMP COLD PERVADED THE NOBLES . . . . .   141 FRENCH REVOLTN   158
    WHAT DAMP ALL OUR FIRES O SPECTRE OF HENRY . . . . . .   142 FRENCH REVOLTN   171
    AND SNAKE AND DAMP TOAD ON THE KINGLY FOOT CRAWL . . . .   147 FRENCH REVOLTN   298
    . . . [WITH FLAMES] [HOAR FROSTS] DAMP MISTS . . . . .   205 AMERICA CANC C   5
    A DAMP COLD CAME OER HER HER BLUSHES ALL FLED . . . . .   428 MARY   19
    TWILL MAKE A GREAT SPLUTTER WITH SMOKE & DAMP   . . . .   549 ENGL ENCOU/N 1   6
    TWILL HOLD FORTH A HUGE SPLUTTER WITH SMOKE & DAMP   . .   550 ENGL ENCOU/N 2   6
    DAMP COUCH THE FLAMES BENEATH AND SILENT SICK STAND   666 JERUSALEM 40   6
        SHUDDERING
DAMPS
    THE DAMPS OF DEATH FALL THICK UPON ME HORRORS STARE ME   35D COUCH DEATH/PS   PROSE
        IN THE FACE
    AND FEELING THE DAMPS OF DEATH THEY WITH ONE ACCORD   674 JERUSALEM 44   28
        DELEGATED LOS
    UPON THE WHITE ROCK ENGLAND A FEMALE SHADOW AS DEADLY DAMPS   741 JERUSALEM 94   7
DAMSEL
    FOR IF A DAMSEL S BLIND OR LAME   . . . .   56 HAIL MATRIM/IM   13
    IN DAMSEL OR IN WIDOW GAY . . . .   56 HAIL MATRIM/IM   21
    BEAUTIFUL BLOOMING DAMSEL AND H(HOPPNER) SAYS . . . . .   574B DESC CAT 3   *PROSE
DAN
    HAR OCHIM IJIM ADAM REUBEN SIMEON LEVI JUDAH DAN NAPHTALI   350 FOUR ZOAS 8   360
    THEN DAN THEN NAPHTALI THEN GAD THEN ASHER THEN ISSACHAR   350 FOUR ZOAS 8   376
    THE GATE OF JUDAH MERIONETHSHIRE THE GATE OF DAN   637 JERUSALEM 16   37
        FLINTSHIRE
    DAN CORNWAL DEVON DORSET NAPTHALI WARWICK LEICESTER   637 JERUSALEM 16   46
        WORCESTER
    DIVIDED IN THE THE GATES OF REUBEN JUDAH DAN & JOSEPH . .   637 JERUSALEM 16   51
    DAN BUTE CAITNES CLAKMANAN NAPTHALI NAIRN INVERNES   638 JERUSALEM 16   55
        LINLITHGO
    THEY DRINK UP DAN & GAD TO FEED WITH MILK SKOFELD & KOTOPE   704 JERUSALEM 67   22
    AND THOSE UNDER DAN ASHER & NAPTHALI ARE THESE   . . . .   711 JERUSALEM 72   25
    DAN NAPTHALI GAD ASHER ISSACHAR ZEBULUN ROLL APART   . .   715 JERUSALEM 74 * 50
    LEVI AND JUDAH & ISSACHAR EPHRAM MANASSEH GAD AND DAN   720 JERUSALEM 79   30
DANCD
    THE ENEMY HE HAS DANCD IN THE FIELD . . . .   22 EDW THIRD/PS 3   30
    GIVING HIMSELF FOR THE NATIONS HE DANCD THE DANCE   160 ALBION ROSE   2
        OF ETERNAL DEATH
    INFECTED MAD HE DANCD ON HIS MOUNTAINS HIGH & DARK   305 FOUR ZOAS 5   1
        AS HEAVEN
    BESIDE THE ANVIL COLD HE DANCD WITH THE HAMMER OF URTHONA   305 FOUR ZOAS 5   4
DANCE
    OUR MAIDENS FAIRER IN THE SPRIGHTLY DANCE . . . . . .   2 TO SUMMER/PS   16
    AND ALL THE DAUGHTERS OF THE YEAR SHALL DANCE . . . . .   2 TO AUTUMN/PS   5
    I LOVE THE JOCUND DANCE . . . .   7 LOVE JOCUND/PS   1
    AND LEAP AND DANCE TO HEAR THE TRUMPET SOUND . . . . .   25 EDW THIRD/PS 3   171
    AND DANCE TO THE NEIGHING OF OUR STEEDS . . . . . .   26 EDW THIRD/PS 3   227

	PAGE	TITLE	LINE

DANCE   (CONTINUED)
THAT SING AND DANCE ROUND REASON'S FINE-WROUGHT THRONE . . . 28 EDW THIRD/PS 3 291
THE DANCE WAS BROKE THE CIRCLE JUST BEGUN . . . . . . 43C WOE CRIED MUSE PROSE
GIVING HIMSELF FOR THE NATIONS HE DANCD THE DANCE 160 ALBION ROSE 2
   OF ETERNAL DEATH
AND BECAUSE I AM HAPPY & DANCE & SING . . . . 180 CHIMNEY SWP/N 9
FOR I DANCE . . . . 183 THE FLY/N 17
WITH MANY AN ALLURING DANCE . . . . 185 LET BROTHELS/N 2
AND BECAUSE I AM HAPPY & DANCE & SING . . . . 212 CHIMNEY SWP/SE 9
FOR I DANCE . . . . 213 THE FLY/SE 9
IN RIVERS RUSH & SHOUT & DANCE . . . . 248 SONG OF LOS 7 39
OR WISDOM FOR A DANCE IN THE STREET NO IT IS BOUGHT WITH 290 FOUR ZOAS 2 398
   THE PRICE
BEGAN A DISMAL DANCE THE WINDS AROUND ON POINTED ROCKS . . 306 FOUR ZOAS 5 34
DANCE ON THE RIVERS & THE ROCKS HOWLING & DRUNK WITH FURY 320 FOUR ZOAS 7 13
BUT IN THE WINE PRESSES THE HUMAN GRAPES SING NOT NOR DANCE 377 FOUR ZOAS 9 748
DANCE ROUND THE WINE PRESSES OF LUVAH THE CENTIPEDE IS 377 FOUR ZOAS 9 757
   THERE
THEY DANCE AROUND THE DYING & THEY DRINK THE HOWL & GROAN 377 FOUR ZOAS 9 767
DANCE BEFORE DEAD ENGLAND'S HEARSE . . . . 433 AUGURIES 118
AND ANVILS DANCE THE DANCE OF TEARS & PAIN LOUD LIGHTNINGS 484 MILTON 5 16
LOUD SPORT THE DANCERS IN THE DANCE OF DEATH REJOICING 509 MILTON 24 62
   IN CARNAGE
THOU SEEST THE GORGEOUS CLOTHED FLIES THAT DANCE & SPORT 512 MILTON 26 2
   IN SUMMER
UPON THE SUNNY BROOKS & MEADOWS EVERY ONE THE DANCE . . . 512 MILTON 26 3
EACH ONE TO SOUND HIS INSTRUMENTS OF MUSIC IN THE DANCE 512 MILTON 26 5
DANCE ROUND THE WINE-PRESSES OF LUVAH THE CENTIPEDE IS 513 MILTON 27 13
   THERE
BUT IN THE WINE-PRESSES THE HUMAN GRAPES SING NOT NOR DANCE 513 MILTON 27 30
THEY DANCE AROUND THE DYING & THEY DRINK THE HOWL & GROAN 514 MILTON 27 37
LIGHT SPRINGING ON THE AIR LEAD THE SWEET DANCE THEY WAKE 520 MILTON 31 53
AND FLOWER & HERB SOON FILL THE AIR WITH AN INNUMERABLE 521 MILTON 31 61
   DANCE
ON WHICH HE USD TO DANCE & SPORT & CAPER . . . . . 537 AND HIS LEGS/N 19
BY FAIRIES AS THEY DANCE ON THE BED THE CIELING & THE FLOOR 618C ILLUS MILTON *PROSE
DANCE THE DANCE OF DEATH CONTENDING WITH JEHOVAH AMONG 697 JERUSALEM 63 10
   THE CHERUBIM
THE GIANTS & THE WITCHES & THE GHOSTS OF ALBION DANCE WITH 697 JERUSALEM 63 13
DRINKING HIS EMANATION IN INTOXICATING BLISS REJOICING 701 JERUSALEM 65 58
   IN GIANT DANCE
TAUGHT TO TOUCH THE HARP TO DANCE IN THE CIRCLE OF WARRIORS 706 JERUSALEM 68 56
WITH CAMBEL & GWENDOLEN IN DANCE AND SOLEMN SONG . . . 722 JERUSALEM 80 39
DOUBT NOT YET TO MAKE A FIGURE IN THE GREAT DANCE OF LIFE 835A LETTER 34 PROSE
A CIRCULAR DANCE . . . . SUPP ILLUS GRAY *TITLE
DANCED
DANCED AROUND HER SHINING HEAD . . . . 435 WILLIAM BOND 42
THEY DANCED OVER THE PILLOW WHITE . . . . 435 WILLIAM BOND 43
WE REARED MIGHTY STONES WE DANCED NAKED AROUND THEM . . . 647 JERUSALEM 24 4
DANCERS
LOUD SPORT THE DANCERS IN THE DANCE OF DEATH REJOICING 509 MILTON 24 62
   IN CARNAGE
DANCES
NOW MY HEART DANCES AND I AM AS LIGHT . . . . 24 EDW THIRD/PS 3 144
IN THE IMMENSE AS WHEN THE SUN DANCES UPON THE MOUNTAINS 366 FOUR ZOAS 9 349
DANCING
MAIDENS DANCING LOVES ASPORTING . . . . 53 PHEBE DREST/IM 5
SINGING & DANCING MERRILY . . . . 188 A FAIRY SKIPD 2
THEY VIEWD THE DANCING HOURS QUICK SPORTING THRO THE SKY 274 FOUR ZOAS 1 357
INTO UNUSUAL FORMS DANCING & HOWLING STAMPING THE ABYSS 305 FOUR ZOAS 4 295
WHEN VOCAL MAY COMES DANCING FROM THE EAST AHANIA CAME . . 362 FOUR ZOAS 9 194
NAKED IN ALL THEIR BEAUTY DANCING ROUND THE WINE PRESSES 377 FOUR ZOAS 9 766
WHERE I WAS DANCING MERRILY . . . . 429 CRYSTL CABINET 2
THE SERVANTS OF THE MILLS DRUNKEN WITH WINE AND DANCING 488 MILTON 8 8
   WILD
NAKED IN ALL THEIR BEAUTY DANCING ROUND THE WINE-PRESSES 513 MILTON 27 29
AND WHAT IS THE SECOND THEN DANCING A JIG . . . . . . 553 ASKD PRIGG/N 3
THE DANCING FAWN FOR YOUR UGLY MAN NOW HE COMES TO HIS 579B DESC CAT 5 PROSE
   TRIAL
NAKED & DRUNK WITH BLOOD GWENDOLEN DANCING TO THE TIMBREL 689 JERUSALEM 58 2
DANCING AROUND IN HOWLING PAIN CLOTHED IN THE BLOODY VEIL 704 JERUSALEM 67 16
DANDELION
MR FINCHAM'S PRACTISE WITH ME THE ADDITION IS DANDELION 874B LETTER 79 PROSE
DANGER
THAT PLAYS WITH DANGER AS THE INNOCENT CHILD . . . . . 27 EDW THIRD/PS 3 241
DO I SLEEP AMIDST DANGER TO FRIENDS O MY CITIES & COUNTIES 744 JERUSALEM 96 33
NOTE THE DANGER IS IN NOT COVERING THE PLATE ALL OVER . . 790C LETTER 2 PROSE
SOLDIER-LIKE DANGER IS OVER I WILL DO DOUBLE THE WORK I DO 830C LETTER 30 PROSE
THAT MUST BE SATISFACTORY THE ONLY DANGER WILL BE THAT I 853A LETTER 51 *PROSE
DANGEROUS
IS DANGEROUS TO FIGHT NOT GOOD FOR FOOD . . . . . . 27 EDW THIRD/PS 3 266
INTO THE DANGEROUS WORLD I LEAPT . . . . 166 INFANT SORW/N 2
INTO THE DANGEROUS WORLD I LEAPT . . . . 217 INFANT SORW/SE 2
DANGERS
THOSE DANGERS ARE NOW PASSED & I CAN SEE THEM BENEATH . . 862D LETTER 60 PROSE
DANK
I HEARD AMONG THE RUSHES DANK . . . . 162 LAID ME DOWN/N 3
DAN'S
ULSTER NORTH IN DAN'S GATE LEINSTER EAST IN JUDAH'S GATE 711 JERUSALEM 72 4
DANTE
AND FROM THOSE OF DANTE OR SHAKESPEAR AN INFINITE NUMBER 158A MARRIAGE HH 21 PROSE
SHAKESPEAR OR DANTE . . . . 411B ANNO BOYD MARG

428

```
                                                              PAGE     TITLE           LINE
DANTE   (CONTINUED)
    EVERY SENTIMENT & OPINION AS WELL AS EVERY PRINCIPLE       413A ANNO BOYD         MARG
      IN DANTE
    DANTE WAS A FOOL OR HIS [TRANSLATION] TRANSLATOR WAS NOT    413B ANNO BOYD       * MARG
    THAT IS DANTE WAS HIRED OR (TRANSLATOR) WAS NOT      . .    413B ANNO BOYD         MARG
    BUT DANTE GIVES TOO MUCH ?CAESAR HE IS NOT A REPUBLICAN     413B ANNO BOYD         MARG
    DANTE WAS AN EMPEROR'S A CAESAR'S MAN    . . . . . . .      413B ANNO BOYD         MARG
    HOW MUCH OF HIS HOMER & DANTE HE WILL ALLOW TO BE MINE . .  592D PUB ADDRESS/N     PROSE
    [PYTHAGORAS SOCRATES EURIPEDES VIRGIL DANTE MILTON] . . .   714 JERUSALEM 73    *  42
    CENTAURS MOST LIKELY DANTE DESCRIBES THE...CIRCLES IN CANTO 786A ILLS DANTE 101   PROSE
      XI...
    DANTE CALLS THEM CERCHIETTI . . . . . . . . . . .           786A ILLS DANTE 101   PROSE
    BUT THE CRITIC MUST BE A FOOL WHO HAS NOT READ DANTE   . .  864B LETTER 61        PROSE
    I AM GOING ON WITH DANTE & PLEASE MYSELF I AM DR SIR YOURS  869A LETTER 68        PROSE
      SINCERELY
    APPAREL ONLY MY BOOK OF DRAWINGS FROM DANTE & ONE PLATE     873A LETTER 76        PROSE
    I GO ON AS I THINK IMPROVING MY ENGRAVINGS OF DANTE . . .   876A LETTER 83        PROSE
    OF DANTE WHICH YOU HAVE THAT I MAY FINISH THEM SUFFICIENTLY 876A LETTER 83        PROSE
    THE DANTE HE EXPRESSD HIMSELF VERY MUCH PLEASD WITH    . .  877A LETTER 85        PROSE
    AIR YET I LOSE NOTHING BY IT DANTE GOES ON THE BETTER   . . 877D LETTER 88        PROSE
    FINISHD STATE I AM TOO MUCH ATTACHD TO DANTE TO THINK MUCH  879C LETTER 89        PROSE
DANTE'S
    EVERY THING IN DANTE'S COMEDIA SHEWS THAT  . . . . . . .    785A ILLUS DANTE 7    PROSE
    IT SEEMS AS IF DANTE'S SUPREME GOOD WAS  . . . . . . .      785C ILLS DANTE 101   PROSE
    HE COULD NEVER HAVE BUILT DANTE'S HELL NOR  . . . . . .     785C ILLS DANTE 101   PROSE
    ?LEAH & RACHEL ?DANTE'S ?DREAM  . . . . . . . . .           SUPP ILLUS DANTE 86  *PROSE
DANUBE
    THE DANUBE ROLLD A PURPLE TIDE . . . . . . . . .            651 FIELDS FROM/J      46
    LOUD THE CRIES OF WAR ON THE RHINE & DANUBE WITH ALBION'S   677 JERUSALEM 47        9
      SONS
    TILL CANAAN ROLLD APART FROM ALBION ACROSS THE RHINE ALONG  698 JERUSALEM 63       41
      THE DANUBE
    OVER FRANCE & GERMANY UPON THE RHINE & DANUBE . . . . .     706 JERUSALEM 68       46
DAPHNE
    "AS DAPHNE WAS ROOT BOUND" MILTON . . . . . . . . .         SUPP LEGEND/N36       *
DAPPLED
    THE DAWN WITH HER DAPPLED HORSES ARISES ABOVE THE EARTH     618A ILLUS MILTON     PROSE
DARE
    IN RIBBED STEEL I DARE NOT LIFT MINE EYES  . . . . . . .      3 TO WINTER/PS       7
    IN YOU I DARE NOT OWN THE PLAN TIS NOT  . . . . . . .        21 EDW THIRD/PS 2     92
    ELSE HE WOULD NEVER DARE TO ATTACK US NOW  . . . . . . .     24 EDW THIRD/PS 3    141
    [WHAT YOU SKIPPING FLEA HOW DARE YE] . . . . . . .          57A ISLAND MOON 9     PROSE
    ("LETTING I DARE NOT WAIT UPON I WOULD") UNEASY    . . .    70B ANNO LAVATER      MARG
    SOME CANNOT TELL WHAT THEY CAN WRITE THO THEY DARE  . .     72A ANNO LAVATER      MARG
    ONLY GOOD HEARTS CAN OR DARE COURT  . . . . . . . .         85B ANNO LAVATER      MARG
    ("SEEN THROUGH MICROSCOPE...IN PASSION") & SUCH A ONE I     85D ANNO LAVATER      MARG
      DARE LOVE
    WHO SHALL DARE TO SAY AFTER THIS THAT ALL ELEVATION IS      94B ANNO SWED LOVE    MARG
      OF SELF
    COME THOU DARK FIEND I DARE THY CUNNING KNOW THAT IJIM     104 TIRIEL 4           17
      SCORNS
    RISE UP FOR I DISCERN THEE & I DARE THY ELOQUENT TONGUE    104 TIRIEL 4           19
    THAT NONE DID DARE TO ENTER IN . . . . . . . . .          163 I SAW CHAPEL/N      2
    THAT NONE DARE EAT THE FRUIT BUT FROM  . . . . . .        171 TO NOBODADDY/N      7
    [COULD] [DARE] FRAME THY FEARFUL SYMMETRY  . . . . . .    172 THE TYGER/N 1       4
    ON WHAT WINGS DARE HE ASPIRE . . . . . . . . .           172 THE TYGER/N 1        7
    WHAT THE HAND DARE SIEZE THE FIRE  . . . . . . . .        172 THE TYGER/N 1        8
    [AND IN [THY] THE HORRID RIBS DARE STEEP] . . . . .       172 THE TYGER/N 1     * 14
    [COULD] DARE ITS DEADLY TERRORS [CLASP] [GRASP] CLASP      172 THE TYGER/N 1      21
    DARE [FORM] FRAME THY FEARFUL SYMMETRY   . . . . . .       173 THE TYGER/N 1      25
    AND [[IS] DID HE LAUGH] DARE HE [SMILE] [LAUGH] HIS WORK   173 THE TYGER/N 1    * 26
      TO SEE
    [DID] DARE HE WHO MADE THE LAMB MAKE THEE  . . . . . .     173 THE TYGER/N 1      28
    DARE FRAME THY FEARFUL SYMMETRY  . . . . . . . .           173 THE TYGER/N 2       4
    WHAT THE HAND DARE SIEZE THE FIRE  . . . . . . . .         173 THE TYGER/N 2       8
    DARE FRAME THY FEARFUL SYMMETRY  . . . . . . . .           173 THE TYGER/N 2      20
    NOW A NYMPH I DARE NOT PLUCK THEE FROM THY DEWY BED . . .  189 V DAU ALBION 1      7
    ON WHAT WINGS DARE HE ASPIRE . . . . . . . . .            214 THE TYGER/SE        7
    WHAT THE HAND DARE SIEZE THE FIRE  . . . . . . . .         214 THE TYGER/SE        8
    DARE ITS DEADLY TERRORS CLASP  . . . . . . . . .           214 THE TYGER/SE       16
    DARE FRAME THY FEARFUL SYMMETRY  . . . . . . . .           214 THE TYGER/SE       24
    THE SPECTRE THUS SPOKE [ART THOU NOT MY SLAVE & SHALT THOU 268 FOUR ZOAS 1       147
      DARE]
    WHAT SOVEREIGN ARCHITECT SAID THARMAS DARE MY WILL CONTROLL 299 FOUR ZOAS 4       53
    HE WILL GIVE IT THEE FOR WE ARE WEAK WOMEN & DARE NOT LIFT  304 FOUR ZOAS 4      255
    HIS WILL WHERE NONE SHOULD DARE OPPOSE HIS WILL HIMSELF     317 FOUR ZOAS 6      232
      BEING KING
    DARE THY MOST TERRIBLE WRATH ABIDE BOUND HERE TO WASTE      321 FOUR ZOAS 7       47
      IN PAIN
    I ALONE DARE THE LASH ABIDE TO SIT BENEATH THE BLAST  . .   344 FOUR ZOAS 8      148
    UNHURT & DARE THE INCLEMENT FOREHEAD OF THE KING OF LIGHT   345 FOUR ZOAS 8      149
    BY PAINE & ALSO THE PERVERSIONS OF THE BIBLE WHO DARE  . .  383B ANNO WATSON      MARG
    CONDEMN PAINE'S HATRED OF PRIESTS IF YOU DARE   . . . .     384A ANNO WATSON      MARG
    WHO DARE TO JUDGE BUT GOD ALONE  . . . . . . . .           396A ANNO WATSON       MARG
    FOR WHO DARE TOUCH THE FROWNING FORM . . . . . . .         427 MENTAL TRAVLER     97
    WHO WILL DARE TO SAY THAT [FINE] POLITE ART IS ENCOURAGED   446A ANNO REYNOLDS   * MARG
    FINDS NOTHING OF INSPIRATION OUGHT NOT TO DARE TO BE AN     458B ANNO REYNOLDS    MARG
      ARTIST
    ("COMPETITION BY PAINTING") [WHAT BUT A PUPPY WILL DARE    SUPP ANNO REYNOLDS   * MARG
      TO DO THIS]
    WHICH FEW DARE UNBAR BECAUSE DREAD OG & ANAK GUARD THE      502 MILTON 20         35
      GATES
```

	PAGE	TITLE	LINE

DARE   (CONTINUED)
NONE DARE TO WAKE HER SOON SHE BURSTS HER CRIMSON CURTAIND   520 MILTON 31   57
  BED
DARE TO ENTER & THEY SHALL ENTER TRIUMPHANT OVER DEATH   522 MILTON 32   28
OF ALL THAT LIVE DARE UTTER THIS OTHERS TREMBLE & BOW . .   530 MILTON 38   57
THAT IT NO LONGER SHALL DARE TO MOCK WITH THE ASPERSION   533 MILTON 41   8
  OF MADNESS
WHO SHALL I DARE TO SHEW THEM TO . . . .   558 THE CAVERNS/N   4
SHALL [DARE IS TO] DAUNTLESS VIEW THE INFERNAL STORM   . .   558 THE CAVERNS/N   6
EGREMONT'S COUNTESS [DARE] CAN CONTROLL . . . .   558 THE CAVERNS/N   7
LESS BUT I DARE SAY THAT CHAUCER . . . .   572A DESC CAT 3   PROSE
FOR I AM ONE OF THE LIVING DARE NOT TO MOCK MY INSPIRED   627 JERUSALEM 8   35
  FURY
DARE NOT APPROACH THE DAUGHTERS OPENLY LEST HE BE CONSUMED   638 JERUSALEM 17   7
I COULD NOT DARE TO TAKE VENGEANCE FOR ALL THINGS ARE SO   657 JERUSALEM 31   30
  CONSTRUCTED
IF I SHOULD DARE TO LAY MY FINGER ON A GRAIN OF SAND   . .   657 JERUSALEM 31   33
ZOAS OF ALBION WHERE A MAN DARE HARDLY TO EMBRACE . . .   663 JERUSALEM 36   45
DARE TOUCH OXFORD IMMORTAL BARD WITH ELOQUENCE . . . .   676 JERUSALEM 46   7
IF YOU DARE REND THEIR VEIL WITH YOUR SPEAR YOU ARE HEALED   706 JERUSALEM 68   42
  OF LOVE
SO DREAD IS LOS'S FURY THAT NONE DARE HIM TO APPROACH . .   732 JERUSALEM 86   48
THOSE WHO DARE APPROPRIATE TO THEMSELVES UNIVERSAL   736 JERUSALEM 90   32
  ATTRIBUTES
I SHOULD NOT DARE TO SAY TO ANY ONE ELSE THAT I CAN ALONE   822C LETTER 26   PROSE
I MAY PRAISE IT SINCE I DARE NOT PRETEND TO BE . . . .   825A LETTER 27   PROSE
WILL YOU YOURSELF FOR I DARE SAY HE WILL BE MUCH PLEASD TO   856D LETTER 54   PROSE
I KNOW IT FOR I SEE IT & DARE NOT HELP . . . .   863B LETTER 60   PROSE
CANNOT BECAUSE THEY DARE NOT LOOK UPON . . . .   864B LETTER 61   PROSE
COURAGE TO SAY SO PUBLICKLY & TO DARE ALL THE POWER ON   866B LETTER 64   PROSE
  EARTH
TOO MUCH TO DARE VENTURE BEYOND MY PRESENT PRECINCTS   . .   872D LETTER 76   PROSE
SO THAT I CONCLUDE ANOTHER WEEK MUST PASS BEFORE I DARE   873A LETTER 76   PROSE
NOT DARE TO LEAVE HIS ROOM BY ANY MEANS HE HAD ANOTHER   SUPP LETTER 81A *PROSE
I AM STILL FAR FROM RECOVERED & DARE NOT GET OUT IN THE   877D LETTER 87   PROSE
  COLD
DARED
THEY DARED SO ROUNDLY TO ASSERT THAT GOD SPAKE TO THEM . .   153B MARRIAGE HH 12 *PROSE
NONE OF WHICH THE BISHOP HAS DARED TO CONSIDER . . . .   390C ANNO WATSON   MARG
AND THEREFORE PALAMABRON DARED NOT TO CALL A SOLEMN   492 MILTON 11   24
  ASSEMBLY
FEW FRIENDS I HAVE DARED TO VISIT IN MY STUPID MELANCHOLY   798C LETTER 10   PROSE
DARES
WHO IS THIS THAT WITH UNERRING STEP DARES TEMPT THE WILDS   36D CONTEMPLATN/PS PROSE
("ON MODESTY & HONOUR DARES NOT DEPEND ") UNEASY . . .   79C ANNO LAVATER   MARG
DARES STRETCH TO TOUCH HER BABY FORM . . . .   425 MENTAL TRAVLER   47
IS SUCH A MATCH AS HE WHO DARES . . . .   559 WOMAN SCALY/N   2
[WHO DARES ?WORSHIP ?ONE WHOD HAVE DRIVEN YOU LONG AGO   SUPP ANNO REYNOLDS * MARG
  INSANE]
DAREST   SEE DARST
BUT IF THOU DAREST OBSTINATE REFUSE MY STERN BEHEST . . .   360 FOUR ZOAS 9   144
DARGLE
STAND YE UPON THE DARGLE FROM WICKLOW TO DROGHEDA . . .   679 JERUSALEM 49   5
DARING
("WHO HAS A DARING EYE TELLS ...") CONTRARY TO...BUT MOST   70B ANNO LAVATER   MARG
  TRUE
DARING MY POWER WILT ARM MY SONS AGAINST ME IN THE [DEEP]   278 FOUR ZOAS 1   510
  ATLANTIC
NOT DARING TO TOUCH ONE FIBRE HE HOWLD ROUND UPON THE SEA   529 MILTON 38   14
EXPRESSIONS OF ARTICULATE SPEECH IS A BOLD AND DARING . .   576B DESC CAT 4   PROSE
NEITHER DARING TO PUT IN ACT ITS COUNCILS FEARING   708 JERUSALEM 70   6
  EACH-OTHER
ADVANTAGEOUS ACQUAINTANCE I GO ON WITHOUT DARING TO COUNT   879C LETTER 89   PROSE
DARIUS
THE VISION OF ATOSSA FROM ESCHYLUS APPARITION OF DARIUS   848D LETTER 45   PROSE
DARK
THE NORTH IS THINE THERE HAST THOU BUILT THY DARK . . .   2 TO WINTER/PS   2
ROLLING DARK CLOUDS OER FRANCE MUFFLING THE SUN . . . .   31 EDW THIRD/PS 6   3
WHILE IN DARK COUNCIL SAT PHILISTA'S LORDS . . . . . .   37D SAMSON/PS   PROSE
BREEDING DARK PLOTS . . . .   38A SAMSON/PS   PROSE
DARK THOUGHTS ROLLED TO AND FRO IN HIS MIND . . . . .   38C SAMSON/PS   PROSE
& MELANCHOLY SPRUNG FROM HER DARK WOMB . . . .   42A THEN SHE BORE PROSE
IN KNOWLEDGE'S DARK PRISON HOUSE . . . .   42B THEN SHE BORE PROSE
AND WE CANNOT [GO TO] GO TO SLEEP [TILL ITS DARK] . . .   60 NURSES SONG/IM   10
THE NIGHT IT WAS DARK & NO FATHER WAS THERE . . . .·· ·.   60 LIT BOY LST/IM   5
[BUT DARK WERE HIS ONCE PIERCING EYES] . . . .   99 TIRIEL 1   2
HE WANDERD DAY & NIGHT TO HIM BOTH DAY & NIGHT WERE DARK   100 TIRIEL 2   1
[?BUT] AND MNETHA SAID THOU MUST NOT GO TO WANDER DARK   103 TIRIEL 3   * 33
  ALONE
TO HIM THE DAY & NIGHT ALIKE WAS DARK & DESOLATE . . . .   103 TIRIEL 4   2
MET HIM AT ENTRANCE OF THE FOREST IN A DARK & LONELY WAY   103 TIRIEL 4   4
IJIM SHALL REND THY FEEBLE JOINTS THOU TEMPTER OF DARK IJIM   103 TIRIEL 4   6
COME THOU DARK FIEND I DARE THY CUNNING KNOW THAT IJIM   104 TIRIEL 4   17
  SCORNS
TIRIEL IS A KING & THOU THE TEMPTER OF DARK IJIM . . . .   104 TIRIEL 4   38
IT IS AS FALSE & [AS] MATHA & AS DARK AS VACANT ORCUS   106 TIRIEL 4   * 87
[DISPLAY THY] TO RAISE HIS DARK & BURNING VISAGE . . . . .   106 TIRIEL 5   5
RISE FROM THE CENTER BELCHING FLAMES & ROARINGS DARK SMOKE   106 TIRIEL 5   7
HE CEAST HER DARK HAIR UPRIGHT STOOD WHILE SNAKES INFOLDED   108 TIRIEL 6   44
  ROUND
[FLINGING FLAMES OF DISCONTENT & PLAGUES OF DARK DESPAIR]   109 TIRIEL 8   16
DARK BENIGHTED TRAVEL-WORN . . . .   111 A DREAM/SI   6

430

```
                                                   PAGE      TITLE          LINE
DARK   (CONTINUED)
    AND SO TOM AWOKE AND WE ROSE IN THE DARK    . . . . . .  118 CHIMNEY SWP/SI     21
    THE NIGHT WAS DARK NO FATHER WAS THERE    . . . . . . .  121 LIT BOY LST/SI      5
    DARK DISPUTES & ARTFUL TEAZING . . . . . . . . . . .     126 VOICE BARD/SI       5
    MY BOSOM OF ITSELF IS COLD AND OF ITSELF IS DARK    . . .  129 BOOK OF THEL 4     12
    SHE WANDERD IN THE LAND OF CLOUDS THRO VALLEYS DARK       130 BOOK OF THEL 6      6
      LISTNING
    . . . IN DARK FOGS LISTNING THE HORROR    . . . . . .    135 FRENCH REVOLTN     19
    HOWLING AND GIVING THE DARK COMMAND . . . . . . . .      135 FRENCH REVOLTN     24
    . . . AND PIERCING THROUGH THE SEVEN TOWERS DARK AND SICKLY  135 FRENCH REVOLTN  25
    CENTERD AND THE RUSHING OF CHAOS OVERWHELMD HIS DARK SOUL  136 FRENCH REVOLTN    50
      . . .
    . . . AND A LIGHT WALKS ROUND THE DARK TOWERS    . . . . .  136 FRENCH REVOLTN   53
    LIKE A DARK CLOUD NECKER PAUSD . . . . . . . . . . .     139 FRENCH REVOLTN    106
    . . . AND DARK MISTS ROLL ROUND ME AND BLOT THE WRITING   139 FRENCH REVOLTN    113
      OF GOD
    . . . A DARK SHADOWY MAN IN THE FORM    . . . . . . .    141 FRENCH REVOLTN    164
    TO WANDER INSLAVD BLACK DEPREST IN DARK IGNORANCE . . .   143 FRENCH REVOLTN *  214
    SEEST THOU YONDER DARK CASTLE . . . . . . . . . . .      145 FRENCH REVOLTN    248
    OVERSTEP THE DARK RIVER THOU TERRIBLE TOWER . . . .  . .  145 FRENCH REVOLTN    250
    THE AGED SUN RISES APPALLD FROM DARK MOUNTAINS . . .  .   146 FRENCH REVOLTN    270
    LIKE A FLAME OF FIRE HE STOOD BEFORE DARK RANKS . . . .   146 FRENCH REVOLTN    273
    DARK CAVALRY LIKE CLOUDS FRAUGHT WITH THUNDER . . . . .   147 FRENCH REVOLTN    291
    GLANCING HIS BEAMY EYELIDS OVER THE DEEP IN DARK DISMAY   159D SONG LIBERTY    PROSE
    I [ WAS FOND] SLEPT IN THE DARK  . . . . . . . . . .     170 SLEPT DARK/N  *     1
    I SLEPT IN THE [DARK] EARTH &C  . . . . . . . . . .      175 WILD FLOWERS/N      5
    [ O DARK SECRET LOVE]  . . . . . . . . . . . . .        175 SICK ROSE/N         7
    AND [HIS] HER DARK SECRET LOVE  . . . . . . . . . .      175 SICK ROSE/N         9
    TO SPIN A WEB OF AGE AROUND HIM GREY AND HOARY DARK   . . .  194 V DAU ALBION 7   19
    WHEN FOURTEEN SUNS HAD FAINTLY JOURNEYD OER HIS DARK ABODE  195 AMERICA PREL 1    2
    CROWND WITH A HELMET & DARK HAIR THE NAMELESS FEMALE STOOD  195 AMERICA PREL 1    4
    THEIR AWFUL FOLDS IN THE DARK AIR SILENT SHE STOOD AS NIGHT  196 AMERICA PREL 1   8
    DARK VIRGIN SAID THE HAIRY YOUTH THY FATHER STERN ABHORRD  196 AMERICA PREL 1    11
    AROUND THE PILLARS OF URTHONA AND ROUND THY DARK LIMBS  . .  196 AMERICA PREL 1   16
    AND THOU ART FALLN TO GIVE ME LIFE IN REGIONS OF DARK DEATH  196 AMERICA PREL 2    9
    WITH MYRIADS OF CLOUDY TERRORS BANNERS DARK & TOWERS   . .  197 AMERICA 4         10
    AND BOSTON'S ANGEL CRIED ALOUD AS THEY FLEW THRO THE DARK  200 AMERICA 11         3
      NIGHT
    FROM THEIR ENCAMPMENTS AND DARK CASTLES SEEKING WHERE TO   201 AMERICA 13         8
      HIDE
    DARK IS THE HEAVEN ABOVE & COLD & HARD THE EARTH BENEATH   201 AMERICA 14         7
    WEEPING IN DISMAL HOWLING WOE HE DARK DESCENDED HOWLING    203 AMERICA 16         7
    SHUT OUT FROM MORTAL SIGHT THE ANGEL CAME THE VALE WAS DARK  204 AMERICA CANC B   10
    TILL TO THAT VOID IT CAME & FELL SO THE DARK HOUSE WAS RENT  204 AMERICA CANC B   22
    AND HIS DARK SECRET LOVE  . . . . . . . . . . . . .      213 SICK ROSE/SE        7
    TO UNFOLD YOUR DARK VISIONS OF TORMENT  . . . . . . .    222 URIZEN 2            7
    BROODING SECRET THE DARK POWER HID . . . . . . . . .     222 URIZEN 3            7
    DARK REVOLVING IN SILENT ACTIVITY  . . . . . . . . .     223 URIZEN 3           18
    HIS COLD HORRORS SILENT DARK URIZEN . . . . . . . .      223 URIZEN 3           27
    FROM THE DEPTHS OF DARK SOLITUDE FROM  . . . . . . .     224 URIZEN 4            6
    A VOID IMMENSE WILD DARK & DEEP . . . . . . . . . .      224 URIZEN 4           16
    THE SECRETS OF DARK CONTEMPLATION  . . . . . . . . .     224 URIZEN 4           26
    AND OER THE DARK DESARTS OF URIZEN . . . . . . . . .     225 URIZEN 5           14
    AND LOS ROUND THE DARK GLOBE OF URIZEN . . . . . . .     226 URIZEN 5           38
    LOS WEPT HOWLING AROUND THE DARK DEMON  . . . . . . .    226 URIZEN 6            2
    THE DARK CHANGES & BOUND EVERY CHANGE  . . . . . . .     227 URIZEN 8           10
    LIKE A DARK WASTE STRETCHING CHANGABLE . . . . . . .     227 URIZEN 10           3
    IN DARK SECRESY HIDING IN SURGEING . . . . . . . . .     227 URIZEN 10          13
    THE ETERNAL PROPHET HEAVD THE DARK BELLOWS . . . . . .   227 URIZEN 10          15
    SIEZD A COLD SOLITUDE & DARK VOID  . . . . . . . . .     230 URIZEN 13          39
    OF THE DARK SEPERATION APPEARD . . . . . . . . . .       231 URIZEN 15           8
    BEHELD THE DARK VISIONS OF LOS . . . . . . . . . .       231 URIZEN 15          12
    TILL A WEB DARK & COLD THROUGHOUT ALL  . . . . . . .     235 URIZEN 25          15
    BENEATH THE DARK NET OF INFECTION  . . . . . . . . .     236 URIZEN 25          30
    LIKE THE DARK CLOUD DISBURDEND IN THE DAY OF DISMAL THUNDER  238 EUROPE PREL 1    7
    DEVOURING & DEVOURED ROAMING ON DARK AND DESOLATE MOUNTAINS  238 EUROPE PREL 2    5
    BLEAK DARK ABRUPT IT STANDS & OVERSHADOWS LONDON CITY    . .  242 EUROPE 12       9
    MOSES BEHELD UPON MOUNT SINAI FORMS OF DARK DELUSION   . .  245 SONG OF LOS 3    17
    IN CHAOS AND CIRCLING DARK URIZEN  . . . . . . . . .     250 AHANIA 2           39
    FORMD OF RIBS THAT IN HIS DARK SOLITUDE . . . . . . .    250 AHANIA 3            5
    AS HE SAT ON HIS DARK ROOTED OAK . . . . . . . . .       250 AHANIA 3           16
    A WHITE LAKE ON THE DARK BLUE AIR  . . . . . . . . .     252 AHANIA 4           14
    AS THE BONES OF MAN SOLID & DARK . . . . . . . . .       253 AHANIA 4           21
    I SEE THY DARK CLOUDS ASCEND . . . . . . . . . . .       254 AHANIA 4           57
    FORTHWITH WRITHING UPON THE DARK VOID  . . . . . . .     259 BOOK OF LOS 5      13
    CIRCLING ROUND THE DARK DEMON WITH HOWLINGS  . . . . .   259 BOOK OF LOS 5      24
    DARK VACUITY HERE URIZEN LAY . . . . . . . . . . .       260 BOOK OF LOS 5      50
    AND IN THE DARK RECESSES FOUND SIN & CANNOT RETURN  . .   265 FOUR ZOAS 1        45
    NINE DAYS SHE LABOURD AT HER WORK & NINE DARK SLEEPLESS   266 FOUR ZOAS 1        86
      NIGHTS
    [AND THREE DARK NIGHTS REPIND THE SOLITUDE BUT THE THIRD  267 FOUR ZOAS 1       135
      MORN ]
    [[THE JEALOUS] THREE DAYS SHE WAILD & THREE DARK NIGHTS   268 FOUR ZOAS 1  *    143
      . . .
    THAT DARK & DISMAL INFINITE WHERE THOUGHT ROAMS UP & DOWN  268 FOUR ZOAS 1      155
    . . . THO DARK I FEEL MY WORLD WITHIN  . . . . . . .     268 FOUR ZOAS 1       172
    INTO NON ENTITY REVOLVING ROUND IN DARK DESPAIR  . . . .  270 FOUR ZOAS 1      219
    CONVERSING WITH THE VISIONS OF BEULAH IN DARK SLUMBEROUS  271 FOUR ZOAS 1  *    246
      BLISS
    [BRIGHT] DARK AS A DEWY MORNING WHEN THE CRIMSON LIGHT    271 FOUR ZOAS 1  *    253
      APPEARS
    BUT MOST THE POLISHD PALACES [?WEAK] DARK SILENT BOW WITH  275 FOUR ZOAS 1  *   396
      DREAD
```

431

		PAGE	TITLE	LINE

DARK   (CONTINUED)

```
     CALL TO THY DARK ARMD HOSTS FOR ALL THE SONS OF MEN MUSTER      275 FOUR ZOAS 1       406
        TOGETHER
     VALA REMAIND IN DESARTS OF DARK SOLITUDE NOR SUN NOR MOON       275 FOUR ZOAS 1       417
     CONGLOBING IN THE DARK CONFUSION MEAN TIME LOS WAS BORN         275 FOUR ZOAS 1       420
     SMITE THIS DARK SLEEPER IN HIS TENT THEN TRY MY STRENGTH        278 FOUR ZOAS 1       513
        WITH THEE
     BESIDE HIS ANVIL STOOD URTHONA DARK A MASS OF IRON   . . .      278 FOUR ZOAS 1       519
     FOR I AM WEARY & MUST SLEEP IN THE DARK SLEEP OF DEATH          280 FOUR ZOAS 2         6
     THEY BECOME NATIONS FAR REMOTE IN A LITTLE & DARK LAND   . .    281 FOUR ZOAS 2     *  56
     WHEN I CALLD FORTH THE EARTH-WORM FROM THE COLD & DARK          282 FOUR ZOAS 2        83
        OBSCURE
     WHILE THUS THE SPIRITS OF STRONGEST WING ENLIGHTEN THE          284 FOUR ZOAS 2       156
        DARK DEEP
     AND WAKE THE BUBBLING SPRINGS OF LIFE IN REGIONS OF DARK        289 FOUR ZOAS 2       373
        DEATH
     [AND [OFT] THUS SHE] THUS ENION WAILS FROM THE DARK DEEP        290 FOUR ZOAS 2     * 386
        . . .
     O BRIGHT [AHANIA] [SHADOW] A BOY IS BORN OF THE DARK OCEAN      292 FOUR ZOAS 3     *  14
     AND LUVAH IN THE LOINS OF LOS A DARK & FURIOUS DEATH   . .      292 FOUR ZOAS 3        22
     LIKE A DARK LAMP ETERNAL DEATH HAUNTS ALL MY EXPECTATION        293 FOUR ZOAS 3        75
     O CRUEL PITY O DARK DECEIT CAN LOVE SEEK FOR DOMINION   . .     293 FOUR ZOAS 3        78
     AND THE DARK BODY OF [MAN] ALBION LEFT PROSTRATE . . . . .      294 FOUR ZOAS 3        81
     VALA SHRUNK IN LIKE THE DARK SEA THAT LEAVES ITS SLIMY          294 FOUR ZOAS 3        99
        BANKS
     A CAVERN SHAGGD WITH HORRID SHADES DARK COOL & DEADLY WHERE     295 FOUR ZOAS 3       122
     SO LOUD IN THUNDERS SPOKE THE KING FOLDED IN DARK DESPAIR       295 FOUR ZOAS 3       131
     BUT THARMAS RODE ON THE DARK ABYSS THE VOICE OF THARMAS         297 FOUR ZOAS 4         1
        ROLLD
     CAN DIE WHEN DARK DESPAIR COMES OVER CAN I NOT   . . . .        298 FOUR ZOAS 4        22
     AND THARMAS CALLD TO THE DARK SPECTRE WHO UPON THE SHORES       299 FOUR ZOAS 4        63
     DARK DREADFUL ROSE & ENITHARMON LAY AT LOS'S FEET    . . .      300 FOUR ZOAS 4       126
     OF MANY WHEELS RESISTLESS IN THE POWER OF DARK URTHONA   . .    302 FOUR ZOAS 4       183
     WARPING UPON THE WINDS & WHIRLING ROUND IN THE DARK DEEP        302 FOUR ZOAS 4       186
     CIRCLING ROUND THE DARK DEMON WITH HOWLINGS DISMAY & SHARP      302 FOUR ZOAS 4       200
        BLIGHTINGS
     INFECTED MAD HE DANCD ON HIS MOUNTAINS HIGH & DARK             305 FOUR ZOAS 5         1
        AS HEAVEN
     THAT DREW THE BODY OF MAN FROM HEAVEN INTO THIS DARK ABYSS      306 FOUR ZOAS 5        47
     WHEN DARK URTHONA WEPT IN TORMENT OF THE SECRET PAIN   . .      306 FOUR ZOAS 5        53
     AND HIS DARK WIFE THAT ONCE FAIR CRYSTAL FORM DIVINELY          306 FOUR ZOAS 5        60
        CLEAR
     CALL [VALAN] VALA FROM HER CLOSE RECESS IN ALL HER DARK         307 FOUR ZOAS 5     *  64
        DECEIT
     ENITHARMON NURSD HER FIERY CHILD IN THE DARK DEEPS   . . .      307 FOUR ZOAS 5        70
     AND BRASS & SILVER & GOLD FOURFOLD IN DARK PROPHETIC FEAR       307 FOUR ZOAS 5        74
     HE WENT EACH MORNING TO HIS LABOURS WITH THE SPECTRE DARK       307 FOUR ZOAS 5        94
     FELL FROM HIS BOSOM ON THE MOUNTAIN THE SPECTRE DARK    . .     307 FOUR ZOAS 5       100
     BUT WHEN THEY CAME TO THE DARK ROCK & TO THE SPECTROUS CAVE     309 FOUR ZOAS 5       155
     AH HOW SHALL URIZEN THE KING SUBMIT TO THIS DARK MANSION        310 FOUR ZOAS 5       190
     I CALLD THE STARS AROUND MY FEET IN THE NIGHT OF COUNCILS       311 FOUR ZOAS 5       223
        DARK
     WE FELL I SIEZD THEE DARK URTHONA IN MY LEFT HAND FALLING       311 FOUR ZOAS 5       225
     [WAS LUVAH XXX HE STOOD ?GLOWING IN THE DARK FLAME]   . . SUPP FOUR ZOAS 5     *
     HE THREW HIS FLIGHT THRO THE DARK AIR TO WHERE A RIVER          311 FOUR ZOAS 6         2
        FLOWD
     CHAINS OF DARK IGNORANCE & CORDS OF TWISTED SELF CONCEIT        312 FOUR ZOAS 6        41
     POUR DOWN MY FLIGHT THRO DARK IMMENSITY ETERNAL FALLING         313 FOUR ZOAS 6        69
     MAKING A PATH TOWARD THE DARK WORLD OF URTHONA HE ROSE   . .    313 FOUR ZOAS 6        78
     SO IN THE REGIONS OF THE GRAVE NONE KNOWS HIS DARK COMPEER      314 FOUR ZOAS 6        97
     AND IN THE DARK VACUITY CREATED A BOSOM OF [SLIME] CLAY         316 FOUR ZOAS 6       158
     ROUND LAKES OF FIRE IN THE DARK DEEP THE RUINS OF URIZEN'S      316 FOUR ZOAS 6       179
        WORLD
     OFT WOULD HE SIT IN A DARK RIFT & REGULATE HIS BOOKS    . .     316 FOUR ZOAS 6       180
     OR SLEEP SUCH SLEEP AS SPIRITS ETERNAL WEARIED IN HIS DARK      316 FOUR ZOAS 6       181
     WHENCE I MIGHT TRAVEL ROUND THE OUTSIDE OF THIS DARK            317 FOUR ZOAS 6       201
        CONFUSION
     AND IF ETERNAL FALLING I REPOSE ON THE DARK BOSOM   . . .      317 FOUR ZOAS 6       218
     WITHIN THE DARK HORRORS OF THE ABYSSES LION OR TYGER OR         318 FOUR ZOAS 6       251
        SCORPION
     AND NOW HE CAME INTO THE ABHORRED WORLD OF DARK URTHONA         319 FOUR ZOAS 6       281
     OERWEARIED OR IN CUMBEROUS FLIGHT HE VENTURD OER DARK RIFTS     319 FOUR ZOAS 6     * 288
     OR DOWN DARK PRECIPICES OR CLIMBD WITH PAIN & LABOUR HUGE       319 FOUR ZOAS 6     * 289
     BETWEEN THE ENORMOUS IRON WALLS BUILT BY THE SPECTRE DARK       319 FOUR ZOAS 6       295
     DARK GREW HIS GLOBE REDDNING WITH MISTS & FULL BEFORE HIS       319 FOUR ZOAS 6       296
        PATH
     AND WATCHD HIS SWIFT APPROACH COLLECTED DARK THE SPECTRE        319 FOUR ZOAS 6       301
        STOOD
     HOWLING & RENDING HIS DARK CAVES THE AWFUL DEMON LAY    . .     320 FOUR ZOAS 7        20
     PITY FOR THEE MOVD ME TO BREAK MY DARK & LONG REPOSE    . .     321 FOUR ZOAS 7        57
     ENQUIRE OF MY DAUGHTERS WHO ACCURSD IN THE DARK DEPTHS  . .     322 FOUR ZOAS 7        92
     A SELF CONSUMING DARK DEVOURER RISING INTO THE HEAVENS  . .     324 FOUR ZOAS 7       156
     IN THE DARK DEEP THE DARK TREE GREW HER SHADOW WAS DRAWN        324 FOUR ZOAS 7       170
        DOWN
     ALL HEAVEN THEY SAW HIM DARK THEY BUILT A GOLDEN WALL   . .     326 FOUR ZOAS 7       242
     IN DARK CONFUSION MEAN TIME LOS WAS BORN & ENITHARMON   . .     326 FOUR ZOAS 7       259
     BESIDE LOS IN THE CAVERN DARK ENSLAVD TO VEGETATIVE FORMS       326 FOUR ZOAS 7       262
     OF THE ETERNAL MAN & SMOTE HIM BUT THOU SPECTRE DARK    . .     326 FOUR ZOAS 7       264
     A FEMALE BRIGHT I STOOD BESIDE MY ANVIL DARK A MASS   . . .     327 FOUR ZOAS 7       282
     AH POOR DIVIDED DARK URTHONA NOW A SPECTRE WANDERING    . .     327 FOUR ZOAS 7     * 296
     IN DREAMS OF ULRO [SWEET] DARK DELUSIVE DRAWN BY THE LOVELY     328 FOUR ZOAS 7       331
        SHADOW
```

432

		PAGE	TITLE	LINE

DARK   (CONTINUED)

```
                                                                   PAGE    TITLE        LINE
DARK   (CONTINUED)
     PEACE TO THE SOUL OF DARK REVENGE & REPENTANCE TO CRUELTY      329 FOUR ZOAS 7        369
     OF SEPARATION & ON MY DARK HEAD THE CURSE & PUNISHMENT  . .    330 FOUR ZOAS 7        405
     AS LOS A FATHER TO HIS BRETHREN & HE JOYD IN THE DARK LAKE     332 FOUR ZOAS 7        480
     THEIR LIFE EXTINCT THEY TOOK THE SPECTRE FORM IN               333 FOUR ZOAS 7B        15
        DARK DESPAIR
     OF SECRET LUST WHEN HID IN CHAMBERS DARK THE NIGHTLY HARLOT    333 FOUR ZOAS 7B        25
     HIS NAKED LIMBS GLITTRING UPON THE DARK BLUE SKY HIS KNEES     334 FOUR ZOAS 7B   *    42
     I MUST HAVE DIED IN THE DARK DESART AMONG NOXIOUS WORMS        335 FOUR ZOAS 7B        86
     WHILE THE BROAD OAK WREATHD HIS ROOTS ROUND HER FORCING        335 FOUR ZOAS 7B        99
        HIS DARK WAY
     WALKS THRO THE BATTLE DARK & FIERCE THE BULL HIS RAGE   . .    335 FOUR ZOAS 7B       109
     SO ORC ROLLD ROUND HIS CLOUDS UPON THE DEEPS OF DARK          336 FOUR ZOAS 7B       133
        URTHONA
     WILL I ARISE TILL HIM I LOVE IS LOOSD FROM THIS DARK CHAIN     339 FOUR ZOAS 7B       255
     NOT SEEN TO HER LIKE WATERS OR LIKE THIS DARK WORLD OF         340 FOUR ZOAS 7B       273
        DEATH
     IN [ANGUISH FOR] RAGE AGAINST THE DARK DESPAIR THE HOWLING     340 FOUR ZOAS 7B  *    287
        MELANCHOLY
     [SILVERY WHITE SHINING UPON THE DARK BLUE SKY IN SILENCE]      341 FOUR ZOAS 8   *    11
     SURROUNDED BY HIS DARK MACHINES FOR ORC AUGMENTED SWIFT        342 FOUR ZOAS 8        67
     HIS HUMAN BULK WHILE THE DARK SHADOWY FEMALE [BROODS]          343 FOUR ZOAS 8   *    80
        BROODING OVER
     COMMUNING WITH THE SERPENT OF ORC IN DARK DISSIMULATION        343 FOUR ZOAS 8        96
     AND WITH THE SYNAGOGUE OF SATAN IN DARK SANHEDRIM    . . .     343 FOUR ZOAS 8        97
     FROM DARK ABYSSES OF THE TIMES REMOTE FATED TO BE    . . .     345 FOUR ZOAS 8       150
     WHO NOW BEGINNETH TO PUT OFF THE DARK SATANIC BODY   . . .     346 FOUR ZOAS 8       196
     OF DARK DEATH & DESPAIR . . . . . . . . . . .                 347 FOUR ZOAS 8       231
     ASSUME THE DARK SATANIC BODY IN THE VIRGIN'S WOMB   . .        347 FOUR ZOAS 8       241
     COLD DARK OPAKE THE ASSEMBLY MET TWELVEFOLD IN AMALEK   . .    348 FOUR ZOAS 8       275
     THEY ROLLD DOWN A DIM WORLD CRUSTED WITH SNOW DEADLY & DARK    351 FOUR ZOAS 8   *   396
     [IN FORMS OF PRIESTHOOD IN THE DARK DELUSIONS OF              353 FOUR ZOAS 8       461
        REPENTANCE]
     A KING OF WRATH & FURY A DARK ENRAGED HORROR   . . . . .      353 FOUR ZOAS 8       462
     IN FORMS OF PRIESTHOOD IN THE DARK DELUSIONS OF REPENTANCE     353 FOUR ZOAS 8       464
     AND FOR THE DREAD OF THE DARK TERRORS OF ORC & URIZEN   . .    353 FOUR ZOAS 8       480
     LISTEN TO HER WHOSE EYES BEHOLD THE DARK BODY OF              354 FOUR ZOAS 8       505
        CORRUPTIBLE DEATH
     HIS FIERY HALLS ARE DARK & ROUND HIS LIMBS THE SERPENT ORC     354 FOUR ZOAS 8       509
     BUT AN ETERNAL CONSUMMATION IS DARK ENION   . . . . .         355 FOUR ZOAS 8       542
     MORE HAPPY IS THE DARK CONSUMER HOPE DROWNS ALL MY TORMENT     355 FOUR ZOAS 8       544
     TO THE DARK VALLEY WHENCE HE CAME TO BEGIN HIS LABOURS ANEW    355 FOUR ZOAS 8   *   575
     SIEZD THE SUN HIS LEFT HAND LIKE DARK ROOTS COVERD THE MOON    357 FOUR ZOAS 9         8
     IN THIS DARK WORLD A NARROW HOUSE I WANDER UP & DOWN           360 FOUR ZOAS 9       113
     SIT HOVRING OVER MY DARK THRESHOLD THO I ARISE LOOK OUT        360 FOUR ZOAS 9   *   118
     LET LUVAH RAGE IN THE DARK DEEP EVEN TO CONSUMMATION    . .    360 FOUR ZOAS 9       142
     URIZEN WEPT IN THE DARK DEEP ANXIOUS HIS SCALY FORM   . . .    361 FOUR ZOAS 9       162
     TO REASSUME THE HUMAN & HE WEPT IN THE DARK DEEP   . . . .     361 FOUR ZOAS 9       163
     OF DARK MORTALITY NOR CAST MY VIEW INTO THE [PAST] FUTURITY    361 FOUR ZOAS 9   *   165
        NOR TURND
     THEN GO O DARK [REMEMBRANCE] FUTURITY . . . . . . . .         361 FOUR ZOAS 9       180
     LET ORC CONSUME LET THARMAS RAGE LET DARK URTHONA GIVE         362 FOUR ZOAS 9       184
     CALLING UPON THEIR FATHER'S NAME UPON THEIR RIVERS DARK        362 FOUR ZOAS 9       203
     ETERNAL & I THRO HIM AWAKE FROM DEATH'S DARK VALE   . .        362 FOUR ZOAS 9       207
     FROM THE [BLACK] DARK JAWS OF DEATH BENEATH & DESOLATE         363 FOUR ZOAS 9       259
        SHORES REMOTE
     IN DARK OBLIVION WITH INCESSANT PANGS AGES ON AGES    . .      366 FOUR ZOAS 9       369
     LUVAH & VALA DESCENDED & ENTERD THE GATES OF DARK URTHONA      367 FOUR ZOAS 9       375
     FOLDING THE PURE WINGS OF HIS MIND SEEKING THE PLACES DARK     374 FOUR ZOAS 9       630
     AT THE DARK MYRIADS IN SHADOWS IN THE WORLDS BENEATH   . .     374 FOUR ZOAS 9       649
     THEN ENION & AHANIA & VALA & THE WIFE OF DARK URTHONA   . .    377 FOUR ZOAS 9       778
     THEN DARK URTHONA TOOK THE CORN OUT OF THE STORES OF URIZEN    378 FOUR ZOAS 9       806
     OF DARK URTHONA THUNDERS EARTHQUAKES FIRES WATER FLOODS        378 FOUR ZOAS 9       812
     SUCH ARE THE WORKS OF DARK URTHONA THARMAS SIFTED THE CORN     379 FOUR ZOAS 9       821
     THE DARK RELIGIONS ARE DEPARTED & SWEET SCIENCE REIGNS  . .    379 FOUR ZOAS 9       855
     AND DARK URTHONA ROUZD HIS SHADY BRIDE FROM HER DEEP DEN       380 FOUR ZOAS AD 1      7
     . . . ALL THE SYNAGOGUE OF SATAN IN DARK SANHEDRIM   . .       382 FOUR ZOAS AD 6      5
     COLD DARK OPAKE THE ASSEMBLY MET TWELVE FOLD IN AMALEK   . .   382 FOUR ZOAS AD 6      8
     [A DEEP WINTER [NIGHT] DARK & COLD]    . . . . . . .          415 MY SPECTRE/N        13
     [[[TO] IN A DARK COLD WINTER NIGHT]]    . . . . . . .         415 MY SPECTRE/N   *   14
     AND A DARK DESART ALL AROUND    . . . . . . . . .            426 MENTAL TRAVLER     68
     THESE BLOTS OF LIGHT AND DARK AS BEING THE RESULT OF LABOUR   439C REMARKS MALKIN   PROSE
     OR OF ONE IN THE DARK WHO FEELS HIS WAY BUT DOES NOT SEE IT   439C REMARKS MALKIN   PROSE
     & NOT TALK OF DARK AGES OR OF ANY AGE AGES ARE ALL EQUAL      461A ANNO REYNOLDS    MARG
     SOME MEN CANNOT SEE A PICTURE EXCEPT IN A DARK CORNER   . .   476A ANNO REYNOLDS    MARG
     AMONG THESE DARK SATANIC MILLS   . . . . . . . .            481 AND DID FEET/M      8
     THE EYE OF MAN A LITTLE NARROW ORB CLOSD UP & DARK    . .     484 MILTON 5           21
     DARK GLEAMS BEFORE THE FURNACE-MOUTH A HEAP OF BURNING        485 MILTON 6           17
        ASHES
     DRIVING THE HARROW IN PITY'S PATHS TWAS THEN WITH OUR DARK    493 MILTON 12          28
        FIRES
     SICK COUCH BEARS THE DARK SHADES OF ETERNAL DEATH INFOLDING   493 MILTON 13           1
     THUNDERD THE ASSEMBLY DARK & CLOUDED AND THEY RATIFYD   . .   494 MILTON 13          15
     A DISK OF BLOOD DISTANT & HEAVNS & EARTHS ROLL DARK BETWEEN   495 MILTON 14          27
     IN THE DARK ULRO TILL THE JUDGMENT ALSO MILTON KNEW THEY      498 MILTON 17           5
        AND
     AND HE ALSO DARKEND HIS BROWS FREEZING DARK ROCKS BETWEEN     500 MILTON 19           1
     IN A DARK TOMB SO ALL THE FAMILY DIVINE WEPT OVER OLOLON      504 MILTON 21          42
     IT ISSUES THRO THE DARK & INTRICATE CAVES OF THE MUNDANE      507 MILTON 23          22
        SHELL
     WITH POWERS FITTED TO CIRCUMSCRIBE THIS DARK SATANIC DEATH    507 MILTON 23          51
     CREATING FORM & BEAUTY AROUND THE DARK REGIONS OF SORROW      514 MILTON 28           2
```

		PAGE	TITLE	LINE

DARK   (CONTINUED)
```
     THE EIGHT IMMORTAL STARRY-ONES DOWN INTO ULRO DARK    . . .   523 MILTON 34        4
     A LONG JOURNEY & DARK THRO CHAOS IN THE TRACK OF MILTON'S      524 MILTON 34       22
       COURSE
     THEY STOOD IN A DARK LAND OF DEATH OF FIERY CORRODING          524 MILTON 34       44
       WATERS
     TO SHOOTERS HILL AND THENCE TO BLACKHEATH THE DARK WOOF        525 MILTON 35       13
       LOUD
     TERRIBLE DEADLY & POISONOUS HIS PRESENCE IN ULRO DARK   . .    526 MILTON 35       55
     THE MONSTROUS CHURCHES OF BEULAH THE GODS OF ULRO DARK   .     528 MILTON 37       16
     OSIRIS ISIS ORUS IN EGYPT DARK THEIR TABERNACLES ON NILE       528 MILTON 37       27
     LOUD SATAN THUNDERD LOUD & DARK UPON MILD FELPHAM SHORE        529 MILTON 38       13
     LOUD SATAN THUNDERD LOUD & DARK UPON MILD FELPHAM'S SHORE      531 MILTON 39       22
     IN A DARK CORNER THE EYES OF STUPID CUNNING NEVER WILL BE      563D DESC CAT     PROSE
     AND HELD THE EMPIRE OF THE WORLD IN THE DARK AGE  .  .  . .   578C DESC CAT 5    PROSE
     I COURT THE COMPARISON & FEAR NOT THE RESULT BUT NOT IN        598D PUB ADDRESS/N PROSE
       A DARK CORNER
     & CLAP THE PICTURE INTO A DARK CORNER   . . . . . . . .  .    599A PUB ADDRESS/N  PROSE
     ALL BOTH MORNING & NIGHT IS NOW A DARK CAVERN XXX WHEN         599B PUB ADDRESS/N *PROSE
       YOU VIEW
     [OF] OR POINTS OF LIGHT TO BE PUT INTO A DARK HOLE   . . .    599B PUB ADDRESS/N *PROSE
     IN WHAT WE CALL THE DARK AGES . . . . . . . . . .            604A INSC ARIMATHEA PROSE
     IN ALL THE DARK ATLANTIC VALE DOWN FROM THE HILLS OF SURREY    622 JERUSALEM 4        9
     BUT THE PERTURBED MAN AWAY TURNS DOWN THE VALLEYS DARK   . .   622 JERUSALEM 4       22
     A DARK AND UNKNOWN NIGHT INDEFINITE UNMEASURABLE WITHOUT       624 JERUSALEM 5       57
       END
     HOWLING IN PAIN A BLACKNING SHADOW BLACKNING DARK & OPAKE      624 JERUSALEM 6        5
     AND HIS INFANT THOUGHTS & DESIRES INTO COLD DARK CLIFFS        628 JERUSALEM 9        2
       OF DEATH
     SO SPOKE THE SPECTRE SHUDDRING & DARK TEARS RAN DOWN HIS       630 JERUSALEM 10      60
       SHADOWY FACE
     WITHOUT THE GATE OF LOS AMONG THE DARK SATANIC WHEELS   . .    632 JERUSALEM 12      44
     AND AS DARK ROOTS AND STEMS A FOREST OF AFFLICTION GROWING     634 JERUSALEM 14       8
     HERE THE TWELVE SONS OF ALBION JOIND IN DARK ASSEMBLY          640 JERUSALEM 18       5
     BEYOND THE NIGHT OF BEULAH IN A DARK & UNKNOWN NIGHT    . .    641 JERUSALEM 18      45
     IN THE DARK WORLD A NARROW HOUSE HE WANDERS UP AND DOWN        641 JERUSALEM 19      14
     THE DARK INCESSANT SKY SEEKING FOR REST AND FINDING NONE       641 JERUSALEM 19      22
     AND IN THE DARK RECESSES FOUND SIN & CAN NEVER RETURN    . .   645 JERUSALEM 22      15
     BUT DARK DESPAIR & EVERLASTING BROODING MELANCHOLY   . . .     645 JERUSALEM 22      24
     AS I BEHOLD JERUSALEM IN THEE O VALA DARK AND COLD   . . .     645 JERUSALEM 22      32
     TREMBLING STOOD ALBION AT HER WORDS IN JEALOUS DARK DESPAIR    646 JERUSALEM 23      13
     MAY GOD WHO DWELLS IN THIS DARK ULRO & VOIDNESS VENGEANCE      646 JERUSALEM 23      38
       TAKE
     AND WANDERD DISTANT IN A DISMAL NIGHT CLOUDED & DARK    . .    647 JERUSALEM 24       9
     AND IN A DARK LAND GAVE HER BIRTH . . . . . . . . . .          651 FIELDS FROM/J     52
     SLEW IN MY DARK SELF-RIGHTEOUS PRIDE . . . . . . . . .         651 FIELDS FROM/J     66
     ALBION'S DARK ROCKS SETTING BEHIND THE GARDENS OF             653 JERUSALEM 29       2
       KENSINGTON
     O CRUEL PITY O DARK DECEIT CAN LOVE SEEK FOR DOMINION   . .    654 JERUSALEM 29      60
     AND THE DARK BODY OF ALBION LEFT PROSTRATE UPON THE CRYSTAL    655 JERUSALEM 29      63
       PAVEMENT
     VALA SHRUNK IN LIKE THE DARK SEA THAT LEAVES ITS SLIMY         655 JERUSALEM 29      78
       BANKS
     ALBION'S ROCKS & PRECIPICES CAVES OF SOLITUDE & DARK          656 JERUSALEM 31       6
       DESPAIR
     SO SAYING SHE HER DARK THREADS CAST OVER THE TREMBLING         658 JERUSALEM 31      67
       RIVER
     IN HIS DARK SPECTRE RAVENING FROM HIS OPEN SEPULCHER    . .    663 JERUSALEM 36      30
     IRON AND STEEL DARK AND OPAKE WITH CLOUDS & TEMPESTS           664 JERUSALEM 38       5
       BROODING
     HIS STRONG LIMBS SHUDDERD UPON HIS MOUNTAINS HIGH AND DARK     664 JERUSALEM 38       6
     IN THAT DARK VALLEY I HAVE GIRDED ROUND MY CLOKE AND ON        666 JERUSALEM 39      20
       MY FEET
     AND HIS DARK EON THAT ONCE FAIR CRYSTAL FORM DIVINELY CLEAR    667 JERUSALEM 40      41
     THE TWENTY-EIGHT TREMBLED IN DEATH'S DARK CAVES IN COLD        668 JERUSALEM 41      23
       DESPAIR
     ARE BECOME THE SOURCES OF DARK & BITTER DEATH & OF            672 JERUSALEM 43      32
       CORRODING HELL
     THEIR AWFUL CHARGE BACK TO HIS NATIVE HOME BUT ALBION DARK     674 JERUSALEM 44       5
     HIS FRIENDS CUT HIS STRONG CHAINS & OVERWHELMD HIS DARK        675 JERUSALEM 45      21
     THE EYE OF MAN A LITTLE NARROW ORB CLOSD UP & DARK   . . .    680 JERUSALEM 49      34
     MAN DIVIDED FROM HIS EMANATION IS A DARK SPECTRE . . . .      684 JERUSALEM 53      25
     LAMENTATION IT FLEE BACK & HIDE IN NON-ENTITY'S DARK WILD      688 JERUSALEM 56      16
     REMEMBER RECOLLECT WHAT DARK BEFEL IN WINTRY DAYS   . . .      688 JERUSALEM 56      25
     REAR THEIR DARK ROCKS AMONG THE STARS OF GOD STUPENDOUS        690 JERUSALEM 58      49
     BURST FORTH IN STREAMS OF BLOOD UPON THE HEAVENS & DARK        696 JERUSALEM 62      31
       NIGHT
     A DARK HERMAPHRODITE . . . . . . . . . . . . .               699 JERUSALEM 64      31
     IS CAIAPHAS THE DARK PREACHER OF DEATH . . . . . . . .  .    718 STOOD AMONG/J     18
     THEY ARE BECOME NARROW PLACES IN A LITTLE AND DARK LAND        720 JERUSALEM 79      14
     OF THE VALLEYS OF DESTRUCTION INTO A DARK LAND OF PITCH        721 JERUSALEM 79      61
       & BITUMEN
     SHRUNK TO A NARROW DOLEFUL FORM IN THE DARK LAND OF CABUL      721 JERUSALEM 79      63
     HE SAW THEM ISSUE FROM MY BOSOM DARK IN JEALOUSY . . .  .    722 JERUSALEM 80      21
     THE REALMS OF DARK DEATH O PERVERSE TO THYSELF CONTRARIOUS     733 JERUSALEM 88      26
     HIS HEAD DARK DEADLY IN ITS BRAIN INCLOSES A REFLEXION   . .   734 JERUSALEM 89      14
     BUT DARK OPAKE TENDER TO TOUCH & PAINFUL & AGONIZING    .      736 JERUSALEM 90       8
     REASONING UPON ITS OWN DARK FICTION . . . . . . . . .         753 EV GOSPEL(D)/N   97
     AND CREATED HELL'S DARK JAWS . . . . . . . . . . .           754 EV GOSPEL(E)/N   32
     WAS IT LOVE OR DARK DECEIT . . . . . . . . . . .             755 EV GOSPEL(E)/N   58
     TWAS DARK DECEIT TO EARN MY BREAD . . . . . . . . .          755 EV GOSPEL(E)/N   60
     IN DARK PRETENCE TO CHASTITY . . . . . . . . . . .           755 EV GOSPEL(E)/N   71
```

434

```
                                                            PAGE    TITLE           LINE
DARK    (CONTINUED)
      CANST THOU RETURN TO THIS DARK HELL  . . . . . . . .   755 EV GOSPEL(E)/N      77
      A DARK HERMAPHRODITE [I] WE STOOD  . . . . . . . . .   770 OF GATES/GP         13
      THE AMERICAN WAR BEGAN ALL ITS DARK HORRORS PASSED BEFORE  799 TO FLAXMAN/L     9
         MY FACE
      A DARK BLACK ROCK & A GLOOMY CAVE  . . . . . . . . .   817 HAPPINESS/L         40
      DARK BUT VERY PROFITABLE YEARS I THANK GOD THAT  . . . . 852C LETTER 50      PROSE
      CANUTE DARK HAIR & EYES  . . . . . . . . . . . . . . . . SUPP ILLUS HISTORY *TITLE
DARKEN
      AND DARKEN ALL MY PALACE WALLS WITH ENVYINGS & HATE  . . .  310 FOUR ZOAS 5    213
DARKEND      SEE DARKNED
      BUT HE IS DARKEND LIKE THE SUMMER'S NOON  . . . . . .     5 FAIR ELENOR/PS     49
      WALKING ALONG THE DARKEND VALLEY  . . . . . . . . . .     8 MEMORY COME/PS     15
      AND CASTS THEM OUT UPON THE DARKEND EARTH  . . . . . .    34 WAR SONG/PS         4
      AND TAUGHT WONDERS TO DARKEND SOULS . . . . . . . . .   136 FRENCH REVOLTN     43
      TILL MAN RAISE HIS DARKEND LIMBS OUT OF THE CAVES OF NIGHT  144 FRENCH REVOLTN  218
         . . .
      TILL BEAUTY FADES FROM OFF MY SHOULDERS DARKEND AND CAST  194 V DAU ALBION 7    14
         OUT
      DARKEND THE ATLANTIC MOUNTAINS & THEIR TRUMPETS SHOOK THE  201 AMERICA 13       14
         VALLEYS
      TIS THOU HAST DARKEND ALL MY WORLD O WOMAN LOVELY BANE  . . 269 FOUR ZOAS 1     178
      WHY IS THE LIGHT OF [VALA] ENITHARMON DARKEND IN [HER]   271 FOUR ZOAS 1   *  268
         DEWY MORN
      NIGHT DARKEND AS SHE SPOKE A SHUDDRING RAN FROM EAST TO  273 FOUR ZOAS 1       312
         WEST
      THE EMPYREAN GROAND THROUGHOUT ALL EDEN WAS DARKEND  . . . 304 FOUR ZOAS 4     264
      BUT NOW MY LAND IS DARKEND & MY WISE MEN ARE DEPARTED  . 310 FOUR ZOAS 5       205
      DARKEND HIS BROWS WITH HIS COLD HELMET & HIS GLOOMY SPEAR  313 FOUR ZOAS 6      52
      DARKEND BEFORE HIM SILENT ON THE RIDGY WAVES HE TOOK  . 313 FOUR ZOAS 6        53
      [NOT SO CLOSD UP THE PRINCE OF LIGHT NOW DARKEND WANDRING  314 FOUR ZOAS 6  *  100
         AMONG]
      DARKEND & LOST IN DUE TIME ISSUING FORTH FROM ENION'S WOMB  327 FOUR ZOAS 7    294
      DARKNESS & SORROW COVERD ALL FLESH ETERNITY WAS DARKEND  351 FOUR ZOAS 8       414
      URIZEN SITTING IN HIS WEB OF (DECEITFUL) RELIGION [WAS  352 FOUR ZOAS 8    *  415
         [?TORMENTED] ?DARKEND]
      URIZEN DROPT A TEAR THE ETERNAL MAN DARKEND WITH SORROW  362 FOUR ZOAS 9   *  200
      DARKEND LIKE MOULD IN THE DIVIDED FALLOW WHERE THE WEED  364 FOUR ZOAS 9   *  294
      THE UNIVERSAL GROAN WENT UP THE ETERNAL MAN WAS DARKEND  372 FOUR ZOAS 9       578
      THE ETERNAL MAN DARKEND WITH SORROW & A WINTRY MANTLE  . 377 FOUR ZOAS 9       772
      DARKNESS & SORROW COVERD ALL FLESH ETERNITY WAS DARKEND  382 FOUR ZOAS AD 6     30
      IMAGE DIVINE THO DARKEND AND THO WALKING AS ONE WALKS  . 496 MILTON 15           6
      THUS DARKEND THE SHADOWY FEMALE TENFOLD & ORC TENFOLD  . 500 MILTON 18          46
      AND HE ALSO DARKEND HIS BROWS FREEZING DARK ROCKS BETWEEN  500 MILTON 19         1
      THE DARKEND URIZEN AS THE SCULPTOR SILENT STANDS BEFORE  502 MILTON 20           8
      THO DARKEND AND THE SEVEN ANGELS OF THE PRESENCE ATTENDED  502 MILTON 20        14
         HIM
      WEEP AT THY SOUL'S DISEASE AND THE DIVINE VISION IS DARKEND  622 JERUSALEM 4    13
      DARKEND THEY ARE DRAWN THRO UNBOUNDED SPACE SCATTERD UPON  623 JERUSALEM 5       2
      OF MOUNTAIN & RIVER & CITY ARE SMALL & WITHERD & DARKEND  623 JERUSALEM 5        8
      THE FAMILY DIVINE HOVER AROUND THE DARKEND ALBION  . . .  674 JERUSALEM 44      20
      WEAK WITHERD DARKEND & JERUSALEM IS CAST FORTH FROM ALBION  679 JERUSALEM 49      8
      WERE CONTAIN IN THE ALL GLORIOUS IMAGINATION ARE WITHERD  679 JERUSALEM 49      14
         & DARKEND
      AND JEALOUSY IMMINGLED & THE PURPLE OF THE VIOLET DARKEND  699 JERUSALEM 64     29
         DEEP
DARKENED
      MY DAYS ARE COVERED WITH SORROW SHUT UP DARKENED  . . . .  38B SAMSON/PS     PROSE
      HIS POWER OF IMAGINATION WEAKENED SO MUCH AND DARKENED  . 582D DESC CAT 9    PROSE
      BUT NOW ALBION IS DARKENED & JERUSALEM LIES IN RUINS  . . 711 JERUSALEM 71      54
DARKENEST     SEE DARKNEST
      DARKENEST EVERY INTERNAL LIGHT WITH THE ARROWS OF  491 MILTON 10               17
         THY QUIVER
DARKENING     SEE DARKNING
      AND THE OWL AND BAT FLEW ROUND THE DARKENING TREES  . . .  35C COUCH DEATH/PS  PROSE
      ON THE DARKENING GREEN  . . . . . . . . . . . . . . .   116 ECCHOING GR/SI     30
      HIS JEALOUSY BEFORE THE THRONE DIVINE DARKENING COLD  . 622 JERUSALEM 4        35
DARKENS
      AND THE VALE DARKENS AT MY PENSIVE WOE  . . . . . . . .    10 WHEN EARLY/PS      6
DARKEST
      . . . BENEATH THE [TREE] ROOTS OF MYSTERY IN DARKEST NIGHT  333 FOUR ZOAS 7B *  1
      HAVE BEEN THE DARKEST YEARS THAT EVER MORTAL SUFFERD  . . 862D LETTER 60     PROSE
DARK-FROWNING
      . . . LONDON'S DARK-FROWNING TOWERS  . . . . . . . . .   501 MILTON 19         39
DARKLING
      IN LUCENT WORDS MY DARKLING VERSES DIGHT  . . . . . .    14 IMIT SPEN/PS        3
      AND BEAM FORTH LUSTRE ON A DARKLING WORLD  . . . . . .    18 EDW THIRD/PS 1     36
      THOU VISITEST OUR DARKLING WORLD WITH BLESSED FEET  . . .  37D SAMSON/PS      PROSE
      HE CEAST & DARKLING OER THE MOUNTAINS SOUGHT HIS PATHLESS  100 TIRIEL 1        52
         WAY
DARKLY
      . . . ALL HIS [LOVELY CHANGING] DARKLY WAVING COLOURS MIX  381 FOUR ZOAS AD 5    4
DARKNED
      BUT NOW HIS EYES WERE DARKNED & HIS WIFE FADING IN DEATH  99 TIRIEL 1           4
      AMERICA IS DARKNED AND MY PUNISHING DEMONS TERRIFIED  . . 199 AMERICA 9     *   3
DARKNESS
      BY NIGHT DESTRUCTION FLIES AND STRIKES IN DARKNESS  . . .   5 FAIR ELENOR/PS    35
      HOW MANY WALK IN DARKNESS TERRORS ARE ROUND  . . . . .    30 EDW THIRD/PS 5     11
      IN SICKLY DARKNESS LIKE A DIM ECLIPSE  . . . . . . . .    31 EDW THIRD/PS 6      4
      TILL THE CURTAINS OF DARKNESS WERE DRAWN  . . . . . . .    35D COUCH DEATH/PS  PROSE
      AND LOWRING DARKNESS HOVERD OER TH ASSEMBLY  . . . . .    49B ISLAND MOON 5  *PROSE
      ("ITS FALLACIES") WHEN THE FALLACIES OF DARKNESS ARE  . .  92A ANNO SWED LOVE  MARG
```

435

		PAGE	TITLE	LINE
DARKNESS	(CONTINUED)			
CHAIND IN THICK DARKNESS UTTERD CRIES OF MOURNING ALL THE NIGHT		107	TIRIEL 5	28
. . . DARKNESS OF OLD TIMES AROUND THEM		135	FRENCH REVOLTN	17
. . . IN THE TOWER NAMD DARKNESS WAS A MAN		135	FRENCH REVOLTN	29
. . . BUT ANCIENT DARKNESS AND TREMBLING WANDER THRO THE PALACE		137	FRENCH REVOLTN	63
IN THEIR DARKNESS THE KING STOOD HIS HEART FLAMD		137	FRENCH REVOLTN	69
I SEE THRO DARKNESS THRO CLOUDS ROLLING ROUND ME		137	FRENCH REVOLTN	72
. . . A DARKNESS CREPT OVER HIS EYE-LIDS AND CHILL COLD SWEAT		147	FRENCH REVOLTN	295
WHICH WILL SOON APPEAR WHEN THE DARKNESS PASSES AWAY	. .	156A	MARRIAGE HH 17	PROSE
FROM THE DARKNESS DREAD & DREAR		168	EARTHS ANSWR/N	2
OR THE PLOWMAN IN DARKNESS PLOW		169	EARTHS ANSWR/N	20
WHY DARKNESS & OBSCURITY		171	TO NOBODADDY/N	5
WHERE THE HORRIBLE DARKNESS IS IMPRESSED WITH REFLECTIONS OF DESIRE		194	V DAU ALBION 7	11
THOU ART THE IMAGE OF GOD WHO DWELLS IN DARKNESS OF AFRICA		196	AMERICA PREL 2	8
LET THE INCHAINED SOUL SHUT UP IN DARKNESS AND IN SIGHING		198	AMERICA 6	8
I SEE THEE IN THICK CLOUDS AND DARKNESS ON AMERICA'S SHORE		199	AMERICA 9	16
FROM THE DARKNESS DREAD & DREAR		210	EARTHS ANSR/SE	2
OR THE PLOWMAN IN DARKNESS PLOW		211	EARTHS ANSR/SE	20
SPACE BY SPACE IN HIS NINEFOLD DARKNESS		222	URIZEN 3	9
NOW FILLD WITH CLOUDS DARKNESS & WATERS		223	URIZEN 4	2
LO I UNFOLD MY DARKNESS AND ON		224	URIZEN 4	31
EMERGE FROM THE DARKNESS HIS HAND		224	URIZEN 4	42
BUT NO LIGHT FROM THE FIRES ALL WAS DARKNESS		225	URIZEN 5	17
OF DARKNESS THE ETERNAL PROPHET HOWLD		227	URIZEN 10	7
FOR IN CHANGEABLE CLOUDS AND DARKNESS		230	URIZEN 15	3
THEY BEGAN TO WEAVE CURTAINS OF DARKNESS		231	URIZEN 19	5
HE IN DARKNESS CLOSD VIEWD ALL HIS RACE		235	URIZEN 23	22
TO THE JAWS OF DEVOURING DARKNESS		236	URIZEN 28	3
FOR THE DARKNESS OF ASIA WAS STARTLED		247	SONG OF LOS 6	5
FROM HIS WOVEN DARKNESS ABOVE		248	SONG OF LOS 7	25
ORC RAGING IN EUROPEAN DARKNESS		248	SONG OF LOS 7	26
THEN HID HER IN DARKNESS IN SILENCE		250	AHANIA 2	36
A CIRCLE OF DARKNESS THEN FIXED		251	AHANIA 3	32
WERE SMITTEN WITH DARKNESS DEFORMD		251	AHANIA 3	43
ENRAGD IN THE DESOLATE DARKNESS		253	AHANIA 4	28
RENEW IN THESE CHAINS OF DARKNESS		255	AHANIA 5	43
INTO DARKNESS AND SHADOWY OBSCURITY		256	BOOK OF LOS 3	42
DARKNESS ROUND LOS HEAT WAS NOT FOR BOUND UP		257	BOOK OF LOS 4	1
COLDNESS DARKNESS OBSTRUCTION A SOLID		257	BOOK OF LOS 4	4
IN DARKNESS AND DEEP CLOUDS INVOLVD		260	BOOK OF LOS 5	57
LET HER LAY SECRET IN THE SOFT RECESS OF DARKNESS & SILENCE		265	FOUR ZOAS 1	30
A NOTHING LEFT IN DARKNESS YET I AM AN IDENTITY		265	FOUR ZOAS 1	62
[IN DARKNESS & SOLITUDE FORMING SEAS OF [TROUBLE] DOUBT . . .		267	FOUR ZOAS 1	* 114
UTTERING THIS DARKNESS IN MY HALLS IN THE PILLARS OF MY HOLY-ONES		271	FOUR ZOAS 1	270
IN DARKNESS BUILDING THY STRONG THRONE & IN MY ANCIENT NIGHT		278	FOUR ZOAS 1	509
URIZEN CAST DEEP DARKNESS ROUND HIM SILENT BROODING DEATH		278	FOUR ZOAS 1	515
BUT URIZEN WITH DARKNESS OVERSPREADING ALL THE ARMIES . .	279	FOUR ZOAS 1	535
THEIR VENTUROUS FLIGHT IN HUMAN FORMS DISTINCT THRO DARKNESS DEEP		284	FOUR ZOAS 2	151
LIKE PILLARS OF FIRE TRAVELLING THRO DARKNESS & NON ENTITY		286	FOUR ZOAS 2	230
WHOM URIZEN DOTH SERVE WITH LIGHT REPLENISHING HIS DARKNESS		292	FOUR ZOAS 3	15
HIS VISAGE CHANGD TO DARKNESS &		294	FOUR ZOAS 3	110
THE PASSIVE IDLE SLEEP THE ENORMOUS NIGHT & DARKNESS OF DEATH		295	FOUR ZOAS 3	115
A WORLD OF DARKNESS AHANIA FELL FAR INTO NON ENTITY . . .		295	FOUR ZOAS 3	144
AND YET TOO NEAR DASHD DOWN I SEND THEE INTO DISTANT DARKNESS		296	FOUR ZOAS 3	170
A WORLD OF DEEP DARKNESS WHERE ALL THINGS IN HORRORS ARE ROOTED		296	FOUR ZOAS 3	181
DOUBTING STOOD THARMAS IN THE [DISMAL] SOLEMN DARKNESS HIS DIM EYES		298	FOUR ZOAS 4	* 44
LABOUR OF AGES IN THE DARKNESS & THE WAR OF THARMAS . . .		301	FOUR ZOAS 4	167
BENEATH THE DEEPS IN DISMAL DARKNESS BENEATH IMMENSITY		304	FOUR ZOAS 4	279
FAINT & MORE FAINT THE DAYLIGHT WANES THE WHEELS OF TURNING DARKNESS		306	FOUR ZOAS 5	27
[WHEN] URIZEN CAST DEEP DARKNESS ROUND HIM RAGING LUVAH POURD		306	FOUR ZOAS 5	* 43
DOWN ON THE ROCK OF ETERNITY ON DARKNESS OF THE DEEP . .	306	FOUR ZOAS 5	55
LET LOOSE THE ENORMOUS SPIRIT IN THE DARKNESS OF THE DEEP		306	FOUR ZOAS 5	* 59
SITTING IN DARKNESS OVER HER LOS MOURND IN ANGUISH FIERCE		307	FOUR ZOAS 5	71
THE DARKNESS WARRING WITH THE WAVES OF THARMAS & SNOWS OF URIZEN		308	FOUR ZOAS 5	107
URIZEN KNEW THEM NOT & THUS ADDRESSD THE SPIRITS OF DARKNESS		311	FOUR ZOAS 6	* 7
LOS BROODED ON THE DARKNESS NOR SAW URIZEN WITH A GLOBE OF FIRE		314	FOUR ZOAS 6	83
SHUTS UP MY POWERS THEN A SEED IN THE VAST WOMB OF DARKNESS		317	FOUR ZOAS 6	222
TRAVELLING THRO DARKNESS & WHEREEVER HE TRAVELD A DIRE WEB		318	FOUR ZOAS 6	* 243
NORTH STOOD URTHONA'S STEDFAST THRONE A WORLD OF SOLID DARKNESS		318	FOUR ZOAS 6	268
I WAS DIVIDED IN DARKNESS & OBLIVION THOU AN INFANT WOE		327	FOUR ZOAS 7	288
WATCHMAN THE NIGHT IS THICK & DARKNESS CHEATS MY RAYIE SIGHT		335	FOUR ZOAS 7B	94
AND RUNNING THEIR IMMORTAL COURSE THRO SOLID DARKNESS BORNE		336	FOUR ZOAS 7B	143
AND BOWELS HIDDEN [IN DARKNESS] IN HAMMERD STEEL [ARE] . . .		338	FOUR ZOAS 7B	* 207

```
                                                                   PAGE      TITLE          LINE
DARKNESS    (CONTINUED)
    AND SHE IS GONE & HERE ALONE I WAR WITH DARKNESS & DEATH       339  FOUR ZOAS 7B         239
    HIS WOVEN DARKNESS & IN LAWS & DECEITFUL RELIGIONS   . . .     345  FOUR ZOAS 8          172
    DARKNESS & SORROW COVERD ALL FLESH ETERNITY WAS DARKEND        351  FOUR ZOAS 8          414
    DARKNESS & SORROW &C TURN OVER LEAF   . . . . . . .           351D  FOUR ZOAS 8        *PROSE
    THRO DISMAL DARKNESS DRAVE THE PLOW OF AGES OVER CITIES        365  FOUR ZOAS 9          312
    AND DARKNESS COVERD ALL THE DEEP THE LIGHT OF ENION FADED      370  FOUR ZOAS 9          496
    LIKE A (FAINT) FLAME QUIVERING UPON THE SURFACE OF THE         370  FOUR ZOAS 9        *  497
        DARKNESS
    DARKNESS WAS ALL BENEATH THE HEAVENS ONLY A LITTLE LIGHT       372  FOUR ZOAS 9          560
    [WITH] BY BEASTS & WORMS & CREEPING THINGS & DARKNESS &        373  FOUR ZOAS 9          596
        DESPAIR
    LO DARKNESS COVERS THE LONG POMP OF BANNERS ON THE WIND        375  FOUR ZOAS 9          666
    LET THE INCHAIND SOUL SHUT UP IN DARKNESS & IN SIGHING  . .    375  FOUR ZOAS 9        *  672
    THE SEA THAT ROLLD & FOAMD WITH DARKNESS & THE SHADOWS         378  FOUR ZOAS 9          802
        OF DEATH
    THEY BUILD THE OVENS OF URTHONA NATURE IN DARKNESS GROANS      379  FOUR ZOAS 9          816
    MINGLING HIS HORRIBLE [BRIGHTNESS] DARKNESS . . . . . .        381  FOUR ZOAS AD 5         2
    DARKNESS & SORROW COVERD ALL FLESH ETERNITY WAS DARKEND        382  FOUR ZOAS AD 6        30
    NO MAN CAN TAKE DARKNESS FOR LIGHT HE MAY PRETEND TO DO SO    386C  ANNO WATSON          MARG
    PRINCE OF DARKNESS IS A GENTLEMAN & NOT A MAN HE IS A LORD    399C  ANNO BACON           MARG
        CHANCELLOR
    PRINCES' POWERS POWERS OF DARKNESS   . . . . . . . . .        407B  ANNO BACON           MARG
    IN THE DARKNESS OF NIGHT & THE WINTER'S SNOW  . . . . .        436  WILLIAM BOND          51
    URIZEN LAY IN DARKNESS & SOLITUDE IN CHAINS OF THE MIND        482  MILTON 3               6
        LOCKD UP
    SHOT SPIRING OUT IN THE DEEP DARKNESS & PETRIFIED AS THEY      482  MILTON 3              18
        GREW
    HIS FUTURE COURSE THRO DARKNESS AND DESPAIR TO ETERNAL         487  MILTON 7              26
        DEATH
    HID HIM FROM SIGHT IN AN EXTREME BLACKNESS AND DARKNESS        490  MILTON 9              33
    BETWEEN SATAN AND PALAMABRON IN THE TERRIBLE DARKNESS   . .    490  MILTON 9              45
    OF FIRE IN INTERCHANGE OF BEAUTY & PERFECTION IN              500  MILTON 18             40
        THE DARKNESS
    IN THE SHADOWY FEMALE'S BOSOM JEALOUS HER DARKNESS GREW        500  MILTON 18             42
    GLOWD ON HIS ROCKY COUCH AGAINST THE DARKNESS LOUD THUNDERS    500  MILTON 18             47
    SHINING IN DARKNESS GLORIOUS UPON THE DEEPS OF ENTUTHON        501  MILTON 19             35
    IN LONDON'S DARKNESS AND MY TEARS FALL DAY AND NIGHT   . .     623  JERUSALEM 5           36
    HE STOOD OVER THE IMMORTAL IN THE SOLITUDE AND DARKNESS        625  JERUSALEM 7            2
    INVOLVD EIGHT THEIR WEBS ROLLD OUTWARDS INTO DARKNESS   . .    626  JERUSALEM 7           46
    THE LAND OF DARKNESS FLAMED BUT NO LIGHT & NO REPOSE   . .     634  JERUSALEM 13          46
    HEAVES IN THE HAND OF PALAMABRON WHO IN LONDON'S DARKNESS      636  JERUSALEM 16           9
    BUT AS A DISTORTED & REVERSED REFLEXION IN THE DARKNESS        639  JERUSALEM 17          42
    IN HER DARKNESS & WAS COMFORTED YET STILL SHE DIVIDED AWAY     639  JERUSALEM 17          49
    AND THE SPECTROUS DARKNESS FROM HIS BACK DIVIDED              639  JERUSALEM 17          57
        IN TEMPTATIONS
    OUT FROM HIS BOSOM A MIGHTY POLYPUS VEGETATING IN DARKNESS     641  JERUSALEM 18          40
    AND THE DIVINE HAND WAS UPON THEM BEARING THEM THRO            655  JERUSALEM 30          12
        DARKNESS
    SO SPOKE LOS TRAVELLING THRO DARKNESS & HORRID SOLITUDE        657  JERUSALEM 31          39
    NOR DARKNESS IMMINGLED WITH LIGHT ON MY FURROWD FIELD   . .    659  JERUSALEM 33          32
    IN DREAMS OF DARKNESS WHILE MY VEGETATING BLOOD IN VEINY       665  JERUSALEM 38          36
        PIPES
    LET LOOSE THE ENORMOUS SPECTRE ON THE DARKNESS OF THE DEEP     667  JERUSALEM 40          32
    IN THE WEST A WORLD OF RAGING WATERS IN THE NORTH SOLID        691  JERUSALEM 59          19
        DARKNESS
    INTO INDEFINITE CLOUDY SHADOWS IN DARKNESS & SEPARATION        703  JERUSALEM 66          52
    AND THUS HER VOICE WENT FORTH IN THE DARKNESS OF PHILISTHEA    719  JERUSALEM 78          30
    IN THE THICK CLOUD & DARKNESS & THE VOICE WENT FORTH FROM      722  JERUSALEM 80          11
    LOS WALKS UPON HIS ANCIENT MOUNTAINS IN THE DEADLY DARKNESS    730  JERUSALEM 85          10
    INTO A GLOBE OF BLOOD BENEATH HIS BOSOM TREMBLING             732  JERUSALEM 86          52
        IN DARKNESS
    AMONG THE DARKNESS OF HIS FURNACES DIVIDING ASUNDER TILL       732  JERUSALEM 86          56
    SO LOS CRIED AT HIS ANVIL IN THE HORRIBLE DARKNESS WEEPING     738  JERUSALEM 91          32
    IN THE DEEP DARKNESS BROAD LIGHTNINGS GLARE LONG THUNDERS      741  JERUSALEM 94           4
        ROLL
    SO JESUS SPOKE THE COVERING CHERUB COMING ON IN DARKNESS       743  JERUSALEM 96          17
    THE FEMALE FROM HIS DARKNESS ROSE  . . . . . . . . .           770  OF GATES/GP            2
    . . . IN THE MIDST OF THE DARKNESS OF THE OATH ALL CLOTHED     781  GHOST ABEL 2          23
    & DARKNESS NOT UNLIKE A CHAMPION I HAVE CONQUERD  . . . .     816A  LETTER 23           PROSE
    MAY PRAISE HIM & THAT THOSE WHO DWELL IN DARKNESS & IN   .    823C  LETTER 26           PROSE
    GENEROUS EXULTATION IN MY ESCAPE FROM THE ARROWS             833C  LETTER 33           PROSE
        OF DARKNESS
    I COURAGEOUSLY PURSUED MY COURSE THROUGH DARKNESS   . .      852C  LETTER 50           PROSE
    HAIL LOCUSTS DARKNESS FIRST BORN XXX RED SEA EGYPTIANS       SUPP  EXODUS/N           *PROSE
        DROWND
DARKNEST
    AND NOW THOU DARKNEST IN MY PRESENCE NEVER FROM MY SIGHT       269  FOUR ZOAS 1          175
    AND NOW THOU DARKNEST IN MY PRESENCE NEVER FROM MY SIGHT       382  FOUR ZOAS AD 5        17
DARKNING
    AND HOVERING OVER HER IN THE DARKNING STORM   . . . . .        42C  THEN SHE BORE       PROSE
    [HARK] HOW SOON THE WINDS SING ROUND THE DARKNING STORM        43C  WOE CRIED MUSE     *PROSE
    . . . AND EVERY DARKNING CITY  . . . . . . . . . . .           139  FRENCH REVOLTN       117
    SUNDRING DARKNING THUNDRING  . . . . . . . . . . . .           225  URIZEN 5               3
    BEGIN WITH THARMAS PARENT POWER DARKNING IN THE WEST   .       264  FOUR ZOAS 1           24
    [LOS] HE ANSWERD DARKNING MORE WITH [FOUL] INDIGNATION         272  FOUR ZOAS 1          282
        HID IN SMILES
    FOR MESSENGERS FROM BEULAH COME IN TEARS & DARKNING CLOUDS     277  FOUR ZOAS 1          476
    IN WOE HIS BRETHREN & HIS SONS IN DARKNING WOE LAMENTING       283  FOUR ZOAS 2          132
    THIS URIZEN PERCIEVD & SILENT BROODED IN DARKNING CLOUDS       285  FOUR ZOAS 2          207
    URIZEN SAW THY SIN & HID HIS BEAMS IN DARKNING CLOUDS   .      288  FOUR ZOAS 2          329
    WHY WILT THOU LOOK UPON FUTURITY DARKNING PRESENT JOY   . .    291  FOUR ZOAS 3           11
```

437

		PAGE	TITLE		LINE

DARKNING   (CONTINUED)
  [AND COMFORTS SHALL DESCEND FROM HEAVEN INTO THY DARKNING   292 FOUR ZOAS 3   29
    CLOUDS]
  THE [ETERNAL] [FALLEN] DARKNING MAN WALKD . . . .   292 FOUR ZOAS 3   *   44
  FELL DOWN DOWN RUSHING RUINING THUNDERING [DARKNING]   295 FOUR ZOAS 3   * 141
    SHUDDERING
  THE DARKNING SPECTRE OF URTHONA HID BENEATH A ROCK   . . .   320 FOUR ZOAS 7   2
  RECIEVD HER IN THE DARKNING SOUTH THEIR BODIES LOST THEY   358 FOUR ZOAS 9   *   26
    STOOD
  MY BACK DARKNING THE PRESENT CLOUDING WITH A CLOUD   . . .   361 FOUR ZOAS 9   166
  UPON THE DARKNING THAMES ACROSS THE WHOLE ISLAND WESTWARD   625 JERUSALEM 7   3
  ALBION'S CIRCUMFERENCE WAS CLOSD HIS CENTER BEGAN DARKNING   642 JERUSALEM 19   36
  FORTHWITH FROM ALBION'S DARKNING LOCKS CAME TWO IMMORTAL   654 JERUSALEM 29   28
    FORMS
  THEN SPOKE THE SPECTROUS CHAOS TO ALBION DARKNING COLD . .   659 JERUSALEM 33   3
DARKS
  BUT ON WHERE THE LIGHTS AND DARKS ARE PUT . . . . 563D DESC CAT   PROSE
DARKSOM
  WOVEN BY THEIR OWN HANDS TO HIDE THEM IN THE DARKSOM GRAVE   266 FOUR ZOAS 1   65
  [ASTONISHD HE FOUND ENION HIDDEN IN THE DARKSOM CAVE] . .   267 FOUR ZOAS 1   136
  AND MANY SAID WE SEE NO VISIONS IN THE DARKSOM AIR   . .   283 FOUR ZOAS 2   127
  . . . THAT LIGHTS THE [DISMAL] DARKSOM DAY . . .   . .   283 FOUR ZOAS 2   128
  BUT LUVAH CLOSE CONFERRD WITH URIZEN IN DARKSOM NIGHT . .   326 FOUR ZOAS 7   255
  BATHD IN THE CLEAR SPRING OF THE ROCK THEN FROM HER   366 FOUR ZOAS 9   * 346
    DARKSOM CAVE
  THE WIND BLOWS HEAVY LOUD THEY THUNDER THRO THE DARKSOM SKY   512 MILTON 26   8
DARLING
  BUILD WE A BOWER FOR HEAVEN'S DARLING IN THE GRIZZLY DEEP   280 FOUR ZOAS 2   24
DARST
  THOU LITTLE DIMINUTIVE PORTION THAT DARST BE A COUNTERPART   295 FOUR ZOAS 3   117
DART
  AND SHOOK HIS MORTAL DART AGAINST MY HEAD   . . . .   25 EDW THIRD/PS 3   176
  DART FORTH UPON THE WIND IN PIPES WRITHING ABOUT IN THE   353 FOUR ZOAS 8   473
    ABYSS
DARTED
  AND THE PESTILENCE DARTED FROM HER ROBE . . . .   185 LET BROTHELS/N   21
  THEN THUNDERS ROLLD AROUND & LIGHTNINGS DARTED TO & FRO   294 FOUR ZOAS 3   109
  DARTED & DARTED HIGHER & HIGHER TO THE SHRINE OF   320 FOUR ZOAS 7   22
    ENITHARMON
  MALE & HER BROW RADIANT AS DAY DARTED A LOVELY SCORN   . .   381 FOUR ZOAS AD 1   19
DARTING
  THEN DARTING INTO THE ABYSS OF NIGHT HIS VENTUROUS LIMBS   316 FOUR ZOAS 6   184
DARTS
  WITH DARTS OF WINTRY HAIL AGAIN THE BLACK BOW DRAW   . . .   337 FOUR ZOAS 7B   156
  IS TO PICK OUT THE HEADS OF THE DARTS   . . . .   552 WHY CUPID/N   16
  THE WICKED ONWARDS WITH FIERY DARTS   . . . . 608B V LAST JUDG/N   PROSE
  IS SEEN IN THE HEAVENS THROWING HIS DARTS & FLAMES OF FIRE 619B ILLUS MILTON   *PROSE
DASH
  WITH TINKLING SOUNDS TO DASH THY NERVOUS VERSE . . . . .   14 IMIT SPEN/PS   11
  THIS EVENING [WE'D] WE'LL ALL GET DRUNK I SAY DASH AN ANTHEM 54B ISLAND MOON 9 *PROSE
  [I'LL DASH YOU THROUGH YOUR CHAIR SAYS THE CYNIC] . . .   57A ISLAND MOON 9   PROSE
  THEY DASH LIKE FOAM AGAINST THE RIDGES OF THE ARMY . . .   146 FRENCH REVOLTN   277
  HERE BOUND TO FIERY MANGERS FURIOUS DASH THEIR GOLDEN HOOFS   320 FOUR ZOAS 7   7
  TELL HIM I WILL DASH HIM INTO SHIVERS WHERE & AT WHAT TIME   640 JERUSALEM 17   61
  HOWLING WINDS COVER HIM ROARING SEAS DASH FURIOUS AGAINST   741 JERUSALEM 94   3
    HIM
DASHD
  [HIS HARP ALOFT SOUNDING THEN DASHD ITS SHINING FRAME   196 AMERICA PREL 2   19
    AGAINST]
  WHERE NOTHING WAS DASHD WIDE APART   . . . .   256 BOOK OF LOS 3   38
  AND YET TOO NEAR DASHD DOWN I SEND THEE INTO DISTANT   296 FOUR ZOAS 3   170
    DARKNESS
  STIFLING I LIVE IF DASHD IN PIECES FROM A ROCKY HEIGHT . .   298 FOUR ZOAS 4   14
  THOU SHALT HAVE REST IF THOU REFUSEST DASHD ABROAD ON ALL   299 FOUR ZOAS 4   73
  SHALL NOW AVAIL YOU NOUGHT SO SPEAKING HE DASHD HIM WITH   364 FOUR ZOAS 9   277
    HIS FOOT
  TILL BASIRE WAS QUITE DASHD & OUT OF CONCEIT WITH WHAT . . 603C PUB ADDR AD/N   PROSE
  AND THARMAS DASHD ON THE ROCKS OF THE ALTARS OF VICTIMS   672 JERUSALEM 43   7
    IN MEXICO
  MY TENTS ARE FALLN MY PILLARS ARE IN RUINS MY CHILDREN   719 JERUSALEM 79   1
    DASHD
DASHED
  OF URIZEN DASHED IN PIECES FROM HIS PRECIPITANT FALL   . .   296 FOUR ZOAS 3   159
DASHING
  BUILD HER A BOWER IN THE MIDST OF ALL MY DASHING WAVES . .   299 FOUR ZOAS 4   71
  DASHING IN PIECES SELF-RIGHTEOUSNESSES DRIVING THEM FROM   719 JERUSALEM 78   6
    ALBION'S
DATE
  SECTS ARE NOT EVER MENTIOND THERE AS BEING QUITE OUT OF   44B ISLAND MOON 1   PROSE
    DATE
  WHICH IS BUT OF ABOUT TWO MONTHS DATE . . . .   862A LETTER 59   PROSE
DATES
  TO PROCURE DATES OF PREMIUMS PICTURES &C MR READ . . . . 836A LETTER 35   PROSE
DAUBING
  FASHIONABLE DAUBING FOR A POOR PITTANCE OF MONEY . . . . 850B LETTER 49   PROSE
DAUBS   SEE DAWBS
  CANNOT BE LIKE THE SICKLY DAUBS OF TITIAN OR RUBENS . . . 580D DESC CAT 5   PROSE
DAUGHTER
  TIS CONTEMPLATION DAUGHTER OF THE GREY MORNING . . . . . 36D CONTEMPLATN/PS PROSE
  BRINGS TRUE JOY ONCE FLED & CONTEMPLATION IS HER DAUGHTER   42A THEN SHE BORE   PROSE
  LORD OF ALL [HUMILITY HER DAUGHTER] . . . .   42A THEN SHE BORE   PROSE
  THEN [SELF LOVE] BORE A DAUGHTER CALLED EMULATION   . . .   43A THEN SHE BORE   PROSE

438

	PAGE	TITLE	LINE

DAUGHTER   (CONTINUED)

	PAGE	TITLE	LINE
[?HILI] HELA MY YOUNGEST DAUGHTER YOU SHALL LEAD ME FROM THIS PLACE	106	TIRIEL 5	* 24
IS TIRIEL CRUEL LOOK HIS DAUGHTER & HIS YOUNGEST DAUGHTER	107	TIRIEL 6	17
HELA MY DAUGHTER LISTEN THOU [XXX] ART THE DAUGHTER OF TIRIEL	108	TIRIEL 6	* 40
WHAT HAVE I DONE HELA MY DAUGHTER FEARST THOU NOW THE CURSE	108	TIRIEL 6	46
THEIR TYRANT PRINCE BLIND & HIS DAUGHTER HOWLING & LEADING HIM	108	TIRIEL 7	4
SHOUT BEAUTIFUL DAUGHTER OF TIRIEL THOU SINGEST A SWEET SONG	109	TIRIEL 7	10
THE DAUGHTER OF BEAUTY WIPD HER PITYING TEARS WITH HER WHITE VEIL	130	BOOK OF THEL 5	7
THE SHADOWY DAUGHTER OF URTHONA STOOD BEFORE RED ORC .	195	AMERICA PREL 1	1
MY DAUGHTER HOW DO I REJOICE FOR THY CHILDREN FLOCK AROUND	243	EUROPE 14	2
DAUGHTER OF BEULAH SING	264	FOUR ZOAS 1	20
THEN [?ONA] ENO A DAUGHTER OF BEULAH TOOK A MOMENT OF TIME	270	FOUR ZOAS 1	* 222
. . . RESPONDING FROM DAUGHTER TO DAUGHTER	366	FOUR ZOAS 9	* 350
MRS GRINDER AND HER DAUGHTER ALL THE TIME	438B	BLAKES MEMORAN	PROSE
MRS HAYNES & HER DAUGHTER ALL THE TIME MR GRINDER . .	438B	BLAKES MEMORAN	PROSE
BUT WHEN LEUTHA A DAUGHTER OF BEULAH BEHELD SATAN'S CONDEMNATION	492	MILTON 11	28
TO NATURAL RELIGION TO TIRZAH THE DAUGHTER OF RAHAB THE HOLY	501	MILTON 19	54
AND BETWEEN EVERY TWO MOMENTS STANDS A DAUGHTER OF BEULAH	516	MILTON 28	48
SEEKING FOR PLEASURES IN MY PLEASURES O DAUGHTER OF BABYLON	522	MILTON 33	4
THE VIRGIN OLOLON & ADDRESSD HER AS A DAUGHTER OF BEULAH	527	MILTON 36	27
JERUSALEM IS THEIR DAUGHTER LITTLE INFANTS CREEP OUT OF THE	609D	V LAST JUDG/N	PROSE
BY THE DAUGHTER OF BABEL IN A WOVEN MANTLE OF PESTILENCE & WAR	625	JERUSALEM 7	20
THE HARLOT DAUGHTER MOTHER OF PITY AND DISHONOURABLE FORGIVENESS	640	JERUSALEM 18	12
THOU ART MY SISTER AND MY DAUGHTER THY SHAME IS MINE ALSO	642	JERUSALEM 20	19
SLAY NOT MY LITTLE ONES BELOVED VIRGIN DAUGHTER OF BABYLON	643	JERUSALEM 20	27
SLAY NOT MY INFANT LOVES & GRACES BEAUTIFUL DAUGHTER OF MOAB	643	JERUSALEM 20	28
DAUGHTER OF MY PHANTASY UNLAWFUL PLEASURE ALBION'S CURSE	645	JERUSALEM 23	2
FOR SLAVES BUT SET YOUR DAUGHTER BEFORE A MAN & SHE . . .	658	JERUSALEM 31	53
AND THOU O HARLOT DAUGHTER DAUGHTER OF DESPAIR ART ALL	658	JERUSALEM 31	58
ART THOU NATURE MOTHER OF ALL IS JERUSALEM THY DAUGHTER	660	JERUSALEM 34	9
ENITHARMON IS MY DAUGHTER ACCURSED WITH A FATHER'S CURSE	670	JERUSALEM 42	15
NOR DAUGHTER NOR SISTER NOR MOTHER COME FORTH TO EMBOSOM THE SLAIN	673	JERUSALEM 43	44
WEPT FOR THEIR SISTER THE DAUGHTER OF ALBION JERUSALEM .	678	JERUSALEM 48	22
BETWEEN DWELLS A DAUGHTER OF BEULAH TO FEED THE HUMAN VEGETABLE	688	JERUSALEM 56	10
AND ONE DAUGHTER OF LOS SAT AT THE FIERY REEL & ANOTHER	691	JERUSALEM 59	26
AND ANOTHER DAUGHTER OF LOS SAT AT THE SPINNING WHEEL . .	691	JERUSALEM 59	29
SHUAH'S DAUGHTER & TAMAR & RAHAB THE CANAANITES	696	JERUSALEM 62	10
THEN VALA THE WIFE OF ALBION WHO IS THE DAUGHTER OF LUVAH	697	JERUSALEM 63	7
ART THOU VALA THE WIFE OF ALBION O THOU LOVELY DAUGHTER OF LUVAH	698	JERUSALEM 64	19
LOOK THE BEAUTIFUL DAUGHTER OF ALBION SITS NAKED UPON THE STONE	705	JERUSALEM 68	11
OF HER TABERNACLE & HER ARK & SECRET PLACE THE BEAUTIFUL DAUGHTER	705	JERUSALEM 68	15
O BEAUTIFUL DAUGHTER OF ALBION CRUELTY IS THY DELIGHT . .	706	JERUSALEM 68	53
AND A SON OF EDEN WAS SET OVER EACH DAUGHTER OF BEULAH TO GUARD	712	JERUSALEM 72	48
THE CLOUD O RENT IN SUNDER FROM JERUSALEM THE HARLOT DAUGHTER	722	JERUSALEM 80	12
BUT I VALA LUVAH'S DAUGHTER KEEP HIS BODY EMBALMD IN MORAL LAWS	722	JERUSALEM 80	27
YOU ARE ALBION'S VICTIM HE HAS SET HIS DAUGHTER IN YOUR PATH	733	JERUSALEM 87	24
WIFE SISTER DAUGHTER TO THE TOMB	771	OF GATES/GP	46
SOLOMON WHEN HE MARRIED PHAROH'S DAUGHTER	784B	ANNO WW EXCUR	* MARG
JEPHTHAH SACRIFICING HIS DAUGHTER	824A	LETTER 27	PROSE
PROPRIETOR OF MY COTTAGE & HIS WIFE & DAUGHTER	827B	LETTER 28	PROSE
HIS WIFE & DAUGHTER WILL EVIDENCE THE SAME & WILL EVIDENTLY	827D	LETTER 28	PROSE
ALL THE ATTENTION THAT A DAUGHTER COULD PAY TO A MOTHER	833D	LETTER 33	PROSE
WHEN HIS DAUGHTER CAME IN HE GAVE THE PRINT INTO HER HAND	843C	LETTER 43	PROSE
BUT TO SAY THAT SHE IS YOUR DAUGHTER & IS LIKE YOU . . .	853A	LETTER 51	*PROSE
YOUR BEAUTIFUL AND ELEGANT DAUGHTER VENUSIA GROWS IN OUR	853D	LETTER 52	*PROSE
WAT TYLER'S DAUGHTER	SUPP	PENC DRAW 2.32	*TITLE

DAUGHTER'S

	PAGE	TITLE	LINE
THE KNIFE INTO HIS DAUGHTER'S HAND SUCH THING WAS NEVER KNOWN	722	JERUSALEM 80	23

DAUGHTERS

	PAGE	TITLE	LINE
AND ALL THE DAUGHTERS OF THE YEAR SHALL DANCE	2	TO AUTUMN/PS	5
THEIR DAUGHTERS SHALL SING SURROUNDED WITH SHINING SPEARS	33	EDW THIRD/PS 6	54
HER DAUGHTERS SING AS TO THE RISING YEAR	34C	KING JOHN/PS	PROSE
WHERE DOTH HE HIDE HIS TERRIBLE HEAD & HIS SWIFT & FIERY DAUGHTERS	106	TIRIEL 5	2
THE CRY WAS GREAT IN TIRIEL'S PALACE HIS FIVE DAUGHTERS RAN	106	TIRIEL 5	18
IN HASTE THEY FLED WHILE ALL THE SONS & DAUGHTERS OF TIRIEL	107	TIRIEL 5	27
THE FOUR DAUGHTERS [& ALL THE CHILDREN IN THEIR SILENT BEDS]	107	TIRIEL 5	30
THE DAUGHTERS OF MNE SERAPHIM LED ROUND THEIR SUNNY FLOCKS	127	BOOK OF THEL 1	1
VISIONS OF THE DAUGHTERS OF ALBION	189A	V DAU ALBION	TITLE
ENSLAVD THE DAUGHTERS OF ALBION WEEP A TREMBLING LAMENTATION	189	V DAU ALBION 1	1

439

	PAGE	TITLE	LINE
DAUGHTERS (CONTINUED)			
THEIR DAUGHTERS WORSHIP TERRORS AND OBEY THE VIOLENT . .	190	V DAU ALBION 1	23
THE DAUGHTERS OF ALBION HEAR HER WOES & ECCHO BACK HER SIGHS	190	V DAU ALBION 2	20
THE DAUGHTERS OF ALBION HEAR HER WOES & ECCHO BACK HER SIGHS	192	V DAU ALBION 5	2
THE DAUGHTERS OF ALBION HEAR HER WOES & ECCHO BACK HER SIGHS	195	V DAU ALBION 8	13
VISION OF THE DAUGHTERS OF ALBION IN ILLUMINATED PRINTING	207D	PRSPECTUS 1793	PROSE
SONS & DAUGHTERS OF SORROW ON MOUNTAINS	234	URIZEN 23	10
HIS DAUGHTERS FROM GREEN HERBS & CATTLE	234	URIZEN 23	20
BOTH SONS & DAUGHTERS FOR HE SAW	235	URIZEN 23	24
THEN ENITHARMON SAW HER SONS & DAUGHTERS RISE AROUND . .	239	EUROPE 4	5
SHE CALLD HER SONS & DAUGHTERS	243	EUROPE 13	12
THY DAUGHTERS MANY CHANGING	244	EUROPE 14	13
FORTY YEARS ALL HIS SONS & DAUGHTERS	253	AHANIA 4	40
WHEN HE TOOK THE DAUGHTERS OF LIFE	254	AHANIA 5	17
[LIKE SONS & DAUGHTERS]	264	FOUR ZOAS 1	19
THE DAUGHTERS OF BEULAH FOLLOW SLEEPERS	267	FOUR ZOAS 1	99
THE INNUMERABLE SONS & DAUGHTERS OF LUVAH CLOSD IN FURNACES	276	FOUR ZOAS 1	423
THE DAUGHTERS OF BEULAH TERRIFIED HAVE CLOSD THE GATE OF THE TONGUE	277	FOUR ZOAS 1	479
THOU LUVAH SAID THE PRINCE OF LIGHT BEHOLD OUR SONS & DAUGHTERS	277	FOUR ZOAS 1	488
THE DAUGHTERS OF BEULAH BEHELD THE EMANATION THEY PITIED	279	FOUR ZOAS 1	560
WEEPING THE DAUGHTERS OF BEULAH SILENT IN THE PORCHES . .	280	FOUR ZOAS 1	568
THE DAUGHTERS OF ALBION GIRDED AROUND THEIR GARMENTS OF NEEDLEWORK	281	FOUR ZOAS 2	57
INEXTRICABLE LABYRINTHS SHE BORE ME SONS & DAUGHTERS . .	282	FOUR ZOAS 2	97
OF HIS THREE DAUGHTERS WERE ENCOMPASSD BY THE TWELVE BRIGHT HALLS	284	FOUR ZOAS 2	175
FEMALE'S LIMBS IN HIS ABSENCE & HER DAUGHTERS OFT UPON . .	285	FOUR ZOAS 2	189
AND TO HIS SONS IN THEIR DEGREES & TO HIS BEAUTEOUS DAUGHTERS	287	FOUR ZOAS 2	271
THE BEAMY DAUGHTERS OF THE LIGHT STARTING THEY RISE THEY FLEE	288	FOUR ZOAS 2	315
SURROUNDED BY THE EVER CHANGING DAUGHTERS OF THE LIGHT . .	291	FOUR ZOAS 3	9
THE DAUGHTERS OF BEULAH SAW THE DIVINE VISION THEY WERE COMFORTED	304	FOUR ZOAS 4	250
THEY GAVE A SCREAM THEY KNEW THEIR FATHER URIZEN KNEW HIS DAUGHTERS	312	FOUR ZOAS 6	21
THEY POURD THEIR RADIANCE ABOVE ALL THE DAUGHTERS OF LUVAH ENVIED	312	FOUR ZOAS 6	33
GO FORTH SONS OF MY CURSE GO FORTH DAUGHTERS OF MY ABHORRENCE	313	FOUR ZOAS 6	46
GAINING A NEW DOMINION OVER ALL HIS SONS & DAUGHTERS . . .	317	FOUR ZOAS 6	237
. . . & OVER THE SONS & DAUGHTERS OF LUVAH IN THE HORRIBLE ABYSS	317	FOUR ZOAS 6	237
THAT HE MIGHT STARVE THE SONS & DAUGHTERS OF URIZEN ON THE WINDS	318	FOUR ZOAS 6	276
HIS SWIFT WINGD DAUGHTERS SWEEP ACROSS THE VAST BLACK OCEAN	320	FOUR ZOAS 7	26
ENQUIRE OF MY DAUGHTERS WHO ACCURSD IN THE DARK DEPTHS . .	322	FOUR ZOAS 7	92
OF ALL THIS DREADFUL RUIN RISE O DAUGHTERS AT MY STERN COMMAND	322	FOUR ZOAS 7	94
LISTEN O DAUGHTERS TO MY VOICE LISTEN TO THE WORDS OF WISDOM	323	FOUR ZOAS 7	110
AND MANY DAUGHTERS FLOURISHD ROUND THE HOLY TENT OF MAN	326	FOUR ZOAS 7	252
. . . OF [LIFE & LOVE] SACRIFICE OF BROTHERS & SONS & DAUGHTERS	331	FOUR ZOAS 7	443
MY LITTLE DAUGHTERS WERE MADE CAPTIVES & I SAW THEM BEATEN	334	FOUR ZOAS 7B	60
FOLLOWD HER DAUGHTERS TO THE FIELDS OF BLOOD THEY LEFT ME NAKED	334	FOUR ZOAS 7B	66
TO FEED THEIR FRUIT TO GRATIFY THEIR HIDDEN SONS & DAUGHTERS	335	FOUR ZOAS 7B	104
MOURNING THE DAUGHTERS OF BEULAH SAW NOR COULD THEY HAVE SUSTAIN	340	FOUR ZOAS 7B	290
DELUSIVE CRUELTY THEY DESCEND AWAY FROM THE DAUGHTERS OF BEULAH	341	FOUR ZOAS 8	26
IN GOLGONOOZA LOOKING DOWN THE DAUGHTERS OF BEULAH SAW . .	342	FOUR ZOAS 8	42
[ASTONISHD COMFORTED DELIGHTED THE DAUGHTERS OF BEULAH SAW]	342	FOUR ZOAS 8	45
COMPELLD BY THE IRON HEARTED SISTERS DAUGHTERS OF URIZEN	343	FOUR ZOAS 8	83
AND WOVE THEM BODIES CALLING THEM HER BELOVD SONS & DAUGHTERS	345	FOUR ZOAS 8	184
EMPLOYING THE DAUGHTERS IN HER LOOMS & LOS EMPLOYD THE SONS	345	FOUR ZOAS 8	185
[DAUGHTERS OF BEULAH DESCRIBE]	346	FOUR ZOAS 8	* 200
THE DAUGHTERS OF ENITHARMON WEAVE THE OVARIUM & THE INTEGUMENT	346	FOUR ZOAS 8	210
HE AWAKES THE SLEEPERS IN ULRO THE DAUGHTERS OF BEULAH PRAISE HIM	347	FOUR ZOAS 8	* 237
[THE DAUGHTERS &]	348	FOUR ZOAS 8	* 292
WHICH CHRIST MUST REND & HER REVEAL HER DAUGHTERS ARE CALLD	348	FOUR ZOAS 8	293
THE DAUGHTERS &C	348C	FOUR ZOAS 8	*PROSE
THE DAUGHTERS OF AMALEK CANAAN & MOAB BINDING ON THE [STEMS] STONES	348	FOUR ZOAS 8	* 295
SOMETIMES AS TWELVE DAUGHTERS LOVELY & SOMETIMES AS FIVE	349	FOUR ZOAS 8	328
. . . OUR DAUGHTERS OCALYTHRON ELYNITTRIA OOTHOON LEUTHA	350	FOUR ZOAS 8	363
AND MYRIADS MORE OF SONS & DAUGHTERS	350	FOUR ZOAS 8	366
HE TEMPTED MANY OF THE SONS & DAUGHTERS OF LOS TO FLEE .	350	FOUR ZOAS 8	374
AND ALL THY SONS & DAUGHTERS GATHERD ROUND MY AMPLE TABLE	360	FOUR ZOAS 9	127
THE THREE DAUGHTERS OF URIZEN GUARD AHANIA'S DEATH COUCH	362	FOUR ZOAS 9	201
THE DAUGHTERS OF URIZEN STAND WITH CUPS & MEASURES OF FOAMING WINE	365	FOUR ZOAS 9	333

440

		PAGE	TITLE	LINE
DAUGHTERS (CONTINUED)				
HE POURD HIS LIGHT & ALL HIS SONS & DAUGHTERS POURD THEIR LIGHT		372	FOUR ZOAS 9	569
BENEATH THEY SAW THEIR SONS & DAUGHTERS WONDERING INCONCEIVABLE		374	FOUR ZOAS 9	* 648
HOW RED THE SONS & DAUGHTERS OF LUVAH HOW THEY TREAD THE GRAPES		377	FOUR ZOAS 9	743
THE CRUEL JOY OF LUVAH'S DAUGHTERS LACERATING WITH KNIVES		377	FOUR ZOAS 9	753
THARMAS WENT DOWN TO THE WINE PRESSES & BEHELD THE SONS & DAUGHTERS		378	FOUR ZOAS 9	785
LUVAH & VALA WOKE & ALL THE SONS & DAUGHTERS OF LUVAH		378	FOUR ZOAS 9	795
THE DAUGHTERS OF CANAAN & MOAB BINDING ON THE STONES	. .	382	FOUR ZOAS AD 6	11
SOMETIMES AS TWELVE DAUGHTERS LOVELY & SOMETIMES AS FIVE		382	FOUR ZOAS AD 6	16
ORIGINATES IN THE GREEKS' CALLING THE MUSES DAUGHTERS OF MEMORY		452D	ANNO REYNOLDS	MARG
A WORK OF GENIUS IS A WORK "NOT...OF MEMORY &...DAUGHTERS..." MILTON		457C	ANNO REYNOLDS	MARG
WILL HOLD THEIR PROPER RANK & THE DAUGHTERS OF MEMORY	. .	480C	MILTON 1	PROSE
SHALL BECOME THE DAUGHTERS OF INSPIRATION	. . . . .	480C	MILTON 1	PROSE
DAUGHTERS OF BEULAH MUSES WHO INSPIRE THE POET'S SONG	. .	481	MILTON 2	1
AND THIS IS THE MANNER OF THE DAUGHTERS OF ALBION IN THEIR BEAUTY		484	MILTON 5	5
AMONG THE DAUGHTERS OF ALBION AMONG THE ROCKS OF THE DRUIDS		485	MILTON 5	42
WITH THE DAUGHTERS OF MEMORY & NOT WITH THE DAUGHTERS OF INSPIRATION		496	MILTON 14	29
. . . & THOSE THREE WHOM HIS DAUGHTERS	. . . . .	498	MILTON 17	1
CALLD ALL HER DAUGHTERS SAYING SURELY TO UNLOOSE MY BOND		498	MILTON 17	32
TO HIS ADVERSARY AND THEY SENT FORTH ALL THEIR SONS & DAUGHTERS		501	MILTON 19	30
AND ALL THE DAUGHTERS OF LOS PROPHETIC WAIL YET IN DECEIT		506	MILTON 22	37
CONTINUALLY WOVEN IN THE LOOMS OF ENITHARMON'S DAUGHTERS		512	MILTON 26	35
HOW RED THE SONS & DAUGHTERS OF LUVAH HERE THEY TREAD THE GRAPES		513	MILTON 27	3
THE CRUEL JOYS OF LUVAH'S DAUGHTERS LACERATING WITH KNIVES		514	MILTON 27	35
THE DAUGHTERS OF BEAUTY LOOK UP FROM THEIR LOOM & PREPARE		515	MILTON 28	19
BUT ENITHARMON AND HER DAUGHTERS TAKE THE PLEASANT CHARGE		517	MILTON 29	51
THE STAMPING FEET OF ZELOPHEHAD'S DAUGHTERS	. . . .	517	MILTON 29	58
INTO THIS PLACE THE SONS & DAUGHTERS OF OLOLON DESCENDED		518	MILTON 30	4
WEEPING FOR MILTON MUTE WONDER HELD THE DAUGHTERS OF BEULAH		518	MILTON 30	6
AND WHEN THE DAUGHTERS OF BEULAH HEARD THE LAMENTATION	. .	519	MILTON 31	9
AND THE COUCHES OF THE MARTYRS & MANY DAUGHTERS OF BEULAH		524	MILTON 34	20
SEEING MILTON'S SHADOW SOME DAUGHTERS OF BEULAH TREMBLING		524	MILTON 34	47
THE GREEK MUSES ARE DAUGHTERS OF MNEMOSYNE OR MEMORY	.	565D	DESC CAT 2	PROSE
FABLE OR ALLEGORY IS FORMD BY THE DAUGHTERS OF MEMORY	.	604D	V LAST JUDG/N	PROSE
IMAGINATION IS SURROUNDED BY THE DAUGHTERS OF INSPIRATION		604D	V LAST JUDG/N	PROSE
THY NURSES AND THY MOTHERS THY SISTERS AND THY DAUGHTERS		622	JERUSALEM 4	12
BEAMING FORTH WITH HER DAUGHTERS INTO THE DIVINE BOSOM [WHERE]		622	JERUSALEM 4	15
JERUSALEM IS NOT HER DAUGHTERS ARE INDEFINITE	. . . .	622	JERUSALEM 4	27
OF THE TERRIBLE SONS & DAUGHTERS OF ALBION AND THEIR GENERATIONS		623	JERUSALEM 5	26
UPON THE EMANATIONS OF ALBION'S SONS THE DAUGHTERS OF ALBION		624	JERUSALEM 5	37
ESTRILD MEHETABEL & RAGAN LOVELY DAUGHTERS OF ALBION	. .	624	JERUSALEM 5	44
HOWLING IN PAIN REDOUNDING FROM THE ARMS OF BEULAH'S DAUGHTERS		624	JERUSALEM 5	49
O WHAT AVAIL THE LOVES & TEARS OF BEULAH'S LOVELY DAUGHTERS		624	JERUSALEM 5	54
AMONG THE DAUGHTERS OF ALBION AMONG THE STARRY WHEELS	. .	624	JERUSALEM 5	64
LAMENTING FOR HER CHILDREN FOR THE SONS & DAUGHTERS OF ALBION		624	JERUSALEM 5	65
INTO HIS TUNS THY DAUGHTERS ARE TRODDEN IN HIS VINTAGE	. .	625	JERUSALEM 7	12
TILL HE SHOULD BRING THE SONS & DAUGHTERS OF JERUSALEM TO BE		629	JERUSALEM 10	3
THE SONS & DAUGHTERS OF LOS THAT HE MIGHT PROTECT THEM FROM		629	JERUSALEM 10	4
TILL HIS SONS & DAUGHTERS CAME FORTH FROM THE FURNACES	. .	630	JERUSALEM 10	64
THEN ERIN CAME FORTH FROM THE FURNACES & ALL THE DAUGHTERS OF BEULAH		630	JERUSALEM 11	8
AND THE SONS AND DAUGHTERS OF LOS CAME FORTH IN PERFECTION LOVELY		630	JERUSALEM 11	11
AND FROM THEM ALL THE LOVELY BEAMING DAUGHTERS OF ALBION		635	JERUSALEM 14	11
AND LOS BEHELD HIS SONS AND HE BEHELD HIS DAUGHTERS	. .	635	JERUSALEM 14	16
LIKE A PALE CLOUD ARISING FROM THE ARMS OF BEULAH'S DAUGHTERS		635	JERUSALEM 14	33
WALES GIVES HIS DAUGHTERS TO THE LOOMS ENGLAND NURSING MOTHERS		637	JERUSALEM 16	23
TO FOLLOW THE DAUGHTERS OF ALBION AS THE HOUND FOLLOWS THE SCENT		638	JERUSALEM 17	3
DARE NOT APPROACH THE DAUGHTERS OPENLY LEST HE BE CONSUMED		638	JERUSALEM 17	7
FIRST FLED MY SONS & THEN MY DAUGHTERS THEN MY WILD ANIMATIONS		643	JERUSALEM 21	7
AND PEARL & DIAMOND THY DAUGHTERS SANG IN HER COURTS	. .	647	JERUSALEM 24	40
THEY BUY HIS DAUGHTERS THAT THEY MAY HAVE POWER TO SELL HIS SONS		656	JERUSALEM 30	29
SHALL MAKE HIM & HIS SONS & DAUGHTERS YOUR SLAVES FOR EVER		658	JERUSALEM 31	54
THE LOVELIEST OF THE DAUGHTERS OF ETERNITY WHEN IN DAY-BREAK		660	JERUSALEM 33	40
IS THIS THE FEMALE WILL O YE LOVELY DAUGHTERS OF ALBION TO		661	JERUSALEM 34	39
WHILE THE DAUGHTERS OF ALBION DIVIDED LUVAH INTO THREE BODIES		661	JERUSALEM 34	46
BY THE NAME OF MORALITY THEIR DAUGHTERS GOVERN ALL	. . .	663	JERUSALEM 36	47
SUBMITTING TO BE CALLD ENITHARMON'S DAUGHTERS AND BE BORN		668	JERUSALEM 40	55

DAUGHTERS   (CONTINUED)

	PAGE	TITLE		LINE
BY THE DAUGHTERS OF BEULAH GENTLY SNATCHD AWAY AND HID IN BEULAH	668	JERUSALEM	41	14
MY DAUGHTERS ARE HARLOTS MY SONS ARE ACCURSED BEFORE ME	670	JERUSALEM	42	14
O I HAVE UTTERLY BEEN WASTED I HAVE GIVEN MY DAUGHTERS TO DEVILS	670	JERUSALEM	42	16
WEEPING WAS IN ALL BEULAH AND ALL THE DAUGHTERS OF BEULAH	678	JERUSALEM	48	21
ASTONISHD LOVELY EMBRACING THE SUBLIME SHADE THE DAUGHTERS OF BEULAH	678	JERUSALEM	48	29
INTO BEULAH TREMBLING THE DAUGHTERS OF BEULAH DRIED . .	678	JERUSALEM	48	39
THE DAUGHTERS ATTENDED HER SHUDDERINGS WIPING THE DEATH SWEAT	678	JERUSALEM	48	43
WRITHING IN PAIN THE DAUGHTERS OF BEULAH IN KIND ARMS RECIEVD	678	JERUSALEM	48	50
AND THUS ERIN SPOKE TO THE DAUGHTERS OF BEULAH IN SOFT TEARS	678	JERUSALEM	48	53
UPON HIS SONS & DAUGHTERS SELF-EXILED FROM HIS BOSOM . .	679	JERUSALEM	48	61
COME YE O DAUGHTERS OF BEULAH LAMENT FOR OG & SIHON . . .	679	JERUSALEM	49	3
SO ERIN SPOKE TO THE DAUGHTERS OF BEULAH SHUDDERING . . .	681	JERUSALEM	50	18
EXPANDING ON WING THE DAUGHTERS OF BEULAH REPLIED IN SWEET RESPONSE	681	JERUSALEM	50	23
AND THUS HE CHAUNTED HIS SONG THE DAUGHTERS OF ALBION REPLY	687	JERUSALEM	56	2
ENTUNE DAUGHTERS OF ALBION YOUR HYMNING CHORUS MILDLY . .	688	JERUSALEM	56	11
OVER THESE DESOLATE ROCKS OF ALBION O DAUGHTERS OF DESPAIR	688	JERUSALEM	56	21
IN BEAUTY THE DAUGHTERS OF ALBION DIVIDE & UNITE AT WILL	689	JERUSALEM	58	1
THE DAUGHTERS OF ALBION DIVIDE & UNITE IN JEALOUSY & CRUELTY	689	JERUSALEM	58	5
MANY WHEELS & AS MANY LOVELY DAUGHTERS SIT WEEPING . . .	691	JERUSALEM	59	33
OTHER DAUGHTERS WEAVE ON THE CUSHION & PILLOW NETWORK FINE	692	JERUSALEM	59	42
AH THAT IT COULD BE AS THE DAUGHTERS OF BEULAH WISH . . .	692	JERUSALEM	59	44
OTHER DAUGHTERS OF LOS LABOURING AT LOOMS LESS FINE . . .	692	JERUSALEM	59	45
HER FORM WAS HELD BY BEULAH'S DAUGHTERS BUT ALL WITHIN UNSEEN	693	JERUSALEM	60	40
RUTH THE MOABITE & BATHSHEBA OF THE DAUGHTERS OF HETH . .	696	JERUSALEM	62	11
THESE ARE THE DAUGHTERS OF VALA MOTHER OF THE BODY OF DEATH	696	JERUSALEM	62	13
INSTEAD OF HUMAN VICTIMS BY THE DAUGHTERS OF ALBION & CANAAN	697	JERUSALEM	63	31
IN VISIONS OF THE DREAMS OF BEULAH AMONG THE DAUGHTERS OF ALBION	698	JERUSALEM	63	37
THE VAST EXPANSE WHERE THE DAUGHTERS OF ALBION WEAVE THE WEB	698	JERUSALEM	64	2
THEN ALL THE DAUGHTERS OF ALBION BECAME ONE BEFORE LOS EVEN VALA	698	JERUSALEM	64	6
AS REUBEN FLED BEFORE THE DAUGHTERS OF ALBION TAXING THE NATIONS	699	JERUSALEM	64	34
TO THE STERN WARRIORS LOVELY SPORT THE DAUGHTERS ROUND THEIR VICTIMS	701	JERUSALEM	65	64
THE DAUGHTERS OF ALBION CLOTHED IN GARMENTS OF NEEDLE WORK	702	JERUSALEM	66	17
GUSHES & STAINS THE FAIR SIDE OF THE FAIR (DAUGHTERS) OF ALBION	702	JERUSALEM	66	21
THE HUMAN FORM BEGAN TO BE ALTERD BY THE DAUGHTERS OF ALBION	703	JERUSALEM	66	46
IN THE HANDS OF ALBION'S DAUGHTERS AMONG THE DRUID TEMPLES	703	JERUSALEM	66	84
AND THE TWELVE DAUGHTERS OF ALBION UNITED IN RAHAB & TIRZAH	704	JERUSALEM	67	2
THEY DIVIDED INTO MANY LOVELY DAUGHTERS TO BE COUNTERPARTS	704	JERUSALEM	67	8
THE DAUGHTERS WEAVE THEIR WORK IN LOUD CRIES OVER THE ROCK	704	JERUSALEM	67	26
THE TWELVE DAUGHTERS IN RAHAB & TIRZAH HAVE CIRCUMSCRIBD THE BRAIN	705	JERUSALEM	67	41
HE SEES THE TWELVE DAUGHTERS NAKED UPON THE TWELVE STONES	706	JERUSALEM	68	24
MOLECH RUSHES INTO THE KINGS IN LOVE TO THE BEAUTIFUL DAUGHTERS	706	JERUSALEM	68	28
TO THE BEAUTIFUL DAUGHTERS OF ALBION THEY SPORT BEFORE THE KINGS	706	JERUSALEM	68	32
ON THE TWELVE STONES OF POWER & THE BEAUTIFUL DAUGHTERS OF ALBION	706	JERUSALEM	68	41
DEADLY HATE BETWEEN LEAH & RACHEL DAUGHTERS OF DECEIT & FRAUD	707	JERUSALEM	69	11
AS SHE SLEPT IN BEULAH'S NIGHT HID BY THE DAUGHTERS OF BEULAH	708	JERUSALEM	69	46
. . . & OF HIS TWELVE DAUGHTERS	709	JERUSALEM	71	10
ALL WERE HIS FRIENDS & THEIR SONS & DAUGHTERS INTERMARRY IN BEULAH	709	JERUSALEM	71	14
SONS & DAUGHTERS OF LOS IN BOWLAHOOLA & IN CATHEDRON . .	714	JERUSALEM	73	52
IN BEULAH BY THE DAUGHTERS OF BEULAH WITH TEARS & LAMENTATIONS	714	JERUSALEM	74	9
DRAVE THE SONS & DAUGHTERS OF ALBION FROM THEIR ANCIENT MOUNTAINS	714	JERUSALEM	74	21
ON LONDON STONE & THE DAUGHTERS OF ALBION RAN AROUND ADMIRING	715	JERUSALEM	74	34
HOW LOS DRAVE THEM FROM ALBION & THEY BECAME DAUGHTERS OF CANAAN	715	JERUSALEM	74	38
AND I WILL LEAD FORTH THY WORDS TELLING HOW THE DAUGHTERS	715	JERUSALEM	74	41
OF ALBION'S DAUGHTERS IN PHILISTEA BY THE SIDE OF AMALEK	715	JERUSALEM	74	46
HIS CHILDREN TO MY BREASTS HIS SONS & DAUGHTERS TO MY KNEES	720	JERUSALEM	79	26
BY THE TEARS & SMILES OF BEULAH'S DAUGHTERS	721	JERUSALEM	79	77
THE CLOUD OF RAHAB VIBRATING WITH THE DAUGHTERS OF ALBION	722	JERUSALEM	80	40
THE TWELVE DAUGHTERS OF ALBION ATTENTIVE LISTEN IN SECRET SHADES	725	JERUSALEM	82	10
SPOKE TO THE DAUGHTERS OF ALBION STANDING ON SKIDDAW'S TOP	725	JERUSALEM	82	16
I HEARD ENITHARMON SAY TO LOS LET THE DAUGHTERS OF ALBION	725	JERUSALEM	82	22
DISCOVERING HER OWN PERFECT BEAUTY TO THE DAUGHTERS OF ALBION	726	JERUSALEM	82	46

442

```
                                                           PAGE    TITLE          LINE
DAUGHTERS   (CONTINUED)
      ACCORDING TO THE WILL OF THE LOVELY DAUGHTERS OF ALBION    728 JERUSALEM 83      42
      SO LOS SPOKE TO THE DAUGHTERS OF BEULAH WHILE HIS EMANATION 728 JERUSALEM 83     66
      AND THUS HE HEARD THE VOICE OF ALBION'S DAUGHTERS          729 JERUSALEM 83      84
         ON EUPHRATES
      . . . & THE DAUGHTERS OF BEULAH . . . . . . . . .          729 JERUSALEM 83      85
      THUS SANG THE DAUGHTERS IN LAMENTATION UNITING INTO ONE    729 JERUSALEM 84      29
      AT HIS FURNACES HIS DAUGHTERS AT THEIR LOOMS SING WOES  .  .  731 JERUSALEM 86   38
      WITH PULSATIONS WE WILL DIVIDE THEM INTO SONS & DAUGHTERS  732 JERUSALEM 87      10
      IN THE LITTLE LOVELY ALLEGORIC NIGHT OF ALBION'S DAUGHTERS  733 JERUSALEM 88     31
      LOUD SCREAM THE DAUGHTERS OF ALBION BENEATH THE TONGS &    737 JERUSALEM 90      44
         HAMMER
      THE SONS & DAUGHTERS OF ALBION ON SOFT CLOUDS WAKING FROM   744 JERUSALEM 96     39
         SLEEP
      AND YOU MY DAUGHTERS IN GREAT STATE  . . . . . . . .        759 EV GOSPEL (2)    39
      I SAW "MILTON AND HIS DAUGHTERS"  . . . . . . . . . .       831A LETTER 31       PROSE
      AND I BELIEVE TWO DAUGHTERS WITH MAPS INSTRUMENTS &C    .   843C LETTER 43       PROSE
DAUGHTERS'
      IN IRON TABLETS AND HIS WIVES' & DAUGHTERS' NAMES WERE      498 MILTON 17        10
         THESE
DAUGHTERS IN LAW
      DAUGHTERS IN LAW WITH INTENT TO RETURN TO HER OWN COUNTRY   584C DESC CAT 15     PROSE
DAUNTLESS
      SHALL [DARE TO] DAUNTLESS VIEW THE INFERNAL STORM    .  .   558 THE CAVERNS/N     6
DAVID
      KING DAVID DESIRED SO FERVENTLY & INVOKES SO PATHETICLY     153D MARRIAGE HH 12  PROSE
      GAD ASHER ISSACHAR ZEBULUN JOSEPH BENJAMIN DAVID SOLOMON    350 FOUR ZOAS 8      361
      IF HE IS GOOD HE WILL ABHOR WICKEDNESS IN DAVID OR ABRAHAM  393B ANNO WATSON     MARG
      IN THE LOINS OF ABRAHAM & DAVID  . . . . . . . . . .        652B JERUSALEM 27    PROSE
      ADAM WHO IS PELEG & JOKTAN & ESAU & JACOB & SAUL & DAVID    713 JERUSALEM 73      28
      ADAM NOAH ABRAHAM MOSES SAMUEL DAVID EZEKIEL  . . . . .     714 JERUSALEM 73      41
      PLANTING THE SEEDS OF THE TWELVE TRIBES & MOSES & DAVID     730 JERUSALEM 85       5
      OF DAVID OR OF EVE OF THE WOMAN OR OF THE LORD     . . .    736 JERUSALEM 90      30
      BUT JESUS AS ALSO ABRAHAM & DAVID CONSIDERD GOD   . . . .   774A ANNO BERKELEY   MARG
      ORPHAN MOSES ELIAS JESUS DAVID SOLOMON    . . . . .        SUPP INSC HERVEY      *TITLE
DAVIDS
      LITCHFIELD SAINT DAVIDS LANDAFF ASAPH BANGOR SODOR    .  .  676 JERUSALEM 46      19
DAW
      [AND] YORKSHIRE JACK HEMP & GENTLE BLUSHING DAW   . . . .   537 AND HIS LEGS/N    20
DAWB
      TWENTY GUINEAS FOR THIS HORRIBLE DAWB & IF ANY ONE WOULD    451D ANNO REYNOLDS   MARG
         GIVE XXX
DAWBED
      THE DAWBED BLACK & YELLOW SHADOWS THAT ARE FOUND IN MOST    815B LETTER 23       PROSE
         FINE
DAWBER
      THE DAWBER DAWBS HIS DRAWINGS  . . . . . . . . . .          584D DESC CAT 15     PROSE
DAWBING
      A DRAWING ON PAPER TO A DAWBING IN OIL BY THE  . . . . .    585B DESC CAT 15     PROSE
DAWBS
      THE DAWBER DAWBS HIS DRAWINGS  . . . . . . . . . .          584D DESC CAT 15     PROSE
      NO JUDGE OF PAINTING WHEN HE IS SHEWN THESE SMEARS & DAWBS  601C PUB ADDRESS/N   *PROSE
DAWN
      AWAKE THE DAWN THAT SLEEPS IN HEAVEN LET LIGHT   . . . .      3 TO MORNING/PS      3
      AND THE RUSTLING [BEDS] BIRDS OF DAWN  . . . . . . . .        9 MAD SONG/PS        7
      . . . RISE NECKER THE ANCIENT DAWN CALLS US    . . . .      134 FRENCH REVOLTN     7
      . . . TILL THE DAWN OF OUR PEACEFUL MORNING   . . . .       144 FRENCH REVOLTN   216
      TILL DAWN TILL MORNING TILL THE BREAKING OF CLOUDS . . .    144 FRENCH REVOLTN   217
      LET THE PRIESTS OF THE RAVEN OF DAWN NO LONGER IN DEADLY    160A SONG LIBERTY    PROSE
         BLACK
      TILL DAWN WAS WONT TO WAKE THEM THEN MY TRUMPET SOUNDING    278 FOUR ZOAS 1      500
         LOUD
      NIGHT PASSD & ENITHARMON EER THE DAWN RETURND IN BLISS  .  .  289 FOUR ZOAS 2   * 341
      SPREAD THRO HER GOLDEN FRAME SHE ROSE UP EER THE DAWN OF    291 FOUR ZOAS 2      420
         DAY
      OF DAWN OUTSTRETCHING AN EXPANSE WHERE NEER EXPANSE HAD     299 FOUR ZOAS 4       87
         BEEN
      AND WHET THEIR BEAKS & SNUFF THE AIR & WATCH THE OPENING    325 FOUR ZOAS 7      206
         DAWN
      BEFORE THE MORNING'S DAWN THE EAGLE CALLD THE VULTURE   .  .  358 FOUR ZOAS 9     59
      AT DAWN & EER THE SUN AROSE THE RAVEN & VULTURE FOLLOWD     358 FOUR ZOAS 9       63
      LOOK HOW THE OPENING DAWN ADVANCES WITH VOCAL HARMONY   .  .  367 FOUR ZOAS 9    397
      AND WHEN MORNING BEGAN TO DAWN UPON THE DISTANT HILLS   .  .  372 FOUR ZOAS 9    590
      INSPIRED & AT THE DAWN OF DAY SEND OUT ANOTHER LARK   . .    526 MILTON 36         6
      I ROSE UP AT THE DAWN OF DAY   . . . . . . . . . .          558 I ROSE UP AT/N     1
      THE DAWN WITH HER DAPPLED HORSES ARISES ABOVE THE EARTH    618A ILLUS MILTON     PROSE
      AND THE SOFT SMILE OF FRIENDSHIP & THE OPEN DAWN           672 JERUSALEM 43       25
         OF BENEVOLENCE
DAWND
      BUT MORNING DAWND HEAVY UPON ME  . . . . . . . . . .        141 FRENCH REVOLTN   152
      WHEN MORNING DAWND THE ETERNALS ROSE TO LABOUR AT          374 FOUR ZOAS 9      647
         THE VINTAGE
      THE MORNING DAWND URIZEN ROSE & IN HIS HAND THE FLAIL   .  .  374 FOUR ZOAS 9    650
DAWSON
      TO DAWSON TURNER ESQRE YARMOUTH NORFOLK  . . . . . .       SUPP ADDRESS/L 66     *TITLE
DAY      SEE MID-DAY,NOON DAY,TO-DAY
      THE HONIED DEW THAT COMETH ON WAKING DAY    . . . . .         3 TO MORNING/PS      5
      MY LORD WAS LIKE THE OPENING EYES OF DAY    . . . . . .       5 FAIR ELENOR/PS    47
      THERE HE SPORTS ALONG THE DAY  . . . . . . . . . .           7 LOVE HARMNY/PS    19
      THE DAY ALONG  . . . . . . . . . . . . . . . .              8 MEMORY COME/PS    12
      MAKE WEEP THE EYES OF DAY  . . . . . . . . . . . .           9 MAD SONG/PS       14
      IN THE BLEAK WINTRY DAY   . . . . . . . . . . . .          11 GWIN KING/PS      28
```

443

	PAGE	TITLE	LINE
DAY (CONTINUED)			
INTO THREE PARTIES WE DIVIDE BY DAY	19	EDW THIRD/PS 1	50
EXULTINGLY THIS IS A PROMISING DAY	21	EDW THIRD/PS 3	5
IN THE BRIGHT SUNSHINE OF THIS FATAL DAY	24	EDW THIRD/PS 3	143
A RAW-BOND FELLOW T OTHER DAY PASSD BY ME	25	EDW THIRD/PS 3	154
WHILE THE POOR SLAVE DRUDGES ALL DAY IN HOPE	26	EDW THIRD/PS 3	202
BUT NEVER TILL THIS FATAL DAY OF CRESSY	31	EDW THIRD/PS 5	41
THE BIRDS OF DAY WERE HEARD IN THEIR NESTS	35C	COUCH DEATH/PS	PROSE
I SEEM TO WALK THROUGH A DEEP VALLEY FAR FROM THE LIGHT OF DAY	35D	COUCH DEATH/PS	PROSE
HE RUSHES UP THE SKY AND LAYS HOLD ON THE IMMORTAL COURSERS OF DAY	37B	CONTEMPLATN/PS	PROSE
TURNING OUR EARTHLY NIGHT TO HEAVENLY DAY	37C	SAMSON/PS	PROSE
AND THUS SHE DAY BY DAY OPPRESSED HIS SOUL	38C	SAMSON/PS	PROSE
WHEN BUSY DAY WAS FADING AND CALM EVENING	39D	SAMSON/PS	PROSE
AND STRENGTHEN HER WEAK ARM [NOW DAY AROSE]	40D	THEN SHE BORE	PROSE
MY NOTES SHOULD RISE TO MEET THE NEW BORN DAY	41D	THEN SHE BORE	PROSE
CLOSD FROM THE EYE OF DAY TO THE HARD ROCK TRANSFIXT BY FATE	41D	THEN SHE BORE	PROSE
A DAY LIKE THIS LAID ELFRID IN THE DUST	43C	WOE CRIED MUSE	PROSE
& A PAIR OF GLOVES EVERY DAY & THE SORROWS OF WERTER	53A	ISLAND MOON 8	PROSE
JOE BRADLEY & I WAS GOING ALONG ONE DAY IN THE SUGAR HOUSE	55B	ISLAND MOON 9	PROSE
NO NO LET US PLAY FOR IT IS YET DAY	60	NURSES SONG/IM	9
THE WISE MAN FALLETH (SEVEN) TIMES IN A DAY AND RISETH AGAIN &C	83D	ANNO LAVATER	MARG
HE WANDERD DAY & NIGHT TO HIM BOTH DAY & NIGHT WERE DARK	100	TIRIEL 2	1
PLAYING WITH FLOWERS & RUNNING AFTER BIRDS THEY SPENT THE DAY	100	TIRIEL 2	8
[O VENERABLE O MOST PITEOUS O MOST WOEFUL DAY]	101	TIRIEL 2	27
TO HIM THE DAY & NIGHT ALIKE WAS DARK & DESOLATE	103	TIRIEL 4	2
ALL DAY THEY WALKD & ALL THE NIGHT BENEATH THE PLEASANT MOON	104	TIRIEL 4	30
ALL DAY HE BORE HIM & WHEN EVENING DREW HER SOLEMN CURTAIN	104	TIRIEL 4	41
TO THIS DAY THEY DWELL	115	LIT GRL FND/SI	49
HE SHALL FOLLOW HIS SHEEP ALL THE DAY	118	SHEPHERD/SI	3
FROM OUR IMMORTAL DAY	119	NIGHT/SI	40
NO NO LET US PLAY FOR IT IS YET DAY	121	NURSES SONG/SI	9
AND NOT SIT BOTH NIGHT & DAY	122	ON ANOTHERS/SI	21
DAY AND NIGHT	123	SPRING/SI	4
THE LITTLE ONES SPEND THE DAY	124	SCHOOL BOY/SI	9
OF THEIR JOY IN THE SPRINGING DAY	124	SCHOOL BOY/SI	24
AND SITTING DOWN BEFORE THE HEAT OF DAY	125	LIT BLK BOY/SI	6
TO FADE AWAY LIKE MORNING BEAUTY FROM HER MORTAL DAY	127	BOOK OF THEL 1	3
LIKE THE DOVE'S VOICE LIKE TRANSIENT DAY LIKE MUSIC IN THE AIR	127	BOOK OF THEL 1	11
ON MARGIN OF THE SEA SHRIVELD UP BY HEAT OF DAY	136	FRENCH REVOLTN	39
. . . ON HIS HANDS AND KNEES DAY AND NIGHT WITHOUT REST	136	FRENCH REVOLTN	46
AS IN DAY OF HAVOCK AND ROUTED BATTLE	137	FRENCH REVOLTN	64
. . . URGD BY CRIES IN DAY AND PROPHETIC DREAMS HOVERING IN NIGHT	138	FRENCH REVOLTN	98
. . . AND LIKE THUNDER ON THE JUST MAN'S BURIAL DAY HE PAUSD	139	FRENCH REVOLTN	106
IS TURND INTO SONGS OF THE HARLOT IN DAY	140	FRENCH REVOLTN	147
. . . IN DAY OF THE BRITISH FLAG WHEN HEAVY CANNONS	147	FRENCH REVOLTN	280
TO TEND IT BY DAY & BY NIGHT	161	ROSE TREE/N	7
WHEN THE DAY WAS SPRINGING	164	HEARD ANGEL/N	2
THUS HE SUNG ALL DAY	164	HEARD ANGEL/N	5
AND IT GREW BY DAY & NIGHT	165	CHRISTN FORB/N	9
AND I [GREW] [SMILD] SOOTHD DAY AFTER DAY	167	INFANT SORW/N	14
[I BEHELD THE [PRIEST] PRIESTS BY DAY]	167	INFANT SORW/N *	33
LIKE [A [SERPENT]] TO [SERPENTS IN THE] HOLY MEN BY DAY	167	INFANT SORW/N *	38
FOR POSSESSD OF DAY	168	SILENT NIGHT/N	4
YOUR SPRING & YOUR DAY ARE WASTED IN PLAY	171	NURSES SONG/N	7
I WALKED ABROAD IN A SNOWY DAY	176	SOFT SNOW/N	1
DAY	177D	DAY/N	TITLE
THE [DAY] SUN ARISES IN THE EAST	177	DAY/N	1
CLOUDS A SUNSHINY DAY	178	THE FAIRY/N	6
WE'D SING AND WE'D PRAY ALL THE LIVELONG DAY	179	LIT VAGABOND/N	8
AND I WEPT BOTH NIGHT & DAY	182	THE ANGEL/N	5
AND I WEPT BOTH DAY & NIGHT	182	THE ANGEL/N	7
BARKS AT THE BREAKING DAY THE NIGHTINGALE HAS DONE LAMENTING	190	V DAU ALBION 2	24
THEY TOLD ME THAT THE NIGHT & DAY WERE ALL THAT I COULD SEE	191	V DAU ALBION 2	30
SILENT I HOVER ALL THE NIGHT AND ALL DAY COULD BE SILENT	191	V DAU ALBION 3	14
TELL ME WHAT IS THE NIGHT OR DAY TO ONE OERFLOWD WITH WOE	191	V DAU ALBION 3	22
THEN OOTHOON WAITED SILENT ALL THE DAY AND ALL THE NIGHT	192	V DAU ALBION 4	25
OVER HER SHRINKING SHOULDERS ALL THE DAY & ALL THE NIGHT	193	V DAU ALBION 5	26
ERE YET HIS EYELIDS CAN BEHOLD THE ARROWS OF THE DAY	193	V DAU ALBION 5	32
THAT CLOUDS WITH JEALOUSY HIS NIGHTS WITH WEEPINGS ALL THE DAY	194	V DAU ALBION 7	18
BUT DUMB TILL THAT DREAD DAY WHEN ORC ASSAYD HIS FIERCE EMBRACE	196	AMERICA PREL 1	10
AND AS A SEA OERWHELMS A LAND IN THE DAY OF AN EARTHQUAKE	201	AMERICA 14	9
IS GIVN THEE TILL THE BREAK OF DAY	210	INTRODUCTN/SE	20
YOUR SPRING & YOUR DAY ARE WASTED IN PLAY	212	NURSES SONG/SE	7
AND I WEPT BOTH NIGHT AND DAY	214	THE ANGEL/SE	5
AND I WEPT BOTH DAY AND NIGHT	214	THE ANGEL/SE	7
TO TEND HER BY DAY AND BY NIGHT	215	ROSE TREE/SE	6
WE'D SING AND WE'D PRAY ALL THE LIVE-LONG DAY	216	LIT VAGABND/SE	7
AND IT GREW BOTH DAY AND NIGHT	218	POISON TREE/SE	9
THERE IN RISING DAY	219	LIT GRL LST/SE	15
ALL DAY THE WORM LAY ON HER BOSOM	232	URIZEN 19	24

	PAGE	TITLE	LINE

DAY   (CONTINUED)

THE GIRDLE WAS FORMD BY DAY . . . . 233 URIZEN 20   16
AND ON THE SEVENTH DAY THEY RESTED . . . . . . 236 URIZEN 25   40
AND THEY BLESSD THE SEVENTH DAY IN SICK HOPE . . . . 236 URIZEN 25   41
LIKE THE DARK CLOUD DISBURDEND IN THE DAY OF DISMAL THUNDER 238 EUROPE PREL 1   7
DESCENDED THRO THE ORIENT GATES OF THE ETERNAL DAY   . . . 239 EUROPE 4   3
SINCE THAT DREAD DAY WHEN HAR AND HEVA FLED . . . . . 246 SONG OF LOS 4   5
IN THE DAY OF FULL-FEEDING PROSPERITY . . . . 247 SONG OF LOS 6   13
SINCE THE DAY OF THUNDERS IN OLD TIME . . . . 255 BOOK OF LOS 3   3
TIMES ON TIMES NIGHT ON NIGHT DAY ON DAY . . . . . 258 BOOK OF LOS 4   29
FOUND FOR FALLING DAY & NIGHT WITHOUT END . . . . . 258 BOOK OF LOS 4   33
FOR THO DAY OR NIGHT WAS NOT THEIR SPACES . . . . . 258 BOOK OF LOS 4   34
THE BINDING OF URIZEN DAY AND NIGHT . . . . 259 BOOK OF LOS 5   23
MARSHALLD IN ORDER FOR THE DAY OF INTELLECTUAL BATTLE . . 264 FOUR ZOAS 1   6
OF A BRIGHT UNIVERSE EMPERY ATTENDED DAY & NIGHT . . . 264 FOUR ZOAS 1   15
AND SAID RETURN O WANDERER WHEN THE DAY OF CLOUDS IS OER 266 FOUR ZOAS 1   75
[THUS THEY CONTENDED ALL THE DAY AMONG THE CAVES   269 FOUR ZOAS 1   179
    OF THARMAS]
AND LUVAH SIEZD THE HORSES OF LIGHT & ROSE INTO THE CHARIOT 271 FOUR ZOAS 1   264
    OF DAY
. . . & [THE] GOLDEN DAY [?DESCENDED] DESCENDING   . . . 274 FOUR ZOAS 1 * 366
[TO ?LIGHT ?THE] BY NIGHT NOR DAY TO COMFORT HER . . . 275 FOUR ZOAS 1 * 418
[XXX THE LIGHT OF DAY] . . . . SUPP FOUR ZOAS 1 *
[WHEN WILT THOU SMILE ON THARMAS O THOU BRINGER OF GOLDEN SUPP FOUR ZOAS 1 *
    DAY]
[AND SAID RETURN O WANDERER WHEN THE DAY OF CLOUDS IS OER] SUPP FOUR ZOAS 1 *
IN ULRO BENEATH BEULAH WHERE THE DEAD WAIL NIGHT & DAY 282 FOUR ZOAS 2   71
THE EVIL DAY AFAR & IF PERCHANCE WITH IRON POWER . . . 282 FOUR ZOAS 2   75
DAY AFTER DAY SHE FED UPON THE MOUNTAINS IN LUVAH'S SIGHT 282 FOUR ZOAS 2   86
. . . THAT LIGHTS THE [DISMAL] DARKSOM DAY . . . . . 283 FOUR ZOAS 2   128
TO LABOUR NIGHT & DAY AMONG THE FIRES HER LAMENTING VOICE 285 FOUR ZOAS 2   216
THUS SHE LAMENTED DAY & NIGHT COMPELLD TO LABOUR & SORROW 286 FOUR ZOAS 2   231
. . . SPIRITS MOURND THEIR BONDAGE NIGHT & DAY . . . 286 FOUR ZOAS 2   246
SPREAD THRO HER GOLDEN FRAME SHE ROSE UP EER THE DAWN OF 291 FOUR ZOAS 2   420
    DAY
AND ON THE EIGHTH DAY WHEN HIS CLOUDS UNFOLDED FROM HIS 292 FOUR ZOAS 3   25
    THRONE
RED AS THE SUN IN THE HOT MORNING OF THE BLOODY DAY . . 297 FOUR ZOAS 4   5
I SLUMBER HERE IN WEAK REPOSE I WELL REMEMBER THE DAY . . 299 FOUR ZOAS 4   84
THE DAY OF TERROR & ABHORRENCE [ETERNAL] . . . . . 299 FOUR ZOAS 4 * 85
LINKD HOUR TO HOUR & DAY TO NIGHT & NIGHT TO DAY & YEAR 302 FOUR ZOAS 4   181
    TO YEAR
AND THUS BEGAN THE BINDING OF URIZEN DAY & NIGHT IN FEAR 302 FOUR ZOAS 4   199
AROUND HIS BOSOM EVERY DAY HE VIEWD THE FIERY YOUTH . . . 307 FOUR ZOAS 5   86
FORMING A GIRDLE IN THE DAY & BURSTING IT AT NIGHT . . . 307 FOUR ZOAS 5   89
THE GIRDLE WAS FORMD BY DAY BY NIGHT WAS BURST IN TWAIN 307 FOUR ZOAS 5   90
O DID I KEEP THE HORSES OF THE DAY IN SILVER PASTURES . 310 FOUR ZOAS 5   210
O I REFUSD THE LORD OF DAY THE HORSES OF HIS PRINCE . . . 310 FOUR ZOAS 5   211
O THAT I HAD NOT SEEN THE DAY THEN SHOULD I BE AT REST . 325 FOUR ZOAS 7   202
I LABOUR NIGHT & DAY FOR LOS BUT LISTEN THOU MY VISION . 327 FOUR ZOAS 7   298
AND SILENCE BUILD THEIR DAY IN SHADOW OF SOFT CLOUDS & DEWS 331 FOUR ZOAS 7   450
OF DIRE NECESSITY STILL LABORING DAY & NIGHT TILL ALL . . 333 FOUR ZOAS 7B   14
TO LIGHT THE WAR BY DAY TO HIDE HIS SECRET BEAMS BY NIGHT 334 FOUR ZOAS 7B   36
FOR HE DIVIDED DAY & NIGHT IN DIFFERENT ORDERD PORTIONS 334 FOUR ZOAS 7B   37
THE DAY FOR WAR THE NIGHT FOR SECRET RELIGION IN HIS TEMPLE 334 FOUR ZOAS 7B   38
BEAT ROUND HER HEAD ALL NIGHT ALL DAY SHE RIOTS IN EXCESS 334 FOUR ZOAS 7B   74
BUT [DAY BY] NIGHT OR DAY LOS FOLLOWS WAR . . . . . . 335 FOUR ZOAS 7B   75
THE ARROWS FLEW FROM CLOUDY BOW ALL DAY TILL BLOOD . . . 337 FOUR ZOAS 7B   159
OF DAY & NIGHT THE MYRIADS OF ETERNITY THAT THEY MIGHT FILE 337 FOUR ZOAS 7B   181
OF DAY IN JEALOUSY & BLOOD MY CHILDREN ARE LED TO URIZEN'S 339 FOUR ZOAS 7B   251
    WAR
AND WHEN THE REVOLUTION OF THEIR DAY OF BATTLES OVER   . . 344 FOUR ZOAS 8   123
OF HIS ETERNAL DAY & MEMORY STRIVES TO AUGMENT HIS 352 FOUR ZOAS 8   455
    RUTHFULNESS
OR WHERE THE COMETS OF THE NIGHT OR STARS OF [ETERNAL] 358 FOUR ZOAS 9   40
    ASTERIAL DAY
RISE UP O SUN MOST GLORIOUS MINISTER & LIGHT OF DAY . . . 368 FOUR ZOAS 9   434
AND SOFT SLEEP FELL UPON HER EYELIDS IN THE SILENT NOON 369 FOUR ZOAS 9   457
    OF DAY
WHEN WILT THOU SMILE ON THARMAS O THOU BRINGER OF GOLDEN 370 FOUR ZOAS 9   493
    DAY
WAS SERVD ROUND BY THE FLAMES OF LUVAH ALL DAY & ALL THE 372 FOUR ZOAS 9   589
    NIGHT
WAS SERVD ROUND BY THE FLAMES OF LUVAH ALL DAY & ALL THE 373 FOUR ZOAS 9   620
    NIGHT
HIS EYES BEHOLD THE ANGELIC SPHERES ARISING NIGHT & DAY 379 FOUR ZOAS 9   828
CONVERSING WITH THE ANIMAL FORMS OF WISDOM NIGHT & DAY . . 379 FOUR ZOAS 9   836
MALE & HER BROW RADIANT AS DAY DARTED A LOVELY SCORN   . 381 FOUR ZOAS AD 1   19
MY SPECTRE AROUND ME NIGHT & DAY . . . . 415 MY SPECTRE/N   1
[SECRET TREMBLING NIGHT & DAY] . . . . 415 MY SPECTRE/N   21
SEVEN MORE LOVES WEEP NIGHT & DAY . . . . 416 MY SPECTRE/N   39
I SEE THE BREAK OF DAY . . . . 421 MORNING/N   6
[THREE VIRGINS AT THE BREAK OF DAY] . . . . 421 BENEATH/N   2
AND IN TEARS CLOTHD NIGHT & DAY . . . . 422 BENEATH/N   16
OER THE MORNING OF MY DAY . . . . 422 BENEATH/N   22
[THREE VIRGINS AT THE BREAK OF DAY] . . . . 422 BENEATH REWR/N   2
EACH DAY I MOURN ALONG THE WOOD . . . . 423 THE BIRDS/N   11
THREE VIRGINS AT THE BREAK OF DAY . . . . 424 THE GOLDEN NET   1
AND IN TEARS CLOTHD NIGHT & DAY . . . . 424 THE GOLDEN NET   15
OVER THE MORNING OF MY DAY . . . . 424 THE GOLDEN NET   21
YOUNGER & YOUNGER EVERY DAY . . . . 426 MENTAL TRAVLER   74
WHILE HE PURSUES HER NIGHT & DAY . . . . 426 MENTAL TRAVLER   79

DAY   (CONTINUED)

	PAGE	TITLE	LINE
TO THOSE WHO DWELL IN REALMS OF DAY	434	AUGURIES	132
SOME SAID HE HAD A WOLF IN HIS STOMACH DAY & NIGHT . . .	434	LONG JOHN BRWN	13
BUT SHE IS RUDDY & BRIGHT AS DAY	435	WILLIAM BOND	31
I THOUGHT TO FIND LOVE IN THE HEAT OF DAY	436	WILLIAM BOND	47
THIS THE DAY AFTER MY TURNING HIM OUT OF THE GARDEN . .	437B	BLAKES MEMORAN	PROSE
IT WAS A STILL DAY THERE WAS NO WIND STIRRING	437D	BLAKES MEMORAN	PROSE
AND OF THE WHEELS OF HEAVEN TO TURN THE MILLS DAY & NIGHT	483	MILTON 4	10
MILDNESS SATAN LABOUR ALL DAY IT WAS A THOUSAND YEARS .	486	MILTON 7	15
FOR ONE WHOLE DAY UNDER PRETENCE OF PITY AND LOVE TO ME	487	MILTON 7	28
AND MAN UNMANS FOLLOW WITH ME MY PLOW THIS MOURNFUL DAY	488	MILTON 8	20
RESUME YOUR LABOURS & THIS DAY SHALL BE A MOURNFUL DAY .	488	MILTON 8	22
THEY MOURND ALL DAY THIS MOURNFUL DAY OF SATAN & PALAMABRON	488	MILTON 8	24
TILL SATAN HAD ASSUMD RINTRAH'S WRATH IN THE DAY OF MOURNING	492	MILTON 11	25
CUPIDITY UNCONQUERABLE MY FAULT WHEN AT NOON OF DAY . .	492	MILTON 12	8
THE GNOMES IN ALL THAT DAY SPARD NOT THEY CURSD SATAN BITTERLY	493	MILTON 12	31
DAY SUNK AND PALAMABRON RETURND TREMBLING I HID MYSELF . .	493	MILTON 12	40
BUT WHEN THE CLARIONS OF DAY SOUNDED THEY DROWND THE LAMENTATIONS	504	MILTON 21	25
COVERING THE LIGHT OF DAY & ROLLING DOWN UPON THE MOUNTAINS	507	MILTON 23	26
TREMBLE IN SPECTROUS BODIES CONTINUALLY DAY AND NIGHT .	507	MILTON 23	43
AND EVERY DAY & NIGHT HAS WALLS OF BRASS & GATES OF ADAMANT	516	MILTON 28	52
EACH HAS ITS GUARD EACH MOMENT MINUTE HOUR DAY MONTH & YEAR	516	MILTON 28	59
BUT RINTRAH & PALAMABRON GOVERN OVER DAY & NIGHT . . .	517	MILTON 29	27
TO GIVE THEM TO THEIR LOVELY HEAVENS TILL THE GREAT JUDGMENT DAY	517	MILTON 29	52
HE LEADS THE CHOIR OF DAY TRILL TRILL TRILL TRILL . .	520	MILTON 31	31
THE NIGHTINGALE AGAIN ASSAYS HIS SONG & THRO THE DAY . .	520	MILTON 31	42
THERE IS A MOMENT IN EACH DAY THAT SATAN CANNOT FIND . .	526	MILTON 35	42
IT RENOVATES EVERY MOMENT OF THE DAY IF RIGHTLY PLACED .	526	MILTON 35	45
INSPIRED & AT THE DAWN OF DAY SEND OUT ANOTHER LARK . .	526	MILTON 36	6
THAT RAGES ROUND HIM LIKE A WOLF DAY & NIGHT WITHOUT REST	533	MILTON 41	18
HE MADE THEM PAY HIS PRICE ALACK A DAY	537	AND HIS LEGS/N	30
I ROSE UP AT THE DAWN OF DAY	558	I ROSE UP AT/N	1
I AM IN GOD'S PRESENCE NIGHT & DAY	558	I ROSE UP AT/N	13
BLOODY WITH THE DAY OF BATTLE	580D	DESC CAT 5	PROSE
AND GETS INTO BED A REWARD FOR THE LABOURS OF THE DAY .	586A	DESC CAT 16	PROSE
NEVER SUSPENDED HIS LABOURS ON COPPER FOR A SINGLE DAY .	587D	CHAUCER/N	PROSE
AT THIS HOUSE EVEN AT THIS DAY EVERY FRIENDLESS WRETCH .	590A	CHAUCER 2	PROSE
THIS DAY IS PUBLISHD ADVERTIZEMENTS TO BLAKE'S CANTERBURY	591B	PUB ADDRESS/N	PROSE
ART AS IT IS THIS DAY	600B	PUB ADDRESS/N	PROSE
TO WHOM THE ANCIENTS LOOKD AND SAW HIS DAY AFAR OFF . .	621A	JERUSALEM 3	PROSE
TREMBLING I SIT DAY AND NIGHT MY FRIENDS ARE ASTONISHD AT ME	623	JERUSALEM 5	16
IN LONDON'S DARKNESS AND MY TEARS FALL DAY AND NIGHT . .	623	JERUSALEM 5	36
THE EVIL DAY AFAR AND IF PERCHANCE WITH IRON POWER . . .	626	JERUSALEM 7	33
I LABOUR DAY AND NIGHT I BEHOLD THE SOFT AFFECTIONS . . .	628	JERUSALEM 9	26
HE CURSES HEAVEN & EARTH DAY & NIGHT & SUN & MOON . . .	629	JERUSALEM 10	25
BUT ALL CLOSD UP TILL THE LAST DAY	633	JERUSALEM 13	11
GOLGONOOZA LOS WALKS ROUND THE WALLS NIGHT AND DAY . . .	634	JERUSALEM 13	55
FEEDING IT WITH HIS GROANS & TEARS DAY & NIGHT WITHOUT CEASING	639	JERUSALEM 17	56
I BROUGHT LOVE INTO LIGHT OF DAY TO PRIDE IN CHASTE BEAUTY	645	JERUSALEM 22	17
THINKING TO BRING LOVE INTO LIGHT OF DAY TO JERUSALEM'S SHAME	647	JERUSALEM 24	5
THY SEVERE JUDGE ALL THE DAY LONG PROVES THEE O BABYLON	647	JERUSALEM 24	27
KNOT DAY BY DAY NIGHT BY NIGHT LOUD ROLL THE INDIGNANT ATLANTIC	648	JERUSALEM 24	62
& OAK GROVES OVER THE WHOLE EARTH WITNESS TO THIS DAY .	649C	JERUSALEM 27	PROSE
IN THE LOVE OF TIRZAH HE SAID DOUBT IS MY FOOD DAY & NIGHT	662	JERUSALEM 36	7
IN BOWLAHOOLA & ALLAMANDA WHERE THE DEAD WAIL NIGHT & DAY	668	JERUSALEM 40	57
BUT AS THE WILL MUST NOT BE BENDED BUT IN THE DAY OF DIVINE	674	JERUSALEM 44	18
IN THE ENDS OF BEULAH WHERE THE DEAD WAIL NIGHT & DAY . .	678	JERUSALEM 48	52
WAS CAUGHT UP WITH THE SUN IN ONE DAY OF FURY AND WAR . .	679	JERUSALEM 49	16
THE SUN SHALL GO BEFORE YOU IN DAY THE MOON SHALL GO . .	680	JERUSALEM 49	51
TO SIN IN THE OPEN FACE OF DAY IS CRUEL & PITILESS BUT . .	681	JERUSALEM 50	26
A BROODER OF AN EVIL DAY AND A SUN RISING IN BLOOD . . .	681	JERUSALEM 50	29
ROCKD BY YEAR MONTH DAY & HOUR AND EVERY TWO MOMENTS . .	688	JERUSALEM 56	9
DAY & NIGHT IN SUBLIME MAJESTY & SILENCE THEY REVOLVE . .	690	JERUSALEM 58	28
THE WHEEL OF HAND INCESSANT TURNING DAY & NIGHT WITHOUT REST	693	JERUSALEM 60	43
SHALL ALBION ARISE I KNOW HE SHALL ARISE AT THE LAST DAY	696	JERUSALEM 62	15
OF DAY & NIGHT THE MYRIADS OF ETERNITY THAT THEY MAY GRIND	700	JERUSALEM 65	23
AND THUS THE WARRIORS CRY IN THE HOT DAY OF VICTORY IN SONGS	705	JERUSALEM 68	10
WEEPING & SHOUTING TO THE LORD DAY & NIGHT AND HIS CHILDREN	711	JERUSALEM 71	62
THE SUMMER & WINTER DAY & NIGHT THE SUN & MOON & STARS . .	713	JERUSALEM 73	19
WITH LUVAH INTO LIGHT ETERNAL IN HIS ETERNAL DAY . . .	716	JERUSALEM 75	26
IN OPEN DAY TO DRAW THE SOULS OF THE DEAD INTO THE LIGHT	721	JERUSALEM 79	79
IN THE FURNACES OF LOS & IN THE WINE-PRESS TREADING DAY & NIGHT	726	JERUSALEM 82	64
THE RAGING FLAMES THO SHE RETURND [CONSUMD DAY AFTER DAY]	726	JERUSALEM 82	67
ALTERNATE THEY WATCH IN NIGHT ALTERNATE LABOUR IN DAY . .	729	JERUSALEM 83	79
A PILLAR OF A CLOUD BY DAY A PILLAR OF FIRE BY NIGHT . .	731	JERUSALEM 86	27
LIKE THE RED SUN UPON THE MOUNTAINS IN THE BLOODY DAY . .	734	JERUSALEM 88	57
PRIDE MEETS WITH PRIDE UPON THE MOUNTAINS IN THE STORMY DAY	740	JERUSALEM 93	9
IN THAT TERRIBLE DAY OF RINTRAH'S PLOW & OF SATAN'S DRIVING THE TEAM	740	JERUSALEM 93	10

446

```
DAY    (CONTINUED)
     ERIN SITTING IN THE TOMB TO WATCH THEM UNCEASING NIGHT       741 JERUSALEM 94       13
       AND DAY
     FOR LO THE NIGHT OF DEATH IS PAST AND THE ETERNAL DAY  .  .  744 JERUSALEM 97        3
     BOTH READ THE BIBLE DAY & NIGHT  .  .  .  .  .  .  .  .  .   748 EV GOSPEL(A)/N      13
     THERE GATES OF DEATH LET IN THE DAY  .  .  .  .  .  .  .  .  749 EV GOSPEL(B)/N      40
     IN TERRORS AT THE LAST JUDGMENT DAY  .  .  .  .  .  .  .  .  751 EV GOSPEL(C)/N      44
     [WHOM THOU SHALT TORMENT AT THE LAST DAY]  .  .  .  .  .  .  751 EV GOSPEL(C)/N      48
     AND TAKE REVENGE AT THE LAST DAY  .  .  .  .  .  .  .  .  .  751 EV GOSPEL(C)/N      49
     IN TERRORS AT THE LAST JUDGMENT DAY  .  .  .  .  .  .  .  .  753 EV GOSPEL(D)/N      80
     AND TAKE REVENGE AT THE LAST DAY  .  .  .  .  .  .  .  .  .  753 EV GOSPEL(D)/N      84
     TO CLOSE THE LABOURS OF MY DAY  .  .  .  .  .  .  .  .  .  . 771 OF GATES/GP         42
     GIVE [XXX] US THIS ETERNAL DAY [XXX] OUR [GHOSTLY] OWN       788A ANNO THORNTON   * MARG
       RIGHT BREAD
     GIVE US DAY BY DAY OUR REAL TAXED  .  .  .  .  .  .  .  .  . 788D ANNO THORNTON     MARG
     WHICH I HAVE THE PLEASURE TO TELL YOU ARE INCREASING EVERY   794C LETTER 5          PROSE
       DAY
     FEEDS THE VILLAGE OF FELPHAM BY DAY & BY NIGHT  .  .  .  .   800 MRS FLAXMAN/L       14
     TO TAKE BUT WHETHER I COME ON WEDNESDAY OR THURSDAY THAT     801B LETTER 13          PROSE
       DAY
     A MOST BEAUTIFUL COUNTRY ON A MOST GLORIOUS DAY OUR  .  .    803A LETTER 15          PROSE
     INTO THE LIGHT OF DAY I STILL & SHALL TO ETERNITY EMBRACE    815D LETTER 23          PROSE
     MY HANDS ARE LABOUR DAY & NIGHT  .  .  .  .  .  .  .  .  .   818 HAPPINESS/L         59
     BOTH TO GOD & MAN WE LOOK FORWARD EVERY DAY WITH PLEASURE    824B LETTER 27          PROSE
     MY WIFE GETS BETTER EVERY DAY HOPE EARNESTLY THAT YOU  .  .  835A LETTER 34          PROSE
     BUT I WILL CALL AGAIN IN A DAY OR TWO NEITHER MR FLAXMAN     836B LETTER 35          PROSE
       NOR
     HIS WORK & THE DAY AFTER I RECIEVD IT WITH THE NOTE  .  .    836D LETTER 35          PROSE
     CALLD ON HIM EVERY DAY & NOT FINDING HIM I NOW UNDERSTAND    842B LETTER 42         *PROSE
     AS I FIND BY THE THINGS I HAVE IN HAND DAY & NIGHT WE  .     843A LETTER 42         *PROSE
     STRENGTH I NOW ENJOY SUDDENLY ON THE DAY AFTER VISITING      852A LETTER 50          PROSE
     ON THE SAME DAY I RECIEVD MINE & SAID SOMEWHAT I CANNOT      853A LETTER 51         *PROSE
       TELL
     A GENTLEMAN WHO VISITED ME THE OTHER DAY SAID I AM VERY      864D LETTER 61          PROSE
     (TWELVE) OCLOCK IT IS QUITE AS CONVENIENT TO ME AS ANY       868B LETTER 67          PROSE
       OTHER DAY
     & TAKE A MUTTON CHOP WITH US THE DAY YOU GO TO CHELTENHAM    870C LETTER 72          PROSE
     UP THE DAY AFTER & SOMETIMES TWO OR THREE DAYS  .  .  .      871A LETTER 72          PROSE
     & STRONGER EVERY DAY THO WEAKER IN MUSCLE & BONE THAN  .     872D LETTER 76          PROSE
     I AM GOING ON BETTER EVERY DAY AS I THINK BOTH  .  .  .      879B LETTER 89          PROSE
     WHICH I RECIEVED FROM YOU THIS DAY WHICH SHALL BE PUT TO     879B LETTER 89          PROSE
       THE
     SOPHRONIA DIED IN CHILDBED SHE DIED ON THE WEDDING DAY       SUPP INSC HERVEY      *TITLE
     ON ACCOUNT OF TEACHING YOUR SON AT...TO COMMENCE THIS DAY    SUPP LETTER 56A       *PROSE
     TOM DRAWINGS IN FULL TO THIS DAY  .  .  .  .  .  .  .  .     SUPP LETTER 61E       *PROSE
DAY-BREAK
     THE LOVELIEST OF THE DAUGHTERS OF ETERNITY WHEN IN          660 JERUSALEM 33        40
       DAY-BREAK
DAYLIGHT
     FAINT & MORE FAINT THE DAYLIGHT WANES THE WHEELS           306 FOUR ZOAS 5         27
       OF TURNING DARKNESS
DAYS
     MY DAYS ARE COVERED WITH SORROW SHUT UP DARKENED  .  .  .  . 38B SAMSON/PS          PROSE
     O SOON CUT OFF I TH MORNING OF HER DAYS  .  .  .  .  .  .    43C WOE CRIED MUSE     PROSE
     I HAVE NOT EAT THESE TWO DAYS LEAD ME TO HAR & HEVA'S TENT  107 TIRIEL 6            19
     ARM IN ARM SEVEN DAYS  .  .  .  .  .  .  .  .  .  .  .  .    113 LIT GRL FND/SI       7
     I AM BUT TWO DAYS OLD  .  .  .  .  .  .  .  .  .  .  .  .    118 INFANT JOY/SI        2
     SWEET JOY BUT TWO DAYS OLD  .  .  .  .  .  .  .  .  .  .     118 INFANT JOY/SI        8
     THE [DESIRES] DAYS OF YOUTH RISE FRESH IN MY MIND  .  .     171 NURSES SONG/N        3
     THE DAYS OF MY YOUTH RISE FRESH IN MY MIND  .  .  .  .  .   212 NURSES SONG/SE       3
     RESERVD FOR THE DAYS OF FUTURITY  .  .  .  .  .  .  .  .    224 URIZEN 4             9
     NUMBRING WITH LINKS HOURS DAYS & YEARS  .  .  .  .  .  .    227 URIZEN 10           18
     SIX DAYS THEY SHRUNK UP FROM EXISTENCE  .  .  .  .  .  .    236 URIZEN 25           39
     BECAUSE THE DAYS AND NIGHTS OF JOY IN LUCKY HOURS RENEW     239 EUROPE 4            23
     DAYS & NIGHTS OF REVOLVING JOY URTHONA WAS HIS NAME  .  .   264 FOUR ZOAS 1         16
     SHUDDRING SHE WOVE NINE DAYS & NIGHTS SLEEPLESS HER FOOD    266 FOUR ZOAS 1         82
       WAS TEARS
     NINE DAYS SHE LABOURD AT HER WORK & NINE DARK SLEEPLESS     266 FOUR ZOAS 1         86
       NIGHTS
     [THREE DAYS IN SELF ADMIRING RAPTURES ON THE ROCKS         267 FOUR ZOAS 1        134
       HE FLAMD]
     [[THE JEALOUS] THREE DAYS SHE WAILD & THREE DARK NIGHTS     268 FOUR ZOAS 1      * 143
       .  .  .
     HE COULD CONTROLL THE TIMES & SEASONS & THE DAYS & YEARS    270 FOUR ZOAS 1        240
     AHANIA BOWD HER HEAD & WEPT SEVEN DAYS BEFORE THE KING  .  . 292 FOUR ZOAS 3         24
     THE DAYS & YEARS IN CHAINS OF IRON ROUND THE LIMBS         302 FOUR ZOAS 4        180
       OF URIZEN
     [XXX DAYS OF GREAT ETERNITY XXX THE TIME]  .  .  .  .  .   SUPP FOUR ZOAS 4       *
     ENITHARMON BEHELD THE BLOODY CHAIN OF NIGHTS & DAYS  .  .   307 FOUR ZOAS 5         92
     NINE DAYS THEY TRAVELD THRO THE GLOOM OF ENTUTHON BENITHON  309 FOUR ZOAS 5        149
     DAYS OF ETERNITY WITH THARMAS MILD & LUVAH SWEET MELODIOUS  327 FOUR ZOAS 7        274
     KEPT IGNORANT OF THE USE THAT THEY MIGHT SPEND THE DAYS     337 FOUR ZOAS 7B       183
       OF WISDOM
     LISTEN TO HER WHOSE MEMORY BEHOLDS YOUR ANCIENT DAYS  .  .  354 FOUR ZOAS 8        504
     WHEN SHALL THE MAN OF FUTURE TIMES BECOME AS IN DAYS OF OLD 360 FOUR ZOAS 9        115
     THE SPRING THE SUMMER TO BE THINE THEN SLEEP THE WINTRY     362 FOUR ZOAS 9        212
       DAYS
     .  .  . THEY REMEMBERD THE DAYS OF OLD  .  .  .  .  .  .    373 FOUR ZOAS 9        625
     FOR SEVEN DAYS OF ETERNITY AND THE RIVER'S LIVING BANKS     503 MILTON 21          18
     AND DAYS & MONTHS & YEARS & AGES & PERIODS WONDROUS        516 MILTON 28          45
       BUILDINGS
     A SHADOW TO REPOSE IN ALL THE DAYS OF HAPPY ETERNITY  .  .  519 MILTON 31           7
```

DAYS   (CONTINUED)
     INTO DAYS & NIGHTS & YEARS & MONTHS TO TRAVEL WITH MY FEET   688 JERUSALEM 56   20
     REMEMBER RECOLLECT WHAT DARK BEFEL IN WINTRY DAYS   . . .   688 JERUSALEM 56   25
     CALL HER PURE AS HE DID IN THE DAYS OF HER INFANCY WHEN SHE   695 JERUSALEM 61   39
     KEPT IGNORANT OF ITS USE THAT THEY MIGHT SPEND THE DAYS   700 JERUSALEM 65   25
          OF WISDOM
     THE INHABITANTS ARE SICK TO DEATH THEY LABOUR TO DIVIDE   703 JERUSALEM 66   68
          INTO DAYS
     WEPT ROUND HIM AS A FLOCK SILENT SEVEN DAYS OF ETERNITY   711 JERUSALEM 71   63
     INTO THE PLANETARY LIVES OF YEARS MONTHS DAYS & HOURS   747 JERUSALEM 99   3
          REPOSING
     WHEN THEY HAD WANDERD THREE DAYS LONG   . . . .   750 EV GOSPEL(C)/N *   5
     WHEN THEY HAD WANDERD THREE DAYS LONG   . . . .   751 EV GOSPEL(D)/N   7
     REMINISCENCE & BEHOLD OUR ANCIENT DAYS BEFORE THIS EARTH   802C LETTER 14   PROSE
     STILL I RESOLVE NOT TO LOSE HOPE OF SEEING BETTER DAYS .   829D LETTER 30   PROSE
     (THREE) DAYS & TO MY CHAMBER A WEEK I AM NOW SO WELL THANK   834B LETTER 34   PROSE
     PROOFS OF MY PLATES WILL WAIT ON YOU IN A FEW DAYS   . .   853A LETTER 51   PROSE
     HOPE IN A FEW DAYS TO SEND PROOFS OF PLATES WHICH   . .   853A LETTER 51   *PROSE
     IN THE DAYS OF MICHAEL ANGELO AND RAPHAEL   . . . . .   864A LETTER 61   PROSE
     DO NOT VENTURE OUT ON SUCH DAYS AS TO-DAY HAS BEEN   . .   870B LETTER 71   PROSE
     I HOPE A FEW MORE DAYS WILL BRING US TO A CONCLUSION   870B LETTER 71   PROSE
     UP THE DAY AFTER & SOMETIMES TWO OR THREE DAYS   . . .   871A LETTER 72   PROSE
     TWO OR THREE DAYS MAY BE SUFFICIENT OR NOT ALL NOW WILL   875A LETTER 80   PROSE
          DEPEND
     ON MY BONES & SINEWS MUSCLE I HAVE NONE BUT A FEW DAYS .   875A LETTER 80   PROSE
DAYS'
     WHEN AFTER THREE DAYS' SORROW FOUND   . . . .   748 EV GOSPEL(B)/N   5
DAZLING
     THE CLOUD IS BLOOD DAZLING UPON THE HEAVENS & IN THE CLOUD   364 FOUR ZOAS 9   278
     DAZLING BRIGHT BEFORE MY EYES   . . . .   424 THE GOLDEN NET   8
     CRIMSON WITH WRATH & GREEN WITH JEALOUSY DAZLING WITH LOVE   699 JERUSALEM 64   28
     BUT TRANSLUCENT THEIR BLACKNESS AS THE DAZLING OF GEMS . .   735 JERUSALEM 89   37
     DAZLING AROUND THY SKIRTS LIKE A SERPENT OF PRECIOUS STONES   743 JERUSALEM 96   12
          & GOLD
DAZZLE
     AND THE SUN BEAMS DAZZLE FROM HER EYNE   . . . . . .   435 WILLIAM BOND   32
DAZZLING
     DAZZLING BRIGHT BEFORE MY EYES . . . .   422 BENEATH/N   9
     [DAZZLING BRIGHT BEFORE MY EYES] . . . .   422 BENEATH REWR/N   6
DAZZLINGS
     THE DAZZLINGS AS OF GEMS SHONE CLEAR RAPTUROUS IN [JOY]   267 FOUR ZOAS 1   128
          FURY
DE
     [ALIAMET] GRAVELOT ONCE SAID TO MY MASTER BASIRE [YOU]   594D PUB ADDRESS/N   *PROSE
          DE ENGLISH
     BUT [YOU] DEY DO NOT DRAW DE [THE] DRAW   . . . . . .   594D PUB ADDRESS/N   PROSE
DEAD
     THE GRAVES GIVE UP THEIR DEAD FAIR ELENOR   . . . . .   4 FAIR ELENOR/PS   2
     HES DEAD AND HOWLING AFTER ME FOR BLOOD   . . . . . .   4 FAIR ELENOR/PS   24
     O GIVE NOT HIM THY HAND NOW I AM DEAD   . . . . . .   6 FAIR ELENOR/PS   66
     SHE SAT WITH DEAD COLD LIMBS STIFFEND TO STONE   . . .   6 FAIR ELENOR/PS   69
     THE MIGHTY DEAD GIANT BODIES STREAMING BLOOD   . . . .   32 EDW THIRD/PS 6   35
     LIKE THE BUBBLING WATERS OF THE BROOK IN THE DEAD OF NIGHT   36B COUCH DEATH/PS   PROSE
     NOW DEAD I'LL GUARD THEE FROM APPROACHING ILL   . . .   43D WOE CRIED MUSE   PROSE
     HE MET WITH A DEAD WOMAN . . . .   50 WHEN CORRUP/IM   18
     ("DEAD SUN") THE DEAD SUN IS ONLY A PHANTASY OF EVIL MAN   92C ANNO SWED LOVE   MARG
     EXPLAINS HOW THE NATURAL SUN IS DEAD   . . . . . .   94B ANNO SWED LOVE   MARG
     WHAT MYRATANA ART THOU DEAD LOOK HERE YE SERPENTS LOOK   .   100 TIRIEL 1   31
     THE STINK OF YOUR DEAD CARCASES ANNOYING MAN & BEAST   .   100 TIRIEL 1   46
     HERE TAKE THY SEAT IN THIS WIDE COURT LET IT BE STROWN   106 TIRIEL 5   11
          WITH DEAD
     BUT NOW MY WIFE IS DEAD & ALL THE TIME OF GRACE IS PAST   107 TIRIEL 6   11
     THEY STUMBLE ALL NIGHT OVER BONES OF THE DEAD   . . . .   126 VOICE BARD/SI   9
     SHE SAW THE COUCHES OF THE DEAD & WHERE THE FIBROUS ROOTS   130 BOOK OF THEL 6   3
     THE DEAD BROOD OVER EUROPE . . . .   134 FRENCH REVOLTN   1
     WHILE LOUD THUNDERS ROLL TROUBLING THE DEAD . . . . . .   137 FRENCH REVOLTN   61
     THRO THE ARCHED ABODE OF THE HOLY DEAD   . . . . . .   140 FRENCH REVOLTN   142
     . . . AND BY SPIRITS OF THE DEAD THUS THUNDERD   . . .   147 FRENCH REVOLTN   284
     . . . HIS PEERS PALE LIKE MOUNTAINS OF THE DEAD   . . .   147 FRENCH REVOLTN   296
     THE ENORMOUS DEAD LIFT UP THEIR PALE FIRES . . . . .   148 FRENCH REVOLTN   302
     DRIVE YOUR CART AND YOUR PLOW OVER THE BONES OF THE DEAD   150D MARRIAGE HH 7   PROSE
     A DEAD BODY REVENGES NOT INJURIES   . . . .   151B MARRIAGE HH 7   PROSE
     HER [EYES FLED] [ORBS DEAD] LIGHT FLED   . . . . . .   168 EARTHS ANSWR/N   3
     FOR THE FEMALE SPIRITS OF THE DEAD PINING IN BONDS   202 AMERICA 15   23
          OF RELIGION
     [SLEEP LIKE THE DEAD] BUT LIKE A CONSTELLATION RISN AND   205 AMERICA CANC C   23
          BLAZING
     AND LIKE THE VOICES OF RELIGIOUS DEAD HEARD IN THE   205 AMERICA CANC C   29
          MOUNTAINS
     THE DEAD HEARD THE VOICE OF THE CHILD   . . . . . .   233 URIZEN 20   26
     THEN TELL ME WHAT IS THE MATERIAL WORLD AND IS IT DEAD .   237 EUROPE INTRO   13
     THRICE HE ASSAYD PRESUMPTUOUS TO AWAKE THE DEAD TO JUDGMENT   243 EUROPE 13   3
     FORTH FROM THE DEAD DUST RATTLING BONES TO BONES   . . .   248 SONG OF LOS 7   31
     LIFTED ON HIGH THE DEAD CORSE   . . . .   251 AHANIA 3   52
     REGENERATION BY THE RESURRECTION FROM THE DEAD   . . .   264 FOUR ZOAS 1   23
     [I SEE THE [REMEMBRANCE] SHADOW OF THE DEAD . . . . .   267 FOUR ZOAS 1   113
     IN ULRO BENEATH BEULAH WHERE THE DEAD WAIL NIGHT & DAY .   282 FOUR ZOAS 2   71
     STILL DIES FOR ENITHARMON NOR A SPIRIT SPRINGS FROM MY   288 FOUR ZOAS 2   322
          DEAD CORSE
     THEN I AM DEAD TILL THOU REVIVEST ME WITH THY SWEET SONG   288 FOUR ZOAS 2   * 323
     SHE FLED VANISHING ON THE WIND AND LEFT A DEAD COLD CORSE   289 FOUR ZOAS 2   334
     SO SAYING IN DEEP SOBS HE LANGUISHD TILL DEAD HE ALSO FELL   289 FOUR ZOAS 2   340

		PAGE	TITLE	LINE
DEAD	(CONTINUED)			
WHEN THE SHATTERD BONE HATH LAID HIM GROANING AMONG THE HAPPIER DEAD		291	FOUR ZOAS 2	416
THE DEAD REARD UP HIS VOICE & STOOD ON THE RESOUNDING SHORE		296	FOUR ZOAS 3	161
THAT THOU ART RISEN FROM THE DEAD OR THAT MY POWER FORGOT		299	FOUR ZOAS 4	83
WHEN WEARIED DEAD HE FELL HIS LIMBS REPOSD IN THE BOSOM OF SLIME		316	FOUR ZOAS 6	159
THE SPECTRES OF THE DEAD FOR I AM AS THE SPECTRE OF THE LIVING		327	FOUR ZOAS 7	310
TILL MANY OF THE DEAD BURST FORTH FROM THE BOTTOMS OF THEIR TOMBS		328	FOUR ZOAS 7	328
URTHONA'S SPECTRE TERRIFIED BEHELD THE SPECTRES OF THE DEAD		330	FOUR ZOAS 7	401
TO MEET THESE SPECTRES OF THE DEAD I THEREFORE FEAR THAT HE		330	FOUR ZOAS 7	425
WHERE THE SPECTROUS DEAD WAIL & SIGHING THUS HE SPOKE TO ENITHARMON		331	FOUR ZOAS 7	435
I FEEL TO FABRICATE EMBODIED SEMBLANCES IN WHICH THE DEAD		331	FOUR ZOAS 7	440
THE SPECTROUS DEAD WEEPING THE SPECTRES VIEWD THE IMMORTAL WORKS		332	FOUR ZOAS 7	473
THEN MYRIADS OF THE DEAD BURST THRO THE BOTTOMS OF THEIR TOMBS		340	FOUR ZOAS 7B	* 298
[THE SWELLING TIDES THEY BENT OVER THE DEAD CORSE LIKE AN ARCH]		341	FOUR ZOAS 8	13
FOR NOTHING COULD RESTRAIN THE DEAD IN BEULAH FROM DESCENDING		341	FOUR ZOAS 8	24
TO BEULAH & THE DEAD IN ULRO DESCENDED FROM THE WAR	. .	342	FOUR ZOAS 8	56
OF MOST MERCIFUL PITY & COMPASSION TO THE SPECTROUS DEAD		342	FOUR ZOAS 8	60
UNFOLDS IN ALLEGORIC FRUIT WHEN SHALL THE DEAD REVIVE	. .	345	FOUR ZOAS 8	169
FROM THOSE WHO WERE DEAD IN ULRO FROM THE SPECTRES OF THE DEAD		345	FOUR ZOAS 8	189
OF SPECTROUS DEAD THENCE TO THE LOOMS OF CATHEDRON CONVEYD		346	FOUR ZOAS 8	209
LULLING THE WEEPING SPECTRES OF THE DEAD CLOTHING THEIR LIMBS		346	FOUR ZOAS 8	213
[SHE] JERUSALEM SAW THE BODY DEAD UPON THE CROSS SHE FLED AWAY		349	FOUR ZOAS 8	331
BESIDE HIM LIES THE LION DEAD & IN HIS BELLY WORMS	. . .	354	FOUR ZOAS 8	527
A MIGHTY SOUND ARTICULATE AWAKE YE DEAD & COME	. . .	357	FOUR ZOAS 9	12
AND ALL THE WHILE THE TRUMPET SOUNDS [AWAKE YE DEAD & COME]		358	FOUR ZOAS 9	42
FLOAT THE DEAD CARCASES OF MEN & BEASTS DRIVEN TO & FRO ON WAVES		359	FOUR ZOAS 9	77
BURST ITS BRIGHT VESSELS SHE FELL DOWN DEAD AT THE FEET OF URIZEN		362	FOUR ZOAS 9	198
AND EVERY ONE OF THE DEAD APPEARS AS HE HAD LIVD BEFORE		363	FOUR ZOAS 9	245
OVER THE GRAVES & CAVERNS OF THE DEAD OVER THE PLANETS		365	FOUR ZOAS 9	314
THE TREMBLING SOULS OF ALL THE DEAD STOOD BEFORE URIZEN		365	FOUR ZOAS 9	317
SOUNDING HIS TRUMPET TO AWAKE THE DEAD ON HIGH HE SOARD		373	FOUR ZOAS 9	615
TO BEULAH & THE DEAD IN BEULAH DESCENDED THRO THEIR GATES		382	FOUR ZOAS AD 6	26
OF MOST MOURNFUL PITY & COMPASSION TO THE SPECTROUS DEAD		382	FOUR ZOAS AD 6	* 29
AND WHEN DEAD I'LL BE THY GRAVE	. . . .	416	MY SPECTRE/N	54
DANCE BEFORE DEAD ENGLAND'S HEARSE	. . . . .	433	AUGURIES	118
FOUR & TWENTY ELDERS SEATED ON THRONES TO JUDGE THE DEAD		444A	LAST JUDGMNT/L	PROSE
UPON HIS KNEES BEFORE THE LIVING & THE DEAD	. . . .	444C	LAST JUDGMNT/L	PROSE
AND IN IT CAUSD THE SPECTRES OF THE DEAD TO TAKE SWEET FORMS		481	MILTON 2	9
OUT FROM THE ASHES OF THE DEAD LOS LIFTS HIS IRON LADLES		486	MILTON 6	29
UPON THE MOUNTAINS OF ALBION AMONG THE CLIFFS OF THE DEAD		488	MILTON 8	26
THE SEPARATION WAS TERRIBLE THE DEAD WAS REPOSD ON HIS COUCH		490	MILTON 9	49
AND ALL THE SPECTRES OF THE DEAD CALLING THEMSELVES SONS OF GOD		491	MILTON 11	13
FOR HE TOOK THE OUTSIDE COURSE AMONG THE GRAVES OF THE DEAD		496	MILTON 14	34
AND MOVED THE FAST FOUNDATIONS OF THE EARTH TO WAKE THE DEAD		500	MILTON 18	50
THE WITNESSES LIE DEAD IN THE STREET OF THE GREAT CITY	.	506	MILTON 22	59
HOW LONG SHALL WE LAY DEAD IN THE STREET OF THE GREAT CITY		507	MILTON 23	11
WAS NEVER KNOWN THAT ONE OF THE HOLY DEAD SHOULD WILLING RETURN		508	MILTON 23	58
THUS THEY CONVERSE WITH THE DEAD WATCHING ROUND THE COUCH OF DEATH		522	MILTON 32	39
THE RIVER STORGE WHICH IS ARNON INTO THE DEAD SEA	. . .	524	MILTON 34	30
RETURND BUT OLOLON REMAIND BEFORE THE GATES OF THE DEAD		524	MILTON 34	48
AND OLOLON EXAMINED ALL THE COUCHES OF THE DEAD	. . .	525	MILTON 35	26
SAYING I AM GOD THE JUDGE OF ALL THE LIVING & THE DEAD	. .	530	MILTON 38	51
THE DEAD AND THE DYING BRITONS NAKED MINGLED WITH	. .	580C	DESC CAT 5	PROSE
IS SEEN FALLING OUTSTRETCHED AMONG THE DEAD AND THE DYING		580C	DESC CAT 5	PROSE
STRIPPED FROM HIS LOAD OF CLOATHING HE IS LIKE A DEAD CORPSE		581A	DESC CAT 5	PROSE
LIKE DEAD HORSES WHEN REPELLED BY THE CELESTIAL SPHERES		581D	DESC CAT 8	PROSE
I WONDER WHO CAN SAY SPEAK NO ILL OF THE DEAD WHEN IT IS		598B	PUB ADDRESS/N	PROSE
MORE ADAPTED TO SOLEMN ORNAMENT THAN [DEAD] MARBLE CAN BE		601A	PUB ADDRESS/N	*PROSE
MONUMENTS TO THE DEAD PAINTED BY	. . . .	601B	PUB ADDRESS/N	PROSE
WITH FOUR TRUMPETS TO AWAKE THE DEAD	. . . . . .	609A	V LAST JUDG/N	PROSE
ARE OPEND & THE DEAD AWAKE & OBEY THE CALL OF THE TRUMPET		609C	V LAST JUDG/N	PROSE
REPRESENTING THOSE WHO ARE NOT OF THE DEAD	. . . .	610A	V LAST JUDG/N	PROSE
EVERY THING HAS ITS VERMIN O SPECTRE OF THE SLEEPING DEAD		620	JERUSALEM 1	11
THE DEAD DESPISE & SCORN THEE & CAST THEE OUT AS ACCURSED		626	JERUSALEM 7	68
IF THOU WAST CAST FORTH FROM MY LIFE IF I WAS DEAD UPON THE MOUNTAINS		627	JERUSALEM 8	36
TO BE ALL EVIL ALL REVERSED & FOR EVER DEAD KNOWING	. .	630	JERUSALEM 10	57
THAT WHENEVER ANY SPECTRE BEGAN TO DEVOUR THE DEAD	. . .	630	JERUSALEM 11	6
ALBION IS DEAD HIS EMANATION IS DIVIDED FROM HIM	. . . .	631	JERUSALEM 12	6
. . . WHEN THE GRAVES SHALL YIELD THEIR DEAD	. . . .	633	JERUSALEM 13	11
DEAD ON THE ANVIL WHERE THE RED HOT WEDGE GROANS IN PAIN		636	JERUSALEM 16	13

449

		PAGE	TITLE	LINE
DEAD	(CONTINUED)			
	THE SPECTRE OF THE LIVING PURSUING THE EMANATIONS OF THE DEAD	638	JERUSALEM 17	13
	INTO NON-ENTITY AND THEIR THUNDERS HOARSE APPALL THE DEAD	640	JERUSALEM 18	9
	TO MURDER THEIR OWN SOULS TO BUILD A KINGDOM AMONG THE DEAD	640	JERUSALEM 18	10
	ARE THE DEAD CRUEL ARE THOSE WHO ARE INFOLDED IN MORAL LAW	644	JERUSALEM 21	48
	AND CAST IT INTO THE ATLANTIC DEEP TO CATCH THE SOULS OF THE DEAD	646	JERUSALEM 23	23
	DOST THOU APPEAR BEFORE ME WHO LIEST DEAD IN LUVAH'S SEPULCHER	648	JERUSALEM 24	57
	DOST THOU FORGIVE ME THOU WHO WAST DEAD & ART ALIVE . . .	648	JERUSALEM 24	58
	THE DEAD AWAKE TO GENERATION ARISE O LORD & REND THE VEIL	656	JERUSALEM 30	40
	FROM THE BACK & LOINS WHERE DWELL THE SPECTROUS DEAD .	659	JERUSALEM 33	4
	HIDDEN AMONG THE DEAD & MURED UP FROM THE PATHS OF LIFE	661	JERUSALEM 34	35
	UNKNOWN AMONG THE DEAD WHERE NEVER BEFORE EXISTENCE CAME	661	JERUSALEM 34	38
	REUBEN SLEPT IN BASHAN LIKE ONE DEAD IN THE VALLEY . . .	661	JERUSALEM 34	43
	IN BOWLAHOOLA & ALLAMANDA WHERE THE DEAD WAIL NIGHT & DAY	668	JERUSALEM 40	57
	LOS STOOD BEFORE HIS FURNACES AWAITING THE FURY OF THE DEAD	671	JERUSALEM 42	55
	THE SPECTRES OF THE DEAD CRY OUT FROM THE DEEPS BENEATH	671	JERUSALEM 42	57
	THEY ENQUIRE AFTER JERUSALEM IN THE REGIONS OF THE DEAD	671	JERUSALEM 42	68
	WITH THE VOICES OF DEAD MEN LOW SCARCELY ARTICULATE .	671	JERUSALEM 42	69
	THIS IS THE NET & VEIL OF VALA AMONG THE SOULS OF THE DEAD	671	JERUSALEM 42	81
	DEAD CORSES LAY BEFORE THEM & NOT AS IN WARS OF OLD . . .	672	JERUSALEM 43	40
	BUT HERE THE SOLDIER STRIKES & A DEAD CORSE FALLS AT HIS FEET	672	JERUSALEM 43	43
	THE LIVING & THE DEAD SHALL BE GROUND IN OUR RUMBLING MILLS	673	JERUSALEM 43	49
	. . . FAINT AS THE VOICE OF THE DEAD IN THE HOUSE OF DEATH	675	JERUSALEM 44	44
	HAVE PASSED OVER THE DEAD TO AWAKE THE DEAD TO JUDGMENT	676	JERUSALEM 46	15
	AWAY FROM BEULAH'S HILLS & VALES BREAK FORTH THE SOULS OF THE DEAD	677	JERUSALEM 47	10
	AND THE VEIL OF VALA IS COMPOSED OF THE SPECTRES OF THE DEAD	677	JERUSALEM 47	12
	IN THE ENDS OF BEULAH WHERE THE DEAD WAIL NIGHT & DAY .	678	JERUSALEM 48	52
	ALBION THE VORTEX OF THE DEAD ALBION THE GENEROUS . . .	678	JERUSALEM 48	54
	BEHOLD THE FOGGY MORNINGS OF THE DEAD ON ALBION'S CLIFFS	681	JERUSALEM 50	13
	FOR BEING DRIVEN FROM OUR FIELDS WHAT HAVE WE TO DO WITH THE DEAD	686	JERUSALEM 55	6
	BY WHICH THE PRINCES OF THE DEAD ENSLAVE THEIR VOTARIES	686	JERUSALEM 55	12
	THE PLOW WENT OVER HIM & THE LIVING WAS PLOWED IN AMONG THE DEAD	689	JERUSALEM 57	14
	TO CATCH THE SOULS OF THE DEAD BEGAN TO VEGETATE & PETRIFY	691	JERUSALEM 59	3
	THE HABITATION OF THE SPECTRES OF THE DEAD & THE PLACE . .	691	JERUSALEM 59	8
	JERUSALEM REPLIED I AM AN OUTCAST ALBION IS DEAD . . .	695	JERUSALEM 62	2
	AROUND IN THE CLOUDS OF THE FEMALE ON ALBION'S CLIFFS OF THE DEAD	697	JERUSALEM 63	22
	THE DEAD BENEATH BEULAH FROM TYBURN TO GOLGOTHA AND FROM	698	JERUSALEM 63	33
	AND NOW THE SPECTRES OF THE DEAD AWAKE IN BEULAH ALL .	708	JERUSALEM 69	32
	MOCKING THE REMOVER OF LIMITS & THE RESURRECTION OF THE DEAD	713	JERUSALEM 73	30
	THE SPECTRES OF THE DEAD HOWL ROUND THE PORCHES OF LOS .	714	JERUSALEM 73	46
	IN OPEN DAY TO DRAW THE SOULS OF THE DEAD INTO THE LIGHT	721	JERUSALEM 79	79
	COME INTO LUVAH'S TENTS AND SEEK NOT TO REVIVE THE DEAD	722	JERUSALEM 80	31
	SOON SHALL THE SPECTRES OF THE DEAD FOLLOW MY WEAVING THREADS	725	JERUSALEM 82	9
	I SEE THE SPECTRES OF THY DEAD O EMANATION OF ALBION . .	731	JERUSALEM 86	13
	WHOSE CURRENTS FLOW INTO THE DEAD SEA BY SODOM & GOMORRA	735	JERUSALEM 89	27
	HIS STONY MEMBERS HE SAW ENGLAND AH SHALL THE DEAD LIVE AGAIN	742	JERUSALEM 95	4
	AND THE DEAD CORPSE FROM SINAI'S HEAT	761	FOR SEXES/GP	10
	I RENT THE VEIL WHERE THE DEAD DWELL	770	OF GATES/GP	18
	ONE DIES ALAS THE LIVING & DEAD	771	OF GATES/GP	25
	EVE FAINTED OVER THE DEAD BODY OF ABEL WHICH LAYS NEAR A GRAVE	779C	GHOST ABEL 1	PROSE
	SEVEN TIMES O EVE THOU HAST FAINTED OVER THE DEAD AH AH	779	GHOST ABEL 1	5
	ABEL IS DEAD & CAIN SLEW HIM WE SHALL ALSO DIE A DEATH . .	780	GHOST ABEL 1	19
	ALIVE & NOT DEAD WERE IT NOT BETTER TO BELIEVE VISION .	780	GHOST ABEL 2	1
	OF THE DEAD WANDER THIS I ENDEAVOUR TO PREVENT & WITH MY	809A	LETTER 20	PROSE
	THO DEAD THEY APPEAR UPON MY PATH	817	HAPPINESS/L	17
	ALL MY TALENTS I BURY AND DEAD IS MY FAME	829	O WHY BORN/L	8
	TO ME FORGIVE THIS DIRGE-LIKE LAMENTATION OVER A DEAD HORSE	830B	LETTER 30	PROSE
	& NOW I HAVE LAMENTED OVER THE DEAD HORSE LET ME LAUGH & BE	830B	LETTER 30	PROSE
	HOPE THAT AS MR D(DODSLEY) IS DEAD & IF MR H(HAYLEY) HAS NO	856B	LETTER 54	PROSE
	HIS DEAD MASTER FROM THE VULTURES OF THESE FIVE I AM MAKING	859B	LETTER 56	PROSE
	I KNOW THAT THOSE WHO ARE DEAD FROM THE EARTH & WHO MOCKD &	863A	LETTER 60	PROSE
	. . . ASSASSIN LAYING DEAD AT THE FEET OF (EDWARD) IST IN . . .	SUPP	ILLUS HISTORY	*TITLE
	"AND IN DEAD PARENTS BALEFUL ASHES BRED" (SPENSER) .	SUPP	LEGEND/N 19	*
	"YET CAN I NOT PERSWADE ME THOU ART DEAD" MILTON . . .	SUPP	LEGEND/N 73	*
DEADEN				
	NATURAL OBJECTS ALWAYS DID & NOW DO WEAKEN DEADEN . . .	783A	ANNO WW POEMS	MARG
DEADENS				
	OF VERY LITTLE TIME AND OF THE AIR IT DEADENS EVERY COLOUR	565A	DESC CAT 2	PROSE
DEADLY				
	[THE DEADLY CUNNING OF THE [SCALY TRIBE] FLATTERER . . .	110	TIRIEL 8	* 22
	. . . THE PALE MOTHER NOURISHES HER CHILD TO THE DEADLY SLAUGHTER	143	FRENCH REVOLTN	210
	. . . BUT NOW I WILL BLESS THEE NO MORE IN DEADLY BLACK	144	FRENCH REVOLTN	225
	LET THE PRIESTS OF THE RAVEN OF DAWN NO LONGER IN DEADLY BLACK	160A	SONG LIBERTY	PROSE
	[COULD] DARE ITS DEADLY TERRORS [CLASP] [GRASP] CLASP .	172	THE TYGER/N 1	21
	BECAUSE THE NIGHT IS GONE THAT CLOSD ME IN ITS DEADLY BLACK	191	V DAU ALBION 2	29
	DARE ITS DEADLY TERRORS CLASP	214	THE TYGER/SE	16
	SEVEN DEADLY SINS OF THE SOUL	224	URIZEN 4	30

		PAGE	TITLE	LINE

DEADLY (CONTINUED)

	PAGE	TITLE	LINE
ALL THE SEVEN DEADLY SINS OF THE SOUL	225	URIZEN 4	49
THO BOUND IN A DEADLY SLEEP	229	URIZEN 13	27
HE SAW URIZEN DEADLY BLACK	230	URIZEN 13	50
INTO THE DEADLY NIGHT TO SEE THE FORM OF ALBION'S ANGEL	242	EUROPE 12	6
HORRIBLE GHAST & DEADLY NOUGHT SHALT THOU FIND IN IT	265	FOUR ZOAS 1	50
. . . [?ALONE ?POSSESSD BY DEADLY FEARS] LOVE IS CHANGD	267	FOUR ZOAS 1	* 111
TO DEADLY HATE			
AND LIVE THEREBY HE IS SUNK DOWN INTO A DEADLY SLEEP	272	FOUR ZOAS 1	291
A CAVERN SHAGGD WITH HORRID SHADES DARK COOL & DEADLY WHERE	295	FOUR ZOAS 3	122
WITH WHOM I LIVD IN HAPPINESS BEFORE THAT DEADLY NIGHT	300	FOUR ZOAS 4	112
DEADLY BETWEEN THE HAMMER'S BEATING GRATEFUL TO THE EARS	302	FOUR ZOAS 4	190
THE IMMORTAL ENDURD THO BOUND IN A DEADLY SLEEP	304	FOUR ZOAS 4	283
WITH SILENT FEAR & HIS IMMORTAL CHEEKS GREW DEADLY PALE	307	FOUR ZOAS 5	87
. . . BURST OPEN & AGAIN CLOSE WITH A [?DISMAL] DEADLY PAIN	309	FOUR ZOAS 5	* 178
THARMAS HEARD THE DEADLY SCREAM ACROSS HIS WATRY WORLD	313	FOUR ZOAS 6	47
AGE AFTER AGE TILL UNDERNEATH HIS HEEL A DEADLY ROOT	321	FOUR ZOAS 7	31
WITHIN AS IN A TABERNACLE ABOMINABLE DEADLY	343	FOUR ZOAS 8	106
THEY PROPAGATED THE DEADLY [WORLD] WORDS THE SHADOWY FEMALE	344	FOUR ZOAS 8	* 143
ABSORBING			
PERTURBD BLACK & DEADLY IN [THE]	346	FOUR ZOAS 8	* 226
THEY ROLLD DOWN A DIM WORLD CRUSTED WITH SNOW DEADLY & DARK	351	FOUR ZOAS 8	* 396
DRINK IN THE DEADLY DULL DELUSION HORRORS OF ETERNAL DEATH	352	FOUR ZOAS 8	418
AND WHIPS THEIR VICTIMS & THE DEADLY [SPORTING] SPORT OF	377	FOUR ZOAS 9	* 754
LUVAH'S SONS			
GREW DEADLY PALE HE BECAME WHAT HE BEHELD FOR A RED	483	MILTON 3	29
IN DEADLY SICKENING PAIN TILL SEPARATED INTO A FEMALE PALE	483	MILTON 3	33
HE CREATED SEVEN DEADLY SINS DRAWING OUT HIS INFERNAL	489	MILTON 9	21
SCROLL			
BOUND UP IN THE HORNS OF JEALOUSY TO A DEADLY FADING MOON	491	MILTON 10	18
DEADLY PALE OUTSTRETCHD AND SNOWY COLD STORM COVERD	497	MILTON 15	37
AND WHIPS THEIR VICTIMS & THE DEADLY SPORT OF LUVAH'S SONS	514	MILTON 27	36
IN THE STOMACH & INTESTINES TERRIBLE DEADLY UNUTTERABLE	524	MILTON 34	16
HERE RENDERD DEADLY WITHIN THE LIFE & INTERIOR VISION	525	MILTON 34	52
ARE HERE FROZEN TO UNEXPANSIVE DEADLY DESTROYING TERRORS	525	MILTON 35	1
TERRIBLE DEADLY & POISONOUS HIS PRESENCE IN ULRO DARK	526	MILTON 35	55
BEYOND THE OUTLINE OF IDENTITY IN THE SELFHOOD DEADLY	527	MILTON 37	10
CALLD DEATH A MADMAN [DEADLY THE AFFRONT] TREMBLING FOR THE	537	AND HIS LEGS/N	17
AFFRONT			
ASSIST IN WEAVING THE DEADLY WOOF "...IN DREADFUL HARMONY"	576C	DESC CAT 4	PROSE
IN ITS DEADLY DREAMS OF GOOD & EVIL	614C	V LAST JUDG/N	PROSE
CONSTELLATIONS OVER THE DEADLY DEEPS OF INDEFINITE	625	JERUSALEM 7	22
UDAN-ADAN			
THE EASTERN GATE FOURFOLD TERRIBLE & DEADLY ITS ORNAMENTS	633	JERUSALEM 13	12
THE FOREST AND THE MARSH AND THE PITS OF BITUMEN DEADLY	634	JERUSALEM 13	39
I SEE THE FOUR-FOLD MAN THE HUMANITY IN DEADLY SLEEP	635	JERUSALEM 15	6
I SEE IN DEADLY FEAR IN LONDON LOS RAGING ROUND HIS ANVIL	636	JERUSALEM 15	21
IN GNAWING PAIN FROM LOS'S BOSOM IN THE DEADLY NIGHT	639	JERUSALEM 17	50
IN SELF-DENIAL BUT WAR AND DEADLY CONTENTION BETWEEN	640	JERUSALEM 18	20
OF HATERS MET IN DEADLY STRIFE RENDING THE HOUSE & GARDEN	640	JERUSALEM 18	22
EVERY BOIL UPON MY BODY IS A SEPARATE & DEADLY SIN	643	JERUSALEM 21	4
THE ARMIES I HEAR THEIR LOUD CYMBALS & THEIR DEADLY CRIES	644	JERUSALEM 21	47
HORRIBLE GHAST & DEADLY NOUGHT SHALT THOU FIND IN IT	645	JERUSALEM 22	23
ALBION GAVE HIS DEADLY GROAN	650	FIELDS FROM/J	35
A DEADLY TREE HE NAMD IT MORAL VIRTUE AND THE LAW	652	JERUSALEM 28	15
THUNDERS OF DEADLY WAR THE FEVER OF THE HUMAN SOUL	664	JERUSALEM 38	9
. . . IS CLOSD IN BY DEADLY TEETH	672	JERUSALEM 43	24
HERE TURN INTO POISONOUS STUPOR & DEADLY INTOXICATION	672	JERUSALEM 43	29
I SEE A CAVE A ROCK A TREE DEADLY AND POISONOUS	673	JERUSALEM 43	60
UNIMAGINATIVE			
THE SILENT BROODINGS OF DEADLY REVENGE SPRINGING FROM THE	685	JERUSALEM 54	9
HE WEPT IN DEADLY WRATH OF THE SPECTRE	699	JERUSALEM 64	27
IN SELF-CONTRADICTING AGONY			
SUDDEN THEY BECOME LIKE WHAT THEY BEHOLD IN HOWLINGS &	701	JERUSALEM 65	75
DEADLY PAIN			
ACROSS EUROPE ACROSS AFRICA IN HOWLINGS & DEADLY WAR	706	JERUSALEM 68	20
DEADLY HATE BETWEEN LEAH & RACHEL DAUGHTERS OF DECEIT &	707	JERUSALEM 69	11
FRAUD			
AND JEALOUSY & ABHORRENCE & REVENGE & DEADLY MURDER	707	JERUSALEM 69	13
IN OPPOSITION DEADLY AND THEIR WHEELS IN POISONOUS	714	JERUSALEM 74	5
AND DEADLY STUPOR TURND AGAINST EACH OTHER LOUD & FIERCE	714	JERUSALEM 74	6
LOS WALKS UPON HIS ANCIENT MOUNTAINS IN THE DEADLY DARKNESS	730	JERUSALEM 85	10
AND DEADLY CUNNING & MEAN ABJECTNESS ONLY SHALL ENJOY THEM	734	JERUSALEM 88	38
HIS HEAD DARK DEADLY IN ITS BRAIN INCLOSES A REFLEXION	734	JERUSALEM 89	14
UPON THE WHITE ROCK ENGLAND A FEMALE SHADOW AS DEADLY DAMPS	741	JERUSALEM 94	7
I BEHOLD THE VISIONS OF MY DEADLY SLEEP OF SIX THOUSAND	743	JERUSALEM 96	11
YEARS			
FIBRES OF A DEADLY NIGHT	753	EV GOSPEL(D)/N	96
BUT MORAL VIRTUES' DEADLY GIN	758	EV GOSPEL (2)	8

DEAF

	PAGE	TITLE	LINE
MAKES HIM DEAF	23	EDW THIRD/PS 3	70
OR IF SHES DEAF OR IS WALL EYED	56	HAIL MATRIM/IM	15
BLIND TO THE PLEASURES OF THE SIGHT & DEAF TO WARBLING	104	TIRIEL 4	29
BIRDS			
AYE NOW YOU FEEL THE CURSE YOU CRY BUT MAY ALL EARS BE DEAF	106	TIRIEL 5	20
BUT HE HEALS THE DEAF & THE DUMB & THE BLIND	755	EV GOSPEL(E)/N	88

DEAFEND

	PAGE	TITLE	LINE
WERE WITHERD & DEAFEND & COLD	236	URIZEN 28	16
THAN ALL THE WRACKING ELEMENTS DEAFEND & RENDED WORSE	195	FOUR ZOAS 3	151

DEAL

	PAGE	TITLE	LINE
MAY DO A GREAT DEAL OF HARM WITHOUT KNOWING IT	29A	EDW THIRD/PS 4	PROSE
GREAT DEAL MORE THAT WE SHALL ALL HEAR BY AND BY AND I CAME	29C	EDW THIRD/PS 4	PROSE

```
                                                          PAGE       TITLE          LINE
DEAL    (CONTINUED)
      THE BAD ARTIST SEEMS TO COPY A GREAT DEAL  . . . . .   456A ANNO REYNOLDS    MARG
      THE GOOD ONE REALLY DOES COPY A GREAT DEAL . . . . .   456A ANNO REYNOLDS    MARG
      HERE IS A GREAT DEAL TO DO TO PROVE THAT ALL TRUTH     475A ANNO REYNOLDS    MARG
         IS PREJUDICE
      A GREAT DEAL BETTER THAN I WAS BEFORE  . . . . . . .   554 TO VENETIAN/N       15
      THE PASSIONS THAT WITH SINNERS DEAL  . . . . . . . .   756 EV GOSPEL(I)/N      14
      & THO WE HAD A GREAT DEAL OF LUGGAGE NO GRUMBLING  . . 802B LETTER 14        PROSE
      A GREAT DEAL OF WORK IN THEM THAT MUST & WILL HAVE TIME 837A LETTER 35       PROSE
      GREAT DEAL OF HONOUR IN LOSING THE FIRST PUBLICATION OF ANY 856C LETTER 54   PROSE
DEALERS
      INTO WHICH BOOKSELLERS & TRADING DEALERS HAVE THROWN YOU 595B PUB ADDRESS/N  PROSE
      IGNORANT PICTURE DEALERS AN ENGLISHMAN MAY WELL SAY I AM 601C PUB ADDRESS/N  PROSE
DEALST
      CRIES IN VAIN POOR LITTLE WRETCH THAT DEALST  . . . . .  3 TO WINTER/PS        14
DEAN
      TILLY LALLY THE SIPTIPPIDIST ARADOBO THE DEAN OF MOROCCO  46B ISLAND MOON 2  PROSE
      ABILITIES AS ALSO FOR THE D(DEAN) OF C(CANTERBURY) BUT  .  868D LETTER 68     PROSE
DEAR
      AH MY DEAR LORD AH WRETCHED ELENOR . . . . . . . .    5 FAIR ELENOR/PS        40
      OF HER DEAR LORD ALL GHASTLY PALE CLOTTED  . . . . .    5 FAIR ELENOR/PS      59
      AND GAIN BUT SCANTY FARE THEN MY DEAR LORD . . . . .   19 EDW THIRD/PS 2      33
      DEAR SIR A PRINCE SHOULD ALWAYS KEEP HIS STATE  . . .  20 EDW THIRD/PS 2      46
      O EDWARD MY DEAR SON LEARN TO THINK LOWLY OF  . . . .  26 EDW THIRD/PS 3     216
      O MY DEAR FRIENDS PRAY YE FOR ME  . . . . . . . . .    36A COUCH DEATH/PS   PROSE
      THAT I TOOK UP IN THE BOG HOUSE O DEAR  . . . . . .    58C ISLAND MOON 10  *PROSE
      O DEAR THE WATER S GOT INTO THE SLIDERS LOOK HERE  . . 58C ISLAND MOON 10   PROSE
      O DEAR SIR HO HO HO I AM NO SINGER I MUST BEG  . . . . 61D ISLAND MOON 11  *PROSE
      MY DEAR THEY HATE PEOPLE WHO ARE OF HIGHER ABILITIES  . 63A ISLAND MOON 11  PROSE
      IS GOD OUR FATHER DEAR . . . . . . . . . . . .       117 DIVNE IMAGE/SI        6
      [O] DEAR MOTHER DEAR MOTHER THE CHURCH IS COLD . . . . 179 LIT VAGABOND/N *   1
      OOTHOON SHALL VIEW HIS DEAR DELIGHT NOR EER WITH JEALOUS 195 V DAU ALBION 7   28
         CLOUD
      DEAR MOTHER DEAR MOTHER THE CHURCH IS COLD  . . . . . 216 LIT VAGABND/SE       1
      I CAN INFUSE MY DEAR REVENGE INTO HIS GLOWING BREAST  . . 289 FOUR ZOAS 2    337
      THEN O MY DEAR LORD LISTEN TO AHANIA LISTEN TO THE VISION 292 FOUR ZOAS 3     41
      AS OUR DEAR REDEEMER SAID  . . . . . . . . . . .     417 MY SPECTRE/N         73
      DEAR CHILD I ALSO BY PLEASANT STREAMS  . . . . . . .  427 LAND OF DREAMS       13
      ON THE RIGHT HAND OF HER WILLIAM BOND  . . . . . . .  435 WILLIAM BOND         38
      SUCH IS THE DESIGN WHICH YOU MY DEAR SIR  . . . . . . 444C LAST JUDGMNT/L   PROSE
      FAITH IN GOD THE DEAR SAVIOUR WHO TOOK ON THE LIKENESS 506 MILTON 22          57
         OF MEN
      O MY DEAR SONS LEAVE NOT YOUR FATHER AS YOUR BRETHREN LEFT 508 MILTON 23      61
         ME
      THY LOVE DEPENDS ON HIM THOU LOVEST & ON HIS DEAR LOVES 522 MILTON 33          8
      I'LL ALSO WRITE MY OWN DEAR EPITAPH  . . . . . . . . 537 AND HIS LEGS/N       49
      AND SO [SWEET] DEAR [CHRISTIANS] CHRISTIAN FRIENDS HOW 551 ONLY MAN/N     *    4
         DO YOU DO
      I ASKD MY DEAR FRIEND ORATOR PRIGG  . . . . . . . .  553 ASKD PRIGG/N    *    1
      O DEAR MOTHER OUTLINE [BE NOT IN A RAGE] OF KNOWLEDGE MOST 554 ASKD PRIGG/N *  16
         SAGE
      THEREFORE [DEAR] READER [FORGIVE] WHAT YOU DO NOT APPROVE 621B JERUSALEM 3   PROSE
      O SPECTRE OF URTHONA REASON NOT AGAINST THEIR DEAR APPROACH 629 JERUSALEM 10  32
      BY OUR DEAR LORD I SEE WORLDS CRUSTED WITH SNOWS & ICE  . . 673 JERUSALEM 43  64
      AND DEAR MUTUAL FORGIVENESS & TO BECOME ONE GREAT SATAN 679 JERUSALEM 49      29
      THO SHE HATES HE CALLS HER AGAIN IN LOVE I LOVE MY DEAR 694 JERUSALEM 61       8
         JOSEPH
      TO YOU FOR YOUR REMARKS YOUR SORROWS AND YOUR DEAR SON'S 796C LETTER 8      PROSE
      I REMAIN DEAR SIR YOUR HUMBLE SERVANT  . . . . . . . 797B LETTER 9          PROSE
      DEAR CUMBERLAND I HAVE TO CONGRATULATE YOU ON . . . . 797C LETTER 10         PROSE
      TO MY DEAR FRIEND MRS ANNA FLAXMAN  . . . . . . . .  800B MRS FLAXMAN/L      TITLE
      LEADER OF MY ANGELS MY DEAR & TOO CAREFUL & OVER JOYOUS 801B LETTER 13       PROSE
      RECIEVE MY HEARTY LOVE & RESPECT I AM DEAR SIR YOUR SINCERE 801C LETTER 13   PROSE
      DEAR SCULPTOR OF ETERNITY WE ARE SAFE ARRIVED AT     801D LETTER 14          PROSE
         OUR COTTAGE
      YOU O DEAR FLAXMAN ARE A SUBLIME ARCHANGEL MY FRIEND & . . 802C LETTER 14    PROSE
      FRIENDSHIP TO OUR DEAR MRS FLAXMAN WHOM WE ARDENTLY  . . 802D LETTER 14      PROSE
      DEAR FRIEND OF MY ANGELS WE ARE SAFE ARRIVED AT OUR COTTAGE 803A LETTER 15   PROSE
      OUR DEAR FRIEND FLAXMAN IS THE THEME OF MY EMULATION  . 807A LETTER 17       PROSE
      SPIRIT OF ABSTRACTION & IMPROVIDENCE SUCH MY DEAR SIR  . 809B LETTER 20      PROSE
      I REMAIN DEAR SIR EVER YOURS SINCERELY  . . . . . . . 810A LETTER 20         PROSE
      DEAR FLAXMAN I REJOICE TO HEAR THAT YOUR GREAT WORK IS 810C LETTER 21        PROSE
         ACCOMPLISHD
      CAN COMPREHEND IN A FORTNIGHT BE ASSURED MY DEAR FRIEND 814D LETTER 23       PROSE
         THAT
      MUST MY DEAR BUTTS FEEL COLD NEGLECT . . . . . . . .  817 HAPPINESS/L         45
      DEAR BROTHER YOUR LETTER MENTIONING MR BUTTS'S ACCOUNT OF 819B LETTER 25   *PROSE
         MY AGUE
      AND NOW MY DEAR SIR CONGRATULATE ME ON MY RETURN TO  . . 822C LETTER 26      PROSE
      AS YOU MY DEAR FRIEND HAVE ALWAYS LEFT ME  . . . . . 826A LETTER 27          PROSE
      THUS YOU SEE MY DEAR FRIEND THAT I CANNOT LEAVE THIS PLACE 828A LETTER 28    PROSE
      DEAR SIR THIS PERHAPS WAS SUFFERD TO CLEAR UP SOME DOUBTS 828C LETTER 28     PROSE
      AND REMAIN DEAR SIR YOUR SINCERE AND DEVOTED SERVANTS  . 832A LETTER 31      PROSE
      BUT MY ARRIVAL HAS DISPELLD THE FORMIDABLE MALADY & MY 833D LETTER 33        PROSE
         DEAR &
      PRAY MY DEAR SIR FAVOUR ME WITH A LINE CONCERNING YOUR  . 833D LETTER 33     PROSE
      ABOVE ALL YOU MY DEAR FRIEND & BENEFACTOR IN THE LORD  . 834A LETTER 33      PROSE
      I REMAIN DEAR SIR YOUR SINCERE  . . . . . . . . . .  837B LETTER 35          PROSE
      I AM DEAR SIR YOUR SINCERELY AFFECTIONATE  . . . . . 841A LETTER 40          PROSE
      PLACE IN HIM I AM DEAR SIR YOUR ANXIOUSLY DEVOTED  . . 842A LETTER 41        PROSE
      RESPECTS I AM DEAR SIR YOURS MOST SINCERELY  . . . . . 845A LETTER 43        PROSE
      I AM DEAR SIR YOURS SINCERELY  . . . . . . . . . . . 849C LETTER 45          PROSE
```

```
                                                            PAGE    TITLE           LINE
DEAR    (CONTINUED)
     WHO WAS MY ENEMY DEAR SIR EXCUSE MY ENTHUSIASM OR RATHER    852C LETTER 50      PROSE
     DEAR SIR I HAVE OMITTED SO LONG TO THANK YOU FOR YOUR KIND  853A LETTER 51     *PROSE
     MY WIFE JOINS ME IN LOVE TO YOU & TO OUR DEAR FRIEND &  .   853A LETTER 51     *PROSE
     FRIENDS AT LAVANT & IN ALL SUSSEX I REMAIN DEAR SIR  . .    853A LETTER 51     *PROSE
     NOW MY DEAR SIR I WILL THANK YOU FOR THE TRANSMISSION       854C LETTER 53      PROSE
     OUR DEAR FRIEND HAWKINS IS OUT OF TOWN & WILL NOT RETURN    855B LETTER 53      PROSE
        TILL APRIL
     CONTINUED HEALTH I AM DEAR SIR YOURS SINCERELY   . . . .    855C LETTER 53      PROSE
     I REMAIN DEAR SIR YOUR OBLIGED AND AFFECTIONATE      . . .  858D LETTER 55      PROSE
     GRATEFUL WISH TO YOU & TO OUR DEAR RESPECTED MISS POOLE     860B LETTER 56      PROSE
     OF YOUR GOOD HEALTH & THAT OF OUR DEAR FRIEND OF LAVANT &   862A LETTER 59      PROSE
     REMEMBERD IN SUSSEX I AM DEAR SIR YOURS EVER AFFECTIONATELY 862B LETTER 59      PROSE
     ALL HITHERTO YOU DEAR SIR ARE ONE WHO HAS MY PARTICULAR     862C LETTER 60      PROSE
     LET US GO ON DEAR SIR FOLLOWING HIS CROSS LET US TAKE       863B LETTER 60      PROSE
        IT UP
     DEAR CUMBERLAND I AM VERY MUCH OBLIGED BY YOUR KIND ARDOUR  865C LETTER 63      PROSE
     I REMAIN DEAR SIR YOURS TRULY  . . . . . . . . . . .        868B LETTER 67      PROSE
     I AM DEAR SIR YOURS SINCERELY  . . . . . . . . . . .        870B LETTER 71      PROSE
     I AM DEAR SIR YOURS SINCERELY  . . . . . . . . . . .        871B LETTER 72      PROSE
     LONDON SUNDAY MORNING DEAR MADAM . . . . . . . . . .        871C LETTER 73      PROSE
     I AM DEAR SIR YOURS SINCERELY  . . . . . . . . . . .        872A LETTER 74      PROSE
     I AM DEAR SIR YOURS MOST GRATEFULLY  . . . . . . . .        873B LETTER 76      PROSE
     WITH WHOM HE MAKES HIS FIRST EFFORT DEAR SIR YOURS EVER     875A LETTER 80      PROSE
     I AM DEAR SIR YOURS SINCERELY  . . . . . . . . . . .        875C LETTER 81      PROSE
     I AM DEAR SIR YOURS SINCERELY  . . . . . . . . . . .        875D LETTER 82      PROSE
     I AM DEAR SIR YOURS SINCERELY  . . . . . . . . . . .        877A LETTER 85      PROSE
     DEAR CUMBERLAND I HAVE BEEN VERY NEAR THE GATES OF DEATH    878A LETTER 88      PROSE
     I AM DEAR SIR YOURS AFFECTIONATELY . . . . . . . . .        879A LETTER 88      PROSE
     ACCOMPANIED BY ALL THE OLD SYMPTOMS I AM DEAR SIR YOURS     880A LETTER 90      PROSE
        SINCERELY
DEAREST
     MY DEAREST FRIEND IT IS TO YOU I OWE ALL MY PRESENT  . .    799A LETTER 11      PROSE
     TO MY DEAREST FRIEND JOHN FLAXMAN THESE LINES  . . . . .    799B TO FLAXMAN/L   TITLE
     "MY DEAREST FRIEND I HOPE YOU WILL NOT THINK WE COULD"  .   800A LETTER 12      PROSE
     MY DEAREST FRIEND THIS SUDDEN COLD WEATHER HAS CUT UP  .    872D LETTER 76      PROSE
DEARTH
     BRING OUT NUMBER WEIGHT & MEASURE IN A YEAR OF DEARTH  . .  151B MARRIAGE HH 7  PROSE
     FELT AFFLICTION & SORROW & SICKNESS & DEARTH   . . . . .    818 HAPPINESS/L      76
DEATH
     OF DEATH ISSUE AS FROM A SEPULCHRE   . . . . . . . .          4 FAIR ELENOR/PS    7
     CHILL DEATH WITHDRAWS HIS HAND AND SHE REVIVES   . . . .      4 FAIR ELENOR/PS    9
     AND GRINNING SKULLS AND CORRUPTIBLE DEATH  . . . . . .        4 FAIR ELENOR/PS   14
     PALE DEATH AND FOLLOWD ON THE WINGS OF FEAR  . . . . .        4 FAIR ELENOR/PS   28
     O GHASTLY DEATH WITHDRAW THY CRUEL HAND  . . . . . . .        5 FAIR ELENOR/PS   43
     A HIRED VILLAIN TURND MY SLEEP TO DEATH  . . . . . . .        5 FAIR ELENOR/PS   64
     FAMINE AND DEATH DOTH CRY  . . . . . . . . . .               13 GWIN KING/PS     78
     LIKE BLAZING COMETS SCATTERING DEATH   . . . . . . .         13 GWIN KING/PS     83
     NOW DEATH IS SICK AND RIVEN MEN  . . . . . . . . .           13 GWIN KING/PS     89
     THE REST DID FILL THE VALE OF DEATH  . . . . . . . .         14 GWIN KING/PS    111
     AND YELLING DEATH RUNS UP AND DOWN THE RANKS   . . . . .     18 EDW THIRD/PS 1    8
     WE SPRING TO BATTLE OER THE FLOODS OF DEATH  . . . . . .     18 EDW THIRD/PS 1   16
     THAT DEATH CAN NEVER RAVISH FROM THY BROW  . . . . . .       18 EDW THIRD/PS 1   22
     SHAKE HANDS WITH DEATH AND STRIKE A BARGAIN FOR  . . . .     22 EDW THIRD/PS 3   29
     NOW THE QUARRY S SET AND DEATH DOTH SPORT  . . . . . .       24 EDW THIRD/PS 3  142
     IF PHILIP CAME ARMD IN THE RIBS OF DEATH   . . . . . .       25 EDW THIRD/PS 3  175
     DEATH WONS IN CITIES' SMOKE AND IN STILL NIGHT   . . . .     30 EDW THIRD/PS 5    6
     TALKING WITH DEATH ANSWERING HIS HARD DEMANDS  . . . . .     30 EDW THIRD/PS 5   10
     YET DEATH IS TERRIBLE THO BORNE ON ANGELS' WINGS . . . .     30 EDW THIRD/PS 5   17
     HOW TERRIBLE THEN IS THE FIELD OF DEATH  . . . . . . .       30 EDW THIRD/PS 5   18
     HAS MY SOUL FAINTED WITH THESE VIEWS OF DEATH  . . . .       31 EDW THIRD/PS 5   42
     I SEEM TO HEAR THE DISMAL YELLS OF DEATH   . . . . . .       31 EDW THIRD/PS 5   45
     OR I LAY STRETCHD UPON THE FIELD OF DEATH  . . . . . .       31 EDW THIRD/PS 5   66
     DREAD VISAGES FROWNING IN SILENT DEATH   . . . . . . .       32 EDW THIRD/PS 6   36
     AND SAILS REJOICING IN THE FLOOD OF DEATH  . . . . . .       33 EDW FOURTH/PS    10
     BROTHER IN BROTHER'S BLOOD MUST BATHE RIVERS OF DEATH  .     34A KING JOHN/PS    PROSE
     OLD AGE MUST WORK THE WORK OF DEATH AGAINST THEIR PROGENY    34B KING JOHN/PS    PROSE
     ANGELS OF DEATH STAND IN THE LOWRING HEAVENS   . . . . .     35 WAR SONG/PS      17
     THE COUCH OF DEATH . . . . . . . . . . . . . . .            35C COUCH DEATH/PS  TITLE
     PARTING IS HARD AND DEATH IS TERRIBLE  . . . . . . .        35D COUCH DEATH/PS  PROSE
     THE DAMPS OF DEATH FALL THICK UPON ME HORRORS STARE ME      35D COUCH DEATH/PS  PROSE
        IN THE FACE
     I LOOK BEHIND THERE IS NO RETURNING DEATH FOLLOWS AFTER ME  35D COUCH DEATH/PS  PROSE
     I WALK IN REGIONS OF DEATH WHERE NO TREE IS  . . . . .      35D COUCH DEATH/PS  PROSE
     AS THE VOICE OF THE ANGEL OF DEATH   . . . . . . . .        36B COUCH DEATH/PS  PROSE
     VOICES OF COMFORT ARE HEARD OVER THE COUCH OF DEATH  . . .  36D COUCH DEATH/PS  PROSE
     MY FLESH IS A PRISON MY BONES THE BARS OF DEATH  . . . .    37B CONTEMPLATN/PS  PROSE
     BY A FALSE WIFE BROUGHT TO THE GATES OF DEATH  . . . .      37C SAMSON/PS       PROSE
     BRINGING GOOD NEWS OF SIN AND DEATH DESTROYED  . . . .      37D SAMSON/PS       PROSE
     O WEAK WOMAN IT IS DEATH CLOATHED IN FLESH THOU LOVEST  .   38B SAMSON/PS       PROSE
     COME HITHER DEATH ART THOU NOT SAMSON'S SERVANT  . . . .    38B SAMSON/PS       PROSE
     THOU WOULDST MY DEATH AND DEATH APPROACHES FAST  . . .      38C SAMSON/PS       PROSE
     MY LIFE IS DEATH I AM A TRAITOR TO MY NATION AND DESPISED   38D SAMSON/PS       PROSE
     MY CUP IS FILLD WITH ENVY'S RANKEST DRAUGHT [ AND DEATH]    41C THEN SHE BORE   PROSE
     SUNK BY THE HAND OF DEATH IN WATRY TOMB OER YONDER          43D WOE CRIED MUSE *PROSE
        [ RUFFLING ] LAKE
     UNTIMELY LOST THY CONRADE ONCE WHEN LIVING THEE I LOVD      43D WOE CRIED MUSE  PROSE
        EVN UNTO DEATH
     OR SHERLOCK UPON DEATH   . . . . . . . . . . . .            57 TO BE OR/IM       5
     OR SHERLOCK UPON DEATH   . . . . . . . . . . . .            57 TO BE OR/IM      29
     HOW COULD LIFE CREATE DEATH  . . . . . . . . . . .          92B ANNO SWED LOVE  MARG
     BUT NOW HIS EYES WERE DARKNED & HIS WIFE FADING IN DEATH    99 TIRIEL 1          4
```

		PAGE	TITLE		LINE
DEATH (CONTINUED)					
COME FORTH SONS OF THE CURSE COME FORTH SEE THE DEATH OF MYRATANA		99	TIRIEL 1		10
ARE CRUEL AS DEATH & AS OBDURATE AS THE DEVOURING PIT		99	TIRIEL 1		15
. . . [HEAVING] SHRINKING IN PANGS OF DEATH		99	TIRIEL 1	*	20
YE WORMS OF DEATH FEASTING UPON YOUR AGED PARENTS FLESH		99	TIRIEL 1		23
THESE ARE THE GROANS OF DEATH YE SERPENTS		99	TIRIEL 1		26
. . . THESE ARE THE GROANS OF DEATH		99	TIRIEL 1		26
FOR HE IS THE KING OF ROTTEN WOOD & OF THE BONES OF DEATH		101	TIRIEL 2		24
AND I WILL BRING THEE FOOD OLD MAN TILL DEATH SHALL CALL THEE HENCE		103	TIRIEL 3		35
AND IN THE MORNING LO AN HUNDRED MEN IN GHASTLY DEATH . .		107	TIRIEL 5		29
DESOLATE LOATHED DUMB [CON] ASTONISHD WAITING FOR BLACK DEATH		107	TIRIEL 5	*	35
THAT OUR FEET MAKE REMEMBER [?HILI] HELA I HAVE SAVD THEE FROM DEATH		107	TIRIEL 6	*	6
TRUE I WAS BORN THY [CHILD] SLAVE WHO ASKD THEE TO SAVE ME FROM DEATH		107	TIRIEL 6		14
PLANT WORMS OF DEATH TO FEAST UPON THE TONGUE OF TERRIBLE CURSES		108	TIRIEL 6		39
STAND STILL OR FROM MY BOW RECIEVE A SHARP & WINGED DEATH		109	TIRIEL 8		2
. . . WHOSE TEETH THE GATES OF ETERNAL DEATH]		109	TIRIEL 8		17
HE CEAST OUTSTRETCHD AT HAR & HEVA'S FEET IN AWFUL DEATH		110	TIRIEL 8		42
AND GENTLE SLEEP THE SLEEP OF DEATH AND GENTLE HEAR THE VOICE		127	BOOK OF THEL 1		13
OR DID SHE ONLY LIVE TO BE AT DEATH THE FOOD OF WORMS . .		129	BOOK OF THEL 3		23
("THAT MEN LIVE AFTER DEATH") IT WAS NOT KNOWN & YET ALL KNOW		132D	ANNO SWED PROV		MARG
OF THE RULER WITHER AMONG BONES OF DEATH		140	FRENCH REVOLTN		145
SAT ROUND HIS BROWS FADED IN FAINT DEATH		147	FRENCH REVOLTN		296
THE VALE OF DEATH		148	MARRIAGE HH 2		5
OR SATAN AND HIS CHILDREN ARE CALLD SIN & DEATH . . .		150A	MARRIAGE HH 5		PROSE
KNOW THAT AFTER CHRIST'S DEATH HE BECAME JEHOVAH . . .		150B	MARRIAGE HH 5		PROSE
GIVING HIMSELF FOR THE NATIONS HE DANCD THE DANCE OF ETERNAL DEATH		160	ALBION ROSE		2
THE SWORD HE SUNG A SONG OF DEATH		178	SWORD SUNG/N		3
THEY CLOTHED ME IN THE CLOTHES OF DEATH		180	CHIMNEY SWP/N		7
[OF THOUGHT IS DEATH]		183	THE FLY/N		28
OF THOUGHT IS DEATH		183	THE FLY/N		32
LOVE TO CURL ROUND THE BONES OF DEATH AND ASK THE RAVNOUS SNAKE		191	V DAU ALBION 3		11
AND THOU ART FALLN TO GIVE ME LIFE IN REGIONS OF DARK DEATH		196	AMERICA PREL 2		9
THIS IS ETERNAL DEATH AND THIS THE TORMENT LONG FORETOLD		196	AMERICA PREL 2		17
THE BONES OF DEATH THE COVRING CLAY THE SINEWS SHRUNK & DRYD		198	AMERICA 6		3
AND EYES OF DEATH THE HARLOT WOMB OFT OPENED IN VAIN . .		199	AMERICA 9		18
THEY CLOTHED ME IN THE CLOTHES OF DEATH		212	CHIMNEY SWP/SE		7
OF THOUGHT IS DEATH		213	THE FLY/SE		16
BUT MERCY CHANGD DEATH INTO SLEEP		220	TO TIRZAH/SE		7
THE DEATH OF JESUS SET ME FREE		220	TO TIRZAH/SE		15
DEATH WAS NOT BUT ETERNAL LIFE SPRUNG		223	URIZEN 3		39
IN DESPAIR AND THE SHADOWS OF DEATH		225	URIZEN 5		27
THE ETERNALS SAID WHAT IS THIS DEATH		226	URIZEN 6		11
AT THE FORMLESS UNMEASURABLE DEATH		226	URIZEN 7		9
FOR HE SAW THAT LIFE LIVD UPON DEATH		235	URIZEN 23		27
IN FORESTS OF ETERNAL DEATH SHRIEKING IN HOLLOW TREES .		238	EUROPE PREL 2		6
AND LEAVE ME VOID AS DEATH		238	EUROPE PREL 2		11
OVER DENS & THRO VALLEYS OF DEATH		254	AHANIA 4		61
DEATH & HELL TEAM WITH LIFE		261D	SMALL BK DSGNS		TITLE
THE FOUR ZOAS VALA OR THE DEATH AND JUDGEMENT . . .		263A	FOUR ZOAS		TITLE
THE DEATH AND JUDGEMENT OF ALBION THE ANCIENT MAN . . .		263C	FOUR ZOAS		TITLE
HIS FALL INTO THE GENERATION OF DECAY & DEATH & HIS . .		264	FOUR ZOAS 1		22
THE MEN HAVE RECIEVED THEIR DEATH WOUNDS & THEIR EMANATIONS ARE FLED		265	FOUR ZOAS 1	*	33
BUT DEATH DESPAIR & EVERLASTING BROODING MELANCHOLY . . .		265	FOUR ZOAS 1		51
CREATING SPACES LEST THEY FALL INTO ETERNAL DEATH . . .		267	FOUR ZOAS 1		100
IS ETERNAL DEATH WHAT SHALL WE DO O GOD [HELP] PITY & HELP		267	FOUR ZOAS 1		107
. . . TO THE PLACE [OF DEATH & HELL] WHENCE I EMERGD . .		268	FOUR ZOAS 1		157
HEAR I WILL SING A SONG OF DEATH IT IS A SONG OF VALA .		271	FOUR ZOAS 1		260
AND WILT THOU SLAY WITH DEATH HIM WHO DEVOTES HIMSELF TO THEE		271	FOUR ZOAS 1		275
I DIE NOT ENITHARMON [THOU] THO THOU SINGST THY SONG OF DEATH		272	FOUR ZOAS 1	*	283
ETERNITY GROAND & WAS TROUBLED AT THE IMAGE OF ETERNAL DEATH		273	FOUR ZOAS 1		315
ETERNITY GROAND & WAS TROUBLED AT THE IMAGE OF ETERNAL DEATH		277	FOUR ZOAS 1	*	462
. . . THUS RECOUNTING THE WARS OF DEATH ETERNAL . . .		277	FOUR ZOAS 1		483
URIZEN CAST DEEP DARKNESS ROUND HIM SILENT BROODING DEATH		278	FOUR ZOAS 1		515
ETERNAL DEATH TO LUVAH RAGING LUVAH POURD		278	FOUR ZOAS 1		516
IN EDEN THAT ONE DIED A DEATH NEVER TO BE REVIVD . . .		278	FOUR ZOAS 1		529
DOWNWARDS & OUTWARDS [TENDING] CONSUMING IN THE WARS OF ETERNAL DEATH		280	FOUR ZOAS 1	*	574
RISING UPON HIS COUCH OF DEATH ALBION BEHELD HIS SONS .		280	FOUR ZOAS 2		1
FOR I AM WEARY & MUST SLEEP IN THE DARK SLEEP OF DEATH .		280	FOUR ZOAS 2		6
FIRST HE BEHELD THE BODY OF MAN PALE COLD THE HORRORS OF DEATH		280	FOUR ZOAS 2		11
NO MORE EXULTING FOR HE SAW ETERNAL DEATH BENEATH . . .		280	FOUR ZOAS 2		14
SHE FELL COLD FROM LAMBETH'S VALES IN GROANS & DEWY DEATH		281	FOUR ZOAS 2		46
OF DEATH ETERNAL THAT WE ALL GO TO ETERNAL DEATH . . .		282	FOUR ZOAS 2		101
BENEATH THE FURNACES A WOFUL HEAP IN LIVING DEATH . . .		283	FOUR ZOAS 2		116
PERMITTED ALL LEST MAN SHOULD FALL INTO ETERNAL DEATH . .		287	FOUR ZOAS 2		262

454

```
                                                            PAGE    TITLE          LINE
DEATH    (CONTINUED)
     HOWL THOU OVER THE BODY OF DEATH TIS THINE BUT IF AMONG   288 FOUR ZOAS 2       312
        THE VIRGINS
     IN LOS'S ARMS HOWLINGS BEGAN OVER THE BODY OF DEATH  .  . 289 FOUR ZOAS 2       335
     THE JOY OF WOMAN IS THE DEATH OF HER MOST BEST BELOVED  . 289 FOUR ZOAS 2       349
     AND WAKE THE BUBBLING SPRINGS OF LIFE IN REGIONS OF DARK  289 FOUR ZOAS 2       373
        DEATH
     MY SUN A PESTILENCE BURNING AT NOON & A VAPOUR OF DEATH   290 FOUR ZOAS 2       396
        IN NIGHT
     AND LUVAH IN THE LOINS OF LOS A DARK & FURIOUS DEATH   .  . 292 FOUR ZOAS 3      22
     LIKE A DARK LAMP ETERNAL DEATH HAUNTS ALL MY EXPECTATION  293 FOUR ZOAS 3       75
     SAYING GO & DIE THE DEATH OF MAN FOR VALA THE SWEET       294 FOUR ZOAS 3       85
        WANDERER
     THE PASSIVE IDLE SLEEP THE ENORMOUS NIGHT & DARKNESS OF   295 FOUR ZOAS 3       115
        DEATH
     REFLECTING ALL MY INDOLENCE MY WEAKNESS & MY DEATH   .  . . 295 FOUR ZOAS 3     126
     LOUD STRONG A UNIVERSAL GROAN OF DEATH LOUDER . . . . . . 195 FOUR ZOAS 3       150
     ARE THOSE WHO LOVE LIKE THOSE WHO DIED RISEN AGAIN FROM   298 FOUR ZOAS 4        19
        DEATH
     IS IT NOT POSSIBLE THAT ONE RISEN AGAIN FROM DEATH   .  . 298 FOUR ZOAS 4        21
     A UNIVERSE OF DEATH & DECAY LET ENITHARMON'S HANDS   .  . . 298 FOUR ZOAS 4      28
     AGAINST ME WHO THEE GUARDED IN THE NIGHT OF DEATH FROM HARM 300 FOUR ZOAS 4     110
     FROM DEATH IN WRATH & FURY BUT NOW COME BEAR BACK  .  . . 300 FOUR ZOAS 4       116
     LEST HE SHOULD RISE AGAIN FROM DEATH IN ALL HIS [DISMAL]  300 FOUR ZOAS 4    *  121
        DREARY POWER
     AND LUVAH HIDDEN IN THE ELEMENTAL FORMS OF LIFE & DEATH   301 FOUR ZOAS 4       130
     AND I WHAT CAN I NOW BEHOLD BUT AN ETERNAL DEATH  .  .  . . 301 FOUR ZOAS 4     143
     DEATH CHOOSE OR LIFE THOU STRUGGLEST IN MY WATERS         301 FOUR ZOAS 4       152
        NOW CHOOSE LIFE
     A HORRIBLE CHAOS TO HIS EYES A FORMLESS UNMEASURABLE DEATH 301 FOUR ZOAS 4      162
     AND LIVE BEHOLD ETERNAL DEATH IS IN BEULAH BEHOLD    .  . . 304 FOUR ZOAS 4     258
     IN MONSTROUS FORMS OF DEATH A HUMAN POLYPUS OF DEATH  .  . 304 FOUR ZOAS 4      268
     THE SAVIOUR MILD & GENTLE BENT OVER THE CORSE OF DEATH  . 304 FOUR ZOAS 4       269
     WAS PUT TO ETERNAL DEATH LOS FELT THE LIMIT & SAW    .  . . 304 FOUR ZOAS 4     276
     [ THE XXX ETERNAL DEATH]  . . . . . . . . . . . . SUPP FOUR ZOAS 4    *
     SHADOWS OF ETERNAL DEATH SIT IN THE LEADEN AIR  .  .  .  . 305 FOUR ZOAS 5       22
     CRYING LUVAH KING OF LOVE THOU ART THE KING OF RAGE &     306 FOUR ZOAS 5        42
        DEATH
     FOR NOW HE FEARD ETERNAL DEATH & UTTERMOST EXTINCTION  .  . 307 FOUR ZOAS 5      75
     IN HIS YOUNG EYES DISCERNING PLAIN THAT ORC PLOTTED HIS   307 FOUR ZOAS 5        82
        DEATH
     EVEN IF HIS OWN DEATH RESULTED SO MUCH PITY HIM PAIND  .  . 309 FOUR ZOAS 5     154
     TO MELT THE CHAIN OF JEALOUSY NOT ENITHARMON'S DEATH   .  . 309 FOUR ZOAS 5     161
     ART THOU LIKE ME RISEN AGAIN FROM DEATH OR ART THOU       313 FOUR ZOAS 6        56
        DEATHLESS
     IF THOU ART HE MY DESPERATE PURPOSE HEAR & GIVE ME DEATH  313 FOUR ZOAS 6        57
     FOR DEATH TO ME IS BETTER FAR THAN LIFE DEATH MY DESIRE   313 FOUR ZOAS 6        58
     LIGHTING HIS DISMAL JOURNEY THRO THE PATHLESS WORLD OF    314 FOUR ZOAS 6        84
        DEATH
     AS THE SEED FALLS FROM THE SOWER'S HAND SO URIZEN FELL    316 FOUR ZOAS 6       160
        & DEATH
     ONWARD THO FALLING THRO THE WASTE OF NIGHT & ENDING IN    316 FOUR ZOAS 6       165
        DEATH
     . . . FOR WRAPD IN HIS DEATH CLOTHES . . . . . . . . . 316 FOUR ZOAS 6          169
     HE HID THEM WHEN HE SLEPT IN DEATH WHEN HE REVIVD         316 FOUR ZOAS 6       170
        THE CLOTHES
     I LOSE MY POWERS WEAKEND EVERY REVOLUTION TILL A DEATH  .  . 317 FOUR ZOAS 6    221
     LEST DEATH ETERNAL SHOULD BE THE RESULT . . . . . . . . 319 FOUR ZOAS 6         283
     ON CLOUDS OF DEATH & SANG THEIR SONGS KNEADING THE BREAD  322 FOUR ZOAS 7        98
        OF ORC
     LOS SAW HER STRETCHD THE IMAGE OF DEATH UPON HIS WITHERD  324 FOUR ZOAS 7       172
        VALLEYS
     THE CAUSE OF HER DIRE ANGUISH FOR SHE LAY THE IMAGE OF    328 FOUR ZOAS 7       320
        DEATH
     THAT WITHOUT A RANSOM I COULD NOT BE SAVD FROM ETERNAL    329 FOUR ZOAS 7       389
        DEATH
     THAT LIFE LIVES UPON DEATH & BY DEVOURING APPETITE   .  . . 330 FOUR ZOAS 7     390
     AND MUST HAVE GIVEN HIMSELF TO DEATH ETERNAL BUT  .  .  . . 330 FOUR ZOAS 7     396
     FOR WITHOUT A CREATED BODY THE SPECTRE IS ETERNAL DEATH   330 FOUR ZOAS 7       410
     WILL GIVE US TO ETERNAL DEATH FIT PUNISHMENT FOR SUCH  .  . 330 FOUR ZOAS 7     426
     THEY RATHER CHOSE TO MEET ETERNAL DEATH THAN TO DESTROY   332 FOUR ZOAS 7       484
     THRO CAVES OF DEATH INTO EXISTENCE THE BEECH LONG LIMBD   335 FOUR ZOAS 7B   *  100
        ADVANCD
     OF DEATH O NORTHERN DRUM AWAKE O HAND OF IRON SOUND    .  . 336 FOUR ZOAS 7B    154
     OF LIFE UPON THE PLAINS OF DEATH & VALLEYS OF DESPAIR  .  . 337 FOUR ZOAS 7B    161
     THEY VOTE THE DEATH OF LUVAH & THEY NAILD HIM TO THE TREE 337 FOUR ZOAS 7B      166
     TO DIE A DEATH OF SIX THOUSAND YEARS BOUND ROUND         337 FOUR ZOAS 7B       168
        WITH DESOLATION
     AND ALL THE ARTS OF LIFE THEY CHANGD INTO THE ARTS OF    337 FOUR ZOAS 7B       174
        DEATH
     AND SHE IS GONE & HERE ALONE I WAR WITH DARKNESS & DEATH  339 FOUR ZOAS 7B      239
     NOT SEEN TO HER LIKE WATERS OR LIKE THIS DARK WORLD OF    340 FOUR ZOAS 7B      273
        DEATH
     WOO'D & SUBDUD INTO ?ETERNAL DEATH THE DEMON ?LAY    .  . . 340 FOUR ZOAS 7B    286
     THE HORRID SIGHT OF DEATH & TORMENT BUT THE ETERNAL PROMISE 340 FOUR ZOAS 7B    291
     TO WAKE UPON THE COUCH OF DEATH HE SNEEZED SEVEN TIMES  .  . 341 FOUR ZOAS 8     17
     ALL BEULAH STOOD ASTONISHD LOOKING DOWN TO ETERNAL DEATH  342 FOUR ZOAS 8        47
     THEY SAW THE SAVIOUR BEYOND THE PIT OF DEATH & DESTRUCTION 342 FOUR ZOAS 8       48
     SURROUNDING THEM ON ALL SIDES BEYOND SIN & DEATH & HELL   342 FOUR ZOAS 8        51
     THE BATTLE HOWLS THE TERRORS FIRD RAGE IN THE WORK OF DEATH 343 FOUR ZOAS 8     107
     THAT ONLY THRO THE GATES OF DEATH THEY CAN ENTER         344 FOUR ZOAS 8        110
        TO ENITHARMON
```

455

	PAGE	TITLE		LINE
DEATH (CONTINUED)				
IS AUGHT BUT DEATH IN INDIVIDUAL WEAKNESS SORROW & PAIN	346	FOUR ZOAS 8		199
OF DARK DEATH & DESPAIR	347	FOUR ZOAS 8		231
WHERE DEATH IS PUT OFF ETERNALLY	347	FOUR ZOAS 8		240
ABHORRD ACCURSED EVER DYING AN ETERNAL DEATH	347	FOUR ZOAS 8	*	256
TO JUDGE THE LAMB OF GOD TO DEATH AS A MURDERER & ROBBER	348	FOUR ZOAS 8		273
FROM DEATH ETERNAL & TO PUT OFF SATAN ETERNALLY	348	FOUR ZOAS 8		286
THUS WAS THE LAMB OF GOD CONDEMND TO DEATH	349	FOUR ZOAS 8		325
SAYING IS THIS ETERNAL DEATH WHERE SHALL I HIDE FROM DEATH	349	FOUR ZOAS 8		332
A SEPULCHER & WORSHIP DEATH IN FEAR WHILE YET WE LIVE . .	349	FOUR ZOAS 8		334
DEATH GOD OF ALL FROM WHOM WE RISE TO WHOM WE ALL RETURN	349	FOUR ZOAS 8		335
JERUSALEM PITYING THEM WOVE THEM MANTLES OF LIFE & DEATH	351	FOUR ZOAS 8		397
[HE] FELT THE FEMALE DEATH A DULL & NUMMING STUPOR SUCH AS NEER	352	FOUR ZOAS 8		416
DRINK IN THE DEADLY DULL DELUSION HORRORS OF ETERNAL DEATH	352	FOUR ZOAS 8		418
THUS IN A LIVING DEATH THE NAMELESS SHADOW ALL THINGS BOUND	353	FOUR ZOAS 8		481
LISTEN TO HER WHOSE EYES BEHOLD THE DARK BODY OF CORRUPTIBLE DEATH	354	FOUR ZOAS 8		505
UPON THE OOZY ROCK INWRAPPED WITH THE WEEDS OF DEATH . .	354	FOUR ZOAS 8		514
O HOW THE HORRORS OF ETERNAL DEATH TAKE HOLD ON MAN . . .	354	FOUR ZOAS 8		519
FEAST ON HIS DEATH TILL UNIVERSAL DEATH DEVOURS ALL . . .	354	FOUR ZOAS 8		528
THE SPECTRE QUITE AWAY FROM ENION THAT I DIE A DEATH . . .	355	FOUR ZOAS 8		546
AND IN THE CRIES OF BIRTH & IN THE GROANS OF DEATH HIS VOICE	356	FOUR ZOAS 8		580
FOR SUCH THEY DEEMD THE DEATH OF THE BODY LOS HIS VEGETABLE HANDS	357	FOUR ZOAS 9		6
ENWRAPPED ROUND WITH WEEDS OF DEATH PALE COLD IN SORROW & WOE	359	FOUR ZOAS 9		96
TO INDOLENCE TO THE NIGHT OF DEATH WHEN INDOLENCE & MOURNING	360	FOUR ZOAS 9		117
ARISE O STONY FORM OF DEATH O DRAGON OF THE DEEPS . . .	360	FOUR ZOAS 9		138
SHALL REFLOURISH THEN BRIGHT AHANIA SHALL AWAKE FROM DEATH	362	FOUR ZOAS 9		210
BY A NEW SPIRITUAL BIRTH REGENERATED FROM DEATH	363	FOUR ZOAS 9		224
FROM THE [BLACK] DARK JAWS OF DEATH BENEATH & DESOLATE SHORES REMOTE	363	FOUR ZOAS 9		259
THE PRISONER ANSWERS YOU SCOURGD MY FATHER TO DEATH BEFORE MY FACE	364	FOUR ZOAS 9		275
IN DENS OF DEATH TO FORGE THE SPADE THE MATTOCK & THE AX	365	FOUR ZOAS 9		306
RISE FROM THE DEWS OF DEATH FOR THE ETERNAL MAN IS RISEN	367	FOUR ZOAS 9		389
O ENION MY WEARY HEAD IS IN THE BED OF DEATH	370	FOUR ZOAS 9		487
FOR WEEDS OF DEATH HAVE WRAPD AROUND MY LIMBES IN THE HOARY DEEPS	370	FOUR ZOAS 9		488
O DREAMS OF DEATH THE HUMAN FORM DISSOLVING COMPANIED . .	373	FOUR ZOAS 9		595
HOW LOVELY THE DELIGHTS OF THOSE RISEN AGAIN FROM DEATH	376	FOUR ZOAS 9		729
. . . THAN PAINS OF ETERNAL [DEATH] BIRTH	377	FOUR ZOAS 9		739
ETERNAL DEATH WHO CAN ENDURE LET US CONSUME IN FIRES . .	377	FOUR ZOAS 9		740
. . . ARE BETTER THAN THE PANGS OF ETERNAL DEATH	377	FOUR ZOAS 9		742
IN PITS & DENS & SHADES OF DEATH IN SHAPES OF TORMENT & WOE	377	FOUR ZOAS 9		751
THE SEA THAT ROLLD & FOAMD WITH DARKNESS & THE SHADOWS OF DEATH	378	FOUR ZOAS 9		802
FROM ENION POURS THE SEED OF LIFE & DEATH IN ALL HER LIMBS	381	FOUR ZOAS AD 4		1
TO JUDGE THE LAMB OF GOD TO DEATH AS A MURDERER & ROBBER	382	FOUR ZOAS AD 6		6
OVER THEIR VICTIMS THUS WAS THE LAMB OF GOD CONDEMND TO DEATH	382	FOUR ZOAS AD 6		13
& THE AFFAIRS OF LIFE & DEATH TRIFLES SPORTS OF TIME . .	383C	ANNO WATSON		MARG
DOST THOU O PRIEST WISH THY BROTHER'S DEATH	384D	ANNO WATSON		MARG
AND SUBMISSION TO DEATH BENEATH HIS FEET	420	I SAW A MONK/N		54
WRITES REVENGE IN REALMS OF DEATH	432	AUGURIES		74
SHALL BE MOCKD IN AGE & DEATH	433	AUGURIES		86
TRIUMPHS OVER HELL & DEATH	433	AUGURIES		90
SATAN NOW AWAKES SIN DEATH & HELL TO CELEBRATE WITH HIM	441D	INSC FALL MAN		PROSE
THE DOOR OF DEATH IS MADE OF GOLD	442	DEDICATN BLAIR		1
& BEFORE THE BOOK OF DEATH WHICH IS OPEND ON CLOUDS . . .	443C	LAST JUDGMNT/L		PROSE
FOR DEATH ETERNAL IN THE HEAVENS OF ALBION & BEFORE THE GATES	481	MILTON 2		14
THY WORK IS ETERNAL DEATH WITH MILLS & OVENS & CAULDRONS	483	MILTON 4		17
HIS FUTURE COURSE THRO DARKNESS AND DESPAIR TO ETERNAL DEATH	487	MILTON 7		26
PITYING HIS YOUTH AND BEAUTY TREMBLING AT ETERNAL DEATH	488	MILTON 8		31
DEATH COUCH IN THE CAVERNS OF DEATH IN THE CORNER OF THE ATLANTIC	489	MILTON 9		3
HE SUNK DOWN A DREADFUL DEATH UNLIKE THE SLUMBERS OF BEULAH	490	MILTON 9		48
SAYING IF THE GUILTY SHOULD BE CONDEMND HE MUST BE AN ETERNAL DEATH	491	MILTON 11		17
THE HORSES OF PALAMABRON CALLD FOR REST AND PLEASANT DEATH	492	MILTON 12		9
SICK COUCH BEARS THE DARK SHADES OF ETERNAL DEATH INFOLDING	493	MILTON 13		1
FOR THEN THE BODY OF DEATH WAS PERFECTED IN HYPOCRITIC HOLINESS	494	MILTON 13		25
OUR VIRTUES & CRUEL GOODNESSES HAVE DESERVD ETERNAL DEATH	494	MILTON 13		34
IN DREAMS SHE BORE THE SHADOWY SPECTRE OF SLEEP & NAMD HIM DEATH	494	MILTON 13		40
AND IN HIS LINEAMENTS DIVINE THE SHADES OF DEATH & ULRO	495	MILTON 14	*	12
AND MILTON SAID I GO TO ETERNAL DEATH THE NATIONS STILL	495	MILTON 14		14
TARRY NO LONGER FOR MY SOUL LIES AT THE GATES OF DEATH . .	495	MILTON 14		19
I WILL GO DOWN TO SELF ANNIHILATION AND ETERNAL DEATH . .	495	MILTON 14		22
TO CLAIM THE HELLS MY FURNACES I GO TO ETERNAL DEATH . .	496	MILTON 14		32
AND MILTON SAID I GO TO ETERNAL DEATH ETERNITY SHUDDERD	496	MILTON 14		33
A MOURNFUL SHADE ETERNITY SHUDDERD AT THE IMAGE OF ETERNAL DEATH	496	MILTON 14		35
OF DEATH FOR WHEN HE ENTERD INTO HIS SHADOW HIMSELF . . .	496	MILTON 15		10
IN SOLEMN DEATH THE SEA OF TIME & SPACE THUNDERD ALOUD . .	497	MILTON 15		39
AGAINST THE ROCK WHICH WAS INWRAPPED WITH THE WEEDS OF DEATH	497	MILTON 15		40

```
                                                         PAGE    TITLE        LINE
DEATH    (CONTINUED)
    TO THE BOSOM OF DEATH WHAT WAS UNDERNEATH SOON SEEMD ABOVE    497 MILTON 15      42
    AND THE PRECIOUS STONES OF ANXIETY & CARE & DESPERATION       499 MILTON 18      23
      & DEATH
    THE ENORMOUS STRIFE ONE GIVING LIFE THE OTHER GIVING DEATH    501 MILTON 19      29
    DRUNK WITH THE SPIRIT BURNING ROUND THE COUCH OF DEATH        502 MILTON 20      44
      THEY STOOD
    SAYING MILTON GOES TO ETERNAL DEATH SO SAYING THEY GROAND     504 MILTON 21      43
      IN SPIRIT
    OURSELVES TO DEATH IN ULRO AMONG THE TRANSGRESSORS   . . .    504 MILTON 21      46
    BUT YOU CANNOT RENEW MILTON HE GOES TO ETERNAL DEATH   . .    504 MILTON 21      57
    BECOMING OBEDIENT TO DEATH EVEN THE DEATH OF THE CROSS        506 MILTON 22      58
    THEIR LIFE'S WHOLE COMFORT TO INTIRE SCORN & INJURY & DEATH   506 MILTON 23       2
    I HAVE EMBRACD THE FALLING DEATH HE IS BECOME ONE WITH ME     507 MILTON 23      33
    WITH POWERS FITTED TO CIRCUMSCRIBE THIS DARK SATANIC DEATH    507 MILTON 23      51
    ARISE O SONS GIVE ALL YOUR STRENGTH AGAINST ETERNAL DEATH     509 MILTON 24      34
    LEST WE ARE VEGETATED FOR CATHEDRON'S LOOMS WEAVE ONLY        509 MILTON 24      35
      DEATH
    A WEB OF DEATH & WERE IT NOT FOR BOWLAHOOLA & ALLAMANDA       509 MILTON 24      36
    LOUD SPORT THE DANCERS IN THE DANCE OF DEATH REJOICING        509 MILTON 24      62
      IN CARNAGE
    THAT WE MAY PREACH RIGHTEOUSNESS & PUNISH THE SINNER WITH     510 MILTON 25      14
      DEATH
    SINCE ALBION'S DEATH & SATAN'S CUTTING-OFF FROM OUR AWFUL     510 MILTON 25      30
      FIELDS
    BUT THE ELECT MUST BE SAVED (FROM ) FIRES OF ETERNAL DEATH    511 MILTON 25      38
    ENDING IN DEATH WHICH WOULD OF ITSELF BE ETERNAL DEATH  . .   513 MILTON 26      42
    IN PITS & DENS & SHADES OF DEATH IN SHAPES OF TORMENT & WOE   514 MILTON 27      33
    HERE THE SONS OF LOS LABOUR AGAINST DEATH ETERNAL THROUGH     514 MILTON 27      44
      ALL
    THE LITTLE WEEPING SPECTRE STANDS ON THE THRESHOLD OF DEATH   515 MILTON 28      10
    TO DEATH IN OLD TIME BY SATAN THE FATHER OF SIN & DEATH       517 MILTON 29      33
    DEATH TO DELUDE WHO ALL IN TERROR AT THEIR SPLENDOR LEAVES    517 MILTON 29      43
    THE SOULS CLEAR FROM THE ROCK OF DEATH THAT DEATH HIMSELF     517 MILTON 29      45
      MAY WAKE
    WEAVE THE BLACK WOOF OF DEATH UPON ENTUTHON BENYTHON    . .   517 MILTON 29      56
    AND MILTON OFT SAT UP ON THE COUCH OF DEATH & OFT CONVERSED   521 MILTON 32  *   1
    THEN HILLEL WHO IS LUCIFER REPLIED OVER THE COUCH OF DEATH    521 MILTON 32       8
    YOU CANNOT GO TO ETERNAL DEATH IN THAT WHICH CAN NEVER DIE    521 MILTON 32      24
    DARE TO ENTER & THEY SHALL ENTER TRIUMPHANT OVER DEATH        522 MILTON 32      28
    THUS THEY CONVERSE WITH THE DEAD WATCHING ROUND THE COUCH     522 MILTON 32      39
      OF DEATH
    THEREFORE I SHEW MY JEALOUSY & SET BEFORE YOU DEATH  . . .    522 MILTON 33      10
    FROM DEATH ETERNAL SUCH YOUR LOT TO BE CONTINUALLY REDEEMD    522 MILTON 33      12
    BY DEATH & MISERY OF THOSE YOU LOVE & BY ANNIHILATION   . .   522 MILTON 33      13
    SHE SHALL RELENT IN FEAR OF DEATH SHE SHALL BEGIN TO GIVE     522 MILTON 33      17
    A SELF-DEVOURING MONSTROUS HUMAN DEATH TWENTY SEVEN FOLD      524 MILTON 34      26
    THEY STOOD IN A DARK LAND OF DEATH OF FIERY CORRODING         524 MILTON 34      44
      WATERS
    WHERE LIE IN EVIL DEATH THE FOUR IMMORTALS PALE AND COLD      524 MILTON 34      45
    HERE FIXD INTO A FROZEN BULK SUBJECT TO DECAY & DEATH   . .   525 MILTON 34      54
    ARE BECOME FOUNTAINS OF BITTER DEATH & OF CORRODING HELL      525 MILTON 35       3
    O DREADFUL LOOM OF DEATH O PITEOUS FEMALE FORMS COMPELLD      525 MILTON 35       7
    TO WEAVE THE WOOF OF DEATH ON CAMBERWELL TIRZAH'S COURTS      525 MILTON 35       8
    OF DEATH ACROSS THE ATLANTIC TO AMERICA NORTH & SOUTH   . .   525 MILTON 35      17
    AND HIS FOUR ZOAS TERRIFIED & ON THE VERGE OF DEATH   . . .   525 MILTON 35      28
    LUVAH SLEPT HERE IN DEATH & HERE IS LUVAH'S EMPTY TOMB  . .   526 MILTON 35      59
    IS TO IMPRESS ON MEN THE FEAR OF DEATH TO TEACH   . . . .     530 MILTON 38      38
    MINE IS TO TEACH MEN TO DESPISE DEATH & TO GO ON  . . . .     530 MILTON 38      40
    LEST HE SHOULD FALL APART IN HIS ETERNAL DEATH TO IMITATE     531 MILTON 39      26
    BENEATH SAT CHAOS SIN ON HIS RIGHT HAND DEATH ON HIS LEFT     531 MILTON 39      29
    O IMMORTAL HOW WERE WE LED TO WAR THE WARS OF DEATH  . . .    534 MILTON 41      36
    THOU GOEST TO ETERNAL DEATH & ALL MUST GO WITH THEE   . . .   534 MILTON 42       2
    ALBION'S BOSOM THE BOSOM OF DEATH & THE FOUR SURROUNDED       534 MILTON 42      21
      HIM
    CALLD DEATH A MADMAN [DEADLY THE AFFRONT] TREMBLING FOR THE   537 AND HIS LEGS/N  17
      AFFRONT
    CLAPD DEATH INTO THE CORNER OF THEIR JAW   . . . . .          537 AND HIS LEGS/N  21
    HORSEBACK WITH DEATH OVER THE FIELDS OF CORN   . . . . .      537 AND HIS LEGS/N  23
    BOTH WENT TO LAW WITH DEATH TO KEEP OUR EARS ON   . . . .     537 AND HIS LEGS/N  27
    FOR HOW TO STARVE DEATH WE HAD LAID A PLOT   . . . . . .      537 AND HIS LEGS/N  28
    AGAINST HIS PRICE BUT DEATH WAS IN THE POT   . . . . . .      537 AND HIS LEGS/N  29
    OR COULD FROM DEATH ASSASSINETTI WAKE    . . . . . . .        537 AND HIS LEGS/N  33
    TWAS NOT A MOUSE TWAS DEATH IN A DISGUISE    . . . . .        537 AND HIS LEGS/N  40
    AND DEATH SITS [MOCKING] LAUGHING ON THEIR MONUMENTS    . .   537 AND HIS LEGS/N  42
    OR POOR SCHIAVONETTI WHOM THEY TO DEATH BOTHERD   . . . .     538 WAS I ANGRY/N   5
    SEND BATTLE MURDER SUDDEN DEATH [WE] O PRAY    . . . . .      550 WHEN I SEE/N    6
    OF HIS DEATH OR SLEEP AND PROMISE TO RETURN AGAIN  . . . .  577D DESC CAT 5     PROSE
    ABOVE THE SHADOWS OF GENERATION AND DEATH    . . . . . .  . 578C DESC CAT 5     PROSE
    SINGING TO HIS HARP IN THE PAINS OF DEATH    . . . . . .  . 580D DESC CAT 5     PROSE
    CONTINUE TO GOVERN MANKIND AFTER DEATH   . . . . . . .  . . 581D DESC CAT 8     PROSE
    AFTER THE DEATH OF THE VEGETATED BODY    . . . . . . . .  . 605D V LAST JUDG/N  PROSE
    DEATH IS CHAIND TO THE CROSS & TIME FALLS TOGETHER WITH     606C V LAST JUDG/N  PROSE
      DEATH
    SIN & DEATH ARE TO BE CLOSED ETERNALLY BY   . . . . .  . . 608B V LAST JUDG/N *PROSE
    THE ETERNAL CONSUMMATION OF VEGETABLE LIFE & DEATH  . . . . 609A V LAST JUDG/N  PROSE
    ARE OPEND THE BOOKS OF REMEMBRANCE OF LIFE & OF DEATH   . . 612B V LAST JUDG/N  PROSE
    IN HUMILIATION BEFORE THAT OF DEATH ON THE LEFT  . . . .  . 612B V LAST JUDG/N  PROSE
    WE ARE IN A WORLD OF GENERATION & DEATH & THIS WORLD   . .  613C V LAST JUDG/N  PROSE
    SPACE IS A WOMAN & HER MASCULINE PORTION IS DEATH   . . .   614D V LAST JUDG/N  PROSE
    THAT ORIGINATED WITH THE FALL & WAS CALLD DEATH    . . . .  616A V LAST JUDG/N  PROSE
    AS HE ENTERD THE DOOR OF DEATH FOR ALBION'S SAKE INSPIRED    620 JERUSALEM 1      9
```

		PAGE	TITLE	LINE
DEATH (CONTINUED)				
ETERNAL DEATH AND OF THE AWAKING TO ETERNAL LIFE . . .		622	JERUSALEM 4	2
A HORRIBLE SHADOW OF DEATH AMONG THE FURNACES BENEATH . .		625	JERUSALEM 7	4
I WILL BREAK THEE INTO SHIVERS & MELT THEE IN THE FURNACES OF DEATH		627	JERUSALEM 8	10
THESE HYPOCRITIC SELFHOODS ON THE ANVILS OF BITTER DEATH		627	JERUSALEM 8	16
AND HIS INFANT THOUGHTS & DESIRES INTO COLD DARK CLIFFS OF DEATH		628	JERUSALEM 9	2
I SAW DISEASE FORMING A BODY OF DEATH AROUND THE LAMB . .		628	JERUSALEM 9	9
INTO THE FURNACES & INTO THE VALLEYS OF THE ANVILS OF DEATH		629	JERUSALEM 10	1
OF FORMS OF DEATH AND THAT TOWARD BEULAH STONE		633	JERUSALEM 13	16
AROUND GOLGONOOZA LIES THE LAND OF DEATH ETERNAL A LAND		633	JERUSALEM 13	30
HIS EMANATION YET HIS WIFE TILL THE SLEEP OF DEATH IS PAST		635	JERUSALEM 14	14
OF DEATH FORMING AN AX OF GOLD THE FOUR SONS OF LOS . . .		636	JERUSALEM 15	22
AND AT THE PLACE OF DEATH WHEN ALBION SAT IN ETERNAL DEATH		636	JERUSALEM 15	33
ALBION GROANS IN THE DEEP SLUMBERS OF DEATH UPON HIS ROCK		637	JERUSALEM 16	27
THEIR LOOMS IN A GENERATION OF DEATH & RESURRECTION TO FORGETFULNESS		638	JERUSALEM 17	9
FACE IN TERRORS & PAINS OF HELL & ETERNAL DEATH THE . . .		639	JERUSALEM 17	54
ON THE GULPH OF DEATH IN SELF-RIGHTEOUSNESS THAT ROLLD . .		642	JERUSALEM 19	31
ALL IS ETERNAL DEATH UNLESS YOU CAN WEAVE A CHASTE .		643	JERUSALEM 21	11
SIX MONTHS THEY LIE EMBALMD IN SILENT DEATH WORSHIPPED . .		644	JERUSALEM 21	44
REVENGEFUL O THAT DEATH & ANNIHILATION WERE THE SAME . .		644	JERUSALEM 21	49
IN AN ETERNAL DEATH FOR ALBION'S SAKE OUR BEST BELOVED . .		646	JERUSALEM 23	10
LIKE ME THY VICTIM O THAT DEATH & ANNIHILATION WERE THE SAME		646	JERUSALEM 23	40
O WHAT IS LIFE & WHAT IS MAN O WHAT IS DEATH WHEREFORE		647	JERUSALEM 24	12
HER STREETS ARE PAVED WITH DESTRUCTION HER HOUSES BUILT WITH DEATH		647	JERUSALEM 24	33
IN WAR & HOWLING DEATH & WOE		650	FIELDS FROM/J	44
AND PASSING THRO THE GATES OF DEATH		651	FIELDS FROM/J	64
THE SLEEP OF DEATH TILL THE MAN OF SIN & REPENTANCE BE REVEALD		653	JERUSALEM 29	12
SAYING GO AND DIE THE DEATH OF MAN FOR VALA THE SWEET WANDERER		655	JERUSALEM 29	66
THE ROCKY LAW OF CONDEMNATION & DOUBLE GENERATION & DEATH		656	JERUSALEM 30	37
HIS WESTERN HEAVEN WITH ROCKY CLOUDS OF DEATH & DESPAIR		656	JERUSALEM 31	1
OF DESPAIR & DEATH TO SEARCH THE TEMPTERS OUT WALKING AMONG		656	JERUSALEM 31	5
THAT MAN MAY BE PURIFIED BY THE DEATH OF THY DELUSIONS . .		658	JERUSALEM 31	66
AT THY WORD & AT THY LOOK DEATH ENROBES ME ABOUT		660	JERUSALEM 34	5
FROM HEAD TO FEET A GARMENT OF DEATH & ETERNAL FEAR . . .		660	JERUSALEM 34	6
FROM GROT & CAVE BENEATH THE MOON DIM REGION OF DEATH .		660	JERUSALEM 34	11
OF DEATH IN ALBION'S CLOUDS DREADFUL UTTERD OVER ALL THE EARTH		661	JERUSALEM 34	24
IN PITY OF THE PUNISHER WHOSE STATE IS ETERNAL DEATH .		662	JERUSALEM 35	7
ALBION GOES TO ETERNAL DEATH IN ME ALL ETERNITY . . .		662	JERUSALEM 35	9
NO INDIVIDUAL CAN KEEP THESE LAWS FOR THEY ARE DEATH .		662	JERUSALEM 35	11
THEN THOSE IN GREAT ETERNITY WHO CONTEMPLATE ON DEATH .		663	JERUSALEM 36	50
TORMENTS DESPAIR ETERNAL DEATH BUT THE DIVINE MERCY . . .		663	JERUSALEM 36	54
AND A DEATH OF EIGHT THOUSAND YEARS FORGD BY THYSELF UPON		664	JERUSALEM 37	7
SO LOS SPOKE BUT WHEN HE SAW [PALE] BLUE DEATH IN ALBION'S FEET		664	JERUSALEM 37	10
MORTALITY BEGINS TO ROLL THE BILLOWS OF ETERNAL DEATH		666	JERUSALEM 39	8
I DIE I GO TO ETERNAL DEATH THE SHADES OF DEATH . . .		666	JERUSALEM 39	16
WILL NONE ACCOMPANY ME IN MY DEATH OR BE A RANSOM FOR ME		666	JERUSALEM 39	19
BOUND THESE BLACK SHOES OF DEATH & ON MY HANDS DEATH'S IRON GLOVES		666	JERUSALEM 39	21
THE FRIENDS OF ALBION TREMBLING AT THE SIGHT OF ETERNAL DEATH		666	JERUSALEM 40	3
AND EVERY RIVER OUR BROTHER ALBION IS SICK TO DEATH . . .		667	JERUSALEM 40	12
O HOW THE TORMENTS OF ETERNAL DEATH WAITED ON MAN . . .		667	JERUSALEM 40	25
THE SHUTTLES OF DEATH SING IN THE SKY TO ISLINGTON & PANCRASS		668	JERUSALEM 41	7
WHERE MILD JERUSALEM SOUGHT TO REPOSE IN DEATH & BE NO MORE		668	JERUSALEM 41	10
THEY KNEELD AROUND THE COUCH OF DEATH IN DEEP HUMILIATION		668	JERUSALEM 41	24
ALSO LOS SICK & TERRIFIED BEHELD THE FURNACES OF DEATH . .		669	JERUSALEM 42	5
TO ATONE FOR YOU FOR SPIRITUAL DEATH MAN LIVES BY DEATHS OF MEN		670	JERUSALEM 42	49
OF DEATH THEY CURB THEIR SPECTRES AS WITH IRON CURBS . .		671	JERUSALEM 42	67
ARE BECOME THE SOURCES OF DARK & BITTER DEATH & OF CORRODING HELL		672	JERUSALEM 43	32
THEY FIGHT & CONTEND FOR LIFE & NOT FOR ETERNAL DEATH . .		672	JERUSALEM 43	42
BUT DEATH ETERNAL DEATH REMAINS IN THE VALLEYS OF PEOR		673	JERUSALEM 43	45
I WILL NOT ENDURE THIS THING I ALONE WITHSTAND TO DEATH		673	JERUSALEM 43	71
SO LOS SPOKE PALE THEY STOOD AROUND THE HOUSE OF DEATH .		673	JERUSALEM 43	80
LOUD ROLL THE STARRY WHEELS OF ALBION INTO THE WORLD OF DEATH		674	JERUSALEM 44	7
CLIFF AFTER CLIFF & OVER VALLEYS OF DESPAIR & DEATH .		674	JERUSALEM 44	13
AND FEELING THE DAMPS OF DEATH THEY WITH ONE ACCORD DELEGATED LOS		674	JERUSALEM 44	28
THE SLUMBERS OF DEATH CAME OVER THEM AROUND THE COUCH OF DEATH		674	JERUSALEM 44	35
. . . FAINT AS THE VOICE OF THE DEAD IN THE HOUSE OF DEATH		675	JERUSALEM 44	44
ALBION'S WESTERN GATE IS CLOSD HIS DEATH IS COMING APACE		675	JERUSALEM 45	17
ASSIMILATED AND EMBRACD ETERNAL DEATH FOR ALBION'S SAKE		676	JERUSALEM 45	39
ETERNITY GROAND & WAS TROUBLED AT THE IMAGE OF ETERNAL DEATH		677	JERUSALEM 48	12
BECAUSE DEATH IS FOR A PERIOD AND THEY RENEW TENFOLD		677	JERUSALEM 48	17
ARE BECOME WEAK VISIONS OF TIME & SPACE FIXD INTO FURROWS OF DEATH		679	JERUSALEM 49	22
O POLYPUS OF DEATH O SPECTRE OVER EUROPE AND ASIA . . .		679	JERUSALEM 49	24

```
                                                        PAGE      TITLE           LINE
DEATH    (CONTINUED)
    SATAN IS THE STATE OF DEATH & NOT A HUMAN EXISTENCE   . . .   680 JERUSALEM 49      67
    A MURDEROUS PROVIDENCE A CREATION THAT GROANS LIVING ON       681 JERUSALEM 50       5
       DEATH
    LIVE BY DEVOURING GOING INTO ETERNAL DEATH CONTINUALLY  . .   681 JERUSALEM 50       7
    SHE WILL BECOME AN ETERNAL DEATH AN AVENGER OF SIN   . . .    681 JERUSALEM 50      15
    ASCENDING AND DESCENDING INTO ALBION'S SEA OF DEATH   . .     681 JERUSALEM 50      21
    OF DEATH THUNDER INCESSANT AROUND THE FLAMING COUCHES OF      684 JERUSALEM 53      21
    TO CREATE A WORLD OF GENERATION FROM THE WORLD OF DEATH       690 JERUSALEM 58      18
    THY VALLEYS PLAINS OF BURNING SAND THY RIVERS WATERS OF       693 JERUSALEM 60      26
       DEATH
    AND BY THESE VISIONS OF PITY & LOVE BECAUSE OF ALBION'S       693 JERUSALEM 60      64
       DEATH
    ONLY BELIEVE IN ME THAT I HAVE POWER TO RAISE FROM DEATH      694 JERUSALEM 60      68
    THESE ARE THE DAUGHTERS OF VALA MOTHER OF THE BODY OF DEATH   696 JERUSALEM 62      13
    ON DEATH ETERNAL IN FIERCE SHUDDERS UPON THE MOUNTAINS        696 JERUSALEM 62      40
       OF ALBION
    DANCE THE DANCE OF DEATH CONTENDING WITH JEHOVAH AMONG        697 JERUSALEM 63      10
       THE CHERUBIM
    THE SEXUAL DEATH LIVING ON ACCUSATION OF SIN & JUDGMENT       699 JERUSALEM 64      22
    WITHOUT FORGIVENESS OF SIN LOVE IS ITSELF ETERNAL DEATH       699 JERUSALEM 64      24
    THEY VOTE THE DEATH OF LUVAH  . . .  .  .  .  .  .  .  .  .   699 JERUSALEM 65       8
    TO DIE A DEATH OF SIX THOUSAND YEARS BOUND ROUND             699 JERUSALEM 65      10
       WITH VEGETATION
    AND ALL THE ARTS OF LIFE THEY CHANGD INTO THE ARTS OF DEATH   700 JERUSALEM 65      16
       IN ALBION
    A BUILDING OF ETERNAL DEATH WHOSE PROPORTIONS ARE ETERNAL     702 JERUSALEM 66       9
       DESPAIR
    THE INHABITANTS ARE SICK TO DEATH THEY LABOUR TO DIVIDE       703 JERUSALEM 66      68
       INTO DAYS
    A POLYPUS OF ROOTS OF REASONING DOUBT DESPAIR & DEATH  . .    707 JERUSALEM 69       3
    BECOMING A GENERATED MORTAL A VEGETATING DEATH   . .  . .     708 JERUSALEM 69      31
    AGAINST THE DIVINE VISION & FALL OVER THE PRECIPICE OF        711 JERUSALEM 71      59
       ETERNAL DEATH
    OF DEATH BUT HOW THEY CAME FORTH FROM THE FURNACES & HOW      713 JERUSALEM 73       7
       LONG
    THESE TO PRESERVE THEM FROM ETERNAL DEATH LOS CREATES  . .    714 JERUSALEM 73      40
    DISSIPATING THE ROCKY FORMS OF DEATH BY HIS THUNDEROUS        714 JERUSALEM 73      43
       HAMMER
    THIS I BEHOLD THE SHUDDERINGS OF DEATH ATTEND MY STEPS  . .   714 JERUSALEM 74      18
    BABYLON THE RATIONAL MORALITY DELUDING TO DEATH THE LITTLE    715 JERUSALEM 74      32
       ONES
    BUT JESUS BREAKING THRO THE CENTRAL ZONES OF DEATH & HELL     716 JERUSALEM 75      21
    TO AWAKE THE PRISONERS OF DEATH TO BRING ALBION AGAIN  . .    716 JERUSALEM 75      25
    IS CAIAPHAS THE DARK PREACHER OF DEATH  .  .  .  .  .  .  .   718 STOOD AMONG/J     18
    WHY WILT THOU SLEEP THE SLEEP OF DEATH  .  .  .  .  .  .  .   718 ENGLND AWAKE/J     3
    IN UNREVIVING DEATH MY LOVE MY LUVAH ORDERD ME IN NIGHT       722 JERUSALEM 80      17
     . . .  THAT ONE SHOULD DIE A DEATH NEVER TO BE REVIVD        722 JERUSALEM 80      24
    THAT LOVE MAY ONLY BE OBTAIND IN THE PASSAGES OF DEATH  . .   724 JERUSALEM 81       7
    TO JUDGE THE FRIEND OF SINNERS TO DEATH WITHOUT THE VEIL      725 JERUSALEM 82      33
    ETERNAL DEATH STANDS AT THE DOOR O GOD PITY OUR LABOURS       728 JERUSALEM 83      65
    THE REALMS OF DARK DEATH O PERVERSE TO THYSELF CONTRARIOUS    733 JERUSALEM 88      26
    IN THREE NIGHTS HE DEVOURD THE REJECTED CORSE OF DEATH  . .   734 JERUSALEM 89      13
    WHERE THE RED SEA TERMINATES THE WORLD OF GENERATION &        735 JERUSALEM 89      49
       DEATH
    APPROPRIATE INDIVIDUALITY THEY BECOME AN ETERNAL DEATH  . .   737 JERUSALEM 90      54
    FEAR NOT MY SONS THIS WAKING DEATH HE IS BECOME ONE WITH ME   741 JERUSALEM 93      18
    THE WEEDS OF DEATH INWRAP HIS HANDS & FEET BLOWN INCESSANT    741 JERUSALEM 94       5
    AND ENGLAND WHO IS BRITTANNIA AWOKE FROM DEATH ON ALBION'S    742 JERUSALEM 94      20
       BOSOM
    AS GOD IS LOVE EVERY KINDNESS TO ANOTHER IS A LITTLE DEATH    743 JERUSALEM 96      27
    DO YOU SLEEP ROUZE UP ROUZE UP ETERNAL DEATH IS ABROAD        744 JERUSALEM 96      34
    FOR LO THE NIGHT OF DEATH IS PAST AND THE ETERNAL DAY  . .    744 JERUSALEM 97       3
    DRIVING OUTWARD THE BODY OF DEATH IN AN ETERNAL DEATH         745 JERUSALEM 98      20
       & RESURRECTION
    OF DEATH WAS SEEN IN (REGENERATIONS) TERRIFIC OR COMPLACENT   746 JERUSALEM 98    *  34
       VARYING
    THERE GATES OF DEATH LET IN THE DAY  .  .  .  .  .  .  .  .   749 EV GOSPEL(B)/N    40
    MOSES COMMANDS SHE BE STONED TO DEATH   .  .  .  .  .  .  .   754 EV GOSPEL(E)/N     9
    AND DEATH & HELL WHICH NOW BEGIN  .  .  .  .  .  .  .  .  .   759 EV GOSPEL (2)     42
    THE DOOR OF DEATH I OPEN FOUND  .  .  .  .  .  .  .  .  .  .   771 OF GATES/GP       43
    PROPAGATING GENERATION & DEATH  .  .  .  .  .  .  .  .  .  .   776B INSC LAOCOON   PROSE
    SCIENCE IS THE TREE OF DEATH   .  .  .  .  .  .  .  .  .  .    777C INSC LAOCOON   PROSE
    IS THIS DEATH  .  .  .  .  .  .  .  .  .  .  .  .  .  .  .  .  779 GHOST ABEL 1       2
    THIS DEATH & THIS LIFE & THIS JEHOVAH  .  .  .  .  .  .  .    779 GHOST ABEL 1       7
    ABEL IS DEAD & CAIN SLEW HIM WE SHALL ALSO DIE A DEATH  . .   780 GHOST ABEL 1      19
    THAT THOU THYSELF GO TO ETERNAL DEATH  .  .  .  .  .  .  .    781 GHOST ABEL 2      19
     . . .  DEATH O HOLY IS THIS BROTHERHOOD  .  .  .  .  .  .    781 GHOST ABEL 2      24
    THE DEATH OF DEMOSTHENES...HAS BEEN APPROVED BY MR FLAXMAN    796B LETTER 7        PROSE
    YOU THRO LIFE & AFTER DEATH SHAME & CONFUSION OF FACE  . .    813B LETTER 22       PROSE
    THE THREE MARIES AT THE SEPULCHER...THE DEATH OF JOSEPH       824A LETTER 27       PROSE
    THE DEATH OF THE VIRGIN MARY...ST PAUL PREACHING &  .  .      824A LETTER 27       PROSE
    AFTERNOON MY POOR WIFE HAS BEEN NEAR THE GATE OF DEATH  . .   833D LETTER 33       PROSE
    BUT THAT OF LEFEVRE'S DEATH HE SPEAKS OF AS INCOMPARABLE      844C LETTER 43       PROSE
    THE DEATH OF SO EXCELLENT A MAN AS MY GENEROUS ADVOCATE       854B LETTER 53       PROSE
    AT THE ROYAL ACADEMY ON THE OCCASION OF BANKS'S DEATH  . .    859D LETTER 56      *PROSE
    & THE USE OF THAT TALENT WHICH IT IS DEATH TO BURY  .  .  .   863B LETTER 60       PROSE
    PERHAPS & I VERILY BELIEVE IT EVERY DEATH IS AN IMPROVEMENT   868D LETTER 68       PROSE
    DEAR CUMBERLAND I HAVE BEEN VERY NEAR THE GATES OF DEATH      878A LETTER 88       PROSE
    HOUSE OF DEATH MILTON  .  .  .  .  .  .  .  .  .  .  .  .  .   SUPP COLOR PRT TATE *TITLE
    CHAPTER III OF THE SEXUAL NATURE & ITS FALL INTO             SUPP ILLUS GENESIS  *TITLE
       GENERATION & DEATH
```

```
                                                                PAGE    TITLE            LINE
DEATH      (CONTINUED)
        CHAPTER IV HOW GENERATION & DEATH TOOK POSSESSION OF THE   SUPP ILLUS GENESIS   *TITLE
          NATURAL MAN
        THE DEATH OF EDWARD'S QUEEN ELEANOR FROM THIS LINE  . . .  SUPP ILLUS GRAY      *TITLE
        THE DEATH OF EARL GOODWIN  . . . . . . . . . . . . . .     SUPP ILLUS HISTORY   *TITLE
        WIDOW FATHER BABE BAPTISM HERVEY ANGEL OF DEATH     . .    SUPP INSC HERVEY     *TITLE
        GUARDIAN ANGEL CHILD ANGEL OF DEATH MOTHER    . . . .      SUPP INSC HERVEY     *TITLE
        GOOD & EVIL ANGEL HOUSE OF DEATH GOD JUDGING ADAM LAMECH   SUPP LETTER 56A      *PROSE
        MIRTH THE THREE TABERNACLES THE CHURCH YARD DEATH HOPE     SUPP PENC DRAW 2.19  *TITLE
DEATH-BED
        AS THE PALE FAINTING MAN ON HIS DEATH-BED  . . . . . .     30  EDW THIRD/PS 5      23
DEATH CLOTHES
        AND LO LIKE THE HARVEST MOON AHANIA CAST OFF HER DEATH     366 FOUR ZOAS 9        344
          CLOTHES
        I SHALL CAST OFF MY DEATH CLOTHES & EMBRACE THARMAS AGAIN  373 FOUR ZOAS 9        599
DEATH COUCH
        THE THREE DAUGHTERS OF URIZEN GUARD AHANIA'S DEATH COUCH   362 FOUR ZOAS 9        201
        DEATH COUCH IN THE CAVERNS OF DEATH IN THE CORNER OF THE   489 MILTON 9             3
          ATLANTIC
        BECOMES A WOMB & IS THIS THE DEATH COUCH OF ALBION   . .   534 MILTON 42            1
DEATH-CUP
        YOU O LOVELY FORMS YOU HAVE PREPARED MY DEATH-CUP   . . .  643 JERUSALEM 21         2
DEATHFUL
        THOU LOVEST ME NOT LOOK NOT UPON ME WITH THOSE DEATHFUL    38C SAMSON/PS         PROSE
          EYES
        BENEATH URIZEN'S DEATHFUL SHADOW  . . . . . . . . . .      233 URIZEN 20            25
        THUS LIVD LOS DRIVING ENION FAR INTO THE DEATHFUL INFINITE 290 FOUR ZOAS 2        383
        TO TYBURN'S DEATHFUL SHADES ADMITS THE WANDERING SOULS  .. 665 JERUSALEM 38        58
DEATH GROAN
        ALBION GAVE HIS LOUD DEATH GROAN THE ATLANTIC MOUNTAINS    281 FOUR ZOAS 2         41
          TREMBLED
DEATH-IMAGE
        BEFORE THE DEATH-IMAGE OF URIZEN   . . . . . . . . . .     230 URIZEN 15            2
DEATHLESS
        DEATHLESS FOR EVER NOW I WANDER SEEKING OBLIVION   . . .   298 FOUR ZOAS 4         12
        ART THOU LIKE ME RISEN AGAIN FROM DEATH OR ART THOU        313 FOUR ZOAS 6         56
          DEATHLESS
DEATHLIKE
        AND THEY DIVIDED INTO FOUR RAVENING DEATHLIKE FORMS  . . . 663 JERUSALEM 36        36
        AROUND THE WORMY GARMENTS OF ALBION THEN PAUSING           741 JERUSALEM 94        17
          IN DEATHLIKE SILENCE
DEATHLY
        & SOON SPREAD A DEATHLY FEEL ALL OVER THE LIMBS WHICH  . . 872B LETTER 75        PROSE
        ACCOMPANYING DEATHLY FEEL I GOT AGAIN INTO A PERSPIRATION  872B LETTER 75        PROSE
DEATH'S
        PREPARE YOUR HEARTS FOR DEATH'S COLD HAND PREPARE   . . .  34  WAR SONG/PS          6
        THE TRAVELLER HASTETH IN THE EVENING DEATH'S DOOR   . . .  209D FOR CHILDRN/GP   TITLE
        FROM DEATH'S COLD SLEEP [UPON]  . . . . . . . . . . . .    298 FOUR ZOAS 4         16
        ETERNAL & I THRO HIM AWAKE FROM DEATH'S DARK VALE   . . .  362 FOUR ZOAS 9        207
        HIMSELF WAS HUMAN THO NOW WANDERING THRO DEATH'S VALE  . . 498 MILTON 17            6
        FOR GOD HIMSELF ENTERS DEATH'S DOOR ALWAYS WITH THOSE THAT 522 MILTON 32           40
          ENTER
        BOUND THESE BLACK SHOES OF DEATH & ON MY HANDS DEATH'S     666 JERUSALEM 39        21
          IRON GLOVES
        THE TWENTY-EIGHT TREMBLED IN DEATH'S DARK CAVES IN COLD    668 JERUSALEM 41        23
          DESPAIR
        AH ME PITIABLE ONES DO YOU ALSO GO TO DEATH'S VALE  . . .  673 JERUSALEM 43        73
        DEATH'S DOOR  . . . . . . . . . . . . . . . . . . . .      769D FOR SEXES/GP     TITLE
        DEATH'S DOOR  . . . . . . . . . . . . . . . . . . . .      SUPP LEGEND/N71      *TITLE
DEATHS
        WHEN THOUSAND DEATHS FOR VENGEANCE CRY  . . . . . . . .    13  GWIN KING/PS        99
        WHERE THOUSAND DEATHS ARE POSTING UP AND DOWN   . . . .    26  EDW THIRD/PS 3     222
        [DESIRES OUR DEATHS O IJIM [?TIS ?ONE ?WHOSE AGED TONGUE]  105 TIRIEL 4            78
        BUT MALES IMMORTAL LIVE RENEWD BY FEMALE DEATHS IN SOFT    266 FOUR ZOAS 1         66
        REVIVES ME TO NEW DEATHS I FADE EVEN LIKE A WATER LILLY    371 FOUR ZOAS 9     *  540
        PUNISHMENTS & DEATHS MUSTERD & NUMBERD SAYING I AM GOD     490 MILTON 9            25
          ALONE
        WOVEN IN LOOMS OF EDEN IN SPIRITUAL DEATHS OF MIGHTY MEN   665 JERUSALEM 38        53
        TO ATONE FOR YOU FOR SPIRITUAL DEATH MAN LIVES BY DEATHS   670 JERUSALEM 42        49
          OF MEN
        WITH BLOOD WEAVING THE DEATHS OF THE MIGHTY INTO           704 JERUSALEM 67        33
          A TABERNACLE
DEATH-SHADOW
        HOPELESS ABHORRD A DEATH-SHADOW   . . . . . . . . . .      250 AHANIA 2            41
DEATH-SWEAT,DEATH SWEAT
        THE DEW OF ANXIOUS SOULS THE DEATH-SWEAT OF THE DYING  . . 281 FOUR ZOAS 2         47
        . . . & DEATH SWEAT OF THE VICTIMS   . . . . . . . . .     347 FOUR ZOAS 8        228
        TEARS OF THE GRAPE THE DEATH SWEAT OF THE CLUSTER THE LAST 377 FOUR ZOAS 9        770
          SIGH
        TEARS OF THE GRAPE THE DEATH SWEAT OF THE CLUSTER THE LAST 514 MILTON 27           40
          SIGH
        THE DAUGHTERS ATTENDED HER SHUDDERINGS WIPING THE DEATH    678 JERUSALEM 48        43
          SWEAT
DEATHY
        IN EARTH COVERD WITH STONES AND DEATHY DUST  . . . . .     30  EDW THIRD/PS 5      14
        WAVES BEFORE HIS DEATHY FACE  . . . . . . . . . . . .      231 URIZEN 18            8
DEBATE
        BUT WE IMMORTAL IN OUR OWN STRENGTH SURVIVE BY STERN DEBATE 272 FOUR ZOAS 1       292
DEBT
        SAYING DOTH JEHOVAH FORGIVE A DEBT ONLY ON CONDITION THAT  694 JERUSALEM 61        17
          IT SHALL
        THAT DEBT IS NOT FORGIVEN THAT POLLUTION IS NOT FORGIVEN   694 JERUSALEM 61        19
```

	PAGE	TITLE	LINE

DEBT   (CONTINUED)
[THY XXX & A TAX] MONEY OR DEBT OR TAX A VALUE OR PRICE AS	788A	ANNO THORNTON	* MARG
WHATEVER CANNOT BE TAXED [DEBT THAT WAS OWING TO HIM XXX]	788D	ANNO THORNTON	* MARG
ACCOUNT I AM THEREFORE THAT (TWELVE) GUINEAS IN YOUR DEBT	854D	LETTER 53	PROSE
WHOSE DEBT I HAVE BEEN TOO LONG BUT PERCIEVE THAT . . .	863B	LETTER 60	PROSE

DEBTOR
| PERSEVERANCE BY WHICH WANT I AM STILL SO MUCH YOUR DEBTOR | 808D | LETTER 20 | PROSE |

DEBTS
| FOR ALL IS DEBTS & TAXES BETWEEN [XXX] CAESAR & US   . . . | 788D | ANNO THORNTON | * MARG |

DECALOGUE
| THE FIVE BOOKS OF THE DECALOGUE THE BOOKS OF JOSHUA & JUDGES | 677 | JERUSALEM 48 | 9 |

DECAY
LOS SUFFERD HIS FIRES TO DECAY	230	URIZEN 13	44
HIS FALL INTO THE GENERATION OF DECAY & DEATH & HIS . .	264	FOUR ZOAS 1	22
A UNIVERSE OF DEATH & DECAY LET ENITHARMON'S HANDS . . .	298	FOUR ZOAS 4	28
FOREHEAD & EYES THY LIPS DECAY LIKE ROSES IN [EARLY] THE SPRING	325	FOUR ZOAS 7	189
. . . THAT THE KING & PRIEST MAY STILL FEAST ON YOUR DECAY	354	FOUR ZOAS 8	498
HE DROOPS HIS HEAD & TREMBLING STANDS & HIS BRIGHT EYES DECAY	354	FOUR ZOAS 8	531
YON SUN SHALL WAX OLD & DECAY BUT THOU SHALT EVER FLOURISH	368	FOUR ZOAS 9	419
HERE FIXD INTO A FROZEN BULK SUBJECT TO DECAY & DEATH . .	525	MILTON 34	54
SUBSTANCE CAN NEVER SUFFER CHANGE NOR DECAY	567C	DESC CAT 3	PROSE
AND AS IT IS VALUED SO DOES SOCIETY FLOURISH OR DECAY . .	587A	CHAUCER 1	PROSE
SUBSTANCE CAN NEVER SUFFER CHANGE NOR DECAY	589A	CHAUCER/N	PROSE

DECAYD
WERE FORGD SMALLER AS THE FLESH DECAYD	135	FRENCH REVOLTN	31
FOR LIBERTY VAIN HOPES HIS REASON DECAYD	136	FRENCH REVOLTN	49
FADED & HER BRIGHT EYES DECAYD MELTED WITH PITY & LOVE .	270	FOUR ZOAS 1	213
THARMAS I KNOW THEE HOW ARE WE ALTERD OUR BEAUTY DECAYD	299	FOUR ZOAS 4	79
AND [ALL MY] STEWHARD'S EGGS ARE ADDLED & DECAYD . . .	537	AND HIS LEGS/N	15
HE IS VERY THIN AND DECAYD AND BUT THE SHADOW OF WHAT HE WAS	844A	LETTER 43	PROSE

DECAYING
AS PLANTS WITHERD BY WINTER LEAVES & STEMS & ROOTS DECAYING	305	FOUR ZOAS 5	9
LONDON CONTINUALLY BUILDING & CONTINUALLY DECAYING DESOLATE	684	JERUSALEM 53	19
CONTINUALLY BUILDING CONTINUALLY DECAYING BECAUSE OF LOVE & JEALOUSY	712A	JERUSALEM 72	PROSE

DECAYS
| THE MORNING COMES THE NIGHT DECAYS THE WATCHMEN LEAVE THEIR STATIONS | 198 | AMERICA 6 | 1 |
| BODY DECAYS I THANK YOU FOR THE PAINS YOU HAVE TAKEN   . . | 878A | LETTER 88 | PROSE |

DECEASD
| ALL SPIRITS DECEASD LET LOOSE FROM REPTILE PRISONS COME IN SHOALS | 363 | FOUR ZOAS 9 | 235 |

DECEASED
| AND ON THE MOUNTAINS OF LEBANON ROUND THE DECEASED GODS | 246 | SONG OF LOS 4 | 19 |
| I KNOW THAT OUR DECEASED FRIENDS ARE MORE REALLY WITH US | 797A | LETTER 9 | PROSE |

DECEIT   SEE SELF DECEIT
MY VOICE HATH USED DECEIT HOW SHOULD I CALL ON HIM WHO IS TRUTH	36A	COUCH DEATH/PS	PROSE
PUT ON THY COUNTRY'S PRIDE DECEIT AND EYES OF LOVE . . .	38A	SAMSON/PS	PROSE
USING DECEIT TO THE WIFE OF HIS BOSOM	38D	SAMSON/PS	PROSE
[IN SILENT DECEIT POISONS INHALING FROM THE MORNING ROSE]	109	TIRIEL 8	13
USED WITH DECEIT	168	SILENT NIGHT/N	8
AND IT BEARS THE FRUIT OF DECEIT	174	HUMAN IMAGE/N	18
[HOW TO KNOW LOVE FROM DECEIT]	175A	HOW TO KNOW/N	TITLE
DECEIT TO SECRESY [INCLIND] CONFIND	175	HOW TO KNOW/N	5
BUT THE LOOK OF SOFT DECEIT	182	LOOK OF LOVE/N	3
SOFT DECEIT & IDLENESS	182	WHICH ARE/N	2
BUT THE LOOK OF SOFT DECEIT	184	SEVRL QUESTN/N	7
SOFT DECEIT & IDLENESS	184	SEVRL QUESTN/N	9
AND IT BEARS THE FRUIT OF DECEIT	217	HUMAN ABSTR/SE	17
[O SLAY ME NOT THOU ART HIS WRATH EMBODIED IN DECEIT] .	268	FOUR ZOAS 1	162
O CRUEL PITY O DARK DECEIT CAN LOVE SEEK FOR DOMINION .	293	FOUR ZOAS 3	78
CALL [VALAN] VALA FROM HER CLOSE RECESS IN ALL HER DARK DECEIT	307	FOUR ZOAS 5	* 64
IS IT IN STRONG DECEIT THAT MAN IS BORN IN STRONG DECEIT	323	FOUR ZOAS 7	140
FLAME HIGH IN PRIDE & LAUGH TO SCORN THE SOURCE OF HIS DECEIT	324	FOUR ZOAS 7	158
CALL FORTH THY SMILES OF SOFT DECEIT CALL FORTH THY CLOUDY TEARS	338	FOUR ZOAS 7B	208
TO ALL HIS ENGINES OF DECEIT THAT LINKED CHAINS MIGHT RUN	344	FOUR ZOAS 8	132
IS A DECEIT SO DETESTABLE THAT I WILL CAST THEE OUT . . .	361	FOUR ZOAS 9	* 155
WHICH ARE ONLY AN EXAMPLE OF THE WICKEDNESS & DECEIT .	387B	ANNO WATSON	MARG
AND THERE IS A SMILE OF DECEIT	423	THE SMILE	2
& THAT ALL PRETENCE TO INSPIRATION IS A LIE & A DECEIT .	452D	ANNO REYNOLDS	MARG
FOR IF IT IS A DECEIT THE WHOLE BIBLE IS MADNESS THIS OPINION	452D	ANNO REYNOLDS	MARG
TO ANNIHILATE THE SELF-HOOD OF DECEIT & FALSE FORGIVENESS	497	MILTON 16	1
AND ALL THE DAUGHTERS OF LOS PROPHETIC WAIL YET IN DECEIT	506	MILTON 22	37
UNDER PERPETUAL TERRORS & VAIN DREAMS PLOTS & SECRET DECEIT	608D	V LAST JUDG/N	PROSE
BOTH OF DECEIT & OF OPEN VIOLENCE THE DEIST & THE CHRISTIAN	615A	V LAST JUDG/N	PROSE
BECAUSE OF ALBION BECAUSE OF DECEIT AND FRIENDSHIP FOR LO	625	JERUSALEM 7	17
I KNOW THY DECEIT & THY REVENGES AND UNLESS THOU DESIST	627	JERUSALEM 8	7
THY HOLY WRATH & DEEP DECEIT CANNOT AVAIL AGAINST ME . .	627	JERUSALEM 8	33
O CRUEL PITY O DARK DECEIT CAN LOVE SEEK FOR DOMINION .	654	JERUSALEM 29	60
IN HIDDEN DECEIT THEY ARE VEGETABLE ONLY FIT FOR BURNING	663	JERUSALEM 36	48
TO SIN & TO HIDE THE SIN IN SWEET DECEIT IS LOVELY . . .	681	JERUSALEM 50	25
CALL FORTH THY SMILES OF SOFT DECEIT CALL FORTH THY CLOUDY TEARS	701	JERUSALEM 65	54

                                                              PAGE   TITLE   LINE
DECEIT   (CONTINUED)
     DEADLY HATE BETWEEN LEAH & RACHEL DAUGHTERS OF DECEIT &   707 JERUSALEM 69   11
          FRAUD
     MUTUAL HATE RETURNS & MUTUAL DECEIT & MUTUAL FEAR . . .   708 JERUSALEM 69   37
     UPON HER BACK BEHIND HER LOINS & THUS UTTERD HER DECEIT   725 JERUSALEM 82   21
     IN GRACEFUL HIDINGS OF ERROR IN MERCIFUL DECEIT . . . .   727 JERUSALEM 83   29
     ALL THEIR JEALOUSIES REVENGES MURDERS HIDINGS OF CRUELTY   739 JERUSALEM 92   16
          IN DECEIT
     WAS IT LOVE OR DARK DECEIT . . . .   755 EV GOSPEL(E)/N   58
     TWAS DARK DECEIT TO EARN MY BREAD . . . .   755 EV GOSPEL(E)/N   60
DECEITFUL
     AND WITH SOFT DECEITFUL WILES . . . .   165 CHRISTN FORB/N   8
     AND WITH SOFT DECEITFUL WILES . . . .   218 POISON TREE/SE   8
     TO GIVE THE IMMORTAL STEEDS OF LIGHT TO HIS DECEITFUL HANDS 292 FOUR ZOAS 3   32
     HIS WOVEN DARKNESS & IN LAWS & DECEITFUL RELIGIONS . . .   345 FOUR ZOAS 8   172
     URIZEN SITTING IN HIS WEB OF (DECEITFUL) RELIGION [WAS   352 FOUR ZOAS 8   * 415
          [?TORMENTED] ?DARKEND]
     URIZEN SITTING IN HIS WEB OF DECEITFUL RELIGION WAS   382 FOUR ZOAS AD 6   31
          TORMENTED
     MAN THE ENEMY OF MAN INTO DECEITFUL FRIENDSHIPS . . . .   622 JERUSALEM 4   26
     TILL THY LIFE IS ALL TAKEN AWAY BY THIS DECEITFUL   625 JERUSALEM 7   10
          FRIENDSHIP
     ALBION SPOKE IN HIS DISMAL DREAMS O THOU DECEITFUL FRIEND   669 JERUSALEM 42   9
     MARCHES AGAINST THEE DECEITFUL FROM SINAI & FROM EDOM . .   743 JERUSALEM 96   9
DECEITS
     STAND FROM MY PATH FOUL FIEND IS THIS THE LAST OF   103 TIRIEL 4   8
          THY DECEITS
     TO DISPLAY NATURE'S CRUEL HOLINESS THE DECEITS OF NATURAL   527 MILTON 36   25
          RELIGION
     POISONS ROSE UP & HIS SWEET DECEITS COVERD THEM ALL OVER   627 JERUSALEM 8   5
     IN CHASTE APPEARANCES FOR SWEET DECEITS OF LOVE & MODESTY   727 JERUSALEM 83   31
DECEIVED   SEE DECIEVD
     BY NIGHT I AM DECEIVED WHO SAYS THAT THOU WAST BORN OF   38B SAMSON/PS   PROSE
          MORTAL KIND
DECEIVING
     ("STEP BEYOND REAL FAITH IS IN DANGER OF DECEIVING")   77C ANNO LAVATER   MARG
          UNEASY
DECEPTION
     SINEWY DECEPTION & OF THE WARRIOR'S (OUTBRAVING)   363 FOUR ZOAS 9   * 248
          & THOUGHTLESSNESS
     & HE COPIES THAT SO NEAT AS TO MAKE IT A DECEPTION NOW . .   597B PUB ADDRESS/N   PROSE
DECEPTIONS
     DECEPTIONS O NO SO I'LL LEARN TO PAINT . . . . . .   546 RUBENS HAD/N   4
DECIDE
     OF THEM TO DO ME THE JUSTICE TO EXAMINE BEFORE THEY DECIDE   561B EXHIBITION ADV   PROSE
     TO DECIDE TWO WORLDS WITH A GREAT DECISION A WORLD OF MERCY 699 JERUSALEM 65   1
          AND
     SOON RECIEVE SUCH DOCUMENTS AS WILL ENABLE YOU TO DECIDE   849B LETTER 45   PROSE
DECIDED
     IS NOW TO BE DECIDED BY THE PUBLIC MR B'S(BLAKE'S)   591B PUB ADDRESS/N   PROSE
          INVENTIVE
     BUT DRAWN WITH A FIRM & DECIDED HAND AT ONCE [WITH ALL ITS] 595C PUB ADDRESS/N   PROSE
     CHRIST IS VERY DECIDED ON THIS POINT "HE WHO IS NOT WITH"   822D LETTER 26   PROSE
     DECIDED ON THE SHIPWRECK & IT WAS HIS OPINION & HE SAYS IT   855A LETTER 53   PROSE
DECIDES
     AND THE FIRST BLOW DECIDES . . . .   14 GWIN KING/PS   106
DECIEVD   SEE SELF-DECIEVD
     AHANIA'S IMAGE I DECIEVD THEE & WILL STILL DECIEVE . . .   288 FOUR ZOAS 2   328
DECIEVE
     A MAN MUST FIRST DECIEVE HIMSELF BEFORE HE IS THUS . . .   75A ANNO LAVATER   MARG
     [[DECIEVE THE NOBLE &] IF THE ELOQUENT VOICE OF TIRIEL]   105 TIRIEL 4   79
     AHANIA'S IMAGE I DECIEVD THEE & WILL STILL DECIEVE . . .   288 FOUR ZOAS 2   328
     TO DECIEVE THARMAS IN HIS RAGE TO SOOTHE HIS FURIOUS SOUL   338 FOUR ZOAS 7B   226
DECIEVER
     HOW IS THIS POSSIBLE EVERY BODY MUST BE A LIAR & DECIEVER   397B ANNO BACON   MARG
     HIS AWFUL BEAUTY WITH MORAL VIRTUE THE FAIR DECIEVER   715 JERUSALEM 74   35
          OFFSPRING
DECIEVING   SEE SELF-DECIEVING
     FOR A SPECTRE HAS NO EMANATION BUT WHAT HE IMBIBES FROM   701 JERUSALEM 65   59
          DECIEVING
     CHARGE VISIONARIES WITH DECIEVING . . . .   756 EV GOSPEL(H)/N   3
DECISION
     THE KIND DECISION OF ENITHARMON & GAVE A TIME TO THE SPACE   494 MILTON 13   16
     WALKETH AMONG US GIVE DECISION BRING FORTH ALL YOUR FIRES   686 JERUSALEM 55   18
     TO DECIDE TWO WORLDS WITH A GREAT DECISION A WORLD OF MERCY 699 JERUSALEM 65   1
          AND
     WITH MORAL LAW AN EQUAL BALANCE NOT GOING DOWN WITH   708 JERUSALEM 69   35
          DECISION
     & WILL REMAIN SO TILL YOU HAVE GIVEN YOUR DECISION . . .   841C LETTER 41   PROSE
     DECISION ON WHAT WOULD BE SAFE & NOT TOO VENTURESOME IN   849B LETTER 45   PROSE
     MATTERS AND LEAVE ALL TO YOUR DECISION . . . . . .   861B LETTER 58   PROSE
     BUT NOT AT ALL IN WHAT IS OF WEIGHT & MOMENT TO OUR   868B LETTER 67   PROSE
          DECISION
     THIS IS HIS OWN DECISION QUITE IN CHARACTER . . . . .   877D LETTER 88   PROSE
DECK
     O DECK HER FORTH WITH THY FAIR FINGERS POUR . . . . .   1 TO SPRING/PS   13
     SEEKST THOU THAT FLOWR TO DECK THY HORRID TEMPLES . . . .   5 FAIR ELENOR/PS   44
     BRINGS ME YEW TO DECK MY GRAVE . . . .   6 MY SILKS/PS   5
DECKED
     GRIM WAR SHALL LAUGH AND SHOUT DECKED IN TEARS . . . .   31 EDW THIRD/PS 5   53
     DECKED IN MILD SORROW AND SELL THY LORD FOR GOLD FOR . .   38A SAMSON/PS   PROSE

```
                                                        PAGE     TITLE            LINE
DECKS
    WHEN SILVER SNOW DECKS SUSAN'S CLOATHS  . . . . . . .   15 BLIND-MANS/PS        1
    WHEN SILVER SNOW DECKS SYLVIO'S CLOTHES  . . . . . . .  64 SHEPHERD OLD         1
DECLARE
    I HEREBY DECLARE THAT MR JOHN LINNELL HAS PURCHASED OF ME  874A LETTER 78    PROSE
DECLARES
    FLAXMAN DECLARES TO ME THAT HE WILL NOT PRETEND TO SET   855A LETTER 53      PROSE
        A PRICE
DECLINE
    THE SON OF MORN IN WEARY NIGHT'S DECLINE  . . . . . .  771 EPILOGUE/GP          7
DECLINED
    THEY ALL DECLINED & HE WAS FORCED TO SING HIMSELF   . . .  61D ISLAND MOON 11 PROSE
    THEM ON A SMALLER SCALE WHICH HE DECLINED ON ACCOUNT OF ITS 831C LETTER 31   PROSE
DECLIVITIES
    ITS PITS & DECLIVITIES FLOWING WITH MOLTEN ORE & FOUNTAINS  529 MILTON 38       18
DECOLLATE
    I WILLIAM BLAKE A MENTAL PRINCE SHOULD DECOLLATE  . . . .599D PUB ADDRESS/N  PROSE
DECOY
    TO THE BLOSSOM OF HOPE FOR A SWEET DECOY  . . . . . .  800 MRS FLAXMAN/L        2
DECREE
    . . . [& ALL MY KINGLY POWER] BUT HEAR MY DETERMIND DECREE  292 FOUR ZOAS 3    19
    "SENDS OVER TO IMAGINATION BEFORE THE DECREE CAN BE ACTED" 794A LETTER 5     PROSE
DECREES
    AND MARCHES ON IN FEARLESS DEPENDANCE ON THE DIVINE DECREES 580B DESC CAT 5  PROSE
DEDICATE
    TO DEDICATE TO ENGLAND'S QUEEN  . . . . . . . . . .  442 DEDICATN BLAIR       11
DEDICATED
    WAS DEDICATED TO THOMAS A BECKET THE PILGRIMS IF SICK OR   590B CHAUCER 2     PROSE
        LAME
    PLEASE TO TELL MRS BUTTS THAT WE HAVE DEDICATED A CHAMBER  803B LETTER 15     PROSE
DEDUCE
    NONE COULD DEDUCE A FOURTH OR FIFTH  . . . . . . . .  97A NAT RELIGION 1     PROSE
DEDUCT
    DEDUCT FROM A ROSE ITS REDNESS FROM A LILLY ITS WHITENESS  81C ANNO LAVATER   MARG
DEDUCTION
    KNOWLEDGE IS NOT BY DEDUCTION BUT IMMEDIATE BY PERCEPTION  774C ANNO BERKELEY MARG
        OR
DEED
    THE WRETCH APPROACHES CRYING THE DEED IS DONE  . . . . .   4 FAIR ELENOR/PS     21
    AND LET THY MASTER DO THE DEED ONE BLOW OF THAT STRONG ARM  38C SAMSON/PS     PROSE
    TO TEAR HIM FROM HIS THRONE BLACK WAS THE DEED  . . . . .  42B THEN SHE BORE  PROSE
    A DEED WHICH IS NOT COMMON  . . . . . . . . . . . .  50 WHEN CORRUP/IM        20
    TILL THE CHILD DWELL WITH ONE HE HATES AND DO THE DEED    193 V DAU ALBION 5    30
        HE LOATHS
    [WHAT HAVE I DONE SAID ENION ACCURSED WRETCH WHAT DEED]   267 FOUR ZOAS 1      109
    [IS THIS A DEED OF LOVE I KNOW WHAT I HAVE DONE I KNOW  ] 267 FOUR ZOAS 1      110
    WHAT CAUSE AT LENGTH MOVD MILTON TO THIS UNEXAMPLED DEED  482 MILTON 2       *  21
    THEIR CONSIDERATION OF MY PLAN AS A GREAT PUBLIC [DEED]   601B PUB ADDRESS/N *PROSE
        MEANS
    SO SAYING AN ETERNAL DEED WAS DONE IN FIERY FLAMES  . . .  686 JERUSALEM 55     19
DEEDS
    WERE BASE WHO WERE NOT FIRD TO DEEDS  . . . . . . . .  23 EDW THIRD/PS 3       79
    I AM ALREADY DISTRACTED AT THEIR DEEDS & IF I LOOK   . . .  265 FOUR ZOAS 1     55
    ALL THY PAST DEEDS HEAR WHAT I TELL THEE MARK IT          268 FOUR ZOAS 1      153
        WELL REMEMBER
    AND THOU THE DELUSIVE TEMPTER TO THESE DEEDS SITTST BEFORE 268 FOUR ZOAS 1     169
        ME
    THE BARDS WHO WERE CAPABLE OF ATTENDING WARLIKE DEEDS  . . 580C DESC CAT 5    PROSE
DEEM
    FOR WHICH HIMSELF MIGHT DEEM HIM NEER THE WORSE  . . . .  14 IMIT SPEN/PS       16
DEEMD
    AND NONE IMPURE WERE DEEMD  . . . . . . . . . . . .  256 BOOK OF LOS 3         9
    FOR SUCH THEY DEEMD THE DEATH OF THE BODY LOS HIS VEGETABLE 357 FOUR ZOAS 9     6
        HANDS
DEEP
    RODE OER THE DEEP OF HEAVEN BESIDE OUR SPRINGS  . . . .    2 TO SUMMER/PS        9
    HE HEARS ME NOT BUT OER THE YAWNING DEEP  . . . . . .    3 TO WINTER/PS         5
    DEEP SIGHS AND SEES PALE SICKLY GHOSTS GLIDING  . . . .    4 FAIR ELENOR/PS     16
    AND OER THE SURFACE OF THE SILENT DEEP DOST FLY  . . . .  15 IMIT SPEN/PS       26
    SHE WAS SEATED IN THE DEEP THE OCEAN CEASD  . . . . . .  21 EDW THIRD/PS 2      81
    ROUND HIS MAJESTIC FEET DEEP THUNDERS ROLL  . . . . . .  34A KING JOHN/S      PROSE
    I SEEM TO WALK THROUGH A DEEP VALLEY FAR FROM THE LIGHT   35D COUCH DEATH/PS  PROSE
        OF DAY
    THE MIRE WAS DEEP & THE CHILD DID WEEP  . . . . . . . .  60 LIT BOY LST/IM      7
    MADNESS & DEEP DISMAY (POSSESS) THE HEART OF THE BLIND MAN 103 TIRIEL 3      *  37
    [SET AGED TIRIEL IN DEEP THOUGHT WHETHER THESE THINGS WERE 106 TIRIEL 4        82
        SO]
    GRAVE THE SENTENCE DEEP  . . . . . . . . . . . . .  112 LIT GRL LST/SI        4
    COME FROM CAVERNS DEEP  . . . . . . . . . . . . . .  113 LIT GRL LST/SI       35
    OVER VALLIES DEEP  . . . . . . . . . . . . . . . .  113 LIT GRL FND/SI        3
    AMONG SHADOWS DEEP  . . . . . . . . . . . . . . . .  114 LIT GRL FND/SI       10
    FILLD WITH DEEP SURPRISE  . . . . . . . . . . . . .  114 LIT GRL FND/SI       34
    IN MY PALACE DEEP  . . . . . . . . . . . . . . . .  114 LIT GRL FND/SI       43
    THE MIRE WAS DEEP & THE CHILD DID WEEP  . . . . . . . .  121 LIT BOY LST/SI     7
    OF EVERY HEART ON EARTH INFIXES DEEP ITS RESTLESS TWISTS  130 BOOK OF THEL 6    4
    FROM THE DEEP AND THE SOLID . . . . . . . . . . . .  138 FRENCH REVOLTN      96
    THRO THE CLOUD A DEEP THUNDER . . . . . . . . . . .  145 FRENCH REVOLTN     247
    HUNGRY CLOUDS SWAG ON THE DEEP  . . . . . . . . . . .  148 MARRIAGE HH 2       2
    HUNGRY CLOUDS SWAG ON THE DEEP  . . . . . . . . . . .  149 MARRIAGE HH 2      22
    WHICH HUNG WITH THE HEAD DOWNWARD INTO THE DEEP  . . . .  156A MARRIAGE HH 17 PROSE
    WHICH FLEW OR RATHER SWUM IN THE INFINITE DEEP  . . . . .  156A MARRIAGE HH 17 PROSE
    FIRE BURST AND ROLLED THRO THE DEEP BLACKNING ALL BENEATH 156B MARRIAGE HH 17 PROSE
```

463

```
                                                       PAGE      TITLE         LINE
DEEP     (CONTINUED)
     SO THAT THE NETHER DEEP GREW BLACK AS A SEA    . . . . .  156B MARRIAGE HH 17   PROSE
     TINGING THE BLACK DEEP WITH BEAMS OF BLOOD . . . . . .    156C MARRIAGE HH 17   PROSE
     AND LO IT WAS A DEEP PIT INTO WHICH I DESCENDED    . . . 157A MARRIAGE HH 17   PROSE
     CAST THY KEYS O ROME INTO THE DEEP DOWN FALLING   . . .  159B SONG LIBERTY     PROSE
     THE JEALOUS WINGS WAVD OVER THE DEEP . . . . . . .       159B SONG LIBERTY     PROSE
     GLANCING HIS BEAMY EYELIDS OVER THE DEEP IN DARK DISMAY  159D SONG LIBERTY     PROSE
     [ COULD FETCH IT FROM THE FURNACE DEEP ] . . . . . . .   172 THE TYGER/N 1       13
     AS WHEN A BLACK CLOUD SHEWS ITS LIGHTNINGS TO THE SILENT 196 AMERICA PREL 2       5
        DEEP
     ENDURD BY ROOTS THAT WRITHE THEIR ARMS INTO THE NETHER DEEP 196 AMERICA PREL 2   11
     CROUCH HOWLING BEFORE THEIR CAVERNS DEEP LIKE SKINS DRYD 199 AMERICA 9            4
        IN THE WIND
     OF TRUMPETS BLEW A LOUD ALARM ACROSS THE ATLANTIC DEEP . . 200 AMERICA 10         2
     FIERY THE ANGELS ROSE & AS THEY ROSE DEEP THUNDER ROLLD  200 AMERICA 11           1
     IN THE DEEP GLOOM BY WASHINGTON & PAINE & WARREN THEY STOOD 200 AMERICA 12        7
     BREAKING IN SMOKY WREATHS FROM THE WILD DEEP & GATHRING  201 AMERICA 12          11
        THICK
     FALLING INTO THE DEEP SUBLIME FLAGD WITH GREY-BROWD SNOWS 203 AMERICA 16          5
     AND THUNDEROUS VISAGES HIS JEALOUS WINGS WAVD OVER THE DEEP 203 AMERICA 16        6
     HE OPEND ON THE DEEP AND ON THE ATLANTIC SEA WHITE      203 AMERICA 16           10
        SHIVRING
     TO THIS DEEP VALLEY SITUATED BY THE FLOWING THAMES   . . 204 AMERICA CANC B       8
     HE TOOK DOWN FROM ITS TREMBLING PILLAR FROM ITS CAVERN  205 AMERICA CANC C        3
        DEEP
     WAVES OER HEAVEN'S DEEP . . . . . . . . . . . . .       219 LIT GRL LST/SE       23
     BROODING SHUT IN THE DEEP ALL AVOID . . . . . . . . .   223 URIZEN 3             25
     INWARDS INTO A DEEP WORLD WITHIN  . . . . . . . . .     224 URIZEN 4             15
     A VOID IMMENSE WILD DARK & DEEP   . . . . . . . . .     224 URIZEN 4             16
     ROUND GLOBE HOT BURNING DEEP  . . . . . . . . . .       228 URIZEN 11             3
     DEEP DOWN INTO THE ABYSS . . . . . . . . . . . . .      228 URIZEN 11             4
     HIS EYES BEHELD THE DEEP . . . . . . . . . . . . .      228 URIZEN 11            16
     TWO NOSTRILS BENT DOWN TO THE DEEP  . . . . . . . . .   229 URIZEN 13             1
     SHOOTING OUT IN ANGUISH DEEP . . . . . . . . . . .      229 URIZEN 13            15
     GRODNA RENT THE DEEP EARTH HOWLING  . . . . . . . . .   234 URIZEN 23            15
     THE DEEP OF WINTER CAME  . . . . . . . . . . . . .      239 EUROPE 4              1
     AWAKE THE THUNDERS OF THE DEEP . . . . . . . . . .      239 EUROPE 4             14
     ARISE O ORC FROM THY DEEP DEN . . . . . . . . . .       239 EUROPE 4             24
     AND RINTRAH HUNG WITH ALL HIS LEGIONS IN THE NETHER DEEP 242 EUROPE 12           24
     DEEP GROAND URIZEN STRETCHING HIS AWFUL HAND  . . . . . 249 AHANIA 2             31
     AROSE IN THE PENDULOUS DEEP . . . . . . . . . . .       253 AHANIA 4             42
     I LIE ON THE VERGE OF THE DEEP . . . . . . . . . .      254 AHANIA 4             56
     THE WILD DEEP WITH HIS TERRIBLE WRATH  . . . . . . .    259 BOOK OF LOS 5         4
     WHIRLING ABOUT IN THE DEEP  . . . . . . . . . . .       259 BOOK OF LOS 5        17
     BUT NO LIGHT FOR THE DEEP FLED AWAY  . . . . . . . .    260 BOOK OF LOS 5        48
     IN DARKNESS AND DEEP CLOUDS INVOLVD  . . . . . . . .    260 BOOK OF LOS 5        57
     AND STRETCHING OUT HIS HOLY HAND IN THE VAST DEEP SUBLIME 266 FOUR ZOAS 1        73
     THUS ENION GAVE THEM ALL HER SPECTROUS LIFE [ IN DEEP   270 FOUR ZOAS 1         221
        DESPAIR ]
     FROM HEAVENS OF JOY INTO THIS DEEP NOW RAGE BUT RAGE IN 276 FOUR ZOAS 1         433
        VAIN
     THUS SANG THE DEMONS OF THE DEEP THE CLARIONS OF WAR BLEW 276 FOUR ZOAS 1       434
        LOUD
     SUMMERS & WINTERS ROUND REVOLVING IN THE FRIGHTFUL DEEP 276 FOUR ZOAS 1         443
     WE MAY ERECT A THRONE DEEP IN THE NORTH I PLACE MY LOT . . 278 FOUR ZOAS 1      491
     DARING MY POWER WILT ARM MY SONS AGAINST ME IN THE [ DEEP] 278 FOUR ZOAS 1      510
        ATLANTIC
     MY DEEP MY NIGHT WHICH THOU ASSUMING HAST ASSUMD MY CROWN 278 FOUR ZOAS 1       511
     URIZEN CAST DEEP DARKNESS ROUND HIM SILENT BROODING DEATH 278 FOUR ZOAS 1       515
     DEEP HORRIBLE WITHOUT END SEPARATED FROM BEULAH FAR BENEATH 279 FOUR ZOAS 1     542
     BUILD WE A BOWER FOR HEAVEN'S DARLING IN THE GRIZLY DEEP 280 FOUR ZOAS 2         24
     AND I COMMANDED THE GREAT DEEP TO HIDE HER IN HIS HAND . . 282 FOUR ZOAS 2       91
     CASTING THEIR SPARKLES DIRE ABROAD INTO THE DISMAL DEEP 283 FOUR ZOAS 2         140
     WITH COMPASSES DIVIDE THE DEEP THEY THE STRONG SCALES ERECT 283 FOUR ZOAS 2     142
     THE ENORMOUS WARP & WOOF RAGE DIREFUL IN THE AFFRIGHTED 284 FOUR ZOAS 2         149
        DEEP
     THEIR VENTUROUS FLIGHT IN HUMAN FORMS DISTINCT THRO     284 FOUR ZOAS 2         151
        DARKNESS DEEP
     WHILE THUS THE SPIRITS OF STRONGEST WING ENLIGHTEN THE  284 FOUR ZOAS 2         156
        DARK DEEP
     AND MEASURE MATHEMATIC MOTION WONDROUS ALONG THE DEEP  . . 287 FOUR ZOAS 2      274
     IN THEIR AMAZING [ FRUCTIFYING ] HARD SUBDUED COURSE IN THE 287 FOUR ZOAS 2   * 286
        VAST DEEP
     SO SAYING IN DEEP SOBS HE LANGUISHD TILL DEAD HE ALSO FELL 289 FOUR ZOAS 2      340
     AT THE FIRST SOUND THE GOLDEN SUN ARISES FROM THE DEEP . . 289 FOUR ZOAS 2      344
     THE DEEP LIFTS UP HIS RUGGED HEAD  . . . . . . . . .    289 FOUR ZOAS 2         360
     [ AND [ OFT ] THUS SHE ] THUS ENION WAILS FROM THE DARK DEEP 290 FOUR ZOAS 2  * 386
        . . .
     AND AS THEY WENT IN FOLDING FIRES & THUNDERS OF THE DEEP 294 FOUR ZOAS 3         98
     . . . DEEP DESPAIRING STAMPING STRUGGLING  . . . . . .  296 FOUR ZOAS 3         156
     A WORLD OF DEEP DARKNESS WHERE ALL THINGS IN HORRORS ARE 296 FOUR ZOAS 3        181
        ROOTED
     DRIVEN BY THY RAGE I WANDER LIKE A CLOUD INTO THE DEEP . . 296 FOUR ZOAS 3      188
     AND HE IS FALLN INTO THE DEEP ROUGH DEMON OF THE WATERS 298 FOUR ZOAS 4          40
     FROM VULTURES OF THE DEEP THEN WHEREFORE SHOULDST THOU RAGE 300 FOUR ZOAS 4     109
     THE SEA ENCOMPASSES HIM & MONSTERS OF THE DEEP ARE HIS  301 FOUR ZOAS 4         134
        COMPANIONS
     SO SAYING THARMAS ON HIS FURIOUS CHARIOTS OF THE DEEP . . 301 FOUR ZOAS 4       157
     WARPING UPON THE WINDS & WHIRLING ROUND IN THE DARK DEEP 302 FOUR ZOAS 4        186
     THE LOVELY FEMALE HOWLD & URIZEN BENEATH DEEP GROAND   . . 302 FOUR ZOAS 4      189
     A RED ROUND GLOBE HOT BURNING DEEP DEEP DOWN INTO THE   303 FOUR ZOAS 4         224
        ABYSS
```

464

	PAGE	TITLE		LINE

DEEP   (CONTINUED)

```
HIDING CAREFULLY FROM THE WIND HIS EYES BEHELD THE DEEP        303 FOUR ZOAS 4        230
HIS LEFT ARM TO THE SOUTH SHOOTING OUT IN ANGUISH DEEP  . .    303 FOUR ZOAS 4        244
THEN WONDROUSLY THE [DEEP BENEATH] . . . . . . . . .           304 FOUR ZOAS 4        275
HIS FEET SHRINK WITHRING FROM THE DEEP SHRINKING              305 FOUR ZOAS 5     *    7
  & WITHERING
THE HORRID TRUMPETS OF THE DEEP BELLOW WITH BITTER BLASTS     306 FOUR ZOAS 5        40
[WHEN] URIZEN CAST DEEP DARKNESS ROUND HIM RAGING LUVAH       306 FOUR ZOAS 5     *   43
  POURD
DOWN ON THE ROCK OF ETERNITY ON DARKNESS OF THE DEEP   .  .   306 FOUR ZOAS 5        55
LET LOOSE THE ENORMOUS SPIRIT IN THE DARKNESS OF THE DEEP     306 FOUR ZOAS 5     *   59
SO SUNG THE DEMONS [OF THE DEEP] ROUND RED ORC . . .          307 FOUR ZOAS 5     *   66
SUCH IS THE DEMON SUCH HIS TERROR IN THE NETHER DEEP   .  .   308 FOUR ZOAS 5     *  142
THO THEY EACH MORNING DRAG THE UNWILLING SUN OUT OF THE       309 FOUR ZOAS 5        165
  DEEP
AND WHEN THE GATE WAS OPEN SHE BEHELD THAT [DISMAL] DREARY    309 FOUR ZOAS 5     *  180
  DEEP
THE WOES OF URIZEN SHUT UP IN THE DEEP DENS OF URTHONA  .  .  310 FOUR ZOAS 5        189
HEARD ON MY MOUNTAINS & DEEP SIGHS UNDER MY PALACE ROOFS      310 FOUR ZOAS 5        207
WAS A REFLECTION OF HIS FACE WHO CALLD ME FROM THE DEEP       310 FOUR ZOAS 5        217
SAYING [S] O LIGHT SPRING UP & SHINE & I SPRANG UP FROM       310 FOUR ZOAS 5     *  219
  THE DEEP
I WILL ARISE EXPLORE THESE DENS & FIND THAT DEEP PULSATION    311 FOUR ZOAS 5        238
DRAWN OUT FROM DEEP TO DEEP WOVEN BY RIBBD  . . . . .   .     314 FOUR ZOAS 6        119
ROUND LAKES OF FIRE IN THE DARK DEEP THE RUINS OF URIZEN'S    316 FOUR ZOAS 6        179
  WORLD
CREATING MANY A VORTEX FIXING MANY A SCIENCE IN THE DEEP      316 FOUR ZOAS 6        187
WHEN I BEND DOWNWARD BENDING MY HEAD DOWNWARD INTO THE        317 FOUR ZOAS 6        202
  DEEP
ABOVE BENEATH ON ALL SIDES ROUND IN THE VAST DEEP            318 FOUR ZOAS 6        275
  OF IMMENSITY
IN INTRICATE LABYRINTHS OERSPREADING MANY A GRIZZLY DEEP      321 FOUR ZOAS 7        35
ORC ANSWERD CURSE THY HOARY BROWS WHAT DOST THOU IN THIS      322 FOUR ZOAS 7        69
  DEEP
I RAGE IN THE DEEP FOR LO . . . . . . . . . .  .              322 FOUR ZOAS 7        71
IN TORTURES OF DIRE COLDNESS NOW A LAKE OF WATERS DEEP  .  .  322 FOUR ZOAS 7        74
I RAGE FURIOUS IN THE DEEP FOR LO MY FEET & HANDS ARE NAILD   322 FOUR ZOAS 7        87
THAT WISDOM REACHES HIGH & DEEP & THEREFORE HE MADE ORC       324 FOUR ZOAS 7        162
IN THE DARK DEEP THE DARK TREE GREW HER SHADOW WAS DRAWN      324 FOUR ZOAS 7        170
  DOWN
TO SWIM THE DEEP & ON THE LAND CHILDREN ARE SOLD TO TRADES    333 FOUR ZOAS 7B       13
AND SLAVES IN MYRIADS IN SHIP LOADS BURDEN THE HOARSE         333 FOUR ZOAS 7B       16
  SOUNDING DEEP
AND HE COMMANDED HIS SONS FOUND A CENTER IN THE DEEP   .  .   333 FOUR ZOAS 7B       18
WITH SIGHS & HOWLING & DEEP SOBS THAT HE MIGHT LOSE HIS       336 FOUR ZOAS 7B       127
  RAGE
SO SUNG THE DEMONS OF THE DEEP THE CLARIONS OF WAR BLEW       338 FOUR ZOAS 7B       210
  LOUD
. . . RODE UPON THE STORMY DEEP  . . . . . . . .             339 FOUR ZOAS 7B       259
AND ALL THE HOLLOW DEEP REBELLOWD WITH THE WONDEROUS WAR      343 FOUR ZOAS 8     *   89
[BUT ?IN] BUT URIZEN HIS MIGHTY RAGE LET LOOSE IN THE MID     343 FOUR ZOAS 8     *   90
  DEEP
THE DIVINE VISION SEEN WITHIN THE INMOST DEEP RECESS   .  .   346 FOUR ZOAS 8        192
INTO THE DEEP TO SIEZE THE SHADOW SCALES HIS NECK & BOSOM     352 FOUR ZOAS 8        424
WITH DEEP REPENTANCE FOR THE LOSS OF THAT FAIR FORM OF MAN    352 FOUR ZOAS 8        435
LASHES HIS TAIL IN THE [WIDE] WILD DEEP HIS EYELIDS LIKE      352 FOUR ZOAS 8     *  439
  THE SUN
AND OF THE NAMELESS SHADOWY FEMALE IN THE NETHER DEEP   .  .  353 FOUR ZOAS 8        479
VOMIT OUT THE SCALY MONSTERS OF THE RESTLESS DEEP  . . .      354 FOUR ZOAS 8        511
SCREAMING IN BIRDS OVER THE DEEP & HOWLING IN THE WOLF  . .   355 FOUR ZOAS 8     *  577
THE SPECTRE OF ENITHARMON LET LOOSE ON THE TROUBLED DEEP      358 FOUR ZOAS 9        24
AND DEEP DESPAIR RATTLING GO UP THE FLAMES AROUND            359 FOUR ZOAS 9        68
  THE SYNAGOGUE
HE CALLD THE DEEP BURIED HIS VOICE & ANSWER NONE RETURND      360 FOUR ZOAS 9        136
LET LUVAH RAGE IN THE DARK DEEP EVEN TO CONSUMMATION  .  .    360 FOUR ZOAS 9        142
URIZEN WEPT IN THE DARK DEEP ANXIOUS HIS SCALY FORM  . . .    361 FOUR ZOAS 9        162
TO REASSUME THE HUMAN & HE WEPT IN THE DARK DEEP  . . . .     361 FOUR ZOAS 9        163
CHOKD THE BRIGHT RIVERS BURDNING WITH MY SHIPS THE ANGRY      361 FOUR ZOAS 9        169
  DEEP
AND DARKNESS COVERD ALL THE DEEP THE LIGHT OF ENION FADED     370 FOUR ZOAS 9        496
DEEP IN THE SOUTH GUARDED BY A FEW SOLITARY STARS  . . .      372 FOUR ZOAS 9        581
OF HUMAN FAMILIES THRO THE DEEP THE WINE PRESSES WERE FILLD   376 FOUR ZOAS 9        725
IN THE DEEP CAVES BENEATH HIS LIMBS RENEWD HIS LIONS ROAR     379 FOUR ZOAS 9        841
AND DARK URTHONA ROUZD HIS SHADY BRIDE FROM HER DEEP DEN      380 FOUR ZOAS AD 1      7
[A DEEP WINTER [NIGHT] DARK & COLD]  . . . . . . . .          415 MY SPECTRE/N       13
[A FATHOMLESS & BOUNDLESS DEEP]  . . . . . . . . .            415 MY SPECTRE/N       17
A FATHOMLESS & BOUNDLESS DEEP  . . . . . . . . .              415 MY SPECTRE/N       23
IN THE STUDIOUS HOURS OF DEEP MIDNIGHT  . . . . . .           419 I SAW A MONK/N     29
FOR IT STICKS IN THE HEART'S DEEP CORE  . . . . . .           423 THE SMILE          9
AND IT STICKS IN THE DEEP BACK BONE  . . . . . . .            423 THE SMILE          10
IN THE STUDIOUS HOURS OF DEEP MIDNIGHT  . . . . . .           430 GREY MONK          14
VIEWING HIS SIXFOLD EMANATION SCATTERD THRO THE DEEP   .  .   481 MILTON 2           19
IN TORMENT TO GO INTO THE DEEP HER TO REDEEM & HIMSELF        481 MILTON 2           20
  PERISH
DOWN SUNK WITH FRIGHT A RED ROUND GLOBE HOT BURNING DEEP      482 MILTON 3           11
DEEP DOWN INTO THE ABYSS PANTING CONGLOBING TREMBLING  .      482 MILTON 3           12
SHOT SPIRING OUT IN THE DEEP DARKNESS & PETRIFIED AS THEY     482 MILTON 3           18
  GREW
HANGING UPON THE WIND TWO NOSTRILS BENT DOWN INTO THE DEEP    482 MILTON 3           20
ROUND GLOBE SUNK DOWN FROM HIS BOSOM INTO THE DEEP IN PANGS   483 MILTON 3           30
LIKE AS A POLYPUS THAT VEGETATES BENEATH THE DEEP  . . .      496 MILTON 15          8
THE FOOTSTEPS AND INFIXING DEEP THE FEET IN MARBLE BEDS       500 MILTON 19          2
```

		PAGE	TITLE	LINE

DEEP   (CONTINUED)

WHEN LUVAH'S BULLS EACH MORNING DRAG THE SULPHUR SUN OUT OF THE DEEP	503 MILTON 21	20
HE WEEPS INTO THE ATLANTIC DEEP YET STILL IN DISMAL DREAMS	506 MILTON 23	9
THOU SEEST THE CONSTELLATIONS IN THE DEEP & WONDROUS NIGHT	511 MILTON 25	66
AND EVERY AGE IS MOATED DEEP WITH BRIDGES OF SILVER & GOLD	516 MILTON 28	56
HE STROVE TO RISE TO WALK INTO THE DEEP BUT STRENGTH FAILING	531 MILTON 39	50
THY HOLY WRATH & DEEP DECEIT CANNOT AVAIL AGAINST ME . .	627 JERUSALEM 8	33
IN ENTUTHON BENYTHON'S DEEP VALES BENEATH GOLGONOOZA . .	635 JERUSALEM 14	34
ALBION GROANS IN THE DEEP SLUMBERS OF DEATH UPON HIS ROCK	637 JERUSALEM 16	27
LIKE WHEELS FROM A GREAT WHEEL REFLECTED IN THE DEEP . .	641 JERUSALEM 18	43
THAT THE DEEP WOUND OF SIN MIGHT BE CLOSD UP WITH THE NEEDLE	643 JERUSALEM 21	13
AND ALL MY CHILDREN FOLLOWD HIS LOUD HOWLINGS INTO THE DEEP	643 JERUSALEM 21	17
AND CAST IT INTO THE ATLANTIC DEEP TO CATCH THE SOULS OF THE DEAD	646 JERUSALEM 23	23
AND AS THEY FLED IN FOLDING FIRES & THUNDERS OF THE DEEP	655 JERUSALEM 29	77
AMONG THE WINDING PLACES OF DEEP CONTEMPLATION INTRICATE	657 JERUSALEM 31	22
LET LOOSE THE ENORMOUS SPECTRE ON THE DARKNESS OF THE DEEP	667 JERUSALEM 40	32
THEY KNEELD AROUND THE COUCH OF DEATH IN DEEP HUMILIATION	668 JERUSALEM 41	24
TO ME THEIR BENEFACTOR CALLS ALOUD FOR VENGEANCE DEEP	671 JERUSALEM 42	54
THEIR EMANATIONS RETURN NOT THEIR SPECTRES RAGE IN THE DEEP	674 JERUSALEM 44	34
TILL DEEP DISSIMULATION IS THE ONLY DEFENCE AN HONEST MAN HAS LEFT	679 JERUSALEM 49	23
AMONG THE FIRES OF THE DRUID & THE DEEP BLACK RETHUNDERING WATERS	689 JERUSALEM 57	3
FOR THE VEIL OF VALA WHICH ALBION CAST INTO THE ATLANTIC DEEP	691 JERUSALEM 59	2
WHEN THE CHERUBIM HID THEIR HEADS UNDER THEIR WINGS IN DEEP SLUMBERS	697 JERUSALEM 63	24
AND JEALOUSY IMMINGLED & THE PURPLE OF THE VIOLET DARKEND DEEP	699 JERUSALEM 64	29
FROM EACH OTHER AND YET ARE A MIGHTY POLYPUS IN THE DEEP	703 JERUSALEM 66	54
SAT DEEP WITHIN HIM HID HIS FEMININE POWER UNREVEALD . .	709 JERUSALEM 70	18
IN THE DEEP DARKNESS BROAD LIGHTNINGS GLARE LONG THUNDERS ROLL	741 JERUSALEM 94	4
THEM HOWLS THE WOLF OF FAMINE DEEP HEAVES THE OCEAN BLACK THUNDERING	741 JERUSALEM 94	16
I BEGIN TO EMERGE FROM A DEEP PIT OF MELANCHOLY	798A LETTER 10	PROSE
ON THE SIDES OF THE DEEP	805 TO BUTTS/L	64
THE LOUD SEA & DEEP GULF	805 TO BUTTS/L	68
WILL I SING FORTH HIS PRAISES THAT THE DRAGONS OF THE DEEP	823C LETTER 26	PROSE

DEEPER

| AND THERE A WORLD OF DEEPER ULRO WAS OPEND IN THE MIDST | 490 MILTON 9 | 34 |
| IS IT AGAIN TO PLUNGE INTO DEEPER AFFLICTION BEHOLD ME   .   . | 527 MILTON 36 | 30 |

DEEPEST

THE MUSE THEN STRUCK HER DEEPEST [NOTE] STRING & SYMPATHY CAME FORTH	43C WOE CRIED MUSE	PROSE
BUT FROM THE CAVES OF DEEPEST NIGHT ASCENDING IN CLOUDS OF MIST	306 FOUR ZOAS 5	31
. . . THEN LOVE SHALL SHEW ITS ROOT IN DEEPEST HELL . . .	311 FOUR ZOAS 5	241
SO SPOKE ALBION IN GLOOMY MAJESTY AND DEEPEST NIGHT . . .	670 JERUSALEM 42	17
THE HILLS OF JUDEA ARE FALLEN WITH ME INTO THE DEEPEST HELL	720 JERUSALEM 79	8
BY LAND ASTOUNDING ERECTING PILLARS IN THE DEEPEST HELL	738 JERUSALEM 91	41

DEEP-FOUNDED

| DEEP-FOUNDED HABITATION SHAKE NOT THY ROOFS   .   .   .   .   . | 2 TO WINTER/PS | 3 |

DEEPLY

| HORRID TO THINK OF WHEN ENQUIRED DEEPLY INTO AND ALL   .   . | 652 JERUSALEM 28 | 8 |

DEEPS

[IN WHAT] [BURNT IN] DISTANT DEEPS OR SKIES	172 THE TYGER/N 1	5
BURNT IN DISTANT DEEPS OR SKIES	173 THE TYGER/N 2	5
SWELLING BELCHING FROM ITS DEEPS RED CLOUDS & RAGING FIRES	197 AMERICA 4	3
BUT THEY SHALL ROT ON DESART SANDS & CONSUME IN BOTTOMLESS DEEPS	199 AMERICA 8	7
TO MAKE THE DESARTS BLOSSOM & THE DEEPS SHRINK TO THEIR FOUNTAINS	199 AMERICA 8	8
LIKE WHITE CLOUDS RISING FROM THE DEEPS HIS FIFTY-TWO ARMIES	205 AMERICA CANC C	16
IN WHAT DISTANT DEEPS OR SKIES	214 THE TYGER/SE	5
OFT HE QUENCHD IT BENEATH IN THE DEEPS	260 BOOK OF LOS 5	35
IT DOWN INTO THE DEEPS FLED	260 BOOK OF LOS 5	43
IS FORMD & THROWN DOWN THUNDRING INTO THE DEEPS OF NON ENTITY	283 FOUR ZOAS 2	137
FURIOUS & TERRIBLE THEY SPORT & ?REND THE NETHER DEEPS .	289 FOUR ZOAS 2	* 359
TWO NOSTRILS BENT DOWN TO THE DEEPS	303 FOUR ZOAS 4	237
BENEATH THE DEEPS IN DISMAL DARKNESS BENEATH IMMENSITY	304 FOUR ZOAS 4	279
SHUDDRING & WEEPING THRO THE GLOOM & DOWN INTO THE DEEPS	307 FOUR ZOAS 5	69
ENITHARMON NURSD HER FIERY CHILD IN THE DARK DEEPS . . .	307 FOUR ZOAS 5	70
THEN LED HER DOWN INTO THE DEEPS & INTO HIS LABYRINTH .	308 FOUR ZOAS 5	111
AND BACK RETURN WITH WINE & FOOD OR DIVE INTO THE DEEPS	308 FOUR ZOAS 5	119
FOR STILL IT SURGES FORTH IN FISH & MONSTERS OF THE DEEPS	313 FOUR ZOAS 6	61
IN VAIN FOR HIDEOUS MONSTERS OF THE DEEPS ANNOYD HIM SORE	313 FOUR ZOAS 6	75
WARRING WITH MONSTERS OF THE DEEPS IN HIS MOST HIDEOUS PILGRIMAGE	318 FOUR ZOAS 6	261
GOLD SILVER BRASS & IRON CLANGORS CLAMORING REND THE [DEEPS] SHORES	319 FOUR ZOAS 6	311
THARMAS THREW HIS IMPETUOUS FLIGHT THRO THE DEEPS OF IMMENSITY	320 FOUR ZOAS 7	3
THE WATRY NATIONS COUCH & HIDE IN THE PROFOUNDEST DEEPS	320 FOUR ZOAS 7	24
THE DEEPS OF LOS THE SLAVE OF THAT CREATION I CREATED . .	327 FOUR ZOAS 7	297
TILL ENITHARMON'S SHADOW PREGNANT IN THE DEEPS BENEATH . .	328 FOUR ZOAS 7	316

```
                                                               PAGE     TITLE           LINE
DEEPS    (CONTINUED)
    WHEN IN THE DEEPS BENEATH I GATHERD OF THIS RUDDY FRUIT     329 FOUR ZOAS 7          387
    LOS DREW THEM FORTH OUT OF THE DEEPS PLANTING HIS RIGHT     332 FOUR ZOAS 7          464
        FOOT FIRM
    ORC WAS COMFORTED IN THE DEEPS HIS SOUL REVIVD IN THEM  . . 332 FOUR ZOAS 7          478
    BUT IN THE DEEPS . . . . . . . . .                         333 FOUR ZOAS 7B           1
    SO ORC ROLLD ROUND HIS CLOUDS UPON THE DEEPS OF DARK       336 FOUR ZOAS 7B         133
        URTHONA
    ARISING IN HIS PRIDE ENLIGHTEN ALL THE GRIZLY DEEPS  . . . 352 FOUR ZOAS 8          440
    COVERS THE DEEPS AT HIS VAST FURY (MOANING) IN HIS ROCK     352 FOUR ZOAS 8      *   450
    ARISE O STONY FORM OF DEATH O DRAGON OF THE DEEPS   . . .  360 FOUR ZOAS 9          138
    REDEEMD FROM ERROR'S POWER WAKE THOU DRAGON OF THE DEEPS    361 FOUR ZOAS 9          161
    FOR WEEDS OF DEATH HAVE WRAPD AROUND MY LIMBS IN THE HOARY  370 FOUR ZOAS 9          488
        DEEPS
    SUCH AS GLOWS OUT FROM SLEEPING SPIRITS APPEARD IN THE      372 FOUR ZOAS 9          561
        DEEPS BENEATH
    OVER THE DEEPS OUTSTRETCHING HER TWENTY SEVEN HEAVENS OVER  499 MILTON 18             3
        ALBION
    SHINING IN DARKNESS GLORIOUS UPON THE DEEPS OF ENTUTHON     501 MILTON 19            35
    INTO A TABERNACLE AND FLEE WITH CRIES DOWN TO THE DEEPS     503 MILTON 20            48
    IS MOSES CASTING HIS TABLES OF STONE INTO THE DEEPS  . . . 607B V LAST JUDG/N     PROSE
    THEY SCOURGE A GROUPE OF FIGURES DOWN INTO THE DEEPS    .  608A V LAST JUDG/N     PROSE
    WITH WHICH THEY HOVERING OVER THE DEEPS BENEATH  . . . . . 612A V LAST JUDG/N     PROSE
    BUT ALL WITHIN IS OPEND INTO THE DEEPS OF ENTUTHON BENYTHON 624 JERUSALEM 5          56
    LOS HEARD HER LAMENTATIONS IN THE DEEPS AFAR HIS TEARS FALL 624 JERUSALEM 5          66
    CONSTELLATIONS OVER THE DEADLY DEEPS OF INDEFINITE         625 JERUSALEM 7          22
        UDAN-ADAN
    WAVES OF THE ERYTHREAN TURNING UP THE BOTTOMS OF THE DEEPS  648 JERUSALEM 24         63
    OF MAN FOR EVER BE POSSESSD BY MONSTERS OF THE DEEPS    .  667 JERUSALEM 40         28
    THE SPECTRES OF THE DEAD CRY OUT FROM THE DEEPS BENEATH     671 JERUSALEM 42         57
    YE TWENTY-FOUR INTO THE DEEPS LET US DEPART TO GLORY   .   671 JERUSALEM 42         65
    THEY WEPT INTO THE DEEPS A LITTLE SPACE AT LENGTH WAS HEARD 675 JERUSALEM 44         43
DEER
    AS THE DEER WOUNDED ELLEN FLEW OVER . . . . . . .           5 FAIR ELENOR/PS         33
    AS THE DEER WOUNDED BY THE BROOKS OF WATER . . . . . .      36B COUCH DEATH/PS    PROSE
    THE WILD DEER WANDRING HERE & THERE . . . . . . .          431 AUGURIES             21
DEFACD
    AND THE GATES [BURST] BROKE IN SUNDER & THEIR ORNAMENTS     328 FOUR ZOAS 7      *  325
        DEFACD
DEFACE
    WHY WILT THOU DEFACE THY BEAUTY & THE BEAUTY OF            693 JERUSALEM 60         29
        THY LITTLE-ONES
    TO SEE JERUSALEM DEFACE HER LINEAMENTS WITH BITTER BLOWS    693 JERUSALEM 60         46
DEFACED
    I AM DEFACED WITH BLOWS & WITH THE DIRT OF THE PRISON  . . 695 JERUSALEM 62          5
DEFACING
    CALLING THE DEFINITE SIN DEFACING EVERY DEFINITE FORM   .  723 JERUSALEM 80         53
DEFECTIVE
    LIKENESSES FROM MEMORY BEING NECESSARILY VERY VERY         824B LETTER 27        PROSE
        DEFECTIVE
DEFECTS
    PRINCIPLES ACCORDING TO SR JOSHUA BECOME DEFECTS . . . . . 477A ANNO REYNOLDS     MARG
    MR ROSE'S OBSERVING SOME DEFECTS IN SEAGRAVE'S WORK  . . . 847A LETTER 44        PROSE
DEFENCE    SEE SELF-DEFENCE
    FALSE WITNESS WHEN HE OMITTED MAKING A DEFENCE BEFORE      158C MARRIAGE HH 22   PROSE
        PILATE
    . . . O LOS MY DEFENCE & GUIDE . . . . . . . . . . .       331 FOUR ZOAS 7         447
    A DEFENCE OF THE WICKEDNESS OF THE ISRAELITES IN MURDERING  387B ANNO WATSON       MARG
    I IN MY OWN DEFENCE CHALLENGE A COMPETITION . . . . . .    602A PUB ADDRESS/N     PROSE
    ASSERTING IN MY OWN DEFENCE THAT THIS PRINT IS THE FINEST   602A PUB ADDRESS/N     PROSE
    TILL DEEP DISSIMULATION IS THE ONLY DEFENCE AN HONEST MAN   679 JERUSALEM 49         23
        HAS LEFT
    IT MAY BE CALLD A DEFENCE OF LITERATURE AGAINST THOSE PESTS 841D LETTER 41       PROSE
        OF
    DEFENCE BUT I SHOULD BE ASHAMED NOT TO SET MY HAND AND  . . 864A LETTER 61       PROSE
DEFEND
    CAN IF THEY WILL DEFEND THEMSELVES AGAINST . . . . . . .    21 EDW THIRD/PS 2       87
    A SPOT OF GROUND THIS HE'LL DEFEND TIS HIS . . . . . .      26 EDW THIRD/PS 3      198
    TO DEFEND THE BIBLE IN THIS YEAR...WOULD COST A MAN HIS    383B ANNO WATSON       MARG
        LIFE
    DEFEND EITHER THE ACTS OF CHRIST OR THE BIBLE UNPERVERTED   383B ANNO WATSON       MARG
    THAT HE WHO WILL NOT DEFEND TRUTH MAY BE COMPELLED TO  . . 489 MILTON 8             47
    DEFEND A LIE THAT HE MAY BE SNARED & CAUGHT & TAKEN  . .   489 MILTON 8             48
    TO DEFEND ME FROM THY TERRORS O ORC MY ONLY BELOVED  . . . 499 MILTON 18            25
    THEN GOD DEFEND US FROM THE ARTS I SAY . . . . . . .       550 WHEN I SEE/N          5
    THAT HE WHO WILL NOT DEFEND TRUTH MAY BE COMPELLD TO DEFEND 628 JERUSALEM 9          29
    I HAVE INNOCENCE TO DEFEND AND IGNORANCE TO INSTRUCT   .   670 JERUSALEM 42         26
    SPECTRE TO DEFEND HER FROM MAN I WILL CREATE SECRET PLACES  733 JERUSALEM 88         17
    PERMIT ME IN RETURN TO DEFEND IT AGAINST A MISTAKEN ONE     793B LETTER 5        PROSE
    TO DEFEND MYSELF AGAINST A VERY UNWARRANTABLE WARRANT   .  826D LETTER 28        PROSE
DEFENDED
    DEFENDED PALAMABRON & RAGE FILLD THE UNIVERSAL TENT  . . . 351 FOUR ZOAS 8         390
    WATSON HAS DEFENDED ANTICHRIST . . . . . . . . . .         383D ANNO WATSON       MARG
DEFENDING
    BUT FOR THE SAKE OF DEFENDING THOSE WHO DO . . . . . .     597D PUB ADDRESS/N     PROSE
    NUMBER OF THE DOG & CROCODILE & THAT OF THE DOG DEFENDING   859B LETTER 56       PROSE
DEFERENCE
    SIRE WITH RESPECT AND DEFERENCE I LOOK . . . . . . .        23 EDW THIRD/PS 3       81
DEFIANCE
    BESIDE (HIM) THARMAS STAYD HIS FLIGHT & STOOD IN STERN     319 FOUR ZOAS 6         302
        DEFIANCE
    IN STERN DEFIANCE CAME FROM ALBION'S BOSOM HAND HYLE KOBAN  658 JERUSALEM 32         10
```

		PAGE	TITLE	LINE

DEFIANCE   (CONTINUED)
    WHEN I HAD MY DEFIANCE GIVEN   . . . .   818 HAPPINESS/L   71
    BUT HE TURNING ABOUT PUT HIMSELF INTO A POSTURE OF DEFIANCE 827A LETTER 28   PROSE
DEFIANTLY
    [AROUND THE ABYSS (DEFIANTLY) ?SHOUTING ALL HIS DEMONS]   SUPP FOUR ZOAS 5   *
DEFICIENCY
    ITS DEFICIENCY OR TO NEW CREATE IT ACCORDING TO YOUR WISH   860C LETTER 56   PROSE
DEFIED   SEE DEFYD
    WHEN KLOPSTOCK ENGLAND DEFIED   . . . .   186 WHEN KLOPSTK/N   1
DEFIES
    HE DEFIES COMPETITION IN COLOURING   . . . .   581A DESC CAT 5   PROSE
DEFILD
    THE SOUL OF SWEET DELIGHT CAN NEVER BE DEFILD   . . . . . 152B MARRIAGE HH 9   PROSE
    HOW CAN I BE DEFILD WHEN I REFLECT THY IMAGE PURE   . . 191 V DAU ALBION 3   16
    BECAUSE THE SOUL OF SWEET DELIGHT CAN NEVER BE DEFILD   . . 199 AMERICA 8   14
DEFILE
    RETURND WITH CHILDREN OF POLLUTION TO ?EFILE OUR HOUSE . . 640 JERUSALEM 18   31
DEFILED
    REND AWAY THIS DEFILED BOSOM THAT I MAY REFLECT   . . . . 190 V DAU ALBION 2   15
DEFIND
    IT IS ALSO SOMEWHAT IN THE SAME MANNER DEFIND BY PLATO   . . 825A LETTER 27   PROSE
DEFINE
    TO BLEND & NOT DEFINE THE PARTS   . . . .   547 LET BE TOLD/N   7
DEFINITE
    NIGGLING WITHOUT THE CORRECT & DEFINITE OUTLINE   . . . 448D ANNO REYNOLDS   MARG
    IN ART & THAT EVERY THING IN ART IS DEFINITE & DETERMINATE 457B ANNO REYNOLDS   MARG
    WITHOUT FATIGUE EVERY THING BEING DEFINITE & DETERMINATE   457B ANNO REYNOLDS   MARG
    [THIS IS ENCOURAGEMENT FOR ARTISTS (?ONLY ?BY) ?DEFINITION] SUPP ANNO REYNOLDS * MARG
    REFUSING ALL DEFINITE FORM THE ABSTRACT HORROR ROOFD STONY 482 MILTON 3   9
      HARD
    BUT THE DEFINITE AND DETERMINATE WHAT IS IT THAT   . . . 585C DESC CAT 15   PROSE
    THE INFINITE ALONE RESIDES IN DEFINITE & DETERMINATE   687 JERUSALEM 55   64
      IDENTITY
    WHERE DWELLS THE SPECTRE OF ALBION DESTROYER OF DEFINITE   688 JERUSALEM 56   17
      FORM
    REFUSD TO TAKE A DEFINITE FORM SHE HOVERD OVER ALL THE   723 JERUSALEM 80   52
      EARTH
    CALLING THE DEFINITE SIN DEFACING EVERY DEFINITE FORM   . . 723 JERUSALEM 80   53
DEFINITION
    THE MONK'S DEFINITION OF TRAGEDY IN THE PROEM TO HIS TALE 569B DESC CAT 3   PROSE
    AND IS SERVED BY NONE HE IS ACCORDING TO CHRIST'S   570B DESC CAT 3   PROSE
      DEFINITION
    IS MY DEFINITION OF THE MOST SUBLIME POETRY   . . . . . 825A LETTER 27   PROSE
DEFORM
    WITH FIRES OF HELL DEFORM THEIR ANCIENT HEAVENS WITH SHAME 202 AMERICA 15   15
      & WOE
    O HOW COULDST THOU DEFORM THOSE BEAUTIFUL PROPORTIONS   . . 360 FOUR ZOAS 9   140
    NOUGHT CAN DEFORM THE HUMAN RACE   . . . .   433 AUGURIES   99
    HIS SHADOWS WOULD DESTROY IT & DEFORM ITS APPEARANCE   . . 464A ANNO REYNOLDS   MARG
DEFORMD
    WERE SMITTEN WITH DARKNESS DEFORMD   . . . .   251 AHANIA 3   43
    DEFORMD THRO THE THREE HEAVENS DESCENDING IN FURY & FIRE   267 FOUR ZOAS 1   104
    DEFORMD I SEE THESE LINEAMENTS OF UNGRATIFIED DESIRE   . . 298 FOUR ZOAS 4   24
    DEFORMD [(BRUTISH)] . . . .   327 FOUR ZOAS 7   * 305
    ARE THUS DEFORMD WITH HARDNESS WITH THE [PLOW] SWORD &   361 FOUR ZOAS 9   * 175
      WITH THE SPEAR
    ENLARGD INTO DIMENSION & DEFORMD INTO INDEFINITE SPACE   498 MILTON 17   23
    THE SPECTRE IS IN GIANT MAN INSANE AND MOST DEFORMD . . . 664 JERUSALEM 37   4
DEFORMED
    FROM ENION'S BRAIN IN THIS DEFORMED FORM LEAVING THEE THERE 327 FOUR ZOAS 7   291
    OF FORTY-EIGHT DEFORMED HUMAN WONDERS OF THE ALMIGHTY   . . 529 MILTON 37   54
DEFORMITY
    VARIETY DOES NOT NECESSARILY SUPPOSE DEFORMITY FOR A ROSE   81C ANNO LAVATER   MARG
    INTO HORRIBLE FORMS OF DEFORMITY   . . . .   230 URIZEN 13   43
    I WILL GIVE BLACKNESS FOR JEWELS HOARY FROST FOR ORNAMENT   312 FOUR ZOAS 6   37
      DEFORMITY
    IT DOES NOT THEREFORE FOLLOW THAT ALL OTHER FORMS   459C ANNO REYNOLDS   MARG
      ARE DEFORMITY
    THE SYMMETRY OF DEFORMITY IS A PRETTY FOOLERY   . . . . 460C ANNO REYNOLDS   MARG
    LEANNESS OR FATNESS IS NOT DEFORMITY BUT   . . . . . 460C ANNO REYNOLDS   MARG
    REYNOLDS THOUGHT CHARACTER ITSELF EXTRAVAGANCE & DEFORMITY 460C ANNO REYNOLDS   MARG
    THE FACE THAT IS INCAPABLE OF PASSION & EXPRESSION   466A ANNO REYNOLDS   MARG
      IS DEFORMITY
    ETERNITY LOOKD UPON AS DEFORMITY & LOVELINESS AS A DRY   628 JERUSALEM 9   8
      TREE
    (DEFORMITY) SHE GAVE HER BEAUTY TO ANOTHER BEARING ABROAD 726 JERUSALEM 82   69
    IN THE WAY SOME SEE NATURE ALL RIDICULE & DEFORMITY &   . . 793D LETTER 5   PROSE
DEFY
    WITH THE FINEST ENGRAVINGS & DEFY THE MOST CRITICAL JUDGE   602A PUB ADDRESS/N   PROSE
    I DEFY ANY MAN TO CUT CLEANER STROKES THAN I DO OR   . . . 602A PUB ADDRESS/N   PROSE
    AND I WILL RETURN IT OTHERWISE I DEFY THY WORST REVENGE   670 JERUSALEM 42   39
    MADE ME VERY UNEASY BUT IT IS OVER & I NOW DEFY THE WORST   819D LETTER 25   PROSE
      & FEAR NOT
DEFYD
    DEFYD THE STORM THAT HOWLED OER THEIR HEADS   . . . . .   32 EDW THIRD/PS 6   33
DEGRADE
    DEGRADE FIRST THE ARTS IF YOUD MANKIND DEGRADE   . . . 445 ANNO REYNOLDS   1
    REMOVE THEM OR DEGRADE THEM & THE EMPIRE IS NO MORE   . . . 445D ANNO REYNOLDS   MARG
    & ITS LAST NOW HE BEGINS TO DEGRADE [&] TO DENY [DESTROY]   458B ANNO REYNOLDS * MARG
      & TO MOCK
    DO NOT DEGRADE BUT RENDER HIM AN OBJECT OF DIGNIFIED MIRTH 568D DESC CAT 3   PROSE
    MY PERSON DEGRADE & MY TEMPER CHASTISE   . . . .   829 O WHY BORN/L   6

DEGRADED

ALL NATURE WAS DEGRADED	451 ANNO REYNOLDS	2
INSULTED & DEGRADED BY THE REPUTATION OF THESE DISCOURSES	452B ANNO REYNOLDS	MARG
AS MUCH AS THEY WERE DEGRADED BY THE REPUTATION OF . .	452B ANNO REYNOLDS	MARG
NIGGLING & POCO PEN AS DRYDEN HAS DEGRADED MILTON WITH .	600D PUB ADDRESS/N	PROSE
AND SAW EVERY MINUTE PARTICULAR OF ALBION DEGRADED	656 JERUSALEM 31	7
& MURDERD		
ART DEGRADED IMAGINATION DENIED WAR GOVERNED THE NATIONS	775D INSC LAOCOON	PROSE
I HAVE BEEN VERY MUCH DEGRADED & INJURIOUSLY TREATED .	828D LETTER 28	PROSE

DEGREE

IS IT TO ASSERT THAT MAN IS BORN IN ONLY ONE DEGREE . . .	93A ANNO SWED LOVE	MARG
WHEN THAT ONE DEGREE IS RECEPTION	93A ANNO SWED LOVE	MARG
IS IT NOT ALSO EVIDENT THAT ONE DEGREE WILL NOT OPEN THE	93A ANNO SWED LOVE	MARG
OTHER		
FOR YOU CANNOT DEMONSTRATE ONE DEGREE BY THE OTHER . .	93B ANNO SWED LOVE	MARG
("IN THE WORLD...THE NATURAL DEGREE") SEE SECT...OF THE	93D ANNO SWED LOVE	MARG
NEXT NUMBER		
IN THE GREATEST DEGREE NOW HEAR HOW HE HAS GIVEN . .	158C MARRIAGE HH 22	PROSE
IN THE HIGHEST DEGREE FOR HE HAS EVERY [PERQUISITE] THING	472A ANNO REYNOLDS	* MARG
OF BOTH		
GRAND IN THE HIGHEST DEGREE THE ARTIST HAS ENDEAVOURED .	565D DESC CAT 2	PROSE
IN A SUBLIME DEGREE BEING DERIVED FROM REAL VISION IN .	607A V LAST JUDG/N	PROSE
("TO HC SIX YEARS OLD") THIS IS ALL IN THE HIGHEST DEGREE	783A ANNO WW POEMS	MARG
IMAGINATIVE		
IN SOME DEGREE & THAT ITS ONCE STUPID INHABITANTS SHOULD	798C LETTER 10	PROSE
WOMAN HAS EXHAUSTED HER STRENGTH TO SUCH A DEGREE WITH .	801B LETTER 13	PROSE
TILL NOW IN ANY DEGREE PLEASED MYSELF & NOW I MUST .	815C LETTER 23	PROSE
PROGRESS CALLD THE PILES WHICH WHEN TO THE DEGREE I HAVE	874D LETTER 80	PROSE
HAD		

DEGREES

OF THE (THREE) DEGREES TWO OF WHICH HE MUST DESTROY . . .	93A ANNO SWED LOVE	MARG
AND BEING RESTRAIND IT BY DEGREES BECOMES PASSIVE . .	150A MARRIAGE HH 5	PROSE
BY DEGREES WE BEHELD THE INFINITE ABYSS FIERY AS THE SMOKE	156A MARRIAGE HH 17	PROSE
AT LAST TO THE EAST DISTANT ABOUT THREE DEGREES APPEARD	156C MARRIAGE HH 17	PROSE
OF SIGHT BY DEGREES UNFOLD	230 URIZEN 13	32
AND TO HIS SONS IN THEIR DEGREES & TO HIS BEAUTEOUS	287 FOUR ZOAS 2	271
DAUGHTERS		

DEIGND

AND THE STRONG LION DEIGND IN HIS MOUTH TO WEAR THE GOLDEN	340 FOUR ZOAS 7B	282
BIT		

DEIGNS

OF TWENTY WHO SCARCELY HAS TAKEN OR DEIGNS TO TAKE A PENCIL	830A LETTER 30	PROSE

DEIR

MAY BE VERY CLEVER IN [YOUR] DEIR OWN OPINIONS	594D PUB ADDRESS/N	PROSE

DEISM

THE ASHES OF MYSTERY BEGAN TO ANIMATE THEY CALLD IT DEISM	357 FOUR ZOAS 8	618
THE KNAVE WHO IS CONVERTED TO [CHRISTIANITY] DEISM . .	615B V LAST JUDG/N	PROSE
DEISM IS THE WORSHIP OF THE GOD OF THIS WORLD BY THE MEANS	682C JERUSALEM 52	PROSE
DEISM IS THE SAME & ENDS IN THE SAME	682C JERUSALEM 52	PROSE
HAS ARISEN FROM DEISM WHICH IS NATURAL RELIGION	683A JERUSALEM 52	PROSE

DEIST

("NOT HONEST PUBLICLY CHRISTIAN PRIVATELY DEIST") BRAVO	72C ANNO LAVATER	MARG
BOTH OF DECEIT & OF OPEN VIOLENCE THE DEIST & THE CHRISTIAN	615A V LAST JUDG/N	PROSE
HEBREW ART IS CALLED SIN BY THE DEIST SCIENCE	776C INSC LAOCOON	PROSE

DEISTICAL

WHO IN THIS DEISTICAL AGE ARE DEISTS	567D DESC CAT 3	PROSE
IT IS DEISTICAL VIRTUE I SUPPOSE BUT AS I HAVE NONE OF THIS	598C PUB ADDRESS/N	PROSE

DEISTS

[THE DEISTS SAY] PAINE SAYS THAT CHRISTIANITY PUT A STOP	388D ANNO WATSON	* MARG
WHO IN THIS DEISTICAL AGE ARE DEISTS	567D DESC CAT 3	PROSE
MANY ARE DEISTS WHO WOULD IN CERTAIN CIRCUMSTANCES . .	615A V LAST JUDG/N	PROSE
TO THE DEISTS	681D JERUSALEM 52	TITLE
YOU O DEISTS PROFESS YOURSELVES THE ENEMIES OF CHRISTIANITY	682A JERUSALEM 52	PROSE
NAMED BY THE DIVINE NAME YOUR RELIGION O DEISTS . . .	682B JERUSALEM 52	PROSE
THOSE WHO MARTYR OTHERS OR WHO CAUSE WAR ARE DEISTS . .	683A JERUSALEM 52	PROSE
COLLUSION CALLING THEMSELVES DEISTS WORSHIPPING THE	737 JERUSALEM 90	65
MATERNAL		

DEITIES

MENTAL DEITIES FROM THEIR OBJECTS THUS BEGAN PRIESTHOOD	153A MARRIAGE HH 11	PROSE
THUS MEN FORGOT THAT ALL DEITIES RESIDE IN THE HUMAN BREAST	153B MARRIAGE HH 11	PROSE
THE DEITIES OF SURROUNDING NATIONS AND ASSERTED THAT THEY	153D MARRIAGE HH 12	PROSE
THE HEATHEN DEITIES WROTE THEM ALL	758 EV GOSPEL (2)	5

DEITY

COUNTRY PLACING IT UNDER ITS MENTAL DEITY	153A MARRIAGE HH 11	PROSE

DELAY

IF AN AMOROUS DELAY	178 THE FAIRY/N	5
TO BRING THEM TO PERFECTION HAS CAUSED THIS DELAY AS ALSO	840B LETTER 39	PROSE
THE DELAY I HAVE SEEN OUR EXCELLENT FLAXMAN LATELY HE IS	842D LETTER 42	PROSE
WELL		
I HOPE YOU WILL EXCUSE MY DELAY IN SENDING THE BOOKS . .	850A LETTER 49	PROSE

DELAYED

EXCUSE THE WRITING I HAVE DELAYED TOO LONG	871D LETTER 73	PROSE

DELECTABLE

DELECTABLE REPOSEST RUDDY IN MY ABSENCE FLAMING WITH BEAUTY	325 FOUR ZOAS 7	187

DELEGATED

AND FEELING THE DAMPS OF DEATH THEY WITH ONE ACCORD	674 JERUSALEM 44	28
DELEGATED LOS		

DELICATE

THAT THE DELICATE EAR IN ITS INFANCY	247 SONG OF LOS 7	5
IMMENSE UPON THE HEAVENS WITH BREAD & DELICATE REPASTS .	366 FOUR ZOAS 9	334
HER DELICATE WOMEN & CHILDREN SHRIEK UPON THE BITTER WIND	375 FOUR ZOAS 9	664
DELICATE HANDS & HEADS WILL NEVER APPEAR	551 DELICATE/N	1

```
                                                    PAGE      TITLE              LINE
DELICATE    (CONTINUED)
    COLOUR IT IS MIXED WITH ESPECIALLY EVERY DELICATE COLOUR    566B DESC CAT 2       PROSE
    SHE HAS CERTAIN PECULIARITIES AND LITTLE DELICATE           568B DESC CAT 3       PROSE
      AFFECTATIONS
    THE EYE THE LITTLE NOSTRILS & THE DELICATE TONGUE & EARS     728 JERUSALEM 83       36
    RIBBD DELICATE & CLOTHD WITH FEATHERD GOLD & AZURE & PURPLE  731 JERUSALEM 86        6
DELICIOUS
    FLATTERY IS DELICIOUS EVEN FROM THE LIPS OF A BABBLER        29D EDW THIRD/PS 4   PROSE
      EXIT PETER
    AND THE NIGHT OF DELICIOUS SONGS              .  .  .  .    247 SONG OF LOS 6       14
    DELICIOUS VIANDS DEMONS OF WAVES THEIR WATRY ECCHOS WOKE   . 274 FOUR ZOAS 1    *   378
    O HOW DELICIOUS ARE THE GRAPES FLOURISHING IN THE SUN   .  . 369 FOUR ZOAS 9       447
DELIGHT
    FETCH HITHER MYRATANA & DELIGHT YOURSELVES WITH SCOFFS   .  . 105 TIRIEL 4          65
    GAVE THEE CLOTHING OF DELIGHT      .  .  .  .  .  .  .  .  .  115 THE LAMB/SI        5
    AND TO THESE VIRTUES OF DELIGHT        .  .  .  .  .  .  .  . 117 DIVNE IMAGE/SI     3
    WITH SILENT DELIGHT     .  .  .  .         .  .  .  .  .  .  . 118 NIGHT/SI          7
    WHERE FLOCKS HAVE TOOK DELIGHT     .  .  .  .  .  .  .  .  .  119 NIGHT/SI          10
    HOVER OVER MY DELIGHT          .  .  .  .  .  .  .  .  .  .  120 CRADLE SONG/SI     10
    BIRDS DELIGHT                  .  .  .  .  .  .  .  .  .  .  123 SPRING/SI          3
    NOR IN MY BOOK CAN I TAKE DELIGHT      .  .  .  .  .  .  .  . 124 SCHOOL BOY/SI     13
    YOUTH OF DELIGHT COME HITHER       .  .  .  .  .  .  .  .  .  126 VOICE BARD/SI      1
    ENERGY IS ETERNAL DELIGHT          .  .  .  .  .  .  .  .  .  149D MARRIAGE HH 4   PROSE
    IS AN IMMENSE WORLD OF DELIGHT CLOSD BY YOUR SENSES FIVE     150D MARRIAGE HH 6   PROSE
    THE SOUL OF SWEET DELIGHT CAN NEVER BE DEFILD   .  .  .  .  . 152B MARRIAGE HH 9   PROSE
    AND HER THORNS WERE MY ONLY DELIGHT        .  .  .  .  .  .  . 161 ROSE TREE/N      10
    TO BIND ANOTHER TO ITS DELIGHT     .  .  .  .  .  .  .  .  .  162 CLOD PEBBLE/N     10
    SEEKING ONLY FOR DELIGHT       .  .  .  .  .  .  .  .  .  .  167 INFANT SORW/N     17
    [NO DELIGHT WAS TO BE FOUND]       .  .  .  .  .  .  .  .  .  167 INFANT SORW/N     19
    [CAN DELIGHT]          .  .  .  .  .  .  .  .  .  .  .  .  .  169 EARTHS ANSWR/N    13
    DOES SPRING HIDE ITS [DELIGHT] JOY     .  .  .  .  .  .  .  . 169 EARTHS ANSWR/N    16
    AND I FELT DELIGHT             .  .  .  .  .  .  .  .  .  .  170 SLEPT DARK/N       4
    WHILE THE LILLY WHITE SHALL IN LOVE DELIGHT     .  .  .  .  . 171 THE LILLY/N       3
    AND HID FROM HIM MY HEART'S DELIGHT        .  .  .  .  .  .  . 182 THE ANGEL/N       8
    ANOTHER FLOWER SHALL SPRING BECAUSE THE SOUL OF SWEET        189 V DAU ALBION 1     9
      DELIGHT
    OVER THE WAVES SHE WENT IN WINGD EXULTING SWIFT DELIGHT      189 V DAU ALBION 1    14
    INFANCY FEARLESS LUSTFUL HAPPY NESTLING FOR DELIGHT   .  .  . 193 V DAU ALBION 6    4
    OPEN TO JOY AND TO DELIGHT WHERE EVER BEAUTY APPEARS  .  .  . 194 V DAU ALBION 6   22
    OOTHOON SHALL VIEW HIS DEAR DELIGHT NOR EER WITH JEALOUS     195 V DAU ALBION 7    28
      CLOUD
    BECAUSE THE SOUL OF SWEET DELIGHT CAN NEVER BE DEFILD  .  .  . 199 AMERICA 8        14
    CAN DELIGHT                   .  .  .  .  .  .  .  .  .  .  211 EARTHS ANSR/SE     13
    TO BIND ANOTHER TO ITS DELIGHT     .  .  .  .  .  .  .  .  .  211 CLOD PEBBLE/SE    10
    AND HID FROM HIM MY HEART'S DELIGHT        .  .  .  .  .  .  . 214 THE ANGEL/SE      8
    AND HER THORNS WERE MY ONLY DELIGHT        .  .  .  .  .  .  . 215 ROSE TREE/SE      8
    WHILE THE LILLY WHITE SHALL IN LOVE DELIGHT     .  .  .  .  . 215 THE LILLY/SE      3
    NAKED IN THE SUNNY BEAMS DELIGHT       .  .  .  .  .  .  .  . 219 LIT GRL LST/SE    9
    HIS PROLIFIC DELIGHT OBSCURD MORE & MORE   .  .  .  .  .  .  . 227 URIZEN 10        12
    IN PERVERSE AND CRUEL DELIGHT          .  .  .  .  .  .  .  . 231 URIZEN 19
    THY GOLDEN WINGS ARE MY DELIGHT & THY FLAMES OF SOFT        244 EUROPE 14          8
      DELUSION
    SO ANTAMON CALLD UP LEUTHA FROM HER VALLEYS OF DELIGHT   .  . 246 SONG OF LOS 3    28
    THE GRAVE SHRIEKS WITH DELIGHT & SHAKES    .  .  .  .  .  .  . 248 SONG OF LOS 7    35
    SELF-DESTROYING HOW CAN DELIGHT        .  .  .  .  .  .  .  . 255 AHANIA 5         42
    DELIGHT THEY DIE & THEY REVIVE IN SPRING WITH MUSIC & SONGS  266 FOUR ZOAS 1       67
    A TABERNACLE OF [DELIGHT] FOR [ENITHARMON] JERUSALEM  .  .  . 266 FOUR ZOAS 1    *   70
    THAT I SHOULD HIDE THEE WITH MY POWER & DELIGHT THEE WITH    269 FOUR ZOAS 1      174
      MY BEAUTY
    AND NINE BRIGHT SPACES WANDERD WEAVING MAZES OF DELIGHT      270 FOUR ZOAS 1      234
    TO FOREGO EACH HIS OWN DELIGHT TO WAR AGAINST HIS SPECTRE    273 FOUR ZOAS 1      340
    AND VALA FED IN CRUEL DELIGHT THE FURNACES WITH FIRE  .  .  . 282 FOUR ZOAS 2      73
    I LOVED HER I GAVE HER ALL MY SOUL & MY DELIGHT   .  .  .  . 282 FOUR ZOAS 2      94
    WEAVING MAZES OF DELIGHT ALONG THE SUNNY PARADISE    .  .  . 282 FOUR ZOAS 2      96
    IN CRUEL DELIGHT THEY TRAP THE LISTENERS & IN CRUEL         284 FOUR ZOAS 2      162
      DELIGHT
    EVERY HALL SURROUNDED BY BRIGHT PARADISES OF DELIGHT   .     284 FOUR ZOAS 2      176
    FLOW INTO RIVERS OF DELIGHT THERE THE SPONTANEOUS FLOWERS    308 FOUR ZOAS 5      132
    ONCE HOW I WALKED FROM MY PALACE IN GARDENS OF DELIGHT  .  . 310 FOUR ZOAS 5      198
    I TAUGHT THEM SONGS OF SWEET DELIGHT I GAVE THEIR TENDER     312 FOUR ZOAS 6       30
      VOICES
    FOR VOICES OF DELIGHT HOARSE CROAKINGS INARTICULATE THRO     312 FOUR ZOAS 6       39
      FROST
    MINGLE TOGETHER TO CREATE A WORLD FOR LOS IN CRUEL DELIGHT   313 FOUR ZOAS 6       82
    AND BOOKS & INSTRUMENTS OF SONG & PICTURES OF DELIGHT   .   317 FOUR ZOAS 6      216
    SURE THOU ART BATHD IN RIVERS OF DELIGHT ON VERDANT FIELDS   321 FOUR ZOAS 7       63
    WITH VISIONS OF DELIGHT SO LOVELY THAT THEY URGE THY RAGE    321 FOUR ZOAS 7       65
    LOVELIEST DELIGHT OF MEN ENITHARMON SHADY HIDING    .  .  . 325 FOUR ZOAS 7      222
    ROUND BEULAH THERE HE REVELD IN DELIGHT AMONG THE FLOWERS    326 FOUR ZOAS 7      243
    IMBODIED THOU MY GARDEN OF DELIGHT & I THE SPIRIT IN THE     327 FOUR ZOAS 7      272
      GARDEN
    LISTEN O VISION OF DELIGHT ONE DREAD MORN OF GOARY BLOOD     327 FOUR ZOAS 7    *  278
    LOVELY DELIGHT OF MEN ENITHARMON SHADY  .  .  .  .  .  .  . 331 FOUR ZOAS 7      436
    BEFORE MY FACE ASCENDING WITH DELIGHT AS IN ANCIENT TIMES    331 FOUR ZOAS 7    *  445
    THEY FORMD THE SECRET PLACE REVERSING ALL THE ORDER OF       333 FOUR ZOAS 7B      22
      DELIGHT
    THIS WAS TO HER SUPREME DELIGHT THE WARRIORS MOURND         338 FOUR ZOAS 7B     219
      DISAPPOINTED
    THE SHADOWY FEMALE VARIED IN THE WAR IN HER DELIGHT   .  .  . 338 FOUR ZOAS 7B     223
    THARMAS REPLID O VALA ONCE I LIVD IN A GARDEN OF DELIGHT     339 FOUR ZOAS 7B     232
    AMONG THE APPLE TREES & ALL THE GARDENS OF DELIGHT   .  .  . 339 FOUR ZOAS 7B  *  234
    I HEAR THY VOICE BUT NOT THY FORM SEE THOU & ALL DELIGHT     339 FOUR ZOAS 7B     240
```

	PAGE	TITLE	LINE

DELIGHT   (CONTINUED)
```
        AND SHE WENT FORTH & SAW THE FORMS OF LIFE & OF DELIGHT      340 FOUR ZOAS 7B      269
        FOR HER DELIGHT THE HORSE HIS PROUD NECK BOWD & HIS WHITE     340 FOUR ZOAS 7B      281
          MANE
        TO BRING HER FRUITS OF SWEET DELIGHT FROM TREES OF RICHEST    340 FOUR ZOAS 7B      .284
          WONDERS
        RESIDES THAT GOD OF MY DELIGHT O MIGHT MY EYES BEHOLD   . .   345 FOUR ZOAS 8       156
        IN SOFT SILK DRAWN FROM THEIR OWN BOWELS IN LASCIVIOUS        346 FOUR ZOAS 8       211
          DELIGHT
        WITH GIFTS & GOLD OF EDEN ASTONISHD STUPIFIED WITH DELIGHT    346 FOUR ZOAS 8     * 214
        THESE NOSTRILS THAT EXPANDED WITH DELIGHT IN MORNING SKIES    349 FOUR ZOAS 8       303
        THRO CHAOS SEEKING FOR DELIGHT & IN SPACES REMOTE   . . .     361 FOUR ZOAS 9       170
        THAT SPRING MAY SEE THEM RISE IN TENFOLD JOY & SWEET          362 FOUR ZOAS 9       218
          DELIGHT
        TO ONE ANOTHER WHAT ARE WE & WHENCE IS OUR JOY & DELIGHT      373 FOUR ZOAS 9       609
        AND THUS HER VOICE GLORY DELIGHT & SWEET ENJOYMENT BORN       381 FOUR ZOAS AD 5     11
        THAT I SHOULD HIDE THEE WITH MY POWER & [DELIGHT THEE WITH    382 FOUR ZOAS AD 5 *   16
          MY BEAUTY]
        AND BINDS HER DOWN FOR HIS DELIGHT  . . . . . . . .           425 MENTAL TRAVLER     24
        SHE WALKD WITH HER THOMAS IN SWEET DELIGHT . . . . .          427 LAND OF DREAMS     10
        MARY MOVES IN SOFT BEAUTY & CONSCIOUS DELIGHT . . . .         428 MARY                9
        IN THE MORNING THE VILLAGERS ROSE WITH DELIGHT    . .         428 MARY               13
        AND RETURND TO ITS OWN DELIGHT  . . . . . . . . .             432 AUGURIES           70
        SOME ARE BORN TO SWEET DELIGHT  . . . . . . . . .             433 AUGURIES          122
        SOME ARE BORN TO SWEET DELIGHT  . . . . . . . . .             433 AUGURIES          123
        WHOSE WHOLE DELIGHT IS IN DESTROYING . . . . . . .            480C MILTON 1        PROSE
        OF VARIED BEAUTY TO DELIGHT THE WANDERER AND REPOSE  . .      481 MILTON 2            4
        THEY TAKE UP INTO THEIR HEAVENS IN INTOXICATING DELIGHT       484 MILTON 5           10
        OUGHT BUT THE VEGETABLE RATIO & LOATHE THE FAINT DELIGHT      485 MILTON 5           35
        SHADOW OF MY DELIGHT WHO WANDEREST SEEKING FOR THE PREY       499 MILTON 18          38
        KNOWS IN ITS INTRICATE MAZES OF DELIGHT ARTFUL TO WEAVE       512 MILTON 26           4
        IS A GARDEN OF DELIGHT & A BUILDING OF MAGNIFICENCE  . .      512 MILTON 26          32
        THE INTEGUMENT SOFT FOR ITS CLOTHING WITH JOY & DELIGHT       515 MILTON 28          20
        HER MAIDENS TO HER HUSBAND DELIGHTING IN HIS DELIGHT    .     522 MILTON 33          18
        SPINNING IT FROM THEIR BOWELS WITH SONGS OF AMOROUS DELIGHT   524 MILTON 34          28
        READY TO OBEY BUT PITY THOU MY SHADOW OF DELIGHT  . . . .     527 MILTON 36          31
        FROM HENCE SHE COMES FORTH ON THE CHURCHES IN DELIGHT   .     529 MILTON 38          24
        AND MY SWEET SHADOW OF DELIGHT STOOD TREMBLING BY MY SIDE     534 MILTON 42          28
        AS THERE IS A CLASS OF MEN WHOSE WHOLE DELIGHT IS   . .       573B DESC CAT 3      PROSE
        UGLY MAN ACTS FROM LOVE OF CARNAGE AND DELIGHT IN   . .       580C DESC CAT 5      PROSE
        MOST CRUEL DEMON WHOSE WHOLE DELIGHT IS TO CAUSE  . . .       583A DESC CAT 9      PROSE
        AND VALA FED IN CRUEL DELIGHT THE FURNACES WITH FIRE   .      625 JERUSALEM 7        31
        CONCERNING MY CHIEF DELIGHT BUT THOU HAST BROKEN SILENCE      630 JERUSALEM 10       41
        WHERE WE DELIGHT IN INNOCENCE BEFORE THE FACE OF THE LAMB     642 JERUSALEM 20        9
        O VALA O JERUSALEM DO YOU DELIGHT IN MY GROANS   . . .        643 JERUSALEM 21        1
        THE PONDS WHERE BOYS TO BATHE DELIGHT  . . . . . .            650 FIELDS FROM/J      14
        . . . WE DELIGHT IN THEIR BLOOD ON OUR ALTARS  . . . .        673 JERUSALEM 43       48
        YET THE INTOXICATING DELIGHT THAT THEY TAKE IN THEIR WORK     691 JERUSALEM 59       34
        THESE NOSTRILS THAT EXPANDED WITH DELIGHT IN MORNING SKIES    705 JERUSALEM 67       49
        BUT THEY FROWN & DELIGHT IN CRUELTY REFUSING ALL OTHER JOY    706 JERUSALEM 68       29
        O BEAUTIFUL DAUGHTER OF ALBION CRUELTY IS THY DELIGHT   .     706 JERUSALEM 68       53
        IS A HOUSE OF (PLEASANTNESS) & A GARDEN OF DELIGHT BUILT      714 JERUSALEM 73       51
          BY THE
        THAT GAVE ME SWEET DELIGHT BY HIS TORMENTS BENEATH MY VEIL    726 JERUSALEM 82       39
        WEAVING BOWERS OF DELIGHT ON THE CURRENT OF INFANT THAMES     728 JERUSALEM 83       50
        LET MAN'S DELIGHT BE LOVE BUT WOMAN'S DELIGHT BE PRIDE        732 JERUSALEM 87       16
        INTO EACH OTHER'S BOSOM WHICH ARE UNIVERSES OF DELIGHT  .     733 JERUSALEM 88        4
        ELUCIDATED BY CHILDREN WHO HAVE TAKEN A GREATER DELIGHT       794A LETTER 5        PROSE
        "O HOW WE DELIGHT IN TALKING OF THE PLEASURE WE SHALL HAVE"   800B LETTER 12       PROSE
        THE BREAD OF SWEET THOUGHT & THE WINE OF DELIGHT . . . .      800 MRS FLAXMAN/L     13
        OF ETERNITY BEFORE MY MORTAL LIFE & THOSE WORKS ARE THE       802C LETTER 14       PROSE
          DELIGHT
        SOFT CONSUMD IN DELIGHT  . . . . . . . . . . .                805 TO BUTTS/L         57
        IT WILL GIVE ME THE UTMOST DELIGHT TO DO MY BEST . . . .      808C LETTER 19       PROSE
        TIS FOURFOLD IN MY SUPREME DELIGHT  . . . . . . .             818 HAPPINESS/L        85
        SMALLER POEMS & WILL READ WITH GREAT DELIGHT I HAVE GIVEN     824A LETTER 27       PROSE
        TO ME FOR NOW O GLORY AND O DELIGHT I HAVE ENTIRELY          851D LETTER 50       PROSE
          REDUCED
DELIGHTED
        DELIGHTED TO SEE THEM IN SUCH A SERIOUS HUMOUR MR SCOPPRELL   61C ISLAND MOON 11   PROSE
        AND IN THE NIGHT LIKE INFANTS SLEPT DELIGHTED WITH INFANT     100 TIRIEL 2           9
          DREAMS
        DELIGHTED WITH THE ENJOYMENTS OF GENIUS  . . . . . .          150C MARRIAGE HH 6   PROSE
        BUT LOS & ENITHARMON DELIGHTED IN THE MOONY SPACES OF [ONA]   270 FOUR ZOAS 1       232
          ENO
        OF SUMMER I HAVE SEEN THEE SLEEP & TURN THY CHEEK DELIGHTED   288 FOUR ZOAS 2       313
        TILL HE FORGOT ETERNITY DELIGHTED IN HIS SWEET JOY   . . .    326 FOUR ZOAS 7       253
        AND DRAWING THEM FORTH DELIGHTED UPON THE WINDS OF            331 FOUR ZOAS 7       460
          GOLGONOOZA
        [ASTONISHD COMFORTED DELIGHTED THE DAUGHTERS OF BEULAH SAW]   342 FOUR ZOAS 8        45
        ASTONISHD COMFORTED DELIGHTED IN NOTES OF RAPTUROUS EXTACY    342 FOUR ZOAS 8        46
        APPEARS DELIGHTED TO RIDE IN HIS COMPANY  . . . . .           570C DESC CAT 3      PROSE
        WILLIAM BLAKE ONE WHO IS VERY MUCH DELIGHTED WITH BEING       781D INSC UPCOTT     PROSE
        YOU WOULD BE MUCH DELIGHTED WITH THE MAN  . . . . .           836D LETTER 35       PROSE
        TO WEAR & THAT WE ARE BOTH HIGHLY DELIGHTED   . . . .         853A LETTER 51      *PROSE
DELIGHTFUL    SEE ONCE DELIGHTFUL
        THE FRUIT OF THIS DELIGHTFUL TREE I CANNOT FLEE AWAY    .     326 FOUR ZOAS 7       234
        THE SPECTRE SAID THOU LOVELY VISION THIS DELIGHTFUL TREE      326 FOUR ZOAS 7       267
        IS NOT THE WOUND OF THE SWORD SWEET & THE BROKEN              337 FOUR ZOAS 7B      189
          BONE DELIGHTFUL
        AS FOOD OR DRINK OR ORNAMENT OR IN DELIGHTFUL WORKS  . . .    340 FOUR ZOAS 7B      276
        BUT THE HUMAN WINE STOOD WONDERING IN ALL THEIR DELIGHTFUL    378 FOUR ZOAS 9       799
          EXPANSES
```

	PAGE	TITLE	LINE

DELIGHTFUL   (CONTINUED)
TO MILD ETERNITY SHUT IN A THREEFOLD SHAPE DELIGHTFUL   . .   381 FOUR ZOAS AD 5   12
DELIGHTFUL WITH BOUNDS TO THE INFINITE PUTTING OFF THE   515 MILTON 28   4
   INDEFINITE
IS NOT THE WOUND OF THE SWORD SWEET & THE BROKEN   700 JERUSALEM 65   31
   BONE DELIGHTFUL
AND DELIGHTFUL FOOD OF THE WARRIOR THE WELL FED WARRIOR'S   706 JERUSALEM 68   34
   FLESH
AND SPENSER WHOSE PHYSIOGNOMIES HAVE BEEN MY DELIGHTFUL   806D LETTER 17   PROSE
   STUDY
DELIGHTFUL THEN I AM DETERMIND THAT MRS BUTTS SHALL HAVE   824B LETTER 27   PROSE
WITH RECOVERD STRENGTH TO HER DELIGHTFUL VILLA   . . . 849B LETTER 45   PROSE
INTENDED FLIGHT INTO YOUR DELIGHTFUL COUNTRY CONCUR IN . 872D LETTER 76   PROSE
DELIGHTING
DREAD TERRORS DELIGHTING IN BLOOD . . . .   234 URIZEN 23   7
DRIVING THE STORMS BEFORE THEM OR DELIGHTING IN SUNNY BEAMS 288 FOUR ZOAS 2   300
RUNNING AMONG MY GREEN PASTURES DELIGHTING AMONG MY TREES   368 FOUR ZOAS 9   442
HER MAIDENS TO HER HUSBAND DELIGHTING IN HIS DELIGHT   .   522 MILTON 33   18
DELIGHTING IN CRIES & TEARS & CLOTHED IN HOLINESS   630 JERUSALEM 10   49
   & SOLITUDE
DELIGHTS
DELIGHTS BLOSSOM AROUND NUMBERLESS BEAUTIES BLOW THE   . . 37B CONTEMPLATN/PS   PROSE
BUT THEL DELIGHTS IN THESE NO MORE BECAUSE I FADE AWAY . . 129 BOOK OF THEL 3   21
. . . MINE NEVER YET FADED FOR FIRE DELIGHTS IN ITS FORM 142 FRENCH REVOLTN   189
THE DEVOURER AS A SEA RECIEVED THE EXCESS OF HIS DELIGHTS   155B MARRIAGE HH 15 PROSE
HOW CAN THE GIVER OF GIFTS EXPERIENCE THE DELIGHTS OF THE   193 V DAU ALBION 5   12
   MERCHANT
FOR EVERY THING THAT LIVES IS HOLY LIFE DELIGHTS IN LIFE   199 AMERICA 8   13
LEUTHA THE MANY COLOURD BOW DELIGHTS UPON THY WINGS . .   244 EUROPE 14   10
WHILE WE DRAW IN THEIR SWEET DELIGHTS WHILE WE RETURN   271 FOUR ZOAS 1   255
   THEM SCORN
OF VALA & THE WOES OF LUVAH TO DRAW IN THEIR DELIGHTS   . 285 FOUR ZOAS 2   213
ALL THINGS BESIDE THE WOFUL LOS ENJOY THE DELIGHTS   325 FOUR ZOAS 7   198
   OF BEAUTY
ONCE HOW I SANG & CALLD THE BEASTS & BIRDS TO THEIR   325 FOUR ZOAS 7   * 199
   DELIGHTS
THY WORKS ARE ALL MY JOY & IN THY FIRES MY SOUL DELIGHTS   331 FOUR ZOAS 7   448
BUT IN VAIN DELIGHTS WERE POURED FORTH ON THE HOWLING   340 FOUR ZOAS 7B   280
   MELANCHOLY
THE TIMES REVOLVE THE TIME IS COMING WHEN ALL THESE   362 FOUR ZOAS 9   208
   DELIGHTS
HOW LOVELY THE DELIGHTS OF THOSE RISEN AGAIN FROM DEATH   376 FOUR ZOAS 9   729
. . . & THESE THE SWEET DELIGHTS OF AMOROUS PLAY . . . 377 FOUR ZOAS 9   769
CRAVE NOT FOR THE MORTAL & PERISHING DELIGHTS BUT LEAVE   511 MILTON 25   56
   THEM
. . . & THESE THE SWEET DELIGHTS OF AMOROUS PLAY . . . 514 MILTON 27   39
THEY GIVE DELIGHTS TO THE MAN UNKNOWN ARTIFICIAL RICHES   515 MILTON 28   31
I THOUGHT THAT YOU WOULD LOVE MY LOVES & JOY IN MY DELIGHTS 522 MILTON 33   3
MENTAL DELIGHTS HERE THEY ARE &C AS THREE LEAVES ON . . . 613C V LAST JUDG/N PROSE
RECIEVE HER LITTLE-ONES FOR SACRIFICES AND THE DELIGHTS   623 JERUSALEM 5   15
   OF CRUELTY
GOVERNING ALL BY THE SWEET DELIGHTS OF SECRET AMOROUS   638 JERUSALEM 16   59
   GLANCES
OR IN THE PORCH OR GARDEN NO MORE THE SINFUL DELIGHTS   . 640 JERUSALEM 18   16
OUR EMANATIONS AND TO ATTACK OUR SECRET SUPREME DELIGHTS   664 JERUSALEM 37   9
TO MALDEN & CANTERBURY IN THE DELIGHTS OF CRUELTY   . . . 668 JERUSALEM 41   6
OF UNCONQUERABLE FEAR AMIDST DELIGHTS OF REVENGE   702 JERUSALEM 66   39
   EARTH-SHAKING
OF ALBION DELIGHTS THE EYES OF THE KINGS THEIR HEARTS & THE 706 JERUSALEM 68   16
WHERE EVERY FEMALE DELIGHTS TO GIVE HER MAIDEN TO   707 JERUSALEM 69   15
   HER HUSBAND
TILL THE TIME OF LOVE IS PASSED IN EVER VARYING DELIGHTS   707 JERUSALEM 69   24
DELIGHTS OF THE TURRET OF LOVELY FELPHAM PLEASE TO GIVE   850C LETTER 49   PROSE
DELILAH   SEE DALILA
DELINEATE
AND DESIGNING WHOSE METHOD ALONE CAN DELINEATE CHARACTER   586D CHAUCER 1   PROSE
DELINEATED
PERFECTLY DELINEATED IN THOSE PARTS OF CHAUCER'S WORK   . . 568C DESC CAT 3   PROSE
DELINEATED BY ANY ENGRAVER WHO KNOWS HOW TO   . . . . . 592B PUB ADDRESS/N PROSE
ORGANIZED & MINUTELY DELINEATED & ARTICULATED EITHER BY   595C PUB ADDRESS/N   PROSE
   GOD OR MAN
DELIRIUM
IN A SPECIES OF DELIRIUM & IN PAIN TOO MUCH FOR THOUGHT   874B LETTER 79   PROSE
DELIVER
THAT HUMAN [TERROR] DELUSION TO DELIVER ALL THE SONS OF GOD 282 FOUR ZOAS 2   107
MY LUVAH THEN COULD I DELIVER ALL THE SONS OF GOD   . . 345 FOUR ZOAS 8   157
WHEN WILL THE RESURRECTION COME TO DELIVER THE SLEEPING   495 MILTON 14   17
   BODY
CRYING O GOD DELIVER US TO THE HEAVENS OR TO THE EARTHS   510 MILTON 25   13
BY (ONE) FOOT HIGH THE ARTIST ENGAGES TO DELIVER IT . . . 587A CHAUCER 1   PROSE
CHRIST COMES AS HE CAME AT FIRST TO DELIVER THOSE   . . . 615B V LAST JUDG/N PROSE
WHO WERE BOUND UNDER THE KNAVE NOT TO DELIVER THE KNAVE   615B V LAST JUDG/N   PROSE
HE COMES TO DELIVER MAN THE [FORGIVEN] ACCUSED   . . . . 615B V LAST JUDG/N *PROSE
STRIVING WITH SYSTEMS TO DELIVER INDIVIDUALS FROM THOSE   630 JERUSALEM 11   5
   SYSTEMS
STATES TO DELIVER INDIVIDUALS EVERMORE AMEN   . . . . . 662 JERUSALEM 35   16
O GOD OF ALBION DESCEND DELIVER JERUSALEM FROM THE OAKEN   672 JERUSALEM 43   11
   GROVES
O GOD DESCEND GATHER OUR BRETHREN DELIVER JERUSALEM . . . 675 JERUSALEM 45   28
[XXX] KINGDOM [BUT DELIVER] LIBERATE US US . . . . . . 788B ANNO THORNTON * MARG
DELIVER FROM THE HOLY GHOST SO WE CALL NATURE . . . . . 788D ANNO THORNTON * MARG
& DELIVER US FROM POVERTY IN JESUS THAT EVIL ONE . . . . 789A ANNO THORNTON   MARG

```
                                                            PAGE      TITLE          LINE
DELIVER   (CONTINUED)
     TIME'S MOMENTS THAT I AM WHO SHALL DELIVER ME FROM THIS    809B LETTER 20      PROSE
     GOD TO KEEP YOU & ALL MEN FROM IT & TO DELIVER ME IN HIS   829A LETTER 28      PROSE
     SAYS THAT HE HAS ORDERS FROM MR ROMNEY TO DELIVER THE   .  839D LETTER 38      PROSE
     IF YOU DO NOT WISH ANY MORE DONE BEFORE I DELIVER THEN PRAY 840C LETTER 39     PROSE
DELIVERANCE
     THE LAST JUDGMENT A DELIVERANCE FROM SATAN'S ACCUSATION    615C V LAST JUDG/N  PROSE
     . . . THE DELIVERANCE OF INDIVIDUALS EVERMORE AMEN  . . .  648 JERUSALEM 25       13
     SUFFERING TILL THE TIME OF COMPLETE DELIVERANCE IN THE  .  863A LETTER 60      PROSE
DELIVERD
     AND SHEPHERD DELIVERD FROM CLOUDS OF WAR . . . . .         144 FRENCH REVOLTN     233
     IMMORTAL IN IMMORTAL TORMENT NEVER TO BE DELIVERD   . . .  298 FOUR ZOAS 4        20
     OF GOARY BLOOD STRUGGLING TO BE DELIVERD FROM OUR BONDS    300 FOUR ZOAS 4       103
     IS GOD THE ETERNAL MAN IS SEALD NEVER TO BE DELIVERD   .   301 FOUR ZOAS 4       132
     AND THOU O URIZEN ART FALLN NEVER TO BE DELIVERD  . . . .  313 FOUR ZOAS 6        63
     MOVD BY STRONG SHUDDERS TILL HER SHADOW WAS DELIVERD THEN  328 FOUR ZOAS 7  *    321
       SHE RAN
     THE ETERNAL MAN IS SEALD BY THEE NEVER TO BE DELIVERD   .  345 FOUR ZOAS 8       161
     ON PATMOS ISLE & HEARD THE SOULS CRY OUT TO BE DELIVERD    356 FOUR ZOAS 8       601
     NAKED & PALE STANDING ON THE EXPECTING AIR TO BE DELIVERD  363 FOUR ZOAS 9       254
     CRIED OUT TO BE DELIVERD & THE SPIRIT OF LUVAH WEPT  . . . 372 FOUR ZOAS 9       575
     OF LOS & THOSE DELIVERD FROM THE BODY ON THE LEFT HAND  .  512 MILTON 26          17
     THE WHOLE CREATION GROANS TO BE DELIVERD . . . . . .       616A V LAST JUDG/N  PROSE
     THROUGHOUT THE WHOLE CREATION WHICH GROANS TO BE DELIVERD  637 JERUSALEM 16       26
     TO THE STATE THEY ARE ENTERD INTO THAT THEY MAY BE DELIVERD 680 JERUSALEM 49      66
     MAY BE DELIVERD TIME AFTER TIME EVERMORE AMEN   . . . . .  680 JERUSALEM 49       71
     SPIRITUAL WAR ISRAEL DELIVERD FROM EGYPT    . . . . . .    776A INSC LAOCOON   PROSE
     IS ART DELIVERD FROM NATURE & IMITATION    . . . . . .     776A INSC LAOCOON   PROSE
     DELIVERD THIS IS A SMALL SPECIMEN OF HOW WE GO ON   . . .  821A LETTER 25      PROSE
     TO BEG OF YOU TO CAUSE THE ENCLOSD LETTER TO BE DELIVERD   829B LETTER 28      PROSE
     DELIVERD A DOZEN COPIES AT STATIONER'S HALL   . . . . .    846D LETTER 44      PROSE
     I HAVE DELIVERD TO MR SANDERS THE (THREE) WORKS OF ROMNEY  863C LETTER 60      PROSE
DELIVERED
     SWAM ROUND THEM WATCHING TO BE DELIVERED . . . . . .       141 FRENCH REVOLTN     159
     TWELVE MONTHS WHEN IT WILL BE DELIVERED TO THE BUYER   .   563B DESC CAT       PROSE
     DELIVERED THE LETTER TO MR EDWARDS WHO WILL GIVE IT  . .   845D LETTER 44      PROSE
DELIVERER
     BUT FROM HER THE LONG-WISHED DELIVERER SHALL SPRING  . . . 39D SAMSON/PS       PROSE
     AND HE SHALL BE CALLED ISRAEL'S DELIVERER    . . . . .     39D SAMSON/PS       PROSE
     THE OX GOAD IS TURNED INTO A SPEAR O WHEN SHALL OUR        40B SAMSON/PS       PROSE
       DELIVERER COME
DELIVERING
     ONE OF RAFAEL'S GRANDEST SUBJECTS NAMELY CHRIST DELIVERING 465C ANNO REYNOLDS   MARG
     AS A MIGHTY TEMPLE DELIVERING FORM OUT OF CONFUSION  . . . 690 JERUSALEM 58       22
     I COULD NOT THINK OF DELIVERING THE (TWELVE) COPIES WITHOUT 840B LETTER 39     PROSE
       GIVING
DELIVERS
     . . . THE DUKE OF BURGUNDY DELIVERS THE KING'S COMMAND  .  145 FRENCH REVOLTN     247
DELIVERY
     AT THE TIME OF PURCHASE AND THE REMAINDER ON DELIVERY  .   563B DESC CAT       PROSE
     TIME OF SUBSCRIBING THE OTHER TWO ON DELIVERY OF THE PRINT 587A CHAUCER 1      PROSE
DELL
     IN A LONELY DELL   . . . . . . . . . . .                   115 LIT GRL FND/SI     50
DELUDE
     DEATH TO DELUDE WHO ALL IN TERROR AT THEIR SPLENDOR LEAVES 517 MILTON 29          43
DELUDED
     DELUDED BY [THE] SUMMER'S HEAT THEY SPORT IN ENORMOUS LOVE 276 FOUR ZOAS 1       452
     AND THE HARLOT OF LOS & THE DELUDED HARLOT OF THE KINGS    336 FOUR ZOAS 7B  *   138
       OF EARTH
     BECAUSE THOU KNOWEST I AM DELUDED BY THE TURNING MILLS  .  693 JERUSALEM 60       63
DELUDING
     AND VALA WALKD WITH HIM IN DREAMS OF SOFT DELUDING SLUMBER 292 FOUR ZOAS 3        45
     JERUSALEM JERUSALEM DELUDING SHADOW OF ALBION    . . . .   645 JERUSALEM 23        1
     BUT THOU DELUDING IMAGE BY WHOM IMBUD THE VEIL I RENT  .   646 JERUSALEM 23       31
     AND VALA WALKD WITH HIM IN DREAMS OF SOFT DELUDING SLUMBER 654 JERUSALEM 29       34
     SOFT DELUDING ODOURS IN SPIRAL VOLUTIONS INTRICATELY       701 JERUSALEM 65  *    66
       WINDING
     BABYLON THE RATIONAL MORALITY DELUDING TO DEATH THE LITTLE 715 JERUSALEM 74       32
       ONES
DELUGE
     FROM OUT HIS HOLY SHRINE HIS TEARS IN DELUGE PITEOUS   .   203 AMERICA 16          4
     IN DELUGE OER THE EARTH-BORN MAN THEN TURND THE FLUXILE    241 EUROPE 10          11
       EYES
     OVER THE HEAVING DELUGE HE SAW LOS & ENITHARMON EMERGE  .  297 FOUR ZOAS 4         2
     THEY ROSE IN STRENGTH ABOVE THE HEAVING DELUGE IN MIGHTY   297 FOUR ZOAS 4         4
       SCORN
     HIGH SPIRES & CASTLES DROWND IN THE BLACK DELUGE SHOAL     359 FOUR ZOAS 9        76
       ON SHOAL
     THE BLOODY DELUGE LIVING FLAMES WINGED WITH INTELLECT  .   359 FOUR ZOAS 9        86
     TREMBLING HE LAY SWELLD WITH THE DELUGE STIFLING IN THE    381 FOUR ZOAS AD 4      3
       ANGUISH
     DELUGE ALL THE COUNTRY ROUND SUCH IS A VISION OF LOS   .   507 MILTON 23          27
     ONE THOUSAND YEARS AND ALL THE EARTH WAS IN A WATRY DELUGE 508 MILTON 24           5
     WITH MY DELUGE OF FORGOTTEN REMEMBRANCES OVER THE TABLET   659 JERUSALEM 33       16
DELUSION     SEE SELF-DELUSION,SELF DELUSION
     THY GOLDEN WINGS ARE MY DELIGHT & THY FLAMES OF SOFT       244 EUROPE 14           8
       DELUSION
     MOSES BEHELD UPON MOUNT SINAI FORMS OF DARK DELUSION   .   245 SONG OF LOS 3      17
     ART THOU A VISIONARY OF JESUS THE SOFT DELUSION OF ETERNITY 273 FOUR ZOAS 1      337
     THE SPECTRE IS THE MAN THE REST IS ONLY DELUSION & FANCY   273 FOUR ZOAS 1       341
     [XXX BUT MONSTROUS DELUSION] . . . . . . . . .             SUPP FOUR ZOAS 1   *
     THAT HUMAN [TERROR] DELUSION TO DELIVER ALL THE SONS OF GOD 282 FOUR ZOAS 2      107
```

		PAGE	TITLE	LINE

DELUSION   (CONTINUED)
```
    BUT THE NEXT JOY OF THINE SHALL BE IN SWEET DELUSION    .  .   326 FOUR ZOAS 7         229
    DELUSION & I CANNOT CRAVE FOR ANY THING BUT THEE [& TILL]     327 FOUR ZOAS 7         307
    DRINK IN THE DEADLY DULL DELUSION HORRORS OF ETERNAL DEATH    352 FOUR ZOAS 8         418
    IN A FEMININE DELUSION OF FALSE PRIDE SELF-DECIEVD    .  .  .  492 MILTON 11           26
    IN MOMENTS NEW CREATED FOR DELUSION INTERWOVEN ROUND ABOUT    494 MILTON 13           39
    A NATURAL FOR A NATURAL CAUSE ONLY SEEMS IT IS A DELUSION     513 MILTON 26           45
    AS OF A GLOBE ROLLING THRO VOIDNESS IT IS A DELUSION OF       516 MILTON 29           16
       ULRO
    BEFORE MY COTTAGE STOOD FOR THE SATANIC SPACE IS DELUSION     527 MILTON 36           20
    OPPOSD TO MERCY AND THE DIVINE DELUSION JESUS BE NO MORE      530 MILTON 39            2
    BLASPHEMOUS SONS OF FEMININE DELUSION GOD IN THE DREARY       646 JERUSALEM 23        29
       VOID
    THOU ART A DELUSION AND JERUSALEM IS MY SIN O MY CHILDREN     648 JERUSALEM 24        54
    A DELUSION BUT I KNOW THEE O LORD WHEN THOU ARISEST UPON      693 JERUSALEM 60        58
    OVER ALBION'S MOUNTAINS A FEMININE INDEFINITE CRUEL          701 JERUSALEM 65        67
       DELUSION
    WHEREFORE THEN DO YOU REALIZE THESE NETS OF BEAUTY           721 JERUSALEM 79        78
       & DELUSION
    OF TORMENT UNENDURABLE AND IF ONCE A DELUSION BE FOUND   .  .  722 JERUSALEM 80        14
    LOOK I HAVE WROUGHT WITHOUT DELUSION LOOK I HAVE WEPT    .  .  725 JERUSALEM 82         5
    HUMANITY THE GREAT DELUSION IS CHANGD TO WAR & SACRIFICE      726 JERUSALEM 82        42
    TO REIGN IN PRIDE & TO OPRESS & TO MIX THE CUP OF DELUSION    730 JERUSALEM 85        31
    OF THREEFOLD WORKMANSHIP IN ALLEGORIC DELUSION & WOE    .  .  735 JERUSALEM 89        45
    EVE IS THIS THE PROMISE OF JEHOVAH O IT IS ALL A             779 GHOST ABEL 1          6
       VAIN DELUSION
    ADAM IT IS ALL A VAIN DELUSION OF THE ALL CREATIVE           780 GHOST ABEL 1         17
       IMAGINATION
DELUSIONS
    AND ITS BIRTH IN FAINTING & SLEEP & [WOE] SWEET DELUSIONS     326 FOUR ZOAS 7       * 230
       OF VALA
    [IN FORMS OF PRIESTHOOD IN THE DARK DELUSIONS OF             353 FOUR ZOAS 8         461
       REPENTANCE]
    IN FORMS OF PRIESTHOOD IN THE DARK DELUSIONS OF REPENTANCE    353 FOUR ZOAS 8         464
    THE LAND OF DOUBTS & SHADOWS SWEET DELUSIONS UNFORMD HOPES    367 FOUR ZOAS 9         379
    OF TERROR & MILD MOONY LUSTRE IN SOFT SEXUAL DELUSIONS   .  .  481 MILTON 2             3
    CRUEL HIPOCRISY UNLIKE THE LOVELY DELUSIONS OF BEULAH         639 JERUSALEM 17        27
    CAST CAST YE JERUSALEM FORTH THE SHADOW OF DELUSIONS    .  .  640 JERUSALEM 18        11
    THAT MAN MAY BE PURIFIED BY THE DEATH OF THY DELUSIONS   .  .  658 JERUSALEM 31        66
    EMBRACE WE SHALL PERISH ANNIHILATE DISCOVERD OUR DELUSIONS    725 JERUSALEM 82         4
    EVE COME AWAY & LET US NOT BELIEVE THESE VAIN DELUSIONS       780 GHOST ABEL 1         18
DELUSIVE
    IN SECRET SOFT WINGS IN MAZES OF DELUSIVE BEAUTY    .  .  .  265 FOUR ZOAS 1          43
    AND THOU THE DELUSIVE TEMPTER TO THESE DEEDS SITTST BEFORE    268 FOUR ZOAS 1         169
       ME
    .  .  . ALL THY SOFT DELUSIVE BEAUTY CANNOT               268 FOUR ZOAS 1         170
    THUS SANG THE LOVELY ONE IN RAPTUROUS DELUSIVE TRANCE    .  .  290 FOUR ZOAS 2         379
    LOS HEARD REVIVING HE SIEZD HER IN HIS ARMS DELUSIVE HOPES    290 FOUR ZOAS 2         380
    WEAVE SOFT DELUSIVE FORMS OF MAN ABOVE MY WATRY WORLD    .  .  298 FOUR ZOAS 4          29
    IN DREAMS OF ULRO [SWEET] DARK DELUSIVE DRAWN BY THE LOVELY   328 FOUR ZOAS 7         331
       SHADOW
    DELUSIVE CRUELTY THEY DESCEND AWAY FROM THE DAUGHTERS OF      341 FOUR ZOAS 8          26
       BEULAH
    A FALSE FEMININE COUNTERPART LOVELY OF DELUSIVE BEAUTY   .  .  348 FOUR ZOAS 8       * 278
    DIVIDING & UNITING IN DELUSIVE FEMININE POMP QUESTIONING      350 FOUR ZOAS 8       * 346
       HIM
    TO THE DELUSIVE FEMALE FORMS SHINING AMONG HIS FURNACES       350 FOUR ZOAS 8         350
    CAPTIVE A WILLING CAPTIVE BY DELUSIVE ARTS IMPELLD    .  .  .  356 FOUR ZOAS 8         598
    WHERE IS THE SPECTRE OF PROPHECY WHERE THE DELUSIVE PHANTOM   379 FOUR ZOAS 9         851
    ("GENERAL COPYING...DELUSIVE") HERE HE CONDEMNS             448C ANNO REYNOLDS      MARG
       GENERALIZING
    NOT BUT A DELUSIVE SHADOW A THOUGHT THAT LIVETH NOT    .  .  693 JERUSALEM 60       *  55
    APPEAR IN STRONG DELUSIVE LIGHT OF TIME & SPACE DRAWN OUT     715 JERUSALEM 75          5
    AND HER DELUSIVE LIGHT BEAMD FIERCE ABOVE THE MOUNTAIN   .  .  723 JERUSALEM 80        59
    OWN ETERNAL HOUSE LEAVING THE DELUSIVE GODDESS NATURE & HER  879A LETTER 88          PROSE
DELUSORY
    DELUSORY LOVE TO PALAMABRON ADMIRATION JOIND WITH ENVY   .  .  492 MILTON 12            7
DELVING
    DELVING EARTH IN HIS RESISTLESS WAY    .  .  .  .  .  .  .  232 URIZEN 19            44
    WHICH NOW OUR RIVERS WERE BECOME DELVING THRO CAVERNS HUGE    300 FOUR ZOAS 4         102
    AND BROKE HIM UP FROM HIS DELVING ROOT    .  .  .  .  .  .  817 HAPPINESS/L         42
DEMAND
    & PROPORTIONATE VALUE & A GENERAL DEMAND FOR ART    .  .  .  446D ANNO REYNOLDS      MARG
    AND IRREGULAR ECCENTRICITY A MADMAN'S SCRAWLS I DEMAND   .  .  561B EXHIBITION ADV    PROSE
    I DEMAND THEREFORE OF THE AMATEURS OF ART    .  .  .  .  .  600C PUB ADDRESS/N      PROSE
    TELL HIM TO BE NO MORE DUBIOUS DEMAND EXPLICIT WORDS    .  .  640 JERUSALEM 17        60
    I DEMAND RIGHTEOUSNESS & JUSTICE O THOU INGRATITUDE    .  .  669 JERUSALEM 42        12
    THE ETERNAL PARENTS DEMAND FROM THEIR CHILDREN    .  .  .  791B LETTER 3            PROSE
    AGAINST FORMER CONDUCT & TO DEMAND JUSTICE & TRUTH    .  .  .  825D LETTER 27          PROSE
    WOULD CUT OFF TEN GUINEAS FROM MY NEXT DEMAND ON PHILLIPS     861B LETTER 58          PROSE
    BETWEEN YOU & ME YOU DEMAND OF ME TO MIX TWO THINGS    .  .  866A LETTER 64          PROSE
DEMANDED
    WHEN THE DRUIDS DEMANDED CHASTITY FROM WOMAN & ALL WAS LOST   697 JERUSALEM 63        25
DEMANDING
    CLOTHD IN THE SERPENT'S FOLDS IN SELFISH HOLINESS DEMANDING   493 MILTON 12           46
       PURITY
DEMANDS
    TALKING WITH DEATH ANSWERING HIS HARD DEMANDS    .  .  .  .  .   30 EDW THIRD/PS 5      10
    AND STERN DEMANDS OF RIGHT & DUTY INSTEAD OF LIBERTY    .  .  265 FOUR ZOAS 1          37
    WHICH IS THE SCIENCE OF SCIENCES DEMANDS    .  .  .  .  .  .  600B PUB ADDRESS/N      PROSE
    AND STERN DEMANDS OF RIGHT & DUTY INSTEAD OF LIBERTY    .  .  645 JERUSALEM 22        11
    ENGAGED IN THE WORK AS ITS MAGNITUDE DEMANDS ALL THE    .  .  848D LETTER 45          PROSE
```

                                                           PAGE   TITLE   LINE
DEMANDS   (CONTINUED)
    [AND STERN DEMANDS OF RIGHT & DUTY INSTEAD OF LIBERTY] . . SUPP FOUR ZOAS 1   *
DEMOCRACIES
    ("DEMOCRACIES...COMMONLY ...QUIET ") SELF CONTRADICTION   401B ANNO BACON   MARG
       KNAVE & FOOL
DEMOCRITUS
    THE ATOMS OF DEMOCRITUS . . . . 418 MOCK ON/N   9
DEMOLISHD
    PERMANENTLY CREATING TO BE IN TIME REVEALD & DEMOLISHD . . 713 JERUSALEM 73   34
DEMOLISHES
    WHICH LOS WITH HIS MIGHTY HAMMER DEMOLISHES TIME ON TIME   713 JERUSALEM 73   32
DEMON   SEE DAEMON
    WHICH BY THE ANCIENTS WAS CALLD AN ANGEL & SPIRIT & DEMON   98B ALL RELIGIONS PROSE
    O URIZEN CREATOR OF MEN MISTAKEN DEMON OF HEAVEN . . . . 192 V DAU ALBION 5   3
    BLASPHEMOUS DEMON ANTICHRIST HATER OF DIGNITIES . . . . 198 AMERICA 7   5
    BEFORE THE DEMON RED WHO BURNT TOWARDS AMERICA . . . . 201 AMERICA 12   9
    HIDING THE DEMON RED WITH CLOUDS & COLD MISTS FROM THE   203 AMERICA 16   13
       EARTH
    IN THE RED AIR BEFORE THE DEMON [SEEN EVEN BY MORTAL MEN] 205 AMERICA CANC C   21
    SUCH WAS THE HOLLOW VOICE THAT OER [THE RED DEMON] AMERICA 205 AMERICA CANC C   31
       LAMENTED
    SELF-CLOSD ALL-REPELLING WHAT DEMON . . . . 222 URIZEN 3   3
    LOS WEPT HOWLING AROUND THE DARK DEMON . . . . . . 226 URIZEN 6   2
    THE HORRENT DEMON ROSE SURROUNDED WITH RED STARS OF FIRE   240 EUROPE 4   29
    SHALL WE WORSHIP THIS DEMON OF SMOKE . . . . 249 AHANIA 2   10
    CIRCLING ROUND THE DARK DEMON WITH HOWLINGS . . . . . 259 BOOK OF LOS 5   24
    OBEY MY VOICE YOUNG DEMON I AM GOD FROM ETERNITY   273 FOUR ZOAS 1   336
       TO ETERNITY
    . . . DEMON OF FURY   288 FOUR ZOAS 2   309
    BEWARE LEST WE ALSO DRINK UP THEE ROUGH DEMON OF THE WATERS 298 FOUR ZOAS 4   37
    AND HE IS FALLN INTO THE DEEP ROUGH DEMON OF THE WATERS   298 FOUR ZOAS 4   40
    THOU RASH ABHORRED DEMON IN THY FURY HAST OERTHROWN . . . 299 FOUR ZOAS 4   52
    CIRCLING ROUND THE DARK DEMON WITH HOWLINGS DISMAY & SHARP 302 FOUR ZOAS 4   200
       BLIGHTINGS
    AND AS HE BEAT ROUND THE HURTLING DEMON TERRIFIED AT THE   302 FOUR ZOAS 4   202
       SHAPES
    THE HURTLING DEMON TERRIFIED AT THE SHAPES . . . . . 305 FOUR ZOAS 4   285
    CRACKLING THE FLAMES WENT UP WITH FURY FROM THE IMMORTAL   308 FOUR ZOAS 5   108
       DEMON
    SURROUNDED WITH FLAMES THE DEMON GREW LOUD HOWLING IN HIS 308 FOUR ZOAS 5   109
       FIRES
    OF LIFE [REJOICE] LAMENT AROUND THE DEMON GOING FORTH &   308 FOUR ZOAS 5   * 117
       RETURNING
    SUCH IS THE DEMON SUCH HIS TERROR IN THE NETHER DEEP   . . 308 FOUR ZOAS 5   * 142
    THAT THEY MAY CURSE & WORSHIP THE OBSCURE DEMON OF   313 FOUR ZOAS 6   44
       DESTRUCTION
    CRYING WHAT & WHO ART THOU COLD DEMON ART THOU URIZEN . . 313 FOUR ZOAS 6   55
    HOWLING & RENDING HIS DARK CAVES THE AWFUL DEMON LAY   . . 320 FOUR ZOAS 7   20
    . . . WHY SHOULDST THOU SIT COLD GROVELLING DEMON OF WOE   322 FOUR ZOAS 7   73
    THOU WILT NOT CEASE FROM RAGE GREY DEMON SILENCE ALL THY   323 FOUR ZOAS 7   144
       STORMS
    REDDNING THE DEMON STRONG PREPARD THE POISON OF SWEET LOVE 325 FOUR ZOAS 7   219
    THOU & THAT DEMON LOS [WERE] WERT BORN AH JEALOUSY & WOE   327 FOUR ZOAS 7   * 295
    THOU NEVER CANST EMBRACE SWEET ENITHARMON TERRIBLE DEMON   328 FOUR ZOAS 7   342
       TILL
    SO CRIED THE DEMON OF THE WATERS IN THE CLOUDS OF LOS . . 334 FOUR ZOAS 7B   72
    WOO'D & SUBDUD INTO ?ETERNAL DEATH THE DEMON ?LAY   . . . 340 FOUR ZOAS 7B   286
    HIS HOLY HANDS RECIEVD THE FLAMING DEMON & DEMONESS OF   366 FOUR ZOAS 9   361
       SMOKE
    PITYING THEY VIEWD THE NEW BORN DEMON FOR THEY COULD NOT   380 FOUR ZOAS AD 1   9
       LOVE
    MALE FORMD THE DEMON MILD ATHLETIC FORCE HIS SHOULDERS   380 FOUR ZOAS AD 1   11
       SPREAD
    AND THARMAS DEMON OF THE WATERS & ORC WHO IS LUVAH . . . 499 MILTON 18   1
    CREATING NEW FLESH ON THE DEMON COLD AND BUILDING HIM . . 500 MILTON 19   13
    THE MAN AND DEMON STROVE MANY PERIODS RAHAB BEHELD . . . 501 MILTON 19   27
    THE WILD THYME IS LOS'S MESSENGER TO EDEN A MIGHTY DEMON   526 MILTON 35   54
    BUT BELIAL OF SODOM & GOMORRHA OBSCURE DEMON OF BRIBES . 528 MILTON 37   30
    HE STOOD UPON THE WAVES A TWENTY-SEVEN FOLD MIGHTY DEMON   529 MILTON 38   11
    RUBENS IS A MOST OUTRAGEOUS DEMON AND BY INFUSING . . . 582D DESC CAT 9   PROSE
    SO THAT THE MAN WHO IS POSSESSED BY THIS DEMON . . . . 583A DESC CAT 9   PROSE
    MOST CRUEL DEMON WHOSE WHOLE DELIGHT IS TO CAUSE . . . 583A DESC CAT 9   PROSE
    DRAGGED DOWN BY [AN ANGEL] A DEMON CROWND WITH LAUREL . . 606C V LAST JUDG/N PROSE
    ANOTHER DEMON WITH A KEY HAS THE CHARGE OF SIN   . . . . 606C V LAST JUDG/N PROSE
    AND SAW HIS FURNACES IN RUINS FOR LOS IS THE DEMON OF THE 658 JERUSALEM 32   6
       FURNACES
DEMONESS
    HIS HOLY HANDS RECIEVD THE FLAMING DEMON & DEMONESS OF   366 FOUR ZOAS 9   361
       SMOKE
DEMON'S
    AND THEN THEIR END SHOULD COME WHEN FRANCE RECIEVD THE   203 AMERICA 16   15
       DEMON'S LIGHT
    TENFOLD THE DEMON'S RAGE FLAMD TENFOLD FORTH RENDING   . . 308 FOUR ZOAS 5   105
    SUSTAINED BY THE DEMON'S LIFE DESPAIR & TERROR & WOE & RAGE 309 FOUR ZOAS 5   170
DEMONS
    AMERICA IS DARKNED AND MY PUNISHING DEMONS TERRIFIED   . . 199 AMERICA 9   *   3
    HIS SHIELD THAT BOUND TWELVE DEMONS & THEIR CITIES IN ITS 205 AMERICA CANC C   2
       ORB
    FILLD WITH IMMORTAL DEMONS OF FUTURITY . . . . 241 EUROPE 9   10
    DELICIOUS VIANDS DEMONS OF WAVES THEIR WATRY ECCHOS WOKE   274 FOUR ZOAS 1   * 378
    THUS SANG THE DEMONS OF THE DEEP THE CLARIONS OF WAR BLEW 276 FOUR ZOAS 1   434
       LOUD

DEMONS   (CONTINUED)
    [ORBITS HIGH] [DEMONS BY THE THOUSANDS OUT OF A GOLDEN   SUPP FOUR ZOAS 1   *
        CLOUD XXX]
    STRIPPING JERUSALEM'S CURTAINS FROM MILD DEMONS OF THE   281 FOUR ZOAS 2   58
        HILLS
    BECOME A PREY TO ALL MY DEMONS OF DESPAIR & HOPE . . . .   299 FOUR ZOAS 4   75
    THE ENORMOUS DEMONS WOKE & HOWLD AROUND THE [YOUTHFUL]   306 FOUR ZOAS 5   41
        NEW BORN KING
    SO SUNG THE DEMONS [OF THE DEEP] ROUND RED ORC . . .   .   307 FOUR ZOAS 5   * 66
    [THEN DEMONS ?HOWLD ROUND HIS CHARIOT ?RAGING ?LUVAH   SUPP FOUR ZOAS 5   *
        (EMPTIED)]
    [AROUND THE ABYSS (DEFIANTLY) ?SHOUTING ALL HIS DEMONS]   SUPP FOUR ZOAS 5   *
    SO SUNG THE DEMONS OF THE DEEP THE CLARIONS OF WAR BLEW   338 FOUR ZOAS 7B   210
        LOUD
    TEN THOUSAND DEMONS LABOUR AT THE FORGES CREATING   346 FOUR ZOAS 8   205
        CONTINUALLY
    WITH BEAUTIFUL ART THE STUDY OF ANGELS THE WORKMANSHIP   365 FOUR ZOAS 9   297
        OF DEMONS
    FOOL & A CUNNING KNAVE SUITED TO THE PURPOSES OF   458B ANNO REYNOLDS   MARG
        EVIL DEMONS
    TREMBLING PALAMABRON STOOD THE STRONGEST OF DEMONS TREMBLED   487 MILTON 7   47
    DEMONS BUT HE WAS ALSO COMPELLED TO LEAVE IT UNFINISHED   581B DESC CAT 6   PROSE
    BECAUSE CORPOREAL DEMONS HAVE GAINED A PREDOMINANCE . .   581D DESC CAT 8   PROSE
    VENETIAN AND FLEMISH DEMONS WHOSE ENMITY TO THE PAINTER   582C DESC CAT 9   PROSE
        HIMSELF
    BY TWO STRONG DEMONS THEY ARE GOG & MAGOG WHO HAVE . .   609B V LAST JUDG/N   PROSE
    OF UNBELIEVING DEMONS ETERNITY EXISTS AND ALL THINGS IN   614B V LAST JUDG/N   PROSE
    AND GOLDEN DEMONS THAT NONE CAN STAY . . . .   817 HAPPINESS/L   12
DEMONSTRATE
    FOR YOU CANNOT DEMONSTRATE ONE DEGREE BY THE OTHER   . . .   93B ANNO SWED LOVE MARG
    FOR HOW CAN SCIENCE BE BROUGHT TO DEMONSTRATE INTELLECT   93B ANNO SWED LOVE MARG
    PENMAENMAWR & DHINAS-BRAN DEMONSTRATE IN UNBELIEF   . . .   644 JERUSALEM 21   35
    MALDEN & COLCHESTER DEMONSTRATE I HEAR MY CHILDREN'S VOICES   644 JERUSALEM 21   37
    CRYING COMPELL THE REASONER TO DEMONSTRATE WITH UNHEWN   687 JERUSALEM 55   56
        DEMONSTRATIONS
DEMONSTRATION
    WORLDLY WISDOM OR DEMONSTRATION BY THE SENSES IS THE CAUSE   90D ANNO SWED LOVE MARG
        OF THIS
    DEMONSTRATION IS ONLY BY BODILY SENSES . . . .   91C ANNO SWED LOVE MARG
    BY CORRESPONDENCE WHICH HAS NOTHING TO DO WITH   93B ANNO SWED LOVE MARG
        DEMONSTRATION
    PLAIN THAT SELF DERIVED INTELLIGENCE IS WORLDLY   94B ANNO SWED LOVE   MARG
        DEMONSTRATION
    AND CALL IT DEMONSTRATION BLIND TO ALL THE SIMPLE RULES   337 FOUR ZOAS 7B   186
        OF LIFE
    DEMONSTRATION SIMILITUDE & HARMONY ARE OBJECTS OF REASONING 474C ANNO REYNOLDS   MARG
    THAT TRUTH SHOULD BE CONFINED TO MATHEMATICAL DEMONSTRATION 474D ANNO REYNOLDS   MARG
    INTO SUBSTANCE & PRINCIPLE BY THE CRUELTIES   517 MILTON 29   36
        OF DEMONSTRATION
    TO CAST OFF RATIONAL DEMONSTRATION BY FAITH IN THE SAVIOUR   533 MILTON 41   3
    BY DEMONSTRATION MAN ALONE CAN LIVE AND NOT BY FAITH . .   622 JERUSALEM 4   28
    I HAVE EDUCATED YOU IN THE CRUCIFYING CRUELTIES OF   648 JERUSALEM 24   55
        DEMONSTRATION
    THEY ARE OF FAITH & NOT OF DEMONSTRATION WHEREFORE IS VALA   657 JERUSALEM 31   46
    RATIONAL PHILOSOPHY AND MATHEMATIC DEMONSTRATION . . . .   690 JERUSALEM 58   13
    AND CALL IT DEMONSTRATION BLIND TO ALL THE SIMPLE RULES   700 JERUSALEM 65   28
        OF LIFE
    INTO THE INDEFINITE REFUSING TO BELIEVE WITHOUT   738 JERUSALEM 91   36
        DEMONSTRATION
    PROMISE YOU OCULAR DEMONSTRATION OF MY ALTERED STATE . .   852B LETTER 50   PROSE
DEMONSTRATIONS
    BY DEMONSTRATIONS THE CRUEL SONS OF QUALITY & NEGATION .   673 JERUSALEM 43   67
    CRYING COMPELL THE REASONER TO DEMONSTRATE WITH UNHEWN   687 JERUSALEM 55   56
        DEMONSTRATIONS
    BY HIS OWN WORKS LET ALL INDEFINITES BE THROWN INTO   687 JERUSALEM 55   58
        DEMONSTRATIONS
    AND NOT IN GENERALIZING DEMONSTRATIONS OF THE RATIONAL   687 JERUSALEM 55   63
        POWER
    O DEMONSTRATIONS OF REASON DIVIDING FAMILIES IN CRUELTY   689 JERUSALEM 57   11
        & PRIDE
    OF ROCKS ROUND LONDON STONE OF REASONINGS OF UNHEWN   702 JERUSALEM 66   3
        DEMONSTRATIONS
    THESE ARE THE DEMONSTRATIONS OF LOS & THE BLOWS OF   737 JERUSALEM 90   57
        MY MIGHTY HAMMER
DEMONSTRATIVE
    DEMONSTRATIVE SCIENCE SUCH AS IS WEIGHED OR MEASURED   . . 475A ANNO REYNOLDS   MARG
    WITH DEMONSTRATIVE SCIENCE PIERCING APOLLYON WITH HIS OWN   631 JERUSALEM 12   14
        BOW
    A FOUNDATION AND CERTAINTY AND DEMONSTRATIVE TRUTH . . .   652 JERUSALEM 28   11
DEMOSTHENES
    THE DEATH OF DEMOSTHENES...HAS BEEN APPROVED BY MR FLAXMAN 796B LETTER 7   PROSE
    FOR MY DEMOSTHENES WHICH IS NOW BECOME A NOBLE SUBJECT .   835A LETTER 34   PROSE
DEMURE
    WITH NARROW SOUL & LOOKS DEMURE . . . .   756 EV GOSPEL(I)/N   2
DEN
    UNTHINKING PLAYS UPON THE VIPER'S DEN . . . .   27 EDW THIRD/PS 3   242
    AND STRIFE BROUGHT FORTH REVENGE HATE BROODING IN   42C THEN SHE BORE   PROSE
        HER DISMAL DEN
    EARTH THUS I STAMP THY BOSOM ROUSE THE EARTHQUAKE FROM   106 TIRIEL 5   4
        HIS DEN
    . . . AND THE DEN NAMD HORROR HELD A MAN . . . .   135 FRENCH REVOLTN   26
    CREPT IN THE SKELETON IN THE DEN NAMD RELIGION . . .   . .   135 FRENCH REVOLTN   35

```
                                                       PAGE    TITLE           LINE
DEN    (CONTINUED)
   . . . AND COLD OF NIGHT HIS DEN WAS SHORT    . . . . . .   136 FRENCH REVOLTN    39
   . . . IN THE DEN NAMD DESTINY A STRONG MAN SAT.   . . . .  136 FRENCH REVOLTN    43
   . . . FANCY GAVE HIM TO SEE AN IMAGE OF DESPAIR IN HIS DEN 136 FRENCH REVOLTN    45
   THEN LAUGH IN THE DISMAL DEN THEN ARE SILENT . . . . . .   136 FRENCH REVOLTN    53
   [STARRY] STARRY JEALOUSY DOES KEEP MY DEN   . . . . . .    169 EARTHS ANSWR/N *   7
   WHO WEPT OVER A DEN IN WHICH HIS ONLY SON OUTSTRETCHD  .   205 AMERICA CANC C    26
   STARRY JEALOUSY DOES KEEP MY DEN   . . . . . . . . .       211 EARTHS ANSR/SE     7
   ARISE O ORC FROM THY DEEP DEN   . . . . . . . . . . .      239 EUROPE 4          24
   EVERY HOUSE A DEN EVERY MAN BOUND THE SHADOWS ARE FILLD    243 EUROPE 12         26
   FROM HIS ANCIENT WOVEN DEN   . . . . . . . . . . . .       247 SONG OF LOS 6      4
   AS WHEN THE EARTHQUAKE ROUZES FROM HIS DEN HIS SHOULDERS   336 FOUR ZOAS 7B     129
      HUGE
   [TO JUDGMENT] FROM THE CLOTTED GORE & FROM THE HOLLOW DEN  358 FOUR ZOAS 9       43
   FROM THE CLOTTED GORE & FROM THE HOLLOW DEN   . . . . .    359 FOUR ZOAS 9       88
   AND DARK URTHONA ROUZD HIS SHADY BRIDE FROM HER DEEP DEN   380 FOUR ZOAS AD 1     7
   WINCHESTER IN HIS DEN & CAVERN THEY LAMENT AGAINST  . . .  671 JERUSALEM 42      59
   [OF ?MORAL] PRAISE WORTHY & THE LIONS DEN   . . . . . .    758 EV GOSPEL (1) *    4
DENBIGHSHIRE
   THE GATE OF JOSEPH DENBIGHSHIRE THE GATE OF BENJAMIN       637 JERUSALEM 16      41
      GLAMORGANSHIRE
DENIAL      SEE SELF-DENIAL,SELF DENIAL
DENIED      SEE DENYD
   WHAT CANST THOU GIVE WHEN SUCH A TRIFLE IS DENIED ME BUT    39A SAMSON/PS       PROSE
   HE WHO SAYS THERE ARE SECOND CAUSES HAS ALREADY DENIED    403B ANNO BACON       MARG
      A FIRST
   TILL THE EXISTENCE OF FRIENDSHIP & BENEVOLENCE IS DENIED   672 JERUSALEM 43      27
   ART DEGRADED IMAGINATION DENIED WAR GOVERNED THE NATIONS   775D INSC LAOCOON    PROSE
DENIES
   PAINE NEVER DENIES HE ONLY DENIES   . . . . . . . . .     389A ANNO WATSON       MARG
   DENIES MENTAL HEALTH AND PERFECTION   . . . . . . . .     772B ANNO SPURZHEIM    MARG
DENMAN
   MR BLAKE'S RESPECTFUL COMPLIMENTS TO MISS DENMAN  . . .   877B LETTER 86        PROSE
   TO MISS DENMAN BUCKINGHAM STREET FITZROY SQUARE   . . .   SUPP ADDRESS/L 86    *TITLE
DENMAN'S
   MISS DENMAN'S SERVICE IF SHE WILL ACCEPT OF THEM WHAT  .  877B LETTER 86        PROSE
DENMARK
   FRANCE & SPAIN & ITALY & DENMARK & HOLLAND & GERMANY  .   690 JERUSALEM 58      41
DENS
   LIKE LIONS ROUZD BY LIGHTNING FROM THEIR DENS  . . . . .   32 EDW THIRD/PS 6      8
   BUT THE DENS SHOOK AND TREMBLED . . . . . . . . . . .     136 FRENCH REVOLTN    52
   IN STONES AMONG ROOTS OF TREES THE PRISONERS HAVE BURST   137 FRENCH REVOLTN    77
      THEIR DENS
   . . . HONESTY BOUND IN THE DENS OF SUPERSTITION  . . .    144 FRENCH REVOLTN   228
   FALLING RUSHING RUINING BURIED IN THE RUINS ON URTHONA'S  159D SONG LIBERTY    PROSE
      DENS
   LOOSING THE ETERNAL HORSES FROM THE DENS OF NIGHT CRYING  160A SONG LIBERTY    PROSE
   EXPLORD HIS DENS AROUND  . . . . . . . . . . . . . .      233 URIZEN 20         32
   URIZEN EXPLORD HIS DENS   . . . . . . . . . . . . . .     234 URIZEN 20         46
   OVER DENS & THRO VALLEYS OF DEATH   . . . . . . . . .     254 AHANIA 4          61
   HIDING THEIR BOOKS & PICTURES UNDERNEATH THE DENS OF EARTH 275 FOUR ZOAS 1     397
   I WAKE SWEET JOY IN DENS OF SORROW & I PLANT A SMILE  .   289 FOUR ZOAS 2      371
   OUT OF THE HALLS OF JUSTICE TILL THESE DENS THY WISDOM    292 FOUR ZOAS 3       38
      FRAMD
   THE WOES OF URIZEN SHUT UP IN THE DEEP DENS OF URTHONA .  310 FOUR ZOAS 5      189
   I WILL ARISE EXPLORE THESE DENS & FIND THAT DEEP PULSATION 311 FOUR ZOAS 5     238
   SO URIZEN AROSE & LEANING ON HIS SPEAR EXPLORD HIS DENS   311 FOUR ZOAS 6        1
   HOWL IN THE BURNING DENS HIS TYGERS ROAM IN THE REDOUNDING 320 FOUR ZOAS 7       9
      SMOKE
   IN DENS OF DEATH TO FORGE THE SPADE THE MATTOCK & THE AX  365 FOUR ZOAS 9      306
   IN PITS & DENS & SHADES OF DEATH IN SHAPES OF TORMENT & WOE 377 FOUR ZOAS 9    751
   ALL THE WISDOM WHICH WAS HIDDEN IN CAVES & DENS FROM      510 MILTON 25         20
      ANCIENT
   IN PITS & DENS & SHADES OF DEATH IN SHAPES OF TORMENT & WOE 514 MILTON 27       33
   HERE IS JERUSALEM BOUND IN CHAINS IN THE DENS OF BABYLON  529 MILTON 38         27
   DENS OF DESPAIR IN THE HOUSE OF BREAD ENQUIRING IN VAIN   657 JERUSALEM 31      26
   AND DENS THEY LOOKED ON ONE-ANOTHER & BECAME WHAT THEY    661 JERUSALEM 34      50
      BEHELD
DENTANT
   [THE HARD DENTANT HAMMERS ARE LULLD BY THE FLUTE LULA LULA] 346 FOUR ZOAS 8 * 203
   THE HARD DENTANT HAMMERS ARE LULLD BY THE FLUTES' LULA LULA 509 MILTON 24      63
DENY
   ("SNATCH FOAM DENY STREAM") UNEASY THIS I LAMENT THAT I    79D ANNO LAVATER     MARG
      HAVE DONE
   O WAS NO DENY  . . . . . . . . . . . . . . . . . . .      161 NEVER PAIN/N      13
   & ITS LAST NOW HE BEGINS TO DEGRADE [&] TO DENY [DESTROY] 458B ANNO REYNOLDS  * MARG
      & TO MOCK
   IN ALBION & TO DENY THE VALUE OF THE SAVIOUR'S BLOOD  . . 506 MILTON 22         54
   HE SEES HIS CHILDREN MOCK AT FAITH AND DENY PROVIDENCE  . 510 MILTON 25         25
   OF JESUS WHO DENY THE FAITH & MOCK AT ETERNAL LIFE  . .   533 MILTON 41         22
   FLAXMAN CANNOT DENY THAT ONE OF THE VERY FIRST MONUMENTS HE 592D PUB ADDRESS/N PROSE
   THEY DENY THAT THEY EVER KNEW JERUSALEM OR EVER DWELT     679 JERUSALEM 49       9
      IN SHILOH
   DENY A CONSCIENCE IN MAN & THE COMMUNION OF SAINTS & ANGELS 741 JERUSALEM 93    22
   & YOU DENY THAT HE IS ARISEN & ARE BLIND TO SPIRIT  . . . 757D EV GOSPEL       PROSE
DENYD
   DESIRE STILL PINES BUT FOR ONE COOLING DROP AND TIS DENYD  41C THEN SHE BORE   PROSE
   INSPIRATION DENYD GENIUS FORBIDDEN BY LAWS OF PUNISHMENT  628 JERUSALEM 9       16
DENYING
   TO JUSTICE IN HIS OWN CITY OF PARIS DENYING              697 JERUSALEM 63        6
      THE RESURRECTION
   CALLING THE ROCKS ATOMIC ORIGINS OF EXISTENCE DENYING   704 JERUSALEM 67       12
      ETERNITY
```

477

DENYING   (CONTINUED)
    DENYING IN PRIVATE MOCKING GOD & ETERNAL LIFE & IN PUBLIC   737 JERUSALEM 90   64
    DIVINE UNION DERIDING AND DENYING IMMEDIATE COMMUNION . . 776D INSC LAOCOON   PROSE
DEPART
    SO SEEMED HE TO DEPART SHE WONDERED WITH EXCEEDING JOY . . 40A SAMSON/PS   PROSE
    DEPART ANSWER NOT FOR THE TEMPEST MUST FALL . . . .   139 FRENCH REVOLTN   120
    . . . DEPART O CLOUDS OF NIGHT AND NO MORE . . . .   145 FRENCH REVOLTN   238
    . . . TROOPS OF WARRIORS DEPART NOR AROUND OUR PEACEABLE   145 FRENCH REVOLTN   239
        CITY
    . . . SAYING BASTILE DEPART AND TAKE THY SHADOWY COURSE   145 FRENCH REVOLTN   249
    . . . AND IF IT OBEY AND DEPART THEN THE KING WILL DISBAND   145 FRENCH REVOLTN   252
    DEPART AND THE STERN CAPTAIN STROKES HIS PROUD STEED . . .   147 FRENCH REVOLTN   288
    AH SHE DOTH DEPART   161 NEVER PAIN/N   8
    SHALT THOU DEPART TO WEEP IN SECRET IN MY JEALOUS WINGS   269 FOUR ZOAS 1   176
    HE CRIED OUT TO HIS FATHER DEPART DEPART BUT SUDDEN SIEZD   275 FOUR ZOAS 1   411
    REPOSD ON BEDS LET THEM SLEEP ON DO THOU ALONE DEPART   277 FOUR ZOAS 1   489
    SENT ROUND HIS HERALDS SECRETLY COMMANDING TO DEPART .   279 FOUR ZOAS 1   536
    FAREWELL THE GOD CALLS ME AWAY I DEPART IN MY SWEET BLISS   288 FOUR ZOAS 2   333
    I NEVER WILL DEPART FROM MY GREAT WRATH . . . .   339 FOUR ZOAS 7B   258
    SAW THEM DEPART IN DISMAL DROVES THE TRUMPET SOUNDED LOUD   359 FOUR ZOAS 9   65
    IN ALL THEIR ANCIENT INNOCENCE THE FLOODS DEPART THE CLOUDS 372 FOUR ZOAS 9   572
    PONDERING HE KNEW THAT RINTRAH & PALAMABRON MIGHT DEPART   503 MILTON 20   52
    DEPART BUT DWELL FOR EVER HERE . . . .   651 FIELDS FROM/J   70
    WITH HER IN POMP AND GLORY OF VICTORY DEPART . . . . .   671 JERUSALEM 42   64
    YE TWENTY-FOUR INTO THE DEEPS LET US DEPART TO GLORY .   671 JERUSALEM 42   65
    KINGS OF CANAAN THEN TO LET THE SPIES DEPART TO MERIBAH   707 JERUSALEM 68   61
        KADESH
DEPARTED
    FOR BIRDS TO EAT BUT I HAVE SCARCE DEPARTED FROM THE PLACE   105 TIRIEL 4   *   52
    HE INDIGNANT DEPARTED ON HORSES OF HEAVN . . . .   143 FRENCH REVOLTN   201
    DEPARTED FAR INTO THE UNKNOWN & LEFT A WONDROUS VOID   . . 301 FOUR ZOAS 4   158
    BUT NOW MY LAND IS DARKEND & MY WISE MEN ARE DEPARTED . . 310 FOUR ZOAS 5   205
    RAHAB BURNING WITH PRIDE & REVENGE DEPARTED FROM LOS   . . 351 FOUR ZOAS 8   410
    DEPARTED & URTHONA RISES FROM THE RUINOUS WALLS . . . .   379 FOUR ZOAS 9   852
    FOR INTELLECTUAL WAR THE WAR OF SWORDS DEPARTED NOW   . .   379 FOUR ZOAS 9   854
    THE DARK RELIGIONS ARE DEPARTED & SWEET SCIENCE REIGNS .   379 FOUR ZOAS 9   855
    I SEND THE SHADOW OF THE DEPARTED ANGEL HOPE THE LIKENESS   797A LETTER 9   PROSE
    OF THE STATE OF THE DEPARTED I CAN DRAW AS WELL A-BED AS   869A LETTER 68   PROSE
        UP
DEPARTING
    . . . FURROWD WITH PLOWS WHOSE SEED IS DEPARTING FROM HER   138 FRENCH REVOLTN   99
    DEPARTING DEPARTING DEPARTING . . . .   225 URIZEN 5   8
DEPARTS
    WHEN HIS EVENING TALE IS TOLD DEPARTS HIS BLESSING LEAVING   40A SAMSON/PS   PROSE
    . . . AND GOD SO LONG WORSHIPPD DEPARTS AS A LAMP   . . . 140 FRENCH REVOLTN   137
DEPARTURE
    BUT THE NOBLES BURND WRATHFUL AT NECKER'S DEPARTURE . . .   139 FRENCH REVOLTN   125
    LOS DROPD A TEAR AT HER DEPARTURE BUT HE WIPD IT AWAY IN   351 FOUR ZOAS 8   411
        HOPE
    DEPARTURE HE THEN THREATEND TO KNOCK OUT MY EYES . . . .   827A LETTER 28   PROSE
    & THEY EXPRESS THEIR SORROW AT OUR DEPARTURE . . . . .   828A LETTER 28   PROSE
DEPEND
    OF THE ARTS & YOUR FALL WILL DEPEND ON [YOUR] THEIR NEGLECT 452C ANNO REYNOLDS   MARG
    DEPEND THY PLEASURES WHICH THOU HAST CUT OFF BY JEALOUSY   522 MILTON 33   9
    COLOURING DOES NOT DEPEND ON WHERE THE COLOURS ARE PUT .   563D DESC CAT   PROSE
    SUCH THINGS AS THESE DEPEND ON THE FASHION OF THE AGE .   787A ANNO THORNTON   MARG
    DEPEND UPON IT IT IS THE TREE YOUR PLEASURES ARE THE FRUIT   795B LETTER 6   PROSE
    IT IS BECAUSE SUCH THINGS DEPEND [XXX] ON THE SPIRITUAL &   812A LETTER 22   *PROSE
    I WILL ZEALOUSLY PERFORM & DEPEND UPON IT I WILL NEITHER   857B LETTER 54   PROSE
    TWO OR THREE DAYS MAY BE SUFFICIENT OR NOT ALL NOW WILL   875A LETTER 80   PROSE
        DEPEND
DEPENDANCE
    AND MARCHES ON IN FEARLESS DEPENDANCE ON THE DIVINE DECREES 580B DESC CAT 5   PROSE
DEPENDANTS
    SEE A MAN'S FEMALE DEPENDANTS YOU KNOW THE MAN   . . . .   82C ANNO LAVATER   MARG
DEPENDED
    DEPENDED ON MORTAL THINGS BOTH MYSELF & MY WIFE MUST   . . 825D LETTER 27   PROSE
DEPENDENCE   SEE SELF-DEPENDENCE
    ("ALL MORAL DEPENDENCE ON GUILTY") IS BEING LIKE   68A ANNO LAVATER   MARG
        HIM RATHER
    AS MY DEPENDENCE IS ON ENGRAVING AT PRESENT & PARTICULARLY   812C LETTER 22   PROSE
DEPENDENT
    THE PHILOSOPHER IS DEPENDENT & GOOD . . . .   412C ANNO BOYD   MARG
    THE TRUE CHRISTIAN CHARITY NOT DEPENDENT ON   . . . . .   776B INSC LAOCOON   PROSE
DEPENDING
    DEPENDING FROM THE BOSOM OF LOS & HOW WITH [DISMAL] GRIDING 307 FOUR ZOAS 5   93
        PAIN
DEPENDS
    DEPENDS ALONE UPON THE UNIVERSAL HAND & NOT IN US   . . . 346 FOUR ZOAS 8   198
    WEEP NOT SO SISTERS WEEP NOT SO OUR LIFE DEPENDS ON THIS   349 FOUR ZOAS 8   319
    [WHAT DOUBT IS VIRTUOUS EVEN HONEST ?THAT DEPENDS ?UPON   386C ANNO WATSON   * MARG
        EXAMINATION]
    INVENTION DEPENDS ALTOGETHER UPON EXECUTION   . . . . .   446D ANNO REYNOLDS   MARG
    DESTROY ART MICHAEL ANGELO'S ART DEPENDS . . . .   447A ANNO REYNOLDS   MARG
    YOUR OWN REAL GREATNESS DEPENDS ON YOUR ENCOURAGEMENT .   452C ANNO REYNOLDS   MARG
    [& SHADOW DEPENDS] IS NECESSARY TO THE ORNAMENTAL STYLE   463A ANNO REYNOLDS   * MARG
    WHICH ALTOGETHER DEPENDS ON DISTINCTNESS OF FORM . . .   463A ANNO REYNOLDS   MARG
    THY LOVE DEPENDS ON HIM THOU LOVEST & ON HIS DEAR LOVES   522 MILTON 33   8
    AND ALL DEPENDS ON FORM OR OUTLINE ON WHERE THAT IS PUT   563D DESC CAT   PROSE
    ESTABLISHMENT OF TRUTH DEPENDS ON DESTRUCTION OF FALSHOOD   687 JERUSALEM 55   * 65
        CONTINUALLY
    WEEP NOT SO SISTERS WEEP NOT SO OUR LIFE DEPENDS ON THIS   705 JERUSALEM 68   7

	PAGE	TITLE	LINE

DEPENDS   (CONTINUED)
    DEPENDS ON THE ORGAN THAT BEHOLDS IT . . . . 760 FOR SEXES/GP   2
DEPICT
    BUT THEY DEPICT HIM BALD & AGED WHO IS IN ETERNAL YOUTH   509 MILTON 24   69
DEPICTED
    DEPICTED IN HIS JOLLY FACE DIRECTS THEM TO THE   . . . . 588C CHAUCER/N   PROSE
    OF ALL THE MISCHIEFS IN THE WORLD ARE HERE DEPICTED . . 616B V LAST JUDG/N   PROSE
DEPOPULATED
    WOULD HAVE DEPOPULATED THE EARTH ALL THESE THINGS   578A DESC CAT 5   PROSE
      ARE WRITTEN
DEPOPULATION
    THE BRITONS' DISTRESS & DEPOPULATION . . . . 208D SUBJCTS HIST/N   TITLE
DEPRECIATES
    THUS REYNOLDS DEPRECIATES THE EFFORTS OF INVENTIVE GENIUS   455D ANNO REYNOLDS   MARG
DEPRESS
    THIS MAN WAS HIRED TO DEPRESS ART . . . . 445A ANNO REYNOLDS   MARG
    TO DEPRESS WHAT IS ITS CHIEF & ONLY SUPPORT   . . . . 445C ANNO REYNOLDS   MARG
    WERE ENDEAVOURING TO DEPRESS BARRY TOLD ME . . . . . . 446A ANNO REYNOLDS   MARG
    WHO WOULD IF THEY COULD FOR EVER DEPRESS MENTAL & PROLONG   480C MILTON 1   PROSE
    TO DEPRESS YOUR POWERS BY THE PRICES THEY PRETEND   . . 480C MILTON 1   PROSE
    HIS IMBECILE ATTEMPTS TO DEPRESS ME ONLY DESERVE LAUGHTER 825C LETTER 27   PROSE
    IT IS THE GREATEST OF CRIMES TO DEPRESS TRUE ART & SCIENCE 863A LETTER 60   PROSE
DEPRESSD
    & ARE DEPRESSD UNDER FOOLISH RULERS . . . . 612C V LAST JUDG/N   PROSE
    TO BE BOASTED OF & THEREFORE I CANNOT FEEL DEPRESSD . . 821C LETTER 25   PROSE
DEPRESSION
    ARE AT ALL TIMES HIRED BY THE SATANS FOR THE DEPRESSION   452B ANNO REYNOLDS   MARG
      OF ART
    & DEPRESSION WHAT YOU FEAR IS YOUR TRUE INTEREST   . . . 452C ANNO REYNOLDS   MARG
DEPREST
    TO WANDER INSLAVD BLACK DEPREST IN DARK IGNORANCE . . . 143 FRENCH REVOLTN *   214
    HEADS DEPREST VOICES WEAK EYES DOWNCAST HANDS WORK-BRUISD   197 AMERICA 3   10
    HEADS DEPREST VOICES WEAK EYES DOWNCAST HANDS WORK BRUISED   204 AMERICA CANC A   10
DEPRIVED
    WORK OF MR HAYLEY'S & THE PUBLIC LIKEWISE ARE DEPRIVED OF   856C LETTER 54   PROSE
    THAT HE IS DEPRIVED OF THE HAPPINESS OF VISITING AGAIN &   SUPP LETTER 81A   *PROSE
DEPTH
    THAT BEAM AND TWINKLE IN THE DEPTH OF NIGHT   . . . . . 18 EDW THIRD/PS 1   33
    THE GREAT STRENGTH OF COLOURING & DEPTH OF WORK   . . . . 588A CHAUCER/N   PROSE
    . . . FROM THE STARRY HEIGHTH TO THE STARRY DEPTH   630 JERUSALEM 11   12
    FOR THE SPACES REACHD FROM THE STARRY HEIGHTH TO THE STARRY 631 JERUSALEM 12   23
      DEPTH
    AND THE NORTH IS BREADTH THE SOUTH IS HEIGHTH & DEPTH   . . 635 JERUSALEM 14   29
DEPTHS
    [HIS LITTLE HANDS INTO THE DEPTHS OF THE SEA TO BRING   110 TIRIEL 8   21
      FORTH]
    FROM THE DEPTHS OF DARK SOLITUDE FROM   . . . . . . 224 URIZEN 4   6
    A SHADOWY HUMAN FORM WINGED & IN HIS DEPTHS   . . . . . 267 FOUR ZOAS 1   127
    . . . FROM THE DEPTHS OF HELL THY BLACK BOW DRAW . . . . 306 FOUR ZOAS 5   50
    ENQUIRE OF MY DAUGHTERS WHO ACCURSD IN THE DARK DEPTHS . 322 FOUR ZOAS 7   92
    GO DOWN INTO THE DEPTHS GO DOWN & HIDE YOURSELVES BENEATH   374 FOUR ZOAS 9   660
    THE EXPANDING EYES OF MAN BEHOLDS THE DEPTHS OF WONDROUS   379 FOUR ZOAS 9   *   830
      WORLDS
    REACHD TO THE DEPTHS OF (DIREST) HELL & THENCE TO ALBION'S   496 MILTON 14   *   40
      LAND
    THESE ARE THE STARRY VOIDS OF NIGHT & THE DEPTHS & CAVERNS   514 MILTON 27   51
      OF EARTH
    AWAY FROM OLOLON SHE DIVIDED & FLED INTO THE DEPTHS . . 534 MILTON 42   5
    EVEN FROM THE DEPTHS OF HELL HIS VOICE I HEAR . . . . . 621 READER LOVER/J   7
    GOD IS WITHIN & WITHOUT HE IS EVEN IN THE DEPTHS OF HELL   631 JERUSALEM 12   15
    BEFORE THE GATE OF LOS & IN THE DEPTHS OF NON ENTITY   . 674 JERUSALEM 44   36
    FOR IN THE DEPTHS OF ALBION'S BOSOM IN THE EASTERN HEAVEN   699 JERUSALEM 65   5
    AND IN DEPTHS OF MY DUNGEONS   . . . . 771 OF GATES/GP   37
DERBY
    JOSEPH STAFFORD SHROPS HEREF BENJAMIN DERBY CHESHIRE   637 JERUSALEM 16   49
      MONMOUTH
    DERBY PEAK YAWND A HORRID CHASM AT THE CRIES OF GWENDOLEN   699 JERUSALEM 64   35
      & AT
    SLADE HAD LINCOLN STAFFORD DERBY NOTTINGHAM & HIS LOVELY   710 JERUSALEM 71   34
DERBYSHIRE
    CORNWALL WALES DERBYSHIRE AND SCOTLAND   . . . . 577D DESC CAT 5   PROSE
    LINCOLNSHIRE DERBYSHIRE NOTTINGHAMSHIRE LEICESTERSHIRE . . 636 JERUSALEM 16   18
    HOARSE FROM HIS ROCKS FROM CAVERNS OF DERBYSHIRE & WALES   646 JERUSALEM 23   27
    ROUND THE ROCKY PEAK OF DERBYSHIRE LONDON STONE & ROSAMONDS   689 JERUSALEM 57   7
      BOWER
    HYLE ON EAST MOOR IN ROCKY DERBYSHIRE RAVD TO THE MOON . 723 JERUSALEM 80   66
    UPON EAST MOOR IN DERBYSHIRE & ALONG THE VALLEYS OF CHEVIOT   740 JERUSALEM 93   6
    OF THE MINES OF CORNWALL & DERBYSHIRE LAYS UPON HIS BOSOM   741 JERUSALEM 94   8
      HEAVY
DEREHAM
    ST EDMUNDS CHAPEL EAST DEREHAM MAY BE UNDERSTOOD TO . . . 838B LETTER 37   PROSE
    MEAN A CHAPEL IN EAST DEREHAM TOWN & NOT TO EXPRESS . . . 838B LETTER 37   PROSE
    SUFFICIENTLY THAT THE MONUMENT IS IN EAST DEREHAM CHURCH   838B LETTER 37   PROSE
DERIDING
    MOCKING AND DERIDING AT THE WRITHINGS OF THEIR VICTIM ON   701 JERUSALEM 65   *   57
      SALISBURY
    DIVINE UNION DERIDING AND DENYING IMMEDIATE COMMUNION   . 776D INSC LAOCOON   PROSE
DERISION
    LIVING IN A COTTAGE AND IN CONTEMPT AND DERISION . . . . 575D DESC CAT 3   PROSE
DERIVATION
    ARE AN ORIGINAL DERIVATION FROM THE POETIC GENIUS THIS . . 98D ALL RELIGIONS   PROSE

479

```
                                                                PAGE     TITLE          LINE
DERIVATIVE
     WAS THE FIRST PRINCIPLE AND ALL THE OTHERS MERELY          153D MARRIAGE HH 12   PROSE
        DERIVATIVE
DERIVED     SEE SELF DERIVED
     OF MAN IS DERIVED FROM THE POETIC GENIUS LIKEWISE    . .    98B ALL RELIGIONS    PROSE
     THAT THE FORMS OF ALL THINGS ARE DERIVED FROM THEIR GENIUS  98B ALL RELIGIONS    PROSE
     THE (RELIGIONS) OF ALL NATIONS ARE DERIVED  . . . . .       98C ALL RELIGIONS   *PROSE
     & UNSUBSTANTIAL THAN THOSE WHICH ARE DERIVED FROM EARTH     474B ANNO REYNOLDS    MARG
     IN A SUBLIME DEGREE BEING DERIVED FROM REAL VISION IN  .   607A V LAST JUDG/N    PROSE
     DERIVED FROM THE MODERN BONDAGE OF RHYMING  . . . . .      621D JERUSALEM 3      PROSE
     NOT ONLY OF THE SUBSTANCE FROM WHICH IT IS DERIVED    . .   629 JERUSALEM 10       11
     YOUR ANCESTORS DERIVED THEIR ORIGIN FROM  . . . . .       649C JERUSALEM 27     PROSE
DERIVES
     AND FROM THESE THREE SCIENCE DERIVES EVERY OCCUPATION OF    514 MILTON 27          62
        MEN
DEROGATE
     DEROGATE FROM HIM IN THE TRIFLES & SMALL ARTICLES OF THAT   673 JERUSALEM 43       57
        GOODNESS
DEROGATION
     REASONING & DEROGATION FROM ME AN OBJECTING & CRUEL SPITE   639 JERUSALEM 17       37
DEROGATORY
     AS HE THINKS IT SOMEWHAT DEROGATORY AS WELL AS             858A LETTER 55        PROSE
        UNPROFITABLE
DESART     SEE DESERT
     AND THE DESART WILD     . . . . . . . . . . . . .          112 LIT GRL LST/SI      7
     LOST IN DESART WILD     . . . . . . . . . . . . .          112 LIT GRL LST/SI     21
     OER THIS DESART BRIGHT   . . . . . . . . . . . . .         113 LIT GRL LST/SI     30
     THEY TRACD THE DESART WAYS  . . . . . . . . . . .          113 LIT GRL FND/SI      8
     STARVD IN DESART WILD . . . . . . . . . . . . .            114 LIT GRL FND/SI     12
     . . . TO PLANT BEAUTY IN THE DESART CRAVING ABYSS THEY      136 FRENCH REVOLTN     55
        GLEAM
     . . . DRIVEN BACK BY THE SANDY DESART    . . . . . .        144 FRENCH REVOLTN    235
     WITH SECRET TEARS BENEATH HIM SOUND LIKE WAVES ON A DESART  190 V DAU ALBION 2      7
        SHORE
     OR POISON FROM THE DESART WILDS FROM THE EYES OF           192 V DAU ALBION 4      11
        THE ENVIER
     BUT THEY SHALL ROT ON DESART SANDS & CONSUME IN BOTTOMLESS  199 AMERICA 8           7
        DEEPS
     THAT MEN GET RICH BY & THE SANDY DESART IS GIVN TO THE      200 AMERICA 11         11
        STRONG
     WEEPS SHE IN DESART SHADES   . . . . . . . . . . .         240 EUROPE 8            6
     AND ALL THE REST A DESART    . . . . . . . . . . .         246 SONG OF LOS 4       3
     A FROWNING CONTINENT APPEARD WHERE ENION IN THE DESART  .   266 FOUR ZOAS 1        89
     [WHERE IS THE VOICE THAT LATELY WOKE THE DESART WHERE THE   268 FOUR ZOAS 1       139
        FACE]
     SHE COULD CONTROLL THE SPACES REGIONS DESART FLOOD & FOREST 271 FOUR ZOAS 1       241
     AND I COMMANDED SPRINGS TO RISE FOR HER IN THE BLACK DESART 282 FOUR ZOAS 2        88
     DESART AMONG THE STARS THEM WITHERING WITH ITS RIDGES COLD  319 FOUR ZOAS 6       306
     VALA THE LILLY OF THE DESART MELTING IN HIGH NOON    . .    326 FOUR ZOAS 7       240
     I MUST HAVE DIED IN THE DARK DESART AMONG NOXIOUS WORMS     335 FOUR ZOAS 7B       86
     AND OF THE WATERS & THE SCORPION OF THE DESART IRRITATE     335 FOUR ZOAS 7B      112
     ON THE GOLDEN PALACE SONGS & JOY ON THE DESART THE COLD     363 FOUR ZOAS 9       251
        BABE
     HE RESTED ON THE DESART WILD & ON THE RAGING SEA    . .     380 FOUR ZOAS AD 1     15
     A DESART VAST WITHOUT A BOUND   . . . . . . . . .          426 MENTAL TRAVLER     66
     AND A DARK DESART ALL AROUND    . . . . . . . . .          426 MENTAL TRAVLER     68
     AND ON THE DESART WILD THEY BOTH   . . . . . . . .         426 MENTAL TRAVLER     75
     TILL THE WIDE DESART PLANTED OER   . . . . . . . .         426 MENTAL TRAVLER     82
     TO ALL WHO IN THE DESART ROAM   . . . . . . . . .          427 MENTAL TRAVLER     90
     CITY & SANDY DESART INTERMINGLED BEYOND MORTAL KEN    . .   532 MILTON 40          27
     HE CURSES FOREST SPRING & RIVER DESART & SANDY WASTE   . .  629 JERUSALEM 10       26
     COME HITHER INTO THE DESART & TURN THESE STONES TO BREAD    685 JERUSALEM 54       21
     CLOSED IN BY A SANDY DESART & A NIGHT OF STARS SHINING  .   707 JERUSALEM 69       21
     IN MIRACLES & WONDERS IN THE FOUR-FOLD DESART OF ALBION     713 JERUSALEM 73       33
     JERUSALEM HUNGERS IN THE DESART AFFECTION TO HER CHILDREN   727 JERUSALEM 83        7
     "HUNDRED FOR THE TERRIBLE DESART OF LONDON WAS BETWEEN"    800B LETTER 12        PROSE
DESARTS
     WHILE THE DESARTS WEEP                                     113 LIT GRL FND/SI      4
     TO MAKE THE DESARTS BLOSSOM & THE DEEPS SHRINK TO THEIR     199 AMERICA 8           8
        FOUNTAINS
     MUSTER AROUND THE BLEAK DESARTS    . . . . . . . .         223 URIZEN 4            1
     AND OER THE DARK DESARTS OF URIZEN   . . . . . . .         225 URIZEN 5           14
     TO THE DESARTS AND ROCKS [THEY] HE RAN RAGING  . . . .     225 URIZEN 5        *  20
     OF ASIA & ON THE DESARTS OF AFRICA ROUND THE FALLEN ANGELS  246 SONG OF LOS 4      20
     THOSE THAT REMAIN HAVE FLED FROM MY CRUELTY INTO           268 FOUR ZOAS 1       167
        THE DESARTS
     VALA REMAIN IN DESARTS OF DARK SOLITUDE NOR SUN NOR MOON    275 FOUR ZOAS 1       417
     AND CAST THEIR YOUNG OUT TO THE HUNGRY WILDS & SANDY        276 FOUR ZOAS 1       453
        DESARTS
     HE TOOK HIGH BOUNDING OVER HILLS & DESARTS FLOODS          313 FOUR ZOAS 6        73
        & HORRIBLE CHASMS
     OVER THE BURNING DESARTS THEN THE DESARTS PASSD INVOLVD     314 FOUR ZOAS 6       110
        IN CLOUDS
     BEATING THE DESARTS & THE ROCKS THE DESARTS FEEL HIS POWER  352 FOUR ZOAS 8       443
     THE TYGERS FROM THE FORESTS & THE LIONS [OF] FROM THE       365 FOUR ZOAS 9    * 301
        SANDY DESARTS
     SEVEN ROCKY MASSES TERRIBLE IN THE DESARTS OF MIDIAN   . .  498 MILTON 17          17
     THE SUN ROLLS INTO CHAOS & THE STARS INTO THE DESARTS  . .  507 MILTON 23          24
     THE DESARTS TREMBLE AT HIS WRATH THEY SHRINK THEMSELVES     726 JERUSALEM 82       51
        IN FEAR
     VIEWING THE WINDING WORM ON THE DESARTS OF GREAT TARTARY    731 JERUSALEM 86       46
     FROM ENION IN THE DESARTS TERRIFIED AT EACH OTHER'S BEAUTY  732 JERUSALEM 86       63
```

480

DESARTS   (CONTINUED)
          DESARTS LOS FIRST BROKE SILENCE & BEGAN TO UTTER HIS LOVE   732 JERUSALEM 87   2
DESCEND
          THAT WISDOM MAY DESCEND IN FAIRY DREAMS . . . .   14 IMIT SPEN/PS   5
          ON THESE PLAINS AND IN THESE SILENT WOODS TRUE JOYS DESCEND   37A CONTEMPLATN/PS   PROSE
          LET YOUR BOUNTY DESCEND TO OUR FAIR EARS   55C ISLAND MOON 9   PROSE
          HE WHO LOVES FEELS LOVE DESCEND INTO HIM & IF HE HAS WISDOM   908 ANNO SWED LOVE   MARG
          OR CLOSE UP OR THEY WILL DESCEND IF HE CLOSES UP THE TWO   93A ANNO SWED LOVE   MARG
          THE SUN DOES DESCEND   116 ECCHOING GR/SI   23
          DESCEND O LITTLE CLOUD & HOVER BEFORE THE EYES OF THEL . .   128 BOOK OF THEL 2   16
          DESCEND FROM THE GLOOM AND WANDER THRO THE PALACE . . .   136 FRENCH REVOLTN   60
          . . . THEY DESCEND AND LOOK INTO THEIR GRAVES . . . . .   137 FRENCH REVOLTN   71
          COULD HEART DESCEND OR WINGS ASPIRE . . . .   173 THE TYGER/N 2   7
          THE EAGLES AT HER CALL DESCEND & REND THEIR BLEEDING PREY   190 V DAU ALBION 2   17
          DESCEND TO GENERATIONS THAT IN FUTURE TIMES FORGET   197 AMERICA 3   12
          DESCEND TO GENERATIONS THAT IN FUTURE TIMES FORGET . . .   204 AMERICA CANC A   12
          I SEE INVISIBLE DESCEND INTO THE GARDENS OF VALA . . . .   272 FOUR ZOAS 1   299
          DESCEND O URIZEN DESCEND WITH HORSE & CHARIOTS . . . .   272 FOUR ZOAS 1   * 308
          DESCEND THEY COULD NOT NOR FROM EACH OTHER AVERT THEIR EYES   274 FOUR ZOAS 1   362
          [AND COMFORTS SHALL DESCEND FROM HEAVEN INTO THY DARKNING   292 FOUR ZOAS 3   29
             CLOUDS]
          GIRD ON THY FLAMING ZONE DESCEND INTO THE SEPULCHER . . .   337 FOUR ZOAS 7B   * 193
          DELUSIVE CRUELTY THEY DESCEND AWAY FROM THE DAUGHTERS OF   341 FOUR ZOAS 8   26
             BEULAH
          GATES BROKEN DOWN THEY DESCEND THRO THE GATE OF PITY . .   341 FOUR ZOAS 8   28
          FOLLOW ME O MY FLOCKS WE WILL NOW DESCEND INTO THE VALLEY   368 FOUR ZOAS 9   446
          DID NOT JESUS DESCEND & BECOME A SERVANT THE . . . . .   399C ANNO BACON   MARG
          WHO DESCEND WITH THE FOUR TRUMPETS . . . .   443A LAST JUDGMNT/L *PROSE
          [WHO DESCEND BEFORE HIS FEET WITH THEIR FOUR TRUMPETS] .   443A LAST JUDGMNT/L PROSE
          THAT THE NEW JERUSALEM IS READY TO DESCEND UPON EARTH .   444A LAST JUDGMNT/L PROSE
          AND OLOLON SAID LET US DESCEND ALSO AND LET US GIVE . .   504 MILTON 21   45
          OF WAR & RELIGION LET US DESCEND & BRING HIM CHAINED . .   507 MILTON 23   17
          THERE ARE TWO GATES THRO WHICH ALL SOULS DESCEND   512 MILTON 26   13
             ONE SOUTHWARD
          AND LEST THEY SHOULD DESCEND BEFORE THE NORTH & SOUTH GATES . 512 MILTON 26   21
          THE PASSIONS & DESIRES DESCEND UPON THE HUNGRY WINDS . .   512 MILTON 26   28
          THEY TOUCH THEIR PINIONS TIP TIP AND EACH DESCEND . . .   526 MILTON 36   3
          INTO ETERNITY THAT WAY BUT ALL DESCEND TO LOS . . . . .   529 MILTON 37   58
          THEN SAID DESCEND THOU UPON EARTH . . . .   557 ART HAS LOST/N   4
          THOSE [WHO] FIGURES THAT DESCEND INTO THE FLAMES . . .   608D V LAST JUDG/N *PROSE
          IN THIS CATARACT FOUR ANGELS DESCEND HEADLONG . . . . .   609A V LAST JUDG/N   PROSE
          HER KINGS & COUNCELLORS & WARRIORS DESCEND IN FLAMES . .   609B V LAST JUDG/N   PROSE
          TO DESCEND FROM THE THRONE OF GOD & OF THE LAMB . . . .   612A V LAST JUDG/N   PROSE
          EVER DESCEND INTO THEE BUT THOU SHALT BE A NON ENTITY FOR   639 JERUSALEM 17   44
             EVER
          DESCEND O LAMB OF GOD & TAKE AWAY THE IMPUTATION OF SIN   648 JERUSALEM 25   12
          O GOD OF ALBION DESCEND DELIVER JERUSALEM FROM THE OAKEN   672 JERUSALEM 43   11
             GROVES
          THIS DREAD DISEASE NONE BUT JESUS O LORD DESCEND AND SAVE   675 JERUSALEM 45   16
          O GOD DESCEND GATHER OUR BRETHREN DELIVER JERUSALEM . . .   675 JERUSALEM 45   28
          COME LORD JESUS LAMB OF GOD DESCEND FOR IF O LORD . . .   681 JERUSALEM 50   10
          GIRD ON THY FLAMING ZONE DESCEND INTO THE SEPULCHER OF   700 JERUSALEM 65   39
             CANTERBURY
          O WHEN SHALL THE LAMB OF GOD DESCEND AMONG THE REPROBATE   727 JERUSALEM 83   15
          FOR MULTITUDES OF THOSE WHO SLEEP IN ALLA DESCEND . . .   736 JERUSALEM 89   58
          ON THE TURRET ITS SPIRAL DOES SOFTLY DESCEND . . . . .   800 MRS FLAXMAN/L   7
          DESCEND & ASCEND WITH THE BREAD & THE WINE . . . . .   800 MRS FLAXMAN/L   12
          WE LIKE INFANTS DESCEND . . . .   805 TO BUTTS/L   42
DESCENDED
          THE CLOUD DESCENDED AND THE LILLY BOWD HER MODEST HEAD . .   128 BOOK OF THEL 2   17
          ENDLESS THE SHADY TRAIN SHIVRING DESCENDED . . . .   140 FRENCH REVOLTN   135
          AND LO IT WAS A DEEP PIT INTO WHICH I DESCENDED . . . .   157A MARRIAGE HH 17 PROSE
          [AND MERCY & PITY & PEACE DESCENDED] . . . .   164 HEARD ANGEL/N   20
          DOWN ON THE LAND OF AMERICA INDIGNANT THEY DESCENDED . .   200 AMERICA 12   4
          WEEPING IN DISMAL HOWLING WOE HE DARK DESCENDED HOWLING   203 AMERICA 16   7
          DESCENDED THRO THE ORIENT GATES OF THE ETERNAL DAY . . .   239 EUROPE 4   3
          THEN ENITHARMON DOWN DESCENDED INTO HIS RED LIGHT . . .   240 EUROPE 4   31
          THE WANDERING MAN BOWD HIS FAINT HEAD AND URIZEN DESCENDED   273 FOUR ZOAS 1   316
          AND THE ONE MUST HAVE MURDERD THE OTHER IF HE HAD   273 FOUR ZOAS 1   * 317
             NOT DESCENDED
          INDIGNANT MUTTERING LOW THUNDERS URIZEN DESCENDED . . .   273 FOUR ZOAS 1   318
          . . . & [THE] GOLDEN DAY [?DESCENDED] DESCENDING . . .   274 FOUR ZOAS 1   * 366
          WHEN URIZEN [DESCENDED] RETURND FROM HIS IMMENSE LABOURS   285 FOUR ZOAS 2   201
             & TRAVELS
          LUVAH DESCENDED FROM THE CLOUD . . . .   293 FOUR ZOAS 3   69
          WITH PAIN UPON THE [DISMAL] DREARY MOUNTAINS & WITH PAIN   313 FOUR ZOAS 6   *   79
             DESCENDED
          BUT URIZEN SILENT DESCENDED TO THE CAVES OF ORC & SAW . .   320 FOUR ZOAS 7   5
          FOR THE SHADOW OF ENITHARMON DESCENDED DOWN THE TREE OF   325 FOUR ZOAS 7   210
             MYSTERY
          DESCENDED TO THE SOUND OF INSTRUMENTS THAT DROWND THE NOISE   333 FOUR ZOAS 7B   32
          TO BEULAH & THE DEAD IN ULRO DESCENDED FROM THE WAR . . .   342 FOUR ZOAS 8   56
          PITYING THE LAMB OF GOD DESCENDED THRO JERUSALEM'S GATES   347 FOUR ZOAS 8   260
          THE LAMB OF GOD DESCENDED THRO THE TWELVE PORTIONS OF LUVAH   349 FOUR ZOAS 8   323
          BUT WHEN LUVAH IN ORC BECAME A SERPENT HE (DESCENDED) INTO   351 FOUR ZOAS 8   * 382
          SHADDAI WAS ANGRY PACHAD DESCENDED PACHAD WAS TERRIFIED   351 FOUR ZOAS 8   404
          AND ALL THE SONS OF ETERNITY DESCENDED INTO BEULAH . . .   359 FOUR ZOAS 9   66
          LUVAH & VALA DESCENDED & ENTERD THE GATES OF DARK URTHONA   367 FOUR ZOAS 9   375
          SHE EMBRACD THEM IN TEARS TILL THE SUN DESCENDED   370 FOUR ZOAS 9   512
             THE WESTERN HILLS
          TO BEULAH & THE DEAD IN BEULAH DESCENDED THRO THEIR GATES   382 FOUR ZOAS AD 6   26
          AND ALL EDEN DESCENDED INTO PALAMABRON'S TENT . . . . .   489 MILTON 9   1

481

```
                                                          PAGE      TITLE            LINE
DESCENDED     (CONTINUED)
       HIS SPECTRE RAGING FURIOUS DESCENDED INTO ITS SPACE   .  .   490 MILTON 9          52
       SHE DOWN DESCENDED INTO THE MIDST OF THE GREAT SOLEMN       492 MILTON 11         29
          ASSEMBLY
       SHADDAI ANGRY PAHAD DESCENDED PAHAD TERRIFIED THEY SENT     494 MILTON 13         23
          JEHOVAH
       AND DOWN DESCENDED INTO UDAN-ADAN IT WAS NIGHT    .  .  .   503 MILTON 21          1
       ON TO WALK FORWARD THRO ETERNITY LOS DESCENDED TO ME    .  . 505 MILTON 22          5
       SO LOS SPOKE FURIOUS THEY DESCENDED TO BOWLAHOOLA          509 MILTON 24         44
          & ALLAMANDA
       LOUD SHOUT THE SONS OF LUVAH AT THE WINE-PRESSES AS LOS    510 MILTON 25          1
          DESCENDED
       INTO THIS PLACE THE SONS & DAUGHTERS OF OLOLON DESCENDED   518 MILTON 30          4
       INTO THIS PLEASANT SHADOW BEULAH ALL OLOLON DESCENDED   .   519 MILTON 31          8
       BEHOLD MILTON DESCENDED TO REDEEM THE FEMALE SHADE    .  .  522 MILTON 33         11
       O HOW THE STARRY EIGHT REJOICD TO SEE OLOLON DESCENDED  .   525 MILTON 35         34
       IN THIS MOMENT OLOLON DESCENDED TO LOS & ENITHARMON    .  . 526 MILTON 35         46
       THE VIRGIN ANSWERD KNOWEST THOU OF MILTON WHO DESCENDED    527 MILTON 37          1
       DESCENDED DOWN A PAVED WORK OF ALL KINDS OF PRECIOUS STONES 529 MILTON 38          6
       GARDEN CLOTHED IN BLACK SEVERE & SILENT HE DESCENDED   .    529 MILTON 38          8
       THEN AS A MOONY ARK OLOLON DESCENDED TO FELPHAM'S VALE  .   534 MILTON 42          7
       LUVAH DESCENDED FROM THE CLOUD IN TERROR ALBION ROSE   .    654 JERUSALEM 29       56
       DESCENDED AND FELL DOWN UPON THEIR KNEES ROUND ALBION'S     666 JERUSALEM 40        8
          KNEES
       AND MUST HAVE DIED BUT THE DIVINE SAVIOUR DESCENDED   .  .  669 JERUSALEM 42        6
       WHEN OUT OF BEULAH THE EMANATION OF THE SLEEPER DESCENDED   678 JERUSALEM 48       23
       THEN DESCENDED THE CRUEL ROD   .  .  .  .  .  .  .  .  .  . 750 EV GOSPEL(C)/N     36
       THEN DESCENDED THE CRUEL ROD   .  .  .  .  .  .  .  .  .  . 752 EV GOSPEL(D)/N     72
DESCENDENTS
       AGES AFTER AGES IN THY DESCENDENTS  .  .  .  .  .  .  .  789A ANNO THORNTON   * MARG
DESCENDETH
       WHICH NOW DESCENDETH OUT OF HEAVEN A CITY YET A WOMAN   .   362 FOUR ZOAS 9       222
DESCENDING
       GOD DESCENDING ACCORDING TO THE WEAKNESS OF MAN   .  .  .    87B ANNO LAVATER      MARG
       THE SUN DESCENDING IN THE WEST  .  .  .  .  .  .  .  .  .   118 NIGHT/SI            1
       UNSEEN DESCENDING WEIGH MY LIGHT WINGS UPON BALMY FLOWERS   128 BOOK OF THEL 3     12
       .  .  . MYRIADS DESCENDING AND WEEPING THRO DISMAL WINDS .  140 FRENCH REVOLTN    134
       DESCENDING TO BEASTS  .  .  .  .  .  .  .  .  .  .  .  .    140 FRENCH REVOLTN    139
       .  .  . TILL GRADUAL A MURMUR IS HEARD DESCENDING INTO THE  145 FRENCH REVOLTN    243
          VALLEY
       HEADLONG FROM OUT THEIR HEAVENLY HEIGHTS DESCENDING SWIFT   200 AMERICA 12          5
          AS FIRES
       DEFORMD THRO THE THREE HEAVENS DESCENDING IN FURY & FIRE    267 FOUR ZOAS 1       104
       .  .  . & [THE] GOLDEN DAY [?DESCENDED] DESCENDING     .    274 FOUR ZOAS 1    *  366
       DESCENDING SHE REPOSD BESIDE HIM FOLDING HIM AROUND    .  . 285 FOUR ZOAS 2       202
       DESCENDING SWEET UPON THE WIND AMONG SOFT HARPS & VOICES    287 FOUR ZOAS 2       288
       DESCENDING OVER BEULAH'S MILD MOON COVERD REGIONS     .  .  304 FOUR ZOAS 4       249
       BORE ON THRO THE AFFRIGHTED VALES ASCENDING & DESCENDING    319 FOUR ZOAS 6       287
       WITH DIFFICULTY DOWN DESCENDING GUIDED BY HIS EAR    .  .   319 FOUR ZOAS 6       293
       SHUT UP WITHIN THEMSELVES DESCENDING DOWN I SUNK ALONG  .   327 FOUR ZOAS 7       286
       CLOTHED IN LUVAH'S ROBES OF BLOOD DESCENDING TO REDEEM  .   330 FOUR ZOAS 7       416
       ENITHARMON ANSWERD I BEHOLD THE LAMB OF GOD DESCENDING  .   330 FOUR ZOAS 7       424
       DESCENDING ON THE SHADOWY FEMALE'S CLOUDS IN SPECTROUS      340 FOUR ZOAS 7B      299
          TERROR
       FOR NOTHING COULD RESTRAIN THE DEAD IN BEULAH FROM          341 FOUR ZOAS 8        24
          DESCENDING
       DESCENDING FROM JERUSALEM WITH POWER AND GREAT GLORY   .  . 364 FOUR ZOAS 9       273
       SOUNDING THE SONG OF LOS DESCENDING TO THE VINEYARDS BRIGHT 376 FOUR ZOAS 9       713
       ARE DESCENDING INTO THE ABYSS IN WAILING & DESPAIR    .  . 443A LAST JUDGMNT/L    PROSE
       INTO WHICH THE WICKED ARE DESCENDING  .  .  .  .  .  .  . 443B LAST JUDGMNT/L    PROSE
       HOWLING & [DESCENDING INTO THE FLAMES & IN THE ACT OF] .  443C LAST JUDGMNT/L    PROSE
       BY YOUR MILD POWER DESCENDING DOWN THE NERVES OF MY RIGHT   481 MILTON 2           6
          ARM
       DESCENDING PERPENDICULAR SWIFT AS THE SWALLOW OR SWIFT  .   497 MILTON 15         48
       THE SOULS DESCENDING TO THE BODY WAIL ON THE RIGHT HAND     512 MILTON 26         16
       LARK MET THE FEMALE OLOLON DESCENDING INTO MY GARDEN   .    527 MILTON 36         10
       DESCENDING DOWN INTO MY GARDEN A HUMAN WONDER OF GOD    .   528 MILTON 37         13
       OUT FROM THE EASTERN SKY DESCENDING DOWN INTO MY COTTAGE    529 MILTON 38          7
       DESCENDING [AS A SCROLL] THE JUST ARISE  .  .  .  .  .  .  606B V LAST JUDG/N   *PROSE
       HELL IS OPENED & MANY FIGURES ARE DESCENDING INTO IT   .  608B V LAST JUDG/N    PROSE
       ARE DESCENDING [INTO HELL] DOWN THE STEPS INTO THE PIT    608C V LAST JUDG/N    PROSE
       DESCENDING FROM THE SEA OF FIRE BEFORE THE THRONE    .  .  609A V LAST JUDG/N    PROSE
       THE OTHER LIVING CREATURES ARE DESCENDING WITH A SHOUT  .  612A V LAST JUDG/N    PROSE
       MILTON SLEEPING ON A BANK SLEEP DESCENDING WITH A     .  . 619C ILLUS MILTON    PROSE
       SO SPOKE THE VOICE FROM THE FURNACES DESCENDING INTO        662 JERUSALEM 35       17
          NON-ENTITY
       AND ALBION'S SONS ASCENDING & DESCENDING IN THE HORRID VOID 674 JERUSALEM 44       17
       ASCENDING AND DESCENDING INTO ALBION'S SEA OF DEATH   .  .  681 JERUSALEM 50       21
       OF WALES & SCOTLAND BEHELD THE DESCENDING WAR THE ROUTED    703 JERUSALEM 66       60
          FLYING
       TREMBLING & DESCENDING DOWN SEEKING TO REST UPON HIGH MONA  703 JERUSALEM 66    *  79
       I SEE THE NEW JERUSALEM DESCENDING OUT OF HEAVEN    .  .  . 731 JERUSALEM 86       19
       IN THE SUN HE APPEARD DESCENDING BEFORE  .  .  .  .  .  .   818 HAPPINESS/L        56
DESCENDS
       SUPERIOR THEN HE IS NOT TRULY IN THE (THIRD) BUT DESCENDS   93A ANNO SWED LOVE     MARG
       .  .  . THE CLOUD AND VISION DESCENDS OVER CHEARFUL FRANCE  134 FRENCH REVOLTN     1
       TROUBLED LEANING ON NECKER DESCENDS THE KING  .  .  .  .  . 134 FRENCH REVOLTN    10
       DESCENDS LINK BY LINK FROM ALBION'S CLIFFS ACROSS THE       197 AMERICA 3          8
          SEA TO BIND
       DESCENDS LINK BY LINK FROM ALBION'S CLIFFS ACROSS THE       204 AMERICA CANC A     8
          SEA TO BIND
       DESCENDS TO BE A WEEPING BABE  .  .  .  .  .  .  .  .  .  . 289 FOUR ZOAS 2       367
```

482

		PAGE	TITLE	LINE

DESCENDS (CONTINUED)

THEN WEEPING HE DESCENDS IN WRATH DRAWING ALL THINGS IN HIS FURY — 353 FOUR ZOAS 8 — 456

DESCENDS [OP] DOWN ON THE SAND THE THIRSTY SAND DRINKS & REJOICES — 373 FOUR ZOAS 9 — * 602

BUT AS A WINTRY GLOBE DESCENDS PRECIPITANT THRO BEULAH BURSTING — 497 MILTON 15 — 44

A FEMALE DESCENDS TO MEET HER LOVER OR HUSBAND . . . . . 610D V LAST JUDG/N PROSE

THE LADDER OF ANGELS DESCENDS THRO THE AIR . . . . . . 800 MRS FLAXMAN/L 6

DESCENT

FEELING THE ELECTRIC FLAME OF MILTON'S AWFUL PRECIPITATE DESCENT — 502 MILTON 20 — 26

IN ULRO BENEATH BEULAH THE VAST BREACH OF MILTON'S DESCENT — 503 MILTON 21 — 7

SOUTHWARD & BY THE EAST WITHIN THE BREACH OF MILTON'S DESCENT — 524 MILTON 34 — 42

BY OLOLON'S DESCENT THRO BEULAH TO LOS & ENITHARMON . . . 525 MILTON 35 — 36

DESCRIBE

[DAUGHTERS OF BEULAH DESCRIBE] . . . . 346 FOUR ZOAS 8 — * 200

IS TAKEN OF THIS CIRCUMSTANCE TO DESCRIBE THE SUBJECT . . 567B DESC CAT 3 PROSE

THE PROPHETS DESCRIBE WHAT THEY SAW IN VISION . . . . . 576D DESC CAT 4 PROSE

IS TAKEN OF THIS CIRCUMSTANCE TO DESCRIBE THE SUBJECT . . 588D CHAUCER/N PROSE

IS TAKEN OF THIS CIRCUMSTANCE TO DESCRIBE THE SUBJECT . . 590C CHAUCER 2 PROSE

CANNOT PREVIOUSLY DESCRIBE IN WORDS WHAT I MEAN TO DESIGN 792B LETTER 4 PROSE

WHO CAN DESCRIBE THE DISMAL TORMENTS OF SUCH A STATE . . 813A LETTER 22 PROSE

WHEN WE MEET I WILL PERFECTLY DESCRIBE TO YOU MY CONDUCT & 826A LETTER 27 PROSE

& FOUND HIM QUITE AS CHEARFUL AS YOU DESCRIBE HIM & BY HIS 835C LETTER 35 PROSE

DESCRIBED

& DESCRIBED SOMETHING THAT NOBODY LISTEND TO SO THEY . . 44B ISLAND MOON 1 PROSE

& ITS VARIOUS PARTS OUGHT TO BE DESCRIBED FOR THE . . . 442D LAST JUDGMNT/L PROSE

CHAUCER HIMSELF AND THE REEVE COMES AS CHAUCER HAS DESCRIBED — 567A DESC CAT 3 — PROSE

OF CHAUCER'S CHARACTERS AS DESCRIBED IN HIS CANTERBURY TALES — 567C DESC CAT 3 — PROSE

LADY IS DESCRIBED ALSO AS OF THE FIRST RANK RICH AND HONOURED — 568B DESC CAT 3 — PROSE

CHAUCER HAS DESCRIBED WITH MINUTENESS IT IS VERY ELEGANT 568B DESC CAT 3 PROSE

FOR THE MONK IS DESCRIBED BY CHAUCER AS A MAN OF THE . 568C DESC CAT 3 PROSE

OF CHAUCER THE DOCTOR OF PHYSIC IS DESCRIBED AS THE FIRST OF — 570D DESC CAT 3 — PROSE

CHAUCER HIMSELF & THE REEVE COMES AS CHAUCER HAS DESCRIBED 588C CHAUCER/N PROSE

CHAUCER HIMSELF AND THE REEVE COMES AS CHAUCER HAS DESCRIBED — 590A CHAUCER 2 — PROSE

OF CHAUCER'S CHARACTERS AS DESCRIBED IN HIS CANTERBURY TALES — 590C CHAUCER 2 — PROSE

ARE REPRESENTATIONS OF THOSE STATES DESCRIBED IN THE BIBLE 609D V LAST JUDG/N PROSE

IS NOT EVERY VICE POSSIBLE TO MAN DESCRIBED IN THE BIBLE OPENLY — 777D INSC LAOCOON — PROSE

DESCRIBES

SUCH AS CHRIST DESCRIBES BY RAVENING WOLVES . . . . . 401D ANNO BACON MARG

CHAUCER DESCRIBES HERE A MIGHTY MAN . . . . 568A DESC CAT 3 PROSE

CENTAURS MOST LIKELY DANTE DESCRIBES THE...CIRCLES IN CANTO XI... — 786A ILLS DANTE 101 PROSE

DESCRIPTION

BETTER THAN ANY DESCRIPTION OF BUILDINGS OR GARMENTS . . 150C MARRIAGE HH 6 PROSE

READ CHAUCER'S DESCRIPTION OF THE GOOD PARSON AND BOW . . 570C DESC CAT 3 PROSE

A DESCRIPTION OF THE ETERNAL PRINCIPLES THAT EXIST IN ALL AGES — 571A DESC CAT 3 — PROSE

QUERY THE ABOVE OUGHT TO FOLLOW THE DESCRIPTION . . . . 606A V LAST JUDG/N PROSE

HERE FOLLOWS THE DESCRIPTION OF THE PICTURE . . . . . 606A V LAST JUDG/N PROSE

TO PROCEED [IN THE] WITH THE DESCRIPTION OF THOSE ON THE LEFT HAND — 607C V LAST JUDG/N — *PROSE

DESCRIPTIONS

PERSONAGES ACCORDING TO THE DESCRIPTIONS IN THE PROPHETS 608C V LAST JUDG/N PROSE

DESCRIPTIVE SEE DISCRIPTIVE

A DESCRIPTIVE CATALOGUE OF BLAKE'S EXHIBITION . . . . . 562A DESC CAT ADV TITLE

THE DESCRIPTIVE CATALOGUE PRICE...CONTAINING MR B'S(BLAKE'S) — 562B DESC CAT ADV — PROSE

A DESCRIPTIVE CATALOGUE OF PICTURES POETICAL AND HISTORICAL 563A DESC CAT TITLE

ABEL KNEELS ON A BLOODY CLOUD DESCRIPTIVE OF THOSE CHURCHES 606D V LAST JUDG/N PROSE

ALL DESCRIPTIVE OF CHARACTER & NOT A LINE IS DRAWN . . . 611B V LAST JUDG/N PROSE

OR UNLESS HE SHOULD READ MY LONG POEM DESCRIPTIVE OF THOSE ACTS — 823A LETTER 26 — PROSE

DESCRY

SWELLD LIMBS WITH NO OUTLINE THAT YOU CAN DESCRY . . . . 546 SWELLD LIMBS/N 1

BUT WHEN ONCE I DID DESCRY . . . . 771 OF GATES/GP 39

DESERT SEE DESART

THE WEARY WANDERER THRO THE DESERT ROVE . . . . 15 IMIT SPEN/PS 52

LIKE ROLLING WAVES UPON A DESERT SHORE SIGHS SUCCEEDED SIGHS — 36B COUCH DEATH/PS — PROSE

TRUE [?HILI] HELA THIS IS THE DESERT OF ALL THOSE CRUEL ONES — 107 TIRIEL 6 — * 16

THE PICTURE OF "CHRIST IN THE DESERT" HE SUPPOSES TO BE 831B LETTER 31 PROSE

DESERVD

OUR VIRTUES & CRUEL GOODNESSES HAVE DESERVD ETERNAL DEATH 494 MILTON 13 34

DESERVE

OF THE MINISTERS YOU DESERVE TO HAVE YOUR EARS BOXED YOU DO 48C ISLAND MOON 4 PROSE

WILL BE IGNORANT FOOLS & WILL NOT DESERVE TO LIVE . . . 62D ISLAND MOON 11 PROSE

HIS IMBECILE ATTEMPTS TO DEPRESS ME ONLY DESERVE LAUGHTER 825C LETTER 27 PROSE

EMINENCE AS AN ENGRAVER MAKES HIS OPINION DESERVE NOTICE 848A LETTER 45 PROSE

UNDERTAKING IT IS CERTAIN THAT THE PICTURES DESERVE TO BE 848C LETTER 45 PROSE

DESERVES

IF YOU TREAT HIM AS HE DESERVES . . . . 380B FOUR ZOAS NOTE PROSE

DESERVES   (CONTINUED)
        THE MAN WHO PERMITS YOU TO INJURE HIM DESERVES YOUR   737 JERUSALEM 91   3
            VENGEANCE
DESIGN
        WAS THE UNNATURAL DESIGN OF WICKED MEN . . . .   388B ANNO WATSON   MARG
        THE DESIGN OF THE LAST JUDGMENT WHICH I HAVE COMPLETED . 442D LAST JUDGMNT/L   PROSE
        THE RIGHT HAND OF THE DESIGN IS APPROPRIATED TO . . .   443B LAST JUDGMNT/L   PROSE
        DESIGN IS APPROPRIATED TO THE RESURRECTION & FALL OF THE 443B LAST JUDGMNT/L   PROSE
            WICKED
        THE WHOLE UPPER PART OF THE DESIGN IS A VIEW OF HEAVEN . 444A LAST JUDGMNT/L   PROSE
        SUCH IS THE DESIGN WHICH YOU MY DEAR SIR . . . .   444C LAST JUDGMNT/L   PROSE
        LEARN TO DESIGN FROM RAFAEL & TO EXECUTE FROM RUBENS XXX 449A ANNO REYNOLDS   MARG
        THIS IS MOST FALSE FOR NO ONE CAN EVER DESIGN TILL HE HAS 455D ANNO REYNOLDS   MARG
        AN IDEAL DESIGN SUGGESTED BY THE FIRST PUBLICATION OF . 583D DESC CAT 10   PROSE
        THIS DESIGN IS TAKEN FROM THAT MOST PATHETIC PASSAGE .   584C DESC CAT 15   PROSE
        SAY GIVE ME THE DESIGN IT IS NO MATTER FOR THE EXECUTION 596A PUB ADDRESS/N   PROSE
        WORDS NOR CAN A DESIGN BE . . . .   596A PUB ADDRESS/N   PROSE
        HE WHO MAKES A DESIGN MUST KNOW THE EFFECT & COLOURING . 603A PUB ADDR AD/N   PROSE
        PROPER TO BE PUT TO THAT DESIGN & WILL NEVER TAKE THAT . 603A PUB ADDR AD/N   PROSE
        TO BE AN ERROR & TO BE CAST OUT IS A PART OF GOD'S DESIGN 613A V LAST JUDG/N   PROSE
        BUT IN COOL BLOODED DESIGN & INTENTION . . . .   615D V LAST JUDG/N   PROSE
        THESE PERSONIFICATIONS ARE ALL BROUGHT TOGETHER IN THE   618A ILLUS MILTON   PROSE
            FIRST DESIGN
        IN THIS DESIGN IS INTRODUCED . . . .   618B ILLUS MILTON   PROSE
        IN THIS DESIGN SURROUNDING THE PRINCIPAL FIGURE . . .   619A ILLUS MILTON   PROSE
        BY THIS DISPLAY OF PRETENDED VIRTUE CHIEFLY DESIGN   682D JERUSALEM 52   PROSE
            TO EXPOSE
        BUT BY DESIGN BY THE KINGS OF PERSIA & THEIR GENERALS . 785B ILLUS DANTE 7   PROSE
        THE DESIGN I HAVE SENT IS . . . .   792B LETTER 4   PROSE
        CANNOT PREVIOUSLY DESCRIBE IN WORDS WHAT I MEAN TO DESIGN 792B LETTER 4   PROSE
        BUT AS YOU HAVE FAVORD ME WITH YOUR REMARKS ON MY DESIGN 793B LETTER 5   PROSE
        PLEASE ME SO WELL THAT I HAVE CHOSEN THAT DESIGN IN OUR   859B LETTER 56   PROSE
            LAST
DESIGND
        DID I GRATUITOUSLY DESIGND FOR HIM AT THE SAME TIME HE . 592D PUB ADDRESS/N   PROSE
        OF MILTON'S FOR TILL I HAD DESIGND IT MILTON'S POEM .   823D LETTER 27   PROSE
DESIGNED
        THE HISTORY OF JOB DESIGNED & ENGRAVED BY WILLIAM BLAKE   SUPP LETTER 67F   *PROSE
DESIGNEDLY
        IGNORANTLY & NOT DESIGNEDLY SURELY I OUGHT TO CONSIDER HIM 828C LETTER 28   PROSE
DESIGNER
        THE DESIGNER PROPOSES TO ENGRAVE IN A CORRECT AND FINISHED 586C CHAUCER 1   PROSE
DESIGNING
        THAT NONE BUT DESIGNING VILLAINS EVER PRETENDED TO BELIEVE 390C ANNO WATSON   MARG
        ON THE BIBLE ARE DISHONEST DESIGNING KNAVES . . . . .   390C ANNO WATSON   MARG
        AND DESIGNING WHOSE METHOD ALONE CAN DELINEATE CHARACTER 586D CHAUCER 1   PROSE
        MY STYLE OF DESIGNING IS A SPECIES BY ITSELF . . . . .   791D LETTER 4   PROSE
        PRAY LET ME INTREAT YOU TO PERSEVERE IN YOUR DESIGNING . 795B LETTER 6   PROSE
        HISTORICAL DESIGNING IS ONE THING & PORTRAIT PAINTING   810B LETTER 20   PROSE
            ANOTHER
        CONTRARY TO DESIGNING & HISTORICAL PAINTING IN EVERY   815D LETTER 23   PROSE
            RESPECT
        THO I KNOW THAT AS FAR AS DESIGNING & POETRY ARE CONCERND 821C LETTER 25   PROSE
        & WILL RELINQUISH ANY ENGAGEMENT OF DESIGNING AT ALL .   826A LETTER 27   PROSE
        DESIGNING AND TO RELIEVE MY MORE LABORIOUS [EMPLOYMENT]   860C LETTER 56   PROSE
        BE DEVOTED TO DESIGNING & PAINTING [ALONE] WHEN I HAVE GOT 866A LETTER 63   PROSE
DESIGNS
        AMERICA A PROPHECY IN ILLUMINATED PRINTING FOLIO   207D PRSPECTUS 1793 PROSE
            WITH...DESIGNS PRICE
        & A DESTRUCTION FROM THE DESIGNS OF ANOTHER THE . . .   388B ANNO WATSON   MARG
        THAT BLAKE'S DESIGNS SHOULD BE BY US DISPLAYED . . . .   537 AND HIS LEGS/N *   37
        BECAUSE HE MAKES DESIGNS SO VERY CHEAP . . . .   537 AND HIS LEGS/N   38
        MY DESIGNS [SHALL STILL] UNCHANGD REMAIN . . . . . .   558 THE CAVERNS/N   15
        THE EXECUTION OF MY DESIGNS . . . .   561B EXHIBITION ADV PROSE
        AN EXHIBITION OF MY OWN MY DESIGNS PAINTED IN WATER-COLOURS 561C EXHIBITION ADV PROSE
        FROM THE PROFITS OF HIS DESIGNS IN THAT WELL-KNOWN WORK   572D DESC CAT 3   PROSE
        DESIGNS FOR BLAIR'S GRAVE HAVE LEFT HIM TO SHIFT   572D DESC CAT 3   PROSE
            FOR HIMSELF
        BECAUSE I KNOW THAT THE GENIUS THAT PRODUCES THE DESIGNS 790B LETTER 2   PROSE
        NONE OF MY DESIGNS WILL BE DESTITUTE OF INFINITE   792B LETTER 4   PROSE
            PARTICULARS
        I SENT YOU AS A SPECIMEN BUT AFTER MY OWN DESIGNS I COULD 794B LETTER 5   PROSE
            DO
        IF ORDERS HAD NOT COME IN FOR MY DESIGNS & PAINTINGS .   794C LETTER 5   PROSE
        WILL SOON BE WELL ENOUGH TO MAKE HUNDREDS OF DESIGNS .   796B LETTER 7   PROSE
        I AM STILL EMPLOYD IN MAKING DESIGNS & LITTLE PICTURES . 798B LETTER 10   PROSE
        I CAN BE GRATEFUL & I CAN SOON SEND YOU SOME OF YOUR   808D LETTER 20   PROSE
            DESIGNS
        MY DESIGNS FOR COMUS WHEN I HAVE DONE THEM DIRECTED TO YOU 810D LETTER 21   PROSE
        TO DO FOR YOU ARE INCOMPATIBLE WITH THE DESIGNS . . .   814C LETTER 23   PROSE
        FAMILY & I AM NOW LABOURING IN MY THOUGHTS DESIGNS FOR . 821C LETTER 25   PROSE
        DESIGNS FROM ROMNEY FLAXMAN & YR HBLE SERVT . . . . .   824C LETTER 27   PROSE
        APPROVES OF MY DESIGNS AS LITTLE AS HE DOES OF MY POEMS   825C LETTER 27   PROSE
            AND
        OF THE MOST DISTINGUISHD DESIGNS OF MR ROMNEY OF WHICH . 832C LETTER 32   PROSE
        & THE MERIT OF THE DESIGNS AN OBJECT OF CONSEQUENCE . .   832D LETTER 32   PROSE
        BEEN ABLE TO CONSULT MR FLAXMAN ABOUT THE DESIGNS OF MR   838B LETTER 37   PROSE
        FLAXMAN'S HOMER WITH ADDITIONAL DESIGNS TWO OF WHICH .   841A LETTER 40   PROSE
        IS NECESSARY TO THE EXECUTION OF ROMNEY'S DESIGNS . .   844B LETTER 43   PROSE
        TO COPY ANY OF HIS FATHER'S DESIGNS THAT MR FLAXMAN MAY   846A LETTER 44   PROSE
        I HAVE GOT THE THREE SUBLIME DESIGNS OF ROMNEY NOW IN MY 848A LETTER 45   PROSE
        WITH ROMNEY'S DESIGNS MRS C(CHETWYND) SENT TO ME THE .   850C LETTER 49   PROSE

	PAGE	TITLE	LINE

DESIGNS   (CONTINUED)

FOR NOT BEING ABLE TO FURNISH ANY DESIGNS YOU WILL READILY   853A LETTER 51   *PROSE
OVERLOOK & ADVISE & DO ALL THAT HE CAN TO MAKE MY DESIGNS   853A LETTER 51   *PROSE
SHALL PUT MY NAME TO HIS DESIGNS BUT IF IT SHOULD FALL   853A LETTER 51   *PROSE
    OUT SO
WHAT YOU HAD SAID ABOUT THE DESIGNS FOR EDWARD THE FIRST &   853A LETTER 51   *PROSE
TWO BALLADS ARE SO PREEMINENT & MY DESIGNS FOR THEM . . .   859B LETTER 56   PROSE
OUT OF A NUMBER OF DESIGNS I HAVE SELECTED FIVE . . . .   860C LETTER 56   PROSE
OF MY DESIGNS HE NAMD HIS PRICE & WISHD ME TO PRODUCE .   861C LETTER 59   PROSE
IN CONSEQUENCE OF THIS I PRODUCED ABOUT TWENTY DESIGNS .   861C LETTER 59   PROSE
THE DESIGNS AS WELL AS THE ENGRAVINGS I AM GETTING ON WITH   877A LETTER 85   PROSE
TO ENGRAVE...PLATES FROM HIS OWN DESIGNS OF JOB'S CAPTIVITY   SUPP LETTER 67D   *PROSE

DESIRABLE

AND SEE WHETHER YOUR LOT OR MINE IS MOST DESIRABLE . . .   155D MARRIAGE HH 17   PROSE
ON WHAT IS TO BE DONE IN OUR DESIRABLE & ARDUOUS TASK OF   849B LETTER 45   PROSE
YOUR DESIRABLE POETICAL PRESENT FOR MRS HAWKINS . . . .   855B LETTER 53   PROSE

DESIRE

AMBITION IS THE DESIRE OR PASSION THAT ONE MAN . . . .   28 EDW THIRD/PS 4   14
THEN SHE BORE PALE DESIRE FATHER OF CURIOSITY . . . . .   40D THEN SHE BORE   PROSE
DESIRE STILL PINES BUT FOR ONE COOLING DROP AND TIS DENYD   41C THEN SHE BORE   PROSE
WILL DESIRE LOVE RAGE ENVY & ?ALL ?OTHER . . . .   89B ANNO SWED LOVE   * MARG
NONE CAN DESIRE WHAT HE HAS NOT PERCIEVD . . . .   97B NAT RELIGION 1   PROSE
IF ANY COULD DESIRE WHAT HE IS INCAPABLE OF POSSESSING .   97D NAT RELIGION 2   PROSE
THE DESIRE OF MAN BEING INFINITE THE POSSESSION IS INFINITE   97D NAT RELIGION 2   PROSE
WHY A LITTLE CURTAIN OF FLESH ON THE BED OF OUR DESIRE . .   130 BOOK OF THEL 6   20
WHOSE EVRY FUNCTION IS FILLD WITH ITS FIERY DESIRE . . .   142 FRENCH REVOLTN   183
. . . BRED FROM THE BLOOD OF REVENGE AND BREATH OF DESIRE   144 FRENCH REVOLTN   215
THOSE WHO RESTRAIN DESIRE DO SO BECAUSE THEIRS . . . .   149D MARRIAGE HH 5   PROSE
TILL IT IS ONLY THE SHADOW OF DESIRE . . . .   150A MARRIAGE HH 5   PROSE
IT INDEED APPEARD TO REASON AS IF DESIRE WAS CAST OUT .   150A MARRIAGE HH 5   PROSE
TO SEND THE COMFORTER OR DESIRE . . . .   150B MARRIAGE HH 5   PROSE
RIGHT & LEFT SIDE HE ANSWERD THE DESIRE OF RAISING OTHER   154B MARRIAGE HH 12   PROSE
    MEN
BUT DESIRE GRATIFIED . . . .   178 ABSTINENCE/N   3
IN A WIFE I WOULD DESIRE . . . .   178 IN A WIFE/N   1
THE LINEAMENTS OF GRATIFIED DESIRE . . . .   178 IN A WIFE/N   3
THE LINEAMENTS OF GRATIFIED DESIRE . . . .   180 QUESTN ANSRD/N   2
THE LINEAMENTS OF GRATIFIED DESIRE . . . .   180 QUESTN ANSRD/N   4
THE LINEAMENTS OF GRATIFIED DESIRE . . . .   184 SEVRL QUESTN/N   2
THE LINEAMENTS OF GRATIFIED DESIRE . . . .   184 SEVRL QUESTN/N   4
TO TURN THE WHEEL OF FALSE DESIRE AND LONGINGS THAT WAKE   193 V DAU ALBION 5   27
    HER WOMB
THE MOMENT OF DESIRE THE MOMENT OF DESIRE THE VIRGIN .   194 V DAU ALBION 7   3
WHERE THE HORRIBLE DARKNESS IS IMPRESSED WITH REFLECTIONS   194 V DAU ALBION 7   11
    OF DESIRE
THAT PLAY AROUND THE GOLDEN ROOFS IN WREATHS OF FIERCE   202 AMERICA 15   21
    DESIRE
WHERE THE YOUTH PINED AWAY WITH DESIRE . . . .   215 AH SUNFLOWR/SE   5
ONE COMMAND ONE JOY ONE DESIRE . . . .   224 URIZEN 4   38
THEN HE LOOKD BACK WITH ANXIOUS DESIRE . . . .   230 URIZEN 13   45
WITH LINEAMENTS OF GRATIFIED DESIRE . . . .   244 EUROPE 14   19
HER BOSOM SWELLS WITH WILD DESIRE . . . .   248 SONG OF LOS 7   37
RAGING FURIOUS THE FLAMES OF DESIRE . . . .   256 BOOK OF LOS 3   27
THE SPECTRE SAID THOU SINFUL WOMAN WAS IT THY DESIRE . .   269 FOUR ZOAS 1   173
[BEAUTY ALL BLUSHING WITH DESIRE MOCKING HER FELL DESPAIR]   269 FOUR ZOAS 1   189
DEFORMD I SEE THESE LINEAMENTS OF UNGRATIFIED DESIRE .   298 FOUR ZOAS 4   24
FOR DEATH TO ME IS BETTER FAR THAN LIFE DEATH MY DESIRE   313 FOUR ZOAS 6   58
TENFOLD WITH FIERCE DESIRE TO REND THY CHAIN & HOWL IN FURY   321 FOUR ZOAS 7   66
BY GRATIFIED DESIRE BY STRONG DEVOURING APPETITE SHE FILLS   323 FOUR ZOAS 7   133
NOR FELT THE STINGINGS OF DESIRE NOR LONGINGS AFTER LIFE   325 FOUR ZOAS 7   203
THEY FEED UPON OUR LIFE WE ARE THEIR VICTIMS STERN DESIRE   331 FOUR ZOAS 7   439
MISPLACING EVERY CENTER HUNGRY DESIRE & LUST BEGAN . . .   345 FOUR ZOAS 8   178
TREMBLING & WEAK A FAINT EMBRACE A FIERCE DESIRE AS WHEN   358 FOUR ZOAS 9   27
NO MORE BUT A DESIRE OF BEING A DISTRACTED RAVENING DESIRE   376 FOUR ZOAS 9   734
BEAUTY ALL BLUSHING WITH DESIRE A SELF ENJOYING WONDER .   381 FOUR ZOAS AD 5   9
HE WHO HAS FEW THINGS TO DESIRE CANNOT HAVE MANY TO FEAR   405B ANNO BACON   MARG
THE OTHER [IN] CLOTHD IN [SWEET DESIRE] IRON WIRE . . .   421 BENEATH/N   * 7
NOW INTREATING [SWEET DESIRE] IRON WIRE . . . . . .   422 BENEATH/N   25
[THE OTHER CLOTHD IN [SWEET DESIRE] IRON WIRE] . . . .   422 BENEATH REWB/N   4
BRING ME MY ARROWS OF DESIRE . . . .   481 AND DID FEET/M   10
THUNDER OF THOUGHT & FLAMES OF FIERCE DESIRE . . . . .   621 READER LOVER/J   6
WHERE THEY DESIRE TO PLACE THE ABOMINATION OF DESOLATION   626 JERUSALEM 7   70
SUBDUED BY THE SPECTRE OF THE LIVING & TERRIFIED   638 JERUSALEM 17   15
    BY UNDISGUISD DESIRE
TORMENTED WITH SWEET DESIRE FOR THESE BEAUTIES OF ALBION   639 JERUSALEM 17   22
WITH PROVINGS OF DESTRUCTION WITH GIVING THEE THY HEART'S   647 JERUSALEM 24   28
    DESIRE
WHEN JERUSALEM WAS THY HEART'S DESIRE IN TIMES OF YOUTH   647 JERUSALEM 24   37
    & LOVE
REASON PITY WRATH THIS WORLD DESIRE . . . .   685B JERUSALEM 54   TITLE
BUT NOW MY SOUL IS HARROWD WITH GRIEF & FEAR & LOVE   707 JERUSALEM 68   66
    & DESIRE
THERE IS NO TIME FOR ANY THING BUT THE TORMENTS OF LOVE   707 JERUSALEM 68   68
    & DESIRE
BABYLON IS OUR CHIEF DESIRE MOAB OUR BATH IN SUMMER . . .   725 JERUSALEM 82   31
FILLING WITH FIBRES FROM HIS LOINS WHICH REDDEND   732 JERUSALEM 86   51
    WITH DESIRE
HE ALSO WILL RECIEVE IT GO SPECTRE OBEY MY MOST SECRET   737 JERUSALEM 91   4
    DESIRE
AGAINST THE ACCUSER'S CHIEF DESIRE . . . .   761 FOR SEXES/GP   3
AS THOU HAST SAID SO IS IT COME TO PASS MY DESIRE IS UNTO   780 GHOST ABEL 2   7
    CAIN

485

```
                                                          PAGE     TITLE        LINE
DESIRE    (CONTINUED)
     THE ABOVE WAS WRITTEN & THE DRAWING ANNEXED BY THE DESIRE   781D INSC UPCOTT   PROSE
     DESIRE TO ENTERTAIN BENEATH OUR THATCHED ROOF OF RUSTED     802D LETTER 14     PROSE
        GOLD
     REMOTE FROM DESIRE . . . . . . . . . . . . . . . . .   804 TO BUTTS/L        12
     & HE HAS READ PART BY HIS OWN DESIRE & HAS LOOKED WITH  .  825B LETTER 27     PROSE
     I DID BUT EXPRESS TO HIM MY DESIRE OF SENDING YOU A COPY OF 836D LETTER 35     PROSE
     ACCORDING TO YOUR DESIRE I SEND PROOFS OF THE  . . . . .  838A LETTER 37     PROSE
     AGO BY HIS DESIRE I WRITE TO HIM BY THIS POST TO INQUIRE    841A LETTER 40     PROSE
     I SEND INCLOSD HIS TERMS AS MR HOARE BY MY DESIRE HAS  .   841D LETTER 41     PROSE
     LEAR AND CORDELIA TO COPY IF YOU DESIRE IT SHOULD BE DONE   845D LETTER 44     PROSE
     READINESS TO SEND ANY OF THE CARTOONS TO LONDON YOU DESIRE  846A LETTER 44     PROSE
     WITH DESIRE AND CURIOSITY BUT HOWEVER CHRISTMAS IS A-COMING 851D LETTER 50     PROSE
     & TO DESIRE YOU IF YOU COULD TO GET FLAXMAN TO DO THE WHOLE 853A LETTER 51    *PROSE
     TO YOU EXPRESSING HIS DESIRE THAT I WILL REPEAT TO YOU      856A LETTER 54     PROSE
        HIS REGRET
     P S YOUR DESIRE THAT I SHOULD WRITE A LITTLE ADVERTISEMENT  860B LETTER 56     PROSE
     [OF] ALL OUR FRIENDS TO WHOM WE ARE GRATEFUL & DESIRE TO BE 862A LETTER 59     PROSE
     MY DESIRE IS THAT YOU WOULD ENQUIRE INTO THIS AFFAIR &  .   865B LETTER 62     PROSE
     ON TWO ACCOUNTS FIRST I OMITTED TO DESIRE YOU WOULD COME    870C LETTER 72     PROSE
     VENTURE UPON WHAT I ARDENTLY DESIRE THE SEEING YOU WITH     873A LETTER 76     PROSE
     EXPECTATION & DESIRE OF VISITING HAMPSTEAD                  873D LETTER 78     PROSE
        I AM NEVERTHELESS
DESIRED
     KING DAVID DESIRED SO FERVENTLY & INVOKES SO PATHETICLY     153D MARRIAGE HH 12 PROSE
     I DESIRED THE GENTLEMAN TO SET GAINSBOROUGH ABOUT   . . .   465C ANNO REYNOLDS  MARG
     WHICH YOU DESIRED ME TO GET MADE FOR YOU   . . . . . .   791B LETTER 3       PROSE
     BUT YOU HAVE SO GENEROUSLY & OPENLY DESIRED THAT I WILL     812B LETTER 22     PROSE
     DESIRED HIM AS POLITELY AS WAS POSSIBLE TO GO OUT OF THE    827A LETTER 28     PROSE
        GARDEN
     I TOOK MY PORTRAIT OF ROMNEY AS YOU DESIRED TO SHEW HIM     834B LETTER 34     PROSE
     I CALLD YESTERDAY ON MR BRAITHWAITE AS YOU DESIRED  . .   835C LETTER 35     PROSE
     SUCH HANDS THE PICTURE FROM STERNE WHICH YOU DESIRED  .   835D LETTER 35     PROSE
     YOU DESIRED HE HAS SENT A CATALOGUE OF ALL HIS COLLECTION   844A LETTER 43     PROSE
     BUT DESIRED ME TO INCLOSE IT FOR YOU WITH WASHINGTON'S LIFE 845C LETTER 44     PROSE
     MR CARR CALLED ON ME AND I AS YOU DESIRED GAVE HIM  . .   845C LETTER 44     PROSE
     HE DESIRED I WOULD EXPRESSING FOR WHICH I THANK HIM  . .   856D LETTER 54     PROSE
     IF POSSIBLE HE DESIRED I WOULD PRESENT YOU FROM HIM WITH    857B LETTER 54     PROSE
     ABOUT IT IMMEDIATELY AND HAS DESIRED THAT I  . . . . .   858D LETTER 55     PROSE
     SIMPLICITY AS YOU DESIRED HAS BEEN MY FIRST OBJECT I SEND   860B LETTER 56     PROSE
        IT
     BEFORE NOW I DO AS MR LINNELL DESIRED I WOULD DO BY THE     871C LETTER 73     PROSE
     YOU DESIRED I WOULD SEND AN ACKNOWLEDGD IT I DID NOT  .   875D LETTER 82     PROSE
DESIRES
     HELL IS THE BEING SHUT UP IN THE POSSESSION OF CORPOREAL     74B ANNO LAVATER   MARG
        DESIRES
     MAN'S DESIRES ARE LIMITED BY HIS PERCEPTIONS . . . . .    97B NAT RELIGION 1 PROSE
     THE DESIRES & PERCEPTIONS OF MAN UNTAUGHT  . . . . . .    97B NAT RELIGION 1 PROSE
     [DESIRES OUR DEATHS O IJIM [?TIS ?ONE ?WHOSE AGED TONGUE]   105 TIRIEL 4        78
     HE WHO DESIRES BUT ACTS NOT BREEDS PESTILENCE  . . . .   151A MARRIAGE HH 7  PROSE
     SOONER MURDER AN INFANT IN ITS CRADLE THAN NURSE UNACTED   152D MARRIAGE HH 10 PROSE
        DESIRES
     AND BINDING WITH BRIARS MY JOYS & DESIRES  . . . . . .   163 GARDEN LOVE/N    12
     SOFT DESIRES I CAN TRACE . . . . . . . . . . . . .   165 CRADLE SONG/N    19
     THE [DESIRES] DAYS OF YOUTH RISE FRESH IN MY MIND  . .   171 NURSES SONG/N     3
     CROWND WITH WARLIKE FIRES & RAGING DESIRES . . . . . .   177 DAY/N             5
     THEY FEEL THE NERVES OF YOUTH RENEW AND DESIRES OF ANCIENT  202 AMERICA 15      25
        TIMES
     AND BINDING WITH BRIARS MY JOYS & DESIRES  . . . . . .   215 GARDEN LOVE/SE   12
     AND LOS & ENITHARMON WERE DRAWN DOWN BY THEIR DESIRES  .   287 FOUR ZOAS 2     287
     [AND IN UNGRATIFIED DESIRES] . . . . . . . . . . .   422 BENEATH/N         15
     AND IN UNGRATIFIED DESIRES . . . . . . . . . . . .   424 THE GOLDEN NET    14
     WHERE SOULS INCESSANT WAIL BEING PITEOUS PASSIONS & DESIRES 512 MILTON 26       26
     THE PASSIONS & DESIRES DESCEND UPON THE HUNGRY WINDS  .   512 MILTON 26       28
     AND HIS INFANT THOUGHTS & DESIRES INTO COLD DARK CLIFFS    628 JERUSALEM 9       2
        OF DEATH
     IN THE FIERCE DESIRES OF BEAUTY & IN THE TORTURES          638 JERUSALEM 17     12
        OF REPULSE HE IS
     PITEOUS IMAGE OF MY SOFT DESIRES & LOVES O ENITHARMON  .   639 JERUSALEM 17     19
     WE ARE TOLD TO ABSTAIN FROM FLESHLY DESIRES  . . . .   716D JERUSALEM 77    PROSE
     WIFE WHO DESIRES HER KINDEST LOVE TO MRS BUTTS & YOURSELF  808C LETTER 19     PROSE
     BECAUSE OF NATURAL FEARS OF NATURAL DESIRES  . . . . .   813A LETTER 22     PROSE
     MY WIFE DESIRES HER KINDEST LOVE TO MRS BUTTS & I HAVE  .  813B LETTER 22     PROSE
     DESIRES ME TO COPY OUT & SEND YOU WITH HER KIND LOVE  .   816D LETTER 24     PROSE
     MR B(BRAITHWAITE) DESIRES I WILL PRESENT HIS COMPLIMENTS   836A LETTER 35     PROSE
        TO YOU
     & IN HIS BEST STYLE HE ALSO DESIRES ME TO EXPRESS TO YOU   836A LETTER 35     PROSE
        HIS
     & DESIRES WITH MINE TO PRESENT HERS TO MISS POOLE   . .   837B LETTER 35     PROSE
     MY WIFE DESIRES ME TO EXPRESS HER LOVE TO YOU  . . . .   837D LETTER 36     PROSE
     DESIRES MAY BE SENT TO YOU WITH HIS COMPLIMENTS WHICH  .   838D LETTER 37     PROSE
     IT IS NOW BETTER HE DESIRES TO BE MOST AFFECTIONATELY  .   842D LETTER 42     PROSE
     I FORGOT TO MENTION THAT MR HOARE DESIRES HIS MOST  . .   843A LETTER 42     PROSE
     SCHEME OF HIS LOTTERY DESIRES HIS COMPLIMENTS TO YOU  .   844A LETTER 43     PROSE
     WITH IT HE DESIRES ME TO EXPRESS TO YOU THAT HE WOULD  .   845C LETTER 44     PROSE
     A LINE FROM YOU DESIRES ME TO ASSURE YOU OF HIS WISH TO    845D LETTER 44     PROSE
        GIVE
     CONTINUED RECOVERY MY WIFE DESIRES WITH ME HER RESPECTS    851A LETTER 49     PROSE
        TO YOU
     MY WIFE CONTINUES IN HEALTH & DESIRES TO JOIN ME IN EVERY  860B LETTER 56     PROSE
     FIRST STAGE MY WIFE DESIRES HER KINDEST REMEMBRANCES TO YOU 871C LETTER 73     PROSE
```

	PAGE	TITLE	LINE
DESIRING			
DESIRING LIKE THE HUNGRY WORM & LIKE THE [SILENT] GAPING GRAVE	376	FOUR ZOAS 9	735
ENVYING EACH OTHER YET DESIRING IN ALL DEVOURING LOVE . .	732	JERUSALEM 86	64
THE GARDEN HE REFUSED I STILL PERSISTED IN DESIRING HIS	827A	LETTER 28	PROSE
J ROMNEY IMMEDIATELY DESIRING HIM TO GIVE US LIBERTY . .	846A	LETTER 44	PROSE
I ASSURED HIM THAT HE DID AND HERE HE LEFT OFF DESIRING ME	846D	LETTER 44	PROSE
& ON MY DESIRING HIM TO TELL ME FOR WHAT HE WOULD UNDERTAKE	848B	LETTER 45	PROSE
BY THE PENNY THAT IS THE TWOPENNY POST DESIRING THAT I .	861B	LETTER 58	PROSE
MR CROMEK THE ENGRAVER CAME TO ME DESIRING TO HAVE SOME	861C	LETTER 59	PROSE
HAPPINESS DESIRING TO BE PARTICULARLY REMEMBERD BY YOU .	862A	LETTER 59	PROSE
DESIROUS			
TO HAVE BEEN DESIROUS OF ENQUIRING INTO THE WORKS OF NATURE	45B	ISLAND MOON 1	PROSE
YOU ARE DESIROUS I KNOW TO DISPOSE OF SOME OF MY WORKS &	878B	LETTER 88	PROSE
DESIST			
OLD CRUELTY DESIST & LET US DIG A GRAVE FOR THEE	100	TIRIEL 1	36
I KNOW THY DECEIT & THY REVENGES AND UNLESS THOU DESIST	627	JERUSALEM 8	7
DESIST NOT FROM THINE OWN WILL & OBEY NOT MY STERN COMMAND	627	JERUSALEM 8	12
DESOLATE			
THE LAND IS DESOLATE OUR WIVES	11	GWIN KING/PS	9
AND THE RED SCOURGE FOLLOWS HER DESOLATE SONS	34A	KING JOHN/PS	PROSE
TO HIM THE DAY & NIGHT ALIKE WAS DARK & DESOLATE . . .	103	TIRIEL 4	2
KISS ME MY BROTHER & THEN LEAVE ME TO WANDER DESOLATE . .	104	TIRIEL 4	22
THE [GLOOM] SECRET FORESTS & ALL NIGHT WANDERD IN DESOLATE WAYS	106	TIRIEL 4	* 90
DESOLATE LOATHED DUMB [CON] ASTONISHD WAITING FOR BLACK DEATH	107	TIRIEL 5	* 35
I DWELT WITH MYRATANA FIVE YEARS IN THE DESOLATE ROCK .	107	TIRIEL 6	8
SHALL [FALL] FAIL IF THOU REFUSE HOWL IN THE DESOLATE MOUNTAINS	108	TIRIEL 6	& 49
THE GIRDLE OF WAR FROM THE DESOLATE EARTH	144	FRENCH REVOLTN	223
[LIKE] IN HIS DESOLATE MOUNTAINS RIFTED FURIOUS	222	URIZEN 3	* 11
TOMBS IN THE DESOLATE PLACES	236	URIZEN 28	5
DEVOURING & DEVOURED ROAMING ON DARK AND DESOLATE MOUNTAINS	238	EUROPE PREL 2	5
ENRAGD IN THE DESOLATE DARKNESS	253	AHANIA 4	28
[AND ENION DESOLATE WHERE ART THOU THARMAS O RETURN] . .	268	FOUR ZOAS 1	142
[WANDERING DESOLATE A WONDER ABHORRD BY GODS & MEN] . . .	269	FOUR ZOAS 1	190
. . . UPON THE DESOLATE WIND	269	FOUR ZOAS 1	192
THEY STOOD ABOVE THE HEAVENS FORSAKEN DESOLATE SUSPENDED IN BLOOD	274	FOUR ZOAS 1	361
TO DESOLATE THEIR CITIES MAN SHALL BE NO MORE AWAKE O HOSTS	275	FOUR ZOAS 1	407
[AND] ENION BLIND & AGE-BENT WEPT UPON THE DESOLATE WIND	276	FOUR ZOAS 1	* 444
HIS WEB IS LEFT ALL DESOLATE THAT HIS LITTLE ANXIOUS HEART	277	FOUR ZOAS 1	459
WISDOM IS SOLD IN THE DESOLATE MARKET WHERE NONE COME TO BUY	290	FOUR ZOAS 2	400
AND NOW LIKE ME PARTAKING DESOLATE THY MASTER'S LOT . . .	317	FOUR ZOAS 6	211
HIS FAINT GROANS SHAKE THE CAVES & ISSUE THRO THE DESOLATE ROCKS	354	FOUR ZOAS 8	520
ONCE I WAILD DESOLATE LIKE THEE MY FALLOW FIELDS IN FEAR	354	FOUR ZOAS 8	536
FROM THE [BLACK] DARK JAWS OF DEATH BENEATH & DESOLATE SHORES REMOTE	363	FOUR ZOAS 9	259
. . . FROM THE SOUL THAT WANDERS DESOLATE	370	FOUR ZOAS 9	502
CHRIST PRONOUNCD THEM THE ABOMINATION THAT MAKETH DESOLATE	393D	ANNO WATSON	* MARG
HOWLINGS FILLD ALL THE DESOLATE PLACES IN ACCUSATIONS OF SIN	500	MILTON 18	43
BECAUSE AHANIA RENT APART INTO A DESOLATE NIGHT	501	MILTON 19	41
THEY WAR TO DESTROY THE FURNACES TO DESOLATE GOLGONOOZA	623	JERUSALEM 5	29
LONDON CONTINUALLY BUILDING & CONTINUALLY DECAYING DESOLATE	684	JERUSALEM 53	19
OVER THESE DESOLATE ROCKS OF ALBION O DAUGHTERS OF DESPAIR	688	JERUSALEM 56	21
THEY RETURN NOT BUT GENERATE IN ROCKY PLACES DESOLATE . .	703	JERUSALEM 66	72
THAT DESOLATE EUROPE WITH WARS	778C	HOMERS POETRY	PROSE
DESOLATED			
BUILDING CASTLES IN DESOLATED PLACES AND STRONG FORTIFICATIONS	641	JERUSALEM 18	38
HIS EON WEEPING IN THE COLD AND DESOLATED EARTH . . .	641	JERUSALEM 19	16
DESOLATING			
[TO] INFOLDING THE BRIGHT WOMAN [FROM THE DESOLATING WINDS . . .	381	FOUR ZOAS AD 5 *	15
HAS NOT YET SWEPT ITS DESOLATING WING	18	EDW THIRD/PS 1	49
[INFOLDING THE BRIGHT INFANTS FROM THE DESOLATING WINDS]	270	FOUR ZOAS 1	210
DESOLATION			
AND DESOLATION SPREADS HIS WINGS OVER THE LAND OF PALESTINE	37D	SAMSON/PS	*PROSE
AND ON WHOSE TOPS THE VIRGINS SANG ARE ROCKS OF DESOLATION	310	FOUR ZOAS 5	193
TO DIE A DEATH OF SIX THOUSAND YEARS BOUND ROUND WITH DESOLATION	337	FOUR ZOAS 7B	168
. . . TO SNUFF UP THE WINDS OF DESOLATION	338	FOUR ZOAS 7B	202
WITH TENFOLD ROUT & DESOLATION ROARD THE CHASMS BENEATH	378	FOUR ZOAS 9	783
BABYLON THE GREAT THE ABOMINATION OF DESOLATION	506	MILTON 22	49
THESE ARE THE SEXUAL GARMENTS THE ABOMINATION OF DESOLATION	533	MILTON 41	25
WHERE THEY DESIRE TO PLACE THE ABOMINATION OF DESOLATION	626	JERUSALEM 7	70
AND IN ITS HOLINESS IS CLOSED THE ABOMINATION OF DESOLATION	629	JERUSALEM 10	16
THERE BABYLON IS BUILDED IN THE WASTE FOUNDED IN HUMAN DESOLATION	647	JERUSALEM 24	25
. . . TO SNUFF UP THE WINDS OF DESOLATION	700	JERUSALEM 65	48
MYSTERY BABYLON THE GREAT THE ABOMINATION OF DESOLATION	716	JERUSALEM 75	19
LET ALBION REMAIN A DESOLATION WITHOUT AN INHABITANT .	725	JERUSALEM 82	25
THE LAND IS MARKD FOR DESOLATION & UNLESS WE PLANT . . .	728	JERUSALEM 83	54
. . . ALL THEIR GLORY THAT GREW ON DESOLATION	746	JERUSALEM 98	51
OF ALBION TAXED THE NATIONS INTO DESOLATION	746	JERUSALEM 98	53
DESOLATIONS			
I ALSO STOOD IN SATAN'S BOSOM & BEHELD ITS DESOLATIONS . .	529	MILTON 38	15

```
                                                               PAGE      TITLE       LINE
DESPAIR
    AND MOURNFUL LEAN DESPAIR  . . . . . . . . . . .           6 MY SILKS/PS          4
    DESPAIR MUST BE HIS ETERNAL LOT  . . . . . . . .         97D NAT RELIGION 2     PROSE
    [FLINGING FLAMES OF DISCONTENT & PLAGUES OF DARK DESPAIR] 109 TIREL 8            16
    UTTERS LOUD DESPAIR SHADOWING PARIS . . . . . . .        135 FRENCH REVOLTN      18
    SUDDEN SEIZD WITH HOWLINGS DESPAIR AND BLACK NIGHT . . .  135 FRENCH REVOLTN      21
    . . . FANCY GAVE HIM TO SEE AN IMAGE OF DESPAIR IN HIS DEN 136 FRENCH REVOLTN     45
    AND BUILDS A HEAVEN IN HELL'S DESPAIR  . . . . . .        162 CLOD PEBBLE/N        4
    AND HER LOCKS COVERD WITH GREY DESPAIR  . . . . . .       168 EARTHS ANSWR/N       5
    DRUNKEN WITH WOE FORGOTTEN AND SHUT UP FROM COLD DESPAIR  192 V DAU ALBION 4       2
    FILLED WITH BLASTING FANCIES AND WITH MILDEWS OF DESPAIR  203 AMERICA 16          20
    AND HER LOCKS COVERD WITH GREY DESPAIR  . . . . . .       210 EARTHS ANSR/SE       5
    AND BUILDS A HEAVEN IN HELL'S DESPAIR  . . . . . .        211 CLOD PEBBLE/SE       4
    IN DESPAIR AND THE SHADOWS OF DEATH  . . . . . . .        225 URIZEN 5            27
    HOWLINGS & HISSINGS SHRIEKS & GROANS & VOICES OF DESPAIR  243 EUROPE 12           34
    DRAWING CLOUDS OF DESPAIR THRO THE HEAVENS . . . . .      248 SONG OF LOS 7       12
    I HAVE HIDDEN [THEE ENION IN JEALOUS DESPAIR] . . . . .   264 FOUR ZOAS 1         27
    BUT DEATH DESPAIR & EVERLASTING BROODING MELANCHOLY  . .  265 FOUR ZOAS 1         51
    UPON THEM MORE DESPAIR WILL BRING SELF MURDER ON MY SOUL  265 FOUR ZOAS 1         56
    [BEAUTY ALL BLUSHING WITH DESIRE MOCKING HER FELL DESPAIR] 269 FOUR ZOAS 1       189
    INTO NON ENTITY REVOLVING ROUND IN DARK DESPAIR  . . .    270 FOUR ZOAS 1        219
    THUS ENION GAVE THEM ALL HER SPECTROUS LIFE [IN DEEP      270 FOUR ZOAS 1        221
        DESPAIR]
    HE MIGHT AVERT HIS OWN DESPAIR IN WOE & FEAR HE SAW . . . 282 FOUR ZOAS 2         76
    A SHADOW OF DESPAIR THEREFORE TOWARD THE WEST URIZEN FORMD 285 FOUR ZOAS 2       187
    SO LOUD IN THUNDERS SPOKE THE KING FOLDED IN DARK DESPAIR 295 FOUR ZOAS 3        131
    WHERE THE IMPRESSIONS OF DESPAIR & HOPE ENROOT FOREVER  . 295 FOUR ZOAS 3        143
    THAN URIZEN & ALL HIS HOSTS IN CURST DESPAIR DOWN RUSHING 296 FOUR ZOAS 3        152
    THE NETHER ABYSS & GNASHING IN FIERCE DESPAIR PANTING     296 FOUR ZOAS 3    *   155
        IN SOBS
    THESE ARE THE WORDS OF ENION HEARD FROM THE COLD WAVES    296 FOUR ZOAS 3        182
        OF DESPAIR
    IN TORRENTS OF DESPAIR IN VAIN FOR IF I PLUNGE BENEATH  . 298 FOUR ZOAS 4         13
    CAN DIE WHEN DARK DESPAIR COMES OVER CAN I NOT  . . .     298 FOUR ZOAS 4         22
    BECOME A PREY TO ALL MY DEMONS OF DESPAIR & HOPE . . .    299 FOUR ZOAS 4         75
    IN VAIN AM DRIVEN ON FALSE HOPE HOPE SISTER OF DESPAIR    300 FOUR ZOAS 4        123
    SUSTAINED BY THE DEMON'S LIFE DESPAIR & TERROR & WOE & RAGE 309 FOUR ZOAS 5      170
    TERRIFIC VOYAGE HILLS & VALES OF TORMENT & DESPAIR  . .   315 FOUR ZOAS 6        151
    SHUT UP IN STIFLING OBSTRUCTION ROOTED IN DUMB DESPAIR  . 318 FOUR ZOAS 6        269
    TO BEAR THEE DOWN BENEATH THE WAVES IN STIFLING DESPAIR   321 FOUR ZOAS 7         56
    [SHE SECRET JOYD TO SEE SHE FED HERSELF ON HIS DESPAIR]   324 FOUR ZOAS 7        177
    ALL THINGS SUBSIST ON ONE ANOTHER THENCEFORTH IN DESPAIR  330 FOUR ZOAS 7        391
    THEN LOS PLUCKED THE FRUIT & EAT & SAT DOWN IN DESPAIR  . 330 FOUR ZOAS 7        395
    THEIR LIFE EXTINCT THEY TOOK THE SPECTRE FORM IN          333 FOUR ZOAS 7B        15
        DARK DESPAIR
    OF LIFE UPON THE PLAINS OF DEATH & VALLEYS OF DESPAIR  . . 337 FOUR ZOAS 7B      161
    IN [ANGUISH FOR] RAGE AGAINST THE DARK DESPAIR THE HOWLING 340 FOUR ZOAS 7B   *  287
        MELANCHOLY
    DESPAIR FROM THE POOR WANDERING SPECTRES AND LOS LOVED THEM 342 FOUR ZOAS 8   *   39
    HIS OWN DESPAIR EVEN AT THE COST OF EVERY THING THAT      344 FOUR ZOAS 8        139
        BREATHES
    MANTLES OF DESPAIR GIRDLES OF BITTER COMPUNCTION SHOES    346 FOUR ZOAS 8        221
        OF INDOLENCE
    OF DARK DEATH & DESPAIR . . . . . . . . . . . . .        347 FOUR ZOAS 8        231
    FOR HIMSELF IN THE ROCK OF ETERNITY TREMBLING & IN [FEAR] 356 FOUR ZOAS 8        595
        DESPAIR
    FELL DOWN & SHADOWY FORMS OF JOY MIXD WITH DESPAIR & GRIEF 358 FOUR ZOAS 9        29
    AND DEEP DESPAIR RATTLING GO UP THE FLAMES AROUND         359 FOUR ZOAS 9         68
        THE SYNAGOGUE
    RISING FROM THE CONFUSION IN TEARS & HOWLINGS & DESPAIR   362 FOUR ZOAS 9        202
    WHERE THE IMPRESSIONS OF DESPAIR & HOPE FOR EVER VEGETATE 367 FOUR ZOAS 9        377
    [WITH] BY BEASTS & WORMS & CREEPING THINGS & DARKNESS &   373 FOUR ZOAS 9        596
        DESPAIR
    DOWN DOWN THRO THE IMMENSE WITH OUTCRY FURY & DESPAIR  . . 376 FOUR ZOAS 9       723
    BUT IN THE WINE PRESSES IS WAILING TERROR & DESPAIR  . .  376 FOUR ZOAS 9        732
    AND THINE IS A FACE OF SWEET LOVE IN DESPAIR . . . . .    429 MARY               45
    TUESDAY JANRY...BETWEEN TWO & SEVEN IN THE EVENING DESPAIR 440A MEMORANDUM/N 1   PROSE
    ARE DESCENDING INTO THE ABYSS IN WAILING & DESPAIR  . . . 443A LAST JUDGMNT/L    PROSE
    IN VARIOUS ATTITUDES OF DESPAIR & HORROR FALL THRO THE AIR 443C LAST JUDGMNT/L   PROSE
    HIS FUTURE COURSE THRO DARKNESS AND DESPAIR TO ETERNAL    487 MILTON 7           26
        DEATH
    SEEING THE CHURCHES AT THEIR PERIOD IN TERROR & DESPAIR   506 MILTON 22          40
    WHO PUBLISHES DOUBT & CALLS IT KNOWLEDGE WHOSE SCIENCE    533 MILTON 41          15
        IS DESPAIR
    THEN TREMBLED THE VIRGIN OLOLON & REPLYD IN CLOUDS        533 MILTON 41          29
        OF DESPAIR
    THE VOID IN (INCOHERENT) DESPAIR CAMBRIDGE & OXFORD       623 JERUSALEM 5         3
        & LONDON
    HE MIGHT AVERT HIS OWN DESPAIR IN WOE & FEAR HE SAW . . . 626 JERUSALEM 7        34
    HE STAMPS AROUND THE ANVIL BEATING BLOWS OF STERN DESPAIR 629 JERUSALEM 10       24
    NOR THEM OBSTRUCT WITH THY TEMPTATIONS OF DOUBT & DESPAIR 629 JERUSALEM 10       33
    O THAT I COULD CEASE TO BE DESPAIR I AM DESPAIR  . . . .  630 JERUSALEM 10       51
    YET WHY DESPAIR I SAW THE FINGER OF GOD GO FORTH . . . .  631 JERUSALEM 12       10
    OF PAIN AND MISERY AND DESPAIR AND EVER BROODING MELANCHOLY 633 JERUSALEM 13     31
    THOSE THAT THOU TORMENTEST A HELL & DESPAIR FOR EVER & EVER 639 JERUSALEM 17     47
    AN ORBED VOID OF DOUBT DESPAIR HUNGER & THIRST & SORROW   640 JERUSALEM 18        4
    WEEPING IN PLEADINGS OF LOVE IN THE WEB OF DESPAIR  . . . 642 JERUSALEM 20        4
    MANCHESTER & LIVERPOOL ARE IN TORTURES OF DOUBT & DESPAIR 644 JERUSALEM 21       36
    BUT DARK DESPAIR & EVERLASTING BROODING MELANCHOLY  . .   645 JERUSALEM 22       24
    TREMBLING STOOD ALBION AT HER WORDS IN JEALOUS DARK DESPAIR 646 JERUSALEM 23     13
    OF EVER-HARDENING DESPAIR SQUARD & POLISHD WITH CRUEL SKILL 647 JERUSALEM 24     35
    HIS WESTERN HEAVEN WITH ROCKY CLOUDS OF DEATH & DESPAIR   656 JERUSALEM 31        1
```

```
                                                            PAGE      TITLE        LINE
DESPAIR   (CONTINUED)
      OF DESPAIR & DEATH TO SEARCH THE TEMPTERS OUT WALKING AMONG   656 JERUSALEM 31      5
      ALBION'S ROCKS & PRECIPICES CAVES OF SOLITUDE & DARK          656 JERUSALEM 31      6
         DESPAIR
      DENS OF DESPAIR IN THE HOUSE OF BREAD ENQUIRING IN VAIN       657 JERUSALEM 31     26
      I FEEL THE IRON THREADS OF LOVE & JEALOUSY & DESPAIR    . .   657 JERUSALEM 31     49
      AND THOU O HARLOT DAUGHTER DAUGHTER OF DESPAIR ART ALL        658 JERUSALEM 31     58
      REUBEN RETURND TO BASHAN IN DESPAIR HE SLEPT ON THE STONE     661 JERUSALEM 34     51
      TORMENTS DESPAIR ETERNAL DEATH BUT THE DIVINE MERCY  . . .    663 JERUSALEM 36     54
      BY THE WAVES OF DESPAIR WHOSE EMANATION ROSE ABOVE    . .     667 JERUSALEM 40     49
      ALBION'S MELANCHOLY WHO MUST ELSE HAVE BEEN A DUMB DESPAIR    668 JERUSALEM 40     60
      AND DESPAIR AS MESHES CLOSELY WOVE OVER THE WEST OF LONDON    668 JERUSALEM 41      9
      THE TWENTY-EIGHT TREMBLED IN DEATH'S DARK CAVES IN COLD       668 JERUSALEM 41     23
         DESPAIR
      DRIVEN ON THE VOID IN INCOHERENT DESPAIR INTO NON ENTITY      673 JERUSALEM 43     68
      IN THE MIDST OF TEMPTATIONS & DESPAIR AMONG THE ROOTED OAKS   673 JERUSALEM 43     81
      OF BLACK DESPAIR THAT THE IMMORTAL WINGS LABOURD AGAINST      674 JERUSALEM 44     12
      CLIFF AFTER CLIFF & OVER VALLEYS OF DESPAIR & DEATH    . .    674 JERUSALEM 44     13
      FOOD OF DESPAIR THEY DRINK THE CONDEMND SOUL & REJOICE  . .   680 JERUSALEM 49     63
      OVER THESE DESOLATE ROCKS OF ALBION O DAUGHTERS OF DESPAIR    688 JERUSALEM 56     21
      OF DESPAIR WHILE THE SATANIC HOLINESS TRIUMPHD IN VALA  . .   693 JERUSALEM 60     47
      OF ALBION'S SPECTRES THAT LOS IN DESPAIR OFT SAT & OFTEN      696 JERUSALEM 62     39
         PONDERD
      A BUILDING OF ETERNAL DEATH WHOSE PROPORTIONS ARE ETERNAL     702 JERUSALEM 66      9
         DESPAIR
      OF AFFLICTION OF LOVE OF SWEET DESPAIR OF TORMENT             705 JERUSALEM 67     51
         UNENDURABLE
      A POLYPUS OF ROOTS OF REASONING DOUBT DESPAIR & DEATH   . .   707 JERUSALEM 69      3
      WITH FURY & DESPAIR & THEY STRETCH FROM SOUTH TO NORTH  . .   713 JERUSALEM 73      3
      AMONG PRECIPICES OF DESPAIR IN GOSHEN I SEEK FOR LIGHT  . .   720 JERUSALEM 79     11
      THE LABOURER OF AGES IN THE VALLEYS OF DESPAIR    . . . .     728 JERUSALEM 83     53
      I DESPAIR OF EVER PLEASING ONE CLASS OF MEN   . . . . .       795A LETTER 6       PROSE
DESPAIRD
      BUT MANY DOUBTED & DESPAIRD & IMPUTED SIN & RIGHTEOUSNESS     648 JERUSALEM 25     15
DESPAIRING
      SILENT AS DESPAIRING LOVE AND STRONG AS JEALOUSY   . . .      196 AMERICA PREL 2    1
      . . . DEEP DESPAIRING STAMPING STRUGGLING  . . . . .  . .     296 FOUR ZOAS 3     156
      SILENT AS DESPAIRING LOVE & STRONG AS JEALOUSY    . . . .     336 FOUR ZOAS 7B    136
      OF ETERNITY FOR HIMSELF HE HEWD IT DESPAIRING OF             349 FOUR ZOAS 8     340
         LIFE ETERNAL
      THARMAS INDOLENT & SULLEN URTHONA DOUBTING & DESPAIRING       671 JERUSALEM 43      3
DESPERATE
      IF THOU ART HE MY DESPERATE PURPOSE HEAR & GIVE ME DEATH      313 FOUR ZOAS 6      57
      AND DIM OBLIVION OF ALL WOE & DESPERATE REPOSE    . . . .     321 FOUR ZOAS 7      67
      DESPERATE REMORSE SWALLOWS THE PRESENT IN A QUENCHLESS RAGE   343 FOUR ZOAS 8     101
      WHAT CAN BE DONE WITH SUCH DESPERATE FOOLS   . . . . .  .     751 EV GOSPEL(D)/N   21
      I HAVE HAD ANOTHER DESPERATE SHIVERING FIT IT CAME ON  . .    872B LETTER 75      PROSE
      DESPERATE ATTACK OF THE ANGUISH (&) TREMBLING LAST NIGHT &    SUPP LETTER 81A    *PROSE
DESPERATION
      SHEWD THEIR IMMORTAL ENERGIES IN WARLIKE DESPERATION    . .   335 FOUR ZOAS 7B    102
      AND THE PRECIOUS STONES OF ANXIETY & CARE & DESPERATION       499 MILTON 18        23
         & DEATH
      AT LAST WHEN DESPERATION ALMOST TORE HIS HEART IN TWAIN       503 MILTON 20        56
      DRIVEN TO DESPERATION BY LOS'S TERRORS & THREATNING FEARS     629 JERUSALEM 10     28
      SHOULD WANT NATURAL BREAD SORROW & DESPERATION PURSUES  . .   813B LETTER 22      PROSE
DESPISD
      STILL SHE DESPISD HIM CALLING ON HIS NAME & KNOWING HIM NOT   286 FOUR ZOAS 2     234
      ALL THE GIFTS OF THE HOLY GHOST ARE [DESPISD] LOOKD UPON      604C V LAST JUDG/N  PROSE
      WHEN ELATE I AM ENVYD WHEN MEEK I'M DESPISD   . . . . .       829 O WHY BORN/L     10
DESPISE
      DOES NOT THE EAGLE SCORN THE EARTH & DESPISE THE TREASURES    193 V DAU ALBION 5   39
         BENEATH
      WHY DIDST THOU DESPISE AHANIA  . . . . . . . . . .            254 AHANIA 4         62
      MINE IS TO TEACH MEN TO DESPISE DEATH & TO GO ON  . . .       530 MILTON 38        40
      [WHICH HE] THAT MAN DOES MOST DESPISE   . . . . . . . .       539 CAN THERE BE/N    4
      HIS [EXECUTION] EXECUTIVE POWER MUST I DESPISE    . . . .     547 RAFAEL SUBLI/N *  2
      A MASTER OF ART AND LEARNING THOUGH AFFECTING TO DESPISE IT   569C DESC CAT 3     PROSE
      THEY DESPISE DRAWING WHICH DESPISES THEM IN RETURN    . . .   596C PUB ADDRESS/N  PROSE
      WHILE THEY DESPISE & LAUGH AT WHAT OTHERS FEAR    . . . .     609B V LAST JUDG/N  PROSE
      THEY DO NOT ENVY ONE ANOTHER THEY CONTEMN & DESPISE  . . .    616C V LAST JUDG/N  PROSE
      THE DEAD DESPISE & SCORN THEE & CAST THEE OUT AS ACCURSED     626 JERUSALEM 7      68
      WHO SHALL PRETEND TO DESPISE ART & SCIENCE   . . . . .  .     717B JERUSALEM 77   PROSE
      THOSE WHO PRETEND TO DESPISE THE LABOURS OF ART & SCIENCE     717B JERUSALEM 77   PROSE
      TO DESPISE KNOWLEDGE IS TO DESPISE JERUSALEM & HER            717C JERUSALEM 77   PROSE
         BUILDERS
      AS IF I WAS NOT THEIR MOTHER THEY DESPISE ME & CAST ME OUT    720 JERUSALEM 79     21
      THEN MY VERSE I DISHONOUR MY PICTURES DESPISE    . . . . .    829 O WHY BORN/L      5
      [I NOW DESPISE & MOCK IN TURN ?ALTHOUGH SUFFRING ?POVERTY]    SUPP ANNO REYNOLDS * MARG
DESPISED
      MY LIFE IS DEATH I AM A TRAITOR TO MY NATION AND DESPISED     38D SAMSON/PS       PROSE
      & ALL MEN OF SENSE HAVE DESPISED THE BOOK AS MUCH AS I DO     397A ANNO BACON      MARG
      MICH ANG KNEW & DESPISED ALL THAT TITIAN COULD DO    . . .    464A ANNO REYNOLDS   MARG
      THOSE WHO GIVE THEIR LIVES FOR HIM ARE DESPISED   . . . .     667 JERUSALEM 40     15
      THE MAN WHO RESPECTS WOMAN SHALL BE DESPISED BY WOMAN  . .    734 JERUSALEM 88     37
      DESPISED THE MEEKNESS OF TRUE ART AND SUCH I FIND HAVE BEEN   863B LETTER 60      PROSE
      [BARRY WAS POOR & INDEPENDENT ?MORTIMER WAS DESPISED &        SUPP ANNO REYNOLDS * MARG
         MOCKED]
DESPISES
      WHO CALLS THE INDIVIDUAL LAW HOLY AND DESPISES THE SAVIOUR    493 MILTON 13         5
      THEY DESPISE DRAWING WHICH DESPISES THEM IN RETURN    . . .   596C PUB ADDRESS/N  PROSE
      AND REMEMBER HE WHO DESPISES & MOCKS A MENTAL GIFT    . . .   717C JERUSALEM 77   PROSE
```

```
                                                      PAGE      TITLE          LINE
DESPISING
      WAS THE CAUSE OF OUR DESPISING THE PRIESTS & PHILOSOPHERS   153D MARRIAGE HH 12  PROSE
      DESPISING TOIL AND CARE                          .   .   .  239 EUROPE 4           22
      DESPISING URIZEN'S LIGHT & TURNING IT INTO FLAMING FIRE     324 FOUR ZOAS 7       153
DESPITE
      AND BUILDS A HELL IN HEAVEN'S DESPITE      .   .   .   .   . 162 CLOD PEBBLE/N      12
      AND BUILDS A HELL IN HEAVEN'S DESPITE      .   .   .   .   . 211 CLOD PEBBLE/SE     12
DESPONDENCY
      OUT OF DESPONDENCY EVEN IF IT LIFTS ME TOO HIGH    .   .   . 822C LETTER 26        PROSE
DESTINATIONS
      HENCE THE THREE CLASSES OF MEN TAKE THEIR FIXD DESTINATIONS  484 MILTON 5           13
      HERE THE THREE CLASSES OF MORTAL MEN TAKE THEIR FIXD         486 MILTON 6           32
          DESTINATIONS
      AND HERE THE SUN & MOON RECIEVE THEIR FIXED DESTINATIONS     514 MILTON 27          54
DESTIND
      OF FIRE FAR SHINING TRAVELLING ALONG EVEN TO ITS DESTIND     287 FOUR ZOAS 2       276
          END
      MY FEEBLE LIMBS INFOLD MY DESTIND MISERY     .   .   .   .   344 FOUR ZOAS 8       147
      BUT LEAVE THEIR DESTIND LINEAMENTS PERMANENT FOR EVER &      505 MILTON 22          25
          EVER
DESTINED
      THAT ONE OF THE DRAWINGS WHICH MR ROMNEY DESTINED FOR YOU    839C LETTER 38        PROSE
DESTINIES
      THE THREE DESTINIES SIT ON THE CIRCLES OF PLATO'S HEAVENS    619B ILLUS MILTON     PROSE
DESTINY
      ("A SCORPION WHIP OF DESTINY") & NEVER FORGIVE HIM TILL      79B ANNO LAVATER      MARG
          HE MENDS
      .   .   IN THE DEN NAMD DESTINY A STRONG MAN SAT    .   .   . 136 FRENCH REVOLTN     43
      BUT IN MILTON THE FATHER IS DESTINY    .   .   .   .   .   . 150B MARRIAGE HH 5     PROSE
      TURND ROUND THE CIRCLE OF DESTINY WITH TEARS & BITTER SIGHS  266 FOUR ZOAS 1        74
      .   .   .   THE CIRCLE OF DESTINY COMPLETE                   266 FOUR ZOAS 1        87
      THE CIRCLE OF DESTINY COMPLETE THEY GAVE TO IT A SPACE   .   267 FOUR ZOAS 1       101
      [ ?TURND ?ROUND THE CIRCLE OF ?DESTINY XXX SIGHS ]    .   .  SUPP FOUR ZOAS 1        *
      A CRASH RAN THRO THE IMMENSE THE BOUNDS OF DESTINY WERE      295 FOUR ZOAS 3       135
          BROKEN
      THE BOUNDS OF DESTINY CRASHD DIREFUL & THE SWELLING SEA      295 FOUR ZOAS 3       136
      THE BOUNDS OF DESTINY WERE BROKEN & HATRED NOW BEGAN    .   . 296 FOUR ZOAS 3       177
      AND CUT THE WINDS LIKE ARROWS SHOT BY TROOPS OF DESTINY      325 FOUR ZOAS 7       208
      THE GODDESSES OF DESTINY THIS SHEWS HOW CHAUCER HAS BEEN     569D DESC CAT 3       PROSE
      AND HAS ALSO HIS GREAT USE AND HIS GRAND LEADING DESTINY     570A DESC CAT 3       PROSE
      IN THE RANK OF WHICH HE HOLDS THE DESTINY THE USES TO    .   570B DESC CAT 3       PROSE
      THE HERMAPHRODITIC SATANIC WORLD OF ROCKY DESTINY           690 JERUSALEM 58        51
      LABOUR UNPARALLELLD A WONDROUS ROCKY WORLD OF CRUEL DESTINY  702 JERUSALEM 66         6
DESTITUTE
      NONE OF MY DESIGNS WILL BE DESTITUTE OF INFINITE            792B LETTER 4          PROSE
          PARTICULARS
      NOT SO DESTITUTE OF ACCOMODATIONS TO OUR WANTS AS          806B LETTER 16         PROSE
          I EXPECTED
DESTROY
      OF THE (THREE) DEGREES TWO OF WHICH HE MUST DESTROY    .   .  93A ANNO SWED LOVE    MARG
      THAT OUR GRIEF HE MAY DESTROY                              123 ON ANOTHERS/SI      34
      OR HOW SHALL WE GATHER WHAT GRIEFS DESTROY     .   .   .   . 124 SCHOOL BOY/SI      28
      WE HAVE CALLD AN ASSEMBLY BUT NOT TO DESTROY   .   .   .   . 139 FRENCH REVOLTN    115
      WHOEVER TRIES TO RECONCILE THEM SEEKS TO DESTROY EXISTENCE  155B MARRIAGE HH 15    PROSE
      DOES ITSELF DESTROY    .   .   .   .   .   .   .   .   .   . 168 SILENT NIGHT/N     11
      [ DOTH LIFE DESTROY ]    .   .   .   .   .   .   .   .   .   . 175 SICK ROSE/N        8
      DOES THY LIFE DESTROY    .   .   .   .   .   .   .   .   .   . 175 SICK ROSE/N       10
      DOES THE WINGED LIFE DESTROY     .   .   .   .   .   .   .   . 179 ETERNITY/N         2
      DOTH THE WINGED LIFE DESTROY     .   .   .   .   .   .   .   . 184 SEVRL QUESTN/N    12
      DOES THY LIFE DESTROY    .   .   .   .   .   .   .   .   .   . 213 SICK ROSE/SE    *  8
      DESTROY THESE OPRESSORS OF JERUSALEM & THOSE WHO           279 FOUR ZOAS 1    * 549
          RUIN SHILOH
      O THARMAS DO NOT THOU DESTROY ME QUITE BUT LET            296 FOUR ZOAS 3       184
      TO WASTE IN ENDLESS CORRUPTION RENEW THOU I WILL DESTROY   298 FOUR ZOAS 4    *  31
      NOW HE RESOLVD TO DESTROY LOS & NOW HIS TEARS FLOWD DOWN   298 FOUR ZOAS 4        47
      THE BODY OF MAN IS GIVEN TO ME I SEEK IN VAIN TO DESTROY   313 FOUR ZOAS 6        60
      TO THE EMBRACES OF THIS TERROR & I WILL DESTROY    .   .   . 327 FOUR ZOAS 7       300
      HE IN HIS TURN GAVE TASKS TO LOS ENORMOUS TO DESTROY       329 FOUR ZOAS 7       375
      SUCH IS OUR STATE NOR WILL THE SON OF GOD REDEEM US BUT    331 FOUR ZOAS 7       431
          DESTROY
      THEY RATHER CHOSE TO MEET ETERNAL DEATH THAN TO DESTROY    332 FOUR ZOAS 7       484
      TIMES UPON TIMES THINKING TO DESTROY THE LAMB BLESSED      347 FOUR ZOAS 8       235
          FOR EVER
      AS TO DESTROY AN INDIVIDUAL BY MEANS OF ANOTHER    .   .   . 388B ANNO WATSON      MARG
      PRETENCE TO RELIGION TO DESTROY RELIGION     .   .   .   .   398A ANNO BACON       MARG
      TO BE TRUE PERSIANS DESTROY THE TEMPLES & ARE PRAISED FOR  413D ANNO BOYD        MARG
          IT
      DESTROY ART MICHAEL ANGELO'S ART DEPENDS     .   .   .   .   447A ANNO REYNOLDS    MARG
      A PRETENCE OF ART TO DESTROY ART XXX   .   .   .   .   .   . 452B ANNO REYNOLDS  * MARG
      & ITS LAST NOW HE BEGINS TO DEGRADE [ & ] TO DENY [ DESTROY ] 458B ANNO REYNOLDS  * MARG
          & TO MOCK
      HIS SHADOWS WOULD DESTROY IT & DEFORM ITS APPEARANCE   .   464A ANNO REYNOLDS    MARG
      [ THE RASCALS WHO ?SEE PAINTING WANT TO DESTROY ART       SUPP ANNO REYNOLDS  * MARG
          & LEARNING ]
      [ FOOLS' OPINIONS & ENDEAVOURS DESTROY INVENTION ]    .   .  SUPP ANNO REYNOLDS  * MARG
      HE SET HIS FACE AGAINST JERUSALEM TO DESTROY THE EON OF    491 MILTON 11          1
          ALBION
      PITYING AND PERMITTING EVIL THO STRONG & MIGHTY TO DESTROY  505 MILTON 22         30
      TO DESTROY JERUSALEM AS A HARLOT & HER SONS AS REPROBATES   506 MILTON 22         47
      THO STRONG AND MIGHTY TO DESTROY O LOS OUR BELOVED FATHER   507 MILTON 23         20
      .   .   .   THAT THEY DESTROY NOT THE EARTH    .   .   .   . 511 MILTON 25         39
      LEST THOSE THREE HEAVENS OF BEULAH SHOULD THE CREATION     512 MILTON 26         20
          DESTROY
```

490

	PAGE	TITLE	LINE

DESTROY (CONTINUED)

WHO CREEPS INTO STATE GOVERNMENT LIKE A CATTERPILLER TO DESTROY — 533 MILTON 41 — 11

TO DESTROY THE WISDOM OF AGES TO GRATIFY RAVENOUS ENVY . . — 533 MILTON 41 — 17

WHO PRETEND TO POETRY THAT THEY MAY DESTROY IMAGINATION — 533 MILTON 41 — 23

. . . TO DESTROY PICTURE [NOR] OR TUNE . . . . . . — 548 ON GREAT ENC/N * — 4

AS THAT WHICH IS FABRICATED FOR THE PURPOSE TO DESTROY ART — 563D DESC CAT — PROSE

LABOURING TO DESTROY IMAGINATIVE POWER BY MEANS OF . . . — 582B DESC CAT 9 — PROSE

& DESTROY ONE ANOTHER BY EVERY MEANS IN THEIR POWER . . — 615A V LAST JUDG/N — PROSE

THEY WAR TO DESTROY THE FURNACES TO DESOLATE GOLGONOOZA — 623 JERUSALEM 5 — 29

OF GOD TO DESTROY JERUSALEM & TO DEVOUR THE BODY OF ALBION — 628 JERUSALEM 9 — 10

THEY WOULD NEVER LOVE MY POWER IF THEY DID NOT SEEK TO DESTROY — 639 JERUSALEM 17 — 23

IF SHE HAD NOT SOUGHT TO DESTROY JERUSALEM SUCH IS THAT FALSE — 639 JERUSALEM 17 — 25

AND GENERATING LOVE A PRETENCE OF LOVE TO DESTROY LOVE — 639 JERUSALEM 17 — 26

LITTLE-ONES TO DESTROY THE DIVINE SAVIOUR THE FRIEND OF SINNERS — 641 JERUSALEM 18 — 37

OF ACTION FOR OBEDIENCE TO DESTROY THE CONTRARIES OF MAN — 653 JERUSALEM 29 — 15

TO DESTROY HIS EMANATION IS THEIR INTENTION . . . . . — 667 JERUSALEM 40 — 17

THEY SAW ALBION ENDEAVOURING TO DESTROY THEIR EMANATIONS — 669 JERUSALEM 41 — 31

THREE THOU HAST SLAIN I AM THE FOURTH THOU CANST NOT DESTROY ME — 670 JERUSALEM 42 — 24

BUT DESTROY NOT THESE LITTLE ONES NOR MOCK THE LORD'S ANOINTED — 670 JERUSALEM 42 — 41

DESTROY NOT BY MORAL VIRTUE THE LITTLE ONES WHOM HE HATH CHOSEN — 670 JERUSALEM 42 — 42

IF WE ARE WRATHFUL ALBION WILL DESTROY JERUSALEM WITH ROOTY GROVES — 672 JERUSALEM 43 — 8

A PRETENCE OF ART TO DESTROY ART A PRETENCE OF LIBERTY — 672 JERUSALEM 43 — 35

TO DESTROY LIBERTY A PRETENCE OF RELIGION TO DESTROY RELIGION — 672 JERUSALEM 43 — 36

ONE ERROR NOT REMOVD WILL DESTROY A HUMAN SOUL . . . . — 676 JERUSALEM 46 — 11

OF GENERATION TO DESTROY BY SIN AND ATONEMENT HAPPY JERUSALEM — 676 JERUSALEM 46 — 27

BROODING ABSTRACT PHILOSOPHY TO DESTROY . . . . — 709 JERUSALEM 70 — 19

TO DESTROY IMAGINATION THE DIVINE BODY BY MARTYRDOMS & WARS — 714 JERUSALEM 74 — 13

AND ON HIS ANVILS LEST THEY DESTROY THE FEMININE AFFECTIONS — 719 JERUSALEM 78 — 8

SURROUNDING THEM WITH ARMIES TO DESTROY THE LAMB OF GOD — 719 JERUSALEM 78 — 14

OF GOD AND THE LAMB TO DESTROY THE LAMB & USURP THE THRONE OF GOD — 719 JERUSALEM 78 — 19

OF MILD JERUSALEM TO DESTROY THE LAMB OF GOD JERUSALEM . . — 726 JERUSALEM 82 — 54

LEST HAND THE TERRIBLE DESTROY HIS AFFECTION THOU HIDEST HER — 727 JERUSALEM 83 — 30

WHO FIRST SPOIL & THEN DESTROY IMAGINATIVE ART . . . . — 777A INSC LAOCOON — PROSE

DESTROYD

FOR NOTHING IS DESTROYD . . . . — SUPP ANNO SWED HELL * MARG

OUR LUNGS ARE DESTROYD WITH THE FLOGISTON . . . . . . — 59A ISLAND MOON 10 — PROSE

FAR IN THE NORTH BUT THEY WERE WICKED & WERE ALL DESTROYD — 102 TIRIEL 2 — 51

WHOSE SMOKE DESTROYD THE PLEASANT [GARDENS] GARDEN . . . — 361 FOUR ZOAS 9 * 168

ARE MOCKD & DESTROYD BY THIS PRESIDENT OF FOOLS . . . . — 458C ANNO REYNOLDS — MARG

BACON'S (PHILOSOPHY) HAS DESTROYD (ALL) ART & SCIENCE . . — 470A ANNO REYNOLDS * MARG

THE NEGATION MUST BE DESTROYD TO REDEEM THE CONTRARIES . . — 533 MILTON 40 — 33

IS PUNISHD & IF POSSIBLE DESTROYD NOT THRO ENVY . . . . — 616C V LAST JUDG/N — PROSE

NATIONS ARE DESTROYD OR FLOURISH IN PROPORTION AS THEIR — 621D JERUSALEM 3 — PROSE

POETRY PAINTING AND MUSIC ARE DESTROYD OR FLOURISH . . . — 621D JERUSALEM 3 — PROSE

I HAVE DESTROYD WANDRING REUBEN WHO STROVE TO BIND MY WILL — 724 JERUSALEM 81 — 10

THEIR WORKS WERE DESTROYD BY THE SEVEN ANGELS . . . . . — 777B INSC LAOCOON — PROSE

ROME & GREECE SWEPT ART INTO THEIR MAW & DESTROYD IT . — 778D HOMERS POETRY — PROSE

TILL THE VENETIAN & FLEMISH ARE DESTROYD THE FLORENTINE — 866B LETTER 64 — PROSE

[FUNERAL GRANTED TO SIR JOSHUA FOR HAVING ?DESTROYD ART] — SUPP ANNO REYNOLDS * MARG

DESTROYED

BRINGING GOOD NEWS OF SIN AND DEATH DESTROYED . . . . . — 37D SAMSON/PS — PROSE

WHO MADE HIMSELF A GOD & DESTROYED THE HUMAN FORM DIVINE — 521 MILTON 32 — 13

THE LABOUR HAS DESTROYED THE LINEAMENTS . . . . — 582B DESC CAT 9 — PROSE

WHICH HE FORESEES SHALL SHORTLY BE DESTROYED . . . . . — 682A JERUSALEM 52 — PROSE

AND RAHAB BABYLON THE GREAT HATH DESTROYED JERUSALEM . — 715 JERUSALEM 75 — 1

WHAT CAN BE CREATED CAN BE DESTROYED . . . . — 776C INSC LAOCOON — PROSE

DESTROYER

O CRUEL O DESTROYER O CONSUMER O AVENGER . . . . . — 107 TIRIEL 6 — 23

LO I AM GOD THE TERRIBLE DESTROYER & NOT THE SAVIOUR . . — 273 FOUR ZOAS 1 — 338

I AM THE NOURISHER THOU THE DESTROYER IN MY BOSOM IS MILK & WINE — 354 FOUR ZOAS 8 — 500

AND HAS COMPELLED THE USE OF THAT DESTROYER OF COLOUR . — 566B DESC CAT 2 — PROSE

BUT VENGEANCE IS THE DESTROYER OF GRACE & REPENTANCE IN THE BOSOM — 648 JERUSALEM 25 — 10

WHERE DWELLS THE SPECTRE OF ALBION DESTROYER OF DEFINITE FORM — 688 JERUSALEM 56 — 17

THE UNPRODUCTIVE MAN IS NOT A CHRISTIAN MUCH LESS THE DESTROYER — 777D INSC LAOCOON — PROSE

DESTROYERS

THESE ARE THE DESTROYERS OF JERUSALEM THESE ARE THE MURDERERS — 533 MILTON 41 — 21

THEY ARE THIEVES AND REBELS THEY ARE DESTROYERS . . . — 571C DESC CAT 3 — PROSE

& SCIENCES AS THEY PRETEND WERE DESTROYERS OF ALL ART . — 778C HOMERS POETRY — PROSE

DESTROYING SEE SELF-DESTROYING,SELF DESTROYING

WHOSE WHOLE DELIGHT IS IN DESTROYING . . . . — 480C MILTON 1 — PROSE

ARE HERE FROZEN TO UNEXPANSIVE DEADLY DESTROYING TERRORS — 525 MILTON 35 — 1

OF DESTROYING ART WHO THESE ARE . . . . — 573B DESC CAT 3 — PROSE

DESTROYING ALL THE WORLD BESIDE . . . . — 651 FIELDS FROM/J — 80

DESTROYING BY SELFISH AFFECTIONS THE THINGS THAT THEY MOST ADMIRE — 669 JERUSALEM 41 — 28

		PAGE	TITLE	LINE

DESTROYING   (CONTINUED)

THEE FROM DESTROYING THESE LITTLE ONES AM I TO BE ONLY . . 670 JERUSALEM 42   21
CALLING THE PRINCE OF THIS WORLD GOD AND DESTROYING ALL   682B JERUSALEM 52   PROSE
CONTINUALLY BUILDING CONTINUALLY DESTROYING IN FAMILY   734 JERUSALEM 88   40
  FEUDS
IN DESTROYING THE SINNERS FRIEND . . . .   759 EV GOSPEL (2)   37
THAT IT IS IMPOSSIBLE FOR ME TO RETURN TO IT WITHOUT   865C LETTER 63   PROSE
  DESTROYING

DESTROYS

. . . THAT DESTROYS OUR ENEMIES' HOUSE . . . . . .   291 FOUR ZOAS 2   411
SHE SMITES WITH HER KNIFE OF FLINT SHE DESTROYS HER OWN   347 FOUR ZOAS 8   234
  WORK
AND CHANGING YELLOW AND AT LENGTH BROWN DESTROYS EVERY . . 566B DESC CAT 2   PROSE
NO IT IS MORAL SEVERITY & DESTROYS MERCY IN ITS VICTIM . . 666 JERUSALEM 39   26
FOR IT IS IDOLATRY & DESTROYS THE SOUL I OUGHT TO TELL YOU 824C LETTER 27   PROSE

DESTRUCTION

BY NIGHT DESTRUCTION FLIES AND STRIKES IN DARKNESS . . .   5 FAIR ELENOR/PS   35
A COUNTRY NOT YET SOWN WITH DESTRUCTION . . . . . . 18 EDW THIRD/PS 1   47
THE CURTAINS OF THEIR BEDS DESTRUCTION IS . . . . . . 30 EDW THIRD/PS 5   12
AND DESTRUCTION HOVERS IN THE CITY'S SMOAK BUT . . . . 37A CONTEMPLATN/PS PROSE
DESTRUCTION WAS THY FATHER A LIONESS SUCKLED THEE . . . 38B SAMSON/PS   PROSE
ON DUSKY WING BREATHING FORTH CLAMOUR & DESTRUCTION . . . 42D THEN SHE BORE   PROSE
("SIN AND DESTRUCTION OF ORDER...") A GOLDEN SENTENCE . . 65D ANNO LAVATER   MARG
WHY CANNOT THE EAR BE CLOSED TO ITS OWN DESTRUCTION . . . 130 BOOK OF THEL 6   11
WITH DESTRUCTION & PLAGUES IN THE MIDST . . . . . . 256 BOOK OF LOS 3   30
THO THUS HEAVENLY BEAUTIFUL TO DRAW ME TO DESTRUCTION . . 265 FOUR ZOAS 1   58
HE MAY BE DEVOTED TO DESTRUCTION FROM HIS MOTHER'S WOMB   272 FOUR ZOAS 1   298
CRYING FURY IN MY LIMBS DESTRUCTION IN MY BONES & MARROW 296 FOUR ZOAS 3   162
THAT THEY MAY CURSE & WORSHIP THE OBSCURE DEMON OF   313 FOUR ZOAS 6   44
  DESTRUCTION
. . . IN HORRIBLE [CONFUSION] DESTRUCTION . . . . . . 317 FOUR ZOAS 6   217
THEY SAW BEYOND THE PIT OF DEATH & DESTRUCTION . . . 342 FOUR ZOAS 8   48
SEEMS TEEMING WITH ENDLESS DESTRUCTION NEVER TO BE REPELLD 343 FOUR ZOAS 8 * 100
TO GRATE THE SOUL INTO DESTRUCTION OR TO INFLAME WITH FURY 344 FOUR ZOAS 8   136
INTO THEIR OWN DESTRUCTION IF PERHAPS HE MIGHT [INVERT]   344 FOUR ZOAS 8 * 138
  AVERT
THE FELL DESTRUCTION AND SHE SAID O URIZEN PRINCE OF LIGHT 344 FOUR ZOAS 8   145
TRIUMPHS IN ITS OWN DESTRUCTION THEY TOOK DOWN THE HARNESS 365 FOUR ZOAS 9   295
THEY BEAT THE IRON ENGINES OF DESTRUCTION INTO WEDGES . . 365 FOUR ZOAS 9   304
& A DESTRUCTION FROM THE DESIGNS OF ANOTHER THE . . . . 388B ANNO WATSON   MARG
BUT THE DESTRUCTION OF THE CANAANITES BY JOSHUA . . . 388B ANNO WATSON * MARG
YOU CANNOT REGULATE THE PRICE OF NECESSARIES WITHOUT   402C ANNO BACON   MARG
  DESTRUCTION
THE ARTS & SCIENCES ARE THE DESTRUCTION OF TYRANNIES . . 445C ANNO REYNOLDS   MARG
DESTRUCTION OF ALL FORM OR OUTLINE PURPOSELY   463D ANNO REYNOLDS   MARG
  & INTENTIONALLY
TO DESTRUCTION FROM THE MOTHER'S WOMB [THE REPROBATE ARE 486 MILTON 7   * 4
  THE FIRST]
BUT RINTRAH WHO IS OF THE REPROBATE OF THOSE FORMD   488 MILTON 8   34
  TO DESTRUCTION
MILTON'S RELIGION IS THE CAUSE THERE IS NO END TO   506 MILTON 22   39
  DESTRUCTION
THE NATURAL POWER CONTINUALLY SEEKS & TENDS TO DESTRUCTION 513 MILTON 26   41
FROM FELL DESTRUCTION IN THE SPECTROUS CUNNING OR RAGE   515 MILTON 28   41
  HE CREATES
SOME MEN CREATED FOR DESTRUCTION COME . . . . . . 544 SOME MEN/N   1
INTEREST BUT FROM MALICE EVEN TO YOUR OWN DESTRUCTION . . 573A DESC CAT 3   PROSE
THE DESTRUCTION OF MEN SO THERE IS A CLASS OF ARTISTS . . 573B DESC CAT 3   PROSE
MUST BE THE DESTRUCTION OF ALL CHARACTER AND EXPRESSION 575B DESC CAT 3   PROSE
MUSIC TRADERS & RHIME TRADERS TO THE DESTRUCTION OF ALL 600B PUB ADDRESS/N PROSE
  TRUE
TO YOUR OWN DESTRUCTION WOOLETT I KNEW VERY INTIMATELY . . 603B PUB ADDR AD/N PROSE
AND THUS THE SPECTRE SPOKE WILT THOU STILL GO ON   625 JERUSALEM 7   9
  TO DESTRUCTION
AND THE RELIGION OF GENERATION WHICH WAS MEANT FOR THE   626 JERUSALEM 7   63
  DESTRUCTION
OR ARE YOU BORN TO FEED THE HUNGRY RAVENINGS OF DESTRUCTION 647 JERUSALEM 24 14
WITH PROVINGS OF DESTRUCTION WITH GIVING THEE THY HEART'S 647 JERUSALEM 24   28
  DESIRE
HER STREETS ARE PAVED WITH DESTRUCTION HER HOUSES BUILT   647 JERUSALEM 24   33
  WITH DEATH
IF WE ARE MERCIFUL OURSELVES MUST SUFFER DESTRUCTION ON   672 JERUSALEM 43   9
  HIS OAKS
MACHINES IN FURY & DESTRUCTION AND THE MAN REVIVING   675 JERUSALEM 45   22
  REPENTED
ALL THE DESTRUCTION THEREFORE IN CHRISTIAN EUROPE . . . 683A JERUSALEM 52   PROSE
ESTABLISHMENT OF TRUTH DEPENDS ON DESTRUCTION OF FALSHOOD 687 JERUSALEM 55 * 65
  CONTINUALLY
HERE VALA STOOD TURNING THE IRON SPINDLE OF DESTRUCTION 702 JERUSALEM 66   10
THE TERRIBLE BALL THE WEDGE THE LOUD SOUNDING HAMMER OF 713 JERUSALEM 73   12
  DESTRUCTION
OF THE VALLEYS OF DESTRUCTION INTO A DARK LAND OF PITCH   721 JERUSALEM 79   61
  & BITUMEN
ALONG THE VALLEY OF DESTRUCTION AMONG THESE DRUID TEMPLES 721 JERUSALEM 79   66
WITH RAHAB AS SHE TURND THE IRON SPINDLE OF DESTRUCTION 729 JERUSALEM 84   30

DESTRUCTIVE

THE RAGING OF THE STORMY SEA AND THE DESTRUCTIVE SWORD . 151C MARRIAGE HH 8 PROSE
COLOURING FORMED UPON THESE PRINCIPLES IS DESTRUCTIVE . . 478C ANNO REYNOLDS MARG
SUCH HARMONY OF COLOURING IS DESTRUCTIVE OF ART . . . . 478D ANNO REYNOLDS   MARG
ALL THIS IS DESTRUCTIVE OF ART . . . . 479A ANNO REYNOLDS   MARG
WHEN ERECTED INTO GODS BECOME DESTRUCTIVE TO HUMANITY . . 571C DESC CAT 3   PROSE
TO EMPIRE THAT IT IS DESTRUCTIVE OF BOTH AS ALL . . . 593D PUB ADDRESS/N *PROSE

		PAGE	TITLE	LINE

DESTRUCTIVE   (CONTINUED)
        A POINT OF LIGHT IS A WITTICISM MANY ARE DESTRUCTIVE OF   599A PUB ADDRESS/N   PROSE
            ALL ART
        BECAUSE THEY AVOID IT AS A DESTRUCTIVE MACHINE AS IT IS   599A PUB ADDRESS/N   PROSE
        AS DESTRUCTIVE OF THE TRUE ARTIST AS IT IS FALSE BY ALL   601D PUB ADDRESS/N   PROSE
            EXPERIENCE
        A MACHINE IS NOT A MAN NOR A WORK OF ART IT IS DESTRUCTIVE   603B PUB ADDR AD/N   PROSE
        AND SNOWY CLOUD BROODER OF TEMPESTS & DESTRUCTIVE WAR   . .   738 JERUSALEM 91   24
DETAIL
        A FOLLY SINGULAR & PARTICULAR DETAIL IS . . . . . .   459A ANNO REYNOLDS   MARG
DETAIN
        LET US DETAIN THEE WHILE I MAKE READY A KID THAT   40B SAMSON/PS   PROSE
            THOU MAYEST
DETECTED
        THE COMPARISON IS EASILY MADE & THE COPY DETECTED   . . .   598A PUB ADDRESS/N   PROSE
DETERMINATE
        THEY ARE ALL FIRM DETERMINATE OUTLINE OR IDENTICAL FORM   439C REMARKS MALKIN   PROSE
        OF ST PAUL PREACHING IS A FIRM DETERMINATE OUTLINE . .   439C REMARKS MALKIN   PROSE
        DETERMINATE ALL HIS EFFORTS PROVE THIS LITTLE BOY TO HAVE   439C REMARKS MALKIN   PROSE
            HAD
        A CLEAR IDEA AND A DETERMINATE VISION OF THINGS IN HIS   439D REMARKS MALKIN   PROSE
            OWN MIND
        UNLESS THEY ARE BORN WITH DETERMINATE ORGANS . . . . .   447C ANNO REYNOLDS   MARG
        I E THE MOST MINUTELY DISCRIMINATING & DETERMINATE . . .   453D ANNO REYNOLDS   * MARG
        IN ART & THAT EVERY THING IN ART IS DEFINITE & DETERMINATE   457B ANNO REYNOLDS   MARG
        BECAUSE VISION IS DETERMINATE & PERFECT & HE COPIES THAT   457B ANNO REYNOLDS   MARG
        WITHOUT FATIGUE EVERY THING BEING DEFINITE & DETERMINATE   457B ANNO REYNOLDS   MARG
        HERE HE IS FOR DETERMINATE & YET FOR INDETERMINATE . .   461A ANNO REYNOLDS   MARG
        FOR THE VARIOUS CLASSES OF MEN ARE ALL MARKD OUT   512 MILTON 26   37
            DETERMINATE
        SO THEY ARE BORN ON EARTH & EVERY CLASS IS DETERMINATE . .   512 MILTON 26   39
        AND FIRM AND DETERMINATE LINEAMENTS UNBROKEN BY SHADOWS   564D DESC CAT 1   PROSE
        WITHOUT FIRM AND DETERMINATE OUTLINE FRESCO PAINTING IS   585A DESC CAT 15   PROSE
        THIS ALONE THE WANT OF THIS DETERMINATE AND BOUNDING FORM   585B DESC CAT 15   PROSE
        BUT THE DEFINITE AND DETERMINATE WHAT IS IT THAT . . .   585C DESC CAT 15   PROSE
        A FIRM & DETERMINATE CONDUCT ON THE PART OF ARTISTS . .   600B PUB ADDRESS/N   PROSE
        THE INFINITE ALONE RESIDES IN DEFINITE & DETERMINATE   687 JERUSALEM 55   64
            IDENTITY
DETERMINATELY
        IF THEY ARE NOT DETERMINATELY WRONG THEY MUST BE RIGHT . .   386B ANNO WATSON   MARG
DETERMINATION
        [?THEY EXCELL BOTH IN MINUTE & DISCRIMINATING   453D ANNO REYNOLDS   * MARG
            DETERMINATION]
        BUT FOR A DETERMINATION WHICH WE HAVE LATELY MADE . . .   819C LETTER 25   PROSE
        TOO MUCH THE CAUSE OF OUR DETERMINATION TO LEAVE FELPHAM   819D LETTER 25   PROSE
        OWING TO MY DETERMINATION OF SENDING YOU PROOFS I HAVE NOT   838B LETTER 37   PROSE
        THAT I PERCEIVE A DETERMINATION IN THE LONDON BOOKSELLERS   846C LETTER 44   PROSE
        DETERMINATION TO DO EVERY THING TO ENGAGE HIMSELF TO YOU   857A LETTER 54   PROSE
DETERMINATIONS
        OPINIONS AND DETERMINATIONS ON ART VERY NECESSARY TO BE   562B DESC CAT ADV   PROSE
            KNOWN
DETERMIND
        . . . [& ALL MY KINGLY POWER] BUT HEAR MY DETERMIND DECREE   292 FOUR ZOAS 3   19
        THIS WILL PRODUCE CERTAIN & DETERMIND FORMS ON THE PLATE   440B MEMORANDUM/N 2   PROSE
        DISTANT WHEN WE SHALL DO SO BEING DETERMIND NOT TO . . .   813C LETTER 22   PROSE
        DELIGHTFUL THEN I AM DETERMIND THAT MRS BUTTS SHALL HAVE   824B LETTER 27   PROSE
        MY OWN SELF WILL FOR I AM DETERMIND TO BE NO LONGER PESTERD   825C LETTER 27   PROSE
        & I AM DETERMIND TO MAKE IT SO AT LEAST . . . .   855D LETTER 53   PROSE
DETERMINE
        SURROUNDED WITH MASSES OF STONE IN ORDERD FORMS DETERMINE   727 JERUSALEM 83   10
            THEN
        WE DETERMINE THEREFORE TO BE HAPPY AND DO ALL THAT WE CAN   807A LETTER 17   PROSE
DETERMINED
        FULFILLED IN ME & IN FUTURE I AM THE DETERMINED ADVOCATE   804A LETTER 16   PROSE
        DETERMINED TO PAINT ANOTHER PORTRAIT OF YOU FROM LIFE IN MY   810B LETTER 20   PROSE
        IN HEAVEN IS CERTAIN & DETERMINED & TO THIS I HAVE LONG   812C LETTER 22   PROSE
        A LINE IN WHICH HE IS DETERMINED NEVER TO ENGAGE . . . .   831C LETTER 31   PROSE
        FOR WHICH I HAVE PROCURED A PUBLISHER & AM DETERMINED . .   865D LETTER 63   PROSE
DETEST
        PERCIEVE THAT I NOT ONLY DETEST FALSE ART BUT HAVE THE . .   866B LETTER 64   PROSE
DETESTABLE
        PERPETUALLY VEGETATING IN DETESTABLE BIRTHS . . . . .   348 FOUR ZOAS 8   289
        IS A DECEIT SO DETESTABLE THAT I WILL CAST THEE OUT . . .   361 FOUR ZOAS 9   * 155
        WHAT SUCH MEN CALL GREAT IS INDEED DETESTABLE . . . . .   407A ANNO BACON   MARG
        FOLLOW AFTER THE DETESTABLE GODS OF PRIAM IN POMP   . . .   495 MILTON 14   15
        TO THE DETESTABLE GODS OF PRIAM TO APOLLO AND AT THE ASYLUM   511 MILTON 25   49
        THIS EVEN HOGARTH'S WORKS PROVE A DETESTABLE FALSHOOD . .   595C PUB ADDRESS/N   PROSE
DETRACTION
        ("LAMENT TALENTS NOT MORE USEFUL") CONTEMPTIBLE FALSHOOD   384D ANNO WATSON   * MARG
            & DETRACTION
DEUS
        CONTEMNING THE DIVINE VISION & FRUITION WORSHIPING THE DEUS   741 JERUSALEM 93   23
DEUT(ERONOMY)
        IF THIS IS PROVED FALSE THE HISTORY IS FALSE DEUT   391C ANNO WATSON   MARG
            XXXI...BUT PERHAPS
DEVASTATION
        IDLENESS & DEVASTATION OF THE THINGS OF THE SPIRIT   . . .   717B JERUSALEM 77   PROSE
DEVIATE
        LOS CRIES OBEY MY VOICE & NEVER DEVIATE FROM MY WILL   . .   629 JERUSALEM 10   29
DEVIATED
        OFTEN DEVIATED FROM THE HABITS TO PRESERVE THE MANNERS . .   583D DESC CAT 10   PROSE

	PAGE	TITLE	LINE

DEVIATES

LIMBS THAT DEVIATES OR ALTERS LEAST FROM INFANCY TO OLD AGE — 580A DESC CAT 5 — PROSE

DEVIL

BE QUIET WHAT THE DEVIL SHOULD THE PEOPLE IN THE HOSPITAL — 50A ISLAND MOON 6 — PROSE
FOR MY ENEMY IS NOT MAN BUT BEAST AND DEVIL IF I HAVE ANY — 72B ANNO LAVATER — * MARG
THERE IS NO OTHER DEVIL HE WHO BITES WITHOUT PRAYING IS — 73D ANNO LAVATER — MARG
  ONLY A BEAST
("THE JEALOUS IS POSSESSED BY A "FINE MAD DEVIL"") — 75B ANNO LAVATER — MARG
  SHAKSPEARE
THE VOICE OF THE DEVIL . . . . — 149C MARRIAGE HH 4 — TITLE
OR POSSESSOR OF THE COMMAND OF THE HEAVENLY HOST IS CALLD — 150A MARRIAGE HH 5 — PROSE
  THE DEVIL
BEING NO OTHER THAN [THE DEVIL] HE WHO DWELLS IN FLAMING — 150B MARRIAGE HH 5 — *PROSE
  FIRE
I SAW A MIGHTY DEVIL FOLDED IN BLACK CLOUDS . . . . — 150C MARRIAGE HH 6 — PROSE
ONCE I SAW A DEVIL IN A FLAME OF FIRE . . . . . . — 158B MARRIAGE HH 22 — PROSE
AND THE DEVIL UTTERED THESE WORDS . . . . — 158B MARRIAGE HH 22 — PROSE
THE DEVIL ANSWERD BRAY A FOOL IN A MORTER WITH WHEAT . — 158C MARRIAGE HH 22 — PROSE
NOTE THIS ANGEL WHO IS NOW BECOME A DEVIL . . . . . — 158D MARRIAGE HH 22 — PROSE
I HEARD A DEVIL CURSE . . . . — 164 HEARD ANGEL/N — 9
WOULD HAVE NO MORE QUARREL WITH THE DEVIL OR THE BARREL — 180 LIT VAGABOND/N — 16
WOULD HAVE NO MORE QUARREL WITH THE DEVIL OR THE BARREL — 216 LIT VAGABND/SE — 15
PAINE IS EITHER A DEVIL OR AN INSPIRED MAN . . . . . — 386B ANNO WATSON — MARG
GOOD ADVICE FOR THE DEVIL . . . . — 402D ANNO BACON — MARG
("MIND") THE DEVIL IS THE MIND OF THE NATURAL FRAME . — 403B ANNO BACON — MARG
BACON WAS ALWAYS A POOR DEVIL IF HISTORY SAYS TRUE . . — 409A ANNO BACON — * MARG
IS THE DEVIL GREAT CONSIDER . . . . — 410D ANNO BACON — MARG
[YOUNG] LONG JOHN BROWN HAD THE DEVIL IN HIS GUT . . . — 434 LONG JOHN BRWN — 2
AND THE FAIRY DREW THE DEVIL INTO THE NUT-SHELL . . . — 434 LONG JOHN BRWN — 4
HE LAUGHD AT THE DEVIL SAYING LOVE IS A SIN . . . . — 434 LONG JOHN BRWN — 6
THE DEVIL HE RAGED & THE DEVIL HE WAS WROTH . . . . — 434 LONG JOHN BRWN — 7
AND THE DEVIL ENTERD INTO THE YOUNG MAN'S BROTH . . . — 434 LONG JOHN BRWN — 8
SOME SAID HE HAD THE DEVIL & THEY GUESSD RIGHT . . . — 434 LONG JOHN BRWN — 14
AND HE LAUGHD AT THE DEVIL TILL POOR JOHN BROWN DIED . — 434 LONG JOHN BRWN — 16
FOR THE DEVIL CREPT IN WHEN THE FAIRY SKIPD OUT . . . — 434 LONG JOHN BRWN — 19
MUST BE A POOR DEVIL . . . . — 451A ANNO REYNOLDS — MARG
("FRESNOY PRINCIPAL FIGURE IN THE MIDST ") WHAT A DEVIL — 478B ANNO REYNOLDS — MARG
  OF A RULE
AND THE DEVIL IS A BLACK OUTLINE ALL OF US KNOW . . . — 554 TO VENETIAN/N — 2
MAY BE GIFTS FROM THE DEVIL & EARTHLY KINGS . . . . — 557 SINCE RICHES/N — 2
I SHOULD SUSPECT THAT I WORSHIPD THE DEVIL . . . . . — 557 SINCE RICHES/N — 3
BE ASSURD MR DEVIL I WON'T PRAY TO YOU . . . . . . — 559 I ROSE UP AT/N — 20
YOU MUST DO MR DEVIL JUST AS GOD PLEASE . . . . . . — 559 I ROSE UP AT/N — 28
HIS COMPANION THE SOMPNOUR IS ALSO A DEVIL . . . . . — 570A DESC CAT 3 — PROSE
SOCIETY ARE PERHAPS EQUAL OF THE DEVIL AND OF THE ANGEL — 570B DESC CAT 3 — PROSE
HE HAD ONLY TO SAY THAT GOD WAS THE DEVIL . . . . . — 752 EV GOSPEL(D)/N — 35
AND THE DEVIL WAS GOD LIKE A CHRISTIAN CIVIL . . . . — 752 EV GOSPEL(D)/N — 36
MILD CHRISTIAN REGRETS TO THE DEVIL CONFESS . . . . — 752 EV GOSPEL(D)/N — 37
A [GOD] DEVIL OR ELSE A PHARISEE . . . . — 754 EV GOSPEL(E)/N — 28
WHERE THE DEVIL COMBS HIS LICE . . . . — 757 EV GOSPEL(I)/N — 26
IT MUST HAVE BEEN ORIGINALLY FORMED BY THE DEVIL HIMSELF — 785C ILLS DANTE 101 — PROSE
SAYING THE LORD'S PRAYER BACKWARDS WHICH THEY SAY RAISES — 788C ANNO THORNTON — MARG
  THE DEVIL
NOW FOR IT WILL HANG HEAVY ON MY DEVIL WHO TERRIBLY RESENTS — 830C LETTER 30 — PROSE
I SOOTHE HIM TO PEACE & INDEED HE IS A GOOD NATURD DEVIL — 830C LETTER 30 — PROSE
OF RESENTMENT AGAINST MAN AND DEVIL AND OF HUMILIATION — 864B LETTER 61 — PROSE
  BEFORE GOD

DEVILISH

BY DEVILISH ARTS ABOMINABLE UNLAWFUL UNUTTERABLE . . . . — 348 FOUR ZOAS 8 — 288
IF THIS IS TRUE IT IS A DEVILISH FOOLISH THING TO BE AN — 476D ANNO REYNOLDS — MARG
  ARTIST

DEVIL'S

BUT THE DEVIL'S ACCOUNT IS THAT THE MESSIAH FELL . . . — 150A MARRIAGE HH 5 — PROSE
A TRUE POET AND OF THE DEVIL'S PARTY WITHOUT KNOWING IT — 150B MARRIAGE HH 5 — PROSE
THE DEVIL'S ARSE A KING . . . . — 400D ANNO BACON — MARG
THE GODDESS FORTUNE IS THE DEVIL'S SERVANT . . . . . — 785C ILLUS DANTE 16 — PROSE

DEVILS

HOW I WILL WORK THOSE POOR MILKSOP DEVILS . . . . . — 52A ISLAND MOON 7 — PROSE
BUT THEIR NASTY HEARTS POOR DEVILS ARE EAT UP WITH ENVY — 62D ISLAND MOON 11 — PROSE
("PLACE FORESEEN ...TIME PROVIDED") DEVILS & ANGELS ARE — 132B ANNO SWED PROV — MARG
  PREDESTINATED
AND AT LIBERTY WHEN OF DEVILS & HELL IS BECAUSE HE WAS . — 150B MARRIAGE HH 5 — PROSE
THESE ARE DEVILS AND ARE CALLED POWERS OF THE AIR . . — 156B MARRIAGE HH 17 — PROSE
ARE ALL RELIGIOUS & CONVERSED NOT WITH DEVILS WHO ALL — 157D MARRIAGE HH 21 — PROSE
  HATE RELIGION
AND ALL THE DEVILS THAT WERE IN HELL . . . . — 187 WHEN KLOPSTK/N — 13
THEY HEAL THE SICK HE CASTS OUT DEVILS . . . . . . — 545 COSWAY FRAZR/N — 4
EVEN THE DEVILS LOVE ONE ANOTHER IN THEIR WAY . . . . — 616B V LAST JUDG/N — PROSE
THE BIBLE NEVER TELLS US THAT DEVILS TORMENT ONE ANOTHER — 616B V LAST JUDG/N — PROSE
  THRO ENVY
IT IS NOT BECAUSE ANGELS ARE HOLIER THAN MEN OR DEVILS . — 616D V LAST JUDG/N — PROSE
ANGELS ARE HAPPIER THAN MEN & DEVILS BECAUSE . . . . — 616D V LAST JUDG/N — PROSE
O I HAVE UTTERLY BEEN WASTED I HAVE GIVEN MY DAUGHTERS — 670 JERUSALEM 42 — 16
  TO DEVILS
DEVILS ARE FALSE RELIGIONS . . . . — 716C JERUSALEM 77 — PROSE
GO THEREFORE CAST OUT DEVILS IN CHRIST'S NAME . . . . — 718 STOOD AMONG/J — 24
THE SEVEN DEVILS THAT TORMENT THEE . . . . — 754 EV GOSPEL(E)/N — 44
WHEN FIRST I LET THESE DEVILS IN . . . . — 755 EV GOSPEL(E)/N — 70
WITH SEVEN DEVILS IN HER PEN . . . . — 756 EV GOSPEL(I)/N — 6
AND MORE SUCKING DEVILS NURST . . . . — 756 EV GOSPEL(I)/N — 8
HE TURND THE DEVILS INTO SWINE . . . . — 757 EV GOSPEL(I)/N — 27
ALL GENIUS VARIES THUS DEVILS ARE VARIOUS ANGELS ARE ALL — 773A NOTE NINE HEAD — PROSE
  ALIKE

	PAGE	TITLE	LINE

DEVILS   (CONTINUED)
    AND LITTLE DEVILS WHO FIGHT FOR THEMSELVES . . . . . .   816 HAPPINESS/L   6
    ALL THE DEVILS IN HELL WILL NEVER DO I MUST OWN THAT SEEING   819C LETTER 25   PROSE
    BUT I WAS A SLAVE BOUND IN A MILL AMONG BEASTS AND DEVILS   852A LETTER 50   PROSE
    THESE BEASTS AND THESE DEVILS ARE NOW TOGETHER WITH MYSELF   852A LETTER 50   PROSE
    THE FIGHTING DEVILS READY FOR THE COPPER I COUNT MYSELF   879C LETTER 89   PROSE
DEVON
    DAN CORNWAL DEVON DORSET NAPTHALI WARWICK LEICESTER   637 JERUSALEM 16   46
        WORCESTER
    HYLE DWELT IN WINCHESTER COMPREHENDING HANTS DORSET DEVON   710 JERUSALEM 71   20
        CORNWALL
    SUSSEX SHUTS UP HER VILLAGES HANTS DEVON & WILTS . . . .   727 JERUSALEM 83   9
DEVOTE
    CAN YOU HAVE GREATER MIRACLES THAN THESE MEN WHO DEVOTE   506 MILTON 23   1
    HEARTILY DEVOTE HIMSELF TO THE BUSINESS IN ALL ITS   845C LETTER 44   PROSE
        LABORIOUS
DEVOTED
    HE MAY BE DEVOTED TO DESTRUCTION FROM HIS MOTHER'S WOMB   272 FOUR ZOAS 1   298
    TO LOVE DEVOTED FEMALE ALL ASTONISHD STOOD THE HOSTS   . .   380 FOUR ZOAS AD 1   13
    [AN UNABATED STUDY & PRACTISE OF FORTY YEARS FOR I DEVOTED]   591C PUB ADDRESS/N   PROSE
    BOWING THEIR HEADS DEVOTED AND THE FURNACES OF LOS . . . .   676 JERUSALEM 46   20
    ACCEPT MINE ALSO & BELIEVE ME TO REMAIN YOUR DEVOTED   . .   808C LETTER 19   PROSE
    YOUR GENEROUS & TENDER SOLICITUDE ABOUT YOUR DEVOTED REBEL   829C LETTER 30   PROSE
    AND REMAIN DEAR SIR YOUR SINCERE AND DEVOTED SERVANTS . .   832A LETTER 31   PROSE
    HIS & YOUR MILD & HAPPY TEMPERS OF SOUL YOUR DEVOTED   . .   835B LETTER 34   PROSE
    PLACE IN HIM I AM DEAR SIR YOUR ANXIOUSLY DEVOTED   . . .   842A LETTER 41   PROSE
    BE DEVOTED TO DESIGNING & PAINTING [ALONE] WHEN I HAVE GOT   866A LETTER 63   PROSE
DEVOTES
    AND WILT THOU SLAY WITH DEATH HIM WHO DEVOTES HIMSELF TO   271 FOUR ZOAS 1   275
        THEE
DEVOTING   SEE SELF-DEVOTING
    WINCHESTER STOOD DEVOTING HIMSELF FOR ALBION HIS TENTS . .   668 JERUSALEM 40   53
DEVOTION
    THE CIELINGS DEVOTION THE HEARTHS THANKSGIVING   . . . .   632 JERUSALEM 12   37
DEVOUR
    NOW THAT THE CURSE SHALL CLEAN DEVOUR ALL THOSE GUILTY SONS   107 TIRIEL 6   4
    OF ETERNITY WHERE THE ETERNAL LION AND EAGLE REMAIN TO   138 FRENCH REVOLTN   97
        DEVOUR
    . . . LET THE BASTILE DEVOUR   141 FRENCH REVOLTN   156
    DEVOUR THY LABOUR NOR LIFT UP A CLOUD IN THY HEAVENS . . .   144 FRENCH REVOLTN   226
    STANDS AT THE GATE OF ENITHARMON TO DEVOUR HER CHILDREN   198 AMERICA 7   4
    LOS WITH AMBITIOUS FURY THAT HIS RACE SHALL ALL DEVOUR . .   323 FOUR ZOAS 7   134
    TO DEVOUR ALBION AND JERUSALEM THE EMANATION OF ALBION . .   493 MILTON 12   27
    HOWLING IN HIS SPECTRE ROUND HIS BODY HUNGRING TO DEVOUR   531 MILTON 39   18
    HIS TORMENT IS UNENDURABLE THEREFORE HE CANNOT DEVOUR . .   531 MILTON 39   20
    AND TO DEVOUR THE SLEEPING HUMANITY OF ALBION IN RAGE &   623 JERUSALEM 5   30
        HUNGER
    TO DEVOUR LOS'S HUMAN PERFECTION BUT WHEN HE SAW THAT LOS   625 JERUSALEM 6   *   14
    OF GOD TO DESTROY JERUSALEM & TO DEVOUR THE BODY OF ALBION   628 JERUSALEM 9   10
    THAT WHENEVER ANY SPECTRE BEGAN TO DEVOUR THE DEAD   . . .   630 JERUSALEM 11   6
    BE LOST & LEST HE SHOULD DEVOUR ENITHARMON AH ME . . . .   638 JERUSALEM 17   18
    THOSE WHO DEVOUR HIS SOUL ARE TAKEN INTO HIS BOSOM   . . .   667 JERUSALEM 40   16
    PLOTTING TO DEVOUR ALBION'S BODY OF HUMANITY & LOVE   . . .   708 JERUSALEM 70   9
    TO DEVOUR THE BODY OF ALBION HUNGRING & THIRSTING & RAVNING   714 JERUSALEM 73   48
    OVER THE TOMB & OVER THE BODY RAVNING TO DEVOUR   . . . .   718 JERUSALEM 78   2
    TO DEVOUR THE HUMAN WHY DOST THOU WEEP UPON THE WIND AMONG   721 JERUSALEM 79   72
    PLOTTING TO DEVOUR ALBION & LOS THE FRIEND OF ALBION   . .   737 JERUSALEM 90   63
DEVOURD
    AND WITH A GRINNING ASPECT FIRST COUPLED WITH & THEN   157B MARRIAGE HH 17   PROSE
        DEVOURD
    WITH SEEMING FONDNESS THEY DEVOURD TOO . . . .   157B MARRIAGE HH 17   PROSE
    SCALED & FINND WITH IRON & BRASS THEY DEVOURD THE PATH   313 FOUR ZOAS 6   76
        BEFORE HIM
    KNEADED IN OVETH'S KNEADING TROUGH STILL ORC DEVOURD THE   343 FOUR ZOAS 8   *   77
        FOOD
    SOON HAND MIGHTILY DEVOURD & ABSORBD ALBION'S TWELVE SONS   641 JERUSALEM 18   39
    SELSEY TRUE FRIEND WHO AFTERWARDS SUBMITTED TO BE DEVOURD   667 JERUSALEM 40   48
    CREATION AND DEVOURD ALL THINGS IN ITS LOUD   . . . . .   717 STOOD AMONG/J   5
    IN THREE NIGHTS HE DEVOURD THE REJECTED CORSE OF DEATH . .   734 JERUSALEM 89   13
    IN THREE NIGHTS HE DEVOURD HIS PREY   . . . .   755 EV GOSPEL(E)/N   93
DEVOURED
    DEVOURING & DEVOURED ROAMING ON DARK AND DESOLATE MOUNTAINS   238 EUROPE PREL 2   5
DEVOURER
    TO THE DEVOURER IT SEEMS AS IF THE PRODUCER WAS IN HIS   155B MARRIAGE HH 15   PROSE
        CHAINS
    THE DEVOURER AS A SEA RECIEVED THE EXCESS OF HIS DELIGHTS   155B MARRIAGE HH 15   PROSE
    DEVOURER OF THY PARENT NOW THY UNUTTERABLE TORMENT RENEWS   199 AMERICA 9   20
    A SELF CONSUMING DARK DEVOURER RISING INTO THE HEAVENS   .   324 FOUR ZOAS 7   156
DEVOURING   SEE ALL DEVOURING,EVER DEVOURING,SELF-DEVOURING
    INFEST OUR ENGLISH SEAS DEVOURING ALL   . . . .   20 EDW THIRD/PS 2   67
    ARE CRUEL AS DEATH & AS OBDURATE AS THE DEVOURING PIT   .   99 TIRIEL 1   15
    THUS ONE PORTION OF BEING IS THE PROLIFIC THE OTHER THE   155B MARRIAGE HH 15   PROSE
        DEVOURING
    TO THE JAWS OF DEVOURING DARKNESS . . . .   236 URIZEN 28   3
    AND BRING FORTH HOWLING TERRORS ALL DEVOURING FIERY KINGS   238 EUROPE PREL 2   4
    DEVOURING & DEVOURED ROAMING ON DARK AND DESOLATE MOUNTAINS   238 EUROPE PREL 2   5
    TO A DEVOURING FLAME AND MAN FLED FROM ITS FACE AND HID   241 EUROPE 10   17
    BY GRATIFIED DESIRE BY STRONG DEVOURING APPETITE SHE FILLS   323 FOUR ZOAS 7   133
    . . . THAT I AM THUS A RAVENING DEVOURING LUST CONTINUALLY   327 FOUR ZOAS 7   305
    CRAVING & DEVOURING BUT MY EYES ARE ALWAYS UPON THEE O   327 FOUR ZOAS 7   306
        LOVELY
    THAT LIFE LIVES UPON DEATH & BY DEVOURING APPETITE   . . .   330 FOUR ZOAS 7   390

495

```
                                                             PAGE      TITLE          LINE
DEVOURING    (CONTINUED)
      BUT FINDS THE POOLS FILLED WITH SERPENTS DEVOURING ONE     354 FOUR ZOAS 8       530
         ANOTHER
      BUT ANIMATED AND VEGETATED SHE IS A DEVOURING WORM  . . .  631 JERUSALEM 12        3
      THARMAS THE VEGETATED TONGUE EVEN THE DEVOURING TONGUE  . .634 JERUSALEM 14        4
      WHO BECOMES HIS FOOD SUCH IS THE WAY OF THE DEVOURING POWER 659 JERUSALEM 33       24
      AT ENMITY WITH THE MERCIFUL & FILLD WITH DEVOURING FIRE     667 JERUSALEM 40       33
      LIVE BY DEVOURING GOING INTO ETERNAL DEATH CONTINUALLY  . . 681 JERUSALEM 50        7
      A WORLD OF SHAPES IN CRAVING LUST & DEVOURING APPETITE  . . 685 JERUSALEM 54       24
      TILL SHE VEGETATED INTO A HUNGRY STOMACH & A DEVOURING      698 JERUSALEM 64        8
         TONGUE
      DEVOURING JERUSALEM FROM EVERY NATION OF THE EARTH   . . .  707 JERUSALEM 69        5
      THIS TERRIBLE DEVOURING SWORD TURNING EVERY WAY   . . . .   718 STOOD AMONG/J      15
      BUT IN THE MIDST OF A DEVOURING STOMACH JERUSALEM    . . .  735 JERUSALEM 89       43
      SHOULD GROW A DEVOURING WINDING SHEET    . . . . . . .      771 OF GATES/GP        24
DEVOURS
      FEAST ON HIS DEATH TILL UNIVERSAL DEATH DEVOURS ALL     . . 354 FOUR ZOAS 8       528
      AND STILL HE DEVOURS THE BODY OF CLAY  . . . . . . .        755 EV GOSPEL(E)/N     94
DEVOUT
      DEVOUT AND PAID RESPECT TO TRUE ENTHUSIASTIC SUPERSTITION   575A DESC CAT 3       PROSE
      OR AMAZEMENT OR DEVOUT WONDER AND UNRESISTING AWE    . . .  580C DESC CAT 5       PROSE
DEW
      BLUE CURTAINS OF THE SKY SCATTER THY SILVER DEW     . . .     3 EVNING STAR/PS      6
      THY SACRED DEW PROTECT THEM WITH THINE INFLUENCE  . . . .     3 EVNING STAR/PS     14
      THE HONIED DEW THAT COMETH ON WAKING DAY   . . . . . .        3 TO MORNING/PS       5
      RAIN FRESHNING DEW UPON HIS BRANCHES AND   . . . . . .       26 EDW THIRD/PS 3     215
      THE BOSOM OF THE LOFTY HILL DRANK IN THE SILENT DEW  . . .   36C COUCH DEATH/PS   PROSE
      AND THE CHILD WAS WET WITH DEW  . . . . . . . . . .          60 LIT BOY LST/IM      6
      THE CHILD WAS WET WITH DEW  . . . . . . . . . . .           121 LIT BOY LST/SI      6
      AND THUS HER GENTLE LAMENTATION FALLS LIKE MORNING DEW  .   127 BOOK OF THEL 1      5
      AND COURT THE FAIR EYED DEW TO TAKE ME TO HER SHINING TENT  128 BOOK OF THEL 3     13
      AND WEEPING IN THE EVENING DEW  . . . . . . . . .          210 INTRODUCTN/SE       7
      LIKE THE GAY FISHES ON THE WAVE WHEN THE COLD MOON DRINKS   243 EUROPE 14           3
         THE DEW
      WHERE IS THE YOUTHFUL ANTAMON PRINCE OF THE PEARLY DEW  . . 244 EUROPE 14          15
      FROM MY SOFT CLOUD OF DEW TO FALL  . . . . . . . .          254 AHANIA 5           13
      THE DEW OF ANXIOUS SOULS THE DEATH-SWEAT OF THE DYING   . . 281 FOUR ZOAS 2        47
      BE NOT PERSWADED THAT THE AIR KNOWS THIS OR THE FALLING DEW 339 FOUR ZOAS 7B      231
      COME FORTH O VALA FROM THE GRASS & FROM THE SILENT DEW  .   367 FOUR ZOAS 9       388
      . . . & HER HAIR GLISTENS WITH DEW  . . . . . . . .         367 FOUR ZOAS 9       392
      I MUST HAVE SLEPT ETERNALLY NOR HAVE FELT THE DEW OF THY    367 FOUR ZOAS 9       396
         MORNING
      OR I MUST HAVE SLEPT ETERNALLY NOR HAVE FELT THE DEW OF     367 FOUR ZOAS 9       403
         MORNING
      ETERNALLY THOU MUST HAVE SLEPT NOR HAVE FELT THE MORNING    367 FOUR ZOAS 9       404
         DEW
      THOU RISEST IN THE DEW OF MORNING & AT NIGHT ART FOLDED UP  367 FOUR ZOAS 9       409
      WHERE IS THE VOICE OF GOD THAT CALLD ME FROM THE SILENT DEW 370 FOUR ZOAS 9       500
      LIKE EVENING DEW ON EVERY HERB UPON THE BREATHING GROUND    669 JERUSALEM 42        8
      MOUNT ZION IS BECOME A CRUEL ROCK & NO MORE DEW   . . . .   719 JERUSALEM 79        4
      BUT WHEN HE TOUCHES THE FIRST FIBROUS THREAD LIKE FILMY DEW 739 JERUSALEM 92       10
DEWS
      WITH SWEET MAY DEWS MY WINGS WERE WET  . . . . . . .          6 HOW SWEET/PS        9
      AND THE DEWS OF NIGHT ARISE . . . . . . . . . .              60 NURSES SONG/IM      6
      AND THE DEWS OF NIGHT ARISE . . . . . . . . . .             121 NURSES SONG/SI      6
      COVERD WITH DEWS OF NIGHT . . . . . . . . . . .             147 FRENCH REVOLTN    297
      AND THE DEWS OF NIGHT ARISE . . . . . . . . . .             171 NURSES SONG/N       6
      WILT THOU BRING COMFORTS ON THY WINGS AND DEWS AND HONEY    192 V DAU ALBION 4     10
         AND BALM
      AND THE DEWS OF NIGHT ARISE . . . . . . . . . .             212 NURSES SONG/SE      6
      I NURTURD HER I FED HER WITH MY RAINS & DEWS SHE GREW  . .  282 FOUR ZOAS 2        84
      COLD DEWS & HOARY FROST CREEPS THO I LIE ON BANKS OF SUMMER 288 FOUR ZOAS 2     *  320
      AND SILENCE BUILD THEIR DAY IN SHADOW OF SOFT CLOUDS & DEWS 331 FOUR ZOAS 7       450
      RISE FROM THE DEWS OF DEATH FOR THE ETERNAL MAN IS RISEN    367 FOUR ZOAS 9       389
      FELL DOWN AS DEWS OF NIGHT & A LOUD SOLEMN UNIVERSAL GROAN  490 MILTON 9           37
DEWY
      O THOU WITH DEWY LOCKS WHO LOOKEST DOWN   . . . . . .         1 TO SPRING/PS        1
      FRESH FROM THE DEWY HILL THE MERRY YEAR  . . . . . . .        9 FRESH FROM/PS       1
      MY FEET ARE WINGD WHILE OER THE DEWY LAWN  . . . . . .        9 FRESH FROM/PS       5
      THEN THEL ASTONISHD VIEWD THE WORM UPON ITS DEWY BED   . .  129 BOOK OF THEL 4      1
      DOLOURS & LAMENTATIONS WAITING OFT BESIDE A DEWY GRAVE  . . 130 BOOK OF THEL 6      7
      NOW A NYMPH I DARE NOT PLUCK THEE FROM THY DEWY BED  . . .  189 V DAU ALBION 1      7
      ARISE FROM OUT THE DEWY GRASS  . . . . . . . . .            210 INTRODUCTN/SE      12
      [BRIGHT] DARK AS A DEWY MORNING WHEN THE CRIMSON LIGHT      271 FOUR ZOAS 1     *  253
         APPEARS
      WHY IS THE LIGHT OF [VALA] ENITHARMON DARKEND IN [HER]      271 FOUR ZOAS 1     *  268
         DEWY MORN
      SHE FELL COLD FROM LAMBETH'S VALES IN GROANS & DEWY DEATH   281 FOUR ZOAS 2        46
      WHY DOST THOU WEEP [?O] AS VALA & WET THY VEIL WITH DEWY    271 FOUR ZOAS 1     *  271
         TEARS
      [NOW] FOR LOS & ENITHARMON WALKD FORTH ON THE DEWY EARTH    288 FOUR ZOAS 2       295
      BUT THOU SHALT STILL SURVIVE ARISE O DRY THY DEWY TEARS     368 FOUR ZOAS 9       421
      AWAKE THARMAS AWAKE AWAKE THOU CHILD OF DEWY TEARS   . . .  371 FOUR ZOAS 9       521
      THE SUN ARISES FROM HIS DEWY BED & THE FRESH AIRS   . . .   379 FOUR ZOAS 9       846
      BENEATH THE VEIL OF [?ENION] VALA ROSE THARMAS FROM DEWY    380 FOUR ZOAS AD 1 *    1
         TEARS
      MELTED BY DEWY TEARS  . . . . . . . . . . . .              421 MORNING/N           8
      A DEWY GARMENT COVERS ME ALL OVER ALL MANHOOD IS GONE  . . 660 JERUSALEM 34        4
      IN A CLOUD THAT DEWY SWEETNESS DISTILLS  . . . . . . .      816 HAPPINESS/L         2
DEXTERITY
      OF DEXTERITY IN CERTAIN POINTS EMBOLDENS ME [TH ] TO HOPE   808A LETTER 19       *PROSE
         THAT
```

```
                                                      PAGE      TITLE        LINE
DEY
      BUT [YOU] DEY DO NOT DRAW DE [THE] DRAW  . . . . . .  594D PUB ADDRESS/N   PROSE
DHINAS-BRAN
      PENMAENMAWR & DHINAS-BRAN DEMONSTRATE IN UNBELIEF   . . .  644 JERUSALEM 21   35
DIABOLICAL
      READ THE BIBLE TOGETHER IN ITS INFERNAL OR DIABOLICAL SENSE 158D MARRIAGE HH 22  PROSE
DIAGRAM
      ("ARISTOTLE...HIS METAPHYSICS") GOD IS NOT A MATHEMATICAL  774D ANNO BERKELEY    MARG
         DIAGRAM
DIAGRAMS
      THE GODS OF GREECE & EGYPT WERE MATHEMATICAL DIAGRAMS  . . 776D INSC LAOCOON    PROSE
DIAL     SEE SUN DIAL
DIAMOND
      OR SHINING GLASS AND A WROUGHT DIAMOND SET IN RICH GOLD AND   29D EDW THIRD/PS 4  PROSE
      FROM A DIAMOND ITS HARDNESS FROM A SPUNGE ITS SOFTNESS    81C ANNO LAVATER   MARG
      WHILE THE POOR INDIGENT IS LIKE THE DIAMOND WHICH     515 MILTON 28       36
         THO CLOTHD
      & IN HIM SEES ALL REFLECTED AS IN A GLASS OF ETERNAL   610D V LAST JUDG/N   PROSE
         DIAMOND
      AND PEARL & DIAMOND THY DAUGHTERS SANG IN HER COURTS   . . 647 JERUSALEM 24    40
DIANA
      THE "VIEWS IN KEW GARDENS" "FOOTS CRAY" & "DIANA"     594A PUB ADDRESS/N   PROSE
         & "ACTEON"
DICK
      AT HOB-NAIL DICK WHO GRIEVD THE CHANCE  . . . . . . .   16 BLIND-MANS/PS    16
      THEN PAUSES ERE HE STARTS BUT DICK  . . . . . . . .   16 BLIND-MANS/PS    45
      POOR PITEOUS DICK SUPPORTS HIS HEAD  . . . . . . .   17 BLIND-MANS/PS    55
      THAT THOUSANDS OF SWEEPERS DICK JOE NED & JACK   . . . .  117 CHIMNEY SWP/SI   11
DICKINS
      I WOULD RUN LIKE THE DICKINS TILL I WAS ALL IN A HEAT   . .  48B ISLAND MOON 4   PROSE
DICTATE
      DICTATE SWIFT WINGED WORDS & FEAR NOT  . . . . . .  222 URIZEN 2         6
      LUVAH REPLIED DICTATE TO THY EQUALS AM NOT I  . . . . .  278 FOUR ZOAS 1    504
      HIS DICTATE AND HIS BODY WAS THE ROCK SINAI THAT BODY  . .  498 MILTON 17      14
      THE UNIVERSAL DICTATE AND YOU ALSO FEEL THIS DICTATE   . .  504 MILTON 21      53
      THE DICTATE WATCH OVER THIS WORLD AND WITH YOUR BROODING   504 MILTON 21      55
         WINGS
      DICTATE TO MY ETERNAL WILL & TO MY DICTATE BOW   . . . .  530 MILTON 38      53
      YOU MUST MY DICTATE OBEY FROM YOUR GOLD-BEAMD LOOMS TRILL   688 JERUSALEM 56    31
      YOUR DICTATE BUT WHEN I FOUND MY ATTEMPTS WERE IN VAIN  . .  792A LETTER 4     PROSE
      I HEAR HIS ADVICE & EVEN NOW WRITE FROM HIS DICTATE  . .  797B LETTER 9     PROSE
DICTATED
      MY FAIRY SAT UPON THE TABLE AND DICTATED EUROPE  . . . .  238 EUROPE INTRO     24
      I THINK (THAT) BARRY OR FUSELI WROTE IT OR [?SAID] DICTATED  463C ANNO REYNOLDS * MARG
         IT
      WHEN THIS VERSE WAS FIRST DICTATED TO ME I CONSIDERD   . .  621C JERUSALEM 3   PROSE
DICTATES
      ("CRIMINALS FOLLOW DICTATES OF CONSCIENCE") CONTEMPTIBLE   386B ANNO WATSON     MARG
      VIRTUE & HONESTY OR THE DICTATES OF CONSCIENCE ARE   . . .  386B ANNO WATSON     MARG
      GENEROUS KNIGHT IS IN THE COMPASSIONATE DICTATES OF HIS   569A DESC CAT 3     PROSE
         SOUL
      BUT IF WE FEAR TO DO THE DICTATES OF OUR ANGELS & TREMBLE  813A LETTER 22    PROSE
DICTATING
      SPREADING HIS BEAMS OF LOVE & DICTATING THE WORDS OF THIS  622 JERUSALEM 4     5
         MILD SONG
DICTATION
      FROM IMMEDIATE DICTATION TWELVE OR SOMETIMES TWENTY  . . .  823A LETTER 26    PROSE
DICTATOR
      A PROPHET IS A SEER NOT AN ARBITRARY DICTATOR  . . . . .  392B ANNO WATSON     MARG
DIDO
      AS ENEAS IS HERE SHEWN A WORSE MAN THAN ACHILLES IN LEAVING  412A ANNO BOYD      MARG
         DIDO
DIDST
      DIDST THOU NOT TELL ME WITH GREEN WITHS(WITHES) TO BIND THY   38D SAMSON/PS    PROSE
      I KNEW THOU DIDST BUT MOCK ME ALAS WHEN IN THY SLEEP   . .   39A SAMSON/PS    PROSE
      HOW DIDST THOU REND THE FEEBLE TIES THOU FEAREST NOUGHT    39A SAMSON/PS    PROSE
      THE PHILISTINES BE UPON THEE THEN DIDST THOU LEAVE ME   . .   39B SAMSON/PS    PROSE
      HOW DIDST THOU LOSE THY EYES OLD TIRIEL BLESS THY WRINKLED  101 TIRIEL 2       43
         FACE
      THOU LITTLE KID DIDST PLAY &C  . . . . . . . . . .  179 THE KID/N        1
      WITH CRUELTY DIDST MOULD MY HEART  . . . . . . . .  220 TO TIRZAH/SE     10
      DIDST BIND MY NOSTRILS EYES & EARS  . . . . . . . .  220 TO TIRZAH/SE     12
      DIDST CLOSE MY TONGUE IN SENSELESS CLAY  . . . . . .  220 TO TIRZAH/SE     13
      WHY DIDST THOU DESPISE AHANIA  . . . . . . . . .  254 AHANIA 4         62
      ENITHARMON ANSWERD WHEREFORE DIDST THOU THROW THINE ARMS   288 FOUR ZOAS 2    327
         AROUND
      WHY DIDST THOU LISTEN TO THE VOICE OF LUVAH THAT DREAD MORN  292 FOUR ZOAS 3     31
      WHEN THOU DIDST BEAR THE GOLDEN CUP AT THE IMMORTAL TABLES  311 FOUR ZOAS 5    228
      THEN THOU DIDST KEEP WITH STRONG URTHONA THE LIVING GATES  311 FOUR ZOAS 5    232
         OF HEAVEN
      THOU DIDST SUBDUE ME IN OLD TIMES BY THY IMMORTAL STRENGTH  328 FOUR ZOAS 7    349
      [WITHIN MY HEART THOU DIDST UNFOLD]  . . . . . . .  415 MY SPECTRE/N     16
      [THOU DIDST CALL THAT LOVE A SIN]  . . . . . . . .  415 MY SPECTRE/N     20
      [DIDST] DOST THOU NOT IN PRIDE & SCORN  . . . . . .  416 MY SPECTRE/N     31
      O DIVINE VISION WHO DIDST CREATE THE FEMALE TO REPOSE   . .  493 MILTON 12      49
      THE CROSS O ALBION WHY DIDST THOU A FEMALE WILL CREATE   . .  688 JERUSALEM 56    43
      THAT DIDST CREATE THIS BODY OF MINE  . . . . . . .  754 EV GOSPEL(E)/N    30
      [THOU] THO THOU DIDST ALL TO CHAOS ROLL  . . . . . .  754 EV GOSPEL(E)/N *  39
DIE
      AND THEN ID DIE IN PEACE AND BE FORGOT  . . . . . .   10 WHEN EARLY/PS     20
      BENEATH HIS ARM LIKE SHEEP THEY DIE  . . . . . . .   13 GWIN KING/PS     85
      'TWILL BE A GALLANT THING TO FIGHT OR DIE  . . . . .   25 EDW THIRD/PS 3   152
```

497

DIE   (CONTINUED)
    AND HE IS TO WRITE ANOTHER ABOUT ALL US THAT ARE TO DIE   29C EDW THIRD/PS 4   PROSE
    OVER THE MEN THAT ARE TO DIE TO-DAY . . . .   30 EDW THIRD/PS 5   2
    UPON THE CLOUDS OF HEAVEN TO DIE NO MORE . . . . . .   30 EDW THIRD/PS 5   16
    BUT O THE SOULS THAT ARE TO DIE TO-DAY . . . .   31 EDW THIRD/PS 5   48
    THE SUCKING INFANT LIVES TO DIE IN BATTLE . . . . . .   34B KING JOHN/PS   PROSE
    HAD I THREE LIVES ID DIE IN SUCH A CAUSE . . . . . .   35 WAR SONG/PS   13
    ERE LONG TO BLEED & DIE A SACRIFICE DONE BY A PRIESTLY HAND 418 THEN SHE BORE   PROSE
    DIE IF I WAS TO LIVE HERE SAID SCOPPRELL HO HO HO HO HO   54C ISLAND MOON 9   PROSE
    [BUT STILL HE FEARD THAT HAR & HEVA WOULD DIE OF JOY &   102 TIRIEL 3   8
        GRIEF]
    TO BEAR ME FURTHER URGE ME NOT LEST I SHOULD DIE   104 TIRIEL 4   33
        WITH TRAVEL
    OR IF I DIE   . . . .   183 THE FLY/N   24
    THAT LIVE A PESTILENCE & DIE A METEOR & ARE NO MORE . . .   193 V DAU ALBION 5   29
    OR IF I DIE   . . . .   213 THE FLY/SE   20
    WHY WILL YOU DIE O ETERNALS . . . .   224 URIZEN 4   12
    DELIGHT THEY DIE & THEY REVIVE IN SPRING WITH MUSIC & SONGS 266 FOUR ZOAS 1   67
    ENION SAID FAREWELL I DIE I HIDE FROM THY SEARCHING EYES   266 FOUR ZOAS 1   68
    I DIE NOT ENITHARMON [THOU] THO THOU SINGST THY SONG OF   272 FOUR ZOAS 1   * 283
        DEATH
    THEY HAVE SURROUNDED ME WITH WALLS OF IRON & BRASS [I ?DIE] 282 FOUR ZOAS 2   *   99
        O LAMB
    IF THOU WITHDRAW THY BREATH I DIE & VANISH INTO HADES . . 293 FOUR ZOAS 3   61
    RENT FROM ETERNAL BROTHERHOOD WE DIE & ARE NO MORE . . .   293 FOUR ZOAS 3   76
    SAYING GO & DIE THE DEATH OF MAN FOR VALA THE SWEET   294 FOUR ZOAS 3   85
        WANDERER
    CAN DIE WHEN DARK DESPAIR COMES OVER CAN I NOT . . . .   298 FOUR ZOAS 4   22
    AND WHEN HIS CHILDREN SICKEN LET THEM DIE THERE ARE ENOUGH 323 FOUR ZOAS 7   120
    SHUT UP IN LITTLE PURPLE COVERING FAINTLY BUD & DIE . .   325 FOUR ZOAS 7   191
    THE FRUIT & GIVE ME PROOF OF LIFE ETERNAL OR I DIE . . .   330 FOUR ZOAS 7   394
    TO DIE A DEATH OF SIX THOUSAND YEARS BOUND ROUND   337 FOUR ZOAS 7B   168
        WITH DESOLATION
    LUCIFER REFUSD TO DIE FOR SATAN IN PRIDE HE FORSOOK HIS   351 FOUR ZOAS 8   399
        CHARGE
    TO DIE FOR SATAN ADAM REFUSD BUT WAS COMPELLD TO DIE   351 FOUR ZOAS 8   402
    AND THE PALE HORSE SEEKS FOR THE POOL TO LIE HIM DOWN & DIE 354 FOUR ZOAS 8   529
    THE SPECTRE QUITE AWAY FROM ENION THAT I DIE A DEATH . .   355 FOUR ZOAS 8   546
    MY BIRDS ARE SILENT ON MY HILLS FLOCKS DIE BENEATH   359 FOUR ZOAS 9   101
        MY BRANCHES
    I DIE I DIE THE MOTHER SAID . . . .   419 I SAW A MONK/N   19
    MY CHILDREN WILL DIE FOR LACK OF BREAD . . . .   419 I SAW A MONK/N   20
    I DIE I DIE THE MOTHER SAID . . . .   430 GREY MONK   1
    MY CHILDREN DIE FOR LACK OF BREAD . . . .   430 GREY MONK   2
    AND I WONDER IF WILLIAM BOND WILL DIE . . . .   434 WILLIAM BOND   3
    BUT LOS HID THULLOH FROM HER SIGHT LEST SHE SHOULD DIE   488 MILTON 8   41
        OF GRIEF
    AND ONE MUST DIE FOR ANOTHER THROUGHOUT ALL ETERNITY . .   491 MILTON 11   18
    BUT LUCIFER REFUSD TO DIE & IN PRIDE HE FORSOOK HIS CHARGE 494 MILTON 13   18
    YOU CANNOT GO TO ETERNAL DEATH IN THAT WHICH CAN NEVER DIE 521 MILTON 32   24
    WHEN HE IS DOOMD TO DIE . . . .   542 PITIFUL CASE/N   2
    SO REYNOLDS WHEN HE CAME TO DIE . . . .   542 PITIFUL CASE/N   5
    THEY KNOW NOT WHY THEY LOVE NOR WHEREFORE THEY SICKEN & DIE 639 JERUSALEM 17   29
    HIS BIRDS ARE SILENT ON HIS HILLS FLOCKS DIE BENEATH HIS   641 JERUSALEM 19   2
        BRANCHES
    I SEE THEM DIE BENEATH THE WHIPS OF THE CAPTAINS THEY ARE 644 JERUSALEM 21   42
        TAKEN
    I DIE I DIE IN THY ARMS THO HOPE IS BANISHD FROM ME . .   648 JERUSALEM 24   60
    BY HIS OWN LAW SHALL SURELY DIE . . . .   652 FIELDS FROM/J   84
    IF THOU WITHDRAW THY BREATH I DIE & VANISH INTO HADES . . 654 JERUSALEM 29   48
    SAYING GO AND DIE THE DEATH OF MAN FOR VALA THE SWEET   655 JERUSALEM 29   66
        WANDERER
    OF MULTITUDES WHO DIE FROM EARTH THIS GATE CANNOT BE FOUND 665 JERUSALEM 38   59
    I DIE I GO TO ETERNAL DEATH THE SHADES OF DEATH . . . .   666 JERUSALEM 39   16
    MUST THE WISE DIE FOR AN ATONEMENT DOES MERCY ENDURE   666 JERUSALEM 39   25
        ATONEMENT
    WHERE FRIENDS DIE FOR EACH OTHER WILL BECOME THE PLACE . . 678 JERUSALEM 48   56
    THY VILLAGES DIE OF THE FAMINE AND THY CITIES . . . . .   693 JERUSALEM 60   27
    I DIE & PASS THE LIMITS OF POSSIBILITY AS IT APPEARS . .   696 JERUSALEM 62   19
    TO DIE A DEATH OF SIX THOUSAND YEARS BOUND ROUND   699 JERUSALEM 65   10
        WITH VEGETATION
    . . . THAT ONE SHOULD DIE A DEATH NEVER TO BE REVIVD . .   722 JERUSALEM 80   24
    BEHOLD HIM HERE WE SHALL NOT DIE WE SHALL BE UNITED IN   741 JERUSALEM 93   19
        JESUS
    JESUS REPLIED FEAR NOT ALBION UNLESS I DIE THOU CANST NOT 743 JERUSALEM 96   14
        LIVE
    BUT IF I DIE I SHALL ARISE AGAIN & THOU WITH ME . . . .   743 JERUSALEM 96   15
    FOR THEE OR EVER DIE FOR ONE WHO HAD NOT DIED FOR THEE . . 743 JERUSALEM 96   24
    HE DID NOT DIE WITH CHRISTIAN EASE . . . .   751 EV GOSPEL(D)/N   31
    AND CANST THOU DIE THAT I MAY LIVE . . . .   755 EV GOSPEL(E)/N   79
    THE IMMORTAL MAN THAT CANNOT DIE . . . .   771 OF GATES/GP   40
    JEHOVAH HE WHO SHALL TAKE CAIN'S LIFE MUST ALSO DIE O ABEL 780 GHOST ABEL 1   15
    ABEL IS DEAD & CAIN SLEW HIM WE SHALL ALSO DIE A DEATH . . 780 GHOST ABEL 1   19
    HE MUST DIE WITHOUT ENCOURAGEMENT MY PICTURES ARE . . . 815B LETTER 23   PROSE
    KING WILL LIVE TO FULFIL THE PROPHECY AND DIE IN PEACE . . 844D LETTER 43   PROSE
    IN THE MOMENT OF HIS AGONY BUT WOULD RATHER RETIRE AND DIE 864B LETTER 61   PROSE
    SOON GET ABOUT AGAIN GREAT MEN DIE EQUALLY WITH THE LITTLE 868D LETTER 68   PROSE
DIED
    & WHAT WAS THAT THAT HE TOOK [XXX] FISSIC OR SOMETHINK   49C ISLAND MOON 5   PROSE
        & SO DIED
    WHEN MY MOTHER DIED I WAS VERY YOUNG . . . .   117 CHIMNEY SWP/SI   1
    BLOWD IN THE MORN IN EVENING DIED . . . .   220 TO TIRZAH/SE   6

```
                                                          PAGE      TITLE            LINE
DIED    (CONTINUED)
    IN EDEN THAT ONE DIED A DEATH NEVER TO BE REVIVD  . . . .   278 FOUR ZOAS 1        529
    ARE THOSE WHO LOVE LIKE THOSE WHO DIED RISEN AGAIN FROM     298 FOUR ZOAS 4         19
        DEATH
    LORD SAVIOUR IF THOU HADST BEEN HERE OUR BROTHER HAD NOT    304 FOUR ZOAS 4        253
        DIED
    FOR WHEN HE DIED THEY LAY BESIDE [HIM] HIS GRAVE & WHEN     316 FOUR ZOAS 6      *  168
        HE ROSE
    WHY SHOULDST THOU REMEMBER & BE AFRAID I SURELY HAVE DIED   330 FOUR ZOAS 7        420
        IN PAIN
    I MUST HAVE DIED IN THE DARK DESART AMONG NOXIOUS WORMS     335 FOUR ZOAS 7B        86
    THEN JESUS CAME & DIED WILLING BENEATH TIRZAH & RAHAB   .   351 FOUR ZOAS 8        406
    TIME AFTER TIME BY THE DIVINE LAMB WHO DIED FOR ALL    . .  353 FOUR ZOAS 8        483
    WHO DIED IN INFANCY RAGE FURIOUS A MIGHTY MULTITUDE RAGE    363 FOUR ZOAS 9        253
        FURIOUS
    CHRIST DIED AS AN UNBELIEVER & IF THE BISHOPS HAD THEIR     387C ANNO WATSON       MARG
        WILL
    AND HE LAUGHD AT THE DEVIL TILL POOR JOHN BROWN DIED    . . 434 LONG JOHN BRWN      16
    WHEN SR JOSHUA REYNOLDS DIED                               451 ANNO REYNOLDS        1
    THE LIVES OF PAINTERS SAY THAT RAFAEL DIED OF DISSIPATION   454B ANNO REYNOLDS     MARG
    HE WAS BORN QUITE A FOOL BUT HE DIED QUITE A KNAVE  . .   . 470 ANNO REYNOLDS        2
    HE DIED AS A REPROBATE HE WAS PUNISHD AS A TRANSGRESSOR     494 MILTON 13           27
    WHO DIED FROM EARTH & HE IS RETURND BEFORE THE JUDGMENT     508 MILTON 23           57
        THIS THING
    THUS POOR SCHIAVONETTI DIED OF THE CROMEK  . . . . . .   .  555 BLAKES APL/N 1      10
    THUS POOR SCHIAVONETTI DIED OF THE CROMEK  . . . . . .   .  556 BLAKES APL/N 2      19
    AND HIS OWN BELOVEDS THEN HE TURND SICK HIS SOUL           669 JERUSALEM 42         4
        DIED WITHIN HIM
    AND MUST HAVE DIED BUT THE DIVINE SAVIOUR DESCENDED  . . .  669 JERUSALEM 42         6
    IF THOU HADST BEEN HERE OUR BROTHER ALBION HAD NOT DIED     681 JERUSALEM 50        11
    HE ANSWERD JESUS DIED BECAUSE HE STROVE  . . . . . .   .    718 STOOD AMONG/J       16
    JESUS SAID WOULDEST THOU LOVE ONE WHO NEVER DIED  . .   .   743 JERUSALEM 96        23
    FOR THEE OR EVER DIE FOR ONE WHO HAD NOT DIED FOR THEE  . . 743 JERUSALEM 96        24
    AND THIS IS THE REASON JESUS DIED  . . . . . . . .   .      750 EV GOSPEL(C)/N      24
    I WAS STANDING BY WHEN JESUS DIED  . . . . . . .   . .      751 EV GOSPEL(D)/N      23
    AND THIS IS THE CAUSE THAT JESUS DIED  . . . . . .   . .    751 EV GOSPEL(D)/N      30
    BORN... (NOVEMBER)...IN LONDON & HAS DIED SEVERAL TIMES     781D INSC UPCOTT       PROSE
        SINCE
    AND I AM NOW SEVEN YEARS OLDER THAN RAFAEL WAS WHEN HE DIED 814D LETTER 23         PROSE
    HE DIED AT THE AGE OF (SEVENTY-FIVE) OF A PARALYTIC STROKE  860A LETTER 56         PROSE
    SOPHRONIA DIED IN CHILDBED SHE DIED ON THE WEDDING DAY      SUPP INSC HERVEY       *TITLE
    THESE DIED FOR LOVE MINISTERING ANGELS  . . . . . .   .     SUPP INSC HERVEY       *TITLE
DIES
    [AND DIES IN PEACE]                                        183 THE FLY/N           11
    STILL DIES FOR ENITHARMON NOR A SPIRIT SPRINGS FROM MY      288 FOUR ZOAS 2        322
        DEAD CORSE
    WHO DIES FOR LOVE OF HER  . . . . . . . . .   .            289 FOUR ZOAS 2        350
    AND ALL IN HIM DIES & HE PUT OFF ALL MORTALITY  . . .   .   353 FOUR ZOAS 8        484
    BUT IT IS NOT SO GENIUS DIES WITH ITS POSSESSOR  . . . .    470D ANNO REYNOLDS     MARG
    YET THE OAK DIES AS WELL AS THE LETTUCE  . . . . .   .      605B V LAST JUDG/N     PROSE
    BUT ITS ETERNAL IMAGE & INDIVIDUALITY NEVER DIES  . . .     605B V LAST JUDG/N     PROSE
    WHAT IS MORTALITY BUT THE THINGS RELATING TO THE BODY WHICH 717B JERUSALEM 77      PROSE
        DIES
    ONE DIES ALAS THE LIVING & DEAD  . . . . . . . .   .       771 OF GATES/GP         25
    THE FLAME SOON DIES AGAIN & I AM LEFT STUPIFIED AND        830B LETTER 30         PROSE
        ASTONISHD
DIET
    I AM GETTING BETTER EVERY HOUR MY PLAN IS DIET ONLY &  . . 873C LETTER 77         PROSE
DIETH
    AND IF GOD DIETH NOT FOR MAN & GIVETH NOT HIMSELF   . . .   743 JERUSALEM 96        25
DIFFER
    DIFFER IN THE MEANING OF THE WORDS INFINITY & ETERNAL   . . 91C ANNO SWED LOVE     MARG
    SORRY THAT YOUR IDEAS & MINE ON MORAL PAINTING DIFFER SO    793A LETTER 5         PROSE
        MUCH
DIFFERENCE
    THERES AS MUCH DIFFERENCE BETWEEN HIM AND ME  . . . . .     29D EDW THIRD/PS 4     PROSE
    THE DIFFERENCE BETWEEN STATES & INDIVIDUALS OF THOSE STATES 351 FOUR ZOAS 8        380
    THERE IS A VAST DIFFERENCE BETWEEN AN  . . . . . .   .      388B ANNO WATSON       MARG
    I KNEW IMMEDIATELY THE DIFFERENCE BETWEEN RAFAEL & RUBENS   447C ANNO REYNOLDS     MARG
    THE DIFFERENCE BETWEEN A BAD ARTIST & A GOOD ONE IS   . .   456A ANNO REYNOLDS     MARG
    SHOULD THAT MAKE DIFFERENCE TWIXT ME & THEE  . . . .   .    539 TO NANCY F/N        2
    IS NO DIFFERENCE BETWEEN RAFAEL'S CARTOONS AND HIS FRESCOS  584D DESC CAT 15       PROSE
    THERE IS NOT BECAUSE THERE CANNOT BE ANY DIFFERENCE   . .   598D PUB ADDRESS/N     PROSE
    REMEMBERD & CALLD REALITY IS THE MIGHTY DIFFERENCE         605C V LAST JUDG/N     PROSE
    WHICH WILL ACCOUNT FOR THE DIFFERENCE OF PRICE AS ALSO THAT 794B LETTER 5         PROSE
    DIFFERENCE BETWEEN THE DOCTRINES OF DR TRUSLER & THOSE      795A LETTER 6         PROSE
        OF CHRIST
    THE LITTLE DIFFERENCE THAT SUBSISTED BETWEEN YOU SPEAKING   846A LETTER 44         PROSE
        OF
    YOU WILL SEE IN THIS LITTLE WORK THE CAUSE OF DIFFERENCE    866A LETTER 64         PROSE
    REAL DIFFERENCE AS TO PERFECT INDEPENDENCE OF JUDGMENT  . . 868B LETTER 67         PROSE
DIFFERENCES
    BY DIFFERENCES BETWEEN IDEAS THAT IDEAS THEMSELVES WHICH    525 MILTON 35           5
        ARE
DIFFERENT
    IS OF A DIFFERENT KIND THEN FROM THE KING'S  . . . . .      22 EDW THIRD/PS 3       40
    A QUERY & AN ANSWER ARE AS DIFFERENT  . . . . . . . .       45D ISLAND MOON 1      PROSE
    IN DIFFERENT ?PERIODS OF TIME WISDOM OF ANGELS XXX   . .  . 89B ANNO SWED LOVE   * MARG
    USES AND SUBSTANCES ARE SO DIFFERENT AS NOT TO CORRESPOND   95B ANNO SWED LOVE     MARG
    FROM EACH NATION'S DIFFERENT RECEPTION OF THE POETIC GENIUS 98C ALL RELIGIONS     PROSE
    AND THEIR PURSUITS AS DIFFERENT AS THEIR FORMS AND AS       191 V DAU ALBION 3      6
        THEIR JOYS
```

499

DIFFERENT   (CONTINUED)

	PAGE	TITLE	LINE
HOW CAN ONE JOY ABSORB ANOTHER ARE NOT DIFFERENT JOYS . .	192	V DAU ALBION 5	5
HOW DIFFERENT FAR THE FAT FED HIRELING WITH HOLLOW DRUM	193	V DAU ALBION 5	14
HOW DIFFERENT THEIR EYE AND EAR HOW DIFFERENT THE WORLD TO THEM	193	V DAU ALBION 5	16
FOR HE DIVIDED DAY & NIGHT IN DIFFERENT ORDERD PORTIONS	334	FOUR ZOAS 7B	37
WHILE RAHAB & TIRZAH FAR DIFFERENT MANTLES PREPARE WEBS OF TORTURE	346	FOUR ZOAS 8	220
FOUR PILLARS OF DIFFERENT HEIGHTS AND SIZES . . .	402A	ANNO BACON	MARG
A LORD CHANCELLOR'S OPINIONS AS DIFFERENT FROM CHRIST . .	407A	ANNO BACON	MARG
O WHY WAS I BORN WITH A DIFFERENT FACE	428	MARY	21
MORE THAN ANIMAL FROM ANIMAL OF DIFFERENT SPECIES . . .	470B	ANNO REYNOLDS	MARG
AS ONE AGE FALLS ANOTHER RISES DIFFERENT TO MORTAL SIGHT	567C	DESC CAT 3	PROSE
AS HIS DRESS IS DIFFERENT AND HIS CHARACTER IS MORE MARKED	572A	DESC CAT 3	PROSE
IDEAS OF STRENGTH AND BEAUTY HAVE NOT BEEN GREATLY DIFFERENT	579C	DESC CAT 5	PROSE
EACH SHEW A DIFFERENT CHARACTER AND A DIFFERENT	580C	DESC CAT 5	PROSE
AS ONE AGE FALLS ANOTHER RISES DIFFERENT TO MORTAL SIGHT	589A	CHAUCER/N	PROSE
MICH ANG EVERY PICTURE OF THEIRS HAS A DIFFERENT & APPROPRIATE EFFECT	598D	PUB ADDRESS/N	PROSE
MINE ARE IN EVERY PICTURE DIFFERENT	598D	PUB ADDRESS/N	PROSE
TO DIFFERENT PEOPLE IT APPEARS DIFFERENTLY AS EVERYTHINC ELSE	605A	V LAST JUDG/N	PROSE
DIFFERENT FROM THAT WHICH A MAN DOES WITH HIS THOUGHT & MIND	782A	INSC UPCOTT	PROSE
FROM ONE CHAISE TO ANOTHER FOR WE HAD SEVEN DIFFERENT .	802B	LETTER 14	PROSE
CHAISES & AS MANY DIFFERENT DRIVERS WE (SET) OUT BETWEEN	802B	LETTER 14	*PROSE
FROM ONE CHAISE TO ANOTHER WE HAD SEVEN DIFFERENT . .	803A	LETTER 15	PROSE
CHAISES & AS MANY DIFFERENT DRIVERS ALL UPON THE ROAD WAS	803A	LETTER 15	PROSE
O WHY WAS I BORN WITH A DIFFERENT FACE	828	O WHY BORN/L	1
I SEND YOU A LIST OF THE DIFFERENT WORKS YOU HAVE DONE ME	867A	LETTER 66	PROSE
ARE A SELECTION FROM THE DIFFERENT BOOKS OF SUCH AS COULD BE	867A	LETTER 66	PROSE

DIFFERENTLY

	PAGE	TITLE	LINE
NONSENSE EVERY EYE SEES DIFFERENTLY	456B	ANNO REYNOLDS	MARG
TO DIFFERENT PEOPLE IT APPEARS DIFFERENTLY AS EVERYTHING ELSE	605A	V LAST JUDG/N	PROSE

DIFFICULT

	PAGE	TITLE	LINE
POISONOUS SOURCE PLACD WITH ART LIFTING DIFFICULT . . .	251	AHANIA 3	34
AND TAKE THEIR COUNSEL ESPECIALLY IN ALL DIFFICULT POINTS	570D	DESC CAT 3	PROSE
TO BE SURE CHAUCER IS A LITTLE DIFFICULT TO HIM WHO HAS ONLY	574A	DESC CAT 3	PROSE
SEARCHD IN VAIN CLOSD FROM THE MINUTIA HE WALKD DIFFICULT	657	JERUSALEM 31	13
WILL NOT BE SO DIFFICULT AS IT HAS BEEN IT IS VERY . .	798B	LETTER 10	PROSE
PATH IS DIFFICULT I HAVE NO FEAR OF STUMBLING WHILE I KEEP IT	813B	LETTER 22	PROSE

DIFFICULTIES

	PAGE	TITLE	LINE
PROJECTED WORK IT BIDS FAIR TO SET ME ABOVE THE DIFFICULTIES	862C	LETTER 60	PROSE

DIFFICULTY

	PAGE	TITLE	LINE
IS CUT OFF FROM THE WEEPING MOUTH WITH DIFFICULTY & PAIN	110	TIRIEL 8	28
THIS DIFFICULTY HAS BEEN OBVIATED BY THE AUTHOR OF THE . .	207B	PRSPECTUS 1793	PROSE
WITH DIFFICULTY & GREAT PAIN URIZEN	251	AHANIA 3	51
HE WITH DIFFICULTY AND GREAT PAIN	252	AHANIA 3	72
WITH DIFFICULTY DOWN DESCENDING GUIDED BY HIS EAR . . .	319	FOUR ZOAS 6	293
STOOD SO THICK HE WITH DIFFICULTY & GREAT PAIN BROUGHT .	321	FOUR ZOAS 7	38
IT WAS WITH DIFFICULTY BROUGHT BACK AGAIN TO A CERTAIN EFFECT	582B	DESC CAT 9	PROSE
BLACK & IMMENSE A ROCK OF DIFFICULTY & A CLIFF	674	JERUSALEM 44	11
THAT BOTH HE & I WISH THAT IS TO LIFT ME OUT OF DIFFICULTY	811D	LETTER 22	PROSE
MY ONLY DIFFICULTY IS TO PRODUCE FAST ENOUGH	821D	LETTER 25	PROSE
FOR OR TAKE SO LONG A RIDE WE WITH SOME DIFFICULTY MADE THE	869D	LETTER 70	PROSE

DIFFIDENT

	PAGE	TITLE	LINE
ON THE RIGHT HAND OF THESE RISE THE DIFFIDENT & HUMBLE .	610D	V LAST JUDG/N	PROSE

DIFFUSAL

	PAGE	TITLE	LINE
THE ADVANTAGE OF SO EXTENSIVE A DIFFUSAL AS WOULD BE PROMOTED	856C	LETTER 54	PROSE

DIFFUSED

	PAGE	TITLE	LINE
TO COUNTERACT THE WIDELY DIFFUSED MALICE WHICH HAS FOR . .	863D	LETTER 61	PROSE

DIG

	PAGE	TITLE	LINE
SO SAYING HE BEGAN TO DIG A GRAVE WITH HIS AGED HANDS . .	100	TIRIEL 1	34
BUT HEUXOS CALLD A SON OF ZAZEL TO [XXX] DIG THEIR MOTHER A GRAVE	100	TIRIEL 1	* 35
OLD CRUELTY DESIST & LET US DIG A GRAVE FOR THEE . . .	100	TIRIEL 1	36
AND NOW YOU FEEL IT DIG A GRAVE & LET US BURY OUR MOTHER	100	TIRIEL 1	42
SO [SAYING] HE BEGAN TO [FORM] ?DIG OF GOLD SILVER & [BRASS] IRON	317	FOUR ZOAS 6	* 229
AND [DIG] ROOT UP THE INFERNAL GROVE	417	MY SPECTRE/N	60

DIGESTION

	PAGE	TITLE	LINE
THE FURNACES THE STOMACH FOR DIGESTION TERRIBLE THEIR FURY	509	MILTON 24	59
EVERY THING IS CONDUCTED BY SPIRITS NO LESS THAN DIGESTION OR SLEEP	621C	JERUSALEM 3	PROSE
THE FURNACES THE STOMACH FOR DIGESTION TERRIBLE THEIR FURY	684	JERUSALEM 53	13

DIGHT

	PAGE	TITLE	LINE
IN LUCENT WORDS MY DARKLING VERSES DIGHT	14	IMIT SPEN/PS	3

DIGNIFIED

	PAGE	TITLE	LINE
DO NOT DEGRADE BUT RENDER HIM AN OBJECT OF DIGNIFIED MIRTH	568D	DESC CAT 3	PROSE

DIGNITIES

	PAGE	TITLE	LINE
BLASPHEMOUS DEMON ANTICHRIST HATER OF DIGNITIES	198	AMERICA 7	5

DIGNITY

	PAGE	TITLE	LINE
BUT KEEP A PROPER DIGNITY FOR NOW	20	EDW THIRD/PS 2	50
TO DIGNITY THAT IM SICK ONT	20	EDW THIRD/PS 2	61

		PAGE	TITLE	LINE

DIGNITY   (CONTINUED)
```
        TITIAN AS WELL AS THE OTHER VENETIANS SO FAR FROM        464B ANNO REYNOLDS   MARG
            SENATORIAL DIGNITY
        DIGNITY AN ADJUNCT . . . . . . . . . . . . . . .        477C ANNO REYNOLDS   MARG
        GO ASSUME PAPAL DIGNITY THOU SPECTRE THOU MALE HARLOT    698 JERUSALEM 64      15
            ARTHUR
        DIGNITY WHO WOULD NOT SIT LOOKING IN THEIR PARENT'S FACE 864A LETTER 61       PROSE
DIKE
        AND I'LL BE BURIED NEAR A DIKE . . . . . . . . . .       537 AND HIS LEGS/N     50
        I WAS BURIED NEAR THIS DIKE . . . . . . . . . . .        546 ANOTHER/N 1         1
DILBURY
        CATALANI DU CROWE & DILBURY DOODLE   . . . . . . .       548B ON GREAT ENC/N  TITLE
DILEMMA
        YOUR LABOURS CALL YOU PALAMABRON IS ALSO IN SAD DILEMMA  488 MILTON 8           17
DILIGENT
        HIS THUNDEROUS WHEELS FROM FURNACE TO FURNACE TENDING    302 FOUR ZOAS 4       176
            DILIGENT
DIM
        IN SICKLY DARKNESS LIKE A DIM ECLIPSE  . . . . . .        31 EDW THIRD/PS 6      4
        . . . SICK SICK THE PRINCE ON HIS COUCH WREATHD IN DIM   134 FRENCH REVOLTN      2
        DIM THE FORM ALMOST FADED . . . . . . . . . . . .        140 FRENCH REVOLTN    132
        LIKE A VOICE FROM THE DIM PILLARS MIRABEAU ROSE . . . .  146 FRENCH REVOLTN    259
        ROUND THE DIM ROCKS OF URIZEN SO NAMD  . . . . . .       223 URIZEN 3           42
        LIKE A SPIDER'S WEB MOIST COLD & DIM  . . . . . .        235 URIZEN 25          10
        DIM & GLUTINOUS AS THE WHITE POLYPUS . . . . . . .       258 BOOK OF LOS 4      57
        IS BOUGHT & SOLD & IN DIM NIGHT MY WORD SHALL BE THEIR LAW 278 FOUR ZOAS 1     503
        A SLUGGISH CURRENT OF DIM WATERS ON WHOSE VERDANT MARGIN 295 FOUR ZOAS 3       121
        DOUBTING STOOD THARMAS IN THE [DISMAL] SOLEMN DARKNESS   298 FOUR ZOAS 4    *   44
            HIS DIM EYES
        I DWELL IN DIM OBLIVION BROODING OVER ME THE ENORMOUS    317 FOUR ZOAS 6      223
            WORLDS
        AND DIM OBLIVION OF ALL WOE & DESPERATE REPOSE   . . .   321 FOUR ZOAS 7       67
        IN THE DIM AIR THEY TOOK THE BOOK OF IRON & PLACD ABOVE  322 FOUR ZOAS 7       97
        CRUSTED WITH SNOW IN A DIM VOID HERE BY THE ARTS OF URIZEN 350 FOUR ZOAS 8  * 373
        THEY ROLLD DOWN A DIM WORLD CRUSTED WITH SNOW DEADLY & DARK 351 FOUR ZOAS 8 * 396
        HIS LIPS WITH FOOD OF EDEN IN HIS COLD AND DIM REPOSE  . . 496 MILTON 15        15
        FROM GROT & CAVE BENEATH THE MOON DIM REGION OF DEATH    660 JERUSALEM 34       11
        AND THE DIM CHAOS BRIGHTEND BENEATH ABOVE AROUND EYED AS 745 JERUSALEM 98       14
            THE PEACOCK
        THIS LIFE'S DIM WINDOWS OF THE SOUL . . . . . . . .      753 EV GOSPEL(D)/N    103
DIMENSION
        ENLARGD INTO DIMENSION & DEFORMD INTO INDEFINITE SPACE   498 MILTON 17          23
        SUCH ARE THE SPACES CALLED EARTH & SUCH ITS DIMENSION  . .  516 MILTON 29        14
        FROM STAR TO STAR MOUNTAINS & VALLEYS TERRIBLE DIMENSION 528 MILTON 37          52
        IN CHASMS & ABYSSES OF SORROW ENLARGD WITHOUT DIMENSION  623 JERUSALEM 5         5
            TERRIBLE
DIMENSIONS
        OF DIMENSIONS EVER SO LARGE OR EVER SO SMALL WHICH MAY BE 560D EXHIBITION ADV  PROSE
        PRINCE OF THE AIR & OUR DIMENSIONS COMPASS ZENITH & NADIR 780 GHOST ABEL 1      11
        I WOULD RATHER PAINT PICTURES IN OIL OF THE SAME DIMENSIONS 792C LETTER 4      PROSE
DIMINUTIVE
        WHO ART THOU DIMINUTIVE HUSK & SHELL . . . . . . .       268 FOUR ZOAS 1       149
        THOU LITTLE DIMINUTIVE PORTION THAT DARST BE A COUNTERPART 295 FOUR ZOAS 3     117
DIMLY
        THE DIVINE VISION DIMLY APPEARD IN CLOUDS OF BLOOD WEEPING 685 JERUSALEM 54     32
DIMMD
        GLORY MAY NOT BE DIMMD WITH CLOUDS OF CARE . . . . . .    19 EDW THIRD/PS 2     15
DIMPLING
        AND THE DIMPLING STREAM RUNS LAUGHING BY   . . . . .      63 SHEPHERD YOUNG      6
        AND THE DIMPLING STREAM RUNS LAUGHING BY   . . . . .     124 LAUGHING/SI         2
DIN
        SWALLOWING UP THE HORRIBLE DIN IN AGONY ON AGONY . . . .  295 FOUR ZOAS 3      148
DINAH
        ROOTED IN SHECHEM THIS IS DINAH THE YOUTHFUL FORM OF ERIN 715 JERUSALEM 74      54
DINE
        TO DINE TO-MORROW WITH THE MAYOR OF LONDON . . . . . .    20 EDW THIRD/PS 2     42
        THAT HE MIGHT TEMPT THE JEWS TO DINE . . . . . . . .     757 EV GOSPEL(I)/N     28
DINED
        THE PROPHETS ISAIAH AND EZEKIEL DINED WITH ME AND I ASKED 153B MARRIAGE HH 12  PROSE
DINNER
        AND AFTER DINNER WE WILL WALK INTO THE CAGE OF HAR   . . 102 TIRIEL 3           14
        AFTER DINNER I ASKD ISAIAH TO FAVOUR THE WORLD WITH  . . 154A MARRIAGE HH 12   PROSE
        THO HE EAT & DRANK AS MUCH AS TEN MEN FOR HIS DINNER  . . 434 LONG JOHN BRWN    12
        BEFORE DINNER I MEAN IF YOU SET OFF BEFORE THAT & SECOND 870D LETTER 72        PROSE
DIOCESE
        IF INDUSTRY IS IN MY DIOCESE   . . . . . . . . . .       19 EDW THIRD/PS 2     24
DIOGENES
        THE SAME THAT MADE OUR FRIEND DIOGENES THE GRECIAN   . . 154A MARRIAGE HH 12 *PROSE
DIP
        DIP HIM IN THE RIVER WHO LOVES WATER . . . . . . . .     151A MARRIAGE HH 7   PROSE
        THEY STRIP OFF JOSEPH'S COAT & DIP IT IN THE BLOOD      704 JERUSALEM 67        23
            OF BATTLE
DIPPED
        THE CLOUDS OF OLOLON FOLDED AS A GARMENT DIPPED IN BLOOD 534 MILTON 42          12
DIPS
        & DIPS HIS HAND UP TO THE SHOULDER IN TREACLE . . . . .  55B ISLAND MOON 9     PROSE
DIRALADA
        BECAUSE OF DIRALADA THINKING TO RECLAIM HIS JOY   . . . .  246 SONG OF LOS 3    31
DIRE
        UPON THE MARGIND OCEAN CONVERSING WITH SHADOWS DIRE  . . . 195 V DAU ALBION 8  12
        IN OPPOSITION DIRE A WARLIKE CLOUD THE MYRIADS STOOD    . . 205 AMERICA CANC C 20
        FOR HE STROVE IN BATTLES DIRE . . . . . . . . . .       222 URIZEN 3           13
```

	PAGE	TITLE	LINE

DIRE   (CONTINUED)

BY FIGHTINGS AND CONFLICTS DIRE	224	URIZEN 4	27
DIRE SHRIEKD HIS INVISIBLE LUST	249	AHANIA 2	30
AROSE FOR HIS DIRE CONTEMPLATIONS	250	AHANIA 3	7
WITH EASE SEARCHING THE DIRE VACUITY	258	BOOK OF LOS 4	53
TEND THE DIRE ANVILS MOUNTAINS MOURN & RIVERS FAINT & FAIL	276	FOUR ZOAS 1	425
JERUSALEM CAME DOWN IN A DIRE RUIN OVER ALL THE EARTH . .	281	FOUR ZOAS 2	45
CASTING THEIR SPARKLES ABROAD INTO THE DISMAL DEEP	283	FOUR ZOAS 2	140
THEN FALLING DOWN A TERRIBLE SPACE RECOVRING IN WINTER DIRE	287	FOUR ZOAS 2	* 277
OF LOS ABSORBD IN DIRE REVENGE HE DRANK WITH JOY THE CRIES	302	FOUR ZOAS 4	191
THE SPECTRE WEPT AT HIS DIRE LABOURS WHEN FROM [?LABLES] LADLES HUGE	302	FOUR ZOAS 4	* 194
TILL MANY A MORN & MANY A NIGHT PASSD OVER IN DIRE WOE	307	FOUR ZOAS 5	88
THO HE PARTAKES OF HIS DIRE WOES & MUTUAL RETURNS THE PANG	314	FOUR ZOAS 6	98
FOR INFINITE THE DISTANCE & OBSCURD BY COMBUSTIONS DIRE	316	FOUR ZOAS 6	177
A LABOURER OF AGES A DIRE DISCONTENT A LIVING WOE . .	317	FOUR ZOAS 6	226
TRAVELLING THRO DARKNESS & WHEREEVER HE TRAVELD A DIRE WEB	318	FOUR ZOAS 6	* 243
THE CAVE OF ORC STOOD TO THE SOUTH A FURNACE OF DIRE FLAMES	318	FOUR ZOAS 6	265
RETIRING INTO HIS DIRE WEB SCATTERING FLEECY SNOWS . . .	319	FOUR ZOAS 6	* 317
THE DISMAL SQUADRONS OF URTHONA WEAVING THE DIRE WEB . .	320	FOUR ZOAS 6	324
IN TORTURES OF DIRE COLDNESS NOW A LAKE OF WATERS DEEP . .	322	FOUR ZOAS 7	74
SINGING AT THEIR DIRE WORK THE WORDS OF URIZEN'S BOOK OF IRON	322	FOUR ZOAS 7	104
THE CAUSE OF HER DIRE ANGUISH FOR SHE LAY THE IMAGE OF DEATH	328	FOUR ZOAS 7	320
THAT THIS DIRE STATE COMMENCES I BEGAN THE DREADFUL STATE	330	FOUR ZOAS 7	404
TO COMFORT ORC IN HIS DIRE SUFFERINGS LOOK MY FIRES ENLUME AFRESH	331	FOUR ZOAS 7	444
OF DIRE NECESSITY STILL LABORING DAY & NIGHT TILL ALL . .	333	FOUR ZOAS 7B	14
HIS FURIOUS NECK (WRITHING) CONTORTIVE IN DIRE BUDDING PAINS	343	FOUR ZOAS 8	* 72
[AMONG THE STARS] HIS HURTLING HAND GAVE THE DIRE SIGNAL	343	FOUR ZOAS 8	88
SPARKLES OF DIRE AFFLICTION ISSUD [FROM] ROUND HIS FROZEN LIMBS	343	FOUR ZOAS 8	* 91
THE DIRE CONFUSION TILL THE BATTLE FAINTS THOSE THAT REMAIN	344	FOUR ZOAS 8	118
RELAPSING IN DIRE TORMENT THEY RETURN TO FORMS OF WOE . .	344	FOUR ZOAS 8	124
WEAKEND THEY STRETCH BEYOND THEIR POWER IN DIRE DROVES	344	FOUR ZOAS 8	129
URIZEN CALLD TOGETHER THE SYNAGOGUE OF SATAN IN DIRE SANHEDRIM	348	FOUR ZOAS 8	272
THEIR DREAD FORMS TENDING THE DIRE MILLS	378	FOUR ZOAS 9	814
THAT WAS BEGOTTEN IN DIRE WOE	424	MENTAL TRAVLER	6
WROUGHT WITH THE NEEDLE WITH DIRE SUFFERINGS POVERTY PAIN & WOE	499	MILTON 18	8
ALL FELL TOWARDS THE CENTER IN DIRE RUIN SINKING DOWN . .	500	MILTON 19	21
ALL FELL TOWARDS THE CENTER SINKING DOWNWARD IN DIRE RUIN	524	MILTON 34	39
THE LAND OF SNARES & TRAPS & WHEELS & PIT-FALLS & DIRE MILLS	634	JERUSALEM 13	49
AND THERE BEHOLD THE LOOM OF LOCKE WHOSE WOOF RAGES DIRE	636	JERUSALEM 15	15
SHE ALSO TOOK AN ATOM OF SPACE WITH DIRE PAIN OPENING IT A CENTER	678	JERUSALEM 48	38
THE FOUR ZOAS RUSH AROUND ON ALL SIDES IN DIRE RUIN . . .	690	JERUSALEM 58	47
ALL FELL TOWARDS THE CENTER SINKING DOWNWARDS IN DIRE RUIN	691	JERUSALEM 59	17
AND THY ARK & HOLY PLACE AT THY FROWNS AT THY DIRE REVENGE	706	JERUSALEM 68	50
TRAVELLING THRO THE NIGHT FOR FROM ITS DIRE	717	STOOD AMONG/J	9
WHILE LOS LAMENTS AT HIS DIRE LABOURS VIEWING JERUSALEM	719	JERUSALEM 78	10
ABSORB ME NOT IN SUCH DIRE GRIEF O ALBION MY BROTHER . .	727	JERUSALEM 83	6
OF DREADFUL POWER SITTING UPON HOREB PONDERING DIRE . . .	735	JERUSALEM 89	55
AND EAR UNBINDING IN DIRE PAIN WITH MANY BLOWS	738	JERUSALEM 91	46
HE ALTERD TIME AFTER TIME WITH DIRE PAIN & MANY TEARS . .	739	JERUSALEM 91	52
O RINTRAH O PALAMABRON WHAT ARE YOUR DIRE & AWFUL PURPOSES	740	JERUSALEM 93	2

DIRECT

WITHOUT A LANTERN TO DIRECT MY STEPS WITHOUT A STAFF TO SUPPORT ME	35D	COUCH DEATH/PS	PROSE
UPON THE EASTERN SEA DIRECT THEY TAKE THEIR COURSE . . .	336	FOUR ZOAS 7B	151
IF TO THE MIDDLE CLASS IT IS THE DIRECT CONTRARY TO CHRIST'S ADVICE	406D	ANNO BACON	MARG
THE KINGDOM OF HEAVEN IS THE DIRECT NEGATION OF EARTHLY DOMINATION	407B	ANNO BACON	MARG
& MUST CONTINUALLY BE CHANGED INTO HIS DIRECT CONTRARY . .	682A	JERUSALEM 52	PROSE
MISCHIEVOUS & DIRECT CONTRARY TO WORDSWORTH'S OWN PRACTISE	783B	ANNO WW POEMS	MARG
DIRECT TO MR BLAKE FELPHAM NEAR CHICHESTER SUSSEX . . .	803D	LETTER 15	*PROSE
INTREAT YOU TO EXCUSE FAULTS FOR PORTRAIT PAINTING IS THE DIRECT	815C	LETTER 23	PROSE
YOUR ANSWER TO THE PROPOSAL YOU WILL IF YOU THINK FIT DIRECT	842A	LETTER 41	PROSE
DO NOR SAY BUT AS YOU DIRECT I FEEL EXTREMELY HAPPY . . .	857B	LETTER 54	PROSE

DIRECTED

MY DESIGNS FOR COMUS WHEN I HAVE DONE THEM DIRECTED TO YOU	810D	LETTER 21	PROSE
WITH IT I SEALD & SENT IT IMMEDIATELY AS DIRECTED BY .	834C	LETTER 34	PROSE
WHICH I GOT AS YOU DIRECTED OF MR JOHNSON I HAVE SEEN .	844D	LETTER 43	PROSE

DIRECTING

RIDES ON THE WHIRLWIND DIRECTING THE STORMS OF WAR . . .	565A	DESC CAT 2	TITLE
DIRECTING THE COMBATS IN THE UPPER ELEMENTS	612A	V LAST JUDG/N	PROSE
URIZEN WRATHFUL STRODE ABOVE DIRECTING THE AWFUL BUILDING	690	JERUSALEM 58	21
AMONG HIS FURNACES DIRECTING HIS LABORIOUS MYRIADS WATCHFUL	730	JERUSALEM 85	11
AS HE WALKS FROM FURNACE TO FURNACE DIRECTING THE LABOURERS	730	JERUSALEM 85	20

DIRECTION

THAT BEATEN MASS KEEPING ITS DIRECTION	249	AHANIA 2	28
AS A DIRECTION FOR YOUR GRAVER	440C	MEMORANDUM/N 3	PROSE

			PAGE	TITLE	LINE

DIRECTION   (CONTINUED)
AND THOSE WHO HAVE THE DIRECTION OF PUBLIC WORKS . . . .   560D EXHIBITION ADV   PROSE
TO BE TOLD THAT I AM UNDER THE DIRECTION OF MESSENGERS . . 812A LETTER 22   PROSE
LADY HAMILTON'S DIRECTION WAS SO UNFORTUNATE AS TO FIND HIM 834D LETTER 34   PROSE
PARTS IF YOU WOULD TAKE ON YOU THE DIRECTION AND HE . . . 845C LETTER 44   PROSE
FAVOR ME WITH A LINE OF DIRECTION HOW TO PROCEED . . . . 853A LETTER 51   *PROSE
DIRECTIONS
AND DIRECTIONS ARE EMPLOYED AT A GREAT EXPENCE . . . . . 572D DESC CAT 3   PROSE
DIRECTIONS AND COMMANDS CONCERNING IT FOR HE WISHES TO SET 858C LETTER 55   PROSE
DIRECTLY
DIRECTLY IN THE BLIND-MAN'S WAY . . . .   16 BLIND-MANS/PS   48
THEN I FLUNG MYSELF WITH HIM DIRECTLY INTO THE BODY OF   156D MARRIAGE HH 17   PROSE
  THE SUN
THE EGYPTIAN GODS AND THO NOT DIRECTLY TAKEN FROM A POEM   823D LETTER 27   PROSE
GIVEN THEM & WE DIRECTLY GO TO PRINTING CONSEQUENTLY IT   840C LETTER 39   PROSE
MR P(PHILLIPS) SAYS HE WILL SEND MR SEAGRAVE THE PAPER   859B LETTER 56   PROSE
  DIRECTLY
DIRECTORS
AND THE ROYAL ACADEMY'S DIRECTORS . . . .   543 TO ROYL ACAD/N   4
DIRECTS
("WITH WISDOM DIRECTS OBSTINACY") THIS MUST BE A GRAND   79B ANNO LAVATER   MARG
  FELLOW
DIRECTS THEM TO THE KNIGHT AS THE PERSON WHO WOULD   566D DESC CAT 3   PROSE
  BE LIKELY
THE DISPOSITION OF FORMS ALWAYS DIRECTS COLOURING . . .   580D DESC CAT 5   PROSE
DEPICTED IN HIS JOLLY FACE DIRECTS THEM TO THE . . . .   588C CHAUCER/N   PROSE
DIRECTS THEM TO THE KNIGHT AS THE PERSON WHO WILL BE LIKELY 589D CHAUCER 2   PROSE
AS HE WATCHES THE FURNACES BY NIGHT & DIRECTS THE LABOURERS 730 JERUSALEM 85   13
DIREFUL
LO NOW THE DIREFUL MONSTER WHOSE SKIN CLINGS . . . . .   3 TO WINTER/PS   9
NOW DIREFUL PAINS ACCOST HER AND STILL PREGNANT . . . .   41C THEN SHE BORE   PROSE
FAR IN A DIREFUL CAVE SHE LIVES UNSEEN . . . . . .   41D THEN SHE BORE   PROSE
WAS BORN ENVY IN DIREFUL PAINS HIM BORE THEN ENVY BROUGHT   42C THEN SHE BORE   PROSE
  FORTH CARE
RIPTED WITH DIREFUL CHANGES . . . .   226 URIZEN 7   6
AT DISTANCE FAR IN NIGHT REPELLD IN DIREFUL HUNGER CRAVING   276 FOUR ZOAS 1   442
WHERE ENION BLIND & AGE BENT WEPT IN DIREFUL HUNGER CRAVING   280 FOUR ZOAS 2   16
THE ENORMOUS WARP & WOOF RAGE DIREFUL IN THE AFFRIGHTED   284 FOUR ZOAS 2   149
  DEEP
THE BOUNDS OF DESTINY CRASHD DIREFUL & THE SWELLING SEA   295 FOUR ZOAS 3   136
AND THE WEB OF URIZEN (STRETCHD) DIREFUL SHIVRING IN CLOUDS   318 FOUR ZOAS 6   * 247
SHE BURST THE GATES OF ENITHARMON'S HEART WITH DIREFUL   328 FOUR ZOAS 7   323
  CRASH
THEY HUMANIZE IN THE FIERCE BATTLE WHERE IN DIREFUL PAIN   344 FOUR ZOAS 8   115
STEEPING THE DIREFUL WEB OF RELIGION SWAGGING HEAVY IT FELL   345 FOUR ZOAS 8   176
IN DIREFUL PAIN FOR THE DREAD SHADOW TWENTY-SEVEN-FOLD . .   496 MILTON 14   39
AND IN GRINDING AGONIES IN THREATS STIFLINGS & DIREFUL   639 JERUSALEM 17   58
  STRUGGLINGS
OF FIRE SPEAKING THE WORDS OF ETERNITY IN HUMAN FORMS IN   742 JERUSALEM 95   9
  DIREFUL
DIREST
REACHD TO THE DEPTHS OF (DIREST) HELL & THENCE TO ALBION'S   496 MILTON 14   * 40
  LAND
DIRGE
[THIS IS THE [DIRGE OF ENO] SONG OF ENITHARMON WHICH . . .   264 FOUR ZOAS 1   * 1
DIRGE-LIKE
TO ME FORGIVE THIS DIRGE-LIKE LAMENTATION OVER A DEAD HORSE   830B LETTER 30   PROSE
DIRT
THEY LAUGHD & MOCKED SOME THREW DIRT & STONES AS THEY PASSD   108 TIRIEL 7   5
  BY
THEY THREW DIRT AFTER THEM TILL TO THE COVERT OF A WOOD   109 TIRIEL 7   15
IT IS AS THE DIRT UPON MY FEET NO PART OF ME . . . . .   617B V LAST JUDG/N   PROSE
I AM DEFACED WITH BLOWS & WITH THE DIRT OF THE PRISON . .   695 JERUSALEM 62   5
DIRTY
I WANDER THRO EACH DIRTY STREET . . . .   170 LONDON/N   1
NEAR WHERE THE DIRTY THAMES DOES FLOW . . . . . .   170 LONDON/N   2
HE PUT A DIRTY PAPER SCROLL . . . .   541 FLORENTINE/N   4
BUT AS I CANNOT PAINT DIRTY RAGS & OLD SHOES . . . .   795A LETTER 6   PROSE
DIS
CITY OF DIS QUEEN OF ENDLESS WOE [XXX] FURIES & . . . .   786A ILLS DANTE 101 *PROSE
MINOTAUR THE CITY OF DIS SEEMS TO OCCUPY THE SPACE . .   786A ILLS DANTE 101   PROSE
DISAGREE
IT IS NOT IN TERMS THAT REYNOLDS & I DISAGREE TWO . .   474B ANNO REYNOLDS   MARG
DISAGREEMENTS
TO CONSIST IN THE AGREEMENTS & (DISAGREEMENTS) OF IDEAS   708 JERUSALEM 70   8
DISAPPEARS
WHEN THE MORTAL DISAPPEARS IN IMPROVED KNOWLEDGE CAST AWAY   355 FOUR ZOAS 8   552
DISAPPOINTED
THIS WAS TO HER SUPREME DELIGHT THE WARRIORS MOURND   338 FOUR ZOAS 7B   219
  DISAPPOINTED
DISAPPOINTMENT
I OUGHT ALSO TO MENTION MY EXTREME DISAPPOINTMENT AT . .   809C LETTER 20   PROSE
THE EXTREME LOSS AND DISAPPOINTMENT WHICH I SHOULD HAVE   861A LETTER 58   PROSE
DISAPPROBATION
WITH HIS GENTEEL IGNORANCE & POLITE DISAPPROBATION . . .   825C LETTER 27   PROSE
DISARRANGE
ARTIFICE TURN OR TWIST ONE FACT OR DISARRANGE SELF EVIDENT   579A DESC CAT 5   PROSE
DIS-ARRANGED
DIS-ARRANGED IMITATIONS AND BLUNDERING MISAPPLIED COPIES   585D DESC CAT 15   PROSE
DISARRANGING
WITHOUT DISARRANGING MY TIME WHICH IN FUTURE MUST ALONE   865D LETTER 63   PROSE

                                                       PAGE   TITLE   LINE

DISBAND
    . . . AND IF IT OBEY AND DEPART THEN THE KING WILL DISBAND   145 FRENCH REVOLTN   252
DISBELIEVD
    LUCIAN DISBELIEVD HEATHEN GODS . . . . 403C ANNO BACON   MARG
DISBELIEVE
    HE DID NOT PERHAPS DISBELIEVE FOR ALL THAT BACON DID   . . 403C ANNO BACON   MARG
    TO DISBELIEVE WHAT YOU THINK IMPROBABLE OR IMPOSSIBLE   . . 579B DESC CAT 5   PROSE
    YOU MAY DISBELIEVE ALL THIS BUT IT SHALL BE AT YOUR OWN   582A DESC CAT 8   PROSE
        PERIL
    I SAY AGAIN O ARTIST YOU MAY DISBELIEVE ALL THIS . . . . 583C DESC CAT 9   PROSE
DISBELIEVED
    DISBELIEVED WHILE THOSE OF THE JEWS ARE COLLECTED AND   . . 578D DESC CAT 5   PROSE
DISBURDEND
    LIKE THE DARK CLOUD DISBURDEND IN THE DAY OF DISMAL THUNDER   238 EUROPE PREL 1   7
DISCARDED
    BEEN PUBLISHD EVEN JOHNSON & FUSELI HAVE DISCARDED   795C LETTER 6   PROSE
        MY GRAVER
DISCERN
    RISE UP FOR I DISCERN THEE & I DARE THY ELOQUENT TONGUE   104 TIRIEL 4   19
    DRAW IN THE OCEAN DOES HIS EYE DISCERN THE FLYING CLOUD   193 V DAU ALBION 5   35
    AND THEIR EYES COULD NOT DISCERN . . . .   236 URIZEN 28   17
    CAN ANGLUS NEVER DISCERN PERFECTION BUT IN THE JOURNEYMAN'S 601D PUB ADDRESS/N   PROSE
        LABOUR
DISCERND
    FOR THAT CALLD BODY IS A PORTION OF SOUL DISCERND BY   . . 149D MARRIAGE HH 4   PROSE
    DISCERND NOT THE WOVEN HIPOCRISY . . . .   236 URIZEN 25   32
    THEY DISCERND MY COUNTENANCE WITH JOY THEY SHEWD ME TO   720 JERUSALEM 79   28
        THEIR SONS
DISCERNING
    IN HIS YOUNG EYES DISCERNING PLAIN THAT ORC PLOTTED HIS   307 FOUR ZOAS 5   82
        DEATH
    TO THE AUTHOR AND HE THINKS WILL PROVE TO ANY DISCERNING   585D DESC CAT 16   PROSE
        EYE
DISCERNMENT
    TRUTH OR DISCERNMENT IN ANOTHER & IN SOME IT IS FOLLY   . . 408D ANNO BACON   MARG
DISCHARGING
    DISCHARGING THEIR ENORMOUS VOICES AT THE FATHER'S CURSE   106 TIRIEL 5   15
DISCIPLE
    & FELLOW DISCIPLE HOW GREAT MUST BE YOUR FAITH . . . . 822B LETTER 26   PROSE
DISCIPLES
    COVET WHEN HE PRAYD FOR HIS DISCIPLES . . . .   158C MARRIAGE HH 22   PROSE
    HIS SEVENTY DISCIPLES SENT . . . .   757 EV GOSPEL(I)/N   37
    JESUS & HIS APOSTLES & DISCIPLES WERE ALL ARTISTS . . . 777B INSC LAOCOON   PROSE
DISCIPLINE
    DISCIPLINE IN MOUNTAINOUS PLACES SR FRANCIS BACON IS A LIAR 871A LETTER 72   PROSE
    NO DISCIPLINE WILL TURN ONE MAN INTO ANOTHER EVEN IN   . . 871A LETTER 72   PROSE
    THE LEAST PARTICLE & SUCH DISCIPLINE I CALL PRESUMPTION   871A LETTER 72   PROSE
        & FOLLY
DISCLOSD
    OR WERT THOU NOT AWAKE WHEN ALL THIS MYSTERY WAS DISCLOSD   193 V DAU ALBION 6   9
DISCLOSE
    DISCLOSE A HIDEOUS ORIFICE THENCE ISSUING THE GIANT-BROOD   708 JERUSALEM 70   13
DISCLOSED
    THY TABERNACLE TAKEN DOWN THY SECRET CHERUBIM DISCLOSED   644 JERUSALEM 21   21
DISCLOSING
    DISCLOSING TO HER SIGHT THE MURDERD HEAD . . . . . .   5 FAIR ELENOR/PS   58
DISCONSOLATE
    LOS SECRET BURIED THULLOH WEEPING DISCONSOLATE OVER THE   489 MILTON 8   45
        MOONY SPACE
    TO HESHBON DISCONSOLATE HE WALKD THRO MOAB & HE STOOD   . . 662 JERUSALEM 36   10
    POURING DISCONSOLATE FROM BEHIND . . . .   817 HAPPINESS/L   22
DISCONTENT
    WITHIN ITSELF AND FINDETH DISCONTENT . . . .   27 EDW THIRD/PS 3   253
    MISERY BUILDS OVER OUR COTTAGE ROOFS AND DISCONTENT RUNS   37B CONTEMPLATN/PS PROSE
        LIKE A BROOK
    [FLINGING FLAMES OF DISCONTENT & PLAGUES OF DARK DESPAIR]   109 TIRIEL 8   16
    . . . AMONG THICK SHADES OF DISCONTENT . . . .   137 FRENCH REVOLTN   64
    . . . FROM COLD FROM SLANDER DISCONTENT AND SLOTH   . . 144 FRENCH REVOLTN   234
    WAVE SHADOWS OF DISCONTENT AND IN WHAT HOUSES DWELL THE   192 V DAU ALBION 4   1
        WRETCHED
    ON SCORN TO FEED OUR DISCONTENT FOR IF WE GRATEFUL PROVE   271 FOUR ZOAS 1   256
    AND LOS & ENITHARMON SAT IN DISCONTENT & SCORN   . . . 274 FOUR ZOAS 1   374
    BUT LOS & ENITHARMON SAT IN DISCONTENT & SCORN   . . . 276 FOUR ZOAS 1   439
    A LABOURER OF AGES A DIRE DISCONTENT A LIVING WOE   . . 317 FOUR ZOAS 6   226
    HOWLING IN DISCONTENT BLACK & HEAVY UTTERING BRUTE SOUNDS   338 FOUR ZOAS 7B   224
    CLOUDED WITH DISCONTENT & BROODING IN THEIR MINDS TERRIBLE 505 MILTON 22   28
        THINGS
    SO LOS SPOKE BUT LIGHTNINGS OF DISCONTENT BROKE ON ALL   511 MILTON 25   63
        SIDES ROUND
DISCONTINUED
    WHICH SHE HAS DISCONTINUED THESE THREE MONTHS . . . . 854A LETTER 52   PROSE
DISCORD
    DISCORD BEGAN & YELLS & CRIES SHOOK THE WIDE FIRMAMENT . . 278 FOUR ZOAS 1   518
    THEN DISCORD BEGAN [&] THEN YELLS & CRIES SHOOK THE WIDE   306 FOUR ZOAS 5   *   45
        (FIRMAMENT)
    ALL MELODIES & COMPREHENDING ONLY DISCORD AND HARMONY . . 484 MILTON 5   24
DISCORDANT
    DISCORDANT PRINCIPLES OF LOVE & HATE I SUFFER AFFLICTION   282 FOUR ZOAS 2   103
    BECAUSE OF ORC BECAUSE HE RENT HIS DISCORDANT WAY   . . 325 FOUR ZOAS 7   225
    OVER THEE & THE TERRIBLE ORC RENT HIS DISCORDANT WAY   . . 326 FOUR ZOAS 7   228
DISCORDS
    I TELL HOW ALBION'S SONS BY HARMONIES OF CONCORDS   715 JERUSALEM 74   24
        & DISCORDS

	PAGE	TITLE	LINE
DISCOUNTENANCE			
O YE RELIGIOUS DISCOUNTENANCE EVERY ONE AMONG YOU . . .	717B	JERUSALEM 77	PROSE
DISCOURAGE			
WHILE THEY DISCOURAGE & LOOK WITH CONTEMPT ON FALSE ART	601C	PUB ADDRESS/N	*PROSE
DISCOURAGE YOU FROM THE PURSUIT OF SO EXPENSIVE AN . . .	848C	LETTER 45	PROSE
DISCOURAGING			
[?HOWEVER ?DISCOURAGING TO THOSE WHO ARE BORN FOR IT] . .	SUPP	ANNO REYNOLDS	* MARG
DISCOURSE			
THE FOLLOWING [LETTER] DISCOURSE IS PARTICULARLY . . .	457D	ANNO REYNOLDS	* MARG
THE [FOLLOWING DISCOURSE IS] [(TWO) DISCOURSES]	461C	ANNO REYNOLDS	* MARG
IN A DISCOURSE ON ART SUCH IDIOTS ARE NOT ARTISTS . . .	464B	ANNO REYNOLDS	MARG
THE FOLLOWING DISCOURSE IS WRITTEN WITH THE SAME END IN VIEW	465D	ANNO REYNOLDS	MARG
THE PURPOSE OF THE FOLLOWING DISCOURSE IS TO PROVE THAT	473A	ANNO REYNOLDS	MARG
BUT MOST ESPECIALLY FOR THIS DISCOURSE IN WHICH IT IS PROVED	473A	ANNO REYNOLDS	MARG
IN ANOTHER DISCOURSE HE SAYS	477B	ANNO REYNOLDS	MARG
ACCORDING TO THE SUBJECT OF DISCOURSE & EVERY WORD & EVERY CHARACTER	746	JERUSALEM 98	35
DISCOURSES			
LISTEND WITH OPEN MOUTHS TO THE EDIFYING DISCOURSES . .	44D	ISLAND MOON 1	PROSE
TO THIS SCOPPRELL ANSWERD I THINK THE LADIES' DISCOURSES	53C	ISLAND MOON 8	PROSE
WE MAY HOPE TO SEE CHRIST'S DISCOURSES EXPUNGD . . .	384D	ANNO WATSON	MARG
THE CONTRADICTIONS IN REYNOLDS'S DISCOURSES ARE STRONG .	449B	ANNO REYNOLDS	MARG
I CONSIDER REYNOLDS'S DISCOURSES TO THE ROYAL ACADEMY .	452A	ANNO REYNOLDS	MARG
INSULTED & DEGRADED BY THE REPUTATION OF THESE DISCOURSES	452B	ANNO REYNOLDS	MARG
THE [FOLLOWING DISCOURSE IS] [(TWO) DISCOURSES] . . .	461C	ANNO REYNOLDS	* MARG
TWO FOLLOWING DISCOURSES ARE PARTICULARLY CALCULATED . .	461C	ANNO REYNOLDS	MARG
HIS ASSERTIONS IN ALL HIS DISCOURSES	476D	ANNO REYNOLDS	MARG
SINCE THE AGE OF RAFAEL ALL SR J REYNOLDS'S DISCOURSES .	814B	LETTER 23	PROSE
DISCOVER			
HE PERCIEVES MORE THAN SENSE THO EVER SO ACUTE CAN DISCOVER	97C	NAT RELIGION 2	PROSE
OR I SHALL SOON DISCOVER THAT I AM A MORTAL MAN	104	TIRIEL 4	35
AS GLASSES DISCOVER WORLDS	231	URIZEN 15	9
I COME TO DISCOVER BEFORE HEAVN & HELL THE SELF RIGHTEOUSNESS	530	MILTON 38	43
I DISCOVER THY SECRET PLACES CORDELLA I BEHOLD . . .	644	JERUSALEM 21	19
DISCOVERD			
HE FIRST DISCOVERD GUTS	51	WHEN CORRUP/IM	36
AY NOW THOU ART DISCOVERD I WILL USE THEE LIKE A SLAVE .	104	TIRIEL 4	25
BUT MY SENSES DISCOVERD THE INFINITE IN EVERY THING . .	153C	MARRIAGE HH 12	PROSE
GOLDEN ROCKS TILL WE DISCOVERD TWO GLOBES OF CRIMSON FIRE	156C	MARRIAGE HH 17	PROSE
THE FOUNDATIONS OF THE ETERNAL HILLS DISCOVERD	357	FOUR ZOAS 9	17
COLUMBUS DISCOVERD AMERICA BUT AMERICUS VESPUTIUS FINISHD &	598C	PUB ADDRESS/N	*PROSE
THEY TORMENT A HYPOCRITE WHEN HE IS DISCOVERD	616C	V LAST JUDG/N	PROSE
EMBRACE WE SHALL PERISH ANNIHILATE DISCOVERD OUR DELUSIONS	725	JERUSALEM 82	4
FOR I HAVE NOW DISCOVERD THAT	810B	LETTER 20	PROSE
DISCOVERED			
BEFORE DISCOVERED	207B	PRSPECTUS 1793	PROSE
I HAVE FORTUNATELY I OUGHT TO SAY PROVIDENTIALLY DISCOVERED	861A	LETTER 58	PROSE
THE WAY IN WHICH I DISCOVERED THIS MISTAKE IS ODD ENOUGH	861B	LETTER 58	PROSE
DISCOVEREST			
LOS THOU NOW DISCOVEREST THY TURPITUDE TO THE HEAVENS . .	669	JERUSALEM 42	11
DISCOVERING			
DISCOVERING HER OWN PERFECT BEAUTY TO THE DAUGHTERS OF ALBION	726	JERUSALEM 82	46
("NEITHER DISCOVERING NOT HIDING HIMSELF") A FEMALE GOD	788C	ANNO THORNTON	MARG
DISCOVERY			
TREMBLED AT DISCOVERY OF LOVE	753	EV GOSPEL(E)/N	6
I SHALL GLORY IN THE DISCOVERY	853A	LETTER 51	*PROSE
DISCRETE			
DISCRETE & NOT CONTINUOUS SO AS TO EXPLAIN EACH OTHER EXCEPT	93A	ANNO SWED LOVE	MARG
WITHOUT MAKING THEM CONTINUOUS & NOT DISCRETE	93B	ANNO SWED LOVE	MARG
DISCRETION			
BACON HATED TALENTS OF ALL KINDS ELOQUENCE IS DISCRETION OF SPEECH	409A	ANNO BACON	MARG
CONFIDENCE IN MY DISCRETION SUCH WAS OUR CONVERSATION . .	856D	LETTER 54	PROSE
DISCRIMINATE			
WITHOUT INTENTION & THAT MOST DISCRIMINATE & PARTICULAR	611B	V LAST JUDG/N	PROSE
DISCRIMINATES			
BUT HE WHO ENTERS INTO & DISCRIMINATES MOST MINUTELY .	611B	V LAST JUDG/N	PROSE
DISCRIMINATING			
[?THEY EXCELL BOTH IN MINUTE & DISCRIMINATING DETERMINATION]	453D	ANNO REYNOLDS	* MARG
I E THE MOST MINUTELY DISCRIMINATING & DETERMINATE . . .	453D	ANNO REYNOLDS	* MARG
DISCRIMINATION			
SEE N...THIS APHORISM SEEMS TO ME TO WANT DISCRIMINATION	82B	ANNO LAVATER	MARG
MINUTE DISCRIMINATION IS NOT ACCIDENTAL	453B	ANNO REYNOLDS	MARG
ALL SUBLIMITY IS FOUNDED ON MINUTE DISCRIMINATION . . .	453B	ANNO REYNOLDS	MARG
& MINUTE DISCRIMINATION OF CHARACTER IT IS THE WHOLE OF ART	466B	ANNO REYNOLDS	MARG
& ON THIS DISCRIMINATION ALL ART IS FOUNDED I INTREAT THEN	611B	V LAST JUDG/N	PROSE
DISCRIPTIVE SEE DESCRIPTIVE			
ADMITTANCE...EACH PERSON A DISCRIPTIVE CATALOGUE INCLUDED	560C	EXHIBITION ADV	PROSE
DISDAIN			
A COLD ORB OF DISDAIN REVOLVD ROUND HIM	143	FRENCH REVOLTN	199
ON HATE ETERNAL IN HIS VAST DISDAIN HE LABOURD BEATING . .	302	FOUR ZOAS 4	206
INCESSANT STERN DISDAIN HIS SCALY FORM GNAWS INWARDLY . .	352	FOUR ZOAS 8	434
AND THERE IS A FROWN OF DISDAIN	423	THE SMILE	6
WITH FACES OF SCORN & WITH EYES OF DISDAIN	429	MARY	41
CONTEMNED AND REJECTED ALL HE DID WITH THE UTMOST DISDAIN	563C	DESC CAT	PROSE

		PAGE	TITLE	LINE
DISDAINING				
	SHALL MOUNT ON NATIVE WINGS DISDAINING	27	EDW THIRD/PS 3	273
DISDAINS				
	THAT DISDAINS TO FOLLOW THIS WORLD'S FASHION	752	EV GOSPEL(D)/N	48
DISEASD				
	IS THE BODY DISEASD WHEN THE MEMBERS ARE HEALTHFUL . . .	142	FRENCH REVOLTN	182
DISEASE				
	AND WHAT WOULD TURN INTO DISEASE	188	A FAIRY SKIPD	15
	WITH FIERCE DISEASE AND LUST UNABLE TO STEM THE FIRE OF ORC	203	AMERICA 16	21
	THE CLOUDS OF DISEASE HOVERD WIDE	253	AHANIA 4	22
	DISEASE ON DISEASE SHAPE ON SHAPE	253	AHANIA 4	25
	HE SPOKE NOT HE WAS SILENT TILL HE FELT THE COLD DISEASE	324	FOUR ZOAS 7	182
	A TYRANT IS THE WORST DISEASE & THE CAUSE OF ALL OTHERS	402B	ANNO BACON	MARG
	WITH THUNDER OF WAR & TRUMPETS SOUND WITH ARMIES OF DISEASE	489	MILTON 9	24
	THE FLEA LOUSE BUG THE TAPE-WORM ALL THE ARMIES OF DISEASE	513	MILTON 27	17
	ANNEXED TO IMBECILITY AND DISEASE IS A SUBJECT FOR BURLESQUE	580A	DESC CAT 5	PROSE
	BY ENTERING INTO DISEASE AND EXCREMENT DRUNKENNESS . . .	582A	DESC CAT 8	PROSE
	WEEP AT THY SOUL'S DISEASE AND THE DIVINE VISION IS DARKEND	622	JERUSALEM 4	13
	I SAW DISEASE FORMING A BODY OF DEATH AROUND THE LAMB . .	628	JERUSALEM 9	9
	THE DISEASE OF SHAME COVERS ME FROM HEAD TO FEET I HAVE NO HOPE	643	JERUSALEM 21	3
	THE SEA THE STARS THE SUN THE MOON DRIVN FORTH BY MY DISEASE	643	JERUSALEM 21	10
	LEANING AGAINST THE PILLARS & HIS DISEASE ROSE FROM HIS SKIRTS	658	JERUSALEM 32	1
	LOS SHUDDERD AT BEHOLDING ALBION FOR HIS DISEASE . . .	666	JERUSALEM 40	1
	THUS ALBION SAT STUDIOUS OF OTHERS IN HIS PALE DISEASE .	669	JERUSALEM 42	1
	I SEE DISEASE ARISE UPON YOU YET SPEAK TO ME AND GIVE . .	673	JERUSALEM 43	76
	STRUCKEN WITH ALBION'S DISEASE THEY BECOME WHAT THEY BEHOLD	674	JERUSALEM 44	32
	THIS DREAD DISEASE NONE BUT JESUS O LORD DESCEND AND SAVE	675	JERUSALEM 45	16
	SCATTERING HER LEPROUS SNOWS IN FLAKES OF DISEASE OVER ALBION	703	JERUSALEM 66	80
	HEAL THOU THE SICK OF SPIRITUAL DISEASE	718	STOOD AMONG/J	25
	YE SMITERS WITH DISEASE MAKE WAY	749	EV GOSPEL(B)/N	28
	IS GOD A SMITER WITH DISEASE	749	EV GOSPEL(B)/N	30
	CORPOREAL DISEASE TO WHICH I READILY AGREE	772B	ANNO SPURZHEIM	MARG
	MELANCHOLY WITHOUT ANY REAL REASON FOR IT A DISEASE WHICH	798A	LETTER 10	PROSE
	JUST AS I HAD BECOME WELL THAT IS SUBDUED THE DISEASE . .	874D	LETTER 80	PROSE
	& HAVE GREAT HOPES THAT THE DISEASE IS GONE	875C	LETTER 81	PROSE
DISEASED				
	AND THE DISEASED ONLY PROPAGATED	246	SONG OF LOS 3	27
DISEASES				
	TO A BED OF STRAW THE SEVEN DISEASES OF EARTH	135	FRENCH REVOLTN	36
	ARMD WITH DISEASES OF THE EARTH TO CAST UPON THE ABYSS . .	201	AMERICA 13	15
	IN SWIFT DISEASES AND TORMENTS	235	URIZEN 25	26
	IN ALL THE DISEASES OF MAN FALLING UPON THY GREY ACCURSED FRONT	322	FOUR ZOAS 7	89
	TAKE THOU THE SEVEN DISEASES OF MAN STORE THEM FOR TIMES TO COME	336	FOUR ZOAS 7B	118
	THE SEVEN DISEASES OF THE EARTH ARE CARVED TERRIBLE . . .	633	JERUSALEM 13	17
	SUSPITION & REVENGE & THE SEVEN DISEASES OF THE SOUL . .	641	JERUSALEM 19	26
	OF SEVEN DISEASES ONCE A CONTINUAL CLOUD OF SALVATION ROSE	721	JERUSALEM 79	57
	AND TRACED DISEASES TO THEIR SOURCE	749	EV GOSPEL(B)/N	36
	ALL MENTAL POWERS BY DISEASES WE BIND	755	EV GOSPEL(E)/N	87
	DISEASES OF THE MIND I PITY HIM	772B	ANNO SPURZHEIM	MARG
DISGRACD				
	DO NOT SUFFER YOURSELVES TO BE DISGRACD	597C	PUB ADDRESS/N	*PROSE
DISGRACE				
	THIS DISGRACE IF SO WE ARE NOT SOVEREIGNS	20	EDW THIRD/PS 2	78
	GIVE HIGH PRICE FOR THE WORST LEAVE THE BEST IN DISGRACE	445	ANNO REYNOLDS	3
	HAS THE COURAGE TO SUFFER POVERTY AND DISGRACE	582D	DESC CAT 9	PROSE
DISGRACED				
	DISGRACED SERGEANT HIS NAME IS JOHN SCHOLFIELD	828B	LETTER 28	PROSE
DISGRACING				
	HIS COUNTRY WILL REFRAIN FROM DISGRACING EITHER BY SUCH	864D	LETTER 61	PROSE
DISGUISE				
	["O WHAT A SCENE IS HERE WHAT A DISGUISE"]	52B	ISLAND MOON 8	
	AND YOUR WINTER & NIGHT IN DISGUISE	171	NURSES SONG/N	8
	AND YOUR WINTER AND NIGHT IN DISGUISE	212	NURSES SONG/SE	8
	PLAYS IN DISGUISE IN WHISPERD HYMN & MUMBLING PRAYER THE PRIESTS	333	FOUR ZOAS 7B	26
	TWAS NOT A MOUSE TWAS DEATH IN A DISGUISE	537	AND HIS LEGS/N	40
	MORE MALICE IN DISGUISE	539	CAN THERE BE/N	2
	ITS DISGUISE IN THE CLASSICAL & SCOTCH LANGUAGE	788D	ANNO THORNTON	* MARG
	UNLESS QUESTIOND & THEN I NEVER DISGUISE THE TRUTH . . .	813A	LETTER 22	PROSE
DISGUISER				
	DISGUISER OF THE FEMALE FORM	188	A FAIRY SKIPD	5
DISGUISES				
	HE ORDAIND & PRIESTESSES CLOTHD IN DISGUISES BEASTIAL . .	333	FOUR ZOAS 7B	27
	WHO DISGUISES HIS PRINCIPLES & CALLS THAT CHANGE	386B	ANNO WATSON.	MARG
DISGUST				
	& DISGUST [A] & ACCORDINGLY	596B	PUB ADDRESS/N	*PROSE
DISH				
	& OUR GOOD LADY PAULINA OVER A DISH OF COFFEE I LONG TO HEAR	862A	LETTER 59	PROSE
DISHES				
	AND DISHES OF PAINTED CLAY GLOWING WITH BEAUTY & CRUELTY	702	JERUSALEM 66	33
	OF LAMBS AND DOVES MINGLED TOGETHER IN CUPS AND DISHES . .	725	JERUSALEM 82	7
DISHONEST				
	("LITTLE OR NO NOVELTY ") DISHONEST MISREPRESENTATION	384D	ANNO WATSON	MARG
	ON THE BIBLE ARE DISHONEST DESIGNING KNAVES	390C	ANNO WATSON	MARG

506

```
                                                      PAGE     TITLE        LINE
DISHONEST   (CONTINUED)
    [EITHER HE IS DISHONEST ?OR HE IS ?INSANE]    . . . . . . SUPP ANNO REYNOLDS  * MARG
DISHONOUR
    THEN MY VERSE I DISHONOUR MY PICTURES DESPISE . . . . .  829 O WHY BORN/L        5
DISHONOURABLE
    THE HARLOT DAUGHTER MOTHER OF PITY AND DISHONOURABLE     640 JERUSALEM 18       12
        FORGIVENESS
DISHUMANIZD
    THEN HE BEHELD THE FORMS OF TYGERS & OF LIONS DISHUMANIZD 314 FOUR ZOAS 6      116
        MEN
    SONS OF PERDITION TERRIBLE HIS FORM DISHUMANIZD MONSTROUS 347 FOUR ZOAS 8   *  252
    TWELVE MONSTROUS DISHUMANIZD TERRORS SYNAGOGUES OF SATAN  528 MILTON 37        17
DISK
    THY CRIMSON DISK SO EER THE SUN WAS RENT FROM THY         198 AMERICA 5         5
        RED SPHERE
    THE BROAD DISK OF URIZEN UPHEAVD  . . . . . . . . .       249 AHANIA 2         21
    BEATS INCESSANT TEN WINTERS THE DISK . . . . . . . .      249 AHANIA 2         24
    HIS DISK INTO A TERRIBLE VISION TO THE EYES OF TREMBLING  335 FOUR ZOAS 7B  *  80
        MORTALS
    A DISK OF BLOOD DISTANT & HEAVNS & EARTHS ROLL DARK BETWEEN 495 MILTON 14      27
    DO YOU NOT SEE A ROUND DISK OF FIRE SOMEWHAT LIKE A GUINEA 617B V LAST JUDG/N  PROSE
DISKS
    ENLARGING AND ENLARGING TILL THEIR DISKS APPROACHD EACH   504 MILTON 21        39
        OTHER
DISLIKE
    WITH DISTASTE AND DISLIKE  . . . . . . . . . .            27 EDW THIRD/PS 3    261
    SO IF BOTH POETS & PAINTERS SHOULD ALTERNATELY DISLIKE  . 825B LETTER 27       PROSE
    MUCH SURPRISED AT THE DISLIKE THAT SOME CONNOISSEURS SHEW  864D LETTER 61      PROSE
DISLOCATED
    WITH DISLOCATED LIMBS HAD FALLN THE SPECTRE ROSE IN PAIN  299 FOUR ZOAS 4      64
DISMAL
    AND OFTEN HEARD THE DISMAL CLANG OF ARMS  . . . . . .     31 EDW THIRD/PS 5    40
    I SEEM TO HEAR THE DISMAL YELLS OF DEATH  . . . . . .     31 EDW THIRD/PS 5    45
    AND STRIFE BROUGHT FORTH REVENGE HATE BROODING IN         42C THEN SHE BORE    PROSE
        HER DISMAL DEN
    WERE FRIGHTED BY THE DISMAL CRIES OF HELA ON THE MOUNTAINS 109 TIRIEL 7        20
    THEN LAUGH IN THE DISMAL DEN THEN ARE SILENT . . . . .    136 FRENCH REVOLTN   53
    IN DISMAL VOLUMES AS RISEN FROM BENEATH THE ARCHBISHOP    139 FRENCH REVOLTN  126
        OF PARIS AROSE
    . . . MYRIADS DESCENDING AND WEEPING THRO DISMAL WINDS  . . 140 FRENCH REVOLTN 134
    [FROM EVERY DISMAL STREET I HEAR] . . . . . . . . .       170 LONDON/N         15
    SOON SPREADS THE DISMAL SHADE . . . . . . . . .           174 HUMAN IMAGE/N    14
    WEEPING IN DISMAL HOWLING WOE HE DARK DESCENDED HOWLING   203 AMERICA 16        7
    WEEPING IN DISMAL HOWLINGS BEFORE THE STERN AMERICANS  . . 203 AMERICA 16      12
    BETWEEN THE MOUNTAINS DISMAL VISIONS MOPE AROUND THE HOUSE 204 AMERICA CANC B  12
    SOON SPREADS THE DISMAL SHADE . . . . . . . . .           217 HUMAN ABSTR/SE   13
    O THE DISMAL CARE  . . . . . . . .                        219 LIT GRL LST/SE   33
    LOS HOWLD IN A DISMAL STUPOR  . . . . . . . . . .         226 URIZEN 7          1
    AND A STATE OF DISMAL WOE  . . . . . . .                  228 URIZEN 10        43
    AND A STATE OF DISMAL WOE  . . . . . . .                  228 URIZEN 11         9
    AND A STATE OF DISMAL WOE  . . . . . . .                  228 URIZEN 11        18
    AND A STATE OF DISMAL WOE  . . . . . . .                  229 URIZEN 11        25
    AND A STATE OF DISMAL WOE  . . . . . . .                  229 URIZEN 13         3
    AND A STATE OF DISMAL WOE  . . . . . . .                  229 URIZEN 13        11
    AND A STATE OF DISMAL WOE  . . . . . . .                  229 URIZEN 13        19
    MANY SORROWS AND DISMAL THROES  . . . . . . . .           232 URIZEN 19        33
    LIKE THE DARK CLOUD DISBURDEN IN THE DAY OF DISMAL THUNDER 238 EUROPE PREL 1    7
    WITH DISMAL TORMENT SICK HANGING UPON THE WIND HE FLED  . . 242 EUROPE 12      18
    OF IRON FROM THE DISMAL SHADE . . . . . . . . .           252 AHANIA 4          1
    IN PERTURBD PAIN AND DISMAL TORMENT . . . . . . . .       252 AHANIA 4         15
    RAN THRO ALL HIS DISMAL WORLD . . . . . . . .             253 AHANIA 4         39
    . . . WAILD IN DISMAL FEAR . . . . . . . . .              264 FOUR ZOAS 1       8
    IN [DISMAL] GNAWING PAIN DRAWN OUT BY HER LOVD FINGERS    266 FOUR ZOAS 1      79
        EVERY NERVE
    THAT DARK & DISMAL INFINITE WHERE THOUGHT ROAMS UP & DOWN 268 FOUR ZOAS 1     155
    [TILL ?FAR DISMAL XXX ?FOUR XXX ALL XXX] . . . . . . SUPP FOUR ZOAS 1   *
    HIS CLOUDY BELLOWS & THE SOUTH & EAST & DISMAL WEST  . . . 282 FOUR ZOAS 2     69
    . . . THAT LIGHTS THE [DISMAL] DARKSOM DAY . . . . .      283 FOUR ZOAS 2     128
    CASTING THEIR SPARKLES DIRE ABROAD INTO THE DISMAL DEEP   283 FOUR ZOAS 2     140
    THE DISMAL VISION OF MINE EYES O LOVE & LIFE & LIGHT  .   293 FOUR ZOAS 3      73
    DOWN FROM THE DISMAL NORTH THE PRINCE IN THUNDERS & THICK 295 FOUR ZOAS 3     139
        CLOUDS
    FOR NOW NO MORE REMAIND OF ENION IN THE DISMAL AIR  . . . 297 FOUR ZOAS 3     205
    DOUBTING STOOD THARMAS IN THE [DISMAL] SOLEMN DARKNESS    298 FOUR ZOAS 4   *  44
        HIS DIM EYES
    WHERE ENITHARMON JOIND TO HIS LEFT SIDE IN [DISMAL] GRIDING 299 FOUR ZOAS 4 *  60
        PAIN
    A SHADOW BLUE OBSCURE & DISMAL LIKE A STATUE OF LEAD  .   299 FOUR ZOAS 4      65
    A SHADOW BLUE OBSCURE & DISMAL FROM THE BREATHING NOSTRILS 300 FOUR ZOAS 4    105
    LEST HE SHOULD RISE AGAIN FROM DEATH IN ALL HIS [DISMAL]  300 FOUR ZOAS 4   * 121
        DREARY POWER
    WHIRLING UP BROKEN ROCKS ON HIGH INTO THE DISMAL AIR  . . 301 FOUR ZOAS 4    163
    A FIRST AGE PASSED A STATE OF DISMAL WOE . . . . . .      303 FOUR ZOAS 4    222
    AND A THIRD AGE PASSED A STATE OF DISMAL WOE . . . .      303 FOUR ZOAS 4    231
    AGE PASSED OVER & A STATE OF DISMAL WOE . . . . . .       303 FOUR ZOAS 4    235
    AND A FIFTH AGE PASSED & A STATE OF DISMAL WOE  . . .     303 FOUR ZOAS 4    238
    AND THIRST APPEARD AND A SIXTH AGE PASSED OF DISMAL WOE   303 FOUR ZOAS 4  * 242
    AND A SEVENTH AGE PASSED OVER & A STATE OF DISMAL WOE  . . 303 FOUR ZOAS 4   246
    BENEATH THE DEEPS IN DISMAL DARKNESS BENEATH IMMENSITY    304 FOUR ZOAS 4    279
    TERRIFIC PALE ENITHARMON STRETCHED ON THE [DISMAL] DREARY 305 FOUR ZOAS 5      5
        EARTH
    THE NIGHT BLEW COLD AND ENITHARMON SHRIEKD ON THE DISMAL  305 FOUR ZOAS 5     20
        WIND
```

507

	PAGE	TITLE		LINE
DISMAL (CONTINUED)				
BEGAN A DISMAL DANCE THE WINDS AROUND ON POINTED ROCKS . .	306	FOUR ZOAS	5	34
DEPENDING FROM THE BOSOM OF LOS & HOW WITH [DISMAL] GRIDING PAIN	307	FOUR ZOAS	5	93
WHILE ENITHARMON FOLLOWD HIM WEEPING IN DISMAL WOE . . .	307	FOUR ZOAS	5	98
THE [DISMAL] ACCURSED CHAIN O HOW BRIGHT ENITHARMON HOWLD & CRIED	308	FOUR ZOAS	5	102
THE DISMAL VALES & UP TO THE IRON MOUNTAIN'S TOP WHERE ORC	309	FOUR ZOAS	5	151
. . . BURST OPEN & AGAIN CLOSE WITH A [?DISMAL] DEADLY PAIN	309	FOUR ZOAS	5 *	178
AND WHEN THE GATE WAS OPEN SHE BEHELD THAT [DISMAL] DREARY DEEP	309	FOUR ZOAS	5 *	180
WITH PAIN UPON THE [DISMAL] DREARY MOUNTAINS & WITH PAIN DESCENDED	313	FOUR ZOAS	6 *	79
LIGHTING HIS DISMAL JOURNEY THRO THE PATHLESS WORLD OF DEATH	314	FOUR ZOAS	6	84
THIS DISMAL WORLD HE STOOD A WHILE & LOOKD BACK OER HIS FORMER	315	FOUR ZOAS	6 *	150
HIMSELF INTO THE DISMAL VOID FALLING HE FELL & FELL . . .	315	FOUR ZOAS	6	153
HE SIEZD THEM WITH A [DISMAL] GLOOMY SMILE	316	FOUR ZOAS	6	169
HIS DISMAL VOYAGE EYEING THE NEXT SPHERE THO FAR REMOTE	316	FOUR ZOAS	6	183
THE DISMAL SQUADRONS OF URTHONA WEAVING THE DIRE WEB . .	320	FOUR ZOAS	6	324
HIS BOOKS OUT OF THE DISMAL SHADE ALL BUT THE BOOK OF IRON	321	FOUR ZOAS	7	39
THEN LOS MOURND ON THE DISMAL WIND IN HIS JEALOUS LAMENTATION	324	FOUR ZOAS	7	183
BENEATH THE TREE OF MYSTERY WHICH IN THE DISMAL ABYSS .	325	FOUR ZOAS	7	212
WHERE URIZEN SAT ON HIS ROCK THE SHADOW BROODED [DISMAL]	333	FOUR ZOAS	7B *	2
. . . & THE DISMAL MOON ROLLS OVER HER	335	FOUR ZOAS	7B	75
THE SHADOW REARD HER DISMAL HEAD OVER THE FLAMING YOUTH	336	FOUR ZOAS	7B	126
BUT BLOOD & WOUNDS & DISMAL CRIES & CLARIONS OF WAR . .	338	FOUR ZOAS	7B	205
CRIED TO THE CHURCHYARDS & THE EARTHWORM CAME IN DISMAL STATE	355	FOUR ZOAS	8	537
AND WEEPING OVER ORC & URIZEN IN CLOUDS & [DISMAL] FLAMING FIRES	355	FOUR ZOAS	8	579
THEIR RIVERS CRY WITH A DISMAL CRY THE CATTLE GATHER TOGETHER	358	FOUR ZOAS	9	54
SAW THEM DEPART IN DISMAL DROVES THE TRUMPET SOUNDED LOUD	359	FOUR ZOAS	9	65
BEGAN TO ENTER THE HOLY CITY ENTRING THE DISMAL CLOUDS .	359	FOUR ZOAS	9	84
THRO DISMAL DARKNESS DRAVE THE PLOW OF AGES OVER CITIES	365	FOUR ZOAS	9	312
WHEN WILL THE TIME OF CLOUDS BE PAST & THE DISMAL NIGHT OF THARMAS	370	FOUR ZOAS	9	490
DISMAL LOUD REDOUNDING THE NETHER FLOOR SHAKES WITH THE SOUND	374	FOUR ZOAS	9	652
AND A FIRST AGE PASSED OVER & A STATE OF DISMAL WOE . . .	482	MILTON	3	10
AND A SECOND AGE PASSED OVER & A STATE OF DISMAL WOE . .	482	MILTON	3	13
AND A THIRD AGE PASSED OVER & A STATE OF DISMAL WOE . . .	482	MILTON	3	16
AND A FOURTH AGE PASSED OVER & A STATE OF DISMAL WOE . .	482	MILTON	3	19
AND A FIFTH AGE PASSED OVER & A STATE OF DISMAL WOE . . .	482	MILTON	3	21
AND A SIXTH AGE PASSED OVER & A STATE OF DISMAL WOE . . .	482	MILTON	3	23
AND A SEVENTH AGE PASSED OVER & A STATE OF DISMAL WOE .	483	MILTON	3	27
UPON HIS FIBROUS LEFT FOOT BLACK MOST DISMAL TO OUR EYES	506	MILTON	22	35
HE WEEPS INTO THE ATLANTIC DEEP YET STILL IN DISMAL DREAMS	506	MILTON	23	9
FOR BACON & NEWTON SHEATHD IN DISMAL STEEL THEIR TERRORS HANG	635	JERUSALEM	15	11
THE SOLDIER'S FIFE THE HARLOT'S SHRIEK THE VIRGIN'S DISMAL GROAN	636	JERUSALEM	16	6
AND WANDERED DISTANT IN A DISMAL NIGHT CLOUDED & DARK .	647	JERUSALEM	24	9
INTO HIS BOSOM FROM WHICH ALBION SHRUNK IN DISMAL PAIN .	656	JERUSALEM	30	17
ALBION SPOKE IN HIS DISMAL DREAMS O THOU DECEITFUL FRIEND	669	JERUSALEM	42	9
BONIFYING INTO A SCULL THE MARROW EXUDING IN DISMAL PAIN	689	JERUSALEM	58	8
BUT BLOOD AND WOUNDS AND DISMAL CRIES AND SHADOWS OF THE OAK	701	JERUSALEM	65	51
HERSELF IN CHAINS THIS FROM WITHIN WAS SEEN IN A DISMAL NIGHT	719	JERUSALEM	78	24
AND RAHAB LIKE A DISMAL AND INDEFINITE HOVERING CLOUD .	723	JERUSALEM	80	51
WHO CAN DESCRIBE THE DISMAL TORMENTS OF SUCH A STATE .	813A	LETTER	22	PROSE
AND HIS DISMAL TERRORS MAKE ME AFRAID	818	HAPPINESS/L		52
DISMAY				
I MUST NOT SLEEP NOR REST BECAUSE Or MADNESS & DISMAY . .	103	TIRIEL	3	29
MADNESS & DEEP DISMAY (POSSESS) THE HEART OF THE BLIND MAN	103	TIRIEL	3 *	37
IN SIGHING AND DISMAY	124	SCHOOL BOY/SI		10
BY SORROW AND CARE'S DISMAY	124	SCHOOL BOY/SI		25
GLANCING HIS BEAMY EYELIDS OVER THE DEEP IN DARK DISMAY	159D	SONG LIBERTY		PROSE
IN TREMBLING & HOWLING & DISMAY	229	URIZEN	13	17
AND ENITHARMON GROANS & CRIES IN ANGUISH AND DISMAY . . .	245	EUROPE	15	8
TO RESTRAIN TO DISMAY TO THIN	247	SONG OF LOS	6	11
DISMAY & SHARP BLIGHTINGS THE PROPHET	259	BOOK OF LOS	5	25
TERRIFIC URIZEN STRODE ABOVE IN FEAR & PALE DISMAY . . .	280	FOUR ZOAS	2	19
CIRCLING ROUND THE DARK DEMON WITH HOWLINGS DISMAY & SHARP BLIGHTINGS	302	FOUR ZOAS	4	200
AND HIS FEET STAMPD THE NETHER ABYSS IN TREMBLING HOWLING & DISMAY	303	FOUR ZOAS	4	245
WANDER IN TERROR & DISMAY	426	MENTAL TRAVLER		76
STAMPD THE NETHER ABYSS IN TREMBLING & HOWLING & DISMAY	483	MILTON	3	26
AND LEFT HIS PARENTS IN DISMAY	748	EV GOSPEL(B)/N		4
AND LEFT HIS PARENTS IN DISMAY	750	EV GOSPEL(C)/N		4
AND LEFT HIS PARENTS IN DISMAY	751	EV GOSPEL(D)/N		6
DISMAYD				
. . . NOR BE YOU DISMAYD WITH SORROWS WHICH FLEE AT THE MORNING	142	FRENCH REVOLTN		180
DISOBEDIENCE				
JOHN FOR DISOBEDIENCE BLED	749	EV GOSPEL(B)/N		17

```
                                                              PAGE      TITLE            LINE
DISOBEDIENT
    HENCE THE INFERNAL VEIL GROWS IN THE DISOBEDIENT FEMALE    708 JERUSALEM 69          38
DISORDER
    IVE TOLD HIM BEFORE BUT HIS DISORDER  . . . . . . . .       23 EDW THIRD/PS 3        69
    HERE WAS GREAT CONFUSION & DISORDER  . . . . . . .          54D ISLAND MOON 9      PROSE
DISORGANIZD
    DISORGANIZD RENT FROM ETERNITY  . . . . . . . . . .        228 URIZEN 10            27
    OVER THE DISORGANIZD IMMORTAL  . . . . . . . . . .         253 AHANIA 4             19
    IN FETTERS OF ICE SHRINKING DISORGANIZD RENT FROM ETERNITY 303 FOUR ZOAS 4         212
    THEY MUST RENEW THEIR BRIGHTNESS & THEIR DISORGANIZD       366 FOUR ZOAS 9         371
        FUNCTIONS
    DISORGANIZD AN EVANESCENT SHADE SCARCE SEEN OR HEARD AMONG 719 JERUSALEM 78         28
    DISORGANIZD & THERE IS PHAROH IN HIS IRON COURT  . . . .   735 JERUSALEM 89         18
DISORGANIZED
    O FIEND OF RIGHTEOUSNESS PRETENDEST THINE IS A DISORGANIZED 738 JERUSALEM 91        23
DISPATCHD
    THUS ARE THE MESSENGERS DISPATCHD TILL THEY REACH THE EARTH 526 MILTON 36            8
        AGAIN
DISPEL
    SUCH IS SWEET ELOQUENCE THAT DOES DISPEL  . . . . . .       15 IMIT SPEN/PS         31
DISPELLD
    BUT MY ARRIVAL HAS DISPELLD THE FORMIDABLE MALADY & MY    833D LETTER 33          PROSE
        DEAR &
DISPENSING
    DISPENSING UNCEASING TO ALL THE WHOLE LAND  . . . . . .   800 MRS FLAXMAN/L         16
DISPERSD
    BUT LOS DISPERSD THE CLOUDS EVEN AS THE STRONG WINDS OF   507 MILTON 23             31
        JEHOVAH
DISPERSE
    DISPERSE THOSE REBELLIOUS SPIRITS OF ENVY & MALIGNITY  . . 842A LETTER 41         PROSE
    BY THE METHODS WHICH THEY USE TO PUBLISH & DISPERSE COPIES 856C LETTER 54         PROSE
DISPLACD
    HE DISPLACD CONTINENTS THE OCEANS FLED BEFORE HIS FACE  . . 489 MILTON 9            16
DISPLAY
    [DISPLAY THY] TO RAISE HIS DARK & BURNING VISAGE . . . . .  106 TIRIEL 5             5
    BUT DOES A HUMAN FORM DISPLAY  . . . . . . . . . . .        434 AUGURIES            131
    TO DISPLAY NATURE'S CRUEL HOLINESS THE DECEITS OF NATURAL   527 MILTON 36            25
        RELIGION
    WHICH OUGHT TO DISPLAY AND NOT TO HIDE FORM  . . . . .      564D DESC CAT 1       PROSE
    GARDENS & GROVES DISPLAY PARADISE WITH ITS INHABITANTS  . . 613C V LAST JUDG/N    PROSE
    I AGAIN DISPLAY MY GIANT FORMS TO THE PUBLIC MY FORMER  .   620D JERUSALEM 3      PROSE
    BY THIS DISPLAY OF PRETENDED VIRTUE CHIEFLY DESIGN          682D JERUSALEM 52     PROSE
        TO EXPOSE
    AND THY REVENGE ABROAD DISPLAY  . . . . . . . . . .        750 EV GOSPEL(C)/N      43
    AND THY REVENGE ABROAD DISPLAY  . . . . . . . . . . .      753 EV GOSPEL(D)/N      79
    OF THE ART WHICH I NEGLECTED TO DISPLAY IN THOSE  . . . .  814C LETTER 23        PROSE
DISPLAYD
    . . . DISPLAYD GREEN FIELDS AMONG  . . . . . . . .         274 FOUR ZOAS 1        367
    THRO THE CLEAR CHANGING ATMOSPHERE DISPLAYD GREEN FIELDS   274 FOUR ZOAS 1        367
        AMONG
    & THE NATURE OF ETERNAL THINGS DISPLAYD  . . . . . .       612D V LAST JUDG/N    PROSE
    ART & SCIENCE CANNOT EXIST BUT BY NAKED BEAUTY DISPLAYD    663 JERUSALEM 36        49
    DISPLAYD IN THE EMANATIVE VISIONS OF CANAAN IN JERUSALEM   739 JERUSALEM 92        21
        & IN SHILOH
DISPLAYED
    THAT BLAKE'S DESIGNS SHOULD BE BY US DISPLAYED  . . . .    537 AND HIS LEGS/N *     37
    ART CAN NEVER EXIST WITHOUT NAKED BEAUTY DISPLAYED  . . .  776D INSC LAOCOON     PROSE
DISPLAYING
    DISPLAYING THE INFINITE WHICH WAS HID  . . . . . . .       154C MARRIAGE HH 14   PROSE
    DISPLAYING NAKED BEAUTY WITH FLUTE & HARP & SONG . . . .   484 MILTON 4             28
    LIKE DISPLAYING OIL & WATER INTO A LAMP  . . . . . .       550 ENGL ENCOU/N 2       5
    OF DISPLAYING UP A LIGHT WHEN WE WANT NOT TO SEE  . . .    550 ENGL ENCOU/N 2       8
    DISPLAYING OUR GIANT LIMBS TO ALL THE WINDS OF HEAVEN      647 JERUSALEM 24         6
        SUDDEN
    DISPLAYING THE ETERNAL VISION THE DIVINE SIMILITUDE  . . . 664 JERUSALEM 38        11
DISPLAYS
    WHICH BY ITS ROLLING AWAY DISPLAYS THE OPENING SEATS OF    444A LAST JUDGMNT/L   PROSE
    THAT UNAFFECTED SIMPLICITY WHEN IN HIGH RANK ALWAYS        568A DESC CAT 3       PROSE
        DISPLAYS
DISPLEASD
    & IF ANY OTHERS ARE DISPLEASD IT IS ALSO AN ARGUMENT OF    862A LETTER 59        PROSE
        THEIR
DISPLEASING
    SATAN THINKS THAT SIN IS DISPLEASING TO GOD  . . . . .     615C V LAST JUDG/N    PROSE
    HE OUGHT TO KNOW THAT NOTHING IS DISPLEASING TO GOD  . . . 615C V LAST JUDG/N    PROSE
DISPOSD
    FROM THE SUPPORTING ARMS OF THE ETERNAL SAVIOUR WHO DISPOSD 277 FOUR ZOAS 1       466
DISPOSE
    HAYLEY IS WILLING TO DISPOSE OF THIS HIS NEW POEM I WILL   856C LETTER 54        PROSE
    YOU ARE DESIROUS I KNOW TO DISPOSE OF SOME OF MY WORKS &   878B LETTER 88        PROSE
DISPOSED
    BEING DISPOSED OF BY MEANS OF A RAFFLE HE SUPPOSES IT IS.  844C LETTER 43        PROSE
DISPOSITION
    THE DISPOSITION OF FORMS ALWAYS DIRECTS COLOURING  . . .   580D DESC CAT 5       PROSE
    THEIR WOMEN LIKE CHALK FOR THE DISPOSITION OF THEIR FORMS  581A DESC CAT 5       PROSE
DISPRAISES
    PRAISES YOU & DISPRAISES WITH THE SAME BREATH . . . . .    798B LETTER 10        PROSE
DISPROVE
    REYNOLDS IS TO DISPROVE & CONTEMN SPIRITUAL PERCEPTION  . . 473D ANNO REYNOLDS    MARG
DISPUTE
    WHERE NO DISPUTE CAN COME BECAUSE OF THOSE WHO SLEEP  . .  518 MILTON 30            3
    THEIR SUBLIMITY WHO CAN DISPUTE  . . . . . . . . . .       570B DESC CAT 3       PROSE
```

509

```
                                                          PAGE      TITLE           LINE
DISPUTE    (CONTINUED)
    WHERE NO DISPUTE CAN COME CREATED FOR THOSE WHO SLEEP   .  .   678 JERUSALEM 48       20
DISPUTED
    TO MY INVENTIONS THE EXECUTIVE PART THEY NEVER DISPUTED      601D PUB ADDRESS/N    PROSE
DISPUTES
    DARK DISPUTES & ARTFUL TEAZING  . . . . . . . . . .          126 VOICE BARD/SI       5
DISREGARD
    WHEN THOSE WHO DISREGARD ALL MORTAL THINGS SAW A MIGHTY-ONE  686 JERUSALEM 55        1
DISSEMBLE
    [TIRIEL COULD SCARCE DISSEMBLE MORE . . . . . . . .          102 TIRIEL 3            7
    WHEN THOU AWAKEST WILT THOU DISSEMBLE ALL THY SECRET JOYS    193 V DAU ALBION 6      8
    THEN COMST THOU FORTH A MODEST VIRGIN KNOWING TO DISSEMBLE   194 V DAU ALBION 6     10
DISSEMBLER
    SUPPOSES THAT HIS PRINCIPLES ARE TO BE CHANGED IS          386B ANNO WATSON       MARG
        A DISSEMBLER
    JERUSALEM DISSEMBLER JERUSALEM I LOOK INTO THY BOSOM  .  .   643 JERUSALEM 21       18
DISSEMBLERS
    THOU EYELESS FIEND & YOU DISSEMBLERS IS THIS TIRIEL'S HOUSE  106 TIRIEL 4           86
DISSEMBLING
    UPON THE THAMES AND MEDWAY RIVERS OF BEULAH DISSEMBLING      622 JERUSALEM 4         34
DISSEMBLINGLY
    I AM NOT OF THIS REGION SAID TIRIEL DISSEMBLINGLY     .  .   102 TIRIEL 2           48
DISSEMINATED
    NOTWITHSTANDING ARTFULLY DISSEMINATED INSINUATIONS  .  .   586D CHAUCER 1        *PROSE
DISSIMULATION
    COMMUNING WITH THE SERPENT OF ORC IN DARK DISSIMULATION      343 FOUR ZOAS 8        96
    THE GLITTERING DISSIMULATION ACHILLES' WRATH IS BLUNT ABUSE 384D ANNO WATSON       MARG
    SERPENTINE DISSIMULATION  . . . . . . . . . . . .          386C ANNO WATSON     * MARG
    IN INDIGNATION FOR SATAN'S SOFT DISSIMULATION OF FRIENDSHIP  488 MILTON 8           35
    TILL DEEP DISSIMULATION IS THE ONLY DEFENCE AN HONEST MAN    679 JERUSALEM 49       23
        HAS LEFT
DISSIMULATIONS
    DISSIMULATIONS BUT TIME & SPACE ARE REAL BEINGS   .  .  .   614D V LAST JUDG/N    PROSE
DISSIPATE
    DISSIPATE OR SINK INTO THE SEAS OF THARMAS LUVAH SAT    .    372 FOUR ZOAS 9       573
    HE WHO HAS NOTHING TO DISSIPATE CANNOT DISSIPATE THE    .  454B ANNO REYNOLDS      MARG
    FROM ALL THE NATIONS OF THE EARTH TO DISSIPATE INTO NON     715 JERUSALEM 74       51
        ENTITY
DISSIPATED
    PAINTERS ARE NOTED FOR BEING DISSIPATED & WILD    .  .  .  454B ANNO REYNOLDS      MARG
    [WHAT PAINTERS HAVE ONLY BEEN DISSIPATED WITHOUT WILDNESS] 454C ANNO REYNOLDS    * MARG
    ARE DRIVEN AMONG THE STARRY WHEELS RENT AWAY AND DISSIPATED  623 JERUSALEM 5         4
    AND THE PERCEPTIONS TO BE DISSIPATED INTO THE INDEFINITE     703 JERUSALEM 66       47
        BECOMING
DISSIPATING
    DISSIPATING THE ROCKY FORMS OF DEATH BY HIS THUNDEROUS       714 JERUSALEM 73       43
        HAMMER
DISSIPATION
    THE LIVES OF PAINTERS SAY THAT RAFAEL DIED OF DISSIPATION   454B ANNO REYNOLDS      MARG
    IDLENESS IS ONE THING & DISSIPATION ANOTHER   .  .  .  .   454B ANNO REYNOLDS      MARG
    A KIND OF CRIMINAL DISSIPATION & NEGLECT OF THE MAIN CHANCE 798C LETTER 10         PROSE
DISSOLVD
    FROM THY FIERCE LOVE FOR THO I AM DISSOLVD IN THE BRIGHT     288 FOUR ZOAS 2       316
        GOD
    LOS ANSWERD THEREFORE FADE I THUS DISSOLVD IN RAPTURD        288 FOUR ZOAS 2       318
        TRANCE
    TILL MICHAEL SAT DOWN IN THE FURROW WEARY DISSOLVD IN TEARS  488 MILTON 8           37
DISSOLVED
    "BEFORE HIM AND DISSOLVED IN HIS PRESENCE"  .  .  .  .  .  560B EXHIBITION ADV    PROSE
DISSOLVES
    NATURE HAS NO SUPERNATURAL & DISSOLVES IMAGINATION          779C GHOST ABEL 1     PROSE
        IS ETERNITY
DISSOLVING
    IN CLOUDS OF SWEET OBSCURITY MY BEAUTEOUS FORM DISSOLVING    288 FOUR ZOAS 2       311
    O DREAMS OF DEATH THE HUMAN FORM DISSOLVING COMPANIED   .    373 FOUR ZOAS 9       595
DISTAFF
    THERE THE WINGD SHUTTLE SANG THE SPINDLE & THE DISTAFF       378 FOUR ZOAS 9       780
        & THE REEL
    THUNDEROUS RAGE THE SPINDLES OF IRON & THE IRON DISTAFF      692 JERUSALEM 59       53
    AND THE DISTAFF & SPINDLE IN THE HANDS OF VALA WITH THE      699 JERUSALEM 64       32
        FLAX OF
    WERE CAUGHT INTO THE FLAX OF HER DISTAFF & IN HER CLOUD      722 JERUSALEM 80       34
DISTANCE
    ("FORGET IT FORGIVE IT BUT KEEP HIM AT DISTANCE") THIS       87D ANNO LAVATER     MARG
        IS A PARADOX
    OF A BURNING CITY BENEATH US AT AN IMMENSE DISTANCE  .  .   156A MARRIAGE HH 17   PROSE
    AT DISTANCE FAR IN NIGHT REPELLD IN DIREFUL HUNGER CRAVING   276 FOUR ZOAS 1       442
    FOR INFINITE THE DISTANCE & OBSCURD BY COMBUSTIONS DIRE      316 FOUR ZOAS 6       177
    THE WHOLE DISTANCE THAT WILLIAM COULD BE AT ANY TIME   .   437D BLAKES MEMORAN    PROSE
    I HAVE SEEN WHEN AT A DISTANCE  . . . . . . . . . .         607C V LAST JUDG/N    PROSE
    BY EARTHQUAKES A GREAT CITY ON FIRE IS SEEN IN THE DISTANCE 608B V LAST JUDG/N    PROSE
    CONVERSE CONCERNING WEIGHT & DISTANCE IN THE WILDS          661 JERUSALEM 34       40
        OF NEWTON & LOCKE
    AT A DISTANCE THE SOUTH BOUNDS ON HIGH OVER OUR THATCH AND  807B LETTER 17        PROSE
    WIND SINGING ABOVE OUR ROOF & THE SEA ROARING AT A DISTANCE 820B LETTER 25        PROSE
    AM PERSUADED THAT DISTANCE IS NOTHING BUT A PHANTASY  .  .  854A LETTER 52        PROSE
    EVER TO LAMENT YOUR DISTANCE FROM LONDON AS THAT ALONE  .   861D LETTER 59        PROSE
DISTANT    SEE FAR DISTANT
    STRETCHING HER MIGHTY SPEAR OER DISTANT LANDS  .  .  .  .    33 EDW THIRD/PS 6      58
    EYES THE DISTANT COUNTRY WITH JOY  . . . . . . . . .         36C COUCH DEATH/PS   PROSE
    HIPOCRISY IS AS DISTANT FROM SUPERSTITION AS THE WOLF        75A ANNO LAVATER     MARG
        FROM THE LAMB

                                  510
```

	PAGE	TITLE	LINE
DISTANT (CONTINUED)			
THE DISTANT HUNTSMAN WINDS HIS HORN	124	SCHOOL BOY/SI	3
AT LAST TO THE EAST DISTANT ABOUT THREE DEGREES APPEARD	156C	MARRIAGE HH 17	PROSE
[IN WHAT] [BURNT IN] DISTANT DEEPS OR SKIES `.	172	THE TYGER/N 1	5
BURNT IN DISTANT DEEPS OR SKIES	173	THE TYGER/N 2	5
IN WHAT DISTANT DEEPS OR SKIES	214	THE TYGER/SE	5
GLOWS LIKE A METEOR IN THE DISTANT NORTH	239	EUROPE 4	12
AND THUS HER VOICE ROSE TO HER CHILDREN THE DISTANT HEAVENS	240	EUROPE 4	32
REPLY			
DISTANT IN SOLITARY NIGHT	253	AHANIA 4	48
AND OF AHANIA HIS PURE BRIDE BUT SHE WAS DISTANT FAR . .	276	FOUR ZOAS 1	438
AND YET TOO NEAR DASHD DOWN I SEND THEE INTO DISTANT	296	FOUR ZOAS 3	170
DARKNESS			
RESTS ON THE DISTANT MOUNTAIN'S TOP SO LOS & ENITHARMON	305	FOUR ZOAS 5	11
WHOM HE HAD SEEN WANDRING HIS NETHER WORLD WHEN DISTANT FAR	319	FOUR ZOAS 6	* 300
SUCH SEEMD THE SYNAGOGUE TO DISTANT VIEW	348	FOUR ZOAS 8	277
THESE FIBRES OF THINE EYES THAT USED TO WANDER IN DISTANT	348	FOUR ZOAS 8	301
HEAVENS			
AND WHEN MORNING BEGAN TO DAWN UPON THE DISTANT HILLS . .	372	FOUR ZOAS 9	590
FOR LO THE WINTER MELTED AWAY UPON THE DISTANT HILLS . .	373	FOUR ZOAS 9	600
SUCH SEEMD THE SYNAGOGUE TO DISTANT VIEW AROUND THEM STOOD	382	FOUR ZOAS AD 6	10
A DISK OF BLOOD DISTANT & HEAVNS & EARTHS ROLL DARK BETWEEN	495	MILTON 14	27
BY GIVING UP OF SELFHOOD & THEY DISTANT VIEWD HIS JOURNEY	498	MILTON 17	* 3
DISTANT AMONG THE MOUNTAINS ARE DRUID TEMPLES	580D	DESC CAT 5	PROSE
WHEN DISTANT THEY APPEAR AS ONE MAN	607C	V LAST JUDG/N	PROSE
THRO HEAVEN THE DISTANT STEEPLE SEEN ACROSS A WIDE WATER	619B	ILLUS MILTON	PROSE
THE DISTANT FOREST THEN THE SLAVE GROANS IN THE DUNGEON	642	JERUSALEM 20	15
OF STONE			
I SEE THEM DISTANT FROM MY BOSOM SCOURGD ALONG THE ROADS	644	JERUSALEM 21	40
AND WANDERD DISTANT IN A DISMAL NIGHT CLOUDED & DARK . .	647	JERUSALEM 24	9
THE LUNGS THE HEART THE LIVER SHRUNK AWAY FAR DISTANT FROM	679	JERUSALEM 49	17
MAN			
AND BECAME AN OPAKE GLOBE FAR DISTANT CLAD WITH MOONY BEAMS	679	JERUSALEM 49	20
OF STARS FOR ALL THE SONS OF ALBION APPEARD DISTANT STARS	681	JERUSALEM 50	20
AND THEN A GLOBE OF BLOOD WANDERING DISTANT IN AN UNKNOWN	702	JERUSALEM 66	43
NIGHT			
THESE FIBRES OF THINE EYES THAT USED TO BEAM IN DISTANT	705	JERUSALEM 67	47
HEAVENS			
HOW DISTANT FAR FROM ALBION HIS HILLS & HIS VALLEYS NO MORE	720	JERUSALEM 79	15
OR HOW UPON THE DISTANT HILLS SEE MY BELOVEDS' TENTS . .	740	JERUSALEM 93	16
DISTANT WHEN WE SHALL DO SO BEING DETERMIND NOT TO . . .	813C	LETTER 22	PROSE
LIKE THE DISTANT APPROACH OF THINGS MIGHTY & MAGNIFICENT	835B	LETTER 34	PROSE
WINDSOR TERRACE A BOY CONTEMPLATING A DISTANT VIEW OF ETON	SUPP	ILLUS GRAY	*TITLE
COLLEGE			
DISTASTE			
WITH DISTASTE AND DISLIKE	27	EDW THIRD/PS 3	261
DISTEMPER			
THE PRINCE MAY NOT CATCH THE DISTEMPER TOO	22	EDW THIRD/PS 3	52
DISTEMPER SIR THOMAS WHAT DISTEMPER	22	EDW THIRD/PS 3	53
I KNOW YOU UNDERSTAND ME A DISTEMPER	22	EDW THIRD/PS 3	56
DISTILLS			
IN A CLOUD THAT DEWY SWEETNESS DISTILLS	816	HAPPINESS/L	2
DISTINCT			
OF HOLINESS DISTINCT FROM MAN IS IMPOSSIBLE TO THE	90C	ANNO SWED LOVE	MARG
AFFECTIONS			
MAN HAS NO BODY DISTINCT FROM HIS SOUL	149D	MARRIAGE HH 4	PROSE
FIRST THE NOTION THAT MAN HAS A BODY DISTINCT FROM HIS SOUL	154C	MARRIAGE HH 14	PROSE
SUBLIME DISTINCT THEIR LINEAMENTS DIVINE OF HUMAN BEAUTY	281	FOUR ZOAS 2	34
IN HUMAN FORMS DISTINCT THEY STOOD ROUND URIZEN PRINCE	281	FOUR ZOAS 2	37
OF LIGHT			
THEIR VENTUROUS FLIGHT IN HUMAN FORMS DISTINCT THRO	284	FOUR ZOAS 2	151
DARKNESS DEEP			
THERE IS A STATE NAMD SATAN LEARN DISTINCT TO KNOW	351	FOUR ZOAS 8	379
O [MORTALS] RAHAB			
DISTINCT GENERAL FORM CANNOT EXIST	461B	ANNO REYNOLDS	MARG
SO OLOLON UTTERD IN WORDS DISTINCT THE ANXIOUS THOUGHT . .	527	MILTON 37	4
MILD WAS THE VOICE BUT MORE DISTINCT THAN ANY EARTHLY . .	527	MILTON 37	5
THE CLEARER THE ORGAN THE MORE DISTINCT THE OBJECT . .	576D	DESC CAT 4	PROSE
THAT THE MORE DISTINCT SHARP AND WIREY THE BOUNDING LINE	585B	DESC CAT 15	PROSE
AS IT IS IN THIS PICTURE WHERE ALL THE LINEAMENTS	586D	CHAUCER 1	PROSE
ARE DISTINCT			
FABLE OR ALLEGORY ARE A TOTALLY DISTINCT & INFERIOR KIND	604D	V LAST JUDG/N	PROSE
AS TWO DISTINCT THINGS & SO CALLD FOR THE SAKE OF ETERNAL	605A	V LAST JUDG/N	PROSE
LIFE			
AS OPPOSD TO & DISTINCT FROM DIVINE VENGEANCE	611A	V LAST JUDG/N	PROSE
OR DISTINCT FROM THE IMAGINATIVE WORLD	774A	ANNO BERKELEY	MARG
DISTINCT SHONE & CLEAR	804	TO BUTTS/L	17
& THEY ARE AS DISTINCT AS ANY TWO ARTS CAN BE	810B	LETTER 20	PROSE
DISTINCTER			
AND HEARD THE HOWLINGS OF RED ORC DISTINCTER & DISTINCTER	319	FOUR ZOAS 6	* 291
DISTINCTION			
("MERELY NATURAL IDEA") OBSERVE THE DISTINCTION HERE . .	90A	ANNO SWED LOVE	MARG
THOUGHT WITHOUT AFFECTION MAKES A DISTINCTION BETWEEN . .	90D	ANNO SWED LOVE	MARG
TO PARTICULARIZE IS THE ALONE DISTINCTION OF MERIT . .	451A	ANNO REYNOLDS	MARG
HE MAKES A WIDE DISTINCTION BETWEEN THE SHEEP & THE GOATS	556D	JESUS NOT/N	PROSE
AND BOND OF SOCIETY THE DISTINCTION MY WORKS HAVE OBTAINED	561C	EXHIBITION ADV	PROSE
THE DISTINCTION THAT IS MADE IN MODERN TIMES BETWEEN .	584D	DESC CAT 15	PROSE
DISTINCTLY			
VOICES OF CELESTIAL INHABITANTS ARE MORE DISTINCTLY HEARD	802A	LETTER 14	PROSE
& THEIR FORMS MORE DISTINCTLY SEEN	802A	LETTER 14	PROSE
MORE DISTINCTLY THAN IN ANY PRINCE OR HERO	845C	LETTER 44	PROSE

DISTINCTNESS
    DISTINCTNESS IS PARTICULAR NOT GENERAL . . . . 461B ANNO REYNOLDS MARG
    WHICH ALTOGETHER DEPENDS ON DISTINCTNESS OF FORM . . 463A ANNO REYNOLDS MARG
DISTINGUISH
    DISTINGUISH THEREFORE STATES FROM INDIVIDUALS IN THOSE 521 MILTON 32 22
      STATES
    DISTINGUISH HIM FROM THE FRIAR OR THE PARDONER . . 570C DESC CAT 3 PROSE
    HOW DO WE DISTINGUISH THE OAK FROM THE BEECH . . . . 585C DESC CAT 15 PROSE
    DO WE DISTINGUISH ONE FACE OR COUNTENANCE FROM ANOTHER . 585C DESC CAT 15 PROSE
    LEARN THEREFORE O SISTERS TO DISTINGUISH THE ETERNAL HUMAN 680 JERUSALEM 49 72
    DISTINGUISH BETWEEN THE MAN & HIS PRESENT STATE . . . 681D JERUSALEM 52 PROSE
DISTINGUISHD
    CONSIDERD AS ONE DISTINGUISHD BY SOME MENTAL PERFECTION 830B LETTER 30 PROSE
    OF COURSE THAT SHALL BE DISTINGUISHD . . . . 832B LETTER 32 PROSE
    OF THE MOST DISTINGUISHD DESIGNS OF MR ROMNEY OF WHICH . 832C LETTER 32 PROSE
DISTINGUISHED
    THAT MANKIND ARE IN A LESS DISTINGUISHED SITUATION . . . 388D ANNO WATSON MARG
DISTINGUISHES
    DISTINGUISHES HONESTY FROM KNAVERY BUT THE HARD AND WIREY 585C DESC CAT 15 PROSE
DISTINGUISHING
    WHILE YOU EXALT ME BY SUCH DISTINGUISHING COMMENDATIONS I 822B LETTER 26 PROSE
DISTORTED
    BUT AS A DISTORTED & REVERSED REFLEXION IN THE DARKNESS 639 JERUSALEM 17 42
    TERRIFIED AT THE SIGHT OF THE VICTIM AT HIS DISTORTED 701 JERUSALEM 65 72
      SINEWS
DISTORTS
    DISTORTS THE HEAVENS FROM POLE TO POLE . . . . 753 EV GOSPEL(D)/N 104
DISTRACTED
    I AM ALREADY DISTRACTED AT THEIR DEEDS & IF I LOOK . . . 265 FOUR ZOAS 1 55
    IMPATIENCE NOW NO LONGER CAN ENDURE DISTRACTED LUVAH . 276 FOUR ZOAS 1 429
    NO MORE BUT A DESIRE OF BEING A DISTRACTED RAVENING DESIRE 376 FOUR ZOAS 9 734
    THESE AWFUL FORMS IN OUR SOFT BANDS DISTRACTED WITH 723 JERUSALEM 80 85
      TREMBLING
DISTRACTING
    THE FIRST AUTHOR OF THIS WAR & THE DISTRACTING OF HONEST 361 FOUR ZOAS 9 153
      MINDS
DISTRACTION
    THO PAINED TO DISTRACTION CRY O LET US EXIST FOR . . . . 376 FOUR ZOAS 9 738
DISTRACTS
    DISTRACTS HER A RUSHING SOUND AND THE FEET . . . . . . 4 FAIR ELENOR/PS 18
DISTRESS
    ACQUIRED BY MEANS OF SUFFERING & DISTRESS I E EXPERIENCE 89B ANNO SWED LOVE * MARG
    ALL PRAY IN THEIR DISTRESS . . . . 117 DIVNE IMAGE/SI 2
    THAT PRAYS IN HIS DISTRESS . . . . 117 DIVNE IMAGE/SI 14
    BURGUNDY THOU WAST BORN A LION MY SOUL IS OERGROWN WITH 139 FRENCH REVOLTN 112
      DISTRESS
    [AND BY DISTRESS INCREASE] . . . . 164 HEARD ANGEL/N 26
    THE BRITONS' DISTRESS & DEPOPULATION . . . . 208D SUBJCTS HIST/N TITLE
    HE GROUND IT IN HIS RUMBLING MILLS TERRIBLE THE DISTRESS 378 FOUR ZOAS 9 807
    HE CANNOT FEEL DISTRESS HE FEEDS ON SACRIFICE & OFFERING 630 JERUSALEM 10 48
    WAYWARD LOVE & EVERY SORROW & DISTRESS IS CARVED HERE . 638 JERUSALEM 16 64
    TERRIBLE THEIR DISTRESS & THEIR SORROW CANNOT BE UTTERD 691 JERUSALEM 59 28
    MEN UNDERSTAND NOT THE DISTRESS & THE LABOUR & SORROW . 692 JERUSALEM 59 50
    TO GREAT QUEEN STREET & LINCOLNS INN ALL IS DISTRESS & WOE 729 JERUSALEM 84 16
    CRYING [IVE FOUND HI] CRUCIFY THIS CAUSE OF DISTRESS . 755 EV GOSPEL(E)/N * 85
    BUT WANT OF MONEY & THE DISTRESS OF A THIEF CAN NEVER . 793B LETTER 5 PROSE
    HEAVIER TO ME & PITT WOULD PRESCRIBE DISTRESS FOR A . . 809B LETTER 20 PROSE
    MENTAL DISTRESS & I KNOW THAT ALL DISTRESS INFLICTED BY 809B LETTER 20 PROSE
    HEAVEN IS A MERCY A FIG FOR ALL CORPOREAL SUCH DISTRESS IS 809B LETTER 20 PROSE
    THE LIGHT OF ART O THE DISTRESS I HAVE UNDERGONE AND MY 852B LETTER 50 PROSE
DISTRESSED
    HIS VISAGE WAS TROUBLED HIS SOUL WAS DISTRESSED . . . . 38D SAMSON/PS PROSE
DISTREST
    TILL THOU DOST ?INJURE THE DISTREST . . . . 380 FOUR ZOAS NOTE 1
    OFT BLIND & AGE-BENT SORE DISTREST . . . . 426 MENTAL TRAVLER 55
DISTRICT
    BUT BEULAH TO ITS INHABITANTS APPEARS WITHIN EACH DISTRICT 518 MILTON 30 10
DISTRICTS
    HAST THOU FORGOT THAT THE AIR LISTENS THRO ALL ITS 339 FOUR ZOAS 7B 242
      DISTRICTS TELLING
    OG HAS TWENTY-SEVEN DISTRICTS SIHON'S DISTRICTS TWENTY-ONE 528 MILTON 37 51
    WITH THEIR DISTRICTS HAND DWELT IN SELSEY & HAD SUSSEX 709 JERUSALEM 71 11
      & SURREY
DITCHES
    IS IT A LITTLE CREEPING ROOT THAT GROWS IN DITCHES . . . 28 EDW THIRD/PS 4 11
DITTO
    HAYLEY'S BALLADS PER BROTHER DITTO MR BIRCH . . . . . SUPP LETTER 56A *PROSE
    ECCHOING GREEN DITTO THE LAMB THE SHEPHERD INFANT JOY SUPP LETTER 66A *PROSE
    LITTLE BLACK BOY DITTO LAUGHING SONG SPRING DITTO . SUPP LETTER 66A *PROSE
    CRADLE SONG DITTO NURSE'S SONG HOLY THURSDAY . . . SUPP LETTER 66A *PROSE
    LITTLE GIRL LOST DITTO DITTO THE CLOD & PEBBLE . . SUPP LETTER 66A *PROSE
DITTY
    HIS DROPPING EYES THE DITTY WAS IF HE . . . . 25 EDW THIRD/PS 3 165
DIVE
    AND BACK RETURN WITH WINE & FOOD OR DIVE INTO THE DEEPS 308 FOUR ZOAS 5 119
DIVESTED
    STATE DIVESTED OF HIS SPECTROUS SHADOW WHICH IS THE MILLER 571C DESC CAT 3 PROSE
DIVIDE
    INTO THREE PARTIES WE DIVIDE BY DAY . . . . 19 EDW THIRD/PS 1 50
    THEY MURMURING DIVIDE WHILE THE WIND SLEEPS BENEATH . . . 146 FRENCH REVOLTN 266
    TO DIVIDE THE ABYSS BENEATH . . . . 233 URIZEN 20 34
    DIVIDE THE HEAVENS OF EUROPE . . . . 241 EUROPE 9 7

```
                                                              PAGE    TITLE          LINE
DIVIDE    (CONTINUED)
    AND HEARD HIS WORD DIVIDE YE BANDS INFLUENCE BY INFLUENCE   280 FOUR ZOAS 2        23
    WITH COMPASSES DIVIDE THE DEEP THEY THE STRONG SCALES ERECT 283 FOUR ZOAS 2       142
    TRIGONS & CUBES DIVIDE THE ELEMENTS IN FINITE BONDS . . .   284 FOUR ZOAS 2       169
    WITH LABOUR & CARE THOU DOST DIVIDE THE [RIVER] CURRENT     312 FOUR ZOAS 6        18
      INTO FOUR
    I WILL DIVIDE THEM IN MY ANGER & THOU O MY KING  . . . .    334 FOUR ZOAS 7B       69
    SINCE THEY WILL DIVIDE THEM IN TWO . . . . . . . .         396D ANNO BACON       MARG
    TO DIVIDE INTO RAHAB & TIRZAH THAT MILTON MAY COME TO OUR   499 MILTON 18          18
      TENTS
    DIVIDE FOUR-FOLD INTO FOUR CHURCHES WHEN LAZARUS AROSE .    508 MILTON 24          31
    I COULD DIVIDE WESTMINSTER HALL OR THE WALLS OF ANY OTHER  560D EXHIBITION ADV   PROSE
    A BLIGHT FOR A TRIAL OF MEN TO DIVIDE THE CLASSES OF MEN   570A DESC CAT 3       PROSE
    HIS SPECTRE DIVIDES & LOS IN FURY COMPELLS IT TO DIVIDE     638 JERUSALEM 17        1
    THEN LOST IN CLOUDS I HEAR THEIR TENDER VOICES CLOUDS       644 JERUSALEM 21       41
      DIVIDE
    ALBION GROANS HE SEES THE ELEMENTS DIVIDE BEFORE HIS FACE   663 JERUSALEM 36       27
    IN BEAUTY THE DAUGHTERS OF ALBION DIVIDE & UNITE AT WILL    689 JERUSALEM 58        1
    THE DAUGHTERS OF ALBION DIVIDE & UNITE IN JEALOUSY          689 JERUSALEM 58        5
      & CRUELTY
    DIVIDE INTO THE KINGS OF EUROPE IN TIMES REMOTE O           698 JERUSALEM 64       16
      WOMAN-BORN
    THEY PUT ASIDE HIS CURLS THEY DIVIDE HIS SEVEN LOCKS UPON   702 JERUSALEM 66       22
    THE INHABITANTS ARE SICK TO DEATH THEY LABOUR TO DIVIDE     703 JERUSALEM 66       68
      INTO DAYS
    THEY DIVIDE TO TWELVE THE KEY-BONES & THE CHEST DIVIDING    708 JERUSALEM 70       12
      IN PAIN
    DIVIDE THEM INTO THREE NAME THEM AMALEK CANAAN & MOAB  .    725 JERUSALEM 82       24
    DIVIDE US FROM THESE TERRORS & GIVE US POWER THEM TO SUBDUE 729 JERUSALEM 84       26
    WITH PULSATIONS WE WILL DIVIDE THEM INTO SONS & DAUGHTERS   732 JERUSALEM 87       10
    DIVIDE MY GRIEFS WITH YOU THAT I CANNOT HIDE WHAT IT IS NOW 812B LETTER 22       PROSE
DIVIDED    SEE SELF-DIVIDED
    HIS FOREHEAD WAS DIVIDED INTO STREAKS OF GREEN & PURPLE    156C MARRIAGE HH 17   PROSE
    TIMES ON TIMES HE DIVIDED & MEASURD . . . . . . .          222 URIZEN 3            8
    THUS THE ETERNAL PROPHET WAS DIVIDED . . . . . . . .       230 URIZEN 15           1
    ON HIS OWN DIVIDED IMAGE . . . . . . . . . . .             232 URIZEN 19          16
    AND THEIR THIRTY CITIES DIVIDED . . . . . . . . .          236 URIZEN 25          43
    IN FORESTS OF NIGHT THEN ALL THE ETERNAL FORESTS WERE       241 EUROPE 10          18
      DIVIDED
    OF ENION I ISSUED INTO THE AIR DIVIDED FROM ENITHARMON .  . 300 FOUR ZOAS 4       106
    SHE IS DIVIDED SHE IS VANISHD EVEN LIKE LUVAH & [VALAN]     301 FOUR ZOAS 4    *  140
      VALA
    AND THEE O LUVAH PRINCE OF LOVE TILL THARMAS WAS DIVIDED    301 FOUR ZOAS 4       142
    HE WEPT & HE DIVIDED & HE LAID HIS GLOOMY HEAD  . . . .     306 FOUR ZOAS 5        54
    MY DIVIDED SPIRIT LIKE A WORM I RISE IN PEACE UNBOUND  . .  323 FOUR ZOAS 7       137
    THE MANHOOD WAS DIVIDED FOR THE GENTLE PASSIONS MAKING WAY  327 FOUR ZOAS 7       279
    I WAS DIVIDED IN DARKNESS & OBLIVION THOU AN INFANT WOE     327 FOUR ZOAS 7       288
    AH POOR DIVIDED DARK URTHONA NOW A SPECTRE WANDERING  . .   327 FOUR ZOAS 7    *  296
    THO THUS DIVIDED FROM THEE & THE SLAVE OF EVERY PASSION     328 FOUR ZOAS 7       346
    THEN HE DIVIDED THIRIEL THE ELDEST OF URIZEN'S SONS . . .   332 FOUR ZOAS 7       493
    FOR HE DIVIDED DAY & NIGHT IN DIFFERENT ORDERD PORTIONS     334 FOUR ZOAS 7B       37
    AND WHAT I LOVED BEST WAS DIVIDED AMONG MY ENEMIES . . .    334 FOUR ZOAS 7B       59
    IN SIGHS & SOBBINGS [TILL] ALL DIVIDING TILL I WAS DIVIDED  334 FOUR ZOAS 7B    *  64
    EVEN RAHAB IN ALL HER TURPITUDE RAHAB DIVIDED HERSELF  . .  350 FOUR ZOAS 8       344
    FELL FROM MY STATION IN THE ETERNAL BOSOM I DIVIDED . . .   350 FOUR ZOAS 8       352
    SATAN DIVIDED AGAINST SATAN RESOLVD IN OPEN SANHEDRIM  .    357 FOUR ZOAS 8       615
    DARKEND LIKE MOULD IN THE DIVIDED FALLOW WHERE THE WEED     364 FOUR ZOAS 9    *  294
    AND HEARTHS PROTECT THE SELFISH TERROR TILL DIVIDED ALL     374 FOUR ZOAS 9       636
    DIVIDED FROM ENITHARMON NO LONGER THE SPECTRE LOS  . . .    379 FOUR ZOAS 9       850
    OTHER & DIVIDED ALL THE ENGLISH WORLD BETWEEN THEM  . .    445C ANNO REYNOLDS    MARG
    SO LOS LAMENTED OVER SATAN WHO TRIUMPHANT DIVIDED          491 MILTON 10          21
      THE NATIONS
    AND SCIENCE IS DIVIDED INTO BOWLAHOOLA & ALLAMANDA  . . .   514 MILTON 27          63
    AFFECTION OR LOVE BECOMES A STATE WHEN DIVIDED FROM         522 MILTON 32          33
      IMAGINATION
    OF PHILISTEA INTO TWELVE DIVIDED CALLD AFTER THE NAMES  .   532 MILTON 40          25
    SO SAYING THE VIRGIN DIVIDED SIX-FOLD & WITH A SHRIEK  .    534 MILTON 42           3
    AWAY FROM OLOLON SHE DIVIDED & FLED INTO THE DEPTHS  . .    534 MILTON 42           5
    FOR ITS STAMINA CHAUCER HAS DIVIDED THE ANCIENT CHARACTER  571B DESC CAT 3       PROSE
    THE CHARACTERS OF WOMEN CHAUCER HAS DIVIDED INTO          572B DESC CAT 3       PROSE
      TWO CLASSES
    WAS IN THE WARS OF EDEN DIVIDED INTO MALE AND FEMALE  .    578A DESC CAT 5       PROSE
    HOW HE BECAME DIVIDED IS A SUBJECT OF GREAT SUBLIMITY  .   578B DESC CAT 5       PROSE
    DIVIDED INTO MALE AND FEMALE FORMS TIME AFTER TIME . .      623 JERUSALEM 5        32
    INCESSANT BEFORE THE FURNACES AND HIS EMANATION DIVIDED     624 JERUSALEM 5        67
      IN PAIN
    OPAKE DIVIDED FROM HIS BACK HE LABOURS AND HE MOURNS  .     624 JERUSALEM 6         2
    FOR AS HIS EMANATION DIVIDED HIS SPECTRE ALSO DIVIDED  .    624 JERUSALEM 6         3
    BUT STILL THE SPECTRE DIVIDED AND STILL HIS PAIN INCREASD   625 JERUSALEM 6        12
    IN PAIN THE SPECTRE DIVIDED IN PAIN OF HUNGER AND THIRST    625 JERUSALEM 6        13
    THIS HAS DIVIDED THEE IN SUNDER AND WILT THOU STILL FORGIVE 625 JERUSALEM 7        27
    I KNOW THAT ALBION HATH DIVIDED ME AND THAT THOU           626 JERUSALEM 7        52
      O MY SPECTRE
    THEY HAVE DIVIDED THEMSELVES BY WRATH THEY MUST BE UNITED   626 JERUSALEM 7        57
      BY
    AND THOU MY SPECTRE ART DIVIDED AGAINST ME BUT MARK . . .   627 JERUSALEM 8        14
    ALBION IS DEAD HIS EMANATION IS DIVIDED FROM HIM . . . .    631 JERUSALEM 12        6
    WHAT SHALL I DO OR HOW EXIST DIVIDED FROM ENITHARMON  .     631 JERUSALEM 12        9
    BUT FIRST ALBION MUST SLEEP DIVIDED FROM THE NATIONS  . .   636 JERUSALEM 15       29
    THE GATE OF ZEBULUN IN ANGLESEA & SODOR SO IS WALES DIVIDED 637 JERUSALEM 16       40
    AND THE FORTY COUNTIES OF ENGLAND ARE THUS DIVIDED IN THE   637 JERUSALEM 16       43
      GATES
```

```
DIVIDED   (CONTINUED)
    DIVIDED IN THE THE GATES OF REUBEN JUDAH DAN & JOSEPH   .   .   637 JERUSALEM 16      51
    AND THE THIRTY-SIX COUNTIES OF SCOTLAND DIVIDED IN THE       638 JERUSALEM 16      52
      GATES
    FOR LOS SAID THO MY SPECTRE IS DIVIDED AS I AM A LIVING MAN  638 JERUSALEM 17      16
    IN HER DARKNESS & WAS COMFORTED YET STILL SHE DIVIDED AWAY   639 JERUSALEM 17      49
    AND THE SPECTROUS DARKNESS FROM HIS BACK DIVIDED             639 JERUSALEM 17      57
      IN TEMPTATIONS
    SHAME DIVIDES FAMILIES SHAME HATH DIVIDED ALBION IN SUNDER   643 JERUSALEM 21       6
    WHILE THE DAUGHTERS OF ALBION DIVIDED LUVAH INTO THREE       661 JERUSALEM 34      46
      BODIES
    THEN GWENDOLEN DIVIDED INTO RAHAB & TIRZA IN TWELVE          661 JERUSALEM 34      52
      PORTIONS
    AND ENGLAND WHO IS BRITTANNIA DIVIDED INTO JERUSALEM & VALA  663 JERUSALEM 36      28
    AND THEY DIVIDED INTO FOUR RAVENING DEATHLIKE FORMS   .   .   .  663 JERUSALEM 36      36
    MAN DIVIDED FROM HIS EMANATION IS A DARK SPECTRE   .   .   .   .  684 JERUSALEM 53      25
    THE HERMAPHRODITIC CONDENSATIONS ARE DIVIDED BY THE KNIFE    689 JERUSALEM 58      11
    IS DIVIDED IN THE INTOXICATIONS OF PLEASURE & AFFECTION      690 JERUSALEM 58      14
    THEY DIVIDED INTO MANY LOVELY DAUGHTERS TO BE COUNTERPARTS   704 JERUSALEM 67       8
    TO THOSE THEY WOVE FOR WHEN THEY WOVE A MALE THEY DIVIDED    704 JERUSALEM 67       9
    ARE THUS DIVIDED THE FOUR COUNTIES ARE IN THE FOUR CAMPS     711 JERUSALEM 72       2
    BY CRUEL LAWS DIVIDED SIXTEEN INTO TWELVE DIVISIONS   .   .   .  715 JERUSALEM 74      27
    OF GOOD & EVIL THEY DIVIDED HIM IN LOVE UPON THE THAMES      715 JERUSALEM 74      36
      & SENT
    THEY HAVE DIVIDED SIMEON HE ALSO ROLLD APART IN BLOOD   .   .  715 JERUSALEM 74      44
    THEY HAVE DIVIDED LEVI HE HATH SHOT OUT INTO FORTY EIGHT     715 JERUSALEM 74      47
      ROOTS
    OVER THE LAND OF CANAAN THEY HAVE DIVIDED JUDAH   .   .   .   .  715 JERUSALEM 74      48
    LOS SAW TERRIFIED MELTED WITH PITY & DIVIDED IN WRATH   .   .  722 JERUSALEM 80      41
    CAMBEL HIS BRIGHT BEAMING COUNTERPART DIVIDED FROM HIM   .   .  723 JERUSALEM 80      58
    TOUCHING ITS SUMMITS & SOMETIMES DIVIDED ROLL APART   .   .   .  728 JERUSALEM 83      44
    THO DIVIDED BY THE CROSS & NAILS & THORNS & SPEAR   .   .   .  734 JERUSALEM 89       1
    TILL HE HAD COMPLETELY DIVIDED HIM INTO A SEPARATE SPACE     739 JERUSALEM 91      53
    HEBREW WHOM SHE DIVIDED INTO TWELVE & SOLD INTO EGYPT   .   .  739 JERUSALEM 92       4
    SO SAYING THE CLOUD OVERSHADOWING DIVIDED THEM ASUNDER   .   .  743 JERUSALEM 96      29
    KNOW BUT MYSELF IN A DIVIDED EXISTENCE   .   .   .   .   .   .   .  853A LETTER 51    PROSE
    NOW NO LONGER DIVIDED NOR AT WAR WITH MYSELF I SHALL TRAVEL  853A LETTER 51    PROSE
    CHAPTER II THE NATURAL MAN DIVIDED INTO MALE & FEMALE &      SUPP ILLUS GENESIS *TITLE
DIVIDES
    GORDRED HIS HEAD DIVIDES   .   .   .   .   .   .   .   .   .   .   .   .   14 GWIN KING/PS    108
    FOR PITY DIVIDES THE SOUL   .   .   .   .   .   .   .   .   .   .   .  230 URIZEN 13        53
    WHEN VIEWD REMOTE SHE IS ONE WHEN VIEWD NEAR SHE DIVIDES     348 FOUR ZOAS 8     283
    MINE IS THE FAULT I SHOULD HAVE REMEMBERD THAT PITY DIVIDES  488 MILTON 8         19
      THE SOUL
    HIS SPECTRE DIVIDES & LOS IN FURY COMPELLS IT TO DIVIDE      638 JERUSALEM 17       1
    SHAME DIVIDES FAMILIES SHAME HATH DIVIDED ALBION IN SUNDER   643 JERUSALEM 21       6
    OF WAR REELING UP THE STREET OF LONDON SHE DIVIDES IN TWAIN  689 JERUSALEM 58    *   3
    JERUSALEM DIVIDES THY CARE WHILE THOU CAREST FOR JERUSALEM   732 JERUSALEM 87      21
    HE DIVIDES INTO MALE & FEMALE & WHEN THE MALE & FEMALE       737 JERUSALEM 90      53
DIVIDING     SEE SELF-DIVIDING
    POURING SODOR OF IRON DIVIDING   .   .   .   .   .   .   .   .   .   .  227 URIZEN 10         9
    IN ANGUISH DIVIDING & DIVIDING   .   .   .   .   .   .   .   .   .   .  230 URIZEN 13        52
    HE FORMD A DIVIDING RULE   .   .   .   .   .   .   .   .   .   .   .  233 URIZEN 20        35
    THE DUNGEON-LIKE HEAVEN DIVIDING   .   .   .   .   .   .   .   .   .  235 URIZEN 25        12
    THE COLD LOINS OF URIZEN DIVIDING   .   .   .   .   .   .   .   .  249 AHANIA 2         29
    HE DROPD HIS HAMMER DIVIDING FROM HIS AKING BOSOM FLED   .   .  278 FOUR ZOAS 1     523
    DIVIDING & DIVIDING FROM MY LOINS A WEAK & PITEOUS   .   .   .  300 FOUR ZOAS 4      98
    THE GOARY TIDE EVEN TO THE PLACE OF SEED & THERE DIVIDING    327 FOUR ZOAS 7     287
    DIVIDING INTO JUST PROPORTIONS LOS UNWEARIED LABOURD   .   .  332 FOUR ZOAS 7     470
    THUS DIVIDING THE POWERS OF EVERY WARRIOR   .   .   .   .   .   .  332 FOUR ZOAS 7    *  495
    IN SIGHS & SOBBINGS [TILL] ALL DIVIDING TILL I WAS DIVIDED   334 FOUR ZOAS 7B    *   64
    DIVIDING & UNITING AT WILL IN THE CRUELTIES OF HOLINESS      348 FOUR ZOAS 8     279
    DIVIDING & UNITING IN DELUSIVE FEMININE POMP QUESTIONING     350 FOUR ZOAS 8    *  346
      HIM
    SURROUNDED HIM DIVIDING & UNITING WITHOUT END OR NUMBER      498 MILTON 17         8
    I AM CLOSD UP FROM MY CHILDREN MY EMANATION IS DIVIDING      627 JERUSALEM 8       13
    BUT I AM LIVING YET I FEEL MY EMANATION ALSO DIVIDING        631 JERUSALEM 12       7
    DIVIDING AND UNITING INTO MANY FEMALE FORMS JERUSALEM   .   .  642 JERUSALEM 19      45
    [ ?WEST ?WEIGHING ?EAST & ?NORTH DIVIDING ?GENERATION XXX ]  663 JERUSALEM 36    *  34
    IN GNAWING PAIN DIVIDING HIM FROM HIS EMANATION   .   .   .   .  684 JERUSALEM 53       6
    O DEMONSTRATIONS OF REASON DIVIDING FAMILIES IN CRUELTY      689 JERUSALEM 57      11
      & PRIDE
    DIVIDING THE MASCULINE & FEMININE FOR THE COMINGLING   .   .  690 JERUSALEM 58      19
    DIVIDING IN FIERCE PAIN ALSO THE VISION OF GOD WAS CLOSD     696 JERUSALEM 62      38
      IN CLOUDS
    IN THE DIVIDING OF REUBEN & BENJAMIN BLEEDING FROM          697 JERUSALEM 63      12
      CHESTER'S RIVER
    THEY DIVIDE TO TWELVE THE KEY-BONES & THE CHEST DIVIDING     708 JERUSALEM 70      12
      IN PAIN
    CLIFFS DIVIDING THEM INTO MALE & FEMALE FORMS IN            719 JERUSALEM 78       7
      HIS FURNACES
    AMONG THE DARKNESS OF HIS FURNACES DIVIDING ASUNDER TILL     732 JERUSALEM 86      56
    AND HATE DIVIDING THE SPACE OF LOVE WITH BRAZEN COMPASSES    734 JERUSALEM 88      47
DIVINE
    ("A MANNER OF FORGIVING SO DIVINE THAT") THIS I CANNOT       76D ANNO LAVATER    MARG
      CONCEIVE
    THE DIVINE IMAGE   .   .   .   .   .   .   .   .   .   .   .   .   .   .  117A DIVNE IMAGE/SI TITLE
    AND LOVE THE HUMAN FORM DIVINE   .   .   .   .   .   .   .   .   .  117 DIVNE IMAGE/SI    11
    PRAYS TO THE HUMAN FORM DIVINE   .   .   .   .   .   .   .   .   .  117 DIVNE IMAGE/SI    15
    A DIVINE IMAGE   .   .   .   .   .   .   .   .   .   .   .   .   .  221A DIVNE IMAGE/SE TITLE
    TERROR THE HUMAN FORM DIVINE   .   .   .   .   .   .   .   .   .   .  221 DIVNE IMAGE/SE    3
    THEY SAW NOT YET THE HAND DIVINE FOR IT WAS NOT YET         270 FOUR ZOAS 1     230
      REVEALD
```

```
                                                              PAGE    TITLE          LINE
DIVINE    (CONTINUED)
    REFUSING TO BEHOLD THE DIVINE IMAGE WHICH ALL BEHOLD    .    .   272 FOUR ZOAS 1        290
    WILL SO RECIEVE THE DIVINE IMAGE THAT AMONGST THE REPROBATE     272 FOUR ZOAS 1        297
    WHY SHOULD THE DIVINE VISION COMPELL THE SONS OF EDEN   .    .   273 FOUR ZOAS 1        339
    THEY WERE INTRODUCD TO THE DIVINE PRESENCE & THEY KNEELED       277 FOUR ZOAS 1        482
        DOWN
    THE FAMILY DIVINE DREW UP THE UNIVERSAL TENT   .    .    .    .   279 FOUR ZOAS 1        551
    HIS INWARD EYES CLOSING FROM THE DIVINE VISION & ALL    .    .   279 FOUR ZOAS 1        558
    TURNING HIS EYES OUTWARD TO SELF LOSING THE DIVINE VISION       280 FOUR ZOAS 2          2
    SUBLIME DISTINCT THEIR LINEAMENTS DIVINE OF HUMAN BEAUTY        281 FOUR ZOAS 2         34
    THEN ROSE THE BUILDERS FIRST THE ARCHITECT DIVINE HIS PLAN      284 FOUR ZOAS 2        166
    AND THE DIVINE VISION APPEARD IN LUVAH'S ROBES OF BLOOD         286 FOUR ZOAS 2        247
    FOR THE DIVINE LAMB EVEN JESUS WHO IS THE DIVINE VISION         287 FOUR ZOAS 2        261
    LEST THE STATE CALLD LUVAH SHOULD CEASE & THE DIVINE VISION     287 FOUR ZOAS 2        264
    TILL THE DIVINE VISION & FRUITION IS QUITE OBLITERATED  .    .   292 FOUR ZOAS 3         36
    BUILT BY THE ARCHITECT DIVINE WHOSE LOVE TO LOS &              298 FOUR ZOAS 4         51
        ENITHARMON
    THE DAUGHTERS OF BEULAH SAW THE DIVINE VISION THEY WERE         304 FOUR ZOAS 4        250
        COMFORTED
    OUR EYES TO THE DIVINE PAVILIONS THEREFORE IN MERCY THOU        304 FOUR ZOAS 4        256
    . . . STARRY WHEELS FELT THE DIVINE HAND LIMIT    .    .    .   304 FOUR ZOAS 4        275
    THY PURE FEET STEPD ON THE STEPS DIVINE TOO PURE FOR OTHER      311 FOUR ZOAS 5        230
        FEET
    AND THY FAIR LOCKS SHADOWD THINE EYES FROM THE DIVINE           311 FOUR ZOAS 5        231
        EFFULGENCE
    WITH JEWELS & PRECIOUS ORNAMENT LABOURD WITH ART DIVINE         312 FOUR ZOAS 6         27
    ENDLESS HAD BEEN HIS TRAVEL BUT THE DIVINE HAND HIM LED         316 FOUR ZOAS 6        176
    BY PROVIDENCE DIVINE CONDUCTED NOT BENT FROM HIS OWN WILL       319 FOUR ZOAS 6        282
    ART NOTHING BEING CREATED CONTINUALLY BY MERCY &               329 FOUR ZOAS 7        360
        LOVE DIVINE
    SO ENITHARMON SPOKE & LOS HIS HANDS DIVINE INSPIRED BEGAN       331 FOUR ZOAS 7    *   456
    WAITING WITH PATIENCE [OF] FOR THE FULFILMENT OF               340 FOUR ZOAS 7B       295
        THE PROMISE DIVINE
    . . . I BEHOLD THE DIVINE VISION THRO THE BROKEN GATES  .    .   341 FOUR ZOAS 8         20
    WONDRING WITH LOVE & [XXX] AWE THEY FELT THE DIVINE HAND        341 FOUR ZOAS 8    *    23
        UPON THEM
    WITH A PARENTAL LOVE FOR THE DIVINE HAND WAS UPON HIM   .    .   342 FOUR ZOAS 8         40
    AND UPON ENITHARMON & THE DIVINE COUNTENANCE SHONE    .    .   342 FOUR ZOAS 8         41
    FOR WHETHER THEY LOOKD UPWARD STILL THEY SAW THE DIVINE VISION  342 FOUR ZOAS 8         49
    OR WHETHER THEY LOOKD DOWNWARD STILL THEY SAW THE DIVINE        342 FOUR ZOAS 8         50
        VISION
    THE DIVINE VISION SEEN WITHIN THE INMOST DEEP RECESS   .    .   346 FOUR ZOAS 8        192
    O LAMB (DIVINE) IT CANNOT THEE ANNOY O PITYING ONE    .    .   347 FOUR ZOAS 8    *   242
    AGAINST THE DIVINE IMAGE CONGREGATED ASSEMBLIES OF WICKED       347 FOUR ZOAS 8        258
        MEN
    TIME AFTER TIME BY THE DIVINE LAMB WHO DIED FOR ALL    .    .   353 FOUR ZOAS 8        483
    SAW NOT AS YET THE DIVINE VISION HER EYES ARE TOWARD URIZEN    353 FOUR ZOAS 8        491
    [FROM THE DIVINE LAMB WEPT OVER THE SEPULCHER WEAVING]  .    .   356 FOUR ZOAS 8        587
    [SHE TURND & SAW THE DIVINE VISION & HER]   .    .    .    .   356 FOUR ZOAS 8        592
    ISSUD IN MAJESTY DIVINE URIZEN ROSE UP FROM HIS COUCH  .    .   366 FOUR ZOAS 9        347
    HIS BODY WAS REDEEMD TO BE PERMANENT THRO THE MERCY DIVINE     366 FOUR ZOAS 9    *   357
    THE HUMAN FORM DIVINE THROWN DOWN FROM THEIR HIGH STATION      366 FOUR ZOAS 9        367
    IN ALL ITS TURPITUDE BENEATH THE DIVINE LIGHT & OF LUVAH'S     382 FOUR ZOAS AD 6      22
        ROBES
    ALL OTHER CODES GIVEN UNDER PRETENCE OF DIVINE COMMAND  .    . 393C ANNO WATSON       MARG
    WITH HANDS DIVINE HE MOVD THE GENTLE SOD   .    .    .    .   414 TO MRS FLAXMAN        7
    REFLECTED IN THE BEAMS DIVINE    .    .    .    .    .    .   418 MOCK ON/N             6
    SHE REMEMBERS NO FACE LIKE THE HUMAN DIVINE    .    .    .   429 MARY                 43
    A CLOTHING FOR THE SOUL DIVINE    .    .    .    .    .    .   432 AUGURIES             60
    THE ETERNAL CREATION FLOWING FROM THE DIVINE HUMANITY   .    . 444C LAST JUDGMNT/L   PROSE
    AND DID THE COUNTENANCE DIVINE    .    .    .    .    .    .   481 AND DID FEET/M        5
    THE ETERNAL GREAT HUMANITY DIVINE PLANTED HIS PARADISE  .    .   481 MILTON 2           8
    AND IN HIS TENT THRO ENVY OF LIVING FORM EVEN OF THE DIVINE     482 MILTON 3           2
        VISION
    WHICH IS THE DIVINE BODY OF THE LORD JESUS BLESSED FOR EVER     482 MILTON 3           4
    JUDGE OF THE PURE MELODIOUS HARP STRUCK BY A HAND DIVINE        485 MILTON 5          31
    TO PERVERT THE DIVINE VOICE IN ITS ENTRANCE TO THE EARTH        489 MILTON 9          23
    OPAKE AGAINST THE DIVINE VISION THE PAVED TERRACES OF   .    .   490 MILTON 9          31
    THE DIVINE MERCY FOR PROTECTING PALAMABRON IN HIS TENT  .    .   490 MILTON 9          42
    A MIGHTY FIEND AGAINST THE DIVINE HUMANITY MUSTRING TO WAR     491 MILTON 10         11
    O DIVINE VISION WHO DIDST CREATE THE FEMALE TO REPOSE   .    .   493 MILTON 12         49
    I HUMBLY BOW IN ALL MY SIN BEFORE THE THRONE DIVINE    .    .   493 MILTON 13          3
    NOW LEUTHA CEASD TEARS FLOWD BUT THE DIVINE PITY SUPPORTED      493 MILTON 13          7
        HER
    THE DIVINE HAND FOUND THE TWO LIMITS   .    .    .    .    .   494 MILTON 13         20
    AND THE ELECT SHALL SAY TO THE REDEEMD WE BEHOLD IT IS         494 MILTON 13         32
        OF DIVINE
    WHO IS THE ETERNAL ALL-PROTECTING DIVINE HUMANITY     .    .   495 MILTON 14          2
    AND IN HIS LINEAMENTS DIVINE THE SHADES OF DEATH & ULRO        495 MILTON 14    *     12
    IMAGE DIVINE THO DARKEND AND THO WALKING AS ONE WALKS   .    .   496 MILTON 15          6
    LOS THE VEHICULAR TERROR BEHELD HIM & DIVINE ENITHARMON        498 MILTON 17         31
    THEY ARE THE FOUR ZOAS THAT STOOD AROUND THE THRONE DIVINE     500 MILTON 19         18
    HE HEARD THEM CALL IN PRAYER ALL THE DIVINE FAMILY    .    .   504 MILTON 21         35
    BUT ALL THE FAMILY DIVINE COLLECTED AS FOUR SUNS   .    .    .   504 MILTON 21         37
    IN A DARK TOMB SO ALL THE FAMILY DIVINE WEPT OVER OLOLON       504 MILTON 21         42
    AND WERE TROUBLED AND AGAIN THE DIVINE FAMILY GROANED IN       504 MILTON 21         44
        SPIRIT
    THEN THE DIVINE FAMILY SAID SIX THOUSAND YEARS ARE NOW         504 MILTON 21         51
    SO SPAKE THE FAMILY DIVINE AS ONE MAN EVEN JESUS   .    .    .   505 MILTON 21         58
    YET THE DIVINE VISION REMAINS EVERY-WHERE FOR-EVER AMEN        505 MILTON 22          2
    HE IS THE FOURTH ZOA THAT STOOD (AROUND) THE THRONE DIVINE     510 MILTON 24         76
    IT BECAME OPAKE & INDEFINITE BUT THE DIVINE SAVIOUR   .    .   517 MILTON 29         37
```

515

		PAGE	TITLE	LINE

DIVINE   (CONTINUED)

ON THROAT & BREAST & WINGS VIBRATES WITH THE EFFLUENCE DIVINE — 520 MILTON 31 — 35

WE WERE ANGELS OF THE DIVINE PRESENCE & WERE DRUIDS IN ANNANDALE — 521 MILTON 32 — 11

WHO MADE HIMSELF A GOD & DESTROYED THE HUMAN FORM DIVINE — 521 MILTON 32 — 13

BUT THE DIVINE HUMANITY & MERCY GAVE US A HUMAN FORM · · 521 MILTON 32 — 14

CALLING THE HUMAN IMAGINATION WHICH IS THE DIVINE VISION & FRUITION — 521 MILTON 32 — 19

AND THE DIVINE VOICE WAS HEARD IN THE SONGS OF BEULAH SAYING — 522 MILTON 33 — 1

THE DIVINE MEMBERS MAY BE SLAIN IN OFFERINGS FOR SIN · · 525 MILTON 35 — 6

BUT THE DIVINE SAVIOUR CAN PASS IT WITHOUT ANNIHILATION — 525 MILTON 35 — 21

OPPOSD TO MERCY AND THE DIVINE DELUSION JESUS BE NO MORE — 530 MILTON 39 — 2

HIM TO THE DIVINE MERCY CAST HIM DOWN INTO THE LAKE · · · 530 MILTON 39 — 11

THE ETERNAL GREAT HUMANITY DIVINE SURROUNDED BY · · · · 531 MILTON 39 — 27

IS THE DIVINE REVELATION IN THE LITTERAL EXPRESSION · · · 534 MILTON 42 — 14

THE ETERNAL ATTRIBUTES OR DIVINE NAMES WHICH , · · · · · 571C DESC CAT 3 — PROSE

AND THE DIVINE ALL HAD ORIGINALLY ONE LANGUAGE AND · · · 579A DESC CAT 5 — PROSE

AND MARCHES ON IN FEARLESS DEPENDANCE ON THE DIVINE DECREES 580B DESC CAT 5 — PROSE

SUBLIME & DIVINE IMAGES AS SEEN IN THE WORLDS OF VISION — 605B V LAST JUDG/N — PROSE

IT IS THE DIVINE BOSOM INTO WHICH WE SHALL ALL GO · · · 605D V LAST JUDG/N — PROSE

IN THE DIVINE BODY OF THE SAVIOUR THE TRUE VINE OF ETERNITY 606A V LAST JUDG/N — PROSE

WITH THE WORD OF DIVINE REVELATION ON HIS KNEES · · · 606B V LAST JUDG/N — PROSE

TO MORTAL MAN IN THE SERIES OF DIVINE REVELATIONS · · · 607B V LAST JUDG/N — PROSE

ANGEL OF THE DIVINE PRESENCE MENTIOND IN EXODUS XIV... — 610A V LAST JUDG/N — PROSE

THESE THREE AGED MEN REPRESENT DIVINE PROVIDENCE · · · · 611A V LAST JUDG/N — PROSE

AS OPPOSD TO & DISTINCT FROM DIVINE VENGEANCE · · · · · 611A V LAST JUDG/N — PROSE

ALL SPRINGING FROM THE DIVINE HUMANITY · · · · · · · 612D V LAST JUDG/N — PROSE

THE ETERNAL BIRTHS OF INTELLECT FROM THE DIVINE HUMANITY — 613D V LAST JUDG/N — PROSE

SAVIOUR'S KINGDOM THE DIVINE BODY WILL NEVER ENTER THERE — 621A JERUSALEM 3 — PROSE

I AM IN YOU AND YOU IN ME MUTUAL IN LOVE DIVINE · · · · 622 JERUSALEM 4 — 7

WEEP AT THY SOUL'S DISEASE AND THE DIVINE VISION IS DARKEND 622 JERUSALEM 4 — 13

BEAMING FORTH WITH HER DAUGHTERS INTO THE DIVINE BOSOM [WHERE] — 622 JERUSALEM 4 — 15

HIS JEALOUSY BEFORE THE THRONE DIVINE DARKENING COLD · · 622 JERUSALEM 4 — 35

WHICH IS THE DIVINE BODY OF THE LORD JESUS BLESSED FOR EVER 624 JERUSALEM 5 — 59

OF EVERY DIVINE MEMBER IT IS THE REASONING POWER · · · · 629 JERUSALEM 10 — 13

SELF-RIGHTEOUSNESSES CONGLOMERATING AGAINST THE DIVINE VISION — 634 JERUSALEM 13 — * 52

BEFORE ME O DIVINE SPIRIT SUSTAIN ME ON THY WINGS · · · 635 JERUSALEM 15 — 9

WHEN THE DIVINE HAND WENT FORTH ON ALBION IN THE MID WINTER 636 JERUSALEM 15 — 32

SUCH IS THE DIVINE WRITTEN LAW OF HOREB & SINAI · · · · 638 JERUSALEM 16 — 68

LITTLE-ONES TO DESTROY THE DIVINE SAVIOUR THE FRIEND OF SINNERS — 641 JERUSALEM 18 — 37

APPEARD A ROCKY FORM AGAINST THE DIVINE HUMANITY · · · · 642 JERUSALEM 19 — 35

REMOTE FROM THE DIVINE VISION MY LORD AND SAVIOUR · · · 646 JERUSALEM 23 — 12

O HUMAN IMAGINATION O DIVINE BODY I HAVE CRUCIFIED · · · 647 JERUSALEM 24 — 23

DONE TO THE DIVINE LORD & SAVIOUR WHO SUFFERS WITH THOSE THAT SUFFER — 648 JERUSALEM 25 — 7

OF THE INJURER IN WHICH THE DIVINE LAMB IS CRUELLY SLAIN — 648 JERUSALEM 25 — 11

THE DIVINE VISION STILL WAS SEEN · · · · · · · · · · · 651 FIELDS FROM/J — 57

STILL WAS THE HUMAN FORM DIVINE · · · · · · · · · · · 651 FIELDS FROM/J — 58

FORTIFICATION AGAINST THE DIVINE HUMANITY AND MERCY · · · 653 JERUSALEM 28 — 26

THEN THE DIVINE VISION LIKE A SILENT SUN APPEARD ABOVE · 653 JERUSALEM 29 — 1

AND THUS THE VOICE DIVINE WENT FORTH UPON THE ROCKS OF ALBION — 653 JERUSALEM 29 — 5

· · · THEY JOIND THE DIVINE FAMILY [?ALBION ?SLEPT] TREMBLING — 655 JERUSALEM 29 — * 83

AND THE DIVINE HAND WAS UPON THEM BEARING THEM THRO DARKNESS — 655 JERUSALEM 30 — 12

BECAUSE HE KEPT THE DIVINE VISION IN TIME OF TROUBLE · · 655 JERUSALEM 30 — 15

INCLOSING LOS BUT THE DIVINE VISION APPEARD WITH LOS · · 656 JERUSALEM 30 — 19

AND LOS PRAYED AND SAID O DIVINE SAVIOUR ARISE · · · · 656 JERUSALEM 30 — 21

FEARING THAT ALBION SHOULD TURN HIS BACK AGAINST THE DIVINE VISION — 656 JERUSALEM 31 — 2

AND BUILDED BY THE DIVINE HAND THAT THE SINNER SHALL ALWAYS ESCAPE — 657 JERUSALEM 31 — 31

UPON THE VALLEYS OF MIDDLESEX SHOUTING LOUD FOR AID DIVINE 658 JERUSALEM 32 — 9

TURNING HIS BACK TO THE DIVINE VISION HIS SPECTROUS · · · 659 JERUSALEM 33 — 1

YOU CALL DIVINE IS BUT A WORM SEVENTY INCHES LONG · · · 659 JERUSALEM 33 — 6

INVOLVING THE DIVINE VISION IN COLOURS OF AUTUMN RIPENESS 659 JERUSALEM 33 — 30

WHENCE CAMEST THOU WHO ART THOU O LOVELIEST THE DIVINE VISION — 659 JERUSALEM 33 — 33

IMMINGLED GOD & MAN WHEN THOU & I HID THE DIVINE VISION — 660 JERUSALEM 33 — 46

FOR THE DIVINE APPEARANCE IS BROTHERHOOD BUT I AM LOVE · 660 JERUSALEM 33 — 52

THEN THE DIVINE HAND FOUND THE TWO LIMITS SATAN AND ADAM — 662 JERUSALEM 35 — 1

AND THE DIVINE VOICE CAME FROM THE FURNACES AS MULTITUDES WITHOUT — 662 JERUSALEM 35 — 3

THESE ARE STATES PERMANENTLY FIXED BY THE DIVINE POWER · 663 JERUSALEM 36 — 38

TORMENTS DESPAIR ETERNAL DEATH BUT THE DIVINE MERCY · · 663 JERUSALEM 36 — 54

AND LENGTH BREDTH HIGHTH AGAIN OBEY THE DIVINE VISION HALLELUJAH — 664 JERUSALEM 36 — 56

AND ONE STOOD FORTH FROM THE DIVINE FAMILY & SAID · · · 664 JERUSALEM 37 — 1

AGAIN HE JOIND THE DIVINE BODY FOLLOWING MERCIFUL · · · 664 JERUSALEM 37 — 11

DISPLAYING THE ETERNAL VISION THE DIVINE SIMILITUDE · · · 664 JERUSALEM 38 — 11

THUS SPEAKING THE DIVINE FAMILY FOLLOW ALBION · · · · · 665 JERUSALEM 38 — 27

SEEING ALBION HAD TURND HIS BACK AGAINST THE DIVINE VISION 666 JERUSALEM 39 — 14

AND THE DIVINE FAMILY WEPT OVER HIM AS ONE MAN · · · · 667 JERUSALEM 40 — 44

AND THESE THE TWENTY-FOUR IN WHOM THE DIVINE FAMILY · · 667 JERUSALEM 40 — 45

HUMAN DIVINE JESUS THE SAVIOUR BLESSED FOR EVER AND EVER — 667 JERUSALEM 40 — 47

AND MUST HAVE DIED BUT THE DIVINE SAVIOUR DESCENDED · · 669 JERUSALEM 42 — 6

```
                                                                PAGE      TITLE          LINE
DIVINE     (CONTINUED)
     AMONG THE INFANT LOVES & AFFECTIONS AND THE DIVINE VISION    669 JERUSALEM 42       7
       WEPT
     THY SELFHOOD IS FOR EVER ACCURSED FROM THE DIVINE PRESENCE   670 JERUSALEM 42      45
     AND THE DIVINE HAND WAS UPON HIM STRENGTHENING HIM MIGHTILY  671 JERUSALEM 42      56
     BUT AS THE WILL MUST NOT BE BENDED BUT IN THE DAY OF DIVINE  674 JERUSALEM 44      18
     THE FAMILY DIVINE HOVER AROUND THE DARKEND ALBION    . .     674 JERUSALEM 44      20
     IN WHOM THE OTHER TEN SHONE MANIFEST A DIVINE VISION         676 JERUSALEM 45      38
     DIVINE HE WEPT OVER ALBION SPEAKING THE WORDS OF GOD     .   676 JERUSALEM 46       8
     IN SILENCE THE DIVINE LORD BUILDED WITH IMMORTAL LABOUR      677 JERUSALEM 48       5
     INSLAVD TO THE MOST POWERFUL SELFHOOD TO MURDER THE DIVINE   679 JERUSALEM 49      30
       HUMANITY
     OF DIVINE ANALOGY AND OG & SIHON IN THE TEARS OF BALAAM      680 JERUSALEM 49      58
     SWAYD BY A PROVIDENCE OPPOSD TO THE DIVINE LORD JESUS    .   681 JERUSALEM 50       4
     NAMED BY THE DIVINE NAME YOUR RELIGION O DEISTS     . . .    682B JERUSALEM 52    PROSE
     ITS OWN PECULIAR LIGHT & THEE FORM IS THE DIVINE VISION  .   684 JERUSALEM 54       2
     THE DIVINE VISION DIMLY APPEARD IN CLOUDS OF BLOOD WEEPING   685 JERUSALEM 54      32
     DIVINE BENEVOLENCE & JOY FOR THE ETERNAL MAN     . . . .     686 JERUSALEM 55       9
     THE DIVINE VISION WITH CURTAIN & VEIL & FLESHLY TABERNACLE   688 JERUSALEM 56    *  40
     BUT ALBION FLED FROM THE DIVINE VISION . . . . . . . .       689 JERUSALEM 57      12
     WONDER SIEZD ALL IN ETERNITY TO BEHOLD THE DIVINE VISION     689 JERUSALEM 57      17
       OPEN
     THEY ARE THE FOUR ZOAS THAT STOOD AROUND THE THRONE DIVINE   691 JERUSALEM 59      13
     IN FLAMING FIRE WITHIN THE FURNACES THE DIVINE VISION        692 JERUSALEM 60       5
       APPEARD
     BUT THE DIVINE LAMB STOOD BESIDE JERUSALEM OFT SHE SAW  .    693 JERUSALEM 60      50
     THE LINEAMENTS DIVINE & OFT THE VOICE HEARD & OFT SHE SAID   693 JERUSALEM 60      51
     THAT THOU O HUMAN IMAGINATION O DIVINE BODY ART ALL      .   693 JERUSALEM 60      57
     THUS SPAKE JERUSALEM & THUS THE DIVINE VOICE REPLIED     .   694 JERUSALEM 60      65
     THAT THERE WAS A GOD OF MERCY O MERCY O DIVINE HUMANITY      695 JERUSALEM 61      43
     BUT LOS BEHELD THE DIVINE VISION AMONG THE FLAMES OF THE     696 JERUSALEM 62      35
       FURNACES
     THE HUMAN DIVINE IS WOMAN'S SHADOW A VAPOR IN THE SUMMER'S   698 JERUSALEM 64      14
       HEAT
     THE DIVINE VISION BECAME FIRST A BURNING FLAME THEN          702 JERUSALEM 66      41
       A COLUMN
     HIS IMMORTAL CHEEKS REARING HIS HANDS TO HEAVEN FOR AID      711 JERUSALEM 71      57
       DIVINE
     AGAINST THE DIVINE VISION & FALL OVER THE PRECIPICE OF       711 JERUSALEM 71      59
       ETERNAL DEATH
     TO DESTROY IMAGINATION THE DIVINE BODY BY MARTYRDOMS & WARS  714 JERUSALEM 74      13
     COMPREHEND WONDEROUS THINGS OUT OF THE DIVINE LAW    . . .   714 JERUSALEM 74      15
     THEY BECAME THE TWELVE GODS OF ASIA OPPOSING THE DIVINE      714 JERUSALEM 74      22
       VISION
     ON ACCOUNT OF OUR LEAVING THE DIVINE HARVEST TO THE ENEMY    716D JERUSALEM 77   *PROSE
     OF BODY & MIND TO EXERCISE THE DIVINE ARTS OF IMAGINATION    716D JERUSALEM 77    PROSE
     WHAT WERE ALL THEIR SPIRITUAL GIFTS WHAT IS THE DIVINE       717A JERUSALEM 77    PROSE
       SPIRIT
     I HAVE SINNED AND AM AN OUTCAST FROM THE DIVINE PRESENCE     719 JERUSALEM 78      33
     HE CALLD IT DIVINE ANALOGY FOR IN BEULAH THE FEMININE    .   730 JERUSALEM 85       7
     THE DIVINE NAMES SEEKING TO VEGETATE THE DIVINE VISION   .   737 JERUSALEM 90      41
     THE DIVINE NAMES SEEKING TO VEGETATE THE DIVINE VISION   .   737 JERUSALEM 90      41
     ONE FIRST IN FRIENDSHIP & LOVE THEN A DIVINE FAMILY & IN     738 JERUSALEM 91      20
       THE MIDST
     PARTICULAR IS A MAN A DIVINE MEMBER OF THE DIVINE JESUS      738 JERUSALEM 91      31
     CONTEMNING THE DIVINE VISION & FRUITION WORSHIPING THE DEUS  741 JERUSALEM 93      23
     TIME WAS FINISHED THE BREATH DIVINE BREATHED OVER ALBION     742 JERUSALEM 94      18
     THE BREATH DIVINE WENT FORTH UPON THE MORNING HILLS ALBION   742 JERUSALEM 95       2
       MOVD
     THE BREATH DIVINE WENT FORTH OVER THE MORNING HILLS ALBION   742 JERUSALEM 95       5
       ROSE
     BECAUSE HE KEPT THE DIVINE VISION IN TIME OF TROUBLE    .    742 JERUSALEM 95      20
     AND THE DIVINE APPEARANCE WAS THE LIKENESS & SIMILITUDE      743 JERUSALEM 96       7
       OF LOS
     I KNOW IT IS MY SELF O MY DIVINE CREATOR & REDEEMER     . .  743 JERUSALEM 96      13
     IN THE DIVINE IMAGE NOR CAN MAN EXIST BUT BY BROTHERHOOD     743 JERUSALEM 96      28
     DIVINE & SELF WAS LOST IN THE CONTEMPLATION OF FAITH    . .  743 JERUSALEM 96      31
     AND WONDER AT THE DIVINE MERCY & AT LOS'S SUBLIME HONOUR     743 JERUSALEM 96      32
     FOUNTAINS OF LIVING WATERS FLOWING FROM THE HUMANITY DIVINE  744 JERUSALEM 96      37
     . . . CHARIOTS OF HUMANITY DIVINE INCOMPREHENSIBLE   . . .   745 JERUSALEM 98      24
     CREATING SPACE CREATING TIME ACCORDING TO THE WONDERS        746 JERUSALEM 98      31
       DIVINE
     . . . & SAW THE WORDS OF THE MUTUAL COVENANT DIVINE   . . .  746 JERUSALEM 98      41
     ON SINAI FELT THE HAND DIVINE . . . . . . . . . .           754 EV GOSPEL(E)/N    17
     THOU ANGEL OF THE PRESENCE DIVINE . . . . . . . . . .       754 EV GOSPEL(E)/N    29
     STILL THE BREATH DIVINE DOES MOVE . . . . . . . . . .       754 EV GOSPEL(E)/N    41
     AND THE BREATH DIVINE IS LOVE . . . . . . . . . . .         754 EV GOSPEL(E)/N    42
     THE NAKED HUMAN FORM DIVINE . . . . . . . . . . .           755 EV GOSPEL(E)/N    66
     BUT IF YOU AVENGE YOU MURDER THE DIVINE IMAGE    . . . . .   757D EV GOSPEL       PROSE
     IS SHE ALSO THE DIVINE IMAGE    . . . . . . . . .           765D FOR SEXES/GP    TITLE
     THO THOU ART WORSHIPD BY THE NAMES DIVINE    . . . . . .     771 EPILOGUE/GP        5
     IMAGINATION OR THE DIVINE BODY IN EVERY MAN    . . . . .     773D ANNO BERKELEY  * MARG
     THE ALL IN MAN THE DIVINE IMAGE OR IMAGINATION     . . . .   773D ANNO BERKELEY    MARG
     THE ANGEL OF THE DIVINE PRESENCE (MALAKH YHWH)     . . .     775C INSC LAOCOON    TITLE
     GOD HIMSELF THE DIVINE BODY (YESHUA) JESUS WE ARE           776B INSC LAOCOON    PROSE
       HIS MEMBERS
     DIVINE UNION DERIDING AND DENYING IMMEDIATE COMMUNION   . .  776D INSC LAOCOON    PROSE
     THIS O WHAT SHALL I CALL THEE FORM DIVINE FATHER OF MERCIES  780 GHOST ABEL 1      21
     ONE POWER ALONE MAKES A POET IMAGINATION THE DIVINE VISION   782D ANNO WW POEMS    MARG
     IMAGINATION IS THE DIVINE VISION NOT OF THE WORLD NOR OF     783D ANNO WW POEMS  * MARG
       MAN
     INTO THE ABSTRACT VOID IT IS CALLED THE DIVINE MERCY    . .  784B ANNO WW EXCUR    MARG
```

517

		PAGE	TITLE	LINE

DIVINE (CONTINUED)
DIVINE WHENCE THEY CAME OR WHITHER THEY WERE BOUND . . 791B LETTER 3 PROSE
& IF IT IS CONSISTENT WITH HIS DIVINE PROVIDENCE RESTORE 796C LETTER 8 PROSE
HIM
US & WITH US ACCORDING TO HIS DIVINE WILL FOR OUR GOOD . . 802C LETTER 14 PROSE
COMPANION FROM ETERNITY IN THE DIVINE BOSOM IN . . . . 802C LETTER 14 PROSE
ARE ORGANIZED BY DIVINE PROVIDENCE FOR SPIRITUAL COMMUNION 813A LETTER 22 *PROSE
WE SHALL RETURN BUT WHILE CLOTHD WITH THE DIVINE MERCY . 813C LETTER 22 PROSE
IN OUR DIVINE MASTER YOU ARE TO ME A LESSON OF HUMILITY 822B LETTER 26 PROSE
THE ANGEL OF THE DIVINE PRESENCE . . . . 824A LETTER 27 PROSE
THIS POEM SHALL BY DIVINE ASSISTANCE BE PROGRESSIVELY . 825A LETTER 27 PROSE
THE DIVINE COUNTENANCE IN SUCH MEN AS COWPER AND MILTON 845C LETTER 44 PROSE
I THROW MYSELF & ALL THAT I HAVE ON OUR SAVIOUR'S DIVINE 863A LETTER 60 PROSE
I HAVE ASKED & INTREATED DIVINE HELP BUT FEAR CONTINUES 876B LETTER 83 PROSE
THE BLOSSOM THE CHIMNEY SWEEPER THE DIVINE IMAGE NIGHT SUPP LETTER 66A *PROSE

DIVINE-HUMANITY
. . . DIVINE-HUMANITY WHO IS THE ONLY GENERAL AND UNIVERSAL 672 JERUSALEM 43 20
FORM
. . . IMAGINATION THE DIVINE-HUMANITY . . . . 709 JERUSALEM 70 19

DIVINELY
AND HIS DARK WIFE THAT ONCE FAIR CRYSTAL FORM DIVINELY 306 FOUR ZOAS 5 60
CLEAR
IT REMAIND PERMANENT A LOVELY FORM INSPIRD DIVINELY HUMAN 332 FOUR ZOAS 7 469
AND HIS DARK EON THAT ONCE FAIR CRYSTAL FORM DIVINELY CLEAR 667 JERUSALEM 40 41

DIVINES
AND TURND FISHERMEN TO DIVINES . . . . 756 EV GOSPEL(I)/N 20

DIVING
WONDERING BEHELD THE CENTER OPEND BY DIVING MERCY INSPIRD 329 FOUR ZOAS 7 374

DIVINITY
I CANNOT CONCIEVE THE DIVINITY OF THE BOOKS IN THE BIBLE 393B ANNO WATSON MARG
HE WHO WOULD SEE THE DIVINITY MUST SEE HIM IN HIS CHILDREN 738 JERUSALEM 91 19
NOT AGREE GOD KEEP ME FROM THE DIVINITY OF YES & NO TOO 878B LETTER 88 PROSE

DIVISION
HIS FALL INTO DIVISION & HIS RESURRECTION TO UNITY . . . 264 FOUR ZOAS 1 21
AND MANY A DIVISION LET IN & OUT INTO THE VAST UNKNOWN . 286 FOUR ZOAS 2 244
SOWD WAR AND STERN DIVISION BETWEEN PAPISTS & PROTESTANTS 507 MILTON 23 48

DIVISIONS
TO PLANT DIVISIONS IN THE SOUL OF URIZEN & AHANIA . . . 286 FOUR ZOAS 2 239
TO PLANT DIVISIONS IN THE SOUL OF URIZEN & AHANIA . . . 287 FOUR ZOAS 2 289
TIRZAH SHE IS [CALLD] NAMD RAHAB THEIR VARIOUS DIVISIONS 348 FOUR ZOAS 8 * 294
ARE CALLD
A DOUBLE TWELVE & THRICE NINE SUCH THEIR DIVISIONS . . . 528 MILTON 37 18
FOURFOLD THE SONS OF LOS IN THEIR DIVISIONS AND FOURFOLD 632 JERUSALEM 12 45
AND SIXTY WINTERS LOS RAGED IN THE DIVISIONS OF REUBEN . 662 JERUSALEM 36 3
SUCH THE APPEARANCE IN CHEVIOT IN THE DIVISIONS OF REUBEN 697 JERUSALEM 63 23
AND AS THEY MOVE & CUT FROM THE LOOMS IN VARIOUS DIVISIONS 704 JERUSALEM 67 6
BY CRUEL LAWS DIVIDED SIXTEEN INTO TWELVE DIVISIONS . . . 715 JERUSALEM 74 27
KNOWING HIMSELF THE AUTHOR OF THEIR DIVISIONS & SHRINKINGS 733 JERUSALEM 88 35
GRATIFIED

DIVORCE
OF THE PRIDE OF DOMINION THAT WILL DIVORCE OCALYTHRON & 740 JERUSALEM 93 5
ELYNITTRIA

DIZZY
A RAGING WHIRLPOOL DRAWS THE DIZZY ENQUIRER TO HIS GRAVE 242 EUROPE 10 31

DOCTOR SEE DR
LIKE DOCTOR JOHNSON . . . . 54 LO THE BAT/IM 5
O NO SAID DOCTOR JOHNSON . . . . 54 LO THE BAT/IM * 6
A MA TO DOCTOR JOHNSON . . . . 54 LO THE BAT/IM * 10
OR LOCKE OR DOCTOR SOUTH . . . . 57 TO BE OR/IM 4
AS LOCKE OR DOCTOR SOUTH . . . . 57 TO BE OR/IM 28
THERES DOCTOR CLASH . . . . 61 DR CLASH/IM * 1
WORKMANSHIP HE WAS THE QUACK DOCTOR OF PAINTING . 468C ANNO REYNOLDS MARG
THE DOCTOR OF PHYSIC IS IN THIS GROUPE AND THE FRANKLIN 570D DESC CAT 3 PROSE
OF CHAUCER THE DOCTOR OF PHYSIC IS DESCRIBED AS THE FIRST 570D DESC CAT 3 PROSE
OF
DOCTOR IN HIS ART THUS THE READER WILL OBSERVE . . . 570D DESC CAT 3 PROSE
AS THE DOCTOR OF PHYSIC IS THE ESCULAPIUS . . . . . 571A DESC CAT 3 PROSE
DOCTOR THORNTON'S TORY TRANSLATION TRANSLATED OUT OF . 788D ANNO THORNTON MARG

DOCTRINE
BY NEWTON'S DOCTRINE OF THE FLUXIONS OF AN ATOM A THING 878A LETTER 88 PROSE
THAT

DOCTRINES
DIFFERENCE BETWEEN THE DOCTRINES OF DR TRUSLER & THOSE 795A LETTER 6 PROSE
OF CHRIST

DOCUMENTS
SOON RECIEVE SUCH DOCUMENTS AS WILL ENABLE YOU TO DECIDE 849B LETTER 45 PROSE

DODGING
HIS CLUMSY HOLD AND DODGING ROUND . . . . 16 BLIND-MANS/PS 35

DODSLEY
HE SAID I KNEW THAT DODSLEY WAS MR HAYLEY'S PUBLISHER BUT 856B LETTER 54 PROSE
HOPE THAT AS MR D(DODSLEY) IS DEAD & IF MR H(HAYLEY) HAS NO 856B LETTER 54 PROSE

DOEST SEE DOST
WHAT DOEST THOU HERE ELIJAH . . . . 779C GHOST ABEL 1 PROSE

DOG
THE DOG DOTH SEIZE THE WOLF THE FORESTER THE LION . . . 24 EDW THIRD/PS 3 119
ANY MORE THAN [?ANY ?BIRD THE] A DOG OR A CAT . . . 61 SAY YOU JOE/IM * 13
A DOG GET A STICK TO HIM . . . . 74C ANNO LAVATER MARG
THE INFANT HEAD WHILE THE MOTHER IDLE PLAYS WITH HER DOG 110 TIRIEL 8 26
ON HER COUCH
[FOR THE DOG AT THE WINTRY DOOR] . . . . 186 LET BROTHELS/N 53
FOR THE DOG AT THE WINTRY DOOR . . . . 186 LET BROTHELS/N 71
I CRY ARISE O THEOTORMON FOR THE VILLAGE DOG . . . . 190 V DAU ALBION 2 23

518

```
                                                           PAGE     TITLE        LINE
DOG    (CONTINUED)
      FOR THY COUNCELLOR OR THE DOG FOR A SCHOOLMASTER TO THY      192 V DAU ALBION 5      9
         CHILDREN
      DOES THE WHALE WORSHIP AT THY FOOTSTEPS AS THE HUNGRY DOG    193 V DAU ALBION 5     33
      THE DOG AT THE WINTRY DOOR  . . . . . . . . . . .  .  235 URIZEN 25        2
      I HAVE CHOSEN THE SERPENT FOR A COUNCELLOR & THE DOG   .  .  290 FOUR ZOAS 2    389
      TO HEAR THE DOG HOWL AT THE WINTRY DOOR . . . . . . .     290 FOUR ZOAS 2    409
      A DOG STARVD AT HIS MASTER'S GATE . . . . . . . . . .  431 AUGURIES        9
      THE BEGGER'S DOG & WIDOW'S CAT  . . . . . . . . . .  .  432 AUGURIES       43
      A SLY DOG SO CAN EVERY BODY  . . . . . . . . . . .  .  450D ANNO REYNOLDS  MARG
      THE SHEEP ENDEAVOURING TO WALK LIKE THE DOG  . . . . .  470B ANNO REYNOLDS  MARG
      A DOG WENT OVER THE WATER WITHOUT A WHERRY . . . . .    554 TO VENETIAN/N     5
      A DOG WILL ENVY A CAT WHO IS PAMPERD AT [HIS] THE  . . .  616B V LAST JUDG/N  PROSE
      MY CATTLE NEXT LAST EVN THE DOG OF MY GATE THE FORESTS FLED  643 JERUSALEM 21    8
      THE EAGLE THE HORSE THE DOG OF THE DOG SPECIES THE  . . . 859B LETTER 56     PROSE
      NUMBER OF THE DOG & CROCODILE & THAT OF THE DOG DEFENDING    859B LETTER 56     PROSE
      THE SERPENT & THE WOLFISH DOG  . . . . . . . . . .  SUPP ILLUS GRAY    *TITLE
DOGS
      THAT YOU MAY LIE AS NOW YOUR MOTHER LIES LIKE DOGS CAST OUT  100 TIRIEL 1       45
      TO THRUST THESE TOWERS WITH HIS SHOULDERS LET HIS FIERY      106 TIRIEL 5        6
         DOGS
      THE FIERY DOGS ARISE THE SHOULDERS HUGE APPEAR  . . . .  336 FOUR ZOAS 7B   132
      OF LEUTHA'S DOGS THENCE THRO THE NARROWS OF THE RIVER'S      657 JERUSALEM 31    16
         SIDE
      WITH HIM WENT DOWN THE DOGS OF LEUTHA AT HIS FEET  . . . 729 JERUSALEM 83    82
      AND NOT USED THE ELDERS & PRIESTS LIKE DOGS  . . . . .  750 EV GOSPEL(C)/N   28
      AND NOT USD THE ELDERS & PRIESTS LIKE DOGS . . . . .  .  752 EV GOSPEL(D)/N   62
      I AM ENVIED IN MANY QUARTERS BUT I WILL CRAM THE DOGS   .  821C LETTER 25     PROSE
DOING
      GUILTY OF DOING WRONG WITHOUT KNOWING IT WAS WRONG  . .   29A EDW THIRD/PS 4  PROSE
      HE BECAME WHAT HE WAS DOING HE WAS HIMSELF TRANSFORMD  .  305 FOUR ZOAS 4    287
      WHETHER REYNOLDS KNEW WHAT HE WAS DOING IS NOTHING TO ME    452A ANNO REYNOLDS  MARG
      THAN PRAISE A MAN FOR DOING [THAT] WHAT  . . . . . . .  539 CAN THERE BE/N    3
      FROM DOING MY DUTY TO MY ART  . . . . . . . .  .  .  .  561A EXHIBITION ADV  PROSE
      THE ENGLISH ARTIST MAY BE ASSURED THAT HE IS DOING  .  .  597C PUB ADDRESS/N  PROSE
      WHAT ARE THOSE GOLDEN BUILDERS DOING WHERE WAS THE          632 JERUSALEM 12    25
         BURYING-PLACE
      WHAT ARE THOSE GOLDEN BUILDERS DOING . . . . . . .  .  650 FIELDS FROM/J    25
      I AM DOING MY FATHER'S BUSINESS  . . . . . . . .  .  .  750 EV GOSPEL(C)/N    8
      I AM DOING MY FATHER'S BUSINESS  . . . . . . . .  .  .  751 EV GOSPEL(D)/N   10
      WHAT WAS HE DOING ALL THAT TIME  . . . . . . . .  .  .  752 EV GOSPEL(D)/N   51
      I AM DOING MY FATHER'S BUSINESS  . . . . . . . .  .  .  757 EV GOSPEL(I)/N   34
      AS SUCH [?A ?MAN] AN ONE WILL CONSIDER WHAT HE IS DOING     781D INSC UPCOTT   *PROSE
      & I FIND ON ALL HANDS GREAT OBJECTIONS TO MY DOING ANY      812C LETTER 22     PROSE
         THING
      I CANNOT LIVE WITHOUT DOING MY DUTY TO LAY UP TREASURES     812C LETTER 22     PROSE
      OF WHAT WAS DOING IN LONDON IN WORKS OF ART BUT I DID  .  820C LETTER 25     PROSE
      IT IS DOING NOTHING THAT IS TO BE REPENTED OF  . . . .  821B LETTER 25     PROSE
      & NOT DOING SUCH THINGS AS THESE  . . . . . . . . .  821B LETTER 25     PROSE
      OF MY FRIENDS AS I PERCIEVE HE IS NOW DOING THE SAME WORK   830D LETTER 30     PROSE
         BY
      THE WRITING LOOKS VERY PRETTY I WAS FORTUNATE IN DOING IT   834C LETTER 34     PROSE
      DOING JUSTICE TO OUR ADMIRED SUBLIME ROMNEY I HAVE NOT .  849B LETTER 45     PROSE
      THE ENGRAVINGS & HOPE SOON TO GET PROOFS OF WHAT I AM DOING  877A LETTER 85     PROSE
      I HAVE LITTLE HOPE OF DOING ANY MORE OF SUCH THINGS  . . . 878C LETTER 88     PROSE
DOLEFUL
      INTO TWO NARROW DOLEFUL FORMS  . . . . . . . . .  .  246 SONG OF LOS 4     8
      INTO THE DOLEFUL VALES WHERE NO TREE GREW NOR RIVER PLOWD    319 FOUR ZOAS 6    284
      AH WEAK & WIDE ASTRAY AH SHUT IN NARROW DOLEFUL FORM   .  484 MILTON 5       19
      AH WEAK & WIDE ASTRAY AH SHUT IN NARROW DOLEFUL FORM   .  679 JERUSALEM 49    32
      SHRUNK TO A NARROW DOLEFUL FORM IN THE DARK LAND OF CABUL   721 JERUSALEM 79    63
DOLL
      PRONOUNCD BY ENGLISH CONNOISSEURS & REYNOLDS THEIR DOLL     599D PUB ADDRESS/N  PROSE
DOLLIES
      IN THIS MANNER HE HAS JUMBLED HIS DUMB DOLLIES TOGETHER     574B DESC CAT 3     PROSE
DOLLY
      ROGER FROM DOLLY TWITCHD THE STOOL  . . . . . . .  .   16 BLIND-MANS/PS    13
DOLOR
      IN DREADFUL DOLOR & PAIN & I AM LIKE AN ATOM  . . . .  265 FOUR ZOAS 1     61
      THEN THE GROAN & THE DOLOR ARE QUITE FORGOTTEN . . . .  291 FOUR ZOAS 2    414
      HE FALLING ON THE ROCKS BELLOWD HIS DOLOR TILL THE BLOOD    299 FOUR ZOAS 4     61
      THE THROB THE DOLOR THE CONVULSION IN SOUL SICKENING WOES    314 FOUR ZOAS 6     99
DOLOROUS
      HEAVING DOLOROUS ANGUISHD UNBEARABLE . . . . . . . .  228 URIZEN 10       32
      WITH DOLOROUS HISSINGS & POISONS  . . . . . . . . .  232 URIZEN 19       27
      A DOLOROUS GROAN THAT STRUCK WITH DUMBNESS ALL CONFUSION    295 FOUR ZOAS 3    147
      BUT FROM THE DOLOROUS GROAN ONE LIKE A SHADOW OF SMOKE      296 FOUR ZOAS 3    153
         APPEARD
      BENT BY ITS FALL FROM A HIGH TOWER THE DOLOROUS SHADOW ROSE  299 FOUR ZOAS 4     66
      THE DOLOROUS SHADOW JOYD WEAK HOPE APPEARD AROUND HIS HEAD   300 FOUR ZOAS 4    127
      RESTLESS THE IMMORTAL INCHAIND HEAVING DOLOROUS  . . .  303 FOUR ZOAS 4    215
      MINGLED WITH HER DOLOROUS MEMBERS STREWN THRO THE ABYSS     338 FOUR ZOAS 7B   212
      A DOLOROUS GROAN & FROM THE DOLOROUS GROAN IN TEARS   .  373 FOUR ZOAS 9    593
      DOLOROUS THAT RAN THRO ALL CREATION A DOUBLE SIX-FOLD       534 MILTON 42       4
         WONDER
      AND DOLOROUS SOBS THE WINE OF LOVERS IN THE WINE-PRESS      723 JERUSALEM 80    82
         OF LUVAH
      BEGAN HER DOLOROUS TASK OF LOVE IN THE WINE-PRESS OF LUVAH   726 JERUSALEM 82    75
      DOLOROUS ARE THEIR LAMENTATIONS IN THE BURNING FORGE   . . 737 JERUSALEM 90    45
DOLOURS
      DOLOURS & LAMENTATIONS WAITING OFT BESIDE A DEWY GRAVE  . . 130 BOOK OF THEL 6    7
```

519

	PAGE	TITLE	LINE

DOLPHINS
AND LET THE JEALOUS DOLPHINS SPORT AROUND THE LOVELY MAID — 190 V DAU ALBION 1 — 19
DOMAIN
AND WHEN THOU YIELDS TO NIGHT THY WIDE DOMAIN . . . . . — 14 IMIT SPEN/PS — 8
DOME
TILL INTO THE HIGH DOME OF PAUL'S THEY LIKE THAMES' WATERS FLOW — 59 HOLY THURS/IM — 4
TILL INTO THE HIGH DOME OF PAUL'S THEY LIKE THAMES WATERS FLOW — 121 HOLY THURS/SI — 4
EACH DOME OPEND TOWARD FOUR HALLS & THE THREE DOMES ENCOMPASSD — 284 FOUR ZOAS 2 — 178
IN BRIGHT CATHEDRON'S GOLDEN DOME WITH CARE & LOVE & TEARS — 512 MILTON 26 — 36
JOYD IN THE MANY WEAVING THREADS IN BRIGHT CATHEDRON'S DOME — 728 JERUSALEM 83 — 72
DOMENICHINO
IS FIVE GUINEAS EACH I SEND THE DOMENICHINO WHICH IS VERY — 844B LETTER 43 — PROSE
DOMES
. . . THREE CENTRAL DOMES AFTER THE NAMES . . . . . . — 284 FOUR ZOAS 2 — 174
EACH DOME OPEND TOWARD FOUR HALLS & THE THREE DOMES ENCOMPASSD — 284 FOUR ZOAS 2 — 178
AND DOMES TERRIFIC IN THE NETHER HEAVENS FOR BENEATH . — 329 FOUR ZOAS 7 — 379
AND BUILDING ARCHES HIGH & CITIES TURRETS & [HIGH] TOWERS & DOMES — 361 FOUR ZOAS 9 — 167
THEN YOU BEHOLD ITS MIGHTY SPIRES & DOMES OF IVORY & GOLD — 525 MILTON 35 — 25
ARCHES & PYRAMIDS & PORCHES COLONADES & DOMES . . . . — 529 MILTON 38 — 22
DOMESTIC
THAT PEACE & PLENTY & DOMESTIC HAPPINESS IS THE SOURCE OF SUBLIME ART — 790D LETTER 2 — PROSE
DOMINATION
THE KINGDOM OF HEAVEN IS THE DIRECT NEGATION OF EARTHLY DOMINATION — 407B ANNO BACON — MARG
UNDER THE DOMINATION OF INSECTS RAISED BY THE SUN'S HEAT — 619C ILLUS MILTON — PROSE
DOMINEER
TO DOMINEER OVER & PROVE TO OTHERS MY SUPERIOR POWER . — 391D ANNO WATSON — MARG
DOMINEERED
SERVANT WHO DOMINEERED OVER ME HE IS EVEN AS A BROTHER . — 852C LETTER 50 — PROSE
DOMINEERING
IN SELF ABASEMENT GIVING UP HIS DOMINEERING LUST . . . . — 328 FOUR ZOAS 7 — 341
DOMINEERS
AND DOMINEERS OVER THE HIGH AND LOW VULGAR THIS MAN . . . — 570A DESC CAT 3 — PROSE
DOMINENCY
OF SIN & PROMOTE ETERNAL WARS & DOMINENCY OVER OTHERS . . — 774D ANNO BERKELEY — MARG
DOMINION
. . . BREATHING RED CLOUDS OF POWER AND DOMINION . . . — 135 FRENCH REVOLTN — 20
TILL THE POWER AND DOMINION IS RENT FROM THE POLE . . . — 138 FRENCH REVOLTN — 94
ARE THE LINEN CLOTHES FOLDED UP NOW IS THE DOMINION OF EDOM — 149B MARRIAGE HH 3 — PROSE
THAT WOMAN LOVELY WOMAN MAY HAVE DOMINION . . . . . . — 240 EUROPE 5 — 3
O CRUEL PITY O DARK DECEIT CAN LOVE SEEK FOR DOMINION . — 293 FOUR ZOAS 3 — 78
AND LUVAH STROVE TO GAIN DOMINION OVER . . . . — 293 FOUR ZOAS 3 — 79
GAINING A NEW DOMINION OVER ALL HIS SONS & DAUGHTERS . . . — 317 FOUR ZOAS 6 — 237
AND LET HIM HAVE DOMINION OVER LOS THE TERRIBLE SHADE . . — 323 FOUR ZOAS 7 — 116
MUST HAVE GIVEN SATAN BY THESE MILD ARTS DOMINION OVER ALL — 351 FOUR ZOAS 8 — 387
IF GODS COMBINE AGAINST MAN SETTING THEIR DOMINION ABOVE — 366 FOUR ZOAS 9 — 366
TO WHOM BE GLORY & POWER & DOMINION EVERMORE AMEN . . . — 495 MILTON 14 — 3
TO WHOM BE GLORY & DOMINION EVERMORE AMEN . . . . . . — 519 MILTON 30 — 16
FROM SLEEP AND RESUME HIS DOMINION OVER EARTH AND OCEAN — 577C DESC CAT 5 — TITLE
O CRUEL PITY O DARK DECEIT CAN LOVE SEEK FOR DOMINION . . — 654 JERUSALEM 29 — 60
AND LUVAH STROVE TO GAIN DOMINION OVER ALBION . . . . . — 655 JERUSALEM 29 — 61
WHILE THOU MY EMANATION REFUSEST MY FIBRES OF DOMINION . — 733 JERUSALEM 88 — 13
WHILE YOU ARE UNDER THE DOMINION OF A JEALOUS FEMALE . — 734 JERUSALEM 88 — 41
OF THE PRIDE OF DOMINION THAT WILL DIVORCE OCALYTHRON & ELYNITTRIA — 740 JERUSALEM 93 — 5
FOR THEIR GLORY IS WAR AND DOMINION . . . . — 777A INSC LAOCOON — PROSE
"ROME HAS SOMEWHAT BETTER TO DO NAMELY WAR & DOMINION" . — 778D HOMERS POETRY — PROSE
DOMINIONS
SATURN MARY SCEPTER LOOKING GLASS THRONES (DOMINIONS) — SUPP ILLUS DANTE 99 *PROSE
DONE
THE WRETCH APPROACHES CRYING THE DEED IS DONE . . . . — 4 FAIR ELENOR/PS — 21
AND HEARD A GLOOMY VOICE CRY IS IT DONE . . . . — 4 FAIR ELENOR/PS — 32
MAY SEE WHATS DONE WITHIN . . . . — 25 EDW THIRD/PS 3 — 188
THE KINGS AND NOBLES OF THE LAND HAVE DONE IT . . . . — 33 EDW FOURTH/PS — 15
HEAR IT NOT HEAVEN THY MINISTERS HAVE DONE IT . . . . — 33 EDW FOURTH/PS — 16
ERE LONG TO BLEED & DIE A SACRIFICE DONE BY A PRIESTLY HAND — 41B THEN SHE BORE — PROSE
THAT HAVE IT DONE FOR NOTHING MAKE SUCH A PIECE OF WORK FOR — 50B ISLAND MOON 6 — PROSE
("SNATCH FOAM DENY STREAM") UNEASY THIS I LAMENT THAT I HAVE DONE — 79D ANNO LAVATER — MARG
WHAT HAVE I DONE HELA MY DAUGHTER FEARST THOU NOW THE CURSE — 108 TIRIEL 6 — 46
BUT WHEN HE HAS DONE THIS LET HIM NOT SAY THAT HE KNOWS — 158A MARRIAGE HH 21 — PROSE
ARE SUCH THINGS [ARE] DONE ON ALBION'S SHORE . . . . — 177 LIT BOY LST/N * — 29
THEY THINK THEY HAVE DONE ME NO INJURY . . . . . . — 180 CHIMNEY SWP/N — 10
BARKS AT THE BREAKING DAY THE NIGHTINGALE HAS DONE LAMENTING — 190 V DAU ALBION 2 — 24
THEY THINK THEY HAVE DONE ME NO INJURY . . . . . . — 212 CHIMNEY SWP/SE — 10
WHERE THE TRAVELLER'S JOURNEY IS DONE . . . . . . — 215 AH SUNFLOWR/SE — 4
ARE SUCH THINGS DONE ON ALBION'S SHORE . . . . . . — 219 LIT BOY LST/SE — 24
[WHAT HAVE I DONE SAID ENION ACCURSED WRETCH WHAT DEED] — 267 FOUR ZOAS 1 — 109
[IS THIS A DEED OF LOVE I KNOW WHAT I HAVE DONE I KNOW] — 267 FOUR ZOAS 1 — 110
HIS SECRET LOVES & GRACES AH ME WRETCHED WHAT HAVE I DONE — 268 FOUR ZOAS 1 — 164
WHAT HAVE I DONE BOTH RAGE & MERCY ARE ALIKE TO ME . . . — 297 FOUR ZOAS 3 — 196
BONIFY & THOU SHALT HAVE REST WHEN THIS THY LABOUR IS DONE — 299 FOUR ZOAS 4 — 69
LEST ANY SHOULD IN FUTURITY DO AS WE HAVE DONE IN HEAVEN — 331 FOUR ZOAS 7 — 430
LISTEN I WILL TELL THEE WHAT IS DONE IN THE CAVERNS OF THE GRAVE — 355 FOUR ZOAS 8 — 555

520

```
                                                           PAGE    TITLE         LINE
DONE   (CONTINUED)
BROTHER OF JESUS WHAT HAVE I DONE INTREAT THY LORD FOR ME    364 FOUR ZOAS 9       270
& COMMANDS THAT IT SHALL NOT BE DONE  . . . . . . . .       388B ANNO WATSON      MARG
FIND THAT YOU HAVE BOTH DONE SUCH MIRACLES &  . . . . .   . 391D ANNO WATSON      MARG
PAINE SAYS THAT KINGS & PRIESTS HAVE DONE HIM HARM FROM      393A ANNO WATSON      MARG
   HIS BIRTH
WELL DONE PAINE  . . . . . . . . . . . . . . . . . .        395D ANNO WATSON      MARG
WHATEER IS DONE TO HER SHE CANNOT KNOW  . . . . . . . .      418 ON VIRGINITY/N       1
AND ALL IS DONE AS I HAVE TOLD  . . . . . . . . . . .        427 MENTAL TRAVLER      104
SAYS THAT EVERY THING MUST BE DONE BY EXPERIMENT  . . . .  . 459D ANNO REYNOLDS    MARG
[?WHY SHOUD ?COMPARING GREAT MASTERS ?BE ?DONE PAINFULLY]   SUPP ANNO REYNOLDS  * MARG
NOT SO THE SICK-ONE ALAS WHAT SHALL BE DONE HIM TO RESTORE   493 MILTON 13           4
FOR IN THIS PERIOD THE POET'S WORK IS DONE AND ALL THE       516 MILTON 29           1
   GREAT
AS IT IS DONE IN BEULAH & THOU O VIRGIN BABYLON MOTHER       523 MILTON 33          20
   OF WHOREDOMS
GREAT THINGS ARE DONE WHEN MEN & MOUNTAINS MEET  . . . .     550 GREAT THINGS/N      1
THIS IS NOT DONE BY JOSTLING IN THE STREET  . . . . . .      550 GREAT THINGS/N      2
LISTEN PATIENT & WHEN JOSEPH HAS DONE  . . . . . . .         552 TELL YOU WHA/N      5
HOW THIS WAS DONE WILL BE TOLD TOGETHER WITH  . . . .   .  . 561A EXHIBITION ADV  PROSE
IT IS OF MALICE AND ENVY THAT YOU HAVE DONE THIS HENCE  .  . 573A DESC CAT 3      PROSE
THAT HE SHOULD NOT SUFFER SUCH THINGS TO BE DONE  . . . .  . 573A DESC CAT 3      PROSE
NOTHING NEED BE DONE BUT TO EXAMINE MY RIVAL'S PROSPECTUS    573C DESC CAT 3      PROSE
IT IS THE SAME WITH ALL HIS CHARACTERS HE HAS DONE ALL  .  . 574A DESC CAT 3      PROSE
MANNER THAT MR S(STOTHARD) HAS DONE  . . . . . . . .        575A DESC CAT 3      PROSE
REPRESENTED HIM AND SAYS THAT THE PICTURE HAS DONE SO TOO    575A DESC CAT 3      PROSE
DONE BY ANY OTHER POWER THAN THAT OF THE POETIC VISIONARY    576C DESC CAT 4      PROSE
MR B(BLAKE) HAS DONE AS ALL THE ANCIENTS DID  . . . . .     578C DESC CAT 5      PROSE
GO BEYOND EITHER WHAT HE DOES OR WHAT THEY HAVE DONE  . .    579C DESC CAT 5      PROSE
HE HAS DONE SO AND THE RESULT YOU BEHOLD HIS  . . . . .     579C DESC CAT 5      PROSE
THIS PICTURE WAS DONE MANY YEARS AGO AND WAS ONE OF  . .  . 581B DESC CAT 6      PROSE
ADOPTS THE VENETIAN PRACTICE OR DOES AS MR B(BLAKE) HAS      582D DESC CAT 9      PROSE
   DONE
LAID TO OUR CHARGE THE ARTIST WHO HAS DONE THESE PICTURES    584B DESC CAT 14     PROSE
SAME MASTER SUPPOSING BOTH TO BE DONE WITH EQUAL CARE  .     585B DESC CAT 15     PROSE
THIS DRAWING WAS DONE ABOVE THIRTY YEARS AGO AND PROVES      585D DESC CAT 16     PROSE
STRANGE'S PRINTS WERE WHEN I KNEW HIM ALL DONE BY ALIAMET    594A PUB ADDRESS/N   PROSE
CAN BE DONE WITHOUT PREMIUMS  . . . . . . . . . . .         597A PUB ADDRESS/N   PROSE
THIS WHEN DONE BY [THIS IN] GRAND WORKS  . . . . . . .      599A PUB ADDRESS/N   PROSE
THIS ABSURD ASSERTION HAS DONE ME & MAY STILL DO ME  . .    602A PUB ADDRESS/N   PROSE
THAT HAS BEEN DONE OR IS LIKELY TO BE DONE IN ENGLAND  .  . 602A PUB ADDRESS/N   PROSE
BY SUCH PRACTISE & HAVE ALREADY DONE SO THAT YOU WILL RAGE   603B PUB ADDR AD/N  PROSE
DONE SO WELL IF HE HAD BEEN PROPERLY [ (PATRONIZED) ]        612C V LAST JUDG/N  *PROSE
   ENCOURAGD
ARE COMPELLD TO ALLOW IS NOT DONE IN PASSION  . . . .  .  . 615D V LAST JUDG/N   PROSE
O THOU SEEST NOT WHAT I SEE WHAT IS DONE IN THE FURNACES     625 JERUSALEM 7        28
LISTEN I WILL TELL THEE WHAT IS DONE IN MOMENTS TO THEE      625 JERUSALEM 7        29
   UNKNOWN
WHAT HAVE I SAID WHAT HAVE I DONE O ALL-POWERFUL HUMAN       646 JERUSALEM 24        1
   WORDS
AS THE SONS OF ALBION HAVE DONE TO LUVAH SO THEY HAVE IN     648 JERUSALEM 25        6
   HIM
DONE TO THE DIVINE LORD & SAVIOUR WHO SUFFERS WITH THOSE     648 JERUSALEM 25        7
   THAT SUFFER
SO SAYING AN ETERNAL DEED WAS DONE IN FIERY FLAMES  . . .  . 686 JERUSALEM 55       19
LOS KNEW NOT YET WHAT WAS DONE HE THOUGHT IT WAS ALL IN      698 JERUSALEM 63       36
   VISION
HE'D HAVE DONE ANY THING TO PLEASE US  . . . . . . .        750 EV GOSPEL(C)/N      26
WHAT CAN BE DONE WITH SUCH DESPERATE FOOLS  . . . . . .  .   751 EV GOSPEL(D)/N      21
HE'D HAVE DONE ANY THING TO PLEASE US  . . . . . . .   .     752 EV GOSPEL(D)/N      60
WITHOUT UNCEASING PRACTISE NOTHING CAN BE DONE  . . .  .    777B INSC LAOCOON    PROSE
AM APT TO BELIEVE THAT WHAT IS DONE WITHOUT MEANING IS VERY  782A INSC UPCOTT     PROSE
NOR THY WILL DONE BUT [BEELZEBUB XXX ?UNJUST ?JEALOUS]  .  . 788A ANNO THORNTON  * MARG
I HAVE DONE THE CORRECTIONS MY PAPER NOT BEING IN ORDER      791A LETTER 2       PROSE
& DONE A GOOD MANY OTHER SOFTENINGS TO THE WHOLE  . . . .  . 797A LETTER 9       PROSE
MY DESIGNS FOR COMUS WHEN I HAVE DONE THEM DIRECTED TO YOU   810D LETTER 21      PROSE
& SUPERIOR IN ONE TO ANY THING THAT HAS BEEN DONE  . . .    814D LETTER 23      PROSE
WORKS I HAVE DONE FOR YOU ARE EQUAL TO CARRACHE OR RAFAEL    814D LETTER 23      PROSE
BECAUSE THEY WERE DONE IN THE HEAT OF MY SPIRITS  . . .     815C LETTER 23      PROSE
EXPECT A LIKENESS BUT NOW I HAVE DONE ALL I COULD & KNOW     815D LETTER 23      PROSE
I HAVE INCLOSED THE ACCOUNT OF MONEY RECIEVD & WORK DONE     816A LETTER 23      PROSE
BEFORE NOW BUT COULD NOT GET ANY THING DONE FOR YOU  . .     819A LETTER 24      PROSE
& WHY SHOULD WE REPENT OF HAVING DONE THEM  . . . . . .     821B LETTER 25      PROSE
A MONTH AFTER MY ARRIVAL HERE I SHOULD HAVE DONE SO BUT      825D LETTER 27      PROSE
WHICH I HAVE DONE IN SO EFFECTUAL A MANNER  . . . . . .     825D LETTER 27      PROSE
WHOSE EYES HAVE DONE ME SO MUCH GOOD I OMITTED  . . . .     826C LETTER 28      PROSE
WHICH WAS VERY QUICKLY DONE WE WERE MET AT THE GATE BY  .    827B LETTER 28      PROSE
WITH MY ACTIVE PHYSIOGNOMY HAD DONE ME MUCH MISCHIEF  .  .   828C LETTER 28      PROSE
TO WRITE IMMEDIATELY THO I HAVE NOT DONE HALF THE BUSINESS   834B LETTER 34      PROSE
IF YOU DO NOT WISH ANY MORE DONE BEFORE I DELIVER THEN PRAY  840C LETTER 39      PROSE
THE EARLIEST POSSIBLE NOTICE OF WHAT ENGRAVING IS TO BE      842D LETTER 42      PROSE
   DONE
NEATLY DONE HIS MERIT WAS BUT LITTLE IN LIGHT AND SHADE      844B LETTER 43      PROSE
THAT WASHINGTON DID ALL THAT WAS DONE BEFORE HE WAS BORN     845B LETTER 44      PROSE
THINKS IT MIGHT BE DONE WITH VERY LITTLE TROUBLE TO YOU      845C LETTER 44      PROSE
LEAR AND CORDELIA TO COPY IF YOU DESIRE IT SHOULD BE DONE    845D LETTER 44      PROSE
IF THIS CAN BE DONE IT WILL BE ALL THAT COULD BE WISHED      846A LETTER 44      PROSE
WHICH MR JOHNSON WAS TO GET DONE FOR OUR FRIEND DALLY  .    847A LETTER 44      PROSE
HAS ADVISED THAT (FOUR) SHOULD BE DONE  . . . . . . .       848B LETTER 45      PROSE
BE DONE IN A CARELESS OR TOO HASTY MANNER THE PRICE  . .    848C LETTER 45      PROSE
THE INFERIOR ONES CANNOT BE DONE AT ANY RATE UNDER          848C LETTER 45      PROSE
   (FIFTEEN)
```

		PAGE	TITLE	LINE

DONE (CONTINUED)

ON WHAT IS TO BE DONE IN OUR DESIRABLE & ARDUOUS TASK OF — 849B LETTER 45 — PROSE
MAKE A VERY BEAUTIFUL ENGRAVING DONE IN THE SAME MANNER AS — 850D LETTER 49 — PROSE
SPOILING WHAT I HAD DONE WELL EVERY ONE OF MY FRIENDS WAS — 852B LETTER 50 — PROSE
HE ADVISED IT TO BE DONE AS ABOVE RELATED — 853A LETTER 51 — *PROSE
I MUST SAY ARE FAR BEYOND ANY THING I HAVE EVER DONE — 853A LETTER 51 — *PROSE
DONE MY DUTY AND PUT FORTH MY WHOLE STRENGTH — 853D LETTER 52 — PROSE
THAT I HAD BEEN PAID FOR ALL I HAVE DONE BUT WHEN I WROTE — 854D LETTER 53 — PROSE
UPON ENGRAVING I THINK IT CAN ONLY BE DONE BY SOME — 855A LETTER 53 — PROSE
STILL IS SO THAT A PRINT OF THAT SIZE CANNOT BE DONE UNDER — 855A LETTER 53 — PROSE
EXECUTED & COULD NOT BE BETTER DONE — 857B LETTER 54 — PROSE
I SEND YOU A LIST OF THE DIFFERENT WORKS YOU HAVE DONE ME — 867A LETTER 66 — PROSE
ON THE ABOVE TERMS & I WILL TAKE CARE THAT THEY SHALL BE DONE — 867C LETTER 66 — PROSE
I COULD NOT HAVE DONE IF THEY HAD TAKEN ME TO GLOUCESTER — 870A LETTER 70 — PROSE
I HAVE I BELIEVE DONE NEARLY ALL THAT WE AGREED ON &C — 870B LETTER 71 — PROSE
MAY DO & HAVE DONE MIRACLES IN THE CASE OF A CONVALESCENT — 875A LETTER 80 — PROSE
"HAD HE NOT RESEMBLED MY FATHER I HAD DONE IT" MACBETH — SUPP PENC DRAW 2.2 — *TITLE

DONNE

"WHOSE CHANGELESS BROW NEER SMILES NOR FROWNS" DONNE — SUPP LEGEND/N85 — *

DONNEGAL

DONNEGAL ANTRIM TYRONE FERMANAGH ARMAGH LONDONDERRY — 711 JERUSALEM 72 — 26

DONT

WHY MY LORD AUDLEY I DONT KNOW — 21 EDW THIRD/PS 3 — 6
I DONT KNOW PERHAPS HE TAKES IT BY FITS — 22 EDW THIRD/PS 3 — 48
WHAT IS THE TREE YOU MENTIONED I DONT THINK — 28 EDW THIRD/PS 4 — 8
BUT I DONT THINK YOU HAVE ANY OF IT — 28 EDW THIRD/PS 4 — 16
AND GIVEN HIM I DONT KNOW WHAT AND I CAN'T TELL — 29C EDW THIRD/PS 4 — PROSE
WHETHER HE DONT MENTION US ALL ONE BY ONE — 29C EDW THIRD/PS 4 — PROSE
I DONT KNOW THAT — 29D EDW THIRD/PS 4 — PROSE
THE CORNERS OF HER MOUTH SEEMD I DONT KNOW HOW — 44B ISLAND MOON 1 — PROSE
I DONT LIKE HIS EYES SAID ETRUSCAN COLUMN — 44C ISLAND MOON 1 — PROSE
I DONT THINK THERES ANY HARM IN IT SAID TILLY LALLY — 47C ISLAND MOON 3 — PROSE
DONT BE PROPHANE MRS [SISTAGATIST] SIGTAGATIST — 47D ISLAND MOON 4 — *PROSE
WHY SAID MRS NANNICANTIPOT I DONT THINK ITS PROPHANE TO SAY — 48A ISLAND MOON 4 — PROSE
HA HA SAID INFLAMMABLE GASS WHAT DONT YOU LIKE TO GO TO CHURCH — 48A ISLAND MOON 4 — PROSE
POO POO SAID OBTUSE ANGLE DONT BE A FOOL — 49B ISLAND MOON 5 — PROSE
THEM THAT HE'LL SCRAPE THEIR BONES IF THEY DONT LAY STILL & — 50A ISLAND MOON 6 — PROSE
WHEN I THINK OF SURGERY I DONT KNOW I DO IT — 51C ISLAND MOON 6 — PROSE
IF I DONT KNOCK THEM ALL UP NEXT YEAR IN THE EXHIBITION — 51D ISLAND MOON 7 — PROSE
AND NEVER THINK AT ALL ABOUT IT IM HANGD IF I DONT GET UP — 51D ISLAND MOON 7 — PROSE
I DONT FIND IT HERE SAID HE — 52C ISLAND MOON 8 — PROSE
IF YOU DONT OWN ME A PHILOSOPHER — 54 LO THE BAT/IM — 8
DONT YOU THINK I HAVE SOMETHING OF THE GOAT'S FACE SAYS HE — 62D ISLAND MOON 11 — PROSE
BECAUSE I DONT WANT YOU TO SHEAR MY FLEECE — 181 ANSWR PARSON/N — 2
TIS YOUR OWN FAULT IF YOU DONT FLOURISH NOW WILLIAM BLAKE — 414 TO MRS FLAXMAN — 10
YOU DONT BELIEVE I [WOUD] WON'T ATTEMPT TO MAKE YE — 536 DONT BELIEVE/N — * 1
DOUBT DOUBT & DONT BELIEVE WITHOUT EXPERIMENT — 536 DONT BELIEVE/N — 9
OF LIGHTING A LAMP WHEN YOU DONT WISH TO SEE — 549 ENGL ENCOU/N 1 — 8
SO AS I DONT VALUE SUCH THINGS AS THESE — 559 I ROSE UP AT/N — 27
[YOU] WHO DONT KEEP THE SECRETS OF HOLINESS — 755 EV GOSPEL(E)/N — 86
OF VIRGINS WAX I DONT KNOW WHAT ANIMAL PRODUCES IT — 790C LETTER 2 — PROSE

DOODLE

CATALANI DU CROWE & DILBURY DOODLE — 548B ON GREAT ENC/N — TITLE

DOOM

SEEKING THE TRUMP OF THE LAST DOOM — 242 EUROPE 12 — 13
THE TRUMP OF THE LAST DOOM BUT HE COULD NOT BLOW THE IRON TUBE — 243 EUROPE 13 — 2
THY RIGHTEOUS DOOM UPON ME ONLY LET ME HEAR THY VOICE — 296 FOUR ZOAS 3 — 187
[AND ON THE CROSS HE SEALD ITS DOOM] — 749 EV GOSPEL(B)/N — 56

DOOMD

WHEN HE IS DOOMD TO DIE — 542 PITIFUL CASE/N — 2

DOOR SEE NEXT DOOR

THE NEEDY FROM THEIR DOOR — 11 GWIN KING/PS — 8
READY AT THE DOOR HOW MANY SLEEP — 30 EDW THIRD/PS 5 — 13
THEN CHERISH PITY LEST YOU DRIVE AN ANGEL FROM YOUR DOOR — 59 HOLY THURS/IM — 18
[BUT I CAN KNEEL DOWN AT YOUR DOOR I AM A HARMLESS MAN] — 101 TIRIEL 2 — 29
[THEN MNETHA LED HIM TO THE DOOR & GAVE TO HIM HIS STAFF] — 103 TIRIEL 3 — 30
THEN MNETHA TREMBLING AT HIS FROWNS LED HIM TO THE TENT DOOR — 103 TIRIEL 3 — 39
MNETHA AWOKE SHE RAN & STOOD AT THE TENT DOOR [IN] & SAW — 109 TIRIEL 7 — * 22
RAN TO THE DOOR WHEN TIRIEL FELT THE ANKLES OF AGED HAR — 109 TIRIEL 8 — 6
THEN CHERISH PITY LEST YOU DRIVE AN ANGEL FROM YOUR DOOR — 122 HOLY THURS/SI — 12
AND THOU SHALT NOT WRIT OVER THE DOOR — 162 GARDEN LOVE/N — 6
THE WHITE PILLARS OF THE DOOR — 163 I SAW CHAPEL/N — 6
[TILL HE BROKE THE PEARLY DOOR] — 163 I SAW CHAPEL/N — 8
THAT PICKS UP CRUMBS AROUND THE DOOR — 177 LIT BOY LST/N — 8
FOR THE STEPS OF ANOTHER'S DOOR — 186 LET BROTHELS/N — 47
[FOR THE DOG AT THE WINTRY DOOR] — 186 LET BROTHELS/N — 53
FOR THE [STEPS] STONE OF ANOTHER'S DOOR — 186 LET BROTHELS/N — 65
FOR THE DOG AT THE WINTRY DOOR — 186 LET BROTHELS/N — 71
THE TRAVELLER HASTETH IN THE EVENING DEATH'S DOOR — 209F FOR CHILDRN/GP — TITLE
AND THOU SHALT NOT WRIT OVER THE DOOR — 215 GARDEN LOVE/SE — 6
THAT PICKS UP CRUMBS AROUND THE DOOR — 218 LIT BOY LST/SE — 8
THE DOG AT THE WINTRY DOOR — 235 URIZEN 25 — 2
A WONDROUS GOLDEN BUILDING MANY A WINDOW MANY A DOOR — 286 FOUR ZOAS 2 — 243
AND I HAVE CAUSED THE EARTH WORM TO BEG FROM DOOR TO DOOR — 290 FOUR ZOAS 2 — 392
TO HEAR THE DOG HOWL AT THE WINTRY DOOR — 290 FOUR ZOAS 2 — 409
WHILE OUR OLIVE & VINE SING & LAUGH ROUND OUR DOOR — 291 FOUR ZOAS 2 — 413
[RENT & A DOOR WAS OPEND THRO THE BOTTOM OF THE SEPULCHER] — 356 FOUR ZOAS 8 — 590
AND THEN FROM HER WHITE DOOR SHE LOOKD TO SEE HER BLEATING LAMBS — 369 FOUR ZOAS 9 — 472

		PAGE	TITLE	LINE

DOOR   (CONTINUED)

INTO THE BARN WHILE CHILDREN GLEAN THE EARS AROUND THE DOOR   376 FOUR ZOAS 9   702
HIS GOLDEN FOOD AND IN THE EVENING SLEEP BEFORE.THE DOOR   376 FOUR ZOAS 9   708
BUT PITY STANDS BEFORE THE DOOR . . . .   421 TERROR IN/N   2
FOR EVER OPEN IS HIS DOOR   425 MENTAL TRAVLER   40
A BEGGAR AT ANOTHER'S DOOR   . . . .   426 MENTAL TRAVLER   52
AND SOME WHEN SHE PASSED BY SHUT TO THE DOOR . . . .   428 MARY   18
DOWN THE ROAD & ALL THE WHILE WE WERE AT THE STABLE DOOR   437B BLAKES MEMORAN   PROSE
AT THE STABLE DOOR AND IN PARTICULAR SAID THAT HE HEARD ME   437C BLAKES MEMORAN   PROSE
PRESENT AT THE STABLE DOOR TO WITNESS THAT NO WORD RELATING   437C BLAKES MEMORAN   PROSE
AT THE STABLE DOOR THAT WE MAY NOT HAVE ANY WITNESSES . .   438B BLAKES MEMORAN   PROSE
ALL THE PERSONS PRESENT AT THE STABLE DOOR WERE . . . .   438B BLAKES MEMORAN   PROSE
CONTENTION AT THE STABLE DOOR & GOING TO THE COMRADE . .   438D BLAKES MEMORAN   1
THE DOOR OF DEATH IS MADE OF GOLD   442 DEDICATN BLAIR   1
FOR GOD HIMSELF ENTERS DEATH'S DOOR ALWAYS WITH THOSE THAT   522 MILTON 32   40
    ENTER
MICHAEL ANGELO'S NAME WRIT ON REMBRANDT'S DOOR   . . . .   542 FLORENTINE/N   14
TO WRITE MCH ANG ON REMBRANDT'S DOOR   . . . . . .   542 FLORENTINE/N *   25
AS HE ENTERD THE DOOR OF DEATH FOR ALBION'S SAKE INSPIRED   620 JERUSALEM 1   9
IN ITS EXTENSION EVERY TWO HUNDRED YEARS HAS A DOOR TO EDEN   678 JERUSALEM 48   37
AND WEPT AT OUR WINTRY DOOR LOOK LOOK BEHOLD GWENDOLEN   688 JERUSALEM 56   27
PRIMROSE HILL IS THE MOUTH OF THE FURNACE & THE IRON DOOR   714 JERUSALEM 73   54
ETERNAL DEATH STANDS AT THE DOOR O GOD PITY OUR LABOURS   728 JERUSALEM 83   65
DEATH'S DOOR . . . .   769D FOR SEXES/GP   TITLE
THE DOOR OF DEATH I OPEN FOUND   771 OF GATES/GP   43
AND AT HIS OWN DOOR THE BLESSD HERMIT DOES STAND . . .   800 MRS FLAXMAN/L   15
EXACTLY TWENTY YEARS BEEN CLOSED FROM ME AS BY A DOOR .   852B LETTER 50   PROSE
OVER MY DOOR AS THE POOR BARBER DID MONEY FOR LIVE HERE   858C LETTER 55   PROSE
DEATH'S DOOR   SUPP LEGEND/N71   *TITLE

DOORS

O WINTER BAR THINE ADAMANTINE DOORS . . . .   2 TO WINTER/PS   1
THE BLIND MAN FELT HIS WAY & CRIED PEACE TO THESE OPEN   101 TIRIEL 2   13
    DOORS
HE WANDERS WITHOUT EYES & PASSES THRO THICK WALLS & DOORS   101 TIRIEL 2   25
IF THE DOORS OF PERCEPTION WERE CLEANSED   . . . . .   154C MARRIAGE HH 14   PROSE
RISE AND LOOK OUT HIS CHAINS ARE LOOSE HIS DUNGEON DOORS   198 AMERICA 6   10
    ARE OPEN
THE DOORS OF MARRIAGE ARE OPEN AND THE PRIESTS IN RUSTLING   202 AMERICA 15   19
    SCALES
OVER THE DOORS THOU SHALT NOT & OVER THE CHIMNEYS FEAR   243 EUROPE 12   28
    IS WRITTEN
AND SLEPT WITH OPEN DOORS   . . . .   256 BOOK OF LOS 3   21
FROZEN DOORS TO MOCK   . . . .   262C LARGE BK DSGNS   TITLE
RISE & LOOK OUT HIS CHAINS ARE LOOSE HIS DUNGEON DOORS   375 FOUR ZOAS 9   674
    ARE OPEN
THIS TO PREVENT ENTERING THE DOORS OF SATAN'S BRAIN NIGHT   492 MILTON 12   4
    AFTER NIGHT
ME FROM HIS INMOST BRAIN & THE DOORS CLOSD WITH THUNDERS   493 MILTON 12   48
    SOUND
ITS EVER DURING DOORS THAT OG & ANAK FIERCELY GUARD . . .   520 MILTON 31   49
OF MORTAL MEN AND SHUT THE DOORS OF MIND AND OF THOUGHT   582A DESC CAT 8   PROSE
THE GOBLIN CROP FULL FLINGS OUT OF DOORS FROM . . . . .   618C ILLUS MILTON   PROSE
[I] THY HEAVEN DOORS ARE MY HELL GATES   . . . . .   748 EV GOSPEL(A)/N *   8
MY LANDLORD COMPELLD THE SOLDIERS TO GO IN DOORS . . .   827B LETTER 28   PROSE

DOORSTONE

THRESHOLD THO EVERY OTHER MAN'S DOORSTONE IS WORN DOWN .   849D LETTER 47   PROSE

DOOR WAY

AND SAW IN THE DOOR WAY BENEATH THE TREES TWO LITTLE   370 FOUR ZOAS 9   507
    CHILDREN PLAYING

DORICK

[DORICK (OR) ?ONE ?COLUMN FROM ANOTHER] . . . .   SUPP ANNO REYNOLDS * MARG

DORMAN

THE RIVER DORMAN ROLLD THEIR BLOOD   . . . .   14 GWIN KING/PS   113

DORSET

DAN CORNWAL DEVON DORSET NAPTHALI WARWICK LEICESTER   637 JERUSALEM 16   46
    WORCESTER
HYLE DWELT IN WINCHESTER COMPREHENDING HANTS DORSET DEVON   710 JERUSALEM 71   20
    CORNWALL

DOSE

TO GIVE THESE RASCALS A DOSE OF CAWDLE . . . . . .   548 ON GREAT ENC/N   6

DOST   SEE DOEST

DOST THOU WITHDRAW THEN THE WOLF RAGES WIDE   . . . . .   3 EVNING STAR/PS   11
THOU THE GOLDEN FRUIT DOST BEAR . . . .   7 LOVE HARMNY/PS   9
DOST MOUNT ALOFT INTO THE YIELDING SKY   . . . . . .   15 IMIT SPEN/PS   20
AND THRO HEAVN'S HALLS THY AIRY FLIGHT DOST THROW . . .   15 IMIT SPEN/PS   21
THEN LADEN WITH ETERNAL FATE DOST GO . . . .   15 IMIT SPEN/PS   24
AND OER THE SURFACE OF THE SILENT DEEP DOST FLY . . .   15 IMIT SPEN/PS   26
THOU DOST NOT UNDERSTAND ME WILLIAM . . . .   28 EDW THIRD/PS 4   12
NOW WILLIAM THOU DOST THRUST THE QUESTION HOME   . . .   29A EDW THIRD/PS 4   PROSE
AND WHO IS THIS MINSTREL PETER DOST KNOW   . . . . .   29C EDW THIRD/PS 4   PROSE
& GOLDEN PLEASURES BEAM AROUND MY HEAD WHY GRIEF DOST THOU   43B WOE CRIED MUSE   PROSE
    ACCOST ME
WHY DOST THOU CURSE IS NOT THE CURSE NOW COME UPON YOUR   100 TIRIEL 1   40
    HEAD
IF THOU DOST GO SAID HAR I WISH THINE EYES MAY SEE THY   102 TIRIEL 3   17
    FOLLY
FOR THOU DOST MAKE MY HEART TO BLEED MY SONS WERE NOT LIKE   103 TIRIEL 3   20
    THINE
NO ARTFUL FIEND BUT I WILL LEAD THEE DOST THOU WANT TO GO   104 TIRIEL 4   23
OR WHEREFORE DOST THOU CRY AH WRETCH TO CURSE THY AGED   108 TIRIEL 6   47
    FATHER
[DOST THOU NOT SEE THAT MEN CANNOT BE FORMED ALL ALIKE]   109 TIRIEL 8   11

		PAGE	TITLE	LINE
DOST	(CONTINUED)			
DOST THOU KNOW WHO MADE THEE		115	THE LAMB/SI	2
DOST THOU KNOW WHO MADE THEE		115	THE LAMB/SI	10
THOU DOST SMILE		118	INFANT JOY/SI	10
WHICH THOU DOST SCATTER ON EVERY LITTLE BLADE OF GRASS THAT SPRINGS		128	BOOK OF THEL 2	9
DOST THOU O LITTLE CLOUD I FEAR THAT I AM NOT LIKE THEE		129	BOOK OF THEL 3	17
WHY DOST THOU NOT FLY AMONG THE CORN FIELDS		168	O LAPWING/N	3
WHY DOST THOU NOT CAST THY SEED		168	HAST LAP/N	3
WHY DOST THOU HIDE THYSELF IN CLOUDS		171	TO NOBODADDY/N	3
[YET THOU DOST EXCHANGE THY PITYING TEARS]		186	LET BROTHELS/N	54
THE SELF ENJOYINGS OF SELF-DENIAL WHY DOST THOU SEEK RELIGION		194	V DAU ALBION 7	9
WHY DOST THOU COME TO ANGELS EYES IN THIS TERRIFIC FORM		198	AMERICA 7	7
AND THOU DOST STAMP THEM WITH A SIGNET THEN THEY ROAM ABROAD		238	EUROPE PREL 2	10
THOU WILT GO MAD WITH HORROR IF THOU DOST EXAMINE THUS . .		265	FOUR ZOAS 1	52
WHY DOST THOU WEEP [?O] AS VALA & WET THY VEIL WITH DEWY TEARS		271	FOUR ZOAS 1	* 271
[AS THOU DOST SMILE UPON THE BARREN MOUNTAINS AND THEY REJOICE]		SUPP	FOUR ZOAS 1	*
IF THOU DOST LAY THINE HAND UPON ME BEHOLD I AM SILENT . .		293	FOUR ZOAS 3	62
DOST THOU REFUSE MIND I THE SPARKS THAT ISSUE FROM THY HAIR		301	FOUR ZOAS 4	150
NOW THOU DOST KNOW WHAT TIS TO STRIVE AGAINST THE GOD OF WATERS		301	FOUR ZOAS 4	156
AND WHEREFORE DOST THOU POUR THIS WATER FORTH IN SIGHS & CARE		312	FOUR ZOAS 6	10
WITH LABOUR & CARE THOU DOST DIVIDE THE [RIVER] CURRENT INTO FOUR		312	FOUR ZOAS 6	18
YET THOU DOST LAUGH AT ALL THESE TORTURES & THIS HORRIBLE PLACE		321	FOUR ZOAS 7	59
ORC ANSWERD CURSE THY HOARY BROWS WHAT DOST THOU IN THIS DEEP		322	FOUR ZOAS 7	69
RENDS THY WHITE HAIR YET THOU DOST FIXD OBDURATE BROODING SIT		322	FOUR ZOAS 7	80
THOU DOST RESTRAIN MY FURY THAT THE WORM MAY FOLD THE TREE		323	FOUR ZOAS 7	141
BUT IF THOU DOST REFUSE ANOTHER BODY WILL BE PREPARED . .		329	FOUR ZOAS 7	357
WHY DOST THOU WANDER AWAY FROM TIRZAH WHY ME COMPELL TO BIND THEE		348	FOUR ZOAS 8	299
IF THOU DOST GO AWAY FROM ME I SHALL CONSUME UPON THE ROCKS		348	FOUR ZOAS 8	300
WHERE DOST THOU DWELL FOR IT IS THEE I SEEK & BUT FOR THEE		367	FOUR ZOAS 9	395
WHERE DOST THOU FLEE O FAIR ONE		367	FOUR ZOAS 9	401
. . . WHERE DOST THOU SEEK THY HAPPY PLACE		367	FOUR ZOAS 9	* 401
RISE SLUGGISH SOUL WHY SITST THOU HERE WHY DOST THOU SIT & WEEP		368	FOUR ZOAS 9	418
AS THOU DOST SMILE UPON THE BARREN MOUNTAINS AND THEY REJOICE		370	FOUR ZOAS 9	492
WHERE IS THE LORD OF VALA DOST THOU HIDE IN CLEFTS OF THE ROCK		370	FOUR ZOAS 9	501
WHY DOST THOU TURN THYSELF AWAY FROM HIS SWEET WATRY EYES		371	FOUR ZOAS 9	526
AND THOU DOST WANDER WITH MY LAMBS & [WITH] WET THEIR INNOCENT FACES		371	FOUR ZOAS 9	532
TILL THOU DOST ?INJURE THE DISTREST		380	FOUR ZOAS NOTE	1
DOST THOU O PRIEST WISH THY BROTHER'S DEATH		384D	ANNO WATSON	MARG
WHERESOEVER THOU DOST GO		416	MY SPECTRE/N	28
[DIDST] DOST THOU NOT IN PRIDE & SCORN		416	MY SPECTRE/N	31
WHERE THOU THY CHARMING NEST DOST BUILD		422	THE BIRDS/N	3
SHE DOST THOU TRULY LONG FOR ME		423	THE BIRDS/N	13
WHY DOST THOU WEEP IN THY GENTLE SLEEP		427	LAND OF DREAMS	3
O WILLIAM IF THOU DOST ANOTHER LOVE		435	WILLIAM BOND	21
DOST ANOTHER LOVE BETTER THAN POOR MARY		435	WILLIAM BOND	22
WHEREFORE DOST THOU CREATE & WEAVE THIS SATAN FOR A COVERING		499	MILTON 18	30
WHENCE IS THIS SHADOW TERRIBLE WHEREFORE DOST THOU REFUSE		505	MILTON 22	31
DOST THOU APPEAR BEFORE ME WHO LIEST DEAD IN LUVAH'S SEPULCHER		648	JERUSALEM 24	57
DOST THOU FORGIVE ME THOU WHO WAST DEAD & ART ALIVE . . .		648	JERUSALEM 24	58
IF THOU DOST LAY THINE HAND UPON ME BEHOLD I AM SILENT . .		654	JERUSALEM 29	49
WHY DOST THOU THUNDER WITH FROZEN SPECTROUS WRATH AGAINST US		664	JERUSALEM 37	3
DOST THOU BLACKEN THEIR BEAUTY BY A SECLUDED PLACE OF REST		693	JERUSALEM 60	32
DOST THOU NOT MURDER ME JOSEPH SPOKE IN ANGER & FURY SHOULD I		694	JERUSALEM 61	5
IF THOU DOST GO AWAY FROM ME I SHALL CONSUME UPON THESE ROCKS		705	JERUSALEM 67	46
TO DEVOUR THE HUMAN WHY DOST THOU WEEP UPON THE WIND AMONG		721	JERUSALEM 79	72
THE VISION OF CHRIST THAT THOU DOST SEE		748	EV GOSPEL(A)/N	1
[WHY DOST THOU HUMBLE THYSELF TO ME]		750	EV GOSPEL(C)/N	37
AND DOST NOT KNOW THE GARMENT FROM THE MAN		771	EPILOGUE/GP	2
JEHOVAH WHAT VENGEANCE DOST THOU REQUIRE		780	GHOST ABEL 1	14
BECAUSE THOU BACKWARD DOST RETURN		817	HAPPINESS/L	36
DOT				
HAVING A WHITE DOT CALLD A CENTER FROM WHICH BRANCHES OUT		659	JERUSALEM 33	19
DOTH				
TRUE LOVE DOTH PASS AWAY		7	MY SILKS/PS	18
THERE HIS CHARMING NEST DOTH LAY		7	LOVE HARMNY/PS	17
AND DOTH AMONG OUR BRANCHES PLAY		7	LOVE HARMNY/PS	20
FOR LIGHT DOTH SEIZE MY BRAIN		9	MAD SONG/PS	23
DOTH DROP A TEAR BENEATH THE SILENT SHADE		10	WHEN EARLY/PS	8
A YOUTH DOTH WALK IN STOLEN JOY AND PRIDE		10	WHEN EARLY/PS	14
FAMINE AND DEATH DOTH CRY		13	GWIN KING/PS	78
OVER THE FIELD DOTH FLY		13	GWIN KING/PS	80

	PAGE	TITLE	LINE

DOTH   (CONTINUED)

	PAGE	TITLE	LINE
THE EARTH DOTH FAINT AND FAIL	13	GWIN KING/PS	94
THE HEART DOTH FAIL YOU SAY MY LORD THE MERCHANTS . . .	21	EDW THIRD/PS 2	86
THE EAGLE THAT DOTH GAZE UPON THE SUN	24	EDW THIRD/PS 3	116
THE DOG DOTH SEIZE THE WOLF THE FORESTER THE LION . . .	24	EDW THIRD/PS 3	119
DOTH SEIZE THE SOARING EAGLE UNDONE BY FLIGHT	24	EDW THIRD/PS 3	121
THE SNAKE DOTH TURN AND BITE THE PADDING FOOT	24	EDW THIRD/PS 3	129
NOW THE QUARRY S SET AND DEATH DOTH SPORT	24	EDW THIRD/PS 3	142
WHILE VACANT YOUTH DOTH CRAVE AND SEEK ABOUT	27	EDW THIRD/PS 3	252
WHERE HE DOTH REND THE VAULT OF HEAVEN	30	EDW THIRD/PS 5	19
THE HUSBANDMAN DOTH LEAVE HIS BENDING HARVEST	34B	KING JOHN/PS	PROSE
BLOOD CRIES AFAR THE LAND DOTH SOW ITSELF	34B	KING JOHN/PS	PROSE
DOTH IT NOT SEEM ASHAMED OF SUCH A PLACE	37A	CONTEMPLATN/PS	PROSE
HE SAT AND HEARD WITH JOY AND PRAISED GOD WHO ISRAEL STILL DOTH KEEP	40A	SAMSON/PS	PROSE
LIKE FABLED HECATE SHE DOTH BIND THEM TO HER LAW . . .	41D	THEN SHE BORE	PROSE
AND WHERE SHE GOES HEAVEN STILL DOTH FOLLOW HER SHE . .	42A	THEN SHE BORE	PROSE
BUT POLICY DOTH DRUDGE FOR HATE AS WELL AS SLANDER . .	42D	THEN SHE BORE	PROSE
[[SUSPITION MIXT] & POLICY DOTH DWELL WITH HER BY WHOM]	43A	THEN SHE BORE	*PROSE
[SHE HAD A SON CALLED SUSPITION] CONCEIT & & POLICY DOTH	43A	THEN SHE BORE	*PROSE
AND TUNES HER [?CHAUNTANT] NOTES WHEN BUXOM JOY DOTH FAN HIS WINGS	43B	WOE CRIED MUSE	*PROSE
& EVRY PIECE OF FLESH DOTH CRY OUT WOE	43C	WOE CRIED MUSE	PROSE
WHERE JOY DOTH SIT ON EVERY BOUGH	63	SHEPHERD FIRST	2
INNOCENCE DOTH LIKE A ROSE	63	SHEPHERD FIRST	5
MY HAIR IS VERY LONG MY BEARD DOTH COVER ALL MY BREAST .	102	TIRIEL 3	4
WHERE DOTH HE HIDE HIS TERRIBLE HEAD & HIS SWIFT & FIERY DAUGHTERS	106	TIRIEL 5	2
HE DOTH GIVE HIS JOY TO ALL	122	ON ANOTHERS/SI	25
HE DOTH FEEL THE SORROW TOO	122	ON ANOTHERS/SI	28
HE DOTH SIT BY US AND MOAN	123	ON ANOTHERS/SI	36
THY BREATH DOTH NOURISH THE INNOCENT LAMB	128	BOOK OF THEL 2	5
THY WINE DOTH PURIFY THE GOLDEN HONEY THY PERFUME . . .	128	BOOK OF THEL 2	8
WHERE LUVAH DOTH RENEW HIS HORSES LOOKST THOU ON MY YOUTH	128	BOOK OF THEL 3	8
AH SHE DOTH DEPART	161	NEVER PAIN/N	8
[DOTH LIFE DESTROY]	175	SICK ROSE/N	8
DOTH THE WINGED LIFE DESTROY	184	SEVRL QUESTN/N	12
WHOM URIZEN DOTH SERVE WITH LIGHT REPLENISHING HIS DARKNESS	292	FOUR ZOAS 3	15
DOTH ENION AVOID THE SIGHT OF THY BLUE WATRY EYES . . .	339	FOUR ZOAS 7B	230
OFT DOTH HIS EYES EMERGE FROM THE ABYSS INTO THE REALMS .	352	FOUR ZOAS 8	* 454
I SEE THE HAND THAT LEADETH ME DOTH ALSO LEAD MY FLOCKS	369	FOUR ZOAS 9	474
DOTH ENION AVOID THE SIGHT OF THY BLUE HEAVENLY EYES . .	371	FOUR ZOAS 9	531
DOTH PUT THE LIGHT OF KNOWLEDGE OUT	433	AUGURIES	96
O WHEREFORE DOTH A DRAGON-FORM FORTH ISSUE FROM MY LIMBS	492	MILTON 12	2
HIS ARMS DOTH HE FORGIVE JERUSALEM & NOT EXACT PURITY FROM HER WHO IS	694	JERUSALEM 61	15
SAYING DOTH JEHOVAH FORGIVE A DEBT ONLY ON CONDITION THAT IT SHALL	694	JERUSALEM 61	17
BE PAYED DOTH HE FORGIVE POLLUTION ONLY ON CONDITIONS OF PURITY	694	JERUSALEM 61	18
AND HE DOTH RULE OVER ME THEREFORE MY SOUL IN FUMES OF BLOOD	780	GHOST ABEL 2	8

DOTS

	PAGE	TITLE	LINE
CUT DOTS & LOZENGES EQUALLY WELL WITH THOSE LITTLE PRINTS	592B	PUB ADDRESS/N	PROSE
ABSURD NONSENSE ABOUT DOTS & LOZENGES & CLEAN STROKES . .	602A	PUB ADDRESS/N	PROSE

DOUBLE

	PAGE	TITLE	LINE
WITH DOUBLE VIOLENCE IT IS NOT WORTH QUARRELING ABOUT . .	45D	ISLAND MOON 1	PROSE
AND AS A DOUBLE FEMALE FORM LOVELINESS & PERFECTION OF BEAUTY	304	FOUR ZOAS 4	251
OF THE NOW FALLEN MAN A DOUBLE FORM VALA APPEARD A MALE	326	FOUR ZOAS 7	246
THE DOUBLE ROOTED LABYRINTH SOON WAVD AROUND THEIR HEADS	328	FOUR ZOAS 7	335
A MOURNFUL FORM DOUBLE HERMAPHRODITIC MALE & FEMALE . . .	496	MILTON 14	37
THE DOUBLE DRUM DROWNS HOWLS & GROANS THE SHRILL FIFE SHRIEKS & CRIES	509	MILTON 24	65
A DOUBLE TWELVE & THRICE NINE SUCH THEIR DIVISIONS . . .	528	MILTON 37	18
DOLOROUS THAT RAN THRO ALL CREATION A DOUBLE SIX-FOLD WONDER	534	MILTON 42	4
THE ROCKY LAW OF CONDEMNATION & DOUBLE GENERATION & DEATH	656	JERUSALEM 30	37
SAMUEL A DOUBLE BOOK & KINGS A DOUBLE BOOK THE PSALMS & PROPHETS	677	JERUSALEM 48	10
THE VIOLENT MAN-SLAUGHTER THESE ARE THE SPECTRE'S DOUBLE CAVE	699	JERUSALEM 64	21
AND NERVES INTO TWO KNOTS & THE SEED INTO A DOUBLE KNOT	703	JERUSALEM 66	49
A DOUBLE FEMALE AND THEY DREW OUT FROM THE ROCKY STONES	704	JERUSALEM 67	3
O CHEMOSH O BACCHUS O VENUS O DOUBLE GOD OF GENERATION	706	JERUSALEM 68	18
HE COMBINES INTO A MIGHTY-ONE THE DOUBLE MOLECH & CHEMOSH	729	JERUSALEM 84	21
A WINE-PRESS OF LOVE & WRATH DOUBLE (HERMAPHRODITIC) . .	734	JERUSALEM 89	* 4
THE ARCHIEREUS THE IEREUS THE SADDUSAION DOUBLE	734	JERUSALEM 89	7
A DOUBLE FEMALE NOW APPEARD WITHIN THE TABERNACLE	735	JERUSALEM 89	52
TO BROCKLEY HILLS ACROSS THE THAMES HE WITH DOUBLE BOADICEA	736	JERUSALEM 90	24
BY DOUBLE SPECTRES SELF ACCURST	771	OF GATES/GP	28
FOR DOUBLE THE VISION MY EYES DO SEE	817	HAPPINESS/L	27
AND A DOUBLE VISION IS ALWAYS WITH ME	817	HAPPINESS/L	28
MY FACE IN FIERCE FLAMES IN MY DOUBLE SIGHT	818	HAPPINESS/L	57
SOLDIER-LIKE DANGER IS OVER I WILL DO DOUBLE THE WORK I DO	830C	LETTER 30	PROSE
HEALTH & HOW YOU HAVE ESCAPED THE DOUBLE BLOW BOTH . . .	833D	LETTER 33	PROSE
DOUBLE OF YOUR LETTER NEVERTHELESS I OUGHT TO HAVE SENT IT	875D	LETTER 82	PROSE

DOUBLE ELEPHANT

	PAGE	TITLE	LINE
ID SOON MAKE DOUBLE ELEPHANT LOOK FOOLISH	52B	ISLAND MOON 8	PROSE

DOUBLE ELEPHANT'S

	PAGE	TITLE	LINE
THERES DOUBLE ELEPHANT'S GIRLS THEY HAVE THEIR OWN WAY . .	52D	ISLAND MOON 8	PROSE

		PAGE	TITLE	LINE

DOUBLE-FORMD
WHO ARE THE SPECTRES OF THE TWENTYFOUR EACH DOUBLE-FORMD 641 JERUSALEM 19 20
DOUBLE-SEXED
THE TWOFOLD FORM HERMAPHRODITIC AND THE DOUBLE-SEXED . . 501 MILTON 19 32
DOUBLING
WITH DOUBLING VOICES & LOUD HORNS WOUND ROUND SOUNDING . . 274 FOUR ZOAS 1 382
DOUBLY
WHOM I AM DOUBLY BOUND TO OBEY MY PARENT . . . . . . 19 EDW THIRD/PS 2 2
IT IS THEREFORE DOUBLY INTERESTING MR WALKER IS TRULY AN 845D LETTER 44 PROSE
   AMIABLE
MY REQUEST MAKES ME DOUBLY THANK YOU . . . . 854D LETTER 53 PROSE
DOUBT
DOUBT NO MORE OF SAMSON'S LOVE FOR THAT FAIR BREAST WAS 39B SAMSON/PS PROSE
   MADE
("BLUNDERER'S FRIENDSHIP THAN CALUMNIATOR'S ENMITY") I 69C ANNO LAVATER MARG
   DOUBT THIS
DOUBT IS FLED & CLOUDS OF REASON . . . . 126 VOICE BARD/SI 4
AND TEMPESTS OF DOUBT ROLL AROUND ME . . . . 139 FRENCH REVOLTN 119
IF THOU CANST NOT DO THIS DOUBT THY THEORIES . . . . . 143 FRENCH REVOLTN 193
[IN DARKNESS & SOLITUDE FORMING SEAS OF [TROUBLE] DOUBT 267 FOUR ZOAS 1 * 114
   . . .
AND URIZEN WHO WAS FAITH & CERTAINTY IS CHANGD TO DOUBT 282 FOUR ZOAS 2 105
NOT SUFFRING DOUBT TO RISE UP FROM THE CLOUDS OF 340 FOUR ZOAS 7B * 297
   THE SHADOWY FEMALE
[WHAT DOUBT IS VIRTUOUS EVEN HONEST ?THAT DEPENDS ?UPON 386C ANNO WATSON * MARG
   EXAMINATION]
EVER DOUBT CHRIST'S IN THE ABOVE SENSE OF THE WORD MIRACLE 391D ANNO WATSON MARG
TO ALL & EQUALLY PLAIN TO ALL NONE CAN DOUBT . . . . . 393B ANNO WATSON MARG
YES I HAVE NO DOUBT HE DID . . . . 395D ANNO WATSON MARG
HE WHO SHALL TEACH THE CHILD TO DOUBT . . . . . . 433 AUGURIES 87
HE WHO REPLIES TO WORDS OF DOUBT . . . . 433 AUGURIES 95
IS TO DOUBT A FIT REPLY . . . . 433 AUGURIES 104
IF THE SUN & MOON SHOULD DOUBT . . . . 433 AUGURIES 109
AMONG INDEFINITE DRUID ROCKS & SNOWS OF DOUBT & REASONING 482 MILTON 3 8
WHO PUBLISHES DOUBT & CALLS IT KNOWLEDGE WHOSE SCIENCE 533 MILTON 41 15
   IS DESPAIR
REASON SAYS MIRACLE NEWTON SAYS DOUBT . . . . . . 536 DONT BELIEVE/N 7
DOUBT DOUBT & DONT BELIEVE WITHOUT EXPERIMENT . . . . 536 DONT BELIEVE/N 9
HAYLEY FLAXMAN & STOTHARD ARE ALSO IN DOUBT . . . . . 545 COSWAY FRAZR/N 5
[HIS PAINS ARE MORE THAN OTHERS' THERES NO DOUBT] . . 548 CRIPPLE EVRY/N 4
SEE WHAT GREAT LABOUR PAIN HIM & MODEST DOUBT . . . 548 CRIPPLE EVRY/N * 5
[XXX FOR TO ?.DOUBT] . . . . 551 WILLM COWPER/N * 3
AND TO DOUBT ITS OWN POWERS CONNOISSEURS TALK AS IF RAFAEL 563C DESC CAT PROSE
THEN HE SHOULD NOT DOUBT OF HAVING A NATIONAL COMMISSION 566A DESC CAT 2 PROSE
HER COMPANION AND HER THREE PRIESTS WERE NO DOUBT ALL . 568C DESC CAT 3 PROSE
O WHO CAN DOUBT THIS . . . . 577A DESC CAT 4 PROSE
FEAR AND DOUBT OF HIS OWN ORIGINAL CONCEPTION THE . . 582C DESC CAT 9 PROSE
AND WHEN ONCE HE HAD RAISED THE DOUBT IT BECAME . . . 582C DESC CAT 9 PROSE
SUITED TO THE PURPOSES OF COMMERCE NO DOUBT . . . . 593D PUB ADDRESS/N PROSE
IS TO BE [BLESSED] I CANNOT DOUBT THAT THIS MORE . . . 620D JERUSALEM 3 PROSE
NOR THEM OBSTRUCT WITH THY TEMPTATIONS OF DOUBT & DESPAIR 629 JERUSALEM 10 33
AN ORBED VOID OF DOUBT DESPAIR HUNGER & THIRST & SORROW 640 JERUSALEM 18 4
DOUBT FIRST ASSAILD ME THEN SHAME TOOK POSSESSION OF ME 643 JERUSALEM 21 5
MANCHESTER & LIVERPOOL ARE IN TORTURES OF DOUBT & DESPAIR 644 JERUSALEM 21 36
IN THE LOVE OF TIRZAH HE SAID DOUBT IS MY FOOD DAY & NIGHT 662 JERUSALEM 36 7
WHO TEACH DOUBT & EXPERIMENT & MY TWO WINGS VOLTAIRE 685 JERUSALEM 54 18
   ROUSSEAU
A POLYPUS OF ROOTS OF REASONING DOUBT DESPAIR & DEATH . . 707 JERUSALEM 69 3
WILL YOU SUFFER THIS SATAN THIS BODY OF DOUBT THAT SEEMS 741 JERUSALEM 93 20
   BUT IS NOT
TO TEACH DOUBT & EXPERIMENT . . . . 752 EV GOSPEL(D)/N 49
IN DOUBT WHICH IS SELF CONTRADICTION . . . . 753 EV GOSPEL(D)/N 98
HUMILITY IS ONLY DOUBT . . . . 753 EV GOSPEL(D)/N 99
DID JESUS TEACH DOUBT OR DID HE . . . . 756 EV GOSPEL(H)/N 1
DOUBT SELF JEALOUS WATRY FOLLY . . . . 770 OF GATES/GP 7
IN DOUBT WHICH IS SELF CONTRADICTION . . . . 770 OF GATES/GP 12
CAN A POET DOUBT THE VISIONS OF JEHOVAH . . . . . . 779C GHOST ABEL 1 PROSE
I HAVE NO DOUBT OF GIVING YOU BENEVOLENCE WITH EQUAL VIGOR 792B LETTER 4 PROSE
& MR H(HAYLEY) I DOUBT NOT WILL DO ULTIMATELY ALL . . . 811D LETTER 22 PROSE
& I DOUBT NOT THAT ALL YOUR KIND WISHES IN MY BEHALF . . 811D LETTER 22 PROSE
NOT ON THE NATURAL WORLD & IF IT WAS FIT FOR ME I DOUBT NOT 812A LETTER 22 PROSE
NO DOUBT THEY THOUGHT THE SAME OF THEIRS . . . . . 815B LETTER 23 PROSE
DOUBT IT IS WE NEED NOT DOUBT OF ITS HAVING BEEN . . . 821D LETTER 25 PROSE
ARE ALWAYS PERNICIOUS ESPECIALLY WHEN WE DOUBT OUR FRIENDS 822D LETTER 26 PROSE
DOUBT NOT THAT I SHALL RECIEVE JUSTICE & AM ONLY SORRY FOR 828B LETTER 28 PROSE
DOUBT NOT YET TO MAKE A FIGURE IN THE GREAT DANCE OF LIFE 835A LETTER 34 PROSE
TO MR ROSE IN AN UNFAIR LIGHT AS I HAVE NO DOUBT . . . 847B LETTER 44 PROSE
BUT A PLEASURE IN EMPLOYING HIS PRINTER & HAVE NO DOUBT I 856C LETTER 54 PROSE
PRODUCTIVE I HAVE NO DOUBT IN THE WAY NOW PROPOSED AND I 858C LETTER 55 PROSE
BEING SUCCESSFUL AS WELL AS RIGHT OF WHICH I HAVE NO DOUBT 862A LETTER 59 PROSE
LAST TIME WE MET I HAVE NO DOUBT THAT THE PLATES WOULD 870B LETTER 71 PROSE
   BE ALL
ON FUTURITY WHICH I CANNOT DO WITHOUT DOUBT & FEAR THAT 879C LETTER 89 PROSE
DOUBTED
BUT MANY DOUBTED & DESPAIRD & IMPUTED SIN & RIGHTEOUSNESS 648 JERUSALEM 25 15
OF WHAT I HAVE LONG DOUBTED VIZ . . . . 819C LETTER 25 PROSE
& TO GIVE OPPORTUNITY TO THOSE WHOM I DOUBTED . . . . 828C LETTER 28 PROSE
DOUBTFUL
("THE UNLOVED CANNOT LOVE") DOUBTFUL . . . . . . 76C ANNO LAVATER MARG
("GLANCE IS THE GREATEST GIFT") UNEASY DOUBTFUL . . . 77C ANNO LAVATER MARG
OF NO DOUBTFUL SIGNIFICATION TO ANYONE . . . . . . 386B ANNO WATSON MARG
TO PLEASE LADY H(HESKETH) WAS A DOUBTFUL CHANCE . . . 820C LETTER 25 PROSE

	PAGE	TITLE	LINE

DOUBTFULNESS
    SHAKING THE ROOTS & FAST FOUNDATIONS OF THE EARTH   495 MILTON 14   8
        IN DOUBTFULNESS
DOUBTING
    TILL HOPE GREW FEEBLE AND WAS READY TO GIVE PLACE   40A SAMSON/PS   PROSE
        TO DOUBTING
    DOUBTING STOOD THARMAS IN THE [DISMAL] SOLEMN DARKNESS   298 FOUR ZOAS 4   * 44
        HIS DIM EYES
    HE WHO STANDS DOUBTING OF WHAT HE INTENDS WHETHER . . . 386C ANNO WATSON   MARG
    THE HUMILIATION OF THE REASONING & DOUBTING SELFHOOD . . 614C V LAST JUDG/N *PROSE
    THARMAS INDOLENT & SULLEN URTHONA DOUBTING & DESPAIRING   671 JERUSALEM 43   3
DOUBTS
    FILLED WITH DOUBTS IN SELF ACCUSATION [GATHERD] BEHELD   329 FOUR ZOAS 7   * 385
        THE FRUIT
    THE LAND OF DOUBTS & SHADOWS SWEET DELUSIONS UNFORMD HOPES 367 FOUR ZOAS 9   379
    HE TOOK HER HAND RELUCTANT SHE FOLLOWD IN INFANT DOUBTS   371 FOUR ZOAS 9   552
    HE WHO DOUBTS FROM WHAT HE SEES . . . . 433 AUGURIES   107
    WHO LIVE IN DOUBTS & FEARS PERPETUALLY TORMENTED BY THE   511 MILTON 25   36
        ELECT
    FOR DOUBTS & FEARS UNFORMD & WRETCHED & MELANCHOLY . . . 515 MILTON 28   9
    IT IS IMPROBABLE MUST REJECT ALL HISTORY AND RETAIN DOUBTS 579B DESC CAT 5   PROSE
        ONLY
    SPIRIT OF TITIAN WAS PARTICULARLY ACTIVE IN RAISING DOUBTS 582C DESC CAT 9   PROSE
    WHICH DOUBTS & HESITATES IN THE MIDST OF ITS COURSE . . . 603C PUB ADDR AD/N PROSE
    AIR ON CLOUDY DOUBTS & REASONING CARES . . . . 763C FOR SEXES/GP   TITLE
    AND ALL MY FRIENDS BE WITH DOUBTS BEGUILD . . . . . . 818 HAPPINESS/L   48
    UNOBSERVD & AT LIBERTY FROM THE DOUBTS OF OTHER MORTALS   822D LETTER 26   PROSE
    PERHAPS DOUBTS PROCEEDING FROM KINDNESS BUT DOUBTS . . . 822D LETTER 26   PROSE
    DEAR SIR THIS PERHAPS WAS SUFFERD TO CLEAR UP SOME DOUBTS 828C LETTER 28   PROSE
    SELECT FOR THAT PURPOSE DOUBTS NOT AT ALL OF MR ROMNEY'S   846A LETTER 44   PROSE
DOUGH
    THAT SWAGGD HEAVY WITH THE ACCURSED DOUGH THE HOAR FROST   322 FOUR ZOAS 7   100
        RAGD
DOVE
    I HAVE BLOTTED OUT FROM LIGHT & LIVING THE DOVE &   290 FOUR ZOAS 2   391
        NIGHTINGALE
    I WEPT FOR JOY LIKE A DOVE I MOURN . . . . 427 LAND OF DREAMS   11
    TO BE WEAK AS A LAMB & SMOOTH AS A DOVE . . . . . . 428 MARY   25
    A DOVE HOUSE FILLD WITH DOVES & PIGEONS . . . . . . 431 AUGURIES   7
    OF MILTON'S SHADOW AS A DOVE UPON THE STORMY SEA . . . 534 MILTON 42   6
    LIKE A DOVE IS SURROUNDED BY A BLUE HEAVEN . . . . . 613B V LAST JUDG/N PROSE
    & THE ARK OF THE COVENANT IS AS A DOVE OF PEACE . . . 613B V LAST JUDG/N PROSE
    A GLORIFICATION OF ANGELS WITH HARPS SURROUND THE DOVE . 613B V LAST JUDG/N PROSE
    THEY SEND THE DOVE & RAVEN & IN VAIN THE SERPENT OVER THE 703 JERUSALEM 66   70
        MOUNTAINS
    WITH EVERY COLOUR LION TYGER HORSE ELEPHANT EAGLE DOVE   746 JERUSALEM 98   43
        FLY WORM
    AND DRIVEN AWAY MY TREMBLING DOVE . . . . 754 EV GOSPEL(E)/N   52
DOVEDALE
    SO SAYING SHE DREW ASIDE HER VEIL FROM MAM-TOR TO DOVEDALE 726 JERUSALEM 82   45
DOVELIKE
    SWEET MOANS DOVELIKE SIGHS . . . . 120 CRADLE SONG/SI   13
    ALL THE DOVELIKE MOANS BEGUILES . . . . 120 CRADLE SONG/SI   16
    OF DOVELIKE SOFTNESS & SHADOWY HABITATIONS PREPARED FOR   519 MILTON 31   3
        THEM
DOVER
    FROM CAITHNESS IN THE NORTH TO LIZARD-POINT & DOVER IN   485 MILTON 6   7
        THE SOUTH
    FROM DOVER CLIFF TO LIZARD POINT THE OTHER TOWARD THE NORTH 512 MILTON 26   14
    HIS RIGHT FOOT STRETCHES TO THE SEA ON DOVER CLIFFS HIS   531 MILTON 39   40
        HEEL
    OF ULRO ROLLD ROUND HIS SKIRTS FROM DOVER TO CORNWALL . . 670 JERUSALEM 42   18
    TO LIZARD-POINT & DOVER IN THE SOUTH HIS EMANATION . . . 728 JERUSALEM 83   71
DOVE'S
    LIKE THE DOVE'S VOICE LIKE TRANSIENT DAY LIKE MUSIC IN   127 BOOK OF THEL 1   11
        THE AIR
DOVES
    THEN LIKE THE DOVES FROM PILLARS OF SMOKE THE TREMBLING   358 FOUR ZOAS 9   46
        FAMILIES
    A DOVE HOUSE FILLD WITH DOVES & PIGEONS . . . . . . 431 AUGURIES   7
    BACK SAFE TO THEIR HUMANITY AS DOVES TO THEIR WINDOWS . . 655 JERUSALEM 30   13
    OF LAMBS AND DOVES MINGLED TOGETHER IN CUPS AND DISHES . . 725 JERUSALEM 82   7
DOWN
    O THOU WITH DEWY LOCKS WHO LOOKEST DOWN . . . .   1 TO SPRING/PS   1
    SIT DOWN AND IN OUR MOSSY VALLIES ON . . . .   2 TO SUMMER/PS   10
    FLOURISH DOWN THE BRIGHT CHEEK OF MODEST EVE . . . . .   2 TO AUTUMN/PS   10
    DRAWN DOWN TO EARTH BY SPELLS AND WICKEDNESS . . . . .   5 FAIR ELENOR/PS   46
    CLOUDED FALLN LIKE THE STATELY TREE CUT DOWN . . . . .   5 FAIR ELENOR/PS   50
    THEN DOWN I'LL LIE AS COLD AS CLAY . . . .   7 MY SILKS/PS   17
    ARISE AND PULL THE TYRANT DOWN . . . . 11 GWIN KING/PS   11
    DOWN BLERON'S HILLS THEY DREADFUL RUSH . . . . 11 GWIN KING/PS   21
    PULL DOWN THE TYRANT TO THE DUST . . . . 12 GWIN KING/PS   29
    THE WORKMAN THROWS HIS HAMMER DOWN . . . . 12 GWIN KING/PS   51
    DOWN FROM THE BROW UNTO THE BREAST . . . . 14 GWIN KING/PS   107
    DOWN LIKE A FALLING STAR FROM AUTUMN SKY . . . . . . 15 IMIT SPEN/PS   25
    DOWN ON HIS HANDS AND KNEES HE LAY . . . . 16 BLIND-MANS/PS   47
    BUT DOWN HE CAME ALAS HOW FRAIL . . . . 17 BLIND-MANS/PS   51
    AND DOWN HIS BACK THEY STRAIT CONVEY . . . . 17 BLIND-MANS/PS   58
    AND YELLING DEATH RUNS UP AND DOWN THE RANKS . . . . . 18 EDW THIRD/PS 1   8
    DOWN GOES OUR RIGHT TO FRANCE . . . . 23 EDW THIRD/PS 3   72
    THE WOLF IS HUNTED DOWN BY CAUSELESS FEAR . . . . . . 24 EDW THIRD/PS 3   113
    WHERE THOUSAND DEATHS ARE POSTING UP AND DOWN . . . . . 26 EDW THIRD/PS 3   222

```
                                                      PAGE     TITLE          LINE
DOWN     (CONTINUED)
  WE SIT US DOWN AND VIEW OUR FORMER JOYS  . . . . . .    27  EDW THIRD/PS 3    260
  THAT MURMUR DOWN THEIR PEBBLY CHANNELS AND  . . . . .    31  EDW THIRD/PS 5     55
  SHALL LAUGH WHOSE FRUITFUL LAPS BEND DOWN WITH FULNESS . .   33  EDW THIRD/PS 6     48
  THE VEILED EVENING WALKED SOLITARY DOWN THE WESTERN HILLS   35C  COUCH DEATH/PS  PROSE
  WHEN THE EVENING DROPS TRICKLE DOWN  . . . . . . . .    35D  COUCH DEATH/PS  PROSE
  HE FOLLOWED ME UP AND DOWN IN THE HOUSE WHEN I GREW UP  .   37C  CONTEMPLATN/PS  PROSE
  SHE SAW THE WORLD FALL DOWN IN ADORATION [NOR COULD        41B  THEN SHE BORE   PROSE
     REFRAIN]
  TWAS CONSCIENCE WHO BROUGHT MELANCHOLY DOWN  . . . . .    42B  THEN SHE BORE   PROSE
  THEN DOWN CAME CONSCIENCE WITH HIS LOVELY BAND THE  . .    42B  THEN SHE BORE   PROSE
  & OVERCAME DOWN HIS WHITE BEARD THE SILVER TORRENTS ROLL   42B  THEN SHE BORE   PROSE
  AN ABUNDANCE OF ENQUIRIES TO NO PURPOSE SAT HIMSELF DOWN   44B  ISLAND MOON 1   PROSE
  OF A VAST NUMBER OF PAPERS TURNED ABOUT & SAT DOWN  . . .   45B  ISLAND MOON 1   PROSE
  OF THE PULPIT STAIRS & KNOCK HIM DOWN & RUN AWAY  . . . .   48B  ISLAND MOON 4   PROSE
  HE'LL SWEAR AT THEM & KEEP THEM DOWN WITH HIS FIST & TELL   50A  ISLAND MOON 6   PROSE
  WITH THAT HE TIED POOR SCURVY DOWN  . . . . . . . .    51  WHEN CORRUP/IM     27
  AND THE CELLAR GOES DOWN WITH A STEP  . . . . . . . .    54  LO THE BAT/IM      14
  INFLAMMABLE GASS TURND SHORT ROUND & THREW DOWN THE TABLE   58D  ISLAND MOON 10  PROSE
  THEN COME HOME MY CHILDREN THE SUN IS GONE DOWN  . . . .    60  NURSES SONG/IM      5
  HE HAS KNOCKD DOWN THE WICKET  . . . . . . . . . .    61  SAY YOU JOE/IM     14
  [BUT I CAN KNEEL DOWN AT YOUR DOOR I AM A HARMLESS MAN]   101  TIRIEL 2           29
  AND I KNEEL DOWN THAT YOU MAY SEE I AM A HARMLESS MAN  . .  101  TIRIEL 2           31
  HE KNEELED DOWN & MNETHA SAID COME HAR & HEVA RISE  . . .  101  TIRIEL 2           32
  THEN MNETHA GAVE HIM MILK & FRUITS & THEY SAT DOWN TOGETHER  102  TIRIEL 2           58
  BUT FAR HE HAD NOT GONE WHEN IJIM FROM HIS WOODS COME DOWN  103  TIRIEL 4       *    3
  THE BLIND MAN HEARD HIS BROTHER'S VOICE & KNEELD DOWN ON   104  TIRIEL 4          10
     HIS KNEE
  PIPING DOWN THE VALLEYS WILD  . . . . . . . . . .   111  INTRODUCTN/SI       1
  PIPER SIT THEE DOWN AND WRITE  . . . . . . . . . .   111  INTRODUCTN/SI      13
  ON HIS SHOULDERS DOWN  . . . . . . . . . . . .   114  LIT GRL FND/SI     38
  THEN DOWN A GREEN PLAIN LEAPING LAUGHING THEY RUN  . . .  117  CHIMNEY SWP/SI     15
  AND SIT DOWN BY THEIR BED  . . . . . . . . . . .   119  NIGHT/SI           24
  I CAN LIE DOWN AND SLEEP  . . . . . . . . . . .   119  NIGHT/SI           42
  SWEET SLEEP WITH SOFT DOWN  . . . . . . . . . . .   120  CRADLE SONG/SI      5
  THEN COME HOME MY CHILDREN THE SUN IS GONE DOWN  . . . .   121  NURSES SONG/SI      5
  AND SITTING DOWN BEFORE THE HEAT OF DAY  . . . . . .   125  LIT BLK BOY/SI      6
  DOWN BY THE RIVER OF ADONA HER SOFT VOICE IS HEARD  . . .  127  BOOK OF THEL 1      4
  AH GENTLE MAY I LAY ME DOWN AND GENTLE REST MY HEAD  . .  127  BOOK OF THEL 1     12
  SHE CEASD & SMILD IN TEARS THEN SAT DOWN IN HER SILVER    128  BOOK OF THEL 2      2
     SHRINE
  AND LAY ME DOWN IN THY COLD BED AND LEAVE MY SHINING LOT  130  BOOK OF THEL 5     13
  AND ALL THY MOANS FLEW OER MY ROOF BUT I HAVE CALLD THEM  130  BOOK OF THEL 5     15
     DOWN
  TILL TO HER OWN GRAVE PLOT SHE CAME & THERE SHE SAT DOWN  130  BOOK OF THEL 6      9
  . . . FROM HIS SHOULDER DOWN THE BONE  . . . . . .   134  FRENCH REVOLTN      3
  PINIOND DOWN TO THE STONE FLOOR  . . . . . . . .   135  FRENCH REVOLTN     30
  . . . A LOATHSOME SICK WOMAN BOUND DOWN  . . . . .   135  FRENCH REVOLTN     35
  MAD WITH CHAINS LOOSE WHICH HE DRAGGD UP AND DOWN  . . .  136  FRENCH REVOLTN     48
  . . . EACH STRONG LIMB BOUND DOWN AS WITH MARBLE  . . .  137  FRENCH REVOLTN     66
  EXPANDED LIKE STARRY HEAVEN HE SAT DOWN . . . . . .   138  FRENCH REVOLTN     82
  . . . NOW DOWN ALL THIS GREAT STARRY HARVEST OF SIX      138  FRENCH REVOLTN     90
     THOUSAND YEARS
  . . . AND MAN LAY HIS FADED HEAD DOWN ON THE ROCK  . .   138  FRENCH REVOLTN     96
  . . . TEARS FELL DOWN THE SHADY CHEEKS AT HIS FEET MANY   140  FRENCH REVOLTN    132
     CLOTHD
  . . . TO ROOT UP AND PULL DOWN AND REMOVE  . . . . .   140  FRENCH REVOLTN    142
  HE SAT DOWN A DAMP COLD PERVADED THE NOBLES . . . . .   141  FRENCH REVOLTN    158
  . . . THROW DOWN THY SWORD AND MUSKET  . . . . . .   144  FRENCH REVOLTN    220
  . . . BLOOD RAN DOWN THE ANCIENT PILLARS  . . . . .   145  FRENCH REVOLTN    246
  SO HE TOOK ME THRO A STABLE & THRO A CHURCH & DOWN . . .  155D  MARRIAGE HH 17  PROSE
  DOWN THE WINDING CAVERN WE GROPED OUR TEDIOUS WAY  . . .  155D  MARRIAGE HH 17  PROSE
  AND MUTTER ACROSS THE OCEAN FRANCE REND DOWN THY DUNGEON  159A  SONG LIBERTY    PROSE
  CAST THY KEYS O ROME INTO THE DEEP DOWN FALLING  . . .  159B  SONG LIBERTY    PROSE
  EVEN TO ETERNITY DOWN FALLING  . . . . . . . . .   159B  SONG LIBERTY    PROSE
  DOWN RUSHD BEATING HIS WINGS IN VAIN THE JEALOUS KING  .  159C  SONG LIBERTY    PROSE
  I LAID ME DOWN UPON A BANK  . . . . . . . . . .   162  LAID ME DOWN/N      1
  DOWN THE GOLDEN HINGES TORE  . . . . . . . . . .   163  I SAW CHAPEL/N      9
  AND LAID ME DOWN AMONG THE SWINE  . . . . . . . .   163  I SAW CHAPEL/N     17
  I ASKD A LITHE LADY TO LIE HER DOWN  . . . . . . .   163  ASKED THIEF/N       3
  TILL THE SUN WENT DOWN  . . . . . . . . . . . .   164  HEARD ANGEL/N       7
  AT HIS CURSE THE SUN WENT DOWN  . . . . . . . . .   164  HEARD ANGEL/N      16
  [[AND] DOWN POURD THE HEAVY RAIN]  . . . . . . . .   164  HEARD ANGEL/N      18
  RUNS IN BLOOD DOWN PALACE WALLS  . . . . . . . .   170  LONDON/N           13
  THEN COME HOME MY CHILDREN THE SUN IS GONE DOWN  . . . .   171  NURSES SONG/N       5
  WHEN THE STARS THREW DOWN THEIR SPEARS  . . . . . .   173  THE TYGER/N 1      29
  WHEN THE STARS THREW DOWN THEIR SPEARS  . . . . . .   173  THE TYGER/N 2      13
  HE SITS DOWN WITH HOLY FEARS  . . . . . . . . .   174  HUMAN IMAGE/N      10
  THE STARS THREW DOWN THEIR CUPS & FLED  . . . . . .   187  WHEN KLOPSTK/N     12
  IF BLAKE COULD DO THIS WHEN HE [SAT DOWN TO] ROSE UP FROM  187  WHEN KLOPSTK/N     33
     SHITE
  WHAT MIGHT HE NOT DO IF HE SAT DOWN TO WRITE  . . . . .  187  WHEN KLOPSTK/N     34
  [AND WANDERD DOWN THE VALES OF KENT IN SICK & DREAR      196  AMERICA PREL 2     21
     LAMENTINGS]
  SO CRIED HE RENDING OFF HIS ROBE & THROWING DOWN        200  AMERICA 12          1
     HIS SCEPTER
  DOWN ON THE LAND OF AMERICA INDIGNANT THEY DESCENDED  .   200  AMERICA 12          4
  TO QUENCH THEIR ANGUISH AT THE FEET OF WASHINGTON DOWN    201  AMERICA 13          4
     FALLN
  THE BUILDER OF VIRGINIA THROWS HIS HAMMER DOWN IN FEAR  .  201  AMERICA 14     *   16
  HIS SNOWY BEARD THAT STREAMS LIKE LAMBENT FLAMES DOWN HIS  204  AMERICA CANC B     16
     WIDE BREAST
```

```
                                                                PAGE      TITLE          LINE
DOWN   (CONTINUED)
        AND ITS ROOFS CRACK ACROSS DOWN FALLING ON TH ANGELIC SEATS   204 AMERICA CANC B      24
        HE TOOK DOWN FROM ITS TREMBLING PILLAR FROM ITS CAVERN        205 AMERICA CANC C       3
          DEEP
        THEN COME HOME MY CHILDREN THE SUN IS GONE DOWN   . . . .     212 NURSES SONG/SE       5
        WHEN THE STARS THREW DOWN THEIR SPEARS   . . . . . . .        214 THE TYGER/SE        17
        RUNS IN BLOOD DOWN PALACE WALLS   . . . . . . . . . .         216 LONDON/SE           12
        HE SITS DOWN WITH HOLY FEARS   . . . . . . . . . .            217 HUMAN ABSTR/SE       9
        OF BLOOD POUR DOWN THE MOUNTAINS TO COOL   . . . . . .        225 URIZEN 5            31
        DOWN SUNK WITH FRIGHT A RED   . . . . . . . . . .             228 URIZEN 11            2
        DEEP DOWN INTO THE ABYSS   . . . . . . . . . . .              228 URIZEN 11            4
        TWO NOSTRILS BENT DOWN TO THE DEEP   . . . . . . .            229 URIZEN 13            1
        LIFE IN CATARACTS POURD DOWN HIS CLIFFS   . . . . . .         230 URIZEN 13           55
        THEY BEAT DOWN THE STAKES THE CORDS   . . . . . . .           232 URIZEN 19           48
        THESE FALLING DOWN ON THE ROCK   . . . . . . . . .            233 URIZEN 20           18
        AND HIS TEARS FLOWED DOWN ON THE WINDS   . . . . . .          235 URIZEN 25            4
        IN THE INFINITE VOID BUT BOUND DOWN   . . . . . . .           236 URIZEN 25           46
        AND CAUGHT HIM IN MY HAT AS BOYS KNOCK DOWN A BUTTERFLY       237 EUROPE INTRO         9
        INTO MY PARLOUR AND SAT DOWN AND TOOK MY PEN TO WRITE   . .   238 EUROPE INTRO        23
        AND ALL THE OVERFLOWING STARS RAIN DOWN PROLIFIC PAINS   . .  238 EUROPE PREL 1       15
        THEN ENITHARMON DOWN DESCENDED INTO HIS RED LIGHT   . . .     240 EUROPE 4            31
        THE CLOUD BEARS HARD UPON THE COUNCIL HOUSE DOWN RUSHING      241 EUROPE 9            12
        BUT PALAMABRON SHOT HIS LIGHTNINGS TRENCHING DOWN HIS WIDE    242 EUROPE 12           23
          BACK
        DOWN THE STEPS OF MY CRYSTAL HOUSE   . . . . . . .            244 EUROPE 14           25
        ORC ON MOUNT ATLAS HOWLD CHAIND DOWN WITH THE CHAIN OF        246 SONG OF LOS 3       21
          JEALOUSY
        SHOT DOWN HIS WIDE BOSOM AND SHOULDERS   . . . . . . .        249 AHANIA 2             4
        SHE FELL DOWN A FAINT SHADOW WANDRING   . . . . . .           250 AHANIA 2            38
        RUSHD DOWN LIKE FLOODS FROM HIS MOUNTAINS   . . . . . .       250 AHANIA 3             8
        THE OINTMENT FLOWD DOWN ON THE VOID   . . . . . . .           251 AHANIA 3            49
        THE SWEAT POURED DOWN THY TEMPLES   . . . . . . .            255 AHANIA 5            35
        WRATH WAS FOLLOWD UP AND DOWN   . . . . . . . . .            256 BOOK OF LOS 3       23
        SUNK PRECIPITANT HEAVY DOWN DOWN   . . . . . . . .            258 BOOK OF LOS 4       28
        DOWN THE HEAVY SUNK CLEAVING AROUND   . . . . . . .           259 BOOK OF LOS 5        6
        THE LIGHT THAT FLOWD DOWN ON THE WINDS   . . . . . .          260 BOOK OF LOS 5       28
        IT DOWN INTO THE DEEPS THE DEEPS FLED   . . . . . .           260 BOOK OF LOS 5       43
        AND BOUND DOWN TO THE GLOWING ILLUSION   . . . . . .          260 BOOK OF LOS 5       47
        FLOWING DOWN INTO NIGHT TILL A FORM   . . . . . . .           260 BOOK OF LOS 5       55
        I ASKD A LITHE LADY TO LIE HER DOWN   . . . . . . .           261 ASKED THIEF          3
        SO SAYING HE SUNK DOWN INTO THE SEA A PALE WHITE CORSE   . .  266 FOUR ZOAS 1         76
        [SO SAYING] IN TORMENT HE SUNK DOWN & FLOWD AMONG HER FILMY   266 FOUR ZOAS 1         77
          WOOF
        [ALIGHTING DOWN FROM] ALIGHTING IN HIS DRUNKEN JOY   . . .    266 FOUR ZOAS 1      *  93
        THAT DARK & DISMAL INFINITE WHERE THOUGHT ROAMS UP & DOWN     268 FOUR ZOAS 1        155
        THEY WANDERD LONG TILL THEY SAT DOWN UPON THE MARGIND SEA     271 FOUR ZOAS 1        245
        AND LIVE THEREBY HE IS SUNK DOWN INTO A DEADLY SLEEP   . .    272 FOUR ZOAS 1        291
        AS THE SUN SHINES DOWN ON THE MISTY EARTH SUCH WAS THE        274 FOUR ZOAS 1        365
          VISION
        HARROW BURN ALL THESE CORN FIELDS THROW DOWN ALL THESE        274 FOUR ZOAS 1        388
          FENCES
        HIS HEAD SHRILL SOUNDING IN THE SKY DOWN RUSHD THE SUN        275 FOUR ZOAS 1        415
          WITH NOISE
        THARMAS ENDURD NOT HE FLED HOWLING THEN A BARREN WASTE        275 FOUR ZOAS 1        419
          SUNK DOWN
        SMITE SPECTRE OF URTHONA MOCK THE FIEND WHO DREW US DOWN      276 FOUR ZOAS 1        432
        WHICH STAND UPON THE EDGE OF BEULAH & HE SUNK DOWN   . . .    277 FOUR ZOAS 1        465
        THEY WERE INTRODUCD TO THE DIVINE PRESENCE & THEY KNEELED     277 FOUR ZOAS 1        482
          DOWN
        SUDDEN DOWN FELL THEY ALL TOGETHER INTO AN UNKNOWN SPACE      279 FOUR ZOAS 1        541
        JERUSALEM CAME DOWN IN A DIRE RUIN OVER ALL THE EARTH   . .   281 FOUR ZOAS 2         45
        IS FORMD & THROWN DOWN THUNDRING INTO THE DEEPS OF NON        283 FOUR ZOAS 2        137
          ENTITY
        HEATED RED HOT THEY HIZZING REND THEIR WAY DOWN MANY A        283 FOUR ZOAS 2        138
          LEAGUE
        LOS JOYD & ENITHARMON LAUGHD SAYING LET US GO DOWN   . . .    285 FOUR ZOAS 2        211
        AND SEE THIS LABOUR & SORROW THEY WENT DOWN TO SEE THE        285 FOUR ZOAS 2        212
          WOES
        FOR WHEN LUVAH SUNK DOWN HIMSELF PUT ON THE ROBES OF BLOOD    287 FOUR ZOAS 2        263
        THEN FALLING DOWN A TERRIBLE SPACE RECOVRING IN WINTER DIRE   287 FOUR ZOAS 2      *  277
        AND LOS & ENITHARMON WERE DRAWN DOWN BY THEIR DESIRES   . .   287 FOUR ZOAS 2        287
        IN GOLDEN WREATHES THE SORROW OF MAN & THE BALMY DROPS        293 FOUR ZOAS 3         67
          FELL DOWN
        WENT DOWN THE HUMAN HEART WHERE PARADISE & ITS JOYS           294 FOUR ZOAS 3         95
          ABOUNDED
        TO WEIGH ME DOWN BENEATH THE GRAVE INTO NON ENTITY   . . .    295 FOUR ZOAS 3        127
        DOWN FROM THE DISMAL NORTH THE PRINCE IN THUNDERS & THICK     295 FOUR ZOAS 3        139
          CLOUDS
        AS WHEN THE THUNDERBOLT DOWN FALLETH ON THE APPOINTED PLACE   295 FOUR ZOAS 3        140
        FELL DOWN DOWN RUSHING RUINING THUNDERING [DARKNING]          295 FOUR ZOAS 3      *  141
          SHUDDERING
        THAN URIZEN & ALL HIS HOSTS IN CURST DESPAIR DOWN RUSHING     296 FOUR ZOAS 3        152
        AND YET TOO NEAR DASHD DOWN I SEND THEE INTO DISTANT          296 FOUR ZOAS 3        170
          DARKNESS
        WEIGHS DOWN HER EYELIDS THEN SHE FALLS THEN STARTING WAKES    297 FOUR ZOAS 3        210
          IN FEARS
        FLOW DOWN INTO THE SEA & SLUMBER IN OBLIVION AH ENION   . .   298 FOUR ZOAS 4         23
        NOW HE RESOLVD TO DESTROY LOS & NOW HIS TEARS FLOWD DOWN      298 FOUR ZOAS 4         47
        THY EDDYING SPIRIT DOWN THE HILLS OF BEULAH ALL MY SONS       300 FOUR ZOAS 4         89
        BUT FOUND MYSELF & HER TOGETHER ISSUING DOWN THE TIDE   . .   300 FOUR ZOAS 4        101
        FROM THE CAVERNS OF HIS JOINTED SPINE DOWN SUNK WITH FRIGHT   303 FOUR ZOAS 4        223
        A RED ROUND GLOBE HOT BURNING DEEP DEEP DOWN INTO THE         303 FOUR ZOAS 4        224
          ABYSS
```

		PAGE	TITLE	LINE

DOWN   (CONTINUED)

TWO NOSTRILS BENT DOWN TO THE DEEPS . . . .   303 FOUR ZOAS 4   237
DOWN ON THE ROCK OF ETERNITY ON DARKNESS OF THE DEEP . .   306 FOUR ZOAS 5   55
WITHIN HIS BREAST HIS FIERY SONS CHAIND DOWN & FILLD WITH   306 FOUR ZOAS 5   57
    CURSINGS
SHUDDRING & WEEPING THRO THE GLOOM & DOWN INTO THE DEEPS   307 FOUR ZOAS 5   69
FALLING DOWN ON THE ROCK AN IRON CHAIN LINK BY LINK LOCKD   307 FOUR ZOAS 5   91
HELD THE FIERCE BOY LOS NAILD HIM DOWN BINDING AROUND HIS   307 FOUR ZOAS 5   101
    LIMBS
OVER HER SON OBDURATE LOS BOUND DOWN HER LOVED JOY . . .   308 FOUR ZOAS 5   103
THEN LED HER DOWN INTO THE DEEPS & INTO HIS LABYRINTH . .   308 FOUR ZOAS 5   111
HIS LIMBS BOUND DOWN MOCK AT HIS CHAINS FOR OVER THEM A   308 FOUR ZOAS 5   114
    FLAME
THE STARS THREW DOWN THEIR SPEARS & FLED NAKED AWAY . . .   311 FOUR ZOAS 5   224
BUT NOW THOU ART BOUND DOWN WITH HIM EVEN TO THE GATES   311 FOUR ZOAS 5 * 233
    OF HELL
POUR DOWN MY FLIGHT THRO DARK IMMENSITY ETERNAL FALLING   313 FOUR ZOAS 6   69
WHIRLING IN UNRESISTIBLE REVOLUTIONS DOWN & DOWN . . . .   315 FOUR ZOAS 6   154
NOR DOWN NOR UP REMAIND THEN IF HE TURND & LOOKD BACK . .   316 FOUR ZOAS 6   191
IS NOT DOWN FALLING THRO IMMENSITY EVER & EVER . . . .   317 FOUR ZOAS 6   220
OR DRAWN UP OR LET DOWN AT THE WILL OF THE IMMORTAL MAN .   318 FOUR ZOAS 6   255
FOR URIZEN FELL AS THE MIDDAY SUN FALLS DOWN INTO THE WEST   318 FOUR ZOAS 6   267
OR DOWN DARK PRECIPICES OR CLIMBD WITH PAIN & LABOUR HUGE   319 FOUR ZOAS 6 * 289
WITH DIFFICULTY DOWN DESCENDING GUIDED BY HIS EAR . . .   319 FOUR ZOAS 6   293
AND [WITH] BY HIS GLOBE OF FIRE HE WENT DOWN THE VALE OF   319 FOUR ZOAS 6   294
    URTHONA
FALLING WITH WHEEL IMPETUOUS DOWN AMONG URTHONA'S VALES   320 FOUR ZOAS 6   321
BRANCHES INTO THE HEAVEN OF LOS THEY PIPE FORMD BENDING   321 FOUR ZOAS 7   33
    DOWN
TO BEAR THEE DOWN BENEATH THE WAVES IN STIFLING DESPAIR   321 FOUR ZOAS 7   56
WITH A CRASH BREAKING ACROSS THE HORRIBLE MASS COMES DOWN   322 FOUR ZOAS 7   78
CUT THEE IN GASHES THO THE BLOOD POURS DOWN AROUND THY   322 FOUR ZOAS 7   84
    ANKLES
DRAW DOWN ENITHARMON TO THE SPECTRE OF URTHONA . . . .   323 FOUR ZOAS 7   115
HIS BROODINGS RUSH DOWN TO HIS FEET PRODUCING EGGS THAT   324 FOUR ZOAS 7   167
    HATCHING
IN THE DARK DEEP THE DARK TREE GREW HER SHADOW WAS DRAWN   324 FOUR ZOAS 7   170
    DOWN
DOWN TO THE ROOTS IT WEPT OVER ORC THE SHADOW OF ENITHARMON   324 FOUR ZOAS 7   171
THY OLIVE TREES THAT POURD DOWN OIL UPON A THOUSAND HILLS   325 FOUR ZOAS 7   192
FOR THE SHADOW OF ENITHARMON DESCENDED DOWN THE TREE OF   325 FOUR ZOAS 7   210
    MYSTERY
FROM THE ENORMITY & CALLD THEM LUVAH & VALA TURNING DOWN   326 FOUR ZOAS 7   248
TO BRING HER DOWN SUBJECTED TO THE RAGE OF MY FIERCE BOY   326 FOUR ZOAS 7   266
OF IRON GLOWD BRIGHT PREPARD FOR SPADES & PLOWSHARES SUDDEN   327 FOUR ZOAS 7 * 283
    DOWN
SHUT UP WITHIN THEMSELVES DESCENDING DOWN I SUNK ALONG . .   327 FOUR ZOAS 7   286
I VIEW FUTURITY IN THEE I WILL BRING DOWN SOFT VALA . . .   327 FOUR ZOAS 7   299
THEN LOS PLUCKED THE FRUIT & EAT & SAT DOWN IN DESPAIR . .   330 FOUR ZOAS 7   395
OR ORC BENDING DOWN AS THE BINDER OF THE SHEAVES FOLLOWS   332 FOUR ZOAS 7   462
AND ALL THE SONS OF ?EVERLASTING SHALL BOW DOWN AT MY FEET   333 FOUR ZOAS 7B   10
AND WITH IMMENSE MACHINES DOWN ROLLING THE TERRIFIC ORB   333 FOUR ZOAS 7B   30
TO LABOUR & BEHOLD MY HEART SUNK DOWN BENEATH . . . . .   334 FOUR ZOAS 7B   63
TO RISE ON HIGH YET LOVE HERE BINDS ME DOWN & NEVER NEVER   339 FOUR ZOAS 7B   254
[THEY HAD WHICH CLOTHD THEIR BODIES LIKE A GARMENT OF SOFT   341 FOUR ZOAS 8   10
    DOWN]
GATES BROKEN DOWN THEY DESCEND THRO THE GATE OF PITY . .   341 FOUR ZOAS 8   28
IN GOLGONOOZA LOOKING DOWN THE DAUGHTERS OF BEULAH SAW . .   342 FOUR ZOAS 8   42
ALL BEULAH STOOD ASTONISHD LOOKING DOWN TO ETERNAL DEATH   342 FOUR ZOAS 8   47
BENEATH DOWN TO HIS EYELIDS SCALES OF PEARL THEN GOLD &   342 FOUR ZOAS 8   70
    SILVER
IMMINGLED WITH THE RUBY OVERSPREAD HIS VISAGE DOWN . . .   342 FOUR ZOAS 8   71
THE SCALY ARMOUR SHOT OUT STUBBORN DOWN HIS BACK & BOSOM   343 FOUR ZOAS 8   73
WE LOOK DOWN INTO ULRO WE BEHOLD THE WONDERS OF THE GRAVE   346 FOUR ZOAS 8   223
SO SANG THEY IN ETERNITY LOOKING DOWN INTO BEULAH . . .   347 FOUR ZOAS 8   246
VALA DRAWN DOWN INTO A VEGETATED BODY NOW TRIUMPHANT . .   348 FOUR ZOAS 8   280
[I HAVE] AWAY FROM ME I HAVE BOUND DOWN WITH A HOT IRON   349 FOUR ZOAS 8 * 302
BIND HIM DOWN SISTERS BIND HIM DOWN ON EBAL MOUNT OF   349 FOUR ZOAS 8   315
    CURSING
AND HE ROLLD DOWN BENEATH THE FIRES OF ORC A GLOBE IMMENSE   350 FOUR ZOAS 8   372
CALLD DOWN A GREAT SOLEMN ASSEMBLY RINTRAH IN FURY & FIRE   351 FOUR ZOAS 8 * 389
THEY ROLLD DOWN A DIM WORLD CRUSTED WITH SNOW DEADLY & DARK   351 FOUR ZOAS 8 * 396
BOW DOWN BEFORE HER YOU HER CHILDREN & SET JERUSALEM FREE   351 FOUR ZOAS 8   409
LOS FELT THE STONY STUPOR & HIS HEAD ROLLD DOWN BENEATH   353 FOUR ZOAS 8   471
AND THE PALE HORSE SEEKS FOR THE POOL TO LIE HIM DOWN & DIE   354 FOUR ZOAS 8   529
DOWN FROM THE CROSS & PLACD IT IN A SEPULCHER WHICH LOS   356 FOUR ZOAS 8   594
    HAD HEWN
AND TORE THEM DOWN . . . .   357 FOUR ZOAS 9   9
THE NAKED WARRIORS RUSH TOGETHER DOWN TO THE SEA SHORE .   357 FOUR ZOAS 9   20
FELL DOWN & SHADOWY FORMS OF JOY MIXD WITH DESPAIR & GRIEF   358 FOUR ZOAS 9   29
FROM OUT THE FLOOD GATES OF THE SKY THE GATES ARE BURST   359 FOUR ZOAS 9   72
    DOWN POUR
THE TORRENTS BLACK UPON THE EARTH THE BLOOD POURS DOWN   359 FOUR ZOAS 9   73
    INCESSANT
ROLL DOWN THE MOUNTAINS IN BLACK TORRENTS CITIES VILLAGES   359 FOUR ZOAS 9   75
IN THIS DARK WORLD A NARROW HOUSE I WANDER UP & DOWN . .   360 FOUR ZOAS 9   113
LIE DOWN BEFORE MY FEET O DRAGON LET URIZEN ARISE . . .   360 FOUR ZOAS 9   139
REND DOWN THIS FABRIC AS A WALL RUIND & FAMILY EXTINCT .   362 FOUR ZOAS 9   186
BURST ITS BRIGHT VESSELS SHE FELL DOWN DEAD AT THE FEET   362 FOUR ZOAS 9   198
    OF URIZEN
TRIUMPHS IN ITS OWN DESTRUCTION THEY TOOK DOWN THE HARNESS   365 FOUR ZOAS 9   295
THE NAKED WARRIORS RUSH TOGETHER DOWN TO THE SEA SHORES   365 FOUR ZOAS 9   326

```
                                                    PAGE      TITLE          LINE
DOWN    (CONTINUED)
    THEN URIZEN SITS DOWN TO REST & ALL HIS WEARIED SONS  . .   366  FOUR ZOAS 9      340
    THE ETERNAL MAN ALSO SAT DOWN UPON THE COUCHES OF BEULAH    366  FOUR ZOAS 9      354
    THE HUMAN FORM DIVINE THROWN DOWN FROM THEIR HIGH STATION   366  FOUR ZOAS 9      367
    THEN O THOU FAIR ONE SIT THEE DOWN FOR THOU ART AS THE      367  FOUR ZOAS 9      408
        GRASS
    ALAS AM I BUT AS A FLOWER THEN WILL I SIT ME DOWN  . . .    368  FOUR ZOAS 9      410
    SO SAYING SHE SAT DOWN & WEPT BENEATH THE APPLE TREES  . .  368  FOUR ZOAS 9      413
    THE FRUIT SHALL RIPEN & FALL DOWN & THE FLOWERS CONSUME     368  FOUR ZOAS 9      420
        AWAY
    MY LUVAH SMILD I KNEELED DOWN HE LAID HIS HAND ON MY HEAD   369  FOUR ZOAS 9      468
    THEN LAST HERSELF LAID DOWN & CLOSD HER EYELIDS IN SOFT     370  FOUR ZOAS 9      516
        SLUMBERS
    SHE PRESD THEM TO HER BOSOM & HER PEARLY TEARS DROPD DOWN   371  FOUR ZOAS 9      524
    SO SAYING THEY WENT DOWN INTO THE GARDEN AMONG THE FRUITS   371  FOUR ZOAS 9      535
    THEN MY LOINS FADE & IN THE HOUSE I SIT ME DOWN & WEEP  . . 371  FOUR ZOAS 9      544
    THRO ALL THE IMMENSE BORNE DOWN BY CLOUDS SWAGGING         372  FOUR ZOAS 9      563
        IN AUTUMNAL HEAT
    DOWN POUR THE TORRENT FLOODS OF HEAVEN ON ALL THE HUMAN     372  FOUR ZOAS 9      566
        HARVEST
    DESCENDS [OF] DOWN ON THE SAND THE THIRSTY SAND DRINKS      373  FOUR ZOAS 9    * 602
        & REJOICES
    CALLING HIM BROTHER IMAGE OF THE ETERNAL FATHER THEY SAT    374  FOUR ZOAS 9      644
        DOWN
    GO DOWN YE KINGS & COUNCELLORS & GIANT WARRIORS  . . . .    374  FOUR ZOAS 9      659
    GO DOWN INTO THE DEPTHS GO DOWN & HIDE YOURSELVES BENEATH   374  FOUR ZOAS 9      660
    GO DOWN WITH HORSE & CHARIOTS & TRUMPETS OF HOARSE WAR  . . 374  FOUR ZOAS 9      661
    LO HOW THE POMP OF MYSTERY GOES DOWN INTO THE CAVES  . .    375  FOUR ZOAS 9      662
    THE LION OF TERROR SHALL COME DOWN & BENDING HIS BRIGHT     376  FOUR ZOAS 9      706
        MANE
    DOWN DOWN THRO THE IMMENSE WITH OUTCRY FURY & DESPAIR  . .  376  FOUR ZOAS 9      723
    THERE IS THE NETTLE THAT STINGS WITH SOFT DOWN & THERE  .   377  FOUR ZOAS 9      762
    WHERE THE WIDE WOOF FLOWD DOWN . . . . . . . . . .         378  FOUR ZOAS 9      784
    THARMAS WENT DOWN TO THE WINE PRESSES & BEHELD THE SONS     378  FOUR ZOAS 9      785
        & DAUGHTERS
    IT APPEARS TO ME THAT MEN ARE HIRED TO RUN DOWN MEN OF      413B ANNO BOYD       MARG
        GENIUS
    THE MONK SAT DOWN ON HER STONY BED  . . . . . . . .        419  I SAW A MONK/N    22
    [THEY WOULD LET THEM DOWN AT WILL]  . . . . . . . . .      422  BENEATH AD/N       3
    WHO NAILS HIM DOWN UPON A ROCK  . . . . . . . . . .        425  MENTAL TRAVLER    11
    AND BINDS HER DOWN FOR HIS DELIGHT  . . . . . . . .        425  MENTAL TRAVLER    24
    SHE NAILS HIM DOWN UPON THE ROCK  . . . . . . . .         427  MENTAL TRAVLER   103
    AND THEN SET ME DOWN IN AN ENVIOUS LAND  . . . . . .       428  MARY              24
    THE MONK SAT DOWN ON THE STONY BED  . . . . . . . .        430  GREY MONK          4
    AND TOOK TO HIS BED & THERE LAY DOWN  . . . . . . .        435  WILLIAM BOND      12
    AND MARY FELL DOWN ON THE RIGHT HAND FLOOR  . . . . .      435  WILLIAM BOND      34
    DOWN THE ROAD & ALL THE WHILE WE WERE AT THE STABLE DOOR   437B BLAKES MEMORAN  PROSE
    HE THEN WENT & TOOK DOWN LE BRUN'S & RUBENS'S GALLERIES    449C ANNO REYNOLDS    MARG
    HE WHO CAN BE BOUND DOWN IS NO GENIUS  . . . . . . .       472D ANNO REYNOLDS    MARG
    AS WELL SAY THAT IF MAN DOES NOT LAY DOWN SETTLED          475C ANNO REYNOLDS    MARG
        PRINCIPLES
    THO IT GOES DOWN ON THE HEAVIEST SIDE  . . . . . .        476B ANNO REYNOLDS    MARG
    BY YOUR MILD POWER DESCENDING DOWN THE NERVES OF MY RIGHT   481  MILTON 2           6
        ARM
    DOWN SUNK WITH FRIGHT A RED ROUND GLOBE HOT BURNING DEEP    482  MILTON 3          11
    DEEP DOWN INTO THE ABYSS PANTING CONGLOBING TREMBLING  .    482  MILTON 3          12
    HANGING UPON THE WIND TWO NOSTRILS BENT DOWN INTO THE DEEP  482  MILTON 3          20
    ROUND GLOBE SUNK DOWN FROM HIS BOSOM INTO THE DEEP IN PANGS 483  MILTON 3          30
    TILL MICHAEL SAT DOWN IN THE FURROW WEARY DISSOLVD IN TEARS 488  MILTON 8          37
    BUT PALAMABRON CALLED DOWN A GREAT SOLEMN ASSEMBLY  . .     489  MILTON 8          46
    FELL DOWN AS DEWS OF NIGHT & A LOUD SOLEMN UNIVERSAL GROAN  490  MILTON 9          37
    HE SUNK DOWN A DREADFUL DEATH UNLIKE THE SLUMBERS OF BEULAH 490  MILTON 9          48
    DRAWN DOWN BY ORC & THE SHADOWY FEMALE INTO GENERATION  .   490  MILTON 10          2
    TO THOSE WITHOUT BUT INFINITE TO THOSE WITHIN IT FELL DOWN  491  MILTON 10          9
        AND
    SHE DOWN DESCENDED INTO THE MIDST OF THE GREAT SOLEMN       492  MILTON 11         29
        ASSEMBLY
    AND THREW ASIDE HER ARROWS AND LAID DOWN HER SOUNDING BOW   494  MILTON 13         37
    I WILL GO DOWN TO THE SEPULCHER TO SEE IF MORNING BREAKS    495  MILTON 14         21
    I WILL GO DOWN TO SELF ANNIHILATION AND ETERNAL DEATH  . .  495  MILTON 14         22
    HOVERING OVER THE COLD BOSOM IN ITS VORTEX MILTON BENT DOWN 497  MILTON 15         41
    HE SAW THE CRUELTIES OF ULRO AND HE WROTE THEM DOWN  . .    498  MILTON 17          9
    EVEN TO MAHANAIM WHEN WITH COLD HAND URIZEN STOOPD DOWN     500  MILTON 19          7
    ALL FELL TOWARDS THE CENTER IN DIRE RUIN SINKING DOWN  .    500  MILTON 19         21
    LOOKING DOWN INTO BEULAH WRATHFUL FILLD WITH RAGE  . . .    502  MILTON 20         45
    INTO A TABERNACLE AND FLEE WITH CRIES DOWN TO THE DEEPS     503  MILTON 20         48
    HE SAT DOWN ON HIS ANVIL-STOCK AND LEAND UPON THE TROUGH    503  MILTON 20         54
    AND DOWN DESCENDED INTO UDAN-ADAN IT WAS NIGHT  . . . .     503  MILTON 21          1
    I STOOPED DOWN & BOUND IT ON TO WALK FORWARD THRO ETERNITY  503  MILTON 21         14
    DOWN INTO ULRO AND THEY WEPT IN LONG RESOUNDING SONG  . .   503  MILTON 21         17
    LOS STOOD IN THAT FIERCE GLOWING FIRE & HE ALSO STOOPD DOWN 505  MILTON 22          8
    I IN SIX THOUSAND YEARS WALK UP AND DOWN FOR NOT ONE MOMENT 505  MILTON 22         18
    COVERING THE LIGHT OF DAY & ROLLING DOWN UPON THE MOUNTAINS 507  MILTON 23         26
    WHO CARRIED HIM DOWN INTO EGYPT WHERE EPHRAIM & MENASSHEH   508  MILTON 24         20
    THERE IS THE NETTLE THAT STINGS WITH SOFT DOWN AND THERE    513  MILTON 27         25
    THE OAK IS CUT DOWN BY THE AX THE LAMB FALLS BY THE KNIFE   522  MILTON 32         37
    AND LAYS DOWN IN THE GRAVE WITH THEM IN VISIONS OF ETERNITY 522  MILTON 32         41
    THE EIGHT IMMORTAL STARRY-ONES DOWN INTO ULRO DARK  . .     523  MILTON 34          4
    ACCOMPANY THEM DOWN TO THE ULRO WITH SOFT MELODIOUS TEARS   524  MILTON 34         21
    OF LIVING FIBRES DOWN INTO THE SEA OF TIME & SPACE GROWING  524  MILTON 34         25
    AND MELTING CADENCES THAT LURE THE SLEEPERS OF BEULAH DOWN  524  MILTON 34         29
    AND OLOLON LOOKED DOWN INTO THE HEAVENS OF ULRO IN FEAR     524  MILTON 34         49
```

531

	PAGE	TITLE	LINE

DOWN   (CONTINUED)

LOUD ROLL THE WEIGHTS & SPINDLES OVER THE WHOLE EARTH LET DOWN — 525 MILTON 35 — 14
THEY THUNDEROUS UTTERD ALL A UNIVERSAL GROAN FALLING DOWN — 525 MILTON 35 — 31
HE SET ME DOWN IN FELPHAM'S VALE & PREPARD A BEAUTIFUL — 527 MILTON 36 — 23
DESCENDING DOWN INTO MY GARDEN A HUMAN WONDER OF GOD — 528 MILTON 37 — 13
DESCENDED DOWN A PAVED WORK OF ALL KINDS OF PRECIOUS STONES — 529 MILTON 38 — 6
OUT FROM THE EASTERN SKY DESCENDING DOWN INTO MY COTTAGE — 529 MILTON 38 — 7
THY LAWS & TERRORS SHAKING DOWN THY SYNAGOGUES AS WEBS — 530 MILTON 38 — 42
FALL THEREFORE DOWN & WORSHIP ME SUBMIT THY SUPREME — 530 MILTON 38 — 52
AS THE CLEAR SUN & MILTON SILENT CAME DOWN ON MY PATH — 530 MILTON 39 — 5
HIM TO THE DIVINE MERCY CAST HIM DOWN INTO THE LAKE — 530 MILTON 39 — 11
HE VIEWS JERUSALEM & BABYLON HIS TEARS FLOW DOWN — 531 MILTON 39 — 48
FORBAD & DOWN WITH DREADFUL GROANS HE SUNK UPON HIS COUCH — 531 MILTON 39 — 51
TURN THRO THE IRON GATE DOWN SNEAKING LANE — 541 MR CROMEK/N — 4
TOM COOKE CUT HOGARTH DOWN WITH HIS CLEAN GRAVING — 554 BLAKES APL/N 1 — 3
TOM COOKE CUT HOGARTH DOWN WITH HIS CLEAN GRAVING — 555 BLAKES APL/N 2 — 7
AND FRANCE SHALL FALL DOWN & ADORE — 557 ART HAS LOST/N — 6
LOOKS DOWN ON THEIR LITTLE FOLLIES FROM THE EMPEROR TO THE MILLER — 569A DESC CAT 3 — PROSE
WHICH GAINED THAT PATRONAGE CRIED DOWN AS ECCENTRICITY — 572D DESC CAT 3 — PROSE
HE IS WORN DOWN WITH LABOUR BUT NOT WITH AGE — 575A DESC CAT 3 — PROSE
WHAT FINE ART IS YE ENGLISH ENGRAVERS MUST COME DOWN — 593C PUB ADDRESS/N — PROSE
TOM COOKE CUT HOGARTH DOWN WITH HIS CLEAN GRAVING — 595 BLAKES APOL/PA — 3
EVERY THING IS TONED DOWN BUT ONE SPOT OF LIGHT — 596C PUB ADDRESS/N — PROSE
A MAN SETS HIMSELF DOWN WITH COLOURS & WITH — 597B PUB ADDRESS/N — PROSE
WILL SIT ME DOWN & CRY I I — 600 MELODIOUS/PA — 2
DRAGGED DOWN BY [AN ANGEL] A DEMON CROWND WITH LAUREL — 606C V LAST JUDG/N — PROSE
& IS DRAGGING HER DOWN BY THE HAIR — 606C V LAST JUDG/N — PROSE
HE DRAGS SATAN DOWN HEADLONG HE IS CROWND WITH OAK — 607D V LAST JUDG/N — PROSE
THEY ARE WEIGHED DOWN BY TWO FIENDS — 607D V LAST JUDG/N — PROSE
THEY SCOURGE A GROUPE OF FIGURES DOWN INTO THE DEEPS — 608A V LAST JUDG/N — PROSE
DOWN STONE STEPS & BESIDE A GATE — 608B V LAST JUDG/N — PROSE
DRAGS THEM DOWN WITH THE OTHER ON THE ROCK & — 608B V LAST JUDG/N — PROSE
ARE DESCENDING [INTO HELL] DOWN THE STEPS INTO THE PIT — 608C V LAST JUDG/N — PROSE
WALKING UP & DOWN IN CONVERSATIONS CONCERNING — 613C V LAST JUDG/N — PROSE
IN ALL THE DARK ATLANTIC VALE DOWN FROM THE HILLS OF SURREY — 622 JERUSALEM 4 — 9
BUT THE PERTURBED MAN AWAY TURNS DOWN THE VALLEYS DARK — 622 JERUSALEM 4 — 22
HE STOOD AND STAMPD THE EARTH THEN HE THREW DOWN HIS HAMMER IN RAGE & — 625 JERUSALEM 6 — 9
IN FURY THEN HE SAT DOWN AND WEPT TERRIFIED THEN AROSE — 625 JERUSALEM 6 — 10
BUT STILL I LABOUR IN HOPE THO STILL MY TEARS FLOW DOWN — 628 JERUSALEM 9 — 28
SO SPOKE THE SPECTRE SHUDDRING & DARK TEARS RAN DOWN HIS SHADOWY FACE — 630 JERUSALEM 10 — 60
SAKE WALKING UP AND DOWN AMONG THE SPACES OF ERIN — 630 JERUSALEM 11 — 10
ROUND FROM HEAVEN TO EARTH DOWN FALLING WITH HEAVY BLOW — 636 JERUSALEM 16 — 12
HERE LOS FIXD DOWN THE FIFTY-TWO COUNTIES OF ENGLAND & WALES — 637 JERUSALEM 16 — 28
IN THE DARK WORLD A NARROW HOUSE HE WANDERS UP AND DOWN — 641 JERUSALEM 19 — 14
THY TABERNACLE TAKEN DOWN THY SECRET CHERUBIM DISCLOSED — 644 JERUSALEM 21 — 21
WITH CUSH HIS SON & TOOK ME DOWN HE IN A GOLDEN ARK — 644 JERUSALEM 22 — 4
DOWN IN SICK PALLID LANGUOR THESE WERE HIS LAST WORDS RELAPSING — 646 JERUSALEM 23 — 26
AND DRAW THEE DOWN INTO THIS ABYSS OF SORROW AND TORTURE — 646 JERUSALEM 23 — 39
DOWN THRO POPLAR & OLD BOW — 650 FIELDS FROM/J — 42
THEY BENT DOWN THEY FELT THE EARTH AND AGAIN ENROOTING — 653 JERUSALEM 28 — 18
IN GOLDEN WREATHES THE SORROW OF MAN & THE BALMY DROPS FELL DOWN — 654 JERUSALEM 29 — 54
WENT DOWN THE HUMAN HEART WHERE PARADISE & ITS JOYS ABOUNDED — 655 JERUSALEM 29 — 74
IN BEULAH THE FEMALE LETS DOWN HER BEAUTIFUL TABERNACLE — 656 JERUSALEM 30 — 34
THE ARTICULATIONS OF A MAN'S SOUL AND LAUGHING THROW IT DOWN — 656 JERUSALEM 31 — 10
HE CAME DOWN FROM HIGHGATE THRO HACKNEY & HOLLOWAY TOWARDS LONDON — 657 JERUSALEM 31 — 14
AND SAW EVERY MINUTE PARTICULAR THE JEWELS OF ALBION RUNNING DOWN — 657 JERUSALEM 31 — 17
O HOW I TREMBLE HOW MY MEMBERS POUR DOWN MILKY FEAR — 660 JERUSALEM 34 — 3
LOS BENDED HIS NOSTRILS DOWN TO THE EARTH THEN SENT HIM OVER — 661 JERUSALEM 34 — 47
LET DOWN AT WILL AROUND AND CALLD THE UNIVERSAL TENT — 665 JERUSALEM 38 — 50
DESCENDED AND FELL DOWN UPON THEIR KNEES ROUND ALBION'S KNEES — 666 JERUSALEM 40 — 8
FOR HAD THE BODY OF ALBION FALLN DOWN AND FROM ITS DREADFUL RUINS — 667 JERUSALEM 40 — 31
THERE TO ETERNITY CHAIND DOWN AND ISSUING IN RED FLAMES — 667 JERUSALEM 40 — 36
WITHIN HIS BREAST HIS MIGHTY SONS CHAIND DOWN & FILLD WITH CURSINGS — 667 JERUSALEM 40 — 40
ROSE IN THE NIGHT OF BEULAH AND BOUND DOWN THE SUN & MOON — 675 JERUSALEM 45 — 20
THE NOSTRILS BENT DOWN TO THE EARTH & CLOSD WITH SENSELESS FLESH — 680 JERUSALEM 49 — 38
TO RECORD THE SIN FOR A REPROACH TO LET THE SUN GO DOWN — 681 JERUSALEM 50 — 27
BUT ALBION FELL DOWN A ROCKY FRAGMENT FROM ETERNITY HURLD — 685 JERUSALEM 54 — 6
TOGETHER INTO AN ASSEMBLY THEY SAID LET US GO DOWN — 686 JERUSALEM 55 — 4
SUCH ARE THESE ULRO VISIONS FOR THO WE SIT DOWN WITHIN — 687 JERUSALEM 55 — 42
AND THOU HAST BOUND ME DOWN UPON THE STEMS OF VEGETATION — 692 JERUSALEM 60 — 11
CUT WITH THE FLINTS HER TEARS RUN DOWN HER REASON GROWS LIKE — 693 JERUSALEM 60 — 42
TREMBLING & DESCENDING DOWN SEEKING TO REST UPON HIGH MONA — 703 JERUSALEM 66 * — 79
AWAY FROM ME I HAVE BOUND DOWN WITH A HOT IRON — 705 JERUSALEM 67 — 48
BIND HIM DOWN SISTERS BIND HIM DOWN ON EBAL MOUNT OF CURSING — 705 JERUSALEM 68 — 3

```
                                                              PAGE     TITLE         LINE
DOWN    (CONTINUED)
    A SHEET & VEIL & CURTAIN OF BLOOD IS LET DOWN FROM HEAVEN    706 JERUSALEM 68      21
    ACROSS THE HILLS OF EPHRAIM & DOWN MOUNT OLIVET TO  . . .    706 JERUSALEM 68      22
    WITH MORAL LAW AN EQUAL BALANCE NOT GOING DOWN WITH          708 JERUSALEM 69      35
        DECISION
    AND LOS SHOUTED WITH CEASELESS SHOUTINGS & HIS TEARS POURED  711 JERUSALEM 71      56
        DOWN
    DOWN MONAGHAN CAVAN THESE ARE THE LAND OF ERIN   . . . .     711 JERUSALEM 72    * 27
    I WALK UP AND DOWN IN SIX THOUSAND YEARS . . . . . . .       714 JERUSALEM 74      19
    FOR LOS IN SIX THOUSAND YEARS WALKS UP & DOWN CONTINUALLY    716 JERUSALEM 75       7
    HER TWELVE GATES THROWN DOWN HER CHILDREN CARRIED INTO       719 JERUSALEM 78      23
        CAPTIVITY
    ALBION GAVE ME TO THE WHOLE EARTH TO WALK UP & DOWN TO POUR  720 JERUSALEM 79      36
    BUT PANGS OF LOVE DRAW ME DOWN TO MY LOINS WHICH ARE  . .    727 JERUSALEM 82      83
    A FORM OF VEGETATION NAIL THEM DOWN ON THE STEMS OF MYSTERY  727 JERUSALEM 83      13
    DOWN FLOWING INTO ENTUTHON'S VALES GLISTENS WITH            728 JERUSALEM 83      74
        SOFT AFFECTIONS
    WHILE LOS AROSE UPON HIS WATCH AND DOWN FROM GOLGONOOZA      728 JERUSALEM 83      75
    WITH HIM WENT DOWN THE DOGS OF LEUTHA AT HIS FEET  . . .     729 JERUSALEM 83      82
    WALKED UP AND DOWN IN ITS GREEN MOUNTAINS BUT HAND IS FLED   729 JERUSALEM 83      86
    OF BABYLON LED BY A CHILD HIS TEARS RUN DOWN HIS BEARD  . .  729 JERUSALEM 84      12
    STARTS FROM HIS LOFTY PLACES & CASTS DOWN HIS TENTS & FLEES  729 JERUSALEM 84      24
        AWAY
    BABEL & SHINAR LOOK TOWARD THE WESTERN GATE THEY SIT DOWN    730 JERUSALEM 85      18
    REFLECTS ETERNITY BENEATH THY AZURE WINGS OF FEATHERY DOWN   730 JERUSALEM 86       5
    SO SPEAKING SHE SAT DOWN ON SUSSEX SHORE SINGING LULLING     733 JERUSALEM 88      23
    REPEATING THE SMARAGDINE TABLE OF HERMES TO DRAW LOS DOWN    738 JERUSALEM 91      35
    IN UNPITYING RUIN DRIVING DOWN THE PYRAMIDS OF PRIDE  . .    738 JERUSALEM 91      44
    OBEDIENT FALL DOWN WORSHIP ME  . . . . . . . . .            749 EV GOSPEL(B)/N    24
    TRAMPLING DOWN HIPOCRISY  . . . . . . . . . . .             749 EV GOSPEL(B)/N    38
    BROKE DOWN FROM EVERY CHAIN & BAR  . . . . . . . .          749 EV GOSPEL(B)/N    41
    ABEL SINKS DOWN INTO THE GRAVE FROM WHICH ARISES SATAN  . .  780C GHOST ABEL 2   PROSE
    YOU SHALL NOT BRING ME DOWN TO BELIEVE SUCH FITTING         784C ANNO WW EXCUR   MARG
        & FITTED
    THIS IS UPSIDE DOWN WHEN VIEWD FROM HELL'S GATE BUT  . . .   785D ILLS DANTE 101 *PROSE
    IN EQUIVOCAL WORLDS UP & DOWN ARE EQUIVOCAL  . . . .        785D ILLS DANTE 101  PROSE
    FOR I SO FAR FROM BEING BOUND DOWN  . . . . . . . .         809A LETTER 20       PROSE
    WHEN I CAME DOWN HERE I WAS MORE SANGUINE THAN I AM  . .     811C LETTER 22       PROSE
    THIS FROM JOHNSON & FUSELI BROUGHT ME DOWN HERE  . . .      812C LETTER 22       PROSE
    CANVAS WHICH I BROUGHT DOWN WITH ME FOR THERE WERE THREE     816C LETTER 24       PROSE
    I THINK THE GRAND REASON OF MY BEING BROUGHT DOWN HERE  .    823B LETTER 26       PROSE
    FIRMNESS I HAVE BROUGHT DOWN HIS AFFECTED LOFTINESS  . .     825C LETTER 27       PROSE
    PRAY TELL ME HOW YOUR EYES DO I NEVER SIT DOWN TO WORK  .    826C LETTER 28       PROSE
    PUSHED HIM FORWARDS DOWN THE ROAD ABOUT FIFTY YARDS  . .     827B LETTER 28       PROSE
    SAW ME TURN HIM BEFORE ME DOWN THE ROAD & SAW & HEARD  .     827C LETTER 28       PROSE
    WROTE DOWN THE ACCUSATION TOLD ME IN PRIVATE ARE COMPELLD    827D LETTER 28       PROSE
    TAKE THEM DOWN AND UNROLL THEM BUT CANNOT DO IT EASILY AS    831B LETTER 31       PROSE
    FALLING DOWN ON THEIR KNEES RUNNING SIDEWAYS & IN  . .      833B LETTER 33       PROSE
    ONE OTHER WHICH I OMITTED TO WRITE DOWN & HAVE FORGOT  .     849A LETTER 45       PROSE
    THRESHOLD THO EVERY OTHER MAN'S DOORSTONE IS WORN DOWN  .    849D LETTER 47       PROSE
    IN WHICH I HAVE REGULARLY WRITTEN DOWN EVERY SUM I HAVE      854C LETTER 53       PROSE
    I HOPE THIS LETTER WILL OUTSTRIP MR PHILLIPS' AS I SIT DOWN  857D LETTER 55       PROSE
    THE YEA NAY CREEPING JESUS FROM SUPPOSING UP & DOWN  . .     878B LETTER 88       PROSE
    [SO SAYING HE ?SANK ?DOWN XXX ?INTO XXX SO SHE XXX]  . . .   SUPP FOUR ZOAS 1    *
    INTRODUCTION PIPING DOWN THE VALLEYS &C  . . . . .          SUPP LETTER 66A    *PROSE
DOWNCAST
    HEADS DEPREST VOICES WEAK EYES DOWNCAST HANDS WORK-BRUISD    197 AMERICA 3         10
    HEADS DEPREST VOICES WEAK EYES DOWNCAST HANDS WORK BRUISED   204 AMERICA CANC A    10
DOWNRIGHT
    DOWNRIGHT PLAIN TRUTH IS SOMETHING BUT REASONING IS NOTHING  394A ANNO WATSON     MARG
    LIKE WHAT SR FRANCIS BACON [SHOULD DOWNRIGHT ASSERT] SAYS    599D PUB ADDRESS/N  PROSE
DOWNS
    AND LET US GO TO THE HIGHEST DOWNS  . . . . . . . .         417 MY SPECTR AD/N  *  13
    NEAR TWENTY YEARS IN UPS & DOWNS I AM USED TO THEM  . . .    795D LETTER 6        PROSE
DOWNSTAIRS
    HE WAS DOWNSTAIRS THE VERY FIRST  . . . . . . . . .          59A ISLAND MOON 10  PROSE
DOWNWARD
    . . . THEY LOOK DOWNWARD AND LABOUR AND FORGET MY HOLY LAW   140 FRENCH REVOLTN   139
    WHICH HUNG WITH THE HEAD DOWNWARD INTO THE DEEP  . . . .     156A MARRIAGE HH 17 PROSE
    WERE BENDED DOWNWARD AND THE NOSTRILS GOLDEN GATES SHUT      241 EUROPE 10         14
    DOWNWARD TIS SUNK BENEATH TH ATTRACTIVE NORTH THAT ROUND     242 EUROPE 10         30
        THE FEET
    DOWNWARD & YOUR FLUXILE EYES ENGLOBD ROLL ROUND IN FEAR      294 FOUR ZOAS 3       87
    STEMMING HIS DOWNWARD FALL LABOURING UP AGAINST FUTURITY     316 FOUR ZOAS 6      186
    WHEN I BEND DOWNWARD BENDING MY HEAD DOWNWARD INTO THE       317 FOUR ZOAS 6      202
        DEEP
    MY WEARIED SPIRITS WAKING THEN TIS DOWNWARD ALL WHICH WAY    317 FOUR ZOAS 6      206
    I SUNK WITH CRIES OF BLOOD ISSUING DOWNWARD IN THE VEINS     327 FOUR ZOAS 7      284
    OR WHETHER THEY LOOKD DOWNWARD STILL THEY SAW THE DIVINE     342 FOUR ZOAS 8       50
        VISION
    I HAVE BENT DOWNWARD WITH LEAD MOLTEN IN MY ROARING          349 FOUR ZOAS 8      304
        FURNACES
    ALL FELL TOWARDS THE CENTER SINKING DOWNWARD IN DIRE RUIN    524 MILTON 34         39
    HIS BROTHER FALLING WITH THE HEAD DOWNWARD  . . . . .       606B V LAST JUDG/N  PROSE
    DOWNWARD AND YOUR FLUXILE EYES ENGLOBD ROLL ROUND IN FEAR    655 JERUSALEM 29      68
    I HAVE BENT DOWNWARD WITH LEAD MELTED IN MY ROARING          705 JERUSALEM 67      50
        FURNACES
DOWNWARD-BORNE
    AND HIS DOWNWARD-BORNE FALL CHANGD OBLIQUE  . . . . .        258 BOOK OF LOS 4     42
DOWNWARDS
    MRS GIMBLET DREW HER MOUTH DOWNWARDS  . . . . . . .          46A ISLAND MOON 1   PROSE
    DOWNWARDS & OUTWARDS [TENDING] CONSUMING IN THE WARS OF      280 FOUR ZOAS 1    * 574
        ETERNAL DEATH
```

	PAGE	TITLE	LINE

DOWNWARDS   (CONTINUED)
FOUR CAVERNS ROOTING DOWNWARDS THEIR FOUNDATIONS THRUSTING   318 FOUR ZOAS 6   263
  FORTH
THE MODERN CHURCH CRUCIFIES CHRIST WITH THE HEAD DOWNWARDS   615D V LAST JUDG/N   PROSE
ALL FELL TOWARDS THE CENTER SINKING DOWNWARDS IN DIRE RUIN   691 JERUSALEM 59   17
AND REUBEN FLED WITH HIS HEAD DOWNWARDS AMONG THE CAVERNS   698 JERUSALEM 63   44

DOWNY
WHILE OTHERS IN CONTENTMENT'S DOWNY NEST DO SLEEP   . . .   41D THEN SHE BORE   PROSE
SO SPOKE THE SINLESS SOUL & LAID HER HEAD ON THE DOWNY   369 FOUR ZOAS 9   455
  FLEECE
BENEATH HER ROSE A DOWNY BED & A CIELING COVERD ALL   . . .   369 FOUR ZOAS 9   463
AS BY DOWNY PINIONS SOFT . . . .   422 BENEATH/N   21
AS ON DOWNY PINIONS SOFT . . . .   424 THE GOLDEN NET   20
AND MEADOW-SWEET DOWNY & SOFT WAVING AMONG THE REEDS   .   520 MILTON 31   52
AND OTHERS CREATE THE WOOLY LAMB & THE DOWNY FOWL   .   .   692 JERUSALEM 59   48
TO CREATE THE WOOLY LAMB & DOWNY FOWL & SCALY SERPENT   . .   713 JERUSALEM 73   18

DOZEN
DELIVERD A DOZEN COPIES AT STATIONER'S HALL   . . . . .   846D LETTER 44   PROSE

DR   SEE DOCTOR
LIKE DR PRIESTLY & [SIR ISAAC] BACON & NEWTON   . . . . .   752 EV GOSPEL(D)/N   39
THRO THE INSTRUMENTALITY OF DR THORNTON . . . .   786C ANNO THORNTON   MARG
SEE ECLOGUE I FOR ALL THIS WE THANK DR THORNTON   . . . .   789B ANNO THORNTON   MARG
TO THE REVD DR TRUSLER REVD SIR I FIND MORE & MORE THAT   791D LETTER 4   PROSE
KIND RECOMMENDATION TO DR TRUSLER WHICH THO IT HAS FAILD OF   794D LETTER 6   PROSE
DR TRUSLER SAYS...I COULD NOT HELP SMILING AT THE   .   .   795A LETTER 6   PROSE
DIFFERENCE BETWEEN THE DOCTRINES OF DR TRUSLER & THOSE   795A LETTER 6   PROSE
  OF CHRIST
I HAVE BEEN EVER SINCE TAKING DR YOUNG'S ADDITION TO   .   874B LETTER 79   PROSE
REVD DR TRUSLER ENGLEFIELD GREEN EGHAM SURREY   . . . . .   SUPP ADDRESSES/L   *TITLE

DRAG
IN SPELLS OF LAW TO ONE SHE LOATHES AND MUST SHE DRAG THE   193 V DAU ALBION 5   22
  CHAIN
THO THEY EACH MORNING DRAG THE UNWILLING SUN OUT OF THE   309 FOUR ZOAS 5   165
  DEEP
MAY COME & DRAG ME AND MY WIFE OUT OF OUR HOUSE   . . .   439A BLAKES MEMORAN   PROSE
WHEN LUVAH'S BULLS EACH MORNING DRAG THE SULPHUR SUN OUT   503 MILTON 21   20
  OF THE DEEP
THEY DRAG THE UNWILLING ORB AT THIS TIME ALL THE FAMILY   504 MILTON 21   23

DRAGD
FLED FROM HIS SIGHT HE DRAGD HIS TORMENTS TO THE WILDERNESS   242 EUROPE 12   20
IN MANY A VALLEY FOR THE BULLS OF LUVAH DRAGD THE PLOW   .   283 FOUR ZOAS 2   120
THAT DRAGD THE WHEELS OF THE SUN'S CHARIOT & THEY PUT THE   333 FOUR ZOAS 7B   34
  SUN
DRAGD AT HIS CHARIOT WHEELS LOUD HOWLD . . . .   749 EV GOSPEL(B)/N   43

DRAGGD
. . . FROM COURT TO COURT RESTLESS HE DRAGGD . . . . .   135 FRENCH REVOLTN   22
MAD WITH CHAINS LOOSE WHICH HE DRAGGD UP AND DOWN . . .   136 FRENCH REVOLTN   48

DRAGGED
DRAGGED DOWN BY [AN ANGEL] A DEMON CROWND WITH LAUREL   .   606C V LAST JUDG/N   PROSE

DRAGGING
DRAGGING EACH OTHER INTO HELL & [OF] IN CONTENDING IN   .   443D LAST JUDGMNT/L   *PROSE
& IS DRAGGING HER DOWN BY THE HAIR   . . . .   606C V LAST JUDG/N   PROSE
THE FIGURE DRAGGING UP A WOMAN BY HER HAIR   . . . . .   608C V LAST JUDG/N   PROSE

DRAGON
A DRAGON FORM CLASHING HIS SCALES AT MIDNIGHT HE AROSE   .   197 AMERICA 3   15
A DRAGON FORM CLASHING HIS SCALES AT MIDNIGHT HE AROSE   .   204 AMERICA CANC A   15
REVEAL THE DRAGON THRO THE HUMAN COURSING SWIFT AS FIRE   204 AMERICA CANC B   1
[TILL] [BUT] SHE BECAME A [DE] DRAGON WINGED BRIGHT   282 FOUR ZOAS 2   *   89
  & POISONOUS
TO WORSHIP URIZEN'S DRAGON FORM TO OFFER HER OWN CHILDREN   356 FOUR ZOAS 8   599
AROUND THE DRAGON FORM OF URIZEN & ROUND HIS STONY FORM   359 FOUR ZOAS 9   81
ARISE O STONY FORM OF DEATH O DRAGON OF THE DEEPS   . . .   360 FOUR ZOAS 9   138
LIE DOWN BEFORE MY FEET O DRAGON LET URIZEN ARISE   .   .   360 FOUR ZOAS 9   139
REDEEMD FROM ERROR'S POWER WAKE THOU DRAGON OF THE DEEPS   361 FOUR ZOAS 9   161
BACON SUPPOSES THAT THE DRAGON BEAST & HARLOT ARE WORTHY OF   404D ANNO BACON   MARG
IN THE CAVERNS OF THE EARTH IS THE DRAGON WITH SEVEN HEADS   443A LAST JUDGMNT/L   PROSE
LUTHER THESE SEVEN ARE THE MALE-FEMALES THE DRAGON FORMS   528 MILTON 37   42
RELIGION HID IN WAR A DRAGON RED & HIDDEN HARLOT   . .   528 MILTON 37   43
A DRAGON RED & HIDDEN HARLOT WHICH JOHN IN PATMOS SAW   . .   532 MILTON 40   22
THE GREAT RED DRAGON WITH SEVEN HEADS & TEN HORNS   .   609B V LAST JUDG/N   PROSE
ORC THE FIRST BORN COILD IN THE SOUTH THE DRAGON URIZEN   634 JERUSALEM 14   3
HIS FIRES REDOUND FROM HIS DRAGON ALTARS IN ERRORS   646 JERUSALEM 23   21
  RETURNING
PLANTING THESE OAKEN GROVES ERECTING THESE DRAGON TEMPLES   648 JERUSALEM 25   4
ANIMATING THE DRAGON TEMPLES SOON TO BECOME THAT HOLY FIEND   677 JERUSALEM 47   6
THE NIGHT WITH DRAGON WINGS COVERD WITH STARS & IN THE   685 JERUSALEM 54   30
  WINGS
LUTHER THESE SEVEN ARE THE MALE FEMALES THE DRAGON FORMS   716 JERUSALEM 75   17
RELIGION HID IN WAR A DRAGON RED & HIDDEN HARLOT   . . . .   716 JERUSALEM 75   20
A DRAGON FORM ON ZION HILL'S MOST ANCIENT PROMONTORY   .   722 JERUSALEM 80   36
COVERD WITH PRECIOUS STONES A HUMAN DRAGON TERRIBLE   . .   734 JERUSALEM 89   11
AND THE DRAGON OF THE RIVER & THE FURNACES OF IRON   .   735 JERUSALEM 89   19
RELIGION HID IN WAR A DRAGON RED & HIDDEN HARLOT   . . . .   735 JERUSALEM 89   53
MYSTERY BABYLON THE GREAT THE DRUID DRAGON & HIDDEN HARLOT   741 JERUSALEM 93   25

DRAGON-FORM
O WHEREFORE DOTH A DRAGON-FORM FORTH ISSUE FROM MY LIMBS   492 MILTON 12   2

DRAGON-MAN
IN THE FIRST CHAMBER WAS A DRAGON-MAN CLEARING AWAY THE   154D MARRIAGE HH 15   PROSE

DRAGON'S
BENEATH THE DRAGON'S CAVERN A SKELETON BEGINS TO ANIMATE   609C V LAST JUDG/N   PROSE
DRAGON'S CAVERN REPRESENTS THE LATTER STATE OF THE CHURCH   610C V LAST JUDG/N   PROSE

		PAGE	TITLE	LINE

DRAGONS
WITHIN A NUMBER OF DRAGONS WERE HOLLOWING THE CAVE . . . 154D MARRIAGE HH 15 PROSE
THE DRAGONS OF THE NORTH PUT ON THEIR ARMOUR . . . . . 336 FOUR ZOAS 7B 150
WILL I SING FORTH HIS PRAISES THAT THE DRAGONS OF THE DEEP 823C LETTER 26 PROSE

DRAGOON
THE EARS OF BILLY'S LAWYER & DRAGOON . . . . 537 AND HIS LEGS/N 25

DRAGOONS
ROYAL DRAGOONS FOR AN ASSAULT & SEDITIOUS WORDS . . . . 826D LETTER 28 PROSE
WAS UTTERD IN THE HEAT OF THEIR FURY BY EITHER OF 827C LETTER 28 PROSE
  THE DRAGOONS

DRAGS
HE DRAGS SATAN DOWN HEADLONG HE IS CROWND WITH OAK . . . 607D V LAST JUDG/N PROSE
THAT FIEND WHO CARRIES THE KEY [& DRAGS] IN ONE HAND & . . 608B V LAST JUDG/N PROSE
DRAGS THEM DOWN WITH THE OTHER ON THE ROCK & . . . . . 608B V LAST JUDG/N PROSE

DRAIN
BUT COME O VALA WITH KNIFE & CUP DRAIN MY BLOOD . . . . 645 JERUSALEM 22 29

DRAIND
THE SERPENTS SPRUNG FROM HER OWN BOWELS HAVE DRAIND HER 100 TIRIEL 1 32
  DRY AS THIS

DRAMAS
THE PROPOSAL CONCERNING THE THREE DRAMAS I FOUND IT . . . 858A LETTER 55 PROSE

DRAMATIC
PROLOGUE INTENDED FOR A DRAMATIC PIECE OF KING EDWARD THE 33C EDW FOURTH/PS TITLE
  FOURTH
AND THEY CONVERSED TOGETHER IN VISIONARY FORMS DRAMATIC 746 JERUSALEM 98 28
  WHICH BRIGHT

DRANK
THE BOSOM OF THE LOFTY HILL DRANK IN THE SILENT DEW . . . 36C COUCH DEATH/PS PROSE
HE DRANK & IJIM RAISD HIM UP & BORE HIM ON HIS SHOULDERS 104 TIRIEL 4 40
THEY EAT THE [XXX] FLESHLY BREAD THEY DRANK THE NERVOUS 274 FOUR ZOAS 1 * 355
  [BLOODY] WINE
[AND LOS & ENITHARMON JOYD THEY DRANK IN TENFOLD JOY] . . 286 FOUR ZOAS 2 236
OF LOS ABSORBD IN DIRE REVENGE HE DRANK WITH JOY THE CRIES 302 FOUR ZOAS 4 191
AND TAKING OFF HIS SILVER HELMET FILLED IT & DRANK . . . 311 FOUR ZOAS 6 3
SAYING O THAT I HAD NEVER DRANK THE WINE NOR EAT THE BREAD 361 FOUR ZOAS 9 * 164
FOR JOHN EAT & DRANK TO DRIVE AWAY LOVE'S PAIN . . . . . 434 LONG JOHN BRWN 10
THO HE EAT & DRANK AS MUCH AS TEN MEN FOR HIS DINNER . . 434 LONG JOHN BRWN 12
OF ALBION DRANK & IMBIBED THE LIFE & ETERNAL FORM OF LUVAH 736 JERUSALEM 90 17

DRANTHON
ENITHARMON ON THE ROAD OF DRANTHON FELT THE INMOST GATE 309 FOUR ZOAS 5 177
[TO HEW THE CAVERND ROCKS OF DRANTHON INTO FORMS OF BEAUTY] 331 FOUR ZOAS 7 457

DRAPERIES
SILK DRAPERIES OFF AND RUSH INTO THE STREAM . . . . . 2 TO SUMMER/PS 12
THEY BEAR THE WOVEN DRAPERIES ON GOLDEN HOOKS THEY HANG 284 FOUR ZOAS 2 152
  ABROAD
THE DRAPERIES PUT IN BY SOMEBODY ELSE . . . . 843C LETTER 43 PROSE

DRAPERY
THE DRAPERY IS FORMED ALONE BY THE SHAPE OF THE NAKED . . 462D ANNO REYNOLDS MARG

DRAUGHT
MY CUP IS FILLD WITH ENVY'S RANKEST DRAUGHT [AND DEATH] 41C THEN SHE BORE PROSE
MIGHTY WAS THE DRAUGHT OF VOIDNESS TO DRAW EXISTENCE IN 280 FOUR ZOAS 2 18
AND DRUNKEN WITH THE IMMORTAL DRAUGHT FELL FROM MY THRONE 311 FOUR ZOAS 5 237
  SUBLIME
AND THE WIFE OF BATH ARE BOTH TAKING THEIR MORNING'S 567A DESC CAT 3 PROSE
  DRAUGHT
& WIFE OF BATH ARE BOTH TAKING THEIR MORNING'S DRAUGHT . . 588D CHAUCER/N PROSE
AND THE WIFE OF BATH ARE BOTH TAKING THEIR MORNING'S 590A CHAUCER 2 PROSE
  DRAUGHT

DRAUGHTSMAN
& BY WHICH HE GOT HIS REPUTATION AS A DRAUGHTSMAN . . . 592B PUB ADDRESS/N PROSE

DRAVE
SHE DRAVE THE FEMALES ALL AWAY FROM LOS . . . . 271 FOUR ZOAS 1 243
[?&] AND LOS DRAVE ALL THE MALES FROM HER AWAY . . . . 271 FOUR ZOAS 1 * 244
HE DRAVE THE MALE SPIRITS ALL AWAY FROM AHANIA . . . . 285 FOUR ZOAS 2 209
AND SHE DRAVE ALL THE FEMALES FROM HIM AWAY . . . . . 285 FOUR ZOAS 2 210
GROANING THE TERROR ROSE & DRAVE HIS [SOLD] SOLID ROCKS 300 FOUR ZOAS 4 * 124
  BEFORE
THRO DISMAL DARKNESS DRAVE THE PLOW OF AGES OVER CITIES 365 FOUR ZOAS 9 312
SATAN WHO DRAVE THE TEAM BESIDE HIM STOOD ANGRY & RED . . 488 MILTON 8 38
DRAVE THE SONS & DAUGHTERS OF ALBION FROM THEIR ANCIENT 714 JERUSALEM 74 21
  MOUNTAINS
HOW LOS DRAVE THEM FROM ALBION & THEY BECAME DAUGHTERS 715 JERUSALEM 74 38
  OF CANAAN

DRAW
I'LL DRAW MY SWORD NOR EVER SHEATH IT UP . . . . . . 31 EDW THIRD/PS 5 64
WHY AN EAR A WHIRLPOOL FIERCE TO DRAW CREATIONS IN . . . 130 BOOK OF THEL 6 17
DRAW IN THE OCEAN DOES HIS EYE DISCERN THE FLYING CLOUD 193 V DAU ALBION 5 35
SIT ON A BANK AND DRAW THE PLEASURES OF THIS FREE BORN JOY 194 V DAU ALBION 7 2
MY WEARY EYELIDS DRAW TOWARDS THE EVENING MY BLISS IS YET 240 EUROPE 5 10
  BUT NEW
THO THUS HEAVENLY BEAUTIFUL TO DRAW ME TO DESTRUCTION . . 265 FOUR ZOAS 1 58
WHILE WE DRAW IN THEIR SWEET DELIGHTS WHILE WE RETURN 271 FOUR ZOAS 1 255
  THEM SCORN
MIGHTY WAS THE DRAUGHT OF VOIDNESS TO DRAW EXISTENCE IN 280 FOUR ZOAS 2 18
OF VALA & THE WOES OF LUVAH TO DRAW IN THEIR DELIGHTS . . 285 FOUR ZOAS 2 213
THAT HE MAY ALSO DRAW AHANIA'S SPIRIT INTO HER VORTEX . . 290 FOUR ZOAS 2 384
DRAW THY BOW [VALAN] VALA . . . . 306 FOUR ZOAS 5 * 50
. . . FROM THE DEPTHS OF HELL THY BLACK BOW DRAW . . . 306 FOUR ZOAS 5 50
DRAW DOWN ENITHARMON TO THE SPECTRE OF URTHONA . . . . 323 FOUR ZOAS 7 115
HE SUFFERD HIM TO CLIMB THAT HE MIGHT DRAW ALL HUMAN FORMS 324 FOUR ZOAS 7 164
WITH DARTS OF WINTRY HAIL AGAIN THE BLACK BOW DRAW . . . 337 FOUR ZOAS 7B 156
AGAIN THE ELEMENTAL STRINGS TO YOUR RIGHT BREASTS DRAW . . 337 FOUR ZOAS 7B 157

```
                                                            PAGE      TITLE          LINE
DRAW    (CONTINUED)
     [BEGAN TO DRAW NEAR TO THE EARTH] . . . . . . . .      359 FOUR ZOAS 9          83
     LET THE BULLS OF LUVAH TREAD THE CORN & DRAW THE LOADED 376 FOUR ZOAS 9         701
         WAGGON
     THEN TRACE YOUR OUTLINES [& DRAW THEM IN WITH A NEEDLE] 440B MEMORANDUM/N 3     PROSE
     BECAUSE THEY COULD NOT DRAW . . . . . . . . . . .      456D ANNO REYNOLDS       MARG
     LABOURED FABRICATION OF JOURNEY-WORK THEY COULD NOT DRAW 457A ANNO REYNOLDS   * MARG
     THE SOFT HANDS OF ANTAMON DRAW THE INDELIBLE LINE  . .  515 MILTON 28           16
     THAT BLAKE WOULD ETCH FOR HIM & DRAW FOR ME . . . . .  537 AND HIS LEGS/N       35
     WHEN MEN WILL DRAW OUTLINES BEGIN YOU TO JAW THEM . .  549 ALL PICTURES/N        7
     MADMEN SEE OUTLINES & THEREFORE THEY DRAW THEM  . . .  549 ALL PICTURES/N        8
     HE WHO DOES NOT KNOW HOW TO DRAW A HAND OR A FOOT  . . 563D DESC CAT           PROSE
     MODERNS WISH TO DRAW FIGURES WITHOUT LINES . . . . . . 577A DESC CAT 4         PROSE
     IF TO INVENT & TO DRAW WELL HINDERS THE EXECUTIVE POWER IN 591B PUB ADDRESS/N  PROSE
     HE DID NOT KNOW HOW TO DRAW THE LEAF OF A TREE  . . . 593A PUB ADDRESS/N       PROSE
     BUT [YOU] DEY DO NOT DRAW DE [THE] DRAW  . . . . . . . 594D PUB ADDRESS/N       PROSE
     IT IS ONLY FUMBLE & BUNGLE WHICH CANNOT DRAW A LINE . . 603C PUB ADDR AD/N     PROSE
     AND DRAW THEM DOWN INTO THIS ABYSS OF SORROW AND TORTURE 646 JERUSALEM 23       39
     DRAW YE JERUSALEM AWAY FROM ALBION'S MOUNTAINS  . . .  679 JERUSALEM 48         62
     ASUNDER & OPPOSED TO THOUGHT TO DRAW JERUSALEM'S SONS . 715 JERUSALEM 74        29
     IN OPEN DAY TO DRAW THE SOULS OF THE DEAD INTO THE LIGHT 721 JERUSALEM 79       79
     BUT PANGS OF LOVE DRAW ME DOWN TO MY LOINS WHICH ARE  . 727 JERUSALEM 82        83
     THE SMALL FIBRES AS THEY SHOOT AROUND ME DRAW OUT IN PITY 732 JERUSALEM 87       8
     REPEATING THE SMARAGDINE TABLE OF HERMES TO DRAW LOS DOWN 738 JERUSALEM 91      35
     DRAW A FEATHER OVER IT & YOU WILL GET AN EVEN SURFACE  . 790C LETTER 2         PROSE
     OF THE STATE OF THE DEPARTED I CAN DRAW AS WELL A-BED AS 869A LETTER 68        PROSE
         UP
DRAWEST
     SMILE ON OUR LOVES AND WHILE THOU DRAWEST THE . . . . .   3 EVNING STAR/PS       5
DRAWETH
     FOR THE LAST JUDGMENT DRAWETH NIGH  . . . . . . . .    432 AUGURIES             40
DRAWING
     [AND SAID I LOVE HANGING & DRAWING & QUARTERING] . . .  185 LET BROTHELS/N       11
     DRAWING OUT FROM HIS SORROWING SOUL  . . . . . . . .   235 URIZEN 25            11
     DRAWING CLOUDS OF DESPAIR THRO THE HEAVENS . . . . . . 248 SONG OF LOS 7        12
     DRAWING FORTH DROOPING MOTHER'S PITY DROOPING MOTHER'S  269 FOUR ZOAS 1        197
         SORROW
     . . . DRAWING HER [LIFE INGRATE] SPECTROUS LIFE  . . . 270 FOUR ZOAS 1        217
     AND DRAWING IN THE SPECTROUS LIFE IN PRIDE AND HAUGHTY JOY 270 FOUR ZOAS 1     220
     CRAVING THE MORE THE MORE ENJOYING DRAWING OUT SWEET BLISS 276 FOUR ZOAS 1     440
     AND DRAWING THEM FORTH DELIGHTED UPON THE WINDS OF      331 FOUR ZOAS 7        460
         GOLGONOOZA
     THEN DRAWING INTO WIRES THE TERRIFIC PASSIONS & AFFECTIONS 346 FOUR ZOAS 8     208
     THEN WEEPING HE DESCENDS IN WRATH DRAWING ALL THINGS IN 353 FOUR ZOAS 8        456
         HIS FURY
     FOR I AM NOW SURROUNDED BY A SHADOWY VORTEX DRAWING . . 355 FOUR ZOAS 8        545
     LET THERE BE FIRST A DRAWING MADE . . . . . . . . . . 440B MEMORANDUM/N 2     PROSE
     HE CREATED SEVEN DEADLY SINS DRAWING OUT HIS INFERNAL  489 MILTON 9            21
         SCROLL
     DRAWING A THIRD PART IN THE FIRES AS STUBBLE NORTH & SOUTH 493 MILTON 12        26
     CRY BLAKIFIED DRAWING SPOILS PAINTER & ENGRAVER  . . . 555 BLAKES APL/N 1      15
     CRY BLAKIFIED DRAWING SPOILS PAINTER & ENGRAVER  . . . 556 BLAKES APL/N 2      14
     THE VENETIAN IS NOT BECAUSE HE DOES NOT UNDERSTAND DRAWING 563D DESC CAT       PROSE
     AND THE ANTIQUE THOSE WHO SEPARATE PAINTING FROM DRAWING 573B DESC CAT 3       PROSE
     AND HINDER ALL CORRECT DRAWING FROM APPEARING TO BE CORRECT 583C DESC CAT 9    PROSE
     NUMBER X THE BRAMINS A DRAWING . . . . . . . . . .    583D DESC CAT 10         TITLE
     FLEEING FROM THE FACE OF HIS PARENTS A DRAWING  . . . 584A DESC CAT 11         TITLE
     NUMBER XII THE SOLDIERS CASTING LOTS FOR CHRIST'S GARMENT 584A DESC CAT 12     TITLE
         A DRAWING
     NUMBER XIII JACOB'S LADDER A DRAWING  . . . . . . . . 584B DESC CAT 13         TITLE
     THE BODY OF JESUS IN THE SEPULCHRE A DRAWING . . . . . 584B DESC CAT 14        TITLE
     NUMBER XV RUTH A DRAWING . . . . . . . . . . . .     584C DESC CAT 15          TITLE
     A PAINTING AND A DRAWING PROCEEDS FROM IGNORANCE OF ART 584D DESC CAT 15       PROSE
     MERIT OF A PICTURE IS THE SAME AS THE MERIT OF A DRAWING 584D DESC CAT 15      PROSE
     SUSCEPTIBLE OF HIGHER FINISHING THAN DRAWING ON PAPER  . 585A DESC CAT 15      PROSE
     A DRAWING ON PAPER TO A DAWBING IN OIL BY THE . . . . 585B DESC CAT 15         PROSE
     NUMBER XVI THE PENANCE OF JANE SHORE IN ST PAULS CHURCH 585D DESC CAT 16       TITLE
         A DRAWING
     THIS DRAWING WAS DONE ABOVE THIRTY YEARS AGO AND PROVES 585D DESC CAT 16       PROSE
     ARE UNACQUAINTED WITH DRAWING [& THE ACCOMPANYING] . . 591B PUB ADDRESS/N      PROSE
     POWERS & HIS SCIENTIFIC KNOWLEDGE OF DRAWING IS  . . . 591B PUB ADDRESS/N      PROSE
     ARTFULLY PROPAGATED OPINION THAT DRAWING SPOILS AN ENGRAVER 591D PUB ADDRESS/N *PROSE
     TO INSPECT MY PRINT OF WHICH DRAWING IS THE FOUNDATION  591D PUB ADDRESS/N     PROSE
     & INDEED THE SUPERSTRUCTURE IT IS DRAWING ON COPPER . . 591D PUB ADDRESS/N     PROSE
     AS PAINTING OUGHT TO BE DRAWING ON CANVAS OR ANY OTHER  591D PUB ADDRESS/N     PROSE
     ENGRAVING BY LOSING DRAWING HAS LOST ALL CHARACTER  . . 592A PUB ADDRESS/N     *PROSE
     UNDERSTAND DRAWING & WHICH ACCORDING TO HEATH & STOTHARD 592B PUB ADDRESS/N    PROSE
     DRAWING SUCH A MAN MUST KNOW THAT I LOOKD UPON HIM . . 593A PUB ADDRESS/N      PROSE
     & ALL BECAUSE I UNDERSTAND DRAWING WHICH THEY UNDERSTOOD 594C PUB ADDRESS/N    PROSE
         NOT
     & PAINTING ARE SOMEWHAT ELSE BESIDES DRAWING  . . . . 594C PUB ADDRESS/N       PROSE
     PAINTING IS DRAWING ON CANVAS . . . . . . . . . .    594C PUB ADDRESS/N        PROSE
     & ENGRAVING IS DRAWING ON COPPER & NOTHING ELSE  . . . 594C PUB ADDRESS/N      PROSE
     WITHOUT BEING A MASTER OF DRAWING IS AN IMPOSTOR . . . 594D PUB ADDRESS/N      *PROSE
     THEY DESPISE DRAWING WHICH DESPISES THEM IN RETURN  . . 596C PUB ADDRESS/N     PROSE
     FOR INVENTION & DRAWING HAS GENERALLY BEEN ACCOMPANIED BY 602A PUB ADDRESS/N   PROSE
     WHERE DRAWING ITS FOUNDATION IS CONTEMND AND  . . . . 602A PUB ADDRESS/N       PROSE
     ENGRAVE OR PAINT EITHER WITHOUT BEING A MASTER OF DRAWING 602B PUB ADDRESS/N   PROSE
         IS
     A FOOL [?& HE] PAINTING IS DRAWING ON CANVAS  . . . . 602B PUB ADDRESS/N      *PROSE
     & ENGRAVING IS DRAWING ON COPPER & NOTHING ELSE  . . . 602B PUB ADDRESS/N      PROSE
     DRAWING IS EXECUTION & NOTHING ELSE  . . . . . . . . 602B PUB ADDRESS/N        PROSE
```

	PAGE	TITLE	LINE

DRAWING   (CONTINUED)
```
          DID NOT UNDERSTAND DRAWING  . . . . . . . .   . 602D PUB ADDR AD/N   PROSE
          THEY DID NOT UNDERSTAND DRAWING   . . . . . . . 602D PUB ADDR AD/N   PROSE
          LET A MAN WHO HAS MADE A DRAWING GO ON & ON  . . . 603A PUB ADDR AD/N  PROSE
          ENGRAVED BY W BLAKE...FROM AN OLD ITALIAN DRAWING  . 604A INSC ARIMATHEA  TITLE
          HE IS ONLY ACCUSED OF UNBELIEF & THEREBY DRAWING MAN  . 615B V LAST JUDG/N  PROSE
          DRAWING JERUSALEM IN ANGUISH OF MATERNAL LOVE  . . .   624 JERUSALEM 5    47
          A MOMENT OF TIME DRAWING IT OUT WITH MANY TEARS &     678 JERUSALEM 48    31
            AFFLICTIONS
          DRAWING THE FREE LOVES OF JERUSALEM INTO INFERNAL BONDAGE  707 JERUSALEM 69    9
          AGE AFTER AGE DRAWING THEM AWAY TOWARDS BABYLON  . . . 715 JERUSALEM 74   31
          DRAWING THEIR ULRO VOIDNESS ROUND THE FOUR-FOLD HUMANITY  719 JERUSALEM 78   20
          DRAWING OUT FIBRE BY FIBRE RETURNING TO ALBION'S TREE  . 723 JERUSALEM 80   61
          OR THROWING THE WINGD SHUTTLE OR DRAWING THE CORDS WITH  725 JERUSALEM 82   13
            SOFTEST SONGS
          THE ABOVE WAS WRITTEN & THE DRAWING ANNEXED BY THE DESIRE  781D INSC UPCOTT   PROSE
          I HAVE MADE HIM A DRAWING IN MY BEST MANNER  . . . . . 794D LETTER 6   PROSE
          TO PRODUCE THESE THINGS I WOULD NOT SEND YOU A DRAWING OR  815A LETTER 23  PROSE
          I HAD OF THE LETTER OR OF THE DRAWING I HAVE FETCHD THE  832B LETTER 32  PROSE
          DRAWING FROM MR ROSE & HAVE SHEWD IT TO MR FLAXMAN WHO  . 832B LETTER 32  PROSE
          THE DRAWING OF THE MONUMENT WHICH MR JOHNSON SENT HAS  . 838B LETTER 37  PROSE
          THE LOST DRAWING YOU SHALL HAVE CHOICE OF EITHER OF THE  839C LETTER 38  PROSE
          TROUBLE AS FLAXMAN WAS NOT WITH ME THE DRAWING I SAW IS  839C LETTER 38  PROSE
          IT IS A VERY SUBLIME DRAWING & WOULD MAKE AN EXCELLENT  839C LETTER 38  PROSE
            PRINT
          THE DRAWING OF PLINY IN THE ERUPTION OF VESUVIUS IS  . . . 839D LETTER 38  PROSE
          MR FLAXMAN ADVISES THAT THE DRAWING OF MR ROMNEY'S  . . . 840D LETTER 40  PROSE
          P S I MADE A VERY FINISHD DRAWING OF ROMNEY AS A  . . . 855D LETTER 53  PROSE
          COMPANION TO MY DRAWING OF THE HEAD OF COWPER YOU  . . . 855D LETTER 53  PROSE
          FROM A DRAWING BY SALVIATI AFTER MICHAEL ANGELO  . . . . SUPP INSC JOSEPH   *TITLE
          [?UNTIL ?THEY (BECAME) THE LORDS ?OF ?DRAWING]  . . . . SUPP ANNO REYNOLDS  * MARG
DRAWINGS
          UNCHANGEABLE AND PERMANENT IN FRESCO AND DRAWINGS  . . 560C EXHIBITION ADV  PROSE
          THE ANCIENT METHOD OF FRESCO PAINTING RESTORED AND DRAWINGS  563A DESC CAT  TITLE
          THE PICTURES AND DRAWINGS TO REMAIN IN THE EXHIBITION  . 563B DESC CAT  PROSE
          THE ABOVE FOUR DRAWINGS THE ARTIST WISHES WERE IN FRESCO  584B DESC CAT 14  PROSE
          AND DRAWINGS WILL TAKE CARE OF THAT  . . . . . . . 584C DESC CAT 14  PROSE
          THE DAWBER DAWBS HIS DRAWINGS  . . . . . . . . . 584D DESC CAT 15  PROSE
          HE WHO DRAWS HIS DRAWINGS DRAWS HIS PICTURES THERE  . . 584D DESC CAT 15  PROSE
          DRAWINGS ON CANVASS BUT NOT PICTURES  . . . . . . . 585A DESC CAT 15  PROSE
          THAN MAKE DRAWINGS & ON THE SAME TERMS  . . . . . . 792C LETTER 4  PROSE
          NEW EDITION OF MR HAYLEY'S TRIUMPHS OF TEMPER FROM DRAWINGS  811D LETTER 22  PROSE
          LITTLE PICTURES & DRAWINGS WHICH I HAD THE PLEASURE   814C LETTER 23  PROSE
            & PROFIT
          THERE IS NOT ONE TOUCH IN THOSE DRAWINGS & PICTURES BUT  814D LETTER 23  PROSE
          AND TO TELL YOU THAT SEVERAL OF THE DRAWINGS  . . . . 816C LETTER 24  PROSE
          ACCOUNT THAT THE REMAINING NUMBER OF DRAWINGS  . . . . 816C LETTER 24  PROSE
          I HAVE NOW ON THE STOCKS THE FOLLOWING DRAWINGS FOR YOU  824A LETTER 27  PROSE
          I SEND (SEVEN) DRAWINGS WHICH I HOPE WILL PLEASE YOU  . 826B LETTER 28  PROSE
          I HAVE BEEN TO LOOK AT THE DRAWINGS & PICTURE BUT FLAXMAN  839C LETTER 38  PROSE
          THAT ONE OF THE DRAWINGS WHICH MR ROMNEY DESTINED FOR YOU  839C LETTER 38  PROSE
          PICTURE & TWO DRAWINGS TO ANY PERSON WHOM YOU SHALL  . 839D LETTER 38  PROSE
          WHICH HE THINKS ONE OF THE FINEST DRAWINGS THE TWELVE  . 840D LETTER 40  PROSE
          WHICH HE SET ME ABOUT THE DRAWINGS HAS NOW SET ME TO  . 861D LETTER 59  PROSE
          I SEND TWO MORE DRAWINGS WITH THE FIRST THAT I DID ALTERED  866C LETTER 65  PROSE
          IT WILL BE MORE CONVENIENT TO ME TO MAKE ALL THE DRAWINGS  866C LETTER 65  PROSE
          APPAREL ONLY MY BOOK OF DRAWINGS FROM DANTE & ONE PLATE  873A LETTER 76  PROSE
          DRAWINGS &C SENT FROM FELPHAM  . . . . . . . . . SUPP LETTER 56A  *PROSE
          TOM DRAWINGS IN FULL TO THIS DAY  . . . . . . . . SUPP LETTER 61E  *PROSE
DRAWN      SEE ILL DRAWN,LONG DRAWN
          DRAWN DOWN TO EARTH BY SPELLS AND WICKEDNESS  . . . .   5 FAIR ELENOR/PS   46
          THE ARROWS OF ALMIGHTY GOD ARE DRAWN  . . . . . . .  35 WAR SONG/PS   16
          TILL THE CURTAINS OF DARKNESS WERE DRAWN  . . . . .  35D COUCH DEATH/PS  PROSE
          WHY ARE EYELIDS STORD WITH ARROWS READY DRAWN  . . . . 130 BOOK OF THEL 6   13
          DRAWN HE THREW ON THE EARTH  . . . . . . . . . . 141 FRENCH REVOLTN  169
          IN THE FLAMES STOOD & VIEWD THE ARMIES DRAWN OUT IN THE SKY  201 AMERICA 14    1
          IN [DISMAL] GNAWING PAIN DRAWN OUT BY HER LOVD FINGERS  266 FOUR ZOAS 1   79
            EVERY NERVE
          TILL WE HAVE DRAWN THE LAMB OF GOD INTO A MORTAL FORM  . 272 FOUR ZOAS 1  293
          NOT LONG IN HARMONY THEY DWELL THEIR LIFE IS DRAWN AWAY  274 FOUR ZOAS 1  371
          WHERE ENION CRAVES SUCCESSIVE DRAWN INTO THE GOLDEN FEAST  274 FOUR ZOAS 1  373
          [TILL THEY HAD ?DRAWN THE SPECTRE QUITE AWAY FROM ENION]  SUPP FOUR ZOAS 1   *
          THE THREADS ARE SPUN & THE CORDS TWISTED & DRAWN OUT THEN  284 FOUR ZOAS 2  157
            THE WEAK
          AND LOS & ENITHARMON WERE DRAWN DOWN BY THEIR DESIRES  . 287 FOUR ZOAS 2  287
          WHEN URIZEN SLEPT ON HIS COUCH DRAWN THRO UNBOUNDED SPACE  291 FOUR ZOAS 2  421
          DRAWN OUT FROM DEEP TO DEEP WOVEN BY RIBBD  . . . . . 314 FOUR ZOAS 6  119
          . . . DRAWN OUT FROM HIS MANTLE OF YEARS  . . . . . 318 FOUR ZOAS 6  245
          OR DRAWN UP OR LET DOWN AT THE WILL OF THE IMMORTAL MAN  318 FOUR ZOAS 6  255
          TILL OVERBURDEND WITH ITS OWN WEIGHT DRAWN OUT THRO   322 FOUR ZOAS 7   77
            IMMENSITY
          IN THE DARK DEEP THE DARK TREE GREW HER SHADOW WAS DRAWN  324 FOUR ZOAS 7  170
            DOWN
          IN DREAMS OF ULRO [SWEET] DARK DELUSIVE DRAWN BY THE LOVELY  328 FOUR ZOAS 7  331
            SHADOW
          FIRST RINTRAH & THEN PALAMABRON DRAWN FROM OUT THE RANKS  332 FOUR ZOAS 7  476
            OF WAR
          LEAVING HIS SPECTROUS FORM WHICH COULD NOT BE DRAWN AWAY  332 FOUR ZOAS 7  492
          INVISIBLE OR VISIBLE DRAWN OUT IN LENGTH OR STRETCHD IN  338 FOUR ZOAS 7B  * 222
            BREADTH
          NO MORE ERECT THO STRONG DRAWN OUT IN LENGTH THEY RAVIN  344 FOUR ZOAS 8  126
          IN SOFT SILK DRAWN FROM THEIR OWN BOWELS IN LASCIVIOUS  346 FOUR ZOAS 8  211
            DELIGHT
```

DRAWN   (CONTINUED)
VALA DRAWN DOWN INTO A VEGETATED BODY NOW TRIUMPHANT   . .   348 FOUR ZOAS 8   280
. . . THEN HIS BREATHING NOSTRILS DRAWN FORTH   . . . . .   352 FOUR ZOAS 8   422
DRAWN DOWN BY ORC & THE SHADOWY FEMALE INTO GENERATION   .   490 MILTON 10   2
THE MISERY OF UNHAPPY FAMILIES SHALL BE DRAWN OUT INTO   499 MILTON 18   7
   ITS BORDER
BY IMITATION OF NATURE'S IMAGES DRAWN FROM REMEMBRANCE   . .   533 MILTON 41   24
WITH THANKS & COMPLIMENTS ARE QUITE DRAWN DRY   . . . . .   549 H PICK THANK/N   2
TO BE DRAWN FROM THE WORKS OF TWO MANIFEST FOOLS   . . .   550 WHEN I SEE/N   4
WHO LOOK IF A PICTURE IS WELL DRAWN AND IF IT IS   573B DESC CAT 3   PROSE
   IMMEDIATELY
DRAWN OUT UPON IT BEFORE MAN OR BEAST CAN EXIST   . . . .   585C DESC CAT 15   PROSE
BUT THE LAME IMITATORS OF LINES DRAWN BY THEIR PREDECESSORS 585D DESC CAT 15   PROSE
BUT DRAWN WITH A FIRM & DECIDED HAND AT ONCE [WITH ALL ITS] 595C PUB ADDRESS/N   PROSE
ALL DESCRIPTIVE OF CHARACTER & NOT A LINE IS DRAWN   . . .   611B V LAST JUDG/N   PROSE
THE CURTAINS ARE DRAWN APART CHRIST HAVING RENT THE VEIL   613B V LAST JUDG/N   PROSE
DARKEND THEY ARE DRAWN THRO UNBOUNDED SPACE SCATTERD UPON   623 JERUSALEM 5   2
AND LUVAH HATH DRAWN THE CURTAINS AROUND ALBION IN VALA'S   656 JERUSALEM 30   39
   BOSOM
APPEAR IN STRONG DELUSIVE LIGHT OF TIME & SPACE DRAWN OUT   715 JERUSALEM 75   5
HAND SLEPT ON SKIDDAW'S TOP DRAWN BY THE LOVE OF BEAUTIFUL   723 JERUSALEM 80   57
DRAWN & ENGRAVED BY WILLIAM BLAKE . . . .   775C INSC LAOCOON   *TITLE
WHOSE HEART & SOUL ARE MORE & MORE DRAWN OUT TOWARDS YOU &   833D LETTER 33   PROSE
WHICH I HAVE DRAWN FROM MR FLAXMAN'S MODEL   . . . . . .   838A LETTER 37   PROSE
THE CHILD IS AS BEAUTIFULLY DRAWN AS IT IS COLOURED IN   864B LETTER 61   PROSE
   BOTH
DRAWS
A RAGING WHIRLPOOL DRAWS THE DIZZY ENQUIRER TO HIS GRAVE   242 EUROPE 10   31
DRAWS ALL INTO A FOUNTAIN AT THE ROCK OF THY ATTRACTION   312 FOUR ZOAS 6   14
HE WHO DRAWS HIS DRAWINGS DRAWS HIS PICTURES THERE   . . .   584D DESC CAT 15   PROSE
& HE WHO DRAWS BEST MUST BE THE BEST ARTIST   . . . . .   602B PUB ADDRESS/N   PROSE
THE POET'S SONG DRAWS TO ITS PERIOD & ENITHARMON IS NO MORE 739 JERUSALEM 92   8
OUR RETURN TO LONDON DRAWS ON APACE OUR EXPECTATION OF   .   826B LETTER 28   PROSE
IT DRAWS THE SOUL TOWARDS ETERNAL LIFE & CONJUNCTION WITH   834A LETTER 33   PROSE
DRAYMAN
HE WHO COULD REPRESENT CHRIST UNIFORMLY LIKE A DRAYMAN   .   596C PUB ADDRESS/N   PROSE
DREAD
DREAD VISAGES FROWNING IN SILENT DEATH   . . . .   32 EDW THIRD/PS 6   36
FROM THE DARKNESS DREAD & DREAR   . . . .   168 EARTHS ANSWR/N   2
STONY DREAD   . . . .   168 EARTHS ANSWR/N   4
WHAT DREAD HAND & WHAT DREAD FEET   . . . .   172 THE TYGER/N 1   12
WHAT THE ANVIL WHAT [THE ARM] [ARM] [GRASP] [CLASP] DREAD 172 THE TYGER/N 1   20
   GRASP
WHAT DREAD HAND & WHAT DREAD FEET   . . . .   173 THE TYGER/N 2   12
BUT DUMB TILL THAT DREAD DAY WHEN ORC ASSAYD HIS FIERCE   196 AMERICA PREL 1   10
   EMBRACE
IN THAT DREAD NIGHT WHEN URIZEN CALLD THE STARS ROUND HIS   204 AMERICA CANC B   5
   FEET
FROM THE DARKNESS DREAD & DREAR   . . . .   210 EARTHS ANSR/SE   2
STONY DREAD   . . . .   210 EARTHS ANSR/SE   4
WHAT DREAD HAND & WHAT DREAD FEET   . . . .   214 THE TYGER/SE   12
WHAT DREAD HAND FORMD THY DREAD FEET   . . . . . .   214 THE TYGER/SE   12
WHAT THE ANVIL WHAT DREAD GRASP   . . . .   214 THE TYGER/SE   15
THE DREAD WORLD & THE ROLLING OF WHEELS   . . . . . .   223 URIZEN 3   30
DREAD TERRORS DELIGHTING IN BLOOD   . . . .   234 URIZEN 23   7
SINCE THAT DREAD DAY WHEN HAR AND HEVA FLED   . . . . .   246 SONG OF LOS 4   5
OF THESE AN ENORMOUS DREAD SERPENT   . . . .   250 AHANIA 3   13
SAT IN A [SWEET] DREAD INTOXICATION OF [FALSE WOVEN BLISS] 266 FOUR ZOAS 1   91
   . . .
REPELLING HER AWAY [FROM ?THEM] & AWAY BY A DREAD   270 FOUR ZOAS 1   * 218
   REPULSIVE POWER
BUT MOST THE POLISHD PALACES [?WEAK] DARK SILENT BOW WITH 275 FOUR ZOAS 1   * 396
   DREAD
THAT HIS DREAD FANCY FORMD BEFORE HIM IN THE UNFORMD VOID 287 FOUR ZOAS 2   294
ALAS FOR ME WHAT WILL BECOME OF ME AT THAT DREAD TIME   . 292 FOUR ZOAS 3   23
WHY DIDST THOU LISTEN TO THE VOICE OF LUVAH THAT DREAD MORN 292 FOUR ZOAS 3   31
DREWST ALL THE SONS OF BEULAH INTO THY [GREAT] DREAD VORTEX 299 FOUR ZOAS 4   88
   FOLLOWING
THO TERRIBLE HIS DREAD OF THAT INFERNAL CHAIN THEY ROSE   309 FOUR ZOAS 5   147
BLACK SCALES OF IRON ARM THE DREAD VISAGE IRON SPIKES   319 FOUR ZOAS 6   307
   INSTEAD
COMPULSIVE ROLLD THE COMETS AT HIS DREAD COMMAND THE DREARY 320 FOUR ZOAS 6   320
   WAY
IMAGE OF DREAD WHENCE ART THOU WHENCE IS THIS MOST WOFUL   321 FOUR ZOAS 7   44
   PLACE
INTO SUBMISSION TO HIS WILL NOR KNEW THE DREAD RESULT   . 324 FOUR ZOAS 7   165
DRINKING THE JOYS OF UNIVERSAL MANHOOD ONE DREAD MORN   . 327 FOUR ZOAS 7   277
LISTEN O VISION OF DELIGHT ONE DREAD MORN OF GOARY BLOOD   327 FOUR ZOAS 7   * 278
WHAT WORDS OF DREAD PIERCE MY FAINT EAR WHAT FALLING SNOWS 344 FOUR ZOAS 8   146
   AROUND
HIS MURDER ON ANOTHER SILENT I BOW WITH DREAD   . . .   345 FOUR ZOAS 8   166
THE DREAD SLEEP OF ULRO IS PAST BUT SATAN [?RECIEVES] OG   346 FOUR ZOAS 8   * 217
   & SIHON
AND FOR THE DREAD OF THE DARK TERRORS OF ORC & URIZEN   . 353 FOUR ZOAS 8   480
THE DREAD I FEEL UNKNOWN BEFORE MY VOICE REFUSES TO ROAR   358 FOUR ZOAS 9   57
THAT THOU DREAD FORM OF CERTAINTY MAIST SIT IN TOWN   360 FOUR ZOAS 9   133
   & VILLAGE
UPON THE WHEELS THE STORMY SEAS HOWL AT HIS DREAD COMMAND 378 FOUR ZOAS 9   810
THEIR DREAD FORMS TENDING THE DIRE MILLS . . . .   378 FOUR ZOAS 9   814
DREAD TOMB IMMORTAL ON HIS ROCK OVERSHADOWD THE WHOLE EARTH 491 MILTON 11   9
IN DIREFUL PAIN FOR THE DREAD SHADOW TWENTY-SEVEN-FOLD   . 496 MILTON 14   39
WHICH FEW DARE UNBAR BECAUSE DREAD OG & ANAK GUARD THE   502 MILTON 20   35
   GATES

```
                                                           PAGE    TITLE        LINE
DREAD    (CONTINUED)
    ALBION'S DREAD SONS HAND HYLE & COBAN SURROUND HIM AS  . .  507 MILTON 23       15
    OF DREAD REPOSE SEEN BY THE VISIONARY EYE HIS FACE         531 MILTON 39       33
       IS TOWARD
    I SEE THEE STRIVE UPON THE BROOKS OF ARNON THERE A DREAD   532 MILTON 40        4
    ALBION'S DREAD SPECTRES STORMING LOUD THUNDEROUS & MIGHTY  629 JERUSALEM 10     5
    FEEDS THE DREAD FORGE TREMBLING & SHUDDERING ALONG THE     636 JERUSALEM 16    15
       VALLEYS
    . . . FROM THY DREAD [COUTENANCE] COUNTENANCE & SEARCHING  645 JERUSALEM 22  *  13
       EYES
    ALBION'S DREAD WHEELS STRETCHING OUT SPACES IMMENSE BETWEEN 674 JERUSALEM 44    9
    THIS DREAD DISEASE NONE BUT JESUS O LORD DESCEND AND SAVE  675 JERUSALEM 45    16
    ALBION'S DREAD TOMB EIGHT THOUSAND AND FIVE HUNDRED YEARS  678 JERUSALEM 48    36
    INTO TWO IRREGULAR FORMS AND LOOKING ON ALBION'S DREAD TREE 723 JERUSALEM 80   73
    SO DREAD IS LOS'S FURY THAT NONE DARE HIM TO APPROACH  . . 732 JERUSALEM 86    48
    HEATED IN THE SMITH'S FORGE BUT COLD THE WIND OF THEIR     735 JERUSALEM 89    42
       DREAD FURY
    TO BE WHEN ALBION ARISES FROM HIS DREAD REPOSE O LOVELY    739 JERUSALEM 92    14
       ENITHARMON
DREADFUL
    DOWN BLERON'S HILLS THEY DREADFUL RUSH  . . . . . . . .     11 GWIN KING/PS    21
    AND DREADFUL THUNDER OF THE BATTLE HEARD AFAR . . . . .    34B KING JOHN/PS PROSE
    THIS IS THE HYPOCRITE THAT SOMETIMES ROARS A DREADFUL LION 105 TIRIEL 4        50
    BUT IF THEY RUSH DREADFUL  . . . . . . . . . . . . .       119 NIGHT/SI        29
    O HORRIBLE O DREADFUL STATE CONSIDER THE HOT BURNING  .  155C MARRIAGE HH 17 PROSE
    THEN THE DREADFUL LIGHTNINGS BREAK  . . . . . . . . .      165 CRADLE SONG/N   17
    AND THE WINTER CALLD IT A DREADFUL CRIME  . . . . . . .    176 SOFT SNOW/N      5
    INFINITE LONDON'S AWFUL SPIRES CAST A DREADFUL [GLEAM] COLD 205 AMERICA CANC C  7
    IN DREADFUL DOLOR & PAIN & I AM LIKE AN ATOM  . . . . .    265 FOUR ZOAS 1     61
    AND ALL THE WHILE THE PLOW OF IRON CUT THE DREADFUL FURROWS 282 FOUR ZOAS 2    70
    DARK DREADFUL ROSE & ENITHARMON LAY AT LOS'S FEET  . .     300 FOUR ZOAS 4    126
    QUEEN OF THESE DREADFUL RIVERS SPEAK & LET ME HEAR THY     312 FOUR ZOAS 6     19
       VOICE
    O HORRIBLE O DREADFUL STATE THOSE WHOM I LOVED BEST    . . 312 FOUR ZOAS 6     25
    . . . IN THEIR DREADFUL [BOWELS] BOSOMS  . . . . . . .     317 FOUR ZOAS 6  * 228
    HIS BOOK OF IRON ON HIS KNEES HE TRACD THE DREADFUL LETTERS 321 FOUR ZOAS 7    29
    OF ALL THIS DREADFUL RUIN RISE O DAUGHTERS AT MY STERN     322 FOUR ZOAS 7     94
       COMMAND
    WHILE THE ENORMOUS SCROLLS ROLLD DREADFUL IN THE HEAVENS   322 FOUR ZOAS 7    105
       ABOVE
    THAT THIS DIRE STATE COMMENCES I BEGAN THE DREADFUL STATE  330 FOUR ZOAS 7    404
    WITH THUNDEROUS NOISE & DREADFUL SHAKINGS ROCKING TO & FRO 357 FOUR ZOAS 9     15
    THE BOOKS OF URIZEN UNROLL WITH DREADFUL NOISE THE FOLDING 358 FOUR ZOAS 9     33
       SERPENT
    . . . WHAT NOISE WHAT DREADFUL ROUT  . . . . . . . .       364 FOUR ZOAS 9    262
    BENEATH THICK CLOUDS DREADFUL LIGHTNINGS BURST & THUNDERS  372 FOUR ZOAS 9    565
       ROLL
    THIS DREADFUL NON EXISTENCE IS WORSE . . . . . . . . .     377 FOUR ZOAS 9    739
    AND HEARD & SAW SUCH DREADFUL THINGS . . . . . . . . .     424 MENTAL TRAVLER   3
    HE SUNK DOWN A DREADFUL DEATH UNLIKE THE SLUMBERS OF BEULAH 490 MILTON 9       48
    BUT THE FOURTH STATE IS DREADFUL IT IS NAMED OR-ULRO   .   524 MILTON 34       13
    O DREADFUL LOOM OF DEATH O PITEOUS FEMALE FORMS COMPELLD   525 MILTON 35        7
    FORBAD & DOWN WITH DREADFUL GROANS HE SUNK UPON HIS COUCH  531 MILTON 39       51
    IN CLOUDS OF BLOOD IN STREAMS OF GORE WITH DREADFUL        534 MILTON 42        8
       THUNDERINGS
    ASSIST IN WEAVING THE DEADLY WOOF "...IN DREADFUL HARMONY" 576C DESC CAT 4   PROSE
    AND EVERY ONE A GATE OF IRON DREADFUL AND WONDERFUL  . .   635 JERUSALEM 14    23
    HUMBER & TRENT ROLL DREADFUL BEFORE THE SEVENTH FURNACE    636 JERUSALEM 16    16
    TO WHERE THE TOWER OF LONDON FROWND DREADFUL OVER JERUSALEM 657 JERUSALEM 31   23
    OF DEATH IN ALBION'S CLOUDS DREADFUL UTTERD OVER ALL THE   661 JERUSALEM 34    24
       EARTH
    IT SEEMS TO BE & IS PRODUCTIVE OF THE MOST DREADFUL  . .   663 JERUSALEM 36    52
    ROLLS DREADFUL THRO THE FURNACES OF LOS AND THE MILLS OF   665 JERUSALEM 38    37
       SATAN
    IT IS THE GATE OF LOS WITHOUTSIDE IS THE MILL INTRICATE    666 JERUSALEM 39     3
       DREADFUL
    FOR HAD THE BODY OF ALBION FALLN DOWN AND FROM ITS DREADFUL 667 JERUSALEM 40   31
       RUINS
    IN DREADFUL PAIN THE SPECTROUS UNCIRCUMCISED VEGETATION    674 JERUSALEM 44    24
    WHICH IS THE VALE OF REPHAIM DREADFUL FROM EAST TO WEST    678 JERUSALEM 48    33
    WHEN WITH A DREADFUL GROAN THE EMANATION MILD OF ALBION    678 JERUSALEM 48    47
    AND SHE PUT FORTH HER HAND UPON THE LOOMS IN DREADFUL      698 JERUSALEM 64     7
       HOWLINGS
    WHEREFORE IN DREADFUL MAJESTY & BEAUTY OUTSIDE APPEARS  .  .  721 JERUSALEM 79  70
    OF DREADFUL POWER SITTING UPON HOREB PONDERING DIRE  . .   735 JERUSALEM 89    55
    MUST BE SO TO A MAN JUST OUT OF SO DREADFUL A FEVER I ALSO 844D LETTER 43    PROSE
DREADFULLY
    VICTIMS TO ONE ANOTHER & DREADFULLY PLOTTING AGAINST EACH  671 JERUSALEM 43     4
       OTHER
DREADS
    PROPHETIC DREADS URGE ME TO SPEAK FUTURITY IS BEFORE ME    293 FOUR ZOAS 3     74
DREAM
    WHERE SIGHING LOVERS DREAM  . . . . . . . . . . . . .        8 MEMORY COME/PS   6
    AND THERE I'LL LIE AND DREAM  . . . . . . . . . . . .        8 MEMORY COME/PS  11
    A DREAM  . . . . . . . . . . . . . . . . . . . . .        111D A DREAM/SI    TITLE
    ONCE A DREAM DID WEAVE A SHADE  . . . . . . . . . . .      111 A DREAM/SI       1
    AND DREAM THEY SEE THEIR CHILD  . . . . . . . . . . .      114 LIT GRL FND/SI  11
    I DREAMT A DREAM WHAT CAN IT MEAN . . . . . . . . . .      182 THE ANGEL/N      1
    OF LIFE ARE HARLOTS AND THEOTORMON IS A SICK MAN'S DREAM   194 V DAU ALBION 6  19
    THEY LOOK BEHIND AT EVERY STEP & BELIEVE IT IS A DREAM  .  198 AMERICA 6       12
    AS WHEN A DREAM OF THIRALATHA FLIES THE MIDNIGHT HOUR   .  206 THIRALATHA       1
    I DREAMT A DREAM WHAT CAN IT MEAN . . . . . . . . . .      213 THE ANGEL/SE     1
```

```
                                                                PAGE      TITLE        LINE
DREAM    (CONTINUED)
     LIKE A DREAM WAS OBLITERATED  . . . . . . . . .  .       230 URIZEN 13           34
     EIGHTEEN HUNDRED YEARS MAN WAS A DREAM   . . . . .       240 EUROPE 9             2
     EIGHTEEN HUNDRED YEARS A FEMALE DREAM    . . . . . .     240 EUROPE 9             5
     TILL LIKE A DREAM ETERNITY WAS OBLITERATED & ERASED . . 246 SONG OF LOS 4        4
     A DREAM OF NINE NIGHTS BY WILLIAM BLAKE... . . . . .  .  263B FOUR ZOAS        TITLE
     THE VOICE CAME & WENT LIKE A DREAM I AWOKE IN MY SWEET   272 FOUR ZOAS 1         280
        BLISS
     SWAM LIKE A DREAM BEFORE MY EYES I WENT TO SEEK THE STEPS 339 FOUR ZOAS 7B       235
     SWIMS LIKE A DREAM BEFORE MY EYES BUT THE SWEET SMELLING 371 FOUR ZOAS 9         539
        FRUIT
     THEY LOOK BEHIND AT EVERY STEP & BELIEVE IT IS A DREAM . . 375 FOUR ZOAS 9       676
     END OF THE DREAM . . . . . . . . . . . . . . . .  . 379D FOUR ZOAS 9          TITLE
     TRAVELLER REPOSE & DREAM AMONG MY LEAVES WILL BLAKE   .  414 ILLUS GRAY           2
     WILD WITH PROPHETIC FURY HIS FORMER LIFE BECAME LIKE A   493 MILTON 12           45
        DREAM
     IN VISION & DREAM BEATIFIC WITH THE SEVEN ANGELS OF THE  521 MILTON 32            2
        PRESENCE
     BY THE HAUNTED STREAM BY SUN SET SEES IN HIS DREAM  . . 618D ILLUS MILTON     PROSE
     STRANGE [INSTRUMENT] MYSTERIOUS DREAM UPON HIS WINGS OF  619C ILLUS MILTON    *PROSE
        SCROLLS &
     POLLUTED I HEARD HIS VOICE IN MY SLEEP & HIS ANGEL IN MY 694 JERUSALEM 61       16
        DREAM
     O PITIOUS SLEEP O PITIOUS DREAM O GOD O GOD AWAKE        742 JERUSALEM 94       22
        I HAVE SLAIN
     ALL WAS A VISION ALL A DREAM THE FURNACES BECAME   . . . 744 JERUSALEM 96       36
     THE LOST TRAVELLER'S DREAM UNDER THE HILL . . . . . .  . 771 EPILOGUE/GP          8
     SEE VISIONS DREAM DREAMS & PROPHECY & SPEAK PARABLES  . 822C LETTER 26         PROSE
     FOR I CERTAINLY AM THAT DREAMER BUT THO I DREAM OVER MY  854C LETTER 53         PROSE
     OWN FORTUNES I OUGHT NOT TO DREAM OVER THOSE OF OTHER .  854C LETTER 53         PROSE
     ?LEAH & RACHEL ?DANTE'S ?DREAM  . . . . . . . .  .     SUPP ILLUS DANTE 86    *PROSE
     A DREAM ON ANOTHER'S SORROW THE LITTLE BOY LOST   . .  SUPP LETTER 66A        *PROSE
DREAMER
     IN VAIN THE DREAMER GRASPS THE JOYFUL IMAGES THEY FLY  . 206 THIRALATHA           2
     DREAMER OF FURIOUS OCEANS COLD SLEEPER OF WEEDS & SHELLS 301 FOUR ZOAS 4         135
     OF TEN POUNDS TO THE DREAMER OVER HIS OWN FORTUNES  . . 854C LETTER 53         PROSE
     FOR I CERTAINLY AM THAT DREAMER BUT THO I DREAM OVER MY  854C LETTER 53         PROSE
DREAMFUL
     IN A HORRIBLE DREAMFUL SLUMBER . . . . . . . . . .      228 URIZEN 10           35
     SOTHA & THIRALATHA SECRET DWELLERS OF DREAMFUL CAVES  . 244 EUROPE 14           26
     A DREAMFUL HORRIBLE STATE IN TOSSINGS ON HIS ICY BED  . 302 FOUR ZOAS 4         171
     IN A HORRIBLE DREAMFUL SLUMBER LIKE THE LINKED CHAIN  . 303 FOUR ZOAS 4         218
     BEFORE THE FURNACES OF LOS IN A HORRIBLE DREAMFUL SLUMBER 662 JERUSALEM 36       11
DREAMING
     DREAMING OER THE JOYS OF NIGHT . . . . . . . . .        165 CRADLE SONG/N        7
DREAMLESS
     HE LAY IN A DREAMLESS NIGHT . . . . . . . . . . .       226 URIZEN 7             7
DREAMS
     THAT WISDOM MAY DESCEND IN FAIRY DREAMS . . . . . .      14 IMIT SPEN/PS         5
     AND IN THE NIGHT LIKE INFANTS SLEPT DELIGHTED WITH INFANT 100 TIRIEL 2            9
        DREAMS
     SWEET DREAMS FORM A SHADE  . . . . . . . . . . .        120 CRADLE SONG/SI       1
     SWEET DREAMS OF PLEASANT STREAMS . . . . . . . .        120 CRADLE SONG/SI       3
     LIKE DREAMS OF INFANTS LIKE A SMILE UPON AN INFANT'S FACE 127 BOOK OF THEL 1     10
     . . . I AWAKE BUT MY SOUL IS IN DREAMS  . . . . . .     134 FRENCH REVOLTN       8
     . . . URGD BY CRIES IN DAY AND PROPHETIC DREAMS HOVERING 138 FRENCH REVOLTN      98
        IN NIGHT
     FEAR NOT DREAMS FEAR NOT VISIONS . . . . . . . .        142 FRENCH REVOLTN      180
     RELIGIOUS DREAMS AND HOLY VESPERS LIGHT THY SMOKY FIRES  194 V DAU ALBION 6      14
     . . . IN ALL THEIR [WANDERINGS] DREAMS  . . . . . .     267 FOUR ZOAS 1     *    99
     AND VALA WALKD WITH HIM IN DREAMS OF SOFT DELUDING SLUMBER 292 FOUR ZOAS 3       45
     TILL ON MY SILVER BED I SLEPT & SWEET DREAMS ROUND      310 FOUR ZOAS 5         204
        ME HOVERD
     IN DREAMS OF ULRO [SWEET] DARK DELUSIVE DRAWN BY THE LOVELY 328 FOUR ZOAS 7     331
        SHADOW
     THAT MOVD WITH HORRIBLE DREAMS & (HOVRING) HIGH OVER HIS 341 FOUR ZOAS 8     *    6
        HEAD
     AND THOSE UPON THE COUCHES VIEWD THEM IN THE DREAMS OF   367 FOUR ZOAS 9         383
        BEULAH
     O DREAMS OF DEATH THE HUMAN FORM DISSOLVING COMPANIED . . 373 FOUR ZOAS 9        595
     THE LAND OF DREAMS . . . . . . . . . . . . . . .      427B LAND OF DREAMS     TITLE
     O WHAT LAND IS THE LAND OF DREAMS . . . . . . . .      427 LAND OF DREAMS        5
     HAVE WANDERD ALL NIGHT IN THE LAND OF DREAMS . . . .   427 LAND OF DREAMS       14
     THE LAND OF DREAMS IS BETTER FAR  . . . . . . . .      427 LAND OF DREAMS       19
     CANAAN THEN SHE RETURND TO LOS WEARY FRIGHTED AS        490 MILTON 10       *    5
        FROM DREAMS
     IN DREAMS SHE BORE THE SHADOWY SPECTRE OF SLEEP & NAMD  494 MILTON 13           40
        HIM DEATH
     IN DREAMS SHE BORE RAHAB THE MOTHER OF TIRZAH & HER SISTERS 494 MILTON 13        41
     AS WHEN A MAN DREAMS HE REFLECTS NOT THAT HIS BODY SLEEPS 496 MILTON 15           1
     HE WEEPS INTO THE ATLANTIC DEEP YET STILL IN DISMAL DREAMS 506 MILTON 23          9
     SLEEP ON SLEEP ON WHILE IN THY PLEASANT DREAMS    . . . 536 DONT BELIEVE/N       3
     UNDER PERPETUAL TERRORS & VAIN DREAMS PLOTS & SECRET DECEIT 608D V LAST JUDG/N PROSE
     IN ITS DEADLY DREAMS OF GOOD & EVIL . . . . . . .  . 614C V LAST JUDG/N       PROSE
     AND VALA WALKD WITH HIM IN DREAMS OF SOFT DELUDING SLUMBER 654 JERUSALEM 29      34
     IN THE VISIONS OF THE DREAMS OF BEULAH ON THE EDGE      663 JERUSALEM 36         22
        OF NON-ENTITY
     IN DREAMS OF DARKNESS WHILE MY VEGETATING BLOOD IN VEINY 665 JERUSALEM 38        36
        PIPES
     ALBION SPOKE IN HIS DISMAL DREAMS O THOU DECEITFUL FRIEND 669 JERUSALEM 42        9
     IN THE DREAMS OF ULRO THEY REPENT OF THEIR HUMAN KINDNESS 671 JERUSALEM 42       62
     IN VISIONS OF THE DREAMS OF BEULAH AMONG THE DAUGHTERS  698 JERUSALEM 63         37
        OF ALBION
```

```
                                                             PAGE     TITLE           LINE
DREAMS   (CONTINUED)
    WHERE SEXES WANDER IN DREAMS OF BLISS AMONG THE EMANATIONS    721 JERUSALEM 79      75
    IN DREAMS OF (CHASTITY) & MORAL LAW I HAVE MURDERED ALBION    742 JERUSALEM 94      23
      AH
    WEAVING TO DREAMS THE SEXUAL STRIFE  . . . . . . . . .        771 OF GATES/GP       47
    SEE VISIONS DREAM DREAMS & PROPHECY & SPEAK PARABLES   .  . 822C LETTER 26        PROSE
    I COULD TELL YOU OF VISIONS & DREAMS UPON THE SUBJECT  .  . 876B LETTER 83        PROSE
DREAMT
    I DREAMT A DREAM WHAT CAN IT MEAN  . . . . . . . . . .        182 THE ANGEL/N        1
    I DREAMT A DREAM WHAT CAN IT MEAN  . . . . . . . . . .        213 THE ANGEL/SE       1
DREAR
    AND NOW MY PARADISE IS FALLN & A DREAR SANDY PLAIN  . . .     110 TIRIEL 8          39
    FROM THE DARKNESS DREAD & DREAR  . . . . . . . . . .         168 EARTHS ANSWR/N     2
    [AND WANDERD DOWN THE VALES OF KENT IN SICK & DREAR          196 AMERICA PREL 2    21
      LAMENTINGS]
    FROM THE DARKNESS DREAD & DREAR  . . . . . . . . . .         210 EARTHS ANSR/SE     2
DREARY
    A HOLLOW GROAN RAN THRO THE DREARY VAULTS  . . . . . .         4 FAIR ELENOR/PS     4
    AND RATTLING GUNS AND BLACK AND DREARY WAR . . . . . .        31 EDW THIRD/PS 5    60
    I WALKED THROUGH DREARY PLACES WITH HIM AND IN CHURCH-YARDS  37C CONTEMPLATN/PS  PROSE
    WORN THRO WITH THE DREARY SHOWER . . . . . . . . . .         124 SCHOOL BOY/SI     15
    LEST HE SHOULD RISE AGAIN FROM DEATH IN ALL HIS [DISMAL]     300 FOUR ZOAS 4     * 121
      DREARY POWER
    TERRIFIC PALE ENITHARMON STRETCHED ON THE [DISMAL] DREARY    305 FOUR ZOAS 5        5
      EARTH
    AND WHEN THE GATE WAS OPEN SHE BEHELD THAT [DISMAL] DREARY   309 FOUR ZOAS 5     * 180
      DEEP
    A DREARY WASTE OF SOLID WATERS FOR THE KING OF LIGHT  .  .   313 FOUR ZOAS 6       51
    WITH PAIN UPON THE [DISMAL] DREARY MOUNTAINS & WITH PAIN     313 FOUR ZOAS 6     *  79
      DESCENDED
    THEY WANDER MOPING IN THEIR HEART A SUN A DREARY MOON  .  .  314 FOUR ZOAS 6       90
    THUS URIZEN IN SORROWS WANDERD MANY A DREARY WAY  . . . .    318 FOUR ZOAS 6      260
    COMPULSIVE ROLLD THE COMETS AT HIS DREAD COMMAND THE DREARY  320 FOUR ZOAS 6      320
      WAY
    BUT TO HIMSELF HE SEEMD A WANDERER LOST IN DREARY NIGHT      496 MILTON 15         16
    BLASPHEMOUS SONS OF FEMININE DELUSION GOD IN THE DREARY      646 JERUSALEM 23      29
      VOID
DREGS
    OF THE WHEAT-FLOOR OR AS THE DREGS OF THE SWEET WINE-PRESS   687 JERUSALEM 55      41
DRESS
    LOOSD HER SLENDER DRESS  . . . . . . . . . .                 113 LIT GRL LST/SI    50
    AND PEACE THE HUMAN DRESS  . . . . . . . . . .               117 DIVNE IMAGE/SI    12
    [WHICH ARE BEAUTIES SWEETEST DRESS]  . . . . . . . . .       182 WHICH ARE/N        1
    THESE ARE BEAUTIES SWEETEST DRESS  . . . . . . . . .         182 WHICH ARE/N        3
    THESE ARE BEAUTY'S SWEETEST DRESS  . . . . . . . . .         184 SEVRL QUESTN/N    10
    AND SECRECY THE HUMAN DRESS  . . . . . . . . . . .           221 DIVNE IMAGE/SE     4
    THE HUMAN DRESS IS FORGED IRON . . . . . . . . . .           221 DIVNE IMAGE/SE     5
    I WILL HUMBLE MY BEAUTY I WILL NOT DRESS FINE  .  . . .      428 MARY              29
    THEIR DRESS AND THEIR HORSES ARE OF THE FIRST RATE  . .     568A DESC CAT 3      PROSE
    MACBETH THOSE WHO DRESS THEM FOR THE STAGE CONSIDER   . .   569D DESC CAT 3      PROSE
    AS HIS DRESS IS DIFFERENT AND HIS CHARACTER IS MORE MARKED  572A DESC CAT 3      PROSE
    EVERY PARTICULAR OF DRESS OR COSTUME  . . . . . . . .       588A CHAUCER/N       PROSE
DRESSED
    THE SAVAGE GIRLS HAD DRESSED THEMSELVES WITH VINE LEAVES    581C DESC CAT 7      PROSE
DREST
    PHEBE DREST LIKE BEAUTIE'S QUEEN  . . . . . . . . .           53 PHEBE DREST/IM     1
DREW
    AND DREW THE CURTAINS OF HEAVEN  . . . . . . . . .           39D SAMSON/PS       PROSE
    SO ONCE THE SUN HIS CHARIOT DREW BACK TO PROLONG A GOOD     41B THEN SHE BORE    PROSE
      KING'S LIFE
    MRS GIMBLET DREW HER MOUTH DOWNWARDS  . . . . . . .         46A ISLAND MOON 1    PROSE
    HE DREW OUT OF THE STOCKS  . . . . . . . . . . .             57 TO BE OR/IM       13
    ALL DAY HE BORE HIM & WHEN EVENING DREW HER SOLEMN CURTAIN  104 TIRIEL 4         41
    ALL HIS SLIMY LENGTH HE DREW  . . . . . . . . . .           163 I SAW CHAPEL/N    12
    BEGAN INTRICATE PIPES THAT DREW IN . . . . . . . .          259 BOOK OF LOS 4     69
    SHE DREW THE SPECTRE FORTH FROM THARMAS . . . . . . .       267 FOUR ZOAS 1      122
    AND DREW IT OUT TO [TWENTY YEARS] SEVEN THOUSAND YEARS      270 FOUR ZOAS 1      223
      . . .
    SMITE SPECTRE OF URTHONA MOCK THE FIEND WHO DREW US DOWN    276 FOUR ZOAS 1      432
    THE FAMILY DIVINE DREW UP THE UNIVERSAL TENT . . . . .      279 FOUR ZOAS 1      551
    THAT DREW THE BODY OF MAN FROM HEAVEN INTO THIS DARK ABYSS  306 FOUR ZOAS 5       47
    LOS DREW THEM FORTH OUT OF THE DEEPS PLANTING HIS RIGHT     332 FOUR ZOAS 7      464
      FOOT FIRM
    AND FIRST HE DREW A LINE UPON THE WALLS OF SHINING HEAVEN   332 FOUR ZOAS 7      467
    FIRST HIS IMMORTAL SPIRIT DREW URIZEN [SPECTRE] SHADOW AWAY 332 FOUR ZOAS 7    * 490
    SHE DREW NEAR TO HER HOUSE & HER FLOCKS FOLLOWD HER         370 FOUR ZOAS 9      508
      FOOTSTEPS
    THY FATHER DREW HIS SWORD IN THE NORTH  . . . . . .         419 I SAW A MONK/N    36
    THY FATHER DREW HIS SWORD IN THE NORTH  . . . . . .         430 GREY MONK         21
    AND THE FAIRY DREW THE DEVIL INTO THE NUT-SHELL  . . .      434 LONG JOHN BRWN     4
    HUDSON DREW CORRECTLY  . . . . . . . . . . . .             447B ANNO REYNOLDS    MARG
    AND IF BEZALEEL & AHOLIAB DREW  . . . . . . . . .           543 IF TRUE/N          5
    THAT LAYS OPEN THE HIDDEN HEART I DREW FORTH THE PANG       628 JERUSALEM 9       19
    OF AFFLICTION AND LOS DREW THEM FORTH COMPELLING THE HARSH  628 JERUSALEM 9       35
      SPECTRE
    HE DREW THE VEIL OF MORAL VIRTUE WOVEN FOR CRUEL LAWS  .    646 JERUSALEM 23      22
    AND LOS DREW HIS SEVEN FURNACES AROUND ALBION'S ALTARS  .   671 JERUSALEM 42      77
    IN EDEN IN LOVELY JERUSALEM DREW EVEN FROM ENVY  . . . .    675 JERUSALEM 45       6
    THEN ALBION DREW ENGLAND INTO HIS BOSOM IN GROANS & TEARS   685 JERUSALEM 54      27
    THEN THE SPECTRE DREW VALA INTO HIS BOSOM MAGNIFICENT       699 JERUSALEM 64      25
      TERRIFIC
    A DOUBLE FEMALE AND THEY DREW OUT FROM THE ROCKY STONES     704 JERUSALEM 67       3
```

```
                                                                  PAGE      TITLE          LINE
DREW     (CONTINUED)
     SO SAYING SHE DREW ASIDE HER VEIL FROM MAM-TOR TO DOVEDALE    726  JERUSALEM 82         45
     ON LONDON'S TOWER ON THE THAMES HE DREW CAMBEL IN WRATH       726  JERUSALEM 82         57
     CONWENNA SAT ABOVE WITH SOLEMN CADENCES SHE DREW  . . . .     736  JERUSALEM 90         21
     THEY DREW FOURFOLD THE UNREPROVABLE STRING . . . . . . .      744  JERUSALEM 98          2
     & RAGING & CURSING WHICH DREW OUT SEVERAL NEIGHBOURS   . .   827B  LETTER 28         PROSE
DREWST
     DREWST ALL THE SONS OF BEULAH INTO THY [GREAT] DREAD VORTEX   299  FOUR ZOAS 4          88
        FOLLOWING
DRIED     SEE DRYD
     I DRIED MY TEARS & ARMD MY FEARS  . . . . . . . . . .         182  THE ANGEL/N          11
     I DRIED MY TEARS & ARMD MY FEARS  . . . . . . . . . .         214  THE ANGEL/SE         11
     DRIED LAID THEM APART TILL WINTER . . . . . . . . . .         251  AHANIA 3             22
     IN ALL MY RIVERS & ON DRIED SHELLS THAT THE FISH  . . . .     296  FOUR ZOAS 3         167
     THOU HANGST A DRIED SKIN SHRUNK UP WEAK WAILING IN THE WIND   313  FOUR ZOAS 6          71
     THAT CREEPS FORTH IN A NIGHT & IS DRIED IN THE MORNING SUN    659  JERUSALEM 33          7
     INTO BEULAH TREMBLING THE DAUGHTERS OF BEULAH DRIED   . .     678  JERUSALEM 48         39
DRIES
     JOY EVEN TO TEARS WHICH THE SUN RISING DRIES FIRST THE        520  MILTON 31            51
        WILD THYME
DRIFT
     "THE DRIFT OF HOLLOW STATES HARD TO BE SPELLD" MILTON   . . SUPP LEGEND/N27            *
DRIFTED
     COLD SNOWS DRIFTED AROUND HIM ICE COVERD HIS LOINS AROUND     652  JERUSALEM 28         13
DRINK
     I'LL DRINK OF THE CLEAR STREAM . . . . . . . . . .              8  MEMORY COME/PS        9
     TO DRINK HER CHILDREN'S GORE . . . . . . . . . . .             13  GWIN KING/PS         74
     THOU FEAR I DRINK MY TEARS LIKE WATER I LIVE UPON SORROW      39A  SAMSON/PS         PROSE
     THAT I SHOULD DRINK NO WINE NOR EAT OF ANY UNCLEAN THING      39C  SAMSON/PS         PROSE
     NOW THEREFORE DRINK NO WINE AND EAT NOT ANY UNCLEAN THING     39D  SAMSON/PS         PROSE
     AND I REMAIN AN OUTCAST HAST THOU ANY THING TO DRINK   .     102  TIRIEL 2             57
     DRINK OF THIS RUNNING BROOK & I WILL BEAR THEE ON            104  TIRIEL 4             39
        MY SHOULDERS
     WHERE ARE YOU GOING COME & EAT SOME ROOTS & DRINK SOME       109  TIRIEL 7             11
        WATER
     O VIRGIN KNOWST THOU NOT OUR STEEDS DRINK OF THE GOLDEN      128  BOOK OF THEL 3        7
        SPRINGS
     . . . AND LET THY SOUL DRINK OF MY COUNSEL  . . . . .        140  FRENCH REVOLTN      128
     THEN THE PARSON MIGHT PREACH & DRINK & SING  . . . . .       179  LIT VAGABOND/N       10
     BUT KISS HIM & GIVE HIM BOTH [FOOD] DRINK & APPAREL  . .     180  LIT VAGABOND/N       18
     AND DRINK & SING  . . . . . . . . . . . . . .               183  THE FLY/N            18
     ARISE AND DRINK YOUR BLISS FOR EVERY THING THAT LIVES IS     195  V DAU ALBION 8       10
        HOLY
     HIS FOOD SHE BROUGHT IN IRON BASKETS HIS DRINK IN CUPS       195  AMERICA PREL 1        3
        OF IRON
     AND DRINK & SING  . . . . . . . . . . . . . .               213  THE FLY/SE           10
     THEN THE PARSON MIGHT PREACH & DRINK & SING  . . . . .       216  LIT VAGABND/SE        9
     BUT KISS HIM & GIVE HIM BOTH DRINK AND APPAREL  . . . .      216  LIT VAGABND/SE       16
     TO GIVE US BLISS THAT WE MAY DRINK THE SPARKLING WINE OF     239  EUROPE 1             20
        LOS
     . . . NOW BORN TO DRINK UP ALL HIS POWERS  . . . . .        272  FOUR ZOAS 1         278
     BUT CLOUDS OF HUMAN SOULS MY NOSTRILS DRINK THE LIVES OF     275  FOUR ZOAS 1         393
        MEN
     ARISE & DRINK YOUR BLISS . . . . . . . . . . . .            289  FOUR ZOAS 2         365
     BEWARE LEST WE ALSO DRINK UP THEE ROUGH DEMON OF THE WATERS  298  FOUR ZOAS 4          37
     DRINK LAUGH & SING THE GRASSHOPPER THE EMMET & THE FLY  .    308  FOUR ZOAS 5       * 133
     ARMED WITH SPEAR & SHIELD THEY DRINK & REJOICE OVER THE      308  FOUR ZOAS 5         141
        SLAIN
     IN STRONG DRINK THO YOU KNOW THAT BREAD & WATER ARE ALL      323  FOUR ZOAS 7         127
     WITH LUST & MURDER FOR OUR DRINK THE DRUNKEN RAVEN SHALL     334  FOUR ZOAS 7B         47
        WANDER
     AS FOOD OR DRINK OR ORNAMENT OR IN DELIGHTFUL WORKS   .      340  FOUR ZOAS 7B        276
     DRINK IN THE DEADLY DULL DELUSION HORRORS OF ETERNAL DEATH   352  FOUR ZOAS 8         418
     TAKE THEIR REPOSE ON BEDS THEY DRINK THEY SING THEY VIEW     366  FOUR ZOAS 9         341
        THE FLAMES
     SHE [D] STOPD TO DRINK OF THE CLEAR SPRING & EAT THE GRAPES  369  FOUR ZOAS 9       * 476
        & APPLES
     I DRINK NEW LIFE & FEEL THE BREATH OF SLEEPING ENION   . .   371  FOUR ZOAS 9         542
     . . . BUT BORN TO DRINK UP ALL HIS POWERS  . . . . .        373  FOUR ZOAS 9         623
     THEY DANCE AROUND THE DYING & THEY DRINK THE HOWL & GROAN    377  FOUR ZOAS 9         767
     THEY ARE HIS MEAT THEY ARE HIS DRINK . . . . . . .          425  MENTAL TRAVLER       37
     AND NOTHING LEFT TO EAT OR DRINK . . . . . . . .            426  MENTAL TRAVLER       67
     THEY DANCE AROUND THE DYING & THEY DRINK THE HOWL & GROAN    514  MILTON 27            37
     OF REASON YOU MAY DRINK OF LIFE'S CLEAR STREAMS   . . .      536  DONT BELIEVE/N        4
     OIL WILL NOT DRINK OR ABSORB COLOUR ENOUGH TO STAND THE     561A  EXHIBITION ADV    PROSE
        TEST
     OIL WILL NOT DRINK OR ABSORB COLOUR ENOUGH TO STAND THE     565A  DESC CAT 2        PROSE
        TEST
     ITSELF WILL DRINK OR ABSORB VERY LITTLE COLOUR  . . . .    566B  DESC CAT 2        PROSE
     CHILDREN OF WHOREDOMS BORN FOR SACRIFICE FOR THE MEAT &      658  JERUSALEM 31         64
        DRINK
     FOOD OF DESPAIR THEY DRINK THE CONDEMND SOUL & REJOICE  . .  680  JERUSALEM 49         63
     BY THOSE WHO DRINK THEIR BLOOD & THE BLOOD OF THEIR          704  JERUSALEM 67          1
        COVENANT
     THEY DRINK UP DAN & GAD TO FEED WITH MILK SKOFELD & KOTOPE   704  JERUSALEM 67         22
     SHRIEK NOT SO MY ONLY LOVE I REFUSE THY JOYS I DRINK        705  JERUSALEM 67         61
     IS IT MEAT & DRINK IS NOT THE BODY MORE THAN RAIMENT   .   717B  JERUSALEM 77      PROSE
     THEY DRINK REUBEN & BENJAMIN AS THE IRON DRINKS THE FIRE     737  JERUSALEM 90         46
     WE EAT LITTLE WE DRINK LESS . . . . . . . . . .             818  HAPPINESS/L          63
DRINKING
     WITH FACE AS BROWN AS ANY NUT WITH DRINKING OF STRONG ALE     58  THIS CITY/IM          3
     WITH EATING BEEF & DRINKING BEER O THEY WERE STOUT & HALE     58  THIS CITY/IM          7
```

```
                                                     PAGE    TITLE        LINE
DRINKING    (CONTINUED)
      I SEE A WHALE IN THE SOUTH-SEA DRINKING MY SOUL AWAY    . .  196 AMERICA PREL 2    14
      HER WOOF OF TERROR TERRIFIED & DRINKING TEARS OF WOE    . .  266 FOUR ZOAS 1       81
      DRINKING THE JOYS OF UNIVERSAL MANHOOD ONE DREAD MORN  .     327 FOUR ZOAS 7      277
      RENDING THE HEAVENS & EARTHS & DRINKING BLOOD IN THE HOT     335 FOUR ZOAS 7B     103
        BATTLE
      . . . GRATIFIED & DRINKING TEARS OF WOE    . . . . . . . .   338 FOUR ZOAS 7B     213
      WHENCE IS THIS SOUND OF RAGE OF MEN DRINKING EACH OTHER'S    360 FOUR ZOAS 9      121
        BLOOD
      WHO IS THE GENIUS OF EATING AND DRINKING THE BACCHUS   . .  571A DESC CAT 3      PROSE
      DRINKING THE SHUDDERING FEARS & LOVES OF ALBION'S FAMILIES   669 JERUSALEM 41      27
      DRINKING & EATING & PITYING & WEEPING AS AT A TRAJIC SCENE   669 JERUSALEM 41      29
      BROODING IN HOLY HYPOCRITIC LUST DRINKING THE CRIES OF PAIN  672 JERUSALEM 43      17
      DRINKING HIS EMANATION IN INTOXICATING BLISS REJOICING       701 JERUSALEM 65      58
        IN GIANT DANCE
      DRINKING THEIR LIVES IN SWEET INTOXICATION HENCE AROSE       701 JERUSALEM 65      65
        FROM BATH
      OVER THE TEMPLES DRINKING GROANS OF VICTIMS WEEPING IN PITY  723 JERUSALEM 80      55
      SOFT INVISIBLE DRINKING HIS SIGHS IN SWEET INTOXICATION      723 JERUSALEM 80      60
DRINKS
      CAN THAT BE LOVE THAT DRINKS ANOTHER AS A SPONGE DRINKS      194 V DAU ALBION 7    17
        WATER
      LIKE THE GAY FISHES ON THE WAVE WHEN THE COLD MOON DRINKS    243 EUROPE 14          3
        THE DEW
      AND YET IT DRINKS THE SUMMER JOY & FEARS THE WINTER SORROW   314 FOUR ZOAS 6       96
      DESCENDS [OF] DOWN ON THE SAND THE THIRSTY SAND DRINKS       373 FOUR ZOAS 9    *  602
        & REJOICES
      THE SLOW SLUG THE GRASSHOPPER THAT SINGS & LAUGHS & DRINKS   377 FOUR ZOAS 9      760
        MORNING DRINKS MY SILENT TEAR . . . . . . . . . . .       423 THE BIRDS/N        7
      FOR AS HE EATS & DRINKS HE GROWS    . . . . . . . . . .     426 MENTAL TRAVLER    73
      THE SLOW SLUG THE GRASSHOPPER THAT SINGS & LAUGHS & DRINKS   513 MILTON 27         19
      HE DRINKS THEE UP LIKE WATER LIKE WINE HE POURS THEE   . .   625 JERUSALEM 7       11
      THE SOUL DRINKS MURDER & REVENGE & APPLAUDS ITS OWN          669 JERUSALEM 41      30
        HOLINESS
      THEY DRINK REUBEN & BENJAMIN AS THE IRON DRINKS THE FIRE     737 JERUSALEM 90      46
      THE PLAYHOUSES WHO EATS & DRINKS FOR BUSINESS NOT FOR NEED  830A LETTER 30       PROSE
DRIVE
      THEY TEAR THE POOR MAN'S LAMB AND DRIVE . . . . . . .   .    11 GWIN KING/PS       7
      DRIVE THE NATIONS TOGETHER WHO CAN STAND   . . . . . . .     33 EDW FOURTH/PS      8
      HE'LL PLUNGE HIS KNIFE UP TO THE HILT IN A SINGLE DRIVE     50A ISLAND MOON 6    PROSE
      THEN CHERISH PITY LEST YOU DRIVE AN ANGEL FROM YOUR DOOR     59 HOLY THURS/IM     18
      SEEKING TO DRIVE THEIR THIRST AWAY    . . . . . . . .       119 NIGHT/SI          27
      THEN CHERISH PITY LEST YOU DRIVE AN ANGEL FROM YOUR DOOR    122 HOLY THURS/SI     12
      TO WALK IN PERILOUS PATHS AND DRIVE    . . . . . . . .      148 MARRIAGE HH 2     15
      DRIVE YOUR CART AND YOUR PLOW OVER THE BONES OF THE DEAD    150D MARRIAGE HH 7   PROSE
      . . . FROM [VALA] LUVAH I WILL DRIVE ALL]  . . . . . .      272 FOUR ZOAS 1    *  276
      BODIES OF VEGETATION SINGING LULLING CADENCES TO DRIVE AWAY  342 FOUR ZOAS 8      38
      THEY SOON DRIVE OUT THE AGED HOST    . . . . . . . . . .    426 MENTAL TRAVLER    51
      FOR JOHN EAT & DRANK TO DRIVE AWAY LOVE'S PAIN    . . . .   434 LONG JOHN BRWN    10
      TO DRIVE AWAY THE SICK MAN'S PAIN    . . . . . . . . . .    435 WILLIAM BOND      20
      ANGER ME NOT THOU CANST NOT DRIVE THE HARROW IN PITY'S      483 MILTON 4          16
        PATHS
      THEY PUT FORTH THEIR SPECTROUS CLOUDY SAILS WHICH DRIVE      625 JERUSALEM 7       21
        THEIR IMMENSE
      OF THE WILD INHABITANT OF THE FOREST TO DRIVE THEM FROM      638 JERUSALEM 17       4
        HIS OWN
      AND PUT ON INTELLECT OR MY THUNDROUS HAMMER SHALL DRIVE      739 JERUSALEM 91      57
        THEE
      TO DRIVE THEM OFF & BEFORE MY WAY    . . . . . . . . . .    817 HAPPINESS/L       23
DRIVEN       SEE DRIVN
      MY NOTES ARE DRIVEN    . . . . . . . . . . . . . . . .       9 MAD SONG/PS       12
      ARE SHAKEN AND THE SOUL IS DRIVEN TO MADNESS   . . . . .    33 EDW FOURTH/PS       3
      IS DRIVEN AWAY   . . . . . . . . . . . . . . . . . . .      119 NIGHT/SI          39
      . . . DRIVEN BACK BY THE SANDY DESERT   . . . . . . . .     144 FRENCH REVOLTN   235
      AND THE PALACE APPEARD LIKE A CLOUD DRIVEN ABROAD . . .     145 FRENCH REVOLTN   246
      IN WINDS DRIVEN OUT OF THE ABBEYS . . . . . . . . . . .     146 FRENCH REVOLTN   275
      DRIVEN OUT BY THE FIERY CLOUD OF VOLTAIRE . . . . . . .     146 FRENCH REVOLTN   276
      DRIVEN OUT & COMPELD TO BE CHASTE    . . . . . . . . .      162 LAID ME DOWN/N     8
      THE PLAGUES CREEP ON THE BURNING WINDS DRIVEN BY FLAMES     202 AMERICA 15        11
        OF ORC
      DRIVEN OER THE GUARDIANS OF IRELAND AND SCOTLAND AND WALES   202 AMERICA 15       13
      "WHEN THE SENSES ARE SHAKEN AND THE SOUL IS DRIVEN         SUPP INSC OUR END   *TITLE
        TO MADNESS"
      DRIVEN OUT BY THE FLAMES OF ORC HIS FURRD ROBES & FALSE     242 EUROPE 12         16
        LOCKS
      AND WINTRY WOES SUCCEED SUCCESSIVE DRIVEN INTO THE VOID     274 FOUR ZOAS 1      372
      LISTEN TO HER WHO LOVES THEE LEST WE ALSO ARE DRIVEN AWAY   294 FOUR ZOAS 3       92
      DRIVEN BY THY RAGE I WANDER LIKE A CLOUD INTO THE DEEP  . . 296 FOUR ZOAS 3      188
      IN VAIN AM DRIVEN ON FALSE HOPE HOPE SISTER OF DESPAIR      300 FOUR ZOAS 4      123
      ARE DRIVEN AWAY & ANNIHILATED WE NEVER CAN REPASS THE GATES 327 FOUR ZOAS 7      303
      MARROWLESS BLOODLESS FALLING INTO DUST DRIVEN BY THE WINDS  354 FOUR ZOAS 8      518
      FLOAT THE DEAD CARCASES OF MEN & BEASTS DRIVEN TO & FRO     359 FOUR ZOAS 9       77
        ON WAVES
      INTO THEIR OWN APPOINTED PLACES DRIVEN BACK BY THE WINDS    365 FOUR ZOAS 9      325
      DRIVEN ON THE UNPRODUCING SANDS & ON THE HARDEND ROCKS      365 FOUR ZOAS 9      329
      ABOVE VEERD ROUND BY THE VIOLENT WHIRLWIND DRIVEN WEST      374 FOUR ZOAS 9    *  655
        & SOUTH
      THE SAVIOUR WHILE THE EVIL ANGELS ARE DRIVEN GENTLY        441D INSC FALL MAN   PROSE
        CONDUCTS
      DRIVEN MILTON INTO THE ULRO FOR NOW THEY KNEW TOO LATE  . . 504 MILTON 21         32
      THO DRIVEN AWAY WITH THE SEVEN STARRY ONES INTO THE ULRO    505 MILTON 22          1
      DRIVEN FROM ETERNITY HIM I SEEK TERRIFIED AT MY ACT  . . .  527 MILTON 37          2
```

543

		PAGE	TITLE	LINE

DRIVEN   (CONTINUED)
    [IS DRIVEN OUT TO MAKE ROOM FOR A PACK OF IDLE SYCOPHANTS]   595B PUB ADDRESS/N   *PROSE
    DRIVEN INTO THE WILDERNESS SHE HAS THE MOON UNDER HER FEET   610A V LAST JUDG/N   PROSE
    ARE DRIVEN AMONG THE STARRY WHEELS RENT AWAY AND DISSIPATED   623 JERUSALEM 5   4
    THEY REVOLVE INTO THE FURNACES SOUTHWARD & ARE DRIVEN FORTH   623 JERUSALEM 5   31
      NORTHWARD
    DRIVEN TO DESPERATION BY LOS'S TERRORS & THREATNING FEARS   629 JERUSALEM 10   28
    DRIVEN ON THE VOID IN INCOHERENT DESPAIR INTO NON ENTITY   673 JERUSALEM 43   68
    I SEE AMERICA CLOSD APART & JERUSALEM DRIVEN IN TERROR .   673 JERUSALEM 43   69
    FOR BEING DRIVEN FROM OUR FIELDS WHAT HAVE WE TO DO WITH   686 JERUSALEM 55   6
      THE DEAD
    AND DRIVEN AWAY MY TREMBLING DOVE . . . .   754 EV GOSPEL(E)/N   52
    [WHO DARES ?WORSHIP ?ONE WHOD HAVE DRIVEN YOU LONG AGO   SUPP ANNO REYNOLDS * MARG
      INSANE]
DRIVERS
    CHAISES & AS MANY DIFFERENT DRIVERS WE (SET) OUT BETWEEN   802B LETTER 14   *PROSE
    CHAISES & AS MANY DIFFERENT DRIVERS ALL UPON THE ROAD WAS   803A LETTER 15   PROSE
DRIVES
    O IT DRIVES ALL JOY AWAY   124 SCHOOL BOY/SI   7
    [SHADOWS ME OER & DRIVES ME OUTWARD TO A WORLD OF WOE] .   267 FOUR ZOAS 1   117
    WHO DRIVES ABROAD ALL THOSE WHO REBELL AGAINST THEIR   608B V LAST JUDG/N   PROSE
      SAVIOUR
    HE DRIVES THEM THRO THE STREETS OF BABYLON BEFORE MY FACE   644 JERUSALEM 21   30
    VENTURE OUT THE CHILL OF THE WEATHER SOON DRIVES ME BACK   871D LETTER 74   PROSE
      INTO
DRIVETH
    BUT HE DRIVETH ME AWAY FROM HIS PRESENCE YET I HEAR THE   694 JERUSALEM 61   9
      VOICE OF GOD
DRIVING
    DRIVING THE ANGEL BEFORE ME SOON WE SAW SEVEN HOUSES OF   157A MARRIAGE HH 17   PROSE
      BRICK
    DRIVING THE FEMALE EMANATIONS ALL AWAY FROM LOS . . . .   271 FOUR ZOAS 1   273
    DRIVING THE STORMS BEFORE THEM OR DELIGHTING IN SUNNY BEAMS   288 FOUR ZOAS 2   300
    THUS LIVD LOS DRIVING ENION FAR INTO THE DEATHFUL INFINITE   290 FOUR ZOAS 2   383
    TERRIFIC WITH THEIR IRON VESSELS DRIVING THEM ACROSS   . .   322 FOUR ZOAS 7   96
    ARE GATHERD IN THE SCORCHING HEAT & IN THE DRIVING RAIN   359 FOUR ZOAS 9   105
    [DRIVING ALL MY LOVES AWAY] . . . .   415 MY SPECTRE/N   22
    DRIVING THE HARROW IN PITY'S PATHS TWAS THEN WITH OUR DARK   493 MILTON 12   28
      FIRES
    IS GATHERD IN THE SCORCHING HEAT & IN THE DRIVING RAIN .   641 JERUSALEM 19   6
    DASHING IN PIECES SELF-RIGHTEOUSNESSES DRIVING THEM FROM   719 JERUSALEM 78   6
      ALBION'S
    IN UNPITYING RUIN DRIVING DOWN THE PYRAMIDS OF PRIDE   .   738 JERUSALEM 91   44
    IN THAT TERRIBLE DAY OF RINTRAH'S PLOW & OF SATAN'S DRIVING   740 JERUSALEM 93   10
      THE TEAM
    DRIVING OUTWARD THE BODY OF DEATH IN AN ETERNAL DEATH   745 JERUSALEM 98   20
      & RESURRECTION
    A GENIUS DRIVING AWAY "COMUS & HIS MIDNIGHT CREW"   . . .   SUPP ILLUS GRAY   *TITLE
DRIVN
    IS DRIVN YELLING TO HIS CAVES BENEATH MOUNT HECLA   . . .   3 TO WINTER/PS   16
    BY LOVE ARE DRIVN AWAY . . . .   6 MY SILKS/PS   3
    OF A HARSH TERROR DRIVN TO MADNESS BOUND TO HOLD A ROD . .   193 V DAU ALBION 5   25
    THEY STOOD WIDE APART DRIVN BY HIS HANDS . . . . . .   257 BOOK OF LOS 3   46
    DRIVN BY WAVES & ENGLOBD ON THE TIDE . . . . . .   258 BOOK OF LOS 4   58
    MELT INTO THIN AIR WHILE THE SEED DRIVN BY THE FURIOUS WIND   305 FOUR ZOAS 5   10
    HIS SPECTRE DRIVN BY THE STARRY WHEELS OF ALBION'S SONS   624 JERUSALEM 6   1
      BLACK AND
    THE SEA THE STARS THE SUN THE MOON DRIVN FORTH BY   643 JERUSALEM 21   10
      MY DISEASE
    JERUSALEM TREMBLED SEEING HER CHILDREN DRIVN BY LOS'S   663 JERUSALEM 36   21
      HAMMER
    DRIVN FORTH BY LOS TIME AFTER TIME FROM ALBION'S CLIFFY   707 JERUSALEM 69   8
      SHORE
DRIVST
    [IF THOU DRIVST ALL THE [MALES] FEMALES AWAY . . . .   272 FOUR ZOAS 1   * 276
DROGHEDA
    STAND YE UPON THE DARGLE FROM WICKLOW TO DROGHEDA   . . .   679 JERUSALEM 49   5
DRONE
    UPON THE SAND &C AND WHEN THE [FOOLISH ?CRAWLING] DRONE   110 TIRIEL 8   * 33
      . . .
DROOP
    BUT DROOP HIS TENDER WING   . . . .   124 SCHOOL BOY/SI   19
DROOPING
    AH THEN AT TIMES I DROOPING SIT   . . . .   124 SCHOOL BOY/SI   11
    DRAWING FORTH DROOPING MOTHER'S PITY DROOPING MOTHER'S   269 FOUR ZOAS 1   197
      SORROW
    DROOPING & THE BIRDS HIDE IN THEIR SILENT NESTS . . . . .   355 FOUR ZOAS 8   567
DROOPS
    HE DROOPS HIS HEAD & TREMBLING STANDS & HIS BRIGHT EYES   354 FOUR ZOAS 8   531
      DECAY
DROP
    DOTH DROP A TEAR BENEATH THE SILENT SHADE . . . . . .   10 WHEN EARLY/PS   8
    WHICH DROP LIKE FRUIT UNTO THE EARTH . . . .   14 GWIN KING/PS   103
    STOP BRAVE SIR WALTER LET ME DROP A TEAR . . . . . .   31 EDW THIRD/PS 5   49
    DESIRE STILL PINES BUT FOR ONE COOLING DROP AND TIS DENYD   41C THEN SHE BORE   PROSE
    DROP FROM THY GARMENTS AS THOU WALKEST WRAPT IN YELLOW   106 TIRIEL 5   10
      CLOUDS
    DROP THY PIPE THY HAPPY PIPE . . . .   111 INTRODUCTN/SI   9
    THEY SHALL DROP AT THE PLOW AND FAINT AT THE HARROW . . .   140 FRENCH REVOLTN   148
    WHERE THE COLD MISER SPREADS HIS GOLD OR DOES THE BRIGHT   195 V DAU ALBION 8   1
      CLOUD DROP
    AND PARCHED LIPS DROP WITH FRESH GORE NOW ROLL THOU IN   199 AMERICA 9   24
      THE CLOUDS

544

```
                                                      PAGE      TITLE          LINE
DROP    (CONTINUED)
      THE MARINERS OF BOSTON DROP THEIR ANCHORS AND UNLADE    . .  201 AMERICA 14          14
      AND ON THE BONES I DROP MY TEARS & WATER THEM IN VAIN   . .  310 FOUR ZOAS 5        197
      TO THE LAST DROP THEN HIDE ME IN THY SCARLET TABERNACLE      645 JERUSALEM 22        30
      THAT DROP WITH CRIMSON GORE WITH THE LOVES OF ALBION &       699 JERUSALEM 64        37
        CANAAN
      DROP WITH THE GORE OF THE SLAIN WHY EUPHRATES IS RED WITH    721 JERUSALEM 79        69
        BLOOD
      THEY BEG THEY INTREAT THEY DROP THEIR TEARS    . . . . .     817 HAPPINESS/L         19
      THE HEAVENS DROP WITH HUMAN GORE    . . . . . . . . .        818 HAPPINESS/L         82
DROPD
      PITYING I DROPD A TEAR    . . . . . . . .                    112 A DREAM/SI          13
      HE DROPD HIS HAMMER DIVIDING FROM HIS AKING BOSOM FLED . .   278 FOUR ZOAS 1        523
      LOS DROPD A TEAR AT HER DEPARTURE BUT HE WIPD IT AWAY IN     351 FOUR ZOAS 8        411
        HOPE
      SHE PRESD THEM TO HER BOSOM & HER PEARLY TEARS DROPD DOWN    371 FOUR ZOAS 9        524
      THE KING DROPD A TEAR INTO THE QUEEN'S EAR  . . . . . .      451 ANNO REYNOLDS        3
      HIS UNDER JAW DROPD AS THOSE EGGS HE LAID  . . . . . .       537 AND HIS LEGS/N      14
DROPPED
      A TEAR OF BLOOD DROPPED FROM EITHER EYE AGAIN HE REPOSD      341 FOUR ZOAS 8         18
      WHILE HE HAS EVERY NIGHT DROPPED INTO HIS SHOE   . . . .    586A DESC CAT 16      PROSE
      JEHOVAH DROPPED A TEAR & FOLLOWD HIM BY HIS SPIRIT  . . .  784B ANNO WW EXCUR      MARG
DROPPING
      HIS DROPPING EYES THE DITTY WAS IF HE    . . . . . .          25 EDW THIRD/PS 3     165
      LIKE LILIES DROPPING TEARS IN EACH OTHER'S BOSOM  . . . .    35D COUCH DEATH/PS   PROSE
      DROPPING A TEAR THE OLD MAN HIS PLACE LEFT AND WHEN HE       139 FRENCH REVOLTN     121
        WAS GONE OUT
      ON GOLDEN CHARIOTS RAGING WITH RED WHEELS DROPPING WITH      245 EUROPE 15           5
        BLOOD
      BUT ENITHARMON ANSWERD WITH A DROPPING TEAR & [?SMILING]     271 FOUR ZOAS 1       * 252
      . . .
      HIS LABORIOUS TASK DROPPING HIS FLAIL & CREAM BOWL  . . .  618C ILLUS MILTON     PROSE
      HER CHILDREN'S DRUID TEMPLES DROPPING WITH BLOOD WANDERD     719 JERUSALEM 78        29
        WEEPING
DROPS
      WITH CRIMSON DROPS HE STAINS THE GROUND  . . . . . . .        17 BLIND-MANS/PS      53
      O MY GOOD LORD TRUE WISDOM DROPS LIKE HONEY  . . . . . .      20 EDW THIRD/PS 2      36
      WHILE THE BLACK GORE DROPS FROM HIS HORRID JAWS  . . . .      31 EDW THIRD/PS 5      46
      WHEN THE EVENING DROPS TRICKLE DOWN  . . . . . . . . .        35D COUCH DEATH/PS   PROSE
      AND THE DROPS OF RAIN GLISTEN THE YELLOW HARVEST BREATHES    36C COUCH DEATH/PS   PROSE
      [FOR THE DROPS OF A HARLOT'S EYE]  . . . . . . . . .          186 LET BROTHELS/N      51
      IN GOLDEN WREATHES THE SORROW OF MAN & THE BALMY DROPS       293 FOUR ZOAS 3        67
        FELL DOWN
      IN GOLDEN WREATHES THE SORROW OF MAN & THE BALMY DROPS       654 JERUSALEM 29        54
        FELL DOWN
DROPSY
      IVE FOUND THE DROPSY OUT & SOON    . . . . . . . . .          51 WHEN CORRUP/IM      31
DROPT
      URIZEN DROPT A TEAR THE ETERNAL MAN DARKEND WITH SORROW      362 FOUR ZOAS 9       * 200
DROSS
      [IMAGINATION IS MY WORLD THIS WORLD OF DROSS IS BENEATH]    600C PUB ADDRESS/N    PROSE
      THE SERPENT BULK OF NATURE'S DROSS   . . . . . . . . .       749 EV GOSPEL(B)/N      53
      LIKE DROSS PURGD AWAY    . . . . . . . . . . . .             805 TO BUTTS/L          55
      MUST EVERY JOY BE DUNG & DROSS   . . . . . . . . . .         817 HAPPINESS/L         44
DROVE    SEE DRAVE
      WHEN ALMOST SINGLY HE DROVE SIX THOUSAND   . . . . . . .      21 EDW THIRD/PS 3      11
      FOR KNOWLEDGE DROVE SWEET INNOCENCE AWAY   . . . . . .       42B THEN SHE BORE    PROSE
      TO THY WIDE GATES HOW GREAT A DROVE  . . . . . . . .          56 HAIL MATRIM/IM       2
      THE SONS OF WAR ASTONISHD AT THE GLITTRING MONSTER DROVE     279 FOUR ZOAS 1       533
      WHO WOULD NOT SUFFER HIM TO APPROACH BUT DROVE HIM BACK      311 FOUR ZOAS 6         6
        WITH STORMS
      IN MENTAL FLAMES THE FLAMES REFUSD THEY DROVE HIM BACK       366 FOUR ZOAS 9       356
        TO BEULAH
      BUT THE ANGELS OF PROVIDENCE DROVE THEM AWAY   . . . . .     434 WILLIAM BOND         7
      DROVE THE FIERCE HARROW AMONG THE CONSTELLATIONS OF JEHOVAH  493 MILTON 12          25
      BEING MOST IMPURE SELF-CONDEMND TO ETERNAL TEARS HE DROVE    493 MILTON 12          47
      NAMD OLOLON ON WHOSE MILD BANKS DWELT THOSE WHO MILTON       503 MILTON 21          16
        DROVE
      ARE YOU THE FIERY CIRCLE THAT LATE DROVE IN FURY & FIRE      523 MILTON 34           3
DROVES
      TROOP BY TROOP THE BEASTIAL DROVES REND ONE ANOTHER         344 FOUR ZOAS 8       116
        SOUNDING LOUD
      WEAKEND THEY STRETCH BEYOND THEIR POWER IN DIRE DROVES       344 FOUR ZOAS 8       129
      . . .
      SAW THEM DEPART IN DISMAL DROVES THE TRUMPET SOUNDED LOUD    359 FOUR ZOAS 9        65
DROWN
      TO DROWN THE THROAT OF WAR WHEN THE SENSES   . . . . . .      33 EDW FOURTH/PS       2
      THEN LIKE A RIVER HE WOULD SEEK TO DROWN ME IN HIS WAVES     105 TIRIEL 4           54
      OF ENITHARMON BUT HER GROANS DROWN THE IMMORTAL HARPS  . .   306 FOUR ZOAS 5        25
DROWND
      AH I AM DROWND IN SHADY WOE AND VISIONARY JOY  . . . . .     238 EUROPE PREL 2      12
      DESCENDED TO THE SOUND OF INSTRUMENTS THAT DROWND THE NOISE  333 FOUR ZOAS 7B       32
      KINGS IN THEIR PALACES LIE DROWND SHEPHERDS THEIR FLOCKS     359 FOUR ZOAS 9        74
        THEIR TENTS
      HIGH SPIRES & CASTLES DROWND IN THE BLACK DELUGE SHOAL       359 FOUR ZOAS 9        76
        ON SHOAL
      DROWND IN THE WINE IS MANY A YOUTH & MAIDEN THOSE AROUND     377 FOUR ZOAS 9       745
      BUT WHEN THE CLARIONS OF DAY SOUNDED THEY DROWND            504 MILTON 21          25
        THE LAMENTATIONS
      DROWND IN THE WINE IS MANY A YOUTH & MAIDEN THOSE AROUND     513 MILTON 27           5
      IN TIME'S OCEAN FALLING DROWND   . . . . . . . . . .        771 OF GATES/GP         33
      HAIL LOCUSTS DARKNESS FIRST BORN XXX RED SEA EGYPTIANS      SUPP EXODUS/N        *PROSE
        DROWND
```

```
                                                             PAGE     TITLE        LINE
DROWNING
      SING A NEW SONG DROWNING CONFUSION IN ITS HAPPY NOTES    .   .   375 FOUR ZOAS 9     683
      DROWNING PEOPLE IS A BEAUTIFUL PERFORMANCE MR SAUNDERS   .   .   839D LETTER 38     PROSE
DROWS
      PREACH TEMPERANCE SAY HE IS OVERGORGD & DROWNS HIS WIT   .   .   323 FOUR ZOAS 7     126
      MORE HAPPY IS THE DARK CONSUMER HOPE DROWNS ALL MY TORMENT     355 FOUR ZOAS 8     544
      THE DOUBLE DRUM DROWNS HOWLS & GROANS THE SHRILL              509 MILTON 24       65
         FIFE SHRIEKS & CRIES
DRUDGE
      TO DO THE WORK OF HATE HER DRUDGE & ELF .   .   .   .   .   .   42D THEN SHE BORE  PROSE
      BUT POLICY DOTH DRUDGE FOR HATE AS WELL AS SLANDER   .   .   .   42D THEN SHE BORE  PROSE
      DRUDGE AND A MISERABLE MAN COMPELLED TO SOFTNESS BY POVERTY   583C DESC CAT 9      PROSE
DRUDGERY
      IN SORROWFUL DRUDGERY TO OBTAIN A SCANTY PITTANCE OF BREAD    337 FOUR ZOAS 7B     184
      AND SHALL PAINTING BE CONFINED TO THE SORDID DRUDGERY   .   . 576B DESC CAT 4      PROSE
      IN SORROWFUL DRUDGERY TO OBTAIN A SCANTY PITTANCE OF BREAD    700 JERUSALEM 65      26
      BUT THE MEER DRUDGERY OF BUSINESS & INTIMATIONS   .   .   . .812C LETTER 22        PROSE
      THAT YOU SHOULD YOURSELF TAKE ON YOU THE DRUDGERY   .   .   .842C LETTER 42        PROSE
      AMUSEMENT THAN HE COULD EVER BE IF EMPLOYD IN THE DRUDGERY   850B LETTER 49        PROSE
         OF
DRUDGES
      WHILE THE POOR SLAVE DRUDGES ALL DAY IN HOPE   .   .   .   .   .   26 EDW THIRD/PS 3  202
      THE CRIPPLE EVERY STEP DRUDGES & LABOURS   .   .   .   .   .   . 548 CRIPPLE EVRY/N    1
DRUID
      AMONG THE DRUID TEMPLES ALBION GROAND ON TYBURN'S BROOK       281 FOUR ZOAS 2       40
      WHILE THE PRINCE OF LIGHT ON SALISBURY PLAIN AMONG THE        281 FOUR ZOAS 2       65
         DRUID STONES
      AMONG INDEFINITE DRUID ROCKS & SNOWS OF DOUBT & REASONING     482 MILTON 3          8
      THUS THEY SING CREATING THE THREE CLASSES AMONG DRUID ROCKS   485 MILTON 5         38
      THENCE STONY DRUID TEMPLES OVERSPREAD THE ISLAND WHITE   .  . 485 MILTON 6         20
      ALL THINGS BEGIN & END IN ALBION'S ANCIENT DRUID ROCKY        486 MILTON 6         25
         SHORE
      STANDING ON ALBION'S ROCKS AMONG HIGH-REARD DRUID TEMPLES     489 MILTON 9         14
      AMONG THE ROCKS OF ALBION'S TEMPLES AND SATAN'S DRUID SONS    491 MILTON 11         7
      THESE TWELVE GODS ARE THE TWELVE SPECTRE SONS OF THE DRUID    528 MILTON 37        34
         ALBION
      OF THE DRUID MONUMENTS OR TEMPLES OF THE PAVEMENT   .   .   . 577D DESC CAT 5      PROSE
      HIGHEST ANTIQUITY ADAM WAS A DRUID AND NOAH   .   .   .   .   . 578A DESC CAT 5     PROSE
      DISTANT AMONG THE MOUNTAINS ARE DRUID TEMPLES   .   .   .   . 580D DESC CAT 5      PROSE
      SHUDDRING THEY FLEE THEY HIDE IN THE DRUID TEMPLES IN COLD    638 JERUSALEM 17      14
         CHASTITY
      ALL THINGS BEGIN & END IN ALBION'S ANCIENT DRUID ROCKY        649B JERUSALEM 27    PROSE
         SHORE
      AS THE DRUID TEMPLES WHICH ARE THE PATRIARCHAL PILLARS   .  . 649C JERUSALEM 27    PROSE
      HE STRETCHD HIS DRUID PILLARS FAR .   .   .   .   .   .   .   . 650 FIELDS FROM/J    40
      REARING THEIR DRUID PATRIARCHAL ROCKY TEMPLES AROUND HIS      658 JERUSALEM 32      14
         LIMBS
      ALL THINGS BEGIN & END IN ALBION'S ANCIENT DRUID ROCKY        658 JERUSALEM 32      15
         SHORE
      CONSTRICTING INTO DRUID ROCKS ROUND CANAAN AGAG & ARAM        685 JERUSALEM 54      26
         & PHAROH
      AMONG THE FIRES OF THE DRUID & THE DEEP BLACK RETHUNDERING    689 JERUSALEM 57       3
         WATERS
      AND THE GREAT VOICE OF THE ATLANTIC HOWLED OVER THE DRUID     689 JERUSALEM 57       5
         ALTARS
      THE CLOUDS OF ALBION'S DRUID TEMPLES RAGE IN THE EASTERN      692 JERUSALEM 60       1
         HEAVEN
      AND FLAMES AMONG THE DRUID TEMPLES & THE STARRY WHEELS   .  . 692 JERUSALEM 60       7
      WILT THOU MAKE ROME THY PATRIARCH DRUID & THE KINGS OF        695 JERUSALEM 61      50
         EUROPE HIS
      OVER THE MOUNTAINS & THE FIRES BLAZD ON DRUID ALTARS   .   . 696 JERUSALEM 62      33
      THE DRUID SONS OF ALBION & THE HEAVENS A VOID AROUND          697 JERUSALEM 63      19
         UNFATHOMABLE
      HOW CAN THE FEMALE BE CHASTE O THOU STUPID DRUID CRIED LOS    697 JERUSALEM 63      26
      HE SAW IN VALA'S HAND THE DRUID KNIFE OF REVENGE & THE        698 JERUSALEM 63      39
         POISON CUP
      HOWLING THE VICTIMS ON THE DRUID ALTARS YIELD THEIR SOULS     701 JERUSALEM 65      63
      IN THE HANDS OF ALBION'S DAUGHTERS AMONG THE DRUID TEMPLES    703 JERUSALEM 66      84
      WHICH JESUS RENDS & THE WHOLE DRUID LAW REMOVES AWAY   .   . 708 JERUSALEM 69      39
      HER CHILDREN'S DRUID TEMPLES DROPPING WITH BLOOD WANDERD      719 JERUSALEM 78      29
         WEEPING
      ALONG THE VALLEY OF DESTRUCTION AMONG THESE DRUID TEMPLES     721 JERUSALEM 79      66
      THESE CRUEL DRUID TEMPLES O VALA HUMANITY IS FAR ABOVE   .  . 721 JERUSALEM 79      73
      ALONG THE ISLAND WHITE AMONG THE DRUID TEMPLES WHILE          725 JERUSALEM 82      15
         GWENDOLEN
      FROWN OVER EACH RIVER STUPENDOUS WORKS OF ALBION'S DRUID      735 JERUSALEM 89      22
         SONS
      IN DRUID TEMPLES OVER THE WHOLE EARTH WITH VICTIMS            735 JERUSALEM 89      32
         SACRIFICE
      OF THE DRUID ALONG THE VALLEY OF REPHAIM FROM CAMBERWELL      740 JERUSALEM 92      26
         TO GOLGOTHA
      MYSTERY BABYLON THE GREAT THE DRUID DRAGON & HIDDEN HARLOT    741 JERUSALEM 93      25
      I HAVE SLAIN HIM IN MY SLEEP WITH THE KNIFE OF THE DRUID      742 JERUSALEM 94      25
         O ENGLAND
      THE DRUID SPECTRE WAS ANNIHILATE .   .   .   .   .   .   .   . 745 JERUSALEM 98       6
      OF ALBION'S SPECTRE THE PATRIARCH DRUID   .   .   .   .   .   . 746 JERUSALEM 98      48
      FOR SIN IN WAR & IN THE DRUID TEMPLES OF THE ACCUSER OF       746 JERUSALEM 98      49
         SIN BENEATH
      BY THE ROCK & OAK OF THE DRUID CREEPING MISTLETOE & THORN     781 GHOST ABEL 2      16
DRUIDICAL
      MOCKING DRUIDICAL MATHEMATICAL PROPORTION OF LENGTH BREDTH    484 MILTON 4         27
         HIGHTH
```

546

```
                                                                PAGE       TITLE          LINE
DRUIDICAL   (CONTINUED)
     ALSO ABRAHAM WAS CALLED TO SUCCEED THE DRUIDICAL AGE    .  . 578A DESC CAT 5        PROSE
DRUIDISM
     BUT YOUR GREEK PHILOSOPHY WHICH IS A REMNANT OF DRUIDISM    682A JERUSALEM 52       PROSE
DRUID'S
     WHERE THE VICTIM NIGHTLY HOWLS BENEATH THE DRUID'S KNIFE    727 JERUSALEM 83         12
DRUIDS
     THE DRUIDS THE LANDING OF JULIUS CAESAR   .   .   .   .   . . 208D SUBJCTS HIST/N  TITLE
     AMONG THE DAUGHTERS OF ALBION AMONG THE ROCKS OF            485 MILTON 5             42
        THE DRUIDS
     AMONG ALBION'S DRUIDS & BARDS IN THE CAVES BENEATH ALBION'S 489 MILTON 9              2
     WE WERE ANGELS OF THE DIVINE PRESENCE & WERE DRUIDS IN      521 MILTON 32            11
        ANNANDALE
     ABRAHAM HEBER SHEM AND NOAH WHO WERE DRUIDS    .   .   .   . 649C JERUSALEM 27      PROSE
     THIS YOU RECIEVED FROM THE DRUIDS .   .   .   .   .   .   . . 649C JERUSALEM 27      PROSE
     ALBION WAS THE PARENT OF THE DRUIDS   .   .   .   .   .   . . 649D JERUSALEM 27      PROSE
     AND THE DRUIDS GOLDEN KNIFE   .   .   .   .   .   .   .   . . 650 FIELDS FROM/J       30
     NOW GIVEN TO STONY DRUIDS AND ALLEGORIC GENERATION    .   . . 681 JERUSALEM 50        2
     JEHOVAH STOOD AMONG THE DRUIDS IN THE VALLEY OF ANNANDALE   696 JERUSALEM 63          1
     TOOK VENGEANCE TWELVE-FOLD AMONG THE CHAOTIC ROCKS OF THE   697 JERUSALEM 63          8
        DRUIDS
     WHEN THE DRUIDS DEMANDED CHASTITY FROM WOMAN & ALL WAS LOST 697 JERUSALEM 63         25
     WHERE THE DRUIDS REARD THEIR ROCKY CIRCLES .   .   .   .   . 740 JERUSALEM 92        24
DRUM
     WELL LET THE TRUMPET SOUND AND THE DRUM BEAT   .   .   .   . . 31 EDW THIRD/PS 5      62
     TO HEAR THE HORSE NEIGH TO THE DRUM AND TRUMPET .   .   . . 138 FRENCH REVOLTN      102
     . . . CAPTAINS OF FOOT STAND EACH BY HIS CLOUDY DRUM    . . 147 FRENCH REVOLTN      289
     THEN THE DRUM BEATS .   .   .   .   .   .   .   .   .   . . 147 FRENCH REVOLTN      290
     BEHIND RANK TO THE SOUL SHAKING DRUM AND SHRILL FIFE . . . 147 FRENCH REVOLTN      292
     ARISE & COME BOTH FIFE & DRUM  .   .   .   .   .   .   . . 185 LET BROTHELS/N        7
     HOW DIFFERENT FAR THE FAT FED HIRELING WITH HOLLOW DRUM    193 V DAU ALBION 5       14
     THEN AS ARMD CLOUDS ARISE TERRIFIC ROUND THE NORTHERN DRUM 204 AMERICA CANC B       18
     SOUND THE SHRILL FIFE SERPENTS OF WAR I HEAR THE NORTHERN   336 FOUR ZOAS 7B       148
        DRUM
     OF DEATH O NORTHERN DRUM AWAKE O HAND OF IRON SOUND    .  . 336 FOUR ZOAS 7B       154
     THE NORTHERN DRUM NOW GIVE THE CHARGE BRAVELY OBSCURD   .  . 337 FOUR ZOAS 7B       155
     AND LET THE THUNDRING DRUM SPEED ON THE ARROWS BLACK   .  . 337 FOUR ZOAS 7B  *    158
     OF FLUTE & HARP & DRUM & TRUMPET HORN & CLARION    .   .  . 372 FOUR ZOAS 9        586
     THE DOUBLE DRUM DROWNS HOWLS & GROANS THE SHRILL           509 MILTON 24           65
        FIFE SHRIEKS & CRIES
DRUNK
     THE GOD OF WAR IS DRUNK WITH BLOOD   .   .   .   .   .   . . 13 GWIN KING/PS         93
     THIS EVENING [ WE'D ] WE'LL ALL GET DRUNK I SAY DASH AN ANTHEM 54B ISLAND MOON 9  *PROSE
     FATTEND ON HUMAN BLOOD & DRUNK WITH WINE OF LIFE IS BETTER  274 FOUR ZOAS 1        389
        FAR
     WE HAVE DRUNK UP THE [ (ANCIENT) ] ETERNAL MAN BY OUR       298 FOUR ZOAS 4   *     36
        UNBOUNDED POWER
     DANCE ON THE RIVERS & THE ROCKS HOWLING & DRUNK WITH FURY   320 FOUR ZOAS 7         13
     DRUNK WITH THE SMOKING GORE & RED BUT NOT WITH NOURISHING   360 FOUR ZOAS 9        122
        WINE
     ART THOU SHE THAT MADE THE NATIONS DRUNK WITH THE CUP OF    374 FOUR ZOAS 9        658
        RELIGION
     AS HE AROSE FROM THE BRIGHT FEAST DRUNK WITH THE WINE OF    376 FOUR ZOAS 9        710
        AGES
     LAUGHING & SHOUTING DRUNK WITH ODORS MANY FALL OERWEARIED   377 FOUR ZOAS 9        744
     SAID TO HIM IS YOUR COMRADE DRUNK A PROOF THAT HE    .   . . 438D BLAKES MEMORAN  PROSE
     BEHELD THE SIGNAL THEY IN SILENCE STOOD THO DRUNK WITH WINE 488 MILTON 8           13
     DRUNK WITH THE SPIRIT BURNING ROUND THE COUCH OF DEATH      502 MILTON 20          44
        THEY STOOD
     LAUGHING & SHOUTING DRUNK WITH ODOURS MANY FALL OERWEARIED  513 MILTON 27           4
     AROUND THE WINE-PRESSES OF LUVAH NAKED & DRUNK WITH WINE    513 MILTON 27          24
     WERE NOT THE WORK OF SKETCHERS DRUNK WITH WINE    .   .   . . 542 FLORENTINE/N      27
     AND WHEN THEY ARE DRUNK THEY ALWAYS PANT BEST  .   .   .  . 549 ALL PICTURES/N *    4
     NAKED & DRUNK WITH BLOOD GWENDOLEN DANCING TO THE TIMBREL   689 JERUSALEM 58         2
     RED RUN THE STREAMS OF ALBION THAMES IS DRUNK WITH BLOOD    703 JERUSALEM 66        61
     THE HUMBER & THE SEVERN ARE DRUNK WITH THE BLOOD OF THE     703 JERUSALEM 66        63
        SLAIN
     HER PANTING VICTIM BESIDE HER HER HEART IS DRUNK WITH BLOOD 705 JERUSALEM 68        12
     THO HER BRAIN IS NOT DRUNK WITH WINE SHE GOES FORTH FROM    705 JERUSALEM 68        13
        ALBION
     TO THE PLACE OF THE AMALEKITE I AM DRUNK WITH UNSATIATED    707 JERUSALEM 68        62
        LOVE
     IN TERRIBLE CONVULSIONS PITYING & GRATIFIED DRUNK WITH PITY 723 JERUSALEM 80        70
     MADNESS FOR I AM REALLY DRUNK WITH INTELLECTUAL VISION  .  . 852C LETTER 50        PROSE
DRUNKEN
     DRUNKEN WITH WOE FORGOTTEN AND SHUT UP FROM COLD DESPAIR    192 V DAU ALBION 4       2
     [ ALIGHTING DOWN FROM ] ALIGHTING IN HIS DRUNKEN JOY   .  . 266 FOUR ZOAS 1   *    93
     AND DRUNKEN WITH THE IMMORTAL DRAUGHT FELL FROM MY THRONE   311 FOUR ZOAS 5        237
        SUBLIME
     WITH LUST & MURDER FOR OUR DRINK THE DRUNKEN RAVEN SHALL    334 FOUR ZOAS 7B        47
        WANDER
     THE SERVANTS OF THE MILLS DRUNKEN WITH WINE AND DANCING     488 MILTON 8            8
        WILD
     INDEED A HARLOT DRUNKEN WITH THE SACRIFICE OF IDOLS DOES HE 695 JERUSALEM 61        38
     THE SUN FORGETS HIS COURSE LIKE A DRUNKEN MAN HE HESITATES  703 JERUSALEM 66        74
DRUNKENNESS
     BY ENTERING INTO DISEASE AND EXCREMENT DRUNKENNESS   .   . . 582A DESC CAT 8        PROSE
     TO ME WHILE DRUNKENNESS LEWDNESS GLUTTONY & EVEN  .   .   . . 812C LETTER 22        PROSE
DRY
     HAD PUMPD INFLAMMABLE GASS QUITE DRY THEY  .   .   .   .  . . 59A ISLAND MOON 11    PROSE
     IT IS NOT THE EXUBERANCE OF BEAUTY SO IF RAFAEL IS HARD     81D ANNO LAVATER        MARG
        & DRY
```

		PAGE	TITLE	LINE

DRY   (CONTINUED)

THE SERPENTS SPRUNG FROM HER OWN BOWELS HAVE DRAIND HER DRY AS THIS . . . . 100 TIRIEL 1 . . . 32

THY CROWN IS BALD OLD MAN THE SUN WILL DRY THY BRAINS AWAY . . . 109 TIRIEL 7 . . . 12

SPREADING THEM OUT BEFORE THE SUN LIKE STALKS OF FLAX TO DRY . . . 265 FOUR ZOAS 1 . . . 48

I BROUGHT HER THRO THE WILDERNESS A DRY & THIRSTY LAND . . 282 FOUR ZOAS 2 . . . 87

THEY SHRUNK INTO THEIR CHANNELS DRY THE ROCKY STRAND BENEATH HIS FEET . . . 312 FOUR ZOAS 6 . . . 22

BUT THOU SHALT STILL SURVIVE ARISE O DRY THY DEWY TEARS . . . 368 FOUR ZOAS 9 . . . 421

HIS EYE WAS DRY NO TEAR COULD FLOW . . . . 419 I SAW A MONK/N . . . 23

[FROM HIS DRY TONGUE THESE ACCENTS FLOW] . . . . 419 I SAW A MONK/N * . . 25

HIS EYE WAS DRY NO TEAR COULD FLOW . . . . 430 GREY MONK . . . 9

OLD HARD STIFF & DRY UNFINISHD WORKS OF ART . . . 449C ANNO REYNOLDS . MARG

WITH THANKS & COMPLIMENTS ARE QUITE DRAWN DRY . . . . 549 H PICK THANK/N . . 2

ETERNITY LOOKD UPON AS DEFORMITY & LOVELINESS AS A DRY TREE . . . 628 JERUSALEM 9 . . . 8

SPREADING THEM OUT BEFORE THE SUN LIKE STALKS OF FLAX TO DRY . . . 645 JERUSALEM 22 . . . 21

AT GETS WET & DRY AS THE WEATHER GETS SO . . . . . . 816B LETTER 23 . . PROSE

DRYD

THE BONES OF DEATH THE COVRING CLAY THE SINEWS SHRUNK & DRYD . . . 198 AMERICA 6 . . . 3

CROUCH HOWLING BEFORE THEIR CAVERNS DEEP LIKE SKINS DRYD IN THE WIND . . . 199 AMERICA 9 . . . 4

DRYDEN

DRYDEN IN RHYME CRIES MILTON ONLY PLANND . . . . . . 554 BLAKES APL/N 1 . . 1

DRYDEN IN RHYME CRIES MILTON ONLY PLANND . . . . . . 555 BLAKES APL/N 2 . . 5

WHILE THE WORKS [OF TRANSLATORS] OF POPE & DRYDEN ARE LOOKD 595A PUB ADDRESS/N *PROSE

DRYDEN IN RHYME CRIES MILTON ONLY PLANND . . . . . 595 BLAKES APOL/PA * . 1

OF MILTON & DRYDEN AS THEY ARE WRITTEN IN A POEM SIGNED 600D PUB ADDRESS/N . PROSE

& DRYDEN HAS FINISHD IT NOW LET DRYDEN'S FALL & . . . . 600D PUB ADDRESS/N . PROSE

NIGGLING & POCO PEN AS DRYDEN HAS DEGRADED MILTON WITH . 600D PUB ADDRESS/N . PROSE

STUPIDITY WILL PREFER DRYDEN BECAUSE IT IS IN RHYME . . 600D PUB ADDRESS/N . PROSE

I DO NOT CONDEMN POPE OR DRYDEN BECAUSE THEY DID NOT . . 602D PUB ADDR AD/N . PROSE

"AT LENGTH FOR HATCHING RIPE HE BREAKS THE SHELL" DRYDEN SUPP LEGEND/N68 . *

DRYDEN'S

I WOULD TRY MY OWN & OPEND THE FOLLOWING...DRYDEN'S VIRGIL 441B MEMORANDUM/N 5 . PROSE

& DRYDEN HAS FINISHD IT NOW LET DRYDEN'S FALL & . . . . 600D PUB ADDRESS/N . PROSE

DUBIOUS

TELL HIM TO BE NO MORE DUBIOUS DEMAND EXPLICIT WORDS . . 640 JERUSALEM 17 . . 60

DUBLIN

EASTMEATH WESTMEATH DUBLIN KILDARE KINGS COUNTY . . . . 711 JERUSALEM 72 . . 19

DU CROWE

CATALANI DU CROWE & DILBURY DOODLE . . . . 548B ON GREAT ENC/N . TITLE

DUE

DARKEND & LOST IN DUE TIME ISSUING FORTH FROM ENION'S WOMB 327 FOUR ZOAS 7 . . 294

THE ENCOURAGEMENT WHICH IS MY DUE . . . . 600C PUB ADDRESS/N . PROSE

GIVE US THE BREAD THAT IS OUR DUE & RIGHT . . . . . 788A ANNO THORNTON . MARG

ALL YOUR WISHES SHALL IN DUE TIME BE FULFILLED . . . . 797C LETTER 10 . . PROSE

INTREAT YOU TO TAKE DUE CARE OF BOTH IT IS A PART OF OUR DUTY . . 811C LETTER 22 . . PROSE

TO GOD & MAN TO TAKE DUE CARE OF HIS GIFTS & . . . . 811C LETTER 22 . . PROSE

SHALL IN DUE TIME BE FULFILLED . . . . 811D LETTER 22 . . PROSE

BECAUSE I GIVE HAYLEY HIS DUE RESPECT . . . . . . 817 HAPPINESS/L . . 46

LAST REQUESTING TEN POUNDS I THOUGHT IT WAS DUE ON . 854D LETTER 53 . . PROSE

BALANCE DUE FROM ME PREVIOUS TO MY GOING TO FELPHAM . . SUPP LETTER 56A . *PROSE

DUG

AND NARROW AS A GRAVE DUG FOR A CHILD . . . . . . 136 FRENCH REVOLTN . 40

[THEY] HE DUG MOUNTAINS & HILLS IN VAST STRENGTH . . . 225 URIZEN 5 . * . 22

THEY DUG THE CHANNELS FOR THE RIVERS & THEY POURD ABROAD 286 FOUR ZOAS 2 . . 250

DUKE

AH WOMAN'S FEAR SHE CRYD AH CURSED DUKE . . . . . . 5 FAIR ELENOR/PS . 39

WAS REFT OF LIFE BY THE ACCURSED DUKE . . . . . . 5 FAIR ELENOR/PS . 63

O ELENOR BEWARE THE CURSED DUKE . . . . 6 FAIR ELENOR/PS . 65

DUKE OF CLARENCE SIR JOHN CHANDOS SIR THOMAS DAGWORTH . 17C EDW THIRD/PS . TITLE

SCENE ENGLISH COURT LIONEL DUKE OF CLARENCE . . . 19A EDW THIRD/PS 2 . PROSE

GOD BLESS THE DUKE & HIS ALDERMEN ALL . . . . . . 55 CRY MATCHES/IM * . 2

THEN THE ANCIENTEST PEER DUKE OF BURGUNDY . . . . . 138 FRENCH REVOLTN . 83

THE FIERCE DUKE HUNG OVER THE COUNCIL . . . . . . 138 FRENCH REVOLTN . 87

UP ROSE AWFUL IN HIS MAJESTIC BEAMS BOURBON'S STRONG DUKE . . . 141 FRENCH REVOLTN . 168

. . . THE DUKE OF BRETAGNE AND THE EARL OF BORGOGNE . . 141 FRENCH REVOLTN . 169

. . . THE STRONG DUKE HIS SWORD TO ITS GOLDEN SCABBARD RETURND . . . 143 FRENCH REVOLTN . 195

. . . THE DUKE OF BURGUNDY DELIVERS THE KING'S COMMAND . 145 FRENCH REVOLTN . 247

DULL

("PROOFS OF DULL FRIGIDITY HARDNESS OR...EGOTISM") RATHER UNEASY . . . 70C ANNO LAVATER . MARG

("AND A DULL SPIRIT AT ONCE ") PITY THE JEALOUS . . . 75B ANNO LAVATER . MARG

TO DO OTHER THAN REPEAT THE SAME DULL ROUND OVER AGAIN . 97B NAT RELIGION 1 . PROSE

THE SAME DULL ROUND EVEN OF A UNIVERSE . . . . . 97D NAT RELIGION 2 . PROSE

THE LUNGS HEAVE INCESSANT DULL AND HEAVY . . . . . 258 BOOK OF LOS 4 . 54

WERE HEAVY & DULL & THEIR EYES & NOSTRILS CLOSED UP . . 315 FOUR ZOAS 6 . 125

FOR HIS FRAIL EYES WERE FADED & HIS EARS HEAVY & DULL . 326 FOUR ZOAS 7 . 250

[HE] FELT THE FEMALE DEATH A DULL & NUMMING STUPOR SUCH AS NEER . . . 352 FOUR ZOAS 8 . 416

DRINK IN THE DEADLY DULL DELUSION HORRORS OF ETERNAL DEATH 352 FOUR ZOAS 8 . 418

BUT THOU ART STILL HEAVY AND DULL AWAKE ALBION AWAKE . 506 MILTON 23 . . 5

IT WOULD HAVE BEEN AS DULL AS HIS ADVERSARY'S . . . . 576C DESC CAT 4 . *PROSE

SO AS IT ALWAYS HAPPENS AND NOT IN THAT DULL WAY THAT SOME 578D DESC CAT 5 . PROSE

A DULL ROUND OF PROBABILITIES AND POSSIBILITIES . . . 578D DESC CAT 5 . PROSE

```
                                                      PAGE      TITLE           LINE
DULL    (CONTINUED)
     DULL NIGHT STARTS FROM HIS WATCH TOWER ON A CLOUD   . . . 618A ILLUS MILTON     PROSE
DULLD
     MAY BE DULLD AND THE NOSTRILS CLOSD UP  . . . . . .  247 SONG OF LOS 7        6
DULWICH
     THE SCENE OF MR S'S (STOTHARD'S) PICTURE IS BY DULWICH HILLS 575B DESC CAT 3   PROSE
DULY
     TILL TIMES & SPACES HAVE PASSD OVER HIM DULY EVERY MORN   374 FOUR ZOAS 9      633
DUMB
     LIKE A DUMB STATUE FROZE TO STONE WITH FEAR    . . . . .    4 FAIR ELENOR/PS    20
     THEIR ELOQUENT TONGUES WERE DUMB  . . . . . . . . . .  105 TIRIEL 4            47
     DESOLATE LOATHED DUMB [CON] ASTONISHD WAITING FOR BLACK    107 TIRIEL 5     *  35
        DEATH
     BUT DUMB TILL THAT DREAD DAY WHEN ORC ASSAYD HIS FIERCE    196 AMERICA PREL 1   10
        EMBRACE
     SHUT UP IN STIFLING OBSTRUCTION ROOTED IN DUMB DESPAIR  . . 318 FOUR ZOAS 6    269
     IN THIS MANNER HE HAS JUMBLED HIS DUMB DOLLIES TOGETHER   574B DESC CAT 3     PROSE
     ALBION'S MELANCHOLY WHO MUST ELSE HAVE BEEN A DUMB DESPAIR  668 JERUSALEM 40    60
     BUT HE HEALS THE DEAF & THE DUMB & THE BLIND   . . . . .  755 EV GOSPEL(E)/N    88
DUMBARTN
     ISSACHAR SELKIRK DUMBARTN GLASGO ZEBULUN ORKNEY SHETLAND   638 JERUSALEM 16     57
        SKYE
DUMBNESS
     FORGETFULNESS DUMBNESS NECESSITY  . . . . . . . . . .  228 URIZEN 10           24
     A DOLOROUS GROAN THAT STRUCK WITH DUMBNESS ALL CONFUSION   295 FOUR ZOAS 3     147
     FORGETFULNESS DUMBNESS NECESSITY IN CHAINS OF THE MIND    303 FOUR ZOAS 4      211
        LOCKD UP
DUMFRIES
     LEVI EDINBURH ROXBRO ROSS JUDAH ABRDEEN BERWIK DUMFRIES    638 JERUSALEM 16  *  54
DUN
     AND THE LION GLARES THRO THE DUN FOREST  . . . . . . .    3 EVNING STAR/PS     12
DUNCE
     TRULY MY SATAN THOU ART BUT A DUNCE  . . . . . . . .  771 EPILOGUE/GP           1
DUNG
     I THEN ASKED EZEKIEL WHY HE EAT DUNG & LAY SO LONG ON HIS 154A MARRIAGE HH 12  PROSE
     LIKE TO DUNG UPON THE GROUND  . . . . . . . . . . .  169 MIRTLE SHADE/N        5
     [LIKE TO DUNG UPON THE GROUND]  . . . . . . . . . .  176 TO MY MIRTLE/N        7
     AND LUVAH WAS PUT FOR DUNG ON THE GROUND . . . . . .  378 FOUR ZOAS 9         791
     MUST EVERY JOY BE DUNG & DROSS  . . . . . . . . . .  817 HAPPINESS/L           44
DUNGEON
     DUNGEON THOU ART PREPARING FOR THYSELF TO ALL ETERNITY  . . 155C MARRIAGE HH 17 PROSE
     AND MUTTER ACROSS THE OCEAN FRANCE REND DOWN THY DUNGEON   159A SONG LIBERTY   PROSE
     FOR THE LINKS OF A DUNGEON FLOOR  . . . . . . . . .  186 LET BROTHELS/N        49
     [FOR THE LINKS OF A DUNGEON FLOOR]  . . . . . . . .  186 LET BROTHELS/N        55
     FOR THE LINKS OF A DUNGEON FLOOR  . . . . . . . . .  186 LET BROTHELS/N        67
     RISE AND LOOK OUT HIS CHAINS ARE LOOSE HIS DUNGEON DOORS   198 AMERICA 6        10
        ARE OPEN
     RISE & LOOK OUT HIS CHAINS ARE LOOSE HIS DUNGEON DOORS    375 FOUR ZOAS 9      674
        ARE OPEN
     THE PRISONER IN THE STONE DUNGEON & THE SLAVE AT THE MILL  499 MILTON 18        11
     OIL BECAME A FETTER TO GENIUS AND A DUNGEON TO ART BUT ONE 566C DESC CAT 2    PROSE
     THE DISTANT FOREST THEN THE SLAVE GROANS IN THE DUNGEON    642 JERUSALEM 20     15
        OF STONE
     MY WEARY EYES EVEN IN THIS DUNGEON & THIS IRON MILL  . . . 693 JERUSALEM 60     59
DUNGEON-LIKE
     THE DUNGEON-LIKE HEAVEN DIVIDING  . . . . . . . . .  235 URIZEN 25             12
DUNGEONS
     BINDING JERUSALEM'S CHILDREN IN THE DUNGEONS OF BABYLON    281 FOUR ZOAS 2      63
     THE HORRID SHAPES & SIGHTS OF TORMENT IN BURNING DUNGEONS  314 FOUR ZOAS 6     103
        & IN
     IN CHAINS OF IRON & IN DUNGEONS CIRCLED WITH CEASELESS    377 FOUR ZOAS 9      750
        FIRES
     IN CHAINS OF IRON & IN DUNGEONS CIRCLED WITH CEASELESS    514 MILTON 27         32
        FIRES
     BUT JERUSALEM FAINTLY SAW HIM CLOSD IN THE DUNGEONS OF    693 JERUSALEM 60      39
        BABYLON
     THE DUNGEONS BURST & THE PRISONERS SET FREE    . . . . .  718 STOOD AMONG/J     35
     AND IN DEPTHS OF MY DUNGEONS  . . . . . . . . . . .  771 OF GATES/GP           37
DUNG HILL
     NOT AS YOU MISTAKENLY CALL IT DUNG HILL  . . . . . . . 812B LETTER 22         PROSE
DUPLICATES
     DUPLICATES TO OTHERS WHICH HE HAS THEY ARE INTIRELY AT  . . 877B LETTER 86     PROSE
DURA
     RESTING IN A CIRCLE IN MALDEN OR IN STRATHNESS OR DURA  . . 737 JERUSALEM 90    62
DURANCE
     AND TIMES A NIGHT OF VAST DURANCE  . . . . . . . . .  257 BOOK OF LOS 4        13
DURER
     FIRST PAINTERS OF HIS AGE ALBERT DURER IS NOT WOULD HAVE  461A ANNO REYNOLDS   MARG
        BEEN
     & CONTEMPT OF ALB DURER  . . . . . . . . . . . . .  472B ANNO REYNOLDS       MARG
     AS IT WAS LEFT US BY RAPHAEL AND ALBERT DURER MICHAEL     562B DESC CAT ADV    PROSE
        ANGELO
     RAFAEL AND ALBERT DURER MICHAEL ANGELO AND JULIO ROMANO   564A DESC CAT        PROSE
     RAFAEL AND MICHAEL ANGELO AND ALBERT DURER ARE KNOWN BY   585B DESC CAT 15     PROSE
        THIS
     COPPER PLATES OF ALBERT DURER LUCAS HISBEN ALDEGRAVE AND   586D CHAUCER 1      PROSE
        THE
     MARC ANTONIO & ALBERT DURER YE MUST BEGIN BEFORE  . . . . 593C PUB ADDRESS/N   PROSE
     OR JULIO ROMANO OR ALB DURER BUT I DO PRETEND TO  . . . . 594C PUB ADDRESS/N   PROSE
     THAN ALB DURER GOLTZIUS SADELER OR EDELINCK BUT          594C PUB ADDRESS/N    PROSE
        I DO PRETEND
     AS THE SAME ART WITH THOSE OF RAFAEL & ALBERT DURER  . . . 595B PUB ADDRESS/N  PROSE
```

549

```
                                                          PAGE      TITLE            LINE
DURER    (CONTINUED)
    IT IS NOT SO WITH RAFAEL JULIO (ROMANO) ALB D(DURER)    .  . 598D PUB ADDRESS/N    PROSE
    RAFAEL MICH ANG ALB D(DURER) JUL R(ROMANO) ARE    .  .  .  . 599A PUB ADDRESS/N    PROSE
    OF ART SUCH AS MICHAEL ANGELO RAFAEL JUL R(ROMANO) ALB      600B PUB ADDRESS/N    PROSE
        DURER LEFT IT
    [ALBERT DURER WOULD NEVER HAVE GOT HIS MANNERS FROM THE     SUPP ANNO REYNOLDS   * MARG
        NOBILITY]
DURER'S
    STYLE OF ALB DURER'S (HISTORIES) & THE OLD ENGRAVERS    .  . 592B PUB ADDRESS/N   *PROSE
DURHAM
    YORK EDINBURGH DURHAM & CARLISLE & ON THE FRONT    .  .  .   531 MILTON 39             43
    AND CUMBERLAND NORTHUMBERLAND WESTMORELAND & DURHAM ARE      637 JERUSALEM 16          50
    LINCOLN DURHAM & CARLISLE COUNCELLORS OF LOS   .  .  .  .  . 676 JERUSALEM 46           5
    BRERTUN HAD YORKSHIRE DURHAM WESTMORELAND & HIS EMANATION    710 JERUSALEM 71          32
DURING    SEE EVER DURING
    PAINTING & ENGRAVING & DURING A PERIOD OF FORTY YEARS    .  587D CHAUCER/N        PROSE
DURNESS
    CAITHNESS & ROCKY DURNESS PENTLAND & JOHN GROATS HOUSE  .  . 512 MILTON 26             15
DURST
    WHO DURST T OPPOSE BUT SHAME OPPOSING FIERCE   .  .  .  .  .  42C THEN SHE BORE   PROSE
DUSK
    AND WASH THE DUSK WITH SILVER SOON FULL SOON   .  .  .  .  .   3 EVNING STAR/PS        10
DUSKY
    WHEN EVENING SITS BENEATH HER DUSKY BOWR   .  .  .  .  .  .   10 WHEN EARLY/PS          3
    ON DUSKY WING BREATHING FORTH CLAMOUR & DESTRUCTION   .  .   42D THEN SHE BORE   PROSE
    A WORM OF SIXTY WINTERS CREEPING ON THE DUSKY GROUND   .  . 110 TIRIEL 8               24
    . . . MOVE ALONG THE DUSKY ROAD TO VERSAILLES THERE   .  .  145 FRENCH REVOLTN        251
    . . . AND GLEAMS A DUSKY BEAM   .  .  .  .  .  .  .  .  .  . 146 FRENCH REVOLTN        270
    FOLLOWD BEHIND HIM AS THE WEB OF A SPIDER DUSKY & COLD   .  318 FOUR ZOAS 6           244
    AND FLAMES OF DUSKY FIRE TO AMALEK CANAAN AND MOAB   .  .   723 JERUSALEM 80           50
    THUS JOYD THE SPECTRE IN THE DUSKY FIRES OF LOS'S FORGE     734 JERUSALEM 88           44
        EYEING
DUST
    PULL DOWN THE TYRANT TO THE DUST   .  .  .  .  .  .  .  .  .  12 GWIN KING/PS          29
    AND DUST ASCENDS THE SKIES   .  .  .  .  .  .  .  .  .  .  .  13 GWIN KING/PS          72
    BUT AS DUST MAINTAIN THY SERVANT'S RIGHT   .  .  .  .  .  .   17 EDW THIRD/PS 1         2
    A CROWN OF GLORY BUT FROM THY VERY DUST   .  .  .  .  .  .   18 EDW THIRD/PS 1         23
    IN EARTH COVERD WITH STONES AND DEATHY DUST   .  .  .  .  .   30 EDW THIRD/PS 5        14
    IF I LAY MY FACE IN THE DUST THE GRAVE OPENS ITS MOUTH       36A COUCH DEATH/PS  PROSE
        FOR ME
    THEIR HELMED YOUTH AND AGED WARRIORS IN DUST TOGETHER        37D SAMSON/PS       PROSE
        LY(LIE)
    A DAY LIKE THIS LAID ELFRID IN THE DUST   .  .  .  .  .  .   43C WOE CRIED MUSE  PROSE
    . . . ROUND THEM THEIR COUNSELLORS LOOK UP FROM THE DUST    137 FRENCH REVOLTN         73
    LET US HIDE LET US HIDE IN THE DUST   .  .  .  .  .  .  .   137 FRENCH REVOLTN         78
    AND WHEN HE BID THEM SHAKE OFF THE DUST OF THEIR FEET   .  158C MARRIAGE HH 22   PROSE
    STAMPS THE STONY LAW TO DUST   .  .  .  .  .  .  .  .  .  . 160A SONG LIBERTY     PROSE
    [XXX] SHAKING THE DUST FROM HIS IMMORTAL PINIONS TO AWAKE   190 V DAU ALBION 2  *     27
    THAT STONY LAW I STAMP TO DUST AND SCATTER RELIGION ABROAD  198 AMERICA 8               5
    THE WORLD WHERE EVERY PARTICLE OF DUST BREATHES FORTH ITS   237 EUROPE INTRO           18
        JOY
    FORTH FROM THE DEAD DUST RATTLING BONES TO BONES   .  .  .  248 SONG OF LOS 7          31
    HURLS APART STAMPING FURIOUS TO DUST   .  .  .  .  .  .  .  257 BOOK OF LOS 4          20
    . . . & THE DUST FROM THY WHITE GARMENTS   .  .  .  .  .  . 338 FOUR ZOAS 7B          195
    MARROWLESS BLOODLESS FALLING INTO DUST DRIVEN BY THE WINDS  354 FOUR ZOAS 8           518
    EACH SPECK OF DUST TO THE EARTH'S CENTER NESTLES ROUND      363 FOUR ZOAS 9           233
        & ROUND
    HIDING HIS FACE IN THE DUST BENEATH [A] THE PRISONER'S      364 FOUR ZOAS 9      *    269
        FEET & SAYING
    THE CLOUDS FALL OFF FROM MY WET BROW THE DUST FROM MY       373 FOUR ZOAS 9           597
        COLD LIMBS
    HER GREAT MEN HOWL & THROW THE DUST & REND THEIR HOARY HAIR 375 FOUR ZOAS 9           663
    O HOW CAN I WITH MY GROSS TONGUE THAT CLEAVETH TO THE DUST  502 MILTON 20             15
    ONE HAIR NOR PARTICLE OF DUST NOT ONE CAN PASS AWAY   .  .  634 JERUSALEM 14           1
    HIS GIANT BEAUTY AND PERFECTION FALLEN INTO DUST   .  .  .  641 JERUSALEM 19           8
    LONDON IS A STONE OF HER RUINS OXFORD IS THE DUST OF HER    653 JERUSALEM 29          19
        WALLS
    THE NATIONS ARE HER DUST GROUND BY THE CHARIOT WHEELS   .  653 JERUSALEM 29          23
    OF HER LORDLY CONQUERORS HER PALACES LEVELLD WITH THE DUST  653 JERUSALEM 29          24
    CONSIDER SEXUAL ORGANIZATION & HIDE THEE IN THE DUST   .  . 661 JERUSALEM 34          58
    IN WHOSE SIGHT ALL ARE AS THE DUST . . .  .  .  .  .  .  .  679 JERUSALEM 49          31
    THEN AS THE MOSS UPON THE TREE OR DUST UPON THE PLOW   .  . 687 JERUSALEM 55          39
    TO BE POUNDED TO DUST & MELTED IN THE FURNACES OF           687 JERUSALEM 55          59
        AFFLICTION
    . . . & THE DUST FROM THY WHITE GARMENTS   .  .  .  .  .  . 700 JERUSALEM 65          41
    THE HILL OF GIANTS ALL HER FOUNDATIONS LEVELLD WITH THE     719 JERUSALEM 78          22
        DUST
    OF SAND & HIS PILLARS DUST ON THE FLY'S WING & HIS STARRY   739 JERUSALEM 91          49
    YOU SHALL LICK THE DUST FOR MEAT   .  .  .  .  .  .  .  .  . 755 EV GOSPEL(E)/N        54
    FOR DUST & CLAY IS THE SERPENT'S MEAT   .  .  .  .  .  .  . 755 EV GOSPEL(E)/N        95
DUSTY
    THY GOLDEN ROD THROWN ON THE DUSTY FLOOR   .  .  .  .  .  .  15 IMIT SPEN/PS          29
DUTCH
    [IN ROME (?WAS NOT) CAESAR (A) DUTCH PAINTER]   .  .  .  . SUPP ANNO REYNOLDS   * MARG
    THE FLORENTINES SAID TIS A DUTCH ENGLISH BORE   .  .  .  . 542 FLORENTINE/N          13
    IT WILL SET HIS DUTCH FRIENDS ALL IN A ROAR   .  .  .  .  . 542 FLORENTINE/N          24
    IT IS A COPY FROM A DUTCH PICTURE DUTCH BOOR SMOKING   .  843C LETTER 43        PROSE
DUTIES
    HOW SHOULD HE HE KNOW THE DUTIES OF ANOTHER O FOOLISH      487 MILTON 7              30
        FORBEARANCE
    MY EXHIBITION AS THE GREATEST OF DUTIES TO MY COUNTRY   . 561C EXHIBITION ADV   PROSE
    MUST THE DUTIES OF LIFE EACH OTHER CROSS   .  .  .  .  .  . 817 HAPPINESS/L           43
```

		PAGE	TITLE	LINE

DUTIES   (CONTINUED)
PRAY GIVE MY & MY WIFE'S DUTIES TO MISS POOLE ACCEPT THEM   834A LETTER 33   PROSE
DUTY
THIS IS MY PRIVATE DUTY AND MY PLEASURE . . . . . .   19 EDW THIRD/PS 2   27
TIS THE BEST POLICY AND TIS OUR DUTY . . . .   26 EDW THIRD/PS 3   218
AND MAY OUR DUTY CHANDOS BE OUR PLEASURE . . . . . .   26 EDW THIRD/PS 3   219
LET THE MEN DO THEIR DUTY & THE WOMEN WILL BE SUCH WONDERS   82C ANNO LAVATER   MARG
HE WHO HINDERS ANOTHER OMITS HIS OWN DUTY AT THE SAME TIME   88D ANNO LAVATER   MARG
SO IF ALL DO THEIR DUTY THEY NEED NOT FEAR HARM . . . .   118 CHIMNEY SWP/SI   24
AND STERN DEMANDS OF RIGHT & DUTY INSTEAD OF LIBERTY . .   265 FOUR ZOAS 1   37
SO SHALL (?YOU) GOVERN OVER ALL LET MORAL DUTY TUNE YOUR   323 FOUR ZOAS 7   * 111
  TONGUE
DUTY TO HIS COUNTRY IS THE FIRST CONSIDERATION & SAFETY   383C ANNO WATSON   MARG
  THE LAST
THE CONSIDERATION OF THESE THINGS IS THE WHOLE DUTY OF MAN   383C ANNO WATSON   MARG
DOES NOT KNOW EITHER HIS OWN INTEREST OR HIS DUTY . . .   452C ANNO REYNOLDS   MARG
WHO SET PLEASURE AGAINST DUTY WHO CREATE OLYMPIC CROWNS   511 MILTON 25   51
THE GUARD ARE ANGELS OF PROVIDENCE ON DUTY EVERMORE . .   516 MILTON 28   61
FROM DOING MY DUTY TO MY ART . . . .   561A EXHIBITION ADV   PROSE
BECOME A DUTY WHICH MR B(BLAKE) OWES TO THE PUBLIC . .   573A DESC CAT 3   PROSE
THE BEAUTIFUL MAN ACTS FROM DUTY AND ANXIOUS SOLICITUDE   580B DESC CAT 5   PROSE
ENGLAND EXPECTS THAT EVERY MAN SHOULD DO HIS DUTY . .   584C DESC CAT 14   PROSE
I ACCOUNT IT A PUBLIC DUTY RESPECTFULLY TO ADDRESS MYSELF   591C PUB ADDRESS/N PROSE
WITH [DUTY &] RESPECTFUL DUTY [&] REQUESTING . . . .   601B PUB ADDRESS/N *PROSE
[MR B(BLAKE) THINKS IT HIS DUTY TO CAUTION THE PUBLIC]   601C PUB ADDRESS/N PROSE
[&] TO THIS I SUBSCRIBE MY NAME AS A PUBLIC DUTY WILLIAM   602B PUB ADDRESS/N *PROSE
  BLAKE
AND STERN DEMANDS OF RIGHT & DUTY INSTEAD OF LIBERTY . .   645 JERUSALEM 22   11
IF WE DO BUT OUR DUTY LABOUR WELL THE TEEMING EARTH . . .   687 JERUSALEM 55   53
EVERY PLEASURE THAT INTERMINGLES WITH THE DUTY OF   716D JERUSALEM 77   PROSE
  OUR STATION
OBEDIENCE IS A DUTY THEN . . . .   748 EV GOSPEL(B)/N   11
I NEGLECT MY DUTY TO MY FRIENDS BUT IT IS NOT WANT . .   798D LETTER 10   PROSE
"PROPER DUTY TO YOU & MR FLAXMAN WE INTEND TO CALL" . .   800A LETTER 12   PROSE
PAST THE TURRET MY WIFE JOINS WITH ME IN DUTY AND AFFECTION   807B LETTER 17   PROSE
THE NECESSARY APPLICATION TO MY DUTY AS WELL TO MY OLD .   808A LETTER 19   PROSE
I WISH TO DO MY DUTY ESPECIALLY TO YOU . . . . . .   808A LETTER 19   PROSE
WHOLE MIGHT CHAIN MY FEET TO THE WORLD OF DUTY & REALITY   809A LETTER 20   PROSE
THAT TILL NOW I HAVE NOT BEEN ABLE TO DO THIS DUTY THE .   811B LETTER 22   PROSE
INTREAT YOU TO TAKE DUE CARE OF BOTH IT IS A PART OF OUR   811C LETTER 22   PROSE
  DUTY
BECOME MY DUTY TO EXPLAIN MY UNHAPPINESS HAS ARISEN . .   812B LETTER 22   PROSE
I CANNOT LIVE WITHOUT DOING MY DUTY TO LAY UP TREASURES   812C LETTER 22   PROSE
ESPECIALLY IF I MYSELF OMIT ANY DUTY TO MY [SELF] STATION   812D LETTER 22   PROSE
INCAPABLE OF MANY ATTENTIONS WHICH IT IS MY DUTY TO OBSERVE   816A LETTER 23   PROSE
IS NECESSARY TO ME BUT TO DO MY DUTY & TO REJOICE IN THE   830B LETTER 30   PROSE
THEREFORE AS IT IS MY DUTY BEG & INTREAT YOU NEVER TO MOUNT   833C LETTER 33   PROSE
MYSELF VERY MUCH SATISFIED THAT I SHALL DO MY DUTY . .   837A LETTER 35   PROSE
ON THE SCORE OF PARENTAL DUTY LITERATURE IS YOUR CHILD .   842A LETTER 41   PROSE
BUT TO BALANCE ALL THIS I MUST IN DUTY TO MY FRIEND   846C LETTER 44   PROSE
  SEAGRAVE
DONE MY DUTY AND PUT FORTH MY WHOLE STRENGTH . . . .   853D LETTER 52   PROSE
I CONSIDERD IT MY DUTY TO INTERFERE I EXPRESSD MY   856B LETTER 54   PROSE
  OWN RESPECT
FOR I DO ASSURE YOU I FEEL IT A DUTY TO MY PROFESSION THAT   856C LETTER 54   PROSE
  I
RECIEVING A PROPHET AS A PROPHET IS A DUTY WHICH   863A LETTER 60   PROSE
  IF OMITTED
[AND STERN DEMANDS OF RIGHT & DUTY INSTEAD OF LIBERTY] . .   SUPP FOUR ZOAS 1   *
DWELL
WHERE NOUGHT BUT ENVIOUS HISSING ADDERS DWELL . . . . .   15 IMIT SPEN/PS   28
AND CAUSE IN SWEET SOCIETY TO DWELL . . . .   15 IMIT SPEN/PS   33
ENGLAND SHALL DWELL IN PEACE THAT WHILE MY FATHER . . .   19 EDW THIRD/PS 2   7
[[SUSPITION MIXT] & POLICY DOTH DWELL WITH HER BY WHOM]   43A THEN SHE BORE *PROSE
DWELL WITH HER BY WHOM SHE (HAD) MISTRUST & SUSPITION . .   43A THEN SHE BORE *PROSE
BUT DWELL WITH US & LET US BE TO THEE INSTEAD OF EYES . .   103 TIRIEL 3   34
NOW [?HILI] HELA I CAN GO WITH PLEASURE & DWELL WITH HAR   107 TIRIEL 6   *   3
  & HEVA
TO THIS DAY THEY DWELL . . . .   115 LIT GRL FND/SI   49
WHERE MERCY LOVE & PITY DWELL . . . .   117 DIVNE IMAGE/SI   19
AND I AM VERY SMALL AND LOVE TO DWELL IN LOWLY VALES . .   127 BOOK OF THEL 1   17
BOUND BACK TO BACK IN BROMION'S CAVES TERROR & MEEKNESS   190 V DAU ALBION 2   5
  DWELL
WAVE SHADOWS OF DISCONTENT AND IN WHAT HOUSES DWELL THE   192 V DAU ALBION 4   1
  WRETCHED
TELL ME WHERE DWELL THE THOUGHTS FORGOTTEN TILL THOU CALL   192 V DAU ALBION 4   3
  THEM FORTH
TELL ME WHERE DWELL THE JOYS OF OLD & WHERE THE ANCIENT   192 V DAU ALBION 4   4
  LOVES
TO BUILD HIM CASTLES AND HIGH SPIRES WHERE KINGS & PRIESTS   193 V DAU ALBION 5   20
  MAY DWELL
TILL THE CHILD DWELL WITH ONE HE HATES AND DO THE DEED   193 V DAU ALBION 5   30
  HE LOATHS
WHERE DWELL THE CHILDREN OF THE ELEMENTAL WORLDS IN HARMONY   274 FOUR ZOAS 1   370
NOT LONG IN HARMONY THEY DWELL THEIR LIFE IS DRAWN AWAY   274 FOUR ZOAS 1   371
I DWELL IN DIM OBLIVION BROODING OVER ME THE ENORMOUS   317 FOUR ZOAS 6   223
  WORLDS
WHERE DOST THOU DWELL FOR IT IS THEE I SEEK & BUT FOR THEE   367 FOUR ZOAS 9   395
AND IN THY CELL THOU SHALL EVER DWELL . . . .   419 I SAW A MONK/N   13
TO THOSE POOR SOULS WHO DWELL IN NIGHT . . . . . .   434 AUGURIES   130
TO THOSE WHO DWELL IN REALMS OF DAY . . . .   434 AUGURIES   132
WHO DWELL IN IMMORTALITY AS ONE SLEEPING ON A COUCH . . .   496 MILTON 15   12

DWELL   (CONTINUED)
    MALAH'S ON BLACKHEATH RAHAB & NOAH DWELL ON WINDSOR'S   525 MILTON 35   9
        HEIGHTS
    ON SNOWDON THERE THEY DWELL IN NAKED SIMPLICITY   . . . . 578C DESC CAT 5   PROSE
    WE WHO DWELL ON EARTH CAN DO NOTHING OF OURSELVES   . . . 621C JERUSALEM 3   PROSE
    SHADOWY TO THOSE WHO DWELL NOT IN THEM MEER POSSIBILITIES   634 JERUSALEM 13   64
    DEPART BUT DWELL FOR EVER HERE . . . .   651 FIELDS FROM/J   70
    FROM THE BACK & LOINS WHERE DWELL THE SPECTROUS DEAD   .   659 JERUSALEM 33   4
    AND IN YOUR CELL YOU SHALL EVER DWELL   683 I SAW A MONK/J   11
    THAT HE HIMSELF MAY DWELL AMONG YOU FEAR NOT THEN TO TAKE   695 JERUSALEM 61   26
    DWELL OVER THE FOUR PROVINCES OF IRELAND IN HEAVENLY LIGHT 710 JERUSALEM 71   52
    AND THIRTY-TWO THE NATIONS TO DWELL IN JERUSALEM'S GATES   712 JERUSALEM 72   32
    RETURN JERUSALEM & DWELL TOGETHER AS OF OLD RETURN   . .   712 JERUSALEM 72   34
    RECIEVE THE LAMB OF GOD TO DWELL   .   .   .   .   .   .   718 ENGLND AWAKE/J   11
    AND IN MY BURNING BOSOM DWELL   .   755 EV GOSPEL(E)/N   78
    THAT HE HIMSELF MAY DWELL AMONG YOU   .   .   .   .   .   757D EV GOSPEL   PROSE
    & HE CANNOT DWELL AMONG YOU [BY HIS]   .   .   .   .   . 757D EV GOSPEL   *PROSE
    I RENT THE VEIL WHERE THE DEAD DWELL   .   .   .   .   .   770 OF GATES/GP   18
    SATAN DWELLS IN IT BUT MERCY DOES NOT DWELL IN HIM   . . 784B ANNO WW EXCUR   MARG
    MAY PRAISE HIM & THAT THOSE WHO DWELL IN DARKNESS & IN   823C LETTER 26   PROSE
DWELLER
    WHY HAVE THOU ELEVATE INWARD O DWELLER OF OUTWARD CHAMBERS   660 JERUSALEM 34   10
    BEEN A GLORIOUS & TRIUMPHANT DWELLER IN IMMORTALITY PLEASE 830C LETTER 30   PROSE
DWELLERS
    SOTHA & THIRALATHA SECRET DWELLERS OF DREAMFUL CAVES   .   244 EUROPE 14   26
    CAVERNOUS DWELLERS FILLD THE ENORMOUS REVELRY RESPONSING   274 FOUR ZOAS 1   383
    THE FULL HISTORY OF MY SPIRITUAL SUFFERINGS TO THE DWELLERS 862D LETTER 60   PROSE
DWELLEST   SEE DWELLST,DWELST
    O VOICE THAT DWELLEST IN MY BREAST   .   .   .   .   .   . 36B COUCH DEATH/PS PROSE
    [THIS WORLD IS [MINE] THINE IN WHICH THOU DWELLEST . . .   268 FOUR ZOAS 1   * 154
    HE WHERE THOU DWELLEST IN WHAT GROVE   .   .   .   .   .   422 THE BIRDS/N   1
    O VIRGIN OF TERRIBLE EYES WHO DWELLEST BY VALLEYS   706 JERUSALEM 68   54
        OF SPRINGS
    O THOU THAT DWELLEST WITH BABYLON COME FORTH O LOVELY-ONE   730 JERUSALEM 85   32
DWELLETH
    "WHOSO DWELLETH IN LOVE DWELLETH IN GOD & GOD IN HIM"   87A ANNO LAVATER
    [THE] LOVE'S TEMPLE [WHERE] THAT GOD DWELLETH IN . . . .   755 EV GOSPEL(E)/N   64
DWELLING
    THOU HAST REFUSD OUR CLOTHES OUR BEDS OUR HOUSES FOR THY   100 TIRIEL 1   38
        DWELLING
    THERE GOD IS DWELLING TOO   .   .   .   .   117 DIVNE IMAGE/SI   20
    EXPAND WHERE IS SPACE WHERE O SUN IS THY DWELLING . . .   144 FRENCH REVOLTN   219
    AND INTENSE FIRES FOR HIS DWELLING   .   226 URIZEN 6   6
    A MAN'S DWELLING & ROBS HIM OR MISUSES HIS WIFE OR .' . 439A BLAKES MEMORAN   PROSE
    MAKES IT A DWELLING FOR IMMORTALS WORK WILL GO ON HERE . 803C LETTER 15   PROSE
    A DWELLING IN THE NORTH MR FLAXMAN SUPPOSES THAT IF SOME 832C LETTER 32   PROSE
DWELLING-PLACE,DWELLING PLACE
    AND SAID LET A PLEASANT HOUSE ARISE TO BE THE DWELLING   369 FOUR ZOAS 9   459
        PLACE
    AND SHE BECOMES HIS DWELLING PLACE   .   .   .   .   .   . 425 MENTAL TRAVLER   27
    REMAIN MY ELEMENT MY ETERNAL DWELLING PLACE HOW CAN I   477A ANNO REYNOLDS   MARG
    AND EVERY SPACE THAT A MAN VIEWS AROUND HIS DWELLING-PLACE 516 MILTON 29   5
    AND IF HE MOVE HIS DWELLING-PLACE HIS HEAVENS ALSO MOVE   516 MILTON 29   12
    WHAT IS CALLD CORPOREAL NOBODY KNOWS OF ITS DWELLING PLACE 617A V LAST JUDG/N   PROSE
    OUR DWELLING PLACE I LOOK BACK INTO THE REGIONS OF   . . 802C LETTER 14   PROSE
DWELLS
    IN THIS ISLAND DWELLS THREE PHILOSOPHERS   .   .   .   .   44A ISLAND MOON 1   PROSE
    BEING NO OTHER THAN [THE DEVIL] HE WHO DWELLS IN FLAMING   150B MARRIAGE HH 5   *PROSE
        FIRE
    THOU ART THE IMAGE OF GOD WHO DWELLS IN DARKNESS OF AFRICA 196 AMERICA PREL 2   8
    REPOSES WHERE THE SUN'S HEAT DWELLS HE RISES TO THE SUN   355 FOUR ZOAS 8   570
    INNOCENCE DWELLS WITH WISDOM BUT NEVER WITH IGNORANCE . 380B FOUR ZOAS NOTE   PROSE
    THERE CHAOS DWELLS & ANCIENT NIGHT & OG & ANAK OLD . .   502 MILTON 20   33
    IN WHICH DWELLS MYSTERY BABYLON HERE IS HER SECRET PLACE   529 MILTON 38   23
    [ALL DWELLS IN HIM] HE IS THE BREAD & THE WINE   . . . 612D V LAST JUDG/N   PROSE
    DWELLS FROM ETERNITY WIDE SEPARATED FROM THE HUMAN SOUL   646 JERUSALEM 23   30
    MAY GOD WHO DWELLS IN THIS DARK ULRO & VOIDNESS VENGEANCE   646 JERUSALEM 23   38
        TAKE
    OF GOD WHO DWELLS IN CHAOS HIDDEN FROM THE HUMAN SIGHT .   652 JERUSALEM 28   16
    CALLING ON GOD FOR HELP AND NOT OURSELVES IN WHOM GOD   672 JERUSALEM 43   13
        DWELLS
    LO SHILOH DWELLS OVER FRANCE AS JERUSALEM DWELLS OVER   680 JERUSALEM 49   48
        ALBION
    BETWEEN DWELLS A DAUGHTER OF BEULAH TO FEED THE HUMAN   688 JERUSALEM 56   10
        VEGETABLE
    WHERE DWELLS THE SPECTRE OF ALBION DESTROYER OF DEFINITE   688 JERUSALEM 56   17
        FORM
    BENDS OVER THY IMMORTAL HEAD IN WHICH ETERNITY DWELLS   .   731 JERUSALEM 86   10
    SATAN DWELLS IN IT BUT MERCY DOES NOT DWELL IN HIM   . . 784B ANNO WW EXCUR   MARG
DWELLST
    THOU ALSO DWELLST IN ETERNITY   .   .   .   .   752 EV GOSPEL(D)/N   74
DWELST
    [THOU ALSO DWELST IN ETERNITY] . . . .   750 EV GOSPEL(C)/N   38
    THOU ALSO DWELST IN ETERNITY   .   .   .   .   750 EV GOSPEL(C)/N   40
DWELT
    THE BREATH OF HEAVEN DWELT AMONG HIS LEAVES   .   .   . .   5 FAIR ELENOR/PS   51
    I DWELT WITH MYRATANA FIVE YEARS IN THE DESOLATE ROCK   .   107 TIRIEL 6   8
    [[OF] IN A SOFT CLOUD OUTSTRETCHD ACROSS & LUVAH DWELT   292 FOUR ZOAS 3   48
        IN THE CLOUD]
    THE MOUNTAINS OF URIZEN ONCE OF SILVER WHERE THE SONS OF   310 FOUR ZOAS 5   192
        WISDOM DWELT
    MUTUAL THERE WE DWELT IN ONE ANOTHER'S JOY REVOLVING   .   327 FOUR ZOAS 7   273

	PAGE	TITLE	LINE

DWELT   (CONTINUED)
      NAMD OLOLON ON WHOSE MILD BANKS DWELT THOSE WHO MILTON   503 MILTON 21   16
        DROVE
      THEY DENY THAT THEY EVER KNEW JERUSALEM OR EVER DWELT   679 JERUSALEM 49   9
        IN SHILOH
      THE ATLANTIC MOUNTAINS WHERE GIANTS DWELT IN INTELLECT . .   681 JERUSALEM 50   1
      WITH THEIR DISTRICTS HAND DWELT IN SELSEY & HAD SUSSEX   709 JERUSALEM 71   11
        & SURREY
      HYLE DWELT IN WINCHESTER COMPREHENDING HANTS DORSET DEVON   710 JERUSALEM 71   20
        CORNWALL
      COBAN DWELT IN BATH SOMERSET WILTSHIRE GLOUCESTERSHIRE . .   710 JERUSALEM 71   26
DYD
      FOR ALBION'S SINS ARE CRIMSON DYD . . . .   34A KING JOHN/PS   PROSE
D'YE
      WHAT D'YE SAY WHAT D'YE SAY SAID INFLAMMABLE GASS   . . .   44D ISLAND MOON 1   PROSE
      OF AN HUNDRED JOURNEYMEN'S HOW D'YE DO NEIGHBOUR . . . .   546 SWELLD LIMBS/N   4
DYER
      THE DYER THE FRANKLIN THE PHYSICIAN THE PLOWMAN . . . .   566D DESC CAT 3   PROSE
      WROTE "A WEBBE DYER" THAT IS A CLOTH DYER   . . . . . .   572A DESC CAT 3   PROSE
      THE DYER THE FRANKLIN THE PHYSICIAN THE PLOWMAN . . . .   588C CHAUCER/N   PROSE
      THE DYER THE FRANKLIN THE PHYSICIAN THE PLOWMAN . . . .   589D CHAUCER 2   PROSE
DYING   SEE EVER DYING,NEVER DYING
      IN MY WEAK [AGED] ARMS I HERE HAVE BORNE YOUR DYING MOTHER   99 TIRIEL 1   9
      THE DEW OF ANXIOUS SOULS THE DEATH-SWEAT OF THE DYING . .   281 FOUR ZOAS 2   47
      THE FADING CRY IS EVER DYING . . . .   289 FOUR ZOAS 2   362
      ABHORRD ACCURSED EVER DYING AN ETERNAL DEATH . . . . .   347 FOUR ZOAS 8   * 256
      THEY DANCE AROUND THE DYING & THEY DRINK THE HOWL & GROAN   377 FOUR ZOAS 9   767
      THEY DANCE AROUND THE DYING & THEY DRINK THE HOWL & GROAN   514 MILTON 27   37
      THE DEAD AND THE DYING BRITONS NAKED MINGLED WITH   . . .   580C DESC CAT 5   PROSE
      IS SEEN FALLING OUTSTRETCHED AMONG THE DEAD AND THE DYING   580C DESC CAT 5   PROSE
      MY DYING LIMBS THEREFORE C MANHOOD IF THOU ART AUGHT   . .   646 JERUSALEM 23   36
      BUT A MEER PHANTASY HEAR DYING ALBION'S CURSE . . . . .   646 JERUSALEM 23   37
      GIVE ME MY EMANATIONS BACK FOOD FOR MY DYING SOUL   . . .   670 JERUSALEM 42   13
      INTO EGYPT FOR NEGATION A VEIL THE SAVIOUR BORN & DYING   686 JERUSALEM 55   16
        RENDS
      TIRZAH SITS WEEPING TO HEAR THE SHRIEKS OF THE DYING HER   704 JERUSALEM 67   24
        KNIFE
      RESOUND WITH CRIES OF VICTIMS SHOUTS & SONGS & DYING GROANS   723 JERUSALEM 80   49
EACH-OTHER   SEE OTHER
      NEITHER DARING TO PUT IN ACT ITS COUNCILS FEARING   708 JERUSALEM 70   6
        EACH-OTHER
EAGER
      EAGER SONG GOES ON TELLING HOW PRIDE AGAINST HER FATHER   42B THEN SHE BORE   PROSE
        WARRD
      THE SPIDER SITS IN HIS LABOURD WEB EAGER WATCHING FOR THE   277 FOUR ZOAS 1   457
        FLY
      HOVERS WITH BLASTED WINGS ALOFT WATCHING WITH EAGER EYE   354 FOUR ZOAS 8   523
      YOUR EAGER EXPECTATION OF HEARING FROM ME COMPELLS ME   . .   834B LETTER 34   PROSE
EAGERLY
      AS THE SEED WAITS EAGERLY WATCHING FOR ITS FLOWER & FRUIT   355 FOUR ZOAS 8   * 558
      OF HOREB STILL EYEING ALBION'S CLIFFS EAGERLY SIEZING &   704 JERUSALEM 67   27
        TWISTING
EAGLE
      AS THE WINGD EAGLE SCORNS THE TOWRY FENCE . . . . . .   15 IMIT SPEN/PS   37
      THE EAGLE THAT DOTH GAZE UPON THE SUN   . . . .   24 EDW THIRD/PS 3   116
      DOTH SEIZE THE SOARING EAGLE UNDONE BY FLIGHT . . . . .   24 EDW THIRD/PS 3   121
      WHILE WITH HER EAGLE WINGS SHE COVERETH . . . .   33 EDW THIRD/PS 6   59
      DOES THE EAGLE KNOW WHAT IS IN THE PIT . . . .   127 THELS MOTTO/BT   1
      OF ETERNITY WHERE THE ETERNAL LION AND EAGLE REMAIN TO   138 FRENCH REVOLTN   97
        DEVOUR
      THE EAGLE NEVER LOST SO MUCH TIME AS WHEN HE SUBMITTED . .   151D MARRIAGE HH 8   PROSE
      WHEN THOU SEEST AN EAGLE THOU SEEST A PORTION OF GENIUS   152B MARRIAGE HH 9   PROSE
      IN THE THIRD CHAMBER WAS AN EAGLE WITH WINGS AND FEATHERS   154D MARRIAGE HH 15 PROSE
      AND THE EAGLE IS KNOWN FROM THE OWL . . . .   183 MOTTO SONGS/N   8
      THE LARK DOES RUSTLE IN THE RIPE CORN AND THE EAGLE RETURNS   190 V DAU ALBION 2   25
      WHERE SHE GETS POISON & THE WINGD EAGLE WHY HE LOVES THE   191 V DAU ALBION 3   12
        SUN
      DOES NOT THE EAGLE SCORN THE EARTH & DESPISE THE TREASURES   193 V DAU ALBION 5   39
        BENEATH
      SOMETIMES AN EAGLE SCREAMING IN THE SKY SOMETIMES A LION   196 AMERICA PREL 1   13
      IN MEXICO AN EAGLE AND A LION IN PERU . . . .   196 AMERICA PREL 2   13
      LIKE A FAMISHD EAGLE EYELESS RAGING IN THE VAST EXPANSE   297 FOUR ZOAS 4   10
      AND THERE THE EAGLE HIDES HER YOUNG IN CLIFFS & PRECIPICES   308 FOUR ZOAS 5   129
      AND THE STRONG PINIOND EAGLE BORE THE FIRE OF HEAVEN . . .   340 FOUR ZOAS 7B   285
      AND THE STRONG EAGLE NOW WITH NUMMING COLD BLIGHTED OF   354 FOUR ZOAS 8   521
        FEATHERS
      WHEREVER THE EAGLE HAS EXPLORD OR LION OR TYGER TROD   . .   358 FOUR ZOAS 9   *   39
      BEFORE THE MORNING'S DAWN THE EAGLE CALLD THE VULTURE . .   358 FOUR ZOAS 9   59
      A TERROR COMING FROM THE SOUTH THE EAGLE & HAWK FLED AWAY   358 FOUR ZOAS 9   62
      AND FROM THE OX & ASS COME MOPING TERRORS FROM THE EAGLE   363 FOUR ZOAS 9   237
      TIGER THE HORSE THE VULTURE AND THE EAGLE CONTEND FOR THE   441D INSC FALL MAN   PROSE
        LAMB
      AND IN VAIN THE EAGLE & LION OVER THE FOUR-FOLD WILDERNESS   703 JERUSALEM 66   71
      OVER THEM THE FAMISHD EAGLE SCREAMS ON BONEY WINGS AND   741 JERUSALEM 94   15
        AROUND
      THE EAGLE & THE WOLF & MONKEY & OWL & THE KING & PRIEST   742 JERUSALEM 94   27
        WERE THERE
      WITH EVERY COLOUR LION TYGER HORSE ELEPHANT EAGLE DOVE   746 JERUSALEM 98   43
        FLY WORM
      THE EAGLE THE HORSE THE DOG OF THE DOG SPECIES THE   . . .   859B LETTER 56   PROSE
EAGLE LIKE
      AROUND WERE NUMBERS OF EAGLE LIKE MEN   . . . .   154D MARRIAGE HH 15 PROSE

553

		PAGE	TITLE	LINE

EAGLE'S
THE EMMET'S INCH & EAGLE'S MILE . . . . 433 AUGURIES 105
EAGLES
FOR THEM THE EAGLES STRIVE . . . . 14 GWIN KING/PS 112
LIKE EAGLES FOR THE PREY NOR SHALL THE YOUNG . . . 33 EDW THIRD/PS 6 45
STRETCH THE HAND THAT BECKONS THE EAGLES OF HEAVEN . . . 138 FRENCH REVOLTN 103
. . . THE EAGLES OF HEAVEN MUST HAVE THEIR PREY . . 138 FRENCH REVOLTN 104
AND CALLING THEOTORMON'S EAGLES TO PREY UPON HER FLESH . 190 V DAU ALBION 2 13
THE EAGLES AT HER CALL DESCEND & REND THEIR BLEEDING PREY 190 V DAU ALBION 2 17
DOES THE STILL SPIDER VIEW THE CLIFFS WHERE EAGLES HIDE 193 V DAU ALBION 5 37
THEIR YOUNG
LIGHT OF THY MOTHER'S SOUL I SEE THY LOVELY EAGLES ROUND 244 EUROPE 14 7
WHILE FAR INTO THE VAST UNKNOWN THE STRONG WINGD EAGLES 284 FOUR ZOAS 2 150
BEND
AND SWORDS RAGE WHERE THE EAGLES CRY & THE VULTURES LAUGH 334 FOUR ZOAS 7B 44
SAYING
EAR
THEY STRIKE THE EAR OF NIGHT . . . . 9 MAD SONG/PS 13
NOW LOWLY BENDING WHISPERS IN MINE EAR . . . . . . 36D CONTEMPLATN/PS PROSE
TILL MUTE ATTENTION STRUCK MY [TREMBLING] LISTNING EAR . 43D WOE CRIED MUSE PROSE
WHY CANNOT THE EAR BE CLOSED TO ITS OWN DESTRUCTION . . . 130 BOOK OF THEL 6 11
WHY AN EAR A WHIRLPOOL FIERCE TO DRAW CREATIONS IN . . 130 BOOK OF THEL 6 17
THAT THE HIRELING BLOWS INTO MY EAR . . . . 166 WHY CARE FOR/N 4
WHY HE LOVES MAN IS IT BECAUSE OF EYE EAR MOUTH OR SKIN . 191 V DAU ALBION 3 8
HOW DIFFERENT THEIR EYE AND EAR HOW DIFFERENT THE WORLD 193 V DAU ALBION 5 16
TO THEM
THAT THE DELICATE EAR IN ITS INFANCY . . . . 247 SONG OF LOS 7 5
HIDE ME SOME SHADOWY SEMBLANCE SECRET WHISPRING IN MY EAR 265 FOUR ZOAS 1 42
WITH DIFFICULTY DOWN DESCENDING GUIDED BY HIS EAR . . . 319 FOUR ZOAS 6 293
LOS FURIOUS ANSWERD SPECTRE HORRIBLE THY WORDS ASTOUND 329 FOUR ZOAS 7 361
MY EAR
WHAT WORDS OF DREAD PIERCE MY FAINT EAR WHAT FALLING SNOWS 344 FOUR ZOAS 8 146
AROUND
FASTEN THIS EAR INTO THE ROCK MILCAH THE TASK IS THINE . . 349 FOUR ZOAS 8 318
THE KING DROPD A TEAR INTO THE QUEEN'S EAR . . . . . 451 ANNO REYNOLDS 3
THE EAR A LITTLE SHELL IN SMALL VOLUTIONS SHUTTING OUT . . 484 MILTON 5 23
CAN SUCH AN EAR FILLD WITH THE VAPOURS OF THE YAWNING PIT 485 MILTON 5 30
AND IN THE NERVES OF THE EAR FOR THE NERVES OF THE TONGUE 517 MILTON 29 40
ARE CLOSED
WITHIN THE UNFATHOMD CAVERNS OF MY EAR . . . . . . 621 READER LOVER/J 8
AND THE TONGUE IS THE WEST AND THE EAR IS THE NORTH . . . 632 JERUSALEM 12 60
HIS EAR IN A SPIRAL CIRCLE OUTWARD THEN SENT HIM 662 JERUSALEM 36 13
OVER JORDAN
BRISTOL & BATH LISTEN TO MY WORDS & YE SEVENTEEN GIVE EAR 673 JERUSALEM 43 55
THE EAR A LITTLE SHELL IN SMALL VOLUTIONS SHUTTING OUT . . 680 JERUSALEM 49 36
THEIR EAR BENT OUTWARDS AS THEIR VICTIM SO ARE THEY IN 702 JERUSALEM 66 38
THE PANGS
AND AS THEIR EYE & EAR SHRUNK THE HEAVENS SHRUNK AWAY . . 702 JERUSALEM 66 40
FASTEN THIS EAR INTO THE ROCK MILCAH THE TASK IS THINE . 705 JERUSALEM 68 6
AND EAR UNBINDING IN DIRE PAIN WITH MANY BLOWS . . . . 738 JERUSALEM 91 46
HER VOICE PIERCD ALBION'S CLAY COLD EAR HE MOVED UPON THE 742 JERUSALEM 95 1
ROCK
THE LABYRINTHINE EAR . . . . 745 JERUSALEM 98 18
WHOSE VERSES [SH] STILL SOUND UPON MY EAR . . . . . 835A LETTER 34 *PROSE
EARL
AND THE EARL OF WARWICK WAS TUMBLED OVER . . . . . 29D EDW THIRD/PS 4 PROSE
FOR NOT FLATTERING THE EARL OF WARWICK EXEUNT . . . . 30A EDW THIRD/PS 4 PROSE
. . . THE DUKE OF BRETAGNE AND THE EARL OF BORGOGNE . . . 141 FRENCH REVOLTN 169
THE DEATH OF EARL GOODWIN . . . . SUPP ILLUS HISTORY *TITLE
EARLIER
THAT COULD SHEW ITSELF BY THE SIDE OF AN EARLIER PRODUCTION 565B DESC CAT 2 PROSE
EARLIEST
THERE ARE NO PROOFS THAT MATTHEW THE EARLIEST . . . . . 394B ANNO WATSON * MARG
FROM MY EARLIEST CHILDHOOD HIDDEN FROM ME I SAW & . . . 447C ANNO REYNOLDS MARG
& OF WHATEVER COMES IN HIS WAY FROM EARLIEST CHILDHOOD . . 455D ANNO REYNOLDS MARG
[MYSELF TO ENGRAVING IN MY EARLIEST YOUTH ARE SUFFICIENT] 591C PUB ADDRESS/N PROSE
THE EARLIEST POSSIBLE NOTICE OF WHAT ENGRAVING IS TO BE 842D LETTER 42 PROSE
DONE
COLLECT FROM HIM BE SO GOOD AS TO GIVE ME YOUR EARLIEST 849B LETTER 45 PROSE
EARLY
WHEN EARLY MORN WALKS FORTH IN SOBER GREY . . . . . 10 WHEN EARLY/PS 1
FOR [SOON] EARLY I IN LOVE WAS CROST . . . . 184 O I CANNOT/N * 3
AN OLD MAID EARLY EER I KNEW . . . . 184 O I CANNOT/N 5
MR BLAKE'S POWERS OF INVENTION VERY EARLY ENGAGED . . . 207C PRSPECTUS 1793 PROSE
FOREHEAD & EYES THY LIPS DECAY LIKE ROSES IN [EARLY] THE 325 FOUR ZOAS 7 189
SPRING
THE TIME CHOSEN IS EARLY MORNING BEFORE SUNRISE . . . . 566C DESC CAT 3 PROSE
MR B(BLAKE) HAVING FROM EARLY YOUTH CULTIVATED THE TWO ARTS 587D CHAUCER/N PROSE
THE TIME CHOSEN IS EARLY MORNING BEFORE SUNRISE . . . . 588B CHAUCER/N PROSE
THE TIME CHOSEN IS EARLY MORNING BEFORE SUN-RISE . . . . 589C CHAUCER 2 PROSE
I DID NOT BEGIN TO LEARN LANGUAGES EARLY IN LIFE AS I FIND 821D LETTER 25 PROSE
IT
I HAVE SEEN FLAXMAN ALREADY AS I TOOK TO HIM EARLY THIS 833C LETTER 33 PROSE
EARN
TWAS DARK DECEIT TO EARN MY BREAD . . . . 755 EV GOSPEL(E)/N 60
EARNEST
[AND TWIXT EARNEST & [GAME] JOKE] . . . . 163 ASKED THIEF/N * 10
THEIR BELIEF IN VISION & REVELATION PLATO WAS IN EARNEST 473D ANNO REYNOLDS MARG
MILTON WAS IN EARNEST THEY BELIEVD THAT GOD DID VISIT MAN 473D ANNO REYNOLDS MARG
EARNESTLY
MY WIFE GETS BETTER EVERY DAY HOPE EARNESTLY THAT YOU . . 835A LETTER 34 PROSE

554

		PAGE	TITLE	LINE
EARS				
MIDAS THE PRAISE HATH GAIND OF LENGTHEND [CARES] EARS	. .	14	IMIT SPEN/PS	15
AND PIERCE THE EARS O TH GODS O SAMSON HOLD ME NOT	. .	38C	SAMSON/PS	PROSE
OF THE MINISTERS YOU DESERVE TO HAVE YOUR EARS BOXED YOU DO		48C	ISLAND MOON 4	PROSE
LET YOUR BOUNTY DESCEND TO OUR FAIR EARS	. . . . . .	55C	ISLAND MOON 9	PROSE
A PAIR OF VERY GOOD EARS		62	DR CLASH/IM	14
THEN LIKE A TOAD OR LIKE A NEWT WOULD WHISPER IN MY EARS		105	TIRIEL 4	59
AYE NOW YOU FEEL THE CURSE YOU CRY BUT MAY ALL EARS BE DEAF		106	TIRIEL 5	20
EYES AND EARS AND SENSE OF TOUCH YET ARE THEIR HABITATIONS		191	V DAU ALBION 3	5
WHOSE EARS HAVE HEARD		210	INTRODUCTN/SE	3
DIDST BIND MY NOSTRILS EYES & EARS		220	TO TIRZAH/SE	12
TWO EARS IN CLOSE VOLUTIONS		229	URIZEN 11	21
FOR THE EARS OF THE INHABITANTS		236	URIZEN 28	15
WHENCE IS THIS VOICE OF ENION THAT SOUNDETH IN MY [EARS] PORCHES		280	FOUR ZOAS 2	4
THEIR EYES THEIR EARS NOSTRILS & TONGUES ROLL OUTWARD THEY BEHOLD		281	FOUR ZOAS 2	54
WHENCE IS THIS VOICE CRYING ENION THAT SOUNDETH IN MY EARS		293	FOUR ZOAS 3	77
I WILL TURN THE VOLUTIONS OF YOUR EARS OUTWARD & BEND YOUR NOSTRILS		294	FOUR ZOAS 3	86
DEADLY BETWEEN THE HAMMER'S BEATING GRATEFUL TO THE EARS		302	FOUR ZOAS 4	190
TWO EARS IN CLOSE VOLUTIONS FROM BENEATH HIS ORBS OF VISION		303	FOUR ZOAS 4	233
HIS VOICE TO THEM WAS BUT AN INARTICULATE THUNDER FOR THEIR EARS		315	FOUR ZOAS 6	124
THE EYELIDS EXPANSIVE AS MORNING & THE EARS	. . . . .	318	FOUR ZOAS 6	249
FOR HIS FRAIL EYES WERE FADED & HIS EARS HEAVY & DULL	. .	326	FOUR ZOAS 7	250
INTO THE BARN WHILE CHILDREN GLEAN THE EARS AROUND THE DOOR		376	FOUR ZOAS 9	702
FROM BENEATH HIS ORBS OF VISION TWO EARS IN CLOSE VOLUTIONS		482	MILTON 3	17
THE EARS OF BILLY'S LAWYER & DRAGOON		537	AND HIS LEGS/N	25
BOTH WENT TO LAW WITH DEATH TO KEEP OUR EARS ON	. . .	537	AND HIS LEGS/N	27
HOW LONG SHALL I BE FORCED TO BEAT THIS INTO MEN'S EARS		602D	PUB ADDR AD/N	PROSE
WHENCE IS THIS VOICE CRYING ENION THAT SOUNDETH IN MY EARS		654	JERUSALEM 29	59
I WILL TURN THE VOLUTIONS OF YOUR EARS OUTWARD AND BEND YOUR NOSTRILS		655	JERUSALEM 29	67
THE EYE THE LITTLE NOSTRILS & THE DELICATE TONGUE & EARS		728	JERUSALEM 83	36
EARTH				
UNCLOTHES THE EARTH AND FREEZES UP FRAIL LIFE	. . . .	3	TO WINTER/PS	12
DRAWN DOWN TO EARTH BY SPELLS AND WICKEDNESS	. . . . .	5	FAIR ELENOR/PS	46
THE EARTH DO SCORN		9	MAD SONG/PS	8
OR THE GREEN CORNERS OF THE EARTH		10	TO MUSES/PS	6
EARTH SMOKES WITH BLOOD AND GROANS AND SHAKES	. . . . .	13	GWIN KING/PS	73
THE EARTH DOTH FAINT AND FAIL		13	GWIN KING/PS	94
WHICH DROP LIKE FRUIT UNTO THE EARTH		14	GWIN KING/PS	103
THE FACE OF THE EARTH		25	EDW THIRD/PS 3	193
IN EARTH COVERD WITH STONES AND DEATHY DUST	. . . . .	30	EDW THIRD/PS 5	14
AND CASTS THEM OUT UPON THE DARKEND EARTH	. . . . . .	34	WAR SONG/PS	4
YOUR SOULS FOR FLIGHT YOUR BODIES FOR THE EARTH	. . . .	34	WAR SONG/PS	7
THE REMAINS OF A FAMILY OF THE TRIBES OF EARTH A MOTHER		35C	COUCH DEATH/PS	PROSE
OVER THE SILENT EARTH SPREADS HER PAVILION	. . . . .	37D	SAMSON/PS	PROSE
[REFRESHING THE COLD EARTH WITH BEAMING JOY] BUT PRIDE AWOKE		40D	THEN SHE BORE	PROSE
OER THE EARTH PRIDE FEARED FOR HER CITY BUT NOT LONG	. .	41B	THEN SHE BORE	PROSE
CARE BROUGHT FORTH COVET EYELESS & PRONE TO TH EARTH	. .	42C	THEN SHE BORE	PROSE
I WOULD STAND TILL I WAS READY TO SINK INTO THE EARTH	. .	48B	ISLAND MOON 4	PROSE
OF THE EARTH [?TALK] TALK OF HAPPINESS		52B	ISLAND MOON 8	*PROSE
A PHANTOM OF THE EARTH & OF THE WATER		82B	ANNO LAVATER	MARG
THING ON EARTH IS THE WORD OF GOD & IN ITS ESSENCE IS GOD		87B	ANNO LAVATER	MARG
AND AS ALL OF US ON EARTH ARE UNITED IN THOUGHT FOR IT IS		88B	ANNO LAVATER	MARG
IMPOSSIBLE TO THINK WITHOUT IMAGES OF SOMEWHAT ON EARTH		88B	ANNO LAVATER	MARG
THEY EXIST LITERALLY ABOUT THE SUN & NOT ABOUT THE EARTH		92B	ANNO SWED LOVE	MARG
THAT NO MAN ON EARTH HAS A SPIRITUAL IDEA AFTER READING N...		94C	ANNO SWED LOVE	MARG
THEREFORE THE NATURAL EARTH & ATMOSPHERE IS A PHANTASY	. .	94D	ANNO SWED LOVE	MARG
LIE STINKING ON THE EARTH THE BURIERS SHALL ARISE FROM THE EAST		100	TIRIEL 1	49
MORE HUMAN CREATURES ON THIS EARTH BESIDE THE SONS OF HAR		102	TIRIEL 2	55
THO IT IS WRINKLED LIKE THE EARTH PARCHD WITH THE SUMMER HEAT		103	TIRIEL 3	25
EARTH THUS I STAMP THY BOSOM ROUSE THE EARTHQUAKE FROM HIS DEN		106	TIRIEL 5	4
THE EARTH TREMBLED [XXX] FIRES BELCHED FROM THE YAWNING CLEFTS		106	TIRIEL 5	* 16
THAT THE EARTH FROM SLEEP		112	LIT GRL LST/SI	3
HEAVEN & EARTH TO PEACE BEGUILES		120	CRADLE SONG/SI	32
AND WE ARE PUT ON EARTH A LITTLE SPACE		125	LIT BLK BOY/SI	13
OF EVERY HEART ON EARTH INFIXES DEEP ITS RESTLESS TWISTS		130	BOOK OF THEL 6	4
. . . WAS HID FROM THE OPPRESSED EARTH		135	FRENCH REVOLTN	32
TO A BED OF STRAW THE SEVEN DISEASES OF EARTH		135	FRENCH REVOLTN	36
. . . KINGS ARE SICK THROUGHOUT ALL THE EARTH		137	FRENCH REVOLTN	61
HIDE IN THE NETHER EARTH HIDE IN THE BONES		137	FRENCH REVOLTN	75
. . . THIS EARTH AN OAK STOOL AND THESE MOWERS		138	FRENCH REVOLTN	89
. . . AND THE KINGDOMS OF EARTH BOUND IN SHEAVES		138	FRENCH REVOLTN	92
TO ENRICH THE LEAN EARTH THAT CRAVES		138	FRENCH REVOLTN	99
DRAWN HE THREW ON THE EARTH		141	FRENCH REVOLTN	169
THE GIRDLE OF WAR FROM THE DESOLATE EARTH		144	FRENCH REVOLTN	223
SHALL WEEP BENDING TO EARTH EMBRACING THE VALLEYS . . .		144	FRENCH REVOLTN	224
. . . AND THE HAPPY EARTH SING IN ITS COURSE		144	FRENCH REVOLTN	236
. . . AND OF SULPHUR THE EARTH FROM FAYETTE AS HE LIFTED HIS HAND		146	FRENCH REVOLTN	278
PERCIEVED BY THE MINDS OF MEN & READ BY THEM ON EARTH	. .	150D	MARRIAGE HH 6	PROSE
THE MOUTH OF WATER THE BEARD OF EARTH		152B	MARRIAGE HH 9	PROSE
THESE TWO CLASSES OF MEN ARE ALWAYS UPON EARTH	. . .	155B	MARRIAGE HH 15	PROSE

EARTH   (CONTINUED)
      & HIMSELF THE SINGLE ONE ON EARTH THAT EVER BROKE A NET   157D MARRIAGE HH 21   PROSE
      THE ETERNAL FEMALE GROAND IT WAS HEARD OVER ALL THE EARTH   159A SONG LIBERTY   PROSE
      HEAVEN & EARTH OF PEACE BEGUILES . . . .   165 CRADLE SONG/N   27
      EARTH RAISD UP HER HEAD . . . .   168 EARTHS ANSWR/N   1
      [HIS EARTH] . . . .   173 HOW CAME/N   5
      THE GODS OF THE EARTH & SEA . . . .   174 HUMAN IMAGE/N   22
      I SLEPT IN THE [DARK] EARTH &C   175 WILD FLOWERS/N   5
      OF LUST THAT BELCH INCESSANT FROM THE SUMMITS OF THE EARTH   190 V DAU ALBION 2   10
      BY THE RED EARTH OF OUR IMMORTAL RIVER I BATHE MY WINGS   191 V DAU ALBION 3   19
      BUT KNOWEST THOU THAT TREES AND FRUITS FLOURISH UPON THE   192 V DAU ALBION 4   14
         EARTH
      DOES NOT THE EAGLE SCORN THE EARTH & DESPISE THE TREASURES   193 V DAU ALBION 5   39
         BENEATH
      FATHER OF JEALOUSY BE THOU ACCURSED FROM THE EARTH . . .   194 V DAU ALBION 7   12
      THEY CANNOT SMITE THE WHEAT NOR QUENCH THE FATNESS OF THE   199 AMERICA 9   5
         EARTH
      OF ANGUISH THREW THEIR SWORDS & MUSKETS TO THE EARTH & RAN   201 AMERICA 13   7
      ARMD WITH DISEASES OF THE EARTH TO CAST UPON THE ABYSS .   201 AMERICA 13   15
      DARK IS THE HEAVEN ABOVE & COLD & HARD THE EARTH BENEATH   201 AMERICA 14   7
      THE SCRIBE OF PENSYLVANIA CASTS HIS PEN UPON THE EARTH . .   201 AMERICA 14   15
      AND EARTH HAD LOST ANOTHER PORTION OF THE INFINITE . . .   202 AMERICA 14   18
      AND CAST THEIR SWORDS & SPEARS TO EARTH & STOOD A NAKED   202 AMERICA 15   5
         MULTITUDE
      HIDING THE DEMON RED WITH CLOUDS & COLD MISTS FROM THE   203 AMERICA 16   13
         EARTH
      AND EARTH CONGLOBD IN NARROW ROOM ROLLD ROUND ITS SULPHUR   204 AMERICA CANC B   7
         SUN
      AND SO THE PRINCES FADE FROM EARTH SCARCE SEEN BY SOULS   206 THIRALATHA   5
         OF MEN
      WATER EARTH AIR FIRE   . . . .   209C FOR CHILDRN/GP   TITLE
      O EARTH O EARTH RETURN   210 INTRODUCTN/SE   11
      EARTH RAISD UP HER HEAD . . . .   210 EARTHS ANSR/SE   1
      THE GODS OF THE EARTH AND SEA . . . .   217 HUMAN ABSTR/SE   21
      MUST BE CONSUMED WITH THE EARTH . . . .   220 TO TIRZAH/SE   2
      EARTH WAS NOT NOR GLOBES OF ATTRACTION . . . . . .   223 URIZEN 3   36
      AS THE STARS ARE APART FROM THE EARTH . . . . . .   226 URIZEN 6   1
      DELVING EARTH IN HIS RESISTLESS WAY . . . .   232 URIZEN 19   44
      GRODNA RENT THE DEEP EARTH HOWLING . . . .   234 URIZEN 23   15
      TO EARTH BY THEIR NARROWING PERCEPTIONS . . . . . .   236 URIZEN 25   47
      AND THEY LEFT THE PENDULOUS EARTH . . . .   237 URIZEN 28   21
      MY ROOTS ARE BRANDISHD IN THE HEAVENS MY FRUITS IN EARTH   238 EUROPE PREL 1   8
         BENEATH
      BIND ALL THE NOURISHING SWEETS OF EARTH . . . . . .   239 EUROPE 4   19
      OF COLOURS TWELVE FEW KNOWN ON EARTH GIVE LIGHT IN THE   241 EUROPE 10   9
         OPAKE
      THAT KINGS & PRIESTS HAD COPIED ON EARTH . . . . .   242 EUROPE 11   4
      AND MORE TO EARTH CLOSING AND RESTRAINING . . . . .   246 SONG OF LOS 4   15
      THE SULLEN EARTH . . . .   248 SONG OF LOS 7   29
      AS THE MOON ANGUISHD CIRCLES THE EARTH . . . . . .   250 AHANIA 2   40
      FIVE HUNDRED YEARS WANDRING ON EARTH . . . .   250 AHANIA 2   46
      BUT THE ROCK FELL UPON THE EARTH . . . .   251 AHANIA 3   45
      GREW TO ROOTS WHEN IT FELT THE EARTH . . . . . .   252 AHANIA 3   66
      THEY REPTILIZE UPON THE EARTH . . . .   253 AHANIA 4   43
      TREMBLED AND SHOOK THE STEDFAST EARTH . . . . . .   256 BOOK OF LOS 3 *   5
      RAN THRO HEAVEN & EARTH LIVING FLAMES . . . . . .   256 BOOK OF LOS 3   28
      THE HEAVENS [SHALL] QUAKE THE EARTH [SHALL MOVE] [MOVES]   264 FOUR ZOAS 1   *   7
         . . .
      LOS WAS THE FOURTH IMMORTAL STARRY ONE & IN THE EARTH . .   264 FOUR ZOAS 1   14
      WHICH IS THE EARTH OF EDEN HE HIS EMANATIONS PROPAGATED   264 FOUR ZOAS 1   18
      [AND ?COURTING THAT THE EARTH WOULD OPE HER EYELIDS   267 FOUR ZOAS 1   131
         & BEHOLD]
      [NO OTHER LIVING THING IS HERE THE SEA THE EARTH   268 FOUR ZOAS 1   141
         THE HEAVEN]
      A MONSTER LOVELY IN THE HEAVENS OR WANDERING ON THE EARTH   269 FOUR ZOAS 1   187
      THEN LOS SMOTE HER UPON THE EARTH TWAS LONG EER SHE REVIVD   272 FOUR ZOAS 1   281
      THE EARTH SPREAD FORTH HER TABLE WIDE THE NIGHT A SILVER   273 FOUR ZOAS 1   347
         CUP
      AS THE SUN SHINES DOWN ON THE MISTY EARTH SUCH WAS THE   274 FOUR ZOAS 1   365
         VISION
      OVER THE JOYFUL EARTH & SEA & ASCENDED INTO THE HEAVENS   274 FOUR ZOAS 1   376
      AND WITH IMMORTAL VOICE SOFT WARBLING FILL ALL EARTH &   274 FOUR ZOAS 1   381
         HEAVEN
      HIDING THEIR BOOKS & PICTURES UNDERNEATH THE DENS OF EARTH   275 FOUR ZOAS 1   397
      FROM ALBION'S LOINS FLED ALL PEOPLES AND NATIONS OF THE   281 FOUR ZOAS 2   *   43
         EARTH [FLED]
      JERUSALEM CAME DOWN IN A DIRE RUIN OVER ALL THE EARTH . .   281 FOUR ZOAS 2   45
      STOOD ON THE INFINITE EARTH & SAW THESE VISIONS IN THE AIR   283 FOUR ZOAS 2   122
      IN WATERS & IN EARTH BENEATH THEY CRIED TO ONE ANOTHER .   283 FOUR ZOAS 2   123
      WAS THIS WIDE EARTH SPREAD ALL ABROAD NOT FOR WILD BEASTS   283 FOUR ZOAS 2   125
         TO ROAM
      SET STATIONS ON THIS BREEDING EARTH & LET US BUY & SELL   283 FOUR ZOAS 2   129
      [NOW] FOR LOS & ENITHARMON WALKD FORTH ON THE DEWY EARTH   288 FOUR ZOAS 2   295
      OR STANDING ON THE EARTH ERECT OR ON THE STORMY WAVES .   288 FOUR ZOAS 2   299
      NOW MY LEFT HAND I STRETCH TO EARTH BENEATH . . . . .   289 FOUR ZOAS 2   369
      I HAVE PLANTED A FALSE OATH IN THE EARTH . . .   290 FOUR ZOAS 2   388
      MY HEAVENS ARE BRASS MY EARTH IS IRON MY MOON A CLOD OF   290 FOUR ZOAS 2   395
         CLAY
      TO CAST AHANIA TO THE EARTH HE SIEZD HER BY THE HAIR .   294 FOUR ZOAS 3   111
      RENEW THESE RUIND SOULS OF MEN THRO EARTH SEA AIR & FIRE   298 FOUR ZOAS 4   30
      TERRIFIC PALE ENITHARMON STRETCHED ON THE [DISMAL] DREARY   305 FOUR ZOAS 5   5
         EARTH

		PAGE	TITLE		LINE
EARTH	(CONTINUED)				
BEGAN IN SOLEMN REVOLUTIONS EARTH CONVULSD WITH RENDING PANGS		306	FOUR ZOAS 5		28
THE GROANS OF ENITHARMON SHAKE THE SKIES THE LABRING EARTH		306	FOUR ZOAS 5		36
INTO THE IRON ROCK & GREW A CHAIN BENEATH THE EARTH	. .	309	FOUR ZOAS 5		167
RENDING THE CAVERNS LIKE A MIGHTY WIND PENT IN THE EARTH		309	FOUR ZOAS 5		183
AN EARTH OF WINTRY WOE BENEATH THEIR FEET & ROUND THEIR LOINS		314	FOUR ZOAS 6		92
ALL THRO THE CAVERNS OF FIRE & AIR & EARTH SEEKING	. . .	318	FOUR ZOAS 6		272
BORN EVEN TOO MANY & OUR EARTH WILL BE OVERRUN	. . . .	323	FOUR ZOAS 7		121
WAS OPEND NEW HEAVENS & A NEW EARTH BENEATH & WITHIN	. .	329	FOUR ZOAS 7		380
LOS REARD HIS MIGHTY [FOREHEAD] STATURE ON EARTH STOOD HIS FEET ABOVE		334	FOUR ZOAS 7B		40
PROPAGATES THRO THE WARRING EARTH THE [LIONS] LION RAGING IN FLAMES		335	FOUR ZOAS 7B	*	110
AND THE HARLOT OF LOS & THE DELUDED HARLOT OF THE KINGS OF EARTH		336	FOUR ZOAS 7B	*	138
OR LIKE AN EARTHQUAKE RUMBLING IN THE BOWELS OF THE EARTH		339	FOUR ZOAS 7B		264
IS BORN ON EARTH SO WAS HE BORN OF FAIR JERUSALEM	. . .	347	FOUR ZOAS 8		262
AND LET ALL NATIONS [IN] OF THE EARTH WORSHIP AT THE SEPULCHER		349	FOUR ZOAS 8	*	336
AND ALL ON EARTH THE TEMPLE & THE SYNAGOGUE OF SATAN & MYSTERY		350	FOUR ZOAS 8		343
AMONG THE STARS THE EARTH & ALL THE ABYSSES FEEL ?HIS FURY		352	FOUR ZOAS 8	*	448
MOVING IN ROOT-LIKE FIBRES TREMBLING IN FEAR UPON THE EARTH		353	FOUR ZOAS 8	*	476
FOR SHE SPOKE OF ALL IN HEAVEN & ALL UPON THE EARTH	. .	353	FOUR ZOAS 8		490
THE ETERNAL MAN SLEEPS IN THE EARTH NOR FEELS THE VIGROUS SUN		354	FOUR ZOAS 8		507
HE SAW THE HARLOT OF THE KINGS OF EARTH & SAW HER CUP	. .	356	FOUR ZOAS 8		602
FOLDING LIKE SCROLLS OF THE ENORMOUS VOLUME OF HEAVEN & EARTH		357	FOUR ZOAS 9		14
THE HEAVENS ARE SHAKEN & THE EARTH REMOVED FROM ITS PLACE		357	FOUR ZOAS 9		16
THE TORRENTS BLACK UPON THE EARTH THE BLOOD POURS DOWN INCESSANT		359	FOUR ZOAS 9		73
MYSTERY'S TYRANTS ARE CUT OFF & NOT ONE LEFT ON EARTH	. .	359	FOUR ZOAS 9		79
AND WHEN ALL TYRANNY WAS CUT OFF FROM THE FACE OF EARTH	.	359	FOUR ZOAS 9	*	80
[BEGAN TO DRAW NEAR TO THE EARTH]		359	FOUR ZOAS 9		83
AND REASON ROUND THE EARTH THEY MARCH IN ORDER FLAME BY FLAME		359	FOUR ZOAS 9		87
THESE COVERING VAULTS OF HEAVEN & THESE TREMBLING GLOBES OF EARTH		364	FOUR ZOAS 9		260
THE KINGS & PRINCES OF THE EARTH CRY WITH A FEEBLE CRY	. .	365	FOUR ZOAS 9		328
THRO NIGHT SHOULD SING SOFT WARBLING FILLING EARTH & HEAVEN		366	FOUR ZOAS 9		352
IN WALLS OF GOLD WE CAST HIM LIKE A SEED INTO THE EARTH		374	FOUR ZOAS 9		632
THEN ALL THE SLAVES FROM EVERY EARTH IN THE WIDE UNIVERSE		375	FOUR ZOAS 9		682
COMPOSED BY AN AFRICAN BLACK FROM THE LITTLE EARTH OF SOTHA		375	FOUR ZOAS 9		686
AND ALL THY SONS O LUVAH BEAR AWAY THE FAMILIES OF EARTH		375	FOUR ZOAS 9		695
IN WATERS STIFLING OR IN AIR CORRODING OR IN EARTH SHUT UP		377	FOUR ZOAS 9		741
OF ALL THE NATIONS OF EARTH GROUND IN THE MILLS OF URTHONA		378	FOUR ZOAS 9		808
ONE EARTH ONE SEA BENEATH NOR ERRING GLOBES WANDER BUT STARS		379	FOUR ZOAS 9		831
THAT RISEN FROM THE SEA OF FIRE RENEWD WALK OER THE EARTH		379	FOUR ZOAS 9		837
THEY RAISE THEIR FACES FROM THE EARTH CONVERSING WITH THE MAN		379	FOUR ZOAS 9		843
AND THE FRESH EARTH BEAMS FORTH		379	FOUR ZOAS 9		848
A [MONSTER] WONDER LOVELY IN THE HEAVENS OR WANDRING ON THE EARTH		381	FOUR ZOAS AD 5		7
THRO THE HEAVEN & EARTH & HELL		416	MY SPECTRE/N		55
THE BANE OF ALL THAT ON EARTH I LOVE		419	I SAW A MONK/N		31
AS COLD EARTH WANDERERS NEVER KNEW		424	MENTAL TRAVLER		4
AND THE FLAT EARTH BECOMES A BALL		426	MENTAL TRAVLER		64
THE BANE OF ALL THAT ON EARTH I LOVD		430	GREY MONK		16
SOUNDING TO THE FOUR WINDS BENEATH [THE EARTH IS CONVULSD]		443A	LAST JUDGMNT/L		PROSE
EARTH IS CONVULSED WITH THE LABOURS OF THE RESURRECTION		443A	LAST JUDGMNT/L	*	PROSE
IN THE CAVERNS OF THE EARTH IS THE DRAGON WITH SEVEN HEADS		443A	LAST JUDGMNT/L		PROSE
THAT THE NEW JERUSALEM IS READY TO DESCEND UPON EARTH	.	444A	LAST JUDGMNT/L		PROSE
STAND UPON THE EARTH EMBRACING & SHOUTING TO THE LAMB	.	444A	LAST JUDGMNT/L		PROSE
& INSUBSTANTIAL THAN THOSE WHICH ARE DERIVED FROM EARTH		474B	ANNO REYNOLDS		MARG
ARE BUILT BENEATH THE EARTH & WATERS OF THE MUNDANE SHELL		483	MILTON 4		3
THRO ALBION'S FOUR FORESTS WHICH OVERSPREAD ALL THE EARTH		485	MILTON 6		3
AND PRAISE THRO THE WHOLE EARTH WERE REARD FROM IRELAND		486	MILTON 6		22
AND HENCE THEY OVERSPREAD THE NATIONS OF THE WHOLE EARTH & HENCE		486	MILTON 6		33
LOS IN HIS WRATH CURSD HEAVEN & EARTH HE RENT UP NATIONS		489	MILTON 9		13
TO PERVERT THE DIVINE VOICE IN ITS ENTRANCE TO THE EARTH		489	MILTON 9		23
OFFER THE HUMAN VICTIMS THROUGHOUT ALL THE EARTH AND ALBION'S		491	MILTON 11		8
DREAD TOMB IMMORTAL ON HIS ROCK OVERSHADOWD THE WHOLE EARTH		491	MILTON 11		9
SHAKING THE ROOTS & FAST FOUNDATIONS OF THE EARTH IN DOUBTFULNESS		495	MILTON 14		8
WHICH IS THIS EARTH OF VEGETATION ON WHICH NOW I WRITE	. .	496	MILTON 14		41
WHILE HE KEEPS ONWARDS IN HIS WONDROUS JOURNEY ON THE EARTH		497	MILTON 15		26
THUS IS THE EARTH ONE INFINITE PLANE AND NOT AS APPARENT		497	MILTON 15		32
THUS IS THE HEAVEN A VORTEX PASSD ALREADY AND THE EARTH		497	MILTON 15		34
BY HIM ON EARTH IN HIS BRIGHT PILGRIMAGE OF SIXTY YEARS		497	MILTON 15		52
WHICH WAS ON EARTH BORN TO CORRUPTION & THE SIX FEMALES		498	MILTON 17		15
THE MUNDANE SHELL IS A VAST CONCAVE EARTH AN IMMENSE	. .	498	MILTON 17		21
HARDEND SHADOW OF ALL THINGS UPON OUR VEGETATED EARTH	. .	498	MILTON 17		22
AND ANCIENT NIGHT & PURGATORY IT IS A CAVERNOUS EARTH	. .	498	MILTON 17		25
ALONG THE ROCKY ISLAND & THENCE THROUGHOUT THE WHOLE EARTH		499	MILTON 18		9
THAT EVERY INFANT THAT IS BORN UPON THE EARTH SHALL READ		499	MILTON 18		13
AND MOVED THE FAST FOUNDATIONS OF THE EARTH TO WAKE THE DEAD		500	MILTON 18		50

557

EARTH   (CONTINUED)
      REGIONS OF THE IMAGINATION ALSO ALL MEN ON EARTH . . . .   503 MILTON 21   5
      REMAINS PERMANENT THO ON THE EARTH WHERE SATAN   . . . .   505 MILTON 22   21
      NO FAITH IS IN ALL THE EARTH THE BOOK OF GOD IS TRODDEN   506 MILTON 22   60
         UNDER FOOT
      WHILE ON THE EARTH THEY LIVE IN SORROWFUL VEGETATIONS   . - 507 MILTON 23   44
      OUR WHEAT WITH SHOUTINGS OF JOY AND LEAVE THE EARTH IN   507 MILTON 23   46
         PEACE
      WHO DIED FROM EARTH & HE IS RETURND BEFORE THE JUDGMENT   508 MILTON 23   57
         THIS THING
      ONE THOUSAND YEARS AND ALL THE EARTH WAS IN A WATRY DELUGE 508 MILTON 24   5
      NOR VEGETATION MAY GO ON TILL ALL THE EARTH IS REAPD   .   509 MILTON 24   43
      ALL THE GODS OF THE KINGDOMS OF EARTH LABOUR IN LOS'S HALLS 510 MILTON 24   74
      SHALL NO MORE BE SOWN UPON EARTH TILL ALL THE VINTAGE IS   510 MILTON 25   9
         OVER
      BUT LOS REFUSED TILL ALL THE VINTAGE OF EARTH WAS GATHERD   510 MILTON 25   *   15
         IN
      FELLOW LABOURERS THE GREAT VINTAGE & HARVEST IS NOW UPON   510 MILTON 25   17
         EARTH
      . . . THAT THEY DESTROY NOT THE EARTH   . . . .   511 MILTON 25   39
      AND IN EVERY SPECIES OF EARTH METAL TREE FISH BIRD & BEAST 511 MILTON 25   4*
      AND YOU SHALL REAP THE WHOLE EARTH FROM POLE TO POLE FROM   511 MILTON 25   4,
         SEA TO SEA
      SO THEY ARE BORN ON EARTH & EVERY CLASS IS DETERMINATE . . 512 MILTON 26   _
      THIS WINE-PRESS IS CALLD WAR ON EARTH IT IS   513 MILTON 27   8
         THE PRINTING-PRESS
      BUT ALLAMANDA CALLD ON EARTH COMMERCE IS THE CULTIVATED   514 MILTON 27   42
         LAND
      THESE ARE THE STARRY VOIDS OF NIGHT & THE DEPTHS & CAVERNS 514 MILTON 27   51
         OF EARTH
      THAT MAN MAY LIVE UPON EARTH TILL THE TIME OF HIS AWAKING   514 MILTON 27   61
      TO MEET THE FLAT EARTH & THE SEA IN SUCH AN ORDERD SPACE   516 MILTON 29   9
      SUCH ARE THE SPACES CALLED EARTH & SUCH ITS DIMENSION   . . 516 MILTON 29   14
      INTO ETERNITY OF WHICH THIS VEGETABLE EARTH IS BUT A SHADOW 517 MILTON 29   22
      THESE ARE THE GODS OF THE KINGDOMS OF THE EARTH IN   520 MILTON 31   23
         CONTRARIOUS
      LOUD ROLL THE WEIGHTS & SPINDLES OVER THE WHOLE EARTH LET   525 MILTON 35   14
         DOWN
      THUS ARE THE MESSENGERS DISPATCHD TILL THEY REACH THE EARTH 526 MILTON 36   8
         AGAIN
      REACHING FROM HEAVEN TO EARTH A CLOUD & HUMAN FORM   . . . 528 MILTON 37   14
      THESE WONDERS OF SATAN'S HOLINESS SHEWING TO THE EARTH . . 530 MILTON 38   45
      BUT I ALONE AM GOD & I ALONE IN HEAVN & EARTH   . . . .   530 MILTON 38   56
      ARISE UPON THEIR THRONES TO JUDGE THE NATIONS OF THE EARTH 534 MILTON 42   17
      ALL ANIMALS UPON THE EARTH ARE PREPARD IN ALL THEIR   535 MILTON 42   39
         STRENGTH
      GO LOVE WITHOUT THE HELP OF ANY [THING] ?KING ON EARTH . . 541 ANGEL PRESID/N *   3
      SINCE ALL THE RICHES OF THIS [EARTH] WORLD . . . . . .   557 SINCE RICHES/N   1
      THEN SAID DESCEND THOU UPON EARTH . . . .   557 ART HAS LOST/N   4
      TILL THE HEAVENS & EARTH ARE GONE . . . .   558 THE CAVERNS/N   10
      IN WHOSE WREATHINGS ARE INFOLDED THE NATIONS OF THE EARTH   564D DESC CAT 1   TITLE
      HE IS ORDERING THE REAPER TO REAP THE VINE OF THE EARTH   565A DESC CAT 2   TITLE
      FROM SLEEP AND RESUME HIS DOMINION OVER EARTH AND OCEAN   577C DESC CAT 5   TITLE
      WOULD HAVE DEPOPULATED THE EARTH ALL THESE THINGS   578A DESC CAT 5   PROSE
         ARE WRITTEN
      POETRY AS IT EXISTS NOW ON EARTH IN THE VARIOUS REMAINS OF 579C DESC CAT 5   PROSE
      DOES FOR THO ON EARTH THINGS SEEM PERMANENT THEY . . . . 605A V LAST JUDG/N   PROSE
      AROUND HIS THRONE THE OLD (HEAVEN) & (OLD) EARTH ARE . . 606B V LAST JUDG/N   PROSE
      PASSING AWAY & THE (NEW) (HEAVEN) & (NEW) EARTH . . . . 606B V LAST JUDG/N   PROSE
      AS MULTITUDES OF CHILDREN ASCENDING FROM THE EARTH . . . 607C V LAST JUDG/N   PROSE
      FEET OF ABRAHAM & RECIEVE THEIR CHILDREN FROM THE EARTH   607C V LAST JUDG/N   PROSE
      WHICH ALAS EVERY ONE ON EARTH IS LIABLE TO ENTER INTO . . 608A V LAST JUDG/N   PROSE
      THE EARTH BENEATH THESE FALLING GROUPES OF FIGURES . . . 608A V LAST JUDG/N   PROSE
      THEY ASCEND FROM THE EARTH WHERE FIGURES KNEEL   . . . . 610B V LAST JUDG/N   PROSE
      & BEFORE THE NEW HEAVEN & THE NEW EARTH   . . . . 612A V LAST JUDG/N   PROSE
      REMOVING THE [?FORMER] OLD HEAVENS & THE OLD EARTH   . . . 612A V LAST JUDG/N   PROSE
      TO MAKE WAY FOR THE NEW HEAVEN & THE NEW EARTH   . . . . 612A V LAST JUDG/N   PROSE
      THE DAWN WITH HER DAPPLED HORSES ARISES ABOVE THE EARTH   618A ILLUS MILTON   PROSE
      THE EARTH BENEATH AWAKES AT THE LARK'S VOICE . . . . . 618B ILLUS MILTON   PROSE
      AIR WATER & EARTH SURROUND MILTON'S CHAIR . . . . . . 619B ILLUS MILTON   PROSE
      HIS SUBLIME & PATHOS BECOME TWO ROCKS PIXD IN THE EARTH   620 JERUSALEM 1   4
      HEAVEN EARTH & HELL HENCEFORTH SHALL LIVE IN HARMONY   . . 621 READER LOVER/J   10
      WE WHO DWELL ON EARTH CAN DO NOTHING OF OURSELVES . . . 621C JERUSALEM 3   PROSE
      LOS RAGD AND STAMPD THE EARTH IN HIS MIGHT & TERRIBLE WRATH 625 JERUSALEM 6   8
      HE STOOD AND STAMPD THE EARTH THEN HE THREW DOWN HIS HAMMER 625 JERUSALEM 6   9
         IN RAGE &
      WHIRLD ROUND FROM HEAVEN TO EARTH TREMBLING HE SAT HIS COLD 627 JERUSALEM 8   4
      AND THE EMANATIONS BURIED ALIVE IN THE EARTH WITH POMP   628 JERUSALEM 9   15
         OF RELIGION
      HE CURSES HEAVEN & EARTH DAY & NIGHT & SUN & MOON   . . . 629 JERUSALEM 10   25
      HE IS LIKE A MANDRAKE IN THE EARTH BEFORE REUBEN'S GATE   631 JERUSALEM 11   22
      THE SEVEN DISEASES OF THE EARTH ARE CARVED TERRIBLE   . . . 633 JERUSALEM 13   17
      FROM THE BLUE MUNDANE SHELL REACHING TO THE VEGETATIVE   633 JERUSALEM 13   33
         EARTH
      A CONCAVE EARTH WONDROUS CHASMAL ABYSSAL INCOHERENT   . . . 634 JERUSALEM 13   53
      OF ALL THE INHABITANTS OF EARTH WAILING TO BE CREATED   . . 634 JERUSALEM 13   63
      IN EVERY NATION OF THE EARTH TILL THE TWELVE SONS OF ALBION 635 JERUSALEM 15   3
      FROM ALBION OVER THE WHOLE EARTH SUCH IS MY AWFUL VISION   635 JERUSALEM 15   5
      ROUND FROM HEAVEN TO EARTH DOWN FALLING WITH HEAVY BLOW   636 JERUSALEM 16   12
      FROM THE BLUE MUNDANE SHELL EVEN TO THE EARTH OF VEGETATION 637 JERUSALEM 16   25
      AND THENCE TO ALL THE KINGDOMS & NATIONS & FAMILIES OF   637 JERUSALEM 16   34
         THE EARTH

EARTH   (CONTINUED)
        ALL THINGS ACTED ON EARTH ARE SEEN IN THE BRIGHT SCULPTURES   638 JERUSALEM 16   61
            OF
        TO LABOUR IN THE FIRE IN THE WATER IN THE EARTH IN THE AIR   638 JERUSALEM 17   2
        HIS EON WEEPING IN THE COLD AND DESOLATED EARTH   . . . .   641 JERUSALEM 19   16
        ALBION COVERD THE WHOLE EARTH ENGLAND ENCOMPASSD   648 JERUSALEM 24   44
            THE NATIONS
        AND THE MOUNT OF OLIVES WAS BEHELD OVER THE WHOLE EARTH   648 JERUSALEM 24   49
        YE ARE UNITED O YE INHABITANTS OF EARTH IN ONE RELIGION   649B JERUSALEM 27   PROSE
        & OAK GROVES OVER THE WHOLE EARTH WITNESS TO THIS DAY   . .   649C JERUSALEM 27   PROSE
        IN HIS MIGHTY LIMBS ALL THINGS IN HEAVEN & EARTH   . . . .   649C JERUSALEM 27   PROSE
        FROM EVERY NATION OF THE EARTH . . . .   651 FIELDS FROM/J   50
        THE LAMB OF GOD THE SAVIOUR BECAME APPARENT ON EARTH   . .   652B JERUSALEM 27   PROSE
        THEY BENT DOWN THEY FELT THE EARTH AND AGAIN ENROOTING . .   653 JERUSALEM 28   18
        OF THE WHOLE EARTH HE WAS THE ANGEL OF MY PRESENCE AND ALL   653 JERUSALEM 29   7
        IT PLOWS THE EARTH IN ITS OWN CONCEIT IT OVERWHELMS THE   659 JERUSALEM 33   9
            HILLS
        THE ANCIENT CITIES OF THE EARTH REMOVE AS A TRAVELLER   . .   659 JERUSALEM 33   14
        SATAN WORSHIPD AS GOD BY THE MIGHTY ONES OF THE EARTH   . .   659 JERUSALEM 33   18
        OF DEATH IN ALBION'S CLOUDS DREADFUL UTTERD OVER ALL THE   661 JERUSALEM 34   24
            EARTH
        LOS BENDED HIS NOSTRILS DOWN TO THE EARTH THEN SENT HIM   661 JERUSALEM 34   47
            OVER
        KOTOPE & BOWEN BECAME WHAT THEY BEHELD FLEEING OVER THE   663 JERUSALEM 36   19
            EARTH
        OF MULTITUDES WHO DIE FROM EARTH THIS GATE CANNOT BE FOUND   665 JERUSALEM 38   59
        OF SAND ON EARTH EVERY NIGHT THEY NEVER FIND THIS GATE . .   666 JERUSALEM 39   2
        . . . COVERD THE WHOLE EARTH   671 JERUSALEM 42   80
        THE VEGETATING CITIES ARE BURNED & CONSUMED FROM THE EARTH   679 JERUSALEM 49   12
        AND THE BODIES IN WHICH ALL ANIMALS & VEGETATIONS THE EARTH   679 JERUSALEM 49   13
            & HEAVEN
        THE NOSTRILS BENT DOWN TO THE EARTH & CLOSD WITH SENSELESS   680 JERUSALEM 49   38
            FLESH
        WHICH OVERSPREAD ALL THE EARTH HE GROANS AMONG HIS RUIND   685 JERUSALEM 54   14
            PORCHES
        THE STARS IN THEIR COURSES FOUGHT THE SUN MOON HEAVEN EARTH   686 JERUSALEM 55   27
        IF WE DO BUT OUR DUTY LABOUR WELL THE TEEMING EARTH . . .   687 JERUSALEM 55   53
        AROUND THE EARTH OF ALBION AMONG THE ROOTS OF HIS TREE . .   691 JERUSALEM 59   4
        A SHEPHERD IN THE NIGHT OF ALBION WHICH OVERSPREAD ALL   692 JERUSALEM 60   9
            THE EARTH
        FROM HEAVEN TO EARTH HOWLING INVISIBLE BUT NOT INVISIBLE   702 JERUSALEM 66   11
        OF FIRE THEN AN AWFUL FIERY WHEEL SURROUNDING EARTH   702 JERUSALEM 66   42
            & HEAVEN
        THE STARS FLEE REMOTE THE HEAVEN IS IRON THE EARTH   703 JERUSALEM 66   81
            IS SULPHUR
        OVER THE WHOLE EARTH LOUD THE WARRIORS RAGE IN BETH PEOh   704 JERUSALEM 67   29
        . . . TILL THE GREAT POLYPUS OF GENERATION COVERED THE   704 JERUSALEM 67   34
            EARTH
        SHOOTING OUT FIBRES ROUND THE EARTH THRO GAUL & ITALY   . .   704 JERUSALEM 67   38
        DEVOURING JERUSALEM FROM EVERY NATION OF THE EARTH   . . .   707 JERUSALEM 69   5
        IN THE OAK GROVES OF ALBION WHICH OVERSPREAD ALL THE EARTH   708 JERUSALEM 70   16
        AND EARTH & ALL YOU BEHOLD THO IT APPEARS WITHOUT IT IS   709 JERUSALEM 71   18
            WITHIN
        THE INHABITANTS OF THE WHOLE EARTH REJOICE IN THEIR   710 JERUSALEM 71   25
            BEAUTIFUL LIGHT
        AND FROM THEM ARE CREATED ALL THE NATIONS OF THE EARTH . .   712 JERUSALEM 72   30
        ALL THE NATIONS PEOPLES & TONGUES THROUGHOUT ALL THE EARTH   712 JERUSALEM 72   44
        WITHOUT & WHATEVER IS VISIBLE IN THE VEGETABLE EARTH THE   712 JERUSALEM 72   46
            SAME
        OVER THE FOUR FOLD MONARCHY FROM EARTH TO THE MUNDANE SHELL   713 JERUSALEM 73   15
        AND ALL THE KINGS & NOBLES OF THE EARTH & ALL THEIR   713 JERUSALEM 73   38
            GLORIES
        FROM ALL THE NATIONS OF THE EARTH TO DISSIPATE INTO NON   715 JERUSALEM 74   51
            ENTITY
        FURY & THUNDERING COURSE ROUND HEAVEN & EARTH . . . . .   717 STOOD AMONG/J   6
        THEY NAMD HER RAHAB & GAVE HER POWER OVER THE EARTH . . .   719 JERUSALEM 78   16
        THE CONCAVE EARTH ROUND GOLGONOOZA IN ENTUTHON BENYTHON   719 JERUSALEM 78   17
        AWAY FROM THE NATIONS OF THE EARTH & FROM THE CITIES OF   720 JERUSALEM 79   9
            THE NATIONS
        LONDON COVERD THE WHOLE EARTH ENGLAND ENCOMPASSD   720 JERUSALEM 79   22
            THE NATIONS
        AND ALL THE NATIONS OF THE EARTH WERE SEEN IN THE CITIES   720 JERUSALEM 79   23
            OF ALBION
        ALBION GAVE ME TO THE WHOLE EARTH TO WALK UP & DOWN TO POUR   720 JERUSALEM 79   36
        WHICH OVERSPREAD ALL THE EARTH IN PATRIARCHAL POMP & CRUEL   721 JERUSALEM 79   67
            PRIDE
        AMONG THE FOUR FORESTS OF ALBION WHICH OVERSPREAD ALL THE   722 JERUSALEM 80   43
            EARTH
        THE SERPENT TEMPLES THRO THE EARTH FROM THE WIDE PLAIN   723 JERUSALEM 80   48
            OF SALISBURY
        REFUSD TO TAKE A DEFINITE FORM SHE HOVERD OVER ALL THE   723 JERUSALEM 80   52
            EARTH
        BUT IF YOU ON EARTH FORGIVE . . . .   724 IN HEAVEN/J   4
        BE SEEN UPON THE FLUCTUATING EARTH WOVEN BY THE SISTERS   728 JERUSALEM 83   39
        AND SOMETIMES THE EARTH SHALL ROLL IN THE ABYSS & SOMETIMES   728 JERUSALEM 83   40
        ACCORDING TO THEIR WILL THE OUTSIDE SURFACE OF THE EARTH   728 JERUSALEM 83   46
        LOOKING TO THE EAST & HIS VOICE IS HEARD OVER THE WHOLE   730 JERUSALEM 85   12
            EARTH
        ON EARTH OF THOSE WHOSE EMANATIONS WEAVE THE LOVES . . .   731 JERUSALEM 86   43
        CAN THERE BE ANY SECRET JOY ON EARTH GREATER THAN THIS . .   733 JERUSALEM 88   * 15
        TWELVE RIDGES OF STONE FROWN OVER ALL THE EARTH IN TYRANT   735 JERUSALEM 89   21
            PRIDE

EARTH   (CONTINUED)

AND ALBION'S FORESTS OF OAKS COVERD THE EARTH FROM POLE TO POLE	735 JERUSALEM 89	23
IN DRUID TEMPLES OVER THE WHOLE EARTH WITH VICTIMS SACRIFICE	735 JERUSALEM 89	32
TERRIFIED ROCKING TO & FRO UPON THE EARTH & SOMETIMES . .	737 JERUSALEM 90	61
O ALL YE NATIONS OF THE EARTH BEHOLD YE THE JEALOUS WIFE	742 JERUSALEM 94	26
AS THE SUN & MOON LEAD FORWARD THE VISIONS OF HEAVEN & EARTH	743 JERUSALEM 95	21
AS THE SUN & MOON LEAD FORWARD THE VISIONS OF HEAVEN & EARTH	743 JERUSALEM 96	1
. . . THAT COVERD THE WHOLE EARTH BENEATH HIS SPECTRE . .	746 JERUSALEM 98	50
SUCH IS THE CRY FROM ALL THE EARTH	746 JERUSALEM 98	54
. . . FROM THE LIVING CREATURES OF THE EARTH	746 JERUSALEM 98	54
AND FROM THE THIRTY-TWO NATIONS OF THE EARTH	746 JERUSALEM 98	56
ALL HUMAN FORMS IDENTIFIED EVEN TREE METAL EARTH & STONE ALL	747 JERUSALEM 99	1
EARTH GROAND BENEATH & HEAVEN ABOVE	753 EV GOSPEL(E)/N	5
THE EARTH TREMBLING & NAKED LAY	754 EV GOSPEL(E)/N	15
EARTH HE STRUGGLES INTO LIFE	762D FOR SEXES/GP	TITLE
VOICE O EARTH COVER NOT THOU MY BLOOD COVER NOT THOU MY BLOOD	780 GHOST ABEL 1	8
OF BLOOD O EARTH COVER NOT THOU THE BLOOD OF ABEL . . .	780 GHOST ABEL 1	13
ABEL COMPELLED I CRY O EARTH COVER NOT THE BLOOD OF ABEL	780 GHOST ABEL 2	12
THE HOLY GHOST THY KINGDOM ON EARTH IS NOT [THY XXX] . .	788A ANNO THORNTON	* MARG
THY KINGSHIP COME UPON EARTH FIRST & THENCE IN HEAVEN . .	788D ANNO THORNTON	* MARG
IT ON EARTH & IF YOU APPROVE OF THIS	792B LETTER 4	PROSE
I BLESS THEE O FATHER OF HEAVEN & EARTH	799 TO FLAXMAN/L	1
. . . THE BLESSED OF HEAVEN ARE MY FRIENDS UPON EARTH .	799 TO FLAXMAN/L	2
. . . TO BE MINE SUCH MY LOT UPON EARTH	799 TO FLAXMAN/L	4
AND IN HELL BENEATH & A MIGHTY & AWFUL CHANGE THREATENED THE EARTH	799 TO FLAXMAN/L	8
. . . I COULD NOT SUBSIST ON THE EARTH	799 TO FLAXMAN/L	11
A NEW LIFE BECAUSE ANOTHER COVERING OF EARTH IS SHAKEN OFF	802B LETTER 14	PROSE
REMINISCENCE & BEHOLD OUR ANCIENT DAYS BEFORE THIS EARTH	802C LETTER 14	PROSE
MOUNTAIN HILL EARTH & SEA	805 TO BUTTS/L	30
IN OUR SHADOWS ON EARTH	805 TO BUTTS/L	43
THE SWEETEST SPOT ON EARTH AT LEAST IT IS SO TO ME & MY GOOD	808C LETTER 19	PROSE
MEDICINAL POTION BUT AS NONE ON EARTH CAN GIVE ME . . .	809B LETTER 20	PROSE
REFUSE & BURY YOUR TALENT IN THE EARTH EVEN THO YOU . . .	813A LETTER 22	PROSE
THIS EARTH BREEDS NOT OUR HAPPINESS	818 HAPPINESS/L	64
AND EVERY SOUL OF MEN ON THE EARTH	818 HAPPINESS/L	75
MEAN TIME I MUST NOT BURY THE TALENTS IN THE EARTH BUT DO MY	822C LETTER 26	PROSE
PERSONS & MACHINERY INTIRELY NEW TO THE INHABITANTS OF EARTH	823A LETTER 26	PROSE
YET I LAUGH & SING FOR IF ON EARTH NEGLECTED I AM IN HEAVEN	830A LETTER 30	PROSE
A PRINCE AMONG PRINCES & EVEN ON EARTH BELOVED BY THE GOOD	830A LETTER 30	PROSE
INTO THE VERY EARTH BY THE FOOTSTEPS OF THE FIENDS OF COMMERCE	849D LETTER 47	PROSE
NOT KNOWN TO MEN ON EARTH IT IS THE PASSAGE THRO THESE . .	862D LETTER 60	PROSE
UPON EARTH & OF THE SPIRITUAL VICTORIES OBTAIND FOR ME BY MY	862D LETTER 60	PROSE
I KNOW THAT THOSE WHO ARE DEAD FROM THE EARTH & WHO MOCKD &	863A LETTER 60	PROSE
COURAGE TO SAY SO PUBLICKLY & TO DARE ALL THE POWER ON EARTH	866B LETTER 64	PROSE
GOD SEND IT SO ON EARTH AS IT IS IN HEAVEN	879A LETTER 88	PROSE
THE SERPENT WHO GIRDS THE EARTH SPECTRES	SUPP ILLUS GRAY	*TITLE

EARTHAM

EARTHAM WILL BE MY FIRST TEMPLE & ALTAR	801B LETTER 13	PROSE
WILLIAM HAYLEY ESQR EARTHAM NEAR CHICHESTER SUSSEX . . .	SUPP ADDRESSES/L	*TITLE

EARTH-BORN

IN DELUGE OER THE EARTH-BORN MAN THEN TURND THE FLUXILE EYES	241 EUROPE 10	11

EARTH-BREATHING

AND THEY NESTLE IN EARTH-BREATHING BOSOMS	136 FRENCH REVOLTN	57

EARTHLY

TURNING OUR EARTHLY NIGHT TO HEAVENLY DAY	37C SAMSON/PS	PROSE
HE SPEAKS OF MEN AS MEER EARTHLY MEN NOT AS RECEPTACLES OF SPIRIT	92C ANNO SWED LOVE	MARG
FIRES INWRAP THE EARTHLY GLOBE YET MAN IS NOT CONSUMD . .	199 AMERICA 8	15
THE KINGDOM OF HEAVEN IS THE DIRECT NEGATION OF EARTHLY DOMINATION	407B ANNO BACON	MARG
WANDRING ROUND AN EARTHLY COT	425 MENTAL TRAVLER	30
IN MILD REPOSE FROM EARTHLY STRIFE	442 DEDICATN BLAIR	19
THAN ANY OTHER EARTHLY THINGS ARE MAN'S EARTHLY LINEAMENTS	503 MILTON 21	11
MILD WAS THE VOICE BUT MORE DISTINCT THAN ANY EARTHLY . .	527 MILTON 37	5
MAY BE GIFTS FROM THE DEVIL & EARTHLY KINGS	557 SINCE RICHES/N	2
IF I THANKD MY GOD FOR [WORLDLY]]EARTHLY] WORLDLY THINGS	557 SINCE RICHES/N	4
IN HEAVEN LOVE BEGETS LOVE BUT FEAR IS THE PARENT OF EARTHLY LOVE	725 JERUSALEM 81	15
WHY WILT THOU REND THYSELF APART & BUILD AN EARTHLY KINGDOM	730 JERUSALEM 85	30
NO EARTHLY PARENTS I CONFESS	748 EV GOSPEL(B)/N	7
NO EARTHLY PARENTS I CONFESS	750 EV GOSPEL(C)/N	7
NO EARTHLY PARENTS I CONFESS	751 EV GOSPEL(D)/N	9
NO EARTHLY PARENTS I CONFESS	757 EV GOSPEL(I)/N	33

EARTHQUAKD

HIS BOSOM EARTHQUAKD WITH SIGHS	230 URIZEN 13	49

EARTHQUAKE

EARTH THUS I STAMP THY BOSOM ROUSE THE EARTHQUAKE FROM HIS DEN	106 TIRIEL 5	4

		PAGE	TITLE	LINE

EARTHQUAKE   (CONTINUED)
    AND AS A SEA OERWHELMS A LAND IN THE DAY OF AN EARTHQUAKE   201 AMERICA 14   9
    TREMBLING SUNK AN EARTHQUAKE ROLLD ALONG THE MOSSY PILE   205 AMERICA CANC C   12
    THEN I HEARD THE EARTHQUAKE &C . . . .   336 FOUR ZOAS 7B   123
    AS WHEN THE EARTHQUAKE ROUZES FROM HIS DEN HIS SHOULDERS   336 FOUR ZOAS 7B   129
        HUGE
    OR LIKE AN EARTHQUAKE RUMBLING IN THE BOWELS OF THE EARTH   339 FOUR ZOAS 7B   264
    [HEAVING XXX] HEAVD LIKE AN EARTHQUAKE LABRING WITH   347 FOUR ZOAS 8   * 249
        CONVULSIVE GROANS
    TOLD OF THE ENORMOUS CONFLICT EARTHQUAKE BENEATH AROUND   500 MILTON 18   48
    STORMS & PESTILENCE IN HER LOCKS & IN HER LOINS EARTHQUAKE   698 JERUSALEM 64   10
EARTHQUAKES
    BY EARTHQUAKES RIVN BELCHING SULLEN FIRES . . . . .   227 URIZEN 10   4
    THRO LIGHTNINGS THUNDERS EARTHQUAKES & CONCUSSIONS FIRES   316 FOUR ZOAS 6   185
        & FLOODS
    OF DARK URTHONA THUNDERS EARTHQUAKES FIRES WATER FLOODS   378 FOUR ZOAS 9   812
    EARTHQUAKES AT LISBON ETC WERE THE NATURAL RESULT OF SIN   388B ANNO WATSON   MARG
    BY EARTHQUAKES A GREAT CITY ON FIRE IS SEEN IN THE DISTANCE   608B V LAST JUDG/N   PROSE
    THE LAND OF EARTHQUAKES AND THE LAND OF WOVEN LABYRINTHS   634 JERUSALEM 13   48
    OF EARTHQUAKES & CONSUMING FIRES THEY ROLL APART IN FEAR   733 JERUSALEM 88   9
EARTH'S
    TILL WE WERE ELEVATED ABOVE THE EARTH'S SHADOW . . . .   156D MARRIAGE HH 17   PROSE
    [THE] EARTH'S ANSWER . . . .   168D EARTHS ANSWR/N   TITLE
    EARTH'S ANSWER . . . .   210D EARTHS ANSR/SE   TITLE
    EACH SPECK OF DUST TO THE EARTH'S CENTER NESTLES ROUND   363 FOUR ZOAS 9   233
        & ROUND
    & ABOVE HIS [CAVERNS] CAVERN ON THE EARTH'S SURFACE . .   443A LAST JUDGMNT/L   PROSE
    THE VEGETATIVE UNIVERSE OPENS LIKE A FLOWER FROM   633 JERUSALEM 13   34
        THE EARTH'S CENTER
    CUT OFF FROM ALBION'S MOUNTAINS & FROM ALL THE EARTH'S   661 JERUSALEM 34   44
        SUMMITS
    BENEATH THE BOTTOMS OF THE GRAVES WHICH IS EARTH'S CENTRAL   677 JERUSALEM 48   13
        JOINT
    AND SOMETIMES IT TOUCHES THE EARTH'S SUMMITS & SOMETIMES   698 JERUSALEM 64   4
        SPREADS
    HE SCORND [HIS] EARTH'S PARENTS SCORND [HIS] EARTH'S GOD   757 EV GOSPEL(I)/N   35
    STRUGGLING THRO EARTH'S MELANCHOLY . . . .   770 OF GATES/GP   8
    EARTH'S ANSWER NURSE'S SONG THE FLY THE TYGER . . . .   SUPP LETTER 66A   *PROSE
EARTHS
    INTO EARTHS ROLLING IN CIRCLES OF SPACE THAT LIKE AN OCEAN   241 EUROPE 10   19
        RUSHD
    RENDING THE HEAVENS & EARTHS & DRINKING BLOOD IN THE HOT   335 FOUR ZOAS 7B   103
        BATTLE
    STRENGTH FROM THE EARTHS CONSUMD & HEAVENS & ALL HIDDEN   358 FOUR ZOAS 9   * 38
        ABYSSES
    A DISK OF BLOOD DISTANT & HEAVNS & EARTHS ROLL DARK BETWEEN   495 MILTON 14   27
    MUST TREMBLE IN THE HEAVENS & EARTHS THRO ALL THE ULRO   509 MILTON 24   39
        SPACE
    CRYING O GOD DELIVER US TO THE HEAVENS OR TO THE EARTHS   510 MILTON 25   13
    TO THEIR RESPECTIVE EARTHS & THERE ALL NIGHT CONSULT WITH   526 MILTON 36   4
        ANGELS
    IN HEAVENS & EARTHS AS IN YOUR OWN BOSOM YOU BEAR YOUR   709 JERUSALEM 71   17
        HEAVEN
EARTH-SHAKING
    OF UNCONQUERABLE FEAR AMIDST DELIGHTS OF REVENGE   702 JERUSALEM 66   39
        EARTH-SHAKING
EARTHWORM
    FOR THE EARTHWORM RENEWS THE MOISTURE OF THE SANDY PLAIN   289 FOUR ZOAS 2   368
    CRIED TO THE CHURCHYARDS & THE EARTHWORM CAME IN DISMAL   355 FOUR ZOAS 8   537
        STATE
    THE SPORTIVE ROOT THE EARTHWORM THE SMALL BEETLE THE WISE   377 FOUR ZOAS 9   756
        EMMET
EARTH-WORM,EARTH WORM
    ARISE ETHINTHUS THO THE EARTH-WORM CALL . . . . . .   243 EUROPE 13   16
    WHEN I CALLD FORTH THE EARTH-WORM FROM THE COLD & DARK   282 FOUR ZOAS 2   83
        OBSCURE
    AND I HAVE CAUSED THE EARTH WORM TO BEG FROM DOOR TO DOOR   290 FOUR ZOAS 2   392
    THE SPORTIVE ROOT THE EARTH-WORM THE GOLD BEETLE THE WISE   513 MILTON 27   12
        EMMET
    THE EMMET AND [EARTH-WORM] EARTH-WORMS ARE HIS SUPERIORS   688 JERUSALEM 56   * 37
        & HIS LORDS
EARTH-WORMS
    THE EMMET AND [EARTH-WORM] EARTH-WORMS ARE HIS SUPERIORS   688 JERUSALEM 56   * 37
        & HIS LORDS
EARTHY
    AND WASH MY EARTHY MIND IN THY CLEAR STREAMS . . . . .   14 IMIT SPEN/PS   4
    SO ENITHARMON CRIED UPON HER TERRIBLE EARTHY BED . . . .   335 FOUR ZOAS 7B   98
    THE LARK SITTING UPON HIS EARTHY BED JUST AS THE MORN . .   520 MILTON 31   29
EARWIG
    THE EARWIG ARMD THE TENDER MAGGOT EMBLEM OF IMMORTALITY   377 FOUR ZOAS 9   759
    THE EARWIG ARMD THE TENDER MAGGOT EMBLEM OF IMMORTALITY   513 MILTON 27   16
EASE
    AND RUNS AT SAM WHO SLIPS WITH EASE . . . .   16 BLIND-MANS/PS   34
    WOULD EASE MY PAIN THEN SHOULD I LAY AT QUIET AND HAVE REST   38C SAMSON/PS   PROSE
    TILL THE VILLAIN LEFT THE PATHS OF EASE . . . . . .   148 MARRIAGE HH 2   14
    ONLY FOR THE SAKE OF PRESENT EASE OR GRATIFICATION . . .   154B MARRIAGE HH 12   PROSE
    BUT FOR ANOTHER GIVES ITS EASE . . . .   162 CLOD PEBBLE/N   3
    JOYS IN ANOTHER'S LOSS OF EASE . . . .   162 CLOD PEBBLE/N   11
    BLAKE WAS GIVING HIS BODY EASE . . . .   187 WHEN KLOPSTK/N   7
    AND EASE POOR KLOPSTOCK'S NINE FOLD PAIN . . . . . .   187 WHEN KLOPSTK/N   28
    AND ARE THERE OTHER JOYS BESIDE THE JOYS OF RICHES AND   192 V DAU ALBION 4   21
        EASE

		PAGE	TITLE	LINE

EASE   (CONTINUED)
```
        BUT FOR ANOTHER GIVES ITS EASE . . . . . . . . .     211 CLOD PEBBLE/SE      3
        JOYS IN ANOTHER'S LOSS OF EASE . . . . . . . . .     211 CLOD PEBBLE/SE     11
        WITH EASE SEARCHING THE DIRE VACUITY . . . . . .     258 BOOK OF LOS 4      53
        TO EASE MY PANGS OF HEART & TO RESTORE SOME PEACE    298 FOUR ZOAS 4        33
            TO THARMAS
        . . . WANDERING IN VAIN SEEKING FOR EASE   . . . .   315 FOUR ZOAS 6       123
        IF THE PICTURE OUGHT TO BE SEEN WITH EASE . . . . . 479B ANNO REYNOLDS    MARG
        I OFT HAVE WISHD FOR HELL FOR EASE FROM HEAVEN . .   552 GROWN OLD IN/N      2
        HE DID NOT DIE WITH CHRISTIAN EASE . . . . . . .     751 EV GOSPEL(D)/N     31
        MR HAYLEY ACTS LIKE A PRINCE I AM AT COMPLETE EASE BUT .  808A LETTER 19   PROSE
        I KNOW MY COTTAGE IS TOO NARROW FOR YOUR EASE & COMFORT  808B LETTER 19    PROSE
        & HOW THEN COULD I BE AT EASE BUT I AM NOW NO LONGER IN  813B LETTER 22    PROSE
            THAT STATE
        AND EASE COMES NEVER IN MY SIGHT . . . . . . . .     818 HAPPINESS/L        60
        HOWEVER THIS I KNOW WILL SET YOU AT EASE I AM NOW SO FULL  820C LETTER 25  PROSE
        BUSINESS COMES IN & I SHALL BE AT EASE . . . . . .  832C LETTER 32         PROSE
        IT IS NOW PASSED AS I HOPE BUT THE MOMENT I GOT EASE OF  874B LETTER 79     PROSE
            BODY
```
EASED
```
        COME & BE EASED OF ALL YOUR PAINS . . . . . . .      56 HAIL MATRIM/IM     26
```
EASEL
```
        REMOVED WITH THE SAME CONVENIENCE AS SO MANY EASEL PICTURES  560D EXHIBITION ADV  PROSE
        NOTE I MEAN FRESCO EASEL OR CABINET PICTURES . . . . . 598A PUB ADDRESS/N  PROSE
```
EASIER
```
        THE MILLS OF SATAN AS THE EASIER TASK FOUND ALL CONFUSION  488 MILTON 8      5
        IT IS EASIER TO FORGIVE AN ENEMY THAN TO FORGIVE A FRIEND  737 JERUSALEM 91  2
        FEEL MUCH EASIER TO HEAR THAT YOU HAVE PARTED WITH YOUR  843A LETTER 42      PROSE
            HORSE
```
EASILY
```
        BE EASILY OUTDONE CHATTERTON NEVER WRIT THOSE POEMS . . .  51D ISLAND MOON 7  PROSE
        OF SOCIETY ARE EASILY EXCLUDED BUT NOT SO EASILY        561C EXHIBITION ADV   PROSE
            OBSTRUCTED
        SHALL THE GOLDEN AGE RETURN BUT ALAS YOU WILL NOT EASILY  570C DESC CAT 3    PROSE
        SUCH IMITATION WHICH ANY ONE MAY EASILY PERFORM . . . .  597B PUB ADDRESS/N  PROSE
        THE COMPARISON IS EASILY MADE & THE COPY DETECTED . . .  598A PUB ADDRESS/N  PROSE
        & ROOMS & ACCOMODATIONS ARE EASILY PROCURD BY ONE . .   808B LETTER 19       PROSE
        TAKE THEM DOWN AND UNROLL THEM BUT CANNOT DO IT EASILY AS  831B LETTER 31    PROSE
        AS YOURS TO HIM HE WILL NOT EASILY MEET FROM ANYONE ELSE  858A LETTER 55     PROSE
        CONSEQUENTLY OUR COUNTRYMEN ARE EASILY BROW-BEAT ON THE   864C LETTER 61     PROSE
        EASILY REMOVED BUT EXCRUCIATING WHILE IT LASTS & ENFEEBLING  871A LETTER 72  PROSE
```
EAST
```
        RISE FROM THE CHAMBERS OF THE EAST AND BRING . . . . .    3 TO MORNING/PS     4
        I TURN MY BACK TO THE EAST . . . . . . . . . . .      9 MAD SONG/PS         21
        OR IN THE CHAMBERS OF THE EAST . . . . . . . . .     10 TO MUSES/PS          2
        THEIR MIGHTY WINGS SHALL STRETCH FROM EAST TO WEST . .   33 EDW THIRD/PS 6   43
        TIME FOR CONTEMPLATION ROSE FROM THE FORSAKEN EAST . . .  39D SAMSON/PS      PROSE
        BUT NOW A CLOUD OERCASTS AND BACK TO TH EAST . . . . .   41B THEN SHE BORE   PROSE
        LIE STINKING ON THE EARTH THE BURIERS SHALL ARISE FROM  100 TIRIEL 1         49
            THE EAST
        AND POINTING TO THE EAST BEGAN TO SAY  . . . . . .    125 LIT BLK BOY/SI      8
        THEN EZEKIEL SAID THE PHILOSOPHY OF THE EAST TAUGHT . .  153D MARRIAGE HH 12  PROSE
        TO BE SEEN BUT A BLACK TEMPEST TILL LOOKING EAST . . .  156B MARRIAGE HH 17  PROSE
        AT LAST TO THE EAST DISTANT ABOUT THREE DEGREES APPEARD  156C MARRIAGE HH 17  PROSE
        THE [DAY] SUN ARISES IN THE EAST . . . . . . . .    177 DAY/N               1
        FROM NIGHTLY PREY AND LIFTS HIS GOLDEN BEAK TO THE PURE  190 V DAU ALBION 2   26
            EAST
        AND PAINE AND WARREN WITH THEIR FOREHEADS REARD TOWARD  199 AMERICA 9        11
            THE EAST
        BUT TERRIBLE ORC WHEN HE BEHELD THE MORNING IN THE EAST  244 EUROPE 14       37
        WHEN RINTRAH GAVE ABSTRACT PHILOSOPHY TO BRAMA IN THE EAST  245 SONG OF LOS 3  11
        NIGHT DARKEND AS SHE SPOKE A SHUDDRING RAN FROM EAST TO  273 FOUR ZOAS 1     312
            WEST
        HIS CLOUDY BELLOWS THE SOUTH & EAST & DISMAL WEST . . .  282 FOUR ZOAS 2     69
        ON THE EAST SIDE REVIVD HER SOUL WITH LIVES OF BEASTS &  285 FOUR ZOAS 2    195
            BIRDS
        AND FROM HER BOSOM LUVAH FELL FAR AS THE EAST & WEST  .  294 FOUR ZOAS 3    100
        THEY FLED TO EAST & WEST & LEFT THE NORTH & SOUTH OF HEAVEN  295 FOUR ZOAS 3  134
        WHEN HE HAD PASSD THESE SOUTHERN TERRORS HE APPROACHD THE  315 FOUR ZOAS 6   147
            EAST
        THE EAST WAS VOID BUT THARMAS ROLLD HIS BILLOWS IN      318 FOUR ZOAS 6     270
            CEASELESS EDDIES
        URTHONA IN THE NORTH LUVAH IN EAST THARMAS IN WEST . . .  319 FOUR ZOAS 6   280
        FROM EAST TO WEST FLOWD LIKE THE HUMAN VEINS IN RIVERS . .  337 FOUR ZOAS 7B  160
        TOWARD THE EAST ONE STANDING AT HIS HEAD TOWARD THE WEST  341 FOUR ZOAS 8      8
        THE SULTRY SOUTH WHEN THE SUN RISES & THE ANGRY EAST . .  355 FOUR ZOAS 8    565
        WHEN VOCAL MAY COMES DANCING FROM THE EAST AHANIA CAME . .  362 FOUR ZOAS 9  194
        WEAK WAILING IN THE TROUBLED AIR EAST WEST & NORTH & SOUTH  365 FOUR ZOAS 9   318
        FROM LONDON STONE TO BLACKHEATH EAST TO HOUNSLOW WEST . .  485 MILTON 6       4
        TO MEXICO & PERU WEST & EAST TO CHINA & JAPAN TILL BABEL  486 MILTON 6        23
        HE ALTERD THE POLES OF THE WORLD EAST WEST & NORTH & SOUTH  489 MILTON 9      17
        WAS UTTERD FROM THE EAST & FROM THE WEST & FROM THE SOUTH  490 MILTON 9       38
        COVERING THE EAST WITH SOLID BLACKNESS ROUND HIS HIDDEN  490 MILTON 9        40
            HEART
        AS THE EYE OF MAN VIEWS BOTH THE EAST & WEST ENCOMPASSING  497 MILTON 15      28
        ONE TO THE EAST NAMED LUVAH ONE TO THE WEST NAMED THARMAS  500 MILTON 19      17
        AND IN THE SOUTH REMAINS A BURNING FIRE IN THE EAST A VOID  500 MILTON 19     22
        IN THE FOUR POINTS OF HEAVEN EAST WEST & NORTH & SOUTH . .  504 MILTON 21     38
        UNWAKEND AND THE COVERING CHERUB ADVANCES FROM THE EAST  506 MILTON 23       10
        FOR LOS AGAINST THE EAST HIS FORCE CONTINUALLY BENDS  . .  512 MILTON 26      18
        IN BLIGHTS OF THE EAST THE HEAVY ROLLER FOLLOWS IN HOWLINGS  514 MILTON 27    48
            OF WOE
```

```
                                                               PAGE      TITLE          LINE
EAST    (CONTINUED)
     N(NORTH) URTHONA W(WEST) THARMAS S(SOUTH) URIZEN E(EAST)   523B MILTON 33       TITLE
        LUVAH
     ONE TO THE EAST OF LUVAH ONE TO THE WEST OF THARMAS     .  -  524 MILTON 34          37
     SOUTHWARD & BY THE EAST WITHIN THE BREACH OF MILTON'S        524 MILTON 34          42
        DESCENT
     IN THE EAST GATE OF GOLGONOOZA & THE TWENTY-EIGHTH BRIGHT    527 MILTON 36           9
     THE EAST TOWARD JERUSALEM'S GATES GROANING HE SAT ABOVE      531 MILTON 39          34
     AND TOWARD THE SOUTH FOURFOLD & FOURFOLD TOWARD THE EAST     632 JERUSALEM 12       47
        & WEST
     THE NADIR EAST THE CENTER UNAPPROACHABLE FOR EVER     .   .  632 JERUSALEM 12       56
     AND THE EYES ARE THE SOUTH AND THE NOSTRILS ARE THE EAST     632 JERUSALEM 12       59
     THE EAST IS INWARDS & THE WEST IS OUTWARDS EVERY WAY    .  .  635 JERUSALEM 14       30
     AND FROM HER BOSOM LUVAH FELL FAR AS THE EAST AND WEST   . .  655 JERUSALEM 29       79
     IS GREAT IN THE EAST THEIR SPEARS OF BLOOD RAGE IN THE       658 JERUSALEM 31       56
        EASTERN HEAVEN
     AND THE FOUR ZOAS CLOUDED RAGE EAST & WEST & NORTH & SOUTH   663 JERUSALEM 36       25
     AND URIZEN ASSUMES THE EAST LUVAH ASSUMES THE SOUTH     .  .  663 JERUSALEM 36       29
     [?WEST ?WEIGHING ?EAST & ?NORTH DIVIDING ?GENERATION XXX]    663 JERUSALEM 36     *  34
     HID FROM THE TERRIBLE EAST SHUT UP IN THE SOUTH & WEST   . .  668 JERUSALEM 41       22
     IN THE FOUR REGIONS OF HUMANITY EAST & WEST & NORTH & SOUTH  671 JERUSALEM 42       79
     WHICH IS THE VALE OF REPHAIM DREADFUL FROM EAST TO WEST      678 JERUSALEM 48       33
     ONE TO THE EAST LUVAH ONE TO THE WEST THARMAS         .   .  691 JERUSALEM 59       12
     IN THE SOUTH REMAINS A BURNING FIRE IN THE EAST A VOID   . .  691 JERUSALEM 59       18
     BEAUTIFUL SHE BEAMS TOWARDS THE EAST ALL KINDS OF PRECIOUS   710 JERUSALEM 71       40
        STONES
     ULSTER NORTH IN DAN'S GATE LEINSTER EAST IN JUDAH'S GATE     711 JERUSALEM 72        4
     THEY ARE CREATED CONTINUALLY EAST & WEST & NORTH & SOUTH     712 JERUSALEM 72       29
     FROM WEST TO EAST AGAINST THE CURRENT OF    .    .    .   .  717 STOOD AMONG/J       4
     FROM MY EAST & FROM MY WEST HE BLESSED ME AND GAVE     .  .  720 JERUSALEM 79       25
     HYLE ON EAST MOOR IN ROCKY DERBYSHIRE RAVD TO THE MOON    .  723 JERUSALEM 80       66
     LANGUISHD UPON MOUNT OLIVET EAST OF MILD ZION'S HILL      .  726 JERUSALEM 82       55
     MARCHING THRO EGYPT IN HIS FURY THE EAST IS PALE AT HIS      729 JERUSALEM 84       22
        COURSE
     LOOKING TO THE EAST & HIS VOICE IS HEARD OVER THE WHOLE      730 JERUSALEM 85       12
        EARTH
     WHICH STRETCHD ABROAD EXPANDING EAST & WEST & NORTH & SOUTH  733 JERUSALEM 88       32
     UPON EAST MOOR IN DERBYSHIRE & ALONG THE VALLEYS OF CHEVIOT  740 JERUSALEM 93        6
     ONE TOWARD THE EAST ONE TO THE SOUTH ONE TO THE NORTH        744 JERUSALEM 97        9
                                                                 745 JERUSALEM 98       13
        .  .  .
     .  .  . EAST IN RIVERS OF BLISS THE NERVES OF THE     .  .  745 JERUSALEM 98       16
     & GOVERNS HIS SONG WHEN MORN PURPLES THE EAST      .    .  . 792C LETTER 4       PROSE
     INJURE AS TO THE EAST AND NORTH I BELIEVE THEY CANNOT GET    807B LETTER 17      PROSE
     ST EDMUNDS CHAPEL EAST DEREHAM MAY BE UNDERSTOOD TO   .  .  838B LETTER 37      PROSE
     MEAN A CHAPEL IN EAST DEREHAM TOWN & NOT TO EXPRESS    .  .  838B LETTER 37      PROSE
     SUFFICIENTLY THAT THE MONUMENT IS IN EAST DEREHAM CHURCH     838B LETTER 37      PROSE
EASTERN
     COME OER THE EASTERN HILLS AND LET OUR WINDS     .  .  .  .  .   1 TO SPRING/PS       9
     OVER THE EASTERN STEEPS    .   .   .   .   .   .   .   .   .     9 MAD SONG/PS        6
     .  .  . FOR A CLOUD ON THE EASTERN HILLS     .  .  .  .  .   146 FRENCH REVOLTN     271
     WHERE THE SON OF FIRE IN HIS EASTERN CLOUD    .  .  .  .  .  160A SONG LIBERTY    PROSE
     IN THE EASTERN CLOUD INSTEAD OF NIGHT A SICKLY CHARNEL       191 V DAU ALBION 2      36
        HOUSE
     THE EASTERN CLOUD RENT ON HIS CLIFFS STOOD ALBION'S          197 AMERICA 3          14
        WRATHFUL PRINCE
     THE EASTERN SKY SPREADING HIS AWFUL WINGS ACROSS             201 AMERICA 13         12
        THE HEAVENS
     THEIR NUMBERS FORTY MILLIONS MUSTRING IN THE EASTERN SKY     201 AMERICA 13         16
     ALBION'S GUARDIAN WRITHED IN TORMENT ON THE EASTERN SKY      202 AMERICA 15          6
     THE EASTERN CLOUD RENT ON HIS CLIFFS STOOD ALBION'S FIERY    204 AMERICA CANC A     14
        PRINCE
     TILL MORNING OPED THE EASTERN GATE [AND THE ANGEL TRUMPET    244 EUROPE 14       *  35
        BLEW]
     INTO THE EASTERN VACUITY THE EMPTY WORLD OF LUVAH    .  .  .  315 FOUR ZOAS 6       156
     UPON THE EASTERN SEA DIRECT THEY TAKE THEIR COURSE    .  .  .  336 FOUR ZOAS 7B     151
     IN RADIANT YOUTH WHEN LO LIKE GARLANDS IN THE EASTERN SKY    362 FOUR ZOAS 9       193
     SHE RISES AMONG FLOWERS & LOOKS TOWARD THE EASTERN           367 FOUR ZOAS 9       390
        CLEARNESS
     BUT THE LARK'S NEST IS AT THE GATE OF LOS AT THE EASTERN     526 MILTON 35          66
     OUT FROM THE EASTERN SKY DESCENDING DOWN INTO MY COTTAGE     529 MILTON 38           7
     IN THE EASTERN PORCH OF SATAN'S UNIVERSE MILTON STOOD &      529 MILTON 38          28
        SAID
     VARIOUS OFFICES AT THE EASTERN GATE BENEATH IN SMALL         618B ILLUS MILTON   PROSE
        FIGURES
     THE FURNACE OF LOS BEFORE THE EASTERN GATE BENDING THEIR     623 JERUSALEM 5        28
        FURY
     THE EASTERN GATE FOURFOLD TERRIBLE & DEADLY ITS ORNAMENTS    633 JERUSALEM 13       12
     AND SIXTY-FOUR THOUSAND GENII GUARD THE EASTERN GATE     .  .  633 JERUSALEM 13       26
     A BUILDING OF LUVAH BUILDED IN JERUSALEM'S EASTERN GATE      657 JERUSALEM 31       24
        TO BE
     IS GREAT IN THE EAST THEIR SPEARS OF BLOOD RAGE IN THE       658 JERUSALEM 31       56
        EASTERN HEAVEN
     OF ETERNITY PALE STOOD ALBION AT HIS EASTERN GATE    .   .  658 JERUSALEM 31       70
     THE CLOUDS OF ALBION'S DRUID TEMPLES RAGE IN THE EASTERN     692 JERUSALEM 60        1
        HEAVEN
     FOR IN THE DEPTHS OF ALBION'S BOSOM IN THE EASTERN HEAVEN    699 JERUSALEM 65        5
     EACH WITHOUTSIDE OF THE OTHER COVERING EASTERN HEAVEN    .  .  734 JERUSALEM 89        8
EASTMEATH
     EASTMEATH WESTMEATH DUBLIN KILDARE KINGS COUNTY    .  .  .  .  711 JERUSALEM 72       19
EASTWARD
     EASTWARD OF GOLGONOOZA STANDS THE LAKE OF [?UAAN] UDAN       346 FOUR ZOAS 8     *  224
        ADAM IN
```

EASTWARD   (CONTINUED)
BUT THE WINE-PRESS OF LOS IS EASTWARD OF GOLGONOOZA BEFORE   513 MILTON 27   1
  THE SEAT
ON ALL SIDES ROUND TO THE FOUR QUARTERS OF THE WORLD   525 MILTON 35   15
  EASTWARD ON
AN AWFUL FORM EASTWARD FROM MIDST OF A BRIGHT PAVED-WORK   531 MILTON 39   24
EASTWARD UPON THE PAVED WORK ACROSS EUROPE & ASIA   . . .   532 MILTON 40   18
THE LANDSCAPE IS AN EASTWARD VIEW OF THE COUNTRY . . . .   567A DESC CAT 3   PROSE
THE LANDSCAPE IS AN EASTWARD VIEW OF THE COUNTRY . . . .   588D CHAUCER/N   PROSE
THE LANDSCAPE IS AN EASTWARD VIEW OF THE COUNTRY . . . .   590B CHAUCER 2   PROSE
EASTWARD A PILLAR OF A CLOUD WITH VALA UPON THE MOUNTAINS   624 JERUSALEM 5   48
EASTWARD TOWARD THE STARRY WHEELS BUT WESTWARD A BLACK   624 JERUSALEM 5   68
  HORROR
EASTWARD & SOUTHWARD & NORTHWARD ARE INCIRCLED WITH FLAMING   635 JERUSALEM 14   28
  FIRES
AND LOS BEHELD THE MILD EMANATION JERUSALEM EASTWARD   635 JERUSALEM 14   31
  BENDING
FROM HIS VALLEYS EASTWARD FROM AMALEK CANAAN & MOAB   . .   654 JERUSALEM 29   31
REMOVE EASTWARD TO BASHAN AND GILEAD AND LEAVE   . . . .   679 JERUSALEM 48   64
WITH BLOOD FROM JAPAN EASTWARD TO THE GIANTS CAUSWAY WEST   719 JERUSALEM 78   26
SEE HOW THE FIRES OF OUR LOINS POINT EASTWARD TO BABYLON   725 JERUSALEM 82   36
FIBRES OF LOS SENDING THEM OVER THE OCEAN EASTWARD INTO   733 JERUSALEM 88   25
EASTWARD INTO HER OWN CENTER CREATING THE FEMALE WOMB   . . 734 JERUSALEM 88   52
EASY
AN EASY OF [HUMAN] HUMING UNDERSTANDING . . . .   52D ISLAND MOON 8 *PROSE
("NOT MUCH RECTITUDE IF UNEASY IN PRESENCE OF THE GOOD")   82C ANNO LAVATER   MARG
  EASY
IT IS AN EASY THING TO TRIUMPH IN THE SUMMER'S SUN   . . .   290 FOUR ZOAS 2   402
IT IS AN EASY THING TO TALK OF PATIENCE TO THE AFFLICTED   290 FOUR ZOAS 2   404
IT IS AN EASY THING TO LAUGH AT WRATHFUL ELEMENTS   . . .   290 FOUR ZOAS 2   408
IT IS AN EASY THING TO REJOICE IN THE TENTS OF PROSPERITY   291 FOUR ZOAS 2   417
IT IS AN EASY MATTER FOR A BISHOP TO TRIUMPH OVER PAINE'S   383B ANNO WATSON   MARG
ATTACK BUT IT IS NOT SO EASY FOR ONE WHO LOVES THE BIBLE   383B ANNO WATSON   MARG
EASY FOR HIM TO SNATCH AWAY THE VISION TIME AFTER TIME FOR   582C DESC CAT 9   PROSE
IT IS EASY TO ACKNOWLEDGE A MAN TO BE GREAT & GOOD WHILE WE   673 JERUSALEM 43   56
BUT THIS IS NO EASY MATTER TO A MAN WHO . . . .   811D LETTER 22   PROSE
VERY EASY AM NOW LEARNING MY HEBREW (ALEPH BETH GIMMEL)   821D LETTER 25   PROSE
IN THIS WORLD AS EASY AS I CAN IN THAT OF AFFECTION &   . . 857C LETTER 54   PROSE
EAT
THAT I SHOULD DRINK NO WINE NOR EAT OF ANY UNCLEAN THING   39C SAMSON/PS   PROSE
NOW THEREFORE DRINK NO WINE AND EAT NOT ANY UNCLEAN THING   39D SAMSON/PS   PROSE
SIT AND EAT AND TELL US OF THY NAME AND WARFARE(?WAYFARE)   40B SAMSON/PS   PROSE
HE EAT WERY LITTLE WICKLY THAT IS . . . .   49C ISLAND MOON 5   PROSE
WERE FIT TO GIVE LAW TO THE CITY EACH EAT AS MUCH AS TEN   58 THIS CITY/IM   10
THE HUNGRY POOR ENTERD THE HALL TO EAT GOOD BEEF & ALE   . .   58 THIS CITY/IM   11
BUT THEIR NASTY HEARTS POOR DEVILS ARE EAT UP WITH ENVY   62D ISLAND MOON 11 PROSE
THEY SAT & EAT & HAR & HEVA SMILD ON TIRIEL   . . . . . .   102 TIRIEL 3   1
TIRIEL I NEVER SAW BUT ONCE I SAT WITH HIM & EAT . . . . .   102 TIRIEL 3   9
FOR BIRDS TO EAT BUT I HAVE SCARCE DEPARTED FROM THE PLACE   105 TIRIEL 4   * 52
I HAVE NOT EAT THESE TWO DAYS LEAD ME TO HAR & HEVA'S TENT   107 TIRIEL 6   19
WHERE ARE YOU GOING COME & EAT SOME ROOTS & DRINK SOME   109 TIRIEL 7   11
  WATER
EAT IN THE EVENING SLEEP IN THE NIGHT . . . .   152A MARRIAGE HH 9   PROSE
I THEN ASKED EZEKIEL WHY HE EAT DUNG & LAY SO LONG ON HIS   154A MARRIAGE HH 12 PROSE
THAT NONE DARE EAT THE FRUIT BUT FROM . . . .   171 TO NOBODADDY/N   7
RUDDY & SWEET TO EAT . . . .   174 HUMAN IMAGE/N   19
AND THE [FAMINE] SHALL EAT BOTH CRUST & CRUMB . . . . . .   185 LET BROTHELS/N   8
RUDDY AND SWEET TO EAT . . . .   217 HUMAN ABSTR/SE   18
SNARING THE WILD GOATS FOR THEIR MILK THEY EAT THE FLESH   270 FOUR ZOAS 1   235
  OF LAMBS
THEY EAT THE [XXX] FLESHLY BREAD THEY DRANK THE NERVOUS   274 FOUR ZOAS 1   * 355
  [BLOODY] WINE
AND DO MY MINISTRY TO THOSE WHO EAT OF MY WIDE TABLE   . .   292 FOUR ZOAS 3   17
TO BEAR THIS SELF CONVICTION TAKE THEN EAT THOU ALSO OF   330 FOUR ZOAS 7   393
THEN LOS PLUCKED THE FRUIT & EAT & SAT DOWN IN DESPAIR . .   330 FOUR ZOAS 7   395
SAYING O THAT I HAD NEVER DRANK THE WINE NOR EAT THE BREAD   361 FOUR ZOAS 9   * 164
SHE [D] STOPD TO DRINK OF THE CLEAR SPRING & EAT THE GRAPES   369 FOUR ZOAS 9   * 476
  & APPLES
AND COUCHING AT THEIR SIDE SHALL EAT FROM THE CURLD BOY'S   376 FOUR ZOAS 9   * 707
  WHITE LAP
AND NOTHING LEFT TO EAT OR DRINK . . . .   426 MENTAL TRAVLER   67
FOR JOHN EAT & DRINK TO DRIVE AWAY LOVE'S PAIN . . . . .   434 LONG JOHN BRWN   10
THO HE EAT & DRANK AS MUCH AS TEN MEN FOR HIS DINNER   . .   434 LONG JOHN BRWN   12
I SHALL EAT COARSER FOOD & GO WORSE SHOD . . . .   559 I ROSE UP AT/N   26
WHICH NEVER WAS MADE FOR MAN TO EAT . . . .   755 EV GOSPEL (E)/N   96
WE EAT LITTLE WE DRINK LESS . . . .   818 HAPPINESS/L   63
EATEN
FOR STOLEN JOYS ARE SWEET & BREAD EATEN IN SECRET PLEASANT   237 EUROPE INTRO   6
EATING
WITH EATING BEEF & DRINKING BEER O THEY WERE STOUT & HALE   58 THIS CITY/IM   7
WHO IS THE GENIUS OF EATING AND DRINKING THE BACCHUS   . .   571A DESC CAT 3   PROSE
OR EATING OF THE TREE OF THOSE KNOWLEDGES OR REASONINGS   604C V LAST JUDG/N   PROSE
[ARE THE SAME THING] IS EATING OF THE TREE OF KNOWLEDGE   615A V LAST JUDG/N   PROSE
THE COMBATS OF TRUTH & ERROR IS EATING OF THE TREE OF LIFE   615A V LAST JUDG/N   PROSE
BUT UNBELIEF & EATING OF THE TREE OF KNOWLEDGE OF GOOD   615C V LAST JUDG/N   PROSE
  & EVIL
& EATING THE TREE OF KNOWLEDGE FOR SATAN'S GRATIFICATION   616D V LAST JUDG/N   PROSE
IN WHICH IS SEEN QUEEN MAB EATING THE JUNKETS . . . . .   618C ILLUS MILTON   PROSE
DRINKING & EATING & PITYING & WEEPING AS AT A TRAJIC SCENE   669 JERUSALEM 41   29
BECAME A RAVENING EATING CANCER GROWING IN THE FEMALE   . .   707 JERUSALEM 69   2
THE ANCIENTS CALLD IT EATING OF THE TREE OF GOOD & EVIL   778C HOMERS POETRY   PROSE

EATS
     FOR AS HE EATS & DRINKS HE GROWS . . . .   426 MENTAL TRAVLER   73
     THE PLAYHOUSES WHO EATS & DRINKS FOR BUSINESS NOT FOR NEED 830A LETTER 30   PROSE
EBAL
     BIND HIM DOWN SISTERS BIND HIM DOWN ON EBAL MOUNT OF   349 FOUR ZOAS 8   315
        CURSING
     BIND HIM DOWN SISTERS BIND HIM DOWN ON EBAL MOUNT OF   705 JERUSALEM 68   3
        CURSING
ECCENTRIC   SEE EXCENTRIC
     THE ELEMENTAL PLANETS & THE ORBS OF ECCENTRIC FIRE . . . 308 FOUR ZOAS 5   126
ECCENTRICITY
     AND IRREGULAR ECCENTRICITY A MADMAN'S SCRAWLS I DEMAND . . 561B EXHIBITION ADV PROSE
     WHICH GAINED THAT PATRONAGE CRIED DOWN AS ECCENTRICITY . 572D DESC CAT 3   PROSE
ECCHO
     THE DAUGHTERS OF ALBION HEAR HER WOES & ECCHO BACK HER   190 V DAU ALBION 2   20
        SIGHS
     THE DAUGHTERS OF ALBION HEAR HER WOES & ECCHO BACK HER   192 V DAU ALBION 5   2
        SIGHS
     THE DAUGHTERS OF ALBION HEAR HER WOES & ECCHO BACK HER   195 V DAU ALBION 8   13
        SIGHS
     THE ECCHO WAKES THE MOON TO UNBIND HER SILVER LOCKS . . . 289 FOUR ZOAS 2   346
     SHE CALLD BUT NONE COULD ANSWER HER & THE ECCHO OF HER   370 FOUR ZOAS 9   499
        VOICE RETURND
ECCHOED
     AND ALL THE HILLS ECCHOED . . . .   60 NURSES SONG/IM   17
     AND ALL THE HILLS ECCHOED . . . . 121 NURSES SONG/SI   16
ECCHOES
     THE VOICE OF WANDERING REUBEN ECCHOES FROM STREET TO STREET 729 JERUSALEM 84   13
ECCHOING
     THE ECCHOING GREEN . . . . 116A ECCHOING GR/SI   TITLE
     ON THE ECCHOING GREEN . . . . 116 ECCHOING GR/SI   10
     ON THE ECCHOING GREEN . . . . 116 ECCHOING GR/SI   20
     WITH ECCHOING CONFUSION THO THE SUN WAS RISEN ON HIGH . 488 MILTON 8   10
     AND SILVER OARS REFLECT ON ITS PILLARS & SOUND ON   690 JERUSALEM 58   25
        ITS ECCHOING
     ECCHOING GREEN DITTO THE LAMB THE SHEPHERD INFANT JOY   SUPP LETTER 66A   *PROSE
ECCHOS
     DELICIOUS VIANDS DEMONS OF WAVES THEIR WATRY ECCHOS WOKE 274 FOUR ZOAS 1   * 378
ECHARD
     VOLTAIRE ECHARD RAPIN PLUTARCH NOR HERODOTUS . . . . . 579A DESC CAT 5   PROSE
ECHOD   SEE RE-ECHOD
ECHOES
     NOR ECHOES SWEET NOR WATERS CLEAR AS HEAVEN . . . . .   2 TO SUMMER/PS   18
     THE ECHOES OF SLAUGHTER REACH FROM HILL TO HILL . . . . 40B SAMSON/PS   PROSE
ECHOING
     I LOVE THE ECHOING HILL . . . .   7 LOVE JOCUND/PS   6
ECLIPSE
     IN SICKLY DARKNESS LIKE A DIM ECLIPSE . . . . 31 EDW THIRD/PS 6   4
     THEN PALAMABRON REDDENING LIKE THE MOON IN AN ECLIPSE . . 487 MILTON 7   22
ECLOGUE
     SEE ECLOGUE I FOR ALL THIS WE THANK DR THORNTON . . . . 789B ANNO THORNTON   MARG
EDDA
     READ THE EDDA OF ICELAND THE SONGS OF FINGAL . . . . . 389C ANNO WATSON   MARG
EDDIES
     EDDIES OF WRATH CEASELESS ROUND & ROUND . . . . 227 URIZEN 10   20
     AND FLUCTUATING ALL BENEATH IN EDDIES OF MOLTEN FLUID . . 301 FOUR ZOAS 4   164
     THE ETERNAL MIND BOUNDED BEGAN TO ROLL EDDIES OF WRATH   303 FOUR ZOAS 4   208
        CEASELESS
     THE EAST WAS VOID BUT THARMAS ROLLD HIS BILLOWS IN   318 FOUR ZOAS 6   270
        CEASELESS EDDIES
EDDYING
     THY EDDYING SPIRIT DOWN THE HILLS OF BEULAH ALL MY SONS 300 FOUR ZOAS 4   89
     AND EDDYING FIERCE REJOICE IN THE FIERCE AGITATION OF   378 FOUR ZOAS 9   811
        THE WHEELS
     REPENTANT AND SHE ALSO IN THE EDDYING WIND OF LOS'S BELLOWS 726 JERUSALEM 82   74
EDELINCK
     THAN ALB DURER GOLTZIUS SADELER OR EDELINCK BUT   594C PUB ADDRESS/N   PROSE
        I DO PRETEND
EDEN
     [IN EDEN IN THE GARDEN OF GOD & IN HEAVENLY JERUSALEM] . . SUPP FOUR ZOAS 8   *
     EACH FIELD SEEMS EDEN AND EACH CALM RETREAT . . . . .   9 FRESH FROM/PS   15
     WHERE IS MY LUREING BIRD OF EDEN LEUTHA SILENT LOVE . . . 244 EUROPE 14   9
     ADAM STOOD IN THE GARDEN OF EDEN . . . . 245 SONG OF LOS 3   6
     LAY BLEACHD ON THE GARDEN OF EDEN . . . . 248 SONG OF LOS 7   21
     CANNOT EXIST BUT FROM THE UNIVERSAL BROTHERHOOD OF EDEN 264 FOUR ZOAS 1   10
     IN EDEN IN THE AURICULAR NERVES OF HUMAN LIFE . . . . . 264 FOUR ZOAS 1   17
     WHICH IS THE EARTH OF EDEN HE HIS EMANATIONS PROPAGATED 264 FOUR ZOAS 1   18
     IN [BEULAH] EDEN FEMALES SLEEP THE WINTER IN SOFT SILKEN 266 FOUR ZOAS 1   64
        VEILS
     . . . VISIONS TOWARD HEAVEN] MADE WINDOWS INTO EDEN . . . 270 FOUR ZOAS 1   224
     WHY SHOULD THE DIVINE VISION COMPELL THE SONS OF EDEN . . 273 FOUR ZOAS 1   339
     LIVE IN PERFECT HARMONY IN EDEN THE LAND OF LIFE . . . . 277 FOUR ZOAS 1   474
     IN EDEN THAT ONE DIED A DEATH NEVER TO BE REVIVD . . . . 278 FOUR ZOAS 1   529
     THE EMPYREAN GROUND THROUGHOUT ALL EDEN WAS DARKEND . . . 304 FOUR ZOAS 4   264
     THEN SANG THE SONS OF EDEN ROUND THE LAMB OF GOD & SAID 346 FOUR ZOAS 8   194
     WITH GIFTS & GOLD OF EDEN ASTONISHD STUPIFIED WITH DELIGHT 346 FOUR ZOAS 8   * 214
     (FORLORN) OF EDEN & REPUGNANT TO THE FORMS OF LIFE . . . 347 FOUR ZOAS 8   254
     HE STOOD IN FAIR JERUSALEM TO AWAKE UP INTO EDEN . . . . 348 FOUR ZOAS 8   264
     TO MULTITUDE AS IT IS IN EDEN SO PERMITTED BECAUSE . . . 348 FOUR ZOAS 8   284
     TIMES AFTER TIMES AND THOSE IN EDEN SENT LUCIFER FOR THEIR 351 FOUR ZOAS 8   398
        GUARD
     OUR FIRST PARENTS OUT OF EDEN THROUGH A GUARD OF WEEPING 441D INSC FALL MAN   PROSE
        ANGELS

		PAGE	TITLE	LINE
EDEN	(CONTINUED)			
AND ALL EDEN DESCENDED INTO PALAMABRON'S TENT		489	MILTON 9	1
AND PALAMABRON APPEALD TO ALL EDEN AND RECIEVD . . .		489	MILTON 9	9
TILL IT BECAME A PROVERB IN EDEN SATAN IS AMONG THE REPROBATE		489	MILTON 9	12
WHICH NOW AROSE AND WALKD WITH THEM IN EDEN AS AN EIGHTH		496	MILTON 15	5
HIS LIPS WITH FOOD OF EDEN IN HIS COLD AND DIM REPOSE .		496	MILTON 15	15
HE RECOLLECTED AN OLD PROPHECY IN EDEN RECORDED		503	MILTON 20	57
THERE IS IN EDEN A SWEET RIVER OF MILK & LIQUID PEARL . .		503	MILTON 21	15
OF EDEN HEARD THE LAMENTATION AND PROVIDENCE BEGAN . .		504	MILTON 21	24
I RECOLLECT AN OLD PROPHECY IN EDEN RECORDED IN GOLD AND OFT		507	MILTON 23	35
THIS MIGHTY ONE IS COME FROM EDEN HE IS OF THE ELECT . .		508	MILTON 23	56
TO THE INHABITANTS OF EDEN AROUND THEM ON ALL SIDES . . .		518	MILTON 30	9
THE SONS OF EDEN THE MOONY HABITATIONS OF BEULAH . .		518	MILTON 30	13
AND THRO BEULAH TO EDEN BENEATH LOS'S WESTERN WALL . .		526	MILTON 35	51
THE WILD THYME IS LOS'S MESSENGER TO EDEN A MIGHTY DEMON		526	MILTON 35	54
OF ISRAEL AS THEY ARE IN EDEN MOUNTAIN RIVER & PLAIN .		532	MILTON 40	26
IN EDEN THE ARTIST IS AN INHABITANT OF THAT HAPPY COUNTRY		578A	DESC CAT 5	PROSE
TO BE OPENED AGAIN TO HEAVEN THROUGH EDEN		578A	DESC CAT 5	PROSE
WAS IN THE WARS OF EDEN DIVIDED INTO MALE AND FEMALE .		578A	DESC CAT 5	PROSE
LEARNING & SCIENCE WHICH ACCOMPANIED ADAM OUT OF EDEN .		611D	V LAST JUDG/N	PROSE
EDEN AND THAT TOWARD THE WORLD OF GENERATION		632	JERUSALEM 12	49
BUT THAT TOWARD EDEN IS WALLED UP TILL TIME OF RENOVATION		632	JERUSALEM 12	52
AND THAT TOWARD EDEN FOUR FORMD OF GOLD SILVER BRASS & IRON		633	JERUSALEM 13	1
THAT TOWARD EDEN FOUR IMMORTAL GOLD SILVER BRASS & IRON		633	JERUSALEM 13	5
THAT TOWARD ULRO CLAY THAT TOWARD EDEN METALS . . .		633	JERUSALEM 13	10
THAT TOWARD EDEN ETERNAL ICE FROZEN IN SEVEN FOLDS . .		633	JERUSALEM 13	15
MOVING BY COMPULSION EACH OTHER NOT AS THOSE IN EDEN WHICH		636	JERUSALEM 15	19
IN ALL THE GARDEN OF EDEN & IN ALL THE GOLDEN MOUNTAINS		652	JERUSALEM 28	2
THEREFORE THE SONS OF EDEN PRAISE URTHONA'S SPECTRE IN SONGS		655	JERUSALEM 30	14
HIS COLD AGAINST THE WARMTH OF EDEN RAGD WITH LOUD . .		664	JERUSALEM 38	8
LIVE IN PERFECT HARMONY IN EDEN THE LAND OF LIFE		665	JERUSALEM 38	21
IN EDEN IN THE GARDEN OF GOD AND IN HEAVENLY JERUSALEM .		665	JERUSALEM 38	25
WOVEN IN LOOMS OF EDEN IN SPIRITUAL DEATHS OF MIGHTY MEN		665	JERUSALEM 38	53
AGAINST HIS WILL THRO LOS'S GATE TO EDEN FOUR-FOLD LOUD		674	JERUSALEM 44	3
O ALBION MILDEST SON OF EDEN CLOSD IS THY WESTERN GATE .		675	JERUSALEM 45	3
IN EDEN IN LOVELY JERUSALEM DREW EVEN FROM ENVY . . .		675	JERUSALEM 45	6
OF EDEN THAT HOWEVER GREAT AND GLORIOUS HOWEVER LOVING		675	JERUSALEM 45	10
BUILT THE MOUNTAIN PALACES OF EDEN STUPENDOUS WORKS . .		676	JERUSALEM 46	4
WHERE THE HUMAN HARVEST WAVES ABUNDANT IN THE BEAMS OF EDEN		678	JERUSALEM 48	34
IN ITS EXTENSION EVERY TWO HUNDRED YEARS HAS A DOOR TO EDEN		678	JERUSALEM 48	37
FOLLOWING THEE AS A SHEPHERD BY THE FOUR RIVERS OF EDEN		692	JERUSALEM 60	21
IN AWFUL POMP & GOLD IN ALL THE PRECIOUS UNHEWN STONES OF EDEN		701	JERUSALEM 66	1
AND FEEDS HER WITH THE FOOD OF EDEN HENCE ALL HER BEAUTY BEAMS		707	JERUSALEM 69	18
FOR THE SANCTUARY OF EDEN IS IN THE CAMP IN THE OUTLINE		708	JERUSALEM 69	41
AND A SON OF EDEN WAS SET OVER EACH DAUGHTER OF BEULAH TO GUARD		712	JERUSALEM 72	48
SEE SISTERS CANAAN IS PLEASANT EGYPT IS AS THE GARDEN OF EDEN		725	JERUSALEM 82	30
IN EDEN OUR LOVES WERE THE SAME HERE THEY ARE OPPOSITE . .		732	JERUSALEM 87	17
OF EDEN ALL PERVERTED EGYPT ON THE GIHON MANY TONGUED . .		734	JERUSALEM 89	15
THEREFORE THE SONS OF EDEN PRAISE URTHONA'S SPECTRE IN SONGS		742	JERUSALEM 95	19
HEAVEN HAVILAH EDEN & ALL THE COUNTRIES WHERE JEWELS ABOUND	837D	LETTER 36		PROSE
EDEN'S				
AS SHE HEARD BY EDEN'S FLOOD		754	EV GOSPEL(E)/N	20
EDESSA				
WHEN EDESSA AND LYCA AND EMILIE		63	SHEPHERD YOUNG	7
EDGE				
AND OUTSTRETCHD ON THE EDGE OF THE FOREST		251	AHANIA 3	44
WHICH STAND UPON THE EDGE OF BEULAH & HE SUNK DOWN . . .		277	FOUR ZOAS 1	465
WHICH STAND UPON THE EDGE OF BEULAH AND THERE ALBION SUNK		646	JERUSALEM 23	25
IN THE VISIONS OF THE DREAMS OF BEULAH ON THE EDGE OF NON-ENTITY		663	JERUSALEM 36	22
EDIFYING				
LISTEND WITH OPEN MOUTHS TO THE EDIFYING DISCOURSES . . .		44D	ISLAND MOON 1	PROSE
EDINBURGH				
HIS ROCKS LONDON & BATH & LEGIONS & EDINBURGH		531	MILTON 39	35
YORK EDINBURGH DURHAM & CARLISLE & ON THE FRONT		531	MILTON 39	43
FROM LINCOLN & NORWICH FROM EDINBURGH & MONMOUTH . . .		644	JERUSALEM 21	39
YORK CROWND WITH LOVING KINDNESS EDINBURGH CLOTHD . .		665	JERUSALEM 38	51
VERULAM LONDON YORK EDINBURGH MOURNING ONE TOWARDS ANOTHER		676	JERUSALEM 46	24
AND THE VOICES OF BATH & CANTERBURY & YORK & EDINBURGH CRY		689	JERUSALEM 57	1
VERULAM LONDON YORK & EDINBURGH THEIR ENGLISH NAMES . .		691	JERUSALEM 59	14
FROM LONDON TO YORK & EDINBURGH THE FURNACES RAGE TERRIBLE		714	JERUSALEM 73	53
THESE FOUR ARE VERULAM & LONDON & YORK & EDINBURGH . . .		714	JERUSALEM 74	3
EDINBURGH'S				
LONDON FEELS HIS BRAIN CUT ROUND EDINBURGH'S HEART IS CIRCUMSCRIBED		703	JERUSALEM 66	64
EDINBURH				
LEVI EDINBURH ROXBRO ROSS JUDAH ABRDEEN BERWIK DUMFRIES		638	JERUSALEM 16 *	54
EDITION				
SEE ADVANCEMT OF LEARNING PART...P...OF FIRST EDITION . .		794A	LETTER 5	PROSE
NEW EDITION OF MR HAYLEY'S TRIUMPHS OF TEMPER FROM DRAWINGS		811D	LETTER 22	PROSE
FOR PRINTING THERE IS NOW IN HAND A NEW EDITION OF . . .		841A	LETTER 40	PROSE
CONSIDERS AS IMPOLITIC AND THAT A HANDSOME GENERAL EDITION		858A	LETTER 55	PROSE
SMALL EDITION OF THE TRIUMPHS OF TEMPER WITH SIX OR SEVEN PLATES		858B	LETTER 55	PROSE

	PAGE	TITLE	LINE

EDITION   (CONTINUED)
THAT ONE THOUSAND COPIES SHOULD BE THE FIRST EDITION AND   858B LETTER 55   PROSE
    IF WE CHOOSE
WE MIGHT ADD TO THE NUMBER OF PLATES IN A SECOND EDITION   858B LETTER 55   PROSE
    AND HE
WE CAN APPLY SOME OF THE PLATES TO THE NEW EDITION   858B LETTER 55   PROSE
    I CONSIDER
SETTLED WITH HIM THE PLAN OF ENGRAVING FOR THE NEW EDITION   859A LETTER 56   PROSE
WHICH IS OMITTED IN THE NEW EDITION TIME ENOUGH TO SAVE   861A LETTER 58   PROSE
EDITIONS
A STRANGE ERRATUM IN ALL THE EDITIONS . . . .   543 TO ROYL ACAD/N   1
ATTACHING HIMSELF WHOLLY TO THE SALE OF FINE EDITIONS OF   831C LETTER 31   PROSE
EDITOR
TO THE EDITOR OF THE MONTHLY MAGAZINE . . . .   SUPP ADDRESS/L 61   *TITLE
EDITORS
IN BEAUFORT BUILDINGS WE ALL KNOW THAT EDITORS OF   592C PUB ADDRESS/N   PROSE
    NEWSPAPERS
EDMUNDS
ST EDMUNDS CHAPEL EAST DEREHAM MAY BE UNDERSTOOD TO . . .   838B LETTER 37   PROSE
EDOM
ARE THE LINEN CLOTHES FOLDED UP NOW IS THE DOMINION OF EDOM   149B MARRIAGE HH 3   PROSE
OF EDOM & ARAM & MOAB & MIDIAN & AMALEK . . . .   498 MILTON 17   20
THE HIGHLY CULTIVATED STATES OF EGYPT MOAB EDOM ARAM   .   565C DESC CAT 2   PROSE
. . . IN EDOM I SAW IT INDIGNANT & THOU ART NOT MOVED   .   625 JERUSALEM 7   26
IN EGYPT & PHILISTEA IN MOAB & EDOM & ARAM . . . . . .   680 JERUSALEM 49   43
AMALEK EDOM EGYPT MOAB AMMON ASHUR PHILISTEA AROUND   740 JERUSALEM 92   23
    JERUSALEM
MARCHES AGAINST THEE DECEITFUL FROM SINAI & FROM EDOM   .   743 JERUSALEM 96   9
EDUCATE
OR THINK TO EDUCATE [AN IDIOT] A FOOL . . . .   598C PUB ADDRESS/N   *PROSE
EDUCATED   SEE WOMAN-EDUCATED
MEN WHO HAVE BEEN EDUCATED WITH WORKS OF VENETIAN ARTISTS   447B ANNO REYNOLDS   MARG
I HAVE EDUCATED YOU IN THE CRUCIFYING CRUELTIES OF   648 JERUSALEM 24   55
    DEMONSTRATION
SO EDUCATED GOD OUR SAVIOUR WATCH OVER YOU & PRESERVE YOU   833C LETTER 33   PROSE
EDUCATION
THE ARGUMENT MAN HAS NO NOTION OF MORAL FITNESS BUT FROM   97A NAT RELIGION 1   PROSE
    EDUCATION
THEY REPRESENT EDUCATION ON THE SIDE NEXT THE LORD'S SUPPER   614A V LAST JUDG/N   PROSE
EDWARD
KING EDWARD THE THIRD . . . .   17C EDW THIRD/PS   TITLE
PERSONS KING EDWARD THE BLACK PRINCE QUEEN PHILIPPA   .   17C EDW THIRD/PS   TITLE
SCENE THE COAST OF FRANCE KING EDWARD AND NOBLES BEFORE   17D EDW THIRD/PS 1   PROSE
    IT THE ARMY
THAT NEVER TARNISHES WHETHER THIRD EDWARD . . . . .   18 EDW THIRD/PS 1   28
I THINK YOU DO NOT KNOW EDWARD S AFRAID OF PHILIP . .   21 EDW THIRD/PS 3   8
THAT EDWARD RUNS AWAY FROM PHILIP . . . .   22 EDW THIRD/PS 3   23
ENTER KING EDWARD AND BLACK PRINCE . . . .   23A EDW THIRD/PS 3   PROSE
EDWARD MY SON THOU ART . . . .   23 EDW THIRD/PS 3   77
WHAT CAN SIR THOMAS DAGWORTH ASK THAT EDWARD   .   . . . .   23 EDW THIRD/PS 3   96
O EDWARD MY DEAR SON LEARN TO THINK LOWLY OF . . . . .   26 EDW THIRD/PS 3   216
[EXEUNT] EXIT KING EDWARD . . . .   26C EDW THIRD/PS 3   PROSE
PROLOGUE INTENDED FOR A DRAMATIC PIECE OF KING EDWARD THE   33C EDW FOURTH/PS   TITLE
    FOURTH
AND LION HEART AND BLACK-BROWD EDWARD WITH . . . . .   35 WAR SONG/PS   28
EDWARD AND ELINOR A HISTORICAL ENGRAVING SIZE...PRICE...   207D PRSPECTUS 1793   PROSE
A FAMINE OCCASIOND BY THE POPISH INTERDICT EDWARD   208D SUBJCTS HIST/N   TITLE
    AT CALAIS
EDWARD THE BLACK PRINCE BRINGS HIS CAPTIVES TO HIS FATHER   209A SUBJCTS HIST/N   TITLE
KING EDWARD AND HIS QUEEN ELENOR ARE PROSTRATED . . .   577A DESC CAT 4   PROSE
ARMIES OF EDWARD ARE SEEN WINDING AMONG THE MOUNTAINS   .   577A DESC CAT 4   PROSE
[EDWARD HENRY ELIZABETH JAMES CHARLES WILLIAM GEORGE]   .   713 JERUSALEM 73   *   37
MY MUCH ADMIRED & RESPECTED EDWARD THE BARD OF OXFORD   .   835A LETTER 34   PROSE
WHAT YOU HAD SAID ABOUT THE DESIGNS FOR EDWARD THE FIRST &   853A LETTER 51   *PROSE
EDWARD & HIS QUEEN & NOBLES ASTONISHD AT THE BARD'S SONG   SUPP ILLUS GRAY   *TITLE
...ASSASSIN LAYING DEAD AT THE FEET OF (EDWARD) IST IN...   SUPP ILLUS HISTORY   *TITLE
KING EDWARD AND QUEEN ELENOR . . . .   SUPP ILLUS HISTORY   *TITLE
EDWARD'S
MAYHAP YOU MAY LOOK UPON EDWARD'S FACE . . . . .   21 EDW THIRD/PS 3   16
WEAVING THE WINDING SHEET OF EDWARD'S RACE BY MEANS   . .   576B DESC CAT 4   PROSE
THE BARD WEAVING EDWARD'S FATE . . . .   SUPP ILLUS GRAY   *TITLE
THE DEATH OF EDWARD'S QUEEN ELEANOR FROM THIS LINE   . .   SUPP ILLUS GRAY   *TITLE
EDWARDS
I HASTEN TO WRITE TO YOU BY THE FAVOUR OF MR EDWARDS I HAVE   831A LETTER 31   PROSE
A MASTER IN CHANCERY THO I HAVE CALLD ON MR EDWARDS TWICE   834D LETTER 34   PROSE
MR EDWARDS KNOW LADY HAMILTON'S ADDRESS THE . . . . .   836B LETTER 35   PROSE
AGO MR EDWARDS WILL PROCURE HER ADDRESS FOR YOU . . .   836C LETTER 35   PROSE
DELIVERED THE LETTER TO MR EDWARDS WHO WILL GIVE IT . . .   845D LETTER 44   PROSE
NEAR NORTHAMPTON MR EDWARDS IS OUT OF TOWN LIKEWISE . . .   855B LETTER 53   PROSE
EDWD
EDWD (FIRST) OR THE BALLADS HAVING COME FROM YOU . . . .   857A LETTER 54   PROSE
EDWIN
EDWIN & MORCAR STIRRING UP THE LONDONERS . . . . . .   208D SUBJCTS HIST/N   TITLE
EEN
SO EEN LET IGNORANCE DO IT ALL . . . .   549 ENGL ENCOU/N 1   12
EER   SEE WHERE-EER,WHERE EER,ERE
O SHOULD SHE EER PROVE FALSE HIS LIMBS ID TEAR . . . .   10 WHEN EARLY/PS   17
DID YOU (EER) SEE HIM FEAR AT BLANCHETAQUE . . . . . .   21 EDW THIRD/PS 3 *   10
AN OLD MAID EARLY EER I KNEW . . . .   184 O I CANNOT/N   5
OOTHOON SHALL VIEW HIS DEAR DELIGHT NOR EER WITH JEALOUS   195 V DAU ALBION 7   28
    CLOUD
THY CRIMSON DISK SO EER THE SUN WAS RENT FROM THY   198 AMERICA 5   5
    RED SPHERE

567

EER   (CONTINUED)
     THEN LOS SMOTE HER UPON THE EARTH TWAS LONG EER SHE REVIVD   272 FOUR ZOAS 1   281
     NIGHT PASSD & ENITHARMON EER THE DAWN RETURND IN BLISS . . 289 FOUR ZOAS 2   * 341
     SPREAD THRO HER GOLDEN FRAME SHE ROSE UP EER THE DAWN OF*   291 FOUR ZOAS 2   420
          DAY
     AT DAWN & EER THE SUN AROSE THE RAVEN & VULTURE FOLLOWD   358 FOUR ZOAS 9   63
     FIRST EER THE MORNING BREAKS JOY OPENS IN THE FLOWERY   520 MILTON 31   50
          BOSOMS
     BE THEY AS VILE & BASE AS EER THEY CAN . . . . 544 SOME MEN/N   4
     IF I EER GROW TO MAN'S ESTATE . . . . 547 IF I GROW/N   1
     THE ONLY MAN THAT EER I KNEW . . . .   551 ONLY MAN/N   1
     VAST & SEVERE THE ANGUISH EER THEY KNEW THEIR FATHER WERE   713 JERUSALEM 73   8
EFFECT
     THEY TAME SUBMIT SUCH THE EFFECT FLIGHT HAS . . . . .   24 EDW THIRD/PS 3   122
     IS THE EFFECT OF YOUTH AND WANT OF USE . . . . . .   27 EDW THIRD/PS 3   246
     & ITS OWN EFFECT ACCIDENT IS THE OMISSION OF ACT IN SELF &   88D ANNO LAVATER   MARG
     IF SUCH A PERJURY AS THIS CAN TAKE EFFECT ANY VILLAIN IN   438D BLAKES MEMORAN   PROSE
          FUTURE
     ARE ALWAYS CLUMSY AND INDEFINITE THE EFFECT OF RUBBING OUT 439C REMARKS MALKIN   PROSE
     A LIE WORKING UP EFFECT IS MORE AN OPERATION OF INDOLENCE   450A ANNO REYNOLDS   MARG
     I SPEAK HERE OF REMBRANDT'S & RUBENS'S & REYNOLDS'S EFFECT 450A ANNO REYNOLDS   * MARG
     FOR REAL EFFECT IS MAKING OUT THE PARTS & IT IS NOTHING   450A ANNO REYNOLDS   MARG
          ELSE BUT THAT
     THIS IS NOT A SATISFACTORY ANSWER TO PRODUCE AN EFFECT OF   463A ANNO REYNOLDS   MARG
     IDENTITIES OR THINGS ARE NEITHER CAUSE NOR EFFECT THEY   470D ANNO REYNOLDS   MARG
          ARE ETERNAL
     AND EVERY NATURAL EFFECT HAS A SPIRITUAL CAUSE AND NOT .   513 MILTON 26   44
     IT WAS WITH DIFFICULTY BROUGHT BACK AGAIN TO A CERTAIN   582B DESC CAT 9   PROSE
          EFFECT
     OF EFFECT IN THE PICTURES OF RUBENS & REMBRANDT . . . . 598D PUB ADDRESS/N   PROSE
     MICH ANG EVERY PICTURE OF THEIRS HAS A DIFFERENT   598D PUB ADDRESS/N   PROSE
          & APPROPRIATE EFFECT
     HAS INTIRELY PUT AN END TO ALL GENUINE & APPROPRIATE EFFECT 599B PUB ADDRESS/N   *PROSE
     EVERY PICTURE HAS THE SAME EFFECT A PIECE OF MACHINERY .   599B PUB ADDRESS/N   PROSE
     HE WHO MAKES A DESIGN MUST KNOW THE EFFECT & COLOURING .   603A PUB ADDR AD/N   PROSE
     HE HIMSELF KNEW BUT HIS IMPUDENCE HAD A CONTRARY EFFECT   603C PUB ADDR AD/N   PROSE
          ON ME
     RUINOUS TO EFFECT THO CONNOISSEURS MAY THINK OTHERWISE .   815B LETTER 23   PROSE
     MY ZEAL WITH GOOD EFFECT AM IN HOPES THAT MISS POOLE IS   841A LETTER 40   PROSE
     THO ADMIRABLY CONTRIVED FOR AN EFFECT EQUAL TO REMBRANDT   855A LETTER 53   PROSE
     INIMITABLE AND THE EFFECT OF THE WHOLE IS TRULY SUBLIME   864B LETTER 61   PROSE
EFFECTED
     HOW THEN IS REGENERATION EFFECTED WHICH TURNS THE EVIL   80A ANNO LAVATER   MARG
          TO GOOD
     WAS NOT TO BE EFFECTED WITHOUT CARES & SORROWS & TROUBLES   330 FOUR ZOAS 7   399
EFFECTS
     GOD IS IN THE LOWEST EFFECTS AS WELL AS IN THE HIGHEST   87A ANNO LAVATER   MARG
          CAUSES
     & IMITATES THE EFFECTS OF NATURE . . . . 597C PUB ADDRESS/N   PROSE
     THEIR EFFECTS ARE IN EVERY PICTURE THE SAME . . . . . 598D PUB ADDRESS/N   PROSE
     THO NOT ITS EFFECTS WEAKNESS &C COMES ANOTHER TO HINDER MY 874D LETTER 80   PROSE
EFFECTUAL
     WHICH I HAVE DONE IN SO EFFECTUAL A MANNER . . . . . . 825D LETTER 27   PROSE
EFFECTUALLY
     AND HAS EFFECTUALLY EXCLUDED ME BY THIS RESOLUTION . . . 561B EXHIBITION ADV   PROSE
EFFEMINATE
     CORREGGIO IS A SOFT AND EFFEMINATE AND CONSEQUENTLY A .   583A DESC CAT 9   PROSE
EFFLUENCE
     ON THROAT & BREAST & WINGS VIBRATES WITH THE EFFLUENCE   520 MILTON 31   35
          DIVINE
EFFLUVIA
     EFFLUVIA VAPORD ABOVE . . . . 253 AHANIA 4   17
     WHEREAS GOD EXISTS NOT EXCEPT FROM THEIR EFFLUVIA . . . 789A ANNO THORNTON   MARG
EFFORT
     THE FURIOUS WIND STILL RENDS AROUND THEY FLEE IN SLUGGISH   363 FOUR ZOAS 9   256
          EFFORT
     & IN MY NEXT EFFORT I PROMISE MORE EXPEDITION . . . .   792C LETTER 4   PROSE
     WITH WHOM HE MAKES HIS FIRST EFFORT DEAR SIR YOURS EVER   875A LETTER 80   PROSE
EFFORTS
     THE WEAK BREEZE IN EFFORTS OERWEARIED . . . . 258 BOOK OF LOS 4   48
     REDOUBLING HIS IMMORTAL EFFORTS THRO THE NARROW VALES .   319 FOUR ZOAS 6   292
     DETERMINATE ALL HIS EFFORTS PROVE THIS LITTLE BOY TO HAVE   439C REMARKS MALKIN   PROSE
          HAD
     THUS REYNOLDS DEPRECIATES THE EFFORTS OF INVENTIVE GENIUS   455D ANNO REYNOLDS   MARG
     [HOGARTH'S TIME WE HAVE HAD VERY FEW EFFORTS   595C PUB ADDRESS/N   PROSE
          OF ORIGINALITY]
EFFULGENCE
     AND THY FAIR LOCKS SHADOWD THINE EYES FROM THE DIVINE   311 FOUR ZOAS 5   231
          EFFULGENCE
EFFUSION
     SPONTANEOUS EFFUSION OF HUMANITY CONGENIAL TO THE WANTS   802A LETTER 14   PROSE
     FRIENDS EXCUSE THIS EFFUSION OF THE SPIRIT FROM ONE WHO   862D LETTER 60   PROSE
EFFUSIONS
     BALLADS WERE THE EFFUSIONS OF FRIENDSHIP TO COUNTENANCE   860C LETTER 56   PROSE
EGG
     FOUR UNIVERSES ROUND THE MUNDANE EGG REMAIN CHAOTIC . .   500 MILTON 19   15
     WE FORM THE MUNDANE EGG THAT SPECTRES COMING BY FURY OR   511 MILTON 25   42
          AMITY
     FOR FOUR UNIVERSES ROUND THE MUNDANE EGG REMAIN CHAOTIC   691 JERUSALEM 59   10
     [XXX MUNDANE EGG] . . . . SUPP FOUR ZOAS 2   *
EGG FORMD
     FOUR INTERSECTING GLOBES & THE EGG FORMD WORLD OF LOS . . 524 MILTON 34   33

| | PAGE | TITLE | LINE |

EGGS

HER EGGS ON SO THE PRIEST LAYS HIS CURSE ON THE FAIREST JOYS   152C MARRIAGE HH 9   PROSE
WITH EGGS OF UNNATURAL PRODUCTION . . . . 250 AHANIA 3   10
HIS BROODINGS RUSH DOWN TO HIS FEET PRODUCING EGGS THAT HATCHING   324 FOUR ZOAS 7   167
THAT HE MIGHT TURN IT INTO EGGS OF GOLD . . . . 537 AND HIS LEGS/N   12
BUT NEITHER BACK NOR MOUTH THOSE EGGS COULD HOLD . . . . 537 AND HIS LEGS/N   13
HIS UNDER JAW DROPD AS THOSE EGGS HE LAID . . . . . . 537 AND HIS LEGS/N   14
AND [ALL MY] STEWHARD'S EGGS ARE ADDLED & DECAYD . . . . 537 AND HIS LEGS/N   15

EGHAM

REVD DR TRUSLER ENGLEFIELD GREEN EGHAM SURREY . . . . . SUPP ADDRESSES/L   *TITLE
G CUMBERLAND ESQ BISHOPSGATE NEAR EGHAM SURREY . . . . SUPP ADDRESS/L 2   *TITLE

EGIS

OR BEARST THY EGIS OER THE BURNING FIELD . . . . . . 15 IMIT SPEN/PS   49

EGOTISM

("LET THE DEGREE OF EGOTISM BE THE MEASURE OF CONFIDENCE") UNEASY   66D ANNO LAVATER   MARG
("PROOFS OF DULL FRIGIDITY HARDNESS OR...EGOTISM") RATHER UNEASY   70C ANNO LAVATER   MARG

EGREMONT

FOR THE COUNTESS OF EGREMONT [BY A HAPPY ACCIDENT] . . . 442D LAST JUDGMNT/L PROSE

EGREMONT'S

[EGR(EGREMONT'S)] WHAT MIGHTY SOUL IN BEAUTY'S FORM . . . 558 THE CAVERNS/N   *   5
EGREMONT'S COUNTESS [DARE] CAN CONTROLL . . . . 558 THE CAVERNS/N   7

EGYPT

AFRICA ITS NAME WAS THEN EGYPT . . . . 236 URIZEN 28   10
THEY CALLED IT EGYPT & LEFT IT . . . . 237 URIZEN 28   22
WAS A PILLAR OF FIRE TO EGYPT . . . . 250 AHANIA 2   45
BLACK AS MARBLE OF EGYPT IMPENETRABLE . . . . 257 BOOK OF LOS 4   6
THE LAMB THE SAVIOUR ALBION TREMBLED TO ITALY GREECE & EGYPT   495 MILTON 14   6
WHO CARRIED HIM DOWN INTO EGYPT WHERE EPHRAIM & MENASSHEH 508 MILTON 24   20
OSIRIS ISIS ORUS IN EGYPT DARK THEIR TABERNACLES ON NILE 528 MILTON 37   27
FLOATING WITH SOLEMN SONGS & ON THE LAKES OF EGYPT NIGHTLY 528 MILTON 37   28
THE HIGHLY CULTIVATED STATES OF EGYPT MOAB EDOM ARAM . 565C DESC CAT 2   PROSE
SUCH AS EGYPT & BABYLON IN WHICH WERE MULTITUDES . . . 610B V LAST JUDG/N   PROSE
MOAB & AMMON & AMALEK & CANAAN & EGYPT & ARAM . . . . . 623 JERUSALEM 5   14
BRERETON & SLADE IN EGYPT HUTTON & SKOFELD & KOX . . . . 662 JERUSALEM 36   17
IN EGYPT & PHILISTEA IN MOAB & EDOM & ARAM . . . . . . 680 JERUSALEM 49   43
INTO EGYPT FOR NEGATION A VEIL THE SAVIOUR BORN & DYING RENDS   686 JERUSALEM 55   16
EGYPT IS THE EIGHT STEPS WITHIN ETHIOPIA SUPPORTS HIS PILLARS   690 JERUSALEM 58   35
THY SONS ARE LOVELIER THAN EGYPT OR ASSYRIA WHEREFORE . . 693 JERUSALEM 60   31
THE SPIES FROM EGYPT TO RAISE JEALOUSY IN THE BOSOMS OF THE TWELVE   707 JERUSALEM 68   60
EGYPT LYBIA ETHIOPIA GUINEA CAFFRARIA NEGROLAND MOROCCO 712 JERUSALEM 72   40
THEY SOUNDED THANKSGIVINGS IN MY COURTS EGYPT & LYBIA HEARD 721 JERUSALEM 79   50
CREATE JERUSALEM & BABYLON & EGYPT & MOAB & AMALEK . . . 725 JERUSALEM 82   27
SEE SISTERS CANAAN IS PLEASANT EGYPT IS AS THE GARDEN OF EDEN   725 JERUSALEM 82   30
MARCHING THRO EGYPT IN HIS FURY THE EAST IS PALE AT HIS COURSE   729 JERUSALEM 84   22
SANDALS OF GOLD & PEARL & EGYPT & ASSYRIA BEFORE ME . . . 731 JERUSALEM 86   31
OF EDEN ALL PERVERTED EGYPT ON THE GIHON MANY TONGUED . . 734 JERUSALEM 89   15
HEBREW WHOM SHE DIVIDED INTO TWELVE & SOLD INTO EGYPT . . 739 JERUSALEM 92   4
AMALEK EDOM EGYPT MOAB AMMON ASHUR PHILISTEA AROUND JERUSALEM   740 JERUSALEM 92   23
SPIRITUAL WAR ISRAEL DELIVERD FROM EGYPT . . . . 776A INSC LAOCOON   PROSE
THE GODS OF GREECE & EGYPT WERE MATHEMATICAL DIAGRAMS . 776D INSC LAOCOON   PROSE
THESE ARE NOT THE WORKS OF EGYPT NOR BABYLON . . . . . 777A INSC LAOCOON   PROSE
AS BABYLON & EGYPT SO FAR FROM BEING PARENTS OF ARTS . . 778C HOMERS POETRY   PROSE
IN EGYPT GUARDED IN THEIR REPOSE FROM THOSE FIENDS . . 823D LETTER 27   PROSE
THE THUNDER OF EGYPT CAESAR . . . . SUPP ILLUS DANTE 3   *PROSE

EGYPTIAN

APOTHEOSES OF PERSIAN HINDOO AND EGYPTIAN ANTIQUITY . . 565C DESC CAT 2   PROSE
GOTHIC GRECIAN HINDOO AND EGYPTIAN ARE THE EXTENT OF THE HUMAN MIND   579D DESC CAT 5   PROSE
THE AMALEKITE THE CANAANITE THE MOABITE THE EGYPTIAN . . 634 JERUSALEM 13   58
THE CANAANITE THE AMALEKITE THE MOABITE THE EGYPTIAN . . 673 JERUSALEM 43   66
UPON THE EGYPTIAN NILE WITH SOLEMN SONGS TO GRECIA . . 692 JERUSALEM 60   19
THEN SCATTERD THE EGYPTIAN & HEBREW TO THE FOUR WINDS . 739 JERUSALEM 92   5
THE EGYPTIAN GODS AND THO NOT DIRECTLY TAKEN FROM A POEM 823D LETTER 27   PROSE
THE EGYPTIAN TASKMASTER WHO WAS KILLED AND BURIED BY MOSES SUPP DRAWING WGR   *TITLE

EGYPTIANS   SEE AEGYPTIANS

HAIL LOCUSTS DARKNESS FIRST BORN XXX RED SEA EGYPTIANS DROWND   SUPP EXODUS/N   *PROSE

EGYPT'S

COSWAY FRAZER & BALDWIN OF EGYPT'S LAKE . . . . 545 COSWAY FRAZR/N   1
UPON EGYPT'S IRON FLOORS & THE MARBLE PAVEMENTS OF ASSYRIA 719 JERUSALEM 79   2

EIGHT   SEE FORTY-EIGHT,FORTY EIGHT,SEVENTY-EIGHT,TWENTY-EIGHT

AND ROUND THE SHADOWY EIGHTH THE EIGHT CLOSE UP THE COUCH 502 MILTON 20   47
AND THE NUMBER OF HIS SONS IS EIGHT MILLIONS & EIGHT . . 515 MILTON 28   30
THE EIGHT IMMORTAL STARRY-ONES DOWN INTO ULRO DARK . . . 523 MILTON 34   4
IN MIDST OF THESE WAS MILTON'S COUCH & WHEN THEY SAW EIGHT 525 MILTON 35   29
PROSTRATE BEFORE THE STARRY EIGHT ASKING WITH TEARS FORGIVENESS   525 MILTON 35   32
O HOW THE STARRY EIGHT REJOICD TO SEE OLOLON DESCENDED . . 525 MILTON 35   34
AROUND THE STARRY EIGHT WITH ONE ACCORD THE STARRY EIGHT BECAME   534 MILTON 42   10
INVOLVD EIGHT THEIR WEBS ROLLD OUTWARDS INTO DARKNESS . . 626 JERUSALEM 7   46

569

```
                                                            PAGE     TITLE           LINE
EIGHT    (CONTINUED)
    AND SCOFIELD THE NINTH REMAIND ON THE OUTSIDE OF THE EIGHT    626 JERUSALEM 7        47
    INVOLVD THE EIGHT SUCH ARE THE GENERATIONS OF THE GIANT       626 JERUSALEM 7        49
        ALBION
    LIKE MEN HERMAPHRODITIC EACH WINGED WITH EIGHT WINGS    .   . 633 JERUSALEM 13        8
    AND A DEATH OF EIGHT THOUSAND YEARS FORGD BY THYSELF UPON     664 JERUSALEM 37        7
    ALBION'S DREAD TOMB EIGHT THOUSAND AND FIVE HUNDRED YEARS     678 JERUSALEM 48       36
    EGYPT IS THE EIGHT STEPS WITHIN ETHIOPIA SUPPORTS            690 JERUSALEM 58       35
        HIS PILLARS
    RETAIN MY YOUTH EIGHT THOUSAND AND FIVE HUNDRED YEARS   .   . 728 JERUSALEM 83       52
    MR FLAXMAN NAMED THE FOLLOWING EIGHT AS PROPER SUBJECTS      848D LETTER 45       PROSE
        FOR PRINTS
    THE TIME I NOW WRITE HE SET OFF LAST NIGHT BEFORE EIGHT      871C LETTER 73       PROSE
        OCLOCK
EIGHTEEN
    EIGHTEEN HUNDRED YEARS MAN WAS A DREAM    . . . . . . .       240 EUROPE 9           2
    EIGHTEEN HUNDRED YEARS A FEMALE DREAM     . . . . . . .       240 EUROPE 9           5
    AND EIGHTEEN HUNDRED YEARS WERE FLED      . . . . . . .       243 EUROPE 13         10
    AND THESE THE NAMES OF THE EIGHTEEN COMBINING WITH THOSE      676 JERUSALEM 45       40
        TEN
    WHICH YOU GAVE ME ORDERS FOR IS EIGHTEEN I WILL FINISH       816C LETTER 24       PROSE
        THESE
    SUPPOSES THAT ROMNEY WAS ABOUT EIGHTEEN WHEN HE PAINTED IT   845D LETTER 44       PROSE
EIGHTH     SEE TWENTY-EIGHTH
    AND ON THE EIGHTH DAY WHEN HIS CLOUDS UNFOLDED FROM HIS       292 FOUR ZOAS 3       25
        THRONE
    VALA NIGHT THE EIGHTH    . . . . . . . . . . . . .            341A FOUR ZOAS 8      TITLE
    [THE END OF THE EIGHTH NIGHT]    . . . . . . . . . . .        356A FOUR ZOAS 8      TITLE
    [END OF THE EIGHTH NIGHT]    . . . . . . . . . . . .          356C FOUR ZOAS 8      TITLE
    WHICH NOW AROSE AND WALKD WITH THEM IN EDEN AS AN EIGHTH      496 MILTON 15          5
    AND ROUND THE SHADOWY EIGHTH THE EIGHT CLOSE UP THE COUCH     502 MILTON 20         47
    THEY NAMD THE EIGHTH HE CAME NOT HE HID IN ALBION'S FORESTS   686 JERUSALEM 55       33
EIGHTY-FIVE
    A VERY STOUT MAN AT EIGHTY-FIVE WHICH AGE HE TELLS ME HE     844B LETTER 43       PROSE
EITHER
    GUARD IT ON EITHER SIDE & IN THE MIDST IS THE HOLY LAW  .    82A ANNO LAVATER      MARG
    MAN IS EITHER THE ARK OF GOD OR    . . . . . . . . .         82B ANNO LAVATER      MARG
    WHO EXPERIENCE EITHER PLEASURE OR PAIN THRO US    . . .      88B ANNO LAVATER      MARG
    A TEAR OF BLOOD DROPPED FROM EITHER EYE AGAIN HE REPOSD      341 FOUR ZOAS 8        18
    TO YOU BUT THAT EVERY ONE IS EITHER YOUR FRIEND OR YOUR     380B FOUR ZOAS NOTE   PROSE
        ENEMY
    HE MUST NECESSARILY BE EITHER THE ONE OR THE OTHER    . .   380B FOUR ZOAS NOTE   PROSE
    DEFEND EITHER THE ACTS OF CHRIST OR THE BIBLE UNPERVERTED   383B ANNO WATSON      MARG
    PAINE IS EITHER A DEVIL OR AN INSPIRED MAN   . . . . .      386B ANNO WATSON      MARG
    MUST EITHER BE THE ACTOR OR A FABLE WRITER OR A LIAR        390D ANNO WATSON      MARG
    TO CONSIST EITHER IN WHO THEY WERE WRITTEN BY    . . . .    393B ANNO WATSON      MARG
    WHAT MUST OUR CLERGY BE WHO ALLOW BACON TO BE EITHER WISE   404B ANNO BACON       MARG
    EITHER RELATING TO SEDITION OR ANY THING ELSE    . . . .    437B BLAKES MEMORAN   PROSE
    TO SEDITIOUS SUBJECTS WAS UTTERED EITHER BY ONE PARTY OR    437C BLAKES MEMORAN   PROSE
    OR EITHER WISHED OR TOLERATED IN A NATION WHERE    . . .    446A ANNO REYNOLDS    MARG
    THE MAN EITHER PAINTER OR PHILOSOPHER WHO LEARNS           449B ANNO REYNOLDS    MARG
        OR ACQUIRES
    DOES NOT KNOW EITHER HIS OWN INTEREST OR HIS DUTY    . .    452C ANNO REYNOLDS    MARG
    THAT HE WANTS EITHER COLOURING OR ORNAMENTAL PARTS OF ART   472A ANNO REYNOLDS    MARG
    [EITHER HE IS DISHONEST ?OR HE IS ?INSANE]    . . . .      SUPP ANNO REYNOLDS  * MARG
    WE DO NOT WANT EITHER GREEK OR ROMAN MODELS   . . . .      480D MILTON 1         PROSE
    TO MAKE [EITHER SENSE OR] MEER COMMON HONESTY    . . . .    543 TO ROYL ACAD/N      9
    NO MAN CAN BELIEVE THAT EITHER HOMER'S MYTHOLOGY    . .     565D DESC CAT 2       PROSE
    CAN BE EITHER YOUNG OR OLD I CANNOT SEE    . . . . .        575A DESC CAT 3       PROSE
    CANNOT SEE EITHER MIRACLE OR PRODIGY ALL IS TO THEM   . .   578D DESC CAT 5       PROSE
    GO BEYOND EITHER WHAT HE DOES OR WHAT THEY HAVE DONE   .    579C DESC CAT 5       PROSE
    SHOULD HE BE ABLE TO MAKE USE OF EITHER LABOUR OR CARE  .   593A PUB ADDRESS/N    PROSE
    & HE WHO PRETENDS TO BE EITHER PAINTER OR ENGRAVER    .     594D PUB ADDRESS/N    PROSE
    ORGANIZED & MINUTELY DELINEATED & ARTICULATED EITHER BY     595C PUB ADDRESS/N    PROSE
        GOD OR MAN
    FROM THE COMPARISON IN EITHER RELIEF OR STRENGTH OF COLOUR  598D PUB ADDRESS/N    PROSE
    WITH EITHER REMBRANDT OR RUBENS ON THE CONTRARY    . . .    598D PUB ADDRESS/N    PROSE
    EVEN HOGARTH CANNOT BE EITHER COPIED OR IMPROVED    . .     601D PUB ADDRESS/N    PROSE
    ENGRAVE OR PAINT EITHER WITHOUT BEING A MASTER OF DRAWING   602B PUB ADDRESS/N    PROSE
        IS
    THAT IS NOT EITHER COLOURING GRAVING OR VERSE WHICH IS  .   603A PUB ADDR AD/N    PROSE
    WHERE THE MAN IS EITHER IN AFFLUENCE OR IS ABOVE THE CARE   612C V LAST JUDG/N    PROSE
        OF IT
    & THEIR INCAPABILITY OF ART THO ART IS ABOVE EITHER    .    612C V LAST JUDG/N    PROSE
    THAT I DO NOT CONSIDER EITHER THE JUST OR THE WICKED   .    614C V LAST JUDG/N    PROSE
    BUT HOW A MONK OR A METHODIST EITHER CAN BE A HYPOCRITE     682C JERUSALEM 52     PROSE
    EITHER FOR ENGLISHMAN OR JEW    . . . . . . . . .           756 EV GOSPEL(F)/N      2
    ARISTOTLE SAYS CHARACTERS ARE EITHER GOOD OR BAD    . .     778B HOMERS POETRY    PROSE
    THAT IT CAN BE IMPROVED EITHER IN BEAUTY OR USE    . .      802A LETTER 14        PROSE
    ON THE SPOT PERMIT ME TO OFFER MY SERVICE IN EITHER WAY     808C LETTER 19        PROSE
    EITHER IN MY COTTAGE OR IN A (LODGING) IN THE VILLAGE       808C LETTER 19        PROSE
    CONVINCD THAT EITHER MY UNDERSTANDING IS INCAPABLE OF  .    814A LETTER 23        PROSE
    GOVERNMENT WAS SPOKEN BY EITHER HIM OR ME HIS ENMITY   .    826D LETTER 28        PROSE
    WAS UTTERD IN THE HEAT OF THEIR FURY BY EITHER OF          827C LETTER 28        PROSE
        THE DRAGOONS
    I AM EITHER TOO LOW OR TOO HIGHLY PRIZD    . . . . .        829 O WHY BORN/L        9
    HAVING A NUMBER OF ARTICLES RELATING TO ROMNEY EITHER  .    836A LETTER 35        PROSE
    THE LOST DRAWING YOU SHALL HAVE CHOICE OF EITHER OF THE     839C LETTER 38        PROSE
    HIS COUNTRY WILL REFRAIN FROM DISGRACING EITHER BY SUCH     864D LETTER 61        PROSE
ELATE
    WHEN ELATE I AM ENVYD WHEN MEEK I'M DESPISD    . . . .      829 O WHY BORN/L       10
```

	PAGE	TITLE	LINE

ELBOW
BATH OXFORD CAMBRIDGE NORWICH HIS RIGHT ELBOW . . . . . 531 MILTON 39 44
ELBOWS
HER KNEES & ELBOWS ARE ONLY . . . . 418 WHEN MAN HAS/N 3
I THEREFORE TOOK HIM BY THE ELBOWS & PUSHED HIM BEFORE ME 827A LETTER 28 PROSE
TOOK HIM AGAIN BY THE ELBOWS & KEEPING HIS BACK TO ME . 827B LETTER 28 PROSE
ELDER
IN MANY POINTS I HAVE SEEN THE ELDER MR WALKER HE KNEW . 843B LETTER 43 PROSE
ELDERS
FOUR & TWENTY ELDERS SEATED ON THRONES TO JUDGE THE DEAD 444A LAST JUDGMNT/L PROSE
& ON EACH SIDE THE FOUR & TWENTY ELDERS SITTING IN JUDGMENT 606B V LAST JUDG/N PROSE
AND NOT USED THE ELDERS & PRIESTS LIKE DOGS . . . . . 750 EV GOSPEL(C)/N 28
AND NOT USD THE ELDERS & PRIESTS LIKE DOGS . . . . . . 752 EV GOSPEL(D)/N 62
CHRIST GIRDING HIMSELF WITH STRENGTH FOUR & TWENTY ELDERS SUPP LETTER 56A *PROSE
ELDEST
AND THUS THE ELDEST SON OF TIRIEL RAISD HIS MIGHTY VOICE 99 TIRIEL 1 12
AND I MAY SEE THEE IN THE HOUR OF BLISS MY ELDEST BORN . . 239 EUROPE 4 28
ARISE O RINTRAH ELDEST BORN SECOND TO NONE BUT ORC . . . 240 EUROPE 8 1
I AM GOD SAID HE ELDEST OF THINGS . . . . 251 AHANIA 3 38
WHO ART THOU ELDEST WOMAN SITTING IN THY CLOUDS . . . . 312 FOUR ZOAS 6 8
AS THE ELDEST BROTHER IS THE [SECOND] FATHER'S IMAGE SO 332 FOUR ZOAS 7 * 479
  ORC BECAME
THEN HE DIVIDED THIRIEL THE ELDEST OF URIZEN'S SONS . . . 332 FOUR ZOAS 7 493
SO CRY HAND & HYLE THE ELDEST OF THE FATHERS OF ALBION'S 641 JERUSALEM 18 36
TO THE SONS OF ALBION & TO HAND THE ELDEST SON OF ALBION 660 JERUSALEM 34 22
PRODUCES BY HER ELDEST SON HOWEVER SUCH AS THEY ARE . . 804B LETTER 16 PROSE
ELEANOR   SEE ELENOR, ELINOR
THE DEATH OF EDWARD'S QUEEN ELEANOR FROM THIS LINE . . . SUPP ILLUS GRAY *TITLE
ELECT
FOR THE ELECT CANNOT BE REDEEMD BUT CREATED CONTINUALLY 484 MILTON 5 11
THE FIRST THE ELECT FROM BEFORE THE FOUNDATION OF THE WORLD 486 MILTON 7 2
AND ALL THE ELECT & ALL THE REDEEMD MOURND ONE TOWARD 488 MILTON 8 25
  ANOTHER
AND THEREFORE THE CLASS OF SATAN SHALL BE CALLD THE ELECT 492 MILTON 11 21
  & THOSE
THE ELECT SHALL MEET THE REDEEMD ON ALBION'S ROCKS THEY 494 MILTON 13 30
  SHALL MEET
AND THE ELECT SHALL SAY TO THE REDEEMD WE BEHOLD IT IS 494 MILTON 13 32
  OF DIVINE
IF THOU CHUSE TO ELECT A WORM IT SHALL REMOVE THE MOUNTAINS 502 MILTON 20 19
FOR THAT PORTION NAMD THE ELECT THE SPECTROUS BODY 502 MILTON 20 20
  OF MILTON
THIS MIGHTY ONE IS COME FROM EDEN HE IS OF THE ELECT . . 508 MILTON 23 56
WHEN UNDER PRETENCE TO BENEVOLENCE THE ELECT SUBDUD ALL 510 MILTON 25 31
FROM THE FOUNDATION OF THE WORLD THE ELECT IS ONE CLASS YOU 511 MILTON 25 32
WHO LIVE IN DOUBTS & FEARS PERPETUALLY TORMENTED BY THE 511 MILTON 25 36
  ELECT
BUT THE ELECT MUST BE SAVED (FROM) FIRES OF ETERNAL DEATH 511 MILTON 25 38
ELECTED
TILL THE TIME OF THE END THEN THEY ELECTED SEVEN CALLED 279 FOUR ZOAS 1 553
  THE SEVEN
AND THEY ELECTED MOLECH AND WHEN MOLECH WAS IMPATIENT . . 494 MILTON 13 19
TRIPLE ELOHIM CAME ELOHIM WEARIED FAINTED THEY ELECTED 494 MILTON 13 22
  SHADDAI
BUT AS TO THIS ELECTED FORM WHO IS RETURND AGAIN . . . . 509 MILTON 24 41
I ELECTED ALBION FOR MY GLORY I GAVE TO HIM THE NATIONS 653 JERUSALEM 29 6
AND THEY ELECTED SEVEN CALLD THE SEVEN EYES OF GOD . . . 686 JERUSALEM 55 31
ELECTION
MERCY ALONE OF FREE GIFT AND ELECTION THAT WE LIVE . . . 494 MILTON 13 33
ELECTRIC
FEELING THE ELECTRIC FLAME OF MILTON'S AWFUL PRECIPITATE 502 MILTON 20 26
  DESCENT
ELECTRICAL
THANKS TO MR BIRCH'S ELECTRICAL MAGIC . . . . 854A LETTER 52 PROSE
ELECTRICITY
ELECTRICITY IS THE WONDERFUL CAUSE THE SWELLING OF HER LEGS 851C LETTER 50 PROSE
ELEGANCE
PROVIDED THAT IT EXCEEDS IN ELEGANCE ALL FORMER METHODS 207B PRSPECTUS 1793 PROSE
AS TO ELEGANCE THEY HAVE NOT A SPARK . . . . 462D ANNO REYNOLDS MARG
VULGARITY & NOT ELEGANCE THE . . . . 464C ANNO REYNOLDS MARG
WORD ELEGANCE OUGHT TO BE APPLIED TO FORMS NOT TO COLOURS 464C ANNO REYNOLDS MARG
AND LOVELY & HER MOTH-LIKE ELEGANCE SHONE OVER THE ASSEMBLY 492 MILTON 11 33
ORDER OF LUXURIES SHOULD HAVE BECOME A CITY OF ELEGANCE 798C LETTER 10 PROSE
THE FIRST RATE ELEGANCE IN PRINTING & PAPER AS THEY HOLD 856D LETTER 54 PROSE
ELEGANCES
AND JUDGE OF TINKLING RHIMES AND ELEGANCES TERSE . . . . 14 IMIT SPEN/PS 18
ELEGANT
CHARMING TRULY ELEGANT SAID SCOPPRELL . . . . 55D ISLAND MOON 9 PROSE
CHAUCER HAS DESCRIBED WITH MINUTENESS IT IS VERY ELEGANT 568B DESC CAT 3 PROSE
WITH SPACES OF SWEET GARDENS & A TENT OF ELEGANT BEAUTY 707 JERUSALEM 69 20
GOES ON BRISKLY THIS WORK IS TO BE A VERY ELEGANT ONE . 824C LETTER 27 PROSE
THE SHOPS IN LONDON IMPROVE EVERY THING IS ELEGANT CLEAN 831D LETTER 31 PROSE
STRAND NEAR ST CLEMENTS IS WIDENED AND BECOME VERY ELEGANT 831D LETTER 31 PROSE
& PRODUCE TWO ELEGANT PLATES THERE IS HOWEVER . . . . . 837A LETTER 35 PROSE
I CALLD ON MR HOARE WITH YOUR ELEGANT & HEART LIFTING . 838C LETTER 37 PROSE
YOUR ELEGANT & PATHETIC POEM . . . . 853A LETTER 51 *PROSE
YOUR BEAUTIFUL AND ELEGANT DAUGHTER VENUSIA GROWS IN OUR 853D LETTER 52 *PROSE
ELEMENT
WAKD FROM HIS ETERNAL SLEEP THE HOARY ELEMENT ROARING FLED 159C SONG LIBERTY PROSE
  AWAY
OF BEAST BIRD FISH SERPENT & ELEMENT . . . . 222 URIZEN 3 16
THE TORMENTED ELEMENT STRETCHD . . . . 235 URIZEN 25 16

		PAGE	TITLE	LINE

ELEMENT   (CONTINUED)
    BECAME ELEMENT PLIANT TO RISE . . . .   258 BOOK OF LOS 4   51
    THUNDRING & HAIL & FROZEN IRON HAILD FROM THE ELEMENT   . . 322 FOUR ZOAS 7   79
    BACON IS IN HIS ELEMENT ON USURY IT IS HIMSELF &   409D ANNO BACON   MARG
        HIS PHILOSOPHY
    CONTEMPT IS THE ELEMENT OF THE CONTEMPTIBLE   . . . . .   410B ANNO BACON   MARG
    REMAIN MY ELEMENT MY ETERNAL DWELLING PLACE HOW CAN I   . 477A ANNO REYNOLDS   MARG
    AND CRUEL OPPOSITION ELEMENT AGAINST ELEMENT OPPOSED IN   520 MILTON 31   24
        WAR
    OUTLINE WAS HIS ELEMENT AND YET THESE OUTLINES GIVE BUT A 844C LETTER 43   PROSE
    "A FAIRY VISION OF SOME GAY CREATURES OF THE ELEMENT"   SUPP LEGEND/N30   *
        (MILTON)
ELEMENTAL
    STRETCH FORTH YOUR HANDS AND STRIKE THE ELEMENTAL STRINGS 239 EUROPE 4   13
    THEY LISTEND TO THE ELEMENTAL HARPS & SPHERY SONG   . . . 274 FOUR ZOAS 1   356
    WHERE DWELL THE CHILDREN OF THE ELEMENTAL WORLDS IN HARMONY 274 FOUR ZOAS 1   370
    FOR ELEMENTAL GODS THEIR THUNDEROUS ORGANS BLEW CREATING 274 FOUR ZOAS 1   377
    WHILE ROUND THEIR HEADS THE ELEMENTAL GODS KEPT HARMONY   288 FOUR ZOAS 2   301
    AND LUVAH HIDDEN IN THE ELEMENTAL FORMS OF LIFE & DEATH   301 FOUR ZOAS 4   130
    THE ELEMENTAL PLANETS & THE ORBS OF ECCENTRIC FIRE   . . 308 FOUR ZOAS 5   126
    OR SINKING THRO THESE ELEMENTAL WONDERS SWIFT TO FALL . 317 FOUR ZOAS 6   199
    WHEN ALL THE ELEMENTAL GODS JOIND IN THE WONDROUS SONG . 336 FOUR ZOAS 7B   146
    AGAIN THE ELEMENTAL STRINGS TO YOUR RIGHT BREASTS DRAW . 337 FOUR ZOAS 7B   157
    INTO THE ELEMENTAL FORMS OF EVERY THING THAT GROWS . .   355 FOUR ZOAS 8   563
    ELEMENTAL BEINGS CALLED BY US BY THE GENERAL NAME   577D DESC CAT 5   PROSE
        OF FAIRIES
    ITS GUARDS LIVING THE WORK OF ELEMENTAL HANDS LABORIOUS   633 JERUSALEM 13   7
        TASK
ELEMENTS
    FROM A PERCEPTION OF ONLY (THREE) SENSES OR (THREE   97A NAT RELIGION 1 PROSE
) ELEMENTS
    PAINTING UPON THE ELEMENTS SMITTEN WITH THEIR OWN PLAGUES 203 AMERICA 16   18
    AGAINST ONE ANOTHER SO LET THEM WAR ON SLAVES TO   245 SONG OF LOS 3   14
        THE ETERNAL ELEMENTS
    BRIGHT SOULS [?ELEMENTS] OF VEGETATIVE LIFE BUDDING AND   274 FOUR ZOAS 1   * 379
        BLOSSOMING
    TRIGONS & CUBES DIVIDE THE ELEMENTS IN FINITE BONDS . . 284 FOUR ZOAS 2   169
    IT IS AN EASY THING TO LAUGH AT WRATHFUL ELEMENTS   . . 290 FOUR ZOAS 2   408
    THAN ALL THE WRACKING ELEMENTS DEAFEND & RENDED WORSE . 195 FOUR ZOAS 3   151
    ONLY A VOICE ETERNAL WAILING IN THE ELEMENTS . . . . .   297 FOUR ZOAS 3   206
    AND ALL THE ELEMENTS SHALL SERVE THEE TO THEIR SOOTHING   301 FOUR ZOAS 4   153
        FLUTES
    NOR COULD HE CALM THE ELEMENTS BECAUSE HIMSELF WAS SUBJECT 315 FOUR ZOAS 6   145
    WHEN I RETURN FROM CLOUDS OF GRIEF IN THE WANDRING ELEMENTS 324 FOUR ZOAS 7   185
    RAVING ABOUT THE UPPER ELEMENTS IN MADDNING FURY . . . . 328 FOUR ZOAS 7   * 322
    DOES NOT THE GOD OF WATERS IN THE WRACKING ?ELEMENTS   . 335 FOUR ZOAS 7B   90
    TO BUILD HER BOWERS FOR THE ELEMENTS BROUGHT FORTH   340 FOUR ZOAS 7B   277
        ABUNDANTLY
    FOR THE MONSTERS OF THE ELEMENTS LIONS OR TYGERS OR WOLVES 344 FOUR ZOAS 8   120
    SHALL BE RENEWD & ALL THESE ELEMENTS THAT NOW CONSUME . 362 FOUR ZOAS 9   209
    FORSAKEN OF THEIR ELEMENTS THEY VANISH & ARE NO MORE .   376 FOUR ZOAS 9   733
    THEY PLUNGE INTO THE ELEMENTS THE ELEMENTS CAST THEM FORTH 376 FOUR ZOAS 9   736
    THE ELEMENTS SUBSIDE THE HEAVENS ROLLD ON WITH VOCAL   378 FOUR ZOAS 9   800
        HARMONY
    THE ELEMENTS ARE FILLD WITH THE PRINCE OF EVIL   . . . . 388A ANNO WATSON   MARG
    ALL ARE THE WORK OF FAIRY HANDS OF THE FOUR ELEMENTS .   516 MILTON 28   60
    AND ALL THE LIVING CREATURES OF THE FOUR ELEMENTS WAILD   519 MILTON 31   17
    THE FAIRIES NYMPHS GNOMES & GENII OF THE FOUR ELEMENTS . 520 MILTON 31   20
    DIRECTING THE COMBATS IN THE UPPER ELEMENTS   . . . . . 612A V LAST JUDG/N PROSE
    ALBION GROANS HE SEES THE ELEMENTS DIVIDE BEFORE HIS FACE 663 JERUSALEM 36   27
    BECAME FOUR ELEMENTS SEPARATING FROM THE LIMBS OF ALBION 663 JERUSALEM 36   32
    FAIRIES & GENII & NYMPHS & GNOMES OF THE ELEMENTS . .   663 JERUSALEM 36   37
    REVOLUTIONS OF ACTION & PASSION THRO THE FOUR ELEMENTS   742 JERUSALEM 95   10
        ON ALL SIDES
ELENOR   SEE ELEANOR
    FAIR ELENOR . . . .   4A FAIR ELENOR/PS TITLE
    THE GRAVES GIVE UP THEIR DEAD FAIR ELENOR   . . . . 4 FAIR ELENOR/PS   2
    IT IS MY LIFE SEND IT TO ELENOR   . . . .   4 FAIR ELENOR/PS   23
    AH MY DEAR LORD AH WRETCHED ELENOR . . . .   5 FAIR ELENOR/PS   40
    O ELENOR WEAK WOMAN FILLD WITH WOE . . . .   5 FAIR ELENOR/PS   52
    O ELENOR [I AM] BEHOLD THY HUSBAND'S HEAD   . . . . . .   5 FAIR ELENOR/PS   61
    O ELENOR BEWARE THE CURSED DUKE . . . .   6 FAIR ELENOR/PS   65
    KING EDWARD AND HIS QUEEN ELENOR ARE PROSTRATED   . .   577A DESC CAT 4   PROSE
    KING EDWARD AND QUEEN ELENOR . . . .   SUPP ILLUS HISTORY *TITLE
ELEPHANT   SEE DOUBLE ELEPHANT
    THE LION THE TYGER THE HORSE THE ELEPHANT WATCH THE FRUITS 151D MARRIAGE HH 8 PROSE
    THE ELEPHANT THE WOLF THE BEAR THE LAMIA THE [SATUR] SATYR 352 FOUR ZOAS 8 * 446
    WITH EVERY COLOUR LION TYGER HORSE ELEPHANT EAGLE DOVE   746 JERUSALEM 98   43
        FLY WORM
ELEPHANTS
    HORSES ELEPHANTS BANNERS CASTLES SLINGS AND ROCKS   . . 159D SONG LIBERTY   PROSE
ELETH
    RENDING THE ROCKS ELETH & UVETH ROSE & ONA ROSE   . . .   322 FOUR ZOAS 7   95
    OF ELETH & THE ICY HANDS OF UVETH KNEADED THE BREAD . . 322 FOUR ZOAS 7   102
ELEVATE
    [TO ELEVATE ME ABOVE THE MEDIOCRITY TO WHICH I HAVE   591C PUB ADDRESS/N PROSE
        HITHERTO]
    ELEVATE INTO THE REGION OF BROTHERHOOD WITH MY RED FIRES 660 JERUSALEM 34   1
    WHY HAVE THOU ELEVATE INWARD O DWELLER OF OUTWARD CHAMBERS 660 JERUSALEM 34   10
ELEVATED
    ("UNDERSTANDING BY...LOVE CAN BE ELEVATED") MARK THIS .   96B ANNO SWED LOVE MARG
    ("LOVE...UNDERSTANDING") MARK THIS THEY ARE ELEVATED   96C ANNO SWED LOVE MARG
        TOGETHER

```
                                                        PAGE     TITLE          LINE
ELEVATED     (CONTINUED)
    TILL WE WERE ELEVATED ABOVE THE EARTH'S SHADOW·  . . . . 156D MARRIAGE HH 17   PROSE
    ONCE OPEN TO THE HEAVENS AND ELEVATED ON THE HUMAN NECK   242 EUROPE 10         28
    ELEVATED INTO ITS OWN PROPER SPHERE OF INVENTION . . . . 576B DESC CAT 4        PROSE
    ABOVE HIM ARE TWO FIGURES ELEVATED ON A CLOUD . . . . . 607D V LAST JUDG/N     PROSE
ELEVATION
    WHO SHALL DARE TO SAY AFTER THIS THAT ALL ELEVATION IS    94B ANNO SWED LOVE    MARG
        OF SELF
ELEVEN
    COULD NOT ARRIVE AT OUR COTTAGE BEFORE HALF PAST ELEVEN   802B LETTER 14        PROSE
    WITHOUT ACCIDENT OR HINDRANCE THO IT WAS BETWEEN ELEVEN   803A LETTER 15        PROSE
ELEVENTH
    LESSER CIRCLE POINT OF THE UNIVERSE CANTO ELEVENTH LINE... 786A ILLS DANTE 101  PROSE
ELF
    TO DO THE WORK OF HATE HER DRUDGE & ELF . . . . . . .  42D THEN SHE BORE        PROSE
    THIS IS THE TRICK OF THE ANCIENT ELF . . . . . . . .  750 EV GOSPEL(C)/N        32
    HE HAD SOON BEEN BLOODY CAESAR'S ELF . . . . . . . .  752 EV GOSPEL(D)/N        41
    THIS IS THE TRICK OF THE ANCIENT ELF . . . . . . . .  752 EV GOSPEL(D)/N        66
ELFRID
    A DAY LIKE THIS LAID ELFRID IN THE DUST . . . . . .  43C WOE CRIED MUSE         PROSE
    SWEET ELFRID FAIRER THAN THE BEAMING SUN . . . . . .  43C WOE CRIED MUSE        PROSE
ELGIN
    JOSEPH ELGIN LANERK KINROS BENJAMIN KROMARTY MURRA        638 JERUSALEM 16       58
        KIRKUBRIHT
ELIAKIM
    THE PERSON NAMD IN ISAIAH XXII ... ELIAKIM THE SON       607D V LAST JUDG/N     PROSE
        OF HILKIAH
ELIAS
    HE IS THE SPIRIT OF PROPHECY THE EVER APPARENT ELIAS  . . 510 MILTON 24          71
    ORPHAN MOSES ELIAS JESUS DAVID SOLOMON . . . . .   SUPP INSC HARVEY           *TITLE
ELIJAH
    & HE WAS CONSUMED AND AROSE AS ELIJAH . . . . . . . 158D MARRIAGE HH 22         PROSE
    BY THE SIDE OF SETH IS ELIJAH . . . . . . . . . . 611C V LAST JUDG/N           PROSE
    & THE MORNING STARS SANG TOGETHER BETWEEN SETH & ELIJAH   611D V LAST JUDG/N   *PROSE
    NEITHER CAN SETH ENVY NOAH OR ELIJAH ENVY ABRAHAM  . . 616B V LAST JUDG/N       PROSE
    NAMING HIM THE SPIRIT OF PROPHECY CALLING HIM ELIJAH  . 674 JERUSALEM 44         31
    WHAT DOEST THOU HERE ELIJAH . . . . . . . . . . . 779C GHOST ABEL 1            PROSE
ELINOR    SEE ELEANOR
    EDWARD AND ELINOR A HISTORICAL ENGRAVING SIZE...PRICE...  207D PRSPECTUS 1793   PROSE
ELIZABETH
    IT WAS A COMMON OPINION IN THE COURT OF QUEEN ELIZABETH   397B ANNO BACON        MARG
    ZACHARIAS & ELIZABETH RECIEVING THE BREAD & WINE  . . 614A V LAST JUDG/N         PROSE
    [EDWARD HENRY ELIZABETH JAMES CHARLES WILLIAM GEORGE]  . . 713 JERUSALEM 73    *  37
    ELIZABETH "GIRT WITH MANY A BARON BOLD" . . . . . . .   SUPP ILLUS GRAY        *TITLE
ELIZABETH'S
    WAS THE BEAUTY OF OUR ANCESTORS TILL AFTER ELIZABETH'S TIME 568B DESC CAT 3     PROSE
ELLAYOL
    SOTHA MYDON ELLAYOL NATHO GON HARHATH SATAN  . . . . .  350 FOUR ZOAS 8         359
ELLEN
    OF ONE THAT FLED APPROACHES ELLEN STOOD . . . . . . .   4 FAIR ELENOR/PS        19
    STIFLING IN MUD FAIR ELLEN PASSD THE BRIDGE  . . . . .   4 FAIR ELENOR/PS        31
    AS THE DEER WOUNDED ELLEN FLEW OVER . . . . . . . .   5 FAIR ELENOR/PS        33
ELM
    THE OAK FROWNS TERRIBLE THE BEECH & ASH & ELM ENROOT  . . 636 JERUSALEM 16        4
ELMS
    MILTON WALKING BY ELMS ON HILLOCKS GREEN THE PLOWMAN  . . 618B ILLUS MILTON    PROSE
ELOHIM
    MOLECH IMPATIENT THEY SENT ELOHIM WHO CREATED ADAM  . . . 351 FOUR ZOAS 8        401
    TRIPLE ELOHIM CAME ELOHIM WEARIED FAINTED THEY ELECTED    494 MILTON 13          22
        SHADDAI
    OVER THE SEPULCHERS IN CLOUDS OF JEHOVAH & WINDS OF ELOHIM 495 MILTON 14          26
    THUS NATURE IS A VISION OF THE SCIENCE OF THE ELOHIM  . 518 MILTON 29            65
    NAME OF JEHOVAH ELOHIM THE I AM OF THE OAKS OF ALBION  . 610A V LAST JUDG/N      PROSE
    SATAN & ADAM & THE WHOLE WORLD WAS CREATED BY THE ELOHIM  649D JERUSALEM 27      PROSE
    LUCIFER MOLECH ELOHIM SHADDAI PAHAD JEHOVAH JESUS  . . . 686 JERUSALEM 55        32
    BEHOLD IN THE VISIONS OF ELOHIM JEHOVAH BEHOLD JOSEPH     694 JERUSALEM 61        1
        & MARY
    AND BE COMFORTED O JERUSALEM IN THE VISIONS OF JEHOVAH    694 JERUSALEM 61        2
        ELOHIM
    ACCUMULATING WITHOUT END HERE LOS WHO IS OF THE ELOHIM  . 713 JERUSALEM 73        24
    ABEL AMONG THE ELOHIM A HUMAN VICTIM I WANDER I AM THEIR  780 GHOST ABEL 1        10
        HOUSE
    AND NO ATONEMENT O JEHOVAH THE ELOHIM LIVE ON SACRIFICE   780 GHOST ABEL 2        14
    THE ELOHIM OF THE HEATHEN SWORE VENGEANCE FOR SIN THEN    781 GHOST ABEL 2        22
        THOU STOODST
    FORTH O ELOHIM JEHOVAH . . . . . . . . . . . . . . . 781 GHOST ABEL 2          23
    THE ELOHIM SAW THEIR OATH ETERNAL FIRE . . . . . . . . 781 GHOST ABEL 2          25
    ELOHIM CREATING ADAM . . . . . . . . . . . . . . SUPP COLOR PRT TATE        *TITLE
ELOQUENCE
    SUCH IS SWEET ELOQUENCE THAT DOES DISPEL  . . . . . .  15 IMIT SPEN/PS          31
    BACON HATED TALENTS OF ALL KINDS ELOQUENCE IS DISCRETION  409A ANNO BACON        MARG
        OF SPEECH
    OXFORD TAKE THOU THESE LEAVES OF THE TREE OF LIFE WITH    675 JERUSALEM 45        30
        ELOQUENCE
    DARE TOUCH OXFORD IMMORTAL BARD WITH ELOQUENCE  . . .   676 JERUSALEM 46         7
ELOQUENT
    RISE UP FOR I DISCERN THEE & I DARE THY ELOQUENT TONGUE   104 TIRIEL 4           19
    IMPUDENT FIEND SAID IJIM HOLD THY GLIB & ELOQUENT TONGUE  104 TIRIEL 4           37
    THEIR ELOQUENT TONGUES WERE DUMB . . . . . . . . . .  105 TIRIEL 4             47
    [[DECIEVE THE NOBLE &] IF THE ELOQUENT VOICE OF TIRIEL]   105 TIRIEL 4           79
    OF URIZEN IN VAIN THE ELOQUENT TONGUE A ROCK A CLOUD A    315 FOUR ZOAS 6        134
        MOUNTAIN
```

ELOQUENT   (CONTINUED)
    ELOQUENT AMOROUS WITTY AND SATYRICAL YOUNG HANDSOME AND   568D DESC CAT 3   PROSE
    RICH
ELSE
    FOSTERS HIS PARENT WHO ELSE MUST SWEAT AND TOIL . . . .   19 EDW THIRD/PS 2   32
    ELSE HE WOULD NEVER DARE TO ATTACK US NOW . . . . .   24 EDW THIRD/PS 3   141
    BUT EVERY BODY ELSE DOES . . . .   29D EDW THIRD/PS 4   PROSE
    & MY COUSIN GIBBLE GABBLE SAYS THAT I AM LIKE NOBODY ELSE   53A ISLAND MOON 8   PROSE
    AND EVERY THING ELSE IS STILL . . . .   60 NURSES SONG/IM   4
    OR ELSE I SHALL BE LOST . . . .   60 LIT BOY LST/IM   4
    I DO NOT UNDERSTAND THIS OR ELSE I DO NOT AGREE TO IT . .   78D ANNO LAVATER   MARG
    OR ELSE HE CONTRADICTS N... . . . .   92C ANNO SWED LOVE   MARG
    OR ELSE THOU WOULDEST NOT HAVE LIVD TO CURSE THY HELPLESS   108 TIRIEL 6   28
    CHILDREN
    OR ELSE I SHALL BE LOST . . . .   120 LIT BOY LST/SI   4
    AND EVERY THING ELSE IS STILL . . . .   121 NURSES SONG/SI   4
    HIS EYES THE LIGHTS OF HIS LARGE SOUL CONTRACT OR ELSE   308 FOUR ZOAS 5   121
    EXPAND
    FROM THY EMBRACE ELSE BE ASSURD SO HORRIBLE A FORM . . .   326 FOUR ZOAS 7   235
    OR ELSE CONSUME THEIR SHADOWY SEMBLANCE YET THEY OBSTINATE   376 FOUR ZOAS 9   737
    THERE IS & CAN BE NO OTHER TO [?MEN] MAN WHAT ELSE CAN BE   398B ANNO BACON   * MARG
    A LIE IT MAKES MERCHANTS & NOTHING ELSE . . . . .   409C ANNO BACON   MARG
    EITHER RELATING TO SEDITION OR ANY THING ELSE . . . .   437B BLAKES MEMORAN   PROSE
    FOR REAL EFFECT IS MAKING OUT THE PARTS & IT IS NOTHING   450A ANNO REYNOLDS   MARG
    ELSE BUT THAT
    CANNOT EVEN KNOW OR SEE MICH ANGO OR RAFAEL OR ANY THING   456B ANNO REYNOLDS   MARG
    ELSE
    SOMEBODY ELSE WROTE THIS PAGE FOR REYNOLDS . . . .   463C ANNO REYNOLDS   MARG
    OF ANY THING ELSE . . . .   473B ANNO REYNOLDS   MARG
    ELSE HE WOULD WAKE SO SEEMD HE ENTERING HIS SHADOW BUT .   496 MILTON 15   2
    AND THEN THE POET WILL BE UNDERSTOOD AND NOT ELSE . .   570A DESC CAT 3   PROSE
    BUT THE HISTORY OF ALL TIMES AND PLACES IS NOTHING ELSE   578D DESC CAT 5   PROSE
    [TABLE] SURFACE & NOTHING ELSE . . . .   591D PUB ADDRESS/N   PROSE
    FOR THESE THIRTY TWO YEARS I AM MAD OR ELSE YOU ARE SO .   593D PUB ADDRESS/N   PROSE
    & PAINTING ARE SOMEWHAT ELSE BESIDES DRAWING . . . .   594C PUB ADDRESS/N   PROSE
    & ENGRAVING IS DRAWING ON COPPER & NOTHING ELSE . . .   594C PUB ADDRESS/N   PROSE
    LET US TEACH BUONAPARTE & WHOMSOEVER ELSE IT MAY CONCERN   597A PUB ADDRESS/N   PROSE
    THEY SEEM TO ME TO BE SOMETHING ELSE BESIDES HUMAN LIFE   600A PUB ADDRESS/N   PROSE
    I KNOW MY EXECUTION IS NOT LIKE ANY BODY ELSE I DO NOT .   601D PUB ADDRESS/N   PROSE
    & ENGRAVING IS DRAWING ON COPPER & NOTHING ELSE . . .   602B PUB ADDRESS/N   PROSE
    DRAWING IS EXECUTION & NOTHING ELSE . . . .   602B PUB ADDRESS/N   PROSE
    TO DIFFERENT PEOPLE IT APPEARS DIFFERENTLY AS EVERYTHING   605A V LAST JUDG/N   PROSE
    ELSE
    BUT HE HIMSELF WILL NOT KNOW IT THO EVERY BODY ELSE DOES   615C V LAST JUDG/N   PROSE
    ALBION'S MELANCHOLY WHO MUST ELSE HAVE BEEN A DUMB DESPAIR   668 JERUSALEM 40   60
    A [GOD] DEVIL OR ELSE A PHARISEE . . . .   754 EV GOSPEL(E)/N   28
    FOR GOD IS ONLY AN ALLEGORY OF KINGS & NOTHING ELSE AMEN   789A ANNO THORNTON   MARG
    WEIGHED & TAXED & MEASURED ALL ELSE . . . .   789B ANNO THORNTON   MARG
    & SHOULD NEVER HAVE ATTEMPTED TO LIVE BY ANY THING ELSE   794C LETTER 5   PROSE
    ACCOUNT & WHATEVER ELSE I CAN FINISH . . . . . .   803D LETTER 15   PROSE
    I SAY THEY ARE EQUAL TO CARRACHE OR RAFAEL OR ELSE I AM   814D LETTER 23   PROSE
    I SHOULD NOT DARE TO SAY TO ANY ONE ELSE THAT I CAN ALONE   822C LETTER 26   PROSE
    THE DRAPERIES PUT IN BY SOMEBODY ELSE . . . . . .   843C LETTER 43   PROSE
    AS YOURS TO HIM HE WILL NOT EASILY MEET FROM ANYONE ELSE   858A LETTER 55   PROSE
    ANY THING ELSE SUCH IS JOB BUT SINCE THE FRENCH REVOLUTION   878B LETTER 88   PROSE
    OF ANYTHING ELSE I HAVE PROVED THE SIX PLATES & REDUCED   879C LETTER 89   PROSE
ELSEWHERE
    THY PITY I CONTEMN SCATTER THY SNOWS ELSEWHERE . . .   322 FOUR ZOAS 7   70
    WE MUST THEREFORE SEEK THE CAUSE ELSEWHERE THAN IN . .   793C LETTER 5   PROSE
ELUCIDATE
    YOU SAY THAT I WANT SOMEBODY TO ELUCIDATE MY IDEAS BUT YOU   793A LETTER 5   PROSE
    WHO CAN ELUCIDATE MY VISIONS & PARTICULARLY THEY HAVE BEEN   794A LETTER 5   PROSE
ELUCIDATED
    ELUCIDATED BY CHILDREN WHO HAVE TAKEN A GREATER DELIGHT   794A LETTER 5   PROSE
ELVES
    AND TO CAGE THE FAIRIES & ELVES . . . .   183 MOTTO SONGS/N   4
    WITH TREES & FIELDS FULL OF FAIRY ELVES . . . . . .   816 HAPPINESS/L   5
ELY
    CAM IS A LITTLE STREAM ELY IS ALMOST SWALLOWD UP . . . .   623 JERUSALEM 5   9
    AND ELY SCRIBE OF LOS WHOSE PEN NO OTHER HAND . . . .   676 JERUSALEM 46   6
    SKOFELD HAD ELY RUTLAND CAMBRIDGE HUNTINGDON NORFOLK . .   710 JERUSALEM 71   38
ELYNITTRIA
    AND SILENT ELYNITTRIA THE SILVER BOWED QUEEN . . . . .   240 EUROPE 8   4
    . . . OUR DAUGHTERS OCALYTHRON ELYNITTRIA OOTHOON LEUTHA   350 FOUR ZOAS 8   363
    WHEN SATAN FAINTED BENEATH THE ARROWS OF ELYNITTRIA . . .   485 MILTON 5   43
    ELYNITTRIA WHENCE IS THIS JEALOUSY RUNNING ALONG   491 MILTON 10   14
    THE MOUNTAINS
    BUT BEAUTIFUL ELYNITTRIA WITH HER SILVER ARROWS REPELLD ME   492 MILTON 11   38
    AS ELYNITTRIA USED TO DO BUT TOO WELL THOSE LIVING   492 MILTON 12   12
    CREATURES
    KNEW THAT I WAS NOT ELYNITTRIA AND THEY BRAKE THE TRACES   492 MILTON 12   13
    FOR ELYNITTRIA MET SATAN WITH ALL HER SINGING WOMEN . . .   493 MILTON 12   42
    BUT ELYNITTRIA MET LEUTHA IN THE PLACE WHERE SHE WAS HIDDEN   494 MILTON 13   36
    OF THE PRIDE OF DOMINION THAT WILL DIVORCE OCALYTHRON &   740 JERUSALEM 93   5
    ELYNITTRIA
ELYTHIRIA
    [ELYTHYRIA] ELYTHIRIA ENANTO MANATHU VORCYON ETHINTHUS   350 FOUR ZOAS 8   * 364
    MOAB MIDIAN
    MOAB MIDIAN
EMANATE
    EMANATE UNCURBED IN THEIR ETERNAL GLORY . . . . . .   615C V LAST JUDG/N   PROSE

	PAGE	TITLE	LINE
EMANATED			
I EMANATED FROM LUVAH OVER THE TOWERS OF JERUSALEM . . .	660	JERUSALEM 33	41
EMANATES			
IN GREAT ETERNITY EVERY PARTICULAR FORM GIVES FORTH OR	684	JERUSALEM 54	1
EMANATES			
TILL SWEET JERUSALEM EMANATES AGAIN INTO ETERNITY . . .	728	JERUSALEM 83	60
EMANATING			
AROUND HIM INFANTS EMANATING FROM HIM THESE REPRESENT . .	613D	V LAST JUDG/N	PROSE
LIKE MANY WATERS AND EMANATING INTO GARDENS & PALACES UPON	695	JERUSALEM 61	30
EMANATION			
WILL LAY MY SCEPTER ON JERUSALEM THE EMANATION	278	FOUR ZOAS 1	498
THE EMANATION & HER SONS THE SATAN & THE ANAK	278	FOUR ZOAS 1	507
JERUSALEM HIS EMANATION [WILL SOON] IS BECOME A RUIN . .	279	FOUR ZOAS 1	545
THE DAUGHTERS OF BEULAH BEHELD THE EMANATION THEY PITIED	279	FOUR ZOAS 1	560
THE EMANATION STOOD BEFORE THE GATES OF ENITHARMON . .	280	FOUR ZOAS 1	567
SUCH WERE THE WORDS OF BEULAH OF THE FEMININE EMANATION	304	FOUR ZOAS 4	263
[I] MY EMANATION FAR WITHIN	415	MY SPECTRE/N *	3
OF JERUSALEM HIS EMANATION IN THE HEAVENS BENEATH BEULAH	481	MILTON 2	15
VIEWING HIS SIXFOLD EMANATION SCATTERD THRO THE DEEP . .	481	MILTON 2	19
TO DEVOUR ALBION AND JERUSALEM THE EMANATION OF ALBION .	493	MILTON 12	27
WHAT DO I HERE BEFORE THE JUDGMENT WITHOUT MY EMANATION .	495	MILTON 14	28
MY SPECTRE STILL WANDERING THRO THEM FOLLOWS MY EMANATION	521	MILTON 32	4
IS NOT LIKE A COAT MADE BY ANOTHER BUT IS AN EMANATION .	593B	PUB ADDRESS/N	PROSE
& IN WHOSE SLEEP OR CHAOS CREATION BEGAN [HIS EMANATION	609C	V LAST JUDG/N	PROSE
OR WIFE IS]			
IN ETERNITY WOMAN IS THE EMANATION OF MAN	613D	V LAST JUDG/N	PROSE
JERUSALEM THE EMANATION OF THE GIANT ALBION	620A	JERUSALEM	TITLE
JERUSALEM HIS EMANATION IS A STONE LAYING BENEATH . .	620	JERUSALEM 1	6
THY EMANATION THAT WAS WONT TO PLAY BEFORE THY FACE . .	622	JERUSALEM 4	14
WHERE HAST THOU HIDDEN THY EMANATION LOVELY JERUSALEM . .	622	JERUSALEM 4	16
SO SPOKE ALBION IN JEALOUS FEARS HIDING HIS EMANATION . .	622	JERUSALEM 4	33
INCESSANT BEFORE THE FURNACES AND HIS EMANATION DIVIDED	624	JERUSALEM 5	67
IN PAIN			
FOR AS HIS EMANATION DIVIDED HIS SPECTRE ALSO DIVIDED . .	624	JERUSALEM 6	3
AND HARROWD FOR HIS PROFIT LO THY STOLEN EMANATION . .	625	JERUSALEM 7	14
I AM CLOSD UP FROM MY CHILDREN MY EMANATION IS DIVIDING	627	JERUSALEM 8	13
ALBION IS DEAD HIS EMANATION IS DIVIDED FROM HIM . . .	631	JERUSALEM 12	6
BUT I AM LIVING YET I FEEL MY EMANATION ALSO DIVIDING .	631	JERUSALEM 12	7
HIS EMANATION YET HIS WIFE TILL THE SLEEP OF DEATH IS PAST	635	JERUSALEM 14	14
AND LOS BEHELD THE MILD EMANATION JERUSALEM EASTWARD	635	JERUSALEM 14	31
BENDING			
AND ITS FALLEN EMANATION THE SPECTRE & ITS CRUEL SHADOW	635	JERUSALEM 15	7
AND MALICE & ENVY BUT MY EMANATION ALAS WILL BECOME . .	639	JERUSALEM 17	38
JERUSALEM HIS EMANATION SHUT WITHIN HIS BOSOM	641	JERUSALEM 19	29
JERUSALEM THE EMANATION OF THE GIANT ALBION CAN IT BE .	649B	JERUSALEM 27	PROSE
THAT JERUSALEM WAS & IS THE EMANATION OF THE GIANT ALBION	649B	JERUSALEM 27	PROSE
AND THE TWO THAT ESCAPED WERE THE EMANATION OF LOS & HIS	655	JERUSALEM 30	1
SPECTRE FOR WHEREEVER THE EMANATION GOES THE SPECTRE .	655	JERUSALEM 30	2
ATTENDS HER AS HER GUARD & LOS'S EMANATION IS NAMED . .	655	JERUSALEM 30	3
AND THEY STROVE TO WEAVE A SHADOW OF THE EMANATION . .	655	JERUSALEM 30	6
ALBION'S EMANATION WHICH HE HAD HIDDEN IN JEALOUSY . .	659	JERUSALEM 33	26
HIS HIDDEN HEART HIS EMANATION WEPT & TREMBLED WITHIN HIM	664	JERUSALEM 38	3
FOR ALBION'S SAKE AND FOR JERUSALEM THY EMANATION . .	665	JERUSALEM 38	38
TO DESTROY HIS EMANATION IS THEIR INTENTION	667	JERUSALEM 40	17
BY THE WAVES OF DESPAIR WHOSE EMANATION ROSE ABOVE . .	667	JERUSALEM 40	49
WHEN OUT OF BEULAH THE EMANATION OF THE SLEEPER DESCENDED	678	JERUSALEM 48	23
WHEN WITH A DREADFUL GROAN THE EMANATION MILD OF ALBION	678	JERUSALEM 48	47
SHILOH THE MASCULINE EMANATION AMONG THE FLOWERS OF BEULAH	680	JERUSALEM 49	47
OF ENVY ALBION IS BECOME AND HIS EMANATION CAST OUT . .	681	JERUSALEM 50	9
YE KNOW THAT IF THE EMANATION REMAINS IN THEM	681	JERUSALEM 50	14
IN GNAWING PAIN DIVIDING HIM FROM HIS EMANATION . . .	684	JERUSALEM 53	6
THE MYSTIC UNION OF THE EMANATION IN THE LORD BECAUSE .	684	JERUSALEM 53	24
MAN DIVIDED FROM HIS EMANATION IS A DARK SPECTRE . . .	684	JERUSALEM 53	25
HIS EMANATION IS AN EVER-WEEPING MELANCHOLY SHADOW . .	684	JERUSALEM 53	26
CONTENDING FOR ALBION & FOR JERUSALEM HIS EMANATION . .	686	JERUSALEM 55	28
AND FOR SHILOH THE EMANATION OF FRANCE & FOR LOVELY VALA	686	JERUSALEM 55	29
DRINKING HIS EMANATION IN INTOXICATING BLISS REJOICING	701	JERUSALEM 65	58
IN GIANT DANCE			
FOR A SPECTRE HAS NO EMANATION BUT WHAT HE IMBIBES FROM	701	JERUSALEM 65	59
DECIEVING			
THEIR OWN PARENT THE EMANATION OF THEIR MURDERD ENEMY . .	701	JERUSALEM 65	69
BECOME THEIR EMANATION AND THEIR TEMPLE AND TABERNACLE .	701	JERUSALEM 65	70
ARE TO THE SONS OF ALBION AND JERUSALEM IS ALBION'S	709	JERUSALEM 71	5
EMANATION			
OBEYD HIS AWFUL VOICE IGNOGE IS HIS LOVELY EMANATION .	710	JERUSALEM 71	27
HIS EMANATION IS MEHETABEL TERRIBLE & LOVELY UPON . .	710	JERUSALEM 71	31
THE MOUNTAINS			
BRERTUN HAD YORKSHIRE DURHAM WESTMORELAND & HIS EMANATION	710	JERUSALEM 71	32
EMANATION GONORILL REJOICES OVER HILLS & ROCKS & WOODS	710	JERUSALEM 71	35
& RIVERS			
LEICESTER & BERKSHIRE & HIS EMANATION IS GWINEFRED	710	JERUSALEM 71	37
BEAUTIFUL			
SUFFOLK HARTFORD & ESSEX & HIS EMANATION IS GWINEVERA . .	710	JERUSALEM 71	39
KOX HAD OXFORD WARWICK WILTS HIS EMANATION IS ESTRILD . .	710	JERUSALEM 71	42
KOTOPE HAD HEREFORD STAFFORD WORCESTER & HIS EMANATION . .	710	JERUSALEM 71	44
HIS EMANATION IS CONWENNA SHE SHINES A TRIPLE FORM . .	710	JERUSALEM 71	47
OPENS THE FURNACES OF AFFLICTION IN THE EMANATION . . .	713	JERUSALEM 73	25
SO LOS SPOKE TO THE DAUGHTERS OF BEULAH WHILE HIS EMANATION	728	JERUSALEM 83	66
TO LIZARD-POINT & DOVER IN THE SOUTH HIS EMANATION . .	728	JERUSALEM 83	71
I SEE THE SPECTRES OF THY DEAD O EMANATION OF ALBION .	731	JERUSALEM 86	13
HIS EMANATION SEPARATES IN MILKY FIBRES AGONIZING . .	731	JERUSALEM 86	39
WHILE THOU MY EMANATION REFUSEST MY FIBRES OF DOMINION . .	733	JERUSALEM 88	13

575

	PAGE	TITLE	LINE

EMANATION (CONTINUED)
OR TO HIS EMANATION ANY OF THE UNIVERSAL CHARACTERISTICS — 736 JERUSALEM 90 — 29
AWAKE AWAKE JERUSALEM O LOVELY EMANATION OF ALBION . . — 744 JERUSALEM 97 — 1
EMANATION OF THE GIANT ALBION BUT FIND THAT TO PRINT IT — 878C LETTER 88 — PROSE
WILL

EMANATIONS
WHICH IS THE EARTH OF EDEN HE HIS EMANATIONS PROPAGATED — 264 FOUR ZOAS 1 — 18
LOST LOST LOST ARE MY EMANATIONS ENION [COME FORTH] O — 264 FOUR ZOAS 1 — 25
ENION
THE MEN HAVE RECIEVED THEIR DEATH WOUNDS & THEIR EMANATIONS — 265 FOUR ZOAS 1 — * 33
ARE FLED
THAT I HAVE SINND & THAT MY EMANATIONS ARE BECOME HARLOTS — 265 FOUR ZOAS 1 — 54
I THOUGHT THARMAS A SINNER & I MURDERD HIS EMANATIONS . . — 268 FOUR ZOAS 1 — 163
[BUT] FOR NOW I FIND THAT ALL THOSE EMANATIONS . . . — 268 FOUR ZOAS 1 — * 165
DRIVING THE FEMALE EMANATIONS ALL AWAY FROM LOS . . . . — 271 FOUR ZOAS 1 — 273
IN MALE FORMS WITHOUT FEMALE COUNTERPARTS OR EMANATIONS — 328 FOUR ZOAS 7 — 329
OF GOLD AND THOSE IN IMMORTALITY GAVE FORTH THEIR — 496 MILTON 15 — 13
EMANATIONS
HOW LONG BENEATH THE COVERING CHERUB GIVE OUR EMANATIONS — 507 MILTON 23 — 12
BUT THE EMANATIONS TREMBLED EXCEEDINGLY NOR COULD THEY . — 519 MILTON 30 — 21
SO SPAKE THE LOVELY EMANATIONS & THERE APPEARD A PLEASANT — 519 MILTON 30 — 32
ITS FURNACES OF AFFLICTION IN WHICH HIS ANGELS & EMANATIONS — 529 MILTON 38 — 20
UPON THE EMANATIONS OF ALBION'S SONS THE DAUGHTERS — 624 JERUSALEM 5 — 37
OF ALBION
THEY ARE THE BEAUTIFUL EMANATIONS OF THE TWELVE SONS OF — 624 JERUSALEM 5 — 45
ALBION
IN THE WARS OF BABEL & SHINAR ALL THEIR EMANATIONS WERE — 628 JERUSALEM 8 — 42
CONDENSD HIS EMANATIONS INTO HARD OPAKE SUBSTANCES . . . — 628 JERUSALEM 9 — 1
AND THE EMANATIONS BURIED ALIVE IN THE EARTH WITH POMP — 628 JERUSALEM 9 — 15
OF RELIGION
TO PROTECT THE EMANATIONS OF ALBION'S MIGHTY ONES FROM — 631 JERUSALEM 11 — 18
CRUELTY
FOR THE PROTECTION OF THE TWELVE EMANATIONS OF ALBION'S — 637 JERUSALEM 16 — 42
SONS
THE SPECTRE OF THE LIVING PURSUING THE EMANATIONS OF THE — 638 JERUSALEM 17 — 13
DEAD
AND THE TWELVE FEMALE EMANATIONS FLED WITH THEM AGONIZING — 663 JERUSALEM 36 — 20
OUR EMANATIONS AND TO ATTACK OUR SECRET SUPREME DELIGHTS — 664 JERUSALEM 37 — 9
SEEN ONLY BY EMANATIONS BY VEGETATIONS VIEWLESS . . . . — 665 JERUSALEM 38 — 56
THE FOUR APPEARD WITH THEIR EMANATIONS IN FIERY . . . . — 666 JERUSALEM 40 — 4
OUTSPREAD WITH ABUNDANT RICHES AND HIS EMANATIONS . . — 668 JERUSALEM 40 — 54
THEY SAW ALBION ENDEAVOURING TO DESTROY THEIR EMANATIONS — 669 JERUSALEM 41 — 31
GIVE ME MY EMANATIONS BACK FOOD FOR MY DYING SOUL . . . — 670 JERUSALEM 42 — 13
THEIR EMANATIONS RETURN NOT THEIR SPECTRES RAGE IN THE DEEP — 674 JERUSALEM 44 — 34
THE EMANATIONS OF THE GRIEVOUSLY AFFLICTED FRIENDS — 678 JERUSALEM 48 — 27
OF ALBION
FOR THE PROTECTION OF THE TWELVE EMANATIONS OF ALBION'S — 684 JERUSALEM 53 — 23
SONS
I KNOW THAT IN MY FLESH I SHALL SEE GOD BUT EMANATIONS . — 696 JERUSALEM 62 — 16
WHERE SEXES WANDER IN DREAMS OF BLISS AMONG THE EMANATIONS — 721 JERUSALEM 79 — 75
SEPARATE ALBION'S SONS GENTLY FROM THEIR EMANATIONS . . — 728 JERUSALEM 83 — 49
EMANATIONS CREATE SPACE THE MASCULINE CREATE TIME & PLANT — 730 JERUSALEM 85 — 8
ON EARTH OF THOSE WHOSE EMANATIONS WEAVE THE LOVES . . — 731 JERUSALEM 86 — 43
IN MUTUAL INTERCHANGE AND FIRST THEIR EMANATIONS MEET . — 733 JERUSALEM 88 — 5
BUT IF THE EMANATIONS MINGLE NOT WITH STORMS & AGITATIONS — 733 JERUSALEM 88 — 8
FOR MAN CANNOT UNITE WITH MAN BUT BY THEIR EMANATIONS . — 733 JERUSALEM 88 — 10
CEASING TO BE HIS EMANATIONS LIFE TO THEMSELVES ASSUMING — 736 JERUSALEM 90 — 2
AND I HEARD THE NAME OF THEIR EMANATIONS THEY ARE NAMED — 747 JERUSALEM 99 — 5
JERUSALEM

EMANATIVE
EVERY EMANATIVE JOY FORBIDDEN AS A CRIME . . . . . . — 628 JERUSALEM 9 — 14
MAN IS ADJOIND TO MAN BY HIS EMANATIVE PORTION . . . . — 675 JERUSALEM 44 — 38
DISPLAYD IN THE EMANATIVE VISIONS OF CANAAN IN JERUSALEM — 739 JERUSALEM 92 — 21
& IN SHILOH

EMANUEL
THIS SUBJECT IS TAKEN FROM THE VISIONS OF EMANUEL — 581D DESC CAT 8 — *PROSE
SWEDENBORG

EMBALMD
SHE SHOULD ARISE AGAIN TO LIFE EMBALMD IN ENION'S BOSOM — 278 FOUR ZOAS 1 — 527
WITHIN HER BOSOM ALBION LIES EMBALMD NEVER TO AWAKE . . — 501 MILTON 19 — 57
SIX MONTHS THEY LIE EMBALMD IN SILENT DEATH WORSHIPPED . . — 644 JERUSALEM 21 — 44
FATHER ONCE PITEOUS IS PITY A SIN EMBALMD IN VALA'S BOSOM — 646 JERUSALEM 23 — 9
BUT I VALA LUVAH'S DAUGHTER KEEP HIS BODY EMBALMD IN MORAL — 722 JERUSALEM 80 — 27
LAWS

EMBALMING
MURDERD HER & HID HER IN HER BOSOM EMBALMING HER FOR FEAR — 278 FOUR ZOAS 1 — 526

EMBARRASD
EMBARRASD AT THE IDEA OF SETTING A VALUE ON ANY WORK OF MR — 860A LETTER 56 — PROSE

EMBLEM
EMBLEM OF PRIDE SHE SAW THE ARTS THEIR TREASURES BRING . . — 41B THEN SHE BORE — PROSE
THE EARWIG ARMD THE TENDER MAGGOT EMBLEM OF IMMORTALITY — 377 FOUR ZOAS 9 — 759
THE EARWIG ARMD THE TENDER MAGGOT EMBLEM OF IMMORTALITY — 513 MILTON 27 — 16

EMBLEMATIC
OF EMBLEMATIC TEXTURE WAS SOLD TO THE AMALEKITE . . . . — 508 MILTON 24 — 19

EMBLEMS
WITH SIXTEEN PILLARS CANOPIED WITH EMBLEMS & WRITTEN VERSE — 677 JERUSALEM 48 — 7
BE ERECTING MONUMENTS IN PARIS EMBLEMS OF PEACE . . . . — 811A LETTER 21 — PROSE

EMBODIED   SEE IMBODIED
[O SLAY ME NOT THOU ART HIS WRATH EMBODIED IN DECEIT] . . — 268 FOUR ZOAS 1 — 162
I FEEL TO FABRICATE EMBODIED SEMBLANCES IN WHICH THE DEAD — 331 FOUR ZOAS 7 — 440
OF LOS ASSIMILATING TO THOSE FORMS EMBODIED & LOVELY . . — 332 FOUR ZOAS 7 — 474
HIS HEAD BENDS OVER LONDON HE SEES HIS EMBODIED SPECTRE — 531 MILTON 39 — 46

		PAGE	TITLE	LINE

EMBODIED   (CONTINUED)
      AND YET THEY ARE EMBODIED AND ORGANIZED IN SOLID MARBLE   576D DESC CAT 4   PROSE
      CITIES NOT YET EMBODIED IN TIME AND SPACE PLANT YE . . . 730 JERUSALEM 85   27
EMBOLDENS
      OF DEXTERITY IN CERTAIN POINTS EMBOLDENS ME [TH] TO HOPE 808A LETTER 19   *PROSE
         THAT
EMBOSOM
      . . . THE WOODS OF FRANCE EMBOSOM THE SOUND   . . . . .   134 FRENCH REVOLTN   11
      NOR DAUGHTER NOR SISTER NOR MOTHER COME FORTH TO EMBOSOM   673 JERUSALEM 43   44
         THE SLAIN
EMBOSSD
      WITH GIFTS & SPICES WITH LAMPS RICH EMBOSSD JEWELS & GOLD 349 FOUR ZOAS 8   337
EMBRACD
      GRIEF PERCHT UPON MY BROW AND THOUGHT EMBRACD HER   . .   43B WOE CRIED MUSE   PROSE
      [[HE] THEY EMBRACD [MY MIRTLE] THE BLOSSOMS BRIGHT] . . . 167 INFANT SORW/N   * 32
      [[HE] THEY EMBRACD MY [MIRTLE] BLOSSOMS BRIGHT] . . . .   167 INFANT SORW/N   * 37
      HE EMBRACD HER SHE WEPT SHE REFUSD   . . . .   231 URIZEN 19   11
      IN EMBRYON PASSIONS THEY KISSD NOT NOR EMBRACD FOR SHAME   270 FOUR ZOAS 1   238
         & FEAR
      SOFT CLOUD OF SNOW A FEMALE PALE & WEAK I SOFT EMBRACD   300 FOUR ZOAS 4   99
      HE TURND FROM SIDE TO SIDE IN [VAIN] TEARS HE WEPT & HE   325 FOUR ZOAS 7   * 220
         EMBRACD
      OF URTHONA LOS EMBRACD THE SPECTRE FIRST AS A BROTHER .   328 FOUR ZOAS 7   339
      AND WITH IT LOSE HIMSELF IN MEEKNESS SHE EMBRACD HIS FIRE 336 FOUR ZOAS 7B   128
      THE CHILDREN CLUNG AROUND HER KNEES SHE EMBRACD THEM &   370 FOUR ZOAS 9   509
         WEPT OVER THEM
      SHE EMBRACD THEM IN TEARS TILL THE SUN DESCENDED   370 FOUR ZOAS 9   512
         THE WESTERN HILLS
      THIS SICKLE URIZEN TOOK THE SCYTHE HIS SONS EMBRACD . .   372 FOUR ZOAS 9   582
      MILD HE EMBRACD HER WHOM HE SOUGHT HE RAISD HER THRO THE   373 FOUR ZOAS 9   614
         HEAVENS
      SO SPOKE THE ETERNAL AT THE FEAST THEY EMBRACD THE NEW   374 FOUR ZOAS 9   643
         BORN MAN
      EMBRACD SOFT WITH A BROTHER'S TEARS PALAMABRON WHO ALSO   486 MILTON 7   17
         WEPT
      I HAVE EMBRACD THE FALLING DEATH HE IS BECOME ONE WITH ME 507 MILTON 23   33
      ALBION LOVD THEE HE RENT THY VEIL HE EMBRACD THEE HE LOVD 643 JERUSALEM 20   36
         THEE
      ASSIMILATED AND EMBRACD ETERNAL DEATH FOR ALBION'S SAKE   676 JERUSALEM 45   39
      HER TEARS SHE ARDENT EMBRACD HER SORROWS OCCUPIED   678 JERUSALEM 48   40
         IN LABOURS
EMBRACE
      . . . AND THEIR WORMS EMBRACE TOGETHER   . . . .   141 FRENCH REVOLTN   150
      AND RUN AND EMBRACE THE MEEK PEASANT . . . .   144 FRENCH REVOLTN   221
      BUT DUMB TILL THAT DREAD DAY WHEN ORC ASSAYD HIS FIERCE   196 AMERICA PREL 1   10
         EMBRACE
      TO EMBRACE AHANIA'S JOY   . . . .   254 AHANIA 5   11
      IN THE BRIGHT SANDS OF LOS EVADING MY EMBRACE THEN I ALONE 288 FOUR ZOAS 2   305
      I [EMBRACES] EMBRACE ROUND THY KNEES & . . . .   291 FOUR ZOAS 3   4
      FROM THY EMBRACE ELSE BE ASSURD SO HORRIBLE A FORM   . .   326 FOUR ZOAS 7   235
      THOU NEVER CANST EMBRACE SWEET ENITHARMON TERRIBLE DEMON   328 FOUR ZOAS 7   342
         TILL
      FORGETFUL OF HIS OWN LAWS PITYING HE BEGAN TO EMBRACE .   352 FOUR ZOAS 8   420
      TREMBLING & WEAK A FAINT EMBRACE A FIERCE DESIRE AS WHEN   358 FOUR ZOAS 9   27
      I SHALL CAST OFF MY DEATH CLOTHES & EMBRACE THARMAS AGAIN 373 FOUR ZOAS 9   599
      WE FALL ON ONE ANOTHER'S NECKS MORE CLOSELY WE EMBRACE . 374 FOUR ZOAS 9   639
      WILL NEVER EMBRACE YOUR SMILES . . . .   417 MY SPECTR AD/N * 16
      PARENTS & CHILDREN WIVES & HUSBANDS EMBRACE & ARISE   443D LAST JUDGMNT/L PROSE
         TOGETHER
      EMBRACE & ASCEND TO MEET ETERNITY . . . . . .   609D V LAST JUDG/N   PROSE
      NO MAN CAN EMBRACE TRUE ART TILL HE HAS EXPLORD & CAST OUT 613A V LAST JUDG/N   PROSE
      EMBRACE HIM TENFOLD BRIGHT RISING FROM HIS TOMB IN   626 JERUSALEM 7   56
         IMMORTALITY
      BUT WHEN THE JOY OF MEETING WAS EXHAUSTED IN LOVING EMBRACE 631 JERUSALEM 11   16
      ZOAS OF ALBION WHERE A MAN DARE HARDLY TO EMBRACE   . . . 663 JERUSALEM 36   45
      AND FEET LEST ANY SHOULD ENTER HIS BOSOM & EMBRACE   . . 664 JERUSALEM 38   2
      THREE-FOLD EMBRACE RETURNS CONSUMING LIVES OF GODS & MEN   709 JERUSALEM 70   27
      EMBRACE WE SHALL PERISH ANNIHILATE DISCOVERD OUR DELUSIONS 725 JERUSALEM 82   4
      SURROUNDED BY THEIR CHILDREN IF THEY EMBRACE & COMINGLE   733 JERUSALEM 88   6
      TO THE EMBRACE OF LOVE & TO THE MINGLING OF SOFT FIBRES   736 JERUSALEM 90   9
      HE IS GLAD TO EMBRACE THE OFFER OF ENGRAVING SUCH BEAUTIFUL 790A LETTER 1   PROSE
         THINGS
      WIFE & SISTER ARE BOTH WELL COURTING NEPTUNE FOR AN EMBRACE 802A LETTER 14   PROSE
      MY WIFE & SISTER ARE BOTH VERY WELL & COURTING NEPTUNE   803B LETTER 15   PROSE
         FOR AN EMBRACE
      INTO THE LIGHT OF DAY I STILL & SHALL TO ETERNITY EMBRACE 815D LETTER 23   PROSE
      & WILL EMBRACE THEM WHENEVER THEY SEE THEM . . . . . .   321D LETTER 25   PROSE
      & EMBRACE IT COMES THRO MR HOARE . . . .   841B LETTER 41   PROSE
      IN SHORT IF YOU SEE IT AS I SEE IT YOU WILL EMBRACE THIS   842A LETTER 41   PROSE
         PROPOSAL
EMBRACED
      MOST MASTERLY CONCEPTION THAT THE PUBLIC HAVE EMBRACED . 576B DESC CAT 4   PROSE
      HIMSELF CAST OUT BY THOSE WHO HAVE ALREADY EMBRACED TRUE   613A V LAST JUDG/N   PROSE
         ART
EMBRACES
      I [EMBRACES] EMBRACE ROUND THY KNEES & . . . .   291 FOUR ZOAS 3   4
      TO THE EMBRACES OF THIS TERROR & I WILL DESTROY   . . .   327 FOUR ZOAS 7   300
      WHENEVER ANY INDIVIDUAL REJECTS ERROR & EMBRACES TRUTH . 613A V LAST JUDG/N   PROSE
      EMBRACES ARE COMINGLINGS FROM THE HEAD EVEN TO THE FEET   708 JERUSALEM 69   43
EMBRACING
      SHE SEEMED A SILVER STREAM HIS FEET EMBRACING . . . . .   38C SAMSON/PS   PROSE
      SHALL WEEP BENDING TO EARTH EMBRACING THE VALLEYS . . .   144 FRENCH REVOLTN   224

577

	PAGE	TITLE	LINE

EMBRACING   (CONTINUED)
    WHO STRETCHED OUT HIS ARMS EMBRACING THE FLAME OF FIRE   . . 158D MARRIAGE HH 22   PROSE
    EMBRACING HIS BRIGHT MOTHER & BEHELD MALIGNANT FIRES   .   . 307 FOUR ZOAS 5   81
    AND HEARD THE SPECTRE BITTERLY SHE WEPT EMBRACING FERVENT   327 FOUR ZOAS 7   312
    SO SPOKE LOS & EMBRACING ENITHARMON & THE SPECTRE   . . . 329 FOUR ZOAS 7   370
    THE REAPER IN BOTH ARMS EMBRACING THE FURIOUS RAGING FLAMES   332 FOUR ZOAS 7   463
    STAND UPON THE EARTH EMBRACING & SHOUTING TO THE LAMB   . . 444A LAST JUDGMNT/L   PROSE
    EMBRACING ABOVE THE GRAVES & REPRESENT RELIGION   . . . . 610C V LAST JUDG/N   PROSE
    VALA REPLIED IN CLOUDS OF TEARS ALBION'S GARMENT EMBRACING   659 JERUSALEM 33   35
    WHY WAS I ONE WITH HER EMBRACING IN THE VISION OF JESUS   660 JERUSALEM 33   44
    ASTONISHD LOVELY EMBRACING THE SUBLIME SHADE THE DAUGHTERS   678 JERUSALEM 48   29
        OF BEULAH
    AH MY MARY SAID JOSEPH WEEPING OVER & EMBRACING HER CLOSELY   694 JERUSALEM 61   14
        IN
    BLACK EYD SUSAN A FIGURE ON THE SEA SHORE EMBRACING A CORSE   848D LETTER 45   PROSE
EMBRIO
    AND THE WEB IS A FEMALE IN EMBRIO   . . . . 235 URIZEN 25   18
EMBROIDERD
    AS THERE MAY BE A FOOL OR A KNAVE IN AN EMBROIDERD COAT   593B PUB ADDRESS/N   PROSE
EMBROIDERY
    ARTIST HIMSELF EVEN TO THE STUFFS & EMBROIDERY   . . . . 588A CHAUCER/N   PROSE
    BUT I SAY THAT THE EMBROIDERY OF THE IGNORANT FINISHER   . 593B PUB ADDRESS/N   PROSE
EMBRYON
    IN EMBRYON PASSIONS THEY KISSD NOT NOR EMBRACD FOR SHAME   270 FOUR ZOAS 1   238
        & FEAR
    THEY SAW THE SEXUAL RELIGION IN ITS EMBRYON UNCIRCUMCISION   655 JERUSALEM 30   11
    ACCORDING AS THEY WEAVE THE LITTLE EMBRYON NERVES & VEINS   728 JERUSALEM 83   35
EMERALD
    HIS KNEES ARE ROCKS OF ADAMANT & RUBIE & EMERALD   . . . . 308 FOUR ZOAS 5   * 139
    THE EMERALD ONYX SAPPHIRE JASPER BERYL AMETHYST   . . . . 343 FOUR ZOAS 8   74
    TRANSLUCENT THE FURNACES OF BERYLL & EMERALD IMMORTAL   . . 684 JERUSALEM 53   9
EMERGD
    THE CLOUD THEN SHEWD HIS GOLDEN HEAD & HIS BRIGHT FORM   128 BOOK OF THEL 3   5
        EMERGD
    ABOVE ALL HEAVENS IN THUNDERS WRAPD EMERGD HIS LEPROUS HEAD   203 AMERICA 16   3
    . . . TO THE PLACE [OF DEATH & HELL] WHENCE I EMERGD   . . 268 FOUR ZOAS 1   157
EMERGE
    THEIR SULLEN FLAMES FADED EMERGE ROUND THE GLOOMY KING   . . 159D SONG LIBERTY   PROSE
    EMERGE FROM THE DARKNESS HIS HAND   . . . . 224 URIZEN 4   42
    OVER THE HEAVING DELUGE HE SAW LOS & ENITHARMON EMERGE   . . 297 FOUR ZOAS 4   2
    OFT DOTH HIS EYES EMERGE FROM THE ABYSS INTO THE REALMS   352 FOUR ZOAS 8   * 454
    I BEGIN TO EMERGE FROM A DEEP PIT OF MELANCHOLY   . . . . 798A LETTER 10   PROSE
EMERGED
    URIZEN EMERGED FROM HIS ROCKY FORM & FROM HIS SNOWS   . . . 500 MILTON 18   51
    BEEN VERY UNHAPPY I AM SO NO LONGER I AM AGAIN EMERGED   . . 815D LETTER 23   PROSE
EMERGING
    FROM THE WATERS EMERGING LAMENTS   . . . . 234 URIZEN 23   14
    TO TAKE THE LIMBS OF MAN AT LENGTH EMERGING FROM THE SMOKE   296 FOUR ZOAS 3   158
    AS SUDDENLY EMERGING FROM THE BLUE SKY FOR THEIR HELP   . . 610D V LAST JUDG/N   PROSE
EMILIE
    WHEN EDESSA AND LYCA AND EMILIE   . . . . 63 SHEPHERD YOUNG   7
EMILY
    WHEN MARY AND SUSAN AND EMILY   . . . . 125 LAUGHING/SI   7
EMIM
    SIHON & OG THE ANAKIM & EMIM NEPHILIM & GIBBORIM   . . . . 735 JERUSALEM 89   47
EMINENCE
    THE ATTENTION OF MANY PERSONS OF EMINENCE AND FORTUNE   . . 207C PRSPECTUS 1793   PROSE
    EMINENCE AS AN ENGRAVER MAKES HIS OPINION DESERVE NOTICE   848A LETTER 45   PROSE
EMINENT
    EMINENT IN THE ART OF MASSING HIS LIGHTS AND SHADES   . . . 844B LETTER 43   PROSE
    AS THEY ARE THE MOST EMINENT AMONG ANIMALS VIZ THE LION   . 859B LETTER 56   PROSE
EMISSARIES
    AND HYLE & COBAN WERE HIS TWO CHOSEN ONES FOR EMISSARIES   641 JERUSALEM 18   41
EMIT
    VIOLENT PASSIONS EMIT THE REAL GOOD & PERFECT TONES   . . . 476A ANNO REYNOLDS   MARG
    MY FINGERS EMIT SPARKS OF FIRE WITH EXPECTATION OF   801C LETTER 13   PROSE
        MY FUTURE LABOURS
EMITTING
    THE SUN WAS EMITTING   . . . . 804 TO BUTTS/L   4
EMMA
    THE ORDEAL OF QUEEN EMMA   . . . . SUPP ILLUS HISTORY   *TITLE
EMMET
    THAT AN EMMET LOST ITS WAY   . . . . 111 A DREAM/SI   3
    THE EMMET & THE BEETLE HARK THEY LAUGH & MOCK AT LOS   . . 288 FOUR ZOAS 2   308
    DRINK LAUGH & SING THE GRASSHOPPER THE EMMET & THE FLY   . . 308 FOUR ZOAS 5   * 133
    WONDERING TO BEHOLD THE EMMET THE GRASSHOPPER THE JOINTED   373 FOUR ZOAS 9   603
        WORM
    THE SPORTIVE ROOT THE EARTHWORM THE SMALL BEETLE THE WISE   377 FOUR ZOAS 9   756
        EMMET
    THE SPORTIVE ROOT THE EARTH-WORM THE GOLD BEETLE THE WISE   513 MILTON 27   12
        EMMET
    THE EMMET AND [EARTH-WORM] EARTH-WORMS ARE HIS SUPERIORS   688 JERUSALEM 56   * 37
        & HIS LORDS
EMMET'S
    THE EMMET'S INCH & EAGLE'S MILE   . . . . 433 AUGURIES   105
EMPERIES
    AN ANCIENT PALACE ARCHETYPE OF MIGHTY EMPERIES   . . . . 200 AMERICA 10   8
EMPEROR
    FITTED TO THE FINGER OF AN EMPEROR SUCH IS THAT WORTHY   29D EDW THIRD/PS 4   PROSE
        CHANDOS
    LOOKS DOWN ON THEIR LITTLE FOLLIES FROM THE EMPEROR TO   569A DESC CAT 3   PROSE
        THE MILLER

		PAGE	TITLE	LINE
EMPEROR'S				
	DANTE WAS AN EMPEROR'S A CAESAR'S MAN	413B	ANNO BOYD	MARG
EMPERY				
	OF A BRIGHT UNIVERSE EMPERY ATTENDED DAY & NIGHT	264	FOUR ZOAS 1	15
EMPIRE				
	OUR SONS SHALL RULE THE EMPIRE OF THE SEA	32	EDW THIRD/PS 6	42
	TO CONSTANTINE'S GREAT CITY EMPIRE FLED	41B	THEN SHE BORE	PROSE
	EMPIRE IS NO MORE AND NOW THE LION & WOLF SHALL CEASE .	160A	SONG LIBERTY	PROSE
	FOR EMPIRE IS NO MORE AND NOW THE LION & WOLF SHALL CEASE	198	AMERICA 6	15
	RATTLING WITH CLANKING CHAINS THE UNIVERSAL EMPIRE GROANS	333	FOUR ZOAS 7B	17
	THE FOUNDATION OF EMPIRE IS ART & SCIENCE	445C	ANNO REYNOLDS	MARG
	REMOVE THEM OR DEGRADE THEM & THE EMPIRE IS NO MORE . .	445D	ANNO REYNOLDS	MARG
	EMPIRE FOLLOWS ART & NOT VICE VERSA AS ENGLISHMEN SUPPOSE	445D	ANNO REYNOLDS	MARG
	AND HELD THE EMPIRE OF THE WORLD IN THE DARK AGE . . .	578C	DESC CAT 5	PROSE
	TO EMPIRE THAT IT IS DESTRUCTIVE OF BOTH AS ALL	593D	PUB ADDRESS/N	*PROSE
	THAT IT IS NOT ARTS THAT FOLLOW & ATTEND UPON [EMPIRES] EMPIRE	597A	PUB ADDRESS/N	*PROSE
	BUT [EMPIRES] EMPIRE THAT ATTENDS UPON	597A	PUB ADDRESS/N	*PROSE
	THAT IS ON CAESAR OR EMPIRE OR NATURAL RELIGION	776B	INSC LAOCOON	PROSE
	EMPIRE AGAINST ART SEE VIRGIL'S ENEID LIB VI...	777A	INSC LAOCOON	PROSE
	SUCH ARE GREECE & ROME SUCH IS EMPIRE OR TAX SEE LUKE...	777B	INSC LAOCOON	PROSE
EMPIRES				
	AND EMPIRES OF CHAOS INVISIBLE TO THE VEGETABLE MAN . .	528	MILTON 37	49
	EMPIRES FLOURISH TILL THEY BECOME COMMERCIAL	594A	PUB ADDRESS/N	PROSE
	LET IT NO MORE BE SAID THAT EMPIRES ENCOURAGE ARTS . .	597A	PUB ADDRESS/N	PROSE
	FOR IT IS ARTS THAT ENCOURAGE EMPIRES	597A	PUB ADDRESS/N	PROSE
	THAT IT IS NOT ARTS THAT FOLLOW & ATTEND UPON [EMPIRES] EMPIRE	597A	PUB ADDRESS/N	*PROSE
	BUT [EMPIRES] EMPIRE THAT ATTENDS UPON	597A	PUB ADDRESS/N	*PROSE
EMPLOY				
	HOW TO EMPLOY THE HAND THAT LACKETH BREAD	19	EDW THIRD/PS 2	23
	PRETEND TO ENCOURAGE ART HE WILL EMPLOY HIMSELF . . .	586A	DESC CAT 16	PROSE
	IT SO MUCH H'S(HAYLEY'S) INTEREST TO EMPLOY ME	819D	LETTER 25	PROSE
	EMPLOY ME AS HIS PUBLISHER I SHOULD HAVE NO OBJECTION .	856C	LETTER 54	PROSE
EMPLOYD				
	WERE EMPLOYD WHEN MRS GIMBLET CAME IN [?HOPING]	44B	ISLAND MOON 1	*PROSE
	BUT THEIR THOUGHTS WERE OTHERWISE EMPLOYD	44C	ISLAND MOON 1	PROSE
	FOR THE LADIES TO VIEW THE PICTURES THUS HE WAS EMPLOYD	58D	ISLAND MOON 10	PROSE
	EMPLOYING THE DAUGHTERS IN HER LOOMS & LOS EMPLOYD THE SONS	345	FOUR ZOAS 8	185
	THE LABOURD WORKS OF JOURNEYMEN EMPLOYD BY CORREGGIO .	455A	ANNO REYNOLDS	MARG
	LABOUR & TRICK SALVATORE ROSA EMPLOYD JOURNEYMEN . . .	468D	ANNO REYNOLDS	MARG
	THESE ARE ONLY EMPLOYD AGAINST THE JUST	616B	V LAST JUDG/N	PROSE
	I AM STILL EMPLOYD IN MAKING DESIGNS & LITTLE PICTURES .	798B	LETTER 10	PROSE
	THAT I SHOULD BE EMPLOYD IN GREATER THINGS & WHEN IT IS	812A	LETTER 22	PROSE
	UNEASY FOR I AM FULLY EMPLOYD & WELL PAID I HAVE MADE .	819D	LETTER 25	PROSE
	BEING FULLY EMPLOYD IN ENGRAVING FOR HIS PROJECTED WORKS	824C	LETTER 27	PROSE
	AMUSEMENT THAN HE COULD EVER BE IF EMPLOYD IN THE DRUDGERY OF	850B	LETTER 49	PROSE
	FROM OTHER PLATES FOR BOOKSELLERS WHICH HE WAS EMPLOYD .	877B	LETTER 86	PROSE
EMPLOYED				
	AND DIRECTIONS ARE EMPLOYED AT A GREAT EXPENCE	572D	DESC CAT 3	PROSE
	I HAVE NO OBJECTION TO RUBENS AND REMBRANDT BEING EMPLOYED	575D	DESC CAT 3	PROSE
	PETTY PRINCE IN ITALY AND EMPLOYED NUMEROUS JOURNEYMEN .	583B	DESC CAT 9	PROSE
	THAT HE IS SO AND IF HE IS NOT EMPLOYED BY THOSE WHO .	586A	DESC CAT 16	PROSE
	ENGAGED SHOULD BE EMPLOYED ON THE WORK OF ROMNEY'S LIFE	849D	LETTER 47	PROSE
EMPLOYER				
	BLASTING MY CHARACTER AS AN ARTIST TO MACKLIN MY EMPLOYER	592D	PUB ADDRESS/N	PROSE
	EMPLOYER & I HAVE AN ORDER FOR FIFTY SMALL PICTURES AT ONE	795C	LETTER 6	PROSE
	THEIR AUTHOR AND GRATEFUL TO YOU MY EMPLOYER & THAT I LOOK	814D	LETTER 23	PROSE
EMPLOYER'S				
	WHILE OTHERS MORE OBEDIENT TO AN EMPLOYER'S OPINIONS .	572D	DESC CAT 3	PROSE
EMPLOYERS				
	EMPLOYERS OF FOOLS TO BE EXECRATED IN	452C	ANNO REYNOLDS	MARG
	TO THEIR EMPLOYERS WHILE THEY THEMSELVES	583B	DESC CAT 9	PROSE
EMPLOYERS'				
	OUGHT NOT THE [?ARTISTS ?& ?EMPLOYERS' ?IMBECILITY] . .	452C	ANNO REYNOLDS	* MARG
EMPLOYING				
	EMPLOYING THE DAUGHTERS IN HER LOOMS & LOS EMPLOYD THE SONS	345	FOUR ZOAS 8	185
	EMPLOYING HIM WERE (FIRST) TO ENCOURAGE A WORTHY MAN & .	856B	LETTER 54	PROSE
	BUT A PLEASURE IN EMPLOYING HIS PRINTER & HAVE NO DOUBT I	856C	LETTER 54	PROSE
EMPLOYMENT				
	WITHOUT EMPLOYMENT & AS MUCH AS COULD POSSIBLY BE WITHOUT BREAD	445B	ANNO REYNOLDS	MARG
	WHILE THE SCULPTORS HAVE CONTINUAL & SUPERABUNDANT EMPLOYMENT	601A	PUB ADDRESS/N	PROSE
	MISERIES ARE LEADEN LEGGED AND THEIR WHOLE EMPLOYMENT IS	807A	LETTER 17	PROSE
	TOWARDS YOU THRO MULTITUDE OF EMPLOYMENT & THRO HOPE .	816A	LETTER 23	PROSE
	FROM HIS SUPERABUNDANT EMPLOYMENT YET NO ONE BRINGS . .	829D	LETTER 30	PROSE
	OF EMPLOYMENT THIS WISH I FEAR IS NOT TO BE ACCOMPLISHD	830B	LETTER 30	PROSE
	AS HE WAS OUT OF THE WAY ALL THE TIME ON OTHER EMPLOYMENT	830D	LETTER 30	PROSE
	YOUR WORDS "DO NOT FEAR YOU CAN WANT EMPLOYMENT" WERE .	831B	LETTER 31	PROSE
	DESIGNING AND TO RELIEVE MY MORE LABORIOUS [EMPLOYMENT]	860C	LETTER 56	PROSE
	UPON BY THEM AS INCAPABLE OF EMPLOYMENT IN THOSE WORKS IT	862C	LETTER 60	PROSE
EMPTIED				
	[THEN DEMONS ?HOWLD ROUND HIS CHARIOT ?RAGING ?LUVAH (EMPTIED)]	SUPP	FOUR ZOAS 5	*
EMPTIING				
	EMPTIING OUT THE VANITIES OF RICHES & WORLDLY HONOURS .	607D	V LAST JUDG/N	*PROSE
EMPTY				
	HAVING MADE A GENTLE BOW PROCEEDED TO EMPTY HIS POCKETS	45B	ISLAND MOON 1	PROSE
	INTO THE EASTERN VACUITY THE EMPTY WORLD OF LUVAH . . .	315	FOUR ZOAS 6	156
	LUVAH SLEPT HERE IN DEATH & HERE IS LUVAH'S EMPTY TOMB .	526	MILTON 35	59

579

		PAGE	TITLE	LINE

EMPYREAN
THE EMPYREAN GROAND THROUGHOUT ALL EDEN WAS DARKEND . . . 304 FOUR ZOAS 4 264
[THEN ALL THE SPACE OF ?EMPYREAN ?PLAYD IN XXX SONG] . . SUPP FOUR ZOAS 4 *

EMULATE
MAY EMULATE THEIR FATHERS' VIRTUES . . . . 18 EDW THIRD/PS 1 20
TO EMULATE THE GRANDEUR OF THOSE SEEN IN HIS VISION . . . 565D DESC CAT 2 PROSE
HAD RESOLVED TO EMULATE THOSE PRECIOUS REMAINS OF ANTIQUITY 579C DESC CAT 5 PROSE

EMULATION
SHE WAS A GODDESS POWERFUL & BORE [CONCEIT & EMULATION] 43A THEN SHE BORE *PROSE
THEN [SELF LOVE] BORE A DAUGHTER CALLED EMULATION . 43A THEN SHE BORE PROSE
STROVE IN TERRIFIC EMULATION WHICH SHOULD GAIN A PLACE . . 343 FOUR ZOAS 8 75
WHEN HEAVEN & HELL IN EMULATION STROVE IN SPORTS OF GLORY 365 FOUR ZOAS 9 298
ENTER INTO AN EMULATION OF GRECIAN MANNERS THERE ARE NOW I 798C LETTER 10 PROSE
OUR DEAR FRIEND FLAXMAN IS THE THEME OF MY EMULATION . . 807A LETTER 17 PROSE

EMULATOR
AROUND YOUR HERMIT & BARD SO PRAYS THE EMULATOR OF BOTH 835B LETTER 34 PROSE

ENABLE
AMERICA ENABLE HIM TO CIRCULATE PUBLICATIONS TO AN IMMENSE 841C LETTER 41 PROSE
SOON RECIEVE SUCH DOCUMENTS AS WILL ENABLE YOU TO DECIDE 849B LETTER 45 PROSE
FIRST BEFORE I BEGIN ENGRAVING THEM AS IT WILL ENABLE ME 866C LETTER 65 PROSE

ENABLED
BY WHOSE MEANS HE HAS BEEN REGULARLY ENABLED TO BRING . 207C PRSPECTUS 1793 PROSE
I SHALL BE ENABLED TO THROW OFF ALL OBSTRUCTIONS TO SUCCESS 808A LETTER 19 PROSE
TO PLEASE BECAUSE YOU AMONG ALL MEN HAVE ENABLED ME . . . 815A LETTER 23 PROSE
WILL BE ENABLED BY IT TO JUDGE OF THE PATHOS OF THE PICTURE 850B LETTER 49 PROSE
GREAT JOY HENCE I AM NOW ENABLED TO TELL YOU THAT I . . . 869D LETTER 70 PROSE

ENAMEL
FRESCO PAINTING IS PROPERLY MINIATURE OR ENAMEL PAINTING 561A EXHIBITION ADV PROSE
OR ENAMEL ALTHOUGH IN WORKS LARGER THAN LIFE . . . . . 561A EXHIBITION ADV PROSE

ENAMELD
ENAMELD WITH LOVE & KINDNESS & THE TILES ENGRAVEN GOLD . . 632 JERUSALEM 12 31
CLAY BAKD & ENAMELD ETERNAL GLOWING AS FOUR FURNACES . . 632 JERUSALEM 12 64

ENAMELS
ALL FRESCOES ARE AS HIGH FINISHED AS MINIATURES OR ENAMELS 566B DESC CAT 2 PROSE

ENAMOURD
SHOULD BE SO ENAMOURD OF ROWLANDSON'S CARICATURES . . . 795B LETTER 6 PROSE

ENANTO
[ELYTHYRIA] ELYTHIRIA ENANTO MANATHU VORCYON ETHINTHUS 350 FOUR ZOAS 8 * 364
    MOAB MIDIAN

ENCAMPMENTS
FROM THEIR ENCAMPMENTS AND DARK CASTLES SEEKING WHERE TO 201 AMERICA 13 8
    HIDE

ENCIRCLED   SEE INCIRCLED
BUT LOS ENCIRCLED ENITHARMON . . . . 234 URIZEN 20 42

ENCLOSD   SEE INCLOSD,ETC
OBSCURE ENCLOSD THE STONE OF NIGHT OBLIQUE IT STOOD OERHUNG 241 EUROPE 10 26
AND ERIN'S LOVELY BOW ENCLOSD THE WHEELS OF ALBION'S SONS 681 JERUSALEM 50 22
TO BEG OF YOU TO CAUSE THE ENCLOSD LETTER TO BE DELIVERD 829b LETTER 28 PROSE

ENCLOSE
I ENCLOSE ALSO NO...OF THE SHAKSPEARE . . . . 839A LETTER 37 PROSE

ENCLOSED
MR DALLY TO WHOM I ENCLOSED...IN A LETTER A FORTNIGHT . 841A LETTER 40 PROSE

ENCOMPASSD
OF HIS THREE DAUGHTERS WERE ENCOMPASSD BY THE TWELVE BRIGHT 284 FOUR ZOAS 2 175
    HALLS
EACH DOME OPEND TOWARD FOUR HALLS & THE THREE DOMES 284 FOUR ZOAS 2 178
    ENCOMPASSD
[XXX THARMAS ?THOUGHT THUNDRING SEAS ENCOMPASSD THEE] SUPP FOUR ZOAS 4 *
ALBION COVERD THE WHOLE EARTH ENGLAND ENCOMPASSD 648 JERUSALEM 24 44
    THE NATIONS
LONDON COVERD THE WHOLE EARTH ENGLAND ENCOMPASSD 720 JERUSALEM 79 22
    THE NATIONS
ENCOMPASSD BY THE FROZEN NET AND BY THE ROOTED TREE . . . 721 JERUSALEM 80 1

ENCOMPASSES
THE SEA ENCOMPASSES HIM & MONSTERS OF THE DEEP ARE HIS 301 FOUR ZOAS 4 134
    COMPANIONS
FOLD WITHOUT FOLD ENCOMPASSES HIM AND HIS CORRUPTING 354 FOUR ZOAS 8 510
    MEMBERS
WHAT CHAIN ENCOMPASSES IN WHAT LOCK IS THE RIVER OF LIGHT 363 FOUR ZOAS 9 226
    CONFIND

ENCOMPASSING
SWEET INSTRUMENTS OF SOUND IN PRIDE ENCOMPASSING MY KNEES 312 FOUR ZOAS 6 32
AS THE EYE OF MAN VIEWS BOTH THE EAST & WEST ENCOMPASSING 497 MILTON 15 28
CRUCIFYING & ENCOMPASSING SEA & LAND . . . . 718 STOOD AMONG/J 29

ENCOUNTERD
I HAVE HITHERTO ENCOUNTERD BUT MY FATE HAS BEEN SO UNCOMMON 862C LETTER 60 PROSE

ENCOURAGD
DONE SO WELL IF HE HAD BEEN PROPERLY [(PATRONIZED)] 612C V LAST JUDG/N *PROSE
    ENCOURAGD

ENCOURAGE
LEO X WAS ADVISED NOT TO ENCOURAGE THE ARTS . . . . . 452C ANNO REYNOLDS MARG
PRETEND TO ENCOURAGE ART HE WILL EMPLOY HIMSELF . . . . 586A DESC CAT 16 PROSE
[ENCOURAGE A BLOCKHEAD & HE IS COUNTED THE GREATEST GENIUS] 595B PUB ADDRESS/N PROSE
LET THEM ENCOURAGE WHAT EXISTS ALREADY . . . . 597A PUB ADDRESS/N PROSE
LET IT NO MORE BE SAID THAT EMPIRES ENCOURAGE ARTS . . . 597A PUB ADDRESS/N PROSE
FOR IT IS ARTS THAT ENCOURAGE EMPIRES . . . . 597A PUB ADDRESS/N PROSE
EMPLOYING HIM WERE (FIRST) TO ENCOURAGE A WORTHY MAN & . 856B LETTER 54 PROSE

ENCOURAGED
WHO WILL DARE TO SAY THAT [FINE] POLITE ART IS ENCOURAGED 446A ANNO REYNOLDS * MARG
PRETEND THAT ART IS ENCOURAGED BY THAT NATION . . . . . 446D ANNO REYNOLDS MARG
THEM WAS TO BE ENCOURAGED TILL HE DID LIKE ANY OF 815B LETTER 23 PROSE
    THE OTHERS

		PAGE	TITLE	LINE
ENCOURAGEMENT				
THE SOCIETY FOR THE ENCOURAGEMENT OF ART SUFFERD BARRY	. .	446A	ANNO REYNOLDS	MARG
O SOCIETY FOR ENCOURAGEMENT OF ART	. . . .	446A	ANNO REYNOLDS	MARG
IN A COUNTRY PRETENDING TO THE ENCOURAGEMENT OF ART	. . .	452B	ANNO REYNOLDS	MARG
YOUR OWN REAL GREATNESS DEPENDS ON YOUR ENCOURAGEMENT	. .	452C	ANNO REYNOLDS	MARG
[THIS IS ENCOURAGEMENT FOR ARTISTS (?ONLY ?BY) ?DEFINITION]	SUPP	ANNO REYNOLDS	* MARG
ON THE GREAT ENCOURAGEMENT [SHEWN] GIVEN BY ENGLISH NOBILITY &		548B	ON GREAT ENC/N	*TITLE
ENGLISH ENCOURAGEMENT OF ART CROMEK'S OPINIONS PUT INTO RHYME		549C	ENGL ENCOU/N 1	TITLE
FOR THE ENCOURAGEMENT OF ART WHEN SUCH PICTURES AS THESE		596D	PUB ADDRESS/N	PROSE
THE ENCOURAGEMENT WHICH IS MY DUE	. . . .	600C	PUB ADDRESS/N	PROSE
TO THE SOCIETY FOR ENCOURAGEMENT OF ARTS I ADDRESS MYSELF		601A	PUB ADDRESS/N	PROSE
THAT THE KING SHEWS IT A GREAT COUNTENANCE & ENCOURAGEMENT		797D	LETTER 10	PROSE
HE MUST DIE WITHOUT ENCOURAGEMENT MY PICTURES ARE	. . .	815B	LETTER 23	PROSE
ENCOURAGERS				
I SAY THE ENGLISH PUBLIC ARE TRUE ENCOURAGERS OF REAL ART		601C	PUB ADDRESS/N	PROSE
ENCOURAGING				
WHAT THEY UNDER PRETENCE OF ENCOURAGING		446A	ANNO REYNOLDS	MARG
VERY BEAUTIFUL & ENCOURAGING VERSES WHICH I ACCOUNT	. .	804A	LETTER 16	PROSE
END	**SEE MILE-END**			
SUCH END TRUE LOVERS HAVE	. . . .	6	MY SILKS/PS	6
THE END	. . . .	40C	SAMSON/PS	*TITLE
TO THINK HIS RACE SHOULD NEVER END	. . . .	50	WHEN CORRUP/IM	7
BEFORE TEN YEARS ARE AT AN END SAID QUID	. . . . . .	52A	ISLAND MOON 7	PROSE
IS NOT INFINITE THEY SHALL COME TO AN END WHICH GOD FORBID		91A	ANNO SWED LOVE	MARG
HOPING TO END HER [LIFE] WOES BUT FROM HER CRIES THE TYGERS FLED		109	TIRIEL 7	17
THY LAWS O HAR & TIRIEL'S WISDOM END TOGETHER IN A CURSE		109	TIRIEL 8	8
AND OUR SPORTS HAVE AN END	. . . .	116	ECCHOING GR/SI	24
THE END	. . . .	130D	BOOK OF THEL 6	TITLE
QUERY DOES HE ALSO OCCUPY THAT PLACE IN HEAVEN SEE N...AT THE END		131D	ANNO SWED PROV	MARG
FINAL PORTION IS PREDESTINATION SEE N...AT THE END &...		132A	ANNO SWED PROV	MARG
END OF THE FIRST BOOK	. . . .	148B	FRENCH REVOLTN	TITLE
END OF SIX THOUSAND YEARS IS TRUE AS I HAVE HEARD FROM HELL		154B	MARRIAGE HH 14	PROSE
INTO THE CHURCH VAULT AT THE END OF WHICH WAS A MILL	.	155D	MARRIAGE HH 17	PROSE
I TOLD MY WRATH MY WRATH DID END	. . . .	165	CHRISTN FORB/N	2
PLATTED QUITE NEAT TO CATCH APPLAUSE WITH A SLIDING NOOSE AT THE END		184	HER LIFE IS/N	2
THE END	. . . .	195C	V DAU ALBION 8	TITLE
AND THEN THEIR END SHOULD COME WHEN FRANCE RECIEVD THE DEMON'S LIGHT		203	AMERICA 16	15
I TOLD MY WRATH MY WRATH DID END	. . . .	218	POISON TREE/SE	2
THE END OF THE [FIRST] BOOK OF URIZEN	. . . . . .	237A	URIZEN 28	TITLE
FOUND FOR FALLING DAY & NIGHT WITHOUT END	. . . . .	258	BOOK OF LOS 4	33
THE END OF THE BOOK OF LOS	. . . .	260D	BOOK OF LOS 5	TITLE
END OF THE FIRST NIGHT	. . . .	277B	FOUR ZOAS 1	TITLE
DEEP HORRIBLE WITHOUT END SEPARATED FROM BEULAH FAR BENEATH		279	FOUR ZOAS 1	542
TILL THE TIME OF THE END THEN THEY ELECTED SEVEN CALLED THE SEVEN		279	FOUR ZOAS 1	553
END OF THE FIRST NIGHT	. . . .	279D	FOUR ZOAS 1	TITLE
OF FIRE FAR SHINING TRAVELLING ALONG EVEN TO ITS DESTIND END		287	FOUR ZOAS 2	276
END OF THE SECOND NIGHT	. . . .	291C	FOUR ZOAS 2	TITLE
CONSUMING ALL TO THE END CONSUMING LOVE AND [JOY] HOPE ARE ENDED		297	FOUR ZOAS 3	204
THE END OF THE THIRD NIGHT	. . . .	297C	FOUR ZOAS 3	TITLE
END OF THE FOURTH [BOOK] NIGHT	. . . .	305B	FOUR ZOAS 4	*TITLE
END OF THE FIFTH [BOOK] NIGHT	. . . .	311C	FOUR ZOAS 5	*TITLE
[CEASE] END & THE ETERNAL MAN NO MORE RENEW BENEATH OUR POWER		313	FOUR ZOAS 6	66
INFINITE WAS HIS LABOUR WITHOUT END HIS TRAVEL HE STROVE		313	FOUR ZOAS 6	74
I THOUGHT PERHAPS TO FIND AN END A WORLD BENEATH OF VOIDNESS		317	FOUR ZOAS 6	200
SO EVER I MY SPIRITS TURN NO END I FIND OF ALL	. . . .	317	FOUR ZOAS 6	207
END OF THE SIXTH NIGHT	. . . .	320A	FOUR ZOAS 6	TITLE
[END OF THE SEVENTH NIGHT]	. . . .	328C	FOUR ZOAS 7	*TITLE
THIS NIGHT BEGINS AT LINE...THE FOLLOWING COMES IN AT THE END		333A	FOUR ZOAS 7B	*TITLE
END OF THE SEVENTH NIGHT	. . . .	340D	FOUR ZOAS 7B	TITLE
[THE END OF THE EIGHTH NIGHT]	. . . .	356A	FOUR ZOAS 8	TITLE
[END OF THE EIGHTH NIGHT]	. . . .	356C	FOUR ZOAS 8	TITLE
O MYSTERY FIERCE THARMAS CRIES BEHOLD THY END IS COME	.	374	FOUR ZOAS 9	657
END OF THE DREAM	. . . .	379D	FOUR ZOAS 9	TITLE
BACON PUT AN END TO FAITH	. . . .	398B	ANNO BACON	MARG
& SHALL IN THE END ANNIHILATE THEM	. . . .	407D	ANNO BACON	MARG
[?I] AND TO END THY CRUEL MOCKS	. . . .	417	MY SPECTRE/N	* 63
SORROW NOW IS AT AN END	. . . .	423	THE BIRDS/N	15
THERES AN END TO ALL MISERY	. . . .	424	THE SMILE	16
DOES NOT KNOW THE BEGINNING NEVER CAN KNOW THE END OF ART		449C	ANNO REYNOLDS	MARG
THERE IS NO END TO THE FOLLIES OF THIS MAN	. . . . .	460B	ANNO REYNOLDS	MARG
THE FOLLOWING DISCOURSE IS WRITTEN WITH THE SAME END IN VIEW		465D	ANNO REYNOLDS	MARG
SUCH IS THE END OF EPICUREAN OR NEWTONIAN PHILOSOPHY IT IS ATHEISM		475D	ANNO REYNOLDS	MARG
ALL THINGS BEGIN & END IN ALBION'S ANCIENT DRUID ROCKY SHORE		486	MILTON 6	25
SURROUNDED HIM DIVIDING & UNITING WITHOUT END OR NUMBER		498	MILTON 17	8
UNFATHOMABLE WITHOUT END BUT IN THE MIDST OF THESE	. . .	500	MILTON 19	24
MILTON'S RELIGION IS THE CAUSE THERE IS NO END TO DESTRUCTION		506	MILTON 22	39

		PAGE	TITLE	LINE

END (CONTINUED)

SIX THOUSAND YEARS ARE PASSD AWAY THE END APPROACHES FAST 508 MILTON 23 55
AS IT WAS SO IT REMAIND & NO HOPE OF AN END . . . . . 509 MILTON 24 47
END OF THE FIRST BOOK . . . . 518A MILTON 29 TITLE
I [HAVE GIVN] GIVE YOU THE END OF A GOLDEN STRING . . . 551 GIVE YOU END/N * 1
THERE WOULD SOON BE AN END OF PROPORTION AND STRENGTH . . 583C DESC CAT 9 PROSE
IT MAY BE WORKED BACKWARDS AND FORWARDS WITHOUT END . . 587A CHAUCER 1 PROSE
BE WORSE THAN IT WAS AT THE END OF THE FIRST TWELVE MONTHS 587A CHAUCER 1 PROSE
HAS INTIRELY PUT AN END TO ALL GENUINE & APPROPRIATE EFFECT 599B PUB ADDRESS/N *PROSE
SING SONG FROM BEGINNING TO END . . . . . . 600D PUB ADDRESS/N PROSE
A DARK AND UNKNOWN NIGHT INDEFINITE UNMEASURABLE WITHOUT 624 JERUSALEM 5 57
  END
OF JERUSALEM BECOME HER COVERING TILL THE TIME OF THE END 626 JERUSALEM 7 64
BUT HIS GRIEFS ADVANCE ALSO FOR EVER & EVER WITHOUT END 630 JERUSALEM 10 50
[END OF THE (FIRST) CHAP] . . . . 635C JERUSALEM 14 *TITLE
ALL THINGS BEGIN & END IN ALBION'S ANCIENT DRUID ROCKY 649B JERUSALEM 27 PROSE
  SHORE
ALL THINGS BEGIN & END IN ALBION'S ANCIENT DRUID ROCKY 658 JERUSALEM 32 15
  SHORE
END OF CHAP (SECOND) . . . . 681C JERUSALEM 50 TITLE
UNFATHOMABLE WITHOUT END BUT IN THE MIDST OF THESE . . 691 JERUSALEM 59 20
THEY HAVE PERSWADED THEE TO THIS THEREFORE THEIR END SHALL 693 JERUSALEM 60 35
  COME
IN THE END OF HIS SLEEP WHEN JESUS CALLS HIM FROM HIM HIS 701 JERUSALEM 65 * 62
  GRAVE
ACCUMULATING WITHOUT END HERE LOS WHO IS OF THE ELOHIM . . 713 JERUSALEM 73 24
I GIVE YOU THE END OF A GOLDEN STRING . . . . . . 716 I GIVE YOU/J 1
THE END OF THE SONG OF JERUSALEM . . . . . . 747B JERUSALEM 99 TITLE
AND [MORAL] ALL THE HEROIC VIRTUES [ALL] END . . . . 759 EV GOSPEL (2) 36
FIRE THAT END IN ENDLESS STRIFE . . . . . . 764C FOR SEXES/GP TITLE
FROM END TO END & NOT WITH MORAL VIRTUES . . . . 774D ANNO BERKELEY MARG
& WILL DO WHAT HE CAN BY THE END OF JANUARY . . . . 790A LETTER 1 PROSE
THRO THE VILLAGE THEN WINDS AT MY COT IT DOES END . . . 800 MRS FLAXMAN/L 8
PROPOSED TO THE PUBLIC AT THE END OF COWPER'S LIFE WHICH 821C LETTER 25 PROSE
I BEGIN WITH THE LATTER END OF YOUR LETTER & GRIEVE MORE 837C LETTER 36 PROSE
  FOR
THIS BUSINESS ARE NOT WHOLLY AT AN END BUT THAT ON HIS 845C LETTER 44 PROSE
  RETURN
FOR MANY VERY MANY YEARS BUT NOW I SAY NOW ITS END IS COME 864A LETTER 61 PROSE
FROM BEGINNING TO END ANY REMARKS THAT YOU MAY BE PLEASED 866C LETTER 65 PROSE
  TO
MR LINNELL WILL HAVE ARRIVED AT HIS JOURNEY'S END BEFORE 871C LETTER 73 PROSE
PROSPECT AT NORTH END MRS HURD'S I SHOULD LIKE AS WELL 873A LETTER 76 PROSE
  AS ANY
MRS LINNELL COLLINS'S FARM NORTH END HAMPSTEAD . . . . SUPP ADDRESS/L 70 *TITLE
OUR END IS COME . . . . SUPP INSC OUR END *TITLE
THE LITTLE BOY FOUND END OF SONGS OF INNOCENCE . . . SUPP LETTER 66A *PROSE

ENDEARING

HIS PRIMITIVE TYRANNICAL ATTEMPTS ON LOS WITH MOST 486 MILTON 7 7
  ENDEARING LOVE

ENDEAVORING

ENDEAVORING TO INCORPORATE THEIR SOULS WITH THEIR BODIES 45C ISLAND MOON 1 PROSE

ENDEAVOUR

WELL I'LL ENDEAVOUR TO TAKE . . . . 20 EDW THIRD/PS 2 59
RELIGION IS AN ENDEAVOUR TO RECONCILE THE TWO . . . . 155B MARRIAGE HH 15 PROSE
OR BAD GOVERNMENTS WHY SHOULD A GOOD GOVERNMENT ENDEAVOUR 445C ANNO REYNOLDS MARG
IF YOU ENDEAVOUR TO PLEASE THE WORST YOU WILL NEVER PLEASE 478A ANNO REYNOLDS MARG
  THE BEST
ENDEAVOUR TO RAISE UP A STYLE AGAINST RAFAEL MICH ANGELO 573B DESC CAT 3 PROSE
& NOT ENDEAVOUR TO COUNTERACT BY TRICKS . . . . . . 597A PUB ADDRESS/N PROSE
ENDEAVOUR TO RESTORE WHAT THE ANCIENTS CALLD THE GOLDEN AGE 605D V LAST JUDG/N PROSE
OF THE DEAD WANDER THIS I ENDEAVOUR TO PREVENT & WITH MY 809A LETTER 20 PROSE
UPON YOU AS THE CHIEF OF MY FRIENDS WHOM I WOULD ENDEAVOUR 815A LETTER 23 PROSE
SHE WILL FORGIVE ANY FAILURE IN CONSIDERATION OF 815D LETTER 23 PROSE
  THE ENDEAVOUR
ENDEAVOUR TO LIVE TO THE GLORY OF OUR LORD & SAVIOUR & I 822C LETTER 26 PROSE
HIS MANNER OF WORKING IS WHAT I SHALL ENDEAVOUR TO ADOPT 843B LETTER 43 PROSE
SHOULD DO MY ENDEAVOUR TO GIVE MR HAYLEY'S WORKS . . . 856D LETTER 54 PROSE
HOWEVER IF THE WEATHER SHOULD BE WARM I WILL ENDEAVOUR TO 872A LETTER 74 PROSE

ENDEAVOURED

WERE EACH [ENDEAVOURED] ENDEAVOURING TO CONCEAL . . . 44C ISLAND MOON 1 *PROSE
GRAND IN THE HIGHEST DEGREE THE ARTIST HAS ENDEAVOURED . 565D DESC CAT 2 PROSE
THIS IMPUTATION MOST ARTFULLY AND INDUSTRIOUSLY ENDEAVOURED 572C DESC CAT 3 PROSE
NO VULGAR CHARACTER AS HE HAS ENDEAVOURED TO MAKE HIM . 574A DESC CAT 3 PROSE

ENDEAVOURING

WERE EACH [ENDEAVOURED] ENDEAVOURING TO CONCEAL . . . 44C ISLAND MOON 1 *PROSE
WERE ENDEAVOURING TO DEPRESS BARRY TOLD ME . . . . 446A ANNO REYNOLDS MARG
THE SHEEP ENDEAVOURING TO WALK LIKE THE DOG . . . . 470B ANNO REYNOLDS MARG
THEY SAW ALBION ENDEAVOURING TO DESTROY THEIR EMANATIONS 669 JERUSALEM 41 31
HE ALL THE WHILE ENDEAVOURING TO TURN ROUND & STRIKE ME 827B LETTER 28 PROSE
VARIOUS & INNUMERABLE WAYS ENDEAVOURING TO THROW THE RIDER 833C LETTER 33 PROSE

ENDEAVOURS

INTERESTING TO BLOCK HEADS AS IT ENDEAVOURS TO PROVE . 457D ANNO REYNOLDS MARG
YOU HAVE FAITH IN THE ENDEAVOURS OF ME YOUR WEAK BROTHER 822B LETTER 26 PROSE
AM ALSO GRATEFUL TO THE KIND HAND THAT ENDEAVOURS TO LIFT 822C LETTER 26 PROSE
  ME
BUT HOPES TO DO SOMEWHAT BY PERSEVERANCE IN HIS ENDEAVOURS 877A LETTER 85 PROSE
[FOOLS' OPINIONS & ENDEAVOURS DESTROY INVENTION] . . . . SUPP ANNO REYNOLDS * MARG

ENDED

[?THEN XXX LABOUR ENDED XXX LOVE FOR VALA] . . . . . SUPP FOUR ZOAS 3 *
HE ENDED THE WIND OF CONTENTION AROSE . . . . . . 145 FRENCH REVOLTN 241
[THE FARMERS WERE RUIND & HARVEST WAS ENDED] . . . . . 164 HEARD ANGEL/N 21

```
                                                          PAGE      TITLE           LINE
ENDED    (CONTINUED)
   THE TIMES ARE ENDED SHADOWS PASS THE MORNING GINS TO BREAK   198 AMERICA 8          2
   THE VOICE ENDED THEY SAW HIS PALE VISAGE    . . . . . .     224 URIZEN 4           41
   THE SONG OF LOS IS ENDED URIZEN WEPT                         248D SONG OF LOS 7   TITLE
   SHE ENDED FOR HIS WRATHFUL THRONE BURST FORTH . . . . .     294 FOUR ZOAS 3       104
   CONSUMING ALL TO THE END CONSUMING LOVE AND [JOY] HOPE      297 FOUR ZOAS 3       204
      ARE ENDED
   CRIED TIMES ARE ENDED HE EXULTED HE AROSE IN JOY HE EXULTED  372 FOUR ZOAS 9       568
   [ (ENDED) ] OERTURND THE TENT OF SECRET SINS   . . . . .    756 EV GOSPEL(I)/N *   21
ENDING
   ONWARD THO FALLING THRO THE WASTE OF NIGHT & ENDING IN      316 FOUR ZOAS 6       165
      DEATH
   ENDING IN DEATH WHICH WOULD OF ITSELF BE ETERNAL DEATH  . . 513 MILTON 26          42
ENDLESS
   THOU ART AN ENDLESS MORALIST   . . . . . . . . . . . .      29B EDW THIRD/PS 4   PROSE
   FOLLY IS AN ENDLESS MAZE . . . . . . . . . . . . . .        126 VOICE BARD/SI       6
   ENDLESS THE SHADY TRAIN SHIVRING DESCENDED . . . . . . .    140 FRENCH REVOLTN     135
   IN THE ENDLESS ABYSS OF SPACE  . . . . . . . . . . .        231 URIZEN 15          10
   AN ENDLESS LABYRINTH OF WOE  . . . . . . . . . . . .        252 AHANIA 4            4
   I REUNITE IN ENDLESS TORMENT WOULD I HAD NEVER RISEN   . .  298 FOUR ZOAS 4        15
   TO WASTE IN ENDLESS CORRUPTION RENEW THOU I WILL DESTROY    298 FOUR ZOAS 4    *   31
   THE LINKS OF FATE LINK AFTER LINK AN ENDLESS CHAIN OF       302 FOUR ZOAS 4       207
      SORROWS
   ENDLESS HAD BEEN HIS TRAVEL BUT THE DIVINE HAND HIM LED     316 FOUR ZOAS 6       176
   I WILL WALK FORTH THRO THOSE WIDE FIELDS OF ENDLESS         333 FOUR ZOAS 7B        8
      ETERNITY
   SEEMS TEEMING WITH ENDLESS DESTRUCTION NEVER TO BE REPELLD  343 FOUR ZOAS 8    *  100
   WEAVES A BOWER IN ENDLESS NIGHT   . . . . . . . . .         431 AUGURIES           36
   SOME ARE BORN TO ENDLESS NIGHT   . . . . . . . . . .        433 AUGURIES          124
   ENDLESS LABOUR TO WHOEVER SUFFERS HIM TO ENTER HIS MIND     583A DESC CAT 9      PROSE
   AND OF ENDLESS REFLECTED LIGHTS THAT CONFUSE ONE ANOTHER    583B DESC CAT 9      PROSE
   SHOT INTO MANY A TREE AN ENDLESS LABYRINTH OF WOE   . . .   653 JERUSALEM 28       19
   AND MAN HIMSELF BECOME A FIEND WRAPD IN AN ENDLESS CURSE    667 JERUSALEM 40       29
   ENDLESS THEIR LABOUR WITH BITTER FOOD VOID OF SLEEP   . . . 691 JERUSALEM 59       30
   FIRE THAT END IN ENDLESS STRIFE                             764C FOR SEXES/GP    TITLE
   CITY OF DIS QUEEN OF ENDLESS WOE [XXX] FURIES &   . . . .   786A ILLS DANTE 101 *PROSE
   THOU ART TO ENDLESS WOE BETRAYD   . . . . . . . . . .       817 HAPPINESS/L        32
   BUT HE IS ALSO A LABORIOUS VOTARY OF ENDLESS WORK   . . .   842D LETTER 42       PROSE
   LIFE OF ROMNEY ENDLESS WORK IS THE TRUE TITLE OF ENGRAVING  843A LETTER 42       PROSE
ENDLONG
   ENDLONG A RAGING SERPENT ROLLING ROUND THE HOLY TENT   . .  279 FOUR ZOAS 1       532
ENDS
   GREAT ENDS NEVER LOOK AT MEANS BUT PRODUCE                  81B ANNO LAVATER     MARG
      THEM SPONTANEOUSLY
   AND ALL HIS GOOD FRIENDS SHEW THEIR PRIVATE ENDS . . . .    183 MOTTO SONGS/N       7
   IN THUNDERS ENDS THE VOICE THEN ALBION'S ANGEL WRATHFUL     198 AMERICA 7           1
      BURNT
   THE ENDS OF HEAVEN LIKE A GARMENT WILL I FOLD THEM ROUND ME 333 FOUR ZOAS 7B        6
   AND I WILL GIVE THEE ALL THE ENDS OF HEAVEN FOR THY         334 FOUR ZOAS 7B       56
      POSSESSION
   WE NOW BEHOLD THE ENDS OF BEULAH & WE NOW BEHOLD  . . . .   347 FOUR ZOAS 8       239
   IN HIS APPOINTED SEASON WHEN THE ENDS OF HEAVEN MEET   . .  517 MILTON 29          46
   SNEAKING & [CALUMNY] BACKBITING & ODDS & ENDS . . . . .     541 MR STOTHARD/N       4
   THE GENEROUS TO ENEMIES PROMOTES THEIR ENDS   . . . . .     541 HOMERS HERO/N       5
   FOR HE LOVD THEM FOR GAIN TO SERVE HIS ENDS   . . . . .     544 P LOVED NOT/N       2
   THAT I MAY PUT THEM IN MIND OF THEIR LATTER ENDS . . . .    556 BLAKES APL/N 2     22
   AND HE IS SUFFERED BY PROVIDENCE FOR WISE ENDS   . . . .    570A DESC CAT 3       PROSE
   WHICH STAND UPON THE ENDS OF BEULAH AND WITHOUTSIDE ALL     642 JERUSALEM 19       34
   IN THE ENDS OF BEULAH WHERE THE DEAD WAIL NIGHT & DAY   .   678 JERUSALEM 48       52
   DEISM IS THE SAME & ENDS IN THE SAME . . . . . . . .        682C JERUSALEM 52     PROSE
   AND WHERE LUTHER ENDS ADAM BEGINS AGAIN IN ETERNAL CIRCLE   716 JERUSALEM 75       24
   WHOM GOD HAS AFFLICTED FOR SECRET ENDS   . . . . . . .      755 EV GOSPEL(E)/N     89
   SIX GUINEAS THUS I HOPE THAT ALL OUR THREE YEARS' TROUBLE   824D LETTER 27       PROSE
      ENDS
   METAL RULES AT THE ENDS OF THE CANTOS BUT HE CONFESSD   . . 857B LETTER 54       PROSE
ENDURD
   ENDURD BY ROOTS THAT WRITHE THEIR ARMS INTO THE NETHER DEEP 196 AMERICA PREL 2     11
   THE IMMORTAL ENDURD HIS CHAINS . . . . . . . . . . .        229 URIZEN 13          26
   UNREMITTING ENDURD THE COLD HAMMER  . . . . . . . . .       249 AHANIA 4           25
   ENDURD THE VAST HAMMER BUT UNWEARIED   . . . . . . . .      260 BOOK OF LOS 5      32
   WHILE ROARING HIS FURNACES ENDURD . . . . . . . . . .       260 BOOK OF LOS 5      39
   THARMAS ENDURD NOT HE FLED HOWLING THEN A BARREN WASTE      275 FOUR ZOAS 1       419
      SUNK DOWN
   THE IMMORTAL ENDURD THO BOUND IN A DEADLY SLEEP   . . . .   304 FOUR ZOAS 4       283
   WILLING THE FRIENDS ENDURD FOR ALBION'S SAKE AND FOR   . . 641 JERUSALEM 19       28
ENDURE
   IMPATIENCE NOW NO LONGER CAN ENDURE DISTRACTED LUVAH   . .  276 FOUR ZOAS 1       429
   ETERNAL DEATH WHO CAN ENDURE LET US CONSUME IN FIRES   . .  377 FOUR ZOAS 9       740
   THOSE THAT PUT THEIR BODIES TO ENDURE ARE FOOLS   . . . .   408C ANNO BACON      MARG
   FOR COMMERCE CANNOT ENDURE INDIVIDUAL MERIT   . . . . .     593D PUB ADDRESS/N   PROSE
   TO WHAT THOU SHALT ENDURE IF THOU OBEY NOT MY GREAT WILL    629 JERUSALEM 10       36
   MUST THE WISE DIE FOR AN ATONEMENT DOES MERCY ENDURE        666 JERUSALEM 39       25
      ATONEMENT
   I WILL NOT ENDURE THIS THING I ALONE WITHSTAND TO DEATH     673 JERUSALEM 43       71
   IN CRUELTIES OF RAHAB & TIRZAH PERMANENT ENDURE   . . . .   734 JERUSALEM 89        2
   MANY HONEST PEOPLE ENDURE GREATER HARDSHIPS WITH FORTITUDE  793B LETTER 5        PROSE
   [WHO WILL OR CAN ?ENDURE ?SUCH HUMILIATION]   . . . . .     SUPP ANNO REYNOLDS * MARG
ENEAS
   AS ENEAS IS HERE SHEWN A WORSE MAN THAN ACHILLES IN LEAVING 412A ANNO BOYD        MARG
      DIDO
ENEID
   EMPIRE AGAINST ART SEE VIRGIL'S ENEID LIB VI... . . . . .   777A INSC LAOCOON    PROSE
```

ENEID   (CONTINUED)
    VIRGIL IN THE ENEID BOOK VI LINE...SAYS "LET OTHERS STUDY   778D HOMERS POETRY   PROSE
    ART"
ENEMIES
    DO WITH ME WHAT THOU WILT MY FRIENDS ARE ENEMIES . . .   38D SAMSON/PS   PROSE
    BY BANDS OF ENEMIES STRETCH FORTH THY HAND AND SAVE . .   40B SAMSON/PS   PROSE
    ("AS YOUR ENEMIES AND YOUR FRIENDS SO ARE YOU")   70C ANNO LAVATER   MARG
    VERY UNEASY
    UNEASY I FEAR I HAVE NOT MANY ENEMIES   70C ANNO LAVATER   MARG
    FORGIVENESS OF ENEMIES CAN ONLY COME UPON THEIR REPENTANCE   77A ANNO LAVATER   MARG
    ("QUALITIES OF FRIENDS...ENEMIES") VERY UNEASY INDEED BUT   80D ANNO LAVATER   MARG
    TRUTH
    SAYING BY THIS HE CONQUERS ENEMIES & GOVERNS KINGDOMS . . 153D MARRIAGE HH 12 PROSE
    & THEY SHOULD BE ENEMIES . . . . 155B MARRIAGE HH 15 PROSE
    TO SCORN AND NOW ARE SCORNED BY THE SLAVES OF OUR ENEMIES   286 FOUR ZOAS 2   224
    I WILL PRESERVE THO ENEMIES ARISE AROUND THEE NUMBERLESS   334 FOUR ZOAS 7B   53
    AND WHAT I LOVED BEST WAS DIVIDED AMONG MY ENEMIES . .   334 FOUR ZOAS 7B   59
    AS IT IS WHAT OUR ENEMIES WISH . . . . 383C ANNO WATSON   MARG
    MARK WELL MY WORDS CORPOREAL FRIENDS ARE SPIRITUAL ENEMIES   484 MILTON 4   26
    THOU HAST GIVN ME POWER TO PROTECT MYSELF FROM MY BITTEREST   489 MILTON 9   6
    ENEMIES
    THE ENEMIES OF HUMANITY EXCEPT IN A FEMALE FORM . . .   527 MILTON 36   15
    IN SELF ANNIHILATION GIVING THY LIFE TO THY ENEMIES . . 532 MILTON 40   8
    THE GENEROUS TO ENEMIES PROMOTES THEIR ENDS . . . .   541 HOMERS HERO/N   5
    TO FORGIVE ENEMIES H(HAYLEY) DOES PRETEND . . . .   544 TO FORGIVE/N   1
    IN ALL PROFESSIONS THESE ARE THE GREATEST ENEMIES OF GENIUS 601C PUB ADDRESS/N PROSE
    ARE SUBDUING THEIR ENEMIES . . . . 612B V LAST JUDG/N PROSE
    WHETHER A GOOD OR EVIL MAN THESE ARE ENEMIES . . . . 615A V LAST JUDG/N PROSE
    O POINT OF MUTUAL FORGIVENESS BETWEEN ENEMIES . . .   626 JERUSALEM 7   66
    A MAN'S WORST ENEMIES ARE THOSE . . . . 652 FIELDS FROM/J   81
    FROM WILLING SACRIFICE OF SELF TO SACRIFICE OF MISCALLD   653 JERUSALEM 28   20
    ENEMIES
    THEY PERCIEVED THAT CORPOREAL FRIENDS ARE SPIRITUAL ENEMIES 655 JERUSALEM 30   10
    HE FROWND ON ALL HIS FRIENDS COUNTING THEM ENEMIES IN HIS   676 JERUSALEM 45   36
    SORROW
    ALAS THE TIME WILL COME WHEN A MAN'S WORST ENEMIES . .   676 JERUSALEM 46   25
    OF MURDER & UNFORGIVING NEVER-AWAKING SACRIFICE OF ENEMIES   678 JERUSALEM 48   57
    THIS IS THE ONLY MEANS TO FORGIVENESS OF ENEMIES . .   680 JERUSALEM 49   75
    YOU O DEISTS PROFESS YOURSELVES THE ENEMIES OF CHRISTIANITY 682A JERUSALEM 52 PROSE
    AND YOU ARE SO YOU ARE ALSO THE ENEMIES OF THE HUMAN RACE 682A JERUSALEM 52 PROSE
    [FORGIVENESS OF ENEMIES ?CAN XXX ONLY XXX GOD XXX] .   737 JERUSALEM 91 *   1
    MADE ENEMIES I NEVER MADE FRIENDS BUT BY SPIRITUAL GIFTS   738 JERUSALEM 91   17
    HE WHO LOVES HIS ENEMIES HATES HIS FRIENDS . . . . 750 EV GOSPEL(C)/N 19
    HE WHO LOVES HIS ENEMIES [HATES] BETRAYS HIS FRIENDS .   751 EV GOSPEL(D)/N 25
    ASKING PARDON OF HIS ENEMIES . . . . 752 EV GOSPEL(D)/N 32
    AGUE & RHEUMATISM HAVE BEEN ALMOST HER CONSTANT ENEMIES   811B LETTER 22   PROSE
    HAVING SPIRITUAL ENEMIES OF SUCH FORMIDABLE MAGNITUDE . 811D LETTER 22   PROSE
    BY HIS BRETHREN & BETRAYD THEIR CAUSE TO THEIR ENEMIES . 813B LETTER 22   PROSE
ENEMIES'
    . . . THAT DESTROYS OUR ENEMIES' HOUSE . . . . .   291 FOUR ZOAS 2   411
ENEMY
    THE ENEMY FIGHT IN CHAINS INVISIBLE CHAINS BUT HEAVY .   18 EDW THIRD/PS 1   13
    I CANNOT BEAR THE ENEMY AT MY BACK . . . . . .   22 EDW THIRD/PS 3   20
    THE ENEMY HE HAS DANCD IN THE FIELD . . . . .   22 EDW THIRD/PS 3   30
    THE THRONGED ENEMY IN TRUTH I AM TOO FULL . . . .   26 EDW THIRD/PS 3 231
    I AM BUT A WEAK WOMAN ALAS I AM WEDDED TO YOUR ENEMY .   38C SAMSON/PS   PROSE
    NONE CAN SEE THE MAN IN THE ENEMY . . . . 72B ANNO LAVATER   MARG
    IF HE IS IGNORANTLY SO HE IS NOT TRULY AN ENEMY . .   72B ANNO LAVATER   MARG
    IF MALICIOUSLY NOT A MAN I CANNOT LOVE MY ENEMY . .   72B ANNO LAVATER   MARG
    FOR MY ENEMY IS NOT MAN BUT BEAST AND DEVIL IF I HAVE ANY   72B ANNO LAVATER * MARG
    O URIZEN MY ENEMY I WEEP FOR THY STERN AMBITION . .   283 FOUR ZOAS 2   109
    STARTLED WAS LOS HE FOUND HIS ENEMY URIZEN NOW . .   332 FOUR ZOAS 7   496
    TO YOU BUT THAT EVERY ONE IS EITHER YOUR FRIEND OR YOUR   380C FOUR ZOAS NOTE PROSE
    ENEMY
    WHICH I INTENDED TO SEND TO THE ENEMY . . . . . 438A BLAKES MEMORAN PROSE
    WAS SATAN'S ENEMY & THAT THE GNOMES BEING PALAMABRON'S   487 MILTON 7   39
    FRIENDS
    IN MIGHTY & MYSTERIOUS COMINGLING ENEMY WITH ENEMY .   529 MILTON 38   3
    AND BECOMES THE ENEMY & BETRAYER OF HIS FRIENDS . .   541 HOMERS HERO/N   6
    DO BE MY ENEMY FOR FRIENDSHIP'S SAKE . . . . .   545 TO H(AYLEY)/N   2
    HE HAS NOT LEFT ONE ENEMY BEHIND . . . . 546 ANOTHER/N 2   2
    INTO THE VERY TEETH OF THE AFFRIGHTED ENEMY . . . 580C DESC CAT 5   *PROSE
    YOUR ENEMY HE ALWAYS BEGINS WITH BEING YOUR FRIEND .   592C PUB ADDRESS/N PROSE
    MAN THE ENEMY OF MAN INTO DECEITFUL FRIENDSHIPS . .   622 JERUSALEM 4   26
    O THOU MY ENEMY WHERE IS MY GREAT SIN SHE IS ALSO THINE   630 JERUSALEM 10   43
    CONSIDER ME AS THINE ENEMY ON ME TURN ALL THY FURY .   670 JERUSALEM 42   40
    FOR THE SOLDIER WHO FIGHTS FOR TRUTH CALLS HIS ENEMY HIS   672 JERUSALEM 43   41
    BROTHER
    A WORLD IN WHICH MAN IS BY NATURE THE ENEMY OF MAN .   673 JERUSALEM 43   52
    A WORLD WHERE MAN IS BY NATURE THE ENEMY OF MAN . .   680 JERUSALEM 49   69
    IS THE RELIGION OF THE ENEMY & AVENGER AND . . . . 682B JERUSALEM 52 PROSE
    OF OUR CAPTAINS FEARING OUR OFFICERS MORE THAN THE ENEMY   700 JERUSALEM 65   36
    THEIR OWN PARENT THE EMANATION OF THEIR MURDERD ENEMY .   701 JERUSALEM 65   69
    ON ACCOUNT OF OUR LEAVING THE DIVINE HARVEST TO THE ENEMY 716D JERUSALEM 77 *PROSE
    IT IS EASIER TO FORGIVE AN ENEMY THAN TO FORGIVE A FRIEND   737 JERUSALEM 91   2
    IS MY VISION'S GREATEST ENEMY . . . . 748 EV GOSPEL(A)/N   2
    IF A MAN IS THE ENEMY OF MY SPIRITUAL LIFE WHILE HE .   822D LETTER 26   PROSE
    PRETENDS TO BE THE FRIEND OF MY CORPOREAL HE IS A REAL   822D LETTER 26   PROSE
    ENEMY
    WHILE HE SEEMS THE ENEMY OF MY CORPOREAL BUT NOT VICE VERSA 822D LETTER 26   PROSE
    OF MY LIFE HE IS THE ENEMY OF CONJUGAL LOVE AND IS THE . 852A LETTER 50   PROSE
    WHO WAS MY ENEMY DEAR SIR EXCUSE MY ENTHUSIASM OR RATHER   852C LETTER 50   PROSE

		PAGE	TITLE	LINE

ENERGETIC
          MEN WHO GIVE THEMSELVES TO THEIR ENERGETIC GENIUS [AS]   386B ANNO WATSON   * MARG
             IN THE MANNER
          & [LOVE] ME FOR THIS ENERGETIC EXERTION OF MY TALENT   . . 621B JERUSALEM 3   PROSE
ENERGIES
          THAT GOD WILL TORMENT MAN IN ETERNITY FOR FOLLOWING HIS   149C MARRIAGE HH 4   PROSE
             ENERGIES
          ONE OF THE ANTEDILUVIANS WHO ARE OUR ENERGIES . . . . . . 155C MARRIAGE HH 15 PROSE
          ARE UNRESTRAIND PERFORMERS OF THE ENERGIES OF NATURE   . . 200 AMERICA 11   9
          BIND THEM [TOGETHER] CONDENSING THE STRONG ENERGIES . . .   284 FOUR ZOAS 2   * 163
          SHEWD THEIR IMMORTAL ENERGIES IN WARLIKE DESPERATION   . . 335 FOUR ZOAS 7B   102
          ONCE MAN WAS OCCUPIED IN INTELLECTUAL PLEASURES & ENERGIES   707 JERUSALEM 68   65
ENERGIZER
          OF WISDOM A SUBLIME ENERGIZER HIS FEATURES AND LIMBS   . . 580B DESC CAT 5   PROSE
ENERGY
          ("UNDERSTAND TO CONNECT ENERGY WITH PATIENCE") UNEASY   72D ANNO LAVATER   MARG
          REASON AND ENERGY LOVE AND HATE ARE NECESSARY TO HUMAN   149B MARRIAGE HH 3 PROSE
             EXISTENCE
          EVIL IS THE ACTIVE SPRINGING FROM ENERGY   . . . . 149B MARRIAGE HH 3   PROSE
          THAT ENERGY CALLD EVIL IS ALONE FROM THE BODY   . . . . . 149C MARRIAGE HH 4   PROSE
          ENERGY IS THE ONLY LIFE AND IS FROM THE BODY AND   . . . . 149D MARRIAGE HH 4   PROSE
          REASON IS THE BOUND OR OUTWARD CIRCUMFERENCE OF ENERGY   . . 149D MARRIAGE HH 4 PROSE
          ENERGY IS ETERNAL DELIGHT . . . . 149D MARRIAGE HH 4   PROSE
          WEAK AND TAME MINDS WHICH HAVE POWER TO RESIST ENERGY   . . 155A MARRIAGE HH 15 PROSE
          AND ENORMOUS FORMS OF ENERGY   . . . . 225 URIZEN 4   48
          FOR WAR IS [HONEST] [AN] ENERGY ENSLAVD BUT THY RELIGION   361 FOUR ZOAS 9   * 152
          EXPENDING ALL HIS ENERGY AGAINST THE FUEL OF FIRE   . . .   366 FOUR ZOAS 9   359
          UNEMPLOYD EXCEPT BY HIS OWN ENERGY   . . . . 445C ANNO REYNOLDS   MARG
          ALL IS THE SAME & EVERY ONE REMAINS IN HIS OWN ENERGY   . . 511 MILTON 25   43
          TO EVERY ENERGY OF MAN AND FORBID THE SPRINGS OF LIFE   . . 662 JERUSALEM 35   12
          BECOME A NET & A TRAP & EVERY ENERGY RENDERD CRUEL   . . . 672 JERUSALEM 43   26
ENERVE
          ENERVE MY SOLDIERS LET LIBERTY . . . .   18 EDW THIRD/PS 1   11
ENFEEBLING
          EASILY REMOVED BUT EXCRUCIATING WHILE IT LASTS & ENFEEBLING 871A LETTER 72   PROSE
ENFLAME   SEE INFLAME
          THROUGHOUT THE CAMP ENFLAME THE TIMOROUS . . . . . .   25 EDW THIRD/PS 3   179
ENFLAMING
          . . . WITH THE PLOW OF NATIONS ENFLAMING . . . . . .   689 JERUSALEM 57   12
ENGAGE
          AND WHAT IS THE SECOND TO PLEASE & ENGAGE . . . . . .   554 ASKD PRIGG/N   18
          ENGAGE HIMSELF OPENLY & PUBLICLY BEFORE ALL THE WORLD   . . 717C JERUSALEM 77   PROSE
          OF VARIETY SHALL ENGAGE IN OTHER LITTLE WORKS AS THEY ARISE 831C LETTER 31   PROSE
          A LINE IN WHICH HE IS DETERMINED NEVER TO ENGAGE   . . . 831C LETTER 31   PROSE
          DETERMINATION TO DO EVERY THING TO ENGAGE HIMSELF TO YOU   857A LETTER 54   PROSE
          IN MY CAUSE & SHOULD IMMEDIATELY ENGAGE IN REVIVING . . 865C LETTER 63   *PROSE
ENGAGED
          MR BLAKE'S POWERS OF INVENTION VERY EARLY ENGAGED   . . 207C PRSPECTUS 1793   PROSE
          I AM NOW ENGAGED IN ENGRAVING (SIX) SMALL PLATES FOR A   . 811D LETTER 22   PROSE
          ENGAGED IN THE WORK AS ITS MAGNITUDE DEMANDS ALL THE   . . 848D LETTER 45   PROSE
          ENGAGED SHOULD BE EMPLOYED ON THE WORK OF ROMNEY'S LIFE   849D LETTER 47   PROSE
          OF THE BALLADS THE PRINTS (FIVE) IN NUMBER I HAVE ENGAGED   859A LETTER 56   PROSE
ENGAGEMENT
          & WILL RELINQUISH ANY ENGAGEMENT OF DESIGNING AT ALL   . 826A LETTER 27   PROSE
          ENGAGEMENT WITH ANY LONDON BOOKSELLER I MAY MYSELF   . . 856B LETTER 54   PROSE
          ENGAGEMENT OF ENGRAVING THOSE . . . .   860C LETTER 56   PROSE
ENGAGEMENTS
          MY PRESENT ENGAGEMENTS ARE IN MINIATURE PAINTING . . . . 808B LETTER 19   PROSE
          BELIEVE HE SAYS HIS ENGAGEMENTS ARE SO MULTIFORM THAT HE   853A LETTER 51   *PROSE
          TEMPTING THAT I HAVE ALREADY INVOLVED MYSELF IN ENGAGEMENTS 865C LETTER 63   PROSE
ENGAGES
          BY (ONE) FOOT HIGH THE ARTIST ENGAGES TO DELIVER IT   . . 587A CHAUCER 1   PROSE
ENGINES
          TO ALL HIS ENGINES OF DECEIT THAT LINKED CHAINS MIGHT RUN   344 FOUR ZOAS 8   132
          THEY BEAT THE IRON ENGINES OF DESTRUCTION INTO WEDGES   . . 365 FOUR ZOAS 9   304
ENGLAND
          AND THESE FAIR YOUTHS THE FLOWR OF ENGLAND . . . . . . 18 EDW THIRD/PS 1   17
          ENGLAND SHALL DWELL IN PEACE THAT WHILE MY FATHER   . . . 19 EDW THIRD/PS 2   7
          AND ENGLAND IS THE LAND FAVOURD BY COMMERCE . . . . .   19 EDW THIRD/PS 2   30
          TO ENGLAND WHEN AT THE BIRTH OF NATURE . . . .   21 EDW THIRD/PS 2   80
          OF ENGLAND'S QUEEN AND WILL ERE LONG OF ENGLAND   . . .   21 EDW THIRD/PS 2   99
          THEREFORE I BEG I MAY RETURN TO ENGLAND . . . .   23 EDW THIRD/PS 3   104
          THEREFORE I BEG I MAY RETURN TO ENGLAND . . . .   24 EDW THIRD/PS 3   132
          THEN GO TO ENGLAND TELL THEM HOW WE FIGHT . . . . . .   24 EDW THIRD/PS 3   138
          DOES IT GROW IN ENGLAND SIR . . . .   28 EDW THIRD/PS 4   3
          ARE FINER THAN ANY WE HAVE IN ENGLAND . . . .   28 EDW THIRD/PS 4   6
          THAT WE MAY BE REMEMBERED IN OLD ENGLAND . . . . 29C EDW THIRD/PS 4   PROSE
          WHY YOU KNOW SIR WHEN WE WERE IN ENGLAND AT THE TOURNAMENT   29D EDW THIRD/PS 4 PROSE
             AT WINDSOR
          TILL ENGLAND BLOW THE TRUMP OF VICTORY . . . .   31 EDW THIRD/PS 5   65
          WHICH SMALL ISLAND SEEMS TO HAVE SOME AFFINITY TO ENGLAND   44A ISLAND MOON 1   *PROSE
          WHEN KLOPSTOCK ENGLAND DEFIED . . . . 186 WHEN KLOPSTK/N   1
          THE KING OF ENGLAND LOOKING WESTWARD TREMBLES AT THE VISION 197 AMERICA 4   12
          WHAT TIME THE THIRTEEN GOVERNORS THAT ENGLAND SENT CONVENE   201 AMERICA 13   1
          AND ANOTHER FROM THE HISTORY OF ENGLAND . . . . 207C PRSPECTUS 1793   PROSE
          THE HISTORY OF ENGLAND A SMALL BOOK OF ENGRAVINGS PRICE...   208A PRSPECTUS 1793 PROSE
          GIANTS ANCIENT INHABITANTS OF ENGLAND THE LANDING   208C SUBJCTS HIST/N TITLE
             OF BRUTUS
          THE YOUTH OF ENGLAND HID IN GLOOM CURSE THE PAIND HEAVENS   242 EUROPE 12   5
             COMPELLD
          ANOTHER ENGLAND THERE I SAW . . . .   429 CRYSTL CABINET   9
          O KING & NOBILITY OF ENGLAND WHERE HAVE . . . . 446A ANNO REYNOLDS   MARG

585

```
                                                              PAGE      TITLE           LINE
ENGLAND    (CONTINUED)
     THE RICH MEN OF ENGLAND FORM THEMSELVES INTO A SOCIETY  .  .  452C  ANNO REYNOLDS     MARG
     THE ENQUIRY IN ENGLAND IS NOT WHETHER A MAN HAS TALENTS      452D  ANNO REYNOLDS     MARG
     BACON'S PHILOSOPHY HAS RUIND ENGLAND  .  .  .  .  .  .  .  . 456C  ANNO REYNOLDS     MARG
     GERMANY WEPT TOWARDS FRANCE & ITALY ENGLAND WEPT            519   MILTON 31          13
       & TREMBLED
     .  .  .  FROM ENGLAND [& POLITENESS] [WAS SENT] WE FETCH]    541   FLORENTINE/N    *    7
     WE MIGHT PERHAPS HAVE THEM NOW IN ENGLAND  .  .  .  .  .  . 560D  EXHIBITION ADV    PROSE
     WATER-COLOUR PAINTING AND ENGLAND PROTECTED  .  .  .  .  .  562B  DESC CAT ADV      PROSE
     AND TO MAKE ENGLAND LIKE ITALY RESPECTED  .  .  .  .  .  .  584B  DESC CAT 14       PROSE
     ENGLAND EXPECTS THAT EVERY MAN SHOULD DO HIS DUTY  .  .  .  584C  DESC CAT 14       PROSE
     [FROM AN] AS AN ART IS LOST IN ENGLAND OWING TO AN  .  .  . 591D  PUB ADDRESS/N    *PROSE
     EQUALLY WELL AT LEAST IT IS SO IN ENGLAND  .  .  .  .  .  . 593D  PUB ADDRESS/N     PROSE
     ENGLAND WILL NEVER RIVAL ITALY WHILE WE SERVILELY COPY  .  .597C  PUB ADDRESS/N     PROSE
     THE GREATEST PART OF WHAT ARE CALLD IN ENGLAND OLD PICTURES 598A  PUB ADDRESS/N     PROSE
     THE PAINTERS OF ENGLAND ARE UNEMPLOYD IN PUBLIC WORKS  .  . 601A  PUB ADDRESS/N     PROSE
     I SAY MONUMENTS SO PAINTED MUST MAKE ENGLAND  .  .  .  .  . 601B  PUB ADDRESS/N     PROSE
     THAT HAS BEEN DONE OR IS LIKELY TO BE DONE IN ENGLAND  .  . 602A  PUB ADDRESS/N     PROSE
     [TO BE THE GOOD KINGS] & QUEENS [OF ENGLAND]  .  .  .  .  . 614A  V LAST JUDG/N    *PROSE
     FROM THESE TWELVE ALL THE FAMILIES OF ENGLAND SPREAD ABROAD 623   JERUSALEM 5         33
     WALES GIVES HIS DAUGHTERS TO THE LOOMS ENGLAND NURSING      637   JERUSALEM 16       23
       MOTHERS
     HERE LOS FIXD DOWN THE FIFTY-TWO COUNTIES OF ENGLAND &      637   JERUSALEM 16       28
       WALES
     TO THE FOUR POINTS CONDUCT TO ENGLAND & SCOTLAND & IRELAND  637   JERUSALEM 16       33
     AND THE FORTY COUNTIES OF ENGLAND ARE THUS DIVIDED IN THE   637   JERUSALEM 16       43
       GATES
     ALBION COVERD THE WHOLE EARTH ENGLAND ENCOMPASSD            648   JERUSALEM 24       44
       THE NATIONS
     FROM BRIGHT JAPAN & CHINA TO HESPERIA FRANCE & ENGLAND  .  .648   JERUSALEM 24       47
     AND ENGLAND WHO IS BRITTANNIA DIVIDED INTO JERUSALEM & VALA 663   JERUSALEM 36       28
     THEN ENGLAND DREW ENGLAND INTO HIS BOSOM IN GROANS & TEARS  685   JERUSALEM 54       27
     OF ENGLAND & IN THE THIRTY-SIX COUNTIES OF SCOTLAND  .  .  .711   JERUSALEM 72       16
     ENGLAND AWAKE AWAKE AWAKE  .  .  .  .  .  .  .  .  .  .  .  .718   ENGLND AWAKE/J      1
     THE FIFTY-TWO COUNTIES OF ENGLAND ARE HARDEND AGAINST ME    720   JERUSALEM 79       20
     LONDON COVERD THE WHOLE EARTH ENGLAND ENCOMPASSD            720   JERUSALEM 79       22
       THE NATIONS
     UPON THE WHITE ROCK ENGLAND A FEMALE SHADOW AS DEADLY DAMPS 741   JERUSALEM 94        7
     AND ENGLAND WHO IS BRITTANNIA AWOKE FROM DEATH ON ALBION'S  742   JERUSALEM 94       20
       BOSOM
     I HAVE SLAIN HIM IN MY SLEEP WITH THE KNIFE OF THE DRUID    742   JERUSALEM 94       25
       O ENGLAND
     HIS STONY MEMBERS HE SAW ENGLAND AH SHALL THE DEAD LIVE     742   JERUSALEM 95        4
       AGAIN
     ENGLAND WHO IS BRITTANNIA ENTERD ALBION'S BOSOM REJOICING   743   JERUSALEM 95       22
     ENGLAND WHO IS BRITTANNIA ENTERED ALBION'S BOSOM REJOICING  743   JERUSALEM 96        2
     CARRIED INTO EXECUTION AS IT MUST BE IF ENGLAND CONTINUES   797C  LETTER 10         PROSE
     BROUGHT INTO ENGLAND OR CAN BE PURCHASD ABROAD AS ITS  .  . 797D  LETTER 10        *PROSE
     MUST BE THE PLAN IF ENGLAND WISHES TO CONTINUE AT ALL WORTH 798A  LETTER 10         PROSE
     BUT I HOPE THAT FRANCE & ENGLAND WILL HENCEFORTH BE  .  .  .811C  LETTER 21         PROSE
     HIS CONNECTIONS THROUGHOUT ENGLAND & INDEED EUROPE &  .  .  841C  LETTER 41         PROSE
     CONFESSEDLY THE FIRST POET OF ENGLAND OUGHT TO BE GIVEN     856B  LETTER 54         PROSE
ENGLAND'S
     BE ENGLAND'S TRADE OUR CARE AND WE AS TRADESMEN  .  .  .  .  19   EDW THIRD/PS 2     34
     OF ENGLAND'S QUEEN AND WILL ERE LONG OF ENGLAND  .  .  .  .  21   EDW THIRD/PS 2     99
     THEN SHALL ENGLAND'S VERDURE SHOOT HER FIELDS SHALL SMILE    31   EDW THIRD/PS 5     57
     SHALL WEAVE OLD ENGLAND'S WINDING SHEET  .  .  .  .  .  .  . 433   AUGURIES         116
     DANCE BEFORE DEAD ENGLAND'S HEARSE  .  .  .  .  .  .  .  .  .433   AUGURIES         118
     O SHEPHERDESS OF ENGLAND'S FOLD  .  .  .  .  .  .  .  .  .  .442   DEDICATN BLAIR     9
     TO DEDICATE TO ENGLAND'S QUEEN  .  .  .  .  .  .  .  .  .  . 442   DEDICATN BLAIR    11
     WALK UPON ENGLAND'S MOUNTAINS GREEN  .  .  .  .  .  .  .  .  480   AND DID FEET/M     2
     ON ENGLAND'S PLEASANT PASTURES SEEN  .  .  .  .  .  .  .  .  480   AND DID FEET/M     4
     IN ENGLAND'S GREEN & PLEASANT LAND  .  .  .  .  .  .  .  .  .481   AND DID FEET/M    16
     AND THESE I SHEWD TO ENGLAND'S QUEEN  .  .  .  .  .  .  .  . 558   THE CAVERNS/N      2
     IN ENGLAND'S GREEN & PLEASANT BOWERS  .  .  .  .  .  .  .  . 718   ENGLND AWAKE/J    12
ENGLEFIELD
     REVD DR TRUSLER ENGLEFIELD GREEN EGHAM SURREY  .  .  .  .  .SUPP  ADDRESSES/L      *TITLE
ENGLISH
     SCENE ENGLISH COURT LIONEL DUKE OF CLARENCE  .  .  .  .  .   19A  EDW THIRD/PS 2    PROSE
     INFEST OUR ENGLISH SEAS DEVOURING ALL  .  .  .  .  .  .  .   20   EDW THIRD/PS 2     67
     GOOD MORROW GENERALS WHEN ENGLISH COURAGE FAILS  .  .  .  .  23   EDW THIRD/PS 3     71
     METHINKS I SEE THEM PERCH ON ENGLISH CRESTS  .  .  .  .  .   26   EDW THIRD/PS 3    229
     ITS A NEW SONG ABOUT THE FRENCH AND ENGLISH  .  .  .  .  .   29B  EDW THIRD/PS 4    PROSE
     HANG ITALIAN SONGS LET'S HAVE ENGLISH SAID QUID  .  .  .  .  56A  ISLAND MOON 9     PROSE
     ENGLISH GENIUS FOR EVER HERE I GO  .  .  .  .  .  .  .  .  . 56A   ISLAND MOON 9     PROSE
     GOOD ENGLISH HOSPITALITY O THEN IT DID NOT FAIL  .  .  .  .  58   THIS CITY/IM       4
     GOOD ENGLISH HOSPITALITY O THEN IT DID NOT FAIL  .  .  .  .  58   THIS CITY/IM       8
     GOOD ENGLISH HOSPITALITY O THEN IT DID NOT FAIL  .  .  .  .  58   THIS CITY/IM      12
     WHITE AS AN ANGEL IS THE ENGLISH CHILD  .  .  .  .  .  .  .  125   LIT BLK BOY/SI     3
     AND THUS I SAY TO LITTLE ENGLISH BOY  .  .  .  .  .  .  .  . 125   LIT BLK BOY/SI    22
     AND CALLD ALOUD TO ENGLISH BLAKE  .  .  .  .  .  .  .  .  .  187   WHEN KLOPSTK/N     6
     TO WHAT DOES THE BISHOP ATTRIBUTE THE ENGLISH CRUSADE  .  . 385C  ANNO WATSON       MARG
     OTHER & DIVIDED ALL THE ENGLISH WORLD BETWEEN THEM  .  .  . 445C  ANNO REYNOLDS     MARG
     OF THE FLOWER OF THE ENGLISH NOBILITY & GENTRY [A SOCIETY]  446A  ANNO REYNOLDS    * MARG
     [AND TIS ENGLISH POLITENESS AS FAIR AS [YOUR] MY AUNT]      542   FLORENTINE/N     *   10
     THE FLORENTINES SAID TIS A DUTCH ENGLISH BORE  .  .  .  .   542   FLORENTINE/N      13
     THE FLORENTINES CALL IT AN ENGLISH FETCH  .  .  .  .  .  .  542   FLORENTINE/N      15
     TIS THE TRADING ENGLISH VENETIAN CANT  .  .  .  .  .  .  .  542   FLORENTINE/N      20
     TO ENGLISH CONNOISSEURS  .  .  .  .  .  .  .  .  .  .  .  .  546C  ENGLISH CONN/N   TITLE
     ON THE GREAT ENCOURAGEMENT [SHEWN] GIVEN BY ENGLISH         548B  ON GREAT ENC/N   *TITLE
       NOBILITY &
     ENGLISH ENCOURAGEMENT OF ART CROMEK'S OPINIONS PUT INTO     549C  ENGL ENCOU/N 1   TITLE
       RHYME
```

ENGLISH   (CONTINUED)

	PAGE	TITLE	LINE
WITH THE OLD ENGLISH PORTRAITS [CO] THAT IS	592A	PUB ADDRESS/N	*PROSE
INTO THIS COUNTRY SINCE WHICH ENGLISH ENGRAVING IS LOST	592A	PUB ADDRESS/N	PROSE
WHAT IS CALLD THE ENGLISH STYLE OF ENGRAVING	593B	PUB ADDRESS/N	PROSE
WHAT FINE ART IS YE ENGLISH ENGRAVERS MUST COME DOWN .	593C	PUB ADDRESS/N	PROSE
IN THIS MANNER THE ENGLISH PUBLIC HAVE BEEN IMPOSED UPON	594C	PUB ADDRESS/N	PROSE
[ALIAMET] GRAVELOT ONCE SAID TO MY MASTER BASIRE [YOU] DE ENGLISH	594D	PUB ADDRESS/N	*PROSE
AS AN ORIGINAL [BELYING] BE-LYING THE ENGLISH CHARACTER IN	595C	PUB ADDRESS/N	PROSE
BY ENGLISH TRADERS MUST [LOA] FEEL A LOATHING	596B	PUB ADDRESS/N	*PROSE
INVITES THE ADMIRERS OF OLD ENGLISH PORTRAITS TO LOOK AT HIS PRINT	596C	PUB ADDRESS/N	PROSE
THE ITALIANS LAUGH AT ENGLISH CONNOISSEURS WHO ARE . . .	597B	PUB ADDRESS/N	PROSE
THE ENGLISH ARTIST MAY BE ASSURED THAT HE IS DOING . .	597C	PUB ADDRESS/N	PROSE
THE ENGLISH PUBLIC WILL BE CONVINCD THAT SUCH A . . .	598B	PUB ADDRESS/N	PROSE
SMOOTHD IT OVER LIKE AN ENGLISH ENGRAVER OR CORREGIO & TITIAN	598C	PUB ADDRESS/N	PROSE
PRONOUNCD BY ENGLISH CONNOISSEURS & REYNOLDS THEIR DOLL	599D	PUB ADDRESS/N	PROSE
IT HAS BEEN SAID OF LATE YEARS THE ENGLISH PUBLIC HAVE .	601B	PUB ADDRESS/N	PROSE
ENGLISH ARE AS GOOD JUDGES [AS] OF PAINTING AS OF POETRY	601B	PUB ADDRESS/N	*PROSE
I SAY THE ENGLISH PUBLIC ARE TRUE ENCOURAGERS OF REAL ART	601C	PUB ADDRESS/N	PROSE
& SHAKSPEARE & ALL WRITERS OF ENGLISH BLANK VERSE . . .	621C	JERUSALEM 3	PROSE
AND EVERY ENGLISH CHILD IS SEEN	650	FIELDS FROM/J	19
I CALL THEM BY THEIR ENGLISH NAMES ENGLISH THE ROUGH BASEMENT	668	JERUSALEM 40	58
THE ENGLISH ARE SCATTERD OVER THE FACE OF THE NATIONS ARE THESE	673	JERUSALEM 43	46
WE SMELL THE BLOOD OF THE ENGLISH	673	JERUSALEM 43	48
VERULAM LONDON YORK & EDINBURGH THEIR ENGLISH NAMES . .	691	JERUSALEM 59	14
O WHEN SHALL THE SAXON RETURN WITH THE ENGLISH HIS REDEEMED BROTHER	727	JERUSALEM 83	14
IN MY FURNACES INTO ONE NATION THE ENGLISH & TAKING REFUGE	739	JERUSALEM 92	2
INTO [PLAIN] THE VULGAR ENGLISH	788D	ANNO THORNTON	MARG
THE ENGLISH TRANSLATION IT IS ALMOST WORD FOR WORD & . .	821D	LETTER 25	PROSE
AS THE FRENCH NOW ADORE BUONAPARTE AND THE ENGLISH OUR POOR GEORGE	845B	LETTER 44	PROSE
BEEN ASSIDUOUSLY SOWN AND PLANTED AMONG THE ENGLISH PUBLIC	864A	LETTER 61	PROSE
THE TASTE OF ENGLISH AMATEURS HAS BEEN TOO MUCH FORMED . .	864C	LETTER 61	PROSE

ENGLISHMAN

HE IS A GENUINE ENGLISHMAN MY CHANDOS	25	EDW THIRD/PS 3	189
SO THE [WISE] [LEARNED] TAUGHT SAVAGE ENGLISHMAN	548	ON GREAT ENC/N	3
THIS I THOUGHT THE ONLY PURSUIT WORTHY OF [AN ENGLISHMAN] A MAN	600B	PUB ADDRESS/N	PROSE
IGNORANT PICTURE DEALERS AN ENGLISHMAN MAY WELL SAY I AM	601C	PUB ADDRESS/N	PROSE
EITHER FOR ENGLISHMAN OR JEW	756	EV GOSPEL (F)/N	2

ENGLISHMEN

LET LIBERTY THE CHARTERD RIGHT OF ENGLISHMEN	18	EDW THIRD/PS 1	9
MY ENGLISHMEN THE BRAVEST PEOPLE ON	25	EDW THIRD/PS 3	192
A WAR SONG TO ENGLISHMEN	34C	WAR SONG/PS	TITLE
EMPIRE FOLLOWS ART & NOT VICE VERSA AS ENGLISHMEN SUPPOSE	445D	ANNO REYNOLDS	MARG
O ENGLISHMEN WHY ARE YOU STILL OF THIS FOOLISH CARDINAL'S OPINION	445D	ANNO REYNOLDS	MARG
PRETENCES OF ENGLISHMEN TO IMPROVE [E] ART BEFORE THEY EVEN	593C	PUB ADDRESS/N	*PROSE
SHEW THAT IT IS ONLY SOME ENGLISHMEN AND NOT ALL	593C	PUB ADDRESS/N	PROSE
ENGLISHMEN ROUZE YOURSELVES FROM THE FATAL SLUMBER . . .	595B	PUB ADDRESS/N	PROSE
THAT WELL KNOWN SAYING ENGLISHMEN IMPROVE WHAT OTHERS INVENT	595C	PUB ADDRESS/N	PROSE
MOST ENGLISHMEN HAVE A CONTEMPT FOR ART [WHICH WILL] . .	596B	PUB ADDRESS/N	PROSE
MOST ENGLISHMEN WHEN THEY LOOK AT A PICTURE	599A	PUB ADDRESS/N	PROSE
ENGLISHMEN HAVE BEEN SO USED TO JOURNEYMEN'S UNDECIDED BUNGLING	603C	PUB ADDR AD/N	PROSE
A MAN SAY I AM NO JUDGE OF PICTURES BUT O ENGLISHMEN . .	864C	LETTER 61	PROSE
ENGLISHMEN ARE FOND OF THE INDEFINITE WHICH THEY MEASURE	878A	LETTER 88	PROSE
ENGLISHMEN ARE ALL INTERMEASURABLE ONE BY ANOTHER . . .	878B	LETTER 88	PROSE

ENGLOBD

AND THE SALT OCEAN ROLLED ENGLOBD	237	URIZEN 28	23
DRIVN BY WAVES & ENGLOBD ON THE TIDE	258	BOOK OF LOS 4	58
DOWNWARD & YOUR FLUXILE EYES ENGLOBD ROLL ROUND IN FEAR	294	FOUR ZOAS 3	87
DOWNWARD AND YOUR FLUXILE EYES ENGLOBD ROLL ROUND IN FEAR	655	JERUSALEM 29	68

ENGLOBES

| [THE SPACE ?BECOMES ?SERPENT-FORMD & THE WOMB ?ENGLOBES] | 490 | MILTON 10 | * 7 |
| ENGLOBES ITSELF & BECOMES A WOMB SUCH WAS ALBION'S COUCH | 620 | JERUSALEM 1 | 2 |

ENGLOBING

ROUND ROLLD THE SEA ENGLOBING IN A WATRY GLOBE SELF BALANCD	266	FOUR ZOAS 1	88
BEFORE ME IN THE WIND ENGLOBING TREMBLING WITH STRONG VIBRATIONS	300	FOUR ZOAS 4	95
SOMETIMES IN [BREADTH] LENGTH SOMETIMES ENGLOBING . . .	315	FOUR ZOAS 6	123

ENGRAVD

FOURSQUARE SCULPTURD & SWEETLY ENGRAVD TO PLEASE THEIR SHADOWY MOTHER	285	FOUR ZOAS 2	191
& TO BE ENGRAVD ALSO BY THE LAST MENTIOND THE	824C	LETTER 27	PROSE
MR SAUNDERS HAS A GOOD MANY WERE ENGRAVD THEY	832C	LETTER 32	PROSE
XXX PILGRIMS ENGRAVD	SUPP	PILGRIMS/N	*PROSE

ENGRAVE

MEMORANDUM TO ENGRAVE ON PEWTER	440B	MEMORANDUM/N 2	PROSE
THE DESIGNER PROPOSES TO ENGRAVE IN A CORRECT AND FINISHED	586C	CHAUCER 1	PROSE
CORREGGIO OR TITIAN I DO NOT PRETEND TO ENGRAVE FINER .	594C	PUB ADDRESS/N	PROSE
TO ENGRAVE FINER THAN STRANGE WOOLETT HALL OR BARTOLOZZI	594C	PUB ADDRESS/N	PROSE
ENGRAVE OR PAINT EITHER WITHOUT BEING A MASTER OF DRAWING IS	602B	PUB ADDRESS/N	PROSE
TO ENGRAVE AFTER ANOTHER PAINTER IS INFINITELY MORE LABORIOUS	794B	LETTER 5	PROSE

587

ENGRAVE   (CONTINUED)
    THAN TO ENGRAVE ONE'S OWN INVENTIONS AND   . . . . . 794B LETTER 5   PROSE
    BEG OF YOU TO SEND TO ME THAT I MAY ENGRAVE THEM   838A LETTER 37   PROSE
        IMMEDIATELY
    TO ENGRAVE ONE IN EACH MANNER THE SIZE TO BE ABOUT (SEVEN) 848B LETTER 45   PROSE
        INCHES
    ENGRAVE THEM HE MEANS TO PUBLISH THEM BY SUBSCRIPTION . . 861D LETTER 59   PROSE
    & PERHAPS BETTER BUT I CANNOT ENGRAVE . . . . 869A LETTER 68   PROSE
    TO ENGRAVE...PLATES FROM HIS OWN DESIGNS OF JOB'S CAPTIVITY SUPP LETTER 67D   *PROSE
ENGRAVED
    THEN SAID HE I WOULD HAVE ALL THE WRITING ENGRAVED INSTEAD   62D ISLAND MOON 11 PROSE
    TWO [PRINTS] I ENGRAVED FROM FOR J R SMITH . . . . . 553B BELLS WEEKLY/N   *PROSE
    PICTURE OF THE CANTERBURY PILGRIMS WHICH IS TO BE ENGRAVED   563B DESC CAT   PROSE
    WHICH I ENGRAVED AFTER HIM FIVE & TWENTY YEARS AGO . . . 592B PUB ADDRESS/N PROSE
    I ALSO KNEW SOMETHING OF TOM COOKE WHO ENGRAVED . . . . 594B PUB ADDRESS/N   PROSE
    ENGRAVED BY W BLAKE...FROM AN OLD ITALIAN DRAWING . . . 604A INSC ARIMATHEA   TITLE
    DRAWN & ENGRAVED BY WILLIAM BLAKE . . . . 775C INSC LAOCOON   *TITLE
    FOR THE PURPOSE OF BEING ENGRAVED FOR THE EUROPEAN MAGNE   838D LETTER 37   PROSE
    ENGRAVED BY THE HANDS OF ANGELS & MUST NOT BY ANY MEANS   848C LETTER 45   PROSE
    OUGHT TO BE ENGRAVED FOR YOUR WORK . . . . 857C LETTER 54   PROSE
    HAVE ENGRAVED ONE OF THE PLATES FOR THAT BALLAD OF THE   861A LETTER 58   PROSE
        HORSE
    ENGRAVED WHEN I WAS A BEGINNER AT BASIRE'S . . . . . SUPP INSC JOSEPH   *TITLE
    THE HISTORY OF JOB DESIGNED & ENGRAVED BY WILLIAM BLAKE   SUPP LETTER 67F   *PROSE
ENGRAVEN
    ENAMELD WITH LOVE & KINDNESS & THE TILES ENGRAVEN GOLD . . 632 JERUSALEM 12   31
ENGRAVER
    CRY BLAKIFIED DRAWING SPOILS PAINTER & ENGRAVER . . . . 555 BLAKES APL/N 1   15
    CRY BLAKIFIED DRAWING SPOILS PAINTER & ENGRAVER . . . . 556 BLAKES APL/N 2   14
    AN OLD WELL-KNOWN AND ACKNOWLEDGED ENGRAVER . . . . . 586D CHAUCER 1   PROSE
    ARTFULLY PROPAGATED OPINION THAT DRAWING SPOILS AN ENGRAVER 591D PUB ADDRESS/N *PROSE
    FLAXMAN & EVEN ROMNEY SPOILS AN ENGRAVER FOR EACH OF . . 592B PUB ADDRESS/N   PROSE
    DELINEATED BY ANY ENGRAVER WHO KNOWS HOW TO . . . . . 592B PUB ADDRESS/N   PROSE
    & HE WHO PRETENDS TO BE EITHER PAINTER OR ENGRAVER . . 594D PUB ADDRESS/N   PROSE
    SMOOTHD IT OVER LIKE AN ENGLISH ENGRAVER OR CORREGIO &   598C PUB ADDRESS/N PROSE
        TITIAN
    BOTH FOR THE ENGRAVER AND THE SCULPTOR . . . . . . 796B LETTER 7   PROSE
    EVERY ENGRAVER TURNS AWAY WORK THAT HE CANNOT EXECUTE . . 829D LETTER 30   PROSE
    EMINENCE AS AN ENGRAVER MAKES HIS OPINION DESERVE NOTICE . 848A LETTER 45   PROSE
    ENGRAVER I CONSULTED MR PARKER ON THE SUBJECT BEFORE I . 855A LETTER 53   PROSE
    MR CROMEK THE ENGRAVER CAME TO ME DESIRING TO HAVE SOME   861C LETTER 59   PROSE
ENGRAVER'S
    I REMAIN IN ENGRAVER'S HURRY WHICH IS THE WORST & . . 840C LETTER 39   PROSE
    ALL THE ENGRAVER'S NICEST ATTENTION INDEED IT IS   855A LETTER 53   PROSE
        MORE FINISHD
ENGRAVERS
    OLD ORIGINAL ENGRAVERS WHO WERE GREAT MASTERS IN PAINTING   586D CHAUCER 1   PROSE
    STYLE OF ALB DURER'S (HISTORIES) & THE OLD ENGRAVERS . . 592B PUB ADDRESS/N   *PROSE
    WHAT FINE ART IS YE ENGLISH ENGRAVERS MUST COME DOWN . . 593C PUB ADDRESS/N   PROSE
    ART IN LONDON FLOURISHES ENGRAVERS IN PARTICULAR ARE WANTED 829D LETTER 30   PROSE
    IN WANT OF HANDS OTHER ENGRAVERS ARE COURTED I SUPPOSE . 829D LETTER 30   PROSE
    OF THE SAME TRADE IS THOUGHT FAIR PLAY ENGRAVERS PAINTERS   847B LETTER 44   PROSE
    MR FLAXMAN ADVISES THAT THE BEST ENGRAVERS SHOULD BE . 848C LETTER 45   PROSE
ENGRAVING
    HERE ARADOBO LOOKD ASTONISHD & ASKD IF HE UNDERSTOOD   46D ISLAND MOON 3   PROSE
        ENGRAVING
    INVENTED A METHOD OF PRINTING BOTH LETTER-PRESS AND   207B PRSPECTUS 1793   PROSE
        ENGRAVING
    JOB A HISTORICAL ENGRAVING SIZE...PRICE... . . . . . 207D PRSPECTUS 1793   PROSE
    EDWARD AND ELINOR A HISTORICAL ENGRAVING SIZE...PRICE...   207D PRSPECTUS 1793 PROSE
    LINE MANNER OF ENGRAVING SIMILAR TO THOSE ORIGINAL . . . 586C CHAUCER 1   PROSE
    THE SIZE OF THE ENGRAVING WILL BE (THREE) FEET (ONE) INCH   587A CHAUCER 1   PROSE
        LONG
    BLAKE'S CHAUCER AN ORIGINAL ENGRAVING BY WILLIAM BLAKE . 587D CHAUCER/N   TITLE
    PAINTING & ENGRAVING & DURING A PERIOD OF FORTY YEARS . . 587D CHAUCER/N   PROSE
    ATTENTION OF THE AMATEUR IN A LARGE [WORK] STROKE ENGRAVING 587D CHAUCER/N   *PROSE
    BLAKE'S CHAUCER AN ORIGINAL ENGRAVING BY HIM . . . . . 589C CHAUCER 2   TITLE
    [MYSELF TO ENGRAVING IN MY EARLIEST YOUTH ARE SUFFICIENT]   591C PUB ADDRESS/N PROSE
    THAT ENGRAVING [IS IN A MOST WRETCHED STATE OF INJURY] . 591D PUB ADDRESS/N   *PROSE
    INTO THIS COUNTRY SINCE WHICH ENGLISH ENGRAVING IS LOST . 592A PUB ADDRESS/N PROSE
    ENGRAVING BY LOSING DRAWING HAS LOST ALL CHARACTER . . 592A PUB ADDRESS/N   *PROSE
    WHAT IS CALLD THE ENGLISH STYLE OF ENGRAVING . . . . . 593B PUB ADDRESS/N   PROSE
    FOR MANY YEARS UNDER THE IMPRESSION THAT ENGRAVING . . 594C PUB ADDRESS/N   PROSE
    & ENGRAVING IS DRAWING ON COPPER & NOTHING ELSE . . . . 594C PUB ADDRESS/N   PROSE
    OF ENGRAVING THAT HAVE BEEN PUBLISHD . . . . 596B PUB ADDRESS/N   PROSE
    & ENGRAVING IS DRAWING ON COPPER & NOTHING ELSE . . . . 602B PUB ADDRESS/N   PROSE
    HE IS GLAD TO EMBRACE THE OFFER OF ENGRAVING SUCH BEAUTIFUL 790A LETTER 1   PROSE
        THINGS
    CHALK ENGRAVING IS AT LEAST SIX TIMES AS LABORIOUS AS   794C LETTER 5   PROSE
        AQUA TINTA
    I HAVE NO OBJECTION TO ENGRAVING AFTER ANOTHER ARTIST . . 794C LETTER 5   PROSE
    ENGRAVING IS THE PROFESSION I WAS APPRENTICED TO . . . . 794C LETTER 5   PROSE
    BUT I AM CONTENTED WHETHER I LIVE BY PAINTING OR ENGRAVING   794C LETTER 5   PROSE
    FOR AS TO ENGRAVING IN WHICH ART I CANNOT REPROACH MYSELF   795C LETTER 6   PROSE
    WITH NOW & THEN AN ENGRAVING & FIND THAT IN FUTURE TO LIVE   798B LETTER 10   PROSE
    AT THIS TIME IS ENGRAVING PLATES FOR COWPER'S LIFE . . . 809D LETTER 20   PROSE
    I AM NOW ENGAGED IN ENGRAVING (SIX) SMALL PLATES FOR A . 811D LETTER 22   PROSE
    PAINTING & ENGRAVING WHICH IN THE CONFUSION OF LONDON . . 812B LETTER 22   PROSE
    AS MY DEPENDENCE IS ON ENGRAVING AT PRESENT & PARTICULARLY   812C LETTER 22   PROSE
    FOLLY NOT TO VENTURE PUBLISHING I AM NOW ENGRAVING SIX   820B LETTER 25   PROSE
        LITTLE
    BEING FULLY EMPLOYD IN ENGRAVING FOR HIS PROJECTED WORKS   824C LETTER 27   PROSE

	PAGE	TITLE	LINE

ENGRAVING   (CONTINUED)

WISH THAT YOU WOULD GIVE THE PUBLIC AN ENGRAVING OF THAT   836A LETTER 35   PROSE
ENGRAVING IS ETERNAL WORK THE TWO PLATES ARE ALMOST FINISHD   837C LETTER 36   PROSE
I CURSE & BLESS ENGRAVING ALTERNATELY BECAUSE IT TAKES   837D LETTER 36   PROSE
  SO MUCH TIME
WHICH I AM NOW ENGRAVING & WHICH WAS LENT BY MR LONG   .   .   838D LETTER 37   PROSE
I AM NOW ENGRAVING I AM UNEASY AT NOT HEARING FROM   .   .   841A LETTER 40   PROSE
ENGRAVING IS OF SO SLOW PROCESS I MUST BEG OF YOU TO GIVE   842D LETTER 42   PROSE
  ME
THE EARLIEST POSSIBLE NOTICE OF WHAT ENGRAVING IS TO BE   842D LETTER 42   PROSE
  DONE
LIFE OF ROMNEY ENDLESS WORK IS THE TRUE TITLE OF ENGRAVING   843A LETTER 42   PROSE
THEY HAVE GIVEN ME SOME EXCELLENT HINTS IN ENGRAVING   .   843B LETTER 43   PROSE
PRICE I RECEIVE FOR ENGRAVING FLAXMAN'S OUTLINES OF HOMER   844B LETTER 43   PROSE
MAKE A VERY BEAUTIFUL ENGRAVING DONE IN THE SAME MANNER AS   850D LETTER 49   PROSE
ON THE PLATES I AM NOW ENGRAVING AFTER ROMNEY WHOSE   .   .   852B LETTER 50   PROSE
CONNOISSEUR IN ENGRAVING HAS GIVEN HER WARM APPROBATION   853B LETTER 52   PROSE
UPON ENGRAVING I THINK IT CAN ONLY BE DONE BY SOME   .   .   855A LETTER 53   PROSE
SETTLED WITH HIM THE PLAN OF ENGRAVING FOR THE NEW EDITION   859A LETTER 56   PROSE
AN ENGRAVING OF COWPER BY THE HAND OF CAROLINE WATSON IS I   859C LETTER 56   PROSE
ENGAGEMENT OF ENGRAVING THOSE   .   .   .   .   860C LETTER 56   PROSE
FIRST BEFORE I BEGIN ENGRAVING THEM AS IT WILL ENABLE ME   866C LETTER 65   PROSE
RECIEVD...OF MR FLAXMAN THE SUM...FOR ENGRAVING   .   .   .   SUPP LETTER 6A   *PROSE
FOR LAYING IN THE ENGRAVING OF MR UPTON'S PORTRAIT   .   .   .   SUPP LETTER 66D   *PROSE

ENGRAVINGS

HIGHLY FINISHED ENGRAVINGS AND TWO MORE ARE NEARLY READY   207C PRSPECTUS 1793   PROSE
THE HISTORY OF ENGLAND A SMALL BOOK OF ENGRAVINGS PRICE...   208A PRSPECTUS 1793   PROSE
THE GATES OF PARADISE A SMALL BOOK OF ENGRAVINGS PRICE...   208A PRSPECTUS 1793   PROSE
ANY MORE THAN THE ENGRAVINGS OF STRANGE BARTOLLOZZI   .   .   455A ANNO REYNOLDS   MARG
WITH THE FINEST ENGRAVINGS & DEFY THE MOST CRITICAL JUDGE   602A PUB ADDRESS/N   PROSE
ON THE ENGRAVINGS I HAVE IN HAND FOR MR H(HAYLEY)   .   .   812C LETTER 22   PROSE
THESE WORKS WILL BE ORNAMENTED WITH ENGRAVINGS FROM   .   .   824C LETTER 27   PROSE
FINISHD ENGRAVINGS WILL DO AS OUTLINE INTIRELY OMITS   .   848A LETTER 45   PROSE
THE NUMBER OF PROJECTED ENGRAVINGS   .   .   .   .   849B LETTER 45   PROSE
BEING AT FLAXMAN'S TAKING HIS ADVICE ABOUT OUR ENGRAVINGS   853A LETTER 51   *PROSE
LITTLE HIGH FINISHD PICTURES THE SIZE THE ENGRAVINGS ARE   859B LETTER 56   PROSE
  TO BE
I GO ON AS I THINK IMPROVING MY ENGRAVINGS OF DANTE   .   .   876A LETTER 83   PROSE
THE DESIGNS AS WELL AS THE ENGRAVINGS I AM GETTING ON WITH   877A LETTER 85   PROSE
THE ENGRAVINGS & HOPE SOON TO GET PROOFS OF WHAT I AM DOING   877A LETTER 85   PROSE

ENGROSSED

SO ENGROSSED HIS MIND THAT HE DID NOT SALUTE THE COMPANY   46A ISLAND MOON 1   PROSE

ENION

[AND THARMAS ?SAID ALL MY HOPE I ?SOUGHT ENION FOR EVER   297 FOUR ZOAS 4   *   9
  GONE]
LOST LOST LOST ARE MY EMANATIONS ENION [COME FORTH] O   264 FOUR ZOAS 1   25
  ENION
I HAVE HIDDEN [THEE ENION IN JEALOUS DESPAIR]   .   .   .   .   .   264 FOUR ZOAS 1   27
.   .   .   [WHERE WE MAY REMAIN FOR EVER ALONE] ALSO O PITY   265 FOUR ZOAS 1   28
  ME O ENION
ENION SAID [HIS] THY FEAR HAS MADE ME TREMBLE   .   .   .   .   .   .   265 FOUR ZOAS 1   *   35
O ENION THOU ART THYSELF A ROOT GROWING IN HELL   .   .   .   265 FOUR ZOAS 1   57
ENION SAID FAREWELL I DIE I HIDE FROM THY SEARCHING EYES   266 FOUR ZOAS 1   68
OF ITS OWN PERVERSE & WAYWARD ENION LOVD & WEPT   .   .   .   266 FOUR ZOAS 1   85
A FROWNING CONTINENT APPEARD WHERE ENION IN THE DESART   .   .   266 FOUR ZOAS 1   89
[HE SPURND ENION WITH HIS FOOT HE SPRANG ALOFT IN CLOUDS]   266 FOUR ZOAS 1   92
[WHAT HAVE I DONE SAID ENION ACCURSED WRETCH WHAT DEED]   267 FOUR ZOAS 1   109
[THAT NOUGHT BUT ENION COULD BE FOUND TO PRAISE ADORE &   267 FOUR ZOAS 1   133
  LOVE]
[ASTONISHD HE FOUND ENION HIDDEN IN THE DARKSOM CAVE]   .   .   267 FOUR ZOAS 1   136
[AND ENION DESOLATE WHERE ART THOU THARMAS O RETURN]   .   268 FOUR ZOAS 1   142
.   .   .   TILL STRENGTH FROM ENION LIKE RICHEST SUMMER [SHINES]   269 FOUR ZOAS 1   *   195
  SHINING
ENION BROODED OER THE ROCKS   .   .   .   .   269 FOUR ZOAS 1   202
THUS ENION GAVE THEM ALL HER SPECTROUS LIFE [IN DEEP   270 FOUR ZOAS 1   221
  DESPAIR]
TO ENION & HER CHILDREN & THEY PONDERD THESE THINGS   270 FOUR ZOAS 1   228
  WONDRING
WHERE ENION CRAVES SUCCESSIVE DRAWN INTO THE GOLDEN FEAST   274 FOUR ZOAS 1   373
[AND] ENION BLIND & AGE-BENT UPON THE DESOLATE WIND   276 FOUR ZOAS 1   *   444
THIS WAS THE LAMENTATION OF ENION ROUND THE GOLDEN FEAST   277 FOUR ZOAS 1   461
AND THARMAS TOOK HER IN PITYING THEN ENION IN JEALOUS FEAR   278 FOUR ZOAS 1   525
TO ENION & HIS BODY FELL THARMAS BEHELD HIM FALL   .   .   .   279 FOUR ZOAS 1   531
[?ENION XXX OF ?SLAVERY]   .   .   .   .   SUPP FOUR ZOAS 1   *
[ARISE O ENION ARISE & SMILE UPON MY HEAD]   .   .   .   .   .   SUPP FOUR ZOAS 1   *
[ARISE O ENION ARISE FOR LO I HAVE CALMD MY SEAS]   .   .   SUPP FOUR ZOAS 1   *
[TILL THEY HAD ?DRAWN THE SPECTRE QUITE AWAY FROM ENION]   SUPP FOUR ZOAS 1   *
WHENCE IS THIS VOICE OF ENION THAT SOUNDETH IN MY [EARS]   280 FOUR ZOAS 2   4
  PORCHES
WHERE ENION BLIND & AGE BENT WEPT IN DIREFUL HUNGER CRAVING   280 FOUR ZOAS 2   16
TO CONDUCT THE VOICE OF ENION TO AHANIA'S MIDNIGHT PILLOW   287 FOUR ZOAS 2   290
NOW TAKING ON AHANIA'S FORM & NOW THE FORM OF ENION   .   288 FOUR ZOAS 2   324
THUS LIVD LOS DRIVING ENION FAR INTO THE DEATHFUL INFINITE   290 FOUR ZOAS 2   383
AH HAPPY BLINDNESS [SHE] ENION SEES NOT THE TERRORS OF   290 FOUR ZOAS 2   *   385
  THE UNCERTAIN
[AND [OFT] THUS SHE] THUS ENION WAILS FROM THE DARK DEEP   290 FOUR ZOAS 2   *   386
  .   .   .
THERE SHE BEHELD THE [TERRIBLE] SPECTROUS FORM OF ENION   291 FOUR ZOAS 2   423
  IN THE VOID
WHENCE IS THIS VOICE CRYING ENION THAT SOUNDETH IN MY EARS   293 FOUR ZOAS 3   77
WHERE ART THOU ENION AH TOO NEAR TO CUNNING TOO FAR OFF   296 FOUR ZOAS 3   169
INSTEAD OF LOVE TO ENION ENION BLIND & AGE BENT   .   .   .   296 FOUR ZOAS 3   178

		PAGE	TITLE	LINE

ENION   (CONTINUED)
```
    THESE ARE THE WORDS OF ENION HEARD FROM THE COLD WAVES        296 FOUR ZOAS 3        182
      OF DESPAIR
    A LITTLE SHADOW BUT A LITTLE SHOWERY FORM OF ENION    .  .  .  296 FOUR ZOAS 3        185
    FROM MY FIERCE RAGE INTO THY SEMBLANCE ENION RETURN   .  .    297 FOUR ZOAS 3        198
    MELTING A SHOWER OF FALLING TEARS NOTHING BUT TEARS ENION     297 FOUR ZOAS 3        200
    SUBSTANCELESS VOICELESS WEEPING VANISHD NOTHING BUT TEARS     297 FOUR ZOAS 3        201
      ENION
    FOR NOW NO MORE REMAIND OF ENION IN THE DISMAL AIR   .  .  .  297 FOUR ZOAS 3        205
    WHERE ENION BLIND & AGE BENT WANDERD AHANIA WANDERS NOW       297 FOUR ZOAS 3        207
    AH ENION AH ENION AH LOVELY LOVELY ENION        .  .  .  .    297 FOUR ZOAS 4          8
    HOW IS THIS ALL MY HOPE IS GONE [ENION] FOR EVER FLED   .  .  297 FOUR ZOAS 4          9
    FLOW DOWN INTO THE SEA & SLUMBER IN OBLIVION AH ENION    .    298 FOUR ZOAS 4         23
    PERHAPS ENION MAY RESUME SOME LITTLE SEMBLANCE    .  .  .  .  298 FOUR ZOAS 4         32
    OF ENION I ISSUED INTO THE AIR DIVIDED FROM ENITHARMON   .  . 300 FOUR ZOAS 4        106
    BUT MY SWEET ENION IS VANISHD & I NEVER MORE     .  .  .  .   300 FOUR ZOAS 4        118
    OF ENION & HIM ASSIST TO BIND THE FALLEN KING    .  .  .  .   300 FOUR ZOAS 4        120
    [AND THARMAS ?SAID ALL MY HOPE I THOUGHT ENION FOR EVER      SUPP FOUR ZOAS 4      *
      GONE]
    VOID PATHLESS BEAT WITH [?ENION] SNOWS ETERNAL & IRON HAIL    318 FOUR ZOAS 6      *  271
      & RAIN
    AND I AN INFANT TERROR IN THE WOMB OF ENION     .  .  .  .  . 327 FOUR ZOAS 7        289
    HE SAID ART THOU BRIGHT ENION IS THE SHADOW OF HOPE RETURND   339 FOUR ZOAS 7B       228
    DOTH ENION AVOID THE SIGHT OF THY BLUE WATRY EYES    .  .  .  339 FOUR ZOAS 7B       230
    I WAKEND ENION IN THE MORNING & SHE TURND AWAY   .  .  .  .   339 FOUR ZOAS 7B       233
    OF ENION IN THE GARDENS & THE SHADOWS COMPASSD ME   .  .  .   339 FOUR ZOAS 7B       236
    AND CLOSD ME IN A WATRY WORLD OF WOE WHERE ENION STOOD   .  . 339 FOUR ZOAS 7B     *  237
    SHALL SEE HIM ENITHARMON & AHANIA COMBIND WITH ENION  .,  .   339 FOUR ZOAS 7B       248
    THUS CRIES AHANIA ENION REPLIES FROM THE CAVERNS OF THE       354 FOUR ZOAS 8        533
      GRAVE
    BUT AN ETERNAL CONSUMMATION IS DARK ENION    .  .  .  .  .    355 FOUR ZOAS 8        542
    THE SPECTRE QUITE AWAY FROM ENION THAT I DIE A DEATH    .  .  355 FOUR ZOAS 8        546
    SUCH ARE THE WORDS OF AHANIA & ENION LOS HEARS & WEEPS   .  . 356 FOUR ZOAS 8        584
    [THAT ENION HAD NUMBERD AWAY FROM HEAVEN]     .  .  .  .  .  SUPP FOUR ZOAS 8      *
    O ENION MY WEARY HEAD IS IN THE BED OF DEATH     .  .  .  .   370 FOUR ZOAS 9        487
    ARISE O ENION ARISE & SMILE UPON MY HEAD     .  .  .  .  .    370 FOUR ZOAS 9        491
    ARISE O ENION ARISE FOR LO I HAVE CALMD MY SEAS     .  .  .   370 FOUR ZOAS 9        494
    AND DARKNESS COVERD ALL THE DEEP THE LIGHT OF ENION FADED     370 FOUR ZOAS 9        496
    THEN VALA LIFTED UP HER HANDS TO HEAVEN TO CALL ON ENION      370 FOUR ZOAS 9        498
    THOU LITTLE BOY ART THARMAS & THOU BRIGHT GIRL ENION    .  .  370 FOUR ZOAS 9        510
    AWAKE O ENION AWAKE & LET THINE INNOCENT EYES    .  .  .  .   371 FOUR ZOAS 9        519
    O MY SWEET CHILDREN ENION LET THARMAS KISS THY CHEEK    .  .  371 FOUR ZOAS 9        525
    O BLESS THE LOVELY EYES OF THARMAS & THE EYES OF ENION        371 FOUR ZOAS 9        528
    DOTH ENION AVOID THE SIGHT OF THY BLUE HEAVENLY EYES    .  .  371 FOUR ZOAS 9        531
    WITH THY BRIGHT TEARS BECAUSE THE STEPS OF ENION ARE IN       371 FOUR ZOAS 9        533
      THE GARDENS
    ARISE SWEET BOY & LET US FOLLOW THE PATH OF ENION    .  .  .  371 FOUR ZOAS 9        534
    AND ENION SANG AMONG THE FLOWERS THAT GREW AMONG THE TREES    371 FOUR ZOAS 9        536
    AND VALA SAID GO THARMAS WEEP NOT GO TO ENION    .  .  .  .   371 FOUR ZOAS 9        537
    IN THE SUN'S HEAT TILL IN THE NIGHT ON THE COUCH OF ENION     371 FOUR ZOAS 9        541
    I DRINK NEW LIFE & FEEL THE BREATH OF SLEEPING ENION    .  .  371 FOUR ZOAS 9        542
    CHEAR UP THY COUNTENANCE BRIGHT BOY & GO TO ENION    .  .  .  371 FOUR ZOAS 9        545
    HE WENT WITH TIMID STEPS & ENION LIKE THE RUDDY MORN    .  .  371 FOUR ZOAS 9        547
    BEHIND HER VEIL WITHDRAWS SO ENION TURND HER MODEST HEAD      371 FOUR ZOAS 9        549
    BUT THARMAS SPOKE VALA SEEKS THEE SWEET ENION IN THE SHADES   371 FOUR ZOAS 9        550
    IN INFANT SORROW & JOY ALTERNATE ENION & THARMAS PLAYD   .  . 372 FOUR ZOAS 9        554
    THEY ARE THE SHADOWS OF THARMAS & OF ENION IN VALA'S WORLD    372 FOUR ZOAS 9        556
    ROSE ENION LIKE A GENTLE LIGHT & ENION SPOKE SAYING     .  .  373 FOUR ZOAS 9        594
    THEN ENION & AHANIA & VALA & THE WIFE OF DARK URTHONA   .  .  377 FOUR ZOAS 9        778
    BENEATH THE VEIL OF [?ENION] VALA ROSE THARMAS FROM DEWY      380 FOUR ZOAS AD 1  *    1
      TEARS
    THE WOMB IMPRESSD ENION FLED & HID IN VERDANT MOUNTAINS       381 FOUR ZOAS AD 3       1
    FROM ENION POURS THE SEED OF LIFE & DEATH IN ALL HER LIMBS    381 FOUR ZOAS AD 4       1
    FOR ENION BROODED GROANING LOUD THE ROUGH SEAS VEGETATE       381 FOUR ZOAS AD 5      10
      .  .  .
    .  .  .  ENION BROODED GROANING THE GOLDEN ROCKS VEGETATE     381 FOUR ZOAS AD 5  *   14
      THE (?VORTEX)]
    LAMENTS & ENION WANDERS LIKE A WEEPING INARTICULATE VOICE     501 MILTON 19           42
    AHANIA AND ENION AND VALA AND ENITHARMON LOVELY    .  .  .  . 634 JERUSALEM 14        10
    AHANIA & ENION & VALA ARE THREE EVANESCENT SHADES    .  .  .  635 JERUSALEM 14        12
    WHENCE IS THIS VOICE CRYING ENION THAT SOUNDETH IN MY EARS    654 JERUSALEM 29        59
    I SHALL BECOME AN INFANT HORROR ENION THARMAS FRIENDS    .  . 727 JERUSALEM 83         5
    FROM ENION IN THE DESARTS TERRIFIED AT EACH OTHER'S BEAUTY    732 JERUSALEM 86        63
    REPELLING WEEPING ENION BLIND & AGE-BENT INTO THE FOURFOLD    732 JERUSALEM 87         1
```
ENION'S
```
    SHE SHOULD ARISE AGAIN TO LIFE EMBALMD IN ENION'S BOSOM       278 FOUR ZOAS 1        527
    FOR ENION'S LIMBS .  .  .  .  .  .  .  .  .  .  .  .  .  .  .  318 FOUR ZOAS 6        273
    FROM ENION'S BRAIN IN THIS DEFORMED FORM LEAVING THEE THERE   327 FOUR ZOAS 7        291
    DARKEND & LOST IN DUE TIME ISSUING FORTH FROM ENION'S WOMB    327 FOUR ZOAS 7        294
    BUT THARMAS MOST REJOICD IN HOPE OF ENION'S RETURN   .  .  .  332 FOUR ZOAS 7        486
    AND HEARD ENION'S VOICE SOUND FROM THE CAVERNS OF THE GRAVE   356 FOUR ZOAS 8        605
    FROZEN IN THE WOMB OF THARMAS RUSH THE RIVERS OF ENION'S      381 FOUR ZOAS AD 4  *    2
      PAIN
```
ENITHARMON
```
    STANDS AT THE GATE OF ENITHARMON TO DEVOUR HER CHILDREN       198 AMERICA 7            4
    WHEN ENITHARMON SICK   .  .  .  .  .  .  .  .  .  .  .  .  .   232 URIZEN 19           19
    WHEN ENITHARMON GROANING   .  .  .  .  .  .  .  .  .  .  .  .  232 URIZEN 19           39
    ISSUD FROM ENITHARMON  .  .  .  .  .  .  .  .  .  .  .  .  .   232 URIZEN 19           46
    HE GAVE HIM TO ENITHARMON  .  .  .  .  .  .  .  .  .  .  .  .  233 URIZEN 20            5
    FED WITH MILK OF ENITHARMON    .  .  .  .  .  .  .  .  .  .  . 233 URIZEN 20         *   7
    O HOW ENITHARMON WEPT  .  .  .  .  .  .  .  .  .  .  .  .  .   233 URIZEN 20           22
    BUT LOS ENCIRCLED ENITHARMON   .  .  .  .  .  .  .  .  .  .  . 234 URIZEN 20           42
```

```
                                                        PAGE    TITLE        LINE
ENITHARMON   (CONTINUED)
    HER SNAKY HAIR BRANDISHING IN THE WINDS OF ENITHARMON   . .  238 EUROPE PREL 1      2
    O MOTHER ENITHARMON WILT THOU BRING FORTH OTHER SONS    . .  238 EUROPE PREL 1      4
    AH MOTHER ENITHARMON  . . . . . . . . . .               . .  238 EUROPE PREL 2      7
    THEN ENITHARMON SAW HER SONS & DAUGHTERS RISE AROUND    . .  239 EUROPE 4           5
    FIRST BORN OF ENITHARMON RISE . . . . . . . . .         . .  239 EUROPE 4          25
    THEN ENITHARMON DOWN DESCENDED INTO HIS RED LIGHT       . .  240 EUROPE 4          31
    ENITHARMON SLEPT  . . . . . . . . . .                   . .  240 EUROPE 9           1
    AND THE CLOUDS & FIRES PALE ROLLD ROUND IN THE NIGHT OF      242 EUROPE 12          1
      ENITHARMON
    ROUND ALBION'S CLIFFS & LONDON'S WALLS STILL ENITHARMON      242 EUROPE 12          2
      SLEPT
    ENITHARMON LAUGHD IN HER SLEEP TO SEE O WOMAN'S TRIUMPH      243 EUROPE 12         25
    THEN ENITHARMON WOKE NOR KNEW THAT SHE HAD SLEPT . . . .     243 EUROPE 13          9
    FOR NOW THY WATERS WARBLE ROUND THE FEET OF ENITHARMON  . .  243 EUROPE 14          5
    O ANTAMON WHY WILT THOU LEAVE THY MOTHER ENITHARMON     . .  244 EUROPE 14         16
    THEN EVERY ONE FLED TO HIS STATION & ENITHARMON WEPT    . .  244 EUROPE 14         36
    SHOT FROM THE HEIGHTS OF ENITHARMON [BEFORE THE TRUMPET      245 EUROPE 15          1
      BLEW]
    AND ENITHARMON GROANS & CRIES IN ANGUISH AND DISMAY  . . .   245 EUROPE 15          8
    THUS THE TERRIBLE RACE OF LOS & ENITHARMON GAVE  . . . . .   246 SONG OF LOS 4     13
    [THIS IS THE [DIRGE OF ENO] SONG OF ENITHARMON WHICH . . .   264 FOUR ZOAS 1    *   1
    . . .[ENITHARMON] JERUSALEM IN SILENT CONTRITION O PITY ME   264 FOUR ZOAS 1    *  27
    . . . SWEET [ENITHARMON] JERUSALEM FROM MY INMOST SOUL  . .  265 FOUR ZOAS 1    *  29
    IT IS NOT LOVE I BEAR TO ENITHARMON IT IS PITY  . . . .      265 FOUR ZOAS 1       31
    A TABERNACLE OF [DELIGHT] FOR [ENITHARMON] JERUSALEM . . .   266 FOUR ZOAS 1    *  70
    BUT LOS & ENITHARMON DELIGHTED IN THE MOONY SPACES OF [ONA]  270 FOUR ZOAS 1      232
      ENO
    THY NAME IS ENITHARMON SAID THE [BRIGHT] FIERCE PROPHETIC    271 FOUR ZOAS 1      249
      BOY
    BUT ENITHARMON ANSWERD WITH A DROPPING TEAR & [?SMILING]     271 FOUR ZOAS 1    * 252
      . . .
    WHY IS THE LIGHT OF [VALA] ENITHARMON DARKEND IN [HER]       271 FOUR ZOAS 1    * 268
      DEWY MORN
    WHY IS THE SILENCE OF [VALA LIGHTNING] ENITHARMON . . .      271 FOUR ZOAS 1    * 269
    I DIE NOT ENITHARMON [THOU] THO THOU SINGST THY SONG OF      272 FOUR ZOAS 1    * 283
      DEATH
    SO SPOKE LOS SCORN & INDIGNATION ROSE UPON ENITHARMON   . .  272 FOUR ZOAS 1      306
    THEN ENITHARMON REDDNING FIERCE STRETCHD HER IMMORTAL HANDS  272 FOUR ZOAS 1      307
    SMILE BROKE FROM URIZEN FOR ENITHARMON BRIGHTEND MORE &      273 FOUR ZOAS 1      322
      MORE
    SULLEN HE LOWERD ON ENITHARMON BUT HE SMILD ON LOS  . . .    273 FOUR ZOAS 1      323
    LOS NOW REPENTED THAT HE HAD SMITTEN ENITHARMON HE FELT      274 FOUR ZOAS 1      352
      LOVE
    AND LOS & ENITHARMON SAT IN DISCONTENT & SCORN  . . . .      274 FOUR ZOAS 1      374
    AND THIS THE SONG SUNG AT THE FEAST OF LOS & ENITHARMON      274 FOUR ZOAS 1    * 385
    AND THOU O ENITHARMON HARK I HEAR THE HAMMERS OF LOS  . .    275 FOUR ZOAS 1      421
    BURSTING FORTH FROM THE LOINS OF ENITHARMON THOU FIERCE      276 FOUR ZOAS 1      430
      TERROR
    BUT LOS & ENITHARMON SAT IN DISCONTENT & SCORN  . . . .      276 FOUR ZOAS 1      439
    ENITHARMON REMAINS A CORSE SUCH THING WAS NEVER KNOWN   . .  278 FOUR ZOAS 1      528
    THE EMANATION STOOD BEFORE THE GATES OF ENITHARMON  . . .    280 FOUR ZOAS 1      567
    SPREAD HER A COUCH UNKNOWN TO ENITHARMON HERE REPOSD   . .   280 FOUR ZOAS 1      569
    LOS JOYD & ENITHARMON LAUGHD SAYING LET US GO DOWN  . . .    285 FOUR ZOAS 2      211
    [AND LOS & ENITHARMON JOYD THEY DRANK IN TENFOLD JOY]   . .  286 FOUR ZOAS 2      236
    AND ENITHARMON JOYD PLOTTING TO REND THE SECRET CLOUD  . .   286 FOUR ZOAS 2      238
    AND LOS & ENITHARMON WERE DRAWN DOWN BY THEIR DESIRES  . .   287 FOUR ZOAS 2      287
    [NOW] FOR LOS & ENITHARMON WALKD FORTH ON THE DEWY EARTH     288 FOUR ZOAS 2      295
    ENITHARMON ANSWERD SECURE NOW FROM THE SMITINGS OF THY       288 FOUR ZOAS 2      309
      POWER . . .
    STILL DIES FOR ENITHARMON NOR A SPIRIT SPRINGS FROM MY       288 FOUR ZOAS 2      322
      DEAD CORSE
    ENITHARMON ANSWERD WHEREFORE DIDST THOU THROW THINE ARMS     288 FOUR ZOAS 2      327
      AROUND
    NIGHT PASSD & ENITHARMON EER THE DAWN RETURND IN BLISS  . .  289 FOUR ZOAS 2    * 341
    [BUT SAW NOT LOS NOR ENITHARMON FOR LUVAH HID THEM           292 FOUR ZOAS 3       47
      IN SHADOW]
    OVER THE HEAVING DELUGE HE SAW LOS & ENITHARMON EMERGE  . .  297 FOUR ZOAS 4        2
    FOR ENITHARMON SHRIEKD AMAIN CRYING O MY SWEET WORLD   . .   298 FOUR ZOAS 4       50
    BUILT BY THE ARCHITECT DIVINE WHOSE LOVE TO LOS &           298 FOUR ZOAS 4       51
      ENITHARMON
    SO SAYING IN A WAVE HE RAPD BRIGHT ENITHARMON FAR   . . .    299 FOUR ZOAS 4       56
    WHERE ENITHARMON JOIND TO HIS LEFT SIDE IN [DISMAL] GRIDING  299 FOUR ZOAS 4    *  60
      PAIN
    GO FORTH BEAR ENITHARMON BACK TO THE ETERNAL PROPHET   . .   299 FOUR ZOAS 4       70
    MAKE FIRST A RESTING PLACE FOR LOS & ENITHARMON THEN   . .   299 FOUR ZOAS 4       72
    THE SPECTRE OF URTHONA [ANSWERS] SEEING ENITHARMON WRITHD    299 FOUR ZOAS 4       76
    MY COUNTER PART & CALLD IT LOVE I NAMD HER ENITHARMON  . .   300 FOUR ZOAS 4      100
    OF ENION I ISSUED INTO THE AIR DIVIDED FROM ENITHARMON  . .  300 FOUR ZOAS 4      106
    THY LOVED ENITHARMON FOR THOU HAST HER HERE BEFORE THINE     300 FOUR ZOAS 4      117
      EYES
    BIND HIM TAKE ENITHARMON FOR THY SWEET REWARD WHILE I  . .   300 FOUR ZOAS 4      122
    DARK DREADFUL ROSE & ENITHARMON LAY AT LOS'S FEET   . . .    300 FOUR ZOAS 4      126
    BUT ENITHARMON WRAPD IN CLOUDS WAILD LOUD FOR AS LOS BEAT    302 FOUR ZOAS 4      184
    LASHD ON THE LIMBS OF ENITHARMON & THE SULPHUR FIRES   . .   302 FOUR ZOAS 4      187
    OF ENITHARMON & THE GROANS OF URIZEN FUEL FOR HIS WRATH      302 FOUR ZOAS 4      192
    HE POURD THE MOLTEN IRON ROUND THE LIMBS OF ENITHARMON  . .  302 FOUR ZOAS 4      195
    INVOLUNTARY TO LAY THE COUCH WHERE ENITHARMON LAY   . . .    305 FOUR ZOAS 4      292
    TERRIFIC PALE ENITHARMON STRETCHED ON THE [DISMAL] DREARY    305 FOUR ZOAS 5        5
      EARTH
    AND ENITHARMON SHRUNK UP ALL THEIR FIBRES WITHRING BENEATH   305 FOUR ZOAS 5        8
    RESTS ON THE DISTANT MOUNTAIN'S TOP SO LOS & ENITHARMON      305 FOUR ZOAS 5       11
```

		PAGE	TITLE	LINE
ENITHARMON	(CONTINUED)			
HE STOOD TREMBLING & ENITHARMON CLUNG AROUND HIS KNEES . .		305	FOUR ZOAS 5	18
THE NIGHT BLEW COLD AND ENITHARMON SHRIEKD ON THE DISMAL WIND		305	FOUR ZOAS 5	20
OF ENITHARMON BUT HER GROANS DROWN THE IMMORTAL HARPS . .		306	FOUR ZOAS 5	25
ROCKD TO & FRO & [&] CRIED SORE AT THE GROANS OF ENITHARMON		306	FOUR ZOAS 5	* 29
THE GROANS OF ENITHARMON SHAKE THE SKIES THE LABRING EARTH		306	FOUR ZOAS 5	36
. . . & ROUND FAINT ENITHARMON		307	FOUR ZOAS 5	66
ENITHARMON NURSD HER FIERY CHILD IN THE DARK DEEPS . .		307	FOUR ZOAS 5	70
OF ENITHARMON LOS AROUND HER BUILDED PILLARS OF IRON		307	FOUR ZOAS 5	73
ENITHARMON BEHELD THE BLOODY CHAIN OF NIGHTS & DAYS . .		307	FOUR ZOAS 5	92
HIS WOES ALOUD TO ENITHARMON SINCE HE COULD NOT HIDE . .		307	FOUR ZOAS 5	96
WHILE ENITHARMON FOLLOWD HIM WEEPING IN DISMAL WOE . . .		307	FOUR ZOAS 5	98
THE [DISMAL] ACCURSED CHAIN O HOW BRIGHT ENITHARMON HOWLD & CRIED		308	FOUR ZOAS 5	102
LOS FOLDED ENITHARMON IN A COLD WHITE CLOUD IN FEAR . . .		308	FOUR ZOAS 5	110
BUT WHEN RETURND TO GOLGONOOZA LOS & ENITHARMON		309	FOUR ZOAS 5	143
LOS TAKING ENITHARMON BY THE HAND LED HER ALONG . . .		309	FOUR ZOAS 5	150
HOWLD IN THE FURIOUS WIND HE THOUGHT TO GIVE TO ENITHARMON		309	FOUR ZOAS 5	152
ENITHARMON ON THE ROAD OF DRANTHON FELT THE INMOST GATE		309	FOUR ZOAS 5	177
OF PROPHECY & LUVAH HATH BURST HIS WAY FROM ENITHARMON . .		311	FOUR ZOAS 5	240
DARTED & DARTED HIGHER & HIGHER TO THE SHRINE OF ENITHARMON		320	FOUR ZOAS 7	22
TO BRING THE SHADOW OF ENITHARMON BENEATH OUR WONDROUS TREE		323	FOUR ZOAS 7	113
DRAW DOWN ENITHARMON TO THE SPECTRE OF URTHONA . . .		323	FOUR ZOAS 7	115
OF ENITHARMON HOW IT BUDS WITH LIFE & FORMS THE BONES . .		323	FOUR ZOAS 7	131
LOS SAT IN SHOWERS OF URIZEN'S [COLD] WATCHING COLD ENITHARMON		324	FOUR ZOAS 7	* 166
ENITHARMON LAY ON HIS KNEES URIZEN TRACD HIS VERSES . . .		324	FOUR ZOAS 7	169
DOWN TO THE ROOTS IT WEPT OVER ORC THE SHADOW OF ENITHARMON		324	FOUR ZOAS 7	171
SILENT HE STOOD OER ENITHARMON WATCHING HER PALE FACE . .		324	FOUR ZOAS 7	181
WHY CAN I NOT ENJOY THY BEAUTY LOVELY ENITHARMON		324	FOUR ZOAS 7	184
THUS LOS LAMENTED IN THE NIGHT UNHEARD BY ENITHARMON . .		325	FOUR ZOAS 7	209
FOR THE SHADOW OF ENITHARMON DESCENDED DOWN THE TREE OF MYSTERY		325	FOUR ZOAS 7	210
THE SPECTRE OF URTHONA SAW THE SHADOW OF ENITHARMON . . .		325	FOUR ZOAS 7	217
LOVELIEST DELIGHT OF MEN ENITHARMON SHADY HIDING . . .		325	FOUR ZOAS 7	222
THE SHADOW OF ENITHARMON ANSWERD ART THOU TERRIBLE SHADE		326	FOUR ZOAS 7	231
IN DARK CONFUSION MEAN TIME LOS WAS BORN & ENITHARMON . .		326	FOUR ZOAS 7	259
ASTONISHD FILLD WITH TEARS THE SPIRIT OF ENITHARMON BEHELD		327	FOUR ZOAS 7	311
BROUGHT FORTH A WONDER HORRIBLE WHILE ENITHARMON SHRIEKD		328	FOUR ZOAS 7	317
AT THE SHRIEKS OF ENITHARMON AT HER TOSSINGS		328	FOUR ZOAS 7	319
OF ENITHARMON BORE URTHONA'S SPECTRE ON ITS WINGS . . .		328	FOUR ZOAS 7	337
OBDURATE LOS FELT PITY ENITHARMON TOLD THE TALE . . .		328	FOUR ZOAS 7	338
THOU NEVER CANST EMBRACE SWEET ENITHARMON TERRIBLE DEMON TILL		328	FOUR ZOAS 7	342
MY LOVELY ENITHARMON I WILL QUELL MY FURY & TEACH . . .		329	FOUR ZOAS 7	368
SO SPOKE LOS & EMBRACING ENITHARMON & THE SPECTRE . .		329	FOUR ZOAS 7	370
BUT ENITHARMON TREMBLING FLED & HID BENEATH URIZEN'S TREE		329	FOUR ZOAS 7	372
OF URIZEN'S MYSTERIOUS TREE FOR ENITHARMON THUS SPAKE . .		329	FOUR ZOAS 7	386
BEING A MEDIUM BETWEEN HIM & ENITHARMON BUT THIS UNION .		330	FOUR ZOAS 7	398
TREMBLE NOT SO MY ENITHARMON AT THE AWFUL GATES . . .		330	FOUR ZOAS 7	412
O SPECTRE OF URTHONA TAKE COMFORT O ENITHARMON		330	FOUR ZOAS 7	417
ENITHARMON ANSWERD I BEHOLD THE LAMB OF GOD DESCENDING .		330	FOUR ZOAS 7	424
SO ENITHARMON SPOKE TREMBLING & IN TORRENTS OF TEARS . .		331	FOUR ZOAS 7	432
WHERE THE SPECTROUS DEAD WAIL & SIGHING THUS HE SPOKE TO ENITHARMON		331	FOUR ZOAS 7	435
LOVELY DELIGHT OF MEN ENITHARMON SHADY		331	FOUR ZOAS 7	436
ENITHARMON SPREAD HER BEAMING LOCKS UPON THE WIND & SAID		331	FOUR ZOAS 7	* 446
SO ENITHARMON SPOKE & LOS HIS HANDS DIVINE INSPIRED BEGAN		331	FOUR ZOAS 7	* 456
INTO THE HEAVENS OF ENITHARMON IN A MIGHTY CIRCLE . . .		332	FOUR ZOAS 7	466
AND ENITHARMON TINCTURD IT WITH BEAMS OF BLUSHING LOVE . .		332	FOUR ZOAS 7	468
SWEET ENITHARMON MILD ENTRANCD BREATHD FORTH UPON THE WIND		332	FOUR ZOAS 7	472
IN YOUTH & BEAUTY IN THE ARMS OF ENITHARMON MILD REPOSING		332	FOUR ZOAS 7	475
MORTAL & NOT AS ENITHARMON WITHOUT A COVERING VEIL . . .		332	FOUR ZOAS 7	489
LOVELY BREATHD FROM ENITHARMON HE TREMBLED WITHIN HIMSELF		332	FOUR ZOAS 7	499
OUTSTRETCHD UPON THE HILLS LAY ENITHARMON CLOUDS & TEMPESTS		334	FOUR ZOAS 7B	73
OF HIS IMMORTAL HEAD INTO THE NORTH UPON FAINT ENITHARMON		335	FOUR ZOAS 7B	77
AND ENITHARMON TREMBLING & IN FEAR UTTERD THESE WORDS . .		335	FOUR ZOAS 7B	81
SO ENITHARMON CRIED UPON HER TERRIBLE EARTHY BED . . .		335	FOUR ZOAS 7B	98
INTO THE WORLDS OF ENITHARMON LOUD THE ROARING WINDS . .		335	FOUR ZOAS 7B	107
SHALL SEE HIM ENITHARMON & AHANIA COMBIND WITH ENION . .		339	FOUR ZOAS 7B	248
AND ENITHARMON SAID I SEE THE LAMB OF GOD UPON MOUNT ZION		341	FOUR ZOAS 8	22
AND ENTER URIZEN'S TEMPLE ENITHARMON PITYING & HER HEART		341	FOUR ZOAS 8	27
THE BROKEN HEART GATE OF ENITHARMON [WHICH JOINS TO URIZEN'S TEMPLE]		341	FOUR ZOAS 8	* 29
INTO HIS HANDS THEN ENITHARMON ERECTED LOOMS IN LUBAN'S GATE		342	FOUR ZOAS 8	36
AND UPON ENITHARMON & THE DIVINE COUNTENANCE SHONE . .		342	FOUR ZOAS 8	41
ENITHARMON WOVE IN TEARS SINGING SONGS OF LAMENTATION . .		342	FOUR ZOAS 8	52
ALSO THE VEGETATED BODIES WHICH ENITHARMON WOVE . . .		342	FOUR ZOAS 8	54
TO UNDERMINE THE WORLD OF LOS & TEAR BRIGHT ENITHARMON . .		343	FOUR ZOAS 8	98
THAT ONLY THRO THE GATES OF DEATH THEY CAN ENTER TO ENITHARMON		344	FOUR ZOAS 8	110
OF ENITHARMON SINGING LULLING CADENCES ON THE WIND . . .		344	FOUR ZOAS 8	114
SOUND LOUD THE HOWLING MUSIC INSPIRD BY LOS & ENITHARMON . . .		344	FOUR ZOAS 8	121
ENITHARMON WOVE IN TEARS SINGING SONGS OF LAMENTATIONS . .		345	FOUR ZOAS 8	182
AND ENITHARMON NAMED THE FEMALE (JERUSALEM) THE HOLY . .		346	FOUR ZOAS 8	* 190
THE DAUGHTERS OF ENITHARMON WEAVE THE OVARIUM & THE INTEGUMENT		346	FOUR ZOAS 8	210
LOS SAID TO ENITHARMON PITYING I SAW		347	FOUR ZOAS 8	259

		PAGE	TITLE		LINE
ENITHARMON (CONTINUED)					
AND THESE [WERE] ARE THE SONS OF LOS & ENITHARMON RINTRAH PALAMABRON		350	FOUR ZOAS	8	357
CUT HIM OFF FROM GOLGONOOZA BUT ENITHARMON IN TEARS . . .		350	FOUR ZOAS	8	370
THAT STATE CALLD SATAN ENITHARMON BREATHD FORTH ON THE WINDS		351	FOUR ZOAS	8	383
LO ENITHARMON TERRIBLE & BEAUTIFUL IN ETERNAL YOUTH . . .		351	FOUR ZOAS	8	408
AND ENITHARMON PALE & COLD IN MILKY JUICES FLOWD . . .		353	FOUR ZOAS	8	474
INTO THE YOUTHFUL PROPHET FOR THE LOVE OF ENITHARMON . . .		353	FOUR ZOAS	8	478
AND LOS & ENITHARMON TOOK THE BODY OF THE LAMB		356	FOUR ZOAS	8	593
THAT ENITHARMON HAD NUMBERD AWAY FROM THE HEAVENS . . .		356	FOUR ZOAS	8	608
AND LOS & ENITHARMON BUILDED JERUSALEM WEEPING		357	FOUR ZOAS	9	1
THE SPECTRE OF ENITHARMON LET LOOSE ON THE TROUBLED DEEP		358	FOUR ZOAS	9	24
ALL STRENGTH TO LOS & ENITHARMON & LET LOS SELF CURSD .		362	FOUR ZOAS	9	185
DIVIDED FROM ENITHARMON NO LONGER THE SPECTRE LOS . .		379	FOUR ZOAS	9	850
ALSO THE VEGETATED BODIES WHICH ENITHARMON WOVE IN HER LOOMS		382	FOUR ZOAS AD 6		24
AT LAST ENITHARMON BROUGHT FORTH SATAN REFUSING FORM IN VAIN		483	MILTON	3	41
LOUD SOUNDS THE HAMMER OF LOS LOUD TURN THE WHEELS OF ENITHARMON		486	MILTON	6	27
LOS WEPT BUT RINTRAH ALSO CAME AND ENITHARMON ON		488	MILTON	8	14
URGING HIM TO ARISE HE WEPT ENITHARMON SAW HIS TEARS . .		488	MILTON	8	40
BUT HE CLOSD UP ENITHARMON FROM THE SIGHT OF ALL THESE THINGS		489	MILTON	9	18
THEN LOS & ENITHARMON KNEW THAT SATAN IS URIZEN		490	MILTON	10 *	1
OFT ENITHARMON ENTERD WEEPING INTO THE SPACE THERE APPEARING		490	MILTON	10	3
BUT LOS HID ENITHARMON FROM THE SIGHT OF ALL THESE THINGS		491	MILTON	11	2
SO LEUTHA SPOKE BUT WHEN SHE SAW THAT ENITHARMON HAD .		494	MILTON	13	12
THE KIND DECISION OF ENITHARMON & GAVE A TIME TO THE SPACE		494	MILTON	13	16
LOS THE VEHICULAR TERROR BEHELD HIM & DIVINE ENITHARMON		498	MILTON	17	31
IS BUILT ETERNALLY THE UNIVERSE OF LOS AND ENITHARMON .		500	MILTON	19	25
BOUND WITH THE CHAIN OF JEALOUSY BY LOS & ENITHARMON .		501	MILTON	19	38
HEARS ITS IMPATIENT PARENT BIRD AND ENITHARMON HEARD THEM		504	MILTON	21	29
THEY LEFT ME WANDERING WITH TIRZAH ENITHARMON WEPT . .		508	MILTON	24	4
LOS IS BY MORTALS NAMD TIME ENITHARMON IS NAMD SPACE .		509	MILTON	24	68
BUT ENITHARMON AND HER DAUGHTERS TAKE THE PLEASANT CHARGE		517	MILTON	29	51
ORC HOWLS ON THE ATLANTIC ENITHARMON TREMBLES ALL BEULAH WEEPS		520	MILTON	31	27
EVEN OF LOS & ENITHARMON & ALL THE SONS OF ALBION . . .		525	MILTON	35	27
BY OLOLON'S DESCENT THRO BEULAH TO LOS & ENITHARMON . .		525	MILTON	35	36
IN THIS MOMENT OLOLON DESCENDED TO LOS & ENITHARMON . .		526	MILTON	35	46
AND LOS & ENITHARMON ROSE OVER THE HILLS OF SURREY . .		534	MILTON	42	31
NOW I WILL SPEAK MY MIND WHERE IS MY LOVELY ENITHARMON .		630	JERUSALEM	10	42
WHAT SHALL I DO OR HOW EXIST DIVIDED FROM ENITHARMON .		631	JERUSALEM	12	9
AHANIA AND ENION AND VALA AND ENITHARMON LOVELY . . .		634	JERUSALEM	14	10
ENITHARMON IS A VEGETATED MORTAL WIFE OF LOS		635	JERUSALEM	14	13
SUCH ARE THE BUILDINGS OF LOS & SUCH ARE THE WOOFS OF ENITHARMON		635	JERUSALEM	14	15
I MUST COMPELL HIM TO OBEY ME WHOLLY THAT ENITHARMON MAY NOT		638	JERUSALEM	17	17
BE LOST & LEST HE SHOULD DEVOUR ENITHARMON AH ME . . .		638	JERUSALEM	17	18
PITEOUS IMAGE OF MY SOFT DESIRES & LOVES O ENITHARMON .		639	JERUSALEM	17	19
ENITHARMON VALA WOULD NEVER HAVE SOUGHT & LOVED ALBION .		639	JERUSALEM	17	24
SO LOS IN SECRET WITH HIMSELF COMMUNED & ENITHARMON HEARD		639	JERUSALEM	17	48
ENITHARMON & HIS SPECTRE IS NAMED URTHONA THEY KNEW . .		655	JERUSALEM	30	4
ENITHARMON IS MY DAUGHTER ACCURSED WITH A FATHER'S CURSE		670	JERUSALEM	42	15
IS BUILT ETERNALLY THE SUBLIME UNIVERSE OF LOS & ENITHARMON		691	JERUSALEM	59	21
BECAUSE HIS CHILDREN WERE CLOSD FROM HIM APART & ENITHARMON		696	JERUSALEM	62	37
MULTITUDINOUS IN THE LOOKING GLASS OF ENITHARMON ON ALL SIDES		697	JERUSALEM	63	21
THEREFORE THE MURDER WAS PUT APART IN THE LOOKING-GLASS OF ENITHARMON		698	JERUSALEM	63	38
I HEARD ENITHARMON SAY TO LOS LET THE DAUGHTERS OF ALBION		725	JERUSALEM	82	22
AND LET THE LOOMS OF ENITHARMON & THE FURNACES OF LOS . .		725	JERUSALEM	82	26
LOS SMILD WITH JOY THINKING ON ENITHARMON & HE BROUGHT .		730	JERUSALEM	85	3
AND ENITHARMON LIKE A FAINT RAINBOW WAVED BEFORE HIM .		732	JERUSALEM	86	50
EVEN ENITHARMON SEPARATED OUTSIDE & HIS LOINS CLOSED .		732	JERUSALEM	86	58
O LOVELY ENITHARMON I BEHOLD THY GRACEFUL FORMS		732	JERUSALEM	87	3
ENITHARMON ANSWERD NO I WILL SIEZE THY FIBRES & WEAVE .		732	JERUSALEM	87	12
ENITHARMON ANSWERD THIS IS WOMAN'S WORLD NOR NEED SHE ANY		733	JERUSALEM	88	16
ENITHARMON WHO AT HER SHINING LOOMS SINGS LULLING CADENCES		734	JERUSALEM	88	45
THE FURNACES OF LOS LOUD ROLL THE WHEELS OF ENITHARMON . .		734	JERUSALEM	88	54
SO LOS SPOKE ENITHARMON ANSWERD IN GREAT TERROR IN LAMBETH'S VALE		739	JERUSALEM	92	7
THE POET'S SONG DRAWS TO ITS PERIOD & ENITHARMON IS NO MORE		739	JERUSALEM	92	8
TO BE WHEN ALBION ARISES FROM HIS DREAD REPOSE O LOVELY ENITHARMON		739	JERUSALEM	92	14
ENITHARMON HEARD SHE RAISD HER HEAD LIKE THE MILD MOON . .		740	JERUSALEM	93	1
THEN LOS AGAIN TOOK UP HIS SPEECH AS ENITHARMON CEAST . .		741	JERUSALEM	93	17
ENITHARMON'S					
ROUND ENITHARMON'S LOINS FOLDING		232	URIZEN	19	28
COILD WITHIN ENITHARMON'S WOMB		232	URIZEN	19	29
NOW COMES THE NIGHT OF ENITHARMON'S JOY		240	EUROPE	5	1
I HEAR THE SOFT OOTHOON IN ENITHARMON'S TENTS . . .		244	EUROPE	14	21
THEY WEPT BEFORE THE INNER GATES OF ENITHARMON'S BOSOM . .		279	FOUR ZOAS	1	561
FROM ENITHARMON'S INWARD PARTS BUT THE BRIGHT FEMALE TERROR		279	FOUR ZOAS	1	564
[?THAT] BUT VALA [?MAY] SHALL BECOME A WORM IN ENITHARMON'S WOMB		292	FOUR ZOAS	3 *	20
A UNIVERSE OF DEATH & DECAY LET ENITHARMON'S HANDS . . .		298	FOUR ZOAS	4	28
AT ENITHARMON'S [SHRIEKS] SHRIEK		305	FOUR ZOAS	4 *	290

	PAGE	TITLE	LINE

ENITHARMON'S (CONTINUED)
BUT NOW THE TIMES RETURN UPON THEE ENITHARMON'S WOMB . . 307 FOUR ZOAS 5 62
AND ENITHARMON'S TEARS PREVAILD PARENTAL LOVE RETURND . . 309 FOUR ZOAS 5 146
TO MELT THE CHAIN OF JEALOUSY NOT ENITHARMON'S DEATH . 309 FOUR ZOAS 5 161
MY GOLDEN LIPS NOR TOOK THE BAR FROM ENITHARMON'S BREAST 326 FOUR ZOAS 7 238
TILL ENITHARMON'S SHADOW PREGNANT IN THE DEEPS BENEATH . 328 FOUR ZOAS 7 316
SHE BURST THE GATES OF ENITHARMON'S HEART WITH DIREFUL 328 FOUR ZOAS 7 323
   CRASH
. . . BENEATH ENITHARMON'S COUCH 328 FOUR ZOAS 7 334
IN INFANT INNOCENCE REPOSD ON ENITHARMON'S BOSOM . . . 332 FOUR ZOAS 7 477
AND ENITHARMON'S SMILES & TEARS PREVAILD OVER SELF 332 FOUR ZOAS 7 483
   PROTECTION
OF [ENITHARMON'S] THY POOR BROKEN HEART ASTONISHD . . . 341 FOUR ZOAS 8 21
FOR LOS COULD ENTER INTO ENITHARMON'S BOSOM & EXPLORE . 342 FOUR ZOAS 8 32
. . . WE BEHOLD WITH WONDER ENITHARMON'S LOOMS & LOS'S 346 FOUR ZOAS 8 200
   FORGES
ENITHARMON'S MOONY SPACE & IN IT SATAN & HIS COMPANIONS 351 FOUR ZOAS 8 395
BY ENITHARMON'S LOOMS WHEN ALBION WAS SLAIN UPON 482 MILTON 3 1
   HIS MOUNTAINS
OF ENITHARMON'S LOOM PLAY LULLING CADENCES ON THE WINDS 485 MILTON 6 6
   OF ALBION
[BY ENITHARMON'S LOOMS & SPUN BENEATH THE SPINDLE 486 MILTON 7 * 1
   OF TIRZAH]
SHE FLED TO ENITHARMON'S TENT & HID HERSELF LOUD RAGING 494 MILTON 13 14
LOS HEARD IN TERROR ENITHARMON'S WORDS IN FIBROUS STRENGTH 498 MILTON 17 34
CONTINUALLY WOVEN IN THE LOOMS OF ENITHARMON'S DAUGHTERS 512 MILTON 26 35
IN ENITHARMON'S HALLS BUILT BY LOS & HIS MIGHTY CHILDREN 638 JERUSALEM 16 60
SUBMITTING TO BE CALLD ENITHARMON'S DAUGHTERS AND BE BORN 668 JERUSALEM 40 55
FORSAKEN SURREY AND SUSSEX ARE ENITHARMON'S CHAMBER . . . 727 JERUSALEM 83 25
ENITHARMON'S NAME IS NOTHING BEFORE YOU YOU FORGET ALL 740 JERUSALEM 93 3
   MY LOVE
AND HERE IS ENITHARMON'S BOWER . . . . 817 HAPPINESS/L 34
ENJOINED
TWICE A SACRED VOW ENJOINED ME . . . . 39C SAMSON/PS PROSE
ENJOY
COME FLAMMABLE SAID GIBBLE GABBLE & LET'S ENJOY OURSELVES 58C ISLAND MOON 10 PROSE
IN SEED TIME LEARN IN HARVEST TEACH IN WINTER ENJOY . . . 150D MARRIAGE HH 7 PROSE
WHY CAN I NOT ENJOY THY BEAUTY LOVELY ENITHARMON . . . 324 FOUR ZOAS 7 184
ALL THINGS BESIDE THE WOFUL LOS ENJOY THE DELIGHTS 325 FOUR ZOAS 7 198
   OF BEAUTY
ALONE ENJOY NOT I ALONE IN MISERY SUPREME . . . . . . 361 FOUR ZOAS 9 178
AND DEADLY CUNNING & MEAN ABJECTNESS ONLY SHALL ENJOY THEM 734 JERUSALEM 88 38
FAMILY ENJOY HEALTH MY MUCH TERRIFIED WIFE JOINS ME IN LOVE 829A LETTER 28 PROSE
WISH THAT YOU MAY LONG ENJOY YOUR BEAUTIFUL RETIREMENT . 847C LETTER 44 PROSE
STRENGTH I NOW ENJOY SUDDENLY ON THE DAY AFTER VISITING 852A LETTER 50 PROSE
ENJOYD
THAT BARDS OF OLD ENJOYD IN YOU . . . . 11 TO MUSES/PS 14
[HE] ENJOYD THE [(DAME)] LADY . . . . 163 ASKED THIEF/N * 12
ENJOYD THE LADY . . . . 261 ASKED THIEF 12
ENJOYED
NOR MATCHLESS MIGHT NOR WISDOM NOR EVERY GIFT ENJOYED . 39B SAMSON/PS PROSE
WITH THE LIGHT I ENJOYED IN MY YOUTH AND WHICH HAS FOR . 852B LETTER 50 PROSE
ENJOYING   SEE SELF ENJOYING
CRAVING THE MORE THE MORE ENJOYING DRAWING OUT SWEET BLISS 276 FOUR ZOAS 1 440
TO CONVEY THEM SAFE HE IS NOW I SUPPOSE ENJOYING THE . . 850C LETTER 49 PROSE
ENJOYINGS   SEE SELF ENJOYINGS
ENJOYMENT
THIS WILL COME TO PASS BY AN IMPROVEMENT OF SENSUAL 154C MARRIAGE HH 14 PROSE
   ENJOYMENT
AND THUS HER VOICE GLORY DELIGHT & SWEET ENJOYMENT BORN 381 FOUR ZOAS AD 5 11
THAT ENJOYMENT & NOT ABSTINENCE IS THE FOOD OF INTELLECT 790D LETTER 2 PROSE
ENJOYMENTS
DELIGHTED WITH THE ENJOYMENTS OF GENIUS . . . . . . 150C MARRIAGE HH 6 PROSE
ENLABYRINTHS
HER BRAIN ENLABYRINTHS THE WHOLE HEAVEN OF HER BOSOM & 709 JERUSALEM 70 29
   LOINS
ENLARGD
ENLARGD INTO DIMENSION & DEFORMD INTO INDEFINITE SPACE 498 MILTON 17 23
IN CHASMS & ABYSSES OF SORROW ENLARGD WITHOUT DIMENSION 623 JERUSALEM 5 5
   TERRIBLE
ENLARGE
TILL GLORY FIRES HIS BREAST TO ENLARGE HIS CASTLE . . . 26 EDW THIRD/PS 3 201
LOOK UP LOOK UP O CITIZEN OF LONDON ENLARGE THY 159C SONG LIBERTY PROSE
   COUNTENANCE
THEY CRY O SPIDER SPREAD THY WEB ENLARGE THY BONES & FILLD 275 FOUR ZOAS 1 404
ENLARGED
IN THAT ENLARGED BREAST OF HIS THAT ALL . . . . 25 EDW THIRD/PS 3 187
AND WHATEVER THEIR ENLARGED & NUMEROUS SENSES COULD 153A MARRIAGE HH 11 PROSE
   PERCIEVE
ON AN ENLARGED SCALE TO ORNAMENT THE ALTARS OF CHURCHES 584B DESC CAT 14 PROSE
EXTENDED & ENLARGED TO TAKE IN ORIGINALS BOTH OF PAINTING & 797D LETTER 10 PROSE
EVER BUILD A PALACE IT WOULD BE ONLY MY COTTAGE ENLARGED 803B LETTER 15 PROSE
WHAT IT WAS ONLY ENLARGED AND CONFIRMD . . . . 816A LETTER 23 PROSE
CORRECT & ENLARGED COPIES FROM ANTIQUE GEMS OF WHICH THE 836B LETTER 35 PROSE
ENLARGING
ENLARGING AND ENLARGING TILL THEIR DISKS APPROACHD EACH 504 MILTON 21 39
   OTHER
OF MAGNIFICENCE ONLY ENLARGING NOT ALTERING ITS PROPORTIONS 801D LETTER 14 PROSE
ENLIGHT
LET RAYS OF TRUTH ENLIGHT HIS SLEEPING BRAIN . . . . . 14 IMIT SPEN/PS 9
ENLIGHTEN
WHILE THUS THE SPIRITS OF STRONGEST WING ENLIGHTEN THE 284 FOUR ZOAS 2 156
   DARK DEEP

```
                                                             PAGE      TITLE       LINE
ENLIGHTEN   (CONTINUED)
    ARISING IN HIS PRIDE ENLIGHTEN ALL THE GRIZLY DEEPS  . . .  352 FOUR ZOAS 8      440
    ENLIGHTEN ALL THE CRYSTAL HOUSE OF VALA AWAKE AWAKE  . . .  371 FOUR ZOAS 9      520
ENLIGHTENED
    TRUCHSESSIAN GALLERY OF PICTURES I WAS AGAIN ENLIGHTENED    852B LETTER 50      PROSE
ENLUME
    TO COMFORT ORC IN HIS DIRE SUFFERINGS LOOK MY FIRES ENLUME  331 FOUR ZOAS 7      444
        AFRESH
ENMITIES
    & TO ITS LAWS OF GOOD & EVIL & ITS ENMITIES AGAINST MIND    784D ANNO WW EXCUR   MARG
ENMITY
    ("BLUNDERER'S FRIENDSHIP THAN CALUMNIATOR'S ENMITY") I       69C ANNO LAVATER    MARG
        DOUBT THIS
    TO THE HARD ROCK OR THOU SHOULDST FEEL MY ENMITY & HATE     322 FOUR ZOAS 7       88
    CRUEL AND RAVENING WITH ENMITY & HATRED & WAR . . . . .  328 FOUR ZOAS 7      330
    IN ENMITY & WAR FIRST WEAKEND THEN IN STERN REPENTANCE . .  366 FOUR ZOAS 9      370
    SHALL FEEL THE SPIDER'S ENMITY . . . . . . . . . .  431 AUGURIES            34
    AND SUCH IS HIS ENMITY                                  458A ANNO REYNOLDS    MARG
    WERE LEAGUED TOGETHER AGAINST SATAN THRO ANCIENT ENMITY     487 MILTON 7         40
    VENETIAN AND FLEMISH DEMONS WHOSE ENMITY TO THE PAINTER     582C DESC CAT 9     PROSE
        HIMSELF
    HALF FRIENDSHIP IS THE BITTEREST ENMITY SAID LOS . . . .  620 JERUSALEM 1        8
    ABSTRACT PHILOSOPHY WARRING IN ENMITY AGAINST IMAGINATION   624 JERUSALEM 5       58
    THE UNFORGIVING PORCHES THE TABLES OF ENMITY AND BEDS  .  640 JERUSALEM 18       23
    AT ENMITY WITH THE MERCIFUL & FILLD WITH DEVOURING FIRE     667 JERUSALEM 40      33
    TO HIM WHOM HE HAS MURDERD BOUND IN VENGEANCE & ENMITY  .  677 JERUSALEM 47       16
    AT ENMITY AGAINST ALL TRUE POETRY OR INSPIRATION . . .  782D ANNO WW POEMS    MARG
    THE NATURAL MAN IS AT ENMITY WITH GOD . . . . . .  782D ANNO WW POEMS    MARG
    GOVERNMENT WAS SPOKEN BY EITHER HIM OR ME HIS ENMITY  . 826D LETTER 28       PROSE
ENO
    ENO AGED MOTHER . . . . . . . . . . . . . .  255 BOOK OF LOS 3        1
    [THIS IS THE [DIRGE OF ENO] SONG OF ENITHARMON WHICH . . .  264 FOUR ZOAS 1    *    1
    THEN [?ONA] ENO A DAUGHTER OF BEULAH TOOK A MOMENT OF TIME  270 FOUR ZOAS 1    *  222
    BUT LOS & ENITHARMON DELIGHTED IN THE MOONY SPACES OF [ONA] 270 FOUR ZOAS 1       232
        ENO
ENOCH
    ADAM SETH ENOS CAINAN MAHALALEEL JARED ENOCH . . . . .  528 MILTON 37          36
    FROM ENOCH TO ADAM SCHOFIELD IS ADAM WHO WAS NEW-CREATED    625 JERUSALEM 7        25
        . . .
    ADAM SETH ENOS CAINAN MAHALALEEL JARED ENOCH . . . . .  716 JERUSALEM 75        11
    THE YOUNG & VERY AMIABLE MRS ENOCH WHO GAVE MY WIFE . . .  833D LETTER 33       PROSE
    RECORDING ANGELS PROTECTING ANGEL NOAH ENOCH . . . .  SUPP INSC HERVEY    *TITLE
ENORMITIES
    BY CRUEL ENORMITIES FORMS . . . . . . . . . .  234 URIZEN 20          50
    AND HIS WORLD TEEMD VAST ENORMITIES . . . . . . .  234 URIZEN 23           2
    AND THAT TOWARD ULRO FORMS OF WAR SEVEN ENORMITIES . .  633 JERUSALEM 13       18
ENORMITY
    FROM THE ENORMITY & CALLD THEM LUVAH & VALA TURNING DOWN    326 FOUR ZOAS 7      248
    THE HEADS OF THE GREAT POLYPUS FOUR-FOLD TWELVE ENORMITY    529 MILTON 38          2
ENORMOUS
    ARE HEARD FROM THE HILLS THE ENORMOUS SONS . . . . .   32 EDW THIRD/PS 6      20
    DISCHARGING THEIR ENORMOUS VOICES AT THE FATHER'S CURSE     106 TIRIEL 5          15
    THE ENORMOUS DEAD LIFT UP THEIR PALE FIRES . . . . . .  148 FRENCH REVOLTN     302
    THAT PINES FOR MAN SHALL AWAKEN HER WOMB TO ENORMOUS JOYS   194 V DAU ALBION 7      4
    HEAVES IN ENORMOUS CIRCLES NOW THE TIMES ARE RETURND UPON   199 AMERICA 9          19
        THEE
    HID IN HIS CAVES THE BARD OF ALBION FELT THE ENORMOUS       202 AMERICA 15         16
        PLAGUES
    IN ENORMOUS LABOURS OCCUPIED . . . . . . . . .  223 URIZEN 3           22
    AND ENORMOUS FORMS OF ENERGY . . . . . . . . .  225 URIZEN 4           48
    AND SHE BORE AN ENORMOUS RACE . . . . . . . . .  234 URIZEN 20          45
    NAMD NEWTON HE SIEZD THE TRUMP & BLOWD THE ENORMOUS BLAST   243 EUROPE 13           5
    THAT NATURE FELT THRO ALL HER PORES THE ENORMOUS REVELRY    244 EUROPE 14          34
    WENT ENORMOUS ABOVE THE RED FLAMES . . . . . . .  248 SONG OF LOS 7      11
    OF THESE AN ENORMOUS DREAD SERPENT . . . . . . .  250 AHANIA 3           13
    HE BENT THE ENORMOUS RIBS SLOWLY . . . . . . . .  251 AHANIA 3           31
    BEATEN ALONG ITS SIGHTLESS WAY GROWING ENORMOUS IN ITS      269 FOUR ZOAS 1      194
        MOTION TO
    CAVERNOUS DWELLERS FILLD THE ENORMOUS REVELRY RESPONSING    274 FOUR ZOAS 1      383
    THE ENORMOUS BRIDE & BRIDEGROOM SAT BESIDE THEM URIZEN  .  276 FOUR ZOAS 1      436
    DELUDED BY [THE] SUMMER'S HEAT THEY SPORT IN ENORMOUS LOVE  276 FOUR ZOAS 1      452
    THE ENORMOUS WARP & WOOF RAGE DIREFUL IN THE AFFRIGHTED     284 FOUR ZOAS 2      149
        DEEP
    THE PASSIVE IDLE SLEEP THE ENORMOUS NIGHT & DARKNESS OF     295 FOUR ZOAS 3      115
        DEATH
    OF URIZEN ENORMOUS WORK HE BUILDED THEM ANEW . . . .  301 FOUR ZOAS 4      166
    THE ENORMOUS DEMONS WOKE & HOWLD AROUND THE [YOUTHFUL]      306 FOUR ZOAS 5       41
        NEW BORN KING
    LET LOOSE THE ENORMOUS SPIRIT IN THE DARKNESS OF THE DEEP   306 FOUR ZOAS 5    *   59
    AT HIS ENORMOUS CALL THEY FLEE INTO THE HEAVENS OF HEAVENS  308 FOUR ZOAS 5      118
    THE ENORMOUS WONDERS OF THE ABYSSES ONCE HIS BRIGHTEST JOY  314 FOUR ZOAS 6       86
    MANY IN SERPENTS & IN WORMS STRETCHD OUT ENORMOUS LENGTH    314 FOUR ZOAS 6    *  117
    I DWELL IN DIM OBLIVION BROODING OVER ME THE ENORMOUS       317 FOUR ZOAS 6      223
        WORLDS
    BETWEEN THE ENORMOUS IRON WALLS BUILT BY THE SPECTRE DARK   319 FOUR ZOAS 6      295
    WHILE IN HIS TURN GAVE TASKS TO LOS ENORMOUS TO DESTROY  .  322 FOUR ZOAS 7      105
        ABOVE
    HE IN HIS TURN GAVE TASKS TO LOS ENORMOUS TO DESTROY  .  329 FOUR ZOAS 7      375
    ENORMOUS WORKS LOS CONTEMPLATED INSPIRD BY THE HOLY SPIRIT  343 FOUR ZOAS 8      108
    THE ENORMOUS SCIENCES OF URIZEN AGES AFTER AGES EXPLORING   344 FOUR ZOAS 8      144
    IN MOTHER'S TENDERNESS THE ENORMOUS WORLDS ROLLING         351 FOUR ZOAS 8      386
        IN URIZEN'S POWER
```

		PAGE	TITLE	LINE

ENORMOUS   (CONTINUED)
    AND NOW HE BEATS THE HEAVY AIR WITH HIS ENORMOUS WINGS . .   354 FOUR ZOAS 8   526
    FOLDING LIKE SCROLLS OF THE ENORMOUS VOLUME OF HEAVEN &   357 FOUR ZOAS 9   14
       EARTH
    TOLD OF THE ENORMOUS CONFLICT EARTHQUAKE BENEATH AROUND   500 MILTON 18   48
    THE ENORMOUS STRIFE ONE GIVING LIFE THE OTHER GIVING DEATH   501 MILTON 19   29
    TURNING UPON THE WHEELS OF ALBION'S SONS WITH ENORMOUS   632 JERUSALEM 12   65
       POWER
    LET LOOSE THE ENORMOUS SPECTRE ON THE DARKNESS OF THE DEEP   667 JERUSALEM 40   32
    A NETHER-WORLD MUST HAVE RECIEVD THE FOUL ENORMOUS SPIRIT   667 JERUSALEM 40   34
    ENVYING STOOD THE ENORMOUS FORM AT VARIANCE WITH ITSELF   707 JERUSALEM 69   6
    ON THEIR ENORMOUS ALTARS BUILT IN THE TERRIBLE NORTH . .   727 JERUSALEM 83   20
    FOUND YE LONDON ENORMOUS CITY WEEPS THY RIVER . . . . .   727 JERUSALEM 83   23
    AND BEHEMOTH THE WAR BY SEA ENORMOUS & THE WAR . . . .   738 JERUSALEM 91   40
ENOS
    ADAM SETH ENOS CAINAN MAHALALEEL JARED ENOCH   528 MILTON 37   36
    ADAM SETH ENOS CAINAN MAHALALEEL JARED ENOCH . . . . .   716 JERUSALEM 75   11
ENOUGH
    THE MERCHANTS ARE RICH ENOUGH . . . .   20 EDW THIRD/PS 2   70
    BURND OUT HE ANSWERD HE WAS PIG ENOUGH . . . .   25 EDW THIRD/PS 3   159
    HM SAID THE LAWGIVER FUNNY ENOUGH . . . .   62B ISLAND MOON 11   PROSE
    THOU HAST THE FORM OF TIRIEL BUT I KNOW THEE WELL ENOUGH   103 TIRIEL 4   7
    IS WEAK ENOUGH TO BE RESTRAINED . . . .   149D MARRIAGE HH 5   PROSE
    YOU NEVER KNOW WHAT IS ENOUGH . . . .   152A MARRIAGE HH 9   PROSE
    UNLESS YOU KNOW WHAT IS MORE THAN ENOUGH . . . . . .   152A MARRIAGE HH 9   PROSE
    ENOUGH OR TOO MUCH . . . .   152D MARRIAGE HH 10   PROSE
    HERE HE HAD TIME ENOUGH TO REPENT OF HIS RASHLY THREATEND   315 FOUR ZOAS 6   141
       CURSE
    AND WHEN HIS CHILDREN SICKEN LET THEM DIE THERE ARE ENOUGH   323 FOUR ZOAS 7   120
    OFTEN ENOUGH TO CONVINCE THY JEALOUSY & FEAR & TERROR . .   330 FOUR ZOAS 7   421
    WEAK MAN MAY BE VIRTUOUS ENOUGH BUT WILL NEVER BE AN ARTIST   454B ANNO REYNOLDS   MARG
    WELL SAID ENOUGH . . . .   464D ANNO REYNOLDS   MARG
    OIL WILL NOT DRINK OR ABSORB COLOUR ENOUGH TO STAND THE   561A EXHIBITION ADV   PROSE
       TEST
    OIL WILL NOT DRINK OR ABSORB COLOUR ENOUGH TO STAND THE   565A DESC CAT 2   PROSE
       TEST
    HE IS A COMPLETE ROGUE WITH CONSTITUTIONAL GAIETY ENOUGH   568D DESC CAT 3   PROSE
    THIS MAKES A GOOD EPIGRAM ENOUGH . . . .   575C DESC CAT 3   PROSE
    I HAVE BEEN SCORNED LONG ENOUGH BY THESE FELLOWS . . .   575D DESC CAT 3   PROSE
    PAY THEIR JOURNEYMEN LITTLE ENOUGH BUT THOUGH . . . .   583B DESC CAT 9   PROSE
    OPEN PROFESSIONS OF FRIENDSHIP ARE COMMON ENOUGH . .   592C PUB ADDRESS/N   PROSE
    I DO NOT KNOW AS HE WENT FAR ENOUGH OFF TO PUBLISH THEM   592D PUB ADDRESS/N   PROSE
    THESE PEOPLE KNOW ENOUGH OF ARTIFICE BUT NOTHING OF ART   596A PUB ADDRESS/N   PROSE
    I HAVE ENOUGH IN THE APPROBATION OF FELLOW LABOURERS .   600C PUB ADDRESS/N   PROSE
    TILL THEY HAVE HAD PUNISHMENT ENOUGH TO MAKE THEM COMMIT   707 JERUSALEM 69   27
       CRIMES
    TO CONSIDER THIS TO ALL ETERNITY WILL BE COMMENT ENOUGH   787A ANNO THORNTON   MARG
    THE PLATE MUST BE WARM ENOUGH TO MELT THE WAX . . . .   790C LETTER 2   PROSE
    WILL SOON BE WELL ENOUGH TO MAKE HUNDREDS OF DESIGNS .   796B LETTER 7   PROSE
    YOU FOR AT PRESENT BECAUSE I HAVE ENOUGH TO SERVE   811D LETTER 22   PROSE
       MY PRESENT
    INTO THE COUNTRY WHICH IS TO ME CONSOLATION ENOUGH . . .   812A LETTER 22   PROSE
    OR IF YOU WOULD RATHER CRY OUT ENOUGH OFF OFF . . . .   816C LETTER 24   PROSE
    MY ONLY DIFFICULTY IS TO PRODUCE FAST ENOUGH . . . .   821D LETTER 25   PROSE
    MR HAYLEY WAS KIND ENOUGH TO COME FORWARDS . . . . .   828A LETTER 28   PROSE
    I ONLY SUGGEST WHAT I KNOW YOU WILL BE KIND ENOUGH   828B LETTER 28   PROSE
       TO EXCUSE
    IF IT IS POSSIBLE YOU WILL BE KIND ENOUGH TO DO IN THIS   828B LETTER 28   PROSE
       MATTER
    BECAUSE I HAD NOT ENOUGH PAPER IN PROPER ORDER FOR PRINTING   839B LETTER 38   PROSE
    FIFTEEN OF EACH BUT I HAD NOT PAPER ENOUGH IN PROPER ORDER   840D LETTER 40   PROSE
    HE HAS ENOUGH & TO SPARE & THE WORLD WILL KNOW HIS AT ONCE   853A LETTER 51   *PROSE
       &
    FOR O HAPPINESS NEVER ENOUGH TO BE GRATEFUL FOR . . .   853A LETTER 51   *PROSE
    WHICH IS OMITTED IN THE NEW EDITION TIME ENOUGH TO SAVE   861A LETTER 58   PROSE
    THE WAY IN WHICH I DISCOVERED THIS MISTAKE IS ODD ENOUGH   861B LETTER 58   PROSE
    THE HONOUR TO ENQUIRE AFTER UNPROFITABLE ENOUGH TO ME THO   867A LETTER 66   PROSE
    ENOUGH TO GO ON WITH MY WORK BUT NOT WELL ENOUGH TO . .   871D LETTER 74   PROSE
    PLEASE TO LET ME KNOW BUT FINDING MYSELF WELL ENOUGH TO   875B LETTER 81   PROSE
       COME
    ENOUGH ASHAMD OF & HOPE TO MEND . . . .   875D LETTER 82   PROSE
ENQUIRD
    AND IT WAS ENQUIRD WHY IN A GREAT SOLEMN ASSEMBLY . .   491 MILTON 11   15
    I HAVE SEEN MR SAUNDERS & ENQUIRD OF HIM WHETHER HE HAS ANY   832C LETTER 32   PROSE
ENQUIRE   SEE INQUIRE
    ENQUIRE NOT AFTER IT SEEING IT IS A SECRET . . . . .   40C SAMSON/PS   PROSE
    ENQUIRE OF MY SONS & THEY SHALL TEACH THEE HOW TO WAR .   322 FOUR ZOAS 7   91
    ENQUIRE OF MY DAUGHTERS WHO ACCURSD IN THE DARK DEPTHS . .   322 FOUR ZOAS 7   92
    THEY ENQUIRE AFTER JERUSALEM IN THE REGIONS OF THE DEAD   671 JERUSALEM 42   68
    AS TO ENQUIRE FOR I NEVER OBTRUDE SUCH THINGS ON OTHERS   813A LETTER 22   PROSE
    BUT YOU WILL JUSTLY ENQUIRE WHY I HAVE NOT WRITTEN ALL THIS   815C LETTER 23   PROSE
    OF SOON SEEING YOU AGAIN I OFTEN OMIT TO ENQUIRE OF YOU   816A LETTER 23   PROSE
    WITH SR ALLAN CHAMBRE RECOMMENDS ME TO ENQUIRE CONCERNING   834D LETTER 34   PROSE
    MY DESIRE IS THAT YOU WOULD ENQUIRE INTO THIS AFFAIR & .   865B LETTER 62   PROSE
    THE HONOUR TO ENQUIRE AFTER UNPROFITABLE ENOUGH TO ME THO   867A LETTER 66   PROSE
ENQUIRED
    IS TO BE ENQUIRED IN ANOTHER WORK ON PAINTING . . . . .   565B DESC CAT 2   PROSE
    HORRID TO THINK OF WHEN ENQUIRED DEEPLY INTO AND ALL . .   652 JERUSALEM 28   8
ENQUIRER
    A RAGING WHIRLPOOL DRAWS THE DIZZY ENQUIRER TO HIS GRAVE   242 EUROPE 10   31
    MODEST ENQUIRER INTO THE TRUTH OF A SELF EVIDENT THING   386C ANNO WATSON   MARG
       IS A KNAVE

```
ENQUIRER    (CONTINUED)
    & MAY PRETEND TO BE A MODEST ENQUIRER BUT HE IS A KNAVE      386C ANNO WATSON      MARG
ENQUIRERS
    THAT PAINE DOES [IS] ARE NO [MODEST ENQUIRERS] EXAMINERS     386B ANNO WATSON    * MARG
    AS TO [MODEST ENQUIRERS] EXAMINERS IN THESE POINTS THEY      386C ANNO WATSON    * MARG
ENQUIRES
    ONE PLANET [CRIES] CALLS TO ANOTHER & ONE STAR ENQUIRES      364 FOUR ZOAS 9    *  261
        OF ANOTHER
ENQUIRIES
    AN ABUNDANCE OF ENQUIRIES TO NO PURPOSE SAT HIMSELF DOWN     44B ISLAND MOON 1    PROSE
ENQUIRING
    TO HAVE BEEN DESIROUS OF ENQUIRING INTO THE WORKS OF NATURE  45B ISLAND MOON 1    PROSE
    DENS OF DESPAIR IN THE HOUSE OF BREAD ENQUIRING IN VAIN      657 JERUSALEM 31       26
    ENQUIRING FOR JERUSALEM HE LED THEM UP MY STEPS TO MY ALTAR  721 JERUSALEM 79       52
ENQUIRY      SEE INQUIRY
    THE ENQUIRY IN ENGLAND IS NOT WHETHER A MAN HAS TALENTS      452D ANNO REYNOLDS   MARG
    ARRANGED IS AN ENQUIRY WORTHY OF BOTH THE ANTIQUARIAN   . .  578D DESC CAT 5     *PROSE
    EVERY ENQUIRY OF HIM IF YOU THINK BEST MR SANDERS HAS   . .  834C LETTER 34       PROSE
ENRAGD
    [THE STERN BARD CEASD ASHAMD OF HIS OWN SONG ENRAGD HE       196 AMERICA PREL 2     18
        SWUNG]
    ALBION IS SICK AMERICA FAINTS ENRAGD THE ZENITH GREW    . .  197 AMERICA 4          4
    OF ALBION'S ANGEL WHO ENRAGD HIS SECRET CLOUDS OPEND    . .  201 AMERICA 13        10
    ENRAGD IN THE DESOLATE DARKNESS                              253 AHANIA 4          28
    HIS HORSES ARE MAD HIS HARROW CONFOUNDED HIS COMPANIONS      488 MILTON 8          18
        ENRAGD
ENRAGE
    THAT WOULD ENRAGE THEE AS IT HAS ENRAGED ME EVEN  . . . .    300 FOUR ZOAS 4      115
ENRAGED
    ENRAGED & STIFLED WITH TORMENT                               229 URIZEN 13         12
    THAT WOULD ENRAGE THEE AS IT HAS ENRAGED ME EVEN  . . . .    300 FOUR ZOAS 4      115
    ENRAGED & STIFLED WITH TORMENT HE THREW HIS RIGHT ARM TO     303 FOUR ZOAS 4      243
        THE NORTH
    A KING OF WRATH & FURY A DARK ENRAGED HORROR  . . . . .      353 FOUR ZOAS 8      462
    ENRAGED & STIFLED WITHOUT & WITHIN IN TERROR & WOE HE THREW  483 MILTON 3          24
        HIS
    OPAKE AND LIKE THE BLACK PEBBLE ON THE ENRAGED BEACH   . .   515 MILTON 28         35
    OF ENRAGED THUNDERS AROUND THEM THE STARRY WHEELS OF THEIR   741 JERUSALEM 94      11
        GIANT SONS
ENRAPTURD
    TO WANDER IN SWEET SOLITUDE ENRAPTURD AT EVERY WIND  . . .   381 FOUR ZOAS AD 5    13
    ENRAPTURD WITH AFFECTION SWEET AND MILD BENEVOLENCE  . . .   518 MILTON 30          7
ENRAPTURED
    IF THE GOD ENRAPTURED ME INFOLDS . . . . . . . .            288 FOUR ZOAS 2     *  310
ENRICH
    TO ENRICH THE LEAN EARTH THAT CRAVES . . . . . . . .        138 FRENCH REVOLTN     99
ENRICHED
    IF ITALY IS ENRICHED AND MADE GREAT BY RAPHAEL    . . . .   561C EXHIBITION ADV  PROSE
ENROBES
    AT THY WORD & AT THY LOOK DEATH ENROBES ME ABOUT  . . . .   660 JERUSALEM 34        5
ENROLLING
    WHAT IS ENROLLING BUT PREDESTINATION . . . . . . . .        131D ANNO SWED PROV   MARG
ENROOT
    WHERE THE IMPRESSIONS OF DESPAIR & HOPE ENROOT FOREVER  . .  295 FOUR ZOAS 3       143
    THE OAK FROWNS TERRIBLE THE BEECH & ASH & ELM ENROOT    . .  636 JERUSALEM 16        4
ENROOTED
    ENROOTED INTO EVERY NATION A MIGHTY POLYPUS GROWING  . . .   635 JERUSALEM 15        4
ENROOTING
    ENROOTING ITSELF ALL AROUND . . . . . . . . . .            252 AHANIA 4            3
    THEY BENT DOWN THEY FELT THE EARTH AND AGAIN ENROOTING  . .  653 JERUSALEM 28       18
    HAND ART THOU NOT REUBEN ENROOTING THYSELF INTO BASHAN  . .  661 JERUSALEM 34       36
ENROOTS
    WHILE REUBEN ENROOTS HIS BRETHREN IN THE NARROW CANAANITE    636 JERUSALEM 15       25
ENSIGNS
    THEIR HEADS ON SNOWY HILLS THEIR ENSIGNS SICKNING IN THE     202 AMERICA 15         10
        SKY
ENSLAVD      SEE INSLAVD
    WAS IT NOT YOU ENSLAVD THE SONS OF ZAZEL & THEY HAVE CURSD   100 TIRIEL 1           41
    ENSLAVD THE VULGAR BY ATTEMPTING TO REALIZE OR ABSTRACT THE  153A MARRIAGE HH 11  PROSE
    ENSLAVD THE DAUGHTERS OF ALBION WEEP A TREMBLING             189 V DAU ALBION 1      1
        LAMENTATION
    ENSLAVD HUMANITY PUT ON HE BECAME WHAT HE BEHELD  . . . .    302 FOUR ZOAS 4       203
    ENSLAVD HUMANITY PUT ON HE BECAME WHAT HE BEHELD  . . . .    305 FOUR ZOAS 4       286
    BESIDE LOS IN THE CAVERN DARK ENSLAVD TO VEGETATIVE FORMS    326 FOUR ZOAS 7       262
    FOR WAR IS [HONEST] [AN] ENERGY ENSLAVD BUT THY RELIGION     361 FOUR ZOAS 9     *  152
    I MUST CREATE A SYSTEM OR BE ENSLAVD BY ANOTHER MAN'S   . .  629 JERUSALEM 10       20
ENSLAVE
    TO BIND THE FATHER & ENSLAVE THE BRETHREN NOUGHT HE KNEW     326 FOUR ZOAS 7       256
    BY WHICH THE PRINCES OF THE DEAD ENSLAVE THEIR VOTARIES      686 JERUSALEM 55       12
ENSLAVED
    MINGLES WITH HIS VICTIM'S SPECTRE ENSLAVED AND TORMENTED     677 JERUSALEM 47       15
ENT
    ONLY ENT SO GOOD NATURD . . . . . . . . . . .             29C EDW THIRD/PS 4    PROSE
ENTANGLED
    AND WIELDING KNOTTY CLUBS LIKE OAKS ENTANGLED . . . . .      32 EDW THIRD/PS 6      23
ENTER
    WHENEER I ENTER MORE THAN MORTAL FIRE   . . . . . .         10 FRESH FROM/PS       19
    ENTER SIR JOHN CHANDOS . . . . . . . . . . .             22C EDW THIRD/PS 3    PROSE
    ENTER KING EDWARD AND BLACK PRINCE . . . . . . .           23A EDW THIRD/PS 3    PROSE
    ENTER PETER BLUNT . . . . . . . . . . . .               29B EDW THIRD/PS 4    PROSE
    SIR THOMAS DAGWORTH TO HIM ENTER SIR WALTER MANNY  . . .    30A EDW THIRD/PS 5    PROSE
    WILT THOU O QUEEN ENTER MY HOUSE TIS GIVEN THEE TO ENTER     130 BOOK OF THEL 5     16
```

ENTER   (CONTINUED)
AND TO RETURN FEAR NOTHING ENTER WITH THY VIRGIN FEET   . . 130 BOOK OF THEL 5   17
. . . ENTER INTO THE INFINITE LABYRINTH OF ANOTHER'S BRAIN 142 FRENCH REVOLTN   190
THAT NONE DID DARE TO ENTER IN . . . . 163 I SAW CHAPEL/N   2
LEST LOS SHOULD ENTER INTO BEULAH THRO HER BEAUTIFUL GATES 279 FOUR ZOAS 1   566
O I AM NOTHING WHEN I ENTER INTO JUDGMENT WITH THEE   . . . 293 FOUR ZOAS 3   60
AND ENTER URIZEN'S TEMPLE ENITHARMON PITYING & HER HEART   341 FOUR ZOAS 8   27
FOR LOS COULD ENTER INTO ENITHARMON'S BOSOM & EXPLORE   . 342 FOUR ZOAS 8   32
THAT ONLY THRO THE GATES OF DEATH THEY CAN ENTER   344 FOUR ZOAS 8   110
   TO ENITHARMON
BEGAN TO ENTER THE HOLY CITY ENTRING THE DISMAL CLOUDS   . 359 FOUR ZOAS 9   84
STILL TO THE ROCK IN VAIN THEY STROVE TO ENTER THE   364 FOUR ZOAS 9   289
   CONSUMMATION
. . . COULD NOT ENTER THE CONSUMMATION . . . .   364 FOUR ZOAS 9   290
OR ARE THESE THE PANGS OF REPENTANCE LET US ENTER INTO THEM 504 MILTON 21   50
DARE TO ENTER & THEY SHALL ENTER TRIUMPHANT OVER DEATH   . 522 MILTON 32   28
FOR GOD HIMSELF ENTERS DEATH'S DOOR ALWAYS WITH THOSE THAT 522 MILTON 32   40
   ENTER
VIRGIN OF PROVIDENCE FEAR NOT TO ENTER INTO MY COTTAGE   . . 527 MILTON 36   28
ENTER MY COTTAGE COMFORT HER FOR SHE IS SICK WITH FATIGUE   527 MILTON 36   32
FROM FELPHAM'S VALE CLOTHED IN CLOUDS OF BLOOD TO ENTER   534 MILTON 42   20
   INTO
ENDLESS LABOUR TO WHOEVER SUFFERS HIM TO ENTER HIS MIND   583A DESC CAT 9   PROSE
WHO PERMITS HIM TO ENTER HIS MIND . . . . 583B DESC CAT 9   PROSE
WHICH ALAS EVERY ONE ON EARTH IS LIABLE TO ENTER INTO   . . 608A V LAST JUDG/N PROSE
IF THE SPECTATOR COULD ENTER INTO THESE IMAGES   . . . . 611A V LAST JUDG/N PROSE
IF HE COULD ENTER INTO NOAH'S RAINBOW OR INTO HIS BOSOM   611A V LAST JUDG/N PROSE
THAT CAN ENTER THE MIND AS IT TAKES AWAY ALL SUBLIMITY   . . 614B V LAST JUDG/N PROSE
THE FOOL SHALL NOT ENTER INTO HEAVEN LET HIM BE EVER SO   615D V LAST JUDG/N PROSE
   HOLY
SAVIOUR'S KINGDOM THE DIVINE BODY WILL NEVER ENTER THERE   621A JERUSALEM 3   PROSE
BUT TO THOSE WHO ENTER INTO THEM THEY SEEM THE ONLY   634 JERUSALEM 13   65
   SUBSTANCES
AND IF ANY ENTER INTO THEE THOU SHALT BE AN UNQUENCHABLE   639 JERUSALEM 17   45
   FIRE
O I AM NOTHING WHEN I ENTER INTO JUDGMENT WITH THEE   . . . 654 JERUSALEM 29   47
AND FEET LEST ANY SHOULD ENTER HIS BOSOM & EMBRACE   . . . 664 JERUSALEM 38   2
WHY SHOULD WE ENTER INTO OUR SPECTRES TO BEHOLD OUR OWN   672 JERUSALEM 43   10
   CORRUPTIONS
THEIR CRUEL FINGERS FOR HIS HEART & THERE THEY ENTER IN   702 JERUSALEM 66   28
   POMP
ALL ARE HUMAN & WHEN YOU ENTER INTO THEIR BOSOMS YOU WALK   709 JERUSALEM 71   16
WHEN IN ETERNITY MAN CONVERSES WITH MAN THEY ENTER   . . . 733 JERUSALEM 88   3
ENTER THE GHOST OF ABEL . . . .   780A GHOST ABEL 1   PROSE
ENTER INTO AN EMULATION OF GRECIAN MANNERS THERE ARE NOW I 798C LETTER 10   PROSE
ENTER AGAIN WITH GREAT PLEASURE AND HOPE SOON TO SHOW YOU 841A LETTER 40   PROSE
"LEAVE EVERY HOPE YOU WHO IN ENTER" . . . . SUPP ILLUS DANTE 4   *
ENTERANCE   SEE ENTRANCE
IT IS THE ENTERANCE OF THE FIRST HEAVEN NAMED LUTHER FOR   526 MILTON 35   62
PREVIOUS TO THE ENTERANCE OF VANDYKE & RUBENS . . . . . . 592A PUB ADDRESS/N *PROSE
HOLINESS IS NOT THE PRICE OF ENTERANCE INTO HEAVEN   . . . 615D V LAST JUDG/N PROSE
AND FORMED INTO FOUR PRECIOUS STONES FOR ENTERANCE FROM   691 JERUSALEM 59   1
   BEULAH
ENTERD
IN A GREAT HURRY INFLAMMABLE GASS THE WIND FINDER ENTERD   44C ISLAND MOON 1 PROSE
[THE PYTHAGOREAN & SUCTION THE EPICUREAN ENTERD THE ROOM &] 46B ISLAND MOON 2 *PROSE
GIBBLE GABBLE THE WIFE OF INFLAMMABLE GASS [ENTERD THE   46B ISLAND MOON 2 PROSE
   ROOM]
& LITTLE SCOPPRELL ENTERD THE ROOM . . . . 46B ISLAND MOON 2 PROSE
AT THIS MOMENT THE THREE PHILOSOPHERS ENTERD . . . . 49B ISLAND MOON 5 PROSE
SO ALL THE PEOPLE IN THE BOOK ENTERD INTO THE ROOM   . . . 49C ISLAND MOON 5 PROSE
OBTUSE ANGLE ENTERD THE ROOM WHAT NEWS MR STEELYARD . . . 52C ISLAND MOON 8 PROSE
THE HUNGRY POOR ENTERD THE HALL TO EAT GOOD BEEF & ALE   . . 58 THIS CITY/IM   11
SOON AS THE BLIND WANDERER ENTERD THE PLEASANT GARDENS   100 TIRIEL 2   10
   OF HAR
[AND HAR & HEVA STOOD & WATCHD HIM TILL HE ENTERD THE WOOD] 103 TIRIEL 3   31
BUT HAR & HEVA STOOD & WATCHD HIM TILL HE ENTERD THE WOOD   103 TIRIEL 3   41
ENTERD THE GATES OF TIRIEL'S PALACE & STOOD & CALLD ALOUD   104 TIRIEL 4   42
THEY ENTERD ON THE MOUNTAINS OF HAR AT NOON THE HAPPY TENTS 109 TIRIEL 7   19
THEL ENTERD IN & SAW THE SECRETS OF THE LAND UNKNOWN   . . 130 BOOK OF THEL 6   2
. . . PALE ENTERD THE CHAMBER . . . . 141 FRENCH REVOLTN   160
ONE WE ENTERD IN IT WERE A NUMBER OF MONKEYS BABOONS   . 157A MARRIAGE HH 17 PROSE
ON FUZON FLEW ENTERD HIS BOSOM . . . . 251 AHANIA 3   40
BUT THEN THE SPECTRE ENTERD LOS'S BOSOM EVERY SIGH & GROAN 328 FOUR ZOAS 7   336
THAT WHOSOEVER ENTERD INTO THE TEMPLE MIGHT NOT BEHOLD   . 333 FOUR ZOAS 7B   23
LUVAH & VALA DESCENDED & ENTERED THE GATES OF DARK URTHONA 367 FOUR ZOAS 9   375
VALA AWOKE WHEN IN THE PLEASANT GATES OF SLEEP I ENTERD   369 FOUR ZOAS 9   464
AND THEN SHE ENTERD HER BRIGHT HOUSE LEADING HER MIGHTY   370 FOUR ZOAS 9   513
   CHILDREN
AND THE DEVIL ENTERD INTO THE YOUNG MAN'S BROTH   . . . . 434 LONG JOHN BRWN   8
OFT ENITHARMON ENTERD WEEPING INTO THE SPACE THERE   490 MILTON 10   3
   APPEARING
IN ONE WONDERFUL BODY AND HE ENTERD INTO IT   . . . . . 496 MILTON 14   38
OF DEATH FOR WHEN HE ENTERD INTO HIS SHADOW HIMSELF . . . 496 MILTON 15   10
AND ON MY LEFT FOOT FALLING ON THE TARSUS ENTERD THERE   497 MILTON 15   49
TWAS TOO LATE NOW TO RECEDE LOS HAD ENTERD INTO MY SOUL   505 MILTON 22   13
HE HATH ENTERD INTO THE COVERING CHERUB BECOME ONE WITH   507 MILTON 23   14
IS THIS THE VOID OUTSIDE OF EXISTENCE WHICH IF ENTERD INTO 534 MILTON 41   37
THERE IS A VOID OUTSIDE OF EXISTENCE WHICH IF ENTERD INTO   620 JERUSALEM 1   1
AS HE ENTERD THE DOOR OF DEATH FOR ALBION'S SAKE INSPIRED   620 JERUSALEM 1   9
ALBION HATH ENTERD THE LOINS THE PLACE OF THE LAST JUDGMENT 656 JERUSALEM 30   38
ALBION HATH ENTERD THE STATE SATAN BE PERMANENT O STATE   662 JERUSALEM 35   13

	PAGE	TITLE	LINE

ENTERD   (CONTINUED)
TO THE STATE THEY ARE ENTERD INTO THAT THEY MAY BE DELIVERD   680 JERUSALEM 49   66
BUT LUVAH IS NAMED SATAN BECAUSE HE HAS ENTERD THAT STATE   680 JERUSALEM 49   68
AND THE ROOTS OF ALBION'S TREE ENTERD THE SOUL OF LOS . .   684 JERUSALEM 53   4
ENGLAND WHO IS BRITTANNIA ENTERD ALBION'S BOSOM REJOICING   743 JERUSALEM 95   22
ENTERD INTO ME AS INTO HIS HOUSE & I LOATHE THY   780 GHOST ABEL 2   6
    TABERNACLES
BY THE MILITARY TO SUFFER A PROSECUTION TO BE ENTERD INTO   827D LETTER 28   PROSE
IN TOGETHER & WITH ANOTHER PASSENGER ENTERD INTO   869C LETTER 70   PROSE
    CONVERSATION
ENTERED
THE POISON HATH ENTERED INTO MY MARROW . . . .   36B COUCH DEATH/PS   PROSE
WHEN LO AN ANGEL FROM THE FIELDS OF LIGHT ENTERED THE HOUSE   39D SAMSON/PS   PROSE
ENGLAND WHO IS BRITTANNIA ENTERED ALBION'S BOSOM REJOICING   743 JERUSALEM 96   2
ENTERING
ENTERING WITH HOLY FEET TO WHERE ON HIGH . . . . . .   15 IMIT SPEN/PS   22
BUT (OBTUSE) ANGLE ENTERING THE ROOM . . . .   45B ISLAND MOON 1   PROSE
OF ORC ENTERING WITH FIBRES BECAME ONE WITH HIM A LIVING   309 FOUR ZOAS 5   * 169
    CHAIN
THIS TO PREVENT ENTERING THE DOORS OF SATAN'S BRAIN NIGHT   492 MILTON 12   4
    AFTER NIGHT
ELSE HE WOULD WAKE SO SEEMD HE ENTERING HIS SHADOW BUT . .   496 MILTON 15   2
ENTERING THEY GAVE HIM STILL PERCEPTIONS OF HIS SLEEPING   496 MILTON 15   4
    BODY
BUT MILTON ENTERING MY FOOT I SAW IN THE NETHER . . . .   503 MILTON 21   4
BY ENTERING INTO DISEASE AND EXCREMENT DRUNKENNESS . . .   582A DESC CAT 8   PROSE
ENTERING THRO THE GATES OF BIRTH . . . .   651 FIELDS FROM/J   63
BOSOM IN ALL THE TERRORS OF FRIENDSHIP ENTERING THE CAVES   656 JERUSALEM 31   4
FOR FEAR AT ENTERING THE GATE INTO OUR WORLD OF CRUEL .   688 JERUSALEM 56   15
AND NOT A POMPOUS HIGH PRIEST ENTERING BY A SECRET PLACE   708 JERUSALEM 69   44
ENTERING INTO THE REASONING POWER FORSAKING IMAGINATION   714 JERUSALEM 74   7
ON EACH SIDE A CHORUS OF ANGELS ENTERING SING THE FOLLOWING   781A GHOST ABEL 2   PROSE
ENTERPRIZE
MR PHILLIPS IS A MAN OF VAST SPIRIT & ENTERPRIZE WITH A   841C LETTER 41   PROSE
    SOLIDITY
ENTERPRIZING
THIS ENTERPRIZING MAN THAT ALL PARTIES I MEAN OUR FRIEND   857A LETTER 54   PROSE
ENTERS
IS IT NOT IN THE POWER OF ANY THIEF WHO ENTERS . . . .   439A BLAKES MEMORAN   PROSE
FOR GOD HIMSELF ENTERS DEATH'S DOOR ALWAYS WITH THOSE THAT   522 MILTON 32   40
    ENTER
BUT HE WHO ENTERS INTO & DISCRIMINATES MOST MINUTELY . .   611B V LAST JUDG/N   PROSE
HE WHO WAITS TO BE RIGHTEOUS BEFORE HE ENTERS INTO THE . .   621A JERUSALEM 3   PROSE
WHICH THE MALE ENTERS MAGNIFICENT BETWEEN HER CHERUBIM . .   656 JERUSALEM 30   35
SUCH IS THE NATURE OF THE ULRO THAT WHATEVER ENTERS . . .   674 JERUSALEM 44   21
WHEN WEARY MAN ENTERS HIS CAVE . . . .   771 OF GATES/GP   19
ENTERTAIN
DESIRE TO ENTERTAIN BENEATH OUR THATCHED ROOF OF RUSTED   802D LETTER 14   PROSE
    GOLD
ENTERTAIND
THUS WERE THE SLEEPERS ENTERTAIND UPON THE COUCHES   372 FOUR ZOAS 9   558
    OF BEULAH
IT CONFIRMS THE SUSPITION I ENTERTAIND CONCERNING THOSE   553B BELLS WEEKLY/N   MARG
ENTERTAIND AND INSTRUCTED BUT HAVE NOT YET COME TO THE .   845B LETTER 44   PROSE
ENTERTAINING
BUT HERE COMES ONE WHO IS AS ENTERTAINING AS A GOOD STORY   29B EDW THIRD/PS 4   PROSE
WHY IS THE BIBLE MORE ENTERTAINING & INSTRUCTIVE THAN ANY   794A LETTER 5   PROSE
    OTHER BOOK
ENTERTAINMENT
HE WAS AS CHEARFUL AS A PRINCE & GAVE ME ENTERTAINMENT   102 TIRIEL 3   10
A PRETTY EPIGRAM FOR [THOSE] THE ENTERTAINMENT OF THOSE WHO   547A PRETTY EPIGR/N   TITLE
CHINA & INDIA & SIBERIA ARE HIS TEMPLES FOR ENTERTAINMENT   690 JERUSALEM 58   39
ENTERTAINS
& LEAVES THE MAN WHO ENTERTAINS SUCH AN IDEA THE HABITATION   614B V LAST JUDG/N   PROSE
ENTHUSIASM
& IS ENTHUSIASM & MADNESS & IS [TH] IT NOT . . . . . .   94B ANNO SWED LOVE   * MARG
WHY ARE [VENETIANS TREATED MORE ?KINDLY XXX ENTHUSIASM]   450B ANNO REYNOLDS   * MARG
[DAMN THE FOOL] MEER ENTHUSIASM IS THE ALL IN ALL . . .   456C ANNO REYNOLDS   * MARG
THE ENTHUSIASM OF THE FOLLOWING POEM THE AUTHOR HOPES . .   620D JERUSALEM 3   PROSE
THAT ENTHUSIASM AND LIFE MAY NOT CEASE ARISE SPECTRE ARISE   628 JERUSALEM 9   31
FORGIVE ME FOR EXPRESSING TO YOU MY ENTHUSIASM WHICH I WISH   797B LETTER 9   PROSE
& IN THE ABYSSES OF THE ACCUSER MY ENTHUSIASM IS STILL .   816A LETTER 23   PROSE
EXCUSE MY PERHAPS TOO GREAT ENTHUSIASM PLEASE TO ACCEPT OF   823C LETTER 26   PROSE
WHO WAS MY ENEMY DEAR SIR EXCUSE MY ENTHUSIASM OR RATHER   852C LETTER 50   PROSE
ENTHUSIAST
WILL LEAD [?THEM] THE POOR ENTHUSIAST IN THE PATHS   85C ANNO LAVATER   * MARG
    OF HOLINESS
("MORAL ENTHUSIAST WHO LOSES PLAIN PATHS OF HONESTY")   88A ANNO LAVATER   MARG
    MOST TRUE
ENTHUSIASTIC
ENTHUSIASTIC ADMIRATION IS THE FIRST PRINCIPLE OF KNOWLEDGE   458B ANNO REYNOLDS   MARG
DEVOUT AND PAID RESPECT TO TRUE ENTHUSIASTIC SUPERSTITION   575A DESC CAT 3   PROSE
ENTHUSIASTIC HOPE-FOSTERED VISIONARY . . . .   807C LETTER 17   PROSE
ENTHUSIASTICALLY
[TO THE FULL AS ENTHUSIASTICALLY AS I HAVE WHO ACKNOWLEDGE   621A JERUSALEM 3   *PROSE
    MINE]
ENTHUSIASTS
YET SIMPLE COUNTRY HINDS ARE MORAL ENTHUSIASTS . . . .   414A ANNO BOYD   MARG
& ENTHUSIASTS FOR CUNNING & ARTIFICE . . . .   414B ANNO BOYD   MARG
HE CALLS ALL OTHERS VAGUE ENTHUSIASTS OR MADMEN . . . .   458C ANNO REYNOLDS   MARG
ENTICE
IN ALL THEIR BEAUTY TO ENTICE MILTON ACROSS THE RIVER . .   501 MILTON 19   31

ENTICE   (CONTINUED)
     TO ENTICE HER SISTERS AWAY TO BABYLON ON EUPHRATES   .   .   .   725 JERUSALEM 82   18
     SERPENT REASONINGS US ENTICE   .   .   .   .   770 OF GATES/GP   5
     TO ENTICE HIM TO FELPHAM & FAR AWAY   .   .   .   .   800 MRS FLAXMAN/L   4
ENTIRE   SEE INTIRE
     ("GREATER WHO PRODUCES ONE THING ENTIRE THAN MANY   78C ANNO LAVATER   MARG
         BY HALVES") UNEASY
     THE PROOFS OF INDUSTRY IN MY WORKS I THANK GOD WITH ENTIRE   852C LETTER 50   PROSE
ENTIRELY   SEE INTIRELY
     WHICH WE INFORMD HIM VIZ TO LEAVE FELPHAM ENTIRELY   .   .   .   820C LETTER 25   PROSE
     HAVE ENTIRELY ESCAPED THE BRUSH OF MY EVIL STAR   .   .   .   835A LETTER 34   PROSE
     AND KNEES IS ENTIRELY REDUCED SHE IS VERY NEAR AS FREE   .   851C LETTER 50   PROSE
     TO ME FOR NOW O GLORY AND O DELIGHT I HAVE ENTIRELY   851D LETTER 50   PROSE
         REDUCED
     THIS MORNING I HAVE BEEN WITH MR PHILLIPS & HAVE ENTIRELY   859A LETTER 56   PROSE
     ENTIRELY PREVENTS ME FROM THE PLEASURE OF SEEING YOU ON   872B LETTER 75   PROSE
     THO I SEEM WELL BEING ENTIRELY FREE FROM BOTH PAIN &   .   875C LETTER 81   PROSE
ENTITLED
     EVERY PURCHASER OF A CATALOGUE WILL BE ENTITLED   .   .   .   562B DESC CAT ADV   PROSE
     THE LAST WORK I PRODUCED IS A POEM ENTITLED JERUSALEM THE   878C LETTER 88   PROSE
ENTITY   SEE NON ENTITY
ENTRANCD
     SWEET ENITHARMON MILD ENTRANCD BREATHD FORTH UPON THE WIND   332 FOUR ZOAS 7   472
ENTRANCE   SEE ENTERANCE
     MET HIM AT ENTRANCE OF THE FOREST IN A DARK & LONELY WAY   103 TIRIEL 4   4
     AT ENTRANCE THEOTORMON SITS WEARING THE THRESHOLD HARD   .   190 V DAU ALBION 2   6
     AND WAS ERECTED AT THE CHIEF ENTRANCE OF URIZEN'S HALL   .   285 FOUR ZOAS 2   200
     TO PERVERT THE DIVINE VOICE IN ITS ENTRANCE TO THE EARTH   489 MILTON 9   23
ENTRANCING
     A SWEET ENTRANCING SELF DELUSION A WATRY VISION OF MAN   .   293 FOUR ZOAS 3   52
     A SWEET ENTRANCING SELF-DELUSION A WATRY VISION OF ALBION   654 JERUSALEM 29   39
ENTREAT   SEE INTREAT
     I ENTREAT YOUR IMMEDIATE ADVICE WHAT I AM TO DO FOR I   .   858C LETTER 55   PROSE
     INSERTION I WRITE TO ENTREAT THAT YOU WOULD CONTRIVE SO AS   861A LETTER 58   PROSE
ENTRING
     BEGAN TO ENTER THE HOLY CITY ENTRING THE DISMAL CLOUDS   .   359 FOUR ZOAS 9   84
ENTRUSTED
     [IS REMINDED THAT THE ANCIENTS ENTRUSTED THEIR LOVE TO   621A JERUSALEM 3   *PROSE
         THEIR WRITING]
ENTUNE
     ENTUNE DAUGHTERS OF ALBION YOUR HYMNING CHORUS MILDLY   .   .   688 JERUSALEM 56   11
ENTUTHON
     UPON THE HEIGHTS OF [ENTUTHON THAT] AMALEK TAKING REFUGE   382 FOUR ZOAS AD 6   3
         IN HIS ARMS
     SHINING IN DARKNESS GLORIOUS UPON THE DEEPS OF ENTUTHON   501 MILTON 19   35
     AROUND THE CITY OF GOLGONOOZA IN THE FORESTS OF ENTUTHON   514 MILTON 27   43
     . . . & OF THE TERRORS OF ENTUTHON   .   .   .   .   623 JERUSALEM 5   24
     IN GOLGONOOZA & IN UDAN-ADAN & IN ENTUTHON OF URIZEN   .   734 JERUSALEM 88   48
ENTUTHON BENITHON
     IN TERRORS SHE WITHERD AWAY TO ENTUTHON BENITHON   .   .   .   .   296 FOUR ZOAS 3   180
     NINE DAYS THEY TRAVELD THRO THE GLOOM OF ENTUTHON BENITHON   309 FOUR ZOAS 5   149
     ENTUTHON BENITHON [IT IS] A LAKE NOT OF WATERS BUT   346 FOUR ZOAS 8   225
         OF SPACES
     IN ENTUTHON BENITHON IN THE SHADOWS OF TORMENTS & WOE   .   348 FOUR ZOAS 8   * 269
     IN ENTUTHON BENITHON IN THE SHADOWS OF TORMENT & WOE   .   382 FOUR ZOAS AD 6   2
ENTUTHON BENYTHON
     THE LAKE OF UDAN-ADAN IN THE FORESTS OF ENTUTHON BENYTHON   512 MILTON 26   25
     IN ALLAMANDA & ENTUTHON BENYTHON WHERE SOULS WAIL   .   .   517 MILTON 29   28
     WEAVE THE BLACK WOOF OF DEATH UPON ENTUTHON BENYTHON   .   517 MILTON 29   56
     TO BOWLAHOOLA & ALLAMANDA & TO ENTUTHON BENYTHON   .   .   529 MILTON 37   59
     MOURNING FOR FEAR OF THE WARRIORS IN THE VALE OF   623 JERUSALEM 5   12
         ENTUTHON-BENYTHON
     BUT ALL WITHIN IS OPEND INTO THE DEEPS OF ENTUTHON BENYTHON   624 JERUSALEM 5   56
     THE CONCAVE EARTH ROUND GOLGONOOZA IN ENTUTHON BENYTHON   719 JERUSALEM 78   17
ENTUTHON BENYTHON'S
     IN ENTUTHON BENYTHON'S DEEP VALES BENEATH GOLGONOOZA   .   .   635 JERUSALEM 14   34
ENTUTHON'S
     DOWN FLOWING INTO ENTUTHON'S VALES GLISTENS WITH   728 JERUSALEM 83   74
         SOFT AFFECTIONS
ENVENOMD
     ENVENOMD THOU ROLLST INWARDS . . .   .   268 FOUR ZOAS 1   157
ENVIABLE
     ENVIABLE AND THE COUNTRY IS NOT ONLY MORE BEAUTIFUL ON   .   847C LETTER 44   PROSE
ENVIED   SEE ENVYD
     URIZEN SAW & ENVIED & HIS IMAGINATION WAS FILLED   .   .   .   287 FOUR ZOAS 2   291
     THEY POURD THEIR RADIANCE ABOVE ALL THE DAUGHTERS OF LUVAH   312 FOUR ZOAS 6   33
         ENVIED
     WHAT ITALY IS AN ENVIED STOREHOUSE OF INTELLECTUAL RICHES   601B PUB ADDRESS/N   PROSE
     WAS BECOME AN ENVIED HORROR AND A REMEMBRANCE OF JEALOUSY   652 JERUSALEM 28   3
     CAMBEL TREMBLED WITH JEALOUSY SHE TREMBLED SHE ENVIED   .   726 JERUSALEM 82   52
     I AM ENVIED IN MANY QUARTERS BUT I WILL CRAM THE DOGS   .   821C LETTER 25   PROSE
ENVIER
     OR POISON FROM THE DESART WILDS FROM THE EYES OF   192 V DAU ALBION 4   11
         THE ENVIER
ENVIES
     SUCH IS SELF-LOVE THAT ENVIES ALL A CREEPING SKELETON   .   194 V DAU ALBION 7   21
     NO ONE ENVIES OR HATES ONE OF HIS OWN PARTY   .   .   .   .   616B V LAST JUDG/N   PROSE
     OR OF OG OR MOLECH THE HORSE NEVER ENVIES THE PEACOCK   .   616B V LAST JUDG/N   PROSE
     HE WHO ENVIES OR CALUMNIATES WHICH IS MURDER & CRUELTY   .   738 JERUSALEM 91   12
ENVIOUS
     WHERE NOUGHT BUT ENVIOUS HISSING ADDERS DWELL   .   .   .   .   15 IMIT SPEN/PS   28
     THE [ROSE PUTS ENVIOUS] [LUSTFUL] MODEST ROSE PUTS FORTH   171 THE LILLY/N   1
         A THORN

600

                                                        PAGE   TITLE   LINE

ENVIOUS   (CONTINUED)
        AND RANGD HIS BOOKS AROUND HIM BROODING ENVIOUS OVER ORC   320 FOUR ZOAS 7   19
        URIZEN ENVIOUS BROODING SAT & SAW THE SECRET TERROR . . .   324 FOUR ZOAS 7   157
        WHY WAS I NOT BORN LIKE THIS ENVIOUS RACE . . . . . .   428 MARY   22
        AND THEN SET ME DOWN IN AN ENVIOUS LAND . . . . . .   428 MARY   24
        THESE VERSES WERE WRITTEN BY A VERY ENVIOUS MAN . . . .   542 FLORENTINE/N   32
        ENVIOUS IMPUTATION OF UNFITNESS FOR FINISHED AND SCIENTIFIC   572C DESC CAT 3   PROSE
            ART
        IT BECAME THE INTEREST OF CERTAIN ENVIOUS KNAVES . . . .   602C PUB ADDRESS/N   PROSE
        LOS SAW THE ENVIOUS BLIGHT ABOVE HIS SEVENTH FURNACE .   726 JERUSALEM 82   56
        POOR FUSELI SORE FROM THE LASH OF ENVIOUS TONGUES . . .   798B LETTER 10   PROSE
        H(HAYLEY) LIKE S(STOTHARD) ENVIOUS & THAT HE IS I AM NOW   819C LETTER 25   PROSE
            CERTAIN
ENVIRONS
        OR PERHAPS IT OCCUPIES BOTH CIRCLES WITH ITS ENVIRONS . .   786A ILLS DANTE 101 PROSE
ENVY
        ENVY AND HATE THAT THIRST FOR HUMAN GORE . . . . . .   15 IMIT SPEN/PS   32
        SO ENVY CAME & HATE TWIN PROGENY . . . .   41C THEN SHE BORE   PROSE
        ENVY HATH A SERPENT'S HEAD OF FEARFUL BULK . . . . . .   41C THEN SHE BORE   PROSE
        HOWEVER SWEET TIS ENVY THAT INSPIRES MY SONG . . . . .   41D THEN SHE BORE   PROSE
        BUT O COULD I AT ENVY SHAKE MY HANDS . . . .   41D THEN SHE BORE   PROSE
        HATE MEAGER HAG SETS ENVY ON UNABLE TO DO OUGHT HERSELF   41D THEN SHE BORE   PROSE
        NOW ENVY SHE CONTROLLS WITH NUMMING TRANCE . . . . .   41D THEN SHE BORE   PROSE
        WAS BORN ENVY IN DIREFUL PAINS HIM BORE THEN ENVY BROUGHT   42C THEN SHE BORE   PROSE
            FORTH CARE
        BUT THEIR NASTY HEARTS POOR DEVILS ARE EAT UP WITH ENVY   62D ISLAND MOON 11   PROSE
        THEY ENVY ME MY ABILITIES & ALL THE WOMEN ENVY YOUR   63A ISLAND MOON 11   PROSE
            ABILITIES
        WILL DESIRE LOVE RAGE ENVY & ?ALL ?OTHER . . . . .   89B ANNO SWED LOVE * MARG
        THOSE WHO ENVY OR CALUMNIATE GREAT MEN HATE GOD . . . .   158B MARRIAGE HH 22 PROSE
        TILL ALL THE SONS OF URIZEN LOOK OUT AND ENVY LOS . . .   239 EUROPE 4   16
        NOR THIN-LIPD ENVY . . . .   256 BOOK OF LOS 3   11
        ENVY FED WITH FAT OF LAMBS . . . .   256 BOOK OF LOS 3   15
        ENVY SUNG AT THE RICH MAN'S FEAST . . . .   256 BOOK OF LOS 3   22
        . . . FROM THE FEAST OF [ENVY] [LOVE] ENVY . . . . .   280 FOUR ZOAS 2   * 10
        . . . FROM THE FEAST OF [ENVY] [LOVE] ENVY . . . . .   280 FOUR ZOAS 2   * 10
        AMBIGUOUS WORDS BLASPHEMOUS FILLD WITH ENVY FIRM RESOLVD   302 FOUR ZOAS 4   205
        LOS FELT THE ENVY IN HIS LIMBS LIKE TO A DLIGHTED TREE .   321 FOUR ZOAS 7   27
        FOR URIZEN FIXD IN ENVY SAT BROODING & COVERD WITH SNOW   321 FOUR ZOAS 7   28
        WITH ENVY HE SAW LOS WITH ENVY THARMAS & [URTHONA] THE   352 FOUR ZOAS 8   436
            SPECTRE
        WITH ENVY & IN VAIN HE SWAM AROUND HIS STONY FORM . .   352 FOUR ZOAS 8   437
        THE ENVY WAS UPON A KING BUT IS THIS ENVY OR INDIGNATION   400B ANNO BACON   MARG
        AND NOT TO RAISE ENVY IS CALLD CHRISTIAN LOVE . . . .   428 MARY   26
        BUT IF YOU RAISE ENVY YOUR MERIT S TO BLAME . . . .   428 MARY   27
        I'LL REFUSE HIM MY HAND & FROM ENVY BE FREE . . . .   428 MARY   32
        ALL FACES HAVE ENVY SWEET MARY BUT THINE . . . . .   429 MARY   44
        TO PEACEFUL ARTS SHALL ENVY BOW . . . .   433 AUGURIES   102
        AND IN HIS TENT THRO ENVY OF LIVING FORM EVEN OF THE DIVINE   482 MILTON 3   2
            VISION
        DELUSORY LOVE TO PALAMABRON ADMIRATION JOIND WITH ENVY . .   492 MILTON 12   7
        WHOSE PRETENCE TO KNOWLEDGE IS ENVY WHOSE WHOLE SCIENCE IS   533 MILTON 41   16
        TO DESTROY THE WISDOM OF AGES TO GRATIFY RAVENOUS ENVY .   533 MILTON 41   17
        I WONDER WHICH THEY ENVY THEE OR ME . . . .   538 MADMAN CALLD/N   2
        FOLLOWD BY ENVY ON THE WINDS . . . .   558 THE CAVERNS/N   12
        IT IS OF MALICE AND ENVY THAT YOU HAVE DONE THIS HENCE .   573A DESC CAT 3   PROSE
        EXPRESSION OF FEAR OR REVENGE OR ENVY OR BLANK HORROR .   580C DESC CAT 5   PROSE
        THE NATURE OF HATRED & ENVY & . . . .   616B V LAST JUDG/N   PROSE
        THEY TORMENT ONE ANOTHER FOR OTHER REASONS THAN HATE OR   616B V LAST JUDG/N   PROSE
            ENVY
        NEITHER CAN SETH ENVY NOAH OR ELIJAH ENVY ABRAHAM . .   616B V LAST JUDG/N   PROSE
        BUT THEY MAY BOTH OF THEM ENVY THE SUCCESS OF SATAN . .   616B V LAST JUDG/N   PROSE
        NOR THE SHEEP THE GOAT BUT THEY ENVY A RIVAL IN LIFE . .   616B V LAST JUDG/N   PROSE
        A DOG WILL ENVY A CAT WHO IS PAMPERD AT [HIS] THE . .   616B V LAST JUDG/N   PROSE
        THE BIBLE NEVER TELLS US THAT DEVILS TORMENT ONE ANOTHER   616B V LAST JUDG/N   PROSE
            THRO ENVY
        IS PUNISHD & IF POSSIBLE DESTROYD NOT THRO ENVY . . .   616C V LAST JUDG/N   PROSE
        THEY DO NOT ENVY ONE ANOTHER THEY CONTEMN & DESPISE .   616C V LAST JUDG/N   PROSE
        CALLING THAT HOLY LOVE WHICH IS ENVY REVENGE & CRUELTY .   639 JERUSALEM 17   30
        AND MALICE & ENVY BUT MY EMANATION ALAS WILL BECOME .   639 JERUSALEM 17   38
        THE REACTOR HATH HID HIMSELF THRO ENVY I BEHOLD HIM . .   653 JERUSALEM 29   9
        OF UNBELIEF ENVY HOVERS OVER HIM HIS FRIENDS ARE . .   667 JERUSALEM 40   14
            HIS ABHORRENCE
        IN EDEN IN LOVELY JERUSALEM DREW EVEN FROM ENVY . . .   675 JERUSALEM 50   6
        OF ENVY ALBION IS BECOME AND HIS EMANATION CAST OUT . .   681 JERUSALEM 50   9
        THE ENVY RAN THRO CATHEDRON'S LOOMS INTO THE HEART . .   726 JERUSALEM 82   53
        THE ENVY LOUD SHE LABOURD IN THE FURNACE OF FIRE . .   726 JERUSALEM 82   62
        IS NOT MERIT IN ONE A CAUSE OF ENVY IN ANOTHER . . .   793B LETTER 5   PROSE
        POVERTY ENVY OLD AGE & FEAR . . . .   817 HAPPINESS/L   37
        DISPERSE THOSE REBELLIOUS SPIRITS OF ENVY & MALIGNITY .   842A LETTER 41   PROSE
        BY WILLIAM BLAKE ?THO NOW SURROUNDED BY CALUMNY & ENVY .   SUPP PILGRIMS/N   *PROSE
ENVYD
        WHEN ELATE I AM ENVYD WHEN MEEK I'M DESPISD . . . . .   829 O WHY BORN/L   10
ENVYING
        SUCH A LIAR AS QUID THINKS HE IS [BUT HE IS ALWAYS ENVYING]   53A ISLAND MOON 8   PROSE
        ENVYING STOOD THE ENORMOUS FORM AT VARIANCE WITH ITSELF   707 JERUSALEM 69   6
        ENVYING EACH OTHER YET DESIRING IN ALL DEVOURING LOVE .   732 JERUSALEM 86   64
ENVYINGS
        AND DARKEN ALL MY PALACE WALLS WITH ENVYINGS & HATE . . .   310 FOUR ZOAS 5   213
ENVY'S
        MY CUP IS FILLD WITH ENVY'S RANKEST DRAUGHT [AND DEATH]   41C THEN SHE BORE   PROSE
        IS THE SWEAT OF ENVY'S FOOT . . . .   432 AUGURIES   48

```
                                                           PAGE      TITLE        LINE
ENWOVEN      SEE INWOVEN
     WHAT YOU HAVE ENWOVEN WITH SO MUCH TEARS & CARE SO MUCH    688 JERUSALEM 56      23
ENWRAPPED      SEE INWRAPPED
     ENWRAPPED ROUND WITH WEEDS OF DEATH PALE COLD IN SORROW    359 FOUR ZOAS 9      96
        & WOE
EON
     HE SET HIS FACE AGAINST JERUSALEM TO DESTROY THE EON OF    491 MILTON 11        1
        ALBION
     HIS EON WEEPING IN THE COLD AND DESOLATED EARTH  . . . .   641 JERUSALEM 19     16
     AND HIS DARK EON THAT ONCE FAIR CRYSTAL FORM DIVINELY CLEAR 667 JERUSALEM 40    41
EPHESIANS
     EPHESIANS III C IOV    . . . . . . . . . .              374B FOUR ZOAS 9      PROSE
EPHRAIM
     [THE MOUNTAIN] EPHRAIM CALLD OUT [TO THE MOUNTAIN ] . . .  274 FOUR ZOAS 1     386
     WHO WANDERD IN MOUNT EPHRAIM SEEKING A SEPULCHER  . . . .  279 FOUR ZOAS 1     557
     EPHRAIM WAS A WILDERNESS OF JOY WHERE ALL MY WILD BEASTS   349 FOUR ZOAS 8     309
        RAN
     SAYING COME THOU TO EPHRAIM BEHOLD THE KINGS OF CANAAN . . 501 MILTON 19        36
     COME THEN TO EPHRAIM & MANASSEH O BELOVED-ONE . . . . .    501 MILTON 20         3
     AND EPHRAIM & JUDAH WERE GENERATED BECAUSE  . . . . . .    508 MILTON 24         3
     WHO CARRIED HIM DOWN INTO EGYPT WHERE EPHRAIM & MENASSHEH  508 MILTON 24        20
     EPHRAIM WAS A WILDERNESS OF JOY WHERE ALL MY WILD BEASTS   705 JERUSALEM 67     56
        RAN
     ACROSS THE HILLS OF EPHRAIM & DOWN MOUNT OLIVET TO  . . .  706 JERUSALEM 68     22
     OF HIM WHO IS SLAIN IN WAR FILLS THE VALLEYS OF EPHRAIM    706 JERUSALEM 68     35
        WITH
     AND THOSE UNDER EPHRAIM MANASSEH & BENJAMIN ARE THESE  . . 711 JERUSALEM 72     23
     I WALK TO EPHRAIM I SEEK FOR SHILOH I WALK LIKE A LOST     720 JERUSALEM 79     10
        SHEEP
     O LOVELY MILD JERUSALEM O SHILOH OF MOUNT EPHRAM  . . .    730 JERUSALEM 85     22
EPHRAM
     LEVI AND JUDAH & ISSACHAR EPHRAM MANASSEH GAD AND DAN  . . 720 JERUSALEM 79     30
EPHRATAH
     THE CITY OF THE WOODS IN THE FOREST OF EPHRATAH IS TAKEN   653 JERUSALEM 29     18
EPICUREAN
     SUCTION THE EPICUREAN QUID THE CYNIC & SIPSOP THE          44A ISLAND MOON 1  PROSE
        PYTHAGOREAN
     THE EPICUREAN SEEMING [NOT] STUDYING THE FLAME OF          44C ISLAND MOON 1  PROSE
        THE CANDLE
     YES SAID THE EPICUREAN & HAVING A BIT OF FUN WITH HIM  . . 45C ISLAND MOON 1  PROSE
     AYE SECONDLY VOLTAIRE S A FOOL SAYS THE EPICUREAN   . . .  45D ISLAND MOON 1  PROSE
     [THE PYTHAGOREAN & SUCTION THE EPICUREAN ENTERD THE ROOM &] 46B ISLAND MOON 2 *PROSE
     THE TRUMPETER SHIT IN HIS HAT SAID THE EPICUREAN . . . .   46C ISLAND MOON 3  PROSE
     IT WAS PHEBUS SAID THE EPICUREAN . . . . . . . . . .       47B ISLAND MOON 3  PROSE
     COME SAID THE EPICUREAN LET'S HAVE SOME RUM & WATER . . .  49B ISLAND MOON 5  PROSE
     AH HANG YOUR REASONING SAID THE EPICUREAN . . . . . .      50A ISLAND MOON 6  PROSE
     BACON WAS A CONTEMPLATIVE ATHEIST EVIDENTLY AN EPICUREAN  403C ANNO BACON      MARG
     THE ARTIFICE OF THE EPICUREAN PHILOSOPHERS IS  . . . . . 474A ANNO REYNOLDS    MARG
     SUCH IS THE END OF EPICUREAN OR NEWTONIAN PHILOSOPHY IT   475D ANNO REYNOLDS    MARG
        IS ATHEISM
     BY THE ATHEISTICAL EPICUREAN PHILOSOPHY OF ALBION'S TREE   704 JERUSALEM 67     13
EPICURISM
     ("THE MOST REFINED EPICURISM") TRUE CHRISTIAN PHILOSOPHY    75D ANNO LAVATER    MARG
EPICURUS
     EVERY BODY KNOWS THAT THIS IS EPICURUS AND LUCRETIUS  . . 397B ANNO BACON      MARG
     BACON IS ONLY EPICURUS OVER AGAIN . . . . . . . . .       456C ANNO REYNOLDS    MARG
EPIGRAM
     HER WHOLE LIFE IS AN EPIGRAM SMACK SMOOTH & NEATLY PEND    184 HER LIFE IS/N     1
     [A PRETTY EPIGRAM FOR THOSE WHO HAVE GIVEN HIGH PRICES]   547A PRETTY EPIGR/N  TITLE
     A PRETTY EPIGRAM FOR [THOSE] THE ENTERTAINMENT OF THOSE WHO 547A PRETTY EPIGR/N TITLE
     THIS MAKES A GOOD EPIGRAM ENOUGH . . . . . . . . .        575C DESC CAT 3      PROSE
     ONE IS AN EPIGRAM ONLY . . . . . . . . . . . . .         599A PUB ADDRESS/N   PROSE
     THAT VULGAR EPIGRAM IN ART REMBRANDT'S "HUNDRED GUELDERS" 599B PUB ADDRESS/N   PROSE
EPIGRAMMATIC
     ACCOUNTED IGNORANT OF THAT EPIGRAMMATIC WIT IN ART  . . . 599A PUB ADDRESS/N   PROSE
EPIGRAMS
     IS LIKE LOOKING FOR EPIGRAMS IN HOMER  . . . . . . .     599A PUB ADDRESS/N   PROSE
EPISTLES
     TO [EPISTLES ON SCULPTURE] AN ESSAY ON SCULPTURE IN SIX    798B LETTER 10      PROSE
        EPISTLES
EPITAPH
     HIS EPITAPH [WITH] FOR MY TEARS [OF] ARE AQUA FORTIS  . . 537 AND HIS LEGS/N *  45
     I'LL ALSO WRITE MY OWN DEAR EPITAPH  . . . . . . . .      537 AND HIS LEGS/N    49
     AN EPITAPH . . . . . . . . . . . . . . . . .            545D AN EPITAPH/N    TITLE
     [EPITAPH FOR] WILLIAM COWPER ESQRE  . . . . . . . .      551C WILLM COWPER/N *TITLE
     A SHEPHERD READING THE EPITAPH . . . . . . . . .        SUPP ILLUS GRAY     *TITLE
EQUAL
     OF YOUTH UNBORN OUR NAMES ARE WRITTEN EQUAL  . . . . .     18 EDW THIRD/PS 1    25
     IS IN HIS HAND TO WHOM ALL MEN ARE EQUAL  . . . . . .      18 EDW THIRD/PS 1    31
     CAST THEIR RIVERS IN EQUAL TIDES THRO THE GREAT PARADISE   142 FRENCH REVOLTN  184
        . . .
     HIS LOST WORKS HE SAID NONE OF EQUAL VALUE WAS LOST  . . 154A MARRIAGE HH 12  PROSE
     PRODUCE TEN THOUSAND VOLUMES OF EQUAL VALUE WITH         158A MARRIAGE HH 21  PROSE
        SWEDENBORG'S
     OF EQUAL MAGNITUDE AND CONSEQUENCE WITH THE PRODUCTIONS   207C PRSPECTUS 1793  PROSE
     THE PRINCE OF ALL THE HOSTS OF MEN NOR EQUAL KNOW IN HEAVEN 278 FOUR ZOAS 1    505
     AM I NOT GOD SAID URIZEN WHO IS EQUAL TO ME  . . . . .     294 FOUR ZOAS 3     106
     BARRY PAINTED A PICTURE FOR BURKE EQUAL TO RAFAEL OR  . . 451D ANNO REYNOLDS    MARG
     & NOT TALK OF DARK AGES OR OF ANY AGE AGES ARE ALL EQUAL  461A ANNO REYNOLDS    MARG
     THAT THE STUPID ARE BORN WITH FACULTIES EQUAL TO OTHER MEN 473A ANNO REYNOLDS   MARG
     IS EQUAL IN ITS PERIOD & VALUE TO SIX THOUSAND YEARS  . . 516 MILTON 28        63
     CORREGGIO RUBENS AND REMBRANDT WE NEVER SHALL EQUAL . . . 564A DESC CAT        PROSE
```

PAGE   TITLE   LINE

EQUAL   (CONTINUED)
    SOCIETY ARE PERHAPS EQUAL OF THE DEVIL AND OF THE ANGEL   570B DESC CAT 3   PROSE
    AND ITS MISEXECUTION IS EQUAL TO ITS MISCONCEPTION . . .   575D DESC CAT 3   PROSE
    SAME MASTER SUPPOSING BOTH TO BE DONE WITH EQUAL CARE .   585B DESC CAT 15   PROSE
    ARE EQUAL IN ALL ESSENTIAL POINTS . . . .   585D DESC CAT 16   PROSE
    JUST EQUAL IN INVENTION & IN EXECUTION AS MY WORKS SHEW   602A PUB ADDRESS/N   PROSE
    SUPERIOR NONE WE KNOW INFERIOR NONE ALL EQUAL SHARE   .   686 JERUSALEM 55   8
    WITH MORAL LAW AN EQUAL BALANCE NOT GOING DOWN WITH   708 JERUSALEM 69   35
        DECISION
    & EQUAL TO ANY POET BUT NOT SUPERIOR . . . .   783A ANNO WW POEMS   MARG
    I HAVE NO DOUBT OF GIVING YOU BENEVOLENCE WITH EQUAL VIGOR   792B LETTER 4   PROSE
    BUT WHOSE MILDNESS IS OFTEN EQUAL TO HIS TERRORS THE .   803B LETTER 15   PROSE
    WHICH I PAINTED FOR YOU ARE EQUAL IN EVERY PART OF THE ART   814A LETTER 23   PROSE
    WORKS I HAVE DONE FOR YOU ARE EQUAL TO CARRACHE OR RAFAEL   814D LETTER 23   PROSE
    I SAY THEY ARE EQUAL TO CARRACHE OR RAFAEL OR ELSE I AM   814D LETTER 23   PROSE
    HIS INDUSTRY IS EQUAL TO HIS OTHER GREAT POWERS   . .   829B LETTER 29   PROSE
    WITH ALL THE FIDELITY I COULD & WILL FINISH WITH EQUAL CARE   838A LETTER 37   PROSE
    THO ADMIRABLY CONTRIVED FOR AN EFFECT EQUAL TO REMBRANDT   855A LETTER 53   PROSE
    WILL GO EQUAL SHARES WITH ME IN THE EXPENSE AND THE PROFITS   858B LETTER 55   PROSE
EQUALLY
    WHOM SMILES AND FROWNS MAKE EQUALLY LOVELY   . . . .   85B ANNO LAVATER   MARG
    AND THAT HE WILL BE EQUALLY PROFITABLE BOTH WAYS . . .   380B FOUR ZOAS NOTE   PROSE
    WHETHER TRUE OR PARABOLIC ARE EQUALLY USEFUL . . . .   393B ANNO WATSON   MARG
    CONSEQUENT GOOD THIS SENSE OF THE BIBLE IS EQUALLY TRUE   393B ANNO WATSON   MARG
    TO ALL & EQUALLY PLAIN TO ALL NONE CAN DOUBT . . .   393B ANNO WATSON   MARG
    CHILDHOOD AND AGE ARE EQUALLY BELONGING TO EVERY CLASS .   460B ANNO REYNOLDS   MARG
    ARE EQUALLY SUBVERSIVE OF THE SUBLIME . . . . . .   464C ANNO REYNOLDS   MARG
    THERE IS A PLACE WHERE CONTRARIETIES ARE EQUALLY TRUE .   518 MILTON 30   1
    AND EQUALLY FREE WITH THE LORD AND THE PEASANT THEY ARE   569D DESC CAT 3   PROSE
    WIFE OF BATH IN WHOSE CHARACTER CHAUCER HAS BEEN EQUALLY   572B DESC CAT 3   PROSE
    AND HIS FRIEND ARE EQUALLY MASTERS OF CHAUCER'S LANGUAGE   574B DESC CAT 3   PROSE
    CUT DOTS & LOZENGES EQUALLY WELL WITH THOSE LITTLE PRINTS   592B PUB ADDRESS/N   PROSE
    EQUALLY WELL AT LEAST IT IS SO IN ENGLAND . . . .   593D PUB ADDRESS/N   PROSE
    I FORBEAR TO NAME [A LI] LIVING ARTISTS THO EQUALLY WORTHY   601B PUB ADDRESS/N   *PROSE
    TWO BLEEDING CONTRARIES EQUALLY TRUE ARE HIS WITNESSES   646 JERUSALEM 24   3
        AGAINST ME
    THERE IS A PLACE WHERE CONTRARIETIES ARE EQUALLY TRUE .   677 JERUSALEM 48   14
    TO BE THEIR INFERIORS OR SUPERIORS WE EQUALLY ABHOR   .   686 JERUSALEM 55   7
    I OWN MYSELF AN ADMIRER OF OSSIAN EQUALLY . . . .   783C ANNO WW POEMS   MARG
    IN A BOOK THAT ALL MAY READ ARE EQUALLY RIGHT . .   787A ANNO THORNTON   MARG
    THAT MAN WHO &C IS EQUALLY SO THE MAN THAT & THE MAN   787B ANNO THORNTON   MARG
        WHICH
    THIS & OTHER WORKS EQUALLY CREDITABLE THESE ARE WORKS .   821C LETTER 25   PROSE
    THERE IS A REAL REASON EQUALLY GOOD WHY I HAVE NOT YET SENT   840B LETTER 39   PROSE
    SOON GET ABOUT AGAIN GREAT MEN DIE EQUALLY WITH THE LITTLE   868D LETTER 68   PROSE
EQUALS
    . . . LEARN TO CONSIDER ALL MEN AS THY EQUALS . . . .   143 FRENCH REVOLTN   193
    LUVAH REPLIED DICTATE TO THY EQUALS AM NOT I . . . . .   278 FOUR ZOAS 1   504
    A MOMENT EQUALS A PULSATION OF THE ARTERY . . . . .   516 MILTON 28   47
    AND IS PRAISED BY HIS EQUALS FOR IT FOR BOTH HIMSELF .   574B DESC CAT 3   PROSE
    THE LIFE'S LABOUR OF MENTAL WEAKNESS SCARCELY EQUALS .   593A PUB ADDRESS/N   PROSE
EQUILIBRIUM
    THE MIDST BETWEEN AN EQUILIBRIUM GREY OF AIR SERENE   . . .   316 FOUR ZOAS 6   194
EQUIVOCAL
    IN EQUIVOCAL WORLDS UP & DOWN ARE EQUIVOCAL   . . . . .   785D ILLS DANTE 101   PROSE
EQUIVOCATED
    WHO HESITATED & EQUIVOCATED WITH ME UPON THE SAME SUBJECT   593A PUB ADDRESS/N   PROSE
EQUIVOCATION
    ALL EQUIVOCATION & SELF-CONTRADICTION . . . . . .   465C ANNO REYNOLDS   MARG
ERADICATED
    THEY WILL SOON BE ERADICATED & FORGOTTEN YOU WHO WAS   .   838C LETTER 37   PROSE
ERASED
    TILL ALL FROM LIFE I WAS OBLITERATED AND ERASED   . . . .   191 V DAU ALBION 2   34
    TILL LIKE A DREAM ETERNITY WAS OBLITERATED & ERASED . .   246 SONG OF LOS 4   4
ERCILLA
    ABSORBED BY THE POETS MILTON HOMER CAMOENS ERCILLA ARIOSTO   806D LETTER 17   PROSE
ERE   SEE EER
    THEN PAUSES ERE HE STARTS BUT DICK . . . .   16 BLIND-MANS/PS   45
    OF ENGLAND'S QUEEN AND WILL ERE LONG OF ENGLAND . . .   21 EDW THIRD/PS 2   99
    ERE ONCE AGAIN THE CHANGING MOON HER CIRCUIT HATH PERFORMED   38A SAMSON/PS   PROSE
    ERE LONG TO BLEED & DIE A SACRIFICE DONE BY A PRIESTLY HAND   41B THEN SHE BORE   PROSE
    ERE THOU MEASURE THE CIRCLE THAT HE SHALL RUN . . . . .   142 FRENCH REVOLTN   191
    ERE YET HIS EYELIDS CAN BEHOLD THE ARROWS OF THE DAY   .   193 V DAU ALBION 5   32
    SHE NUMBERS WITH HER FINGERS EVERY FIBRE ERE IT GROW   .   501 MILTON 19   49
    ON HIS ROCK ERE YET THE STARRY HEAVENS WERE FLED AWAY .   660 JERUSALEM 34   20
    AS ONE COUNTRY AND THEIR ARTS ONE & THAT YOU WILL ERE LONG   811A LETTER 21   PROSE
ERECT
    DOES NOT THE WORM ERECT A PILLAR IN THE MOULDERING CHURCH   193 V DAU ALBION 5   41
        YARD
    BEGAN TO ERECT THE TENT . . . .   232 URIZEN 19   18
    WE MAY ERECT A THRONE DEEP IN THE NORTH I PLACE MY LOT . .   278 FOUR ZOAS 1   491
    WITH COMPASSES DIVIDE THE DEEP THEY THE STRONG SCALES ERECT   283 FOUR ZOAS 2   142
    OR STANDING ON THE EARTH ERECT OR ON THE STORMY WAVES .   288 FOUR ZOAS 2   299
    NO MORE ERECT THO STRONG DRAWN OUT IN LENGTH THEY RAVIN   344 FOUR ZOAS 8   126
    NO LONGER NOW ERECT THE KING OF LIGHT OUTSTRETCHD IN FURY   352 FOUR ZOAS 8   438
    THAT NOT OF HIS OWN POWER HE BORE THE HUMAN FORM ERECT .   353 FOUR ZOAS 8   458
    WILL YOU ERECT A LASTING HABITATION IN THE MOULDERING   353 FOUR ZOAS 8   495
        CHURCH YARD
    [THE] YET PALE THE JUST MAN STANDS ERECT & LOOKING UP TO   358 FOUR ZOAS 9   51
        HEAVN
    FOR ATONEMENT ALBION BEGAN TO ERECT TWELVE ALTARS . . .   653 JERUSALEM 28   21
    & WILL ERECT THE SYNAGOGUE OF SATAN . . . .   682B JERUSALEM 52   PROSE

603

		PAGE	TITLE	LINE
ERECT	**(CONTINUED)**			
	IN MANY TEARS & THERE THEY ERECT A TEMPLE & AN ALTAR . .	702	JERUSALEM 66	29
	WHILE HAND & HYLE CONDENSE THE LITTLE-ONES & ERECT THEM INTO	737	JERUSALEM 90	49
	PROFITS OF THE WORK ARE INTENDED TO BE APPROPRIATED TO ERECT	824D	LETTER 27	PROSE
ERECTED				
	THEY ERECTED LARGE PILLARS ROUND THE VOID	231	URIZEN 19	6
	SOME FIXD THE ANVIL SOME THE LOOM ERECTED SOME THE PLOW	281	FOUR ZOAS 2	27
	THEY ERECTED THE FURNACES	281	FOUR ZOAS 2	30
	OTHERS AROSE & SCHOOLS ERECTED FORMING INSTRUMENTS . .	283	FOUR ZOAS 2	130
	AND ALL THE TIME IN CAVERNS SHUT THE GOLDEN LOOMS ERECTED	284	FOUR ZOAS 2	145
	AND WAS ERECTED AT THE CHIEF ENTRANCE OF URIZEN'S HALL .	285	FOUR ZOAS 2	200
	HE HAD ERECTED MANY PORCHES [WHICH]	331	FOUR ZOAS 7	434
	INTO HIS HANDS THEN ENITHARMON ERECTED LOOMS IN LUBAN'S GATE	342	FOUR ZOAS 8	36
	ON WALLS OF TEMPLES TOWERS CITIES PALACES AND ERECTED IN	565C	DESC CAT 2	PROSE
	WHEN ERECTED INTO GODS BECOME DESTRUCTIVE TO HUMANITY .	571C	DESC CAT 3	PROSE
ERECTING				
	PLANTING THESE OAKEN GROVES ERECTING THESE DRAGON TEMPLES	648	JERUSALEM 25	4
	BY LAND ASTOUNDING ERECTING PILLARS IN THE DEEPEST HELL	738	JERUSALEM 91	41
	BE ERECTING MONUMENTS IN PARIS EMBLEMS OF PEACE	811A	LETTER 21	PROSE
EREWHILE				
	ERE WHILE SO FAIR AND NOW THEY FALL & BEG THE SKIES WILL WEEP	43C	WOE CRIED MUSE	PROSE
ERIN				
	TILL THE SPACES OF ERIN WERE PERFECTED IN THE FURNACES .	628	JERUSALEM 9	34
	THEN ERIN CAME FORTH FROM THE FURNACES & ALL THE DAUGHTERS OF BEULAH	630	JERUSALEM 11	8
	SAKE WALKING UP AND DOWN AMONG THE SPACES OF ERIN . .	630	JERUSALEM 11	10
	AND THE SPACES OF ERIN REACHD	630	JERUSALEM 11	12
	JERUSALEM WEEPING OVER HER AMONG THE SPACES OF ERIN . .	678	JERUSALEM 48	51
	AND THUS ERIN SPOKE TO THE DAUGHTERS OF BEULAH IN SOFT TEARS	678	JERUSALEM 48	53
	SO ERIN SPOKE TO THE DAUGHTERS OF BEULAH SHUDDERING . .	681	JERUSALEM 50	18
	DOWN MONAGHAN CAVAN THESE ARE THE LAND OF ERIN . . .	711	JERUSALEM 72 *	27
	ROOTED IN SHECHEM THIS IS DINAH THE YOUTHFUL FORM OF ERIN	715	JERUSALEM 74	54
	ALBION'S TWELVE SONS SURROUND THE FORTY-TWO GATES OF ERIN	719	JERUSALEM 78	12
	CONCENTERING IN THE MAJESTIC FORM OF ERIN IN ETERNAL TEARS	731	JERUSALEM 86	45
	THRO ALL THE WORLD OF ERIN & OF LOS & ALL THEIR CHILDREN	733	JERUSALEM 88	33
	ERIN SITTING IN THE TOMB TO WATCH THEM UNCEASING NIGHT AND DAY	741	JERUSALEM 94	13
ERIN'S				
	LEANS ON THE ROCKS OF ERIN'S LAND IRELAND ANCIENT NATION	531	MILTON 39	45
	AND THEY STOOD AROUND TERRIFIED WITH ADMIRATION AT ERIN'S SPACES	631	JERUSALEM 12	22
	IN ERIN'S LAND TOWARD THE NORTH JOINT AFTER JOINT & BURNING	674	JERUSALEM 44	26
	AND ERIN'S LOVELY BOW ENCLOSD THE WHEELS OF ALBION'S SONS	681	JERUSALEM 50	22
	IN ERIN'S CONTINENT AND JERUSALEM WEPT UPON EUPHRATES' BANKS	719	JERUSALEM 78	27
ERMINE				
	IS CLOSD AS WITH A THREEFOLD CURTAIN OF IVORY & FINE LINEN & ERMINE	633	JERUSALEM 13	23
ERRANT				
	THE AUTHOR IS AN ERRANT BLOCKHEAD	44D	ISLAND MOON 1	PROSE
ERRATIC				
	BY ROCKY MASSES FROWNING IN THE ABYSSES REVOLVING ERRATIC	316	FOUR ZOAS 6	178
ERRATUM				
	("TO MEN'S BUSINESS AND BOSOMS") ERRATUM TO MEN'S POCKETS	397B	ANNO BACON	MARG
	A STRANGE ERRATUM IN ALL THE EDITIONS	543	TO ROYL ACAD/N	1
ERRED				
	URIZEN SAID I HAVE ERRED & MY ERROR REMAINS WITH ME . .	363	FOUR ZOAS 9	225
	I HAVE ERRED I AM ASHAMED AND WILL NEVER RETURN MORE .	646	JERUSALEM 23	16
	THIS WORLD IS ALL A CRADLE FOR THE ERRED WANDERING PHANTOM	688	JERUSALEM 56	8
ERRING				
	ONE EARTH ONE SEA BENEATH NOR ERRING GLOBES WANDER BUT STARS	379	FOUR ZOAS 9	831
ERROR				
	TRUTH HAS BOUNDS ERROR NONE FALLING FALLING	258	BOOK OF LOS 4	30
	ERROR CAN NEVER BE REDEEMD IN ALL ETERNITY	361	FOUR ZOAS 9 *	158
	URIZEN SAID I HAVE ERRED & MY ERROR REMAINS WITH ME . .	363	FOUR ZOAS 9	225
	("ERROR IS ON THE SIDE OF MINUTENESS") HERE IS NONSENSE	462A	ANNO REYNOLDS	MARG
	GENIUS HAS NO ERROR IT IS IGNORANCE THAT IS ERROR . .	465B	ANNO REYNOLDS	MARG
	NEITHER DID ANY LACK OR FAIL INTO ERROR WITHOUT . . .	519	MILTON 31	6
	LAMENTABLE ACCIDENT AND ERROR OF THE MORTAL AND . . .	579D	DESC CAT 5	PROSE
	CALL THAT THE PUBLIC VOICE WHICH IS THEIR ERROR . . .	597	PUBLC VOICE/PA	1
	ALL LIFE CONSISTS OF THESE TWO THROWING OFF ERROR & KNAVES	612D	V LAST JUDG/N	PROSE
	TO BE AN ERROR & TO BE CAST OUT IS A PART OF GOD'S DESIGN	613A	V LAST JUDG/N	PROSE
	WHENEVER ANY INDIVIDUAL REJECTS ERROR & EMBRACES TRUTH .	613A	V LAST JUDG/N	PROSE
	THO WILLING WERE TOO WEAK TO REJECT ERROR WITHOUT . .	614A	V LAST JUDG/N	PROSE
	FOR A MAN CAN ONLY REJECT ERROR BY THE ADVICE OF A FRIEND	614A	V LAST JUDG/N	PROSE
	THE COMBATS OF GOOD & EVIL [& OF TRUTH & ERROR WHICH] .	615A	V LAST JUDG/N	PROSE
	THE COMBATS OF TRUTH & ERROR IS EATING OF THE TREE OF LIFE	615A	V LAST JUDG/N	PROSE
	NOT AN ERROR BUT IT HAS A MAN FOR ITS [ACTOR] AGENT .	615A	V LAST JUDG/N	PROSE
	THAT ERROR OR EXPERIMENT WILL MAKE A PART OF TRUTH . .	617A	V LAST JUDG/N	PROSE
	ERROR IS CREATED TRUTH IS ETERNAL	617B	V LAST JUDG/N	PROSE
	ERROR OR CREATION WILL BE BURNED UP	617B	V LAST JUDG/N	PROSE
	WHERE WE LIVE FORGETTING ERROR NOT PONDERING ON EVIL .	642	JERUSALEM 20	7
	ERROR & FAULT THAT IS SOON FORGIVEN BUT MERCY IS NOT A SIN	643	JERUSALEM 20	24
	SO SPEAKING NOT YET INFECTED WITH THE ERROR & ILLUSION .	666	JERUSALEM 39	27
	THOU ART IN ERROR TROUBLE ME NOT WITH THY RIGHTEOUSNESS	670	JERUSALEM 42	25

	PAGE	TITLE	LINE
ERROR (CONTINUED)			
THOU ART IN ERROR ALBION THE LAND OF ULRO	676	JERUSALEM 46	10
ONE ERROR NOT REMOVD WILL DESTROY A HUMAN SOUL . . .	676	JERUSALEM 46	11
REPOSE IN BEULAH'S NIGHT TILL THE ERROR IS REMOVD . . .	676	JERUSALEM 46	12
IT IS BETTER TO PREVENT ERROR THAN TO FORGIVE THE CRIMINAL	687	JERUSALEM 55	50
IN GRACEFUL HIDINGS OF ERROR IN MERCIFUL DECEIT	727	JERUSALEM 83	29
WE ARE ALL SUBJECT TO ERROR	865B	LETTER 62	PROSE
ERROR'S			
REDEEMD FROM ERROR'S POWER WAKE THOU DRAGON OF THE DEEPS	361	FOUR ZOAS 9	161
ERRORS			
("UNHAPPINESS AT ANOTHER'S ERRORS") EXCELLENT	73A	ANNO LAVATER	MARG
BECAUSE IT REPROACHES HIM WITH THE ERRORS OF ACQUIRED FOLLY	87C	ANNO LAVATER	MARG
OF THE FOLLOWING ERRORS	149C	MARRIAGE HH 4	PROSE
AT A FRIEND'S ERRORS ANGER SHEW	538	WAS I ANGRY/N	8
MIRTH AT THE ERRORS OF A FOE	538	WAS I ANGRY/N	9
I THOUGHT THEM THE ERRORS OF FRIENDS	538	ANGER WRATH/N	2
I FIND THEM THE ERRORS OF THE FOE	538	ANGER WRATH/N	4
THE ERRORS OF A WISE MAN MAKE YOUR RULE	550	SAY PICTURES/N	6
HIS FIRES REDOUND FROM HIS DRAGON ALTARS IN ERRORS RETURNING	646	JERUSALEM 23	21
THEY HAVE SOWN ERRORS OVER ALL HIS FRUITFUL FIELDS . . .	667	JERUSALEM 40	20
& ESPECIALLY THE RELIGIOUS WHOSE ERRORS YOU	682D	JERUSALEM 52	PROSE
PRAY FORGIVE ERRORS IN OMISSIONS OF THIS KIND I AM . . .	816A	LETTER 23	PROSE
ERST			
THAT BED OF JOY WHERE ERST HER LORD HATH PRESSD	5	FAIR ELENOR/PS	38
ERUPTION			
THE DRAWING OF PLINY IN THE ERUPTION OF VESUVIUS IS . . .	839D	LETTER 38	PROSE
ERYTHREAN			
FROM THE ATLANTIC TO THE GREAT SOUTH SEA THE ERYTHREAN . .	518	MILTON 29	63
JERUSALEM COVERD THE ATLANTIC MOUNTAINS & THE ERYTHREAN .	648	JERUSALEM 24	46
WAVES & THE ERYTHREAN TURNING UP THE BOTTOMS OF THE DEEPS	648	JERUSALEM 24	63
IN THE ERYTHREAN SEA THEIR (UNCIRCUMCISION) IN HEART & LOINS	680	JERUSALEM 49	* 44
FROM THE ATLANTIC SEA TO THE UNIVERSAL ERYTHREAN	727	JERUSALEM 83	22
ESAU			
ADAM WHO IS PELEG & JOKTAN & ESAU & JACOB & SAUL & DAVID	713	JERUSALEM 73	28
ESCAPE			
ESCAPE YE FIENDS FOR IJIM WILL NOT LIFT HIS HAND AGAINST YE	106	TIRIEL 4	88
. . . & NONE [?IS] FROM ETERNITY TO ETERNITY COULD ESCAPE	347	FOUR ZOAS 8	* 231
THE OPRESSED PURSUE LIKE THE WIND THERE IS NO ROOM FOR ESCAPE	357	FOUR ZOAS 9	* 23
HAS SUFFERD THE SUBJECT OF HIS TORTURE TO ESCAPE . . .	616C	V LAST JUDG/N	PROSE
AND BUILDED BY THE DIVINE HAND THAT THE SINNER SHALL ALWAYS ESCAPE	657	JERUSALEM 31	31
VOLTAIRE ROUSSEAU YOU CANNOT ESCAPE MY CHARGE THAT . . .	682D	JERUSALEM 52	PROSE
AS THAT IS THE ONLY WAY TO ESCAPE	750	EV GOSPEL(C)/N	17
AS THAT IS THE ONLY WAY TO ESCAPE	751	EV GOSPEL(D)/N	19
GENEROUS EXULTATION IN MY ESCAPE FROM THE ARROWS OF DARKNESS	833C	LETTER 33	PROSE
ESCAPED			
WHO SURPRISED ASKED ME HOW I ESCAPED	156D	MARRIAGE HH 17	PROSE
ALL IS CONFUSION ALL IS TUMULT & WE ALONE ARE ESCAPED .	294	FOUR ZOAS 3	103
IN THE LAST BATTLE OF KING ARTHUR ONLY THREE BRITONS ESCAPED	577B	DESC CAT 5	TITLE
REMNANT STRENGTH BEAUTY AND UGLINESS ESCAPED THE WRECK .	577C	DESC CAT 5	PROSE
AND OF THESE THREE WHO ESCAPED NAMELY BEAUTY STRENGTH .	578A	DESC CAT 5	PROSE
SAYING WE ALONE ARE ESCAPED O MERCIFUL LORD AND SAVIOUR	654	JERUSALEM 29	29
ALL IS CONFUSION ALL IS TUMULT & WE ALONE ARE ESCAPED .	655	JERUSALEM 29	82
AND THE TWO THAT ESCAPED WERE THE EMANATION OF LOS & HIS	655	JERUSALEM 30	1
ESCAPED THE CONTAGION OF THE COURT OF JUSTICE I FEAR THAT	829C	LETTER 30	PROSE
HEALTH & HOW YOU HAVE ESCAPED THE DOUBLE BLOW BOTH . .	833D	LETTER 33	PROSE
HAVE ENTIRELY ESCAPED THE BRUSH OF MY EVIL STAR	835A	LETTER 34	PROSE
ESCAPES			
THAT IT IS A MIRACLE IF A STRANGER ESCAPES WITH LIFE .	833C	LETTER 33	PROSE
ESCHYLUS			
THE VISION OF ATOSSA FROM ESCHYLUS APPARITION OF DARIUS	848D	LETTER 45	PROSE
ESCULAPIUS			
AS THE DOCTOR OF PHYSIC IS THE ESCULAPIUS	571A	DESC CAT 3	PROSE
ESHER			
OF WALTON & ESHER FROM STONE-HENGE & FROM MALDEN'S COVE	706	JERUSALEM 68	44
ESOP			
I NAME MOSES SOLOMON ESOP HOMER PLATO	793B	LETTER 5	PROSE
ESPECIALLY			
ESPECIALLY AS HE WAS SURE THAT NO SEDITIOUS WORDS WERE SPOKEN	438C	BLAKES MEMORAN	PROSE
BUT MOST ESPECIALLY FOR THIS DISCOURSE IN WHICH IT IS PROVED	473A	ANNO REYNOLDS	MARG
COLOUR IT IS MIXED WITH ESPECIALLY EVERY DELICATE COLOUR	566B	DESC CAT 2	PROSE
AND TAKE THEIR COUNSEL ESPECIALLY IN ALL DIFFICULT POINTS	570D	DESC CAT 3	PROSE
AS THE PAINTER HIMSELF ESPECIALLY AS MR B(BLAKE) IS .	586D	CHAUCER 1	PROSE
& ESPECIALLY THE RELIGIOUS WHOSE ERRORS YOU	682D	JERUSALEM 52	PROSE
ESPECIALLY TO THE FEMALE	724	IN HEAVEN/J	3
I DO NOT THINK AN ARTIST CAN WRITE AN AUTOGRAPH ESPECIALLY	781D	INSC UPCOTT	PROSE
SPIRITS ARE LAWFUL BUT NOT GHOSTS ESPECIALLY ROYAL GIN IS	787D	ANNO THORNTON	MARG
WORLD ESPECIALLY IF I SHOULD HAVE TO ANSWER FOR IT I FEEL VERY	793A	LETTER 5	PROSE
& ESPECIALLY THAT YOU WOULD NOT REGRET THAT SPECIES . .	793A	LETTER 5	PROSE
I WISH TO DO MY DUTY ESPECIALLY TO YOU	808A	LETTER 19	PROSE
ESPECIALLY IF I MYSELF OMIT ANY DUTY TO MY [SELF] STATION	812D	LETTER 22	PROSE
ARE ALWAYS PERNICIOUS ESPECIALLY WHEN WE DOUBT OUR FRIENDS	822D	LETTER 26	PROSE
THE LAST TOUCHES ESPECIALLY THE PLATE OF THE MONUMENT .	838A	LETTER 37	PROSE
WOULD BE ACCEPTABLE AT ALL TIMES BUT ESPECIALLY AT THE PRESENT	844A	LETTER 43	PROSE

ESPECIALLY   (CONTINUED)
    THE PAPER & SO ARE UNFIT FOR TO MAKE UP A SET ESPECIALLY AS   877B LETTER 86   PROSE
    BE UNLUCKY TO MY FRIENDS & ESPECIALLY THAT I MAY NOT BE   879C LETTER 89   PROSE
        SO TO YOU
ESPOUSED
    HIS ESPOUSED WIFE AND MARY SAID IF THOU PUT ME AWAY FROM   694 JERUSALEM 61   4
        THEE
ESQ
    LANDLORD ROBERT BRISTOW ESQ OF BROXMORE NEAR RUMSEY . . . 590A CHAUCER 2   PROSE
    G CUMBERLAND ESQ BISHOPSGATE NEAR EGHAM SURREY   . . . . SUPP ADDRESS/L 2   *TITLE
ESQR
    HIS ADDRESS IS THIS TO JOHN HAWKINS ESQR DALLINGTON . . 855B LETTER 53   PROSE
    WILLIAM HAYLEY ESQR EARTHAM NEAR CHICHESTER SUSSEX   . . SUPP ADDRESSES/L   *TITLE
    RICHARD PHILLIPS ESQR...BRIDGE STREET BLACK FRIARS   . . SUPP ADDRESS/L 62   *TITLE
ESQRE
    TO OZIAS HUMPHRY ESQRE   . . . . 442D LAST JUDGMNT/L   TITLE
    [EPITAPH FOR] WILLIAM COWPER ESQRE   . . . . 551C WILLM COWPER/N *TITLE
    MR HOARE'S ADDRESS IS TO PRINCE HOARE ESQRE BUCKINGHAM   842B LETTER 41   PROSE
        STREET STRAND
    WILLIAM HAYLEY ESQRE FELPHAM NEAR CHICHESTER SUSSEX . . SUPP ADDRESSES/L   *TITLE
    WILLIAM HAYLEY ESQRE FELPHAM NEAR BOGNOR SUSSEX . . . . SUPP ADDRESSES/L   *TITLE
    JOHN LINNELL ESQRE CIRENCESTER PLACE FITZROY SQUARE . . SUPP ADDRESSES/L   *TITLE
    WILLIAM HAYLEY ESQRE AT MISS POOLE'S LAVANT NEAR CHICHESTER SUPP ADDRESS/L 13 *TITLE
        SUSSEX
    OZIAS HUMPHREY ESQRE   . . . . SUPP ADDRESS/L 64   *TITLE
    TO JOSIAH WEDGWOOD ESQRE . . . . SUPP ADDRESS/L 65   *TITLE
    TO DAWSON TURNER ESQRE YARMOUTH NORFOLK . . . . SUPP ADDRESS/L 66   *TITLE
    GEORGE CUMBERLAND ESQRE CULVER STREET BRISTOL . . . . SUPP ADDRESS/L 88   *TITLE
ESSAY
    TO [EPISTLES ON SCULPTURE] AN ESSAY ON SCULPTURE IN SIX   798B LETTER 10   PROSE
        EPISTLES
ESSAYS
    IS IN THESE PRELIMINARY ESSAYS CONTROVERTED & PROVED   413A ANNO BOYD   MARG
        FOOLISH
ESSENCE
    FOR THUS (TWO) CONTRARIES WOULD SPRING FROM ONE ESSENCE   80A ANNO LAVATER   MARG
    CAN SUBSTANCE AND ACCIDENT BE PREDICATED OF THE SAME   81D ANNO LAVATER   MARG
        ESSENCE
    THING ON EARTH IS THE WORD OF GOD & IN ITS ESSENCE IS GOD   87B ANNO LAVATER   MARG
    ANSWER ESSENCE IS NOT IDENTITY BUT FROM ESSENCE PROCEEDS   91A ANNO SWED LOVE   MARG
        IDENTITY
    & FROM ONE ESSENCE MAY PROCEED MANY IDENTITIES   . . . .   91A ANNO SWED LOVE   MARG
    IF THE ESSENCE WAS THE SAME AS THE IDENTITY   . . . . .   91B ANNO SWED LOVE   MARG
    BUT ONE & THE SAME ESSENCE IS THEREFORE ESSENCE & NOT   91B ANNO SWED LOVE   MARG
        IDENTITY
    WHERE THOU & I IN UNDIVIDED ESSENCE WALKD ABOUT . . . .   327 FOUR ZOAS 7   271
ESSENTIAL
    ARE EQUAL IN ALL ESSENTIAL POINTS . . . . 585D DESC CAT 16   PROSE
ESSEX
    OF REUBEN NORFOLK SUFFOLK ESSEX SIMEON LINCOLN YORK   637 JERUSALEM 16   44
        LANCASHIRE
    SUFFOLK HARTFORD & ESSEX & HIS EMANATION IS GWINEVERA   . .   710 JERUSALEM 71   39
ESTABLISHD
    ESTABLISHD BY SUCH CONTEMPTIBLE POLITICIANS AS LOUIS XIV &   600B PUB ADDRESS/N   PROSE
    THE TEMPORAL THAT THE ETERNAL MIGHT BE ESTABLISHD   . . .   606A V LAST JUDG/N   PROSE
ESTABLISHMENT
    ESTABLISHMENT OF TRUTH DEPENDS ON DESTRUCTION OF FALSHOOD   687 JERUSALEM 55   *   65
        CONTINUALLY
ESTATE
    I'LL SET MY WHOLE ESTATE . . . .   21 EDW THIRD/PS 2   96
    IF I EER GROW TO MAN'S ESTATE . . . . 547 IF I GROW/N   1
    OF THIS BEAUTIFUL LITTLE ESTATE FOR THAT IT WILL BE HIGHLY 858C LETTER 55   PROSE
ESTIMATE
    IS A PUBLIC LOSS WHICH THOSE WHO KNEW HIM CAN BEST ESTIMATE 854B LETTER 53   PROSE
ESTIMATING
    THE MEASURE OF ESTIMATING THE PROFITS & . . . . 860A LETTER 56   PROSE
ESTIMATION
    THE ESTIMATION YOU ARE HELD IN AMONG ARTISTS & CONNOISSEURS 798B LETTER 10   PROSE
    ESTIMATION ON A SECOND AND THIRD PERUSAL I HAVE NOT . . . 853D LETTER 52   PROSE
ESTRILD
    BOADICEA CONWENNA ESTRILD GWINEFRID IGNOGE CAMBEL   . . .   281 FOUR ZOAS 2   62
    ESTRILD MEHETABEL & RAGAN LOVELY DAUGHTERS OF ALBION . .   624 JERUSALEM 5   44
    HACKNEY AND HOLLOWAY SICKEN FOR ESTRILD & IGNOGE . . . .   644 JERUSALEM 21   33
    KOX HAD OXFORD WARWICK WILTS HIS EMANATION IS ESTRILD . . 710 JERUSALEM 71   42
ETCH
    INSTEAD OF ETCHING THE BLACKS ETCH THE WHITES & BITE IT IN   440C MEMORANDUM/N 4   PROSE
    THAT BLAKE WOULD ETCH FOR HIM & DRAW FOR ME   . . . . .   537 AND HIS LEGS/N   35
    I SHOULD PROPOSE TO ETCH THEM IN A RAPID BUT FIRM MANNER   844B LETTER 43   PROSE
ETCHD
    WOOLETT'S BEST WORKS WERE ETCHD BY JACK BROWN . . . . .   594A PUB ADDRESS/N   PROSE
    WOOLETT ETCHD VERY BAD HIMSELF . . . . 594A PUB ADDRESS/N   PROSE
    & IN SHORT ALL THAT ARE CALLD WOOLETT'S WERE ETCHD   . . . 594A PUB ADDRESS/N   PROSE
ETCHING
    LAY A GROUND ON THE PLATE & SMOKE IT AS FOR ETCHING . . 440B MEMORANDUM/N 3   PROSE
    [& INSTEAD OF ETCHING THE SHADOWY STROKES]   . . . . . 440C MEMORANDUM/N 3   PROSE
    LAY A GROUND AS FOR ETCHING TRACE &C & . . . . . . 440C MEMORANDUM/N 4   PROSE
    INSTEAD OF ETCHING THE BLACKS ETCH THE WHITES & BITE IT IN 440C MEMORANDUM/N 4   PROSE
    BY JACK BROWNE & IN WOOLETT'S WORKS THE ETCHING IS ALL .   594A PUB ADDRESS/N   PROSE
ETERNAL
    THEN LADEN WITH ETERNAL FATE DOST GO . . . .   15 IMIT SPEN/PS   24
    BENEATH ME BURNS ETERNAL FIRE O FOR A HAND TO PLUCK ME   36B COUCH DEATH/PS   PROSE
        FORTH

```
                                                           PAGE    TITLE        LINE
ETERNAL    (CONTINUED)
    & MOUTH & HE WAS THINKING OF HIS ETERNAL FAME . . . . .  44C ISLAND MOON 1   PROSE
    ("THE HUMBLE...THE LOVING...ETERNAL LOVE") SWEET . . . .  68C ANNO LAVATER    MARG
    A VISION OF THE ETERNAL NOW . . . . . . . . . . . . . .   77B ANNO LAVATER    MARG
    DIFFER IN THE MEANING OF THE WORDS INFINITY & ETERNAL .   91C ANNO SWED LOVE   MARG
    DESPAIR MUST BE HIS ETERNAL LOT . . . . . . . . . . . .   97D NAT RELIGION 2  PROSE
    VISIT YOU BUT ETERNAL FOGS HOVER AROUND YOUR WALLS . . . 106 TIRIEL 5           23
    . . . WHOSE TEETH THE GATES OF ETERNAL DEATH] . . . . .  109 TIRIEL 8           17
    TO FLOURISH IN ETERNAL VALES THEN WHY SHOULD THEL COMPLAIN 127 BOOK OF THEL 1   25
    THE ETERNAL GATES' TERRIFIC PORTER LIFTED THE NORTHERN BAR 130 BOOK OF THEL 6    1
    OF ANCIENT KINGS AND THE FROWN OF THE ETERNAL LION . . . 135 FRENCH REVOLTN     32
    . . . THE ETERNAL WORM . . . . . . . . . . . . . . . .   135 FRENCH REVOLTN     34
    THE LAW AND GOSPEL FROM FIRE AND AIR AND ETERNAL REASON  138 FRENCH REVOLTN     95
       AND SCIENCE
    OF ETERNITY WHERE THE ETERNAL LION AND EAGLE REMAIN TO   138 FRENCH REVOLTN     97
       DEVOUR
    . . . AND COVERED HIS SOUL WITH SNOWS ETERNAL . . . . .  143 FRENCH REVOLTN    199
    SINCE ITS ADVENT THE ETERNAL HELL REVIVES AND LO . . . . 149A MARRIAGE HH 3    PROSE
    ENERGY IS ETERNAL DELIGHT . . . . . . . . . . . . . .    149D MARRIAGE HH 4    PROSE
    SAID PERHAPS YOU WILL BE WILLING TO SHEW ME MY ETERNAL LOT 155D MARRIAGE HH 17 PROSE
    I NOW ASKED MY COMPANION WHICH WAS MY ETERNAL LOT . . .  156B MARRIAGE HH 17   PROSE
    HEARING A HARPER BUT NOW WE HAVE SEEN MY ETERNAL LOT . . 156D MARRIAGE HH 17   PROSE
    THE ETERNAL FEMALE GROAND IT WAS HEARD OVER ALL THE EARTH 159A SONG LIBERTY    PROSE
    WAKD FROM HIS ETERNAL SLEEP THE HOARY ELEMENT ROARING FLED 159C SONG LIBERTY   PROSE
       AWAY
    LOOSING THE ETERNAL HORSES FROM THE DENS OF NIGHT CRYING 160A SONG LIBERTY     PROSE
    GIVING HIMSELF FOR THE NATIONS HE DANCD THE DANCE       160 ALBION ROSE          2
       OF ETERNAL DEATH
    [THOU MY] ETERNAL BANE . . . . . . . . . . . . . . . .   169 EARTHS ANSWR/N     24
    LIVES IN [AN ETERNAL] ETERNITY'S SUN RISE . . . . . . .  179 ETERNITY/N          4
    TIS ETERNAL WINTER THERE . . . . . . . . . . . . . . .   181 HOLY THURS/N       12
    AND IS THERE NOT ETERNAL FIRE AND ETERNAL CHAINS . . .   192 V DAU ALBION 4     23
    TO BIND THE PHANTOMS OF EXISTENCE FROM ETERNAL LIFE . .  192 V DAU ALBION 4     24
    HOLY ETERNAL INFINITE AND EACH JOY IS A LOVE . . . . .   192 V DAU ALBION 5      6
    THE CLEAR HEAVEN OF HER ETERNAL SPRING TO BEAR THE WINTRY 193 V DAU ALBION 5    24
       RAGE
    AND TREES & BIRDS & BEASTS & MEN BEHOLD THEIR ETERNAL JOY 195 V DAU ALBION 8     8
    THIS IS ETERNAL DEATH AND THIS THE TORMENT LONG FORETOLD 196 AMERICA PREL 2     17
    BESIDE THE STONE OF NIGHT AND LIKE THE ETERNAL LION'S HOWL 198 AMERICA 7          2
    LOUD HOWLS THE ETERNAL WOLF THE ETERNAL LION LASHES HIS  199 AMERICA 9           2
       TAIL
    HEAVENS ETERNAL VIPER SELF-RENEWD ROLLING IN CLOUDS . .  199 AMERICA 9          15
    LOUD HOWLS THE ETERNAL WOLF THE ETERNAL LION LASHES HIS  199 AMERICA 9          27
       TAIL
    IN A SWEET VALE SHELTERD WITH CEDARS THAT ETERNAL STRETCH 204 AMERICA CANC B     3
    . . . TH [ETERNAL] (ANCIENT) PILLAR . . . . . . . . .    205 AMERICA CANC C *   11
    ETERNAL BANE . . . . . . . . . . . . . . . . . . . . .   211 EARTHS ANSR/SE     24
    IT IS ETERNAL WINTER THERE . . . . . . . . . . . . . .   212 HOLY THURS/SE      12
    DEATH WAS NOT BUT ETERNAL LIFE SPRUNG . . . . . . . . .  223 URIZEN 3           39
    THE ETERNAL ABODE IN MY HOLINESS . . . . . . . . . . .   224 URIZEN 4            7
    OF ETERNAL BRASS WRITTEN IN MY SOLITUDE . . . . . . . .  224 URIZEN 4           33
    IN THE FLAMES OF ETERNAL FURY . . . . . . . . . . . . .  225 URIZEN 5            2
    IN THE FLAMES OF ETERNAL FURY . . . . . . . . . . . . .  225 URIZEN 5           18
    THE ETERNAL FIRES BEATING WITHOUT . . . . . . . . . . .  226 URIZEN 5           32
    OF DARKNESS THE ETERNAL PROPHET HOWLD . . . . . . . . .  227 URIZEN 10           7
    AND URIZEN SO HIS ETERNAL NAME . . . . . . . . . . . .   227 URIZEN 10          11
    THE ETERNAL PROPHET HEAVD THE DARK BELLOWS . . . . . .   227 URIZEN 10          15
    THE ETERNAL MIND BOUNDED BEGAN TO ROLL . . . . . . . .   227 URIZEN 10          19
    AND NOW HIS ETERNAL LIFE . . . . . . . . . . . . . . .   230 URIZEN 13          33
    SHUDDRING THE ETERNAL PROPHET SMOTE . . . . . . . . . .  230 URIZEN 13          35
    THE ETERNAL PROPHET & URIZEN CLOSD . . . . . . . . . .   230 URIZEN 13          40
    THUS THE ETERNAL PROPHET WAS DIVIDED . . . . . . . . .   230 URIZEN 15           1
    PETRIFY THE ETERNAL MYRIADS . . . . . . . . . . . . . .  231 URIZEN 18          14
    HIS ETERNAL CREATIONS APPEAR . . . . . . . . . . . . .   234 URIZEN 23           9
    ALL HIS ETERNAL SONS IN LIKE MANNER . . . . . . . . . .  234 URIZEN 23          19
    AND FORGOT THEIR ETERNAL LIFE . . . . . . . . . . . . .  236 URIZEN 25          42
    THE ETERNAL LAWS OF GOD . . . . . . . . . . . . . . . .  236 URIZEN 28           7
    THRO ONE HEARS MUSIC OF THE SPHERES THRO ONE THE ETERNAL 237 EUROPE INTRO        2
       VINE
    AND SEE SMALL PORTIONS OF THE ETERNAL WORLD THAT        237 EUROPE INTRO         4
       EVER GROWETH
    WILD FLOWERS I GATHERD & HE SHEWD ME EACH ETERNAL FLOWER 238 EUROPE INTRO       20
    IN FORESTS OF ETERNAL DEATH SHRIEKING IN HOLLOW TREES .  238 EUROPE PREL 2       6
    AND WHO SHALL BIND THE INFINITE WITH AN ETERNAL BAND . . 239 EUROPE PREL 2      13
    DESCENDED THRO THE ORIENT GATES OF THE ETERNAL DAY . .   239 EUROPE 4            3
    THAT AN ETERNAL LIFE AWAITS THE WORMS OF SIXTY WINTERS . 240 EUROPE 5            6
    WITH TOOL STONES PRECIOUS SUCH ETERNAL IN THE HEAVENS .  241 EUROPE 10           8
    IN FORESTS OF NIGHT THEN ALL THE ETERNAL FORESTS WERE   241 EUROPE 10           18
       DIVIDED
    I WILL SING YOU A SONG OF LOS THE ETERNAL PROPHET . . .  245 SONG OF LOS 3       1
    AGAINST ONE ANOTHER SO LET THEM WAR ON SLAVES TO       245 SONG OF LOS 3        14
       THE ETERNAL ELEMENTS
    THE ETERNAL PROPHET BEAT ON HIS ANVILS . . . . . . . .   253 AHANIA 4           27
    ETERNAL FELL ROUND THE TREE . . . . . . . . . . . . . .  253 AHANIA 4           51
    TO THE BLISS OF ETERNAL VALLEYS . . . . . . . . . . . .  254 AHANIA 5            9
    TO THE SONS OF ETERNAL JOY . . . . . . . . . . . . . .   254 AHANIA 5           16
    FILLD WITH ETERNAL SEED . . . . . . . . . . . . . . . .  255 AHANIA 5           21
    O ETERNAL BIRTHS SUNG ROUND AHANIA . . . . . . . . . .   255 AHANIA 5           22
    THE SEED OF ETERNAL SCIENCE . . . . . . . . . . . . . .  255 AHANIA 5           34
    SITTING BENEATH THE ETERNAL OAK . . . . . . . . . . . .  256 BOOK OF LOS 3       4
    THE ETERNAL PROPHET BOUND IN A CHAIN . . . . . . . . .   256 BOOK OF LOS 3      31
    HIS FEET STAMP THE ETERNAL FIERCE-RAGING . . . . . . .   256 BOOK OF LOS 3      39
```

```
                                                          PAGE      TITLE          LINE
ETERNAL    (CONTINUED)
   OF THE [ETERNAL] ANCIENT MAN  . . . . . . . . . . . .  263B FOUR ZOAS          *TITLE
   CREATING SPACES LEST THEY FALL INTO ETERNAL DEATH  . . 267 FOUR ZOAS 1           100
   IS ETERNAL DEATH WHAT SHALL WE DO O GOD [HELP] PITY & HELP  267 FOUR ZOAS 1      107
   THE [?ETERNAL] FALLEN MAN TAKES HIS REPOSE URIZEN SLEEPS  271 FOUR ZOAS 1    *  261
      IN THE PORCH
   NOR SHALT THOU ME TORMENT FOR I BEHOLD THE [ETERNAL] FALLEN  272 FOUR ZOAS 1  *  284
      MAN
   SICKNING LIES THE [ETERNAL] FALLEN MAN HIS HEAD SICK HIS  272 FOUR ZOAS 1     *  288
      HEART FAINT
   ETERNITY GROAND & WAS TROUBLED AT THE IMAGE OF ETERNAL  273 FOUR ZOAS 1          315
      DEATH
   PITY NOT VALA FOR SHE PITIED NOT THE ETERNAL MAN  . .  273 FOUR ZOAS 1          326
   AFAR OFF RUSHING BACK REDDNING WITH RAGE THE [ETERNAL]  275 FOUR ZOAS 1       *  413
      MIGHTY FATHER
   ETERNITY GROAND & WAS TROUBLED AT THE IMAGE OF ETERNAL  277 FOUR ZOAS 1       *  462
      DEATH
   FROM THE SUPPORTING ARMS OF THE ETERNAL SAVIOUR WHO DISPOSD  277 FOUR ZOAS 1    466
   THE PALE LIMBS OF HIS ETERNAL INDIVIDUALITY  . . . . . 277 FOUR ZOAS 1          467
   . . . THUS RECOUNTING THE WARS OF DEATH ETERNAL  . . . 277 FOUR ZOAS 1          483
   THE ETERNAL MAN WEPT IN THE HOLY TENT OUR BROTHER  . . 277 FOUR ZOAS 1          484
      IN ETERNITY
   I WILL INFOLD THE ETERNAL TENT IN CLOUDS OPAKE WHILE THOU  278 FOUR ZOAS 1      493
   ETERNAL DEATH TO LUVAH RAGING LUVAH POURD  . . . . . . 278 FOUR ZOAS 1          516
   THE ETERNAL VOICE HE STOOD THE SWEAT CHILLD ON HIS MIGHTY  278 FOUR ZOAS 1      522
      LIMBS
   TO POUR ITS FURY ON HIMSELF & ON THE ETERNAL MAN  . .  279 FOUR ZOAS 1          540
   TERRIFIC RAGD THE ETERNAL WHEELS OF INTELLECT TERRIFIC  280 FOUR ZOAS 1         571
      RAGD
   THE LIVING CREATURES OF THE WHEELS IN THE WARS OF ETERNAL  280 FOUR ZOAS 1      572
      LIFE
   DOWNWARDS & OUTWARDS [TENDING] CONSUMING IN THE WARS OF  280 FOUR ZOAS 1      *  574
      ETERNAL DEATH
   [?SAYING XXX OF XXX FOR XXX OF ETERNAL LIFE]  . . . .  SUPP FOUR ZOAS 1       *
   NO MORE EXULTING FOR HE SAW ETERNAL DEATH BENEATH  . . 280 FOUR ZOAS 2           14
   OF DEATH ETERNAL THAT WE ALL GO TO ETERNAL DEATH  . . . 282 FOUR ZOAS 2         101
   . . . THE FAINT HEART OF THE [ETERNAL] FALLEN [ANCIENT] MAN  283 FOUR ZOAS 2  *  143
   AND PILLARD HALLS & ROOMS RECIEVD THE ETERNAL WANDERING  286 FOUR ZOAS 2        242
      STARS
   PERMITTED ALL LEST MAN SHOULD FALL INTO ETERNAL DEATH  . 287 FOUR ZOAS 2        262
   . . . WITH [SONGS & JOY] SORROW & CARE [?ETERNAL FEAR]  . 287 FOUR ZOAS 2     *  268
   O PRINCE THE ETERNAL ONE HATH SET THEE LEADER OF HIS HOSTS  292 FOUR ZOAS 3      27
   WHERE LIBERTY WAS JUSTICE & ETERNAL SCIENCE WAS MERCY  . 292 FOUR ZOAS 3         40
   . . . & THE [ETERNAL] ANCIENT MAN WAS SMITTEN  . . . . . 292 FOUR ZOAS 3      *   43
   THE [ETERNAL] [FALLEN] DARKNING MAN WALKD  . . . . . . 292 FOUR ZOAS 3        *   44
   . . . OF THE [?ETERNAL] SLUMBEROUS MAN & THUS HE SPOKE  . 293 FOUR ZOAS 3     *   58
   . . . OF THE [ETERNAL] FALLEN ONE ALBION  . . . . . .  293 FOUR ZOAS 3        *   68
   . . . [THE ETERNAL MAN] AROSE IN TERROR ALBION ROSE  . . 293 FOUR ZOAS 3      *   69
   INDIGNANT ROSE THE [ETERNAL] [FALLEN] AWFUL MAN . . . .  293 FOUR ZOAS 3      *   70
   . . . THE [ETERNAL] [FALLN ONE] ALBION STARTING FROM HIS  293 FOUR ZOAS 3     *   71
      SLEEP
   LIKE A DARK LAMP ETERNAL DEATH HAUNTS ALL MY EXPECTATION  293 FOUR ZOAS 3        75
   RENT FROM ETERNAL BROTHERHOOD WE DIE & ARE NO MORE  . . 293 FOUR ZOAS 3          76
   . . . THE [ETERNAL] ANCIENT MAN MIGHTY ALBION . . . . . 293 FOUR ZOAS 3       *   79
   THEN FROWND THE [ETERNAL] FALLEN MAN ALBION . . . . .  294 FOUR ZOAS 3           83
   ONLY A VOICE ETERNAL WAILING IN THE ELEMENTS  . . . .  297 FOUR ZOAS 3          206
   SHE WANDERS IN ETERNAL FEAR OF FALLING INTO THE INDEFINITE  297 FOUR ZOAS 3     208
   WE HAVE DRUNK UP THE [(ANCIENT)] ETERNAL MAN BY OUR  . . 298 FOUR ZOAS 4         36
      UNBOUNDED POWER
   GO FORTH BEAR ENITHARMON BACK TO THE ETERNAL PROPHET  . . 299 FOUR ZOAS 4        70
   THE DAY OF TERROR & ABHORRENCE [ETERNAL]  . . . . . .  299 FOUR ZOAS 4        *   85
   IS GOD THE ETERNAL MAN IS SEALD NEVER TO BE DELIVERD  . 301 FOUR ZOAS 4         132
   THY ETERNAL FORM SHALL NEVER RENEW MY UNCERTAIN PREVAILS  301 FOUR ZOAS 4       136
      AGAINST THEE
   THAT IN ETERNAL FIELDS IN COMFORT WANDERD WITH MY FLOCKS  301 FOUR ZOAS 4       138
   AND I WHAT CAN I NOW BEHOLD BUT AN ETERNAL DEATH  . . . 301 FOUR ZOAS 4         143
   BEFORE MY EYES & AN ETERNAL WEARY WORK TO STRIVE  . . . 301 FOUR ZOAS 4         144
   ON HATE ETERNAL IN HIS VAST DISDAIN HE LABOURD BEATING  . 302 FOUR ZOAS 4       206
   THE ETERNAL MIND BOUNDED BEGAN TO ROLL EDDIES OF WRATH  303 FOUR ZOAS 4         208
      CEASELESS
   AND LIVE BEHOLD ETERNAL DEATH IS IN BEULAH BEHOLD  . . 304 FOUR ZOAS 4         258
   WAS PUT TO ETERNAL DEATH LOS FELT THE LIMIT & SAW  . . 304 FOUR ZOAS 4         276
   [THE XXX ETERNAL DEATH]  . . . . . . . . . . . . . . . SUPP FOUR ZOAS 4      *
   SHADOWS OF ETERNAL DEATH SIT IN THE LEADEN AIR  . . .  305 FOUR ZOAS 5           22
   THE SPEARS OF URIZEN FROM CHARIOTS ROUND THE ETERNAL TENT  306 FOUR ZOAS 5       44
   FOR NOW HE FEARD ETERNAL DEATH & UTTERMOST EXTINCTION  . 307 FOUR ZOAS 5          75
   THE VIRTUES OF THE ETERNAL WORLDS TEN THOUSAND THOUSAND  308 FOUR ZOAS 5         116
      SPIRITS
   THE ROCKS SHOOK THE ETERNAL BARS TUGGD TO & FRO WERE RIFTED  310 FOUR ZOAS 5    186
   AND IN THESE MONSTROUS FORMS I [?LINE] LIVE IN AN ETERNAL  313 FOUR ZOAS 6    *   62
      WOE
   [CEASE] END & THE ETERNAL MAN NO MORE RENEW BENEATH OUR  313 FOUR ZOAS 6         66
      POWER
   IF THOU REFUSEST IN ETERNAL FLIGHT THY BEAMS IN VAIN  . . 313 FOUR ZOAS 6        67
   POUR DOWN MY FLIGHT THRO DARK IMMENSITY ETERNAL FALLING  313 FOUR ZOAS 6         69
   OR GOLD A GLITTERING TORMENT SHINING & HISSING IN ETERNAL  315 FOUR ZOAS 6      121
      PAIN
   VOID PATHLESS BEATEN WITH [ETERNAL] IRON SLEET . . . .   315 FOUR ZOAS 6     *  148
   . . . & ETERNAL HAIL & [SNOW] RAIN  . . . . . . . . .  315 FOUR ZOAS 6          148
   OR SLEEP SUCH SLEEP AS SPIRITS ETERNAL WEARIED IN HIS DARK  316 FOUR ZOAS 6     181
   AND IF ETERNAL FALLING I REPOSE ON THE DARK BOSOM  . .  317 FOUR ZOAS 6         218
   VOID PATHLESS BEAT WITH [?ENION] SNOWS ETERNAL & IRON HAIL  318 FOUR ZOAS 6  *  271
      & RAIN
```

608

ETERNAL   (CONTINUED)

	PAGE	TITLE	LINE
BUT IN ETERNAL TIMES THE SEAT OF URIZEN IS IN THE SOUTH	319 FOUR ZOAS 6		279
LEST DEATH ETERNAL SHOULD BE THE RESULT	319 FOUR ZOAS 6		283
THE RIPE FRUIT BLUSHES INTO JOY IN HEAVEN'S ETERNAL HALLS	324 FOUR ZOAS 7		176
AMONG THE FLOWERS OF BEULAH WALKD THE ETERNAL MAN & SAW	326 FOUR ZOAS 7		239
OF THE ETERNAL MAN & SMOTE HIM BUT THOU SPECTRE DARK	326 FOUR ZOAS 7		264
FOR TILL THESE TERRORS PLANTED ROUND THE GATES OF ETERNAL LIFE	327 FOUR ZOAS 7		302
TO LIFE ETERNAL BE ASSURD I AM THY REAL SELF	328 FOUR ZOAS 7		345
THAT WITHOUT A RANSOM I COULD NOT BE SAVD FROM ETERNAL DEATH	329 FOUR ZOAS 7		389
THE FRUIT & GIVE ME PROOF OF LIFE ETERNAL OR I DIE	330 FOUR ZOAS 7		394
AND MUST HAVE GIVEN HIMSELF TO DEATH ETERNAL BUT	330 FOUR ZOAS 7		396
FOR WITHOUT A CREATED BODY THE SPECTRE IS ETERNAL DEATH	330 FOUR ZOAS 7		410
WILL GIVE US TO ETERNAL DEATH FIT PUNISHMENT FOR SUCH	330 FOUR ZOAS 7		426
HIDEOUS OFFENDERS UTTERMOST EXTINCTION IN ETERNAL PAIN .	330 FOUR ZOAS 7		427
THEY RATHER CHOSE TO MEET ETERNAL DEATH THAN TO DESTROY	332 FOUR ZOAS 7		484
TO ETERNAL TORMENT IN THESE FLAMES FOR THO I HAVE THE POWER	339 FOUR ZOAS 7B		253
WOO'D & SUBDUD INTO ?ETERNAL DEATH THE DEMON ?LAY .	340 FOUR ZOAS 7B		286
THE HORRID SIGHT OF DEATH & TORMENT BUT THE ETERNAL PROMISE	340 FOUR ZOAS 7B		291
THE [ETERNAL] FALLEN MAN STRETCHD LIKE A CORSE UPON THE OOZY ROCK	341 FOUR ZOAS 8		4
ALL BEULAH STOOD ASTONISHD LOOKING DOWN TO ETERNAL DEATH	342 FOUR ZOAS 8		47
AS ONCE IN THOSE ETERNAL FIELDS IN BROTHERHOOD & LOVE .	345 FOUR ZOAS 8		159
THE ETERNAL MAN IS SEALD BY THEE NEVER TO BE DELIVERD .	345 FOUR ZOAS 8		161
NOW WE BEHOLD REDEMPTION NOW WE KNOW THAT LIFE ETERNAL .	346 FOUR ZOAS 8		197
WHERE DEATH ETERNAL IS PUT OFF ETERNALLY	347 FOUR ZOAS 8		240
ABHORRD ACCURSED EVER DYING AN ETERNAL DEATH	347 FOUR ZOAS 8	*	256
FROM DEATH ETERNAL & TO PUT OFF SATAN ETERNALLY	348 FOUR ZOAS 8		286
SAYING IS THIS ETERNAL DEATH WHERE SHALL I HIDE FROM DEATH	349 FOUR ZOAS 8		332
OF ETERNITY FOR HIMSELF HE HEWD IT DESPAIRING OF LIFE ETERNAL	349 FOUR ZOAS 8		340
FELL FROM MY STATION IN THE ETERNAL BOSOM I DIVIDED . .	350 FOUR ZOAS 8		352
LO ENITHARMON TERRIBLE & BEAUTIFUL IN ETERNAL YOUTH . . .	351 FOUR ZOAS 8		408
DRINK IN THE DEADLY DULL DELUSION HORRORS OF ETERNAL DEATH	352 FOUR ZOAS 8		418
OF HIS ETERNAL DAY & MEMORY STRIVES TO AUGMENT HIS RUTHFULNESS	352 FOUR ZOAS 8		455
THE ETERNAL MAN SLEEPS IN THE EARTH NOR FEELS THE VIGROUS SUN	354 FOUR ZOAS 8		507
O HOW THE HORRORS OF ETERNAL DEATH TAKE HOLD ON MAN . .	354 FOUR ZOAS 8		519
BUT AN ETERNAL CONSUMMATION IS DARK ENION	355 FOUR ZOAS 8		542
OR A LEAF BUDS THE ETERNAL MAN IS SEEN IS HEARD IS FELT	356 FOUR ZOAS 8		582
THE FOUNDATIONS OF THE ETERNAL HILLS DISCOVERD	357 FOUR ZOAS 9		17
OR WHERE THE COMETS OF THE NIGHT OR STARS OF [ETERNAL] ASTERIAL DAY	358 FOUR ZOAS 9		40
ON THIS ROCK LAY THE FADED HEAD OF THE ETERNAL MAN .	359 FOUR ZOAS 9		95
THE ETERNAL MAN SAT ON THE ROCKS & CRIED WITH AWFUL VOICE	360 FOUR ZOAS 9		123
IN THOSE ETERNAL FIELDS IN CLOUDS OF MORNING STEPPING FORTH	360 FOUR ZOAS 9		125
ARISE TO ETERNAL BIRTHS SHAKE OFF THY COLD REPOSE . .	360 FOUR ZOAS 9		130
THAT THE ETERNAL WORLDS MAY SEE THY FACE IN PEACE & JOY	360 FOUR ZOAS 9		132
THEN WRATH BURST ROUND THE ETERNAL MAN WAS WRATH AGAIN HE CRIED	360 FOUR ZOAS 9		137
THY SELF DESTROYING BEAST FORMD SCIENCE SHALL BE THY ETERNAL LOT	361 FOUR ZOAS 9		150
SEEKING THE ETERNAL WHICH IS ALWAYS PRESENT TO THE WISE	361 FOUR ZOAS 9		171
URIZEN DROPT A TEAR THE ETERNAL MAN DARKEND WITH SORROW	362 FOUR ZOAS 9	*	200
AND THE ETERNAL MAN SAID HEAR MY [VOICE] WORDS O PRINCE OF LIGHT	362 FOUR ZOAS 9		204
ETERNAL & I THRO HIM AWAKE FROM DEATH'S DARK VALE . .	362 FOUR ZOAS 9		207
IN PANGS OF AN ETERNAL BIRTH IN TORMENT & AWE & FEAR .	363 FOUR ZOAS 9		234
THE SONS OF URIZEN SHOUT THEIR FATHER ROSE THE ETERNAL HORSES	365 FOUR ZOAS 9		308
THE ETERNAL MAN ALSO SAT DOWN UPON THE COUCHES OF BEULAH	366 FOUR ZOAS 9		354
IN THE ETERNAL HEAVENS OF HUMAN [THOUGHT] IMAGINATION BURIED BENEATH	366 FOUR ZOAS 9		368
SERVANTS TO THE INFINITE & ETERNAL OF THE HUMAN FORM . .	366 FOUR ZOAS 9		374
RISE FROM THE DEWS OF DEATH FOR THE ETERNAL MAN IS RISEN	367 FOUR ZOAS 9		389
THUS IN ETERNAL CHILDHOOD STRAYING AMONG VALA'S FLOCKS .	371 FOUR ZOAS 9		553
THE UNIVERSAL GROAN WENT UP THE ETERNAL MAN WAS DARKEND	372 FOUR ZOAS 9		578
OVER THE RUIND WORLDS THE SMOKING TOMB OF THE ETERNAL PROPHET	373 FOUR ZOAS 9		616
THE ETERNAL MAN AROSE HE WELCOMD THEM TO THE FEAST . . .	373 FOUR ZOAS 9		617
THE FEAST WAS SPREAD IN THE BRIGHT SOUTH & THE ETERNAL MAN	373 FOUR ZOAS 9		618
AND MANY ETERNAL MEN SAT AT THE GOLDEN FEAST TO SEE . .	373 FOUR ZOAS 9		621
NOT FOR OURSELVES BUT FOR THE ETERNAL FAMILY WE LIVE . .	374 FOUR ZOAS 9		640
EACH SHALL BEHOLD THE ETERNAL FATHER & LOVE & JOY ABOUND	374 FOUR ZOAS 9		642
SO SPOKE THE ETERNAL AT THE FEAST THEY EMBRACD THE NEW BORN MAN	374 FOUR ZOAS 9		643
CALLING HIM BROTHER IMAGE OF THE ETERNAL FATHER THEY SAT DOWN	374 FOUR ZOAS 9		644
CALLING THE MORNING INTO BEULAH THE ETERNAL MAN REJOICD	374 FOUR ZOAS 9		646
THE SONG AROSE TO THE GOLDEN FEAST THE ETERNAL MAN REJOICD	375 FOUR ZOAS 9		692
THEN THE ETERNAL MAN SAID LUVAH THE VINTAGE IS RIPE ARISE	375 FOUR ZOAS 9		693
BEHIND THE SEAT OF THE ETERNAL MAN & TOOK HIS WAY . .	376 FOUR ZOAS 9		712
. . . THAN PAINS OF ETERNAL [DEATH] BIRTH	377 FOUR ZOAS 9		739
ETERNAL DEATH WHO CAN ENDURE LET US CONSUME IN FIRES .	377 FOUR ZOAS 9		740
THE PANGS OF ETERNAL BIRTH	377 FOUR ZOAS 9		742
. . . ARE BETTER THAN THE PANGS OF ETERNAL DEATH . . .	377 FOUR ZOAS 9		742
THE ETERNAL MAN DARKEND WITH SORROW & A WINTRY MANTLE .	377 FOUR ZOAS 9		772
TO THE ETERNAL MAN IN WOE HE CAST THEM WAILING INTO . . .	378 FOUR ZOAS 9		797
HE WALKS UPON THE ETERNAL MOUNTAINS RAISING HIS HEAVENLY VOICE	379 FOUR ZOAS 9		835

ETERNAL   (CONTINUED)

	PAGE	TITLE	LINE
AROUND THE ETERNAL MAN'S BRIGHT TENT THE LITTLE CHILDREN PLAY	379	FOUR ZOAS 9	839
THE [ANCIENT] ETERNAL MAN BOWD HIS BRIGHT HEAD	380	FOUR ZOAS AD 1	2
HIS GRIEF IS THEIR ETERNAL JOY	425	MENTAL TRAVLER	41
THE BLOSSOMS OF ETERNAL LIFE	442	DEDICATN BLAIR	20
THE TWO INTRODUCERS INTO ETERNAL LIFE WOMEN WITH INFANTS	444B	LAST JUDGMNT/L	PROSE
THE ETERNAL CREATION FLOWING FROM THE DIVINE HUMANITY .	444C	LAST JUDGMNT/L	PROSE
IDENTITIES OR THINGS ARE NEITHER CAUSE NOR EFFECT THEY ARE ETERNAL	470D	ANNO REYNOLDS	MARG
REMAIN MY ELEMENT MY ETERNAL DWELLING PLACE HOW CAN I .	477A	ANNO REYNOLDS	MARG
THE ETERNAL GREAT HUMANITY DIVINE PLANTED HIS PARADISE . .	481	MILTON 2	8
FOR DEATH ETERNAL IN THE HEAVENS OF ALBION & BEFORE THE GATES	481	MILTON 2	14
A BARD'S PROPHETIC SONG FOR SITTING AT ETERNAL TABLES . .	482	MILTON 2	22
MARK WELL MY WORDS THEY ARE OF YOUR ETERNAL SALVATION .	482	MILTON 2	25
MARK WELL MY WORDS THEY ARE OF YOUR ETERNAL SALVATION .	482	MILTON 3	5
THY WORK IS ETERNAL DEATH WITH MILLS & OVENS & CAULDRONS	483	MILTON 4	17
TROUBLE ME NO MORE THOU CANST NOT HAVE ETERNAL LIFE . .	483	MILTON 4	18
MARK WELL MY WORDS THEY ARE OF YOUR ETERNAL SALVATION .	484	MILTON 4	20
FROM GOLGONOOZA THE SPIRITUAL FOUR-FOLD LONDON ETERNAL .	485	MILTON 6	1
MARK WELL MY WORDS THEY ARE OF YOUR ETERNAL SALVATION .	486	MILTON 7	18
HIS FUTURE COURSE THRO DARKNESS AND DESPAIR TO ETERNAL DEATH	487	MILTON 7	26
MARK WELL MY WORDS THEY ARE OF YOUR ETERNAL SALVATION .	487	MILTON 7	50
PITYING HIS YOUTH AND BEAUTY TREMBLING AT ETERNAL DEATH	488	MILTON 8	31
MARK WELL MY WORDS THEY ARE OF YOUR ETERNAL SALVATION .	489	MILTON 9	7
OF MY ETERNAL MIND TRANSGRESSORS I WILL REND OFF FOR EVER	490	MILTON 9	28
THE INNOCENT SHOULD BE CONDEMND FOR THE GUILTY THEN AN ETERNAL ROSE	491	MILTON 11	16
SAYING IF THE GUILTY SHOULD BE CONDEMND HE MUST BE AN ETERNAL DEATH	491	MILTON 11	17
SO SPAKE THE ETERNAL AND CONFIRMD IT WITH A THUNDEROUS OATH	492	MILTON 11	27
MARK WELL MY WORDS THEY ARE OF YOUR ETERNAL SALVATION . .	492	MILTON 11	31
WHICH NOW GIRD ROUND US O ETERNAL TORMENT I FORMD THE SERPENT	493	MILTON 12	29
BEING MOST IMPURE SELF-CONDEMND TO ETERNAL TEARS HE DROVE	493	MILTON 12	47
SICK COUCH BEARS THE DARK SHADES OF ETERNAL DEATH INFOLDING	493	MILTON 13	1
GLORYING TO INVOLVE ALBION'S BODY IN FIRES OF ETERNAL WAR	493	MILTON 13	6
OUR VIRTUES & CRUEL GOODNESSES HAVE DESERVD ETERNAL DEATH	494	MILTON 13	34
WHO IS THE ETERNAL ALL-PROTECTING DIVINE HUMANITY . .	495	MILTON 14	2
AND MILTON SAID I GO TO ETERNAL DEATH THE NATIONS STILL	495	MILTON 14	14
I WILL GO DOWN TO SELF ANNIHILATION AND ETERNAL DEATH .	495	MILTON 14	22
TO CLAIM THE HELLS MY FURNACES I GO TO ETERNAL DEATH .	496	MILTON 14	32
AND MILTON SAID I GO TO ETERNAL DEATH ETERNITY SHUDDERD	496	MILTON 14	33
A MOURNFUL SHADE ETERNITY SHUDDERD AT THE IMAGE OF ETERNAL DEATH	496	MILTON 14	35
IN THEIR ETERNAL SPHERES NOW HUMAN THO THEIR BODIES REMAIN CLOSD	498	MILTON 17	4
BUT MANY OF THE ETERNALS ROSE UP FROM ETERNAL TABLES .	502	MILTON 20	43
SAYING MILTON GOES TO ETERNAL DEATH SO SAYING THEY GROAND IN SPIRIT	504	MILTON 21	43
RENEW IT TO ETERNAL LIFE LO I AM WITH YOU ALWAY	504	MILTON 21	56
BUT YOU CANNOT RENEW MILTON HE GOES TO ETERNAL DEATH .	504	MILTON 21	57
FELL FROM MY STATION IN THE ETERNAL BOSOM SIX THOUSAND YEARS	505	MILTON 22	16
ARISE O SONS GIVE ALL YOUR STRENGTH AGAINST ETERNAL DEATH	509	MILTON 24	34
BUT THEY DEPICT HIM BALD & AGED WHO IS IN ETERNAL YOUTH	509	MILTON 24	69
WHICH IS THE SWIFTEST OF ALL THINGS ALL WERE ETERNAL TORMENT	510	MILTON 24	73
SHALL BIND THEM SEPARATE THEY CANNOT BELIEVE IN ETERNAL LIFE	511	MILTON 25	33
BUT THE ELECT MUST BE SAVED (FROM) FIRES OF ETERNAL DEATH	511	MILTON 25	38
ENDING IN DEATH WHICH WOULD OF ITSELF BE ETERNAL DEATH . .	513	MILTON 26	42
HERE THE SONS OF LOS LABOUR AGAINST DEATH ETERNAL THROUGH ALL	514	MILTON 27	44
ETERNAL AND SOMETIMES TWO SPECTRES LIKE LAMPS QUIVERING	515	MILTON 28	11
WHERE ORC INCESSANT HOWLS BURNING IN FIRES OF ETERNAL YOUTH	517	MILTON 29	29
AND IT IS THUS CREATED LO THE ETERNAL GREAT HUMANITY . .	519	MILTON 30	15
THE ETERNAL WHO IS BLESSED FOR EVER & EVER AMEN	519	MILTON 30	31
YOU CANNOT GO TO ETERNAL DEATH IN THAT WHICH CAN NEVER DIE	521	MILTON 32	24
CALLED ETERNAL ANNIHILATION THAT NONE BUT THE LIVING SHALL	522	MILTON 32	27
JUDGE THEN OF THY OWN SELF THY ETERNAL LINEAMENTS EXPLORE	522	MILTON 32	30
WHAT IS ETERNAL & WHAT CHANGEABLE & WHAT ANNIHILABLE .	522	MILTON 32	31
BUT THEIR FORMS ETERNAL EXIST FOR-EVER AMEN HALLELUJAH .	522	MILTON 32	* 38
FROM DEATH ETERNAL SUCH YOUR LOT TO BE CONTINUALLY REDEEMD	522	MILTON 33	12
AND THE ETERNAL MAN EVEN ALBION UPON THE ROCK OF AGES .	524	MILTON 34	46
DICTATE TO MY ETERNAL WILL & TO MY DICTATE BOW	530	MILTON 38	53
LEST HE SHOULD FALL APART IN HIS ETERNAL DEATH TO IMITATE	531	MILTON 39	26
THE ETERNAL GREAT HUMANITY DIVINE SURROUNDED BY . . .	531	MILTON 39	27
BEFORE OLOLON MILTON STOOD & PERCIEVD THE ETERNAL FORM .	532	MILTON 40	1
OF JESUS WHO DENY THE FAITH & MOCK AT ETERNAL LIFE . . .	533	MILTON 41	22
THOU GOEST TO ETERNAL DEATH & ALL MUST GO WITH THEE . .	534	MILTON 42	2
A DESCRIPTION OF THE ETERNAL PRINCIPLES THAT EXIST IN ALL AGES	571A	DESC CAT 3	PROSE
VISIONS OF THESE ETERNAL PRINCIPLES OR	571B	DESC CAT 3	PROSE
THE ETERNAL ATTRIBUTES OR DIVINE NAMES WHICH	571C	DESC CAT 3	PROSE
THE PLOWMAN OF CHAUCER IS HERCULES IN HIS SUPREME ETERNAL	571C	DESC CAT 3	PROSE
IS INSPIRATION AND CANNOT BE SURPASSED IT IS PERFECT AND ETERNAL	579C	DESC CAT 5	PROSE
BUT ETERNAL VISION OR IMAGINATION OF ALL THAT EXISTS .	604D	V LAST JUDG/N	PROSE
AS TWO DISTINCT THINGS & SO CALLD FOR THE SAKE OF ETERNAL LIFE	605A	V LAST JUDG/N	PROSE

	PAGE	TITLE	LINE

ETERNAL   (CONTINUED)

KNOWN & THE ETERNAL NATURE & PERMANENCE . . . . . . 605B V LAST JUDG/N   PROSE
BUT ITS ETERNAL IMAGE & INDIVIDUALITY NEVER DIES . . . 605B V LAST JUDG/N   PROSE
THIS WORLD OF IMAGINATION IS INFINITE & ETERNAL WHEREAS   605D V LAST JUDG/N   PROSE
& [FOR A SMALL MOMENT] TEMPORAL THERE EXIST IN THAT ETERNAL 605D V LAST JUDG/N   PROSE
   WORLD
ALL THINGS ARE COMPREHENDED IN THEIR ETERNAL FORMS . . . 605D V LAST JUDG/N   PROSE
THE TEMPORAL THAT THE ETERNAL MIGHT BE ESTABLISHD . . 606A V LAST JUDG/N   PROSE
EXIST NO MORE EVERY THING IS ETERNAL . . . . 606D V LAST JUDG/N   PROSE
EACH IDENTITY [&] IS ETERNAL CONSEQUENTLY . . . . . . 607A V LAST JUDG/N   *PROSE
BUT ETERNAL IDENTITY IS ONE THING & CORPOREAL VEGETATION IS 607A V LAST JUDG/N   PROSE
THE ETERNAL CONSUMMATION OF VEGETABLE LIFE & DEATH . . . 609A V LAST JUDG/N   PROSE
REPRESENTS ETERNAL FIRE WHICH IS THE FIRE OF GENERATION OR 609A V LAST JUDG/N   PROSE
VEGETATION IT IS AN ETERNAL CONSUMMATION . . . . . . 609A V LAST JUDG/N   PROSE
THIS ETERNAL FEMALE & TREMBLE AT WHAT OTHERS FEAR NOT . . 609B V LAST JUDG/N   PROSE
& IN HIM SEES ALL REFLECTED AS IN A GLASS OF ETERNAL   610D V LAST JUDG/N   PROSE
   DIAMOND
& THE NATURE OF ETERNAL THINGS DISPLAYD . . . . . . 612D V LAST JUDG/N   PROSE
ETERNAL REALITIES AS THEY EXIST IN THE HUMAN IMAGINATION   613C V LAST JUDG/N   PROSE
THE ETERNAL BIRTHS OF INTELLECT FROM THE DIVINE HUMANITY   613D V LAST JUDG/N   PROSE
BUT THE REAL VISION OF TIME IS IN ETERNAL YOUTH . . . 614D V LAST JUDG/N   PROSE
EMANATE UNCURBED IN THEIR ETERNAL GLORY . . . . . . 615C V LAST JUDG/N   PROSE
ERROR IS CREATED TRUTH IS ETERNAL . . . . 617B V LAST JUDG/N   PROSE
ETERNAL DEATH AND OF THE AWAKING TO ETERNAL LIFE . . . 622 JERUSALEM 4   2
TO OPEN THE ETERNAL WORLDS TO OPEN THE IMMORTAL EYES . . 623 JERUSALEM 5   18
I WILL CERTAINLY CREATE AN ETERNAL HELL FOR THEE LISTEN   627 JERUSALEM 8   8
THOU ABSTAIN RAVENING I WILL CREATE AN ETERNAL HELL FOR   627 JERUSALEM 8   38
   THEE
AND THEY BUILDED GOLGONOOZA TERRIBLE ETERNAL LABOUR . . 631 JERUSALEM 12   24
CLAY BAKD & ENAMELD ETERNAL GLOWING AS FOUR FURNACES . . 632 JERUSALEM 12   64
THAT TOWARD EDEN ETERNAL ICE FROZEN IN SEVEN FOLDS . . 633 JERUSALEM 13   15
AROUND GOLGONOOZA LIES THE LAND OF DEATH ETERNAL A LAND   633 JERUSALEM 13   30
AND AT THE PLACE OF DEATH WHEN ALBION SAT IN ETERNAL DEATH 636 JERUSALEM 15   33
FACE IN TERRORS & PAINS OF HELL & ETERNAL DEATH THE . . 639 JERUSALEM 17   54
TREMBLING THEN IN ONE COMINGLING IN ETERNAL TEARS . . 642 JERUSALEM 19   46
ALL IS ETERNAL DEATH UNLESS YOU CAN WEAVE A CHASTE . . 643 JERUSALEM 21   11
IN AN ETERNAL DEATH FOR ALBION'S SAKE OUR BEST BELOVED . . 646 JERUSALEM 23   10
THE ETERNAL & THE EVERLASTING GOSPEL . . . . 649B JERUSALEM 27   PROSE
FROM HEAD TO FEET A GARMENT OF DEATH & ETERNAL FEAR . . 660 JERUSALEM 34   6
IN PITY OF THE PUNISHER WHOSE STATE IS ETERNAL DEATH . . 662 JERUSALEM 35   7
ALBION GOES TO ETERNAL DEATH IN ME ALL ETERNITY . . . 662 JERUSALEM 35   9
AND THE FOUR ZOAS WHO ARE THE FOUR ETERNAL SENSES OF MAN   663 JERUSALEM 36   31
AND MANY OF THE ETERNAL ONES LAUGHED AFTER THEIR MANNER   663 JERUSALEM 36   43
TORMENTS DESPAIR ETERNAL DEATH BUT THE DIVINE MERCY . . 663 JERUSALEM 36   54
DISPLAYING THE ETERNAL VISION THE DIVINE SIMILITUDE . . 664 JERUSALEM 38   11
MORTALITY BEGINS TO ROLL THE BILLOWS OF ETERNAL DEATH . . 666 JERUSALEM 39   8
HIS ETERNAL STATION HE IS THE TWENTY-EIGHTH & IS FOUR-FOLD 666 JERUSALEM 39   13
I DIE I GO TO ETERNAL DEATH THE SHADES OF DEATH . . . 666 JERUSALEM 39   16
THE FRIENDS OF ALBION TREMBLING AT THE SIGHT OF ETERNAL   666 JERUSALEM 40   3
   DEATH
O HOW THE TORMENTS OF ETERNAL DEATH WAITED ON MAN . . 667 JERUSALEM 40   25
THEY FIGHT & CONTEND FOR LIFE & NOT FOR ETERNAL DEATH . . 672 JERUSALEM 43   42
BUT DEATH ETERNAL DEATH REMAINS IN THE VALLEYS OF PEOR   673 JERUSALEM 43   45
ASSIMILATED AND EMBRACD ETERNAL DEATH FOR ALBION'S SAKE   676 JERUSALEM 45   39
THE PALE LIMBS OF HIS ETERNAL INDIVIDUALITY . . . . 677 JERUSALEM 48   3
ETERNITY GROAND & WAS TROUBLED AT THE IMAGE OF ETERNAL   677 JERUSALEM 48   12
   DEATH
LEARN THEREFORE O SISTERS TO DISTINGUISH THE ETERNAL HUMAN 680 JERUSALEM 49   72
LIVE BY DEVOURING GOING INTO ETERNAL DEATH CONTINUALLY . . 681 JERUSALEM 50   7
SHE WILL BECOME AN ETERNAL DEATH AN AVENGER OF SIN . . . 681 JERUSALEM 50   15
RAHAB IS AN ETERNAL STATE . . . . 681D JERUSALEM 52   PROSE
THE SPIRITUAL STATES OF THE SOUL ARE ALL ETERNAL . . . 681D JERUSALEM 52   PROSE
IN ETERNAL LABOURS LOUD THE [FURNAES] FURNACES & LOUD   684 JERUSALEM 53   * 20
   THE ANVILS
WHO TEACHES BELIEF TO THE NATIONS & AN UNKNOWN ETERNAL LIFE 685 JERUSALEM 54   20
DIVINE BENEVOLENCE & JOY FOR THE ETERNAL MAN . . . . 686 JERUSALEM 55   9
SO SAYING AN ETERNAL DEED WAS DONE IN FIERY FLAMES . . 686 JERUSALEM 55   19
AND ROCK THE CRADLE WHILE AH ME OF THAT ETERNAL MAN . . 688 JERUSALEM 56   33
ON DEATH ETERNAL IN FIERCE SHUDDERS UPON THE MOUNTAINS   696 JERUSALEM 62   40
   OF ALBION
WITHOUT FORGIVENESS OF SIN LOVE IS ITSELF ETERNAL DEATH   699 JERUSALEM 64   24
A BUILDING OF ETERNAL DEATH WHOSE PROPORTIONS ARE ETERNAL   702 JERUSALEM 66   9
   DESPAIR
IN ALL ITS MEMBERS IN ETERNAL TORMENT OF LOVE & JEALOUSY   707 JERUSALEM 69   7
AND THE CENTER HAS ETERNAL STATES THESE STATES WE NOW   709 JERUSALEM 71   9
   EXPLORE
AGAINST THE DIVINE VISION & FALL OVER THE PRECIPICE OF   711 JERUSALEM 71   59
   ETERNAL DEATH
THESE TO PRESERVE THEM FROM ETERNAL DEATH LOS CREATES . . 714 JERUSALEM 73   40
IN SHADOWY POMP BY THE ETERNAL PROPHET CREATED EVERMORE   716 JERUSALEM 75   6
AND WHERE LUTHER ENDS ADAM BEGINS AGAIN IN ETERNAL CIRCLE   716 JERUSALEM 75   24
WITH LUVAH INTO LIGHT ETERNAL IN HIS ETERNAL DAY . . . 716 JERUSALEM 75   26
IMAGINATION THE REAL & ETERNAL WORLD . . . . 717A JERUSALEM 77   PROSE
& IN WHICH WE SHALL LIVE IN OUR ETERNAL OR IMAGINATIVE   717A JERUSALEM 77   PROSE
   BODIES
A WORM GOING TO ETERNAL TORMENT RAISD UP IN A NIGHT . . . 721 JERUSALEM 80   4
TO AN ETERNAL NIGHT OF PAIN LOST LOST LOST FOR EVER . . 721 JERUSALEM 80   5
IN AN ETERNAL CONDEMNATION IN FIERCE BURNING FLAMES . . 722 JERUSALEM 80   13
I GATHER OUR ETERNAL FATE OUTCASTS FROM LIFE AND LOVE . . 725 JERUSALEM 82   2
ETERNAL DEATH STANDS AT THE DOOR O GOD PITY OUR LABOURS   728 JERUSALEM 83   65
CONCENTERING IN THE MAJESTIC FORM OF ERIN IN ETERNAL TEARS 731 JERUSALEM 86   45
TO LIVE IN THY BOSOM'S TRANSLUCENCE AS IN AN ETERNAL   732 JERUSALEM 87   11
   MORNING

		PAGE	TITLE	LINE

ETERNAL (CONTINUED)
THE FORCE OF LOS'S HAMMER IS ETERNAL FORGIVENESS BUT	734	JERUSALEM 88	50
OF ALBION DRANK & IMBIBED THE LIFE & ETERNAL FORM OF LUVAH	736	JERUSALEM 90	17
APPROPRIATE INDIVIDUALITY THEY BECOME AN ETERNAL DEATH . .	737	JERUSALEM 90	54
DENYING IN PRIVATE MOCKING GOD & ETERNAL LIFE & IN PUBLIC	737	JERUSALEM 90	64
TO OCCUPY THE VERY THRESHOLD OF ETERNAL LIFE IF BACON NEWTON LOCKE	741	JERUSALEM 93	21
DO YOU SLEEP ROUZE UP ROUZE UP ETERNAL DEATH IS ABROAD	744	JERUSALEM 96	34
FOR LO THE NIGHT OF DEATH IS PAST AND THE ETERNAL DAY . .	744	JERUSALEM 97	3
DRIVING OUTWARD THE BODY OF DEATH IN AN ETERNAL DEATH & RESURRECTION	745	JERUSALEM 98	20
MY ETERNAL MAN SET IN REPOSE	770	OF GATES/GP	1
IMAGINATION OR THE HUMAN ETERNAL BODY IN EVERY MAN . . .	773C	ANNO BERKELEY	MARG
OF SIN & PROMOTE ETERNAL WARS & DOMINENCY OVER OTHERS . .	774D	ANNO BERKELEY	MARG
THE ETERNAL BODY OF MAN IS THE IMAGINATION THAT IS . . .	776B	INSC LAOCOON	PROSE
MATHEMATIC FORM IS ETERNAL IN THE REASONING MEMORY . . .	778D	HOMERS POETRY	PROSE
LIVING FORM IS ETERNAL EXISTENCE	778D	HOMERS POETRY	PROSE
THAT THOU THYSELF GO TO ETERNAL DEATH	781	GHOST ABEL 2	19
THE ELOHIM SAW THEIR OATH ETERNAL FIRE	781	GHOST ABEL 2	25
GIVE [XXX] US THIS ETERNAL DAY [XXX] OUR [GHOSTLY] OWN RIGHT BREAD	788A	ANNO THORNTON	* MARG
EVERY THING HAS AS MUCH RIGHT TO ETERNAL LIFE	788B	ANNO THORNTON	MARG
THE ETERNAL PARENTS DEMAND FROM THEIR CHILDREN	791B	LETTER 3	PROSE
YOUR HARVEST SPRINGING TO ETERNAL LIFE	806	TO MRS BUTTS/L	5
IT DRAWS THE SOUL TOWARDS ETERNAL LIFE & CONJUNCTION WITH	834A	LETTER 33	PROSE
ENGRAVING IS ETERNAL WORK THE TWO PLATES ARE ALMOST FINISHD	837C	LETTER 36	PROSE
SURELY THESE THINGS ARE REAL AND ETERNAL IN OUR ETERNAL MIND	854A	LETTER 52	PROSE
BANKS THE SCULPTOR IS GONE TO HIS ETERNAL HOME	859D	LETTER 56	PROSE
AGAINST THEIR ETERNAL EXISTENCE ITSELF BECAUSE IT IS . .	871A	LETTER 72	PROSE
OWN ETERNAL HOUSE LEAVING THE DELUSIVE GODDESS NATURE & HER	879A	LETTER 88	PROSE

ETERNALLY
(ETERNALLY) RUSHING ROUND LIKE A MAN	136	FRENCH REVOLTN	* 46
ETERNALLY WANDRING A COMET AND SWIFT-FALLING FIRE . . .	141	FRENCH REVOLTN	160
ETERNALLY I LABOUR ON	262B	SMALL BK DSGNS	TITLE
ETERNALLY CREATED BY THE LAMB OF GOD AROUND	266	FOUR ZOAS 1	97
WHERE DEATH ETERNAL IS PUT OFF ETERNALLY	347	FOUR ZOAS 8	240
FROM DEATH ETERNAL & TO PUT OFF SATAN ETERNALLY	348	FOUR ZOAS 8	286
I MUST HAVE SLEPT ETERNALLY NOR HAVE FELT THE DEW OF THY MORNING	367	FOUR ZOAS 9	396
OR I MUST HAVE SLEPT ETERNALLY NOR HAVE FELT THE DEW OF MORNING	367	FOUR ZOAS 9	403
ETERNALLY THOU MUST HAVE SLEPT NOR HAVE FELT THE MORNING DEW	367	FOUR ZOAS 9	404
IS BUILT ETERNALLY THE UNIVERSE OF LOS AND ENITHARMON . .	500	MILTON 19	25
IN WHICH MAN LIVETH ETERNALLY MADNESS & BLASPHEMY AGAINST	521	MILTON 32	20
THERE THEY SHINE ETERNALLY	558	THE CAVERNS/N	20
OF WHAT ETERNALLY EXISTS REALLY & UNCHANGEABLY	604D	V LAST JUDG/N	PROSE
SIN & DEATH ARE TO BE CLOSED ETERNALLY BY	608B	V LAST JUDG/N	*PROSE
IS BUILT ETERNALLY THE SUBLIME UNIVERSE OF LOS & ENITHARMON	691	JERUSALEM 59	21
WHICH LIVES ETERNALLY	717B	JERUSALEM 77	PROSE
AND HIS MATERNAL HUMANITY MUST BE PUT OFF ETERNALLY . . .	737	JERUSALEM 90	36
ETERNALLY FOR MAN MAN COULD NOT EXIST FOR MAN IS LOVE . .	743	JERUSALEM 96	26
OF IMMORTAL FRIENDSHIP TO THEE I AM ETERNALLY INDEBTED . .	852A	LETTER 50	PROSE

ETERNALS
WHEN ETERNALS SPURND BACK HIS RELIGION	222	URIZEN 2	2
ETERNALS I HEAR YOUR CALL GLADLY	222	URIZEN 2	5
BUT ETERNALS BEHELD HIS VAST FORESTS	223	URIZEN 3	23
WHY WILL YOU DIE O ETERNALS	224	URIZEN 4	12
FROM ETERNALS & LIKE A BLACK GLOBE	226	URIZEN 5	33
KEPT WATCH FOR ETERNALS TO CONFINE	226	URIZEN 5	39
THE ETERNALS SAID WHAT IS THIS DEATH	226	URIZEN 6	11
OF ETERNALS THE VISIONS REMOTE	231	URIZEN 15	7
THAT ETERNALS MAY NO MORE BEHOLD THEM	231	URIZEN 19	4
WITH INFINITE LABOUR THE ETERNALS	231	URIZEN 19	8
A TIME PASSED OVER THE ETERNALS	232	URIZEN 19	17
THE ETERNALS THEIR TENT FINISHED	232	URIZEN 19	37
THE ETERNALS CLOSED THE TENT	232	URIZEN 19	47
FROM ETERNALS HE SAT ON A ROCK	252	AHANIA 3	56
BY SATAN'S ARTS THEN THE ETERNALS SENT SHADDAI	351	FOUR ZOAS 8	403
AND ONE OF THE ETERNALS SPOKE ALL WAS SILENT AT THE FEAST	374	FOUR ZOAS 9	626
WHEN MORNING DAWND THE ETERNALS ROSE TO LABOUR AT THE VINTAGE	374	FOUR ZOAS 9	647
BUT MANY OF THE ETERNALS ROSE UP FROM ETERNAL TABLES . .	502	MILTON 20	43
I WILL HIDE IT FROM ETERNALS I WILL GIVE MYSELF FOR MY CHILDREN	646	JERUSALEM 23	18

ETERNITY
THROUGH THE VOID SPACE I WALK BETWEEN THE SINFUL WORLD AND ETERNITY	36A	COUCH DEATH/PS	PROSE
AND THE YOUTH BREATHES OUT HIS SOUL WITH JOY INTO ETERNITY	36D	COUCH DEATH/PS	PROSE
O MAN SLAVE OF EACH MOMENT LORD OF ETERNITY	37A	CONTEMPLATN/PS	PROSE
OF ETERNITY WHERE THE ETERNAL LION AND EAGLE REMAIN TO DEVOUR	138	FRENCH REVOLTN	97
THAT GOD WILL TORMENT MAN IN ETERNITY FOR FOLLOWING HIS ENERGIES	149C	MARRIAGE HH 4	PROSE
ETERNITY IS IN LOVE WITH THE PRODUCTIONS OF TIME . . .	151A	MARRIAGE HH 7	PROSE
ARE PORTIONS OF ETERNITY TOO GREAT FOR THE EYE OF MAN .	151C	MARRIAGE HH 8	PROSE
DUNGEON THOU ART PREPARING FOR THYSELF TO ALL ETERNITY .	155C	MARRIAGE HH 11	PROSE
EVEN TO ETERNITY DOWN FALLING	159B	SONG LIBERTY	PROSE
ETERNITY	179A	ETERNITY/N	TITLE
AND A PALACE OF ETERNITY IN THE JAWS OF THE HUNGRY GRAVE	193	V DAU ALBION 6	1
IN ETERNITY UNKNOWN UNPROLIFIC	222	URIZEN 3	2

		PAGE	TITLE	LINE

ETERNITY   (CONTINUED)

	PAGE	TITLE	LINE
SHRILL THE TRUMPET & MYRIADS OF ETERNITY	223	URIZEN 3	44
ON THE ROCK OF ETERNITY UNCLASPING	224	URIZEN 4	43
ETERNITY ROLLD WIDE APART	225	URIZEN 5	5
VIEWD BY SONS OF ETERNITY STANDING	226	URIZEN 5	34
FOR ETERNITY STOOD WIDE APART	226	URIZEN 5	41
UNORGANIZD RENT FROM ETERNITY	226	URIZEN 6	8
DISORGANIZD RENT FROM ETERNITY	228	URIZEN 10	27
ALL THE MYRIADS OF ETERNITY	230	URIZEN 13	28
IN PANGS ETERNITY ON ETERNITY	230	URIZEN 13	54
IN PANGS ETERNITY ON ETERNITY	231	URIZEN 18	5
ALL ETERNITY SHUDDERD AT SIGHT	231	URIZEN 18	9
ETERNITY SHUDDERD WHEN THEY SAW	232	URIZEN 19	14
A SHRIEK RAN THRO ETERNITY	232	URIZEN 19	41
STRETCHD FOR A WORK OF ETERNITY	233	URIZEN 20	1
NO MORE LOS BEHELD ETERNITY	233	URIZEN 20	2
HE SUNG IT TO FOUR HARPS AT THE TABLES OF ETERNITY	245	SONG OF LOS 3	2
LIKE NETS & GINS & TRAPS TO CATCH THE JOYS OF ETERNITY	246	SONG OF LOS 4	2
TILL LIKE A DREAM ETERNITY WAS OBLITERATED & ERASED	246	SONG OF LOS 4	4
IN THE INFINITE AGES OF ETERNITY	252	AHANIA 4	12
WHERE THE SONS OF ETERNITY SINGING	254	AHANIA 5	6
THE VAST ROCK OF ETERNITY TIMES	257	BOOK OF LOS 4	12
OF ETERNITY BEAT ON HIS IRON LINKS	259	BOOK OF LOS 5	26
. . . KNOWETH [NOT] NOR CAN KNOW IN ALL ETERNITY	264	FOUR ZOAS 1	13
THERE IS FROM GREAT ETERNITY A MILD & PLEASANT REST	266	FOUR ZOAS 1	94
[BUT THOSE IN GREAT ETERNITY MET IN THE COUNCIL OF GOD]	269	FOUR ZOAS 1	198
ETERNITY GROAND & WAS TROUBLED AT THE IMAGE OF ETERNAL DEATH	273	FOUR ZOAS 1	315
GLOOMY SOUNDING NOW I AM GOD FROM ETERNITY TO ETERNITY	273	FOUR ZOAS 1	319
OBEY MY VOICE YOUNG DEMON I AM GOD FROM ETERNITY TO ETERNITY	273	FOUR ZOAS 1	336
ART THOU A VISIONARY OF JESUS THE SOFT DELUSION OF ETERNITY	273	FOUR ZOAS 1	337
ETERNITY APPEARD ABOVE THEM AS ONE MAN INFOLDED	274	FOUR ZOAS 1	363
ETERNITY GROAND & WAS TROUBLED AT THE IMAGE OF ETERNAL DEATH	277	FOUR ZOAS 1	* 462
THEN THOSE IN GREAT ETERNITY MET IN THE COUNCIL OF GOD	277	FOUR ZOAS 1	469
WHOM THOU LOVEST IS SICK HE WANDERS FROM HIS HOUSE OF ETERNITY	277	FOUR ZOAS 1	478
THE ETERNAL MAN WEPT IN THE HOLY TENT OUR BROTHER IN ETERNITY	277	FOUR ZOAS 1	484
THREE GATES WITHIN GLORIOUS & BRIGHT OPEN INTO [ETERNITY] BEULAH	279	FOUR ZOAS 1	* 563
IDOLATROUS TO HIS OWN SHADOW WORDS OF ETERNITY UTTERING	293	FOUR ZOAS 3	59
THE PROPHET OF ETERNITY BEAT ON HIS IRON LINKS & LINKS OF BRASS	302	FOUR ZOAS 4	201
IN FETTERS OF ICE SHRINKING DISORGANIZD RENT FROM ETERNITY	303	FOUR ZOAS 4	212
BEHOLD THESE WONDERS OF ETERNITY WE SHALL CONSUME	304	FOUR ZOAS 4	262
[XXX DAYS OF GREAT ETERNITY XXX THE TIME]	SUPP	FOUR ZOAS 4	*
DOWN ON THE ROCK OF ETERNITY ON DARKNESS OF THE DEEP	306	FOUR ZOAS 5	55
AT THEIR EXCEEDING BRIGHTNESS & THE SONS OF ETERNITY SENT THEM GIFTS	312	FOUR ZOAS 6	34
WERE NOW NOT VOCAL AS IN CLIMES OF HAPPY ETERNITY	315	FOUR ZOAS 6	135
FOR EVERY ONE OPEND WITHIN INTO ETERNITY AT WILL	318	FOUR ZOAS 6	252
THEE SECRETS OF ETERNITY WHICH NEER BEFORE UNLOCKD	326	FOUR ZOAS 7	237
TILL HE FORGOT ETERNITY DELIGHTED IN HIS SWEET JOY	326	FOUR ZOAS 7	253
OF SWEET ETERNITY THE BLOOD FLOWD ROUND THE HOLY TENT & RIVN	326	FOUR ZOAS 7	257
TO REUNITE IN THOSE MILD FIELDS OF HAPPY ETERNITY	326	FOUR ZOAS 7	270
DAYS OF ETERNITY WITH THARMAS MILD & LUVAH SWEET MELODIOUS	327	FOUR ZOAS 7	274
THREEFOLD AS IT WAS IN ETERNITY & THIS THE FOURTH UNIVERSE	329	FOUR ZOAS 7	355
O [LOVELY] LOVELY TERRIBLE LOS WONDER OF ETERNITY	331	FOUR ZOAS 7	447
I WILL WALK FORTH THRO THOSE WIDE FIELDS OF ENDLESS ETERNITY	333	FOUR ZOAS 7B	8
OF DAY & NIGHT THE MYRIADS OF ETERNITY THAT THEY MIGHT FILE	337	FOUR ZOAS 7B	181
AND WHENCE THEY NEVER CAN BE BROUGHT IN ALL ETERNITY	339	FOUR ZOAS 7B	245
IS HIDDEN FROM ME & I NEVER IN ALL ETERNITY	339	FOUR ZOAS 7B	247
THEN ALL IN GREAT ETERNITY [WHICH IS CALLED]	341	FOUR ZOAS 8	1
THE SORROWER OF ETERNITY IN LOVE WITH TEARS SUBMISS I REAR	345	FOUR ZOAS 8	151
. . . & NONE [?IS] FROM ETERNITY TO ETERNITY COULD ESCAPE	347	FOUR ZOAS 8	* 231
BEGUN ALREADY IN ETERNITY COME THEN O LAMB OF GOD	347	FOUR ZOAS 8	244
SO SANG THEY IN ETERNITY LOOKING DOWN INTO BEULAH	347	FOUR ZOAS 8	246
OF ETERNITY FOR HIMSELF HE HEWD IT DESPAIRING OF LIFE ETERNAL	349	FOUR ZOAS 8	340
THE STATE NAMD SATAN NEVER CAN BE REDEEMD IN ALL ETERNITY	351	FOUR ZOAS 8	381
AND THEN THEY SENT JEHOVAH WHO LEPROUS STRETCHD HIS HAND TO ETERNITY	351	FOUR ZOAS 8	405
DARKNESS & SORROW COVERD ALL FLESH ETERNITY WAS DARKEND	351	FOUR ZOAS 8	414
OR A PILLAR & PALACE OF ETERNITY IN THE JAWS OF THE HUNGRY GRAVE	354	FOUR ZOAS 8	496
[BUT RAHAB [BUILT] HEWD A SEPULCHER IN THE ROCK OF ETERNITY]	356	FOUR ZOAS 8	* 585
[INTO ETERNITY AND AS SHE WOVE	356	FOUR ZOAS 8	591
FOR HIMSELF IN THE ROCK OF ETERNITY TREMBLING & IN [FEAR] DESPAIR	356	FOUR ZOAS 8	595
THEN FELL THE FIRES OF ETERNITY WITH LOUD & SHRILL	357	FOUR ZOAS 9	10
BATHING THEIR LIMBS IN THE BRIGHT VISIONS OF ETERNITY	358	FOUR ZOAS 9	45
AND ALL THE SONS OF ETERNITY DESCENDED INTO BEULAH	359	FOUR ZOAS 9	66
BATHING THEIR LIMBS IN THE BRIGHT VISIONS OF ETERNITY	359	FOUR ZOAS 9	90
AGAINST THEE TO ETERNITY & NEVER RECIEVE THEE MORE	361	FOUR ZOAS 9	149
ERROR CAN NEVER BE REDEEMD IN ALL ETERNITY	361	FOUR ZOAS 9	* 158
THUS SHALL THE MALE & FEMALE LIVE THE LIFE OF ETERNITY	362	FOUR ZOAS 9	219
FOURFOLD EACH IN THE OTHER REFLECTED THEY ARE NAMED LIVES IN ETERNITY	364	FOUR ZOAS 9	283

	PAGE	TITLE	LINE

ETERNITY   (CONTINUED)

	PAGE	TITLE	LINE
FOUR STARRY UNIVERSES GOING FORWARD FROM ETERNITY TO ETERNITY	364	FOUR ZOAS 9	284
SAT AT THE FEAST REJOICING & THE WINE OF ETERNITY . . .	372	FOUR ZOAS 9	588
SAT AT THE FEAST REJOICING & THE WINE OF ETERNITY . . .	373	FOUR ZOAS 9	619
TO MILD ETERNITY SHUT IN A THREEFOLD SHAPE DELIGHTFUL . .	381	FOUR ZOAS AD 5	12
DARKNESS & SORROW COVERD ALL FLESH ETERNITY WAS DARKEND	382	FOUR ZOAS AD 6	30
BUT THESE CONSIDERATIONS (ARE THE) BUSINESS OF ETERNITY	383C	ANNO WATSON	MARG
TO STEP INTO ETERNITY	417	MY SPECTRE/N	62
THE WORLDS OF HAPPY ETERNITY	417	MY SPECTRE/N	70
& THROUGHOUT ALL ETERNITY	417	MY SPECTRE/N	71
AND THERE TO ETERNITY ASPIRE	421	EACH MAN/N	5
AND ETERNITY IN AN HOUR	431	AUGURIES	4
BECOMES A BABE IN ETERNITY	432	AUGURIES	68
OF ETERNITY IN WHICH WE SHALL LIVE FOR EVER IN JESUS OUR LORD	480D	MILTON 1	PROSE
SAY FIRST WHAT MOVD MILTON WHO WALKD ABOUT IN ETERNITY . .	481	MILTON 2	16
THE MILLER OF ETERNITY MADE SUBSERVIENT TO THE GREAT HARVEST	483	MILTON 3	42
PERSWADED THE PROPHET OF ETERNITY THAT PALAMABRON . . .	487	MILTON 7	38
BECAME CANAAN CLOSING LOS FROM ETERNITY IN ALBION'S CLIFFS	491	MILTON 10	10
EVERY THING IN ETERNITY SHINES BY ITS OWN INTERNAL LIGHT BUT THOU	491	MILTON 10	16
AND ONE MUST DIE FOR ANOTHER THROUGHOUT ALL ETERNITY . . .	491	MILTON 11	18
THE SIN WAS BEGUN IN ETERNITY AND WILL NOT REST TO ETERNITY	494	MILTON 13	10
AND JEHOVAH WAS LEPROUS LOUD HE CALLD STRETCHING HIS HAND TO ETERNITY	494	MILTON 13	24
AND MILTON SAID I GO TO ETERNAL DEATH ETERNITY SHUDDERD	496	MILTON 14	33
A MOURNFUL SHADE ETERNITY SHUDDERD AT THE IMAGE OF ETERNAL DEATH	496	MILTON 14	35
OWN VORTEX AND WHEN ONCE A TRAVELLER THRO ETERNITY . . .	497	MILTON 15	22
A VORTEX NOT YET PASSD BY THE TRAVELLER THRO ETERNITY . .	497	MILTON 15	35
FOR TRAVELLERS FROM ETERNITY PASS OUTWARD TO SATAN'S SEAT	498	MILTON 17	29
BUT TRAVELLERS TO ETERNITY PASS INWARD TO GOLGONOOZA . .	498	MILTON 17	30
REVEAL THE SECRETS OF ETERNITY FOR MORE EXTENSIVE . . .	503	MILTON 21	10
I STOOPED DOWN & BOUND IT ON TO WALK FORWARD THRO ETERNITY	503	MILTON 21	14
FOR SEVEN DAYS OF ETERNITY AND THE RIVER'S LIVING BANKS	503	MILTON 21	18
OF GREAT ETERNITY UNNATURAL REFUGE UNKNOWN BY US TILL NOW	504	MILTON 21	49
ON TO WALK FORWARD THRO ETERNITY LOS DESCENDED TO ME . . .	505	MILTON 22	5
AWAKE THOU SLEEPER ON THE ROCK OF ETERNITY ALBION AWAKE	506	MILTON 23	3
THE WATCHMAN OF ETERNITY THE THREE ARE NOT & I AM PRESERVED	508	MILTON 24	9
TIME IS THE MERCY OF ETERNITY WITHOUT TIME'S SWIFTNESS . .	510	MILTON 24	72
STILL ABSTAIN FROM PLEASURE & REST IN THE LABOURS OF ETERNITY	511	MILTON 25	46
OF MEN THESE ARE THE SONS OF LOS THESE THE VISIONS OF ETERNITY	512	MILTON 26	10
BUT IN ETERNITY THE FOUR ARTS POETRY PAINTING MUSIC . . .	514	MILTON 27	55
AND IN HIS HALLOWD CENTER HOLDS THE HEAVENS OF BRIGHT ETERNITY	515	MILTON 28	38
INTO ETERNITY OF WHICH THIS VEGETABLE EARTH IS BUT A SHADOW	517	MILTON 29	22
BEULAH IS EVERMORE CREATED AROUND ETERNITY APPEARING . .	518	MILTON 30	8
ARE FROM GREAT ETERNITY A MILD & PLEASANT REST	518	MILTON 30	14
IN THE GREAT WARS OF ETERNITY IN FURY OF POETIC INSPIRATION	519	MILTON 30	19
BEHOLD THESE WONDERS OF ETERNITY WE SHALL CONSUME . . .	519	MILTON 30	27
BUT YOU O OUR FATHERS & BROTHERS REMAIN IN ETERNITY . . .	519	MILTON 30	28
THE BOSOM OF THE FATHER IN ETERNITY ON ETERNITY	519	MILTON 31	5
A SHADOW TO REPOSE IN ALL THE DAYS OF HAPPY ETERNITY . .	519	MILTON 31	7
NOT MENTAL AS THE WARS OF ETERNITY BUT A CORPOREAL STRIFE	520	MILTON 31	25
FORGETTING THAT WITHIN THAT CENTER ETERNITY EXPANDS . . .	520	MILTON 31	48
IS TERROR CHANGD TO PITY O WONDER OF ETERNITY	522	MILTON 32	41
THEY SAID HOW ARE THE WARS OF MAN WHICH IN GREAT ETERNITY	523	MILTON 34	7
AND NOW THAT A WIDE ROAD WAS OPEN TO ETERNITY	524	MILTON 34	50
OF THEIR GREAT SWAY REACHING FROM ULRO TO ETERNITY . . .	525	MILTON 35	35
DRIVEN FROM ETERNITY HIM I SEEK TERRIFIED AT MY ACT . . .	526	MILTON 35	38
IN GREAT ETERNITY WHICH THOU KNOWEST I COME HIM TO SEEK	527	MILTON 37	2
INTO ETERNITY THAT WAY BUT ALL DESCEND TO LOS	527	MILTON 37	3
SUCH ARE THE LAWS OF THY FALSE HEAVNS BUT LAWS OF ETERNITY	529	MILTON 37	58
SUCH ARE THE LAWS OF ETERNITY THAT EACH SHALL MUTUALLY . .	530	MILTON 38	33
HIS CHERUBIM & SERAPHIM IN EVER HAPPY ETERNITY	530	MILTON 38	35
HENCE AROSE ALL OUR TERRORS IN ETERNITY & NOW REMEMBRANCE	531	MILTON 41	28
THE SAVIOUR THE VINE OF ETERNITY	534	MILTON 41	34
THIS WORLD OF IMAGINATION IS THE WORLD OF ETERNITY . . .	571C	DESC CAT 3	PROSE
IN THE DIVINE BODY OF THE SAVIOUR THE TRUE VINE OF ETERNITY	605D	V LAST JUDG/N	PROSE
IN ETERNITY ONE THING NEVER CHANGES INTO ANOTHER THING	606A	V LAST JUDG/N	PROSE
EMBRACE & ASCEND TO MEET ETERNITY	607A	V LAST JUDG/N	PROSE
SURROUNDED BY INFANTS THERE IS SUCH A STATE IN ETERNITY	609D	V LAST JUDG/N	PROSE
IN ETERNITY WOMAN IS THE EMANATION OF MAN	610A	V LAST JUDG/N	PROSE
IN ETERNITY AS A FEMALE WILL	613D	V LAST JUDG/N	*PROSE
OF UNBELIEVING DEMONS ETERNITY EXISTS AND ALL THINGS IN	613D	V LAST JUDG/N	PROSE
ETERNITY INDEPENDENT OF CREATION WHICH WAS AN ACT OF MERCY	614B	V LAST JUDG/N	PROSE
I HAVE REPRESENTED THOSE WHO ARE IN ETERNITY BY SOME . . .	614B	V LAST JUDG/N	PROSE
& THEN & NOT TILL THEN TRUTH OR ETERNITY WILL APPEAR . . .	614C	V LAST JUDG/N	PROSE
OF MAN INWARDS INTO THE WORLDS OF THOUGHT INTO ETERNITY	617B	V LAST JUDG/N	PROSE
ETERNITY LOOKD UPON AS DEFORMITY & LOVELINESS AS A DRY TREE	623	JERUSALEM 5	19
IT CONTINUES ACCUMULATING TO ETERNITY THE JOYS OF GOD ADVANCE	628	JERUSALEM 9	8
WAS BUILT IN FROM ETERNITY IN THE CLIFFS OF ALBION . . .	630	JERUSALEM 10	46
AND THE FOUR POINTS ARE THUS BEHELD IN GREAT ETERNITY . .	631	JERUSALEM 11	15
IN WHICH IS ETERNITY IT EXPANDS IN STARS TO THE MUNDANE SHELL	632	JERUSALEM 12	54
	633	JERUSALEM 13	35

		PAGE	TITLE	LINE

ETERNITY   (CONTINUED)

	PAGE	TITLE	LINE
AND THERE IT MEETS ETERNITY AGAIN BOTH WITHIN AND WITHOUT	633	JERUSALEM 13	36
AND LOS WAS ROOFD IN FROM ETERNITY IN ALBION'S CLIFFS . .	642	JERUSALEM 19	33
AND SCOTLAND UTTERD FROM THE CIRCUMFERENCE INTO ETERNITY	646	JERUSALEM 23	28
DWELLS FROM ETERNITY WIDE SEPARATED FROM THE HUMAN SOUL	646	JERUSALEM 23	30
IDOLATROUS TO HIS OWN SHADOW WORDS OF ETERNITY UTTERING	654	JERUSALEM 29	46
OF ETERNITY PALE STOOD ALBION AT HIS EASTERN GATE . . .	658	JERUSALEM 31	70
VALA WAS ALBION'S BRIDE & WIFE IN GREAT ETERNITY	660	JERUSALEM 33	39
THE LOVELIEST OF THE DAUGHTERS OF ETERNITY WHEN IN DAY-BREAK	660	JERUSALEM 33	40
IN ETERNITY THEY NEITHER MARRY NOR ARE GIVEN IN MARRIAGE	660	JERUSALEM 34	15
NUMBER THE VOICES OF THE INNUMERABLE MULTITUDES OF ETERNITY	662	JERUSALEM 35	4
ALBION GOES TO ETERNAL DEATH IN ME ALL ETERNITY	662	JERUSALEM 35	9
THEN THOSE IN GREAT ETERNITY WHO CONTEMPLATE ON DEATH . .	663	JERUSALEM 36	50
CHARIOTS BLACK THEIR FIRES ROLL BEHOLDING ALBION'S HOUSE OF ETERNITY	666	JERUSALEM 40	5
THERE TO ETERNITY CHAIND DOWN AND ISSUING IN RED FLAMES	667	JERUSALEM 40	36
IN THE BOSOM OF MAN FOR EVER FROM ETERNITY TO ETERNITY . .	670	JERUSALEM 42	36
AND THE TWO SOURCES OF LIFE IN ETERNITY HUNTING AND WAR	672	JERUSALEM 43	31
BROTHERS OF ETERNITY THIS MAN WHOSE GREAT EXAMPLE . . .	675	JERUSALEM 45	4
BATH MILD PHYSICIAN OF ETERNITY MYSTERIOUS POWER	676	JERUSALEM 46	1
ETERNITY GROAND & WAS TROUBLED AT THE IMAGE OF ETERNAL DEATH	677	JERUSALEM 48	12
THE VISIONS OF ETERNITY BY REASON OF NARROWED PERCEPTIONS	679	JERUSALEM 49	21
IN GREAT ETERNITY EVERY PARTICULAR FORM GIVES FORTH OR EMANATES	684	JERUSALEM 54	1
BUT ALBION FELL DOWN A ROCKY FRAGMENT FROM ETERNITY HURLD	685	JERUSALEM 54	6
AND THE GREAT VOICE OF ETERNITY ROLLED ABOVE TERRIBLE IN CLOUDS	687	JERUSALEM 55	68
WONDER SIEZD ALL IN ETERNITY TO BEHOLD THE DIVINE VISION OPEN	689	JERUSALEM 57	17
OF REDEMPTION & OF AWAKING AGAIN INTO ETERNITY	691	JERUSALEM 59	9
IN THE PERPETUAL MUTUAL SACRIFICE IN GREAT ETERNITY FOR BEHOLD	694	JERUSALEM 61	23
OF DAY & NIGHT THE MYRIADS OF ETERNITY THAT THEY MAY GRIND	700	JERUSALEM 65	23
THE HEAVENS MIGHT REVOLVE & ETERNITY BE BOUND IN THEIR CHAIN	702	JERUSALEM 66	5
AS THE MISTLETOE GROWS ON THE OAK SO ALBION'S TREE ON ETERNITY LO	703	JERUSALEM 66	55
CALLING THE ROCKS ATOMIC ORIGINS OF EXISTENCE DENYING ETERNITY	704	JERUSALEM 67	12
HER NAME IS VALA IN ETERNITY IN TIME HER NAME IS RAHAB	709	JERUSALEM 70	31
WHAT IS ABOVE IS WITHIN FOR EVERY-THING IN ETERNITY IS TRANSLUCENT	709	JERUSALEM 71	6
AND THE CIRCUMFERENCE STILL EXPANDS GOING FORWARD TO ETERNITY	709	JERUSALEM 71	8
FOR ALL ARE MEN IN ETERNITY RIVERS MOUNTAINS CITIES VILLAGES	709	JERUSALEM 71	15
WEPT ROUND HIM AS A FLOCK SILENT SEVEN DAYS OF ETERNITY	711	JERUSALEM 71	63
FOR ALBION IN ETERNITY HAS SIXTEEN GATES AMONG HIS PILLARS	711	JERUSALEM 72	5
OPENS ETERNITY IN TIME & SPACE TRIUMPHANT IN MERCY . .	716	JERUSALEM 75	22
THAT APPARENT TO ALL IN ETERNITY GLOWS LIKE THE SUN IN THE BREAST	723	JERUSALEM 80	68
TILL THY AWAKING YET ALAS I SHALL FORGET ETERNITY . . .	727	JERUSALEM 83	3
TILL SWEET JERUSALEM EMANATES AGAIN INTO ETERNITY . . .	728	JERUSALEM 83	60
REFLECTS ETERNITY BENEATH THY AZURE WINGS OF FEATHERY DOWN	730	JERUSALEM 86	5
BENDS OVER THY IMMORTAL HEAD IN WHICH ETERNITY DWELLS . .	731	JERUSALEM 86	10
IN FLAMING FIRE UNCEASING BURNS FROM ETERNITY TO ETERNITY	731	JERUSALEM 86	25
WHEN IN ETERNITY MAN CONVERSES WITH MAN THEY ENTER . . .	733	JERUSALEM 88	3
OF FIRE SPEAKING THE WORDS OF ETERNITY IN HUMAN FORMS IN DIREFUL	742	JERUSALEM 95	9
A MAN & THEY CONVERSED AS MAN WITH MAN IN AGES OF ETERNITY	743	JERUSALEM 96	6
OVERSHADOWD THEM & JESUS SAID THUS DO MEN IN ETERNITY . .	743	JERUSALEM 96	18
OF HEAVEN FOURFOLD AMONG THE VISIONS OF GOD IN ETERNITY	744	JERUSALEM 96	43
. . . IRRESISTIBLE FROM ETERNITY TO ETERNITY	745	JERUSALEM 98	27
TO & FRO IN ETERNITY AS ONE MAN	746	JERUSALEM 98	39
[THOU ALSO DWELST IN ETERNITY]	750	EV GOSPEL(C)/N	38
THOU ALSO DWELST IN ETERNITY	750	EV GOSPEL(C)/N	40
THOU ALSO DWELLST IN ETERNITY	752	EV GOSPEL(D)/N	74
IN ETERNITY ALL IS VISION	776B	INSC LAOCOON	PROSE
ALL THE LOVES & GRACES OF ETERNITY	777D	INSC LAOCOON	PROSE
NATURE HAS NO SUPERNATURAL & DISSOLVES IMAGINATION IS ETERNITY	779C	GHOST ABEL 1	PROSE
ABEL ARE THESE THE SACRIFICES OF ETERNITY O JEHOVAH A BROKEN SPIRIT	780	GHOST ABEL 2	4
TO CONSIDER THIS TO ALL ETERNITY WILL BE COMMENT ENOUGH	787A	ANNO THORNTON	MARG
OR WHETHER THEY WERE TO LIE THERE TO ETERNITY	791B	LETTER 3	PROSE
WHICH GIVES EXISTENCE TO EVERY OTHER NAMELY VISIONS OF ETERNITY	793A	LETTER 5	PROSE
THE RUINS OF TIME BUILDS MANSIONS IN ETERNITY	797B	LETTER 9	PROSE
DEAR SCULPTOR OF ETERNITY WE ARE SAFE ARRIVED AT OUR COTTAGE	801D	LETTER 14	PROSE
OF ETERNITY BEFORE MY MORTAL LIFE & THOSE WORKS ARE THE DELIGHT	802C	LETTER 14	PROSE
COMPANION FROM ETERNITY IN THE DIVINE BOSOM IN . . .	802C	LETTER 14	PROSE
I SEE OUR HOUSES OF ETERNITY WHICH CAN NEVER BE SEPARATED	802C	LETTER 14	PROSE
TO ETERNITY EVERY ONE IN ETERNITY WILL LEAVE YOU AGHAST	813B	LETTER 22	PROSE
INTO THE LIGHT OF DAY I STILL & SHALL TO ETERNITY EMBRACE	815D	LETTER 23	PROSE
SHALL BE MADE FULLY APPARENT & PERFECT IN ETERNITY IN THE	822C	LETTER 26	PROSE
& THAT I MAY CONVERSE WITH MY FRIENDS IN ETERNITY . .	822C	LETTER 26	PROSE
ANY OTHER THAN THE SECRETARY THE AUTHORS ARE IN ETERNITY	825A	LETTER 27	PROSE

```
                                                            PAGE    TITLE           LINE

ETERNITY    (CONTINUED)
    HEALTH & JOY IN GOD OUR SAVIOUR TO ETERNITY YOURS    . . .  830D LETTER 30        PROSE
    WITH THE GOOD THINGS BOTH OF THIS LIFE & OF ETERNITY & WITH  835A LETTER 34        PROSE
    A LOSS THAT ONLY CAN BE REPAIRD IN ETERNITY WHERE IT WILL    854B LETTER 53        PROSE
    THAT SUCH MOCKERS ARE MOST SEVERELY PUNISHD IN ETERNITY      863B LETTER 60        PROSE
ETERNITY'S
    LIVES IN [AN ETERNAL] ETERNITY'S SUN RISE . . . . . .   179 ETERNITY/N          4
    LIVES IN ETERNITY'S SUN RISE . . . . . . . . . .   184 SEVRL QUESTN/N      14
ETERNITYS
    TILL TWO ETERNITYS MEET TOGETHER AH LOST LOST LOST FOR      494 MILTON 13          11
        EVER
ETERNIZE
    WHO IN EVERY AGE IS BORN TO RECORD AND ETERNIZE ITS ACTS    569A DESC CAT 3       PROSE
ETHINTHUS
    ARISE ETHINTHUS THO THE EARTH-WORM CALL . . . . . .   243 EUROPE 13          16
    ETHINTHUS QUEEN OF WATERS HOW THOU SHINEST IN THE SKY   . .   243 EUROPE 14           1
    ETHINTHUS THOU ART SWEET AS COMFORTS TO MY FAINTING SOUL     243 EUROPE 14           4
    [ELYTHRIA] ELYTHIRIA ENANTO MANATHU VORCYON ETHINTHUS       350 FOUR ZOAS 8    *  364
        MOAB MIDIAN
    OF SOFT ETHINTHUS NEAR TYBURN'S FATAL TREE IS THAT   . . .   632 JERUSALEM 12        26
ETHIOPIA
    EGYPT IS THE EIGHT STEPS WITHIN ETHIOPIA SUPPORTS           690 JERUSALEM 58        35
        HIS PILLARS
    EGYPT LYBIA ETHIOPIA GUINEA CAFFRARIA NEGROLAND MOROCCO     712 JERUSALEM 72        40
    THE SWARTHY SONS OF ETHIOPIA STOOD ROUND THE LAMB OF GOD    721 JERUSALEM 79        51
    AND MANY MOUTHD ETHIOPIA LYBIA THE SEA OF REPHAIM   . . .   734 JERUSALEM 89        16
ETON
    WINDSOR TERRACE A BOY CONTEMPLATING A DISTANT VIEW OF ETON  SUPP ILLUS GRAY     *TITLE
        COLLEGE
    TWO BOYS WANDERING IN THE WOODS BY ETON COLLEGE  . . . .  SUPP ILLUS GRAY     *TITLE
ETRUSCAN COLUMN
    IN COMES ETRUSCAN COLUMN THE ANTIQUARIAN & AFTER . . . .   44B ISLAND MOON 1     PROSE
    ETRUSCAN COLUMN & INFLAMMABLE GASS FIXD THEIR EYES   . . .   44C ISLAND MOON 1     PROSE
    I DONT LIKE HIS EYES SAID ETRUSCAN COLUMN . . . . . . .   44C ISLAND MOON 1     PROSE
    HERE ETRUSCAN COLUMN LEFT OFF . . . . . . . . . .   45A ISLAND MOON 1     PROSE
    ETRUSCAN COLUMN THEN (STARTING) UP & CLENCHING BOTH HIS      45B ISLAND MOON 1     PROSE
        FISTS
EULER
    SOMEWHAT PERHAPS AS I DID THE HEAD OF EULER THE  . . . .  844B LETTER 43        PROSE
EUPHRATES
    EUROPE TO EUPHRATES & HINDU TO NILE & BACK IN CLOUDS   . .   525 MILTON 35          16
    AND THESE UNITED INTO RAHAB IN THE COVERING CHERUB         624 JERUSALEM 5         42
        ON EUPHRATES
    ON THE EUPHRATES SATAN STOOD . . . . . . . . . .   651 FIELDS FROM/J        47
    THIS CAUSE OF THESE SHAKINGS OF MY TOWERS ON EUPHRATES  .   658 JERUSALEM 31        59
    ITS PILLARS EUPHRATES RAN UNDER ITS ARCHES WHITE SAILS  .   690 JERUSALEM 58        24
    EUPHRATES & TO FORESTS & FLOODS & ANIMALS WILD & TAME FROM   695 JERUSALEM 61        31
    DROP WITH THE GORE OF THE SLAIN WHY EUPHRATES IS RED WITH    721 JERUSALEM 79        69
        BLOOD
    AND JORDAN TO EUPHRATES JERUSALEM FOLLOWD TREMBLING  . . .   722 JERUSALEM 80         9
    TO ENTICE HER SISTERS AWAY TO BABYLON ON EUPHRATES   . . .   725 JERUSALEM 82        18
    THAT THEY RETURN NO MORE THAT A PLACE BE PREPARD           728 JERUSALEM 83        63
        ON EUPHRATES
    AND THUS HE HEARD THE VOICE OF ALBION'S DAUGHTERS          729 JERUSALEM 83        84
        ON EUPHRATES
    BUT HERE WE BUILD BABYLON ON EUPHRATES COMPELLD TO BUILD    729 JERUSALEM 84         8
    ON ALBION'S ROCKS & LET THY VOICE BE HEARD UPON EUPHRATES   729 JERUSALEM 84        28
    HIS LOINS INCLOSE BABYLON ON EUPHRATES BEAUTIFUL  . . . .   735 JERUSALEM 89        38
EUPHRATES'
    IN ERIN'S CONTINENT AND JERUSALEM WEPT UPON EUPHRATES'      719 JERUSALEM 78        27
        BANKS
EURIPEDES
    [PYTHAGORAS SOCRATES EURIPEDES VIRGIL DANTE MILTON]  . . .   714 JERUSALEM 73    *   42
EUROPE
    THE DEAD BROOD OVER EUROPE . . . . . . . . . . .   134 FRENCH REVOLTN       1
    TO ROUZE UP THE ANCIENT FORESTS OF EUROPE . . . . . . .   138 FRENCH REVOLTN     101
    EUROPE A PROPHECY LAMBETH PRINTED BY WILL BLAKE ... . . .  237B EUROPE           TITLE
    MY FAIRY SAT UPON THE TABLE AND DICTATED EUROPE . . . .   238 EUROPE INTRO       24
    DIVIDE THE HEAVENS OF EUROPE . . . . . . . . . .   241 EUROPE 9            7
    THUS WAS THE HOWL THRO EUROPE . . . . . . . . . .   242 EUROPE 12          21
    THE HOWL RISE UP FROM EUROPE . . . . . . . . . .   247 SONG OF LOS 6        2
    OF EUROPE AS HE WENT . . . . . . . . . . . . .   248 SONG OF LOS 7       13
    ACROSS EUROPE & ASIA TO CHINA & JAPAN LIKE LIGHTENINGS  .   281 FOUR ZOAS 2    *   59
    OVERTHROW ALL THE ARMIES OF EUROPE WITH A SMALL PAMPHLET   391C ANNO WATSON      MARG
    WHEN FRANCE GOT FREE EUROPE TWIXT FOOLS & KNAVES . . . .   451 ANNO REYNOLDS       1
    BUT FROM MY LEFT FOOT A BLACK CLOUD REDOUNDING SPREAD OVER   497 MILTON 15          50
        EUROPE
    LAMENT UPON THE WINDS OF EUROPE IN REPHAIM'S VALE   . . .   501 MILTON 19          40
    AND HE BEHELD THE CLOUD OF MILTON STRETCHING OVER EUROPE    504 MILTON 21          36
    STRETCHD OVER EUROPE & ASIA COME O SONS COME COME AWAY      509 MILTON 24          33
    THE AWAKENER IS COME OUTSTRETCHD OVER EUROPE . . . . .   510 MILTON 25          22
    EUROPE TO EUPHRATES & HINDU TO NILE & BACK IN CLOUDS   . .   525 MILTON 35          16
    EASTWARD UPON THE PAVED WORK ACROSS EUROPE & ASIA   . . .   532 MILTON 40          18
    TO A PRINCE OF THE FIFTH CENTURY WHO CONQUERED EUROPE  .  578C DESC CAT 5        PROSE
    IF ALL THE PRINCES IN EUROPE LIKE LOUIS XIV  . . . . .  599D PUB ADDRESS/N     PROSE
    THE WRETCHED STATE OF THE ARTS IN THIS COUNTRY & IN EUROPE  600B PUB ADDRESS/N     PROSE
    ACROSS ALL EUROPE & ASIA HE SAW THE TORTURES OF THE VICTIMS  627 JERUSALEM 8         24
    I TURN MY EYES TO THE SCHOOLS & UNIVERSITIES OF EUROPE  .   636 JERUSALEM 15        14
    IN SOLEMN POMP INTO CHALDEA ACROSS THE BREDTHS OF EUROPE    644 JERUSALEM 21        43
    SO LOS SPOKE STANDING ON MAM-TOR LOOKING OVER EUROPE & ASIA  661 JERUSALEM 34        41
    THE CLOUDS OF EUROPE & ASIA AMONG THE SERPENT TEMPLES   .   671 JERUSALEM 42        76
    OF BLOOD OVER EUROPE A VEGETATING ROOT IN GRINDING PAIN     677 JERUSALEM 47         5
```

		PAGE	TITLE	LINE

EUROPE   (CONTINUED)

O POLYPUS OF DEATH O SPECTRE OVER EUROPE AND ASIA . . . 679 JERUSALEM 49 24
ALL THE DESTRUCTION THEREFORE IN CHRISTIAN EUROPE . . . 683A JERUSALEM 52 PROSE
SPREADING IN BLOODY VEINS IN TORMENTS OVER EUROPE & ASIA 692 JERUSALEM 60 3
WILT THOU MAKE ROME THY PATRIARCH DRUID & THE KINGS OF 695 JERUSALEM 61 50
  EUROPE HIS
DIVIDE INTO THE KINGS OF EUROPE IN TIMES REMOTE O 698 JERUSALEM 64 16
  WOMAN-BORN
STRETCHING OVER EUROPE & ASIA FROM IRELAND TO JAPAN . . . 704 JERUSALEM 67 7
ACROSS EUROPE ACROSS AFRICA IN HOWLINGS & DEADLY WAR . . 706 JERUSALEM 68 20
LO THEY SHOOT FORTH IN TENDER NERVES ACROSS EUROPE & ASIA 706 JERUSALEM 68 26
EUROPE & ASIA & AFRICA & AMERICA IN FURY FOURFOLD . . . 712 JERUSALEM 72 31
HIM OVER EUROPE IN STREAMS OF GORE OUT OF CATHEDRON'S LOOMS 715 JERUSALEM 74 37
AGAINST JERUSALEM THEY RAGE THRO ALL THE NATIONS OF EUROPE 722 JERUSALEM 80 46
HE RAN IN TENDER NERVES ACROSS EUROPE TO JERUSALEM'S SHADE 723 JERUSALEM 80 64
AND BRIGHT STRETCHD OVER EUROPE & ASIA GORGEOUS . . . . 734 JERUSALEM 89 12
THAT DESOLATE EUROPE WITH WARS . . . . 778C HOMERS POETRY PROSE
ON EUROPE WILL MORE THAN REALIZE OUR WARMEST WISHES . . . 797C LETTER 10 PROSE
HIS CONNECTIONS THROUGHOUT ENGLAND & INDEED EUROPE & . 841C LETTER 41 PROSE
AMERICA EUROPE VISIONS &C THEL SONGS OF INNOCENCE . 867B LETTER 66 PROSE
AMERICA EUROPE VISIONS &C THEL . . . . 878D LETTER 88 PROSE

EUROPEAN

ORC RAGING IN EUROPEAN DARKNESS . . . . 248 SONG OF LOS 7 26

EUROPEAN MAGNE

FOR THE PURPOSE OF BEING ENGRAVED FOR THE EUROPEAN MAGNE 838D LETTER 37 PROSE

EUROPE'S

OF JAVAN THRO THE ISLES OF GRECIA & ALL EUROPE'S KINGS . . 735 JERUSALEM 89 34

EURYDICE

[?HE WERE LOST (?EURYDICE)] . . . . SUPP ANNO REYNOLDS * MARG

EVADING

IN THE BRIGHT SANDS OF LOS EVADING MY EMBRACE THEN I ALONE 288 FOUR ZOAS 2 305

EVANESCENT

AN EVANESCENT SHADOW LAST SHE FELL A HEAP OF ASHES . . . 283 FOUR ZOAS 2 115
AHANIA & ENION & VALA ARE THREE EVANESCENT SHADES . . . 635 JERUSALEM 14 12
DISORGANIZD AN EVANESCENT SHADE SCARCE SEEN OR HEARD AMONG 719 JERUSALEM 78 28

EVANISH

WHY DOES THY PITEOUS FACE EVANISH LIKE A RAINY CLOUD . . 297 FOUR ZOAS 3 199

EVANS

EVANS THE BOOKSELLER IN PALLMALL SAYS THEY GO OFF VERY WELL 821B LETTER 25 PROSE
I CALLED ON MR EVANS WHO GIVES SMALL HOPES OF OUR BALLADS 831C LETTER 31 PROSE
  HE

EVAPORATE

THAT LOS MAY EVAPORATE LIKE SMOKE & BE NO MORE . . . . 323 FOUR ZOAS 7 114
FOR ME & THOU ANNIHILATE EVAPORATE & BE NO MORE . . . . 329 FOUR ZOAS 7 358
FOR FEAR I SHOULD EVAPORATE THE SPIRIT OF MY INVENTION . 792B LETTER 4 PROSE

EVAPORATED

WHITE LEAD WHICH WHEN ITS PROTECTING OIL IS EVAPORATED WILL 566B DESC CAT 2 PROSE

EVAPORATING

HUSK & COVERING INTO VACUUM EVAPORATING . . . . 745 JERUSALEM 98 19

EVE   (EVENING)

FLOURISH DOWN THE BRIGHT CHEEK OF MODEST EVE . . . . . . 2 TO AUTUMN/PS 10
SWEETER THAN MUSIC IN A SUMMER'S EVE . . . . 28 EDW THIRD/PS 3 286
THE BAT THAT FLITS AT CLOSE OF EVE . . . . 431 AUGURIES 25

EVE

SINCE EVE FIRST CHOSE HER HELL FIRE SPARK . . . . 187 WHEN KLOPSTK/N 24
IMMEDIATELY BEFORE THE THRONE OF CHRIST IS ADAM & EVE . . 443B LAST JUDGMNT/L PROSE
FROM THE CLOUD ON WHICH EVE KNEELS [& BENEATH MOSES] . 443B LAST JUDGMNT/L PROSE
NUMBER XI THE BODY OF ABEL FOUND BY ADAM AND EVE . . 584A DESC CAT 11 TITLE
ADAM & EVE APPEAR FIRST BEFORE THE [THRONE] . . . . 606B V LAST JUDG/N PROSE
FROM THE CLOUD ON WHICH EVE STANDS SATAN IS SEEN . . 606B V LAST JUDG/N PROSE
BETWEEN THE FIGURES OF ADAM & EVE APPEARS A FIERY GULPH 609A V LAST JUDG/N PROSE
FORBIDDING US THAT VEIL WHICH SATAN PUTS BETWEEN EVE & ADAM 686 JERUSALEM 55 11
OF DAVID OR OF EVE OF THE WOMAN OR OF THE LORD . . . . 736 JERUSALEM 90 30
A VEGETATED CHRIST & A VIRGIN EVE ARE THE HERMAPHRODITIC 736 JERUSALEM 90 34
EVE FAINTED OVER THE DEAD BODY OF ABEL WHICH LAYS NEAR 779C GHOST ABEL 1 PROSE
  A GRAVE
SEVEN TIMES O EVE THOU HAST FAINTED OVER THE DEAD AH AH 779 GHOST ABEL 1 5
EVE REVIVES . . . . 779D GHOST ABEL 1 PROSE
EVE IS THIS THE PROMISE OF JEHOVAH O IT IS ALL A 779 GHOST ABEL 1 6
  VAIN DELUSION
EVE THOU VISIONARY PHANTASM THOU ART NOT THE REAL ABEL . . 780 GHOST ABEL 1 9
AND WHO IS HE ADAM WILT THOU OR EVE THOU DO THIS . . . . 780 GHOST ABEL 1 16
EVE COME AWAY & LET US NOT BELIEVE THESE VAIN DELUSIONS 780 GHOST ABEL 1 18
THAT APPEAREST TO MY SPIRITUAL VISION EVE SEEST THOU ALSO 780 GHOST ABEL 1 22
EVE I SEE HIM PLAINLY WITH MY MIND'S EYE I SEE ALSO ABEL 780 GHOST ABEL 1 23
  LIVING
ADAM EVE THOU HAST SPOKEN TRULY LET US KNEEL BEFORE HIS 780 GHOST ABEL 2 3
  FEET
CLOTHING ADAM & EVE WITH COATS OF SKINS . . . . . . 824A LETTER 27 PROSE
CAIN SERPENT ABEL EVE ADAM . . . . SUPP INSC HERVEY *TITLE
ADAM & EVE . . . . SUPP PENC DRAW 2.13 *TITLE

EVEN   SEE EVN

FLATTERY IS DELICIOUS EVEN FROM THE LIPS OF A BABBLER 29D EDW THIRD/PS 4 PROSE
  EXIT PETER
EVEN IN CHILDHOOD SORROW SLEPT WITH ME IN MY CRADLE . . . 37B CONTEMPLATN/PS PROSE
I DID EVEN THAT TO TRY THY TRUTH BUT WHEN I CRIED . . . 39B SAMSON/PS PROSE
FOR HOLY UNTO ISRAEL'S GOD I AM A NAZARITE EVEN FROM MY 39C SAMSON/PS PROSE
  MOTHER'S WOMB
THE SAME DULL ROUND EVEN OF A UNIVERSE . . . . 97D NAT RELIGION 2 PROSE
CURSE ON YOUR [XXX] RUTHLESS HEADS FOR I WILL BURY HER 100 TIRIEL 1 * 33
  EVEN HERE
EVEN TO ETERNITY DOWN FALLING . . . . 159B SONG LIBERTY PROSE

EVEN   (CONTINUED)

EVEN [TO] ON RATIONAL THINGS BENEATH AND FROM THE PALACE   205 AMERICA CANC C   8
    WALLS
. . . [?TILL ?BY THE] ?FROZEN CHILL & HEAVY EVEN TO THE   205 AMERICA CANC C *   9
    CITY GATE
IN THE RED AIR BEFORE THE DEMON [SEEN EVEN BY MORTAL MEN]   205 AMERICA CANC C   21
EVEN MILTON AND SHAKESPEARE COULD NOT PUBLISH THEIR OWN   207B PRSPECTUS 1793 PROSE
    WORKS
I ALONE EVEN I THE WINDS MERCILESS   . . . .   224 URIZEN 4   19
APPROACHD URIZEN EVEN TO HIS KNEES   . . . .   250 AHANIA 3   15
EVEN [SHILOH] ALBION WHOM THOU LOVEST WEPT IN PAIN HIS   277 FOUR ZOAS 1   *   485
    FAMILY
WANDERING EVEN TO THE SUNNY [ORBS] CUBES OF LIGHT & HEAT   286 FOUR ZOAS 2   254
FOR THE DIVINE LAMB EVEN JESUS WHO IS THE DIVINE VISION   287 FOUR ZOAS 2   261
OF FIRE FAR SHINING TRAVELLING ALONG EVEN TO ITS DESTIND   287 FOUR ZOAS 2   276
    END
TRIUMPHING EVEN TO THE STARS AT BRIGHT AHANIA'S FALL   . .   295 FOUR ZOAS 3   138
THAT WOULD ENRAGE THEE AS IT HAS ENRAGED ME EVEN . . . .   300 FOUR ZOAS 4   115
SHE IS DIVIDED SHE IS VANISHD EVEN LIKE LUVAH & [VALAN]   301 FOUR ZOAS 4   *   140
    VALA
EVEN IF HIS OWN DEATH RESULTED SO MUCH PITY HIM PAIND . .   309 FOUR ZOAS 5   154
EVEN TO THE CENTER WRAPPING ROUND THE CENTER & THE LIMBS   309 FOUR ZOAS 5   168
BUT NOW THOU ART BOUND DOWN WITH HIM EVEN TO THE GATES   311 FOUR ZOAS 5   *   233
    OF HELL
BORN EVEN TOO MANY & OUR EARTH WILL BE OVERRUN   . . . .   323 FOUR ZOAS 7   121
THE GOARY TIDE EVEN TO THE PLACE OF SEED & THERE DIVIDING   327 FOUR ZOAS 7   287
BY REASON'S POWER EVEN I ALREADY FEEL A WORLD WITHIN   . .   329 FOUR ZOAS 7   364
[MET] AS ONE MAN EVEN JESUS UPON GILEAD & HERMON . . . .   341 FOUR ZOAS 8   2
AND KNEW HE WAS THE SAVIOUR EVEN JESUS & THEY WORSHIPPED   342 FOUR ZOAS 8   44
HIS OWN DESPAIR EVEN AT THE COST OF EVERY THING THAT   344 FOUR ZOAS 8   139
    BREATHES
THEY STOOD IN BEAMING BEAUTY & SOMETIMES AS ONE EVEN RAHAB   349 FOUR ZOAS 8   329
EVEN RAHAB IN ALL HER TURPITUDE RAHAB DIVIDED HERSELF   . .   350 FOUR ZOAS 8   344
LET LUVAH RAGE IN THE DARK DEEP EVEN TO CONSUMMATION   360 FOUR ZOAS 9   142
BUT SIN EVEN RAHAB IS REDEEMD IN BLOOD & FURY & JEALOUSY   361 FOUR ZOAS 9   159
REVIVES ME TO NEW DEATHS I FADE EVEN LIKE A WATER LILLY   371 FOUR ZOAS 9   *   540
HOW IS IT THAT ALL THINGS ARE CHANGD EVEN AS IN ANCIENT   379 FOUR ZOAS 9   845
    TIMES
THEY STOOD IN BEAMING BEAUTY & SOMETIMES AS ONE EVEN RAHAB   382 FOUR ZOAS AD 6   17
[WHAT DOUBT IS VIRTUOUS EVEN HONEST ?THAT DEPENDS ?UPON   386C ANNO WATSON   * MARG
    EXAMINATION]
OR EVEN OF COMMON CAPACITY I CANNOT   . . . .   404B ANNO BACON   MARG
THESE ARE NOT SO EVEN THE COPY FROM RAPHAEL'S CARTOON . .   439C REMARKS MALKIN   PROSE
NOT EVEN BEGUN HOW CAN THEY THEN BE FINISHD THE MAN WHO   449C ANNO REYNOLDS   MARG
[GENERAL PRINCIPLES YOU CANNOT EVEN KNOW OR SEE MICH ANG]   456B ANNO REYNOLDS * MARG
CANNOT EVEN KNOW OR SEE MICH ANGO OR RAFAEL OR ANY THING   456B ANNO REYNOLDS   MARG
    ELSE
NOT ADMIRE RAFAEL'S EXECUTION DOES NOT EVEN SEE RAFAEL   .   467A ANNO REYNOLDS   MARG
ITS OFFERINGS EVEN TILL JESUS THE IMAGE OF THE INVISIBLE   481 MILTON 2   12
    GOD
AND IN HIS TENT THRO ENVY OF LIVING FORM EVEN OF THE DIVINE   482 MILTON 3   2
    VISION
SEEMING A BROTHER BEING A TYRANT EVEN THINKING HIMSELF   487 MILTON 7   24
    A BROTHER
EVEN SIX THOUSAND YEARS AND SENT LUCIFER FOR ITS GUARD . .   494 MILTON 13   17
EVEN PITY & HUMANITY BUT MY CLOTHING SHALL BE CRUELTY   . .   499 MILTON 18   20
EVEN TO MAHANAIM WHEN WITH COLD HAND URIZEN STOOPD DOWN   500 MILTON 19   7
HER SHADOWY SISTERS FORM THE BONES EVEN THE BONES OF HOREB   501 MILTON 19   51
EVEN AS REUBEN & AS GAD GAVE UP HIMSELF TO TEARS   . . . .   503 MILTON 20   53
SO SPAKE THE FAMILY DIVINE AS ONE MAN EVEN JESUS . . . .   505 MILTON 21   58
BECOMING OBEDIENT TO DEATH EVEN THE DEATH OF THE CROSS   506 MILTON 22   58
BUT LOS DISPERSD THE CLOUDS EVEN AS THE STRONG WINDS OF   507 MILTON 23   31
    JEHOVAH
JOY EVEN TO TEARS WHICH THE SUN RISING DRIES FIRST THE   520 MILTON 31   51
    WILD THYME
AND THE ETERNAL MAN EVEN ALBION UPON THE ROCK OF AGES   . .   524 MILTON 34   46
EVEN OF LOS & ENITHARMON & ALL THE SONS OF ALBION   . . .   525 MILTON 35   27
THAT THE SEVEN EYES OF GOD WHO WALK EVEN TO SATAN'S SEAT   526 MILTON 35   64
WITH POMP EVEN TILL MORNING BREAK & OSIRIS APPEAR IN THE   528 MILTON 37   29
    SKY
INTEREST BUT FROM MALICE EVEN TO YOUR OWN DESTRUCTION   . .   573A DESC CAT 3   PROSE
YET A LITTLE PAINS OUGHT TO BE TAKEN EVEN BY THE IGNORANT   574A DESC CAT 3   PROSE
    AND WEAK
OR EVEN TO THEIR LIVING IN A PALACE BUT IT SHALL NOT BE   575D DESC CAT 3   PROSE
HE INFUSES A LOVE OF SOFT AND EVEN TINTS WITHOUT BOUNDARIES   583B DESC CAT 9   PROSE
ARTIST HIMSELF EVEN TO THE STUFFS & EMBROIDERY . . . . .   588A CHAUCER/N   PROSE
AT THIS HOUSE EVEN AT THIS DAY EVERY FRIENDLESS WRETCH   .   590B CHAUCER 2   PROSE
FLAXMAN & EVEN ROMNEY SPOILS AN ENGRAVER FOR EACH OF   . .   592B PUB ADDRESS/N   PROSE
EVEN TO ITALY BUT THE PUBLIC WILL KNOW & POSTERITY WILL   592D PUB ADDRESS/N   PROSE
    KNOW
THEY COULD NOT WOUND EVEN MR BARRY SO . . . .   592D PUB ADDRESS/N   PROSE
PRETENCES OF ENGLISHMEN TO IMPROVE [E] ART BEFORE THEY EVEN   593C PUB ADDRESS/N *PROSE
THO EVEN IN THESE A SINGLE LEAF OF A TREE IS NEVER CORRECT   594A PUB ADDRESS/N   PROSE
THIS EVEN HOGARTH'S WORKS PROVE A DETESTABLE FALSHOOD   . .   595C PUB ADDRESS/N   PROSE
EVEN HOGARTH'S EXECUTION CANNOT BE COPIED OR IMPROVED . .   599C PUB ADDRESS/N   PROSE
THEIR [BEAUTY IS CONFESSD EVEN BY THE LIPS OF PASCH   601A PUB ADDRESS/N *PROSE
    HIMSELF]
[EVEN MORE LIFELIKE THAN CANVAS] . . . .   601A PUB ADDRESS/N *PROSE
EVEN HOGARTH CANNOT BE EITHER COPIED OR IMPROVED . . . .   601D PUB ADDRESS/N   PROSE
OR EVEN VANLOO THAT THERE IS IN RAFAEL OR MICH ANGELO . .   602C PUB ADDR AD/N   PROSE
AN EVEN TINT IS NOT IN NATURE IT PRODUCES HEAVINESS   . . .   603B PUB ADDR AD/N   PROSE
THAT IS QUITE EVEN NEVER CAN PRODUCE A NATURAL SKY   . . .   603B PUB ADDR AD/N   PROSE

```
                                                          PAGE    TITLE         LINE
EVEN    (CONTINUED)
    & VAPOUR OF SMOKE EVEN TILL ABRAHAM'S TIME THE VAPOR    .  . 606D V LAST JUDG/N   PROSE
    WO WO WO TO YOU HYPOCRITES EVEN MURDER                   .  . 615D V LAST JUDG/N   PROSE
    EVEN THE DEVILS LOVE ONE ANOTHER IN THEIR WAY  . . . .     616B V LAST JUDG/N   PROSE
    EVEN FROM THE DEPTHS OF HELL HIS VOICE I HEAR      .  .    621 READER LOVER/J       7
    GOD IS WITHIN & WITHOUT HE IS EVEN IN THE DEPTHS OF HELL  631 JERUSALEM 12        15
    THARMAS THE VEGETATED TONGUE EVEN THE DEVOURING TONGUE  .  634 JERUSALEM 14         4
    FROM THE BLUE MUNDANE SHELL EVEN TO THE EARTH OF VEGETATION 637 JERUSALEM 16       25
    TO HIDE THE MOST EVIDENT GOD IN A HIDDEN COVERT EVEN   .  . 661 JERUSALEM 34       32
    CONSEQUENCES TO THOSE TO WHOM IT SEEMS TO BE EVEN OF   .  . 663 JERUSALEM 36       53
    IN EDEN IN LOVELY JERUSALEM DREW EVEN FROM ENVY   . . . .  675 JERUSALEM 45         6
    SUBSERVIENT TO THE CLODS OF THE FURROW THE CATTLE AND EVEN  688 JERUSALEM 56       36
    AND SWEET HESPERIA EVEN TO GREAT CHALDEA & TESSHINA   .  . 692 JERUSALEM 60        20
    MY WEARY EYES EVEN IN THIS DUNGEON & THIS IRON MILL  .  .  693 JERUSALEM 60        59
    EVEN A LONG SEASON & A HARD JOURNEY & A HOWLING WILDERNESS  696 JERUSALEM 62       27
    THEN ALL THE DAUGHTERS OF ALBION BECAME ONE BEFORE LOS     698 JERUSALEM 64         6
        EVEN VALA
    EMBRACES ARE COMINGLINGS FROM THE HEAD EVEN TO THE FEET    708 JERUSALEM 69        43
    EACH WITHIN OTHER ON HER WHITE MARBLE & EVEN NECK HER HEART 709 JERUSALEM 70       21
    AND SAW A FLAME OF FIRE EVEN AS A WHEEL  . . . . . . .     717 STOOD AMONG/J        2
    EVEN TO THE STARS EXALTING HER THRONE TO BUILD BEYOND THE  719 JERUSALEM 78        18
        THRONE
    EVEN ENITHARMON SEPARATED OUTSIDE & HIS LOINS CLOSED   .   732 JERUSALEM 86        58
    A MIGHTY TEMPLE EVEN TO THE STARS BUT THEY VEGETATE   . .  737 JERUSALEM 90        50
    ALL HUMAN FORMS IDENTIFIED EVEN TREE METAL EARTH & STONE   747 JERUSALEM 99         1
        ALL
    EVEN TO THE TEMPLE'S HIGHEST STEEPLE  . . . . . . . .      752 EV GOSPEL(D)/N      70
    BROUGHT TO LIGHT BY JESUS EVEN THE COVENANT OF JEHOVAH  .  757D EV GOSPEL         PROSE
    IN SELF ANNIHILATION EVEN TILL SATAN SELF-SUBDUD PUT OFF   781 GHOST ABEL 2        20
        SATAN
    DRAW A FEATHER OVER IT & YOU WILL GET AN EVEN SURFACE  .   790C LETTER 2          PROSE
    IN CONTEMPLATING MY PICTURES THAN I EVEN HOPED    . . .    794B LETTER 5          PROSE
    BEEN PUBLISHD EVEN JOHNSON & FUSELI HAVE DISCARDED         795C LETTER 6          PROSE
        MY GRAVER
    I HEAR HIS ADVICE & EVEN NOW WRITE FROM HIS DICTATE  . .   797B LETTER 9          PROSE
    EVEN IN THIS WORLD BY IT I AM THE COMPANION OF ANGELS  .   797B LETTER 9          PROSE
    VERY ILL NATURED YET EVEN FROM HIM I LEARN      . . . .    798B LETTER 10         PROSE
    "REMEMBER WITH AFFECTION EVEN THE HEM OF YOUR GARMENT"  .  800A LETTER 12         PROSE
    TO ME WHILE DRUNKENNESS LEWDNESS GLUTTONY & EVEN   . . .   812C LETTER 22         PROSE
    REFUSE & BURY YOUR TALENT IN THE EARTH EVEN THO YOU   . .  813A LETTER 22         PROSE
    OUT OF DESPONDENCY EVEN IF IT LIFTS ME TOO HIGH   . . .    822C LETTER 26         PROSE
    OR THIRTY LINES AT A TIME WITHOUT PREMEDITATION & EVEN  .  823A LETTER 26         PROSE
    A PRINCE AMONG PRINCES & EVEN ON EARTH BELOVED BY THE GOOD 830A LETTER 30         PROSE
    EVEN SNOW HILL IS BECOME ALMOST LEVEL   . . . . . . .      831D LETTER 31         PROSE
    ME I LEARNED THAT [XXX] NO ONE NOT EVEN THE MOST EXPERT    833B LETTER 33        *PROSE
        HORSEMAN
    SERVANT WHO DOMINEERED OVER ME HE IS EVEN AS A BROTHER  .  852C LETTER 50         PROSE
    WHENEVER I TAKE A PENCIL OR GRAVER INTO MY HAND EVEN AS I  852C LETTER 50         PROSE
    EVEN ISLINGTON & ALL PLACES NORTH OF LONDON ALWAYS LAID ME 871A LETTER 72         PROSE
    NO DISCIPLINE WILL TURN ONE MAN INTO ANOTHER EVEN IN   .   871A LETTER 72         PROSE
EVENING
    THY MORN AND EVENING BREATH SCATTER THY PEARLS    . . . .    1 TO SPRING/PS       11
    TO THE EVENING STAR  . . . . . . . . . . .                  3B EVNING STAR/PS   TITLE
    THOU FAIR-HAIRD ANGEL OF THE EVENING  . . . . . . . .        3 EVNING STAR/PS       1
    PUT ON AND SMILE UPON OUR EVENING BED   . . . . . . .        3 EVNING STAR/PS       4
    WHEN EVENING SITS BENEATH HER DUSKY BOWR    . . . . .       10 WHEN EARLY/PS        3
    AND EVENING HEAR THEIR SONG OF VICTORY  . . . . . .         33 EDW THIRD/PS 6      52
    THE VEILED EVENING WALKED SOLITARY DOWN THE WESTERN HILLS   35C COUCH DEATH/PS   PROSE
    IN FORMER TIMES ON SUCH AN EVENING    . . . . . . .         35C COUCH DEATH/PS   PROSE
    WHEN THE EVENING DROPS TRICKLE DOWN   . . . . . . .         35D COUCH DEATH/PS   PROSE
    THUS HE LAMENTS THROUGH THE STILL EVENING   . . . . .       35D COUCH DEATH/PS   PROSE
    TO THEE I POUR MY TEARS FOR SACRIFICE MORNING AND EVENING   38B SAMSON/PS        PROSE
    WHEN BUSY DAY WAS FADING AND CALM EVENING   . . . . .       39D SAMSON/PS        PROSE
    HIS SPACIOUS BROW SHOT TERRORS THROUGH THE EVENING SHADE    39D SAMSON/PS        PROSE
    WHEN HIS EVENING TALE IS TOLD DEPARTS HIS BLESSING LEAVING  40A SAMSON/PS        PROSE
    THIS EVENING [WE'D] WE'LL ALL GET DRUNK I SAY DASH AN ANTHEM 54B ISLAND MOON 9  *PROSE
    ALL DAY HE BORE HIM & WHEN EVENING DREW HER SOLEMN CURTAIN  104 TIRIEL 4          41
    FROM THE MORN TO THE EVENING HE STRAYS    . . . . . .       118 SHEPHERD/SI        2
    THE EVENING STAR DOES SHINE  . . . . . . . . .             118 NIGHT/SI            2
    OF HIM THAT WALKETH IN THE GARDEN IN THE EVENING TIME  .   127 BOOK OF THEL 1     14
    EAT IN THE EVENING SLEEP IN THE NIGHT   . . . . . .       152A MARRIAGE HH 9     PROSE
    IN HAPPY COPULATION IF IN EVENING MILD WEARIED WITH WORK   194 V DAU ALBION 7      1
    THE TRAVELLER HASTETH IN THE EVENING DEATH'S DOOR   . .    209D FOR CHILDRN/GP   TITLE
    AND WEEPING IN THE EVENING DEW   . . . . . . . .           210 INTRODUCTN/SE       7
    BLOWD IN THE MORN IN EVENING DIED  . . . . . . . .         220 TO TIRZAH/SE        6
    MY WEARY EYELIDS DRAW TOWARDS THE EVENING MY BLISS IS YET  240 EUROPE 5           10
        BUT NEW
    TO AHANIA RETURND IN EVENING    . . . . . . . .            255 AHANIA 5           36
    URIZEN ROSE FROM THE BRIGHT FEAST LIKE A STAR THRO THE     280 FOUR ZOAS 2         9
        EVENING SKY
    MEASURD HIS FOOD MORNING & EVENING IN CUPS & BASKETS OF    343 FOUR ZOAS 8        81
        IRON
    . . . & THE EVENING BY CAREFULNESS    . . . . . . .        363 FOUR ZOAS 9     *  227
    HIS GOLDEN FOOD AND IN THE EVENING SLEEP BEFORE THE DOOR   376 FOUR ZOAS 9       708
    AROUND THE FURNACES & IN EVENING SPORT UPON THE PLAINS     379 FOUR ZOAS 9       842
    AND EVENING WINDS MY SORROWS BEAR   . . . . . . .          423 THE BIRDS/N         8
    AND CAME HOME IN EVENING BESPATTERD WITH MIRE  . . . .     428 MARY               36
    TUESDAY JANRY...BETWEEN TWO & SEVEN IN THE EVENING DESPAIR 440A MEMORANDUM/N 1   PROSE
    FOR PALAMABRON RETURND WITH LABOUR WEARIED EVERY EVENING   486 MILTON 7            9
    IN THE EVENING RETURNING TERRIFIED OVERLABOURD & ASTONISHD 486 MILTON 7           16
    AND WHEN UNWEARIED IN THE EVENING HE CREATES THE MOON  .   517 MILTON 29          42
    MY MORN & EVENING FOOD WERE PREPARD IN BATTLES OF MEN  .   644 JERUSALEM 22        7
```

619

		PAGE	TITLE	LINE

EVENING   (CONTINUED)
```
      LIKE EVENING DEW ON EVERY HERB UPON THE BREATHING GROUND    669 JERUSALEM 42      8
      THIS IS THE SONG OF THE LAMB SUNG BY SLAVES IN EVENING TIME  693 JERUSALEM 60     38
      THE TRAVELLER HASTETH IN THE EVENING  . . . . . . . . .    769B FOR SEXES/GP   TITLE
      THRO EVENING SHADES I HASTE AWAY  . . . . . . . . .         771 OF GATES/GP      41
      I SHALL WISH FOR YOU ON TUESDAY EVENING AS USUAL PRAY GIVE 803C LETTER 15       PROSE
      THUS THE TRAVELLER HASTETH IN THE EVENING  . . . . .       SUPP LEGEND/N15     *TITLE
```
EVENING'S
```
      TO SIT IN THE HOUSE AND TAKE HIS EVENING'S REST FROM LABOUR  40A SAMSON/PS      PROSE
```
EVENNESS
```
      HAVE SOFTNESS AND EVENNESS BY A TWELVEMONTH'S LABOUR    . . 583C DESC CAT 9     PROSE
```
EVENT
```
      OF TIME IS LOST NOR ONE EVENT OF SPACE UNPERMANENT  . . .   505 MILTON 22        19
```
EVENTIDE
```
      TILL TO THE CAVES OF ZAZEL THEY APPROACHD AT EVEN TIDE  . . 108 TIRIEL 7          2
```
EVENTS
```
      LOOK OVER THE EVENTS OF YOUR OWN LIFE & IF YOU DO NOT  . . 391C ANNO WATSON      MARG
      EVENTS OF TIME START FORTH & ARE CONCIEVD IN SUCH A PERIOD  516 MILTON 29         2
      . . . THEIR EVENTS ARE PRESENT BEFORE ME  . . . . .        714 JERUSALEM 74      19
```
EVER   SEE FOR-EVER,SO EVER,WHERE-EVER,WHERE EVER
```
      AND LOVE THEM I EVER SHALL  . . . . . . . . . . . . .        8 LOVE JOCUND/PS    19
      I EVER SAW IT  . . . . . . . . . . . . . . . . . . .        28 EDW THIRD/PS 4     9
      I'LL DRAW MY SWORD NOR EVER SHEATH IT UP  . . . . . .       31 EDW THIRD/PS 5    64
      A VIRGIN EVER YOUNG AND AFTER LEADEN SLOTH  . . . . .      40D THEN SHE BORE    PROSE
      IT SAID NO MORE BUT VANISHED EVER FROM MY SIGHT  . . .     43D WOE CRIED MUSE   PROSE
      SECTS ARE NOT EVER MENTIOND THERE AS BEING QUITE OUT OF    44B ISLAND MOON 1    PROSE
         DATE
      THEY SEEM TO ME TO BE THE MOST WRETCHED PALTRY FLIMSY STUFF 44D ISLAND MOON 1   PROSE
         THAT EVER
      HE DOES NOT MIND THEIR CRYING THO THEY CRY EVER SO  . .    50A ISLAND MOON 6    PROSE
      AND SAID IM MADE FOR EVER  . . . . . . . . . . . . .       51 WHEN CORRUP/IM    24
      EVERY PROVOKING SPEECH THAT EVER SHE COULD & HE BORE IT    53B ISLAND MOON 8    PROSE
      ENGLISH GENIUS FOR EVER HERE I GO  . . . . . . . . .       56A ISLAND MOON 9    PROSE
      WHICH SMEARD THE GLASS WORSE THAN EVER THEN HE SCREWD IT ON 58D ISLAND MOON 10  PROSE
      NO MAN WAS EVER TRULY SUPERSTITIOUS WHO WAS NOT  . . .     75A ANNO LAVATER     MARG
      HE PERCIEVES MORE THAN SENSE THO EVER SO ACUTE CAN DISCOVER 97C NAT RELIGION 2  PROSE
      MY BRIGHT MANE FOR EVER  . . . . . . . . . . . . . .       119 NIGHT/SI         46
      THOU HIS IMAGE EVER SEE  . . . . . . . . . . . . . .       120 CRADLE SONG/SI   27
      BEGAN TO CRY BUT GOD EVER NIGH  . . . . . . . . . .        121 LIT BOY FND/SI    3
      CAN THE FIRES OF NOBILITY EVER BE QUENCHD  .  . . . .      142 FRENCH REVOLTN   181
      & HIMSELF THE SINGLE ONE ON EARTH THAT EVER BROKE A NET   157D MARRIAGE HH 21   PROSE
      NOR EVER ONCE WISH FROM THE CHURCH TO STRAY  . . . .      179 LIT VAGABOND/N     9
      NOR EVER ONCE WISH FROM THE CHURCH TO STRAY  . . . .      216 LIT VAGABND/SE     8
      AND SEE SMALL PORTIONS OF THE ETERNAL WORLD THAT         237 EUROPE INTRO        4
         EVER GROWETH
      . . . [WHERE WE MAY REMAIN FOR EVER ALONE] ALSO O PITY    265 FOUR ZOAS 1       28
         ME O ENION
      THE LAMB OF GOD BLESSED FOR EVER & HE FOLLOWD THE MAN  .  279 FOUR ZOAS 1      556
      THE FADING CRY IS EVER DYING  . . . . . . . . . .        289 FOUR ZOAS 2      362
      THE LIVING VOICE IS EVER LIVING IN ITS INMOST JOY  . .   289 FOUR ZOAS 2      363
      ART THOU FOR EVER VANISHD FROM THE WATRY EYES OF THARMAS  297 FOUR ZOAS 3      202
      HOW IS THIS ALL MY HOPE IS GONE [ENION] FOR EVER FLED    297 FOUR ZOAS 4        9
      DEATHLESS FOR EVER NOW I WANDER SEEKING OBLIVION  . . .   298 FOUR ZOAS 4       12
      AND CANNOT THOSE WHO ONCE HAVE LOVD EVER FORGET THEIR LOVE 298 FOUR ZOAS 4      17
      [AND THARMAS ?SAID ALL MY HOPE I THOUGHT ENION FOR EVER  SUPP FOUR ZOAS 4        *
         GONE]
      NOR THE CONSUMMATION OF LOS COULD EVER MELT THE CHAIN  .  309 FOUR ZOAS 5      162
      WITHHOLD THY LIGHT FROM ME FOR EVER & I WILL WITHHOLD  .  313 FOUR ZOAS 6       64
      IS NOT DOWN FALLING THRO IMMENSITY EVER & EVER  . . .    317 FOUR ZOAS 6      220
      NOR COULD THEY EVER BE CLOSD AGAIN THE GOLDEN HINGES WERE 328 FOUR ZOAS 7      324
         BROKEN
      BUT [ALL] THOU O UNIVERSAL HUMANITY WHO IS ONE MAN BLESSED 347 FOUR ZOAS 8     232
         FOR EVER
      TIMES UPON TIMES THINKING TO DESTROY THE LAMB BLESSED    347 FOUR ZOAS 8      235
         FOR EVER
      ABHORRD ACCURSED EVER DYING AN ETERNAL DEATH  . . . .    347 FOUR ZOAS 8    * 256
      WITH MYSTERY THE HARLOT & WITH SATAN FOR EVER & EVER  .  361 FOUR ZOAS 9      157
      WHERE THE IMPRESSIONS OF DESPAIR & HOPE FOR EVER VEGETATE 367 FOUR ZOAS 9      377
      YON SUN SHALL WAX OLD & DECAY BUT THOU SHALT EVER FLOURISH 368 FOUR ZOAS 9     419
      IS FOR EVER REMOVED & HENCEFORTH EVERY MAN MAY  . . .   389C ANNO WATSON       MARG
      THAT NONE BUT DESIGNING VILLAINS EVER PRETENDED TO BELIEVE 390C ANNO WATSON    MARG
      CEASED PUTS IT OUT OF HIS OWN POWER TO EVER WITNESS ONE  391C ANNO WATSON      MARG
      NEITHER DID JESUS EVER DO SUCH A MIRACLE IS IT A  . .   391C ANNO WATSON       MARG
      EVER DOUBT CHRIST'S IN THE ABOVE SENSE OF THE WORD MIRACLE 391D ANNO WATSON    MARG
      HOW CAN WATSON EVER BELIEVE THE ABOVE SENSE OF A MIRACLE 391D ANNO WATSON      MARG
      AS THIS BOOK CONTAINS CAN EVER HAVE BEEN CALLD WISDOM  . 397A ANNO BACON       MARG
      EXCEPT IS CHRIST YOU LIE EXCEPT DID ANYONE EVER DO THIS 400D ANNO BACON        MARG
      AND IN THY CELL THOU SHALL EVER DWELL  . . . . . . .    419 I SAW A MONK/N     13
      THEY CRY & TEARS FOR EVER FLOW  . . . . . . . . . .     421 BENEATH/N           5
      AND NO SMILE THAT EVER WAS SMILD  . . . . . . . . .     423 THE SMILE          11
      THEY CRY & TEARS FOR EVER FLOW  . . . . . . . . . .     424 THE GOLDEN NET      4
      FOR EVER OPEN IS HIS DOOR  . . . . . . . . . . . .      425 MENTAL TRAVLER     40
      SWEET MARY THE FIRST TIME SHE EVER WAS THERE  . . . .   428 MARY                1
      THE STRONGEST POISON EVER KNOWN  . . . . . . . . .      433 AUGURIES           97
      TO LEARN THE LANGUAGE OF ART COPY FOR EVER IS MY RULE  . 446B ANNO REYNOLDS    MARG
      I AM HAPPY I CANNOT SAY THAT RAFAEL EVER WAS  . . . .   447C ANNO REYNOLDS     MARG
      THIS IS MOST FALSE FOR NO ONE CAN EVER DESIGN TILL HE HAS 455D ANNO REYNOLDS   MARG
      & ADVERTISED FOR EVER IT WILL ONLY BE ADMIRED BY FOOLS . 466A ANNO REYNOLDS    MARG
      BUT HE OUGHT TO PUT ALL MEN OF GENIUS WHO EVER PAINTED  469A ANNO REYNOLDS     MARG
      WHO EVER SAID THIS  . . . . . . . . . . . . . . .      474A ANNO REYNOLDS      MARG
      WHO WOULD IF THEY COULD FOR EVER DEPRESS MENTAL & PROLONG 480C MILTON 1        PROSE
      OF ETERNITY IN WHICH WE SHALL LIVE FOR EVER IN JESUS OUR 480D MILTON 1        PROSE
         LORD
```

		PAGE	TITLE	LINE
EVER	(CONTINUED)			
WHICH IS THE DIVINE BODY OF THE LORD JESUS BLESSED FOR EVER		482	MILTON 3	4
IN IMMENSE LABOURS & SORROWS EVER BUILDING EVER FALLING		485	MILTON 6	2
OF MY ETERNAL MIND TRANSGRESSORS I WILL REND OFF FOR EVER		490	MILTON 9	28
TILL TWO ETERNITYS MEET TOGETHER AH LOST LOST LOST FOR EVER		494	MILTON 13	11
BUT LEAVE THEIR DESTIND LINEAMENTS PERMANENT FOR EVER & EVER		505	MILTON 22	25
THE ETERNAL WHO IS BLESSED FOR EVER & EVER AMEN		519	MILTON 30	31
TO PUT OFF SELF & ALL I HAVE EVER & EVER AMEN		530	MILTON 38	49
OF LOS THAT EVER BURNETH WITH FIRE EVER & EVER AMEN		530	MILTON 39	12
NO REAL STYLE OF COLOURING EVER APPEARS		536	NO REAL STYL/N	1
THIS IS ONE OF THE BEST COMPLIMENTS HE EVER HAD		538	TO H(UNT)/N	2
[FOR NOW] IN SPITE WE WILL BE GREATER FRIENDS THAN EVER		556	IF MEN ACT/N	6
EVER IN THEIR YOUTHFUL PRIME		558	THE CAVERNS/N	14
OF DIMENSIONS EVER SO LARGE OR EVER SO SMALL WHICH MAY BE		560D	EXHIBITION ADV	PROSE
NOTHING NEW OCCURS IN IDENTICAL EXISTENCE ACCIDENT EVER VARIES		567C	DESC CAT 3	PROSE
BUT THE CHARACTERS THEMSELVES FOR EVER REMAIN UNALTERED		567C	DESC CAT 3	PROSE
HAS EVER BEEN A CONQUEROR AND IS THAT SPECIES OF CHARACTER		567D	DESC CAT 3	PROSE
AND REMAIN FOR EVER UNSUBDUED AGE AFTER AGE		577D	DESC CAT 5	PROSE
THE FIRST MR B(BLAKE) EVER DID IN FRESCO FORTUNATELY OR		581B	DESC CAT 6	PROSE
NOTHING NEW OCCURS IN IDENTICAL EXISTENCE ACCIDENT EVER VARIES		589A	CHAUCER/N	PROSE
BUT THE CHARACTERS THEMSELVES FOR EVER REMAIN UNALTERED		590D	CHAUCER 2	PROSE
NOR CAN THEIR METHOD EVER EXPRESS IDEAS OR IMAGINATIONS		596A	PUB ADDRESS/N	PROSE
NO MAN OF SENSE EVER SUPPOSES THAT COPYING FROM NATURE		598A	PUB ADDRESS/N	PROSE
P S I DO NOT BELIEVE THAT THIS ABSURD OPINION EVER WAS		602B	PUB ADDRESS/N	PROSE
NATURE'S SHADOWS ARE EVER VARYING & A RULED SKY		603B	PUB ADDR AD/N	PROSE
ONE OF THE MOST IGNORANT FELLOWS THAT I EVER KNEW		603B	PUB ADDR AD/N	PROSE
MAN PASSES ON BUT STATES REMAIN FOR EVER HE PASSES THRO		606D	V LAST JUDG/N	PROSE
THE FOOL SHALL NOT ENTER INTO HEAVEN LET HIM BE EVER SO HOLY		615D	V LAST JUDG/N	PROSE
THE LONG SUFFERINGS OF GOD ARE NOT FOR EVER THERE IS A JUDGMENT		620	JERUSALEM 1	10
EVER EXPANDING IN THE BOSOM OF GOD THE HUMAN IMAGINATION		623	JERUSALEM 5	20
WHICH IS THE DIVINE BODY OF THE LORD JESUS BLESSED FOR EVER		624	JERUSALEM 5	59
NOR SHALT THOU EVER ASSUME THE TRIPLE-FORM OF ALBION'S SPECTRE		627	JERUSALEM 8	34
BUT MY GRIEFS ADVANCE ALSO FOR EVER & EVER WITHOUT END		630	JERUSALEM 10	50
AND IRON BOUND IT OVER ME FOR EVER LIFE LIVES ON MY		630	JERUSALEM 10	55
TO BE ALL EVIL ALL REVERSED & FOR EVER DEAD KNOWING		630	JERUSALEM 10	57
GIVING A BODY TO FALSHOOD THAT IT MAY BE CAST OFF FOR EVER		631	JERUSALEM 12	* 13
THE NADIR EAST THE CENTER UNAPPROACHABLE FOR EVER		632	JERUSALEM 12	56
IN THOSE CHURCHES EVER CONSUMING & EVER BUILDING BY THE SPECTRES		634	JERUSALEM 13	62
EXIST NOT NOR SHALL THEY EVER BE ORGANIZED FOR EVER & EVER		639	JERUSALEM 17	35
EVER DESCEND INTO THEE BUT THOU SHALT BE A NON ENTITY FOR EVER		639	JERUSALEM 17	44
THOSE THAT THOU TORMENTEST A HELL & DESPAIR FOR EVER & EVER		639	JERUSALEM 17	47
TO BE FOR A SHAME & A CURSE AND TO BE OUR SLAVES FOR EVER		640	JERUSALEM 18	35
DEPART BUT DWELL FOR EVER HERE		651	FIELDS FROM/J	70
SHALL MAKE HIM & HIS SONS & DAUGHTERS YOUR SLAVES FOR EVER		658	JERUSALEM 31	54
AND BE THOU FOR EVER ACCURSED THAT ALBION MAY ARISE AGAIN		662	JERUSALEM 35	14
OF MAN FOR EVER BE POSSESSD BY MONSTERS OF THE DEEPS		667	JERUSALEM 40	28
HUMAN DIVINE JESUS THE SAVIOUR BLESSED FOR EVER AND EVER		667	JERUSALEM 40	47
IN THE BOSOM OF MAN FOR EVER FROM ETERNITY TO ETERNITY		670	JERUSALEM 42	36
HE HATH CAST THEE OFF FOR EVER THE LITTLE ONES HE HATH ANOINTED		670	JERUSALEM 42	44
THY SELFHOOD IS FOR EVER ACCURSED FROM THE DIVINE PRESENCE		670	JERUSALEM 42	45
PITS OF BITUMEN EVER BURNING ARTIFICIAL RICHES OF THE CANAANITE		673	JERUSALEM 43	62
THEY DENY THAT THEY EVER KNEW JERUSALEM OR EVER DWELT IN SHILOH		679	JERUSALEM 49	9
BE LOST FOR EVER & EVER THEN THEY SHALL ARISE FROM SELF		680	JERUSALEM 49	45
AND IN YOUR CELL YOU SHALL EVER DWELL		683	I SAW A MONK/J	11
EVERY ONE KNOWS WE ARE ONE FAMILY ONE MAN BLESSED FOR EVER		687	JERUSALEM 55	46
O IT WAS LOST FOR EVER AND WE FOUND IT NOT IT CAME		688	JERUSALEM 56	26
BEFORE I HAD EVER BEHELD WITH LOVE THE FACE OF JEHOVAH OR KNOWN		695	JERUSALEM 61	42
THE FEMININE & MASCULINE SHADOWS SOFT MILD & EVER VARYING		707	JERUSALEM 68	69
SO MEN PASS ON BUT STATES REMAIN PERMANENT FOR EVER		714	JERUSALEM 73	45
TO AN ETERNAL NIGHT OF PAIN LOST LOST LOST FOR EVER		721	JERUSALEM 80	5
WHICH IS UNCHANGEABLE FOR EVER & EVER AMEN SO BE IT		728	JERUSALEM 83	48
HOW THEN CAN I EVER AGAIN BE UNITED AS MAN WITH MAN		733	JERUSALEM 88	12
UNPERMANENT FOR EVER BECAUSE OF LOVE & JEALOUSY		734	JERUSALEM 88	42
MY LOOMS WILL BE NO MORE & I ANNIHILATE VANISH FOR EVER		739	JERUSALEM 92	11
FOR THEE OR EVER DIE FOR ONE WHO HAD NOT DIED FOR THEE		743	JERUSALEM 96	24
IN THE FOUR SENSES IN THE OUTLINE THE CIRCUMFERENCE & FORM FOR EVER		745	JERUSALEM 98	22
NOR CANST THOU EVER CHANGE KATE INTO NAN		771	EPILOGUE/GP	4
OF THE TRANSGRESOR OR NO FLESH OR SPIRIT COULD EVER LIVE		780	GHOST ABEL 2	* 11
INTO THE BOTTOMLESS ABYSS WHOSE TORMENT ARISES FOR EVER & EVER		781	GHOST ABEL 2	21
I DESPAIR OF EVER PLEASING ONE CLASS OF MEN		795A	LETTER 6	PROSE
BETTER THINGS THAN I HAVE EVER SEEN MY WORK PLEASES MY		795C	LETTER 6	PROSE
& BELIEVE ME TO BE FOR EVER YOURS		798D	LETTER 10	PROSE
. . . THAT EVER I SAW FLAXMAN'S FACE		799	TO FLAXMAN/L	1
I REMAIN FOR EVER YOURS		799D	LETTER 11	PROSE
OF MAN NO OTHER FORMED HOUSE CAN EVER PLEASE ME SO WELL		802A	LETTER 14	PROSE
NOR SHALL I EVER BE PERSWADED I BELIEVE		802A	LETTER 14	PROSE

	PAGE	TITLE	LINE

EVER   (CONTINUED)

& BELIEVE ME FOR EVER TO REMAIN YOUR GRATEFUL   802D LETTER 14   PROSE
  & AFFECTIONATE
EVER BUILD A PALACE IT WOULD BE ONLY MY COTTAGE ENLARGED   803B LETTER 15   PROSE
& FIND THAT I CAN WORK WITH GREATER PLEASURE THAN EVER . . 803C LETTER 15 PROSE
ACCEPT THEM YOURSELF & BELIEVE ME FOR EVER . . . . . .   803C LETTER 15   PROSE
ALL I EVER HAD KNOWN   . . . .   806 TO BUTTS/L   73
I AM FOR EVER YOURS   . . . .   806C LETTER 16   PROSE
OR RATHER CERTAINLY THE VERY BEST LETTERS THAT EVER WERE   810A LETTER 20   PROSE
  PUBLISHED
I REMAIN DEAR SIR EVER YOURS SINCERELY . . . .   810A LETTER 20   PROSE
& WE SHALL REIGN WITH HIM FOR EVER & EVER   . . . . . . 810D LETTER 21   PROSE
WHICH SHE HAS COMBATED IN VAIN EVER SINCE WE HAVE BEEN HERE 811C LETTER 22   PROSE
& RHEUMATISMS ALMOST EVER SINCE SHE HAS BEEN HERE   . . . 819C LETTER 25   PROSE
& BELIEVE ME TO BE EVER YOURS AFFECTIONATELY . . . . . 823C LETTER 26   PROSE
YOU HAVE & MUST SUFFER MORE ON MY ACCOUNT THAN I SHALL EVER 829C LETTER 30   PROSE
OUGHT EVER TO MOUNT A TROOPER'S HORSE THEY ARE TAUGHT SO   833B LETTER 33   PROSE
THE TWO ANGELS WHO STAND AT HEAVEN'S GATE EVER OPEN . . 834A LETTER 33   PROSE
EVER INVITING GUESTS TO THE MARRIAGE O FOOLISH PHILOSOPHY 834A LETTER 33   PROSE
WHICH I BELIEVE IS NOW FOR EVER FALLEN INTO THE ABYSS . . 835A LETTER 34   PROSE
OPINION THE MOST EXACT RESEMBLANCE OF ROMNEY HE EVER SAW   836B LETTER 35   PROSE
& BELIEVE ME TO REMAIN EVER YOURS   . . . .   840A LETTER 38   PROSE
IT IS THE FIRST PORTRAIT ROMNEY EVER PAINTED BUT ABOVE ALL 843D LETTER 43   PROSE
IT IS ONE OF THE PRETTIEST THINGS I EVER READ AND I HOPE   844D LETTER 43   PROSE
  THE
AND TIMES THREATEN WORSE THAN EVER I MUST NOW EXPRESS . . 845A LETTER 43   PROSE
AMUSEMENT THAN HE COULD EVER BE IF EMPLOYD IN THE DRUDGERY 850B LETTER 49   PROSE
  OF
I EVER EXPECTED THEM TO BE   . . . .   852C LETTER 50   PROSE
SHOULD THEY EVER BE ATTEMPTED WHAT HE CAN & I KNOW . . 853A LETTER 51   *PROSE
I MUST SAY ARE FAR BEYOND ANY THING I HAVE EVER DONE . . 853A LETTER 51   *PROSE
COPYRIGHT IS FOR EVER YOURS I THEREFORE BEG THAT YOU WILL 858B LETTER 55   PROSE
EVER TO LAMENT YOUR DISTANCE FROM LONDON AS THAT ALONE . . 861D LETTER 59   PROSE
REMEMBERD IN SUSSEX I AM DEAR SIR YOURS EVER AFFECTIONATELY 862B LETTER 59   PROSE
HAVE BEEN THE DARKEST YEARS THAT EVER MORTAL SUFFERD   . . 862D LETTER 60   PROSE
A HAPPY CHRISTMAS I REMAIN EVER   . . . .   863C LETTER 60   PROSE
THE MOST WRETCHED TASTE EVER PRODUCED HAS BEEN UPHELD . . 864A LETTER 61   PROSE
ON ONE OF THE STRONGEST & HANDSOMEST BUILT STAGES I EVER   871C LETTER 73   PROSE
  SAW
YESTERDAY AFTERNOON AFTER AS GOOD A MORNING AS I EVER . . 872B LETTER 75   PROSE
THAN I HAD EVER HOPED IN MY HEALTHFULL HOURS . . . . . 873A LETTER 76   PROSE
I HAVE BEEN EVER SINCE TAKING DR YOUNG'S ADDITION TO . . 874B LETTER 79   PROSE
WITH WHOM HE MAKES HIS FIRST EFFORT DEAR SIR YOURS EVER   875A LETTER 80   PROSE
FOR EVER IN THAT I AM STRONGER & STRONGER AS THIS FOOLISH 878A LETTER 88   PROSE

EVER APPARENT
HE IS THE SPIRIT OF PROPHECY THE EVER APPARENT ELIAS . . 510 MILTON 24   71
EVER BROODING
OF PAIN AND MISERY AND DESPAIR AND EVER BROODING MELANCHOLY 633 JERUSALEM 13   31
EVER CHANGING
WITH WINGED RADIANCE SCATTERING JOYS THRO THE EVER CHANGING 274 FOUR ZOAS 1 358
  LIGHT
SURROUNDED BY THE EVER CHANGING DAUGHTERS OF THE LIGHT . . 291 FOUR ZOAS 3   9
EVER DEVOURING
AN EVER DEVOURING APPETITE   . . . .   755 EV GOSPEL(E)/N   83
EVER DURING
OER WHELMD BY EVER DURING THIRST SHE SWALLOWETH . . . . 41C THEN SHE BORE PROSE
ITS EVER DURING DOORS THAT OG & ANAK FIERCELY GUARD . . 520 MILTON 31   49
EVER DYING
AN EVER DYING LIFE OF STIFLING & OBSTRUCTION SHUT OUT . . 331 FOUR ZOAS 7   428
IN A CORPOREAL & EVER DYING VEGETATION & CORRUPTION . . . 737 JERUSALEM 90   42
EVER EXISTENT
OF ITS EVER EXISTENT IMAGES IS CONSIDERD AS LESS PERMANENT 605B V LAST JUDG/N PROSE
EVER EXPANDING
PRESS IT AROUND THE LOINS OF THIS EVER EXPANDING CRUELTY   705 JERUSALEM 67   60
EVER HAPPY
HIS CHERUBIM & SERAPHIM IN EVER HAPPY ETERNITY   . . . . 531 MILTON 39   28
EVER-HARDENING
OF EVER-HARDENING DESPAIR SQUARD & POLISHD WITH CRUEL SKILL 647 JERUSALEM 24   35
EVER-HISSING
AND WHERE THE MOTHER'S MILK INSTEAD THOSE EVER-HISSING JAWS 199 AMERICA 9   23
EVERLASTING
WHEN SOULS ARE TORN TO EVERLASTING FIRE . . . .   33 EDW FOURTH/PS   11
. . . SEAL THEM UP O ANOINTED IN EVERLASTING CHAINS . . . 141 FRENCH REVOLTN 157
BUT DEATH DESPAIR & EVERLASTING BROODING MELANCHOLY . . . 265 FOUR ZOAS 1   51
THE WORKMANSHIP OF LUVAH'S HANDS IN TIMES OF EVERLASTING   282 FOUR ZOAS 2   82
AND ALL THE SONS OF ?EVERLASTING SHALL BOW DOWN AT MY FEET 333 FOUR ZOAS 7B   10
BECAUSE IN TIMES OF EVERLASTING I WAS RENT IN SUNDER . . 334 FOUR ZOAS 7B   58
THIS COWL UPON MY HEAD HE PLACD IN TIMES OF EVERLASTING   336 FOUR ZOAS 7B   115
HE WHO ASSUMD MY LUVAH'S THRONE IN TIMES OF EVERLASTING   345 FOUR ZOAS 8 * 154
NOR OF HIS OWN WILL GAVE HIS LAWS IN TIMES OF EVERLASTING 353 FOUR ZOAS 8   459
THE BISHOP NEVER SAW THE EVERLASTING GOSPEL ANY MORE THAN 394D ANNO WATSON * MARG
  TOM PAINE
ONE RELIGION THIS WAS THE RELIGION OF JESUS THE   579A DESC CAT 5   PROSE
  EVERLASTING GOSPEL
BUT DARK DESPAIR & EVERLASTING BROODING MELANCHOLY . . . 645 JERUSALEM 22   24
THE ETERNAL & THE EVERLASTING GOSPEL . . . .   649B JERUSALEM 27   PROSE
THE FOUR-FOLD GOSPEL AND THE REVELATIONS EVERLASTING . . 677 JERUSALEM 48   11
THE EVERLASTING GOSPEL   . . . .   751B EV GOSPEL(D)/N TITLE
"O THAT THE EVERLASTING HAD NOT FIXD" (SHAKESPEARE) . . . SUPP LEGEND/N95   *
EVER LOVELY
OF LOVE & HARMONY IN MAN EXPAND THY EVER LOVELY GATES . . 675 JERUSALEM 44   42

		PAGE	TITLE	LINE

EVERMORE   SEE FOR-EVERMORE
    THE UNIVERSAL MAN TO WHOM BE GLORY EVERMORE AMEN . . . . 264 FOUR ZOAS 1   11
    I EVERMORE WILL HOLD THEE WHEN THOU GOEST OUT OR COMEST IN 269 FOUR ZOAS 1   177
    THAT WE HIS CHILDREN EVERMORE MAY LIVE IN JERUSALEM . . . 362 FOUR ZOAS 9   221
    TO WHOM BE GLORY & POWER & DOMINION EVERMORE AMEN . . . . 495 MILTON 14   3
    THE GUARD ARE ANGELS OF PROVIDENCE ON DUTY EVERMORE . . . 516 MILTON 28   61
    BEULAH IS EVERMORE CREATED AROUND ETERNITY APPEARING   . . 518 MILTON 30   8
    TO WHOM BE GLORY & DOMINION EVERMORE AMEN . . . . 519 MILTON 30   16
    . . . THE DELIVERANCE OF INDIVIDUALS EVERMORE AMEN . . . 648 JERUSALEM 25   13
    STATES TO DELIVER INDIVIDUALS EVERMORE AMEN . . . . . 662 JERUSALEM 35   16
    MAY BE DELIVERD TIME AFTER TIME EVERMORE AMEN . . . . 680 JERUSALEM 49   71
    IN SHADOWY POMP BY THE ETERNAL PROPHET CREATED EVERMORE . 716 JERUSALEM 75   6
EVER MOURNING
    AND FOR VALA THE SHADOW OF JERUSALEM THE EVER MOURNING 631 JERUSALEM 12   19
      SHADE
EVER PAINFUL
    THE METAL ROCK & STONE IN EVER PAINFUL THROES OF VEGETATION 318 FOUR ZOAS 6   264
EVER PITYING
    THE EVER PITYING ONE WHO SEETH ALL THINGS SAW HIS FALL . 316 FOUR ZOAS 6   157
EVER-PROLIFIC
    FIXING THE SEXUAL INTO AN EVER-PROLIFIC GENERATION . . . 713 JERUSALEM 73   26
EVER STREAMING
    WITH EVER STREAMING FIRES BEAMING FROM HIS AWFUL LIMBS . . 284 FOUR ZOAS 2   180
EVER-VARYING,EVER VARYING
    THE EVER-VARYING SPIRAL ASCENTS TO THE HEAVENS OF HEAVENS 241 EUROPE 10   13
    TILL THE TIME OF LOVE IS PASSED IN EVER VARYING DELIGHTS 707 JERUSALEM 69   24
EVER-WEEPING,EVER WEEPING
    EVER WEEPING PADDINGTON IS THAT CALVARY AND GOLGOTHA   . . 632 JERUSALEM 12   28
    NEAR MOURNFUL EVER-WEEPING PADDINGTON . . . . . . 650 FIELDS FROM/J   26
    HIS EMANATION IS AN EVER-WEEPING MELANCHOLY SHADOW . . . 684 JERUSALEM 53   26
EVERY   SEE EVRY
    ON EVERY FLOWER THAT SHUTS ITS SWEET EYES . . . . . . 3 EVNING STAR/PS   7
    BUT WE ARE CONQUERORS EVERY WHERE NOTHING . . . . . 23 EDW THIRD/PS 3   73
    IT IS A ROOT THAT GROWS IN EVERY BREAST . . . . . . 28 EDW THIRD/PS 4   13
    YES I HAVE I HAVE A GREAT AMBITION TO KNOW EVERY THING SIR 28D EDW THIRD/PS 4   PROSE
    BUT EVERY BODY ELSE DOES . . . . 29D EDW THIRD/PS 4   PROSE
    WITH HER PURE QUILL ON EVERY FLOWER WRITETH WISDOM'S NAME 36D CONTEMPLATN/PS   PROSE
    IT IS A FLOWER THAT GROWS IN EVERY VALE . . . . . . 37A CONTEMPLATN/PS   PROSE
    NOR MATCHLESS MIGHT NOR WISDOM NOR EVERY GIFT ENJOYED . 39B SAMSON/PS   PROSE
    IF I HAVE NOT PRESENTED YOU WITH EVERY CHARACTER IN THE 46B ISLAND MOON 2   PROSE
      PIECE
    EVERY ART & SCIENCE ADORND HIM AS BEADS ROUND HIS NECK . . 46D ISLAND MOON 3   PROSE
    & HAPPINESS ITS NO SUCH THING EVERY PERSON HAS AS SOMETHING 528 ISLAND MOON 8   PROSE
    & A PAIR OF GLOVES EVERY DAY & THE SORROWS OF WERTER . . 53A ISLAND MOON 8   PROSE
    EVERY PROVOKING SPEECH THAT EVER SHE COULD & HE BORE IT 53B ISLAND MOON 8   PROSE
    PLEASURE AS I HAVE THERE I STAND & BEAR EVERY FOOL'S INSULT 53C ISLAND MOON 8   PROSE
    PLAYD AT FORFEITS & TRYD EVERY METHOD TO GET GOOD HUMOUR 59B ISLAND MOON 11   PROSE
    AND EVERY THING ELSE IS STILL . . . . 60 NURSES SONG/IM   4
    OF PRINTED & AT EVERY OTHER [?SHEET CA] LEAF A HIGH FINISHD 62D ISLAND MOON 11 *PROSE
      PRINT
    WHERE JOY DOTH SIT ON EVERY BOUGH . . . . . . 63 SHEPHERD FIRST   2
    PALENESS FLIES FROM EVERY FACE . . . . 63 SHEPHERD FIRST   3
    BLOOM ON EVERY MAIDEN'S CHEEK . . . . 63 SHEPHERD FIRST   6
    WOULD TO GOD THAT EVERY ONE WOULD CONSIDER THIS . . . 73C ANNO LAVATER   MARG
    & RECTIFY EVERY THING IN NATURE AS THE PHILOSOPHERS DO . 81C ANNO LAVATER   MARG
    FOR OUR LORD IS THE WORD OF GOD & EVERY . . . . . 87B ANNO LAVATER   MARG
    & THAT IS HE MAKES EVERY THING ORIGINATE IN ITS ACCIDENT 88C ANNO LAVATER   MARG
    EVERY MAN'S LEADING PROPENSITY OUGHT TO BE CALLD . . 88C ANNO LAVATER   MARG
    ADAPTED TO THE WEAKNESSES OF EVERY INDIVIDUAL . . . 98C ALL RELIGIONS   PROSE
    WHICH IS EVERY WHERE CALLD THE SPIRIT OF PROPHECY . . 98C ALL RELIGIONS   PROSE
    EVERY CHILD MAY JOY TO HEAR . . . . 111 INTRODUCTN/SI   20
    THEN EVERY MAN OF EVERY CLIME . . . . 117 DIVNE IMAGE/SI   13
    THEY LOOK IN EVERY THOUGHTLESS NEST . . . . . 119 NIGHT/SI   17
    THEY VISIT CAVES OF EVERY BEAST . . . . . . 119 NIGHT/SI   19
    AND EVERY THING ELSE IS STILL . . . . 121 NURSES SONG/SI   4
    WHEN THE BIRDS SING ON EVERY TREE . . . . . . 124 SCHOOL BOY/SI   2
    WHICH THOU DOST SCATTER ON EVERY LITTLE BLADE OF GRASS 128 BOOK OF THEL 2   9
      THAT SPRINGS
  HOW GREAT THY USE HOW GREAT THY BLESSING EVERY THING THAT 129 BOOK OF THEL 3   26
      LIVES
    OF EVERY HEART ON EARTH INFIXES DEEP ITS RESTLESS TWISTS 130 BOOK OF THEL 6   4
    WHY A TONGUE IMPRESSD WITH HONEY FROM EVERY WIND . . 130 BOOK OF THEL 6   16
    UNDER EVERY GOOD IS A HELL I E HELL IS THE OUTWARD . . SUPP ANNO SWED HELL * MARG
    SEE...WHERE HE SAYS THAT A PLACE FOR EVERY MAN IS FORESEEN 131D ANNO SWED PROV   MARG
    . . . AND EVERY DARKNING CITY . . . . 139 FRENCH REVOLTN   117
    ON EVERY CLIFF AND TOMB . . . . 148 MARRIAGE HH 2   11
    EVERY THING POSSIBLE TO BE BELIEVD IS AN IMAGE OF TRUTH 151D MARRIAGE HH 8   PROSE
    THE CROW WISHD EVERY THING WAS BLACK . . . . . 152D MARRIAGE HH 10 PROSE
    THE OWL THAT EVERY THING WAS WHITE . . . . . 152D MARRIAGE HH 10 PROSE
    BUT MY SENSES DISCOVERD THE INFINITE IN EVERY THING . 153C MARRIAGE HH 12 PROSE
    EVERY THING WOULD APPEAR TO MAN AS IT IS INFINITE . . 154C MARRIAGE HH 14 PROSE
    FOR EVERY THING THAT LIVES IS HOLY . . . . . . 160B SONG LIBERTY   PROSE
    [THOU WILT EVERY SECRET KEEP] . . . . . . 164 CRADLE SONG/N   3
    AND [SEE] MARK IN EVERY FACE I MEET . . . . . . 170 LONDON/N   3
    IN EVERY CRY OF EVERY MAN . . . . 170 LONDON/N   5
    IN [EVERY VOICE OF EVERY CHILD] EVERY INFANT'S CRY OF 170 LONDON/N   6
      FEAR
    IN EVERY VOICE IN EVERY BAN . . . . 170 LONDON/N   7
    EVERY BLACKNING CHURCH APPALLS . . . . 170 LONDON/N   11
    [FROM EVERY DISMAL STREET I HEAR] . . . . . . 170 LONDON/N   15
    BUT MOST [FROM EVERY STREET] THRO WINTRY STREETS I HEAR 170 LONDON/N   * 18
    FROM EVERY SEARCHING EYE . . . . 171 TO NOBODADDY/N   4

		PAGE	TITLE	LINE
EVERY	(CONTINUED)			
AND BREAKS ALL CHAINS FROM EVERY MIND	. . . . .	175	HOW TO KNOW/N	4
[NEVER IS TO] TO EVERY THING BUT INTEREST BLIND	. . . .	175	HOW TO KNOW/N	8
[AND CHAINS & FETTERS EVERY MIND]	. . . .	175	HOW TO KNOW/N *	9
[SO] EVERY BIT AS WELL AS WAR & SLAUGHTERING	. . .	185	LET BROTHELS/N *	12
ARISE AND DRINK YOUR BLISS FOR EVERY THING THAT LIVES IS HOLY		195	V DAU ALBION 8	10
THUS EVERY MORNING WAILS OOTHOON BUT THEOTORMON SITS	. .	195	V DAU ALBION 8	11
THEY LOOK BEHIND AT EVERY STEP & BELIEVE IT IS A DREAM	.	198	AMERICA 6	12
FOR EVERY THING THAT LIVES IS HOLY LIFE DELIGHTS IN LIFE		199	AMERICA 8	13
AND MARK IN EVERY FACE I MEET	. . . .	216	LONDON/SE	3
IN EVERY CRY OF EVERY MAN	. . . .	216	LONDON/SE	5
IN EVERY INFANT'S CRY OF FEAR	. . . .	216	LONDON/SE	6
IN EVERY VOICE IN EVERY BAN	. . . .	216	LONDON/SE	7
EVERY BLACKNING CHURCH APPALLS	. . . .	216	LONDON/SE	10
THE DARK CHANGES & BOUND EVERY CHANGE	. . . . . .	227	URIZEN 8	10
THE WORLD WHERE EVERY PARTICLE OF DUST BREATHES FORTH ITS JOY		237	EUROPE INTRO	18
SPREAD NETS IN EVERY SECRET PATH	. . . . . .	240	EUROPE 5	9
EVERY HOUSE A DEN EVERY MAN BOUND THE SHADOWS ARE FILLD	.	243	EUROPE 12	26
THEN EVERY ONE FLED TO HIS STATION & ENITHARMON WEPT	. .	244	EUROPE 14	36
A FLAMING SWORD REVOLVING EVERY WAY	. . . .	261D	SMALL BK DSGNS	TITLE
FOUR MIGHTY ONES ARE IN EVERY MAN A PERFECT UNITY	. . .	264	FOUR ZOAS 1	9
WHY WILT THOU EXAMINE EVERY LITTLE FIBRE OF MY SOUL	. .	265	FOUR ZOAS 1	47
EVERY MOMENT OF MY SECRET HOURS YEA I KNOW	. . . .	265	FOUR ZOAS 1	53
IN [DISMAL] GNAWING PAIN DRAWN OUT BY HER LOVD FINGERS EVERY NERVE		266	FOUR ZOAS 1	79
SHE COUNTED EVERY VEIN & LACTEAL THREADING THEM AMONG	. .	266	FOUR ZOAS 1	80
THEY SAID THE SPECTRE IS IN EVERY MAN INSANE & MOST	. . .	267	FOUR ZOAS 1	103
AND MANY TEARS & IN THE [TWENTY] EVERY YEARS [GAVE . . .		270	FOUR ZOAS 1	224
HER LITTLE ONES [WILL BE] ARE SLAIN ON THE TOP OF EVERY STREET		279	FOUR ZOAS 1	546
IN EVERY PILLARD HALL & ARCHED ROOF OF ALBION'S SKIES	.	281	FOUR ZOAS 2	48
SOME BECAME SEED OF EVERY PLANT THAT SHALL BE PLANTED SOME		284	FOUR ZOAS 2	164
EVERY HALL SURROUNDED BY BRIGHT PARADISES OF DELIGHT	. .	284	FOUR ZOAS 2	176
AND EVERY ONE SEEKS FOR HIS MATE TO PROVE HIS INMOST JOY		289	FOUR ZOAS 2	358
FOR EVERY THING THAT LIVES IS HOLY FOR THE SOURCE OF LIFE		289	FOUR ZOAS 2	366
TO SEE A GOD ON EVERY WIND & A BLESSING ON EVERY BLAST	.	291	FOUR ZOAS 2	410
IN ALBION'S BOSOM FOR IN EVERY HUMAN BOSOM THESE LIMITS STAND		304	FOUR ZOAS 4	272
AROUND HIS BOSOM EVERY DAY HE VIEWD THE FIERY YOUTH	. .	307	FOUR ZOAS 5	86
SOOTHING OR FURIOUS NO ONE ANSWERD EVERY ONE WRAPD UP	.	315	FOUR ZOAS 6	127
I LOSE MY POWERS WEAKEND EVERY REVOLUTION TILL A DEATH	.	317	FOUR ZOAS 6	221
ON ALL THE SONS OF MEN & EVERY HUMAN SOUL TERRIFIED	. .	317	FOUR ZOAS 6	235
FOR EVERY ONE OPEND WITHIN INTO ETERNITY AT WILL	. . .	318	FOUR ZOAS 6	252
WITH POMP GIVE EVERY CRUST OF BREAD YOU GIVE WITH GRACIOUS CUNNING		323	FOUR ZOAS 7	123
THOU KNOWEST THAT THE SPECTRE IS IN EVERY MAN INSANE BRUTISH		327	FOUR ZOAS 7	304
BUT THEN THE SPECTRE ENTERD LOS'S BOSOM EVERY SIGH & GROAN		328	FOUR ZOAS 7	336
THO THUS DIVIDED FROM THEE & THE SLAVE OF EVERY PASSION	.	328	FOUR ZOAS 7	346
THUS DIVIDING THE POWERS OF EVERY WARRIOR	. . . .	332	FOUR ZOAS 7 *	495
WITH HARSH SONGS EVERY LIVING SOUL THE PRESTER SERPENT RUNS		335	FOUR ZOAS 7B	113
BEFORE MY EYES & FOR EVERY ONE OF THESE I AM CONDEMND	.	339	FOUR ZOAS 7B	252
THE LIVING SOUL IN GLORIOUS FORMS & EVERY ONE CAME FORTH		340	FOUR ZOAS 7B	278
THEY WROTE ON ALL THEIR TOMBS & PILLARS & ON EVERY URN		340	FOUR ZOAS 7B	292
HIS OWN DESPAIR EVEN AT THE COST OF EVERY THING THAT BREATHES		344	FOUR ZOAS 8	139
FOR HE WAS SOURCE OF EVERY JOY THAT THIS MYSTERIOUS TREE		345	FOUR ZOAS 8	168
MISPLACING EVERY CENTER HUNGRY DESIRE & LUST BEGAN	. .	345	FOUR ZOAS 8	178
INTO THE ELEMENTAL FORMS OF EVERY THING THAT GROWS	. .	355	FOUR ZOAS 8	563
OF WOMEN & CHILDREN THROUGHOUT EVERY NATION UNDER HEAVEN		358	FOUR ZOAS 9	47
AND RAVEN NUMEROUS AS THE LEAVES OF AUTUMN EVERY SPECIES		363	FOUR ZOAS 9	238
AND EVERY ONE OF THE DEAD APPEARS AS HE HAD LIVD BEFORE		363	FOUR ZOAS 9	245
AND EVERY FLOWER & EVERY LEAF REJOICES IN HIS LIGHT	. .	367	FOUR ZOAS 9	407
TILL TIMES & SPACES HAVE PASSD OVER HIM DULY EVERY MORN		374	FOUR ZOAS 9	633
THEY LOOK BEHIND AT EVERY STEP & BELIEVE IT IS A DREAM	.	375	FOUR ZOAS 9	676
THEN ALL THE SLAVES FROM EVERY EARTH IN THE WIDE UNIVERSE		375	FOUR ZOAS 9	682
TO YOU BUT THAT EVERY ONE IS EITHER YOUR FRIEND OR YOUR ENEMY		380B	FOUR ZOAS NOTE	PROSE
TO WANDER IN SWEET SOLITUDE ENRAPTURD AT EVERY WIND	. .	381	FOUR ZOAS AD 5	13
THE STING OF THE SERPENT IS IN EVERY SENTENCE AS WELL AS		384C	ANNO WATSON	MARG
HIS PRINCIPLES EVERY MAN CHANGES HIS OPINIONS HE WHO	.	386B	ANNO WATSON	MARG
IS FOR EVER REMOVED & HENCEFORTH EVERY MAN MAY	. . .	389C	ANNO WATSON	MARG
EVERY HONEST MAN IS A PROPHET HE UTTERS HIS OPINION	. .	392B	ANNO WATSON	MARG
EVERY BODY KNOWS THAT THIS IS EPICURUS AND LUCRETIUS	.	397B	ANNO BACON	MARG
& YET EVERY BODY SAYS THAT IT IS CHRISTIAN PHILOSOPHY	.	397B	ANNO BACON	MARG
HOW IS THIS POSSIBLE EVERY BODY MUST BE A LIAR & DECIEVER		397B	ANNO BACON	MARG
BUT EVERY BODY DOES NOT DO THIS BUT THE HIRELINGS	. . .	397B	ANNO BACON	MARG
OF KINGS & COURTS WHO MAKE THEMSELVES EVERY BODY	. . .	397B	ANNO BACON	MARG
A LIE EVERY BODY HATES A KING BACON WAS AFRAID TO SAY THAT		400B	ANNO BACON	MARG
EVERY BODY NATURALLY HATES A PERFECT CHARACTER BECAUSE	.	412A	ANNO BOYD	MARG
EVERY SENTIMENT & OPINION AS WELL AS EVERY PRINCIPLE IN DANTE		413A	ANNO BOYD	MARG
AND EVERY SAND BECOMES A GEM	. . . .	418	MOCK ON/N	5
AND EVERY WOUND IT HAS MADE SHALL HEAL	. . . . .	420	I SAW A MONK/N	56
O THOU PRIDE OF EVERY FIELD	. . . .	422	THE BIRDS/N	4
HER FINGERS NUMBER EVERY NERVE	. . . . . .	425	MENTAL TRAVLER	17
YOUNGER & YOUNGER EVERY DAY	. . . . . .	426	MENTAL TRAVLER	74
AND FLEE AWAY ON EVERY SIDE	. . . . . .	427	MENTAL TRAVLER	96
AND EVERY TREE DOES SHED ITS FRUIT	. . . . . .	427	MENTAL TRAVLER	100
AND THESE ARE THE WORDS UPON EVERY TONGUE	. . . . .	428	MARY	4

624

		PAGE	TITLE	LINE

EVERY   (CONTINUED)

```
        HER EYES OUTSHINE EVERY BRILLIANT RAY  . . . . . . .   428 MARY                      7
        EVERY WOLF'S & LION'S HOWL  . . . . . . . . . . .     431 AUGURIES                  19
        UNDER EVERY GRIEF & PINE  . . . . . . . . . . . . .   432 AUGURIES                  61
        EVERY FARMER UNDERSTANDS  . . . . . . . . . . . . .   432 AUGURIES                  66
        EVERY TEAR FROM EVERY EYE  . . . . . . . . . . . .    432 AUGURIES                  67
        EVERY NIGHT & EVERY MORN  . . . . . . . . . . . . .   433 AUGURIES                 119
        EVERY MORN & EVERY NIGHT  . . . . . . . . . . . .     433 AUGURIES                 121
        AND WITH LABOURS OF IGNORANCE FILL EVERY PLACE  . . . . 445 ANNO REYNOLDS             4
        A SLY DOG SO CAN EVERY BODY  . . . . . . . . . . .   450D ANNO REYNOLDS          MARG
        AND COMMERCE SETTLES ON EVERY TREE  . . . . . . . .   452 ANNO REYNOLDS             2
        NONSENSE EVERY EYE SEES DIFFERENTLY  . . . . . . . .  456B ANNO REYNOLDS          MARG
        IN ART & THAT EVERY THING IN ART IS DEFINITE & DETERMINATE  457B ANNO REYNOLDS    MARG
        WITHOUT FATIGUE EVERY THING BEING DEFINITE & DETERMINATE   457B ANNO REYNOLDS     MARG
        IT IS BORN WITH US INNATE IDEAS ARE IN EVERY MAN  . . .  459B ANNO REYNOLDS       MARG
        SAYS THAT EVERY THING MUST BE DONE BY EXPERIMENT  . . .  459D ANNO REYNOLDS        MARG
        EVERY CLASS IS INDIVIDUAL  . . . . . . . . . . . .   460A ANNO REYNOLDS          MARG
        CHILDHOOD AND AGE ARE EQUALLY BELONGING TO EVERY CLASS  . 460B ANNO REYNOLDS       MARG
        (GENERALIZING) IN EVERY (THING) THE MAN (WOULD) SOON BE  460D ANNO REYNOLDS  * MARG
           A FOOL
        RUBENS & THE VENETIANS ARE OPPOSITE IN EVERY THING TO TRUE  469A ANNO REYNOLDS    MARG
           ART
        WHY THEN DOES HE TALK IN OTHER PLACES OF PLEASING EVERY  469D ANNO REYNOLDS        MARG
           BODY
        IN THE HIGHEST DEGREE FOR HE HAS EVERY [PERQUISITE] THING  472A ANNO REYNOLDS  * MARG
           OF BOTH
        ON EVERY ONE OF THESE BOOKS I WROTE MY OPINIONS &       476D ANNO REYNOLDS        MARG
           ON LOOKING THEM
        EVERY MAN'S WISDOM IS PECULIAR TO HIS OWN (INDIVIDUALITY)  483 MILTON 4       *       8
        TO MORTALS THY MILLS SEEM EVERY THING & THE HARROW     483 MILTON 4                 12
           OF SHADDAI
        EVERY ONE IS THREEFOLD IN HEAD & HEART & REINS & EVERY ONE  484 MILTON 5             6
        THEY TOUCH NOT OUGHT BUT PALLID TURN & TREMBLE AT EVERY  485 MILTON 5               37
           WIND
        WHERE THEY WERE LAID IN RUINS FROM EVERY NATION &      485 MILTON 6                 16
           OAK GROVES ROOTED
        FOR PALAMABRON RETURND WITH LABOUR WEARIED EVERY EVENING  486 MILTON 7               9
        EVERY THING IN ETERNITY SHINES BY ITS OWN INTERNAL LIGHT  491 MILTON 10            16
           BUT THOU
        DARKENEST EVERY INTERNAL LIGHT WITH THE ARROWS OF     491 MILTON 10                17
           THY QUIVER
        THAT EVERY THING IS FIXD OPAKE WITHOUT INTERNAL LIGHT  . .  491 MILTON 10           20
        THE NATURE OF INFINITY IS THIS THAT EVERY THING HAS ITS  497 MILTON 15             21
        THAT EVERY INFANT THAT IS BORN UPON THE EARTH SHALL READ  499 MILTON 18            13
        SHE NUMBERS WITH HER FINGERS EVERY FIBRE ERE IT GROW  .  501 MILTON 19             49
        FOR EVERY HUMAN HEART HAS GATES OF BRASS & BARS OF ADAMANT  502 MILTON 20          34
        THE MOUNTAINS WAILD & EVERY PLANT THAT GREW IN SOLEMN SIGHS  503 MILTON 21         19
           LAMENTED
        BUT ALL REMAIN EVERY FABRIC OF SIX THOUSAND YEARS     . . .  505 MILTON 22         20
        BOWLAHOOLA IS THE STOMACH IN EVERY INDIVIDUAL MAN  . . .  509 MILTON 24            67
        EVERY ONE IS A FALLEN SON OF THE SPIRIT OF PROPHECY  . .  510 MILTON 24            75
        THE WHOLE EXTENT OF THE GLOBE IS EXPLORED EVERY SCATTERD  510 MILTON 25            18
           ATOM
        FOR IN EVERY NATION & EVERY FAMILY THE THREE CLASSES ARE  511 MILTON 25            40
           BORN
        AND IN EVERY SPECIES OF EARTH METAL TREE FISH BIRD & BEAST  511 MILTON 25          41
        ALL IS THE SAME & EVERY ONE REMAINS IN HIS OWN ENERGY  . .  511 MILTON 25          43
        UPON THE SUNNY BROOKS & MEADOWS EVERY ONE THE DANCE  . . .  512 MILTON 26           3
        AND EVERY GENERATED BODY IN ITS INWARD FORM  . . . . .  512 MILTON 26             31
        SO THEY ARE BORN ON EARTH & EVERY CLASS IS DETERMINATE  . .  512 MILTON 26          39
        AND EVERY NATURAL EFFECT HAS A SPIRITUAL CAUSE AND NOT  .  513 MILTON 26           44
        AND FROM THESE THREE SCIENCE DERIVES EVERY OCCUPATION OF  514 MILTON 27            62
           MEN
        AND EVERY MOMENT HAS A COUCH OF GOLD FOR SOFT REPOSE  . .  516 MILTON 28           46
        AND BETWEEN EVERY TWO MOMENTS STANDS A DAUGHTER OF BEULAH  516 MILTON 28           48
        AND EVERY MINUTE HAS AN AZURE TENT WITH SILKEN VEILS  . .  516 MILTON 28           50
        AND EVERY HOUR HAS A BRIGHT GOLDEN GATE CARVED WITH SKILL  516 MILTON 28           51
        AND EVERY DAY & NIGHT HAS WALLS OF BRASS & GATES OF ADAMANT  516 MILTON 28         52
        AND EVERY MONTH A SILVER PAVED TERRACE BUILDED HIGH  . .  516 MILTON 28            54
        AND EVERY YEAR INVULNERABLE BARRIERS WITH HIGH TOWERS  . .  516 MILTON 28          55
        AND EVERY AGE IS MOATED DEEP WITH BRIDGES OF SILVER & GOLD  516 MILTON 28          56
        AND EVERY SEVEN AGES IS INCIRCLED WITH A FLAMING FIRE  . .  516 MILTON 28          57
        EVERY TIME LESS THAN A PULSATION OF THE ARTERY  . . . .  516 MILTON 28            62
        AND EVERY SPACE THAT A MAN WALKS AROUND HIS DWELLING-PLACE  516 MILTON 29           5
        FOR EVERY SPACE LARGER THAN A RED GLOBULE OF MAN'S BLOOD  516 MILTON 29            19
        AND EVERY SPACE SMALLER THAN A GLOBULE OF MAN'S BLOOD OPENS  516 MILTON 29         21
        TO MEASURE TIME AND SPACE TO MORTAL MEN EVERY MORNING  .  517 MILTON 29            24
        WITHIN THE VEGETATED MORTAL NERVES FOR EVERY MAN BORN IS  517 MILTON 29            30
           JOINED
        WALKS AMONG ALL HIS AWFUL FAMILY SEEN IN EVERY FACE  . . .  519 MILTON 30          17
        BUT EVERY MAN RETURND & WENT STILL GOING FORWARD THRO  . .  519 MILTON 31           4
        HIS LITTLE THROAT LABOURS WITH INSPIRATION EVERY FEATHER  520 MILTON 31            34
        AND THRO THE NIGHT WARBLES LUXURIANT EVERY BIRD OF SONG  520 MILTON 31             43
        AND COMES FORTH IN THE MAJESTY OF BEAUTY EVERY FLOWER  . .  520 MILTON 31          58
        THE JONQUIL THE MILD LILLY OPES HER HEAVENS EVERY TREE  . .  521 MILTON 31          60
        IT RENOVATES EVERY MOMENT OF THE DAY IF RIGHTLY PLACED  . .  526 MILTON 35          45
        IN ALL ITS HYPOCRITIC TURPITUDE OPENING TO EVERY EYE  . .  530 MILTON 38           44
        AND FELPHAM BILLY RODE OUT EVERY MORN  . . . . . . .  537 AND HIS LEGS/N         22
        EVERY LINE OF HIS HAS MEANING  . . . . . . . . . .   542 FLORENTINE/N           17
        BUT NOW THEY STAND IN EVERY BODIES WAY  . . . . . .   546 ANOTHER/N 2             4
        THE CRIPPLE EVERY STEP DRUDGES & LABOURS  . . . . . .  548 CRIPPLE EVRY/N          1
        AND HOW HIGH LABOURD IS EVERY STEP  . . . . . . . .   548 CRIPPLE EVRY/N          9
```

EVERY   (CONTINUED)

IF YOU MEAN TO PLEASE EVERY BODY YOU WILL   .   .   .   .   .   .   549 ENGL ENCOU/N 1   1
IF YOU MEAN TO PLEASE EVERY BODY YOU WILL   .   .   .   .   .   .   549 ENGL ENCOU/N 2   1
AND AWAY FLED EVERY JOY   .   .   .   .   552 WHY CUPID/N   20
EVERY FOOL SHOOK HIS BELLS THROUGHOUT THE LAND   .   .   .   .   554 BLAKES APL/N 1   2
EVERY FOOL SHOOK HIS BELLS THROUGHOUT THE LAND   .   .   .   .   555 BLAKES APL/N 2   6
FOR EVERY THING BESIDES I HAVE   .   .   .   .   558 I ROSE UP AT/N   7
EVERY THING IN FRESCO IS AS HIGH FINISHED AS MINIATURE   561A EXHIBITION ADV   PROSE
EVERY PURCHASER OF A CATALOGUE WILL BE ENTITLED   .   .   .   .   562B DESC CAT ADV   PROSE
OF VERY LITTLE TIME AND OF THE AIR IT DEADENS EVERY COLOUR   565A DESC CAT 2   PROSE
AND CHANGING YELLOW AND AT LENGTH BROWN DESTROYS EVERY   .   566B DESC CAT 2   PROSE
COLOUR IT IS MIXED WITH ESPECIALLY EVERY DELICATE COLOUR   566B DESC CAT 2   PROSE
IT TURNS EVERY PERMANENT WHITE TO A YELLOW AND BROWN PUTTY   566B DESC CAT 2   PROSE
WHICH IN EVERY AGE STANDS AS THE GUARDIAN   .   .   .   .   .   .   568A DESC CAT 3   PROSE
WHO IN EVERY AGE IS BORN TO RECORD AND ETERNIZE ITS ACTS   569A DESC CAT 3   PROSE
IS SENT IN EVERY AGE FOR A ROD AND SCOURGE AND FOR   .   .   570A DESC CAT 3   PROSE
AN APOSTLE A REAL MESSENGER OF HEAVEN SENT IN EVERY AGE   570B DESC CAT 3   PROSE
THE HEAD AND THE KNEE TO HIM WHO IN EVERY AGE SENDS US   .   570C DESC CAT 3   PROSE
EVERY AGE IS A CANTERBURY PILGRIMAGE WE   .   .   .   .   .   .   570D DESC CAT 3   PROSE
THAT CHAUCER MAKES EVERY ONE OF HIS CHARACTERS PERFECT IN   570D DESC CAT 3   PROSE
HIS KIND EVERY ONE IS AN ANTIQUE STATUE   .   .   .   .   .   .   571A DESC CAT 3   PROSE
FOR THE TRIAL OF MEN TO ASTONISH EVERY NEIGHBOURHOOD WITH   571D DESC CAT 3   PROSE
AS IT IS OF EVERY LINEAMENT   .   .   .   .   575B DESC CAT 3   PROSE
AS EVERY MASTER OF A BOAT IS BUT THIS DOES NOT MAKE HIM A   575C DESC CAT 3   PROSE
AND IF EVERY THING GOES ON AS IT HAS BEGUN   .   .   .   .   .   578A DESC CAT 5   PROSE
THE ANTIQUITIES OF EVERY NATION UNDER HEAVEN   .   .   .   .   .   578D DESC CAT 5   PROSE
NARROW AND CUNNING AND EVERY THING TENDING   .   .   .   .   .   580B DESC CAT 5   PROSE
THEY CAUSE THAT EVERY THING IN ART SHALL BECOME A MACHINE   582C DESC CAT 9   PROSE
THE TIMES REQUIRE THAT EVERY ONE SHOULD SPEAK OUT BOLDLY   584C DESC CAT 14   PROSE
ENGLAND EXPECTS THAT EVERY MAN SHOULD DO HIS DUTY   .   .   584C DESC CAT 14   PROSE
WHILE HE HAS EVERY NIGHT DROPPED INTO HIS SHOE   .   .   .   .   586A DESC CAT 16   PROSE
ON HORSEBACK OF CHAUCER'S CHARACTERS WHERE EVERY CHARACTER   587D CHAUCER/N   PROSE
   &
EVERY EXPRESSION EVERY LINEAMENT OF HEAD HAND & FOOT   .   .   588A CHAUCER/N   PROSE
EVERY PARTICULAR OF DRESS OR COSTUME   .   .   .   .   588A CHAUCER/N   PROSE
WHERE EVERY HORSE IS APPROPRIATE TO HIS RIDER   .   .   .   .   588A CHAUCER/N   PROSE
AT THIS HOUSE EVEN AT THIS DAY EVERY FRIENDLESS WRETCH   590B CHAUCER 2   PROSE
EVERY FOOL SHOOK HIS BELLS THROUGHOUT THE LAND   .   .   .   .   595 BLAKES APOL/PA   2
EVERY THING IS. TONED DOWN BUT ONE SPOT OF LIGHT   .   .   .   596C PUB ADDRESS/N   PROSE
MICH ANG EVERY PICTURE OF THEIRS HAS A DIFFERENT   598D PUB ADDRESS/N   PROSE
   & APPROPRIATE EFFECT
THEIR EFFECTS ARE IN EVERY PICTURE THE SAME   .   .   .   .   .   598D PUB ADDRESS/N   PROSE
MINE ARE IN EVERY PICTURE DIFFERENT   .   .   .   .   598D PUB ADDRESS/N   PROSE
EVERY PICTURE HAS THE SAME EFFECT A PIECE OF MACHINERY   .   599B PUB ADDRESS/N   PROSE
MILTON'S PARADISE BE READ & I WILL ASSERT THAT EVERY BODY   600D PUB ADDRESS/N   PROSE
LIKE ALL THAT THEY SAY FOR THERE IS EVERY LINE IN NATURE   603B PUB ADDR AD/N   PROSE
THE SAME WITH EVERY OBJECT IN A PICTURE ITS SPOTS ARE ITS   603B PUB ADDR AD/N   PROSE
EVERY LINE IS THE LINE OF BEAUTY   .   .   .   .   603C PUB ADDR AD/N   PROSE
IS SEEN BY THE [IMAGINATIVE EYE] OF EVERY ONE   .   .   .   .   604C V LAST JUDG/N   PROSE
THE PERMANENT REALITIES OF EVERY THING   .   .   .   .   .   .   605D V LAST JUDG/N   PROSE
EXIST NO MORE EVERY THING IS ETERNAL   .   .   .   .   606D V LAST JUDG/N   PROSE
WHICH ALAS EVERY ONE ON EARTH IS LIABLE TO ENTER INTO   .   608A V LAST JUDG/N   PROSE
EVERY MAN HAS EYES NOSE & MOUTH THIS EVERY IDIOT KNOWS   611B V LAST JUDG/N   PROSE
TO BE IN A SUPREME STATE BUT TO BE EVERY ONE OF THEM   .   614C V LAST JUDG/N   PROSE
GOOD & EVIL ARE QUALITIES IN EVERY MAN   .   .   .   .   .   .   615A V LAST JUDG/N   PROSE
& DESTROY ONE ANOTHER BY EVERY MEANS IN THEIR POWER   .   .   615A V LAST JUDG/N   PROSE
BUT HE HIMSELF WILL NOT KNOW IT THO EVERY BODY ELSE DOES   615B V LAST JUDG/N   PROSE
EVERY THING HAS ITS VERMIN O SPECTRE OF THE SLEEPING DEAD   620 JERUSALEM 1   11
EVERY THING IS CONDUCTED BY SPIRITS NO LESS THAN DIGESTION   621C JERUSALEM 3   PROSE
   OR SLEEP
VARIETY IN EVERY LINE BOTH OF CADENCES & NUMBER OF   621D JERUSALEM 3   PROSE
   SYLLABLES
EVERY WORD AND EVERY LETTER IS STUDIED AND PUT INTO ITS   621D JERUSALEM 3   PROSE
   FIT PLACE
RESOUND INTO THE UNBOUNDED NIGHT EVERY HUMAN PERFECTION   623 JERUSALEM 5   7
ALTHOUGH IN EVERY BOSOM THEY CONTROLL OUR VEGETATIVE POWERS   624 JERUSALEM 5   39
TERRORS IN EVERY NERVE BY SPASMS & EXTENDED PAINS   .   .   .   625 JERUSALEM 7   7
EVERY EMANATIVE JOY FORBIDDEN AS A CRIME   628 JERUSALEM 9   14
THE CRYSOLITE THE TOPAZ THE JACINTH & EVERY PRECIOUS STONE   628 JERUSALEM 9   24
EVERY SUBSTANCE IS CLOTHED THEY NAME THEM GOOD & EVIL   .   .   629 JERUSALEM 10   9
OF EVERY DIVINE MEMBER IS THE REASONING POWER   .   .   .   .   629 JERUSALEM 10   13
AN ABSTRACT OBJECTING POWER THAT NEGATIVES EVERY THING   .   629 JERUSALEM 10   14
SURPASSED BUT EVERY MOMENT IT ACCUMULATES MORE & MORE   .   .   630 JERUSALEM 10   45
IN EVERY MAN EZEKIEL SAW THEM BY CHEBAR'S FLOOD   .   .   .   .   632 JERUSALEM 12   58
AND EVERY PART OF THE CITY IS FOURFOLD & EVERY INHABITANT   633 JERUSALEM 13   20
   FOURFOLD
AND EVERY POT & VESSEL & GARMENT & UTENSIL OF THE HOUSES   633 JERUSALEM 13   21
AND EVERY HOUSE FOURFOLD BUT THE THIRD GATE IN EVERY ONE   633 JERUSALEM 13   22
PERMANENT & NOT LOST NOT LOST NOR VANISHD & EVERY LITTLE   634 JERUSALEM 13   60
   ACT
FOR EVERY THING EXISTS & NOT ONE SIGH NOR SMILE NOR TEAR   634 JERUSALEM 13   66
BENEATH BEULAH AS A WATRY FLAME REVOLVING EVERY WAY   .   .   634 JERUSALEM 14   7
EVERY ONE A TRANSLUCENT WONDER A UNIVERSE WITHIN   .   .   .   635 JERUSALEM 14   17
STARRY & GLORIOUS AND THEY EVERY ONE IN THEIR BRIGHT LOINS   635 JERUSALEM 14   19
AND EVERY ONE A GATE OF RUBIES & ALL SORTS OF PRECIOUS   635 JERUSALEM 14   21
   STONES
AND EVERY ONE A GATE OF IRON DREADFUL AND WONDERFUL   .   .   635 JERUSALEM 14   23
AND EVERY ONE HAS THE THREE REGIONS CHILDHOOD MANHOOD & AGE   635 JERUSALEM 14   25
THE EAST IS INWARDS & THE WEST IS OUTWARDS EVERY WAY   .   .   635 JERUSALEM 14   30
IN EVERY NATION OF THE EARTH TILL THE TWELVE SONS OF ALBION   635 JERUSALEM 15   3
ENROOTED INTO EVERY NATION A MIGHTY POLYPUS GROWING   .   .   635 JERUSALEM 15   4
IN HEAVY WREATHES FOLDS OVER EVERY NATION CRUEL WORKS   .   .   636 JERUSALEM 15   17

```
                                                              PAGE      TITLE          LINE
EVERY    (CONTINUED)
    IN THE TWELVE COUNTIES OF WALES & THENCE GATES LOOKING      637  JERUSALEM 16       32
    EVERY WAY
    LOS'S HALLS & EVERY AGE RENEWS ITS POWERS FROM THESE WORKS  638  JERUSALEM 16       62
    WITH EVERY PATHETIC STORY POSSIBLE TO HAPPEN FROM HATE OR   638  JERUSALEM 16       63
    WAYWARD LOVE & EVERY SORROW & DISTRESS IS CARVED HERE   . . 638  JERUSALEM 16       64
    EVERY AFFINITY OF PARENTS MARRIAGES & FRIENDSHIPS ARE HERE  638  JERUSALEM 16       65
    EVERY BOIL UPON MY BODY IS A SEPARATE & DEADLY SIN   . . .  643  JERUSALEM 21        4
    NOR THAT THEIR EVERY THOUGHT WAS SIN & SECRET APPETITE  . . 644  JERUSALEM 21       27
    WHY WILT THOU NUMBER EVERY LITTLE FIBRE OF MY SOUL   . . .  645  JERUSALEM 22       20
    IN THE EXCHANGES OF LONDON EVERY NATION WALKD   . . . . .   647  JERUSALEM 24       42
    AND LONDON WALKD IN EVERY NATION MUTUAL IN LOVE & HARMONY   647  JERUSALEM 24       43
    MOUNT ZION LIFTED HIS HEAD IN EVERY NATION UNDER HEAVEN     648  JERUSALEM 24       48
    AND EVERY ENGLISH CHILD IS SEEN   . . . . . . . . .         650  FIELDS FROM/J      19
    FROM EVERY NATION OF THE EARTH  . . . . . . . . . .         651  FIELDS FROM/J      50
    IN MY EXCHANGES EVERY LAND  . . . . . . . . . . .           652  FIELDS FROM/J      85
    SHALL WALK & MINE IN EVERY LAND   . . . . . . . .           652  FIELDS FROM/J      86
    EVERY ORNAMENT OF PERFECTION AND EVERY LABOUR OF LOVE   . . 652  JERUSALEM 28        1
    AND EVERY ACT A CRIME AND ALBION THE PUNISHER & JUDGE   . . 652  JERUSALEM 28        4
    BECAUSE OF THE OPRESSORS OF ALBION IN EVERY CITY & VILLAGE  656  JERUSALEM 30       27
    AND SAW EVERY MINUTE PARTICULAR OF ALBION DEGRADED          656  JERUSALEM 31        7
    & MURDERD
    AND SAW EVERY MINUTE PARTICULAR THE JEWELS OF ALBION        657  JERUSALEM 31       17
    RUNNING DOWN
    EVERY UNIVERSAL FORM WAS BECOME BARREN MOUNTAINS OF MORAL   657  JERUSALEM 31       19
    VIRTUE AND EVERY MINUTE PARTICULAR HARDEND INTO GRAINS      657  JERUSALEM 31       20
    OF SAND
    THERE IS A THRONE IN EVERY MAN IT IS THE THRONE OF GOD      661  JERUSALEM 34       27
    IN ALBION'S BOSOM FOR IN EVERY HUMAN BOSOM THOSE LIMITS     662  JERUSALEM 35        2
    STAND
    TO EVERY ENERGY OF MAN AND FORBID THE SPRINGS OF LIFE   . . 662  JERUSALEM 35       12
    FLED OVER CHALDEA IN TERROR IN PAINS IN EVERY NERVE   . . . 663  JERUSALEM 36       18
    ARE ALSO MEN EVERY THING IS HUMAN MIGHTY SUBLIME   . . . .  665  JERUSALEM 38       48
    IN EVERY BOSOM A UNIVERSE EXPANDS AS WINGS  . . . . . .     665  JERUSALEM 38       49
    BY SATAN'S WATCH-FIENDS THO THEY SEARCH NUMBERING EVERY     666  JERUSALEM 39        1
    GRAIN
    OF SAND ON EARTH EVERY NIGHT THEY NEVER FIND THIS GATE  . . 666  JERUSALEM 39        2
    BEFORE THE PORCH OF SIXTEEN PILLARS WEEPING EVERY ONE   . . 666  JERUSALEM 40        7
    ALBION IS SICK SAID EVERY VALLEY EVERY MOURNFUL HILL    . . 667  JERUSALEM 40       11
    AND EVERY RIVER OUR BROTHER ALBION IS SICK TO DEATH    . .  667  JERUSALEM 40       12
    OPENING INTO BEULAH EVERY ANGLE IS A LOVELY HEAVEN   . . .  668  JERUSALEM 41       18
    LIKE EVENING DEW ON EVERY HERB UPON THE BREATHING GROUND    669  JERUSALEM 42        8
    IN EVERY INDIVIDUAL MAN AND THE LIMIT OF OPAKENESS   . . .  670  JERUSALEM 42       30
    WHO PROTECTS MINUTE PARTICULARS EVERY ONE IN THEIR OWN      672  JERUSALEM 43       23
    IDENTITY
    BECOME A NET & A TRAP & EVERY ENERGY RENDERD CRUEL   . . .  672  JERUSALEM 43       26
    THAT EVERY LITTLE PARTICLE OF LIGHT & AIR BECAME OPAKE  . . 674  JERUSALEM 44       10
    WHO IS JERUSALEM IN EVERY INDIVIDUAL MAN AND HER   . . . .  675  JERUSALEM 44       39
    IN ITS EXTENSION EVERY TWO HUNDRED YEARS HAS A DOOR TO EDEN 678  JERUSALEM 48       37
    EVERY RELIGION THAT PREACHES VENGEANCE FOR SIN   . . . .    682B JERUSALEM 52     PROSE
    IN GREAT ETERNITY EVERY PARTICULAR FORM GIVES FORTH OR      684  JERUSALEM 54        1
    EMANATES
    AND THE LIGHT IS HIS GARMENT THIS IS JERUSALEM IN EVERY MAN 684  JERUSALEM 54        3
    BY HIS OWN SPECTRE WHO IS THE REASONING POWER IN EVERY MAN  685  JERUSALEM 54        7
    EVERY ONE KNOWS WE ARE ONE FAMILY ONE MAN BLESSED FOR       687  JERUSALEM 55       46
    EVER
    SILENCE REMAIND & EVERY ONE RESUMD HIS HUMAN MAJESTY    . . 687  JERUSALEM 55       47
    LET THE INDEFINITE BE EXPLORED AND LET EVERY MAN BE JUDGED  687  JERUSALEM 55       57
    ROCKD BY YEAR MONTH DAY & HOUR AND EVERY TWO MOMENTS    . . 688  JERUSALEM 56        9
    OBLITERATES EVERY OTHER EVIL NONE PITIES THEIR TEARS    . . 691  JERUSALEM 59       35
    THEY ARE MOCKD BY EVERY ONE THAT PASSES BY THEY REGARD NOT  692  JERUSALEM 59       39
    EVERY HARLOT WAS ONCE A VIRGIN EVERY CRIMINAL AN INFANT     695  JERUSALEM 61       52
    LOVE
    FIBRES OF LIFE TO WEAVE FOR EVERY FEMALE IS A GOLDEN LOOM   704  JERUSALEM 67        4
    THEN ALL THE MALES [CONJOINED] COMBINED INTO ONE MALE &     707  JERUSALEM 69    *   1
    EVERY ONE
    DEVOURING JERUSALEM FROM EVERY NATION OF THE EARTH   . . .  707  JERUSALEM 69        5
    WHERE EVERY FEMALE DELIGHTS TO GIVE HER MAIDEN TO           707  JERUSALEM 69       15
    HER HUSBAND
    IN THE CIRCUMFERENCE & EVERY MINUTE PARTICULAR IS HOLY  . . 708  JERUSALEM 69       42
    AND EVERY HUMAN VEGETATED FORM IN ITS INWARD RECESSES   . . 714  JERUSALEM 73       50
    THAT NOT ONE MOMENT OF TIME BE LOST & EVERY REVOLUTION  . . 716  JERUSALEM 75        8
    EVERY MOMENT LOST IS A MOMENT THAT CANNOT BE REDEEMED   . . 716D JERUSALEM 77     PROSE
    EVERY PLEASURE THAT INTERMINGLES WITH THE DUTY OF           716D JERUSALEM 77     PROSE
    OUR STATION
    O YE RELIGIOUS DISCOUNTENANCE EVERY ONE AMONG YOU   . . .   717B JERUSALEM 77     PROSE
    MOCKS JESUS THE GIVER OF EVERY MENTAL GIFT  . . . . . .     717C JERUSALEM 77     PROSE
    LET EVERY CHRISTIAN AS MUCH AS IN HIM LIES  . . . . .       717C JERUSALEM 77     PROSE
    THIS TERRIBLE DEVOURING SWORD TURNING EVERY WAY  . . . .    718  STOOD AMONG/J      15
    HIS AGED PARENTS SOUGHT ME OUT IN EVERY CITY & VILLAGE  . . 720  JERUSALEM 79       27
    JOY UPON EVERY MOUNTAIN TO TEACH SONGS TO THE SHEPHERD      720  JERUSALEM 79       37
    & PLOWMAN
    TILL ALBION IS SHUT OUT FROM EVERY NATION UNDER HEAVEN  . . 721  JERUSALEM 79       80
    CALLING THE DEFINITE SIN DEFACING EVERY DEFINITE FORM   . . 723  JERUSALEM 80       53
    HE SIEZES HIS HAMMER EVERY HOUR FLAMES SURROUND HIM AS  . . 731  JERUSALEM 86       34
    BUT GENERAL FORMS HAVE THEIR VITALITY IN PARTICULARS &      738  JERUSALEM 91       30
    EVERY
    THUS LOS ALTERD HIS SPECTRE & EVERY RATIO OF HIS REASON     739  JERUSALEM 91       51
    ONE FOR ANOTHER TO PUT OFF BY FORGIVENESS EVERY SIN   . . . 743  JERUSALEM 96       19
    AS GOD IS LOVE EVERY KINDNESS TO ANOTHER IS A LITTLE DEATH  743  JERUSALEM 96       27
    AND EVERY MAN STOOD FOURFOLD EACH FOUR FACES HAD ONE TO     745  JERUSALEM 98       12
    THE WEST
```

```
                                                              PAGE       TITLE          LINE
EVERY    (CONTINUED)
    ACCORDING TO THE SUBJECT OF DISCOURSE & EVERY WORD & EVERY   746 JERUSALEM 98        35
        CHARACTER
    WITH EVERY COLOUR LION TYGER HORSE ELEPHANT EAGLE DOVE       746 JERUSALEM 98        43
        FLY WORM
    BROKE DOWN FROM EVERY CHAIN & BAR . . . . . . . . .          749 EV GOSPEL(B)/N      41
    ON EVERY ONE WHO FORGIVES SIN . . . . . . . . . . .          759 EV GOSPEL (2)       43
    EVERY HARLOT WAS A VIRGIN ONCE . . . . . . . . . .           771 EPILOGUE/GP          3
    IMAGINATION OR THE HUMAN ETERNAL BODY IN EVERY MAN  . . .    773C ANNO BERKELEY    MARG
    IMAGINATION OR THE DIVINE BODY IN EVERY MAN  . . . .         773D ANNO BERKELEY  * MARG
    THOSE OF A BULL EVERY THING HAS ITS OWN HARMONY &            774B ANNO BERKELEY    MARG
        PROPORTION
    JESUS SUPPOSES EVERY THING TO BE EVIDENT TO THE CHILD  .     774D ANNO BERKELEY    MARG
    FOR EVERY PLEASURE MONEY IS USELESS  . . . . . . . .         777A INSC LAOCOON    PROSE
    IS NOT EVERY VICE POSSIBLE TO MAN DESCRIBED IN THE BIBLE     777D INSC LAOCOON    PROSE
        OPENLY
    EVERY POEM MUST NECESSARILY BE A PERFECT UNITY   . . . .     778A HOMERS POETRY   PROSE
    EVERY THING IN DANTE'S COMEDIA SHEWS THAT  . . . . .         785A ILLUS DANTE 7   PROSE
    EVERY THING HAS AS MUCH RIGHT TO ETERNAL LIFE  . . . .       788B ANNO THORNTON    MARG
    I ATTEMPTED EVERY MORNING FOR A FORTNIGHT TOGETHER          792A LETTER 4        PROSE
        TO FOLLOW
    WHICH GIVES EXISTENCE TO EVERY OTHER NAMELY VISIONS OF       793A LETTER 5        PROSE
        ETERNITY
    I SEE EVERY THING I PAINT IN THIS WORLD  . . . . . .         793D LETTER 5        PROSE
    BUT EVERY BODY DOES NOT SEE ALIKE TO THE EYES OF A MISER     793D LETTER 5        PROSE
    WHICH I HAVE THE PLEASURE TO TELL YOU ARE INCREASING EVERY   794C LETTER 5        PROSE
        DAY
    OF EVERY THING YOU VALUE GO ON IF NOT FOR YOUR OWN SAKE      795B LETTER 6        PROSE
        YET FOR OURS
    MORE & MORE PERSWADED THAT EVERY MORTAL LOSS IS             797B LETTER 9        PROSE
        AN IMMORTAL GAIN
    SCULPTURE BY CONSIDERING EVERY VALUABLE ORIGINAL THAT IS     797D LETTER 10       PROSE
    EVERY THING IS NEARLY COMPLETED FOR OUR REMOVAL TO FELPHAM   799A LETTER 11       PROSE
    EVERY STONE ON THE LAND  . . . . . . . . . . . . . .         804 TO BUTTS/L         26
    LEFT WITH US THEY KEEP OFF EVERY WIND WE HEAR THE WEST HOWL  807B LETTER 17       PROSE
    NOW LET ME INTREAT YOU TO GIVE ME ORDERS TO FURNISH EVERY    808B LETTER 19       PROSE
    TO ETERNITY EVERY ONE IN ETERNITY WILL LEAVE YOU AGHAST      813B LETTER 22       PROSE
    WHICH I PAINTED FOR YOU ARE EQUAL IN EVERY PART OF THE ART   814A LETTER 23       PROSE
    CONTRARY TO DESIGNING & HISTORICAL PAINTING IN EVERY         815D LETTER 23       PROSE
        RESPECT
    IF YOU HAVE NOT NATURE BEFORE YOU FOR EVERY TOUCH            815D LETTER 23       PROSE
        YOU CANNOT
    MUST EVERY JOY BE DUNG & DROSS . . . . . . . . . .           817 HAPPINESS/L        44
    AND EVERY SOUL OF MEN ON THE EARTH   . . . . . . . .         818 HAPPINESS/L        75
    EVERY ASSISTANCE IN HIS POWER WITHOUT KNOWING MY INTENTION   820B LETTER 25       PROSE
    FRENCH PRINTS & PLEASE EVERY ONE IN SHORT I HAVE GOT   .     821A LETTER 25       PROSE
    EVERY THING SO UNDER MY THUMB THAT IT IS MORE PROFITABLE     821B LETTER 25       PROSE
    & THIS WE MUST PREVENT BY EVERY MEANS IN OUR POWER   . .     821B LETTER 25       PROSE
    WHAT IS VERY PLEASANT EVERY ONE WHO HEARS OF MY GOING   .    822D LETTER 26       PROSE
    BOTH TO GOD & MAN WE LOOK FORWARD EVERY DAY WITH PLEASURE    824B LETTER 27       PROSE
    BY PRESENCE FOR RECOLLECTION OFTEN SURPASSES EVERY THING     824B LETTER 27       PROSE
    WITHOUT THE ORIGINAL SITTING BEFORE YOU FOR EVERY TOUCH ALL  824B LETTER 27       PROSE
    HAVE BEEN LOST I SHALL LEAVE EVERY ONE IN THIS COUNTRY  .    825D LETTER 27       PROSE
    TO EVERY ONE THAT THE WHOLE ACCUSATION IS A WILFUL PERJURY   828A LETTER 28       PROSE
    ALL THE VILLAGES ROUND EVERY MAN IS NOW AFRAID OF SPEAKING   828A LETTER 28       PROSE
    EVERY ONE HERE IS MY EVIDENCE FOR PEACE & GOOD              828B LETTER 28       PROSE
        NEIGHBOURHOOD
    THEN I'M SILENT & PASSIVE & LOSE EVERY FRIEND . . . . .      828 O WHY BORN/L        4
    EVERY ENGRAVER TURNS AWAY WORK THAT HE CANNOT EXECUTE   .    829D LETTER 30       PROSE
    EVERY BODY COMPLAINS YET ALL GO ON CHEERFULLY AND WITH       831D LETTER 31       PROSE
        SPIRIT
    THE SHOPS IN LONDON IMPROVE EVERY THING IS ELEGANT CLEAN     831D LETTER 31       PROSE
    MR SAUNDERS WILL SHORTLY WRITE TO YOU GIVING YOU EVERY  .    832D LETTER 32       PROSE
    & OTHER ARTICLES COLLECTED FROM EVERY FOUNTAIN HE CAN VISIT  832D LETTER 32       PROSE
    EVERY ENQUIRY OF HIM IF YOU THINK BEST MR SANDERS HAS   .    834C LETTER 34       PROSE
    GOING ON BRISKLY WITH THE PLATES FIND EVERY THING PROMISING  835A LETTER 34       PROSE
    MY WIFE GETS BETTER EVERY DAY HOPE EARNESTLY THAT YOU   .    835A LETTER 34       PROSE
    TO MR HOARE WHO IS WORTHY OF EVERY CONFIDENCE YOU CAN   .    842A LETTER 41       PROSE
    CALLD ON HIM EVERY DAY & NOT FINDING HIM I NOW UNDERSTAND    842B LETTER 42      *PROSE
    IN WESTMORELAND PROMISES TO MAKE EVERY INQUIRY ABOUT IT      844C LETTER 43       PROSE
    EVERY INFORMATION IN HIS POWER SAYS THAT I SHALL HAVE   .    845D LETTER 44       PROSE
    PERSUADED TO PRINT IN LONDON YOU WILL BE CHEATED EVERY WAY   847B LETTER 44       PROSE
    IN LONDON EVERY CALUMNY AND FALSEHOOD UTTERD AGAINST         847B LETTER 44       PROSE
        ANOTHER
    THRESHOLD THO EVERY OTHER MAN'S DOORSTONE IS WORN DOWN  .    849D LETTER 47       PROSE
    SPOILING WHAT I HAD DONE WELL EVERY ONE OF MY FRIENDS WAS    852B LETTER 50       PROSE
    THEY KNEW MY INDUSTRY AND ABSTINENCE FROM EVERY PLEASURE     852B LETTER 50       PROSE
    IN WHICH I HAVE REGULARLY WRITTEN DOWN EVERY SUM I HAVE      854C LETTER 53       PROSE
    THAN THE SHIPWRECK IT IS EVERY BODY FAVOURITE WHO HAVE  .    855A LETTER 53       PROSE
    DETERMINATION TO DO EVERY THING TO ENGAGE HIMSELF TO YOU     857A LETTER 54       PROSE
    HE IS AGREEABLE TO EVERY PROPOSAL YOU HAVE MADE AND WILL     857D LETTER 55       PROSE
    TALK OF EVERY BODY I HAVE NOT SEEN HIM & PERHAPS NEVER MAY   859C LETTER 56       PROSE
    MY WIFE CONTINUES IN HEALTH & DESIRES TO JOIN ME IN EVERY    860B LETTER 56       PROSE
    IS MORE SEVERELY AVENGED THAN EVERY SIN & WICKEDNESS BESIDE  863A LETTER 60       PROSE
    KNOW THAT EVERY MAN OUGHT TO BE A JUDGE OF PICTURES AND      864C LETTER 61       PROSE
    EVERY MAN IS SO WHO HAS NOT BEEN CONNOISSEURED OUT OF HIS    864C LETTER 61       PROSE
        SENSES
    PERHAPS & I VERILY BELIEVE IT EVERY DEATH IS AN IMPROVEMENT  868D LETTER 68       PROSE
    ALL MY HOPES BY THE ROOTS EVERY ONE WHO KNOWS OF OUR    .    872D LETTER 76       PROSE
    & STRONGER EVERY DAY THO WEAKER IN MUSCLE & BONE THAN   .    872D LETTER 76       PROSE
    I AM GETTING BETTER EVERY HOUR MY PLAN IS DIET ONLY &   .    873C LETTER 77       PROSE
    BETTER EVERY MORNING BUT SLOWLY AS I AM STILL FEEBLE &  .    876A LETTER 83       PROSE
```

```
                                                           PAGE     TITLE        LINE
EVERY   (CONTINUED)
     FLAXMAN IS GONE & WE MUST ALL SOON FOLLOW EVERY ONE TO HIS   879A LETTER 88      PROSE
     THE MIND IN WHICH EVERY ONE IS KING & PRIEST IN HIS OWN      879A LETTER 88      PROSE
        HOUSE
     I AM GOING ON BETTER EVERY DAY AS I THINK BOTH     . . . .   879B LETTER 89      PROSE
     "LEAVE EVERY HOPE YOU WHO IN ENTER"  . . . . . . . . . SUPP ILLUS DANTE 4    *
     EVERY THING WHICH IS IN HARMONY WITH ME I CALL     . . . . SUPP IN HARMONY/N   *PROSE
     "EVERY THING THAT GROWS" (SHAKESPEARE)  . . . . . . . SUPP LEGEND/N21      *
EVERY-ONE
     FROM EVERY-ONE OF THE FOUR REGIONS OF HUMAN MAJESTY  . . .   640 JERUSALEM 18       1
     JORDAN TO THE LAND OF THE HITTITE EVERY-ONE THAT SAW HIM     661 JERUSALEM 34      48
EVERYTHING
     I HATE REASONING I DO EVERYTHING BY MY FEELINGS AH SAID      50A ISLAND MOON 6    PROSE
        SIPSOP I ONLY
     RESOLVED TO GO CONTRARY IN EVERYTHING TO CHAUCER WHO SAYS    574A DESC CAT 3      PROSE
     TO DIFFERENT PEOPLE IT APPEARS DIFFERENTLY AS EVERYTHING     605A V LAST JUDG/N   PROSE
        ELSE
     MY WAY TO MAKE THE BEST OF EVERYTHING I NEVER MAKE MYSELF    819B LETTER 25      PROSE
EVERY-THING
     WHAT IS ABOVE IS WITHIN FOR EVERY-THING IN ETERNITY IS       709 JERUSALEM 71       6
        TRANSLUCENT
     AND ARE NOT THE GIFTS OF THE SPIRIT EVERY-THING TO MAN  . . 717B JERUSALEM 77    PROSE
EVERY-WHERE
     YET THE DIVINE VISION REMAINS EVERY-WHERE FOR-EVER AMEN      505 MILTON 22        2
EVIDENCE
     BUT THE EVIDENCE IS NOTHING FOR HOW CAN HE WHO    . . . . . 392D ANNO WATSON     MARG
     BE AN EVIDENCE OF THE TRUTH OF HIS HISTORY  . . . . . . . . 392D ANNO WATSON     MARG
     OR AT WHAT TIME OR IN THE HISTORICAL EVIDENCE WHICH MAY BE   393B ANNO WATSON     MARG
     HOSIER SAYS HE IS READY TO GIVE EVIDENCE OF THIS    437B BLAKES MEMORAN PROSE
        IF NECESSARY
     WILLIAM'S TIMIDITY IN GIVING HIS EVIDENCE BEFORE THE    . . 438D BLAKES MEMORAN PROSE
     THE GREATER IS THE EVIDENCE OF WEAK IMITATION PLAGIARISM     585B DESC CAT 15     PROSE
     SUFFICIENT EVIDENCE IN THE WORKS OF OUR OWN HOGARTH  . .     586D CHAUCER 1       PROSE
     [BECAUSE IT BEARS THE [EVIDENT] EVIDENCE AT FIRST VIEW]      599C PUB ADDRESS/N  *PROSE
        TO BE
     THE WORK OF A BLOCKHEAD IT BEARS THIS EVIDENCE IN ITS FACE   599C PUB ADDRESS/N   PROSE
     HIS WIFE & DAUGHTER WILL EVIDENCE THE SAME & WILL EVIDENTLY  827D LETTER 28      PROSE
     EVERY ONE HERE IS MY EVIDENCE FOR PEACE & GOOD      828B LETTER 28      PROSE
        NEIGHBOURHOOD
EVIDENCES
     MRS HAYNES EVIDENCES THAT SHE SAW ME TURN HIM  . . . . .     437B BLAKES MEMORAN PROSE
     EVIDENCES THE [IDEA OF WANT] WANT OF IDEA IN THE ARTIST'S    585B DESC CAT 15     PROSE
     AT THE FOX & WHO EVIDENCES THAT TO HIS KNOWLEDGE NO WORD     827C LETTER 28      PROSE
     ALL THAT HAPPEND AT THE GATE OF THE INN WHO EVIDENCES THAT   827C LETTER 28      PROSE
EVIDENT    SEE SELF EVIDENT
     IS IT NOT ALSO EVIDENT THAT ONE DEGREE WILL NOT OPEN THE     93A ANNO SWED LOVE  MARG
        OTHER
     NEEDS NO ONE TO PROVE IT IT IS EVIDENT AS THE SUN & MOON     386C ANNO WATSON    MARG
     IT IS EVIDENT THAT REYNOLDS WISHD NONE BUT FOOLS    . . .    458C ANNO REYNOLDS  MARG
     [BECAUSE IT BEARS THE [EVIDENT] EVIDENCE AT FIRST VIEW]      599C PUB ADDRESS/N  *PROSE
        TO BE
     [AMONG THE ANCIENTS IS EVIDENT FROM THE WORDS OF THE]   . .  601A PUB ADDRESS/N  *PROSE
     TO HIDE THE MOST EVIDENT GOD IN A HIDDEN COVERT EVEN  . .    661 JERUSALEM 34      32
     JESUS SUPPOSES EVERY THING TO BE EVIDENT TO THE CHILD   . .  774D ANNO BERKELEY  MARG
EVIDENTLY
     BACON WAS A CONTEMPLATIVE ATHEIST EVIDENTLY AN EPICUREAN     403C ANNO BACON     MARG
     ALL THE REST ARE EVIDENTLY COPIES THOUGH FINE ONES   . . .  565D DESC CAT 2      PROSE
     HIS WIFE & DAUGHTER WILL EVIDENCE THE SAME & WILL EVIDENTLY  827D LETTER 28      PROSE
EVIL
     NOBLE BUT MARK ACTIVE EVIL IS BETTER THAN PASSIVE GOOD  . .  77B ANNO LAVATER    MARG
     MAN IS A TWOFOLD BEING ONE PART CAPABLE OF EVIL  . .    . .  80A ANNO LAVATER    MARG
     THAT WHICH IS CAPABLE OF GOOD IS NOT ALSO CAPABLE OF EVIL    80A ANNO LAVATER    MARG
        BUT
     THAT WHICH IS CAPABLE OF EVIL IS ALSO CAPABLE OF GOOD        80A ANNO LAVATER    MARG
        THIS APHORISM
     SEEMS TO CONSIDER MAN AS SIMPLE & YET CAPABLE OF EVIL   .    80A ANNO LAVATER    MARG
     NOW BOTH EVIL & GOOD CANNOT EXIST IN A SIMPLE BEING  . .     80A ANNO LAVATER    MARG
     BUT IF MAN IS CONSIDERD AS ONLY EVIL & GOD ONLY GOOD    .    80A ANNO LAVATER    MARG
     HOW THEN IS REGENERATION EFFECTED WHICH TURNS THE EVIL       80A ANNO LAVATER    MARG
        TO GOOD
     BY CASTING OUT THE EVIL BY THE GOOD SEE MATTHEW XII... .  .  80A ANNO LAVATER    MARG
     THERE CAN BE NO GOOD-WILL WILL IS ALWAYS EVIL  . . . . .     89A ANNO SWED LOVE  MARG
     BUT NEVER ?CAN ?THE TRUTH ?BE ?EVIL . . . . . . .    .       89B ANNO SWED LOVE * MARG
     BECAUSE MAN IS ONLY EVIL ?WHEN ?HE ?WILLS ?AN ?UNTRUTH  .    89B ANNO SWED LOVE * MARG
     GOOD & EVIL ARE HERE BOTH GOOD & THE TWO CONTRARIES          91D ANNO SWED LOVE  MARG
        MARRIED
     ("DEAD SUN") THE DEAD SUN IS ONLY A PHANTASY OF EVIL MAN     92C ANNO SWED LOVE  MARG
     O LEAGUED WITH EVIL SPIRITS THOU ACCURSED MAN OF SIN   . .   107 TIRIEL 6        13
     SILENCE THY EVIL TONGUE THOU MURDERER OF THY HELPLESS        108 TIRIEL 6        35
        CHILDREN
     THAT GOD WOULD LOVE A WORM I KNEW AND PUNISH THE EVIL FOOT   130 BOOK OF THEL 5   9
     FROM THESE CONTRARIES SPRING WHAT THEY RELIGIOUS CALL GOOD   149B MARRIAGE HH 3
        & EVIL
     EVIL IS THE ACTIVE SPRINGING FROM ENERGY    . . . . . .  .   149B MARRIAGE HH 3  PROSE
     GOOD IS HEAVEN EVIL IS HELL . . . . . . . .    .    . . .    149B MARRIAGE HH 3  PROSE
     THAT ENERGY CALLD EVIL IS ALONE FROM THE BODY  . . . .  .    149C MARRIAGE HH 4  PROSE
     THE EVIL DAY AFAR & IF PERCHANCE WITH IRON POWER   . . . .   282 FOUR ZOAS 2      75
     WHILE YET THOSE BEINGS WERE NOT BORN NOR KNEW OF GOOD OR     304 FOUR ZOAS 4     274
        EVIL
     AND MAN WALKS FORTH FROM MIDST OF THE FIRES THE EVIL IS      379 FOUR ZOAS 9     827
        ALL CONSUMD
     THE ELEMENTS ARE FILLD WITH THE PRINCE OF EVIL   . . . . .  388A ANNO WATSON     MARG
```

```
                                                           PAGE     TITLE         LINE
EVIL     (CONTINUED)
         & ITS CONSEQUENT EVIL & THE HONESTY OF OTHERS & ITS . . .  393B ANNO WATSON      MARG
         DO OR ACT TO DO GOOD OR TO DO EVIL . . . . . . . . . .     396A ANNO WATSON      MARG
         IT IS THE TREE OF THE KNOWLEDGE OF GOOD & EVIL . . . . .   397C ANNO BACON       MARG
         & OF SWEET SOWER & OF GOOD EVIL & OF NOTHING SOMETHING . . 414B ANNO BOYD        MARG
         WHETHER TIS GOOD OR EVIL NONE S TO BLAME . . . . . .       418  ON VIRGINITY/N    3
         THE SAVIOUR WHILE THE EVIL ANGELS ARE DRIVEN GENTLY        441D INSC FALL MAN    PROSE
            CONDUCTS
         FOOL & A CUNNING KNAVE SUITED TO THE PURPOSES OF           458B ANNO REYNOLDS    MARG
            EVIL DEMONS
         I IN MY SELPHOOD AM THAT SATAN I AM THAT EVIL ONE . . .    496  MILTON 14         30
         PITYING AND PERMITTING EVIL THO STRONG & MIGHTY TO DESTROY 505  MILTON 22         30
         CRUEL IN THY MILDNESS PITYING AND PERMITTING EVIL . . .    507  MILTON 23         19
         WHERE LIE IN EVIL DEATH THE FOUR IMMORTALS PALE AND COLD   524  MILTON 34         45
         WHO TROUBLE RELIGION WITH QUESTIONS CONCERNING GOOD & EVIL 604C V LAST JUDG/N    PROSE
         HERE THEY ARE NO LONGER TALKING OF WHAT IS GOOD & EVIL . . 613C V LAST JUDG/N    PROSE
         IN ITS DEADLY DREAMS OF GOOD & EVIL . . . . . . . . .      614C V LAST JUDG/N    PROSE
         THE COMBATS OF GOOD & EVIL [& OF TRUTH & ERROR WHICH]  .   615A V LAST JUDG/N    PROSE
         GOOD & EVIL ARE QUALITIES IN EVERY MAN . . . . . . .       615A V LAST JUDG/N    PROSE
         WHETHER A GOOD OR EVIL MAN THESE ARE ENEMIES . . . . .     615A V LAST JUDG/N    PROSE
         BUT UNBELIEF & EATING OF THE TREE OF KNOWLEDGE OF GOOD     615C V LAST JUDG/N    PROSE
            & EVIL
         WE WILL NOT CONVERSE CONCERNING GOOD & EVIL . . . . . .    615D V LAST JUDG/N    PROSE
         THEY ARE NOT ALWAYS PRYING AFTER GOOD & EVIL IN ONE ANOTHER 616D V LAST JUDG/N   PROSE
         LO WE ARE ONE FORGIVING ALL EVIL NOT SEEKING RECOMPENSE    622  JERUSALEM 4       20
         THE EVIL DAY AFAR AND IF PERCHANCE WITH IRON POWER  . .    626  JERUSALEM 7       33
         EVERY SUBSTANCE IS CLOTHED THEY NAME THEM GOOD & EVIL  . . 629  JERUSALEM 10       9
         TO BE ALL EVIL ALL REVERSED & FOR EVER DEAD KNOWING  .     630  JERUSALEM 10      57
         I PLEASE TELL HAND & SKOFIELD THEY ARE MY MINISTERS OF EVIL 640 JERUSALEM 17      62
         WHERE WE LIVE FORGETTING ERROR NOT PONDERING ON EVIL  .    642  JERUSALEM 20       7
         [TO GOVERN THE EVIL BY GOOD AND ?STATES ABOLISH ?SYSTEMS]  662  JERUSALEM 35    *  18
         BROODING ON EVIL BUT WHEN LOS OPEND THE FURNACES BEFORE HIM 669 JERUSALEM 42       2
         BECAUSE THE EVIL IS CREATED INTO A STATE THAT MEN  . . .   680  JERUSALEM 49      70
         A BROODER OF AN EVIL DAY AND A SUN RISING IN BLOOD   .     681  JERUSALEM 50      29
         IS ALTOGETHER AN EVIL & REQUIRES A NEW SELPHOOD CONTINUALLY 682A JERUSALEM 52    PROSE
         ROUSSEAU THOUGHT MEN GOOD BY NATURE HE FOUND THEM EVIL &   682D JERUSALEM 52     PROSE
         OBLITERATES EVERY OTHER EVIL NONE PITIES THEIR TEARS  .    691  JERUSALEM 59      35
         OF GOOD & EVIL THEY DIVIDED HIM IN LOVE UPON THE THAMES    715  JERUSALEM 74      36
            & SENT
         PITY THE EVIL FOR THOU ART NOT SENT . . . . . . . .        718  STOOD AMONG/J     26
         I CARE NOT WHETHER A MAN IS GOOD OR EVIL ALL THAT I CARE   739  JERUSALEM 91      55
         OF SIN & THE TREE OF GOOD & EVIL SPRANG FROM THE ROCKY     740  JERUSALEM 92      25
            CIRCLE & SNAKE
         WHERE IS THE TREE OF GOOD & EVIL THAT ROOTED BENEATH THE   746  JERUSALEM 98      47
            CRUEL HEEL
         GOOD & EVIL ARE NO MORE  . . . . . . . . . . . . .         754  EV GOSPEL(E)/N    21
         THE EVIL SPIRITS FROM THEIR SHRINES . . . . . . . .        756  EV GOSPEL(I)/N    19
         OF GOOD & EVIL & MISERY . . . . . . . . . . . .            759  EV GOSPEL (2)     41
         OF GOOD & EVIL VIRTUE & VICE . . . . . . . . . .           770  OF GATES/GP        6
         RATIONAL TRUTH ROOT OF EVIL & GOOD . . . . . . . .         770  OF GATES/GP       14
         EVIL GOOD  . . . . . . . . . . . . . . . . . .             775C INSC LAOCOON     TITLE
         THE ROOT OF GOOD & EVIL IN THE ACCUSATION OF SIN . . .     776B INSC LAOCOON     PROSE
         GOOD & EVIL ARE RICHES & POVERTY A TREE OF MISERY  . .     776B INSC LAOCOON     PROSE
         THE ANCIENTS CALLD IT EATING OF THE TREE OF GOOD & EVIL    778C HOMERS POETRY    PROSE
         & TO ITS LAWS OF GOOD & EVIL & ITS ENMITIES AGAINST MIND   784D ANNO WW EXCUR     MARG
         [?AS] FOR IF HE GIVES HIS RAIN TO THE EVIL & THE GOOD  .   785C ILLS DANTE 101   *PROSE
         [?EVIL GOD OF THIS WORLD] [HIS] SATAN'S WILL . . . . .     788A ANNO THORNTON   * MARG
         & DELIVER US FROM POVERTY IN JESUS THAT EVIL ONE  . .      789A ANNO THORNTON     MARG
         AND MY BROTHER JOHN THE EVIL ONE . . . . . . . .           817  HAPPINESS/L       15
         ALL IS COME FROM THE SPIRITUAL WORLD FOR GOOD & NOT FOR    828C LETTER 28        PROSE
            EVIL
         HAVE ENTIRELY ESCAPED THE BRUSH OF MY EVIL STAR  . . .     835A LETTER 34        PROSE
         THINGS KNOWN ONLY TO MYSELF & TO SPIRITS GOOD & EVIL BUT   862D LETTER 60        PROSE
         IDEAS OF GOOD & EVIL . . . . . . . . . . . . .             889C IDEAS/N4         PROSE
         THE GOOD AND EVIL ANGELS . . . . . . . . . . .            SUPP  COLOR PRT TATE  *TITLE
         OF THE TREE OF LIFE & OF THE TREE OF GOOD & EVIL  . .     SUPP  ILLUS GENESIS   *TITLE
         GOOD & EVIL ANGEL HOUSE OF DEATH GOD JUDGING ADAM LAMECH  SUPP  LETTER 56A      *PROSE
         SAUL KING OF ISRAEL SOMEWHAT INFLUENCED BY XXX EVIL SPIRIT SUPP PENC DRAW 1.42  *TITLE
EVIL-ONE
         BLASPHEMY BY HIS MATERNAL BIRTH HE IS THAT EVIL-ONE . . .  736  JERUSALEM 90      35
EVILS
         NOT IF EVILS ARE PAST SINS . . . . . . . . . . .           81A  ANNO LAVATER     MARG
         THIS LIFE IS A WARFARE AGAINST EVILS . . . . . . . .       545  COSWAY FRAZR/N    3
EVN
         OR EVN THE LEAST BY BIRTH SHALL GAIN THE BRIGHTEST FAME    18   EDW THIRD/PS 1    30
         THEN NINEVA & BABYLON AND COSTLY TYRE AND EVN JERUSALEM    41A  THEN SHE BORE   *PROSE
         UNTIMELY LOST THY CONRADE ONCE WHEN LIVING THEE I LOVD     43D  WOE CRIED MUSE   PROSE
            EVN UNTO DEATH
         IN SILENCE EVN WITHOUT A WHISPER AND IN SEEMING SLEEP  .   194  V DAU ALBION 6    13
         MY CATTLE NEXT LAST EVN THE DOG OF MY GATE THE FORESTS FLED 643 JERUSALEM 21       8
EVRY
         AMBITION IS THE GROWTH OF EVRY CLIME . . . . . . . .       28   EDW THIRD/PS 4     2
         TIS AT THIS RIVER'S FOUNT WHERE EVRY MORTAL'S CUP IS MIXT  41C  THEN SHE BORE    PROSE
         & EVRY PIECE OF FLESH DOTH CRY OUT WOE . . . . . . .       43C  WOE CRIED MUSE   PROSE
         FOR EVRY ONE OF THOSE THY WRINKLES EACH OF THOSE GREY HAIRS 99  TIRIEL 1        *  14
         WHOSE EVRY FUNCTION IS FILLD WITH ITS FIERY DESIRE . . .   142  FRENCH REVOLTN   183
         HOW DO YOU KNOW BUT EVRY BIRD THAT CUTS THE AIRY WAY  .    150D MARRIAGE HH 6    PROSE
         THIS THEME CALLS ME IN SLEEP NIGHT AFTER NIGHT & EVRY MORN 622  JERUSALEM 4        3
EWE
         BY A LITTLE EWE LAMB  . . . . . . . . . . . . .            256  BOOK OF LOS 3     24
EWES
         AND HE HEARS THE EWE'S TENDER REPLY . . . . . . . .        118  SHEPHERD/SI        6
```

```
                                                      PAGE      TITLE          LINE
EXACT
    MINUTE AND EXACT BECAUSE SHE IS ALSO A SCOURGE AND A BLIGHT   572B DESC CAT 3      PROSE
    HIS ARMS DOTH HE FORGIVE JERUSALEM & NOT EXACT PURITY FROM    694 JERUSALEM 61      15
        HER WHO IS
    OPINION THE MOST EXACT RESEMBLANCE OF ROMNEY HE EVER SAW      836B LETTER 35       PROSE
EXACTLY
    OVER FIND THAT MY NOTES ON REYNOLDS IN THIS BOOK             477A ANNO REYNOLDS    MARG
        ARE EXACTLY
    [THIS] REYNOLDS LECTURES [PLAINLY SHEW] EXACTLY SO  . . .     539 CAN THERE BE/N     5
    TALKED EXACTLY IN THIS WAY ("I PASS THEM UNALARMED")  .  .   784B ANNO WW EXCUR    MARG
    IT IS NOW EXACTLY TWENTY YEARS SINCE I WAS UPON THE OCEAN     795D LETTER 6        PROSE
        OF
    THE WRITING BEING EXACTLY COPIED FROM THE TRACING PAPER       838A LETTER 37       PROSE
    MR PARKER HAS AFFIXD TO EACH IS EXACTLY WHAT I MYSELF   .  .  848C LETTER 45       PROSE
    & THE FIGURES LEFT EXACTLY  .  .  .  .  .  .  .  .  .  .      850D LETTER 49       PROSE
    EXACTLY TWENTY YEARS BEEN CLOSED FROM ME AS BY A DOOR   .  .  852B LETTER 50       PROSE
EXALT
    WITH MARROW SINEWS & FLESH EXALT THYSELF ATTAIN A VOICE       275 FOUR ZOAS 1       405
    WHILE YOU EXALT ME BY SUCH DISTINGUISHING COMMENDATIONS I     822B LETTER 26       PROSE
EXALTED
    TO BE EXALTED TO THOSE HEAVENLY FIELDS  .  .  .  .  .  .       30 EDW THIRD/PS 5     28
    GLORYING IN HIS OWN EYES EXALTED IN TERRIFIC PRIDE  .  .  .   267 FOUR ZOAS 1       129
    AS ONE MAN FOR CONTRACTING THEIR EXALTED SENSES  .  .  .  .   277 FOUR ZOAS 1       470
EXALTING
    EVEN TO THE STARS EXALTING HER THRONE TO BUILD BEYOND THE     719 JERUSALEM 78      18
        THRONE
EXAMINATION     SEE SELF-EXAMINATION
    [WHAT DOUBT IS VIRTUOUS EVEN HONEST ?THAT DEPENDS ?UPON      386C ANNO WATSON    * MARG
        EXAMINATION]
EXAMINE
    WHY WILT THOU EXAMINE EVERY LITTLE FIBRE OF MY SOUL  .  .  .  265 FOUR ZOAS 1       47
    THOU WILT GO MAD WITH HORROR IF THOU DOST EXAMINE THUS  .  .  265 FOUR ZOAS 1       52
    OF THEM TO DO ME THE JUSTICE TO EXAMINE BEFORE THEY DECIDE    561B EXHIBITION ADV  PROSE
    NOTHING NEED BE DONE BUT TO EXAMINE MY RIVAL'S PROSPECTUS     573C DESC CAT 3      PROSE
    TO ROAST THE FLESH IN FIRE TO EXAMINE THE INFANT'S LIMBS      707 JERUSALEM 68      58
    LET US LOOK LET US EXAMINE IS THE CRUEL BECOME AN INFANT      724 JERUSALEM 81       8
EXAMINED
    AND OLOLON EXAMINED ALL THE COUCHES OF THE DEAD  .  .  .  .   525 MILTON 35         26
EXAMINER
    THE EXAMINER WHOSE VERY NAME IS HUNT  .  .  .  .  .  .  .  .   537 AND HIS LEGS/N    16
    PARTICULARLY IN A SUNDAY PAPER CALD THE EXAMINER PUBLISHD     592C PUB ADDRESS/N   PROSE
EXAMINER'S
    A THING THATS TIED ABOUT THE EXAMINER'S NECK       .  .  .  . 555 BLAKES APL/N 1    11
    A THING THATS TIED AROUND THE EXAMINER'S NECK  .  .  .  .  .  556 BLAKES APL/N 2    20
EXAMINERS
    THAT PAINE DOES [IS] ARE NO [MODEST ENQUIRERS] EXAMINERS     386B ANNO WATSON    * MARG
    AS TO [MODEST ENQUIRERS] EXAMINERS IN THESE POINTS THEY      386C ANNO WATSON    * MARG
EXAMINING
    [EXAMINING THE SINS OF THARMAS I [HAVE] SOON FOUND MY OWN]    268 FOUR ZOAS 1       161
    THE MAN WHO ON EXAMINING HIS OWN MIND  .  .  .  .  .  .  .    458B ANNO REYNOLDS  * MARG
EXAMPLE
    EXAMPLE FOR YOUR REASON AS I WAS WALKING ALONG THE STREET     45A ISLAND MOON 1    PROSE
    ("THE PUBLIC SELDOM FORGIVE TWICE ") LET US TAKE THEIR        85D ANNO LAVATER     MARG
        EXAMPLE
    GIVE ME EXAMPLE OF THY MILDNESS KING OF FURIOUS HAIL STORMS   323 FOUR ZOAS 7       145
    WHICH ARE ONLY AN EXAMPLE OF THE WICKEDNESS & DECEIT   .  .  387B ANNO WATSON      MARG
    OF THE JEWS & WERE WRITTEN AS AN EXAMPLE OF  .  .  .  .  .   387C ANNO WATSON      MARG
    THE FRIENDSHIP OF THESE ROMAN VILLAINS IS A STRANGE EXAMPLE   406D ANNO BACON      MARG
    THE BRITISH INSTITUTION HAS THIS YEAR FOLLOWED ITS EXAMPLE    561B EXHIBITION ADV  PROSE
    INTO AN ORNAMENT & AN EXAMPLE TO BE AVOIDED BY SOME   .  .  . 598C PUB ADDRESS/N   PROSE
    EXAMPLE OF THESE CONTRARY ARTS IS GIVEN US IN THE            600D PUB ADDRESS/N   PROSE
        CHARACTERS
    PITY LET US THEREFORE TAKE EXAMPLE & WARNING O MY SPECTRE     626 JERUSALEM 7       58
    CREATED TO BE THE GREAT EXAMPLE OF HORROR & AGONY ALSO MY     630 JERUSALEM 10      52
    BROTHERS OF ETERNITY THIS MAN WHOSE GREAT EXAMPLE  .  .  .   675 JERUSALEM 45        4
    A PITEOUS EXAMPLE OF OBLIVION TO TEACH THE SONS  .  .  .  .   675 JERUSALEM 45        9
EXAMPLES
    ABOVE HEROIC HAVING SUCH EXAMPLES  .  .  .  .  .  .  .  .  .    23 EDW THIRD/PS 3     80
    ANOTHER BUT IN THE SENTIMENTS & EXAMPLES WHICH  .  .  .  .  . 393B ANNO WATSON      MARG
    AS EXAMPLES GIVEN TO US OF THE PERVERSENESS OF SOME   .  .  . 393B ANNO WATSON      MARG
    THE IMPRESSION WHICH HE RECIEVES FROM A BOOK OF EXAMPLES      393B ANNO WATSON      MARG
EXCEED
    & EXISTENCE WHOSE WAYS & MEANS EXCEED THEIR OWN  .  .  .  .   616B V LAST JUDG/N    PROSE
EXCEEDING
    SO SEEMED HE TO DEPART SHE WONDERED WITH EXCEEDING JOY  .  .   40A SAMSON/PS       PROSE
    AT THEIR EXCEEDING BRIGHTNESS & THE SONS OF ETERNITY SENT     312 FOUR ZOAS 6       34
        THEM GIFTS
    LIVE BECAUSE THE LIFE OF MAN WAS TOO EXCEEDING UNBOUNDED      519 MILTON 30         22
    HE TREMBLED WITH EXCEEDING GREAT TREMBLING & ASTONISHMENT     531 MILTON 39         17
    HE TREMBLED WITH EXCEEDING GREAT TREMBLING & ASTONISHMENT     531 MILTON 39         31
    TREMBLING BEFORE HIM WITH EXCEEDING GREAT TREMBLING & FEAR    531 MILTON 39         47
    THIS IS MY GLORY & EXCEEDING GREAT REWARD  .  .  .  .  .  .  600C PUB ADDRESS/N    PROSE
    LOS WEPT WITH EXCEEDING JOY & ALL WEPT WITH JOY TOGETHER      631 JERUSALEM 11      13
    EXCEEDING JOY THAT IS ALWAYS POURED OUT ON MY SPIRIT   .  .   830B LETTER 30       PROSE
EXCEEDINGLY
    EXCEEDINGLY WITH FEAR & TERROR STANDING IN THE VALE  .  .  .  505 MILTON 22         10
    BUT THE EMANATIONS TREMBLED EXCEEDINGLY NOR COULD THEY  .  .  519 MILTON 30         21
    GUIDE THOU MY HAND WHICH TREMBLES EXCEEDINGLY UPON THE        623 JERUSALEM 5       23
        ROCK OF AGES
    PLEASD HIS RELATIONS EXCEEDINGLY  .  .  .  .  .  .  .  .  .  820C LETTER 25        PROSE
    MY INDIGNATION WAS EXCEEDINGLY MOVED AT READING A  .  .  .  863D LETTER 61        PROSE
```

EXCEEDS
    PROVIDED THAT IT EXCEEDS IN ELEGANCE ALL FORMER METHODS   207B PRSPECTUS 1793 PROSE
EXCELL
    [?THEY EXCELL BOTH IN MINUTE & DISCRIMINATING   453D ANNO REYNOLDS * MARG
      DETERMINATION]
    WHOM I HAVE CONTENDED IN ART HAVE STROVE NOT TO EXCELL BUT 596D PUB ADDRESS/N PROSE
    IN SUSSEX SAY THAT I [?EXCESS] EXCELL IN THE PURSUIT . . 808B LETTER 19   *PROSE
EXCELLENCE
    MECHANICAL EXCELLENCE IS THE ONLY VEHICLE OF GENIUS . 453D ANNO REYNOLDS   MARG
    OF WHICH GROSS VULGARITY FORMS·THE PRINCIPAL EXCELLENCE   464D ANNO REYNOLDS   MARG
EXCELLENCIES
    ("RELISH FOR EXCELLENCIES AN ACQUIRED TASTE") [FOOL] . . SUPP ANNO REYNOLDS * MARG
EXCELLENT
    AY SAID SHE THAT WOULD BE EXCELLENT . . . . 62D ISLAND MOON 11 PROSE
    ("WHO ADHERES TO TRUTH NOR BETRAYS TRUST IS NEAR SUMMIT") 67B ANNO LAVATER   MARG
      EXCELLENT
    ("UNHAPPINESS AT ANOTHER'S ERRORS") EXCELLENT . . . . 73A ANNO LAVATER   MARG
    ("BE NOT THE FOURTH FRIEND OF HIM WHO LOST ") AN   74A ANNO LAVATER   MARG
      EXCELLENT RULE
    ("JUDGE OF YOURSELF...OTHERS") MOST EXCELLENT . . . . 76B ANNO LAVATER   MARG
    ("YOU BEG AS YOU QUESTION AS YOU ANSWER")   77D ANNO LAVATER   MARG
      EXCELLENT
    ("LOVE SEES WHAT NO EYE SEES ") MOST EXCELLENT   77D ANNO LAVATER   MARG
    ("IF YOUR TURN BE PROFUSE AVOID AVARICE") EXCELLENT . 78B ANNO LAVATER   MARG
    ("POET COMPOSES...INSPIRATION...FOR ALL MEN ") MOST   80C ANNO LAVATER   MARG
      EXCELLENT
    ("CROWD OF NOISY IMPOTENT PATRIOTS") EXCELLENT   . . 81A ANNO LAVATER   MARG
    ("NO GIFTS CAN EXHAUST GENIUS IMPOVERISH CHARITY") MOST 84B ANNO LAVATER   MARG
      EXCELLENT
    ("KNOWS HIMSELF WHO NEVER OPPOSES HIS GENIUS")   84C ANNO LAVATER   MARG
      MOST EXCELLENT
    ("FOOL AT BIT OF BREAD TREMBLES POISONED") EXCELLENT   84C ANNO LAVATER   MARG
    ("HATE AS IF YOU COULD LOVE OR SHOULD BE") BETTER THAN 84D ANNO LAVATER   MARG
      EXCELLENT
    ("AVOID CHARACTERS WHOSE GOOD & BAD SIDES UNMIXED")   86D ANNO LAVATER   MARG
      MOST EXCELLENT
    ("AFTER PERFORMING PASSES ON LIKE SAMSON") THIS IS   86D ANNO LAVATER   MARG
      EXCELLENT
    ("THOUGHTS OF ANGELS NOTHING FROM SPACE AND TIME")   92A ANNO SWED LOVE   MARG
      EXCELLENT
    A PLACE IN THE NEW JERUSALEM EXCELLENT TRAVELLER GO ON 404D ANNO BACON   * MARG
      & BE DAMND
    EXCELLENT . . . .   454C ANNO REYNOLDS   MARG
    EXCELLENT . . . .   454D ANNO REYNOLDS   MARG
    EXCELLENT REMARKS . . . .   462D ANNO REYNOLDS   MARG
    THESE REMARKS ON POUSSIN ARE EXCELLENT . . . . . 469C ANNO REYNOLDS   MARG
    EXCELLENT . . . .   476C ANNO REYNOLDS   MARG
    THESE ARE EXCELLENT REMARKS ON (PROPORTIONAL) COLOUR . 479B ANNO REYNOLDS * MARG
    EXCELLENT & CONTRARY TO HIS USUAL OPINIONS .   479C ANNO REYNOLDS   MARG
    TIS EXCELLENT TO TURN A THORN TO A PIN . . . . 544 ON F AND S/N   3
    IT WILL GIVE YOU A GOOD IDEA OF THIS GOOD & EXCELLENT MAN 839B LETTER 38   PROSE
    IT IS A VERY SUBLIME DRAWING & WOULD MAKE AN EXCELLENT   839C LETTER 38   PROSE
      PRINT
    THE DELAY I HAVE SEEN OUR EXCELLENT FLAXMAN LATELY HE IS 842D LETTER 42   PROSE
      WELL
    THEY HAVE GIVEN ME SOME EXCELLENT HINTS IN ENGRAVING . 843B LETTER 43   PROSE
    IT IS A VERY EXCELLENT PICTURE BUT UNFINISHED . . . . . 843C LETTER 43   PROSE
    IF OUR EXCELLENT AND MANLY FRIEND MEYER IS YET WITH YOU 852D LETTER 50   PROSE
    THE DEATH OF SO EXCELLENT A MAN AS MY GENEROUS ADVOCATE 854B LETTER 53   PROSE
EXCELLENTLY
    MYSELF & HIT IT OFF EXCELLENTLY I HAVE NOT SEEN MR ROSE   .834D LETTER 34   PROSE
EXCENTRIC   SEE ECCENTRIC
    TO BE EXCENTRIC IF HE CREATES O HAPPY PHILOSOPHER . . 81C ANNO LAVATER * MARG
    FROM HEAVEN TO HEAVEN FROM GLOBE TO GLOBE IN VAST   320 FOUR ZOAS 6   319
      EXCENTRIC PATHS
EXCEPT
    EXCEPT WHEN I GO TO MR JACKO'S HE KNOWS WHAT RIDING IS . . 53A ISLAND MOON 8 PROSE
    DISCRETE & NOT CONTINUOUS SO AS TO EXPLAIN EACH OTHER   93A ANNO SWED LOVE   MARG
      EXCEPT
    EXCEPT WHAT HIS LITTLE ORBS . . . .   230 URIZEN 13   31
    AND OVERWHELMED ALL EXCEPT THIS FINITE WALL OF FLESH . 241 EUROPE 10   20
    EXCEPT IS CHRIST YOU LIE EXCEPT DID ANYONE EVER DO THIS 400D ANNO BACON   MARG
    & NEVER CAN BE EXCEPT FACTIOUS IS CHRISTIANITY . . . 403A ANNO BACON   MARG
    EXCEPT PRETENCE TO BE RICH IF THAT IS IT . . . . 409A ANNO BACON   MARG
    EXCEPT IT BE A WOMAN OLD . . . .   427 MENTAL TRAVLER   102
    UNEMPLOYD EXCEPT BY HIS OWN ENERGY . . . .   445C ANNO REYNOLDS   MARG
    SOME MEN CANNOT SEE A PICTURE EXCEPT IN A DARK CORNER . 476A ANNO REYNOLDS   MARG
    NEVER IS THE CASE EXCEPT IN THE ROMAN & FLORENTINE SCHOOLS 479B ANNO REYNOLDS   MARG
    EXCEPT BY MIRACLE & A NEW BIRTH THE OTHER TWO CLASSES . 511 MILTON 25   34
    THE ENEMIES OF HUMANITY EXCEPT IN A FEMALE FORM . . . 527 MILTON 36   15
    EXCEPT REMOTELY AND I HEARD OLOLON SAY TO MILTON . . . . 532 MILTON 40   3
    EXCEPT BY BLUNDERING IGNORANCE TILL AFTER VANDYKE'S TIME 566C DESC CAT 2   PROSE
    AND BLOCKS UP ALL ITS GATES OF LIGHT EXCEPT ONE . . . . 583A DESC CAT 9   PROSE
    OR PICTURES EXCEPT THAT THE FRESCOS OR PICTURES ARE . . 584D DESC CAT 15   PROSE
    WHEREAS GOD EXISTS NOT EXCEPT FROM THEIR EFFLUVIA . . 789A ANNO THORNTON   MARG
    EXCEPT WHAT COMES TO HER FROM HEAVEN . . . .   818 HAPPINESS/L   62
    EXCEPT PAPER WHICH IS JOHNSON'S FAULT COWPER IS FAR THE 847A LETTER 44   PROSE
      BEST
    EXCEPT AT PRIVATE PRESSES I HOPE THIS WILL BECOME A SOURCE 859C LETTER 56   PROSE
    WHO SHALL SAY EXCEPT THE NATURAL RELIGIONISTS . . . . . 865B LETTER 62   *PROSE
    THIS EXCEPT IT BE THE MORNING AIR & THAT IN MY COUSIN'S 870D LETTER 72   PROSE
      TIME

	PAGE	TITLE	LINE

EXCEPT   (CONTINUED)
    I GO ON JUST AS IF PERFECTLY WELL WHICH INDEED I· AM EXCEPT   873C LETTER 77   PROSE
    CANNOT PRINT MORE EXCEPT AT A GREAT LOSS FOR AT THE TIME   878C LETTER 88   PROSE
EXCEPTED
    SOME OF THE PERSONS EXCEPTED I HAVE WRITTEN THIS POEM   . . 823A LETTER 26   PROSE
EXCEPTION
    TO EXCEPTION & NOT TO RULE TO ACCIDENT & NOT TO SUBSTANCE   778C HOMERS POETRY   PROSE
EXCEPTIONS
    OR GO INTO A MODERN EXHIBITON WITH A VERY FEW EXCEPTIONS   599B PUB ADDRESS/N   PROSE
    BUT NEGATIONS EXIST NOT EXCEPTIONS & OBJECTIONS & UNBELIEFS   639 JERUSALEM 17   34
EXCESS
    THE ROAD OF EXCESS LEADS TO THE PALACE OF WISDOM . . . . 150D MARRIAGE HH 7   PROSE
    EXCESS OF SORROW LAUGHS EXCESS OF JOY WEEPS   . . . . . 151C MARRIAGE HH 8   PROSE
    THE DEVOURER AS A SEA RECIEVED THE EXCESS OF HIS DELIGHTS   155B MARRIAGE HH 15   PROSE
    HOW ART THOU SHRUNK THY GRAPES THAT BURST IN SUMMER'S VAST   325 FOUR ZOAS 7   190
        EXCESS
    BEAT ROUND HER HEAD ALL NIGHT ALL DAY SHE RIOTS IN EXCESS   334 FOUR ZOAS 7B   74
    EXCESS OF JOY IS WORSE THAN GRIEF HER HEART BEAT HIGH HER   362 FOUR ZOAS 9   197
        BLOOD
    O TREMBLING JOY EXCESS OF JOY IS LIKE EXCESS OF GRIEF   376 FOUR ZOAS 9   730
    EXCESS IN YOUTH IS NECESSARY TO LIFE . . . . 408B ANNO BACON   MARG
    OF GRATITUDE OR FRIENDSHIP BUT PERHAPS AN EXCESS OF BOTH   798D LETTER 10   PROSE
    IN SUSSEX SAY THAT I [?EXCESS] EXCELL IN THE·PURSUIT   . . 808B LETTER 19   *PROSE
    I WISH HER A CONTINUED EXCESS OF HAPPINESS SOME SAY THAT   830C LETTER 30   PROSE
EXCESSIVE
    HE IS THIN WITH EXCESSIVE LABOUR . . . . 571B DESC CAT 3   PROSE
EXCHANGD
    [OF PITY ARE EXCHANGD FOR THOSE] . . . . 186 LET BROTHELS/N *   41
EXCHANGE
    WHO WILL EXCHANGE HIS OWN FIRE SIDE   . . . . . . 186 LET BROTHELS/N   46
    WHO WILL EXCHANGE HIS WHEATEN LOAF   . . . . . . 186 LET BROTHELS/N   48
    [WHO WILL EXCHANGE HIS OWN HEART'S BLOOD] . . . . 186 LET BROTHELS/N   50
    [WILL THE MOTHER EXCHANGE HER NEW BORN BABE] . . . 186 LET BROTHELS/N   52
    [YET THOU DOST EXCHANGE THY PITYING TEARS] . . . . 186 LET BROTHELS/N   54
    [IN EXCHANGE FOR THE TEARS OF SORROW] . . ..· . . 186 LET BROTHELS/N   59
    WHO WILL EXCHANGE HIS OWN FIRE SIDE   . . . . . . 186 LET BROTHELS/N   64
    WHO WILL EXCHANGE HIS WHEATEN LOAF   . . . . . . 186 LET BROTHELS/N   66
    OR WHO WILL EXCHANGE HIS NEW BORN CHILD . . .· . . 186 LET BROTHELS/N   70
EXCHANGES
    IN THE EXCHANGES OF LONDON EVERY NATION WALKD . . . 647 JERUSALEM 24   42
    IN MY EXCHANGES EVERY LAND . . . . 652 FIELDS FROM/J   85
EXCLUDED
    AND HAS EFFECTUALLY EXCLUDED ME BY THIS RESOLUTION   . . 561B EXHIBITION ADV   PROSE
    SUBSCRIBERS TO INSPECT WHAT THEY HAVE EXCLUDED AND THOSE   561B EXHIBITION ADV   PROSE
    OF SOCIETY ARE EASILY EXCLUDED BUT NOT SO EASILY   561C EXHIBITION ADV   PROSE
        OBSTRUCTED
    THEY HAVE (EXCLUDED) WATER-COLOURS IT IS THEREFORE   . . 561C EXHIBITION ADV   PROSE
    THEIR PRODUCING FOR AGES BACK WHILE PAINTING IS EXCLUDED   601A PUB ADDRESS/N   PROSE
EXCLUSIVE
    EXCLUSIVE OF CONSCIENCE OR THE WORD OF GOD UNIVERSAL   . . 389C ANNO WATSON   MARG
    THESE ARE NEITHER THE EXCLUSIVE PROPERTY OF HUME GIBBON NOR 579A DESC CAT 5   PROSE
EXCLUSIVELY
    THAT THE JEWS ASSUMED A RIGHT EXCLUSIVELY TO THE BENEFITS   389A ANNO WATSON   MARG
    THOSE WHO WILL HAVE UNITY EXCLUSIVELY IN HOMER   . . . 778B HOMERS POETRY   PROSE
EXCREMENT
    HIS SHADOWS ARE OF A FILTHY BROWN SOMEWHAT OF THE COLOUR   469A ANNO REYNOLDS   MARG
        OF EXCREMENT
    BY ENTERING INTO DISEASE AND EXCREMENT DRUNKENNESS   . . 582A DESC CAT 8   PROSE
EXCREMENTITIOUS
    FOR I WILL MAKE THEIR PLACES OF JOY & LOVE EXCREMENTITIOUS   734 JERUSALEM 88   39
    . . .CIRCUMSCRIBING & CIRCUMCISING THE EXCREMENTITIOUS   745 JERUSALEM 98   18
EXCRUCIATING
    EASILY REMOVED BUT EXCRUCIATING WHILE IT LASTS & ENFEEBLING   871A LETTER 72   PROSE
EXCULPATING
    HIMSELF EXCULPATING WITH MILDEST SPEECH FOR HIMSELF BELIEVD   487 MILTON 8   2
EXCUSE
    I HOPE THEIR LORDSHIPS WILL EXCUSE YOUR GIDDINESS   . . . 20 EDW THIRD/PS 2   64
    CHRIST'S CRUCIFIX SHALL BE MADE AN EXCUSE FOR EXECUTING   380A FOUR ZOAS NOTE PROSE
        CRIMINALS
    IF HE IS WICKED HE WILL MAKE THEIR WICKEDNESS AN EXCUSE   393C ANNO WATSON   MARG
    POETRY IS TO EXCUSE VICE & SHEW ITS REASON & NECESSARY   412C ANNO BOYD   MARG
        PURGATION
    I HOPE MY COUNTRYMEN WILL EXCUSE ME IF I TELL THEM   599A PUB ADDRESS/N   PROSE
        A WHOLESOME TRUTH
    HOWEVER ADMIRABLE THAT TRACK MAY BE AT ANY RATE MY EXCUSE   792A LETTER 4   PROSE
    EXCUSE I INTREAT YOU MY NOT RETURNING THANKS AT THE PROPER   798A LETTER 10   PROSE
    FEAR THEY WILL NOT EXCUSE & I KNOW NOT HOW TO [XXX]   798B LETTER 10   *PROSE
        APOLOGIZE FOR
    EXCUSE THIS COMMUNICATION OF SENTIMENTS WHICH I FELT   . . 798C LETTER 10   PROSE
    YOU A FEW LINES WHICH I HOPE YOU WILL EXCUSE AND AS THE   799A LETTER 11   PROSE
        TIME
    WHENEVER SHE HEARS IT NAMED EXCUSE MY HASTE & . . . . 801C LETTER 13   PROSE
    MRS BUTTS WILL I HOPE EXCUSE MY NOT HAVING FINISHD THE   806A LETTER 16   PROSE
        PORTRAIT I
    MRS BUTTS WILL EXCUSE THE FOLLOWING LINES . . . . . 806B LETTER 16   PROSE
    I HOPE YOU WILL CONTINUE TO EXCUSE MY WANT OF STEADY   . . 808D LETTER 20   PROSE
    INTREAT YOU TO EXCUSE FAULTS FOR PORTRAIT PAINTING IS THE   815C LETTER 23   PROSE
        DIRECT
    EXCUSE MY PERHAPS TOO GREAT ENTHUSIASM PLEASE TO ACCEPT OF   823C LETTER 26   PROSE
    I ONLY SUGGEST WHAT I KNOW YOU WILL BE KIND ENOUGH   828B LETTER 28   PROSE
        TO EXCUSE
    WITH AN ACCOUNT OF HIS SAFE ARRIVAL WHICH WILL EXCUSE HIS   829C LETTER 30   PROSE

```
                                                             PAGE      TITLE          LINE
EXCUSE    (CONTINUED)
     BUT HOWEVER AS SOME LITTLE EXCUSE I MUST SAY THAT   . . .  847B LETTER 44        PROSE
     I HOPE YOU WILL EXCUSE MY DELAY IN SENDING THE BOOKS  .   850A LETTER 49         PROSE
     WHO WAS MY ENEMY DEAR SIR EXCUSE MY ENTHUSIASM OR RATHER  852C LETTER 50         PROSE
     EXCUSE FOR TROUBLING YOU BEFORE IT CAN BE PROPERLY CALLED 853C LETTER 52         PROSE
     FRIENDS EXCUSE THIS EFFUSION OF THE SPIRIT FROM ONE WHO   862D LETTER 60         PROSE
     EXCUSE THE WRITING I HAVE DELAYED TOO LONG  . . . . .  871D LETTER 73            PROSE
     PRAY EXCUSE THIS HEARTY EXPOSTULATION   . . . . . .  874B LETTER 79              PROSE
     BUT MUST BEG YOU TO EXCUSE SUCH FOLLIES WHICH THO I AM  . 875D LETTER 82         PROSE
EXCUSES
     YOU CAN FIND FRIENDLY EXCUSES FOR ME CHANDOS  . . . . .  27 EDW THIRD/PS 3        277
EXECRATED
     EMPLOYERS OF FOOLS TO BE EXECRATED IN   . . . . . .  452C ANNO REYNOLDS          MARG
EXECUTE
     LEARN TO DESIGN FROM RAFAEL & TO EXECUTE FROM RUBENS XXX  449A ANNO REYNOLDS      MARG
     HOW TO EXECUTE WHAT THEY COULD NOT THINK OR INVENT  .  467C ANNO REYNOLDS        MARG
     TO EXECUTE THESE TWO PICTURES ON A SCALE THAT IS SUITABLE 566A DESC CAT 2        PROSE
     WHEN THE ARTIST TOOK HIS PENCIL TO EXECUTE HIS IDEAS  . 582C DESC CAT 9          PROSE
     CAUSES TO THE FLORENTINE AND ROMAN ARTIST FEAR TO EXECUTE 583A DESC CAT 9        PROSE
     AFFECTATION & FOPPERY HE WHO COPIES DOES NOT EXECUTE  . 596B PUB ADDRESS/N        PROSE
     THAT GREAT INVENTORS CANNOT EXECUTE THIS OPINION IS  . . 601D PUB ADDRESS/N      PROSE
     THIS HE CAN CONCIEVE BUT HE CANNOT EXECUTE  . . . . . 602A PUB ADDRESS/N         PROSE
     CAN EXECUTE THEM IN ANY MANNER  . . . . . . . . . .  790B LETTER 2               PROSE
     & I SAY HE WHO INVENT CAN EXECUTE   . . . . . . . .  790C LETTER 2               PROSE
     COMMISSION TO (EXECUTE) FOR YOU BUT SHALL NOT BE  . . . 826D LETTER 28          *PROSE
     EVERY ENGRAVER TURNS AWAY WORK THAT HE CANNOT EXECUTE  . 829D LETTER 30          PROSE
     TO EXECUTE ANY WORK I NEED ONLY REFER TO THE LITTLE JOB  847A LETTER 44          PROSE
EXECUTED
     HAND WHICH EXECUTED THESE LITTLE IDEAS BEEN THAT         439C REMARKS MALKIN     PROSE
         OF A PLAGIARY
     AND ALL THE GRAND WORKS OF ANCIENT ART THEY WERE EXECUTED 565D DESC CAT 2        PROSE
     AFTERWARD EXECUTED FOR A LADY OF HIGH RANK AN EXPERIMENT 582B DESC CAT 9         TITLE
         PICTURE
     BETTER AND HIGHER AND THE POOR WRETCH WHO EXECUTED IT  . 583C DESC CAT 9         PROSE
     HE ONLY IMITATES WHAT IS ALREADY EXECUTED   . . . . .  596B PUB ADDRESS/N        PROSE
     HIS CHIEF BEAUTIES BUT THERE ARE SOME WHICH MAY BE EXECUTED 848A LETTER 45       PROSE
     THAT I MAY PUT IT INTO A TRAIN TO BE PROPERLY EXECUTED  . 849B LETTER 45         PROSE
     EXECUTED & COULD NOT BE BETTER DONE   . . . . . . . .  857B LETTER 54            PROSE
     THEY NEVER COULD HAVE BEEN EXECUTED   . . . . . . . .  867A LETTER 66            PROSE
EXECUTING
     CHRIST'S CRUCIFIX SHALL BE MADE AN EXCUSE FOR EXECUTING  380A FOUR ZOAS NOTE     PROSE
         CRIMINALS
     CONCERNING THE POSSIBILITY OF EXECUTING WITHOUT A MODEL  582C DESC CAT 9         PROSE
EXECUTION
     INVENTION DEPENDS ALTOGETHER UPON EXECUTION   . . . . .  446D ANNO REYNOLDS      MARG
     WHOEVER IS SET TO UNDERMINE THE EXECUTION OF ART IS SET TO 447A ANNO REYNOLDS    MARG
     ON MICHAEL ANGELO'S EXECUTION ALTOGETHER   . . . . .  447A ANNO REYNOLDS         MARG
     IMITATION OF FACILITY IN EXECUTION OR ARE WE TO UNDERSTAND 453D ANNO REYNOLDS    MARG
     EXECUTION IS THE CHARIOT OF GENIUS   . . . . . . . .  454A ANNO REYNOLDS         MARG
     WITHOUT MINUTE NEATNESS OF EXECUTION THE SUBLIME CANNOT  457D ANNO REYNOLDS      MARG
     OF EXECUTION IN ART LET HIM WHO WILL FOLLOW SUCH ADVICE  461C ANNO REYNOLDS      MARG
     KNOW THAT THE MAN'S EXECUTION IS AS HIS CONCEPTION & NO  461C ANNO REYNOLDS      MARG
         BETTER
     NOT ADMIRE RAFAEL'S EXECUTION DOES NOT EVEN SEE RAFAEL  . 467A ANNO REYNOLDS     MARG
     THE STUDY OF RAFAEL & MICH ANGELO'S EXECUTION   . . . .  468A ANNO REYNOLDS      MARG
     HE WHO ADMIRES RAFAEL MUST ADMIRE RAFAEL'S EXECUTION  . 472A ANNO REYNOLDS       MARG
     HE WHO DOES NOT ADMIRE RAFAEL'S EXECUTION CANNOT ADMIRE  472A ANNO REYNOLDS      MARG
         RAFAEL
     HIS [EXECUTION] EXECUTIVE POWER MUST I DESPISE   . . . .  547 RAFAEL SUBLI/N *      2
     HIS POWER OF EXECUTION I MUST GRANT   . . . . . . .  547 RAFAEL SUBLI/N            4
     THE EXECUTION OF MY DESIGNS . . . . . . . . . . . .  561B EXHIBITION ADV         PROSE
     EXECUTION OF THIS PICTURE IS ALSO IN WATER COLOURS      577B DESC CAT 4          PROSE
         OR FRESCO
     THEY CAUSE THAT THE EXECUTION SHALL BE ALL BLOCKED UP  . 582C DESC CAT 9         PROSE
     OF APPROPRIATE EXECUTION RESULTING FROM THE INVENTIONS  . 582D DESC CAT 9         PROSE
     THE REMEMBRANCES OF HIS PICTURES AND STYLE OF EXECUTION  582D DESC CAT 9         PROSE
     OF EXECUTION IN ART MR B(BLAKE) HAS NOW PUT TO THE TEST  591B PUB ADDRESS/N       PROSE
     NOR CAN AN ORIGINAL INVENTION EXIST WITHOUT EXECUTION  . 595C PUB ADDRESS/N      PROSE
     SAY GIVE ME THE DESIGN IT IS NO MATTER FOR THE EXECUTION 596A PUB ADDRESS/N      PROSE
     MADE WITHOUT ITS MINUTELY APPROPRIATE EXECUTION   . . .  596A PUB ADDRESS/N      PROSE
     UNAPPROPRIATE EXECUTION IS THE MOST NAUSEOUS OF ALL  . . 596B PUB ADDRESS/N      PROSE
     EXECUTION IS ONLY THE RESULT OF INVENTION   . . . . .  596B PUB ADDRESS/N        PROSE
     CONSEQUENTLY HIS (EXECUTION) MUST HAVE BEEN AS QUEER  . 596C PUB ADDRESS/N       *PROSE
     WITH THE EXECUTION OF TITIAN RUBENS COREGGIO REMBRANT  . 599B PUB ADDRESS/N      *PROSE
     EVEN HOGARTH'S EXECUTION CANNOT BE COPIED OR IMPROVED  . 599C PUB ADDRESS/N      PROSE
     CAN ITS EXECUTION BE ANY OTHER THAN THE WORK OF A BLOCKHEAD 599C PUB ADDRESS/N   PROSE
     OF THE MOST PROFOUND SENSE A GENIUS & YET HIS EXECUTION  599D PUB ADDRESS/N      PROSE
     & WE ARE [WE] TO IMITATE THEIR EXECUTION THIS IS [AS IF]  599D PUB ADDRESS/N     PROSE
     I KNOW MY EXECUTION IS NOT LIKE ANY BODY ELSE I DO NOT  . 601D PUB ADDRESS/N     PROSE
     TO BE SUPERIOR MY EXECUTION WILL BE FOUND SO TOO  . . . 601D PUB ADDRESS/N       PROSE
     JUST EQUAL IN INVENTION & IN EXECUTION AS MY WORKS SHEW  602A PUB ADDRESS/N      PROSE
     DRAWING IS EXECUTION & NOTHING ELSE   . . . . . . . .  602B PUB ADDRESS/N        PROSE
     THAT EXECUTION IS THE POWER OF ONE & INVENTION OF ANOTHER 790B LETTER 2          PROSE
     YOUR PLAN FOR A NATIONAL GALLERY BEING PUT INTO EXECUTION 797C LETTER 10         PROSE
     CARRIED INTO EXECUTION AS IT MUST BE IF ENGLAND CONTINUES 797C LETTER 10         PROSE
     & RESUMED MY PRIMITIVE & ORIGINAL WAYS OF EXECUTION IN BOTH 812B LETTER 22       PROSE
     IS NECESSARY TO THE EXECUTION OF ROMNEY'S DESIGNS  . . . 844B LETTER 43          PROSE
EXECUTIONER
     SATAN'S HOLY TRINITY THE ACCUSER THE JUDGE & THE        SUPP INSC OUR END        *TITLE
         EXECUTIONER
EXECUTIVE
     TO REPRESENT VULGAR ARTISTS AS THE MODELS OF EXECUTIVE  465D ANNO REYNOLDS        MARG
         MERIT
```

```
                                                              PAGE    TITLE          LINE
EXECUTIVE    (CONTINUED)
    HIS [EXECUTION] EXECUTIVE POWER MUST I DESPISE   . . . .   547 RAFAEL SUBLI/N *    2
    IF TO INVENT & TO DRAW WELL HINDERS THE EXECUTIVE POWER IN 591B PUB ADDRESS/N   PROSE
    TO MY INVENTIONS THE EXECUTIVE PART THEY NEVER DISPUTED    601D PUB ADDRESS/N   PROSE
EXEMPLARS
    IN NEW EXPANSES CREATING EXEMPLARS OF MEMORY AND          746 JERUSALEM 98      30
        OF INTELLECT
EXEMPTED
    NOR KNEW THAT I ALONE EXEMPTED FROM THE JOYS OF LOVE  . .  325 FOUR ZOAS 7      200
    FROM NEITHER PAIN NOR GRIEF EXEMPTED . . . . . . . . .     756 EV GOSPEL(I)/N    12
EXERCISE
    I SAW THE LIMBS FORMD FOR EXERCISE CONTEMND & THE BEAUTY OF 628 JERUSALEM 9       7
    OF BODY & MIND TO EXERCISE THE DIVINE ARTS OF IMAGINATION 716D JERUSALEM 77    PROSE
EXERCISED
    PROPER MY TALENTS SHALL BE PROPERLY EXERCISED IN PUBLIC   812A LETTER 22       PROSE
EXERTION
    & [LOVE] ME FOR THIS ENERGETIC EXERTION OF MY TALENT   .  621B JERUSALEM 3     PROSE
    FOR ALL SUCH WHO MAY BE LED TO SUCH OSTENTATIOUS EXERTION 871A LETTER 72       PROSE
EXERTIONS
    ("DURABILITY TO HIS EXERTIONS") UNEASY STERLING  . . . .   69D ANNO LAVATER     MARG
    TO PROMOTE THE SPIRITED EXERTIONS OF MY FRIEND CROMEK  .  861D LETTER 59       PROSE
EXETER
    GLOUCESTER AND EXETER AND SALISBURY AND BRISTOL AND       668 JERUSALEM 40      61
        BENEVOLENT BATH
    THRO ROCHESTER AND CHICHESTER & EXETER & SALISBURY   . .  704 JERUSALEM 67      36
EXEUNT
    EXEUNT  . . . . . . . . . . . . . . . . . . . . . . . .    19A EDW THIRD/PS 1  PROSE
    EXEUNT  . . . . . . . . . . . . . . . . . . . . . . . .    21B EDW THIRD/PS 2  PROSE
    [EXEUNT] EXIT KING EDWARD  . . . . . . . . . . . . . .     26C EDW THIRD/PS 3  PROSE
    EXEUNT  . . . . . . . . . . . . . . . . . . . . . . . .    28A EDW THIRD/PS 3  PROSE
    FOR NOT FLATTERING THE EARL OF WARWICK EXEUNT   . . . .    30A EDW THIRD/PS 4  PROSE
    EXEUNT  . . . . . . . . . . . . . . . . . . . . . . . .    31C EDW THIRD/PS 5  PROSE
EXHALATIONS
    IN BEAUTEOUS ORDER THENCE AROSE SOFT CLOUDS & EXHALATIONS 286 FOUR ZOAS 2      253
EXHALD
    SHE BOWD OVER THE WEEPING INFANT AND HER LIFE EXHALD   .  129 BOOK OF THEL 4     8
    AND LUVAH & VALA SAW THE LIGHT THEIR SPIRITS WERE EXHALD  372 FOUR ZOAS 9      571
EXHALE
    TO EXHALE THE SPIRITS OF LUVAH & VALA THRO THE ATMOSPHERE 372 FOUR ZOAS 9      570
EXHALES
    EXHALES ON HIGH  . . . . . . . . . . . . . . . . . . .    421 MORNING/N          9
EXHAUST
    ("NO GIFTS CAN EXHAUST GENIUS IMPOVERISH CHARITY") MOST    84B ANNO LAVATER     MARG
        EXCELLENT
    AND THE FURY OF MAN EXHAUST IN WAR WOMAN PERMANENT REMAIN 725 JERUSALEM 82      35
EXHAUSTED
    OF LUVAH QUITE EXHAUSTED WITH THE LABOUR & QUITE FILLD    378 FOUR ZOAS 9      786
    BUT WHEN THE JOY OF MEETING WAS EXHAUSTED IN LOVING EMBRACE 631 JERUSALEM 11    16
    WOMAN HAS EXHAUSTED HER STRENGTH TO SUCH A DEGREE WITH  . 801B LETTER 13       PROSE
EXHIBIT
    BECOME NECESSARY THAT I SHOULD EXHIBIT TO THE PUBLIC IN   561C EXHIBITION ADV  PROSE
    OFFERING TO EXHIBIT MY (TWO) LAST PICTURES IN THE GALLERY 826C LETTER 28       PROSE
EXHIBITED
    ARE REGULARLY REFUSED TO BE EXHIBITED BY THE ROYAL ACADEMY 561B EXHIBITION ADV PROSE
        AND
    THE WORKS NOW EXHIBITED WILL GIVE THE LIE TO SUCH        572D DESC CAT 3       PROSE
        ASPERSIONS
    THE FUN AFTERWARDS EXHIBITED ON THE ROAD MAY BE SEEN   .  588C CHAUCER/N       PROSE
EXHIBITING
    GOLDEN-SQUARE WHERE THE PICTURE IS NOW EXHIBITING   . . . 587B CHAUCER 1       PROSE
    P S YOUR OBLIGING PROPOSAL OF EXHIBITING MY TWO  . . . . 813D LETTER 22       PROSE
    YOU FOR YOUR KIND OFFER OF EXHIBITING MY (TWO) PICTURES THE 826C LETTER 28     PROSE
EXHIBITION
    IF I DONT KNOCK THEM ALL UP NEXT YEAR IN THE EXHIBITION    51D ISLAND MOON 7   PROSE
    EXHIBITION OF PAINTINGS IN FRESCO POETICAL AND HISTORICAL 560A EXHIBITION ADV  TITLE
        INVENTIONS
    AN EXHIBITION OF MY OWN MY DESIGNS PAINTED IN WATER-COLOURS 561C EXHIBITION ADV PROSE
    MY EXHIBITION AS THE GREATEST OF DUTIES TO MY COUNTRY  .  561C EXHIBITION ADV  PROSE
    A DESCRIPTIVE CATALOGUE OF BLAKE'S EXHIBITION  . . . . .  562A DESC CAT ADV    TITLE
    IN THIS EXHIBITION WILL BE SEEN REAL ART   . . . . . .    562B DESC CAT ADV    PROSE
    AT THE TIME OF PURCHASE TO VIEW THE EXHIBITION   . . . .  562C DESC CAT ADV    PROSE
    ADMITTANCE TO THE EXHIBITION (ONE) SHILLING   . . . . .   562C DESC CAT ADV    PROSE
    THE PICTURES AND DRAWINGS TO REMAIN IN THE EXHIBITION     563B DESC CAT        PROSE
    OR BE HINDERED FROM THE PUBLIC EXHIBITION  . . . . . .    573A DESC CAT 3      PROSE
    ROMAN SCHOOLS MAY BE REMOVED BY AN EXHIBITION  . . . .    582C DESC CAT 9      PROSE
    ANOTHER OF THE EXHIBITION WHICH I HAVE NOT YET SEEN   . .  844C LETTER 43      PROSE
    COUNT UGOLINO BY MR FUSELI IN THE ROYAL ACADEMY EXHIBITION 863D LETTER 61      PROSE
    MY EXHIBITION WITH A VISIT  . . . . . . . . . . . . .     866B LETTER 64       PROSE
EXHIBITIONS
    DOES NOT THROW HIS CONTEMPT ON SUCH TRADING EXHIBITIONS   452C ANNO REYNOLDS    MARG
EXHIBITON
    OR GO INTO A MODERN EXHIBITON WITH A VERY FEW EXCEPTIONS  599B PUB ADDRESS/N   PROSE
EXILD
    HIS CHILDREN EXILD FROM HIS BREAST PASS TO AND FRO BEFORE 641 JERUSALEM 19       1
        HIM
EXILED    SEE SELF-EXILED
    MY SONS EXILED FROM MY BREAST PASS TO & FRO BEFORE ME  .  359 FOUR ZOAS 9      100
    AND ALL EXILED FROM THE FACE OF LIGHT & SHINE OF MORNING  360 FOUR ZOAS 9      112
EXIST
    NOW BOTH EVIL & GOOD CANNOT EXIST IN A SIMPLE BEING  . .   80A ANNO LAVATER     MARG
    THEY EXIST LITERALLY ABOUT THE SUN & NOT ABOUT THE EARTH   92B ANNO SWED LOVE   MARG
    NO VIRTUE CAN EXIST WITHOUT BREAKING THESE TEN COMMANDMENTS 158C MARRIAGE HH 22 PROSE
```

```
                                                              PAGE    TITLE          LINE
EXIST     (CONTINUED)
     CANNOT EXIST BUT FROM THE UNIVERSAL BROTHERHOOD OF EDEN    264  FOUR ZOAS 1        10
     THO PAINED TO DISTRACTION CRY O LET US EXIST FOR  . . .    376  FOUR ZOAS 9       738
     EXIST GRANDEUR OF IDEAS IS FOUNDED ON PRECISION OF IDEAS   457D ANNO REYNOLDS    MARG
     DISTINCT GENERAL FORM CANNOT EXIST  . . . . . . . . .      461B ANNO REYNOLDS    MARG
     BUT THEIR FORMS ETERNAL EXIST FOR-EVER AMEN HALLEUJAH      522  MILTON 32       *  38
     A DESCRIPTION OF THE ETERNAL PRINCIPLES THAT EXIST IN ALL  571A DESC CAT 3      PROSE
       AGES
     EXPRESSION CANNOT EXIST WITHOUT CHARACTER AS ITS STAMINA   585A DESC CAT 15     PROSE
     AND NEITHER CHARACTER NOR EXPRESSION CAN EXIST  . . . .    585A DESC CAT 15     PROSE
     DRAWN OUT UPON IT BEFORE MAN OR BEAST CAN EXIST . . . .    585C DESC CAT 15     PROSE
     NOR CAN AN ORIGINAL INVENTION EXIST WITHOUT EXECUTION .    595C PUB ADDRESS/N   PROSE
     & [FOR A SMALL MOMENT] TEMPORAL THERE EXIST IN THAT ETERNAL 605D V LAST JUDG/N  PROSE
       WORLD
     & HEAT WAS NOT EXTINGUISHD THESE STATES EXIST NOW  . . .   606D V LAST JUDG/N   PROSE
     THE PLACES HE HAS PASSED THRO EXIST NO MORE . . . . .      606D V LAST JUDG/N   PROSE
     EXIST NO MORE EVERY THING IS ETERNAL . . . . . . . .       606D V LAST JUDG/N   PROSE
     ETERNAL REALITIES AS THEY EXIST IN THE HUMAN IMAGINATION   613C V LAST JUDG/N   PROSE
     MORAL VIRTUES DO NOT EXIST THEY ARE [EL ] ALLEGORIES & .   614D V LAST JUDG/N  *PROSE
     WHAT SHALL I DO OR HOW EXIST DIVIDED FROM ENITHARMON  .    631  JERUSALEM 12       9
     NEGATIONS ARE NOT CONTRARIES CONTRARIES MUTUALLY EXIST     639  JERUSALEM 17      33
     BUT NEGATIONS EXIST NOT EXCEPTIONS & OBJECTIONS & UNBELIEFS 639 JERUSALEM 17      34
     EXIST NOT NOR SHALL THEY EVER BE ORGANIZED FOR EVER & EVER 639  JERUSALEM 17      35
     ART & SCIENCE CANNOT EXIST BUT BY NAKED BEAUTY DISPLAYD    663  JERUSALEM 36      49
     WHICH IF MAN CEASES TO BEHOLD HE CEASES TO EXIST  . . .    664  JERUSALEM 38      13
     FOUND NO FRIEND FRIENDSHIP CANNOT EXIST WITHOUT FORGIVENESS 682D JERUSALEM 52    PROSE
     FOR ART & SCIENCE CANNOT EXIST BUT IN MINUTELY ORGANIZED   687  JERUSALEM 55      62
       PARTICULARS
     IS A THEATRE ARE THEY TWO & NOT ONE CAN THEY EXIST SEPARATE 689 JERUSALEM 57       9
     THAT RAHAB & TIRZAH MAY EXIST & LIVE & BREATHE & LOVE  .   692  JERUSALEM 59      43
     FOR ALL THINGS EXIST IN THE HUMAN IMAGINATION . . . .      707  JERUSALEM 69      25
     ALBION REPLYD CANNOT MAN EXIST WITHOUT MYSTERIOUS  . .     743  JERUSALEM 96      20
     ETERNALLY CAN MAN COULD NOT EXIST FOR MAN IS LOVE  . .     743  JERUSALEM 96      26
     IN THE DIVINE IMAGE NOR CAN MAN EXIST BUT BY BROTHERHOOD   743  JERUSALEM 96      28
     ART CAN NEVER EXIST WITHOUT NAKED BEAUTY DISPLAYED . . .   776D INSC LAOCOON     PROSE
     & GOD IS THE GHOST OF THE PRIEST & KING WHO EXIST  . .     789A ANNO THORNTON    MARG
     AS IF I DID NOT EXIST & SINCE MY YOUNG'S NIGHT THOUGHTS    795C LETTER 6         PROSE
       HAVE
     TO OPPOSE FLORENTINE & VENETIAN ART CANNOT EXIST TOGETHER  866B LETTER 64        PROSE
     & ROMAN CANNOT EXIST THIS WILL BE SHORTLY ACCOMPLISHD .    866B LETTER 64        PROSE
     DOES NOT EXIST THESE ARE POLITICIANS & THINK  . . . .      878A LETTER 88        PROSE
EXISTED
     CAN THAT WHICH HAS EXISTED CEASE OR CAN LOVE & LIFE EXPIRE 345  FOUR ZOAS 8       170
     EXISTED JONAH WAS NO PROPHET IN THE MODERN SENSE . . .     392A ANNO WATSON      MARG
     SUPPOSING SUCH CONVERSATION TO HAVE EXISTED . . . . .      437D BLAKES MEMORAN   PROSE
     THE BIBLE SAYS THAT CULTIVATED LIFE EXISTED FIRST  . .     446C ANNO REYNOLDS    MARG
     COMPARE THE MODERN ART WITH THE ART AS IT EXISTED  . .     592A PUB ADDRESS/N    PROSE
     AND ALL THAT HAS EXISTED IN THE SPACE OF SIX THOUSAND YEARS 634 JERUSALEM 13      59
     WORD WORK & WISH THAT HAS EXISTED ALL REMAINING STILL .    634  JERUSALEM 13      61
     AGAINST TRUE ART SUCH AS IT EXISTED . . . . . . . .        864A LETTER 61        PROSE
     MY WIFE ALONE IS ANSWERABLE FOR THEIR HAVING EXISTED IN ANY 879C LETTER 89       PROSE
EXISTENCE     SEE NON EXISTENCE
     REASON AND ENERGY LOVE AND HATE ARE NECESSARY TO HUMAN     149B MARRIAGE HH 3    PROSE
       EXISTENCE
     GIANTS WHO FORMED THIS WORLD INTO ITS SENSUAL EXISTENCE    155A MARRIAGE HH 15   PROSE
     HE ONLY TAKES PORTIONS OF EXISTENCE AND FANCIES THAT THE   155B MARRIAGE HH 15   PROSE
       WHOLE
     WHOEVER TRIES TO RECONCILE THEM SEEKS TO DESTROY EXISTENCE 155B MARRIAGE HH 15   PROSE
     ADVANCING TOWARD US WITH ALL THE FURY OF A SPIRITUAL       156C MARRIAGE HH 17   PROSE
       EXISTENCE
     TO BIND THE PHANTOMS OF EXISTENCE FROM ETERNAL LIFE . .    192  V DAU ALBION 4    24
     BUT THE SPACE UNDIVIDED BY EXISTENCE . . . . . . . .       230  URIZEN 13         46
     TO BE MOULDED INTO EXISTENCE  . . . . . . . . . .          232  URIZEN 19         23
     ASTONISHD AT HIS OWN EXISTENCE  . . . . . . . . . .        234  URIZEN 23         12
     SIX DAYS THEY SHRUNK UP FROM EXISTENCE . . . . . . .       236  URIZEN 25         39
     IN AN ALLEGORICAL ABODE WHERE EXISTENCE HATH NEVER COME    240  EUROPE 5           7
     MIGHTY WAS THE DRAUGHT OF VOIDNESS TO DRAW EXISTENCE IN    280  FOUR ZOAS 2       18
     SOFT EXULTING IN EXISTENCE ALL THE MAN ABSORBING  . . .    293  FOUR ZOAS 3       53
     WHERE NEVER YET EXISTENCE CAME THERE LOSING ALL MY LIFE    296  FOUR ZOAS 3      189
     AS ON THE OUTSIDE OF EXISTENCE BUT LOOK BEHOLD TAKE COMFORT 330 FOUR ZOAS 7      414
     OF EXISTENCE TO BE A SIGN & TERROR TO ALL WHO BEHOLD  .    331  FOUR ZOAS 7      429
     THRO CAVES OF DEATH INTO EXISTENCE THE BEECH LONG LIMBD    335  FOUR ZOAS 7B    * 100
       ADVANCD
     THEY VIEW THE LIGHT & WONDER CRYING OUT IN TERRIBLE        352  FOUR ZOAS 8      452
       EXISTENCE
     WEEPING AT THE THRESHOLD OF EXISTENCE I WILL STEEL MY HEART 361 FOUR ZOAS 9      148
     THEY CRY OUT IN JOYS OF EXISTENCE THE BROAD STEMS  . .     373  FOUR ZOAS 9      605
     THE IMAGINATION IS NOT A STATE IT IS THE HUMAN EXISTENCE   522  MILTON 32         32
       ITSELF
     IS THIS THE VOID OUTSIDE OF EXISTENCE WHICH IF ENTERD INTO 534  MILTON 41         37
     NOTHING NEW OCCURS IN IDENTICAL EXISTENCE ACCIDENT EVER    567C DESC CAT 3       PROSE
       VARIES
     NOTHING NEW OCCURS IN IDENTICAL EXISTENCE ACCIDENT EVER    589A CHAUCER/N        PROSE
       VARIES
     VEGETATIVE EXISTENCE AS IT IS WRITTEN IN REVELATIONS  .  . 609A V LAST JUDG/N    PROSE
     FROM THE BIBLE & LIMITS ALL EXISTENCE TO CREATION & TO     614B V LAST JUDG/N    PROSE
       CHAOS
     & EXISTENCE WHOSE WAYS & MEANS EXCEED THEIR OWN  . . . .   616B V LAST JUDG/N    PROSE
     IT IS IN FALLACY & ITS EXISTENCE AN IMPOSTURE  . . . .     617A V LAST JUDG/N    PROSE
     WHERE IS THE EXISTENCE OUT OF MIND OR THOUGHT . . . .  .   617A V LAST JUDG/N    PROSE
     THERE IS A VOID OUTSIDE OF EXISTENCE WHICH IF ENTERD INTO  620  JERUSALEM 1        1
     SOFT EXULTING IN EXISTENCE ALL THE MAN ABSORBING  . . .    654  JERUSALEM 29      40
```

		PAGE	TITLE	LINE

EXISTENCE   (CONTINUED)

UNKNOWN AMONG THE DEAD WHERE NEVER BEFORE EXISTENCE CAME . . . 661 JERUSALEM 34   38
TILL THE EXISTENCE OF FRIENDSHIP & BENEVOLENCE IS DENIED . . 672 JERUSALEM 43   27
SATAN IS THE STATE OF DEATH & NOT A HUMAN EXISTENCE . . . 680 JERUSALEM 49   67
CALLING THE ROCKS ATOMIC ORIGINS OF EXISTENCE DENYING   704 JERUSALEM 67   12
    ETERNITY
LIVING FORM IS ETERNAL EXISTENCE . . . . 778D HOMERS POETRY PROSE
WHICH GIVES EXISTENCE TO EVERY OTHER NAMELY VISIONS OF   793A LETTER 5   PROSE
    ETERNITY
KNOW BUT MYSELF IN A DIVIDED EXISTENCE . . . . 853A LETTER 51   PROSE
AGAINST THEIR ETERNAL EXISTENCE ITSELF BECAUSE IT IS . . 871A LETTER 72   PROSE

EXISTENCES

ARE ALL OF THEM REPRESENTATIONS OF SPIRITUAL EXISTENCES   576C DESC CAT 4   PROSE
AROUND HIM WERE SEEN THE IMAGES OF EXISTENCES . . . . 606A V LAST JUDG/N   PROSE

EXISTENT   SEE EVER EXISTENT,NON EXISTENT

EXISTING

THAT MAN HAS TWO REAL EXISTING PRINCIPLES VIZ A BODY &   149C MARRIAGE HH 4 PROSE
    A SOUL
GOD ONLY ACTS & IS IN EXISTING BEINGS OR MEN . . . . 155B MARRIAGE HH 15 PROSE
AS REAL AND EXISTING MEN . . . . 576D DESC CAT 4   PROSE
I SEE THE PAST PRESENT & FUTURE EXISTING ALL AT ONCE . . 635 JERUSALEM 15   8

EXISTS

("THOUGHT INDEED EXISTS FIRST ...BUT") NOTE THIS . . . 95B ANNO SWED LOVE MARG
THEREFORE AN UNIVERSAL POETIC GENIUS EXISTS . . . . . 98C ALL RELIGIONS PROSE
A TERRIBLE FELLOW SUCH AS EXISTS IN ALL TIMES AND PLACES   571C DESC CAT 3   PROSE
AS IT ONLY EXISTS IN CERTAIN PERIODS IT IS THE SOLDIER   575C DESC CAT 3   PROSE
    BY SEA
PAINTING AS WELL AS POETRY AND MUSIC EXISTS AND EXULTS   576B DESC CAT 4   PROSE
POETRY AS IT EXISTS NOW ON EARTH IN THE VARIOUS REMAINS OF 579C DESC CAT 5   PROSE
ANCIENT AUTHORS MUSIC AS IT EXISTS IN OLD TUNES OR MELODIES 579C DESC CAT 5   PROSE
PAINTING AND SCULPTURE AS IT EXISTS IN THE REMAINS . . 579C DESC CAT 5   PROSE
LET THEM ENCOURAGE WHAT EXISTS ALREADY . . . . 597A PUB ADDRESS/N   PROSE
OF WHAT ETERNALLY EXISTS REALLY & UNCHANGEABLY . . . 604D V LAST JUDG/N   PROSE
BUT ETERNAL VISION OR IMAGINATION OF ALL THAT EXISTS . 604D V LAST JUDG/N   PROSE
OF UNBELIEVING DEMONS ETERNITY EXISTS AND ALL THINGS IN   614B V LAST JUDG/N   PROSE
FOR EVERY THING EXISTS & NOT ONE SIGH NOR SMILE NOR TEAR   634 JERUSALEM 13   66
MAN IS ALL IMAGINATION GOD IS MAN & EXISTS IN US & WE   775A ANNO BERKELEY MARG
    IN HIM
WHERE ANY VIEW OF MONEY EXISTS ART CANNOT BE CARRIED ON   776C INSC LAOCOON   PROSE
WHEREAS GOD EXISTS NOT EXCEPT FROM THEIR EFFLUVIA . . 789A ANNO THORNTON MARG
RENDERD NON EXISTENT & AN IMMENSE POEM EXISTS . . . . 823B LETTER 26   PROSE

EXIT

EXIT DAGWORTH . . . . 25C EDW THIRD/PS 3 PROSE
[EXEUNT] EXIT KING EDWARD . . . . 26C EDW THIRD/PS 3 PROSE
FLATTERY IS DELICIOUS EVEN FROM THE LIPS OF A BABBLER   29D EDW THIRD/PS 4 PROSE
    EXIT PETER

EXODUS

MILTON'S PARADISE LOST IS AS TRUE AS GENESIS OR EXODUS   392D ANNO WATSON   MARG
ANGEL OF THE DIVINE PRESENCE MENTIOND IN EXODUS XIV... . 610A V LAST JUDG/N   PROSE
EXODUS VII . . . . SUPP EXODUS/N   *TITLE
?EXODUS AARON XXX ?MOSES XXX RIVER XXX FROGS LICE . . SUPP EXODUS/N   *PROSE

EXPAND

EXPAND WHERE IS SPACE WHERE O SUN IS THY DWELLING . . . 144 FRENCH REVOLTN   219
HIS EYES THE LIGHTS OF HIS LARGE SOUL CONTRACT OR ELSE   308 FOUR ZOAS 5   121
    EXPAND
AWAKE AWAKE O SLEEPER OF THE LAND OF SHADOWS WAKE EXPAND   622 JERUSALEM 4   6
OF LOVE & HARMONY IN MAN EXPAND THY EVER LOVELY GATES . . 675 JERUSALEM 44   42
THAT ODOURS CANNOT THEM EXPAND NOR JOY ON THEM EXULT . 680 JERUSALEM 49   39
CONTRACT OR EXPAND SPACE AT WILL OR IF WE RAISE OURSELVES 687 JERUSALEM 55   44
IN BEAUTIFUL PARADISES EXPAND THESE ARE THE FOUR RIVERS   745 JERUSALEM 98   25
    OF PARADISE
MY EYES DID EXPAND . . . . 804 TO BUTTS/L   8

EXPANDED

EXPANDED LIKE STARRY HEAVEN HE SAT DOWN . . . . 138 FRENCH REVOLTN   82
THE WILL OF THE IMMORTAL EXPANDED . . . . 223 URIZEN 3   37
EXPANDED FROM NORTH TO SOUTH . . . . 242 EUROPE 11   5
EXPANDED THEY BEHOLD THE TERRORS OF THE SUN & MOON . . 308 FOUR ZOAS 5   125
HIS BOSOM IS LIKE STARRY HEAVEN EXPANDED ALL THE STARS . 308 FOUR ZOAS 5   130
THY ROSES THAT EXPANDED IN THE FACE OF GLOWING MORN . . 325 FOUR ZOAS 7   194
THESE NOSTRILS THAT EXPANDED WITH DELIGHT IN MORNING SKIES 349 FOUR ZOAS 8   303
THESE NOSTRILS THAT EXPANDED WITH DELIGHT IN MORNING SKIES 705 JERUSALEM 67   49
ACCOUNT OF ITS EXPANDED MEADOWS BUT ALSO ON ACCOUNT OF ITS 847C LETTER 44   PROSE

EXPANDING   SEE EVER EXPANDING

SO THE EXPANDING EYES OF IMMORTALS . . . . 231 URIZEN 15   11
BOUND IN HIS EXPANDING CLEAR SENSES . . . . 257 BOOK OF LOS 4   10
SOMETIMES I THINK THOU ART A FLOWER EXPANDING . . . . 265 FOUR ZOAS 1   59
THEY BEHOLD MULTITUDE OR EXPANDING THEY BEHOLD AS ONE . 277 FOUR ZOAS 1   471
CONTRACTING OR EXPANDING THEIR ALL FLEXIBLE SENSES . . 288 FOUR ZOAS 2   296
PRESS IT AROUND THE LOINS OF THIS EXPANDING CRUELTY . . 349 FOUR ZOAS 8   313
THE EXPANDING EYES OF MAN BEHOLDS THE DEPTHS OF WONDROUS   379 FOUR ZOAS 9 * 830
    WORLDS
EVER EXPANDING IN THE BOSOM OF GOD THE HUMAN IMAGINATION   623 JERUSALEM 5   20
WE BEHOLD MULTITUDE OR EXPANDING WE BEHOLD AS ONE . . 664 JERUSALEM 38   18
EXPANDING ON WING THE DAUGHTERS OF BEULAH REPLIED IN SWEET 681 JERUSALEM 50   23
    RESPONSE
AT WILL CONTRACTING INTO WORMS OR EXPANDING INTO GODS . 686 JERUSALEM 55   37
UPON THE CHARIOTS OF THE MORNING CONTRACTING OR EXPANDING 687 JERUSALEM 55   45
    TIME
WHICH STRETCHD ABROAD EXPANDING EAST & WEST & NORTH & SOUTH 733 JERUSALEM 88   32
CONTINUE EXPANDING . . . . 805 TO BUTTS/L   47

EXPANDS

FORGETTING THAT WITHIN THAT CENTER ETERNITY EXPANDS . . . 520 MILTON 31   48

	PAGE	TITLE	LINE

EXPANDS   (CONTINUED)
    IN WHICH IS ETERNITY IT EXPANDS IN STARS TO THE MUNDANE   633 JERUSALEM 13   35
        SHELL
    IN EVERY BOSOM A UNIVERSE EXPANDS AS WINGS . . . . . .   665 JERUSALEM 38   49
    AND THE CIRCUMFERENCE STILL EXPANDS GOING FORWARD   709 JERUSALEM 71   8
        TO ETERNITY
    ON WHICH THE SOUL EXPANDS ITS WING . . . .   755 EV GOSPEL(E)/N   68
EXPANSE
    WHICH CAST THE METALS INTO THE EXPANSE . . . .   155A MARRIAGE HH 15   PROSE
    WITH WHAT SENSE DOES THE TAME PIGEON MEASURE OUT   191 V DAU ALBION 3   3
        THE EXPANSE
    AS THE RAVEN'S EYE OR DOES HE MEASURE THE EXPANSE LIKE   193 V DAU ALBION 5   36
        THE VULTURE
    THAT GLOWD FURIOUS IN THE EXPANSE . . . .   259 BOOK OF LOS 5   9
    THOU NEER SHALT LEAVE THIS COLD EXPANSE WHERE WATRY THARMAS   272 FOUR ZOAS 1   305
        MOURNS
    BUT THE BRIGHT SUN WAS NOT AS YET HE FILLING ALL   273 FOUR ZOAS 1   349
        THE EXPANSE
    THE VARYING CLOUDS LIKE PARADISES STRETCHD IN THE EXPANSE   274 FOUR ZOAS 1   368
    LIKE A FAMISHD EAGLE EYELESS RAGING IN THE VAST EXPANSE   297 FOUR ZOAS 4   10
    OF DAWN OUTSTRETCHING AN EXPANSE WHERE NEER EXPANSE HAD   299 FOUR ZOAS 4   87
        BEEN
    INTO THE BLUE EXPANSE & I INVENTED WITH LABORIOUS ART . .   312 FOUR ZOAS 6   31
    WALKING ON MOUNTAINS OR FLYING IN THE OPEN EXPANSE   340 FOUR ZOAS 7B   270
        OF HEAVEN
    ANXIOUS ITS LITTLE SOUL LOOKS OUT INTO THE CLEAR EXPANSE   355 FOUR ZOAS 8   559
    MOUNTING UPON THE WINGS OF LIGHT INTO THE GREAT EXPANSE   520 MILTON 31   32
    THE CENTER INTO AN EXPANSE & THE CENTER ROLLED OUT INTO   689 JERUSALEM 57   18
        AN EXPANSE
    THE VAST EXPANSE WHERE THE DAUGHTERS OF ALBION WEAVE THE   698 JERUSALEM 64   2
        WEB
    STAND IN THE CENTER & SOMETIMES STRETCH FLAT IN THE EXPANSE   728 JERUSALEM 83   41
EXPANSES
    WALKING IN JOY IN BRIGHT EXPANSES SLEEPING ON BRIGHT   321 FOUR ZOAS 7   64
        CLOUDS
    IN ABSTRACT FALSE EXPANSES THAT HE MAY NOT HEAR THE VOICE   353 FOUR ZOAS 8   487
    BUT THE HUMAN WINE STOOD WONDERING IN ALL THEIR DELIGHTFUL   378 FOUR ZOAS 9   799
        EXPANSES
    IN NEW EXPANSES CREATING EXEMPLARS OF MEMORY AND   746 JERUSALEM 98   30
        OF INTELLECT
EXPANSION
    EXPANSION TO THE EYE OF PITY OR WILL HE BIND HIMSELF . .   195 V DAU ALBION 8   3
    BUT THERE IS NO LIMIT OF EXPANSION . . . .   670 JERUSALEM 42   35
    WAS HUMAN ACCORDING TO THE EXPANSION OR CONTRACTION . . .   746 JERUSALEM 98   36
EXPANSIVE
    THE EYELIDS EXPANSIVE AS MORNING & THE EARS . . . . .   318 FOUR ZOAS 6   249
    WEAK & WEAKER THEIR EXPANSIVE ORBS BEGAN SHRINKING . . .   318 FOUR ZOAS 6   257
    WITHINSIDE WONDROUS & EXPANSIVE ITS GATES ARE NOT CLOSD   502 MILTON 20   29
    EXPANSIVE NOSTRILS WEST FLOWD THE PARENT SENSE THE TONGUE   745 JERUSALEM 98   17
        NORTH STOOD
EXPATIATE
    AND THAT I CAN AT WILL EXPATIATE IN THE GARDENS OF BLISS   727 JERUSALEM 82   82
EXPECT
    IF YOU EXPECT HIS RESENTMENT YOU DO NOT FORGIVE HIM NOW   77A ANNO LAVATER   MARG
    EXPECT POISON FROM THE STANDING WATER . . . .   152A MARRIAGE HH 9   PROSE
    IF WE ARE TO EXPECT CRIMES FROM PAINE & HIS FOLLOWERS . .   385C ANNO WATSON   MARG
    SHOULD EXPECT THAT THE MAN WHO WROTE THIS SNEAKING SENTENCE   385C ANNO WATSON   MARG
    THE READER MUST EXPECT TO READ IN ALL MY REMARKS . . .   445B ANNO REYNOLDS   MARG
    HE MUST EXPECT TO BE CALLD A FOOL BY MEN OF UNDERSTANDING   469D ANNO REYNOLDS   MARG
    THE WORLD OF VEGETATION AND GENERATION MAY EXPECT . .   578A DESC CAT 5   PROSE
    EXPECT HOLINESS FROM ONE ANOTHER BUT FROM GOD ONLY . .   616D V LAST JUDG/N   PROSE
    YET THEY REGARD NOT PITY & THEY EXPECT NO ONE TO PITY .   691 JERUSALEM 59   36
    YOU MAY EXPECT SOON I SHOULD HAVE SENT THEM BY MY SISTER   809B LETTER 20   PROSE
        BUT
    CANNOT EXPECT TO WANT NATURAL HIDDEN ONES . . . . .   811D LETTER 22   PROSE
    EXPECT A LIKENESS BUT NOW I HAVE DONE ALL I COULD & KNOW   815D LETTER 23   PROSE
    SO HE IS NOW A SHADOW'S SHADOW BUT HOW CAN WE EXPECT .   844B LETTER 43   PROSE
    EXPECT A FULL ACCOUNT OF ALL HE CAN COLLECT MR SANDERS .   847D LETTER 44   PROSE
    THAT I EXPECT NOTHING I WAS ALIVE & IN HEALTH & WITH THE   862C LETTER 60   PROSE
    A PRICE FOR THEM THAT I SCARCE EXPECT TO GET FROM   878C LETTER 88   PROSE
        A STRANGER
EXPECTANT
    STAMPD THE HARD ROCKS EXPECTANT OF THE UNKNOWN WANDERER   319 FOUR ZOAS 6   299
EXPECTATION
    AND WING THEIR BROWS WITH HOPE AND EXPECTATION . . .   25 EDW THIRD/PS 3   182
    LIKE A DARK LAMP ETERNAL DEATH HAUNTS ALL MY EXPECTATION   293 FOUR ZOAS 3   75
    EXPECTATION & GLADNESS ADDED TO LABOUR IN OUR REMOVAL THAT   801B LETTER 13   PROSE
    MY FINGERS EMIT SPARKS OF FIRE WITH EXPECTATION OF   801C LETTER 13   PROSE
        MY FUTURE LABOURS
    OUR RETURN TO LONDON DRAWS ON APACE OUR EXPECTATION OF .   826B LETTER 28   PROSE
    YOUR EAGER EXPECTATION OF HEARING FROM ME COMPELLS ME .   834B LETTER 34   PROSE
    EXPECTATION & DESIRE OF VISITING HAMPSTEAD   873D LETTER 78   PROSE
        I AM NEVERTHELESS
EXPECTED
    OR BUT EXPECTED AS A THING OF COURSE . . . .   27 EDW THIRD/PS 3   249
    NOT SO DESTITUTE OF ACCOMODATIONS TO OUR WANTS AS   806B LETTER 16   PROSE
        I EXPECTED
    BUT NOT SO MUCH AS I EXPECTED FOR I REMEMBER & SAUNDERS   839D LETTER 38   PROSE
        SAYS
    I EVER EXPECTED THEM TO BE . . . .   852C LETTER 50   PROSE
    WAS IN SOME MEASURE TO BE EXPECTED BUT THAT HE HAS REASONS   853A LETTER 51   *PROSE

```
                                                        PAGE    TITLE        LINE
EXPECTING
    . . . AND BEFORE EXPECTING CAPTAINS  . . . . . . . 146 FRENCH REVOLTN    273
    EXPECTING TO RECIEVE AHANIA IN THE SPRING WITH JOY . . . 362 FOUR ZOAS 9  215
    NAKED & PALE STANDING ON THE EXPECTING AIR TO BE DELIVERD 363 FOUR ZOAS 9 254
EXPECTS
    ENGLAND EXPECTS THAT EVERY MAN SHOULD DO HIS DUTY   . . . 584C DESC CAT 14 PROSE
    HOW FAR HE EXPECTS TO PLEASE I CANNOT TELL . . . . . . 795A LETTER 6       PROSE
    MR SANDERS TO KENDALL WESTMORELAND MR SANDERS EXPECTS  . 834C LETTER 34    PROSE
EXPEDITION
    & IN MY NEXT EFFORT I PROMISE MORE EXPEDITION   . . . 792C LETTER 4        PROSE
    WITH ALL POSSIBLE EXPEDITION I SEND YOU A PROOF OF MY  . . 796C LETTER 8   PROSE
    WITH ALL POSSIBLE EXPEDITION IF INDEED I HAVE NOT TIRED YOU 816C LETTER 24 PROSE
EXPEDITIOUS
    HIS PICTURES ARE HIGH LABOURD PRETENSIONS TO EXPEDITIOUS  468B ANNO REYNOLDS MARG
EXPEL
    ANSWER THIS TO YOURSELVES & EXPEL FROM AMONG YOU  . . . . 717B JERUSALEM 77 PROSE
EXPENCE
    AND DIRECTIONS ARE EMPLOYED AT A GREAT EXPENCE   . . . . 572D DESC CAT 3    PROSE
    AT THE EXPENCE OF RAFAEL AND MICHAEL ANGELO  . . . . . 575D DESC CAT 3      PROSE
EXPEND
    TO EXPEND (TWO THOUSAND) A YEAR MR PHILLIPS CONSIDERS YOU 841C LETTER 41    PROSE
        AS
EXPENDING
    EXPENDING ALL HIS ENERGY AGAINST THE FUEL OF FIRE   . . . 366 FOUR ZOAS 9  359
EXPENSE    SEE EXPENCE
    WHILE IT PRODUCES WORKS AT LESS THAN ONE FOURTH OF THE   207B PRSPECTUS 1793 PROSE
        EXPENSE
    STATES ARE NOT IMPROVED AT THE EXPENSE OF FOREIGNERS  . . 402D ANNO BACON   MARG
    EXPENSE OF HIS COMFORT AS I HAVE OFTEN SEEN  . . . . . 616B V LAST JUDG/N   PROSE
    A BOOK PRICE HALF A GUINEA MAY BE GOT OUT AT THE EXPENSE OF 820A LETTER 25  PROSE
    THE TROUBLE & EXPENSE I HAVE HEARD THAT MY ACCUSER IS A  828B LETTER 28     PROSE
    THE EXPENSE WOULD NOT BE VERY GREAT  . . . . . . . . 832D LETTER 32         PROSE
    WILL GO EQUAL SHARES WITH ME IN THE EXPENSE AND THE PROFITS 858B LETTER 55  PROSE
    BUT THINK OF THE EXPENSE & HOW IT MAY BE SPARED  . . . 873A LETTER 76       PROSE
EXPENSES
    PURPOSE HERE OUR EXPENSES ARE SMALL & OUR INCOME FROM  . . 811D LETTER 22   PROSE
    GOING ON WOULD BE A CERTAIN LOSS OF ALMOST ALL THE EXPENSES 831C LETTER 31  PROSE
EXPENSIVE
    EXPENSIVE ADVERTIZING BOASTS THAT THEY MAKE OF SUCH WORKS 480C MILTON 1     PROSE
    WHOEVER LOOKS AT ANY OF THE GREAT & EXPENSIVE WORKS  . . 596B PUB ADDRESS/N PROSE
    DISCOURAGE YOU FROM THE PURSUIT OF SO EXPENSIVE AN  . . . 848C LETTER 45    PROSE
    EXPENSIVE TO THE BUYER THOSE I PRINTED FOR MR HUMPHRY  . 867A LETTER 66     PROSE
EXPENSIVELY
    FIRST RANK IN SOCIETY NOBLE RICH AND EXPENSIVELY ATTENDED 568C DESC CAT 3   PROSE
EXPERIENCE
    SEIZES THE FRUITS OF TIME ATTACKS EXPERIENCE  . . . . .  27 EDW THIRD/PS 3  255
    THEN IF WE MUST TUG FOR EXPERIENCE   . . . . . . . .  27 EDW THIRD/PS 3     262
    ("WARM ATTACHMENT OR DEEP DISLIKE ") TRUE EXPERIENCE    86B ANNO LAVATER    MARG
    AS WE CANNOT EXPERIENCE PLEASURE BUT BY MEANS OF OTHERS  88B ANNO LAVATER  * MARG
        [SO WE ARE]
    WHO EXPERIENCE EITHER PLEASURE OR PAIN THRO US   . . .  88B ANNO LAVATER    MARG
    ACQUIRED BY MEANS OF SUFFERING & DISTRESS I E EXPERIENCE  89B ANNO SWED LOVE * MARG
    FOR IT IS FALSE BY ALL EXPERIENCE  . . . . . . . . .  92D ANNO SWED LOVE    MARG
    MOTTO TO THE SONGS OF INNOCENCE & OF EXPERIENCE  . . . . 183D MOTTO SONGS/N TITLE
    TILL EXPERIENCE TEACHES THEM TO CATCH  . . . . . . . 183 MOTTO SONGS/N       3
    HOW CAN THE GIVER OF GIFTS EXPERIENCE THE DELIGHTS OF THE 193 V DAU ALBION 5 12
        MERCHANT
    TO KEEP THE GENROUS FROM EXPERIENCE TILL THE UNGENEROUS   200 AMERICA 11     8
    SONGS OF EXPERIENCE IN ILLUMINATED PRINTING OCTAVO...  . 208A PRSPECTUS 1793 PROSE
    SONGS OF INNOCENCE AND OF EXPERIENCE . . . . . . . . 210A SONGS OF EXPER    TITLE
    SONGS OF EXPERIENCE THE AUTHOR & PRINTER W BLAKE  . . . 210B SONGS OF EXPER TITLE
    WHAT IS THE PRICE OF EXPERIENCE DO MEN BUY IT FOR A SONG  290 FOUR ZOAS 2   397
    ("ONLY BY EXPERIENCE") A LIE   . . . . . . . . . .  459A ANNO REYNOLDS      MARG
    KNOWLEDGE AND EXPERIENCE HENRY BAILLIE THE KEEPER   . .  569D DESC CAT 3     PROSE
    AND WHAT CONNOISSEURS CALL TOUCH I KNOW BY EXPERIENCE  . 575B DESC CAT 3     PROSE
    & EXPERIENCE OF MANY YEARS   . . . . . . . . . . .  591D PUB ADDRESS/N      PROSE
    AS DESTRUCTIVE OF THE TRUE ARTIST AS IT IS FALSE BY ALL  601D PUB ADDRESS/N PROSE
        EXPERIENCE
    TOO MUCH EXPERIENCE TO BE ANY LONGER IMPOSED UPON   . . 821A LETTER 25      PROSE
    SONGS OF EXPERIENCE URIZEN MILTON PRINTS FOLIO QUARTO   867B LETTER 66      PROSE
        OCTAVO
    EXPERIENCE FOR A FRIEND AT TEN GUINEAS WHICH I CANNOT DO  878C LETTER 88    PROSE
    URIZEN HEAVEN &C & SONGS OF EXPERIENCE FOR BALANCE  . . SUPP LETTER 56A    *PROSE
    THE ORDER IN WHICH THE SONGS OF INNOCENCE & OF EXPERIENCE SUPP LETTER 66A  *PROSE
    THEN BEGINS SONGS OF EXPERIENCE  . . . . . . . . . . SUPP LETTER 66A       *PROSE
    TITLE PAGE OF SONGS OF EXPERIENCE  . . . . . . . . . SUPP LETTER 66A       *PROSE
    OF MR LINNELL FOR SONGS OF INNOCENCE & EXPERIENCE ONE COPY SUPP LETTER 66G *PROSE
EXPERIENCED
    EXPERIENCED IT BEGAN BY A GNAWING PAIN IN THE STOMACH  . 872B LETTER 75     PROSE
EXPERIENCES
    THE FACULTY WHICH EXPERIENCES THIS FACULTY I TREAT OF  . . 98B ALL RELIGIONS PROSE
EXPERIMENT
    THE ARGUMENT AS THE TRUE METHOD OF KNOWLEDGE IS EXPERIMENT 98B ALL RELIGIONS PROSE
    TRUE I CANNOT DO A MIRACLE THRO EXPERIMENT &  . . . . . 391D ANNO WATSON    MARG
    SAYS THAT EVERY THING MUST BE DONE BY EXPERIMENT   . . . 459D ANNO REYNOLDS MARG
    DOUBT DOUBT & DONT BELIEVE WITHOUT EXPERIMENT   . . . . 536 DONT BELIEVE/N   9
    NUMBER VII THE GOATS AN EXPERIMENT PICTURE   . . . . . 581C DESC CAT 7      TITLE
    FOR EXPERIMENT WITH THE COLOURS AND IS LABOURED   . . . 581C DESC CAT 7     PROSE
    NUMBER VIII THE SPIRITUAL PRECEPTOR AN EXPERIMENT PICTURE 581D DESC CAT 8   TITLE
    AFTERWARD EXECUTED FOR A LADY OF HIGH RANK AN EXPERIMENT  582B DESC CAT 9   TITLE
        PICTURE
    FOR EXPERIMENT ON COLOURS WITHOUT ANY OILY VEHICLE IT MAY 582B DESC CAT 9   PROSE
```

```
                                                              PAGE      TITLE        LINE
EXPERIMENT   (CONTINUED)
      EXPERIMENT WERE THE RESULT OF TEMPTATIONS AND PERTURBATIONS  582B DESC CAT 9     PROSE
      NOTE THESE EXPERIMENT PICTURES HAVE BEEN BRUIZED  . . . .   583D DESC CAT 9      PROSE
      THAT ERROR OR EXPERIMENT WILL MAKE A PART OF TRUTH  . . .   617A V LAST JUDG/N   PROSE
      WHO TEACH DOUBT & EXPERIMENT & MY TWO WINGS VOLTAIRE        685 JERUSALEM 54       18
         ROUSSEAU
      VAIN FOOLISH MAN WILT THOU BELIEVE WITHOUT EXPERIMENT  . .  685 JERUSALEM 54       22
      TO TEACH DOUBT & EXPERIMENT  . . . . . . . . . . . .        752 EV GOSPEL(D)/N     49
      A FOOLISH EXPERIMENT HAPPINESSES HAVE WINGS AND WHEELS  .   807A LETTER 17        PROSE
      EXPERIMENT RICHES IF YOU TRAP &C  . . . . . . . . .         SUPP ON PLATE/N101  *PROSE
EXPERIMENTAL
      OR PROPHETIC CHARACTER THE PHILOSOPHIC & EXPERIMENTAL  . .  97B NAT RELIGION 1   PROSE
      TO THE INTIRE ABROGATION OF EXPERIMENTAL THEORY  . . . .    682B JERUSALEM 52    PROSE
EXPERIMENTALISTS
      TO BE THE SAME THING AS ALL EXPERIMENTALISTS MUST SUPPOSE   878B LETTER 88       PROSE
EXPERIMENTS
      I'LL TRY EXPERIMENTS  . . . . . . . . . . . . . .          51 WHEN CORRUP/IM      26
      HA HA HA SHE CALLS THE EXPERIMENTS PUPPETS  . . . . .   .   58C ISLAND MOON 10   PROSE
      OF ALL HIS WANDERING EXPERIMENTS IN THE HORRIBLE ABYSS  .   324 FOUR ZOAS 7      160
      IN NATURAL RELIGION IN EXPERIMENTS ON MEN  . . . . . .      501 MILTON 19         47
      HE IS ALL EXPERIMENTS FROM LAST TO FIRST  . . . . . .       548 CRIPPLE EVRY/N     7
      AND KNOCKED ABOUT WITHOUT MERCY TO TRY ALL EXPERIMENTS  .   583D DESC CAT 9      PROSE
      IS OPRESSED BY HIS OWN REASONINGS & EXPERIMENTS  . . . .    865B LETTER 62       PROSE
EXPERT
      ME I LEARNED THAT [XXX] NO ONE NOT EVEN THE MOST EXPERT     833B LETTER 33      *PROSE
         HORSEMAN
EXPIRE                          •
      CAN THAT WHICH HAS EXISTED CEASE OR CAN LOVE & LIFE EXPIRE  345 FOUR ZOAS 8      170
EXPLAIN
      DISCRETE & NOT CONTINUOUS SO AS TO EXPLAIN EACH OTHER       93A ANNO SWED LOVE   MARG
         EXCEPT
      THE PROSPECTUS DOES NOT EXPLAIN BUT IT TAKES CARE  . . .    575C DESC CAT 3      PROSE
      THE HELL OF THE BIBLE NEITHER IN THE WAY OUR PARSONS        785C ILLS DANTE 101  PROSE
         EXPLAIN IT
      BECOME MY DUTY TO EXPLAIN MY UNHAPPINESS HAS ARISEN  . .    812B LETTER 22       PROSE
      IDLENESS ITSELF DOES NOT HURT OTHER MEN LET SATAN HIMSELF   812C LETTER 22       PROSE
         EXPLAIN
      THAT HE WOULD IN HIS LETTER TO YOU EXPLAIN HIS REASONS FOR  858A LETTER 55       PROSE
EXPLAIND
      HE SENT A GREAT PART OF THEM TO THE NORTH & EXPLAIND   . .  832C LETTER 32       PROSE
EXPLAINING
      MY SPIRITUAL STATE UNLESS IT HAD BEEN NECESSARY IN          813A LETTER 22       PROSE
         EXPLAINING
EXPLAINS
      MARK THIS IT EXPLAINS N... . . . . . . . . . .            93C ANNO SWED LOVE * MARG
      EXPLAINS HOW THE NATURAL SUN IS DEAD . . . . . . . .      94B ANNO SWED LOVE   MARG
EXPLICIT
      TELL HIM TO BE NO MORE DUBIOUS DEMAND EXPLICIT WORDS  .     640 JERUSALEM 17       60
      THAT WHICH CAN BE MADE EXPLICIT TO THE IDIOT IS NOT WORTH   793B LETTER 5        PROSE
      CONSIDERD WHAT IS NOT TOO EXPLICIT AS THE FITTEST          793B LETTER 5         PROSE
         FOR INSTRUCTION
      BUT MY LETTER TO MR BUTTS APPEARS TO ME NOT TO BE          820B LETTER 25        PROSE
         SO EXPLICIT
      & HE HAS IN THE MOST OPEN & EXPLICIT MANNER OFFERD HIS     856A LETTER 54        PROSE
         SERVICE
EXPLODES
      HE CEASD FOR RIVN LINK FROM LINK THE BURSTING UNIVERSE     363 FOUR ZOAS 9        230
         EXPLODES
EXPLORD
      EXPLORD HIS DENS AROUND  . . . . . . . . . . . .          233 URIZEN 20            32
      URIZEN EXPLORD HIS DENS  . . . . . . . . . . . .          234 URIZEN 20            46
      SO URIZEN AROSE & LEANING ON HIS SPEAR EXPLORD HIS DENS    311 FOUR ZOAS 6         1
      WHEREVER THE EAGLE HAS EXPLORD OR LION OR TYGER TROD  .    358 FOUR ZOAS 9   *    39
      NO MAN CAN EMBRACE TRUE ART TILL HE HAS EXPLORD & CAST OUT 613A V LAST JUDG/N    PROSE
      FROM A SOURCE WHICH IF EXPLORD TOO NARROWLY  . . . . .     812B LETTER 22        PROSE
EXPLORE
      AND BEGAN TO EXPLORE THE ABYSS . . . . . . . . . .        234 URIZEN 20            40
      I WILL ARISE EXPLORE THESE DENS & FIND THAT DEEP PULSATION 311 FOUR ZOAS 5        238
      URIZEN ANSWERD READ MY BOOKS EXPLORE MY CONSTELLATIONS . . 322 FOUR ZOAS 7         90
      FOR LOS COULD ENTER INTO ENITHARMON'S BOSOM & EXPLORE  .   342 FOUR ZOAS 8         32
      ABOMINABLE TO THE EYES OF MORTALS WHO EXPLORE HIS BOOKS    352 FOUR ZOAS 8        430
      JUDGE THEN OF THY OWN SELF THY ETERNAL LINEAMENTS EXPLORE  522 MILTON 32           30
      EXPLORE IN ALL ITS SELFISH NATURAL VIRTUE & PUT OFF  . .   530 MILTON 33           47
      AND THE CENTER HAS ETERNAL STATES THESE STATES WE NOW      709 JERUSALEM 71         9
         EXPLORE
      SO PLAIN I TOLD MR BUTTS THAT I DID NOT WISH TO EXPLORE    819D LETTER 25        PROSE
EXPLORED
      THE WHOLE EXTENT OF THE GLOBE IS EXPLORED EVERY SCATTERD   510 MILTON 25           18
         ATOM
      IS IT A TRUTH THAT THE LEARNED HAVE EXPLORED  . . . . .    649B JERUSALEM 27     PROSE
      LET THE INDEFINITE BE EXPLORED AND LET EVERY MAN BE JUDGED 687 JERUSALEM 55        57
EXPLORING
      THE ENORMOUS SCIENCES OF URIZEN AGES AFTER AGES EXPLORING  344 FOUR ZOAS 8        144
      EXPLORING THE THREE STATES OF ULRO CREATION REDEMPTION     663 JERUSALEM 36        42
         & JUDGMENT
EXPOSD
      UNLESS EXPOSD BY THEIR VAIN PARENTS LO HIM WHOM I LOVE  .   . 339 FOUR ZOAS 7B    246
EXPOSE
      SAY NO MORE OF HER NOR EXPOSE WHAT CHAUCER HAS LEFT HIDDEN  572B DESC CAT 3       PROSE
      BY THIS DISPLAY OF PRETENDED VIRTUE CHIEFLY DESIGN          682D JERUSALEM 52     PROSE
         TO EXPOSE
      SO HONEST AS TO EXPOSE TO YOU HIS WHOLE ABSURD PREJUDICE    838C LETTER 37       PROSE
```

	PAGE	TITLE	LINE

EXPOSED
THE FLUSH OF HEALTH IN FLESH EXPOSED TO THE OPEN AIR . . 580D DESC CAT 5   PROSE
EXPOSES
& EXPOSES HYPOCRITES TILL HE IMAGINES THAT ALL ARE   157D MARRIAGE HH 21 PROSE
    RELIGIOUS
EXPOSTULATION
PRAY EXCUSE THIS HEARTY EXPOSTULATION . . . . 874B LETTER 79   PROSE
EXPOSURE
YOU HID FUSELI'S MILTON IS SATAN TROUBLED AT HIS EXPOSURE 446A ANNO REYNOLDS   MARG
AND EXPOSURE OF THEIR VILE TRICKS . . . . 582C DESC CAT 9   PROSE
EXPRESS
SAID THE ANGELS COULD NOT EXPRESS THEMSELVES AT ALL TO HIM 94C ANNO SWED LOVE   MARG
TO THE CHALCOGRAPHIC SOCIETY & TO EXPRESS TO THEM   591D PUB ADDRESS/N PROSE
    MY OPINION
NOR CAN THEIR METHOD EVER EXPRESS IDEAS OR IMAGINATIONS   596A PUB ADDRESS/N   PROSE
ATTEMPT TO EXPRESS YOUR & OUR MUCH BELOVED'S COUNTENANCE   796C LETTER 8   PROSE
THANKING YOU FOR THE KINDNESS WITH WHICH YOU EXPRESS THEM   797B LETTER 9   PROSE
OF WHICH I HAVE NEED & NOW I MUST EXPRESS MY WISHES . . . 809C LETTER 20   PROSE
CHRISTIANITY AND ADORE HIM WHO IS THE EXPRESS IMAGE OF GOD 815D LETTER 23   PROSE
& THEY EXPRESS THEIR SORROW AT OUR DEPARTURE . . . . 828A LETTER 28   PROSE
I MUST NOW EXPRESS TO YOU MY CONVICTION THAT . . . . 828C LETTER 28   PROSE
ACKNOWLEDGMENTS TO EXPRESS PARTICULARLY FOR YOUR TENS WHICH 832B LETTER 32   PROSE
& IN HIS BEST STYLE HE ALSO DESIRES ME TO EXPRESS TO YOU   836A LETTER 35   PROSE
    HIS
I DID BUT EXPRESS TO HIM MY DESIRE OF SENDING YOU A COPY OF 836D LETTER 35   PROSE
MY WIFE DESIRES ME TO EXPRESS HER LOVE TO YOU . . . . 837D LETTER 36   PROSE
MEAN A CHAPEL IN EAST DEREHAM TOWN & NOT TO EXPRESS . . 838B LETTER 37   PROSE
AND TIMES THREATEN WORSE THAN EVER I MUST NOW EXPRESS . . 845A LETTER 43   PROSE
WITH IT HE DESIRES ME TO EXPRESS TO YOU THAT HE WOULD . . 845C LETTER 44   PROSE
BUT CAN NO LONGER WAIT FOR THEM BUT MUST EXPRESS MY OWN & 853A LETTER 51   *PROSE
I WAS ABOUT TO HAVE WRITTEN TO YOU TO EXPRESS MY WISH THAT 853A LETTER 51   *PROSE
I MUST NOW EXPRESS MY THANKS FOR YOUR GENEROUS MANNER OF 858A LETTER 55   PROSE
EXPRESSD
I CONSIDERD IT MY DUTY TO INTERFERE I EXPRESSD MY   856B LETTER 54   PROSE
    OWN RESPECT
THE DANTE HE EXPRESSD HIMSELF VERY MUCH PLEASD WITH . . . 877A LETTER 85   PROSE
EXPRESSED
ONLY BE EXPRESSED BY THOSE WHO FEEL THEM . . . . . . 599C PUB ADDRESS/N PROSE
EXPRESSED HIS WISH THAT YOU SHOULD YOURSELF SET A PRICE AND 858A LETTER 55   PROSE
TAKEN OUT THAT PART WHICH EXPRESSED THE HOLE FOR THE LADLE 866C LETTER 65   PROSE
EXPRESSING
FORGIVE ME FOR EXPRESSING TO YOU MY ENTHUSIASM WHICH I WISH 797B LETTER 9   PROSE
ALWAYS BEEN FORWARD IN EXPRESSING THEIR KINDNESS FOR US   828A LETTER 28   PROSE
EXPRESSING HIS PLEASURE [OF YOUR] IN YOUR WISH TO SEE IT   836D LETTER 35   PROSE
I TAKE THE EXTREME PLEASURE OF EXPRESSING MY JOY AT OUR   851C LETTER 50   PROSE
    GOOD
EXPRESSING PRIVATE OPINION WHICH WILL VARY IN EACH   853A LETTER 51   *PROSE
    INDIVIDUAL
TO YOU EXPRESSING HIS DESIRE THAT I WILL REPEAT TO YOU   856A LETTER 54   PROSE
    HIS REGRET
HE DESIRED I WOULD EXPRESSING FOR WHICH I THANK HIM . . . 856D LETTER 54   PROSE
EXPRESSION
WHAT NONSENSE PASSION & EXPRESSION IS BEAUTY ITSELF . . . 466A ANNO REYNOLDS   MARG
THE FACE THAT IS INCAPABLE OF PASSION & EXPRESSION   466A ANNO REYNOLDS   MARG
    IS DEFORMITY
REYNOLDS CANNOT BEAR EXPRESSION . . . . 466B ANNO REYNOLDS   MARG
IS THE DIVINE REVELATION IN THE LITTERAL EXPRESSION . . 534 MILTON 42   14
THE CHARACTER AND EXPRESSION IN THIS PICTURE COULD NEVER   573A DESC CAT 3   PROSE
MUST BE THE DESTRUCTION OF ALL CHARACTER AND EXPRESSION   575B DESC CAT 3   PROSE
EXPRESSION OF FEAR OR REVENGE OR ENVY OR BLANK HORROR . 580C DESC CAT 5   PROSE
CALL EXPRESSION BUT THIS IS A FALSE NOTION OF EXPRESSION   585A DESC CAT 15   PROSE
EXPRESSION CANNOT EXIST WITHOUT CHARACTER AS ITS STAMINA   585A DESC CAT 15   PROSE
AND NEITHER CHARACTER NOR EXPRESSION CAN EXIST . . . 585A DESC CAT 15   PROSE
EVERY EXPRESSION EVERY LINEAMENT OF HEAD HAND & FOOT . 588A CHAUCER/N   PROSE
& ALL EXPRESSION WITHOUT WHICH THE ART IS LOST . . . . 592A PUB ADDRESS/N   PROSE
CAN NEVER PRODUCE CHARACTER & EXPRESSION . . . . . 593B PUB ADDRESS/N   PROSE
OR EXPRESSION IN THIS PRINT WHICH COULD BE PRODUCED . . 599B PUB ADDRESS/N   PROSE
OR ANY OF THAT CLASS CHARACTER & EXPRESSION CAN . . . 599B PUB ADDRESS/N   PROSE
THE [EXPRESSION] CHARACTERS IN ALL THEIR BRANCHES . . . 611B V LAST JUDG/N   PROSE
YOU WITH A LETTER OF MEER COMPLIMENT & EXPRESSION OF THANKS 798A LETTER 10   PROSE
NO EXPRESSION OF THREATENING ON ACCOUNT OF SEDITION . . . 827C LETTER 28   PROSE
AND EXQUISITE FOR EXPRESSION INDEED IT IS MOST PATHETIC   843D LETTER 43   PROSE
IN IMITATION OF THE FIRST STROKES OF THE PAINTER   850D LETTER 49   PROSE
    THE EXPRESSION
EXPRESSIONS
EXPRESSIONS OF ARTICULATE SPEECH IS A BOLD AND DARING . 576B DESC CAT 4   PROSE
TO KEEP HIS OWN CHARACTERS AND EXPRESSIONS HAVING HAD . 586D CHAUCER 1   PROSE
EXPRESSIVE
ALWAYS SUBSTANTIALLY AND WEIGHTILY EXPRESSIVE OF . . . . 569C DESC CAT 3   PROSE
& NOT ARE AS MOST EXPRESSIVE & CORRECT TOO . . . . . 786C ANNO THORNTON   MARG
EXPUNGD
WE MAY HOPE TO SEE CHRIST'S DISCOURSES EXPUNGD . . . 384D ANNO WATSON   MARG
EXPUNGED
IS TO BE EXPUNGED . . . . 154C MARRIAGE HH 14 PROSE
EXQUISITE
WITHIN IS ASIA & GREECE ORNAMENTED WITH EXQUISITE ART . 690 JERUSALEM 58   37
AND EXQUISITE FOR EXPRESSION INDEED IT IS MOST PATHETIC 843D LETTER 43   PROSE
EXQUISITELY
DOES NOT THIS FIT & IS IT NOT FITTING MOST EXQUISITELY TOO 784D ANNO WW EXCUR   MARG
EXTACY
CLOUDS WOULD HAVE FOLDED ROUND IN EXTACY & LOVE UNITING   329 FOUR ZOAS 7   371
ASTONISHD COMFORTED DELIGHTED IN NOTES OF RAPTUROUS EXTACY 342 FOUR ZOAS 8   46

		PAGE	TITLE	LINE

EXTACY   (CONTINUED)
   THE TREES BRING FORTH SWEET EXTACY . . . . 427 MENTAL TRAVLER   89
EXTANT
   THE INN IS YET EXTANT UNDER THE NAME OF THE TALBOT AND . . 590A CHAUCER 2   PROSE
EXTATIC
   CORD OF AFFECTION THRILLING EXTATIC ON THE IRON REEL . . 688 JERUSALEM 56   12
EXTENDED
   THE BLIND-MAN'S ARMS EXTENDED WIDE . . . . 16 BLIND-MANS/PS   23
   IN LINEAMENTS TOO EXTENDED & IN BONES TOO STRAIT & LONG . 363 FOUR ZOAS 9   249
   CONSOLIDATED & EXTENDED WORK WILL BE AS KINDLY RECIEVED 620D JERUSALEM 3   PROSE
   TERRORS IN EVERY NERVE BY SPASMS & EXTENDED PAINS . . . 625 JERUSALEM 7   7
   EXTENDED & ENLARGED TO TAKE IN ORIGINALS BOTH OF PAINTING & 797D LETTER 10   PROSE
EXTENSION
   IN ITS EXTENSION EVERY TWO HUNDRED YEARS HAS A DOOR TO EDEN 678 JERUSALEM 48   37
EXTENSIONS
   IN PULSATIONS OF TIME & EXTENSIONS OF SPACE LIKE URNS OF 630 JERUSALEM 11   2
     BEULAH
EXTENSIVE
   REVEAL THE SECRETS OF ETERNITY FOR MORE EXTENSIVE . . . 503 MILTON 21   10
   EXTENSIVE WAY I SPEAK HIS OWN WORDS THAT A POEM OF . . . 856B LETTER 54   PROSE
   THE ADVANTAGE OF SO EXTENSIVE A DIFFUSAL AS WOULD 856C LETTER 54   PROSE
     BE PROMOTED
   AND YOUR MAGAZINE BEING AS EXTENSIVE IN ITS CIRCULATION 863D LETTER 61   PROSE
EXTENSIVELY
   PUBLIC MAY BE MUTUALLY & EXTENSIVELY BENEFITTED HIS . . . 857A LETTER 54   PROSE
EXTENT
   THE WHOLE EXTENT OF THE GLOBE IS EXPLORED EVERY SCATTERD 510 MILTON 25   18
     ATOM
   FOR MIGHTY WERE THE MULTITUDES OF OLOLON VAST THE EXTENT 526 MILTON 35   37
   GOTHIC GRECIAN HINDOO AND EGYPTIAN ARE THE EXTENT OF THE 579D DESC CAT 5   PROSE
     HUMAN MIND
   SUBORDINATION STRENGTH IS COMPACTNESS NOT EXTENT NOR BULK 580B DESC CAT 5   PROSE
   EXTENT & HE TOLD MR HOARE THAT ON THE PRESENT WORK WHICH 841C LETTER 41   PROSE
EXTERIORS
   THE MAN'S EXTERIORS ARE BECOME INDEFINITE OPEND TO PAIN 279 FOUR ZOAS 1   543
EXTERMINATE
   ("GOD'S MORAL JUSTICE EXTERMINATE SO WICKED A PEOPLE 388B ANNO WATSON   MARG
   ") HORRIBLE
EXTERNAL
   OR EXTERNAL OF HEAVEN & IS OF THE BODY OF THE LORD . . . SUPP ANNO SWED HELL * MARG
   MAN MAY COMPREHEND BUT NOT THE NATURAL OR EXTERNAL MAN . . 90A ANNO SWED LOVE   MARG
   APPEAR AROUND IN THE EXTERNAL SPHERES OF VISIONARY LIFE 524 MILTON 34   51
EXTINCT
   I AM ALMOST EXTINCT & SOON SHALL BE A SHADOW IN OBLIVION 265 FOUR ZOAS 1   40
   THEIR LIFE EXTINCT THEY TOOK THE SPECTRE FORM IN 333 FOUR ZOAS 7B   15
     DARK DESPAIR
   REND DOWN THIS FABRIC AS A WALL RUIND & FAMILY EXTINCT . . 362 FOUR ZOAS 9   186
EXTINCTION
   FOR NOW HE FEARD ETERNAL DEATH & UTTERMOST EXTINCTION . . 307 FOUR ZOAS 5   75
   HIDEOUS OFFENDERS UTTERMOST EXTINCTION IN ETERNAL PAIN . . 330 FOUR ZOAS 7   427
EXTINGUISH
   MR PAINE HAS NOT EXTINGUISHD & CANNOT EXTINGUISH . . . . 384D ANNO WATSON   MARG
EXTINGUISHD
   MR PAINE HAS NOT EXTINGUISHD & CANNOT EXTINGUISH . . . . 384D ANNO WATSON   MARG
   MORAL RECTITUDE HE HAS EXTINGUISHD SUPERSTITION WHICH TOOK 384D ANNO WATSON   MARG
   & HEAT WAS NOT EXTINGUISHD THESE STATES EXIST NOW . . . 606D V LAST JUDG/N   PROSE
EXTIRPATE
   TO EXTIRPATE A NATION BY MEANS OF ANOTHER NATION IS 388B ANNO WATSON   * MARG
     AS WICKED
EXTRACTS
   TAKING EXTRACTS FROM HERVEY'S MEDITATIONS AMONG THE TOMBS 52A ISLAND MOON 8   PROSE
EXTRAORDINARY
   & WHAT IS MORE EXTRAORDINARY THE PEOPLE ARE SO MUCH ALIKE 44A ISLAND MOON 1   PROSE
   EXTRAORDINARY THAT LONDON IN SO FEW YEARS FROM A CITY OF 798B LETTER 10   PROSE
EXTRAVAGANCE
   HETEROGENEOUS WHICH ALL EXTRAVAGANCE IS BUT EXUBERANCE NOT 81D ANNO LAVATER   MARG
   REYNOLDS THOUGHT CHARACTER ITSELF EXTRAVAGANCE & DEFORMITY 460C ANNO REYNOLDS   MARG
EXTRAVAGANT
   THY CARE PRUNE ALL EXTRAVAGANT SHOOTS AND GUIDE . . . . 26 EDW THIRD/PS 3   212
   PROVES THERE IS TRUTH IN HIS EXTRAVAGANT CLAIM . . . . 551 WILLM COWPER/N   8
EXTREME
   ("BOUNDS...TO LIBERTY") IF IT IS THUS THE EXTREME OF BLACK 414B ANNO BOYD   MARG
     IS WHITE
   INGRATITUDE & LOS BELIEVE THE ACCUSATION THRO SATAN'S 486 MILTON 7   14
     EXTREME
   HID HIM FROM SIGHT IN AN EXTREME BLACKNESS AND DARKNESS 490 MILTON 9   33
   WAS EXTREME OLD & MOST EXTREMELY POOR . . . . 539 IN CHILDHOOD/N   2
   HE IS EXTREME OLD & EXTREME POOR STILL . . . . 539 IN CHILDHOOD/N   4
   TERRIBLE TO BEHOLD FOR THY EXTREME BEAUTY & PERFECTION . . 731 JERUSALEM 86   16
   I OUGHT ALSO TO MENTION MY EXTREME DISAPPOINTMENT AT . . 809C LETTER 20   PROSE
   EXTREME PLEASURE OF TRANSMITTING TO YOU ONE PROOF OF THIS 841B LETTER 41   PROSE
   I TAKE THE EXTREME PLEASURE OF EXPRESSING MY JOY AT OUR 851C LETTER 50   PROSE
     GOOD
   THE EXTREME LOSS AND DISAPPOINTMENT WHICH I SHOULD HAVE 861A LETTER 58   PROSE
EXTREMELY
   WAS EXTREME OLD & MOST EXTREMELY POOR . . . . 539 IN CHILDHOOD/N   2
   DO NOR SAY BUT AS YOU DIRECT I FEEL EXTREMELY HAPPY . . . 857B LETTER 54   PROSE
EXTREMES
   REPRESENT [OUR PRESENT CHANGES OF EXTREMES] . . . . . 611C V LAST JUDG/N   PROSE
EXTREMITIES
   AND HIS EXTREMITIES LARGE HIS EYES WITH SCARCE ANY WHITES 580A DESC CAT 5   PROSE
   AND BETTER TYPE THAN THE TWO EXTREMITIES ALSO IT 847A LETTER 44   PROSE
     IS CAREFULLY

642

```
                                                                PAGE     TITLE            LINE
EXUBERANCE
      IT IS NOT THE EXUBERANCE OF BEAUTY SO IF RAFAEL IS HARD    81D ANNO LAVATER         MARG
        & DRY
      HETEROGENEOUS WHICH ALL EXTRAVAGANCE IS BUT EXUBERANCE NOT 81D ANNO LAVATER         MARG
      EXUBERANCE IS BEAUTY . . . . . . . . . . . .    . . . . 152D MARRIAGE HH 10         PROSE
EXUBERANT
      & A LILLY ARE VARIOUS & BOTH BEAUTIFUL BEAUTY IS EXUBERANT  81C ANNO LAVATER         MARG
EXUDATION
      WITHOUT THE BODY OF MAN AN EXUDATION FROM HIS SICKNING      277 FOUR ZOAS 1           463
        LIMBS
EXUDED
      AND THAT BY THESE ARTS THE SERPENT FORM EXUDED FROM HIS     336 FOUR ZOAS 7B          135
        LIMBS
      EXUDED ROUND HIS AWFUL LIMBS STRETCHING TO SERPENT LENGTH   343 FOUR ZOAS 8           79
      THE SHADOWY FEMALE SINCE LIFE CANNOT BE QUENCHD LIFE        352 FOUR ZOAS 8           421
        EXUDED
      A BLUE FLUID EXUDED IN SINEWS HARDENING IN THE ABYSS    . . 483 MILTON 3              35
EXUDING
      BONIFYING INTO A SCULL THE MARROW EXUDING IN DISMAL PAIN    689 JERUSALEM 58           8
EXULT
      THAT ODOURS CANNOT THEM EXPAND NOR JOY ON THEM EXULT     .  680 JERUSALEM 49           39
      OUR SOULS EXULT & LONDON'S TOWERS . . . . . . . . .      .  718 ENGLND AWAKE/J         10
EXULTATION
      HEAVEN RANG WITH WINGED EXULTATION ALL BENEATH HOWLD LOUD   378 FOUR ZOAS 9            782
      HUMILIATION & IN EXULTATION RISE THRO THE AIR WITH THEIR   443D LAST JUDGMNT/L        PROSE
        CHILDREN
      MANY GROUPES ARISE [WITH] IN EXULTATION [IN JOY] . . . .   443D LAST JUDGMNT/L       *PROSE
      GENEROUS EXULTATION IN MY ESCAPE FROM THE ARROWS           833C LETTER 33             PROSE
        OF DARKNESS
EXULTED
      CRIED TIMES ARE ENDED HE EXULTED HE AROSE IN JOY HE EXULTED 372 FOUR ZOAS 9            568
EXULTING
      OVER THE WAVES SHE WENT IN WINGD EXULTING SWIFT DELIGHT     189 V DAU ALBION 1         14
      OPPOSD TO THE EXULTING FLAMD BEAM . . . . . . . . . .    .  249 AHANIA 2               20
      [EXULTING] [INDIGNANT] EXULTING AT THE VOICE THAT CALLD     280 FOUR ZOAS 2      *    10
        HIM . . .
      NO MORE EXULTING FOR HE SAW ETERNAL DEATH BENEATH     . .   280 FOUR ZOAS 2           14
      SOFT EXULTING IN EXISTENCE ALL THE MAN ABSORBING . . . .    293 FOUR ZOAS 3           53
      INTO THE FIRES THEN GLORIOUS BRIGHT EXULTING IN HIS JOY     362 FOUR ZOAS 9           191
      EXULTING IN HER FLIGHT AS WHEN A BUBBLE RISES UP . . . .    362 FOUR ZOAS 9           195
      & IN EXULTING ATTITUDES OF GREAT JOY TELL EACH OTHER     . 443D LAST JUDGMNT/L        PROSE
      SOFT EXULTING IN EXISTENCE ALL THE MAN ABSORBING . . . .    654 JERUSALEM 29          40
EXULTINGLY
      EXULTINGLY THIS IS A PROMISING DAY . . . . . . . . .     .   21 EDW THIRD/PS 3         5
      AND RAISE HER GOLDEN HEAD EXULTINGLY . . . . . . . .     .  34C KING JOHN/PS          PROSE
EXULTS
      PAINTING AS WELL AS POETRY AND MUSIC EXISTS AND EXULTS     576B DESC CAT 4            PROSE
EYD       SEE BLACK-EYD,BLACK EYD,BLEAR-EYD,EYED
EYE
      A SEA OF BLOOD NOR CAN THE EYE . . . . . . . . . . .     .   13 GWIN KING/PS          75
      CLOSD FROM THE EYE OF DAY TO THE HARD ROCK TRANSFIXT BY     41D THEN SHE BORE         PROSE
        FATE
      JOE BRADLEY SAW FOR HE HAD BUT ONE EYE [?COME] . . . .     55B ISLAND MOON 9         *PROSE
      FOR HE HAD BUT ONE EYE HA HA HA HO THEN SUNG SCOPPRELL     55C ISLAND MOON 9          PROSE
      HE HAS GIVEN ME A BLACK EYE . . . . . . . . . . . .     .   61 SAY YOU JOE/IM         11
      ("WHO HAS A DARING EYE TELLS ...") CONTRARY TO...BUT MOST  70B ANNO LAVATER           MARG
        TRUE
      ("LOVE SEES WHAT NO EYE SEES ") MOST EXCELLENT . . . .     77D ANNO LAVATER           MARG
      UNDER A CRUEL EYE OUTWORN . . . . . . . . . . . . . .      124 SCHOOL BOY/SI          8
      OR THE GLISTNING EYE TO THE POISON OF A SMILE . . . .      130 BOOK OF THEL 6         12
      OR AN EYE OF GIFTS & GRACES SHOWRING FRUITS & COINED GOLD  130 BOOK OF THEL 6         15
      ARE PORTIONS OF ETERNITY TOO GREAT FOR THE EYE OF MAN  . . 151C MARRIAGE HH 8         PROSE
      FROM THY CHEEK & FROM THY EYE . . . . . . . . . . .       165 CRADLE SONG/N          16
      FROM EVERY SEARCHING EYE . . . . . . . . . . . . .        171 TO NOBODADDY/N         4
      WHAT IMMORTAL HAND OR EYE . . . . . . . . . . . . .       172 THE TYGER/N 1          3
      WHAT IMMORTAL HAND & EYE . . . . . . . . . . . . .        173 THE TYGER/N 1          24
      WHAT IMMORTAL HAND [OR] & EYE . . . . . . . . . . .       173 THE TYGER/N 2      *   3
      WHAT IMMORTAL HAND & EYE . . . . . . . . . . . . .        173 THE TYGER/N 2          19
      THE RUBIES & PEARLS OF A LOVING EYE . . . . . . . .       181 RICHES/N               2
      [AND WINK HER LOVELY EYE] . . . . . . . . . . . . .       185 LET BROTHELS/N         32
      [FOR THE DROPS OF A HARLOT'S EYE] . . . . . . . . .       186 LET BROTHELS/N         51
      THE EYE SEES MORE THAN THE HEART KNOWS . . . . . .       189A V DAU ALBION           TITLE
      INSTEAD OF MORN ARISES A BRIGHT SHADOW LIKE AN EYE  . .   191 V DAU ALBION 2         35
      WHY HE LOVES MAN IS IT BECAUSE OF EYE EAR MOUTH OR SKIN   191 V DAU ALBION 3         8
      HOW DIFFERENT THEIR EYE AND EAR HOW DIFFERENT THE WORLD   193 V DAU ALBION 5         16
        TO THEM
      DRAW IN THE OCEAN DOES HIS EYE DISCERN THE FLYING CLOUD   193 V DAU ALBION 5         35
      AS THE RAVEN'S EYE OR DOES HE MEASURE THE EXPANSE LIKE    193 V DAU ALBION 5         36
        THE VULTURE
      ON HIS STONE THRESHOLD DOES HIS EYE BEHOLD THE BEAM THAT  195 V DAU ALBION 8         2
        BRINGS
      EXPANSION TO THE EYE OF PITY OR WILL HE BIND HIMSELF   . . 195 V DAU ALBION 8         3
      WHAT IMMORTAL HAND OR EYE  . . . . . . . . . . . .       214 THE TYGER/SE           3
      WHAT IMMORTAL HAND OR EYE . . . . . . . . . . . . .      214 THE TYGER/SE           23
      OR A HEART OR AN EYE THEY SWAM MISCHEVOUS . . . . .      234 URIZEN 23              6
      WHY DOES THE RAVEN CRY ALOUD AND NO EYE PITIES HER  . .  276 FOUR ZOAS 1            445
      IN SECRET PLACES WHERE NO EYE CAN TRACE THY WATRY WAY . . 325 FOUR ZOAS 7           223
      A TEAR OF BLOOD DROPPED FROM EITHER EYE AGAIN HE REPOSD   341 FOUR ZOAS 8           18
      HOVERS WITH BLASTED WINGS ALOFT WATCHING WITH EAGER EYE   354 FOUR ZOAS 8           523
      BLOWN BACK THEY [MO] BLIND THE [MOCKERS] MOCKING EYE   .  418 MOCK ON/N        *     7
      HIS EYE WAS DRY NO TEAR COULD FLOW . . . . . . . .       419 I SAW A MONK/N         23
      THE RUBIES & PEARLS OF A LOVESICK EYE . . . . . . .      425 MENTAL TRAVLER         34
```

	PAGE	TITLE	LINE

EYE   (CONTINUED)

FOR THE EYE ALTERING ALTERS ALL	426	MENTAL TRAVLER	62
THE WILD GAME OF HER ROVING EYE	426	MENTAL TRAVLER	71
HIS EYE WAS DRY NO TEAR COULD FLOW	430	GREY MONK	9
EVERY TEAR FROM EVERY EYE	432	AUGURIES	67
WHEN WE SEE [WITH] NOT THRO THE EYE	433	AUGURIES	126
[TO GOOD ARTISTS] THE STYLE THAT STRIKES THE EYE IS THE TRUE STYLE	448C	ANNO REYNOLDS	* MARG
BUT A FOOL'S EYE IS NOT TO BE A CRITERION	448C	ANNO REYNOLDS	MARG
UNLESS IT WAS TO CAST [AN EYE] A STIGMA UPON REAL FACILITY IN	453D	ANNO REYNOLDS	* MARG
NONSENSE EVERY EYE SEES DIFFERENTLY	456B	ANNO REYNOLDS	MARG
AS THE EYE SUCH THE OBJECT	456B	ANNO REYNOLDS	MARG
TO MY EYE RUBENS'S COLOURING IS MOST CONTEMPTIBLE . . .	469A	ANNO REYNOLDS	MARG
HIS EYE IS ON THE MANY OR RATHER ON THE MONEY	469D	ANNO REYNOLDS	* MARG
REYNOLDS'S EYE COULD NOT BEAR CHARACTERISTIC COLOURING OR	475D	ANNO REYNOLDS	MARG
THE EYE OF MAN A LITTLE NARROW ORB CLOSD UP & DARK . .	484	MILTON 5	21
CAN SUCH AN EYE JUDGE OF THE STARS & LOOKING THRO ITS TUBES	485	MILTON 5	28
AS THE EYE OF MAN VIEWS BOTH THE EAST & WEST ENCOMPASSING	497	MILTON 15	28
IN ALL ITS HYPOCRITIC TURPITUDE OPENING TO EVERY EYE .	530	MILTON 38	44
OF DREAD REPOSE SEEN BY THE VISIONARY EYE HIS FACE IS TOWARD	531	MILTON 39	33
AND THE GIRL SHOOTS WITH HER EYE	552	WHY CUPID/N	6
WITH A LEAR IN HIS EYE HE'LL REPLY A PAINT BRUSH . . .	553	ASKD PRIGG/N	12
THE EYE THAT CAN PREFER THE COLOURING OF TITIAN AND RUBENS	563C	DESC CAT	PROSE
WHERE MORE IS MEANT THAN MEETS THE EYE THE ARTIST . .	566A	DESC CAT 2	PROSE
BETTER LIGHT THAN HIS PERISHING MORTAL EYE CAN SEE . .	576D	DESC CAT 4	*PROSE
THAN ANY THING SEEN BY HIS MORTAL EYE	577A	DESC CAT 4	PROSE
TO THE AUTHOR AND HE THINKS WILL PROVE TO ANY DISCERNING EYE	585D	DESC CAT 16	PROSE
IS SEEN BY THE [IMAGINATIVE EYE] OF EVERY ONE	604C	V LAST JUDG/N	PROSE
SUITED TO MY IMAGINATIVE EYE [IN THE FOLLOWING ORDER] AS FOLLOWS	606A	V LAST JUDG/N	PROSE
TO THE TIME & SPACE FIXED BY THE CORPOREAL VEGETATIVE EYE	614B	V LAST JUDG/N	PROSE
I QUESTION NOT MY CORPOREAL OR VEGETATIVE EYE	617B	V LAST JUDG/N	PROSE
TOUCHD BY THE HAND NOR SEEN WITH THE EYE O JERUSALEM	645	JERUSALEM 22	27
THE EYE OF MAN A LITTLE NARROW ORB CLOSD UP & DARK .	680	JERUSALEM 49	34
THEY OBSCURE THE SUN & THE MOON NO EYE CAN LOOK UPON THEM	702	JERUSALEM 66	34
AND AS THEIR EYE & EAR SHRUNK THE HEAVENS SHRUNK AWAY .	702	JERUSALEM 66	40
THE EYE THE LITTLE NOSTRILS & THE DELICATE TONGUE & EARS	728	JERUSALEM 83	36
SMITING THE SPECTRE ON HIS ANVIL & THE INTEGUMENTS OF HIS EYE	738	JERUSALEM 91	45
SOUTH STOOD THE NERVES OF THE EYE	745	JERUSALEM 98	16
WHEN YOU SEE WITH NOT THRO THE EYE	753	EV GOSPEL(D)/N	106
FORMS MUST BE APPREHENDED BY SENSE OR THE EYE OF IMAGINATION	775A	ANNO BERKELEY	MARG
WHICH BLINDS THE EYE OF IMAGINATION THE REAL MAN . . .	775B	ANNO BERKELEY	MARG
EVE I SEE HIM PLAINLY WITH MY MIND'S EYE I SEE ALSO ABEL LIVING	780	GHOST ABEL 1	23
THE BEST LIVING MODELS I PERCIEVE THAT YOUR EYE IS PERVERTED	793C	LETTER 5	PROSE
AS THE EYE IS FORMED SUCH ARE ITS POWERS	793D	LETTER 5	PROSE
WITHOUT NATURE BEFORE THE PAINTER'S EYE HE CAN NEVER PRODUCE	810B	LETTER 20	PROSE
WITH MY INWARD EYE TIS AN OLD MAN GREY	817	HAPPINESS/L	29
& BEING UNDER MY OWN EYE THE PRINTS ARE AS FINE AS THE	821A	LETTER 25	PROSE
THE FLEMINGS THEY CALL IT BURNT BONE HAS POSSESSED THE EYE	864C	LETTER 61	PROSE

EYED   SEE FAIR EYED,WALL EYED

[OR EYED WITH LITTLE SPARKS OF HELL OR WITH INFERNAL BRANDS]	109	TIRIEL 8	15
SULLEN SAT LOS PLOTTING REVENGE SILENT HE [URIZEN] EYED THE PRINCE	273	FOUR ZOAS 1	320
AND THE DIM CHAOS BRIGHTEND BENEATH ABOVE AROUND EYED AS THE PEACOCK	745	JERUSALEM 98	14

EYEING

HIS DISMAL VOYAGE EYEING THE NEXT SPHERE THO FAR REMOTE	316	FOUR ZOAS 6	183
OF HOREB STILL EYEING ALBION'S CLIFFS EAGERLY SIEZING & TWISTING	704	JERUSALEM 67	27
THUS JOYD THE SPECTRE IN THE DUSKY FIRES OF LOS'S FORGE EYEING	734	JERUSALEM 88	44

EYELESS

CARE BROUGHT FORTH COVET EYELESS & PRONE TO TH EARTH .	42C	THEN SHE BORE	PROSE
THOU SHALT NOT SMITE MY MOTHER MNETHA O THOU EYELESS MAN	101	TIRIEL 2	26
WHO ART THOU EYELESS WRETCH THAT THUS OBSTRUCTST THE LIONS PATH	103	TIRIEL 4	5
TO SMITE (THEE) IN THE FORM OF HELPLESS AGE & EYELESS POLICY	104	TIRIEL 4	* 18
THOU EYELESS FIEND & YOU DISSEMBLERS IS THIS TIRIEL'S HOUSE	106	TIRIEL 4	86
NOT EYELESS COVET	256	BOOK OF LOS 3	10
LIKE A FAMISHD EAGLE EYELESS RAGING IN THE VAST EXPANSE	297	FOUR ZOAS 4	10
INCLOSED BY EYELESS WINGS GLOWING WITH FIRE AS THE IRON	735	JERUSALEM 89	41

EYELIDS

WHY ARE EYELIDS STORD WITH ARROWS READY DRAWN	130	BOOK OF THEL 6	13
GLANCING HIS BEAMY EYELIDS OVER THE DEEP IN DARK DISMAY	159D	SONG LIBERTY	PROSE
DOES NOT THE GREAT MOUTH LAUGH AT A GIFT & THE NARROW EYELIDS MOCK	192	V DAU ALBION 5	7
ERE YET HIS EYELIDS CAN BEHOLD THE ARROWS OF THE DAY .	193	V DAU ALBION 5	32
MY WEARY EYELIDS DRAW TOWARDS THE EVENING MY BLISS IS YET BUT NEW	240	EUROPE 5	10
[AND ?COURTING THAT THE EARTH WOULD OPE HER EYELIDS & BEHOLD]	267	FOUR ZOAS 1	131
[THEN SLEEP FELL ON HER EYELIDS IN A CHASM OF THE VALLEY]	268	FOUR ZOAS 1	145

	PAGE	TITLE	LINE

EYELIDS   (CONTINUED)

IMAGE OF GRIEF THY FADING LINEAMENTS MAKE MY EYELIDS FAIL	297	FOUR ZOAS 3	195
WEIGHS DOWN HER EYELIDS THEN SHE FALLS THEN STARTING WAKES IN FEARS	297	FOUR ZOAS 3	210
SWEAT & BLOOD STOOD ON THE LIMBS OF LOS IN GLOBES HIS FIERY EYELIDS	307	FOUR ZOAS 5	67
THE EYELIDS EXPANSIVE AS MORNING & THE EARS	318	FOUR ZOAS 6	249
VIBRATED IN SUCH ANGUISH THE EYELIDS QUIVERD	318	FOUR ZOAS 6	256
THY EYELIDS ARE A TERROR TO ME & THE FLAMING OF THY CREST	335	FOUR ZOAS 7B	83
BENEATH DOWN TO HIS EYELIDS SCALES OF PEARL THEN GOLD & SILVER	342	FOUR ZOAS 8	70
LASHES HIS TAIL IN THE [WIDE] WILD DEEP HIS EYELIDS LIKE THE SUN	352	FOUR ZOAS 8 *	439
HIS EYELIDS GIVE THEIR LIGHT AROUND HIS FOLDING TAIL ASPIRES	352	FOUR ZOAS 8	447
AND SOFT SLEEP FELL UPON HER EYELIDS IN THE SILENT NOON OF DAY	369	FOUR ZOAS 9	457
THEN LAST HERSELF LAID DOWN & CLOSD HER EYELIDS IN SOFT SLUMBERS	370	FOUR ZOAS 9	516
FOR HIS EYELIDS WERE NARROWD & HIS NOSTRILS SCENTED THE GROUND	662	JERUSALEM 36	2
UPON THE ROCK HE OPEND HIS EYELIDS IN PAIN IN PAIN HE MOVD	742	JERUSALEM 95	3

EYE-LIDS

| . . . A DARKNESS CREPT OVER HIS EYE-LIDS AND CHILL COLD SWEAT | 147 | FRENCH REVOLTN | 295 |

EYE'S

| TO THE VEGETATED MORTAL EYE'S PERVERTED & SINGLE VISION | 684 | JERUSALEM 53 | 11 |

EYES

THINE ANGEL EYES UPON OUR WESTERN ISLE	1	TO SPRING/PS	3
VALLIES HEAR ALL OUR LONGING EYES ARE TURNED	1	TO SPRING/PS	6
IN RIBBED STEEL I DARE NOT LIFT MINE EYES	3	TO WINTER/PS	7
ON EVERY FLOWER THAT SHUTS ITS SWEET EYES	3	EVNING STAR/PS	7
THE LAKE SPEAK (SILENCE) WITH THY GLIMMERING EYES . .	3	EVNING STAR/PS *	9
MY LORD WAS LIKE THE OPENING EYES OF DAY	5	FAIR ELENOR/PS	47
HER EYES WERE FIXD THE BLOODY CLOTH UNFOLDS	5	FAIR ELENOR/PS	57
WHERE INNOCENT EYES DO GLANCE	7	LOVE JOCUND/PS	3
MAKE WEEP THE EYES OF DAY	9	MAD SONG/PS	14
CLOSES HER EYES IN SLEEP BENEATH NIGHT'S SHADE	10	FRESH FROM/PS	18
I TURN MY EYES AND PENSIVE AS I GO	10	WHEN EARLY/PS	9
OR HAVE THY SOFT PITEOUS EYES BEHELD	15	IMIT SPEN/PS	51
AND NOW WILL'S EYES BEHELD THE PLAY	16	BLIND-MANS/PS	27
HIS OWN HEAD UP BUT NOT HIS EYES	16	BLIND-MANS/PS	32
THAT THE ASTONISHD WORLD WITH UP-TURND EYES	18	EDW THIRD/PS 1	40
TOILS IN HIS WARS AND TURNS HIS EYES ON THIS	19	EDW THIRD/PS 2	8
FROM HIS EYES ACROSS THE FIELD I HAVE SEEN HIM	22	EDW THIRD/PS 3	28
HIS DROPPING EYES THE DITTY WAS IF HE	25	EDW THIRD/PS 3	165
WHOSE EYES DO GLARE AGAINST THE STORMY FIRES	32	EDW THIRD/PS 6	9
CASTING HER BLUE EYES OVER THE GREEN OCEAN	33	EDW THIRD/PS 6	56
PREPARE YOUR EYES TO MEET A HOLY GOD	34	WAR SONG/PS	9
MY WAYS ARE SINFUL HOW SHOULD I RAISE MINE EYES	36A	COUCH DEATH/PS	PROSE
CAN I NOT CRY AND LIFT MY EYES TO HEAVEN	36B	COUCH DEATH/PS	PROSE
AND THE THANKFUL EYES OF THE VILLAGERS ARE TURNED UP IN SMILES	36C	COUCH DEATH/PS	PROSE
EYES THE DISTANT COUNTRY WITH JOY	36C	COUCH DEATH/PS	PROSE
PUT ON THY COUNTRY'S PRIDE DECEIT AND EYES OF LOVE . . .	38A	SAMSON/PS	PROSE
THOU LOVEST ME NOT LOOK NOT UPON ME WITH THOSE DEATHFUL EYES	38C	SAMSON/PS	PROSE
TWAS THE RUDE THUNDER STROKE THAT CLOSD HER EYES	43C	WOE CRIED MUSE	PROSE
BUT IT WAS NOT SO SHE WAS THINKING OF THE SHAPE OF HER EYES	44B	ISLAND MOON 1	PROSE
ETRUSCAN COLUMN & INFLAMMABLE GASS FIXD THEIR EYES . . .	44C	ISLAND MOON 1	PROSE
I DONT LIKE HIS EYES SAID ETRUSCAN COLUMN	44C	ISLAND MOON 1	PROSE
& SHUTTING HIS EYES BEGAN TO SCRATCH HIS HEAD	45B	ISLAND MOON 1	PROSE
OBTUSE ANGLE SHUTTING HIS EYES & SAYING THAT HE ALWAYS .	45D	ISLAND MOON 1	PROSE
UNDERSTOOD BETTER WHEN HE SHUT HIS EYES [?SAID]	45D	ISLAND MOON 1	*PROSE
BEFORE HIS EYES LIKE THE ANIMAL UPON THE PYTHAGOREAN'S LAP	46A	ISLAND MOON 1	PROSE
[BUT DARK WERE HIS ONCE PIERCING EYES]	99	TIRIEL 1	2
BUT NOW HIS EYES WERE DARKNED & HIS WIFE FADING IN DEATH	99	TIRIEL 1	4
THE ORBS OF HIS LARGE EYES HE OPEND & THUS HIS VOICE WENT FORTH	99	TIRIEL 1	21
LOOK AT MY EYES BLIND AS THE ORBLESS [XXX] SCULL AMONG THE STONES	99	TIRIEL 1 *	28
HE WANDERS WITHOUT EYES & PASSES THRO THICK WALLS & DOORS	101	TIRIEL 2	25
GOD BLESS [XXX] THY POOR BALD PATE GOD BLESS THY HOLLOW WINKING EYES	101	TIRIEL 2 *	35
BLESS THY POOR EYES OLD MAN & BLESS THE OLD FATHER OF TIRIEL	101	TIRIEL 2	40
HOW DIDST THOU LOSE THY EYES OLD TIRIEL BLESS THY WRINKLED FACE	101	TIRIEL 2	43
IF THOU DOST GO SAID HAR I WISH THINE EYES MAY SEE THY FOLLY	102	TIRIEL 3	17
BUT DWELL WITH US & LET US BE TO THEE INSTEAD OF EYES . .	103	TIRIEL 3	34
LOOK KNOWST THOU AUGHT OF THIS GREY BEARD OR OF THESE BLINDED EYES	104	TIRIEL 4	44
[O NOBLE IJIM THOU HAST BROUGHT OUR FATHER TO [THE GATES] OUR EYES]	105	TIRIEL 4	75
AS TIRIEL'S & ALL EYES AS BLIND AS TIRIEL'S TO YOUR WOES	106	TIRIEL 5	21
TWAS FOR THY SELF THOU CRUEL MAN BECAUSE THOU WANTEST EYES	107	TIRIEL 6	15
LOOK ON MY EYES HELA & SEE FOR THOU HAST EYES TO SEE . .	108	TIRIEL 6	29
TWAS THOU THAT CHAIND THY BROTHER ZAZEL WHERE ARE NOW THINE EYES	108	TIRIEL 7	9
WHILE I CLOSE MY EYES	113	LIT GRL LST/SI	32
FROM HIS EYES OF FLAME	113	LIT GRL LST/SI	47

645

EYES   (CONTINUED)

THEY LOOK UPON HIS EYES . . . .   114 LIT GRL FND/SI   33
AND THERE THE LION'S RUDDY EYES   . . . .   119 NIGHT/SI   33
CHASE NOT SLUMBER FROM THY EYES   . . . .   120 CRADLE SONG/SI   14
DESCEND O LITTLE CLOUD & HOVER BEFORE THE EYES OF THEL . .   128 BOOK OF THEL 2   16
IN MILKY FONDNESS THEN ON THEL SHE FIXD HER HUMBLE EYES   129 BOOK OF THEL 4   9
. . . IN THE EYES OF THE KINGLY MOURNER . . . .   134 FRENCH REVOLTN   6
HIS FEET AND HANDS CUT OFF AND HIS EYES BLINDED . . .   .   136 FRENCH REVOLTN   44
. . . OR MIRABEAU'S EYES OR THE SHOULDERS OF TARGET . . .   142 FRENCH REVOLTN   187
. . . HIS EYES AND HIS HEART   . . . .   144 FRENCH REVOLTN   218
THE EYES OF FIRE THE NOSTRILS OF AIR . . . .   152B MARRIAGE HH 9   PROSE
[AND] HE [TURND] TURNED UP HIS EYES   . . . .   163 ASKED THIEF/N * 2
HER [EYES FLED] [ORBS DEAD] LIGHT FLED   . . . . . .   168 EARTHS ANSWR/N   3
[BURNT THE] [THE CRUEL] FIRE OF THINE EYES   . . . . .   172 THE TYGER/N 1   6
[WERE THY EYES OF FURY ROLLD]   . . . .   172 THE TYGER/N 1   17
THE CRUEL FIRE OF THINE EYES   . . . .   173 THE TYGER/N 2 * 6
EYES AND EARS AND SENSE OF TOUCH YET ARE THEIR HABITATIONS   191 V DAU ALBION 3   5
IF THEOTORMON ONCE WOULD TURN HIS LOVED EYES UPON ME   . .   191 V DAU ALBION 3   15
OR POISON FROM THE DESART WILDS FROM THE EYES OF   192 V DAU ALBION 4   11
THE ENVIER
THOU KNOWEST THAT THE ANCIENT TREES SEEN BY THINE EYES   192 V DAU ALBION 4   13
HAVE FRUIT
ONCE WERE THY FIRES LIGHTED BY THE EYES OF HONEST MORN   . .   194 V DAU ALBION 6   15
IF IN THE MORNING SUN I FIND IT THERE MY EYES ARE FIXD   . .   194 V DAU ALBION 6   23
TILL HIS EYES SICKEN AT THE FRUIT THAT HANGS BEFORE HIS   194 V DAU ALBION 7   20
SIGHT
WITH LAMPLIKE EYES WATCHING AROUND THE FROZEN MARRIAGE BED   194 V DAU ALBION 7   22
I HOWL MY JOY AND MY RED EYES SEEK TO BEHOLD THY FACE   . .   196 AMERICA PREL 1   19
HEADS DEPREST VOICES WEAK EYES DOWNCAST HANDS WORK-BRUISD   197 AMERICA 3   10
HIS VOICE HIS LOCKS HIS AWFUL SHOULDERS AND HIS GLOWING   197 AMERICA 3   17
EYES
WHY DOST THOU COME TO ANGELS EYES IN THIS TERRIFIC FORM   198 AMERICA 7   7
AND EYES OF DEATH THE HARLOT WOMB OFT OPENED IN VAIN   . .   199 AMERICA 9   18
PALE QUIVRING TOWARD THE BRAIN HIS GLIMMERING EYES TEETH   202 AMERICA 15   7
CHATTERING
HEADS DEPREST VOICES WEAK EYES DOWNCAST HANDS WORK BRUISED   204 AMERICA CANC A   10
HIS VOICE HIS LOCKS HIS AWFUL SHOULDERS & HIS GLOWING EYES   204 AMERICA CANC A   17
BURNT THE FIRE OF THINE EYES   . . . .   214 THE TYGER/SE   6
DIDST BIND MY NOSTRILS EYES & EARS   . . . .   220 TO TIRZAH/SE   12
HIS EYES BEHELD THE DEEP   . . . .   228 URIZEN 11   16
AND NOW SEEN NOW OBSCURD TO THE EYES   . . . . . .   230 URIZEN 15   6
SO THE EXPANDING EYES OF IMMORTALS   . . . .   231 URIZEN 15   11
TILL THE SHRUNKEN EYES CLOUDED OVER   . . . .   236 URIZEN 25   31
APPEARD TRANSPARENT AIR FOR THEIR EYES   . . . . . .   236 URIZEN 25   35
GREW SMALL LIKE THE EYES OF A MAN   . . . .   236 URIZEN 25   36
AND THEIR EYES COULD NOT DISCERN   . . . .   236 URIZEN 28   17
AND THINE EYES REJOICE BECAUSE OF STRENGTH O RINTRAH   240 EUROPE 8   12
FURIOUS KING
IN DELUGE OER THE EARTH-BORN MAN THEN TURND THE FLUXILE   241 EUROPE 10   11
EYES
BEFORE THEIR SHRUNKEN EYES   . . . .   246 SONG OF LOS 4   12
THAT THE LUST OF THE EYES MAY BE QUENCHD   . . . . .   247 SONG OF LOS 7   4
AND HIS EYES PALE WITH ANGUISH HIS LIPS . . . . . .   250 AHANIA 3   2
A HORRIBLE WASTE TO MY EYES   . . . .   254 AHANIA 4   59
HIS VOICE & BOW NOR SEE HIS EYES   . . . .   254 AHANIA 4   67
HE TURNED UP HIS EYES   . . . .   261 ASKED THIEF   2
ENION SAID FAREWELL I DIE I HIDE FROM THY SEARCHING EYES   266 FOUR ZOAS 1   68
. . . WITHIN MY [EYES] SOUL WANDERING] . . . .   267 FOUR ZOAS 1   113
[ALREADY ARE MY EYES REVERTED ALL THAT I BEHOLD] . . . .   267 FOUR ZOAS 1   115
GLORYING IN HIS OWN EYES EXALTED IN TERRIFIC PRIDE   . . .   267 FOUR ZOAS 1   129
[SEARCHING FOR GLORY WISHING THAT THE HEAVENS HAD EYES   267 FOUR ZOAS 1   130
TO SEE]
FADED & HER BRIGHT EYES DECAYD MELTED WITH PITY & LOVE   . .   270 FOUR ZOAS 1   213
DESCEND THEY COULD NOT NOR FROM EACH OTHER AVERT THEIR EYES   274 FOUR ZOAS 1   362
EYES OF GOD & THE SEVEN LAMPS OF THE ALMIGHTY . . . . .   279 FOUR ZOAS 1   554
HIS INWARD EYES CLOSING FROM THE DIVINE VISION & ALL   . .   279 FOUR ZOAS 1   558
TURNING HIS EYES OUTWARD TO SELF LOSING THE DIVINE VISION   280 FOUR ZOAS 2   2
THEIR EYES THEIR EARS NOSTRILS & TONGUES ROLL OUTWARD THEY   281 FOUR ZOAS 2   54
BEHOLD
[RAISE THEN THY RADIANT EYES TO HIM RAISE THY OBEDIENT   292 FOUR ZOAS 3   28
HANDS]
THE DISMAL VISION OF MINE EYES O LOVE & LIFE & LIGHT   . .   293 FOUR ZOAS 3   73
DOWNWARD & YOUR FLUXILE EYES ENGLOBD ROLL ROUND IN FEAR   294 FOUR ZOAS 3   87
MY SKULL RIVEN INTO FILAMENTS MY EYES INTO SEA JELLIES   296 FOUR ZOAS 3   163
ART THOU FOR EVER VANISHED FROM THE WATRY EYES OF THARMAS   297 FOUR ZOAS 3   202
FOR HER BRIGHT EYES BEHOLD THE ABYSS SOMETIMES A LITTLE   297 FOUR ZOAS 3   209
SLEEP
DOUBTING STOOD THARMAS IN THE [DISMAL] SOLEMN DARKNESS   298 FOUR ZOAS 4 * 44
HIS DIM EYES
THY LOVED ENITHARMON FOR THOU HAST HER HERE BEFORE THINE   300 FOUR ZOAS 4   117
EYES
BEFORE MY EYES & AN ETERNAL WEARY WORK TO STRIVE . . . .   301 FOUR ZOAS 4   144
A HORRIBLE CHAOS TO HIS EYES A FORMLESS UNMEASURABLE DEATH   301 FOUR ZOAS 4   162
HIDING CAREFULLY FROM THE WIND HIS EYES BEHELD THE DEEP   303 FOUR ZOAS 4   230
OUR EYES TO THE DIVINE PAVILIONS THEREFORE IN MERCY THOU   304 FOUR ZOAS 4   256
PALE TERROR SIEZD THE EYES OF LOS AS HE BEAT ROUND   . . .   305 FOUR ZOAS 4 * 284
[ON] WITH STONY EYES ON URIZEN & THEN SWIFT WRITHD HIS   305 FOUR ZOAS 4 * 291
NECK
FROM HIS MOUTH CURSES & FROM HIS EYES SPARKS OF BLIGHTING   305 FOUR ZOAS 5   3
SOON AS HIS BURNING EYES WERE OPEND ON THE ABYSS . . . .   306 FOUR ZOAS 5   39
IN HIS YOUNG EYES DISCERNING PLAIN THAT ORC PLOTTED HIS   307 FOUR ZOAS 5   82
DEATH

```
                                                       PAGE      TITLE           LINE
EYES    (CONTINUED)
        HIS EYES THE LIGHTS OF HIS LARGE SOUL CONTRACT OR ELSE      308 FOUR ZOAS 5        121
           EXPAND
        O FOOL TO THINK THAT I COULD HIDE FROM HIS ALL PIERCING     310 FOUR ZOAS 5        214
           EYES
        AND THY FAIR LOCKS SHADOWD THINE EYES FROM THE DIVINE       311 FOUR ZOAS 5        231
           EFFULGENCE
        HIDING THEMSELVES IN ROCKY FORMS FROM THE EYES OF URIZEN    312 FOUR ZOAS 6         23
        AND SAW THEIR GRIZLY FEARS & HIS EYES SICKEND AT THE SIGHT  313 FOUR ZOAS 6         80
        WERE HEAVY & DULL & THEIR EYES & NOSTRILS CLOSED UP    . .  315 FOUR ZOAS 6        125
        OF HAIR SHOOT FROM HIS ORBED SCULL HIS GLOWING EYES  . . .  319 FOUR ZOAS 6        308
        FOREHEAD & EYES THY LIPS DECAY LIKE ROSES IN [EARLY] THE    325 FOUR ZOAS 7        189
           SPRING
        FIRST BORN OF GENERATION THEN BEHOLD A WONDER TO THE EYES   326 FOUR ZOAS 7        245
        FOR HIS FRAIL EYES WERE FADED & HIS EARS HEAVY & DULL  . .  326 FOUR ZOAS 7        250
        IN ODOROUS STUPEFACTION STOOD BEFORE THE EYES OF MAN    . . 327 FOUR ZOAS 7        281
        CRAVING & DEVOURING BUT MY EYES ARE ALWAYS UPON THEE O      327 FOUR ZOAS 7        306
           LOVELY
        . . . NOR COULD HIS EYES PERCIEVE   . . . . . . . . . . .   328 FOUR ZOAS 7        319
        THO HORRIBLE & GHASTLY TO THINE EYES THO BURIED BENEATH     329 FOUR ZOAS 7        351
        TURN INWARDLY THINE EYES & THERE BEHOLD THE LAMB OF GOD     330 FOUR ZOAS 7        415
        HIS DISK INTO A TERRIBLE VISION TO THE EYES OF TREMBLING    335 FOUR ZOAS 7B   *   80
           MORTALS
        LIFT UP THY BLUE EYES VALA & PUT ON THY SAPPHIRE SHOES  . . 337 FOUR ZOAS 7B      191
        DOTH ENION AVOID THE SIGHT OF THY BLUE WATRY EYES   . . .   339 FOUR ZOAS 7B      230
        SWAM LIKE A DREAM BEFORE MY EYES I WENT TO SEEK THE STEPS   339 FOUR ZOAS 7B      235
        BEFORE MY EYES & FOR EVERY ONE OF THESE I AM CONDEMND   .   339 FOUR ZOAS 7B      252
        MY EYES TO THY PAVILIONS HEAR MY PRAYER FOR LUVAH'S SAKE    345 FOUR ZOAS 8       152
        RESIDES THAT GOD OF MY DELIGHT O MIGHT MY EYES BEHOLD       345 FOUR ZOAS 8       156
        THESE FIBRES OF THINE EYES THAT USED TO WANDER IN DISTANT   348 FOUR ZOAS 8       301
           HEAVENS
        HIS EYES [HIS] THEN SHOT OUTWARDS . . . . . . . . . . .     352 FOUR ZOAS 8   *  422
        ABOMINABLE TO THE EYES OF MORTALS WHO EXPLORE HIS BOOKS     352 FOUR ZOAS 8       430
        OFT DOTH HIS EYES EMERGE FROM THE ABYSS INTO THE REALMS     352 FOUR ZOAS 8   *  454
        SAW NOT AS YET THE DIVINE VISION HER EYES ARE TOWARD URIZEN 353 FOUR ZOAS 8       491
        LISTEN TO HER WHOSE EYES BEHOLD THE DARK BODY OF            354 FOUR ZOAS 8       505
           CORRUPTIBLE DEATH
        HIS EYES SINK HOLLOW IN HIS HEAD HIS FLESH COVERD WITH      354 FOUR ZOAS 8       515
           SLIME
        HE DROOPS HIS HEAD & TREMBLING STANDS & HIS BRIGHT EYES     354 FOUR ZOAS 8       531
           DECAY
        THESE ARE THE VISIONS OF MY EYES THE VISIONS OF AHANIA      354 FOUR ZOAS 8       532
        WHICH TO THEIR PHANTOM EYES APPEARD STILL IN THE SEPULCHER  357 FOUR ZOAS 9         3
        HE LIFTS THE BLUE LAMPS OF HIS EYES & CRIES WITH HEAVENLY   359 FOUR ZOAS 9        97
           VOICE
        A GLORIOUS VISION [OF] TO THINE EYES A SELF RENEWING VISION 362 FOUR ZOAS 9       211
        OR WHERE ARE HUMAN FEET FOR LO OUR EYES ARE IN THE HEAVENS  363 FOUR ZOAS 9       229
        WILD FURIES FROM THE TYGER'S BRAIN & FROM THE LION'S EYES   363 FOUR ZOAS 9       236
        AND AS SHE ROSE HER EYES WERE OPEND TO THE WORLD OF WATERS  369 FOUR ZOAS 9       483
        AMONG HER FLOCKS & SHE TURND HER EYES TOWARD HER PLEASANT   370 FOUR ZOAS 9       506
           HOUSE
        AWAKE O ENION AWAKE & LET THINE INNOCENT EYES      . . . .  371 FOUR ZOAS 9       519
        OPEN THE ORBS OF THY BLUE EYES & SMILE UPON MY GARDENS  . . 371 FOUR ZOAS 9       522
        WHY DOST THOU TURN THYSELF AWAY FROM HIS SWEET WATRY EYES   371 FOUR ZOAS 9       526
        O BLESS THE LOVELY EYES OF THARMAS & THE EYES OF ENION      371 FOUR ZOAS 9       528
        DOTH ENION AVOID THE SIGHT OF THY BLUE HEAVENLY EYES    . . 371 FOUR ZOAS 9       531
        SWIMS LIKE A DREAM BEFORE MY EYES BUT THE SWEET SMELLING    371 FOUR ZOAS 9       539
           FRUIT
        BUT IN THE MORNING SHE ARISES TO AVOID MY EYES     . . . .  371 FOUR ZOAS 9       543
        THE GROUND SPIDER WITH MANY EYES THE MOLE CLOTHED IN VELVET 377 FOUR ZOAS 9       758
        HIS EYES BEHOLD THE ANGELIC SPHERES ARISING NIGHT & DAY     379 FOUR ZOAS 9       828
        THE EXPANDING EYES OF MAN BEHOLDS THE DEPTHS OF WONDROUS    379 FOUR ZOAS 9   *  830
           WORLDS
        ALL FALSE IN THE EYES OF ONE MAN & TRUE IN THE EYES OF      393B ANNO WATSON      MARG
        DAZZLING BRIGHT BEFORE MY EYES . . . . . . . . . . .        422 BENEATH/N           9
        [DAZZLING BRIGHT BEFORE MY EYES]  . . . . . . . . . .       422 BENEATH REWR/N      6
        DAZLING BRIGHT BEFORE MY EYES  . . . . . . . . . . .        424 THE GOLDEN NET      8
        HER EYES OUTSHINE EVERY BRILLIANT RAY   . . . . . .         428 MARY                7
        I WILL KEEP FROM THE BALL & MY EYES SHALL NOT SHINE  . . .  428 MARY               30
        WITH FACES OF SCORN & WITH EYES OF DISDAIN . . . . . .      429 MARY               41
        TAPROOM THREATENED TO KNOCK WILLIAM'S EYES OUT     . . . .  438C BLAKES MEMORAN   PROSE
        THAT MORTAL EYES CANNOT BEHOLD  . . . . . . . . . .         442 DEDICATN BLAIR      2
        BUT WHEN THE MORTAL EYES ARE CLOSD    . . . . . . . .       442 DEDICATN BLAIR      3
        FILLED WITH EYES ATTENDED BY SEVEN ANGELS   . . . . . .     444A LAST JUDGMNT/L   PROSE
        UNDER THEIR EYES CANNOT SEE RAFAEL . . . . . . . . .        447C ANNO REYNOLDS    MARG
        THE EYES BEHELD THE ABYSS LEST BONES OF SOLIDNESS FREEZE    482 MILTON 3           15
           OVER ALL
        UPON HIS FIBROUS LEFT FOOT BLACK MOST DISMAL TO OUR EYES    506 MILTON 22          35
        AND THAT THE SEVEN EYES OF GOD MAY HAVE SPACE FOR           507 MILTON 23          52
           REDEMPTION
        BECAUSE OF SATAN & THE SEVEN EYES OF GOD CONTINUALLY   . .  508 MILTON 24           7
        WHEN WITH OUR VEGETABLE EYES WE VIEW THESE WONDROUS VISIONS 512 MILTON 26          12
        THE GROUND SPIDER WITH MANY EYES THE MOLE CLOTHED IN VELVET 513 MILTON 27          14
        THEIR MILD INFLUENCES THEREFORE THE SEVEN EYES OF GOD WALK  517 MILTON 29          54
           ROUND
        WITH EYES OF SOFT HUMILITY & WONDER LOVE & AWE     . . .    520 MILTON 31          38
        OPENS HER MANY LOVELY EYES LISTENING THE ROSE STILL SLEEPS  520 MILTON 31          56
        THAT THE SEVEN EYES OF GOD WHO WALK EVEN TO SATAN'S SEAT    526 MILTON 35          64
        OF PROVIDENCE & WITH THE EYES OF GOD ALL NIGHT IN SLUMBERS  526 MILTON 36           5
        THUS IT APPEARS TO MORTAL EYES & THOSE OF THE ULRO HEAVENS  527 MILTON 36          11
        AND I ALAS LIVE TO WEEP OUT MINE EYES    . . . . . . . .    537 AND HIS LEGS/N     41
        NARROW BLINKING EYES THAT HAVE TOO LONG GOVERNED ART   . .  563D DESC CAT         PROSE
```

647

		PAGE	TITLE	LINE
EYES	(CONTINUED)			
	IN A DARK CORNER THE EYES OF STUPID CUNNING NEVER WILL BE	563 D	DESC CAT	PROSE
	WAS IMPOSSIBLE IF WE DID NOT SEE IT ALWAYS BEFORE OUR EYES	578 D	DESC CAT 5	PROSE
	AND HIS EXTREMITIES LARGE HIS EYES WITH SCARCE ANY WHITES	580 A	DESC CAT 5	PROSE
	WHO COULD NOT DO THIS WHAT MAN WHO HAS EYES	597 B	PUB ADDRESS/N	PROSE
	WHO THAT HAS EYES CANNOT SEE THAT RUBENS & CORREGGIO	599 D	PUB ADDRESS/N	*PROSE
	EVERY MAN HAS EYES NOSE & MOUTH THIS EVERY IDIOT KNOWS	611 B	V LAST JUDG/N	PROSE
	TO OPEN THE ETERNAL WORLDS TO OPEN THE IMMORTAL EYES	623	JERUSALEM 5	18
	WATCHING HIS TIME WITH GLOWING EYES TO LEAP UPON HIS PREY	627	JERUSALEM 8	22
	AND THE EYES ARE THE SOUTH AND THE NOSTRILS ARE THE EAST	632	JERUSALEM 12	59
	I TURN MY EYES TO THE SCHOOLS & UNIVERSITIES OF EUROPE	636	JERUSALEM 15	14
	THEN MOURNS THE WANDERER THEN HE REPENTS HIS WANDERINGS & EYES	642	JERUSALEM 20	14
	THE VEIL SHONE WITH THY BRIGHTNESS IN THE EYES OF ALBION	643	JERUSALEM 20	34
	. . . FROM THY DREAD [COUTENANCE] COUNTENANCE & SEARCHING EYES	645	JERUSALEM 22 *	13
	DOWNWARD AND YOUR FLUXILE EYES ENGLOBD ROLL ROUND IN FEAR	655	JERUSALEM 29	68
	LOS ROLLED HIS EYES INTO TWO NARROW CIRCLES THEN SENT HIM	661	JERUSALEM 34	53
	O SEARCH & SEE TURN YOUR EYES INWARD OPEN O THOU WORLD	675	JERUSALEM 44	41
	AND THEY ELECTED SEVEN CALLD THE SEVEN EYES OF GOD	686	JERUSALEM 55	31
	MY WEARY EYES EVEN IN THIS DUNGEON & THIS IRON MILL	693	JERUSALEM 60	59
	THE CHARIOT WHEELS FILLED WITH EYES RAGE ALONG THE HOWLING VALLEY	697	JERUSALEM 63	11
	LIFT UP THY BLUE EYES VALA & PUT ON THY SAPPHIRE SHOES	700	JERUSALEM 65	37
	LIDS TO GROW OVER HIS EYES IN VEILS OF TEARS AND CAVERNS	702	JERUSALEM 66	31
	ALL WHO SEE BECOME WHAT THEY BEHOLD THEIR EYES ARE COVERD	702	JERUSALEM 66	36
	THESE FIBRES OF THINE EYES THAT USED TO BEAM IN DISTANT HEAVENS	705	JERUSALEM 67	47
	OF ALBION DELIGHTS THE EYES OF THE KINGS THEIR HEARTS & THE	706	JERUSALEM 68	16
	O VIRGIN OF TERRIBLE EYES WHO DWELLEST BY VALLEYS OF SPRINGS	706	JERUSALEM 68	54
	FOR HELL IS OPEND TO HEAVEN THINE EYES BEHELD	718	STOOD AMONG/J	34
	ABOVE HIS HEAD HIGH ARCHING WINGS BLACK FILLD WITH EYES	735	JERUSALEM 89	28
	JEHOVAH WOMAN LIFT THINE EYES	779	GHOST ABEL 1	7
	BUT EVERY BODY DOES NOT SEE ALIKE TO THE EYES OF A MISER	793 D	LETTER 5	PROSE
	OF JOY IS IN THE EYES OF OTHERS ONLY A GREEN THING THAT STANDS	793 D	LETTER 5	PROSE
	SEE NATURE AT ALL BUT TO THE EYES OF THE MAN OF IMAGINATION	793 D	LETTER 5	PROSE
	APPEARD IN ITS VEGETATED MORTALITY TO MY MORTAL VEGETATED EYES	802 C	LETTER 14	PROSE
	MY EYES DID EXPAND	804	TO BUTTS/L	8
	MY EYES MORE & MORE	805	TO BUTTS/L	45
	MINIATURE (IS) BECOME A GODDESS IN MY EYES & MY FRIENDS	808 B	LETTER 19	*PROSE
	FOR DOUBLE THE VISION MY EYES DO SEE	817	HAPPINESS/L	27
	A GOOD LIKENESS OF YOU IF I HAVE HANDS & EYES LEFT	824 B	LETTER 27	PROSE
	PRAY TELL ME HOW YOUR EYES DO I NEVER SIT DOWN TO WORK	826 C	LETTER 28	PROSE
	WHOSE EYES HAVE DONE ME SO MUCH GOOD I OMITTED	826 C	LETTER 28	PROSE
	DEPARTURE HE THEN THREATEND TO KNOCK OUT MY EYES	827 A	LETTER 28	PROSE
	NOTWITHSTANDING HE WAS SHADED BY A GREEN SHADE OVER HIS EYES	835 C	LETTER 35	PROSE
	HIS EYES LIGHT UP AT THE MENTION OF YOUR NAME	844 B	LETTER 43	PROSE
	READING IN THE BIBLE OF THE EYES OF THE ALMIGHTY	860 D	LETTER 57	PROSE
	I AM SURE THAT ANY PERSON CONSULTING HIS OWN EYES MUST	864 D	LETTER 61	PROSE
	CANUTE DARK HAIR & EYES	SUPP	ILLUS HISTORY	*TITLE
EYNE				
	AND THE SUN BEAMS DAZZLE FROM HER EYNE	435	WILLIAM BOND	32
EZEKIEL				
	OF SODOM SEE EZEKIEL CH XVI...	79 D	ANNO LAVATER	MARG
	THE PROPHETS ISAIAH AND EZEKIEL DINED WITH ME AND I ASKED	153 B	MARRIAGE HH 12	PROSE
	THEN EZEKIEL SAID THE PHILOSOPHY OF THE EAST TAUGHT	153 D	MARRIAGE HH 12	PROSE
	EZEKIEL SAID THE SAME OF HIS I ALSO ASKED ISAIAH WHAT	154 A	MARRIAGE HH 12	PROSE
	I THEN ASKED EZEKIEL WHY HE EAT DUNG & LAY SO LONG ON HIS	154 A	MARRIAGE HH 12	PROSE
	BEEN COMPELLD TO SUBDUE THEIR MASTER EZEKIEL XXXVIII...	609 B	V LAST JUDG/N	PROSE
	IN EVERY MAN EZEKIEL SAW THEM BY CHEBAR'S FLOOD	632	JERUSALEM 12	58
	ADAM NOAH ABRAHAM MOSES SAMUEL DAVID EZEKIEL	714	JERUSALEM 73	41
	I HAVE ORDERS TO SET MY FACE LIKE A FLINT EZEKIEL...	825 B	LETTER 27	PROSE
	"THOU HAST SET THY HEART AS THE HEART OF GOD" EZEKIEL	SUPP	LEGEND/N94	*
EZEKIEL'S				
	FAMINE WAR MOSES STRIKING THE ROCK EZEKIEL'S WHEELS	SUPP	LETTER 56A	*PROSE
EZRA				
	EZRA CAME WITH ISAIAH THE PROPHET	799	TO FLAXMAN/L	6
FA				
	FA RA SO BO RO	56	FA RA SO BO/IM	1
	FA RA BO RA	56	FA RA SO BO/IM	2
	[FA] SA BA RA RA BA RARE RORO	56	FA RA SO BO/IM *	3
	FA ME LA SOL LA ME FA SOL	61	DR CLASH/IM	5
	FA ME LA SOL LA ME FA SOL	62	DR CLASH/IM	12
	FA ME LA SOL LA ME FA SOL	62	DR CLASH/IM	17
	FA ME LA SOL LA ME FA SOL	62	DR CLASH/IM	22
FABLE				
	PERHAPS THIS LITTLE FABLE &C	554	TO VENETIAN/N	3
	PERHAPS THIS LITTLE FABLE MAY MAKE US MERRY	554	TO VENETIAN/N	4
	THE LAST JUDGMENT IS NOT FABLE OR ALLEGORY BUT VISION	604 D	V LAST JUDG/N	PROSE
	FABLE OR ALLEGORY IS A TOTALLY DISTINCT & INFERIOR KIND	604 D	V LAST JUDG/N	PROSE
	FABLE OR ALLEGORY IS FORMD BY THE DAUGHTERS OF MEMORY	604 D	V LAST JUDG/N	PROSE
	WHO IN THE AGGREGATE ARE CALLD JERUSALEM FABLE IS ALLEGORY	604 D	V LAST JUDG/N	PROSE
	BUT WHAT CRITICS CALL THE FABLE IS VISION ITSELF	604 D	V LAST JUDG/N	PROSE
	NOTE HERE THAT FABLE OR (ALLEGORY) IS SELDOM WITHOUT	604 D	V LAST JUDG/N	*PROSE
	THE SAME BUT [FABLE & ALLEGORY] ALLEGORY & VISION	604 D	V LAST JUDG/N	PROSE
	BETWEEN ALLEGORIC FABLE & SPIRITUAL MYSTERY LET IT HERE BE	605 C	V LAST JUDG/N	PROSE
	IN FABLE & ALLEGORY [WHICH]	605 C	V LAST JUDG/N	PROSE
	OTHERS OF THE LIKE KIND ARE FABLE YET THEY CONTAIN VISION	607 A	V LAST JUDG/N	PROSE

		PAGE	TITLE	LINE

FABLE   (CONTINUED)
    WILL BE PLEASD TO REMEMBER THAT MINE IS VISION & NOT FABLE   608A V LAST JUDG/N   PROSE
    THE GREEKS REPRESENT CHRONOS OR TIME AS A VERY AGED MAN   614D V LAST JUDG/N   PROSE
       THIS IS FABLE
FABLED
    LIKE FABLED HECATE SHE DOTH BIND THEM TO HER LAW . . . . 41D THEN SHE BORE   PROSE
FABLES
    OF THE NORTH POLE AND ALL THE FABLES OF ARTHUR AND HIS . . 577D DESC CAT 5   PROSE
    NOTED THAT THE GREEK FABLES ORIGINATED IN SPIRITUAL MYSTERY 605C V LAST JUDG/N   PROSE
FABLE WRITER
    MUST EITHER BE THE ACTOR OR A FABLE WRITER OR A LIAR . . 390D ANNO WATSON   MARG
FABRIC
    REND DOWN THIS FABRIC AS A WALL RUIND & FAMILY EXTINCT . . 362 FOUR ZOAS 9   186
    BUT ALL REMAIN EVERY FABRIC OF SIX THOUSAND YEARS . . 505 MILTON 22   20
FABRICATE
    I FEEL TO FABRICATE EMBODIED SEMBLANCES IN WHICH THE DEAD 331 FOUR ZOAS 7   440
    WILT IN SWEET MODERATED FURY FABRICATE [SWEET] FORMS 331 FOUR ZOAS 7   453
       SUBLIME
    OTHERS CABINETS RICHLY FABRICATE OF GOLD & IVORY . . . . 515 MILTON 28   8
    THEY CONTEND WITH THE WEAK SPECTRES THEY FABRICATE SOOTHING 515 MILTON 28   23
       FORMS
FABRICATED
    THUS URIZEN IN SELF DECEIT HIS WARLIKE PREPARATIONS 343 FOUR ZOAS 8   *   86
       FABRICATED
    AND CHAINS & PULLIES FABRICATED ALL ROUND THE HEAVENS OF 343 FOUR ZOAS 8   95
       LOS
    FABRICATED FOR PLEASURE AS MODERNS SAY BUT I SAY 390D ANNO WATSON   MARG
       BY INSPIRATION
    CHARGE MUST HAVE BEEN FABRICATED IN THE STABLE AFTERWARDS 437C BLAKES MEMORAN PROSE
    AS THAT WHICH IS FABRICATED FOR THE PURPOSE TO DESTROY ART 563D DESC CAT   PROSE
    WHOSE WHOLE ART AND SCIENCE IS FABRICATED FOR THE PURPOSE 573B DESC CAT 3   PROSE
    A FABRICATED PERJURY I HAVE BEEN FORCED TO FIND BAIL . . 827D LETTER 28   *PROSE
FABRICATION
    LABOURED FABRICATION OF JOURNEY-WORK THEY COULD NOT DRAW 457A ANNO REYNOLDS * MARG
FACE
    HIS FACE IS FAIR AS HEAVN . . . . 6 MY SILKS/PS   7
    HE THOUGHT HIS FACE WAS T OTHER WAY . . . . 16 BLIND-MANS/PS   28
    MAYHAP YOU MAY LOOK UPON EDWARD'S FACE . . . . . . 21 EDW THIRD/PS 3   16
    HIS BACK THEN I WILL SAY IT TO HIS FACE . . . . . . 21 EDW THIRD/PS 3   18
    HE FEARS TO TURN HIS FACE AND YOU TO TURN YOUR BACK . . . 22 EDW THIRD/PS 3   41
    I SAW A LITTLE WELCHMAN WITH A FIERY FACE . . . . . . 25 EDW THIRD/PS 3   157
    THE FACE OF THE EARTH . . . . 25 EDW THIRD/PS 3   193
    WHOSE FACE IS SHEWN BY LIGHT OF SICKLY TAPER . . . . . 30 EDW THIRD/PS 5   24
    THE DAMPS OF DEATH FALL THICK UPON ME HORRORS STARE ME 35D COUCH DEATH/PS PROSE
       IN THE FACE
    IF I LAY MY FACE IN THE DUST THE GRAVE OPENS ITS MOUTH 36A COUCH DEATH/PS PROSE
       FOR ME
    SUCH SMILES WERE SEEN UPON THE FACE OF THE YOUTH . . . 36C COUCH DEATH/PS PROSE
    ALAS IN CITIES WHERES THE MAN WHOSE FACE IS NOT A MASK 42D THEN SHE BORE   PROSE
       UNTO HIS HEART
    WIPED HIS [HEAD] FACE WITH HIS POCKET HANDKERCHIEF . . 45B ISLAND MOON 1   PROSE
    HOW CAN YOU HAVE THE FACE TO MAKE GAME OF MATRIMONY . . . 57A ISLAND MOON 9   PROSE
    WIPING HIS FACE & LOOKING ON THE CORNER OF THE CIELING SANG 57A ISLAND MOON 9   *PROSE
    WITH FACE AS BROWN AS ANY NUT WITH DRINKING OF STRONG ALE 58 THIS CITY/IM   3
    DONT YOU THINK I HAVE SOMETHING OF THE GOAT'S FACE SAYS HE 62D ISLAND MOON 11 PROSE
    VERY LIKE A GOAT'S FACE SHE ANSWERD . . . . 62D ISLAND MOON 11 PROSE
    I THINK YOUR FACE SAID HE IS LIKE THAT NOBLE BEAST THE 62D ISLAND MOON 11 PROSE
       TYGER
    PALENESS FLIES FROM EVERY FACE . . . . 63 SHEPHERD FIRST   3
    HOW DIDST THOU LOSE THY EYES OLD TIRIEL BLESS THY WRINKLED 101 TIRIEL 2   43
       FACE
    HOW CAME THINE HAIR TO LEAVE THY FOREHEAD HOW CAME THY 102 TIRIEL 3   3
       FACE SO BROWN
    GOD BLESS THY PITEOUS FACE TO COUNT THE WRINKLES IN THY 102 TIRIEL 3   5
       FACE
    WOULD PUZZLE [HAR] MNETHA BLESS THY FACE FOR THOU 102 TIRIEL 3   6
       ART TIRIEL
    TIS NOW SEVEN YEARS SINCE IN MY PALACE I BEHELD THY FACE 104 TIRIEL 4   15
    FELL SHAKING AGONIES & IN EACH WRINKLE OF THAT FACE . . . 108 TIRIEL 6   38
    PITY A HUMAN FACE . . . . 117 DIVNE IMAGE/SI   10
    SWEET BABE IN THY FACE . . . . 120 CRADLE SONG/SI   21
    HEAVENLY FACE THAT SMILES ON THEE . . . . 120 CRADLE SONG/SI   28
    YOUR SOFT FACE . . . . 123 SPRING/SI   26
    AND THESE BLACK BODIES AND THIS SUN-BURNT FACE . . . . 125 LIT BLK BOY/SI   15
    LIKE DREAMS OF INFANTS LIKE A SMILE UPON AN INFANT'S FACE 127 BOOK OF THEL 1   10
    HE CROPS THY FLOWERS WHILE THOU SITTEST SMILING IN HIS FACE 128 BOOK OF THEL 2   6
    HOVERING AND GLITTERING ON THE AIR BEFORE THE FACE OF THEL 128 BOOK OF THEL 3   6
    . . . A MASK OF IRON ON HIS FACE HID THE LINEAMENTS . . 135 FRENCH REVOLTN   31
    HE SET HIS FACE TOWARD GENEVA TO FLEE . . . . 139 FRENCH REVOLTN * 122
    HE WHOSE FACE GIVES NO LIGHT SHALL NEVER BECOME A STAR . . 151A MARRIAGE HH 7   PROSE
    SWEET BABE IN THY FACE . . . . 165 CRADLE SONG/N   18
    AND [SEE] MARK IN EVERY FACE I MEET . . . . 170 LONDON/N   3
    MY FACE TURNS GREEN & PALE . . . . 171 NURSES SONG/N   4
    AND THUS I TURN MY FACE TO WHERE MY WHOLE SOUL SEEKS . . 189 V DAU ALBION 1   13
    I HOWL MY JOY AND MY RED EYES SEEK TO BEHOLD THY FACE . . 196 AMERICA PREL 1   19
    WHOSE FACE HAS NEVER SEEN A SMILE IN THIRTY WEARY YEARS 198 AMERICA 6   9
    MY FACE TURNS GREEN AND PALE . . . . 212 NURSES SONG/SE   4
    AND MARK IN EVERY FACE I MEET . . . . 216 LONDON/SE   3
    AND JEALOUSY A HUMAN FACE . . . . 221 DIVNE IMAGE/SE   2
    THE HUMAN FACE A FURNACE SEALD . . . . 221 DIVNE IMAGE/SE   7
    WAVES BEFORE HIS DEATHY FACE . . . . 231 URIZEN 18   8
    WAVING BEFORE THE FACE OF LOS . . . . 231 URIZEN 18   12

		PAGE	TITLE	LINE

FACE   (CONTINUED)

		PAGE	TITLE		LINE
TO A DEVOURING FLAME AND MAN FLED FROM ITS FACE AND HID		241	EUROPE 10		17
[WHERE IS THE VOICE THAT LATELY WOKE THE DESART WHERE THE FACE]		268	FOUR ZOAS 1		139
MAN FELL UPON HIS FACE PROSTRATE BEFORE THE WATRY SHADOW		293	FOUR ZOAS 3		54
AND VALA TREMBLED & COVERD HER FACE		293	FOUR ZOAS 3		56
WHY DOES THY PITEOUS FACE EVANISH LIKE A RAINY CLOUD		297	FOUR ZOAS 3		199
WAS A REFLECTION OF HIS FACE WHO CALLD ME FROM THE DEEP		310	FOUR ZOAS 5		217
SILENT HE STOOD OER ENITHARMON WATCHING HER PALE FACE		324	FOUR ZOAS 7		181
THY ROSES THAT EXPANDED IN THE FACE OF GLOWING MORN		325	FOUR ZOAS 7		194
PALE GREW THY FACE [THY SON'S] [& HIS]		325	FOUR ZOAS 7	*	227
BEFORE MY FACE ASCENDING WITH DELIGHT AS IN ANCIENT TIMES		331	FOUR ZOAS 7	*	445
THE NAMELESS SHADOWY VORTEX STOOD BEFORE THE FACE OF ORC		336	FOUR ZOAS 7B		125
AND SHE SAID THARMAS I AM VALA BLESS THY INNOCENT FACE		339	FOUR ZOAS 7B		229
WALKING BEFORE HER SHADOWY FACE & BOWING AT HER FEET		340	FOUR ZOAS 7B		279
REVEALD BEFORE THE FACE OF HEAVEN HIS SECRET HOLINESS		351	FOUR ZOAS 8		413
AND WHEN ALL TYRANNY WAS CUT OFF FROM THE FACE OF EARTH		359	FOUR ZOAS 9	*	80
AND ALL EXILED FROM THE FACE OF LIGHT & SHINE OF MORNING		360	FOUR ZOAS 9		112
WITH HARPS & SONGS WHERE BRIGHT AHANIA SANG BEFORE THY FACE		360	FOUR ZOAS 9	*	126
THAT THE ETERNAL WORLDS MAY SEE THY FACE IN PEACE & JOY		360	FOUR ZOAS 9		132
HIDING HIS FACE IN THE DUST BENEATH [A] THE PRISONER'S FEET & SAYING		364	FOUR ZOAS 9	*	269
THE PRISONER ANSWERS YOU SCOURGD MY FATHER TO DEATH BEFORE MY FACE		364	FOUR ZOAS 9		275
O THAT I COULD BEHOLD HIS FACE & FOLLOW HIS PURE FEET		368	FOUR ZOAS 9		426
MAN LIVETH NOT BY SELF ALONE BUT IN HIS BROTHER'S FACE		374	FOUR ZOAS 9		641
WHOSE FACE HAS NEVER SEEN A SMILE IN THIRTY WEARY YEARS		375	FOUR ZOAS 9		673
O WHY WAS I BORN WITH A DIFFERENT FACE		428	MARY		21
SHE REMEMBERS NO FACE LIKE THE HUMAN DIVINE		429	MARY		43
AND THINE IS A FACE OF SWEET LOVE IN DESPAIR		429	MARY		45
AND THINE IS A FACE OF MILD SORROW & CARE		429	MARY		46
AND THINE IS A FACE OF WILD TERROR & FEAR		429	MARY		47
THE FACE THAT IS INCAPABLE OF PASSION & EXPRESSION IS DEFORMITY		466A	ANNO REYNOLDS	MARG
HE DISPLACD CONTINENTS THE OCEANS FLED BEFORE HIS FACE		489	MILTON 9		16
HE SET HIS FACE AGAINST JERUSALEM TO DESTROY THE EON OF ALBION		491	MILTON 11		1
THE WHOLE ASSEMBLY WEPT PROPHETIC SEEING IN MILTON'S FACE		495	MILTON 14		11
WHEN RINTRAH & PALAMABRON SPOKE AND SUCH HIS STORMY FACE		507	MILTON 23	*	28
APPEARD AS DOES THE FACE OF HEAVEN WHEN COVERD WITH THICK STORMS		507	MILTON 23		29
WALKS AMONG ALL HIS AWFUL FAMILY SEEN IN EVERY FACE		519	MILTON 30		17
OF DREAD REPOSE SEEN BY THE VISIONARY EYE HIS FACE IS TOWARD		531	MILTON 39		33
IS OLOLON THE CAUSE OF THIS O WHERE SHALL I HIDE MY FACE		532	MILTON 40		14
TO CLEANSE THE FACE OF MY SPIRIT BY SELF-EXAMINATION		533	MILTON 40		37
[HIS] WHOSE HEART IS IRON HIS HEAD WOOD & HIS FACE BRASS		545	ON S(TOTHRD)/N		2
AND HE NEVER TURNS HIS FACE AWAY		558	I ROSE UP AT/N		14
WHAT IS TRULY GRAND AND REALLY POLITE HER PERSON AND FACE		568B	DESC CAT 3		PROSE
HIS OWN IDEA OF INTELLECTUAL BEAUTY THE FACE AND		580A	DESC CAT 5		PROSE
IS THE FACE AND LIMBS OF GREATEST BEAUTY AND PERFECTION		580A	DESC CAT 5		PROSE
FLEEING FROM THE FACE OF HIS PARENTS A DRAWING		584A	DESC CAT 11		TITLE
DO WE DISTINGUISH ONE FACE OR COUNTENANCE FROM ANOTHER		585C	DESC CAT 15		PROSE
DEPICTED IN HIS JOLLY FACE DIRECTS THEM TO THE		588C	CHAUCER/N		PROSE
THE WORK OF A BLOCKHEAD IT BEARS THIS EVIDENCE IN ITS FACE		599C	PUB ADDRESS/N		PROSE
THY EMANATION THAT WAS WONT TO PLAY BEFORE THY FACE		622	JERUSALEM 4		14
SO SPOKE THE SPECTRE SHUDDRING & DARK TEARS RAN DOWN HIS SHADOWY FACE		630	JERUSALEM 10		60
FACE IN TERRORS & PAINS OF HELL & ETERNAL DEATH THE		639	JERUSALEM 17		54
AND SELF-EXILED FROM THE FACE OF LIGHT & SHINE OF MORNING		641	JERUSALEM 19		13
WHERE WE DELIGHT IN INNOCENCE BEFORE THE FACE OF THE LAMB		642	JERUSALEM 20		9
HE DRIVES THEM THRO THE STREETS OF BABYLON BEFORE MY FACE		644	JERUSALEM 21		30
THEN ALBION TURND HIS FACE TOWARD JERUSALEM & SPOKE		645	JERUSALEM 22		25
AND THINE THE HUMAN FACE & THINE		651	FIELDS FROM/J		61
ALBION FELL UPON HIS FACE PROSTRATE BEFORE THE WATRY SHADOW		654	JERUSALEM 29		41
AND VALA TREMBLED & COVERD HER FACE		654	JERUSALEM 29		43
THE CITIES OF ALBION SEEK THY FACE LONDON GROANS IN PAIN		656	JERUSALEM 30		23
CHAOS BEFORE HIS FACE APPEARD AN UNFORMED MEMORY		659	JERUSALEM 33		2
ALBION GROANS HE SEES THE ELEMENTS DIVIDE BEFORE HIS FACE		663	JERUSALEM 36		27
HIS FACE AND BOSOM WITH PETRIFIC HARDNESS AND HIS HANDS		664	JERUSALEM 38		1
SO LOS SPOKE THEN TURND HIS FACE & WEPT FOR ALBION		670	JERUSALEM 42		46
THE ENGLISH ARE SCATTERD OVER THE FACE OF THE NATIONS ARE THESE		673	JERUSALEM 43		46
TO SIN IN THE OPEN FACE OF DAY IS CRUEL & PITILESS BUT		681	JERUSALEM 50		26
SAYING WHO WILL GO FORTH FOR US & WHO SHALL WE SEND BEFORE OUR FACE		687	JERUSALEM 55		69
BEFORE I HAD EVER BEHELD WITH LOVE THE FACE OF JEHOVAH OR KNOWN		695	JERUSALEM 61		42
BEFORE THE FACE OF ALBION A MIGHTY THREATNING FORM		708	JERUSALEM 70		2
ALWAYS BEHOLD THE FACE OF THE ?HEAVENLY FATHER		774A	ANNO BERKELEY		MARG
WHICH I HID MY FACE FOR NOT BEING ABLE TO ABANDON		798C	LETTER 10		PROSE
. . . THAT EVER I SAW FLAXMAN'S FACE		799	TO FLAXMAN/L		1
. . . MILTON LOVD ME IN CHILDHOOD & SHEWD ME HIS FACE		799	TO FLAXMAN/L		5
THE AMERICAN WAR BEGAN ALL ITS DARK HORRORS PASSED BEFORE MY FACE		799	TO FLAXMAN/L		9
WILL NEXT SUMMER JOKE US FACE TO FACE GOD BLESS YOU ALL		810C	LETTER 20		PROSE
YOU THRO LIFE & AFTER DEATH SHAME & CONFUSION OF FACE		813B	LETTER 22		PROSE
MY FACE IN FIERCE FLAMES IN MY DOUBLE SIGHT		818	HAPPINESS/L		57
YOUR ADVICE I SEE THE FACE OF MY HEAVENLY FATHER HE LAYS HIS		823B	LETTER 26		PROSE
I HAVE ORDERS TO SET MY FACE LIKE A FLINT EZEKIEL...		825B	LETTER 27		PROSE
O WHY WAS I BORN WITH A DIFFERENT FACE		828	O WHY BORN/L		1

		PAGE	TITLE	LINE

FACE (CONTINUED)
DIGNITY WHO WOULD NOT SIT LOOKING IN THEIR PARENT'S FACE — 864A LETTER 61 — PROSE

FACES
THEY COVERED THEIR FACES AND WEPT THE YOUTH LAY SILENT . . — 36C COUCH DEATH/PS — PROSE
UPON A HOLY THURSDAY THEIR INNOCENT FACES CLEAN . . . — 59 HOLY THURS/IM — 1
TWAS ON A HOLY THURSDAY THEIR INNOCENT FACES CLEAN . . . — 121 HOLY THURS/SI — 1
BROTHERS & SONS OF AMERICA TILL OUR FACES PALE AND YELLOW — 197 AMERICA 3 — 9
BROTHERS & SONS OF AMERICA TILL OUR FACES PALE AND YELLOW — 204 AMERICA CANC A — 9
AND DOST THOU WANDER WITH MY LAMBS & [WITH] WET THEIR — 371 FOUR ZOAS 9 — 532
  INNOCENT FACES
THEY RAISE THEIR FACES FROM THE EARTH CONVERSING WITH THE — 379 FOUR ZOAS 9 — 843
  MAN
HER SOFT MEMORY IMPRINTED WITH FACES OF SCORN . . . . . — 429 MARY — 40
WITH FACES OF SCORN & WITH EYES OF DISDAIN . . . . . — 429 MARY — 41
ALL FACES HAVE ENVY SWEET MARY BUT THINE . . . . . . — 429 MARY — 44
AND ARCHITECTURE WHICH IS SCIENCE ARE THE FOUR FACES OF MAN — 514 MILTON 27 — 56
THESE ARE THE FOUR FACES TOWARDS THE FOUR WORLDS — 632 JERUSALEM 12 — 57
  OF HUMANITY
I SEE THEIR PITEOUS FACES GLEAM OUT UPON THE CRUEL WINDS — 644 JERUSALEM 21 — 38
AND EVERY MAN STOOD FOURFOLD EACH FOUR FACES HAD ONE TO — 745 JERUSALEM 98 — 12
  THE WEST
AND THE FOUR FACES OF HUMANITY FRONTING THE FOUR CARDINAL — 745 JERUSALEM 98 — 26
  POINTS
THE FOUR SENSES ARE THE FOUR FACES OF MAN & . . . . . — 773D ANNO BERKELEY — MARG
BUT IF ALL THE WORLD SHOULD SET THEIR FACES AGAINST THIS — 825B LETTER 27 — PROSE
AGAINST THEIR FACES & MY FOREHEAD AGAINST THEIR FOREHEADS — 825B LETTER 27 — PROSE

FACILITIES
NOR OF THE CITY CLARK'S IDLE FACILITIES . . . . — 542 FLORENTINE/N — 30

FACILITY
BEGUN BY THE WORDS "A FACILITY IN COMPOSING" I CANNOT TELL — 453C ANNO REYNOLDS — MARG
UNLESS IT WAS TO CAST [AN EYE] A STIGMA UPON REAL FACILITY — 453D ANNO REYNOLDS — * MARG
  IN
IMITATION OF FACILITY IN EXECUTION OR ARE WE TO UNDERSTAND — 453D ANNO REYNOLDS — MARG
HIM TO MEAN THAT FACILITY IN COMPOSING IS A FRIVOLOUS — 453D ANNO REYNOLDS — MARG
  PURSUIT
A FACILITY IN COMPOSING IS THE GREATEST POWER OF ART . . — 453D ANNO REYNOLDS — MARG

FAC-SIMILE
OF FAC-SIMILE REPRESENTATIONS OF MERELY MORTAL AND . . . — 576B DESC CAT 4 — PROSE

FACT
NOW HEAR A PLAIN FACT SWEDENBORG HAS NOT WRITTEN ONE NEW — 157D MARRIAGE HH 21 — PROSE
  TRUTH
HAVE NOW ANOTHER PLAIN FACT ANY MAN OF MECHANICAL TALENTS — 158A MARRIAGE HH 21 — PROSE
WITH OPINIONS CONCERNING HISTORICAL FACT . . . . . — 384D ANNO WATSON — MARG
THIS IS NO CERTAIN FACT PRESUMPTION IS NO PROOF . . . . — 395B ANNO WATSON — MARG
GIVEN THE HISTORICAL FACT IN ITS POETICAL VIGOUR . . . . — 578D DESC CAT 5 — PROSE
ARTIFICE TURN ONE FACT OR DISARRANGE SELF EVIDENT — 579A DESC CAT 5 — PROSE
IS NOT WORTH ANY MAN'S READING HE WHO REJECTS A FACT — 579B DESC CAT 5 — PROSE
  BECAUSE
VARIED FROM THE LITERAL FACT FOR THE SAKE OF PICTURESQUE — 581C DESC CAT 7 — PROSE
  SCENERY
NATURAL FACT OR HISTORY OF ILIUM . . . . — 775D INSC LAOCOON — TITLE
BAD USE OF IT BUT IT IS A FACT TOO TRUE THAT IF I HAD ONLY — 825D LETTER 27 — PROSE
CERTAINTY OF THE FACT WHICH HAS PASSED UPON ME . . . . — 852A LETTER 50 — PROSE

FACTIOUS
FACTIOUS IS NOT POPULAR . . . . — 403A ANNO BACON — MARG
& NEVER CAN BE EXCEPT FACTIOUS IS CHRISTIANITY . . . . — 403A ANNO BACON — MARG

FACTS
FOR THE FACTS ARE SUCH AS NONE BUT THE ACTOR COULD TELL — 392D ANNO WATSON — MARG
IF HISTORICAL FACTS CAN BE WRITTEN BY INSPIRATION . . . — 392D ANNO WATSON — MARG
COULD NOT BE REPRESENTED BY ANY HISTORICAL FACTS BUT . . — 577C DESC CAT 5 — PROSE

FACULTIES
THE SPIRITS OF LIFE TO PERVERT ALL THE FACULTIES OF SENSE — 344 FOUR ZOAS 8 — 137
THAT THE STUPID ARE BORN WITH FACULTIES EQUAL TO OTHER MEN — 473A ANNO REYNOLDS — MARG
BECAUSE IT ROUZES THE FACULTIES TO ACT . . . . — 793B LETTER 5 — PROSE

FACULTY
THE TRUE FACULTY OF KNOWING MUST BE . . . . — 98B ALL RELIGIONS — PROSE
THE FACULTY WHICH EXPERIENCES THIS FACULTY I TREAT OF . . — 98B ALL RELIGIONS — PROSE
LOCKE SAYS IT SAME FACULTY THAT INVENTS JUDGES . . . . — 790C LETTER 2 — PROSE

FADE
HERE I'LL SIT & FADE AWAY . . . . — 61 LEAVE O/IM — 2
TO FADE AWAY LIKE MORNING BEAUTY FROM HER MORTAL DAY . . — 127 BOOK OF THEL 1 — 3
WHY FADE THESE CHILDREN OF THE SPRING BORN BUT TO SMILE — 127 BOOK OF THEL 1 — 7
  & FALL
WHY THOU COMPLAINEST NOT WHEN IN ONE HOUR THOU FADE AWAY — 128 BOOK OF THEL 3 — 2
BUT THEL DELIGHTS IN THESE NO MORE BECAUSE I FADE AWAY . . — 129 BOOK OF THEL 3 — 21
AND I COMPLAIND IN THE MILD AIR BECAUSE I FADE AWAY . . . — 130 BOOK OF THEL 5 — 12
THE BRITISH COLONIES BENEATH THE WOFUL PRINCES FADE . . — 206 THIRALATHA — 4
AND SO THE PRINCES FADE FROM EARTH SCARCE SEEN BY SOULS — 206 THIRALATHA — 5
  OF MEN
LOS ANSWERD THEREFORE FADE I THUS DISSOLVD IN RAPTURD — 288 FOUR ZOAS 2 — 318
  TRANCE
THE FORMER THINGS SO SHALL THE MORTAL GENTLY FADE AWAY . . — 355 FOUR ZOAS 8 — 553
REVIVES ME TO NEW DEATHS I FADE EVEN LIKE A WATER LILLY — 371 FOUR ZOAS 9 — * 540
THEN MY LOINS FADE & IN THE HOUSE I SIT ME DOWN & WEEP . . — 371 FOUR ZOAS 9 — 544
FOR HER LIGHT IS TERRIBLE TO ME I FADE BEFORE HER IMMORTAL — 492 MILTON 12 — 1
  BEAUTY
IN SELFHOOD WE ARE NOTHING BUT FADE AWAY IN MORNING'S — 675 JERUSALEM 45 — 13
  BREATH

FADED
TILL OUR PURPLE AND CRIMSON IS FADED TO RUSSET . . . — 138 FRENCH REVOLTN — 92
. . . AND MAN LAY HIS FADED HEAD DOWN ON THE ROCK . . . — 138 FRENCH REVOLTN — 96
DIM THE FORM ALMOST FADED . . . . — 140 FRENCH REVOLTN — 132

```
                                                                  PAGE    TITLE          LINE
FADED   (CONTINUED)
    . . . MINE NEVER YET FADED FOR FIRE DELIGHTS IN ITS FORM       142  FRENCH REVOLTN      189
    SAT ROUND HIS BROWS FADED IN FAINT DEATH . . . . . . . .  .    147  FRENCH REVOLTN      296
    THEIR SULLEN FLAMES FADED EMERGE ROUND THE GLOOMY KING   .    159D  SONG LIBERTY      PROSE
    URIZEN FADED ARISTON SHUDDERD    . . . . . . . . . . .         245  SONG OF LOS 3         4
    ADAM SHUDDERD NOAH FADED BLACK GREW THE SUNNY AFRICAN   .      245  SONG OF LOS 3        10
    FADED & HER BRIGHT EYES DECAYD MELTED WITH PITY & LOVE  .      270  FOUR ZOAS 1         213
    WITH FADED RADIANCE SIGHD FORGETFUL OF THE FLOWING WINE        276  FOUR ZOAS 1         437
    [ THE XXX ?FADED XXX ?SLEPT XXX ]   . . . . . . . . .         SUPP  FOUR ZOAS 1           *
    THE FIRES OF VALA FADED LIKE A SHADOW COLD & PALE    . .  .    283  FOUR ZOAS 2         114
    . . . PRINCE OF LIGHT [WITH] THY SPLENDOR FADED     . .  .     292  FOUR ZOAS 3          46
    FADED HE ROUZD HE SIEZD THE WONDER IN HIS HANDS & WENT  .      307  FOUR ZOAS 5          68
    I SIEZD THEE BEAUTEOUS LUVAH THOU ART FADED LIKE A FLOWER      311  FOUR ZOAS 5         226
    FOR HIS FRAIL EYES WERE FADED & HIS EARS HEAVY & DULL   .  .   326  FOUR ZOAS 7         250
    OF MAN WHO LAYS UPON THE SHORES LEANING HIS FADED HEAD  .  .   354  FOUR ZOAS 8         513
    ON THIS ROCK LAY THE FADED HEAD OF THE ETERNAL MAN   . .  .    359  FOUR ZOAS 9          95
    AND DARKNESS COVERD ALL THE DEEP THE LIGHT OF ENION FADED      370  FOUR ZOAS 9         496
    AND ALL HIS PICTURES FADED   . . . . . . . . . .    .         451  ANNO REYNOLDS         4
    HE LOOKED UP & SAW THE PRINCE OF LIGHT WITH SPLENDOR FADED     654  JERUSALEM 29         35
    IS AS NOTHING BEFORE THEE FADED IS ALL LIFE AND JOY   . . .    659  JERUSALEM 33         34
    BY IT THE MOON FADED INTO A GLOBE    . . . . . . . .   .       717  STOOD AMONG/J         8
    THE FOUR ZOAS IN ALL THEIR FADED MAJESTY BURST OUT IN FURY     734  JERUSALEM 88         55
    AND THE VOICE FADED MILD   . . . . . . . . .   .    .         805  TO BUTTS/L           71
    "SWEET ROSE FAIR FLOWER UNTIMELY PLUCKD SOON FADED"          SUPP  LEGEND/N83            *
      (SHAKESPEARE)
    "PLUCKD IN THE BUD & FADED IN THE SPRING" SHAKESPEARE    .  . SUPP  LEGEND/N83            *
FADES
    WELL WELL GO & PLAY TILL THE LIGHT FADES AWAY     . .  . .      60  NURSES SONG/IM       14
    NEVER FADES AWAY   . . . . . . . . . . .    .   .    .         112  LIT GRL LST/SI       11
    WELL WELL GO & PLAY TILL THE LIGHT FADES AWAY     . .  . .     121  NURSES SONG/SI       13
    O LIFE OF THIS OUR SPRING WHY FADES THE LOTUS OF THE WATER     127  BOOK OF THEL 1        6
    TILL BEAUTY FADES FROM OFF MY SHOULDERS DARKEND AND CAST       194  V DAU ALBION 7       14
      OUT
    WHEN THE MAN GENTLY FADES AWAY IN HIS IMMORTALITY    .   . .   355  FOUR ZOAS 8         551
    AN AGED SHADOW SOON HE FADES    . . . . . . . .   .   .        425  MENTAL TRAVLER       29
    THE COTTAGE FADES BEFORE HIS SIGHT    . . . . . .   .  .       426  MENTAL TRAVLER       59
FADING
    WHEN BUSY DAY WAS FADING AND CALM EVENING     . . .  . .       39D  SAMSON/PS         PROSE
    BUT NOW HIS EYES WERE DARKNED & HIS WIFE FADING IN DEATH        99  TIRIEL 1              4
    . . . THE OLD MOUNTAINS OF FRANCE LIKE AGED MEN FADING AWAY    134  FRENCH REVOLTN        9
    THE FADING CRY IS EVER DYING    . . . . . . . . .  .           289  FOUR ZOAS 2         362
    UPON THE IMMENSE LIKE A BRIGHT RAINBOW WEEPING & SMILING       290  FOUR ZOAS 2         382
      & FADING
    IMAGE OF GRIEF THY FADING LINEAMENTS MAKE MY EYELIDS FAIL      297  FOUR ZOAS 3         195
    BOUND UP IN THE HORNS OF JEALOUSY TO A DEADLY FADING MOON      491  MILTON 10            18
FAIL
    WHERE MIRTH DOES NEVER FAIL . . . . . . . . . . .    .           7  LOVE JOCUND/PS        7
    THE EARTH DOTH FAINT AND FAIL  . . . . . . . . . .              13  GWIN KING/PS         94
    OUR BEST OF HOPES HOW SOON THEY FAIL  . . . . . . . .           17  BLIND-MANS/PS        52
    THE HEART DOTH FAIL YOU SAY MY LORD THE MERCHANTS     . . .     21  EDW THIRD/PS 2       86
    GOOD ENGLISH HOSPITALITY O THEN IT DID NOT FAIL   . . .  .      58  THIS CITY/IM          4
    GOOD ENGLISH HOSPITALITY O THEN IT DID NOT FAIL   . . .  .      58  THIS CITY/IM          8
    GOOD ENGLISH HOSPITALITY O THEN IT DID NOT FAIL   . . .  .      58  THIS CITY/IM         12
    SHALL [FALL] FAIL IF THOU REFUSE HOWL IN THE DESOLATE          108  TIRIEL 6           *  49
      MOUNTAINS
    AND NOBLES AND CLERGY SHALL FAIL FROM BEFORE ME . . . . .      140  FRENCH REVOLTN      143
    THAT THE PRIDE OF THE HEART MAY FAIL   . . . . . . .  .        247  SONG OF LOS 7         3
    TEND THE DIRE ANVILS MOURN & RIVERS FAINT & FAIL              276  FOUR ZOAS 1         425
    IMAGE OF GRIEF THY FADING LINEAMENTS MAKE MY EYELIDS FAIL      297  FOUR ZOAS 3         195
FAILD
    KIND RECOMMENDATION TO DR TRUSLER WHICH THO IT HAS FAILD OF    794D  LETTER 6         PROSE
FAILED
    AND WHERE STRENGTH FAILED BLACK THOUGHTS IN AMBUSH LAY  .  .    37D  SAMSON/PS         PROSE
    FOR HIS PROPHECY OF NINEVEH FAILED    . . . . . . .  .        392A  ANNO WATSON        MARG
FAILING
    HE STROVE TO RISE TO WALK INTO THE DEEP BUT STRENGTH          531  MILTON 39            50
      FAILING
FAILS
    GOOD MORROW GENERALS WHEN ENGLISH COURAGE FAILS    . . .  .     23  EDW THIRD/PS 3       71
    THE SOUND OF PRAYER FAILS FROM LIPS OF FLESH . . . . .   . .   140  FRENCH REVOLTN      140
FAILURE
    THEY PUNISH A FAILURE IN THE TORMENTOR WHO . . . . .  .  .    616C  V LAST JUDG/N     PROSE
    SHE WILL FORGIVE ANY FAILURE IN CONSIDERATION OF             815D  LETTER 23         PROSE
      THE ENDEAVOUR
    MISS POOLE'S ILL-HEALTH THAN FOR MY FAILURE IN SENDING       837C  LETTER 36         PROSE
      PROOFS
FAIN
    AND FAIN WOULD CURE THE HURT HE MADE . . . . . . . .            17  BLIND-MANS/PS        56
FAINT
    WHISPRING FAINT MURMURS TO THE SCANTY BREEZE   . . . . .  .     10  WHEN EARLY/PS        12
    THE EARTH DOTH FAINT AND FAIL  . . . . . . . . . .             13  GWIN KING/PS         94
    WHEN THE THIN BEAMS OF THE MOON GIVE A FAINT LIGHT   . . .     36B  COUCH DEATH/PS    PROSE
    JELLICOE IN FAINT PEA GREEN   . . . . . . . . . .    .         53  PHEBE DREST/IM        2
    O IJIM I AM FAINT & WEARY FOR MY KNEES FORBID   . . .  .       104  TIRIEL 4             32
    AND YOU WILL LOSE YOUR ONCE LOVD TIRIEL ALAS HOW FAINT I AM    104  TIRIEL 4             36
    BUT THEL IS LIKE A FAINT CLOUD KINDLED AT THE RISING SUN       128  BOOK OF THEL 2       11
    THEY SHALL DROP AT THE PLOW AND FAINT AT THE HARROW  . . .     140  FRENCH REVOLTN      148
    . . . WHERE THY TENT O FAINT SLUMBROUS MOON    . . . . .      144  FRENCH REVOLTN      219
    . . . UTTERING A FAINT FEEBLE CRY  . . . . . . . .   .         146  FRENCH REVOLTN      277
    SAT ROUND HIS BROWS FADED IN FAINT DEATH . . . . . .  .        147  FRENCH REVOLTN      296
    A FAINT HEAT FROM THEIR FIRES REVIVD THE COLD LOUVRE   . . .   148  FRENCH REVOLTN      303
    ALBION'S COAST IS SICK SILENT THE AMERICAN MEADOWS FAINT      159A  SONG LIBERTY      PROSE
```

FAINT   (CONTINUED)
         LAY THE FAINT MAID AND SOON HER WOES APPALLD HIS THUNDERS   190 V DAU ALBION 1   17
            HOARSE
         FOR I AM FAINT WITH TRAVEL . . . .   238 EUROPE PREL 1   6
         SHE FELL DOWN A FAINT SHADOW WANDRING . . . .   250 AHANIA 2   38
         SICKNING LIES THE [ETERNAL] FALLEN MAN HIS HEAD SICK HIS   272 FOUR ZOAS 1   * 288
            HEART FAINT
         THE WANDERING MAN BOWD HIS FAINT HEAD AND URIZEN DESCENDED   273 FOUR ZOAS 1   316
         THE VILLAGES LAMENT THEY FAINT OUTSTRETCHD UPON THE PLAIN   275 FOUR ZOAS 1   394
         TEND THE DIRE ANVILS MOUNTAINS MOURN & RIVERS FAINT & FAIL   276 FOUR ZOAS 1   425
         FAINT SHIVERING THEY SIT ON LEAFLESS BUSH OR FROZEN STONE   276 FOUR ZOAS 1   447
         . . . THE FAINT HEART OF THE [ETERNAL] FALLEN [ANCIENT] MAN   283 FOUR ZOAS 2   * 143
         O I AM WEARY LAY THINE HAND UPON ME OR I FAINT . . . .   290 FOUR ZOAS 2   374
         I FAINT BENEATH THESE BEAMS OF THINE . . . .   290 FOUR ZOAS 2   375
         LOOKING UPON THEE IMAGE OF FAINT WATERS I RECOIL . . . .   297 FOUR ZOAS 3   197
         AND THEY TO THEE ONLY REMIT NOT FAINT NOT THOU MY SON . .   301 FOUR ZOAS 4   155
         FAINT & MORE FAINT THE DAYLIGHT WANES THE WHEELS   306 FOUR ZOAS 5   27
            OF TURNING DARKNESS
         STILL THE FAINT HARPS & SILVER VOICES CALM THE WEARY COUCH   306 FOUR ZOAS 5   30
         . . . & ROUND FAINT ENITHARMON . . . .   307 FOUR ZOAS 5   66
         AND MOUNTAINS FAINT WEARY HE WANDERD WHERE MULTITUDES   314 FOUR ZOAS 6   * 113
            (WERE) SHUT
         THE FLEETING IMAGE & IN WHISPERS MILD WOO'D THE FAINT SHADE   325 FOUR ZOAS 7   221
         OF HIS IMMORTAL HEAD INTO THE NORTH UPON FAINT ENITHARMON   335 FOUR ZOAS 7B   77
         WHAT WORDS OF DREAD PIERCE MY FAINT EAR WHAT FALLING SNOWS   344 FOUR ZOAS 8   146
            AROUND
         HIS FAINT GROANS SHAKE THE CAVES & ISSUE THRO THE DESOLATE   354 FOUR ZOAS 8   520
            ROCKS
         TREMBLING & WEAK A FAINT EMBRACE A FIERCE DESIRE AS WHEN   358 FOUR ZOAS 9   27
         AND MY HEAD FAINT YET WILL I LOOK AGAIN UNTO THE MORNING   360 FOUR ZOAS 9   120
         . . . & MOURND FAINT THRO THE SUMMER VALES . . . .   369 FOUR ZOAS 9   485
         SO SAYING HIS FAINT HEAD HE LAID UPON THE OOZY ROCK . .   370 FOUR ZOAS 9   495
         LIKE A (FAINT) FLAME QUIVERING UPON THE SURFACE OF THE   370 FOUR ZOAS 9   * 497
            DARKNESS
         OUGHT BUT THE VEGETABLE RATIO & LOATHE THE FAINT DELIGHT   485 MILTON 5   35
         THULLOH THE FRIEND OF SATAN ALSO REPROVD HIM FAINT THEIR   488 MILTON 8   33
            REPROOF
         . . . FAINT AS THE VOICE OF THE DEAD IN THE HOUSE OF DEATH   675 JERUSALEM 44   44
         AND SWORD FAINT IN HIS HAND FROM ALBION ACROSS GREAT   706 JERUSALEM 68   52
            TARTARY
         OF WHICH THIS VEGETABLE UNIVERSE IS BUT A FAINT SHADOW .   717A JERUSALEM 77   PROSE
         LIKE A FAINT RAINBOW WAVED BEFORE HIM IN THE AWFUL GLOOM   728 JERUSALEM 83   67
         AND ENITHARMON LIKE A FAINT RAINBOW WAVED BEFORE HIM . .   732 JERUSALEM 86   50
         FAINT IDEA OF THE FINISHED PRINTS FROM HIS WORKS SEVERAL OF   844C LETTER 43   PROSE
         REGARDLESS OF THAT FAINT SHADOW CALLD NATURAL LIFE . . .   863A LETTER 60   PROSE
FAINTED
         HAS MY SOUL FAINTED WITH THESE VIEWS OF DEATH . . . . .   31 EDW THIRD/PS 5   42
         UPON HER BOSOM IN SWEET BLISS HE FAINTED WONDER SIEZD . .   326 FOUR ZOAS 7   241
         FROM BREATHING FIELDS SATAN FAINTED BENEATH THE ARTILLERY   484 MILTON 5   *   2
         WHEN SATAN FAINTED BENEATH THE ARROWS OF ELYNITTRIA . .   485 MILTON 5   43
         TRIPLE ELOHIM CAME ELOHIM WEARIED FAINTED THEY ELECTED   494 MILTON 13   22
            SHADDAI
         OXFORD TREMBLED WHILE HE SPOKE THEN FAINTED IN THE ARMS   676 JERUSALEM 46   17
         JERUSALEM FAINTED OVER THE CROSS & SEPULCHER SHE HEARD   695 JERUSALEM 61   49
            THE VOICE
         SHE AWOKE PALE & COLD SHE FAINTED SEVEN TIMES ON THE BODY   742 JERUSALEM 94   21
            OF ALBION
         EVE FAINTED OVER THE DEAD BODY OF ABEL WHICH LAYS NEAR   779C GHOST ABEL 1   PROSE
            A GRAVE
         SEVEN TIMES O EVE THOU HAST FAINTED OVER THE DEAD AH AH   779 GHOST ABEL 1   5
FAINTING
         AS THE PALE FAINTING MAN ON HIS DEATH-BED . . . . . .   30 EDW THIRD/PS 5   23
         FAINTING UPON THE ELEMENTS SMITTEN WITH THEIR OWN PLAGUES   203 AMERICA 16   18
         ETHINTHUS THOU ART SWEET AS COMFORTS TO MY FAINTING SOUL   243 EUROPE 14   4
         THE MAIDEN'S FATHER & HER MOTHER FAINTING OVER THE BODY   281 FOUR ZOAS 2   51
         THE TERRIBLE BOY TILL FAINTING BY HIS SIDE THE PARENTS FELL   309 FOUR ZOAS 5   172
         AND ITS BIRTH IN FAINTING & SLEEP & [WOE] SWEET DELUSIONS   326 FOUR ZOAS 7   * 230
            OF VALA
         A STANDARD BEARER FAINTING IN THE ROUTED BATTLE . . . .   SUPP ILLUS GRAY   *TITLE
FAINTLY
         AND THE STARS FAINTLY GLIMMERED IN THE SUMMER SKY . . .   36C COUCH DEATH/PS   PROSE
         WHEN FOURTEEN SUNS HAD FAINTLY JOURNEYD OER HIS DARK ABODE   195 AMERICA PREL 1   2
         SHUT UP IN LITTLE PURPLE COVERING FAINTLY BUD & DIE . . .   325 FOUR ZOAS 7   191
         HID IN A LITTLE SILKEN VEIL SCARCE BREATHE & FAINTLY SHINE   325 FOUR ZOAS 7   195
         HID IN THE VALES FAINTLY LAMENT & NO ONE HEARS THEIR VOICE   325 FOUR ZOAS 7   197
         A LITTLE SOUND IT UTTERS & ITS CRIES ARE FAINTLY HEARD . .   484 MILTON 5   26
         A LITTLE SOUND IT UTTERS & ITS CRIES ARE FAINTLY HEARD . .   680 JERUSALEM 49   41
         BUT JERUSALEM FAINTLY SAW HIM CLOSD IN THE DUNGEONS OF   693 JERUSALEM 60   39
            BABYLON
FAINTS
         THE BATTLE FAINTS AND BLOODY MEN . . . .   13 GWIN KING/PS   87
         ALBION IS SICK AMERICA FAINTS ENRAGD THE ZENITH GREW   197 AMERICA 4   4
         THE DIRE CONFUSION TILL THE BATTLE FAINTS THOSE THAT REMAIN   344 FOUR ZOAS 8   118
         URIZEN FAINTS IN TERROR STRIVING AMONG THE BROOKS OF ARNON   531 MILTON 39   53
FAIR   SEE ONCE FAIR
         O DECK HER FORTH WITH THY FAIR FINGERS POUR . . . .   1 TO SPRING/PS   13
         FAIR ELENOR . . . .   4A FAIR ELENOR/PS   TITLE
         THE GRAVES GIVE UP THEIR DEAD FAIR ELENOR . . . . .   4 FAIR ELENOR/PS   2
         STIFLING IN MUD FAIR ELLEN PASSD THE BRIDGE . . . . .   4 FAIR ELENOR/PS   31
         HE LED ME THROUGH HIS GARDENS FAIR . . . .   6 HOW SWEET/PS   7
         HIS FACE IS FAIR AS HEAVN . . . .   6 MY SILKS/PS   7
         I AM CLAD IN FLOWERS FAIR . . . .   7 LOVE HARMNY/PS   10

		PAGE	TITLE	LINE

FAIR   (CONTINUED)

WHETHER IN HEAVN YE WANDER FAIR	10 TO MUSES/PS	5
FAIR NINE FORSAKING POETRY	11 TO MUSES/PS	12
WITH HEARTH SO RED AND WALLS SO FAIR	15 BLIND-MANS/PS	4
WITH LAD AND LASS HOW FAIR THE SHOW	16 BLIND-MANS/PS	8
THEN LAWS WERE MADE TO KEEP FAIR PLAY	17 BLIND-MANS/PS	70
AND THESE FAIR YOUTHS THE FLOWR OF ENGLAND	18 EDW THIRD/PS 1	17
FAIR ALBION'S SHORE AND ALL HER FAMILIES	33 EDW THIRD/PS 6	60
TYRANNY HATH STAIND FAIR ALBION'S BREAST WITH HER OWN CHILDREN'S GORE	34A KING JOHN/PS	PROSE
FOR DALILA'S FAIR ARTS HAVE LONG BEEN TRIED IN VAIN . . .	38A SAMSON/PS	PROSE
GO ON FAIR TRAITRESS DO THY GUILEFUL WORK	38A SAMSON/PS	PROSE
PUT ON FAIR LINEN THAT WITH THE LILY VIES PURPLE AND SILVER	38A SAMSON/PS	PROSE
WITH HER FAIR ARMS THOU LOVST ME NOT	38B SAMSON/PS	PROSE
DOUBT NO MORE OF SAMSON'S LOVE FOR THAT FAIR BREAST WAS MADE	39B SAMSON/PS	PROSE
PRIDE MADE A GODDESS FAIR OR IMAGE RATHER	42D THEN SHE BORE	PROSE
ERE WHILE SO FAIR AND NOW THEY FALL & BEG THE SKIES WILL WEEP	43C WOE CRIED MUSE	PROSE
LET YOUR BOUNTY DESCEND TO OUR FAIR EARS	55C ISLAND MOON 9	PROSE
WOULD BLIGHT ALL BLOSSOMS FAIR & TRUE	166 I FEARD FURY/N	2
BUT A BLOSSOM FAIR OR TRUE	166 I FEARD FURY/N	5
FRUITLESS FALSE THO FAIR TO SEE	166 I FEARD FURY/N	8
AND THE FAIR MOON REJOICES IN THE CLEAR & CLOUDLESS NIGHT	198 AMERICA 6	14
WILL PRODUCE HIS WORKS AND OFFER THEM TO SALE AT A FAIR PRICE	208A PRSPECTUS 1793	PROSE
WITH HER FAIR CRYSTAL CLEARNESS IN HER LIPS & CHEEKS HIS POISONS ROSE	269 FOUR ZOAS 1	185
ARE MY ABHORRENCE WHEREFORE HAST THOU TAKEN THAT FAIR FORM	295 FOUR ZOAS 3	* 119
AND HIS DARK WIFE THAT ONCE FAIR CRYSTAL FORM DIVINELY CLEAR	306 FOUR ZOAS 5	60
AND THY FAIR LOCKS SHADOWD THINE EYES FROM THE DIVINE EFFULGENCE	311 FOUR ZOAS 5	231
THO ALL THOSE FAIR PERFECTIONS WHICH MEN KNOW ONLY BY NAME	340 FOUR ZOAS 7B	274
[THEIR WINGS TOUCHD THE HEAVENS THEIR FAIR FEET HOVERD ABOVE]	341 FOUR ZOAS 8	12
OF FAIR JERUSALEM'S BOSOM IN A GENTLY BEAMING ?FIRE . . .	346 FOUR ZOAS 8	193
IS BORN ON EARTH SO WAS HE BORN OF FAIR JERUSALEM . . .	347 FOUR ZOAS 8	262
HE STOOD IN FAIR JERUSALEM TO AWAKE UP INTO EDEN	348 FOUR ZOAS 8	264
WITH DEEP REPENTANCE FOR THE LOSS OF THAT FAIR FORM OF MAN	352 FOUR ZOAS 8	435
WHERE DOST THOU FLEE O FAIR ONE	367 FOUR ZOAS 9	401
THEN O THOU FAIR ONE SIT THEE DOWN FOR THOU ART AS THE GRASS	367 FOUR ZOAS 9	408
WITH HER FAIR CRYSTAL CLEARNESS	381 FOUR ZOAS AD 5	5
TELL ME FAIR ONE TELL ME LOVE	422 THE BIRDS/N	2
AMONG THE LILLIES BY WATERS FAIR	427 LAND OF DREAMS	8
CAME INTO THE BALL ROOM AMONG THE FAIR	428 MARY	2
NOR ONCE BLUSHES TO OWN TO THE REST OF THE FAIR . . .	428 MARY	11
LIBERALITY WE WANT NOT LIBERALITY WE WANT A FAIR PRICE	446D ANNO REYNOLDS	MARG
[AND TIS ENGLISH POLITENESS AS FAIR AS [YOUR] MY AUNT]	542 FLORENTINE/N	* 10
BUT AH MORE WONDROUS STILL THE CHARMING FAIR	545 IMIT POPE/N	4
THAT SHE IS THE FAIR WIFE OF BATH AND THAT THE SPRING .	574B DESC CAT 3	PROSE
AND FAIR JERUSALEM HIS BRIDE	649 FIELDS FROM/J	7
GUSHES & STAINS THE FAIR SIDE OF THE FAIR (DAUGHTERS) OF ALBION	702 JERUSALEM 66	21
BLOOD HATH STAIND HER FAIR SIDE BENEATH HER BOSOM . .	705 JERUSALEM 67	43
HIS AWFUL BEAUTY WITH MORAL VIRTUE THE FAIR DECIEVER OFFSPRING	715 JERUSALEM 74	35
AND IN HER FAIR ARMS	805 TO BUTTS/L	38
OF THE SAME TRADE IS THOUGHT FAIR PLAY ENGRAVERS PAINTERS	847B LETTER 44	PROSE
PROJECTED WORK IT BIDS FAIR TO SET ME ABOVE THE DIFFICULTIES	862C LETTER 60	PROSE
UNDER PRETENCE OF FAIR CRITICISM AND CANDOUR	864A LETTER 61	PROSE
"SWEET ROSE FAIR FLOWER UNTIMELY PLUCKD SOON FADED" (SHAKESPEARE)	SUPP LEGEND/N83	*

FAIRER

OUR MAIDENS FAIRER IN THE SPRIGHTLY DANCE	2 TO SUMMER/PS	16
FAIRER THAN SNOW AND RICH AS MIDSUMMER	25 EDW THIRD/PS 3	167
REASON ONCE FAIRER THAN THE LIGHT TILL FOULD	42B THEN SHE BORE	PROSE
SWEET ELFRID FAIRER THAN THE BEAMING SUN	43C WOE CRIED MUSE	PROSE

FAIREST

| AS THE CATTERPILLER CHOOSES THE FAIREST LEAVES TO LAY . . | 152C MARRIAGE HH 9 | PROSE |
| HER EGGS ON SO THE PRIEST LAYS HIS CURSE ON THE FAIREST JOYS | 152C MARRIAGE HH 9 | PROSE |

FAIR EYED

| AND COURT THE FAIR EYED DEW TO TAKE ME TO HER SHINING TENT | 128 BOOK OF THEL 3 | 13 |

FAIR-HAIRD

| THOU FAIR-HAIRD ANGEL OF THE EVENING . . . . | 3 EVNING STAR/PS | 1 |

FAIRIES

AND TO CAGE THE FAIRIES & ELVES	183 MOTTO SONGS/N	4
. . . FAIRIES OF ALBION AFTERWARDS GODS OF THE HEATHEN . .	264 FOUR ZOAS 1	19
ATTENDED BY FAIRIES ONE TWO & THREE	434 WILLIAM BOND	6
THE FAIRIES THAT FLED FROM WILLIAM BOND	435 WILLIAM BOND	41
THE FAIRIES NYMPHS GNOMES & GENII OF THE FOUR ELEMENTS . .	520 MILTON 31	20
SHAKSPEARE'S FAIRIES ALSO ARE THE RULERS OF THE VEGETABLE WORLD	570A DESC CAT 3	PROSE
ELEMENTAL BEINGS CALLED BY US BY THE GENERAL NAME OF FAIRIES	577D DESC CAT 5	PROSE
THE SPORTS OF THE FAIRIES ARE SEEN	618C ILLUS MILTON	PROSE
BY FAIRIES AS THEY DANCE ON THE RED THE CIELING & THE FLOOR	618C ILLUS MILTON	*PROSE
AROUND MILTON ARE SIX SPIRITS OR FAIRIES HOVERING ON THE AIR	619C ILLUS MILTON	PROSE

```
                                                         PAGE      TITLE          LINE
FAIRIES    (CONTINUED)
    GIANTS & FAIRIES HAVING RECIEVD THE HIGHEST REWARD POSSIBLE  620D JERUSALEM 3    PPOSE
    AND SIXTY-FOUR THOUSAND FAIRIES GUARD THE SOUTHERN GATE      633 JERUSALEM 13    29
    FAIRIES & GENII & NYMPHS & GNOMES OF THE ELEMENTS    . .     663 JERUSALEM 36    37
    THOR & FRIGA & THE FAIRIES LEAD THE MOON ALONG THE VALLEY    697 JERUSALEM 63    14
        OF CHERUBIM
    ASSISTANCE OF BRUNO'S FAIRIES BUT I INVOKE THE GOOD GENII    801B LETTER 13      PROSE
    FAIRIES RIDING ON FLIES  . . . . . . . . . . . .  .         SUPP ILLUS GRAY     *TITLE
    SPENSER CREATING HIS FAIRIES  . . . . . . . . . .          SUPP ILLUS GRAY     *TITLE
FAIRIES'
    KNOWEST THOU NOT O FAIRIES' LORD  . . . . . . . . .          188 A FAIRY SKIPD     9
FAIRLY
    BE FAIRLY SEPERATED & THEN SUPERSTITION WILL BE HONEST       85C ANNO LAVATER    MARG
        FEELING
FAIRY
    THAT WISDOM MAY DESCEND IN FAIRY DREAMS  . . . . . . .        14 IMIT SPEN/PS      5
    [THE MARRIAGE RING] THE FAIRY  . . . . . . . . . .          178A THE FAIRY/N     TITLE
    MAKES EACH FAIRY A KING  . . . . . . . . . . . .            178 THE FAIRY/N      10
    SO A FAIRY SUNG  . . . . . . . . . . . . . . .              178 THE FAIRY/N      11
    A FAIRY [LEAPT] SKIPD UPON MY KNEE  . . . . . . . .          188 A FAIRY SKIPD  *  1
    SO SANG A FAIRY MOCKING AS HE SAT ON A STREAKD TULIP  . .    237 EUROPE INTRO      7
    MY FAIRY SAT UPON THE TABLE AND DICTATED EUROPE  . . . .     238 EUROPE INTRO     24
    [PRETTY] LITTLE MARY BELL HAD A FAIRY IN A NUT  . . . .      434 LONG JOHN BRWN    1
    AND THE FAIRY DREW THE DEVIL INTO THE NUT-SHELL  . . . .     434 LONG JOHN BRWN    4
    HER FAIRY SKIPD OUT & HER FAIRY SKIPD IN  . . . . . .        434 LONG JOHN BRWN    5
    THE FAIRY SKIPD ABOUT IN HIS GLORY JOY & PRIDE  . . . .      434 LONG JOHN BRWN   15
    THEN THE FAIRY SKIPD OUT OF THE OLD NUT SHELL  . . . .       434 LONG JOHN BRWN   17
    FOR THE DEVIL CREPT IN WHEN THE FAIRY SKIPD OUT  . . . .     434 LONG JOHN BRWN   19
    ALL ARE THE WORK OF FAIRY HANDS OF THE FOUR ELEMENTS  . .    516 MILTON 28        60
    SAID TO MY FAIRY WAS NOT IT VERY QUEER  . . . . . . .        552 TELL YOU WHA/N    2
    TWILL MAKE A FOOL LAUGH & A FAIRY FUN  . . . . . . .         552 TELL YOU WHA/N    6
    WITH TREES & FIELDS FULL OF FAIRY ELVES  . . . . . .         816 HAPPINESS/L       5
    "A FAIRY VISION OF SOME GAY CREATURES OF THE ELEMENT"       SUPP LEGEND/N30     *
        (MILTON)
FAITH
    ("STEP BEYOND REAL FAITH IS IN DANGER OF DECEIVING")         77C ANNO LAVATER    MARG
        UNEASY
    AND URIZEN WHO WAS FAITH & CERTAINTY IS CHANGD TO DOUBT      282 FOUR ZOAS 2     105
    BACON PUT AN END TO FAITH  . . . . . . . . . . .           398B ANNO BACON      MARG
    HE WHO MOCKS THE INFANT'S FAITH  . . . . . . . . .           433 AUGURIES         85
    HE WHO RESPECTS THE INFANT'S FAITH  . . . . . . . .          433 AUGURIES         89
    FAITH IN GOD THE DEAR SAVIOUR WHO TOOK ON THE LIKENESS       506 MILTON 22        57
        OF MEN
    NO FAITH IS IN ALL THE EARTH THE BOOK OF GOD IS TRODDEN      506 MILTON 22        60
        UNDER FOOT
    HE SEES HIS CHILDREN MOCK AT FAITH AND DENY PROVIDENCE  . .  510 MILTON 25        25
    TO CAST OFF RATIONAL DEMONSTRATION BY FAITH IN THE SAVIOUR   533 MILTON 41         3
    OF JESUS WHO DENY THE FAITH & MOCK AT ETERNAL LIFE  . . .    533 MILTON 41        22
    BY DEMONSTRATION MAN ALONE CAN LIVE AND NOT BY FAITH  . .    622 JERUSALEM 4      28
    THEY ARE OF FAITH & NOT OF DEMONSTRATION WHEREFORE IS VALA   657 JERUSALEM 31     46
    AND IS THIS FAITH BEHOLD THE STRIFE OF ALBION & LUVAH  . .   658 JERUSALEM 31     55
    DIVINE & SELF WAS LOST IN THE CONTEMPLATION OF FAITH  . .    743 JERUSALEM 96     31
    YOU HAVE FAITH IN THE ENDEAVOURS OF ME YOUR WEAK BROTHER    822B LETTER 26       PROSE
    & FELLOW DISCIPLE HOW GREAT MUST BE YOUR FAITH  . . . .     822B LETTER 26       PROSE
FAITHLESS
    FRIGHTNING FAITHLESS FAWNING  . . . . . . . . . .            234 URIZEN 23         3
FALALASOLE
    AND SIGNIOR PALALASOLE  . . . . . . . . . . . .              61 DR CLASH/IM        2
FALCONER
    I THANK YOU SINCERELY FOR FALCONER AN ADMIRABLE POET  . .    843B LETTER 43      PROSE
FALCONET'S
    ("ON TIMANTHES") I AM OF FALCONET'S OPINION  . . . . .      479D ANNO REYNOLDS   MARG
FALL
    AND ROUZE THE STRONGEST PREY THEN IF WE FALL  . . . . .       27 EDW THIRD/PS 3  264
    WE FALL WITH GLORY I KNOW THE WOLF  . . . . . . .             27 EDW THIRD/PS 3  265
    WHY BRAVE SIR WALTER YOU OR I MAY FALL  . . . . . .           30 EDW THIRD/PS 5    3
    THOUSANDS MUST FALL TO-DAY  . . . . . . . . . .               30 EDW THIRD/PS 5   26
    AND THOSE THAT FALL SHALL RISE IN VICTORY  . . . . . .        31 EDW THIRD/PS 5   38
    PREPARE O TROOPS THAT ARE TO FALL TO-DAY  . . . . . .         35 WAR SONG/N       24
    THE DAMPS OF DEATH FALL THICK UPON ME HORRORS STARE ME       35D COUCH DEATH/PS  PROSE
        IN THE FACE
    SHE SAW THE WORLD FALL DOWN IN ADORATION [NOR COULD         41B THEN SHE BORE    PROSE
        REFRAIN]
    ERE WHILE SO FAIR AND NOW THEY FALL & BEG THE SKIES WILL     43C WOE CRIED MUSE  PROSE
        WEEP
    AND I WILL FALL INTO SUCH A PASSION I'LL HOLLOW AND STAMP    63A ISLAND MOON 11  PROSE
    AND LET THE CURSE FALL ON THE REST & WRAP THEM UP TOGETHER   106 TIRIEL 5         25
    AND ALL THAT TIME WE WAITED FOR THE FIRE TO FALL            107 TIRIEL 6          9
        FROM HEAVEN
    SHALL [FALL] FAIL IF THOU REFUSE HOWL IN THE DESOLATE        108 TIRIEL 6      *  49
        MOUNTAINS
    WHY FADE THESE CHILDREN OF THE SPRING BORN BUT TO SMILE      127 BOOK OF THEL 1    7
        & FALL
    . . . HIS WORDS FALL LIKE PURPLE AUTUMN ON THE SHEAVES  . .  138 FRENCH REVOLTN   88
    DEPART ANSWER NOT FOR THE TEMPEST MUST FALL . . . . .        139 FRENCH REVOLTN  120
    AND WHEREEER THE RAIN DOES FALL  . . . . . . . . .           181 HOLY THURS/N  *  14
    AND WHERE-EER THE RAIN DOES FALL  . . . . . . . .            212 HOLY THURS/SE    14
    THEY FALL & FALL STRONG I REPELLD  . . . . . . . .           224 URIZEN 4         21
    FROM MY SOFT CLOUD OF DEW TO FALL  . . . . . . . .           254 AHANIA 5         13
    AND HIS DOWNWARD-BORNE FALL CHANGD OBLIQUE  . . . . .        258 BOOK OF LOS 4    42
    OR TO FALL OR TO SWIM OR TO FLY  . . . . . . . . .           258 BOOK OF LOS 4    52
    HIS FALL INTO DIVISION & HIS RESURRECTION TO UNITY  . . .    264 FOUR ZOAS 1      21
```

		PAGE	TITLE	LINE

FALL   (CONTINUED)

```
          HIS FALL INTO THE GENERATION OF DECAY & DEATH & HIS  . . .    264 FOUR ZOAS 1      22
          CREATING SPACES LEST THEY FALL INTO ETERNAL DEATH    . . .    267 FOUR ZOAS 1     100
          WHY FALL THE SPARROW & THE ROBIN IN THE FOODLESS WINTER .     276 FOUR ZOAS 1     446
          TO ENION & HIS BODY FELL THARMAS BEHELD HIM FALL   . . . .    279 FOUR ZOAS 1     531
          PERMITTED ALL LEST MAN SHOULD FALL INTO ETERNAL DEATH   .     287 FOUR ZOAS 2     262
          TRIUMPHING EVEN TO THE STARS AT BRIGHT AHANIA'S FALL   . .    295 FOUR ZOAS 3     138
          OF URIZEN DASHED IN PIECES FROM HIS PRECIPITANT FALL   . .    296 FOUR ZOAS 3     159
          FALL OFF AFAR FROM THARMAS COME NOT TOO NEAR MY STRONG FURY   296 FOUR ZOAS 3     173
          SCREAM & FALL OFF & LAUGH AT THARMAS LOVELY SUMMER BEAUTY     296 FOUR ZOAS 3     174
          BENT BY ITS FALL FROM A HIGH TOWER THE DOLOROUS SHADOW ROSE   299 FOUR ZOAS 4      66
          THE EVER PITYING ONE WHO SEETH ALL THINGS SAW HIS FALL  .     316 FOUR ZOAS 6     157
          STEMMING HIS DOWNWARD FALL LABOURING UP AGAINST FUTURITY      316 FOUR ZOAS 6     186
          OR SINKING THRO THESE ELEMENTAL WONDERS SWIFT TO FALL   .     317 FOUR ZOAS 6     199
          OF WINDS & WATERS OR THENCE FALL INTO A VOID WHERE AIR  .     317 FOUR ZOAS 6     219
          I AM REGENERATED TO FALL OR RISE AT WILL OR TO REMAIN   .     317 FOUR ZOAS 6     225
          MUST FALL UNLESS A WAY BE FOUND [THE] TO RANSOM & REDEEM      330 FOUR ZOAS 7    * 406
          FOR FROM THE HAND OF URIZEN THE MYRIADS FALL LIKE STARS       365 FOUR ZOAS 9     324
          AND CHIDE MY MAKER THEE O SUN THAT RAISEDST ME TO FALL  .     368 FOUR ZOAS 9     412
          THE FRUIT SHALL RIPEN & FALL DOWN & THE FLOWERS CONSUME       368 FOUR ZOAS 9     420
            AWAY
          THE CLOUDS FALL OFF FROM MY WET BROW THE DUST FROM MY         373 FOUR ZOAS 9     597
            COLD LIMBS
          WE FALL ON ONE ANOTHER'S NECKS MORE CLOSELY WE EMBRACE  .     374 FOUR ZOAS 9     639
          LAUGHING & SHOUTING DRUNK WITH ODORS MANY FALL OERWEARIED     377 FOUR ZOAS 9     744
          WITH MIRTH & JOY URTHONA LIMPING FROM HIS FALL ON THARMAS     377 FOUR ZOAS 9     775
            LEAND
          AT THE FALL OF ADAM & THAT  . . . . . . . . . .              390A ANNO WATSON      MARG
          THE FATHER INDIGNANT AT THE FALL  . . . . . . . .            441D INSC FALL MAN    PROSE
          DESIGN IS APPROPRIATED TO THE RESURRECTION & FALL OF THE     443B LAST JUDGMNT/L   PROSE
            WICKED
          IN VARIOUS ATTITUDES OF DESPAIR & HORROR FALL THRO THE AIR   443C LAST JUDGMNT/L   PROSE
          OF THE ARTS & YOUR FALL WILL DEPEND ON [YOUR] THEIR NEGLECT   452C ANNO REYNOLDS    MARG
          LAUGHING & SHOUTING DRUNK WITH ODOURS MANY FALL OERWEARIED    513 MILTON 27         4
          NEITHER DID ANY LACK OR FALL INTO ERROR WITHOUT    . . .      519 MILTON 31         6
          FALL THEREFORE DOWN & WORSHIP ME SUBMIT THY SUPREME  . . .    530 MILTON 38        52
          LEST HE SHOULD FALL APART IN HIS ETERNAL DEATH TO IMITATE     531 MILTON 39        26
          THESE TEARS FALL FOR THE LITTLE-ONES THE CHILDREN            532 MILTON 40        15
            OF JERUSALEM
          BUT TO REJOICE & TRIUMPH IN MY FALL   . . . . . . .           544 P LOVED NOT/N     4
          AND FRANCE SHALL FALL DOWN & ADORE    . . . . . . .           557 ART HAS LOST/N    6
          WHICH IS THE GREATEST CURSE THAT CAN FALL UPON A NATION      596B PUB ADDRESS/N    PROSE
          & DRYDEN HAS FINISHD IT NOW LET DRYDEN'S FALL &    . . .     600D PUB ADDRESS/N    PROSE
          PRETENDERS FALL SOME PEOPLE & NOT A FEW ARTISTS HAVE  .      612C V LAST JUDG/N    PROSE
          STATES OF THE SLEEP [OF] WHICH THE SOUL MAY FALL INTO  .     614C V LAST JUDG/N    PROSE
          THAT ORIGINATED WITH THE FALL & WAS CALLD DEATH   . . .      616A V LAST JUDG/N    PROSE
          IN LONDON'S DARKNESS AND MY TEARS FALL DAY AND NIGHT   .      623 JERUSALEM 5      36
          LOS HEARD HER LAMENTATIONS IN THE DEEPS AFAR HIS TEARS FALL   624 JERUSALEM 5      66
          HIS SNOWS FALL ON ME AND COVER ME WHILE IN THE VEIL I FOLD    646 JERUSALEM 23     35
          UPON THE PRECIPICE HE STOOD READY TO FALL INTO NON-ENTITY     658 JERUSALEM 32      2
          BEHOLDING ALBION UPON THE PRECIPICE READY TO FALL INTO        672 JERUSALEM 43     15
            NON-ENTITY
          AMONG THE INHABITANTS OF ALBION THE PEOPLE FALL AROUND  .     689 JERUSALEM 58      4
          JERUSALEM'S PILLARS FALL IN THE RENDINGS OF FIERCE WAR  .     706 JERUSALEM 68     45
          AGAINST THE DIVINE VISION & FALL OVER THE PRECIPICE OF        711 JERUSALEM 71     59
            ETERNAL DEATH
          WALKS ROUND LOUD HIS THREATS LOUD HIS BLOWS FALL    . . .     719 JERUSALEM 78      4
          OBEDIENT FALL DOWN WORSHIP ME    . . . . . . . . .            749 EV GOSPEL(B)/N   24
          SHALL PUT MY NAME TO HIS DESIGNS BUT IF IT SHOULD FALL       853A LETTER 51       *PROSE
            OUT SO
          THE PUBLIC THEY WILL FALL FAR SHORT OF THIS FIRST SPECIMEN   860D LETTER 57        PROSE
          CHAPTER III OF THE SEXUAL NATURE & ITS FALL INTO            SUPP ILLUS GENESIS    *TITLE
            GENERATION & DEATH
```

FALLACIES
```
          ("ITS FALLACIES") WHEN THE FALLACIES OF DARKNESS ARE   . .    92A ANNO SWED LOVE   MARG
```
FALLACIOUS
```
          ARE ARTFUL OPINIONS & FALLACIOUS ALSO    . . . . . . .       474C ANNO REYNOLDS    MARG
          AND (RAHAB) IN AN OUTSIDE WHICH IS FALLACIOUS WITHIN   .      527 MILTON 37         9
```
FALLACIOUSNESS
```
          LOCKE'S OPINIONS OF WORDS & THEIR FALLACIOUSNESS   . . . .   474C ANNO REYNOLDS    MARG
```
FALLACY
```
          ("BUT THIS ALSO IS A FALLACY") MARK THIS    . . . . . .       95D ANNO SWED LOVE   MARG
          THO SEEN IN FALLACY OUTSIDE A FALLACY OF SATAN'S CHURCHES     532 MILTON 39        61
          A LITTLE CONSIDERATION MUST SHEW THE FALLACY OF THIS         565A DESC CAT 2       PROSE
            OPINION
          IT IS IN FALLACY & ITS EXISTENCE AN IMPOSTURE   . . . . .    617A V LAST JUDG/N    PROSE
```
FALLEN   SEE FALLN
```
          HOW MANY HAVE FALLEN THERE   . . . . . . . . . .             126 VOICE BARD/SI      8
          AND FALLEN FALLEN LIGHT RENEW    . . . . . . . .             210 INTRODUCTN/SE     10
          OF ASIA & ON THE DESARTS OF AFRICA ROUND THE FALLEN ANGELS   246 SONG OF LOS 4     20
          THE [?ETERNAL] FALLEN MAN TAKES HIS REPOSE URIZEN SLEEPS     271 FOUR ZOAS 1     * 261
            IN THE PORCH
          FOR IN THE VISIONS OF VALA I WALKD WITH THE MIGHTY FALLEN    271 FOUR ZOAS 1      266
            ONE
          NOR SHALT THOU ME TORMENT FOR I BEHOLD THE [ETERNAL] FALLEN  272 FOUR ZOAS 1     * 284
            MAN
          SICKNING LIES THE [ETERNAL] FALLEN MAN HIS HEAD SICK HIS     272 FOUR ZOAS 1     * 288
            HEART FAINT
          . . . THE FAINT HEART OF THE [ETERNAL] FALLEN [ANCIENT] MAN  283 FOUR ZOAS 2     * 143
          [XXX OF FALLEN MAN]  . . . . . . . . . . . .               SUPP FOUR ZOAS 2      *
          THE [ETERNAL] [FALLEN] DARKNING MAN WALKD . . . . . . .      292 FOUR ZOAS 3     *  44
          IF THOU WITHHOLD THINE HAND I PERISH LIKE A FALLEN LEAF      293 FOUR ZOAS 3        63
```

		PAGE	TITLE	LINE
FALLEN	(CONTINUED)			
. . . OF THE [ETERNAL] FALLEN ONE ALBION	.	293	FOUR ZOAS 3	* 68
INDIGNANT ROSE THE [ETERNAL] [FALLEN] AWFUL MAN	.	293	FOUR ZOAS 3	* 70
THEN FROWND THE [ETERNAL] FALLEN MAN ALBION	. .	294	FOUR ZOAS 3	* 83
OF ENION & HIM ASSIST TO BIND THE FALLEN KING	.	300	FOUR ZOAS 4	120
OF THE NOW FALLEN MAN A DOUBLE FORM VALA APPEARD A MALE		326	FOUR ZOAS 7	246
AND FEMALE SHUDDRING PALE THE FALLEN MAN RECOILD	.	326	FOUR ZOAS 7	247
UPON THE LIMIT OF CONTRACTION TO CREATE THE FALLEN MAN .	.	341	FOUR ZOAS 8	3
THE [ETERNAL] FALLEN MAN STRETCHD LIKE A CORSE UPON THE OOZY ROCK		341	FOUR ZOAS 8	4
THE FALLEN MAN BUT FIRST	. .	348	FOUR ZOAS 8	265
MY TENTS ARE FALLEN MY TRUMPETS & THE SWEET SOUNDS OF MY HARP		359	FOUR ZOAS 9	* 102
TOGETHER FOR THE [FALLEN] REDEEMD MAN	. .	364	FOUR ZOAS 9	290
[THE FALLEN MAN WONDRING BEHELD] HE LAID HIS (HAND) ON THE PLOW		365	FOUR ZOAS 9	* 311
EVERY ONE IS A FALLEN SON OF THE SPIRIT OF PROPHECY . . .		510	MILTON 24	75
AND ITS FALLEN EMANATION THE SPECTRE & ITS CRUEL SHADOW		635	JERUSALEM 15	7
HIS GIANT BEAUTY AND PERFECTION FALLEN INTO DUST .	. .	641	JERUSALEM 19	8
IF THOU WITHHOLD THINE HAND I PERISH LIKE A FALLEN LEAF		654	JERUSALEM 29	50
THEN FROWND THE FALLEN MAN AND PUT FORTH LUVAH FROM HIS PRESENCE		655	JERUSALEM 29	* 65
THE HILLS OF JUDEA ARE FALLEN WITH ME INTO THE DEEPEST HELL		720	JERUSALEM 79	8
FALLEN FIENDS OF HEAVNLY BIRTH		754	EV GOSPEL(E)/N	50
WITH ALL OUR MIGHT & STRENGTH THO WE ARE FALLEN & LOST .	.	780	GHOST ABEL 2	2
WHICH I BELIEVE IS NOW FOR EVER FALLEN INTO THE ABYSS .	.	835A	LETTER 34	PROSE
FALLETH				
THE WISE MAN FALLETH (SEVEN) TIMES IN A DAY AND RISETH AGAIN &C		83D	ANNO LAVATER	MARG
AS WHEN THE THUNDERBOLT DOWN FALLETH ON THE APPOINTED PLACE		295	FOUR ZOAS 3	140
FALLING	SEE SWIFT-FALLING			
DOWN LIKE A FALLING STAR FROM AUTUMN SKY	.	15	IMIT SPEN/PS	25
SHE FALLING KISSD THE GROUND POOR FOOL	.	16	BLIND-MANS/PS	14
CAN I SEE A FALLING TEAR	.	122	ON ANOTHERS/SI	5
FROM FALLING FROM STIFLING FROM HUNGER		144	FRENCH REVOLTN	234
CAST THY KEYS O ROME INTO THE DEEP DOWN FALLING . . .	.	159B	SONG LIBERTY	PROSE
EVEN TO ETERNITY DOWN FALLING	.	159B	SONG LIBERTY	PROSE
THE FIRE THE FIRE IS FALLING	.	159C	SONG LIBERTY	PROSE
FALLING RUSHING RUINING BURIED IN THE RUINS ON URTHONA'S DENS		159D	SONG LIBERTY	PROSE
FALLING UPON AMERICA AS A STORM TO CUT THEM OFF . . .	.	201	AMERICA 14	5
FALLING INTO THE DEEP SUBLIME FLAGD WITH GREY-BROWD SNOWS		203	AMERICA 16	5
AND ITS ROOFS CRACK ACROSS DOWN FALLING ON TH ANGELIC SEATS		204	AMERICA CANC B	24
THESE FALLING DOWN ON THE ROCK	.	233	URIZEN 20	18
HURLD APART ON ALL SIDES AS A FALLING	.	257	BOOK OF LOS 4	23
FALLING FALLING LOS FELL & FELL	.	258	BOOK OF LOS 4	27
TRUTH HAS BOUNDS ERROR NONE FALLING FALLING	.	258	BOOK OF LOS 4	30
FOUND FOR FALLING DAY & NIGHT WITHOUT END	.	258	BOOK OF LOS 4	33
TILL IN PROCESS FROM FALLING HE BORE	.	258	BOOK OF LOS 4	46
INCESSANT THE FALLING MIND LABOURD	.	258	BOOK OF LOS 4	49
HEAVY FALLING HIS ORGANS LIKE ROOTS	.	259	BOOK OF LOS 4	64
TO BIND THE BODY OF MAN TO HEAVEN FROM FALLING INTO THE ABYSS		287	FOUR ZOAS 2	267
THEN FALLING DOWN A TERRIBLE SPACE RECOVRING IN WINTER DIRE		287	FOUR ZOAS 2	* 277
SHE CONTINUED FALLING LOUD THE CRASH CONTINUD LOUD & HOARSE		295	FOUR ZOAS 3	145
MELTING A SHOWER OF FALLING TEARS NOTHING BUT TEARS ENION		297	FOUR ZOAS 3	200
SHE WANDERS IN ETERNAL FEAR OF FALLING INTO THE INDEFINITE		297	FOUR ZOAS 3	208
HE FALLING ON THE ROCKS BELLOWD HIS DOLOR TILL THE BLOOD		299	FOUR ZOAS 4	61
FALLING DOWN ON THE ROCK AN IRON CHAIN LINK BY LINK LOCKD		307	FOUR ZOAS 5	91
WE FELL I SIEZD THEE DARK URTHONA IN MY LEFT HAND FALLING		311	FOUR ZOAS 5	225
POUR DOWN MY FLIGHT THRO DARK IMMENSITY ETERNAL FALLING		313	FOUR ZOAS 6	69
HIMSELF INTO THE DISMAL VOID FALLING HE FELL & FELL . .	.	315	FOUR ZOAS 6	153
IN THE HORRID BOTTOMLESS VACUITY FALLING FALLING FALLING		315	FOUR ZOAS 6	155
ONWARD THO FALLING THRO THE WASTE OF NIGHT & ENDING IN DEATH		316	FOUR ZOAS 6	165
AND IF ETERNAL FALLING I REPOSE ON THE DARK BOSOM . . .		317	FOUR ZOAS 6	218
IS NOT DOWN FALLING THRO IMMENSITY EVER & EVER . . .	.	317	FOUR ZOAS 6	220
FALLING WITH WHEEL IMPETUOUS DOWN AMONG URTHONA'S VALES		320	FOUR ZOAS 6	321
IN ALL THE DISEASES OF MAN FALLING UPON THY GREY ACCURSED FRONT		322	FOUR ZOAS 7	89
IN THROES OF BIRTH & NOW THE BLOSSOMS FALLING SHINING FRUIT		325	FOUR ZOAS 7	214
BE NOT PERSWADED THAT THE AIR KNOWS THIS OR THE FALLING DEW		339	FOUR ZOAS 7B	231
STAMPING THE HILLS WADING OR SWIMMING FLYING FURIOUS OR FALLING		339	FOUR ZOAS 7B	263
LIKE TO A RUSHING TORRENT BENEATH & A FALLING ROCK ABOVE		340	FOUR ZOAS 7B	267
WHAT WORDS OF DREAD PIERCE MY FAINT EAR WHAT FALLING SNOWS AROUND		344	FOUR ZOAS 8	146
COVERD & SCALES HIS HANDS & FEET UPON HIS BELLY FALLING		352	FOUR ZOAS 8	425
MARROWLESS BLOODLESS FALLING INTO DUST DRIVEN BY THE WINDS		354	FOUR ZOAS 8	518
THE FALLING GRAPES THAT ODOROUS BURST UPON THE WINDS ARISE		376	FOUR ZOAS 9	698
WITH CHAINS WHILE HER PALACES ARE FALLING INTO [IN] RUINS		443A	LAST JUDGMNT/L	PROSE
IS SEEN SATAN WOUND ROUND BY THE SERPENT & FALLING HEADLONG		443B	LAST JUDGMNT/L	PROSE
BY TWO ANGELS & MANY GROUPES OF FIGURES ARE FALLING . .	.	443C	LAST JUDGMNT/L	PROSE
IN IMMENSE LABOURS & SORROWS EVER BUILDING EVER FALLING		485	MILTON 6	2
FOR HE IS REDEEMD FROM SATAN'S LAW THE WRATH FALLING ON RINTRAH		492	MILTON 11	23
THEN FIRST I SAW HIM IN THE ZENITH AS A FALLING STAR .	.	497	MILTON 15	47
AND ON MY LEFT FOOT FALLING ON THE TARSUS ENTERD THERE		497	MILTON 15	49
I HAVE EMBRACD THE FALLING DEATH HE IS BECOME ONE WITH ME		507	MILTON 23	33
THEY THUNDEROUS UTTERD ALL A UNIVERSAL GROAN FALLING DOWN		525	MILTON 35	31
IS SEEN FALLING OUTSTRETCHED AMONG THE DEAD AND THE DYING		580C	DESC CAT 5	PROSE

657

		PAGE	TITLE	LINE

FALLING   (CONTINUED)
    HIS BROTHER FALLING WITH THE HEAD DOWNWARD . . . . . 606B V LAST JUDG/N   PROSE
    FALLING HEADLONG WOUND ROUND BY THE TAIL OF THE SERPENT 606C V LAST JUDG/N   PROSE
    FALLING INTO THE ABYSS SIN IS ALSO REPRESENTED AS A FEMALE 606C V LAST JUDG/N   PROSE
    BENEATH THE FALLING FIGURE OF CAIN . . . . 607B V LAST JUDG/N   PROSE
    FALLING HEADLONG BY THE SIDE OF THEM IS A MIGHTY FIEND . 607D V LAST JUDG/N   PROSE
    THE EARTH BENEATH THESE FALLING GROUPES OF FIGURES . . . 608A V LAST JUDG/N   PROSE
    ROUND FROM HEAVEN TO EARTH DOWN FALLING WITH HEAVY BLOW 636 JERUSALEM 16   12
    STRETCHING A HAND TO SAVE THE FALLING MAN ARE WE NOT FOUR 672 JERUSALEM 43   14
    IN TIME'S OCEAN FALLING DROWND . . . . 771 OF GATES/GP   33
    FALLING DOWN ON THEIR KNEES RUNNING SIDEWAYS & IN   . . . 833B LETTER 33   PROSE
FALLN
    CLOUDED FALLN LIKE THE STATELY TREE CUT DOWN . . . . .   5 FAIR ELENOR/PS   50
    [AND] FALLN BY THE PESTILENCE THE REST MOPED ROUND . . . 107 TIRIEL 5   32
    AND NOW MY PARADISE IS FALLN & A DREAR SANDY PLAIN . . . 110 TIRIEL 8   39
    AND THOU ART FALLN TO GIVE ME LIFE IN REGIONS OF DARK DEATH 196 AMERICA PREL 2   9
    TO QUENCH THEIR ANGUISH AT THE FEET OF WASHINGTON DOWN 201 AMERICA 13   4
        FALLN
    . . . THE [ETERNAL] [FALLN ONE] ALBION STARTING FROM HIS 293 FOUR ZOAS 3   * 71
        SLEEP
    AND HE IS FALLN INTO THE DEEP ROUGH DEMON OF THE WATERS 298 FOUR ZOAS 4   40
    WITH DISLOCATED LIMBS HAD FALLN THE SPECTRE ROSE IN PAIN 299 FOUR ZOAS 4   64
    NOW ALL COMES INTO THE POWER OF THARMAS URIZEN IS FALLN 301 FOUR ZOAS 4   129
    AND THOU O URIZEN ART FALLN NEVER TO BE DELIVERD . . . . 313 FOUR ZOAS 6   63
    THEIR OPRESSORS ARE FALLN THEY HAVE STRICKEN THEM THEY 358 FOUR ZOAS 9   * 50
        AWAKE TO LIFE
    AND THE FALLEN MAN WHO WAS ARISEN UPON THE ROCK OF AGES . 364 FOUR ZOAS 9   285
    SATAN IS FALLN FROM HIS STATION & NEVER CAN BE REDEEMD . 491 MILTON 11   19
    HIS TENTS ARE FALLN HIS TRUMPETS AND THE SWEET SOUND OF 641 JERUSALEM 19   3
        HIS HARP
    BUT WHEN THEY SAW ALBION FALLN UPON MILD LAMBETH'S VALE 642 JERUSALEM 20   1
    FOR HAD THE BODY OF ALBION FALLN DOWN AND FROM ITS DREADFUL 667 JERUSALEM 40   31
        RUINS
    MY TENTS ARE FALLN MY PILLARS ARE IN RUINS MY CHILDREN 719 JERUSALEM 79   1
        DASHD
    REVD SIR I REALLY AM SORRY THAT YOU ARE FALLN OUT WITH 793A LETTER 5   PROSE
        THE SPIRITUAL
FALLOW
    ONCE I WAILD DESOLATE LIKE THEE MY FALLOW FIELDS IN FEAR 354 FOUR ZOAS 8   536
    DARKEND LIKE MOULD IN THE DIVIDED FALLOW WHERE THE WEED 364 FOUR ZOAS 9   * 294
FALLS   SEE PIT-FALLS
    HER MAIDS AWAIT HER ON HER BED SHE FALLS . . . . . .   5 FAIR ELENOR/PS   37
    AND THUS HER GENTLE LAMENTATION FALLS LIKE MORNING DEW . 127 BOOK OF THEL 1   5
    WEIGHS DOWN HER EYELIDS THEN SHE FALLS THEN STARTING WAKES 297 FOUR ZOAS 3   210
        IN FEARS
    AS THE SEED FALLS FROM THE SOWER'S HAND SO URIZEN FELL 316 FOUR ZOAS 6   160
        & DEATH
    FOR URIZEN FELL AS THE MIDDAY SUN FALLS DOWN INTO THE WEST 318 FOUR ZOAS 6   267
    AS SNOW THAT FALLS AROUND A LEAFLESS TREE UPON THE GREEN 358 FOUR ZOAS 9   49
    SEEKING FOR PLEASURE WHICH UNSOUGHT FALLS ROUND THE 361 FOUR ZOAS 9   172
        INFANT'S PATH
    I BELIEVE THE WHOLE CHARGE FALLS TO THE GROUND   . . . . 437C BLAKES MEMORAN PROSE
    THE OAK IS CUT DOWN BY THE AX THE LAMB FALLS BY THE KNIFE 522 MILTON 32   37
    AS ONE AGE FALLS ANOTHER RISES DIFFERENT TO MORTAL SIGHT 567C DESC CAT 3   PROSE
    AS ONE AGE FALLS ANOTHER RISES DIFFERENT TO MORTAL SIGHT 589A CHAUCER/N   PROSE
    DEATH IS CHAIND TO THE CROSS & TIME FALLS TOGETHER WITH 606C V LAST JUDG/N PROSE
        DEATH
    WHEN WINTER RENDS THE HUNGRY FAMILY AND THE SNOW FALLS . 642 JERUSALEM 20   12
    BUT HERE THE SOLDIER STRIKES & A DEAD CORSE FALLS AT HIS 672 JERUSALEM 43   43
        FEET
    THEREFORE WHEN A RELIGIOUS MAN FALLS INTO SIN . . . . . 682C JERUSALEM 52   PROSE
    MORE PROPERLY TO BE GIVEN TO A PLAYER WHO FALLS INTO SIN 682C JERUSALEM 52   PROSE
    THE NIGHT FALLS THICK I GO UPON MY WATCH BE ATTENTIVE   . 728 JERUSALEM 83   61
    THE NIGHT FALLS THICK HAND COMES FROM ALBION IN HIS 729 JERUSALEM 84   20
        STRENGTH
    THE CURTAIN FALLS . . . . 781B GHOST ABEL 2   PROSE
FALSE
    O SHOULD SHE EER PROVE FALSE HIS LIMBS ID TEAR . . . .   10 WHEN EARLY/PS   17
    BY A FALSE WIFE BROUGHT TO THE GATES OF DEATH . . . . .   37C SAMSON/PS   PROSE
    THUS IN FALSE TEARS SHE BATHD HIS FEET . . . .   38C SAMSON/PS   PROSE
    FALSE FOR WEAK IS THE JOY THAT IS NEVER WEARIED   . . . .   65D ANNO LAVATER   MARG
    FALSE SEVERITY OF JUDGMENT IS A GREAT VIRTUE . . . . .   67A ANNO LAVATER   MARG
    FALSE APHORISMS SHOULD BE UNIVERSALLY TRUE . . . . . .   67A ANNO LAVATER   MARG
    UNEASY FALSE A MAN MAY LIE FOR HIS OWN PLEASURE . . . .   67B ANNO LAVATER   MARG
    ("WHO LOVES WILL NOT BE ADORED ") FALSE . . . . . .   75C ANNO LAVATER   MARG
    CANNOT RESIST THE IMPULSE I FEEL TO RECTIFY WHAT I THINK   88A ANNO LAVATER   MARG
        FALSE
    THERE COULD BE BUT ONE IDENTITY WHICH IS FALSE   . . . .   91B ANNO SWED LOVE MARG
    FALSE TAKE IT SO OR THE CONTRARY IT COMES TO THE SAME   .   91C ANNO SWED LOVE MARG
    FALSE PHILOSOPHY ACCORDING TO THE LETTER . . . .   92B ANNO SWED LOVE MARG
    FOR IT IS FALSE BY ALL EXPERIENCE . . . .   92D ANNO SWED LOVE MARG
    IS IT NOT FALSE THEN THAT LOVE RECIEVES INFLUX THRO . .   96B ANNO SWED LOVE MARG
    IT IS AS FALSE & [AS] MATHA & AS DARK AS VACANT ORCUS 106 TIRIEL 4   * 87
    FALSE WITNESS WHEN HE OMITTED MAKING A DEFENCE BEFORE 158C MARRIAGE HH 22 PROSE
        PILATE
    FRUITLESS FALSE THO FAIR TO SEE . . . . 166 I FEARD FURY/N   8
    [HIS CAPTAINS FALSE AROUND] . . . . 186 LET BROTHELS/N   44
    TO TURN THE WHEEL OF FALSE DESIRE AND LONGINGS THAT WAKE 193 V DAU ALBION 5   27
        HER WOMB
    AND WITH FALSE SELF-DECIEVING TEARS . . . . 220 TO TIRZAH/SE   11
    DRIVEN OUT BY THE FLAMES OF ORC HIS FURRD ROBES & FALSE 242 EUROPE 12   16
        LOCKS

<pre>
                                                             PAGE   TITLE   LINE
FALSE   (CONTINUED)
    IN SLUMBERS OF MY NIGHT-REPOSE INFUSING A FALSE MORNING   271 FOUR ZOAS 1   272
    . . . YOUR [YOUR] FALSE MORNING . . . .   272 FOUR ZOAS 1   *   287
    MY SPIRIT STILL PURSUES THY FALSE LOVE OVER ROCKS & VALLEYS 288 FOUR ZOAS 2   317
    I HAVE PLANTED A FALSE OATH IN THE EARTH . . . .   290 FOUR ZOAS 2   388
    IN VAIN AM DRIVEN ON FALSE HOPE HOPE SISTER OF DESPAIR   300 FOUR ZOAS 4   123
    AND LIFE APPEAR & VANISH MOCKING ME WITH SHADOWS OF FALSE 339 FOUR ZOAS 7B   241
      HOPE
    CURSING THE VOICE THAT MOCKD HIM WITH FALSE HOPE IN FURIOUS 339 FOUR ZOAS 7B   260
      MOOD
    A FALSE FEMININE COUNTERPART LOVELY OF DELUSIVE BEAUTY . . 348 FOUR ZOAS 8   *   278
    WHICH GIVE A TINCTURE TO FALSE BEAUTY . . . .   348 FOUR ZOAS 8   291
    . . . THE BOSOM OF SATAN THE FALSE FEMALE AS IN AN ARK   348 FOUR ZOAS 8   292
      & VEIL
    IN ABSTRACT FALSE EXPANSES THAT HE MAY NOT HEAR THE VOICE 353 FOUR ZOAS 8   487
    ("ON ALL OCCASIONS ACT RIGHT ") ALWAYS OR THE BIBLE   386B ANNO WATSON   MARG
      IS FALSE
    OR THE BIBLE IS FALSE . . . .   386B ANNO WATSON   MARG
    IS FALSE WHEN IT IS ATTRIBUTED TO A WRONG AUTHOR HES A FOOL 391B ANNO WATSON   MARG
    IF THIS IS PROVED FALSE THE HISTORY IS FALSE DEUT   391C ANNO WATSON   MARG
      XXXI...BUT PERHAPS
    THE REASON ALLEDGED BY PRIESTS FOR MIRACLES IS FALSE . . 391D ANNO WATSON   MARG
    ALL FALSE IN THE EYES OF ONE MAN & TRUE IN THE EYES OF   393B ANNO WATSON   MARG
    IS IT TRUE OR IS IT FALSE THAT . . . .   396D ANNO BACON   MARG
    THIS IS CERTAIN IF WHAT BACON SAYS IS TRUE WHAT CHRIST   396D ANNO BACON   MARG
      SAYS IS FALSE
    ("UNKNOWN TO THE HEATHEN") FALSE O SATAN   . . . . .   398D ANNO BACON   MARG
    FALSE . . . .   399A ANNO BACON   MARG
    ALL FALSE . . . .   402C ANNO BACON   MARG
    FALSE . . . .   408B ANNO BACON   MARG
    FALSE CONTEMPTIBLE . . . .   410A ANNO BACON   MARG
    FALSE ALL POETRY GIVES THE LIE TO THIS . . . . . .   411C ANNO BOYD   MARG
    ("NATURE TEACHES") FALSE . . . .   412D ANNO BOYD   MARG
    A FALSE OATH FOR THAT HE HEARD ME SAY NOTHING OF THE KIND 438C BLAKES MEMORAN   PROSE
    THIS IS ALL FALSE & SELF-CONTRADICTORY . . . . . .   454A ANNO REYNOLDS   MARG
    THIS IS FALSE . . . .   454C ANNO REYNOLDS   MARG
    THIS IS MOST FALSE FOR NO ONE CAN EVER DESIGN TILL HE HAS 455D ANNO REYNOLDS   MARG
    FALSE THE ANCIENTS WERE CHIEFLY ATTENTIVE TO COMPLICATED 466B ANNO REYNOLDS   MARG
    THIS IS FALSE FRESCO PAINTING IS THE MOST MINUTE . . . 466D ANNO REYNOLDS   MARG
    THIS IS FALSE THE FAULT IS NOT IN WORDS BUT IN THINGS . 474C ANNO REYNOLDS   MARG
    ("REYNOLDS ANTIPATHY TO ALL FALSE PRETENTIONS") [O SHAME SUPP ANNO REYNOLDS   * MARG
      FALSE]
    IN LIKENESS OF HIMSELF TELL ALSO OF THE FALSE TONGUE   481 MILTON 2   10
      VEGETATED
    KEEP NOR IN PITY FALSE NOR IN OFFICIOUS BROTHERHOOD WHERE 487 MILTON 7   44
    IN A FEMININE DELUSION OF FALSE PRIDE SELF-DECIEVD . . 492 MILTON 11   26
    TO ANNIHILATE THE SELF-HOOD OF DECEIT & FALSE FORGIVENESS 497 MILTON 16   1
    WHICH IS THE FALSE TONGUE BENEATH BEULAH IT IS THE SENSE 514 MILTON 27   46
      OF TOUCH
    AS TO THAT FALSE APPEARANCE WHICH APPEARS TO THE REASONER 516 MILTON 29   15
    SUCH ARE THE LAWS OF THY FALSE HEAVNS BUT LAWS OF ETERNITY 530 MILTON 38   33
    THIS IS A FALSE BODY AN INCRUSTATION OVER MY IMMORTAL . 533 MILTON 40   35
    AND NOW I'LL LEAD MY FALSE FRIENDS BY THE NOSE . . .   555 BLAKES APL/N 1   23
    AND THAT NOW I LEAD MY FALSE FRIENDS BY THE [TOES] NOSE 556 BLAKES APL/N 2 *   12
    FALSE FRIENDS [O NO] FIE FIE . . . .   556 IF MEN ACT/N   5
    FOR HIS PICTURES IS ALTOGETHER FALSE HE WAS A . . . .   583B DESC CAT 9   PROSE
    CALL EXPRESSION BUT THIS IS A FALSE NOTION OF EXPRESSION 585A DESC CAT 15   PROSE
    WHILE THEY DISCOURAGE & LOOK WITH CONTEMPT ON FALSE ART 601C PUB ADDRESS/N   *PROSE
    AS DESTRUCTIVE OF THE TRUE ARTIST AS IT IS FALSE BY ALL 601D PUB ADDRESS/N   PROSE
      EXPERIENCE
    FALSE ART SUCH IS THE NATURE OF MORTAL THINGS OR HE WILL BE 613A V LAST JUDG/N PROSE
    A THREEFOLD REGION A FALSE BRAIN A FALSE HEART . . .   634 JERUSALEM 14   5
    AND FALSE BOWELS ALTOGETHER COMPOSING THE FALSE TONGUE   634 JERUSALEM 14   6
    IF SHE HAD NOT SOUGHT TO DESTROY JERUSALEM SUCH IS THAT 639 JERUSALEM 17   25
      FALSE
    FROM THE INNER SANCTUARY A FALSE HOLINESS HID WITHIN THE 708 JERUSALEM 69   40
      CENTER
    DEVILS ARE FALSE RELIGIONS . . . .   716C JERUSALEM 77   PROSE
    SEEING THIS FALSE CHRIST IN FURY & PASSION . . . .   756 EV GOSPEL(G)/N   1
    PERCIEVE THAT I NOT ONLY DETEST FALSE ART BUT HAVE THE . 866B LETTER 64   PROSE
FALSEHOOD
    MAGISTRATES AND HIS FEAR OF UTTERING A FALSEHOOD UPON OATH 438D BLAKES MEMORAN PROSE
    IN LONDON EVERY CALUMNY AND FALSEHOOD UTTERD AGAINST   847B LETTER 44   PROSE
      ANOTHER
FALSELY
    OIL HAS FALSELY BEEN SUPPOSED TO GIVE STRENGTH TO COLOURS 565A DESC CAT 2   PROSE
      BUT
FALSE-WOVEN
    SAT IN A [SWEET] DREAD INTOXICATION OF [FALSE WOVEN BLISS] 266 FOUR ZOAS 1   91
      . . .
FALSHOOD
    NERVOUS ARMS AND AFTER THAT WHEN I HAD FOUND THY FALSHOOD 38D SAMSON/PS   *PROSE
    ("LAMENT TALENTS NOT MORE USEFUL") CONTEMPTIBLE FALSHOOD 384D ANNO WATSON   * MARG
      & DETRACTION
    FALSHOOD & WICKEDNESS . . . .   386B ANNO WATSON   MARG
    & KNOWINGLY PROPAGATE FALSHOOD . . . .   397B ANNO BACON   MARG
    ALL SELF-CONTRADICTORY TRUTH & FALSHOOD JUMBLED TOGETHER 454B ANNO REYNOLDS * MARG
    FOLLY & FALSHOOD THE MAN WHO CAN SAY THAT RAFAEL . . . 467A ANNO REYNOLDS * MARG
    ("PECULIARITIES ARE BLEMISHES ") INFERNAL FALSHOOD . . 471C ANNO REYNOLDS   MARG
    HE THEREFORE TAKES A FALSHOOD FOR GRANTED TO SET OUT WITH 475B ANNO REYNOLDS   MARG
    WHAT FALSHOOD . . . .   479C ANNO REYNOLDS   MARG
    AND WHO FIRST FORGED THE SILLY STORY AND KNOWN FALSHOOD 565B DESC CAT 2   PROSE
</pre>

FALSHOOD (CONTINUED)
  THIS EVEN HOGARTH'S WORKS PROVE A DETESTABLE FALSHOOD . . 595C PUB ADDRESS/N PROSE
  NO TASTE FOR PAINTING THIS IS A FALSHOOD . . . . . 601B PUB ADDRESS/N *PROSE
  THIS IS A MOST PERNICIOUS FALSHOOD . . . . 605A V LAST JUDG/N PROSE
  GIVING A BODY TO FALSHOOD THAT IT MAY BE CAST OFF FOR EVER 631 JERUSALEM 12 * 13
  ESTABLISHMENT OF TRUTH DEPENDS ON DESTRUCTION OF FALSHOOD 687 JERUSALEM 55 * 65
   CONTINUALLY
  SO SAYING SHE TOOK A FALSHOOD & HID IT IN HER LEFT HAND 725 JERUSALEM 82 * 17
  AND THUS SHE CLOSED HER LEFT HAND AND UTTERD HER FALSHOOD 725 JERUSALEM 82 * 19
  FORGETTING THAT FALSHOOD IS PROPHETIC SHE HID HER HAND 725 JERUSALEM 82 * 20
   BEHIND HER
  TERRIFIED AT THE SONS OF ALBION THEY TOOK THE FALSHOOD 729 JERUSALEM 84 * 31
   WHICH
  THIS IS THE MOST DAMNABLE FALSHOOD OF SATAN & HIS 785B ILLUS DANTE 7 PROSE
   ANTICHRIST
FALSHOODS
  NOW HEAR ANOTHER HE HAS WRITTEN ALL THE OLD FALSHOODS . . 157D MARRIAGE HH 21 *PROSE
  THEY HAVE PERSWADED HIM OF HORRIBLE FALSHOODS . . . . . 667 JERUSALEM 40 * 19
FAMD
  OUR BARDS ARE FAMD WHO STRIKE THE SILVER WIRE . . . . . 2 TO SUMMER/PS 14
FAME
  OR EVN THE LEAST BY BIRTH SHALL GAIN THE BRIGHTEST FAME 18 EDW THIRD/PS 1 30
  PRICKT BY THE FAME OF OTHERS HOW I MOURN . . . . . . 41D THEN SHE BORE *PROSE
  & MOUTH & HE WAS THINKING OF HIS ETERNAL FAME . . . . . 44C ISLAND MOON 1 PROSE
  TILL SOME BOOKSELLER & THE PUBLIC FAME . . . . 551 WILLM COWPER/N 7
  AND AS ALL THE MODERNS WHO ARE WORTHY OF FAME . . . . 578C DESC CAT 5 PROSE
  UNWORTHY MEN WHO GAIN FAME AMONG MEN . . . . 581D DESC CAT 8 PROSE
  THE ROMAN VIRTUES WARLIKE FAME . . . . 758 EV GOSPEL (1) 9
  RICHES OR FAME OF MORTALITY THE LORD OUR FATHER WILL DO FOR 802C LETTER 14 PROSE
  ALL MY TALENTS I BURY AND DEAD IS MY FAME . . . . . . 829 O WHY BORN/L 8
  INTERESTING HIMSELF IN THE GREAT OBJECT OF HIS FATHER'S 835C LETTER 35 PROSE
   FAME
  FOR FRIENDSHIP WITH SUCH A ONE IS BETTER THAN FAME . . . 853A LETTER 51 *PROSE
  FAME A BIRD SINGING . . . . SUPP ILLUS GRAY *TITLE
FAMED
  I AM MORE FAMED IN HEAVEN FOR MY WORKS THAN I COULD WELL 802B LETTER 14 PROSE
FAME'S
  IN FAME'S WIDE TROPHIED HALL TIS OURS TO GILD . . . . . 18 EDW THIRD/PS 1 26
FAMILIES
  FAIR ALBION'S SHORE AND ALL HER FAMILIES . . . . . . 33 EDW THIRD/PS 6 60
  ANGELS OF CITIES AND OF PARISHES AND VILLAGES AND FAMILIES 205 AMERICA CANC C 18
  BUT MANY STOOD SILENT & BUSIED IN THEIR FAMILIES . . . . 283 FOUR ZOAS 2 126
  THEN LIKE THE DOVES FROM PILLARS OF SMOKE THE TREMBLING 358 FOUR ZOAS 9 46
   FAMILIES
  IN FAMILIES WE SEE OUR SHADOWS BORN & THENCE WE KNOW . . 374 FOUR ZOAS 9 637
  AND ALL THY SONS O LUVAH BEAR AWAY THE FAMILIES OF EARTH 375 FOUR ZOAS 9 695
  OF HUMAN FAMILIES THRO THE DEEP THE WINE PRESSES WERE FILLD 376 FOUR ZOAS 9 725
  & FAMILIES SOME OF WHOM ARE BOWING BEFORE THE BOOK OF LIFE 443D LAST JUDGMNT/L PROSE
  THE MISERY OF UNHAPPY FAMILIES SHALL BE DRAWN OUT INTO 499 MILTON 18 7
   ITS BORDER
  THEREFORE YOU MUST BIND THE SHEAVES NOT BY NATIONS 510 MILTON 25 26
   OR FAMILIES
  FROM THESE TWELVE ALL THE FAMILIES OF ENGLAND SPREAD ABROAD 623 JERUSALEM 5 33
  CITIES & NATIONS FAMILIES & PEOPLES TONGUES & LAWS . . . 629 JERUSALEM 10 27
  AND THENCE TO ALL THE KINGDOMS & NATIONS & FAMILIES OF 637 JERUSALEM 16 34
   THE EARTH
  SHAME DIVIDES FAMILIES SHAME HATH DIVIDED ALBION IN SUNDER 643 JERUSALEM 21 6
  OF NATIONS HER TOWERS ARE THE MISERIES OF ONCE HAPPY 647 JERUSALEM 24 32
   FAMILIES
  DRINKING THE SHUDDERING FEARS & LOVES OF ALBION'S FAMILIES 669 JERUSALEM 41 27
  O DEMONSTRATIONS OF REASON DIVIDING FAMILIES IN CRUELTY 689 JERUSALEM 57 11
   & PRIDE
  WEAVING THE SHUDDRING FEARS & LOVES OF ALBION'S FAMILIES 692 JERUSALEM 59 52
  AND FIRE & THE RUIN OF CITIES & NATIONS & FAMILIES 698 JERUSALEM 64 11
   & TONGUES
  MONEY THE LIFE'S BLOOD OF POOR FAMILIES . . . . 776B INSC LAOCOON PROSE
FAMILY
  THE REMAINS OF A FAMILY OF THE TRIBES OF EARTH A MOTHER 35C COUCH DEATH/PS PROSE
  AS ONE MAN ALL THE UNIVERSAL FAMILY & THAT ONE MAN . . . 277 FOUR ZOAS 1 472
  EVEN [SHILOH] ALBION WHOM THOU LOVEST WEPT IN PAIN HIS 277 FOUR ZOAS 1 * 485
   FAMILY
  THE FAMILY DIVINE DREW UP THE UNIVERSAL TENT . . . . . 279 FOUR ZOAS 1 551
  AMONG HIS FAMILY HIS FLOCKS & HERDS & TENTS & PASTURES . . 326 FOUR ZOAS 7 254
  THUS FORMING A VAST FAMILY WONDROUS IN BEAUTY & LOVE . . 345 FOUR ZOAS 8 187
  ORDER THE NATIONS SEPARATING FAMILY BY FAMILY . . . . . 361 FOUR ZOAS 9 177
  REND DOWN THIS FABRIC AS A WALL RUIND & FAMILY EXTINCT . . 362 FOUR ZOAS 9 186
  NOT FOR OURSELVES BUT FOR THE ETERNAL FAMILY WE LIVE . . 374 FOUR ZOAS 9 640
  FIRST ORC WAS BORN THEN THE SHADOWY FEMALE THEN ALL LOS'S 483 MILTON 3 40
   FAMILY
  AS NOW I REND THIS ACCURSED FAMILY FROM MY COVERING . . . 490 MILTON 9 29
  THERE SHALL BE THE SICK FATHER & HIS STARVING FAMILY THERE 499 MILTON 18 10
  THEY DRAG THE UNWILLING ORB AT THIS TIME ALL THE FAMILY 504 MILTON 21 23
  HE HEARD THEM CALL IN PRAYER ALL THE DIVINE FAMILY . . . 504 MILTON 21 35
  BUT ALL THE FAMILY DIVINE COLLECTED AS FOUR SUNS . . . . 504 MILTON 21 37
  IN A DARK TOMB SO ALL THE FAMILY DIVINE WEPT OVER OLOLON 504 MILTON 21 42
  AND WERE TROUBLED AND AGAIN THE DIVINE FAMILY GROANED IN 504 MILTON 21 44
   SPIRIT
  THEN THE DIVINE FAMILY SAID SIX THOUSAND YEARS ARE NOW . . 504 MILTON 21 51
  SO SPAKE THE FAMILY DIVINE AS ONE MAN EVEN JESUS . . . . 505 MILTON 21 58
  FOR IN EVERY NATION & EVERY FAMILY THE THREE CLASSES ARE 511 MILTON 25 40
   BORN
  WALKS AMONG ALL HIS AWFUL FAMILY SEEN IN EVERY FACE . . . 519 MILTON 30 17

	PAGE	TITLE	LINE
FAMILY (CONTINUED)			
AND ALL NATIONS WEPT IN AFFLICTION FAMILY BY FAMILY . . .	519	MILTON 31	12
A MOTHER MEETS HER NUMEROUS FAMILY	610B	V LAST JUDG/N	PROSE
THE HOLY FAMILY CONSISTING OF MARY JOSEPH JOHN THE BAPTIST	614A	V LAST JUDG/N	PROSE
AND RIVER AND MOUNTAIN AND CITY & VILLAGE AND HOUSE & FAMILY	640	JERUSALEM 18	18
AND CITY & VILLAGE AND HOUSE & FAMILY THAT THE PERFECT . .	640	JERUSALEM 18	26
WHEN WINTER RENDS THE HUNGRY FAMILY AND THE SNOW FALLS . .	642	JERUSALEM 20	12
PLANTING THY FAMILY ALONE	651	FIELDS FROM/J	79
OF HIS OWN HOUSE & FAMILY	652	FIELDS FROM/J	82
SO SAYING THE MILD SUN INCLOSD THE HUMAN FAMILY	653	JERUSALEM 29	27
. . . THEY JOIND THE DIVINE FAMILY [?ALBION ?SLEPT] TREMBLING	655	JERUSALEM 29	* 83
AND ONE STOOD FORTH FROM THE DIVINE FAMILY & SAID . . .	664	JERUSALEM 37	1
AS ONE MAN ALL THE UNIVERSAL FAMILY AND THAT ONE MAN . .	664	JERUSALEM 38	19
THUS SPEAKING THE DIVINE FAMILY FOLLOW ALBION	665	JERUSALEM 38	27
AND THE DIVINE FAMILY WEPT OVER HIM AS ONE MAN	667	JERUSALEM 40	44
AND THESE THE TWENTY-FOUR IN WHOM THE DIVINE FAMILY . . .	667	JERUSALEM 40	45
IN THE TERRIBLE FAMILY CONTENTIONS OF THOSE WHO LOVE EACH OTHER	672	JERUSALEM 43	38
THE FAMILY DIVINE HOVER AROUND THE DARKEND ALBION . . .	674	JERUSALEM 44	20
SHALL BE THOSE OF HIS OWN HOUSE AND FAMILY IN A RELIGION	676	JERUSALEM 46	26
TO MAKE ONE FAMILY OF CONTRARIES THAT JOSEPH MAY BE SOLD	686	JERUSALEM 55	15
EVERY ONE KNOWS WE ARE ONE FAMILY ONE MAN BLESSED FOR EVER	687	JERUSALEM 55	46
IN THE TERRIBLE FAMILY FEUDS OF ALBION'S CITIES & VILLAGES	714	JERUSALEM 73	47
CONTINUALLY BUILDING CONTINUALLY DESTROYING IN FAMILY FEUDS	734	JERUSALEM 88	40
ONE FIRST IN FRIENDSHIP & LOVE THEN A DIVINE FAMILY & IN THE MIDST	738	JERUSALEM 91	20
NOW YOU WILL I HOPE SHEW ALL THE FAMILY OF ANTIQUE BORERS	790D	LETTER 2	PROSE
YOURS SINCERELY...HEALTH TO MRS CUMBERLAND & FAMILY . .	790D	LETTER 2	PROSE
COMPLIMENTS TO MRS CUMBERLAND & FAMILY	791C	LETTER 3	PROSE
RESPECTFUL COMPLIMENTS TO MRS CUMBERLAND & FAMILY . . .	798D	LETTER 10	PROSE
IN AN INCREASE OF FAMILY & OF HEALTH & HAPPINESS . . .	810A	LETTER 20	PROSE
PRAY GIVE MY LOVE TO MRS BUTTS & YOUR FAMILY I AM YOURS SINCERELY	813C	LETTER 22	PROSE
WELFARE OF YOUR FAMILY ACCEPT MY SINCERE LOVE & RESPECT	816A	LETTER 23	PROSE
FAMILY & I AM NOW LABOURING IN MY THOUGHTS DESIGNS FOR . .	821C	LETTER 25	PROSE
& GIVE OUR LOVES TO MRS BUTTS & YOUR AMIABLE FAMILY . .	823C	LETTER 26	PROSE
PICTURE IN MANY RESPECTS IT REPRESENTS THE HOLY FAMILY .	823D	LETTER 27	PROSE
& FAMILY & BELIEVE ME TO REMAIN YOURS IN TRUTH & SINCERITY	826A	LETTER 27	PROSE
FAMILY ENJOY HEALTH MY MUCH TERRIFIED WIFE JOINS ME IN LOVE	829A	LETTER 28	PROSE
YOU & MRS BUTTS & ALL YOUR FAMILY I AGAIN TAKE THE LIBERTY	829A	LETTER 28	PROSE
THE LAST PERFORMANCE OF ROMNEY IT IS OF MR WALKER AND FAMILY	843C	LETTER 43	PROSE
YOUR HAPPY FAMILY ONCE AGAIN & THAT FOR A LONGER PERIOD	873A	LETTER 76	PROSE
SOLICITUDE CONCERNING ME AT REST YOU HAVE A FAMILY I HAVE	873C	LETTER 77	PROSE
& HER LOVELY FAMILY YOURS SINCERELY	873D	LETTER 78	PROSE
FAMILY-LOVE			
IS THIS THY SOFT FAMILY-LOVE	651	FIELDS FROM/J	77
FAMILYS			
THEN LAUGHD GWENDOLEN & HER LAUGHTER SHOOK THE NATIONS & FAMILYS OF	698	JERUSALEM 63	32
FAMINE			
FAMINE AND DEATH DOTH CRY	13	GWIN KING/PS	78
AND THE [FAMINE] SHALL EAT BOTH CRUST & CRUMB	185	LET BROTHELS/N	8
[AND SOON HE SAW THE FAMINE RAGE]	185	LET BROTHELS/N	29
IN FAMINE & WAR REPLYD ART THOU NOT ORC WHO SERPENT FORMD	198	AMERICA 7	3
A FAMINE OCCASIOND BY THE POPISH INTERDICT EDWARD AT CALAIS	208D	SUBJCTS HIST/N	TITLE
SHALL NOT THE KING CALL FOR FAMINE FROM THE HEATH . . .	247	SONG OF LOS 6	9
THE FAMINE SHALL CLASP IT TOGETHER WITH BUCKLES & CLASPS	499	MILTON 18	16
THY VILLAGES DIE OF THE FAMINE AND THY CITIES	693	JERUSALEM 60	27
THEM HOWLS THE WOLF OF FAMINE DEEP HEAVES THE OCEAN BLACK THUNDERING	741	JERUSALEM 94	16
FAMINE WAR MOSES STRIKING THE ROCK EZEKIEL'S WHEELS . .	SUPP	LETTER 56A	*PROSE
FAMISHD			
FAMISHD WEEPING WEAK	114	LIT GRL FND/SI	15
PRESENTLY COMES A FAMISHD BIRD & TAKES AWAY THE SPIDER .	277	FOUR ZOAS 1	458
LIKE A FAMISHD EAGLE EYELESS RAGING IN THE VAST EXPANSE	297	FOUR ZOAS 4	10
TILL MAN SHALL LEAVE A CORRUPTIBLE BODY HE FAMISHD HEARS HIM GROAN	354	FOUR ZOAS 8	524
OVER THEM THE FAMISHD EAGLE SCREAMS ON BONEY WINGS AND AROUND	741	JERUSALEM 94	15
FAMOUS			
WHO WORTHILY ARE FAMOUS AND AS SWEDENBORG OBSERVES . .	582A	DESC CAT 8	PROSE
GO ON WITH THE VIGOR I WAS IN MY CHILDHOOD FAMOUS FOR . .	815A	LETTER 23	*PROSE
FAN			
AND TUNES HER [?CHAUNTANT] NOTES WHEN BUXOM JOY DOTH FAN HIS WINGS	43B	WOE CRIED MUSE	*PROSE
THEN THARMAS TOOK THE WINNOWING FAN THE WINNOWING WIND FURIOUS	374	FOUR ZOAS 9	654
FANATIC			
("COLD AND VEHEMENT AT THE SAME TIME A FANATIC") I E HYPOCRITE	73C	ANNO LAVATER	MARG
THE SACRIFICE OF FANATIC LOVE WHY LOVED I JERUSALEM . .	660	JERUSALEM 33	43
FANATICS			
ARE TO BE CONSIDERD AS WEAK HEADED FANATICS	473A	ANNO REYNOLDS	MARG
FANCIED			
THE FANCIED IMAGE STRAYS	114	LIT GRL FND/SI	14
I BROUGHT LOVE INTO LIGHT & FANCIED INNOCENCE IS NO MORE	645	JERUSALEM 22	18

```
                                                          PAGE    TITLE          LINE
FANCIES
     WRAPD IN HIS SHROUD AND NOW FANCIES SHE HEARS  . . . . .    4  FAIR ELENOR/PS    15
     AND FISH FOR FANCIES AS THEY PASS  . . . . . . . . . .     8  MEMORY COME/PS     7
     SCATTER THEIR FANCIES AT THY POET'S FEET  . . . . . .     14  IMIT SPEN/PS       7
     HE FANCIES HE IS GROWN INTO A GIANT  . . . . . . . .     37A  CONTEMPLATN/PS  PROSE
     AND SCOURGES OFF ALL YOUTHFUL FANCIES FROM THE NEW-BORN MAN  110  TIRIEL 8      31
     HE ONLY TAKES PORTIONS OF EXISTENCE AND FANCIES THAT THE  155B  MARRIAGE HH 15  PROSE
        WHOLE
     BUT OOTHOON IS NOT SO A VIRGIN FILLD WITH VIRGIN FANCIES  194  V DAU ALBION 6   21
     FILLED WITH BLASTING FANCIES AND WITH MILDEWS OF DESPAIR  203  AMERICA 16       20
     A CUP OF SPARKLING POETIC FANCIES SO WHEN I AM TIPSIE  . .  237  EUROPE INTRO    16
     FROM REDOUNDING FANCIES HAD PETRIFIED  . . . . . . .    252  AHANIA 3          58
     MY WIFE CONTINUES POORLY BUT FANCIES SHE IS BETTER      832A  LETTER 31       PROSE
        IN HEALTH
FANCY
     FANCY RETURNS AND NOW SHE THINKS OF BONES  . . . . . .     4  FAIR ELENOR/PS    13
     AT LENGTH NO FANCY BUT REALITY  . . . . . . . . . .       4  FAIR ELENOR/PS    17
     . . . FANCY GAVE HIM TO SEE AN IMAGE OF DESPAIR IN HIS DEN  136  FRENCH REVOLTN  45
     A MEMORABLE FANCY  . . . . . . . . . . . . . .          150C  MARRIAGE HH 6   TITLE
     A MEMORABLE FANCY  . . . . . . . . . . . . . .          153B  MARRIAGE HH 12  TITLE
     A MEMORABLE FANCY  . . . . . . . . . . . . . .          154D  MARRIAGE HH 15  TITLE
     A MEMORABLE FANCY  . . . . . . . . . . . . . .          155C  MARRIAGE HH 17  TITLE
     A MEMORABLE FANCY  . . . . . . . . . . . . . .          158A  MARRIAGE HH 21  TITLE
     [WHO CALL IT FANCY [&] OR SHUT THE GATES OF SENSE . . .  205  AMERICA CANC C    22
     THE SPECTRE IS THE MAN THE REST IS ONLY DELUSION & FANCY  273  FOUR ZOAS 1     341
     THAT HIS DREAD FANCY FORMD BEFORE HIM IN THE UNFORMD VOID  287  FOUR ZOAS 2    294
     THE NATURE OF VISIONARY FANCY OR IMAGINATION IS VERY LITTLE  605A  V LAST JUDG/N  PROSE
     CONCEPTIONS OF THE VISIONARY FANCY BY THEIR VARIOUS  . . .  605B  V LAST JUDG/N  PROSE
     THAT THE VISIONS OF FANCY ARE NOT TO BE FOUND IN THIS WORLD  793D  LETTER 5     PROSE
     TO ME THIS WORLD IS ALL ONE CONTINUED VISION OF FANCY OR  793D  LETTER 5       PROSE
     WHICH ARE TO REJECT ALL FANCY FROM HIS WORK  . . . .    794D  LETTER 6        PROSE
     BUT NATURE & FANCY ARE TWO THINGS & CAN NEVER BE JOINED  824C  LETTER 27      PROSE
     BUT FANCY IT MAY HAVE MISCARRIED MY WIFE JOINS ME IN  . .  853D  LETTER 52     PROSE
FANS
     WHAT PITYING ANGEL LUSTS FOR TEARS AND FANS HIMSELF WITH  200  AMERICA 11       13
        SIGHS
FAR
     I SEEM TO WALK THROUGH A DEEP VALLEY FAR FROM THE LIGHT  35D  COUCH DEATH/PS  PROSE
        OF DAY
     O MAN OF GOD SAID HE THOU COMEST FROM FAR  . . . . . .   40B  SAMSON/PS       PROSE
     FAR IN A DIREFUL CAVE SHE LIVES UNSEEN  . . . . . . .    41D  THEN SHE BORE   PROSE
     SHE MONGST MEN WAS SENT AND WORSER ILLS ATTENDED HER BY FAR  43A  THEN SHE BORE  PROSE
     IN [ (TWENTY) ] TEN OR TWELVE YEARS WILL BE A FAR SUPERIOR  49D  ISLAND MOON 6  *PROSE
        GENIUS
     I CRY MY MATCHES AS FAR AS GUILD HALL  . . . . . . .     55  CRY MATCHES/IM     1
     THIS IS TRUE CHRISTIAN PHILOSOPHY FAR ABOVE ALL ABSTRACTION  65C  ANNO LAVATER   MARG
     TRULY RELIGIOUS AS FAR AS HE KNEW  . . . . . . . . .    75A  ANNO LAVATER     MARG
     GIVE IT ME FOR I CANNOT STAY MY JOURNEY IS FAR FROM HENCE  101  TIRIEL 2        22
     FAR IN THE NORTH BUT THEY WERE WICKED & WERE ALL DESTROYD  102  TIRIEL 2        51
     BUT FAR HE HAD NOT GONE WHEN IJIM FROM HIS WOODS COME DOWN  103  TIRIEL 4     *  3
     THAT I MIGHT TRAVERSE TIMES & SPACES FAR REMOTE AND BRING  192  V DAU ALBION 4   6
     HOW DIFFERENT FAR THE FAT FED HIRELING WITH HOLLOW DRUM  193  V DAU ALBION 5    14
     AND THEN THEY WANDERD FAR AWAY SHE SOUGHT FOR THEM IN VAIN  270  FOUR ZOAS 1   214
     FATTEND ON HUMAN BLOOD & DRUNK WITH WINE OF LIFE IS BETTER  274  FOUR ZOAS 1   389
        FAR
     AND OF AHANIA HIS PURE BRIDE BUT SHE WAS DISTANT FAR  . .  276  FOUR ZOAS 1    438
     AT DISTANCE FAR IN NIGHT REPELLD IN DIREFUL HUNGER CRAVING  276  FOUR ZOAS 1    442
     HIM FAR INTO THE WORLD OF THARMAS INTO A CAVERND ROCK  . .  279  FOUR ZOAS 1    534
     DEEP HORRIBLE WITHOUT END SEPARATED FROM BEULAH FAR BENEATH  279  FOUR ZOAS 1   542
     [TILL ?FAR DISMAL XXX ?FOUR XXX ALL XXX]  . . . . .    SUPP  FOUR ZOAS 1      *
     THEY BECOME NATIONS FAR REMOTE IN A LITTLE & DARK LAND  . .  281  FOUR ZOAS 2  *  56
     WHILE FAR INTO THE VAST UNKNOWN THE STRONG WINGD EAGLES  284  FOUR ZOAS 2      150
        BEND
     THUS LIVD LOS DRIVING ENION FAR INTO THE DEATHFUL INFINITE  290  FOUR ZOAS 2   383
     AND FROM HER BOSOM LUVAH FELL FAR AS THE EAST & WEST  . .  294  FOUR ZOAS 3    100
     A WORLD OF DARKNESS AHANIA FELL FAR INTO NON ENTITY  . . .  295  FOUR ZOAS 3   144
     WHERE ART THOU ENION AH TOO NEAR TO CUNNING TOO FAR OFF  296  FOUR ZOAS 3      169
     FAR AS MY STRENGTH CAN HURL THEE WANDER THERE & LAUGH &  296  FOUR ZOAS 3      171
        PLAY
     SO SAYING IN A WAVE HE RAPD BRIGHT ENITHARMON FAR  . . .  299  FOUR ZOAS 4      56
     IS THIS TO BE A GOD FAR RATHER WOULD I BE A MAN  . . . .  301  FOUR ZOAS 4     146
     DEPARTED FAR INTO THE UNKNOWN & LEFT A WONDROUS VOID  . .  301  FOUR ZOAS 4     158
     AS FAR AS HIGHEST ZENITH FROM THE LOWEST (NADIR) SO FAR  305  FOUR ZOAS 5    *  14
        SHRUNK
     FOR DEATH TO ME IS BETTER FAR THAN LIFE DEATH MY DESIRE  313  FOUR ZOAS 6       58
     HIS DISMAL VOYAGE EYEING THE NEXT SPHERE THO FAR REMOTE  316  FOUR ZOAS 6      183
     WHOM HE HAD SEEN WANDRING HIS NETHER WORLD WHEN DISTANT FAR  319  FOUR ZOAS 6  *  300
     WITH VISIONS OF SWEET BLISS FAR OTHER THAN THIS BURNING  321  FOUR ZOAS 7       62
        CLIME
     THAT FAR WITHIN THE CLOSE RECESSES OF THEIR SECRET PALACES  335  FOUR ZOAS 7B  105
     FOR FAR & WIDE SHE STRETCHD THRO ALL THE WORLDS OF URIZEN'S  340  FOUR ZOAS 7B  288
        JOURNEY
     WHILE RAHAB & TIRZAH FAR DIFFERENT MANTLES PREPARE WEBS  346  FOUR ZOAS 8      220
        OF TORTURE
     SAYING LET US GO UP FAR FOR SOON I SMELL UPON THE WIND  . .  358  FOUR ZOAS 9    61
     A HORRIBLE ROCK FAR IN THE SOUTH IT WAS FORSAKEN WHEN  . .  359  FOUR ZOAS 9     93
     [I] MY EMANATION FAR WITHIN  . . . . . . . . . . .      415  MY SPECTRE/N    *  3
     HE WANDERS WEEPING FAR AWAY  . . . . . . . . . . .      426  MENTAL TRAVLER    53
     THE LAND OF DREAMS IS BETTER FAR  . . . . . . . . .     427  LAND OF DREAMS    19
     ANOTHER I LOVE FAR BETTER THAN THEE  . . . . . . . .    435  WILLIAM BOND      26
     AS FAR AS GREATEST IS MORE THAN LEAST  . . . . . . .   450A  ANNO REYNOLDS    MARG
     TITIAN AS WELL AS THE OTHER VENETIANS SO FAR FROM      464B  ANNO REYNOLDS    MARG
        SENATORIAL DIGNITY
```

                                                    PAGE   TITLE   LINE
FAR   (CONTINUED)
    SO FAR FROM BEING ALL OF A PIECE ARE THE MOST WRETCHED   468D ANNO REYNOLDS   MARG
       BUNGLES
    I DO NOT KNOW AS HE WENT FAR ENOUGH OFF TO PUBLISH THEM   592D PUB ADDRESS/N   PROSE
    COMMERCE IS SO FAR FROM BEING BENEFICIAL TO ARTS OR . . .   593D PUB ADDRESS/N   PROSE
    LOS ANSWERD ALTHO I KNOW NOT THIS I KNOW FAR WORSE THAN   626 JERUSALEM 7   51
       THIS
    GO ON BUILDERS IN HOPE THO JERUSALEM WANDERS FAR AWAY   . . 632 JERUSALEM 12   43
    SEEKING FOR REST AND FINDING NONE AND HIDDEN FAR WITHIN   641 JERUSALEM 19   15
    HE STRETCHD HIS DRUID PILLARS FAR . . . .   650 FIELDS FROM/J   40
    AND FROM HER BOSOM LUVAH FELL FAR AS THE EAST AND WEST   . .655 JERUSALEM 29   79
    UPON THE HILLS & VALLEYS AND THE CLOUDY OATH ROLLD FAR   666 JERUSALEM 40   10
       AND WIDE
    AWAY FROM ALBION'S MOUNTAINS FAR AWAY FROM LONDON'S SPIRES   673 JERUSALEM 43   70
    REMOVE FROM ALBION FAR REMOVE THESE TERRIBLE SURFACES . . 680 JERUSALEM 49   60
    THEN FAR THE GREATEST NUMBER WERE ABOUT TO MAKE A   686 JERUSALEM 55   30
       SEPARATION
    AWAY INTO THE FAR REMOTE AND THE TREES & MOUNTAINS WITHERD   703 JERUSALEM 66   51
    HOW DISTANT FAR FROM ALBION HIS HILLS & HIS VALLEYS NO MORE 720 JERUSALEM 79   15
    THESE CRUEL DRUID TEMPLES O VALA HUMANITY IS FAR ABOVE . . 721 JERUSALEM 79   73
    WHEN THEY ARE MURDERERS AS FAR AS MY HAMMER & ANVIL PERMIT   738 JERUSALEM 91   7
    AS BABYLON & EGYPT SO FAR FROM BEING PARENTS OF ARTS   . . 778C HOMERS POETRY   PROSE
    OF MR LEIGH HOW FAR IT IS AN AUTOGRAPH IS A QUESTION   . . 781D INSC UPCOTT   PROSE
    HOW FAR HE EXPECTS TO PLEASE I CANNOT TELL . . . . 795A LETTER 6   PROSE
    TO ENTICE HIM TO FELPHAM & FAR AWAY . . . .   800 MRS FLAXMAN/L   4
    FOR I SO FAR FROM BEING BOUND DOWN   . . . .   809A LETTER 20   PROSE
    THO I KNOW THAT AS FAR AS DESIGNING & POETRY ARE CONCERND   821C LETTER 25   PROSE
    SO FAR AS HIS RECOLLECTION WILL SERVE   . . . .   831A LETTER 31   PROSE
    SO FAR YOU WILL BE REJOICED WITH ME AND . . . .   831B LETTER 31   PROSE
    COPYRIGHT AND AS FAR AS I CAN JUDGE OF THE NATURE OF . .   831C LETTER 31   PROSE
    CENTER ORNAMENT IS WORTHY HE SAYS THAT IT IS BY FAR IN HIS   836B LETTER 35   PROSE
    A HISTORY OF THE REVIEWING BUSINESS AS FAR AS I   845C LETTER 44   PROSE
       AM ACQUAINTED
    FURNISHD BY JOHNSON I LET HIM RUN ON SO FAR AS TO SAY THAT   846D LETTER 44   PROSE
    EXCEPT PAPER WHICH IS JOHNSON'S FAULT COWPER IS FAR THE   847A LETTER 44   PROSE
       BEST
    BOTH AS TO TYPE AND PRINTING PRAY LOOK AT WASHINGTON AS   847A LETTER 44   PROSE
       FAR AS
    I MUST SAY ARE FAR BEYOND ANY THING I HAVE EVER DONE   . . 853A LETTER 51   *PROSE
    I AM VERY FAR FROM SHEWING THE PORTRAIT OF ROMNEY AS A . . 855B LETTER 53   PROSE
    THE PUBLIC THEY WILL FALL SHORT OF THIS FIRST SPECIMEN   860D LETTER 57   PROSE
    SAY THAT HIS ILLNESS IS SO FAR FROM GONE THAT THE LEAST   SUPP LETTER 81A   *PROSE
       THING
    I AM STILL FAR FROM RECOVERED & DARE NOT GET OUT IN THE   877D LETTER 87   PROSE
       COLD
FAR BEAMING
    WHILE THE FAR BEAMING PEACOCK WAITED ON THE FRAGRANT WIND   340 FOUR ZOAS 7B   283
    IS RAGAN SHE ADJOINT TO SLADE & PRODUCED GONORILL   710 JERUSALEM 71   33
       FAR BEAMING
    FAR BEAMING TURRET LIKE THE VILLA OF LAVANT BLESSED & . . 835B LETTER 34   PROSE
FAR DISTANT
    . . . IN A FAR DISTANT GROVE] . . . .   266 FOUR ZOAS 1   93
    THE LUNGS THE HEART THE LIVER SHRUNK AWAY FAR DISTANT FROM   679 JERUSALEM 49   17
       MAN
    AND BECAME AN OPAKE GLOBE FAR DISTANT CLAD WITH MOONY BEAMS 679 JERUSALEM 49   20
FARE
    AND GAIN BUT SCANTY FARE THEN MY DEAR LORD 19   EDW THIRD/PS 2   33
FAREWELL
    IT SPOKE I COME MY FRIEND TO TAKE MY LAST FAREWELL   . . .   43D WOE CRIED MUSE   PROSE
    FAREWELL MY TIME IS GONE . . . .   43D WOE CRIED MUSE   PROSE
    FAREWELL GREEN FIELDS AND HAPPY GROVES . . . .   119 NIGHT/SI   9
    ENION SAID FAREWELL I DIE I HIDE FROM THY SEARCHING EYES   266 FOUR ZOAS 1   68
    FAREWELL THE GOD CALLS ME AWAY I DEPART IN MY SWEET BLISS   288 FOUR ZOAS 2   333
    "ON SUNDAY AFTERNOON IN HAMPSTEAD TO TAKE FAREWELL ALL"   800A LETTER 12   PROSE
    FAREWELL MY BEST FRIEND REMEMBER ME & MY WIFE IN LOVE &   802D LETTER 14   PROSE
    OR UNWILLING & MY PRESS NOT YET BEING PUT UP FAREWELL   . . 833A LETTER 32   PROSE
    FAREWELL SWEET ROSE THOU HAST GOT BEFORE ME INTO THE . .   854C LETTER 53   PROSE
FARM
    THE FIELDS OF COWS BY WILLANS FARM . . . .   650 FIELDS FROM/J   15
    MRS LINNELL COLLINS'S FARM NORTH END HAMPSTEAD . . . . . SUPP ADDRESS/L 70   *TITLE
FARMER
    WITH WHAT SENSE DOES THE PARSON CLAIM THE LABOUR OF THE   193 V DAU ALBION 5   17
       FARMER
    AND IN THE WITHERD FIELD WHERE THE FARMER PLOWS FOR BREAD   290 FOUR ZOAS 2   401
       IN VAIN
    EVERY FARMER UNDERSTANDS . . . .   432 AUGURIES   66
FARMERS
    [THE FARMERS WERE RUIND & HARVEST WAS ENDED] . . . . . .   164 HEARD ANGEL/N   21
FARNESE
    THE GREEKS AND HETRURIANS COPIED HERCULES FARNESE   . . .   565C DESC CAT 2   PROSE
FAR SHINING
    OF FIRE FAR SHINING TRAVELLING ALONG EVEN TO ITS DESTIND   287 FOUR ZOAS 2   276
       END
FARTED
    [FARTED & BELCHD & COUGHD] . . . .   185 LET BROTHELS/N   10
    FARTED & BELCHD & COUGHD . . . .   186 WHEN KLOPSTK/N   4
    TILL TO THE LAST TRUMPET IT WAS FARTED . . . .   187 WHEN KLOPSTK/N   20
FARTHEST
    TO IRELAND'S FARTHEST ROCKS WHERE GIANTS BUILDED THEIR   735 JERUSALEM 89   50
       CAUSEWAY
FARTHING
    I WOULD NOT GIVE A FARTHING FOR IT DO ALL BY YOUR FEELINGS   51D ISLAND MOON 7   PROSE

663

		PAGE	TITLE	LINE

FARTHING (CONTINUED)
THE POOR MAN'S FARTHING IS WORTH MORE . . . . 432 AUGURIES 79
HOW TO BUILD A UNIVERSE WITH FARTHING BALLS . . . . . 598C PUB ADDRESS/N PROSE

FARTHINGS
[ARTISTS XXX ?FOOL THE XXX] (THREE) FARTHINGS . . . . . 453A ANNO REYNOLDS * MARG

FASCINATING
SOMETIMES I CURSE & SOMETIMES BLESS THY FASCINATING BEAUTY 707 JERUSALEM 68 64

FASHION
("AVOID ORIGINALITY AND SACRIFICE TO FASHION") & GO TO HELL . 858 ANNO LAVATER MARG
SINCE TWAS THE FASHION TO GO NAKED . . . . 187 WHEN KLOPSTK/N 25
NOR OF THE CITY CLARK'S MERRY HEARTED FASHION . . . . 542 FLORENTINE/N * 28
WISHES IT WAS NOW THE FASHION TO MAKE SUCH MONUMENTS AND 566A DESC CAT 2 PROSE
TO SUPPOSE THEM SUITABLE ATTENDANTS ON RANK AND FASHION 568C DESC CAT 3 PROSE
SINCE VENETIAN ART [IS] WAS THE FASHION . . . . 599B PUB ADDRESS/N *PROSE
WHO FOLLOW THE FASHION AS THAT IS CALLD WHICH IS . . 610D V LAST JUDG/N *PROSE
WITHOUT SHAPE OR FASHION [BY] ON THE RIGHT HAND OF NOAH 610D V LAST JUDG/N *PROSE
THAT DISDAINS TO FOLLOW THIS WORLD'S FASHION . . . . 752 EV GOSPEL(D)/N 48
SUCH THINGS AS THESE DEPEND ON THE FASHION OF THE AGE 787A ANNO THORNTON MARG
THAN IN THE COLD GALLERY OF FASHION THE SUN . . . . 812B LETTER 22 PROSE
I REGARD FASHION IN POETRY AS LITTLE AS I DO IN PAINTING 825B LETTER 27 PROSE
[IS FASHION THE CONCERN OF ARTISTS] . . . . SUPP ANNO REYNOLDS * MARG

FASHIONABLE
[?FIRST ?TO SERVE NOBILITY & FASHIONABLE TASTE & SR JOSHUA] 451C ANNO REYNOLDS * MARG
SUFFER NOT THE (FASHIONABLE) FOOLS . . . . 480C MILTON 1 PROSE
FASHIONABLE DAUBING FOR A POOR PITTANCE OF MONEY . . . 850B LETTER 49 PROSE

FAST
THOU WOULDST MY DEATH AND DEATH APPROACHES FAST . . . . 38C SAMSON/PS PROSE
WITH NEW ROPES TO BIND THEE FAST . . . . 39A SAMSON/PS PROSE
NOW THEY SURROUND THE GOD AND BIND HIM FAST . . . . . 42C THEN SHE BORE PROSE
OH DO NOT WALK SO FAST . . . . 60 LIT BOY LST/IM 2
O DO NOT WALK SO FAST . . . . 120 LIT BOY LST/SI 2
BUT SPARE MY LIFE BUT HE KNOWS NOT THAT [THE] WINTER COMETH FAST 276 FOUR ZOAS 1 456
REFUSD TO OPEN THE BRIGHT GATES SHE CLOSD AND BARRD THEM FAST 279 FOUR ZOAS 1 565
BEHOLD THE TIME APPROACHES FAST THAT THOU SHALT BE AS A THING 355 FOUR ZOAS 8 549
AND LULL [MY] THY OWN SINS FAST ASLEEP . . . . 417 MY SPECTR AD/N 4
SHAKING THE ROOTS & FAST FOUNDATIONS OF THE EARTH IN DOUBTFULNESS 495 MILTON 14 8
AND MOVED THE FAST FOUNDATIONS OF THE EARTH TO WAKE THE DEAD 500 MILTON 18 50
SIX THOUSAND YEARS ARE PASSD AWAY THE END APPROACHES FAST 508 MILTON 23 55
BOWLAHOOLA THRO ALL ITS PORCHES FEELS THO TOO FAST FOUNDED 509 MILTON 24 54
TIME FLIES VERY FAST AND VERY MERRILY I SOMETIMES . . . 807A LETTER 17 PROSE
MY ONLY DIFFICULTY IS TO PRODUCE FAST ENOUGH . . . . . 821D LETTER 25 PROSE

FASTEN
FASTEN THIS EAR INTO THE ROCK MILCAH THE TASK IS THINE . 349 FOUR ZOAS 8 318
FASTEN THIS EAR INTO THE ROCK MILCAH THE TASK IS THINE . 705 JERUSALEM 68 6

FASTEND
FASTEND INTO THE WALL . . . . 136 FRENCH REVOLTN 45
WITH GOLDEN HOOKS FASTEND IN THE PILLARS . . . . . . 231 URIZEN 19 7
WITH BANDS OF IRON ROUND THEIR NECKS FASTEND INTO THE WALLS 243 EUROPE 12 29

FASTER
TIME FLIES FASTER AS SEEMS TO ME HERE THAN IN LONDON . 809A LETTER 20 PROSE
BUT IN VAIN THE FASTER I BIND THE BETTER IS THE BALLAST 809A LETTER 20 PROSE

FASTING
WOULD NOT HAVE BANDY CHILDREN NOR FASTING NOR BIRCH . . . 179 LIT VAGABOND/N 13
WOULD NOT HAVE BANDY CHILDREN NOR FASTING NOR BIRCH . . . 216 LIT VAGABND/SE 12
FASTING &C ALL RELATE TO ART . . . . 776A INSC LAOCOON PROSE

FAT
WITH HIS FAT BELLY & HIS ROUND CHIN . . . . 46 PHEBUS CAME/IM 2
HOW DIFFERENT FAR THE FAT FED HIRELING WITH HOLLOW DRUM 193 V DAU ALBION 5 14
IN FAT OF LAMBS NO MORE I FOLLOW NO MORE OBEDIENCE PAY 200 AMERICA 11 15
SWELLD WITH RIPENESS & FAT WITH FATNESS . . . . 255 AHANIA 5 24
ENVY FED WITH FAT OF LAMBS . . . . 256 BOOK OF LOS 3 15
FEED THEM & THOU WILT GROW FAT . . . . 432 AUGURIES 44
[ON] BY SWEET RESERVE & MODESTY [FEED FAT] GET FAT . . 545 ON S(TOTHRD)/N * 4
BY SWEET RESERVE AND MODESTY GET FAT . . . . 575 DESC CAT 3 2

FATAL
IN THE BRIGHT SUNSHINE OF THIS FATAL DAY . . . . . . 24 EDW THIRD/PS 3 143
COMMISSIOND TO THIS FATAL FIELD OF CRESSY . . . . . . 26 EDW THIRD/PS 3 223
BUT NEVER TILL THIS FATAL DAY OF CRESSY . . . . . . 31 EDW THIRD/PS 5 41
WHOSE FATAL SCROLL IS THAT METHINKS TIS MINE . . . . 34 WAR SONG/PS 11
THUS THEY WEEP UPON THE FATAL BROOK OF ALBION'S RIVER . 494 MILTON 13 35
ENGLISHMEN ROUZE YOURSELVES FROM THE FATAL SLUMBER . . 595B PUB ADDRESS/N PROSE
OF SOFT ETHINTHUS NEAR TYBURN'S FATAL TREE IS THAT . . 632 JERUSALEM 12 26
WHERE ALBION SLEPT BENEATH THE FATAL TREE . . . . . 650 FIELDS FROM/J 29
AN OPINION OF FATAL & ACCURSED CONSEQUENCE TO MAN . . 682A JERUSALEM 52 PROSE
BENEATH ALBION'S FATAL TREE BEFORE THE GATE OF LOS . . 726 JERUSALEM 82 60
THE THREE FATAL SISTERS . . . . SUPP ILLUS GRAY *TITLE
THE FATAL SISTERS RIDING THRO THE BATTLE THEY ARE . . SUPP ILLUS GRAY *TITLE
OF BAD PERHAPS OF FATAL CONSEQUENCE IS VERY SORRY INDEED SUPP LETTER 81A *PROSE

FATE
THEN LADEN WITH ETERNAL FATE DOST GO . . . . 15 IMIT SPEN/PS 24
THINE IRON HEART IS SMITTEN THOUGH LINGERING FATE IS SLOW 34B KING JOHN/PS PROSE
TH ANGEL OF FATE TURNS THEM WITH MIGHTY HANDS . . . 34 WAR SONG/PS 3
CLOSD FROM THE EYE OF DAY TO THE HARD ROCK TRANSFIXT BY FATE 41D THEN SHE BORE PROSE
AND REASON WOULD HAVE FOLLOWD BUT FATE SUFFERD NOT . . 42B THEN SHE BORE PROSE
HE KNEW TWAS VAIN FOR IJIM'S WORDS WERE AS THE VOICE OF FATE 104 TIRIEL 4 27

```
                                                 PAGE      TITLE        LINE
FATE    (CONTINUED)
    [HATH WORKD OUR RUIN WE SUBMIT NOR STRIVE AGAINST STERN    105 TIRIEL 4        80
      FATE]
    THE LINKS OF FATE LINK AFTER LINK AN ENDLESS CHAIN OF      302 FOUR ZOAS 4    207
      SORROWS
    TO BE SUBSERVIENT TO MY FATE . . . . . . . . . . . 417 MY SPECTRE/N        66
    LICENCD BUILD THAT NATION'S FATE . . . . . . . . 433 AUGURIES           114
    O GIVE TO ME A WOMAN'S FATE . . . . . . . . . 547 IF I GROW/N          2
    I GATHER OUR ETERNAL FATE OUTCASTS FROM LIFE AND LOVE . 725 JERUSALEM 82       2
    SOMEWHAT LIKE MY FATE & SUCH IT IS LIKELY TO REMAIN . . . 830A LETTER 30    PROSE
    I HAVE HITHERTO ENCOUNTERD BUT MY FATE HAS BEEN SO UNCOMMON 862C LETTER 60  PROSE
    THE BARD WEAVING EDWARD'S FATE . . . . . . . . . SUPP ILLUS GRAY     *TITLE
FATED
    FROM DARK ABYSSES OF THE TIMES REMOTE FATED TO BE    . . . 345 FOUR ZOAS 8    150
FATES
    FOR THE FATES OF THOSE FOR WHOM HE COMBATS THE    . . . . 580C DESC CAT 5    PROSE
FATHER
    ENGLAND SHALL DWELL IN PEACE THAT WHILE MY FATHER . . . 19 EDW THIRD/PS 2     7
    YOUR FATHER TIS WITH PRINCES AS TIS WITH THE SUN . . . 20 EDW THIRD/PS 2     52
    ANOTHER WEPT AND WISHD HEALTH TO HIS FATHER    . . . . 25 EDW THIRD/PS 3    168
    IM GLAD MY FATHER DOES NOT HEAR ME TALK . . . . . 27 EDW THIRD/PS 3    276
    FROM PRESENCE OF THE ALMIGHTY FATHER . . . . . . . 37D SAMSON/PS       PROSE
    DESTRUCTION WAS THY FATHER A LIONESS SUCKLED THEE    . . 38B SAMSON/PS       PROSE
    THEN SHE BORE PALE DESIRE FATHER OF CURIOSITY . . . . 40D THEN SHE BORE  PROSE
    EAGER SONG GOES ON TELLING HOW PRIDE AGAINST HER FATHER   42B THEN SHE BORE  PROSE
      WARRD
    THE FATHER GRIN'D & SKIPT ABOUT    . . . . . . . . 51 WHEN CORRUP/IM       23
    BECAUSE I LIKE IT MY FATHER DOES WHAT HE LIKES & SO DO I   51C ISLAND MOON 6  PROSE
    O FATHER FATHER WHERE ARE YOU GOING    . . . . . . 60 LIT BOY LST/IM        1
    OH SPEAK FATHER SPEAK TO YOUR LITTLE BOY    . . . . . 60 LIT BOY LST/IM        3
    THE NIGHT IT WAS DARK & NO FATHER WAS THERE    . . . . 60 LIT BOY LST/IM        5
    [ ("HATES") ] LOVES ("WISEST & BEST [HATES] ") LOVES      82D ANNO LAVATER   MARG
      ("FATHER OF MEN")
    ("FATHER OF MEN SEEN IN MOST PERFECT CHILDREN") THIS IS   82D ANNO LAVATER   MARG
      TRUE WORSHIP
    ACCURSED RACE OF TIRIEL BEHOLD YOUR [AGED] FATHER    . . 99 TIRIEL 1          7
    OLD MAN UNWORTHY TO BE CALLD THE FATHER OF TIRIEL'S RACE   99 TIRIEL 1         13
    [THE AGED FATHER & MOTHER SAW HIM AS THEY SAT AT PLAY] . 100 TIRIEL 2         11
    BLESS THY POOR EYES OLD MAN & BLESS THE OLD FATHER OF     101 TIRIEL 2         40
      TIRIEL
    THOU ART MY TIRIEL'S OLD FATHER I KNOW THEE THRO         101 TIRIEL 2         41
      THY WRINKLES
    I AM AN AGED WANDERER ONCE FATHER OF A RACE    . . . . 102 TIRIEL 2         50
    AND I THEIR FATHER SENT AN OUTCAST I HAVE TOLD YOU ALL . 102 TIRIEL 2         52
    AND SAW THEIR AGED FATHER BORNE UPON HIS MIGHTY SHOULDERS 105 TIRIEL 4         46
    WHAT HEUXOS CALL THY FATHER FOR I [?MUST] MEAN TO SPORT   105 TIRIEL 4         49
      TO NIGHT
    AND SO I'LL KEEP HIM FETCH YOUR FATHER FETCH FORTH        105 TIRIEL 4         62
      MYRATANA
    SERPENTS NOT SONS [YOU SEE ?AND ?KNOW YOUR FATHER] . . . 105 TIRIEL 4      *   64
    MEAN TIME THE OTHER SONS OF TIRIEL RAN AROUND THEIR FATHER 105 TIRIEL 4        68
    [THEN IJIM SAID LOTHO CLITHYMA MAKUTH FETCH YOUR FATHER]  105 TIRIEL 4         73
    [O NOBLE IJIM THOU HAST BROUGHT OUR FATHER TO [THE GATES] 105 TIRIEL 4         75
      OUR EYES]
    HE CEAST & [?HILI] HELA LED HER FATHER FROM THE NOISOM   107 TIRIEL 5      *   26
      PLACE
    AND [?HILI] HELA LED HER FATHER THRO THE SILENT OF THE   107 TIRIEL 6      *    1
      NIGHT
    THEN BE OBEDIENT TO THY FATHER FOR THE CURSE IS TAKEN OFF 107 TIRIEL 6          7
      THEE
    LAUGH FOR THY FATHER TIRIEL SHALL GIVE (THEE) CAUSE TO   108 TIRIEL 6         33
      LAUGH
    THY FATHER CALLS THY FATHER LIFTS HIS HAND UNTO THE [AIR] 108 TIRIEL 6         41
      HEAVENS
    FOR THOU HAST LAUGHED AT MY TEARS & CURST THY AGED FATHER 108 TIRIEL 6         42
    OR WHEREFORE DOST THOU CRY AH WRETCH TO CURSE THY AGED    108 TIRIEL 6         47
      FATHER
    [THEY] THE HOWLING MAIDEN LED HER FATHER WHERE WILD BEASTS 109 TIRIEL 7        16
      RESORT
    HE SAID O WEAK MISTAKEN FATHER OF A LAWLESS RACE . . . . 109 TIRIEL 8          7
    THE CHILD SPRINGS FROM THE WOMB THE FATHER READY STANDS   110 TIRIEL 8         25
      TO FORM
    THE FATHER FORMS A WHIP TO ROUZE THE SLUGGISH SENSES TO ACT 110 TIRIEL 8       30
    MISTAKEN FATHER OF A LAWLESS RACE MY VOICE IS PAST    . . 110 TIRIEL 8         41
    DO THEY HEAR THEIR FATHER SIGH . . . . . . . . . 112 A DREAM/SI        10
    DO FATHER MOTHER WEEP . . . . . . . . . . . 112 LIT GRL LST/SI       19
    IS GOD OUR FATHER DEAR . . . . . . . . . . . 117 DIVNE IMAGE/SI        6
    AND MY FATHER SOLD ME WHILE YET MY TONGUE    . . . . . 117 CHIMNEY SWP/SI       2
    HED HAVE GOD FOR HIS FATHER & NEVER WANT JOY    . . . . 118 CHIMNEY SWP/SI      20
    FATHER FATHER WHERE ARE YOU GOING    . . . . . . . 120 LIT BOY LST/SI       1
    SPEAK FATHER SPEAK TO YOUR LITTLE BOY    . . . . . . 120 LIT BOY LST/SI       3
    THE NIGHT WAS DARK NO FATHER WAS THERE    . . . . . . 121 LIT BOY LST/SI       5
    APPEARD LIKE HIS FATHER IN WHITE . . . . . . . . 121 LIT BOY FND/SI       4
    CAN A FATHER SEE HIS CHILD . . . . . . . . . . 122 ON ANOTHERS/SI       7
    O FATHER & MOTHER IF BUDS ARE NIPD    . . . . . . . 124 SCHOOL BOY/SI       21
    . . . AS A FATHER THAT BOWS TO HIS SON    . . . . . . 143 FRENCH REVOLTN * 203
    THIS IS SHEWN IN THE GOSPEL WHERE HE PRAYS TO THE FATHER  150B MARRIAGE HH 5  PROSE
    BUT IN MILTON THE FATHER IS DESTINY    . . . . . . . 150B MARRIAGE HH 5  PROSE
    MY MOTHER GROAND MY FATHER WEPT . . . . . . . . 166 INFANT SORW/N        1
    MY FATHER THEN WITH HOLY LOOK    . . . . . . . . 167 INFANT SORW/N       26
    I HEAR THE [FATHER OF THE] ANCIENT [?FATHER OF] MEN . . . 169 EARTHS ANSWR/N * 10
    [[CRUEL] SELFISH FATHER OF MEN] . . . . . . . . 169 EARTHS ANSWR/N      11
```

FATHER   (CONTINUED)
    OFT [THE PRIEST BEHELD] MY FATHER SAW US SIGH . . . . .   169 MIRTLE SHADE/N   13
    [MAN] FATHER OF JEALOUSY . . . .   171 TO NOBODADDY/N   2
    [THEN] AND FATHER [I CAN NOT] HOW CAN I LOVE YOU . . .   177 LIT BOY LST/N   5
    THEN GOD LIKE A FATHER [THAT JOYS FOR] REJOICING TO SEE   180 LIT VAGABOND/N   14
    WHERE ARE THY FATHER & MOTHER SAY . . . .   180 CHIMNEY SWP/N   3
    FATHER OF JEALOUSY BE THOU ACCURSED FROM THE EARTH . .   194 V DAU ALBION 7   12
    DARK VIRGIN SAID THE HAIRY YOUTH THY FATHER STERN ABHORRD 196 AMERICA PREL 1   11
    EDWARD THE BLACK PRINCE BRINGS HIS CAPTIVES TO HIS FATHER 209A SUBJCTS HIST/N   TITLE
    I HEAR THE FATHER OF THE ANCIENT MEN . . . .   211 EARTHS ANSR/SE   10
    SELFISH FATHER OF MEN . . . .   211 EARTHS ANSR/SE   11
    WHERE ARE THY FATHER & MOTHER SAY . . . .   212 CHIMNEY SWP/SE   3
    AND GOD LIKE A FATHER REJOICING TO SEE . . . .   216 LIT VAGABND/SE   13
    MY MOTHER GROAND MY FATHER WEPT . . . .   217 INFANT SORW/SE   1
    AND FATHER HOW CAN I LOVE YOU . . . .   218 LIT BOY LST/SE   5
    TO HER FATHER WHITE   . . . .   219 LIT GRL LST/SE   25
    TO THY FATHER SPEAK   . . . .   219 LIT GRL LST/SE   31
    . . . THE HEAVNLY FATHER ONLY . . . .   264 FOUR ZOAS 1   12
    HE CRIED OUT TO HIS FATHER DEPART DEPART BUT SUDDEN SIEZD 275 FOUR ZOAS 1   411
    AFAR OFF RUSHING BACK REDDNING WITH RAGE THE [ETERNAL]   275 FOUR ZOAS 1   * 413
      MIGHTY FATHER
    THE MAIDEN WEEPING BY THE FATHER & THE MOTHER WITH . . . 281 FOUR ZOAS 2   50
    THE MAIDEN'S FATHER & HER MOTHER FAINTING OVER THE BODY   281 FOUR ZOAS 2   51
    WE HAVE NO OTHER GOD BUT HE THOU FATHER OF WORMS & CLAY   298 FOUR ZOAS 4   39
    AND LOS REMAINS GOD OVER ALL WEAK FATHER OF WORMS & CLAY   298 FOUR ZOAS 4   41
    THEY GAVE A SCREAM THEY KNEW THEIR FATHER URIZEN KNEW   312 FOUR ZOAS 6   21
      HIS DAUGHTERS
    THE BREAD IS KNEADED LET US REST O CRUEL FATHER OF CHILDREN 322 FOUR ZOAS 7   107
    TO BIND THE FATHER & ENSLAVE THE BRETHREN NOUGHT HE KNEW   326 FOUR ZOAS 7   256
    AS LOS A FATHER TO HIS BRETHREN & HE JOYD IN THE DARK LAKE 332 FOUR ZOAS 7   480
    THY FURIOUS POWER BE OUR FATHER & OUR LOVED KING . . . .   345 FOUR ZOAS 8   163
    THE PRISONER ANSWERS YOU SCOURGD MY FATHER TO DEATH BEFORE 364 FOUR ZOAS 9   275
      MY FACE
    THE SONS OF URIZEN SHOUT THEIR FATHER ROSE THE ETERNAL   365 FOUR ZOAS 9   308
      HORSES
    EACH SHALL BEHOLD THE ETERNAL FATHER & LOVE & JOY ABOUND   374 FOUR ZOAS 9   642
    CALLING HIM BROTHER IMAGE OF THE ETERNAL FATHER THEY SAT   374 FOUR ZOAS 9   644
      DOWN
    ALL MEN & WAS THEIR FATHER & FORBAD ALL CONTENTION . . . 387B ANNO WATSON   MARG
    THY FATHER DREW HIS SWORD IN THE NORTH . . . .   419 I SAW A MONK/N   36
    AWAKE THY FATHER DOES THEE KEEP   . . . .   427 LAND OF DREAMS   4
    O FATHER I SAW MY MOTHER THERE . . . .   427 LAND OF DREAMS   7
    FATHER O FATHER WHAT DO WE HERE   . . . .   427 LAND OF DREAMS   17
    THY FATHER DREW HIS SWORD IN THE NORTH . . . . . .   430 GREY MONK   21
    THE FATHER INDIGNANT AT THE FALL . . . .   441D INSC FALL MAN   PROSE
    THERE SHALL BE THE SICK FATHER & HIS STARVING FAMILY THERE 499 MILTON 18   10
    SEEK NOT THY HEAVENLY FATHER THEN BEYOND THE SKIES . . . 502 MILTON 20   32
    THEY SAID O FATHER MOST BELOVED O MERCIFUL PARENT   . .   505 MILTON 22   29
    MILTON WILL UTTERLY CONSUME US & THEE OUR BELOVED FATHER   507 MILTON 23   13
    TO BOWLAHOOLA O FATHER MOST BELOVED O MILD PARENT . .   507 MILTON 23   18
    THO STRONG AND MIGHTY TO DESTROY O LOS OUR BELOVED FATHER 507 MILTON 23   20
    O MY DEAR SONS LEAVE NOT YOUR FATHER AS YOUR BRETHREN LEFT 508 MILTON 23   61
      ME
    TO DEATH IN OLD TIME BY SATAN THE FATHER OF SIN & DEATH   517 MILTON 29   33
    THE BOSOM OF THE FATHER IN ETERNITY ON ETERNITY . . .   519 MILTON 31   5
    FATHER & MOTHER I RETURN FROM FLAMES OF FIRE TRIED & PURE 535B FATHER MOTHER   PROSE
      & WHITE
    HIS MOTHER ON HIS FATHER HIM BEGOT . . . .   539 OF HS BIRTH/N   2
    THIS HE DOES AS A MASTER AS A FATHER AND SUPERIOR WHO . 569A DESC CAT 3   PROSE
    USURPED THE THRONE OF HIS FATHER SATURN & BROUGHT ON .   605C V LAST JUDG/N   PROSE
    IN THE ARMS OF THEIR FATHER THESE ARE REPRESENTATIONS OF 610B V LAST JUDG/N   PROSE
      THE
    I CANNOT HELP SAYING THE SON O HOW UNLIKE THE FATHER .   617A V LAST JUDG/N   PROSE
    KOX IS THE FATHER OF SHEM & HAM & JAPHETH HE IS THE NOAH   625 JERUSALEM 7   23
    OF THE FLOOD OF UDAN-ADAN HUTN IS THE FATHER OF THE SEVEN 625 JERUSALEM 7   24
    OF ALBION'S SONS & THE FATHER OF ALL HIS BRETHREN IN THE   626 JERUSALEM 7   43
      SHADOWY
    THEY FEARD THEY NEVER MORE SHOULD SEE THEIR FATHER WHO . . 631 JERUSALEM 11   14
    OUR FATHER ALBION'S SIN AND SHAME BUT FATHER NOW NO MORE   640 JERUSALEM 18   13
    FATHER AND SON AND LIGHT AND LOVE ALL BOLD ASPERITIES .   640 JERUSALEM 18   21
    THEN SPOKE JERUSALEM O ALBION MY FATHER ALBION . . . .   645 JERUSALEM 22   19
    PERFECT AND SHINING WITH BEAUTY BUT THOU O WRETCHED FATHER 645 JERUSALEM 23   7
    FATHER ONCE PITEOUS IS PITY A SIN EMBALMD IN VALA'S BOSOM 646 JERUSALEM 23   9
    THOU ART MY FATHER & MY BROTHER WHY HAST THOU HIDDEN ME   646 JERUSALEM 23   11
    TILL YOU HAVE ASSUMD THE PROVIDENCE OF GOD & SLAIN YOUR   648 JERUSALEM 24   56
      FATHER
    IN ALL ITS REGIONS & ITS FATHER & SAVIOUR NOT PITY AND WEEP 648 JERUSALEM 25   9
    VAST & SEVERE THE ANGUISH EER THEY KNEW THEIR FATHER WERE 713 JERUSALEM 73   8
    MY BROTHER & MY FATHER ARE NO MORE GOD HATH FORSAKEN ME   719 JERUSALEM 78   31
    MY FATHER GAVE TO ME COMMAND TO MURDER ALBION . . . . .   722 JERUSALEM 80   16
    HE CONQUERD LUVAH MY BELOVED HE TOOK ME AND MY FATHER .   722 JERUSALEM 80   19
    OUR FATHER ALBION'S LAND O IT WAS A LOVELY LAND . . . .   729 JERUSALEM 83   85
    THE UNIVERSAL FATHER THEN ALBION STRETCHD HIS HAND INTO   744 JERUSALEM 97   6
      INFINITUDE
    OR OF CHRIST & HIS FATHER ITS ALL A BOAST . . . . . .   752 EV GOSPEL(D)/N   46
    CLOSED THE FATHER & THE SONS . . . .   771 OF GATES/GP   38
    ALWAYS BEHOLD THE FACE OF THE ?HEAVENLY FATHER . . . .   774A ANNO BERKELEY   MARG
    THIS O WHAT SHALL I CALL THEE FORM DIVINE FATHER OF MERCIES 780 GHOST ABEL 1   21
    SOMETHING SUPERIOR TO THE FATHER OR JESUS . . . . . .   785C ILLS DANTE 101   PROSE
    BOOK IS AGAINST THE FORGIVENESS OF SINS IS NOT OF   785D ILLS DANTE 101   PROSE
      THE FATHER
    BUT OF SATAN THE ACCUSER & FATHER OF HELL . . . . . .   785D ILLS DANTE 101   PROSE

                                    666

```
                                                         PAGE    TITLE          LINE
FATHER    (CONTINUED)
     JESUS OUR FATHER WHO ART IN THY HEAVNS CALLD BY THY NAME    788A ANNO THORNTON    * MARG
     OUR FATHER AUGUSTUS CAESAR WHO ART IN THESE    . . . . .    788D ANNO THORNTON    * MARG
     A FATHER TAKING LEAVE OF HIS WIFE & CHILD IS WATCHD . . .   792B LETTER 4         PROSE
     I BLESS THEE O FATHER OF HEAVEN & EARTH . . . . . . . .     799  TO FLAXMAN/L     1
     RICHES OR FAME OF MORTALITY THE LORD OUR FATHER WILL DO FOR  802C LETTER 14       PROSE
     TO THE PLOWMAN "FATHER THE GATE IS OPEN" I HAVE BEGUN TO     803C LETTER 15       PROSE
          WORK
     WITH MY FATHER HOVERING UPON THE WIND    . . . . . . . .    817  HAPPINESS/L      13
     MY BROTHERS & FATHER MARCH BEFORE . . . . . . . . . . .     818  HAPPINESS/L      81
     YOUR ADVICE I SEE THE FACE OF MY HEAVENLY FATHER HE LAYS     823B LETTER 26       PROSE
          HIS
     PRAY TO MY GOD & FATHER FOR THE HEALTH OF MISS POOLE HOPE    833D LETTER 33       PROSE
     GIVES HOPES THAT HE MAY PROVE WORTHY OF HIS FATHER &   . .   838C LETTER 37       PROSE
     FUSELI'S COUNT UGOLINO IS THE FATHER OF SONS OF FEELING AND  864A LETTER 61       PROSE
     AFTER MRS LINNELL'S FATHER IT WILL BE BRUTAL NOT TO SAY      874B LETTER 79       PROSE
     WIDOW FATHER BABE BAPTISM HERVEY ANGEL OF DEATH    . . . .   SUPP INSC HERVEY     *TITLE
     WHERE IS YOUR FATHER THE LOST CHILD ORPHANS   . . . . .     SUPP INSC HERVEY     *TITLE
     "I HAVE SAID TO CORRUPTION THOU ART MY FATHER" (JOB)  . .    SUPP LEGEND/N45      *
     "HAD HE NOT RESEMBLED MY FATHER I HAD DONE IT" MACBETH  . .  SUPP PENC DRAW 2.2   *TITLE
FATHERLY
     FOR LABOURD FATHERLY CARE & SWEET INSTRUCTION I WILL GIVE    312  FOUR ZOAS 6      40
FATHER'S
     DISCHARGING THEIR ENORMOUS VOICES AT THE FATHER'S CURSE      106  TIRIEL 5         15
     OR I WILL WRAP (THEE) UP IN SUCH A TERRIBLE FATHER'S CURSE   107  TIRIEL 6         20
     TO LEAN IN JOY UPON OUR FATHER'S KNEE    . . . . . . . .     125  LIT BLK BOY/SI   26
     STRUGGLING IN MY FATHER'S HANDS    . . . . . . . . . .       166  INFANT SORW/N    5
     STRUGGLING IN MY FATHER'S HANDS    . . . . . . . . . .       217  INFANT SORW/SE   5
     AS THE ELDEST BROTHER IS THE [SECOND] FATHER'S IMAGE SO      332  FOUR ZOAS 7    * 479
          ORC BECAME
     CALLING UPON THEIR FATHER'S NAME UPON THEIR RIVERS DARK      362  FOUR ZOAS 9      203
     WHEN IN MY FATHER'S HOUSE I SAT & HEARD HIS CHEARING VOICE   375  FOUR ZOAS 9      689
     AND IF YOU ALSO FLEE AWAY AND LEAVE YOUR FATHER'S SIDE  . .  508  MILTON 24        22
     BENEATH THE MOON OF ULRO PITY THEN YOUR FATHER'S TEARS  . .  508  MILTON 24        25
     . . . & THE GATES OF THEIR FATHER'S HOUSE  . . . . . .       522  MILTON 32        43
     ENITHARMON IS MY DAUGHTER ACCURSED WITH A FATHER'S CURSE     670  JERUSALEM 42     15
     MY HEAVENLY FATHER'S BUSINESS  . . . . . . . . . . . .       748  EV GOSPEL(B)/N   8
     I AM DOING MY FATHER'S BUSINESS    . . . . . . . . . .       750  EV GOSPEL(C)/N   8
     I AM DOING MY FATHER'S BUSINESS    . . . . . . . . . .       751  EV GOSPEL(D)/N   10
     ABOUT HIS FATHER'S BUSINESS  . . . . . . . . . . . .         752  EV GOSPEL(D)/N   54
     I AM DOING MY FATHER'S BUSINESS    . . . . . . . . . .       757  EV GOSPEL(I)/N   34
     HE LEFT HIS FATHER'S TRADE TO ROAM . . . . . . . . .         757  EV GOSPEL(I)/N   41
     INTERESTING HIMSELF IN THE GREAT OBJECT OF HIS FATHER'S      835C LETTER 35       PROSE
          FAME
     HIS FATHER'S BEST FRIEND WILL I HOPE BECOME THE MOST         838C LETTER 37       PROSE
          RESPECTED
     TO COPY ANY OF HIS FATHER'S DESIGNS THAT MR FLAXMAN MAY      846A LETTER 44       PROSE
FATHERS
     WON BY OUR FATHERS IN MANY A GLORIOUS FIELD    . . . . .     18   EDW THIRD/PS 1   10
     OUR FATHERS SWARM FROM THE SHIPS GIANT VOICES  . . . . .     32   EDW THIRD/PS 6   19
     OUR FATHERS MOVE IN FIRM ARRAY TO BATTLE   . . . . . .       32   EDW THIRD/PS 6   25
     OUR FATHERS SWEATING LEAN ON THEIR SPEARS AND VIEW   . . .   32   EDW THIRD/PS 6   34
     THEN BRUTUS SPOKE INSPIRD OUR FATHERS SIT  . . . . . .       32   EDW THIRD/PS 6   37
     THY AGED FATHERS GIRD THEMSELVES FOR WAR   . . . . . .       34B  KING JOHN/PS    PROSE
     PREPARE TO MEET OUR FATHERS IN THE SKY   . . . . . . .       35   WAR SONG/PS      23
     LIKE OUR ANCIENT FATHERS IN REGIONS OF TWILIGHT . . . .      134  FRENCH REVOLTN   14
     . . . AND MEN WALK WITH THEIR FATHERS IN BLISS    . . . .    145  FRENCH REVOLTN   237
     AND ALL FLESH NAKED STANDS FATHERS AND FRIENDS   . . . .     248  SONG OF LOS 7    33
     FATHERS & FRIENDS MOTHERS & INFANTS KINGS & WARRIORS   .     363  FOUR ZOAS 9      243
     BUT YOU O OUR FATHERS & BROTHERS REMAIN IN ETERNITY  . .     519  MILTON 30        28
     UNDER THE NAMES OF THE FATHERS BEFORE & AFTER THE FLOOD      609D V LAST JUDG/N    PROSE
     THE FIGURES OF SETH & HIS WIFE COMPREHENDS THE FATHERS  .    611C V LAST JUDG/N    PROSE
     NURSING FATHERS & NURSING MOTHERS [THEY HAVE CROWNS]   .     613D V LAST JUDG/N    PROSE
     THY BRETHREN CALL THEE AND THY FATHERS AND THY SONS  . .     622  JERUSALEM 4      11
     SO CRY HAND & HYLE THE ELDEST OF THE FATHERS OF ALBION'S     641  JERUSALEM 18     36
     IN LOVES AND TEARS OF BROTHERS SISTERS SONS FATHERS AND      664  JERUSALEM 38     12
          FRIENDS
     ARE MEN FATHERS OF MULTITUDES AND RIVERS & MOUNTAINS   . .   665  JERUSALEM 38     47
     YOU MUST LEAVE FATHERS & MOTHERS & HOUSES & LANDS    . .     776A INSC LAOCOON    PROSE
FATHERS'
     MAY EMULATE THEIR FATHERS' VIRTUES   . . . . . . . .         18   EDW THIRD/PS 1   20
FATHOM
     INTO A LITTLE ROOT A FATHOM LONG . . . . . . . . .           717  STOOD AMONG/J    11
FATHOMLESS
     THE RAGING FATHOMLESS ABYSS ANON A SERPENT FOLDING   . . .   196  AMERICA PREL 1   15
     AND A FATHOMLESS VOID FOR HIS FEET . . . . . . . .           226  URIZEN 6         5
     SITTING IN FATHOMLESS ABYSS OF MY IMMORTAL SHRINE   . . .    238  EUROPE PREL 2    2
     [A FATHOMLESS & BOUNDLESS DEEP]  . . . . . . . . .           415  MY SPECTRE/N     17
     A FATHOMLESS & BOUNDLESS DEEP  . . . . . . . . . .           415  MY SPECTRE/N     23
FATIGUE
     WITHOUT FATIGUE EVERY THING BEING DEFINITE & DETERMINATE     457B ANNO REYNOLDS   MARG
     ENTER MY COTTAGE COMFORT HER FOR SHE IS SICK WITH FATIGUE    527  MILTON 36        32
FATNESS
     THEY CANNOT SMITE THE WHEAT NOR QUENCH THE FATNESS OF THE    199  AMERICA 9        5
          EARTH
     SWELLD WITH RIPENESS & FAT WITH FATNESS  . . . . . . .       255  AHANIA 5         24
     LEANNESS OR FATNESS IS NOT DEFORMITY BUT   . . . . . .       460C ANNO REYNOLDS   MARG
     OF EACH CLASS SO ARE LEANNESS & FATNESS  . . . . . . .       460C ANNO REYNOLDS   MARG
FATTEND
     FATTEND ON HUMAN BLOOD & DRUNK WITH WINE OF LIFE IS BETTER   274  FOUR ZOAS 1      389
          FAR
```

```
                                                        PAGE      TITLE        LINE
FAULT
    THIS WAS NEVER THE FAULT OF THE PUBLIC  . . . . . .  207A PRSPECTUS 1793  PROSE
    IT IS MAN'S FAULT IF GOD IS NOT ABLE TO DO HIM GOOD FOR HE  392B ANNO WATSON  MARG
    TIS YOUR OWN FAULT IF YOU DONT FLOURISH NOW WILLIAM BLAKE    414 TO MRS FLAXMAN  10
    THIS IS FALSE THE FAULT IS NOT IN WORDS BUT IN THINGS  . .  474C ANNO REYNOLDS  MARG
    MINE IS THE FAULT I SHOULD HAVE REMEMBERD THAT PITY DIVIDES  488 MILTON 8        19
        THE SOUL
    CUPIDITY UNCONQUERABLE MY FAULT WHEN AT NOON OF DAY  . . .  492 MILTON 12         8
    ALL IS MY FAULT WE ARE THE SPECTRE OF LUVAH THE MURDERER    494 MILTON 13         8
    IF YOU BREAK NOT YOUR NECK TIS NOT HIS FAULT  . . . . . .  544 HS FRENDSHIP/N     3
    ERROR & FAULT THAT IS SOON FORGIVEN BUT MERCY IS NOT A SIN  643 JERUSALEM 20      24
    BUT IF IT ALL ARISE FROM MY OWN FAULT I OUGHT TO BLAME     828D LETTER 28      PROSE
        MYSELF
    OF CONSEQUENCE LUCKILY HE FOUND FAULT WITH THE PAPER  . .  846D LETTER 44      PROSE
    EXCEPT PAPER WHICH IS JOHNSON'S FAULT COWPER IS FAR THE    847A LETTER 44      PROSE
        BEST
    PUBLICATION OF HIS LABOURS HE THEN PROCEEDED TO FIND FAULT 856B LETTER 54      PROSE
    CAN ONLY DO SO AT PRESENT BY OWNING THE FAULT  . . . . .  875D LETTER 82      PROSE
FAULTERETH
    WHY SINKS MY HEART WHY FAULTERETH MY TONGUE  . . . . .     34 WAR SONG/PS        12
FAULTS
    LOVE TO FAULTS IS ALWAYS BLIND  . . . . . . . . . . .     175 HOW TO KNOW/N      1
    FOR ALL MY SECRET FAULTS WHICH HE BRINGS FORTH UPON THE   339 FOUR ZOAS 7B     250
        LIGHT
    [ SPOTS & BLEMISHES WHICH ARE BEAUTIES & NOT FAULTS ]  . .  595D PUB ADDRESS/N  PROSE
    FAULTS CARACCHE CORREGIO'S & RAFAEL'S HAVE FAULTS  . . .  815A LETTER 23      *PROSE
    INTREAT YOU TO EXCUSE FAULTS FOR PORTRAIT PAINTING IS THE  815C LETTER 23      PROSE
        DIRECT
    ASTONISHED AT MY FAULTS AND COULD NOT ASSIGN A REASON  .  852B LETTER 50      PROSE
FAVOR
    DID ME THE FAVOR TO CALL ON ME I HAVE PROMISD HIM TO SEND  810D LETTER 21      PROSE
    BEGGING THE FAVOR OF A FEW LINES TO INFORM HIM HOW YOU  .  829C LETTER 30      PROSE
    FAVOR ME WITH A LINE THAT I MAY SEND THE PLATES TO JOHNSON 840C LETTER 39      PROSE
    COWPER FOR THAT SONNET IN FAVOR OF A PRISONER AT LEICESTER 841C LETTER 41      PROSE
    THE FAVOR OF TEN POUNDS MORE WILL CARRY ME THRO THIS PLATE 851A LETTER 49      PROSE
    FAVOR ME WITH A LINE OF DIRECTION HOW TO PROCEED  . . .  853A LETTER 51      *PROSE
FAVORD
    BUT AS YOU HAVE FAVORD ME WITH YOUR REMARKS ON MY DESIGN  793B LETTER 5       PROSE
FAVOUR
    TO ASK WHICH IS THE FAVOUR OF YOUR COMPANY  . . . . .     20 EDW THIRD/PS 2    44
    AND FAVOUR US WITH A FINE SONG THEN SHE SUNG  . . . .     55C ISLAND MOON 9  PROSE
    AFTER DINNER I ASKD ISAIAH TO FAVOUR THE WORLD WITH  . . 154A MARRIAGE HH 12 PROSE
    AND FAVOUR GAINS WITH GOD & MEN  . . . . . . . . .      748 EV GOSPEL(B)/N    12
    WITH FAVOUR & AFFECTION PERHAPS THE SIMPLICITY OF MYSELF   828C LETTER 28      PROSE
    I HASTEN TO WRITE TO YOU BY THE FAVOUR OF MR EDWARDS I HAVE 831A LETTER 31     PROSE
    PRAY MY DEAR SIR FAVOUR ME WITH A LINE CONCERNING YOUR  .  833D LETTER 33      PROSE
    & BEG THE FAVOUR OF SOME MORE OF THE [XXX] NEEDFUL  . . .  851A LETTER 49     *PROSE
    DO SO TO SATISFY YOU THAT I HAVE RECEIVED YOUR KIND FAVOUR 851C LETTER 50      PROSE
    I HAVE & BEG THE FAVOUR OF YOU TO SEND ME THE TWO PLATES   876A LETTER 83      PROSE
FAVOURD
    AND ENGLAND IS THE LAND FAVOURD BY COMMERCE  . . . .      19 EDW THIRD/PS 2    30
    BE NO LESS FAVOURD THO THEY ARE ROUGH LIKE ROUGH SAILORS  807A LETTER 17      PROSE
FAVOURED
    BUT MILD HE HAILED HER HAIL HIGHLY FAVOURED SAID HE  . .   39D SAMSON/PS      PROSE
FAVOURITE
    IN HER FAVOURITE TOPIC & SHE PROCEEDED TO USE  . . . .    53B ISLAND MOON 8  PROSE
    HE WAS FRIEND TO THE FAVOURITE . . . . . . . . . . . .   136 FRENCH REVOLTN    47
    THAN THE SHIPWRECK IT IS EVERY BODY FAVOURITE WHO HAVE  . 855A LETTER 53      PROSE
FAVOURS
    AND GRANT HIS FAVOURS WITH A SPARING HAND  . . . . .      20 EDW THIRD/PS 2    47
    FOR FORTUNE'S FAVOURS YOU YOUR RICHES BRING  . . . .     541 MR STOTHARD/N     1
    FORTUNE FAVOURS THE BRAVE OLD PROVERBS SAY  . . . . .    541 MR CROMEK/N       1
FAWN
    THE DANCING FAWN FOR YOUR UGLY MAN NOW HE COMES TO HIS    579B DESC CAT 5     PROSE
        TRIAL
FAWNING
    HIS MIGHTY ROAR AND FAWNING PLAYD AROUND  . . . .        21 EDW THIRD/PS 2    82
    FRIGHTNING FAITHLESS FAWNING  . . . . . . . . . .       234 URIZEN 23          3
FAYETTE
    TILL FAYETTE POINT HIS FINGER TO VERSAILLES . . . .     138 FRENCH REVOLTN   104
    FAYETTE SPRUNG FROM HIS SEAT SAYING READY . . . . . .   146 FRENCH REVOLTN   263
    SO FAYETTE STOOD SILENT AMONG THE ASSEMBLY . . . . .    146 FRENCH REVOLTN   268
    AND THE VOTE WAS THAT FAYETTE SHOULD ORDER THE ARMY . . 146 FRENCH REVOLTN   269
    ON FAYETTE BUT ON THE WHOLE ARMY A SHADOW . . . . .     146 FRENCH REVOLTN   271
    . . . AND OF SULPHUR THE EARTH FROM FAYETTE AS HE LIFTED 146 FRENCH REVOLTN   278
        HIS HAND
    . . . SILENT LISTNING TOWARD FAYETTE  . . . . . .      147 FRENCH REVOLTN   283
    [ FAYETTE BESIDE KING LEWIS STOOD ] . . . . . . . .     185 LET BROTHELS/N    27
    [ FAYETTE BEHELD THE QUEEN TO SMILE ] . . . . . .      185 LET BROTHELS/N    31
    FAYETTE BEHELD THE KING & QUEEN  . . . . . . . .       185 LET BROTHELS/N    35
    BUT MUTE FAYETTE WEPT TEAR FOR TEAR  . . . . . .       185 LET BROTHELS/N    37
    [ FAYETTE FAYETTE THOURT BOUGHT & SOLD ] . . . . .     186 LET BROTHELS/N    39
    [ FAYETTE BESIDE HIS BANNER STOOD ] . . . . . . . .     186 LET BROTHELS/N    43
    [ FAYETTE FAYETTE THOURT BOUGHT & SOLD ] . . . . .     186 LET BROTHELS/N    56
    FAYETTE BEHELD THE KING & QUEEN  . . . . . . . .       186 LET BROTHELS/N    60
    BUT MUTE FAYETTE WEPT TEAR FOR TEAR  . . . . . .       186 LET BROTHELS/N    62
FAYETTE'S
    HAVE YOU NEVER SEEN FAYETTE'S FOREHEAD . . . . . . .    142 FRENCH REVOLTN   187
FEAR     SEE NIGHT-FEAR
    LIKE A DUMB STATUE FROZE TO STONE WITH FEAR  . . . .      4 FAIR ELENOR/PS    20
    PALE DEATH AND FOLLOWD ON THE WINGS OF FEAR  . . . .      4 FAIR ELENOR/PS    28
    SHE FLED FROM FEAR TILL AT HER HOUSE ARRIVD  . . . .      5 FAIR ELENOR/PS    36
```

FEAR   (CONTINUED)

		PAGE	TITLE	LINE
AH WOMAN'S FEAR SHE CRYD AH CURSED DUKE	. . . .	5	FAIR ELENOR/PS	39
I FEAR LORD PERCY WILL NOT GIVE ME LEAVE	. . . . . .	20	EDW THIRD/PS 2	45
THOU HAST A GALLANT SPIRIT WHICH I FEAR	. . . . . .	20	EDW THIRD/PS 2	57
DID YOU (EER) SEE HIM FEAR AT BLANCHETAQUE	. . . . . .	21	EDW THIRD/PS 3 *	10
FRENCH FROM THE FORD DID HE FEAR THEN	. . . . . .	21	EDW THIRD/PS 3	12
YES FEAR THAT MADE HIM FIGHT SO	. . . . . .	21	EDW THIRD/PS 3	13
BY THE SAME REASON I MIGHT SAY TIS FEAR	. . . . . .	21	EDW THIRD/PS 3	14
AND THIS SIR THOMAS YOU CALL FEAR YOUR FEAR	. . . . .	22	EDW THIRD/PS 3	39
I DO NOT THINK SIR THOMAS YOU KNOW WHAT FEAR IS	. . . .	22	EDW THIRD/PS 3	42
THERE SIR THOMAS DO YOU CALL THAT FEAR	. . . . . .	22	EDW THIRD/PS 3	47
THE WOLF IS HUNTED DOWN BY CAUSELESS FEAR	. . . . . .	24	EDW THIRD/PS 3	113
THE LION FLEES AND FEAR USURPS HIS HEART	. . . . . .	24	EDW THIRD/PS 3	114
IF AT THIS MOMENT OF THEIR IDLE FEAR	. . . . . .	24	EDW THIRD/PS 3	118
LET US NOT FEAR TO BEAT ROUND NATURE'S WILDS	. . . . .	27	EDW THIRD/PS 3	263
YET I NOT FEAR THE MONSTER IN HIS PRIDE	. . . . . .	31	EDW THIRD/PS 5	47
THOUGH I SHOULD TELL HER ALL MY HEART WHAT CAN I FEAR	.	38D	SAMSON/PS	PROSE
WHAT SHOULDST THOU FEAR THY POWER IS MORE THAN MORTAL	. .	39A	SAMSON/PS	PROSE
THOU FEAR I DRINK MY TEARS LIKE WATER I LIVE UPON SORROW	.	39A	SAMSON/PS	PROSE
THESE ARE THE GODS WHICH CAME FROM FEAR FOR	. . . .	40D	THEN SHE BORE	PROSE
AS WELL AS THIS [FOR ALL SHE XXX FEAR AND XXX THE XXX]		41A	THEN SHE BORE	*PROSE
& FILLD HIM WITH CONFUSION FEAR AS A TORRENT WILD	. . .	42B	THEN SHE BORE	PROSE
THEREFORE PRONOUNCE HIM A KNAVE WHY SHOULD HONESTY FEAR A KNAVE		68B	ANNO LAVATER	MARG
UNEASY I FEAR I HAVE NOT MANY ENEMIES	. . . . . .	70C	ANNO LAVATER	MARG
LET NO ONE FEAR FOR POOR BLIND TIRIEL HURTS NONE BUT HIMSELF		101	TIRIEL 2	14
NOR FEAR THE WOLVISH HOWL	. . . . . .	115	LIT GRL FND/SI	51
SO IF ALL DO THEIR DUTY THEY NEED NOT FEAR HARM	. . . .	118	CHIMNEY SWP/SI	24
AN INFANT GROAN AN INFANT FEAR	. . . . . .	122	ON ANOTHERS/SI	10
DOST THOU O LITTLE CLOUD I FEAR THAT I AM NOT LIKE THEE		129	BOOK OF THEL 3	17
LIVES NOT ALONE NOR FOR ITSELF FEAR NOT AND I WILL CALL		129	BOOK OF THEL 3	27
AND TO RETURN FEAR NOTHING ENTER WITH THY VIRGIN FEET	. .	130	BOOK OF THEL 5	17
IN FEAR UTTER VOICES OF THUNDER . . .		134	FRENCH REVOLTN	11
. . . A FEAR AND A WITHRING BLIGHT BLOWN BY THE NORTH	.	141	FRENCH REVOLTN	162
FEAR NOT DREAMS FEAR NOT VISIONS	. . . . . .	142	FRENCH REVOLTN	180
OR SHRINK AT THE LITTLE BLASTS OF FEAR	. . . . . .	166	WHY CARE FOR/N	3
[CRUEL JEALOUS [WINTRY] SELFISH FEAR]	. . . . . .	169	EARTHS ANSWR/N *	12
IN [EVERY VOICE OF EVERY CHILD] EVERY INFANT'S CRY OF FEAR		170	LONDON/N	6
AND MUTUAL FEAR BRINGS PEACE	. . . . . .	174	HUMAN IMAGE/N	6
THE BUILDER OF VIRGINIA THROWS HIS HAMMER DOWN IN FFAR	. .	201	AMERICA 14 *	16
FEAR [OR] & HOPE ARE VISION	. . . . . .	209D	FOR CHILDRN/GP	*TITLE
CRUEL JEALOUS SELFISH FEAR	. . . . . .	211	EARTHS ANSR/SE	12
IN EVERY INFANT'S CRY OF FEAR	. . . . . .	216	LONDON/SE	6
AND MUTUAL FEAR BRINGS PEACE	. . . . . .	217	HUMAN ABSTR/SE	5
AND THE MAIDEN SOON FORGOT HER FEAR	. . . . . .	219	LIT GRL LST/SE	19
O THE TREMBLING FEAR	. . . . . .	219	LIT GRL LST/SE	32
DICTATE SWIFT WINGED WORDS & FEAR NOT	. . . . . .	222	URIZEN 2	6
HE WATCHD IN SHUDDRING FEAR	. . . . . .	227	URIZEN 8	9
IN HARROWING FEAR ROLLING ROUND	. . . . . .	228	URIZEN 11	10
WONDER AWE FEAR ASTONISHMENT	. . . . . .	231	URIZEN 18	13
OVER THE DOORS THOU SHALT NOT & OVER THE CHIMNEYS FEAR IS WRITTEN		243	EUROPE 12	28
CRUEL JEALOUSY SELFISH FEAR	. . . . . .	255	AHANIA 5	41
. . . WAILD IN DISMAL FEAR	. . . . . .	264	FOUR ZOAS 1	8
ENION SAID [HIS] THY FEAR HAS MADE ME TREMBLE		265	FOUR ZOAS 1 *	35
. . . GATE OF [AURICULAR POWER] THE TONGUE [NERVES] IN TREMBLING FEAR		267	FOUR ZOAS 1 *	109
[WITHIN MY SOUL HAS LOST ITS SPLENDOR & A BROODING FEAR]		267	FOUR ZOAS 1	116
A SORROW & A FEAR A LIVING TORMENT & NAKED VICTIM	. . .	268	FOUR ZOAS 1	159
IN EMBRYON PASSIONS THEY KISSD NOT NOR EMBRACD FOR SHAME & FEAR		270	FOUR ZOAS 1	238
AND THARMAS TOOK HER IN PITYING THEN ENION IN JEALOUS FEAR		278	FOUR ZOAS 1	525
MURDERD HER & HID HER IN HER BOSOM EMBALMING HER FOR FEAR		278	FOUR ZOAS 1	526
TERRIFIC URIZEN STRODE ABOVE IN FEAR & PALE DISMAY	. . .	280	FOUR ZOAS 2	19
HE MIGHT AVERT HIS OWN DESPAIR IN WOE & FEAR HE SAW	. . .	282	FOUR ZOAS 2	76
. . . WITH [SONGS & JOY] SORROW & CARE [?ETERNAL FEAR]	. .	287	FOUR ZOAS 2 *	268
DOWNWARD & YOUR FLUXILE EYES ENGLOBD ROLL ROUND IN FEAR		294	FOUR ZOAS 3	87
SHE WANDERS IN ETERNAL FEAR OF FALLING INTO THE INDEFINITE		297	FOUR ZOAS 3	208
HIS CLOUDY FORM IN JEALOUS FEAR & MUTTERING THUNDERS HOARSE		299	FOUR ZOAS 4	77
AND THUS BEGAN THE BINDING OF URIZEN DAY & NIGHT IN FEAR		302	FOUR ZOAS 4	199
IN HARROWING FEAR ROLLING HIS NERVOUS [BRAINS] BRAIN SHOT BRANCHES		303	FOUR ZOAS 4 *	227
AND BRASS & SILVER & GOLD FOURFOLD IN DARK PROPHETIC FEAR		307	FOUR ZOAS 5	74
WITH SILENT FEAR & HIS IMMORTAL CHEEKS GREW DEADLY PALE		307	FOUR ZOAS 5	87
LOS FOLDED ENITHARMON IN A COLD WHITE CLOUD IN FEAR	. . .	308	FOUR ZOAS 5	110
[OF HOPE & FEAR XXX SINGING THE ?SAME SONG AROUND THE ?GLOWING BED]		SUPP	FOUR ZOAS 5 *	
HE SAW THEM CURSD BEYOND HIS CURSE HIS SOUL MELTED WITH FEAR		315	FOUR ZOAS 6	142
TRACES THE WONDERS OF FUTURITY IN HORRIBLE FEAR OF THE FUTURE		322	FOUR ZOAS 7	86
HAVE I FOUND THEE HAVE I FOUND THEE TREMBLEST THOU IN FEAR		325	FOUR ZOAS 7	224
OFTEN ENOUGH TO CONVINCE THY JEALOUSY & FEAR & TERROR	. .	330	FOUR ZOAS 7	421
TO MEET THESE SPECTRES OF THE DEAD I THEREFORE FEAR THAT HE		330	FOUR ZOAS 7	425
MY WATERS LIKE A FLOOD AROUND THEE FEAR NOT TRUST IN ME		334	FOUR ZOAS 7B	55
AND ENITHARMON TREMBLING & IN FEAR UTTERD THESE WORDS	. .	335	FOUR ZOAS 7B	81
A SEPULCHER & WORSHIP DEATH IN FEAR WHILE YET WE LIVE	. .	349	FOUR ZOAS 8	334
THEY SHAKE THEIR SLUMBERS OFF THEY WAVE IN AWFUL FEAR	. .	352	FOUR ZOAS 8	444
MOVING IN ROOT-LIKE FIBRES TREMBLING IN FEAR UPON THE EARTH		353	FOUR ZOAS 8 *	476
FEAR NOT O POOR FORSAKEN ONE O LAND OF BRIARS & THORNS		354	FOUR ZOAS 8	534

		PAGE	TITLE	LINE

FEAR   (CONTINUED)

ONCE I WAILD DESOLATE LIKE THEE MY FALLOW FIELDS IN FEAR   354 FOUR ZOAS 8   536
FOR HIMSELF IN THE ROCK OF ETERNITY TREMBLING & IN [FEAR]   356 FOUR ZOAS 8   595
   DESPAIR
IN PANGS OF AN ETERNAL BIRTH IN TORMENT & AWE & FEAR . .   363 FOUR ZOAS 9   234
PRIESTS & CHAIND CAPTIVES MET TOGETHER IN A HORRIBLE FEAR   363 FOUR ZOAS 9   244
THE MYRIADS & IN SILENT FEAR THEY [F] LOOK OUT FROM THEIR   366 FOUR ZOAS 9   * 339
   GRAVES
FEAR CANNOT LOVE . . . .   401A ANNO BACON   MARG
HE WHO HAS FEW THINGS TO DESIRE CANNOT HAVE MANY TO FEAR   405B ANNO BACON   MARG
ALONE CAN FREE THE [WOLD] WORLD FROM FEAR . . . . .   419 I SAW A MONK/N *   43
THE SENSES ROLL THEMSELVES IN FEAR . . . .   426 MENTAL TRAVLER   63
HER FEAR PLANTS MANY A THICKET WILD . . . .   426 MENTAL TRAVLER   78
IN THIS LAND OF UNBELIEF & FEAR . . . .   427 LAND OF DREAMS   18
AND THINE IS A FACE OF WILD TERROR & FEAR . . . . .   429 MARY   47
O WHAT A PLEASANT TREMBLING FEAR . . . .   429 CRYSTL CABINET   16
ALONE CAN FREE THE WORLD FROM FEAR . . . .   430 GREY MONK   28
MAGISTRATES AND HIS FEAR OF UTTERING A FALSEHOOD UPON OATH   438D BLAKES MEMORAN   PROSE
& DEPRESSION WHAT YOU FEAR IS YOUR TRUE INTEREST . . .   452C ANNO REYNOLDS   MARG
AND REPENTANCE FOR SIN & SORROW & PUNISHMENT & FEAR . .   499 MILTON 18   24
BURNS TO THE TOP OF HEAVEN AGAINST THEE IN JEALOUSY & FEAR   499 MILTON 18   32
WHILE LOS HEARD INDISTINCT IN FEAR WHAT TIME I BOUND MY   505 MILTON 22   4
   SANDALS
EXCEEDINGLY WITH FEAR & TERROR STANDING IN THE VALE . .   505 MILTON 22   10
TERRIFIED THE SPECTRE SCREAMS & RUSHES IN FEAR INTO THEIR   515 MILTON 28   25
   NET
THE BADGER & FOX THEY WORSHIP BEFORE HIS FEET IN TREMBLING   515 MILTON 28   43
   FEAR
SHE SHALL RELENT IN FEAR OF DEATH SHE SHALL BEGIN TO GIVE   522 MILTON 33   17
AND OLOLON LOOKED DOWN INTO THE HEAVENS OF ULRO IN FEAR   524 MILTON 34   49
VIRGIN OF PROVIDENCE FEAR NOT TO ENTER INTO MY COTTAGE   527 MILTON 36   28
IS TO IMPRESS ON MEN THE FEAR OF DEATH TO TEACH . . .   530 MILTON 38   38
TREMBLING & FEAR TERROR CONSTRICTION ABJECT SELFISHNESS   530 MILTON 38   39
TREMBLING BEFORE HIM WITH EXCEEDING GREAT TREMBLING & FEAR   531 MILTON 39   47
FEAR TO ASSOCIATE WITH BLAKE . . . .   545 COSWAY FRAZR/N   2
EXPRESSION OF FEAR OR REVENGE OR ENVY OR BLANK HORROR .   580C DESC CAT 5   PROSE
FEAR AND DOUBT OF HIS OWN ORIGINAL CONCEPTION THE . .   582C DESC CAT 9   PROSE
CAUSES TO THE FLORENTINE AND ROMAN ARTIST FEAR TO EXECUTE   583A DESC CAT 9   PROSE
I COURT THE COMPARISON & FEAR NOT THE RESULT BUT NOT IN   598D PUB ADDRESS/N   PROSE
   A DARK CORNER
THIS ETERNAL FEMALE & TREMBLE AT WHAT OTHERS FEAR NOT .   609B V LAST JUDG/N   PROSE
WHILE THEY DESPISE & LAUGH AT WHAT OTHERS FEAR . . .   609B V LAST JUDG/N   PROSE
MOURNING FOR FEAR OF THE WARRIORS IN THE VALE OF   623 JERUSALEM 5   12
   ENTUTHON-BENYTHON
HE MIGHT AVERT HIS OWN DESPAIR IN WOE & FEAR HE SAW . .   626 JERUSALEM 7   34
LOS OPEND THE FURNACES IN FEAR THE SPECTRE SAW TO BABEL   627 JERUSALEM 8   23
   & SHINAR
COMPELLING HIS SPECTRE TO LABOURS MIGHTY TREMBLING IN FEAR   629 JERUSALEM 10   18
I SEE IN DEADLY FEAR IN LONDON LOS RAGING ROUND HIS ANVIL   636 JERUSALEM 15   21
THE PARENT'S FEAR THE BROTHER'S JEALOUSY THE SISTER'S CURSE   636 JERUSALEM 16   7
THEE WHOM I THOUGHT PURE AS THE HEAVENS IN INNOCENCE & FEAR   644 JERUSALEM 21   20
HYLE SEES IN FEAR HE HOWLS IN FURY OVER THEM HAND SEES .   644 JERUSALEM 21   28
IN JEALOUS FEAR IN STERN ACCUSATION WITH CRUEL STRIPES . .   644 JERUSALEM 21   29
ALBION THY FEAR HAS MADE ME TREMBLE THY TERRORS HAVE   644 JERUSALEM 22   1
   SURROUNDED ME
SUBDUE MY SPECTRE TO THY FEAR . . . .   651 FIELDS FROM/J   72
FEAR NOT O LITTLE FLOCK I COME ALBION SHALL RISE AGAIN . .   653 JERUSALEM 29   26
DOWNWARD AND YOUR FLUXILE EYES ENGLOBD ROLL ROUND IN FEAR   655 JERUSALEM 29   68
O HOW I TREMBLE HOW MY MEMBERS POUR DOWN MILKY FEAR . . .   660 JERUSALEM 34   3
FROM HEAD TO FEET A GARMENT OF DEATH & ETERNAL FEAR . . .   660 JERUSALEM 34   6
FOR FEAR AT ENTERING THE GATE INTO OUR WORLD OF CRUEL . .   688 JERUSALEM 56   15
I MIND NOT YOUR LAUGH AND YOUR FROWN I NOT FEAR AND . . .   688 JERUSALEM 56   30
THAT IN THE INTERIOR WORLDS IS CARRIED ON IN FEAR   692 JERUSALEM 59   51
   & TREMBLING
GIVE FORTH THY PITY & LOVE FEAR NOT LO I AM WITH   694 JERUSALEM 60   67
   THEE ALWAYS
THY BROTHER WHO SLEEPETH IN ALBION FEAR NOT TREMBLING SHADE   694 JERUSALEM 60   69
THAT HE HIMSELF MAY DWELL AMONG YOU FEAR NOT THEN TO TAKE   695 JERUSALEM 61   26
OF UNCONQUERABLE FEAR AMIDST DELIGHTS OF REVENGE   702 JERUSALEM 66   39
   EARTH-SHAKING
IN CHANNELS THRO MY FIERY LIMBS O LOVE O PITY O FEAR . .   705 JERUSALEM 67   54
BUT NOW MY SOUL IS HARROWD WITH GRIEF & FEAR & LOVE   707 JERUSALEM 68   66
   & DESIRE
MUTUAL HATE RETURNS & MUTUAL DECEIT & MUTUAL FEAR . . .   708 JERUSALEM 69   37
IN HEAVEN LOVE BEGETS LOVE BUT FEAR IS THE PARENT   725 JERUSALEM 81   15
   OF EARTHLY LOVE
AND HE WHO WILL NOT BEND TO LOVE MUST BE SUBDUD BY FEAR   725 JERUSALEM 81   16
THE DESARTS TREMBLE AT HIS WRATH THEY SHRINK THEMSELVES   726 JERUSALEM 82   51
   IN FEAR
OF EARTHQUAKES & CONSUMING FIRES THEY ROLL APART IN FEAR   733 JERUSALEM 88   9
FEAR NOT MY SONS THIS WAKING DEATH HE IS BECOME ONE WITH ME   741 JERUSALEM 93   18
JESUS REPLIED FEAR NOT ALBION UNLESS I DIE THOU CANST NOT   743 JERUSALEM 96   14
   LIVE
MARY FEAR NOT LET ME SEE . . . .   754 EV GOSPEL (E)/N   43
THE MORAL VIRTUES IN GREAT FEAR . . . .   759 EV GOSPEL (2)   28
FEAR & HOPE ARE VISION . . . .   768D FOR SEXES/GP   TITLE
NAKED IN AIR IN SHAME & FEAR . . . .   770 OF GATES/GP   9
FOR FEAR I SHOULD EVAPORATE THE SPIRIT OF MY INVENTION .   792B LETTER 4   PROSE
FEAR THEY WILL NOT EXCUSE & I KNOW NOT HOW TO [XXX]   798B LETTER 10   *PROSE
   APOLOGIZE FOR
BUT BY MY CONJUNCTION WITH FLAXMAN WHO KNOWS TO FORGIVE   799 TO FLAXMAN/L   12
   NERVOUS FEAR

	PAGE	TITLE	LINE

FEAR   (CONTINUED)

I FEAR IT WILL BE THURSDAY BEFORE WE CAN GET AWAY FROM . . 801B LETTER 13   PROSE
AMAZD & IN FEAR . . . . 804 TO BUTTS/L   18
SLIDE IN CLAY HOW CAN WE DO OTHERWISE THAN FEAR & TREMBLE   813A LETTER 22   PROSE
BUT IF WE FEAR TO DO THE DICTATES OF OUR ANGELS & TREMBLE   813A LETTER 22   PROSE
PATH IS DIFFICULT I HAVE NO FEAR OF STUMBLING WHILE I KEEP 813B LETTER 22   PROSE
  IT
FEAR SO TOO BECAUSE THERE APPEARS SOME REASON WHY YOU MIGHT 814A LETTER 23   PROSE
POVERTY ENVY OLD AGE & FEAR . . . . 817 HAPPINESS/L   37
MADE ME VERY UNEASY BUT IT IS OVER & I NOW DEFY THE WORST 819D LETTER 25   PROSE
  & FEAR NOT
THEN FEAR NOTHING & LET MY SISTER FEAR NOTHING BECAUSE   821A LETTER 25   PROSE
ESCAPED THE CONTAGION OF THE COURT OF JUSTICE I FEAR THAT 829C LETTER 30   PROSE
OF EMPLOYMENT THIS WISH I FEAR IS NOT TO BE ACCOMPLISHD   830B LETTER 30   PROSE
YOUR WORDS "DO NOT FEAR YOU CAN WANT EMPLOYMENT" WERE   . . 831B LETTER 31   PROSE
SO THAT I SHOULD NOT FEAR TO PRODUCE SOMEWHAT IN THIS WAY 353A LETTER 51   *PROSE
HAYLEY'S & FEAR THAT HE WILL WISH ME TO DO SO I ASKED HIM 860A LETTER 56   PROSE
HAMPSTEAD AIR AS IT ALWAYS DID SO I FEAR IT ALWAYS WILL DO 870D LETTER 72   PROSE
COME TO YOU BEFORE TUESDAY BUT MUCH FEAR THAT MY PRESENT   872A LETTER 74   PROSE
SUNDAY AT HAMPSTEAD AS I FEAR THE ATTACK AGAIN . . . . 872C LETTER 75   PROSE
AT PRESENT WOULD BE A RUMBLE I FEAR I COULD NOT GO THRO   873A LETTER 76   PROSE
IN THE STAGE & SHALL BE I FEAR FOR SOME TIME BEING ONLY   875B LETTER 81   PROSE
MIND OUT OF A STATE OF TERRIBLE FEAR AT SUCH A STEP . . . 876B LETTER 83   PROSE
I HAVE ASKED & INTREATED DIVINE HELP BUT FEAR CONTINUES   876B LETTER 83   PROSE
ON FUTURITY WHICH I CANNOT DO WITHOUT DOUBT & FEAR THAT   879C LETTER 89   PROSE
SUFFICIENTLY PAID IF I LIVE AS I NOW DO & ONLY FEAR THAT   879C LETTER 89   PROSE
  I MAY
A VISION OF FEAR A VISION OF HOPE   . . . . SUPP LEGEND/N75   *TITLE
FEARD

[BUT STILL HE FEARD THAT HAR & HEVA WOULD DIE OF JOY &   102 TIRIEL 3   8
  GRIEF]
I FEARD THE [ROUGHNESS] FURY OF MY WIND   . . . . . . 166 I FEARD FURY/N   1
FOR NOW HE FEARD ETERNAL DEATH & UTTERMOST EXTINCTION . . 307 FOUR ZOAS 5   75
BECAUSE PALAMABRON WAS GOOD NATURD SATAN SUPPOSD HE FEARD 351 FOUR ZOAS 8   391
  HIM
PALAMABRON FEARD TO BE ANGRY LEST SATAN SHOULD ACCUSE HIM 486 MILTON 7   13
  OF
THEY FEARD THEY NEVER MORE SHOULD SEE THEIR FATHER WHO . . 631 JERUSALEM 11 14
FEARED

OER THE EARTH PRIDE FEARED FOR HER CITY BUT NOT LONG   . . 41B THEN SHE BORE PROSE
CIRENCESTER PLACE I FEARED YOU MIGHT BE GONE OR I MIGHT   871B LETTER 72   PROSE
FEAREST   SEE FEARST

HOW DIDST THOU REND THE FEEBLE TIES THOU FEAREST NOUGHT   39A SAMSON/PS   PROSE
AND FEAREST THOU BECAUSE I VANISH AND AM SEEN NO MORE . . 128 BOOK OF THEL 3   9
. . . UNLESS THOU FIRST FEAREST TO HURT THEM . . . . . 143 FRENCH REVOLTN 194
FEARFUL

THE FEARFUL CRANE SPRINGS FROM THE SPLASHY FEN   24 EDW THIRD/PS 3   125
ENVY HATH A SERPENT'S HEAD OF FEARFUL BULK . . . . . . 41C THEN SHE BORE PROSE
[COULD] [DARE] FRAME THY FEARFUL SYMMETRY   . . . . . . 172 THE TYGER/N 1   4
DARE [FORM] FRAME THY FEARFUL SYMMETRY . . . . 173 THE TYGER/N 1   25
DARE FRAME THY FEARFUL SYMMETRY   . . . . 173 THE TYGER/N 2   4
DARE FRAME THY FEARFUL SYMMETRY   . . . . 173 THE TYGER/N 2   20
THIS KNOWING ARTFUL SECRET FEARFUL CAUTIOUS TREMBLING   194 V DAU ALBION 6 17
  HYPOCRITE
COULD FRAME THY FEARFUL SYMMETRY . . . . 214 THE TYGER/SE   4
DARE FRAME THY FEARFUL SYMMETRY   . . . . 214 THE TYGER/SE   24
A FEARFUL JOURNEY ANNOYD . . . . 234 URIZEN 20   49
[TWISTING IN FEARFUL FORMS & HOWLING HOWLING HARSH   269 FOUR ZOAS 1   180
  SHRIEKING
LEST HE SHOULD SLAY JERUSALEM IN HIS FEARFUL JEALOUSY   . . 675 JERUSALEM 45 27
WE WOMEN TREMBLE AT THE LIGHT THEREFORE HIDING FEARFUL . . 688 JERUSALEM 56 39
FEARFULLY

"I AM FEARFULLY & WONDERFULLY MADE" I HAD BEEN READING . . 823B LETTER 26   PROSE
FEARING

[FEARING TO TELL THEM WHO HE WAS BECAUSE OF THE WEAKNESS   102 TIRIEL 2   49
  OF HAR]
SECLUDED PLACES FEARING THE JOYS OF LOVE . . . . 246 SONG OF LOS 3 26
FEARING THY FROWN LOVING THY SMILE O URIZEN PRINCE OF LIGHT 360 FOUR ZOAS 9   135
IN THE STILL NIGHT FEARING LEST THEY SHOULD OTHERS MOLEST 504 MILTON 21   27
BUT FEARING FOR THE PAIN FOR IF HE TOUCHES A VITAL . . . 531 MILTON 39   19
FEARING THAT ALBION SHOULD TURN HIS BACK AGAINST THE DIVINE 656 JERUSALEM 31   2
  VISION
OF OUR CAPTAINS FEARING OUR OFFICERS MORE THAN THE ENEMY   700 JERUSALEM 65   36
NEITHER DARING TO PUT IN ACT ITS COUNCILS FEARING   703 JERUSALEM 70   6
  EACH-OTHER
BUT HE SPOKE NOT TO ALBION FEARING LEST ALBION SHOULD   711 JERUSALEM 71   58
  TURN HIS BACK
FEARLESS

BUT HAR & HEVA SLEPT FEARLESS AS BABES ON LOVING BREASTS   109 TIRIEL 7   21
INFANCY FEARLESS LUSTFUL HAPPY NESTLING FOR DELIGHT . . . 193 V DAU ALBION 6 4
IN FEARLESS MAJESTY ANNIHILATING SELF LAUGHING TO SCORN   530 MILTON 38   41
AND MARCHES ON IN FEARLESS DEPENDANCE ON THE DIVINE DECREES 580B DESC CAT 5   PROSE
& NOW GO ON AGAIN WITH MY TASK FEARLESS AND THO MY . . . 813B LETTER 22   PROSE
FEARS

NO ONE CAN SAY HE FEARS BUT WHEN HE TURNS   . . . . . . 21 EDW THIRD/PS 3 17
HE FEARS TO TURN HIS FACE AND YOU TO TURN YOUR BACK . . . 22 EDW THIRD/PS 3 41
FEARS THE SMALL FIRE THAT PLAYS ABOUT THE FEN   . . . . . 24 EDW THIRD/PS 3 117
. . . IN [GHASTLY FEA] GUILTY FEARS   . . . . 107 TIRIEL 5   * 32
BUT THEIR FEARS ALLAY . . . . 114 LIT GRL FND/SI 30
HOW CAN A CHILD WHEN FEARS ANNOY . . . . 124 SCHOOL BOY/SI 18
TREMBLING COLD IN GHASTLY FEARS   . . . . 161 NEVER PAIN/N   7
AND I WATERD IT IN FEARS . . . . 165 CHRISTN FORB/N 5

		PAGE	TITLE	LINE

FEARS   (CONTINUED)
```
    I MURMURD MY FEARS  . . . . . . . . . . . .        170 SLEPT DARK/N        3
    HE SITS DOWN WITH HOLY FEARS  . . . . . . .        174 HUMAN IMAGE/N      10
    I DRIED MY TEARS & ARMD MY FEARS  . . . . . . .     182 THE ANGEL/N        11
    [OF SELFISH SLAVISH FEARS]  . . . . . . . . .       186 LET BROTHELS/N     42
    I TREMBLED IN MY VIRGIN FEARS  . . . . . . .        189 ARGUMENT V DAU      3
    I DRIED MY TEARS & ARMD MY FEARS  . . . . . .       214 THE ANGEL/SE       11
    HE SITS DOWN WITH HOLY FEARS  . . . . . . .         217 HUMAN ABSTR/SE      9
    AND I WATERD IT IN FEARS  . . . . . . . . .         218 POISON TREE/SE      5
    . . . [?ALONE ?POSSESSD BY DEADLY FEARS] LOVE IS CHANGD   267 FOUR ZOAS 1   *  111
        TO DEADLY HATE
    [A LIFE IS BLOTTED OUT & I ALONE REMAIN POSSESSD    267 FOUR ZOAS 1       112
        WITH FEARS]
    OF HIS WIDE HEAVEN TREMBLING COLD IN PALING FEARS SHE SAT   285 FOUR ZOAS 2  186
    IN JEALOUS FEARS IN FURY & RAGE . . .   . . . . .   294 FOUR ZOAS 3        96
    WEIGHS DOWN HER EYELIDS THEN SHE FALLS THEN STARTING WAKES   297 FOUR ZOAS 3  210
        IN FEARS
    AND SAW THEIR GRIZLY FEARS & HIS EYES SICKEND AT THE SIGHT   313 FOUR ZOAS 6   80
    AND YET IT DRINKS THE SUMMER JOY & FEARS THE WINTER SORROW   314 FOUR ZOAS 6   96
    AND WITH JEALOUSIES & FEARS  . . . . . . . .        416 MY SPECTRE/N       33
    AND WITH COLD & SHUDDERING FEARS  . . . . . . .     416 MY SPECTRE/N       38
    THE SUN IS FREED FROM FEARS  . . . . . . . .        421 MORNING/N          10
    WHO LIVE IN DOUBTS & FEARS PERPETUALLY TORMENTED BY THE   511 MILTON 25       36
        ELECT
    FOR DOUBTS & FEARS UNFORMD & WRETCHED & MELANCHOLY   . . .   515 MILTON 28      9
    SO SPOKE ALBION IN JEALOUS FEARS HIDING HIS EMANATION   .   622 JERUSALEM 4    33
    DRIVEN TO DESPERATION BY LOS'S TERRORS & THREATNING FEARS   629 JERUSALEM 10   28
    IN JEALOUS FEARS & FURY & RAGE & FLAMES ROLL ROUND THEIR   655 JERUSALEM 29   75
        FERVID FEET
    DRINKING THE SHUDDERING FEARS & LOVES OF ALBION'S FAMILIES   669 JERUSALEM 41   27
    IN THE MIDST OF THE ROCKS OF THE ALTARS OF ALBION IN FEARS   684 JERUSALEM 53   17
    WEAVING THE SHUDDRING FEARS & LOVES OF ALBION'S FAMILIES   692 JERUSALEM 59   52
    BECAUSE OF NATURAL FEARS OF NATURAL DESIRES  . . . . .   813A LETTER 22     PROSE
    MY BROTHER TELLS ME THAT HE FEARS YOU ARE OFFENDED WITH   814A LETTER 23     PROSE
        ME I
    FILLD FULL OF HOPES FILLD FULL OF FEARS   . . . . . .   817 HAPPINESS/L     20
    I HAD SOME FEARS TILL MR MEYER OBLIGINGLY UNDERTOOK   . . .  850C LETTER 49   PROSE
```
FEARST
```
    WHAT HAVE I DONE HELA MY DAUGHTER FEARST THOU NOW THE CURSE   108 TIRIEL 6     46
```
FEAST
```
    PLANT WORMS OF DEATH TO FEAST UPON THE TONGUE OF TERRIBLE   108 TIRIEL 6     39
        CURSES
    ENVY SUNG AT THE RICH MAN'S FEAST . . . . . . . .   256 BOOK OF LOS 3      22
    FILLD WITH THE WINE OF ANGUISH WAITED AT THE GOLDEN FEAST   273 FOUR ZOAS 1  348
    WHERE ENION CRAVES SUCCESSIVE DRAWN INTO THE GOLDEN FEAST   274 FOUR ZOAS 1  373
    AND THIS THE SONG SUNG AT THE FEAST OF LOS & ENITHARMON   274 FOUR ZOAS 1   *  385
    THE FEAST REDOUNDS & CROWND WITH ROSES & THE CIRCLING VINE   276 FOUR ZOAS 1  435
    THIS WAS THE LAMENTATION OF ENION ROUND THE GOLDEN FEAST   277 FOUR ZOAS 1  461
    URIZEN ROSE FROM THE BRIGHT FEAST LIKE A STAR THRO THE   280 FOUR ZOAS 2     9
        EVENING SKY
    . . . FROM THE FEAST OF [ENVY] [LOVE] ENVY . . . . .   280 FOUR ZOAS 2   *   40
    . . . THAT THE KING & PRIEST MAY STILL FEAST ON YOUR DECAY   354 FOUR ZOAS 8  498
    FEAST ON HIS DEATH TILL UNIVERSAL DEATH DEVOURS ALL   .   354 FOUR ZOAS 8  528
    THE FEAST WAS SPREAD IN THE BRIGHT SOUTH & THE REGENERATE   372 FOUR ZOAS 9  587
        MAN
    SAT AT THE FEAST REJOICING & THE WINE OF ETERNITY   . . .   372 FOUR ZOAS 9  588
    THE ETERNAL MAN AROSE HE WELCOMD THEM TO THE FEAST   . . .   373 FOUR ZOAS 9  617
    THE FEAST WAS SPREAD IN THE BRIGHT SOUTH & THE ETERNAL MAN   373 FOUR ZOAS 9  618
    SAT AT THE FEAST REJOICING & THE WINE OF ETERNITY   . . .   373 FOUR ZOAS 9  619
    AND MANY ETERNAL MEN SAT AT THE GOLDEN FEAST TO SEE   . . .   373 FOUR ZOAS 9  621
    AND ONE OF THE ETERNALS SPOKE ALL WAS SILENT AT THE FEAST   374 FOUR ZOAS 9  626
    SO SPOKE THE ETERNAL AT THE FEAST THEY EMBRACD THE NEW   374 FOUR ZOAS 9  643
        BORN MAN
    THE SONG AROSE TO THE GOLDEN FEAST THE ETERNAL MAN REJOICD   375 FOUR ZOAS 9  692
    AS HE AROSE FROM THE BRIGHT FEAST DRUNK WITH THE WINE OF   376 FOUR ZOAS 9  710
        AGES
    HIS SONS ARISING FROM THE FEAST WITH GOLDEN BASKETS FOLLOW   376 FOUR ZOAS 9  714
    THEN THARMAS & URTHONA ROSE FROM THE GOLDEN FEAST   . . .   377 FOUR ZOAS 9  774
    ROSE FROM THE FEAST IN JOY ASCENDING TO THEIR GOLDEN LOOMS   378 FOUR ZOAS 9  779
    HIS SOFTNESS & CANDOUR THE HIDDEN TRAP & THE POISONED FEAST   452A ANNO REYNOLDS   MARG
```
FEASTING
```
    YE WORMS OF DEATH FEASTING UPON YOUR AGED PARENTS FLESH   99 TIRIEL 1       23
```
FEASTS
```
    AND OFTEN SUNG TO THE LOUD HARP AT THE IMMORTAL FEASTS   . .   503 MILTON 20    58
```
FEATHER
```
    HIS LITTLE THROAT LABOURS WITH INSPIRATION EVERY FEATHER   520 MILTON 31     34
    I'LL WRITE IN RHYME AS SOFT AS [FEATHER PILLOWS]   555 BLAKES APL/N 1     7
        BARTOLLOZE
    DRAW A FEATHER OVER IT & YOU WILL GET AN EVEN SURFACE   . .   790C LETTER 2    PROSE
```
FEATHERD
```
    AND FEATHERD CLOUDS STREW FLOWERS ROUND HER HEAD . . . .     2 TO AUTUMN/PS   12
    SWEET SYMPHONY TO FEATHERD ANGELS SITTING   . . . . . .     28 EDW THIRD/PS 3   288
    RIBBD DELICATE & CLOTHD WITH FEATHERD GOLD & AZURE & PURPLE   731 JERUSALEM 86    6
    THENCE FEATHERD WITH SOFT CRIMSON OF THE RUBY BRIGHT AS   731 JERUSALEM 86    8
        FIRE
    BETWEEN THY WINGS OF GOLD & SILVER FEATHERD IMMORTAL   . .   731 JERUSALEM 86   20
```
FEATHERS
```
    IN THE THIRD CHAMBER WAS AN EAGLE WITH WINGS AND FEATHERS   154D MARRIAGE HH 15   PROSE
    AND THE STRONG EAGLE NOW WITH NUMMING COLD BLIGHTED OF   354 FOUR ZOAS 8   521
        FEATHERS
    SO FULL OF THE BUSINESS OF SETTLING THE STICKS & FEATHERS   804A LETTER 16   PROSE
        OF
```

	PAGE	TITLE	LINE

FEATHERS   (CONTINUED)
    START FOR HAMPSTEAD LIKE A YOUNG LARK WITHOUT FEATHERS . . 875A LETTER 80   PROSE
FEATHERY
    REFLECTS ETERNITY BENEATH THY AZURE WINGS OF FEATHERY DOWN   730 JERUSALEM 86   5
FEATURE
    HE MAKES THE VICIOUS PROPENSITY NOT ONLY A LEADING FEATURE   88C ANNO LAVATER   MARG
FEATURELESS
    COLD FEATURELESS FLESH OR CLAY . . . .   226 URIZEN 7   5
FEATURES
    . . . OF MAN STRUGGLING TO TAKE THE FEATURES OF MAN   296 FOUR ZOAS 3   157
        STRUGGLING
    NOW FIXD INTO ONE STEDFAST BULK HIS FEATURES STONIFY   . .   305 FOUR ZOAS 5   2
    . . . & HIS [SCALY ARMOUR] ROCKY FEATURES SOFTNING   . . .   381 FOUR ZOAS AD 5   6
    ART IS LINEAMENTS OR FORMS AND FEATURES THAT ARE CAPABLE OF 579D DESC CAT 5   PROSE
    HIS UGLY MAN ONE APPROACHING TO THE BEAST IN FEATURES   .   580A DESC CAT 5   PROSE
    OF WISDOM A SUBLIME ENERGIZER HIS FEATURES AND LIMBS   .   580B DESC CAT 2   PROSE
    IS ONE OF THE MOST AMIABLE FEATURES OF THE CHRISTIAN CHURCH 590B CHAUCER 2   PROSE
    SPASMS SMITE THEIR FEATURES SINEWS & LIMBS . . . .   701 JERUSALEM 65   76
    OVER HER BEAUTIFUL FEMALE FEATURES SOFT FLOURISHING IN   709 JERUSALEM 70   23
        BEAUTY
FEBRUARY
    JANUARY...[FEBRUARY]...WILLIAM BLAKE . . . .   444C LAST JUDGMNT/L PROSE
FED   SEE MILK FED,WELL FED
    HE CALLD HIM SURGERY & FED . . . .   50 WHEN CORRUP/IM   9
    FOR THOU SHALT BE CLOTHED IN LIGHT AND FED WITH MORNING   127 BOOK OF THEL 1   23
        MANNA
    AND FED ON THE BODY SHE REFUSD TO BE WHORE TO THE MINISTER   135 FRENCH REVOLTN   37
        . . .
    . . . FED WITH HOPES YEAR BY YEAR HE PINED   . . . . .   136 FRENCH REVOLTN   48
    FED WITH COLD & USUROUS HAND . . . .   181 HOLY THURS/N   4
    HOW DIFFERENT FAR THE FAT FED HIRELING WITH HOLLOW DRUM   193 V DAU ALBION 5   14
    FED WITH COLD AND USUROUS HAND . . . .   211 HOLY THURS/SE   4
    FED WITH MILK OF ENITHARMON . . . .   233 URIZEN 20   *   7
    ENVY FED WITH FAT OF LAMBS . . . .   256 BOOK OF LOS 3   15
    CHILDREN ARE NOURISHD FOR THE SLAUGHTER ONCE THE CHILD   275 FOUR ZOAS 1   400
        WAS FED
    WITH MILK BUT WHEREFORE NOW ARE CHILDREN FED WITH BLOOD   275 FOUR ZOAS 1   401
    AND VALA FED IN CRUEL DELIGHT THE FURNACES WITH FIRE   .   282 FOUR ZOAS 2   73
    I NURTURD HER I FED HER WITH MY RAINS & DEWS SHE GREW . .   282 FOUR ZOAS 2   84
    A SCALED SERPENT YET I FED HER THO SHE HATED ME . . .   282 FOUR ZOAS 2   85
    DAY AFTER DAY SHE FED UPON THE MOUNTAINS IN LUVAH'S SIGHT   282 FOUR ZOAS 2   86
    HAD WEARIED ME THERE I LAID MY PLOW & THERE MY HORSES FED   295 FOUR ZOAS 3   124
    COVERD WITH GLOOM THE FIERY BOY GREW FED BY THE MILK   .   307 FOUR ZOAS 5   72
    [SHE SECRET JOYD TO SEE SHE FED HERSELF ON HIS DESPAIR]   324 FOUR ZOAS 7   177
    ITS INSATIABLE MAW MUST BE FED BY WHAT ALL CAN DO   . . .   593D PUB ADDRESS/N PROSE
    AND VALA FED IN CRUEL DELIGHT THE FURNACES WITH FIRE   .   625 JERUSALEM 7   31
    THE FLESH OF MULTITUDES FED & NOURISD ME IN MY CHILDHOOD   644 JERUSALEM 22   6
    WHERE I LAID MY PLOW IN THE HOT NOON WHERE MY HOT TEAM FED   660 JERUSALEM 34   12
    BY THE FRUIT OF ALBION'S TREE I HAVE FED HIM WITH SWEET   726 JERUSALEM 82   40
        MILK
    OF ALBION'S CLOUDS HE FED IT WITH HIS TEARS & BITTER GROANS 732 JERUSALEM 86   53
FEEBLE
    MY HAND IS FEEBLE HOW SHOULD I STRETCH IT OUT . . . . .   36A COUCH DEATH/PS PROSE
    HOW DIDST THOU REND THE FEEBLE TIES THOU FEAREST NOUGHT   39A SAMSON/PS   PROSE
    TILL HOPE GREW FEEBLE AND WAS READY TO GIVE PLACE   40A SAMSON/PS   PROSE
        TO DOUBTING
    IJIM SHALL REND THY FEEBLE JOINTS THOU TEMPTER OF DARK IJIM 103 TIRIEL 4   6
    . . . UTTERING A FAINT FEEBLE CRY . . . .   146 FRENCH REVOLTN   277
    ON THE CANADIAN WILDS I FOLD FEEBLE MY SPIRIT FOLDS . . .   196 AMERICA PREL 1   17
    MY FEEBLE LIMBS INFOLD MY DESTIND MISERY . . . .   344 FOUR ZOAS 8   147
    THE KINGS & PRINCES OF THE EARTH CRY WITH A FEEBLE CRY .   365 FOUR ZOAS 9   328
    AT LENGTH WITH A FEEBLE CRY HE SAID . . . .   419 I SAW A MONK/N   27
    AT LENGTH WITH A FEEBLE CRY HE SAID . . . .   430 GREY MONK   12
    BETTER EVERY MORNING BUT SLOWLY AS I AM STILL FEEBLE & .   876A LETTER 83   PROSE
    FEEBLE & TOTTERING BUT NOT IN SPIRIT . . . .   878A LETTER 88   PROSE
FEED
    THE NOBLES OF THE LAND DID FEED . . . .   11 GWIN KING/PS   5
    GAVE THEE LIFE & BID THEE FEED . . . .   115 THE LAMB/SI   3
    BUT I FEED NOT THE LITTLE FLOWERS I HEAR THE WARBLING BIRDS 129 BOOK OF THEL 3   19
    BUT I FEED NOT THE WARBLING BIRDS THEY FLY AND SEEK THEIR   129 BOOK OF THEL 3   20
        FOOD
    FEED ON THE MYSTERY . . . .   174 HUMAN IMAGE/N   17
    FEED ON THE MYSTERY . . . .   217 HUMAN ABSTR/SE   16
    IF YOU WILL FEED ME ON LOVE THOUGHTS & GIVE ME NOW AND THEN 237 EUROPE INTRO   15
    ON SCORN TO FEED OUR DISCONTENT FOR IF WE GRATEFUL PROVE   271 FOUR ZOAS 1   256
    TO FEED THEM WITH INTOXICATION FROM THE WINE PRESSES OF   292 FOUR ZOAS 3   35
        LUVAH
    OF CIRCLING FIRE UNCEASING PLAYS TO FEED THEM WITH LIFE   308 FOUR ZOAS 5   115
        & BRING
    THEY FEED UPON OUR LIFE WE ARE THEIR VICTIMS STERN DESIRE   331 FOUR ZOAS 7   439
    TO FEED THEIR FRUIT TO GRATIFY THEIR HIDDEN SONS   335 FOUR ZOAS 7B   104
        & DAUGHTERS
    GREATER MIRACLE TO FEED FIVE THOUSAND MEN WITH FIVE LOAVES 391C ANNO WATSON   MARG
    FEED THEM & THOU WILT GROW FAT . . . .   432 AUGURIES   44
    LIKE FEMALES OF SWEET BEAUTY TO GUARD ROUND HIM & TO FEED   496 MILTON 15   14
    THE SONS OF LOS CLOTHE THEM & FEED & PROVIDE HOUSES   512 MILTON 26   30
        & FIELDS
    TO FEED THE SLEEPERS ON THEIR COUCHES WITH MATERNAL CARE   516 MILTON 28   49
    FEED THEM WITH THE JUICE OF OUR MARROW BONES . . . . .   543 IF TRUE/N   4
    [ON] BY SWEET RESERVE & MODESTY [FEED FAT] GET FAT   . . .   545 ON S(TOTHRD)/N *   4
    OR ARE YOU BORN TO FEED THE HUNGRY RAVENINGS OF DESTRUCTION 647 JERUSALEM 24   14
    BETWEEN DWELLS A DAUGHTER OF BEULAH TO FEED THE HUMAN   688 JERUSALEM 56   10
        VEGETABLE

		PAGE	TITLE	LINE

FEED   (CONTINUED)
```
      TO FREEZE OVER HIS NOSTRILS WHILE THEY FEED HIS TONGUE        702 JERUSALEM 66       32
        FROM CUPS
      SONS WITHOUT TO FEED WITH THEIR SOULS THE SPECTRES            704 JERUSALEM 67       18
        OF ALBION
      THEY DRINK UP DAN & GAD TO FEED WITH MILK SKOFELD & KOTOPE    704 JERUSALEM 67       22
      THE SONS OF LOS CLOTHE THEM & FEED & PROVIDE HOUSES           714 JERUSALEM 73       49
        & GARDENS
      TO FEED THE AFFLICTED IN THE FURNACES SHE MINDED NOT    . .   726 JERUSALEM 82       66
      FEED WITH THE SACRIFICE & BE                                  749 EV GOSPEL(B)/N     23
FEEDEST
      FOR IF THOU FEEDEST NOT HIS RAGE IT WILL SUBSIDE IN PEACE     360 FOUR ZOAS 9       143
FEEDING     SEE FULL-FEEDING
      FOR URIZEN UNCLASPD HIS BOOK FEEDING HIS SOUL WITH PITY       242 EUROPE 12           4
      NINE TIMES THEY LIVD AMONG THE FORESTS FEEDING ON SWEET       270 FOUR ZOAS 1       233
        FRUITS
      AND FOR HIS PITY SECRET FEEDING ON THOUGHTS OF CRUELTY  . .   302 FOUR ZOAS 4       193
      WHILE THOU REPOSEST THROWING RAGE ON RAGE FEEDING THYSELF     321 FOUR ZOAS 7        61
      FEEDING IT WITH HIS GROANS & TEARS DAY & NIGHT WITHOUT        639 JERUSALEM 17       56
        CEASING
FEEDS
      THERE SHE SITS AND FEEDS HER YOUNG    .  .  .  .  .  .  .  .     7 LOVE HARMNY/PS     13
      THE WEEPING MOTHER FEEDS HIM FOR THE SLAUGHTER     .  .  .   348 KING JOHN/PS     PROSE
      SWEETEST THE FRUIT THAT THE WORM FEEDS ON & THE SOUL PREYD    191 V DAU ALBION 3     17
        ON BY WOE
      HE FEEDS THE BEGGAR & THE POOR .  .  .  .  .  .  .  .  .  .   425 MENTAL TRAVLER     38
      WHO FEEDS ON CONTEMPT OF HIS NEIGHBOUR THERE ALL THE IDLE     513 MILTON 27          27
        WEEDS
      HE CANNOT FEEL DISTRESS HE FEEDS ON SACRIFICE & OFFERING      630 JERUSALEM 10       48
      FEEDS THE DREAD FORGE TREMBLING & SHUDDERING ALONG THE        636 JERUSALEM 16       15
        VALLEYS
      AND FEEDS HER WITH THE FOOD OF EDEN HENCE ALL HER BEAUTY      707 JERUSALEM 69       18
        BEAMS
      FEEDS THE VILLAGE OF FELPHAM BY DAY & BY NIGHT     .  .  .  . 800 MRS FLAXMAN/L      14
      ANOTHER SUN FEEDS OUR LIFE'S STREAMS   .  .  .  .  .  .  .  . 818 HAPPINESS/L        65
FEEL
      I FEEL IT COMING UPON ME SO I STRIVE AGAINST IT   .  .  .  .   22 EDW THIRD/PS 3     62
      CANNOT RESIST THE IMPULSE I FEEL TO RECTIFY WHAT I THINK      88A ANNO LAVATER     MARG
        FALSE
      AND NOW YOU FEEL IT DIG A GRAVE & LET US BURY OUR MOTHER      100 TIRIEL 1           42
      AYE NOW YOU FEEL THE CURSE YOU CRY BUT MAY ALL EARS BE DEAF   106 TIRIEL 5           20
      THAT THOU SHALT FEEL WORMS IN THY MARROW CREEPING THRO        107 TIRIEL 6           21
        THY BONES
      BUT THAT I FEEL THEY WILL CURSE THEE & HANG UPON THY BONES    108 TIRIEL 6           37
      AND NOT FEEL MY SORROW'S SHARE   .  .  .  .  .  .  .  .  .  . 122 ON ANOTHERS/SI      6
      HE DOTH FEEL THE SORROW TOO   .  .  .  .  .  .  .  .  .  .  . 122 ON ANOTHERS/SI     28
      AND FEEL THEY KNOW NOT WHAT BUT CARE   .  .  .  .  .  .  .  . 126 VOICE BARD/SI      10
      AS THY SOFTEST LIMBS I [TOUCH] [STROKE] FEEL   .  .  .  .  . 165 CRADLE SONG/N      10
      FROM USURY FEEL THE SAME PASSION OR ARE THEY MOVED ALIKE      193 V DAU ALBION 5     11
      ON MY AMERICAN PLAINS I FEEL THE STRUGGLING AFFLICTIONS       196 AMERICA PREL 2     10
      O WHAT LIMB RENDING PAINS I FEEL THY FIRE & MY FROST    .  .  196 AMERICA PREL 2     15
      THEY FEEL THE NERVES OF YOUTH RENEW AND DESIRES OF ANCIENT    202 AMERICA 15         25
        TIMES
      I WISH & FEEL & WEEP & GROAN AH TERRIBLE TERRIBLE    .  .  .  265 FOUR ZOAS 1        63
      .  .  . THO DARK I FEEL MY WORLD WITHIN    .  .  .  .  .  .  . 268 FOUR ZOAS 1       172
      AND HE SAID WHEREFORE DO I FEEL SUCH LOVE & PITY   .  .  .  . 297 FOUR ZOAS 4         7
      FELT ALL THE SORROW PARENTS FEEL THEY WEPT TOWARD             309 FOUR ZOAS 5       144
        ONE ANOTHER
      TO THE HARD ROCK OR THOU SHOULDST FEEL MY ENMITY & HATE       322 FOUR ZOAS 7        88
      WITH IRRESISTIBLE CONVICTION I FEEL I AM NOT ONE OF THOSE     329 FOUR ZOAS 7       362
      BY REASON'S POWER EVEN I ALREADY FEEL A WORLD WITHIN    .  .  329 FOUR ZOAS 7       364
      LOS TREMBLING ANSWERD NOW I FEEL THE WEIGHT OF STERN          330 FOUR ZOAS 7       411
        REPENTANCE
      I FEEL TO FABRICATE EMBODIED SEMBLANCES IN WHICH THE DEAD     331 FOUR ZOAS 7       440
      BEATING THE DESARTS & THE ROCKS THE DESARTS FEEL HIS POWER    352 FOUR ZOAS 8       443
      AMONG THE STARS THE EARTH & ALL THE ABYSSES FEEL ?HIS FURY    352 FOUR ZOAS 8     * 448
      THE DREAD I FEEL UNKNOWN BEFORE MY VOICE REFUSES TO ROAR      358 FOUR ZOAS 9        57
      TO FEEL THY HEAT & SEE THY LIGHT & WANDER HERE ALONE    .  .  368 FOUR ZOAS 9       416
      I DRINK NEW LIFE & FEEL THE BREATH OF SLEEPING ENION    .  .  371 FOUR ZOAS 9       542
      METHINKS I SEE HIS FLOCKS & HERDS & FEEL MY LIMBS RENEWD      375 FOUR ZOAS 9       690
      TO REVENGE THE WRONGS THY CHILDREN FEEL    .  .  .  .  .  .  . 419 I SAW A MONK/N    39
      TO MAKE IT FEEL BOTH COLD & HEAT   .  .  .  .  .  .  .  .  .  . 425 MENTAL TRAVLER   16
      TO AVENGE THE WRONGS THY CHILDREN FEEL     .  .  .  .  .  .  . 430 GREY MONK         24
      SHALL FEEL THE SPIDER'S ENMITY .  .  .  .  .  .  .  .  .  .  . 431 AUGURIES          34
      CAN SUCH CLOSED NOSTRILS FEEL A JOY OR TELL OF AUTUMN         485 MILTON 5           32
        FRUITS
      THE UNIVERSAL DICTATE AND YOU ALSO FEEL THIS DICTATE          504 MILTON 21          53
      AND NOW YOU KNOW THIS WORLD OF SORROW AND FEEL PITY OBEY      504 MILTON 21          54
      [BECAUSE WE KNOW] AMIABLE STATE HE CANNOT FEEL AT ALL    .    549 CROMEK SPEAK/N      4
      BY ENGLISH TRADERS MUST [LOA ] FEEL A LOATHING    .  .  .    596B PUB ADDRESS/N  *PROSE
      ONLY BE EXPRESSED BY THOSE WHO FEEL THEM    .  .  .  .  .  .  599C PUB ADDRESS/N   PROSE
      HE CANNOT FEEL DISTRESS HE FEEDS ON SACRIFICE & OFFERING      630 JERUSALEM 10       48
      HE MIGHT FEEL THE PAIN AS IF A MAN GNAWD HIS OWN TENDER       630 JERUSALEM 11        7
        NERVES
      BUT I AM LIVING YET I FEEL MY EMANATION ALSO DIVIDING   .  .  631 JERUSALEM 12        7
      I FEEL THE IRON THREADS OF LOVE & JEALOUSY & DESPAIR    .  .  657 JERUSALEM 31       49
      I FEEL MY SPECTRE RISING UPON ME ALBION AROUZE THYSELF  .  .  664 JERUSALEM 37        2
      FEEL THEIR BRAIN CUT ROUND BENEATH THE TEMPLES SHRIEKING      689 JERUSALEM 58        7
      THEY FLEE OVER THE ROCKS BONIFYING HORSES OXEN FEEL THE       689 JERUSALEM 58        9
        KNIFE
      OR SUCH A BODY AS MIGHT NOT FEEL   .  .  .  .  .  .  .  .  .  . 756 EV GOSPEL(I)/N   13
      WORLD ESPECIALLY IF I SHOULD HAVE TO ANSWER FOR IT I FEEL    793A LETTER 5        PROSE
        VERY
```

FEEL   (CONTINUED)

```
    I FEEL THAT A MAN MAY BE HAPPY IN THIS WORLD AND  .  .  .  .  793C LETTER 5         PROSE
    IMAGINATION & I FEEL FLATTERD WHEN I AM TOLD SO  .  .  .  .  793D LETTER 5         PROSE
    AFTER ANOTHER ARTIST BUT ABOVE ALL I FEEL MYSELF HAPPY &      795C LETTER 6         PROSE
    OF WHAT ALL FEEL IN THIS VALLEY OF MISERY & HAPPINESS MIXED   797A LETTER 9         PROSE
    NECESSARY TO MY REPOSE AT THIS TIME I FEEL VERY STRONGLY      798D LETTER 10        PROSE
       THAT
    MUST MY DEAR BUTTS FEEL COLD NEGLECT  .  .  .  .  .  .  .  .   817 HAPPINESS/L        45
    TO BE BOASTED OF & THEREFORE I CANNOT FEEL DEPRESSD  .  .  .  821C LETTER 25        PROSE
    AS TO MR H(HAYLEY) I FEEL MYSELF AT LIBERTY  .  .  .  .  .  . 825B LETTER 27        PROSE
    BUT I THINK OF YOU & FEEL ANXIOUS FOR THE SIGHT OF THAT       826C LETTER 28        PROSE
       FRIEND
    FELPHAM & ITS KIND INHABITANTS I FEEL ANXIOUS & THEREFORE     833D LETTER 33        PROSE
    I AM THANKFUL THAT I FEEL IT                                  833D LETTER 33        PROSE
    GRATITUDE I FEEL IT & I KNOW IT I THANK GOD & MAN FOR IT &    834A LETTER 33        PROSE
    FEEL MUCH EASIER TO HEAR THAT YOU HAVE PARTED WITH YOUR       843A LETTER 42        PROSE
       HORSE
    INFINITELY BETTER THE NEXT PROOF I FEEL VERY MUCH GRATIFIED   855C LETTER 53        PROSE
    COULD BE OF SERVICE TO HIM IN MANY WAYS BUT I FEEL FOR THE    856C LETTER 54        PROSE
    FOR I DO ASSURE YOU I FEEL IT A DUTY TO MY PROFESSION THAT    856C LETTER 54        PROSE
       I
    DO NOR SAY BUT AS YOU DIRECT I FEEL EXTREMELY HAPPY  .  .  .  857B LETTER 54        PROSE
    REMEMBRANCE I FEEL IT IS NECESSARY TO BE VERY CIRCUMSPECT     857C LETTER 54        PROSE
    COURSE OF OUR CONVERSATION HIS WORDS WERE I FEEL SOMEWHAT     860A LETTER 56        PROSE
    YOU WILL I KNOW FEEL AS YOU ALWAYS DO ON SUCH OCCASIONS       861D LETTER 59        PROSE
    IT IS A PRINT THAT I FEEL PROUD OF ON A NEW INSPECTION  .  .  863C LETTER 60        PROSE
    & SOON SPREAD A DEATHLY FEEL ALL OVER THE LIMBS WHICH  .  .   872B LETTER 75        PROSE
    ACCOMPANYING DEATHLY FEEL I GOT AGAIN INTO A PERSPIRATION     872B LETTER 75        PROSE
    FEEL MYSELF WEAKER THAN I WAS AWARE BEING NOT ABLE AS YET     872D LETTER 76        PROSE
    TO SIT UP LONGER THAN SIX HOURS AT A TIME & ALSO FEEL THE     872D LETTER 76        PROSE
       COLD
    I BEGIN TO AGAIN FEEL RETURNING STRENGTH ON THESE ACCOUNTS    874D LETTER 80        PROSE
    THANK GOD I FEEL NO MORE OF IT  .  .  .  .  .  .  .  .  .  .   875C LETTER 81        PROSE
    THE MORE I THINK THE MORE I FEEL TERROR AT WHAT I WISHD       876B LETTER 83        PROSE
FEELEST
    TREMBLE THE LION SHUDDERING ASKS THE LEOPARD FEELEST THOU     358 FOUR ZOAS 9          56
FEELING
    WALKING FEELING THE COLD WALLS WITH HER HANDS  .  .  .  .  .    4 FAIR ELENOR/PS       12
    BE FAIRLY SEPERATED & THEN SUPERSTITION WILL BE HONEST       85C ANNO LAVATER        MARG
       FEELING
    AND SO FEELING HE BEGD HIM TO TURN AGAIN  .  .  .  .  .  .  . 187 WHEN KLOPSTK/N *     27
    ?FEELING THE HAND OF LOS IN GOLGONOOZA & THE FORCE  .  .  .   344 FOUR ZOAS 8         112
    FEELING THE CRUSHING WHEELS THEY RISE THEY WRITE THE BITTER   379 FOUR ZOAS 9         819
       WORDS
    FEELING THE ELECTRIC FLAME OF MILTON'S AWFUL PRECIPITATE      502 MILTON 20           26
       DESCENT
    KNOWING & FEELING THAT WE ALL HAVE NEED OF BUTTER  .  .  .    556 IF MEN ACT/N          4
    AND FEELING THE DAMPS OF DEATH THEY WITH ONE ACCORD           674 JERUSALEM 44         28
       DELEGATED LOS
    & FEELING HEARTILY YOUR GRIEF WITH A BROTHER'S SYMPATHY       797B LETTER 9          PROSE
    WERE TRULY AMIABLE AND FEELING LIKE HIMSELF  .  .  .  .  .  . 844A LETTER 43         PROSE
    FUSELI'S COUNT UGOLINO IS THE FATHER OF SONS OF FEELING AND   864A LETTER 61         PROSE
FEELINGS
    I HATE REASONING I DO EVERYTHING BY MY FEELINGS AH SAID        50A ISLAND MOON 6      PROSE
       SIPSOP I ONLY
    SHAKESPEARE IS TOO WILD & MILTON HAS NO FEELINGS THEY MIGHT    51D ISLAND MOON 7      PROSE
    I WOULD NOT GIVE A FARTHING FOR IT DO ALL BY YOUR FEELINGS     51D ISLAND MOON 7      PROSE
    FEELINGS WILL BE ATTRACTIONS OR REPULSES SEE APHORISMS...      87A ANNO LAVATER       MARG
    NOT PREJUDICD BY FEELINGS GREAT OR SMALL  .  .  .  .  .  .    549 CROMEK SPEAK/N        3
FEELS
    HE WHO LOVES FEELS LOVE DESCEND INTO HIM & IF HE HAS WISDOM    90B ANNO SWED LOVE      MARG
    THE ETERNAL MAN SLEEPS IN THE EARTH NOR FEELS THE VIGROUS     354 FOUR ZOAS 8         507
       SUN
    OR OF ONE IN THE DARK WHO FEELS HIS WAY BUT DOES NOT SEE IT   439C REMARKS MALKIN    PROSE
    BOWLAHOOLA THRO ALL ITS PORCHES FEELS THO TOO FAST FOUNDED    509 MILTON 24           54
    LONDON FEELS HIS BRAIN CUT ROUND EDINBURGH'S HEART            703 JERUSALEM 66         64
       IS CIRCUMSCRIBED
FEET     SEE SEVEN FEET
    AND LET THY HOLY FEET VISIT OUR CLIME  .  .  .  .  .  .  .      1 TO SPRING/PS          8
    THY BUSKIND FEET APPEAR UPON OUR HILLS  .  .  .  .  .  .  .     3 TO MORNING/PS         8
    AMAZD SHE FINDS HERSELF UPON HER FEET  .  .  .  .  .  .  .      4 FAIR ELENOR/PS       10
    DISTRACTS HER A RUSHING SOUND AND THE FEET  .  .  .  .  .  .    4 FAIR ELENOR/PS       18
    LIKE GENTLE STREAMS BENEATH OUR FEET  .  .  .  .  .  .  .  .    7 LOVE HARMNY/PS        7
    MY FEET ARE WINGD WHILE OER THE DEWY LAWN  .  .  .  .  .  .     9 FRESH FROM/PS         5
    OH BLESS THOSE HOLY FEET LIKE ANGELS' FEET  .  .  .  .  .  .    9 FRESH FROM/PS         7
    EACH VILLAGE SEEMS THE HAUNT OF HOLY FEET  .  .  .  .  .  .     9 FRESH FROM/PS        16
    SCATTER THEIR FANCIES AT THY POET'S FEET  .  .  .  .  .  .     14 IMIT SPEN/PS          7
    ENTERING WITH HOLY FEET TO WHERE ON HIGH  .  .  .  .  .  .     15 IMIT SPEN/PS         22
    HER SNOWY FEET AND OWND HIS AWFUL QUEEN  .  .  .  .  .  .  .    21 EDW THIRD/PS 2       83
    IN THE DAIRY MY FEET ARE WINGD BUT NOT  .  .  .  .  .  .  .    24 EDW THIRD/PS 3      149
    BIND ARDENT HOPE UPON YOUR FEET LIKE SHOES  .  .  .  .  .  .   30 EDW THIRD/PS 5       33
    ROUND HIS MAJESTIC FEET DEEP THUNDERS ROLL  .  .  .  .  .  .   34A KING JOHN/PS       PROSE
    THOU VISITEST OUR DARKLING WORLD WITH BLESSED FEET  .  .  .   37D SAMSON/PS          PROSE
    THUS IN FALSE TEARS SHE BATHD HIS FEET  .  .  .  .  .  .  .    38C SAMSON/PS          PROSE
    SHE SEEMED A SILVER STREAM HER FEET EMBRACING  .  .  .  .  .   38C SAMSON/PS          PROSE
    THAT OUR FEET MAKE REMEMBER [?HILI] HELA I HAVE SAVD THEE     107 TIRIEL 6         *    6
       FROM DEATH
    HE CEAST OUTSTRETCHD AT HAR & HEVA'S FEET IN AWFUL DEATH      110 TIRIEL 8            42
    WITH FEET OF WEARY WOE  .  .  .  .  .  .  .  .  .  .  .  .  .  114 LIT GRL FND/SI      19
    THE FEET OF ANGELS BRIGHT  .  .  .  .  .  .  .  .  .  .  .  .  119 NIGHT/SI            12
    AND TO RETURN FEAR NOTHING ENTER WITH THY VIRGIN FEET  .  .   130 BOOK OF THEL 5      17
    HIS FEET AND HANDS CUT OFF AND HIS EYES BLINDED  .  .  .  .   136 FRENCH REVOLTN      44
```

FEET   (CONTINUED)

	PAGE	TITLE	LINE
. . . TEARS FELL DOWN THE SHADY CHEEKS AT HIS FEET MANY CLOTHD	140	FRENCH REVOLTN	132
. . . THAT THREATEN TO BATHE THEIR FEET	141	FRENCH REVOLTN	155
. . . LANGUISH BECAUSE THE FEET	142	FRENCH REVOLTN	184
. . . THEN THE ABBE DE (SIEYES) RAISD HIS FEET	143	FRENCH REVOLTN *	201
THE GENITALS BEAUTY THE HANDS & FEET PROPORTION . . .	152C	MARRIAGE HH 10	PROSE
AND WHEN HE BID THEM SHAKE OFF THE DUST OF THEIR FEET .	158C	MARRIAGE HH 22	PROSE
TRODDEN WITH THE CATTLE'S FEET	162	CLOD PEBBLE/N	6
WHAT DREAD HAND & WHAT DREAD FEET	172	THE TYGER/N 1	12
WHAT DREAD HAND & WHAT DREAD FEET	173	THE TYGER/N 2	12
AS THE CLEAR SPRING MUDDED WITH FEET OF BEASTS GROWS PURE & SMILES	190	V DAU ALBION 2	19
FEET BLEEDING ON THE SULTRY SANDS AND THE FURROWS OF THE WHIP	197	AMERICA 3	11
AMIDST THE LUSTFUL FIRES HE WALKS HIS FEET BECOME LIKE BRASS	199	AMERICA 8	16
TO QUENCH THEIR ANGUISH AT THE FEET OF WASHINGTON DOWN FALLN	201	AMERICA 13	4
FEET BLEEDING ON THE SULTRY SANDS & THE FURROWS OF THE WHIP	204	AMERICA CANC A	11
IN THAT DREAD NIGHT WHEN URIZEN CALLD THE STARS ROUND HIS FEET	204	AMERICA CANC B	5
TRODDEN WITH THE CATTLE'S FEET	211	CLOD PEBBLE/SE	6
WHAT DREAD HAND & WHAT DREAD FEET	214	THE TYGER/SE	12
WHAT DREAD HAND FORMD THY DREAD FEET	214	THE TYGER/SE	12
AND A FATHOMLESS VOID FOR HIS FEET	226	URIZEN 6	5
AND HIS FEET STAMPD THE NETHER ABYSS	229	URIZEN 13	16
DOWNWARD TIS SUNK BENEATH TH ATTRACTIVE NORTH THAT ROUND THE FEET	242	EUROPE 10	30
THEY SAW HIS BONEY FEET ON THE ROCK THE FLESH CONSUMD IN FLAMES	242	EUROPE 12	10
FOR NOW THY WATERS WARBLE ROUND THE FEET OF ENITHARMON . .	243	EUROPE 14	5
WHEREON HIS BRIGHT FEET HAVE TROD	254	AHANIA 4	71
IN INFANT JOY AT THY FEET	255	AHANIA 5	27
HIS FEET STAMP THE ETERNAL FIERCE-RAGING	256	BOOK OF LOS 3	39
AND HIS FEET WHICH THE NETHER ABYSS	257	BOOK OF LOS 3	47
HIS SPECTRE ISSUING FROM HIS FEET IN FLAMES OF FIRE . .	266	FOUR ZOAS 1	78
BENEATH HIS FEET SHOT THRO HIM AS HE STOOD IN THE HUMAN BRAIN	280	FOUR ZOAS 2	12
HIS FEET UPON THE VERGE OF NON EXISTENCE HIS VOICE WENT FORTH	280	FOUR ZOAS 2	21
I SEE NOT LUVAH AS OF OLD I ONLY SEE HIS FEET . . .	286	FOUR ZOAS 2	229
AND BRIGHT AHANIA BOWD HERSELF BEFORE HIS SPLENDID FEET	291	FOUR ZOAS 3	2
. . . & FLAMES ROLLD ROUND THEIR FERVID FEET	294	FOUR ZOAS 3	96
UPON THE TIDE TILL UNDERNEATH THE FEET OF LOS A WORLD . .	300	FOUR ZOAS 4	125
DARK DREADFUL ROSE & ENITHARMON LAY AT LOS'S FEET . .	300	FOUR ZOAS 4	126
AND HIS FEET STAMPD THE NETHER ABYSS IN TREMBLING HOWLING & DISMAY	303	FOUR ZOAS 4	245
HIS FEET SHRINK WITHRING FROM THE DEEP SHRINKING & WITHERING	305	FOUR ZOAS 5 *	7
I CALLD THE STARS AROUND MY FEET IN THE NIGHT OF COUNCILS DARK	311	FOUR ZOAS 5	223
THY PURE FEET STEPD ON THE STEPS DIVINE TOO PURE FOR OTHER FEET	311	FOUR ZOAS 5	230
THEY SHRUNK INTO THEIR CHANNELS DRY THE ROCKY STRAND BENEATH HIS FEET	312	FOUR ZOAS 6	22
AN EARTH OF WINTRY WOE BENEATH THEIR FEET & ROUND THEIR LOINS	314	FOUR ZOAS 6	92
SIEZING UPON HIS FEET & RENDING THE SINEWS THAT IN CAVES	315	FOUR ZOAS 6	139
WHERE SELF SUSTAINING I MAY VIEW ALL THING BENEATH MY FEET	317	FOUR ZOAS 6	198
TILL A WHITE WOOF COVERD HIS COLD LIMBS FROM HEAD TO [FOOT] FEET	318	FOUR ZOAS 6 *	239
A SPECTRE VAST APPEARD WHOSE FEET & LEGS WITH IRON SCALED	319	FOUR ZOAS 6	298
. . . MY FEET & HANDS ARE NAILD TO THE BURNING ROCK . . .	322	FOUR ZOAS 7	71
FREEZING THY FEET TO THE HARD ROCK STILL THY PEN OBDURATE	322	FOUR ZOAS 7	85
I RAGE FURIOUS IN THE DEEP FOR LO MY FEET & HANDS ARE NAILD	322	FOUR ZOAS 7	87
HIS BROODINGS RUSH DOWN TO HIS FEET PRODUCING EGGS THAT HATCHING	324	FOUR ZOAS 7	167
SORROW SHOT THRO HIM FROM HIS FEET IT SHOT UP TO HIS HEAD	324	FOUR ZOAS 7	179
AND ALL THE SONS OF ?EVERLASTING SHALL BOW DOWN AT MY FEET	333	FOUR ZOAS 7B	10
LOS REARD HIS MIGHTY [FOREHEAD] STATURE ON EARTH STOOD HIS FEET ABOVE	334	FOUR ZOAS 7B	40
MY FEET ARE TURNED BACKWARD & MY FOOTSTEPS SLIDE IN CLAY	335	FOUR ZOAS 7B	88
WALKING BEFORE HER SHADOWY FACE & BOWING AT HER FEET .	340	FOUR ZOAS 7B	279
TWO WINGED IMMORTAL SHAPES ONE STANDING AT HIS FEET . .	341	FOUR ZOAS 8	7
[THEIR WINGS TOUCHD THE HEAVENS THEIR FAIR FEET HOVERD ABOVE]	341	FOUR ZOAS 8	12
VEILS OF IGNORANCE COVERING FROM HEAD TO FEET WITH A COLD WEB	346	FOUR ZOAS 8	222
THEY ANOINT HIS FEET WITH OINTMENT	347	FOUR ZOAS 8	238
COVERD & SCALES HIS HANDS & FEET UPON HIS BELLY FALLING	352	FOUR ZOAS 8	425
WHILE LITTLE CHILDREN PLAY AROUND THY FEET IN GENTLE AWE	360	FOUR ZOAS 9	134
LIE DOWN BEFORE MY FEET O DRAGON LET URIZEN ARISE . . .	360	FOUR ZOAS 9	139
BURST ITS BRIGHT VESSELS SHE FELL DOWN DEAD AT THE FEET OF URIZEN	362	FOUR ZOAS 9	198
OR WHERE ARE HUMAN FEET FOR LO OUR EYES ARE IN THE HEAVENS	363	FOUR ZOAS 9	229
HIDING HIS FACE IN THE DUST BENEATH [A] THE PRISONER'S FEET & SAYING	364	FOUR ZOAS 9 *	269
AND ALL THE WHILE THE FLAMES OF ORC FOLLOW THE VENTROUS FEET	365	FOUR ZOAS 9	330
ON WINGS OF TENFOLD JOY CLAPPING HIS HANDS HIS FEET HIS RADIANT WINGS	366	FOUR ZOAS 9	348

676

FEET   (CONTINUED)

	PAGE	TITLE	LINE
SHE WALKS YEA RUNS HER FEET ARE WINGD	367	FOUR ZOAS 9	391
O THAT I COULD BEHOLD HIS FACE & FOLLOW HIS PURE FEET .	368	FOUR ZOAS 9	426
THAT SING & FLY IN THE BRIGHT AIR BUT YOU DO LICK MY FEET	368	FOUR ZOAS 9	431
AND NOW HER FEET STEP ON THE GRASSY BOSOM OF THE GROUND	370	FOUR ZOAS 9	505
AND MURMURING IN THEIR CHANNELS PLOW & CIRCLE ROUND HIS FEET	378	FOUR ZOAS 9	805
AND HIS BRIGHT FEET FIRM AS A BRAZEN ALTAR BUT THE PARTS	380	FOUR ZOAS AD 1	12
WITH PRINTLESS FEET SCORNING THE CONCAVE OF THE JOYFUL SKY	381	FOUR ZOAS AD 1	17
HIS HANDS & FEET WERE WOUNDED WIDE	419	I SAW A MONK/N	16
AND SUBMISSION TO DEATH BENEATH HIS FEET	420	I SAW A MONK/N	54
SHE PIERCES BOTH HIS HANDS & FEET	425	MENTAL TRAVLER	14
HIS HANDS & FEET WERE WOUNDED WIDE	430	GREY MONK	6
AND AN ANGEL OF PROVIDENCE AT HIS FEET	435	WILLIAM BOND	13
BOWING BEFORE MY SOVREIGN'S FEET	442	DEDICATN BLAIR	17
[WHO DESCEND BEFORE HIS FEET WITH THEIR FOUR TRUMPETS]	443A	LAST JUDGMNT/L	PROSE
BEFORE HIS FEET & AROUND HIM THE HEAVENS IN CLOUDS ARE ROLLING	443A	LAST JUDGMNT/L	*PROSE
& THE MOON BENEATH HER FEET WITH SIX INFANTS AROUND HER	443D	LAST JUDGMNT/L	PROSE
AND DID THOSE FEET IN ANCIENT TIME	480	AND DID FEET/M	1
RIGHT ARM TO THE NORTH HIS LEFT ARM TO THE SOUTH & HIS FEET	483	MILTON 3	25
THE FOOTSTEPS AND INFIXING DEEP THE FEET IN MARBLE BEDS	500	MILTON 19	2
THAT MILTON LABOURD WITH HIS JOURNEY & HIS FEET BLED SORE	500	MILTON 19	3
BEGINNING AT THE FEET OF URIZEN AND ON THE BONES . . .	500	MILTON 19	12
THE BADGER & FOX THEY WORSHIP BEFORE HIS FEET IN TREMBLING FEAR	515	MILTON 28	43
THE STAMPING FEET OF ZELOPHEHAD'S DAUGHTERS	517	MILTON 29	58
A WONDROUS JOURNEY NOT PASSABLE BY IMMORTAL FEET & NONE	525	MILTON 35	20
AND [ARMIES] WAR SHALL SINK BENEATH THY FEET	557	ART HAS LOST/N	8
ONE HUNDRED FEET IN HEIGHT SOME WERE PAINTED AS PICTURES	566A	DESC CAT 2	PROSE
THOUGH THE FIGURES WERE ONE HUNDRED FEET IN HEIGHT . .	566A	DESC CAT 2	PROSE
THE SIZE OF THE ENGRAVING WILL BE (THREE) FEET (ONE) INCH LONG	587A	CHAUCER 1	PROSE
(THREE) FEET (ONE) INCH LONG BY ONE FOOT HIGH CONTAINING	587D	CHAUCER/N	PROSE
THREE FEET 1 INCH LONG AND 1 FOOT HIGH PRICE THREE GUINEAS	589C	CHAUCER 2	TITLE
SCALED WITH IRON SCALES FROM HEAD TO FEET [WITH] . . .	606C	V LAST JUDG/N	PROSE
FEET OF ABRAHAM & RECIEVE THEIR CHILDREN FROM THE EARTH	607C	V LAST JUDG/N	PROSE
A MALE & FEMALE CHAIND [TO] TOGETHER BY THE FEET . . .	607D	V LAST JUDG/N	*PROSE
BENEATH HER FEET IS A FLAMING CAVERN IN WHICH IS SEEN .	609B	V LAST JUDG/N	PROSE
DRIVEN INTO THE WILDERNESS SHE HAS THE MOON UNDER HER FEET	610A	V LAST JUDG/N	PROSE
THAT THE SPECTATOR WILL ATTEND TO THE HANDS & FEET . .	611B	V LAST JUDG/N	PROSE
BENEATH THE FEET OF SETH TWO FIGURES REPRESENT . . .	611C	V LAST JUDG/N	PROSE
WHILE BENEATH THE FEET OF NOAH FOUR SEASONS	611C	V LAST JUDG/N	PROSE
IT IS AS THE DIRT UPON MY FEET NO PART OF ME	617B	V LAST JUDG/N	PROSE
& A GHOST PULLS THE BED CLOTHES AT HER FEET	618C	ILLUS MILTON	PROSE
HIS FEET INDIGNANT SELF-RIGHTEOUSNESS LIKE WHIRLWINDS OF THE NORTH	626	JERUSALEM 7	73
GROANING HE KNEELD BEFORE LOS'S IRON-SHOD FEET ON LONDON STONE	627	JERUSALEM 8	27
BEFORE HIS AWFUL FEET IN PRIDE OF VIRTUE FOR VICTORY .	642	JERUSALEM 19	32
THE DISEASE OF SHAME COVERS ME FROM HEAD TO FEET I HAVE NO HOPE	643	JERUSALEM 21	3
THY SONS HAVE NAILD ME ON THE GATES PIERCING MY HANDS & FEET	644	JERUSALEM 22	2
WITH BLESSINGS ON THEIR HANDS & ON THEIR FEET BLESSINGS OF GOLD	647	JERUSALEM 24	39
THE HUMAN HANDS & FEET & BREATH	651	FIELDS FROM/J	62
IN JEALOUS FEARS & FURY & RAGE & FLAMES ROLL ROUND THEIR FERVID FEET	655	JERUSALEM 29	75
PRODUCING MANY HEADS THREE OR SEVEN OR TEN & HANDS & FEET	659	JERUSALEM 33	22
FROM HEAD TO FEET A GARMENT OF DEATH & ETERNAL FEAR . .	660	JERUSALEM 34	6
THE GRAVES THUNDER BENEATH HIS FEET FROM IRELAND TO JAPAN	661	JERUSALEM 34	42
SO LOS SPOKE BUT WHEN HE SAW [PALE] BLUE DEATH IN ALBION'S FEET	664	JERUSALEM 37	10
AND FEET LEST ANY SHOULD ENTER HIS BOSOM & EMBRACE . .	664	JERUSALEM 38	2
IN THAT DARK VALLEY I HAVE GIRDED ROUND MY CLOKE AND ON MY FEET	666	JERUSALEM 39	20
BUT HERE THE SOLDIER STRIKES & A DEAD CORSE FALLS AT HIS FEET	672	JERUSALEM 43	43
HIS HANDS & FEET WERE WOUNDED WIDE	683	I SAW A MONK/J	14
INTO DAYS & NIGHTS & YEARS & MONTHS TO TRAVEL WITH MY FEET	688	JERUSALEM 56	20
SHE SAT AT THE MILLS HER HAIR UNBOUND HER FEET NAKED . .	693	JERUSALEM 60	41
HER HAND IS A COURT OF JUSTICE HER FEET TWO ARMIES IN BATTLE	698	JERUSALEM 64	9
THE STAMPING FEET OF RAGAN UPON THE FLAMING TREDDLES OF HER LOOM	699	JERUSALEM 64	36
EMBRACES ARE COMINGLINGS FROM THE HEAD EVEN TO THE FEET	708	JERUSALEM 69	43
THY HILLS & VALLEYS FELT HER FEET	718	ENGLND AWAKE/J	5
RECIEVE THE FEET OF JERUSALEM THEY HAVE CAST ME QUITE AWAY	720	JERUSALEM 79	16
I HAVE NAILD HIS HANDS ON BETH RABBIM & HIS (FEET) ON HESHBON'S WALL	726	JERUSALEM 82	* 43
WITH HIM WENT DOWN THE DOGS OF LEUTHA AT HIS FEET . . .	729	JERUSALEM 83	82
COMFORTING SOUNDS OF LOVE & HARMONY & ON THY FEET . . .	731	JERUSALEM 86	30
HE BEATS SEAS ROLL BENEATH HIS FEET TEMPESTS MUSTER . .	731	JERUSALEM 86	35
THUS THEY CONVERSE UPON MAM-TOR THE GRAVES THUNDER UNDER THEIR FEET	741	JERUSALEM 93	27
THE WEEDS OF DEATH INWRAP HIS HANDS & FEET BLOWN INCESSANT	741	JERUSALEM 94	5
YOU SHALL BOW BEFORE HER FEET	754	EV GOSPEL(E)/N	53
ADAM EVE THOU HAST SPOKEN TRULY LET US KNEEL BEFORE HIS FEET	780	GHOST ABEL 2	3
BENEATH MY BRIGHT FEET	805	TO BUTTS/L	36

		PAGE	TITLE	LINE

FEET   (CONTINUED)

WHOLE MIGHT CHAIN MY FEET TO THE WORLD OF DUTY & REALITY   809A LETTER 20   PROSE
OTHER BOTH HELD ABOVE HER HEAD & A FIGURE KNEELING AT HER   839C LETTER 38   PROSE
    FEET
ON A CANVAS ABOUT TWO FEET BY ONE AND A HALF   . . 843D LETTER 43   PROSE
FIVE SHILLINGS AT A BROKER'S SHOP IT IS ABOUT FIVE FEET   843D LETTER 43   PROSE
    BY FOUR
BECOME CHILDREN OF LIGHT AND LIBERTY AND MY FEET AND MY   852A LETTER 50   PROSE
WIFE'S FEET ARE FREE FROM FETTERS O LOVELY FELPHAM PARENT   852A LETTER 50   PROSE
MY FEET IT WILL NOT BE LONG BEFORE I SHALL BE ABLE   862D LETTER 60   PROSE
    TO PRESENT
(TWELVE) LARGE PRINTS SIZE OF EACH ABOUT (TWO) FEET BY...   867B LETTER 66   PROSE
...ASSASSIN LAYING DEAD AT THE FEET OF (EDWARD) IST IN...   SUPP ILLUS HISTORY *TITLE

FEIGNED

REMEMBER ALL THY FEIGNED TERRORS ON THE SECRET COUCH . . 338 FOUR ZOAS 7B   196
REMEMBER ALL THY FEIGNED TERRORS . . . . 700 JERUSALEM 65   42

FELICITY

BUT FELICITY DOES NOT LAST LONG FOR   . . . . 58B ISLAND MOON 10 PROSE
INDEED WITH SUCH ABUNDANT FELICITY IN THE MEETING HIM . 854B LETTER 53   PROSE

FELL

GWIN FELL THE SONS OF NORWAY FLED . . . . 14 GWIN KING/PS   109
BRAVE LORDS WHO FELL BENEATH THE BLOODY AXE   . . . . 18 EDW THIRD/PS 1   44
YOU ASKD ME IF HE DID NOT LOOK WELL WHEN HE FELL . . 29D EDW THIRD/PS 4 PROSE
HE FELL IN LOVE & MARRIED HER . . . . 50 WHEN CORRUP/IM   19
FELL SHAKING AGONIES & IN EACH WRINKLE OF THAT FACE . . 108 TIRIEL 6   38
 . . . TEARS FELL DOWN THE SHADY CHEEKS AT HIS FEET MANY   140 FRENCH REVOLTN   132
    CLOTHD
BUT THE DEVIL'S ACCOUNT IS THAT THE MESSIAH FELL   . . 150A MARRIAGE HH 5   PROSE
LET MAN WEAR THE FELL OF THE LION WOMAN THE FLEECE OF THE   151C MARRIAGE HH 8   PROSE
    SHEEP
WEEPING HE FELL UPON MY THIGH   . . . . 188 A FAIRY SKIPD   7
TILL TO THAT VOID IT CAME & FELL SO THE DARK HOUSE WAS RENT 204 AMERICA CANC B   22
HIS GREAT HAMMER FELL FROM HIS HAND . . . . 229 URIZEN 13   21
FELL THRO THE WINTRY SKIES SEEKING THEIR GRAVES . . . . 243 EUROPE 13   7
SHE FELL DOWN A FAINT SHADOW WANDRING . . . . 250 AHANIA 2   38
WHEN OBSCURD IN HIS FORESTS FELL MONSTERS . . . . . . 250 AHANIA 3   6
BUT THE ROCK FELL UPON THE EARTH   . . . . 251 AHANIA 3   45
MANY TEARS FELL ON THE ROCK . . . . 252 AHANIA 3   59
ETERNAL FELL ROUND THE TREE . . . . 253 AHANIA 4   51
FELL ASUNDER AND HORRIBLE VACUUM   . . . . 257 BOOK OF LOS 4   25
FALLING FALLING LOS FELL & FELL . . . . 258 BOOK OF LOS 4   27
STILL HE FELL THRO THE VOID STILL A VOID . . . . . . 258 BOOK OF LOS 4   32
[THEN SLEEP FELL ON HER EYELIDS IN A CHASM OF THE VALLEY]   268 FOUR ZOAS 1   145
[BEAUTY ALL BLUSHING WITH DESIRE MOCKING HER FELL DESPAIR]   269 FOUR ZOAS 1   189
TO ENION & HIS BODY FELL THARMAS BEHELD HIM FALL . . 279 FOUR ZOAS 1   531
SUDDEN DOWN FELL THEY ALL TOGETHER INTO AN UNKNOWN SPACE   279 FOUR ZOAS 1   541
[?HE ?FELL XXX HID IN ?HORRIBLE ?CAVERNS OF MOUNTAINS]   SUPP FOUR ZOAS 1   *
[SO SAYING HE ?FELL XXX INTO THE RESTLESS SEA]   SUPP FOUR ZOAS 1   *
SHE FELL COLD FROM LAMBETH'S VALES IN GROANS & DEWY DEATH   281 FOUR ZOAS 2   46
AN EVANESCENT SHADOW LAST SHE FELL A HEAP OF ASHES . . 283 FOUR ZOAS 2   115
SO SAYING IN DEEP SOBS HE LANGUISHD TILL DEAD HE ALSO FELL   289 FOUR ZOAS 2   340
MAN FELL UPON HIS FACE PROSTRATE BEFORE THE WATRY SHADOW   293 FOUR ZOAS 3   54
IN GOLDEN WREATHES THE SORROW OF MAN & THE BALMY DROPS   293 FOUR ZOAS 3   67
    FELL DOWN
AND FROM HER BOSOM LUVAH FELL FAR AS THE EAST & WEST . 294 FOUR ZOAS 3   100
AND THREW AHANIA FROM HIS BOSOM OBDURATE SHE FELL LIKE   295 FOUR ZOAS 3   132
    LIGHTNING
FELL DOWN DOWN RUSHING RUINING THUNDERING [DARKNING]   295 FOUR ZOAS 3   * 141
    SHUDDERING
A WORLD OF DARKNESS AHANIA FELL FAR INTO NON ENTITY . . 295 FOUR ZOAS 3   144
FELL FROM HIS HAND HIS FIRES HID THEIR STRONG LIMBS IN   304 FOUR ZOAS 4   281
    SMOKE
FELL FROM HIS BOSOM ON THE MOUNTAIN THE SPECTRE DARK . . 307 FOUR ZOAS 5   100
THE TERRIBLE BOY TILL FAINTING BY HIS SIDE THE PARENTS FELL 309 FOUR ZOAS 5   172
WE FELL I SIEZD THEE DARK URTHONA IN MY LEFT HAND FALLING   311 FOUR ZOAS 5   225
AND DRUNKEN WITH THE IMMORTAL DRAUGHT FELL FROM MY THRONE   311 FOUR ZOAS 5   237
    SUBLIME
HIMSELF INTO THE DISMAL VOID FALLING HE FELL & FELL . . 315 FOUR ZOAS 6   153
WHEN WEARIED DEAD HE FELL HIS LIMBS REPOSD IN THE BOSOM   316 FOUR ZOAS 6   159
    OF SLIME
AS THE SEED FALLS FROM THE SOWER'S HAND SO URIZEN FELL   316 FOUR ZOAS 6   160
    & DEATH
FOR URIZEN FELL AS THE MIDDAY SUN FALLS DOWN INTO THE WEST   318 FOUR ZOAS 6   267
WHILE HIS SNOWS FELL & HIS STORMS BEAT TO COOL THE FLAMES   321 FOUR ZOAS 7   30
    OF ORC
FROM ITS HINGES UTTERING ITS FINAL GROAN ALL BEULAH FELL   326 FOUR ZOAS 7   258
THE FELL DESTRUCTION AND SHE SAID O URIZEN PRINCE OF LIGHT   344 FOUR ZOAS 8   145
STEEPING THE DIREFUL WEB OF RELIGION SWAGGING HEAVY IT FELL 345 FOUR ZOAS 8   176
FELL FROM MY STATION IN THE ETERNAL BOSOM I DIVIDED . . 350 FOUR ZOAS 8   352
THEN FELL THE FIRES OF ETERNITY WITH LOUD & SHRILL . . . 357 FOUR ZOAS 9   10
FELL DOWN & SHADOWY FORMS OF JOY MIXD WITH DESPAIR & GRIEF   358 FOUR ZOAS 9   29
BURST ITS BRIGHT VESSELS SHE FELL DOWN DEAD AT THE FEET   362 FOUR ZOAS 9   198
    OF URIZEN
AND SOFT SLEEP FELL UPON HER EYELIDS IN THE SILENT NOON   369 FOUR ZOAS 9   457
    OF DAY
HIS CROWN OF THORNS FELL FROM HIS HEAD HE HUNG HIS LIVING   376 FOUR ZOAS 9   711
    LYRE
THEN FELL THE LEGIONS OF MYSTERY IN MADDNING CONFUSION . . 376 FOUR ZOAS 9   722
INTO THE WINE PRESSES OF LUVAH HOWLING FELL THE CLUSTERS   376 FOUR ZOAS 9   724
SWEEP OER THE STRUGGLING COPULATION IN FELL WRITHING PANGS   381 FOUR ZOAS AD 2   4
AND THEIR TEARS FELL THRO THE BLACK BLACK CLOUD . . . . 435 WILLIAM BOND   19
AND MARY FELL DOWN ON THE RIGHT HAND FLOOR . . . . . . 435 WILLIAM BOND   34

678

FELL   (CONTINUED)

JUDGMENT AND LO IT FELL ON RINTRAH AND HIS RAGE	489 MILTON 9	10
FELL DOWN AS DEWS OF NIGHT & A LOUD SOLEMN UNIVERSAL GROAN	490 MILTON 9	37
TO THOSE WITHOUT BUT INFINITE TO THOSE WITHIN IT FELL DOWN AND	491 MILTON 10	9
WITH THUNDERS LOUD AND TERRIBLE SO MILTON'S SHADOW FELL	497 MILTON 15	45
ALL FELL TOWARDS THE CENTER IN DIRE RUIN SINKING DOWN . .	500 MILTON 19	21
THUS MILTON FELL THRO ALBION'S HEART TRAVELLING OUTSIDE OF HUMANITY	502 MILTON 20	41
FELL FROM MY STATION IN THE ETERNAL BOSOM SIX THOUSAND YEARS	505 MILTON 22	16
FELL AND WAS CUT OFF ALL THINGS VANISH & ARE SEEN NO MORE	505 MILTON 22	22
FROM FELL DESTRUCTION IN THE SPECTROUS CUNNING OR RAGE HE CREATES	515 MILTON 28	41
ALL FELL TOWARDS THE CENTER SINKING DOWNWARD IN DIRE RUIN	524 MILTON 34	39
MY BONES TREMBLED I FELL OUTSTRETCHD UPON THE PATH . . .	534 MILTON 42	25
WHILE LOS SPOKE THE TERRIBLE SPECTRE FELL SHUDDRING BEFORE HIM	627 JERUSALEM 8	21
JERUSALEM FELL FROM LAMBETH'S VALE	650 FIELDS FROM/J	41
ALBION FELL UPON HIS FACE PROSTRATE BEFORE THE WATRY SHADOW	654 JERUSALEM 29	41
IN GOLDEN WREATHES THE SORROW OF MAN & THE BALMY DROPS FELL DOWN	654 JERUSALEM 29	54
AND FROM HER BOSOM LUVAH FELL FAR AS THE EAST AND WEST . .	655 JERUSALEM 29	79
DESCENDED AND FELL DOWN UPON THEIR KNEES ROUND ALBION'S KNEES	666 JERUSALEM 40	8
BUT ALBION FELL DOWN A ROCKY FRAGMENT FROM ETERNITY HURLD	685 JERUSALEM 54	6
WHO FELL BENEATH HIS INSTRUMENTS OF HUSBANDRY & BECAME . .	688 JERUSALEM 56	35
THE LIVING CREATURES MADDEND AND ALBION FELL INTO THE FURROW AND	689 JERUSALEM 57	13
ALL FELL TOWARDS THE CENTER SINKING DOWNWARDS IN DIRE RUIN	691 JERUSALEM 59	17
THEREFORE HE LIVED & BREATHED IN HOPE BUT HIS TEARS FELL INCESSANT	696 JERUSALEM 62	36
WHEN THE SOUL FELL INTO SLEEP	753 EV GOSPEL(D)/N	93
YES BUT THEY SAY HE NEVER FELL	756 EV GOSPEL(I)/N	15
THEY BY THE SWORD OF JUSTICE FELL	757 EV GOSPEL(I)/N	39

FELLOW   SEE SCHOOL-FELLOW

A RAW-BOND FELLOW T OTHER DAY PASSD BY ME	25 EDW THIRD/PS 3	154
AS I WAS LOOKING UP A LITTLE OUTRE FELLOW PULLING ME . .	45A ISLAND MOON 1	PROSE
TO HAVE THRASHD THE FELLOW ONLY HE WAS BIGGER THAN I . .	45A ISLAND MOON 1	PROSE
AH SAID THE PYTHAGOREAN ARADOBO WILL MAKE A VERY CLEVER FELLOW	49D ISLAND MOON 6	PROSE
WOULD MAKE A CLEVER FELLOW IF HE WAS PROPERLY BROUGHT UP	50A ISLAND MOON 6	PROSE
AND HE IS THE FUNNIEST FELLOW	53A ISLAND MOON 8	PROSE
THAT BILL S A FOOLISH FELLOW	61 SAY YOU JOE/IM	9
("WITH WISDOM DIRECTS OBSTINACY") THIS MUST BE A GRAND FELLOW	79B ANNO LAVATER	MARG
MY HORSES HATH HE MADDEND AND MY FELLOW SERVANTS INJURD	487 MILTON 7	29
FELLOW LABOURERS THE GREAT VINTAGE & HARVEST IS NOW UPON EARTH	510 MILTON 25	17
RESOLVD TO BE A VERY CONTRARY FELLOW	555 BLAKES APL/N 1	17
RESOLVD TO BE A VERY CONTRARY FELLOW	556 BLAKES APL/N 2	16
A TERRIBLE FELLOW SUCH AS EXISTS IN ALL TIMES AND PLACES	571C DESC CAT 3	PROSE
HE HAS PUT THE REEVE A VULGAR FELLOW	574A DESC CAT 3	PROSE
RESOLVD TO BE A VERY CONTRARY FELLOW	596 BLAKES APOL/PA	10
I HAVE ENOUGH IN THE APPROBATION OF FELLOW LABOURERS . .	600C PUB ADDRESS/N	PROSE
BUT I AM HAPPY TO FIND A GREAT MAJORITY OF FELLOW MORTALS	794A LETTER 5	PROSE
SO PRAYS A FELLOW SUFFERER & YOUR HUMBLE SERVANT . . .	796D LETTER 8	PROSE
& FELLOW DISCIPLE HOW GREAT MUST BE YOUR FAITH	822B LETTER 26	PROSE
AS WAS SUPPOSED BY OUR KIND & ATTENTIVE FELLOW INHABITANT	833D LETTER 33	PROSE

FELLOWS

I HAVE BEEN SCORNED LONG ENOUGH BY THESE FELLOWS . . .	575D DESC CAT 3	PROSE
& THOSE MUST BE QUEER FELLOWS WHO GIVE GREAT SUMS . .	596C PUB ADDRESS/N	PROSE
[ALL] MOST OF THEM SUCH SILLY FELLOWS AS TO BELIEVE THIS	597B PUB ADDRESS/N	PROSE
WITH TOO GREAT CONTEMPT OF SUCH CONTEMPTIBLE FELLOWS .	599D PUB ADDRESS/N	PROSE
MUST HAVE BEEN VERY WEAK & VULGAR FELLOWS	599D PUB ADDRESS/N	PROSE
ONE OF THE MOST IGNORANT FELLOWS THAT I EVER KNEW . .	603B PUB ADDR AD/N	PROSE

FELPHAM

MR COSENS OWNER OF THE MILL AT FELPHAM WAS PASSING BY .	437D BLAKES MEMORAN	PROSE
FORWARDS FROM ULRO FROM THE VALE OF FELPHAM AND SET FREE	503 MILTON 20	60
BLAKE'S COTTAGE AT FELPHAM	527C MILTON 36	TITLE
LOUD SATAN THUNDERD LOUD & DARK UPON MILD FELPHAM SHORE	529 MILTON 38	13
AND FELPHAM BILLY RODE OUT EVERY MORN	537 AND HIS LEGS/N	22
CONCERNING MY THREE YEARS' HERCULEAN LABOURS AT FELPHAM	592C PUB ADDRESS/N	PROSE
IN FELPHAM I HEARD AND SAW THE VISIONS OF ALBION . . .	665 JERUSALEM 38	41
EVERY THING IS NEARLY COMPLETED FOR OUR REMOVAL TO FELPHAM	799A LETTER 11	PROSE
"CALLD ON YOU SINCE MY HUSBAND'S FIRST RETURN FROM FELPHAM"	800A LETTER 12	PROSE
"IN PREPARING YOU A SUMMER BOWER AT FELPHAM"	800B LETTER 12	PROSE
TO ENTICE HIM TO FELPHAM & FAR AWAY	800 MRS FLAXMAN/L	4
AWAY TO SWEET FELPHAM FOR HEAVEN IS THERE	800 MRS FLAXMAN/L	5
FEEDS THE VILLAGE OF FELPHAM BY DAY & BY NIGHT	800 MRS FLAXMAN/L	14
I HAVE BEGUN TO WORK FELPHAM IS A SWEET PLACE FOR STUDY	802A LETTER 14	PROSE
VILLAGERS OF FELPHAM ARE NOT MEER RUSTICS THEY ARE POLITE &	803B LETTER 15	PROSE
THAT FELPHAM IS PROPITIOUS TO THE ARTS GOD BLESS YOU .	803C LETTER 15	PROSE
DIRECT TO MR BLAKE FELPHAM NEAR CHICHESTER SUSSEX . . .	803D LETTER 15	*PROSE
VERSES SUCH AS FELPHAM PRODUCES BY ME THO NOT SUCH AS SHE	804B LETTER 16	PROSE
AND SAW FELPHAM SWEET	805 TO BUTTS/L	35
SUSSEX IS CERTAINLY A HAPPY PLACE & FELPHAM IN PARTICULAR IS	808C LETTER 19	PROSE
TO SEE YOU AT FELPHAM & TO SHEW YOU MR HAYLEY'S LIBRARY	809C LETTER 20	PROSE
FELPHAM COTTAGE OF COTTAGES THE PRETTIEST	810A LETTER 20	PROSE
FELPHAM MEN ARE THE MILDEST OF THE HUMAN RACE IF IT IS THE	810C LETTER 20	PROSE
HONOURABLE MENTION OF ME HAS BEEN AT FELPHAM &	810D LETTER 21	PROSE

		PAGE	TITLE	LINE

FELPHAM   (CONTINUED)

SO NEAR TO FELPHAM PARIS BEING SCARCE FURTHER OFF THAN   811A LETTER 21   PROSE
  LONDON
WHILE WALKING FROM FELPHAM TO LAVANT TO MEET MY SISTER   .   . 816D LETTER 24   PROSE
TOO MUCH THE CAUSE OF OUR DETERMINATION TO LEAVE FELPHAM   819D LETTER 25   PROSE
WHICH WE INFORMD HIM VIZ TO LEAVE FELPHAM ENTIRELY   .   .   . 820C LETTER 25   PROSE
FELPHAM & ITS KIND INHABITANTS I FEEL ANXIOUS & THEREFORE   833D LETTER 33   PROSE
ACROSS THE COUNTRY TO FELPHAM AS HE ALWAYS KEEPS A HORSE   843A LETTER 42   PROSE
DELIGHTS OF THE TURRET OF LOVELY FELPHAM PLEASE TO GIVE   850C LETTER 49   PROSE
WIFE'S FEET ARE FREE FROM FETTERS O LOVELY FELPHAM PARENT   852A LETTER 50   PROSE
HAPPY CHRISTMAS AT LOVELY FELPHAM OUR SPIRITS SEEM STILL   853D LETTER 52   PROSE
WHEN I LEFT FELPHAM LAST IN ONE OF HEATH'S SHAKESPEARE   855C LETTER 53   PROSE
  YOU WILL SEE
& AT THE VERY IDEA OF ANOTHER JOURNEY TO SWEET FELPHAM   .   . 857C LETTER 54   PROSE
O THAT I COULD BUT BRING FELPHAM TO ME OR GO TO HER   .   .   . 857C LETTER 54   PROSE
FELPHAM   .   .   .   .   SUPP ADDRESSES/L   *TITLE
WILLIAM HAYLEY ESQRE FELPHAM NEAR CHICHESTER SUSSEX   .   .   . SUPP ADDRESSES/L   *TITLE
WILLIAM HAYLEY ESQRE FELPHAM NEAR BOGNOR SUSSEX   .   .   .   . SUPP ADDRESSES/L   *TITLE
DRAWINGS &C SENT FROM FELPHAM   .   .   .   .   SUPP LETTER 56A   *PROSE
BALANCE DUE FROM ME PREVIOUS TO MY GOING TO FELPHAM   .   .   SUPP LETTER 56A   *PROSE

FELPHAM'S

SHOULD UP ASCEND FORWARD FROM FELPHAM'S VALE & BREAK THE   507 MILTON 23   37
  CHAIN
HE SET ME DOWN IN FELPHAM'S VALE & PREPARD A BEAUTIFUL   .   . 527 MILTON 36   23
SURROUNDING FELPHAM'S VALE REACHING TO THE MUNDANE SHELL   530 MILTON 39   9
  SAYING
LOUD SATAN THUNDERD LOUD & DARK UPON MILD FELPHAM'S SHORE   531 MILTON 39   22
THEN AS A MOONY ARK OLOLON DESCENDED TO FELPHAM'S VALE   .   . 534 MILTON 42   7
INTO THE FIRES OF INTELLECT THAT REJOICD IN FELPHAM'S VALE   534 MILTON 42   9
FROM FELPHAM'S VALE CLOTHED IN CLOUDS OF BLOOD TO ENTER   534 MILTON 42   20
  INTO
IN THE COLUMN OF FIRE IN FELPHAM'S VALE THEN TO THEIR   534 MILTON 42   22
  MOUTHS THE FOUR
IMMEDIATELY THE LARK MOUNTED WITH A LOUD TRILL FROM   534 MILTON 42   29
  FELPHAM'S VALE
OR CAN I BE ANGRY WITH FELPHAM'S OLD MILL .   .   .   .   .   . 538 WAS I ANGRY/N   2
LIKE THE REMEMBRANCE OF FELPHAM'S WAVES & OF THE GLORIOUS &   835B LETTER 34   PROSE

FELT

THE SUN HE FELT BUT THE BRIGHT MOON WAS NOW A USELESS GLOBE   100 TIRIEL 2   2
THE BLIND MAN FELT HIS WAY & CRIED PEACE TO THESE OPEN   101 TIRIEL 2   13
  DOORS
RAN TO THE DOOR WHEN TIRIEL FELT THE ANKLES OF AGED HAR   109 TIRIEL 8   6
AND I FELT DELIGHT .   .   .   .   170 SLEPT DARK/N   4
KLOPSTOCK FELT THE [NINEFOLD] INTRIPLED TURN   .   .   .   .   187 WHEN KLOPSTK/N   15
HID IN HIS CAVES THE BARD OF ALBION FELT THE ENORMOUS   202 AMERICA 15   16
  PLAGUES
FELT A WORM WITHIN HER WOMB .   .   .   .   232 URIZEN 19   20
FELT THEIR NERVES CHANGE INTO MARROW .   .   .   . 235 URIZEN 25   24
THAT NATURE FELT THRO ALL HER PORES THE ENORMOUS REVELRY   244 EUROPE 14   34
GREW TO ROOTS WHEN IT FELT THE EARTH   .   .   .   . 252 AHANIA 3   66
FELT THEIR SKULLS HARDEN THEN ASIA .   .   .   .   253 AHANIA 3   41
LOS NOW REPENTED THAT HE HAD SMITTEN ENITHARMON HE FELT   274 FOUR ZOAS 1   352
  LOVE
.   .   . STARRY WHEELS FELT THE DIVINE HAND LIMIT   304 FOUR ZOAS 4   275
WAS PUT TO ETERNAL DEATH LOS FELT THE LIMIT & SAW   .   .   . 304 FOUR ZOAS 4   276
FELT HER IMMORTAL LIMBS FREEZE STIFFNING PALE INFLEXIBLE   305 FOUR ZOAS 5   * 6
FELT ALL THE SORROW PARENTS FEEL THEY WEPT TOWARD   309 FOUR ZOAS 5   144
  ONE ANOTHER
ENITHARMON ON THE ROAD OF DRANTHON FELT THE INMOST GATE   309 FOUR ZOAS 5   177
OF THE CHAIN OF JEALOUSY & FELT THE RENDINGS OF FIERCE   309 FOUR ZOAS 5   182
  HOWLING ORC
LOS FELT THE ENVY IN HIS LIMBS LIKE TO A BLIGHTED TREE   .   . 321 FOUR ZOAS 7   27
HE SPOKE NOT HE WAS SILENT TILL HE FELT THE COLD DISEASE   324 FOUR ZOAS 7   182
NOR FELT THE STINGINGS OF DESIRE NOR LONGINGS AFTER LIFE   325 FOUR ZOAS 7   203
OBDURATE LOS FELT PITY ENITHARMON TOLD THE TALE   .   .   .   328 FOUR ZOAS 7   338
IN HIS HANDS HE WONDERD THAT HE FELT LOVE & NOT HATE   .   .   332 FOUR ZOAS 7   497
WONDRING WITH LOVE & [XXX] AWE THEY FELT THE DIVINE HAND   341 FOUR ZOAS 8   * 23
  UPON THEM
SITTING WITHIN HIS TEMPLE FURIOUS FELT THE (NUMMING) STUPOR   345 FOUR ZOAS 8   180
[HE] FELT THE FEMALE DEATH A DULL & NUMMING STUPOR SUCH   352 FOUR ZOAS 8   416
  AS NEER
BEFORE ASSAULTED THE BRIGHT HUMAN FORM HE FELT HIS PORES   352 FOUR ZOAS 8   417
THEN THARMAS & URTHONA FELT THE STONY STUPOR RISE   .   .   . 353 FOUR ZOAS 8   467
LOS FELT THE STONY STUPOR & HIS HEAD ROLLD DOWN BENEATH   353 FOUR ZOAS 8   471
OR A LEAF BUDS THE ETERNAL MAN IS SEEN IS HEARD IS FELT   356 FOUR ZOAS 8   582
THEY HEARD NOT SAW NOT FELT NOT ALL THE TERRIBLE CONFUSION   367 FOUR ZOAS 9   381
I MUST HAVE SLEPT ETERNALLY NOR HAVE FELT THE DEW OF THY   367 FOUR ZOAS 9   396
  MORNING
OR I MUST HAVE SLEPT ETERNALLY NOR HAVE FELT THE DEW OF   367 FOUR ZOAS 9   403
  MORNING
ETERNALLY THOU MUST HAVE SLEPT NOR HAVE FELT THE MORNING   367 FOUR ZOAS 9   404
  DEW
HE FELT THE FEMALE &C .   .   .   .   382 FOUR ZOAS AD 6   32
A LIAR HE NEVER WAS ABASHED IN HIS LIFE & NEVER FELT HIS   447D ANNO REYNOLDS MARG
  IGNORANCE
SIMILAR I FELT THE SAME CONTEMPT & ABHORRENCE THEN THAT   477A ANNO REYNOLDS MARG
  I DO
HE SAW NOW FROM THE (OUTSIDE) WHAT HE BEFORE SAW & FELT   627 JERUSALEM 8   * 25
  FROM WITHIN
HE FELT THAT LOVE AND PITY ARE THE SAME A SOFT REPOSE   .   . 646 JERUSALEM 23   14
THEY BENT DOWN THEY FELT THE EARTH AND AGAIN ENROOTING   .   . 653 JERUSALEM 28   18
THY HILLS & VALLEYS FELT HER FEET .   .   .   . 718 ENGLND AWAKE/J   5

```
                                                           PAGE     TITLE          LINE
FELT    (CONTINUED)
     ON SINAI FELT THE HAND DIVINE  . . . . . . . . .    754  EV GOSPEL(E)/N     17
     EXCUSE THIS COMMUNICATION OF SENTIMENTS WHICH I FELT   .   798C LETTER 10    PROSE
     FELT AFFLICTION & SORROW & SICKNESS & DEARTH  . . . . .   918  HAPPINESS/L    76
FEMALE    SEE MALE-FEMALE
     GODS LIKE THESE NOR MALE NOR FEMALE ARE BUT SINGLE PREGNATE   40D  THEN SHE BORE   PROSE
     THE FEMALE LIFE LIVES FROM THE LIGHT OF THE MALE  . . . .    82C  ANNO LAVATER    MARG
     SEE A MAN'S FEMALE DEPENDANTS YOU KNOW THE MAN  . . . .    82C  ANNO LAVATER    MARG
     THE ETERNAL FEMALE GROAND IT WAS HEARD OVER ALL THE EARTH   159A  SONG LIBERTY    PROSE
     [FEMALE] INFANT WILES & [FEMALE ] INFANT SMILES  . . . .   165  CRADLE SONG/N    26
     DISGUISER OF THE FEMALE FORM  . . . . . . . . . .    188  A FAIRY SKIPD     5
     WHATEVER HIDES THE FEMALE FORM  . . . . . . . . .    188  A FAIRY SKIPD    11
     OUR LIVES TO MAKE THE FEMALE LIVE  . . . . . . . .    188  A FAIRY SKIPD    14
     CROWND WITH A HELMET & DARK HAIR THE NAMELESS FEMALE STOOD   195  AMERICA PREL 1    4
     FOR THE FEMALE SPIRITS OF THE DEAD PINING IN BONDS     202  AMERICA 15       23
        OF RELIGION
     A FEMALE FORM TREMBLING AND PALE  . . . . . . . .    231  URIZEN 18         7
     OF THE FIRST FEMALE NOW SEPARATE  . . . . . . . .    231  URIZEN 18        10
     AT THE FIRST FEMALE FORM NOW SEPARATE  . . . . . .    231  URIZEN 18        15
     BUT LOS SAW THE FEMALE & PITIED  . . . . . . . .    231  URIZEN 19        10
     AND THE WEB IS A FEMALE IN EMBRIO  . . . . . . . .    235  URIZEN 25        18
     THE NAMELESS SHADOWY FEMALE ROSE FROM OUT THE BREAST OF ORC   238  EUROPE PREL 1    1
     FORBID ALL JOY & FROM HER CHILDHOOD SHALL THE LITTLE FEMALE   240  EUROPE 5         8
     EIGHTEEN HUNDRED YEARS A FEMALE DREAM  . . . . . .    240  EUROPE 9         5
     BUT MALES IMMORTAL LIVE RENEWD BY FEMALE DEATHS IN SOFT   266  FOUR ZOAS 1      66
     A MALE & FEMALE NAKED & RUDDY AS THE PRIDE OF SUMMER  .    270  FOUR ZOAS 1     236
     DRIVING THE FEMALE EMANATIONS ALL AWAY FROM LOS  . . .    271  FOUR ZOAS 1     273
     FROM ENITHARMON'S INWARD PARTS BUT THE BRIGHT FEMALE TERROR   279  FOUR ZOAS 1     564
     [A MALE & FEMALE WITHERD]  . . . . . . . . . . .   SUPP FOUR ZOAS 1       *
     SEVERE THE LABOUR FEMALE SLAVES THE MORTAR TROD OPPRESSED   284  FOUR ZOAS 2     172
     ONTO THE MARGIN OF NON ENTITY THE BRIGHT FEMALE CAME  . .    291  FOUR ZOAS 2   *  422
     SOFT CLOUD OF SNOW A FEMALE PALE & WEAK I SOFT EMBRACD    300  FOUR ZOAS 4      99
     THE LOVELY FEMALE HOWLD & URIZEN BENEATH DEEP GROAND  . .    302  FOUR ZOAS 4     189
     AND AS A DOUBLE FEMALE FORM LOVELINESS & PERFECTION OF    304  FOUR ZOAS 4     251
        BEAUTY
     AND FEMALE SHUDDRING PALE THE FALLEN MAN RECOILD  . . .    326  FOUR ZOAS 7     247
     A FEMALE BRIGHT I STOOD BESIDE MY ANVIL DARK A MASS  . .    327  FOUR ZOAS 7     282
     IN MALE FORMS WITHOUT FEMALE COUNTERPARTS OR EMANATIONS    328  FOUR ZOAS 7     329
     FOR HE BEHELD NEW FEMALE FORMS BORN FORTH UPON THE AIR  .    332  FOUR ZOAS 7     487
     URIZEN SAW & TRIUMPHD & HE CRIED TO [THE SHADOWY FEMALE]    333  FOUR ZOAS 7B      3
        HIS WARRIORS
     AND ROUND THE NAMELESS SHADOWY FEMALE IN HER HOWLING TERROR   336  FOUR ZOAS 7B    145
     THE SHADOWY FEMALE VARIED IN THE WAR IN HER DELIGHT  . . .    338  FOUR ZOAS 7B    223
     NOT SUFFRING DOUBT TO RISE UP FROM THE CLOUDS OF     340  FOUR ZOAS 7B   *  297
        THE SHADOWY FEMALE
     HIS HUMAN BULK WHILE THE DARK SHADOWY FEMALE [BROODS]    343  FOUR ZOAS 8    *   80
        BROODING OVER
     THEY PROPAGATED THE DEADLY [WORLD] WORDS THE SHADOWY FEMALE   344  FOUR ZOAS 8    *  143
        ABSORBING
     AND THEY APPEARD A UNIVERSAL FEMALE FORM CREATED  . . .    345  FOUR ZOAS 8     188
     AND ENITHARMON NAMED THE FEMALE (JERUSALEM) THE HOLY  . .    346  FOUR ZOAS 8    *  190
     A MALE WITHOUT A FEMALE COUNTERPART A HOWLING FIEND  . . .    347  FOUR ZOAS 8     253
     YET HIDING THE SHADOWY FEMALE VALA AS IN AN ARK & CURTAINS   347  FOUR ZOAS 8     255
     OF FEMALE FORMS BEAUTIFUL THRO POISONS HIDDEN IN SECRET    348  FOUR ZOAS 8     290
     . . . THE BOSOM OF SATAN THE FALSE FEMALE AS IN AN ARK    348  FOUR ZOAS 8     292
        & VEIL
     TO THE DELUSIVE FEMALE FORMS SHINING AMONG HIS FURNACES    350  FOUR ZOAS 8     350
     [HE] FELT THE FEMALE DEATH A DULL & NUMMING STUPOR SUCH    352  FOUR ZOAS 8     416
        AS NEER
     THE SHADOWY FEMALE SINCE LIFE CANNOT BE QUENCHD LIFE    352  FOUR ZOAS 8     421
        EXUDED
     AND OF THE NAMELESS SHADOWY FEMALE IN THE NETHER DEEP  . .    353  FOUR ZOAS 8     479
     THUS SHALL THE MALE & FEMALE LIVE THE LIFE OF ETERNITY  .    362  FOUR ZOAS 9     219
     THE FEMALE FORM NOW SEPARATE THEY SHUDDERD AT THE HORRIBLE   373  FOUR ZOAS 9     622
        THING
     TO LOVE DEVOTED FEMALE ALL ASTONISHD STOOD THE HOSTS  . .    380  FOUR ZOAS AD 1   13
     FEMALE HER FORM BRIGHT AS THE SUMMER BUT THE PARTS OF LOVE   381  FOUR ZOAS AD 1   18
     WITH FEMALE VOICE WARBLING UPON THE [HILLS &] HOLLOW VALES   381  FOUR ZOAS AD 5    8
     HE FELT THE FEMALE &C  . . . . . . . . . . . .    382  FOUR ZOAS AD 6   32
     TILL [THOU] I TURN FROM FEMALE LOVE  . . . . . . .    417  MY SPECTRE/N     59
     A LITTLE FEMALE BABE DOES SPRING  . . . . . . . .    425  MENTAL TRAVLER   44
     IN DEADLY SICKENING PAIN TILL SEPARATED INTO A FEMALE PALE   483  MILTON 3        33
     FIRST ORC WAS BORN THEN THE SHADOWY FEMALE THEN ALL LOS'S   483  MILTON 3        40
        FAMILY
     DRAWN DOWN BY ORC & THE SHADOWY FEMALE INTO GENERATION  . .    490  MILTON 10        2
     THE NATURE OF A FEMALE SPACE IS THIS IT SHRINKS THE ORGANS   490  MILTON 10        6
     O DIVINE VISION WHO DIDST CREATE THE FEMALE TO SERVE  . .    493  MILTON 12       49
     AROUND THE LAMB A FEMALE TABERNACLE WOVEN IN CATHEDRON'S    494  MILTON 13       26
        LOOMS
     A MOURNFUL FORM DOUBLE HERMAPHRODITIC MALE & FEMALE  . . .    496  MILTON 14       37
     IN CONFLICT WITH THOSE FEMALE FORMS WHICH IN BLOOD     498  MILTON 17        7
        & JEALOUSY
     THE SHADOWY FEMALE SEEING MILTON HOWLD IN HER LAMENTATION   499  MILTON 18        2
     AND THUS THE SHADOWY FEMALE HOWLS IN ARTICULATE HOWLINGS   499  MILTON 18        4
     FEMALE & LOVELY THAT CANNOT CONSUME IN MAN'S CONSUMMATION   499  MILTON 18       29
     WHEN WILT THOU PUT ON THE FEMALE FORM AS IN TIMES OF OLD   499  MILTON 18       34
     IN FEMALE BEAUTY SHINING IN THE UNFORMD VOID & ORC IN VAIN   500  MILTON 18       44
     THUS DARKEND THE SHADOWY FEMALE TENFOLD & ORC TENFOLD  . .    500  MILTON 18       46
     THE SHADOWY FEMALE SHUDDERS THRO HEAVEN IN TORMENT     506  MILTON 22       36
        INEXPRESSIBLE
     BEHOLD MILTON DESCENDED TO REDEEM THE FEMALE SHADE  . . .    522  MILTON 33       11
     WHEN THE SIXFOLD FEMALE PERCIEVES THAT MILTON ANNIHILATES   522  MILTON 33       14
```

	PAGE	TITLE	LINE

FEMALE   (CONTINUED)

HER ALSO INTIRELY ABSTRACTING HIMSELF FROM FEMALE LOVES	522 MILTON 33		16
AND THEN & THEN ALONE BEGINS THE HAPPY FEMALE JOY . . .	522 MILTON 33		19
SWEET FEMALE FORMS WINGED OR FLOATING IN THE AIR SPONTANEOUS	524 MILTON 34		11
O DREADFUL LOOM OF DEATH O PITEOUS FEMALE FORMS COMPELLD	525 MILTON 35		7
LARK MET THE FEMALE OLOLON DESCENDING INTO MY GARDEN . .	527 MILTON 36		10
THE ENEMIES OF HUMANITY EXCEPT IN A FEMALE FORM	527 MILTON 36		15
AND AS ONE FEMALE OLOLON AND ALL ITS MIGHTY HOSTS . . .	527 MILTON 36		16
A MALE WITHIN A FEMALE HID AS IN AN ARK & CURTAINS . . .	528 MILTON 37		40
A FEMALE HIDDEN IN A MALE RELIGION HIDDEN IN WAR . . .	532 MILTON 40		20
IS THIS OUR (FEMININE) PORTION THE SIX-FOLD MILTONIC FEMALE	533 MILTON 41		30
THE PRIORESS FOLLOWS THESE WITH HER FEMALE CHAPLAIN . . .	568B DESC CAT 3		PROSE
WAS IN THE WARS OF EDEN DIVIDED INTO MALE AND FEMALE . .	578A DESC CAT 5		PROSE
FALLING INTO THE ABYSS SIN IS ALSO REPRESENTED AS A FEMALE	606C V LAST JUDG/N		PROSE
SOMETIMES IN THE ARMS OF A FEMALE [THEY] THIS REPRESENTED THE CHURCH	607C V LAST JUDG/N		*PROSE
A MALE & FEMALE CHAIND [TO] TOGETHER BY THE FEET	607D V LAST JUDG/N		*PROSE
THIS ETERNAL FEMALE & TREMBLE AT WHAT OTHERS FEAR NOT .	609B V LAST JUDG/N		PROSE
THIS STATE APPEARS LIKE A FEMALE CROWND WITH STARS . . .	610A V LAST JUDG/N		PROSE
A FEMALE DESCENDS TO MEET HER LOVER OR HUSBAND	610D V LAST JUDG/N		PROSE
SETH IS MALE & FEMALE IN A HIGHER STATE OF HAPPINESS . .	611C V LAST JUDG/N		PROSE
A MALE & FEMALE WITH NUMEROUS CHILDREN THESE	611D V LAST JUDG/N		PROSE
BETWEEN SETH & THESE A FEMALE FIGURE [WITH THE BACK TURND]	611D V LAST JUDG/N		PROSE
THREE FEMALE FIGURES CROWND WITH GARLANDS REPRESENT . .	611D V LAST JUDG/N		PROSE
IN ETERNITY AS A FEMALE WILL	613D V LAST JUDG/N		*PROSE
A MALE & A FEMALE TIME IS A MAN	614D V LAST JUDG/N		PROSE
DIVIDED INTO MALE AND FEMALE FORMS TIME AFTER TIME . . .	623 JERUSALEM 5		32
THE MALE IS A FURNACE OF BERYLL THE FEMALE IS A GOLDEN LOOM	623 JERUSALEM 5		34
DIVIDING AND UNITING INTO MANY FEMALE FORMS JERUSALEM . .	642 JERUSALEM 19		45
IN BEULAH THE FEMALE LETS DOWN HER BEAUTIFUL TABERNACLE	656 JERUSALEM 30		34
O ALBION WHY WILT THOU CREATE A FEMALE WILL	661 JERUSALEM 34		31
IS THIS THE FEMALE WILL O YE LOVELY DAUGHTERS OF ALBION TO	661 JERUSALEM 34		39
AND THE TWELVE FEMALE EMANATIONS FLED WITH THEM AGONIZING	663 JERUSALEM 36		20
CONCENTER IN ONE FEMALE FORM AN AGED PENSIVE WOMAN . .	678 JERUSALEM 48		28
FEMALE AND LOVELY STRUGGLING TO PUT OFF THE HUMAN FORM .	678 JERUSALEM 48		49
A TENT & TABERNACLE OF MUTUAL FORGIVENESS MALE & FEMALE CLOTHINGS	684 JERUSALEM 54		4
THE CROSS O ALBION WHY DIDST THOU A FEMALE WILL CREATE .	688 JERUSALEM 56		43
AROUND IN THE CLOUDS OF THE FEMALE ON ALBION'S CLIFFS OF THE DEAD	697 JERUSALEM 63		22
HOW CAN THE FEMALE BE CHASTE O THOU STUPID DRUID CRIED LOS	697 JERUSALEM 63		26
THYSELF FEMALE A MALE A BREEDER OF SEED A SON & HUSBAND & LO	698 JERUSALEM 64		13
A DOUBLE FEMALE AND THEY DREW OUT FROM THE ROCKY STONES	704 JERUSALEM 67		3
FIBRES OF LIFE TO WEAVE FOR EVERY FEMALE IS A GOLDEN LOOM	704 JERUSALEM 67		4
INTO A FEMALE TO THE WOVEN MALE IN OPAKE HARDNESS . . .	704 JERUSALEM 67		10
BECAME A RAVENING EATING CANCER GROWING IN THE FEMALE .	707 JERUSALEM 69		2
WHERE EVERY FEMALE DELIGHTS TO GIVE HER MAIDEN TO HER HUSBAND	707 JERUSALEM 69		15
THE FEMALE SEARCHES SEA & LAND FOR GRATIFICATIONS TO THE	707 JERUSALEM 69		16
FROM MALE & FEMALE LOVES IN BEULAH & THEIR JEALOUSIES . .	708 JERUSALEM 69		29
BUT NO ONE CAN CONSUMMATE FEMALE BLISS IN LOS'S WORLD WITHOUT	708 JERUSALEM 69		30
HENCE THE INFERNAL VEIL GROWS IN THE DISOBEDIENT FEMALE	708 JERUSALEM 69		38
OVER HER BEAUTIFUL FEMALE FEATURES SOFT FLOURISHING IN BEAUTY	709 JERUSALEM 70		23
PELEG REU SERUG NAHOR TERAH THESE ARE THE FEMALE MALES .	716 JERUSALEM 75		14
A MALE WITHIN A FEMALE HID AS IN AN ARK & CURTAINS . . .	716 JERUSALEM 75		15
THE FEMALE HID WITHIN A MALE THUS RAHAB IS REVEALD . . .	716 JERUSALEM 75		18
CLIFFS DIVIDING THEM INTO MALE & FEMALE FORMS IN HIS FURNACES	719 JERUSALEM 78		7
ESPECIALLY TO THE FEMALE	724 IN HEAVEN/J		3
SHE SEPARATED STOOD BEFORE HIM A LOVELY FEMALE WEEPING .	732 JERUSALEM 86		57
WHICH STAND BOTH MALE & FEMALE AT THE GATES OF EACH HUMANITY	733 JERUSALEM 88		11
A TRIPLE FEMALE TABERNACLE FOR MORAL LAW I WEAVE . . .	733 JERUSALEM 88		19
THAT HE WHO LOVES JESUS MAY LOATHE TERRIFIED FEMALE LOVE	733 JERUSALEM 88		20
TILL GOD HIMSELF BECOME A MALE SUBSERVIENT TO THE FEMALE	733 JERUSALEM 88		21
WHILE YOU ARE UNDER THE DOMINION OF A JEALOUS FEMALE . .	734 JERUSALEM 88		41
EASTWARD INTO HER OWN CENTER CREATING THE FEMALE WOMB .	734 JERUSALEM 88		52
A DOUBLE FEMALE NOW APPEARD WITHIN THE TABERNACLE . . .	735 JERUSALEM 89		52
FOR THE MALE IS A FURNACE OF BERYLL THE FEMALE IS A GOLDEN LOOM	736 JERUSALEM 90		27
HE DIVIDES INTO MALE & FEMALE & WHEN THE MALE & FEMALE	737 JERUSALEM 90		53
THEN THOU WILT CREATE ANOTHER FEMALE ACCORDING TO THY WILL	739 JERUSALEM 92		12
UPON THE WHITE ROCK ENGLAND A FEMALE SHADOW AS DEADLY DAMPS	741 JERUSALEM 94		7
AND THE BOW IS A MALE & FEMALE & THE QUIVER OF THE ARROWS OF LOVE	744 JERUSALEM 97		12
AND THE HAND OF MAN GRASPS FIRM BETWEEN THE MALE & FEMALE LOVES	744 JERUSALEM 97		15
WHAT ARE THESE ALAS THE FEMALE MARTYR	765D FOR SEXES/GP		TITLE
THE FEMALE FROM HIS DARKNESS ROSE	770 OF GATES/GP		2
SOME FIND A FEMALE GARMENT THERE	771 OF GATES/GP		21
HE REPENTED THAT HE HAD MADE ADAM OF THE FEMALE THE ADAMAH	776C INSC LAOCOON		PROSE
("NEITHER DISCOVERING NOT HIDING HIMSELF") A FEMALE GOD	788C ANNO THORNTON		MARG
IN SOFT FEMALE CHARMS	805 TO BUTTS/L		37
FEMALE HEAD HE HAS PROMISED TO WRITE A LIST OF ALL THAT HE	831A LETTER 31		PROSE
OF A FEMALE FIGURE WITH A SERPENT IN ONE HAND & A TORCH IN THE	839C LETTER 38		PROSE
CHAPTER II THE NATURAL MAN DIVIDED INTO MALE & FEMALE &	SUPP ILLUS GENESIS		*TITLE

	PAGE	TITLE	LINE

FEMALE-MALE
   THE FEMALE-MALE & THE MALE-FEMALE SELF-DIVIDING STOOD . . 501 MILTON 19   33
FEMALE-MALES
   PELEG REU SERUG NAHOR TERAH THESE ARE THE FEMALE-MALES . 528 MILTON 37   39
FEMALE'S
   FEMALE'S LIMBS IN HIS ABSENCE & HER DAUGHTERS OFT UPON . 285 FOUR ZOAS 2   189
   DESCENDING ON THE SHADOWY FEMALE'S CLOUDS IN SPECTROUS   340 FOUR ZOAS 7B   299
      TERROR
   UNTO ULRO'S NIGHT TEMPTED BY THE SHADOWY FEMALE'S SWEET   341 FOUR ZOAS 8   25
   OF URIZEN & THARMAS & FROM THE SHADOWY FEMALE'S CLOUDS . 342 FOUR ZOAS 8   57
   IN THE SHADOWY FEMALE'S BOSOM JEALOUS HER DARKNESS GREW   500 MILTON 18   42
FEMALES   SEE MALE-FEMALES
   THE FEMALES OF OUR HUMAN NATURES . . . . 56 HAIL MATRIM/IM   8
   LEAVING THE FEMALES NAKED AND GLOWING WITH THE LUSTS OF   202 AMERICA 15   22
      YOUTH
   IN [BEULAH] EDEN FEMALES SLEEP THE WINTER IN SOFT SILKEN   266 FOUR ZOAS 1   64
      VEILS
   SHE DRAVE THE FEMALES ALL AWAY FROM LOS . . . . 271 FOUR ZOAS 1   243
   [IF THOU DRIVST ALL THE [MALES] FEMALES AWAY . . . . . . 272 FOUR ZOAS 1 * 276
   AND SHE DRAVE ALL THE FEMALES FROM HIM AWAY . . . . . 285 FOUR ZOAS 2   210
   OVER THEIR VICTIMS HEAR YE THE SONG OF THE FEMALES   348 FOUR ZOAS 8   297
      OF AMALEK
   THIS IS CAUGHT BY FEMALES BRIGHT . . . . 432 AUGURIES   69
   WHILE THE FEMALES PREPARE THE VICTIMS THE MALES AT FURNACES   484 MILTON 5   15
   LIKE FEMALES OF SWEET BEAUTY TO GUARD ROUND HIM & TO FEED   496 MILTON 15   14
   IN THOSE THREE FEMALES WHOM HIS WIVES . . . . . . 498 MILTON 17   1
   WHICH WAS ON EARTH BORN TO CORRUPTION & THE SIX FEMALES   498 MILTON 17   15
   RENT THE IMMORTAL FEMALES LIMB FROM LIMB & JOINT FROM   500 MILTON 18   49
      JOINT
   THESE LOVELY FEMALES FORM SWEET NIGHT AND SILENCE   507 MILTON 23   39
      AND SECRET
   THAT THE FEMALES HAD WOVEN FOR THEM . . . . 522 MILTON 32   43
   WITHIN IT SIT FIVE FEMALES & THE NAMELESS SHADOWY MOTHER   524 MILTON 34   27
   THE FEMALES BEHIND THEM REPRESENT . . . . 608D V LAST JUDG/N   PROSE
   THE FEMALES BELONGING TO SUCH STATES WHO ARE . . . . 608D V LAST JUDG/N   PROSE
   INTO THE AIR AMONG THESE ARE THREE FEMALES . . . . . 610A V LAST JUDG/N   PROSE
   IN SEAS OF SORROW LOS ALSO VIEWS THE FOUR FEMALES . . 634 JERUSALEM 14   9
   YOUR FIRST BORN OF SEVEN YEARS OLD BE THEY MALES OR FEMALES   706 JERUSALEM 68   31
   LUTHER THESE SEVEN ARE THE MALE FEMALES THE DRAGON FORMS   716 JERUSALEM 75   17
   AS A BEAUTIFUL VEIL SO THESE FEMALES SHALL FOLD & UNFOLD   728 JERUSALEM 83   45
FEMALES'
   OR IS IT BECAUSE SECRESY GAINS [FEMININE] FEMALES' LOUD   171 TO NOBODADDY/N   9
      APPLAUSE
FEMALITY'S
   WHEN WE ARE AT MR FEMALITY'S DO YOU SNAP & TAKE ME UP . 63A ISLAND MOON 11   PROSE
FEMININE
   OR IS IT BECAUSE SECRESY GAINS [FEMININE] FEMALES' LOUD   171 TO NOBODADDY/N   9
      APPLAUSE
   NAMD BEULAH A SOFT MOONY UNIVERSE FEMININE LOVELY   . . . 266 FOUR ZOAS 1   95
   BUT THEY WENT ON IN SILENT HOPE & FEMININE REPOSE   . . . 270 FOUR ZOAS 1   231
   HIS SHADOWY FEMININE SEMBLANCE HERE REPOSD ON A [BRIGHT]   284 FOUR ZOAS 2 * 181
      WHITE COUCH
   SHALL THE FEMININE INDOLENT BLISS THE INDULGENT SELF OF   295 FOUR ZOAS 3   114
      WEARINESS
   SUCH WERE THE WORDS OF BEULAH OF THE FEMININE EMANATION   304 FOUR ZOAS 4   263
   A FALSE FEMININE COUNTERPART LOVELY OF DELUSIVE BEAUTY . 348 FOUR ZOAS 8 * 278
   DIVIDING & UNITING IN DELUSIVE FEMININE POMP QUESTIONING   350 FOUR ZOAS 8 * 346
      HIM
   IN A FEMININE DELUSION OF FALSE PRIDE SELF-DECIEVD   . . 492 MILTON 11   26
   AND KEPT ONLY THE FEMININE AWAKE HENCE ROSE HIS SOFT . . 492 MILTON 12   6
   BECOME IN THEIR (FEMININE) PORTIONS THE CAUSES & PROMOTERS   532 MILTON 40   10
   IS THIS OUR (FEMININE) PORTION THE SIX-FOLD MILTONIC FEMALE   533 MILTON 41   30
   BLASPHEMOUS SONS OF FEMININE DELUSION GOD IN THE DREARY   646 JERUSALEM 23   29
      VOID
   HAD BROUGHT HUMANITY INTO A FEMININE TABERNACLE . . 652B JERUSALEM 27   PROSE
   RENDING THE FIBRES OF BROTHERHOOD & IN FEMININE ALLEGORIES   656 JERUSALEM 30 * 18
   DIVIDING THE MASCULINE & FEMININE FOR THE COMINGLING . . 690 JERUSALEM 58   19
   OVER ALBION'S MOUNTAINS A FEMININE INDEFINITE CRUEL   701 JERUSALEM 65   67
      DELUSION
   FROZEN SONS OF THE FEMININE TABERNACLE OF BACON NEWTON   702 JERUSALEM 66   14
      & LOCKE
   SUCH ARE THE FEMININE & MASCULINE WHEN SEPARATED FROM MAN   704 JERUSALEM 67   14
   THE FEMININE & MASCULINE SHADOWS SOFT MILD & EVER VARYING   707 JERUSALEM 68   69
   SAT DEEP WITHIN HIM HID HIS FEMININE POWER UNREVEALD . . 709 JERUSALEM 70   18
   . . . A THREE-FOLD WONDER FEMININE MOST BEAUTIFUL   709 JERUSALEM 70   20
      THREE-FOLD
   I SEE A FEMININE FORM ARISE FROM THE FOUR TERRIBLE ZOAS   715 JERUSALEM 74   52
   AND ON HIS ANVILS LEST THEY DESTROY THE FEMININE AFFECTIONS   719 JERUSALEM 78   8
   THY MASCULINE FROM THY FEMININE HARDENING AGAINST   721 JERUSALEM 79   71
      THE HEAVENS
   WHERE THE MASCULINE & FEMININE ARE NURSD INTO YOUTH   721 JERUSALEM 79   76
      & MAIDEN
   HE CALLD IT DIVINE ANALOGY FOR IN BEULAH THE FEMININE . 730 JERUSALEM 85   7
   THE FEMININE SEPARATES FROM THE MASCULINE & BOTH FROM MAN   736 JERUSALEM 90   1
   WITH THE FEMININE BUT THE SUBLIME IS SHUT OUT FROM THE   736 JERUSALEM 90   11
      PATHOS
FEN
   FEARS THE SMALL FIRE THAT PLAYS ABOUT THE FEN . . . . . 24 EDW THIRD/PS 3   117
   THE FEARFUL CRANE SPRINGS FROM THE SPLASHY FEN . . . . 24 EDW THIRD/PS 3   125
   THE LITTLE BOY LOST IN THE LONELY FEN . . . . . . 121 LIT BOY FND/SI   1
   NOR THE PRIEST FOR PESTILENCE FROM THE FEN . . . . . 247 SONG OF LOS 6   10

	PAGE	TITLE	LINE

FENCE
    AS THE WINGD EAGLE SCORNS THE TOWRY FENCE . . . . . . 15 IMIT SPEN/PS 37
FENCES
    HARROW BURN ALL THESE CORN FIELDS THROW DOWN ALL THESE 274 FOUR ZOAS 1 388
        FENCES
FENELON
    TOWARDS BEULAH IS TO THE SOUTH FENELON GUION TERESA . . . 712 JERUSALEM 72 50
FENS
    WADING THRO FENS AMONG THE SLIMY WEEDS MAKING LAMENTATIONS 338 FOUR ZOAS 7B 225
FERMANAGH
    DONNEGAL ANTRIM TYRONE FERMANAGH ARMAGH LONDONDERRY . . . 711 JERUSALEM 72 26
FERTILE
    . . . STRETCH OUT HIS CROOKD SICKLE OER FERTILE FRANCE . . 138 FRENCH REVOLTN 91
FERVENT
    HE WAS SO FERVENT . . . . 57 TO BE OR/IM 18
    AND HEARD THE SPECTRE BITTERLY SHE WEPT EMBRACING FERVENT 327 FOUR ZOAS 7 312
FERVENTLY
    KING DAVID DESIRED SO FERVENTLY & INVOKES SO PATHETICLY 153D MARRIAGE HH 12 PROSE
FERVID
    THY VOICE WHEN NOON UPON THY FERVID CAR . . . . . 2 TO SUMMER/PS 8
    . . . & FLAMES ROLLD ROUND THEIR FERVID FEET . . . 294 FOUR ZOAS 3 96
    IN JEALOUS FEARS & FURY & RAGE & FLAMES ROLL ROUND THEIR 655 JERUSALEM 29 75
        FERVID FEET
FERVOR
    FERVOR MILD SPOKE THRO THE WESTERN PORCH IN SOFT GENTLE 675 JERUSALEM 45 2
        TEARS
FESTAL
    A FESTAL BOARD THE BARD SINGING OWEN'S PRAISE . . . . SUPP ILLUS GRAY *TITLE
FESTERING
    WILL YOU SEEK PLEASURE FROM THE FESTERING WOUND OR MARRY 354 FOUR ZOAS 8 497
        FOR A WIFE
    GLITTERING WITH FESTERING VENOMS BRIGHT . . . . . . 755 EV GOSPEL(E)/N 84
FETCH
    AND SO I'LL KEEP HIM FETCH YOUR FATHER FETCH FORTH 105 TIRIEL 4 62
        MYRATANA
    . . . WHY DO YOU STAND FETCH HITHER TIRIEL . . . 105 TIRIEL 4 64
    FETCH HITHER MYRATANA & DELIGHT YOURSELVES WITH SCOFFS . . 105 TIRIEL 4 65
    [THEN IJIM SAID LOTHO CLITHYMA MAKUTH FETCH YOUR FATHER] 105 TIRIEL 4 73
    [COULD FETCH IT FROM THE FURNACE DEEP] . . . . . . 172 THE TYGER/N 1 13
    GO NOAH FETCH THE GIRDLE OF STRONG BRASS [PRE] HEAT IT 349 FOUR ZOAS 8 312
        RED HOT
    . . . FROM ENGLAND [& POLITENESS] [WAS SENT] WE FETCH] 541 FLORENTINE/N * 7
    THE FLORENTINES CALL IT AN ENGLISH FETCH . . . . . 542 FLORENTINE/N 15
    GO NOAH FETCH THE GIRDLE OF STRONG BRASS HEAT IT RED-HOT 705 JERUSALEM 67 59
FETCHD
    I HAD OF THE LETTER OR OF THE DRAWING I HAVE FETCHD THE 832B LETTER 32 PROSE
FETTER
    SHALT GATHER THEM FROM OUT THEIR GRAVES & PUT THY FETTER 334 FOUR ZOAS 7B 70
        ON THEM
    OIL BECAME A FETTER TO GENIUS AND A DUNGEON TO ART BUT ONE 566C DESC CAT 2 PROSE
FETTERD
    THEIR MINDS ARE FETTERD THEN HOW CAN THEY BE FREE . . . 18 EDW THIRD/PS 1 14
    POETRY FETTERD FETTERS THE HUMAN RACE . . . . 621D JERUSALEM 3 PROSE
FETTERS
    . . . AND THE TRIPLE FORGD FETTERS OF TIMES WERE UNLOOSD 137 FRENCH REVOLTN 62
    NOTE THE REASON MILTON WROTE IN FETTERS . . . . 150B MARRIAGE HH 5 PROSE
    [AND CHAINS & FETTERS EVERY MIND] . . . . 175 HOW TO KNOW/N * 9
    AND FORGES FETTERS FOR THE MIND . . . . 175 HOW TO KNOW/N 10
    RUN FROM THEIR FETTERS REDDENING & IN LONG DRAWN ARCHES 202 AMERICA 15 24
        SITTING
    LIKE FETTERS OF ICE SHRINKING TOGETHER . . . . 228 URIZEN 10 26
    LOS BEAT ON HIS FETTERS OF IRON . . . . 228 URIZEN 10 28
    GO HOWL IN VAIN SMITE SMITE HIS FETTERS SMITE O WINTRY 276 FOUR ZOAS 1 431
        HAMMERS
    IN FETTERS OF ICE SHRINKING DISORGANIZD RENT FROM ETERNITY 303 FOUR ZOAS 4 212
    LOS BEAT ON HIS FETTERS & [POURD] HEATED HIS FURNACES . . 303 FOUR ZOAS 4 213
    FETTERS OF RED HOT IRON SOME WITH CROWNS OF SERPENTS & SOME 314 FOUR ZOAS 6 104
    HE COULD NOT TAKE THEIR FETTERS OFF FOR THEY GREW FROM 315 FOUR ZOAS 6 143
        THE SOUL
    STRIKING FIERCE SPARKLES FROM THEIR BRAZEN FETTERS FIERCE 320 FOUR ZOAS 7 8
        HIS LIONS
    PULSE AFTER PULSE BEAT ON HIS FETTERS PULSE AFTER PULSE 320 FOUR ZOAS 7 21
        HIS SPIRIT
    FROM WRATH NOW WHEN I RAGE MY FETTERS BIND ME MORE . . . 323 FOUR ZOAS 7 138
    POETRY FETTERD FETTERS THE HUMAN RACE . . . . 621D JERUSALEM 3 PROSE
    O SHAME O STRONG & MIGHTY SHAME I BREAK THY BRAZEN 629 JERUSALEM 10 34
        FETTERS
    WIFE'S FEET ARE FREE FROM FETTERS O LOVELY FELPHAM PARENT 852A LETTER 50 PROSE
FEUDS
    IN THE TERRIBLE FAMILY FEUDS OF ALBION'S CITIES & VILLAGES 714 JERUSALEM 73 47
    CONTINUALLY BUILDING CONTINUALLY DESTROYING IN FAMILY 734 JERUSALEM 88 40
        FEUDS
FEVER
    SCURVY & SPOTTD FEVER . . . . 51 WHEN CORRUP/IM 22
    HE TOOK UP FEVER BY THE NECK . . . . 51 WHEN CORRUP/IM 33
    ("A STILL RABIES IS MORE DANGEROUS THAN PAROXISMS OF 68A ANNO LAVATER MARG
        FEVER") BRAVO
    THUNDERS OF DEADLY WAR THE FEVER OF THE HUMAN SOUL . . . 664 JERUSALEM 38 9
    MUST BE SO TO A MAN JUST OUT OF SO DREADFUL A FEVER I ALSO 844D LETTER 43 PROSE
FEVROUS
    THRO THE RED FEVROUS NIGHT . . . . 13 GWIN KING/PS 84

```
                                                          PAGE    TITLE          LINE
FEW
    THE SOUND IS FORCD THE NOTES ARE FEW . . . . . . . .   11  TO MUSES/PS          16
    YOU YET ARE WHOLE BUT AFTER A FEW MORE  . . . . . . .   23  EDW THIRD/PS 3       63
    WHEN THE FEW INHABITANTS CLING TREMBLING TOGETHER   . .  36B COUCH DEATH/PS    PROSE
    IF THE MANY BECOME THE SAME AS THE FEW WHEN POSSESSD  . . 97D NAT RELIGION 2   PROSE
    OF COLOURS TWELVE FEW KNOWN ON EARTH GIVE LIGHT IN THE   241 EUROPE 10            9
       OPAKE
    DEEP IN THE SOUTH GUARDED BY A FEW SOLITARY STARS    . . . 372 FOUR ZOAS 9      581
    A LIE FEW BELIEVE IT IS A NEW BIRTH . . . . . . . . .   403C ANNO BACON        MARG
    HE WHO HAS FEW THINGS TO DESIRE CANNOT HAVE MANY TO FEAR   405B ANNO BACON     MARG
    WHAT IS FORTUNE BUT AN OUTWARD ACCIDENT FOR A FEW YEARS    409B ANNO BACON     MARG
    BUT SUCH A HIRED KNAVE CARES NOT FOR THE FEW  . . . . .   469D ANNO REYNOLDS   MARG
    WHICH FEW DARE UNBAR BECAUSE DREAD OG & ANAK GUARD THE   502 MILTON 20           35
       GATES
    "FIT AUDIENCE FIND THO FEW" MILTON  . . . . . . . . . .   560C EXHIBITION ADV  PROSE
    TO SAY A FEW WORDS  . . . . . . . . . . . . . . . . .   595A PUB ADDRESS/N     PROSE
    [HOGARTH'S TIME WE HAVE HAD VERY FEW EFFORTS            595C PUB ADDRESS/N     PROSE
       OF ORIGINALITY]
    OR GO INTO A MODERN EXHIBITON WITH A VERY FEW EXCEPTIONS   599B PUB ADDRESS/N  PROSE
    OR NEAR SO GOOD TILL A FEW YEARS AGO . . . . . . . . .   602C PUB ADDRESS/N    PROSE
    PRETENDERS FALL SOME PEOPLE & NOT A FEW ARTISTS HAVE   . 612C V LAST JUDG/N    PROSE
    HOW FEW PRODUCE THEM IN SUCH PERFECTION                 791B LETTER 3          PROSE
    EXTRAORDINARY THAT LONDON IN SO FEW YEARS FROM A CITY OF   798B LETTER 10      PROSE
    FEW FRIENDS I HAVE DARED TO VISIT IN MY STUPID MELANCHOLY  798C LETTER 10      PROSE
    YOU A FEW LINES WHICH I HOPE YOU WILL EXCUSE AND AS THE   799A LETTER 11       PROSE
       TIME
    MUSTER A FEW IN COLOURS AND SOME IN BLACK WHICH I HOPE WILL  807A LETTER 17    PROSE
    BEGGING THE FAVOR OF A FEW LINES TO INFORM HIM HOW YOU  . 829C LETTER 30       PROSE
    OF CHARACTER WHICH FEW HAVE HE IS THE MAN WHO APPLIED TO   841C LETTER 41      PROSE
    PROOFS OF MY PLATES WILL WAIT ON YOU IN A FEW DAYS  . . . 853A LETTER 51       PPOSE
    HOPE IN A FEW DAYS TO SEND PROOFS OF PLATES WHICH   . . . 853A LETTER 51      *PROSE
    FROM A FEW LUCKY OR WELL ADVISED TOUCHES I CANNOT OMIT  . 853C LETTER 52       PROSE
    CELESTIAL CITY I ALSO HAVE BUT A FEW MORE MOUNTAINS TO PASS  854C LETTER 53    PROSE
    HOPE THAT THE PUBLIC WILL APPROVE OF MY RATHER GIVING FEW   860C LETTER 56     PROSE
    A VERY FEW TOUCHES WILL FINISH THE SHIPWRECK THOSE FEW I   863C LETTER 60      PROSE
    THE FEW I HAVE PRINTED & SOLD ARE SUFFICIENT TO HAVE GAINED  867C LETTER 66    PROSE
    I HOPE A FEW MORE DAYS WILL BRING US TO A CONCLUSION  . .  870B LETTER 71      PROSE
    ON MY BONES & SINEWS MUSCLE I HAVE NONE BUT A FEW DAYS  . . 875A LETTER 80     PROSE
FIBRE
    WHY WILT THOU EXAMINE EVERY LITTLE FIBRE OF MY SOUL  . . .  265 FOUR ZOAS 1      47
    ITS TOPMOST [BRANCHES] BOUGHS SHOOTING A [STEM] FIBRE . . .  328 FOUR ZOAS 7    334
    A FIBRE FROM THE BRAIN DOES TEAR  . . . . . . . . . .   431 AUGURIES             14
    SHE NUMBERS WITH HER FINGERS EVERY FIBRE ERE IT GROW   .   501 MILTON 19         49
    NOT DARING TO TOUCH ONE FIBRE HE HOWLD ROUND UPON THE SEA   529 MILTON 38        14
    AND HAND & HYLE ROOTED INTO JERUSALEM BY A FIBRE  . . . .  635 JERUSALEM 15       1
    WHY WILT THOU NUMBER EVERY LITTLE FIBRE OF MY SOUL  . . .  645 JERUSALEM 22       20
    DRAWING OUT FIBRE BY FIBRE RETURNING TO ALBION'S TREE  . .  723 JERUSALEM 80      61
    MOUNTAINOUS WALES INTO THE LOOM OF CATHEDRON FIBRE BY FIBRE   723 JERUSALEM 80    63
FIBRES
    FIBRES OF BLOOD MILK AND TEARS  . . . . . . . . . . .   231 URIZEN 18             4
    UPFOLDING HIS FIBRES TOGETHER . . . . . . . . . . . .   259 BOOK OF LOS 5        18
    LAYING HER SEED UPON THE FIBRES SOON TO ISSUE FORTH   . .   292 FOUR ZOAS 3      21
    O HOW LOS HOWLD AT THE RENDING ASUNDER ALL THE FIBRES RENT   299 FOUR ZOAS 4     59
    SPASMS SIEZD HIS MUSCULAR FIBRES . . . . . . . . . . .   305 FOUR ZOAS 4        288
    AND ENITHARMON SHRUNK UP ALL THEIR FIBRES WITHRING BENEATH   305 FOUR ZOAS 5      8
    FIBRES HAD FROM THE CHAIN OF JEALOUSY INWOVE THEMSELVES   309 FOUR ZOAS 5       157
    NOR UNROOT THE INFERNAL FIBRES FROM THEIR ROCKY BED  . .   309 FOUR ZOAS 5      163
    OF ORC ENTERING WITH FIBRES BECAME ONE WITH HIM A LIVING   309 FOUR ZOAS 5    * 169
       CHAIN
    THESE FIBRES OF THINE EYES THAT USED TO WANDER IN DISTANT   348 FOUR ZOAS 8     301
       HEAVENS
    MOVING IN ROOT-LIKE FIBRES TREMBLING IN FEAR UPON THE EARTH   353 FOUR ZOAS 8  * 476
    SHE TIES THE KNOT OF NERVOUS FIBRES INTO A WHITE BRAIN  . .  501 MILTON 19       55
    OF LIVING FIBRES DOWN INTO THE SEA OF TIME & SPACE GROWING   524 MILTON 34       25
    THAT MILTON'S SHADOW HEARD & CONDENSING ALL HIS FIBRES  . .  527 MILTON 37        6
    AND MILTON COLLECTING ALL HIS FIBRES INTO IMPREGNABLE   529 MILTON 38             5
       STRENGTH
    FIBRES OF LOVE FROM MAN TO MAN THRO ALBION'S PLEASANT LAND   622 JERUSALEM 4      8
    STAND ROUND HIM CUTTING THE FIBRES FROM ALBION'S HILLS  . .  636 JERUSALEM 15    23
    RENDING THE FIBRES OF BROTHERHOOD & IN FEMININE ALLEGORIES   656 JERUSALEM 30  * 18
    OF LONDON BUT THE INTERIORS OF ALBION'S FIBRES & NERVES   658 JERUSALEM 32        4
       WERE HIDDEN
    LUVAH THEIR LIPS TREMBLE THEIR MUSCULAR FIBRES ARE CRAMPD   701 JERUSALEM 65     78
       & SMITTEN
    FIBRES OF LIFE TO WEAVE FOR EVERY FEMALE IS A GOLDEN LOOM   704 JERUSALEM 67      4
    THEY CUT THE FIBRES FROM THE ROCKS GROANING IN PAIN THEY   704 JERUSALEM 67      11
       WEAVE
    SHOOTING OUT FIBRES ROUND THE EARTH THRO GAUL & ITALY  . .  704 JERUSALEM 67     38
    THESE FIBRES OF THINE EYES THAT USED TO BEAM IN DISTANT   705 JERUSALEM 67       47
       HEAVENS
    CUT THE FIBRES OF REUBEN HOW HE ROLLD APART & TOOK ROOT   715 JERUSALEM 74       42
    SHEWD HER THE FIBRES OF HER BELOVED TO AMELIORATE   . . .   726 JERUSALEM 82     61
    HIS EMANATION SEPARATES IN MILKY FIBRES AGONIZING   . . .  731 JERUSALEM 86      39
    AMONG THE GOLDEN LOOMS OF CATHEDRON SENDING FIBRES OF LOVE   731 JERUSALEM 86    40
    FILLING WITH FIBRES FROM HIS LOINS WHICH REDDEND       732 JERUSALEM 86          51
       WITH DESIRE
    OF BEAUTY & PERFECTION MY WILD FIBRES SHOOT IN VEINS  . .   732 JERUSALEM 87      5
    THE SMALL FIBRES AS THEY SHOOT AROUND ME DRAW OUT IN PITY   732 JERUSALEM 87      8
    ENITHARMON ANSWERD NO I WILL SIEZE THY FIBRES & WEAVE  . .  732 JERUSALEM 87     12
    FROM HER THESE FIBRES SHOOT TO SHUT ME IN A GRAVE  . . .   733 JERUSALEM 87      23
    WHILE THOU MY EMANATION REFUSEST MY FIBRES OF DOMINION  . .  733 JERUSALEM 88    13
    WHEN SOULS MINGLE & JOIN THRO ALL THE FIBRES OF BROTHERHOOD   733 JERUSALEM 88   14
```

FIBRES   (CONTINUED)
    FIBRES OF LOS SENDING THEM OVER THE OCEAN EASTWARD INTO   733 JERUSALEM 88   25
    FLOWD INTO THE ACHING FIBRES OF LOS YET CONTENDING AGAINST   733 JERUSALEM 88   29
      HIM
    IN PRIDE (SENDING) HIS FIBRES OVER TO HER OBJECTS   733 JERUSALEM 88   30
      OF JEALOUSY
    TO THE EMBRACE OF LOVE & TO THE MINGLING OF SOFT FIBRES   736 JERUSALEM 90   9
    BOWEN & CONWENNA STOOD ON SKIDDAW CUTTING THE FIBRES   .   .   736 JERUSALEM 90   14
    AS THEY CUT THE FIBRES FROM THE RIVERS HE SEARS THEM WITH   736 JERUSALEM 90   19
      HOT
    FIBRES OF LIFE OUT FROM THE BONES INTO HER GOLDEN LOOM   .   . 736 JERUSALEM 90   22
    OPAKENESS OF NERVOUS FIBRES SUCH WAS THE VARIATION OF TIME   746 JERUSALEM 98   37
      & SPACE
    FIBRES OF A DEADLY NIGHT .   .   .   . 753 EV GOSPEL(D)/N   96
FIBROUS
    SHE SAW THE COUCHES OF THE DEAD & WHERE THE FIBROUS ROOTS   130 BOOK OF THEL 6   3
    FIBROUS WRITHING UPON THE WINDS   .   .   .   . 231 URIZEN 18   3
    AN IMMENSE FIBROUS FORM STRETCHING OUT .   .   .   .   .   .   259 BOOK OF LOS 5   1
    [XXX POURD FROM FIBROUS VEINY PIPES]   .   .   .   . SUPP FOUR ZOAS 1   *
    INTO THEIR LIMBS URTHONA SHOT FORTH A VAST FIBROUS FORM   353 FOUR ZOAS 8   468
    OUTSTRETCHD HIS RIGHT HAND BRANCHING OUT IN FIBROUS   357 FOUR ZOAS 9   7
      STRENGTH
    LOS HEARD IN TERROR ENITHARMON'S WORDS IN FIBROUS STRENGTH   498 MILTON 17   34
    UPON HIS FIBROUS LEFT FOOT BLACK MOST DISMAL TO OUR EYES   506 MILTON 22   35
    NO HUMAN FORM BUT ONLY A FIBROUS VEGETATION   .   .   .   .   . 509 MILTON 24   37
    LUVAH TORE FORTH FROM ALBION'S LOINS IN FIBROUS VEINS IN   677 JERUSALEM 47   4
      RIVERS
    BUT WHEN HE TOUCHES THE FIRST FIBROUS THREAD LIKE FILMY DEW   739 JERUSALEM 92   10
FICTION
    DO WHAT YOU WILL THIS LIFE S A FICTION .   .   .   .   .   .   751 EV GOSPEL(C)/N   50
    [[ALL] THIS CORPOREAL LIFE S A] [ALL LIFE S A FICTION]   753 EV GOSPEL(D)/N *   85
    REASONING UPON ITS OWN DARK FICTION   .   .   .   . 753 EV GOSPEL(D)/N   97
    TWO HORND REASONING CLOVEN FICTION .   .   .   .   770 OF GATES/GP   11
FICTIONS
    NAMES ANCIENTLY REMEMBERD BUT NOW CONTEMND AS FICTIONS .   . 624 JERUSALEM 5   38
FIDDLE
    FIDDLE FIDDLE FIDDLE .   .   .   . 62 DR CLASH/IM   20
FIDELITY
    WITH ALL THE FIDELITY I COULD & WILL FINISH WITH EQUAL CARE 838A LETTER 37   PROSE
FIE
    FIE FIE LORD CLARENCE YOU PROCEED NOT TO BUSINESS   .   .   . 20 EDW THIRD/PS 2   62
    FALSE FRIENDS [O NO] FIE FIE .   .   .   . 556 IF MEN ACT/N   5
FIELD   SEE CORN-FIELD,CORN FIELD
    HOW SWEET I ROAMD FROM FIELD TO FIELD   .   .   .   . 6 HOW SWEET/PS   1
    EACH FIELD SEEMS EDEN AND EACH CALM RETREAT   .   .   .   .   . 9 FRESH FROM/PS   15
    OVER THE FIELD DOTH FLY .   .   .   . 13 GWIN KING/PS   80
    OR BEARST THY EGIS OER THE BURNING FIELD .   .   .   .   .   . 15 IMIT SPEN/PS   49
    WHEN CONFUSION RAGES WHEN THE FIELD IS IN A FLAME   .   .   . 18 EDW THIRD/PS 1   6
    WON BY OUR FATHERS IN MANY A GLORIOUS FIELD   .   .   .   .   . 18 EDW THIRD/PS 1   10
    FROM HIS EYES ACROSS THE FIELD I HAVE SEEN HIM .   .   .   .   22 EDW THIRD/PS 3   28
    THE ENEMY HE HAS DANCD IN THE FIELD   .   .   .   . 22 EDW THIRD/PS 3   30
    NEER SHOUTED TO THE HEAVNS NOR SHOOK THE FIELD .   .   .   .   23 EDW THIRD/PS 3   76
    HAVE GIVEN ME WHEN I HAVE SEEN THE FIELD GLOW .   .   .   .   . 23 EDW THIRD/PS 3   84
    COMMISSION TO THIS FATAL FIELD OF CRESSY .   .   .   .   .   . 26 EDW THIRD/PS 3   223
    USE MAKES THE ARMED FIELD AND NOISY WAR .   .   .   .   .   .   27 EDW THIRD/PS 3   247
    HOW TERRIBLE THEN IS THE FIELD OF DEATH .   .   .   .   .   .   30 EDW THIRD/PS 5   18
    IVE OFTEN SEEN THE BURNING FIELD OF WAR .   .   .   .   .   .   31 EDW THIRD/PS 5   39
    OR I LAY STRETCHD UPON THE FIELD OF DEATH .   .   .   .   .   . 31 EDW THIRD/PS 5   66
    WHOSE VOICES ARE THE THUNDER OF THE FIELD .   .   .   .   .   . 31 EDW THIRD/PS 6   2
    AND RISE WITH GHOSTS OVER THE WELL-FOUGHT FIELD   .   .   .   . 35 WAR SONG/PS   14
    THUS PRAYED MANOA THE AGED WOMAN WALKED INTO THE FIELD .   . 40B SAMSON/PS   PROSE
    "MY CROP OF CORN IS BUT A FIELD OF TARES"   .   .   .   .   .   . 52B ISLAND MOON 8
    .   .   .   OUR BONDS AND OUR PRISNERS SHOUT IN THE OPEN FIELD   137 FRENCH REVOLTN   74
    .   .   .   THEY SHALL CONSUME FROM THE THISTLY FIELD   140 FRENCH REVOLTN   145
    MOURNING OPPRESSED ON VILLAGE AND FIELD .   .   .   .   .   .   143 FRENCH REVOLTN   208
    .   .   .   TILL THE VILLAGE AND FIELD IS A WASTE   .   .   .   .   143 FRENCH REVOLTN   208
    .   .   .   WHEN BRAZEN CANNONS RAGE IN THE FIELD   .   .   .   .   146 FRENCH REVOLTN   262
    NOR A SOLDIER BE SEEN IN ROAD OR IN FIELD .   .   .   .   .   . 147 FRENCH REVOLTN   286
    THE SICKLE [ON] IN THE FRUITFUL FIELD   .   .   .   . 178 SWORD SUNG/N   *   2
    LET THE SLAVE GRINDING AT THE MILL RUN OUT INTO THE FIELD   198 AMERICA 6   6
    AND IN THE WITHERD FIELD WHERE THE FARMER PLOWS FOR BREAD   290 FOUR ZOAS 2   401
      IN VAIN
    TO REJOICE IN THE BLIGHT THAT COVERS HIS FIELD .   .   .   .   . 291 FOUR ZOAS 2   412
    .   .   .   & THE SOLDIER IN THE FIELD   .   .   .   .   291 FOUR ZOAS 2   415
    THE GARDENS OF WISDOM ARE BECOME A FIELD OF HORRID GRAVES   310 FOUR ZOAS 5   196
    GIVING THEM SWEET INSTRUCTIONS WHERE THE CLOUD THE RIVER   315 FOUR ZOAS 6   137
      & THE FIELD
    ALL NIGHT AMONG THE SLAIN & MOCK THE WOUNDED THAT GROAN   334 FOUR ZOAS 7B   48
      IN THE FIELD
    .   .   .   WHEN THE WOUNDED GROAN IN THE FIELD .   .   .   .   .   337 FOUR ZOAS 7B   * 190
    AND THE GRAVE MOCK & LAUGH AT THE PLOWD FIELD SAYING .   .   . 354 FOUR ZOAS 8   499
    THE FURROWD FIELD REPLIES TO THE GRAVE I HEAR HER REPLY   355 FOUR ZOAS 8   548
      TO ME
    RESHONE ACROSS THE FIELD IMMENSE WHERE ALL THE NATIONS .   . 364 FOUR ZOAS 9   293
    OF THE WIDE UNIVERSAL FIELD THEN STEPD [OUT] FORTH INTO   365 FOUR ZOAS 9   320
      THE IMMENSE
    LET THE SLAVE GRINDING AT THE MILL RUN OUT INTO THE FIELD   375 FOUR ZOAS 9   670
    O THOU PRIDE OF EVERY FIELD .   .   .   . 422 THE BIRDS/N   4
    HE WENT NOT OUT TO THE FIELD NOR FOLD   .   .   .   . 435 WILLIAM BOND   9
    "THE MOST UGLY AND NO OTHER BESIDE RETURND FROM THE BLOODY   560B EXHIBITION ADV   PROSE
      FIELD"
    CANNOT BE SURPASSED HE HAS SPENT HIS LIFE IN THE FIELD .   . 567D DESC CAT 3   PROSE

```
                                                        PAGE     TITLE          LINE
FIELD    (CONTINUED)
     THE UGLIEST MAN THESE THREE MARCHED THROUGH THE FIELD   .  .  577B DESC CAT 5     TITLE
     ARMED ROMANS STREW THE FIELD BENEATH AMONG THESE THE LAST    580C DESC CAT 5     PROSE
        OF
     WITH SIN AND SHAME CAST CAST HER INTO THE POTTER'S FIELD     640 JERUSALEM 18       32
     AND ON THE COUCH REPOSD HIS LIMBS TREMBLING FROM THE BLOODY  658 JERUSALEM 32       13
        FIELD
     NOR DARKNESS IMMINGLED WITH LIGHT ON MY FURROWD FIELD  .  .  659 JERUSALEM 33       32
     THE ARMIES OF BALAAM WEEP NO WOMEN COME TO THE FIELD   .  .  672 JERUSALEM 43       39
     .  .  .  WHEN THE WOUNDED GROAN IN THE FIELD  .  .  .  .  .  700 JERUSALEM 65       32
     AS REUBEN FOUND MANDRAKES IN THE FIELD & GAVE THEM TO HIS    740 JERUSALEM 93        8
        MOTHER
     STATUARIES PRINTERS POETS WE ARE NOT IN A FIELD OF BATTLE    847B LETTER 44       PROSE
        BUT
FIELDS      SEE CORN-FIELDS,CORN FIELDS
     .  .  .  DISPLAYD GREEN FIELDS AMONG  .  .  .  .  .  .  .  .  274 FOUR ZOAS 1      367
     TO WADE THRO FIELDS OF GORE  .  .  .  .  .  .  .  .  .  .  .  12 GWIN KING/PS       46
     MY THOUGHTS ARE ON MY GARDENS AND MY FIELDS  .  .  .  .  .  .  19 EDW THIRD/PS 2    22
     WELCOME TO THE FIELDS OF CRESSY HERE WE STOP  .  .  .  .  .  22 EDW THIRD/PS 3      44
     HERE ON THE FIELDS OF CRESSY WE ARE SETTLED  .  .  .  .  .  .  24 EDW THIRD/PS 3   111
     AND REAP HARVEST IN THE FIELDS OF CRESSY  .  .  .  .  .  .  .  24 EDW THIRD/PS 3   137
     TO BE EXALTED TO THOSE HEAVENLY FIELDS  .  .  .  .  .  .  .  .  30 EDW THIRD/PS 5    28
     THEN SHALL ENGLAND'S VERDURE SHOOT HER FIELDS SHALL SMILE     31 EDW THIRD/PS 5    57
     WHEN LO AN ANGEL FROM THE FIELDS OF LIGHT ENTERED THE HOUSE   39D SAMSON/PS       PROSE
     NOR KNEW HE WAS AN ANGEL MANOA LEFT HIS FIELDS  .  .  .  .  40A SAMSON/PS         PROSE
     TO SEE THE FIELDS SO PLEASANT & SO GAY  .  .  .  .  .  .  .  .  55 MAY MORNING/IM    2
     FAREWELL GREEN FIELDS AND HAPPY GROVES  .  .  .  .  .  .  .  .  119 NIGHT/SI          9
     THEN TURN TOWARDS PENSIVE FIELDS  .  .  .  .  .  .  .  .  .  .  139 FRENCH REVOLTN  109
     WHOSE RICH FIELDS INHERITING SPREAD THEIR OLD GLORY  .  .  .  143 FRENCH REVOLTN  204
     AND THEIR FIELDS ARE BLEAK & BARE  .  .  .  .  .  .  .  .  .  .  181 HOLY THURS/N     10
     AND THEIR FIELDS ARE BLEAK & BARE  .  .  .  .  .  .  .  .  .  .  212 HOLY THURS/SE    10
     THRO THE CLEAR CHANGING ATMOSPHERE DISPLAYD GREEN FIELDS      274 FOUR ZOAS 1      367
        AMONG
     MY CLOUDS ARE NOT THE CLOUDS OF VERDANT FIELDS & GROVES       275 FOUR ZOAS 1      392
        OF FRUIT
     I KNOW THEE NOT AS ONCE I KNEW THEE IN THOSE BLESSED FIELDS   288 FOUR ZOAS 2      325
     LEAVE ALL FUTURITY TO HIM RESUME THY FIELDS OF LIGHT   .  .   292 FOUR ZOAS 3       30
     THEY CALL THY LIONS TO THE FIELDS OF BLOOD THEY ROWZE THY     292 FOUR ZOAS 3   *   37
        TYGERS
     GOLDEN & BEAUTIFUL BUT O HOW UNLIKE THOSE SWEET FIELDS        292 FOUR ZOAS 3       39
        OF BLISS
     THAT IN ETERNAL FIELDS IN COMFORT WANDERD WITH MY FLOCKS      301 FOUR ZOAS 4      138
     SOFT TEARS & SIGHS WHERE ARE YOU COME FORTH SHOUT ON BLOODY   306 FOUR ZOAS 5       48
        FIELDS
     THE PLOW OF AGES & THE GOLDEN HARROW WADE THRO FIELDS   .  .  320 FOUR ZOAS 7       14
     SURE THOU ART BATHD IN RIVERS OF DELIGHT ON VERDANT FIELDS    321 FOUR ZOAS 7       63
     TO REUNITE IN THOSE MILD FIELDS OF HAPPY ETERNITY   .  .  .   326 FOUR ZOAS 7      270
     I WILL WALK FORTH THRO THOSE WIDE FIELDS OF ENDLESS           333 FOUR ZOAS 7B       8
        ETERNITY
     FOLLOWD HER DAUGHTERS TO THE FIELDS OF BLOOD THEY LEFT        334 FOUR ZOAS 7B      66
        ME NAKED
     ALONE & THEY REFUSD TO RETURN FROM THE FIELDS OF THE MIGHTY   334 FOUR ZOAS 7B      67
     AS ONCE IN THOSE ETERNAL FIELDS IN BROTHERHOOD & LOVE   .  .  345 FOUR ZOAS 8      159
     ONCE I WAILD DESOLATE LIKE THEE MY FALLOW FIELDS IN FEAR      354 FOUR ZOAS 8      536
     IN THOSE ETERNAL FIELDS IN CLOUDS OF MORNING STEPPING FORTH   360 FOUR ZOAS 9      125
     FROM BREATHING FIELDS SATAN FAINTED BENEATH THE ARTILLERY     484 MILTON 5      *    2
     SINCE ALBION'S DEATH & SATAN'S CUTTING-OFF FROM OUR AWFUL     510 MILTON 25         30
        FIELDS
     THE SONS OF LOS CLOTHE THEM & FEED & PROVIDE HOUSES           512 MILTON 26         30
        & FIELDS
     HORSEBACK WITH DEATH OVER THE FIELDS OF CORN  .  .  .  .  .  537 AND HIS LEGS/N     23
     [MOULD] [GROUND] FLOWERY MOULD INTO THE GREEN FIELDS OF       609D V LAST JUDG/N  *PROSE
     MULTITUDES ARE SEEN ASCENDING FROM THE GREEN FIELDS  .  .  .  610C V LAST JUDG/N  PROSE
     THE FIELDS FROM ISLINGTON TO MARYBONE  .  .  .  .  .  .  .  .  649 FIELDS FROM/J     1
     HER LITTLE-ONES RAN ON THE FIELDS  .  .  .  .  .  .  .  .  .  .  649 FIELDS FROM/J     5
     THE FIELDS OF COWS BY WILLANS FARM  .  .  .  .  .  .  .  .  .  650 FIELDS FROM/J    15
     THEY HAVE SOWN ERRORS OVER ALL HIS FRUITFUL FIELDS   .  .  .  667 JERUSALEM 40       20
     OUR PALACES AND CITIES AND HOWEVER FRUITFUL ARE OUR FIELDS    675 JERUSALEM 45       12
     FOR BEING DRIVEN FROM OUR FIELDS WHAT HAVE WE TO DO WITH      686 JERUSALEM 55        6
        THE DEAD
     WITH TREES & FIELDS FULL OF FAIRY ELVES  .  .  .  .  .  .  .  816 HAPPINESS/L        5
FIEND
     LIKE A FIEND IN A CLOUD  .  .  .  .  .  .  .  .  .  .  .  .  .  9 MAD SONG/PS        17
     STAND FROM MY PATH FOUL FIEND IS THIS THE LAST OF            103 TIRIEL 4           8
        THY DECEITS
     COME THOU DARK FIEND I DARE THY CUNNING KNOW THAT IJIM       104 TIRIEL 4          17
        SCORNS
     NO ARTFUL FIEND BUT I WILL LEAD THEE DOST THOU WANT TO GO    104 TIRIEL 4          23
     IMPUDENT FIEND SAID IJIM HOLD THY GLIB & ELOQUENT TONGUE     104 TIRIEL 4          37
     HEUXOS COME FORTH I HERE HAVE BROUGHT THE FIEND THAT         104 TIRIEL 4          43
        TROUBLES IJIM
     THOU EYELESS FIEND & YOU DISSEMBLERS IS THIS TIRIEL'S HOUSE  106 TIRIEL 4          86
     LIKE A FIEND HID IN A CLOUD  .  .  .  .  .  .  .  .  .  .  .  .  166 INFANT SORW/N     4
     [O THAT I SUCH A FIEND SHOULD BEAR]  .  .  .  .  .  .  .  .  .  177 LIT BOY LST/N    12
     LO WHAT A FIEND IS HERE SAID HE  .  .  .  .  .  .  .  .  .  .  177 LIT BOY LST/N    17
     LIKE A FIEND HID IN A CLOUD  .  .  .  .  .  .  .  .  .  .  .  .  217 INFANT SORW/SE    4
     LO WHAT A FIEND IS HERE SAID HE  .  .  .  .  .  .  .  .  .  .  218 LIT BOY LST/SE    14
     WHIRLING ABOUT IN FURIOUS CIRCLES ROUND THE IMMORTAL FIEND   240 EUROPE 4          30
     ARISE AND PLEASE THE HORRENT FIEND WITH YOUR MELODIOUS       244 EUROPE 14         27
        SONGS
     SMITE SPECTRE OF URTHONA MOCK THE FIEND WHO DREW US DOWN     276 FOUR ZOAS 1      432
     GIVING THE SPECTRE STERNEST CHARGE OVER THE HOWLING FIEND    308 FOUR ZOAS 5      112
```

687

	PAGE	TITLE	LINE

FIEND (CONTINUED)
- [ON THE IMMORTAL FIEND] UPON THE MIGHTY FIEND . . .   343 FOUR ZOAS 8   76
- A MALE WITHOUT A FEMALE COUNTERPART A HOWLING FIEND . . .   347 FOUR ZOAS 8   253
- A MIGHTY FIEND AGAINST THE DIVINE HUMANITY MUSTRING TO WAR   491 MILTON 10   11
- FALLING HEADLONG BY THE SIDE OF THEM IS A MIGHTY FIEND . .   607D V LAST JUDG/N   PROSE
- THAT FIEND WHO CARRIES THE KEY [& DRAGS] IN ONE HAND &   608B V LAST JUDG/N   PROSE
- ABOVE THE GATE A FIEND WITH WINGS [DR] URGES [THEM] . . .   608B V LAST JUDG/N   *PROSE
- WHILE LOS ANSWERD UNTERRIFIED TO THE OPAKE BLACKENING FIEND   625 JERUSALEM 7   8
- SPECTRE OF ALBION WARLIKE FIEND . . . .   651 FIELDS FROM/J   73
- AND MAN HIMSELF BECOME A FIEND WRAPD IN AN ENDLESS CURSE   667 JERUSALEM 40   29
- ANIMATING THE DRAGON TEMPLES SOON TO BECOME THAT HOLY FIEND   677 JERUSALEM 47   6
- O FIEND OF RIGHTEOUSNESS PRETENDEST THINE IS A DISORGANIZED   738 JERUSALEM 91   23
- THAT SPECTROUS FIEND TO HIS STATION WHOSE ANNOYANCE HAS   851D LETTER 50   PROSE

FIENDS   SEE WATCH-FIENDS,WATCH FIENDS
- AND FIENDS OF HELL REJOICE UPON THE SLAIN . . . . . .   33 EDW FOURTH/PS   12
- ESCAPE YE FIENDS FOR IJIM WILL NOT LIFT HIS HAND AGAINST YE   106 TIRIEL 4   88
- LIKE FOUL FIENDS INHABITING MARY'S MILD BRAIN . . . .   429 MARY   42
- ROUND WHICH THE FIENDS OF COMMERCE [ROAR] SMILE . . . .   557 ART HAS LOST/N   14
- BOUND IN ONE OF THE SERPENT'S FOLDS SURROUNDED BY   606C V LAST JUDG/N   PROSE
    HER FIENDS
- THEY ARE WEIGHED DOWN BY TWO FIENDS . . . .   607D V LAST JUDG/N   PROSE
- BENEATH THE MAN WITH THE BASKET ARE THREE FIERY FIENDS WITH   607D V LAST JUDG/N   PROSE
- . . . GO TO THESE FIENDS OF RIGHTEOUSNESS . . . . .   738 JERUSALEM 91   5
- FALLEN FIENDS OF HEAVNLY BIRTH . . . .   754 EV GOSPEL(E)/N   50
- BY TWO FIENDS INCARNATE WITH INTENTION THAT WHEN . . .   792B LETTER 4   PROSE
- IN EGYPT GUARDED IN THEIR REPOSE FROM THOSE FIENDS . .   823D LETTER 27   PROSE
- INTO THE VERY EARTH BY THE FOOTSTEPS OF THE FIENDS   849D LETTER 47   PROSE
    OF COMMERCE

FIERCE
- THY STRENGTH CURB THY FIERCE STEEDS ALLAY THE HEAT . . .   1 TO SUMMER/PS   2
- THRO THE FIERCE BURNING NIGHT . . . .   14 GWIN KING/PS   104
- AND ROAR THE WILD FLAME OF FIERCE WAR UPON . . . . .   26 EDW THIRD/PS 3   230
- WHO DURST T OPPOSE BUT SHAME OPPOSING FIERCE . . . .   42C THEN SHE BORE   PROSE
- WHY AN EAR A WHIRLPOOL FIERCE TO DRAW CREATIONS IN . .   130 BOOK OF THEL 6   17
- . . . FROM COURT TO COURT CURSD THE FIERCE TORMENT   135 FRENCH REVOLTN   23
    UNQUELLD
- THE FIERCE DUKE HUNG OVER THE COUNCIL . . . . . .   138 FRENCH REVOLTN   87
- . . . AND FIERCE SORROWS BECAUSE OF THE NOBLES OF FRANCE   139 FRENCH REVOLTN   119
- BUT DUMB TILL THAT DREAD DAY WHEN ORC ASSAYD HIS FIERCE   196 AMERICA PREL 1   10
    EMBRACE
- INTENSE NAKED A HUMAN FIRE FIERCE GLOWING AS THE WEDGE . .   197 AMERICA 4   8
- AND THE FLAME FOLDED ROARING FIERCE WITHIN THE PITCHY NIGHT   200 AMERICA 12   8
- AND THE RED FLAMES OF ORC THAT FOLDED ROARING FIERCE AROUND   201 AMERICA 14   11
- THE ANGRY SHORES AND THE FIERCE RUSHING OF TH INHABITANTS   201 AMERICA 14   12
    TOGETHER
- AND BY THE FIERCE AMERICANS RUSHING TOGETHER IN THE NIGHT   202 AMERICA 15   12
- THAT PLAY AROUND THE GOLDEN ROOFS IN WREATHS OF FIERCE   202 AMERICA 15   21
    DESIRE
- OVER THE HILLS THE VALES THE CITIES RAGE THE RED FLAMES   202 AMERICA 16   1
    FIERCE
- WITH FIERCE DISEASE AND LUST UNABLE TO STEM THE FIRE OF ORC   203 AMERICA 16   21
- AND THE FIERCE FLAMES BURNT ROUND THE HEAVENS . . . . .   203 AMERICA 16   23
- AND PLAMD FIERCE METEORS ROUND THE LAND OF ALBION BENEATH   204 AMERICA CANC A *   16
- IN FIERCE ANGUISH & QUENCHLESS FLAMES . . . . . .   225 URIZEN 5   19
- IN HOWLINGS & PANGS & FIERCE MADNESS . . . . . .   225 URIZEN 5   24
- HOWLING THE CHILD WITH FIERCE FLAMES . . . . . .   232 URIZEN 19   45
- BOUND IN THE FIERCE RAGING IMMORTAL . . . .   257 BOOK OF LOS 4   7
- THE THIN FLOWING ROUND THE FIERCE FIRES . . . . .   259 BOOK OF LOS 5   8
- IN FIERCE TORMENTS ON HIS GLOWING BED . . . . . .   260 BOOK OF LOS 5   51
- TILL WITH FIERCE PAIN SHE BROUGHT FORTH ON THE ROCKS HER   269 FOUR ZOAS 1   191
    SORROW & WOE
- RAISD THE [BRIGHT] FIERCE BOY & GIRL . . . .   269 FOUR ZOAS 1   196
- THY NAME IS ENITHARMON SAID THE [BRIGHT] FIERCE PROPHETIC   271 FOUR ZOAS 1   249
    BOY
- THEN ENITHARMON REDDNING FIERCE STRETCHD HER IMMORTAL HANDS   272 FOUR ZOAS 1   307
- ON HIGH REMAIND ALONE FORSAKEN IN FIERCE JEALOUSY . . .   274 FOUR ZOAS 1   360
- THE HORSE IS OF MORE VALUE THAN THE MAN THE TYGER FIERCE   275 FOUR ZOAS 1   402
- BURSTING FORTH FROM THE LOINS OF ENITHARMON THOU FIERCE   276 FOUR ZOAS 1   430
    TERROR
- RETREAT FROM THE FIERCE CONFLICT ALL THE SONS OF URIZEN   279 FOUR ZOAS 1   538
    AT ONCE
- IN A FIERCE HUNGRING VOID & NONE CAN VISIT HIS REGIONS .   279 FOUR ZOAS 1   * 544
- AND LOS SAID LO THE LILLY PALE & THE ROSE REDDNING FIERCE   288 FOUR ZOAS 2   302
- FROM THY FIERCE LOVE FOR THO I AM DISSOLVD IN THE BRIGHT   288 FOUR ZOAS 2   316
    GOD
- IN STRONG VIBRATIONS OF FIERCE JEALOUSY FOR THOU ART MINE   288 FOUR ZOAS 2   331
- IN TORMENTS OF FIERCE JEALOUSY & PANGS OF ADORATION . . .   289 FOUR ZOAS 2   351
- BURST FROM ITS BONDS IN WHIRLPOOLS FIERCE ROARING WITH   295 FOUR ZOAS 3   137
    HUMAN VOICE
- THE NETHER ABYSS & GNASSHING IN FIERCE DESPAIR PANTING   296 FOUR ZOAS 3   * 155
    IN SOBS
- FROM MY FIERCE RAGE INTO THY SEMBLANCE ENION RETURN . . .   297 FOUR ZOAS 3   198
- AND CASTING ROUND THICK GLOOMS THUS UTTERD HIS FIERCE PANGS   299 FOUR ZOAS 4   78
    OF HEART
- THEN RAGE ON RAGE SHALL FIERCE REDOUND OUT OF HER CRYSTAL   307 FOUR ZOAS 5   65
    QUIVER
- SITTING IN DARKNESS OVER HER LOS MOURND IN ANGUISH FIERCE   307 FOUR ZOAS 5   71
- HELD THE FIERCE BOY LOS NAILD HIM DOWN BINDING AROUND HIS   307 FOUR ZOAS 5   101
    LIMBS
- HIS LOINS INWOVE WITH SILKEN FIBES ARE LIKE A FURNACE   308 FOUR ZOAS 5   135
    FIERCE
- OF THE CHAIN OF JEALOUSY & FELT THE RENDINGS OF FIERCE   309 FOUR ZOAS 5   182
    HOWLING ORC

		PAGE	TITLE	LINE

FIERCE   (CONTINUED)

OFT WOULD HE STAND & QUESTION A FIERCE SCORPION GLOWING WITH GOLD — 315 FOUR ZOAS 6 — 131

BY THE FIERCE MANE STAYING [THEIR] HIS HOWLING COURSE . . . — 315 FOUR ZOAS 6 — * 133

REVOLVING ROUND IN WHIRLPOOLS FIERCE ALL ROUND THE CAVERND WORLDS — 320 FOUR ZOAS 7 — 4

STRIKING FIERCE SPARKLES FROM THEIR BRAZEN FETTERS FIERCE HIS LIONS — 320 FOUR ZOAS 7 — 8

THE HOLY OIL RAGES THRO ALL THE CAVERND ROCKS FIERCE FLAMES — 320 FOUR ZOAS 7 — 12

WHENCE THESE FIERCE FIRES BUT FROM THYSELF NO OTHER LIVING THING — 321 FOUR ZOAS 7 — 45

TENFOLD WITH FIERCE DESIRE TO REND THY CHAIN & HOWL IN FURY — 321 FOUR ZOAS 7 — 66

YET MY FIERCE FIRES ARE BETTER THAN THY SNOWS SHUDDRING THOU SITTEST — 322 FOUR ZOAS 7 — 72

BEGAN TO BLOSSOM IN FIERCE PAIN SHOOTING ITS WRITHING BUDS — 325 FOUR ZOAS 7 — 213

TO BRING HER DOWN SUBJECTED TO THE RAGE OF MY FIERCE BOY — 326 FOUR ZOAS 7 — 266

. . . HIS FIERCE SOUL WAS TERRIFID . . . . — 328 FOUR ZOAS 7 — * 318

OF THY FIERCE SOUL UNBAR THE GATES OF MEMORY LOOK UPON ME — 328 FOUR ZOAS 7 — 347

COMPELLD THE SUN REDDNING LIKE A FIERCE LION IN HIS CHAINS — 333 FOUR ZOAS 7B — 31

THAT WHEN LOS WARRD UPON THE SOUTH REFLECTED THE FIERCE FIRES — 335 FOUR ZOAS 7B — * 76

RED RAGE THE FURIES OF FIERCE ORC BLACK THUNDERS ROLL ROUND LOS — 335 FOUR ZOAS 7B — 78

WALKS THRO THE BATTLE DARK & FIERCE THE BULL HIS RAGE . . — 335 FOUR ZOAS 7B — 109

IN THE FIERCE BATTLE & HE SAW THE LAMB OF GOD & THE WORLD OF LOS — 342 FOUR ZOAS 8 — 66

THEY HUMANIZE IN THE FIERCE BATTLE WHERE IN DIREFUL PAIN — 344 FOUR ZOAS 8 — 115

FOR NOW FIERCE ORC IN WRATH & FURY RISES INTO THE HEAVENS — 353 FOUR ZOAS 8 — 460

TREMBLING & WEAK A FAINT EMBRACE A FIERCE DESIRE AS WHEN — 358 FOUR ZOAS 9 — 27

OF ORC BEGAN TO CONSUME IN FIERCE RAVING FIRE HIS PIERCE FLAMES — 358 FOUR ZOAS 9 — 34

IN THE FIERCE FLAMES THE LIMBS OF MYSTERY LAY CONSUMING WITH HOWLING — 359 FOUR ZOAS 9 — 67

BLOOD ISSUD OUT IN MIGHTY VOLUMES POURING IN WHIRLPOOLS FIERCE — 359 FOUR ZOAS 9 — * 71

IN THE FIERCE WIND ROUND HEAVING ROCKS & MOUNTAINS FILLD WITH GROANS — 363 FOUR ZOAS 9 — 240

AS OF FIERCE BATTLE . . .   . — 364 FOUR ZOAS 9 — 264

AND NOW FIERCE ORC HAD QUITE CONSUMD HIMSELF IN MENTAL FLAMES — 366 FOUR ZOAS 9 — 358

O MYSTERY FIERCE THARMAS CRIES BEHOLD THY END IS COME . . — 374 FOUR ZOAS 9 — 657

THEY HOWL & WRITHE IN SHOALS OF TORMENT IN FIERCE FLAMES CONSUMING — 377 FOUR ZOAS 9 — 749

AND EDDYING FIERCE REJOICE IN THE FIERCE AGITATION OF THE WHEELS — 378 FOUR ZOAS 9 — 811

WITH ARDOR FIERCE & HANDS OF FLAME . . . . — 429 CRYSTL CABINET — 22

DROVE THE FIERCE HARROW AMONG THE CONSTELLATIONS OF JEHOVAH — 493 MILTON 12 — 25

LOS STOOD IN THAT FIERCE GLOWING FIRE & HE ALSO STOOPD DOWN — 505 MILTON 22 — 8

STILL RINTRAH FIERCE AND PALAMABRON MILD & PITEOUS . . . — 508 MILTON 24 — 11

THEY HOWL & WRITHE IN SHOALS OF TORMENT IN FIERCE FLAMES CONSUMING — 513 MILTON 27 — 31

THUNDER OF THOUGHT & FLAMES OF FIERCE DESIRE . . . . . . — 621 READER LOVER/J — 6

WHILE LOS PURSUD HIS SPEECH IN THREATNINGS LOUD & FIERCE — 627 JERUSALEM 8 — 29

BEFORE BROMION'S IRON TONGS & GLOWING POKER REDDENING FIERCE — 636 JERUSALEM 16 — 2

HERTFORDSHIRE GLOWS WITH FIERCE VEGETATION IN THE FORESTS — 636 JERUSALEM 16 — 3

IN THE FIERCE DESIRES OF BEAUTY & IN THE TORTURES OF REPULSE HE IS — 638 JERUSALEM 17 — 12

DIVIDING IN FIERCE PAIN ALSO THE VISION OF GOD WAS CLOSD IN CLOUDS — 696 JERUSALEM 62 — 38

ON DEATH ETERNAL IN FIERCE SHUDDERS UPON THE MOUNTAINS OF ALBION — 696 JERUSALEM 62 — 40

WALKING & IN THE VALES IN HOWLINGS FIERCE THEN TO HIS ANVILS — 696 JERUSALEM 62 — 41

HUMAN MISERIES TURND FIERCE WITH THE LIVES OF MEN ALONG THE VALLEY — 699 JERUSALEM 64 — 33

JERUSALEM'S PILLARS FALL IN THE RENDINGS OF FIERCE WAR . . — 706 JERUSALEM 68 — 45

AND DEADLY STUPOR TURND AGAINST EACH OTHER LOUD & FIERCE — 714 JERUSALEM 74 — 6

IN AN ETERNAL CONDEMNATION IN FIERCE BURNING FLAMES . . . — 722 JERUSALEM 80 — 13

TO MURDER ALBION THE KING OF MEN HE FOUGHT IN BATTLES FIERCE — 722 JERUSALEM 80 — 18

AND HER DELUSIVE LIGHT BEAMD FIERCE ABOVE THE MOUNTAIN . . — 723 JERUSALEM 80 — 59

MY FACE IN FIERCE FLAMES IN MY DOUBLE SIGHT . . . . . — 818 HAPPINESS/L — 57

MY BOWSTRING FIERCE WITH ARDOUR BREATHES . . . . — 818 HAPPINESS/L — 79

FIERCELY

ITS EVER DURING DOORS THAT OG & ANAK FIERCELY GUARD . . . — 520 MILTON 31 — 49

FIERCE-RAGING

HIS FEET STAMP THE ETERNAL FIERCE-RAGING . . . . . . — 256 BOOK OF LOS 3 — 39

FIERY

AND WHERE THE FIERY WHIRLWIND OF SWIFT WAR . . . . . . — 18 EDW THIRD/PS 1 — 48

I SAW A LITTLE WELCHMAN WITH A FIERY FACE . . . . . — 25 EDW THIRD/PS 3 — 157

WHERE DOTH HE HIDE HIS TERRIBLE HEAD & HIS SWIFT & FIERY DAUGHTERS — 106 TIRIEL 5 — 2

WHERE DO THEY SHROUD THEIR FIERY WINGS & THE TERRORS OF THEIR HAIR — 106 TIRIEL 5 — 3

TO THRUST THESE TOWERS WITH HIS SHOULDERS·LET HIS FIERY DOGS — 106 TIRIEL 5 — 6

FOR THE BARS OF CHAOS ARE BURST HER MILLIONS PREPARE THEIR FIERY WAY — 140 FRENCH REVOLTN — 141

WHOSE EVRY FUNCTION IS FILLD WITH ITS FIERY DESIRE . . . — 142 FRENCH REVOLTN — 183

DRIVEN OUT BY THE FIERY CLOUD OF VOLTAIRE . . . .   . . — 146 FRENCH REVOLTN — 276

OVER HIS HEAD THE SOUL OF VOLTAIRE SHONE FIERY . . .   . . — 147 FRENCH REVOLTN — 282

689

```
                                                    PAGE      TITLE        LINE
FIERY    (CONTINUED)
     BY DEGREES WE BEHELD THE INFINITE ABYSS FIERY AS THE SMOKE    156A  MARRIAGE HH 17   PROSE
     WAS THE SUN BLACK BUT SHINING ROUND IT WERE FIERY TRACKS      156A  MARRIAGE HH 17   PROSE
     A FIERY CREST ABOVE THE WAVES SLOWLY IT REARED LIKE A RIDGE   156C  MARRIAGE HH 17   PROSE
     THE FIERY LIMBS THE FLAMING HAIR . . . . . . . . .            159C  SONG LIBERTY     PROSE
     MEET ON THE COAST GLOWING WITH BLOOD FROM ALBION'S FIERY      197   AMERICA 3          5
        PRINCE
     THE FIERY JOY THAT URIZEN PERVERTED TO TEN COMMANDS  . . .    198   AMERICA 8          3
     AND TO RENEW THE FIERY JOY AND BURST THE STONY ROOF  . . .    199   AMERICA 8          9
     FIERY THE ANGELS ROSE & AS THEY ROSE DEEP THUNDER ROLLD       200   AMERICA 11         1
     MEET ON THE COAST GLOWING WITH BLOOD FROM ALBION'S FIERY      203   AMERICA CANC A     5
        PRINCE
     THE EASTERN CLOUD RENT ON HIS CLIFFS STOOD ALBION'S FIERY     204   AMERICA CANC A    14
        PRINCE
     THE HUMAN FORM A FIERY FORGE  . . . . . . . . . .             221   DIVNE IMAGE/SE     6
     AND BRING FORTH HOWLING TERRORS ALL DEVOURING FIERY KINGS     238   EUROPE PREL 2      4
     THUS SPEAKING WHILE HIS NUMROUS SONS SHOOK THEIR BRIGHT       239   EUROPE 4           8
        FIERY WINGS
     THE FIERY KING WHO SOUGHT HIS ANCIENT TEMPLE SERPENT-FORMD    241   EUROPE 10          2
     THE SUN GLOWD FIERY RED  . . . . . . . . . . . .              245   EUROPE 15          3
     LIKE A SERPENT OF FIERY FLAME   . . . . . . . . .             248   SONG OF LOS 7     28
     SO HE SPOKE IN A FIERY FLAME  . . . . . . . . . .             249   AHANIA 2          14
     BUT THE FIERY BEAM OF FUZON . . . . . . . . . .               250   AHANIA 2          44
     INTO FIERY SPHERES FROM HIS FURY  . . . . . . . .             257   BOOK OF LOS 4      2
     IN FIERY PYRAMID OR CUBE OR [ORNAMENTED] UNORNAMENTED         287   FOUR ZOAS 2    *  275
        PILLAR [SQUARE]
     AND NINE BRIGHT SPHERES OF HARMONY RISE ROUND THE FIERY       289   FOUR ZOAS 2      348
        KING
     TILL INTO NARROW FORMS YOU CREEP GO TAKE YOUR FIERY WAY       294   FOUR ZOAS 3       89
     WITHIN HIS BREAST HIS FIERY SONS CHAIND DOWN & FILLD WITH     306   FOUR ZOAS 5       57
        CURSINGS
     SWEAT & BLOOD STOOD ON THE LIMBS OF LOS IN GLOBES HIS FIERY   307   FOUR ZOAS 5       67
        EYELIDS
     ENITHARMON NURSD HER FIERY CHILD IN THE DARK DEEPS  . . .     307   FOUR ZOAS 5       70
     COVERD WITH GLOOM THE FIERY BOY GREW FED BY THE MILK   . .    307   FOUR ZOAS 5       72
     AROUND HIS BOSOM EVERY DAY HE VIEWD THE FIERY YOUTH   . .     307   FOUR ZOAS 5       86
     HIS NOSTRILS BREATHE [WITH] A FIERY FLAME . . . . . .         308   FOUR ZOAS 5      127
     AND OVER THE IMMORTAL LIMBS OF THE TERRIBLE FIERY BOY   . .   309   FOUR ZOAS 5      159
     THY CHILDREN SMOTE THEIR FIERY WINGS CROWND WITH THE GOLD     311   FOUR ZOAS 5      229
        OF HEAVEN
     A UNIVERSE OF FIERY CONSTELLATIONS IN THEIR BRAIN  . . .      314   FOUR ZOAS 6       91
     THEN CAME HE AMONG FIERY CITIES & CASTLES BUILT OF BURNING    314   FOUR ZOAS 6      115
        STEEL
     HERE BOUND TO FIERY MANGERS FURIOUS DASH THEIR GOLDEN HOOFS   320   FOUR ZOAS 7        7
     MAIST FIND A WAY TO PUNISH VALA IN THY FIERY SOUTH   . . .    326   FOUR ZOAS 7      265
     FROM OUT THE RANKS OF URIZEN'S WAR & FROM THE FIERY LAKE      331   FOUR ZOAS 7      461
     THE FIERY DOGS ARISE THE SHOULDERS HUGE APPEAR   . . . .      336   FOUR ZOAS 7B     132
     IN CHANNELS THRO MY FIERY LIMBS O LOVE O PITY O PAIN   . .    349   FOUR ZOAS 8      307
     HIS FIERY HALLS ARE DARK & ROUND HIS LIMBS THE SERPENT ORC    354   FOUR ZOAS 8      509
     A FIERY TRAIN AS WHEN THE SUN SINGS IN THE RIPE VINEYARDS     376   FOUR ZOAS 9      715
     THEN LUVAH STOOD BEFORE THE WINE PRESS ALL HIS FIERY SONS     376   FOUR ZOAS 9      716
     THE OCEAN CALM THE CLOUDS FOLD ROUND & FIERY FLAMES OF LOVE   381   FOUR ZOAS AD 2     1
     PALAMABRON WITH THE FIERY HARROW IN MORNING RETURNING   .     484   MILTON 5           1
     AROUND THE FIERY FLAMING HARROW IN LABYRINTHINE FORMS   .     493   MILTON 12         18
     CHAOS & ANCIENT NIGHT FLED FROM BENEATH THE FIERY HARROW      493   MILTON 12         21
     THEY REND THE HEAVENS ROUND THE WATCHERS IN A FIERY CIRCLE    502   MILTON 20         46
     THE SONS OF OZOTH WITHIN THE OPTIC NERVE STAND FIERY          515   MILTON 28         29
        GLOWING
     ARE YOU THE FIERY CIRCLE THAT LATE DROVE IN FURY & FIRE       523   MILTON 34          3
     BUT OLOLON SOUGHT THE OR-ULRO & ITS FIERY GATES   . . . .     524   MILTON 34         19
     THEY STOOD IN A DARK LAND OF DEATH OF FIERY CORRODING         524   MILTON 34         44
        WATERS
     COMING IN A CLOUD WITH TRUMPETS & WITH FIERY FLAME   . . .    531   MILTON 39         23
     FIERY PEGASUS SHAKSPEARE THE HORSE OF INTELLECT IS LEAPING    581B  DESC CAT 6     TITLE
     BENEATH THE MAN WITH THE BASKET ARE THREE FIERY FIENDS WITH   607D  " LAST JUDG/N    PROSE
     THE WICKED ONWARDS WITH FIERY DARTS . . . . . . . .           608B  V LAST JUDG/N   PROSE
     BETWEEN THE FIGURES OF ADAM & EVE APPEARS A FIERY GULPH       609A  V LAST JUDG/N   PROSE
     ON THE FIERY CHARIOT OF HIS CONTEMPLATIVE THOUGHT    . . .    611A  V LAST JUDG/N   PROSE
     HE IS SEEN ON HIS FIERY CHARIOT BOWING BEFORE THE THRONE      611C  V LAST JUDG/N   PROSE
     THE ISLANDS OF THE FIERY LAKES THE TREES OF MALICE REVENGE    634   JERUSALEM 13      42
     TILL INTO NARROW FORMS YOU CREEP GO TAKE YOUR FIERY WAY       655   JERUSALEM 29      70
     THE FOUR APPEARD WITH THEIR EMANATIONS IN FIERY   . . . .     666   JERUSALEM 40       4
     SO SAYING AN ETERNAL DEED WAS DONE IN FIERY FLAMES   . . .    686   JERUSALEM 55      19
     AND ONE DAUGHTER OF LOS SAT AT THE FIERY REEL & ANOTHER       691   JERUSALEM 59      26
     OF FIRE THEN AN AWFUL FIERY WHEEL SURROUNDING EARTH           702   JERUSALEM 66      42
        & HEAVEN
     IN CHANNELS THRO MY FIERY LIMBS O LOVE O PITY O FEAR   . .    705   JERUSALEM 67      54
     CREATING NATURE FROM THIS FIERY LAW . . . . . . . .           718   STOOD AMONG/J     22
     THE MORNING BLUSHD FIERY RED  . . . . . . . . . .             753   EV GOSPEL(E)/N     3
FIFE
     FOR THE HUSBANDMAN WEEPS AT BLIGHTS OF THE FIFE . . . . .     143   FRENCH REVOLTN   209
     BEHIND RANK TO THE SOUL SHAKING DRUM AND SHRILL FIFE . . .    147   FRENCH REVOLTN   292
     ARISE & COME BOTH FIFE & DRUM . . . . . . . . . .             185   LET BROTHELS/N     7
     SOUND THE SHRILL FIFE SERPENTS OF WAR I HEAR THE NORTHERN     336   FOUR ZOAS 7B     148
        DRUM
     THE DOUBLE DRUM DROWNS HOWLS & GROANS THE SHRILL             509   MILTON 24         65
        FIFE SHRIEKS & CRIES
     THE SOLDIER'S FIFE THE HARLOT'S SHRIEK THE VIRGIN'S DISMAL    636   JERUSALEM 16       6
        GROAN
FIFES
     NO TRUMPETS ANSWER NO REPLY OF CLARIONS OR OF FIFES     . .   200   AMERICA 10         3
```

690

		PAGE	TITLE	LINE

FIFTEEN
SAYS HE HAS SOLD BUT FIFTEEN NUMBERS AT THE MOST AND THAT 831C LETTER 31 PROSE
FIFTEEN OF EACH BUT I HAD NOT PAPER ENOUGH IN PROPER ORDER 840D LETTER 40 PROSE
THE INFERIOR ONES CANNOT BE DONE AT ANY RATE UNDER 848C LETTER 45 PROSE
(FIFTEEN)
(THIRTY) GUINEAS IF FINISHD & IF A SKETCH (FIFTEEN) GUINEAS 855B LETTER 53 PROSE
AS
(THIRTY) GUINEAS AS ITS PRICE & THE PLINY (FIFTEEN) GUINEAS 855B LETTER 53 PROSE
HAS FOUND (FIFTEEN) PROOFS OF THE HESIOD AS THEY ARE . . 877B LETTER 86 PROSE
FIFTH
NONE COULD DEDUCE A FOURTH OR FIFTH . . . . 97A NAT RELIGION 1 PROSE
IN THE FIFTH CHAMBER WERE UNNAMD FORMS . . . . 155A MARRIAGE HH 15 PROSE
AND A FIFTH AGE PASSED OVER . . . . 229 URIZEN 13 2
AND A FIFTH AGE PASSED & A STATE OF DISMAL WOE . . . . 303 FOUR ZOAS 4 238
VALA [BOOK] NIGHT THE FIFTH . . . . 305B FOUR ZOAS 5 *TITLE
END OF THE FIFTH [BOOK] NIGHT . . . . 311C FOUR ZOAS 5 *TITLE
AND A FIFTH AGE PASSED OVER & A STATE OF DISMAL WOE . . 482 MILTON 3 21
WHO LIVED IN THE FIFTH CENTURY THERE WERE REMAINS . . . 578B DESC CAT 5 PROSE
TO A PRINCE OF THE FIFTH CENTURY WHO CONQUERED EUROPE . 578C DESC CAT 5 PROSE
BETWEEN THE FIFTH AND SIXTH CIRCLES . . . . 786A ILLS DANTE 101 PROSE
FIFTIES
IN SEVENS & TENS & FIFTIES HUNDREDS THOUSANDS NUMBERD ALL 287 FOUR ZOAS 2 269
OF SAND IN BANDS OF HUNDREDS & OF FIFTIES & OF THOUSANDS 314 FOUR ZOAS 6 107
. . .
CLING ROUND THE MEN IN BANDS OF TWENTIES & OF FIFTIES PALE 358 FOUR ZOAS 9 48
FIFTY
EMPLOYER & I HAVE AN ORDER FOR FIFTY SMALL PICTURES AT ONE 795C LETTER 6 PROSE
PUSHED HIM FORWARDS DOWN THE ROAD ABOUT FIFTY YARDS . . 827B LETTER 28 PROSE
HOW IS IT POSSIBLE THAT A MAN ALMOST (FIFTY) YEARS OF AGE 830A LETTER 30 PROSE
FIFTY-TWO,FIFTY TWO
LIKE WHITE CLOUDS RISING FROM THE DEEPS HIS FIFTY-TWO 205 AMERICA CANC C 16
ARMIES
LIKE WHITE CLOUDS RISING FROM THE VALES HIS FIFTY 319 FOUR ZOAS 6 312
TWO ARMIES
HERE LOS FIXD DOWN THE FIFTY-TWO COUNTIES OF ENGLAND & 637 JERUSALEM 16 28
WALES
THE FIFTY-TWO COUNTIES OF ENGLAND ARE HARDEND AGAINST ME 720 JERUSALEM 79 20
FIG
HEAVEN IS A MERCY A FIG FOR ALL CORPOREAL SUCH DISTRESS IS 809B LETTER 20 PROSE
FIGHT
FIGHT UPON HILLS OF SLAIN . . . . 13 GWIN KING/PS 88
THE ENEMY FIGHT IN CHAINS INVISIBLE CHAINS BUT HEAVY . . 18 EDW THIRD/PS 1 13
YES FEAR THAT MADE HIM FIGHT SO . . . . 21 EDW THIRD/PS 3 13
THAT MAKES YOU FIGHT . . . . 21 EDW THIRD/PS 3 15
HE IS A YOUNG LION O I HAVE SEEN HIM FIGHT . . . . . 22 EDW THIRD/PS 3 26
BETTER THAN FIGHT TO BE PLAIN I THINK RETREATING . . . . 23 EDW THIRD/PS 3 65
AND SHALL WHILE YOU CAN FIGHT AS YOU DID AT . . . . . 23 EDW THIRD/PS 3 93
I HOPE YOULL STAY AND SEE US FIGHT THIS BATTLE . . . . 24 EDW THIRD/PS 3 136
THEN GO TO ENGLAND TELL THEM HOW WE FIGHT . . . . . . 24 EDW THIRD/PS 3 138
'TWILL BE A GALLANT THING TO FIGHT OR DIE . . . . . . 25 EDW THIRD/PS 3 152
IS DANGEROUS TO FIGHT NOT GOOD FOR FOOD . . . . . . 27 EDW THIRD/PS 3 266
THAT BROUGHT OVER OUR KING TO FRANCE TO FIGHT FOR HIS RIGHT 28D EDW THIRD/PS 4 PROSE
LET THOSE THAT FIGHT FIGHT IN GOOD STEDFASTNESS . . . . 31 EDW THIRD/PS 5 37
I'LL FIGHT AND WEEP TIS IN MY COUNTRY'S CAUSE . . . . 31 EDW THIRD/PS 5 51
FIGHT IN THE TROUBLED AIR THAT RAGES WHO CAN STAND . . . 33 EDW FOURTH/PS 5
THE GAME COCK CLIPD & ARMD FOR FIGHT . . . . 431 AUGURIES 17
I WILL NOT CEASE FROM MENTAL FIGHT . . . . 481 AND DID FEET/M 13
OSHEA AND CALEB FIGHT THEY CONTEND IN THE VALLEYS OF OF 672 JERUSALEM 43 37
PEOR
THEY FIGHT & CONTEND FOR LIFE & NOT FOR ETERNAL DEATH . 672 JERUSALEM 43 42
CHAIND HAND & FOOT COMPELLD TO FIGHT UNDER THE IRON WHIPS 700 JERUSALEM 65 35
OVERWEARIED WITH HOWLING WALES & SCOTLAND ALONE SUSTAIN 703 JERUSALEM 66 67
THE FIGHT
AND LITTLE DEVILS WHO FIGHT FOR THEMSELVES . . . . . 816 HAPPINESS/L 6
FIGHTEST
AND THOU MY SON BE STRONG THOU FIGHTEST FOR A CROWN . . . 18 EDW THIRD/PS 1 21
FIGHTETH
THE CRANE OERTAKEN FIGHTETH WITH THE HAWK . . . . . 24 EDW THIRD/PS 3 128
FIGHTING
IN COMING WITH HIM AND IN FIGHTING FOR HIM . . . . . 28D EDW THIRD/PS 4 PROSE
WHERE A THOUSAND FIGHTING MEN IN AMBUSH LIE . . . . . 130 BOOK OF THEL 6 14
[[THE BLOOD OF TEN THOUSAND BY FIGHTING OR SWINGING]] . 185 LET BROTHELS/N 15
FIGHTING WITH EACH OTHER ON THE [VERY] BRINK OF PERDITION 443D LAST JUDGMNT/L PROSE
THE FIGHTING DEVILS READY FOR THE COPPER I COUNT MYSELF 879C LETTER 89 PROSE
FIGHTINGS
BY FIGHTINGS AND CONFLICTS DIRE . . . . 224 URIZEN 4 27
FIGHTS
FOR THE SOLDIER WHO FIGHTS FOR TRUTH CALLS HIS ENEMY HIS 672 JERUSALEM 43 41
BROTHER
FIGS
BECAUSE THOU SMELLEST LIKE THE FIGTREE THOU SMELLEST LIKE 101 TIRIEL 2 42
RIPE FIGS
MY RIPE FIGS AND RICH POMEGRANATES . . . . 255 AHANIA 5 26
WHEN GRAPES & FIGS BURST THEIR COVERING TO THE JOYFUL AIR 485 MILTON 5 33
FIGTREE
BECAUSE THOU SMELLEST LIKE THE FIGTREE THOU SMELLEST LIKE 101 TIRIEL 2 42
RIPE FIGS
FIG-TREE
BENEATH THE OAK & PALM BENEATH THE VINE AND FIG-TREE . . 640 JERUSALEM 18 19
FIGURE
AMONG THEM IS A FIGURE CROWND WITH STARS . . . . . . 443D LAST JUDGMNT/L *PROSE
APPROACH THE FIGURE OF AN AGED APOSTLE WHICH REPRESENTS 444B LAST JUDGMNT/L PROSE
BAPTISM

691

	PAGE	TITLE	LINE

FIGURE   (CONTINUED)

```
       THE PRINCIPAL FIGURE IN THE NEXT GROUPE IS THE GOOD PARSON   570B DESC CAT 3       PROSE
       [ BY ] BESIDE THEM A [ SCALD ] FIGURE IS SEEN  . . . . . .   606C V LAST JUDG/N   *PROSE
       BENEATH THE FALLING FIGURE OF CAIN   . . . . . . . .         607B V LAST JUDG/N    PROSE
       [ & HAS ] BY THE SIDE OF THE SCALED FIGURE   . . . . .       607D V LAST JUDG/N    PROSE
       REPRESENTING OG KING OF BASHAN IS A FIGURE WITH A BASKET     607D V LAST JUDG/N    PROSE
       THE FIGURE DRAGGING UP A WOMAN BY HER HAIR   . . . . . .     608C V LAST JUDG/N    PROSE
       THE AGED FIGURE WITH WINGS HAVING A WRITING TABLET   . . .   610A V LAST JUDG/N    PROSE
       BETWEEN SETH & THESE A FEMALE FIGURE [ WITH THE BACK TURND ] 611D V LAST JUDG/N    PROSE
       I HAVE HOWEVER SOMEWHAT ACCOMODATED MY FIGURE OF TIME   . .  614D V LAST JUDG/N    PROSE
       SURROUNDING THE PRINCIPAL FIGURE WHICH IS MIRTH HERSELF      618A ILLUS MILTON     PROSE
       IN THIS DESIGN SURROUNDING THE PRINCIPAL FIGURE   . . . .    619A ILLUS MILTON     PROSE
       DOUBT NOT YET TO MAKE A FIGURE IN THE GREAT DANCE OF LIFE    835A LETTER 34        PROSE
       OF A FEMALE FIGURE WITH A SERPENT IN ONE HAND & A TORCH      839C LETTER 38        PROSE
          IN THE
       OTHER BOTH HELD ABOVE HER HEAD & A FIGURE KNEELING AT HER    839C LETTER 38        PROSE
          FEET
       BE RECOVERED BE HECATE THE FIGURE WITH THE TORCH AND SNAKE   840D LETTER 40        PROSE
       BLACK EYD SUSAN A FIGURE ON THE SEA SHORE EMBRACING A CORSE  848D LETTER 45        PROSE
       THINK THAT IT WAS A FIGURE WITH CHILDREN WHICH HE CALLD      849A LETTER 45        PROSE
          A CHARITY
       PRAYER AND PARENTAL AFFECTION FILLS THE FIGURE FROM HEAD     864B LETTER 61       *PROSE
          TO FOOT
```

FIGURES

```
       BEHOLD TWO [ LITTLE INFANTS WEPT ] [ ?FIGURES OF ?PAIN HOWLD ]  269 FOUR ZOAS 1     *    192
          . . .
       BY TWO ANGELS & MANY GROUPES OF FIGURES ARE FALLING   . . .   443C LAST JUDGMNT/L  PROSE
       MANY FIGURES [ CHAIND ] CHAINED & BOUND TOGETHER & . . . .    443C LAST JUDGMNT/L *PROSE
       BESIDES LET THEM LOOK AT GOTHIC FIGURES & GOTHIC BUILDINGS    461A ANNO REYNOLDS    MARG
       THE ARMY OF ARMED ROMANS THE FIGURES FULL AS LARGE AS LIFE    560A EXHIBITION ADV   PROSE
       THIRTY FIGURES ON HORSE-BACK IN A BRILLIANT MORNING SCENE     560B EXHIBITION ADV   PROSE
       THOUGH THE FIGURES WERE ONE HUNDRED FEET IN HEIGHT   . . .    566A DESC CAT 2       PROSE
       MODERNS WISH TO DRAW FIGURES WITHOUT LINES   . . . . . .      577A DESC CAT 4       PROSE
       ONE OF RAFAEL OR MICHAEL ANGELO'S FIGURES WAS TO BE TRACED    583C DESC CAT 9       PROSE
       BENEATH THE CLOUD ON WHICH MOSES KNEELS IS TWO FIGURES   .    607C V LAST JUDG/N    PROSE
       ABOVE HIM ARE TWO FIGURES ELEVATED ON A CLOUD   . . . .       607D V LAST JUDG/N    PROSE
       THEY SCOURGE A GROUPE OF FIGURES DOWN INTO THE DEEPS   .      608A V LAST JUDG/N    PROSE
       BENEATH THEM ARE VARIOUS FIGURES IN ATTITUDES   . . . .       608A V LAST JUDG/N    PROSE
       THE EARTH BENEATH THESE FALLING GROUPES OF FIGURES   . .      608A V LAST JUDG/N    PROSE
       HELL IS OPENED & MANY FIGURES ARE DESCENDING INTO IT   .      608B V LAST JUDG/N    PROSE
       THOSE [ WHO ] FIGURES THAT DESCEND INTO THE FLAMES   . . .    608D V LAST JUDG/N   *PROSE
       BETWEEN THE FIGURES OF ADAM & EVE APPEARS A FIERY GULPH       609A V LAST JUDG/N    PROSE
       AROUND NOAH & BENEATH HIM ARE VARIOUS FIGURES RISEN   . .     610A V LAST JUDG/N    PROSE
       REPRESENTED AS A STREAM OF [ LIGHT ] FIGURES   . . . . .      610B V LAST JUDG/N    PROSE
       THEY ASCEND FROM THE EARTH WHERE FIGURES KNEEL   . . . .      610B V LAST JUDG/N    PROSE
       THE TWO FIGURES IN PURIFYING FLAMES BY THE SIDE OF THE   .    610C V LAST JUDG/N    PROSE
       BENEATH THE FEET OF SETH TWO FIGURES REPRESENT   . . . .      611C V LAST JUDG/N    PROSE
       THE FIGURES OF SETH & HIS WIFE COMPREHENDS THE FATHERS   .    611C V LAST JUDG/N    PROSE
       A LITTLE BELOW SETH ON HIS RIGHT ARE TWO FIGURES   . . .      611D V LAST JUDG/N    PROSE
       THREE FEMALE FIGURES CROWND WITH GARLANDS REPRESENT   . .     611D V LAST JUDG/N    PROSE
       IS COMPOSED OF VARIOUS GROUPES OF FIGURES   . . . . . .       612A V LAST JUDG/N    PROSE
       BEFORE THAT OF LIFE ON THE RIGHT SOME FIGURES [ ?BOW ] BOW    612B V LAST JUDG/N   *PROSE
       VARIOUS OFFICES AT THE EASTERN GATE BENEATH IN SMALL          618B ILLUS MILTON    PROSE
          FIGURES
       WHICH YOU CAN NEVER PROVE MY FIGURES TO BE   . . . . . .      793C LETTER 5         PROSE
       THE FIGURES AS LARGE AS LIFE HALF LENGTH MR W(WALKER)         843C LETTER 43        PROSE
          THREE SONS
       & THE FIGURES LEFT EXACTLY   . . . . . . . . . . . .          850D LETTER 49        PROSE
```

FILAMENTS

```
       MY SKULL RIVEN INTO FILAMENTS MY EYES INTO SEA JELLIES        296 FOUR ZOAS 3        163
```

FILD   SEE FILLD

FILE

```
       OF DAY & NIGHT THE MYRIADS OF ETERNITY THAT THEY MIGHT FILE   337 FOUR ZOAS 7B       181
```

FILL

```
       AND THE JOLLY SWAIN LAUGHS HIS FILL   . . . . . . . .          7 LOVE JOCUND/PS        8
       THE REST DID FILL THE VALE OF DEATH   . . . . . . . .         14 GWIN KING/PS         111
       AND WITH IMMORTAL VOICE SOFT WARBLING FILL ALL EARTH &       274 FOUR ZOAS 1          381
          HEAVEN
       HERDS THRONG UP THE VALLEY WILD BEASTS FILL THE FORESTS      373 FOUR ZOAS 9          612
       FILL WITH TEMPESTS ALL MY MORN  . . . . . . . . .            416 MY SPECTRE/N          32
       FILL MY PLEASANT NIGHTS WITH TEARS   . . . . . . .           416 MY SPECTRE/N          34
       AND WITH LABOURS OF IGNORANCE FILL EVERY PLACE   . . . .     445 ANNO REYNOLDS          4
       AND FLOWER & HERB SOON FILL THE AIR WITH AN INNUMERABLE      521 MILTON 31             61
          DANCE
```

FILLD

```
       O ELENOR WEAK WOMAN FILLD WITH WOE   . . . . . . . .           5 FAIR ELENOR/PS        52
       GWIN THOU HAST FILLD THY MEASURE UP   . . . . . . . .         13 GWIN KING/PS          67
       HEATED WITH WAR FILLD WITH THE BLOOD OF GREEKS   . . . .      32 EDW THIRD/PS 6        10
       MY CUP IS FILLD WITH ENVY'S RANKEST DRAUGHT [ AND DEATH ]     41C THEN SHE BORE      PROSE
       & FILLD HIM WITH CONFUSION FEAR AS A TORRENT WILD   . . .     42B THEN SHE BORE      PROSE
       O THEY ARE HOLY & FORGIVING FILLD WITH LOVING MERCY   . . .  108 TIRIEL 6             26
       FILLD WITH DEEP SURPRISE  . . . . . . . . . .                114 LIT GRL FND/SI       34
       WEEP NOR BE WITH SORROW FILLD   . . . . . . . . .            122 ON ANOTHERS/SI        8
       WHOSE EVRY FUNCTION IS FILLD WITH ITS FIERY DESIRE . . .     142 FRENCH REVOLTN       183
       [ WAS FILLD ] TURND AWAY WITH JEALOUSY   . . . . . . .       161 ROSE TREE/N            9
       AND THEIR WAYS ARE FILLD WITH THORNS   . . . . . . .         181 HOLY THURS/N          11
       BECAUSE TIS FILLD WITH FIRE   . . . . . . . . .              182 LOOK OF LOVE/N         2
       BECAUSE TIS FILLD WITH FIRE   . . . . . . . . . .            184 SEVRL QUESTN/N         6
       BUT OOTHOON IS NOT SO A VIRGIN FILLD WITH VIRGIN FANCIES     194 V DAU ALBION 6        21
       AND AS A PLAGUE WIND FILLD WITH INSECTS CUTS OFF MAN &       201 AMERICA 14             8
          BEAST
       AND THEIR WAYS ARE FILLD WITH THORNS   . . . . . . .         212 HOLY THURS/SE         11
```

```
                                                            PAGE      TITLE          LINE
FILLD   (CONTINUED)
    FILLD WITH SOFTEST CARE  . . . . . . . . .        219  LIT GRL LST/SE     11
    NOW FILLD WITH CLOUDS DARKNESS & WATERS  . . . . . . .  223  URIZEN 4        2
    FILLD WITH IMMORTAL DEMONS OF FUTURITY  . . . . . . .    241  EUROPE 9       10
    EVERY HOUSE A DEN EVERY MAN BOUND THE SHADOWS ARE FILLD    243  EUROPE 12      26
    FILLD WITH ETERNAL SEED  . . . . . . . . .        255  AHANIA 5       21
    REJOICING IN THE VICTORY & THE HEAVENS WERE FILLD WITH    273  FOUR ZOAS 1   346
        BLOOD
    FILLD WITH THE WINE OF ANGUISH WAITED AT THE GOLDEN FEAST  273  FOUR ZOAS 1   348
    CAVERNOUS DWELLERS FILLD THE ENORMOUS REVELRY RESPONSING   274  FOUR ZOAS 1   383
    THEY CRY O SPIDER SPREAD THY WEB ENLARGE THY BONES & FILLD  275  FOUR ZOAS 1   404
    WHEN THE RED BLOOD IS FILLD WITH WINE & WITH THE MARROW    290  FOUR ZOAS 2   407
        OF LAMBS
    AMBIGUOUS WORDS BLASPHEMOUS FILLD WITH ENVY FIRM RESOLVD   302  FOUR ZOAS 4   205
    WITHIN HIS BREAST HIS FIERY SONS CHAIND DOWN & FILLD WITH  306  FOUR ZOAS 5    57
        CURSINGS
    SHE ANSWERD NOT BUT FILLD HER URN & POURD IT FORTH ABROAD  312  FOUR ZOAS 6    11
    WRITING THY BOOKS ANON A CLOUD FILLD WITH A WASTE OF SNOWS  322  FOUR ZOAS 7    81
    ASTONISHD FILLD WITH TEARS THE SPIRIT OF ENITHARMON BEHELD  327  FOUR ZOAS 7   311
    DEFENDED PALAMABRON & RAGE FILLD THE UNIVERSAL TENT  . . .  351  FOUR ZOAS 8   390
    IN THE FIERCE WIND ROUND HEAVING ROCKS & MOUNTAINS FILLD   363  FOUR ZOAS 9   240
        WITH GROANS
    WITH A BRIGHT GIRDLE & HIS SKIRT FILLD WITH IMMORTAL SOULS  365  FOUR ZOAS 9   322
    OF HUMAN FAMILIES THRO THE DEEP THE WINE PRESSES WERE FILLD  376  FOUR ZOAS 9   725
    OF LUVAH QUITE EXHAUSTED WITH THE LABOUR & QUITE FILLD     378  FOUR ZOAS 9   786
    THE ELEMENTS ARE FILLD WITH THE PRINCE OF EVIL   . . . . 388A  ANNO WATSON   MARG
    FILLD ME THAT LIKE A FLAME I BURND  . . . . . . .       429  CRYSTL CABINET  18
    I FILLD WITH WOES THE PASSING WIND  . . . . . . .       430  CRYSTL CABINET  28
    A DOVE HOUSE FILLD WITH DOVES & PIGEONS  . . . . . .      431  AUGURIES        7
    THESE ARE FILLD WITH TINTS & (MESSES) OF YELLOW & RED  . 469A  ANNO REYNOLDS  * MARG
    CAN SUCH AN EAR FILLD WITH THE VAPOURS OF THE YAWNING PIT  485  MILTON 5       30
    AND BACK RETURND TO LOS NOT FILLD WITH VENGEANCE BUT WITH  488  MILTON 8        6
        TEARS
    HOWLINGS FILLD ALL THE DESOLATE PLACES IN ACCUSATIONS OF   500  MILTON 18      43
        SIN
    LOOKING DOWN INTO BEULAH WRATHFUL FILLD WITH RAGE   . . .  502  MILTON 20      45
    THEOTORMON FILLD WITH CARE DROMION LOVING SCIENCE   . . .  508  MILTON 24      12
    WITH PLUTE & CLARION WITH CUPS & MEASURES FILLD WITH      511  MILTON 25      69
        FOAMING WINE
    HERE IS HER CUP FILLD WITH ITS POISONS IN THESE HORRID    529  MILTON 38      25
        VALES
    BEFORE THE FLOOD THAT THEY WERE FILLD WITH BLOOD & FIRE   606D  V LAST JUDG/N  PROSE
    SCANDINAVIA FLED WITH ALL HIS MOUNTAINS FILLD WITH GROANS   647  JERUSALEM 24   11
    AND FILLD WITH CRUEL TORTURES BUT NO MORTAL MAN CAN FIND   666  JERUSALEM 39    4
        THE MILL
    AT ENMITY WITH THE MERCIFUL & FILLD WITH DEVOURING FIRE    667  JERUSALEM 40   33
    UNDER PRETENCE OF MORAL VIRTUE FILLD WITH REVENGE AND LAW  667  JERUSALEM 40   35
    WITHIN HIS BREAST HIS MIGHTY SONS CHAIND DOWN & FILLD WITH  667  JERUSALEM 40   40
        CURSINGS
    OF GREY OBSCURITY FILLD WITH CLOUDS & ROCKS & WHIRLING    674  JERUSALEM 44   16
        WATERS
    FILLD WITH THE LITTLE-ONES ARE CONSUMED IN THE FIRES OF   679  JERUSALEM 49   11
        THEIR ALTARS
    THEREFORE THE MALE SEVERE & CRUEL FILLD WITH STERN REVENGE  708  JERUSALEM 69   36
    OUTSIDE UNKNOWN BEFORE IN BEULAH & THE TWELVE GATES WERE   719  JERUSALEM 78   25
        FILLD
    ABOVE HIS HEAD HIGH ARCHING WINGS BLACK FILLD WITH EYES    735  JERUSALEM 89   28
    THE WHOLE BIBLE IS FILLD WITH IMAGINATION & VISIONS  . . 774D  ANNO BERKELEY  MARG
    CONCIEVE IN MY BRAIN ARE STUDIES & CHAMBERS FILLD WITH  . 802B  LETTER 14     PROSE
    FILLD FULL OF HOPES FILLD FULL OF FEARS  . . . . . .      817  HAPPINESS/L    20
FILLED
    AND HIS TONGUE SHALL BE FILLED WITH PRAISE  . . . . . .   118  SHEPHERD/SI     4
    AND I SAW IT WAS FILLED WITH GRAVES  . . . . . . .       163  GARDEN LOVE/N   9
    FILLED WITH BLASTING FANCIES AND WITH MILDEWS OF DESPAIR   203  AMERICA 16     20
    AND I SAW IT WAS FILLED WITH GRAVES  . . . . . . .       215  GARDEN LOVE/SE  9
    URIZEN SAW & ENVIED & HIS IMAGINATION WAS FILLED  . . . .  287  FOUR ZOAS 2   291
    O FOOL COULD I FORGET THE LIGHT THAT FILLED MY BRIGHT     310  FOUR ZOAS 5   216
        SPHERES
    AND TAKING OFF HIS SILVER HELMET FILLED IT & DRANK   . .   311  FOUR ZOAS 6     3
    FILLED WITH DOUBTS IN SELF ACCUSATION [GATHERD] BEHELD    329  FOUR ZOAS 7   * 385
        THE FRUIT
    BUT FINDS THE POOLS FILLED WITH SERPENTS DEVOURING ONE    354  FOUR ZOAS 8   530
        ANOTHER
    FULL FILLED ALL WITH GEMS & GOLD  . . . . . . .          425  MENTAL TRAVLER  31
    FILLED WITH EYES ATTENDED BY SEVEN ANGELS  . . . . . .  444A  LAST JUDGMNT/L PROSE
    THE CHARIOT WHEELS FILLED WITH EYES RAGE ALONG THE HOWLING  697  JERUSALEM 63   11
        VALLEY
    A VINE FILLED WITH GRAPES THE TREE WHICH MOVES SOME TO   793D  LETTER 5      PROSE
        TEARS
FILLIGREE WORK
    & FILLIGREE WORK I HOPE SHALL LIVE TO SEE  . . . . . .    52C  ISLAND MOON 8 PROSE
    & THERES MISS FILLIGREE WORK SHE GOES OUT IN HER COACHES   52D  ISLAND MOON 8 PROSE
FILLING
    BUT THE BRIGHT SUN WAS NOT AS YET HE FILLING ALL         273  FOUR ZOAS 1   349
        THE EXPANSE
    THRO NIGHT SHOULD SING SOFT WARBLING FILLING EARTH & HEAVEN  366  FOUR ZOAS 9   352
    BETWEEN HIS PALMS AND FILLING UP THE FURROWS OF MANY YEARS  500  MILTON 19      11
    FILLING CUPS OF SILVER & CRYSTAL WITH SHRIEKS & CRIES WITH  723  JERUSALEM 80   81
        GROANS
    FILLING WITH FIBRES FROM HIS LOINS WHICH REDDEND         732  JERUSALEM 86   51
        WITH DESIRE
```

		PAGE	TITLE	LINE
FILLS				
WHILE THE AIRY MUSIC FILLS THE WORLD WITH JOYFUL SOUNDS		37B	CONTEMPLATN/PS	PROSE
AND THE SHOUT OF HIS THOUSANDS FILLS HIS HEART		62	CROWND KING/IM	6
AND THE SHOUT OF HIS THOUSANDS FILLS HIS HEART		62	CROWND KING/IM	7
ONE THOUGHT FILLS IMMENSITY		151D	MARRIAGE HH 8	PROSE
WHILE THY MILD VOICE FILLS ALL THESE CAVERNS WITH SWEET HARMONY		271	FOUR ZOAS 1	250
[XXX ?LIVING JOY FILLS ?ALBION]		SUPP	FOUR ZOAS 1	*
BY GRATIFIED DESIRE BY STRONG DEVOURING APPETITE SHE FILLS		323	FOUR ZOAS 7	133
THE TONGUE A LITTLE MOISTURE FILLS A LITTLE FOOD IT CLOYS		484	MILTON 5	25
THE TONGUE A LITTLE MOISTURE FILLS A LITTLE FOOD IT CLOYS		680	JERUSALEM 49	40
ALL POWERFUL PARENTAL AFFECTION FILLS ALBION FROM HEAD TO FOOT		685	JERUSALEM 54	10
OF HIM WHO IS SLAIN IN WAR FILLS THE VALLEYS OF EPHRAIM WITH		706	JERUSALEM 68	35
FILLS ME FULL OF SMILES OR TEARS		817	HAPPINESS/L	26
PRAYER AND PARENTAL AFFECTION FILLS THE FIGURE FROM HEAD		864B	LETTER 61	*PROSE
FILMY				
[SO SAYING] IN TORMENT HE SUNK DOWN & FLOWD AMONG HER FILMY WOOF		266	FOUR ZOAS 1	77
BUT WHEN HE TOUCHES THE FIRST FIBROUS THREAD LIKE FILMY DEW		739	JERUSALEM 92	10
FILTH				
AND ALL THE TENDERNESSES OF THE SOUL CAST FORTH AS FILTH & MIRE		657	JERUSALEM 31	21
FILTHY				
THAN THEIR NASTY FILTHY [SOULS] SELVES		63A	ISLAND MOON 11	PROSE
HIS SHADOWS ARE OF A FILTHY BROWN SOMEWHAT OF THE COLOUR OF EXCREMENT		469A	ANNO REYNOLDS	MARG
TO TAKE OFF HIS FILTHY GARMENTS & CLOTHE HIM WITH IMAGINATION		533	MILTON 41	6
[LIKE A FILTHY INFECTIOUS HEAD OF HAIR]		540	SIR JOSH RUB/N	6
FINAL				
FINAL PORTION IS PREDESTINATION SEE N...AT THE END &...		132A	ANNO SWED PROV	MARG
. . . TO SHUT UP THIS ASSEMBLY IN THEIR FINAL HOME . . .		141	FRENCH REVOLTN	154
FROM ITS HINGES UTTERING ITS FINAL GROAN ALL BEULAH FELL		326	FOUR ZOAS 7	258
FINCHAM				
P S FINCHAM IS A PUPIL OF ABERNETHY'S		874C	LETTER 79	PROSE
I DID NOT KNOW IT BEFORE YESTERDAY FROM MR FINCHAM . . .		874C	LETTER 79	PROSE
FINCHAM'S				
MR FINCHAM'S PRACTISE WITH ME THE ADDITION IS DANDELION		874B	LETTER 79	PROSE
FINCHLEY				
TO FINCHLEY NORTH TO NORWOOD SOUTH AND THE WEIGHTS . . .		485	MILTON 6	5
HAMPSTEAD HIGHGATE FINCHLEY HENDON MUSWELL HILL RAGE LOUD		636	JERUSALEM 16	1
BETWEEN BLACKHEATH & HOUNSLOW BETWEEN NORWOOD & FINCHLEY		670	JERUSALEM 42	51
TILL NORWOOD & FINCHLEY & BLACKHEATH & HOUNSLOW		671	JERUSALEM 42	80
FIND				
WHEN THAT THEY FIND THEY MUST MY LORD THEY WILL		20	EDW THIRD/PS 2	74
FIND PREY TILL TIRD AT LENGTH SATED AND TIRED		27	EDW THIRD/PS 3	258
YOU CAN FIND FRIENDLY EXCUSES FOR ME CHANDOS		27	EDW THIRD/PS 3	277
THOSE WHO WANT HAPPINESS MUST STOOP TO FIND IT		37A	CONTEMPLATN/PS	PROSE
THOU SCARCE SHALL FIND BUT SELF LOVE STANDS BETWEEN . . .		43A	THEN SHE BORE	PROSE
ID FIND IT OUT IN A MINUTE BUT IVE FOUND IT OUT ALREADY		51D	ISLAND MOON 7	PROSE
I DONT FIND IT HERE SAID HE		52C	ISLAND MOON 8	PROSE
OR ANY COMFORT FIND		56	HAIL MATRIM/IM	12
SOME TENDER LOVER SHE SHALL FIND		56	HAIL MATRIM/IM	17
UNLESS YOU FIND IT TO BE HIS ALSO PREVIOUS TO YOUR ACQUAINTANCE		87D	ANNO LAVATER	MARG
CAN FIND OUT THE UNKNOWN SO		98C	ALL RELIGIONS	PROSE
I VANISH FROM MY PEARLY THRONE AND WHO SHALL FIND MY PLACE		128	BOOK OF THEL 2	12
THEN WE SHALL SEEK THEE BUT NOT FIND AH THEL IS LIKE TO THEE		128	BOOK OF THEL 3	3
AND THE BRIGHT CLOUD SAILD ON TO FIND HIS PARTNER IN THE VALE		129	BOOK OF THEL 3	31
SOUGHT THRO NATURE TO FIND THIS TREE		174	HUMAN IMAGE/N	23
O I CANNOT CANNOT FIND		184	O I CANNOT/N	1
IF IN THE MORNING SUN I FIND IT THERE MY EYES ARE FIXD .		194	V DAU ALBION 6	23
MAY FIND IT IN A HARLOT AND IN COARSE-CLAD HONESTY . . .		199	AMERICA 8	11
SOUGHT THRO NATURE TO FIND THIS TREE		217	HUMAN ABSTR/SE	22
HORRIBLE GHAST & DEADLY NOUGHT SHALT THOU FIND IN IT . .		265	FOUR ZOAS 1	50
[BUT] FOR NOW I FIND THAT ALL THOSE EMANATIONS		268	FOUR ZOAS 1	* 165
I WILL ARISE EXPLORE THESE DENS & FIND THAT DEEP PULSATION		311	FOUR ZOAS 5	238
I THOUGHT PERHAPS TO FIND AN END A WORLD BENEATH OF VOIDNESS		317	FOUR ZOAS 6	200
SO EVER I MY SPIRITS TURN NO END I FIND OF ALL		317	FOUR ZOAS 6	207
THE VALES TO FIND HIS WAY BACK INTO HEAVEN BUT FOUND NONE		326	FOUR ZOAS 7	249
MAIST FIND A WAY TO PUNISH VALA IN THY FIERY SOUTH . . .		326	FOUR ZOAS 7	265
THARMAS HENCEFORTH IN VALA'S BOSOM THOU SHALT FIND SWEET PEACE		371	FOUR ZOAS 9	527
FIND THAT YOU HAVE BOTH DONE SUCH MIRACLES &		391D	ANNO WATSON	MARG
I HAVE READ THIS BOOK WITH ATTENTION & FIND THAT THE BISHOP		396B	ANNO WATSON	MARG
[NEVER SHALT THOU A [LOVER] TRUE LOVE FIND]		415	MY SPECTRE/N	11
TO FIND THE WESTERN PATH		421	MORNING/N	1
BUT WHEN THEY FIND THE FROWNING BABE		427	MENTAL TRAVLER	93
I THOUGHT TO FIND LOVE IN THE HEAT OF DAY		436	WILLIAM BOND	47
SOME LOOK TO FIND OUT PATCHES PAINT		447	ANNO REYNOLDS	3
THE KEYS TO ST PETER & HE WOULD FIND THAT		465D	ANNO REYNOLDS	MARG
OVER FIND THAT MY NOTES ON REYNOLDS IN THIS BOOK ARE EXACTLY		477A	ANNO REYNOLDS	MARG
LEST THE LAST JUDGMENT COME & FIND ME UNANNIHILATE . . .		495	MILTON 14	23
THEY SOON FIND THEIR OWN PLACE & JOIN THE WATCHERS OF THE ULRO		503	MILTON 20	50
THERE IS A MOMENT IN EACH DAY THAT SATAN CANNOT FIND . .		526	MILTON 35	42

		PAGE	TITLE	LINE

FIND   (CONTINUED)

NOR CAN HIS WATCH FIENDS FIND IT BUT THE INDUSTRIOUS FIND . . . 526 MILTON 35 43
I FIND THEM THE ERRORS OF THE FOE . . . . 538 ANGER WRATH/N 4
FRIENDS WERE QUITE HARD TO FIND OLD AUTHORS SAY . . . . 546 ANOTHER/N 2 3
WILL FIND THE WOMAN'S SCALES SCRAPE OFF THE MAN'S HAIRS . 559 WOMAN SCALY/N 3
"FIT AUDIENCE FIND THO FEW" MILTON . . . . . . 560C EXHIBITION ADV PROSE
THEIR ART IS TO LOSE FORM HIS ART IS TO FIND FORM . . . 573B DESC CAT 3 PROSE
CANNOT FIND IN CHAUCER WHO HAS ONLY ONE MONK AND THAT . 574A DESC CAT 3 PROSE
I CAN FIND THAT OUT MYSELF AS WELL AS YOU CAN AND I WILL 579B DESC CAT 5 PROSE
   NOT
WHERE WILL THE COPIER OF NATURE AS IT NOW IS FIND . . . 580D DESC CAT 5 PROSE
THEY WILL FIND THEMSELVES MISTAKEN . . . . . . 592D PUB ADDRESS/N PROSE
AS I COPY IMAGINATION THIS THEY WILL FIND IMPOSSIBLE . . 594D PUB ADDRESS/N PROSE
WE DO NOT FIND ANY WHERE THAT SATAN IS ACCUSED OF SIN . 615B V LAST JUDG/N PROSE
HORRIBLE GHAST & DEADLY NOUGHT SHALT THOU FIND IN IT . . 645 JERUSALEM 22 23
I COME THAT I MAY FIND A WAY FOR MY BANISHED ONES TO RETURN 653 JERUSALEM 29 25
WHAT SHALL I DO WHAT COULD I DO IF I COULD FIND THESE 657 JERUSALEM 31 29
   CRIMINALS
OF SAND ON EARTH EVERY NIGHT THEY NEVER FIND THIS GATE . 666 JERUSALEM 39 2
AND FILLD WITH CRUEL TORTURES BUT NO MORTAL MAN CAN FIND 666 JERUSALEM 39 4
   THE MILL
FOR HUMAN BEAUTY KNOWS IT NOT NOR CAN MERCY FIND IT BUT 666 JERUSALEM 39 6
THERE IS A GRAIN OF SAND IN LAMBETH THAT SATAN CANNOT FIND 668 JERUSALEM 41 15
NOR CAN HIS WATCH FIENDS FIND IT TIS TRANSLUCENT & HAS 668 JERUSALEM 41 16
   MANY ANGLES
BUT HE WHO FINDS IT WILL FIND OOTHOON'S PALACE FOR WITHIN 668 JERUSALEM 41 17
BUT SHOULD THE WATCH FIENDS FIND IT THEY WOULD CALL IT SIN 668 JERUSALEM 41 19
YOU SHALL NOT FIND WHERE TO LIVE . . . . 724 IN HEAVEN/J 5
UNLESS WE FIND A WAY TO BIND THESE AWFUL FORMS TO OUR . 725 JERUSALEM 82 3
SOME FIND A FEMALE GARMENT THERE . . . . . 771 OF GATES/GP 21
TO THE REVD DR TRUSLER REVD SIR I FIND MORE & MORE THAT 791D LETTER 4 PROSE
HERE I COUNTED WITHOUT MY HOST I NOW FIND MY MISTAKE . 792A LETTER 4 PROSE
BUT I AM HAPPY TO FIND A GREAT MAJORITY OF FELLOW MORTALS 794A LETTER 5 PROSE
WITH NOW & THEN AN ENGRAVING & FIND THAT IN FUTURE TO LIVE 798B LETTER 10 PROSE
& FIND THAT I CAN WORK WITH GREATER PLEASURE THAN EVER . 803C LETTER 15 PROSE
TRY TO BE MISERABLE THAT I MAY DO MORE WORK BUT FIND IT IS 807A LETTER 17 PROSE
& I FIND ON ALL HANDS GREAT OBJECTIONS TO MY DOING ANY 812C LETTER 22 PROSE
   THING
I DID NOT BEGIN TO LEARN LANGUAGES EARLY IN LIFE AS I FIND 821D LETTER 25 PROSE
   IT
HIS HYMN ON THE NATIVITY WHICH YOU WILL FIND AMONG HIS . 823D LETTER 27 PROSE
TO YOU BY HIM WHO SEETH IN SECRET IF YOU SHOULD FIND IT 826C LETTER 28 PROSE
A FABRICATED PERJURY I HAVE BEEN FORCED TO FIND BAIL . 827D LETTER 29 PROSE
LADY HAMILTON'S DIRECTION WAS SO UNFORTUNATE AS TO FIND HIM 834D LETTER 34 PROSE
GOING ON BRISKLY WITH THE PLATES FIND EVERY THING PROMISING 835A LETTER 34 PROSE
MR WALKER I HAVE BEEN SO UNFORTUNATE AS NOT TO FIND AT HOME 836B LETTER 35 PROSE
YOU WILL FIND INCLOSED ONE IS A COPY FROM THAT MINIATURE 838D LETTER 37 PROSE
AS I FIND BY THE THINGS I HAVE IN HAND DAY & NIGHT WE . 843A LETTER 42 *PROSE
PAGE...YOU WILL FIND THAT THE TYPE IS SMALLER THAN FROM... 847A LETTER 44 PROSE
LODGINGS & FIND THEM ALL TOO GRAND AS WELL AS . . . . 848A LETTER 45 PROSE
IN ALL CIRCUMSTANCES I FIND THAT YOU WAS RIGHT IN SUPPOSING 854C LETTER 53 PROSE
PUBLICATION OF HIS LABOURS HE THEN PROCEEDED TO FIND FAULT 856B LETTER 54 PROSE
DESPISED THE MEEKNESS OF TRUE ART AND SUCH I FIND HAVE BEEN 863B LETTER 60 PROSE
BUT CANNOT AS YET FIND A CUSTOMER FOR ONE . . . . . 876D LETTER 85 PROSE
EMANATION OF THE GIANT ALBION BUT FIND THAT TO PRINT IT 878C LETTER 88 PROSE
   WILL
BROUGHT ON A RELAPSE WHICH IS LASTED TILL NOW I FIND I AM 880A LETTER 90 PROSE
"ARE GLAD WHEN THEY CAN FIND THE GRAVE" . . . . . . SUPP LEGEND/N17 *

FINDER   SEE WIND FINDER

FINDETH
WITHIN ITSELF AND FINDETH DISCONTENT . . . . 27 EDW THIRD/PS 3 253

FINDING
. . . NOUGHT FINDING BUT THE BLACK SEA WEED & SICKNING 318 FOUR ZOAS 6 273
   SLIME
SEEKING FOR REST AND FINDING NONE AND HIDDEN FAR WITHIN 641 JERUSALEM 19 15
THE DARK INCESSANT SKY SEEKING FOR REST AND FINDING NONE 641 JERUSALEM 19 22
CALLD ON HIM EVERY DAY & NOT FINDING HIM I NOW UNDERSTAND 842B LETTER 42 *PROSE
PLEASE TO LET ME KNOW BUT FINDING MYSELF WELL ENOUGH TO 875B LETTER 81 PROSE
   COME

FINDS
AMAZD SHE FINDS HERSELF UPON HER FEET . . . . . . 4 FAIR ELENOR/PS 10
& VICE VERSA GENIUS FINDS THOUGHT WITHOUT SEEKG . . . 80B ANNO LAVATER MARG
& THOUGHT THUS PRODUCD FINDS SENSE . . . . 80B ANNO LAVATER * MARG
TILL RESTING EACH HIS [CENTER] [BASEMENT] FINDS . . . . 283 FOUR ZOAS 2 139
INTO OBEDIENCE TO HIS WILL & NOW HE FINDS IN VAIN . . 353 FOUR ZOAS 8 457
BUT FINDS THE POOLS FILLED WITH SERPENTS DEVOURING ONE 354 FOUR ZOAS 8 530
   ANOTHER
HE FINDS OUT WHETHER . . . . 418 WHEN MAN HAS/N 2
FINDS NOTHING OF INSPIRATION OUGHT NOT TO DARE TO BE AN 458B ANNO REYNOLDS MARG
   ARTIST
WHEN HY (HAYLEY) FINDS OUT WHAT YOU CANNOT DO . . . . . 544 HS FRENDSHIP/N 1
BUT HE WHO FINDS IT WILL FIND OOTHOON'S PALACE FOR WITHIN 668 JERUSALEM 41 17

FINE
MY SILKS AND FINE ARRAY . . . . 6 MY SILKS/PS 1
AND FAVOUR US WITH A FINE SONG THEN SHE SUNG . . . . 55C ISLAND MOON 9 PROSE
AND THIS IS A FINE COUNTRY . . . . 168 HAST LAP/N 2
HUNDREDS OR THOUSANDS OF YEARS O VERY FINE RECORDS . . 394A ANNO WATSON MARG
PIETY & VIRTUE IS SENECA CLASSICAL O FINE BISHOP . . . 394D ANNO WATSON MARG
TO HANG UPON THE BRANCHES FINE . . . . 422 BENEATH/N 11
TO HANG UPON THE BRANCHES FINE . . . . 424 THE GOLDEN NET 10
I WILL HUMBLE MY BEAUTY I WILL NOT DRESS FINE . . . . 428 MARY 29
JOY & WOE ARE WOVEN FINE . . . . 432 AUGURIES 59

695

```
                                                         PAGE      TITLE         LINE
FINE    (CONTINUED)
      WHO WILL DARE TO SAY THAT [FINE] POLITE ART IS ENCOURAGED    446A ANNO REYNOLDS  * MARG
      FINE & JUST NOTIONS WHY DOES HE NOT ALWAYS ALLOW AS MUCH     462C ANNO REYNOLDS    MARG
      A FINE JUMBLE  . . . . . . . . . . . . . . . . . . . . 466C ANNO REYNOLDS    MARG
      OR FINE WAX TO MOULD ARTFUL A MODEL FOR GOLDEN ORNAMENTS     515 MILTON 28        15
      ALL THE REST ARE EVIDENTLY COPIES THOUGH FINE ONES  . .  . 565D DESC CAT 2     PROSE
      [BEEN THE VICTIM] IN A WORK OF ART IT IS NOT FINE TINTS      591C PUB ADDRESS/N  PROSE
      THAT ARE REQUIRED BY FINE FORMS FINE TINTS WITHOUT  . . .  591C PUB ADDRESS/N  PROSE
      ARE LOATHSOM FINE TINTS WITHOUT FINE FORMS  . . . . . . .  591C PUB ADDRESS/N *PROSE
      A MAN WHO PRETENDS TO IMPROVE FINE ART DOES NOT KNOW   .  . 593C PUB ADDRESS/N  PROSE
      WHAT FINE ART IS YE ENGLISH ENGRAVERS MUST COME DOWN  . .  593C PUB ADDRESS/N  PROSE
      FOR SUCH NONSENSE & THINK IT FINE ART  . . . . . . .  .  . 596C PUB ADDRESS/N  PROSE
      OF ADVANCING FINE ART IN PROTESTANT COMMUNITIES  . . . .  601B PUB ADDRESS/N  PROSE
      IS CLOSD AS WITH A THREEFOLD CURTAIN OF IVORY & FINE LINEN   633 JERUSALEM 13     23
           & ERMINE
      THY PILLARS OF IVORY & GOLD THY CURTAINS OF SILK & FINE      647 JERUSALEM 24     18
      OTHER DAUGHTERS WEAVE ON THE CUSHION & PILLOW NETWORK FINE   692 JERUSALEM 59     42
      OTHER DAUGHTERS OF LOS LABOURING AT LOOMS LESS FINE  . . .  692 JERUSALEM 59     45
      THE VEIL OF GOATS-HAIR & PURPLE & SCARLET & FINE TWINED      692 JERUSALEM 59     55
           LINEN
      (TO HER) SERVICE & THAT IT HAS A VERY FINE VIEW OF THE SEA   803B LETTER 15     *PROSE
      THE DAWBED BLACK & YELLOW SHADOWS THAT ARE FOUND IN MOST     815B LETTER 23      PROSE
           FINE
      & BEING UNDER MY OWN EYE THE PRINTS ARE AS FINE AS THE       821A LETTER 25      PROSE
      LONDON AFFORDS OF SEEING FINE PICTURES AND THE VARIOUS  . . 823A LETTER 26      PROSE
      ATTACHING HIMSELF WHOLLY TO THE SALE OF FINE EDITIONS OF     831C LETTER 31      PROSE
      HE SHEWD ME A VERY FINE PORTRAIT OF MRS SIDDONS BY ROMNEY    836A LETTER 35      PROSE
      HECATE A VERY FINE THING INDEED WHICH I HAVE  . . . . .  . 849A LETTER 45      PROSE
      PLINY VERY FINE BUT VERY UNFINISHD WHICH I HAVE  . . . .  849A LETTER 45      PROSE
      CONGRATULATE YOU ON THE RECEIT OF ANOTHER FINE BOY  . . .  873B LETTER 77      PROSE
      GONE AS THE FINE WEATHER IS VERY BENEFICIAL & COMFORTABLE    876A LETTER 83      PROSE
           TO ME
FINER
      ARE FINER THAN ANY WE HAVE IN ENGLAND  . . . . . . .  .   28 EDW THIRD/PS 4      6
      PAINT FINER THAN RUBENS OR (REMBRANDT) OR  . . . . . .  . 594C PUB ADDRESS/N  PROSE
      CORREGGIO OR TITIAN I DO NOT PRETEND TO ENGRAVE FINER  .  . 594C PUB ADDRESS/N  PROSE
      TO ENGRAVE FINER THAN STRANGE WOOLETT HALL OR BARTOLOZZI    594C PUB ADDRESS/N  PROSE
FINERY
      ("ALL FINERY IS A SIGN OF LITTLENESS") NOT ALWAYS  . . .  71B ANNO LAVATER     MARG
FINESSE
      TO THE ROYAL ACADEMY WILL SHEW THAT THE VENETIAN FINESSE     814B LETTER 23      PROSE
FINEST
      THAN YOU WILL GIVE FOR RAFAEL'S FINEST THINGS . . . . .   546 ENGLISH CONN/N     4
      MILTON SHAKSPEARE MICHAEL ANGELO RAFAEL THE FINEST  . . .  579C DESC CAT 5     PROSE
      THE FINEST SPECIMENS OF ART THAT ARE NOW IN THE WORLD IS     579D DESC CAT 5     PROSE
      WITH THE FINEST ENGRAVINGS & DEFY THE MOST CRITICAL JUDGE    602A PUB ADDRESS/N  PROSE
      ASSERTING IN MY OWN DEFENCE THAT THIS PRINT IS THE FINEST    602A PUB ADDRESS/N  PROSE
      AY & THE FINEST PICTURES I ALTOGETHER REJECT AS  . . .  . 815B LETTER 23      PROSE
      WHICH HE THINKS ONE OF THE FINEST DRAWINGS THE TWELVE  .  . 840D LETTER 40      PROSE
FINE-WROUGHT,FINE WROUGHT
      THAT SING AND DANCE ROUND REASON'S FINE-WROUGHT THRONE  . .  28 EDW THIRD/PS 3    291
      AND OF HER FINE WROUGHT BRAIN & OF HER BOWELS WITHIN HER     279 FOUR ZOAS 1     562
           LOINS
      IN SATAN'S INMOST PALACE OF HIS NERVOUS FINE WROUGHT BRAIN   493 MILTON 12       41
FINGAL
      READ THE EDDA OF ICELAND THE SONGS OF FINGAL . . . . .  . 389C ANNO WATSON     MARG
FINGER
      FITTED TO THE FINGER OF AN EMPEROR SUCH IS THAT WORTHY       29D EDW THIRD/PS 4  PROSE
           CHANDOS
      TILL FAYETTE POINT HIS FINGER TO VERSAILLES  . . . .  .  . 138 FRENCH REVOLTN   104
      THE FINGER OF GOD TOUCH THE SEVENTH FURNACE IN TERROR  . .  304 FOUR ZOAS 4     277
      WITH THE FINGER ON THE LIPS & THE BACK TURND TO THE LIGHT    528 MILTON 37       32
      WHAT THE FINGER OF GOD POINTED TO THEIR VIEW  . . . . .   543 IF TRUE/N          6
      AND LOS SAID I BEHOLD THE FINGER OF GOD IN TERRORS  . . .  631 JERUSALEM 12       5
      YET WHY DESPAIR I SAW THE FINGER OF GOD GO FORTH  . . . .  631 JERUSALEM 12      10
      IF I SHOULD DARE TO LAY MY FINGER ON A GRAIN OF SAND  . .  657 JERUSALEM 31      33
      SAW THE FINGER OF GOD GO FORTH UPON HIS SEVENTH FURNACE      678 JERUSALEM 48      45
      CEASE FINGER OF GOD TO WRITE . . . . . . . . . . .  .  . 754 EV GOSPEL(E)/N     23
      JEHOVAH'S FINGER WROTE THE LAW . . . . . . . . . . . .   761 FOR SEXES/GP        6
FINGERFOOTED
      HAIL FINGERFOOTED LOVELY CREATURES  . . . . . . . .  .   56 HAIL MATRIM/IM       7
FINGERS
      O DECK HER FORTH WITH THY FAIR FINGERS POUR  . . . . .  .   1 TO SPRING/PS       13
      AND LONG FINGERS & THUMBS  . . . . . . . . . . . . .  .  62 DR CLASH/IM        15
      IN [DISMAL] GNAWING PAIN DRAWN OUT BY HER LOVD FINGERS       266 FOUR ZOAS 1      79
           EVERY NERVE
      HER FINGERS NUMBER EVERY NERVE . . . . . . . . . . . .   425 MENTAL TRAVLER     17
      SHE NUMBERS WITH HER FINGERS EVERY FIBRE ERE IT GROW  . .  501 MILTON 19         49
      [WITH WHITLORS ON THEIR FINGERS] . . . . . . . . . . .  595B PUB ADDRESS/N *PROSE
      THEIR CRUEL FINGERS FOR HIS HEART & THERE THEY ENTER IN      702 JERUSALEM 66      28
           POMP
      [JEHOVAH'S FINGERS WROTE THE LAW] . . . . . . . . . .  . 761 FOR SEXES/GP        5
      MY FINGERS EMIT SPARKS OF FIRE WITH EXPECTATION OF          801C LETTER 13      PROSE
           MY FUTURE LABOURS
FINIS
      FINIS  . . . . . . . . . . . . . . . . . . . . . . . .  203C AMERICA 16       TITLE
      FINIS  . . . . . . . . . . . . . . . . . . . . . . . .  245B EUROPE 15        TITLE
      FINIS  . . . . . . . . . . . . . . . . . . . . . . . .  255C AHANIA 5         TITLE
      FINIS  . . . . . . . . . . . . . . . . . . . . . . . .  535B MILTON 43        TITLE
      FINIS  . . . . . . . . . . . . . . . . . . . . . . . .  586A DESC CAT 16      TITLE
FINISH
      NO ONE CAN FINISH SO HIGH AS THE ORIGINAL INVENTOR  . . .  555 BLAKES APL/N 1    19
```

```
                                                          PAGE    TITLE           LINE
FINISH   (CONTINUED)
    NO ONE CAN FINISH SO HIGH AS THE ORIGINAL INVENTOR  .  .    556 BLAKES APL/N 2      18
    YOU ATTEMPT TO FINISH OR IMPROVE & WHEN YOU HAVE BEGUN  .  593D PUB ADDRESS/N   PROSE
    NO ONE CAN FINISH SO HIGH AS THE ORIGINAL INVENTOR  .  .    596 BLAKES APOL/PA     12
    WOULD MAKE A NOBLE FINISH PLACED ABOVE THE GREAT PUBLIC     601A PUB ADDRESS/N   PROSE
    "MY HUSBAND HAS BEEN OBLIGED TO FINISH SEVERAL THINGS"  .   800B LETTER 12      PROSE
    ACCOUNT & WHATEVER ELSE I CAN FINISH . . . . . . . .       803D LETTER 15      PROSE
    PICTURES LIKEWISE CALLS FOR MY THANKS I WILL FINISH THE     813D LETTER 22      PROSE
        OTHER
    AND NOW LET ME FINISH WITH ASSURING YOU THAT THO I HAVE     815D LETTER 23      PROSE
    WHICH YOU GAVE ME ORDERS FOR IS EIGHTEEN I WILL FINISH      816C LETTER 24      PROSE
        THESE
    MY LETTER I WILL FINISH IT WISHING YOU  . . . . . . .      830D LETTER 30      PROSE
    WITH ALL THE FIDELITY I COULD & WILL FINISH WITH EQUAL CARE 838A LETTER 37      PROSE
    TO FINISH BY...MAY THEY ARE TO BE AS HIGHLY FINISHD AS      859A LETTER 56      PROSE
        I CAN
    A VERY FEW TOUCHES WILL FINISH THE SHIPWRECK THOSE FEW I    863C LETTER 60      PROSE
    OF DANTE WHICH YOU HAVE THAT I MAY FINISH THEM SUFFICIENTLY 876A LETTER 83      PROSE
FINISHD      SEE HIGH FINISHD
    THARMAS LAID THE FOUNDATIONS & LOS FINISHD IT IN HOWLING    307 FOUR ZOAS 5     *   78
        WOE
    AND WHEN ALL THINGS WERE FINISHD . . .  . . . . . . .      343 FOUR ZOAS 8         87
    FINISHD WHAT DOES HE MEAN . . . . . . . . . . . . . .      448D ANNO REYNOLDS  MARG
    I SAID TO MOSER THESE THINGS THAT YOU CALL FINISHD ARE  .   449C ANNO REYNOLDS  MARG
    NOT EVEN BEGUN HOW CAN THEY THEN BE FINISHD THE MAN WHO     449C ANNO REYNOLDS  MARG
    LEARND THE LANGUAGE OF ART BY MAKING MANY FINISHD COPIES    455D ANNO REYNOLDS  MARG
    ARE FINISHD I RETURN BOTH TIME & SPACE OBEY MY WILL  .  .   505 MILTON 22         17
    OF SATAN LUVAH LAID THE FOUNDATION & URIZEN FINISHD IT      513 MILTON 27          2
        IN HOWLING WOE
    BUT ALL THE PULP WASHD PAINTED FINISHD WITH LABOUR  . . .   546 SWELLD LIMBS/N      3
    COLUMBUS DISCOVERD AMERICA BUT AMERICUS VESPUTIUS FINISHD &  598C PUB ADDRESS/N *PROSE
    & DRYDEN HAS FINISHD IT NOW LET DRYDEN'S FALL & . . . .    600D PUB ADDRESS/N   PROSE
    "NECESSARY TO BE FINISHD BEFORE OUR MIGRATION THE"  . .     800B LETTER 12      PROSE
    MRS BUTTS WILL I HOPE EXCUSE MY NOT HAVING FINISHD THE      806A LETTER 16      PROSE
        PORTRAIT I
    DID NOT SEND & WHY I HAVE NOT BEFORE NOW FINISHD  . . .     815C LETTER 23      PROSE
    AFTER I HAD FINISHD MY LETTER I FOUND THAT I HAD NOT SAID   816C LETTER 24      PROSE
    MANY VERY FORMIDABLE WORKS WHICH I HAVE FINISHD & READY     820A LETTER 25      PROSE
    THE RIPOSO WHICH IS NEARLY FINISHD MUCH TO MY SATISFACTION  822B LETTER 26      PROSE
    BRING SOME WITH ME FINISHD I AM AT PRESENT IN A BUSTLE  .   826D LETTER 28      PROSE
    ENGRAVING IS ETERNAL WORK THE TWO PLATES ARE ALMOST FINISHD 837C LETTER 36      PROSE
    FINISHD ENGRAVINGS WILL DO AS OUTLINE INTIRELY OMITS  .  .  848A LETTER 45      PROSE
    IN THE HIGHLY FINISHED MANNER & (FOUR) IN A LESS FINISHD    848B LETTER 45      PROSE
    THE HEAD OF COWPER AFTER LAWRENCE THE HEADS TO BE FINISHD   850D LETTER 49      PROSE
    BUT THE HECATE IS A FINISHD PRODUCTION WHICH WILL CALL FOR  855A LETTER 53      PROSE
    ALL THE ENGRAVER'S NICEST ATTENTION INDEED IT IS           855A LETTER 53      PROSE
        MORE FINISHD
    (THIRTY) GUINEAS IF FINISHD & IF A SKETCH (FIFTEEN) GUINEAS 855B LETTER 53      PROSE
        AS
    THEREFORE HECATE MUST BE A FINISHD PLATE I CONSIDER  . .    855B LETTER 53      PROSE
    FINISHD PROOF BE ASSURED THAT WITH OUR GOOD FLAXMAN'S  .    855B LETTER 53      PROSE
    TO FINISH BY...MAY THEY ARE TO BE AS HIGHLY FINISHD AS      859A LETTER 56      PROSE
        I CAN
    HIGHLY LABOURD PLATES THAN A GREATER NUMBER & LESS FINISHD  860C LETTER 56      PROSE
    HE TELLS ME THAT IT IS TOO MUCH FINISHD OR OVER LABOURD     877A LETTER 85      PROSE
    COST MY TIME THE AMOUNT OF TWENTY GUINEAS NOW I HAVE        878C LETTER 88      PROSE
        FINISHD
    FINISHD STATE I AM TOO MUCH ATTACHD TO DANTE TO THINK MUCH  879C LETTER 89      PROSE
FINISHED      SEE HIGH FINISHED
    ADVERTISEMENT THE REMAINING BOOKS OF THIS POEM ARE FINISHED 134A FRENCH REVOLTN  TITLE
    HIGHLY FINISHED ENGRAVINGS AND TWO MORE ARE NEARLY READY    207C PROSPECTUS 1793 PROSE
    THE ETERNALS THEIR TENT FINISHED  .  .  .  .  .  .  .  .    232 URIZEN 19          37
    IN HIGH FINISHED FRESCO WHERE THE COLOURS WOULD BE AS PURE  566A DESC CAT 2      PROSE
    ALL FRESCOES ARE AS HIGH FINISHED AS MINIATURES OR ENAMELS  566B DESC CAT 2      PROSE
    ENVIOUS IMPUTATION OF UNFITNESS FOR FINISHED AND SCIENTIFIC 572C DESC CAT 3      PROSE
        ART
    OF HIS FINISHED PRODUCTIONS BY ANY CALUMNIES IN FUTURE  .   573A DESC CAT 3      PROSE
    FINISHED A MORE PERFECT PICTURE . . . . . . . . . . .      582B DESC CAT 9      PROSE
    WHERE A MONTH WOULD WITH JUDGMENT HAVE FINISHED IT  . .     583C DESC CAT 9      PROSE
    MORE FINISHED WHEN MR B(BLAKE) FORMERLY PAINTED IN OIL  .   584D DESC CAT 15     PROSE
    THE DESIGNER PROPOSES TO ENGRAVE IN A CORRECT AND FINISHED  586C CHAUCER 1       PROSE
    FINISHED IN ONE YEAR FROM SEPTEMBER NEXT  . . . . . .      587A CHAUCER 1       PROSE
    TIME WAS FINISHED THE BREATH DIVINE BREATHED OVER ALBION    742 JERUSALEM 94       18
    THE PICTURE IS VERY HIGHLY FINISHED  . . . . . . . .       843D LETTER 43      PROSE
    FAINT IDEA OF THE FINISHED PRINTS FROM HIS WORKS SEVERAL OF 844C LETTER 43      PROSE
    IN THE HIGHLY FINISHED MANNER & (FOUR) IN A LESS FINISHD    848B LETTER 45      PROSE
    SO HIGH FINISHED A STATE I AM SURE MARK MY CONFIDENCE  .    853B LETTER 52      PROSE
    IT MUST BE SOON A HIGHLY FINISHED AND PROPERLY FINISHED     853C LETTER 52      PROSE
        PRINT
    FINISHED THOUGH FLAXMAN HAS ALREADY PRONOUNCED IT SO  .     853C LETTER 52      PROSE
FINISHER     SEE HIGH FINISHER
    BUT I SAY THAT THE EMBROIDERY OF THE IGNORANT FINISHER  .   593B PUB ADDRESS/N   PROSE
FINISHES
    ("PATIENTLY FINISHES WHAT HE BOLDLY BEGAN ") UNEASY    .    74C ANNO LAVATER    MARG
    AND FINISHES WHERE THE LARK MOUNTS HERE MILTON JOURNEYED    498 MILTON 17          27
FINISHING
    SUSCEPTIBLE OF HIGHER FINISHING THAN DRAWING ON PAPER  .    585A DESC CAT 15     PROSE
    FROM IGNORANCE ITSELF & ITS FINISHING IS LIKE ITS MASTER    593B PUB ADDRESS/N   PROSE
    WHICH IS STILL UNFINISHD BUT IS IN A FINISHING WAY & LOOKS  809C LETTER 20      PROSE
        WELL
    BUT I GO ON FINISHING ROMNEY WITH SPIRIT AND FOR THE RELIEF 831C LETTER 31      PROSE
    IT YET WANTS ALL ITS LAST & FINISHING TOUCHES BUT I HOPE    850B LETTER 49      PROSE
        YOU
```

	PAGE	TITLE	LINE

FINISHING (CONTINUED)

VERY UNEQUAL IN POINT OF FINISHING THE PLINY IN(IS) . . . . 855A LETTER 53 . . PROSE
   A SKETCH

FINISHINGS   SEE HIGH FINISHINGS

FINITE

IN A FINITE ORGANICAL PERCEPTION . . . . 153C MARRIAGE HH 12 PROSE
WHEREAS IT NOW APPEARS FINITE & CORRUPT . . . . . . 154B MARRIAGE HH 14 PROSE
AND OVERWHELMED ALL EXCEPT THIS FINITE WALL OF FLESH . . 241 EUROPE 10 20
SHUT UP IN FINITE REVOLUTIONS AND MAN BECAME AN ANGEL . . 241 EUROPE 10 22
INTO FINITE INFLEXIBLE ORGANS . . . . 258 BOOK OF LOS 4 45
TRIGONS & CUBES DIVIDE THE ELEMENTS IN FINITE BONDS . . . 284 FOUR ZOAS 2 169
OF LIFE TILL THEY BECOME FINITE & ITSELF SEEMS INFINITE . 490 MILTON 10 * 7
   [UNTIL]
THE WORLD OF GENERATION OR VEGETATION IS FINITE . . . . 605D V LAST JUDG/N PROSE

FINND

SCALED & FINND WITH IRON & BRASS THEY DEVOURD THE PATH . 313 FOUR ZOAS 6 76
   BEFORE HIM

FIRD

AND PHOEBUS FIRD MY VOCAL RAGE . . . . 6 HOW SWEET/PS 10
WERE BASE WHO WERE NOT FIRD TO DEEDS . . . . 23 EDW THIRD/PS 3 79
ROARING REDOUNDING LOUD LOUD LOUDER & LOUDER & FIRD . . 308 FOUR ZOAS 5 106
THE BATTLE HOWLS THE TERRORS FIRD RAGE IN THE WORK OF DEATH 343 FOUR ZOAS 8 107

FIRE   SEE HELL FIRE

WHENEER I ENTER MORE THAN MORTAL FIRE . . . . 10 FRESH FROM/PS 19
THE OAKEN LOG LAY ON THE FIRE . . . . 16 BLIND-MANS/PS 6
BLAZE IN EACH COUNTENANCE AND FIRE THE BATTLE . . . . 18 EDW THIRD/PS 1 12
SHALL BEAM A RADIANCE TO FIRE THE BREASTS . . . . . 18 EDW THIRD/PS 1 24
OUR BACKS TO THE FIRE TILL WE SHALL BURN OUR SKIRTS . . 22 EDW THIRD/PS 3 38
FEARS THE SMALL FIRE THAT PLAYS ABOUT THE PEN . . . . 24 EDW THIRD/PS 3 117
AND SET ALL HEARTS ON FIRE TO BE WITH US . . . . . 24 EDW THIRD/PS 3 139
THREATENING AS THE RED BROW OF STORMS AS FIRE . . . . 31 EDW THIRD/PS 6 5
THE SAVAGE MONSTERS RUSH LIKE ROARING FIRE . . . . . 32 EDW THIRD/PS 6 26
RAIN FIRE INTO THE MOLTEN RAGING SEA . . . . 32 EDW THIRD/PS 6 30
WHEN SOULS ARE TORN TO EVERLASTING FIRE . . . . . . 33 EDW FOURTH/PS 11
BENEATH ME BURNS ETERNAL FIRE O FOR A HAND TO PLUCK ME . 36B COUCH DEATH/PS PROSE
   FORTH
LIKE SMOULDRING FIRE OR IN THE BUZZ OF CITIES FLIES ABROAD 42C THEN SHE BORE PROSE
& SET HIS WIG ON FIRE & THROW IT AT THE PEOPLE HED CRY . 48B ISLAND MOON 4 PROSE
THEN MR INFLAMMABLE GASS RAN & SHOVD HIS HEAD INTO THE FIRE 48C ISLAND MOON 4 PROSE
WHAT MYRATANA WHAT MY WIFE O SOUL O SPIRIT O FIRE . . . 99 TIRIEL 1 30
THUNDER & FIRE & PESTILENCE (HEAR) YOU NOT TIRIEL'S CURSE 106 TIRIEL 5 13
AND ALL THAT TIME WE WAITED FOR THE FIRE TO FALL . . . 107 TIRIEL 6 9
   FROM HEAVEN
. . . LIKE SPIRITS OF FIRE IN THE BEAUTIFUL . . . . . 136 FRENCH REVOLTN 54
LIKE THE CENTRAL FIRE . . . . 137 FRENCH REVOLTN 80
THE LAW AND GOSPEL FROM FIRE AND AIR AND ETERNAL REASON . 138 FRENCH REVOLTN 95
   AND SCIENCE
ETERNALLY WANDRING A COMET AND SWIFT-FALLING FIRE . . . 141 FRENCH REVOLTN 160
. . . O PRINCES OF FIRE WHOSE FLAMES ARE FOR GROWTH NOT . 142 FRENCH REVOLTN 179
   CONSUMING
. . . MINE NEVER YET FADED FOR FIRE DELIGHTS IN ITS FORM 142 FRENCH REVOLTN 189
. . . A WHIRLWIND AND FIRE TORE FURIOUS FROM HIS ANGRY . 143 FRENCH REVOLTN 200
   BOSOM
SUDDEN AS THE BULLET WRAPPD IN HIS FIRE . . . . . . 146 FRENCH REVOLTN 262
LIKE A FLAME OF FIRE HE STOOD BEFORE DARK RANKS . . . . 146 FRENCH REVOLTN 273
GLEAMS OF FIRE STREAK THE HEAVENS . . . . 146 FRENCH REVOLTN 278
. . . ALONG THE ROADS GLITTER LIKE FIRE . . . . . . 147 FRENCH REVOLTN 292
BEING NO OTHER THAN [THE DEVIL] HE WHO DWELLS IN FLAMING 150B MARRIAGE HH 5 *PROSE
   FIRE
THE EYES OF FIRE THE NOSTRILS OF AIR . . . . 152B MARRIAGE HH 9 PROSE
THE ANCIENT TRADITION THAT THE WORLD WILL BE CONSUMED IN 154B MARRIAGE HH 14 PROSE
   FIRE
IN THE FOURTH CHAMBER WERE LIONS OF FLAMING FIRE . . . 155A MARRIAGE HH 15 PROSE
FIRE BURST AND ROLLED THRO THE DEEP BLACKNING ALL BENEATH 156B MARRIAGE HH 17 PROSE
MIXED WITH FIRE AND NOT MANY STONES' THROW FROM US . . 156B MARRIAGE HH 17 PROSE
GOLDEN ROCKS TILL WE DISCOVERD TWO GLOBES OF CRIMSON FIRE 156C MARRIAGE HH 17 PROSE
ONCE I SAW A DEVIL IN A FLAME OF FIRE . . . . 158B MARRIAGE HH 22 PROSE
WHO STRETCHED OUT HIS ARMS EMBRACING THE FLAME OF FIRE . 158D MARRIAGE HH 22 PROSE
THE NEW BORN FIRE STOOD BEFORE THE STARRY KING . . . . 159B SONG LIBERTY PROSE
THE FIRE THE FIRE IS FALLING . . . . 159C SONG LIBERTY PROSE
WITH THUNDER AND FIRE LEADING HIS STARRY HOSTS . . . . 159D SONG LIBERTY PROSE
WHERE THE SON OF FIRE IN HIS EASTERN CLOUD . . . . . 160A SONG LIBERTY PROSE
[BURNT THE] [THE CRUEL] FIRE OF THINE EYES . . . . 172 THE TYGER/N 1 6
WHAT THE HAND DARE SIEZE THE FIRE . . . . 172 THE TYGER/N 1 8
THE CRUEL FIRE OF THINE EYES . . . . 173 THE TYGER/N 2 * 6
WHAT THE HAND DARE SIEZE THE FIRE . . . . 173 THE TYGER/N 2 8
[THEY] AND BURND HIM IN A HOLY [FIRE] PLACE . . . . 177 LIT BOY LST/N 26
AND A PLEASANT FIRE OUR SOULS TO REGALE . . . . . . 179 LIT VAGABOND/N 7
BECAUSE TIS FILLD WITH FIRE . . . . 182 LOOK OF LOVE/N 2
BECAUSE TIS FILLD WITH FIRE . . . . 184 SEVRL QUESTN/N 6
AH ARE THERE OTHER WARS BESIDE THE WARS OF SWORD AND FIRE 192 V DAU ALBION 4 19
AND IS THERE NOT ETERNAL FIRE AND ETERNAL CHAINS . . . 192 V DAU ALBION 4 23
THE HAIRY SHOULDERS REND THE LINKS FREE ARE THE WRISTS . 196 AMERICA PREL 2 2
   OF FIRE
O WHAT LIMB RENDING PAINS I FEEL THY FIRE & MY FROST . . 196 AMERICA PREL 2 15
INTENSE NAKED A HUMAN FIRE FIERCE GLOWING AS THE WEDGE . 197 AMERICA 4 8
OF IRON HEATED IN THE FURNACE HIS TERRIBLE LIMBS WERE FIRE 197 AMERICA 4 9
BUT ALL RUSH TOGETHER IN THE NIGHT IN WRATH AND RAGING FIRE 202 AMERICA 14 19
WITH FIERCE DISEASE AND LUST UNABLE TO STEM THE FIRE OF ORC 203 AMERICA 16 21
REVEAL THE DRAGON THRO THE HUMAN COURSING SWIFT AS FIRE . 204 AMERICA CANC B 1
THE FIRE OF LONDON [CH(CHARLES) I REHEADED] . . . . . 209A SUBJCTS HIST/N TITLE
WATER EARTH AIR FIRE . . . . 209C FOR CHILDRN/GP TITLE

698

```
                                                         PAGE     TITLE          LINE
FIRE     (CONTINUED)
    BURNT THE FIRE OF THINE EYES          . . . . . . . .  214  THE TYGER/SE        6
    WHAT THE HAND DARE SIEZE THE FIRE  . . . . . . . . .   214  THE TYGER/SE        8
    AND A PLEASANT FIRE OUR SOULS TO REGALE  . . . . . .   216  LIT VAGABND/SE      6
    FIRST I FOUGHT WITH THE FIRE CONSUMD  . . . . . . . . 224  URIZEN 4           14
    IN CATARACTS OF FIRE BLOOD & GALL     . . . . . . . . 225  URIZEN 4           46
    WITH A GLOBE OF FIRE LIGHTING HIS JOURNEY  . . . . .   234  URIZEN 20          48
    NONE COULD BREAK THE WEB NO WINGS OF FIRE  . . . . .   235  URIZEN 25          19
    THE HORRENT DEMON ROSE SURROUNDED WITH RED STARS OF FIRE  240  EUROPE 4        29
    ARISE MY SON BRING ALL THY BRETHREN O THOU KING OF FIRE   240  EUROPE 8         8
    AROSE LIKE A PILLAR OF FIRE ABOVE THE ALPS . . . . . . 248  SONG OF LOS 7      27
    WAS A PILLAR OF FIRE TO EGYPT  . . . . . . . . . . .   250  AHANIA 2           45
    WITH THY HAND FULL OF GENEROUS FIRE  . . . . . . . .   255  AHANIA 5           30
    IN THE VOID BETWEEN FIRE AND FIRE  . . . . . . . . .   257  BOOK OF LOS 3      44
    AN IMMENSE ORB OF FIRE HE FRAMD   . . . . . . . . . . 260  BOOK OF LOS 5      34
    OBSCURING THE IMMENSE ORB OF FIRE  . . . . . . . . .   260  BOOK OF LOS 5      54
    HIS SPECTRE ISSUING FROM HIS FEET IN FLAMES OF FIRE  . . 266  FOUR ZOAS 1      78
    DEFORMD THRO THE THREE HEAVENS DESCENDING IN FURY & FIRE  267  FOUR ZOAS 1    104
    UPON THE SANDY SHORE RESTED HIS CHARIOT OF FIRE   . .   273  FOUR ZOAS 1      330
    AND SPIRITS OF FLAMING FIRE ON HIGH GOVERND THE MIGHTY SONG  274  FOUR ZOAS 1 384
    AND VALA FED IN CRUEL DELIGHT THE FURNACES WITH FIRE  . . 282  FOUR ZOAS 2     73
    LIKE PILLARS OF FIRE TRAVELLING THRO DARKNESS & NON ENTITY  286  FOUR ZOAS 2  230
    OF FIRE FAR SHINING TRAVELLING ALONG EVEN TO ITS DESTIND  287  FOUR ZOAS 2   276
        END
    . . . ON THE STEPS OF FIRE BEFORE HIS HALLS   . . . .  292  FOUR ZOAS 3        44
    . . . BLUE (SULPHUREOUS) FIRE FROM THE FLAME  . . . .  295  FOUR ZOAS 3    *  146
    RENEW THESE RUIND SOULS OF MEN THRO EARTH SEA AIR & FIRE  298  FOUR ZOAS 4     30
    BELCHD FROM THE FURNACES WREATHD ROUND HER CHAIND      302  FOUR ZOAS 4       188
        IN CEASELESS FIRE
    TORN BY BLACK STORMS & CEASELESS TORRENTS OF CONSUMING FIRE  306  FOUR ZOAS 5  56
    WITHIN HIS RIBS PRODUCING SERPENTS WHOSE SOULS ARE FLAMES  306  FOUR ZOAS 5    61
        OF FIRE
    OF CIRCLING FIRE UNCEASING PLAYS TO FEED THEM WITH LIFE  308  FOUR ZOAS 5     115
        & BRING
    THE ELEMENTAL PLANETS & THE ORBS OF ECCENTRIC FIRE   . . 308  FOUR ZOAS 5     126
    VESTS OF THE RADIANT COLOURS OF HEAVEN & CROWNS OF GOLDEN  312  FOUR ZOAS 6     28
        FIRE
    LOS BROODED ON THE DARKNESS NOR SAW URIZEN WITH A GLOBE  314  FOUR ZOAS 6      83
        OF FIRE
    SOME [?AS] COLUMNS OF FIRE [&] OR OF WATER . . . . . . 315  FOUR ZOAS 6    *  122
    ROUND LAKES OF FIRE IN THE DARK DEEP THE RUINS OF URIZEN'S  316  FOUR ZOAS 6  179
        WORLD
    ALL THRO THE CAVERNS OF FIRE & AIR & EARTH SEEKING   . .  318  FOUR ZOAS 6    272
    STILL HE WITH HIS GLOBE OF FIRE IMMENSE IN HIS VENTUROUS  319  FOUR ZOAS 6    286
        HAND
    AND [WITH] BY HIS GLOBE OF FIRE HE WENT DOWN THE VALE OF  319  FOUR ZOAS 6    294
        URTHONA
    A CAVERND UNIVERSE OF FLAMING FIRE THE HORSES OF URIZEN  320  FOUR ZOAS 7       6
    THE BULLS OF LUVAH BREATHING FIRE BELLOW ON BURNING   320  FOUR ZOAS 7         16
        PASTURES
    ROUND HOWLING ORC WHOSE AWFUL LIMBS CAST FORTH RED SMOKE  320  FOUR ZOAS 7     17
        & FIRE
    BENEATH THEE & AROUND ABOVE A SHOWER OF FIRE NOW BEATS  .  321  FOUR ZOAS 7    51
    AND NOW A ROCK MOVES ON THE SURFACE OF THIS LAKE OF FIRE  321  FOUR ZOAS 7     55
    I WELL REMEMBER HOW I STOLE THY LIGHT & IT BECAME FIRE  .  .  323  FOUR ZOAS 7 147
    DESPISING URIZEN'S LIGHT & TURNING IT INTO FLAMING FIRE  324  FOUR ZOAS 7     153
    AND WITH IT LOSE HIMSELF IN MEEKNESS SHE EMBRACD HIS FIRE  336  FOUR ZOAS 7B  128
    THE HAIRY SHOULDERS REND THE LINKS FREE ARE THE WRISTS  336  FOUR ZOAS 7B     140
        OF FIRE
    THAT RAISES WATER INTO CISTERNS BROKEN & BURND IN FIRE  . . 337  FOUR ZOAS 7B 177
    OR LIKE A CLOUD BENEATH & LIKE A FIRE FLAMING IN HIGH  . 339  FOUR ZOAS 7B  *  265
    AND THE STRONG PINIOND EAGLE BORE THE FIRE OF HEAVEN . . . 340  FOUR ZOAS 7B   285
    A CREST OF FIRE ROSE ON HIS FOREHEAD RED AS THE CARBUNCLE  342  FOUR ZOAS 8     69
    OF FAIR JERUSALEM'S BOSOM IN A GENTLY BEAMING ?FIRE  . . . 346  FOUR ZOAS 8    193
    CALLD DOWN A GREAT SOLEMN ASSEMBLY RINTRAH IN FURY & FIRE  351  FOUR ZOAS 8  *  389
    TO BURN MYSTERY WITH FIRE & FORM ANOTHER FROM HER ASHES  357  FOUR ZOAS 8     616
    OF ORC BEGAN TO CONSUME IN FIERCE RAVING FIRE HIS FIERCE  358  FOUR ZOAS 9      34
        FLAMES
    INTO RESISTLESS PILLARS OF FIRE ROLLING ROUND & ROUND   358  FOUR ZOAS 9       37
        GATHERING
    START FORTH THE TREMBLING MILLIONS INTO FLAMES OF MENTAL  358  FOUR ZOAS 9      44
        FIRE
    START FORTH THE TREMBLING MILLIONS INTO FLAMES OF MENTAL  359  FOUR ZOAS 9      89
        FIRE
    EXPENDING ALL HIS ENERGY AGAINST THE FUEL OF FIRE    . . . 366  FOUR ZOAS 9    359
    OF FIRE RISE UP NIGHTLY FROM THE OCEAN & ONE SUN   . . . .  379  FOUR ZOAS 9   832
    THAT RISEN FROM THE SEA OF FIRE RENEWD WALK OER THE EARTH  379  FOUR ZOAS 9    837
    LEAPD FROM THE STEPS OF FIRE & ON THE GRASS  . . . . . .  414  TO MRS FLAXMAN   5
    THE SELFHOOD IN A FLAME OF FIRE   . . . . . . . . . .  421  EACH MAN/N          6
    THE ONE WAS CLOTHD IN FLAMES OF FIRE   . . . . . . . .  421  BENEATH/N           6
    NOW INTREATING [?FLAME] FLAMING FIRE  . . . . . . . .  422  BENEATH/N       *  24
    [THE ONE WAS CLOTHD IN FLAMES OF FIRE]  . . . . . . .  422  BENEATH REWR/N      3
    THE ONE WAS CLOTHD IN FLAMES OF FIRE   . . . . . . . .  424  THE GOLDEN NET      5
    NOW INTREATING BURNING FIRE    . . . . . . . . . . .  424  THE GOLDEN NET      23
    TILL FROM THE FIRE ON THE HEARTH  . . . . . . . . . .  425  MENTAL TRAVLER      43
    AND SHE IS ALL OF SOLID FIRE   . . . . . . . . . . .  425  MENTAL TRAVLER      45
    FROM BEFORE THE THRONE & FROM BEFORE THE SEA OF FIRE  443C  LAST JUDGMNT/L *PROSE
        WHICH
    & SOME ARE SCOURGED BY SPIRITS WITH FLAMES OF FIRE INTO  443C  LAST JUDGMNT/L  PROSE
    BRING ME MY CHARIOT OF FIRE   . . . . . . . . . . .  481  AND DID FEET/M       12
    THE GNOMES ACCUSD SATAN WITH INDIGNATION FURY AND FIRE  . . 487  MILTON 7       21
    OF FIRE ROUND THE WALLS COLUMNS OF FIRE GUARD AROUND   . . 490  MILTON 9        44
```

```
                                                           PAGE      TITLE          LINE
FIRE     (CONTINUED)
    OF CANAAN AND THEY WROTE IN THUNDER SMOKE AND FIRE     . . .  498 MILTON 17          13
    OF FIRE IN INTERCHANGE OF BEAUTY & PERFECTION IN             500 MILTON 18          40
        THE DARKNESS
    STRETCHD OUT HIS HANDS OF FIRE & WOOED THEY TRIUMPH IN       500 MILTON 18          45
        HIS PAIN
    AND IN THE SOUTH REMAINS A BURNING FIRE IN THE EAST A VOID   500 MILTON 19          22
    AND THEY LAMENTED THAT THEY HAD IN WRATH & FURY & FIRE  . .  504 MILTON 21          31
    LOS STOOD IN THAT FIERCE GLOWING FIRE & HE ALSO STOOPD DOWN  505 MILTON 22           8
    LO ORC ARISES ON THE ATLANTIC LO HIS BLOOD AND FIRE     . .  506 MILTON 23           6
    AND EVERY SEVEN AGES IS INCIRCLED WITH A FLAMING FIRE   . .  516 MILTON 28          57
    ARE YOU THE FIERY CIRCLE THAT LATE DROVE IN FURY & FIRE      523 MILTON 34           3
    OF OG & PEALING LOUD THE CRIES OF THE VICTIMS OF FIRE   . .  528 MILTON 37          22
    SATAN HEARD COMING IN A CLOUD WITH TRUMPETS & FLAMING FIRE   530 MILTON 38          50
    BURND TERRIBLE MY PATH BECAME A SOLID FIRE AS BRIGHT    . .  530 MILTON 39           4
    AS THE SEVEN SPAKE AND THEY STOOD IN A MIGHTY COLUMN OF      530 MILTON 39           8
        FIRE
    OF LOS THAT EVER BURNETH WITH FIRE EVER & EVER AMEN          530 MILTON 39          12
    WHICH JESUS RENT & NOW SHALL WHOLLY PURGE AWAY WITH FIRE     533 MILTON 41          27
    IN THE COLUMN OF FIRE IN FELPHAM'S VALE THEN TO THEIR        534 MILTON 42          22
        MOUTHS THE FOUR
    FATHER & MOTHER I RETURN FROM FLAMES OF FIRE TRIED & PURE    535B FATHER MOTHER   PROSE
        & WHITE
    THOUGH THE ORIGINAL CONCEPTION WAS ALL FIRE AND ANIMATION    583A DESC CAT 9     PROSE
    WHICH HINDER THE VISION OF GOD TURNING ALL INTO A CONSUMING  604C V LAST JUDG/N  PROSE
        FIRE
    A SEA OF FIRE ISSUES FROM BEFORE THE THRONE            . . . 606B V LAST JUDG/N  PROSE
    BEFORE THE FLOOD THAT THEY WERE FILLD WITH BLOOD & FIRE      606D V LAST JUDG/N  PROSE
    GREY BEARDS & SCOURGES OF FIRE THEY REPRESENT CRUEL LAWS     608A V LAST JUDG/N  PROSE
    BY EARTHQUAKES A GREAT CITY ON FIRE IS SEEN IN THE DISTANCE  608B V LAST JUDG/N  PROSE
    DESCENDING FROM THE SEA OF FIRE BEFORE THE THRONE      . . . 609A V LAST JUDG/N  PROSE
    THEY STRIP HER NAKED & BURN HER WITH FIRE IT REPRESENTS      609A V LAST JUDG/N  PROSE
    REPRESENTS ETERNAL FIRE WHICH IS THE FIRE OF GENERATION OR   609A V LAST JUDG/N  PROSE
    AMONG THE WICKED WITH SCOURGES OF FIRE     . . . . . . .     611A V LAST JUDG/N  PROSE
    DO YOU NOT SEE A ROUND DISK OF FIRE SOMEWHAT LIKE A GUINEA   617B V LAST JUDG/N  PROSE
    IS SEEN IN THE SKY BENEATH HERMES & THE SPIRITS OF FIRE      619B ILLUS MILTON   PROSE
    IS SEEN IN THE HEAVENS THROWING HIS DARTS & FLAMES OF FIRE   619B ILLUS MILTON  *PROSE
    OUR LORD WHO IS THE GOD [OF FIRE] AND LORD [OF LOVE]    .  . 621A JERUSALEM 3    PROSE
    AGAIN HE SPEAKS IN THUNDER AND IN FIRE     . . . . . . .     621 READER LOVER/J      5
    AND VALA FED IN CRUEL DELIGHT THE FURNACES WITH FIRE    .    625 JERUSALEM 7         31
    AND LUBAN STANDS IN MIDDLE OF THE CITY A MOAT OF FIRE   .    633 JERUSALEM 13        24
    THE ROCKS OF SOLID FIRE THE ICE VALLEYS THE PLAINS     . .   634 JERUSALEM 13        40
    OF BURNING SAND THE RIVERS CATARACT & LAKES OF FIRE    . . . 634 JERUSALEM 13        41
    TO LABOUR IN THE FIRE IN THE WATER IN THE EARTH IN THE AIR   638 JERUSALEM 17         2
    AND IF ANY ENTER INTO THEE THOU SHALT BE AN UNQUENCHABLE     639 JERUSALEM 17        45
        FIRE
    ARE SILENT ON HIS CLOUDED HILLS THAT BELCH FORTH STORMS      641 JERUSALEM 19         4
        & FIRE
    SATAN HIS NAME IN FLAMES OF FIRE     . . . . . . . . .       650 FIELDS FROM/J       39
    ALBION WALKD ON THE STEPS OF FIRE BEFORE HIS HALLS     . . . 654 JERUSALEM 29        33
    LOS TOOK HIS GLOBE OF FIRE TO SEARCH THE INTERIORS          656 JERUSALEM 31         3
        OF ALPION'S
    AT ENMITY WITH THE MERCIFUL & FILLD WITH DEVOURING FIRE      667 JERUSALEM 40        33
    TORN WITH BLACK STORMS & CEASELESS TORRENTS OF HIS OWN       667 JERUSALEM 40        39
        CONSUMING FIRE
    WITHIN HIS RIBS PRODUCING SERPENTS WHOSE SOULS ARE FLAMES    667 JERUSALEM 40        42
        OF FIRE
    THAT WALKS ABOUT AMONG THE STONES OF FIRE IN BLISS & WOE     680 JERUSALEM 49        73
    IN THE SOUTH REMAINS A BURNING FIRE IN THE EAST A VOID  . .  691 JERUSALEM 59        18
    IN FLAMING FIRE WITHIN THE FURNACES THE DIVINE VISION        692 JERUSALEM 60         5
        APPEARD
    . . . IN THE MIDST OF HIS ANGER IN FURNACE OF FIRE     . . . 694 JERUSALEM 61        13
    AND FIRE & THE RUIN OF CITIES & NATIONS & FAMILIES          698 JERUSALEM 64        11
        & TONGUES
    GLITTERING WITH PRECIOUS STONES & GOLD WITH GARMENTS OF      699 JERUSALEM 64        26
        BLOOD & FIRE
    THAT RAISES WATER INTO CISTERNS BROKEN & BURND WITH FIRE     700 JERUSALEM 65        19
    OF FIRE THEN AN AWFUL FIERY WHEEL SURROUNDING EARTH          702 JERUSALEM 66        42
        & HEAVEN
    TO ROAST THE FLESH IN FIRE TO EXAMINE THE INFANT'S LIMBS     707 JERUSALEM 68        58
    AND SAW A FLAME OF FIRE EVEN AS A WHEEL    . . . . . . .     717 STOOD AMONG/J        2
    OF FIRE SURROUNDING ALL THE HEAVENS IT WENT    . . . . .     717 STOOD AMONG/J        3
    THE SPINDLE TURND IN BLOOD & FIRE LOUD SOUND THE TRUMPETS    722 JERUSALEM 80        37
    AND FLAMES OF DUSKY FIRE TO AMALEK CANAAN AND MOAB     . .   723 JERUSALEM 80        50
    THE ENVY LOUD SHE LABOURD IN THE FURNACE OF FIRE     . . .   726 JERUSALEM 82        62
    ARISE UPON THY WATCHES LET US SEE THY GLOBE OF FIRE    . .   729 JERUSALEM 84        27
    SILENT AT HIS VOICE THEY VIEW THE RED GLOBE OF FIRE IN       730 JERUSALEM 85        19
        LOS'S HAND
    THENCE FEATHERD WITH SOFT CRIMSON OF THE RUBY BRIGHT AS      731 JERUSALEM 86         8
        FIRE
    IN FLAMING FIRE UNCEASING BURNS FROM ETERNITY TO ETERNITY    731 JERUSALEM 86        25
    A PILLAR OF A CLOUD BY DAY A PILLAR OF FIRE BY NIGHT    . .  731 JERUSALEM 86        27
    AND FIRE JERUSALEM TOOK THE CUP WHICH FOAMD IN VALA'S HAND   734 JERUSALEM 88        56
    INCLOSED BY EYELESS WINGS GLOWING WITH FIRE AS THE IRON      735 JERUSALEM 89        41
    THEY DRINK REUBEN & BENJAMIN AS THE IRON DRINKS THE FIRE     737 JERUSALEM 90        46
    BY SEVERE CONTENTIONS OF FRIENDSHIP & THE BURNING FIRE       738 JERUSALEM 91        18
        OF THOUGHT
    OF FIRE SPEAKING THE WORDS OF ETERNITY IN HUMAN FORMS IN     742 JERUSALEM 95         9
        DIREFUL
    BECAME A CHARIOT OF FIRE     . . . . . . . . . . . .     .   749 EV GOSPEL(B)/N      34
    WHO WALKD AMONG THE STONES OF FIRE     . . . . . . . .   .   761 FOR SEXES/GP         4
    FIRE THAT END IN ENDLESS STRIFE    . . . . . . . .   . . . . 764C FOR SEXES/GP     TITLE

                                    700
```

```
                                                              PAGE     TITLE            LINE
FIRE    (CONTINUED)
        BLIND IN FIRE WITH SHIELD & SPEAR  . . . . . . . .    770 OF GATES/GP            10
        THE ELOHIM SAW THEIR OATH ETERNAL FIRE . . . . . . .  781 GHOST ABEL 2           25
        MY FINGERS EMIT SPARKS OF FIRE WITH EXPECTATION OF    801C LETTER 13           PROSE
            MY FUTURE LABOURS
        INTO REGIONS OF FIRE  . . . . . . . . . . . . . .     804 TO BUTTS/L            11
        VERY HAPPY SITTING AT TEA BY A WOOD FIRE IN OUR COTTAGE THE  820B LETTER 25    PROSE
        WE ARE OFTEN SITTING BY OUR COTTAGE FIRE  . . . . .   854A LETTER 52           PROSE
        GOD OUT OF CHRIST IS A CONSUMING FIRE MERCY WRATH   . . . SUPP INSC HERVEY    *TITLE
FIRE-BREATHING
        REVIVES THE MILKED COW & TAMES THE FIRE-BREATHING STEED   128 BOOK OF THEL 2    10
FIRED    SEE FIRD
        TILL FIRED WITH ARDOUR FRESH RECRUITED IN ITS HUMBLE   287 FOUR ZOAS 2      *  279
            [SPRING] SEASON
FIRES
        TILL GLORY FIRES HIS BREAST TO ENLARGE HIS CASTLE  . . .   26 EDW THIRD/PS 3    201
        YOUR ANCESTORS CAME FROM THE FIRES OF TROY . . . . . .     32 EDW THIRD/PS 6      7
        WHOSE EYES DO GLARE AGAINST THE STORMY FIRES . . . . .     32 EDW THIRD/PS 6      9
        THE EARTH TREMBLED [XXX] FIRES BELCHED FROM THE YAWNING   106 TIRIEL 5        *  16
            CLEFTS
        BREATHING RED FIRES FROM MAN TO MAN AND FROM HORSE TO    137 FRENCH REVOLTN      81
            HORSE . . .
        OF KING HENRY THE FOURTH WALKS BEFORE HIM IN FIRES . . .  141 FRENCH REVOLTN     165
        WHAT DAMP ALL OUR FIRES O SPECTRE OF HENRY . . . . . . .  142 FRENCH REVOLTN     171
        CAN THE FIRES OF NOBILITY EVER BE QUENCHD . . . . .   .   142 FRENCH REVOLTN     181
        . . . GO THOU COLD RECLUSE INTO THE FIRES  . . . . . .    142 FRENCH REVOLTN     191
        THE PALE FIRES OF AUMONT INTO THE CHAMBER . . . . . . .   143 FRENCH REVOLTN     203
        BREATHE FIRES BUT TEN MILES FROM PARIS LET ALL BE PEACE   145 FRENCH REVOLTN     240
            . . .
        THE ENORMOUS DEAD LIFT UP THEIR PALE FIRES . . . . . .    148 FRENCH REVOLTN     302
        A FAINT HEAT FROM THEIR FIRES REVIVD THE COLD LOUVRE . . . 148 FRENCH REVOLTN    303
        RINTRAH ROARS & SHAKES HIS FIRES IN THE BURDEND AIR . . . 148 MARRIAGE HH 2       1
        RINTRAH ROARS & SHAKES HIS FIRES IN THE BURDEND AIR . . . 149 MARRIAGE HH 2      21
        AS I WAS WALKING AMONG THE FIRES OF HELL  . . . . . .   . 150C MARRIAGE HH 6  PROSE
        WITH CORRODING FIRES HE WROTE THE FOLLOWING SENTENCE NOW  150D MARRIAGE HH 6  PROSE
        CROWND WITH WARLIKE FIRES & RAGING DESIRES . . . . . .    177 DAY/N               5
        THAT SHIVER IN RELIGIOUS CAVES BENEATH THE BURNING FIRES  190 V DAU ALBION 2      9
        RELIGIOUS DREAMS AND HOLY VESPERS LIGHT THY SMOKY FIRES   194 V DAU ALBION 6     14
        ONCE WERE THY FIRES LIGHTED BY THE EYES OF HONEST MORN  . 194 V DAU ALBION 6     15
        SULLEN FIRES ACROSS THE ATLANTIC GLOW TO AMERICA'S SHORE  197 AMERICA 3           2
        SWELLING BELCHING FROM ITS DEEPS RED CLOUDS & RAGING FIRES 197 AMERICA 4          3
        FIRES INWRAP THE EARTHLY GLOBE YET MAN IS NOT CONSUMD  . . 199 AMERICA 8         15
        AMIDST THE LUSTFUL FIRES HE WALKS HIS FEET BECOME LIKE    199 AMERICA 8          16
            BRASS
        AROUND THEIR SHORES INDIGNANT BURNING WITH THE FIRES OF ORC  200 AMERICA 11       2
        HEADLONG FROM OUT THEIR HEAVENLY HEIGHTS DESCENDING SWIFT  200 AMERICA 12         5
            AS FIRES
        THE RED FIRES RAGD THE PLAGUES RECOILD THEN ROLLD THEY    202 AMERICA 14         20
            BACK WITH FURY
        WITH FIRES OF HELL DEFORM THEIR ANCIENT HEAVENS WITH SHAME 202 AMERICA 15        15
            & WOE
        RUSH INTO REPTILE COVERTS HIDING FROM THE FIRES OF ORC  . . 202 AMERICA 15       20
        SULLEN FIRES ACROSS THE ATLANTIC GLOW TO AMERICA'S SHORE  203 AMERICA CANC A      2
        AROUND SAINT JAMES'S [GLOW THE FIRES] . . . . . . . .     205 AMERICA CANC C      9
        IN ARMOUR AS THE NERVES OF WISDOM EACH HIS STATION [FIRES]  205 AMERICA CANC C   19
            HOLDS
        THE ROARING FIRES RAN OER THE HEAVNS . . . . . . . .      225 URIZEN 5           12
        FIRES POUR THRO THE VOID ON ALL SIDES  . . . . . . . .    225 URIZEN 5           15
        BUT NO LIGHT FROM THE FIRES ALL WAS DARKNESS  . . . . .   225 URIZEN 5           17
        LONG PERIODS IN BURNING FIRES LABOURING  . . . . . . .    225 URIZEN 5           25
        THE ETERNAL FIRES BEATING WITHOUT  . . . . . . . . . .    226 URIZEN 5           32
        AND INTENSE FIRES FOR HIS DWELLING  . . . . . . . . .     226 URIZEN 6            6
        TILL LOS ROUZD HIS HIS FIRES AFFRIGHTED  . . . . . . .    226 URIZEN 7       *    8
        BY EARTHQUAKES RIVN BELCHING SULLEN FIRES . . . . . .     227 URIZEN 10           4
        HIS FIRES BEHELD AND SICKENING  . . . . . . . . . . .     229 URIZEN 13          22
        LOS SUFFERD HIS FIRES TO DECAY . . . . . . . . . . . .    230 URIZEN 13          44
        WITH FIRES OF PROPHECY  . . . . . . . . . . . . . . .     234 URIZEN 20          43
        STAMP NOT WITH SOLID FORM THIS VIGROUS PROGENY OF FIRES   238 EUROPE PREL 2       8
        AND THE CLOUDS & FIRES PALE ROLLD ROUND IN THE NIGHT OF   242 EUROPE 12           1
            ENITHARMON
        ABRAM FLED IN FIRES FROM CHALDEA  . . . . . . . . . .     245 SONG OF LOS 3      16
        AT THE THICK-FLAMING THOUGHT-CREATING FIRES OF ORC  . .   247 SONG OF LOS 6       6
        CALL FOR FIRES IN THE CITY . . . . . . . . . . . .   .    247 SONG OF LOS 6      20
        WIDE APART STOOD THE FIRES LOS REMAIND  . . . . . . .     257 BOOK OF LOS 3      43
        BUT NO LIGHT FROM THE FIRES ALL WAS . . . . . . . . .     257 BOOK OF LOS 3      49
        AND THE SEPERATED FIRES FROZE IN . . . . . . . . . .     257 BOOK OF LOS 4       8
        THE THIN FLOWING ROUND THE FIERCE FIRES  . . . . . . .    259 BOOK OF LOS 5       8
        THEN LIGHT FIRST BEGAN FROM THE FIRES  . . . . . . . .    259 BOOK OF LOS 5      10
        AND FIRST FROM THOSE INFINITE FIRES  . . . . . . . . .    260 BOOK OF LOS 5      27
        SIEZING FIRES FROM THE TERRIFIC ORBS  . . . . . . . .     260 BOOK OF LOS 5      37
        JUSTLING TOGETHER IN THE VOID SUSPENDED BY INWARD FIRES   276 FOUR ZOAS 1       428
        WHILE THUS HE SPOKE HIS FIRES REDDEND [ROUND] OER THE HOLY  278 FOUR ZOAS 1      514
            TENT
        AND THE LEOPARDS COVERD WITH SKINS OF BEASTS TENDED THE   281 FOUR ZOAS 2        33
            ROARING FIRES
        THE FIRES OF VALA FADED LIKE A SHADOW COLD & PALE  . . .  283 FOUR ZOAS 2       114
        WITH EVER STREAMING FIRES BEAMING FROM HIS AWFUL LIMBS  . . 284 FOUR ZOAS 2      180
        A RECESS IN THE WALL FOR FIRES TO GLOW UPON THE PALE  . . 285 FOUR ZOAS 2       188
        TO LABOUR NIGHT & DAY AMONG THE FIRES HER LAMENTING VOICE  285 FOUR ZOAS 2      216
        AND AS THEY WENT IN FOLDING FIRES & THUNDERS OF THE DEEP   294 FOUR ZOAS 3       98
        LASHD ON THE LIMBS OF ENITHARMON & THE SULPHUR FIRES  . . 302 FOUR ZOAS 4       187
        FELL FROM HIS HAND HIS FIRES HID THEIR STRONG LIMBS IN    304 FOUR ZOAS 4       281
            SMOKE
```

701

		PAGE	TITLE	LINE

FIRES   (CONTINUED)

	PAGE	TITLE	LINE
SHEW THY SOUL VALA SHEW THY BOW & QUIVER OF SECRET FIRES	306	FOUR ZOAS 5	49
EMBRACING HIS BRIGHT MOTHER & BEHELD MALIGNANT FIRES . .	307	FOUR ZOAS 5	81
SURROUNDED WITH FLAMES THE DEMON GREW LOUD HOWLING IN HIS FIRES	308	FOUR ZOAS 5	109
HIS LOINS INWOVE WITH SILKEN FIRES ARE LIKE A FURNACE FIERCE	308	FOUR ZOAS 5	135
NOR COULD HE QUENCH THE FIRES FOR THEY FLAMD OUT FROM THE HEART	315	FOUR ZOAS 6	144
THRO LIGHTNINGS THUNDERS EARTHQUAKES & CONCUSSIONS FIRES & FLOODS	316	FOUR ZOAS 6	185
ROUND HIS LOINS A GIRDLE GLOWD WITH MANY COLOURD FIRES . .	319	FOUR ZOAS 6	304
ON A ROCK OF IRON FROWNING OVER THE FOAMING FIRES OF ORC	321	FOUR ZOAS 7	41
WHENCE THESE FIERCE FIRES BUT FROM THYSELF NO OTHER LIVING THING	321	FOUR ZOAS 7	45
THY VITAL SUBSTANCE IN THESE FIRES THAT ISSUE NEW & NEW	321	FOUR ZOAS 7	48
OF LIVING PANGS THY HORRIBLE BED GLOWING WITH CEASELESS FIRES	321	FOUR ZOAS 7	50
YET THROW THY LIMBS THESE FIRES ABROAD THAT BACK RETURN UPON THEE	321	FOUR ZOAS 7	60
YET MY FIERCE FIRES ARE BETTER THAN THY SNOWS SHUDDERING THOU SITTEST	322	FOUR ZOAS 7	72
WILL BE RENEWD BY THE THREE & CONSUMMATED IN MENTAL FIRES	329	FOUR ZOAS 7	356
TO COMFORT ORC IN HIS DIRE SUFFERINGS LOOK MY FIRES ENLUME AFRESH	331	FOUR ZOAS 7	444
THY WORKS ARE ALL MY JOY & IN THY FIRES MY SOUL DELIGHTS	331	FOUR ZOAS 7	448
TO MODULATE HIS FIRES STUDIOUS THE LOUD ROARING FLAMES . .	331	FOUR ZOAS 7	458
BATHED IN BLOODY CLOUDS HIS LOINS IN FIRES OF WAR WHERE SPEARS	334	FOUR ZOAS 7B	43
THAT WHEN LOS WARRD UPON THE SOUTH REFLECTED THE FIERCE FIRES	335	FOUR ZOAS 7B *	76
ORC RENT HER & HIS HUMAN FORM CONSUMD IN HIS OWN FIRES . .	338	FOUR ZOAS 7B	211
AND HE ROLLD DOWN BENEATH THE FIRES OF ORC A GLOBE IMMENSE	350	FOUR ZOAS 8	372
IN CLOUDS & FIRES AROUND THE ROCK & THE MYSTERIOUS TREE	355	FOUR ZOAS 8	557
AND WEEPING OVER ORC & URIZEN IN CLOUDS & [DISMAL] FLAMING FIRES	355	FOUR ZOAS 8	579
THEN FELL THE FIRES OF ENTERNITY WITH LOUD & SHRILL . . .	357	FOUR ZOAS 9	10
IS SILENT ON MY CLOUDED HILLS THAT BELCH FORTH STORMS & FIRES	359	FOUR ZOAS 9 *	103
INTO THE FIRES THEN GLORIOUS BRIGHT EXULTING IN HIS JOY	362	FOUR ZOAS 9	191
ON RIFTED ROCKS SUSPENDED IN THE AIR BY INWARD FIRES . .	363	FOUR ZOAS 9	241
THEN FOLLOWS THE GOLDEN HARROW IN THE MIDST OF MENTAL FIRES	366	FOUR ZOAS 9	335
ETERNAL DEATH WHO CAN ENDURE LET US CONSUME IN FIRES . .	377	FOUR ZOAS 9	740
IN CHAINS OF IRON & IN DUNGEONS CIRCLED WITH CEASELESS FIRES	377	FOUR ZOAS 9	750
. . . & CORDS & FIRES & FLOODS	377	FOUR ZOAS 9	752
OF DARK URTHONA THUNDERS EARTHQUAKES FIRES WATER FLOODS	378	FOUR ZOAS 9	812
AND HIS PALE WIFE THE AGED SNOW THEY WATCH OVER THE FIRES	378	FOUR ZOAS 9	815
AND MAN WALKS FORTH FROM MIDST OF THE FIRES THE EVIL IS ALL CONSUMD	379	FOUR ZOAS 9	827
HOW IS IT WE HAVE WALKD THRO FIRES & YET ARE NOT CONSUMD	379	FOUR ZOAS 9	844
[TO BE CONSUMD IN BURNING FIRES]	422	BENEATH/N	14
TO BE CONSUMD IN BURNING FIRES	424	THE GOLDEN NET	13
LIKE A SCROLL READY TO BE CONSUMED IN THE FIRES OF THE ANGELS	443A	LAST JUDGMNT/L	PROSE
SURROUNDED WITH FIRES UNAPPROACHABLE BUT WHOM THEY PLEASE	484	MILTON 5	9
JAMES CALLS FOR FIRES IN GOLGONOOZA FOR HEAPS OF SMOKING RUINS	485	MILTON 5	40
THICK FIRES CONTENDING WITH THE RAIN THUNDERD ABOVE ROLLING	488	MILTON 8	28
HIS BOSOM INWARDS SHONE WITH FIRES BUT THE STONES BECOMING OPAKE	490	MILTON 9	32
THE HARROW CAST THICK FLAMES & ORBD US ROUND IN CONCAVE FIRES	493	MILTON 12	22
DRAWING A THIRD PART IN THE FIRES AS STUBBLE NORTH & SOUTH	493	MILTON 12	26
DRIVING THE HARROW IN PITY'S PATHS TWAS THEN WITH OUR DARK FIRES	493	MILTON 12	28
GLORYING TO INVOLVE ALBION'S BODY IN FIRES OF ETERNAL WAR	493	MILTON 13	6
THE BEAUTIFUL AMALEKITES BEHOLD THE FIRES OF YOUTH . . .	501	MILTON 19	37
WHERE LOS OPENS HIS THREE WIDE GATES SURROUNDED BY RAGING FIRES	503	MILTON 20	49
WITH RINTRAH & PALAMABRON IN HIS FIRES OF RESISTLESS FURY	510	MILTON 25	2
BUT THE ELECT MUST BE SAVED (FROM) FIRES OF ETERNAL DEATH	511	MILTON 25	38
IN CHAINS OF IRON & IN DUNGEONS CIRCLED WITH CEASELESS FIRES	514	MILTON 27	32
THE PLATES & SCREWS & WRACKS & SAWS & CORDS & FIRES & CISTERNS	514	MILTON 27	34
WHERE ORC INCESSANT HOWLS BURNING IN FIRES OF ETERNAL YOUTH	517	MILTON 29	29
IMMORTAL STARRY-ONES GUARDING THE COUCH IN FLAMING FIRES	525	MILTON 35	30
THE MUNDANE SHELL IN GOLGONOOZA BUT THE FIRES OF LOS RAGE	529	MILTON 37	56
INTO THE FIRES OF INTELLECT THAT REJOICD IN FELPHAM'S VALE	534	MILTON 42	9
I BEHOLD THEM AND THEIR RUSHING FIRES OVERWHELM MY SOUL	623	JERUSALEM 5	35
EASTWARD & SOUTHWARD & NORTHWARD ARE INCIRCLED WITH FLAMING FIRES	635	JERUSALEM 14	28
AMONG THE SPIRITUAL FIRES LOUD THE CORN FIELDS THUNDER ALONG	636	JERUSALEM 16	5
LABOUR WITHIN THE FURNACES WALKING AMONG THE FIRES . . .	637	JERUSALEM 16	20
IN THE FIRES OF THEIR BEAUTY & PERFECTION & BE VEGETATED BENEATH	638	JERUSALEM 17	8
HIS FIRES REDOUND FROM HIS DRAGON ALTARS IN ERRORS RETURNING	646	JERUSALEM 23	21
AND AS THEY FLED IN FOLDING FIRES & THUNDERS OF THE DEEP	655	JERUSALEM 29	77
ELEVATE INTO THE REGION OF BROTHERHOOD WITH MY RED FIRES	660	JERUSALEM 34	1

702

	PAGE	TITLE	LINE

FIRES   (CONTINUED)
    FIRES AND CLOUDS OF ROLLING SMOKE BUT MILD THE SAVIOUR   664 JERUSALEM 38   10
        FOLLOWD HIM
    CHARIOTS BLACK THEIR FIRES ROLL BEHOLDING ALBION'S HOUSE   666 JERUSALEM 40   5
        OF ETERNITY
    FILLD WITH THE LITTLE-ONES ARE CONSUMED IN THE FIRES OF   679 JERUSALEM 49   11
        THEIR ALTARS
    WALKETH AMONG US GIVE DECISION BRING FORTH ALL YOUR FIRES   686 JERUSALEM 55   19
    CITIES & NATIONS CONTENDED IN FIRES & CLOUDS & TEMPESTS   686 JERUSALEM 55   25
    AMONG THE FIRES OF THE DRUID & THE DEEP BLACK RETHUNDERING   689 JERUSALEM 57   3
        WATERS
    THO VALA'S CLOUD HIDE THEE & LUVAH'S FIRES FOLLOW THEE . .   696 JERUSALEM 62   28
    OVER THE MOUNTAINS & THE FIRES BLAZD ON DRUID ALTARS   . .   696 JERUSALEM 62   33
    SPOTTED WITH VICTIMS' BLOOD BY THE FIRES OF THY SECRET   706 JERUSALEM 68   49
        TABERNACLE
    IN FIRES OF BEAUTY MELTING THEM AS GOLD & SILVER IN THE   709 JERUSALEM 70   28
        FURNACE
    MY FIRES ARE CORRUPT MY INCENSE IS A CLOUDY PESTILENCE . .   721 JERUSALEM 79   56
    SEE HOW THE FIRES OF OUR LOINS POINT EASTWARD TO BABYLON   725 JERUSALEM 82   36
    OF EARTHQUAKES & CONSUMING FIRES THEY ROLL APART IN FEAR   733 JERUSALEM 88   9
    THUS JOYD THE SPECTRE IN THE DUSKY FIRES OF LOS'S FORGE   734 JERUSALEM 88   44
        EYEING
    SOON ALL AROUND REMOTE THE HEAVENS BURNT WITH FLAMING FIRES   744 JERUSALEM 96   40
FIRE SIDE
    WHO WILL EXCHANGE HIS OWN FIRE SIDE . . . .   186 LET BROTHELS/N   46
    WHO WILL EXCHANGE HIS OWN FIRE SIDE . . . .   186 LET BROTHELS/N   64
FIRM
    THEY LANDED IN FIRM ARRAY UPON THE ROCKS . . . . . .   32 EDW THIRD/PS 6   13
    OUR FATHERS MOVE IN FIRM ARRAY TO BATTLE . . . . . .   32 EDW THIRD/PS 6   25
    THEN I ASKED DOES A FIRM PERSWASION THAT A THING IS SO   153C MARRIAGE HH 12 PROSE
        MAKE IT SO
    AGES OF IMAGINATION THIS FIRM PERSWASION REMOVED MOUNTAINS   153C MARRIAGE HH 12 PROSE
    BUT MANY ARE NOT CAPABLE OF A FIRM PERSWASION OF ANY THING   153C MARRIAGE HH 12 PROSE
    THIS SAID HE LIKE ALL FIRM PERSWASIONS IS COME TO PASS . .   154A MARRIAGE HH 12 PROSE
    WHERE WINTER BEATS INCESSANT FIXING THEM FIRM ON THEIR BASE   281 FOUR ZOAS 2   31
    AMBIGUOUS WORDS BLASPHEMOUS FILLD WITH ENVY FIRM RESOLVD   302 FOUR ZOAS 4   205
    LOS DREW THEM FORTH OUT OF THE DEEPS PLANTING HIS RIGHT   332 FOUR ZOAS 7   464
        FOOT FIRM
    AND HIS BRIGHT FEET FIRM AS A BRAZEN ALTAR BUT THE PARTS   380 FOUR ZOAS AD 1   12
    THEY ARE ALL FIRM DETERMINATE OUTLINE OR IDENTICAL FORM   439C REMARKS MALKIN PROSE
    OF ST PAUL PREACHING IS A FIRM DETERMINATE OUTLINE   . . .   439C REMARKS MALKIN PROSE
    THE MAP OF ALLESTONE HAS THE SAME CHARACTER OF THE FIRM AND   439C REMARKS MALKIN PROSE
    AND FIRM AND DETERMINATE LINEAMENTS UNBROKEN BY SHADOWS   564D DESC CAT 1   PROSE
    WITHOUT FIRM AND DETERMINATE OUTLINE FRESCO PAINTING IS   585A DESC CAT 15   PROSE
    BUT DRAWN WITH A FIRM & DECIDED HAND AT ONCE [WITH ALL ITS]   595C PUB ADDRESS/N   PROSE
    A FIRM & DETERMINATE CONDUCT ON THE PART OF ARTISTS . . .   600B PUB ADDRESS/N   PROSE
    AND WELL CONTRIVED WORDS FIRM FIXING NEVER FORGOTTEN   . .   632 JERUSALEM 12   35
    AND THE HAND OF MAN GRASPS FIRM BETWEEN THE MALE & FEMALE   744 JERUSALEM 97   15
        LOVES
    & TO GO THRO ALL WITHOUT MURMURING & IN FIRM HOPE   . . .   825D LETTER 27   *PROSE
    I SHOULD PROPOSE TO ETCH THEM IN A RAPID BUT FIRM MANNER   844B LETTER 43   PROSE
FIRMAMENT
    DISCORD BEGAN & YELLS & CRIES SHOOK THE WIDE FIRMAMENT . .   278 FOUR ZOAS 1   518
    THEN DISCORD BEGAN [&] THEN YELLS & CRIES SHOOK THE WIDE   306 FOUR ZOAS 5   * 45
        (FIRMAMENT)
    PASSING THE PLANETARY VISIONS & THE WELL ADORNED FIRMAMENT   507 MILTON 23   23
    . . . FIXT IN THE FIRMAMENT BY PEACE BROTHERHOOD AND LOVE   781 GHOST ABEL 2   26
FIRMNESS
    THAT THEY CANNOT BEAR THE FIRMNESS OF A MASTER'S TOUCH . .   603C PUB ADDR AD/N   PROSE
    FIRMNESS I HAVE BROUGHT DOWN HIS AFFECTED LOFTINESS . . .   825C LETTER 27   PROSE
FIRST
    AND THE FIRST BLOW DECIDES . . . .   14 GWIN KING/PS   106
    WHEN MEN WERE FIRST A NATION GROWN . . . .   17 BLIND-MANS/PS   66
    SAY LORDS SHOULD NOT OUR THOUGHTS BE FIRST TO COMMERCE . .   19 EDW THIRD/PS 2   16
    BUT WHEN OUR FIRST IDEAS ARE WRONG WHAT FOLLOWS MUST   . .   28D EDW THIRD/PS 4   PROSE
    VENERABLE SWEETNER OF HIS LIFE RECEIVES THE PROMISE FIRST   39C SAMSON/PS   PROSE
        FROM HEAVEN
    IN THE FIRST PLACE IT IS OF NO USE FOR A MAN TO MAKE   45D ISLAND MOON 1   PROSE
        QUERIES
    OBTUSE ANGLE SAID IN THE FIRST PLACE YOU THOUGHT HE WAS   48D ISLAND MOON 5   PROSE
        [NOT]
    I THINK I DO IN THE FIRST PLACE SAID HE WITH A GRIN . . .   49B ISLAND MOON 5   PROSE
    THEN ARADOBO BEGAN IN THE FIRST PLACE I THINK   . . . .   49C ISLAND MOON 5   PROSE
    I THINK IN THE FIRST PLACE THAT CHATTERTON WAS CLEVER AT   49C ISLAND MOON 5   PROSE
    PHIZOGRAPHY HOGAMY HATOMY & HALL THAT BUT IN THE FIRST   49C ISLAND MOON 5   PROSE
        PLACE
    WHEN OLD CORRUPTION FIRST BEGUN   . . . .   50 WHEN CORRUP/IM   1
    HE FIRST DISCOVERD GUTS . . . .   51 WHEN CORRUP/IM   36
    FIRST VOICE SECOND VOICE   . . . .   54D WANT MATCHS/IM PROSE
    HE WAS DOWNSTAIRS THE VERY FIRST . . . .   59A ISLAND MOON 10   PROSE
    SONG (FIRST) BY A SHEPHERD . . . .   63B SHEPHERD FIRST   TITLE
    A MAN MUST FIRST DECIEVE HIMSELF BEFORE HE IS THUS   . . .   75A ANNO LAVATER   MARG
    BUT I WILL TRY TO DO IT THE FIRST OPPORTUNITY   . . . .   87D ANNO LAVATER   MARG
    PRINCIPLE FIRST THAT THE POETIC GENIUS IS THE TRUE MAN . .   98B ALL RELIGIONS   PROSE
    THE FRENCH REVOLUTION A POEM IN SEVEN BOOKS BOOK THE FIRST   134A FRENCH REVOLTN TITLE
    BOOK THE FIRST . . . .   134A FRENCH REVOLTN TITLE
    . . . ALL CHILDREN NEW-BORN FIRST BEHOLD THEM TEARS ARE   136 FRENCH REVOLTN   56
        FLED
    . . . UNLESS THOU FIRST FEAREST TO HURT THEM . . . .   143 FRENCH REVOLTN   194
    THEN HEAR THE FIRST VOICE OF THE MORNING . . .   .   145 FRENCH REVOLTN   238
    END OF THE FIRST BOOK . . . .   148B FRENCH REVOLTN TITLE
    THE FIRST PRINCIPLES OF HUMAN PERCEPTION . . . .   153D MARRIAGE HH 12 PROSE

FIRST   (CONTINUED)   PAGE   TITLE   LINE

	PAGE	TITLE	LINE
WAS THE FIRST PRINCIPLE AND ALL THE OTHERS MERELY DERIVATIVE	153D	MARRIAGE HH 12	PROSE
FIRST THE NOTION THAT MAN HAS A BODY DISTINCT FROM HIS SOUL	154C	MARRIAGE HH 14	PROSE
IN THE FIRST CHAMBER WAS A DRAGON-MAN CLEARING AWAY THE	154D	MARRIAGE HH 15	PROSE
AND WITH A GRINNING ASPECT FIRST COUPLED WITH & THEN DEVOURD	157B	MARRIAGE HH 17	PROSE
BY PLUCKING OFF FIRST ONE LIMB AND THEN ANOTHER TILL THE BODY	157B	MARRIAGE HH 17	PROSE
SINCE EVE FIRST CHOSE HER HELL FIRE SPARK	187	WHEN KLOPSTK/N	24
THE [FIRST] BOOK OF URIZEN LAMBETH PRINTED BY WILL BLAKE...	222A	URIZEN 1	TITLE
PRELUDIUM TO THE [FIRST] BOOK OF URIZEN	222A	URIZEN 2	TITLE
FIRST I FOUGHT WITH THE FIRE CONSUMD	224	URIZEN 4	14
AND A FIRST AGE PASSED OVER	228	URIZEN 10	42
OF THE FIRST FEMALE NOW SEPARATE	231	URIZEN 18	10
AT THE FIRST FEMALE FORM NOW SEPARATE	231	URIZEN 18	15
WEEPING WAILING FIRST THIRIEL APPEARD	234	URIZEN 23	11
FLAMD OUT FIRST BEGOTTEN LAST BORN	234	URIZEN 23	18
THE END OF THE [FIRST] BOOK OF URIZEN	237A	URIZEN 28	TITLE
SURGE FOAM AND LABOUR INTO LIFE FIRST BORN & FIRST CONSUMD	238	EUROPE PREL 1	9
FIRST BORN OF ENITHARMON RISE	239	EUROPE 4	25
FIRST HE POISOND THE ROCKS WITH HIS BLOOD	251	AHANIA 3	20
FIRST IN WRATH THREW HIS LIMBS LIKE THE BABE	258	BOOK OF LOS 4	38
AND CONTEMPLATIVE THOUGHTS FIRST AROSE	258	BOOK OF LOS 4	40
THEN LIGHT FIRST BEGAN FROM THE FIRES	259	BOOK OF LOS 5	10
AND FIRST FROM THOSE INFINITE FIRES	260	BOOK OF LOS 5	27
VALA NIGHT THE FIRST	264A	FOUR ZOAS 1	TITLE
THE FIRST STATE WEEPING THEY BEGAN & HELPLESS AS A WAVE	269	FOUR ZOAS 1	193
THE LISTNING STARS HEARD & THE FIRST BEAM OF THE MORNING STARTED BACK	275	FOUR ZOAS 1	410
END OF THE FIRST NIGHT	277B	FOUR ZOAS 1	TITLE
END OF THE FIRST NIGHT	279D	FOUR ZOAS 1	TITLE
[?AT FIRST ?AROUND XXX THE SPECTRE]	SUPP	FOUR ZOAS 1	*
VALA NIGHT THE [?THIRD] [FIRST] [FIRST]	280B	FOUR ZOAS 2	*TITLE
FIRST HE BEHELD THE BODY OF MAN PALE COLD THE HORRORS OF DEATH	280	FOUR ZOAS 2	11
FIRST SPUN THEN WOVE THE ATMOSPHERES THERE THE SPIDER & WORM	284	FOUR ZOAS 2	146
THEN ROSE THE BUILDERS FIRST THE ARCHITECT DIVINE HIS PLAN	284	FOUR ZOAS 2	166
AT THE FIRST SOUND THE GOLDEN SUN ARISES FROM THE DEEP . .	289	FOUR ZOAS 2	344
MAKE FIRST A RESTING PLACE FOR LOS & ENITHARMON THEN .	299	FOUR ZOAS 4	72
A FIRST AGE PASSED A STATE OF DISMAL WOE	303	FOUR ZOAS 4	222
AND FIRST HE FOUND THE LIMIT OF OPACITY & NAMD IT SATAN	304	FOUR ZOAS 4	271
AT FIRST AN INFANT WEAKNESS PERIODS PASSD HE GATHERD STRENGTH	316	FOUR ZOAS 6	163
FIRST BORN OF GENERATION THEN BEHOLD A WONDER TO THE EYES	326	FOUR ZOAS 7	245
OF URTHONA LOS EMBRACD THE SPECTRE FIRST AS A BROTHER .	328	FOUR ZOAS 7	339
AND FIRST HE DREW A LINE UPON THE WALLS OF SHINING HEAVEN	332	FOUR ZOAS 7	467
FIRST RINTRAH & THEN PALAMABRON DRAWN FROM OUT THE RANKS OF WAR	332	FOUR ZOAS 7	476
FIRST HIS IMMORTAL SPIRIT DREW URIZEN [SPECTRE] SHADOW AWAY	332	FOUR ZOAS 7 *	490
FIRST TRADES & COMMERCE SHIPS & ARMED VESSELS HE BUILDED LABORIOUS	333	FOUR ZOAS 7B	12
AND URIZEN LAID THE FIRST STONE & ALL HIS MYRIADS . .	333	FOUR ZOAS 7B	19
THEN [FIRST] LOS [BEHELD] SAID	341	FOUR ZOAS 8 *	20
THE FALLEN MAN BUT FIRST	348	FOUR ZOAS 8	265
AWAY FROM [LOS] ME FIRST REUBEN FLED THEN SIMEON THEN LEVI THEN JUDAH	350	FOUR ZOAS 8	375
THE FIRST AUTHOR OF THIS WAR & THE DISTRACTING OF HONEST MINDS	361	FOUR ZOAS 9	153
THE HUMAN HARVEST TO BEGIN TOWARDS THE SOUTH FIRST SPRANG	366	FOUR ZOAS 9	338
IN ENMITY & WAR FIRST WEAKEND THEN IN STERN REPENTANCE . .	366	FOUR ZOAS 9	370
THEN FIRST SHE SAW HIS GLORY & HER HARLOT FORM APPEARD . .	382	FOUR ZOAS AD 6	21
DUTY TO HIS COUNTRY IS THE FIRST CONSIDERATION & SAFETY THE LAST	383C	ANNO WATSON	MARG
IF THIS FIRST LETTER IS WRITTEN WITHOUT RAILING & ILLIBERALITY	384C	ANNO WATSON	MARG
IN THE MOMENT THE FIRST WORDS WERE OUT OF HIS MOUTH CAN	390B	ANNO WATSON	MARG
WAS WRITTEN WITHIN THE FIRST CENTURY SEE P...&... . .	394C	ANNO WATSON	MARG
HE WHO SAYS THERE ARE SECOND CAUSES HAS ALREADY DENIED A FIRST	403B	ANNO BACON	MARG
[WHEN MY LOVE DID FIRST BEGIN]	415	MY SPECTRE/N	19
A HOLLOW GROAN FIRST SPOKE HIS WOE	419	I SAW A MONK/N	24
THE TYRANT WHO FIRST THE BLACK BOW BENT	420	I SAW A MONK/N	50
WHEN SATAN FIRST THE BLACK BOW BENT	420	I SAW MNK AD/N	1
SWEET MARY THE FIRST TIME SHE EVER WAS THERE	428	MARY	1
A HOLLOW GROAN FIRST SPOKE HIS WOE	430	GREY MONK	10
WILLIAM SAYS ON HIS OATH THAT THE FIRST WORDS THAT HE . .	437D	BLAKES MEMORAN	PROSE
LET THERE BE FIRST A DRAWING MADE	440B	MEMORANDUM/N 2	PROSE
OUR FIRST PARENTS OUT OF EDEN THROUGH A GUARD OF WEEPING ANGELS	441D	INSC FALL MAN	PROSE
DEGRADE FIRST THE ARTS IF YOUD MANKIND DEGRADE	445	ANNO REYNOLDS	1
THE BIBLE SAYS THAT CULTIVATED LIFE EXISTED FIRST . . .	446C	ANNO REYNOLDS	MARG
SATAN TOOK AWAY ORNAMENT FIRST NEXT HE TOOK AWAY ACCOMODATIONS	446C	ANNO REYNOLDS	MARG
ART IS FIRST IN INTELLECTUALS & OUGHT TO BE FIRST IN NATIONS	446D	ANNO REYNOLDS	MARG
WERE SAVAGE FIRST TO FRANCE & AFTER SLAVES	451	ANNO REYNOLDS	2
[?FIRST ?TO SERVE NOBILITY & FASHIONABLE TASTE & SR JOSHUA]	451C	ANNO REYNOLDS	* MARG
ENTHUSIASTIC ADMIRATION IS THE FIRST PRINCIPLE OF KNOWLEDGE	458B	ANNO REYNOLDS	MARG
HIS FIRST PRINCIPLE IS UNBELIEF AND YET HERE HE SAYS . .	459D	ANNO REYNOLDS	MARG

	PAGE	TITLE	LINE
FIRST (CONTINUED)			
FIRST PAINTERS OF HIS AGE ALBERT DURER IS NOT WOULD HAVE BEEN	461A	ANNO REYNOLDS	MARG
[?FIRST ?WERE CREATED WINE & (HAPPINESS) ?GOOD ?LOOKS & ?FORTUNE XXX]	446C	ANNO REYNOLDS	* MARG
[SO SATAN TOOK AWAY ORNAMENTS FIRST NECESSARIES LAST] . .	446C	ANNO REYNOLDS	* MARG
[CAESAR SAID HE'D RATHER BE THE (FIRST IN) A VILLAGE (THAN) SECOND]	SUPP	ANNO REYNOLDS	* MARG
MILTON BOOK THE FIRST	481B	MILTON 1	TITLE
SAY FIRST WHAT MOVD MILTON WHO WALKD ABOUT IN ETERNITY . .	481	MILTON 2	16
AND A FIRST AGE PASSED OVER & A STATE OF DISMAL WOE . . .	482	MILTON 3	10
FIRST ORC WAS BORN THEN THE SHADOWY FEMALE THEN ALL LOS'S FAMILY	483	MILTON 3	40
THE FIRST THE ELECT FROM BEFORE THE FOUNDATION OF THE WORLD	486	MILTON 7	2
TO DESTRUCTION FROM THE MOTHER'S WOMB [THE REPROBATE ARE THE FIRST]	486	MILTON 7	* 4
OF THE FIRST CLASS WAS SATAN WITH INCOMPARABLE MILDNESS	486	MILTON 7	6
. . . FIRST OF OPACITY THEN OF CONTRACTION	494	MILTON 13	20
FIRST MILTON SAW ALBION UPON THE ROCK OF AGES . . .	497	MILTON 15	36
THEN FIRST I SAW HIM IN THE ZENITH AS A FALLING STAR . .	497	MILTON 15	47
THEY VANISH NOT FROM ME & MINE WE GUARD THEM FIRST & LAST	505	MILTON 22	23
(?TO) THOR & CRUEL ODIN WHO FIRST REARD THE POLAR CAVES	511	MILTON 25	* 53
END OF THE FIRST BOOK	518A	MILTON 29	TITLE
FIRST EER THE MORNING BREAKS JOY OPENS IN THE FLOWERY BOSOMS	520	MILTON 31	50
JOY EVEN TO TEARS WHICH THE SUN RISING DRIES FIRST THE WILD THYME	520	MILTON 31	51
WHILE THOSE COMBIND BY SATAN'S TYRANNY FIRST IN THE BLOOD OF WAR	521	MILTON 32	16
WHEN I FIRST MARRIED YOU I GAVE YOU ALL MY WHOLE SOUL . .	522	MILTON 33	2
WERE SHEWED THEM FIRST OF BEULAH A MOST PLEASANT SLEEP . .	523	MILTON 34	9
THE FIRST STATE IS IN THE HEAD THE SECOND IS IN THE HEART	524	MILTON 34	14
AND FIRST FROM THE WILD THYME STANDS A FOUNTAIN IN A ROCK	526	MILTON 35	49
IT IS THE ENTERANCE OF THE FIRST HEAVEN NAMED LUTHER FOR	526	MILTON 35	62
HE IS ALL EXPERIMENTS FROM LAST TO FIRST	548	CRIPPLE EVRY/N	7
WHATS THE FIRST PART OF ORATORY HE SAID A GREAT WIG . . .	553	ASKD PRIGG/N	2
WHATS THE FIRST PART OF PAINTING HE'LL SAY A PAINT BRUSH	553	ASKD PRIGG/N	8
WHATS THE FIRST PART OF PAINTING SHE SAID PATRONAGE . . .	554	ASKD PRIGG/N	17
IT IS MIXED WITH AT ITS FIRST MIXTURE AND IN A LITTLE TIME	565B	DESC CAT 2	PROSE
WITNESS THE VILLANY OF SOME ONE AT THAT TIME WHO FIRST .	565B	DESC CAT 2	*PROSE
AND WHO FIRST FORGED THE SILLY STORY AND KNOWN FALSHOOD	565B	DESC CAT 2	PROSE
WITH COTTAGES AND VILLAGES THE FIRST BEAMS OF THE SUN .	567B	DESC CAT 3	PROSE
AS CHAUCER HAS ALSO PLACED THEM FIRST IN HIS PROLOGUE .	567D	DESC CAT 3	PROSE
THEIR DRESS AND THEIR HORSES ARE OF THE FIRST RATE . .	568A	DESC CAT 3	PROSE
LADY IS DESCRIBED ALSO AS OF THE FIRST RANK RICH AND HONOURED	568B	DESC CAT 3	PROSE
FIRST RANK IN SOCIETY NOBLE RICH AND EXPENSIVELY ATTENDED	568C	DESC CAT 3	PROSE
OF THE FIRST MAGNITUDE GRAND TERRIFIC RICH AND HONOURED	570A	DESC CAT 3	PROSE
OF CHAUCER THE DOCTOR OF PHYSIC IS DESCRIBED AS THE FIRST OF	570D	DESC CAT 3	PROSE
TWO FIRST CHARACTERS IN CHAUCER THE KNIGHT AND THE SQUIRE	573C	DESC CAT 3	PROSE
THE FIRST MR B(BLAKE) EVER DID IN FRESCO FORTUNATELY OR	581B	DESC CAT 6	PROSE
WHICH IT HAD AT FIRST WHEN ALL THE LINEAMENTS WERE PERFECT	582B	DESC CAT 9	PROSE
AN IDEAL DESIGN SUGGESTED BY THE FIRST PUBLICATION OF .	583D	DESC CAT 10	PROSE
BE WORSE THAN IT WAS AT THE END OF THE FIRST TWELVE MONTHS	587A	CHAUCER 1	PROSE
WITH COTTAGES & VILLAGES THE FIRST BEAMS OF THE SUN . .	588D	CHAUCER/N	PROSE
WITH COTTAGES AND VILLAGES THE FIRST BEAMS OF THE SUN	590C	CHAUCER 2	PROSE
FLAXMAN CANNOT DENY THAT ONE OF THE VERY FIRST MONUMENTS HE	592D	PUB ADDRESS/N	PROSE
KNOW THE FIRST [LINES] BEGINNINGS OF ART I HOPE THIS PRINT	593C	PUB ADDRESS/N	PROSE
[BECAUSE IT BEARS THE [EVIDENT] EVIDENCE AT FIRST VIEW] TO BE	599C	PUB ADDRESS/N	*PROSE
& CHARLES THE FIRST WERE TO PATRONIZE SUCH BLOCKHEADS . .	599D	PUB ADDRESS/N	PROSE
TO WHAT IS IT THAT GENTLEMEN OF THE FIRST RANK . . .	601D	PUB ADDRESS/N	*PROSE
ADAM & EVE APPEAR FIRST BEFORE THE [THRONE]	606B	V LAST JUDG/N	PROSE
CHRIST COMES AS HE CAME AT FIRST TO DELIVER THOSE . .	615D	V LAST JUDG/N	PROSE
FIRST GOD ALMIGHTY COMES WITH A THUMP ON THE HEAD . .	617A	V LAST JUDG/N	PROSE
THESE PERSONIFICATIONS ARE ALL BROUGHT TOGETHER IN THE FIRST DESIGN	618A	ILLUS MILTON	PROSE
WHEN THIS VERSE WAS FIRST DICTATED TO ME I CONSIDERD .	621C	JERUSALEM 3	PROSE
[END OF THE (FIRST) CHAP]	635C	JERUSALEM 14	*TITLE
BUT FIRST ALBION MUST SLEEP DIVIDED FROM THE NATIONS . .	636	JERUSALEM 15	29
I SEE ALBION SITTING UPON HIS ROCK IN THE FIRST WINTER .	636	JERUSALEM 15	30
FIRST AS A RED GLOBE OF BLOOD TREMBLING BENEATH HIS BOSOM	639	JERUSALEM 17	51
DOUBT FIRST ASSAILD ME THEN SHAME TOOK POSSESSION OF ME	643	JERUSALEM 21	5
FIRST FLED MY SONS & THEN MY DAUGHTERS THEN MY WILD ANIMATIONS	643	JERUSALEM 21	7
WHERE SATAN THE FIRST VICTORY WON	650	FIELDS FROM/J	28
MUST HAVE BECOME THE FIRST VICTIMS BEING THE FIRST TRANSGRESSORS	653	JERUSALEM 28	24
WHOSE SPECTRE FIRST ASSIMILATED WITH LUVAH IN ALBION'S MOUNTAINS	668	JERUSALEM 41	3
WHEN SATAN FIRST THE BLACK BOW BENT	683	I SAW A MONK/J	17
BUT FIRST THEY SAID & THEIR WORDS STOOD IN CHARIOTS IN ARRAY	686	JERUSALEM 55	34
THE DIVINE VISION BECAME FIRST A BURNING FLAME THEN A COLUMN	702	JERUSALEM 66	41
BRING YOUR OFFERINGS YOUR FIRST BEGOTTEN PAMPERD WITH MILK & BLOOD	706	JERUSALEM 68	30
DESARTS LOS FIRST BROKE SILENCE & BEGAN TO UTTER HIS LOVE	732	JERUSALEM 87	2
IN MUTUAL INTERCHANGE AND FIRST THEIR EMANATIONS MEET . .	733	JERUSALEM 88	5
ONE FIRST IN FRIENDSHIP & LOVE THEN A DIVINE FAMILY & IN THE MIDST	738	JERUSALEM 91	20

		PAGE	TITLE	LINE

FIRST   (CONTINUED)
  BUT WHEN HE TOUCHES THE FIRST FIBROUS THREAD LIKE FILMY DEW   739 JERUSALEM 92   10
  WHEN FIRST I LET THESE DEVILS IN . . . .   755 EV GOSPEL(E)/N   70
  THIS TO COME FIRST . . . .   758A EV GOSPEL   PROSE
  WHO FIRST SPOIL & THEN DESTROY IMAGINATIVE ART . . .   777A INSC LAOCCON   PROSE
  JUSTLY STANDS FIRST IN THE BOOK & THAT BEAUTIFUL SPECIMEN   782A INSC UPCOTT   PROSE
  THY KINGSHIP COME UPON EARTH FIRST & THENCE IN HEAVEN .   788D ANNO THORNTON   * MARG
  SEE ADVANCEMT OF LEARNING PART...P...OF FIRST EDITION   794A LETTER 5   PROSE
  "CALLD ON YOU SINCE MY HUSBAND'S FIRST RETURN FROM FELPHAM"   800A LETTER 12   PROSE
  "BUT CAN NEVER THINK OF GOING WITHOUT FIRST PAYING OUR"   800A LETTER 12   PROSE
  SHALL BE MARKED ON MY CALENDAR WITH A STAR OF THE FIRST   801B LETTER 13   PROSE
    MAGNITUDE
  EARTHAM WILL BE MY FIRST TEMPLE & ALTAR . . . . .   801B LETTER 13   PROSE
  I MET A PLOW ON MY FIRST GOING OUT AT MY GATE . . . .   803C LETTER 15   PROSE
  THE FIRST MORNING AFTER MY ARRIVAL & THE PLOWBOY SAID .   803C LETTER 15   PROSE
  MY FIRST VISION OF LIGHT . . . .   804 TO BUTTS/L   2
  NUMEROUS & OF THE FIRST RANK THE PRICE OF THE WORK IS .   824D LETTER 27   PROSE
  AGAINST ME BY A PRIVATE IN CAPTN LEATHES'S TROOP OF (FIRST)   826D LETTER 28   PROSE
    OR
  ME MRS LAMBERT HAS BEEN WITH ME WHICH IS THE FIRST NOTICE   832B LETTER 32   PROSE
  AS WHEN SHE FIRST MOUNTED ME ON MY BELOVED BRUNO . . .   843A LETTER 42   PROSE
  SHOWED ME ROMNEY'S FIRST ATTEMPT AT OIL PAINTING . . .   843C LETTER 43   PROSE
  IT IS THE FIRST PORTRAIT ROMNEY EVER PAINTED BUT ABOVE ALL   843D LETTER 43   PROSE
  OTHER THINGS I SAW OF ROMNEY'S FIRST WORKS . . . . .   844A LETTER 43   PROSE
  IN IMITATION OF THE FIRST STROKES OF THE PAINTER   850D LETTER 49   PROSE
    THE EXPRESSION
  SUDDENLY AS I WAS AT FIRST BY PRODUCING THE HEAD OF ROMNEY   852C LETTER 50   PROSE
  WHAT YOU HAD SAID ABOUT THE DESIGNS FOR EDWARD THE FIRST &   853A LETTER 51   *PROSE
  CONFESSEDLY THE FIRST POET OF ENGLAND OUGHT TO BE GIVEN   856B LETTER 54   PROSE
  EMPLOYING HIM WORTHY (FIRST) TO ENCOURAGE A WORTHY MAN & .   856B LETTER 54   PROSE
  GREAT DEAL OF HONOUR IN LOSING THE FIRST PUBLICATION OF ANY   856C LETTER 54   PROSE
  THE FIRST IN INTERNAL VALUE I THEN SAID IS IT AGREEABLE   856D LETTER 54   PROSE
    TO YOU
  EDWD (FIRST) OR THE BALLADS HAVING COME FROM YOU . . .   857A LETTER 54   PROSE
  TO ME THAT THE FIRST PAGE OF THE POEM WAS BEAUTIFULLY .   857B LETTER 54   PROSE
  THAT ONE THOUSAND COPIES SHOULD BE THE FIRST EDITION AND   858B LETTER 55   PROSE
    IF WE CHOOSE
  SIMPLICITY AS YOU DESIRED HAS BEEN MY FIRST OBJECT I SEND   860B LETTER 56   PROSE
    IT
  THE PUBLIC THEY WILL FALL FAR SHORT OF THIS FIRST SPECIMEN   860D LETTER 57   PROSE
  FOR WHAT IS GOOD MUST SUCCEED FIRST OR LAST BUT WHAT IS BAD   862A LETTER 59   PROSE
  MY WORK PRINTED I WILL SEND IT YOU FIRST OF ANY BODY .   866A LETTER 63   PROSE
  I SEND TWO MORE DRAWINGS WITH THE FIRST THAT I DID ALTERED   866C LETTER 65   PROSE
  FIRST BEFORE I BEGIN ENGRAVING THEM AS IT WILL ENABLE ME   866C LETTER 65   PROSE
  PILGRIMS UNDER YOUR CARE WITH THE TWO FIRST PLATES OF JOB   869B LETTER 69   PROSE
  ON TWO ACCOUNTS FIRST I OMITTED TO DESIRE YOU WOULD COME   870C LETTER 72   PROSE
  FIRST STAGE MY WIFE DESIRES HER KINDEST REMEMBRANCES TO YOU   871C LETTER 73   PROSE
  WITH WHOM HE MAKES HIS FIRST EFFORT DEAR SIR YOURS EVER   875A LETTER 80   PROSE
  AT FIRST & THOUGHT IT A THING OF BENEFIT & GOOD HOPE YOU   876B LETTER 83   PROSE
  PURGATORY FIRST CIRCLE . . . .   SUPP ILLUS DANTE 7   *PROSE
FIRST BEGOTTEN
  THE CORSE OF HIS FIRST BEGOTTEN . . . .   252 AHANIA 4   5
FIRST-BORN,FIRST BORN
  RED AS THE ROSY MORNING LUSTFUL AS THE FIRST BORN BEAM .   195 V DAU ALBION 7   27
  IT JOYD SHE PUT ASIDE HER CLOUDS & SMILED HER FIRST-BORN   196 AMERICA PREL 2   4
    SMILE
  FROM BONDAGE OF THE HUMAN FORM O FIRST BORN SON OF LIGHT   283 FOUR ZOAS 2   108
  ORC THE FIRST BORN COILD IN THE SOUTH THE DRAGON URIZEN   634 JERUSALEM 14   3
  YOUR FIRST BORN OF SEVEN YEARS OLD BE THEY MALES OR FEMALES   706 JERUSALEM 68   31
  HAIL LOCUSTS DARKNESS FIRST BORN XXX RED SEA EGYPTIANS   SUPP EXODUS/N   *PROSE
    DROWND
FIRSTRATE
FIRST RATE
  THE FIRST RATE ELEGANCE IN PRINTING & PAPER AS THEY HOLD   856D LETTER 54   PROSE
FIRY
  FOR WHEN LOS JOIND WITH ME HE TOOK ME IN HIS FIRY WHIRLWIND   527 MILTON 36   21
FISH
  AND FISH FOR FANCIES AS THEY PASS . . . .   8 MEMORY COME/PS   7
  AS THE AIR TO A BIRD OR THE SEA TO A FISH . . . . .   152D MARRIAGE HH 10 PROSE
  OF BEAST BIRD FISH SERPENT & ELEMENT . . . .   222 URIZEN 3   16
  MANY FORMS OF FISH BIRD & BEAST . . . .   232 URIZEN 19   34
  IN ALL MY RIVERS & ON DRIED SHELLS THAT THE FISH . . .   296 FOUR ZOAS 3   167
  FOR STILL IT SURGES FORTH IN FISH & MONSTERS OF THE DEEPS   313 FOUR ZOAS 4   61
  SO MAN LOOKS OUT IN TREE & HERB & FISH & BIRD & BEAST .   355 FOUR ZOAS 8   561
  AND IN EVERY SPECIES OF EARTH METAL TREE FISH BIRD & BEAST   511 MILTON 25   41
  WHERE FISH & BIRD & BEAST & MAN & TREE & METAL & STONE .   681 JERUSALEM 50   6
FISHERMEN
  OF POOR FISHERMEN & A JOURNEYMAN CARPENTER . . . . .   465D ANNO REYNOLDS   MARG
  AND TURND FISHERMEN TO DIVINES . . . .   756 EV GOSPEL(I)/N   20
FISHES
  LIKE THE GAY FISHES ON THE WAVE WHEN THE COLD MOON DRINKS   243 EUROPE 14   3
    THE DEW
  IN FLOWERS IN FRUITS IN FISHES BIRDS & BEASTS & CLOUDS   367 FOUR ZOAS 9   378
    & WATERS
  HOW ARE THE BEASTS & BIRDS & FISHES & PLANTS & MINERALS   525 MILTON 34   53
FISH-POOLS
  THE ROCKS OF RABBATH ON THE ARNON & THE FISH-POOLS   735 JERUSALEM 89   26
    OF HESHBON
FISHY
  AND WITH THE BLAST OF HIS FURNACE UPON FISHY BILLINGSGATE   726 JERUSALEM 82   59
FISSIC
  FISSIC FOLLOGY PISTINOLOGY ARIDOLOGY AROGRAPHY   49C ISLAND MOON 5   PROSE
    TRANSMOGRAPHY

	PAGE	TITLE	LINE

FISSIC   (CONTINUED)
    & WHAT WAS THAT THAT HE TOOK [XXX] FISSIC OR SOMETHINK   49C ISLAND MOON 5   PROSE
    & SO DIED
FIST
    AND THRUST HIS FIST IN AND ALL IN THE SPACE OF A QUARTER   50A ISLAND MOON 6   PROSE
    OF AN HOUR
    HE'LL SWEAR AT THEM & KEEP THEM DOWN WITH HIS FIST & TELL   50A ISLAND MOON 6   PROSE
FISTS
    ETRUSCAN COLUMN THEN (STARTING) UP & CLENCHING BOTH HIS   45B ISLAND MOON 1   PROSE
    PISTS
FIT
    TO PLACES FIT FOR WOE . . . .   8 MEMORY COME/PS   14
    AND GIRD THE SWORD UPON EACH THIGH AND FIT   . . .   26 EDW THIRD/PS 3   225
    THAT YOUTH HAS NEED OF AGE TO POINT FIT PREY   . . . . .   27 EDW THIRD/PS 3   269
    WERE FIT TO GIVE LAW TO THE CITY EACH EAT AS MUCH AS TEN   58 THIS CITY/IM   10
    WILL GIVE US TO ETERNAL DEATH FIT PUNISHMENT FOR SUCH   .   330 FOUR ZOAS 7   426
    ARE FOR THY TRANSGRESSIONS FIT . . . .   417 MY SPECTR AD/N   6
    IS TO DOUBT A FIT REPLY . . . .   433 AUGURIES   104
    READ REMBRANDT [& YOU WILL KNOW] FOR IT IS FIT   . . . .   543 TO ROYL ACAD/N   6
    "FIT AUDIENCE FIND THO FEW" MILTON . . . .   560C EXHIBITION ADV   PROSE
    SHE HAS HAD FOUR HUSBANDS A FIT SUBJECT FOR THIS PAINTER   574D DESC CAT 3   PROSE
    IT IS FIT FOR THE BURLESQUE THE BEAUTY PROPER FOR SUBLIME   579D DESC CAT 5   PROSE
    EVERY WORD AND EVERY LETTER IS STUDIED AND PUT INTO ITS   621D JERUSALEM 3   PROSE
    FIT PLACE
    ARE FORMD IN A WHEEL TO FIT THE COGS OF THE ADVERSE WHEEL   633 JERUSALEM 13   14
    NO ONE BRUISES OR STARVES HIMSELF TO MAKE HIMSELF FIT   639 JERUSALEM 17   21
    FOR LABOUR
    IN HIDDEN DECEIT THEY ARE VEGETABLE ONLY FIT FOR BURNING   663 JERUSALEM 36   48
    DOES NOT THIS FIT & IS IT NOT FITTING MOST EXQUISITELY TOO   784D ANNO WW EXCUR   MARG
    OR FIT THINGS FOR A CLERGYMAN TO WRITE UPON   . . . . .   795B LETTER 6   PROSE
    ALONE IS THE GOVERNOR OF WORLDLY RICHES & WHEN IT IS FIT   796A LETTER 6   PROSE
    NOT ON THE NATURAL WORLD & IF IT WAS FIT FOR ME I DOUBT NOT   812A LETTER 22   PROSE
    THAT SORROW IS NOT FIT FOR IMMORTALS & IS UTTERLY USELESS   830C LETTER 30   PROSE
    TO
    WHICH I BELIEVE YOU THOUGHT FIT NOT TO PRINT   . . . . .   841C LETTER 41   PROSE
    YOUR ANSWER TO THE PROPOSAL YOU WILL IF YOU THINK   842A LETTER 41   PROSE
    FIT DIRECT
    IMMEDIATELY REPLIED IF MR HAYLEY SHOULD THINK FIT TO   .   856C LETTER 54   PROSE
    A RETURN OF THE OLD SHIVERING FIT CAME ON THIS MORNING   .   869B LETTER 69   PROSE
    & FIT ONLY FOR A SOLDIER OF SATAN TO PERFORM   . . . . .   871B LETTER 72   PROSE
    THAT (SHIVERING) FIT WHICH MUST BE AVOIDED TILL THE COLD   871D LETTER 74   *PROSE
    IS GONE
    I HAVE HAD ANOTHER DESPERATE SHIVERING FIT IT CAME ON   .   872B LETTER 75   PROSE
    BRINGS ON THE SHIVERING FIT WHEN I AM FORCED TO GO TO BED   872B LETTER 75   PROSE
    SHIVERING FIT ATTACKED ME AGAIN & THE PAIN WITH ITS   . .   872B LETTER 75   PROSE
    [THE KNAVE CALLS ANY THING ?FOUND IN NATURE FIT FOR ART]   SUPP ANNO REYNOLDS   * MARG
FITLY
    TELL OF THE FOUR-FOLD MAN IN STARRY NUMBERS FITLY ORDERD   502 MILTON 20   16
FITNESS
    THE ARGUMENT MAN HAS NO NOTION OF MORAL FITNESS BUT FROM   97A NAT RELIGION 1   PROSE
    EDUCATION
    AND SEEING ACCORDING TO FITNESS & ORDER AND I HEARD JEHOVAH   746 JERUSALEM 98   40
    SPEAK
FITS
    I DONT KNOW PERHAPS HE TAKES IT BY FITS . . . .   22 EDW THIRD/PS 3   48
FITTED
    MY LORDS THE FRENCH HAVE FITTED OUT MANY   . . . . . .   20 EDW THIRD/PS 2   65
    FITTED TO THE FINGER OF AN EMPEROR SUCH IS THAT WORTHY   29D EDW THIRD/PS 4   PROSE
    CHANDOS
    THE TRUMPET FITTED TO THE BATTLE & THE FLUTE OF SUMMER   . .   337 FOUR ZOAS 7B   173
    WITH POWERS FITTED TO CIRCUMSCRIBE THIS DARK SATANIC DEATH   507 MILTON 23   51
    THE TRUMPET FITTED TO MORTAL BATTLE . . . .   700 JERUSALEM 65   15
    THEN EACH AN ARROW FLAMING FROM HIS QUIVER FITTED CAREFULLY   744 JERUSALEM 98   1
    YOU SHALL NOT BRING ME DOWN TO BELIEVE SUCH FITTING   784C ANNO WW EXCUR   MARG
    & FITTED
FITTEST
    IN HEAD OR HEART OR REINS ACCORDING TO THE FITTEST ORDER   342 FOUR ZOAS 8   59
    IN HEAD OR HEART OR REINS ACCORDING TO THE FITTEST ORDER   382 FOUR ZOAS AD 6   28
    CONSIDERD WHAT IS NOT TOO EXPLICIT AS THE FITTEST   793B LETTER 5   PROSE
    FOR INSTRUCTION
FITTING
    YOU SHALL NOT BRING ME DOWN TO BELIEVE SUCH FITTING   784C ANNO WW EXCUR   MARG
    & FITTED
    DOES NOT THIS FIT & IS IT NOT FITTING MOST EXQUISITELY TOO   784D ANNO WW EXCUR   MARG
FITTLER
    ADMIRABLE PRINTS TO IT BY FITTLER WHETHER YOU INTENDED   843B LETTER 43   PROSE
    IT OR
FITZROY
    MR FLAXMAN SCULPTOR BUCKINGHAM STREET FITZROY SQUARE LONDON   SUPP ADDRESSES/L   *TITLE
    JOHN LINNELL ESQRE CIRENCESTER PLACE FITZROY SQUARE   . . .   SUPP ADDRESSES/L   *TITLE
    TO MISS DENMAN BUCKINGHAM STREET FITZROY SQUARE   . . . .   SUPP ADDRESS/L 86   *TITLE
FIVE   SEE EIGHTY-FIVE,SEVENTY-FIVE,TWENTY-FIVE
    THE CRY WAS GREAT IN TIRIEL'S PALACE HIS FIVE DAUGHTERS RAN   106 TIRIEL 5   18
    I DWELT WITH MYRATANA FIVE YEARS IN THE DESOLATE ROCK   .   107 TIRIEL 6   8
    TO AWAKE FROM SLUMBERS OF FIVE THOUSAND YEARS . . . . .   134 FRENCH REVOLTN   8
    THE NERVES OF FIVE THOUSAND YEARS' ANCESTRY TREMBLE . . .   137 FRENCH REVOLTN   70
    THE FIVE SENSES THE CHIEF INLETS OF SOUL IN THIS AGE   . .   149D MARRIAGE HH 4   PROSE
    THE SON A RATIO OF THE FIVE SENSES & THE HOLY-GHOST VACUUM   150B MARRIAGE HH 5   PROSE
    WHEN I CAME HOME ON THE ABYSS OF THE FIVE SENSES   . . .   150C MARRIAGE HH 6   PROSE
    IS AN IMMENSE WORLD OF DELIGHT CLOSD BY YOUR SENSES FIVE   150D MARRIAGE HH 6   PROSE
    I SAY I SHANT LIVE FIVE YEARS AND . . . .   187C SAY I SHANT/N   PROSE
    THEY TOLD ME THAT I HAD FIVE SENSES TO INCLOSE ME UP   . .   191 V DAU ALBION 2   31

		PAGE	TITLE	LINE

FIVE   (CONTINUED)

THEY SLOW ADVANCE TO SHUT THE FIVE GATES OF THEIR LAW-BUILT HEAVEN — 203 AMERICA 16 — 19

BUT THE FIVE GATES WERE CONSUMD & THEIR BOLTS AND HINGES MELTED — 203 AMERICA 16 — 22

FIVE WINDOWS LIGHT THE CAVERND MAN THRO ONE HE BREATHES THE AIR — 237 EUROPE INTRO — 1

PLACD IN THE ORDER OF THE STARS WHEN THE FIVE SENSES WHELMD — 241 EUROPE 10 — 10

TILL A PHILOSOPHY OF FIVE SENSES WAS COMPLETE . . . . . — 246 SONG OF LOS 4 — 16

FIVE HUNDRED YEARS WANDRING ON EARTH . . . . — 250 AHANIA 2 — 46

FOR THOU HAST TOUCHD MY FIVE SENSES & THEY ANSWERD THEE — 290 FOUR ZOAS 2 — 376

SOMETIMES AS TWELVE DAUGHTERS LOVELY & SOMETIMES AS FIVE — 349 FOUR ZOAS 8 — 328

SOMETIMES AS TWELVE DAUGHTERS LOVELY & SOMETIMES AS FIVE — 382 FOUR ZOAS AD 6 — 16

GREATER MIRACLE TO FEED FIVE THOUSAND MEN WITH FIVE LOAVES — 391C ANNO WATSON — MARG

HIS CORN-FIELDS AND HIS VALLEYS OF FIVE HUNDRED ACRES SQUARE — 497 MILTON 15 — 31

WITHIN IT SIT FIVE FEMALES & THE NAMELESS SHADOWY MOTHER — 524 MILTON 34 — 27

APPEARD THE SEVEN KINGDOMS OF CANAAN & FIVE BAALIM . . . — 532 MILTON 40 — 24

WHILE TITIAN'S &C AS IN THE BOOK OF MOONLIGHT P (FIVE) . — 551A DELICATE/N — PROSE

WHICH I ENGRAVED AFTER HIM FIVE & TWENTY YEARS AGO . . . — 592B PUB ADDRESS/N — PROSE

THE LIFE'S LABOUR OF FIVE HUNDRED IDIOTS . . . . . . — 593B PUB ADDRESS/N — PROSE

THE FIVE BOOKS OF THE DECALOGUE THE BOOKS OF JOSHUA & JUDGES — 677 JERUSALEM 48 — 9

ALBION'S DREAD TOMB EIGHT THOUSAND AND FIVE HUNDRED YEARS — 678 JERUSALEM 48 — 36

RETAIN MY YOUTH EIGHT THOUSAND AND FIVE HUNDRED YEARS . . — 728 JERUSALEM 83 — 52

THERE THE SEVEN KINGS OF CANAAN & FIVE BAALIM OF PHILISTEA — 735 JERUSALEM 89 — 46

MRS FLAXMAN & FIVE MORE TWO OF WHICH YOU WILL BE SO GOOD — 821B LETTER 25 — PROSE

WHO HAS NOT LOST ANY OF HIS LIFE SINCE HE WAS FIVE YEARS OLD — 830A LETTER 30 — PROSE

I SEND THE FIVE COPIES OF COWPER'S PLATES WHICH YOU WILL — 832D LETTER 32 — PROSE

FIVE SHILLINGS AT A BROKER'S SHOP IT IS ABOUT FIVE FEET BY FOUR — 843D LETTER 43 — PROSE

IS FIVE GUINEAS EACH I SEND THE DOMENICHINO WHICH IS VERY — 844B LETTER 43 — PROSE

FIVE HUNDRED WERE OUT THIS IS SWIFT WORK IF LITERALLY TRUE BUT — 846D LETTER 44 — PROSE

I SEND WASHINGTON'S (SECOND) VOL (FIVE) NUMBERS OF FUSELI'S — 850B LETTER 49 — PROSE

FROM RHEUMATISM AS SHE WAS FIVE YEARS AGO AND WE HAVE . — 851C LETTER 50 — PROSE

OF THE BALLADS THE PRINTS (FIVE) IN NUMBER I HAVE ENGAGED — 859A LETTER 56 — PROSE

HIS DEAD MASTER FROM THE VULTURES OF THESE FIVE I AM MAKING — 859B LETTER 56 — PROSE

OUT OF A NUMBER OF DESIGNS I HAVE SELECTED FIVE . . . — 860C LETTER 56 — PROSE

I THANK YOU FOR THE RECEIT OF FIVE POUNDS THIS MORNING & — 873B LETTER 77 — PROSE

I OUGHT TO HAVE ACKNOWLEDGD THE RECEIT OF FIVE POUNDS . — 875D LETTER 82 — PROSE

I THANK YOU FOR THE FIVE POUNDS RECIEVD TO DAY AM GETTING — 876A LETTER 83 — *PROSE

RECIEVD...OF MR LINNELL THE SUM OF FIVE POUNDS ON ACCOUNT — SUPP LETTER 66C — *PROSE

OF TWO POUNDS FIVE SHILLINGS FOR THE SONGS OF INNOCENCE — SUPP LETTER 80A — *PROSE

FIX

HERE BUILD THY NEST HERE FIX THY STAFF . . . . . . — 37B CONTEMPLATN/PS — PROSE

TO FIX THE PRICE OF LABOUR . . . . — 247 SONG OF LOS 6 — 17

. . . THEN FIX THEM IN THEIR AWFUL STATIONS . . . . — 283 FOUR ZOAS 2 — 144

WANDRING IN VAIN HERE WILL I FIX MY FOOT & HERE REBUILD — 317 FOUR ZOAS 6 — * 227

AND BRASS VAST INSTRUMENTS TO MEASURE OUT THE IMMENSE & FIX — 317 FOUR ZOAS 6 — 230

AND LET THEM RUN ON THE WINDS OF THY BOSOM I WILL FIX THEM — 732 JERUSALEM 87 — 9

FIXD

HER EYES WERE FIXD THE BLOODY CLOTH UNFOLDS . . . . . — 5 FAIR ELENOR/PS — 57

ETRUSCAN COLUMN & INFLAMMABLE GASS FIXD THEIR EYES . . . — 44C ISLAND MOON 1 — PROSE

IN MILKY FONDNESS THEN ON THEL SHE FIXD HER HUMBLE EYES — 129 BOOK OF THEL 4 — 9

IF IN THE MORNING SUN I FIND IT THERE MY EYES ARE FIXD . — 194 V DAU ALBION 6 — 23

SOME FIXD THE ANVIL SOME THE LOOM ERECTED SOME THE PLOW — 281 FOUR ZOAS 2 — 27

NOW FIXD INTO ONE STEDFAST BULK HIS FEATURES STONIFY . — 305 FOUR ZOAS 5 — 2

AND THE SCIENCES WERE FIXD & THE VORTEXES BEGAN TO OPERATE — 317 FOUR ZOAS 6 — 234

FOR URIZEN FIXD IN ENVY SAT BROODING & COVERD WITH SNOW — 321 FOUR ZOAS 7 — 28

RENDS THY WHITE HAIR YET THOU DOST FIXD OBDURATE BROODING SIT — 322 FOUR ZOAS 7 — 80

THE LIMIT OF CONTRACTION NOW WAS FIXD & MAN BEGAN . . . — 341 FOUR ZOAS 8 — 16

HENCE THE THREE CLASSES OF MEN TAKE THEIR FIXD DESTINATIONS — 484 MILTON 5 — 13

HERE THE THREE CLASSES OF MORTAL MEN TAKE THEIR FIXD DESTINATIONS — 486 MILTON 6 — 32

THAT EVERY THING IS FIXD OPAKE WITHOUT INTERNAL LIGHT . — 491 MILTON 10 — 20

HERE FIXD INTO A FROZEN BULK SUBJECT TO DECAY & DEATH . — 525 MILTON 34 — 54

HIS SUBLIME & PATHOS BECOME TWO ROCKS FIXD IN THE EARTH — 620 JERUSALEM 1 — 4

HERE LOS FIXD DOWN THE FIFTY-TWO COUNTIES OF ENGLAND & WALES — 637 JERUSALEM 16 — 28

ARE BECOME WEAK VISIONS OF TIME & SPACE FIXD INTO FURROWS OF DEATH — 679 JERUSALEM 49 — 22

ARCHD OVER THE MOON AT MIDNIGHT & LOS FIXD THEM THERE . — 690 JERUSALEM 58 — 31

IN VAIN THEY ROLLD APART THEY ARE FIXD INTO THE LAND OF CABUL — 715 JERUSALEM 74 — 57

"O THAT THE EVERLASTING HAD NOT FIXD" (SHAKESPEARE) . . — SUPP LEGEND/N95 — *

FIXED

BETWEEN SATURN & THE FIXED STARS . . . . — 157A MARRIAGE HH 17 — PROSE

TILL SHE WHO BURNS WITH YOUTH AND KNOWS NO FIXED LOT IS BOUND — 193 V DAU ALBION 5 — 21

AND FIXED IN TWO LITTLE CAVES . . . . — 228 URIZEN 11 — 14

A CIRCLE OF DARKNESS THEN FIXED . . . . — 251 AHANIA 3 — 32

SHRUNK INTO FIXED SPACE STOOD TREMBLING ON A ROCKY CLIFF — 305 FOUR ZOAS 5 — 12

AND HERE THE SUN & MOON RECIEVE THEIR FIXED DESTINATIONS — 514 MILTON 27 — 54

TO THE TIME & SPACE FIXED BY THE CORPOREAL VEGETATIVE EYE — 614B V LAST JUDG/N — PROSE

THESE ARE STATES PERMANENTLY FIXED BY THE DIVINE POWER . — 663 JERUSALEM 36 — 38

FIXES

AND NOW HE FIXES HIS STRONG TALONS IN THE POINTED ROCK . — 354 FOUR ZOAS 8 — 525

KNIGHT WHOSE SOLEMN GALLANTRY NO LESS FIXES ATTENTION . — 588C CHAUCER/N — PROSE

AND LOS FIXES THEM ON HIS ANVIL INCESSANT HIS BLOWS . . — 690 JERUSALEM 58 — 16

		PAGE	TITLE	LINE

FIXES   (CONTINUED)
HE FIXES THEM WITH STRONG BLOWS PLACING THE STONES   690 JERUSALEM 58   17
& TIMBERS
IRON OF HIS FORGE & FIXES THEM INTO BONES OF CHALK & ROCK   736 JERUSALEM 90   20

FIXING
WHERE WINTER BEATS INCESSANT FIXING THEM FIRM ON THEIR BASE   281 FOUR ZOAS 2   31
CREATING MANY A VORTEX FIXING MANY A SCIENCE IN THE DEEP   316 FOUR ZOAS 6   187
FIXING THEIR SYSTEMS PERMANENT BY MATHEMATIC POWER . . .   631 JERUSALEM 12   12
AND WELL CONTRIVED WORDS FIRM FIXING NEVER FORGOTTEN . .   632 JERUSALEM 12   35
AWAY FROM THE CONFLICT OF LUVAH & URIZEN FIXING THE GATES   637 JERUSALEM 16   31
FIXING THE SEXUAL INTO AN EVER-PROLIFIC GENERATION . . .   713 JERUSALEM 73   26

FIXT
. . . FIXT IN THE FIRMAMENT BY PEACE BROTHERHOOD AND LOVE   781 GHOST ABEL 2   26

FLAG
. . .IN DAY OF THE BRITISH FLAG WHEN HEAVY CANNONS . . .   147 FRENCH REVOLTN   280

FLAGD
FLAGD WITH GREY BROWD SNOWS AND THUNDEROUS VISAGES . . .   159B SONG LIBERTY   PROSE
FALLING INTO THE DEEP SUBLIME FLAGD WITH GREY-BROWD SNOWS   203 AMERICA 16   5
FLEW THE KING THO FLAGD HIS POWERS LABRING TILL OVER ROCKS   314 FOUR ZOAS 6   * 112

FLAGGING
ONCE LIKE THE PRIDE OF THE SUN NOW FLAGGING IN COLD NIGHT   354 FOUR ZOAS 8   * 522

FLAGS
REPLY NOT LEST I BIND THEE WITH THE GREEN FLAGS OF THE   104 TIRIEL 4   24
BROOK

FLAIL
THE MORNING DAWND URIZEN ROSE & IN HIS HAND THE FLAIL . .   374 FOUR ZOAS 9   650
WHILE THE FLAIL OF URIZEN SOUNDED LOUD . . . .   375 FOUR ZOAS 9   684
I HEAR THE FLAIL OF URIZEN HIS BARNS ARE FULL NO (ROOM)   375 FOUR ZOAS 9   * 696
HIS LABORIOUS TASK DROPPING HIS FLAIL & CREAM BOWL . . .   618C ILLUS MILTON   PROSE
THE SOUNDING FLAIL TO THRESH THE WINNOW TO WINNOW KINGDOMS   713 JERUSALEM 73   13

FLAKES
SCATTERING HER LEPROUS SNOWS IN FLAKES OF DISEASE OVER   703 JERUSALEM 66   80
ALBION

FLAKY
HAIR WHITE AS SNOW COVERD HIM IN FLAKY LOCKS TERRIFIC . .   318 FOUR ZOAS 6   240

FLAMD
IN THEIR DARKNESS THE KING STOOD HIS HEART FLAMD . . . .   137 FRENCH REVOLTN   69
AND FLAMD RED METEORS ROUND THE LAND OF ALBION BENEATH . .   197 AMERICA 3   16
AND FLAMD FIERCE METEORS ROUND THE LAND OF ALBION BENEATH   204 AMERICA CANC A   * 16
FLAMD OUT FIRST BEGOTTEN LAST BORN . . . .   234 URIZEN 23   18
FLAMD FURIOUS SPARKLES HIS HAIR & BEARD . . . .   249 AHANIA 2   3
OPPOSD TO THE EXULTING FLAMD BEAM . . . .   249 AHANIA 2   20
[THREE DAYS IN SELF ADMIRING RAPTURES ON THE ROCKS   267 FOUR ZOAS 1   134
HE FLAMD]
TENFOLD THE DEMON'S RAGE FLAMD TENFOLD FORTH RENDING . .   308 FOUR ZOAS 5   105
NOR COULD HE QUENCH THE FIRES FOR THEY FLAMD OUT FROM THE   315 FOUR ZOAS 6   144
HEART
FLAMD ABOVE ALL THE PLOWED FURROWS ANGRY RED AND FURIOUS   488 MILTON 8   36
WHICH NOW FLAMD HIGH & FURIOUS IN SATAN AGAINST PALAMBRON   489 MILTON 9   11
LOS FLAMD IN MY PATH & THE SUN WAS HOT . . . .   818 HAPPINESS/L   77

FLAME
WHEN CONFUSION RAGES WHEN THE FIELD IS IN A FLAME . . .   18 EDW THIRD/PS 1   6
WHILE LIKE THE MOUNTING FLAME . . . .   18 EDW THIRD/PS 1   15
AND ROAR THE WILD FLAME OF FIERCE WAR UPON . . . . . .   26 EDW THIRD/PS 3   230
THE EPICUREAN SEEMING [NOT] STUDYING THE FLAME OF   44C ISLAND MOON 1   PROSE
THE CANDLE
& SET HIS [HEAD] HAIR ALL IN A FLAME & RAN ABOUT THE ROOM   48C ISLAND MOON 4   PROSE
FROM HIS EYES OF FLAME . . . .   113 LIT GRL LST/SI   47
LIKE A FLAME OF FIRE HE STOOD BEFORE DARK RANKS . . . . .   146 FRENCH REVOLTN   273
ONCE I SAW A DEVIL IN A FLAME OF FIRE . . . .   158B MARRIAGE HH 22   PROSE
WHO STRETCHED OUT HIS ARMS EMBRACING THE FLAME OF FIRE .   158D MARRIAGE HH 22   PROSE
AND THE FLAME FOLDED ROARING FIERCE WITHIN THE PITCHY NIGHT   200 AMERICA 12   8
AND LIKE A RED FLAME A TONGUE . . . .   229 URIZEN 13   8
TO A DEVOURING FLAME AND MAN FLED FROM ITS FACE AND HID   241 EUROPE 10   17
LIKE A SERPENT OF FIERY FLAME . . . .   248 SONG OF LOS 7   28
SO HE SPOKE IN A FIERY FLAME . . . .   249 AHANIA 2   14
RIVERS OF WIDE FLAME THEY ROLL ROUND . . . .   256 BOOK OF LOS 3   40
FROM THE CRASH [REARED] ROARED A FLAME OF . . . . . .   295 FOUR ZOAS 3   * 146
. . . BLUE (SULPHUREOUS) FIRE FROM THE FLAME . . . . .   295 FOUR ZOAS 3   * 146
THROAT THEN LIKE A RED FLAME A TONGUE OF HUNGER . . . .   303 FOUR ZOAS 4   241
HIS LIMBS BOUND DOWN MOCK AT HIS CHAINS FOR OVER THEM A   308 FOUR ZOAS 5   114
FLAME
HIS NOSTRILS BREATHE [WITH] A FIERY FLAME . . . .   308 FOUR ZOAS 5   127
[WAS LUVAH XXX HE STOOD ?GLOWING IN THE DARK FLAME] .   SUPP FOUR ZOAS 5   *
FLAME HIGH IN PRIDE & LAUGH TO SCORN THE SOURCE OF HIS   324 FOUR ZOAS 7   158
DECEIT
AND REASON ROUND THE EARTH THEY MARCH IN ORDER FLAME BY   359 FOUR ZOAS 9   87
FLAME
LIKE A (PAINT) FLAME QUIVERING UPON THE SURFACE OF THE   370 FOUR ZOAS 9   * 497
DARKNESS
THE SELFHOOD IN A FLAME OF FIRE . . . .   421 EACH MAN/N   6
NOW INTREATING [?FLAME] FLAMING FIRE . . . .   422 BENEATH/N   * 24
FILLD ME THAT LIKE A FLAME I BURND . . . .   429 CRYSTL CABINET   18
WITH ARDOR FIERCE & HANDS OF FLAME . . . .   429 CRYSTL CABINET   22
FEELING THE ELECTRIC FLAME OF MILTON'S AWFUL PRECIPITATE   502 MILTON 20   26
DESCENT
COMING IN A CLOUD WITH TRUMPETS & WITH FIERY FLAME . . .   531 MILTON 39   23
& JUSTICE CAIPHAS HAS A BLUE FLAME LIKE A MITER ON HIS HEAD   608D V LAST JUDG/N   PROSE
BENEATH BEULAH AS A WATRY FLAME REVOLVING EVERY WAY . . .   634 JERUSALEM 14   7
NOR IN HAVILAH WHERE THE CHERUB ROLLD HIS REDOUNDING FLAME   686 JERUSALEM 55   22
THE DIVINE VISION BECAME FIRST A BURNING FLAME THEN   702 JERUSALEM 66   41
A COLUMN

		PAGE	TITLE	LINE

FLAME   (CONTINUED)
  AND SAW A FLAME OF FIRE EVEN AS A WHEEL . . . . 717 STOOD AMONG/J   2
  MY WIFE IS LIKE A FLAME OF MANY COLOURS OF PRECIOUS JEWELS 801B LETTER 13   PROSE
  THE FLAME SOON DIES AGAIN & I AM LEFT STUPIFIED AND   830B LETTER 30   PROSE
    ASTONISHD
FLAMED
  IN GHASTLY TORMENT SICK A TONGUE OF HUNGER & THIRST FLAMED   482 MILTON 3   22
    OUT
  THE LAND OF DARKNESS FLAMED BUT NO LIGHT & NO REPOSE   . . 634 JERUSALEM 13   46
FLAMES
  THAT FLAMES FROM THEIR LARGE NOSTRILS THOU O SUMMER . . .   1 TO SUMMER/PS   3
  LIKE AS A FOREST ROARS WITH CRACKLING FLAMES . . . . . .   32 EDW THIRD/PS 6   27
  RISE FROM THE CENTER BELCHING FLAMES & ROARINGS DARK SMOKE 106 TIRIEL 5   7
  [FLINGING FLAMES OF DISCONTENT & PLAGUES OF DARK DESPAIR]   109 TIRIEL 8   16
  IN FLAMES OF RED WRATH BURNING . . . .   137 FRENCH REVOLTN 67
  CLOTHD IN FLAMES OF CRIMSON . . . .   138 FRENCH REVOLTN 86
  IN THE RUSHING OF SCALES AND HISSING OF FLAMES . . . . . 140 FRENCH REVOLTN 127
  . . . SAID BOURBON AND REND THE FLAMES . . . . 142 FRENCH REVOLTN 171
  . . . O PRINCES OF FIRE WHOSE FLAMES ARE FOR GROWTH NOT   142 FRENCH REVOLTN 179
    CONSUMING
  THEIR SULLEN FLAMES FADED EMERGE ROUND THE GLOOMY KING . 159D SONG LIBERTY PROSE
  WRITHING IN PANGS OF ABHORRED BIRTH RED FLAMES THE CREST   199 AMERICA 9   17
    REBELLIOUS
  IN FLAMES AS OF A FURNACE ON THE LAND FROM NORTH TO SOUTH 201 AMERICA 12   12
  IN BERNARD'S HOUSE THE FLAMES COVERD THE LAND THEY ROUZE   201 AMERICA 13   2
    THEY CRY
  FROM THE GRIM FLAMES AND FROM THE VISIONS OF ORC IN SIGHT 201 AMERICA 13   9
  IN THE FLAMES STOOD & VIEWD THE ARMIES DRAWN OUT IN THE SKY 201 AMERICA 14   1
  AND THE RED FLAMES OF ORC THAT FOLDED ROARING FIERCE AROUND 201 AMERICA 14   11
  THE PLAGUES CREEP ON THE BURNING WINDS DRIVEN BY FLAMES   202 AMERICA 15   11
    OF ORC
  OVER THE HILLS THE VALES THE CITIES RAGE THE RED FLAMES   202 AMERICA 16   1
    FIERCE
  AND THE FIERCE FLAMES BURNT ROUND THE HEAVENS . . . . . . 203 AMERICA 16   23
  HIS SNOWY BEARD THAT STREAMS LIKE LAMBENT FLAMES DOWN HIS 204 AMERICA CANC B 16
    WIDE BREAST
  . . . [WITH FLAMES] [HOAR FROSTS] DAMP MISTS . . . . . . 205 AMERICA CANC C   5
  IN GLITTRING ARMOUR SWIFT AS WINDS INTELLIGENT AS [FLAMES] 205 AMERICA CANC C 13
    CLOUDS
  IN THE FLAMES OF ETERNAL FURY . . . .   225 URIZEN 5   2
  IN THE FLAMES OF ETERNAL FURY . . . .   225 URIZEN 5   18
  IN FIERCE ANGUISH & QUENCHLESS FLAMES . . . .   225 URIZEN 5   19
  HOWLING THE CHILD WITH FIERCE FLAMES . . . . 232 URIZEN 19   45
  I BRING FORTH FROM MY TEEMING BOSOM MYRIADS OF FLAMES .   238 EUROPE PREL 2   9
  THEY SAW HIS BONEY FEET ON THE ROCK THE FLESH CONSUMD IN   242 EUROPE 12   10
    FLAMES
  THEY HEARD THE VOICE OF ALBION'S ANGEL HOWLING IN FLAMES   242 EUROPE 12   12
    OF ORC
  DRIVEN OUT BY THE FLAMES OF ORC HIS FURRD ROBES & FALSE   242 EUROPE 12   16
    LOCKS
  BETWEEN THE CLOUDS OF URIZEN THE FLAMES OF ORC ROLL HEAVY 243 EUROPE 12   32
  THY GOLDEN WINGS ARE MY DELIGHT & THY FLAMES OF SOFT   244 EUROPE 14   8
    DELUSION
  WENT ENORMOUS ABOVE THE RED FLAMES . . . .   248 SONG OF LOS 7   11
  ON SPIKED FLAMES ROSE HIS HOT VISAGE . . . .   249 AHANIA 2   2
  RAGING FURIOUS THE FLAMES OF DESIRE . . . .   256 BOOK OF LOS 3   27
  RAN THRO HEAVEN & EARTH LIVING FLAMES . . . .   256 BOOK OF LOS 3   28
  ROUND THE FLAMES ROLL AS LOS HURLS HIS CHAINS . . . . .   256 BOOK OF LOS 3   34
  THE GIGANTIC FLAMES TREMBLED AND HID . . . .   257 BOOK OF LOS 4   3
  HIS SPECTRE ISSUING FROM HIS FEET IN FLAMES OF FIRE . . . 266 FOUR ZOAS 1   78
  AMONG THESE FLAMES INCESSANT LABOURING OUR HARD MASTERS   285 FOUR ZOAS 2   219
    LAUGH
  . . . & FLAMES ROLLD ROUND THEIR FERVID FEET . . . . .   294 FOUR ZOAS 3   96
  IN THUNDER SMOKE & SULLEN FLAMES & HOWLINGS & FURY & BLOOD 306 FOUR ZOAS 5   38
  WITHIN HIS RIBS PRODUCING SERPENTS WHOSE SOULS ARE FLAMES 306 FOUR ZOAS 5   61
    OF FIRE
  CRACKLING THE FLAMES WENT UP WITH FURY FROM THE IMMORTAL   308 FOUR ZOAS 5   108
    DEMON
  SURROUNDED WITH FLAMES THE DEMON GREW LOUD HOWLING IN HIS 308 FOUR ZOAS 5   109
    FIRES
  THE CAVE OF ORC STOOD TO THE SOUTH A FURNACE OF DIRE FLAMES 318 FOUR ZOAS 6   265
  THE HOLY OIL RAGES THRO ALL THE CAVERND ROCKS FIERCE FLAMES 320 FOUR ZOAS 7   12
  WHILE HIS SNOWS FELL & HIS STORMS BEAT TO COOL THE FLAMES 321 FOUR ZOAS 7   30
    OF ORC
  TO MODULATE HIS FIRES STUDIOUS THE LOUD ROARING FLAMES . 331 FOUR ZOAS 7   458
  THE REAPER IN BOTH ARMS EMBRACING THE FURIOUS RAGING FLAMES 332 FOUR ZOAS 7   463
  PROPAGATES THRO THE WARRING EARTH THE [LIONS] LION RAGING 335 FOUR ZOAS 7B * 110
    IN FLAMES
  TO ETERNAL TORMENT IN THESE FLAMES FOR THO I HAVE THE POWER 339 FOUR ZOAS 7B   253
  HIS NECK FLAMES WITH WRATH & MAJESTY HE LASHES THE ABYSS   352 FOUR ZOAS 8   442
  RAHAB & TIRZAH WAIL ALOUD IN THE WILD FLAMES . . . . . .   358 FOUR ZOAS 9   32
  OF ORC BEGAN TO CONSUME IN FIERCE RAVING FIRE HIS FIERCE   358 FOUR ZOAS 9   34
    FLAMES
  START FORTH THE TREMBLING MILLIONS INTO FLAMES OF MENTAL   358 FOUR ZOAS 9   44
    FIRE
  IN THE FIERCE FLAMES THE LIMBS OF MYSTERY LAY CONSUMING   359 FOUR ZOAS 9   67
    WITH HOWLING
  AND DEEP DESPAIR RATTLING GO UP THE FLAMES AROUND   359 FOUR ZOAS 9   68
    THE SYNAGOGUE
  FOLDS THE TREE OF MYSTERY WENT UP IN FOLDING FLAMES . . . 359 FOUR ZOAS 9   70
  THE FLAMES ROLLING INTENSE THRO THE WIDE UNIVERSE   . . . 359 FOUR ZOAS 9   82
  . . . THE WILD FLAMES ?WHIRRING UP . . . .   359 FOUR ZOAS 9 * 85

710

		PAGE	TITLE	LINE
FLAMES	(CONTINUED)			
THE BLOODY DELUGE LIVING FLAMES WINGED WITH INTELLECT	. .	359	FOUR ZOAS 9	86
START FORTH THE TREMBLING MILLIONS INTO FLAMES OF MENTAL FIRE		359	FOUR ZOAS 9	89
I HEAR MYSTERY HOWLING IN THESE FLAMES OF CONSUMMATION	. .	360	FOUR ZOAS 9	114
THEY VIEW THE FLAMES RED ROLLING ON THRO THE WIDE UNIVERSE		363	FOUR ZOAS 9	258
WHAT FLAMES ARE THESE COMING FROM THE SOUTH	.	364	FOUR ZOAS 9	262
. . . WHILE THEY SPOKE THE FLAMES COME ON INTENSE ROARING		364	FOUR ZOAS 9	264
PERHAPS I MAY BE FORGIVEN WHILE HE SPEAKS THE FLAMES ROLL ON		364	FOUR ZOAS 9	271
AND AFTER THE FLAMES APPEARS THE CLOUD OF THE SON OF MAN		364	FOUR ZOAS 9	272
AND URIZEN AROSE UP WITH HIM WALKING THRO THE FLAMES	. .	364	FOUR ZOAS 9	287
TO MEET THE LORD COMING TO JUDGMENT BUT THE FLAMES REPELLD THEM		364	FOUR ZOAS 9	288
AND ALL THE WHILE THE FLAMES OF ORC FOLLOW THE VENTROUS FEET		365	FOUR ZOAS 9	330
THE SEED IS HARROWD IN WHILE FLAMES HEAT THE BLACK MOULD & CAUSE		366	FOUR ZOAS 9	337
TAKE THEIR REPOSE ON BEDS THEY DRINK THEY SING THEY VIEW THE FLAMES		366	FOUR ZOAS 9	341
IN MENTAL FLAMES THE FLAMES REFUSD THEY DROVE HIM BACK TO BEULAH		366	FOUR ZOAS 9	356
AND NOW FIERCE ORC HAD QUITE CONSUMD HIMSELF IN MENTAL FLAMES		366	FOUR ZOAS 9	358
WAS SERVD ROUND BY THE FLAMES OF LUVAH ALL DAY & ALL THE NIGHT		372	FOUR ZOAS 9	589
WAS SERVD ROUND BY THE FLAMES OF LUVAH ALL DAY & ALL THE NIGHT		373	FOUR ZOAS 9	620
THEY HOWL & WRITHE IN SHOALS OF TORMENT IN FIERCE FLAMES CONSUMING		377	FOUR ZOAS 9	749
THE OCEAN CALM THE CLOUDS FOLD ROUND & FIERY FLAMES OF LOVE		381	FOUR ZOAS AD 2	1
THE ONE WAS CLOTHD IN FLAMES OF FIRE	.	421	BENEATH/N	6
[THE ONE WAS CLOTHD IN FLAMES OF FIRE]	.	422	BENEATH REWR/N	3
THE ONE WAS CLOTHD IN FLAMES OF FIRE	.	424	THE GOLDEN NET	5
& SOME ARE SCOURGED BY SPIRITS WITH FLAMES OF FIRE INTO		443C	LAST JUDGMNT/L	PROSE
HOWLING & [DESCENDING INTO THE FLAMES & IN THE ACT OF]	. .	443C	LAST JUDGMNT/L	PROSE
RAGD WITH THICK FLAMES REDUNDANT & THE HARROW MADDEND WITH FURY		487	MILTON 7	46
THE HARROW CAST THICK FLAMES JEHOVAH THUNDERD ABOVE	. . .	493	MILTON 12	20
THE HARROW CAST THICK FLAMES & ORBD US ROUND IN CONCAVE FIRES		493	MILTON 12	22
A HELL OF OUR OWN MAKING SEE ITS FLAMES STILL GIRD ME ROUND		493	MILTON 12	23
THEY HOWL & WRITHE IN SHOALS OF TORMENT IN FIERCE FLAMES CONSUMING		513	MILTON 27	31
JERUSALEM'S CHILDREN CONSUME IN FLAMES AMONG THE STARS	.	527	MILTON 37	12
FATHER & MOTHER I RETURN FROM FLAMES OF FIRE TRIED & PURE & WHITE		535B	FATHER MOTHER	PROSE
THE [WAVES] FLAMES OF HELL THAT ROUND ME ROLL	.	558	THE CAVERNS/N	8
THOSE [WHO] FIGURES THAT DESCEND INTO THE FLAMES . . .	.	608D	V LAST JUDG/N	*PROSE
HER KINGS & COUNCELLORS & WARRIORS DESCEND IN FLAMES		609B	V LAST JUDG/N	PROSE
THE TWO FIGURES IN PURIFYING FLAMES BY THE SIDE OF THE	. .	610C	V LAST JUDG/N	PROSE
THE GREAT SUN IS REPRESENTED CLOTHED IN FLAMES . . .	.	618B	ILLUS MILTON	PROSE
IS SEEN IN THE HEAVENS THROWING HIS DARTS & FLAMES OF FIRE		619B	ILLUS MILTON	*PROSE
THUNDER OF THOUGHT & FLAMES OF FIERCE DESIRE	.	621	READER LOVER/J	6
IS HOWLING IN THE FURNACES IN FLAMES AMONG ALBION'S SPECTRES		626	JERUSALEM 7	39
I HEATED IT IN THE FLAMES OF HAND & HYLE & COBAN . . .	.	628	JERUSALEM 9	21
BEFORE THE ANVIL WATCHES THE BELLOWING FLAMES THUNDERING		636	JERUSALEM 16	10
SATAN HIS NAME IN FLAMES OF FIRE	.	650	FIELDS FROM/J	39
IN JEALOUS FEARS & FURY & RAGE & FLAMES ROLL ROUND THEIR FERVID FEET		655	JERUSALEM 29	75
DAMP COUCH THE FLAMES BENEATH AND SILENT SICK STAND SHUDDERING		666	JERUSALEM 40	6
CONSUMING AND CONSUMD FOR-EVER IN FLAMES OF MORAL JUSTICE		667	JERUSALEM 40	30
THERE TO ETERNITY CHAIND DOWN AND ISSUING IN RED FLAMES		667	JERUSALEM 40	36
WITHIN HIS RIBS PRODUCING SERPENTS WHOSE SOULS ARE FLAMES OF FIRE		667	JERUSALEM 40	42
THE CAPTIVES REARD TO HEAVEN HOWL IN FLAMES AMONG THE STARS		677	JERUSALEM 47	8
THEY WONDERD CHECKING THEIR WILD FLAMES & MANY GATHERING		686	JERUSALEM 55	3
SO SAYING AN ETERNAL DEED WAS DONE IN FIERY FLAMES . .	.	686	JERUSALEM 55	19
AND FLAMES AMONG THE DRUID TEMPLES & THE STARRY WHEELS	. .	692	JERUSALEM 60	7
BUT LOS BEHELD THE DIVINE VISION AMONG THE FLAMES OF THE FURNACES		696	JERUSALEM 62	35
IN AN ETERNAL CONDEMNATION IN FIERCE BURNING FLAMES . .	.	722	JERUSALEM 80	13
AND FLAMES OF DUSKY FIRE TO AMALEK CANAAN AND MOAB . .	.	723	JERUSALEM 80	50
THE RAGING FLAMES THO SHE RETURND [CONSUMD DAY AFTER DAY]		726	JERUSALEM 82	67
AND SOMETIMES SPREAD ABROAD REVEAL THE FLAMES OF HOLINESS		731	JERUSALEM 86	23
HE SIEZES HIS HAMMER EVERY HOUR FLAMES SURROUND HIM AS	. .	731	JERUSALEM 86	34
HIS AWFUL LIMBS INTO THE HEAVENS HE WALKED CLOTHED IN FLAMES		742	JERUSALEM 95	7
MY FACE IN FIERCE FLAMES IN MY DOUBLE SIGHT	.	818	HAPPINESS/L	57
FLAMING	SEE HIGH FLAMING,THICK-FLAMING			
SMILES ON MY HEAD AND MOUNTS HIS FLAMING CAR	.	9	FRESH FROM/PS	2
BEING NO OTHER THAN [THE DEVIL] HE WHO DWELLS IN FLAMING FIRE		150B	MARRIAGE HH 5	*PROSE
FOR THE CHERUB WITH HIS FLAMING SWORD IS HEREBY COMMANDED		154B	MARRIAGE HH 14	PROSE
IN THE FOURTH CHAMBER WERE LIONS OF FLAMING FIRE . . .	.	155A	MARRIAGE HH 15	PROSE
FORTH WENT THE HAND OF JEALOUSY AMONG THE FLAMING HAIR .	.	159C	SONG LIBERTY	PROSE
THE FIERY LIMBS THE FLAMING HAIR	.	159C	SONG LIBERTY	PROSE
THE RUDDY LIMBS & FLAMING HAIR	.	178	ABSTINENCE/N	2
OVER THE LAND NAKED & FLAMING ARE THEIR LINEAMENTS SEEN		200	AMERICA 12	6
MANATHU-VORCYON I BEHOLD THEE FLAMING IN MY HALLS	. .	244	EUROPE 14	* 6

	PAGE	TITLE	LINE

FLAMING   (CONTINUED)

A FLAMING SWORD REVOLVING EVERY WAY . . . . 261D SMALL BK DSGNS   TITLE
AND SPIRITS OF FLAMING FIRE ON HIGH GOVERND THE MIGHTY SONG   274 FOUR ZOAS 1   384
A CAVERND UNIVERSE OF FLAMING FIRE THE HORSES OF URIZEN   320 FOUR ZOAS 7   6
. . . WITH TERRIBLE VISAGES & FLAMING HAIR . . . . . .   320 FOUR ZOAS 7   25
DESPISING URIZEN'S LIGHT & TURNING IT INTO FLAMING FIRE   324 FOUR ZOAS 7   153
DELECTABLE REPOSEST RUDDY IN MY ABSENCE FLAMING WITH BEAUTY   325 FOUR ZOAS 7   187
FLAMING HIS HEAD LIKE THE BRIGHT SUN SEEN THRO A MIST THAT   335 FOUR ZOAS 7B   79
    MAGNIFIES
THY EYELIDS ARE A TERROR TO ME & THE FLAMING OF THY CREST   335 FOUR ZOAS 7B   83
THE SHADOW REARD HER DISMAL HEAD OVER THE FLAMING YOUTH   336 FOUR ZOAS 7B   126
THEY HOWL AROUND THE FLAMING YOUTH RENDING THE NAMELESS   336 FOUR ZOAS 7B   142
    SHADOW
GIRD ON THY FLAMING ZONE DESCEND INTO THE SEPULCHER . . .   337 FOUR ZOAS 7B * 193
OR LIKE A CLOUD BENEATH & LIKE A FIRE FLAMING IN HIGH . .   339 FOUR ZOAS 7B * 265
UPON MY TERRIBLY FLAMING HEART THE MOLTEN METAL RUNS . .   349 FOUR ZOAS 8   306
AND WEEPING OVER ORC & URIZEN IN CLOUDS & [DISMAL] FLAMING   355 FOUR ZOAS 8   579
    FIRES
HIS HOLY HANDS RECIEVD THE FLAMING DEMON & DEMONESS OF   366 FOUR ZOAS 9   361
    SMOKE
NOW INTREATING [?FLAME] FLAMING FIRE . . . .   422 BENEATH/N   * 24
FOR SATAN FLAMING WITH RINTRAH'S FURY HIDDEN BENEATH HIS   489 MILTON 9   19
    OWN MILDNESS
IN ALL MY BEAUTY THAT I MIGHT UNLOOSE THE FLAMING STEEDS   492 MILTON 12   11
AROUND THE FIERY FLAMING HARROW IN LABYRINTHINE FORMS . .   493 MILTON 12   18
AND LOS BEHIND ME STOOD A TERRIBLE FLAMING SUN JUST CLOSE   505 MILTON 22   6
AND EVERY SEVEN AGES IS INCIRCLED WITH A FLAMING FIRE .   516 MILTON 28   57
IMMORTAL STARRY-ONES GUARDING THE COUCH IN FLAMING FIRES   525 MILTON 35   30
SATAN HEARD COMING IN A CLOUD WITH TRUMPETS & FLAMING FIRE   530 MILTON 38   50
BENEATH HER FEET IS A FLAMING CAVERN IN WHICH IS SEEN . . 609B V LAST JUDG/N   PROSE
ON THE VERGE OF PERDITION YET PROTECTED BY A FLAMING SWORD 610C V LAST JUDG/N   PROSE
EASTWARD & SOUTHWARD & NORTHWARD ARE INCIRCLED WITH FLAMING   635 JERUSALEM 14   28
    FIRES
OF DEATH THUNDER INCESSANT AROUND THE FLAMING COUCHES OF   684 JERUSALEM 53   21
IN FLAMING FIRE WITHIN THE FURNACES THE DIVINE VISION   692 JERUSALEM 60   5
    APPEARD
THE STAMPING FEET OF RAGAN UPON THE FLAMING TREDDLES OF   699 JERUSALEM 64   36
    HER LOOM
GIRD ON THY FLAMING ZONE DESCEND INTO THE SEPULCHER OF   700 JERUSALEM 65   39
    CANTERBURY
UPON MY TERRIBLY FLAMING HEART THE MOLTEN METAL RUNS . .   705 JERUSALEM 67   53
IN FLAMING FIRE UNCEASING BURNS FROM ETERNITY TO ETERNITY   731 JERUSALEM 86   25
IN ANGER THE WRATH OF GOD BREAKING BRIGHT FLAMING ON ALL   742 JERUSALEM 95   6
    SIDES AROUND
LOUD THUNDRING WITH BROAD FLASHES OF FLAMING LIGHTNING   742 JERUSALEM 95   8
    & PILLARS
HE TAKES HIS BOW THEN CHOOSES OUT HIS ARROWS OF FLAMING   742 JERUSALEM 95   13
    GOLD
SOON ALL AROUND REMOTE THE HEAVENS BURNT WITH FLAMING FIRES   744 JERUSALEM 96   40
THARMAS WESTWARD A BOW OF BRASS PURE FLAMING RICHLY WROUGHT   744 JERUSALEM 97   10
THEN EACH AN ARROW FLAMING FROM HIS QUIVER FITTED CAREFULLY   744 JERUSALEM 98   1
. . . LOUD SOUNDING FLEW THE FLAMING ARROW FOURFOLD . . .   744 JERUSALEM 98   3
ON CHARIOTS OF GOLD & JEWELS WITH LIVING CREATURES STARRY   746 JERUSALEM 98   42
    & FLAMING
ROUND ME FLEW THE FLAMING SWORD . . . .   770 OF GATES/GP   15

FLAMMABLE

COME FLAMMABLE SAID GIBBLE GABBLE & LET'S ENJOY OURSELVES   58C ISLAND MOON 10 PROSE

FLANDERS

AS IS THE PRACTICE OF THE LATTER SCHOOLS OF ITALY   564D DESC CAT 1   PROSE
    AND FLANDERS
FLANDERS IT LOSES ALL CHARACTER AND LEAVES WHAT SOME PEOPLE 585A DESC CAT 15   PROSE
OF THOSE PLAGIARIES OF VENICE OR FLANDERS THEY WERE . . . 585C DESC CAT 15   PROSE
UPON PICTURES IMPORTED FROM FLANDERS AND HOLLAND . . . . 864C LETTER 61   PROSE

FLAPPING

THE WORLD IS SILENT AT THE FLAPPING OF THE FOLDING BANNERS   204 AMERICA CANC B   19

FLAPPINGS

AWAKE I HEAR THE FLAPPINGS OF THE FOLDING BANNERS . . .   336 FOUR ZOAS 7B * 149

FLARING

AWAY FROM THE SUN'S FLARING BEAMS WHO . . . . 619B ILLUS MILTON   *PROSE

FLASH

FLASH OF LIGHTNING BUT MORE QUICK THE VIRGIN IN MY GARDEN   527 MILTON 36   19
THEY GO FORTH & RETURN SWIFT AS A FLASH OF LIGHTNING . .   722 JERUSALEM 80   44

FLASHED

AND GIVE COMMAND AND LIGHTNING HAS FLASHED . . . . . .   22 EDW THIRD/PS 3   27

FLASHES

LOUD THUNDERING WITH BROAD FLASHES OF FLAMING LIGHTNING   742 JERUSALEM 95   8
    & PILLARS

FLAT

AND THE FLAT EARTH BECOMES A BALL . . . .   426 MENTAL TRAVLER   64
TO MEET THE FLAT EARTH & THE SEA IN SUCH AN ORDERD SPACE   516 MILTON 29   9
STAND IN THE CENTER & SOMETIMES STRETCH FLAT IN THE EXPANSE   728 JERUSALEM 83   41
UNDER SOMEWHAT TO PRESS THEM FLAT YOU SHOULD HAVE HAD . . 840D LETTER 40   PROSE

FLAT SIDED

WHERE A FLAT SIDED STEEP FROWNS OVER THE PRESENT WORLD . . 150C MARRIAGE HH 6   PROSE

FLATTEN

FLATTEN ABOVE & BENEATH & STRETCH OUT INTO BEASTIAL LENGTH   344 FOUR ZOAS 8   128

FLATTER

I NEVER FLATTER YOUR HONOUR . . . .   29D EDW THIRD/PS 4   PROSE
I HOPE I DO NOT FLATTER MY SELF THAT THIS IS PLEASANT TO ME   71C ANNO LAVATER   MARG
HE CAN AFFORD FLATTER HIS WIFE PITY HIS CHILDREN TILL WE   323 FOUR ZOAS 7   128
    CAN
SOME PEOPLE FLATTER THEMSELVES THAT THERE WILL BE NO LAST   617A V LAST JUDG/N   PROSE
    JUDGMENT

		PAGE	TITLE	LINE

FLATTER   (CONTINUED)

THESE PEOPLE FLATTER THEMSELVES I WILL NOT FLATTER THEM   617B V LAST JUDG/N   PROSE
WHILE YOU ACQUIT & FLATTER THE ALEXANDERS & CAESARS . . . 683A JERUSALEM 52   PROSE
WHICH I FLATTER MYSELF WILL NOT BE . . . .   792C LETTER 4   PROSE

FLATTERD

IMAGINATION & I FEEL FLATTERD WHEN I AM TOLD SO . . . .   793D LETTER 5   PROSE

FLATTERER

[THE DEADLY CUNNING OF THE [SCALY TRIBE] FLATTERER . . .   110   TIRIEL 8   *   22
HE IS A FLATTERER WHO MEANS TO BETRAY . . . . 681D JERUSALEM 52   PROSE
GENERAL GOOD IS THE PLEA OF THE SCOUNDREL HYPOCRITE   687   JERUSALEM 55   61
    & FLATTERER

FLATTERING

AND YOU WAS VERY ANGRY WITH ME FOR NOT FLATTERING YOU . . 30A   EDW THIRD/PS 4   PROSE
FOR NOT FLATTERING THE EARL OF WARWICK EXEUNT . . . .   30A   EDW THIRD/PS 4   PROSE

FLATTERY

FLATTERY IS DELICIOUS EVEN FROM THE LIPS OF A BABBLER   29D   EDW THIRD/PS 4   PROSE
    EXIT PETER
TILL BROTHERHOOD IS CHANGD INTO A CURSE & A FLATTERY . .   525   MILTON 35   4

FLAUNTING

THE HONEYSUCKLE SLEEPING ON THE OAK THE FLAUNTING BEAUTY   520   MILTON 31   54

FLAX

SPREADING THEM OUT BEFORE THE SUN LIKE STALKS OF FLAX TO   265   FOUR ZOAS 1   48
    DRY
SHE COMMUND WITH ORC IN SECRET SHE HID HIM WITH THE FLAX   356   FOUR ZOAS 8   607
SPREADING THEM OUT BEFORE THE SUN LIKE STALKS OF FLAX TO   645   JERUSALEM 22   21
    DRY
AND THE DISTAFF & SPINDLE IN THE HANDS OF VALA WITH THE   699   JERUSALEM 64   32
    FLAX OF
WERE CAUGHT INTO THE FLAX OF HER DISTAFF & IN HER CLOUD   722   JERUSALEM 80   34

FLAXMAN

TO MRS ANN FLAXMAN . . . .   414D TO MRS FLAXMAN   TITLE
OR ANGRY WITH FLAXMAN OR CROMEK OR STOTHARD   538   WAS I ANGRY/N   4
[LOOK XXX FLAXMAN & STOTHARD DO] OLD ACQUAINTANCE WE'LL   538   OLD ACQUAINT/N * 1
    RENEW
TO F(FLAXMAN) . . . .   539A F(LAXMAN)/N 1   TITLE
TO NANCY F(FLAXMAN) . . . .   539C TO NANCY F/N   TITLE
[BECAUSE] AND YET HIS PRAISE OF FLAXMAN WAS THE SMARTEST   540   SIR JOSH RUB/N   3
[TO] ON F(FLAXMAN) & S(STOTHARD) . . . .   543D ON F AND S/N   *TITLE
TO F(FLAXMAN) . . . .   544B F(LAXMAN)/N 2   TITLE
HAYLEY FLAX`AN & STOTHARD ARE ALSO IN DOUBT   545   COSWAY FRAZR/N   5
NOT PRAISD JY HAYLEY NOR BY FLAXMAN LOVD   546   MY TITLE AS/N   2
FLAXMAN & STOTHARD SMELLING A SWEET SAVOUR   555   BLAKES APL/N 1   14
FLAXMAN & STOTHARD SMELLING A SWEET SAVOUR   556   BLAKES APL/N 2   13
[FLAXMAN ROMNEY STOTHARD IT] I REQUEST THE SOCIETY . . . 591D PUB ADDRESS/N   *PROSE
FLAXMAN & EVEN ROMNEY SPOILS AN ENGRAVER FOR EACH OF .   592B PUB ADDRESS/N   PROSE
FLAXMAN CANNOT DENY THAT ONE OF THE VERY FIRST MONUMENTS HE 592D PUB ADDRESS/N   PROSE
THE DEATH OF DEMOSTHENES...HAS BEEN APPROVED BY MR FLAXMAN   796B LETTER 7   PROSE
MR FLAXMAN HAS SEEN IT & APPROVED OF MY NOW SENDING IT .   796C LETTER 8   PROSE
PRAISE YOUR OUTLINES & WISH FOR MORE FLAXMAN IS VERY WARM   798A LETTER 10   PROSE
TO JOHN FLAXMAN I HAVE BEEN TOO LITTLE AMONG FRIENDS WHICH   798B LETTER 10   PROSE
    I
SUNDAY AFTERNOON TO CALL ON MRS FLAXMAN AT HAMPSTEAD I SEND 799A LETTER 11   PROSE
TO MY DEAREST FRIEND JOHN FLAXMAN THESE LINES . . . .   799B TO FLAXMAN/L   TITLE
WHEN FLAXMAN WAS TAKEN TO ITALY FUSELI WAS GIVEN TO ME   799   TO FLAXMAN/L   3
    FOR A SEASON
AND NOW FLAXMAN HATH GIVEN ME HAYLEY HIS FRIEND . . .   799   TO FLAXMAN/L   4
BUT BY MY CONJUNCTION WITH FLAXMAN WHO KNOWS TO FORGIVE   799   TO FLAXMAN/L   12
    NERVOUS FEAR
"PROPER DUTY TO YOU & MR FLAXMAN WE INTEND TO CALL" . . . 800A LETTER 12   PROSE
TO MY DEAR FRIEND MRS ANNA FLAXMAN . . . .   800B MRS FLAXMAN/L   TITLE
YOU O DEAR FLAXMAN ARE A SUBLIME ARCHANGEL MY FRIEND & .   802C LETTER 14   PROSE
FRIENDSHIP TO OUR DEAR MRS FLAXMAN WHOM WE ARDENTLY . .   802D LETTER 14   PROSE
OUR DEAR FRIEND FLAXMAN IS THE THEME OF MY EMULATION .   807A LETTER 17   PROSE
MR AND MRS FLAXMAN AND BELIEVE ME TO BE YOUR AFFECTIONATE   807B LETTER 17   PROSE
DEAR FLAXMAN I REJOICE TO HEAR THAT YOUR GREAT WORK IS   810C LETTER 21   PROSE
    ACCOMPLISHD
MY WIFE JOINS WITH ME IN LOVE TO YOU & MRS FLAXMAN . .   811A LETTER 21   PROSE
BY MARIA FLAXMAN SISTER TO MY FRIEND THE SCULPTOR AND IT   812A LETTER 22   PROSE
MUST FLAXMAN LOOK UPON ME AS WILD   818   HAPPINESS/L   47
MRS FLAXMAN & FIVE MORE TWO OF WHICH YOU WILL BE SO GOOD   821B LETTER 25   PROSE
DESIGNS FROM ROMNEY FLAXMAN & YR HBLE SERVT . . . . .   824C LETTER 27   PROSE
MR FLAXMAN IS NOW OUT OF TOWN WHEN HE RETURNS . . . .   831B LETTER 31   PROSE
DRAWING FROM MR ROSE & HAVE SHEWD IT TO MR FLAXMAN WHO .   832B LETTER 32   PROSE
A DWELLING IN THE NORTH MR FLAXMAN SUPPOSES THAT IF SOME   832C LETTER 32   PROSE
I HAVE SEEN FLAXMAN ALREADY AS I TOOK TO HIM EARLY THIS   833C LETTER 33   PROSE
MR JOHN ROMNEY TO MR FLAXMAN WHO WAS PERFECTLY SATISFIED   834C LETTER 34   PROSE
THO HE IS IN TOWN MR FLAXMAN IS NOT AT ALL ACQUAINTED .   834D LETTER 34   PROSE
BUT I WILL CALL AGAIN IN A DAY OR TWO NEITHER MR FLAXMAN   836B LETTER 35   PROSE
    NOR
THAT ARE OUT & THE BOOK OF ITALIAN LETTERS FROM MRS FLAXMAN 836C LETTER 35   PROSE
TO CALL ON ME MRS FLAXMAN & HER SISTERS GAVE ALSO THEIR   836C LETTER 35   PROSE
TESTIMONY TO MY LIKENESS OF ROMNEY MR FLAXMAN I HAVE . .   836C LETTER 35   PROSE
BEEN ABLE TO CONSULT MR FLAXMAN ABOUT THE DESIGNS OF MR   838B LETTER 37   PROSE
ROMNEY WHICH ARE AT SAUNDERS' I CALLD ONCE OF(ON)   838B LETTER 37   PROSE
    MR F(FLAXMAN)
I HAVE BEEN TO LOOK AT THE DRAWINGS & PICTURE BUT FLAXMAN   839B LETTER 38   PROSE
TROUBLE AS FLAXMAN WAS NOT WITH ME THE DRAWING I SAW IS   839C LETTER 38   PROSE
BUT I WILL NOT ADVISE ANY THING TILL FLAXMAN SEES THEM .   839C LETTER 38   PROSE
MR FLAXMAN ADVISES THAT THE DRAWING OF MR ROMNEY'S . .   840D LETTER 40   PROSE
THE DELAY I HAVE SEEN OUR EXCELLENT FLAXMAN LATELY HE IS   842D LETTER 42   PROSE
    WELL
MR FLAXMAN AGREES WITH ME THAT SOMEWHAT MORE THAN OUTLINE   844B LETTER 43   PROSE

	PAGE	TITLE	LINE
FLAXMAN (CONTINUED)			
YOU BOTH WITH GREAT AFFECTION MR FLAXMAN HAS ALSO PROMISED	846A	LETTER 44	PROSE
TO COPY ANY OF HIS FATHER'S DESIGNS THAT MR FLAXMAN MAY	846A	LETTER 44	PROSE
I SPOKE TO MR FLAXMAN ABOUT CHOOSING OUT PROPER SUBJECTS	846A	LETTER 44	PROSE
MR FLAXMAN TOLD ME THAT MR ROMNEY WAS THREE YEARS . . .	847D	LETTER 44	PROSE
FLAXMAN HAS PROMISED TO PUT PEN TO PAPER YOU MAY	847D	LETTER 44	PROSE
OPINION BUT THAT OF MR FLAXMAN & MR PARKER BOTH OF . . .	848A	LETTER 45	PROSE
MR FLAXMAN ADVISES THAT THE BEST ENGRAVERS SHOULD BE	848C	LETTER 45	PROSE
MR FLAXMAN NAMED THE FOLLOWING EIGHT AS PROPER SUBJECTS	848D	LETTER 45	PROSE
FOR PRINTS			
FLAXMAN HAS NOT YET SEEN IT BUT SHALL SOON & THEN YOU .	849A	LETTER 45	PROSE
THIS TIME FLAXMAN HAS WRITTEN TO YOU & THAT YOU WILL .	849B	LETTER 45	PROSE
BUT I HAVE MENTIOND YOUR PROPOSAL TO OUR NOBLE FLAXMAN .	853A	LETTER 51	*PROSE
& TO DESIRE YOU IF YOU COULD TO GET FLAXMAN TO DO THE WHOLE	853A	LETTER 51	*PROSE
THE ASSISTANCE AND APPROBATION OF OUR GOOD FRIEND FLAXMAN	853B	LETTER 52	PROSE
OF THE SHIPWRECK MRS FLAXMAN ALSO WHO IS A GOOD . . .	853B	LETTER 52	PROSE
FINISHED THOUGH FLAXMAN HAS ALREADY PRONOUNCED IT SO .	853C	LETTER 52	PROSE
FLAXMAN DECLARES TO ME THAT HE WILL NOT PRETEND TO SET	855A	LETTER 53	PROSE
A PRICE			
REMEMBER WITH WHICH FLAXMAN IS VERY MUCH SATISFIED & .	855D	LETTER 53	PROSE
HAVE HEARD THAT FLAXMAN MEANS TO GIVE A LECTURE ON	859D	LETTER 53	PROSE
SCULPTURE			
I CONCIEVE FLAXMAN STANDS WITHOUT A COMPETITOR IN SCULPTURE	860A	LETTER 56	PROSE
FLAXMAN IS GONE & WE MUST ALL SOON FOLLOW EVERY ONE TO HIS	879A	LETTER 88	PROSE
MR FLAXMAN SCULPTOR BUCKINGHAM STREET FITZROY SQUARE LONDON	SUPP	ADDRESSES/L	*TITLE
RECIEVD...OF MR FLAXMAN THE SUM...FOR ENGRAVING	SUPP	LETTER 6A	*PROSE
FLAXMAN'S			
. . . THAT EVER I SAW FLAXMAN'S FACE	799	TO FLAXMAN/L	1
THIS SONG TO THE FLOWER OF FLAXMAN'S JOY	800	MRS FLAXMAN/L	1
MY ADMIRATION OF FLAXMAN'S GENIUS IS MORE AND MORE . .	829B	LETTER 29	PROSE
WHICH I HAVE DRAWN FROM MR FLAXMAN'S MODEL	838A	LETTER 37	PROSE
FLAXMAN'S HOMER WITH ADDITIONAL DESIGNS TWO OF WHICH .	841A	LETTER 40	PROSE
PRICE I RECEIVE FOR ENGRAVING FLAXMAN'S OUTLINES OF HOMER	844B	LETTER 43	PROSE
SEND YOU FLAXMAN'S ADVICE UPON THIS ARTICLE WHEN I REPEATED	846B	LETTER 44	PROSE
BEING AT FLAXMAN'S TAKING HIS ADVICE ABOUT OUR ENGRAVINGS	853A	LETTER 51	*PROSE
WITH FLAXMAN'S ADVICE WHICH HE GIVES	853B	LETTER 52	PROSE
FINISHD PROOF BE ASSURED THAT WITH OUR GOOD FLAXMAN'S .	855B	LETTER 53	PROSE
FLEA			
[WHAT YOU SKIPPING FLEA HOW DARE YE]	57A	ISLAND MOON 9	PROSE
A FLEA OR A BUTTERFLY OR A COCK CHAFER	58C	ISLAND MOON 10	PROSE
THE FLEA LOUSE BUG THE TAPE-WORM ALL THE ARMIES OF DISEASE	513	MILTON 27	17
FLED			
HILLS FLED FROM OUR SIGHT BUT LEFT HIS GOLDEN LOAD . . .	2	TO AUTUMN/PS	18
OF ONE THAT FLED APPROACHES ELLEN STOOD	4	FAIR ELENOR/PS	19
SHE FLED FROM FEAR TILL AT HER HOUSE ARRIVD	5	FAIR ELENOR/PS	36
GWIN FELL THE SONS OF NORWAY FLED	14	GWIN KING/PS	109
TO CONSTANTINE'S GREAT EMPIRE FLED	41B	THEN SHE BORE	PROSE
BRINGS TRUE JOY ONCE FLED & CONTEMPLATION IS HER DAUGHTER	42A	THEN SHE BORE	PROSE
IN HASTE THEY FLED WHILE ALL THE SONS & DAUGHTERS OF TIRIEL	107	TIRIEL 5	27
[THEY] SOME FLED AWAY [& HID THEMSELVES] BUT [SOME] . . .	108	TIRIEL 7	7
HOPING TO END HER [LIFE] WOES BUT FROM HER CRIES THE TYGERS	109	TIRIEL 7	17
FLED			
TILL OUR GRIEF IS FLED & GONE	123	ON ANOTHERS/SI	35
DOUBT IS FLED & CLOUDS OF REASON	126	VOICE BARD/SI	4
FLED BACK UNHINDERD TILL SHE CAME INTO THE VALES OF HAR	130	BOOK OF THEL 6	22
. . . ALL CHILDREN NEW-BORN FIRST BEHOLD THEM TEARS ARE	136	FRENCH REVOLTN	56
FLED			
THEN FLED AND THE WHOLE CITY KNEW HE WAS FLED TO GENEVA	139	FRENCH REVOLTN	124
. . .			
. . . AND THE GUARDS OF THY PALACE ARE FLED	141	FRENCH REVOLTN	167
FROM WHICH THE SEA FLED AWAY IN CLOUDS OF SMOKE	156C	MARRIAGE HH 17	PROSE
WAKD FROM HIS ETERNAL SLEEP THE HOARY ELEMENT ROARING FLED	159C	SONG LIBERTY	PROSE
AWAY			
BUT THE TIME OF YOUTH IS FLED	167	INFANT SORW/N	42
HER [EYES DEAD] [ORBS DEAD] LIGHT FLED	168	EARTHS ANSWR/N	3
BUT THE TIME OF YOUTH IS FLED	169	MIRTLE SHADE/N	17
SO HE TOOK HIS WINGS & FLED	182	THE ANGEL/N	9
[BUT] FOR THE TIME OF YOUTH WAS FLED	182	THE ANGEL/N	15
[SHATTERD FLED]	182	THE FLY/N	4
THE STARS THREW DOWN THEIR CUPS & FLED	187	WHEN KLOPSTK/N	12
HER LIGHT FLED	210	EARTHS ANSR/SE	3
SO HE TOOK HIS WINGS AND FLED	214	THE ANGEL/SE	9
FOR THE TIME OF YOUTH WAS FLED	214	THE ANGEL/SE	15
THEY CALLD HER PITY AND FLED	231	URIZEN 19	1
SHE FLED FROM HIS ARMS YET HE FOLLOWD	231	URIZEN 19	13
WAR CEASD & ALL THE TROOPS LIKE SHADOWS FLED TO THEIR	239	EUROPE 4	4
ABODES			
TILL ALBION'S ANGEL SMITTEN WITH HIS OWN PLAGUES FLED WITH	241	EUROPE 9	8
HIS BANDS			
TO A DEVOURING FLAME AND MAN FLED FROM ITS FACE AND HID	241	EUROPE 10	17
WITH DISMAL TORMENT SICK HANGING UPON THE WIND HE FLED . .	242	EUROPE 12	18
FLED FROM HIS SIGHT HE DRAGD HIS TORMENTS TO THE WILDERNESS	242	EUROPE 12	20
AND EIGHTEEN HUNDRED YEARS WERE FLED	243	EUROPE 13	10
THEN EVERY ONE FLED TO HIS STATION & ENITHARMON WEPT .	244	EUROPE 14	36
ABRAM FLED IN FIRES FROM CHALDEA	245	SONG OF LOS 3	16
SINCE THAT DREAD DAY WHEN HAR AND HEVA FLED	246	SONG OF LOS 4	5
AND AS THEY FLED THEY SHRUNK	246	SONG OF LOS 4	7
IT DOWN INTO THE DEEPS THE DEEPS FLED	260	BOOK OF LOS 5	43
BUT NO LIGHT FOR THE DEEP FLED AWAY	260	BOOK OF LOS 5	48
THE MEN HAVE RECIEVED THEIR DEATH WOUNDS & THEIR EMANATIONS	265	FOUR ZOAS 1	* 33
ARE FLED			
THOSE THAT REMAIN HAVE FLED FROM MY CRUELTY INTO	268	FOUR ZOAS 1	167
THE DESARTS			

714

FLED (CONTINUED)

OF WAR THE MOUNTAINS FLED AWAY THEY SOUGHT A PLACE BENEATH | 275 FOUR ZOAS 1 | 416
THARMAS ENDURD NOT HE FLED HOWLING THEN A BARREN WASTE SUNK DOWN | 275 FOUR ZOAS 1 | 419
HIS SONS FLED FROM HIS SIDE TO JOIN THE CONFLICT PALE HE HEARD | 278 FOUR ZOAS 1 | 521
HE DROPD HIS HAMMER DIVIDING FROM HIS AKING BOSOM FLED . . | 278 FOUR ZOAS 1 | 523
A PORTION OF HIS LIFE SHRIEKING UPON THE WIND SHE FLED . . | 278 FOUR ZOAS 1 | 524
URTHONA STOOD IN TERROR BUT NOT LONG HIS SPECTRE FLED . . | 278 FOUR ZOAS 1 | 530
ALOFT THE MOON FLED WITH A CRY THE SUN WITH STREAMS OF BLOOD | 281 FOUR ZOAS 2 | 42
FROM ALBION'S LOINS FLED ALL PEOPLES AND NATIONS OF THE EARTH [FLED] | 281 FOUR ZOAS 2 * | 43
FLED WITH THE NOISE OF SLAUGHTER & THE STARS OF HEAVEN FLED | 281 FOUR ZOAS 2 | 44
SHE FLED VANISHING ON THE WIND AND LEFT A DEAD COLD CORSE | 289 FOUR ZOAS 2 | 334
KINDLING SHE LED HIM INTO SHADOWS & THENCE FLED OUTSTRETCHD | 290 FOUR ZOAS 2 | 381
THEY HEARD THE VOICE & [THEY] FLED SWIFT AS THE WINTER'S SETTING SUN | 294 FOUR ZOAS 3 * | 93
THEN FLED THE SONS OF URIZEN FROM HIS THUNDEROUS THRONE PETRIFIC | 295 FOUR ZOAS 3 | 133
THEY FLED TO EAST & WEST & LEFT THE NORTH & SOUTH OF HEAVEN | 295 FOUR ZOAS 3 | 134
[WE FLED FROM ?JERUSALEM ?AFTER ?THE MERCIFUL LORD & SAVIOUR] | SUPP FOUR ZOAS 3 * |
HOW IS THIS ALL MY HOPE IS GONE [ENION] FOR EVER FLED . . | 297 FOUR ZOAS 4 | 9
FLED FROM MY SIDE THEN PANGS SMOTE ME UNKNOWN BEFORE I SAW | 300 FOUR ZOAS 4 | 93
THE STARS THREW DOWN THEIR SPEARS & FLED NAKED AWAY . . . | 311 FOUR ZOAS 5 | 224
HIS GLOOMY WAY BEFORE HIM THARMAS FLED & FLYING FOUGHT . . | 313 FOUR ZOAS 6 | 54
THEN URIZEN AROSE THE SPECTRE FLED & THARMAS FLED . . . | 320 FOUR ZOAS 7 | 1
BUT ENITHARMON TREMBLING FLED & HID BENEATH URIZEN'S TREE | 329 FOUR ZOAS 7 | 372
THE VICTIMS FLED FROM PUNISHMENT FOR ALL HIS WORDS WERE PEACE | 348 FOUR ZOAS 8 | 271
OR MERCY & TRUTH ARE FLED AWAY FROM SHECHEM & MOUNT GILEAD | 349 FOUR ZOAS 8 | 320
[SHE] JERUSALEM SAW THE BODY DEAD UPON THE CROSS SHE FLED AWAY | 349 FOUR ZOAS 8 | 331
AWAY FROM [LOS] ME FIRST REUBEN FLED THEN SIMEON THEN LEVI THEN JUDAH | 350 FOUR ZOAS 8 | 375
A TERROR COMING FROM THE SOUTH THE EAGLE & HAWK FLED AWAY | 358 FOUR ZOAS 9 | 62
LET US FLEE ALSO TO THE NORTH THEY FLED THE SONS OF MEN | 359 FOUR ZOAS 9 | 64
THE WOMB IMPRESSD ENION FLED & HID IN VERDANT MOUNTAINS | 381 FOUR ZOAS AD 3 | 1
THE VICTIMS FLED FROM PUNISHMENT [THAT] FOR ALL HIS WORDS WERE PEACE | 382 FOUR ZOAS AD 6 | 4
TO WHICH THE PURPLE TYRANT FLED . . . . | 419 I SAW A MONK/N | 45
A DAMP COLD CAME OER HER HER BLUSHES ALL FLED . . . . . | 428 MARY | 19
TO WHICH THE PURPLE TYRANT FLED . . . . | 431 GREY MONK | 34
THE FAIRIES THAT FLED FROM WILLIAM BOND . . . . | 435 WILLIAM BOND | 41
BUT NOW THE STARRY HEAVENS ARE FLED FROM THE MIGHTY LIMBS OF ALBION | 486 MILTON 6 | 26
HE DISPLACD CONTINENTS THE OCEANS FLED BEFORE HIS FACE . . | 489 MILTON 9 | 16
CHAOS & ANCIENT NIGHT FLED FROM BENEATH THE FIERY HARROW | 493 MILTON 12 | 21
SHE FLED TO ENITHARMON'S TENT & HID HERSELF LOUD RAGING | 494 MILTON 13 | 14
TWELVE SONS SUCCESSIVE FLED AWAY IN THAT THOUSAND YEARS OF SORROW | 508 MILTON 23 | 62
FLED WITH THEIR SISTER MOAB INTO THAT ABHORRED VOID . . . | 508 MILTON 24 | 15
AWAY FROM OLOLON SHE DIVIDED & FLED INTO THE DEPTHS . . . | 534 MILTON 42 | 5
AND AWAY FLED EVERY JOY . . . . | 552 WHY CUPID/N | 20
"THE MOST UGLY THEY FLED WITH OUTCRIES AND CONTORTION OF THEIR LIMBS" | 560B EXHIBITION ADV | PROSE
WITH MIGHTY POWER WHEN THEY FLED OUT AT JERUSALEM'S GATES | 637 JERUSALEM 16 | 30
AND ALBION FLED INWARD AMONG THE CURRENTS OF HIS RIVERS | 642 JERUSALEM 19 | 39
FIRST FLED MY SONS & THEN MY DAUGHTERS THEN MY WILD ANIMATIONS | 643 JERUSALEM 21 | 7
MY CATTLE NEXT LAST EVN THE DOG OF MY GATE THE FORESTS FLED | 643 JERUSALEM 21 | 8
OF OUR IMMORTAL VEINS & ALL THEIR HOSTS FLED FROM OUR LIMBS | 647 JERUSALEM 24 | 8
THE SUN FLED FROM THE BRITON'S FOREHEAD . . . . | 647 JERUSALEM 24 | 10
SCANDINAVIA FLED WITH ALL HIS MOUNTAINS FILLD WITH GROANS | 647 JERUSALEM 24 | 11
BUT NOW THE STARRY HEAVENS ARE FLED FROM THE MIGHTY LIMBS OF ALBION | 649C JERUSALEM 27 | PROSE
BUT THEY FLED TO THE MOUNTAINS TO SEEK RANSOM BUILDING A STRONG | 653 JERUSALEM 28 | 25
THEY HEARD THE VOICE AND FLED SWIFT AS THE WINTER'S SETTING SUN | 655 JERUSALEM 29 | 72
AND AS THEY FLED IN FOLDING FIRES & THUNDERS OF THE DEEP | 655 JERUSALEM 29 | 77
ON HIS ROCK ERE YET THE STARRY HEAVENS WERE FLED AWAY . . | 660 JERUSALEM 34 | 20
FLED THEY FLED AT HIS HORRIBLE FORM THEY HID IN CAVES . . | 661 JERUSALEM 34 | 49
OVER JORDAN ALL TERRIFIED FLED THEY BECAME WHAT THEY BEHELD | 661 JERUSALEM 34 | 54
ALL THAT BEHELD HIM FLED HOWLING AND GNAWED THEIR TONGUES | 662 JERUSALEM 36 | 8
THE SEVEN NATIONS FLED BEFORE HIM THEY BECAME WHAT THEY BEHELD | 662 JERUSALEM 36 | 14
HAND HYLE & COBAN FLED THEY BECAME WHAT THEY BEHELD . . . | 662 JERUSALEM 36 | 15
FLED OVER CHALDEA IN TERROR IN PAINS IN EVERY NERVE . . . | 663 JERUSALEM 36 | 18
AND THE TWELVE FEMALE EMANATIONS FLED WITH THEM AGONIZING | 663 JERUSALEM 36 | 20
WHILE ALBION FLED MORE INDIGNANT REVENGEFUL COVERING . . | 664 JERUSALEM 37 | 12
ALBION FLED THRO THE GATE OF LOS AND HE STOOD IN THE GATE | 666 JERUSALEM 39 | 11
SHE FLED TO LAMBETH'S MILD VALE AND HID HERSELF BENEATH . . | 668 JERUSALEM 41 | 11
BUT ALBION FLED FROM THE DIVINE VISION . . . . | 689 JERUSALEM 57 | 12
. . . ALBION FLED BENEATH THE PLOW . . . . | 689 JERUSALEM 57 | 15
AND REUBEN FLED WITH HIS HEAD DOWNWARDS AMONG THE CAVERNS | 698 JERUSALEM 63 | 44
AS REUBEN FLED BEFORE THE DAUGHTERS OF ALBION TAXING THE NATIONS | 699 JERUSALEM 64 | 34
AFAR INTO THE UNKNOWN NIGHT THE MOUNTAINS FLED AWAY . . . | 702 JERUSALEM 66 | 44
OR MERCY & TRUTH ARE FLED AWAY FROM SHECHEM & MOUNT GILEAD | 705 JERUSALEM 68 | 8
THE STARRY HEAVENS ALL WERE FLED FROM THE MIGHTY LIMBS OF ALBION | 709 JERUSALEM 70 | 32

	PAGE	TITLE	LINE
FLED (CONTINUED)			
BECAUSE TWELVE SONS OF JERUSALEM FLED SUCCESSIVE THRO THE GATES	711	JERUSALEM 72	9
BUT THE FOUR SONS OF JERUSALEM WHO FLED NOT BUT REMAIND	711	JERUSALEM 72	10
BUT NOW THE STARRY HEAVENS ARE FLED FROM THE MIGHTY LIMBS OF ALBION	716	JERUSALEM 75	27
TREMBLING & PITYING SHE SCREAMD & FLED UPON THE WIND	726	JERUSALEM 82	49
WALKED UP AND DOWN IN ITS GREEN MOUNTAINS BUT HAND IS FLED	729	JERUSALEM 83	86
JUDAH WAS LIKE PALAMABRON O SIMEON O LEVI YE FLED AWAY	740	JERUSALEM 93	14
LOVE TOO LONG FROM ME HAS FLED	755	EV GOSPEL(E)/N	59
ONE IS SLAIN & ONE IS FLED	771	OF GATES/GP	26
FLEE			
PHILIP IS PLUMD AND THINKS WE FLEE FROM HIM	24	EDW THIRD/PS 3	140
SHALL FLEE AWAY AND LEAVE [THEM] HIM ALL FORLORN	28	EDW THIRD/PS 3	292
BUT WORSE O NEVER ASK ME MORE OR I MUST FLEE AWAY	103	TIRIEL 3	21
HE SET HIS FACE TOWARD GENEVA TO FLEE	139	FRENCH REVOLTN *	122
. . . NOR BE YOU DISMAYD WITH SORROWS WHICH FLEE AT THE MORNING	142	FRENCH REVOLTN	180
TO FLEE AWAY	178	THE FAIRY/N	14
THE BEAMY DAUGHTERS OF THE LIGHT STARTING THEY RISE THEY FLEE	288	FOUR ZOAS 2	315
AT HIS ENORMOUS CALL THEY FLEE INTO THE HEAVENS OF HEAVENS	308	FOUR ZOAS 5	118
THE FRUIT OF THIS DELIGHTFUL TREE I CANNOT FLEE AWAY	326	FOUR ZOAS 7	234
HOW SHALL I FLEE HOW SHALL I FLEE INTO THE TOWER OF LOS	335	FOUR ZOAS 7B *	87
HE TEMPTED MANY OF THE SONS & DAUGHTERS OF LOS TO FLEE	350	FOUR ZOAS 8	374
LET US FLEE ALSO TO THE NORTH THEY FLED THE SONS OF MEN	359	FOUR ZOAS 9	64
THE FURIOUS WIND STILL RENDS AROUND THEY FLEE IN SLUGGISH EFFORT	363	FOUR ZOAS 9	256
WHERE DOST THOU FLEE O FAIR ONE	367	FOUR ZOAS 9	401
AND FLEE AWAY ON EVERY SIDE	427	MENTAL TRAVLER	96
LIONS BOARS WOLVES ALL HOWLING FLEE	427	MENTAL TRAVLER	99
INTO A TABERNACLE AND FLEE WITH CRIES DOWN TO THE DEEPS	503	MILTON 20	48
AND IF YOU ALSO FLEE AWAY AND LEAVE YOUR FATHER'S SIDE	508	MILTON 24	22
HOWLING THE SPECTRES FLEE THEY TAKE REFUGE IN HUMAN LINEAMENTS	515	MILTON 28	28
SHUDDRING THEY FLEE THEY HIDE IN THE DRUID TEMPLES IN COLD CHASTITY	638	JERUSALEM 17	14
WE FLEE FROM THE INTERIORS OF ALBION'S HILLS AND MOUNTAINS	654	JERUSALEM 29	30
NOT WHERE TO FLEE THEY HAD BEEN ON A VISIT TO ALBION'S CHILDREN	655	JERUSALEM 30	5
LAMENTATION IT FLEE BACK & HIDE IN NON-ENTITY'S DARK WILD	688	JERUSALEM 56	16
THEY FLEE OVER THE ROCKS BONIFYING HORSES OXEN FEEL THE KNIFE	689	JERUSALEM 58	9
WITH HIS THUNDEROUS HAMMER TERRIFIED THE SPECTRES RAGE & FLEE	690	JERUSALEM 58	32
THE STARS FLEE REMOTE THE HEAVEN IS IRON THE EARTH IS SULPHUR	703	JERUSALEM 66	81
REUBEN & BENJAMIN FLEE THEY HIDE IN THE VALLEY OF REPHAIM	706	JERUSALEM 68	47
FLEECE			
LET MAN WEAR THE FELL OF THE LION WOMAN THE FLEECE OF THE SHEEP	151C	MARRIAGE HH 8	PROSE
BECAUSE I DONT WANT YOU TO SHEAR MY FLEECE	181	ANSWR PARSON/N	2
SO SPOKE THE SINLESS SOUL & LAID HER HEAD ON THE DOWNY FLEECE	369	FOUR ZOAS 9	455
FLEECES			
THE FLEECES OF OUR FLOCKS ARE COVERD WITH	3	EVNING STAR/PS	13
AND [HE] HEARD HAR SING IN THE GREAT CAGE & SLEPT UPON OUR FLEECES	103	TIRIEL 3 *	23
AND ON THE FLEECES OF MILD FLOCKS WHO NEITHER CARE NOR LABOUR	361	FOUR ZOAS 9	173
FLEECY			
RETIRING INTO HIS DIRE WEB SCATTERING FLEECY SNOWS	319	FOUR ZOAS 6 *	317
THE FLEECY WHITE RENEWD HE SHOOK HIS AGED MANTLES OFF	362	FOUR ZOAS 9	190
FLEEING			
WOMEN FLEEING FROM WAR WOMEN IN A SIEGE	208B	SUBJCTS HIST/N	TITLE
HIS CHILDREN WANDERING OUTSIDE FROM HIS BOSOM FLEEING AWAY	279	FOUR ZOAS 1	559
AND THE YOUNG MAN THE MURDERER FLEEING OVER THE MOUNTAINS	281	FOUR ZOAS 2	52
WHEN FLEEING FROM THE BATTLE THOU FLEETING LIKE THE RAVEN	299	FOUR ZOAS 4	86
PURSUING THE VAIN SHADOW OF HOPE FLEEING FROM IDENTITY	353	FOUR ZOAS 8	486
FLEEING FROM THE FACE OF HIS PARENTS A DRAWING	584A	DESC CAT 11	TITLE
THE ARMIES ARE FLEEING UPON THE MOUNTAINS ON THE FOREGROUND	608B	V LAST JUDG/N	PROSE
FLEEING FROM THE ROLLING CLOUD WHICH SEPARATES THE WICKED	614A	V LAST JUDG/N	PROSE
OF ALBION'S CHILDREN FLEEING THRO ALBION'S VALES IN STREAMS OF GORE	655	JERUSALEM 30	8
KOTOPE & BOWEN BECAME WHAT THEY BEHELD FLEEING OVER THE EARTH	663	JERUSALEM 36	19
THE HAMMER & THE CHISEL & THE RULE & COMPASSES FROM LONDON FLEEING	699	JERUSALEM 65	13
AH THEN I SAW MY BELOVED ONES FLEEING FROM MY TENT	740	JERUSALEM 93	12
FLEES			
THE LION FLEES AND FEAR USURPS HIS HEART	24	EDW THIRD/PS 3	114
LIKE THE WILD STAG SHE FLEES AWAY	426	MENTAL TRAVLER	77
AS ABRAHAM FLEES FROM CHALDEA SHAKING HIS GOARY LOCKS	636	JERUSALEM 15	28
STARTS FROM HIS LOFTY PLACES & CASTS DOWN HIS TENTS & FLEES AWAY	729	JERUSALEM 84	24
FLEEST			
LOS SAID TO ALBION WHITHER FLEEST THOU ALBION REPLYD	666	JERUSALEM 39	15
FLEETING			
SHADOWS OF MEN IN FLEETING BANDS UPON THE WINDS	241	EUROPE 9	6
WHEN FLEEING FROM THE BATTLE THOU FLEETING LIKE THE RAVEN	299	FOUR ZOAS 4	86
THE FLEETING IMAGE & IN WHISPERS MILD WOO'D THE FAINT SHADE	325	FOUR ZOAS 7	221
"SWALLOWS CALL US FLEETING PAST OUR WINDOW AT THIS MOMENT"	800B	LETTER 12	PROSE

	PAGE	TITLE	LINE

FLEMINGS

THE FLEMINGS THEY CALL IT BURNT BONE HAS POSSESSED THE EYE   864C LETTER 61   PROSE

FLEMISH

A LIE THE FLORID STYLE SUCH AS THE VENETIAN & THE FLEMISH   448B ANNO REYNOLDS   MARG
[PAY] HAVE PAID GREAT SUMS IN THE VENETIAN & FLEMISH OOZE   547A PRETTY EPIGR/N   TITLE
OR WITH REMBRANDT'S OR ANYTHING VENETIAN OR FLEMISH . . . 573A DESC CAT 3   PROSE
THE VENETIAN AND FLEMISH PRACTICE IS BROKEN LINES . . . 573A DESC CAT 3   PROSE
VENETIAN AND FLEMISH DEMONS WHOSE ENMITY TO THE PAINTER   582C DESC CAT 9   PROSE
   HIMSELF
AND ROMAN PRACTICE AND ADOPT THE VENETIAN AND FLEMISH . 583A DESC CAT 9   PROSE
TILL THE VENETIAN & FLEMISH ARE DESTROYD THE FLORENTINE   866B LETTER 64   PROSE
[?WHY ?THEN GRATIFY FLEMISH PAINTERS XXX] . . . . . SUPP ANNO REYNOLDS   * MARG

FLESH

I KNOW THIS BREATHING FLESH MUST LIE AND ROT . . . . 30 EDW THIRD/PS 5   4
SO THE ARROWS OF SIN STICK IN MY FLESH   36B COUCH DEATH/PS   PROSE
MY FLESH IS A PRISON MY BONES THE BARS OF DEATH . . . 37B CONTEMPLATN/PS   PROSE
O WEAK WOMAN IT IS DEATH CLOATHED IN FLESH THOU LOVEST . 38B SAMSON/PS   PROSE
THY YOUNG HANDS TORE HUMAN LIMBS AND GORGED HUMAN FLESH   38B SAMSON/PS   PROSE
GO SEE THE NATURAL TIE OF FLESH & BLOOD . . . . . . 43A THEN SHE BORE   PROSE
& EVRY PIECE OF FLESH DOTH CRY OUT WOE   43C WOE CRIED MUSE   PROSE
HE COMMITTED ON FLESH A WHOREDOM . . . . 50 WHEN CORRUP/IM   3
FOR FLESH & HE COULD NEER AGREE . . . . 50 WHEN CORRUP/IM   11
YE WORMS OF DEATH FEASTING UPON YOUR AGED PARENTS FLESH   99 TIRIEL 1   23
WHY SHOULDEST THOU CONCEAL THYSELF FROM THOSE OF THINE   101 TIRIEL 2   47
   OWN FLESH
REBOUNDED & THE PIERCING SWORD BROKE ON HIS NAKED [LIMBS]   105 TIRIEL 4   72
   FLESH
LAUGH SERPENT YOUNGEST VENOMOUS REPTILE OF THE FLESH OF   108 TIRIEL 6   32
   TIRIEL
WHY A LITTLE CURTAIN OF FLESH ON THE BED OF OUR DESIRE . . 130 BOOK OF THEL 6   20
WERE FORGD SMALLER AS THE FLESH DECAYD . . . . 135 FRENCH REVOLTN   31
OUR FLESH IS CORRUPTED AND WE (WEAR) AWAY . . . . . . 137 FRENCH REVOLTN *   76
THE SOUND OF PRAYER FAILS FROM LIPS OF FLESH . . . . . 140 FRENCH REVOLTN   140
PICKING THE FLESH OFF OF HIS OWN TAIL . . . . . . 157B MARRIAGE HH 17 *PROSE
AND CALLING THEOTORMON'S EAGLES TO PREY UPON HER FLESH . 190 V DAU ALBION 2   13
AND A COWL OF FLESH GREW OER HIS HEAD & SCALES ON HIS BACK   202 AMERICA 15   17
   & RIBS
COLD FEATURELESS FLESH OR CLAY . . . . 226 URIZEN 7   5
THAT NO FLESH NOR SPIRIT COULD KEEP . . . . 235 URIZEN 23   25
AND OVERWHELMED ALL EXCEPT THIS FINITE WALL OF FLESH . . 241 EUROPE 10   20
THEY SAW HIS BONEY FEET ON THE ROCK THE FLESH CONSUMD IN   242 EUROPE 12   10
   FLAMES
ADHERED AND GREW ONE WITH HIS FLESH AND NERVES & VEINS   242 EUROPE 12   17
   SHOT THRO THEM
AROUND THE LIMBS OF ALBION'S GUARDIAN HIS FLESH CONSUMING   243 EUROPE 12   33
CREEPING IN REPTILE FLESH UPON . . . . 246 SONG OF LOS 4   9
AND ALL FLESH NAKED STANDS FATHERS AND FRIENDS . . . . 248 SONG OF LOS 7   33
SNARING THE WILD GOATS FOR THEIR MILK THEY EAT THE FLESH   270 FOUR ZOAS 1   235
   OF LAMBS
WITH MARROW SINEWS & FLESH EXALT THYSELF ATTAIN A VOICE   275 FOUR ZOAS 1   405
FURROWD WITH WHIPS & OUR FLESH BRUISED WITH THE HEAVY   286 FOUR ZOAS 2   226
   BASKET
AMONG THE FROZEN ARROWS THEY WILL TEAR THY TENDER FLESH   296 FOUR ZOAS 3   172
REORGANIZE ME SHOOTING FORTH IN BONES & FLESH & BLOOD . . 317 FOUR ZOAS 6   224
NOW COMES THE NIGHT OF CARNAGE NOW THE FLESH OF KINGS &   334 FOUR ZOAS 7B   45
   PRINCES
DARKNESS & SORROW COVERD ALL FLESH ETERNITY WAS DARKEND   351 FOUR ZOAS 8   414
HIS EYES SINK HOLLOW IN HIS HEAD HIS FLESH COVERD WITH   354 FOUR ZOAS 8   515
   SLIME
DARKNESS & SORROW COVERD ALL FLESH ETERNITY WAS DARKEND   382 FOUR ZOAS AD 6   30
CREEPING IN REPTILE FLESH UPON THE BOSOM OF THE GROUND . . 484 MILTON 5   20
CREATING NEW FLESH ON THE DEMON COLD AND BUILDING HIM . 500 MILTON 19   13
MINE IS THE FLESH THE BONES MAY BE [HIS] [THY] YOUR SHARE   540 S(TOTHAR] D/N *   6
THE PLUSH OF HEALTH IN FLESH EXPOSED TO THE OPEN AIR . 580D DESC CAT 5   PROSE
THE FLESH OF MULTITUDES FED & NOURISD ME IN MY CHILDHOOD   644 JERUSALEM 22   6
CREEPING IN REPTILE FLESH UPON THE BOSOM OF THE GROUND . . 680 JERUSALEM 49   33
THE NOSTRILS BENT DOWN TO THE EARTH & CLOSD WITH SENSELESS   680 JERUSALEM 49   38
   FLESH
I KNOW THAT IN MY FLESH I SHALL SEE GOD BUT EMANATIONS . . 696 JERUSALEM 62   16
AND DELIGHTFUL FOOD OF THE WARRIOR THE WELL FED WARRIOR'S   706 JERUSALEM 68   34
   FLESH
BEFORE THE KINGS OF CANAAN TO CUT THE FLESH FROM THE VICTIM   706 JERUSALEM 68   57
TO ROAST THE FLESH IN FIRE TO EXAMINE THE INFANT'S LIMBS   707 JERUSALEM 68   58
OF THE TRANSGRESOR OR NO FLESH OR SPIRIT COULD EVER LIVE   780 GHOST ABEL 2 *   11
ALSO LET ME OBSERVE THAT THE YELLOW LEATHER FLESH OF OLD   815A LETTER 23   PROSE
   MEN
WHY SHOULD I BE TROUBLED WHY SHOULD MY HEART & FLESH CRY   823C LETTER 26   PROSE
   OUT

FLESHLY

THEY EAT THE [XXX] FLESHLY BREAD THEY DRANK THE NERVOUS   274 FOUR ZOAS 1 *   355
   [BLOODY] WINE
THE DIVINE VISION WITH CURTAIN & VEIL & FLESHLY TABERNACLE   688 JERUSALEM 56 *   40
WE ARE TOLD TO ABSTAIN FROM FLESHLY DESIRES . . . . . 716D JERUSALEM 77   PROSE

FLESHY

IN A FLESHY SLOUGH FORMED FOUR RIVERS . . . . 260 BOOK OF LOS 5   53

FLEW

AS THE DEER WOUNDED ELLEN FLEW OVER . . . . 5 FAIR ELENOR/PS   33
AND THE OWL AND BAT FLEW ROUND THE DARKENING TREES . . . 35C COUCH DEATH/PS   PROSE
AND AWAY THE VAPOUR FLEW . . . . 60 LIT BOY LST/IM   8
AND AWAY THE VAPOUR FLEW . . . . 121 LIT BOY LST/SI   8
AND ALL THY MOANS FLEW OER MY ROOF BUT I HAVE CALLD THEM   130 BOOK OF THEL 5   15
   DOWN

```
                                                                    PAGE      TITLE        LINE
FLEW    (CONTINUED)
    WHICH FLEW OR RATHER SWUM IN THE INFINITE DEEP      . . . .  156A MARRIAGE HH 17   PROSE
    & FLEW WESTERLY THRO THE NIGHT . . . . . . . . . .  156D MARRIAGE HH 17   PROSE
    THEN MARS THOU WAST OUR CENTER & THE PLANETS THREE FLEW      197 AMERICA 5            4
        ROUND
    AND BOSTON'S ANGEL CRIED ALOUD AS THEY FLEW THRO THE DARK    200 AMERICA 11           3
        NIGHT
    HIS PLAGUES OBEDIENT TO HIS VOICE FLEW FORTH OUT OF THEIR    201 AMERICA 14           4
        CLOUDS
    THE FURIOUS TERRORS FLEW AROUND   . . . . . . . .   245 EUROPE 15            4
    MELTED OVER THE LAND AS HE FLEW   . . . . . . . .   248 SONG OF LOS 7       15
    THE HOWLING GLOBE BURNING IT FLEW . . . . . . . .   249 AHANIA 2            18
    SOME IN VALES SOME ALOFT FLEW IN AIR   . . . . . .  250 AHANIA 3            12
    ON FUZON FLEW ENTERD HIS BOSOM . . . . . . . . .    251 AHANIA 3            40
    FORTH FLEW THE ARROWS OF PESTILENCE   . . . . . .   252 AHANIA 4             9
    FORTY YEARS FLEW THE ARROWS OF PESTILENCE   . . . . 253 AHANIA 4            37
    LUVAH AND VALA [WAKE] WOKE & [FLY] FLEW UP FROM THE HUMAN    271 FOUR ZOAS 1   *   262
        HEART
    THE BANDS OF HEAVEN FLEW THRO THE AIR SINGING & SHOUTING     281 FOUR ZOAS 2        26
        TO URIZEN
    FLEW OVER THE WAVES OF THARMAS PITYING THARMAS STAYD HIS     298 FOUR ZOAS 4   *    49
        WAVES
    IN SUCCESSIVE VOLLIES WITH LOUD THUNDERS SWIFT FLEW THE      314 FOUR ZOAS 6   *   109
        KING OF LIGHT
    FLEW THE KING THO FLAGD HIS POWERS LABRING TILL OVER ROCKS   314 FOUR ZOAS 6   *   112
    THE ARROWS FLEW FROM CLOUDY BOW ALL DAY TILL BLOOD   . . .   337 FOUR ZOAS 7B       159
    ALL THINGS REVERSD FLEW FROM THEIR CENTERS RATTLING BONES    363 FOUR ZOAS 9        231
        [TO BONES ]
    . . . THARMAS WITH WINGD SPEED FLEW TO THE SANDY SHORE       380 FOUR ZOAS AD 1 *   14
        [OCEAN]
    . . . LOUD SOUNDING FLEW THE FLAMING ARROW FOURFOLD  . . .   744 JERUSALEM 98        3
    ROUND ME FLEW THE FLAMING SWORD   . . . . . . . .   770 OF GATES/GP         15
FLEXIBLE     SEE ALL FLEXIBLE
    ANTAMON TAKES THEM INTO HIS BEAUTIFUL FLEXIBLE HANDS    .    515 MILTON 28           13
FLIES
    BY NIGHT DESTRUCTION FLIES AND STRIKES IN DARKNESS   . . .     5 FAIR ELENOR/PS      35
    LIKE SMOULDRING FIRE OR IN THE BUZZ OF CITIES FLIES ABROAD   42C THEN SHE BORE    PROSE
    SCORN WAITS ON PRIDE BUT SLANDER FLIES AROUND THE WORLD      42D THEN SHE BORE    PROSE
    PALENESS FLIES FROM EVERY FACE    . . . . . . . .    63 SHEPHERD FIRST        3
    THAT FLIES IN THE NIGHT    . . . . . . . . . . .    175 SICK ROSE/N           3
    BUT HE WHO [JUST] KISSES THE JOY AS IT FLIES   . . . .      179 ETERNITY/N            3
    BUT HE WHO KISSES THE JOY AS IT FLIES   . . . . . .        184 SEVRL QUESTN/N       13
    AS WHEN A DREAM OF THIRALATHA FLIES THE MIDNIGHT HOUR   .   206 THIRALATHA            1
    THAT FLIES IN THE NIGHT    . . . . . . . . . . .    213 SICK ROSE/SE          3
    OF AHANIA WAILING ON THE WINDS IN VAIN HE FLIES FOR STILL   353 FOUR ZOAS 8        488
    THOU SEEST THE GORGEOUS CLOTHED FLIES THAT DANCE & SPORT     512 MILTON 26            2
        IN SUMMER
    OF FRIENDSHIP OUR SEXUAL CANNOT BUT FLIES INTO THE ULRO      534 MILTON 41           33
    THESE HEAVENS ARE VENUS JUPITER & MARS HERMES FLIES BEFORE   619B ILLUS MILTON    PROSE
    TIME FLIES VERY FAST AND VERY MERRILY I SOMETIMES    . . .   807A LETTER 17      PROSE
    TIME FLIES FASTER AS SEEMS TO ME HERE THAN IN LONDON    .    809A LETTER 20      PROSE
    MONEY FLIES FROM ME PROFIT NEVER VENTURES UPON MY    . . .   849D LETTER 47      PROSE
    SUMMER FLIES REPROACHING THE POET . . . . . . . .   SUPP ILLUS GRAY      *TITLE
    FAIRIES RIDING ON FLIES    . . . . . . . . . . .    SUPP ILLUS GRAY      *TITLE
    [PLIES] SWARMS OF FLIES MURRAIN OF BEASTS BOILS & BLAINS     SUPP EXODUS/N       *PROSE
FLIEST
    O LAPWING THOU FLIEST AROUND THE HEATH    . . . . . .      168 O LAPWING/N           1
FLIGHT
    AND THRO HEAVN'S HALLS THY AIRY FLIGHT DOST THROW    . .     15 IMIT SPEN/PS        21
    DOTH SEIZE THE SOARING EAGLE UNDONE BY FLIGHT  . . . .       24 EDW THIRD/PS 3     121
    THEY TAME SUBMIT SUCH THE EFFECT FLIGHT HAS    . . . .       24 EDW THIRD/PS 3     122
    FOR FLIGHT AN PLEASE YOUR GRACE   . . . . . . . .    24 EDW THIRD/PS 3     150
    YOUR SOULS FOR FLIGHT YOUR BODIES FOR THE EARTH  . . . .     34 WAR SONG/PS          7
    WHERE GOEST THOU O THOUGHT TO WHAT REMOTE LAND IS    192 V DAU ALBION 4        8
        THY FLIGHT
    THEIR VENTUROUS FLIGHT IN HUMAN FORMS DISTINCT THRO    284 FOUR ZOAS 2        151
        DARKNESS DEEP
    HE THREW HIS FLIGHT THRO THE DARK AIR TO WHERE A RIVER   311 FOUR ZOAS 6          2
        FLOWD
    IF THOU REFUSEST IN ETERNAL FLIGHT THY BEAMS IN VAIN    .    313 FOUR ZOAS 6         67
    POUR DOWN MY FLIGHT THRO DARK IMMENSITY ETERNAL FALLING      313 FOUR ZOAS 6         69
    SO HE THREW HIS FLIGHT IN TERROR & PAIN & IN REPENTANT       315 FOUR ZOAS 6        146
        TEARS
    BUT STILL IN SOLITUDE HE SAT THEN RISING THREW HIS FLIGHT    316 FOUR ZOAS 6        164
    OERWEARIED ON IN CUMBEROUS FLIGHT HE VENTURD OER DARK RIFTS  319 FOUR ZOAS 6   *   288
    BESIDE (HIM) THARMAS STAYD HIS FLIGHT & STOOD IN STERN       319 FOUR ZOAS 6        302
        DEFIANCE
    THARMAS THREW HIS IMPETUOUS FLIGHT THRO THE DEEPS      320 FOUR ZOAS 7          3
        OF IMMENSITY
    TO STAY HIM IN HIS FLIGHT THAT URIZEN MIGHT LIVE THO IN      339 FOUR ZOAS 7B       227
        PAIN
    EXULTING IN HER FLIGHT AS WHEN A BUBBLE RISES UP  . . . .    362 FOUR ZOAS 9        195
    NIGHT & MORN THE FLIGHT RENEW   . . . . . . . . .   416 MY SPECTRE/N        58
    INTENDED FLIGHT INTO YOUR DELIGHTFUL COUNTRY CONCUR IN  .    872D LETTER 76      PROSE
FLIGHTS
    FROM YOUR HIGH FLIGHTS YE MUST CONDESCEND TO STUDY   . .     593C PUB ADDRESS/N  PROSE
    THE PRECIOUS STONES GLITTER ON FLIGHTS SEVENTY SEVEN    .    800 MRS FLAXMAN/L       10
    TAKE THE WORLD WITH ME IN MY FLIGHTS & OFTEN IT SEEMS   .    809A LETTER 20      PROSE
FLIMSY
    THEY SEEM TO ME TO BE THE MOST WRETCHED PALTRY FLIMSY STUFF  44D ISLAND MOON 1   PROSE
        THAT EVER
```

718

		PAGE	TITLE	LINE

FLINCH
    THEN NEVER FLINCH BUT KEEP UP A JAW . . . . 550 WHEN LOOK AT/N   3
FLINGING
    [FLINGING FLAMES OF DISCONTENT & PLAGUES OF DARK DESPAIR] 109 TIRIEL 8   16
FLINGS
    THE GOBLIN CROP FULL FLINGS OUT OF DOORS FROM . . . . . 618C ILLUS MILTON PROSE
FLINT
    SHE SMITES WITH HER KNIFE OF FLINT SHE DESTROYS HER OWN 347 FOUR ZOAS 8   234
      WORK
    & CAIN WITH THE FLINT IN HIS HAND WITH WHICH HE SLEW . 606B V LAST JUDG/N PROSE
    THE KNIFE OF FLINT PASSES OVER THE HOWLING VICTIM HIS BLOOD 702 JERUSALEM 66   20
    THEY TAKE OFF HIS VESTURE WHOLE WITH THEIR KNIVES OF FLINT 702 JERUSALEM 66   26
    AS THE SENSES OF MEN SHRINK TOGETHER UNDER THE KNIFE OF 703 JERUSALEM 66   83
      FLINT
    OF FLINT IS IN HER HAND SHE PASSES IT OVER THE HOWLING 704 JERUSALEM 67   25
      VICTIM
    I HAVE ORDERS TO SET MY FACE LIKE A FLINT EZEKIEL... . . 825B LETTER 27 PROSE
FLINTS
    CUT WITH THE FLINTS HER TEARS RUN DOWN HER REASON GROWS 693 JERUSALEM 60   42
      LIKE
FLINTSHIRE
    THE GATE OF JUDAH MERIONETHSHIRE THE GATE OF DAN 637 JERUSALEM 16   37
      FLINTSHIRE
FLITS
    THE BAT THAT FLITS AT CLOSE OF EVE . . . . 431 AUGURIES   25
FLOAT
    FLOAT THE DEAD CARCASES OF MEN & BEASTS DRIVEN TO & FRO 359 FOUR ZOAS 9   77
      ON WAVES
FLOATING
    (FLOATING) UPON THE BOSOMD AIR . . . . 244 EUROPE 14   * 18
    FLOATING UPON THE TIDE WANDER BUBBLING & BUBBLING . . . 296 FOUR ZOAS 3   164
    SWEET FEMALE FORMS WINGED OR FLOATING IN THE AIR 524 MILTON 34   11
      SPONTANEOUS
    FLOATING WITH SOLEMN SONGS & ON THE LAKES OF EGYPT NIGHTLY 528 MILTON 37   28
    AND LEFT A LITTLE SLIMY SUBSTANCE FLOATING UPON THE TIDES 679 JERUSALEM 49   18
FLOATS
    YOUR MUSIC FLOATS . . . . 8 MEMORY COME/PS   4
    LOUD & MORE LOUD THE LIVING MUSIC FLOATS UPON THE AIR . . 306 FOUR ZOAS 5   26
FLOCK
    ONE ROTTEN SHEEP SPOILS THE WHOLE FLOCK . . . . . . 22 EDW THIRD/PS 3   50
    THEN PRAYED MANOA O LORD THY FLOCK IS SCATTERED ON THE 40A SAMSON/PS PROSE
      HILLS
    MY DAUGHTER HOW DO I REJOICE FOR THY CHILDREN FLOCK AROUND 243 EUROPE 14   2
    WILL YOU KEEP A FLOCK OF WOLVES & LEAD THEM . . . . . 353 FOUR ZOAS 8   493
    FLOCK TO THE TRUMPET MUTTRING OVER THE SIDES OF THE GRAVE 363 FOUR ZOAS 9   239
      & CRYING
    FEAR NOT O LITTLE FLOCK I COME ALBION SHALL RISE AGAIN . . 653 JERUSALEM 29   26
    WEPT ROUND HIM AS A FLOCK SILENT SEVEN DAYS OF ETERNITY 711 JERUSALEM 71   63
FLOCKING
    OF HUMAN INTELLECT NOW IS FLOCKING TO THE SOUND OF THE 510 MILTON 25   19
      TRUMPET
FLOCKS
    THE FLEECES OF OUR FLOCKS ARE COVERD WITH . . . . . . 3 EVNING STAR/PS   13
    OUR BURDEND VESSELS SPOILING OUR NAVAL FLOCKS . . . . . 20 EDW THIRD/PS 2   68
    AN ARMY OF MIGHTY MEN ARE AS FLOCKS IN THE VALLIES WHAT 39A SAMSON/PS PROSE
      CANST
    TILL VENERABLE AGE CAME ON HIS FLOCKS INCREASED . . . . 39C SAMSON/PS PROSE
    THE PHILISTINE RIOTS ON OUR FLOCKS OUR VINTAGE IS GATHERED 40B SAMSON/PS PROSE
    [THE FLOCKS ARE AT PLAY & WE CAN'T GO AWAY] . . . . . 60 NURSES SONG/IM   11
    WHERE FLOCKS HAVE TOOK DELIGHT . . . . 119 NIGHT/SI   10
    THE DAUGHTERS OF MNE SERAPHIM LED ROUND THEIR SUNNY FLOCKS 127 BOOK OF THEL 1   1
    WHERE MEMORY WISHES TO REPOSE AMONG THE FLOCKS OF THARMAS 288 FOUR ZOAS 2   326
    THAT IN ETERNAL FIELDS IN COMFORT WANDERD WITH MY FLOCKS 301 FOUR ZOAS 4   138
    THE NUMROUS FLOCKS COVER THE MOUNTAIN & SHINE ALONG THE 308 FOUR ZOAS 5   * 138
      VALLEY
    AMONG HIS FAMILY HIS FLOCKS & HERDS & TENTS & PASTURES . . 326 FOUR ZOAS 7   254
    THEY ARE BECOME LIKE WINTRY FLOCKS LIKE FORESTS STRIPD 357 FOUR ZOAS 9   22
      OF LEAVES
    KINGS IN THEIR PALACES LIE DROWND SHEPHERDS THEIR FLOCKS 359 FOUR ZOAS 9   74
      THEIR TENTS
    MY BIRDS ARE SILENT ON MY HILLS FLOCKS DIE BENEATH 359 FOUR ZOAS 9   101
      MY BRANCHES
    AND ON THE FLEECES OF MILD FLOCKS WHO NEITHER CARE NOR 361 FOUR ZOAS 9   173
      LABOUR
    THEY ARE BECOME LIKE WINTRY FLOCKS LIKE FORESTS STRIPD 365 FOUR ZOAS 9   327
      OF LEAVES
    I WALK AMONG HIS FLOCKS & HEAR THE BLEATING OF HIS LAMBS 368 FOUR ZOAS 9   425
    I WALK BY THE FOOTSTEPS OF HIS FLOCKS COME HITHER TENDER 368 FOUR ZOAS 9   427
      FLOCKS
    FOLLOW ME O MY FLOCKS & HEAR ME SING MY RAPTUROUS SONG . . 368 FOUR ZOAS 9   438
    I AM NOT HERE ALONE MY FLOCKS YOU ARE MY BRETHREN . . . 368 FOUR ZOAS 9   443
    FOLLOW ME O MY FLOCKS WE WILL NOW DESCEND INTO THE VALLEY 368 FOUR ZOAS 9   446
    INTO THIS BODILY HOUSE TO TEND MY FLOCKS IN MY PLEASANT 369 FOUR ZOAS 9   470
      GARDEN
    BUT HER FLOCKS WERE GONE UP FROM BENEATH THE TREES INTO 369 FOUR ZOAS 9   473
      THE HILLS
    I SEE THE HAND THAT LEADETH ME DOTH ALSO LEAD MY FLOCKS 369 FOUR ZOAS 9   474
    SHE WENT UP TO HER FLOCKS & TURNED OFT TO SEE HER SHINING 369 FOUR ZOAS 9   475
      HOUSE
    SHE CALLED TO HER FLOCKS SAYING FOLLOW ME O MY FLOCKS . . 369 FOUR ZOAS 9   478
    AMONG HER FLOCKS & SHE TURND HER EYES TOWARD HER PLEASANT 370 FOUR ZOAS 9   505
      HOUSE

	PAGE	TITLE	LINE

FLOCKS (CONTINUED)

SHE DREW NEAR TO HER HOUSE & HER FLOCKS FOLLOWD HER FOOTSTEPS — 370 FOUR ZOAS 9 — 508
AND WHEN NIGHT CAME THE FLOCKS LAID ROUND THE HOUSE BENEATH THE TREES — 370 FOUR ZOAS 9 — 514
THUS IN ETERNAL CHILDHOOD STRAYING AMONG VALA'S FLOCKS — 371 FOUR ZOAS 9 — 553
CREEPS ROUND OUR SECRET NEST FLOCKS BRIGHTEN THE MOUNTAINS — 373 FOUR ZOAS 9 — 611
METHINKS I SEE HIS FLOCKS & HERDS & FEEL MY LIMBS RENEWD — 375 FOUR ZOAS 9 — 690
MY FLOCKS & HERDS TRAMPLE THE CORN MY CATTLE BROWZE UPON — 376 FOUR ZOAS 9 — 699
FOR THARMAS BROUGHT HIS FLOCKS UPON THE HILLS & IN THE VALES — 379 FOUR ZOAS 9 — 838
AMONG THE WOOLY FLOCKS THE HAMMER OF URTHONA SOUNDS — 379 FOUR ZOAS 9 — 840
HIS BIRDS ARE SILENT ON HIS HILLS FLOCKS DIE BENEATH HIS BRANCHES — 641 JERUSALEM 19 — 2
O WHEN SHALL JEHOVAH GIVE US VICTIMS FROM HIS FLOCKS & HERDS — 697 JERUSALEM 63 — 30
YORK & LINCOLN HIDE AMONG THE FLOCKS BECAUSE OF THE GRIDING KNIFE — 703 JERUSALEM 66 — 65
AND KENT & MIDDLESEX ALL THEIR RIVERS & THEIR HILLS OF FLOCKS & HERDS — 709 JERUSALEM 71 — 12
THE PLAINS OF SUSSEX & SURREY THEIR HILLS OF FLOCKS & HERDS — 720 JERUSALEM 79 — 18
ARE SEEN IN OUR HILLS & VALLEYS THEY KEEP OUR FLOCKS & HERDS — 720 JERUSALEM 79 — 31
AND GIVEN SOFT MILK MINGLED TOGETHER WITH THE SPIRITS OF FLOCKS — 725 JERUSALEM 82 — 6

FLOGD

TO BE FLOGD INTO FOLLOWING THE STYLE OF A FOOL — 550 SAY PICTURES/N — 5

FLOGGING

A FLOGGING MAGISTRATE I HAVE SEEN MANY SUCH FLY BLOWS OF BACON — 400D ANNO BACON — MARG

FLOGISTON

OUR LUNGS ARE DESTROYD WITH THE FLOGISTON — 59A ISLAND MOON 10 — PROSE

FLOOD

AND SAILS REJOICING IN THE FLOOD OF DEATH — 33 EDW FOURTH/PS — 10
GIANTS OF MIGHTY ARM BEFORE THE FLOOD CAIN'S CITY — 41A THEN SHE BORE — PROSE
SHE COULD CONTROLL THE SPACES REGIONS DESART FLOOD & FOREST — 271 FOUR ZOAS 1 — 241
LO THREE TERRIFIC WOMEN AT THE VERGE OF THE BRIGHT FLOOD — 311 FOUR ZOAS 6 — 5
AROUND THEE SOMETIMES LIKE A FLOOD & SOMETIMES LIKE A ROCK — 321 FOUR ZOAS 7 — 49
MY WATERS LIKE A FLOOD AROUND THEE FEAR NOT TRUST IN ME — 334 FOUR ZOAS 7B — 55
BEFORE THE FLOOD THAT THEY WERE FILLD WITH BLOOD & FIRE — 606D V LAST JUDG/N — PROSE
THEY REPRESENT THOSE WHO PERISHD BY THE FLOOD — 607D V LAST JUDG/N — PROSE
UNDER THE NAMES OF THE FATHERS BEFORE & AFTER THE FLOOD — 609D V LAST JUDG/N — PROSE
WHICH THE FLOOD DID NOT SWEEP AWAY ABOVE NOAH IS — 609D V LAST JUDG/N — PROSE
THE CHANGED STATE MADE BY THE FLOOD — 611C V LAST JUDG/N — PROSE
BEFORE THE FLOOD & THEIR GENERATIONS — 611D V LAST JUDG/N — PROSE
WHO PREVIOUS TO THE FLOOD WALKED WITH GOD — 611D V LAST JUDG/N — PROSE
OF THE FLOOD OF UDAN-ADAN HUTN IS THE FATHER OF THE SEVEN — 625 JERUSALEM 7 — 24
IN EVERY MAN EZEKIEL SAW THEM BY CHEBAR'S FLOOD — 632 JERUSALEM 12 — 58
THE FLOOD AND WAS NAMD CHICHESTER LOVELY MILD & GENTLE LO — 667 JERUSALEM 40 — 50
AS SHE HEARD BY EDEN'S FLOOD — 754 EV GOSPEL(E)/N — 20
THE IMMENSE FLOOD OF GRECIAN LIGHT & GLORY WHICH IS COMING — 797C LETTER 10 — PROSE

FLOODGATES

I OPEND ALL THE FLOODGATES OF THE HEAVENS TO QUENCH HER THIRST — 282 FOUR ZOAS 2 — 90

FLOOD GATES

FROM OUT THE FLOOD GATES OF THE SKY THE GATES ARE BURST DOWN POUR — 359 FOUR ZOAS 9 — 72

FLOODS SEE WATER FLOODS

LIKE RUSHING MIGHTY FLOODS — 11 GWIN KING/PS — 24
WE SPRING TO BATTLE OER THE FLOODS OF DEATH — 18 EDW THIRD/PS 1 — 16
GROANING SHAKING FORESTS AND FLOODS THE COLD NEWT — 147 FRENCH REVOLTN — 297
WITH COLD FLOODS OF ABSTRACTION AND WITH FORESTS OF SOLITUDE — 193 V DAU ALBION 5 — 19
SURROUNDED BY SALT FLOODS NOW CALLD — 236 URIZEN 28 — 9
RUSHD DOWN LIKE FLOODS FROM HIS MOUNTAINS — 250 AHANIA 3 — 8
I SEE THY BLACK FORESTS AND FLOODS — 254 AHANIA 4 — 58
HE ROSE ON THE FLOODS THEN HE SMOTE — 259 BOOK OF LOS 5 — 3
I ROLL MY FLOODS OVER HIS BODY MY BILLOWS & WAVES PASS OVER HIM — 301 FOUR ZOAS 4 — 133
HE TOOK HIGH BOUNDING OVER HILLS & DESARTS FLOODS & HORRIBLE CHASMS — 313 FOUR ZOAS 6 — 73
THRO LIGHTNINGS THUNDERS EARTHQUAKES & CONCUSSIONS FIRES & FLOODS — 316 FOUR ZOAS 6 — 185
THO FLOODS POUR THO WINDS BLACK AS THE SEA — 322 FOUR ZOAS 7 — 83
DOWN POUR THE TORRENT FLOODS OF HEAVEN ON ALL THE HUMAN HARVEST — 372 FOUR ZOAS 9 — 566
IN ALL THEIR ANCIENT INNOCENCE THE FLOODS DEPART THE CLOUDS — 372 FOUR ZOAS 9 — 572
& CORDS & FIRES & FLOODS — 377 FOUR ZOAS 9 — 752
VOMITED OUT & GAVE UP ALL THE FLOODS LIFT UP THEIR HANDS — 378 FOUR ZOAS 9 — 803
NOURISHED BY THE SPIRITS OF FORESTS AND FLOODS — 580D DESC CAT 5 — PROSE
EUPHRATES & TO FORESTS & FLOODS & ANIMALS WILD & TAME FROM — 695 JERUSALEM 61 — 31
[XXX BLOOD FROM TORRENT FLOODS MELTING [AWAY]] — SUPP FOUR ZOAS 1 — *

FLOOR SEE WHEAT-FLOOR

THY GOLDEN ROD THROWN ON THE DUSTY FLOOR — 15 IMIT SPEN/PS — 29
PINIOND DOWN TO THE STONE FLOOR — 135 FRENCH REVOLTN — 30
WHOSE WHITE BEARD COVERD THE STONE FLOOR LIKE WEEDS — 135 FRENCH REVOLTN — 38
FOR THE LINKS OF A DUNGEON FLOOR — 186 LET BROTHELS/N — 49
[FOR THE LINKS OF A DUNGEON FLOOR] — 186 LET BROTHELS/N — 55
FOR THE LINKS OF A DUNGEON FLOOR — 186 LET BROTHELS/N — 67
DOES THE SUN WALK IN GLORIOUS RAIMENT ON THE SECRET FLOOR — 195 V DAU ALBION 7 — 30
THE STARRY FLOOR — 210 INTRODUCTN/SE — 18

720

		PAGE	TITLE	LINE

FLOOR   (CONTINUED)

SOUNDS ON THE FLOOR HEARD TERRIBLE BY ALL BENEATH   374 FOUR ZOAS 9   651
THE HEAVENS
DISMAL LOUD REDOUNDING THE NETHER FLOOR SHAKES WITH THE   374 FOUR ZOAS 9   652
SOUND
THE WEAK LUVAH & VALA SLEPT ON THE FLOOR OERWEARIED . . .   378 FOUR ZOAS 9   788
AND MARY FELL DOWN ON THE RIGHT HAND FLOOR . . . . .   435 WILLIAM BOND   34
AT LENGTH STANDING UPON THE GOLDEN FLOOR OF PALAMABRON . .   492 MILTON 11   34
S(?STOTHARD) IN CHILDHOOD ON THE NURSERY FLOOR   . . .   539 IN CHILDHOOD/N   1
HE IS ARAUNAH THE JEBUSITE MASTER OF THE THRESHING FLOOR   607D V LAST JUDG/N   PROSE
BY FAIRIES AS THEY DANCE ON THE BED THE CIELING & THE FLOOR   618C ILLUS MILTON   *PROSE

FLOORS

ALWAYS COMFORTING THE REMEMBRANCE THE FLOORS HUMILITY . .   632 JERUSALEM 12   36
UPON EGYPT'S IRON FLOORS & THE MARBLE PAVEMENTS OF ASSYRIA   719 JERUSALEM 79   2

FLORENTINE

FLORENTINE WHAT THEN DOES HE MEAN WHEN HE SAYS THAT . . .   467D ANNO REYNOLDS   MARG
THAT WE CANNOT MIX THE FLORENTINE & VENETIAN . . . . .   477B ANNO REYNOLDS   MARG
NEVER IS THE CASE EXCEPT IN THE ROMAN & FLORENTINE SCHOOLS   479B ANNO REYNOLDS   MARG
NOTE I INCLUDE THE GERMANS IN THE FLORENTINE SCHOOL . .   479B ANNO REYNOLDS   MARG
FLORENTINE INGRATITUDE . . . .   541D FLORENTINE/N   TITLE
OF SELF-DEVOTING GENIUS THE QUARREL OF THE FLORENTINE WITH   563D DESC CAT   PROSE
AND TO ALL ARTISTS WHO STUDY IN THE FLORENTINE AND . . .   582C DESC CAT 9   PROSE
TORMENTING THE TRUE ARTIST TILL HE LEAVES THE FLORENTINE   582D DESC CAT 9   PROSE
AND
CAUSES TO THE FLORENTINE AND ROMAN ARTIST FEAR TO EXECUTE   583A DESC CAT 9   PROSE
TILL THE VICTIM IS OBLIGED TO GIVE UP THE FLORENTINE .   583A DESC CAT 9   PROSE
FLORENTINE ORIGINAL & IF POSSIBLE TO GO BEYOND THAT   600B PUB ADDRESS/N   PROSE
ORIGINAL
ONE WHO HAS STUDIED IN THE FLORENTINE & ROMAN SCHOOLS .   781D INSC UPCOTT   PROSE
TO OPPOSE FLORENTINE & VENETIAN ART CANNOT EXIST TOGETHER   866B LETTER 64   PROSE
TILL THE VENETIAN & FLEMISH ARE DESTROYD THE FLORENTINE   866B LETTER 64   PROSE

FLORENTINES

THE FLORENTINES SAID TIS A DUTCH ENGLISH BORE . . . . .   542 FLORENTINE/N   13
THE FLORENTINES CALL IT AN ENGLISH FETCH . . . . . .   542 FLORENTINE/N   15
IF YOU MEAN THAT THE FLORENTINES [TO] SHOULD BUY . . . .   542 FLORENTINE/N   * 23

FLORID

A LIE THE FLORID STYLE SUCH AS THE VENETIAN & THE FLEMISH   448B ANNO REYNOLDS   MARG
FLOTING UPON THE BOSOMD AIR . . . .   244 EUROPE 14   * 18

FLOURISH

FLOURISH DOWN THE BRIGHT CHEEK OF MODEST EVE . . . . .   2 TO AUTUMN/PS   10
RELIGION WILL FLOURISH EACH MAN'S HEART . . . .   19 EDW THIRD/PS 2   25
TO FLOURISH IN ETERNAL VALES THEN WHY SHOULD THEL COMPLAIN   127 BOOK OF THEL 1   25
THE HARVEST SHALL FLOURISH IN WINTRY WEATHER . . . . .   177 MERLNS PROPH/N   1
BUT KNOWEST THOU THAT TREES AND FRUITS FLOURISH UPON THE   192 V DAU ALBION 4   14
EARTH
YON SUN SHALL WAX OLD & DECAY BUT THOU SHALT EVER FLOURISH   368 FOUR ZOAS 9   419
TIS YOUR OWN FAULT IF YOU DONT FLOURISH NOW WILLIAM BLAKE   414 TO MRS FLAXMAN   10
ALL POWERFUL AND HIS LOCKS FLOURISH LIKE THE BROWS   509 MILTON 24   70
OF MORNING
AND AS IT IS VALUED SO DOES SOCIETY FLOURISH OR DECAY .   587A CHAUCER 1   PROSE
EMPIRES FLOURISH TILL THEY BECOME COMMERCIAL . . . . .   594A PUB ADDRESS/N   PROSE
A LAST JUDGMENT IS NECESSARY BECAUSE FOOLS FLOURISH . .   612B V LAST JUDG/N   PROSE
NATIONS FLOURISH UNDER WISE RULERS . . . .   612C V LAST JUDG/N   PROSE
NATIONS ARE DESTROYD OR FLOURISH IN PROPORTION AS THEIR   621D JERUSALEM 3   PROSE
POETRY PAINTING AND MUSIC ARE DESTROYD OR FLOURISH . .   621D JERUSALEM 3   PROSE

FLOURISHD

AND MANY DAUGHTERS FLOURISHD ROUND THE HOLY TENT OF MAN   326 FOUR ZOAS 7   252
WHERE ONCE THE OLIVE FLOURISHD & THE CEDAR SPREAD HIS WINGS   354 FOUR ZOAS 8   * 535

FLOURISHES

FLOURISHES THAT HE MAY RECIEVE THE GRAPES THRO ONE CAN LOOK   237 EUROPE INTRO   3
ART IN LONDON FLOURISHES ENGRAVERS IN PARTICULAR ARE WANTED   829D LETTER 30   PROSE

FLOURISHING

WITH JOY THY RUDDY LIMBS AND FLOURISHING HAIR . . . . .   1 TO SUMMER/PS   6
. . . NOR IN CRUELTY BRUISE THE MILD FLOURISHING MOUNTAINS   134 FRENCH REVOLTN   5
O HOW DELICIOUS ARE THE GRAPES FLOURISHING IN THE SUN . .   369 FOUR ZOAS 9   447
OVER HER BEAUTIFUL FEMALE FEATURES SOFT FLOURISHING IN   709 JERUSALEM 70   23
BEAUTY

FLOW

AND BLOOD SHALL FLOW LIKE STREAMS ACROSS THE MEADOWS . .   31 EDW THIRD/PS 5   54
TILL INTO THE HIGH DOME OF PAUL'S THEY LIKE THAMES' WATERS   59 HOLY THURS/IM   4
FLOW
SHALL FLOW WITH TEARS OF GOLD . . . .   119 NIGHT/SI   34
TILL INTO THE HIGH DOME OF PAUL'S THEY LIKE THAMES WATERS   121 HOLY THURS/SI   4
FLOW
ON PESTILENT VAPOURS AROUND HIM FLOW . . . .   146 FRENCH REVOLTN   274
NEAR WHERE THE DIRTY THAMES DOES FLOW . . . .   170 LONDON/N   2
NEAR WHERE THE CHARTERD THAMES DOES FLOW . . . . . .   216 LONDON/SE   2
O THEOTORMON ROBBD OF JOY I SEE THY SALT TEARS FLOW . .   244 EUROPE 14   24
THE WONDROUS WORK FLOW FORTH LIKE VISIBLE OUT OF   287 FOUR ZOAS 2   260
THE INVISIBLE
FLOW DOWN INTO THE SEA & SLUMBER IN OBLIVION AH ENION .   298 FOUR ZOAS 4   23
FLOW INTO RIVERS OF DELIGHT THERE THE SPONTANEOUS FLOWERS   308 FOUR ZOAS 5   132
FLOW ON YE GENTLE AIRS & BEAR THE VOICE OF MY REJOICING   368 FOUR ZOAS 9   435
AND MURMURING IN THEIR CHANNELS FLOW & CIRCLE ROUND HIS   378 FOUR ZOAS 9   805
FEET
HIS EYE WAS DRY NO TEAR COULD FLOW . . . .   419 I SAW A MONK/N   23
[FROM HIS DRY TONGUE THESE ACCENTS FLOW] . . . . . .   419 I SAW A MONK/N *   25
THEY CRY & TEARS FOR EVER FLOW . . . .   421 BENEATH/N   5
THEY CRY & TEARS FOR EVER FLOW . . . .   424 THE GOLDEN NET   4
HIS EYE WAS DRY NO TEAR COULD FLOW . . . .   430 GREY MONK   9
HE VIEWS JERUSALEM & BABYLON HIS TEARS FLOW DOWN . . . .   531 MILTON 39   48
BUT STILL I LABOUR IN HOPE THO STILL MY TEARS FLOW DOWN   628 JERUSALEM 9   28

		PAGE	TITLE	LINE

FLOW   (CONTINUED)
        THE RIVER OF LIFE TO FLOW AGAINST MY WALLS & AMONG MY TREES   660 JERUSALEM 33   38
        TO FLOW WITH MILK & WINE THO THOU SEEST ME NOT A SEASON   696 JERUSALEM 62   26
        WHOSE CURRENTS FLOW INTO THE DEAD SEA BY SODOM & GOMORRA   735 JERUSALEM 89   27
FLOWD
        FLOWD HIS GOLDEN HAIR   114 LIT GRL FND/SI   39
        THE OINTMENT FLOWD DOWN ON THE VOID . . . .   251 AHANIA 3   49
        WHEN HIS NERVES OF JOY MELTED & FLOWD . . . .   252 AHANIA 4   13
        FLOWD AROUND THE IMMENSE LOS BEHELD . . . .   259 BOOK OF LOS 5   12
        THE LIGHT THAT FLOWD DOWN ON THE WINDS . . . .   260 BOOK OF LOS 5   28
        [SO SAYING] IN TORMENT HE SUNK DOWN & FLOWD AMONG HER FILMY   266 FOUR ZOAS 1   77
          WOOF
        NOW HE RESOLVD TO DESTROY LOS & NOW HIS TEARS FLOWD DOWN   298 FOUR ZOAS 4   47
        HE THREW HIS FLIGHT THRO THE DARK AIR TO WHERE A RIVER   311 FOUR ZOAS 6   2
          FLOWD
        INTO THE DOLEFUL VALES WHERE NO TREE GREW NOR RIVER FLOWD   319 FOUR ZOAS 6   284
        FROM THY SWEET LOINS OF BLISS RED FLOWD THY BLOOD . . .   325 FOUR ZOAS 7   226
        OF SWEET ETERNITY THE BLOOD FLOWD ROUND THE HOLY TENT &   326 FOUR ZOAS 7   257
          RIVN
        FROM EAST TO WEST FLOWD LIKE THE HUMAN VEINS IN RIVERS . .   337 FOUR ZOAS 7B   160
        AND ENITHARMON PALE & COLD IN MILKY JUICES FLOWD . . . .   353 FOUR ZOAS 8   474
        THE BLOOD OF LIFE FLOWD PLENTIFUL ODORS OF LIFE AROSE . .   376 FOUR ZOAS 9   726
        WHERE THE WIDE WOOF FLOWD DOWN . . . .   378 FOUR ZOAS 9   784
        NOW LEUTHA CEASD TEARS FLOWD BUT THE DIVINE PITY SUPPORTED   493 MILTON 13   7
          HER
        FLOWD INTO THE ACHING FIBRES OF LOS YET CONTENDING AGAINST   733 JERUSALEM 88   29
          HIM
        EXPANSIVE NOSTRILS WEST FLOWD THE PARENT SENSE THE TONGUE   745 JERUSALEM 98   17
          NORTH STOOD
FLOWED
        AND HIS TEARS FLOWED DOWN ON THE WINDS . . . .   235 URIZEN 25   4
        THEN MARY BURST FORTH INTO A SONG SHE FLOWED LIKE A RIVER   695 JERUSALEM 61   28
          OF
FLOWER   SEE SUN-FLOWER,WALL-FLOWER,FLOWR
        ON EVERY FLOWER THAT SHUTS ITS SWEET EYES . . . . .   3 EVNING STAR/PS   7
        MY LORD WAS LIKE A FLOWER UPON THE BROWS . . . . . .   5 FAIR ELENOR/PS   41
        OF LUSTY MAY AH LIFE AS FRAIL AS FLOWER . . . .   5 FAIR ELENOR/PS   42
        WITH HER PURE QUILL ON EVERY FLOWER WRITETH WISDOM'S NAME   36D CONTEMPLATN/PS   PROSE
        IT IS A FLOWER THAT GROWS IN EVERY VALE . . . . . .   37A CONTEMPLATN/PS   PROSE
        THE FLOWER WAS PLUCKD & YET IT WAS NOT BLOWN . . . . .   43C WOE CRIED MUSE   PROSE
        THE MOON LIKE A FLOWER   118 NIGHT/SI   5
        SAYING REJOICE THOU HUMBLE GRASS THOU NEW-BORN LILLY FLOWER   127 BOOK OF THEL 1   21
        TO CREATE A LITTLE FLOWER IS THE LABOUR OF AGES . . . .   152C MARRIAGE HH 9   PROSE
        A FLOWER WAS OFFERD TO ME . . . .   161 ROSE TREE/N   1
        SUCH A FLOWER AS MAY NEVER BORE . . . .   161 ROSE TREE/N   2
        AND I PASSED THE SWEET FLOWER OER . . . .   161 ROSE TREE/N   4
        AND MANY A LOVELY FLOWER & TREE . . . .   167 INFANT SORW/N   23
        I HEARD A WILD [THISTLE] FLOWER . . . .   175 WILD FLOWERS/N   3
        BEFORE MY FLOWER OF LOVE WAS LOST . . . .   184 O I CANNOT/N   4
        I PLUCKED LEUTHA'S FLOWER   189 ARGUMENT V DAU   5
        ART THOU A FLOWER ART THOU A NYMPH I SEE THEE NOW A FLOWER   189 V DAU ALBION 1   6
        THE GOLDEN NYMPH REPLIED PLUCK THOU MY FLOWER OOTHOON THE   189 V DAU ALBION 1   8
          MILD
        ANOTHER FLOWER SHALL SPRING BECAUSE THE SOUL OF SWEET   189 V DAU ALBION 1   9
          DELIGHT
        THEN OOTHOON PLUCKD THE FLOWER SAYING I PLUCK THEE FROM   189 V DAU ALBION 1   11
          THY BED
        SWEET FLOWER AND PUT THEE HERE TO GLOW BETWEEN MY BREASTS   189 V DAU ALBION 1   12
        A FLOWER WAS OFFERD TO ME . . . .   215 ROSE TREE/SE   1
        SUCH A FLOWER AS MAY NEVER BORE . . . .   215 ROSE TREE/SE   2
        AND I PASSED THE SWEET FLOWER OER . . . .   215 ROSE TREE/SE   4
        WILD FLOWERS I GATHERD & HE SHEWD ME EACH ETERNAL FLOWER   238 EUROPE INTRO   20
        FLOWER OF MORNING I WEEP ON THE VERGE . . . . . .   254 AHANIA 4   53
        SOMETIMES I THINK THOU ART A FLOWER EXPANDING . . . .   265 FOUR ZOAS 1   59
        I SIEZD THEE BEAUTEOUS LUVAH THOU ART FADED LIKE A FLOWER   311 FOUR ZOAS 5   226
        AS THE SEED WAITS EAGERLY WATCHING FOR ITS FLOWER & FRUIT   355 FOUR ZOAS 8   * 558
        AND EVERY FLOWER & EVERY LEAF REJOICES IN HIS LIGHT . .   367 FOUR ZOAS 9   407
        ALAS AM I BUT AS A FLOWER THEN WILL I SIT ME DOWN . . .   368 FOUR ZOAS 9   410
        A LITTLE FLOWER GREW IN A LONELY VALE . . . . . .   414 TO MRS FLAXMAN   1
        ALIGHTED WHERE THIS LITTLE FLOWER WAS . . . . . .   414 TO MRS FLAXMAN   6
        AND TOOK THE FLOWER UP IN ITS NATIVE CLOD . . . . .   414 TO MRS FLAXMAN   8
        AND A HEAVEN IN A WILD FLOWER . . . .   431 AUGURIES   2
        OF THE FLOWER OF THE ENGLISH NOBILITY & GENTRY [A SOCIETY]   446A ANNO REYNOLDS   * MARG
        AND COMES FORTH IN THE MAJESTY OF BEAUTY EVERY FLOWER .   520 MILTON 31   58
        AND FLOWER & HERB SOON FILL THE AIR WITH AN INNUMERABLE   521 MILTON 31   61
          DANCE
        THE VEGETATIVE UNIVERSE OPENS LIKE A FLOWER FROM   633 JERUSALEM 13   34
          THE EARTH'S CENTER
        THE TREE THE PLANT THE FLOWER THE ROCK THE STONE THE METAL   713 JERUSALEM 73   20
        & IS PLANTED LIKE THE SEED OF A WILD FLOWER AMONG OUR WHEAT   716D JERUSALEM 77   PROSE
        THIS SONG TO THE FLOWER OF FLAXMAN'S JOY . . . . .   800 MRS FLAXMAN/L   1
        "SWEET ROSE FAIR FLOWER UNTIMELY PLUCKD SOON FADED"   SUPP LEGEND/N83   *
          (SHAKESPEARE)
FLOWER'S
        THE WILD FLOWER'S SONG . . . .   175B WILD FLOWERS/N   TITLE
FLOWERS
        SING NOW THE LUSTY SONG OF FRUITS AND FLOWERS . . . .   2 TO AUTUMN/PS   6
        AND FEATHERD CLOUDS STREW FLOWERS ROUND HER HEAD . . .   2 TO AUTUMN/PS   12
        WHEN WESTERN WINDS CREEP SOFTLY OER THE FLOWERS . . .   5 FAIR ELENOR/PS   48
        I AM CLAD IN FLOWERS FAIR . . . .   7 LOVE HARMNY/PS   10
        FLOWERS OF HEAVEN'S GROWTH OVER THE BANQUET-TABLE . . .   30 EDW THIRD/PS 5   32
        THE FLOWERS OF IMMORTALITY ARE BLOWN . . . .   31 EDW THIRD/PS 5   36

	PAGE	TITLE	LINE

FLOWERS   (CONTINUED)
```
    O WHAT A MULTITUDE THEY SEEMD THESE FLOWERS OF LONDON TOWN     59 HOLY THURS/IM        5
    PLAYING WITH FLOWERS & RUNNING AFTER BIRDS THEY SPENT THE      100 TIRIEL 2             8
      DAY
    CONSUMING ALL BOTH FLOWERS & FRUITS INSECTS & WARBLING         110 TIRIEL 8            38
      BIRDS
    O WHAT A MULTITUDE THEY SEEMD THESE FLOWERS OF LONDON TOWN     122 HOLY THURS/SI        5
    AND FLOWERS AND TREES AND BEASTS AND MEN RECIEVE  . . . .      125 LIT BLK BOY/SI      11
    HE CROPS THY FLOWERS WHILE THOU SITTEST SMILING IN HIS FACE    128 BOOK OF THEL 2       6
    UNSEEN DESCENDING WEIGH MY LIGHT WINGS UPON BALMY FLOWERS      128 BOOK OF THEL 3      12
    BUT WALK UNITED BEARING FOOD TO ALL OUR TENDER FLOWERS  . .    128 BOOK OF THEL 3      16
    FOR I WALK THROUGH THE VALES OF HAR AND SMELL THE SWEETEST     129 BOOK OF THEL 3 *    18
      FLOWERS
    BUT I FEED NOT THE LITTLE FLOWERS I HEAR THE WARBLING BIRDS    129 BOOK OF THEL 3      19
    THAT SO MANY SWEET FLOWERS BORE  . . . . . . . . .             162 GARDEN LOVE/N        8
    AND TOMB-STONES WHERE FLOWERS SHOULD BE . . . . . . .          163 GARDEN LOVE/N       10
    ALONG THE VALES OF LEUTHA SEEKING FLOWERS TO COMFORT HER       189 V DAU ALBION 1       4
    THAT SO MANY SWEET FLOWERS BORE     . . . . . . . . .          215 GARDEN LOVE/SE       8
    AND TOMB-STONES WHERE FLOWERS SHOULD BE . . . . . . .          215 GARDEN LOVE/SE      10
    HE LAUGHING ANSWERD I WILL WRITE A BOOK ON LEAVES              237 EUROPE INTRO        14
      OF FLOWERS
    WILD FLOWERS I GATHERD & HE SHEWD ME EACH ETERNAL FLOWER       238 EUROPE INTRO        20
    WITH PURPLE FLOWERS AND BERRIES RED IMAGE OF THAT SWEET        241 EUROPE 10           27
      SOUTH
    SOFT SOUL OF FLOWERS LEUTHA . . . . . . . . . .                244 EUROPE 14           11
    I HEARD HIS VOICE AMONG THE BRANCHES & AMONG SWEET FLOWERS     271 FOUR ZOAS 1        267
    AT WILL TO MURMUR IN THE FLOWERS SMALL AS THE HONEY BEE        288 FOUR ZOAS 2        297
    . . . & OUR CHILDREN BRING FRUITS & FLOWERS   . . . . .        291 FOUR ZOAS 2        413
    FLOW INTO RIVERS OF DELIGHT THERE THE SPONTANEOUS FLOWERS      308 FOUR ZOAS 5        132
    AND WALKED IN THE SILENT NIGHT AMONG SWEET SMELLING FLOWERS    310 FOUR ZOAS 5        203
    AMONG THE FLOWERS OF BEULAH WALKD THE ETERNAL MAN & SAW        326 FOUR ZOAS 7        239
    ROUND BEULAH THERE HE REVELD IN DELIGHT AMONG THE FLOWERS      326 FOUR ZOAS 7        243
    IN FLOWERS IN FRUITS IN FISHES BIRDS & BEASTS & CLOUDS         367 FOUR ZOAS 9        378
      & WATERS
    SHE RISES AMONG FLOWERS & LOOKS TOWARD THE EASTERN             367 FOUR ZOAS 9        390
      CLEARNESS
    THE FRUIT SHALL RIPEN & FALL DOWN & THE FLOWERS CONSUME        368 FOUR ZOAS 9        420
      AWAY
    AND THOU SWEET SMELLING GROUND PUT FORTH THY LIFE IN FRUITS    368 FOUR ZOAS 9        437
      & FLOWERS
    SHE BORE THE FRUITS IN HER LAP SHE GATHERD FLOWERS FOR         369 FOUR ZOAS 9        477
      HER BOSOM
    AND ENION SANG AMONG THE FLOWERS THAT GREW AMONG THE TREES     371 FOUR ZOAS 9        536
    WHEN INFANT SPRING APPEARS IN SWELLING BUDS & OPENING          371 FOUR ZOAS 9        548
      FLOWERS
    AMONG THE FLOWERS OF BEULAH IN HIS SELFISH COLD REPOSE  . .    374 FOUR ZOAS 9        628
    AND THE HERBS & FLOWERS & FURNITURE & BEDS & CHAMBERS  . .     512 MILTON 26           34
    THOU PERCIEVEST THE FLOWERS PUT FORTH THEIR PRECIOUS ODOURS    520 MILTON 31           46
    ON COUCHES SOFT WITH MILD MUSIC TENDED BY FLOWERS OF BEULAH    523 MILTON 34           10
    SURROUNDED BY THE SPIRITS OF THE HERBS & FLOWERS  . . . .      619C ILLUS MILTON      PROSE
    SHILOH THE MASCULINE EMANATION AMONG THE FLOWERS OF BEULAH     680 JERUSALEM 49        47
    AMONG THE FLOWERS OF BEULAH STILL RETAIN HIS AWFUL STRENGTH    686 JERUSALEM 55         2
    SUCH AS THE FLOWERS OF BEULAH WEAVE TO BE THEIR FUNERAL        736 JERUSALEM 90         7
      MANTLES
    AWAKING IT TO LIFE AMONG THE FLOWERS OF BEULAH REJOICING       745 JERUSALEM 98        21
      IN UNITY
FLOWERY
    FIRST EER THE MORNING BREAKS JOY OPENS IN THE FLOWERY          520 MILTON 31           50
      BOSOMS
    [MOULD] [GROUND] FLOWERY MOULD INTO THE GREEN FIELDS OF        609D V LAST JUDG/N     *PROSE
    & THE HOURS SUCKLING THEIR FLOWERY INFANTS . . . . . .         SUPP ILLUS GRAY        *TITLE
FLOWING
    HEAR YE THE VOICE OF BRUTUS THE FLOWING WAVES  . . . .          32 EDW THIRD/PS 6      39
    TO THIS DEEP VALLEY SITUATED BY THE FLOWING THAMES  . . .      204 AMERICA CANC B       8
    THE THIN FLOWING ROUND THE FIERCE FIRES . . . . . . .          259 BOOK OF LOS 5        8
    FLOWING DOWN INTO NIGHT TILL A FORM   . . . . . . .            260 BOOK OF LOS 5       55
    WITH FADED RADIANCE SIGHD FORGETFUL OF THE FLOWING WINE        276 FOUR ZOAS 1        437
    WAVE FRESHLY CLEAR WATERS FLOWING AROUND THE TENDER GRASS      368 FOUR ZOAS 9        436
    THE ETERNAL CREATION FLOWING FROM THE DIVINE HUMANITY   .      444C LAST JUDGMNT/L    PROSE
    OF CRYSTAL FLOWING INTO TWO STREAMS ONE FLOWS THRO            526 MILTON 35           50
      GOLGONOOZA
    ITS PITS & DECLIVITIES FLOWING WITH MOLTEN ORE & FOUNTAINS     529 MILTON 38           18
    DOWN FLOWING INTO ENTUTHON'S VALES GLISTENS WITH              728 JERUSALEM 83        74
      SOFT AFFECTIONS
    FOUNTAINS OF LIVING WATERS FLOWING FROM THE HUMANITY DIVINE    744 JERUSALEM 96        37
FLOWR
    SEEKST THOU THAT FLOWR TO DECK THY HORRID TEMPLES   . . .        5 FAIR ELENOR/PS      44
    AND THESE FAIR YOUTHS THE FLOWR OF ENGLAND . . . . . .          18 EDW THIRD/PS 1      17
FLOWS
    FLOWS BEFORE THE STEPS OF THE THRONE ON WHICH [ARE] IS SEEN    443C LAST JUDGMNT/L    *PROSE
    OF CRYSTAL FLOWING INTO TWO STREAMS ONE FLOWS THRO            526 MILTON 35           50
      GOLGONOOZA
    THE OTHER FLOWS THRO THE AERIAL VOID & ALL THE CHURCHES        526 MILTON 35           52
    FROM IT FLOWS ON EACH SIDE [OF] THE RIVER OF LIFE   . . .      613B V LAST JUDG/N     *PROSE
FLUCTUATING
    AND FLUCTUATING ALL BENEATH IN EDDIES OF MOLTEN FLUID   .      301 FOUR ZOAS 4       164
    FORMING THE FLUCTUATING GLOBE ACCORDING TO THEIR WILL   . .    727 JERUSALEM 83        34
    BE SEEN UPON THE FLUCTUATING EARTH WOVEN BY THE SISTERS        728 JERUSALEM 83        39
FLUCTUATION
    FOR A SOLID WITHOUT FLUCTUATION    . . . . . . . . .           224 URIZEN 4            11
    WITHOUT FLUCTUATION HARD AS ADAMANT   . . . . . . . .          257 BOOK OF LOS 4        5
    A VAST SOLID WITHOUT FLUCTUATION  . . . . . . . . .            257 BOOK OF LOS 4        9
```

		PAGE	TITLE	LINE

FLUENTLY
    I READ GREEK AS FLUENTLY AS AN OXFORD SCHOLAR & . . . . 821D LETTER 25   PROSE
FLUID
    SULPHUREOUS FLUID HIS PHANTASIES . . . . 227 URIZEN 10   14
    IN A STIFLING BLACK FLUID HE WOKE . . . . 258 BOOK OF LOS 4   62
    BEAMS CONDUCTED BY FLUID SO PURE . . . . 259 BOOK OF LOS 5   11
    ROARING LET OUT THE FLUID THE MOLTEN METAL RAN IN CHANNELS 283 FOUR ZOAS 2   118
    AND FLUCTUATING ALL BENEATH IN EDDIES OF MOLTEN FLUID . . 301 FOUR ZOAS 4   164
    A BLUE FLUID EXUDED IN SINEWS HARDENING IN THE ABYSS . . 483 MILTON 3   35
    TO MILTON'S BRAIN THE ICY FLUID FROM HIS BROAD COLD PALM . 500 MILTON 19   9
FLUIDS
    RAGING AROUND & MELTING THE METALS INTO LIVING FLUIDS . . 155A MARRIAGE HH 15 PROSE
FLUNG
    THEN I FLUNG MYSELF WITH HIM DIRECTLY INTO THE BODY OF   156D MARRIAGE HH 17   PROSE
        THE SUN
FLUSH
    THE FLUSH OF HEALTH IN FLESH EXPOSED TO THE OPEN AIR . . 580D DESC CAT 5   PROSE
FLUTE
    HER MARINERS SHALL USE THE FLUTE AND VIOL . . . . . . 31 EDW THIRD/PS 5   59
    SOUND THE FLUTE . . . . 123 SPRING/SI   1
    INNUMERABLE THE GINS & TRAPS & MANY A SOOTHING FLUTE . . 284 FOUR ZOAS 2   160
    BUT THE SOFT PIPE THE FLUTE THE VIOL ORGAN HARP & CYMBAL 306 FOUR ZOAS 5   23
    THE TRUMPET FITTED TO THE BATTLE & THE FLUTE OF SUMMER . 337 FOUR ZOAS 7B   173
    [THE HARD DENTANT HAMMERS ARE LULLD BY THE FLUTE LULA LULA 346 FOUR ZOAS 8   * 203
    ]
    TO RAVISHING MELODY OF FLUTE & HARPS & SOFTEST VOICE . . 366 FOUR ZOAS 9   336
    OF FLUTE & HARP & DRUM & TRUMPET HORN & CLARION . . . . 372 FOUR ZOAS 9   586
    REPLY TO VIOLINS & TABORS TO THE PIPE FLUTE LYRE & CYMBAL 376 FOUR ZOAS 9   721
    DISPLAYING NAKED BEAUTY WITH FLUTE & HARP & SONG . . . . 484 MILTON 4   28
    WITH FLUTE & CLARION WITH CUPS & MEASURES FILLD WITH   511 MILTON 25   69
        FOAMING WINE
    . . . & THE FLUTE OF SUMMER IN ANNANDALE . . . . . . 700 JERUSALEM 65   15
    THEY SIEZD THE HARP THE FLUTE THE MELLOW HORN OF   721 JERUSALEM 79   49
        JERUSALEM'S JOY
    & HIS FLUTE HEARD FROM HIS SECRET FORESTS CHEARS US TO . . 791C LETTER 3   PROSE
    AND HEAVY THE GERMAN FLUTE COLOUR WHICH WAS USED BY . . . 864C LETTER 61   PROSE
FLUTED
    STRINGED OR FLUTED TO AMELIORATE THE SORROWS OF SLAVERY   509 MILTON 24   61
FLUTES
    AND ALL THE ELEMENTS SHALL SERVE THEE TO THEIR SOOTHING   301 FOUR ZOAS 4   153
        FLUTES
    OF MORTAL OR IMMORTAL ARM AND SOFTLY LILLING FLUTES . . . 509 MILTON 24   56
FLUTES'
    THE HARD DENTANT HAMMERS ARE LULLD BY THE FLUTES' LULA LULA 509 MILTON 24   63
FLUTTERD
    THE SHAPES SCREAMING FLUTTERD VAIN . . . . 253 AHANIA 4   31
FLUTTERING
    THE BEGGAR'S RAGS FLUTTERING IN AIR . . . . 432 AUGURIES   75
FLUXILE
    IN DELUGE OER THE EARTH-BORN MAN THEN TURND THE FLUXILE   241 EUROPE 10   11
        EYES
    DOWNWARD & YOUR FLUXILE EYES ENGLOBD ROLL ROUND IN FEAR   294 FOUR ZOAS 3   87
    DOWNWARD AND YOUR FLUXILE EYES ENGLOBD ROLL ROUND IN FEAR 655 JERUSALEM 29   68
FLUXIONS
    BY NEWTON'S DOCTRINE OF THE FLUXIONS OF AN ATOM A THING   878A LETTER 88   PROSE
        THAT
FLY
    THE PATHLESS PLAIN AS THE ARROWS THAT FLY . . . . . . 5 FAIR ELENOR/PS   34
    WHEN PESTILENCE DOES FLY . . . . 12 GWIN KING/PS   56
    OVER THE FIELD DOTH FLY . . . . 13 GWIN KING/PS   80
    AND OER THE SURFACE OF THE SILENT DEEP DOST FLY . . . . 15 IMIT SPEN/PS   26
    THAT ROUND THE CIRCLE OF THE WORLD WOUD FLY . . . . . 15 IMIT SPEN/PS   36
    AND SEE THE WINGED LIGHTNINGS AS THEY FLY . . . . . . 15 IMIT SPEN/PS   * 41
    HIS NATIVE SHORE AND SEES COMMERCE FLY ROUND . . . . . 19 EDW THIRD/PS 2   9
    HE SAW THE PESTILENCE FLY OUT OF THE BOTTLE & CRIED OUT   58D ISLAND MOON 10   PROSE
    BESIDES IN THE SKY THE LITTLE BIRDS FLY . . . . 60 NURSES SONG/IM   12
    BESIDES IN THE SKY THE LITTLE BIRDS FLY . . . . 121 NURSES SONG/SI   11
    BUT I FEED NOT THE WARBLING BIRDS THEY FLY AND SEEK THEIR 129 BOOK OF THEL 3   20
        FOOD
    WHY DOST THOU NOT FLY AMONG THE CORN FIELDS . . . . . 168 O LAPWING/N   3
    AND THE CATTERPILLER & FLY . . . . 174 HUMAN IMAGE/N   16
    LITTLE FLY . . . . 183 THE FLY/N   5
    A FLY LIKE THEE . . . . 183 THE FLY/N   14
    A HAPPY FLY . . . . 183 THE FLY/N   22
    [FROM STREET TO STREET TO FLY] . . . . 185 LET BROTHELS/N   34
    OR DOES THE FLY REJOICE BECAUSE THE HARVEST IS BROUGHT IN 193 V DAU ALBION 5   38
    IN VAIN THE DREAMER GRASPS THE JOYFUL IMAGES THEY FLY . 206 THIRALATHA   2
    THE FLY . . . . 213B THE FLY/SE   TITLE
    LITTLE FLY . . . . 213 THE FLY/SE   1
    A FLY LIKE THEE . . . . 213 THE FLY/SE   6
    A HAPPY FLY . . . . 213 THE FLY/SE   18
    AND THE CATTERPILLER AND FLY . . . . 217 HUMAN ABSTR/SE   15
    OR TO FALL OR TO SWIM OR TO FLY . . . . 258 BOOK OF LOS 4   52
    TEACH THESE SOULS TO FLY (PLATE II URIZEN) . . . . . 262A SMALL BK DSGNS   TITLE
    LUVAH AND VALA [WAKE] WOKE & [FLY] FLEW UP FROM THE HUMAN 271 FOUR ZOAS 1   * 262
        HEART
    THE SPIDER SITS IN HIS LABOURD WEB EAGER WATCHING FOR THE 277 FOUR ZOAS 1   457
        FLY
    DO THEY NOT FLY INTO THEIR STATIONS & RETURN THEIR LIGHT   291 FOUR ZOAS 3   7
        TO THEE
    SETTLED LIKE BATS INNUMERABLE READY TO FLY ABROAD . . . 306 FOUR ZOAS 5   35
    DRINK LAUGH & SING THE GRASSHOPPER THE EMMET & THE FLY . . 308 FOUR ZOAS 5   * 133

		PAGE	TITLE	LINE

FLY (CONTINUED)

HOWLING & WAILING FLY THE SOULS FROM URIZEN'S STRONG HAND — 365 FOUR ZOAS 9 — 323

WEEPING & WAILING FLY THE SOULS FROM URIZEN'S STRONG HAND — 365 FOUR ZOAS 9 — * 332

THAT SING & FLY IN THE BRIGHT AIR BUT YOU DO LICK MY FEET — 368 FOUR ZOAS 9 — 431

FROM THE STONE & THE ARMED FLY SPRINGS FROM THE ROCKY CREVICE — 373 FOUR ZOAS 9 — 607

I WILL FLY & THOU PURSUE . . . . — 416 MY SPECTRE/N — 57

HE COME ON WINGS OF JOY WE'LL FLY . . . . — 423 THE BIRDS/N — 17

THE WANTON BOY THAT KILLS THE FLY . . . . — 431 AUGURIES — 33

SEEST THOU THE LITTLE WINGED FLY SMALLER THAN A GRAIN OF SAND — 502 MILTON 20 — 27

THAT THE WIDE WORLD MIGHT FLY FROM ITS HINGES & THE IMMORTAL MANSION — 667 JERUSALEM 40 — 27

THE SCORND AND CONTEMND YOUTHFUL GIRL WHERE SHALL SHE FLY — 727 JERUSALEM 83 — 8

WITH EVERY COLOUR LION TYGER HORSE ELEPHANT EAGLE DOVE FLY WORM — 746 JERUSALEM 98 — 43

EARTH'S ANSWER NURSE'S SONG THE FLY THE TYGER . . . . — SUPP LETTER 66A — *PROSE

FLY BLOWS

A FLOGGING MAGISTRATE I HAVE SEEN MANY SUCH FLY BLOWS OF BACON — 400D ANNO BACON — MARG

FLYING

AND BANNERS FLYING . . . . — 62 CROWND KING/IM — 4

DRAW IN THE OCEAN DOES HIS EYE DISCERN THE FLYING CLOUD — 193 V DAU ALBION 5 — 35

HIS GLOOMY WAY BEFORE HIM THARMAS FLED & FLYING FOUGHT . . — 313 FOUR ZOAS 6 — 54

FLYING AWAY FROM URIZEN THAT HE MIGHT NOT GIVE HIM FOOD — 318 FOUR ZOAS 6 — 274

STAMPING THE HILLS WADING OR SWIMMING FLYING FURIOUS OR FALLING — 339 FOUR ZOAS 7B — 263

WALKING ON MOUNTAINS OR FLYING IN THE OPEN EXPANSE OF HEAVEN — 340 FOUR ZOAS 7B — 270

OF WALES & SCOTLAND BEHELD THE DESCENDING WAR THE ROUTED FLYING — 703 JERUSALEM 66 — 60

A BOY FLYING A KITE . . . . — SUPP ILLUS GRAY — *TITLE

FLY'S

OF SAND & HIS PILLARS DUST ON THE FLY'S WING & HIS STARRY — 739 JERUSALEM 91 — 49

FOAM

("SNATCH FOAM DENY STREAM") UNEASY THIS I LAMENT THAT I HAVE DONE — 79D ANNO LAVATER — MARG

THEY DASH LIKE FOAM AGAINST THE RIDGES OF THE ARMY . . . — 146 FRENCH REVOLTN — 277

& RED GILLS HANG JUST ABOVE THE RAGING FOAM . . . . . — 156C MARRIAGE HH 17 — PROSE

AND THE SULPHUREOUS FOAM SURGEING THICK . . . . . . — 227 URIZEN 10 — 21

SURGE FOAM AND LABOUR INTO LIFE FIRST BORN & FIRST CONSUMD — 238 EUROPE PREL 1 — 9

ROUND & ROUND & THE SULPHUREOUS FOAM SURGEING THICK . . — 303 FOUR ZOAS 4 — 209

FOAMD

AND NOW THE HUMAN BLOOD FOAMD HIGH I SAW THAT LUVAH & VALA — 294 FOUR ZOAS 3 — 94

THE SEA THAT ROLLD & FOAMD WITH DARKNESS & THE SHADOWS OF DEATH — 378 FOUR ZOAS 9 — 802

AND NOW THE HUMAN BLOOD FOAMD HIGH THE SPIRITS LUVAH & VALA — 655 JERUSALEM 29 — 73

AND FIRE JERUSALEM TOOK THE CUP WHICH FOAMD IN VALA'S HAND — 734 JERUSALEM 88 — 56

FOAMING

HER SHIPS SHALL SING ACROSS THE FOAMING SEA . . . . . — 31 EDW THIRD/PS 5 — 58

ON A ROCK OF IRON FROWNING OVER THE FOAMING FIRES OF ORC — 321 FOUR ZOAS 7 — 41

OF FOAMING BLOOD BENEATH THE BLACK INCESSANT SKY TILL ALL — 359 FOUR ZOAS 9 — 78

THE DAUGHTERS OF URIZEN STAND WITH CUPS & MEASURES OF FOAMING WINE — 365 FOUR ZOAS 9 — 333

WITH FLUTE & CLARION WITH CUPS & MEASURES FILLD WITH FOAMING WINE — 511 MILTON 25 — 69

AND WASHD INCESSANT BY THE FOR-EVER RESTLESS SEA-WAVES FOAMING ABROAD — 741 JERUSALEM 94 — 6

FOAMY

HIS BILLOWS ROLL WHERE MONSTERS WANDER IN THE FOAMY PATHS — 286 FOUR ZOAS 2 — 257

FOE

I WAS ANGRY WITH MY FOE . . . . — 165 CHRISTN FORB/N — 3

[AND I GAVE IT TO MY FOE] . . . . — 165 CHRISTN FORB/N — 11

AND MY FOE BEHELD IT SHINE . . . . — 165 CHRISTN FORB/N — 12

MY FOE OUTSTRETCHD BENEATH THE TREE . . . . — 166 CHRISTN FORB/N — 17

I WAS ANGRY WITH MY FOE . . . . — 218 POISON TREE/SE — 3

AND MY FOE BEHELD IT SHINE . . . . — 218 POISON TREE/SE — 11

MY FOE OUTSTRETCHD BENEATH THE TREE . . . . — 218 POISON TREE/SE — 16

MIRTH AT THE ERRORS OF A FOE . . . . — 538 WAS I ANGRY/N — 9

I FIND THEM THE ERRORS OF THE FOE . . . . — 538 ANGER WRATH/N — 4

[AND COUNTS IT COURAGE THUS TO PRAISE HIS FOE] . . . . — 539 SIR JOSH MIC/N — 2

TIS CHRISTIAN MILDNESS WHEN [FOOLS] KNAVES PRAISE A FOE — 539 SIR JOSH MIC/N — 4

I PROFESS NOT GENEROSITY TO A FOE . . . . — 541 HOMERS HERO/N — 2

TO SEEK TO TURN A MADMAN TO A FOE . . . . — 544 F(LAXMAN)/N 2 — 2

FOES

IVE GIVEN GREAT PROVISION TO MY FOES . . . . — 555 BLAKES APL/N 1 — 22

SOME SAY IVE GIVEN GREAT PROVISION TO MY FOES . . . . — 556 BLAKES APL/N 2 — 11

FOG

AND WHEN THE SHAKING CEAST A FOG POSSEST THE ACCURSED CLIME — 106 TIRIEL 5 — 17

FOGGY

BEHOLD THE FOGGY MORNINGS OF THE DEAD ON ALBION'S CLIFFS — 681 JERUSALEM 50 — 13

FOGS

AS THICK AS NORTHERN FOGS AROUND YOUR GATES TO CHOKE YOU UP — 100 TIRIEL 1 — 44

[XXX] WHERE ART THOU PESTILENCE THAT BATHEST IN FOGS & STANDING LAKES — 106 TIRIEL 5 — * 8

VISIT YOU BUT ETERNAL FOGS HOVER AROUND YOUR WALLS . . . — 106 TIRIEL 5 — 23

. . . IN DARK FOGS LISTNING THE HORROR . . . . — 135 FRENCH REVOLTN — 19

LIKE PESTILENT FOGS ROUND CITIES OF MEN . . . . — 144 FRENCH REVOLTN — 236

FOILED

HOW HE WAS FOILED BY WOMAN'S ARTS . . . . — 37C SAMSON/PS — PROSE

ON THE LEFT HAND APOLLYON IS FOILED BEFORE THE SWORD . . — 612B V LAST JUDG/N — PROSE

725

```
                                                              PAGE      TITLE              LINE
FOLD      SEE FOUR-FOLD,FOUR FOLD,NINE FOLD,ONE FOLD,SEVEN-FOLD,SEVENTY FOLD,
          SIX-FOLD,THREE-FOLD,THREE FOLD,TWELVE-FOLD,TWELVE FOLD,TWENTY-SEVEN-FOLD
          TWENTY-SEVEN/FOLD,TWENTY/SEVEN/FOLD,TWO-FOLD,TWO/FOLD
     AND WALKING ROUND THE FOLD  . . . . . . . . .          119 NIGHT/SI            36
     AS I GUARD OER THE FOLD  . . . . . . . . . . .          119 NIGHT/SI            48
     . . . COLD WAVING THE NOBLES FOLD ROUND THE KING  . . . .   137 FRENCH REVOLTN      65
     THEN THE KING GLOWD HIS NOBLES FOLD ROUND . . . . . . .   137 FRENCH REVOLTN      68
     APPEARD AND SUNK AGAIN THE SCALY FOLD OF A MONSTROUS         156B MARRIAGE HH 17   PROSE
        SERPENT
     ON THE CANADIAN WILDS I FOLD FEEBLE MY SPIRIT FOLDS  . .   196 AMERICA PREL 1     17
     AND FOLD THE SHEETY WATERS AS A MANTLE ROUND MY LIMBS  . .   238 EUROPE PREL 1      13
     DO I NOT STRETCH THE HEAVENS ABROAD OR FOLD THEM UP LIKE    294 FOUR ZOAS 3       107
        A GARMENT
     TWINGE & HIS IRON SINEWS BEND LIKE LEAD & FOLD  . . .     305 FOUR ZOAS 4       294
     THOU DOST RESTRAIN MY FURY THAT THE WORM MAY FOLD THE TREE   323 FOUR ZOAS 7       141
     THE ENDS OF HEAVEN LIKE A GARMENT WILL I FOLD THEM ROUND ME   333 FOUR ZOAS 7B        6
     FOLD WITHOUT FOLD ENCOMPASSES HIM AND HIS CORRUPTING         354 FOUR ZOAS 8       510
        MEMBERS
     THE OCEAN CALM THE CLOUDS FOLD ROUND & FIERY FLAMES OF LOVE   381 FOUR ZOAS AD 2      1
     HE WENT NOT OUT TO THE FIELD NOR FOLD  . . . . . . .      435 WILLIAM BOND        9
     O SHEPHERDESS OF ENGLAND'S FOLD  . . . . . . . . .        442 DEDICATN BLAIR      9
     HIS SNOWS FALL ON ME AND COVER ME WHILE IN THE VEIL I FOLD   646 JERUSALEM 23       35
     OF LABYRINTHINE INTRICACY SO SHALL THEY FOLD THE WORLD  . .   728 JERUSALEM 83       37
     AS A BEAUTIFUL VEIL SO THESE FEMALES SHALL FOLD & UNFOLD    728 JERUSALEM 83       45
     SAYING THIS IS MY FOLD  . . . . . . . . . . . .          805 TO BUTTS/L         61
     THESE ARE GUARDS OF MY FOLD  . . . . . . . . . .          805 TO BUTTS/L         69
FOLDED
     . . . HIS BROWS FOLDED HEAVY HIS FOREHEAD WAS IN AFFLICTION   137 FRENCH REVOLTN      79
     ARE THE LINEN CLOTHES FOLDED UP NOW IS THE DOMINION OF EDOM   149B MARRIAGE HH 3    PROSE
     I SAW A MIGHTY DEVIL FOLDED IN BLACK CLOUDS  . . . . .    150C MARRIAGE HH 6    PROSE
     AND FOLDED HIS BLACK JEALOUS WATERS ROUND THE ADULTERATE    190 V DAU ALBION 2      4
        PAIR
     AND THE FLAME FOLDED ROARING FIERCE WITHIN THE PITCHY NIGHT   200 AMERICA 12         8
     AND THE RED FLAMES OF ORC THAT FOLDED ROARING FIERCE AROUND   201 AMERICA 14        11
     SO LOUD IN THUNDERS SPOKE THE KING FOLDED IN DARK DESPAIR   295 FOUR ZOAS 3       131
     LOS FOLDED ENITHARMON IN A COLD WHITE CLOUD IN FEAR  . . .   308 FOUR ZOAS 5       110
     CLOUDS WOULD HAVE FOLDED ROUND IN EXTACY & LOVE UNITING     329 FOUR ZOAS 7       371
     SHE FOLDED THEM UP IN CARE IN SILENCE & HER BRIGHTNING     366 FOUR ZOAS 9       345
        LIMBS
     THOU RISEST IN THE DEW OF MORNING & AT NIGHT ART FOLDED UP   367 FOUR ZOAS 9       409
     CAN SUCH GROSS LIPS PERCIEVE ALAS FOLDED WITHIN THEMSELVES   485 MILTON 5          36
     GLOWD BUT IN TERRORS FOLDED ROUND HIS CLOUDS OF BLOOD  . .   502 MILTON 20         24
     THE CLOUDS OF OLOLON FOLDED AS A GARMENT DIPPED IN BLOOD    534 MILTON 42         12
     REUBEN SLEPT IN THE CAVE OF ADAM AND LOS FOLDED HIS TONGUE   662 JERUSALEM 36        5
     THEY ARE FOLDED UP ON THE TOP OF HIS WORKSHOP THE REST  . .   834C LETTER 34       PROSE
FOLDING
     FOLDING ROUND THE ROCK & THE CAVE  . . . . . . . .        154D MARRIAGE HH 15   PROSE
     THE RAGING FATHOMLESS ABYSS ANON A SERPENT FOLDING  . . .   196 AMERICA PREL 1     15
     THE WORLD IS SILENT AT THE FLAPPING OF THE FOLDING BANNERS   204 AMERICA CANC B     19
     ROUND ENITHARMON'S LOINS FOLDING  . . . . . . . .        232 URIZEN 19          28
     DESCENDING SHE REPOSD BESIDE HIM FOLDING HIM AROUND  . .   285 FOUR ZOAS 2       202
     AND AS THEY WENT IN FOLDING FIRES & THUNDERS OF THE DEEP    294 FOUR ZOAS 3        98
     AWAKE I HEAR THE FLAPPINGS OF THE FOLDING BANNERS  . . .   336 FOUR ZOAS 7B     *  149
     HIS EYELIDS GIVE THEIR LIGHT AROUND HIS FOLDING TAIL        352 FOUR ZOAS 8       447
        ASPIRES
     FOLDING LIKE SCROLLS OF THE ENORMOUS VOLUME OF HEAVEN &      357 FOUR ZOAS 9        14
        EARTH
     THE BOOKS OF URIZEN UNROLL WITH DREADFUL NOISE THE FOLDING   358 FOUR ZOAS 9        33
        SERPENT
     FOLDS THE TREE OF MYSTERY WENT UP IN FOLDING FLAMES  . . .   359 FOUR ZOAS 9        70
     FOLDING THE PURE WINGS OF HIS MIND SEEKING THE PLACES DARK   374 FOUR ZOAS 9       630
     THE PILLAR OF FOLDING SMOKE AND HE SOUGHT BY OTHER MEANS    625 JERUSALEM 7         5
     AND AS THEY FLED IN FOLDING FIRES & THUNDERS OF THE DEEP    655 JERUSALEM 29       77
     OF AGES & GENERATIONS FOLDING & UNFOLDING IT LIKE A VEIL    698 JERUSALEM 64        3
        OF CHERUBIM
     A WEEPING INFANT IN RUIND LOVELY JERUSALEM'S FOLDING CLOUD   724 JERUSALEM 81       14
     LIKE TO A CURTAIN & FOLDING THEM ACCORDING TO HIS WILL  . .   738 JERUSALEM 91       34
     MOVED BY THE WIND IN VOLUMES OF THICK CLOUD RETURNING        741 JERUSALEM 94        9
        FOLDING ROUND
FOLDS      SEE SHEEP-FOLDS
     JENNY HER SILKEN KERCHIEF FOLDS  . . . . . . . .          16 BLIND-MANS/PS      19
     . . . IN FOLDS OF THE ROBE THE CROWND ADDER BUILDS AND      147 FRENCH REVOLTN     299
        HISSES
     IN THE SHADOWS OF HIS CURTAINS AND IN THE FOLDS OF HIS      194 V DAU ALBION 7      7
        SILENT PILLOW
     THEIR AWFUL FOLDS IN THE DARK AIR SILENT SHE STOOD AS NIGHT   196 AMERICA PREL 1      8
     ON THE CANADIAN WILDS I FOLD FEEBLE MY SPIRIT FOLDS  . . .   196 AMERICA PREL 1     17
     AS WHEN THE THUNDER FOLDS HIMSELF IN THICKEST CLOUDS  . .   320 FOUR ZOAS 7        23
     FOLDS THE TREE OF MYSTERY WENT UP IN FOLDING FLAMES  . . .   359 FOUR ZOAS 9        70
     THE WINTER COMES HE FOLDS HIS SLENDER BONES WITHOUT         377 FOUR ZOAS 9       761
        A MURMUR
     CLOTHD IN THE SERPENT'S FOLDS IN SELFISH HOLINESS DEMANDING   493 MILTON 12         46
        PURITY
     OF LABYRINTHINE INTRICACY TWENTY-SEVEN FOLDS OF OPAKENESS    498 MILTON 17         26
     WINTER COMES HE FOLDS HIS SLENDER BONES WITHOUT A MURMUR    513 MILTON 27         20
     BOUND IN ONE OF THE SERPENT'S FOLDS SURROUNDED BY         606C V LAST JUDG/N   PROSE
        HER FIENDS
     THAT TOWARD EDEN ETERNAL ICE FROZEN IN SEVEN FOLDS  . . .   633 JERUSALEM 13       15
     IN HEAVY WREATHES FOLDS OVER EVERY NATION CRUEL WORKS  . .   636 JERUSALEM 15       17
FOLIO
     ALL IN THREE VOLUMES FOLIO & SELL THEM  . . . . . .       62D ISLAND MOON 11   PROSE
     AMERICA A PROPHECY IN ILLUMINATED PRINTING FOLIO          207D PRSPECTUS 1793  PROSE
        WITH...DESIGNS PRICE
```

	PAGE	TITLE	LINE
FOLIO (CONTINUED)			
SONGS OF EXPERIENCE URIZEN MILTON PRINTS FOLIO QUARTO	867B	LETTER 66	PROSE
OCTAVO			
FOLK			
AMONG THE OLD FOLK	116	ECCHOING GR/SI	14
FOLKS			
ALL THE COUNTRY FOLKS ACOURTING	53	PHEBE DREST/IM	6
FOLLIES			
THERE IS NO END TO THE FOLLIES OF THIS MAN . . .	460B	ANNO REYNOLDS	MARG
LOOKS DOWN ON THEIR LITTLE FOLLIES FROM THE EMPEROR TO	569A	DESC CAT 3	PROSE
THE MILLER			
OF FOLLIES BY ME FOSTERD YOUR PREDICTION WILL I HOPE BE	804A	LETTER 16	PROSE
BUT MUST BEG YOU TO EXCUSE SUCH FOLLIES WHICH THO I AM .	875D	LETTER 82	PROSE
FOLLOGY			
FISSIC FOLLOGY PISTINOLOGY ARIDOLOGY AROGRAPHY	49C	ISLAND MOON 5	PROSE
TRANSMOGRAPHY			
FOLLOW			
FOLLOW IN WILD ARRAY	11	GWIN KING/PS	26
AND WHERE SHE GOES HEAVEN STILL DOTH FOLLOW HER SHE . . .	42A	THEN SHE BORE	PROSE
WHO MARRIED HONOUR THESE FOLLOW HER AROUND THE WORLD . .	43A	THEN SHE BORE	PROSE
FOLLOW NOW THE BEETLE'S HUM	112	A DREAM/SI	19
FOLLOW ME HE SAID	114	LIT GRL FND/SI	41
HE SHALL FOLLOW HIS SHEEP ALL THE DAY	118	SHEPHERD/SI	3
HANDS HEAD BOSOM AND PARTS OF LOVE FOLLOW THEIR HIGH	142	FRENCH REVOLTN	185
BREATHING JOY			
IN FAT OF LAMBS NO MORE I FOLLOW NO MORE OBEDIENCE PAY	200	AMERICA 11	15
THE DAUGHTERS OF BEULAH FOLLOW SLEEPERS	267	FOUR ZOAS 1	99
LIKE THE PALE VISAGE IN ITS SHEET OF LEAD THAT CANNOT	352	FOUR ZOAS 8	433
FOLLOW			
AND ALL THE WHILE THE FLAMES OF ORC FOLLOW THE VENTROUS	365	FOUR ZOAS 9	330
FEET			
O THAT I COULD BEHOLD HIS FACE & FOLLOW HIS PURE FEET . .	368	FOUR ZOAS 9	426
AND LET ME TOUCH YOUR WOOLY BACKS FOLLOW ME AS I SING .	368	FOUR ZOAS 9	* 432
FOLLOW ME O MY FLOCKS & HEAR ME SING MY RAPTUROUS SONG .	368	FOUR ZOAS 9	438
FOLLOW ME O MY FLOCKS WE WILL NOW DESCEND INTO THE VALLEY	368	FOUR ZOAS 9	446
SHE CALLED TO HER FLOCKS SAYING FOLLOW ME O MY FLOCKS .	369	FOUR ZOAS 9	478
ARISE SWEET BOY & LET US FOLLOW THE PATH OF ENION . . .	371	FOUR ZOAS 9	534
FOLLOW THE STEPS OF THARMAS O THOU BRIGHTNESS OF	371	FOUR ZOAS 9	551
THE GARDENS			
HIS SONS ARISING FROM THE FEAST WITH GOLDEN BASKETS FOLLOW	376	FOUR ZOAS 9	714
& NOT FOLLOW CHRIST WHO DOES BY NATURE	400D	ANNO BACON	MARG
THAT I FOLLOW IN A STORM	417	MY SPECTR AD/N	10
WHY THEN DID HE NOT FOLLOW RAFAEL'S TRACK	447A	ANNO REYNOLDS	MARG
HE IS TO FOLLOW A GREAT MANY FOOLS	455C	ANNO REYNOLDS	MARG
IT DOES NOT THEREFORE FOLLOW THAT ALL OTHER FORMS	459C	ANNO REYNOLDS	MARG
ARE DEFORMITY			
OF EXECUTION IN ART LET HIM WHO WILL FOLLOW SUCH ADVICE	461C	ANNO REYNOLDS	MARG
[WHO XXX] FOLLOW WITH ME MY PLOW	486	MILTON 7	* 5
AND MAN UNMANS FOLLOW WITH ME MY PLOW THIS MOURNFUL DAY	488	MILTON 8	20
MUST BE A BLANK IN NATURE FOLLOW WITH ME AND TOMORROW AGAIN	488	MILTON 8	21
FOLLOW AFTER THE DETESTABLE GODS OF PRIAM IN POMP . . .	495	MILTON 14	15
THE PROCESSION NEXT FOLLOW THE YOUTHFUL ABBESS HER NUN . .	566D	DESC CAT 3	PROSE
NEXT FOLLOW THE FRIAR AND MONK THEN THE TAPISER	566D	DESC CAT 3	PROSE
AFTER THE HOST FOLLOW THE SHIPMAN THE HABERDASHER . . .	566D	DESC CAT 3	*PROSE
ARE AS FOLLOW "THE TABARDE INN BY HENRY BAILLIE THE" . .	567B	DESC CAT 3	PROSE
YOU WILL CONTINUE TO FOLLOW	570C	DESC CAT 3	PROSE
OF THE ARTIST AND CONNOISSEUR FOR REASONS THAT FOLLOW . .	581C	DESC CAT 7	PROSE
NEXT FOLLOW THE FRIAR & MONK THEN THE TAPISER	588B	CHAUCER/N	PROSE
AFTER THE HOST FOLLOW THE SHIPMAN THE HABERDASHER . . .	588C	CHAUCER/N	*PROSE
OVER THE GATEWAY ARE AS FOLLOW "THE TABARDE INNE" . .	589A	CHAUCER/N	PROSE
NEXT FOLLOW THE FRIAR AND MONK THEN THE TAPSTER	589D	CHAUCER 2	PROSE
AFTER THE HOST FOLLOW THE SHIPMAN THE HABERDASHER . . .	589D	CHAUCER 2	PROSE
OVER THE GATEWAY OF THE INN ARE AS FOLLOW	590C	CHAUCER 2	PROSE
THAT IT IS NOT ARTS THAT FOLLOW & ATTEND UPON [EMPIRES]	597A	PUB ADDRESS/N	*PROSE
EMPIRE			
QUERY THE ABOVE OUGHT TO FOLLOW THE DESCRIPTION	606A	V LAST JUDG/N	PROSE
WHO FOLLOW THE FASHION AS THAT IS CALLD WHICH IS . . .	610D	V LAST JUDG/N	*PROSE
TO FOLLOW THE DAUGHTERS OF ALBION AS THE HOUND FOLLOWS	638	JERUSALEM 17	3
THE SCENT			
TAKE UP THE CROSS O ISRAEL & FOLLOW JESUS	652B	JERUSALEM 27	PROSE
THUS SPEAKING THE DIVINE FAMILY FOLLOW ALBION	665	JERUSALEM 38	27
THO VALA'S CLOUD HIDE THEE & LUVAH'S FIRES FOLLOW THEE .	696	JERUSALEM 62	28
SOON SHALL THE SPECTRES OF THE DEAD FOLLOW MY WEAVING	725	JERUSALEM 82	9
THREADS			
THE SONS OF ALBION GO FORTH I FOLLOW FROM MY FURNACES .	728	JERUSALEM 83	62
THEY LAP THE WATER OF THE TREMBLING THAMES THEN FOLLOW	729	JERUSALEM 83	83
SWIFT			
FOLLOW ME I AM MEEK & LOWLY OF HEART	750	EV GOSPEL(C)/N	16
FOLLOW ME I AM MEEK & LOWLY OF HEART	751	EV GOSPEL(D)/N	18
WHO FOLLOW AFTER THE HEATHEN SCHOOLS	751	EV GOSPEL(D)/N	22
THAT DISDAINS TO FOLLOW THIS WORLD'S FASHION	752	EV GOSPEL(D)/N	48
OR ANGEL TO FOLLOW WHERE HE LED IF I WERE TO ACT OTHERWISE	791D	LETTER 4	PROSE
I ATTEMPTED EVERY MORNING FOR A FORTNIGHT TOGETHER	792A	LETTER 4	PROSE
TO FOLLOW			
SEEMS THAT OTHER THINGS WILL FOLLOW IN COURSE IF I DO BUT	812A	LETTER 22	PROSE
FLAXMAN IS GONE & WE MUST ALL SOON FOLLOW EVERY ONE TO HIS	879A	LETTER 88	PROSE
FOLLOWD			
PALE DEATH AND FOLLOWD ON THE WINGS OF FEAR	4	FAIR ELENOR/PS	28
AND REASON WOULD HAVE FOLLOWD BUT FATE SUFFERD NOT . . .	42B	THEN SHE BORE	PROSE
. . . LIKE A VOICE OF GOD FOLLOWING A STORM THE ABBE	143	FRENCH REVOLTN	202
FOLLOWD			
. . . HIM THE PEERS FOLLOWD THEY SAW THE COURTS OF THE	148	FRENCH REVOLTN	304
PALACE			

FOLLOWD (CONTINUED)
 AND FOLLOWD THE ARMY . . . . 148 FRENCH REVOLTN 306
 [THE MOTHER FOLLOWD WEEPING LOUD] . . . . 177 LIT BOY LST/N * 11
 SHE FLED FROM HIS ARMS YET HE FOLLOWD . . . . . . 231 URIZEN 19 13
 A COLD SHADOW FOLLOWD BEHIND HIM . . . . 235 URIZEN 25 9
 WRATH WAS FOLLOWD UP AND DOWN . . . . 256 BOOK OF LOS 3 23
 IN WEEPING BLINDNESS STUMBLING SHE FOLLOWD THEM OER ROCKS 270 FOUR ZOAS 1 215
  & MOUNTAINS
 THE LAMB OF GOD BLESSED FOR EVER & HE FOLLOWD THE MAN . 279 FOUR ZOAS 1 556
 WHILE ENITHARMON FOLLOWD HIM WEEPING IN DISMAL WOE . . 307 FOUR ZOAS 5 98
 THE SONS OF WISDOM STOOD AROUND THE HARPERS FOLLOWD WITH 310 FOUR ZOAS 5 199
  HARPS
 FOLLOWD BEHIND HIM AS THE WEB OF A SPIDER DUSKY & COLD . 318 FOUR ZOAS 6 244
 FOLLOWD HER DAUGHTERS TO THE FIELDS OF BLOOD THEY LEFT 334 FOUR ZOAS 7B 66
  ME NAKED
 AT DAWN & EER THE SUN AROSE THE RAVEN & VULTURE FOLLOWD . 358 FOUR ZOAS 9 63
 THEY FOLLOWD HER TO THE SILENT VALLY BENEATH THE SPREADING 369 FOUR ZOAS 9 * 479
  TREES
 SHE DREW NEAR TO HER HOUSE & HER FLOCKS FOLLOWD HER 370 FOUR ZOAS 9 508
  FOOTSTEPS
 HE TOOK HER HAND RELUCTANT SHE FOLLOWD IN INFANT DOUBTS 371 FOUR ZOAS 9 552
 HE NEVER WOULD HAVE FOLLOWD RUBENS . . . . 450C ANNO REYNOLDS MARG
 WILDLY THEY FOLLOWD LOS AND RINTRAH & THE MILLS WERE SILENT 488 MILTON 8 23
 FOLLOWD BY ENVY ON THE WINDS . . . . 558 THE CAVERNS/N 12
 AND ALL MY CHILDREN FOLLOWD HIS LOUD HOWLINGS INTO THE DEEP 643 JERUSALEM 21 17
 SO LOS IN LAMENTATIONS FOLLOWD ALBION ALBION COVERD . . 656 JERUSALEM 30 41
 FIRES AND CLOUDS OF ROLLING SMOKE BUT MILD THE SAVIOUR 664 JERUSALEM 38 10
  FOLLOWD HIM
 GOSHEN HATH FOLLOWD PHILISTEA GILEAD HATH JOIND WITH OG 720 JERUSALEM 79 13
 AND JORDAN TO EUPHRATES JERUSALEM FOLLOWD TREMBLING . . . 722 JERUSALEM 80 9
 JEHOVAH DROPPED A TEAR & FOLLOWD HIM BY HIS SPIRIT . . . 784B ANNO WW EXCUR MARG
 . . . SHE FOLLOWD THEM OER ROCKS & MOUNTAINS] . . . . . SUPP FOUR ZOAS 1 *
FOLLOWED
 HE FOLLOWED ME UP AND DOWN IN THE HOUSE WHEN I GREW UP . 37C CONTEMPLATN/PS PROSE
 THEN THEY FOLLOWED . . . . 115 LIT GRL FND/SI 45
 THE BRITISH INSTITUTION HAS THIS YEAR FOLLOWED ITS EXAMPLE 561B EXHIBITION ADV PROSE
FOLLOWERS
 IF WE ARE TO EXPECT CRIMES FROM PAINE & HIS FOLLOWERS . 385C ANNO WATSON MARG
FOLLOWING
 THE KING'S TENT WITH A MINSTREL WHO SINGS THE FOLLOWING 31D EDW THIRD/PS 6 PROSE
  SONG
 SCOPPRELL TOOK UP A BOOK & READ THE FOLLOWING PASSAGE . 52D ISLAND MOON 8 PROSE
 THE FOLLOWING AFFAIRS HAPPEND . . . . 58C ISLAND MOON 10 PROSE
 . . . LIKE A VOICE OF GOD FOLLOWING A STORM THE ABBE 143 FRENCH REVOLTN 202
  FOLLOWD
 OF THE FOLLOWING ERRORS . . . . 149C MARRIAGE HH 4 PROSE
 THAT GOD WILL TORMENT MAN IN ETERNITY FOR FOLLOWING HIS 149C MARRIAGE HH 4 PROSE
  ENERGIES
 BUT THE FOLLOWING CONTRARIES TO THESE ARE TRUE . . . 149D MARRIAGE HH 4 PROSE
 WITH CORRODING FIRES HE WROTE THE FOLLOWING SENTENCE NOW 150D MARRIAGE HH 6 PROSE
 FOLLOWING PRODUCTIONS NOW PRESENTED TO THE PUBLIC WHO HAS 207B PRSPECTUS 1793 PROSE
 THE FOLLOWING ARE THE SUBJECTS OF THE SEVERAL WORKS NOW 207C PRSPECTUS 1793 PROSE
 IN THOUGHTS PERTURBD THEY ROSE FROM THE BRIGHT RUINS SILENT 241 EUROPE 10 1
  FOLLOWING
 DREWST ALL THE SONS OF BEULAH INTO THY [GREAT] DREAD VORTEX 299 FOUR ZOAS 4 88
  FOLLOWING
 THIS NIGHT BEGINS AT LINE...THE FOLLOWING COMES IN AT THE 333A FOUR ZOAS 7B *TITLE
  END
 THE TRIFLES WHICH THE BISHOP HAS COMBATED IN THE FOLLOWING 390C ANNO WATSON MARG
 IT WAS BYSSHE'S ART OF POETRY SHE OPEND THE 440D MEMORANDUM/N 5 PROSE
  FOLLOWING...BEHN
 I WOULD TRY MY OWN & OPEND THE FOLLOWING...DRYDEN'S VIRGIL 441B MEMORANDUM/N 5 PROSE
 MY PROOFS OF THIS OPINION ARE GIVEN IN THE FOLLOWING NOTES 445A ANNO REYNOLDS MARG
 I CONSIDER THE FOLLOWING SENTENCE IS SUPREMELY INSOLENT 453C ANNO REYNOLDS MARG
 FOR THE FOLLOWING REASONS WHY THIS SENTENCE SHOULD BE . 453C ANNO REYNOLDS MARG
 INSTEAD OF FOLLOWING ONE GREAT MASTER . . . . 455C ANNO REYNOLDS MARG
 THE FOLLOWING [LETTER] DISCOURSE IS PARTICULARLY . . . 457D ANNO REYNOLDS * MARG
 THE [FOLLOWING DISCOURSE IS] [(TWO) DISCOURSES] . . . 461C ANNO REYNOLDS * MARG
 TWO FOLLOWING DISCOURSES ARE PARTICULARLY CALCULATED . 461C ANNO REYNOLDS MARG
 THE FOLLOWING DISCOURSE IS WRITTEN WITH THE SAME END IN 465D ANNO REYNOLDS MARG
  VIEW
 THE PURPOSE OF THE FOLLOWING DISCOURSE IS TO PROVE THAT 473A ANNO REYNOLDS MARG
 FOLLOWING MILTON INTO ULRO ALTHO YOUR POWER IS GREAT . 508 MILTON 24 23
 TO BE FLOGD INTO FOLLOWING THE STYLE OF A FOOL . . . 550 SAY PICTURES/N 5
 FOR REASONS THAT WILL BE SHEWN IN THE FOLLOWING . . . 581B DESC CAT 6 PROSE
 SHOULD CONSIDER THE FOLLOWING . . . . 599C PUB ADDRESS/N PROSE
 SUITED TO MY IMAGINATIVE EYE [IN THE FOLLOWING ORDER] AS 606A V LAST JUDG/N PROSE
  FOLLOWS
 WHEN IT LEAVES PARADISE [WITH] FOLLOWING THE SERPENT . 614C V LAST JUDG/N PROSE
 "HE" IS SEEN FOLLOWING THE FRIAR'S LANTERN TOWARDS THE 618C ILLUS MILTON PROSE
  CONVENT
 THE ENTHUSIASM OF THE FOLLOWING POEM THE AUTHOR HOPES . 620D JERUSALEM 3 PROSE
 OF THE MEASURE IN WHICH THE FOLLOWING POEM IS WRITTEN . 621C JERUSALEM 3 TITLE
 FOLLOWING ALBION INTO HIS CENTRAL VOID AMONG HIS OAKS . 656 JERUSALEM 30 20
 AGAIN HE JOIND THE DIVINE BODY FOLLOWING MERCIFUL . . . 664 JERUSALEM 37 11
 FOLLOWING THEE AS A SHEPHERD BY THE FOUR RIVERS OF EDEN 692 JERUSALEM 60 21
 ON EACH SIDE A CHORUS OF ANGELS ENTERING SING THE FOLLOWING 781A GHOST ABEL 2 PROSE
 BETTER THAN SLAVISHLY FOLLOWING THE TRACK OF ANOTHER . 792A LETTER 4 PROSE
 MRS BUTTS WILL EXCUSE THE FOLLOWING LINES . . . . . 806B LETTER 16 PROSE
 I HAVE NOW ON THE STOCKS THE FOLLOWING DRAWINGS FOR YOU 824A LETTER 27 PROSE
 THE FOLLOWING INSCRIPTION...BUT IT STRIKES ME THAT . . 838B LETTER 37 PROSE
 FROM HIS SHOP HE MADE A REPLY TO THE FOLLOWING PURPOSE . 846B LETTER 44 PROSE

	PAGE	TITLE	LINE

FOLLOWING   (CONTINUED)
MR FLAXMAN NAMED THE FOLLOWING EIGHT AS PROPER SUBJECTS   848D LETTER 45   PROSE
   FOR PRINTS
& AT LENGTH PRODUCD THE FOLLOWING   . . . .   860B LETTER 56   PROSE
THE PUBLIC OUGHT TO BE INFORMD THAT [THE FOLLOWING] THESE   860C LETTER 56   PROSE
LET US GO ON DEAR SIR FOLLOWING HIS CROSS LET US TAKE   863B LETTER 60   PROSE
   IT UP

FOLLOWS
BUT WHEN OUR FIRST IDEAS ARE WRONG WHAT FOLLOWS MUST   . .   28D EDW THIRD/PS 4   PROSE
AND THE RED SCOURGE FOLLOWS HER DESOLATE SONS . . . . .   34A KING JOHN/PS   PROSE
I LOOK BEHIND THERE IS NO RETURNING DEATH FOLLOWS AFTER ME   35D COUCH DEATH/PS   PROSE
LIKE A TRIUMPH SEASON FOLLOWS SEASON . . . .   37B CONTEMPLATN/PS   PROSE
HANG YOUR SERIOUS SONGS SAID SIPSOP & HI ~UNG AS FOLLOWS   56A ISLAND MOON 9   PROSE
AS THE PLOW FOLLOWS WORDS SO GOD REWARDS PRAYERS . . .   152A MARRIAGE HH 9   PROSE
OR ORC BENDING DOWN AS THE BINDER OF THE SHEAVES FOLLOWS   332 FOUR ZOAS 7   462
BUT [DAY BY] NIGHT OR DAY LOS FOLLOWS WAR . . . . . .   335 FOUR ZOAS 7B   75
THEN FOLLOWS THUS IN THE CAVERNS OF THE GRAVE &C AS IT . .   336B FOUR ZOAS 7B   *PROSE
THEN FOLLOWS THE GOLDEN HARROW IN THE MIDST OF MENTAL FIRES   366 FOUR ZOAS 9   335
[MY SPECTRE FOLLOWS THEE BEHIND] . . . .   415 MY SPECTRE/N   12
MY SPECTRE FOLLOWS THEE BEHIND . . . .   415 MY SPECTRE/N   26
EMPIRE FOLLOWS ART & NOT VICE VERSA AS ENGLISHMEN SUPPOSE   445D ANNO REYNOLDS   MARG
AS FOLLOWS IN THE NEXT PAGE . . . .   448A ANNO REYNOLDS   MARG
IN BLIGHTS OF THE EAST THE HEAVY ROLLER FOLLOWS IN HOWLINGS   514 MILTON 27   48
   OF WOE
MY SPECTRE STILL WANDERING THRO THEM FOLLOWS MY EMANATION   521 MILTON 32   4
THE PRIORESS FOLLOWS THESE WITH HER FEMALE CHAPLAIN . .   568B DESC CAT 3   PROSE
THE MONK FOLLOWS THESE WITH THE FRIAR . . . . . .   568C DESC CAT 3   PROSE
FOR THE HOST WHO FOLLOWS THIS GROUP AND HOLDS THE CENTER   569D DESC CAT 3   PROSE
& FOLLOWS [WHEREVER ART LEADS] THE ARTS . . . . . .   597A PUB ADDRESS/N   *PROSE
SUITED TO MY IMAGINATIVE EYE [IN THE FOLLOWING ORDER] AS   606A V LAST JUDG/N   PROSE
   FOLLOWS
HERE FOLLOWS THE DESCRIPTION OF THE PICTURE . . . . .   606A V LAST JUDG/N   PROSE
TO FOLLOW THE DAUGHTERS OF ALBION AS THE HOUND FOLLOWS   638 JERUSALEM 17   3
   THE SCENT
AS TO LAYING ON THE WAX IT IS AS FOLLOWS TAKE A CAKE .   790C LETTER 2   PROSE
BEHIND THE SEA OF TIME & SPACE ROARS & FOLLOWS SWIFTLY .   812A LETTER 22   PROSE
TO SAY AS FOLLOWS UPON THIS TICKLISH SUBJECT . . . .   825B LETTER 27   PROSE
MY CRITICISM ON THIS PICTURE IS AS FOLLOWS MR . . . .   864A LETTER 61   PROSE
THE PRICES OF THESE THINGS THEY ARE AS FOLLOWS . . . .   878D LETTER 88   PROSE

FOLLY
AND LOVE OF FOLLY NEEDS NONE [OTHERS] OTHER CURSE . . .   14 IMIT SPEN/PS   14
BECAUSE IT REPROACHES HIM WITH THE ERRORS OF ACQUIRED FOLLY   87C ANNO LAVATER   MARG
IF THOU DOST GO SAID HAR I WISH THINE EYES MAY SEE THY   102 TIRIEL 3   17
   FOLLY
[HYPOCRISY THE IDIOT'S WISDOM & THE WISE MAN'S FOLLY] . .   110 TIRIEL 8   35
FOLLY IS AN ENDLESS MAZE . . . .   126 VOICE BARD/SI   6
WITNESS THIS NUMBER & MANY OTHERS...CURSED FOLLY . . .   133A ANNO SWED PROV   MARG
THE HOURS OF FOLLY ARE MEASURD BY THE CLOCK . . . . .   151A MARRIAGE HH 7   PROSE
IF THE FOOL WOULD PERSIST IN HIS FOLLY HE WOULD BECOME WISE   151B MARRIAGE HH 7   PROSE
FOLLY IS THE CLOKE OF KNAVERY . . . .   151B MARRIAGE HH 7   PROSE
IT IS SO WITH SWEDENBORG HE SHEWS THE FOLLY OF CHURCHES   157D MARRIAGE HH 21   PROSE
YET SHALL NOT HIS FOLLY BE BEATEN OUT OF HIM . . . .   158C MARRIAGE HH 22   PROSE
FOLLY & IMPUDENCE DOES THE THOROUGH BELIEF OF POPERY   385C ANNO WATSON   MARG
IT IS FOLLY TO CONFUTE HIM SO SERIOUSLY IN THEM . . .   392D ANNO WATSON   MARG
I AM ASTONISHD HOW SUCH CONTEMPTIBLE KNAVERY & FOLLY . .   397A ANNO BACON   MARG
("NAKEDNESS IS UNCOMELY") THIS IS FOLLY ITSELF . . . .   399D ANNO BACON   MARG
BUT ONLY IMITATION WHAT FOLLY . . . .   400C ANNO BACON   MARG
IS NOT THIS THE GREATEST FOLLY . . . .   408A ANNO BACON   MARG
TRUTH OR DISCERNMENT IN ANOTHER & IN SOME IT IS FOLLY . .   408D ANNO BACON   MARG
A FOLLY SINGULAR & PARTICULAR DETAIL IS . . . . . .   459A ANNO REYNOLDS   MARG
("REDUCED VARIETY OF NATURE TO ABSTRACT IDEA") WHAT FOLLY   460D ANNO REYNOLDS   MARG
FOLLY OF WHAT CONSEQUENCE IS IT TO THE ARTS . . . .   465A ANNO REYNOLDS   MARG
FOLLY & FALSHOOD THE MAN WHO CAN SAY THAT RAFAEL . . .   467A ANNO REYNOLDS   * MARG
NOT TO SHEW IT I DO NOT ACCOUNT THAT WISDOM BUT FOLLY . .   483 MILTON 4   7
YOU CALL ME MAD TIS FOLLY TO DO SO . . . .   544 F(LAXMAN)/N 2   1
VOLUPTUOUSNESS AND FOLLY BEGAN TO BE ACCOUNTED BEAUTIFUL   568B DESC CAT 3   PROSE
THE BEAUTY THAT IS ANNEXED AND APPENDED TO FOLLY IS A .   579D DESC CAT 5   PROSE
AWKWARDNESS ARMD IN STEEL FOLLY IN A HELMET OF GOLD . .   628 JERUSALEM 9   12
. . . & WHO CHARGETH HIS ANGELS WITH FOLLY . . . .   679 JERUSALEM 49   31
IS A FOLLY UNREDEEMABLE . . . .   716B JERUSALEM 77   PROSE
DOUBT SELF JEALOUS WATRY FOLLY . . . .   770 OF GATES/GP   7
AS UNITY IS THE CLOKE OF FOLLY . . . .   778B HOMERS POETRY   PROSE
NEITHER YOUTH NOR CHILDHOOD IS FOLLY OR INCAPACITY . .   794B LETTER 5   PROSE
I INTEND BECAUSE MY ABSTRACT FOLLY HURRIES ME OFTEN AWAY   809A LETTER 20   PROSE
FOLLY NOT TO VENTURE PUBLISHING I AM NOW ENGRAVING SIX   820B LETTER 25   PROSE
   LITTLE
THE LEAST PARTICLE & SUCH DISCIPLINE I CALL PRESUMPTION   871A LETTER 72   PROSE
   & FOLLY

FOLLY'S
FOR IGNORANCE IS FOLLY'S LEESING NURSE . . . . . .   14 IMIT SPEN/PS   * 13

FOND   SEE OVER-FOND
I [WAS FOND] SLEPT IN THE DARK . . . .   170 SLEPT DARK/N   *   1
ENGLISHMEN ARE FOND OF THE INDEFINITE WHICH THEY MEASURE   878A LETTER 88   PROSE

FONDNESS
IN MILKY FONDNESS THEN ON THEL SHE FIXD HER HUMBLE EYES   129 BOOK OF THEL 4   9
WITH SEEMING FONDNESS THEY DEVOURD TOO . . . . . .   157B MARRIAGE HH 17   PROSE

FOOD
SEEKING THEIR NIGHTLY FOOD . . . .   11 GWIN KING/PS   20
IS DANGEROUS TO FIGHT NOT GOOD FOR FOOD . . . . . .   27 EDW THIRD/PS 3   266
THOU HAST REFUSD OUR CHARITY THOU HAST REFUSD OUR FOOD   100 TIRIEL 1   37
MNETHA NOW AGED WAITED ON THEM & BROUGHT THEM FOOD   100 TIRIEL 2   6
   & CLOTHING

	PAGE	TITLE	LINE

FOOD   (CONTINUED)
```
        NO MATTER WHO I AM O MNETHA IF THOU HAST ANY FOOD    . . .    101  TIRIEL 2             21
        A WANDERER I BEG FOR FOOD YOU SEE I CANNOT WEEP   . . . .     101  TIRIEL 2             28
        AND I WILL BRING THEE FOOD OLD MAN TILL DEATH SHALL CALL      103  TIRIEL 3             35
            THEE HENCE
        BUT WALK UNITED BEARING FOOD TO ALL OUR TENDER FLOWERS  . .   128  BOOK OF THEL 3       16
        BUT I FEED NOT THE WARBLING BIRDS THEY FLY AND SEEK THEIR     129  BOOK OF THEL 3       20
            FOOD
        OR DID SHE ONLY LIVE TO BE AT DEATH THE FOOD OF WORMS  . .    129  BOOK OF THEL 3       23
        THEN IF THOU ART THE FOOD OF WORMS O VIRGIN OF THE SKIES      129  BOOK OF THEL 3       25
        ALL WHOLSOM FOOD IS CAUGHT WITHOUT A NET OR A TRAP  . . .     151A MARRIAGE HH 7      *PROSE
        BUT KISS HIM & GIVE HIM BOTH [FOOD] DRINK & APPAREL  . . .    180  LIT VAGABOND/N       18
        HIS FOOD SHE BROUGHT IN IRON BASKETS HIS DRINK IN CUPS        195  AMERICA PREL 1        3
            OF IRON
        FOR CHAIND BENEATH I REND THESE CAVERNS WHEN THOU BRINGEST    196  AMERICA PREL 1       18
            FOOD
        SHUDDRING SHE WOVE NINE DAYS & NIGHTS SLEEPLESS HER FOOD      266  FOUR ZOAS 1          82
            WAS TEARS
        THEY WILL WITHOLD SWEET LOVE WHOSE FOOD IS THORNS & BITTER    271  FOUR ZOAS 1         257
            ROOTS
        WEARIED WITH SEEKING FOOD ACROSS THE SNOWY WASTE THE LITTLE   276  FOUR ZOAS 1         448
        INCESSANT TEARS ARE NOW MY FOOD INCESSANT RAGE & TEARS        298  FOUR ZOAS 4          11
        AND BACK RETURN WITH WINE & FOOD OR DIVE INTO THE DEEPS       308  FOUR ZOAS 5         119
        AND WHIPS OF STERN REPENTANCE & FOOD OF STUBBORN OBSTINACY    313  FOUR ZOAS 6          42
        FROM THEE THY FOOD SO SHALL WE CEASE TO BE & ALL             313  FOUR ZOAS 6          65
            OUR SORROWS
        SHALL PURSUE THARMAS & IN VAIN SHALT CRAVE FOR FOOD I WILL    313  FOUR ZOAS 6          68
        FLYING AWAY FROM URIZEN THAT HE MIGHT NOT GIVE HIM FOOD       318  FOUR ZOAS 6         274
        WITHOUT THE FOOD OF LIFE LET US CREATE THEM (COUNTERPARTS)    330  FOUR ZOAS 7         409
        PAMPERD IN PALACES [OF] FOR OUR FOOD THE BLOOD OF CAPTAINS    334  FOUR ZOAS 7B      *  46
            NURTURD
        AS FOOD OR DRINK OR ORNAMENT OR IN DELIGHTFUL WORKS  . . .    340  FOUR ZOAS 7B        276
        KNEADED IN UVETH'S KNEADING THOUGH STILL ORC DEVOURD THE      343  FOUR ZOAS 8       *  77
            FOOD
        IN RAGING HUNGER STILL THE PESTILENTIAL FOOD IN GEMS & GOLD   343  FOUR ZOAS 8          78
        MEASURD HIS FOOD MORNING & EVENING IN CUPS & BASKETS OF       343  FOUR ZOAS 8          81
            IRON
        WITH TEARS OF SORROW INCESSANT SHE LABOURD THE FOOD OF ORC    343  FOUR ZOAS 8          82
        OF FORNICATION FOOD OF ORC & SATAN PRESSD FROM THE FRUIT      356  FOUR ZOAS 8         603
            OF MYSTERY
        HIS GOLDEN FOOD AND IN THE EVENING SLEEP BEFORE THE DOOR      376  FOUR ZOAS 9         708
        THE TONGUE A LITTLE MOISTURE FILLS A LITTLE FOOD IT CLOYS     484  MILTON 5             25
        HIS LIPS WITH FOOD OF EDEN IN HIS COLD AND DIM REPOSE  . .    496  MILTON 15            15
        I SHALL EAT COARSER FOOD & GO WORSE SHOD  . . . . . .         559  I ROSE UP AT/N       26
        MY MORN & EVENING FOOD WERE PREPARD IN BATTLES OF MEN  . .    644  JERUSALEM 22          7
        WHO BECOMES HIS FOOD SUCH IS THE WAY OF THE DEVOURING POWER   659  JERUSALEM 33         24
        IN THE LOVE OF TIRZAH HE SAID DOUBT IS MY FOOD DAY & NIGHT    662  JERUSALEM 36          7
        GIVE ME MY EMANATIONS BACK FOOD FOR MY DYING SOUL  . . .      670  JERUSALEM 42         13
        THE TONGUE A LITTLE MOISTURE FILLS A LITTLE FOOD IT CLOYS     680  JERUSALEM 49         40
        CIRCLES THE HELLS FOR FOOD TO THE HEAVENS FOOD OF TORMENT     680  JERUSALEM 49         62
        FOOD OF DESPAIR THEY DRINK THE CONDEMND SOUL & REJOICE  . .   680  JERUSALEM 49         63
        ENDLESS THEIR LABOUR WITH BITTER FOOD VOID OF SLEEP  . . .    691  JERUSALEM 59         30
        I WILL COMMAND THE CLOUD TO GIVE THEE FOOD & THE HARD ROCK    696  JERUSALEM 62         25
        AND DELIGHTFUL FOOD OF THE WARRIOR THE WELL FED WARRIOR'S     706  JERUSALEM 68         34
            FLESH
        WITH PLEASURE WITHOUT PAIN FOR THEIR FOOD IS BLOOD OF THE     706  JERUSALEM 68         37
            CAPTIVE
        AND FEEDS HER WITH THE FOOD OF EDEN HENCE ALL HER BEAUTY      707  JERUSALEM 69         18
            BEAMS
        AND TURN THEM OUT INTO THE STREETS FOR HARLOTS TO BE FOOD     724  JERUSALEM 81          4
        THAT ENJOYMENT & NOT ABSTINENCE IS THE FOOD OF INTELLECT     790D LETTER 2            PROSE
FOODLESS
        WHY FALL THE SPARROW & THE ROBIN IN THE FOODLESS WINTER       276  FOUR ZOAS 1         446
FOOL
        SHE FALLING KISSD THE GROUND POOR FOOL  . . . . . . . .        16  BLIND-MANS/PS        14
        I TURND MYSELF ABOUT WITH GREAT CONTEMPT SAID I GO ALONG      45A  ISLAND MOON 1      PROSE
            YOU FOOL
        FOOL SAID HE WHO DO YOU CALL FOOL  . . . . . . . .            45A  ISLAND MOON 1      PROSE
        I DO NOT THINK THE MAN WAS A FOOL FOR HE SEEMS TO ME  . .     45B  ISLAND MOON 1      PROSE
        MUST BE A FOOL I'FAITH NOT TO UNDERSTAND THE MATHEMATICS      45C  ISLAND MOON 1      PROSE
        BUT TO SOLVE THEM FOR A MAN MAY BE A FOOL & MAKE QUERIES      45D  ISLAND MOON 1      PROSE
        AYE SECONDLY VOLTAIRE S A FOOL SAYS THE EPICUREAN  . . .      45D  ISLAND MOON 1      PROSE
        NO NO HE DID NOT I WAS ONLY MAKING A FOOL OF YOU  . . .       48C  ISLAND MOON 4      PROSE
        POO POO SAID OBTUSE ANGLE DONT BE A FOOL  . . . . .           49B  ISLAND MOON 5      PROSE
        WHY SAID QUID I THINK THAT [A] ANY NATURAL FOOL  . . . .      50A  ISLAND MOON 6      PROSE
        TONGUE AS A CITY CLARK BUT A BOY WOULD BE SUCH A FOOL  . .    53B  ISLAND MOON 8      PROSE
        ("FOOL AT BIT OF BREAD TREMBLES POISONED") EXCELLENT          84C  ANNO LAVATER        MARG
        A FOOL SEES NOT THE SAME TREE THAT A WISE MAN SEES  . . .    151A  MARRIAGE HH 7      PROSE
        IF THE FOOL WOULD PERSIST IN HIS POLLY HE WOULD BECOME WISE  151B  MARRIAGE HH 7      PROSE
        THE SELFISH SMILING FOOL & THE SULLEN FROWNING FOOL  . .     151D  MARRIAGE HH 8      PROSE
        THE DEVIL ANSWERD BRAY A FOOL IN A MORTER WITH WHEAT  . .    158C  MARRIAGE HH 22     PROSE
        A FOOL TANGLED IN A RELIGIOUS SNARE  . . . . . . . .          180  LACEDEMONIAN/N        2
        HAVE QUITE FORSAKEN O FOOL FOOL TO LOSE MY SWEETEST BLISS     296  FOUR ZOAS 3         168
        O FOOL TO THINK THAT I COULD HIDE FROM HIS ALL PIERCING       310  FOUR ZOAS 5         214
            EYES
        O FOOL COULD I FORGET THE LIGHT THAT FILLED MY BRIGHT        310  FOUR ZOAS 5         216
            SPHERES
        & YET HE WAS NO FOOL  . . . . . . . . . . . .                389C  ANNO WATSON         MARG
        IS FALSE WHEN IT IS ATTRIBUTED TO A WRONG AUTHOR HES A FOOL  391B  ANNO WATSON         MARG
        READ THEM & JUDGE IF YOU ARE NOT A FOOL OF WHAT  . . . .     392D  ANNO WATSON       * MARG
        HARTLEY A MAN OF JUDGMENT THEN JUDGMENT WAS A FOOL  . . .    394C  ANNO WATSON         MARG
        O FOOL SLIGHT HYPOCRITE & VILLAIN  . . . . . . . .           395D  ANNO WATSON       * MARG
```

	PAGE	TITLE	LINE

FOOL   (CONTINUED)

("DEMOCRACIES...COMMONLY ...QUIET ") SELF CONTRADICTION   401B ANNO BACON   MARG
  KNAVE & FOOL
NONE BUT A FOOL CAN ACT SO . . . .   406A ANNO BACON   MARG
WHAT A CURSED FOOL IS THIS ILL SHAPEN ARE INFANTS OR SMALL   406C ANNO BACON   MARG
  PLANTS
WHAT A CONTEMPTIBLE FOOL IS THIS BACON   406C ANNO BACON   MARG
THE WORK OF A FOOL TO USE PHYSIC BUT FOR NECESSITY   . . .   408B ANNO BACON   MARG
DANTE WAS A FOOL OR HIS [TRANSLATION] TRANSLATOR WAS NOT   413B ANNO BOYD   * MARG
HE CERTAINLY WOULD HAVE BEEN MORE LIKE A FOOL THAN A WISE   450D ANNO REYNOLDS   MARG
  MAN
[ARTISTS XXX ?FOOL THE XXX] (THREE) FARTHINGS . . . .   453A ANNO REYNOLDS   * MARG
AFTER HAVING BEEN A FOOL A STUDENT IS TO AMASS A STOCK .   455B ANNO REYNOLDS   MARG
KNOWING HIMSELF TO BE A FOOL HE IS . . . .   455B ANNO REYNOLDS   MARG
[DAMN THE FOOL] MEER ENTHUSIASM IS THE ALL IN ALL   . . .   456C ANNO REYNOLDS   * MARG
FOOL & A CUNNING KNAVE SUITED TO THE PURPOSES OF   458B ANNO REYNOLDS   MARG
  EVIL DEMONS
A FOOL & KNAVE HAVING NO CON-SCIENCE OR INNATE SCIENCE   .   459B ANNO REYNOLDS   MARG
(GENERALIZING) IN EVERY (THING) THE MAN (WOULD) SOON BE   460D ANNO REYNOLDS   * MARG
  A FOOL
BUT A CUNNING FOOL   460D ANNO REYNOLDS   MARG
CAN ANY MAN BE SUCH A FOOL AS TO BELIEVE THAT RAFAEL & .   467B ANNO REYNOLDS   MARG
DAMND FOOL . . . .   467C ANNO REYNOLDS   * MARG
HE MUST EXPECT TO BE CALLD A FOOL BY MEN OF UNDERSTANDING   469D ANNO REYNOLDS   MARG
HE WAS BORN QUITE A FOOL BUT HE DIED QUITE A KNAVE   . . .   470 ANNO REYNOLDS   2
DAMND FOOL   470C ANNO REYNOLDS   MARG
ANY FOOL MAY (CONCENTRATE) A LIGHT IN THE MIDDLE . . . .   477C ANNO REYNOLDS   * MARG
CALLD HARMONY IT IS LIKE THE SMILE OF A FOOL . . . . .   478D ANNO REYNOLDS   MARG
("RELISH FOR EXCELLENCIES AN ACQUIRED TASTE") [FOOL]   .   SUPP ANNO REYNOLDS   * MARG
MADMAN I HAVE BEEN CALLD FOOL THEY CALL THEE   . . . .   538 MADMAN CALLD/N   1
AND HES A FOOL WHO [SEEKS] TRIES TO MAKE SUCH A BLOCKHEAD   540 BLOCKHEAD/N   2
  BELIEVE
TILL HES BECOME THE GOLDEN FOOL . . . .   540 GOLDEN RULE/N   2
TILL [HES] YOURE AT LAST BECOME THE [OLD] GOLDEN FOOL   .   540 S(TOTHAR)D/N *   2
AND IN THE HAND OF THE SIMPERING FOOL   . . . . .   541 FLORENTINE/N   3
A [KNAVE] FOOL TO A BOLT A [FOOL] KNAVE TO A GLASS OF GIN   544 ON F AND S/N   4
YOU MUST AGREE THAT RUBENS WAS A FOOL . . . . . .   546 ENGLISH CONN/N   1
THE LABORIOUS STUMBLE OF A FOOL . . . .   547 LET BE TOLD/N   5
BUT TO LOSE THEM THE FOOL MAKES HIS FOOLISH GAME . . . .   547 LET BE TOLD/N   9
. . . LABORIOUS STUMBLE OF A FOOL . . . .   547 RAFAEL SUBLI/N   5
FOR THE GREATER THE FOOL IN THE PENCIL MORE BLEST   . . .   548 ALL PICTURES/N   3
I ALWAYS TAKE MY JUDGMENT FROM A FOOL . . . . . .   549 CROMEK SPEAK/N   1
[TO LEARN TO ADMIRE THE WORKS OF A FOOL] . . . . .   550 SAY PICTURES/N   4
TO BE FLOGD INTO FOLLOWING THE STYLE OF A FOOL   . . . .   550 SAY PICTURES/N   5
RATHER THAN THE PERFECTIONS OF A FOOL . . . . . .   550 SAY PICTURES/N   7
RATHER THAN [LET] BE SUCH A BLIND HUMAN FOOL   . . . .   550 WHEN I SEE/N   7
TWILL MAKE A FOOL LAUGH & A FAIRY FUN . . . . . .   552 TELL YOU WHA/N   6
BUT THE GREATER [FOOLS] FOOL THE [GRATER] GREATER LIAR   554 GREAT MEN/N   *   2
EVERY FOOL SHOOK HIS BELLS THROUGHOUT THE LAND   . . .   554 BLAKES APL/N 1   2
EVERY FOOL SHOOK HIS BELLS THROUGHOUT THE LAND   . . .   555 BLAKES APL/N 2   6
SOME PEOPLE ADMIRE THE WORK OF A FOOL . . . . . .   556 SOME PEOPLE/N   1
HE HAS MADE HIM LOOK MORE LIKE A FOOL THAN A KNAVE   . .   574D DESC CAT 3   PROSE
HEATH'S LAME IMITATION STOTHARD BEING SUCH A FOOL   . . .   592B PUB ADDRESS/N   PROSE
AS THERE MAY BE A FOOL OR A KNAVE IN AN EMBROIDERED COAT   593B PUB ADDRESS/N   PROSE
EVERY FOOL SHOOK HIS BELLS THROUGHOUT THE LAND   . . .   595 BLAKES APOL/PA   2
DO IT & THE FOOL OFTEN WILL DO IT BEST AS IT IS A WORK   598A PUB ADDRESS/N   PROSE
  OF NO MIND
OR THINK TO EDUCATE [AN IDIOT] . . . .   598C PUB ADDRESS/N   *PROSE
A FOOL [?& HE] PAINTING IS DRAWING ON CANVAS   . . . .   602B PUB ADDRESS/N   *PROSE
THE FOOL SHALL NOT ENTER INTO HEAVEN LET HIM BE EVER SO   615D V LAST JUDG/N   PROSE
  HOLY
WHERE IS IT BUT IN THE MIND OF A FOOL . . . . . .   617A V LAST JUDG/N   PROSE
IS WHETHER HE IS A WISE MAN OR A FOOL GO PUT OFF HOLINESS   739 JERUSALEM 91   56
BUT THE CRITIC MUST BE A FOOL WHO HAS NOT READ DANTE   .   864B LETTER 61   PROSE

FOOLED
BE FOOLED BY YOU INTO OPINIONS THAT YOU PLEASE TO IMPOSE   579B DESC CAT 5   PROSE

FOOLERY
POLITIC FOOLERY & MOST CONTEMPTIBLE VILLAINY & MURDER   . .   400A ANNO BACON   * MARG
OF IDEAS & [THEN TO BE ?INSOLENT IN HIS FOOLERY] . . .   455B ANNO REYNOLDS * MARG
TO ASSUME THE RIGHT TO PUT OTHER MEN'S IDEAS INTO   455B ANNO REYNOLDS   MARG
  HIS FOOLERY
THE SYMMETRY OF DEFORMITY IS A PRETTY FOOLERY . . . . .   460C ANNO REYNOLDS   MARG

FOOLING
NOW THIS IS SUPREME FOOLING . . . .   475C ANNO REYNOLDS   MARG

FOOLISH
AND I SAID NO HE LOOKD VERY FOOLISH . . . .   29D EDW THIRD/PS 4 PROSE
VAIN FOOLISH MAN THAT ROAMS ON LOFTY ROCKS   . . . . .   37A CONTEMPLATN/PS PROSE
THOURT WAR THOU ART NOT LOVE O FOOLISH DALILA . . . .   38B SAMSON/PS   PROSE
HES A FOOLISH PUPPY SAID INFLAMMABLE GASS SMILING ON HIM   44C ISLAND MOON 1   PROSE
NO SAID OBTUSE ANGLE HOW CAN YOU BE SO FOOLISH AS TO THINK   48D ISLAND MOON 5   PROSE
  HE WAS
ID SOON MAKE DOUBLE ELEPHANT LOOK FOOLISH . . . . .   52B ISLAND MOON 8   PROSE
HAY HAY SAID HE YOU SHO WHY YA YA HOW CAN YOU BE   58C ISLAND MOON 10 PROSE
  SO FOOLISH
THAT BILL S A FOOLISH FELLOW   61   SAY YOU JOE/IM   9
MUCH LESS CAN INTELLECT TEACH AFFECTION HOW FOOLISH THEN   93A ANNO SWED LOVE MARG
AND THOU WILT BE AS FOOLISH AS THY FOOLISH BROTHER ZAZEL   109 TIRIEL 7   13
UPON THE SAND &C AND WHEN THE [FOOLISH ?CRAWLING] DRONE   110 TIRIEL 8   *   33
  . . .
IF OTHERS HAD NOT BEEN FOOLISH WE SHOULD BE SO   . . .   152B MARRIAGE HH 9   PROSE
AN ANGEL CAME TO ME AND SAID O PITIABLE FOOLISH YOUNG MAN   155C MARRIAGE HH 17 PROSE
[[IS A FOOLISH THING] IS A CHILD'S PLAY THING]   . . . .   178 THE FAIRY/N   *   21

731

```
                                                                PAGE      TITLE         LINE
FOOLISH    (CONTINUED)
         FOOLISH & TELLS INTO THE HANDS OF A TYRANT [WHO ?WILL XXX    400B ANNO BACON    * MARG
            HARM]
         THE WORD CAUSE IS A FOOLISH WORD . . . . . . . .         403C ANNO BACON       MARG
         WHAT CAN BE WORSE THAN THIS OR MORE FOOLISH              408A ANNO BACON       MARG
         HOW SHOULD ONE SO FOOLISH KNOW ABOUT RICHES    . . . . . 409A ANNO BACON       MARG
         VERY FOOLISH                                             409B ANNO BACON       MARG
         IS IN THESE PRELIMINARY ESSAYS CONTROVERTED & PROVED     413A ANNO BOYD        MARG
            FOOLISH
         HOW VERY FOOLISH ALL THIS IS  . . . . . . . . . . .      413C ANNO BOYD        MARG
         O ENGLISHMEN WHY ARE YOU STILL OF THIS FOOLISH CARDINAL'S 445D ANNO REYNOLDS   MARG
            OPINION
         FUTURE AGES THEY WILL AND SHALL FOOLISH MEN    . . . .   452C ANNO REYNOLDS    MARG
         IF THIS IS TRUE IT IS A DEVILISH FOOLISH THING TO BE AN  476D ANNO REYNOLDS    MARG
            ARTIST
         HOW SHOULD HE HE KNOW THE DUTIES OF ANOTHER O FOOLISH    487 MILTON 7          30
            FORBEARANCE
         BUT TO LOSE THEM THE FOOL MAKES HIS FOOLISH GAME . . . . 547 LET BE TOLD/N     9
         MR B(BLAKE) WILL NEVER BE SO FOOLISH AS TO DO ONE . . .  585A DESC CAT 15      PROSE
         MANY PEOPLE ARE SO FOOLISH (AS ) TO THINK THAT THEY . .  592D PUB ADDRESS/N    PROSE
         & ARE DEPRESSD UNDER FOOLISH RULERS  . . . . . . . .     612C V LAST JUDG/N    PROSE
         VAIN FOOLISH MAN WILT THOU BELIEVE WITHOUT EXPERIMENT . . 685 JERUSALEM 54     22
         A FOOLISH EXPERIMENT HAPPINESSES HAVE WINGS AND WHEELS .  807A LETTER 17       PROSE
         CONTEMPT FOR MY PERSON IT AFFRONTED MY FOOLISH PRIDE . .  827A LETTER 28       PROSE
         SUCH IS THE PRESENT STATE OF THINGS THIS FOOLISH ACCUSATION 828B LETTER 28     PROSE
         EVER INVITING GUESTS TO THE MARRIAGE O FOOLISH PHILOSOPHY 834A LETTER 33       PROSE
         FOR EVER IN THAT I AM STRONGER & STRONGER AS THIS FOOLISH 878A LETTER 28       PROSE
         NOAH & RAINBOW WISE & FOOLISH VIRGINS  . . . . . .       SUPP LETTER 56A       *PROSE
FOOLISHER
         & WHAT CAN BE FOOLISHER THAN THIS . . . . . . . . .      773B MIRTH AND COMP   PROSE
FOOLISHLY
         THREATENING & SWEARING AT ME I PERHAPS FOOLISHLY & PERHAPS 827A LETTER 28      PROSE
FOOLISHNESS
         THE WISDOM OF THIS WORLD IS FOOLISHNESS WITH GOD . . . . 396D ANNO BACON       MARG
FOOL'S
         PLEASURE AS I HAVE THERE I STAND & BEAR EVERY FOOL'S INSULT 53C ISLAND MOON 8  PROSE
         LISTEN TO THE FOOL'S REPROACH IT IS A KINGLY TITLE . . . 152A MARRIAGE HH 9    PROSE
         BUT A FOOL'S EYE IS NOT TO BE A CRITERION  . . . . . .   448C ANNO REYNOLDS    MARG
         A FOOL'S BALANCE IS NO CRITERION BECAUSE  . . . . . .    476B ANNO REYNOLDS    MARG
         WHETHER [THE FOOL'S HAND OR THE] PHYSIOGNOMIC STRENGTH .  591C PUB ADDRESS/N   PROSE
         POVERTY IS THE FOOL'S ROD WHICH AT LAST IS TURND ON HIS  612C V LAST JUDG/N    PROSE
            OWN BACK
FOOLS
         THUS FOOLS QUOTE SHAKESPEARE THE ABOVE IS THESEUS'S OPINION SUPP ANNO SWED HELL * MARG
         A PARCEL OF FOOLS GOING TO BRISTOL IF I WAS TO GO . . .  51D ISLAND MOON 7     PROSE
         WILL BE IGNORANT FOOLS & WILL NOT DESERVE TO LIVE . . .  62D ISLAND MOON 11    PROSE
         AND ARE NOT ALL OTHER MEN FOOLS SINNERS & NOTHINGS . . . 158B MARRIAGE HH 22   PROSE
         ATHEISM IS THUS THE BEST OF ALL BACON FOOLS US . . . .   404B ANNO BACON       MARG
         BETTER CHOOSE FOOLS AT ONCE  . . . . . . . . . . .       405C ANNO BACON       MARG
         WHAT FOOLS  . . . . . . . . . . . . . . . . . .          406A ANNO BACON       MARG
         THOSE THAT PUT THEIR BODIES TO ENDURE ARE FOOLS . . . .  408C ANNO BACON       MARG
         [AS DO ?FOOLS THAT ADORE THINGS & ?IDEAS XXX OF GENERAL  451A ANNO REYNOLDS    * MARG
            KNOWLEDGE]
         WHEN FRANCE GOT FREE EUROPE TWIXT FOOLS & KNAVES . . . . 451 ANNO REYNOLDS     1
         EMPLOYERS OF FOOLS TO BE EXECRATED IN  . . . . . .       452C ANNO REYNOLDS    MARG
         HE IS TO FOLLOW A GREAT MANY FOOLS  . . . . . . . .      455C ANNO REYNOLDS    MARG
         ARE MOCKD & DESTROYD BY THIS PRESIDENT OF FOOLS . . . .  458C ANNO REYNOLDS    MARG
         IT IS EVIDENT THAT REYNOLDS WISHD NONE BUT FOOLS . . . . 458C ANNO REYNOLDS    MARG
         MAKES BOTH STATESMEN & ARTISTS FOOLS & KNAVES . . . .    461C ANNO REYNOLDS    MARG
         & ADVERTISED FOR EVER IT WILL ONLY BE ADMIRED BY FOOLS . 466A ANNO REYNOLDS    MARG
         SUFFER NOT THE (FASHIONABLE) FOOLS  . . . . . . . .      480C MILTON 1         PROSE
         THE SUSSEX MEN ARE NOTED FOOLS . . . . . . . . .         538 SUSSEX MEN/N      1
         TIS CHRISTIAN MILDNESS WHEN [FOOLS] KNAVES PRAISE A FOE  539 SIR JOSH NIC/N    4
         THAT FOOLS HAVE THEIR HIGH FINISHINGS  . . . . . .       547 LET BE TOLD/N     3
         TO BE DRAWN FROM THE WORKS OF TWO MANIFEST FOOLS . . . . 550 WHEN I SEE/N      4
         GREAT MEN & FOOLS [OF] DO OFTEN ME INSPIRE . . . . . .   554 GREAT MEN/N       * 1
         BUT THE GREATER [FOOLS] FOOL THE [GREATER] GREATER LIAR  554 GREAT MEN/N       * 2
         HE HAS LAUGHED AT HIS KNAVES AND FOOLS AS I DO NOW . . . 575A DESC CAT 3       PROSE
         COMPELLD TO BE A TYRANNY PRINCES APPEAR TO ME TO BE FOOLS 600A PUB ADDRESS/N   PROSE
         HOUSES OF COMMONS & HOUSES OF LORDS APPEAR TO ME TO BE   600A PUB ADDRESS/N    PROSE
            FOOLS
         A LAST JUDGMENT IS NECESSARY BECAUSE FOOLS FLOURISH . .  612B V LAST JUDG/N    PROSE
         WHAT CAN BE DONE WITH SUCH DESPERATE FOOLS . . . . . .   751 EV GOSPEL(D)/N    21
         SOME CHILDREN ARE FOOLS & SO ARE SOME OLD MEN BUT THERE  794B LETTER 5         PROSE
            IS A
FOOLS'
         [FOOLS' OPINIONS & ENDEAVOURS DESTROY INVENTION] . . . . SUPP ANNO REYNOLDS    * MARG
FOOT
         THE SNAKE DOTH TURN AND BITE THE PADDING FOOT  . . . . . 24 EDW THIRD/PS 3     129
         WHERE ONLY NATURE'S FOOT HATH TROD  . . . . . . . .      36D CONTEMPLATN/PS    PROSE
         THAT GOD WOULD LOVE A WORM I KNEW AND PUNISH THE EVIL FOOT 130 BOOK OF THEL 5  9
         CHAIND HAND AND FOOT ROUND HIS NECK AN IRON BAND . . . . 135 FRENCH REVOLTN    27
         OR BAILLY THE STRONG FOOT OF FRANCE . . . . . . . . .    142 FRENCH REVOLTN    188
         THY BRETHREN AND NOT AS THY FOOT OR THY HAND . . . . .   143 FRENCH REVOLTN    194
         . . . CAPTAINS OF FOOT STAND EACH BY HIS CLOUDY DRUM . . 147 FRENCH REVOLTN    289
         AND SNAKE AND DAMP TOAD ON THE KINGLY FOOT CRAWL . . . . 147 FRENCH REVOLTN    298
         UNDERNEATH HIS FOOT  . . . . . . . . . . . . . .         174 HUMAN IMAGE/N     13
         IF THE [TREAD] STEP OF A FOOT  . . . . . . . . . .       178 THE FAIRY/N       7
         UNDERNEATH HIS FOOT  . . . . . . . . . . . . . .         217 HUMAN ABSTR/SE    12
         OF A FOOT OR A HAND OR A HEAD  . . . . . . . . . .       234 URIZEN 23         5
         [HE SPURND ENION WITH HIS FOOT HE SPRANG ALOFT IN CLOUDS] 266 FOUR ZOAS 1      92
         HE STARTS HE HEARS THE FOOT OF MAN HE SAYS TAKE THOU MY  276 FOUR ZOAS 1       455
            WOOL
```

		PAGE	TITLE	LINE
FOOT	**(CONTINUED)**			
	COVERD WITH BOILS FROM HEAD TO FOOT THE TERRIBLE SMITINGS OF LUVAH	294	FOUR ZOAS 3	82
	WANDRING IN VAIN HERE WILL I FIX MY FOOT & HERE REBUILD	317	FOUR ZOAS 6	* 227
	TILL A WHITE WOOF COVERD HIS COLD LIMBS FROM HEAD TO [FOOT] FEET	318	FOUR ZOAS 6	* 239
	LOS DREW THEM FORTH OUT OF THE DEEPS PLANTING HIS RIGHT FOOT FIRM	332	FOUR ZOAS 7	464
	SHALL NOW AVAIL YOU NOUGHT SO SPEAKING HE DASHD HIM WITH HIS FOOT	364	FOUR ZOAS 9	277
	IS NOT THIS THE BISHOP'S CLOVEN FOOT	390B	ANNO WATSON	MARG
	IS THE SWEAT OF ENVY'S FOOT	432	AUGURIES	48
	BETWEEN SOUTH MOLTON STREET & STRATFORD PLACE CALVARY'S FOOT	484	MILTON 4	21
	AND ON MY LEFT FOOT FALLING ON THE TARSUS ENTERD THERE	497	MILTON 15	49
	BUT FROM MY LEFT FOOT A BLACK CLOUD REDOUNDING SPREAD OVER EUROPE	497	MILTON 15	50
	REDOUNDING FROM MY LEFT FOOT INTO LOS'S MUNDANE SPACE .	502	MILTON 20	21
	BUT MILTON ENTERING MY FOOT I SAW IN THE NETHER . . .	503	MILTON 21	4
	AND ALL THIS VEGETABLE WORLD APPEARD ON MY LEFT FOOT .	503	MILTON 21	12
	UPON HIS FIBROUS LEFT FOOT BLACK MOST DISMAL TO OUR EYES	506	MILTON 22	35
	NO FAITH IS IN ALL THE EARTH THE BOOK OF GOD IS TRODDEN UNDER FOOT	506	MILTON 22	60
	ARE THE FOUR PILLARS OF HIS THRONE HIS LEFT FOOT NEAR LONDON	531	MILTON 39	36
	HIS RIGHT FOOT STRETCHES TO THE SEA ON DOVER CLIFFS HIS HEEL	531	MILTON 39	40
	HE MOVD HIS RIGHT FOOT TO CORNWALL HIS LEFT TO THE ROCKS OF BOGNOR	531	MILTON 39	49
	BUT RAFAEL THINKS A HEAD A FOOT A HAND	547	PRETTY EPIGR/N	4
	HE WHO DOES NOT KNOW HOW TO DRAW A HAND OR A FOOT . .	563D	DESC CAT	PROSE
	WITH THEIR HORSES AT THE FOOT OF A ROCK ON WHICH . . .	577A	DESC CAT 4	PROSE
	A CORSE OF A SLAUGHTERED BARD AT THE FOOT OF THE ROCK .	577A	DESC CAT 4	PROSE
	BY (ONE) FOOT HIGH THE ARTIST ENGAGES TO DELIVER IT . .	587A	CHAUCER 1	PROSE
	(THREE) FEET (ONE) INCH LONG BY ONE FOOT HIGH CONTAINING	587D	CHAUCER/N	PROSE
	EVERY EXPRESSION EVERY LINEAMENT OF HEAD HAND & FOOT .	588A	CHAUCER/N	PROSE
	THREE FEET I INCH LONG AND I FOOT HIGH PRICE THREE GUINEAS	589C	CHAUCER 2	TITLE
	HOW TO PUT SO MUCH LABOUR INTO A HEAD OR A FOOT AS DASIRE DID	593A	PUB ADDRESS/N	PROSE
	TO RESIST THE CONTEMPTIBLE COUNTER ARTS [SET ON FOOT] .	600B	PUB ADDRESS/N	PROSE
	[BUT] ORIGINALLY SET ON FOOT BY VENETIAN PICTURE TRADERS	600B	PUB ADDRESS/N	PROSE
	SET ON FOOT TILL IN MY OUTSET INTO LIFE IT WAS ARTFULLY PUBLISHD	602B	PUB ADDRESS/N	PROSE
	COVERD WITH BOILS FROM HEAD TO FOOT THE TERRIBLE SMITINGS OF LUVAH	655	JERUSALEM 29	64
	ALL POWERFUL PARENTAL AFFECTION FILLS ALBION FROM HEAD TO FOOT	685	JERUSALEM 54	10
	I AM LEFT TO THE TRAMPLING FOOT & THE SPURNING HEEL . . .	695	JERUSALEM 62	3
	CHAIND HAND & FOOT COMPELLD TO FIGHT UNDER THE IRON WHIPS	700	JERUSALEM 65	35
	I STRUCK THE THISTLE WITH MY FOOT	817	HAPPINESS/L	41
	PARTICULARLY COWPER'S MILTON A WORK NOW ON FOOT . . .	824C	LETTER 27	PROSE
	PRAYER AND PARENTAL AFFECTION FILL THE FIGURE FROM HEAD TO FOOT	864B	LETTER 61	PROSE
FOOTE				
	FOOTE IN CALLING WHITEFIELD HYPOCRITE WAS HIMSELF ONE .	682D	JERUSALEM 52	PROSE
FOOTMAN				
	& HER FOOTMAN & HER MAIDS & STORMONTS & BALLOON HATS .	52D	ISLAND MOON 8	PROSE
FOOTS				
	THE "VIEWS IN KEW GARDENS" "FOOTS CRAY" & "DIANA" & "ACTEON"	594A	PUB ADDRESS/N	PROSE
FOOTSTEP				
	A WEARINESS TO ME & THE HUMAN FOOTSTEP IS A TERROR TO ME	666	JERUSALEM 39	23
FOOTSTEPS				
	THEN WALKS THE WEAK INFANT IN SORROW COMPELLD TO NUMBER FOOTSTEPS	110	TIRIEL 8	32
	DOES THE WHALE WORSHIP AT THY FOOTSTEPS AS THE HUNGRY DOG	193	V DAU ALBION 5	33
	WHERE EVER THE FOOTSTEPS OF URIZEN	235	URIZEN 25	13
	AND JOY NOR HEAR HIS FOOTSTEPS AND	254	AHANIA 4	68
	MY FEET ARE TURNED BACKWARD & MY FOOTSTEPS SLIDE IN CLAY	335	FOUR ZOAS 7B	88
	I WALK BY THE FOOTSTEPS OF HIS FLOCKS COME HITHER TENDER FLOCKS	368	FOUR ZOAS 9	427
	I'LL WATCH YOU & ATTEND YOUR FOOTSTEPS YOU ARE NOT LIKE THE BIRDS	368	FOUR ZOAS 9	430
	SHE DREW NEAR TO HER HOUSE & HER FLOCKS FOLLOWD HER FOOTSTEPS	370	FOUR ZOAS 9	508
	HE SCENTS THY FOOTSTEPS IN THE SNOW	416	MY SPECTRE/N	27
	THE FOOTSTEPS AND INFIXING DEEP THE FEET IN MARBLE BEDS	500	MILTON 19	2
	HE HUNTS HER FOOTSTEPS THRO THE SNOW & THE WINTRY HAIL & RAIN	521	MILTON 32	5
	THE FOOTSTEPS OF THE LAMB OF GOD WERE THERE BUT NOW NO MORE	648	JERUSALEM 24	50
	GERMANY POLAND & THE NORTH WOOED MY FOOTSTEPS THEY FOUND	720	JERUSALEM 79	45
	HE WHO KEEPS NOT RIGHT ONWARD IS LOST & IF OUR FOOTSTEPS	813A	LETTER 22	PROSE
	INTO THE VERY EARTH BY THE FOOTSTEPS OF THE FIENDS OF COMMERCE	849D	LETTER 47	PROSE
FOP				
	CALLS THE SQUIRE THE FOP OF CHAUCER'S AGE NOW HEAR CHAUCER	573C	DESC CAT 3	PROSE
	WAS THIS A FOP...WAS THIS A FOP ...WAS THIS A FOP . .	573D	DESC CAT 3	PROSE
	HOW IS IT POSSIBLE THAT SUCH A FOP CAN BE SUPERIOR TO THE	830A	LETTER 30	PROSE
FOPPERY				
	AFFECTATION & FOPPERY HE WHO COPIES DOES NOT EXECUTE .	596B	PUB ADDRESS/N	PROSE
FOPS				
	SAVAGES ARE [FRIBBLES & POPS] POPS & FRIBBLES	468C	ANNO REYNOLDS	* MARG

FORBAD
    ALL MEN & WAS THEIR FATHER & FORBAD ALL CONTENTION   . . . 387B ANNO WATSON   MARG
    FORBAD & DOWN WITH DREADFUL GROANS HE SUNK UPON HIS COUCH   531 MILTON 39   51
FORBEAR
    I FORBEAR TO NAME [A LI] LIVING ARTISTS THO EQUALLY WORTHY 601B PUB ADDRESS/N *PROSE
FORBEARANCE
    CHRISTIAN FORBEARANCE . . . . 165C CHRISTN FORB/N TITLE
    HOW SHOULD HE HE KNOW THE DUTIES OF ANOTHER O FOOLISH   487 MILTON 7   30
        FORBEARANCE
    I THANK YOU AGAIN & AGAIN FOR YOUR GENEROUS FORBEARANCE   809C LETTER 20   PROSE
    ASTONISHD AT MY PATIENCE & FORBEARANCE OF INJURIES UPON   825D LETTER 27   PROSE
        INJURIES
FORBID
    NO GOD FORBID IM SURE HE IS NOT   . . . .   22 EDW THIRD/PS 3   25
    AND WOULD AGAIN WERE I NOT FORBID . . . .   23 EDW THIRD/PS 3   100
    IS NOT INFINITE THEY SHALL COME TO AN END WHICH GOD FORBID 91A ANNO SWED LOVE MARG
    O IJIM I AM FAINT & WEARY FOR MY KNEES FORBID . . . . . 104 TIRIEL 4   32
    FORBID ALL JOY & FROM HER CHILDHOOD SHALL THE LITTLE FEMALE 240 EUROPE 5   8
    GOD FORBID . . . . 474D ANNO REYNOLDS MARG
    TO EVERY ENERGY OF MAN AND FORBID THE SPRINGS OF LIFE   . 662 JERUSALEM 35   12
    THE POINT OF HIS SPEAR IF THOU PERSISTEST TO FORBID WITH   664 JERUSALEM 37   8
        LAWS
FORBIDDEN
    OF HEAVENLY SONG SOUND IN THE WILDS ONCE FORBIDDEN . . . 144 FRENCH REVOLTN   232
    EVERY EMANATIVE JOY FORBIDDEN AS A CRIME   . . . . . 628 JERUSALEM 9   14
    INSPIRATION DENYD GENIUS FORBIDDEN BY LAWS OF PUNISHMENT   628 JERUSALEM 9   16
    AS A PASSION WHICH IS FORBIDDEN BY LAW & RELIGION BUT NOW 798C LETTER 10   PROSE
        IT
    IS ALL JOY FORBIDDEN   . . . . SUPP PENC DRAW 1.7 *TITLE
FORBIDDING
    FORBIDDING US THAT VEIL WHICH SATAN PUTS BETWEEN EVE & ADAM 686 JERUSALEM 55   11
FORBORE
    AND THROUGH BEULAH AND ALL SILENT FORBORE TO CONTEND   . . 526 MILTON 35   40
FORCD
    THE SOUND IS FORCD THE NOTES ARE FEW . . . .   11 TO MUSES/PS   16
    BUT LONG I STAID NOT AT HIS PALACE FOR I AM FORCD TO WANDER 102 TIRIEL 3   11
    AND HE FORCD & FORCD & FORCD   . . . . 163 I SAW CHAPEL/N   7
FORCE
    BY FORCE UNCONQUERABLE AND WREST HIS SECRET FROM HIM   . . 38A SAMSON/PS   PROSE
    BUT I BY FORCE SUDDENLY CAUGHT HIM IN MY ARMS . . . . . 156D MARRIAGE HH 17 PROSE
    AND THE IMPURE SCOURGE FORCE HIS SEED INTO ITS UNRIPE BIRTH 193 V DAU ALBION 5   31
    ?WHO ANIMATING TIMES ON TIMES BY THE FORCE OF HER SWEET   267 FOUR ZOAS 1   120
        SONG
    ?FEELING THE HAND OF LOS IN GOLGONOOZA & THE FORCE   . . 344 FOUR ZOAS 8   112
    MALE FORMD THE DEMON MILD ATHLETIC FORCE HIS SHOULDERS   380 FOUR ZOAS AD 1   11
        SPREAD
    THIS HE HAS SHEWN WITH GREAT FORCE   . . . . 390D ANNO WATSON   MARG
    ITS PILLARS & PORTICOES TO TREMBLE AT THE FORCE   . . . 509 MILTON 24   55
    FOR LOS AGAINST THE EAST HIS FORCE CONTINUALLY BENDS   . . 512 MILTON 26   18
    THE FORCE OF LOS'S HAMMER IS ETERNAL FORGIVENESS BUT   . . 734 JERUSALEM 88   50
    AND ANGRY FORCE ME TO OBEY   . . . .   748 EV GOSPEL(B)/N   10
FORCED
    THEY ALL DECLINED & HE WAS FORCED TO SING HIMSELF   . . . 61D ISLAND MOON 11 PROSE
    ONLY BE FORCED TO BRING IT BACK TO WHAT IT WAS AND IT WILL 587A CHAUCER 1   PROSE
    HOW LONG SHALL I BE FORCED TO BEAT THIS INTO MEN'S EARS   602D PUB ADDR AD/N PROSE
    I HAVE BEEN FORCED TO INSIST ON HIS LEAVING ME IN BOTH TO   825C LETTER 27   PROSE
    A FABRICATED PERJURY I HAVE BEEN FORCED TO FIND BAIL   . 827D LETTER 28   PROSE
    I AM FORCED TO WRITE BECAUSE I CANNOT COME TO YOU & THIS   870C LETTER 72   PROSE
    BRINGS ON THE SHIVERING FIT WHEN I AM FORCED TO GO TO BED 872B LETTER 75   PROSE
    NOW I AM SHUT UP IN A CORNER THEREFORE AM FORCED TO ASK   878C LETTER 88   PROSE
FORCES
    IF I HAD NOT A PLACE OF PROFIT THAT FORCES ME TO GO TO   48A ISLAND MOON 4   PROSE
        CHURCH
FORCIBLY
    FORCIBLY THAT THE TOBIT & TOBIAS IN YOUR BEDCHAMBER WOULD 850D LETTER 49   PROSE
FORCING
    WHILE THE BROAD OAK WREATHD HIS ROOTS ROUND HER FORCING   335 FOUR ZOAS 7B   99
        HIS DARK WAY
FORD
    FRENCH FROM THE FORD DID HE FEAR THEN   . . . .   21 EDW THIRD/PS 3   12
    THE FORD   . . . .   23 EDW THIRD/PS 3   94
FOREGO
    TO FOREGO EACH HIS OWN DELIGHT TO WAR AGAINST HIS SPECTRE 273 FOUR ZOAS 1   340
FOREGOING
    CASH ON ACCT OF PLATES IN THE FOREGOING AGREEMENT   . . . SUPP LETTER 67D *PROSE
FOREGROUND
    THE ARMIES ARE FLEEING UPON THE MOUNTAINS ON THE FOREGROUND 608B V LAST JUDG/N PROSE
FOREHEAD
    GOD BLESS THY SHRIVELD BEARD GOD BLESS THY MANY WRINKLED   101 TIRIEL 2   *   36
        FOREHEAD
    HOW CAME THINE HAIR TO LEAVE THY FOREHEAD HOW CAME THY   102 TIRIEL 3   3
        FACE SO BROWN
    . . . HIS BROWS FOLDED HEAVY HIS FOREHEAD WAS IN AFFLICTION 137 FRENCH REVOLTN   79
    HAVE YOU NEVER SEEN FAYETTE'S FOREHEAD . . . . 142 FRENCH REVOLTN   187
    HIS FOREHEAD WAS DIVIDED INTO STREAKS OF GREEN & PURPLE   156C MARRIAGE HH 17 PROSE
    LIKE THOSE ON A TYGER'S FOREHEAD SOON WE SAW HIS MOUTH . . 156C MARRIAGE HH 17 PROSE
    O AFRICAN BLACK AFRICAN GO WINGED THOUGHT WIDEN   159C SONG LIBERTY   PROSE
        HIS FOREHEAD
    BUT THE FOREHEAD OF URIZEN GATHERING . . . . 250 AHANIA 3   1
    WHAT IS THAT NAME WRITTEN ON THY FOREHEAD WHAT ART THOU   312 FOUR ZOAS 6   9
    FOREHEAD & EYES THY LIPS DECAY LIKE ROSES IN [EARLY] THE   325 FOUR ZOAS 7   189
        SPRING

		PAGE	TITLE	LINE

FOREHEAD   (CONTINUED)

LOS REARD HIS MIGHTY [FOREHEAD] STATURE ON EARTH STOOD — 334 FOUR ZOAS 7B — 40
HIS FEET ABOVE

THE MOON HIS FURIOUS FOREHEAD CIRCLED WITH BLACK BURSTING — 334 FOUR ZOAS 7B — 41
THUNDERS

A CREST OF FIRE ROSE ON HIS FOREHEAD RED AS THE CARBUNCLE — 342 FOUR ZOAS 8 — 69

UNHURT & DARE THE INCLEMENT FOREHEAD OF THE KING OF LIGHT — 345 FOUR ZOAS 8 — 149

AND ON HER FOREHEAD WAS HER NAME WRITTEN IN BLOOD MYSTERY — 348 FOUR ZOAS 8 — 282

SCALES COVERD OVER A COLD FOREHEAD & A NECK OUTSTRETCHD — 352 FOUR ZOAS 8 — 423

AND FORM HIS FOREHEAD SMALL WITHOUT FRONTALS HIS JAWS LARGE — 580A DESC CAT 5 — PROSE

THE SUN FLED FROM THE BRITON'S FOREHEAD . . . . — 647 JERUSALEM 24 — 10

HIS FOREHEAD THEY BIND HIS FOREHEAD WITH THORNS OF IRON — 702 JERUSALEM 66 — 23

THY FOREHEAD BRIGHT HOLINESS TO THE LORD WITH GATES OF — 730 JERUSALEM 86 — 4
PEARL

AGAINST THEIR FACES & MY FOREHEAD AGAINST THEIR FOREHEADS — 825B LETTER 27 — PROSE

& OF THE FORGIVENESS OF SINS WRITTEN UPON THE MURDERER'S — SUPP ILLUS GENESIS — *TITLE
FOREHEAD

FOREHEADS

THROBS OF ANGUISH BEAT ON BRAZEN WAR FOREHEADS . . . . . — 137 FRENCH REVOLTN — 71

AND PAINE AND WARREN WITH THEIR FOREHEADS REARD TOWARD — 199 AMERICA 9 — 11
THE EAST

ROUZE UP O YOUNG MEN OF THE NEW AGE SET YOUR FOREHEADS . . — 480C MILTON 1 — PROSE

TRANSLUCENT IN THEIR FOREHEADS & THEIR BOSOMS & THEIR LOINS — 484 MILTON 5 — 8

AGAINST THEIR FACES & MY FOREHEAD AGAINST THEIR FOREHEADS — 825B LETTER 27 — PROSE

FOREIGNERS

STATES ARE NOT IMPROVED AT THE EXPENSE OF FOREIGNERS . . — 402D ANNO BACON — MARG

FORE SAIL

HIS SPRIT SAIL FORE SAIL MAIN SAIL & HIS MIZEN . . . . — 52 HEAR THEN/IM — 2

FORESEE

AND IN THE VISION & IN THE PROPHECY THAT WE MAY FORESEE — 739 JERUSALEM 92 — 19
& AVOID

STARVE I LAUGH AT FORTUNE & GO ON & ON I THINK I FORESEE — 795C LETTER 6 — PROSE

FORESEEN

SEE...WHERE HE SAYS THAT A PLACE FOR EVERY MAN IS FORESEEN — 131D ANNO SWED PROV — MARG

WHERE HE SAYS A PLACE FOR EACH MAN IS FORESEEN . . . . — 132A ANNO SWED PROV — MARG

SEE ALSO...WHERE HE SAYS THAT A PLACE FOR EACH MAN — 133D ANNO SWED PROV — MARG
IS FORESEEN

FORESEES

WHICH HE FORESEES SHALL SHORTLY BE DESTROYED . . . . . — 682A JERUSALEM 52 — PROSE

FORESHEW

LOOK HOW THE BEAMS FORESHEW THE RISING OF SOME GLORIOUS — 367 FOUR ZOAS 9 — 398
POWER

FOREST

AND THE LION GLARES THRO THE DUN FOREST . . . . — 3 EVNING STAR/PS — 12

ROAMS ROUND VAST NATURE'S FOREST WHERE NO BOUNDS . . . . — 27 EDW THIRD/PS 3 — 256

THICK AS A FOREST READY FOR THE AXE . . . . — 32 EDW THIRD/PS 6 — 24

LIKE AS A FOREST ROARS WITH CRACKLING FLAMES . . . . . — 32 EDW THIRD/PS 6 — 27

THE BREATH OF NIGHT SLEPT AMONG THE LEAVES OF THE FOREST — 36C COUCH DEATH/PS — PROSE

THEN IF CHANCE ALONG THIS FOREST . . . . — 61 LEAVE O/IM — 5

MET HIM AT ENTRANCE OF THE FOREST IN A DARK & LONELY WAY — 103 TIRIEL 4 — 4

THEN I HAVE [REND] RENT HIS LIMBS & LEFT HIM ROTTING IN — 105 TIRIEL 4 — * 51
THE FOREST

AS I WANDERD THE FOREST . . . . — 175 WILD FLOWERS/N — 1

REARS ITS IMMORTAL PINNACLES BUILT IN THE FOREST OF GOD — 200 AMERICA 10 — 9

AND OUTSTRETCHD ON THE EDGE OF THE FOREST . . . . . . — 251 AHANIA 3 — 44

SHE COULD CONTROLL THE SPACES REGIONS DESART FLOOD & FOREST — 271 FOUR ZOAS 1 — 241

HE CURSES FOREST SPRING & RIVER DESART & SANDY WASTE . . — 629 JERUSALEM 10 — 26

THE FOREST AND THE MARSH AND THE PITS OF BITUMEN DEADLY — 634 JERUSALEM 13 — 39

AND AS DARK ROOTS AND STEMS A FOREST OF AFFLICTION GROWING — 634 JERUSALEM 14 — 8

OF THE WILD INHABITANT OF THE FOREST TO DRIVE THEM FROM — 638 JERUSALEM 17 — 4
HIS OWN

THE DISTANT FOREST THEN THE SLAVE GROANS IN THE DUNGEON — 642 JERUSALEM 20 — 15
OF STONE

THE CITY OF THE WOODS IN THE FOREST OF EPHRATAH IS TAKEN — 653 JERUSALEM 29 — 18

FORESTER

THE DOG DOTH SEIZE THE WOLF THE FORESTER THE LION . . . — 24 EDW THIRD/PS 3 — 119

FORESTS

THE [GLOOM] SECRET FORESTS & ALL NIGHT WANDERD IN DESOLATE — 106 TIRIEL 4 — * 90
WAYS

AND THE ANCIENT FORESTS OF CHIVALRY HEWN . . . . — 138 FRENCH REVOLTN — 93

TO ROUZE UP THE ANCIENT FORESTS OF EUROPE . . . . — 138 FRENCH REVOLTN — 101

. . . THAT WANDER IN FORESTS AND HOWL IN LAW BLASTED WASTES — 144 FRENCH REVOLTN — 227

. . . GROANING SHAKING FORESTS AND FLOODS THE COLD NEWT — 147 FRENCH REVOLTN — 297

. . . SHAKEN THE FORESTS OF FRANCE SICK THE KINGS OF THE — 147 FRENCH REVOLTN — 300
NATIONS

IN THE FORESTS OF THE NIGHT . . . . — 172 THE TYGER/N 1 — 2

IN (THE) FORESTS OF THE NIGHT . . . . — 173 THE TYGER/N 1 — * 23

IN THE FORESTS OF THE NIGHT . . . . — 173 THE TYGER/N 2 — 2

IN THE FORESTS OF THE NIGHT . . . . — 173 THE TYGER/N 2 — 18

WITH COLD FLOODS OF ABSTRACTION AND WITH FORESTS — 193 V DAU ALBION 5 — 19
OF SOLITUDE

IN THE FORESTS OF THE NIGHT . . . . — 214 THE TYGER/SE — 2

IN THE FORESTS OF THE NIGHT . . . . — 214 THE TYGER/SE — 22

BUT ETERNALS BEHELD HIS VAST FORESTS . . . . — 223 URIZEN 3 — 23

IN FORESTS OF ETERNAL DEATH SHRIEKING IN HOLLOW TREES . . — 238 EUROPE PREL 2 — 6

O LION RINTRAH RAISE THY FURY FROM THY FORESTS BLACK . — 240 EUROPE 8 — 2

IN FORESTS OF NIGHT THEN ALL THE ETERNAL FORESTS WERE — 241 EUROPE 10 — 18
DIVIDED

WHEN OBSCURD IN HIS FORESTS FELL MONSTERS . . . . . . — 250 AHANIA 3 — 6

I SEE THY BLACK FORESTS AND FLOODS . . . . — 254 AHANIA 4 — 58

NINE TIMES THEY LIVD AMONG THE FORESTS FEEDING ON SWEET — 270 FOUR ZOAS 1 — 233
FRUITS

735

```
                                                              PAGE    TITLE         LINE
FORESTS   (CONTINUED)
    IN FORESTS OF AFFLICTION  . . . . . . . . . . .         289 FOUR ZOAS 2        372
    . . . HIS LOCKS ARE LIKE THE FORESTS  . . . . .         308 FOUR ZOAS 5        127
    IN FORESTS OF AFFLICTION THE ADAMANTINE SCALES OF JUSTICE 320 FOUR ZOAS 7       10
    RED RAGE REDOUNDS HE ROUZD HIS LIONS FROM HIS FORESTS BLACK 336 FOUR ZOAS 7B  * 141
    THEY ARE BECOME LIKE WINTRY FLOCKS LIKE FORESTS STRIPD  357 FOUR ZOAS 9         22
        OF LEAVES
    LOWING THEY KNEEL BEFORE THE HEAVENS THE WILD BEASTS OF 358 FOUR ZOAS 9         55
        THE FORESTS
    THE RAVEN CALLD THE HAWK I HEARD THEM FROM MY FORESTS BLACK 358 FOUR ZOAS 9     60
    THE TYGERS FROM THE FORESTS & THE LIONS [OF] FROM THE   365 FOUR ZOAS 9     * 301
        SANDY DESARTS
    THEY ARE BECOME LIKE WINTRY FLOCKS LIKE FORESTS STRIPD  365 FOUR ZOAS 9        327
        OF LEAVES
    HERDS THRONG UP THE VALLEY WILD BEASTS FILL THE FORESTS 373 FOUR ZOAS 9        612
    THRO ALBION'S FOUR FORESTS WHICH OVERSPREAD ALL THE EARTH 485 MILTON 6          3
    WITH SHOUTS AND PALAMABRON'S SONGS RENDING THE FORESTS  488 MILTON 8            9
        GREEN
    THE LAKE OF UDAN-ADAN IN THE FORESTS OF ENTUTHON BENYTHON 512 MILTON 26        25
    AROUND THE CITY OF GOLGONOOZA IN THE FORESTS OF ENTUTHON 514 MILTON 27         43
    NOURISHED BY THE SPIRITS OF FORESTS AND FLOODS  . . . 580D DESC CAT 5        PROSE
    HERTFORDSHIRE GLOWS WITH FIERCE VEGETATION IN THE FORESTS 636 JERUSALEM 16      3
    MY CATTLE NEXT LAST EVN THE DOG OF MY GATE THE FORESTS FLED 643 JERUSALEM 21    8
    HIDDEN IN ALBION'S FORESTS HE LURKS HE ADMITS OF NO REPLY 653 JERUSALEM 29     13
    HIMSELF OF ALBION'S FORESTS & WILDS AND JERUSALEM IS TAKEN 653 JERUSALEM 29    17
    THEY RAGE LIKE WILD BEASTS IN THE FORESTS OF AFFLICTION 671 JERUSALEM 42       61
    WE CANNOT AWAKE AND OUR SPECTRES RAGE IN THE FORESTS  . 671 JERUSALEM 42       73
    LOUD LOUD THE MOUNTAINS LIFTED UP THEIR VOICES LOUD THE 686 JERUSALEM 55       23
        FORESTS
    THEY NAMD THE EIGHTH HE CAME NOT HE HID IN ALBION'S FORESTS 686 JERUSALEM 55   33
    EUPHRATES & TO FORESTS & FLOODS & ANIMALS WILD & TAME FROM 695 JERUSALEM 61    31
    AMONG THE FOUR FORESTS OF ALBION WHICH OVERSPREAD ALL THE 722 JERUSALEM 80     43
        EARTH
    OVER THE FORESTS WITH BITTER TEARS AND OVER THE WINDING 726 JERUSALEM 82       73
        WORM
    AND ALBION'S FORESTS OF OAKS COVERD THE EARTH FROM POLE 735 JERUSALEM 89       23
        TO POLE
    & HIS PLUTE HEARD FROM HIS SECRET FORESTS CHEARS US TO . . 791C LETTER 3     PROSE
FORETOLD
    TWICE WAS MY BIRTH FORETOLD FROM HEAVEN AND  . . . . .  39B SAMSON/PS        PROSE
    THIS IS ETERNAL DEATH AND THIS THE TORMENT LONG FORETOLD 196 AMERICA PREL 2    17
    AS THE PROPHETS HAD FORETOLD  . . . . . . . . . .  652B JERUSALEM 27         PROSE
FOREVER
    WHERE THE IMPRESSIONS OF DESPAIR & HOPE ENROOT FOREVER . . 295 FOUR ZOAS 3    143
    THOU ART FOREVER LOST WHAT CAN I DO TO HINDER THE SONS . 657 JERUSALEM 31      37
FOR-EVER
    YET THE DIVINE VISION REMAINS EVERY-WHERE FOR-EVER AMEN 505 MILTON 22          2
    BUT THEIR FORMS ETERNAL EXIST FOR-EVER AMEN HALLELUJAH  . 522 MILTON 32      * 38
    CONSUMING AND CONSUMD FOR-EVER IN FLAMES OF MORAL JUSTICE 667 JERUSALEM 40     30
    AND WASHD INCESSANT BY THE FOR-EVER RESTLESS SEA-WAVES  741 JERUSALEM 94        6
        FOAMING ABROAD
FOREVERMORE
    IN THE SHADOWS OF POSSIBILITY BY MUTUAL FORGIVENESS     739 JERUSALEM 92       18
        FOREVERMORE
FOR-EVERMORE
    ART THOU ALIVE & LIVEST THOU FOR-EVERMORE OR ART THOU  . . 693 JERUSALEM 60    54
FORFAR
    OF REUBEN KINCARD HADDNTN FORFAR SIMEON AYR ARGYLL BANFF 638 JERUSALEM 16      53
FORFEITS
    PLAYD AT FORFEITS & TRYD EVERY METHOD TO GET GOOD HUMOUR 59B ISLAND MOON 11  PROSE
FORGAVE
    WHO NEVER IN HIS LIFE FORGAVE A FRIEND  . . . . . . . 544 TO FORGIVE/N         2
    GWANTOKE FORGAVE & JOYD OVER SOUTH WALES & ALL ITS     710 JERUSALEM 71       29
        MOUNTAINS
FORGAVEST
    ASTONISHD AT HIS BEAUTY & PERFECTION THOU FORGAVEST HIS 643 JERUSALEM 20       37
        FURIOUS LOVE
FORGD      SEE MIND-FORGD,MIND FORGD,TRIPLE FORGD
    WERE FORGD SMALLER AS THE FLESH DECAYD . . . . . . .   135 FRENCH REVOLTN     31
    IT WAS FORGD IN MILLS WHERE THE WINTER  . . . . . . . 249 AHANIA 2            23
    HE FORGD NETS OF IRON AROUND  . . . . . . . . . . . 253 AHANIA 4             29
    THEY FORGD THE SWORD THE CHARIOT OF WAR THE BATTLE AX  . . 337 FOUR ZOAS 7B   172
    HE FORGD THE LAW INTO A SWORD  . . . . . . . . . . 420 I SAW MNK AD/N         3
    AND A DEATH OF EIGHT THOUSAND YEARS FORGD BY THYSELF UPON 664 JERUSALEM 37     7
    HE FORGD THE LAW INTO A SWORD  . . . . . . . . . . 683 I SAW A MONK/J        19
    THEY FORGD THE SWORD ON CHEVIOT THE CHARIOT OF WAR & THE 699 JERUSALEM 65      14
        BATTLE-AX
FORGE
    THE HUMAN FORM A FIERY FORGE  . . . . . . . . . . .  221 DIVNE IMAGE/SE        6
    THEN SIEZD THE LIONS OF URIZEN THEIR WORK & HEATED IN THE 283 FOUR ZOAS 2     135
        FORGE
    TO FORGE THE CURBS OF IRON & BRASS TO BUILD THE IRON   292 FOUR ZOAS 3        34
        MANGERS
    LOS SAT UPON HIS ANVIL STOCK THEY SAT BESIDE THE FORGE 350 FOUR ZOAS 8       348
    IN DENS OF DEATH TO FORGE THE SPADE THE MATTOCK & THE AX 365 FOUR ZOAS 9      306
    ON TYBURN'S BROOK LOUD GROANS THAMES BENEATH THE IRON FORGE 485 MILTON 6      11
    . . . TO FORGE THE INSTRUMENTS . . . . . . . . . . 485 MILTON 6             12
    HE SIEZD THE BARS OF CONDENSD THOUGHTS TO FORGE THEM  . . 628 JERUSALEM 9      4
    YET CEASD HE NOT FROM LABOURING AT THE ROARINGS OF HIS 630 JERUSALEM 10       62
        FORGE
    HE QUENCHES IT IN THE BLACK TROUGH OF HIS FORGE LONDON'S 636 JERUSALEM 16     14
        RIVER
```

FORGE   (CONTINUED)
     FEEDS THE DREAD FORGE TREMBLING & SHUDDERING ALONG THE   636 JERUSALEM 16   15
          VALLEYS
     ARE THE TEMPLES AMONG HIS PILLARS BRITAIN IS LOS'S FORGE   690 JERUSALEM 58   42
     OF JERUSALEM'S CHERUBIMS & TO FORGE THEM SWORDS OF HER   729 JERUSALEM 84   10
          ALTARS
     THUS JOYD THE SPECTRE IN THE DUSKY FIRES OF LOS'S FORGE   734 JERUSALEM 88   44
          EYEING
     HEATED IN THE SMITH'S FORGE BUT COLD THE WIND OF THEIR   735 JERUSALEM 89   42
          DREAD FURY
     IRON OF HIS FORGE & FIXES THEM INTO BONES OF CHALK & ROCK   736 JERUSALEM 90   20
     DOLOROUS ARE THEIR LAMENTATIONS IN THE BURNING FORGE   . .   737 JERUSALEM 90   45
FORGED   SEE GERMAN FORGED,FORGD
     AND FORGED HELM AND SHIELD OF SEVEN TIMES BEATEN BRASS . .   17 EDW THIRD/PS 1   4
     THE HUMAN DRESS IS FORGED IRON . . . .   221 DIVNE IMAGE/SE   5
     AND WHO FIRST FORGED THE SILLY STORY AND KNOWN FALSHOOD   565B DESC CAT 2   PROSE
     WHERE IMPLEMENTS OF WAR ARE FORGED THE PLOW TO GO OVER   660 JERUSALEM 34   13
          THE NATIONS
FORGES
     AND FORGES FETTERS FOR THE MIND   . . . .   175 HOW TO KNOW/N   10
     . . . WE BEHOLD WITH WONDER ENITHARMON'S LOOMS & LOS'S   346 FOUR ZOAS 8   200
          FORGES
     TEN THOUSAND DEMONS LABOUR AT THE FORGES CREATING   346 FOUR ZOAS 8   205
          CONTINUALLY
FORGET
     AND FORGET HIS YOUTHFUL SPRING . . . .   124 SCHOOL BOY/SI   20
     . . . THEY LOOK DOWNWARD AND LABOUR AND FORGET MY HOLY LAW   140 FRENCH REVOLTN   139
     THE LUSTFUL JOY SHALL FORGET TO GENERATE & CREATE   194 V DAU ALBION 7   6
          AN AMOROUS IMAGE
     DESCEND TO GENERATIONS THAT IN FUTURE TIMES FORGET   . . .   197 AMERICA 3   12
     DESCEND TO GENERATIONS THAT IN FUTURE TIMES FORGET   . . .   204 AMERICA CANC A   12
     AND CANNOT THOSE WHO ONCE HAVE LOVD EVER FORGET THEIR LOVE   298 FOUR ZOAS 4   17
     O FOOL COULD I FORGET THE LIGHT THAT FILLED MY BRIGHT   310 FOUR ZOAS 5   216
          SPHERES
     THAT MAN SHOULD LABOUR & SORROW & LEARN & FORGET & RETURN   355 FOUR ZOAS 8   574
     YOU SHALL FORGET YOUR FORMER STATE RETURN O LOVE IN PEACE   366 FOUR ZOAS 9   * 364
     THEY SEEM TO FORGET THAT THERE IS A GOD OF THIS WORLD A GOD   394C ANNO WATSON   MARG
     WHICH YOU STRIVE TO FORGET IN VAIN   . . . .   423 THE SMILE   8
     & HIS FRENCH JOURNEYMEN WHOSE NAMES I FORGET . . . .   594A PUB ADDRESS/N   PROSE
     TILL THY AWAKING YET ALAS I SHALL FORGET ETERNITY   . . .   727 JERUSALEM 83   3
     ENITHARMON'S NAME IS NOTHING BEFORE YOU YOU FORGET ALL   740 JERUSALEM 93   3
          MY LOVE
     "FORGET YOUR SERVICES TO US OR ANY WAY NEGLECT TO LOVE &"   800A LETTER 12   PROSE
FORGETFUL
     WITH FADED RADIANCE SIGHD FORGETFUL OF THE FLOWING WINE   276 FOUR ZOAS 1   437
     FORGETFUL OF HIS OWN LAWS PITYING HE BEGAN TO EMBRACE   . .   352 FOUR ZOAS 8   420
FORGETFULNESS
     COVERD WITH SILENCE AND FORGETFULNESS   . . . . . .   30 EDW THIRD/PS 5   5
     FORGETFULNESS DUMBNESS NECESSITY . . . .   228 URIZEN 10   24
     FORGETFULNESS DUMBNESS NECESSITY IN CHAINS OF THE MIND   303 FOUR ZOAS 4   211
          LOCKD UP
     BUT HOW I KNOW NOT THEN FORGETFULNESS QUITE WRAPD ME UP   326 FOUR ZOAS 7   260
     THEIR LOOMS IN A GENERATION OF DEATH & RESURRECTION TO   638 JERUSALEM 17   9
          FORGETFULNESS
     MR JOHNSON'S FORGETFULNESS WHO APPOINTD TO CALL ON YOU BUT   809C LETTER 20   *PROSE
FORGETS
     AND URIZEN REPENTANT FORGETS HIS WISDOM IN THE ABYSS   . .   353 FOUR ZOAS 8   463
     THE SUN FORGETS HIS COURSE LIKE A DRUNKEN MAN HE HESITATES   703 JERUSALEM 66   74
FORGETTER
     AS THE MOST INNOCENT FORGETTER OF HIS OWN INTERESTS   . . .   809C LETTER 20   PROSE
FORGETTEST
     WHAT THOU FORGETTEST THEY IN US & WE IN THEM ALTERNATE LIVD   327 FOUR ZOAS 7   276
FORGETTING
     FORGETTING THE OFFENCES OF THEIR MOST REBELLIOUS CHILDREN   108 TIRIEL 6   27
     FORGETTING THAT WITHIN THAT CENTER ETERNITY EXPANDS   . . .   520 MILTON 31   48
     WHERE WE LIVE FORGETTING ERROR NOT PONDERING ON EVIL   . .   642 JERUSALEM 20   7
     IS FORGETTING & FORGIVING . . . .   724 IN HEAVEN/J   2
     FORGETTING THAT FALSHOOD IS PROPHETIC SHE HID HER HAND   725 JERUSALEM 82   *   20
          BEHIND HER
     THE LABOURS OF LIFE & WE PLOW & REAP FORGETTING OUR LABOUR   791C LETTER 3   PROSE
FORGING
     INCESSANT BEAT FORGING CHAINS NEW & NEW . . . .   227 URIZEN 10   17
FORGIVE
     FORGIVE MY LORDS MY TALKATIVE YOUTH THAT SPEAKS   . . . .   20 EDW THIRD/PS 2   38
     FORGIVE MY PREJUDICE SIR JOHN I THINK   . . . . . .   25 EDW THIRD/PS 3   191
     SUCH A ONE I CAN NEVER FORGIVE WHILE HE CONTINUES SUCH   72C ANNO LAVATER   MARG
          A ONE
     IF YOU EXPECT HIS RESENTMENT YOU DO NOT FORGIVE HIM NOW   77A ANNO LAVATER   MARG
     ("A SCORPION WHIP OF DESTINY") & NEVER FORGIVE HIM TILL   79B ANNO LAVATER   MARG
          HE MENDS
     ("FORGIVE A TRESPASS OF MALICE") UNEASY THIS I KNOW NOT   80D ANNO LAVATER   MARG
     ("THE PUBLIC SELDOM FORGIVE TWICE ") LET US TAKE THEIR   85D ANNO LAVATER   MARG
          EXAMPLE
     ("FORGET IT FORGIVE IT BUT KEEP HIM AT DISTANCE") THIS   87D ANNO LAVATER   MARG
          IS A PARADOX
     FORGIVE US O THOU PITEOUS ONE WHOM WE HAVE OFFENDED FORGIVE   286 FOUR ZOAS 2   227
     WHEN WILT THOU PITY [&] AS I FORGIVE . . . .   416 MY SPECTRE/N   50
     I FORGIVE YOU YOU FORGIVE ME . . . .   417 MY SPECTRE/N   72
     AND CAN YOU THUS LAMENT & CAN YOU PITY & FORGIVE   . . . .   523 MILTON 34   6
     TO FORGIVE ENEMIES H(HAYLEY) DOES PRETEND . . . . .   544 TO FORGIVE/N   1
     DOES FORGIVE SIN IS CRUCIFIED AS AN ABETTOR OF CRIMINALS   616C V LAST JUDG/N   PROSE
     THEREFORE [DEAR] READER [FORGIVE] WHAT YOU DO NOT APPROVE   621B JERUSALEM 3   PROSE

		PAGE	TITLE	LINE

FORGIVE   (CONTINUED)

YET THEY FORGIVE MY WANDERINGS I REST NOT FROM MY GREAT TASK — 623 JERUSALEM 5 — 17

THIS HAS DIVIDED THEE IN SUNDER AND WILT THOU STILL FORGIVE — 625 JERUSALEM 7 — 27

FORGIVE & PITY ME O UNFOLD THY VEIL IN MERCY & LOVE . . . — 643 JERUSALEM 20 — 26

DOST THOU FORGIVE ME THOU WHO WAST DEAD & ART ALIVE . . . — 648 JERUSALEM 24 — 58

IF WE HAVE OFFENDED FORGIVE US TAKE NOT VENGEANCE AGAINST US — 665 JERUSALEM 38 — 26

IT IS BETTER TO PREVENT ERROR THAN TO FORGIVE THE CRIMINAL — 687 JERUSALEM 55 — 50

HIS ARMS DOTH HE FORGIVE JERUSALEM & NOT EXACT PURITY FROM HER WHO IS — 694 JERUSALEM 61 — 15

SAYING DOTH JEHOVAH FORGIVE A DEBT ONLY ON CONDITION THAT IT SHALL — 694 JERUSALEM 61 — 17

BE PAYED DOTH HE FORGIVE POLLUTION ONLY ON CONDITIONS OF PURITY — 694 JERUSALEM 61 — 18

OF JEHOVAH IF YOU FORGIVE ONE-ANOTHER SO SHALL JEHOVAH FORGIVE YOU — 695 JERUSALEM 61 — 25

BUT IF YOU ON EARTH FORGIVE . . . . — 724 IN HEAVEN/J — 4

IT IS EASIER TO FORGIVE AN ENEMY THAN TO FORGIVE A FRIEND — 737 JERUSALEM 91 — 2

IF HE HAD CAIPHAS WOULD FORGIVE . . . . — 752 EV GOSPEL(D)/N — 33

CANST THOU FORGIVE MY BLASPHEMY . . . . — 755 EV GOSPEL(E)/N — 76

AND CANST THOU PITY & FORGIVE . . . . — 755 EV GOSPEL(E)/N — 80

WHICH IS THIS IF YOU FORGIVE ONE ANOTHER YOUR TRESPASSES — 757D EV GOSPEL — PROSE

SO SHALL JEHOVAH FORGIVE YOU . . . . — 757D EV GOSPEL — PROSE

AND A CONTRITE HEART O I CANNOT FORGIVE THE ACCUSER HATH — 780 GHOST ABEL 2 — 5

HE KNOWS NOT TO FORGIVE . . . . — 784B ANNO WW EXCUR — MARG

FORGIVE ME FOR EXPRESSING TO YOU MY ENTHUSIASM WHICH I WISH — 797B LETTER 9 — PROSE

& HOPE YOU WILL FORGIVE THE POETRY . . . . — 799B LETTER 11 — PROSE

BUT BY MY CONJUNCTION WITH FLAXMAN WHO KNOWS TO FORGIVE NERVOUS FEAR — 799 TO FLAXMAN/L — 12

SHE WILL FORGIVE ANY FAILURE IN CONSIDERATION OF THE ENDEAVOUR — 815D LETTER 23 — PROSE

PRAY FORGIVE ERRORS IN OMISSIONS OF THIS KIND I AM . . . — 816A LETTER 23 — PROSE

TO ME FORGIVE THIS DIRGE-LIKE LAMENTATION OVER A DEAD HORSE — 830B LETTER 30 — PROSE

FORGIVEN

PERHAPS I MAY BE FORGIVEN WHILE HE SPEAKS THE FLAMES ROLL ON — 364 FOUR ZOAS 9 — 271

SPEAKS A WORD AGAINST THE SON OF MAN SHALL BE FORGIVEN . — 387C ANNO WATSON — MARG

HE COMES TO DELIVER MAN THE [FORGIVEN] ACCUSED . . . . — 615B V LAST JUDG/N — *PROSE

ERROR & FAULT THAT IS SOON FORGIVEN BUT MERCY IS NOT A SIN — 643 JERUSALEM 20 — 24

THAT DEBT IS NOT FORGIVEN THAT POLLUTION IS NOT FORGIVEN — 694 JERUSALEM 61 — 19

MY SIN THOU HAST FORGIVEN ME . . . . — 755 EV GOSPEL(E)/N — 75

THY SINS ARE ALL FORGIVEN THEE . . . . — 758 EV GOSPEL (2) — 18

THY SINS ARE ALL FORGIVEN THEE . . . . — 758 EV GOSPEL (2) — 23

FORGIVENESS

FORGIVENESS OF ENEMIES CAN ONLY COME UPON THEIR REPENTANCE — 77A ANNO LAVATER — MARG

OF PITY COMPASSION FORGIVENESS . . . . — 224 URIZEN 4 — 35

. . . IN FORGIVENESS OF [FORMER INJURIES] ANCIENT INJURIES — 330 FOUR ZOAS 7 — * 419

THE GOSPEL IS FORGIVENESS OF SINS & HAS NO MORAL PRECEPTS — 395C ANNO WATSON — MARG

BUT THE TEAR OF LOVE & FORGIVENESS SWEET . . . . . — 420 I SAW A MONK/N — 53

TO ANNIHILATE THE SELF-HOOD OF DECEIT & FALSE FORGIVENESS — 497 MILTON 16 — 1

PROSTRATE BEFORE THE STARRY EIGHT ASKING WITH TEARS FORGIVENESS — 525 MILTON 35 — 32

THERE IS NO SUCH THING THERE AS FORGIVENESS OF SIN HE WHO — 616C V LAST JUDG/N — PROSE

ONE ANOTHER FORGIVENESS OF SIN IS ONLY AT THE JUDGMENT SEAT — 616D V LAST JUDG/N — PROSE

THE SPIRIT OF JESUS IS CONTINUAL FORGIVENESS OF SIN . . — 621A JERUSALEM 3 — PROSE

O POINT OF MUTUAL FORGIVENESS BETWEEN ENEMIES . . . . — 626 JERUSALEM 7 — 66

LABOUR OF MERCIFUL HANDS THE BEAMS & RAFTERS ARE FORGIVENESS — 632 JERUSALEM 12 — 32

THE HARLOT DAUGHTER MOTHER OF PITY AND DISHONOURABLE FORGIVENESS — 640 JERUSALEM 18 — 12

NOR PITY NOR LOVE NOR KIND FORGIVENESS O IF I HAVE SINNED — 643 JERUSALEM 20 — 25

WHEN FORGIVENESS MIGHT IT WEAVE WITH WINGS OF CHERUBIM . — 645 JERUSALEM 22 — 35

AND DEAR MUTUAL FORGIVENESS & TO BECOME ONE GREAT SATAN — 679 JERUSALEM 49 — 29

THIS IS THE ONLY MEANS TO FORGIVENESS OF ENEMIES . . . — 680 JERUSALEM 49 — 75

FOUND NO FRIEND FRIENDSHIP CANNOT EXIST WITHOUT FORGIVENESS — 682D JERUSALEM 52 — PROSE

ITS ACTORS BUT THE RELIGION OF JESUS FORGIVENESS OF SIN — 683A JERUSALEM 52 — PROSE

THE GLORY OF CHRISTIANITY IS TO CONQUER BY FORGIVENESS . — 683A JERUSALEM 52 — PROSE

A TENT & TABERNACLE OF MUTUAL FORGIVENESS MALE & FEMALE CLOTHINGS — 684 JERUSALEM 54 — 4

OF THE (FORGIVENESS) OF SINS . . . . — 694 JERUSALEM 61 — 12

SUCH IS THE FORGIVENESS OF THE GODS THE MORAL VIRTUES OF THE — 694 JERUSALEM 61 — 20

. . . IN THE CONTINUAL FORGIVENESS OF SINS . . . . — 694 JERUSALEM 61 — 22

O FORGIVENESS & PITY & COMPASSION IF I WERE PURE I SHOULD NEVER — 695 JERUSALEM 61 — 44

WITHOUT THE FORGIVENESS OF SINS IN THE MERCIFUL CLOUDS OF JEHOVAH — 697 JERUSALEM 63 — 27

WITHOUT FORGIVENESS OF SIN LOVE IS ITSELF ETERNAL DEATH — 699 JERUSALEM 64 — 24

BY SELF-DENIAL & FORGIVENESS OF SIN . . . . . . — 718 STOOD AMONG/J — 23

THE FORCE OF LOS'S HAMMER IS ETERNAL FORGIVENESS BUT . — 734 JERUSALEM 88 — 50

[FORGIVENESS OF ENEMIES ?CAN XXX ONLY XXX GOD XXX] . . — 737 JERUSALEM 91 — * 1

IN THE SHADOWS OF POSSIBILITY BY MUTUAL FORGIVENESS FOREVERMORE — 739 JERUSALEM 92 — 18

ONE FOR ANOTHER TO PUT OFF BY FORGIVENESS EVERY SIN . . — 743 JERUSALEM 96 — 19

IN FORGIVENESS OF SINS WHICH IS SELF ANNIHILATION . . . — 745 JERUSALEM 98 — 23

IN THE FORGIVENESS OF SINS . . . . — 746 JERUSALEM 98 — 45

THAT FORGIVENESS THOU MAIST WIN . . . . — 754 EV GOSPEL(E)/N — 46

WHAT THEN DID CHRIST INCULCATE FORGIVENESS OF SINS . . — 757D EV GOSPEL — PROSE

MUTUAL FORGIVENESS OF EACH VICE . . . . — 758 EV GOSPEL (2) — 26

MUTUAL FORGIVENESS OF EACH VICE . . . . — 761 FOR SEXES/GP — 1

IN THY COVENANT OF THE FORGIVENESS OF SINS . . . . . — 781 GHOST ABEL 2 — 24

738

```
                                                             PAGE     TITLE      LINE
FORGIVENESS    (CONTINUED)
      BOOK IS AGAINST THE FORGIVENESS OF SINS IS NOT OF        785D ILLS DANTE 101  PROSE
        THE FATHER
      BE FORGIVENESS THAT HE MAY BE (CONSUMD) IN HIS OWN SHAME  788A ANNO THORNTON   * MARG
      [HIS JUDGMENT] THE ACCUSATION SHALL BE FORGIVENESS  . .  788A ANNO THORNTON   * MARG
      PARTICULAR TO YOU AND YOUR ACCUSTOMED FORGIVENESS OF MY   808A LETTER 19      PROSE
        WANT
      FORGIVENESS TO BE CONTINUED TO ME A LITTLE LONGER WHEN  . . 808A LETTER 19    PROSE
      TELL ME IN A LETTER OF FORGIVENESS IF YOU WERE OFFENDED & 816C LETTER 24      PROSE
      & OF THE FORGIVENESS OF SINS WRITTEN UPON THE MURDERER'S  SUPP ILLUS GENESIS  *TITLE
        FOREHEAD
FORGIVENESSES
      INSTEAD OF THE MUTUAL FORGIVENESSES THE MINUTE PARTICULARS  673 JERUSALEM 43      61
        I SEE
FORGIVER
      NOT OF THE FORGIVER OF SIN AND THEIR GOD IS SATAN   . . . 682B JERUSALEM 52   PROSE
FORGIVERS
      BUT NEVER CAN BE FORGIVERS OF SIN . . . . . . . . . . 683A JERUSALEM 52       PROSE
FORGIVES
      THE CUT WORM FORGIVES THE PLOW . . . . . . . . . . . 151A MARRIAGE HH 7       PROSE
      [FORGIVES THE PLOW] . . . . . . . . . . . . . . . 183 THE FLY/N                 10
      [TILL SHE FORGIVES & COMES TO ME] . . . . . . . . . 415 MY SPECTRE/N             8
      AND YET FORGIVES THE BUTCHER'S KNIFE . . . . . . . . 431 AUGURIES               24
      ON EVERY ONE WHO FORGIVES SIN . . . . . . . . . . . 759 EV GOSPEL (2)          43
FORGIVETH
      THAN THY MAKER WHO FORGIVETH SINS & CALLS AGAIN HER THAT   694 JERUSALEM 61       7
        IS LOST
FORGIVING
      ("A MANNER OF FORGIVING SO DIVINE THAT") THIS I CANNOT     76D ANNO LAVATER    MARG
        CONCEIVE
      O THEY ARE HOLY & FORGIVING FILLD WITH LOVING MERCY  . . 108 TIRIEL 6            26
      PITYING & FORGIVING ALL . . . . . . . . . . . . . 416 MY SPECTRE/N             45
      SCOURGING SIN INSTEAD OF FORGIVING IT . . . . . . . 608A V LAST JUDG/N        PROSE
      LO WE ARE ONE FORGIVING ALL EVIL NOT SEEKING RECOMPENSE    622 JERUSALEM 4       20
      FORGIVING TRESPASSES AND SINS . . . . . . . . . . . 650 FIELDS FROM/J           21
      GIVING RECIEVING AND FORGIVING EACH OTHER'S TRESPASSES . . 665 JERUSALEM 38      22
      IS FORGETTING & FORGIVING . . . . . . . . . . . . 724 IN HEAVEN/J               2
FORGOT
      AND THEN ID DIE IN PEACE AND BE FORGOT . . . . . . .  10 WHEN EARLY/PS          20
      O AYE I FORGOT TO TELL THAT HE HAS GOT THE SAME NAME   . 29C EDW THIRD/PS 4    PROSE
      . . . BUT THEY SOON FORGOT THEIR TEARS]. . . . . . . 103 TIRIEL 3               32
      AND THEN THEY WENT & WEPT TO MNETHA BUT THEY SOON FORGOT  103 TIRIEL 3           42
        THEIR TEARS
      THUS MEN FORGOT THAT ALL DEITIES RESIDE IN THE HUMAN BREAST 153B MARRIAGE HH 11   1
      AND THE MAIDEN SOON FORGOT HER FEAR . . . . . . . . 219 LIT GRL LST/SE         19
      AND FORGOT THEIR ETERNAL LIFE . . . . . . . . . . . 236 URIZEN 25              42
      IN JOY SHE HEARD HIS HOWLINGS & FORGOT HE WAS HER LUVAH   282 FOUR ZOAS 2        78
      THAT THOU ART RISEN FROM THE DEAD OR THAT MY POWER FORGOT 299 FOUR ZOAS 4        83
      TILL HE FORGOT ETERNITY DELIGHTED IN HIS SWEET JOY  . . 326 FOUR ZOAS 7        253
      HAST THOU FORGOT THAT THE AIR LISTENS THRO ALL ITS       339 FOUR ZOAS 7B      242
        DISTRICTS TELLING
      SHE FORGOT IT WAS NIGHT & SHE TREMBLED & CRIED  . . . . 429 MARY                38
      SHE FORGOT IT WAS NIGHT SHE FORGOT IT WAS MORN  . . . . 429 MARY                39
      REALITY WAS FORGOT & THE VANITIES OF TIME & SPACE ONLY . 605C V LAST JUDG/N    PROSE
      WITH JOY SHE HEARD HIS HOWLINGS & FORGOT HE WAS HER LUVAH  626 JERUSALEM 7       36
      AND HEALD AFTER THE SEPARATION HIS PAINS HE SOON FORGOT   732 JERUSALEM 86       59
      THAT HAVE FORGOT YOUR ANCIENT LOVE . . . . . . . . 754 EV GOSPEL(E)/N          51
      IN GOOD LUCK AT LAST & SHALL BE FORGOT BY MY AFFECTIONS & 824D LETTER 27        PROSE
      I FORGOT TO MENTION THAT MR HOARE DESIRES HIS MOST  . . 843A LETTER 42         PROSE
      ONE OTHER WHICH I OMITTED TO WRITE DOWN & HAVE FORGOT . 849A LETTER 45         PROSE
FORGOTTEN
      BUT THEY WERE AS THE SHADOW OF HAR & AS THE YEARS        100 TIRIEL 2            7
        FORGOTTEN
      DRUNKEN WITH WOE FORGOTTEN AND SHUT UP FROM COLD DESPAIR  192 V DAU ALBION 4     2
      TELL ME WHERE DWELL THE THOUGHTS FORGOTTEN TILL THOU CALL 192 V DAU ALBION 4     3
        THEM FORTH
      THEN THE GROAN & THE DOLOR ARE QUITE FORGOTTEN . . . . 291 FOUR ZOAS 2        414
      MAKE ME NOT LIKE THE THINGS FORGOTTEN AS THEY HAD NOT BEEN 297 FOUR ZOAS 3     192
      FORGOTTEN WHEN ONE SPEAKS OF THEE HE WILL NOT BE BELIEVD  355 FOUR ZOAS 8      550
      AND WELL CONTRIVED WORDS FIRM FIXING NEVER FORGOTTEN  . 632 JERUSALEM 12        35
      WITH MY DELUGE OF FORGOTTEN REMEMBRANCES OVER THE TABLET  659 JERUSALEM 33       16
      BE SCATTERD ABROAD AND LET THE NAME OF ALBION BE FORGOTTEN 725 JERUSALEM 82      23
      THE MOTHER'S LOVE OF OBEDIENCE IS FORGOTTEN & YOU SEEK    740 JERUSALEM 93       4
        A LOVE
      THEY WILL SOON BE ERADICATED & FORGOTTEN YOU WHO WAS  . 838C LETTER 37         PROSE
FORK
      AND HIS LEGS CARRIED IT LIKE A LONG FORK . . . . . . 536 AND HIS LEGS/N         1
FORLORN
      SHALL FLEE AWAY AND LEAVE [THEM] HIM ALL FORLORN . . . . 28 EDW THIRD/PS 3     292
      YET NOT FORLORN IF CONSCIENCE IS HIS FRIEND  . . . . .  28 EDW THIRD/PS 3     293
      TROUBLED WILDERD AND (FORLORN) . . . . . . . . . . 111 A DREAM/SI               5
      (FORLORN) OF EDEN & REPUGNANT TO THE FORMS OF LIFE  . . 347 FOUR ZOAS 8       254
FORM     SEE DRAGON-FORM,TRIPLE-FORM
      HIS FORM WAS MANHOOD IN THE PRIME AND FROM . . . . . .  39D SAMSON/PS         PROSE
      AND I LOSE THIS FORM OF CLAY . . . . . . . . . . .  61 LEAVE O/IM              4
      AND THAT THE BODY OR OUTWARD FORM . . . . . . . . .  98B ALL RELIGIONS       PROSE
      AS ALL MEN ARE ALIKE IN OUTWARD FORM SO AND WITH THE  . 98C ALL RELIGIONS     PROSE
      THOU HAST THE FORM OF TIRIEL BUT I KNOW THEE WELL ENOUGH  103 TIRIEL 4           7
      TO SMITE (THEE) IN THE FORM OF HELPLESS AGE & EYELESS    104 TIRIEL 4         *  18
        POLICY
      AT LAST I CAUGHT HIM IN THE FORM OF TIRIEL BLIND & OLD  . 105 TIRIEL 4         61
      AND WHY MEN BOUND BENEATH THE HEAVENS IN A REPTILE FORM   110 TIRIEL 8          23
```

```
                                                            PAGE      TITLE           LINE
FORM    (CONTINUED)
     THE CHILD SPRINGS FROM THE WOMB THE FATHER READY STANDS    110 TIRIEL 8           25
        TO FORM
     AND LOVE THE HUMAN FORM DIVINE  . . . . . . . . .  .    117 DIVNE IMAGE/SI       11
     PRAYS TO THE HUMAN FORM DIVINE  . . . . . . . . .  .    117 DIVNE IMAGE/SI       15
     AND ALL MUST LOVE THE HUMAN FORM  . . . . . . . .  .    117 DIVNE IMAGE/SI       17
     SWEET DREAMS FORM A SHADE   . . . . . . . .  .    120 CRADLE SONG/SI        1
     THE CLOUD THEN SHEWD HIS GOLDEN HEAD & HIS BRIGHT FORM    128 BOOK OF THEL 3        5
        EMERGD
     THAT WILFUL BRUISD ITS HELPLESS FORM BUT THAT HE CHERISHD  130 BOOK OF THEL 5       10
        IT
     AN AGED FORM WHITE AS SNOW HOVRING IN MIST . . . . . .    140 FRENCH REVOLTN      131
     DIM THE FORM ALMOST FADED . . . . . . . .  .  .  .    140 FRENCH REVOLTN      132
     . . . FROM THE GLOOM WHERE THE AGED FORM WEPT  . .  .    140 FRENCH REVOLTN      135
     . . . A DARK SHADOWY MAN IN THE FORM . . . . . . .  .    141 FRENCH REVOLTN      164
     . . . MINE NEVER YET FADED FOR FIRE DELIGHTS IN ITS FORM  142 FRENCH REVOLTN      189
     DARE [FORM] FRAME THY FEARFUL SYMMETRY  . . . . . .  .    173 THE TYGER/N 1        25
     DISGUISER OF THE FEMALE FORM   . . . . . . .  .    188 A FAIRY SKIPD         5
     WHATEVER HIDES THE FEMALE FORM . . . . . . . . .  .    188 A FAIRY SKIPD        11
     WITH WHAT SENSE DOES THE BEE FORM CELLS HAVE NOT THE MOUSE 191 V DAU ALBION 3        4
        & FROG
     THY JOYS ARE TEARS THY LABOUR VAIN TO FORM MEN TO THINE   192 V DAU ALBION 5        4
        IMAGE
     TO THE ABHORRED BIRTH OF CHERUBS IN THE HUMAN FORM  . .    193 V DAU ALBION 5       28
     A DRAGON FORM CLASHING HIS SCALES AT MIDNIGHT HE AROSE .  .  197 AMERICA 3           15
     WHY DOST THOU COME TO ANGELS EYES IN THIS TERRIFIC FORM   198 AMERICA 7            7
     AH VISION FROM AFAR AH REBEL FORM THAT RENT THE ANCIENT   199 AMERICA 9           14
     A DRAGON FORM CLASHING HIS SCALES AT MIDNIGHT HE AROSE .  .  204 AMERICA CANC A      15
     TO THE CLOSE HALL OF COUNSEL WHERE HIS ANGEL FORM RENEWS  204 AMERICA CANC B        2
     BUT THO OBSCURD THIS IS THE FORM OF THE ANGELIC LAND  .    206 THIRALATHA           6
     TERROR THE HUMAN FORM DIVINE   . . . . . . . . .  .    221 DIVNE IMAGE/SE        3
     THE HUMAN FORM A FIERY FORGE   . . . . . . . . .  .    221 DIVNE IMAGE/SE        6
     A FEMALE FORM TREMBLING AND PALE  . . . . . . .  .    231 URIZEN 18            7
     AT THE FIRST FEMALE FORM NOW SEPARATE  . . . . . .  .    231 URIZEN 18           15
     BROUGHT FORTH AN INFANT FORM   . . . . . . . . .  .    232 URIZEN 19           35
     IN FORM OF A HUMAN HEART . . . . . . . . .  .  .  .    236 URIZEN 25           44
     STAMP NOT WITH SOLID FORM THIS VIGROUS PROGENY OF FIRES   238 EUROPE PREL 2        8
     INTO THE DEADLY NIGHT TO SEE THE FORM OF ALBION'S ANGEL   242 EUROPE 12            6
     ALONE I SEE THEE CRYSTAL FORM  . . . . . . . . .  .    244 EUROPE 14           17
     HER VOICE WAS HEARD BUT NO FORM  . . . . . . . .  .    253 AHANIA 4            49
     AN IMMENSE FIBROUS FORM STRETCHING OUT  . . . . .  .    259 BOOK OF LOS 5         1
     TO A FORM OF IMPREGNABLE STRENGTH  . . . . . . .  .    259 BOOK OF LOS 5        19
     FLOWING DOWN INTO NIGHT TILL A FORM . . . . . . .  .    260 BOOK OF LOS 5        55
     TO IT A FORM OF VEGETATION BUT THIS SPECTRE OF THARMAS .  .  267 FOUR ZOAS 1         106
     REARD UP A FORM OF GOLD & STOOD UPON THE GLITTERING ROCK  267 FOUR ZOAS 1         126
     A SHADOWY HUMAN FORM WINGED & IN HIS DEPTHS  . . .  .    267 FOUR ZOAS 1         127
     TILL WE HAVE DRAWN THE LAMB OF GOD INTO A MORTAL FORM  .  .  272 FOUR ZOAS 1         293
     FORM THE [FREE] REBELLIOUS SPIRITS OF HEAVEN . . . .  .    272 FOUR ZOAS 1         311
     LAUGHS AT THE HUMAN FORM THE LION MOCKS & THIRSTS FOR BLOOD 275 FOUR ZOAS 1         403
     TRIUMPHANT IN THE BLOODY SKY & THE HUMAN FORM IS NO MORE  275 FOUR ZOAS 1         409
     FROM BONDAGE OF THE HUMAN FORM O FIRST BORN SON OF LIGHT  283 FOUR ZOAS 2         108
     HER SHADOWY FORM NOW SEPARATE HE SHUDDERD & WAS SILENT .    285 FOUR ZOAS 2         204
     IN CLOUDS OF SWEET OBSCURITY MY BEAUTEOUS FORM DISSOLVING  288 FOUR ZOAS 2         311
     NOW TAKING ON AHANIA'S FORM & NOW THE FORM OF ENION  .    288 FOUR ZOAS 2         324
     THERE SHE BEHELD THE [TERRIBLE] SPECTROUS FORM OF ENION   291 FOUR ZOAS 2         423
        IN THE VOID
     AND THE VAST FORM OF NATURE LIKE A SERPENT PLAYD BEFORE   294 FOUR ZOAS 3          97
        THEM
     AND THE VAST FORM OF NATURE LIKE A SERPENT ROLLD BETWEEN  294 FOUR ZOAS 3         101
     ARE MY ABHORRENCE WHEREFORE HAST THOU TAKEN THAT FAIR FORM 295 FOUR ZOAS 3    *   119
     A LITTLE SHADOW BUT A LITTLE SHOWERY FORM OF ENION  . . .  296 FOUR ZOAS 3         185
     HIS CLOUDY FORM IN JEALOUS FEAR & MUTTERING THUNDERS HOARSE 299 FOUR ZOAS 4          77
     WEPT BITTER TEARS INCESSANT STILL BEHOLDING HOW THE PITEOUS 300 FOUR ZOAS 4          97
        FORM
     THY ETERNAL FORM SHALL NEVER RENEW MY UNCERTAIN PREVAILS  301 FOUR ZOAS 4         136
        AGAINST THEE
     FREEZING TO SOLID ALL BENEATH HIS GREY OBLIVIOUS FORM  .    302 FOUR ZOAS 4         172
     HOLLOW UPON THE HOLLOW WIND HIS SHADOWY FORM OBEYING  .    302 FOUR ZOAS 4         197
     AND AS A DOUBLE FEMALE FORM LOVELINESS & PERFECTION OF  .    304 FOUR ZOAS 4         251
        BEAUTY
     WHERE IS SWEET VALA GLOOMY PROPHET WHERE THE LOVELY FORM  306 FOUR ZOAS 5          46
     AND HIS DARK WIFE THAT ONCE FAIR CRYSTAL FORM DIVINELY    306 FOUR ZOAS 5          60
        CLEAR                          •
     NO FORM WAS THERE NO LIVING THING & YET HIS WAY LAY THRO  315 FOUR ZOAS 6         149
     SO [SAYING] HE BEGAN TO [FORM] ?DIG OF GOLD SILVER  .    317 FOUR ZOAS 6    *   229
        & [BRASS] IRON
     AND TO REVEAL MYSELF BEFORE THEE IN A FORM OF WISDOM  .  .  321 FOUR ZOAS 7          58
     IN SERPENT FORM COMPELLD STRETCH OUT & UP THE MYSTERIOUS  324 FOUR ZOAS 7         163
        TREE
     FROM THY EMBRACE ELSE BE ASSURD SO HORRIBLE A FORM  . .  .  326 FOUR ZOAS 7         235
     OF THE NOW FALLEN MAN A DOUBLE FORM VALA APPEARD A MALE   326 FOUR ZOAS 7         246
     FROM ENION'S BRAIN IN THIS DEFORMED FORM LEAVING THEE THERE 327 FOUR ZOAS 7         291
     FOR THOU ART BUT A FORM & ORGAN OF LIFE & OF THYSELF  .  .  329 FOUR ZOAS 7         359
     TO FORM A WORLD . . . . . . . . .  .  .  .    331 FOUR ZOAS 7         443
     IT REMAIND PERMANENT A LOVELY FORM INSPIRD DIVINELY HUMAN 332 FOUR ZOAS 7         469
     LEAVING HIS SPECTROUS FORM WHICH COULD NOT BE DRAWN AWAY  332 FOUR ZOAS 7         492
     THEIR LIFE EXTINCT THEY TOOK THE SPECTRE FORM IN         333 FOUR ZOAS 7B         15
        DARK DESPAIR
     IN TWAIN & LO MY CRYSTAL FORM THAT LIVED IN MY BOSOM  .    334 FOUR ZOAS 7B         65
     AND BIND THEM TO THEE THAT MY CRYSTAL FORM MAY COME TO ME 334 FOUR ZOAS 7B         71
     AND THAT BY THESE ARTS THE SERPENT FORM EXUDED FROM HIS   336 FOUR ZOAS 7B        135
        LIMBS
```

FORM   (CONTINUED)

	PAGE	TITLE	LINE
ORC RENT HER & HIS HUMAN FORM CONSUMD IN HIS OWN FIRES . .	338	FOUR ZOAS 7B	211
THE FORM OF ORC WAS GONE HE REARD HIS SERPENT BULK AMONG	338	FOUR ZOAS 7B	215
THE STARS OF URIZEN IN [FOR] POWER RENDING THE FORM OF LIFE	338	FOUR ZOAS 7B	* 216
I HEAR THY VOICE BUT NOT THY FORM SEE THOU & ALL DELIGHT	339	FOUR ZOAS 7B	240
HID HIM IN THAT OUTRAGEOUS FORM OF ORC WHICH TORMENTS ME FOR SIN	339	FOUR ZOAS 7B	249
WITH JOY THE BRIGHT LIGHT & IN IT A HUMAN FORM	342	FOUR ZOAS 8	43
WHO ASSUMD LUVAH'S FORM & STOOD BEFORE HIM OPPOSITE . . .	342	FOUR ZOAS 8	64
BUT HE SAW ORC A SERPENT FORM AUGMENTING TIMES ON TIMES	342	FOUR ZOAS 8	65
TERRIFIED & ASTONISHD URIZEN BEHELD THE BATTLE TAKE A FORM	343	FOUR ZOAS 8	102
RAGING THEY TAKE THE HUMAN VISAGE & THE HUMAN FORM . . .	344	FOUR ZOAS 8	111
FROM BONDAGE OF [THE HUMAN FORM] THESE TERRORS	345	FOUR ZOAS 8	158
AND THEY APPEARD A UNIVERSAL FEMALE FORM CREATED . . .	345	FOUR ZOAS 8	188
THE WAR ROARD ROUND JERUSALEM'S GATES IT TOOK A HIDEOUS FORM	347	FOUR ZOAS 8	247
SEEN IN THE AGGREGATE A VAST HERMAPHRODITIC FORM	347	FOUR ZOAS 8	248
SONS OF PERDITION TERRIBLE HIS FORM DISHUMANIZD MONSTROUS	347	FOUR ZOAS 8	* 252
O THOU POOR HUMAN FORM O THOU POOR CHILD OF WOE	348	FOUR ZOAS 8	298
BEFORE ASSAULTED THE BRIGHT HUMAN FORM HE FELT HIS PORES	352	FOUR ZOAS 8	417
AND HIS IMMENSE TAIL LASHD THE ABYSS HIS HUMAN FORM A STONE	352	FOUR ZOAS 8	428
A FORM OF SENSELESS STONE REMAIND IN TERRORS ON THE ROCK	352	FOUR ZOAS 8	429
AND STILL HIS STONY FORM REMAIND IN THE ABYSS IMMENSE . .	352	FOUR ZOAS 8	432
INCESSANT STERN DISDAIN HIS SCALY FORM GNAWS INWARDLY	352	FOUR ZOAS 8	434
WITH DEEP REPENTANCE FOR THE LOSS OF THAT FAIR FORM OF MAN	352	FOUR ZOAS 8	435
WITH ENVY & IN VAIN HE SWAM AROUND HIS STONY FORM . . .	352	FOUR ZOAS 8	437
THAT NOT OF HIS OWN POWER HE BORE THE HUMAN FORM ERECT . .	353	FOUR ZOAS 8	458
INTO THEIR LIMBS URTHONA SHOT FORTH A VAST FIBROUS FORM	353	FOUR ZOAS 8	468
INTO A FORM OF VEGETATION LIVING HAVING A VOICE	353	FOUR ZOAS 8	475
TO WORSHIP URIZEN'S DRAGON FORM TO OFFER HER OWN CHILDREN	356	FOUR ZOAS 8	599
BUT WHEN SHE SAW THE FORM OF AHANIA WEEPING ON THE VOID	356	FOUR ZOAS 8	604
TO BURN MYSTERY WITH FIRE & FORM ANOTHER FROM HER ASHES	357	FOUR ZOAS 8	616
AROUND THE DRAGON FORM OF URIZEN & ROUND HIS STONY FORM	359	FOUR ZOAS 9	81
THAT THOU DREAD FORM OF CERTAINTY MAIST SIT IN TOWN & VILLAGE	360	FOUR ZOAS 9	133
ARISE O STONY FORM OF DEATH O DRAGON OF THE DEEPS . . .	360	FOUR ZOAS 9	138
URIZEN WEPT IN THE DARK DEEP ANXIOUS HIS SCALY FORM . .	361	FOUR ZOAS 9	162
THE HUMAN FORM DIVINE THROWN DOWN FROM THEIR HIGH STATION	366	FOUR ZOAS 9	367
SERVANTS TO THE INFINITE & ETERNAL OF THE HUMAN FORM . .	366	FOUR ZOAS 9	374
O DREAMS OF DEATH THE HUMAN FORM DISSOLVING COMPANIED . .	373	FOUR ZOAS 9	595
JOY THRILLD THRO ALL THE FURIOUS FORM OF THARMAS HUMANIZING	373	FOUR ZOAS 9	* 613
THE FEMALE FORM NOW SEPARATE THEY SHUDDERD AT THE HORRIBLE THING	373	FOUR ZOAS 9	622
IN ALL HIS ANCIENT STRENGTH TO FORM THE GOLDEN ARMOUR OF SCIENCE	379	FOUR ZOAS 9	853
FEMALE HER FORM BRIGHT AS THE SUMMER BUT THE PARTS OF LOVE	381	FOUR ZOAS AD 1	18
THEN FIRST SHE SAW HIS GLORY & HER HARLOT FORM APPEARD . .	382	FOUR ZOAS AD 6	21
ITS FORM WAS LOVELY BUT ITS COLOURS PALE	414	TO MRS FLAXMAN	2
AND ANOTHER FORM CREATE	417	MY SPECTRE/N	65
POOR PALE PITIABLE FORM	417	MY SPECTR AD/N	9
DARES STRETCH TO TOUCH HER BABY FORM	425	MENTAL TRAVLER	47
FOR WHO DARE TOUCH THE FROWNING FORM	427	MENTAL TRAVLER	97
AND NONE CAN TOUCH THAT FROWNING FORM	427	MENTAL TRAVLER	101
I STROVE TO SIEZE THE INMOST FORM	429	CRYSTL CABINET	21
BUT DOES A HUMAN FORM DISPLAY	434	AUGURIES	131
THEY ARE ALL FIRM DETERMINATE OUTLINE OR IDENTICAL FORM	439C	REMARKS MALKIN	PROSE
BLOTS WITHOUT FORM AND THEREFORE WITHOUT MEANING . . .	439C	REMARKS MALKIN	PROSE
THE RICH MEN OF ENGLAND FORM THEMSELVES INTO A SOCIETY . .	452C	ANNO REYNOLDS	MARG
ONE CENTRAL FORM COMPOSED OF ALL OTHER FORMS BEING GRANTED	459C	ANNO REYNOLDS	MARG
HERE HE LOSES SIGHT OF A CENTRAL FORM &	460A	ANNO REYNOLDS	MARG
HERE HE COMES AGAIN TO HIS CENTRAL FORM	460B	ANNO REYNOLDS	MARG
DISTINCT GENERAL FORM CANNOT EXIST	461B	ANNO REYNOLDS	MARG
WHICH ALTOGETHER DEPENDS ON DISTINCTNESS OF FORM	463A	ANNO REYNOLDS	MARG
[??THEIR VENETIAN ATTENTION IS TO A CONTEMPT & NEGLECT OF FORM ITSELF	463D	ANNO REYNOLDS	* MARG
DESTRUCTION OF ALL FORM OR OUTLINE PURPOSELY & INTENTIONALLY	463D	ANNO REYNOLDS	MARG
AND IN HIS TENT THRO ENVY OF LIVING FORM EVEN OF THE DIVINE VISION	482	MILTON 3	2
REFUSING ALL DEFINITE FORM THE ABSTRACT HORROR ROOFD STONY HARD	482	MILTON 3	9
TILL IT SEPARATED INTO A MALE FORM HOWLING IN JEALOUSY . .	483	MILTON 3	36
AT LAST ENITHARMON BROUGHT FORTH SATAN REFUSING FORM IN VAIN	483	MILTON 3	41
AH WEAK & WIDE ASTRAY AH SHUT IN NARROW DOLEFUL FORM . .	484	MILTON 5	19
A MOURNFUL FORM DOUBLE HERMAPHRODITIC MALE & FEMALE . . .	496	MILTON 14	37
OR LIKE A HUMAN FORM A FRIEND WITH WITH WHOM HE LIVD BENEVOLENT	497	MILTON 15	27
A GIANT FORM OF PERFECT BEAUTY OUTSTRETCHD ON THE ROCK . .	497	MILTON 15	38
FOR I WILL PUT ON THE HUMAN FORM & TAKE THE IMAGE OF GOD	499	MILTON 18	19
ORC ANSWERD TAKE NOT THE HUMAN FORM O LOVELIEST TAKE NOT	499	MILTON 18	26
CONSUME IN MY CONSUMMATION BUT THOU MAIST TAKE A FORM . .	499	MILTON 18	28
WHEN THOU ATTEMPTEST TO PUT ON THE HUMAN FORM MY WRATH . .	499	MILTON 18	31
WHEN WILT THOU PUT ON THE FEMALE FORM AS IN TIMES OF OLD	499	MILTON 18	34
URIZEN EMERGED FROM HIS ROCKY FORM & FROM HIS SNOWS . .	500	MILTON 18	51
AS WITH NEW CLAY A HUMAN FORM IN THE VALLEY OF BETH PEOR	500	MILTON 19	14
THE TWOFOLD FORM HERMAPHRODITIC AND THE DOUBLE-SEXED . .	501	MILTON 19	32
HER SHADOWY SISTERS FORM THE BONES EVEN THE BONES OF HOREB	501	MILTON 19	51
THESE LOVELY FEMALES FORM SWEET NIGHT AND SILENCE AND SECRET	507	MILTON 23	39
NO HUMAN FORM BUT ONLY A FIBROUS VEGETATION	509	MILTON 24	37
BUT AS TO THIS ELECTED FORM WHO IS RETURND AGAIN	509	MILTON 24	41

		PAGE	TITLE	LINE
FORM	(CONTINUED)			
WE FORM THE MUNDANE EGG THAT SPECTRES COMING BY FURY OR AMITY		511	MILTON 25	42
WITH NEITHER LINEAMENT NOR FORM BUT LIKE TO WATRY CLOUDS		512	MILTON 26	27
AND EVERY GENERATED BODY IN ITS INWARD FORM		512	MILTON 26	31
CREATING FORM & BEAUTY AROUND THE DARK REGIONS OF SORROW		514	MILTON 28	2
FORM IMMORTAL WITH GOLDEN PEN SUCH AS THE SPECTRE ADMIRING		515	MILTON 28	17
PUTS ON THE SWEET FORM THEN SMILES ANTAMON BRIGHT THRO HIS WINDOWS		515	MILTON 28	18
COMPELLD TO COMBINE INTO FORM BY SATAN THE SPECTRE OF ALBION		521	MILTON 32	12
WHO MADE HIMSELF A GOD & DESTROYED THE HUMAN FORM DIVINE		521	MILTON 32	13
BUT THE DIVINE HUMANITY & MERCY GAVE US A HUMAN FORM		521	MILTON 32	14
THE ENEMIES OF HUMANITY EXCEPT IN A FEMALE FORM		527	MILTON 36	15
REACHING FROM HEAVEN TO EARTH A CLOUD & HUMAN FORM		528	MILTON 37	14
AN AWFUL FORM EASTWARD FROM MIDST OF A BRIGHT PAVED-WORK		531	MILTON 39	24
BEFORE OLOLON MILTON STOOD & PERCIEVD THE ETERNAL FORM		532	MILTON 40	1
AND FROM AN IDIOT'S ACTIONS FORM MY RULE		547	RAFAEL SUBLI/N	6
[EGR(EGREMONT'S)] WHAT MIGHTY SOUL IN BEAUTY'S FORM		558	THE CAVERNS/N *	5
AND ALL DEPENDS ON FORM OR OUTLINE ON WHERE THAT IS PUT		563D	DESC CAT	PROSE
NUMBER I THE SPIRITUAL FORM OF NELSON GUIDING LEVIATHAN		564D	DESC CAT 1	TITLE
WHICH OUGHT TO DISPLAY AND NOT TO HIDE FORM		564D	DESC CAT 1	PROSE
THE SPIRITUAL FORM OF PITT GUIDING BEHEMOTH HE IS		565A	DESC CAT 2	TITLE
THEIR ART IS TO LOSE FORM HIS ART IS TO FIND FORM		573B	DESC CAT 3	PROSE
AND THE FORM OF THE FOURTH WAS LIKE THE SON OF GOD		578B	DESC CAT 5	PROSE
AND FORM HIS FOREHEAD SMALL WITHOUT FRONTALS HIS JAWS LARGE		580A	DESC CAT 5	PROSE
THIS ALONE THE WANT OF THIS DETERMINATE AND BOUNDING FORM		585B	DESC CAT 15	PROSE
AND NEVER ONCE PERCIEVES HIS UGLY FORM		597	PUBLC VOICE/PA	4
THEY HOLD THE IMMORTAL FORM IN GENTLE BANDS & TENDER TEARS		624	JERUSALEM 5	55
I LIFTED THEM INTO MY FURNACES TO FORM THE SPIRITUAL SWORD		628	JERUSALEM 9	18
APPEARD A ROCKY FORM AGAINST THE DIVINE HUMANITY		642	JERUSALEM 19	35
I CANNOT PUT OFF THE HUMAN FORM I STRIVE BUT STRIVE IN VAIN		643	JERUSALEM 20	29
HE WITHERD UP THE HUMAN FORM		651	FIELDS FROM/J	53
STILL WAS THE HUMAN FORM DIVINE		651	FIELDS FROM/J	58
O JESUS STILL THE FORM WAS THINE		651	FIELDS FROM/J	60
MOST ANCIENT PROMONTORY AND IN THE SUN A HUMAN FORM APPEARD		653	JERUSALEM 29	4
AND THE VAST FORM OF NATURE LIKE A SERPENT PLAYD BEFORE THEM		655	JERUSALEM 29	76
AND THE VAST FORM OF NATURE LIKE A SERPENT ROLLD BETWEEN		655	JERUSALEM 29	80
EVERY UNIVERSAL FORM WAS BECOME BARREN MOUNTAINS OF MORAL		657	JERUSALEM 31	19
OF STONES AND ROCKS HE TOOK HIS WAY FOR HUMAN FORM WAS NONE		657	JERUSALEM 31	27
I AM YOUR RATIONAL POWER O ALBION & THAT HUMAN FORM		659	JERUSALEM 33	5
THE IMAGINATIVE HUMAN FORM IS BUT A BREATHING OF VALA		660	JERUSALEM 33	49
FLED THEY FLED AT HIS HORRIBLE FORM THEY HID IN CAVES		661	JERUSALEM 34	49
SHUT FROM MY NERVOUS FORM WHICH SLEEPS UPON THE VERGE OF BEULAH		665	JERUSALEM 38	35
AND HIS DARK EON THAT ONCE FAIR CRYSTAL FORM DIVINELY CLEAR		667	JERUSALEM 40	41
. . . DIVINE-HUMANITY WHO IS THE ONLY GENERAL AND UNIVERSAL FORM		672	JERUSALEM 43	20
FORMING A SEXUAL MACHINE AN AGED VIRGIN FORM		674	JERUSALEM 44	25
CONCENTER IN ONE FEMALE FORM AN AGED PENSIVE WOMAN		678	JERUSALEM 48	28
FEMALE AND LOVELY STRUGGLING TO PUT OFF THE HUMAN FORM		678	JERUSALEM 48	49
WITHERING THE HUMAN FORM BY LAWS OF SACRIFICE FOR SIN		679	JERUSALEM 49	25
AH WEAK & WIDE ASTRAY AH SHUT IN NARROW DOLEFUL FORM		679	JERUSALEM 49	32
THEY ARE BEGINNING TO FORM HEAVENS & HELLS IN IMMENSE		680	JERUSALEM 49	61
BUT LOS WHO IS THE VEHICULAR FORM OF STRONG URTHONA		684	JERUSALEM 53	1
IN GREAT ETERNITY EVERY PARTICULAR FORM GIVES FORTH OR EMANATES		684	JERUSALEM 54	1
ITS OWN PECULIAR LIGHT & THE FORM IS THE DIVINE VISION		684	JERUSALEM 54	2
TEACHING THEM TO FORM THE SERPENT OF PRECIOUS STONES & GOLD		686	JERUSALEM 55	13
WHERE DWELLS THE SPECTRE OF ALBION DESTROYER OF DEFINITE FORM		688	JERUSALEM 56	17
AS A MIGHTY TEMPLE DELIVERING FORM OUT OF CONFUSION		690	JERUSALEM 58	22
HER FORM WAS HELD BY BEULAH'S DAUGHTERS BUT ALL WITHIN UNSEEN		693	JERUSALEM 60	40
NO HUMAN FORM BUT SEXUAL & A LITTLE WEEPING INFANT PALE REFLECTED		697	JERUSALEM 63	20
THE HUMAN FORM BEGAN TO BE ALTERD BY THE DAUGHTERS OF ALBION		703	JERUSALEM 66	46
O THOU POOR HUMAN FORM SAID SHE O THOU POOR CHILD OF WOE		705	JERUSALEM 67	44
ENVYING STOOD THE ENORMOUS FORM AT VARIANCE WITH ITSELF		707	JERUSALEM 69	6
AND THIS THE FORM OF MIGHTY HAND SITTING ON ALBION'S CLIFFS		708	JERUSALEM 70	1
BEFORE THE FACE OF ALBION A MIGHTY THREATNING FORM		708	JERUSALEM 70	2
SUCH FORM THE AGGREGATE OF THE TWELVE SONS OF ALBION TOOK & SUCH		708	JERUSALEM 70	10
FROM THE PRESSD LOVELINESS SO HER WHOLE IMMORTAL FORM THREE-FOLD		709	JERUSALEM 70	26
HIS EMANATION IS CONWENNA SHE SHINES A TRIPLE FORM		710	JERUSALEM 71	47
BECAME A LIMIT A ROCKY HARDNESS WITHOUT FORM & VOID		713	JERUSALEM 73	23
AND EVERY HUMAN VEGETATED FORM IN ITS INWARD RECESSES		714	JERUSALEM 73	50
I SEE A FEMININE FORM ARISE FROM THE FOUR TERRIBLE ZOAS		715	JERUSALEM 74	52
BEAUTIFUL BUT TERRIBLE STRUGGLING TO TAKE A FORM OF BEAUTY		715	JERUSALEM 74	53
ROOTED IN SHECHEM THIS IS DINAH THE YOUTHFUL FORM OF ERIN		715	JERUSALEM 74	54
SHRUNK TO A NARROW DOLEFUL FORM IN THE DARK LAND OF CABUL		721	JERUSALEM 79	63
A DRAGON FORM ON ZION HILL'S MOST ANCIENT PROMONTORY		722	JERUSALEM 80	36
REFUSD TO TAKE A DEFINITE FORM SHE HOVERD OVER ALL THE EARTH		723	JERUSALEM 80	52
CALLING THE DEFINITE SIN DEFACING EVERY DEFINITE FORM		723	JERUSALEM 80	53
THE INVISIBLE LOVELY ONE GIVING HIM A FORM ACCORDING TO		723	JERUSALEM 80	78
HIS LAW A FORM AGAINST THE LAMB OF GOD OPPOSD TO MERCY		723	JERUSALEM 80	79
UPON MY BOSOM LOOK HERE IS THE LOVELY WAYWARD FORM		726	JERUSALEM 82	38

742

		PAGE	TITLE	LINE

FORM   (CONTINUED)

TO FORM THE MIGHTY FORM OF HAND ACCORDING TO HER WILL   . .   726 JERUSALEM 82   63
TO FORM THE WORM INTO A FORM OF LOVE BY TEARS & PAIN   726 JERUSALEM 82   76
A FORM FOR VALA AND A FORM FOR LUVAH HERE ON THE THAMES   727 JERUSALEM 83   11
A FORM OF VEGETATION NAIL THEM DOWN ON THE STEMS OF MYSTERY   727 JERUSALEM 83   13
I SEE THY FORM O LOVELY MILD JERUSALEM WINGD WITH SIX WINGS   730 JERUSALEM 86   1
CONCENTERING IN THE MAJESTIC FORM OF ERIN IN ETERNAL TEARS   731 JERUSALEM 86   45
A TERRIBLE INDEFINITE HERMAPHRODITIC FORM . . . . . .   734 JERUSALEM 89   3
OF ALBION DRANK & IMBIBED THE LIFE & ETERNAL FORM OF LUVAH   736 JERUSALEM 90   17
AND YOU CALL THAT SWELLD & BLOATED FORM A MINUTE PARTICULAR   738 JERUSALEM 91   29
WAS THE LORD THE UNIVERSAL HUMANITY & ALBION SAW HIS FORM   743 JERUSALEM 96   5
IN THE FOUR SENSES IN THE OUTLINE THE CIRCUMFERENCE & FORM   745 JERUSALEM 98   22
    FOR EVER
THE NAKED HUMAN FORM DIVINE . . . .   755 EV GOSPEL(E)/N   66
FOR ITS REALITY IS ITS IMAGINATIVE FORM . . . . . .   774B ANNO BERKELEY   MARG
GRECIAN IS MATHEMATIC FORM GOTHIC IS LIVING FORM . . . .   778D HOMERS POETRY   PROSE
MATHEMATIC FORM IS ETERNAL IN THE REASONING MEMORY   . . .   778D HOMERS POETRY   PROSE
LIVING FORM IS ETERNAL EXISTENCE . . . .   778D HOMERS POETRY   PROSE
THIS O WHAT SHALL I CALL THEE FORM DIVINE FATHER OF MERCIES   780 GHOST ABEL 1   21

FORMAL

WAS PREPARED TO GIVE A FORMAL ANSWER TO THE COMPANY   . . .   458 ISLAND MOON 1   PROSE

FORMATION

ONE THOUSAND MEN OF WONDROUS POWER SPENT THEIR LIVES IN   285 FOUR ZOAS 2   198
    ITS FORMATION

FORMD   SEE BEAST FORMD,DOUBLE-FORMD,EGG FORMD,HUMAN FORMD,LUST FORMD,MALE FORMD
           PIPE/FORMD,SERPENT-FORMD,SERPENT/FORMD

AND FORMD A CROOKED KNIFE . . . .   50 WHEN CORRUP/IM   14
WHAT DREAD HAND FORMD THY DREAD FEET   . . . . . .   214 THE TYGER/SE   12
HATH FORMD THIS ABOMINABLE VOID . . . .   222 URIZEN 3   4
HERE ALONE I IN BOOKS FORMD OF METALS . . . .   224 URIZEN 4   24
THE GIRDLE WAS FORMD BY DAY . . . .   233 URIZEN 20   16
HE FORMD A LINE & A PLUMMET . . . .   233 URIZEN 20   33
HE FORMD A DIVIDING RULE . . . .   233 URIZEN 20   35
AND FORMD LAWS OF PRUDENCE AND CALLD THEM . . . . .   236 URIZEN 28   6
THEIR OAK-SURROUNDED PILLARS FORMD OF MASSY STONES UNCUT   241 EUROPE 10   7
THEN WAS THE SERPENT TEMPLE FORMD IMAGE OF INFINITE   . . . 241 EUROPE 10   21
FORMD OF RIBS THAT IN HIS DARK SOLITUDE . . . . . .   250 AHANIA 3   5
AND HARROW FORMD & FRAMD THE HARNESS OF SILVER & IVORY   . . 281 FOUR ZOAS 2   28
. . . THEY FORMD THE ANVILS OF GOLD BEATEN IN MILLS . .   281 FOUR ZOAS 2   30
IS FORMD & THROWN DOWN THUNDRING INTO THE DEEPS OF NON   283 FOUR ZOAS 2   137
    ENTITY
IS FORMD & MANY A CORDED LYRE OUTSPREAD OVER THE IMMENSE   284 FOUR ZOAS 2   161
A SHADOW OF DESPAIR THEREFORE TOWARD THE WEST URIZEN FORMD   285 FOUR ZOAS 2   187
A GOLDEN ALTAR BURNT PERFUMES WITH ART CELESTIAL FORMD . . 285 FOUR ZOAS 2   190
THAT HIS DREAD FANCY FORMD BEFORE HIM IN THE UNFORMD VOID   287 FOUR ZOAS 2   294
AND LOS FORMD ANVILS OF IRON PETRIFIC FOR HIS BLOWS . . .   301 FOUR ZOAS 4   168
IN PERIODS OF PULSATIVE FUROR MILLS HE FORMD & WORKS   . .   302 FOUR ZOAS 4   182
THE GIRDLE WAS FORMD BY DAY BY NIGHT WAS BURST IN TWAIN   307 FOUR ZOAS 5   90
BUT WHEN A VORTEX FORMD ON HIGH BY LABOUR & SORROW & CARE   317 FOUR ZOAS 6   204
AND FORMD A MALE TO BE A COUNTERPART TO THEE O LOVE . . .   327 FOUR ZOAS 7   293
EACH MALE FORMD WITHOUT A COUNTERPART WITHOUT A   330 FOUR ZOAS 7   402
    CONCENTERING VISION
THEY FORMD THE SECRET PLACE REVERSING ALL THE ORDER OF   333 FOUR ZOAS 7B   22
    DELIGHT
HORRIBLE HOOKS & NETS HE FORMD TWISTING THE CORDS OF IRON   343 FOUR ZOAS 8   92
FOR THIS LAKE IS FORMD FROM THE TEARS & SIGHS . . . . .   . 347 FOUR ZOAS 8   228
BESET WITH GOLD GOLD WERE THE ORNAMENTS FORMD BY SONS   377 FOUR ZOAS 9   777
    OF URIZEN
THIS CABINET IS FORMD OF GOLD . . . .   429 CRYSTL CABINET   5
THE SECOND THE REDEEMD THE THIRD THE REPROBATE & FORMD . . 486 MILTON 7   3
BUT RINTRAH WHO IS OF THE REPROBATE OF THOSE FORMD   488 MILTON 8   34
    TO DESTRUCTION
SHE FORMD A SPACE FOR SATAN & MICHAEL & FOR THE POOR   489 MILTON 8   43
    INFECTED
WHICH NOW GIRD ROUND US O ETERNAL TORMENT I FORMD   493 MILTON 12   29
    THE SERPENT
THUS FORMD THE CLAY OF URIZEN BUT WITHIN THAT PORTION   . . 502 MILTON 20   12
AS A BRIGHT SANDAL FORMD IMMORTAL OF PRECIOUS STONES & GOLD 503 MILTON 21   13
AS COGS ARE FORMD IN A WHEEL TO TURN THE COGS OF   513 MILTON 27   10
    THE ADVERSE WHEEL
SAID LITTLE CREATURE [THOU ART] FORMD [FOR] OF JOY & MIRTH   541 ANGEL PRESID/N   2
IF YOU HAVE FORMD A CIRCLE TO GO INTO . . . . 557 TO GOD/N   1
FABLE OR ALLEGORY IS FORMD BY THE DAUGHTERS OF MEMORY . . 604D V LAST JUDG/N   PROSE
I SAW THE LIMBS FORMD FOR EXERCISE CONTEMND & THE BEAUTY OF 628 JERUSALEM 9   7
AND THAT TOWARD EDEN FOUR FORMD OF GOLD SILVER BRASS & IRON 633 JERUSALEM 13   1
ARE FORMD IN A WHEEL TO FIT THE COGS OF THE ADVERSE WHEEL   633 JERUSALEM 13   14
THUS ARE THE HEAVENS FORMD BY LOS WITHIN THE MUNDANE SHELL   716 JERUSALEM 75   23

FORMED   SEE HEART-FORMED

FORMED TO SUCKLE ALL MANKIND . . . .   56 HAIL MATRIM/IM   9
[DOST THOU NOT SEE THAT MEN CANNOT BE FORMED ALL ALIKE]   109 TIRIEL 8   11
& FORMED A HEAVEN OF WHAT HE STOLE FROM THE ABYSS   . . .   150A MARRIAGE HH 5   PROSE
TILL A SYSTEM WAS FORMED WHICH SOME TOOK ADVANTAGE OF &   153A MARRIAGE HH 11   PROSE
GIANTS WHO FORMED THIS WORLD INTO ITS SENSUAL EXISTENCE   155A MARRIAGE HH 15   PROSE
AND LOS FORMED NETS & GINS . . . .   227 URIZEN 8   7
HE FORMED SCALES TO WEIGH . . . .   234 URIZEN 20   36
HE FORMED MASSY WEIGHTS . . . .   234 URIZEN 20   37
HE FORMED A BRAZEN QUADRANT . . . .   234 URIZEN 20   38
HE FORMED GOLDEN COMPASSES . . . .   234 URIZEN 20   39
FURNACES HE FORMED AN ANVIL . . . .   259 BOOK OF LOS 5   21
IN A FLESHY SLOUGH FORMED FOUR RIVERS . . . .   260 BOOK OF LOS 5   53
LO HOW THE HEART & BRAIN ARE FORMED IN THE BREEDING WOMB   323 FOUR ZOAS 7   130
HE FORMED ALSO HARSH INSTRUMENTS OF SOUND . . . . . .   344 FOUR ZOAS 8   135

```
                                                         PAGE    TITLE           LINE
FORMED    (CONTINUED)
     THEY FORMED HEAVENS OF SWEETEST (?WOODS) OF GOLD & SILVER    378 FOUR ZOAS 9   *  792
          & IVORY
     THE BIBLE SAYS THAT GOD FORMED NATURE PERFECT BUT THAT MAN   388A ANNO WATSON     MARG
     THE DRAPERY IS FORMED ALONE BY THE SHAPE OF THE NAKED   .  . 462D ANNO REYNOLDS   MARG
     COLOURING FORMED UPON THESE PRINCIPLES IS DESTRUCTIVE   .  . 478C ANNO REYNOLDS   MARG
     TO BE FORMED INTO THE CHURCHES OF BEULAH . . . . . . .  .  . 511 MILTON 25        39
     BUT IN THE NERVES OF THE NOSTRILS ACCIDENT BEING FORMED      517 MILTON 29        35
     FORMED IT INTO A SOLID BY LOS'S MATHEMATIC POWER   .  .  .   517 MILTON 29        38
     AND FORMED INTO FOUR PRECIOUS STONES FOR ENTERANCE FROM      691 JERUSALEM 59      1
          BEULAH
     THIS LOS FORMED INTO THE GATES & MIGHTY WALL BETWEEN THE     691 JERUSALEM 59      5
          OAK
     NOT YET FORMED BUT A WRETCHED TORMENT UNFORMED & ABYSSAL     692 JERUSALEM 60      4
     THE CIRCUMFERENCE IS WITHIN WITHOUT IS FORMED THE SELFISH    709 JERUSALEM 71      7
          CENTER
     FORMED THE CROSS & NAILS & SPEAR   .  .  .  .  .  .  .  .  . 759 EV GOSPEL (2)    29
     IT MUST HAVE BEEN ORIGINALLY FORMED BY THE DEVIL HIMSELF     785C ILLS DANTE 101  PROSE
     AS THE EYE IS FORMED SUCH ARE ITS POWERS   .  .  .  .  .  .  793D LETTER 5        PROSE
     OF MAN NO OTHER FORMED HOUSE CAN EVER PLEASE ME SO WELL      802A LETTER 14       PROSE
     THE TASTE OF ENGLISH AMATEURS HAS BEEN TOO MUCH FORMED   .   864C LETTER 61       PROSE
     FOR A LINE OR LINEAMENT IS NOT FORMED BY CHANCE   .  .   .   878B LETTER 88       PROSE
FORMER
     WE SIT US DOWN AND VIEW OUR FORMER JOYS  .  .  .  .  .  .     27 EDW THIRD/PS 3    260
     IN FORMER TIMES ON SUCH AN EVENING    .  .  .  .  .  .  .  . 35C COUCH DEATH/PS   PROSE
     PROVIDED THAT IT EXCEEDS IN ELEGANCE ALL FORMER METHODS      207B PRSPECTUS 1793  PROSE
     KNOW THAT IN A FORMER TIME  .  .  .  .  .  .  .  .  .  .  .   219 LIT GRL LST/SE    3
     THIS DISMAL WORLD HE STOOD A WHILE & LOOKD BACK OER HIS      315 FOUR ZOAS 6   *  150
          FORMER
     . . . IN FORGIVENESS OF [FORMER INJURIES] ANCIENT INJURIES   330 FOUR ZOAS 7   *  419
     I ALSO TREMBLE AT MYSELF & AT ALL MY FORMER LIFE  .  .  .    330 FOUR ZOAS 7       423
     THE FORMER THINGS SO SHALL THE MORTAL GENTLY FADE AWAY   .   355 FOUR ZOAS 8       553
     YOU SHALL FORGET YOUR FORMER STATE RETURN O LOVE IN PEACE    366 FOUR ZOAS 9   *  364
     WILD WITH PROPHETIC FURY HIS FORMER LIFE BECAME LIKE A       493 MILTON 12        45
          DREAM
     REMOVING THE [?FORMER] OLD HEAVENS & THE OLD EARTH    .  .   612A V LAST JUDG/N   PROSE
     I AGAIN DISPLAY MY GIANT FORMS TO THE PUBLIC MY FORMER   .   620D JERUSALEM 3     PROSE
     THEY VIEW THEIR FORMER LIFE THEY NUMBER MOMENTS OVER AND     642 JERUSALEM 20      17
          OVER
     AGAINST FORMER CONDUCT & TO DEMAND JUSTICE & TRUTH    .  .   825D LETTER 27       PROSE
     COURAGE OF CONSCIOUS INDUSTRY WORTHY OF HIS FORMER KINDNESS  851D LETTER 50       PROSE
     MY FORMER PURSUITS OF PRINTING IF I HAD NOT NOW   .  .   .   865C LETTER 63       *PROSE
FORMERLY
     MESSIAH OR SATAN OR TEMPTER WAS FORMERLY THOUGHT TO BE   .   155C MARRIAGE HH 15  PROSE
     IT IS STRANGE THAT GOD SHOULD SPEAK TO MAN FORMERLY &    .   390A ANNO WATSON      MARG
     MORE FINISHED WHEN MR B(BLAKE) FORMERLY PAINTED IN OIL   .   584D DESC CAT 15     PROSE
FORMIDABLE
     HAVING SPIRITUAL ENEMIES OF SUCH FORMIDABLE MAGNITUDE   .    811D LETTER 22       PROSE
     MANY VERY FORMIDABLE WORKS WHICH I HAVE FINISHD & READY      820A LETTER 25       PROSE
     BUT MY ARRIVAL HAS DISPELLD THE FORMIDABLE MALADY & MY       833D LETTER 33       PROSE
          DEAR &
FORMING
     [IN DARKNESS & SOLITUDE FORMING SEAS OF [TROUBLE] DOUBT      267 FOUR ZOAS 1   *  114
          . . .
     OTHERS AROSE & SCHOOLS ERECTED FORMING INSTRUMENTS   .  .    283 FOUR ZOAS 2      130
     HAMMER OF URTHONA FORMING UNDER HIS HEAVY HAND THE HOURS      302 FOUR ZOAS 4      179
     FORMING A GIRDLE IN THE DAY & BURSTING IT AT NIGHT   .  .    307 FOUR ZOAS 5       89
     THUS FORMING A VAST FAMILY WONDROUS IN BEAUTY & LOVE    .    345 FOUR ZOAS 8      187
     HIS FORMING IMAGE HE WALKS ROUND IT PATIENT LABOURING   .    502 MILTON 20         9
     THUS MILTON STOOD FORMING BRIGHT URIZEN WHILE HIS MORTAL     502 MILTON 20        10
          PART
     FORMING THE SPECTRES OF ALBION ACCORDING TO HIS RAGE    .    626 JERUSALEM 7      41
     I SAW DISEASE FORMING A BODY OF DEATH AROUND THE LAMB   .    628 JERUSALEM 9       9
     FORMING THE MUNDANE SHELL ABOVE BENEATH ON ALL SIDES         634 JERUSALEM 13     54
          SURROUNDING
     OF DEATH FORMING AN AX OF GOLD THE FOUR SONS OF LOS   .  .   636 JERUSALEM 15     22
     FORMING A SEXUAL MACHINE AN AGED VIRGIN FORM  .  .  .  .     674 JERUSALEM 44     25
     A RELIGION OF CHASTITY FORMING A COMMERCE TO SELL LOVES      708 JERUSALEM 69     34
     FORMING THE FLUCTUATING GLOBE ACCORDING TO THEIR WILL   .    727 JERUSALEM 83     34
     ROLLING THE SEA IN ROCKY PATHS FORMING LEVIATHAN  .  .  .    738 JERUSALEM 91     39
FORMLESS
     AT THE FORMLESS UNMEASURABLE DEATH   .  .  .  .  .  .  .      226 URIZEN 7          9
     FOR AS YET WERE ALL OTHER PARTS FORMLESS   .  .  .  .  .  .  258 BOOK OF LOS 4     55
     A HORRIBLE CHAOS TO HIS EYES A FORMLESS UNMEASURABLE DEATH   301 FOUR ZOAS 4      162
     INTO A FORMLESS INDEFINITE & STREWING HER ON THE ABYSS   .   338 FOUR ZOAS 7B     217
FORMS
     THAT THE FORMS OF ALL THINGS ARE DERIVED FROM THEIR GENIUS   98B ALL RELIGIONS    PROSE
     THE FATHER FORMS A WHIP TO ROUZE THE SLUGGISH SENSES TO ACT  110 TIRIEL 8         30
     IN BEASTIAL FORMS OR MORE TERRIBLE MEN . . . . . . . .  .    144 FRENCH REVOLTN *  216
     CHOOSING FORMS OF WORSHIP FROM POETIC TALES AND AT LENGTH    153B MARRIAGE HH 11  PROSE
     IN THE FIFTH CHAMBER WERE UNNAMD FORMS   .  .  .  .  .  .    155A MARRIAGE HH 15  PROSE
     AND TOOK THE FORMS OF BOOKS & WERE ARRANGED IN LIBRARIES     155A MARRIAGE HH 15  PROSE
     AND THEIR PURSUITS AS DIFFERENT AS THEIR FORMS AND AS        191 V DAU ALBION 3    6
          THEIR JOYS
     OF LIFE BY MAGIC POWER CONDENSD INFERNAL FORMS ART-BOUND     204 AMERICA CANC B   14
     AND ENORMOUS FORMS OF ENERGY   .  .  .  .  .  .  .  .  .  .   225 URIZEN 4         48
     INTO HORRIBLE FORMS OF DEFORMITY    .  .  .  .  .  .  .  .    230 URIZEN 13        43
     MANY FORMS OF FISH BIRD & BEAST   .  .  .  .  .  .  .  .  .   232 URIZEN 19        34
     BY CRUEL ENORMITIES FORMS   .  .  .  .  .  .  .  .  .  .  .   234 URIZEN 20        50
     AND IN REPTILE FORMS SHRINKING TOGETHER  .  .  .  .  .  .    236 URIZEN 25        37
     MOSES BEHELD UPON MOUNT SINAI FORMS OF DARK DELUSION    .    245 SONG OF LOS 3    17
     INTO TWO NARROW DOLEFUL FORMS   .  .  .  .  .  .  .  .  .     246 SONG OF LOS 4     9
```

		PAGE	TITLE	LINE
FORMS	**(CONTINUED)**			
BRANCHY FORMS ORGANIZING THE HUMAN	. . . .	258	BOOK OF LOS 4	44
[TWISTING IN FEARFUL FORMS & HOWLING HOWLING HARSH SHRIEKING		269	FOUR ZOAS 1	180
[TWO FORMS OF HORROR HOWLD BENEATH IT]	. . . .	SUPP	FOUR ZOAS 1	*
IN HUMAN FORMS DISTINCT THEY STOOD ROUND URIZEN PRINCE OF LIGHT		281	FOUR ZOAS 2	37
[?LOS] REASONING FROM THE LOINS IN THE UNREAL FORMS OF ULRO'S NIGHT		283	FOUR ZOAS 2	* 112
THEIR VENTUROUS FLIGHT IN HUMAN FORMS DISTINCT THRO DARKNESS DEEP		284	FOUR ZOAS 2	151
BROUGHT HIM IN VARIOUS FORMS BEFORE HER STILL SHE KNEW HIM NOT		286	FOUR ZOAS 2	233
TILL INTO NARROW FORMS YOU CREEP GO TAKE YOUR FIERY WAY		294	FOUR ZOAS 3	89
WEAVE SOFT DELUSIVE FORMS OF MAN ABOVE MY WATRY WORLD	. .	298	FOUR ZOAS 4	29
AND LUVAH HIDDEN IN THE ELEMENTAL FORMS OF LIFE & DEATH		301	FOUR ZOAS 4	130
AGAINST THE MONSTROUS FORMS THAT BREED AMONG MY SILENT WAVES		301	FOUR ZOAS 4	145
IN MONSTROUS FORMS OF DEATH A HUMAN POLYPUS OF DEATH	. .	304	FOUR ZOAS 4	268
INTO UNUSUAL FORMS DANCING & HOWLING STAMPING THE ABYSS		305	FOUR ZOAS 4	295
HIDING THEMSELVES IN ROCKY FORMS FROM THE EYES OF URIZEN		312	FOUR ZOAS 6	23
AND IN THESE MONSTROUS FORMS I [?LINE] LIVE IN AN ETERNAL WOE		313	FOUR ZOAS 6	* 62
THEN HE BEHELD THE FORMS OF TYGERS & OF LIONS DISHUMANIZD MEN		314	FOUR ZOAS 6	116
BUT THEY REFUSD BECAUSE THEIR OUTWARD FORMS WERE IN THE ABYSS		318	FOUR ZOAS 6	253
OF ENITHARMON HOW IT BUDS WITH LIFE & FORMS THE BONES	. .	323	FOUR ZOAS 7	131
HE SUFFERD HIM TO CLIMB THAT HE MIGHT DRAW ALL HUMAN FORMS		324	FOUR ZOAS 7	164
BESIDE LOS IN THE CAVERN DARK ENSLAVD TO VEGETATIVE FORMS		326	FOUR ZOAS 7	262
WHICH NOW MY RIVERS WERE BECOME ROLLING IN [TUBLIKE] TUBELIKE FORMS		327	FOUR ZOAS 7	* 285
IN MALE FORMS WITHOUT FEMALE COUNTERPARTS OR EMANATIONS		328	FOUR ZOAS 7	329
THEN I CAN SIGH FORTH ON THE WINDS OF GOLGONOOZA PITEOUS FORMS		331	FOUR ZOAS 7	451
WILT IN SWEET MODERATED FURY FABRICATE [SWEET] FORMS SUBLIME		331	FOUR ZOAS 7	453
[TO HEW THE CAVERND ROCKS OF DRANTHON INTO FORMS OF BEAUTY]		331	FOUR ZOAS 7	457
OF LOS ASSIMILATING TO THOSE FORMS EMBODIED & LOVELY	. .	332	FOUR ZOAS 7	474
FOR HE BEHELD NEW FEMALE FORMS BORN FORTH UPON THE AIR	. .	332	FOUR ZOAS 7	487
AND SHE WENT FORTH & SAW THE FORMS OF LIFE & OF DELIGHT		340	FOUR ZOAS 7B	269
IN BEAUTIFUL SUBSTANTIAL FORMS APPEARD & SERVED HER	. . .	340	FOUR ZOAS 7B	275
THE LIVING SOUL IN GLORIOUS FORMS & EVERY ONE CAME FORTH		340	FOUR ZOAS 7B	278
THE INSTRUMENTS OF SOUND & TROOP BY TROOP IN HUMAN FORMS THEY URGE		344	FOUR ZOAS 8	117
RELAPSING IN DIRE TORMENT THEY RETURN TO FORMS OF WOE	. .	344	FOUR ZOAS 8	124
MIGHT ACT ACCORDING TO THEIR FORMS BY INNATE CRUELTY	. .	344	FOUR ZOAS 8	134
THEY UNWEAVE THE SOFT THREADS THEN THEY WEAVE THEM ANEW IN THE FORMS		347	FOUR ZOAS 8	230
(FORLORN) OF EDEN & REPUGNANT TO THE FORMS OF LIFE	. . .	347	FOUR ZOAS 8	254
TWELVE ROCKY UNSHAPD FORMS TERRIFIC FORMS OF TORTURE & WOE		348	FOUR ZOAS 8	276
OF FEMALE FORMS BEAUTIFUL THRO POISONS HIDDEN IN SECRET		348	FOUR ZOAS 8	290
TO THE DELUSIVE FEMALE FORMS SHINING AMONG HIS FURNACES		350	FOUR ZOAS 8	350
[IN FORMS OF PRIESTHOOD IN THE DARK DELUSIONS OF REPENTANCE]		353	FOUR ZOAS 8	461
IN FORMS OF PRIESTHOOD IN THE DARK DELUSIONS OF REPENTANCE		353	FOUR ZOAS 8	464
INTO THE ELEMENTAL FORMS OF EVERY THING THAT GROWS	. . .	355	FOUR ZOAS 8	563
AS IN A STORE HOUSE IN HIS MEMORY HE REGULATES THE FORMS		355	FOUR ZOAS 8	568
FELL DOWN & SHADOWY FORMS OF JOY MIXD WITH DESPAIR & GRIEF		358	FOUR ZOAS 9	29
WHEN LUVAH & VALA WERE CLOSD UP IN THEIR WORLD OF SHADOWY FORMS		372	FOUR ZOAS 9	559
MUTTERING ALONG FROM HEAVEN TO HEAVEN HOARSE ROLL THE HUMAN FORMS		372	FOUR ZOAS 9	* 564
THEIR DREAD FORMS TENDING THE DIRE MILLS	. . . .	378	FOUR ZOAS 9	814
CONVERSING WITH THE ANIMAL FORMS OF WISDOM NIGHT & DAY	. .	379	FOUR ZOAS 9	836
TWELVE ROCKY UNSHAPD FORMS TERRIFIC FORMS OF TORTURE & WOE		382	FOUR ZOAS AD 6	9
THIS WILL PRODUCE CERTAIN & DETERMIND FORMS ON THE PLATE		440B	MEMORANDUM/N 2	PROSE
AND BEAUTEOUS FORMS THAT LOVE DOES WEAR	. . . .	447	ANNO REYNOLDS	2
WEAKNESS IN THE MARKING OUT OF THE FORMS	. . . . . .	457C	ANNO REYNOLDS	MARG
ONE CENTRAL FORM COMPOSED OF ALL OTHER FORMS BEING GRANTED		459C	ANNO REYNOLDS	MARG
IT DOES NOT THEREFORE FOLLOW THAT ALL OTHER FORMS ARE DEFORMITY		459C	ANNO REYNOLDS	MARG
ALL FORMS ARE PERFECT IN THE POET'S MIND	. . . . . .	459C	ANNO REYNOLDS	MARG
GETS INTO MANY CENTRAL FORMS	. . . .	460A	ANNO REYNOLDS	MARG
WORD ELEGANCE OUGHT TO BE APPLIED TO FORMS NOT TO COLOURS		464C	ANNO REYNOLDS	MARG
OF WHICH GROSS VULGARITY FORMS THE PRINCIPAL EXCELLENCE		464D	ANNO REYNOLDS	MARG
AND IN IT CAUSD THE SPECTRES OF THE DEAD TO TAKE SWEET FORMS		481	MILTON 2	9
AROUND THE FIERY FLAMING HARROW IN LABYRINTHINE FORMS	. .	493	MILTON 12	18
IN CONFLICT WITH THOSE FEMALE FORMS WHICH IN BLOOD & JEALOUSY		498	MILTON 17	7
INTO MOST HOLY FORMS OF THOUGHT SUCH IS THE POWER OF INSPIRATION		515	MILTON 28	5
THEY CONTEND WITH THE WEAK SPECTRES THEY FABRICATE SOOTHING FORMS		515	MILTON 28	23
TO BUILD THE UNIVERSE STUPENDOUS MENTAL FORMS CREATING	. .	519	MILTON 30	20
WHATEVER CAN BE CREATED CAN BE ANNIHILATED FORMS CANNOT		522	MILTON 32	36
BUT THEIR FORMS ETERNAL EXIST FOR-EVER AMEN HALLEUJAH	. .	522	MILTON 32	* 39
SWEET FEMALE FORMS WINGED OR FLOATING IN THE AIR SPONTANEOUS		524	MILTON 34	11
O DREADFUL LOOM OF DEATH O PITEOUS FEMALE FORMS COMPELLD		525	MILTON 35	7
LUTHER THESE SEVEN ARE THE MALE-FEMALES THE DRAGON FORMS		528	MILTON 37	42

		PAGE	TITLE	LINE

FORMS   (CONTINUED)
```
AND THERE WENT FORTH FROM THE STARRY LIMBS OF THE SEVEN        530 MILTON 39           6
    FORMS
THE PAINTER HAS CONSEQUENTLY VARIED THE HEADS AND FORMS        567D DESC CAT 3      PROSE
"AND VERY ORDINARY FORMS" WHICH IS THE TRUEST PART OF ALL      574D DESC CAT 3      PROSE
ART IS LINEAMENTS OR FORMS AND FEATURES THAT ARE CAPABLE OF    579D DESC CAT 5      PROSE
THE DISPOSITION OF FORMS ALWAYS DIRECTS COLOURING    . .  .    580D DESC CAT 5      PROSE
THEIR WOMEN LIKE CHALK FOR THE DISPOSITION OF THEIR FORMS      581A DESC CAT 5      PROSE
THE PAINTER HAS CONSEQUENTLY VARIED THE HEADS AND FORMS        590D CHAUCER 2       PROSE
THAT ARE REQUIRED BY FINE FORMS FINE TINTS WITHOUT   . . .     591C PUB ADDRESS/N   PROSE
ARE LOATHSOM FINE TINTS WITHOUT FINE FORMS   . . . . .         591C PUB ADDRESS/N  *PROSE
SEES ONLY THE COLOURS OF THINGS & NOT THE FORMS OF THINGS      597D PUB ADDRESS/N   PROSE
RIDICULING THE FORMS OF BASIRE'S OTHER GRAVERS   . . . .       603C PUB ADDR AD/N   PROSE
ALL THINGS ARE COMPREHENDED IN THEIR ETERNAL FORMS    . .      605D V LAST JUDG/N   PROSE
I AGAIN DISPLAY MY GIANT FORMS TO THE PUBLIC MY FORMER  .      620D JERUSALEM 3     PROSE
DIVIDED INTO MALE AND FEMALE FORMS TIME AFTER TIME    . .      623 JERUSALEM 5         32
I WILL CAST THEE INTO FORMS OF ABHORRENCE & TORMENT IF THOU    627 JERUSALEM 8         11
CONDENSE BENEATH MY HAMMER INTO FORMS OF CRUELTY   . . . .     628 JERUSALEM 9         27
THE CURTAINS WOVEN TEARS & SIGHS WROUGHT INTO LOVELY FORMS     632 JERUSALEM 12        39
TAKING THEIR FORMS FROM THE WHEELS OF ALBION'S SONS AS COGS    633 JERUSALEM 13        13
OF FORMS OF DEATH AND THAT TOWARD BEULAH STONE   . . .  .      633 JERUSALEM 13        16
AND THAT TOWARD ULRO FORMS OF WAR SEVEN ENORMITIES   . . .     633 JERUSALEM 13        18
AND THAT TOWARD GENERATION SEVEN GENERATIVE FORMS    . . .     633 JERUSALEM 13        19
AND CRUEL FORMS UNLIKE THE MERCIFUL FORMS OF BEULAH'S          639 JERUSALEM 17        28
    NIGHT
DIVIDING AND UNITING INTO MANY FEMALE FORMS JERUSALEM   . .    642 JERUSALEM 19        45
YOU O LOVELY FORMS YOU HAVE PREPARED MY DEATH-CUP    .  .      643 JERUSALEM 21         2
OF NATURAL VIRTUE FOR THEIR SPIRITUAL FORMS WITHOUT A VEIL     643 JERUSALEM 21        15
FORTHWITH FROM ALBION'S DARKNING LOCKS CAME TWO IMMORTAL       654 JERUSALEM 29        28
    FORMS
TILL INTO NARROW FORMS YOU CREEP GO TAKE YOUR FIERY WAY        655 JERUSALEM 29        70
AND THEY DIVIDED INTO FOUR RAVENING DEATHLIKE FORMS   . .      663 JERUSALEM 36        36
CONTRACTION'S LIMIT AND OF THE LIMIT HE FORMS WOMAN THAT       670 JERUSALEM 42        33
THEIR HUMAN MAJESTIC FORMS SIT UP UPON THEIR COUCHES     . .   671 JERUSALEM 42        66
SWELLD & BLOATED GENERAL FORMS REPUGNANT TO THE . . . . .      672 JERUSALEM 43        19
THEIR GIANT FORMS CONDENSING INTO NATIONS & PEOPLES           684 JERUSALEM 53         8
    & TONGUES
THE OBDURATE FORMS ARE CUT ASUNDER BY JEALOUSY & PITY   .      689 JERUSALEM 58        12
AND THERE THEY COMBINE INTO THREE FORMS NAMED BACON           708 JERUSALEM 70        15
    & NEWTON & LOCKE
DISSIPATING THE ROCKY FORMS OF DEATH BY HIS THUNDEROUS         714 JERUSALEM 73        43
    HAMMER
LUTHER THESE SEVEN ARE THE MALE FEMALES THE DRAGON FORMS       716 JERUSALEM 75        17
CLIFFS DIVIDING THEM INTO MALE & FEMALE FORMS IN               719 JERUSALEM 78         7
    HIS FURNACES
INTO TWO IRREGULAR FORMS AND LOOKING ON ALBION'S DREAD TREE    723 JERUSALEM 80        73
THESE AWFUL FORMS IN OUR SOFT BANDS DISTRACTED WITH            723 JERUSALEM 80        85
    TREMBLING
UNLESS WE FIND A WAY TO BIND THESE AWFUL FORMS TO OUR   . .    725 JERUSALEM 82         3
SURROUNDED WITH MASSES OF STONE IN ORDERD FORMS DETERMINE      727 JERUSALEM 83        10
    THEN
O LOVELY ENITHARMON I BEHOLD THY GRACEFUL FORMS   . . . .      732 JERUSALEM 87         3
THE HUMAN FOUR-FOLD FORMS MINGLE ALSO IN THUNDERS              733 JERUSALEM 88         7
    OF INTELLECT
BUT GENERAL FORMS HAVE THEIR VITALITY IN PARTICULARS &         738 JERUSALEM 91        30
    EVERY
OF FIRE SPEAKING THE WORDS OF ETERNITY IN HUMAN FORMS IN       742 JERUSALEM 95         9
    DIREFUL
AND THEY CONVERSED TOGETHER IN VISIONARY FORMS DRAMATIC        746 JERUSALEM 98        28
    WHICH BRIGHT
ALL HUMAN FORMS IDENTIFIED EVEN TREE METAL EARTH & STONE       747 JERUSALEM 99         1
    ALL
HUMAN FORMS IDENTIFIED LIVING GOING FORTH & RETURNING          747 JERUSALEM 99         2
    WEARIED
("SOUL THAT IMPARTETH FORMS TO MATTER") THIS IS MY OPINION     775A ANNO BERKELEY   MARG
    BUT
FORMS MUST BE APPREHENDED BY SENSE OR THE EYE OF              775A ANNO BERKELEY   MARG
    IMAGINATION
& THEIR FORMS MORE DISTINCTLY SEEN    . . . . . . . .  .       802A LETTER 14       PROSE
```
FORNICATION
```
OF FORNICATION FOOD OF ORC & SATAN PRESSD FROM THE FRUIT       356 FOUR ZOAS 8         603
    OF MYSTERY
```
FORSAKEN
```
O LAND MOST HAPLESS O BEAUTEOUS ISLAND HOW FORSAKEN     .      34A KING JOHN/PS     PROSE
TIME FOR CONTEMPLATION ROSE FROM THE FORSAKEN EAST   . . .     39D SAMSON/PS        PROSE
FORSAKEN AND PARIS WITHOUT A SOLDIER SILENT FOR THE NOISE      148 FRENCH REVOLTN     305
    WAS GONE UP
BRED FROM HIS FORSAKEN WILDERNESS . . . . . . . . .  .         222 URIZEN 3            15
OF LIFE ON HIS FORSAKEN MOUNTAINS . . . . . . . . . . .        234 URIZEN 23            1
ON HIGH REMAIND ALONE FORSAKEN IN FIERCE JEALOUSY    . .       274 FOUR ZOAS 1         360
THEY STOOD ABOVE THE HEAVENS FORSAKEN DESOLATE SUSPENDED       274 FOUR ZOAS 1         361
    IN BLOOD
THE POOR FORSAKEN LOS MOCKD BY THE WORM THE SHELLY SNAIL       288 FOUR ZOAS 2         307
HAVE QUITE FORSAKEN O FOOL FOOL TO LOSE MY SWEETEST BLISS      295 FOUR ZOAS 3         168
O THE PANGS THE BITTER PANGS OF LOVE FORSAKEN   . . . .        349 FOUR ZOAS 8         308
FEAR NOT O POOR FORSAKEN ONE O LAND OF BRIARS & THORNS         354 FOUR ZOAS 8         534
A HORRIBLE ROCK FAR IN THE SOUTH IT WAS FORSAKEN WHEN   .      359 FOUR ZOAS 9          93
FORSAKEN OF THEIR ELEMENTS THEY VANISH & ARE NO MORE   .       376 FOUR ZOAS 9         733
O JERUSALEM JERUSALEM I HAVE FORSAKEN THY COURTS    . .        647 JERUSALEM 24        17
TO BUILD BABYLON BECAUSE THEY HAVE FORSAKEN JERUSALEM   .      647 JERUSALEM 24        30
GOD HATH FORSAKEN ME & MY FRIENDS ARE BECOME A BURDEN   .      666 JERUSALEM 39        22
O PAIN O THE PANGS THE BITTER PANGS OF LOVE FORSAKEN    .      705 JERUSALEM 67        55
```

	PAGE	TITLE	LINE

FORSAKEN   (CONTINUED)
```
    MY BROTHER & MY FATHER ARE NO MORE GOD HATH FORSAKEN ME        719 JERUSALEM 78        31
    FORSAKEN SURREY AND SUSSEX ARE ENITHARMON'S CHAMBER  . . .     727 JERUSALEM 83        25
FORSAKES
    AND IF ANY GIRL'S LOVER FORSAKES HER FOR ME    . . . . .       428 MARY                 31
FORSAKING
    FAIR NINE FORSAKING POETRY  . . . . . . . . . .                 11 TO MUSES/PS          12
    FORSAKING BROTHERHOOD & UNIVERSAL LOVE IN SELFISH CLAY  . .    374 FOUR ZOAS 9          629
    ENTERING INTO THE REASONING POWER FORSAKING IMAGINATION        714 JERUSALEM 74          7
FORSOOK
    PITY FORSOOK THEE AT THY BIRTH O DAGON FURIOUS  . . . .        38C SAMSON/PS          PROSE
    THEY SPOTTED WITH PLAGUES FORSOOK THE FRONTIERS & THEIR        202 AMERICA 15           14
        BANNERS SEARD
    THE GUARDIAN OF THE SECRET CODES FORSOOK HIS ANCIENT          242 EUROPE 12             15
        MANSION
    LUCIFER REFUSD TO DIE FOR SATAN & IN PRIDE HE FORSOOK HIS     351 FOUR ZOAS 8          399
        CHARGE
    BUT LUCIFER REFUSD TO DIE & IN PRIDE HE FORSOOK HIS CHARGE    494 MILTON 13             18
    WITH PANGS SHE FORSOOK BEULAH'S PLEASANT LOVELY SHADOWY       678 JERUSALEM 48          19
        UNIVERSE
FORTH
    UP TO THY BRIGHT PAVILLIONS ISSUE FORTH  . . . . . . . .        1 TO SPRING/PS          7
    O DECK HER FORTH WITH THY FAIR FINGERS POUR  . . . . .          1 TO SPRING/PS         13
    TILL CLUSTRING SUMMER BREAKS FORTH INTO SINGING  . . . .        2 TO AUTUMN/PS         11
    UNLOCK HEAVN'S GOLDEN GATES AND ISSUE FORTH  . . . . .          3 TO MORNING/PS         2
    WHEN EARLY MORN WALKS FORTH IN SOBER GREY  . . . . .           10 WHEN EARLY/PS         1
    AND BEAM FORTH LUSTRE ON A DARKLING WORLD  . . . . . .         18 EDW THIRD/PS 1       36
    IS CULTIVATED AND WILL BRING FORTH FRUIT  . . . . . .          19 EDW THIRD/PS 2       26
    BRINGS FORTH FRUIT TO THE MIND'S TREASURE-HOUSE  . . .        27 EDW THIRD/PS 3      251
    CRAVE OR BE HEARD FOR PLENTY SHALL BRING FORTH  . . . .        33 EDW THIRD/PS 6       46
    BRING FORTH THE LOTS CAST IN THE SPACIOUS ORB  . . . .        34 WAR SONG/PS           2
    STRETCH FORTH YOUR HANDS THAT MY HELPER MAY COME  . . .       36A COUCH DEATH/PS     PROSE
    BENEATH ME BURNS ETERNAL FIRE O FOR A HAND TO PLUCK ME       36B COUCH DEATH/PS     PROSE
        FORTH
    FOR CARE WAS I BROUGHT FORTH AND LABOUR IS MY LOT  . . .      39B SAMSON/PS         PROSE
    BY BANDS OF ENEMIES STRETCH FORTH THY HAND AND SAVE  . . .    40B SAMSON/PS         PROSE
    FROM WHOM CAME IGNORANCE WHO BROUGHT FORTH WONDER  . . .      40D THEN SHE BORE     PROSE
    OR IF THEY LIST TOGETHER MINGLING BRING FORTH MIGHTY POWRS    40D THEN SHE BORE     PROSE
    FORTH CAME AMBITION CRAWLING LIKE A TOAD  . . . . . .         41A THEN SHE BORE     PROSE
    AND SWELLING SIGHS BURST FORTH HIS CHILDREN ALL IN ARMS       42B THEN SHE BORE     PROSE
        APPEAR
    SHE BROUGHT FORTH RAGE [THEN] AND SHAME BORE HONOUR &  . .    42C THEN SHE BORE    *PROSE
    WAS BORN ENVY IN DIREFUL PAINS HIM BORE THEN ENVY BROUGHT     42C THEN SHE BORE     PROSE
        FORTH CARE
    CARE BROUGHT FORTH COVET EYELESS & PRONE TO TH EARTH   . .    42C THEN SHE BORE     PROSE
    AND STRIFE BROUGHT FORTH REVENGE HATE BROODING IN            42C THEN SHE BORE     PROSE
        HER DISMAL DEN
    GREW PREGNANT & [BROUGHT FORTH] BORE SCORN & SLANDER   . .    42D THEN SHE BORE     PROSE
    POLICY BROUGHT FORTH GUILE & FRAUD  . . . . . . .             42D THEN SHE BORE     PROSE
    ON DUSKY WING BREATHING FORTH CLAMOUR & DESTRUCTION  . . .    42D THEN SHE BORE     PROSE
    THE MUSE THEN STRUCK HER DEEPEST [NOTE] STRING & SYMPATHY     43C WOE CRIED MUSE    PROSE
        CAME FORTH
    SHE SOON GREW PREGNANT & BROUGHT FORTH  . . . . . . .         51 WHEN CORRUP/IM       21
    AS I WALKD FORTH ONE MAY MORNING  . . . . . . . .             55 MAY MORNING/IM        1
    THIS CITY & THIS COUNTRY HAS BROUGHT FORTH MANY MAYORS  . .   58 THIS CITY/IM          1
    TO SIT IN STATE & GIVE FORTH LAWS OUT OF THEIR OLD OAK        58 THIS CITY/IM          2
        CHAIRS
    ("IMAGE OF CREATION") A GOING FORTH & RETURNING  . . . .      95A ANNO SWED LOVE     MARG
    COME FORTH & LOOK ON HER THAT BORE YOU COME YOU ACCURSED      99 TIRIEL 1              8
        SONS
    COME FORTH SONS OF THE CURSE COME FORTH SEE THE DEATH         99 TIRIEL 1             10
        OF MYRATANA
    THE ORBS OF HIS LARGE EYES HE OPEND & THUS HIS VOICE WENT     99 TIRIEL 1             21
        FORTH
    HEUXOS COME FORTH I HERE HAVE BROUGHT THE FIEND THAT         104 TIRIEL 4             43
        TROUBLES IJIM
    HEUXOS & LOTHO RAN FORTH AT THE SOUND OF IJIM'S VOICE  . .   105 TIRIEL 4             45
    AND SO I'LL KEEP HIM FETCH YOUR FATHER FETCH FORTH          105 TIRIEL 4             62
        MYRATANA
    IS READY FOR YOUR BITTER TAUNTS [XXX] COME FORTH SONS OF    105 TIRIEL 4         *   67
        THE CURSE
    FORTH FROM THEIR CAVES [THE SONS OF ZAZEL] . . . . . .      108 TIRIEL 7              3
    [HIS LITTLE HANDS INTO THE DEPTHS OF THE SEA TO BRING       110 TIRIEL 8             21
        FORTH]
    COME FORTH WORM OF THE SILENT VALLEY TO THY PENSIVE QUEEN   129 BOOK OF THEL 3       29
    . . . AND UTTERD A WITHRING HEAT AND THESE WORDS BURST      137 FRENCH REVOLTN       69
        FORTH
    HEAR MY COUNSEL O KING AND SEND FORTH THY GENERALS . . .    141 FRENCH REVOLTN      153
    . . . AROSE AND UNFOLDED HIS ROBE AND PUT FORTH  . . . .    142 FRENCH REVOLTN      175
    RED CLAY BROUGHT FORTH  . . . . . . . . . .                 148 MARRIAGE HH 2        13
    JOYS IMPREGNATE SORROWS BRING FORTH  . . . . . . . .       151C MARRIAGE HH 8      PROSE
    FORTH WENT THE HAND OF JEALOUSY AMONG THE FLAMING HAIR  . . 159C SONG LIBERTY      PROSE
    THE [ROSE PUTS ENVIOUS] [LUSTFUL] MODEST ROSE PUTS FORTH    171 THE LILLY/N          1
        A THORN
    OF BROMION'S RAGE THAT OOTHOON SHALL PUT FORTH IN NINE      190 V DAU ALBION 2       2
        MOONS' TIME
    TELL ME WHERE DWELL THE THoUGHTS FORGOTTEN TILL THOU CALL   192 V DAU ALBION 4       3
        THEM FORTH
    THEN COMST THOU FORTH A MODEST VIRGIN KNOWING TO DISSEMBLE  194 V DAU ALBION 6      10
    WITH BEAMS OF BLOOD & THUS A VOICE CAME FORTH AND SHOOK     198 AMERICA 5            7
        THE TEMPLE
    HIS PLAGUES OBEDIENT TO HIS VOICE FLEW FORTH OUT OF THEIR   201 AMERICA 14           4
        CLOUDS
```

			PAGE	TITLE	LINE

FORTH   (CONTINUED)
```
                                                            PAGE    TITLE              LINE
FORTH   (CONTINUED)
  HIS STORED SNOWS HE POURED FORTH AND HIS ICY MAGAZINES  .  .  203 AMERICA 16            9
  THEIR UNMOVD BRANCHES STOOD THE HALL BUILT WHEN THE MOON     204 AMERICA CANC B         4
    SHOT FORTH
  THE MODEST ROSE PUTS FORTH A THORN  .  .  .  .  .  .  .  .   215 THE LILLY/SE           1
  BROUGHT FORTH AN INFANT FORM  .  .  .  .  .  .  .  .  .  .   232 URIZEN 19             35
  THE WORLD WHERE EVERY PARTICLE OF DUST BREATHES FORTH ITS    237 EUROPE INTRO          18
    JOY
  O MOTHER ENITHARMON WILT THOU BRING FORTH OTHER SONS    .    238 EUROPE PREL 1          4
  AND BRING FORTH HOWLING TERRORS ALL DEVOURING FIERY KINGS    238 EUROPE PREL 2          4
  I BRING FORTH FROM MY TEEMING BOSOM MYRIADS OF FLAMES   .  . 238 EUROPE PREL 2          9
  STRETCH FORTH YOUR HANDS AND STRIKE THE ELEMENTAL STRINGS    239 EUROPE 4              13
  THEIR PARENTS BROUGHT THEM FORTH & AGED IGNORANCE PREACHES   242 EUROPE 12              7
    CANTING
  SHE CEASD [AND] FOR ALL [WENT] WERE FORTH [TO] AT SPORT      244 EUROPE 14        *     32
    .  .  .
  FORTH FROM THE DEAD DUST RATTLING BONES TO BONES  .  .  .  . 248 SONG OF LOS 7         31
  FORTH PLEW THE ARROWS OF PESTILENCE  .  .  .  .  .  .  .  .  252 AHANIA 4               9
  WALKED FORTH FROM THE CLOUDS OF MORNING  .  .  .  .  .  .  . 255 AHANIA 5              31
  AND THUS HER SPEECH BROKE FORTH  .  .  .  .  .  .  .  .  .   256 BOOK OF LOS 3          6
  LOST LOST LOST ARE MY EMANATIONS ENION [COME FORTH] O        264 FOUR ZOAS 1           25
    ENION
  SHE DREW THE SPECTRE FORTH FROM THARMAS .  .  .  .  .  .  .  267 FOUR ZOAS 1          122
  [SHE SPOKE WHAT AM I WHEREFORE WAS I PUT FORTH ON THESE      268 FOUR ZOAS 1          137
    ROCKS]
  TILL WITH FIERCE PAIN SHE BROUGHT FORTH ON THE ROCKS HER     269 FOUR ZOAS 1          191
    SORROW & WOE
  DRAWING FORTH DROOPING MOTHER'S PITY DROOPING MOTHER'S       269 FOUR ZOAS 1          197
    SORROW
  [THE ROUGH BARK OPENS TWITTERING PEEP FORTH LITTLE BEAKS     270 FOUR ZOAS 1          206
    & WINGS]
  THE EARTH SPREAD FORTH HER TABLE WIDE THE NIGHT A SILVER     273 FOUR ZOAS 1          347
    CUP
  BURSTING FORTH FROM THE LOINS OF ENITHARMON THOU FIERCE      276 FOUR ZOAS 1          430
    TERROR
  TAKE THOU POSSESSION TAKE THIS SCEPTER GO FORTH IN MY        280 FOUR ZOAS 2            5
    MIGHT
  HIS FEET UPON THE VERGE OF NON EXISTENCE HIS VOICE WENT      280 FOUR ZOAS 2           21
    FORTH
  THEY GO FORTH & RETURN TO ALBION ON HIS ROCKY COUCH  .  .  . 281 FOUR ZOAS 2           60
  WHEN I CALLD FORTH THE EARTH-WORM FROM THE COLD & DARK       282 FOUR ZOAS 2           83
    OBSCURE
  [THEN] SORROWING WENT THE PLANTERS FORTH TO PLANT .  .  .    286 FOUR ZOAS 2          249
  .  .  .  THE SOWERS [FORTH] TO SOW  .  .  .  .  .  .  .  .   286 FOUR ZOAS 2          249
  THE WONDROUS WORK FLOW FORTH LIKE VISIBLE OUT OF            287 FOUR ZOAS 2          260
    THE INVISIBLE
  [NOW] FOR LOS & ENITHARMON WALKD FORTH ON THE DEWY EARTH     288 FOUR ZOAS 2          295
  .  .  .  IT HAS BROUGHT FORTH A POISON TREE  .  .  .  .  .   290 FOUR ZOAS 2          388
  INFOLDED IN THICK CLOUDS FROM WHENCE HIS MIGHTY VOICE BURST  292 FOUR ZOAS 3           13
    FORTH
  LAYING HER SEED UPON THE FIBRES SOON TO ISSUE FORTH  .  .  . 292 FOUR ZOAS 3           21
  .  .  .  & PUT FORTH LUVAH FROM HIS PRESENCE  .  .  .  .  .  294 FOUR ZOAS 3           83
  SHE ENDED FOR HIS WRATHFUL THRONE BURST FORTH  .  .  .  .  . 294 FOUR ZOAS 3          104
  .  .  .  HIS STRONG RIGHT [HAD] HAND CAME FORTH  .  .  .  .  294 FOUR ZOAS 3     *    110
  GO FORTH REBUILD THIS UNIVERSE BENEATH MY INDIGNANT POWER    298 FOUR ZOAS 4           27
  GO FORTH SAID THARMAS WORKS OF JOY ARE THINE OBEY & LIVE     299 FOUR ZOAS 4           67
  GO FORTH BEAR ENITHARMON BACK TO THE ETERNAL PROPHET   .  .  299 FOUR ZOAS 4           70
  MY LOINS BEGIN TO BREAK FORTH INTO VEINY PIPES & WRITHE      300 FOUR ZOAS 4           94
  SHE STROVE IN VAIN NOT SO URTHONA STROVE FOR BREAKING        300 FOUR ZOAS 4          104
    FORTH
  TILL FROM HER HEART RENDING HIS WAY A TERRIBLE CHILD SPRANG  306 FOUR ZOAS 5           37
    FORTH
  SOFT TEARS & SIGHS WHERE ARE YOU COME FORTH SHOUT ON BLOODY  306 FOUR ZOAS 5           48
    FIELDS
  NOW HOLDS THEE SOON TO ISSUE FORTH SOUND CLARIONS OF WAR     307 FOUR ZOAS 5           63
  TENFOLD THE DEMON'S RAGE FLAMD TENFOLD FORTH RENDING    .  . 308 FOUR ZOAS 5          105
  OF LIFE [REJOICE] LAMENT AROUND THE DEMON GOING FORTH &      308 FOUR ZOAS 5     *    117
    RETURNING
  [SAYING] & SAID GO FORTH & GUIDE MY SON WHO WANDERS ON       310 FOUR ZOAS 5          221
    THE OCEAN
  I WENT NOT FORTH I HID MYSELF IN BLACK CLOUDS OF MY WRATH    311 FOUR ZOAS 5          222
  AND WHEREFORE DOST THOU POUR THIS WATER FORTH IN SIGHS       312 FOUR ZOAS 6           10
    & CARE
  SHE ANSWERD NOT BUT FILLD HER URN & POURD IT FORTH ABROAD    312 FOUR ZOAS 6           11
  THEN URIZEN WEPT & THUS HIS LAMENTATION POURED FORTH    .  . 312 FOUR ZOAS 6           24
  GO FORTH SONS OF MY CURSE GO FORTH DAUGHTERS OF             313 FOUR ZOAS 6           46
    MY ABHORRENCE
  FOR STILL IT SURGES FORTH IN FISH & MONSTERS OF THE DEEPS    313 FOUR ZOAS 6           61
  SHUT UP HIS POWERS IN OBLIVION THEN AS THE SEED SHOOTS       316 FOUR ZOAS 6          161
    FORTH
  REORGANIZE ME SHOOTING FORTH IN BONES & FLESH & BLOOD   .  . 317 FOUR ZOAS 6          224
  FOUR CAVERNS ROOTING DOWNWARDS THEIR FOUNDATIONS THRUSTING   318 FOUR ZOAS 6          263
    FORTH
  ALL THESE AROUND THE WORLD OF LOS CAST FORTH THEIR          318 FOUR ZOAS 6          278
    MONSTROUS BIRTHS
  ROUND HOWLING ORC WHOSE AWFUL LIMBS CAST FORTH RED SMOKE     320 FOUR ZOAS 7           17
    & FIRE
  TAKE ROOT AGAIN WHEREEVER THEY TOUCH AGAIN BRANCHING FORTH   321 FOUR ZOAS 7           34
  SITTING UPON [HIS] AN IRON CRAG AT LENGTH HIS WORDS BROKE    321 FOUR ZOAS 7           43
    FORTH
  AND STILL THE BURDEN OF THEIR SONG IN TEARS WAS POURED       322 FOUR ZOAS 7     *    106
    FORTH
```

748

FORTH   (CONTINUED)

	PAGE	TITLE		LINE
BURST FORTH UPON THE WINDS ABOVE THE TREE OF MYSTERY . .	324	FOUR ZOAS 7		168
HER SHADOW WENT FORTH & RETURND NOW SHE WAS PALE AS SNOW	324	FOUR ZOAS 7		173
SICKLY LOOK FORTH & SCARCELY STRETCH THEIR BRANCHES TO THE PLAIN	325	FOUR ZOAS 7		193
THY LILLIES THAT GAVE LIGHT WHAT TIME THE MORNING LOOKED FORTH	325	FOUR ZOAS 7		196
[VALAM] VALA WAS PREGNANT & BROUGHT FORTH URIZEN PRINCE OF LIGHT	326	FOUR ZOAS 7	*	244
MY MASCULINE SPIRIT SCORNING THE FRAIL BODY ISSUD FORTH	327	FOUR ZOAS 7	*	290
DARKEND & LOST IN DUE TIME ISSUING FORTH FROM ENION'S WOMB	327	FOUR ZOAS 7		294
BROUGHT FORTH A WONDER HORRIBLE WHILE ENITHARMON SHRIEKD	328	FOUR ZOAS 7		317
BROUGHT FORTH THIS WONDER HORRIBLE A CLOUD SHE GREW & GREW	328	FOUR ZOAS 7		327
TILL MANY OF THE DEAD BURST FORTH FROM THE BOTTOMS OF THEIR TOMBS	328	FOUR ZOAS 7		328
THEN I CAN SIGH FORTH ON THE WINDS OF GOLGONOOZA PITEOUS FORMS	331	FOUR ZOAS 7		451
AND DRAWING THEM FORTH DELIGHTED UPON THE WINDS OF GOLGONOOZA	331	FOUR ZOAS 7		460
LOS DREW THEM FORTH OUT OF THE DEEPS PLANTING HIS RIGHT FOOT FIRM	332	FOUR ZOAS 7		464
SWEET ENITHARMON MILD ENTRANCD BREATHD FORTH UPON THE WIND	332	FOUR ZOAS 7		472
FOR HE BEHELD NEW FEMALE FORMS BORN FORTH UPON THE AIR . .	332	FOUR ZOAS 7		487
I WILL WALK FORTH THRO THOSE WIDE FIELDS OF ENDLESS ETERNITY	333	FOUR ZOAS 7B		8
LIFT UP LIFT UP SHINE FORTH O LIGHT WATCHMAN THY LIGHT IS OUT	335	FOUR ZOAS 7B		96
AND SAID GO FORTH & GUIDE MY BATTLES LIKE THE JOINTED SPINE	336	FOUR ZOAS 7B		116
. . . RIPPD FORTH UPON THE GROUND	338	FOUR ZOAS 7B		207
CALL FORTH THY SMILES OF SOFT DECEIT CALL FORTH THY CLOUDY TEARS	338	FOUR ZOAS 7B		208
FOR ALL MY SECRET FAULTS WHICH HE BRINGS FORTH UPON THE LIGHT	339	FOUR ZOAS 7B		250
AND SHE WENT FORTH & SAW THE FORMS OF LIFE & OF DELIGHT	340	FOUR ZOAS 7B		269
TO BUILD HER BOWERS FOR THE ELEMENTS BROUGHT FORTH ABUNDANTLY	340	FOUR ZOAS 7B		277
THE LIVING SOUL IN GLORIOUS FORMS & EVERY ONE CAME FORTH	340	FOUR ZOAS 7B		278
BUT IN VAIN DELIGHTS WERE POURED FORTH ON THE HOWLING MELANCHOLY	340	FOUR ZOAS 7B		280
[WHICH IS THE SYNAGOGUE OF SATAN] SHE SIGHS THEM FORTH UPON THE WIND	341	FOUR ZOAS 8		30
AND PITYING COMFORT AS SHE SIGHD FORTH ON THE WIND THE SPECTRES	342	FOUR ZOAS 8		53
FOR SENSELESS GRATIFICATION & THEIR VISAGES THRUST FORTH	344	FOUR ZOAS 8		127
AND PITYING COMFORT AS SHE SIGHD FORTH ON THE WIND THE SPECTRES	345	FOUR ZOAS 8		183
MALAH COME FORTH FROM LEBANON & HOGLAH FROM MOUNT SINAI	349	FOUR ZOAS 8		316
THAT STATE CALLD SATAN ENITHARMON BREATHD FORTH ON THE WINDS	351	FOUR ZOAS 8		383
. . . THEN HIS BREATHING NOSTRILS DRAWN FORTH	352	FOUR ZOAS 8		422
HIS SCALES TRANSPARENT GIVE FORTH LIGHT LIKE WINDOWS OF THE MORNING	352	FOUR ZOAS 8		441
INTO THEIR LIMBS URTHONA SHOT FORTH A VAST FIBROUS FORM	353	FOUR ZOAS 8		468
DART FORTH UPON THE WIND IN PIPES WRITHING ABOUT IN THE ABYSS	353	FOUR ZOAS 8		473
START FORTH THE TREMBLING MILLIONS INTO FLAMES OF MENTAL FIRE	358	FOUR ZOAS 9		44
START FORTH THE TREMBLING MILLIONS INTO FLAMES OF MENTAL FIRE	359	FOUR ZOAS 9		89
IS SILENT ON MY CLOUDED HILLS THAT BELCH FORTH STORMS & FIRES	359	FOUR ZOAS 9	*	103
IN THOSE ETERNAL FIELDS IN CLOUDS OF MORNING STEPPING FORTH	360	FOUR ZOAS 9		125
COME FORTH FROM SLUMBERS OF THY COLD ABSTRACTION COME FORTH	360	FOUR ZOAS 9		129
. . . I WILL CAST THEE FORTH FROM THESE	361	FOUR ZOAS 9		180
THAT ISSUES FORTH IN THE MORNING BY MEASURE	363	FOUR ZOAS 9		227
OF THE WIDE UNIVERSAL FIELD THEN STEPD [OUT] FORTH INTO THE IMMENSE	365	FOUR ZOAS 9		320
COME FORTH O VALA FROM THE GRASS & FROM THE SILENT DEW	367	FOUR ZOAS 9		388
THE SUN IS THINE [WHEN] HE GOETH FORTH IN HIS MAJESTIC BRIGHTNESS	367	FOUR ZOAS 9		399
AND THOU SWEET SMELLING GROUND PUT FORTH THY LIFE IN FRUITS & FLOWERS	368	FOUR ZOAS 9		437
AND WENT FORTH & BEGAN TO REAP & ALL HIS JOYFUL SONS . .	372	FOUR ZOAS 9		583
THEY PLUNGE INTO THE ELEMENTS THE ELEMENTS CAST THEM FORTH	376	FOUR ZOAS 9		736
AND MAN WALKS FORTH FROM MIDST OF THE FIRES THE EVIL IS ALL CONSUMD	379	FOUR ZOAS 9		827
AND THE FRESH EARTH BEAMS FORTH	379	FOUR ZOAS 9		848
AWAKEND VALA ARISTON RAN FORTH WITH BRIGHT ?ONANA . . .	380	FOUR ZOAS AD 1	*	6
WITH HIS THOUSANDS STRONG HE IS MARCHED FORTH	419	I SAW A MONK/N		37
THE TREES BRING FORTH SWEET EXTACY	427	MENTAL TRAVLER		89
WITH HIS THOUSANDS STRONG HE MARCHED FORTH	430	GREY MONK		22
SHINE FORTH UPON OUR CLOUDED HILLS	481	AND DID FEET/M		6
A BARD BROKE FORTH ALL SAT ATTENTIVE TO THE AWFUL MAN . .	482	MILTON 2		24
AT LAST ENITHARMON BROUGHT FORTH SATAN REFUSING FORM IN VAIN	483	MILTON 3		41
AROUND THEIR LOINS POURD FORTH THEIR ARROWS & THEIR BOSOMS BEAM	484	MILTON 4		23
THEN BRINGS FORTH MORAL VIRTUE THE CRUEL VIRGIN BABYLON	484	MILTON 5		27
O WHEREFORE DOTH A DRAGON-FORM FORTH ISSUE FROM MY LIMBS	492	MILTON 12		2
I CAME FORTH FROM THE HEAD OF SATAN BACK THE GNOMES RECOILD	493	MILTON 12		38
I WILL ARISE AND LOOK FORTH FOR THE MORNING OF THE GRAVE	495	MILTON 14		20

FORTH   (CONTINUED)

	PAGE	TITLE	LINE
OF GOLD AND THOSE IN IMMORTALITY GAVE FORTH THEIR EMANATIONS	496	MILTON 15	13
HIS LIMBS SHOT FORTH LIKE ROOTS OF TREES AGAINST THE FORWARD PATH	498	MILTON 17	35
TO HIS ADVERSARY AND THEY SENT FORTH ALL THEIR SONS & DAUGHTERS	501	MILTON 19	30
LET IT NOT BE SO NOW O GO NOT FORTH IN MARTYRDOMS & WARS	507	MILTON 23	49
GO FORTH REAPERS WITH REJOICING YOU SOWED IN TEARS . . .	511	MILTON 25	44
FORTH IN YOUR WRATH LEST YOU ALSO ARE VEGETATED BY TIRZAH	511	MILTON 25	58
THE PLOW GOES FORTH IN TEMPESTS & LIGHTNINGS & THE HARROW CRUEL	514	MILTON 27	47
EVENTS OF TIME START FORTH & ARE CONCIEVD IN SUCH A PERIOD	516	MILTON 29	2
THOU PERCIEVEST THE FLOWERS PUT FORTH THEIR PRECIOUS ODOURS	520	MILTON 31	46
AND COMES FORTH IN THE MAJESTY OF BEAUTY EVERY FLOWER . .	520	MILTON 31	58
FROM HENCE SHE COMES FORTH ON THE CHURCHES IN DELIGHT . .	529	MILTON 38	24
AND THERE WENT FORTH FROM THE STARRY LIMBS OF THE SEVEN FORMS	530	MILTON 39	6
AROSE AROUND ALBION'S BODY JESUS WEPT & WALKED FORTH . .	534	MILTON 42	19
TO GO FORTH TO THE GREAT HARVEST & VINTAGE OF THE NATIONS	535	MILTON 43	1
TWILL HOLD FORTH A HUGE SPLUTTER WITH SMOKE & DAMP . . .	550	ENGL ENCOU/N 2	6
HIS NINE AND TWENTY PILGRIMS SETTING FORTH	589C	CHAUCER 2	TITLE
BURSTS FORTH INTO A RAPTUROUS PROPHETIC STRAIN	619C	ILLUS MILTON	PROSE
BEAMING FORTH WITH HER DAUGHTERS INTO THE DIVINE BOSOM [WHERE]	622	JERUSALEM 4	15
THEY REVOLVE INTO THE FURNACES SOUTHWARD & ARE DRIVEN FORTH NORTHWARD	623	JERUSALEM 5	31
THEY PUT FORTH THEIR SPECTROUS CLOUDY SAILS WHICH DRIVE THEIR IMMENSE	625	JERUSALEM 7	21
IF THOU WAST CAST FORTH FROM MY LIFE IF I WAS DEAD UPON THE MOUNTAINS	627	JERUSALEM 8	36
THAT LAYS OPEN THE HIDDEN HEART I DREW FORTH THE PANG . .	628	JERUSALEM 9	19
OF AFFLICTION AND LOS DREW THEM FORTH COMPELLING THE HARSH SPECTRE	628	JERUSALEM 9	35
TILL HIS SONS & DAUGHTERS CAME FORTH FROM THE FURNACES . .	630	JERUSALEM 10	64
THEN ERIN CAME FORTH FROM THE FURNACES & ALL THE DAUGHTERS OF BEULAH	630	JERUSALEM 11	8
AND THE SONS AND DAUGHTERS OF LOS CAME FORTH IN PERFECTION LOVELY	630	JERUSALEM 11	11
YET WHY DESPAIR I SAW THE FINGER OF GOD GO FORTH	631	JERUSALEM 12	10
WHEN THE DIVINE HAND WENT FORTH ON ALBION IN THE MID WINTER	636	JERUSALEM 15	32
TREMBLING GLOBE SHOT FORTH SELF-LIVING & LOS HOWLD OVER IT	639	JERUSALEM 17	55
CAST CAST YE JERUSALEM FORTH THE SHADOW OF DELUSIONS	640	JERUSALEM 18	11
IN WAR FORTH FROM HIS BOSOM THEY WENT AND RETURND . . .	641	JERUSALEM 18	42
ARE SILENT ON HIS CLOUDED HILLS THAT BELCH FORTH STORMS & FIRE	641	JERUSALEM 19	4
THE SEA THE STARS THE SUN THE MOON DRIVN FORTH BY MY DISEASE	643	JERUSALEM 21	10
BUT ALBION IS CAST FORTH TO THE POTTER HIS CHILDREN TO THE BUILDERS	647	JERUSALEM 24	29
TORE FORTH IN ALL THE POMP OF WAR	650	FIELDS FROM/J	38
AND THUS THE VOICE DIVINE WENT FORTH UPON THE ROCKS OF ALBION	653	JERUSALEM 29	5
THEN FROWND THE FALLEN MAN AND PUT FORTH LUVAH FROM HIS PRESENCE	655	JERUSALEM 29	* 65
THEY WEPT & TREMBLED & LOS PUT FORTH HIS HAND & TOOK THEM IN	656	JERUSALEM 30	16
AND ALL THE TENDERNESSES OF THE SOUL CAST FORTH AS FILTH & MIRE	657	JERUSALEM 31	21
AND HERE WE HAVE FOUND THY SINS & HENCE WE TURN THEE FORTH	658	JERUSALEM 31	61
THAT CREEPS FORTH IN A NIGHT & IS DRIED IN THE MORNING SUN	659	JERUSALEM 33	7
I BREATHE HIM FORTH INTO THE HEAVEN FROM MY SECRET CAVE	660	JERUSALEM 33	50
AND BE THOU CREATED INTO A STATE I GO FORTH TO CREATE . .	662	JERUSALEM 35	15
BETWEEN LIPS OF MIRE & CLAY THEN SENT HIM FORTH OVER JORDAN	662	JERUSALEM 36	6
AND ONE STOOD FORTH FROM THE DIVINE FAMILY & SAID . . .	664	JERUSALEM 37	1
TO CAST JERUSALEM FORTH UPON THE WILDS TO POPLAR & BOW . .	668	JERUSALEM 41	5
THAT THE SPEAR THAT LIGHTS IT FORTH MAY SHATTER THE RIBS & BOSOM	672	JERUSALEM 43	34
NOR DAUGHTER NOR SISTER NOR MOTHER COME FORTH TO EMBOSOM THE SLAIN	673	JERUSALEM 43	44
LUVAH TORE FORTH FROM ALBION'S LOINS IN FIBROUS VEINS IN RIVERS	677	JERUSALEM 47	4
AWAY FROM BEULAH'S HILLS & VALES BREAK FORTH THE SOULS OF THE DEAD	677	JERUSALEM 47	10
SAW THE FINGER OF GOD GO FORTH UPON HIS SEVENTH FURNACE	678	JERUSALEM 48	45
WEAK WITHERD DARKEND & JERUSALEM IS CAST FORTH FROM ALBION	679	JERUSALEM 49	8
IN GREAT ETERNITY EVERY PARTICULAR FORM GIVES FORTH OR EMANATES	684	JERUSALEM 54	1
WALKETH AMONG US GIVE DECISION BRING FORTH ALL YOUR FIRES	686	JERUSALEM 55	18
SAYING WHO WILL GO FORTH FOR US & WHO SHALL WE SEND BEFORE OUR FACE	687	JERUSALEM 55	69
THEY SPREAD FORTH LIKE A LOVELY ROOT INTO THE GARDEN OF GOD	692	JERUSALEM 60	15
GIVE FORTH THY PITY & LOVE FEAR NOT LO I AM WITH THEE ALWAYS	694	JERUSALEM 60	67
THEN MARY BURST FORTH INTO A SONG SHE FLOWED LIKE A RIVER OF	695	JERUSALEM 61	28
MANY STREAMS IN THE ARMS OF JOSEPH & GAVE FORTH HER TEARS OF JOY	695	JERUSALEM 61	29
SHALL VALA BRING THEE FORTH SHALL THE CHASTE BE ASHAMED ALSO	696	JERUSALEM 62	7
BURST FORTH IN STREAMS OF BLOOD UPON THE HEAVENS & DARK NIGHT	696	JERUSALEM 62	31

		PAGE	TITLE	LINE

FORTH   (CONTINUED)
AND SHE PUT FORTH HER HAND UPON THE LOOMS IN DREADFUL   698 JERUSALEM 64   7
  HOWLINGS
CALL FORTH THY SMILES OF SOFT DECEIT CALL FORTH   701 JERUSALEM 65   54
  THY CLOUDY TEARS
THEY LOOK FORTH THE SUN IS SHRUNK THE HEAVENS ARE SHRUNK   703 JERUSALEM 66   50
THEY LOOK FORTH FROM STONE-HENGE FROM THE COVE ROUND   703 JERUSALEM 66   57
  LONDON STONE
MALAH COME FORTH FROM LEBANON & HOGLAH FROM MOUNT SINAI   705 JERUSALEM 68   4
THO HER BRAIN IS NOT DRUNK WITH WINE SHE GOES FORTH FROM   705 JERUSALEM 68   13
  ALBION
LO THEY SHOOT FORTH IN TENDER NERVES ACROSS EUROPE & ASIA   706 JERUSALEM 68   26
BREEDING WOMEN WALKING IN PRIDE & BRINGING FORTH UNDER   706 JERUSALEM 68   36
  GREEN TREES
GOING FORTH & RETURNING FROM ALBION'S ROCKS TO CANAAN   . .   707 JERUSALEM 69   4
DRIVN FORTH BY LOS TIME AFTER TIME FROM ALBION'S CLIFFY   707 JERUSALEM 69   8
  SHORE
OF DEATH BUT HOW THEY CAME FORTH FROM THE FURNACES & HOW   713 JERUSALEM 73   7
  LONG
AND I WILL LEAD FORTH THY WORDS TELLING HOW THE DAUGHTERS   715 JERUSALEM 74   41
GO FORTH OUT OF THY MOUTH TO BLIGHT THEIR PEACE   .   718 STOOD AMONG/J   33
AND THUS HER VOICE WENT FORTH IN THE DARKNESS OF PHILISTHEA   719 JERUSALEM 78   30
IN THE THICK CLOUD & DARKNESS & THE VOICE WENT FORTH FROM   722 JERUSALEM 80   11
THEY GO FORTH & RETURN SWIFT AS A FLASH OF LIGHTNING   . .   722 JERUSALEM 80   44
THE SONS OF ALBION GO FORTH I FOLLOW FROM MY FURNACES   . .   728 JERUSALEM 83   62
BUT WE WOO HIM ALL THE NIGHT IN SONGS O LOS COME FORTH   729 JERUSALEM 84   25
  O LOS
O THOU THAT DWELLEST WITH BABYLON COME FORTH O LOVELY-ONE   730 JERUSALEM 85   32
THEN HE SENT FORTH THE SPECTRE ALL HIS PYRAMIDS WERE GRAINS   739 JERUSALEM 91   48
THE BREATH DIVINE WENT FORTH UPON THE MORNING HILLS ALBION   742 JERUSALEM 95   2
  MOVD
THE BREATH DIVINE WENT FORTH OVER THE MORNING HILLS ALBION   742 JERUSALEM 95   5
  ROSE
HUMAN FORMS IDENTIFIED LIVING GOING FORTH & RETURNING   747 JERUSALEM 99   2
  WEARIED
AND BURSTING FORTH [WITH] HIS FURIOUS IRE   . . . .   749 EV GOSPEL(B)/N   33
WHO SHALL ACCUSE THEE COME YE FORTH   . . . .   754 EV GOSPEL(E)/N   49
FORTH O ELOHIM JEHOVAH . . . .   781 GHOST ABEL 2   23
"THINGS BEING NOW NEARLY COMPLETED FOR OUR SETTING FORTH   800B LETTER 12   PROSE
  ON"
WILL I SING FORTH HIS PRAISES THAT THE DRAGONS OF THE DEEP   823C LETTER 26   PROSE
DONE MY DUTY AND PUT FORTH MY WHOLE STRENGTH   . . . . .   853D LETTER 52   PROSE
FORTHWITH
FORTHWITH HATCHING SOME HOWLD ON HIS HILLS   . . . . . .   250 AHANIA 3   11
FORTHWITH WRITHING UPON THE DARK VOID   . . . .   259 BOOK OF LOS 5   13
FORTHWITH FROM ALBION'S DARKNING LOCKS CAME TWO IMMORTAL   654 JERUSALEM 29   28
  FORMS
"[FORTHWITH UPRIGHT] HE REARS FROM OFF THE POOL" (MILTON)   SUPP LEGEND/N91   *
FORTIFICATION
FORTIFICATION AGAINST THE DIVINE HUMANITY AND MERCY   . . .   653 JERUSALEM 28   26
FORTIFICATIONS
. . . THEY LEVEL THE FORTIFICATIONS   . . . .   365 FOUR ZOAS 9   303
BUILDING CASTLES IN DESOLATED PLACES AND STRONG   641 JERUSALEM 18   38
  FORTIFICATIONS
FORTITUDE
TEMPERANCE PRUDENCE JUSTICE FORTITUDE THE FOUR PILLARS   517 MILTON 29   49
  OF TYRANNY
WITH FORTITUDE AS WITH A GARMENT OF IMMORTAL TEXTURE   . .   665 JERUSALEM 38   52
MANY HONEST PEOPLE ENDURE GREATER HARDSHIPS WITH FORTITUDE   793B LETTER 5   PROSE
FORTNIGHT
I ATTEMPTED EVERY MORNING FOR A FORTNIGHT TOGETHER   792A LETTER 4   PROSE
  TO FOLLOW
CAN COMPREHEND IN A FORTNIGHT BE ASSURED MY DEAR FRIEND   814D LETTER 23   PROSE
  THAT
MR DALLY TO WHOM I ENCLOSED...IN A LETTER A FORTNIGHT   . .   841A LETTER 40   PROSE
ONCE WHICH HAS HINDERD HIS WORKING FOR A FORTNIGHT   . . .   842D LETTER 42   *PROSE
HE PROMISED IT IN A FORTNIGHT AND IT IS NOW THREE MONTHS   847A LETTER 44   PROSE
FORTUITOUS
TO OUR PRIMEVAL CHAOS IN FORTUITOUS CONCOURSE OF INCOHERENT   282 FOUR ZOAS 2   102
IN FORTUITOUS CONCOURSE OF MEMORYS ACCUMULATED & LOST   . .   659 JERUSALEM 33   8
FORTUNATE
BY YOUR RECOMMENDATION [UNDER A FORTUNATE STAR]   . . . .   442D LAST JUDGMNT/L   PROSE
THRO THE PETWORTH ROAD WHICH BY YOUR FORTUNATE ADVICE I   801B LETTER 13   PROSE
  MEAN
THE WRITING LOOKS VERY PRETTY I WAS FORTUNATE IN DOING IT   834C LETTER 34   PROSE
FORTUNATELY
THE FIRST MR B(BLAKE) EVER DID IN FRESCO FORTUNATELY OR   581B DESC CAT 6   PROSE
I HAVE FORTUNATELY I OUGHT TO SAY PROVIDENTIALLY DISCOVERED   861A LETTER 58   PROSE
FORTUNE
ID CURSE BRIGHT FORTUNE FOR MY MIXED LOT   . . . . . .   10 WHEN EARLY/PS   19
[O WE ARE BUT THE SLAVES OF FORTUNE & THAT MOST CRUEL MAN]   105 TIRIEL 4   77
THE ATTENTION OF MANY PERSONS OF EMINENCE AND FORTUNE   . .   207C PRSPECTUS 1793   PROSE
WHAT IS FORTUNE BUT AN OUTWARD ACCIDENT FOR A FEW YEARS   409B ANNO BACON   MARG
MY WIFE WAS TOLD BY A SPIRIT TO LOOK FOR HER FORTUNE BY   440D MEMORANDUM/N 5   PROSE
GAINSBOROUGH TOLD A GENTLEMAN OF RANK & FORTUNE   . . . .   465C ANNO REYNOLDS   MARG
[WITH FORTUNE SPORTING MERRY BLITHE & GAY]   . . . . .   540 GOLDEN RULE/N   *   3
I SPORT WITH FORTUNE MERRY BLITHE & GAY   . . . . . .   540 S(TOTHARD)D/N   3
BUT FORTUNE SAYS SHE GAVE YOU NO SUCH THING   . . . . .   541 MR STOTHARD/N   2
FORTUNE FAVOURS THE BRAVE OLD PROVERBS SAY   . . . . . .   541 MR CROMEK/N   1
. . . [GIVES] SPENDS HIS WHOLE FORTUNE   . . . . . .   548 ON GREAT ENC/N *   3
BY CHANCE OR PERHAPS HIS FORTUNE MONEY MONEY   . . . . .   574A DESC CAT 3   PROSE
GENTLEMEN OF FORTUNE WHO GIVE GREAT PRICES FOR PICTURES   599C PUB ADDRESS/N   PROSE

	PAGE	TITLE	LINE

FORTUNE   (CONTINUED)
```
    BOTH IN GENIUS & FORTUNE HAVE SUBSCRIBED THEIR NAMES     .  . 601D PUB ADDRESS/N   PROSE
    THE GODDESS FORTUNE IS THE DEVIL'S SERVANT  .  .   .  .  . . 785C ILLUS DANTE 16  PROSE
    STARVE I LAUGH AT FORTUNE & GO ON & ON I THINK I FORESEE    . 795C LETTER 6        PROSE
    BUSINESS & THO I LAUGH AT FORTUNE I AM PERSWADED THAT SHE     795D LETTER 6        PROSE
    WHO WERE THE PRAECURSOR OF MY PRESENT FORTUNE  .  .  .  .  . . 808B LETTER 19      *PROSE
    A FORTUNE SUCH AS WOULD MAKE ME INDEPENDENT  .  .  .  .  .  . 820B LETTER 25       PROSE
    A LADY OF FORTUNE I SUPPOSE HE SENDS IT AS A SPECIMEN OF      857B LETTER 54       PROSE
       PRINTING
    [?FIRST ?WERE CREATED WINE & (HAPPINESS) ?GOOD ?LOOKS &      SUPP ANNO REYNOLDS   * MARG
       ?FORTUNE XXX ]
FORTUNE'S
    FOR FORTUNE'S FAVOURS YOU YOUR RICHES BRING  .  .  .  .  . . 541 MR STOTHARD/N       1
FORTUNES
    SUCH ARE THE FORTUNES OF THE GAME  .  .  .  .  .  .  .  .  . . 17 BLIND-MANS/PS      61
    OF TEN POUNDS TO THE DREAMER OVER HIS OWN FORTUNES  .  .  . . 854C LETTER 53        PROSE
    OWN FORTUNES I OUGHT NOT TO DREAM OVER THOSE OF OTHER   .  . 854C LETTER 53        PROSE
FORTY
    FORTY MEN EACH CONVERSING WITH WOES .  .  .  .  .  .  .  .    134 FRENCH REVOLTN     13
    THEIR NUMBERS FORTY MILLIONS MUSTRING IN THE EASTERN SKY    201 AMERICA 13          16
    FORTY YEARS FLEW THE ARROWS OF PESTILENCE  .  .  .  .  .  . 253 AHANIA 4            37
    FORTY YEARS ALL HIS SONS & DAUGHTERS   .  .  .  .  .  .  . . 253 AHANIA 4            40
    PAINTING & ENGRAVING & DURING A PERIOD OF FORTY YEARS   .  . 587D CHAUCER/N         PROSE
    [AN UNABATED STUDY & PRACTISE OF FORTY YEARS FOR I DEVOTED]  591C PUB ADDRESS/N     PROSE
    AS I HAVE FOUND TO MY COST THESE FORTY YEARS   .  .  .  . . 593D PUB ADDRESS/N     P-OSE
    AND THE FORTY COUNTIES OF ENGLAND ARE THUS DIVIDED IN THE    637 JERUSALEM 16        43
       GATES
    AND IN TWELVE COUNTIES OF WALES & IN THE FORTY COUNTIES     711 JERUSALEM 72        15
    OLD PARR WHEN YOUNG VIZ (FORTY)  .  .  .  .  .  .  .  .  . . SUPP PENC DRAW 2.38  *TITLE
FORTY-EIGHT,FORTY EIGHT
    OF FORTY-EIGHT DEFORMED HUMAN WONDERS OF THE ALMIGHTY   .  . 529 MILTON 37          54
    AND THE FORTY-EIGHT STARRY REGIONS ARE CITIES OF             529 MILTON 38           1
       THE LEVITES
    THEY HAVE DIVIDED LEVI HE HATH SHOT OUT INTO FORTY EIGHT     715 JERUSALEM 74        47
       ROOTS
FORTY-TWO
    ALBION'S TWELVE SONS SURROUND THE FORTY-TWO GATES OF ERIN    719 JERUSALEM 78        12
FORWARD
    FOUR STARRY UNIVERSES GOING FORWARD FROM ETERNITY            364 FOUR ZOAS 9        284
       TO ETERNITY
    HIS LIMBS SHOT FORTH LIKE ROOTS OF TREES AGAINST            498 MILTON 17          35
       THE FORWARD PATH
    I STOOPED DOWN & BOUND IT ON TO WALK FORWARD THRO ETERNITY   503 MILTON 21          14
    ON TO WALK FORWARD THRO ETERNITY LOS DESCENDED TO ME   .  . 505 MILTON 22           5
    SHOULD UP ASCEND FORWARD FROM FELPHAM'S VALE & BREAK THE     507 MILTON 23          37
       CHAIN
    AND THEN RUSH FORWARD WITH ME INTO THE GLORIOUS SPIRITUAL    511 MILTON 25          60
    BUT EVERY MAN RETURND & WENT STILL GOING FORWARD THRO   .  . 519 MILTON 31           4
    TO COME IN HERE AS TWO LEAVES FORWARD  .  .  .  .  .  .  . . 606D V LAST JUDG/N    PROSE
    AND THE CIRCUMFERENCE STILL EXPANDS GOING FORWARD           709 JERUSALEM 71         8
       TO ETERNITY
    AS THE SUN & MOON LEAD FORWARD THE VISIONS OF HEAVEN &      743 JERUSALEM 95        21
       EARTH
    AS THE SUN & MOON LEAD FORWARD THE VISIONS OF HEAVEN &      743 JERUSALEM 96         1
       EARTH
    OF HEAVEN GOING FORWARD FORWARD .  .  .  .  .  .  .  .  .  . 745 JERUSALEM 98        27
    BOTH TO GOD & MAN WE LOOK FORWARD EVERY DAY WITH PLEASURE    824B LETTER 27        PROSE
    ALWAYS BEEN FORWARD IN EXPRESSING THEIR KINDNESS FOR US     828A LETTER 28        PROSE
    WOULD FORWARD IT TO MR SEAGRAVE BUT I HAVE INCLOSED IT   .  . 861B LETTER 58       PROSE
    WHAT I WAS ABOUT I HAVE GOT ON VERY FORWARD WITH (FOUR)     876D LETTER 84        PROSE
       PLATES
FORWARDER
    MY NEST I HAVE NOT GOT ANY FORWARDER WITH THE THREE MARYS    804A LETTER 16        PROSE
       OR
FORWARDNESS
    ("FORWARDNESS NIPS AFFECTION IN THE BUD") THE MORE IS THE     85A ANNO LAVATER      MARG
       PITY
    WERE IN GREAT FORWARDNESS YOU WILL SEE BY THE INCLOSED   .  . 816C LETTER 24       PROSE
    THESE ARE ALL IN GREAT FORWARDNESS & I AM SATISFIED THAT    824A LETTER 27        PROSE
    FORWARDNESS & YOU SHALL HAVE PROOFS IN ANOTHER WEEK  .  .  . 837A LETTER 35        PROSE
    IN VERY GREAT FORWARDNESS PARKER COMMENDS IT HIGHLY  .  .  . 849A LETTER 45        PROSE
FORWARDS
    HE WAS BACKWARDS AND FORWARDS IN THE GARDEN  .  .  .  .  . . 437D BLAKES MEMORAN   PROSE
    FORWARDS FROM ULRO FROM THE VALE OF FELPHAM AND SET FREE     503 MILTON 20          60
    IT MAY BE WORKED BACKWARDS AND FORWARDS WITHOUT END  .  .  . 587A CHAUCER 1        PROSE
    PUSHED HIM FORWARDS DOWN THE ROAD ABOUT FIFTY YARDS  .  .  . 827B LETTER 28        PROSE
    MR HAYLEY WAS KIND ENOUGH TO COME FORWARDS  .  .  .  .  . . 828A LETTER 28        PROSE
FOSTERD
    OF FOLLIES BY ME FOSTERD YOUR PREDICTION WILL I HOPE BE     804A LETTER 16        PROSE
FOSTERED     SEE HOPE-FOSTERED
FOSTERS
    FOSTERS HIS PARENT WHO ELSE MUST SWEAT AND TOIL  .  .  .  . . 19 EDW THIRD/PS 2     32
FOUGHT     SEE WELL-FOUGHT
    FIRST I FOUGHT WITH THE FIRE CONSUMD  .  .  .  .  .  .  .  . 224 URIZEN 4           14
    HIS GLOOMY WAY BEFORE HIM THARMAS FLED & FLYING FOUGHT  .  . 313 FOUR ZOAS 6        54
    "IN THE LAST BATTLE THAT ARTHUR FOUGHT THE MOST BEAUTIFUL    560B EXHIBITION ADV  PROSE
       WAS ONE"
    RIVERS THUNDERD AGAINST THEIR BANKS LOUD WINDS FURIOUS      686 JERUSALEM 55        24
       FOUGHT
    THE STARS IN THEIR COURSES FOUGHT THE SUN MOON HEAVEN EARTH  686 JERUSALEM 55        27
    TO MURDER ALBION THE KING OF MEN HE FOUGHT IN BATTLES       722 JERUSALEM 80        18
       FIERCE
```

```
                                                            PAGE      TITLE           LINE
FOUGHT    (CONTINUED)
  FOUGHT THRO A HELL OF TERRORS & HORRORS WHICH NONE COULD  853A LETTER 51            PROSE
FOUL
  BREEDS SATIRE FOUL CONTAGION FROM WHICH NONE ARE FREE  . .  41C THEN SHE BORE        PROSE
  STAND FROM MY PATH FOUL FIEND IS THIS THE LAST OF          103 TIRIEL 4                 8
    THY DECEITS
  [LOS] HE ANSWERD DARKNING MORE WITH [FOUL] INDIGNATION     272 FOUR ZOAS 1             282
    HID IN SMILES
  O WHY DID FOUL AMBITION SIEZE THEE [L] URIZEN PRINCE OF    301 FOUR ZOAS 4        *    141
    LIGHT
  LIKE FOUL FIENDS INHABITING MARY'S MILD BRAIN . . . . .    429 MARY                     42
  A NETHER-WORLD MUST HAVE RECIEVD THE FOUL ENORMOUS SPIRIT  667 JERUSALEM 40             34
FOULD
  REASON ONCE FAIRER THAN THE LIGHT TILL FOULD  . . . . .     42B THEN SHE BORE        PROSE
FOUND
  AND I OFT FOUND MYSELF SITTING BY SORROW ON A TOMB-STONE    37C CONTEMPLATN/PS      PROSE
  NERVOUS ARMS AND AFTER THAT WHEN I HAD FOUND THY FALSHOOD   38D SAMSON/PS          *PROSE
  MATHEMATICS HE FOUND OUT A NUMBER OF QUERIES IN PHILOSOPHY  45C ISLAND MOON 1       PROSE
  IVE FOUND THE DROPSY OUT & SOON  . . . . . . . . . .        51 WHEN CORRUP/IM          31
  ID FIND IT OUT IN A MINUTE BUT IVE FOUND IT OUT ALREADY    51D ISLAND MOON 7        PROSE
  THE LITTLE GIRL FOUND  . . . . . . . . . . . . . .        113D LIT GRL FND/SI       TITLE
  THE LITTLE BOY FOUND  . . . . . . . . . . . . . .        121A LIT BOY FND/SI       TITLE
  BUT I FOUND MYSELF SITTING ON A PLEASANT BANK BESIDE A     156C MARRIAGE HH 17      PROSE
    RIVER
  BUT I AROSE AND SOUGHT FOR THE MILL & THERE I FOUND MY     156D MARRIAGE HH 17      PROSE
    ANGEL
  FOR WHEN YOU RAN AWAY I FOUND MYSELF ON A BANK BY MOONLIGHT 156D MARRIAGE HH 17      PROSE
  I HAVE ALWAYS FOUND THAT ANGELS HAVE THE VANITY TO SPEAK   157C MARRIAGE HH 21      PROSE
  WAS NOT FOUND ON ANY TREE  . . . . . . . . . .             166 I FEARD FURY/N            6
  [NO DELIGHT WAS TO BE FOUND]  . . . . . . . . . .          167 INFANT SORW/N            19
  HATH FOUND OUT THY BED  . . . . . . . . . . . .            175 SICK ROSE/N               5
  WHAT IN WHORES IS ALWAYS FOUND  . . . . . . . . .          178 IN A WIFE/N               2
  [THERE IS JUST SUCH A TREE AT JAVA FOUND]  . . . . .       185 LET BROTHELS/N           25
  WITH NETS FOUND UNDER THY NIGHT PILLOW TO CATCH VIRGIN JOY  194 V DAU ALBION 6          11
  I KNOW THEE I HAVE FOUND THEE & I WILL NOT LET THEE GO  . . 196 AMERICA PREL 2           7
  SINGING THE SUN HAS LEFT HIS BLACKNESS & HAS FOUND         198 AMERICA 6                13
    A FRESHER MORNING
  THEN BURST THE CENTER FROM ITS ORB AND FOUND A PLACE       204 AMERICA CANC B           6
    BENEATH
  WHAT IS MAN I FOUND HIM BENEATH A TREE  . . . . . . .     209C FOR CHILDRN/GP       TITLE
  HAS FOUND OUT THY BED  . . . . . . . . . . . .             213 SICK ROSE/SE              5
  TO CAUSE MY NAME TO VANISH THAT MY PLACE MAY NOT BE FOUND  238 EUROPE PREL '1            5
  WHEN I FOUND BABES OF BLISS ON MY BEDS  . . . . . .        255 AHANIA 5                 19
  FOUND FOR FALLING DAY & NIGHT WITHOUT END  . . . . .       258 BOOK OF LOS 4            33
  UNLESS SOME WAY CAN BE FOUND THAT I MAY LOOK UPON THEE     265 FOUR ZOAS 1             41
    & LIVE
  AND IN THE DARK RECESSES FOUND SIN & CANNOT RETURN  . . .  265 FOUR ZOAS 1             45
  [THAT NOUGHT BUT ENION COULD BE FOUND TO PRAISE ADORE &    267 FOUR ZOAS 1            133
    LOVE]
  [ASTONISHD HE FOUND ENION HIDDEN IN THE DARKSOM CAVE]  . . 267 FOUR ZOAS 1            136
  [EXAMINING THE SINS OF THARMAS I [HAVE] SOON FOUND MY OWN]  268 FOUR ZOAS 1            161
  [HIS WOE FOUND XXX THE CRYSTAL SKY]  . . . . . . . . . SUPP FOUR ZOAS 1            *
  O THARMAS I HAD LOST THEE & WHEN I HOPED I HAD FOUND THEE   296 FOUR ZOAS 3            183
  BUT FOUND MYSELF & HER TOGETHER ISSUING DOWN THE TIDE  . .  300 FOUR ZOAS 4            101
  WE PERISH & SHALL NOT BE FOUND UNLESS THOU GRANT A PLACE    304 FOUR ZOAS 4            259
  AND FIRST HE FOUND THE LIMIT OF OPACITY & NAMD IT SATAN     304 FOUR ZOAS 4            271
  AND NEXT HE FOUND THE LIMIT OF CONTRACTION & NAMD IT ADAM   304 FOUR ZOAS 4            273
  NOT LONG THEY LAY URTHONA'S SPECTRE FOUND HERBS OF THE PIT  309 FOUR ZOAS 5            173
  AMAZD STARTED URIZEN WHEN HE FOUND HIMSELF COMPASSD ROUND   321 FOUR ZOAS 7             36
  HAVE I FOUND THEE HAVE I FOUND THEE TREMBLEST THOU IN FEAR  325 FOUR ZOAS 7            224
  THE VALES TO FIND HIS WAY BACK INTO HEAVEN BUT FOUND NONE   326 FOUR ZOAS 7            249
  MUST FALL UNLESS A WAY BE FOUND [THE] TO RANSOM & REDEEM    330 FOUR ZOAS 7        *   406
  STARTLED WAS LOS HE FOUND HIS ENEMY URIZEN NOW  . . . .    332 FOUR ZOAS 7            496
  AND HE COMMANDED HIS SONS FOUND A CENTER IN THE DEEP  . .  333 FOUR ZOAS 7B            18
  I FOUND HIM IN MY BOSOM & I SAID THE TIME OF LOVE  . . .   355 FOUR ZOAS 8            538
  THE SUN HAS LEFT HIS BLACKNESS & HAS FOUND A FRESHER       379 FOUR ZOAS 9            825
    MORNING
  WILL [ALWAYS BE FOUND TO BE NEITHER COLD NOR HOT & WILL]  386C ANNO WATSON           MARG
  WHEN IT IS FOUND REVERENCE IS ALL FOR REVERENCE  . . . .  401D ANNO BACON            MARG
  AND FOUND A THREEFOLD KISS RETURND  . . . . . . . . .      429 CRYSTL CABINET           20
  THE HAND OF VENGEANCE FOUND THE BED  . . . . . . . .       431 GREY MONK                33
  WHEN MARY WOKE & FOUND HER LAID  . . . . . . . . .         435 WILLIAM BOND             37
  I SAY THESE PRINCIPLES COULD NEVER BE FOUND OUT BY  . . . 457C ANNO REYNOLDS         MARG
  [THE KNAVE CALLS ANY THING ?FOUND IN NATURE FIT FOR ART]  SUPP ANNO REYNOLDS       * MARG
  THE MILLS OF SATAN AS THE EASIER TASK FOUND ALL CONFUSION  488 MILTON 8                 5
  THE DIVINE HAND FOUND THE TWO LIMITS . . . . . . . . .     494 MILTON 13               20
  THIS MOMENT & IT MULTIPLY & WHEN IT ONCE IS FOUND  . . .   526 MILTON 35               44
  I FOUND [THEE] THEM BLIND I TAUGHT [THEE] THEM HOW TO SEE   543 ON F AND S/N            1
  ...MAY...FOUND THE WORD GOLDEN  . . . . . . . . . . .     556C FOUND WORD/N          PROSE
  I FOUND THEM BLIND I TAUGHT THEM HOW TO SEE  . . . . .     575 DESC CAT 3               3
  SUCH AS IS FOUND IN THE FRESCOS OF RAFAEL AND MICHAEL     580D DESC CAT 5            PROSE
    ANGELO
  NUMBER XI THE BODY OF ABEL FOUND BY ADAM AND EVE  . . .   584A DESC CAT 11           TITLE
  PECULIAR TO MR B'S(BLAKE'S) PRINTS WILL BE HERE FOUND     588A CHAUCER/N            PROSE
    ACCOMPANIED
  AS I HAVE FOUND TO MY COST THESE FORTY YEARS  . . . . .   593D PUB ADDRESS/N         P-OSE
  TO BE SUPERIOR MY EXECUTION WILL BE FOUND SO TOO  . . . . 601D PUB ADDRESS/N         PROSE
  BUT OF THOSE FOUND ALIVE AT THE LAST JUDGMENT  . . . . .  610B V LAST JUDG/N         PROSE
  BUT I SOON FOUND THAT IN THE MOUTH OF A TRUE ORATOR  . .  621D JERUSALEM 3           PROSE
  THOU ART MY PRIDE & SELF-RIGHTEOUSNESS I HAVE FOUND THEE   627 JERUSALEM 8             30
    OUT
  HE FOUND JERUSALEM UPON THE RIVER OF HIS CITY SOFT REPOSD  642 JERUSALEM 19            40
```

753

```
                                                                     PAGE      TITLE            LINE
FOUND   (CONTINUED)
    AND IN THE DARK RECESSES FOUND SIN & CAN NEVER RETURN    .       645  JERUSALEM 22          15
    WOULD THOU WERT NOT & THAT THY PLACE MIGHT NEVER BE FOUND        645  JERUSALEM 22          28
    AND HERE WE HAVE FOUND THY SINS & HENCE WE TURN THEE FORTH       658  JERUSALEM 31          61
    THEIR PLACE SHALL NOT BE FOUND AS THE WIND PASSES OVER    .   .  659  JERUSALEM 33          13
    THEN THE DIVINE HAND FOUND THE TWO LIMITS SATAN AND ADAM        662  JERUSALEM 35           1
    AND ACCIDENT & CHANCE WERE FOUND HIDDEN IN LENGTH BREDTH        663  JERUSALEM 36          35
        & HIGHTH
    OF MULTITUDES WHO DIE FROM EARTH THIS GATE CANNOT BE FOUND      665  JERUSALEM 38          59
    FOR VICTIMS OF SACRIFICE BUT JERUSALEM CANNOT BE FOUND HID      668  JERUSALEM 41          13
    TILL NOW IN BEULAH UNLESS A REFUGE CAN BE FOUND    .    .    .   679  JERUSALEM 48          59
    ROUSSEAU THOUGHT MEN GOOD BY NATURE HE FOUND THEM EVIL &        682D ANNO REYNOLDS        PROSE
    FOUND NO FRIEND FRIENDSHIP CANNOT EXIST WITHOUT FORGIVENESS     682D JERUSALEM 52         PROSE
    ROCK THE CRADLE AND IN MILD MELODIES TELL ME WHERE FOUND        688  JERUSALEM 56          22
    O IT WAS LOST FOR EVER AND WE FOUND IT NOT IT CAME    .    .    688  JERUSALEM 56          26
    GERMANY POLAND & THE NORTH WOOED MY FOOTSTEPS THEY FOUND        720  JERUSALEM 79          45
    OF TORMENT UNENDURABLE AND IF ONCE A DELUSION BE FOUND    .     722  JERUSALEM 80          14
    FOUND YE LONDON ENORMOUS CITY WEEPS THY RIVER    .    .    .    727  JERUSALEM 83          23
    AS REUBEN FOUND MANDRAKES IN THE FIELD & GAVE THEM TO HIS       740  JERUSALEM 93           8
        MOTHER
    BY THE LOST SHEEP THAT HE HATH FOUND & ALBION KNEW THAT IT      743  JERUSALEM 96           4
    WHEN AFTER THREE DAYS' SORROW FOUND    .    .    .    .    .     748  EV GOSPEL(B)/N         5
    MARY WAS FOUND IN ADULTEROUS BED    .    .    .    .    .    .   753  EV GOSPEL(E)/N         4
    CRYING [IVE FOUND HI] CRUCIFY THIS CAUSE OF DISTRESS    .    .   755  EV GOSPEL(E)/N  *     85
    I FOUND HIM BENEATH A TREE    .    .    .    .    .    .    .    761D FOR SEXES/GP        TITLE
    AND SHE FOUND ME BENEATH A TREE    .    .    .    .    .    .    770  OF GATES/GP            3
    THE DOOR OF DEATH I OPEN FOUND    .    .    .    .    .    .     771  OF GATES/GP           43
    THAT WHAT HE WRITES VALUABLE IS NOT TO BE FOUND IN NATURE       783A ANNO WW POEMS        MARG
    & IT WAS SOME TIME WHEN I FOUND THEM BEFORE I COULD    .    .   791B LETTER 3            PROSE
    YOUR DICTATE BUT WHEN I FOUND MY ATTEMPTS WERE IN VAIN    .     792A LETTER 4            PROSE
    THAT THE VISIONS OF FANCY ARE NOT TO BE FOUND IN THIS WORLD     793D LETTER 5            PROSE
    BLESSED ARE THOSE WHO ARE FOUND STUDIOUS OF LITERATURE &        810D LETTER 21           PROSE
    BUT IT FOUND MY WIFE & MYSELF SO ILL & MY WIFE SO VERY ILL      811B LETTER 22           PROSE
    THE DAWBED BLACK & YELLOW SHADOWS THAT ARE FOUND IN MOST        815B LETTER 23           PROSE
        FINE
    AFTER I HAD FINISHD MY LETTER I FOUND THAT I HAD NOT SAID       816C LETTER 24           PROSE
    FOUND THIS I SHALL HAVE LEARNED A MOST VALUABLE THING    .      828C LETTER 28           PROSE
    WELL WORTH THREE YEARS' PERSEVERANCE I HAVE FOUND IT    .    .  828C LETTER 28           PROSE
    & FOUND HIM QUITE AS CHEARFUL AS YOU DESCRIBE HIM & BY HIS      835C LETTER 35           PROSE
    HIM TO PROCURE FOR YOU HE HAS NOT YET FOUND WHERE IT IS         835D LETTER 35           PROSE
    IS LOST OR AT LEAST CANNOT NOW BE FOUND IT IS THAT OF    .      839C LETTER 38           PROSE
    OF CONSEQUENCE LUCKILLY HE FOUND FAULT WITH THE PAPER    .      846D LETTER 44           PROSE
    IN GENERAL FOUND GREAT BODIES TO BE THEY WERE MUCH PLEASED      850C LETTER 49           PROSE
    ARE ALONE TO BE FOUND IN RELIGION THE SUN & THE MOON OF OUR     854B LETTER 53           PROSE
    THE PROPOSAL CONCERNING THE THREE DRAMAS I FOUND IT    .    .   858A LETTER 55           PROSE
    WHEN AT LENGTH WE FOUND THAT WE WERE ALL THREE PROCEEDING       869C LETTER 70           PROSE
    I FOUND I COULD BEAR WITH SAFETY & PERHAPS BENEFIT    .    .    870D LETTER 72           PROSE
    HAS FOUND (FIFTEEN) PROOFS OF THE HESIOD AS THEY ARE    .       877B LETTER 86           PROSE
    I FOUND HIM BENEATH A TREE IN THE GARDEN    .    .    .    .    SUPP LEGEND/N63          *TITLE
    THE LITTLE BOY FOUND END OF SONGS OF INNOCENCE    .    .    .   SUPP LETTER 66A          *PROSE
FOUNDATION
    THY PITY IS FROM THE FOUNDATION OF THE WORLD & THY             347  FOUR ZOAS 8          243
        REDEMPTION
    THE FOUNDATION OF EMPIRE IS ART & SCIENCE    .    .    .    .   445C ANNO REYNOLDS        MARG
    THE FOUNDATION OF THE SUBLIME    .    .    .    .    .    .     459A ANNO REYNOLDS        MARG
    THE FIRST THE ELECT FROM BEFORE THE FOUNDATION OF THE WORLD     486  MILTON 7              2
    FROM THE FOUNDATION OF THE WORLD THE ELECT IS ONE CLASS YOU     511  MILTON 25            32
    OF SATAN LUVAH LAID THE FOUNDATION & URIZEN FINISHD IT          513  MILTON 27             2
        IN HOWLING WOE
    TO INSPECT MY PRINT OF WHICH DRAWING IS THE FOUNDATION    .    591D PUB ADDRESS/N        PROSE
    WHERE DRAWING ITS FOUNDATION IS CONTEMND AND    .    .    .    602A PUB ADDRESS/N        PROSE
    FOUNDATION OF SOCIETY WHICH IS HUMANITY ITSELF    .    .    .   613A V LAST JUDG/N       *PROSE
    & THEY BOAST THAT IT IS ITS FOUNDATION    .    .    .    .      617B V LAST JUDG/N        PROSE
    A FOUNDATION AND CERTAINTY AND DEMONSTRATIVE TRUTH    .    .    652  JERUSALEM 28          11
    THE FOUNDATION OF ALL & THE GODDESS NATURE    .    .    .    .  785A ILLUS DANTE 7       *PROSE
FOUNDATIONS
    THARMAS LAID THE FOUNDATIONS & LOS FINISHD IT IN HOWLING        307  FOUR ZOAS 5     *    78
        WOE
    FOUR CAVERNS ROOTING DOWNWARDS THEIR FOUNDATIONS THRUSTING      318  FOUR ZOAS 6          263
        FORTH
    THE FOUNDATIONS OF THE ETERNAL HILLS DISCOVERD    .    .    .   357  FOUR ZOAS 9           17
    WHERE JERUSALEM'S FOUNDATIONS BEGAN WHERE THEY WERE LAID        485  MILTON 6             15
        IN RUINS
    SHAKING THE ROOTS & FAST FOUNDATIONS OF THE EARTH              495  MILTON 14             8
        IN DOUBTFULNESS
    AND MOVED THE FAST FOUNDATIONS OF THE EARTH TO WAKE THE         500  MILTON 18            50
        DEAD
    OF PAINTERS AND POETS THEY ARE FOUNDATIONS FOR GRAND THINGS     581D DESC CAT 8          PROSE
    HE SHOOTS BENEATH JERUSALEM'S WALLS TO UNDERMINE                631  JERUSALEM 11         23
        HER FOUNDATIONS
    WHOSE FOUNDATIONS REMAIN IN THE THIRTY-TWO COUNTIES OF          711  JERUSALEM 72         14
        IRELAND
    THE HILL OF GIANTS ALL HER FOUNDATIONS LEVELLD WITH THE         719  JERUSALEM 78         22
        DUST
    WE BEGAN OUR FOUNDATIONS LOVELY LAMBETH O LOVELY HILLS          729  JERUSALEM 84          4
FOUNDED      SEE DEEP-FOUNDED
    OR IS THY JOY FOUNDED ON TORMENT WHICH OTHERS BEAR FOR THEE     321  FOUR ZOAS 7          68
    ALL SUBLIMITY IS FOUNDED ON MINUTE DISCRIMINATION    .    .    453B ANNO REYNOLDS        MARG
    EXIST GRANDEUR OF IDEAS IS FOUNDED ON PRECISION OF IDEAS        457D ANNO REYNOLDS        MARG
    IS FOUNDED ON THE OPINIONS OF NEWTON & LOCKE    .    .    .     476D ANNO REYNOLDS        MARG
    BOWLAHOOLA IS NAMD LAW BY MORTALS THARMAS FOUNDED IT            509  MILTON 24            48
    BOWLAHOOLA THRO ALL ITS PORCHES FEELS THO TOO FAST FOUNDED      509  MILTON 24            54
```

                                                          PAGE   TITLE   LINE
FOUNDED   (CONTINUED)
     & ON THIS DISCRIMINATION ALL ART IS FOUNDED I INTREAT THEN   611B V LAST JUDG/N   PROSE
     THERE BABYLON IS BUILDED IN THE WASTE FOUNDED IN HUMAN   647 JERUSALEM 24   25
       DESOLATION
     FROM ALBION BUT HATH FOUNDED HIS REACTION INTO A LAW   . .   653 JERUSALEM 29   14
FOUNT
     TIS AT THIS RIVER'S FOUNT WHERE EVRY MORTAL'S CUP IS MIXT   41C THEN SHE BORE   PROSE
     BESIDE THE FOUNT ABOVE THE LARK'S NEST IN GOLGONOOZA   . .   526 MILTON 35   58
FOUNTAIN
     THE CISTERN CONTAINS THE FOUNTAIN OVERFLOWS   . . . . .   151D MARRIAGE HH 8   PROSE
     IN AN ORB HIS FOUNTAIN OF THOUGHT   . . . .   228 URIZEN 10   34
     IN AN ORB HIS FOUNTAIN OF THOUGHT   . . . .   303 FOUR ZOAS 4   217
     DRAWS ALL INTO A FOUNTAIN AT THE ROCK OF THY ATTRACTION   312 FOUR ZOAS 6   14
     AND A FOUNTAIN FROM MY BREASTS TO ME COME ALL MULTITUDES   354 FOUR ZOAS 8   501
     AND FIRST FROM THE WILD THYME STANDS A FOUNTAIN IN A ROCK   526 MILTON 35   49
     OLOLON SAT BESIDE THIS FOUNTAIN ON THE ROCK OF ODOURS   .   526 MILTON 35   60
     CANAAN IS HIS PORTICO JORDAN IS A FOUNTAIN IN HIS PORCH   690 JERUSALEM 58   33
     A FOUNTAIN OF MILK & WINE TO RELIEVE THE TRAVELLER   . .   690 JERUSALEM 58   34
     IS THE HOLY GHOST ANY OTHER THAN AN INTELLECTUAL FOUNTAIN   717A JERUSALEM 77   PROSE
     BECOME A FOUNTAIN OF VEINY PIPES O ALBION MY BROTHER   .   727 JERUSALEM 82   84
     GOD THAN THAT GOD WHO IS THE INTELLECTUAL FOUNTAIN OF   738 JERUSALEM 91   11
       HUMANITY
     EACH FOUNTAIN & RILL   . . . .   805 TO BUTTS/L   28
     & OTHER ARTICLES COLLECTED FROM EVERY FOUNTAIN HE CAN VISIT 832D LETTER 32   PROSE
     FOUNTAIN COURT STRAND . . . .   SUPP ADDRESSES/L   *TITLE
FOUNTAINS
     WEEP FROM THY SILVER FOUNTAINS . . . .   34A KING JOHN/PS   PROSE
     THE TEARS SWELL FROM MY STONY FOUNTAINS WHEREFORE DO I WEEP   108 TIRIEL 6   30
     TILL SUMMER'S HEAT MELTS THEE BESIDE THE FOUNTAINS AND   127 BOOK OF THEL 1   24
       THE SPRINGS
     TO MAKE THE DESARTS BLOSSOM & THE DEEPS SHRINK TO THEIR   199 AMERICA 8   8
       FOUNTAINS
     MY FOUNTAINS ONCE THE HAUNT OF SWANS NOW BREED THE SCALY   310 FOUR ZOAS 5   194
       TORTOISE
     AND WAR & HUNTING THE TWO FOUNTAINS OF THE RIVER OF LIFE   525 MILTON 35   2
     ARE BECOME FOUNTAINS OF BITTER DEATH & OF CORRODING HELL   525 MILTON 35   3
     ITS PITS & DECLIVITIES FLOWING WITH MOLTEN ORE & FOUNTAINS   529 MILTON 38   18
     FOR ABOVE TIME'S TROUBLED FOUNTAINS   . . . .   558 THE CAVERNS/N   17
     AMONG THE GODS OF ASIA AMONG THE FOUNTAINS OF PITCH &   693 JERUSALEM 60   24
       NITRE
     FOUNTAINS OF LIVING WATERS FLOWING FROM THE HUMANITY DIVINE   744 JERUSALEM 96   37
     BY THE FOUNTAINS OF LIFE   . . . .   806 TO BUTTS/L   76
FOUR   SEE SIXTY-FOUR,THIRTY-FOUR,TWENTY-FOUR,TWENTY FOUR
     UP IN A MORNING AT FOUR O CLOCK WHEN I WAS A GIRL   . . .   488 ISLAND MOON 4   PROSE
     TO MORROW MORNING BY FOUR O CLOCK & WORK SIR JOSHUA   . .   51D ISLAND MOON 7   PROSE
     ("SANGUINE CHOLERIC PHLEGMATIC MELANCHOLY") (FOUR) MOST   86A ANNO LAVATER   MARG
       HOLY MEN
     THE FOUR DAUGHTERS [& ALL THE CHILDREN IN THEIR SILENT   107 TIRIEL 5   30
       BEDS]
     TO THE FOUR WINDS AS A TORN BOOK & NONE SHALL GATHER THE   198 AMERICA 8   6
       LEAVES
     FOUR WINGED HERALDS MOUNT THE FURIOUS BLASTS & BLOW THEIR   205 AMERICA CANC C   14
       TRUMPS
     FROM THE FOUR CLIFFS OF ALBION RISE . . . .   205 AMERICA CANC C   17
     HE SUNG IT TO FOUR HARPS AT THE TABLES OF ETERNITY   . . . 245 SONG OF LOS 3   2
     IN A FLESHY SLOUGH FORMED FOUR RIVERS   . . . .   260 BOOK OF LOS 5   53
     THE FOUR ZOAS VALA OR THE DEATH AND JUDGEMENT   . . . .   263A FOUR ZOAS   TITLE
     THE FOUR ZOAS THE TORMENTS OF LOVE & JEALOUSY IN   . . . 263C FOUR ZOAS   TITLE
     FOUR MIGHTY ONES ARE IN EVERY MAN A PERFECT UNITY   . . .   264 FOUR ZOAS 1   3
     [TILL ?FAR DISMAL XXX ?FOUR XXX ALL XXX]   . . . . . . SUPP FOUR ZOAS 1   *
     EACH DOME OPEND TOWARD FOUR HALLS & THE THREE DOMES   284 FOUR ZOAS 2   178
       ENCOMPASSD
     WITH LABOUR & CARE THOU DOST DIVIDE THE [RIVER] CURRENT   312 FOUR ZOAS 6   18
       INTO FOUR
     FOUR CAVERNS ROOTING DOWNWARDS THEIR FOUNDATIONS THRUSTING   318 FOUR ZOAS 6   263
       FORTH
     FOUR WINGED HERALDS MOUNT THE FURIOUS BLASTS & BLOW THEIR   319 FOUR ZOAS 6   310
       TRUMPS
     FROM THE FOUR CLIFFS OF URTHONA RISE GLOWING AROUND THE   319 FOUR ZOAS 6   313
       SPECTRE
     FOUR SONS OF URIZEN THE SQUADRONS OF URTHONA LED IN ARMS   319 FOUR ZOAS 6   114
     TO THE FOUR WINDS HOPELESS OF FUTURE ALL FUTURITY   . . .   343 FOUR ZOAS 8   99
     TO JUDGMENT FROM THE FOUR WINDS AWAKE & COME AWAY   . . .   357 FOUR ZOAS 9   13
     AND THESE AGAIN SURROUNDED [OF] BY FOUR WONDERS OF THE   364 FOUR ZOAS 9   * 281
       ALMIGHTY
     FOUR STARRY UNIVERSES GOING FORWARD FROM ETERNITY   364 FOUR ZOAS 9   284
       TO ETERNITY
     FOUR PILLARS OF DIFFERENT HEIGHTS AND SIZES   . . . . . 402A ANNO BACON   MARG
     WHO DESCEND WITH THE FOUR TRUMPETS   . . . . 443A LAST JUDGMNT/L   *PROSE
     [WHO DESCEND BEFORE HIS FEET WITH THEIR FOUR TRUMPETS] .   443A LAST JUDGMNT/L   PROSE
     SOUNDING TO THE FOUR WINDS BENEATH [THE EARTH IS CONVULSD]   443A LAST JUDGMNT/L   PROSE
     IN THE CLOUD WHICH ROLLS AWAY ARE THE FOUR LIVING CREATURES 444A LAST JUDGMNT/L   PROSE
     VOLTAIRE MOEURS DE NATIONS [?VOL] TOME (FOUR)   . . . . 445D ANNO REYNOLDS   * MARG
     THRO ALBION'S FOUR FORESTS WHICH OVERSPREAD ALL THE EARTH   485 MILTON 6   3
     FOUR UNIVERSES ROUND THE MUNDANE EGG REMAIN CHAOTIC   . .   500 MILTON 19   15
     THEY ARE THE FOUR ZOAS THAT STOOD AROUND THE THRONE DIVINE   500 MILTON 19   18
     BUT ALL THE FAMILY DIVINE COLLECTED AS FOUR SUNS   . . .   504 MILTON 21   37
     IN THE FOUR POINTS OF HEAVEN EAST WEST & NORTH & SOUTH . . 504 MILTON 21   38
     STILL MY FOUR MIGHTY ONES ARE LEFT TO ME IN GOLGONOOZA . . 508 MILTON 24   10
     DIVIDE FOUR-FOLD INTO FOUR CHURCHES WHEN LAZARUS AROSE . . 508 MILTON 24   31
     BUT IN ETERNITY THE FOUR ARTS POETRY PAINTING MUSIC   . .   514 MILTON 27   55
     AND ARCHITECTURE WHICH IS SCIENCE ARE THE FOUR FACES OF MAN   514 MILTON 27   56

	PAGE	TITLE	LINE

FOUR   (CONTINUED)

ALL ARE THE WORK OF FAIRY HANDS OF THE FOUR ELEMENTS   .   . 516 MILTON 28   60
GREAT GOLGONOOZA FREE FROM THE FOUR IRON PILLARS OF SATAN'S   517 MILTON 29   48
   THRONE
TEMPERANCE PRUDENCE JUSTICE FORTITUDE THE FOUR PILLARS   517 MILTON 29   49
   OF TYRANNY
AND ALL THE LIVING CREATURES OF THE FOUR ELEMENTS WAILD   519 MILTON 31   17
THE FAIRIES NYMPHS GNOMES & GENII OF THE FOUR ELEMENTS   .   . 520 MILTON 31   20
AND THE FOUR STATES OF HUMANITY IN ITS REPOSE   .   .   .   . 523 MILTON 34   8
FOUR UNIVERSES ROUND THE UNIVERSE OF LOS REMAIN CHAOTIC   524 MILTON 34   32
FOUR INTERSECTING GLOBES & THE EGG FORMD WORLD OF LOS   .   . 524 MILTON 34   33
WHERE LIE IN EVIL DEATH THE FOUR IMMORTALS PALE AND COLD   524 MILTON 34   45
ON ALL SIDES ROUND TO THE FOUR QUARTERS OF THE WORLD   525 MILTON 35   15
   EASTWARD ON
AND HIS FOUR ZOAS TERRIFIED & ON THE VERGE OF DEATH   .   .   . 525 MILTON 35   28
LET THE FOUR ZOAS AWAKE FROM SLUMBERS OF SIX THOUSAND YEARS   530 MILTON 39   13
ARE THE FOUR PILLARS OF HIS THRONE HIS LEFT FOOT   531 MILTON 39   36
   NEAR LONDON
THE FOUR ZOAS OF ALBION & THY SPIRIT WITH THEM STRIVING   532 MILTON 40   7
AND THE IMMORTAL FOUR IN WHOM THE TWENTY-FOUR APPEAR   534 MILTON 42   18
   FOUR-FOLD
ALBION'S BOSOM THE BOSOM OF DEATH & THE FOUR SURROUNDED   534 MILTON 42   21
   HIM
IN THE COLUMN OF FIRE IN FELPHAM'S VALE THEN TO THEIR   534 MILTON 42   22
   MOUTHS THE FOUR
APPLIED THEIR FOUR TRUMPETS & THEM SOUNDED TO THE FOUR   534 MILTON 42   23
   WINDS
TWO YEARS BEFORE MICHAEL ANGELO AND TITIAN BUT FOUR YEARS   563C DESC CAT   PROSE
   AFTER
CHAUCER HAS BEEN SOMEHOW MADE TO NUMBER FOUR CITIZENS   .   . 571D DESC CAT 3   PROSE
SHE HAS HAD FOUR HUSBANDS A FIT SUBJECT FOR THIS PAINTER   574D DESC CAT 3   PROSE
THAT IS THREE OR FOUR TIMES AS MUCH AS WOULD HAVE   .   .   . 582B DESC CAT 9   PROSE
THE ABOVE FOUR DRAWINGS THE ARTIST WISHES WERE IN FRESCO   584B DESC CAT 14   PROSE
THE PRICE TO SUBSCRIBERS FOUR GUINEAS TWO TO BE PAID AT THE   587A CHAUCER 1   PROSE
& THEN THEY ARE SCATTERD ABROAD TO THE FOUR WINDS   .   .   . 594A PUB ADDRESS/N   PROSE
& ON EACH SIDE THE FOUR & TWENTY ELDERS SITTING IN JUDGMENT   606B V LAST JUDG/N   PROSE
IN THIS CATARACT FOUR ANGELS DESCEND HEADLONG   .   .   .   . 609A V LAST JUDG/N   PROSE
WITH FOUR TRUMPETS TO AWAKE THE DEAD   .   .   .   . 609A V LAST JUDG/N   PROSE
WHILE BENEATH THE FEET OF NOAH FOUR SEASONS   .   .   .   .   . 611C V LAST JUDG/N   PROSE
PARTICULARLY THE FOUR LIVING CREATURES   .   .   .   .   .   . 612A V LAST JUDG/N   PROSE
EACH WITHIN OTHER TOWARD THE FOUR POINTS THAT TOWARD   .   . 632 JERUSALEM 12   48
AND THE FOUR POINTS ARE THUS BEHELD IN GREAT ETERNITY   .   . 632 JERUSALEM 12   54
THESE ARE THE FOUR FACES TOWARDS THE FOUR WORLDS   632 JERUSALEM 12   57
   OF HUMANITY
HAS FOUR SCULPTURD BULLS TERRIBLE BEFORE THE GATE OF IRON   632 JERUSALEM 12   62
CLAY BAKD & ENAMELD ETERNAL GLOWING AS FOUR FURNACES   .   . 632 JERUSALEM 12   64
AND THAT TOWARD BEULAH FOUR GOLD SILVER BRASS & IRON   .   . 632 JERUSALEM 12   66
AND THAT TOWARD EDEN FOUR FORMD OF GOLD SILVER BRASS & IRON   633 JERUSALEM 13   1
THE SOUTH A GOLDEN GATE HAS FOUR LIONS TERRIBLE LIVING   .   . 633 JERUSALEM 13   2
THAT TOWARD GENERATION FOUR OF IRON CARVD WONDROUS   .   .   . 633 JERUSALEM 13   3
THAT TOWARD ULRO FOUR CLAY BAKD LABORIOUS WORKMANSHIP   .   . 633 JERUSALEM 13   4
THAT TOWARD EDEN FOUR IMMORTAL GOLD SILVER BRASS & IRON   633 JERUSALEM 13   5
THE WESTERN GATE FOURFOLD IS CLOSD HAVING FOUR CHERUBIM   633 JERUSALEM 13   6
IN SEAS OF SORROW LOS ALSO VIEWS THE FOUR FEMALES   .   .   . 634 JERUSALEM 14   9
OF DEATH FORMING AN AX OF GOLD THE FOUR SONS OF LOS   .   .   . 636 JERUSALEM 15   22
TO THE FOUR POINTS CONDUCT TO ENGLAND & SCOTLAND & IRELAND   637 JERUSALEM 16   33
.   .   . SENDING HIM ABROAD OVER THE FOUR POINTS OF HEAVEN   638 JERUSALEM 17   11
FROM EVERY-ONE OF THE FOUR REGIONS OF HUMAN MAJESTY   .   .   . 640 JERUSALEM 18   1
THUS WEPT THEY IN BEULAH OVER THE FOUR REGIONS OF ALBION   648 JERUSALEM 25   14
HE SAW ALSO THE FOUR POINTS OF ALBION REVERSD INWARDS   .   . 658 JERUSALEM 32   7
AND THE FOUR ZOAS CLOUDED RAGE EAST & WEST & NORTH & SOUTH   663 JERUSALEM 36   25
AND THE FOUR ZOAS WHO ARE THE FOUR ETERNAL SENSES OF MAN   663 JERUSALEM 36   31
BECAME FOUR ELEMENTS SEPARATING FROM THE LIMBS OF ALBION   663 JERUSALEM 36   32
AND THEY DIVIDED INTO FOUR RAVENING DEATHLIKE FORMS   .   .   . 663 JERUSALEM 36   36
THE FOUR APPEARD WITH THEIR EMANATIONS IN FIERY   .   .   .   . 666 JERUSALEM 40   4
THE FOUR ZOAS IN TERRIBLE COMBUSTION CLOUDED RAGE   .   .   . 668 JERUSALEM 41   26
THOU WAST THE IMAGE OF GOD SURROUNDED BY THE FOUR ZOAS   .   . 670 JERUSALEM 42   23
IN THE FOUR REGIONS OF HUMANITY EAST & WEST & NORTH & SOUTH   671 JERUSALEM 42   79
TO PREVENT ALBION WALKING ABOUT IN THE FOUR COMPLEXIONS   671 JERUSALEM 43   5
STRETCHING A HAND TO SAVE THE FALLING MAN ARE WE NOT FOUR   672 JERUSALEM 43   14
AND THESE THE FOUR IN WHOM THE TWENTY-FOUR APPEARD   676 JERUSALEM 46   23
   FOUR-FOLD
THE TWENTYFOUR FRIENDS OF ALBION AND ROUND THE AWFUL FOUR   684 JERUSALEM 53   22
THE FOUR ZOAS RUSH AROUND ON ALL SIDES IN DIRE RUIN   .   .   . 690 JERUSALEM 58   47
AND FORMED INTO FOUR PRECIOUS STONES FOR ENTERANCE FROM   691 JERUSALEM 59   1
   BEULAH
FOR FOUR UNIVERSES ROUND THE MUNDANE EGG REMAIN CHAOTIC   691 JERUSALEM 59   10
THEY ARE THE FOUR ZOAS THAT STOOD AROUND THE THRONE DIVINE   691 JERUSALEM 59   13
FOLLOWING THEE AS A SHEPHERD BY THE FOUR RIVERS OF EDEN   692 JERUSALEM 60   21
WHEN THE FOUR ZOAS OF ALBION THE FOUR LIVING CREATURES   696 JERUSALEM 63   2
   THE CHERUBIM
IN THE TWO CONTRARIES OF HUMANITY & IN THE FOUR REGIONS   699 JERUSALEM 65   4
BUT THE FOUR SONS OF JERUSALEM THAT NEVER WERE GENERATED   710 JERUSALEM 71   50
DWELL OVER THE FOUR PROVINCES OF IRELAND IN HEAVENLY LIGHT   710 JERUSALEM 71   52
THE FOUR UNIVERSITIES OF SCOTLAND .   .   .   . 710 JERUSALEM 71   53
AND THE THIRTY-TWO COUNTIES OF THE FOUR PROVINCES   711 JERUSALEM 72   1
   OF IRELAND
ARE THUS DIVIDED THE FOUR COUNTIES ARE IN THE FOUR CAMPS   711 JERUSALEM 72   2
BUT THE FOUR TOWARDS THE WEST WERE WALLED UP & THE TWELVE   711 JERUSALEM 72   6
THAT FRONT THE FOUR OTHER POINTS WERE TURNED FOUR SQUARE   711 JERUSALEM 72   7
BUT THE FOUR SONS OF JERUSALEM WHO FLED NOT BUT REMAIN   711 JERUSALEM 72   10
THE FOUR THAT REMAIN WITH LOS TO GUARD THE WESTERN WALL   711 JERUSALEM 72   12

	PAGE	TITLE	LINE

FOUR (CONTINUED)

AND THESE FOUR REMAIN TO GUARD THE FOUR WALLS OF JERUSALEM   711 JERUSALEM 72   13
AND THE FOUR GATES OF LOS SURROUND THE UNIVERSE WITHIN AND   712 JERUSALEM 72   45
WHO GUIDE THE GREAT WINE-PRESS OF LOVE FOUR PRECIOUS STONES   712 JERUSALEM 72   52
  THAT GATE
THRO ALL THE FOUR POINTS LO THE LABOURERS AT THE FURNACES   713 JERUSALEM 73   4
THE FOUR ZOAS CLOUDED RAGE URIZEN STOOD BY ALBION . .   714 JERUSALEM 74   1
THESE FOUR ARE VERULAM & LONDON & YORK & EDINBURGH . . .   714 JERUSALEM 74   3
AND THE FOUR ZOAS ARE URIZEN & LUVAH & THARMAS & URTHONA   714 JERUSALEM 74   4
I SEE A FEMININE FORM ARISE FROM THE FOUR TERRIBLE ZOAS   715 JERUSALEM 74   52
JERUSALEM C(CHAPTER) (FOUR) . . . .   718D JERUSALEM 78   TITLE
AMONG THE FOUR FORESTS OF ALBION WHICH OVERSPREAD ALL THE   722 JERUSALEM 80   43
  EARTH
THE FOUR ZOAS IN ALL THEIR FADED MAJESTY BURST OUT IN FURY   734 JERUSALEM 88   55
THEN SCATTERD THE EGYPTIAN & HEBREW TO THE FOUR WINDS . .   739 JERUSALEM 92   5
REVOLUTIONS OF ACTION & PASSION THRO THE FOUR ELEMENTS .   742 JERUSALEM 95   10
  ON ALL SIDES
AND EVERY MAN STOOD FOURFOLD EACH FOUR FACES HAD ONE TO   745 JERUSALEM 98   12
  THE WEST
. . . THE FOUR RIVERS OF THE WATER OF LIFE . . . . . .   745 JERUSALEM 98   15
IN THE FOUR SENSES IN THE OUTLINE THE CIRCUMFERENCE & FORM   745 JERUSALEM 98   22
  FOR EVER
THE FOUR LIVING CREATURES . . .   745 JERUSALEM 98   24
IN BEAUTIFUL PARADISES EXPAND THESE ARE THE FOUR RIVERS   745 JERUSALEM 98   25
  OF PARADISE
AND THE FOUR FACES OF HUMANITY FRONTING THE FOUR CARDINAL   745 JERUSALEM 98   26
  POINTS
THE FOUR SENSES ARE THE FOUR FACES OF MAN & .   773D ANNO BERKELEY   MARG
THE FOUR RIVERS OF THE WATER OF LIFE . . . .   773D ANNO BERKELEY   MARG
(FOUR) NUMBERS FOR MR BIRCH WITH BEST RESPECTS TO HIM .   822B LETTER 26   PROSE
FIVE SHILLINGS AT A BROKER'S SHOP IT IS ABOUT FIVE FEET   843D LETTER 43   PROSE
  BY FOUR
HAS ADVISED THAT (FOUR) SHOULD BE DONE . . . .   848B LETTER 45   PROSE
IN THE HIGHLY FINISHED MANNER & (FOUR) IN A LESS FINISHD   848B LETTER 45   PROSE
PRAY MIGHT I NOT SHEW PHILLIPS THE FOUR NUMBERS OF BALLADS   857B LETTER 54   PROSE
MORE & MORE & SHALL SOON GET PROOFS OF THESE FOUR WHICH   876A LETTER 83   PROSE
WHAT I WAS ABOUT I HAVE GOT ON VERY FORWARD WITH (FOUR)   876D LETTER 84   PROSE
  PLATES

FOUR & TWENTY

FOUR & TWENTY ELDERS SEATED ON THRONES TO JUDGE THE DEAD   444A LAST JUDGMNT/L   PROSE
CHRIST GIRDING HIMSELF WITH STRENGTH FOUR & TWENTY ELDERS   SUPP LETTER 56A   *PROSE

FOURFOLD

AND BRASS & SILVER & GOLD FOURFOLD IN DARK PROPHETIC FEAR   307 FOUR ZOAS 5   74
FOURFOLD EACH IN THE OTHER REFLECTED THEY ARE NAMED LIFES   364 FOUR ZOAS 9   283
  IN ETERNITY
THE SEXUAL IS THREEFOLD THE HUMAN IS FOURFOLD . . . . .   483 MILTON 4   5
WHICH IS THE SPIRITUAL FOURFOLD LONDON IN THE LOINS OF   502 MILTON 20   40
  ALBION
LONDON IS BETWEEN HIS KNEES ITS BASEMENTS FOURFOLD . . .   531 MILTON 39   39
THEY WERE ORIGINALLY ONE MAN WHO WAS FOURFOLD HE   578B DESC CAT 5   PROSE
  WAS SELF-DIVIDED
AND KOX KOTOPE & BOWEN ONE IN HIM A FOURFOLD WONDER . . .   626 JERUSALEM 7   48
FOURFOLD THE SONS OF LOS IN THEIR DIVISIONS AND FOURFOLD   632 JERUSALEM 12   45
THE GREAT CITY OF GOLGONOOZA FOURFOLD TOWARD THE NORTH .   632 JERUSALEM 12   46
AND TOWARD THE SOUTH FOURFOLD & FOURFOLD TOWARD THE EAST   632 JERUSALEM 12   47
  & WEST
THE WESTERN GATE FOURFOLD IS CLOSD HAVING FOUR CHERUBIM   633 JERUSALEM 13   6
THE EASTERN GATE FOURFOLD TERRIBLE & DEADLY ITS ORNAMENTS   633 JERUSALEM 13   12
AND EVERY PART OF THE CITY IS FOURFOLD & EVERY INHABITANT   633 JERUSALEM 13   20
  FOURFOLD
AND EVERY HOUSE FOURFOLD BUT THE THIRD GATE IN EVERY ONE   633 JERUSALEM 13   22
HE BUILDED IT IN RAGE & IN FURY IT IS THE SPIRITUAL   684 JERUSALEM 53   18
  FOURFOLD
EUROPE & ASIA & AFRICA & AMERICA IN FURY FOURFOLD . .   712 JERUSALEM 72   31
REPELLING WEEPING ENION BLIND & AGE-BENT INTO THE FOURFOLD   732 JERUSALEM 87   1
OF HEAVEN FOURFOLD AMONG THE VISIONS OF GOD IN ETERNITY   744 JERUSALEM 96   43
AND TOOK HIS BOW FOURFOLD THE VISION FOR BRIGHT BEAMING   744 JERUSALEM 97   7
  URIZEN
AND HE CLOTHED HIMSELF IN BOW & ARROWS IN AWFUL STATE   744 JERUSALEM 97   16
  FOURFOLD
THEY DREW FOURFOLD THE UNREPROVABLE STRING . . . .   744 JERUSALEM 98   2
THE HORNED BOW FOURFOLD . . . .   744 JERUSALEM 98   3
. . . LOUD SOUNDING FLEW THE FLAMING ARROW FOURFOLD . . .   744 JERUSALEM 98   3
FOURFOLD ANNIHILATION & AT THE CLANGOR OF THE ARROWS OF   745 JERUSALEM 98   7
  INTELLECT
AND EVERY MAN STOOD FOURFOLD EACH FOUR FACES HAD ONE TO   745 JERUSALEM 98   12
  THE WEST
. . . THE HORSES FOURFOLD . . . .   745 JERUSALEM 98   13
NOW I A FOURFOLD VISION SEE . . . .   818 HAPPINESS/L   83
AND A FOURFOLD VISION IS GIVEN TO ME . . . .   818 HAPPINESS/L   84
TIS FOURFOLD IN MY SUPREME DELIGHT . . . .   818 HAPPINESS/L   85

FOUR-FOLD,FOUR FOLD

FROM GOLGONOOZA THE SPIRITUAL FOUR-FOLD LONDON ETERNAL .   485 MILTON 6   1
TELL OF THE FOUR-FOLD MAN IN STARRY NUMBERS FITLY ORDERD   502 MILTON 20   16
DIVIDE FOUR-FOLD INTO FOUR CHURCHES WHEN LAZARUS AROSE .   508 MILTON 24   31
IT IS VIEWED ON ALL SIDES ROUND BY A FOUR-FOLD VISION .   525 MILTON 35   23
THE HEADS OF THE GREAT POLYPUS FOUR-FOLD TWELVE ENORMITY   529 MILTON 38   2
CIRCLING ALBION'S CLIFFS IN WHICH THE FOUR-FOLD WORLD   532 MILTON 39   60
  RESIDES
AND THE IMMORTAL FOUR IN WHOM THE TWENTY-FOUR APPEAR   534 MILTON 42   18
  FOUR-FOLD
I SEE THE FOUR-FOLD MAN THE HUMANITY IN DEADLY SLEEP . .   635 JERUSALEM 15   6

757

FOUR-FOLD   (CONTINUED)
      HIS ETERNAL STATION HE IS THE TWENTY-EIGHTH & IS FOUR-FOLD   666 JERUSALEM 39   13
      AGAINST HIS WILL THRO LOS'S GATE TO EDEN FOUR-FOLD LOUD   674 JERUSALEM 44   3
      AND THESE THE FOUR IN WHOM THE TWENTY-FOUR APPEARD   676 JERUSALEM 46   23
         FOUR-FOLD
      THE FOUR-FOLD GOSPEL AND THE REVELATIONS EVERLASTING   . .   677 JERUSALEM 48   11
      AND IN VAIN THE EAGLE & LION OVER THE FOUR-FOLD WILDERNESS   703 JERUSALEM 66   71
      IN ALBION'S TOMB THE WONDROUS CREATION & THE FOUR-FOLD GATE   712 JERUSALEM 72   49
      OVER THE FOUR FOLD MONARCHY FROM EARTH TO THE MUNDANE SHELL   713 JERUSALEM 73   15
      IN MIRACLES & WONDERS IN THE FOUR-FOLD DESART OF ALBION   713 JERUSALEM 73   33
      DRAWING THEIR ULRO VOIDNESS ROUND THE FOUR-FOLD HUMANITY   719 JERUSALEM 78   20
      FROM ALL MY MYRIADS ONCE THE FOUR-FOLD WORLD REJOICD AMONG   721 JERUSALEM 79   58
      FROM ALBION'S TOMB AFAR AND FROM THE FOUR-FOLD WONDERS   721 JERUSALEM 79   62
         OF GOD
      THE HUMAN FOUR-FOLD FORMS MINGLE ALSO IN THUNDERS   733 JERUSALEM 88   7
         OF INTELLECT
FOURSQUARE
      FOURSQUARE SCULPTURD & SWEETLY ENGRAVD TO PLEASE THEIR   285 FOUR ZOAS 2   191
         SHADOWY MOTHER
      THAT FRONT THE FOUR OTHER POINTS WERE TURNED FOUR SQUARE   711 JERUSALEM 72   7
FOURTEEN
      WHEN FOURTEEN SUNS HAD FAINTLY JOURNEYD OER HIS DARK ABODE   195 AMERICA PREL 1   2
      BUT WHEN FOURTEEN SUMMERS & WINTERS HAD REVOLVED OVER   . .   307 FOUR ZOAS 5   79
      WHO HAVING RECEIVED FOURTEEN HUNDRED GUINEAS AND MORE   . .   572C DESC CAT 3   PROSE
      THE COMPASS OF A BOY OF (FOURTEEN) & . . . .   859C LETTER 56   PROSE
      OF MR LINNELL...FOURTEEN SHILLINGS FOR JERUSALEM CHAP (TWO)   SUPP LETTER 67A   *PROSE
FOURTH
      PROLOGUE INTENDED FOR A DRAMATIC PIECE OF KING EDWARD THE   33C EDW FOURTH/PS   TITLE
         FOURTH
      NONE COULD DEDUCE A FOURTH OR FIFTH . . . .   97A NAT RELIGION 1   PROSE
      OF KING HENRY THE FOURTH WALKS BEFORE HIM IN PIRES . . .   141 FRENCH REVOLTN   165
      IN THE FOURTH CHAMBER WERE LIONS OF FLAMING FIRE . . .   155A MARRIAGE HH 15 PROSE
      WHILE IT PRODUCES WORKS AT LESS THAN ONE FOURTH OF THE   207B PRSPECTUS 1793 PROSE
         EXPENSE
      AS THEY GREW AND A FOURTH AGE PASSED . . . .   229 URIZEN 11   24
      LOS WAS THE FOURTH IMMORTAL STARRY ONE & IN THE EARTH   .   264 FOUR ZOAS 1   14
      VALA NIGHT THE [FOURTH] THIRD   . . . .   291C FOUR ZOAS 3   *TITLE
      VALA NIGHT THE FOURTH   . . . .   297C FOUR ZOAS 4   TITLE
      SHOT SPIRING OUT & PETRIFIED [IN] AS THEY GREW AND A FOURTH   303 FOUR ZOAS 4   * 234
      END OF THE FOURTH [BOOK] NIGHT   . . . .   305B FOUR ZOAS 4   *TITLE
      THREEFOLD AS IT WAS IN ETERNITY & THIS THE FOURTH UNIVERSE   329 FOUR ZOAS 7   355
      AND A FOURTH AGE PASSED OVER & A STATE OF DISMAL WOE   . .   482 MILTON 3   19
      GUARD ROUND THEM BUT I THE FOURTH ZOA AM ALSO SET   . .   508 MILTON 24   8
      HE IS THE FOURTH ZOA THAT STOOD (AROUND) THE THRONE DIVINE   510 MILTON 24   76
      BUT THE FOURTH STATE IS DREADFUL IT IS NAMED OR-ULRO   . .   524 MILTON 34   13
      THE THIRD IN THE LOINS & SEMINAL VESSELS & THE FOURTH   . .   524 MILTON 34   15
      AND THE FORM OF THE FOURTH WAS LIKE THE SON OF GOD   . .   578B DESC CAT 5   PROSE
      IN THE FOURTH REGION OF HUMANITY URTHONA NAMD . . . . .   666 JERUSALEM 39   7
      THREE THOU HAST SLAIN I AM THE FOURTH THOU CANST   670 JERUSALEM 42   24
         NOT DESTROY ME
FOWL   SEE SEA-FOWL,SEA FOWL
      AND OTHERS CREATE THE WOOLY LAMB & THE DOWNY FOWL   . .   692 JERUSALEM 59   48
      TO CREATE THE WOOLY LAMB & DOWNY FOWL & SCALY SERPENT   . .   713 JERUSALEM 73   18
FOWLS   SEE SEA-FOWLS
FOX
      THE FOX CONDEMNS THE TRAP NOT HIMSELF   . . . .   151C MARRIAGE HH 8   PROSE
      THE RAT THE MOUSE THE FOX THE RABBET WATCH THE ROOTS   .   151D MARRIAGE HH 8   PROSE
      THE FOX PROVIDES FOR HIMSELF BUT GOD PROVIDES FOR THE LION   152A MARRIAGE HH 9   PROSE
      IF THE LION WAS ADVISED BY THE FOX HE WOULD BE CUNNING   .   152D MARRIAGE HH 10   PROSE
      THE BADGER & FOX THEY WORSHIP BEFORE HIS FEET IN TREMBLING   515 MILTON 28   43
         FEAR
      THE FOX THE OWL THE BEETLE & THE BAT . . . .   545 ON S(TOTHRD)/N   3
      THE FOX THE OWL THE SPIDER AND THE MOLE   . . . . .   575 DESC CAT 3   1
      THE MASTER OF THE HOUSE THE FOX INN WHO IS [MY] THE . . .   827B LETTER 28   PROSE
      AT THE FOX & WHO EVIDENCES THAT TO HIS KNOWLEDGE NO WORD   827C LETTER 28   PROSE
FRAGMENT
      BUT ALBION FELL DOWN A ROCKY FRAGMENT FROM ETERNITY HURLD   685 JERUSALEM 54   6
FRAGMENTS
      [A RUIND PILLAR IN GLITTRING FRAGMENTS SILENT HE TURND   196 AMERICA PREL 2   20
         AWAY]
      LEAVING RUINOUS FRAGMENTS OF LIFE   . . . .   225 URIZEN 5   9
      CRACKD ACROSS INTO NUMBERLESS FRAGMENTS   . . . .   257 BOOK OF LOS 4   18
      THE BLACK MARBLE ON HIGH INTO FRAGMENTS   . . . .   257 BOOK OF LOS 4   22
      ROCK THE INNUMERABLE FRAGMENTS AWAY   . . . .   257 BOOK OF LOS 4   24
      TO THE FRAGMENTS OF SOLID UP ROSE . . . .   259 BOOK OF LOS 5   7
FRAGRANT
      WHATEVER GROWS FROM ITS PURE BUD OR BREATHES A FRAGRANT   308 FOUR ZOAS 5   124
         SOUL
      WHILE THE FAR BEAMING PEACOCK WAITED ON THE FRAGRANT WIND   340 FOUR ZOAS 7B   . 283
FRAIL
      UNCLOTHES THE EARTH AND FREEZES UP FRAIL LIFE . . . . .   3 TO WINTER/PS   12
      OF LUSTY MAY AH LIFE AS FRAIL AS FLOWER . . . .   5 FAIR ELENOR/PS   42
      BUT DOWN HE CAME ALAS HOW FRAIL   . . . .   17 BLIND-MANS/PS   51
      FRAIL BARK CAN SEE NO SHORE OR BOUND FOR VAST . . . .   26 EDW THIRD/PS 3   237
      A POOR FRAIL MAN GOD WOT I KNOW NONE FRAILER . . . . .   52 HEAR THEN/IM   3
      FOR HIS FRAIL EYES WERE FADED & HIS EARS HEAVY & DULL   .   326 FOUR ZOAS 7   250
      MY MASCULINE SPIRIT SCORNING THE FRAIL BODY ISSUD FORTH   327 FOUR ZOAS 7   * 290
FRAILER
      A POOR FRAIL MAN GOD WOT I KNOW NONE FRAILER . . . . .   52 HEAR THEN/IM   3
FRAMD
      ON ALL SIDES [THEY] HE FRAMD LIKE A WOMB . . . .   225 URIZEN 5   * 29
      AN IMMENSE ORB OF FIRE HE FRAMD   . . . .   260 BOOK OF LOS 5   34

FRAMD   (CONTINUED)
    AND HARROW FORMD & FRAMD THE HARNESS OF SILVER & IVORY . . 281 FOUR ZOAS 2   28
    OUT OF THE HALLS OF JUSTICE TILL THESE DENS THY WISDOM   292 FOUR ZOAS 3   38
       FRAMD
    HE BURND BEFORE ME LUVAH FRAMD THE KNIFE & LUVAH GAVE   . . 722 JERUSALEM 80   22
FRAME
    OR NATURE'S HAND HAS CROOKED HER FRAME . . . .   56 HAIL MATRIM/IM   14
    [COULD] [DARE] FRAME THY FEARFUL SYMMETRY   . . . . . .   172 THE TYGER/N 1   4
    DARE [FORM] FRAME THY FEARFUL SYMMETRY   . . . .   173 THE TYGER/N 1   25
    DARE FRAME THY FEARFUL SYMMETRY   . . . .   173 THE TYGER/N 2   4
    DARE FRAME THY FEARFUL SYMMETRY   . . . .   173 THE TYGER/N 2   20
    [HIS HARP ALOFT SOUNDING THEN DASHD ITS SHINING FRAME   196 AMERICA PREL 2   19
       AGAINST]
    COULD FRAME THY FEARFUL SYMMETRY   . . . .   214 THE TYGER/SE   4
    DARE FRAME THY FEARFUL SYMMETRY   . . . .   214 THE TYGER/SE   24
    SPREAD THRO HER GOLDEN FRAME SHE ROSE UP EER THE DAWN OF   291 FOUR ZOAS 2   420
       DAY
    ("MIND") THE DEVIL IS THE MIND OF THE NATURAL FRAME   . . 403B ANNO BACON   MARG
    INTO THE FRAME THEN KNOCK IT OUT UPON THE PLANK & SOULS   657 JERUSALEM 31   11
       ARE BAKD
FRAMED
    AND FRAMED THE MUNDANE SHELL CAVERNOUS IN LENGTH BREDTH   740 JERUSALEM 92   27
       & HIGHTH
FRAMES
    OF THE THINGS OF MEMORY IT THENCE FRAMES LAWS & MORALITIES   714 JERUSALEM 74   12
    NEVER WERE PROPERLY STRAINED UPON THEIR STRAINING FRAMES   839D LETTER 38   PROSE
FRANCE
    SCENE THE COAST OF FRANCE KING EDWARD AND NOBLES BEFORE   17D EDW THIRD/PS 1   PROSE
       IT THE ARMY
    THE KING CAUGHT HERE IN FRANCE OF RUNNING AWAY   . . . .   22 EDW THIRD/PS 3   57
    DOWN GOES OUR RIGHT TO FRANCE . . . .   23 EDW THIRD/PS 3   72
    THY HEART IS RICHER THAN THE VALES OF FRANCE   . . . . .   25 EDW THIRD/PS 3   173
    THEN IT GROWS MOST IN FRANCE THE VINES HERE   . . . . .   28 EDW THIRD/PS 4   5
    THAT BROUGHT OVER OUR KING TO FRANCE TO FIGHT FOR HIS RIGHT 28D EDW THIRD/PS 4   PROSE
    FOR ALL OUR BLOOD AND BONES ARE IN FRANCE AND A   . . . .   29C EDW THIRD/PS 4   PROSE
    O DAGWORTH FRANCE IS SICK THE VERY SKY   . . . . . .   30 EDW THIRD/PS 5   21
    ROLLING DARK CLOUDS OER FRANCE MUFFLING THE SUN   . . .   31 EDW THIRD/PS 6   3
    HA HA HA SAID INFLAMMABLE GASS HE WAS THE GLORY OF FRANCE   46A ISLAND MOON 1   PROSE
    . . . THE CLOUD AND VISION DESCENDS OVER CHEARFUL FRANCE   134 FRENCH REVOLTN   1
    . . . THE OLD MOUNTAINS OF FRANCE LIKE AGED MEN FADING AWAY 134 FRENCH REVOLTN   9
    . . . THE WOODS OF FRANCE EMBOSOM THE SOUND   . . . . .   134 FRENCH REVOLTN   11
    AGAIN THE LOUD VOICE OF FRANCE CRIES TO THE MORNING . . .   134 FRENCH REVOLTN   15
    . . . FRANCE SHAKES AND THE HEAVENS OF FRANCE   . . . . . 134 FRENCH REVOLTN   16
    A THOUSAND HIS SOLDIERS OLD VETERANS OF FRANCE . . .   135 FRENCH REVOLTN   20
    . . . SHAKING THE HEAVENS OF FRANCE   . . . .   137 FRENCH REVOLTN   70
    . . . STRETCH OUT HIS CROOKD SICKLE OER FERTILE FRANCE .   138 FRENCH REVOLTN   91
    FOR THE NOBLES OF FRANCE . . . .   139 FRENCH REVOLTN   113
    . . . AND FIERCE SORROWS BECAUSE OF THE NOBLES OF FRANCE   139 FRENCH REVOLTN   119
    HEARKEN MONARCH OF FRANCE TO THE TERRORS OF HEAVEN . . .   140 FRENCH REVOLTN   128
    . . . O PRINCES AND GENERALS OF FRANCE   . . . .   141 FRENCH REVOLTN   163
    . . . RISE MONARCH OF FRANCE COMMAND ME AND I WILL LEAD   142 FRENCH REVOLTN   172
    MAY YET BURN IN FRANCE . . .   .   142 FRENCH REVOLTN   174
    OR BAILLY THE STRONG FOOT OF FRANCE . . . .   142 FRENCH REVOLTN   188
    HEAR O HEAVENS OF FRANCE . . . .   143 FRENCH REVOLTN   206
    THE SOULS OF MILD FRANCE . . . .   143 FRENCH REVOLTN   210
    THEN THE VALLEYS OF FRANCE SHALL CRY TO THE SOLDIER . . .   144 FRENCH REVOLTN   220
    LIKE THE MOUNTAINS OF FRANCE . . . .   145 FRENCH REVOLTN   242
    ROUND THE SHORE OF FRANCE . . . .   147 FRENCH REVOLTN   280
    . . . SHAKEN THE FORESTS OF FRANCE SICK THE KINGS OF THE   147 FRENCH REVOLTN   300
       NATIONS
    AND MUTTER ACROSS THE OCEAN FRANCE REND DOWN THY DUNGEON   159A SONG LIBERTY   PROSE
    SAID THE BEAUTIFUL QUEEN OF FRANCE   . . . .   185 LET BROTHELS/N   4
    THE QUEEN OF FRANCE JUST TOUCHD THIS GLOBE   . . . . .   185 LET BROTHELS/N *   20
    AND THEN THEIR END SHOULD COME WHEN FRANCE RECIEVD THE   203 AMERICA 16   15
       DEMON'S LIGHT
    STIFF SHUDDERINGS SHOOK THE HEAVNLY THRONES FRANCE SPAIN   203 AMERICA 16   16
       & ITALY
    AND IN THE VINEYARDS OF RED FRANCE APPEARD THE LIGHT OF   245 EUROPE 15   2
       HIS FURY
    AGAINST FRANCE IS IT NOT TO STATE RELIGION BLUSH FOR SHAME 385C ANNO WATSON   MARG
    WHEN FRANCE GOT FREE EUROPE TWIXT FOOLS & KNAVES   . . . . 451 ANNO REYNOLDS   1
    WERE SAVAGE FIRST TO FRANCE & AFTER SLAVES   . . . . .   451 ANNO REYNOLDS   2
    GERMANY WEPT TOWARDS FRANCE & ITALY ENGLAND WEPT   519 MILTON 31   13
       & TREMBLED
    FRANCE SHALL SUBDUE THE WORLD IN ARMS   . . . .   557 ART HAS LOST/N   2
    AND FRANCE SHALL FALL DOWN & ADORE   . . . .   557 ART HAS LOST/N   6
    FRANCE SHALL THE ARTS OF PEACE RESTORE   . . . .   557 ART HAS LOST/N   11
    FROM BRIGHT JAPAN & CHINA TO HESPERIA FRANCE & ENGLAND . . 648 JERUSALEM 24   47
    LO SHILOH DWELLS OVER FRANCE AS JERUSALEM DWELLS OVER   680 JERUSALEM 49   48
       ALBION
    AND FOR SHILOH THE EMANATION OF FRANCE & FOR LOVELY VALA   686 JERUSALEM 55   29
    FRANCE & SPAIN & ITALY & DENMARK & HOLLAND & GERMANY   . . 690 JERUSALEM 58   41
    FOR LUVAH IS FRANCE THE VICTIM OF THE SPECTRES OF ALBION   702 JERUSALEM 66   15
    OVER FRANCE & GERMANY UPON THE RHINE & DANUBE . . . . .   706 JERUSALEM 68   46
    FRANCE SPAIN ITALY GERMANY POLAND RUSSIA SWEDEN TURKEY . . 712 JERUSALEM 72   38
    ITALY SAW ME IN SUBLIME ASTONISHMENT FRANCE WAS WHOLLY MINE 720 JERUSALEM 79   39
    WE MUST POSSESS ORIGINALS AS WELL AS FRANCE OR BE NOTHING   798A LETTER 10   PROSE
    ACROSS THE ATLANTIC TO FRANCE . . . .   799 TO FLAXMAN/L   10
    BUT I HOPE THAT FRANCE & ENGLAND WILL HENCEFORTH BE . . . 811A LETTER 21   PROSE
FRANCE'S
    & ROBINSONS & THE QUEEN OF FRANCE'S PUSS COLOUR   . . . .   53A ISLAND MOON 8   PROSE

```
                                                                 PAGE      TITLE        LINE
FRANCIS
     LIKE WHAT SR FRANCIS BACON [SHOULD DOWNRIGHT ASSERT] SAYS   599D PUB ADDRESS/N    PROSE
     FOR SOME TIME AFTER SR FRANCIS BACON WOULD SAY IT IS WANT   871A LETTER 72        PROSE
        OF
     DISCIPLINE IN MOUNTAINOUS PLACES SR FRANCIS BACON IS A LIAR 871A LETTER 72        PROSE
FRANKLIN
     WASHINGTON FRANKLIN PAINE & WARREN GATES HANCOCK & GREEN     197 AMERICA 3           4
     WASHINGTON FRANKLIN PAINE & WARREN ALLEN GATES & LEE    .    201 AMERICA 14          2
     WASHINGTON HANCOCK PAINE & WARREN GATES FRANKLIN & GREEN     203 AMERICA CANC A      4
     THE DYER THE FRANKLIN THE PHYSICIAN THE PLOWMAN     .    .  566D DESC CAT 3        PROSE
     THE DOCTOR OF PHYSIC IS IN THIS GROUPE AND THE FRANKLIN     570D DESC CAT 3        PROSE
     THE FRANKLIN IS ONE WHO KEEPS OPEN TABLE     .    .    .  . 571A DESC CAT 3        PROSE
     THE FRANKLIN IS VOLUPTUOUSNESS ITSELF MOST NOBLY POURTRAYED 571A DESC CAT 3        PROSE
     THE DYER THE FRANKLIN THE PHYSICIAN THE PLOWMAN    .    .  . 588C CHAUCER/N        PROSE
     THE DYER THE FRANKLIN THE PHYSICIAN THE PLOWMAN    .    .  . 589D CHAUCER 2        PROSE
FRANTIC
     WITH FRANTIC PAIN    .    .    .    .    .    .    .    .      9 MAD SONG/PS          24
FRAUD
     POLICY BROUGHT FORTH GUILE & FRAUD    .    .    .    .    .   42D THEN SHE BORE     PROSE
     WHO CRIES ALL ART IS A FRAUD & GENIUS A TRICK    .    .    . 555 BLAKES APL/N 1      20
     DEADLY HATE BETWEEN LEAH & RACHEL DAUGHTERS OF DECEIT &     707 JERUSALEM 69         11
        FRAUD
FRAUGHT
     WITH SORROW FRAUGHT    .    .    .    .    .    .    .    .     9 MAD SONG/PS         11
     FRAUGHT WITH THE SWORDS OF LIGHTNING BUT I BRAVD            105 TIRIEL 4       *    56
        THE VENGEANCE TOO
     DARK CAVALRY LIKE CLOUDS FRAUGHT WITH THUNDER    .    .    .  . 147 FRENCH REVOLTN  291
FRAZER
     COSWAY FRAZER & BALDWIN OF EGYPT'S LAKE    .    .    .    .  545 COSWAY FRAZR/N       1
FREDERICKS
     THE LEWISS & FREDERICKS WHO ALONE ARE ITS CAUSES &    .    . 683A JERUSALEM 52     *PROSE
FREE
     THEIR MINDS ARE FETTERD THEN HOW CAN THEY BE FREE     .    .  18 EDW THIRD/PS 1      14
     TEACH MAN TO THINK HES A FREE AGENT    .    .    .    .    .  25 EDW THIRD/PS 3     195
     THE SON OF HIS OLD AGE SHALL SET IT FREE THE    .    .    .  39C SAMSON/PS         PROSE
     BREEDS SATIRE FOUL CONTAGION FROM WHICH NONE ARE FREE    .   41C THEN SHE BORE     PROSE
     THING THAT ACTS OF PARLIAMENT SHOULD BE IN A FREE STATE     46A ISLAND MOON 1      PROSE
        IT HAD
     ("WHO IS FREE MAKES FREE ") RATHER UNEASY    .    .    .    . 69B ANNO LAVATER       MARG
     AND HE OPEND THE COFFINS & SET THEM ALL FREE    .    .    .  117 CHIMNEY SWP/SI      14
     WHEN I FROM BLACK AND HE FROM WHITE CLOUD FREE    .    .    . 125 LIT BLK BOY/SI     23
     AND CAN NOBLES BE BOUND WHEN THE PEOPLE ARE FREE    .    .  . 142 FRENCH REVOLTN    186
     NOR HIS ACCEPTED BRETHREN WHOM TYRANT HE CALLS FREE    .    160A SONG LIBERTY       PROSE
     I WAS BORN A SLAVE BUT I [LONG] GO TO BE FREE    .    .    . 166 WHY CARE FOR/N *     9
     [HAST MY] THAT FREE LOVE WITH BONDAGE BOUND    .    .    .  . 169 EARTHS ANSWR/N     25
     LOVE FREE LOVE CANNOT BE BOUND    .    .    .    .    .    .  169 MIRTLE SHADE/N       9
     [LOVE FREE LOVE CANNOT BE BOUND]    .    .    .    .    .    176 TO MY MIRTLE/N        3
     I CRY LOVE LOVE LOVE HAPPY HAPPY LOVE FREE AS               194 V DAU ALBION 7      16
        THE MOUNTAIN WIND
     THE HAIRY SHOULDERS REND THE LINKS FREE ARE THE WRISTS      196 AMERICA PREL 2       2
        OF FIRE
     THAT FREE LOVE WITH BONDAGE BOUND    .    .    .    .    .  . 211 EARTHS ANSR/SE     25
     FREE FROM WINTER'S COLD    .    .    .    .    .    .    .  . 219 LIT GRL LST/SE      6
     TO RISE FROM GENERATION FREE    .    .    .    .    .    .  . 220 TO TIRZAH/SE        3
     THE DEATH OF JESUS SET ME FREE    .    .    .    .    .    .  220 TO TIRZAH/SE       15
     FORM THE [FREE] REBELLIOUS SPIRITS OF HEAVEN    .    .    .  272 FOUR ZOAS 1        311
     THE HAIRY SHOULDERS REND THE LINKS FREE ARE THE WRISTS      336 FOUR ZOAS 7B       140
        OF FIRE
     BOW DOWN BEFORE HER YOU HER CHILDREN & SET JERUSALEM FREE   351 FOUR ZOAS 8        409
     [AND NEVER WILL FROM SIN BE FREE]    .    .    .    .    .  . 415 MY SPECTRE/N        7
     ALONE CAN FREE THE [WOLD] WORLD FROM FEAR    .    .    .    419 I SAW A MONK/N *     43
     AND MARY AROSE AMONG FRIENDS TO BE FREE    .    .    .    .  428 MARY                15
     I'LL REFUSE HIM MY HAND & FROM ENVY BE FREE    .    .    .  . 428 MARY               32
     ALONE CAN FREE THE WORLD FROM FEAR    .    .    .    .    .  430 GREY MONK           28
     SHOULD HAVE BEEN FREE FROM HIS IMPERTINENCE & INTRUSION    438D BLAKES MEMORAN     PROSE
     WHEN FRANCE GOT FREE EUROPE TWIXT FOOLS & KNAVES    .    .  . 451 ANNO REYNOLDS       1
     MERCY ALONE OF FREE GIFT AND ELECTION THAT WE LIVE    .    . 494 MILTON 13          33
     FORWARDS FROM ULRO FROM THE VALE OF FELPHAM AND SET FREE    503 MILTON 20          60
     GREAT GOLGONOOZA FREE FROM THE FOUR IRON PILLARS OF SATAN'S 517 MILTON 29          48
        THRONE
     AND EQUALLY FREE WITH THE LORD AND THE PEASANT THEY ARE    569D DESC CAT 3        PROSE
     ALL THAT THEY HAVE IS MINE FROM MY FREE GENROUS GIFT    .   671 JERUSALEM 42        52
     DRAWING THE FREE LOVES OF JERUSALEM INTO INFERNAL BONDAGE   707 JERUSALEM 69         9
     THE DUNGEONS BURST & THE PRISONERS SET FREE    .    .    .  . 718 STOOD AMONG/J      35
     AND KNEES IS ENTIRELY REDUCED SHE IS VERY NEAR AS FREE    . 851C LETTER 50        PROSE
     WIFE'S FEET ARE FREE FROM FETTERS O LOVELY FELPHAM PARENT  852A LETTER 50        PROSE
     THO I SEEM WELL BEING ENTIRELY FREE FROM BOTH PAIN &    .  . 875C LETTER 81        PROSE
FREE BORN
     SIT ON A BANK AND DRAW THE PLEASURES OF THIS FREE BORN JOY  194 V DAU ALBION 7       2
FREED
     THE SUN IS FREED FROM FEARS    .    .    .    .    .    .    . 421 MORNING/N         10
FREEDOM
     [AND THE LION INCREASE FREEDOM & PEACE]    .    .    .    .  171 THE LILLY/N          4
     BECAUSE WE WERE COMBINED IN FREEDOM & HOLY BROTHERHOOD    . 521 MILTON 32          15
     ABOUT FREEDOM & JENNY SUCK AWA    .    .    .    .    .    .  550 WHEN LOOK AT/N      4
     WHEEL WITHIN WHEEL IN FREEDOM REVOLVE IN HARMONY & PEACE    636 JERUSALEM 15        20
     & I HAVE COMPELLD WHAT SHOULD HAVE BEEN OF FREEDOM    .    825D LETTER 27        PROSE
     LAWS TO GET INTO FREEDOM FROM ALL LAW OF THE MEMBERS INTO  879A LETTER 88        PROSE
FREEST
     THEM IF THEY ARE NOT WISE THE FREEST GOVERNMENT IS    .    600A PUB ADDRESS/N      PROSE
FREEZE
     THAT DOES [CLOSE] FREEZE MY BONES AROUND    .    .    .    . 169 EARTHS ANSWR/N     .22
```

```
                                                          PAGE    TITLE          LINE
FREEZE    (CONTINUED)
     THAT DOES FREEZE MY BONES AROUND  . . . . . . . .   . 211 EARTHS ANSR/SE      22
     FELT HER IMMORTAL LIMBS FREEZE STIFFNING PALE INFLEXIBLE  305 FOUR ZOAS 5   *   6
     THE EYES BEHELD THE ABYSS LEST BONES OF SOLIDNESS FREEZE  482 MILTON 3          15
        OVER ALL
     FREEZE ROUND HIM TO BARS OF STEEL & TO IRON ROCKS BENEATH 626 JERUSALEM 7       72
     TO FREEZE LOVE & INNOCENCE INTO THE GOLD & SILVER OF THE  699 JERUSALEM 64      23
        MERCHANT
     TO FREEZE OVER HIS NOSTRILS WHILE THEY FEED HIS TONGUE    702 JERUSALEM 66      32
        FROM CUPS
FREEZES
     UNCLOTHES THE EARTH AND FREEZES UP FRAIL LIFE . . . .   . 3 TO WINTER/PS       12
     ("NO ATTRACTION UNLESS IT WARMS") OR FREEZES ("THE      411C ANNO BOYD       MARG
        HEART")
     TO HIDE THEM FROM THE WRATH OF ALBION'S LAW THAT FREEZES  679 JERUSALEM 48      60
        SORE
FREEZING
     FREEZING TO SOLID ALL BENEATH HIS GREY OBLIVIOUS FORM  . . 302 FOUR ZOAS 4     172
     SWEEPS OVER THEE FREEZING TO SOLID STILL THOU SITST CLOSD  322 FOUR ZOAS 7      75
        UP
     FREEZING THY FEET TO THE HARD ROCK STILL THY PEN OBDURATE  322 FOUR ZOAS 7      85
     AND TO ALLAY HIS [XXX] FREEZING AGE . . . . . . . .     . 426 MENTAL TRAVLER * 57
     HIS BURNING THIRST & FREEZING HUNGER COME INTO MY HAND  . . 481 MILTON 2         5
     AND HE ALSO DARKEND HIS BROWS FREEZING DARK ROCKS BETWEEN  500 MILTON 19         1
     FREEZING HER VEIL THE MUNDANE SHELL . . . . . . . .     . 770 OF GATES/GP       17
FRENCH
     MY LORDS THE FRENCH HAVE FITTED OUT MANY . . . . . .    .  20 EDW THIRD/PS 2    65
     FRENCH FROM THE FORD DID HE FEAR THEN . . . . . . .     .  21 EDW THIRD/PS 3    12
     ITS A NEW SONG ABOUT THE FRENCH AND ENGLISH . . . .    .  29B EDW THIRD/PS 4  PROSE
     THE FRENCH REVOLUTION A POEM IN SEVEN BOOKS BOOK THE FIRST 134A FRENCH REVOLTN TITLE
     & HIS FRENCH JOURNEYMEN WHOSE NAMES I FORGET . . . .   . 594A PUB ADDRESS/N   PROSE
     AWKWARD FRENCH PALACE ARE [ALL] THROWN TOGETHER AROUND  . 599C PUB ADDRESS/N  *PROSE
     . . . THEN THE FRENCH REVOLUTION COMMENCD IN THICK CLOUDS  799 TO FLAXMAN/L     10
     FRENCH PRINTS & PLEASE EVERY ONE IN SHORT I HAVE GOT   . 821A LETTER 25       PROSE
     THE BEST OF WHICH I HAVE I SEND ALSO THE FRENCH MONUMENTS 844C LETTER 43       PROSE
     AS THE FRENCH NOW ADORE BUONAPARTE AND THE ENGLISH OUR  845B LETTER 44        PROSE
        POOR GEORGE
     ANY THING ELSE SUCH IS JOB BUT SINCE THE FRENCH REVOLUTION 878B LETTER 88      PROSE
FREQUENT
     . . . FREQUENT SPECTRES OF RELIGIOUS MEN WEEPING . . . . 146 FRENCH REVOLTN     274
FREQUENTLY
     & IN OTHER PLACES THIS ANGEL IS FREQUENTLY CALLD BY THE 610A V LAST JUDG/N    PROSE
FRESCO
     THIS IS FALSE FRESCO PAINTING IS THE MOST MINUTE . . . . 466D ANNO REYNOLDS    MARG
     FRESCO PAINTING IS LIKE MINIATURE PAINTING . . . . .    . 466D ANNO REYNOLDS    MARG
     EXHIBITION OF PAINTINGS IN FRESCO POETICAL AND HISTORICAL 560A EXHIBITION ADV  TITLE
        INVENTIONS
     THE CANTERBURY PILGRIMS FROM CHAUCER A CABINET PICTURE   560B EXHIBITION ADV  PROSE
        IN FRESCO
     UNCHANGEABLE AND PERMANENT IN FRESCO AND DRAWINGS  . . . 560C EXHIBITION ADV  PROSE
     THE INVENTION OF A PORTABLE FRESCO . . . . . . . .      . 560D EXHIBITION ADV  TITLE
     ARE IN FRESCO AND NOT IN OIL . . . . . . . . .          . 561A EXHIBITION ADV  PROSE
     FRESCO PAINTING IS PROPERLY MINIATURE OR ENAMEL PAINTING 561A EXHIBITION ADV  PROSE
     EVERY THING IN FRESCO IS AS HIGH FINISHED AS MINIATURE  561A EXHIBITION ADV  PROSE
     FRESCO PAINTING AS IT IS NOW PRACTISED IS . . . . .     . 561A EXHIBITION ADV  PROSE
     BEING ALL IN WATER-COLOURS THAT IS IN FRESCO . . . .   . 561B EXHIBITION ADV  PROSE
     THE GRAND STYLE OF ART RESTORED IN FRESCO OR . . . .   . 562B DESC CAT ADV    PROSE
     THE ANCIENT METHOD OF FRESCO PAINTING RESTORED AND DRAWINGS 563A DESC CAT     TITLE
     IN HIGH FINISHED FRESCO WHERE THE COLOURS WOULD BE AS PURE 566A DESC CAT 2     PROSE
     ARE IN FRESCO AND NOT IN OIL OIL WAS NOT USED . . . .  . 566B DESC CAT 2      PROSE
     BUT THE ART OF FRESCO PAINTING BEING LOST . . . . .     . 566C DESC CAT 2      PROSE
     EXECUTION OF THIS PICTURE IS ALSO IN WATER COLOURS      577B DESC CAT 4       PROSE
        OR FRESCO
     THE FIRST MR B(BLAKE) EVER DID IN FRESCO FORTUNATELY OR 581B DESC CAT 6       PROSE
     THE ABOVE FOUR DRAWINGS THE ARTIST WISHES WERE IN FRESCO 584B DESC CAT 14     PROSE
     WITHOUT FIRM AND DETERMINATE OUTLINE FRESCO PAINTING IS 585A DESC CAT 15      PROSE
     BLAKE'S CHAUCER THE CANTERBURY PILGRIMS THE FRESCO PICTURE 586C CHAUCER 1     TITLE
     FROM HIS FRESCO PAINTING OF CHAUCER'S CANTERBURY PILGRIMS 587D CHAUCER/N      TITLE
     FROM HIS FRESCO PAINTING OF SIR JEFFREY CHAUCER AND . . . 589C CHAUCER 2      TITLE
     ARE OIL COLOUR COPIES FROM FRESCO ORIGINALS . . . . .   598A PUB ADDRESS/N   PROSE
     NOTE I MEAN FRESCO EASEL OR CABINET PICTURES . . . .  . 598A PUB ADDRESS/N   PROSE
FRESCOES
     ALL FRESCOES ARE AS HIGH FINISHED AS MINIATURES OR ENAMELS 566B DESC CAT 2     PROSE
FRESCOS
     IF THE FRESCOS OF APELLES OF PROTOGENES OF RAPHAEL  . . . 560D EXHIBITION ADV  PROSE
     WITH FRESCOS WHICH WOULD BE REMOVABLE AT PLEASURE  . . . 560D EXHIBITION ADV  PROSE
     AS THEY ARE IN ALL THE OLD PICTURES AND IN MR B'S(BLAKE'S) 566C DESC CAT 2     PROSE
        FRESCOS
     SUCH AS IS FOUND IN THE FRESCOS OF RAFAEL AND MICHAEL   580D DESC CAT 5       PROSE
        ANGELO
     IS NO DIFFERENCE BETWEEN RAFAEL'S CARTOONS AND HIS FRESCOS 584D DESC CAT 15    PROSE
     OR PICTURES EXCEPT THAT THE FRESCOS OR PICTURES ARE  . . 584D DESC CAT 15     PROSE
FRESH
     AND TUNE THY JOLLY VOICE TO MY FRESH PIPE . . . . . .   . 2 TO AUTUMN/PS        4
     FRESH FROM THE DEWY HILL THE MERRY YEAR . . . . . . .    . 9 FRESH FROM/PS      1
     CLAD AS A TRAVELLER FRESH RISEN ON HIS JOURNEY . . . . . 40B SAMSON/PS        PROSE
     THE [DESIRES] DAYS OF YOUTH RISE FRESH IN MY MIND  . . . 171 NURSES SONG/N     3
     ARE BOTH ALIKE A NIGHT OF SIGHS A MORNING OF FRESH TEARS 191 V DAU ALBION 2    38
     AND PARCHED LIPS DROP WITH FRESH GORE NOW ROLL THOU IN  199 AMERICA 9         24
        THE CLOUDS
     THE DAYS OF MY YOUTH RISE FRESH IN MY MIND . . . . .    . 212 NURSES SONG/SE    3
     TILL FIRED WITH ARDOUR FRESH RECRUITED IN ITS HUMBLE    287 FOUR ZOAS 2   *  279
        [SPRING] SEASON
```

FRESH   (CONTINUED)
  SIGHING & WIPING A FRESH TEAR THEN TURNING ROUND HE THREW   315 FOUR ZOAS 6   * 152
  THE SUN ARISES FROM HIS DEWY BED & THE FRESH AIRS   . . . 379 FOUR ZOAS 9   846
  AND THE FRESH EARTH BEAMS FORTH . . .   .   379 FOUR ZOAS 9   848
FRESHER
  SINGING THE SUN HAS LEFT HIS BLACKNESS & HAS FOUND   198 AMERICA 6   13
    A FRESHER MORNING
  THE SUN HAS LEFT HIS BLACKNESS & HAS FOUND A FRESHER   379 FOUR ZOAS 9   825
    MORNING
FRESHLY
  WAVE FRESHLY CLEAR WATERS FLOWING AROUND THE TENDER GRASS   368 FOUR ZOAS 9   436
FRESHNING
  RAIN FRESHNING DEW UPON HIS BRANCHES AND   . . . . . .   26 EDW THIRD/PS 3   215
FRESNOY
  ("FRESNOY PRINCIPAL FIGURE IN THE MIDST ") WHAT A DEVIL   478B ANNO REYNOLDS   MARG
    OF A RULE
FRIAR
  NEXT FOLLOW THE FRIAR AND MONK THEN THE TAPISER   . . . .   566D DESC CAT 3   PROSE
  THE MONK FOLLOWS THESE WITH THE FRIAR   568C DESC CAT 3   PROSE
  THE FRIAR IS A CHARACTER ALSO OF A MIXED KIND   . . . . .   568D DESC CAT 3   PROSE
  DISTINGUISH HIM FROM THE FRIAR OR THE PARDONER   . . . .   570C DESC CAT 3   PROSE
  NEXT FOLLOW THE FRIAR & MONK THEN THE TAPISER   . . . .   588B CHAUCER/N   PROSE
  NEXT FOLLOW THE FRIAR AND MONK THEN THE TAPSTER   . . . .   589D CHAUCER 2   PROSE
  GRAY THE POET FRIAR BACON   . . . .   SUPP PENC DRAW 2.37 *TITLE
FRIAR'S
  "HE" IS SEEN FOLLOWING THE FRIAR'S LANTERN TOWARDS THE   618C ILLUS MILTON   PROSE
    CONVENT
FRIBBLE'S
  FOR THEIRS WERE FRIBBLE'S TOILETTES   . . . .   593B PUB ADDRESS/N   PROSE
FRIBBLES
  SAVAGES ARE [FRIBBLES & FOPS] FOPS & FRIBBLES   . . . .   468C ANNO REYNOLDS   * MARG
FRIEND
  THAN SUCH A SOLDIER AS YOU HAVE BEEN AND SUCH A FRIEND   24 EDW THIRD/PS 3   107
  YET NOT FORLORN IF CONSCIENCE IS HIS FRIEND   . . . . .   28 EDW THIRD/PS 3   293
  IT SPOKE I COME MY FRIEND TO TAKE MY LAST FAREWELL   . .   43D WOE CRIED MUSE   PROSE
  ("BE NOT THE FOURTH FRIEND OF HIM WHO LOST ") AN   74A ANNO LAVATER   MARG
    EXCELLENT RULE
  IT IS THE GOD IN ALL THAT IS OUR COMPANION & FRIEND   . .   87A ANNO LAVATER   MARG
  HE WAS FRIEND TO THE FAVOURITE . . . .   136 FRENCH REVOLTN   47
  THE SAME THAT MADE OUR FRIEND DIOGENES THE GRECIAN   . .   154A MARRIAGE HH 12 *PROSE
  FRIEND THE ANGEL CLIMBD UP FROM HIS STATION INTO THE MILL   156C MARRIAGE HH 17   PROSE
  IS MY PARTICULAR FRIEND WE OFTEN . . . .   158D MARRIAGE HH 22   PROSE
  I WAS ANGRY WITH MY FRIEND   . . . .   165 CHRISTN FORB/N   1
  I WAS ANGRY WITH MY FRIEND   . . . .   218 POISON TREE/SE   1
  THARMAS REPLIED ART THOU URTHONA MY FRIEND MY OLD COMPANION 300 FOUR ZOAS 4   111
  TO YOU BUT THAT EVERY ONE IS EITHER YOUR FRIEND OR YOUR   380B FOUR ZOAS NOTE   PROSE
    ENEMY
  O MY LOVER & MY FRIEND   . . . .   423 THE BIRDS/N   16
  BUT NO FRIEND FROM HENCEFORWARD THOU MARY SHALT SEE   . . . 428 MARY   16
  THULLOH THE FRIEND OF SATAN ALSO REPROVD HIM PAINT THEIR   488 MILTON 8   33
    REPROOF
  OR LIKE A HUMAN FORM A FRIEND WITH WITH WHOM HE LIVD   497 MILTON 15   27
    BENEVOLENT
  AWAKING OF ALBION OUR FRIEND AND ANCIENT COMPANION   . .   511 MILTON 25   62
  WHAT IS THY MESSAGE TO THY FRIEND WHAT AM I NOW TO DO   . . 527 MILTON 36   29
  FOR SORROW THAT [YOUR] OUR FRIEND BOB SCREWMUCH S GONE   .   537 AND HIS LEGS/N   47
  HERE LIES STEWHARD THE [LORD OF] FRIEND OF ALL &C   . .   537 AND HIS LEGS/N *   52
  WHO NEVER IN HIS LIFE FRIEND A FRIEND   . . . . . .   544 TO FORGIVE/N   2
  [FRIEND CAIAPHAS IS ONE DO WHAT HE CAN]   . . . . . .   544 SOME MEN/N   3
  HERE LIES JOHN TROT THE FRIEND OF ALL MANKIND   . . .   546 ANOTHER/N 2   1
  FOR THIS IS BEING A FRIEND JUST IN THE NICK   . . . .   551 WILLM COWPER/N   1
  FOR TIS [MOST WICKED] ATROCIOUS IN A FRIEND YOU LOVE   .   551 WILLM COWPER/N   9
  I ASKD MY DEAR FRIEND ORATOR PRIGG . . . .   553 ASKD PRIGG/N   *   1
  TO GROW SOWER AT WHAT A FRIEND MAY UTTER   . . . . .   556 IF MEN ACT/N   3
  AND HIS FRIEND ARE EQUALLY MASTERS OF CHAUCER'S LANGUAGE   574B DESC CAT 3   PROSE
  HIS FRIEND H(OPPNER) WHO HAS CALLED HIS "A COMMON SCENE"   574D DESC CAT 3   *PROSE
  YOUR ENEMY HE ALWAYS BEGINS WITH BEING YOUR FRIEND   . .   592C PUB ADDRESS/N   PROSE
  OR COULD MAKE A FRIEND & COMPANION OF ONE OF THESE IMAGES   611A V LAST JUDG/N   PROSE
    OF
  FOR A MAN CAN ONLY REJECT ERROR BY THE ADVICE OF A FRIEND   614A V LAST JUDG/N   PROSE
  & THE MORE TO HAVE AN INTEREST IN THE FRIEND OF SINNERS   621A JERUSALEM 3   PROSE
  I AM NOT A GOD AFAR OFF I AM A BROTHER AND FRIEND   . .   622 JERUSALEM 4   18
  LITTLE-ONES TO DESTROY THE DIVINE SAVIOUR THE FRIEND OF   641 JERUSALEM 18   37
    SINNERS
  LOS WAS THE FRIEND OF ALBION WHO MOST LOVD HIM IN   666 JERUSALEM 39   12
    CAMBRIDGESHIRE
  SELSEY TRUE FRIEND WHO AFTERWARDS SUBMITTED TO BE DEVOURD   667 JERUSALEM 40   48
  ALBION SPOKE IN HIS DISMAL DREAMS O THOU DECEITFUL FRIEND   669 JERUSALEM 42   9
  WORSHIPPING MERCY & BEHOLDING THY FRIEND IN SUCH AFFLICTION 669 JERUSALEM 42   10
  ALBION REPLIED GO HAND & HYLE SIEZE THE ABHORRED FRIEND   670 JERUSALEM 42   47
  HE NEVER CAN BE A FRIEND TO THE HUMAN RACE   . . . . .   681D JERUSALEM 52   PROSE
  STATE MUST BE PUT OFF BEFORE HE CAN BE THE FRIEND OF MAN   682A JERUSALEM 52   PROSE
  FOUND NO FRIEND FRIENDSHIP CANNOT EXIST WITHOUT FORGIVENESS 682D JERUSALEM 52   PROSE
  WHERE IS THAT FRIEND OF SINNERS THAT REBEL AGAINST MY LAWS 685 JERUSALEM 54   19
  TO JUDGE THE FRIEND OF SINNERS TO DEATH WITHOUT THE VEIL   725 JERUSALEM 82   33
  PLOTTING TO DEVOUR ALBION & LOS THE FRIEND OF ALBION   .   737 JERUSALEM 90   63
  IT IS EASIER TO FORGIVE AN ENEMY THAN TO FORGIVE A FRIEND   737 JERUSALEM 91   2
  I SEE THEE IN THE LIKENESS & SIMILITUDE OF LOS MY FRIEND   743 JERUSALEM 96   22
  ALBION STOOD IN TERROR NOT FOR HIMSELF BUT FOR HIS FRIEND   743 JERUSALEM 96   30
  THINE IS THE FRIEND OF ALL MANKIND   . . . .   748 EV GOSPEL(A)/N   5
  IN DESTROYING THE SINNERS FRIEND   . . . .   759 EV GOSPEL (2)   37
  IS IN CONJUNCTION WITH SUCH MEN AS MY FRIEND CUMBERLAND   792A LETTER 4   PROSE

```
                                                               PAGE     TITLE          LINE
FRIEND    (CONTINUED)
    MY DEAREST FRIEND IT IS TO YOU I OWE ALL MY PRESENT  . . . 799A LETTER 11          PROSE
    TO MY DEAREST FRIEND JOHN FLAXMAN THESE LINES . . . . .    799B TO FLAXMAN/L       TITLE
    AND NOW FLAXMAN HATH GIVEN ME HAYLEY HIS FRIEND . . .  . . 799 TO FLAXMAN/L           4
    "MY DEAREST FRIEND I HOPE YOU WILL NOT THINK WE COULD" .   800A LETTER 12          PROSE
    TO MY DEAR FRIEND MRS ANNA FLAXMAN    . . . . . . . .      800B MRS FLAXMAN/L      TITLE
    AND MY BROTHER IS THERE & MY FRIEND & THINE     . . . .    800 MRS FLAXMAN/L         11
    YOU O DEAR FLAXMAN ARE A SUBLIME ARCHANGEL MY FRIEND &  .  802C LETTER 14          PROSE
    FAREWELL MY BEST FRIEND REMEMBER ME & MY WIFE IN LOVE &    802D LETTER 14          PROSE
    DEAR FRIEND OF MY ANGELS WE ARE SAFE ARRIVED AT OUR COTTAGE 803A LETTER 15         PROSE
    YOUR AFFECTIONATE & OBLIGED FRIEND     . . . . . . . .     803C LETTER 15          PROSE
    FRIEND OF RELIGION & ORDER I THANK YOU FOR YOUR  . . . .   804A LETTER 16          PROSE
    TO MY FRIEND BUTTS I WRITE   . . . . . . . . . . .         804 TO BUTTS/L             1
    AND MY SISTER & FRIEND   . . . . . . . . . . . . . .       805 TO BUTTS/L            41
    WIFE OF THE FRIEND OF THOSE I MOST REVERE  . . . . . .     806 TO MRS BUTTS/L         1
    OUR DEAR FRIEND FLAXMAN IS THE THEME OF MY EMULATION   .   807A LETTER 17          PROSE
    MR THOMAS YOUR FRIEND TO WHOM YOU WAS SO KIND AS TO MAKE   810D LETTER 21          PROSE
    BY MARIA FLAXMAN SISTER TO MY FRIEND THE SCULPTOR AND IT   812A LETTER 22          PROSE
    YOU WILL BE CALLD THE BASE JUDAS WHO BETRAYD HIS FRIEND    813D LETTER 22          PROSE
    CAN COMPREHEND IN A FORTNIGHT BE ASSURED MY DEAR FRIEND    814D LETTER 23          PROSE
        THAT
    NO FURTHER MY FRIEND THAN HE IS COMPELLD BY CIRCUMSTANCES  819C LETTER 25          PROSE
    PRETENDS TO BE THE FRIEND OF MY CORPOREAL HE IS A REAL     822D LETTER 26          PROSE
        ENEMY
    BUT THE MAN MAY BE THE FRIEND OF MY SPIRITUAL LIFE   . .   822D LETTER 26          PROSE
    AS YOU MY DEAR FRIEND HAVE ALWAYS LEFT ME  . . . . . .     826A LETTER 27          PROSE
    BUT I THINK OF YOU & FEEL ANXIOUS FOR THE SIGHT OF THAT    826C LETTER 28          PROSE
        FRIEND
    THUS YOU SEE MY DEAR FRIEND THAT I CANNOT LEAVE THIS PLACE 828A LETTER 28          PROSE
    BURN WHAT I HAVE PEEVISHLY WRITTEN ABOUT ANY FRIEND  . .   828C LETTER 28          PROSE
    THEN I'M SILENT & PASSIVE & LOSE EVERY FRIEND  . . . .     828 O WHY BORN/L           4
    ABOVE ALL YOU MY DEAR FRIEND & BENEFACTOR IN THE LORD  .   834A LETTER 33          PROSE
    HIS FATHER'S BEST FRIEND WILL I HOPE BECOME THE MOST       838C LETTER 37          PROSE
        RESPECTED
    MAN SPOKE OF MR GREEN AS THE OLDEST FRIEND OF ROMNEY   .   845D LETTER 44          PROSE
    BUT TO BALANCE ALL THIS I MUST IN DUTY TO MY FRIEND       846C LETTER 44          PROSE
        SEAGRAVE
    WHICH MR JOHNSON WAS TO GET DONE FOR OUR FRIEND DALLY  .   847A LETTER 44          PROSE
    OUR GOOD AND KIND FRIEND HAWKINS IS NOT YET IN TOWN  . .   851D LETTER 50          PROSE
    IF OUR EXCELLENT AND MANLY FRIEND MEYER IS YET WITH YOU    852D LETTER 50          PROSE
    AND AFFECTIONATE COMPLIMENTS TO HIM ALSO TO OUR KIND FRIEND 852D LETTER 50         PROSE
    MY WIFE JOINS ME IN LOVE TO YOU & TO OUR DEAR FRIEND &  .  853A LETTER 51         *PROSE
    THE ASSISTANCE AND APPROBATION OF OUR GOOD FRIEND FLAXMAN  853B LETTER 52          PROSE
    OUR DEAR FRIEND HAWKINS IS OUT OF TOWN & WILL NOT RETURN   855B LETTER 53          PROSE
        TILL APRIL
    WITH THE PRINTING OF OUR FRIEND THE CHICHESTER PRINTER HERE 856B LETTER 54         PROSE
    THIS ENTERPRIZING MAN THAT ALL PARTIES I MEAN OUR FRIEND   857A LETTER 54          PROSE
    OF ADVANTAGE TO OUR FRIEND SEAGRAVE THE IDEA OF SEEING  .  859C LETTER 56          PROSE
    TO PROMOTE THE SPIRITED EXERTIONS OF MY FRIEND CROMEK  .   861D LETTER 59          PROSE
    OF YOUR GOOD HEALTH & THAT OF OUR DEAR FRIEND OF LAVANT &  862A LETTER 59          PROSE
    IN THE MEAN TIME BELIEVE ME TO BE YOUR SINCERE FRIEND  .   866A LETTER 63          PROSE
    MY DEAREST FRIEND THIS SUDDEN COLD WEATHER HAS CUT UP  .   872D LETTER 76          PROSE
    EXPERIENCE FOR A FRIEND AT TEN GUINEAS WHICH I CANNOT DO   878C LETTER 88          PROSE
FRIENDLESS
    AT THIS HOUSE EVEN AT THIS DAY EVERY FRIENDLESS WRETCH  .  590B CHAUCER 2          PROSE
FRIENDLY
    YOU CAN FIND FRIENDLY EXCUSES FOR ME CHANDOS  . . . . .     27 EDW THIRD/PS 3        277
    BUT THAT WE MAY OMIT NO OFFICE OF THE FRIENDLY SPIRIT  .   675 JERUSALEM 45           29
FRIEND'S
    AT A FRIEND'S ERRORS ANGER SHEW     . . . . . . . .        538 WAS I ANGRY/N          8
FRIENDS
    O MY DEAR FRIENDS PRAY YE FOR ME    . . . . . . . . .       36A COUCH DEATH/PS    PROSE
    SUCH WAS THIS YOUNG MAN'S VOICE TO HIS FRIENDS  . . . .     36B COUCH DEATH/PS    PROSE
    DO WITH ME WHAT THOU WILT MY FRIENDS ARE ENEMIES  . . .     38D SAMSON/PS         PROSE
    GO SEE THE CITY FRIENDS JOIND HAND IN HAND  . . . . .       43A THEN SHE BORE     PROSE
    THAT YOU WOULD THINK YOU WAS AMONG YOUR FRIENDS  . . .      44A ISLAND MOON 1     PROSE
    ("AS YOUR ENEMIES AND YOUR FRIENDS SO ARE YOU")            70C ANNO LAVATER       MARG
        VERY UNEASY
    ("WANT OF FRIENDS ARGUES WANT OF HUMILITY OR COURAGE")     74A ANNO LAVATER       MARG
        UNEASY
    ("QUALITIES OF FRIENDS...ENEMIES") VERY UNEASY INDEED BUT  80D ANNO LAVATER       MARG
        TRUTH
    TELL ME O FRIENDS WHERE AM I NOW & IN WHAT PLEASANT PLACE  101 TIRIEL 2             15
    AND ALL HIS GOOD FRIENDS SHEW THEIR PRIVATE ENDS  . . .    183 MOTTO SONGS/N         7
    WASHINGTON SPOKE FRIENDS OF AMERICA LOOK OVER THE ATLANTIC 197 AMERICA 3            6
        SEA
    WASHINGTON SPOKE FRIENDS OF AMERICA LOOK OVER THE ATLANTIC 204 AMERICA CANC A       6
        SEA
    AND ALL FLESH NAKED STANDS FATHERS AND FRIENDS  . . . .    248 SONG OF LOS 7       33
    FATHERS & FRIENDS MOTHERS & INFANTS KINGS & WARRIORS  .    363 FOUR ZOAS 9        243
    AND MARY AROSE AMONG FRIENDS TO BE FREE  . . . . . .       428 MARY                 15
    BURKE USED TO SHEW THIS PICTURE TO HIS FRIENDS & TO SAY    451D ANNO REYNOLDS      MARG
        I GAVE
    BAD PICTURES ARE ALWAYS SR JOSHUA'S FRIENDS  . . . . .     478C ANNO REYNOLDS      MARG
    MARK WELL MY WORDS CORPOREAL FRIENDS ARE SPIRITUAL ENEMIES 484 MILTON 4            26
    WOULD I HAD TOLD LOS ALL MY HEART BUT PATIENCE O MY FRIENDS 487 MILTON 7           31
    WAS SATAN'S ENEMY & THAT THE GNOMES BEING PALAMABRON'S     487 MILTON 7            39
        FRIENDS
    O GOD PROTECT ME FROM MY FRIENDS THAT THEY HAVE NOT POWER  489 MILTON 9             5
        OVER ME
    THAT MY FRIENDS MAY WEEP AS MUCH AS THEY LIKE   . . . .    537 AND HIS LEGS/N      51
    I THOUGHT THEM THE ERRORS OF FRIENDS . . . . . . . .       538 ANGER WRATH/N        2
```

	PAGE	TITLE	LINE

FRIENDS   (CONTINUED)

	PAGE	TITLE	LINE
WHY SHOULD YOU BE UNGRATEFUL TO YOUR FRIENDS	541	MR STOTHARD/N	3
MY GENEROSITY IS TO MY FRIENDS	541	HOMERS HERO/N	3
AND BECOMES THE ENEMY & BETRAYER OF HIS FRIENDS	541	HOMERS HERO/N	6
IT WILL SET HIS DUTCH FRIENDS ALL IN A ROAR	542	FLORENTINE/N	24
P(?PHILLIPS) LOVED ME NOT AS HE LOVD HIS FRIENDS	544	P LOVED NOT/N	1
THAT MY FRIENDS MAY WEEP AS MUCH AS THEY LIKE	546	ANOTHER/N 1	2
FRIENDS WERE QUITE HARD TO FIND OLD AUTHORS SAY	546	ANOTHER/N 2	3
AND SO [SWEET] DEAR [CHRISTIANS] CHRISTIAN FRIENDS HOW DO YOU DO	551	ONLY MAN/N *	4
AND NOW I'LL LEAD MY FALSE FRIENDS BY THE NOSE	555	BLAKES APL/N 1	23
AND THAT NOW I LEAD MY FALSE FRIENDS BY THE [TOES] NOSE	556	BLAKES APL/N 2 *	12
THIS IS MY SWEET APOLOGY TO MY FRIENDS	556	BLAKES APL/N 2	21
FALSE FRIENDS [O NO] PIE FIE	556	IF MEN ACT/N	5
[FOR NOW] IN SPITE WE WILL BE GREATER FRIENDS THAN EVER	556	IF MEN ACT/N	6
AND MENTAL [FRIENDSHIP] FRIENDS & MENTAL WEALTH . . .	558	I ROSE UP AT/N *	10
THE PAINTER HOPES THAT HIS FRIENDS ANYTUS [&] MELITUS &	598B	PUB ADDRESS/N	PROSE
TREMBLING I SIT DAY AND NIGHT MY FRIENDS ARE ASTONISHD AT ME	623	JERUSALEM 5	16
WILLING THE FRIENDS ENDURD FOR ALBION'S SAKE AND FOR .	641	JERUSALEM 19	28
THEY PERCIEVED THAT CORPOREAL FRIENDS ARE SPIRITUAL ENEMIES	655	JERUSALEM 30	10
IN LOVES AND TEARS OF BROTHERS SISTERS SONS FATHERS AND FRIENDS	664	JERUSALEM 38	12
GOD HATH FORSAKEN ME & MY FRIENDS ARE BECOME A BURDEN . .	666	JERUSALEM 39	22
THE FRIENDS OF ALBION TREMBLING AT THE SIGHT OF ETERNAL DEATH	666	JERUSALEM 40	3
OF UNBELIEF ENVY HOVERS OVER HIM HIS FRIENDS ARE HIS ABHORRENCE	667	JERUSALEM 40	14
ARISE AWAKE O FRIENDS OF THE GIANT ALBION	667	JERUSALEM 40	18
THOSE ALONE ARE HIS FRIENDS WHO ADMIRE HIS MINUTEST POWERS	673	JERUSALEM 43	58
ALL YOU MY FRIENDS & BROTHERS ALL YOU MY BELOVED COMPANIONS	673	JERUSALEM 43	74
HIS FRIENDS CUT HIS STRONG CHAINS & OVERWHELMD HIS DARK	675	JERUSALEM 45	21
HE FROWND ON ALL HIS FRIENDS COUNTING THEM ENEMIES IN HIS SORROW	676	JERUSALEM 45	36
THE EMANATIONS OF THE GRIEVOUSLY AFFLICTED FRIENDS OF ALBION	678	JERUSALEM 48	27
WHERE FRIENDS DIE FOR EACH OTHER WILL BECOME THE PLACE . .	678	JERUSALEM 48	56
THE TWENTYFOUR FRIENDS OF ALBION AND ROUND THE AWFUL FOUR	684	JERUSALEM 53	22
WALKETH AMONG US CALLING US HIS BROTHERS & HIS FRIENDS . .	686	JERUSALEM 55 *	10
OR HAST THOU BEEN PIERCED IN THE HOUSE OF THY FRIENDS . .	693	JERUSALEM 60	53
ALL WERE HIS FRIENDS & THEIR SONS & DAUGHTERS INTERMARRY IN BEULAH	709	JERUSALEM 71	14
I SHALL BECOME AN INFANT HORROR ENION THARMAS FRIENDS .	727	JERUSALEM 83	5
I HAVE TRIED TO MAKE FRIENDS BY CORPOREAL GIFTS BUT HAVE ONLY	738	JERUSALEM 91	16
MADE ENEMIES I NEVER MADE FRIENDS BUT BY SPIRITUAL GIFTS	738	JERUSALEM 91	17
DO I SLEEP AMIDST DANGER TO FRIENDS O MY CITIES & COUNTIES	744	JERUSALEM 96	33
HE WHO LOVES HIS ENEMIES HATES HIS FRIENDS	750	EV GOSPEL(C)/N	19
HE WHO LOVES HIS ENEMIES [HATES] BETRAYS HIS FRIENDS . .	751	EV GOSPEL(D)/N	25
HE COMFORTS & HEALS & CALLS THEM FRIENDS	755	EV GOSPEL(E)/N	90
THAT SHE IS BUSIED AMONG MY FRIENDS WITH MINE & MY WIFE'S	796A	LETTER 6	PROSE
I KNOW THAT OUR DECEASED FRIENDS ARE MORE REALLY WITH US	797A	LETTER 9	PROSE
TO JOHN FLAXMAN I HAVE BEEN TOO LITTLE AMONG FRIENDS WHICH I	798B	LETTER 10	PROSE
FEW FRIENDS I HAVE DARED TO VISIT IN MY STUPID MELANCHOLY	798C	LETTER 10	PROSE
I NEGLECT MY DUTY TO MY FRIENDS BUT IT IS NOT WANT . .	798D	LETTER 10	PROSE
. . . THE BLESSED OF HEAVEN ARE MY FRIENDS UPON EARTH .	799	TO FLAXMAN/L	2
FRIENDS OUR COTTAGE IS SURROUNDED BY THE SAME GUARDIANS YOU	807B	LETTER 17	PROSE
AS NEW FRIENDS HAS PREVENTED ME FROM THAT RESPECT I OWE IN	808A	LETTER 19	PROSE
MINIATURE (IS) BECOME A GODDESS IN MY EYES & MY FRIENDS	808B	LETTER 19	*PROSE
DID NOT HE IS ALSO A HAPPY ABSTRACT KNOWN BY ALL HIS FRIENDS	809C	LETTER 20	PROSE
AS ALL MY FRIENDS TELL ME BUT MY PRINCIPAL LABOUR . .	809C	LETTER 20	PROSE
AS IT WILL CONTAIN LETTERS OF COWPER TO HIS FRIENDS PERHAPS	810A	LETTER 20	PROSE
UPON YOU AS THE CHIEF OF MY FRIENDS WHOM I WOULD ENDEAVOUR	815A	LETTER 23	PROSE
THINK OF TROUBLING YOU ABOUT IT OR ANY OF MY REAL FRIENDS	815C	LETTER 23	PROSE
AND ALL MY FRIENDS BE WITH DOUBTS BEGUILD	818	HAPPINESS/L	48
NOR MY FRIENDS UNEASY IF I CAN HELP IT MY WIFE HAS HAD AGUES	819C	LETTER 25	PROSE
& ALSO VERY AFRAID THAT MY FRIENDS IN LONDON SHOULD HAVE	820A	LETTER 25	PROSE
FOR I KNOW THAT THE PUBLIC ARE MY FRIENDS & LOVE MY WORKS	821C	LETTER 25	PROSE
& THAT I MAY CONVERSE WITH MY FRIENDS IN ETERNITY . .	822C	LETTER 26	PROSE
ARE ALWAYS PERNICIOUS ESPECIALLY WHEN WE DOUBT OUR FRIENDS	822D	LETTER 26	PROSE
INDEED THE PROSPECT OF RETURNING TO OUR FRIENDS IS SUPREMELY	824B	LETTER 27	PROSE
I WAS COMMANDED BY MY SPIRITUAL FRIENDS TO BEAR ALL TO BE SILENT	825D	LETTER 27	PROSE
TO SEE MY FRIENDS IN TOWN BEFORE THIS CONTEMPTIBLE BUSINESS	828A	LETTER 28	PROSE
MERRY WITH MY FRIENDS TILL CHRISTMAS FOR AS MAN LIVETH NOT BY	830B	LETTER 30	*PROSE
TO PRAY THAT MY FRIENDS & YOU ABOVE THE REST MAY BE MADE	830B	LETTER 30	PROSE
OF MY FRIENDS AS I PERCIEVE HE IS NOW DOING THE SAME WORK BY	830D	LETTER 30	PROSE
THE HEALTH OF MISS POOLE AND FOR ALL OUR FRIENDS IN SUSSEX	832A	LETTER 31	PROSE
& THAT YOU HAD ACCORDINGLY NOMINATED ONE OF YOUR FRIENDS	842C	LETTER 42	*PROSE
IT SEEMS AS IF ALL ROMNEY'S INTIMATE FRIENDS	844A	LETTER 43	PROSE
WE CONSTANTLY SEND WISHES TO OUR SPIRITUAL FRIENDS YOURS SINCERELY	847C	LETTER 44	PROSE
SPOILING WHAT I HAD DONE WELL EVERY ONE OF MY FRIENDS WAS	852B	LETTER 50	PROSE
FRIENDS AT LAVANT & IN ALL SUSSEX I REMAIN DEAR SIR . . .	853A	LETTER 51	*PROSE
[OF] ALL OUR FRIENDS TO WHOM WE ARE GRATEFUL & DESIRE TO BE	862A	LETTER 59	PROSE

	PAGE	TITLE	LINE

FRIENDS (CONTINUED)

FRIENDS EXCUSE THIS EFFUSION OF THE SPIRIT FROM ONE WHO — 862D LETTER 60 — PROSE
WISHING YOU & ALL FRIENDS IN SUSSEX A MERRY & . . . . . 863C LETTER 60 — PROSE
ITS BUSINESS AMONG HIS FRIENDS . . . . 875A LETTER 80 — PROSE
FOR HIS BRISTOL FRIENDS AS THEY THINK I SAW MR TATHAM SENR 877A LETTER 85 — PROSE
BE UNLUCKY TO MY FRIENDS & ESPECIALLY THAT I MAY NOT BE 879C LETTER 89 — PROSE
   SO TO YOU

FRIENDSHIP

("BLUNDERER'S FRIENDSHIP THAN CALUMNIATOR'S ENMITY") I 69C ANNO LAVATER — MARG
   DOUBT THIS
THE BIRD A NEST THE SPIDER A WEB MAN FRIENDSHIP . . . . 151D MARRIAGE HH 8 — PROSE
OPPOSITION IS TRUE FRIENDSHIP . . . . 157C MARRIAGE HH 17 — PROSE
UPON THE GREEN PLAINS & SWEET FRIENDSHIP MET IN PALACES 317 FOUR ZOAS 6 — 215
THE FRIENDSHIP OF THESE ROMAN VILLAINS IS A STRANGE EXAMPLE 406D ANNO BACON — MARG
IN INDIGNATION FOR SATAN'S SOFT DISSIMULATION OF FRIENDSHIP 488 MILTON 8 — 35
OF FRIENDSHIP OUR SEXUAL CANNOT BUT FLIES INTO THE ULRO 534 MILTON 41 — 33
THAT FOR THEIR FRIENDSHIP I MAY MAKE AMENDS . . . . . 541 HOMERS HERO/N — 4
ON HY'S(HAYLEY'S) FRIENDSHIP . . . . 544C HS FRENDSHIP/N — TITLE
THY FRIENDSHIP OFT HAS MADE MY HEART TO AKE . . . . . 545 TO H(AYLEY)/N — 1
. . . OUR FRIENDSHIP [NEER SHALL] YOU SHANT SEVER . . . 556 IF MEN ACT/N — 5
AND MENTAL [FRIENDSHIP] FRIENDS & MENTAL WEALTH . . . 558 I ROSE UP AT/N * 10
OPEN PROFESSIONS OF FRIENDSHIP ARE COMMON ENOUGH . . . . 592C PUB ADDRESS/N — PROSE
REPRESENTATIVE OF THAT LOVE CALLD FRIENDSHIP . . . . . 610D V LAST JUDG/N — PROSE
HALF FRIENDSHIP IS THE BITTEREST ENMITY SAID LOS . . . . 620 JERUSALEM 1 — 8
THE [LOVE] AND [FRIENDSHIP] OF THOSE WITH WHOM TO 620D JERUSALEM 3 — PROSE
   BE CONNECTED
CURSING THE TERRIBLE LOS BITTERLY CURSING HIM FOR HIS 624 JERUSALEM 6 — 6
   FRIENDSHIP
TILL THY LIFE IS ALL TAKEN AWAY BY THIS DECEITFUL 625 JERUSALEM 7 — 10
   FRIENDSHIP
BECAUSE OF ALBION BECAUSE OF DECEIT AND FRIENDSHIP FOR LO 625 JERUSALEM 7 — 17
BOSOM IN ALL THE TERRORS OF FRIENDSHIP ENTERING THE CAVES 656 JERUSALEM 31 — 4
AND THE SOFT SMILE OF FRIENDSHIP & THE OPEN DAWN 672 JERUSALEM 43 — 25
   OF BENEVOLENCE
TILL THE EXISTENCE OF FRIENDSHIP & BENEVOLENCE IS DENIED 672 JERUSALEM 43 — 27
FOUND NO FRIEND FRIENDSHIP CANNOT EXIST WITHOUT FORGIVENESS 682D JERUSALEM 52 — PROSE
BY SEVERE CONTENTIONS OF FRIENDSHIP & THE BURNING FIRE 738 JERUSALEM 91 — 18
   OF THOUGHT
ONE FIRST IN FRIENDSHIP & LOVE THEN A DIVINE FAMILY & IN 738 JERUSALEM 91 — 20
   THE MIDST
THIS IS FRIENDSHIP & BROTHERHOOD WITHOUT IT MAN IS NOT . . 743 JERUSALEM 96 — 16
OFFERING OF SELF FOR ANOTHER IS THIS FRIENDSHIP & 743 JERUSALEM 96 — 21
   BROTHERHOOD
ON ACCOUNT OF NOT ACKNOWLEDGING YOUR FRIENDSHIP TO ME . . 791A LETTER 3 — PROSE
OF GRATITUDE OR FRIENDSHIP BUT PERHAPS AN EXCESS OF BOTH 798D LETTER 10 — PROSE
OF MY LIFE I HAVE PRESUMD ON YOUR FRIENDSHIP IN STAYING SO 799A LETTER 11 — PROSE
FRIENDSHIP TO OUR DEAR MRS FLAXMAN WHOM WE ARDENTLY . . 802D LETTER 14 — PROSE
AND MINE NO LESS HAPPY IN HIS FRIENDSHIP AND IN THAT OF HIS 807B LETTER 17 — PROSE
OF ACCUSTOMD FRIENDSHIP IF YOU WERE NOT . . . . 816D LETTER 24 — PROSE
FRIENDSHIP IN PREFERENCE TO INTEREST THE PUBLISHERS ARE 821A LETTER 25 — PROSE
OF IMMORTAL FRIENDSHIP TO THEE I AM ETERNALLY INDEBTED . . 852A LETTER 50 — PROSE
FOR FRIENDSHIP WITH SUCH A ONE IS BETTER THAN FAME . . 853A LETTER 51 — *PROSE
WITH ALL THE WARMTH OF FRIENDSHIP BOTH TO YOU AND ME . 853B LETTER 52 — PROSE
BALLADS WERE THE EFFUSIONS OF FRIENDSHIP TO COUNTENANCE 860C LETTER 56 — PROSE

FRIENDSHIP'S

DO BE MY ENEMY FOR FRIENDSHIP'S SAKE . . . . 545 TO H(AYLEY)/N — 2

FRIENDSHIPS

MAN THE ENEMY OF MAN INTO DECEITFUL FRIENDSHIPS . . . . 622 JERUSALEM 4 — 26
EVERY AFFINITY OF PARENTS MARRIAGES & FRIENDSHIPS ARE HERE 638 JERUSALEM 16 — 65
OF LOVES OF UNNATURAL CONSANGUINITIES AND FRIENDSHIPS . . 652 JERUSALEM 28 — 7

FRIGA

WHERE THE HUMAN VICTIMS HOWL TO THE MOON & THOR & FRIGA 697 JERUSALEM 63 — 9
THOR & FRIGA & THE FAIRIES LEAD THE MOON ALONG THE VALLEY 697 JERUSALEM 63 — 14
   OF CHERUBIM
HEARTS OF THEIR WARRIORS GLOW HOT BEFORE THOR & FRIGA O 706 JERUSALEM 68 — 17
   MOLECH
WODEN AND THOR AND FRIGA WHOLLY CONSUME MY SAXONS . . . 727 JERUSALEM 83 — 19

FRIGHT

. . . ALL HIS ANGELS FRIGHT THEIR ANCIENT HEAVENS . . . 202 AMERICA 15 — 18
DOWN SUNK WITH FRIGHT A RED . . . . 228 URIZEN 11 — 2
FROM THE CAVERNS OF HIS JOINTED SPINE DOWN SUNK WITH FRIGHT 303 FOUR ZOAS 4 — 223
SPEAKS THE UNBELIEVER'S FRIGHT . . . . 431 AUGURIES — 28
DOWN SUNK WITH FRIGHT A RED ROUND GLOBE HOT BURNING DEEP 482 MILTON 3 — 11

FRIGHTED

THEY RAN WEEPING LIKE FRIGHTED INFANTS FOR REFUGE 100 TIRIEL 2 * 12
   IN MNETHA'S ARMS
SHE HOWLING LED HIM OVER MOUNTAINS & THRO FRIGHTED VALES 108 TIRIEL 7 — 1
WERE FRIGHTED BY THE DISMAL CRIES OF HELA ON THE MOUNTAINS 109 TIRIEL 7 — 20
CANAAN THEN SHE RETURND TO LOS WEARY FRIGHTED AS 490 MILTON 10 * 5
   FROM DREAMS
WAS LIVING PANTING LIKE A FRIGHTED WOLF AND HOWLING . . . 625 JERUSALEM 7 — 1

FRIGHTEN

& FRIGHTEN ALL THE PEOPLE THERE & SHOW THEM WHAT TRUTH IS 63A ISLAND MOON 11 PROSE

FRIGHTEND

FRIGHTEND AT THE HURTLING BONES . . . . 226 URIZEN 8 — 2
THE CONTEMPLATIVE TERROR FRIGHTEND IN HIS SCORNFUL SPHERE 302 FOUR ZOAS 4 — 177
FRIGHTEND WITH COLD INFECTIOUS MADNESS IN HIS HAND THE 302 FOUR ZOAS 4 — 178
   THUNDERING
THE TRUTH IS AS A POET HE IS FRIGHTEND AT ME & AS 819C LETTER 25 — PROSE
   A PAINTER

FRIGHTFUL

SUMMERS & WINTERS ROUND REVOLVING IN THE FRIGHTFUL DEEP 276 FOUR ZOAS 1 — 443

	PAGE	TITLE	LINE

FRIGHTNING
    FRIGHTNING FAITHLESS FAWNING . . . . 234 URIZEN 23   3
FRIGIDITY
    ("PROOFS OF DULL FRIGIDITY HARDNESS OR...EGOTISM") RATHER 70C ANNO LAVATER   MARG
      UNEASY
FRINGE
    AND THE PESTILENCE SHALL BE ITS FRINGE & THE WAR ITS GIRDLE 499 MILTON 18   17
FRIVOLOUS
    HIM TO MEAN THAT FACILITY IN COMPOSING IS A FRIVOLOUS 453D ANNO REYNOLDS   MARG
      PURSUIT
FRO
    DARK THOUGHTS ROLLED TO AND FRO IN HIS MIND . . . . . 38C SAMSON/PS   PROSE
    ROSE INFLAMD TO AND FRO IN THE CHAMBER . . . . 141 FRENCH REVOLTN   170
    IN VAIN THESE CLOUDS ROLL TO & FRO & HIDE THEE FROM MY 196 AMERICA PREL 1   20
      SIGHT
    THEN THUNDERS ROLLD AROUND & LIGHTNINGS DARTED TO & FRO 294 FOUR ZOAS 3   109
    . . . WRITHING TO & [FROM] FRO HIS PALLID LIPS . . . . . 305 FOUR ZOAS 4 * 288
    ROCKD TO & FRO & [&] CRIED SORE AT THE GROANS OF ENITHARMON 306 FOUR ZOAS 5 * 29
    THE ROCKS SHOOK THE ETERNAL BARS TUGGD TO & FRO WERE RIFTED 310 FOUR ZOAS 5   186
    WITH THUNDEROUS NOISE & DREADFUL SHAKINGS ROCKING TO & FRO 357 FOUR ZOAS 9   15
    FLOAT THE DEAD CARCASES OF MEN & BEASTS DRIVEN TO & FRO 359 FOUR ZOAS 9   77
      ON WAVES
    MY SONS EXILED FROM MY BREAST PASS TO & FRO BEFORE ME . 359 FOUR ZOAS 9   100
    HIS CHILDREN EXILD FROM HIS BREAST PASS TO AND FRO BEFORE 641 JERUSALEM 19   1
      HIM
    TERRIFIED ROCKING TO & FRO UPON THE EARTH & SOMETIMES . . 737 JERUSALEM 90   61
    TO & FRO IN ETERNITY AS ONE MAN . . . . 746 JERUSALEM 98   39
FROG
    THIS FROG HE WOULD A WOOING RIDE . . . . 55 THIS FROG/IM   1
    THIS FROG HE WOULD A WOOING RIDE . . . . 55 THIS FROG/IM   3
    [THIS FROG] SING COCK I CARY KITTY ALONE . . . . . 55 THIS FROG/IM * 5
    WITH WHAT SENSE DOES THE BEE FORM CELLS HAVE NOT THE MOUSE 191 V DAU ALBION 3   4
      & FROG
FROGS
    ?EXODUS AARON XXX ?MOSES XXX RIVER XXX FROGS LICE . . SUPP EXODUS/N   *PROSE
FRONT
    . . . AND IN FRONT OF HIS SOLID RANKS . . . . 147 FRENCH REVOLTN   288
    IN ALL THE DISEASES OF MAN FALLING UPON THY GREY ACCURSED 322 FOUR ZOAS 7   89
      FRONT
    YORK EDINBURGH DURHAM & CARLISLE & ON THE FRONT . . . . 531 MILTON 39   43
    THEY POUR COLD WATER ON HIS BRAIN IN FRONT TO CAUSE . . 702 JERUSALEM 66   30
    THAT FRONT THE FOUR OTHER POINTS WERE TURNED FOUR SQUARE 711 JERUSALEM 72   7
FRONTALS
    AND FORM HIS FOREHEAD SMALL WITHOUT FRONTALS HIS JAWS LARGE 580A DESC CAT 5   PROSE
FRONTIERS
    THEY SPOTTED WITH PLAGUES FORSOOK THE FRONTIERS & THEIR 202 AMERICA 15   14
      BANNERS SEARD
FRONTING
    AND THE FOUR FACES OF HUMANITY FRONTING THE FOUR CARDINAL 745 JERUSALEM 98   26
      POINTS
FRONTISPIECE
    THE ANCIENT BRITONS ACCORDING TO CAESAR [THE FRONTISPIECE] 208C SUBJCTS HIST/N   TITLE
    GENERAL TITLE FRONTISPIECE OF PIPER . . . . SUPP LETTER 66A   *PROSE
    FRONTISPIECE OF CHILD ON THE SHEPHERD'S HEAD . . . . . SUPP LETTER 66A   *PROSE
FROST
    O WHAT LIMB RENDING PAINS I FEEL THY FIRE & MY FROST . . 196 AMERICA PREL 2   15
    COLD DEWS & HOARY FROST CREEPS THO 1 LIE ON BANKS OF SUMMER 288 FOUR ZOAS 2 * 320
    GRIM FROST BENEATH & TERRIBLE SNOW LINKD IN A MARRIAGE 306 FOUR ZOAS 5   33
      CHAIN
    I WILL GIVE BLACKNESS FOR JEWELS HOARY FROST FOR ORNAMENT 312 FOUR ZOAS 6   37
      DEFORMITY
    FOR VOICES OF DELIGHT HOARSE CROAKINGS INARTICULATE THRO 312 FOUR ZOAS 6   39
      FROST
    THAT SWAGGD HEAVY WITH THE ACCURSED DOUGH THE HOAR FROST 322 FOUR ZOAS 7   100
      RAGD
    . . . THE GREY HOAR FROST WAS THERE . . . . 378 FOUR ZOAS 9   814
    BUT THE SPECTRE LIKE A HOAR FROST & A MILDEW ROSE OVER 685 JERUSALEM 54   15
      ALBION
FROSTS
    . . . [WITH FLAMES] [HOAR FROSTS] DAMP MISTS . . . . . 205 AMERICA CANC C   5
FROWN
    BLOW BOISTEROUS WIND STERN WINTER FROWN . . . . 64 SHEPHERD OLD   9
    OF ANCIENT KINGS AND THE FROWN OF THE ETERNAL LION . . . 135 FRENCH REVOLTN   32
    ANCIENT WONDERS FROWN OVER THE KINGDOM . . . . 139 FRENCH REVOLTN   118
    FROWN ON THE GARDENS . . . . 145 FRENCH REVOLTN   252
    AND THE HEAVENS GAVE A FROWN . . . . 164 HEARD ANGEL/N   17
    I HEARD HIM FROWN NOT URIZEN BUT LISTEN TO MY VISION . . 294 FOUR ZOAS 3   84
    IN PEACE BENEATH MY AWFUL FROWN MY WILL SHALL BE MY LAW 299 FOUR ZOAS 4   55
    SMILE WHEN THEY FROWN FROWN WHEN THEY SMILE & WHEN A 323 FOUR ZOAS 7   118
      MAN LOOKS PALE
    FEARING THY FROWN LOVING THY SMILE O URIZEN PRINCE OF LIGHT 360 FOUR ZOAS 9   135
    AND THERE IS A FROWN OF HATE . . . . 423 THE SMILE   5
    AND THERE IS A FROWN OF DISDAIN . . . . 423 THE SMILE   6
    AND THERE IS A FROWN OF FROWNS . . . . 423 THE SMILE   7
    I MIND NOT YOUR LAUGH AND YOUR FROWN I NOT FEAR AND . . . 688 JERUSALEM 56   30
    BUT THEY FROWN & DELIGHT IN CRUELTY REFUSING ALL OTHER JOY 706 JERUSALEM 68   29
    TWELVE RIDGES OF STONE FROWN OVER ALL THE EARTH IN TYRANT 735 JERUSALEM 89   21
      PRIDE
    FROWN OVER EACH RIVER STUPENDOUS WORKS OF ALBION'S DRUID 735 JERUSALEM 89   22
      SONS
FROWND
    THEN TIRIEL FROWND & ANSWERD DID I NOT COMMAND YOU SAYING 103 TIRIEL 3   36

766

	PAGE	TITLE	LINE

FROWND   (CONTINUED)

LIKE A BRIGHT CLOUD IN HARVEST BUT WHEN URIZEN FROWND SHE WEPT — 284 FOUR ZOAS 2 — 183

THEN FROWND THE [ETERNAL] FALLEN MAN ALBION — 294 FOUR ZOAS 3 — * 83

IN HIS HAND A KNOTTED CLUB WHOSE KNOTS LIKE MOUNTAINS FROWND — 319 FOUR ZOAS 6 — 305

AND GAVE THEM TO URIZEN'S HANDS THE IMMORTAL FROWND SAYING — 366 FOUR ZOAS 9 — 362

THE SPECTRE OF ALBION FROWND OVER THE NATIONS IN GLORY & WAR — 486 MILTON 6 — 24

SHE FROWND LIKE A FURY & SAID PATRONAGE — 554 ASKD PRIGG/N — 19

THEN FROWND THE FALLEN MAN AND PUT FORTH LUVAH FROM HIS PRESENCE — 655 JERUSALEM 29 — * 65

TO WHERE THE TOWER OF LONDON FROWND DREADFUL OVER JERUSALEM — 657 JERUSALEM 31 — 23

HE OPEND HIS FURNACES BEFORE VALA THEN ALBION FROWND IN ANGER — 660 JERUSALEM 34 — 19

HE FROWND ON ALL HIS FRIENDS COUNTING THEM ENEMIES IN HIS SORROW — 676 JERUSALEM 45 — 36

I MUST RUSH AGAIN TO WAR FOR THE VIRGIN HAS FROWND & REFUSD — 707 JERUSALEM 68 — 63

FROWNED

SO CRIED THEY AT THE PLOW ALBION'S ROCK FROWNED ABOVE — 687 JERUSALEM 55 — 67

FROWNING   SEE DARK-FROWNING

GORDRED APPEARS HIS FROWNING BROW — 12 GWIN KING/PS — 63

DREAD VISAGES FROWNING IN SILENT DEATH — 32 EDW THIRD/PS 6 — 36

FROWNING FROWNING NIGHT — 113 LIT GRL LST/SI — 29

FROWNING AND LOOKING UP FROM BROODING VILLAGES — 139 FRENCH REVOLTN — 117

THE KING FROWNING IN PURPLE BESIDE THE GREY PLOWMAN — 141 FRENCH REVOLTN — 150

THE SELFISH SMILING FOOL & THE SULLEN FROWNING FOOL — 151D MARRIAGE HH 8 — PROSE

[OVER THE] A FROWNING SHADOW LIKE [A] AN AGED KING IN ARMS OF GOLD — 205 AMERICA CANC C — * 25

HANGING FROWNING CLIFFS & ALL BETWEEN — 225 URIZEN 5 — 10

ON URIZEN FROWNING INDIGNANT — 249 AHANIA 2 — 15

A FROWNING CONTINENT APPEARD WHERE ENION IN THE DESART — 266 FOUR ZOAS 1 — 89

[THE PEAR TREE MILD THE FROWNING WALNUT THE SHARP CRAB & APPLE SWEET] . . . FROWNING [FROWNING] — 269 FOUR ZOAS 1 — 205

— 271 FOUR ZOAS 1 — 252

WITH FROWNING BROW THOU SITTEST MISTRESS OF THESE MIGHTY WATERS — 312 FOUR ZOAS 6 — 15

BY ROCKY MASSES FROWNING IN THE ABYSSES REVOLVING ERRATIC — 316 FOUR ZOAS 6 — 178

ON A ROCK OF IRON FROWNING OVER THE FOAMING FIRES OF ORC — 321 FOUR ZOAS 7 — 41

BUT WHEN THEY FIND THE FROWNING BABE — 427 MENTAL TRAVLER — 93

FOR WHO DARE TOUCH THE FROWNING FORM — 427 MENTAL TRAVLER — 97

AND NONE CAN TOUCH THAT FROWNING FORM — 427 MENTAL TRAVLER — 101

AND THIS IS THE CAUSE OF THE APPEARANCE IN THE FROWNING CHAOS — 659 JERUSALEM 33 — 25

APPEARD NOW IN THE FROWNING CHAOS PROLIFIC UPON THE CHAOS — 659 JERUSALEM 33 — 27

. . . THEY STOOD (FROWNING) UPON LONDON'S RIVER — 699 JERUSALEM 64 — 31

TWO FROWNING ROCKS ON EACH SIDE OF THE COVE & STONE OF TORTURE — 702 JERUSALEM 66 — 13

THEY CALL THE ROCKS PARENTS OF MEN & ADORE THE FROWNING CHAOS — 704 JERUSALEM 67 — 15

A FROWNING THISTLE IMPLORES MY STAY — 817 HAPPINESS/L — 24

FROWNS

THRONE OF GOD WHEN THE FROWNS OF HIS COUNTENANCE — 33 EDW FOURTH/PS — 7

WHOM SMILES AND FROWNS MAKE EQUALLY LOVELY — 85B ANNO LAVATER — MARG

THEN MNETHA TREMBLING AT HIS FROWNS LED HIM TO THE TENT DOOR — 103 TIRIEL 3 — 39

WHERE A FLAT SIDED STEEP FROWNS OVER THE PRESENT WORLD — 150C MARRIAGE HH 6 — PROSE

WHY SEEKS HE REFUGE FROM THE FROWNS OF HIS IMMORTAL STATION — 200 AMERICA 11 — 5

THE WOMAN THAT DOES NOT LOVE YOUR FROWNS — 417 MY SPECTR AD/N — 15

AND THERE IS A FROWN OF FROWNS — 423 THE SMILE — 7

PITYING AND LOVING THO IN FROWNS OF TERRIBLE PERTURBATION — 507 MILTON 23 — 30

GROANING THE SPECTRE HEAVD THE BELLOWS OBEYING LOS'S FROWNS — 628 JERUSALEM 9 — * 33

THE OAK FROWNS TERRIBLE THE BEECH & ASH & ELM ENROOT — 636 JERUSALEM 16 — 4

AND THY ARK & HOLY PLACE AT THY FROWNS AT THY DIRE REVENGE — 706 JERUSALEM 68 — 50

SHE WHO ADORES NOT YOUR FROWNS WILL ONLY LOATHE YOUR SMILES — 743 JERUSALEM 95 — 24

"WHOSE CHANGELESS BROW NEER SMILES NOR FROWNS" DONNE — SUPP LEGEND/N85 — *

FROZE

LIKE A DUMB STATUE FROZE TO STONE WITH FEAR — 4 FAIR ELENOR/PS — 20

AND BONES OF SOLIDNESS FROZE — 228 URIZEN 10 — 40

AND THE SEPERATED FIRES FROZE IN — 257 BOOK OF LOS 4 — 8

AND THREW HER FROM THE STEPS OF ICE THAT FROZE AROUND HIS THRONE — 294 FOUR ZOAS 3 — 112

AND BONES OF SOLIDNESS FROZE OVER ALL HIS NERVES OF JOY — 303 FOUR ZOAS 4 — 221

AND HE CAME RIDING IN HIS FURY FROZE TO SOLID WERE HIS WAVES — 313 FOUR ZOAS 6 — 49

OF THE MUNDANE SHELL WHICH FROZE ON ALL SIDES ROUND CANAAN ON — 698 JERUSALEM 64 — 1

FROZEN

. . . THE FROZEN BLOOD REFLOWD — 148 FRENCH REVOLTN — 303

WITH LAMPLIKE EYES WATCHING AROUND THE FROZEN MARRIAGE BED — 194 V DAU ALBION 7 — 22

. . . [?TILL ?BY THE] ?FROZEN CHILL & HEAVY EVEN TO THE CITY GATE — 205 AMERICA CANC C — * 9

CUT OFF FROM LIFE & LIGHT FROZEN — 230 URIZEN 13 — 42

THE IMMORTAL STOOD FROZEN AMIDST — 257 BOOK OF LOS 4 — 11

FROZEN DOORS TO MOCK — 262C LARGE BK DSGNS — TITLE

FAINT SHIVERING THEY SIT ON LEAFLESS BUSH OR FROZEN STONE — 276 FOUR ZOAS 1 — 447

AMONG THE FROZEN ARROWS THEY WILL TEAR THY TENDER FLESH — 296 FOUR ZOAS 3 — 172

THUNDRING & HAIL & FROZEN IRON HAILD FROM THE ELEMENT — 322 FOUR ZOAS 7 — 79

SPARKLES OF DIRE AFFLICTION ISSUD [FROM] ROUND HIS FROZEN LIMBS — 343 FOUR ZOAS 8 — * 91

FROZEN IN THE WOMB OF THARMAS RUSH THE RIVERS OF ENION'S PAIN — 381 FOUR ZOAS AD 4 — * 2

FROZEN   (CONTINUED)
    SAT FROZEN IN THE ROCK OF HOREB AND HIS REDEEMED PORTION   502 MILTON 20   11
    HERE FIXD INTO A FROZEN BULK SUBJECT TO DECAY & DEATH   .   .   525 MILTON 34   54
    ARE HERE FROZEN TO UNEXPANSIVE DEADLY DESTROYING TERRORS   525 MILTON 35   1
    THAT TOWARD EDEN ETERNAL ICE FROZEN IN SEVEN FOLDS   .   .   .   633 JERUSALEM 13   15
    WHY DOST THOU THUNDER WITH FROZEN SPECTROUS WRATH AGAINST   664 JERUSALEM 37   3
        US
    AND AS ALBION BUILT HIS FROZEN ALTARS LOS BUILT   671 JERUSALEM 42   78
        THE MUNDANE SHELL
    THE OPEN HEART IS SHUT UP IN INTEGUMENTS OF FROZEN SILENCE   672 JERUSALEM 43   33
    FROZEN SONS OF THE FEMININE TABERNACLE OF BACON NEWTON   702 JERUSALEM 66   14
        & LOCKE
    ENCOMPASSD BY THE FROZEN NET AND BY THE ROOTED TREE .   .   .   721 JERUSALEM 80   1
FRUCTIFYING
    IN THEIR AMAZING [FRUCTIFYING] HARD SUBDUED COURSE IN THE   287 FOUR ZOAS 2   * 286
        VAST DEEP
FRUIT
    O AUTUMN LADEN WITH FRUIT AND STAINED   .   .   .   .   .   .   2 TO AUTUMN/PS   1
    OF FRUIT AND JOY WITH PINIONS LIGHT ROVES ROUND   .   .   .   .   2 TO AUTUMN/PS   14
    THOU THE GOLDEN FRUIT DOST BEAR   .   .   .   .   7 LOVE HARMNY/PS   9
    OR FRUIT IN THE MID-DAY HOUR   .   .   .   .   8 LOVE JOCUND/PS   12
    WHICH DROP LIKE FRUIT UNTO THE EARTH   .   .   .   .   14 GWIN KING/PS   103
    IS CULTIVATED AND WILL BRING FORTH FRUIT   .   .   .   .   .   19 EDW THIRD/PS 2   26
    BRINGS FORTH FRUIT TO THE MIND'S TREASURE-HOUSE   .   .   .   .   27 EDW THIRD/PS 3   251
    AND OPT THE STANDER-BY SHALL STEAL THE FRUIT   .   .   .   .   27 EDW THIRD/PS 3   270
    [WHO THE FRUIT OR BLOSSOMS SHED]   .   .   .   .   167 INFANT SORW/N   29
    THAT NONE DARE EAT THE FRUIT BUT FROM   .   .   .   .   .   .   171 TO NOBODADDY/N   7
    AND IT BEARS THE FRUIT OF DECEIT   .   .   .   . 174 HUMAN IMAGE/N   18
    SWEETEST THE FRUIT THAT THE WORM FEEDS ON & THE SOUL PREYD   191 V DAU ALBION 3   17
        ON BY WOE
    THOU KNOWEST THAT THE ANCIENT TREES SEEN BY THINE EYES   192 V DAU ALBION 4   13
        HAVE FRUIT
    TILL HIS EYES SICKEN AT THE FRUIT THAT HANGS BEFORE HIS   194 V DAU ALBION 7   20
        SIGHT
    AND IT BEARS THE FRUIT OF DECEIT   .   .   .   . 217 HUMAN ABSTR/SE   17
    SOMETIMES I THINK THOU ART FRUIT BREAKING FROM ITS BUD   .   .   265 FOUR ZOAS 1   60
    MY CLOUDS ARE NOT THE CLOUDS OF VERDANT FIELDS & GROVES   275 FOUR ZOAS 1   392
        OF FRUIT
    THE RIPE FRUIT BLUSHES INTO JOY IN HEAVEN'S ETERNAL HALLS   324 FOUR ZOAS 7   176
    IN THROES OF BIRTH & NOW THE BLOSSOMS FALLING SHINING FRUIT   325 FOUR ZOAS 7   214
    BENEATH THE TREE OF MYSTERY AMONG THE LEAVES & FRUIT   .   .   325 FOUR ZOAS 7   218
    THE FRUIT OF THIS DELIGHTFUL TREE I CANNOT FLEE AWAY   326 FOUR ZOAS 7   234
    FILLED WITH DOUBTS IN SELF ACCUSATION [GATHERD] BEHELD   329 FOUR ZOAS 7   * 385
        THE FRUIT
    WHEN IN THE DEEPS BENEATH I GATHERD OF THIS RUDDY FRUIT   329 FOUR ZOAS 7   387
    THE FRUIT & GIVE ME PROOF OF LIFE ETERNAL OR I DIE   .   .   .   330 FOUR ZOAS 7   394
    THEN LOS PLUCKED THE FRUIT & EAT & SAT DOWN IN DESPAIR   .   .   330 FOUR ZOAS 7   395
    TERRIFIC INTO THE PAIND HEAVENS THE FRUIT TREES HUMANIZING   335 FOUR ZOAS 7B   101
    TO FEED THEIR FRUIT TO GRATIFY THEIR HIDDEN SONS   335 FOUR ZOAS 7B   104
        & DAUGHTERS
    . . . THE FRUIT OF THE MYSTERIOUS TREE   343 FOUR ZOAS 8   76
    GATHRING THE FRUIT OF THAT MYSTERIOUS TREE CIRCLING ITS   343 FOUR ZOAS 8   *   84
        ROOT
    UNFOLDS IN ALLEGORIC FRUIT WHEN SHALL THE DEAD REVIVE   .   .   345 FOUR ZOAS 8   169
    GATHERING THE FRUIT OF THAT MYSTERIOUS TREE TILL URIZEN   345 FOUR ZOAS 8   179
    THE SYNAGOGUE CREATED HER FROM FRUIT OF URIZEN'S TREE   .   .   348 FOUR ZOAS 8   287
    AS THE SEED WAITS EAGERLY WATCHING FOR ITS FLOWER & FRUIT   355 FOUR ZOAS 8   * 558
    OF FORNICATION FOOD OF ORC & SATAN PRESSD FROM THE FRUIT   356 FOUR ZOAS 8   603
        OF MYSTERY
    MY MILK OF COWS & HONEY OF BEES & FRUIT OF GOLDEN HARVEST   359 FOUR ZOAS 9   104
    THE FRUIT SHALL RIPEN & FALL DOWN & THE FLOWERS CONSUME   368 FOUR ZOAS 9   420
        AWAY
    SWIMS LIKE A DREAM BEFORE MY EYES BUT THE SWEET SMELLING   371 FOUR ZOAS 9   539
        FRUIT
    JUST AS WE REAP IN JOY THE FRUIT   .   .   .   . 424 MENTAL TRAVLER   7
    AND EVERY TREE DOES SHED ITS FRUIT   .   .   .   .   427 MENTAL TRAVLER   100
    OR THE APPLE TREE TEACHES THE PEAR TREE HOW TO BEAR FRUIT   453B ANNO REYNOLDS   MARG
    HIS MILK OF COWS & HONEY OF BEES & FRUIT OF GOLDEN HARVEST   641 JERUSALEM 19   5
    BY THE FRUIT OF ALBION'S TREE I HAVE FED HIM WITH SWEET   726 JERUSALEM 82   40
        MILK
    THE FRUIT OF ALBION'S POVERTY TREE   .   .   .   .   746 JERUSALEM 98   52
    THE FRUIT OF MY (MYSTERIOUS) TREE   .   .   .   .   759 EV GOSPEL (2)   *   40
    DEPEND UPON IT IT IS THE TREE YOUR PLEASURES ARE THE FRUIT   795B LETTER 6   PROSE
    KILL NOT A TREE BUT IT STILL BEAR FRUIT LET NONE SAY THAT   830C LETTER 30   PROSE
    THE FRUIT WAS IN CONSEQUENCE OF THE BLIGHT WHEN THIS   .   . 830C LETTER 30   PROSE
FRUITFUL
    AS BETWEEN GLITTERING SAND AND FRUITFUL MOLD   .   .   .   .   29D EDW THIRD/PS 4 *PROSE
    SHALL LAUGH WHOSE FRUITFUL LAPS BEND DOWN WITH FULNESS   .   .   33 EDW THIRD/PS 6   48
    AND [TURND] TURN IT INTO FRUITFUL LAND   .   .   .   .   .   .   168 HAST LAP/N   6
    THE SICKLE [ON] IN THE FRUITFUL FIELD   .   .   .   .   .   .   178 SWORD SUNG/N   *   2
    IN A RICH & FRUITFUL LAND   .   .   .   .   181 HOLY THURS/N   2
    [ABOUT THE FRUITFUL LAND]   .   .   .   .   185 LET BROTHELS/N   30
    IN A RICH AND FRUITFUL LAND   .   .   .   . 211 HOLY THURS/SE   2
    AND GARDEN FRUITFUL SEVENTY FOLD   .   .   .   .   425 MENTAL TRAVLER   28
    THEY HAVE SOWN ERRORS OVER ALL HIS FRUITFUL FIELDS   .   .   .   667 JERUSALEM 40   20
    OUR PALACES AND CITIES AND HOWEVER FRUITFUL ARE OUR FIELDS   675 JERUSALEM 45   12
FRUITION
    TILL THE DIVINE VISION & FRUITION IS QUITE OBLITERATED   .   .   292 FOUR ZOAS 3   36
    CALLING THE HUMAN IMAGINATION WHICH IS THE DIVINE VISION   521 MILTON 32   19
        & FRUITION
    FROM THE VISION AND FRUITION OF THE HOLY-ONE   .   .   .   .   622 JERUSALEM 4   17
    CONTEMNING THE DIVINE VISION & FRUITION WORSHIPING THE DEUS   741 JERUSALEM 93   23

	PAGE	TITLE	LINE

FRUITLESS
FRUITLESS FALSE THO FAIR TO SEE . . . . 166 I FEARD FURY/N 8

FRUITS
SING NOW THE LUSTY SONG OF FRUITS AND FLOWERS . . . . . 2 TO AUTUMN/PS 6
SEIZES THE FRUITS OF TIME ATTACKS EXPERIENCE . . . . . 27 EDW THIRD/PS 3 255
THEN MNETHA GAVE HIM MILK & FRUITS & THEY SAT DOWN TOGETHER 102 TIRIEL 2 58
CONSUMING ALL BOTH FLOWERS & FRUITS INSECTS & WARBLING 110 TIRIEL 8 38
BIRDS
OR THE SUMMER FRUITS APPEAR 124 SCHOOL BOY/SI 27
OR AN EYE OF GIFTS & GRACES SHOWRING FRUITS & COINED GOLD 130 BOOK OF THEL 6 15
THE LION THE TYGER THE HORSE THE ELEPHANT WATCH THE FRUITS 151D MARRIAGE HH 8 PROSE
PLUCK FRUITS BEFORE THE LIGHT . . . . 172 ARE NOT JOYS/N 8
PLANTS FRUITS OF LIFE & BEAUTY THERE . . . . 178 ABSTINENCE/N 4
BUT KNOWEST THOU THAT TREES AND FRUITS FLOURISH UPON THE 192 V DAU ALBION 4 14
EARTH
AND HE PLANTED A GARDEN OF FRUITS . . . . 234 URIZEN 20 41
MY ROOTS ARE BRANDISHD IN THE HEAVENS MY FRUITS IN EARTH 238 EUROPE PREL 1 8
BENEATH
NINE TIMES THEY LIVD AMONG THE FORESTS FEEDING ON SWEET 270 FOUR ZOAS 1 233
FRUITS
. . . & OUR CHILDREN BRING FRUITS & FLOWERS . . . . . 291 FOUR ZOAS 2 413
TO BRING HER FRUITS OF SWEET DELIGHT FROM TREES OF RICHEST 340 FOUR ZOAS 7B 284
WONDERS
IN FLOWERS IN FRUITS IN FISHES BIRDS & BEASTS & CLOUDS 367 FOUR ZOAS 9 378
& WATERS
AND THOU SWEET SMELLING GROUND PUT FORTH THY LIFE IN FRUITS 368 FOUR ZOAS 9 437
& FLOWERS
AND GIVEN ME FRUITS & PLEASANT WATERS & WARM HILLS & COOL 369 FOUR ZOAS 9 452
VALLEYS
SHE BORE THE FRUITS IN HER LAP SHE GATHERD FLOWERS FOR 369 FOUR ZOAS 9 477
HER BOSOM
SO SAYING THEY WENT DOWN INTO THE GARDEN AMONG THE FRUITS 371 FOUR ZOAS 9 535
ARE THE FRUITS OF THE TWO SEASONS . . . . 433 AUGURIES 92
CAN SUCH CLOSED NOSTRILS FEEL A JOY OR TELL OF AUTUMN 485 MILTON 5 32
FRUITS

FUEL
. . . AND THE JOYS OF THE COMBAT BURNT FOR FUEL . . . 138 FRENCH REVOLTN 93
OF ENITHARMON & THE GROANS OF URIZEN FUEL FOR HIS WRATH 302 FOUR ZOAS 4 192
EXPENDING ALL HIS ENERGY AGAINST THE FUEL OF FIRE . . 366 FOUR ZOAS 9 359

FUGITIVE
IN THE LOINS OF ALBION THE CANAANITE UNITED WITH 739 JERUSALEM 92 3
THE FUGITIVE

FUGITIVES
SO SPOKE THE FUGITIVES . . . . 655 JERUSALEM 29 83
I WOO TO AMALEK TO PROTECT MY FUGITIVES AMALEK TREMBLES 727 JERUSALEM 83 16

FULFIL
KING WILL LIVE TO FULFIL THE PROPHECY AND DIE IN PEACE . 844D LETTER 43 PROSE

FULFILL
FOR GOD PUT IT INTO THEIR HEART TO FULFILL ALL HIS WILL 357 FOUR ZOAS 8 617
IT WOULD NOT FULFILL THE PURPOSE FOR WHICH ALONE I LIVE 791D LETTER 4 PROSE
WHICH

FULFILLED
. . . THE VISION OF GOD IS FULFILLED . . . . 510 MILTON 25 22
ALL YOUR WISHES SHALL IN DUE TIME BE FULFILLED . . . 797C LETTER 10 PROSE
FULFILLED IN ME & IN FUTURE I AM THE DETERMINED ADVOCATE 804A LETTER 16 PROSE
SHALL IN DUE TIME BE FULFILLED . . . . 811D LETTER 22 PROSE

FULFILLING
I AM SO MUCH BETTER THAT I HAVE HOPES OF FULFILLING MY . 873D LETTER 78 PROSE

FULFILMENT
WAITING WITH PATIENCE [OF] FOR THE FULFILMENT OF 340 FOUR ZOAS 7B 295
THE PROMISE DIVINE

FULL
WHICH IN FULL CHOIR HAILS THY APPROACH O SPRING . . . . 1 TO SPRING/PS 4
AND WASH THE DUSK WITH SILVER SOON FULL SOON . . . . . 3 EVNING STAR/PS 10
THE THRONGED ENEMY IN TRUTH I AM TOO FULL . . . . . 26 EDW THIRD/PS 3 231
THEN PATRIOT ROSE FULL OFT DID PATRIOT RISE WHEN . . 34A KING JOHN/PS PROSE
BUT NOW FULL TO THE SETTING SUN . . . . 41B THEN SHE BORE PROSE
THEY ARE GENERALLY FULL OF PAPER [FOR XXX ?PERSON] . 86B ANNO LAVATER * MARG
[THE AGED TIRIEL COULD NOT SPEAK HIS HEART WAS FULL OF 101 TIRIEL 2 44
GRIEF]
FULL OF JOY . . . . 123 SPRING/SI 11
& THE AIR WAS FULL OF THEM & SEEMD COMPOSED OF THEM . . 156B MARRIAGE HH 17 PROSE
THOU HAST A LAP FULL OF SEED . . . . 168 HAST LAP/N 1
THEN THOU WITH THY LAP FULL OF SEED . . . . 255 AHANIA 5 29
WITH THY HAND FULL OF GENEROUS FIRE . . . . 255 AHANIA 5 30
BUT COVET WAS POURED FULL . . . . 256 BOOK OF LOS 3 14
DARK GREW HIS GLOBE REDDNING WITH MISTS & FULL BEFORE HIS 319 FOUR ZOAS 6 296
PATH
I HEAR THE FLAIL OF URIZEN HIS BARNS ARE FULL NO (ROOM) 375 FOUR ZOAS 9 * 696
FULL FILLED ALL WITH GEMS & GOLD . . . . 425 MENTAL TRAVLER 31
ALL HE KNOWS FROM OTHERS MUST BE FULL OF CONTRADICTIONS 449B ANNO REYNOLDS MARG
HE IS LIKE SR JOSHUA FULL OF SELF-CONTRADICTION & KNAVERY 459D ANNO REYNOLDS MARG
THE ARMY OF ARMED ROMANS THE FIGURES FULL AS LARGE AS LIFE 560A EXHIBITION ADV PROSE
BUT IN HIS OFFICE HE IS SAID TO BE A "FULL SOLEMN MAN" . 568D DESC CAT 3 PROSE
THEY ALSO ARE "FULL SOLEMN MEN" AND THEIR COUNSEL . . 570C DESC CAT 3 PROSE
OPINION FOR FULL NINE AND TWENTY MAY SIGNIFY ONE MORE OR 572A DESC CAT 3 PROSE
LIKE THE FULL GALLOP OF THE GOUTY MAN TO THE ORDINARY WALK 593A PUB ADDRESS/N PROSE
SOME VISION PILGRIM'S PROGRESS IS FULL OF IT THE GREEK 604D V LAST JUDG/N PROSE
POETS
THE GOBLIN CROP FULL FLINGS OUT OF DOORS FROM . . . . 618C ILLUS MILTON PROSE
[TO THE FULL AS ENTHUSIASTICALLY AS I HAVE WHO ACKNOWLEDGE 621A JERUSALEM 3 *PROSE
MINE]

```
                                                          PAGE       TITLE          LINE
FULL    (CONTINUED)
    MR BLAKE'S COMPTS TO MR REVELEY THO FULL OF WORK  . . . .  790A LETTER 1          PROSE
    HE HAS SENT IT BACK WITH A LETTER FULL OF CRITICISMS  . .  794D LETTER 6         *PROSE
    HEAVY BOXES & PORTFOLIOS FULL OF PRINTS AND NOW BEGINS  .  802B LETTER 14         PROSE
    SO FULL OF THE BUSINESS OF SETTLING THE STICKS & FEATHERS  804A LETTER 16         PROSE
      OF
    GLADLY I HEAR OF HIS FULL HEALTH AND SPIRITS  . . . . .   807B LETTER 17          PROSE
    WITH TREES & FIELDS FULL OF FAIRY ELVES . . . . . . .     816  HAPPINESS/L          5
    FILLD FULL OF HOPES FILLD FULL OF FEARS    . . . . . .    817  HAPPINESS/L         20
    FILLS ME FULL OF SMILES OR TEARS . . . . . . . . .       817  HAPPINESS/L         26
    HOWEVER THIS I KNOW WILL SET YOU AT EASE I AM NOW SO FULL  820C LETTER 25          PROSE
    I WRITE IN GREAT HASTE & WITH A HEAD FULL OF BOTHERATION  821B LETTER 25          PROSE
    LONDON WITH THE FULL APPROBATION OF MR HAYLEY & WITH  . .  822C LETTER 26          PROSE
    MY HEART IS FULL OF FUTURITY I PERCIEVE  . . . . . . .   823B LETTER 26          PROSE
    EXPECT A FULL ACCOUNT OF ALL HE CAN COLLECT MR SANDERS  .  847D LETTER 44          PROSE
    HIS WHAT HE CAN WILL BE FULL AS MUCH AS HE PRETENDS  . .  853A LETTER 51         *PROSE
    BEAUTIFUL POEM MUST NOW AFFORD YOU THEIR FULL REWARD  . .  854B LETTER 53          PROSE
    THE FULL HISTORY OF MY SPIRITUAL SUFFERINGS TO THE DWELLERS  862D LETTER 60        PROSE
    TOM DRAWINGS IN FULL TO THIS DAY . . . . . . . .         SUPP LETTER 61E         *PROSE
FULL-BLOWN
    THAT MY FULL-BLOWN SAILS OVERSET ME NOT . . . . . . .     27 EDW THIRD/PS 3       239
FULL-FEEDING
    IN THE DAY OF FULL-FEEDING PROSPERITY    . . . . . . .   247 SONG OF LOS 6         13
FULLNESS
    "PRIDE FULLNESS OF BREAD & ABUNDANCE OF IDLENESS" WAS THE  79D ANNO LAVATER        MARG
      SIN
FULLY
    OUR INCESSANT LABOUR FULLY ADEQUATE TO [IT] THEM AT PRESENT  811D LETTER 22       PROSE
    UNEASY FOR I AM FULLY EMPLOYD & WELL PAID I HAVE MADE  . .  819D LETTER 25         PROSE
    SHALL BE MADE FULLY APPARENT & PERFECT IN ETERNITY IN THE  822C LETTTR 26         PROSE
    BEING FULLY EMPLOYD IN ENGRAVING FOR HIS PROJECTED WORKS  824C LETTER 27          PROSE
FULNESS
    SHALL LAUGH WHOSE FRUITFUL LAPS BEND DOWN WITH FULNESS  .   33 EDW THIRD/PS 6       48
FUMBLE
    IT IS ONLY FUMBLE & BUNGLE WHICH CANNOT DRAW A LINE  . .  603C PUB ADDR AD/N       PROSE
FUMES
    THUS THEY CONFERRD AMONG THE INTOXICATING FUMES OF MYSTERY  328 FOUR ZOAS 7        315
    INSPIRING SECRECY & LAMPS THEY BORE INTOXICATING FUMES  .   333 FOUR ZOAS 7B        28
    AND HE DOTH RULE OVER ME THEREFORE MY SOUL IN FUMES OF     780 GHOST ABEL 2          8
      BLOOD
FUN
    YES SAID THE EPICUREAN & HAVING A BIT OF FUN WITH HIM  . .  45C ISLAND MOON 1      PROSE
    TWILL MAKE A FOOL LAUGH & A FAIRY FUN   . . . . . . .    552 TELL YOU WHA/N          6
    CONCEPTION OF THE HUMOUR AND FUN THAT OCCURS ON THE JOURNEY  569A DESC CAT 3       PROSE
    THE FUN AFTERWARDS EXHIBITED ON THE ROAD MAY BE SEEN  . .  588C CHAUCER/N          PROSE
    AS THEY DO FUN I LOVE BUT TOO MUCH FUN IS OF ALL THINGS   793C LETTER 5           PROSE
    THE MOST LOATHSOM MIRTH IS BETTER THAN FUN . . . . . .   793C LETTER 5           PROSE
FUNCTION
    WHOSE EVRY FUNCTION IS FILLD WITH ITS FIERY DESIRE . . .  142 FRENCH REVOLTN       183
FUNCTIONS
    THEY MUST RENEW THEIR BRIGHTNESS & THEIR DISORGANIZD      366 FOUR ZOAS 9          371
      FUNCTIONS
FUNERAL
    IN SILKEN GARMENTS SPUN BY HER OWN HANDS AGAINST         362 FOUR ZOAS 9          213
      HER FUNERAL
    IN THE POTTER'S FURNACE AMONG THE FUNERAL URNS OF BEULAH  684 JERUSALEM 53          28
    BURST THE BOTTOMS OF THE GRAVES & FUNERAL ARKS OF BEULAH  736 JERUSALEM 89          60
    SUCH AS THE FLOWERS OF BEULAH WEAVE TO BE THEIR FUNERAL   736 JERUSALEM 90           7
      MANTLES
    [FUNERAL GRANTED TO SIR JOSHUA FOR HAVING ?DESTROYD ART]  SUPP ANNO REYNOLDS  * MARG
FUNGUS
    HE WAS SUSPENDED IN A FUNGUS  . . . . . . . . . .       156A MARRIAGE HH 17   PROSE
FUNNIEST
    AND HE IS THE FUNNIEST FELLOW  . . . . . . . . . .       53A ISLAND MOON 8    PROSE
FUNNY
    VERY PRITTY & FUNNY [ABOUT LONDON O NO] ABOUT MATCHES  . .  54D ISLAND MOON 9   *PROSE
    HM SAID THE LAWGIVER FUNNY ENOUGH . . . . . . . . .       62B ISLAND MOON 11   PROSE
FURBISH
    FURBISH OUR ARMOURS BRIGHT NEW PLUME OUR HELMS   . . . .   24 EDW THIRD/PS 3      147
FURIES
    ("HURRIED ON BY FURIES OF IMMATURE IMPETUOUS WISHES")     85D ANNO LAVATER       MARG
      UNEASY
    RED RAGE THE FURIES OF PIERCE ORC BLACK THUNDERS ROLL ROUND  335 FOUR ZOAS 7B      78
      LOS
    WILD FURIES FROM THE TYGER'S BRAIN & FROM THE LION'S EYES  363 FOUR ZOAS 9        236
    THE FURIES BY THREE MEN & NOT BY THREE WOMEN  . . . . .  608A V LAST JUDG/N     PROSE
    CITY OF DIS QUEEN OF ENDLESS WOE [XXX] FURIES &   . . . .  786A ILLS DANTE 101  *PROSE
FURIOUS
    HOWLING LIKE GHOSTS FURIOUS AS WOLVES   . . . . . . .     11 GWIN KING/PS         27
    WHEN THE RED LIGHTNING BORNE BY FURIOUS STORMS   . . . .   32 EDW THIRD/PS 6       28
    PITY FORSOOK THEE AT THY BIRTH O DAGON FURIOUS   . . . .   38C SAMSON/PS         PROSE
    THROUGH THE LAND IT RUNS ROLLING WITH FURIOUS NOISE  . .   41C THEN SHE BORE     PROSE
    . . . A WHIRLWIND AND FIRE TORE FURIOUS FROM HIS ANGRY    143 FRENCH REVOLTN      200
      BOSOM
    AND CATCH FOR THEE THE GIRLS OF MILD SILVER OR OF FURIOUS GOLD  194 V DAU ALBION 7  24
    FOUR WINGED HERALDS MOUNT THE FURIOUS BLASTS & BLOW THEIR  205 AMERICA CANC C      14
      TRUMPS
    [LIKE] IN HIS DESOLATE MOUNTAINS RIFTED FURIOUS   . . . .  222 URIZEN 3         *   11
    ROUND THE FURIOUS LIMBS OF LOS . . . . . . . . . .       227 URIZEN 8               6
    WHIRLING ABOUT IN FURIOUS CIRCLES ROUND THE IMMORTAL FIEND  240 EUROPE 4           30
    AND THINE EYES REJOICE BECAUSE OF STRENGTH O RINTRAH     240 EUROPE 8             12
      FURIOUS KING
```

```
                                                              PAGE     TITLE            LINE
FURIOUS   (CONTINUED)
     ARISE AROUND HIM IN THE CLOUDY HEAVENS OF ALBION FURIOUS     243 EUROPE 12            35
     THE FURIOUS TERRORS FLEW AROUND    . . . . . . . . .         245 EUROPE 15             4
     FLAMD FURIOUS SPARKLES HIS HAIR & BEARD  . . . . . . .       249 AHANIA 2              3
     WITH HIS HORNS HE PUSHD FURIOUS    . . . . . . . . . .       250 AHANIA 3             17
     RAGING FURIOUS THE FLAMES OF DESIRE  . . . . . . . . .       256 BOOK OF LOS 3        27
     HURLS APART STAMPING FURIOUS TO DUST . . . . . . . . .       257 BOOK OF LOS 4        20
     IN FURIOUS TORRENTS BEGAN    . . . . . . . . . . .           259 BOOK OF LOS 4        67
     THAT GLOWD FURIOUS IN THE EXPANSE  . . . . . . . . .         259 BOOK OF LOS 5         9
     LOS ANSWERD FURIOUS ART THOU ONE OF THOSE WHO WHEN MOST      273 FOUR ZOAS 1         331
        COMPLACENT
     AFAR INTO THE ZENITH HIGH BENDING THY FURIOUS COURSE   .  .  278 FOUR ZOAS 1         495
     GLOWD FURIOUS ON THE ANVIL PREPARD FOR SPADES & COULTERS     278 FOUR ZOAS 1         520
        ALL
     THE VEHICLES OF LIGHT THEY SEPARATE THE FURIOUS PARTICLES    284 FOUR ZOAS 2         154
     FURIOUS & TERRIBLE THEY SPORT & ?REND THE NETHER DEEPS   .   289 FOUR ZOAS 2       * 359
     AND LUVAH IN THE LOINS OF LOS A DARK & FURIOUS DEATH    .  . 292 FOUR ZOAS 3          22
     LOS ANSWERD IN HIS FURIOUS PRIDE SPARKS ISSUING FROM HIS     298 FOUR ZOAS 4          34
        HAIR
     IN SCORN STOOD LOS RED SPARKS OF BLIGHTING FROM HIS FURIOUS  293 FOUR ZOAS 4          48
        HEAD
     OF IRON GLOWD FURIOUS PREPARD FOR SPADES & MATTOCKS  . . .   300 FOUR ZOAS 4          91
     DREAMER OF FURIOUS OCEANS COLD SLEEPER OF WEEDS & SHELLS     301 FOUR ZOAS 4         135
     I WILL COMPELL THEE TO REBUILD BY THESE MY FURIOUS WAVES     301 FOUR ZOAS 4         151
     SO SAYING THARMAS ON HIS FURIOUS CHARIOTS OF THE DEEP   .  . 301 FOUR ZOAS 4         157
     IN MIGHTY POWER ROUND HIM LOS ROLLD FURIOUS    . . . . .     302 FOUR ZOAS 4         175
     MELT INTO THIN AIR WHILE THE SEED DRIVN BY THE FURIOUS WIND  305 FOUR ZOAS 5          10
     HOWLD IN THE FURIOUS WIND HE THOUGHT TO GIVE TO ENITHARMON   309 FOUR ZOAS 5         152
     SOOTHING OR FURIOUS NO ONE ANSWERD EVERY ONE WRAPD UP   .  . 315 FOUR ZOAS 6         127
     FOUR WINGED HERALDS MOUNT THE FURIOUS BLASTS & BLOW THEIR    319 FOUR ZOAS 6         310
        TRUMPS
     HERE BOUND TO FIERY MANGERS FURIOUS DASH THEIR GOLDEN HOOFS  320 FOUR ZOAS 7           7
     I RAGE FURIOUS IN THE DEEP FOR LO MY FEET & HANDS ARE NAILD  322 FOUR ZOAS 7          87
     GIVE ME EXAMPLE OF THY MILDNESS KING OF FURIOUS HAIL STORMS  323 FOUR ZOAS 7         145
     LOS FURIOUS ANSWERD SPECTRE HORRIBLE THY WORDS ASTOUND       329 FOUR ZOAS 7         361
        MY EAR
     WHO WHEN CONVINCD CAN STILL PERSIST THO FURIOUS              329 FOUR ZOAS 7         363
        CONTROLLABLE
     . . . [SWEET] REFUGE FROM FURIOUS WAR    . . . . . . .       331 FOUR ZOAS 7         436
     THE REAPER IN BOTH ARMS EMBRACING THE FURIOUS RAGING FLAMES  332 FOUR ZOAS 7         463
     THE MOON HIS FURIOUS FOREHEAD CIRCLED WITH BLACK BURSTING    334 FOUR ZOAS 7B         41
        THUNDERS
     THARMAS LAUGHD FURIOUS AMONG THE BANNERS CLOTHD IN BLOOD     334 FOUR ZOAS 7B         49
     TO DECIEVE THARMAS IN HIS RAGE TO SOOTHE HIS FURIOUS SOUL    338 FOUR ZOAS 7B        226
     SO THARMAS WAILD [THEN ?FURIOUS] WRATHFUL THEN . . .         339 FOUR ZOAS 7B      * 259
     CURSING THE VOICE THAT MOCKD HIM WITH FALSE HOPE IN FURIOUS  339 FOUR ZOAS 7B        260
        MOOD
     HOWLING IN ALL THE NOTES OF WOE TO STAY HIS FURIOUS RAGE     339 FOUR ZOAS 7B        262
     STAMPING THE HILLS WADING OR SWIMMING FLYING FURIOUS OR      339 FOUR ZOAS 7B        263
        FALLING
     HIS FURIOUS NECK (WRITHING) CONTORTIVE IN DIRE BUDDING       343 FOUR ZOAS 8       *  72
        PAINS
     TO MOPING VISAGES RETURNING INANIMATE THO FURIOUS   . . .    344 FOUR ZOAS 8         125
     THY FURIOUS POWER BE OUR FATHER & OUR LOVED KING  . . . .    345 FOUR ZOAS 8         163
     SITTING WITHIN HIS TEMPLE FURIOUS FELT THE (NUMMING) STUPOR  345 FOUR ZOAS 8         180
     THARMAS [ABOVE] ON HIGH RODE FURIOUS THRO THE AFFLICTED      353 FOUR ZOAS 8         485
        WORLDS
     SEE YOU NOT ALL THIS WRACKING FURIOUS CONFUSION  . . . .     360 FOUR ZOAS 9         128
     STANDS IN THE FURIOUS AIR HE CRIES THE CHILDREN OF SIX       363 FOUR ZOAS 9         252
        THOUSAND YEARS
     WHO DIED IN INFANCY RAGE FURIOUS A MIGHTY MULTITUDE RAGE     363 FOUR ZOAS 9         253
        FURIOUS
     THE FURIOUS WIND STILL RENDS AROUND THEY FLEE IN SLUGGISH    363 FOUR ZOAS 9         256
        EFFORT
     JOY THRILLD THRO ALL THE FURIOUS FORM OF THARMAS HUMANIZING  373 FOUR ZOAS 9       * 613
     THEN THARMAS TOOK THE WINNOWING FAN THE WINNOWING WIND       374 FOUR ZOAS 9         654
        FURIOUS
     THEN SHALL THEY LIFT THEIR INNOCENT HANDS & STROKE HIS       376 FOUR ZOAS 9         703
        FURIOUS NOSE
     IN THE JINGLING TRACES FURIOUS LIONS SOUND THE SONG OF JOY   376 FOUR ZOAS 9         718
     FLAMD ABOVE ALL THE PLOWED FURROWS ANGRY RED AND FURIOUS     488 MILTON 8             36
     WHICH NOW FLAMD HIGH & FURIOUS IN SATAN AGAINST PALAMABRON   489 MILTON 9             11
     HIS SPECTRE RAGING FURIOUS DESCENDED INTO ITS SPACE  . . .   490 MILTON 9             52
     THE SPECTRE OF SATAN HE FURIOUS REFUSES TO REPOSE IN SLEEP   493 MILTON 13             2
     SO LOS SPOKE FURIOUS THEY DESCENDED TO BOWLAHOOLA            509 MILTON 24            44
        & ALLAMANDA
     HAND SITS BEFORE HIS FURNACE SCORN OF OTHERS & FURIOUS       626 JERUSALEM 7          71
        PRIDE
     ASTONISHD AT HIS BEAUTY & PERFECTION THOU FORGAVEST HIS      643 JERUSALEM 20         37
        FURIOUS LOVE
     THEN LOS GREW FURIOUS RAGING WHY STAND WE HERE TREMBLING     672 JERUSALEM 43         12
        AROUND
     RIVERS THUNDERD AGAINST THEIR BANKS LOUD WINDS FURIOUS       686 JERUSALEM 55         24
        FOUGHT
     FURIOUS IN PRIDE OF SELFHOOD THE TERRIBLE SPECTRES           690 JERUSALEM 58         48
        OF ALBION
     IRELAND TO JAPAN FURIOUS HER LIONS & TYGERS & WOLVES SPORT   698 JERUSALEM 63         34
        BEFORE
     SO SANG SHE AND THE SPINDLE TURND FURIOUS AS SHE SANG   .  . 722 JERUSALEM 80         32
     TO REACH THE HEAVENLY ARCHES LOS BEHELD UNDAUNTED FURIOUS    738 JERUSALEM 91         42
     HOWLING WINDS COVER HIM ROARING SEAS DASH FURIOUS AGAINST    741 JERUSALEM 94          3
        HIM
```

FURIOUS   (CONTINUED)
    AND BURSTING FORTH [WITH] HIS FURIOUS IRE . . . . . .   749 EV GOSPEL(B)/N   33
FURNACE
    [COULD FETCH IT FROM THE FURNACE DEEP] . . . .   172 THE TYGER/N 1   13
    IN WHAT FURNACE WAS THY BRAIN . . . .   172 THE TYGER/N 1   19
    OF IRON HEATED IN THE FURNACE HIS TERRIBLE LIMBS WERE FIRE   197 AMERICA 4   9
    IN FLAMES AS OF A FURNACE ON THE LAND FROM NORTH TO SOUTH   201 AMERICA 12   12
    IN WHAT FURNACE WAS THY BRAIN . . . .   214 THE TYGER/SE   14
    THE HUMAN FACE A FURNACE SEALD . . . .   221 DIVNE IMAGE/SE   7
    HIS THUNDEROUS WHEELS FROM FURNACE TO FURNACE TENDING   302 FOUR ZOAS 4   176
       DILIGENT
    THE FINGER OF GOD TOUCH THE SEVENTH FURNACE IN TERROR . 304 FOUR ZOAS 4   277
    HIS LOINS INWOVE WITH SILKEN FIRES ARE LIKE A FURNACE   308 FOUR ZOAS 5   135
       FIERCE
    THE CAVE OF ORC STOOD TO THE SOUTH A FURNACE OF DIRE FLAMES 318 FOUR ZOAS 6   265
    THE SURREY HILLS GLOW LIKE THE CLINKERS OF THE FURNACE 485 MILTON 6   14
       LAMBETH'S VALE
    THE FURNACE OF LOS BEFORE THE EASTERN GATE BENDING THEIR 623 JERUSALEM 5   28
       FURY
    THE MALE IS A FURNACE OF BERYLL THE FEMALE IS A GOLDEN LOOM 623 JERUSALEM 5   34
    VALA COMES FROM THE FURNACE IN A CLOUD BUT WRETCHED LUVAH 626 JERUSALEM 7   38
    HAND SITS BEFORE HIS FURNACE SCORN OF OTHERS & FURIOUS 626 JERUSALEM 7   71
       PRIDE
    HUMBER & TRENT ROLL DREADFUL BEFORE THE SEVENTH FURNACE 636 JERUSALEM 16   16
    OF ROUGH UNHEWN ROCKS BEFORE THE POTTER'S FURNACE .   653 JERUSALEM 28   22
    UPON THE HILLS OF ALBION OXFORD GROANS IN HIS IRON FURNACE 671 JERUSALEM 42   58
    LOS ALSO SAW HER IN HIS SEVENTH FURNACE HE ALSO TERRIFIED 678 JERUSALEM 48   44
    SAW THE FINGER OF GOD GO FORTH UPON HIS SEVENTH FURNACE 678 JERUSALEM 48   45
    WITH THEIR WINGS THEY SAT IN THE FURNACE IN A NIGHT . . . 681 JERUSALEM 50   19
    IN THE POTTER'S FURNACE AMONG THE FUNERAL URNS OF BEULAH 684 JERUSALEM 53   28
    . . . IN THE MIDST OF HIS ANGER IN FURNACE OF FIRE . . . 694 JERUSALEM 61   13
    ARISE AS THE SMOKE OF THE FURNACE SHAKING THE ROCKS FROM 708 JERUSALEM 70   14
       SEA TO SEA
    IN FIRES OF BEAUTY MELTING THEM AS GOLD & SILVER IN THE 709 JERUSALEM 70   28
       FURNACE
    PRIMROSE HILL IS THE MOUTH OF THE FURNACE & THE IRON DOOR 714 JERUSALEM 73   54
    THEY ARE BROKEN LOUD HOWL THE SPECTRES IN HIS IRON FURNACE 719 JERUSALEM 78   9
    LOS SAW THE ENVIOUS BLIGHT ABOVE HIS SEVENTH FURNACE . 726 JERUSALEM 82   56
    AND WITH THE BLAST OF HIS FURNACE UPON FISHY BILLINGSGATE 726 JERUSALEM 82   59
    THE ENVY LOUD SHE LABOURD IN THE FURNACE OF FIRE . . . 726 JERUSALEM 82   62
    AS HE WALKS FROM FURNACE TO FURNACE DIRECTING THE   730 JERUSALEM 85   20
       LABOURERS
    THUS LOS SINGS UPON HIS WATCH WALKING FROM FURNACE   731 JERUSALEM 86   33
       TO FURNACE
    HAND HAD HIS FURNACE ON HIGHGATE'S HEIGHTS & IT REACHD . . 736 JERUSALEM 90   23
    FOR THE MALE IS A FURNACE OF BERYLL THE FEMALE IS A GOLDEN 736 JERUSALEM 90   27
       LOOM
FURNACE-MOUTH
    DARK GLEAMS BEFORE THE FURNACE-MOUTH A HEAP OF BURNING 485 MILTON 6   17
       ASHES
FURNACES
    AND HEATED HIS FURNACES & POURD . . . .   228 URIZEN 10   29
    FURNACES HE FORMED AN ANVIL . . . .   259 BOOK OF LOS 5   21
    WHILE ROARING HIS FURNACES ENDURD . . . .   260 BOOK OF LOS 5   39
    THE INNUMERABLE SONS & DAUGHTERS OF LUVAH CLOSD IN FURNACES 276 FOUR ZOAS 1   423
    THEY ERECTED THE FURNACES . . . .   281 FOUR ZOAS 2   30
    IN MOUNTAINOUS MASSES PLUNGD IN FURNACES & THEY SHUT & 282 FOUR ZOAS 2   67
       SEALD
    THE FURNACES A TIME & TIMES ALL THE WHILE BLEW THE NORTH 282 FOUR ZOAS 2   68
    LUVAH WAS CAST INTO THE FURNACES OF AFFLICTION & SEALED 282 FOUR ZOAS 2   72
    AND VALA FED IN CRUEL DELIGHT THE FURNACES WITH FIRE . 282 FOUR ZOAS 2   73
    VALA INCIRCLE ROUND THE FURNACES WHERE LUVAH WAS CLOSD . 282 FOUR ZOAS 2   77
    HEAR YE THE VOICE OF LUVAH FROM THE FURNACES OF URIZEN . 282 FOUR ZOAS 2   80
    BENEATH THE FURNACES A WOFUL HEAP IN LIVING DEATH . . 283 FOUR ZOAS 2   116
    THEN WERE THE FURNACES UNSEALD WITH SPADES & PICKAXES . 283 FOUR ZOAS 2   117
    TAKE THOU THE HAMMER OF URTHONA REBUILD THESE FURNACES . 301 FOUR ZOAS 4   149
    THEN LOS WITH TERRIBLE HANDS SIEZD ON THE RUIND FURNACES 301 FOUR ZOAS 4   165
    BELCHD FROM THE FURNACES WREATHD ROUND HER CHAIND   302 FOUR ZOAS 4   188
       IN CEASELESS FIRE
    THE VOICE OF LOS COMPELLD HE LABOURD ROUND THE FURNACES 302 FOUR ZOAS 4   198
    LOS BEAT ON HIS FETTERS & [POUR] HEATED HIS FURNACES . 303 FOUR ZOAS 4   213
    AND LOS BEHELD THE HAND OF GOD OVER HIS FURNACES . . . 304 FOUR ZOAS 4   278
    LOS FROM THE FURNACES A SPACE IMMENSE & LEFT THE COLD . 305 FOUR ZOAS 5   15
    PRINCE OF LIGHT BOUND IN CHAINS OF INTELLECT AMONG THE 305 FOUR ZOAS 5   16
       FURNACES
    BUT ALL THE FURNACES WERE OUT & THE BELLOWS HAD CEAST TO 305 FOUR ZOAS 5   17
       BLOW
    BURN LIKE TWO FURNACES HE CALLD WITH VOICE OF THUNDER . 319 FOUR ZOAS 6   309
    IN GOLGONOOZA'S FURNACES AMONG THE ANVILS OF TIME AND SPACE 345 FOUR ZOAS 8   186
    IN GOLGONOOZA LOS'S ANVILS STAND & HIS FURNACES RAGE . 346 FOUR ZOAS 8   202
    I HAVE BENT DOWNWARD WITH LEAD MOLTEN IN MY ROARING   349 FOUR ZOAS 8   304
       FURNACES
    MY SOUL IS SEVEN FURNACES INCESSANT ROARS THE BELLOWS . 349 FOUR ZOAS 8   * 305
    SHE STOOD BEFORE LOS IN HER PRIDE [ABOVE] AMONG THE   350 FOUR ZOAS 8   * 345
       FURNACES
    TO THE DELUSIVE FEMALE FORMS SHINING AMONG HIS FURNACES 350 FOUR ZOAS 8   350
    AROUND THE FURNACES & IN EVENING SPORT UPON THE PLAINS . 379 FOUR ZOAS 9   842
    WHILE THE FEMALES PREPARE THE VICTIMS THE MALES AT FURNACES 484 MILTON 5   15
    THE FURNACES LAMENTING AROUND THE ANVILS & THIS THEIR SONG 484 MILTON 5   18
    TO CLAIM THE HELLS MY FURNACES I GO TO ETERNAL DEATH . 496 MILTON 14   32
    AND VALA LABOURS FOR HER BREAD & WATER AMONG THE FURNACES 501 MILTON 19   43
    TO THROW HIM INTO THE FURNACES KNOWEST THOU NOT THAT HE 505 MILTON 22   32

```
                                                             PAGE    TITLE        LINE
FURNACES    (CONTINUED)
    IN BOWLAHOOLA LOS'S ANVILS STAND & HIS FURNACES RAGE    . .   509 MILTON 24          51
    THE FURNACES THE STOMACH FOR DIGESTION TERRIBLE THEIR FURY     509 MILTON 24          59
    IN LOS'S HALLS CONTINUAL LABOURING IN THE FURNACES            520 MILTON 31          26
        OF GOLGONOOZA
    IN AMMON MOLECH LOUD HIS FURNACES RAGE AMONG THE WHEELS        528 MILTON 37          21
    ITS FURNACES OF AFFLICTION IN WHICH HIS ANGELS & EMANATIONS    529 MILTON 38          20
    THEN LOUD THE FURNACES OF LOS WERE HEARD & SEEN AS SEVEN       531 MILTON 39          14
        HEAVENS
    THEY WAR TO DESTROY THE FURNACES TO DESOLATE GOLGONOOZA        623 JERUSALEM 5        29
    THEY REVOLVE INTO THE FURNACES SOUTHWARD & ARE DRIVEN FORTH    623 JERUSALEM 5        31
        NORTHWARD
    THE STARRY WHEELS REVOLVD HEAVILY OVER THE FURNACES  . . .    624 JERUSALEM 5        46
    OUT FROM THE FURNACES OF LOS ABOVE THE HEAD OF LOS   . . .    624 JERUSALEM 5        50
    WHICH REVOLVE HEAVILY IN THE MIGHTY VOID ABOVE THE FURNACES    624 JERUSALEM 5        53
    INCESSANT BEFORE THE FURNACES AND HIS EMANATION DIVIDED        624 JERUSALEM 5        67
        IN PAIN
    A HORRIBLE SHADOW OF DEATH AMONG THE FURNACES BENEATH   . .    625 JERUSALEM 7         4
    O THOU SEEST NOT WHAT I SEE WHAT IS DONE IN THE FURNACES       625 JERUSALEM 7        28
    LUVAH WAS CAST INTO THE FURNACES OF AFFLICTION AND SEALED      625 JERUSALEM 7        30
    AND VALA FED IN CRUEL DELIGHT THE FURNACES WITH FIRE   . .    625 JERUSALEM 7        31
    VALA INCIRCLE ROUND THE FURNACES WHERE LUVAH WAS CLOSD  . .    626 JERUSALEM 7        35
    IS HOWLING IN THE FURNACES IN FLAMES AMONG ALBION'S           626 JERUSALEM 7        39
        SPECTRES
    BE ATTENTIVE BE OBEDIENT LO THE FURNACES ARE READY            627 JERUSALEM 8         9
        TO RECIEVE THEE
    I WILL BREAK THEE INTO SHIVERS & MELT THEE IN THE FURNACES     627 JERUSALEM 8        10
        OF DEATH
    LOS OPEND THE FURNACES IN FEAR THE SPECTRE SAW TO BABEL        627 JERUSALEM 8        23
        & SHINAR
    HE SAW THAT LOS WAS THE SOLE UNCONTROLLD LORD OF              627 JERUSALEM 8        26
        THE FURNACES
    I LIFTED THEM INTO MY FURNACES TO FORM THE SPIRITUAL SWORD     628 JERUSALEM 9        18
    LOUD ROAR MY FURNACES AND LOUD MY HAMMER IS HEARD   . . .     628 JERUSALEM 9        25
    THUS THEY CONTENDED AMONG THE FURNACES WITH GROANS & TEARS     628 JERUSALEM 9        32
    TILL THE SPACES OF ERIN WERE PERFECTED IN THE FURNACES  . .    628 JERUSALEM 9        34
    INTO THE FURNACES & INTO THE VALLEYS OF THE ANVILS OF         629 JERUSALEM 10         1
        DEATH
    TILL HIS SONS & DAUGHTERS CAME FORTH FROM THE FURNACES  . .    630 JERUSALEM 10        64
    THEN ERIN CAME FORTH FROM THE FURNACES & ALL THE DAUGHTERS     630 JERUSALEM 11         8
        OF BEULAH
    CAME FROM THE FURNACES BY LOS'S MIGHTY POWER FOR              630 JERUSALEM 11         9
        JERUSALEM'S
    UPON MY FURNACES FROM WITHIN THE WHEELS OF ALBION'S SONS       631 JERUSALEM 12        11
    SUCH WERE THE LAMENTATIONS OF THE LABOURERS IN THE FURNACES    631 JERUSALEM 12        16
    TERRIFIED AT THE SUBLIME WONDER LOS STOOD BEFORE             631 JERUSALEM 12        21
        HIS FURNACES
    CLAY BAKD & ENAMELD ETERNAL GLOWING AS FOUR FURNACES   . .    632 JERUSALEM 12        64
    AMONG THE FURNACES OF LOS IN THE VALLEY OF THE SON            636 JERUSALEM 15        34
        OF HINNOM
    LABOUR WITHIN THE FURNACES WALKING AMONG THE FIRES   . .     637 JERUSALEM 16        20
    SCOTLAND POURS OUT HIS SONS TO LABOUR AT THE FURNACES   . .    637 JERUSALEM 16        22
    TO MAKE A WAY FOR THE CHILDREN OF LOS TO COME FROM THE        638 JERUSALEM 17         5
        FURNACES
    AND SAW HIS FURNACES IN RUINS FOR LOS IS THE DEMON OF THE      658 JERUSALEM 32         6
        FURNACES
    HE OPEND HIS FURNACES BEFORE VALA THEN ALBION FROWND IN        660 JERUSALEM 34        19
        ANGER
    AND THE DIVINE VOICE CAME FROM THE FURNACES AS MULTITUDES      662 JERUSALEM 35         3
        WITHOUT
    AND THE APPEARANCE OF A MAN WAS SEEN IN THE FURNACES   . .    662 JERUSALEM 35         5
    SO SPOKE THE VOICE FROM THE FURNACES DESCENDING INTO         662 JERUSALEM 35        17
        NON-ENTITY
    BEFORE THE FURNACES OF LOS IN A HORRIBLE DREAMFUL SLUMBER      662 JERUSALEM 36        11
    ROLLS DREADFUL THRO THE FURNACES OF LOS AND THE MILLS OF       665 JERUSALEM 38        37
        SATAN
    BROODING ON EVIL BUT WHEN LOS OPEND THE FURNACES BEFORE HIM    669 JERUSALEM 42         2
    ALSO LOS SICK & TERRIFIED BEHELD THE FURNACES OF DEATH  . .    669 JERUSALEM 42         5
    LOS STOOD BEFORE HIS FURNACES AWAITING THE FURY OF THE DEAD    671 JERUSALEM 42        55
    THUS MOURN THEY LOUD THE FURNACES OF LOS THUNDER UPON   . .    671 JERUSALEM 42        75
    AND LOS DREW HIS SEVEN FURNACES AROUND ALBION'S ALTARS  . .    671 JERUSALEM 42        77
    AMONG THE FURNACES OF LOS AMONG THE OAKS OF ALBION   . . .    674 JERUSALEM 44        37
    BOWING THEIR HEADS DEVOTED AND THE FURNACES OF LOS   . . .    676 JERUSALEM 46        20
    UPON THE FURNACES AND LOUD THE FURNACES REBELLOW BENEATH       676 JERUSALEM 46        22
    WHERE LOS'S FURNACES STAND WHERE JERUSALEM & VALA HOWL  . .    677 JERUSALEM 47         3
    AS HE SAT BEFORE HIS FURNACES CLOTHD IN SACKCLOTH OF HAIR      684 JERUSALEM 53         5
    TRANSLUCENT THE FURNACES OF BERYLL & EMERALD IMMORTAL   . .    684 JERUSALEM 53         9
    THE FURNACES THE STOMACH FOR DIGESTION TERRIBLE THEIR FURY     684 JERUSALEM 53        13
    IN ETERNAL LABOURS LOUD THE [ FURNAES ] FURNACES & LOUD        684 JERUSALEM 53    *    20
        THE ANVILS
    TO BE POUNDED TO DUST & MELTED IN THE FURNACES OF            687 JERUSALEM 55        59
        AFFLICTION
    CATHEDRON'S LOOMS ARE BUILDED AND LOS'S FURNACES IN THE        691 JERUSALEM 59        23
        SOUTH
    IN FLAMING FIRE WITHIN THE FURNACES THE DIVINE VISION         692 JERUSALEM 60         5
        APPEARD
    ON ALBION'S HILLS OFTEN WALKING FROM THE FURNACES IN CLOUDS    692 JERUSALEM 60         6
    BUT LOS BEHELD THE DIVINE VISION AMONG THE FLAMES OF THE       696 JERUSALEM 62        35
        FURNACES
    LOS BEHELD IN TERROR HE POURD HIS LOUD STORMS ON             702 JERUSALEM 66        16
        THE FURNACES
    I HAVE BENT DOWNWARD WITH LEAD MELTED IN MY ROARING          705 JERUSALEM 67        50
        FURNACES
```

		PAGE	TITLE	LINE

FURNACES (CONTINUED)

MY SOUL IS SEVEN FURNACES INCESSANT ROARS THE BELLOWS . . 705 JERUSALEM 67 52
AND LOS'S FURNACES HOWL LOUD LIVING SELF-MOVING LAMENTING 713 JERUSALEM 73 2
THRO ALL THE FOUR POINTS LO THE LABOURERS AT THE FURNACES 713 JERUSALEM 73 4
OF DEATH BUT HOW THEY CAME FORTH FROM THE FURNACES & HOW 713 JERUSALEM 73 7
LONG
OPENS THE FURNACES OF AFFLICTION IN THE EMANATION . . . 713 JERUSALEM 73 25
FROM LONDON TO YORK & EDINBURGH THE FURNACES RAGE TERRIBLE 714 JERUSALEM 73 53
CLIFFS DIVIDING THEM INTO MALE & FEMALE FORMS IN 719 JERUSALEM 78 7
HIS FURNACES
SITTING BEFORE HIS FURNACES CLOTHED IN SACKCLOTH OF HAIR 719 JERUSALEM 78 11
AND LET THE LOOMS OF ENITHARMON & THE FURNACES OF LOS . . 725 JERUSALEM 82 26
IN THE FURNACES OF LOS & IN THE WINE-PRESS TREADING DAY 726 JERUSALEM 82 64
& NIGHT
TO FEED THE AFFLICTED IN THE FURNACES SHE MINDED NOT . . 726 JERUSALEM 82 66
TOWARDS LONDON THEN THEY SAW THE (FURNACES) OPEND & IN 726 JERUSALEM 82 78
TEARS
BEGAN TO GIVE THEIR SOULS AWAY IN THE (FURNACES) 727 JERUSALEM 82 79
OF AFFLICTION
LOS SAW & WAS COMFORTED AT HIS FURNACES UTTERING THUS HIS 727 JERUSALEM 82 80
VOICE
THE SONS OF ALBION GO FORTH I FOLLOW FROM MY FURNACES . . 728 JERUSALEM 83 62
LISTEN TO YOUR WATCHMAN'S VOICE SLEEP NOT BEFORE 728 JERUSALEM 83 64
THE FURNACES
BEFORE THE FURNACES LABOURING WHILE LOS ALL NIGHT WATCHES 729 JERUSALEM 83 80
FOR JERUSALEM LIES IN RUINS & THE FURNACES OF LOS 729 JERUSALEM 84 6
ARE BUILDED THERE
AMONG HIS FURNACES DIRECTING HIS LABORIOUS MYRIADS WATCHFUL 730 JERUSALEM 85 11
AS HE WATCHES THE FURNACES BY NIGHT & DIRECTS THE LABOURERS 730 JERUSALEM 85 13
AT HIS FURNACES HIS DAUGHTERS AT THEIR LOOMS SING WOES . . 731 JERUSALEM 86 38
WITHOUT BECOMING HIS CHILDREN IN THE FURNACES OF AFFLICTION 732 JERUSALEM 86 49
AMONG THE DARKNESS OF HIS FURNACES DIVIDING ASUNDER TILL 732 JERUSALEM 86 56
RUBIES JACINTHS CRYSOLITES ISSUING FROM THY FURNACES WHILE 732 JERUSALEM 87 20
LOS ANSWERD SIGHING LIKE THE BELLOWS OF HIS FURNACES . . 733 JERUSALEM 88 1
THE FURNACES OF LOS LOUD ROLL THE WHEELS OF ENITHARMON . 734 JERUSALEM 88 54
AND THE DRAGON OF THE RIVER & THE FURNACES OF IRON . . . 735 JERUSALEM 89 19
IN MY FURNACES INTO ONE NATION THE ENGLISH & TAKING REFUGE 739 JERUSALEM 92 2
THIS SINFUL NATION CREATED IN OUR FURNACES & LOOMS 739 JERUSALEM 92 6
IS ALBION
BENEATH THE FURNACES & THE STARRY WHEELS & THE IMMORTAL 741 JERUSALEM 94 2
TOMB
REVOLVE & OVER THEM THE FURNACES OF LOS & THE IMMORTAL 741 JERUSALEM 94 12
TOMB AROUND
BENEATH THE FURNACES & STARRY WHEELS AND IN THE IMMORTAL 742 JERUSALEM 94 19
TOMB
SO ALBION SPOKE & THREW HIMSELF INTO THE FURNACES 744 JERUSALEM 96 35
OF AFFLICTION
ALL WAS A VISION ALL A DREAM THE FURNACES BECAME . . . 744 JERUSALEM 96 36

FURNACES'

[THE BELLOWING ?FURNACES' BLARE BY THE LONG SOUNDING 346 FOUR ZOAS 8 * 204
CLARION]
THE BELLOWING FURNACES' BLARE BY THE LONG SOUNDING CLARION 509 MILTON 24 64

FURNISH

THIS GROUPE ALSO WOULD FURNISH SUBSTANTIAL MATTER . . . 571A DESC CAT 3 PROSE
IMAGINATION ONLY CAN FURNISH US WITH COLOURING APPROPRIATE 580D DESC CAT 5 PROSE
NOW LET ME INTREAT YOU TO GIVE ME ORDERS TO FURNISH EVERY 808B LETTER 19 PROSE
FOR NOT BEING ABLE TO FURNISH ANY DESIGNS YOU WILL READILY 853A LETTER 51 *PROSE

FURNISHD

HE FURNISHD IT WITHIN . . . . 57 TO BE OR/IM 10
FURNISHD BY JOHNSON I LET HIM RUN ON SO FAR AS TO SAY THAT 846D LETTER 44 PROSE
BY ASKING IF HE KNEW WHO FURNISHD THE PAPER HE ANSWERED 846D LETTER 44 PROSE

FURNITURE

AND THE HERBS & FLOWERS & FURNITURE & BEDS & CHAMBERS . 512 MILTON 26 34
PREPARE THE FURNITURE O LAMBETH IN THY PITYING LOOMS . 632 JERUSALEM 12 38
FOR COMFORT THERE THE SECRET FURNITURE OF JERUSALEM'S 632 JERUSALEM 12 40
CHAMBER
THE FURNITURE OF THEIR HOUSES WAS THE FURNITURE OF MY 720 JERUSALEM 79 47
CHAMBER

FUROR

IN PERIODS OF PULSATIVE FUROR MILLS HE FORMD & WORKS . . 302 FOUR ZOAS 4 182
IN PERIODS OF PULSATIVE FUROR BEATING INTO [BARS] WEDGES 346 FOUR ZOAS 8 * 207
& BARS

FURRD

DRIVEN OUT BY THE FLAMES OF ORC HIS FURRD ROBES & FALSE 242 EUROPE 12 16
LOCKS

FURROW

BESIDE THE OX TO THY HARD FURROW DOES NOT THAT MILD BEAM 195 V DAU ALBION 8 4
BLOT
TILL MICHAEL SAT DOWN IN THE FURROW WEARY DISSOLVD IN TEARS 488 MILTON 8 37
THE PLOWED FURROW LISTNING TO THE WEEPING CLODS TILL WE 687 JERUSALEM 55 43
AND MANY CONVERSED ON THESE THINGS AS THEY LABOURD AT THE 687 JERUSALEM 55 48
FURROW
SUBSERVIENT TO THE CLODS OF THE FURROW THE CATTLE AND EVEN 688 JERUSALEM 56 36
THE LIVING CREATURES MADDEND AND ALBION FELL INTO 689 JERUSALEM 57 13
THE FURROW AND
COMPELLING URIZEN TO HIS FURROW & THARMAS TO HIS SHEEPFOLD 742 JERUSALEM 95 16

FURROWD

. . . FURROWD WITH PLOWS WHOSE SEED IS DEPARTING FROM HER 138 FRENCH REVOLTN 99
FURROWD WITH WHIPS & OUR FLESH BRUISED WITH THE HEAVY 286 FOUR ZOAS 2 226
BASKET
THE FURROWD FIELD REPLIES TO THE GRAVE I HEAR HER REPLY 355 FOUR ZOAS 8 548
TO ME

```
                                                          PAGE    TITLE         LINE

FURROWD    (CONTINUED)
     IN FURROWD LIGHTNINGS BREAK THEIR WAY . . .   . . . .   359 FOUR ZOAS 9       85
     NOR DARKNESS IMMINGLED WITH LIGHT ON MY FURROWD FIELD  . .  659 JERUSALEM 33   32
FURROWS
     . . . NOR OUR SHOULDERS BE PLOWD WITH THE FURROWS         142 FRENCH REVOLTN  174
        OF POVERTY
     MINGLE IN HOWLING PAINS IN FURROWS BY THY LIGHTNINGS RENT  196 AMERICA PREL 2  16
     FEET BLEEDING ON THE SULTRY SANDS AND THE FURROWS OF THE   197 AMERICA 3       11
        WHIP
     FEET BLEEDING ON THE SULTRY SANDS & THE FURROWS OF THE WHIP 204 AMERICA CANC A 11
     MELT INTO FURROWS WINTER BLOWS HIS BELLOWS ICE & SNOW  . .  276 FOUR ZOAS 1   424
     AND ALL THE WHILE THE PLOW OF IRON CUT THE DREADFUL FURROWS 282 FOUR ZOAS 2    70
     HE TRIES THE SULLEN NORTH WIND RIDING ON ITS ANGRY FURROWS  355 FOUR ZOAS 8   564
     FLAMD ABOVE ALL THE PLOWED FURROWS ANGRY RED AND FURIOUS    488 MILTON 8       36
     BETWEEN HIS PALMS AND FILLING UP THE FURROWS OF MANY YEARS  500 MILTON 19      11
     ARE BECOME WEAK VISIONS OF TIME & SPACE FIXD INTO FURROWS   679 JERUSALEM 49   22
        OF DEATH
     HARD & OBDURATE ARE THE FURROWS OF THE MOUNTAIN OF WINE     719 JERUSALEM 79    6
        & OIL
FURTHER
     & THE PRIDE OF GREECE AND FURTHER FROM THE RISING SUN  . .   41A THEN SHE BORE PROSE
     TO BEAR ME FURTHER URGE ME NOT LEST I SHOULD DIE           104 TIRIEL 4        33
        WITH TRAVEL
     SHE COULD NO FURTHER GO . . . . . . . . . . .             114 LIT GRL FND/SI   20
     AND AN ANALYSIS OF THE MORE SUBLIME BUT NO FURTHER  . . .  158A MARRIAGE HH 21 PROSE
     HITHERTO SHALT THOU COME NO FURTHER HERE THY PROUD WAVES   298 FOUR ZOAS 4     35
        CEASE
     THE STARRY HEAVENS REACH NO FURTHER BUT HERE BEND AND SET  516 MILTON 29       10
     SO NEAR TO FELPHAM PARIS BEING SCARCE FURTHER OFF THAN     811A LETTER 21     PROSE
        LONDON
     NO FURTHER MY FRIEND THAN HE IS COMPELLD BY CIRCUMSTANCES  819C LETTER 25     PROSE
     TO TAKE A HOUSE IN SOME VILLAGE FURTHER FROM THE SEA  . .  820D LETTER 25     PROSE
FURTHERMORE
     I HAVE FURTHERMORE THE PLEASURE OF INFORMING YOU THAT HE   836B LETTER 35     PROSE
FURTHEST
     . . . AS FURTHEST NORTH IS FROM THE FURTHEST SOUTH  . . .  309 FOUR ZOAS 5    184
FURY
     O THOU TO WHOSE FURY THE NATIONS ARE . . . . . . . . .      17 EDW THIRD/PS 1    1
     THOUDST LAUGH HIS FURY INTO NERVELESS SHAME . . . . .       25 EDW THIRD/PS 3  177
     BURNING UP NATIONS IN YOUR WRATH AND FURY . . . . . .       31 EDW THIRD/PS 6    6
     WHEN THE WHIRLWIND OF FURY COMES FROM THE . . . . . .       33 EDW FOURTH/PS    6
     ADVANCING TOWARD US WITH ALL THE FURY OF A SPIRITUAL       156C MARRIAGE HH 17 PROSE
        EXISTENCE
     I FEARD THE [ROUGHNESS] FURY OF MY WIND . . . . . . .      166 I FEARD FURY/N    1
     [WERE THY EYES OF FURY ROLLD] . . . . . . . . . . .        172 THE TYGER/N 1    17
     SHAKING THEIR MENTAL CHAINS THEY RUSH IN FURY TO THE SEA   201 AMERICA 13        3
     FURY RAGE MADNESS IN A WIND SWEPT THROUGH AMERICA          201 AMERICA 14       10
     THE RED FIRES RAGD THE PLAGUES RECOILD THEN ROLLD THEY     202 AMERICA 14       20
        BACK WITH FURY
     RAGE FURY INTENSE INDIGNATION . . . . . . . . . .          225 URIZEN 4        45
     IN THE FLAMES OF ETERNAL FURY . . . . . . . . . .          225 URIZEN 5         2
     IN THE FLAMES OF ETERNAL FURY . . . . . . . . . .          225 URIZEN 5        18
     O LION RINTRAH RAISE THY FURY FROM THY FORESTS BLACK   .   240 EUROPE 8         2
     AND IN THE VINEYARDS OF RED FRANCE APPEARD THE LIGHT OF    245 EUROPE 15        2
        HIS FURY
     ROARING WITH FURY HE THREW . . . . . . . . . . .          249 AHANIA 2        17
     RAGD WITH CURSES & SPARKLES OF FURY . . . . . . .         256 BOOK OF LOS 3    33
     MOUNTING UP FROM HIS FURY CONDENSD . . . . . . .          256 BOOK OF LOS 3    35
     STAMPD IN FURY AND HOT INDIGNATION . . . . . . .          257 BOOK OF LOS 3    48
     INTO FIERY SPHERES FROM HIS FURY . . . . . . . .          257 BOOK OF LOS 4     2
     DEFORMD THRO THE THREE HEAVENS DESCENDING IN FURY & FIRE   267 FOUR ZOAS 1    104
     THE DAZZLINGS AS OF GEMS SHONE CLEAR RAPTUROUS IN [JOY]    267 FOUR ZOAS 1    128
        FURY
     TO POUR ITS FURY ON HIMSELF & ON THE ETERNAL MAN  . . .   279 FOUR ZOAS 1    540
     . . . DEMON OF FURY . . . . . . . . . . . . .            288 FOUR ZOAS 2    309
     IN JEALOUS FEARS IN FURY & RAGE . . . . . . . .          294 FOUR ZOAS 3     96
     CRYING FURY IN MY LIMBS DESTRUCTION IN MY BONES & MARROW   296 FOUR ZOAS 3    162
     FALL OFF AFAR FROM THARMAS COME NOT TOO NEAR MY STRONG FURY 296 FOUR ZOAS 3    173
     THOU RASH ABHORRED DEMON IN THY FURY HAST OERTHROWN  . .   299 FOUR ZOAS 4     52
     FROM DEATH IN WRATH & FURY BUT NOW COME BEAR BACK  . . .   300 FOUR ZOAS 4    116
     IN THUNDER SMOKE & SULLEN FLAMES & HOWLINGS & FURY & BLOOD  306 FOUR ZOAS 5     38
     CRACKLING THE FLAMES WENT UP WITH FURY FROM THE IMMORTAL   308 FOUR ZOAS 5    108
        DEMON
     NOW WILL I POUR MY FURY ON THEM & I WILL REVERSE  . . .   312 FOUR ZOAS 6     35
     AND HE CAME RIDING IN HIS FURY FROZE TO SOLID WERE HIS    313 FOUR ZOAS 6     49
        WAVES
     DANCE ON THE RIVERS & THE ROCKS HOWLING & DRUNK WITH FURY  320 FOUR ZOAS 7     13
     TENFOLD WITH FIERCE DESIRE TO REND THY CHAIN & HOWL IN FURY 321 FOUR ZOAS 7     66
     LOS WITH AMBITIOUS FURY THAT HIS RACE SHALL ALL DEVOUR  . . 323 FOUR ZOAS 7    134
     THOU DOST RESTRAIN MY FURY THAT THE WORM MAY FOLD THE TREE  323 FOUR ZOAS 7    141
     AND TURNING [WISDOM] AFFECTION INTO FURY & THOUGHT INTO    324 FOUR ZOAS 7    155
        ABSTRACTION
     RAVING ABOUT THE UPPER ELEMENTS IN MADDNING FURY . . . .   328 FOUR ZOAS 7  *  322
     MY LOVELY ENITHARMON I WILL QUELL MY FURY & TEACH  . . .   329 FOUR ZOAS 7    368
     WILT IN SWEET MODERATED FURY FABRICATE [SWEET] FORMS      331 FOUR ZOAS 7    453
        SUBLIME
     LOUD SOUNDS THE WAR SONG ROUND RED ORC IN HIS [TRIUMPHANT] 336 FOUR ZOAS 7B  * 144
        FURY
     IN FURY A SERPENT WONDROUS AMONG THE CONSTELLATIONS OF     342 FOUR ZOAS 8     68
        URIZEN
     TO GRATE THE SOUL INTO DESTRUCTION OR TO INFLAME WITH FURY  344 FOUR ZOAS 8    136
     CALLD DOWN A GREAT SOLEMN ASSEMBLY RINTRAH IN FURY & FIRE  351 FOUR ZOAS 8  * 389
```

775

PAGE TITLE   LINE

FURY (CONTINUED)
 NO LONGER NOW ERECT THE KING OF LIGHT OUTSTRETCHD IN FURY 352 FOUR ZOAS 8   438
 AMONG THE STARS THE EARTH & ALL THE ABYSSES FEEL ?HIS FURY 352 FOUR ZOAS 8 * 448
 COVERS THE DEEPS AT HIS VAST FURY (MOANING) IN HIS ROCK 352 FOUR ZOAS 8 * 450
 THEN WEEPING HE DESCENDS IN WRATH DRAWING ALL THINGS IN 353 FOUR ZOAS 8   456
  HIS FURY
 FOR NOW FIERCE ORC IN WRATH & FURY RISES INTO THE HEAVENS 353 FOUR ZOAS 8   460
 A KING OF WRATH & FURY A DARK ENRAGED HORROR . . . . 353 FOUR ZOAS 8   462
 HAVE SHOT THEIR ARROWS OR LONG BEAMED SPEARS IN WRATH & 358 FOUR ZOAS 9   41
  FURY
 BUT SIN EVEN RAHAB IS REDEEMD IN BLOOD & FURY & JEALOUSY 361 FOUR ZOAS 9   159
 DOWN DOWN THRO THE IMMENSE WITH OUTCRY FURY & DESPAIR . . 376 FOUR ZOAS 9   723
 WERE MADDEND WITH TORMENTING FURY & THE SERVANTS OF THE 487 MILTON 7   20
  HARROW
 THE GNOMES ACCUSD SATAN WITH INDIGNATION FURY AND FIRE . 487 MILTON 7   21
 RAGD WITH THICK FLAMES REDUNDANT & THE HARROW MADDEND WITH 487 MILTON 7   46
  FURY
 THEY BIT IN THEIR WILD FURY WHO ALSO MADDEND LIKE WILDEST 487 MILTON 7   49
  BEASTS
 FOR SATAN FLAMING WITH RINTRAH'S FURY HIDDEN BENEATH HIS 489 MILTON 9   19
  OWN MILDNESS
 WILD WITH PROPHETIC FURY HIS FORMER LIFE BECAME LIKE A 493 MILTON 12   45
  DREAM
 AND THEY LAMENTED THAT THEY HAD IN WRATH & FURY & FIRE . . 504 MILTON 21   31
 HIS TERRORS NOW POSSESD ME WHOLE I AROSE IN FURY & STRENGTH 505 MILTON 22   14
 REMEMBER HOW CALVIN AND LUTHER IN FURY PREMATURE . . . 507 MILTON 23   47
 OF PALAMABRON'S HARROW & OF RINTRAH'S WRATH & FURY . . . 508 MILTON 24   1
 THE FURNACES THE STOMACH FOR DIGESTION TERRIBLE THEIR FURY 509 MILTON 24   59
 WITH RINTRAH & PALAMABRON IN HIS FIRES OF RESISTLESS FURY 510 MILTON 25   2
 WE FORM THE MUNDANE EGG THAT SPECTRES COMING BY FURY OR 511 MILTON 25   42
  AMITY
 THESE MILLS ARE OCEANS CLOUDS & WATERS UNGOVERNABLE IN 514 MILTON 27   52
  THEIR FURY
 IN THE GREAT WARS OF ETERNITY IN FURY OF POETIC INSPIRATION 519 MILTON 30   19
 CUT OFF MY LOVES IN FURY TILL I HAVE NO LOVE LEFT FOR THEE 522 MILTON 33   7
 ARE YOU THE FIERY CIRCLE THAT LATE DROVE IN FURY & FIRE 523 MILTON 34   3
 SHE FROWND LIKE A FURY & SAID PATRONAGE . . . . . . 554 ASKD PRIGG/N   19
 THE FURNACE OF LOS BEFORE THE EASTERN GATE BENDING THEIR 623 JERUSALEM 5   28
  FURY
 IN FURY THEN HE SAT DOWN AND WEPT TERRIFIED THEN AROSE . . 625 JERUSALEM 6   10
 OF GOD WOULD LOOK UPON ME AND PITY ME IN MY FURY . . . 626 JERUSALEM 7   60
 FOR I AM ONE OF THE LIVING DARE NOT TO MOCK MY INSPIRED 627 JERUSALEM 8   35
  FURY
 SO LOS IN FURY & STRENGTH IN INDIGNATION & BURNING WRATH 629 JERUSALEM 10   22
 HIS SPECTRE DIVIDES & LOS IN FURY COMPELLS IT TO DIVIDE 638 JERUSALEM 17   1
 BUT LOS HIMSELF AGAINST ALBION'S SONS HIS FURY BENDS FOR HE 638 JERUSALEM 17   6
 HYLE SEES IN FEAR HE HOWLS IN FURY OVER THEM HAND SEES . . 644 JERUSALEM 21   28
 IN JEALOUS FEARS & FURY & RAGE & FLAMES ROLL ROUND THEIR 655 JERUSALEM 29   75
  FERVID FEET
 THOU WILT CERTAINLY PROVOKE MY SPECTRE AGAINST THINE IN 664 JERUSALEM 37   5
  FURY
 CONSIDER ME AS THINE ENEMY ON ME TURN ALL THY FURY . . . 670 JERUSALEM 42   40
 LOS STOOD BEFORE HIS FURNACES AWAITING THE FURY OF THE DEAD 671 JERUSALEM 42   55
 MACHINES IN FURY & DESTRUCTION AND THE MAN REVIVING 675 JERUSALEM 45   22
  REPENTED
 WAS CAUGHT UP WITH THE SUN IN ONE DAY OF FURY AND WAR . . 679 JERUSALEM 49   16
 THE FURNACES THE STOMACH FOR DIGESTION TERRIBLE THEIR FURY 684 JERUSALEM 53   13
 HE BUILDED IT IN RAGE & IN FURY IT IS THE SPIRITUAL 684 JERUSALEM 53   18
  FOURFOLD
 TWO CONTRARIES WAR AGAINST EACH OTHER IN FURY & BLOOD . . 690 JERUSALEM 58   15
 MADDENS IN THE FURY OF THEIR HANDS WEAVING IN BITTER TEARS 692 JERUSALEM 59   54
 DOST THOU NOT MURDER ME JOSEPH SPOKE IN ANGER & FURY SHOULD 694 JERUSALEM 61   5
  I
 EUROPE & ASIA & AFRICA & AMERICA IN FURY FOURFOLD . . . 712 JERUSALEM 72   31
 WITH FURY & DESPAIR & THEY STRETCH FROM SOUTH TO NORTH . . 713 JERUSALEM 73   3
 FURY & THUNDERING COURSE ROUND HEAVEN & EARTH . . . . . 717 STOOD AMONG/J   6
 AND RESTLESS FURY MAN HIMSELF SHRUNK UP . . . . . . 717 STOOD AMONG/J   10
 AND THE FURY OF MAN EXHAUST IN WAR WOMAN PERMANENT REMAIN 725 JERUSALEM 82   35
 MARCHING THRO EGYPT IN HIS FURY THE EAST IS PALE AT HIS 729 JERUSALEM 84   22
  COURSE
 SO DREAD IS LOS'S FURY THAT NONE DARE HIM TO APPROACH . . 732 JERUSALEM 86   48
 THE FOUR ZOAS IN ALL THEIR FADED MAJESTY BURST OUT IN FURY 734 JERUSALEM 88   55
 HEATED IN THE SMITH'S FORGE BUT COLD THE WIND OF THEIR 735 JERUSALEM 89   42
  DREAD FURY
 SEEING THIS FALSE CHRIST IN FURY & PASSION . . . . . . 756 EV GOSPEL(G)/N   1
 THE FURY OF MY COURSE AMONG THE STARS OF GOD . . . . . 816A LETTER 23   PROSE
 WAS UTTERD IN THE HEAT OF THEIR FURY BY EITHER OF 827C LETTER 28   PROSE
  THE DRAGOONS
 INSANITY AND FURY AND WHATEVER PALTRY COLD HEARTED CRITICS 864B LETTER 61   PROSE
 A MR BLAIR A SURGEON HAS WITH THE COLD FURY OF ROBESPIERRE 865A LETTER 62   PROSE
FURZE
 OVER THE HEATH & THE FURZE . . . . 164 HEARD ANGEL/N   10
FUSELI
 FUSELI INDIGNANT ALMOST HID HIMSELF I [?WAS] AM HID . . . 445C ANNO REYNOLDS * MARG
 I THINK (THAT) BARRY OR FUSELI WROTE IT OR [?SAID] DICTATED 463C ANNO REYNOLDS * MARG
  IT
 YOU THINK FUSELI IS NOT A GREAT PAINTER IM GLAD . . . . 538 TO H(UNT)/N   1
 THEY NEVER CAN RAFAEL IT FUSELI IT NOR BLAKE IT . . . . 549 ALL PICTURES/N   5
 WAS FUSELI HE WAS BOTH TURK & JEW . . . . 551 ONLY MAN/N   3
 CAN WOUND MR FUSELI OVER MY SHOULDER . . . . . . 592D PUB ADDRESS/N   PROSE
 LIKE FUSELI & MICHAEL ANGELO SHAKESPEARE & MILTON . . . 595D PUB ADDRESS/N   PROSE
 BEEN PUBLISHD EVEN JOHNSON & FUSELI HAVE DISCARDED 795C LETTER 6   PROSE
  MY GRAVER

		PAGE	TITLE	LINE
FUSELI	**(CONTINUED)**			
POOR FUSELI SORE FROM THE LASH OF ENVIOUS TONGUES	. . .	798B	LETTER 10	PROSE
WHEN FLAXMAN WAS TAKEN TO ITALY FUSELI WAS GIVEN TO ME FOR A SEASON		799	TO FLAXMAN/L	3
THIS FROM JOHNSON & FUSELI BROUGHT ME DOWN HERE	. . . .	812C	LETTER 22	PROSE
AND BUTTS SHALL GIVE WHAT FUSELI GAVE	. . . . . .	817	HAPPINESS/L	39
I HAVE GOT TO WORK AFTER FUSELI FOR A LITTLE SHAKESPEARE		831B	LETTER 31	PROSE
FUSELI SHAKESPEARE IS WORTH (TWENTY-FIVE) GUINEAS THESE		848C	LETTER 45	PROSE
FUSELI IS MADE MASTER OF THE ROYAL ACADEMY	. . . . . .	859D	LETTER 56	PROSE
COUNT UGOLINO BY MR FUSELI IN THE ROYAL ACADEMY EXHIBITION		863D	LETTER 61	PROSE
SUCH AN ARTIST AS FUSELI IS INVULNERABLE HE NEEDS NOT MY		864A	LETTER 61	PROSE
ON VIEWING THE PICTURES OF MR FUSELI BUT THE TRUTH IS HE		864D	LETTER 61	PROSE
FUSELI'S				
YOU HID FUSELI'S MILTON IS SATAN TROUBLED AT HIS EXPOSURE		446A	ANNO REYNOLDS	MARG
THE NEGLECT OF FUSELI'S MILTON	. . . .	452B	ANNO REYNOLDS	MARG
THE SAME THAT FUSELI'S MILTON GALLERY WAS PAINTED FOR	.	821C	LETTER 25	PROSE
I HAVE INCLOSD FOR YOU THE...NUMBERS OF FUSELI'S SHAKESPEARE		836C	LETTER 35	PROSE
I SEND WASHINGTON'S (SECOND) VOL (FIVE) NUMBERS OF FUSELI'S		850B	LETTER 49	PROSE
OF FUSELI'S SHAKESPEARE THE CONCLUDING NUMBERS OF WHICH		853C	LETTER 52	PROSE
FUSELI'S COUNT UGOLINO IS THE FATHER OF SONS OF FEELING AND		864A	LETTER 61	PROSE
FUSELI'S COUNT UGOLINO IS A MAN OF WONDER AND ADMIRATION		864B	LETTER 61	PROSE
FUSTY				
AND THERE GOES MISS BELL WITH HER FUSTY OLD NUT	. . . .	434	LONG JOHN BRWN	20
FUTURE				
DESCEND TO GENERATIONS THAT IN FUTURE TIMES FORGET	. . .	197	AMERICA 3	12
DESCEND TO GENERATIONS THAT IN FUTURE TIMES FORGET	. . .	204	AMERICA CANC A	12
WHO PRESENT PAST & FUTURE SEES	. . . .	210	INTRODUCTN/SE	2
CHILDREN OF THE FUTURE AGE	. . . .	219	LIT GRL LST/SE	1
TRACES THE WONDERS OF FUTURITY IN HORRIBLE FEAR OF THE FUTURE		322	FOUR ZOAS 7	86
TO THE FOUR WINDS HOPELESS OF FUTURE ALL FUTURITY	. . .	343	FOUR ZOAS 8	99
WHEN SHALL THE MAN OF FUTURE TIMES BECOME AS IN DAYS OF OLD		360	FOUR ZOAS 9	115
IF SUCH A PERJURY AS THIS CAN TAKE EFFECT ANY VILLAIN IN FUTURE		438D	BLAKES MEMORAN	PROSE
FUTURE AGES THEY WILL AND SHALL FOOLISH MEN	. . . . .	452C	ANNO REYNOLDS	MARG
HIS FUTURE COURSE THRO DARKNESS AND DESPAIR TO ETERNAL DEATH		487	MILTON 7	26
OF HIS FINISHED PRODUCTIONS BY ANY CALUMNIES IN FUTURE	.	573A	DESC CAT 3	PROSE
I SEE THE PAST PRESENT & FUTURE EXISTING ALL AT ONCE	. .	635	JERUSALEM 15	8
WITH NOW & THEN AN ENGRAVING & FIND THAT IN FUTURE TO LIVE		798B	LETTER 10	PROSE
MY FINGERS EMIT SPARKS OF FIRE WITH EXPECTATION OF MY FUTURE LABOURS		801C	LETTER 13	PROSE
FULFILLED IN ME & IN FUTURE I AM THE DETERMINED ADVOCATE		804A	LETTER 16	PROSE
TO COME & TO SPEAK TO FUTURE GENERATIONS BY A SUBLIME ALLEGORY		825A	LETTER 27	PROSE
ILL-JUDGED CRITICISMS IN FUTURE YOURS	. . . .	864D	LETTER 61	PROSE
WITHOUT DISARRANGING MY TIME WHICH IN FUTURE MUST ALONE		865D	LETTER 63	PROSE
FUTURITY				
JOVE WEIGHS THE COUNSEL OF FUTURITY	. . . .	15	IMIT SPEN/PS	23
AND MY HEART LABOURS WITH FUTURITY	. . . .	32	EDW THIRD/PS 6	41
IN FUTURITY	. . . .	112	LIT GRL LST/SI	1
RESERVD FOR THE DAYS OF FUTURITY	. . . .	224	URIZEN 4	9
FILLD WITH IMMORTAL DEMONS OF FUTURITY	. . . .	241	EUROPE 9	10
I LABOUR UPWARDS INTO FUTURITY	. . . .	262B	SMALL BK DSGNS	TITLE
I SEE THE SHOWER OF BLOOD I SEE THE SWORDS & SPEARS OF FUTURITY		272	FOUR ZOAS 1	301
PALE HE BEHELD FUTURITY PALE HE BEHELD THE ABYSS	. . .	280	FOUR ZOAS 2	15
TERRIFIED WITH HIS HEART & SPIRIT AT THE VISIONS OF FUTURITY		287	FOUR ZOAS 2	293
WHY WILT THOU LOOK UPON FUTURITY DARKNING PRESENT JOY	. .	291	FOUR ZOAS 3	11
LEAVE ALL FUTURITY TO HIM RESUME THY FIELDS OF LIGHT	. .	292	FOUR ZOAS 3	30
PROPHETIC DREADS URGE ME TO SPEAK FUTURITY IS BEFORE ME		293	FOUR ZOAS 3	74
STEMMING HIS DOWNWARD FALL LABOURING UP AGAINST FUTURITY		316	FOUR ZOAS 6	186
OF ALL & ALL FUTURITY BE BOUND IN HIS VAST CHAIN	. . .	317	FOUR ZOAS 6	233
TRACES THE WONDERS OF FUTURITY IN HORRIBLE FEAR OF THE FUTURE		322	FOUR ZOAS 7	86
I VIEW FUTURITY IN THEE I WILL BRING DOWN SOFT VALA	. .	327	FOUR ZOAS 7	299
LEST ANY SHOULD IN FUTURITY DO AS WE HAVE DONE IN HEAVEN		331	FOUR ZOAS 7	430
TO THE FOUR WINDS HOPELESS OF FUTURE ALL FUTURITY	. . .	343	FOUR ZOAS 8	99
OF DARK MORTALITY NOR CAST MY VIEW INTO THE [PAST] FUTURITY NOR TURND		361	FOUR ZOAS 9	* 165
THEN GO O DARK [REMEMBRANCE] FUTURITY	. . . .	361	FOUR ZOAS 9	180
HEAVENS OF MY BRAIN NOR WILL I LOOK UPON [REMEMBRANCE] FUTURITY MORE		361	FOUR ZOAS 9	181
I CAST [REMEMBRANCE] FUTURITY AWAY & TURN MY BACK UPON THAT VOID		361	FOUR ZOAS 9	182
WHICH I HAVE MADE FOR LO [REMEMBRANCE] FUTURITY IS IN THIS MOMENT		362	FOUR ZOAS 9	183
MY HEART IS FULL OF FUTURITY I PERCIEVE	. . . .	823B	LETTER 26	PROSE
ON FUTURITY WHICH I CANNOT DO WITHOUT DOUBT & FEAR THAT		879C	LETTER 89	PROSE
FUZON				
LIKE THE GROUND PARCHD WITH HEAT THEN FUZON	. . . . .	234	URIZEN 23	17
SO FUZON CALLD ALL TOGETHER	. . . .	237	URIZEN 28	19
FUZON ON A CHARIOT IRON-WINGD	. . . .	249	AHANIA 2	1
SAID FUZON THIS ABSTRACT NON-ENTITY	. . . .	249	AHANIA 2	11
BUT THE FIERY BEAM OF FUZON	. . . .	250	AHANIA 2	44
THE BLACK CLOUDS ON THE BOSOM OF FUZON	. . . .	251	AHANIA 3	29
WHILE FUZON HIS TYGERS UNLOOSING	. . . .	251	AHANIA 3	36
ON FUZON FLEW ENTERD HIS BOSOM	. . . .	251	AHANIA 3	40
FUZON GROAND ON THE TREE	. . . .	253	AHANIA 4	44
AND ROUND THE TREE OF FUZON	. . . .	253	AHANIA 4	47

		PAGE	TITLE	LINE

FUZON'S
URIZEN NAILD FUZON'S CORSE . . . . 252 AHANIA 4   8

GAD
GAD ASHER ISSACHAR ZEBULUN JOSEPH BENJAMIN DAVID SOLOMON   350 FOUR ZOAS 8   361
THEN DAN THEN NAPHTALI THEN GAD THEN ASHER THEN ISSACHAR   350 FOUR ZOAS 8   376
EVEN AS REUBEN & AS GAD GAVE UP HIMSELF TO TEARS   . . . 503 MILTON 20   53
REUBEN & MANAZZOTH & GAD & SIMEON & LEVI   . . . . . . 508 MILTON 24   2
THE GATE OF NAPTHALI RADNORSHIRE THE GATE OF GAD   637 JERUSALEM 16   38
    PEMBROKESHIRE
GAD OXFORD BUCKS HARFORD ASHER SUSSEX HAMPSHIRE BERKSHIRE   637 JERUSALEM 16   47
GAD PEEBLES PERTH RENFRU ASHER SUTHERLAN STERLING WIGTOUN   638 JERUSALEM 16   56
THEY DRINK UP DAN & GAD TO FEED WITH MILK SKOFELD & KOTOPE   704 JERUSALEM 67   22
DAN NAPTHALI GAD ASHER ISSACHAR ZEBULUN ROLL APART   . . . 715 JERUSALEM 74 * 50
LEVI AND JUDAH & ISSACHAR EPHRAM MANASSEH GAD AND DAN   720 JERUSALEM 79   30
THERE IS REUBEN & GAD & JOSEPH & JUDAH & LEVI CLOSD UP   . . 721 JERUSALEM 79   64

GAIETY
HE IS A COMPLETE ROGUE WITH CONSTITUTIONAL GAIETY ENOUGH   568D DESC CAT 3   PROSE

GAIN
OR EVN THE LEAST BY BIRTH SHALL GAIN THE BRIGHTEST FAME   18 EDW THIRD/PS 1   30
AND GAIN BUT SCANTY FARE THEN MY DEAR LORD . . . . . . 19 EDW THIRD/PS 2   33
LOOKING TO THE GAIN OF THIS OUR NATIVE LAND   . . . . . 19 EDW THIRD/PS 2   35
THEY CAN AND MAY BUT HOW TO GAIN THEIR WILL   . . . . . 20 EDW THIRD/PS 2   72
& HAVE NO IDEA OF ANY BUT WORLDLY GAIN   . . . . 94A ANNO SWED LOVE   MARG
AND TO [SUCK] SULK WOULD NOTHING GAIN   . . . . 167 INFANT SORW/N * 10
AND LUVAH STROVE TO GAIN DOMINION OVER . . . . 293 FOUR ZOAS 3   79
STROVE IN TERRIFIC EMULATION WHICH SHOULD GAIN A PLACE   343 FOUR ZOAS 8   75
RESISTANCE & WAR IS THE TYRANT'S GAIN   . . . . 420 I SAW A MONK/N   52
FOR HE LOVD THEM FOR GAIN TO SERVE HIS ENDS   . . . . . 544 P LOVED NOT/N   2
[BUT] HE LOVED ME [BUT] AND FOR NO GAIN AT ALL   . . . . 544 P LOVED NOT/N   3
UNWORTHY MEN WHO GAIN FAME AMONG MEN . . . . 581D DESC CAT 8   PROSE
AND LUVAH STROVE TO GAIN DOMINION OVER ALBION   . . . . 655 JERUSALEM 29   61
MORE & MORE PERSWADED THAT EVERY MORTAL LOSS IS   797B LETTER 9   PROSE
    AN IMMORTAL GAIN

GAIND
MIDAS THE PRAISE HATH GAIND OF LENGTHEND [CARES] EARS   . . 14 IMIT SPEN/PS   15
THEM OVER AGAIN THEY WOULD LOSE AS MUCH AS THEY GAIND   . 815C LETTER 23   PROSE

GAINED
WHICH GAINED THAT PATRONAGE CRIED DOWN AS ECCENTRICITY   . . 572D DESC CAT 3   PROSE
BECAUSE CORPOREAL DEMONS HAVE GAINED A PREDOMINANCE   . . 581D DESC CAT 8   PROSE
THE FEW I HAVE PRINTED & SOLD ARE SUFFICIENT TO HAVE GAINED 867C LETTER 66   PROSE

GAINING
GAINING A NEW DOMINION OVER ALL HIS SONS & DAUGHTERS . . . 317 FOUR ZOAS 6   237

GAINS
OR IS IT BECAUSE SECRESY GAINS [FEMININE] FEMALES' LOUD   171 TO NOBODADDY/N   9
    APPLAUSE
AND FAVOUR GAINS WITH GOD & MEN   . . . . 748 EV GOSPEL(B)/N   12

GAINSBOROUGH
REYNOLDS & GAINSBOROUGH BLOTTED & BLURRED ONE AGAINST THE   445C ANNO REYNOLDS   MARG
GAINSBOROUGH TOLD A GENTLEMAN OF RANK & FORTUNE   . . . 465C ANNO REYNOLDS   MARG
I DESIRED THE GENTLEMAN TO SET GAINSBOROUGH ABOUT   . . . 465C ANNO REYNOLDS   MARG
THAT GAINSBOROUGH HAD IN MAKING THE ABOVE ASSERTION NAMELY   465D ANNO REYNOLDS   MARG
GENTRY TO CORREGGIO RUBENS REMBRANT REYNOLDS GAINSBOROUGH   548B ON GREAT ENC/N *TITLE
[THEN ?WHILE REYNOLDS ?& GAINSBOROUGH PXXXD & DXXX   SUPP ANNO REYNOLDS * MARG
    THEMSELVES]

GAINSBOROUGH'S
IN GAINSBOROUGH'S HANDS IT WOULD BE A VULGAR SUBJECT   . 465D ANNO REYNOLDS   MARG

GAINST
"HIS CANON GAINST SELF SLAUGHTER" SHAKESPEARE . . . . . SUPP LEGEND/N95   *

GALL
IN CATARACTS OF FIRE BLOOD & GALL . . . . 225 URIZEN 4   46

GALLANT
THOU HAST A GALLANT SPIRIT WHICH I FEAR   . . . . . . 20 EDW THIRD/PS 2   57
SMILES ON OUR ARMY AND THE GALLANT SUN   . . . . . . 21 EDW THIRD/PS 3   2
'TWILL BE A GALLANT THING TO FIGHT OR DIE   . . . . . 25 EDW THIRD/PS 3   152
METHINKS I SEE THEM ARM MY GALLANT SOLDIERS   . . . . 26 EDW THIRD/PS 3   224

GALLANTRY
KNIGHT WHOSE SOLEMN GALLANTRY NO LESS FIXES ATTENTION   . 588C CHAUCER/N   PROSE

GALLERIES
HE THEN WENT & TOOK DOWN LE BRUN'S & RUBENS'S GALLERIES   449C ANNO REYNOLDS   MARG

GALLERY
RUBENS'S LUXEMBOURG GALLERY IS CONFESSD ON ALL HANDS   . 599C PUB ADDRESS/N *PROSE
YOUR PLAN FOR A NATIONAL GALLERY BEING PUT INTO EXECUTION   797C LETTER 10   PROSE
THAN IN THE COLD GALLERY OF FASHION THE SUN   . . . . 812B LETTER 22   PROSE
THE SAME THAT FUSELI'S MILTON GALLERY WAS PAINTED FOR   . 821C LETTER 25   PROSE
OFFERING TO EXHIBIT MY (TWO) LAST PICTURES IN THE GALLERY   826C LETTER 28   PROSE
AND INCLOSE WITH THEM A CATALOGUE OF BELL'S GALLERY AND   844C LETTER 43   PROSE
TRUCHSESSIAN GALLERY OF PICTURES I WAS AGAIN ENLIGHTENED   852B LETTER 50   PROSE

GALLIC
BUT WE WILL BRING THESE GALLIC ROVERS UNDER   . . . . 21 EDW THIRD/PS 2   97

GALLOP
LIKE THE FULL GALLOP OF THE GOUTY MAN TO THE ORDINARY WALK   593A PUB ADDRESS/N   PROSE

GALLOWS
THE VILLAIN AT THE GALLOWS TREE   . . . . 542 PITIFUL CASE/N   1

GALWAY
GALWAY ROSCOMMON MAYO SLIGO LEITRIM   . . . . 711 JERUSALEM 72   24

GAMBLER
THE WHORE & GAMBLER BY THE STATE   . . . . 433 AUGURIES   113

GAMBOLD
THEN HE GAMBOLD ROUND . . . . 113 LIT GRL LST/SI   39

GAME
TILL TIRD OF CHAT THE GAME BEGINS . . . . 16 BLIND-MANS/PS   11
SUCH ARE THE FORTUNES OF THE GAME . . . . 17 BLIND-MANS/PS   61

GAME   (CONTINUED)

HOW CAN YOU HAVE THE FACE TO MAKE GAME OF MATRIMONY . . .   57A ISLAND MOON 9   PROSE
[AND TWIXT EARNEST & [GAME] JOKE] . . . . 163 ASKED THIEF/N   *   10
THE WILD GAME OF HER ROVING EYE   . . . . 426 MENTAL TRAVLER   71
THE GAME COCK CLIPD & ARMD FOR FIGHT . . . . 431 AUGURIES   17
BUT TO LOSE THEM THE FOOL MAKES HIS FOOLISH GAME . . . 547 LET BE TOLD/N   9
IF YOU PLAY A GAME OF CHANCE KNOW BEFORE YOU BEGIN   . . 551 IF YOU PLAY/N   1
AMONG HONEST PEOPLE TO MAKE GAME OF AND LAUGH AT THEM . 574D DESC CAT 3   PROSE

GANG

OPRESSION OF SR JOSHUA & HIS GANG OF CUNNING HIRED KNAVES 445B ANNO REYNOLDS   MARG

GAPING

THAN TO THE GAPING WORLD HE CARRIES WINDOWS   . . . . .   25 EDW THIRD/PS 3   186
DESIRING LIKE THE HUNGRY WORM & LIKE THE [SILENT] GAPING 376 FOUR ZOAS 9   735
    GRAVE

GARB

O WHAT AN HUMBLE GARB TRUE JOY PUTS ON . . . .   37A CONTEMPLATN/PS   PROSE

GARDEN

AND MNETHA HASTED & MET THEM AT THE GATE OF THE LOWER   109 TIRIEL 8   1
    GARDEN
BECOME A GARDEN MILD . . . . 112 LIT GRL LST/SI   8
OF HIM THAT WALKETH IN THE GARDEN IN THE EVENING TIME . . 127 BOOK OF THEL 1   14
I WENT TO THE GARDEN OF LOVE   . . . . 162 GARDEN LOVE/N   1
SO I TURND TO THE GARDEN OF LOVE . . . . 162 GARDEN LOVE/N   *   7
AND INTO MY GARDEN STOLE   . . . . 166 CHRISTN FORB/N   14
THE GARDEN OF LOVE   . . . . 215C GARDEN LOVE/SE   TITLE
I WENT TO THE GARDEN OF LOVE   . . . . 215 GARDEN LOVE/SE   1
SO I TURND TO THE GARDEN OF LOVE . . . . 215 GARDEN LOVE/SE   7
AND INTO MY GARDEN STOLE   . . . . 218 POISON TREE/SE   13
MET IN GARDEN BRIGHT   . . . . 219 LIT GRL LST/SE   12
AND HE PLANTED A GARDEN OF FRUITS   . . . . 234 URIZEN 20   41
ADAM STOOD IN THE GARDEN OF EDEN . . . . 245 SONG OF LOS 3   6
LAY BLEACHD ON THE GARDEN OF EDEN   . . . . 248 SONG OF LOS 7   21
SHE RISES FROM HIS THRONE AND SEEKS THE SHADOWS OF HER   272 FOUR ZOAS 1   286
    GARDEN
IMBODIED THOU MY GARDEN OF DELIGHT & I THE SPIRIT IN THE   327 FOUR ZOAS 7   272
    GARDEN
THARMAS REPLID O VALA ONCE I LIVD IN A GARDEN OF DELIGHT   339 FOUR ZOAS 7B   232
[IN EDEN IN THE GARDEN OF GOD & IN HEAVENLY JERUSALEM]   SUPP FOUR ZOAS 8   *
WHOSE SMOKE DESTROYD THE PLEASANT [GARDENS] GARDEN . . . 361 FOUR ZOAS 9   * 168
AND WALKD FROM THE HANDS OF URIZEN IN THE SHADOWS OF VALA'S 367 FOUR ZOAS 9   376
    GARDEN
YOU ANSWER NOT THEN AM I SET YOUR MISTRESS IN THIS GARDEN 368 FOUR ZOAS 9   429
INTO THIS BODILY HOUSE TO TEND MY FLOCKS IN MY PLEASANT   369 FOUR ZOAS 9   470
    GARDEN
SO SAYING THEY WENT DOWN INTO THE GARDEN AMONG THE FRUITS 371 FOUR ZOAS 9   535
HE SAID O VALA I AM SICK & ALL THIS GARDEN OF PLEASURE . . 371 FOUR ZOAS 9   538
TELL HER THAT VALA WAITS HER IN THE SHADOWS OF HER GARDEN 371 FOUR ZOAS 9   546
AND GARDEN FRUITFUL SEVENTY FOLD . . . . 425 MENTAL TRAVLER   28
THE GARDEN & ITS LOVELY CHARMS . . . . 426 MENTAL TRAVLER   60
THIS THE DAY AFTER MY TURNING HIM OUT OF THE GARDEN . . . 437B BLAKES MEMORAN PROSE
HE WAS BACKWARDS AND FORWARDS IN THE GARDEN   . . . . 437D BLAKES MEMORAN PROSE
THE GARDEN THE TRUTH IS I DID NOT SPEAK TO THE SOLDIER . . 438A BLAKES MEMORAN PROSE
TILL THEN & MY ORDERING HIM OUT OF THE GARDEN WAS . . . 438A BLAKES MEMORAN PROSE
THE TIME THAT I & THE SOLDIER WERE TOGETHER IN THE GARDEN 438A BLAKES MEMORAN PROSE
I THINK THAT THIS PROVES HIS HAVING COME INTO THE GARDEN   438A BLAKES MEMORAN PROSE
ALL THE REST OF THE TIME WHAT PASSED IN THE GARDEN THERE IS 438B BLAKES MEMORAN PROSE
TURNED THE SOLDIER OUT OF MY GARDEN I NEVER   . . . . 438D BLAKES MEMORAN PROSE
& BEAT US IN THE GARDEN OR USE US AS HE PLEASE . . . 439A BLAKES MEMORAN PROSE
MAN IS BORN LIKE A GARDEN READY PLANTED & SOWN . . . . 471A ANNO REYNOLDS   MARG
IS A GARDEN OF DELIGHT & A BUILDING OF MAGNIFICENCE . . . 512 MILTON 26   32
STANDING ON HIS OWN ROOF OR IN HIS GARDEN ON A MOUNT . . 516 MILTON 29   6
LARK MET THE FEMALE OLOLON DESCENDING INTO MY GARDEN . . 527 MILTON 36   10
FLASH OF LIGHTNING BUT MORE QUICK THE VIRGIN IN MY GARDEN 527 MILTON 36   19
WALKING IN MY COTTAGE GARDEN SUDDEN I BEHELD . . . . . 527 MILTON 36   26
DESCENDING DOWN INTO MY GARDEN A HUMAN WONDER OF GOD . . 528 MILTON 37   13
GARDEN CLOTHED IN BLACK SEVERE & SILENT HE DESCENDED . . 529 MILTON 38   8
WHAT IS IT THAT BUILDS A HOUSE AND PLANTS A GARDEN . . . 585C DESC CAT 15   PROSE
IS HIS GARDEN OF PLEASURE ALL THE SPECTRES OF HIS SONS   625 JERUSALEM 7   15
    MOCK THEE
OR IN THE PORCH OR GARDEN NO MORE THE SINFUL DELIGHTS . . 640 JERUSALEM 18   16
OF HATERS MET IN DEADLY STRIFE RENDING THE HOUSE & GARDEN 640 JERUSALEM 18   22
IN ALL THE GARDEN OF EDEN & IN ALL THE GOLDEN MOUNTAINS   652 JERUSALEM 28   2
I WAS A GARDEN PLANTED WITH BEAUTY I ALLURED ON HILL &   659 JERUSALEM 33   37
    VALLEY
IN EDEN IN THE GARDEN OF GOD AND IN HEAVENLY JERUSALEM . . 665 JERUSALEM 38   25
THE GOLDEN GATE OF HAVILAH AND ALL THE GARDEN OF GOD . . 679 JERUSALEM 49   15
THEY SPREAD FORTH LIKE A LOVELY ROOT INTO THE GARDEN OF GOD 692 JERUSALEM 60   15
IS A HOUSE OF (PLEASANTNESS) & A GARDEN OF DELIGHT BUILT   714 JERUSALEM 73   51
    BY THE
AS MY GARDEN & AS MY SECRET BATH SPAIN WAS MY HEAVENLY   720 JERUSALEM 79   40
    COUCH
SEE SISTERS CANAAN IS PLEASANT EGYPT IS AS THE GARDEN OF   725 JERUSALEM 82   30
    EDEN
ONCE A DID SO WHEN I PRAYD IN THE GARDEN   . . . . . . 753 EV GOSPEL(D)/N   89
ARISES FROM MY HAVING TURNED HIM OUT OF MY GARDEN . . . 826D LETTER 28   PROSE
DESIRED HIM AS POLITELY AS WAS POSSIBLE TO GO OUT OF THE   827A LETTER 28   PROSE
    GARDEN
THE GARDEN HE REFUSED I STILL PERSISTED IN DESIRING HIS   827A LETTER 28   PROSE
COMBAT HIS ASSERTION AS THE GARDENER REMAIND IN MY GARDEN 827D LETTER 28   PROSE
HE SAYS THAT THERE WERE SEVERAL ONE A GARDEN SCENE . . . 844C LETTER 43   PROSE
WITH UNCLE TOBY AND OBADIAH PLANTING IN THE GARDEN . . 844C LETTER 43   PROSE
I FOUND HIM BENEATH A TREE IN THE GARDEN   . . . . . . SUPP LEGEND/N63   *TITLE

```
                                                  PAGE    TITLE           LINE
GARDEN    (CONTINUED)
    MY PRETTY ROSE TREE THE GARDEN OF LOVE A LITTLE BOY LOST  SUPP LETTER 66A    *PROSE
GARDENER
    O NOBLE CHANDOS THINK THYSELF A GARDENER  . . . . . .    26 EDW THIRD/PS 3    210
    PART OF THE TIME MR HAYLEY'S GARDENER PART OF THE TIME   438B BLAKES MEMORAN  PROSE
    MR HAYLEY'S GARDENER CAME PAST AT THE TIME OF THE   . . . 438D BLAKES MEMORAN  PROSE
    INTO WHICH HE WAS INVITED AS AN ASSISTANT BY A GARDENER  827A LETTER 28       PROSE
       AT WORK
    OUTLINE I HAVE FOR WITNESSES THE GARDENER WHO IS HOSTLER  827C LETTER 28      PROSE
    COMBAT HIS ASSERTION AS THE GARDENER REMAIND IN MY GARDEN 827D LETTER 28      PROSE
GARDENING
    IN THE MOON AS PHEBUS STOOD OVER HIS ORIENTAL GARDENING   46C ISLAND MOON 3   *PROSE
       [ON]
GARDENS
    THE GARDENS OR SITS SINGING IN THE TREES  . . . . . .     2 TO AUTUMN/PS      15
    HE LED ME THROUGH HIS GARDENS FAIR  . . . . . . . .       6 HOW SWEET/PS       7
    MY THOUGHTS ARE ON MY GARDENS AND MY FIELDS  . . . . .   19 EDW THIRD/PS 2    22
    SOON AS THE BLIND WANDERER ENTERD THE PLEASANT GARDENS   100 TIRIEL 2         10
       OF HAR
    . . . AND WOO IN PLEASANT GARDENS  . . . . . . . . .     144 FRENCH REVOLTN   229
    FROWN ON THE GARDENS . . . . . . . . . . . . . .        145 FRENCH REVOLTN   252
    TELL ME WHAT IS A JOY & IN WHAT GARDENS DO JOYS GROW   . 191 V DAU ALBION 3   24
    I SEE INVISIBLE DESCEND INTO THE GARDENS OF VALA  . . .  272 FOUR ZOAS 1     299
    I HID HER IN SOFT GARDENS & IN SECRET BOWERS OF SUMMER   282 FOUR ZOAS 2      95
    REPROACH THEE & THE BEAMY GARDENS SICKEN AT THY BEAUTY . 288 FOUR ZOAS 2     303
    THE GARDENS OF WISDOM ARE BECOME A FIELD OF HORRID GRAVES 310 FOUR ZOAS 5    196
    ONCE HOW I WALKED FROM MY PALACE IN GARDENS OF DELIGHT . 310 FOUR ZOAS 5     198
    . . . & IN OUR GARDENS OF [PLEASURE] LABOUR  . . . . .   331 FOUR ZOAS 7     441
    AMONG THE APPLE TREES & ALL THE GARDENS OF DELIGHT  . . . 339 FOUR ZOAS 7B  *  234
    OF ENION IN THE GARDENS & THE SHADOWS COMPASSD ME   . . . 339 FOUR ZOAS 7B     236
    WHOSE SMOKE DESTROYD THE PLEASANT [GARDENS] GARDEN . . .  361 FOUR ZOAS 9   *  168
    HOW ARE YE THUS RENEWD & BROUGHT INTO THE GARDENS OF VALA 370 FOUR ZOAS 9     511
    OPEN THE ORBS OF THY BLUE EYES & SMILE UPON MY GARDENS .  371 FOUR ZOAS 9     522
    WITH THY BRIGHT TEARS BECAUSE THE STEPS OF ENION ARE IN   371 FOUR ZOAS 9     533
       THE GARDENS
    FOLLOW THE STEPS OF THARMAS O THOU BRIGHTNESS OF         371 FOUR ZOAS 9     551
       THE GARDENS
    ROUND VALA IN THE GARDENS OF VALA & BY HER RIVER'S MARGIN 372 FOUR ZOAS 9     555
    STRATFORD & OLD BOW & ACROSS TO THE GARDENS OF KENSINGTON 485 MILTON 6        10
    THE "VIEWS IN KEW GARDENS" "FOOTS CRAY" & "DIANA"        594A PUB ADDRESS/N   PROSE
       & "ACTEON"
    GARDENS & GROVES DISPLAY PARADISE WITH ITS INHABITANTS . . 613C V LAST JUDG/N  PROSE
    SEEING THE LAMB OF GOD IN THY GARDENS & THY PALACES  . . . 626 JERUSALEM 7    69
    FROM RANELAGH & STRUMBOLO FROM CROMWELLS GARDENS & CHELSEA 627 JERUSALEM 8     2
    THE CORN-FIELDS & THE BREATHING GARDENS OUTSIDE SEPARATED 643 JERUSALEM 21     9
    THEIR SECRET GARDENS WERE MADE PATHS TO THE TRAVELLER  . . 644 JERUSALEM 21    25
    ALBION'S DARK ROCKS SETTING BEHIND THE GARDENS OF       653 JERUSALEM 29     2
       KENSINGTON
    LIKE MANY WATERS AND EMANATING INTO GARDENS & PALACES UPON 695 JERUSALEM 61   30
    WITH SPACES OF SWEET GARDENS & A TENT OF ELEGANT BEAUTY   707 JERUSALEM 69    20
    THEIR VILLAGES CITIES SEA PORTS THEIR CORN FIELDS & GARDENS 710 JERUSALEM 71  21
       SPACIOUS
    THE SONS OF LOS CLOTHE THEM & FEED & PROVIDE HOUSES      714 JERUSALEM 73     49
       & GARDENS
    AND THAT I CAN AT WILL EXPATIATE IN THE GARDENS OF BLISS  727 JERUSALEM 82    82
GARLANDS
    AND WE WILL CROWN THY HEAD WITH GARLANDS OF THE RUDDY VINE 239 EUROPE 4       26
    IN RADIANT YOUTH WHEN LO LIKE GARLANDS IN THE EASTERN SKY 362 FOUR ZOAS 9    193
    THREE FEMALE FIGURES CROWND WITH GARLANDS REPRESENT  . . . 611D V LAST JUDG/N  PROSE
GARMENT
    DO I NOT STRETCH THE HEAVENS ABROAD OR FOLD THEM UP LIKE  294 FOUR ZOAS 3    107
       A GARMENT
    THE ENDS OF HEAVEN LIKE A GARMENT WILL I FOLD THEM ROUND ME 333 FOUR ZOAS 7B  6
    [THEY HAD WHICH CLOTHD THEIR BODIES LIKE A GARMENT OF SOFT 341 FOUR ZOAS 8    10
       DOWN]
    WITH A GARMENT OF PITY & COMPASSION LIKE THE GARMENT OF   499 MILTON 18       35
       GOD
    JERUSALEM IS HIS GARMENT & NOT THY COVERING CHERUB O LOVELY 499 MILTON 18     37
    A GIRDLE GWENDOLEN & CONWENNA AS A GARMENT WOVEN  . . . . 507 MILTON 23       16
    THE CLOUDS OF OLOLON FOLDED AS A GARMENT DIPPED IN BLOOD  534 MILTON 42       12
    A GARMENT OF WAR I HEARD IT NAMD THE WOOF OF SIX THOUSAND 534 MILTON 42       15
       YEARS
    NUMBER XII THE SOLDIERS CASTING LOTS FOR CHRIST'S GARMENT 584A DESC CAT 12    TITLE
       A DRAWING
    AND EVERY POT & VESSEL & GARMENT & UTENSIL OF THE HOUSES  633 JERUSALEM 13    21
    VALA REPLIED IN CLOUDS OF TEARS ALBION'S GARMENT EMBRACING 659 JERUSALEM 33   35
    A DEWY GARMENT COVERS ME ALL OVER ALL MANHOOD IS GONE  . . 660 JERUSALEM 34    4
    FROM HEAD TO FEET A GARMENT OF DEATH & ETERNAL FEAR  . . . 660 JERUSALEM 34    6
    WITH FORTITUDE AS WITH A GARMENT OF IMMORTAL TEXTURE  . . 665 JERUSALEM 38    52
    AND THE LIGHT IS HIS GARMENT THIS IS JERUSALEM IN EVERY MAN 684 JERUSALEM 54   3
    A GARMENT AND CRADLE WEAVING FOR THE INFANTINE TERROR  . . 688 JERUSALEM 56   14
    SOME FIND A FEMALE GARMENT THERE . . . . . . . . . .     771 OF GATES/GP     21
    AND DOST NOT KNOW THE GARMENT FROM THE MAN . . . . . . . 771 EPILOGUE/GP      2
    "REMEMBER WITH AFFECTION EVEN THE HEM OF YOUR GARMENT" . . 800A LETTER 12     PROSE
GARMENTS
    KISS THY PERFUMED GARMENTS LET US TASTE . . . . . . .     1 TO SPRING/PS      10
    WHERE 'CAUSE HIS GARMENTS ARE SWOLN WITH WIND . . . . .  37A CONTEMPLATN/PS  PROSE
    DROP FROM THY GARMENTS AS THOU WALKEST WRAPT IN YELLOW   106 TIRIEL 5        10
       CLOUDS
    AND CAUGHT HIM BY THE GARMENTS WEEPING WITH CRIES OF BITTER 106 TIRIEL 5      19
       WOE
    . . . HE SMELLS THY MILKY GARMENTS  . . . . . . . .     128 BOOK OF THEL 2    5

                                   780
```

GARMENTS   (CONTINUED)

. . . AN ODOR OF WAR LIKE A RIPE VINEYARD ROSE FROM HIS   138 FRENCH REVOLTN   84
GARMENTS
KNEELD ROUND HIM AND KISSED HIS GARMENTS AND WEPT . . .   139 FRENCH REVOLTN   123
BETTER THAN ANY DESCRIPTION OF BUILDINGS OR GARMENTS . . 150C MARRIAGE HH 6   PROSE
WETTING WITH TEARS & HIS WHITE GARMENTS CAST A WINTRY LIGHT   204 AMERICA CANC B   17
AS GARMENTS WOVEN SUBSERVIENT TO HER HANDS BUT HAVING A   266 FOUR ZOAS 1   84
WILL
THE DAUGHTERS OF ALBION GIRDED AROUND THEIR GARMENTS OF   281 FOUR ZOAS 2   57
NEEDLEWORK
OF GOD CLOTHED IN LUVAH'S GARMENTS LITTLE KNOWEST THOU . .   282 FOUR ZOAS 2   100
ASCENDING INTO HER [CLOUDY] MISTY GARMENTS . . . . . .   285 FOUR ZOAS 2   192
APPEAREST CLOTHD IN LUVAH'S GARMENTS THAT WE MAY BEHOLD   304 FOUR ZOAS 4   257
THEE
. . . & THE DUST FROM THY WHITE GARMENTS . . . .   338 FOUR ZOAS 7B   195
IN SILKEN GARMENTS SPUN BY HER OWN HANDS AGAINST   362 FOUR ZOAS 9   213
HER FUNERAL
HER GARMENTS REJOICE IN THE [VOCLE] VOCAL WIND . . .   367 FOUR ZOAS 9   * 392
MY GARMENTS SHALL BE WOVEN OF SIGHS & HEART BROKEN   499 MILTON 18   6
LAMENTATIONS
HIS GARMENTS ARE LONG SUFFERINGS FOR THE CHILDREN OF MEN   499 MILTON 18   36
BUT WE SEE ONLY AS IT WERE THE HEM OF THEIR GARMENTS   .   512 MILTON 26   11
TO TAKE OFF HIS FILTHY GARMENTS & CLOTHE HIM WITH   533 MILTON 41   6
IMAGINATION
THESE ARE THE SEXUAL GARMENTS THE ABOMINATION OF DESOLATION   533 MILTON 41   25
OF THE GARMENTS THE HAIR UPON THE HORSES THE . . . . 588A CHAUCER/N   PROSE
SUSPENDED OVER HER HE HUNG HE INFOLDED HER IN HIS GARMENTS   639 JERUSALEM 17   52
SUSSEX & KENT ARE HER SCATTERD GARMENTS IRELAND HER HOLY   653 JERUSALEM 29   20
PLACE
. . . CHANGES HIS SEXUAL [GARENTS] GARMENTS AT WILL . . .   695 JERUSALEM 61   * 51
GLITTERING WITH PRECIOUS STONES & GOLD WITH GARMENTS OF   699 JERUSALEM 64   26
BLOOD & FIRE
. . . & THE DUST FROM THY WHITE GARMENTS . . . .   700 JERUSALEM 65   41
THE DAUGHTERS OF ALBION CLOTHED IN GARMENTS OF NEEDLE WORK   702 JERUSALEM 66   17
THEIR GARMENTS THEY SIT NAKED UPON THE STONE OF TRIAL . .   702 JERUSALEM 66   19
BUT THEY CUT ASUNDER HIS INNER GARMENTS SEARCHING WITH . . 702 JERUSALEM 66   27
AROUND THE WORMY GARMENTS OF ALBION THEN PAUSING   741 JERUSALEM 94   17
IN DEATHLIKE SILENCE
LEST THE SEXUAL GARMENTS SWEET . . . .   771 OF GATES/GP   23

GARNERS

THE BULBOUS ROOTS THROWN UP TOGETHER INTO BARNS & GARNERS   284 FOUR ZOAS 2   165

GASHES

CUT THEE IN GASHES THO THE BLOOD POURS DOWN AROUND THY   322 FOUR ZOAS 7   84
ANKLES

GASS   SEE INFLAMMABLE GASS

GATE

WALKD BY THE CASTLE GATE AND LOOKED IN . . . .   4 FAIR ELENOR/PS   3
THEY PASSD SWIFT THRO THE OUTER GATE THE WRETCH . . .   4 FAIR ELENOR/PS   29
AND MNETHA HASTED & MET THEM AT THE GATE OF THE LOWER   109 TIRIEL 8   1
GARDEN
AND THE [GATE] GATES OF THE CHAPEL [WAS] WERE SHUT . . .   162 GARDEN LOVE/N   * 5
STANDS AT THE GATE OF ENITHARMON TO DEVOUR HER CHILDREN   198 AMERICA 7   4
. . . [?TILL ?BY THE] ?FROZEN CHILL & HEAVY EVEN TO THE   205 AMERICA CANC C   * 9
CITY GATE
GROVELING ALONG GREAT GEORGE STREET THRO THE PARK GATE   242 EUROPE 12   19
. . .
TILL MORNING OPED THE EASTERN GATE [AND THE ANGEL TRUMPET   244 EUROPE 14   * 35
BLEW]
. . . GATE OF [AURICULAR POWER] THE TONGUE [NERVES] IN   267 FOUR ZOAS 1   * 108
TREMBLING FEAR
THE DAUGHTERS OF BEULAH TERRIFIED HAVE CLOSD THE GATE OF   277 FOUR ZOAS 1   479
THE TONGUE
ALBION CLOSD THE WESTERN GATE & SHUT AMERICA OUT BY THE   294 FOUR ZOAS 3   105
. . .
ENITHARMON ON THE ROAD OF DRANTHON FELT THE INMOST GATE   309 FOUR ZOAS 5   177
AND WHEN THE GATE WAS OPEN SHE BEHELD THAT [DISMAL] DREARY   309 FOUR ZOAS 5   * 180
DEEP
LOS SAT IN GOLGONOOZA IN THE GATE OF LUBAN WHERE . . . .   331 FOUR ZOAS 7   433
GATES BROKEN DOWN THEY DESCEND THRO THE GATE OF PITY   . .   341 FOUR ZOAS 8   28
THE BROKEN HEART GATE OF ENITHARMON [WHICH JOINS   341 FOUR ZOAS 8   * 29
TO URIZEN'S TEMPLE]
OF GOLGONOOZA LOS STOOD [AT THE GATE] RECIEVING THEM   .   341 FOUR ZOAS 8   31
INTO HIS HANDS THEN ENITHARMON ERECTED LOOMS IN LUBAN'S   342 FOUR ZOAS 8   36
GATE
. . . TIMES AFTER TIMES BESIDE JERUSALEM'S GATE] . . .   356 FOUR ZOAS 8   588
A DOG STARVD AT HIS MASTER'S GATE . . . .   431 AUGURIES   9
MRS HAYNES WAS PRESENT FROM MY TURNING HIM OUT AT MY GATE   438B BLAKES MEMORAN   PROSE
THE GRAVE IS HEAVEN'S GOLDEN GATE . . . .   442 DEDICATN BLAIR   7
BEHOLD THIS GATE OF PEARL AND GOLD . . . .   442 DEDICATN BLAIR   10
SCOFIELD IS BOUND IN IRON ARMOUR BEFORE REUBEN'S GATE .   501 MILTON 19   59
RINTRAH AND PALAMABRON MET US AT THE GATE OF GOLGONOOZA   505 MILTON 22   27
BUT THEOTORMON & SOTHA STAND IN THE GATE OF LUBAN ANXIOUS   515 MILTON 28   21
AND EVERY HOUR HAS A BRIGHT GOLDEN GATE CARVED WITH SKILL   516 MILTON 28   51
JUST AT THE PLACE TO WHERE THE LARK MOUNTS IS A CRYSTAL   526 MILTON 35   61
GATE
BUT THE LARK'S NEST IS AT THE GATE OF LOS AT THE EASTERN   526 MILTON 35   66
GATE OF WIDE GOLGONOOZA & THE LARK IS LOS'S MESSENGER .   526 MILTON 35   67
AT THAT BRIGHT GATE ANOTHER LARK MEETS HIM & BACK TO BACK   526 MILTON 36   2
IN THE EAST GATE OF GOLGONOOZA & THE TWENTY-EIGHTH BRIGHT   527 MILTON 36   9
TURN THRO THE IRON GATE DOWN SNEAKING LANE . . . . . .   541 MR CROMEK/N   4
IT WILL LEAD YOU IN AT HEAVEN'S GATE . . . .   551 GIVE YOU END/N   3
DOWN STONE STEPS & BESIDE A GATE . . . .   608B V LAST JUDG/N   PROSE

```
                                                        PAGE      TITLE         LINE
GATE    (CONTINUED)
    ABOVE THE GATE A FIEND WITH WINGS [DR] URGES [THEM]  .  .  . 608B V LAST JUDG/N  *PROSE
    VARIOUS OFFICES AT THE EASTERN GATE BENEATH IN SMALL      618B ILLUS MILTON    PROSE
        FIGURES
    THE FURNACE OF LOS BEFORE THE EASTERN GATE BENDING THEIR    623 JERUSALEM 5        28
        FURY
    HE IS LIKE A MANDRAKE IN THE EARTH BEFORE REUBEN'S GATE     631 JERUSALEM 11       22
    WITHOUT THE GATE OF LOS AMONG THE DARK SATANIC WHEELS  .  . 632 JERUSALEM 12       44
    AND THE NORTH GATE OF GOLGONOOZA TOWARD GENERATION   .  .   632 JERUSALEM 12       61
    HAS FOUR SCULPTURD BULLS TERRIBLE BEFORE THE GATE OF IRON   632 JERUSALEM 12       62
    THE SOUTH A GOLDEN GATE HAS FOUR LIONS TERRIBLE LIVING  .  .633 JERUSALEM 13        2
    THE WESTERN GATE FOURFOLD IS CLOSD HAVING FOUR CHERUBIM     633 JERUSALEM 13        6
    THE EASTERN GATE FOURFOLD TERRIBLE & DEADLY ITS ORNAMENTS   633 JERUSALEM 13       12
    AND EVERY HOUSE FOURFOLD BUT THE THIRD GATE IN EVERY ONE    633 JERUSALEM 13       22
    AND SIXTY-FOUR THOUSAND GENII GUARD THE EASTERN GATE        633 JERUSALEM 13       26
    AND SIXTY-FOUR THOUSAND GNOMES GUARD THE NORTHERN GATE  .   633 JERUSALEM 13       27
    AND SIXTY-FOUR THOUSAND NYMPHS GUARD THE WESTERN GATE  .  . 633 JERUSALEM 13       28
    AND SIXTY-FOUR THOUSAND FAIRIES GUARD THE SOUTHERN GATE     633 JERUSALEM 13       29
    HAVE A BEAUTIFUL GOLDEN GATE WHICH OPENS INTO THE          635 JERUSALEM 14       20
        VEGETATIVE WORLD
    AND EVERY ONE A GATE OF RUBIES & ALL SORTS OF PRECIOUS     635 JERUSALEM 14       21
        STONES
    AND EVERY ONE A GATE OF IRON DREADFUL AND WONDERFUL  .  .  .635 JERUSALEM 14       23
    BUT THE GATE OF THE TONGUE THE WESTERN GATE IN THEM IS     635 JERUSALEM 14       26
        CLOSD
    OF STRONG REVENGE & SKOFELD VEGETATED BY REUBEN'S GATE  .  635 JERUSALEM 15        2
    THE GATE OF REUBEN IN CARMARTHENSHIRE THE GATE OF SIMEON    637 JERUSALEM 16       35
        IN
    CARDIGANSHIRE & THE GATE OF LEVI IN MONTGOMERYSHIRE  .  .  .637 JERUSALEM 16       36
    THE GATE OF JUDAH MERIONETHSHIRE THE GATE OF DAN            637 JERUSALEM 16       37
        FLINTSHIRE
    THE GATE OF NAPTHALI RADNORSHIRE THE GATE OF GAD           637 JERUSALEM 16       38
        PEMBROKESHIRE
    THE GATE OF ASHER CARNARVONSHIRE THE GATE OF ISSACHAR      637 JERUSALEM 16       39
        BRECKNOKSHIRE
    THE GATE OF ZEBULUN IN ANGLESEA & SODOR SO IS WALES DIVIDED 637 JERUSALEM 16       40
    THE GATE OF JOSEPH DENBIGHSHIRE THE GATE OF BENJAMIN        637 JERUSALEM 16       41
        GLAMORGANSHIRE
    MY CATTLE NEXT LAST EVN THE DOG OF MY GATE THE FORESTS FLED 643 JERUSALEM 21        8
    A BUILDING OF LUVAH BUILDED IN JERUSALEM'S EASTERN GATE     657 JERUSALEM 31       24
        TO BE
    OF ETERNITY PALE STOOD ALBION AT HIS EASTERN GATE   .  .  . 658 JERUSALEM 31       70
    THERE IS IN ALBION A GATE OF PRECIOUS STONES AND GOLD  .  . 665 JERUSALEM 38       55
    OF MULTITUDES WHO DIE FROM EARTH THIS GATE CANNOT BE FOUND  665 JERUSALEM 38       59
    OF SAND ON EARTH EVERY NIGHT THEY NEVER FIND THIS GATE  .  .666 JERUSALEM 39        2
    IT IS THE GATE OF LOS WITHOUTSIDE IS THE MILL INTRICATE    666 JERUSALEM 39        3
        DREADFUL
    BEFORE THE GATE OF LOS URTHONA HERE IS NAMED LOS   .  .  .  666 JERUSALEM 39        9
    ALBION FLED THRO THE GATE OF LOS AND HE STOOD IN THE GATE   666 JERUSALEM 39       11
    AGAINST HIS WILL THRO LOS'S GATE TO EDEN FOUR-FOLD LOUD     674 JERUSALEM 44        3
    AND ALL THE GATE OF LOS CLOUDED WITH CLOUDS REDOUNDING FROM 674 JERUSALEM 44        8
    BEFORE THE GATE OF LOS & IN THE DEPTHS OF NON ENTITY  .  .  674 JERUSALEM 44       36
    O ALBION MILDEST SON OF EDEN CLOSD IS THY WESTERN GATE  .   675 JERUSALEM 45        3
    ALBION'S WESTERN GATE IS CLOSD HIS DEATH IS COMING APACE    675 JERUSALEM 45       17
    THE GOLDEN GATE OF HAVILAH AND ALL THE GARDEN OF GOD   .  . 679 JERUSALEM 49       15
    FOR FEAR AT ENTERING THE GATE INTO OUR WORLD OF CRUEL  .  . 688 JERUSALEM 56       15
    AND IN THE NORTH GATE IN THE WEST OF THE NORTH TOWARD      691 JERUSALEM 59       22
        BEULAH
    MUNSTER SOUTH IN REUBEN'S GATE CONNAUT WEST IN JOSEPH'S     711 JERUSALEM 72        3
        GATE
    ULSTER NORTH IN DAN'S GATE LEINSTER EAST IN JUDAH'S GATE    711 JERUSALEM 72        4
    IN ALBION'S TOMB THE WONDROUS CREATION & THE FOUR-FOLD GATE 712 JERUSALEM 72       49
    WHITEFIELD & HERVEY GUARD THAT GATE WITH ALL THE GENTLE    712 JERUSALEM 72       51
        SOULS
    WHO GUIDE THE GREAT WINE-PRESS OF LOVE FOUR PRECIOUS STONES 712 JERUSALEM 72       52
        THAT GATE
    IT WILL LEAD YOU IN AT HEAVEN'S GATE .  .  .  .  .  .  .  . 716 I GIVE YOU/J        3
    BENEATH ALBION'S FATAL TREE BEFORE THE GATE OF LOS   .  .   726 JERUSALEM 82       60
    BABEL & SHINAR LOOK TOWARD THE WESTERN GATE THEY SIT DOWN   730 JERUSALEM 85       18
    SHALL BE BEGGARS AT LOVE'S GATE .  .  .  .  .  .  .  .  .  .755 EV GOSPEL(E)/N     56
    AND RHADAMANTHUS AT THE GATE .  .  .  .  .  .  .  .  .  .  .758 EV GOSPEL (1)      14
    THIS IS UPSIDE DOWN WHEN VIEWD FROM HELL'S GATE BUT  .  .  .785D ILLS DANTE 101 *PROSE
    I MET A PLOW ON MY FIRST GOING OUT AT MY GATE  .  .  .  .  .803C LETTER 15      PROSE
    TO THE PLOWMAN "FATHER THE GATE IS OPEN" I HAVE BEGUN TO    803C LETTER 15      PROSE
        WORK
    NOT STEPPED OUT AT THE GATE & PUTTING ASIDE HIS BLOWS  .   827A LETTER 28      PROSE
    WHICH WAS VERY QUICKLY DONE WE WERE MET AT THE GATE BY  .   827B LETTER 28      PROSE
    ALL THAT HAPPEND AT THE GATE OF THE INN WHO EVIDENCES THAT  827C LETTER 28      PROSE
    AT THE GATE UTTER SEDITIOUS WORDS & (DAMN) THE (KING)  .   827D LETTER 28      PROSE
    AFTERNOON MY POOR WIFE HAS BEEN NEAR THE GATE OF DEATH  .  .833D LETTER 33      PROSE
    THE TWO ANGELS WHO STAND AT HEAVEN'S GATE EVER OPEN   .  .  834A LETTER 33      PROSE
    AND OFTEN WE THINK WE HEAR YOUR VOICE CALLING AT THE GATE   854A LETTER 52      PROSE
GATES      SEE FLOOD GATES
    UNLOCK HEAVN'S GOLDEN GATES AND ISSUE FORTH    .  .  .  .  .  3 TO MORNING/PS       2
    AND SHAKE THE GATES OF HELL .  .  .  .  .  .  .  .  .  .  . 30 EDW THIRD/PS 5      20
    HER CITIZENS SHALL THRONG ABOUT HER GATES  .  .  .  .  .  . 34C KING JOHN/PS   PROSE
    BY A FALSE WIFE BROUGHT TO THE GATES OF DEATH  .  .  .  .  . 37C SAMSON/PS      PROSE
    TO THY WIDE GATES HOW GREAT A DROVE .  .  .  .  .  .  .  . 56 HAIL MATRIM/IM       2
    ("WHILE I AND MINE ARE THE TWO ONLY GATES YOU (USE)        78C ANNO LAVATER    MARG
        ") UNEASY
    AND AGED TIRIEL STOOD BEFORE THE GATES OF HIS BEAUTIFUL    99 TIRIEL 1
        PALACE
```

	PAGE	TITLE	LINE
GATES (CONTINUED)			
OF AGED TIRIEL AROSE THAT HIS SONS MIGHT HEAR IN THEIR GATES	99	TIRIEL 1	6
HIS SONS RAN FROM THEIR GATES & SAW THEIR AGED PARENTS STAND	99	TIRIEL 1	11
AS THICK AS NORTHERN FOGS AROUND YOUR GATES TO CHOKE YOU UP	100	TIRIEL 1	44
ENTERD THE GATES OF TIRIEL'S PALACE & STOOD & CALLD ALOUD	104	TIRIEL 4	42
[O NOBLE IJIM THOU HAST BROUGHT OUR FATHER TO [THE GATES] OUR EYES]	105	TIRIEL 4	75
. . . WHOSE TEETH THE GATES OF ETERNAL DEATH]	109	TIRIEL 8	17
AND THE [GATE] GATES OF THE CHAPEL [WAS] WERE SHUT . .	162	GARDEN LOVE/N *	5
THEY SLOW ADVANCE TO SHUT THE FIVE GATES OF THEIR LAW-BUILT HEAVEN	203	AMERICA 16	19
BUT THE FIVE GATES WERE CONSUMD & THEIR BOLTS AND HINGES MELTED	203	AMERICA 16	22
[WHO CALL IT FANCY [&] OR SHUT THE GATES OF SENSE . . .	205	AMERICA CANC C	22
THE GATES OF PARADISE A SMALL BOOK OF ENGRAVINGS PRICE...	208A	PRSPECTUS 1793	PROSE
FOR CHILDREN THE GATES OF PARADISE	209B	FOR CHILDRN/GP	TITLE
AND THE GATES OF THIS CHAPEL WERE SHUT	215	GARDEN LOVE/SE	5
DESCENDED THRO THE ORIENT GATES OF THE ETERNAL DAY . .	239	EUROPE 4	3
WERE BENDED DOWNWARD AND THE NOSTRILS GOLDEN GATES SHUT	241	EUROPE 10	14
THAT LEADS FROM THE GATES OF THE GRAVE	247	SONG OF LOS 7	8
THEY WEPT BEFORE THE INNER GATES OF ENITHARMON'S BOSOM .	279	FOUR ZOAS 1	561
THREE GATES WITHIN GLORIOUS & BRIGHT OPEN INTO [ETERNITY] BEULAH	279	FOUR ZOAS 1 *	563
REFUSD TO OPEN THE BRIGHT GATES SHE CLOSD AND BARRD THEM FAST	279	FOUR ZOAS 1	565
LEST LOS SHOULD ENTER INTO BEULAH THRO HER BEAUTIFUL GATES	279	FOUR ZOAS 1	566
THE EMANATION STOOD BEFORE THE GATES OF ENITHARMON . . .	280	FOUR ZOAS 1	567
I KNOW I WAS URTHONA KEEPER OF THE GATES OF HEAVEN . .	298	FOUR ZOAS 4	42
THEN THOU DIDST KEEP WITH STRONG URTHONA THE LIVING GATES OF HEAVEN	311	FOUR ZOAS 5	232
BUT NOW THOU ART BOUND DOWN WITH HIM EVEN TO THE GATES OF HELL	311	FOUR ZOAS 5 *	233
FOR TILL THESE TERRORS PLANTED ROUND THE GATES OF ETERNAL LIFE	327	FOUR ZOAS 7	302
ARE DRIVEN AWAY & ANNIHILATED WE NEVER CAN REPASS THE GATES	327	FOUR ZOAS 7	303
SHE BURST THE GATES OF ENITHARMON'S HEART WITH DIREFUL CRASH	328	FOUR ZOAS 7	323
AND THE GATES [BURST] BROKE IN SUNDER & THEIR ORNAMENTS DEFACD	328	FOUR ZOAS 7 *	325
OF THY FIERCE SOUL UNBAR THE GATES OF MEMORY LOOK UPON ME	328	FOUR ZOAS 7	347
OPENING ITS GATES & IN IT ALL THE REAL SUBSTANCES . . .	329	FOUR ZOAS 7	365
TREMBLE NOT SO MY ENITHARMON AT THE AWFUL GATES . . .	330	FOUR ZOAS 7	412
. . . I BEHOLD THE DIVINE VISION THRO THE BROKEN GATES . .	341	FOUR ZOAS 8	20
GATES BROKEN DOWN THEY DESCEND THRO THE GATE OF PITY . .	341	FOUR ZOAS 8	28
THAT ONLY THRO THE GATES OF DEATH THEY CAN ENTER TO ENITHARMON	344	FOUR ZOAS 8	110
THE WAR ROARD ROUND JERUSALEM'S GATES IT TOOK A HIDEOUS FORM	347	FOUR ZOAS 8	247
PITYING THE LAMB OF GOD DESCENDED THRO JERUSALEM'S GATES	347	FOUR ZOAS 8	260
FROM OUT THE FLOOD GATES OF THE SKY THE GATES ARE BURST DOWN POUR	359	FOUR ZOAS 9	72
IS SEEN THO SLAIN BEFORE HER GATES HE SELF-RENEWD REMAINS	362	FOUR ZOAS 9	206
LUVAH & VALA DESCENDED & ENTERD THE GATES OF DARK URTHONA	367	FOUR ZOAS 9	375
VALA AWOKE WHEN IN THE PLEASANT GATES OF SLEEP I ENTERD	369	FOUR ZOAS 9	464
AND WHEN HE LAID HIS HAND UPON ME FROM THE GATES OF SLEEP I CAME	369	FOUR ZOAS 9	469
TO BEULAH & THE DEAD IN BEULAH DESCENDED THRO THEIR GATES	382	FOUR ZOAS AD 6	26
RIGHT THRO THE GATES OF WRATH	421	MORNING/N	2
FOR DEATH ETERNAL IN THE HEAVENS OF ALBION & BEFORE THE GATES	481	MILTON 2	14
HAS THREE GATES INTO THE THREE HEAVENS OF BEULAH WHICH SHINE	484	MILTON 5	7
TARRY NO LONGER FOR MY SOUL LIES AT THE GATES OF DEATH . .	495	MILTON 14	19
WITHINSIDE WONDROUS & EXPANSIVE ITS GATES ARE NOT CLOSD	502	MILTON 20	29
FOR EVERY HUMAN HEART HAS GATES OF BRASS & BARS OF ADAMANT	502	MILTON 20	34
WHICH FEW DARE UNBAR BECAUSE DREAD OG & ANAK GUARD THE GATES	502	MILTON 20	35
GATES OPEN BEHIND SATAN'S SEAT TO THE CITY OF GOLGONOOZA	502	MILTON 20	39
WHERE LOS OPENS HIS THREE WIDE GATES SURROUNDED BY RAGING FIRES	503	MILTON 20	49
THERE ARE TWO GATES THRO WHICH ALL SOULS DESCEND ONE SOUTHWARD	512	MILTON 26	13
AND LEST THEY SHOULD DESCEND BEFORE THE NORTH & SOUTH GATES	512	MILTON 26	21
AND EVERY DAY & NIGHT HAS WALLS OF BRASS & GATES OF ADAMANT	516	MILTON 28	52
. . . & THE GATES OF THEIR FATHER'S HOUSE	522	MILTON 32	43
AND HE WHOSE GATES ARE OPEND IN THOSE REGIONS OF HIS BODY	524	MILTON 34	17
CAN FROM THOSE GATES VIEW ALL THESE WONDROUS IMAGINATIONS	524	MILTON 34	18
BUT OLOLON SOUGHT THE OR-ULRO & ITS FIERY GATES . . .	524	MILTON 34	19
RETURND BUT OLOLON REMAIND BEFORE THE GATES OF THE DEAD	524	MILTON 34	48
THE EAST TOWARD JERUSALEM'S GATES GROANING HE SAT ABOVE	531	MILTON 39	34
AND BLOCKS UP ALL ITS GATES OF LIGHT EXCEPT ONE .	583A	DESC CAT 9	PROSE
HAVING A WALL BUILDED AGAINST IT AND THEREBY THE GATES .	635	JERUSALEM 14	27
WITH MIGHTY POWER WHEN THEY FLED OUT AT JERUSALEM'S GATES	637	JERUSALEM 16	30
AWAY FROM THE CONFLICT OF LUVAH & URIZEN FIXING THE GATES	637	JERUSALEM 16	31
IN THE TWELVE COUNTIES OF WALES & THENCE GATES LOOKING EVERY WAY	637	JERUSALEM 16	32
AND THE FORTY COUNTIES OF ENGLAND ARE THUS DIVIDED IN THE GATES	637	JERUSALEM 16	43
DIVIDED IN THE THE GATES OF REUBEN JUDAH DAN & JOSEPH . .	637	JERUSALEM 16	51

783

		PAGE	TITLE	LINE

GATES   (CONTINUED)
    AND THE THIRTY-SIX COUNTIES OF SCOTLAND DIVIDED IN THE   638 JERUSALEM 16   52
       GATES
    THY SONS HAVE NAILD ME ON THE GATES PIERCING MY HANDS &   644 JERUSALEM 22   2
       FEET
    AND GOLD THY GATES OF THANKSGIVING THY WINDOWS OF PRAISE   647 JERUSALEM 24   20
    THE WALLS OF BABYLON ARE SOULS OF MEN HER GATES THE GROANS   647 JERUSALEM 24   31
    HE WITHERD UP JERUSALEM'S GATES . . . . 651 FIELDS FROM/J   51
    ENTERING THRO THE GATES OF BIRTH . . . . 651 FIELDS FROM/J   63
    AND PASSING THRO THE GATES OF DEATH . . . . 651 FIELDS FROM/J   64
    OF LOVE & HARMONY IN MAN EXPAND THY EVER LOVELY GATES . . 675 JERUSALEM 44   42
    TO THOSE WHOSE WESTERN GATES WERE OPEN AS THEY STOOD   676 JERUSALEM 45   34
       WEEPING
    WITHIN THE HUMAN HEART WHOSE GATES CLOSED WITH SOLEMN SOUND   678 JERUSALEM 48   25
    OUTSIDE OF THE GATES OF THE HUMAN HEART BENEATH BEULAH . . 684 JERUSALEM 53   16
    THIS LOS FORMED INTO THE GATES & MIGHTY WALL BETWEEN THE   691 JERUSALEM 59   5
       OAK
    AND JEHOVAH STOOD IN THE GATES OF THE VICTIM & HE APPEARED   697 JERUSALEM 63   16
    A WEEPING INFANT IN THE GATES OF BIRTH IN THE MIDST OF   697 JERUSALEM 63   17
       HEAVEN
    FOR ALBION IN ETERNITY HAS SIXTEEN GATES AMONG HIS PILLARS   711 JERUSALEM 72   5
    BY LOS FOR JERUSALEM'S SAKE & CALLED THE GATES OF JERUSALEM   711 JERUSALEM 72   8
    BECAUSE TWELVE SONS OF JERUSALEM FLED SUCCESSIVE THRO THE   711 JERUSALEM 72   9
       GATES
    AND THIRTY-TWO THE NATIONS TO DWELL IN JERUSALEM'S GATES   712 JERUSALEM 72   32
    AND THE FOUR GATES OF LOS SURROUND THE UNIVERSE WITHIN AND   712 JERUSALEM 72   45
    HENCE IS MY THEME O LORD MY SAVIOUR OPEN THOU THE GATES   715 JERUSALEM 74   40
    THY GATES BEHELD SWEET ZION'S WAYS . . . . 718 ENGLND AWAKE/J   7
    ALBION'S TWELVE SONS SURROUND THE FORTY-TWO GATES OF ERIN   719 JERUSALEM 78   12
    NAKED JERUSALEM LAY BEFORE THE GATES UPON MOUNT ZION . . 719 JERUSALEM 78   21
    HER TWELVE GATES THROWN DOWN HER CHILDREN CARRIED INTO   719 JERUSALEM 78   23
       CAPTIVITY
    OUTSIDE UNKNOWN BEFORE IN BEULAH & THE TWELVE GATES WERE   719 JERUSALEM 78   25
       FILLD
    MY GATES IN ALL THEIR MOUNTAINS & MY CURTAINS IN ALL THEIR   720 JERUSALEM 79   46
       VALES
    I KNOW I AM URTHONA KEEPER OF THE GATES OF HEAVEN . . . 727 JERUSALEM 82   81
    I SEE THY GATES OF PRECIOUS STONES THY WALLS OF GOLD &   730 JERUSALEM 85   23
       SILVER
    THY FOREHEAD BRIGHT HOLINESS TO THE LORD WITH GATES OF   730 JERUSALEM 86   4
       PEARL
    WHICH STAND BOTH MALE & FEMALE AT THE GATES OF EACH   733 JERUSALEM 88   11
       HUMANITY
    [I] THY HEAVEN DOORS ARE MY HELL GATES . . . . 748 EV GOSPEL(A)/N *   8
    THERE GATES OF DEATH LET IN THE DAY . . . . 749 EV GOSPEL(B)/N   40
    AND OPED THE GATES OF PARADISE . . . . 759 EV GOSPEL (2)   27
    FOR THE SEXES THE GATES OF PARADISE . . . . 760A FOR SEXES/GP   TITLE
    SUCH ARE THE GATES OF PARADISE . . . . 761 FOR SEXES/GP   2
    HEAVEN OPENS HERE ON ALL SIDES HER GOLDEN GATES . . . 802A LETTER 14   PROSE
    DEAR CUMBERLAND I HAVE BEEN VERY NEAR THE GATES OF DEATH   878A LETTER 88   PROSE
GATES (SURNAME)
    WASHINGTON FRANKLIN PAINE & WARREN GATES HANCOCK & GREEN   197 AMERICA 3   4
    WASHINGTON FRANKLIN PAINE & WARREN ALLEN GATES & LEE . . 201 AMERICA 14   2
    WASHINGTON HANCOCK PAINE & WARREN GATES FRANKLIN & GREEN   203 AMERICA CANC A   4
GATES'
    THE ETERNAL GATES' TERRIFIC PORTER LIFTED THE NORTHERN BAR   130 BOOK OF THEL 6   1
GATEWAY
    THESE LAST ARE ISSUING FROM THE GATEWAY OF THE INN THE COOK   567A DESC CAT 3   PROSE
    OF COMFORT SPECTATORS STAND AT THE GATEWAY OF THE INN . . 567A DESC CAT 3   PROSE
    OF THE PICTURE THE WORDS WRITTEN OVER THE GATEWAY OF THE   567B DESC CAT 3   PROSE
       INN
    THESE LAST ARE ISSUING FROM THE GATEWAY OF THE INN THE COOK   588D CHAUCER/N   PROSE
    OF COMFORT SPECTATORS STAND AT THE GATEWAY OF THE INN . . 588D CHAUCER/N   PROSE
    OVER THE GATEWAY ARE AS FOLLOW "THE TABARDE INNE" . . . 589A CHAUCER/N   PROSE
    THESE LAST ARE ISSUING FROM THE GATEWAY OF THE INN THE COOK   590A CHAUCER 2   PROSE
    OF COMFORT SPECTATORS STAND AT THE GATEWAY OF THE INN . . 590A CHAUCER 2   PROSE
    HAS CONTINUED A BOARD OVER THE GATEWAY . . . . . . 590A CHAUCER 2   PROSE
    OVER THE GATEWAY OF THE INN ARE AS FOLLOW . . . . . 590C CHAUCER 2   PROSE
GATHER
    AND THOU SHALT HELP US TO CATCH BIRDS & GATHER THEM RIPE   102 TIRIEL 3   15
       CHERRIES
    OR HOW SHALL WE GATHER WHAT GRIEFS DESTROY . . . . . 124 SCHOOL BOY/SI   28
    TO THE FOUR WINDS AS A TORN BOOK & NONE SHALL GATHER THE   198 AMERICA 8   6
       LEAVES
    IN COUNCIL GATHER THE SMITTEN ANGELS OF ALBION . . . 241 EUROPE 9   11
    BUT WHEN UNSATIATED HIS THIRST HE ASSAYD TO GATHER MORE   311 FOUR ZOAS 6   4
    SHALT GATHER THEM FROM OUT THEIR GRAVES & PUT THY FETTER   334 FOUR ZOAS 7B   70
       ON THEM
    THEIR RIVERS CRY WITH A DISMAL CRY THE CATTLE GATHER   358 FOUR ZOAS 9   54
       TOGETHER
    THE SONS OF URIZEN SHALL GATHER THE VINTAGE WITH SHARP   375 FOUR ZOAS 9   694
       HOOKS
    O GOD DESCEND GATHER OUR BRETHREN DELIVER JERUSALEM . . . 675 JERUSALEM 45   28
    I GATHER OUR ETERNAL FATE OUTCASTS FROM LIFE AND LOVE . . 725 JERUSALEM 82   2
GATHERD
    THY NOBLES HAVE GATHERD THY STARRY HOSTS ROUND THIS   138 FRENCH REVOLTN   100
       REBELLIOUS CITY
    WILD FLOWERS I GATHERD & HE SHEWD ME EACH ETERNAL FLOWER   238 EUROPE INTRO   20
    AT FIRST AN INFANT WEAKNESS PERIODS PASSD HE GATHERD   316 FOUR ZOAS 6   163
       STRENGTH
    WHERE MY SONS GATHERD ROUND MY KNEES O THOU POOR RUIND   317 FOUR ZOAS 6   209
       WORLD

	PAGE	TITLE		LINE

GATHERD   (CONTINUED)

FILLED WITH DOUBTS IN SELF ACCUSATION [GATHERD] BEHELD
  THE FRUIT   329 FOUR ZOAS 7   *   385
WHEN IN THE DEEPS BENEATH I GATHERD OF THIS RUDDY FRUIT   329 FOUR ZOAS 7   387
SHE GATHERD IT TOGETHER TO CONSUME HER HARLOT ROBES   . .   356 FOUR ZOAS 8   609
ARE GATHERD IN THE SCORCHING HEAT & IN THE DRIVING RAIN   359 FOUR ZOAS 9   105
AND ALL THY SONS & DAUGHTERS GATHERD ROUND MY AMPLE TABLE   360 FOUR ZOAS 9   127
SHE BORE THE FRUITS IN HER LAP SHE GATHERD FLOWERS FOR
  HER BOSOM   369 FOUR ZOAS 9   477
. . . & WHERE THE NATIONS ARE GATHERD TOGETHER   . . . .   378 FOUR ZOAS 9   784
GATHERD MY SONS TOGETHER IN THE SANDS OF MIDIAN   . . . .   508 MILTON 24   21
AND ALL GATHERD IN TILL THE PLOW HAS PASSD OVER THE NATIONS   510 MILTON 25   10
BUT LOS REFUSED TILL ALL THE VINTAGE OF EARTH WAS GATHERD
  IN   510 MILTON 25   * 15
IS GATHERD IN THE SCORCHING HEAT & IN THE DRIVING RAIN .   641 JERUSALEM 19   6
GATHERD JERUSALEM'S CHILDREN IN HIS ARMS & BORE THEM LIKE   692 JERUSALEM 60   8
THE SEA COASTS MAY BE GATHERD INTO HIS KINGDOM   . . . . .   823C LETTER 26   PROSE
GATHERED
AND A SISTER WERE GATHERED TO THE SICK BED OF A YOUTH   .   35C COUCH DEATH/PS   PROSE
THE PHILISTINE RIOTS ON OUR FLOCKS OUR VINTAGE IS GATHERED   40B SAMSON/PS   PROSE
GATHERING
. . . WALK GATHERING ROUND THE KING   . . . .   134 FRENCH REVOLTN   14
BUT THE FOREHEAD OF URIZEN GATHERING . . . .   250 AHANIA 3   1
GATHERING THE FRUIT OF THAT MYSTERIOUS TREE TILL URIZEN   345 FOUR ZOAS 8   179
INTO RESISTLESS PILLARS OF FIRE ROLLING ROUND & ROUND
  GATHERING   358 FOUR ZOAS 9   37
THEY WONDERD CHECKING THEIR WILD FLAMES & MANY GATHERING   686 JERUSALEM 55   3
GATHRING
BREAKING IN SMOKY WREATHS FROM THE WILD DEEP & GATHRING
  THICK   201 AMERICA 12   11
GATHRING THE FRUIT OF THAT MYSTERIOUS TREE CIRCLING ITS
  ROOT   343 FOUR ZOAS 8   * 84
ISSUD ON ALL SIDES GATHRING STRENGTH IN ANIMATING VOLUMES   358 FOUR ZOAS 9   * 35
GAUL
SHOOTING OUT FIBRES ROUND THE EARTH THRO GAUL & ITALY . .   704 JERUSALEM 67   38
GAVE
OF THE SEA OUR RIGHT THAT HEAVEN GAVE   . . . .   20 EDW THIRD/PS 2   79
I CHID THEM BOTH BUT GAVE THEM NOBLE HOPES . . . . . .   25 EDW THIRD/PS 3   169
SHE SPRED HER [SHADOWY] AWFUL WINGS & GAVE ME UP . . . .   43C WOE CRIED MUSE   PROSE
HERE THEY GAVE A SHOUT & THE COMPANY BROKE UP . . . . .   58B ISLAND MOON 9   PROSE
THEN MNETHA GAVE HIM MILK & FRUITS & THEY SAT DOWN TOGETHER   102 TIRIEL 2   58
HE WAS AS CHEARFUL AS A PRINCE & GAVE ME ENTERTAINMENT   102 TIRIEL 3   10
[THEN MNETHA LED HIM TO THE DOOR & GAVE TO HIM HIS STAFF]   103 TIRIEL 3   30
AND GAVE TO HIM HIS STAFF & BLEST HIM HE WENT ON HIS WAY   103 TIRIEL 3   40
GAVE THEE LIFE & BID THEE FEED . . . .   115 THE LAMB/SI   3
GAVE THEE CLOTHING OF DELIGHT . . . .   115 THE LAMB/SI   5
GAVE THEE SUCH A TENDER VOICE . . . .   115 THE LAMB/SI   7
. . . FANCY GAVE HIM TO SEE AN IMAGE OF DESPAIR IN HIS DEN   136 FRENCH REVOLTN   45
AND THE HEAVENS GAVE A FROWN . . . .   164 HEARD ANGEL/N   17
[AND I GAVE IT TO MY FOE] . . . .   165 CHRISTN FORB/N   11
AND GAVE HIM A PLACE IN THE NORTH . . . .   222 URIZEN 2   3
HE GAVE HIM TO ENITHARMON . . . .   233 URIZEN 20   5
WHEN RINTRAH GAVE ABSTRACT PHILOSOPHY TO BRAMA IN THE EAST   245 SONG OF LOS 3   11
TO TRISMEGISTUS PALAMABRON GAVE AN ABSTRACT LAW . . . .   246 SONG OF LOS 3   18
AND TO MAHOMET A LOOSE BIBLE GAVE . . . .   246 SONG OF LOS 3   29
BUT IN THE NORTH TO ODIN SOTHA GAVE A CODE OF WAR . . .   246 SONG OF LOS 3   30
THUS THE TERRIBLE RACE OF LOS & ENITHARMON GAVE   . . . .   246 SONG OF LOS 4   13
URIZEN WEPT & GAVE IT INTO THE HANDS OF NEWTON & LOCKE   .   246 SONG OF LOS 4   17
THAT GAVE LIGHT TO THE MORNINGS OF HEAVEN . . . .   251 AHANIA 3   42
WHEN HE GAVE MY HAPPY SOUL . . . .   254 AHANIA 5   15
THE CIRCLE OF DESTINY COMPLETE THEY GAVE TO IT A SPACE . .   267 FOUR ZOAS 1   101
THUS ENION GAVE THEM ALL HER SPECTROUS LIFE [IN DEEP
  DESPAIR]   270 FOUR ZOAS 1   221
AND MANY TEARS & IN THE [TWENTY] EVERY YEARS [GAVE . . .   270 FOUR ZOAS 1   224
GAVE SONGS OF GRATITUDE TO [THE] WAVING CORN FIELDS ROUND   276 FOUR ZOAS 1   * 450
  THEIR NEST
ALBION GAVE HIS LOUD DEATH GROAN THE ATLANTIC MOUNTAINS   281 FOUR ZOAS 2   41
  TREMBLED
I LOVED HER I GAVE HER ALL MY SOUL & MY DELIGHT   . . . .   282 FOUR ZOAS 2   94
WHEN URIZEN GAVE THE HORSES OF LIGHT INTO THE HANDS OF   300 FOUR ZOAS 4   113
  LUVAH
HE GAVE TO ME A SILVER SCEPTER & CROWND ME WITH A GOLDEN   310 FOUR ZOAS 5   220
  CROWN
I GAVE TO THEE THE STEEDS I POURD THE STOLEN WINE . . .   311 FOUR ZOAS 5   236
THEY GAVE A SCREAM THEY KNEW THEIR FATHER URIZEN KNEW   312 FOUR ZOAS 6   21
  HIS DAUGHTERS
I GAVE SWEET LILLIES TO THEIR BREASTS & ROSES TO THEIR HAIR   312 FOUR ZOAS 6   29
I TAUGHT THEM SONGS OF SWEET DELIGHT I GAVE THEIR TENDER   312 FOUR ZOAS 6   30
  VOICES
THY LILLIES THAT GAVE LIGHT WHAT TIME THE MORNING LOOKED   325 FOUR ZOAS 7   196
  FORTH
THE SPECTRE [SMILD] TERRIFIED & GAVE HER CHARGE OVER THE   328 FOUR ZOAS 7   * 332
  HOWLING ORC
HE IN HIS TURN GAVE TASKS TO LOS ENORMOUS TO DESTROY   .   329 FOUR ZOAS 7   375
[AMONG THE STARS] HIS HURTLING HAND GAVE THE DIRE SIGNAL   343 FOUR ZOAS 8   88
  . . .
AND URIZEN GAVE LIFE & SENSE BY HIS IMMORTAL POWER   . . .   344 FOUR ZOAS 8   131
NOR OF HIS OWN WILL GAVE HIS LAWS IN TIMES OF EVERLASTING   353 FOUR ZOAS 8   459
AND THARMAS GAVE HIS POWER TO LOS URTHONA GAVE HIS   353 FOUR ZOAS 8   477
  STRENGTH
URIZEN GAVE THE HORSES OF LIGHT INTO THE HANDS OF LUVAH   359 FOUR ZOAS 9   94
AND GAVE THEM TO URIZEN'S HANDS THE IMMORTAL FROWND SAYING   366 FOUR ZOAS 9   362

785

	PAGE	TITLE	LINE
GAVE (CONTINUED)			
VOMITED OUT & GAVE UP ALL THE FLOODS LIFT UP THEIR HANDS	378	FOUR ZOAS 9	803
WHO GAVE THEM THE NAME OF BOOKS OF SAMUEL	394C	ANNO WATSON	* MARG
BURKE USED TO SHEW THIS PICTURE TO HIS FRIENDS & TO SAY I GAVE	451D	ANNO REYNOLDS	MARG
LOS GAVE TO HIM THE HARROW OF THE ALMIGHTY ALAS BLAMABLE	486	MILTON 7	12
THEY GAVE SATAN THEIR WINE INDIGNANT AT THE BURNING WRATH	493	MILTON 12	44
THE KIND DECISION OF ENITHARMON & GAVE A TIME TO THE SPACE	494	MILTON 13	16
ENTERING THEY GAVE HIM STILL PERCEPTIONS OF HIS SLEEPING BODY	496	MILTON 15	4
OF GOLD AND THOSE IN IMMORTALITY GAVE FORTH THEIR EMANATIONS	496	MILTON 15	13
EVEN AS REUBEN & AS GAD GAVE UP HIMSELF TO TEARS . . .	503	MILTON 20	53
BUT THE DIVINE HUMANITY & MERCY GAVE US A HUMAN FORM . .	521	MILTON 32	14
WHEN I FIRST MARRIED YOU I GAVE YOU ALL MY WHOLE SOUL .	522	MILTON 33	2
BUT FORTUNE SAYS SHE GAVE YOU NO SUCH THING	541	MR STOTHARD/N	2
TO MAN THE WONDROUS ART OF WRITING GAVE	621	READER LOVER/J	4
FOR VALA PRODUCD THE BODIES JERUSALEM GAVE THE SOULS . .	640	JERUSALEM 18	7
HE MADE ME HIS BRIDE & WIFE HE GAVE THEE TO ALBION . . .	643	JERUSALEM 20	40
ALBION GAVE HIS DEADLY GROAN	650	FIELDS FROM/J	35
AND IN A DARK LAND GAVE HER BIRTH	651	FIELDS FROM/J	52
I ELECTED ALBION FOR MY GLORY I GAVE TO HIM THE NATIONS .	653	JERUSALEM 29	6
VALA REPLYD ALBION IS MINE LUVAH GAVE ME TO ALBION . . .	658	JERUSALEM 31	50
TILL JESUS SHALL APPEAR & THEY GAVE THEIR POWER TO LOS .	674	JERUSALEM 44	30
I GAVE THEE LIBERTY AND LIFE O LOVELY JERUSALEM . . .	692	JERUSALEM 60	10
I GAVE THEE SHEEP-WALKS UPON THE SPANISH MOUNTAINS . . .	692	JERUSALEM 60	12
JERUSALEM			
I GAVE THEE PRIAM'S CITY AND THE ISLES OF GRECIA LOVELY .	692	JERUSALEM 60	13
I GAVE THEE HAND & SCOFIELD & THE COUNTIES OF ALBION . .	692	JERUSALEM 60	14
MANY STREAMS IN THE ARMS OF JOSEPH & GAVE FORTH HER TEARS OF JOY	695	JERUSALEM 61	29
THEY NAMD HER RAHAB & GAVE HER POWER OVER THE EARTH . . .	719	JERUSALEM 78	16
FROM MY EAST & FROM MY WEST HE BLESSED ME AND GAVE . . .	720	JERUSALEM 79	25
ALBION GAVE ME TO THE WHOLE EARTH TO WALK UP & DOWN TO POUR	720	JERUSALEM 79	36
MY FATHER GAVE TO ME COMMAND TO MURDER ALBION	722	JERUSALEM 80	16
HE BURND BEFORE ME LUVAH FRAMD THE KNIFE & LUVAH GAVE . .	722	JERUSALEM 80	22
THAT GAVE ME SWEET DELIGHT BY HIS TORMENTS BENEATH MY VEIL	726	JERUSALEM 82	39
(DEFORMITY) SHE GAVE HER BEAUTY TO ANOTHER BEARING ABROAD	726	JERUSALEM 82	69
AND GAVE A TIME & REVOLUTION TO THE SPACE SIX THOUSAND YEARS	730	JERUSALEM 85	6
AS REUBEN FOUND MANDRAKES IN THE FIELD & GAVE THEM TO HIS MOTHER	740	JERUSALEM 93	8
. . . & THEN GAVE THE SPECTROUS OATH	746	JERUSALEM 98	53
. . . BUT SHAKESPEARE IN RIPER YEARS GAVE ME HIS HAND . .	799	TO FLAXMAN/L	6
WHICH YOU GAVE ME ORDERS FOR IS EIGHTEEN I WILL FINISH THESE	816C	LETTER 24	PROSE
AND BUTTS SHALL GIVE WHAT FUSELI GAVE	817	HAPPINESS/L	39
I GO ON WITH THE REMAINING SUBJECTS WHICH YOU GAVE ME . .	826D	LETTER 28	PROSE
THE YOUNG & VERY AMIABLE MRS ENOCH WHO GAVE MY WIFE . .	833D	LETTER 33	PROSE
TO CALL ON ME MRS FLAXMAN & HER SISTERS GAVE ALSO THEIR	836C	LETTER 35	PROSE
WHEN HIS DAUGHTER CAME IN HE GAVE THE PRINT INTO HER HAND	843C	LETTER 43	PROSE
MR CARR CALLED ON ME AND I AS YOU DESIRED GAVE HIM . . .	845C	LETTER 44	PROSE
GAVEST			
[THOU GAVEST THE TEARS OF PITY AWAY]	186	LET BROTHELS/N	58
BECAUSE THOU GAVEST URIZEN THE WINE OF THE ALMIGHTY . . .	311	FOUR ZOAS 5	234
THAT GAVEST ME A HEART TO CRAVE & RAISEDST ME THY PHANTOM	368	FOUR ZOAS 9	415
GAY			
TO SEE THE FIELDS SO PLEASANT & SO GAY	55	MAY MORNING/IM	2
IN DAMSEL OR IN WIDOW GAY	56	HAIL MATRIM/IM	21
LIKE THE GAY FISHES ON THE WAVE WHEN THE COLD MOON DRINKS THE DEW	243	EUROPE 14	3
[IF XXX GAY]	540	GOLDEN RULE/N	* 1
[WITH FORTUNE SPORTING MERRY BLITHE & GAY]	540	GOLDEN RULE/N	* 3
I SPORT WITH FORTUNE MERRY BLITHE & GAY	540	S(TOTHAR)D/N	3
THEY APPEAR TO BE INNOCENTLY GAY & THOUGHTLESS . . .	610B	V LAST JUDG/N	PROSE
"A FAIRY VISION OF SOME GAY CREATURES OF THE ELEMENT" (MILTON)	SUPP	LEGEND/N30	*
GAZA			
FROM BASHAN TO TYRE & FROM TROY TO GAZA OF THE AMALEKITE	698	JERUSALEM 63	43
FROM GAZA TO DAMASCUS TYRE & SIDON & THE GODS	735	JERUSALEM 89	33
GAZE			
STAND ONLY FOR TO GAZE UPON THEIR SPLENDOR	18	EDW THIRD/PS 1	42
THE EAGLE THAT DOTH GAZE UPON THE SUN	24	EDW THIRD/PS 3	116
GAZED			
I EACH PARTICLE GAZED	804	TO BUTTS/L	19
GEETA			
THE SUBJECT IS MR WILKIN TRANSLATING THE GEETA . . .	583D	DESC CAT 10	PROSE
GEM			
AND EVERY SAND BECOMES A GEM	418	MOCK ON/N	5
GEMS			
AND THE WILD SNAKE THE PESTILENCE TO ADORN HIM WITH GEMS & GOLD	195	V DAU ALBION 8	7
THE DAZZLINGS AS OF GEMS SHONE CLEAR RAPTUROUS IN [JOY] FURY	267	FOUR ZOAS 1	128
SIEZD HIS BRIGHT SHEEPHOOK STUDDED WITH GEMS & GOLD HE SWUNG IT ROUND	275	FOUR ZOAS 1	414
IN RAGING HUNGER STILL THE PESTILENTIAL FOOD IN GEMS & GOLD	343	FOUR ZOAS 8	78
THE SYNAGOGUE OF SATAN CLOTHED HER WITH SCARLET ROBES & GEMS	348	FOUR ZOAS 8	281
FULL FILLED ALL WITH GEMS & GOLD	425	MENTAL TRAVLER	31
AND THESE ARE THE GEMS OF THE HUMAN SOUL	425	MENTAL TRAVLER	33
AND GEMS & GOLD THAT NONE HIS HAND	425	MENTAL TRAVLER	46

```
                                                          PAGE     TITLE           LINE
GEMS    (CONTINUED)
    WHEN GOLD & GEMS ADORN THE PLOW    . . . . . . . .     433 AUGURIES            101
    THE GREEK GEMS ARE IN THE SAME STYLE AS THE GREEK STATUES  463B ANNO REYNOLDS   MARG
    THE TOAD & VENOMOUS NEWT THE SERPENT CLOTHD IN GEMS & GOLD  513 MILTON 27        22
    MALE GENIUS WHO IN RETURN CLOTHES HER IN GEMS & GOLD   .  . 707 JERUSALEM 69     17
    THE CRUEL-ONE OF ALBION TO CLOTHE HIM IN GEMS OF MY ZONE  724 JERUSALEM 81       12
    THY BOSOM WHITE TRANSLUCENT COVERD WITH IMMORTAL GEMS  .  . 731 JERUSALEM 86     14
    BUT TRANSLUCENT THEIR BLACKNESS AS THE DAZLING OF GEMS  .  735 JERUSALEM 89      37
    AND THE ALL WONDROUS SERPENT CLOTHED IN GEMS & RICH ARRAY  746 JERUSALEM 98      44
        HUMANIZE
    THE BURIED SOUL & ALL ITS GEMS    . . . . . . . . .    753 EV GOSPEL(D)/N      102
    WHAT WE CALL ANTIQUE GEMS ARE THE GEMS OF AARON'S BREAST  777D INSC LAOCOON    PROSE
        PLATE
    CORRECT & ENLARGED COPIES FROM ANTIQUE GEMS OF WHICH THE  836B LETTER 35       PROSE
GENERAL     SEE GENRAL
    WHERE IS THE GENERAL OF THE NATION . . . . . . .       146 FRENCH REVOLTN      261
    . . . THE WALLS RE-ECHOD WHERE IS THE GENERAL OF THE NATION  146 FRENCH REVOLTN * 261
    & PROPORTIONATE VALUE & A GENERAL DEMAND FOR ART  .  .  .  446D ANNO REYNOLDS   MARG
    GENERAL KNOWLEDGES ARE THOSE KNOWLEDGES THAT IDIOTS       451A ANNO REYNOLDS   MARG
        POSSESS
    [AS DO ?FOOLS THAT ADORE THINGS & ?IDEAS XXX OF GENERAL   451A ANNO REYNOLDS  * MARG
        KNOWLEDGE]
    [GENERAL PRINCIPLES YOU CANNOT EVEN KNOW OR SEE MICH ANG]  456B ANNO REYNOLDS * MARG
    GENERAL PRINCIPLE AGAIN UNLESS YOU CONSULT PARTICULARS  . . 456B ANNO REYNOLDS * MARG
    WHAT IS GENERAL KNOWLEDGE [IS] THERE SUCH A THING  .  .  459D ANNO REYNOLDS    MARG
    DISTINCT GENERAL FORM CANNOT EXIST   . . . . . . .     461B ANNO REYNOLDS     MARG
    DISTINCTNESS IS PARTICULAR NOT GENERAL   . . . . . .   461B ANNO REYNOLDS     MARG
    GENERAL IDEAS AGAIN    . . . . . . . . . . . .         461D ANNO REYNOLDS     MARG
    A HISTORY PAINTER PAINTS THE HERO & NOT MAN IN GENERAL  . 465A ANNO REYNOLDS    MARG
    ONE SPECIES OF GENERAL HUE OVER ALL IS THE CURSED THING  478D ANNO REYNOLDS    MARG
    SHAKSPEARE & MILTON WERE BOTH CURBD BY THE GENERAL MALADY  480C MILTON 1      *PROSE
    BROUGHT OIL PAINTING INTO GENERAL OPINION AND PRACTICE  . 565B DESC CAT 2     PROSE
    THE THREE GENERAL CLASSES OF MEN WHO ARE REPRESENTED BY   577C DESC CAT 5     PROSE
    ELEMENTAL BEINGS CALLED BY US BY THE GENERAL NAME         577D DESC CAT 5     PROSE
        OF FAIRIES
    GENERAL KNOWLEDGE IS REMOTE KNOWLEDGE   . . . . . .    611A V LAST JUDG/N     PROSE
    BOTH IN ART & IN LIFE GENERAL MASSES ARE  . . . . .   611B V LAST JUDG/N     PROSE
    SWELLD & BLOATED GENERAL FORMS REPUGNANT TO THE . . . .  672 JERUSALEM 43       19
    . . . DIVINE-HUMANITY WHO IS THE ONLY GENERAL AND UNIVERSAL  672 JERUSALEM 43     20
        FORM
    ALL BROAD & GENERAL PRINCIPLES BELONG TO BENEVOLENCE  .  . 672 JERUSALEM 43      22
    GENERAL GOOD IS THE PLEA OF THE SCOUNDREL HYPOCRITE       687 JERUSALEM 55       61
        & FLATTERER
    BUT GENERAL FORMS HAVE THEIR VITALITY IN PARTICULARS &    738 JERUSALEM 91       30
        EVERY
    AUTHORS AND CURIOUS BOOKS IN GENERAL HE ADVISES THAT SOME  831C LETTER 31      PROSE
    IN GENERAL FOUND GREAT BODIES TO BE THEY WERE MUCH PLEASED  850C LETTER 49      PROSE
    CONSIDERS AS IMPOLITIC AND THAT A HANDSOME GENERAL EDITION  858A LETTER 55      PROSE
    NUMBER FOR A GENERAL SALE BY MEANS OF A REGULAR PUBLISHER  867C LETTER 66      PROSE
    GENERAL TITLE FRONTISPIECE OF PIPER   . . . . . . .   SUPP LETTER 66A      *PROSE
GENERALIZE
    TO GENERALIZE IS TO BE AN IDIOT   . . . . . . . .     451A ANNO REYNOLDS     MARG
GENERALIZER
    REMBRANDT WAS A GENERALIZER POUSSIN WAS A PARTICULARIZER  477B ANNO REYNOLDS    MARG
GENERALIZING
    ("GENERAL COPYING...DELUSIVE") HERE HE CONDEMNS          448C ANNO REYNOLDS     MARG
        GENERALIZING
    (GENERALIZING) IN EVERY (THING) THE MAN (WOULD) SOON BE   460D ANNO REYNOLDS  * MARG
        A FOOL
    . . . [WHAT A BRILLIANT TONE] ONE GENERALIZING TONE   .  .  554 TO VENETIAN/N      9
    GENERALIZING ART & SCIENCE TILL ART & SCIENCE IS LOST    673 JERUSALEM 43       54
    AND NOT IN GENERALIZING DEMONSTRATIONS OF THE RATIONAL    687 JERUSALEM 55       63
        POWER
    THERE ISRAEL IN BONDAGE TO HIS GENERALIZING GODS  . . .  735 JERUSALEM 89       30
GENERALLY
    THEY ARE GENERALLY FULL OF PAPER [FOR XXX ?PERSON]  .  .   86B ANNO LAVATER    * MARG
    IN A BOOK I LOVE SO MUCH & APPROVE SO GENERALLY  .  .     88A ANNO LAVATER      MARG
    IT WAS NEVER GENERALLY USED TILL AFTER VANDYKE'S TIME  .  561A EXHIBITION ADV  PROSE
    FOR INVENTION & DRAWING HAS GENERALLY BEEN ACCOMPANIED BY  602A PUB ADDRESS/N  PROSE
GENERALS
    GOOD MORROW GENERALS I GIVE YOU JOY   . . . . . . .    22 EDW THIRD/PS 3       43
    GOOD MORROW GENERALS WHEN ENGLISH COURAGE FAILS  . . .   23 EDW THIRD/PS 3       71
    THEM ALL GENERALS   . . . . . . . . . . . .            23 EDW THIRD/PS 3       91
    HEAR MY COUNSEL O KING AND SEND FORTH THY GENERALS . . .  141 FRENCH REVOLTN     153
    . . . O PRINCES AND GENERALS OF FRANCE   . . . . .    141 FRENCH REVOLTN      163
    WITHIN LABOURING BEHOLDING WITHOUT FROM PARTICULARS TO    483 MILTON 3          37
        GENERALS
    BUT BY DESIGN BY THE KINGS OF PERSIA & THEIR GENERALS  . 785B ILLUS DANTE 7    PROSE
GENERATE
    THE LUSTFUL JOY SHALL FORGET TO GENERATE & CREATE        194 V DAU ALBION 7      6
        AN AMOROUS IMAGE
    AND SATAN IS THE SPECTRE OF ORC & ORC IS THE GENERATE    517 MILTON 29         34
        LUVAH
    THEY RETURN NOT BUT GENERATE IN ROCKY PLACES DESOLATE  .  . 703 JERUSALEM 66     72
GENERATED
    AND EPHRAIM & JUDAH WERE GENERATED BECAUSE  . . . . .  508 MILTON 24           3
    AND EVERY GENERATED BODY IN ITS INWARD FORM   . . . .  512 MILTON 26          31
    BUT WHATEVER IS VISIBLE TO THE GENERATED MAN  . . . .  634 JERUSALEM 13       44
    BECOMING A GENERATED MORTAL A VEGETATING DEATH   . . .  708 JERUSALEM 69      31
    BUT THE FOUR SONS OF JERUSALEM THAT NEVER WERE GENERATED  710 JERUSALEM 71     50
    NOR CAN ANY CONSUMMATE BLISS WITHOUT BEING GENERATED   .  731 JERUSALEM 86     42
    FROM GENERATED ORGANS GONE AS SOON AS COME   . . . . . 776D INSC LAOCOON    PROSE
```

	PAGE	TITLE	LINE

GENERATING

AND GENERATING LOVE A PRETENCE OF LOVE TO DESTROY LOVE   639 JERUSALEM 17   26

GENERATION

KNOWLEDGE IS TRANSMITTED FROM GENERATION TO GENERATION . . 154D MARRIAGE HH 15   PROSE
TO RISE FROM GENERATION FREE   220 TO TIRZAH/SE   3
HIS FALL INTO THE GENERATION OF DECAY & DEATH & HIS . . . 264 FOUR ZOAS 1   22
FIRST BORN OF GENERATION THEN BEHOLD A WONDER TO THE EYES   326 FOUR ZOAS 7   245
SUBDUING HIS SPECTRE THEY BUILDED THE LOOMS OF GENERATION   483 MILTON 3   38
DRAWN DOWN BY ORC & THE SHADOWY FEMALE INTO GENERATION .   490 MILTON 10   2
CONCERNING GENERATION & THE VEGETATIVE POWER & CONCERNING   495 MILTON 14   5
AND RAHAB THEY KNOW NOT OF REGENERATION BUT ONLY   520 MILTON 31   19
     OF GENERATION
BUT MUST BE CREATED FOR THEY KNOW ONLY OF GENERATION . . 520 MILTON 31   22
TILL GENERATION IS SWALLOWD UP IN REGENERATION . . . . 533 MILTON 41   28
THE WORLD OF VEGETATION AND GENERATION MAY EXPECT . . . 578A DESC CAT 5   PROSE
AND HIS REAL HUMANITY SLAIN ON THE STEMS OF GENERATION . . 578B DESC CAT 5   PROSE
ABOVE THE SHADOWS OF GENERATION AND DEATH . . . . . 578C DESC CAT 5   PROSE
THE WORLD OF GENERATION OR VEGETATION IS FINITE . . . . 605D V LAST JUDG/N   PROSE
REPRESENTS ETERNAL FIRE WHICH IS THE FIRE OF GENERATION OR   609A V LAST JUDG/N   PROSE
WE ARE IN A WORLD OF GENERATION & DEATH & THIS WORLD . . 613C V LAST JUDG/N   PROSE
GENERATION CAMBEL & GWENDOLEN WOVE WEBS OF WAR & OF . . 626 JERUSALEM 7   44
AND THE RELIGION OF GENERATION WHICH WAS MEANT FOR THE   626 JERUSALEM 7   63
     DESTRUCTION
O HOLY GENERATION [IMAGE] OF REGENERATION . . . . . . 626 JERUSALEM 7   *   65
EDEN AND THAT TOWARD THE WORLD OF GENERATION . . . . . 632 JERUSALEM 12   49
AND THE NORTH GATE OF GOLGONOOZA TOWARD GENERATION . . 632 JERUSALEM 12   61
THAT TOWARD GENERATION FOUR OF IRON CARVD WONDROUS . . 633 JERUSALEM 13   3
THAT TOWARDS GENERATION IRON THAT TOWARD BEULAH STONE . . 633 JERUSALEM 13   9
AND THAT TOWARD GENERATION SEVEN GENERATIVE FORMS . . 633 JERUSALEM 13   19
THEIR LOOMS IN A GENERATION OF DEATH & RESURRECTION TO   638 JERUSALEM 17   9
     FORGETFULNESS
THE ROCKY LAW OF CONDEMNATION & DOUBLE GENERATION & DEATH   656 JERUSALEM 30   37
THE DEAD AWAKE TO GENERATION ARISE O LORD & REND THE VEIL   656 JERUSALEM 30   40
THESE ARE THEIR NAMES IN THE VEGETATIVE GENERATION . . . 663 JERUSALEM 36   33
[?WEST ?WEIGHING ?EAST & ?NORTH DIVIDING ?GENERATION XXX]   663 JERUSALEM 36   *   34
OF GENERATION TO DESTROY BY SIN AND ATONEMENT HAPPY   676 JERUSALEM 46   27
     JERUSALEM
NOW GIVEN TO STONY DRUIDS AND ALLEGORIC GENERATION . . . 681 JERUSALEM 50   2
BUT SHE IS MADE RECEPTIVE OF GENERATION THRO MERCY . . . 684 JERUSALEM 53   27
TO CREATE A WORLD OF GENERATION FROM THE WORLD OF DEATH   690 JERUSALEM 58   18
WORKS A WORLD OF GENERATION CONTINUALLY CREATING OUT OF   690 JERUSALEM 58   50
. . . TILL THE GREAT POLYPUS OF GENERATION COVERED THE   704 JERUSALEM 67   34
     EARTH
O CHEMOSH O BACCHUS O VENUS O DOUBLE GOD OF GENERATION   706 JERUSALEM 68   18
FIXING THE SEXUAL INTO AN EVER-PROLIFIC GENERATION . . . 713 JERUSALEM 73   26
WHERE THE RED SEA TERMINATES THE WORLD OF GENERATION &   735 JERUSALEM 89   49
     DEATH
LEST THE SEXUAL GENERATION SWALLOW UP REGENERATION . . . 737 JERUSALEM 90   37
AND FROM THE GREAT CITY OF GOLGONOOZA IN THE SHADOWY   746 JERUSALEM 98   55
     GENERATION
PROPAGATING GENERATION & DEATH . . . . 776B INSC LAOCOON   PROSE
IS A HUNDRED YEARS BEYOND THE PRESENT GENERATION THOUGH   864D LETTER 61   PROSE
CHAPTER III OF THE SEXUAL NATURE & ITS FALL INTO   SUPP ILLUS GENESIS   *TITLE
     GENERATION & DEATH
CHAPTER IV HOW GENERATION & DEATH TOOK POSSESSION OF THE   SUPP ILLUS GENESIS   *TITLE
     NATURAL MAN

GENERATIONS

DESCEND TO GENERATIONS THAT IN FUTURE TIMES FORGET . . 197 AMERICA 3   12
DESCEND TO GENERATIONS THAT IN FUTURE TIMES FORGET . . . 204 AMERICA CANC A   12
THE HIDDEN WONDERS ALLEGORIC OF THE GENERATIONS . . . 333 FOUR ZOAS 7B   24
HEAR ME REPEAT MY GENERATIONS THAT THOU MAYST ALSO REPENT   350 FOUR ZOAS 8   *   356
THE GENERATIONS OF MEN RUN ON IN THE TIDE OF TIME . . . 505 MILTON 22   24
WE CALLD HIM MENASSEH BECAUSE OF THE GENERATIONS OF TIRZAH   508 MILTON 24   6
BEFORE THE FLOOD & THEIR GENERATIONS . . . . 611D V LAST JUDG/N   PROSE
OF THE TERRIBLE SONS & DAUGHTERS OF ALBION AND THEIR   623 JERUSALEM 5   26
     GENERATIONS
INVOLVD THE EIGHT SUCH ARE THE GENERATIONS OF THE GIANT   626 JERUSALEM 7   49
     ALBION
OF AGES & GENERATIONS FOLDING & UNFOLDING IT LIKE A VEIL   698 JERUSALEM 64   3
     OF CHERUBIM
TO COME & TO SPEAK TO FUTURE GENERATIONS BY A SUBLIME   825A LETTER 27   PROSE
     ALLEGORY

GENERATIVE

THIS IS THE [VEGETATIVE] GENERATIVE WORLD . . . . . . 373 FOUR ZOAS 9   625
THAN THE THINGS OF VEGETATIVE & GENERATIVE NATURE . . 605B V LAST JUDG/N   PROSE
AND THAT TOWARD GENERATION SEVEN GENERATIVE FORMS . . 633 JERUSALEM 13   19

GENEROSITY

TILL PITY IS BECOME A TRADE AND GENEROSITY A SCIENCE . . 200 AMERICA 11   10
I PROFESS NOT GENEROSITY TO A FOE . . . . 541 HOMERS HERO/N   2
MY GENEROSITY IS TO MY FRIENDS . . . . 541 HOMERS HERO/N   3

GENEROUS   SEE GENROUS

HIS GENEROUS AID TO PUT IT INTO PRACTICE . . . . . . 21 EDW THIRD/PS 2   90
("GRATITUDE...OPENS TREASURES WITHIN US") NOBLE & GENEROUS   70A ANNO LAVATER   MARG
THEN ORLEANS GENEROUS AS MOUNTAINS . . . . 142 FRENCH REVOLTN   175
COME IN THE HEAVEN OF GENEROUS LOVE NOR SELFISH BLIGHTINGS   195 V DAU ALBION 7   29
     BRING
MUST THE GENEROUS TREMBLE . . . . 200 AMERICA 11   6
WITH THY HAND FULL OF GENEROUS FIRE . . . . 255 AHANIA 5   30
THE GENEROUS TO ENEMIES PROMOTES THEIR ENDS . . . . 541 HOMERS HERO/N   5
GENEROUS KNIGHT IS IN THE COMPASSIONATE DICTATES OF HIS   569A DESC CAT 3   PROSE
     SOUL
SUCH THING AS GENEROUS CONTENTION I KNOW THAT ALL THOSE   596D PUB ADDRESS/N   PROSE
     WITH

788

	PAGE	TITLE	LINE

GENEROUS   (CONTINUED)
GENEROUS IMMORTAL GUARDIAN GOLDEN CLAD FOR CITIES   . . .   665 JERUSALEM 38   46
ALBION THE VORTEX OF THE DEAD ALBION THE GENEROUS   . . .   678 JERUSALEM 48   54
I THANK YOU AGAIN & AGAIN FOR YOUR GENEROUS FORBEARANCE   809C LETTER 20   PROSE
YOUR GENEROUS & TENDER SOLICITUDE ABOUT YOUR DEVOTED REBEL   829C LETTER 30   PROSE
GENEROUS EXULTATION IN MY ESCAPE FROM THE ARROWS   833C LETTER 33   PROSE
  OF DARKNESS
HIS PROPOSAL WAS BY NO MEANS A GENEROUS ONE   . . . . .   842D LETTER 42   PROSE
BE VERY HONEST AND VERY GENEROUS TOO WHERE HIS OWN   846C LETTER 44   PROSE
  INTEREST
WE BOTH REJOICE IN THE GENEROUS PAULINA'S RETURN   . . .   849B LETTER 45   PROSE
WHOSE HIGH & GENEROUS SPIRIT RELINQUISHING THE WHOLE TO ME   853A LETTER 51   *PROSE
THE DEATH OF SO EXCELLENT A MAN AS MY GENEROUS ADVOCATE   854B LETTER 53   PROSE
HIM MAD IF HE HAD NOT FOR SUCH CLEAR AND GENEROUS PROPOSALS   857D LETTER 55   PROSE
I MUST NOW EXPRESS MY THANKS FOR YOUR GENEROUS MANNER OF   858A LETTER 55   PROSE
JESUS PRESENT ALSO MY THANKS TO THE GENEROUS SEAGRAVE IN   863B LETTER 60   PROSE
GENEROUSLY
BUT YOU HAVE SO GENEROUSLY & OPENLY DESIRED THAT I WILL   812B LETTER 22   PROSE
GENESIS
MILTON'S PARADISE LOST IS AS TRUE AS GENESIS OR EXODUS   392D ANNO WATSON   MARG
GENESIS CHAPTER I THE CREATION OF THE NATURAL MAN   . . .   SUPP ILLUS GENESIS   *TITLE
GENEVA
AND SHALL NECKER THE HIND OF GENEVA . . . .   138 FRENCH REVOLTN   91
HE SET HIS FACE TOWARD GENEVA TO FLEE . . . .   139 FRENCH REVOLTN *   122
THEN FLED AND THE WHOLE CITY KNEW HE WAS FLED TO GENEVA   139 FRENCH REVOLTN   124
  . . .
GENII
AND LOS SAID YE GENII OF THE MILLS THE SUN IS ON HIGH   . .   488 MILTON 8   16
THE FAIRIES NYMPHS GNOMES & GENII OF THE FOUR ELEMENTS   . .   520 MILTON 31   20
AND SIXTY-FOUR THOUSAND GENII GUARD THE EASTERN GATE   . .   633 JERUSALEM 13   26
FAIRIES & GENII & NYMPHS & GNOMES OF THE ELEMENTS   . . .   663 JERUSALEM 36   37
ASSISTANCE OF BRUNO'S FAIRIES BUT I INVOKE THE GOOD GENII   801B LETTER 13   PROSE
GENITALS
THE GENITALS BEAUTY THE HANDS & FEET PROPORTION   . . . .   152C MARRIAGE HH 10   PROSE
GENIUS
HONOUR & GENIUS IS ALL I ASK   . . . .   47 ASK GODS/IM 1   1
IN [(TWENTY)] TEN OR TWELVE YEARS WILL BE A FAR SUPERIOR   49D ISLAND MOON 6   *PROSE
  GENIUS
ENGLISH GENIUS FOR EVER HERE I GO   . . . .   56 ISLAND MOON 9   PROSE
("WHO ...IS A GENIUS AND A HERO AT ONCE ") UNEASY   69B ANNO LAVATER   MARG
("THE DEGREE OF GENIUS IS DETERMINED BY") COPIOUSNESS   69C ANNO LAVATER   MARG
  OF GLANCE
("ALL GENIUS IS THE OFFSPRING OF IMMORTALITY") UNEASY   69D ANNO LAVATER   MARG
  STERLING
& VICE VERSA GENIUS FINDS THOUGHT WITHOUT SEEKG   . . .   80B ANNO LAVATER   MARG
IT IS NOT HIS GENIUS BUT AN ACCIDENT ACQUIRED FOR HOW   . .   81D ANNO LAVATER   MARG
("NO GIFTS CAN EXHAUST GENIUS IMPOVERISH CHARITY") MOST   84B ANNO LAVATER   MARG
  EXCELLENT
("KNOWS HIMSELF WHO NEVER OPPOSES HIS GENIUS")   84C ANNO LAVATER   MARG
  MOST EXCELLENT
MAY PERCIEVE IT IS FROM THE POETIC GENIUS WHICH IS THE LORD   90B ANNO SWED LOVE   MARG
("CONSTITUTES HELL") THE NEGATION OF THE POETIC GENIUS   90D ANNO SWED LOVE   MARG
PRINCIPLE FIRST THAT THE POETIC GENIUS IS THE TRUE MAN   . .   98B ALL RELIGIONS   PROSE
OF MAN IS DERIVED FROM THE POETIC GENIUS LIKEWISE   . . .   98B ALL RELIGIONS   PROSE
THAT THE FORMS OF ALL THINGS ARE DERIVED FROM THEIR GENIUS   98B ALL RELIGIONS   PROSE
SAME INFINITE VARIETY ALL ARE ALIKE IN THE POETIC GENIUS   98C ALL RELIGIONS   PROSE
THUS ALL SECTS OF PHILOSOPHY ARE FROM THE POETIC GENIUS   98C ALL RELIGIONS   PROSE
THEREFORE AN UNIVERSAL POETIC GENIUS EXISTS   . . . . .   98C ALL RELIGIONS   PROSE
FROM EACH NATION'S DIFFERENT RECEPTION OF THE POETIC GENIUS   98C ALL RELIGIONS   PROSE
ARE AN ORIGINAL DERIVATION FROM THE POETIC GENIUS THIS   . .   98D ALL RELIGIONS   PROSE
THE TRUE MAN IS THE SOURCE HE BEING THE POETIC GENIUS   98D ALL RELIGIONS   PROSE
DELIGHTED WITH THE ENJOYMENTS OF GENIUS   . . . .   150C MARRIAGE HH 6   PROSE
WHEN THOU SEEST AN EAGLE THOU SEEST A PORTION OF GENIUS   152B MARRIAGE HH 9   PROSE
BUT THE CROOKED ROADS WITHOUT IMPROVEMENT ARE ROADS OF   152D MARRIAGE HH 10   PROSE
  GENIUS
AND PARTICULARLY THEY STUDIED THE GENIUS OF EACH CITY &   153A MARRIAGE HH 11   PROSE
WE OF ISRAEL TAUGHT THAT THE POETIC GENIUS AS YOU NOW CALL   153D MARRIAGE HH 12   PROSE
  IT
OF THE POETIC GENIUS IT WAS THIS THAT OUR GREAT POET   . . .   153D MARRIAGE HH 12   PROSE
& IS HE HONEST WHO RESISTS HIS GENIUS OR CONSCIENCE   . . .   154B MARRIAGE HH 12   PROSE
EACH ACCORDING TO HIS GENIUS AND LOVING THE GREATEST MEN   158B MARRIAGE HH 22   PROSE
  BEST
SUCH WORKS AS HAVE WHOLLY ABSORBED THE MAN OF GENIUS   . .   207B PRSPECTUS 1793   PROSE
MEN WHO GIVE THEMSELVES TO THEIR ENERGETIC GENIUS [AS]   386B ANNO WATSON   * MARG
  IN THE MANNER
HERE IS NOTHING OF THY OWN ORIGINAL GENIUS   . . . . .   400C ANNO BACON   MARG
IT APPEARS TO ME THAT MEN ARE HIRED TO RUN DOWN MEN OF   413B ANNO BOYD   MARG
  GENIUS
HAVING SPENT THE VIGOUR OF MY YOUTH & GENIUS UNDER THE   . .   445B ANNO REYNOLDS   MARG
ALL THIS CONCESSION IS TO PROVE THAT GENIUS IS ACQUIRED   448A ANNO REYNOLDS   MARG
REYNOLDS'S OPINION WAS THAT GENIUS MAY BE TAUGHT   . . .   452D ANNO REYNOLDS   MARG
& GENIUS BUT WHETHER HE IS PASSIVE & POLITE & A VIRTUOUS   453A ANNO REYNOLDS   MARG
  ASS
MECHANICAL EXCELLENCE IS THE ONLY VEHICLE OF GENIUS   . .   453D ANNO REYNOLDS   MARG
EXECUTION IS THE CHARIOT OF GENIUS   . . . .   454A ANNO REYNOLDS   MARG
THUS REYNOLDS DEPRECIATES THE EFFORTS OF INVENTIVE GENIUS   455D ANNO REYNOLDS   MARG
A WORK OF GENIUS IS A WORK "NOT...OF MEMORY   457C ANNO REYNOLDS   MARG
  &...DAUGHTERS..." MILTON
BUT GENIUS (IS ALWAYS ABOVE THE AGE) . . . .   461A ANNO REYNOLDS * MARG
GENIUS HAS NO ERROR IT IS IGNORANCE THAT IS ERROR   . . .   465B ANNO REYNOLDS   MARG
BUT HE OUGHT TO PUT ALL MEN OF GENIUS WHO EVER PAINTED   .   469A ANNO REYNOLDS   MARG
THE MAN WHO SAYS THAT THE GENIUS IS NOT BORN (BUT) TAUGHT   470A ANNO REYNOLDS * MARG
  IS A KNAVE

	PAGE	TITLE	LINE

GENIUS (CONTINUED)

BUT IT IS NOT SO GENIUS DIES WITH ITS POSSESSOR	470D	ANNO REYNOLDS	MARG
HE WHO CAN BE BOUND DOWN IS NO GENIUS	472D	ANNO REYNOLDS	MARG
GENIUS CANNOT BE BOUND	472D	ANNO REYNOLDS	MARG
TASTE & GENIUS ARE NOT OF HEAVENLY ORIGIN &	473A	ANNO REYNOLDS	MARG
I SAY TASTE & GENIUS ARE NOT TEACHABLE OR ACQUIRABLE .	474B	ANNO REYNOLDS	MARG
THINKS HE HAS PROVED THAT GENIUS & INSPIRATION ARE ALL A HUM	475A	ANNO REYNOLDS	MARG
ACCORDING TO THE INSPIRATION OF THE POETIC GENIUS . . .	495	MILTON 14	1
MY TITLE AS AN [ARTIST] GENIUS THUS IS PROVD . . .	546	MY TITLE AS/N	1
WHO CRIES ALL ART IS A FRAUD & GENIUS A TRICK	555	BLAKES APL/N 1	20
OF A NATION IF GENIUS AND INSPIRATION ARE THE GREAT ORIGIN	561C	EXHIBITION ADV	PROSE
OF SELF-DEVOTING GENIUS THE QUARREL OF THE FLORENTINE WITH	563D	DESC CAT	PROSE
OIL BECAME A FETTER TO GENIUS AND A DUNGEON TO ART BUT ONE	566C	DESC CAT 2	PROSE
WHO IS THE GENIUS OF EATING AND DRINKING THE BACCHUS .	571A	DESC CAT 3	PROSE
THE SHIPMAN OR SAILOR IS A SIMILAR GENIUS OF ULYSSEAN ART	571D	DESC CAT 3	PROSE
CONTEMPLATIVE PHILOSOPHER VARIES FROM THE POETICAL GENIUS	572B	DESC CAT 3	PROSE
OF ANTIQUITY AND IN THE WORKS OF MORE MODERN GENIUS . . .	579C	DESC CAT 5	PROSE
IT IS NOT THE WANT OF GENIUS THAT CAN HEREAFTER BE . .	584B	DESC CAT 14	PROSE
IN PREFERENCE TO THE INSPIRED MOMENTS OF GENIUS & ANIMATION	594B	PUB ADDRESS/N	PROSE
[ENCOURAGE A BLOCKHEAD & HE IS COUNTED THE GREATEST GENIUS]	595B	PUB ADDRESS/N	PROSE
OF THE MOST PROFOUND SENSE A GENIUS & YET HIS EXECUTION	599D	PUB ADDRESS/N	PROSE
IN ALL PROFESSIONS THESE ARE THE GREATEST ENEMIES OF GENIUS	601C	PUB ADDRESS/N	PROSE
BOTH IN GENIUS & FORTUNE HAVE SUBSCRIBED THEIR NAMES .	601D	PUB ADDRESS/N	PROSE
BUT NOT THE SAME GENIUS SCIENCE IS SOON GOT	602D	PUB ADDR AD/N	PROSE
INSPIRATION DENYD GENIUS FORBIDDEN BY LAWS OF PUNISHMENT	628	JERUSALEM 9	16
MALE GENIUS WHO IN RETURN CLOTHES HER IN GEMS & GOLD .	707	JERUSALEM 69	17
TO HIS GENIUS WHICH IS THE HOLY GHOST IN MAN THERE IS NO OTHER	738	JERUSALEM 91	10
ALL GENIUS VARIES THUS DEVILS ARE VARIOUS ANGELS ARE ALL ALIKE	773A	NOTE NINE HEAD	PROSE
BECAUSE I KNOW THAT THE GENIUS THAT PRODUCES THE DESIGNS	790B	LETTER 2	PROSE
& IN THIS WHICH I SEND YOU HAVE BEEN COMPELLD BY MY GENIUS	791D	LETTER 4	PROSE
& HE BEGINS TO THINK I HAVE SOME GENIUS	825C	LETTER 27	PROSE
AS IF GENIUS & ASSURANCE WERE THE SAME THING BUT . .	825C	LETTER 27	PROSE
MY ADMIRATION OF FLAXMAN'S GENIUS IS MORE AND MORE . .	829B	LETTER 29	PROSE
THE PRESS & A BULWARK FOR GENIUS	841D	LETTER 41	PROSE
ROMNEY'S GENIUS NOTHING LESS THAN SOME	848A	LETTER 45	PROSE
IN RETURN FOR THE SACRIFICE OF ART & GENIUS HE SAYS . .	850B	LETTER 49	PROSE
THE PUBLIC A SINGULAR MONUMENT OF ROMNEY'S GENIUS . .	851A	LETTER 49	PROSE
OF GENIUS AS TO THE [PLATES] PRICE OF THE PLATES . .	855A	LETTER 53	PROSE
THE PINDARIC GENIUS RECIEVING HIS LYRE	SUPP	ILLUS GRAY	*TITLE
A GENIUS DRIVING AWAY "COMUS & HIS MIDNIGHT CREW" . .	SUPP	ILLUS GRAY	*TITLE

GENIUSES

OR GENIUSES CALLING THEM BY THE NAMES AND ADORNING THEM	153A	MARRIAGE HH 11	PROSE

GENRAL

MY THOUGHTS TAKE IN THE GENRAL GOOD OF THE WHOLE	19	EDW THIRD/PS 2	29

GENROUS

TO KEEP THE GENROUS FROM EXPERIENCE TILL THE UNGENEROUS	200	AMERICA 11	8
ALL THAT THEY HAVE IS MINE FROM MY FREE GENROUS GIFT .	671	JERUSALEM 42	52

GENT

BY JOHN LOOKYE [?PANTRYMAN] GENT JOHN LOCKE SAID OBTUSE ANGLE	52D	ISLAND MOON 8	PROSE

GENTEEL

WITH HIS GENTEEL IGNORANCE & POLITE DISAPPROBATION . . .	825C	LETTER 27	PROSE

GENTILITY

GIVE ANY MARKS OF GENTILITY	748	EV GOSPEL(B)/N	2

GENTLE

LIKE GENTLE STREAMS BENEATH OUR FEET	7	LOVE HARMNY/PS	7
WEEP FROM THY GENTLE RIVERS THE ANGEL OF THE ISLAND WEEPS	34A	KING JOHN/PS	PROSE
HAVING MADE A GENTLE BOW PROCEEDED TO EMPTY HIS POCKETS	45B	ISLAND MOON 1	PROSE
AND THUS HER GENTLE LAMENTATION FALLS LIKE MORNING DEW .	127	BOOK OF THEL 1	5
AH GENTLE MAY I LAY ME DOWN AND GENTLE REST MY HEAD .	127	BOOK OF THEL 1	12
AND GENTLE SLEEP THE SLEEP OF DEATH AND GENTLE HEAR THE VOICE	127	BOOK OF THEL 1	13
THOU GENTLE MAID OF SILENT VALLEYS AND OF MODEST BROOKS	127	BOOK OF THEL 1	22
. . . NOW BEAMING WITH KNOWLEDGE WITH GENTLE AWE ADORNED	144	FRENCH REVOLTN	230
[FOR THE GENTLE WIND DOES MOVE]	161	NEVER PAIN/N	3
PURE MILD & GENTLE GIVEN IN MERCY TO THOSE WHO SLEEP .	266	FOUR ZOAS 1	96
THE SAVIOUR MILD & GENTLE BENT OVER THE CORSE OF DEATH .	304	FOUR ZOAS 4	269
THE MANHOOD WAS DIVIDED FOR THE GENTLE PASSIONS MAKING WAY	327	FOUR ZOAS 7	279
. . . THIS IS NO GENTLE HARP	338	FOUR ZOAS 7B	203
OF ALL BENEATH & ALL ABOVE & IN THE GENTLE WEST	355	FOUR ZOAS 8	569
WHILE LITTLE CHILDREN PLAY AROUND THY FEET IN GENTLE AWE	360	FOUR ZOAS 9	134
FLOW ON YE GENTLE AIRS & BEAR THE VOICE OF MY REJOICING	368	FOUR ZOAS 9	435
VALA AWOKE & CALLD THE CHILDREN FROM THEIR GENTLE SLUMBERS	370	FOUR ZOAS 9	518
ROSE ENION LIKE A GENTLE LIGHT & ENION SPOKE SAYING . .	373	FOUR ZOAS 9	594
WITH HANDS DIVINE HE MOVD THE GENTLE SOD	414	TO MRS FLAXMAN	7
WHY DOST THOU WEEP IN THY GENTLE SLEEP	427	LAND OF DREAMS	3
IN THE GENTLE RELIEF OF ANOTHER'S CARE	436	WILLIAM BOND	50
THEN THOU WAS LOVELY MILD & GENTLE NOW THOU ART TERRIBLE	522	MILTON 33	5
TO WATCH THE TIME PITYING & GENTLE TO AWAKEN URIZEN . .	524	MILTON 34	43
[AND] YORKSHIRE JACK HEMP & GENTLE BLUSHING DAW . . .	537	AND HIS LEGS/N	20
THE MILD & GENTLE FOR THE MILD & GENTLE PARTS AND THE	621D	JERUSALEM 3	PROSE
THEY HOLD THE IMMORTAL FORM IN GENTLE BANDS & TENDER TEARS	624	JERUSALEM 5	55
THE FLOOD AND WAS NAMD CHICHESTER LOVELY MILD & GENTLE LO	667	JERUSALEM 40	50
FERVOR MILD SPOKE THRO THE WESTERN PORCH IN SOFT GENTLE TEARS	675	JERUSALEM 45	2
GENTLE TO ALBION'S WATCHMAN ON ALBION'S MOUNTAINS REECCHO	688	JERUSALEM 56	32
. . . THIS IS NO GENTLE HARP	700	JERUSALEM 65	49
WHITEFIELD & HERVEY GUARD THAT GATE WITH ALL THE GENTLE SOULS	712	JERUSALEM 72	51

GENTLE   (CONTINUED)
   WAS JESUS GENTLE OR DID HE . . . . 748 EV GOSPEL(B)/N   1
   I MUCH ADMIRED HIS MILD AND GENTLE BENEVOLENT MANNERS . . 844A LETTER 43   PROSE
GENTLEMAN
   WHY SIR SAID HE THE GENTLEMAN THAT THE SONG WAS ABOUT . . 47A ISLAND MOON 3   PROSE
   AH THAT WAS THE GENTLEMAN SAID ARADOBO . . . . 47B ISLAND MOON 3   PROSE
   IF SUCH IS THE CHARACTERISTIC OF A MODERN POLITE GENTLEMAN 384D ANNO WATSON   MARG
   PRINCE OF DARKNESS IS A GENTLEMAN & NOT A MAN HE IS A LORD 399C ANNO BACON   MARG
     CHANCELLOR
   GAINSBOROUGH TOLD A GENTLEMAN OF RANK & FORTUNE . . . . 465C ANNO REYNOLDS   MARG
   I DESIRED THE GENTLEMAN TO SET GAINSBOROUGH ABOUT . . 465C ANNO REYNOLDS   MARG
   THE VOLUPTUOUS COUNTRY GENTLEMAN CONTRASTED WITH . . . 570D DESC CAT 3   PROSE
   A GENTLEMAN WHO VISITED ME THE OTHER DAY SAID I AM VERY . 864D LETTER 61   PROSE
GENTLEMEN
   WELL GENTLEMEN SAID HE WHAT IS THE CAUSE OF STRIFE . . 45C ISLAND MOON 1   PROSE
   HERE LADIES & GENTLEMEN SAID HE I'LL SHEW YOU A LOUSE . 58C ISLAND MOON 10 *PROSE
     [?CLIMING] OR
   GENTLEMEN GENTLEMEN . . . . 62 DR CLASH/IM   18
   SHOULD BE CORRECTED BY THE YOUNG GENTLEMEN . . . 543 TO ROYL ACAD/N   3
   I THEREFORE INVITE THOSE NOBLEMEN AND GENTLEMEN WHO ARE ITS 561B EXHIBITION ADV   PROSE
   IT IS NONSENSE FOR NOBLEMEN & GENTLEMEN TO OFFER PREMIUMS 596D PUB ADDRESS/N   PROSE
   GENTLEMEN OF FORTUNE WHO GIVE GREAT PRICES FOR PICTURES 599C PUB ADDRESS/N   PROSE
   TO WHAT IS IT THAT GENTLEMEN OF THE FIRST RANK . . 601D PUB ADDRESS/N   *PROSE
   BEAUTIES NOW GENTLEMEN CRITICS HOW DO YOU LIKE THIS . 603B PUB ADDR AD/N   PROSE
GENTLEST
   YET WHY THESE SMITINGS OF LUVAH THE GENTLEST MILDEST ZOA 648 JERUSALEM 24   52
GENTLY
   AND GENTLY SIGHS AWAY THE SILENT HOUR . . . . 10 WHEN EARLY/PS   4
   OF FAIR JERUSALEM'S BOSOM IN A GENTLY BEAMING ?FIRE . . 346 FOUR ZOAS 8   193
   WHEN THE MAN GENTLY FADES AWAY IN HIS IMMORTALITY . . 355 FOUR ZOAS 8   551
   THE FORMER THINGS SO SHALL THE MORTAL GENTLY FADE AWAY . 355 FOUR ZOAS 8   553
   THE SAVIOUR WHILE THE EVIL ANGELS ARE DRIVEN GENTLY 441D INSC FALL MAN   PROSE
     CONDUCTS
   BY THE DAUGHTERS OF BEULAH GENTLY SNATCHD AWAY AND HID 668 JERUSALEM 41   14
     IN BEULAH
   GENTLY UPON THEIR BOSOMS MOVE . . . . 718 ENGLND AWAKE/J   6
   SEPARATE ALBION'S SONS GENTLY FROM THEIR EMANATIONS . . 728 JERUSALEM 83   49
GENTRY
   OF THE FLOWER OF THE ENGLISH NOBILITY & GENTRY [A SOCIETY] 446A ANNO REYNOLDS * MARG
   GENTRY TO CORREGGIO RUBENS REMBRANT REYNOLDS GAINSBOROUGH 548B ON GREAT ENC/N *TITLE
GENUINE
   HE IS A GENUINE ENGLISHMAN MY CHANDOS . . . . 25 EDW THIRD/PS 3   189
   AND IN HIS TIME ALL THE GENUINE PICTURES . . . 565B DESC CAT 2   PROSE
   ALL THE GENUINE OLD LITTLE PICTURES CALLED CABINET PICTURES 566B DESC CAT 2   PROSE
   HAS INTIRELY PUT AN END TO ALL GENUINE & APPROPRIATE EFFECT 599B PUB ADDRESS/N   PROSE
   WHILE THE HEBREW BIBLE & THE GREEK GOSPEL ARE GENUINE . 605C V LAST JUDG/N   PROSE
   ARE GENUINE SAXONS HANDSOMER THAN THE PEOPLE [AR] ABOUT 806B LETTER 16   *PROSE
     LONDON
GEOGRAPHY
   PAINTING PERSPECTIVE GEOMETRY GEOGRAPHY ASTRONOMY . . . 46D ISLAND MOON 3   PROSE
GEOMETRY
   PAINTING PERSPECTIVE GEOMETRY GEOGRAPHY ASTRONOMY . . . 46D ISLAND MOON 3   PROSE
GEORGE
   ("MAGNANIMOUSLY A CONQUEROR") THIS WAS OLD GEORGE 82B ANNO LAVATER   MARG
     THE SECOND
   WHERE GEORGE THE THIRD HOLDS COUNCIL & HIS LORDS & COMMONS 204 AMERICA CANC B   9
     MEET
   GROVELING ALONG GREAT GEORGE STREET THRO THE PARK GATE 242 EUROPE 12   19
     . . .
   [EDWARD HENRY ELIZABETH JAMES CHARLES WILLIAM GEORGE] . 713 JERUSALEM 73   * 37
   AS THE FRENCH NOW ADORE BUONAPARTE AND THE ENGLISH OUR 845B LETTER 44   PROSE
     POOR GEORGE
   GEORGE CUMBERLAND ESQRE CULVER STREET BRISTOL . . . . . SUPP ADDRESS/L 88 *TITLE
GERM
   WITH THE GERM OF PERHAPS GREATER PERFECTION STILL . . 568A DESC CAT 3   PROSE
GERMAN
   AND HEAVY THE GERMAN FLUTE COLOUR WHICH WAS USED BY . . 864C LETTER 61   PROSE
GERMAN FORGED
   THE [GERMAN FORGED] MIND FORGD [LINKS I HEAR] MANACLES 170 LONDON/N   * 8
     I HEAR
GERMANS
   NOTE I INCLUDE THE GERMANS IN THE FLORENTINE SCHOOL . . . 479B ANNO REYNOLDS   MARG
GERMANY
   GERMANY WEPT TOWARDS FRANCE & ITALY ENGLAND WEPT 519 MILTON 31   13
     & TREMBLED
   FRANCE & SPAIN & ITALY & DENMARK & HOLLAND & GERMANY . . 690 JERUSALEM 58   41
   OVER FRANCE & GERMANY UPON THE RHINE & DANUBE . . . . 706 JERUSALEM 68   46
   FRANCE SPAIN ITALY GERMANY POLAND RUSSIA SWEDEN TURKEY . 712 JERUSALEM 72   38
   GERMANY POLAND & THE NORTH WOOED MY FOOTSTEPS THEY FOUND 720 JERUSALEM 79   45
GERYON
   GERYON MALEBOLGE CONTAINING (TEN) GULPHS . . . . . . 786A ILLS DANTE 101 *PROSE
GET
   NOW MUST I TO MY SOLDIERS GET THEM READY . . . . . . 24 EDW THIRD/PS 3   146
   HAS TO GET BEFORE ANOTHER IN ANY PURSUIT AFTER GLORY . 28 EDW THIRD/PS 4   15
   GO PETER GET YOU GONE . . . . 29D EDW THIRD/PS 4   PROSE
   AND NEVER THINK AT ALL ABOUT IT IM HANGD IF I DONT GET UP 51D ISLAND MOON 7   PROSE
   THIS EVENING [WE'D] WE'LL ALL GET DRUNK I SAY DASH AN ANTHEM 54B ISLAND MOON 9 *PROSE
   PLAYD AT FORFEITS & TRYD EVERY METHOD TO GET GOOD HUMOUR 59B ISLAND MOON 11 PROSE
   A DOG GET A STICK TO HIM . . . . 74C ANNO LAVATER   MARG
   . . . AND GET THEE UP INTO THE COUNTRY TEN MILES . . . . 145 FRENCH REVOLTN   250
   THAT MEN GET RICH BY & THE SANDY DESART IS GIVN TO THE 200 AMERICA 11   11
     STRONG

GET   (CONTINUED)
    I COULD NOT GET TO THE OTHER SIDE . . . . 427 LAND OF DREAMS   16
    THE ROTTING GRAVE SHALL NEER GET OUT . . . . 433 AUGURIES   88
    HOW MUCH DID BARRY GET . . . . 450B ANNO REYNOLDS   MARG
    GET TO THY LABOURS AT THE MILLS & LEAVE ME TO MY WRATH . 483 MILTON 4   14
    AND GET BY ROTE AS A HARD TASK OF A LIFE OF SIXTY YEARS . 499 MILTON 18   14
    [ON] BY SWEET RESERVE & MODESTY [FEED FAT] GET FAT . . . 545 ON S(TOTHRD)/N *   4
    GET THEE AWAY GET THEE AWAY . . . . 558 I ROSE UP AT/N   2
    RUBENS AND REMBRANDT TILL WE GET RID OF TITIAN AND . . . 564A DESC CAT   PROSE
    TO GET RICH AND POWERFUL TO CURB THE PRIDE OF MAN . . . 571D DESC CAT 3   PROSE
    THIS HAS HITHERTO BEEN HIS LOT TO GET PATRONAGE FOR OTHERS . 572D DESC CAT 3   PROSE
    BY SWEET RESERVE AND MODESTY GET FAT . . . . 575 DESC CAT 3   2
    I ACT WITH BENEVOLENCE & VIRTUE & GET MURDERD TIME AFTER . 738 JERUSALEM 91   26
       TIME
    DRAW A FEATHER OVER IT & YOU WILL GET AN EVEN SURFACE . . 790C LETTER 2   PROSE
    WHICH YOU DESIRED ME TO GET MADE FOR YOU . . . . . . 791B LETTER 3   PROSE
    I FEAR IT WILL BE THURSDAY BEFORE WE CAN GET AWAY FROM . 801B LETTER 13   PROSE
    & TWELVE OCLOCK AT NIGHT BEFORE WE COULD GET HOME . . . 803A LETTER 15   PROSE
    WE CAN GET MOST CONVENIENCES AT THE COUNTRY IS . . . 806B LETTER 16   PROSE
    INJURE AS TO THE EAST AND NORTH I BELIEVE THEY CANNOT GET . 807B LETTER 17   PROSE
    BEFORE NOW BUT COULD NOT GET ANY THING DONE FOR YOU . . 819A LETTER 24   PROSE
    NOT MENTION ILLNESS BECAUSE I HOPED TO GET BETTER FOR I WAS . 820C LETTER 25   PROSE
    I DO NOT SEND A PROOF BECAUSE I CANNOT GET ONE . . . 833A LETTER 32   PROSE
    GOD AS TO GET OUT & HAVE ACCORDINGLY BEEN TO MR WALKER'S . 834B LETTER 34   PROSE
    TO GET THE NUMBER AND PRICES OF ALL ROMNEY'S PRINTS AS . . 844A LETTER 43   PROSE
    WHICH MR JOHNSON WAS TO GET DONE FOR OUR FRIEND DALLY . . 847A LETTER 44   PROSE
    CONTINUES TO GET BETTER & JOINS ME IN MY WARMEST LOVE & . 849C LETTER 45   PROSE
    & TO DESIRE YOU IF YOU COULD TO GET FLAXMAN TO DO THE WHOLE . 853A LETTER 51   *PROSE
    ONE I COULD GET AT JOHNSON'S I LEFT A GOOD IMPRESSION OF IT . 855C LETTER 53   PROSE
    WITH THEIR MASTERS & ARE LIKELY TO GET THE BETTER EACH . 859B LETTER 56   PROSE
       PARTY
    TO PURSUE THE PLAN OF PUBLISHING WHAT I MAY GET PRINTED . 865D LETTER 63   PROSE
    SOON GET ABOUT AGAIN GREAT MEN DIE EQUALLY WITH THE LITTLE . 868D LETTER 68   PROSE
    TO GO WHEN HE OBLIGINGLY PERMITTED ME TO GET OUT TO MY . 869D LETTER 70   PROSE
    THE BETTER FOR IT I CANNOT GET WELL & AM NOW IN BED BUT . 870B LETTER 71   PROSE
       SEEM
    WHERE I CONTRIVE TO GET INTO A LITTLE PERSPIRATION WHICH . 872B LETTER 75   PROSE
    GET UP BUT JUST AS I WAS GOING TO RISE THIS MORNING THE . 872B LETTER 75   PROSE
    & THE TROUBLE YOU WILL YET HAVE WITH ME BUT I GET BETTER . 872D LETTER 76   PROSE
    MORE & MORE & SHALL SOON GET PROOFS OF THESE FOUR WHICH . 876A LETTER 83   PROSE
    I HAVE THOUGHT & THOUGHT OF THE REMOVAL & CANNOT GET MY . 876B LETTER 83   PROSE
    THE ENGRAVINGS & HOPE SOON TO GET PROOFS OF WHAT I AM DOING . 877A LETTER 85   PROSE
    I AM STILL FAR FROM RECOVERED & DARE NOT GET OUT IN THE . 877D LETTER 87   PROSE
       COLD
    A PRICE FOR THEM THAT I SCARCE EXPECT TO GET FROM . 878C LETTER 88   PROSE
       A STRANGER
    CONTAINS (A HUNDRED) PLATES BUT IT IS NOT LIKELY THAT I . 878C LETTER 88   PROSE
       SHALL GET
    LAWS TO GET INTO FREEDOM FROM ALL LAW OF THE MEMBERS INTO . 879A LETTER 88   PROSE
GETS
    WHERE SHE GETS POISON & THE WINGD EAGLE WHY HE LOVES THE . 191 V DAU ALBION 3   12
       SUN
    MIXD WITH BLOOD HERE THE SNAKE GETS HER POISON . . . . 251 AHANIA 3   50
    POISON GETS FROM SLANDER'S TONGUE . . . . 432 AUGURIES   46
    GETS INTO MANY CENTRAL FORMS . . . . 460A ANNO REYNOLDS   MARG
    AND GETS INTO BED A REWARD FOR THE LABOURS OF THE DAY . 586A DESC CAT 16   PROSE
    AT GETS WET & DRY AS THE WEATHER GETS SO . . . . . 816B LETTER 23   PROSE
    MY WIFE GETS BETTER EVERY DAY HOPE EARNESTLY THAT YOU . 835A LETTER 34   PROSE
GETTING
    BECAUSE I AM GETTING BEFORE HAND IN MONEY MATTERS . . 820A LETTER 25   PROSE
    MR ROSE I AM HAPPY TO HEAR IS GETTING QUITE WELL HOPE TO . 838C LETTER 37   PROSE
    I AM GETTING BETTER EVERY HOUR MY PLAN IS DIET ONLY & . 873C LETTER 77   PROSE
    THO GETTING BETTER & STRONGER I AM STILL INCAPABLE . 875B LETTER 81   PROSE
       OF RIDING
    I THANK YOU FOR THE FIVE POUNDS RECIEVD TO DAY AM GETTING . 876A LETTER 83   *PROSE
    & AM GETTING BETTER OR I COULD NOT HAVE COME AT ALL YOURS . 876D LETTER 84   PROSE
    THE DESIGNS AS WELL AS THE ENGRAVINGS I AM GETTING ON WITH . 877A LETTER 85   PROSE
GHAST
    HORRIBLE GHAST & DEADLY NOUGHT SHALT THOU FIND IN IT . 265 FOUR ZOAS 1   50
    HORRIBLE GHAST & DEADLY NOUGHT SHALT THOU FIND IN IT . 645 JERUSALEM 22   23
GHASTLY
    O GHASTLY DEATH WITHDRAW THY CRUEL HAND . . . . . . 5 FAIR ELENOR/PS   43
    OF HER DEAR LORD ALL GHASTLY PALE CLOTTED . . . . . 5 FAIR ELENOR/PS   59
    AND IN THE MORNING LO AN HUNDRED MEN IN GHASTLY DEATH . 107 TIRIEL 5   29
    . . . IN [GHASTLY FEA] GUILTY FEARS . . . . 107 TIRIEL 5   * 32
    TREMBLING COLD IN GHASTLY FEARS . . . . 161 NEVER PAIN/N   7
    ON AGES ROLLD AGES IN GHASTLY . . . . 227 URIZEN 10   5
    IN GHASTLY TORMENT SICK . . . . 229 URIZEN 11   26
    IN GHASTLY TORMENT SICK . . . . 229 URIZEN 13   4
    I PITYING HOVERD OVER THEE I PROTECTED THY GHASTLY CORSE . 300 FOUR ZOAS 4   108
    IN GHASTLY TORMENT SICK HANGING UPON THE WIND . . . . 303 FOUR ZOAS 4   236
    IN GHASTLY TORMENT SICK WITHIN HIS RIBS BLOATED ROUND . 303 FOUR ZOAS 4   239
    THO HORRIBLE & GHASTLY TO THINE EYES THO BURIED BENEATH . 329 FOUR ZOAS 7   351
    IN GHASTLY TORMENT SICK A TONGUE OF HUNGER & THIRST FLAMED . 482 MILTON 3   22
       OUT
    AROSE UPON HIM PALE AND GHASTLY AND HE CALLD AROUND . . . 666 JERUSALEM 40   2
GHIOTTO
    IF PINDAR WAS NOT A BETTER POET THAN GHIOTTO WAS A PAINTER . 49D ISLAND MOON 6   PROSE
    PLUTARCH HAS NOT THE LIFE OF GHIOTTO SAID SIPSOP . . . 49D ISLAND MOON 6   PROSE
GHIOTTO'S
    GHIOTTO'S CIRCLE OR APELLES' LINE . . . . 542 FLORENTINE/N   26

GHOST   SEE HOLY-GHOST,HOLY GHOST
    AND LIKE A GHOST THRO NARROW PASSAGES . . . .   4 FAIR ELENOR/PS   11
    LIKE THE TALL GHOST OF BARRATON   . . . .   12 GWIN KING/PS   53
    & A GHOST PULLS THE BED CLOTHES AT HER FEET . . . . 618C ILLUS MILTON   PROSE
    THE GHOST OF ABEL . . . .   779B GHOST ABEL 1   TITLE
    ENTER THE GHOST OF ABEL . . . .   780A GHOST ABEL 1   PROSE
    & THAT SPIRIT IS THE GHOST OF MATTER OR NATURE . . . 789A ANNO THORNTON   MARG
    & GOD IS THE GHOST OF THE PRIEST & KING WHO EXIST . . 789A ANNO THORNTON   MARG
GHOSTLY
    GIVE [XXX] US THIS ETERNAL DAY [XXX] OUR [GHOSTLY] OWN 788A ANNO THORNTON * MARG
        RIGHT BREAD
GHOSTS
    DEEP SIGHS AND SEES PALE SICKLY GHOSTS GLIDING   . . . .   4 FAIR ELENOR/PS   16
    HOWLING LIKE GHOSTS FURIOUS AS WOLVES   . . . .   11 GWIN KING/PS   27
    GHOSTS GLUT THE THROAT OF HELL . . . .   13 GWIN KING/PS   96
    AND GHOSTS ACCUSING GROAN . . . .   13 GWIN KING/PS   100
    AND RISE WITH GHOSTS OVER THE WELL-FOUGHT FIELD . . . . 35 WAR SONG/PS   14
    THE GIANTS & THE WITCHES & THE GHOSTS OF ALBION DANCE WITH 697 JERUSALEM 63   13
    SPIRITS ARE LAWFUL BUT NOT GHOSTS ESPECIALLY ROYAL GIN IS 787D ANNO THORNTON MARG
GIANT
    GORDRED THE GIANT ROUSD HIMSELF   . . . .   11 GWIN KING/PS   13
    OUR FATHERS SWARM FROM THE SHIPS GIANT VOICES . . . . . 32 EDW THIRD/PS 6   19
    THE MIGHTY DEAD GIANT BODIES STREAMING BLOOD   . . . .   32 EDW THIRD/PS 6   35
    HE FANCIES HE IS GROWN INTO A GIANT . . . .   37A CONTEMPLATN/PS   PROSE
    CORINEUS THROWS GOGMAGOG THE GIANT INTO THE SEA KING LEAR 208C SUBJCTS HIST/N TITLE
    BEGOT A GIANT RACE . . . .   256 BOOK OF LOS 3   26
    GO DOWN YE KINGS & COUNCELLORS & GIANT WARRIORS . .   374 FOUR ZOAS 9   659
    A GIANT FORM OF PERFECT BEAUTY OUTSTRETCHD ON THE ROCK . 497 MILTON 15   38
    THE GIANT ALBION WAS PATRIARCH OF THE ATLANTIC   . . . 578C DESC CAT 5   PROSE
    JERUSALEM THE EMANATION OF THE GIANT ALBION . . . .   620A JERUSALEM   TITLE
    I AGAIN DISPLAY MY GIANT FORMS TO THE PUBLIC MY FORMER . 620D JERUSALEM 3   PROSE
    INVOLVD THE EIGHT SUCH ARE THE GENERATIONS OF THE GIANT 626 JERUSALEM 7   49
        ALBION
    OUTSTRETCHD HIS GIANT BEAUTY ON THE GROUND IN PAIN & TEARS 641 JERUSALEM 18   46
    HIS GIANT BEAUTY AND PERFECTION FALLEN INTO DUST . . . 641 JERUSALEM 19   8
    SIGHING TO MELT HIS GIANT BEAUTY ON THE MOONY RIVER . . 642 JERUSALEM 19   47
    ASTONISHD TERRIFIED THEY HOVERD OVER HIS GIANT LIMBS . 642 JERUSALEM 20   2
    DISPLAYING OUR GIANT LIMBS TO ALL THE WINDS OF HEAVEN   647 JERUSALEM 24   6
        SUDDEN
    JERUSALEM THE EMANATION OF THE GIANT ALBION CAN IT BE . 649B JERUSALEM 27   PROSE
    THAT JERUSALEM WAS & IS THE EMANATION OF THE GIANT ALBION 649B JERUSALEM 27 PROSE
    THE SPECTRE IS IN GIANT MAN INSANE AND MOST DEFORMD . . 664 JERUSALEM 37   4
    ARISE AWAKE O FRIENDS OF THE GIANT ALBION . . . . .   667 JERUSALEM 40   18
    TO PROTECT FROM THE GIANT BLOWS IN THE SPORTS OF INTELLECT 677 JERUSALEM 48   15
    THEIR GIANT FORMS CONDENSING INTO NATIONS & PEOPLES   684 JERUSALEM 53   8
        & TONGUES
    DRINKING HIS EMANATION IN INTOXICATING BLISS REJOICING 701 JERUSALEM 65   58
        IN GIANT DANCE
    HENCE ALBION WAS CALLD THE CANAANITE & ALL HIS GIANT SONS 715 JERUSALEM 74   39
    OF ENRAGED THUNDERS AROUND THEM THE STARRY WHEELS OF THEIR 741 JERUSALEM 94   11
        GIANT SONS
    . . . WHEN THE TRIPLE HEADED GOG-MAGOG GIANT . . . . . 746 JERUSALEM 98   52
    FOR HE OUGHT TO BE RECKOND OF THE GIANT BROOD . . .   824A LETTER 27   PROSE
    HER BROTHER A GIANT IN BODY MILD & POLITE IN SOUL AS I HAVE 850C LETTER 49   PROSE
    EMANATION OF THE GIANT ALBION BUT FIND THAT TO PRINT IT 878C LETTER 88   PROSE
        WILL
GIANT-BROOD
    DISCLOSE A HIDEOUS ORIFICE THENCE ISSUING THE GIANT-BROOD 708 JERUSALEM 70   13
GIANTS
    GIANTS OF MIGHTY ARM BEFORE THE FLOOD CAIN'S CITY   . . 41A THEN SHE BORE   PROSE
    GIANTS WHO FORMED THIS WORLD INTO ITS SENSUAL EXISTENCE 155A MARRIAGE HH 15 PROSE
    GIANTS ANCIENT INHABITANTS OF ENGLAND THE LANDING   208C SUBJCTS HIST/N   TITLE
        OF BRUTUS
    METHUSELAH LAMECH THESE ARE GIANTS MIGHTY HERMAPHRODITIC 528 MILTON 37   37
    OF THE GIANTS OF IRELAND AND BRITAIN OF THE   . . . . . 577D DESC CAT 5   PROSE
    GIANTS & FAIRIES HAVING RECIEVD THE HIGHEST REWARD POSSIBLE 620D JERUSALEM 3 PROSE
    AND THE SEA POURED IN AMAIN UPON THE GIANTS OF ALBION . . 663 JERUSALEM 36   40
    JERUSALEM'S CHILDREN HARK HEAR THE GIANTS OF ALBION CRY 673 JERUSALEM 43   47
        AT NIGHT
    FOR BREAD OF THE SONS OF ALBION OF THE GIANTS HAND   673 JERUSALEM 43   50
        & SCOFIELD
    THE MOUNTAIN OF GIANTS ALL THE GIANTS OF ALBION ARE BECOME 679 JERUSALEM 49   7
    HE HATH PLACED OG & ANAK THE GIANTS OF ALBION FOR THEIR 680 JERUSALEM 49   56
        GUARDS
    THE ATLANTIC MOUNTAINS WHERE GIANTS DWELT IN INTELLECT . . 681 JERUSALEM 50   1
    THE GIANTS & THE WITCHES & THE GHOSTS OF ALBION DANCE WITH 697 JERUSALEM 63   13
    METHUSELAH LAMECH THESE ARE THE GIANTS MIGHTY   716 JERUSALEM 75   12
        HERMAPHRODITIC
    THE HILL OF GIANTS ALL HER FOUNDATIONS LEVELLD WITH THE 719 JERUSALEM 78   22
        DUST
    WITH BLOOD FROM JAPAN EASTWARD TO THE GIANTS CAUSWAY WEST 719 JERUSALEM 78   26
    TO IRELAND'S FARTHEST ROCKS WHERE GIANTS BUILDED THEIR 735 JERUSALEM 89   50
        CAUSEWAY
    SO LOS SPOKE AND THE GIANTS OF ALBION TERRIFIED & ASHAMED 737 JERUSALEM 90   58
    MERLIN WAS LIKE THEE RINTRAH AMONG THE GIANTS OF ALBION 740 JERUSALEM 93   13
GIBBET
    [WILL NOT SUBMIT TO THE GIBBET & HALTER] . . . . . . 185 LET BROTHELS/N   23
GIBBLE GABBLE
    GIBBLE GABBLE THE WIFE OF INFLAMMABLE GASS [ENTERD THE 46B ISLAND MOON 2   PROSE
        ROOM]
    & MY COUSIN GIBBLE GABBLE SAYS THAT I AM LIKE NOBODY ELSE 53A ISLAND MOON 8 PROSE
    COME FLAMMABLE SAID GIBBLE GABBLE & LET'S ENJOY OURSELVES 58C ISLAND MOON 10 PROSE

793

GIBBLE GABBLE   (CONTINUED)
    GIBBLE GABBLE LEND ME YOUR HANDKERCHIEF TILLY LALLY . . .   58C ISLAND MOON 10   PROSE
GIBBON
    GIBBON AROSE WITH A LASH OF STEEL . . . .   418 I SAW A MONK/N   5
    O VOLTAIRE ROUSSEAU GIBBON VAIN . . . .   420 I SAW MNK AD/N   7
    GIBBON PLIED HIS LASH OF STEEL . . . .   420 I SAW MNK AD/N   11
    GIBBON ALOUD HIS LASH DOES PLY . . . .   420 I SAW MNK AD/N   16
    THIS VOLTAIRE & ROUSSEAU THIS HUME & GIBBON & BOLINGBROKE   532 MILTON 40   12
    SUCH AS HUME GIBBON AND VOLTAIRE CANNOT WITH ALL THEIR .   579A DESC CAT 5   PROSE
    THESE ARE NEITHER THE EXCLUSIVE PROPERTY OF HUME GIBBON NOR   579A DESC CAT 5   PROSE
    VOLTAIRE ROUSSEAU GIBBON HUME . . . .   682C JERUSALEM 52   PROSE
    GIBBON AROSE WITH A LASH OF STEEL . . . .   683 I SAW A MONK/J   5
    O VOLTAIRE ROUSSEAU GIBBON VAIN . . . .   683 I SAW A MONK/J   22
GIBBORIM
    SIHON & OG THE ANAKIM & EMIM NEPHILIM & GIBBORIM . . .   735 JERUSALEM 89   47
GIDDINESS
    I HOPE THEIR LORDSHIPS WILL EXCUSE YOUR GIDDINESS . . .   20 EDW THIRD/PS 2   64
GIFT
    NOR MATCHLESS MIGHT NOR WISDOM NOR EVERY GIFT ENJOYED . .   39B SAMSON/PS   PROSE
    ("GLANCE IS THE GREATEST GIFT") UNEASY DOUBTFUL . . . .   77C ANNO LAVATER   MARG
    DOES NOT THE GREAT MOUTH LAUGH AT A GIFT & THE NARROW .   192 V DAU ALBION 5   7
        EYELIDS MOCK
    MAGNIFY SMALL GIFTS REDUCE [THEM] THE MAN TO WANT A GIFT   323 FOUR ZOAS 7   *   124
    . . .
    GIVES TO THE JUST & TO THE UNJUST BUT THE UNJUST REJECT   392B ANNO WATSON   MARG
        HIS GIFT
    MERCY ALONE OF FREE GIFT AND ELECTION THAT WE LIVE . .   494 MILTON 13   33
    IT IS THE GIFT OF GOD IT IS INSPIRATION AND VISION HE .   579C DESC CAT 5   PROSE
    THE HUMAN MIND CANNOT GO BEYOND THE GIFT OF GOD THE HOLY   579D DESC CAT 5   PROSE
        GHOST
    ALL THAT THEY HAVE IS MINE FROM MY FREE GENROUS GIFT .   671 JERUSALEM 42   52
    AND REMEMBER HE WHO DESPISES & MOCKS A MENTAL GIFT . .   717C JERUSALEM 77   PROSE
    MOCKS JESUS THE GIVER OF EVERY MENTAL GIFT . . . . .   717C JERUSALEM 77   PROSE
    PANG OF AFFECTION & GRATITUDE IS THE GIFT OF GOD FOR GOOD   833D LETTER 33   PROSE
GIFTS
    THE GODS ADMIRING LOADED HER WITH GIFTS AS ONCE PANDORA   42D THEN SHE BORE   PROSE
    OR AN EYE OF GIFTS & GRACES SHOWRING FRUITS & COINED GOLD   130 BOOK OF THEL 6   15
    . . . WE HAVE GIVEN GIFTS NOT TO THE WEAK . . . . .   139 FRENCH REVOLTN   115
    THE WORSHIP OF GOD IS HONOURING HIS GIFTS IN OTHER MEN .   158B MARRIAGE HH 22   PROSE
    HOW CAN THE GIVER OF GIFTS EXPERIENCE THE DELIGHTS OF THE   193 V DAU ALBION 5   12
        MERCHANT
    [TO CREATE MAN MORNING BY MORNING TO GIVE GIFTS AT NOON   269 FOUR ZOAS 1   201
        DAY]
    AT THEIR EXCEEDING BRIGHTNESS & THE SONS OF ETERNITY SENT   312 FOUR ZOAS 6   34
        THEM GIFTS
    MAGNIFY SMALL GIFTS REDUCE [THEM] THE MAN TO WANT A GIFT   323 FOUR ZOAS 7   *   124
    . . .
    WITH GIFTS & GOLD OF EDEN ASTONISHD STUPIFIED WITH DELIGHT   346 FOUR ZOAS 8   *   214
    WITH GIFTS & SPICES WITH LAMPS RICH EMBOSSD JEWELS & GOLD   349 FOUR ZOAS 8   337
    [TO CREATE MAN MORNING BY MORNING TO GIVE GIFTS AT NOON   SUPP FOUR ZOAS 8   *
        DAY]
    MAY BE GIFTS FROM THE DEVIL & EARTHLY KINGS . . . . .   557 SINCE RICHES/N   2
    NOT KNOWING WHAT ART IS IT IS BEING BLIND TO THE GIFTS   579D DESC CAT 5   PROSE
        OF THE SPIRIT
    WHEN IMAGINATION ART & SCIENCE & ALL INTELLECTUAL GIFTS   604C V LAST JUDG/N   PROSE
    ALL THE GIFTS OF THE HOLY GHOST ARE [DESPISD] LOOKD UPON   604C V LAST JUDG/N   PROSE
    WHAT ARE ALL THE GIFTS OF THE SPIRIT BUT MENTAL GIFTS .   613A V LAST JUDG/N   PROSE
    THY SONS CAME TO JERUSALEM WITH GIFTS SHE SENT THEM AWAY   647 JERUSALEM 24   38
    WHAT WERE ALL THEIR SPIRITUAL GIFTS WHAT IS THE DIVINE   717A JERUSALEM 77   PROSE
        SPIRIT
    WHAT ARE ALL THE GIFTS OF THE GOSPEL ARE THEY NOT ALL   717A JERUSALEM 77   PROSE
        MENTAL GIFTS
    AND ARE NOT THE GIFTS OF THE SPIRIT EVERY-THING TO MAN .   717B JERUSALEM 77   PROSE
    GO TELL THEM THAT THE WORSHIP OF GOD IS HONOURING HIS GIFTS   738 JERUSALEM 91   8
    I HAVE TRIED TO MAKE FRIENDS BY CORPOREAL GIFTS BUT HAVE   738 JERUSALEM 91   16
        ONLY
    MADE ENEMIES I NEVER MADE FRIENDS BUT BY SPIRITUAL GIFTS   738 JERUSALEM 91   17
    TO GOD & MAN TO TAKE DUE CARE OF HIS GIFTS & . . . . .   811C LETTER 22   PROSE
GIGANTIC
    THE GIGANTIC FLAMES TREMBLED AND HID . . . .   257 BOOK OF LOS 4   3
    THE GIGANTIC ROOTS & TWIGS OF THE VEGETATING SONS OF ALBION   679 JERUSALEM 49   10
GIHON
    GIHON TO HIDDEKEL & TO CORN FIELDS & VILLAGES & INHABITANTS   695 JERUSALEM 61   32
    OF EDEN ALL PERVERTED EGYPT ON THE GIHON MANY TONGUED .   734 JERUSALEM 89   15
GILD
    IN FAME'S WIDE TROPHIED HALL TIS OURS TO GILD . . . . .   18 EDW THIRD/PS 1   26
    AND TO THE PLANETS OF THE NIGHT & TO THE STARS THAT GILD   355 FOUR ZOAS 8   571
GILDED
    SO WEAK THE GILDED BUTTERFLY SCARCE PERCHES ON MY HEAD .   127 BOOK OF THEL 1   18
    [ALL THY GILDED PAINTED PRIDE] . . . .   182 THE FLY/N   3
    THOU PALTRY GILDED POISNOUS WORM . . . .   188 A FAIRY SKIPD *   6
GILEAD
    [AS ONE MAN HOVERING OVER GILEAD & HERMON] . . . . .   269 FOUR ZOAS 1   199
    CONSULTING AS ONE MAN ABOVE [MOUNT GILEAD] . . . . . .   277 FOUR ZOAS 1   475
    ABOVE [MOUNT GILEAD] HIGH SNOWDON . . . .   279 FOUR ZOAS 1   552
    [MET] AS ONE MAN EVEN JESUS UPON GILEAD & HERMON . . .   341 FOUR ZOAS 8   2
    OR MERCY & TRUTH ARE FLED AWAY FROM SHECHEM & MOUNT GILEAD   349 FOUR ZOAS 8   320
    THESE ARE UNITED INTO TIRZAH AND HER SISTERS ON MOUNT   624 JERUSALEM 5   40
        GILEAD
    ON MOUNT GILEAD LOOKING TOWARD GILGAL AND LOS BENDED .   662 JERUSALEM 36   12
    REMOVE EASTWARD TO BASHAN AND GILEAD AND LEAVE . . . .   679 JERUSALEM 48   64
    OR MERCY & TRUTH ARE FLED AWAY FROM SHECHEM & MOUNT GILEAD   705 JERUSALEM 68   8

	PAGE	TITLE	LINE
GILEAD (CONTINUED)			
IN VAIN AND IN GILEAD FOR A PHYSICIAN AND A COMFORTER . .	720	JERUSALEM 79	12
GOSHEN HATH FOLLOWD PHILISTEA GILEAD HATH JOIND WITH OG	720	JERUSALEM 79	13
GILGAL			
ON MOUNT GILEAD LOOKING TOWARD GILGAL AND LOS BENDED . .	662	JERUSALEM 36	12
GILLS			
& RED GILLS HANG JUST ABOVE THE RAGING FOAM	156C	MARRIAGE H8 17	PROSE
GILPIN			
REVD MR GILPIN AUTHOR OF A WORK ON PICTURESQUE SCENERY .	814B	LETTER 23	PROSE
GILT			
A TRIFLE IVE GILT YOUR CAUSE WITH MY BEST BLOOD	23	EDW THIRD/PS 3	99
GIMBLET			
WERE EMPLOYD WHEN MRS GIMBLET CAME IN [?HOPING]	44B	ISLAND MOON 1	*PROSE
MRS GIMBLET DREW HER MOUTH DOWNWARDS	46A	ISLAND MOON 1	PROSE
MRS GIMBLET LOOKD AS IF THEY MEANT HER TILLY LALLY LAUGHT	46D	ISLAND MOON 3	PROSE
GIM CRANK			
[WHAT IS THIS GIM CRANK FOR] IS NOT THIS A SUN DIAL . . .	49B	ISLAND MOON 5	*PROSE
GIMMEL			
VERY EASY AM NOW LEARNING MY HEBREW (ALEPH BETH GIMMEL)	821D	LETTER 25	PROSE
GIN			
A [KNAVE] FOOL TO A BOLT A [FOOL] KNAVE TO A GLASS OF GIN	544	ON F AND S/N	4
BUT MORAL VIRTUES' DEADLY GIN	753	EV GOSPEL (2)	8
SPIRITS ARE LAWFUL BUT NOT GHOSTS ESPECIALLY ROYAL GIN IS	787D	ANNO THORNTON	MARG
GINS			
WHAT ARE HIS NETS & GINS & TRAPS & HOW DOES HE SURROUND HIM	193	V DAU ALBION 5	18
THE TIMES ARE ENDED SHADOWS PASS THE MORNING GINS TO BREAK	198	AMERICA 8	2
AND LOS FORMED NETS & GINS	227	URIZEN 8	7
LIKE NETS & GINS & TRAPS TO CATCH THE JOYS OF ETERNITY .	246	SONG OF LOS 4	2
INNUMERABLE THE GINS & TRAPS & MANY A SOOTHING FLUTE . .	284	FOUR ZOAS 2	160
GIRD			
AND GIRD THE SWORD UPON EACH THIGH AND FIT	26	EDW THIRD/PS 3	225
THY AGED FATHERS GIRD THEMSELVES FOR WAR	348	KING JOHN/PS	PROSE
GIRD ON THY SWORD O THOU MOST MIGHTY IN GLORY & MAJESTY	279	FOUR ZOAS 1	548
GIRD ON THY FLAMING ZONE DESCEND INTO THE SEPULCHER . . .	337	FOUR ZOAS 7B	* 193
A HELL OF OUR OWN MAKING SEE ITS FLAMES STILL GIRD ME ROUND	493	MILTON 12	23
WHICH NOW GIRD ROUND US O ETERNAL TORMENT I FORMD	493	MILTON 12	29
THE SERPENT			
GIRD ON THY FLAMING ZONE DESCEND INTO THE SEPULCHER OF	700	JERUSALEM 65	39
CANTERBURY			
GIRDED			
THEN ROSE GIRDED HIMSELF AND OER THE BLEAK	2	TO AUTUMN/PS	17
THE DAUGHTERS OF ALBION GIRDED AROUND THEIR GARMENTS OF	281	FOUR ZOAS 2	57
NEEDLEWORK			
THEN HE BEGAN TO SOW THE SEED HE GIRDED ROUND HIS LOINS	365	FOUR ZOAS 9	321
AND SHE AROSE OUT OF THE RIVER & GIRDED ON HER GOLDEN	370	FOUR ZOAS 9	* 504
GIRDLE			
IN THAT DARK VALLEY I HAVE GIRDED ROUND MY CLOKE AND ON	666	JERUSALEM 39	20
MY FEET			
GIRDING			
WITH MONSTERS GIRDING ROUND THEIR BOSOMS	314	FOUR ZOAS 6	105
IN PAIN GIRDING ME ROUND LIKE A RIB OF IRON IN HEAVEN O	660	JERUSALEM 34	14
VALA			
HE TAKES HIS WAY GIRDING HIMSELF WITH GOLD & IN HIS HAND	729	JERUSALEM 83	77
CHRIST GIRDING HIMSELF WITH STRENGTH FOUR & TWENTY ELDERS	SUPP	LETTER 56A	*PROSE
GIRDLE			
THE GIRDLE OF WAR FROM THE DESOLATE EARTH	144	FRENCH REVOLTN	223
A TIGHTNING GIRDLE GREW	233	URIZEN 20	9
HE BURST THE GIRDLE IN TWAIN	233	URIZEN 20	11
BUT STILL ANOTHER GIRDLE	233	URIZEN 20	12
ANOTHER GIRDLE SUCCEEDS	233	URIZEN 20	15
THE GIRDLE WAS FORMD BY DAY	233	URIZEN 20	16
GRIEF ROSE UPON HIS RUDDY BROWS A TIGHTENING GIRDLE GREW	307	FOUR ZOAS 5	83
HE BURST IT BUT NEXT MORN ANOTHER GIRDLE SUCCEEDS . . .	307	FOUR ZOAS 5	85
FORMING A GIRDLE IN THE DAY & BURSTING IT AT NIGHT . . .	307	FOUR ZOAS 5	89
THE GIRDLE WAS FORMD BY DAY BY NIGHT WAS BURST IN TWAIN	307	FOUR ZOAS 5	90
ROUND HIS LOINS A GIRDLE GLOWD WITH MANY COLOURD FIRES . .	319	FOUR ZOAS 6	304
GO NOAH FETCH THE GIRDLE OF STRONG BRASS [PRE] HEAT IT	349	FOUR ZOAS 8	312
RED HOT			
WITH A BRIGHT GIRDLE & HIS SKIRT FILLD WITH IMMORTAL SOULS	365	FOUR ZOAS 9	322
AND ON THE RIVER'S MARGIN SHE UNGIRDED HER GOLDEN GIRDLE	369	FOUR ZOAS 9	480
AND SHE AROSE OUT OF THE RIVER & GIRDED ON HER GOLDEN	370	FOUR ZOAS 9	* 504
GIRDLE			
AND THE PESTILENCE SHALL BE ITS FRINGE & THE WAR ITS GIRDLE	499	MILTON 18	17
A GIRDLE GWENDOLEN & CONWENNA AS A GARMENT WOVEN	507	MILTON 23	16
GO NOAH FETCH THE GIRDLE OF STRONG BRASS HEAT IT RED-HOT	705	JERUSALEM 67	59
GIRDLES			
MANTLES OF DESPAIR GIRDLES OF BITTER COMPUNCTION SHOES	346	FOUR ZOAS 8	221
OF INDOLENCE			
GIRDS			
THE SERPENT WHO GIRDS THE EARTH SPECTRES	SUPP	ILLUS GRAY	*TITLE
GIRL			
UP IN A MORNING AT FOUR O CLOCK WHEN I WAS A GIRL . .	48B	ISLAND MOON 4	PROSE
A GIRL HAS ALWAYS MORE TONGUE THAN A BOY I HAVE SEEN . .	53B	ISLAND MOON 8	PROSE
THE LITTLE GIRL LOST	112B	LIT GRL LST/SI	TITLE
THE LITTLE GIRL FOUND	113D	LIT GRL FND/SI	TITLE
LITTLE GIRL	123	SPRING/SI	12
A LITTLE GIRL LOST	219A	LIT GRL LST/SE	TITLE
RAISD THE [BRIGHT] FIERCE BOY & GIRL	269	FOUR ZOAS 1	196
THOU LITTLE BOY ART THARMAS & THOU BRIGHT GIRL ENION . .	370	FOUR ZOAS 9	510
HE SHOULD HAVE BEEN A GIRL	552	WHY CUPID/N	3
AND THE GIRL SHOOTS WITH HER EYE	552	WHY CUPID/N	6
OF AGE AND YOUTH AND BOY AND GIRL AND ANIMAL AND HERB . .	640	JERUSALEM 18	17

```
                                                                PAGE      TITLE        LINE
GIRL   (CONTINUED)
     AND BOY & GIRL & ANIMAL & HERB & RIVER & MOUNTAIN   . . .   640 JERUSALEM 18        25
     THE SCORND AND CONTEMND YOUTHFUL GIRL WHERE SHALL SHE FLY   727 JERUSALEM 93         8
     TO SAY TIS A GIRL PROMISING BOYS HEREAFTER & TO SAY  .  . 853A LETTER 51        *PROSE
     THE CHILD IN HIS ARMS WHETHER BOY OR GIRL SIGNIFIES NOT   864B LETTER 61         PROSE
     AND WHO DOES NOT KNOW A BOY FROM A GIRL I SAY  . . . .    864B LETTER 61         PROSE
     LITTLE GIRL LOST DITTO DITTO THE CLOD & PEBBLE   .  .    SUPP LETTER 66A       *PROSE
     INFANT SORROW THE SCHOOL BOY LONDON LITTLE GIRL LOST     SUPP LETTER 66A       *PROSE
GIRL'S
     AND HE SHALL LICK THE LITTLE GIRL'S WHITE NECK & ON HER   376 FOUR ZOAS 9        704
          HEAD
     AND IF ANY GIRL'S LOVER FORSAKES HER FOR ME  . . . . .    428 MARY               31
     WAS [SURELY A WOMAN'S] THE CUPID GIRL'S MOCKING PLAN  .   552 WHY CUPID/N        10
GIRLS
     THERES DOUBLE ELEPHANT'S GIRLS THEY HAVE THEIR OWN WAY  .  52D ISLAND MOON 8     PROSE
     THOUSANDS OF LITTLE GIRLS & BOYS RAISING THEIR INNOCENT    59 HOLY THURS/IM       9
          HANDS
     WHEN WE ALL GIRLS & BOYS   . . . . . . . .               116 ECCHOING GR/SI      18
     THOUSANDS OF LITTLE BOYS & GIRLS RAISING THEIR INNOCENT   122 HOLY THURS/SI       8
          HANDS
     AND CATCH FOR THEE GIRLS OF MILD SILVER OR OF FURIOUS GOLD 194 V DAU ALBION 7     24
     I WONDER WHETHER THE GIRLS ARE MAD   . . . . . . .        434 WILLIAM BOND         1
     THE SAVAGE GIRLS HAD DRESSED THEMSELVES WITH VINE LEAVES  581C DESC CAT 7        PROSE
GIRT
     GIRT AS A SOWER WITH HIS SEED TO SCATTER LIFE ABROAD  .   338 FOUR ZOAS 7B       199
     HIS LEFT SCOTLAND HIS BOSOM GIRT WITH GOLD INVOLVES  . .  531 MILTON 39           42
     GIRT AS A SOWER WITH HIS SEED TO SCATTER LIFE ABROAD OVER 700 JERUSALEM 65        45
          ALBION
     ELIZABETH "GIRT WITH MANY A BARON BOLD"  . . . . . . .   SUPP ILLUS GRAY       *TITLE
GIT
     WITH STOCKINGS ROLLD ABOVE THEIR KNEES & SHOES AS BLACK    58 THIS CITY/IM    *    6
          AS [GIT] JET
GITTIPIN
     [?AND] MISS GITTIPIN [&] MRS NANNICANTIPOT  . . . . . .    46B ISLAND MOON 2   *PROSE
     THEN SCOPPRELL & MISS GITTIPIN COMING IN   . . . . .      52D ISLAND MOON 8     PROSE
     NOW HERE SAID MISS GITTIPIN I NEVER SAW SUCH COMPANY  .   52D ISLAND MOON 8     PROSE
     THIS QUITE PROVOKD MISS GITTIPIN TO INTERRUPT HER  . .    53B ISLAND MOON 8     PROSE
     THEN SAID MISS GITTIPIN MR SCOPPRELL DO YOU KNOW  . .     53C ISLAND MOON 8     PROSE
     MISS GITTIPIN SAID HE YOU SING LIKE A HARPSICHORD  . .    55C ISLAND MOON 9     PROSE
     [THIS QUID CRIES OUT MISS GITTIPIN]  . . . . . . .        57A ISLAND MOON 9     PROSE
     SAID MISS GITTIPIN PRAY MR OBTUSE ANGLE SING US A SONG    59B ISLAND MOON 11    PROSE
          THEN HE SUNG
     THEN [MISS GITTIPIN TILLY LALLY SUNG QUID] SUNG QUID  .   60C ISLAND MOON 11    PROSE
     HERE A LAUGH BEGAN AND MISS GITTIPIN SUNG   . . . . .     61B ISLAND MOON 11    PROSE
GIVE
     THE GRAVES GIVE UP THEIR DEAD FAIR ELENOR   . . . . . .     4 FAIR ELENOR/PS      2
     O GIVE NOT HIM THY HAND NOW I AM DEAD  . . . . . . .        6 FAIR ELENOR/PS     66
     I FEAR LORD PERCY WILL NOT GIVE ME LEAVE   . . . . . .     20 EDW THIRD/PS 2     45
     THEN YOU WILL GIVE ME LEAVE TO SHINE SOMETIMES  . . . .    20 EDW THIRD/PS 2     55
     GIVE ME YOUR HAND AND NOW I'LL TELL YOU WHAT  . . . . .    21 EDW THIRD/PS 3      7
     AND GIVE COMMAND AND LIGHTNING HAS FLASHED  . . . . .      22 EDW THIRD/PS 3     27
     GOOD MORROW GENERALS I GIVE YOU JOY  . . . . . . .         22 EDW THIRD/PS 3     43
     GIVE BUT A SLAVE HIS LIBERTY HE'LL SHAKE  . . . . . .      26 EDW THIRD/PS 3    196
     THAT I WILL TELL YOUR HONOUR IF YOULL GIVE ME LEAVE  .    29B EDW THIRD/PS 4    PROSE
     WHEN THE THIN BEAMS OF THE MOON GIVE A FAINT LIGHT  . .   36B COUCH DEATH/PS    PROSE
     WHAT CANST THOU GIVE WHEN SUCH A TRIFLE IS DENIED ME BUT  39A SAMSON/PS         PROSE
     TILL HOPE GREW FEEBLE AND WAS READY TO GIVE PLACE         40A SAMSON/PS         PROSE
          TO DOUBTING
     REASON SIR SAID THE ANTIQUARIAN I'LL GIVE YOU AN  . . .   45A ISLAND MOON 1     PROSE
     WAS PREPARED TO GIVE A FORMAL ANSWER TO THE COMPANY  .    45B ISLAND MOON 1     PROSE
     I WOULD NOT GIVE A FARTHING FOR IT DO ALL BY YOUR FEELINGS 51D ISLAND MOON 7    PROSE
     TO SIT IN STATE & GIVE FORTH LAWS OUT OF THEIR OLD OAK     58 THIS CITY/IM        2
          CHAIRS
     WERE FIT TO GIVE LAW TO THE CITY EACH EAT AS MUCH AS TEN   58 THIS CITY/IM       10
     COME OUT [GIVE ME] WE ARE PUTRIFIED WE ARE CORRUPTED  .   58D ISLAND MOON 10  *PROSE
     ("YOU BEG AS YOU QUESTION YOU GIVE AS YOU ANSWER")        77D ANNO LAVATER      MARG
          EXCELLENT
     FROM MILTON & GIVE THEM AS MILTON'S OPINIONS   . . . .   SUPP ANNO SWED HELL * MARG
     GIVE IT ME FOR I CANNOT STAY MY JOURNEY IS FAR FROM HENCE 101 TIRIEL 2          22
     LAUGH FOR THY FATHER TIRIEL SHALL GIVE (THEE) CAUSE TO    108 TIRIEL 6          33
          LAUGH
     HE DOTH GIVE HIS JOY TO ALL  . . . . . . . . .           122 ON ANOTHERS/SI     25
     BUT IF AT THE CHURCH THEY WOULD GIVE US SOME ALE  . . .   179 LIT VAGABOND/N      6
     BUT KISS HIM & GIVE HIM BOTH [FOOD] DRINK & APPAREL  . .  180 LIT VAGABOND/N     18
     THEREFORE IN PITY STILL WE GIVE  . . . . . . . .         188 A FAIRY SKIPD      13
     AND THOU ART FALLN TO GIVE ME LIFE IN REGIONS OF DARK DEATH 196 AMERICA PREL 2    9
     AND HEARD THE VOICE OF ALBION'S ANGEL GIVE THE THUNDEROUS 201 AMERICA 14          3
          COMMAND
     BUT IF AT THE CHURCH THEY WOULD GIVE US SOME ALE  . . .   216 LIT VAGABND/SE      5
     BUT KISS HIM & GIVE HIM BOTH DRINK AND APPAREL  . . . .   216 LIT VAGABND/SE     16
     IF YOU WILL FEED ME ON LOVE THOUGHTS & GIVE ME NOW AND THEN 237 EUROPE INTRO     15
     TO GIVE US BLISS THAT WE MAY DRINK THE SPARKLING WINE OF  239 EUROPE 4           20
          LOS
     OF COLOURS TWELVE FEW KNOWN ON EARTH GIVE LIGHT IN THE    241 EUROPE 10           9
          OPAKE
     WHY WILT THOU GIVE UP WOMAN'S SECRECY MY MELANCHOLY CHILD 244 EUROPE 14          22
     ARISE O ORC AND GIVE OUR MOUNTAINS JOY OF THY RED LIGHT   244 EUROPE 14          31
     THEY SAW URIZEN GIVE HIS LAWS TO THE NATIONS  . . . .    245 SONG OF LOS 3       8
     WE MEET IT WITH OUR SONGS & LOVING BLANDISHMENTS & GIVE   267 FOUR ZOAS 1       105
     [TO CREATE MAN MORNING BY MORNING TO GIVE GIFTS AT NOON   269 FOUR ZOAS 1       201
          DAY]
     SAYING THOU ART THE LORD OF LUVAH INTO THINE HANDS I GIVE 273 FOUR ZOAS 1       324
```

		PAGE	TITLE		LINE
GIVE (CONTINUED)

TO GIVE THE IMMORTAL STEEDS OF LIGHT TO HIS DECEITFUL HANDS	292 FOUR ZOAS 3	32
SET HERSELF UP TO GIVE HER LAWS TO THE ACTIVE MASCULINE VIRTUE	295 FOUR ZOAS 3	116
HE WILL GIVE IT THEE FOR WE ARE WEAK WOMEN & DARE NOT LIFT	304 FOUR ZOAS 4	255
HOWLD IN THE FURIOUS WIND HE THOUGHT TO GIVE TO ENITHARMON	309 FOUR ZOAS 5	152
I WILL GIVE BLACKNESS FOR JEWELS HOARY FROST FOR ORNAMENT DEFORMITY	312 FOUR ZOAS 6	37
FOR LABOURD FATHERLY CARE & SWEET INSTRUCTION I WILL GIVE	312 FOUR ZOAS 6	40
IF THOU ART HE MY DESPERATE PURPOSE HEAR & GIVE ME DEATH	313 FOUR ZOAS 6	57
FLYING AWAY FROM URIZEN THAT HE MIGHT NOT GIVE HIM FOOD	318 FOUR ZOAS 6	274
WITH POMP GIVE EVERY CRUST OF BREAD YOU GIVE WITH GRACIOUS CUNNING	323 FOUR ZOAS 7	123
. . . & THEN GIVE WITH POMP	323 FOUR ZOAS 7	124
GIVE ME EXAMPLE OF THY MILDNESS KING OF FURIOUS HAIL STORMS	323 FOUR ZOAS 7	145
THE FRUIT & GIVE ME PROOF OF LIFE ETERNAL OR I DIE . . .	330 FOUR ZOAS 7	394
WILL GIVE US TO ETERNAL DEATH FIT PUNISHMENT FOR SUCH	330 FOUR ZOAS 7	426
INTO THE TEMPLE OF URIZEN GIVE LIGHT TO THE ABYSS . .	333 FOUR ZOAS 7B	35
AND I WILL GIVE THEE ALL THE ENDS OF HEAVEN FOR THY POSSESSION	334 FOUR ZOAS 7B	56
THE NORTHERN DRUM NOW GIVE THE CHARGE BRAVELY OBSCURD . .	337 FOUR ZOAS 7B	155
THEY GIVE THE OATH OF BLOOD THEY CAST THE LOTS INTO THE HELMET	337 FOUR ZOAS 7B	165
. . . TO [?REND THE VEIL OF MYSTERY] GIVE HIS VEGETATED BODY	348 FOUR ZOAS 8 *	265
WHICH GIVE A TINCTURE TO FALSE BEAUTY	348 FOUR ZOAS 8	291
HIS SCALES TRANSPARENT GIVE FORTH LIGHT LIKE WINDOWS OF THE MORNING	352 FOUR ZOAS 8	441
HIS EYELIDS GIVE THEIR LIGHT AROUND HIS FOLDING TAIL ASPIRES	352 FOUR ZOAS 8	447
[TO CREATE MAN MORNING BY MORNING TO GIVE GIFTS AT NOON DAY]	SUPP FOUR ZOAS 8 *	
. . . THEY GIVE UP THEMSELVES TO CONSUMMATION	358 FOUR ZOAS 9	32
O WEARY LIFE WHY SIT I HERE & GIVE UP ALL MY POWERS . . .	360 FOUR ZOAS 9	116
UNGRATIFIED GIVE ALL MY JOY INTO THIS LUVAH & VALA . . .	361 FOUR ZOAS 9 *	179
LET ORC CONSUME LET THARMAS RAGE LET DARK URTHONA GIVE	362 FOUR ZOAS 9	184
THEY GIVE THEM TO URTHONA'S SONS RINGING THE HAMMERS SOUND	365 FOUR ZOAS 9	305
A TIME THEY GIVE TO SWEET REPOSE TILL ALL THE HARVEST IS RIPE	366 FOUR ZOAS 9	343
MEN WHO GIVE THEMSELVES TO THEIR ENERGETIC GENIUS [AS] IN THE MANNER	386B ANNO WATSON * MARG
[[HER] THY WEEPING [SHE] THOU SHALL NEER GIVE OER] . . .	415 MY SPECTRE/N	5
LET US AGREE TO GIVE UP LOVE	417 MY SPECTRE/N	67
HOSIER SAYS HE IS READY TO GIVE EVIDENCE OF THIS IF NECESSARY	437B BLAKES MEMORAN PROSE
IT IS NECESSARY TO GIVE SOME ACCOUNT OF	442D LAST JUDGMNT/L PROSE
ACCOMODATION OF THOSE WHO GIVE IT THE HONOR OF ATTENTION	442D LAST JUDGMNT/L PROSE
GIVE HIGH PRICE FOR THE WORST LEAVE THE BEST IN DISGRACE	445 ANNO REYNOLDS 3
TO GIVE THEM HIS LABOUR FOR NOTHING A SOCIETY COMPOSED .	446A ANNO REYNOLDS MARG
TWENTY GUINEAS FOR THIS HORRIBLE DAWB & IF ANY ONE WOULD GIVE XXX	451D ANNO REYNOLDS MARG
APPEARS TO ME TO GIVE ALWAYS THE CHARACTERS OF VULGAR STUPIDITY	464B ANNO REYNOLDS MARG
TO GIVE FOR CONTEMPTIBLE WORKS OR THE	480C MILTON 1 PROSE
HE SOFT INTREATED LOS TO GIVE TO HIM PALAMABRON'S STATION	486 MILTON 7 8
AND OLOLON SAID LET US DESCEND ALSO AND LET US GIVE .	504 MILTON 21 45
HOW LONG BENEATH THE COVERING CHERUB GIVE OUR EMANATIONS	507 MILTON 23 12
ARISE O SONS GIVE ALL YOUR STRENGTH AGAINST ETERNAL DEATH	509 MILTON 24 34
THEY GIVE DELIGHTS TO THE MAN UNKNOWN ARTIFICIAL RICHES	515 MILTON 28 31
THEY GIVE TO SCORN & THEIR POSESSORS TO TROUBLE & SORROW & CARE	515 MILTON 28 * 32
TO GIVE THEM TO THEIR LOVELY HEAVENS TILL THE GREAT JUDGMENT DAY	517 MILTON 29 52
CRYING WITH ONE VOICE GIVE US A HABITATION & A PLACE . .	519 MILTON 30 24
SHE SHALL RELENT IN FEAR OF DEATH SHE SHALL BEGIN TO GIVE	522 MILTON 33 17
SHALT GIVE HER INTO THE ARMS OF GOD YOUR LORD & HUSBAND	523 MILTON 33 23
AND GIVE MORE MONEY FOR HIS SLOBBERINGS	546 ENGLISH CONN/N 3
THAN YOU WILL GIVE FOR RAFAEL'S FINEST THINGS	546 ENGLISH CONN/N 4
O GIVE TO ME A WOMAN'S FATE	547 IF I GROW/N 2
TO GIVE THESE RASCALS A DOSE OF CAWDLE	548 ON GREAT ENC/N 6
GIVE PENSIONS TO THE LEARNED PIG	548 GIVE PENSION/N 1
I [HAVE GIVN] GIVE YOU THE END OF A GOLDEN STRING . . .	551 GIVE YOU END/N * 1
OIL HAS FALSELY BEEN SUPPOSED TO GIVE STRENGTH TO COLOURS BUT	565A DESC CAT 2 PROSE
THE WORKS NOW EXHIBITED WILL GIVE THE LIE TO SUCH ASPERSIONS	572D DESC CAT 3 PROSE
THE PAINTER THOUGHT HE WOULD GIVE THEM A RIDE ROUND ABOUT	575B DESC CAT 3 PROSE
TILL THE VICTIM IS OBLIGED TO GIVE UP THE FLORENTINE .	583A DESC CAT 9 PROSE
SUCH AS THE WORLD CANNOT GIVE AND PATIENCE	586A DESC CAT 16 PROSE
AND TIME AWAIT TO GIVE HIM ALL THAT THE WORLD CAN GIVE .	586A DESC CAT 16 PROSE
& POWER IS TO GIVE PLACE TO IMBECILLITY [AND WHETHER] .	591C PUB ADDRESS/N PROSE
AFTER HOGARTH [COGAR] COOKE WISHED TO GIVE TO HOGARTH .	594B PUB ADDRESS/N *PROSE
I HAVE HEARD MANY PEOPLE SAY GIVE ME THE IDEAS . . .	596A PUB ADDRESS/N PROSE
SAY GIVE ME THE DESIGN IT IS NO MATTER FOR THE EXECUTION	596A PUB ADDRESS/N PROSE
& THOSE MUST BE QUEER FELLOWS WHO GIVE GREAT SUMS . .	596C PUB ADDRESS/N PROSE
GENTLEMEN OF FORTUNE WHO GIVE GREAT PRICES FOR PICTURES	599C PUB ADDRESS/N PROSE
WHICH LOS WIPED OFF BUT COMFORT NONE COULD GIVE OR BEAM OF HOPE	630 JERUSALEM 10 61
WHY WILT THOU GIVE TO HER A BODY WHOSE LIFE IS BUT A SHADE	631 JERUSALEM 12 1
AND TWEED & TYNE ANXIOUS GIVE UP THEIR SOULS FOR ALBION'S SAKE	636 JERUSALEM 16 17
I WILL HIDE IT FROM ETERNALS I WILL GIVE MYSELF FOR MY CHILDREN	646 JERUSALEM 23 18

```
                                                         PAGE     TITLE           LINE
GIVE    (CONTINUED)
      THEY REDUCE THE MAN TO WANT THEN GIVE WITH POMP & CEREMONY    656  JERUSALEM 30      31
      HE SAYS RETURN ALBION RETURN I GIVE MYSELF FOR THEE    . .    665  JERUSALEM 38      30
      I GIVE MYSELF AND THESE MY BRETHREN GIVE THEMSELVES FOR       665  JERUSALEM 38      39
        ALBION
      WHO GIVE THEMSELVES IN GOLGOTHA VICTIMS TO JUSTICE WHERE      665  JERUSALEM 38      54
      THOSE WHO GIVE THEIR LIVES FOR HIM ARE DESPISED    . . . .    667  JERUSALEM 40      15
      GIVE ME MY EMANATIONS BACK FOOD FOR MY DYING SOUL    . . .    670  JERUSALEM 42      13
      LOS ANSWERD RIGHTEOUSNESS & JUSTICE I GIVE THEE IN RETURN     670  JERUSALEM 42      19
      BRISTOL & BATH LISTEN TO MY WORDS & YE SEVENTEEN GIVE EAR     673  JERUSALEM 43      55
      I SEE DISEASE ARISE UPON YOU YET SPEAK TO ME AND GIVE   .     673  JERUSALEM 43      76
      TO GIVE A PLACE FOR REDEMPTION LET SIHON AND OG    . . . .    679  JERUSALEM 48      63
      WALKETH AMONG US GIVE DECISION BRING FORTH ALL YOUR FIRES     686  JERUSALEM 55      18
      GIVE FORTH THY PITY & LOVE FEAR NOT LO I AM WITH             694  JERUSALEM 60      67
        THEE ALWAYS
      I WILL COMMAND THE CLOUD TO GIVE THEE FOOD & THE HARD ROCK    696  JERUSALEM 62      25
      O WHEN SHALL JEHOVAH GIVE US VICTIMS FROM HIS FLOCKS &        697  JERUSALEM 63      30
        HERDS
      . . . THEY GIVE THE OATH OF BLOOD IN LAMBETH   . . . . .     699  JERUSALEM 65       7
      ASHAMED TO GIVE LOVE OPENLY TO THE PITEOUS & MERCIFUL MAN     704  JERUSALEM 67      19
      WHERE EVERY FEMALE DELIGHTS TO GIVE HER MAIDEN TO            707  JERUSALEM 69      15
        HER HUSBAND
      I GIVE YOU THE END OF A GOLDEN STRING    . . . . . . . .     716  I GIVE YOU/J       1
      THE CRUEL WARRIOR I HAVE REFUSED TO GIVE LOVE TO MERLIN      723  JERUSALEM 81       2
        THE PITEOUS
      BEGAN TO GIVE THEIR SOULS AWAY IN THE (FURNACES)            727  JERUSALEM 82      79
        OF AFFLICTION
      DIVIDE US FROM THESE TERRORS & GIVE US POWER THEM TO SUBDUE   729  JERUSALEM 84      26
      GIVE ANY MARKS OF GENTILITY . . . . . . . . . . .           748  EV GOSPEL(B)/N     2
      GIVE ANY PROOFS OF HUMILITY . . . . . . . . . . .           750  EV GOSPEL(C)/N     2
      GIVE ANY PROOFS OF HUMILITY . . . . . . . . . . .           751  EV GOSPEL(D)/N     2
      AND GIVE WITH CHARITY A STONE . . . . . . . . . .           751  EV GOSPEL(D)/N     4
      GIVE ANY LESSONS OF CHASTITY . . . . . . . . . .            753  EV GOSPEL(E)/N     2
      GIVE ANY LESSONS OF PHILOSOPHY . . . . . . . . .            756  EV GOSPEL(H)/N     2
      GIVE US THE BREAD THAT IS OUR DUE & RIGHT    . . . . .       788A ANNO THORNTON    MARG
      GIVE [XXX] US THIS ETERNAL DAY [XXX] OUR [GHOSTLY] OWN        788A ANNO THORNTON  * MARG
        RIGHT BREAD
      GIVE US DAY BY DAY OUR REAL TAXED   . . . . . . . .          788D ANNO THORNTON    MARG
      I KNOW I BEGGED OF YOU TO GIVE ME YOUR IDEAS . . . . .       792A LETTER 4        PROSE
      HOPE SOON TO GIVE YOU A PROOF . . . . . . . . . .           803C LETTER 15       PROSE
      I SHALL WISH FOR YOU ON TUESDAY EVENING AS USUAL PRAY GIVE   803C LETTER 15       PROSE
      NOW LET ME INTREAT YOU TO GIVE ME ORDERS TO FURNISH EVERY    808B LETTER 19       PROSE
      IT WILL GIVE ME THE UTMOST DELIGHT TO DO MY BEST  . . .      808C LETTER 19       PROSE
      MEDICINAL POTION BUT AS NONE ON EARTH CAN GIVE ME   . . .    809B LETTER 20       PROSE
      PRAY GIVE MY LOVE TO MRS BUTTS & YOUR FAMILY I AM YOURS      813C LETTER 22       PROSE
        SINCERELY
      & IS MINE PRAY GIVE MY WIFE'S LOVE WITH MINE TO MRS BUTTS    815D LETTER 23       PROSE
      AND BUTTS SHALL GIVE WHAT FUSELI GAVE   . . . . . .          817  HAPPINESS/L       39
      BECAUSE I GIVE HAYLEY HIS DUE RESPECT   . . . . . .          817  HAPPINESS/L       46
      OR GIVE HIM & OBLIGE YOURS . . . . . . . . . . .            819A LETTER 24       PROSE
      AS TO GIVE TO MRS CHETWYND IF SHE SHOULD CALL OR SEND  .     821B LETTER 25       PROSE
      & GIVE OUR LOVES TO MRS BUTTS & YOUR AMIABLE FAMILY  . .     823C LETTER 26       PROSE
      & YOURS & MINE PRAY GIVE MY & MY WIFE'S LOVE TO MRS BUTTS    826A LETTER 27       PROSE
      & TO GIVE OPPORTUNITY TO THOSE WHOM I DOUBTED . . . .        828C LETTER 28       PROSE
      GIVE ME YOUR ADVICE IN MY PERILOUS ADVENTURE  . . . . .      828C LETTER 28       PROSE
      PRAY GIVE MY & MY WIFE'S DUTIES TO MISS POOLE ACCEPT THEM    834A LETTER 33       PROSE
      WISH THAT YOU WOULD GIVE THE PUBLIC AN ENGRAVING OF THAT     836A LETTER 35       PROSE
      I WISH I COULD GIVE YOU A PLEASANT ACCOUNT OF OUR BELOVED    836B LETTER 35       PROSE
      I SEND MY PROOFS TO GIVE AS GOOD AN ACCOUNT OF MR WALKER     837B LETTER 35       PROSE
      IT WILL GIVE YOU A GOOD IDEA OF THIS GOOD & EXCELLENT MAN     839B LETTER 38       PROSE
      BUT I ONLY SAW ONE MORE BECAUSE I WOULD NOT GIVE MUCH  .     839C LETTER 38       PROSE
      ENGRAVING IS OF SO SLOW PROCESS I MUST BEG OF YOU TO GIVE    842D LETTER 42       PROSE
        ME
      OUTLINE WAS HIS ELEMENT AND YET THESE OUTLINES GIVE BUT A    844C LETTER 43       PROSE
      DELIVERED THE LETTER TO MR EDWARDS WHO WILL GIVE IT  . . .   845D LETTER 44       PROSE
      A LINE FROM YOU DESIRES ME TO ASSURE YOU OF HIS WISH TO      845D LETTER 44       PROSE
        GIVE
      J ROMNEY IMMEDIATELY DESIRING HIM TO GIVE US LIBERTY   .     846A LETTER 44       PROSE
      RATHER THAN THE TONGUE OF ULYSSES AND I WILL VENTURE TO      847B LETTER 44       PROSE
        GIVE
      WHOM I HAVE CONSULTED THAT TO GIVE A TRUE IDEA OF   . . .    848A LETTER 45       PROSE
      COLLECT FROM HIM BE SO GOOD AS TO GIVE ME YOUR EARLIEST      849B LETTER 45       PROSE
      DELIGHTS OF THE TURRET OF LOVELY FELPHAM PLEASE TO GIVE      850C LETTER 49       PROSE
      SHOULD DO MY ENDEAVOUR TO GIVE MR HAYLEY'S WORKS  . . . .    856D LETTER 54       PROSE
      SOON GIVE HIM AS NEAR AS I CAN REMEMBER WHAT YOU HAVE  .     856D LETTER 54       PROSE
      WILL GIVE HIM MY PROPOSAL CONCERNING IT IN WRITING  . . .    858D LETTER 55       PROSE
      HAVE HEARD THAT FLAXMAN MEANS TO GIVE A LECTURE ON          859D LETTER 56       PROSE
        SCULPTURE
      IMMEDIATELY HE SAID GIVE MY BEST RESPECTS & TELL MR HAYLEY   860A LETTER 58       PROSE
      I CANNOT GIVE YOU ANY ACCOUNT OF OUR BALLADS  . . . . .      862A LETTER 59       PROSE
GIVEN    SEE GIVN
      HAVE GIVEN ME WHEN I HAVE SEEN THE FIELD GLOW  . . . . .      23  EDW THIRD/PS 3    84
      AND GIVEN HIM I DONT KNOW WHAT AND I CAN'T TELL   . . . .     29C EDW THIRD/PS 4   PROSE
      MY JOY IS GIVEN INTO THE HANDS OF HIM WHO HATES ME   . . .    38D SAMSON/PS        PROSE
      HE HAS GIVEN ME A BLACK EYE . . . . . . . . . . .            61  SAY YOU JOE/IM    11
      WHY IS ONE LAW GIVEN TO THE LION & THE [PA ] PATIENT OX      109  TIRIEL 8       *  10
      AND I HAVE GIVEN THEE A CROWN THAT NONE CAN TAKE AWAY  .     129  BOOK OF THEL 5     4
      WILT THOU O QUEEN ENTER MY HOUSE TIS GIVEN THEE TO ENTER     130  BOOK OF THEL 5    16
      . . . WE HAVE GIVEN GIFTS NOT TO THE WEAK  . . . . .        139  FRENCH REVOLTN   115
      . . . AND THE VOTES WERE GIVEN AND THE NUMBERS NUMBRED  . .  146  FRENCH REVOLTN   268
      GIVEN HIS SANCTION TO THE LAW OF TEN COMMANDMENTS    . . .  158B MARRIAGE HH 22   PROSE
      IN THE GREATEST DEGREE NOW HEAR HOW HE HAS GIVEN   . . . .  158C MARRIAGE HH 22   PROSE
```

		PAGE	TITLE	LINE

GIVEN   (CONTINUED)

PURE MILD & GENTLE GIVEN IN MERCY TO THOSE WHO SLEEP   . . .   266 FOUR ZOAS 1   96
[SUCH POWER WAS GIVEN TO THE SOLITARY WANDERER]   . . . .   269 FOUR ZOAS 1   203
WHY IS THE SHEEP GIVEN TO THE KNIFE THE LAMB PLAYS IN THE   276 FOUR ZOAS 1   454
   SUN
THE TIMES ARE NOW RETURND UPON US WE HAVE GIVEN OURSELVES   286 FOUR ZOAS 2   223
WHENCE IS THIS POWER GIVEN TO THEE ONCE THOU WAST IN MY   295 FOUR ZOAS 3   120
   BREAST
THE BODY OF MAN IS GIVEN TO ME I SEEK IN VAIN TO DESTROY   313 FOUR ZOAS 6   60
IS GIVEN A CRAVING CRY THAT THEY MAY SIT AT NIGHT ON BARREN 325 FOUR ZOAS 7   205
   ROCKS
IS GIVEN US FOR A SHELTER FROM THE TEMPESTS OF VOID & SOLID 326 FOUR ZOAS 7   268
AND MUST HAVE GIVEN HIMSELF TO DEATH ETERNAL BUT . . . .   330 FOUR ZOAS 7   396
MUST HAVE GIVEN SATAN BY THESE MILD ARTS DOMINION OVER ALL 351 FOUR ZOAS 8   367
AND GIVEN ME FRUITS & PLEASANT WATERS & WARM HILLS & COOL   369 FOUR ZOAS 9   452
   VALLEYS
HAS NOT THE BISHOP GIVEN HIMSELF THE LIE   . . . . . .   390A ANNO WATSON   MARG
AS EXAMPLES GIVEN TO US OF THE PERVERSENESS OF SOME . . . 393B ANNO WATSON   MARG
ALL OTHER CODES GIVEN UNDER PRETENCE OF DIVINE COMMAND .   393C ANNO WATSON   MARG
HES GIVEN TO A WOMAN OLD . . . .   425 MENTAL TRAVLER   10
MY PROOFS OF THIS OPINION ARE GIVEN IN THE FOLLOWING NOTES 445A ANNO REYNOLDS   MARG
BEGINING AT JERUSALEM'S INNER COURT LAMBETH RUIND AND GIVEN 511 MILTON 25   48
GIVEN TO HERCULES WHO LABOUR IN TIRZAH'S LOOMS FOR BREAD   511 MILTON 25   50
AND THEIR SUBLIME INTENT GIVEN TO THEIR KINGS . . . . .   543 IF TRUE/N   12
[A PRETTY EPIGRAM FOR THOSE WHO HAVE GIVEN HIGH PRICES]   547A PRETTY EPIGR/N   TITLE
ON THE GREAT ENCOURAGEMENT [SHEWN] GIVEN BY ENGLISH   548B ON GREAT ENC/N *TITLE
   NOBILITY &
HAVING GIVEN GREAT OFFENCE BY WRITING IN PROSE   . . . .   555 BLAKES APL/N 1   6
IVE GIVEN GREAT PROVISION TO MY FOES . . . .   555 BLAKES APL/N 1   22
HAVING GIVEN GREAT OFFENCE BY WRITING IN PROSE   . . . .   555 BLAKES APL/N 2   1
SOME SAY IVE GIVEN GREAT PROVISION TO MY FOES . . . . .   556 BLAKES APL/N 2   11
GIVEN THE HISTORICAL FACT IN ITS POETICAL VIGOUR . . .   578D DESC CAT 5   PROSE
ACCORDINGLY THE PAINTER HAS GIVEN IN HIS BEAUTIFUL MAN . 580A DESC CAT 5   PROSE
IDEAS CANNOT BE GIVEN BUT IN THEIR MINUTELY APPROPRIATE   596A PUB ADDRESS/N   PROSE
EXAMPLE OF THESE CONTRARY ARTS IS GIVEN US IN THE   600D PUB ADDRESS/N   PROSE
   CHARACTERS
AND OF THAT GOD FROM WHOM [ALL BOOKS ARE GIVEN] . . .   621 READER LOVER/J * 2
IN ETERNITY THEY NEITHER MARRY NOR ARE GIVEN IN MARRIAGE   660 JERUSALEM 34   15
O I HAVE UTTERLY BEEN WASTED I HAVE GIVEN MY DAUGHTERS   670 JERUSALEM 42   16
   TO DEVILS
THE SON OF BEOR HAVE GIVEN THEIR POWER TO JOSHUA & CALEB   680 JERUSALEM 49   59
NOW GIVEN TO STONY DRUIDS AND ALLEGORIC GENERATION . .   681 JERUSALEM 50   7
MORE PROPERLY TO BE GIVEN TO A PLAYER WHO FALLS INTO SIN 682C JERUSALEM 52   PROSE
AND GIVEN SOFT MILK MINGLED TOGETHER WITH THE SPIRITS OF   725 JERUSALEM 82   6
   FLOCKS
JEHOVAH LO I HAVE GIVEN YOU A LAMB FOR AN ATONEMENT INSTEAD 780 GHOST ABEL 2   10
WHEN FLAXMAN WAS TAKEN TO ITALY FUSELI WAS GIVEN TO ME   799 TO FLAXMAN/L   3
   FOR A SEASON
AND NOW FLAXMAN HATH GIVEN ME HAYLEY HIS FRIEND . . . .   799 TO FLAXMAN/L   4
I HAVE NOW GIVEN TWO YEARS TO THE INTENSE STUDY OF THOSE 814A LETTER 23   PROSE
MY WIFE HAS NO INDULGENCE GIVEN . . . .   818 HAPPINESS/L   61
WHEN I HAD MY DEFIANCE GIVEN   . . . .   818 HAPPINESS/L   71
AND A FOURFOLD VISION IS GIVEN TO ME . . . .   818 HAPPINESS/L   84
A BAD OPINION OF THE RECEPTION HE HAS GIVEN TO ME . .   821A LETTER 25   PROSE
THAT THE SORE TRAVEL WHICH HAS BEEN GIVEN ME THESE THREE 823B LETTER 26   PROSE
   YEARS
SMALLER POEMS & WILL READ WITH GREAT DELIGHT I HAVE GIVEN 824A LETTER 27   PROSE
PRINTED & ORNAMENTED WITH PRINTS & GIVEN TO THE PUBLIC . 825A LETTER 27   PROSE
GIVEN THEM & WE DIRECTLY GO TO PRINTING CONSEQUENTLY IT   840C LETTER 39   PROSE
& WILL REMAIN SO TILL YOU HAVE GIVEN YOUR DECISION   . . 841C LETTER 41   PROSE
GIVEN THEM TO ME IN WRITING . . . .   841D LETTER 41   PROSE
THEY HAVE GIVEN ME SOME EXCELLENT HINTS IN ENGRAVING .   843B LETTER 43   PROSE
CONNOISSEUR IN ENGRAVING HAS GIVEN HER WARM APPROBATION   853B LETTER 52   PROSE
MEN & ACCORDINGLY HAVE GIVEN A LOOK OVER MY ACCOUNT BOOK 854C LETTER 53   PROSE
CONFESSEDLY THE FIRST POET OF ENGLAND OUGHT TO BE GIVEN   856B LETTER 54   PROSE
ACKNOWLEDGMENTS FOR THE KIND RECEPTION YOU HAVE GIVEN MY 862C LETTER 60   PROSE
   NEW

GIVER

("PROVES HIMSELF AT ONCE A SILLY GIVER") UNEASY   . . .   70D ANNO LAVATER   MARG
HOW CAN THE GIVER OF GIFTS EXPERIENCE THE DELIGHTS OF THE 193 V DAU ALBION 5   12
   MERCHANT
MOCKS JESUS THE GIVER OF EVERY MENTAL GIFT . . . . .   717C JERUSALEM 77   PROSE

GIVES

AND PEGGY POUT GIVES SAM A PLUM . . . .   16 BLIND-MANS/PS   22
I CANNOT CONCIEVE BUT THE SUBSTANCE GIVES TINCTURE TO .   81D ANNO LAVATER   * MARG
   THE ACCIDENT
O HE GIVES TO US HIS JOY . . . .   123 ON ANOTHERS/SI   33
AND GIVES HIS LIGHT AND GIVES HIS HEAT AWAY . . . . .   125 LIT BLK BOY/SI   10
HE WHOSE FACE GIVES NO LIGHT SHALL NEVER BECOME A STAR . 151A MARRIAGE HH 7   PROSE
BUT FOR ANOTHER GIVES ITS EASE . . . .   162 CLOD PEBBLE/N   3
BUT FOR ANOTHER GIVES ITS EASE . . . .   211 CLOD PEBBLE/SE   3
GIVES TO THE JUST & TO THE UNJUST BUT THE UNJUST REJECT   392B ANNO WATSON   MARG
   HIS GIFT
FALSE ALL POETRY GIVES THE LIE TO THIS   . . . . . .   411C ANNO BOYD   MARG
BUT DANTE GIVES TOO MUCH ?CAESAR HE IS NOT A REPUBLICAN   413B ANNO BOYD   MARG
[PRINTING HIS PRAISES ?GIVES (?HIMSELF NO) ?PAIN]   . .   539 SIR JOSH MIC/N *   3
. . . [GIVES] SPENDS HIS WHOLE FORTUNE . . . . . .   548 ON GREAT ENC/N *   3
THAT LIVING CREATURE ON THE LEFT OF THE THRONE GIVES .   612A V LAST JUDG/N   PROSE
WALES GIVES HIS DAUGHTERS TO THE LOOMS ENGLAND NURSING   637 JERUSALEM 16   23
   MOTHERS
GIVES TO THE CHILDREN OF ALBION & TO THE CHILDREN   637 JERUSALEM 16   24
   OF JERUSALEM

```
                                                               PAGE      TITLE        LINE
GIVES    (CONTINUED)
      IN GREAT ETERNITY EVERY PARTICULAR FORM GIVES FORTH OR      684 JERUSALEM 54        1
         EMANATES
      AND THE MALE GIVES A TIME & REVOLUTION TO HER SPACE . . .   707 JERUSALEM 69       23
      [?AS] FOR IF HE GIVES HIS RAIN TO THE EVIL & THE GOOD  .   785C ILLS DANTE 101 *PROSE
      WHICH GIVES EXISTENCE TO EVERY OTHER NAMELY VISIONS OF      793A LETTER 5       PROSE
         ETERNITY
      AS A SOLDIER OF CHRIST IT GIVES ME THE GREATEST OF TORMENTS 812D LETTER 22      PROSE
      HAND UPON MY HEAD & GIVES A BLESSING TO ALL MY WORKS  .    823B LETTER 26      PROSE
      I CALLED ON MR EVANS WHO GIVES SMALL HOPES OF OUR BALLADS  831C LETTER 31      PROSE
      HE
      HE GIVES A VERY SPIRITED ASSURANCE OF MR JOHN ROMNEY'S .   835C LETTER 35      PROSE
      GIVES HOPES THAT HE MAY PROVE WORTHY OF HIS FATHER &   .   838C LETTER 37      PROSE
      WITH FLAXMAN'S ADVICE WHICH HE GIVES . . . . . . . .      853B LETTER 52      PROSE
      OBSERVING THAT THE PRICE MR JOHNSON GIVES FOR THE PLATES   853C LETTER 52      PROSE
      THIS IS WHAT GIVES ME GREAT PLEASURE . . . . . . . .      874C LETTER 79      PROSE
GIVETH
      AND IF GOD DIETH NOT FOR MAN & GIVETH NOT HIMSELF    . . . 743 JERUSALEM 96       25
GIVING
      OBTUSE ANGLE GIVING A GRIN SAID     . . . . . . . . .      45C ISLAND MOON 1   PROSE
      GIVING TO THOSE THAT CANNOT CRAVE THE VOICELESS THE        128 BOOK OF THEL 2      4
         OERTIRED
      HOWLING AND GIVING THE DARK COMMAND . . . . . . . .       135 FRENCH REVOLTN      24
      GIVING HIMSELF FOR THE NATIONS HE DANCD THE DANCE         160 ALBION ROSE        2
         OF ETERNAL DEATH
      BLAKE WAS GIVING HIS BODY EASE . . . . . . . . . .        187 WHEN KLOPSTK/N      7
      GIVING THE SPECTRE STERNEST CHARGE OVER THE HOWLING FIEND  308 FOUR ZOAS 5      112
      GIVING THEM SWEET INSTRUCTIONS WHERE THE CLOUD THE RIVER   315 FOUR ZOAS 6      137
         & THE FIELD
      IN SELF ABASEMENT GIVING UP HIS DOMINEERING LUST . . . .  328 FOUR ZOAS 7      341
      PLAY IN HIS SMILING BEAMS GIVING THE SEEDS OF LIFE TO GROW 379 FOUR ZOAS 9      847
      WILLIAM'S TIMIDITY IN GIVING HIS EVIDENCE BEFORE THE  .  438D BLAKES MEMORAN  PROSE
      BY GIVING UP OF SELFHOOD & THEY DISTANT VIEWD HIS JOURNEY  498 MILTON 17       *   3
      THE ENORMOUS STRIFE ONE GIVING LIFE THE OTHER GIVING DEATH 501 MILTON 19         29
      GIVING TO AIRY NOTHING A NAME AND A HABITATION  . . .     514 MILTON 28          3
      IN SELF ANNIHILATION GIVING THY LIFE TO THY ENEMIES  . .  532 MILTON 40          8
      & THE GIVING ALL UP TO INSPIRATION BY THIS IT WILL BE SEEN 614C V LAST JUDG/N  PROSE
      GIVING A BODY TO FALSHOOD THAT IT MAY BE CAST OFF FOR EVER 631 JERUSALEM 12    *  13
      WITH PROVINGS OF DESTRUCTION WITH GIVING THEE THY HEART'S  647 JERUSALEM 24       28
         DESIRE
      GIVING RECIEVING AND FORGIVING EACH OTHER'S TRESPASSES .   665 JERUSALEM 38       22
      GIVING THEM BENDS OF SELF INTEREST & SELFISH NATURAL VIRTUE 723 JERUSALEM 80      75
      THE INVISIBLE LOVELY ONE GIVING HIM A FORM ACCORDING TO    723 JERUSALEM 80       78
      I HAVE NO DOUBT OF GIVING YOU BENEVOLENCE WITH EQUAL VIGOR 792B LETTER 4       PROSE
      MR SAUNDERS WILL SHORTLY WRITE TO YOU GIVING YOU EVERY .   832D LETTER 32      PROSE
      I COULD NOT THINK OF DELIVERING THE (TWELVE) COPIES WITHOUT 840B LETTER 39     PROSE
         GIVING
      HOPE THAT THE PUBLIC WILL APPROVE OF MY RATHER GIVING FEW  860C LETTER 56      PROSE
GIVN
      O WHY TO HIM WAS'T GIVN . . . . . . . . .                   6 MY SILKS/PS         9
      BABEL WITH THOUSAND TONGUES CONFUSION IT WAS CALLD AND     41A THEN SHE BORE  *PROSE
         GIVN TO SHAME
      BUT KNEW NOT THAT THE REST WAS GIVN TO SHAME  . . . . .    41A THEN SHE BORE   PROSE
      THAT MEN GET RICH BY & THE SANDY DESART IS GIVN TO THE     200 AMERICA 11        11
         STRONG
      IS GIVN THEE TILL THE BREAK OF DAY  . . . . . . . .       210 INTRODUCTN/SE      20
      THOU HAST GIVN ME POWER TO PROTECT MYSELF FROM MY BITTEREST 489 MILTON 9          6
         ENEMIES
      AND I BE SIEZD & GIVN INTO THE HANDS OF MY OWN SELFHOOD    495 MILTON 14         24
      I [HAVE GIVN] GIVE YOU THE END OF A GOLDEN STRING    . . . 551 GIVE YOU END/N *    1
GLAD
      IM GLAD MY FATHER DOES NOT HEAR ME TALK . . . . . . .      27 EDW THIRD/PS 3    276
      THEN SIR I SHOULD BE GLAD TO KNOW IF IT WAS NOT AMBITION   28D EDW THIRD/PS 4  PROSE
      OH I AM GLAD YOU ARE COME SAID QUID . . . . . . . .       63A ISLAND MOON 11  PROSE
      IN THE MORNING GLAD I SEE  . . . . . . . . . . .         166 CHRISTN FORB/N      16
      IN THE MORNING GLAD I SEE  . . . . . . . . . . .         218 POISON TREE/SE      15
      I SING & YOU REPLY TO MY SONG I REJOICE & YOU ARE GLAD .   368 FOUR ZOAS 9      445
      YOU THINK FUSELI IS NOT A GREAT PAINTER IM GLAD  . . .    538 TO H(UNT)/N         1
      AND THEY BOTH ARE MERRY & GLAD . . . . . . . . .         552 WHY CUPID/N         7
      HE IS GLAD TO EMBRACE THE OFFER OF ENGRAVING SUCH BEAUTIFUL 790A LETTER 1      PROSE
         THINGS
      AM GLAD TO HEAR OF MRS LINNELL'S HEALTH & SAFETY  . . .   873B LETTER 77       PROSE
      "ARE GLAD WHEN THEY CAN FIND THE GRAVE" . . . . . .      SUPP LEGEND/N17       *
GLADLY
      ETERNALS I HEAR YOUR CALL GLADLY . . . . . . . .         222 URIZEN 2            5
      GLADLY I HEAR OF HIS FULL HEALTH AND SPIRITS  . . . .    807B LETTER 17       PROSE
      WE ARE RICHLY CLOTHD IN SPIRITUAL & SUFFER ALL THE REST   813C LETTER 22       PROSE
         GLADLY
GLADNESS
      EXPECTATION & GLADNESS ADDED TO LABOUR IN OUR REMOVAL THAT 801B LETTER 13      PROSE
GLAMORGANSHIRE
      THE GATE OF JOSEPH DENBIGHSHIRE THE GATE OF BENJAMIN       637 JERUSALEM 16       41
         GLAMORGANSHIRE
GLANCE
      WHERE INNOCENT EYES DO GLANCE . . . . . . . . . .          7 LOVE JOCUND/PS      3
      SHE BLUSHD SO RED WITH SIDE-LONG GLANCE . . . . .         16 BLIND-MANS/PS      15
      ("THE DEGREE OF GENIUS IS DETERMINED BY") COPIOUSNESS     69C ANNO LAVATER    MARG
         OF GLANCE
      ("GLANCE IS THE GREATEST GIFT") UNEASY DOUBTFUL  . . .    77C ANNO LAVATER    MARG
GLANCES
      GOVERNING ALL BY THE SWEET DELIGHTS OF SECRET AMOROUS      638 JERUSALEM 16       59
         GLANCES
```

	PAGE	TITLE	LINE

GLANCING
    GLANCING HIS BEAMY EYELIDS OVER THE DEEP IN DARK DISMAY   159D SONG LIBERTY   PROSE
    ARISE YOU LITTLE GLANCING WINGS AND SING YOUR INFANT JOY   195 V DAU ALBION 8   9
    ARISE YOU LITTLE GLANCING WINGS & SING YOUR INFANT JOY . .   289 FOUR ZOAS 2   364
GLANDOUS
    AND MILK & BLOOD & GLANDOUS WINE . . . .   248 SONG OF LOS 7   38
GLANDS
    SOME COMBIND INTO MUSCLES & GLANDS . . . .   253 AHANIA 4   32
GLARE
    WHOSE EYES DO GLARE AGAINST THE STORMY FIRES . . . . .   32 EDW THIRD/PS 6   9
    IN THE DEEP DARKNESS BROAD LIGHTNINGS GLARE LONG THUNDERS   741 JERUSALEM 94   4
        ROLL
GLARES
    AND THE LION GLARES THRO THE DUN FOREST . . . .   3 EVNING STAR/PS   12
    OF WILD BEASTS THERE THE LION GLARES THE TYGER & WOLF HOWL   308 FOUR ZOAS 5   128
        THERE
GLASGO
    ISSACHAR SELKIRK DUMBARTN GLASGO ZEBULUN ORKNEY SHETLAND   638 JERUSALEM 16   57
        SKYE
GLASS   SEE HOUR-GLASS,HOUR GLASS,LOOKING-GLASS,LOOKING GLASS
    WITHIN THE WATERY GLASS . . . .   8 MEMORY COME/PS   8
    OR SHINING GLASS AND A WROUGHT DIAMOND SET IN RICH GOLD AND   29D EDW THIRD/PS 4   PROSE
    WHICH SMEARD THE GLASS WORSE THAN EVER THEN HE SCREWD IT ON   58D ISLAND MOON 10   PROSE
    WERE PUMPING AT THE AIRPUMP SMACK WENT THE GLASS . . . .   58D ISLAND MOON 10   PROSE
    LIKE A REFLECTION IN A GLASS LIKE SHADOWS IN THE WATER   127 BOOK OF THEL 1   9
    SHE STOOD IN THE RIVER & VIEWD HERSELF WITHIN THE WATRY   369 FOUR ZOAS 9   481
        GLASS
    OF GLASS & PRECIOUS STONES THEY LOADED ALL THE WAGGONS   378 FOUR ZOAS 9   793
        OF HEAVEN
    A [KNAVE] FOOL TO A BOLT A [FOOL] KNAVE TO A GLASS OF GIN   544 ON F AND S/N   4
    WHICH WE SEE REFLECTED IN THIS VEGETABLE GLASS OF NATURE   605D V LAST JUDG/N   PROSE
    & IN HIM SEES ALL REFLECTED AS IN A GLASS OF ETERNAL   610D V LAST JUDG/N   PROSE
        DIAMOND
GLASSES
    THEN HE WENT UP STAIRS & LOADED THE MAID WITH GLASSES . .   58C ISLAND MOON 10   PROSE
    THEN HE TOOK THE SLIDERS & THEN HE SET UP THE GLASSES . .   58D ISLAND MOON 10   PROSE
    & GLASSES & PICTURES & BROKE THE BOTTLES OF WIND . . . .   58D ISLAND MOON 10   PROSE
    AS GLASSES DISCOVER WORLDS . . . .   231 URIZEN 15   9
GLEAM
    THE GLITTERING YOUTH OF COURTS MUST GLEAM IN ARMS . . .   34B KING JOHN/PS   PROSE
    . . . TO PLANT BEAUTY IN THE DESERT CRAVING ABYSS THEY   136 FRENCH REVOLTN   55
        GLEAM
    INFINITE LONDON'S AWFUL SPIRES CAST A DREADFUL [GLEAM] COLD   205 AMERICA CANC C   7
    I SEE THEIR PITEOUS FACES GLEAM OUT UPON THE CRUEL WINDS   644 JERUSALEM 21   38
GLEAMING
    SHALL BE PREVENTED BY THEIR SWORDS GLEAMING . . . . .   33 EDW THIRD/PS 6   51
GLEAMS
    . . . AND GLEAMS A DUSKY BEAM . . . .   146 FRENCH REVOLTN   270
    GLEAMS OF FIRE STREAK THE HEAVENS . . . .   146 FRENCH REVOLTN   278
    DARK GLEAMS BEFORE THE FURNACE-MOUTH A HEAP OF BURNING   485 MILTON 6   17
        ASHES
GLEAN
    INTO THE BARN WHILE CHILDREN GLEAN THE EARS AROUND THE DOOR   376 FOUR ZOAS 9   702
GLEE
    PIPING SONGS OF PLEASANT GLEE . . . .   111 INTRODUCTN/SI   2
GLEWED
    [GLEWED] GLUED TOGETHER . . . .   418 WHEN MAN HAS/N *   4
GLIB
    IMPUDENT FIEND SAID IJIM HOLD THY GLIB & ELOQUENT TONGUE   104 TIRIEL 4   37
GLIDE
    WHO IN THE SUNNY BEAMS DID GLIDE . . . .   6 HOW SWEET/PS   4
GLIDES
    THE SHINING SNAKE GLIDES OER THE BENDING GRASS . . . .   24 EDW THIRD/PS 3   126
GLIDING
    DEEP SIGHS AND SEES PALE SICKLY GHOSTS GLIDING . . . .   4 FAIR ELENOR/PS   16
GLIMMERED
    AND THE STARS FAINTLY GLIMMERED IN THE SUMMER SKY . . .   36C COUCH DEATH/PS   PROSE
GLIMMERING
    THE LAKE SPEAK (SILENCE) WITH THY GLIMMERING EYES . . .   3 EVNING STAR/PS *   9
    PALE QUIVRING TOWARD THE BRAIN HIS GLIMMERING EYES TEETH   202 AMERICA 15   7
        CHATTERING
    IS NOT THAT SUN THY HUSBAND & THAT MOON THY GLIMMERING VEIL   660 JERUSALEM 34   7
GLISTEN
    AND THE DROPS OF RAIN GLISTEN THE YELLOW HARVEST BREATHES   36C COUCH DEATH/PS   PROSE
GLISTENING
    IMMINGLED INTERWOVEN GLISTENING TO THE SICKENING SIGHT . .   727 JERUSALEM 83   32
    CADENCES & PLAYING IN SWEET INTOXICATION AMONG THE   733 JERUSALEM 88   24
        GLISTENING
GLISTENS
    . . . & HER HAIR GLISTENS WITH DEW . . . .   367 FOUR ZOAS 9   392
    DOWN FLOWING INTO ENTUTHON'S VALES GLISTENS WITH   728 JERUSALEM 83   74
        SOFT AFFECTIONS
GLISTNING
    OR THE GLISTNING EYE TO THE POISON OF A SMILE . . . . .   130 BOOK OF THEL 6   12
GLITTER
    . . . ALONG THE ROADS GLITTER LIKE FIRE . . . .   147 FRENCH REVOLTN   292
    . . . ON THE CLOUDS THAT GLITTER IN THE SUN . . . . .   368 FOUR ZOAS 9   439
    THE PRECIOUS STONES GLITTER ON FLIGHTS SEVENTY SEVEN . .   800 MRS FLAXMAN/L   10
GLITTERING
    AS BETWEEN GLITTERING SAND AND FRUITFUL MOLD . . . . .   29D EDW THIRD/PS 4   *PROSE
    THE GLITTERING YOUTH OF COURTS MUST GLEAM IN ARMS . . .   34B KING JOHN/PS   PROSE
    HOVERING AND GLITTERING ON THE AIR BEFORE THE FACE OF THEL   128 BOOK OF THEL 3   6

	PAGE	TITLE	LINE

GLITTERING   (CONTINUED)
    RUSHING ALONG IRON RANKS GLITTERING THE OFFICERS EACH TO   147 FRENCH REVOLTN   287
        HIS STATION
    REARD UP A FORM OF GOLD & STOOD UPON THE GLITTERING ROCK   267 FOUR ZOAS 1   126
    TEN THOUSAND THOUSAND GLITTERING CHARIOTS SHINING IN THE   273 FOUR ZOAS 1   344
        SKY
    OR GOLD A GLITTERING TORMENT SHINING & HISSING IN ETERNAL   315 FOUR ZOAS 6   121
        PAIN
    I PUT NOT ANY TRUST IN THEE NOR IN THY GLITTERING SCALES   335 FOUR ZOAS 7B   *   82
    THE GLITTERING DISSIMULATION ACHILLES' WRATH IS BLUNT ABUSE   384D ANNO WATSON   MARG
    GLITTERING WITH PRECIOUS STONES & GOLD WITH GARMENTS OF   699 JERUSALEM 64   26
        BLOOD & FIRE
    GLITTERING WITH FESTERING VENOMS BRIGHT . . . .   755 EV GOSPEL(E)/N   84
    ARMED IN GLITTERING SCALES WITH A CROWN & A SPEAR   . . .   780C GHOST ABEL 2   PROSE
GLITTERS
    THE SKY GLITTERS WITH THE JINGLING TRAPPINGS . . . . .   37B CONTEMPLATN/PS   PROSE
    AND IT SHALL TELL THEE WHY IT GLITTERS IN THE MORNING SKY   128 BOOK OF THEL 2   14
GLITTRING
    LIKE AS AN ANGEL GLITTRING IN THE SKY   . . . .   9 FRESH FROM/PS   9
    [A RUIND PILLAR IN GLITTRING FRAGMENTS SILENT HE TURND   196 AMERICA PREL 2   20
        AWAY]
    IN GLITTRING ARMOUR SWIFT AS WINDS INTELLIGENT AS [FLAMES]   205 AMERICA CANC C   13
        CLOUDS
    THE SONS OF WAR ASTONISHD AT THE GLITTRING MONSTER DROVE   279 FOUR ZOAS 1   533
    HIS NAKED LIMBS GLITTRING UPON THE DARK BLUE SKY HIS KNEES   334 FOUR ZOAS 7B   *   42
    THE GLITTRING OF THEIR HORSES' TRAPPINGS STAINS THE VAULT   336 FOUR ZOAS 7B   *   152
        OF NIGHT
    GLITTRING THE STREAMS REFLECT THE VISION OF BEATITUDE . .   511 MILTON 25   70
    THEN WAS PERFECTED HIS GLITTRING PRIDE . . . .   755 EV GOSPEL(E)/N   92
GLOBE
    WHO NOW SLEEP IN THEIR GRAVES WALKED ON THE STEDFAST GLOBE   35C COUCH DEATH/PS   PROSE
    THE SUN HE FELT BUT THE BRIGHT MOON WAS NOW A USELESS GLOBE   100 TIRIEL 2   2
    NO MORE SAID TIRIEL BUT I REMAIN ON ALL THIS GLOBE   . . .   102 TIRIEL 2   56
    THE QUEEN OF FRANCE JUST TOUCHD THIS GLOBE . . . . . .   185 LET BROTHELS/N *   20
    AND SUNK MY HEART INTO THE ABYSS A RED ROUND GLOBE HOT   191 V DAU ALBION 2   33
        BURNING
    FIRES INWRAP THE EARTHLY GLOBE YET MAN IS NOT CONSUMD . .   199 AMERICA 8   15
    SO STILL TERRORS RENT THE HOUSE AS WHEN THE SOLEMN GLOBE   204 AMERICA CANC B   20
    FROM ETERNALS & LIKE A BLACK GLOBE . . . .   226 URIZEN 5   33
    AND LOS ROUND THE DARK GLOBE OF URIZEN . . . .   226 URIZEN 5   38
    ROUND GLOBE HOT BURNING DEEP . . . .   228 URIZEN 11   3
    AND LEFT A ROUND GLOBE OF BLOOD . . . .   230 URIZEN 13   58
    AND THE GLOBE OF LIFE BLOOD TREMBLING . . . .   231 URIZEN 15   13
    THE GLOBE OF LIFE BLOOD TREMBLED . . . .   231 URIZEN 18   1
    WITH A GLOBE OF FIRE LIGHTING HIS JOURNEY . . . . . .   234 URIZEN 20   48
    MOULDING INTO A VAST GLOBE HIS WRATH . . . .   249 AHANIA 2   7
    THE GLOBE OF WRATH SHAKING ON HIGH . . . .   249 AHANIA 2   16
    THE HOWLING GLOBE BURNING IT FLEW . . . .   249 AHANIA 2   18
    THE GLOBE SHOOK AND URIZEN SEATED . . . .   251 AHANIA 3   47
    HE HEATED THE ROUND GLOBE THEN BEAT   . . . .   260 BOOK OF LOS 5   38
    ROUND ROLLD THE SEA ENGLOBING IN A WATRY GLOBE SELF BALANCD   266 FOUR ZOAS 1   88
    [ROUND ROLLD XXX GLOBE SELF BALANCD] . . . . . .   SUPP FOUR ZOAS 1   *
    . . . BEAT THE HAMMERS MANY A [GLOBE] PYRAMID . . .   283 FOUR ZOAS 2   136
    A RED ROUND GLOBE HOT BURNING DEEP DEEP DOWN INTO THE   303 FOUR ZOAS 4   224
        ABYSS
    BRING IN HERE THE GLOBE OF BLOOD AS IN THE (BOOK) OF URIZEN   305A FOUR ZOAS 4   PROSE
    LOS BROODED ON THE DARKNESS NOR SAW URIZEN WITH A GLOBE   314 FOUR ZOAS 6   83
        OF FIRE
    STILL HE WITH HIS GLOBE OF FIRE IMMENSE IN HIS VENTUROUS   319 FOUR ZOAS 6   286
        HAND
    AND [WITH] BY HIS GLOBE OF FIRE HE WENT DOWN THE VALE OF   319 FOUR ZOAS 6   294
        URTHONA
    DARK GREW HIS GLOBE REDDNING WITH MISTS & FULL BEFORE HIS   319 FOUR ZOAS 6   296
        PATH
    FROM HEAVEN TO HEAVEN FROM GLOBE TO GLOBE IN VAST   320 FOUR ZOAS 6   319
        EXCENTRIC PATHS
    THE SUN WAS BLACK & THE MOON ROLLD A USELESS GLOBE THRO   337 FOUR ZOAS 7B   169
        HEAVEN
    AND HE ROLLD DOWN BENEATH THE FIRES OF ORC A GLOBE IMMENSE   350 FOUR ZOAS 8   372
    DOWN SUNK WITH FRIGHT A RED ROUND GLOBE HOT BURNING DEEP   482 MILTON 3   11
    ROUND GLOBE SUNK DOWN FROM HIS BOSOM INTO THE DEEP IN PANGS   483 MILTON 3   30
    AND OCALYTHRON BINDS THE SUN INTO A JEALOUS GLOBE   . . .   491 MILTON 10   19
    HIS PATH INTO A GLOBE ITSELF INFOLDING LIKE A SUN   . . .   497 MILTON 15   24
    BUT AS A WINTRY GLOBE DESCENDS PRECIPITANT THRO BEULAH   497 MILTON 15   44
        BURSTING
    THE WHOLE EXTENT OF THE GLOBE IS EXPLORED EVERY SCATTERD   510 MILTON 25   18
        ATOM
    AS OF A GLOBE ROLLING THRO VOIDNESS IT IS A DELUSION OF   516 MILTON 29   16
        ULRO
    FIRST AS A RED GLOBE OF BLOOD TREMBLING BENEATH HIS BOSOM   639 JERUSALEM 17   51
    TREMBLING GLOBE SHOT FORTH SELF-LIVING & LOS HOWLD OVER IT   639 JERUSALEM 17   55
    LOS TOOK HIS GLOBE OF FIRE TO SEARCH THE INTERIORS   656 JERUSALEM 31   3
        OF ALBION'S
    AND BECAME AN OPAKE GLOBE FAR DISTANT CLAD WITH MOONY BEAMS   679 JERUSALEM 49   20
    THE SUN WAS BLACK & THE MOON ROLLD A USELESS GLOBE THRO   699 JERUSALEM 65   11
        BRITAIN
    AND THEN A GLOBE OF BLOOD WANDERING DISTANT IN AN UNKNOWN   702 JERUSALEM 66   43
        NIGHT
    BY IT THE MOON FADED INTO A GLOBE . . . .   717 STOOD AMONG/J   8
    FORMING THE FLUCTUATING GLOBE ACCORDING TO THEIR WILL . .   727 JERUSALEM 83   34
    ARISE UPON THY WATCHES LET US SEE THY GLOBE OF FIRE . .   729 JERUSALEM 84   27
    SILENT AT HIS VOICE THEY VIEW THE RED GLOBE OF FIRE   730 JERUSALEM 85   19
        LOS'S HAND

GLOBE   (CONTINUED)
    INTO A GLOBE OF BLOOD BENEATH HIS BOSOM TREMBLING   732 JERUSALEM 86   52
      IN DARKNESS
    CELESTIAL GLOBE TERESTRIAL GLOBE . . . . SUPP ILLUS DANTE 16 *PROSE
GLOBES
    GOLDEN ROCKS TILL WE DISCOVERD TWO GLOBES OF CRIMSON FIRE   156C MARRIAGE HH 17 PROSE
    EARTH WAS NOT NOR GLOBES OF ATTRACTION . . . .   223 URIZEN 3   36
    AND WEIGH THE MASSY [GLOBES] CUBES . . . .   283 FOUR ZOAS 2   144
    SWEAT & BLOOD STOOD ON THE LIMBS OF LOS IN GLOBES HIS FIERY 307 FOUR ZOAS 5   67
      EYELIDS
    SLOW ROLL THE MASSY GLOBES AT HIS COMMAND & SLOW OERWHEEL   320 FOUR ZOAS 6   323
    MOULDED TO GLOBES & ARROWY WEDGES RENDING THY BLEEDING   321 FOUR ZOAS 7   52
      LIMBS
    OF PLAGUES HIDDEN IN SHINING GLOBES THAT GREW ON THE LIVING 325 FOUR ZOAS 7   216
      TREE
    AND BRASS & MOLTEN METALS CAST IN HOLLOW GLOBES & BORD . . 343 FOUR ZOAS 8   93
    THESE COVERING VAULTS OF HEAVEN & THESE TREMBLING GLOBES   364 FOUR ZOAS 9   260
      OF EARTH
    ONE EARTH ONE SEA BENEATH NOR ERRING GLOBES WANDER BUT   379 FOUR ZOAS 9   831
      STARS
    FOUR INTERSECTING GLOBES & THE EGG FORMD WORLD OF LOS . . 524 MILTON 34   33
GLOBULE
    FOR EVERY SPACE LARGER THAN A RED GLOBULE OF MAN'S BLOOD   516 MILTON 29   19
    AND EVERY SPACE SMALLER THAN A GLOBULE OF MAN'S BLOOD OPENS 516 MILTON 29   21
    THE RED GLOBULE IS THE UNWEARIED SUN BY LOS CREATED . . . 517 MILTON 29   23
    OF THAT PULSATION & THAT GLOBULE TERRIBLE THEIR POWER . . 517 MILTON 29   26
GLOOM
    IN SOLEMN GLOOM OF BRANCHES INTERWOVE . . . .   15 IMIT SPEN/PS   48
    THRO THE GLOOM HE'LL SEE MY SHADOW . . . .   61 LEAVE O/IM   7
    THE [GLOOM] SECRET FORESTS & ALL NIGHT WANDERD IN DESOLATE 106 TIRIEL 4   *   90
      WAYS
    DESCEND FROM THE GLOOM AND WANDER THRO THE PALACE . . .   136 FRENCH REVOLTN   60
    . . . FROM THE GLOOM WHERE THE AGED FORM WEPT . . . . .   140 FRENCH REVOLTN   135
    IN THE DEEP GLOOM BY WASHINGTON & PAINE & WARREN THEY STOOD 200 AMERICA 12   7
    THE YOUTH OF ENGLAND HID IN GLOOM CURSE THE PAIND HEAVENS 242 EUROPE 12   5
      COMPELLD
    SHUDDRING & WEEPING THRO THE GLOOM & DOWN INTO THE DEEPS   307 FOUR ZOAS 5   69
    COVERD WITH GLOOM THE FIERY BOY GREW FED BY THE MILK . . 307 FOUR ZOAS 5   72
    NINE DAYS THEY TRAVELD THRO THE GLOOM OF ENTUTHON BENITHON 309 FOUR ZOAS 5   149
    IN CLOUD OF SECRET GLOOM WHICH BEHOLD INVOLVE ME ROUND   660 JERUSALEM 33   47
      ABOUT
    LIKE A FAINT RAINBOW WAVED BEFORE HIM IN THE AWFUL GLOOM   728 JERUSALEM 83   67
    COLOURING AND ARE BLIND TO THE GLOOM OF A REAL TERROR . . 864C LETTER 61   PROSE
GLOOMD
    RANGD IN GLOOMD ARRAY STRETCH OUT ACROSS . . . . . .   223 URIZEN 3   29
GLOOMS
    AND CASTING ROUND THICK GLOOMS THUS UTTERD HIS FIERCE PANGS 299 FOUR ZOAS 4   78
      OF HEART
GLOOMY
    AND HEARD A GLOOMY VOICE CRY IS IT DONE . . . . . .   4 FAIR ELENOR/PS   32
    SO SAYING IJIM GLOOMY TURND HIS BACK & SILENT SOUGHT . . 106 TIRIEL 4   89
    THEIR SULLEN FLAMES FADED EMERGE ROUND THE GLOOMY KING . . 159D SONG LIBERTY   PROSE
    SOLEMN HEAVE THE ATLANTIC WAVES BETWEEN THE GLOOMY NATIONS 197 AMERICA 4   2
    ALARMD WITH THESE GLOOMY VISIONS . . . .   232 URIZEN 19   38
    GLOOMY SOUNDING NOW I AM GOD FROM ETERNITY TO ETERNITY . . 273 FOUR ZOAS 1   319
    WHERE IS SWEET VALA GLOOMY PROPHET WHERE THE LOVELY FORM   306 FOUR ZOAS 5   46
    HE WEPT & HE DIVIDED & HE LAID HIS GLOOMY HEAD . . . .   306 FOUR ZOAS 5   54
    DARKEND HIS BROWS WITH HIS COLD HELMET & HIS GLOOMY SPEAR 313 FOUR ZOAS 6   52
    HIS GLOOMY WAY BEFORE HIM THARMAS FLED & FLYING FOUGHT . . 313 FOUR ZOAS 6   54
    HE SIEZD THEM WITH A [DISMAL] GLOOMY SMILE . . . . .   316 FOUR ZOAS 6   169
    THE SPECTRE SAW THE SHADE SHIVRING OVER HIS GLOOMY ROCKS   325 FOUR ZOAS 7   * 211
    ALBION SPOKE WHO ART THOU THAT APPEAREST IN GLOOMY POMP   659 JERUSALEM 33   29
    LIKE ROCKY CLOUDS BUILD ME A GLOOMY MONUMENT OF WOE . . . 666 JERUSALEM 39   18
    SO SPOKE ALBION IN GLOOMY MAJESTY AND DEEPEST NIGHT . . . 670 JERUSALEM 42   17
    A DARK BLACK ROCK & A GLOOMY CAVE . . . .   817 HAPPINESS/L   40
GLORIED
    SATAN GLORIED IN HIS PRIDE . . . .   748 EV GOSPEL(B)/N   14
GLORIES
    AND RISING GLORIES BEAM AROUND MY HEAD . . . .   9 FRESH FROM/PS   4
    LAUGHS AT AFFECTION GLORIES IN REBELLION SCOFFS AT LOVE   107 TIRIEL 6   18
    . . . WITH GLORIES FROM THEIR HEADS OUT BEAMING . . . . 269 FOUR ZOAS 1   196
    WHEN HIS MERIDIAN GLORIES WERE BEGUN . . . .   414 TO MRS FLAXMAN   4
    AND ALL THE KINGS & NOBLES OF THE EARTH & ALL THEIR   713 JERUSALEM 73   38
      GLORIES
    SHALL PLANT THEIR GLORIES IN YOUR BREAST . . . . . .   749 EV GOSPEL(B)/N   20
    OF GOD & HEAVEN & THEIR GLORIES . . . .   758 EV GOSPEL (1)   6
GLORIFICATION
    A GLORIFICATION OF ANGELS WITH HARPS SURROUND THE DOVE . . 613B V LAST JUDG/N   PROSE
GLORIFIED
    GLORIFIED THY HOLINESS OR REJOICED IN THY GREAT SALVATION 695 JERUSALEM 61   46
    A GLORIFIED SAINT WHO WAS A SUFFERING MORTAL THAT . . . . 854B LETTER 53   PROSE
    TO WELCOME THY ARRIVAL AMONG COWPER'S GLORIFIED BAND . . 854C LETTER 53   PROSE
GLORIFY
    I TOUCH THE HEAVENS AS AN INSTRUMENT TO GLORIFY THE LORD   494 MILTON 13   29
GLORIOUS   SEE ALL GLORIOUS,ONCE GLORIOUS
    WON BY OUR FATHERS IN MANY A GLORIOUS FIELD . . . . .   18 EDW THIRD/PS 1   10
    AND NO LESS GLORIOUS THAN THOSE OF WAR . . . .   19 EDW THIRD/PS 2   19
    PERHAPS MORE GLORIOUS IN THE (PHILOSOPHIC) MIND . . . .   19 EDW THIRD/PS 2   20
    TO THIS MOST GLORIOUS VOYAGE ON WHICH CAST . . . . . .   21 EDW THIRD/PS 2   95
    O LIBERTY HOW GLORIOUS ART THOU . . . .   26 EDW THIRD/PS 3   204
    I SHALL WITH PLEASURE VIEW A GLORIOUS ACTION . . . . .   27 EDW THIRD/PS 3   280
    I'LL WEEP AND SHOUT FOR GLORIOUS LIBERTY . . . . . .   31 EDW THIRD/PS 5   52

```
                                                             PAGE     TITLE          LINE
GLORIOUS    (CONTINUED)
    PREPARE YOUR ARMS FOR GLORIOUS VICTORY  . . . . . . .     34 WAR SONG/PS              8
    SUNK FROM THE GLORIOUS CLIME  . . . . . . . . . .       157A MARRIAGE HH 17      PROSE
    DOES THE SUN WALK IN GLORIOUS RAIMENT ON THE SECRET FLOOR  195 V DAU ALBION 7       30
    LOS BEAT ON THE ANVIL TILL GLORIOUS  . . . . . . .       260 BOOK OF LOS 5          33
    THREE GATES WITHIN GLORIOUS & BRIGHT OPEN INTO [ETERNITY]  279 FOUR ZOAS 1       *  563
        BEULAH
    BUT THOU MY SON GLORIOUS IN BRIGHTNESS COMFORTER OF THARMAS  298 FOUR ZOAS 4        26
    THOU HORRIBLE RUIN ONCE LIKE ME THOU WAST ALL GLORIOUS  .  .  317 FOUR ZOAS 6      210
    STOP WE THE RISING OF THE GLORIOUS KING . . . . . . . .  336 FOUR ZOAS 7B        153
    THE LIVING SOUL IN GLORIOUS FORMS & EVERY ONE CAME FORTH   340 FOUR ZOAS 7B       278
    INTO THE FIRES THEN GLORIOUS BRIGHT EXULTING IN HIS JOY    362 FOUR ZOAS 9        191
    A GLORIOUS VISION [OF] TO THINE EYES A SELF RENEWING VISION  362 FOUR ZOAS 9      211
    LOOK HOW THE BEAMS FORESHEW THE RISING OF SOME GLORIOUS    367 FOUR ZOAS 9        398
        POWER
    RISE UP O SUN MOST GLORIOUS MINISTER & LIGHT OF DAY  . . .  368 FOUR ZOAS 9       434
    IN VAIN CONDEMNING GLORIOUS WAR  . . . . . . . . .       419 I SAW A MONK/N        12
    OPENING INTERIORLY INTO JERUSALEM & BABYLON SHINING       500 MILTON 18           41
        GLORIOUS
    SHINING IN DARKNESS GLORIOUS UPON THE DEEPS OF ENTUTHON   501 MILTON 19           35
    AND THEN RUSH FORWARD WITH ME INTO THE GLORIOUS SPIRITUAL  511 MILTON 25          60
    ON ALBION'S ROCK LOS STANDS CREATING THE GLORIOUS SUN EACH  517 MILTON 29         41
        MORNING
    ONE TO THE SOUTH THIS WAS THE GLORIOUS WORLD OF URIZEN  . .  524 MILTON 34        36
    GLORIOUS AS THE MIDDAY SUN IN SATAN'S BOSOM GLOWING  . . .  532 MILTON 40         19
    IS THIS ART OR IS IT GLORIOUS TO A NATION TO PRODUCE  . .  597C PUB ADDRESS/N   PROSE
    STARRY & GLORIOUS AND THEY EVERY ONE IN THEIR BRIGHT LOINS  635 JERUSALEM 14      19
    OFFERING TO SUSTAIN THE GLORIOUS COMBAT & THE BATTLE & WAR  658 JERUSALEM 31      65
    OF EDEN THAT HOWEVER GREAT AND GLORIOUS HOWEVER LOVING      675 JERUSALEM 45      10
    IN VAIN CONDEMNING GLORIOUS WAR  . . . . . . . . . .      683 I SAW A MONK/J      10
    AND SHINE GLORIOUS WITHIN HAND & KOBAN ARCHD OVER THE SUN  690 JERUSALEM 58       29
    GLORIOUS (INCOMPREHENSIBLE) BY MORTAL MAN . . . .  .  .   745 JERUSALEM 98        11
    A MOST BEAUTIFUL COUNTRY ON A MOST GLORIOUS DAY OUR  .  . 803A LETTER 15        PROSE
    HIS GLORIOUS BEAMS  . . . . . . . . . . . . . .          804 TO BUTTS/L            5
    HAPPY SON OF THE IMMORTAL PHIDIAS HIS LOT IS TRULY GLORIOUS  807B LETTER 17     PROSE
    BEEN A GLORIOUS & TRIUMPHANT DWELLER IN IMMORTALITY PLEASE  830C LETTER 30      PROSE
    LIKE THE REMEMBRANCE OF FELPHAM'S WAVES & OF THE GLORIOUS &  835B LETTER 34     PROSE
GLORIOUSLY
    ON BOTH SIDES WITHIN & WITHOUT BEAMING GLORIOUSLY    . . . 631 JERUSALEM 12       20
GLORY    SEE VAIN-GLORY
    A CROWN OF GLORY BUT FROM THY VERY DUST . . . . . . .      18 EDW THIRD/PS 1      23
    EACH CLAD IN GLORY ACCORDING TO HIS SPHERE . . . . . .     18 EDW THIRD/PS 1      34
    GLORY MAY NOT BE DIMMD WITH CLOUDS OF CARE . . . . . .     19 EDW THIRD/PS 2      15
    OF HIS OFFICIOUS GLORY  . . . . . . . . . . . . .         20 EDW THIRD/PS 2      54
    AND SHALL BE STILL MY GLORY I WAS INSPIRD  . . . . . .     23 EDW THIRD/PS 3      88
    THESE ARE THE MINDS THAT GLORY IN THE BATTLE . . . . .     25 EDW THIRD/PS 3     170
    TILL GLORY FIRES HIS BREAST TO ENLARGE HIS CASTLE  . . .   26 EDW THIRD/PS 3     201
    WE FALL WITH GLORY I KNOW THE WOLF . . . . . . . .        27 EDW THIRD/PS 3     265
    LITTLE SPORT AND CUT A PATH INTO THE HEAVEN OF GLORY  .    27 EDW THIRD/PS 3     274
    HAS TO GET BEFORE ANOTHER IN ANY PURSUIT AFTER GLORY  .    28 EDW THIRD/PS 4      15
    PROPHETIC SAW THE KINGDOMS OF THE WORLD & ALL THEIR GLORY  41A THEN SHE BORE   PROSE
    HA HA HA SAID INFLAMMABLE GASS HE WAS THE GLORY OF FRANCE  46A ISLAND MOON 1   PROSE
    WHOSE RICH FIELDS INHERITING SPREAD THEIR OLD GLORY . . .  143 FRENCH REVOLTN    204
    THE PRIDE OF THE PEACOCK IS THE GLORY OF GOD  . . . . .  151C MARRIAGE HH 8    PROSE
    THE UNIVERSAL MAN TO WHOM BE GLORY EVERMORE AMEN . . . .   264 FOUR ZOAS 1       11
    [SEARCHING FOR GLORY WISHING THAT THE HEAVENS HAD EYES     267 FOUR ZOAS 1      130
        TO SEE]
    [SUCH WONDROUS BEAUTY REPINING IN THE MIDST OF ALL HIS     267 FOUR ZOAS 1      132
        GLORY]
    GIRD ON THY SWORD O THOU MOST MIGHTY IN GLORY & MAJESTY    279 FOUR ZOAS 1      548
    THE IMMORTAL ATMOSPHERES ARE THINE THERE THOU ART SEEN     291 FOUR ZOAS 3        8
        IN GLORY
    A GOD & NOT A MAN A CONQUEROR IN TRIUMPHANT GLORY   . . .  333 FOUR ZOAS 7B        9
    GLORY GLORY GLORY TO THE HOLY LAMB OF GOD    . . . . .     346 FOUR ZOAS 8       195
    SHINES WITH IMMORTAL GLORY . . . . . . . . . . . .        364 FOUR ZOAS 9       268
    DESCENDING FROM JERUSALEM WITH POWER AND GREAT GLORY  .    364 FOUR ZOAS 9       273
    WHEN HEAVEN & HELL IN EMULATION STROVE IN SPORTS OF GLORY  365 FOUR ZOAS 9       298
    SHE CEASD & (LIGHT) BEAMD ROUND HER LIKE THE GLORY OF THE  370 FOUR ZOAS 9    *  503
        MORNING
    AND THUS HER VOICE GLORY DELIGHT & SWEET ENJOYMENT BORN    381 FOUR ZOAS AD 5     11
    THEN FIRST SHE SAW HIS GLORY & HER HARLOT FORM APPEARD  .  382 FOUR ZOAS AD 6     21
    [THE GLORY OF WAR THOU CONDEMNST IN VAIN] . . . . . .      419 I SAW A MONK/N     11
    [VICT ] GLORY & VICTORY A [ [?ROMAN] ] [?TROJAN] [PLAITED]  420 I SAW MNK AD/N *  21
      PHALLIC WHIP
    THE FAIRY SKIPD ABOUT IN HIS GLORY JOY & PRIDE   . . . .   434 LONG JOHN BRWN     15
    WHO COMETH IN THE CLOUDS WITH POWER & GREAT GLORY   . .   444A LAST JUDGMNT/L  PROSE
    SURROUNDED BY A GLORY [IN THE GLORY ] . . . . . . .      444B LAST JUDGMNT/L  PROSE
    MANY INFANTS APPEAR IN THE GLORY REPRESENTING  . . . .   444C LAST JUDGMNT/L  PROSE
    THE SPECTRE OF ALBION FRCWND OVER THE NATIONS IN GLORY     486 MILTON 6           24
        & WAR
    GLORY GLORY GLORY TO THE HOLY LAMB OF GOD   . . . . .     494 MILTON 13           28
    TO WHOM BE GLORY & POWER & DOMINION EVERMORE AMEN   . . .  495 MILTON 14           3
    TO PERPETUATE WAR & GLORY TO PERPETUATE THE LAWS OF SIN    506 MILTON 22          45
    TO WHOM BE GLORY & DOMINION EVERMORE AMEN  . . . . . .     519 MILTON 30          16
    IN THE CLOUDS OF OLOLON WITH POWER & GREAT GLORY  . . .    519 MILTON 31          16
    IF MICHAEL ANGELO IS ITS SUPREME GLORY IF ART IS THE GLORY  561C EXHIBITION ADV   PROSE
    AND ITS ANCIENT GLORY WHEN IT WAS AS IT AGAIN SHALL BE  .  577D DESC CAT 5      PROSE
    GLORY [OF] & PRIDE OF A NATION [& THAT THE MAN WHO DOES    597B PUB ADDRESS/N *PROSE
        THIS IS]
    THIS IS MY GLORY & EXCEEDING GREAT REWARD  . . . . . .    600C PUB ADDRESS/N    PROSE
    COMING IN THE CLOUDS WITH POWER & GREAT GLORY  . . . . .  609D V LAST JUDG/N    PROSE
    JESUS IS SURROUNDED BY BEAMS OF GLORY IN WHICH ARE SEEN ALL  613D V LAST JUDG/N  PROSE
```

GLORY   (CONTINUED)

A RAINBOW SURROUNDS THE THRONE & THE GLORY	613D	V LAST JUDG/N	PROSE
EMANATE UNCURBED IN THEIR ETERNAL GLORY	615C	V LAST JUDG/N	PROSE
MAY LIVE IN GLORY REDEEMD BY SACRIFICE OF THE LAMB . . .	640	JERUSALEM 18	27
I ELECTED ALBION FOR MY GLORY I GAVE TO HIM THE NATIONS	653	JERUSALEM 29	6
BUT GLORY TO THE MERCIFUL-ONE FOR HE IS OF TENDER MERCIES	667	JERUSALEM 40	43
WITH HER IN POMP AND GLORY OF VICTORY DEPART	671	JERUSALEM 42	64
YE TWENTY-FOUR INTO THE DEEPS LET US DEPART TO GLORY . .	671	JERUSALEM 42	65
THE GLORY OF CHRISTIANITY IS TO CONQUER BY FORGIVENESS .	683A	JERUSALEM 52	PROSE
OF CAMBERWELL WE SHALL BEHOLD YOU NO MORE IN GLORY & PRIDE	729	JERUSALEM 84	5
. . . ALL THEIR GLORY THAT GREW ON DESOLATION	746	JERUSALEM 98	51
AMIDST THEM IN HIS GLORY BEAMS	758	EV GOSPEL (2)	15
FOR THEIR GLORY IS WAR AND DOMINION	777A	INSC LAOCOON	PROSE
FOR THINE IS THE KINGDOM & THE POWER & THE GLORY	788B	ANNO THORNTON	MARG
& THE POWER OR WAR & THE GLORY OR LAW	789A	ANNO THORNTON	MARG
THE IMMENSE FLOOD OF GRECIAN LIGHT & GLORY WHICH IS COMING	797C	LETTER 10	PROSE
AT THE MAN WHO WAS CROWND WITH GLORY & HONOUR	813B	LETTER 22	PROSE
ENDEAVOUR TO LIVE TO THE GLORY OF OUR LORD & SAVIOUR & I	822C	LETTER 26	PROSE
LEADS TO GLORY & HONOUR I REJOICE & I TREMBLE	823B	LETTER 26	PROSE
TO ME FOR NOW O GLORY AND O DELIGHT I HAVE ENTIRELY REDUCED	851D	LETTER 50	PROSE
I SHALL GLORY IN THE DISCOVERY	853A	LETTER 51	*PROSE

GLORYING   SEE SELF-GLORYING

GLORYING IN HIS OWN EYES EXALTED IN TERRIFIC PRIDE . . .	267	FOUR ZOAS 1	129
GLORYING TO INVOLVE ALBION'S BODY IN FIRES OF ETERNAL WAR	493	MILTON 13	6

GLOSSARY

THE INN IS A GOTHIC BUILDING WHICH THYNNE IN HIS GLOSSARY	567B	DESC CAT 3	PROSE
THE INN IS A GOTHIC BUILDING WHICH THYNNE IN HIS GLOSSARY	588D	CHAUCER/N	PROSE
THE INN IS A GOTHIC BUILDING WHICH THYNNE IN HIS GLOSSARY	590C	CHAUCER 2	PROSE

GLOUCESTER

MORTIMER AND GLOUCESTER LIE SPELL BOUND BEHIND THEIR KING	577B	DESC CAT 4	PROSE
GLOUCESTER AND EXETER AND SALISBURY AND BRISTOL AND BENEVOLENT BATH	668	JERUSALEM 40	61
I COULD NOT HAVE DONE IF THEY HAD TAKEN ME TO GLOUCESTER	870A	LETTER 70	PROSE

GLOUCESTERSHIRE

COBAN DWELT IN BATH SOMERSET WILTSHIRE GLOUCESTERSHIRE . .	710	JERUSALEM 71	26

GLOUSTER

LEVI MIDDLESEX KENT SURREY JUDAH SOMERSET GLOUSTER WILTSHIRE	637	JERUSALEM 16	45

GLOVES

& A PAIR OF GLOVES EVERY DAY & THE SORROWS OF WERTER . .	53A	ISLAND MOON 8	PROSE
BOUND THESE BLACK SHOES OF DEATH & ON MY HANDS DEATH'S IRON GLOVES	666	JERUSALEM 39	21

GLOW

HAVE GIVEN ME WHEN I HAVE SEEN THE FIELD GLOW	23	EDW THIRD/PS 3	84
SWEET FLOWER AND PUT THEE HERE TO GLOW BETWEEN MY BREASTS	189	V DAU ALBION 1	12
SULLEN FIRES ACROSS THE ATLANTIC GLOW TO AMERICA'S SHORE	197	AMERICA 3	2
SULLEN FIRES ACROSS THE ATLANTIC GLOW TO AMERICA'S SHORE	203	AMERICA CANC A	2
AROUND SAINT JAMES'S [GLOW THE FIRES]	205	AMERICA CANC C	9
A RECESS IN THE WALL FOR FIRES TO GLOW UPON THE PALE . .	285	FOUR ZOAS 2	188
THE SURREY HILLS GLOW LIKE THE CLINKERS OF THE FURNACE LAMBETH'S VALE	485	MILTON 6	14
GLOW ON AMERICA'S SHORE ALBION TURNS UPON HIS COUCH . . .	506	MILTON 23	7
BUT ALL MY LIMBS WITH WARMTH GLOW	538	ANGER WRATH/N	3
HEARTS OF THEIR WARRIORS GLOW HOT BEFORE THOR & FRIGA O MOLECH	706	JERUSALEM 68	17
MY ARROWS GLOW IN THEIR GOLDEN SHEAVES	818	HAPPINESS/L	80

GLOWD

THEN THE KING GLOWD HIS NOBLES FOLD ROUND	137	FRENCH REVOLTN	68
THE SPECTRE GLOWD HIS HORRID LENGTH STAINING THE TEMPLE LONG	198	AMERICA 5	6
THE SUN GLOWD FIERY RED	245	EUROPE 15	3
THAT GLOWD FURIOUS IN THE EXPANSE	259	BOOK OF LOS 5	9
GLOWD FURIOUS ON THE ANVIL PREPARD FOR SPADES & COULTERS ALL	278	FOUR ZOAS 1	520
THE GOLDEN HALL OF URIZEN WHOSE WESTERN SIDE GLOWD BRIGHT	284	FOUR ZOAS 2	179
OF IRON GLOWD FURIOUS PREPARD FOR SPADES & MATTOCKS . . .	300	FOUR ZOAS 4	91
ROUND HIS LOINS A GIRDLE GLOWD WITH MANY COLOURD FIRES . .	319	FOUR ZOAS 6	304
OF IRON GLOWD BRIGHT PREPARD FOR SPADES & PLOWSHARES SUDDEN DOWN	327	FOUR ZOAS 7	* 283
ROLL ROUND THE TEMPLE & THEY TOOK THE SUN THAT GLOWD OER LOS	333	FOUR ZOAS 7B	29
GLOWD ON HIS ROCKY COUCH AGAINST THE DARKNESS LOUD THUNDERS	500	MILTON 18	47
GLOWD BUT IN TERRORS FOLDED ROUND HIS CLOUDS OF BLOOD . .	502	MILTON 20	24
THE MOON THAT GLOWD REMOTE BELOW	818	HAPPINESS/L	73

GLOWING

THE BAT THE OWL THE GLOWING TYGER AND THE KING OF NIGHT	195	V DAU ALBION 8	5
MEET ON THE COAST GLOWING WITH BLOOD FROM ALBION'S FIERY PRINCE	197	AMERICA 3	5
HIS VOICE HIS LOCKS HIS AWFUL SHOULDERS AND HIS GLOWING EYES	197	AMERICA 3	17
INTENSE NAKED A HUMAN FIRE FIERCE GLOWING AS THE WEDGE . .	197	AMERICA 4	8
LEAVING THE FEMALES NAKED AND GLOWING WITH THE LUSTS OF YOUTH	202	AMERICA 15	22
MEET ON THE COAST GLOWING WITH BLOOD FROM ALBION'S FIERY PRINCE	203	AMERICA CANC A	5
HIS VOICE HIS LOCKS HIS AWFUL SHOULDERS & HIS GLOWING EYES	204	AMERICA CANC A	17
. . . [GLOWING] MUSTRING AROUND THEIR PRINCE	205	AMERICA CANC C	* 17
WHEN LOS HEATED THE GLOWING MASS CASTING	260	BOOK OF LOS 5	42
AND BOUND DOWN TO THE GLOWING ILLUSION	260	BOOK OF LOS 5	47
IN FIERCE TORMENTS ON HIS GLOWING BED	260	BOOK OF LOS 5	51
[BUT STANDING ON THE ROCKS HER WOVEN SHADOW GLOWING BRIGHT]	267	FOUR ZOAS 1	119

	PAGE	TITLE	LINE

GLOWING   (CONTINUED)
    I CAN INFUSE MY DEAR REVENGE INTO HIS GLOWING BREAST . . 289 FOUR ZOAS 2   337
    [WAS LUVAH XXX HE STOOD ?GLOWING IN THE DARK FLAME] . . SUPP FOUR ZOAS 5 *
    [OF HOPE & FEAR XXX SINGING THE ?SAME SONG AROUND THE   SUPP FOUR ZOAS 5 *
      ?GLOWING BED]
    OFT WOULD HE STAND & QUESTION A FIERCE SCORPION GLOWING   315 FOUR ZOAS 6   131
      WITH GOLD
    OF HAIR SHOOT FROM HIS ORBED SCULL HIS GLOWING EYES . . . 319 FOUR ZOAS 6   308
    FROM THE FOUR CLIFFS OF URTHONA RISE GLOWING AROUND THE   319 FOUR ZOAS 6   313
      SPECTRE
    OF LIVING PANGS THY HORRIBLE BED GLOWING WITH CEASELESS   321 FOUR ZOAS 7   50
      FIRES
    THY ROSES THAT EXPANDED IN THE FACE OF GLOWING MORN . . . 325 FOUR ZOAS 7   194
    I SPEND MY GLOWING TIME BUT THOU ART STRONG & MIGHTY . . 330 FOUR ZOAS 7   392
    WHEN THE SUN ROSE IN GLOWING MORN WITH ARMS OF MIGHTY HOSTS 338 FOUR ZOAS 7B 197
    AND LEUTHA STOOD GLOWING WITH VARYING COLOURS IMMORTAL   492 MILTON 11   32
      HEART-PIERCING
    LOS STOOD IN THAT FIERCE GLOWING FIRE & HE ALSO STOOPD DOWN 505 MILTON 22   8
    THE SONS OF OZOTH WITHIN THE OPTIC NERVE STAND FIERY   515 MILTON 28   29
      GLOWING
    GLORIOUS AS THE MIDDAY SUN IN SATAN'S BOSOM GLOWING . . . 532 MILTON 40   19
    WATCHING HIS TIME WITH GLOWING EYES TO LEAP UPON HIS PREY 627 JERUSALEM 8   22
    CLAY BAKD & ENAMELD ETERNAL GLOWING AS FOUR FURNACES . . 632 JERUSALEM 12   64
    BEFORE BROMION'S IRON TONGS & GLOWING POKER REDDENING   636 JERUSALEM 16   2
      FIERCE
    WHEN THE SUN ROSE IN GLOWING MORN WITH ARMS OF MIGHTY HOSTS 700 JERUSALEM 65   43
    AND DISHES OF PAINTED CLAY GLOWING WITH BEAUTY & CRUELTY   702 JERUSALEM 66   33
    GLOWING WITH LOVELINESS BEFORE HIM BECOMING APPARENT . . 723 JERUSALEM 80   71
    INCLOSED BY EYELESS WINGS GLOWING WITH FIRE AS THE IRON   735 JERUSALEM 89   41
GLOWS
    GLOWS LIKE A METEOR IN THE DISTANT NORTH . . . . 239 EUROPE 4   12
    SUCH AS GLOWS OUT FROM SLEEPING SPIRITS APPEARD IN THE   372 FOUR ZOAS 9   561
      DEEPS BENEATH
    HERTFORDSHIRE GLOWS WITH FIERCE VEGETATION IN THE FORESTS 636 JERUSALEM 16   3
    THAT APPARENT TO ALL IN ETERNITY GLOWS LIKE THE SUN IN   723 JERUSALEM 80   68
      THE BREAST
GLOW-WORM
    BUT I SAW A GLOW-WORM NEAR . . . . 112 A DREAM/SI   14
GLUED
    [GLEWED] GLUED TOGETHER   . . . . 418 WHEN MAN HAS/N *   4
GLUT
    GHOSTS GLUT THE THROAT OF HELL . . . . 13 GWIN KING/PS   96
GLUTINOUS
    DIM & GLUTINOUS AS THE WHITE POLYPUS . . . . 258 BOOK OF LOS 4   57
GLUTTON'S
    THE MISER'S NET & THE GLUTTON'S TRAP . . . . 750 EV GOSPEL(C)/N   18
    THE MISER'S NET & THE GLUTTON'S TRAP . . . . 751 EV GOSPEL(D)/N   20
GLUTTONY
    TO ME WHILE DRUNKENNESS LEWDNESS GLUTTONY & EVEN . . . . 812C LETTER 22   PROSE
GLYCON
    OF HOMER SOCRATES PHIDIAS GLYCON ARISTOTLE ETC . . . . 388D ANNO WATSON   MARG
GNASHING
    GROANING GNASHING GROANING . . . . 226 URIZEN 7   2
    AND BREATHING TERRIBLE BLOOD & VENGEANCE GNASHING HIS TEETH 306 FOUR ZOAS 5   58
      WITH PAIN
    BREATHING CRUELTY BLOOD & VENGEANCE GNASHING HIS TEETH   667 JERUSALEM 40   38
      WITH PAIN
GNASHINGS
    THE HOWLINGS GNASHINGS GROANINGS SHRIEKINGS . . . . . . 313 FOUR ZOAS 6   81
GNASSHING
    THE NETHER ABYSS & GNASSHING IN FIERCE DESPAIR PANTING   296 FOUR ZOAS 3 * 155
      IN SOBS
GNAT
    THE GNAT THAT SINGS HIS SUMMER'S SONG . . . . 432 AUGURIES   45
    THE CRUEL SCORPION IS THERE THE GNAT WASP HORNET & THE   513 MILTON 27   21
      HONEY BEE
GNAWD
    HE MIGHT FEEL THE PAIN AS IF A MAN GNAWD HIS OWN TENDER   630 JERUSALEM 11   7
      NERVES
GNAWED
    ALL THAT BEHELD HIM FLED HOWLING AND GNAWED THEIR TONGUES 662 JERUSALEM 36   8
GNAWING
    IN [DISMAL] GNAWING PAIN DRAWN OUT BY HER LOVD FINGERS   266 FOUR ZOAS 1   79
      EVERY NERVE
    IN GNAWING PAIN FROM LOS'S BOSOM IN THE DEADLY NIGHT . . 639 JERUSALEM 17   50
    IN GNAWING PAIN DIVIDING HIM FROM HIS EMANATION . . . . . 684 JERUSALEM 53   6
    AND VALA FOR I CANNOT LEAVE THEM IN THE GNAWING GRAVE . . 696 JERUSALEM 62   21
    EXPERIENCED IT BEGAN BY A GNAWING PAIN IN THE STOMACH . . 872B LETTER 75   PROSE
GNAWN
    HIS SOUL WAS GNAWN IN SUNDER . . . . 336 FOUR ZOAS 7B   139
GNAWS
    INCESSANT STERN DISDAIN HIS SCALY FORM GNAWS INWARDLY . . 352 FOUR ZOAS 8   434
GNOMES
    THE GNOMES ACCUSD SATAN WITH INDIGNATION FURY AND FIRE . 487 MILTON 7   21
    WAS SATAN'S ENEMY & THAT THE GNOMES BEING PALAMABRON'S   487 MILTON 7   39
      FRIENDS
    CURBING HIS LIVING CREATURES MANY OF THE STRONGEST GNOMES 487 MILTON 7   48
    COMPELLD THE GNOMES TO CURB THE HORSES & TO THROW BANKS   493 MILTON 12   17
      OF SAND
    THE GNOMES IN ALL THAT DAY SPARD NOT THEY CURSD SATAN   493 MILTON 12   31
      BITTERLY
    THE GNOMES LABOURD I WEEPING HID IN SATAN'S INMOST BRAIN 493 MILTON 12   36

		PAGE	TITLE	LINE

GNOMES   (CONTINUED)

	PAGE	TITLE	LINE
BUT WHEN THE GNOMES REFUSD TO LABOUR MORE WITH BLANDISHMENTS	493	MILTON 12	37
I CAME FORTH FROM THE HEAD OF SATAN BACK THE GNOMES RECOILD	493	MILTON 12	38
THE FAIRIES NYMPHS GNOMES & GENII OF THE FOUR ELEMENTS	520	MILTON 31	20
AND SIXTY-FOUR THOUSAND GNOMES GUARD THE NORTHERN GATE	633	JERUSALEM 13	27
FAIRIES & GENII & NYMPHS & GNOMES OF THE ELEMENTS	663	JERUSALEM 36	37

GO

	PAGE	TITLE	LINE
AND WHEN NIGHT COMES I'LL GO	8	MEMORY COME/PS	13
AND WITH NIGHT WILL GO	9	MAD SONG/PS	20
THE VILLAGE BELL ALARMS AWAY I GO	10	WHEN EARLY/PS	5
I TURN MY EYES AND PENSIVE AS I GO	10	WHEN EARLY/PS	9
THEN LADEN WITH ETERNAL FATE DOST GO	15	IMIT SPEN/PS	24
MUST SURER BOUND GO THRO THY PART	16	BLIND-MANS/PS	42
THESE ARE MY THOUGHTS YET IT WERE BEST TO GO	20	EDW THIRD/PS 2	49
THEN GO TO ENGLAND TELL THEM HOW WE FIGHT	24	EDW THIRD/PS 3	138
GO NOW FOR THOU ART SUITED TO THE WORK	25	EDW THIRD/PS 3	178
GO PETER GET YOU GONE	29D	EDW THIRD/PS 4	PROSE
GO ON FAIR TRAITRESS DO THY GUILEFUL WORK	38A	SAMSON/PS	PROSE
I WILL GO MAD AND TEAR MY CRISPED HAIR I'LL RUN ABOUT	38C	SAMSON/PS	PROSE
GO SEE THE CITY FRIENDS JOIND HAND IN HAND	43A	THEN SHE BORE	PROSE
GO SEE THE NATURAL TIE OF FLESH & BLOOD	43A	THEN SHE BORE	PROSE
GO SEE MORE STRONG THE TIES OF MARRIAGE LOVE	43A	THEN SHE BORE	PROSE
I TURND MYSELF ABOUT WITH GREAT CONTEMPT SAID I GO ALONG YOU FOOL	45A	ISLAND MOON 1	PROSE
I WON'T LET IT GO AT ONLY SO & SO	46	PHEBUS CAME/IM	5
HA HA SAID INFLAMMABLE GASS WHAT DONT YOU LIKE TO GO TO CHURCH	48A	ISLAND MOON 4	PROSE
IF I HAD NOT A PLACE OF PROFIT THAT FORCES ME TO GO TO CHURCH	48A	ISLAND MOON 4	PROSE
A PARCEL OF FOOLS GOING TO BRISTOL IF I WAS TO GO	51D	ISLAND MOON 7	PROSE
THERE THEY GO [TO] IN POSTCHAISES & STAGES	53A	ISLAND MOON 8	PROSE
EXCEPT WHEN I GO TO MR JACKO'S HE KNOWS WHAT RIDING IS	53A	ISLAND MOON 8	PROSE
& I DO BELIEVE HE'LL GO IN PARTNERSHIP WITH HIS MASTER	53A	ISLAND MOON 8	PROSE
ENGLISH GENIUS FOR EVER HERE I GO	56A	ISLAND MOON 9	PROSE
[I NONE OF] GO & BE HANGED SAID SCOPPREL	57A	ISLAND MOON 9	*PROSE
SO THEY NEED NOT BIDDING GO	59A	ISLAND MOON 10	PROSE
AND WE CANNOT [GO TO] GO TO SLEEP [TILL ITS DARK]	60	NURSES SONG/IM	10
[THE FLOCKS ARE AT PLAY & WE CAN'T GO AWAY]	60	NURSES SONG/IM	11
WELL WELL GO & PLAY TILL THE LIGHT FADES AWAY	60	NURSES SONG/IM	14
AND THEN GO HOME TO BED	60	NURSES SONG/IM	15
IVE A GOOD MIND TO GO	60	SAY YOU JOE/IM	3
("AVOID ORIGINALITY AND SACRIFICE TO FASHION") & GO TO HELL	85B	ANNO LAVATER	MARG
TELL ME WITH WHOM YOU GO & I'LL TELL YOU WHAT YOU DO	88A	ANNO LAVATER	MARG
IF THOU DOST GO SAID HAR I WISH THINE EYES MAY SEE THY FOLLY	102	TIRIEL 3	17
THOU SHALT NOT GO SAID HEVA TILL THOU HAST SEEN OUR SINGING BIRDS	103	TIRIEL 3	22
GO NOT FOR THOU ART SO LIKE TIRIEL THAT I LOVE THINE HEAD	103	TIRIEL 3	24
[?BUT] AND MNETHA SAID THOU MUST NOT GO TO WANDER DARK ALONE	103	TIRIEL 3 *	33
NO ARTFUL FIEND BUT I WILL LEAD THEE DOST THOU WANT TO GO	104	TIRIEL 4	23
NOW [?HILI] HELA I CAN GO WITH PLEASURE & DWELL WITH HAR & HEVA	107	TIRIEL 6 *	3
LYCA'S PARENTS GO	113	LIT GRL FND/SI	2
SHE COULD NO FURTHER GO	114	LIT GRL FND/SI	20
AND WE CANNOT GO TO SLEEP	121	NURSES SONG/SI	10
WELL WELL GO & PLAY TILL THE LIGHT FADES AWAY	121	NURSES SONG/SI	13
AND THEN GO HOME TO BED	121	NURSES SONG/SI	14
BUT TO GO TO SCHOOL IN A SUMMER MORN	124	SCHOOL BOY/SI	6
OR WILT THOU GO ASK THE MOLE	127	THELS MOTTO/BT	2
BUT GO MERCILESS MAN	142	FRENCH REVOLTN	190
. . . GO THOU COLD RECLUSE INTO THE FIRES	142	FRENCH REVOLTN	191
GO COMMAND YONDER TOWER	145	FRENCH REVOLTN	249
MADE HIM GO NAKED AND BAREFOOT THREE YEARS HE ANSWERD	154A	MARRIAGE HH 12	PROSE
O AFRICAN BLACK AFRICAN GO WINGED THOUGHT WIDEN HIS FOREHEAD	159C	SONG LIBERTY	PROSE
I WAS BORN A SLAVE BUT I [LONG] GO TO BE FREE	166	WHY CARE FOR/N *	9
BUT IF ONCE YOU LET THE RIPE MOMENT GO	179	IF YOU TRAP/N	3
[SUCH USAGE IN HEAVEN MAKES ALL GO TO HELL]	179	LIT VAGABOND/N	4
[BUT IF THEY REBEL THEY MUST GO TO HELL]	185	LET BROTHELS/N	18
SINCE TWAS THE FASHION TO GO NAKED	187	WHEN KLOPSTK/N	25
I KNOW THEE I HAVE FOUND THEE & I WILL NOT LET THEE GO	196	AMERICA PREL 2	7
WHERE MY SUN-FLOWER WISHES TO GO	215	AH SUNFLOWR/SE	8
GO TELL THE HUMAN RACE THAT WOMAN'S LOVE IS SIN	240	EUROPE 5	5
THOU WILT GO MAD WITH HORROR IF THOU DOST EXAMINE THUS	265	FOUR ZOAS 1	52
GO HOWL IN VAIN SMITE SMITE HIS FETTERS SMITE O WINTRY HAMMERS	276	FOUR ZOAS 1	431
SIEZING THE CHARIOTS OF THE MORNING GO OUTFLEETING RIDE	278	FOUR ZOAS 1	494
TAKE THOU POSSESSION TAKE THIS SCEPTER GO FORTH IN MY MIGHT	280	FOUR ZOAS 2	5
THEY GO FORTH & RETURN TO ALBION ON HIS ROCKY COUCH	281	FOUR ZOAS 2	60
OF DEATH ETERNAL THAT WE ALL GO TO ETERNAL DEATH	282	FOUR ZOAS 2	101
LOS JOYD & ENITHARMON LAUGHD SAYING LET US GO DOWN	285	FOUR ZOAS 2	211
SAYING GO & DIE THE DEATH OF MAN FOR VALA THE SWEET WANDERER	294	FOUR ZOAS 3	85
TILL INTO NARROW FORMS YOU CREEP GO TAKE YOUR FIERY WAY	294	FOUR ZOAS 3	89
GO FORTH REBUILD THIS UNIVERSE BENEATH MY INDIGNANT POWER	298	FOUR ZOAS 4	27
GO FORTH SAID THARMAS WORKS OF JOY ARE THINE OBEY & LIVE	299	FOUR ZOAS 4	67
GO FORTH BEAR ENITHARMON BACK TO THE ETERNAL PROPHET	299	FOUR ZOAS 4	70
[SAYING] & SAID GO FORTH & GUIDE MY SON WHO WANDERS ON THE OCEAN	310	FOUR ZOAS 5	221

		PAGE	TITLE	LINE

GO   (CONTINUED)

GO FORTH SONS OF MY CURSE GO FORTH DAUGHTERS OF   313 FOUR ZOAS 6   46
MY ABHORRENCE
AND SAID GO FORTH & GUIDE MY BATTLES LIKE THE JOINTED SPINE   336 FOUR ZOAS 7B   116
THEY GO OUT TO WAR WITH STRONG SHOUTS & LOUD CLARIONS O   338 FOUR ZOAS 7B   *   220
PITY
IF THOU DOST GO AWAY FROM ME I SHALL CONSUME UPON THE ROCKS   348 FOUR ZOAS 8   300
GO NOAH FETCH THE GIRDLE OF STRONG BRASS [PRE] HEAT IT   349 FOUR ZOAS 8   312
RED HOT
SAYING LET US GO UP FAR FOR SOON I SMELL UPON THE WIND . .   358 FOUR ZOAS 9   61
AND DEEP DESPAIR RATTLING GO UP THE FLAMES AROUND   359 FOUR ZOAS 9   68
THE SYNAGOGUE
THEN GO O DARK [REMEMBRANCE] FUTURITY . . . .   361 FOUR ZOAS 9   180
GO ON THY COURSE REJOICING & LET US BOTH REJOICE TOGETHER   368 FOUR ZOAS 9   424
AND VALA SAID GO THARMAS WEEP NOT GO TO ENION   . . . .   371 FOUR ZOAS 9   537
CHEAR UP THY COUNTENANCE BRIGHT BOY & GO TO ENION   . . .   371 FOUR ZOAS 9   545
GO DOWN YE KINGS & COUNCELLORS & GIANT WARRIORS   . .   374 FOUR ZOAS 9   659
GO DOWN INTO THE DEPTHS GO DOWN & HIDE YOURSELVES BENEATH   374 FOUR ZOAS 9   660
GO DOWN WITH HORSE & CHARIOTS & TRUMPETS OF HOARSE WAR . .   374 FOUR ZOAS 9   661
IF YOU ARE THIRSTY THERE IS THE RIVER GO BATHE YOUR PARCHED   375 FOUR ZOAS 9   680
LIMBS
THUS IF YOU GO ON SO THE RESULT IS SO HE NEVER SAYS . . .   392B ANNO WATSON   MARG
A PLACE IN THE NEW JERUSALEM EXCELLENT TRAVELLER GO ON   404D ANNO BACON   * MARG
& BE DAMND
WHERESOEVER THOU DOST GO . . . .   416 MY SPECTRE/N   28
AND LET US GO TO THE HIGHEST DOWNS   . . . .   417 MY SPECTR AD/N *   13
THRO THE WORLD WE SAFELY GO . . . .   432 AUGURIES   58
THEYD [IMMEDIATLY] IMMEDIATELY GO OUT   . . . .   433 AUGURIES   * 110
GO & TAKE THAT OTHER TO BE THY WIFE   . . . .   435 WILLIAM BOND   23
BECAUSE W(WILLIAM) REFUSED TO GO WITH HIM TO CHICHESTER   438C BLAKES MEMORAN   PROSE
THAT W(WILLIAM) SHOULD NOT GO BECAUSE OF THOSE THREATS . .   438C BLAKES MEMORAN   PROSE
OR IS ABLE & AFTERWARDS GO AND SWEAR OUR LIVES AWAY . . .   439A BLAKES MEMORAN   PROSE
CHILDREN TO GO & SWEAR AS THIS MAN HAS SWORN   . . . .   439A BLAKES MEMORAN   PROSE
IN TORMENT TO GO INTO THE DEEP HER TO REDEEM & HIMSELF   481 MILTON 2   20
PERISH
THAT HE MAY GO TO HIS OWN PLACE PRINCE OF THE STARRY WHEELS   483 MILTON 3   43
AND MILTON SAID I GO TO ETERNAL DEATH THE NATIONS STILL   495 MILTON 14   14
I WILL GO DOWN TO THE SEPULCHER TO SEE IF MORNING BREAKS   495 MILTON 14   21
I WILL GO DOWN TO SELF ANNIHILATION AND ETERNAL DEATH . .   495 MILTON 14   22
TO CLAIM THE HELLS MY FURNACES I GO TO ETERNAL DEATH . .   496 MILTON 14   32
AND MILTON SAID I GO TO ETERNAL DEATH ETERNITY SHUDDERD   496 MILTON 14   33
LET IT NOT BE SO NOW O GO NOT FORTH IN MARTYRDOMS & WARS   507 MILTON 23   49
NOR VEGETATION MAY GO ON TILL ALL THE EARTH IS REAPD . .   509 MILTON 24   43
GO FORTH REAPERS WITH REJOICING YOU SOWED IN TEARS . . .   511 MILTON 25   44
YOU CANNOT GO TO ETERNAL DEATH IN THAT WHICH CAN NEVER DIE   521 MILTON 32   24
MINE IS TO TEACH MEN TO DESPISE DEATH & TO GO ON . . .   530 MILTON 38   40
THOU GOEST TO ETERNAL DEATH & ALL MUST GO WITH THEE . . .   534 MILTON 42   2
TO GO FORTH TO THE GREAT HARVEST & VINTAGE OF THE NATIONS   535 MILTON 43   1
GO LOVE WITHOUT THE HELP OF ANY [THING] ?KING ON EARTH . .   541 ANGEL PRESID/N *   3
GO SEND YOUR CHILDREN TO THE SLOBBERING SCHOOL   . . . .   547 RAFAEL SUBLI/N   7
IF YOU HAVE FORMD A CIRCLE TO GO INTO   . . . . . .   557 TO GOD/N   1
GO INTO IT YOURSELF & SEE HOW [YOW] YOU WOULD DO . . . .   557 TO GOD/N   *   2
IF SHE REFUSE I STILL GO ON . . . .   558 THE CAVERNS/N   9
I SHALL EAT COARSER FOOD & GO WORSE SHOD   . . . . . .   559 I ROSE UP AT/N   26
RESOLVED TO GO CONTRARY IN EVERYTHING TO CHAUCER WHO SAYS   574A DESC CAT 3   PROSE
GO BEYOND EITHER WHAT HE DOES OR WHAT THEY HAVE DONE . .   579C DESC CAT 5   PROSE
THE HUMAN MIND CANNOT GO BEYOND THE GIFT OF GOD THE HOLY   579D DESC CAT 5   PROSE
GHOST
TO SUPPOSE THAT ART CAN GO BEYOND . . . .   579D DESC CAT 5   PROSE
A CIVILIZED MAN WHO HAS BEEN ACCUSTOMED TO GO NAKED . .   580D DESC CAT 5   PROSE
THAT GO UNDER HIS NAME   . . . .   583B DESC CAT 9   PROSE
OR GO INTO A MODERN EXHIBITON WITH A VERY FEW EXCEPTIONS   599B PUB ADDRESS/N   PROSE
FLORENTINE ORIGINAL & IF POSSIBLE TO GO BEYOND THAT   600B PUB ADDRESS/N   PROSE
ORIGINAL
I GO ON & NOTHING CAN HINDER MY COURSE . . . .   600C PUB ADDRESS/N   PROSE
LET A MAN WHO HAS MADE A DRAWING GO ON & ON . . . . .   603A PUB ADDR AD/N   PROSE
IT IS THE DIVINE BOSOM INTO WHICH WE SHALL ALL GO . . .   605D V LAST JUDG/N   PROSE
AND THUS THE SPECTRE SPOKE WILT THOU STILL GO ON   625 JERUSALEM 7   9
TO DESTRUCTION
YET WHY DESPAIR I SAW THE FINGER OF GOD GO FORTH . . .   631 JERUSALEM 12   10
GO ON BUILDERS IN HOPE THO JERUSALEM WANDERS FAR AWAY . .   632 JERUSALEM 12   43
GO THOU TO SKOFIELD ASK HIM IF HE IS BATH OR IF HE   640 JERUSALEM 17   59
IS CANTERBURY
OF LOVE THOU REFUSEDST TO LET ME GO ALBION BEHELD   643 JERUSALEM 20   32
THY BEAUTY
ARE YOU MY CHILDREN NATIVES IN THE GRAVE TO WHERE I GO . .   647 JERUSALEM 24   13
SAYING GO AND DIE THE DEATH OF MAN FOR VALA THE SWEET   655 JERUSALEM 29   66
WANDERER
TILL INTO NARROW FORMS YOU CREEP GO TAKE YOUR FIERY WAY   655 JERUSALEM 29   70
WHERE IMPLEMENTS OF WAR ARE FORGED THE PLOW TO GO OVER   660 JERUSALEM 34   13
THE NATIONS
AND BE THOU CREATED INTO A STATE I GO FORTH TO CREATE . .   662 JERUSALEM 35   15
I DIE I GO TO ETERNAL DEATH THE SHADES OF DEATH   . . .   666 JERUSALEM 39   16
ALBION REPLIED GO HAND & HYLE SIEZE THE ABHORRED FRIEND   670 JERUSALEM 42   47
AH ME PITIABLE ONES DO YOU ALSO GO TO DEATH'S VALE . . .   673 JERUSALEM 43   73
SAW THE FINGER OF GOD GO FORTH UPON HIS SEVENTH FURNACE   678 JERUSALEM 48   45
THE SUN SHALL GO BEFORE YOU IN DAY THE MOON SHALL GO . .   680 JERUSALEM 49   51
ARISE SISTERS GO YE & MEET THE LORD WHILE I REMAIN . . .   681 JERUSALEM 50   12
TO RECORD THE SIN FOR A REPROACH TO LET THE SUN GO DOWN   681 JERUSALEM 50   27
TOGETHER INTO AN ASSEMBLY THEY SAID LET US GO DOWN . . .   686 JERUSALEM 55   4
SAYING WHO WILL GO FORTH FOR US & WHO SHALL WE SEND BEFORE   687 JERUSALEM 55   69
OUR FACE

GO   (CONTINUED)

GO ASSUME PAPAL DIGNITY THOU SPECTRE THOU MALE HARLOT ARTHUR	698 JERUSALEM 64	15
IF THOU DOST GO AWAY FROM ME I SHALL CONSUME UPON THESE ROCKS	705 JERUSALEM 67	46
GO NOAH FETCH THE GIRDLE OF STRONG BRASS HEAT IT RED-HOT	705 JERUSALEM 67	59
GWENDOLEN & CAMBEL WHO IS BOADICEA THEY GO ABROAD & RETURN	710 JERUSALEM 71	23
GO THEREFORE CAST OUT DEVILS IN CHRIST'S NAME	718 STOOD AMONG/J	24
BUT TO THE PUBLICANS & HARLOTS GO	718 STOOD AMONG/J	31
GO FORTH OUT OF THY MOUTH TO BLIGHT THEIR PEACE . . .	718 STOOD AMONG/J	33
THEY GO FORTH & RETURN SWIFT AS A FLASH OF LIGHTNING . .	722 JERUSALEM 80	44
THE NIGHT FALLS THICK I GO UPON MY WATCH BE ATTENTIVE . .	728 JERUSALEM 83	61
THE SONS OF ALBION GO FORTH I FOLLOW FROM MY FURNACES . .	728 JERUSALEM 83	62
HE ALSO WILL RECIEVE IT GO SPECTRE OBEY MY MOST SECRET DESIRE	737 JERUSALEM 91	4
. . . GO TO THESE FIENDS OF RIGHTEOUSNESS . . .	738 JERUSALEM 91	5
GO TELL THEM THAT THE WORSHIP OF GOD IS HONOURING HIS GIFTS	738 JERUSALEM 91	8
MURDERS THE HOLY-ONE GO TELL THEM THIS & OVERTHROW THEIR CUP	738 JERUSALEM 91	13
IS WHETHER HE IS A WISE MAN OR A FOOL GO PUT OFF HOLINESS	739 JERUSALEM 91	56
THAT THOU THYSELF GO TO ETERNAL DEATH	781 GHOST ABEL 2	19
GO ON GO ON SUCH WORKS AS YOURS NATURE & PROVIDENCE .	791B LETTER 3	PROSE
I CANNOT GO BEYOND THE COMMAND OF THE LORD	792C LETTER 4	PROSE
OF EVERY THING YOU VALUE GO ON IF NOT FOR YOUR OWN SAKE YET FOR OURS	795B LETTER 6	PROSE
STARVE I LAUGH AT FORTUNE & GO ON & ON I THINK I FORESEE	795C LETTER 6	PROSE
MAKES IT A DWELLING FOR IMMORTALS WORK WILL GO ON HERE .	803C LETTER 15	PROSE
GO ON IN VIRTUOUS SEED SOWING ON MOLD	806 TO MRS BUTTS/L	3
& NOW GO ON AGAIN WITH MY TASK FEARLESS AND THO MY . .	813B LETTER 22	PROSE
GO ON WITH THE VIGOR I WAS IN MY CHILDHOOD FAMOUS FOR .	815A LETTER 23	*PROSE
AND SHALL STILL GO ON CONQUERING NOTHING CAN WITHSTAND .	816A LETTER 23	PROSE
OF WORK THAT I HAVE HAD NO TIME TO GO ON WITH THE BALLADS	820C LETTER 25	PROSE
DELIVERD THIS IS A SMALL SPECIMEN OF HOW WE GO ON . .	821A LETTER 25	PROSE
EVANS THE BOOKSELLER IN PALLMALL SAYS THEY GO OFF VERY WELL	821B LETTER 25	PROSE
I GO ON MERRILY WITH MY GREEK & LATIN AM VERY SORRY THAT	821D LETTER 25	PROSE
PRESSURE OF OTHER BUSINESS BUT THEY WILL GO ON AGAIN SOON	822B LETTER 26	PROSE
I WILL GO ON IN THE STRENGTH OF THE LORD THROUGH HELL .	823C LETTER 26	PROSE
& TO GO THRO ALL WITHOUT MURMURING & IN FIRM HOPE . .	825D LETTER 27	*PROSE
I GO ON WITH THE REMAINING SUBJECTS WHICH YOU GAVE ME .	826D LETTER 28	PROSE
DESIRED HIM AS POLITELY AS WAS POSSIBLE TO GO OUT OF THE GARDEN	827A LETTER 28	PROSE
MY LANDLORD COMPELLD THE SOLDIERS TO GO IN DOORS . . .	827B LETTER 28	PROSE
THAT I MUST GO A COURTING WHICH I SHALL DO AWKWARDLY IN THE MEAN TIME	829D LETTER 30	PROSE
BUT I GO ON FINISHING ROMNEY WITH SPIRIT AND FOR THE RELIEF	831C LETTER 31	PROSE
EVERY BODY COMPLAINS YET ALL GO ON CHEERFULLY AND WITH SPIRIT	831D LETTER 31	PROSE
HAS NOT YET BEEN ABLE TO GO WITH ME AM SORRY TO INFORM YOU	839C LETTER 38	PROSE
GIVEN THEM & WE DIRECTLY GO TO PRINTING CONSEQUENTLY IT	840C LETTER 39	PROSE
O THAT I COULD BUT BRING FELPHAM TO ME OR GO TO HER . .	857C LETTER 54	PROSE
WILL GO EQUAL SHARES WITH ME IN THE EXPENSE AND THE PROFITS	858B LETTER 55	PROSE
LET US GO ON DEAR SIR FOLLOWING HIS CROSS LET US TAKE IT UP	863B LETTER 60	PROSE
TO PERMIT ME TO BE OUT OF BED BUT THEY GO OFF BY REST WHICH	869B LETTER 69	PROSE
TO GO WHEN HE OBLIGINGLY PERMITTED ME TO GET OUT TO MY .	869D LETTER 70	PROSE
& TAKE A MUTTON CHOP WITH US THE DAY YOU GO TO CHELTENHAM	870C LETTER 72	PROSE
& I WILL GO WITH YOU TO THE COACH ALSO I WILL GO . . .	870D LETTER 72	PROSE
ENOUGH TO GO ON WITH MY WORK BUT NOT WELL ENOUGH TO .	871D LETTER 74	PROSE
BRINGS ON THE SHIVERING FIT WHEN I AM FORCED TO GO TO BED	872B LETTER 75	PROSE
SHUT UP IN THE BOOK ALL WILL GO VERY WELL IN THE COACH WHICH	873A LETTER 76	PROSE
AT PRESENT WOULD BE A RUMBLE I FEAR I COULD NOT GO THRO	873A LETTER 76	PROSE
I GO ON JUST AS IF PERFECTLY WELL WHICH INDEED I AM EXCEPT	873C LETTER 77	PROSE
IS CERTAIN THAT AT PRESENT ANY VENTURE TO GO OUT MUST BE	SUPP LETTER 81A	*PROSE
I GO ON AS I THINK IMPROVING MY ENGRAVINGS OF DANTE . .	876A LETTER 83	PROSE
MOST GRATIFYING MAY IT GO ON TO THE PERFECTION YOU WISH	876C LETTER 83	PROSE
ADVANTAGEOUS ACQUAINTANCE I GO ON WITHOUT DARING TO COUNT	879C LETTER 89	PROSE
NOT SO WELL AS I THOUGHT I MUST NOT GO ON IN A YOUTHFUL STYLE	880A LETTER 90	PROSE

GOAD

| THE OX GOAD IS TURNED INTO A SPEAR O WHEN SHALL OUR DELIVERER COME | 40B SAMSON/PS | PROSE |

GOAL

| ITS UTMOST GOAL . . . . | 269 FOUR ZOAS 1 | 195 |

GOARY

OF GOARY BLOOD STRUGGLING TO BE DELIVERD FROM OUR BONDS	300 FOUR ZOAS 4	103
OF GOARY BLOOD THE IMMORTAL SEED IS NOURISHD FOR THE SLAUGHTER	320 FOUR ZOAS 5	15
LISTEN O VISION OF DELIGHT ONE DREAD MORN OF GOARY BLOOD	327 FOUR ZOAS 7	* 278
THE GOARY TIDE EVEN TO THE PLACE OF SEED & THERE DIVIDING	327 FOUR ZOAS 7	287
AS ABRAHAM FLEES FROM CHALDEA SHAKING HIS GOARY LOCKS . .	636 JERUSALEM 15	28

GOAT

THE LUST OF THE GOAT IS THE BOUNTY OF GOD	151C MARRIAGE HH 8	PROSE
[THE GOAT LEAPD FROM THE CRAGGY [?ROCK] CLIFF	270 FOUR ZOAS 1	* 208
NOR THE SHEEP THE GOAT BUT THEY ENVY A RIVAL IN LIFE .	616B V LAST JUDG/N	PROSE

GOATHERD

| A POOR GOATHERD IN WALES . . . . | SUPP ILLUS GRAY | *TITLE |

GOAT'S

| DONT YOU THINK I HAVE SOMETHING OF THE GOAT'S FACE SAYS HE | 62D ISLAND MOON 11 | PROSE |
| VERY LIKE A GOAT'S FACE SHE ANSWERD . . . . | 62D ISLAND MOON 11 | PROSE |

GOATS

| BUT TO SEPERATE THEM AS IN THE PARABLE OF SHEEP AND GOATS | 155C MARRIAGE HH 15 | PROSE |

	PAGE	TITLE	LINE

GOATS   (CONTINUED)
    SNARING THE WILD GOATS FOR THEIR MILK THEY EAT THE FLESH   270 FOUR ZOAS 1   235
        OF LAMBS
    HE MAKES A WIDE DISTINCTION BETWEEN THE SHEEP & THE GOATS   556D JESUS NOT/N   PROSE
    NUMBER VII THE GOATS AN EXPERIMENT PICTURE   .   .   .   . . 581C DESC CAT 7   TITLE
    AND SOME GOATS ON BOARD THE MISSIONARY SHIP STRIPPED   .   . 581C DESC CAT 7   PROSE
    SHEEP TO THE PUBLIC GOATS . . . . 620D JERUSALEM 3   TITLE
    SATAN I WILL HAVE HUMAN BLOOD & NOT THE BLOOD OF BULLS   780 GHOST ABEL 2   13
        OR GOATS
    CAIN'S CITY BUILT WITH HUMAN BLOOD NOT BLOOD OF BULLS   781 GHOST ABEL 2   17
        & GOATS
GOATS-HAIR
    THE VEIL OF GOATS-HAIR & PURPLE & SCARLET & FINE TWINED   692 JERUSALEM 59   55
        LINEN
GOAT SKINS
    WANDERING ABOUT IN SHEEP SKINS & GOAT SKINS OF WHOM THE   604A INSC ARIMATHEA   PROSE
GOBLIN
    THE GOBLIN CROP FULL FLINGS OUT OF DOORS FROM . . . . . . 618C ILLUS MILTON   PROSE
GOD
    THE GOD OF WAR IS DRUNK WITH BLOOD   . . . .   13 GWIN KING/PS   93
    NO GOD FORBID IM SURE HE IS NOT   . . . .   22 EDW THIRD/PS 3   25
    THRONE OF GOD WHEN THE FROWNS OF HIS COUNTENANCE   . . . .   33 EDW FOURTH/PS   7
    O WHO CAN ANSWER AT THE THRONE OF GOD   . . . .   33 EDW FOURTH/PS   14
    PREPARE YOUR EYES TO MEET A HOLY GOD . . . .   34 WAR SONG/PS   9
    THE ARROWS OF ALMIGHTY GOD ARE DRAWN   . . . .   35 WAR SONG/PS   16
    BUT LO THERE IS A GOD WHO MADE THE WORLD STRETCH OUT THY   36A COUCH DEATH/PS   PROSE
        HAND TO HIM
    ALAS MY LORD WHAT AM I CALLING THEE THOU ART MY GOD   . .   38B SAMSON/PS   PROSE
    FOR HOLY UNTO ISRAEL'S GOD I AM A NAZARITE EVEN FROM MY   39C SAMSON/PS   PROSE
        MOTHER'S WOMB
    CHILDLESS HE MOURNED BUT THOUGHT HIS GOD KNEW BEST   . . .   39C SAMSON/PS   PROSE
    BUT GOD HATH OTHER JOYS IN STORE IS BURDENED ISRAEL HIS   39C SAMSON/PS   PROSE
        GRIEF
    AND SILENT PRAYED TO ISRAEL'S GOD . . . .   39D SAMSON/PS   PROSE
    FOR HE SHALL BE A NAZARITE TO GOD THEN AS A NEIGHBOUR   . . 39D SAMSON/PS   PROSE
    THE SWEETEST TIME THAT GOD HAS ALLOTTED MORTAL MAN   . . . 40A SAMSON/PS   PROSE
    HE SAT AND HEARD WITH JOY AND PRAISED GOD WHO ISRAEL STILL   40A SAMSON/PS   PROSE
        DOTH KEEP
    O MAN OF GOD SAID HE THOU COMEST FROM FAR   . . . . . . 40B SAMSON/PS   PROSE
    NOW THEY SURROUND THE GOD AND BIND HIM FAST   . . . . .   42C THEN SHE BORE   PROSE
    OBTUSE ANGLE ANSWERD QUICKLY HE WAS THE GOD OF PHYSIC   . . 46D ISLAND MOON 3   PROSE
    A POOR FRAIL MAN GOD WOT I KNOW NONE FRAILER   . . . . .   52 HEAR THEN/IM   3
    GOD BLESS THE DUKE & HIS ALDERMEN ALL   . . . .   55 CRY MATCHES/IM *   2
    ("AS MAN SO HIS GOD AS HIS GOD SO HE") ALL GOLD   . . . .   65D ANNO LAVATER   MARG
    ("MAN'S INTEREST...HIS GOD...VORTEX...CENTRE") PURE GOLD   66A ANNO LAVATER   MARG
    WOULD TO GOD THAT EVERY ONE WOULD CONSIDER THIS   . . . .   73C ANNO LAVATER   MARG
    & THIS IS BELOVED OF GOD AND MAN . . . . 75A ANNO LAVATER   MARG
    BUT IF MAN IS CONSIDERED AS ONLY EVIL & GOD ONLY GOOD   80A ANNO LAVATER   MARG
    O THAT MEN WOULD CONVERSE WITH GOD   . . . . 80C ANNO LAVATER   MARG
    & THEN WE SHALL RETURN TO CHAOS & GOD WILL BE COMPELLD   . . 81C ANNO LAVATER   MARG
    MAN IS THE ARK OF GOD   . . . . 82A ANNO LAVATER   MARG
    MAN IS EITHER THE ARK OF GOD OR   . . . . 82B ANNO LAVATER   MARG
    & PURE WOULD TO GOD THAT ALL MEN WOULD CONSIDER IT   . . . 82D ANNO LAVATER   MARG
    ("ART IS HIGHEST HUMAN NATURE") HUMAN NATURE IS THE   83A ANNO LAVATER   MARG
        IMAGE OF GOD
    & GOD WHO LOVES ALL HONEST MEN   . . . . 85C ANNO LAVATER   MARG
    IT IS THE GOD IN ALL THAT IS OUR COMPANION & FRIEND   . . . 87A ANNO LAVATER   MARG
    FOR OUR GOD HIMSELF SAYS "YOU ARE MY BROTHER"   . . . . . 87A ANNO LAVATER   MARG
    "WHOSO DWELLETH IN LOVE DWELLETH IN GOD & GOD IN HIM"   87A ANNO LAVATER
    GOD IS IN THE LOWEST EFFECTS AS WELL AS IN THE HIGHEST   87A ANNO LAVATER   MARG
        CAUSES
    GOD DESCENDING ACCORDING TO THE WEAKNESS OF MAN   . . . . 87B ANNO LAVATER   MARG
    FOR OUR LORD IS THE WORD OF GOD & EVERY . . . . 87B ANNO LAVATER   MARG
    THING ON EARTH IS THE WORD OF GOD & IN ITS ESSENCE IS GOD   87B ANNO LAVATER   MARG
    SO IT IS IMPOSSIBLE TO KNOW GOD OR HEAVENLY THINGS WITHOUT   88B ANNO LAVATER   MARG
    CONJUNCTION WITH THOSE WHO KNOW GOD & HEAVENLY THINGS   . . 88B ANNO LAVATER   MARG
    [& THEY CONVERSE WITH THE SPIRIT OF GOD] FOR THESE REASONS   88B ANNO LAVATER   * MARG
        I SAY
    IF GOD IS ANY THING HE IS UNDERSTANDING . . . . 89A ANNO SWED LOVE   MARG
    BUT GOD IS A MAN NOT BECAUSE HE IS SO PERCIEVD BY MAN   . . 90B ANNO SWED LOVE   MARG
    THAT THERE IS BUT ONE OMNIPOTENT UNCREATE & GOD I AGREE   91A ANNO SWED LOVE   MARG
    BUT THAT THERE IS BUT ONE INFINITE I DO NOT FOR IF ALL   91A ANNO SWED LOVE   MARG
        BUT GOD
    IS NOT INFINITE THEY SHALL COME TO AN END WHICH GOD FORBID   91A ANNO SWED LOVE   MARG
    APPLICATION HE WHO SEES THE INFINITE IN ALL THINGS SEES   98A NAT RELIGION 2   PROSE
        GOD
    THEREFORE GOD BECOMES AS WE ARE THAT WE MAY BE AS HE IS   98A NAT RELIGION 2   PROSE
    GOD BLESS [XXX] THY POOR BALD PATE GOD BLESS THY HOLLOW   101 TIRIEL 2   *   35
        WINKING EYES
    GOD BLESS THY SHRIVELD BEARD GOD BLESS THY MANY WRINKLED   101 TIRIEL 2   *   36
        FOREHEAD
    GOD BLESS THY PITEOUS FACE TO COUNT THE WRINKLES IN THY   102 TIRIEL 3   5
        FACE
    THEN TIRIEL ROSE UP FROM THE SEAT & SAID GOD BLESS THESE   103 TIRIEL 3   26
        TENTS
    [GOD BLESS MY BENEFACTORS FOR I CANNOT TARRY LONGER]   . . 103 TIRIEL 3   27
    [THY GOD OF LOVE THY HEAVEN OF JOY]   . . . . 109 TIRIEL 8   *   9
    LITTLE LAMB GOD BLESS THEE   . . . . 115 THE LAMB/SI   19
    LITTLE LAMB GOD BLESS THEE   . . . . 115 THE LAMB/SI   20
    IS GOD OUR FATHER DEAR   . . . . 117 DIVNE IMAGE/SI   6
    THERE GOD IS DWELLING TOO   . . . . 117 DIVNE IMAGE/SI   20
    HED HAVE GOD FOR HIS FATHER & NEVER WANT JOY   . . . . . 118 CHIMNEY SWP/SI   20

```
                                                          PAGE      TITLE        LINE
GOD    (CONTINUED)
  BEGAN TO CRY BUT GOD EVER NIGH  . . . . . . . . .  121 LIT BOY FND/SI     3
  LOOK ON THE RISING SUN THERE GOD DOES LIVE  . . . . .  125 LIT BLK BOY/SI    9
  AND ROUND THE TENT OF GOD LIKE LAMBS WE JOY  . . . .  125 LIT BLK BOY/SI   24
  THAT GOD WOULD LOVE A WORM I KNEW AND PUNISH THE EVIL FOOT  130 BOOK OF THEL 5    9
  . . . IN THE SEVENTH TOWER NAMD THE TOWER OF GOD WAS A MAN  136 FRENCH REVOLTN   47
  . . . AND DARK MISTS ROLL ROUND ME AND BLOT THE WHITING  139 FRENCH REVOLTN  113
      OF GOD
  . . . AND GOD SO LONG WORSHIPPD DEPARTS AS A LAMP   . . .  140 FRENCH REVOLTN  137
  . . . OR GOD WEEP WHEN HIS CHILDREN ARE HAPPY  . . . .  142 FRENCH REVOLTN  186
  . . . LIKE A VOICE OF GOD FOLLOWING A STORM THE ABBE  143 FRENCH REVOLTN  202
      FOLLOWD
  THAT GOD WILL TORMENT MAN IN ETERNITY FOR FOLLOWING HIS  149C MARRIAGE HH 4  PROSE
      ENERGIES
  WHEN HE WROTE OF ANGELS & GOD  . . . . . . . . . .  150B MARRIAGE HH 5  PROSE
  THE PRIDE OF THE PEACOCK IS THE GLORY OF GOD  . . . .  151C MARRIAGE HH 8  PROSE
  THE LUST OF THE GOAT IS THE BOUNTY OF GOD  . . . . .  151C MARRIAGE HH 8  PROSE
  THE WRATH OF THE LION IS THE WISDOM OF GOD  . . . . .  151C MARRIAGE HH 8  PROSE
  THE NAKEDNESS OF WOMAN IS THE WORK OF GOD  . . . . .  151C MARRIAGE HH 8  PROSE
  THE FOX PROVIDES FOR HIMSELF BUT GOD PROVIDES FOR THE LION  152A MARRIAGE HH 9  PROSE
  AS THE PLOW FOLLOWS WORDS SO GOD REWARDS PRAYERS  . .  152A MARRIAGE HH 9  PROSE
  THEY DARED SO ROUNDLY TO ASSERT THAT GOD SPAKE TO THEM .  153B MARRIAGE HH 12 *PROSE
  ISAIAH ANSWERD I SAW NO GOD NOR HEARD ANY  . . . . .  153C MARRIAGE HH 12 PROSE
  THAT THE VOICE OF HONEST INDIGNATION IS THE VOICE OF GOD  153C MARRIAGE HH 12 PROSE
  AND WE SO LOVED OUR GOD THAT WE CURSED IN HIS NAME ALL .  153D MARRIAGE HH 12 PROSE
  WORSHIP THE JEWS' GOD AND WHAT GREATER SUBJECTION CAN BE  154A MARRIAGE HH 12 PROSE
  SOME WILL SAY IS NOT GOD ALONE THE PROLIFIC I ANSWER  .  155B MARRIAGE HH 15 PROSE
  GOD ONLY ACTS & IS IN EXISTING BEINGS OR MEN  . . . .  155B MARRIAGE HH 15 PROSE
  THE WORSHIP OF GOD IS HONOURING HIS GIFTS IN OTHER MEN  158B MARRIAGE HH 22 PROSE
  THOSE WHO ENVY OR CALUMNIATE GREAT MEN HATE GOD  . . .  158B MARRIAGE HH 22 PROSE
  FOR THERE IS NO OTHER GOD  . . . . . . . . . . .  158B MARRIAGE HH 22 PROSE
  THOU IDOLATER IS NOT GOD ONE & IS NOT HE VISIBLE  . .  158B MARRIAGE HH 22 PROSE
  NOT MOCK AT THE SABBATH AND SO MOCK THE SABBATH'S GOD  158C MARRIAGE HH 22 PROSE
  THEN GOD LIKE A FATHER [THAT JOYS FOR] REJOICING TO SEE  180 LIT VAGABOND/N   14
  AND ARE GONE TO PRAISE GOD & HIS PRIEST & KING  . . .  180 CHIMNEY SWP/N    11
  THOU ART THE IMAGE OF GOD WHO DWELLS IN DARKNESS OF AFRICA  196 AMERICA PREL 2    8
  REARS ITS IMMORTAL PINNACLES BUILT IN THE FOREST OF GOD  200 AMERICA 10    9
  THAT MOCK HIM WHO COMMANDED THIS WHAT GOD WHAT ANGEL  .  200 AMERICA 11    7
  WHAT GOD IS HE WRITES LAWS OF PEACE & CLOTHES HIM IN A  200 AMERICA 11   12
      TEMPEST
  DOES THY GOD O PRIEST TAKE SUCH VENGEANCE AS THIS   . .  209D FOR CHILDRN/GP TITLE
  AND ARE GONE TO PRAISE GOD & HIS PRIEST & KING  . . .  212 CHIMNEY SWP/GE   11
  AND GOD LIKE A FATHER REJOICING TO SEE  . . . . . .  216 LIT VAGABND/SE   13
  ONE KING ONE GOD ONE LAW  . . . . . . . . . . .  224 URIZEN 4   40
  THE ETERNAL LAWS OF GOD  . . . . . . . . . . . .  236 URIZEN 28    7
  HEAVEN A MIGHTY CIRCLE TURNING GOD A TYRANT CROWND  . .  241 EUROPE 10   23
  THIS CLOUDY GOD SEATED ON WATERS  . . . . . . . . .  249 AHANIA 2   12
  I AM GOD SAID HE ELDEST OF THINGS  . . . . . . . .  251 AHANIA 3   38
  ETERNALLY CREATED BY THE LAMB OF GOD AROUND  . . . .  266 FOUR ZOAS 1   97
  IS ETERNAL DEATH WHAT SHALL WE DO O GOD [HELP] PITY & HELP  267 FOUR ZOAS 1  107
  [BUT THOSE IN GREAT ETERNITY MET IN THE COUNCIL OF GOD]  269 FOUR ZOAS 1  198
  TILL WE HAVE DRAWN THE LAMB OF GOD INTO A MORTAL FORM  .  272 FOUR ZOAS 1  293
  GLOOMY SOUNDING NOW I AM GOD FROM ETERNITY TO ETERNITY  .  273 FOUR ZOAS 1  319
  OBEY MY VOICE YOUNG DEMON I AM GOD FROM ETERNITY  . .  273 FOUR ZOAS 1  336
      TO ETERNITY
  LO I AM GOD THE TERRIBLE DESTROYER & NOT THE SAVIOUR  .  273 FOUR ZOAS 1  339
  THEN THOSE IN GREAT ETERNITY MET IN THE COUNCIL OF GOD  .  277 FOUR ZOAS 1  469
  EYES OF GOD & THE SEVEN LAMPS OF THE ALMIGHTY  . . . .  279 FOUR ZOAS 1  554
  THE LAMB OF GOD BLESSED FOR EVER & HE FOLLOWD THE MAN  .  279 FOUR ZOAS 1  556
  OF GOD CLOTHED IN LUVAH'S GARMENTS LITTLE KNOWEST THOU  .  282 FOUR ZOAS 2  100
  THAT HUMAN [TERROR] DELUSION TO DELIVER ALL THE SONS OF GOD  282 FOUR ZOAS 2  107
  IF THE GOD ENRAPTURED ME INFOLDS  . . . . . . . . .  288 FOUR ZOAS 2  *  310
  FROM THY FIERCE LOVE FOR THO I AM DISSOLVD IN THE BRIGHT  288 FOUR ZOAS 2  316
      GOD
  FAREWELL THE GOD CALLS ME AWAY I DEPART IN MY SWEET BLISS  288 FOUR ZOAS 2  333
  LOS SPOKE THY GOD IN VAIN SHALL CALL THEE IF BY MY STRONG  289 FOUR ZOAS 2  336
      POWER
  TO SEE A GOD ON EVERY WIND & A BLESSING ON EVERY BLAST  291 FOUR ZOAS 2  410
  [THOU SITST IN HARMONY FOR GOD HATH SET THEE OVER ALL]  . .  291 FOUR ZOAS 3   10
  AM I NOT GOD SAID URIZEN WHO IS EQUAL TO ME  . . . .  294 FOUR ZOAS 3  106
  OUR GOD IS URIZEN THE KING KING OF THE HEAVENLY HOSTS  .  298 FOUR ZOAS 4   38
  WE HAVE NO OTHER GOD BUT HE THOU FATHER OF WORMS & CLAY  298 FOUR ZOAS 4   39
  AND LOS REMAINS GOD OVER ALL WEAK FATHER OF WORMS & CLAY  298 FOUR ZOAS 4   41
  IS GOD THE ETERNAL MAN IS SEALD NEVER TO BE DELIVERD  .  301 FOUR ZOAS 4  132
  YET THO I RAGE GOD OVER ALL A PORTION OF MY LIFE  . . .  301 FOUR ZOAS 4  137
  IS THIS TO BE A GOD FAR RATHER WOULD I BE A MAN  . . .  301 FOUR ZOAS 4  146
  NOW THOU DOST KNOW WHAT TIS TO STRIVE AGAINST THE GOD OF  301 FOUR ZOAS 4  156
      WATERS
  RAGING AGAINST THARMAS HIS GOD & UTTERING  . . . . .  302 FOUR ZOAS 4  204
  THE COUNCIL OF GOD ON HIGH WATCHING OVER THE BODY   . .  304 FOUR ZOAS 4  247
  AND NOW WE KNOW THAT WHATSOEVER THOU WILT ASK OF GOD  .  304 FOUR ZOAS 4  254
  THE FINGER OF GOD TOUCH THE SEVENTH FURNACE IN TERROR  .  304 FOUR ZOAS 4  277
  AND LOS BEHELD THE HAND OF GOD OVER HIS FURNACES  . .  304 FOUR ZOAS 4  278
  THAT THEY MAY CURSE THARMAS THEIR GOD & LOS HIS ADOPTED SON  313 FOUR ZOAS 6   43
  KNEAD BREAD OF SORROW BY MY STERN COMMAND FOR I AM GOD  .  322 FOUR ZOAS 7   93
  TURN INWARDLY THINE EYES & THERE BEHOLD THE LAMB OF GOD  330 FOUR ZOAS 7  415
  ENITHARMON ANSWERD I BEHOLD THE LAMB OF GOD DESCENDING  .  330 FOUR ZOAS 7  424
  SUCH IS OUR STATE NOR WILL THE SON OF GOD REDEEM US BUT  331 FOUR ZOAS 7  431
      DESTROY
  A GOD & NOT A MAN A CONQUEROR IN TRIUMPHANT GLORY   . .  333 FOUR ZOAS 7B    9
  DOES NOT THE GOD OF WATERS IN THE WRACKING ?ELEMENTS  .  335 FOUR ZOAS 7B   90
  AND MUST NOT I OBEY THE GOD THOU SHADOW OF JEALOUSY  . .  335 FOUR ZOAS 7B   92
```

811

			PAGE	TITLE	LINE

GOD   (CONTINUED)

ALONG THE RANKS CRYING LISTEN TO THE PRIEST OF GOD   336 FOUR ZOAS 7B   114
YE WARRIORS
. . . MET IN THE COUNCIL OF GOD   .   341 FOUR ZOAS 8   1
AND ENITHARMON SAID I SEE THE LAMB OF GOD UPON MOUNT ZION   341 FOUR ZOAS 8   22
WHEN URIZEN SAW THE LAMB OF GOD CLOTHED IN LUVAH'S ROBES   342 FOUR ZOAS 8   61
IN THE FIERCE BATTLE & HE SAW THE LAMB OF GOD & THE WORLD   342 FOUR ZOAS 8   66
OF LOS
RESIDES THAT GOD OF MY DELIGHT O MIGHT MY EYES BEHOLD   . .   345 FOUR ZOAS 8   156
MY LUVAH THEN COULD I DELIVER ALL THE SONS OF GOD   . .   345 FOUR ZOAS 8   157
WONDRING SHE SAW THE LAMB OF GOD WITHIN JERUSALEM'S VEIL   346 FOUR ZOAS 8   191
THEN SANG THE SONS OF EDEN ROUND THE LAMB OF GOD & SAID   346 FOUR ZOAS 8   194
GLORY GLORY GLORY TO THE HOLY LAMB OF GOD   . . . .   346 FOUR ZOAS 8   195
RECIEVEST THE INTEGUMENTS WOVEN RAHAB BEHOLDS THE LAMB   347 FOUR ZOAS 8   233
OF GOD
BEGUN ALREADY IN ETERNITY COME THEN O LAMB OF GOD   . .   347 FOUR ZOAS 8   244
PITYING THE LAMB OF GOD DESCENDED THRO JERUSALEM'S GATES   347 FOUR ZOAS 8   260
THE LAMB OF GOD STOOD BEFORE SATAN OPPOSITE   . . . .   348 FOUR ZOAS 8   268
TO JUDGE THE LAMB OF GOD TO DEATH AS A MURDERER & ROBBER   348 FOUR ZOAS 8   273
THE LAMB OF GOD DESCENDED THRO THE TWELVE PORTIONS OF LUVAH   349 FOUR ZOAS 8   323
THUS WAS THE LAMB OF GOD CONDEMND TO DEATH   . . . . .   349 FOUR ZOAS 8   325
DEATH GOD OF ALL FROM WHOM WE RISE TO WHOM WE ALL RETURN   349 FOUR ZOAS 8   335
THE LAMB OF GOD IT ROLLD APART REVEALING TO ALL IN HEAVEN   350 FOUR ZOAS 8   342
OF PRIDE AND I ALSO HAVE PIERCD THE LAMB OF GOD IN PRIDE   350 FOUR ZOAS 8   355
& WRATH
THE LAMB OF GOD HAS RENT THE VEIL OF MYSTERY SOON TO RETURN   355 FOUR ZOAS 8   556
FOR GOD PUT IT INTO THEIR HEART TO FULFILL ALL HIS WILL   357 FOUR ZOAS 8   617
[IN EDEN IN THE GARDEN OF GOD & IN HEAVENLY JERUSALEM]   SUPP FOUR ZOAS 8   *
BEHOLD JERUSALEM IN WHOSE BOSOM THE LAMB OF GOD [IS SEEN]   362 FOUR ZOAS 9   205
BECAUSE THE LAMB OF GOD CREATES HIMSELF A BRIDE & WIFE   . .   362 FOUR ZOAS 9   220
BEHELD THE VISION OF GOD & HE AROSE UP FROM THE ROCK   .   364 FOUR ZOAS 9   286
WHERE IS THE VOICE OF GOD THAT CALLD ME FROM THE SILENT DEW   370 FOUR ZOAS 9   500
THE LAMB OF GOD STOOD BEFORE URIZEN OPPOSITE   . . . .   382 FOUR ZOAS AD 6   1
TO JUDGE THE LAMB OF GOD TO DEATH AS A MURDERER & ROBBER   382 FOUR ZOAS AD 6   6
OVER THEIR VICTIMS THUS WAS THE LAMB OF GOD CONDEMND TO   382 FOUR ZOAS AD 6   13
DEATH
AND RAHAB STRIPD OFF LUVAH'S ROBES FROM OFF THE LAMB OF   382 FOUR ZOAS AD 6   20
GOD
("RICH AND POOR") GOD MADE MAN HAPPY & RICH   . . . .   384A ANNO WATSON   MARG
WHEN GOD HAS PRESERVED HIM   . . . .   384D ANNO WATSON   MARG
IS THE VOICE OF GOD OUR JUDGMENT OF RIGHT & WRONG IS REASON   385D ANNO WATSON   MARG
FROM GOD IS ALTOGETHER ABOMINABLE & BLASPHEMOUS   . . .   387B ANNO WATSON   MARG
WAS NOT CHRIST MURDERD BECAUSE HE TAUGHT THAT GOD LOVED   387B ANNO WATSON   * MARG
THE BIBLE SAYS THAT GOD FORMED NATURE PERFECT BUT THAT MAN   388A ANNO WATSON   MARG
NATURAL RELIGION IS THE VOICE OF GOD &   . . . . . .   388A ANNO WATSON   MARG
GOD NEVER MAKES ONE MAN MURDER ANOTHER NOR ONE NATION   .   388B ANNO WATSON   MARG
INDIVIDUAL WHICH GOD CONSIDERS IN THE BIBLE AS MURDER   .   388B ANNO WATSON   MARG
THAT GOD DOES & ALWAYS DID CONVERSE WITH HONEST MEN   .   389A ANNO WATSON   MARG
THAT GOD CONVERSED WITH MURDERERS & REVENGERS   . . . .   389A ANNO WATSON   MARG
WHICH THEY CALLD GOD & SO WERE LIARS AS CHRIST SAYS   .   389A ANNO WATSON   MARG
OF GOD WILL BE A LASTING WITNESS AGAINST THEM   . . . .   389A ANNO WATSON   MARG
HE KNEW NOTHING OF GOD IN THE BISHOP'S SENSE OF THE WORD   389C ANNO WATSON   MARG
THE BIBLE OR PECULIAR WORD OF GOD   . . . .   389C ANNO WATSON   MARG
EXCLUSIVE OF CONSCIENCE OR THE WORD OF GOD UNIVERSAL   .   389C ANNO WATSON   MARG
CONVERSE WITH GOD & BE A KING & PRIEST IN HIS OWN HOUSE   389C ANNO WATSON   MARG
IT IS STRANGE THAT GOD SHOULD SPEAK TO MAN FORMERLY &   .   390A ANNO WATSON   MARG
IT IS MAN'S FAULT IF GOD IS NOT ABLE TO DO HIM GOOD FOR HE   392B ANNO WATSON   MARG
THEY SEEM TO FORGET THAT THERE IS A GOD OF THIS WORLD A GOD   394C ANNO WATSON   MARG
WORSHIPD IN THIS WORLD AS GOD & SET ABOVE ALL THAT IS CALLD   394C ANNO WATSON   MARG
GOD
WHO DARE TO JUDGE BUT GOD ALONE   . . . .   396A ANNO WATSON   MARG
DOES GOD LOVE THE RIGHTEOUS ACCORDING TO THE GOSPEL   . .   396A ANNO WATSON   MARG
THE WISDOM OF THIS WORLD IS FOOLISHNESS WITH GOD   . . .   396D ANNO BACON   MARG
("A KING IS A MORTAL GOD") O CONTEMPTIBLE & ABJECT SLAVE   401A ANNO BACON   MARG
NONE BUT GOD IS THIS   . . . .   410C ANNO BACON   MARG
WHEN GOD COMMANDED THIS HAND TO WRITE   . . . . . .   419 I SAW A MONK/N   28
TILL THEN THE LAMB OF GOD   . . . .   421 EACH MAN/N   7
WHEN GOD COMMANDED THIS HAND TO WRITE   . . . . . .   430 GREY MONK   13
GOD APPEARS & GOD IS LIGHT   . . . .   434 AUGURIES   129
WITH THE SEVEN VIALS OF THE WRATH OF GOD   . . . . .   444A LAST JUDGMNT/L   PROSE
I CERTAINLY DO THANK GOD THAT I AM NOT LIKE REYNOLDS   .   471A ANNO REYNOLDS   MARG
THIS IS A VERY CLEVER SENTENCE WHO WROTE (IT) GOD KNOWS   471C ANNO REYNOLDS   * MARG
MILTON WAS IN EARNEST THEY BELIEVD THAT GOD DID VISIT MAN   473D ANNO REYNOLDS   MARG
GOD FORBID   . . . .   474D ANNO REYNOLDS   MARG
("ILLUSTRIOUS CHARACTERS") [GOD BLASTS THEM AS THOUGH]   SUPP ANNO REYNOLDS   * MARG
TO JUSTIFY THE WAYS OF GOD TO MEN   . . . .   480A MILTON   TITLE
"WOULD TO GOD THAT ALL THE LORD'S PEOPLE WERE PROPHETS"   481B MILTON 1   PROSE
NUMBERS XI...
AND WAS THE HOLY LAMB OF GOD   . . . .   480 AND DID FEET/M   3
ITS OFFERINGS EVEN TILL JESUS THE IMAGE OF THE INVISIBLE   481 MILTON 2   12
GOD
O GOD PROTECT ME FROM MY FRIENDS THAT THEY HAVE NOT POWER   489 MILTON 9   5
OVER ME
PUNISHMENTS & DEATHS MUSTERD & NUMBERD SAYING I AM GOD   490 MILTON 9   25
ALONE
SATAN AH ME IS GONE TO HIS OWN PLACE SAID LOS THEIR GOD   491 MILTON 10   12
BEING CALLD GOD SETTING HIMSELF ABOVE ALL THAT IS CALLED   491 MILTON 11   12
GOD
AND ALL THE SPECTRES OF THE DEAD CALLING THEMSELVES SONS   491 MILTON 11   13
OF GOD
GLORY GLORY GLORY TO THE HOLY LAMB OF GOD   . . . . .   494 MILTON 13   28
. . . & UNGIRDED HIMSELF FROM THE OATH OF GOD   . . . .   495 MILTON 14   13

	PAGE	TITLE	LINE

GOD   (CONTINUED)

THE LAMB OF GOD IS SEEN THRO MISTS & SHADOWS HOVRING   . .   495 MILTON 14   25
FOR I WILL PUT ON THE HUMAN FORM & TAKE THE IMAGE OF GOD   499 MILTON 18   19
WITH A GARMENT OF PITY & COMPASSION LIKE THE GARMENT OF   499 MILTON 18   35
GOD
WHERE IS THE LAMB OF GOD WHERE IS THE PROMISE OF HIS COMING   501 MILTON 19   50
FAITH IN GOD THE DEAR SAVIOUR WHO TOOK ON THE LIKENESS   506 MILTON 22   57
OF MEN
NO FAITH IS IN ALL THE EARTH THE BOOK OF GOD IS TRODDEN   506 MILTON 22   60
UNDER FOOT
AND THAT THE SEVEN EYES OF GOD MAY HAVE SPACE FOR   507 MILTON 23   52
REDEMPTION
BECAUSE OF SATAN & THE SEVEN EYES OF GOD CONTINUALLY   . .   508 MILTON 24   7
CRYING O GOD DELIVER US TO THE HEAVENS OR TO THE EARTHS   510 MILTON 25   13
. . . THE VISION OF GOD IS FULFILLED . . . .   510 MILTON 25   22
THEIR MILD INFLUENCES THEREFORE THE SEVEN EYES OF GOD WALK   517 MILTON 29   54
ROUND
WHO MADE HIMSELF A GOD & DESTROYED THE HUMAN FORM DIVINE   521 MILTON 32   13
FOR GOD HIMSELF ENTERS DEATH'S DOOR ALWAYS WITH THOSE THAT   522 MILTON 32   40
ENTER
SHALT GIVE HER INTO THE ARMS OF GOD THY OUR LORD & HUSBAND   523 MILTON 33   23
THAT THE SEVEN EYES OF GOD WHO WALK EVEN TO SATAN'S SEAT   526 MILTON 35   64
OF PROVIDENCE & WITH THE EYES OF GOD ALL NIGHT IN SLUMBERS   526 MILTON 36   5
DESCENDING DOWN INTO MY GARDEN A HUMAN WONDER OF GOD   . .   528 MILTON 37   13
A RUIND MAN A RUIND BUILDING OF GOD NOT MADE WITH HANDS   529 MILTON 38   16
IN SELF ANNIHILATION ALL THAT IS NOT OF GOD ALONE   . . .   530 MILTON 38   48
SAYING I AM GOD THE JUDGE OF ALL THE LIVING & THE DEAD   .   530 MILTON 38   51
BUT I ALONE AM GOD & I ALONE IN HEAVN & EARTH   . . . .   530 MILTON 38   56
WHAT THE FINGER OF GOD POINTED TO THEIR VIEW . . . . .   543 IF TRUE/N   6
THANK GOD I NEVER WAS SENT TO SCHOOL . . . .   550 SAY PICTURES/N   3
THEN GOD DEFEND US FROM THE ARTS I SAY . . . .   550 WHEN I SEE/N   5
THAT GOD IS COLOURING NEWTON DOES SHEW   . . . . . .   554 TO VENETIAN/N   1
TO GOD . . . .   557A TO GOD/N   TITLE
IF I THANKD MY GOD FOR [WORLDLY]EARTHLY] WORLDLY THINGS   557 SINCE RICHES/N   4
I TOOK IT TO BE THE THRONE OF GOD . . . .   558 I ROSE UP AT/N   6
FOR [ALL THAT] MY WORLDLY THINGS GOD MAKES HIM PAY   . . . 559 I ROSE UP AT/N   17
GOD KNOWS I LITTLE OF PRAYERS NEED SAY . . . . . .   559 I ROSE UP AT/N   22
HE SAYS IF I DO NOT WORSHIP HIM FOR A GOD   . . . . .   559 I ROSE UP AT/N   25
YOU MUST DO MR DEVIL JUST AS GOD PLEASE . . . .   559 I ROSE UP AT/N   28
AND THE FORM OF THE FOURTH WAS LIKE THE SON OF GOD   . .   578B DESC CAT 5   PROSE
AND WILL IF GOD PLEASE PUBLISH IT IT IS VOLUMINOUS   . .   578B DESC CAT 5   PROSE
IT IS THE GIFT OF GOD IT IS INSPIRATION AND VISION HE   .   579C DESC CAT 5   PROSE
THE HUMAN MIND CANNOT GO BEYOND THE GIFT OF GOD THE HOLY   579D DESC CAT 5   PROSE
GHOST
ORGANIZED & MINUTELY DELINEATED & ARTICULATED EITHER BY   595C PUB ADDRESS/N PROSE
GOD OR MAN
WHICH HINDER THE VISION OF GOD TURNING ALL INTO A CONSUMING 604C V LAST JUDG/N PROSE
FIRE
WHO PREVIOUS TO THE FLOOD WALKED WITH GOD . . . . .   611D V LAST JUDG/N PROSE
TO DESCEND FROM THE THRONE OF GOD & OF THE LAMB   . . .   612A V LAST JUDG/N PROSE
TO THE SEVEN ANGELS THE SEVEN VIALS OF THE WRATH OF GOD   612A V LAST JUDG/N PROSE
THE TEMPLE STANDS ON THE MOUNT OF GOD   . . . . . .   613B V LAST JUDG/N PROSE
OR BY THE IMMEDIATE INSPIRATION OF GOD IT IS . . . .   614A V LAST JUDG/N PROSE
SATAN THINKS THAT SIN IS DISPLEASING TO GOD   . . . .   615C V LAST JUDG/N PROSE
HE OUGHT TO KNOW THAT NOTHING IS DISPLEASING TO GOD   . .   615C V LAST JUDG/N PROSE
THAT THINKS IT DOES GOD SERVICE WHICH GOD IS SATAN   . .   616C V LAST JUDG/N PROSE
EXPECT HOLINESS FROM ONE ANOTHER BUT FROM GOD ONLY   . .   616D V LAST JUDG/N PROSE
FIRST GOD ALMIGHTY COMES WITH A THUMP ON THE HEAD   . .   617A V LAST JUDG/N PROSE
CRYING HOLY HOLY HOLY IS THE [G] LORD GOD ALMIGHTY   .   617B V LAST JUDG/N *PROSE
THE LONG SUFFERINGS OF GOD ARE NOT FOR EVER THERE IS A   620 JERUSALEM 1   10
JUDGMENT
OUR LORD WHO IS THE GOD [OF FIRE] AND LORD [OF LOVE]   .   621A JERUSALEM 3   PROSE
AND OF THAT GOD FROM WHOM [ALL BOOKS ARE GIVEN] . . .   621 READER LOVER/J *   2
I AM NOT A GOD AFAR OFF I AM A BROTHER AND FRIEND   . .   622 JERUSALEM 4   18
EVER EXPANDING IN THE BOSOM OF GOD THE HUMAN IMAGINATION   623 JERUSALEM 5   20
OF GOD WOULD LOOK UPON ME AND PITY ME IN MY FURY . . .   626 JERUSALEM 7   60
BIRTHPLACE OF THE LAMB OF GOD INCOMPREHENSIBLE   . . . .   626 JERUSALEM 7   67
SEEING THE LAMB OF GOD IN THY GARDENS & THY PALACES . .   626 JERUSALEM 7   69
OF GOD TO DESTROY JERUSALEM & TO DEVOUR THE BODY OF ALBION   628 JERUSALEM 9   10
THAT THOU CALLEST THY CHILDREN LO THE LAW OF GOD COMMANDS   629 JERUSALEM 10   38
IT CONTINUES ACCUMULATING TO ETERNITY THE JOYS OF   630 JERUSALEM 10   46
GOD ADVANCE
AND LOS SAID I BEHOLD THE FINGER OF GOD IN TERRORS   . .   631 JERUSALEM 12   5
YET WHY DESPAIR I SAW THE FINGER OF GOD GO FORTH . . .   631 JERUSALEM 12   10
GOD IS WITHIN & WITHOUT HE IS EVEN IN THE DEPTHS OF HELL   631 JERUSALEM 12   15
THE LAMB OF GOD RECIEVD ME IN HIS ARMS HE SMILD UPON US   643 JERUSALEM 20   39
BLASPHEMOUS SONS OF FEMININE DELUSION GOD IN THE DREARY   646 JERUSALEM 23   29
VOID
AND THEREFORE GOD TAKES VENGEANCE ON ME FROM MY CLAY-COLD   646 JERUSALEM 23   33
BOSOM
MAY GOD WHO DWELLS IN THIS DARK ULRO & VOIDNESS VENGEANCE   646 JERUSALEM 23   38
TAKE
THE FOOTSTEPS OF THE LAMB OF GOD WERE THERE BUT NOW NO MORE   648 JERUSALEM 24   50
IF GOD WAS MERCIFUL THIS COULD NOT BE O LAMB OF GOD . .   648 JERUSALEM 24   53
TILL YOU HAVE ASSUMD THE PROVIDENCE OF GOD & SLAIN YOUR   648 JERUSALEM 24   56
FATHER
LOOK NOT SO MERCIFUL UPON ME O THOU SLAIN LAMB OF GOD   . . 648 JERUSALEM 24   59
DESCEND O LAMB OF GOD & TAKE AWAY THE IMPUTATION OF SIN   648 JERUSALEM 25   12
THE LAMB OF GOD AMONG THEM SEEN . . . .   649 FIELDS FROM/J   6
THE LAMB OF GOD WALKS BY HER SIDE . . . .   650 FIELDS FROM/J   18
AND O THOU LAMB OF GOD WHOM I . . . .   651 FIELDS FROM/J   65
THE LAMB OF GOD THE SAVIOUR BECAME APPARENT ON EARTH   .   652B JERUSALEM 27   PROSE

		PAGE	TITLE	LINE

GOD   (CONTINUED)

	PAGE	TITLE	LINE
OF GOD WHO DWELLS IN CHAOS HIDDEN FROM THE HUMAN SIGHT . .	652	JERUSALEM 28	16
THE SONS OF GOD WERE ALBION'S SONS AND JERUSALEM WAS MY JOY	653	JERUSALEM 29	8
BELONG TO GOD ALONE AND ALL THY LITTLE ONES ARE HOLY . .	657	JERUSALEM 31	45
SATAN WORSHIPD AS GOD BY THE MIGHTY ONES OF THE EARTH . .	659	JERUSALEM 33	18
IMMINGLED GOD & MAN WHEN THOU & I HID THE DIVINE VISION	660	JERUSALEM 33	46
THERE IS A THRONE IN EVERY MAN IT IS THE THRONE OF GOD	661	JERUSALEM 34	27
TO HIDE THE MOST EVIDENT GOD IN A HIDDEN COVERT EVEN	661	JERUSALEM 34	32
IN EDEN IN THE GARDEN OF GOD AND IN HEAVENLY JERUSALEM .	665	JERUSALEM 38	25
I SEE THEM IN THE VISION OF GOD UPON MY PLEASANT VALLEYS	665	JERUSALEM 38	28
I BEHOLD LONDON A HUMAN AWFUL WONDER OF GOD	665	JERUSALEM 38	29
GOD HATH FORSAKEN ME & MY FRIENDS ARE BECOME A BURDEN . .	666	JERUSALEM 39	22
SWEARING THE OATH OF GOD WITH AWFUL VOICE OF THUNDERS ROUND	666	JERUSALEM 40	9
THOU WAST THE IMAGE OF GOD SURROUNDED BY THE FOUR ZOAS . .	670	JERUSALEM 42	23
O GOD OF ALBION WHERE ART THOU PITY THE WATCHERS	671	JERUSALEM 42	74
O GOD OF ALBION DESCEND DELIVER JERUSALEM FROM THE OAKEN GROVES	672	JERUSALEM 43	11
CALLING ON GOD FOR HELP AND NOT OURSELVES IN WHOM GOD DWELLS	672	JERUSALEM 43	13
THAT THEY MAY BE CONDEMND BY LAW & THE LAMB OF GOD BE SLAIN	672	JERUSALEM 43	30
IS INCAPABLE AND NOTHING NONE BUT THE LAMB OF GOD CAN HEAL	675	JERUSALEM 45	15
O GOD DESCEND GATHER OUR BRETHREN DELIVER JERUSALEM . . .	675	JERUSALEM 45	28
DIVINE HE WEPT OVER ALBION SPEAKING THE WORDS OF GOD . .	676	JERUSALEM 46	8
THE BRIDE AND WIFE OF THE LAMB O GOD THOU ART NOT AN AVENGER	676	JERUSALEM 46	28
SHUDDER NOT BUT WRITE & THE HAND OF GOD WILL ASSIST YOU	677	JERUSALEM 47	17
SAW THE FINGER OF GOD GO FORTH UPON HIS SEVENTH FURNACE	678	JERUSALEM 48	45
THE GOLDEN GATE OF HAVILAH AND ALL THE GARDEN OF GOD . .	679	JERUSALEM 49	15
COME LORD JESUS LAMB OF GOD DESCEND FOR IF O LORD . . .	681	JERUSALEM 50	10
COME O THOU LAMB OF GOD AND TAKE AWAY THE REMEMBRANCE OF SIN	681	JERUSALEM 50	24
COME THEN O LAMB OF GOD AND TAKE AWAY THE REMEMBRANCE OF SIN	681	JERUSALEM 50	30
CALLING THE PRINCE OF THIS WORLD GOD AND DESTROYING ALL	682B	JERUSALEM 52	PROSE
WHO DO NOT WORSHIP SATAN UNDER THE NAME OF GOD	682B	JERUSALEM 52	PROSE
UNDER THE NAME OF GOD WHERE ARE THEY LISTEN	682B	JERUSALEM 52	PROSE
NOT OF THE FORGIVER OF SIN AND THEIR GOD IS SATAN . . .	682B	JERUSALEM 52	PROSE
DEISM IS THE WORSHIP OF THE GOD OF THIS WORLD BY THE MEANS	682C	JERUSALEM 52	PROSE
SAYING I AM GOD O SONS OF MEN I AM YOUR RATIONAL POWER . .	685	JERUSALEM 54	16
AND THEY ELECTED SEVEN CALLD THE SEVEN EYES OF GOD . . .	686	JERUSALEM 55	31
REAR THEIR DARK ROCKS AMONG THE STARS OF GOD STUPENDOUS	690	JERUSALEM 58	49
THEY SPREAD FORTH LIKE A LOVELY ROOT INTO THE GARDEN OF GOD	692	JERUSALEM 60	15
BABEL MOCKS SAYING THERE IS NO GOD NOR SON OF GOD . . .	693	JERUSALEM 60	56
BUT HE DRIVETH ME AWAY FROM HIS PRESENCE YET I HEAR THE VOICE OF GOD	694	JERUSALEM 61	9
THAT THERE WAS A GOD OF MERCY O MERCY O DIVINE HUMANITY	695	JERUSALEM 61	43
I KNOW THAT IN MY FLESH I SHALL SEE GOD BUT EMANATIONS .	696	JERUSALEM 62	16
SO SPOKE THE LAMB OF GOD WHILE LUVAH'S CLOUD REDDENING ABOVE	696	JERUSALEM 62	30
DIVIDING IN FIERCE PAIN ALSO THE VISION OF GOD WAS CLOSD IN CLOUDS	696	JERUSALEM 62	38
O CHEMOSH O BACCHUS O VENUS O DOUBLE GOD OF GENERATION	706	JERUSALEM 68	18
VOLTAIRE INSINUATES THAT THESE LIMITS ARE THE CRUEL WORK OF GOD	713	JERUSALEM 73	29
IS GOD A SPIRIT WHO MUST BE WORSHIPPED IN SPIRIT & IN TRUTH	717A	JERUSALEM 77	PROSE
IN THE SIGHT OF OUR KIND GOD	717C	JERUSALEM 77	PROSE
RECIEVE THE LAMB OF GOD TO DWELL	718	ENGLND AWAKE/J	11
SURROUNDING THEM WITH ARMIES TO DESTROY THE LAMB OF GOD	719	JERUSALEM 78	14
OF GOD AND THE LAMB TO DESTROY THE LAMB & USURP THE THRONE OF GOD	719	JERUSALEM 78	19
MY BROTHER & MY FATHER ARE NO MORE GOD HATH FORSAKEN ME	719	JERUSALEM 78	31
THEY WATCH THEM IN THE NIGHT AND THE LAMB OF GOD APPEARS AMONG US	720	JERUSALEM 79	32
I SLEPT IN HIS GOLDEN HILLS THE LAMB OF GOD MET ME THERE	720	JERUSALEM 79	41
WITH HOLY RAPTURES OF ADORATION RAPD SUBLIME IN THE VISIONS OF GOD	720	JERUSALEM 79	44
THE SWARTHY SONS OF ETHIOPIA STOOD ROUND THE LAMB OF GOD	721	JERUSALEM 79	51
FROM ALBION'S TOMB AFAR AND FROM THE FOUR-FOLD WONDERS OF GOD	721	JERUSALEM 79	62
PITY ME THEN O LAMB OF GOD O JESUS PITY ME	722	JERUSALEM 80	30
HIS LAW A FORM AGAINST THE LAMB OF GOD OPPOSD TO MERCY .	723	JERUSALEM 80	79
OF MILD JERUSALEM TO DESTROY THE LAMB OF GOD JERUSALEM	726	JERUSALEM 82	54
O WHEN SHALL THE LAMB OF GOD DESCEND AMONG THE REPROBATE	727	JERUSALEM 83	15
ETERNAL DEATH STANDS AT THE DOOR O GOD PITY OUR LABOURS	728	JERUSALEM 83	65
TILL GOD HIMSELF BECOME A MALE SUBSERVIENT TO THE FEMALE	733	JERUSALEM 88	21
IN MILD JERUSALEM AROUND THE LAMB OF GOD LOUD HOWL . . .	734	JERUSALEM 88	53
HERMAPHRODITIC WORSHIPPERS OF A GOD OF CRUELTY & LAW . .	737	JERUSALEM 90	55
YOUR SLAVES & CAPTIVES YOU COMPELL TO WORSHIP A GOD OF MERCY	737	JERUSALEM 90	56
DENYING IN PRIVATE MOCKING GOD & ETERNAL LIFE & IN PUBLIC	737	JERUSALEM 90	64
[FORGIVENESS OF ENEMIES ?CAN XXX ONLY XXX GOD XXX] . . .	737	JERUSALEM 91 *	1
GO TELL THEM THAT THE WORSHIP OF GOD IS HONOURING HIS GIFTS	738	JERUSALEM 91	8
GOD THAN THAT GOD WHO IS THE INTELLECTUAL FOUNTAIN OF HUMANITY	738	JERUSALEM 91	11
OF THE HEATHEN THE GOD OF THIS WORLD & THE GODDESS NATURE	741	JERUSALEM 93	24
O PITIOUS SLEEP O PITIOUS DREAM O GOD O GOD AWAKE I HAVE SLAIN	742	JERUSALEM 94	22
IN ANGER THE WRATH OF GOD BREAKING BRIGHT FLAMING ON ALL SIDES AROUND	742	JERUSALEM 95	6
AND IF GOD DIETH NOT FOR MAN & GIVETH NOT HIMSELF . . .	743	JERUSALEM 96	25

	PAGE	TITLE	LINE

GOD   (CONTINUED)

AS GOD IS LOVE EVERY KINDNESS TO ANOTHER IS A LITTLE DEATH   743 JERUSALEM 96   27
OF HEAVEN FOURFOLD AMONG THE VISIONS OF GOD IN ETERNITY   744 JERUSALEM 96   43
AND FAVOUR GAINS WITH GOD & MEN   . . . .   748 EV GOSPEL(B)/N   12
I COME YOUR KING & GOD TO SIEZE   . . . .   749 EV GOSPEL(B)/N   29
IS GOD A SMITER WITH DISEASE   . . . .   749 EV GOSPEL(B)/N   30
THE GOD OF THIS WORLD RAGED IN VAIN   . . . .   749 EV GOSPEL(B)/N   31
THE GOD OF THIS WORLD LOUDER ROLLD   . . . .   749 EV GOSPEL(B)/N   44
GOD WANTS NOT MAN TO HUMBLE HIMSELF   . . . .   750 EV GOSPEL(C)/N   31
HUMBLE TOWARD GOD HAUGHTY TOWARD MAN   . . . . . .   750 EV GOSPEL(C)/N   33
AND WHEN HE HUMBLED HIMSELF TO GOD   . . . . . .   750 EV GOSPEL(C)/N   35
THOU ART A MAN GOD IS NO MORE   . . . .   750 EV GOSPEL(C)/N   41
HE HAD ONLY TO SAY THAT GOD WAS THE DEVIL   . . . . .   752 EV GOSPEL(D)/N   35
AND THE DEVIL WAS GOD LIKE A CHRISTIAN CIVIL   . . . .   752 EV GOSPEL(D)/N   36
GOD CAN ONLY BE KNOWN BY HIS ATTRIBUTES   . . . . .   752 EV GOSPEL(D)/N   44
GOD WANTS NOT MAN TO HUMBLE HIMSELF   . . . .   752 EV GOSPEL(D)/N   65
HUMBLE TO GOD HAUGHTY TO MAN   . . . .   752 EV GOSPEL(D)/N   68
AND WHEN HE HUMBLED HIMSELF TO GOD   . . . . . .   752 EV GOSPEL(D)/N   71
THOU ART A MAN GOD IS NO MORE   . . . .   752 EV GOSPEL(D)/N   75
AND SHE HEARD THE BREATH OF GOD   . . . .   754 EV GOSPEL(E)/N   19
CEASE FINGER OF GOD TO WRITE   . . . .   754 EV GOSPEL(E)/N   23
A [GOD] DEVIL OR ELSE A PHARISEE   . . . .   754 EV GOSPEL(E)/N   28
[THE] LOVE'S TEMPLE [WHERE] THAT GOD DWELLETH IN   . . .   755 EV GOSPEL(E)/N   64
WHOM GOD HAS AFFLICTED FOR SECRET ENDS   . . . . .   755 EV GOSPEL(E)/N   89
THE SABBATH'S GOD & HE UNLOCKD   . . . .   756 EV GOSPEL(I)/N   18
HE SCORND [HIS] EARTH'S PARENTS SCORND [HIS] EARTH'S GOD   757 EV GOSPEL(I)/N   35
OF GOD & HEAVEN & THEIR GLORIES   . . . .   758 EV GOSPEL (1)   6
THE ACCUSER HOLY GOD OF ALL   . . . .   758 EV GOSPEL (2)   13
DOES THY GOD O PRIEST TAKE SUCH VENGEANCE AS THIS   . .   768B FOR SEXES/GP   TITLE
TO THE ACCUSER WHO IS THE GOD OF THIS WORLD   . . . .   771D EPILOGUE/GP   TITLE
O THAT IN THE BOSOM OF GOD I WAS HID   . . . . . .   772C ANNO SPURZHEIM   MARG
("THE AEGYPTIANS") THEY ALSO CONSIDERD GOD AS ABSTRACTED   774A ANNO BERKELEY   * MARG
BUT JESUS AS ALSO ABRAHAM & DAVID CONSIDERED GOD   . . .   774A ANNO BERKELEY   MARG
("ARISTOTLE...HIS METAPHYSICS") GOD IS NOT A MATHEMATICAL   774D ANNO BERKELEY   MARG
  DIAGRAM
MAN IS ALL IMAGINATION GOD IS MAN & EXISTS IN US & WE   775A ANNO BERKELEY   MARG
  IN HIM
GOD HIMSELF THE DIVINE BODY (YESHUA) JESUS WE ARE   776B INSC LAOCOON   PROSE
  HIS MEMBERS
WITH GOD THE SPOILERS SAY WHERE ARE HIS WORKS THAT HE DID   776D INSC LAOCOON   PROSE
ART IS THE TREE OF LIFE GOD IS JESUS   . . . .   777C INSC LAOCOON   PROSE
& MAKE US REVERENCE THE WORD OF GOD   . . . .   778D HOMERS POETRY   PROSE
OF MEN HENCE I AM GOD OF MEN THOU HUMAN O JEHOVAH   . . .   780 GHOST ABEL 2   15
THOU SHALT THYSELF BE SACRIFICED TO ME THY GOD ON CALVARY   781 GHOST ABEL 2   18
THE NATURAL MAN IS AT ENMITY WITH GOD   . . . . . .   782D ANNO WW POEMS   MARG
[?EVIL GOD OF THIS WORLD] [HIS] SATAN'S WILL   . . . .   788A ANNO THORNTON   * MARG
WHO IS THE GOD OF THIS WORLD THE ACCUSER LET HIS JUDGMENT   788A ANNO THORNTON   MARG
AS GOD WHO IS THE SERVANT OF MAN   . . . .   788B ANNO THORNTON   MARG
("NEITHER DISCOVERING NOT HIDING HIMSELF") A FEMALE GOD   788C ANNO THORNTON   MARG
("WILL") SO YOU SEE THAT GOD IS JUST SUCH A TYRANT   788C ANNO THORNTON   * MARG
  AS AUGUSTUS CAESAR
FOR GOD IS ONLY AN ALLEGORY OF KINGS & NOTHING ELSE AMEN   789A ANNO THORNTON   MARG
& GOD IS THE GHOST OF THE PRIEST & KING WHO EXIST   . . .   789A ANNO THORNTON   MARG
WHEREAS GOD EXISTS NOT EXCEPT FROM THEIR EFFLUVIA   . .   789A ANNO THORNTON   MARG
THUS WE SEE THAT THE REAL GOD IS THE GODDESS NATURE   . .   789B ANNO THORNTON   MARG
& THAT GOD CREATES NOTHING BUT WHAT CAN BE TOUCHD &   . . .   789B ANNO THORNTON   MARG
IS HERESY & REBELLION AGAINST CAESAR VIRGIL'S ONLY GOD   .   789B ANNO THORNTON   * MARG
GOD KEEP YOU FROM & ALL GOOD MEN OUR ARTISTS OF ALL RANKS   798A LETTER 10   PROSE
WITH GOD SPEED A ROLLER & TWO HARROWS LIE BEFORE MY WINDOW   803C LETTER 15   PROSE
THAT FELPHAM IS PROPITIOUS TO THE ARTS GOD BLESS YOU   .   803C LETTER 15   PROSE
WILL NEXT SUMMER JOKE US FACE TO FACE GOD BLESS YOU ALL   810C LETTER 20   PROSE
THIS WORLD ARE NOW BECOME THE KINGDOMS OF GOD & HIS CHRIST   810C LETTER 21   PROSE
TO GOD & MAN TO TAKE DUE CARE OF HIS GIFTS &   . . .   811C LETTER 22   PROSE
CHRISTIANITY AND ADORE HIM WHO IS THE EXPRESS IMAGE OF GOD   815D LETTER 23   PROSE
THE FURY OF MY COURSE AMONG THE STARS OF GOD   . . . .   816A LETTER 23   PROSE
AND GOD HIMSELF IN THE PASSING HOURS   . . . .   817 HAPPINESS/L   10
AND TWOFOLD ALWAYS MAY GOD US KEEP   . . . .   818 HAPPINESS/L   87
OF THE TIME I HAVE SPENT UPON THEM GOD BLESS YOU YOURS   .   819A LETTER 24   PROSE
BOTH TO GOD & MAN WE LOOK FORWARD EVERY DAY WITH PLEASURE   824B LETTER 27   PROSE
TILL WE MEET I BEG OF GOD OUR SAVIOUR TO BE WITH YOU & ME   826A LETTER 27   PROSE
GOD TO KEEP YOU & ALL MEN FROM IT & TO DELIVER ME IN HIS   829A LETTER 28   PROSE
WORK TO ME I AM CONTENT THAT IT SHALL BE SO AS LONG AS GOD   829D LETTER 30   PROSE
HEALTH & JOY IN GOD OUR SAVIOUR TO ETERNITY YOURS   . .   830D LETTER 30   PROSE
THUS THE CASE STANDS AT PRESENT GOD SEND BETTER TIMES   . .   831D LETTER 31   PROSE
GOD BLESS YOU & PRESERVE YOU & REWARD YOUR KINDNESS TO ME   833A LETTER 32   PROSE
SO EDUCATED GOD OUR SAVIOUR WATCH OVER YOU & PRESERVE YOU   833C LETTER 33   PROSE
PRAY TO MY GOD & FATHER FOR THE HEALTH OF MISS POOLE HOPE   833D LETTER 33   PROSE
PANG OF AFFECTION & GRATITUDE IS THE GIFT OF GOD FOR GOOD   833D LETTER 33   PROSE
GRATITUDE I FEEL IT & I KNOW IT I THANK GOD & MAN FOR IT &   834A LETTER 33   PROSE
GOD AS TO GET OUT & HAVE ACCORDINGLY BEEN TO MR WALKER'S   834B LETTER 34   PROSE
WORK IN ABUNDANCE & IF GOD BLESSES ME WITH HEALTH   . .   835A LETTER 34   PROSE
GOD BLESS & PRESERVE YOU AND OUR GOOD LADY PAULINA   . . .   835A LETTER 34   PROSE
BLESSING AMEN GOD BLESS YOU ALL O PEOPLE OF SUSSEX   . .   835B LETTER 34   PROSE
INTERESTING TOPIC IN BOTH YOUR LAST LETTERS GOD BE WITH YOU   841A LETTER 40   PROSE
SO THE AMERICANS WILL CONSIDER WASHINGTON AS THEIR GOD   .   845B LETTER 44   PROSE
HAD TWENTY THANK GOD I WAS NOT ALTOGETHER A BEAST AS HE WAS   852A LETTER 50   PROSE
THE PROOFS OF INDUSTRY IN MY WORKS I THANK GOD WITH ENTIRE   852C LETTER 50   PROSE
DARK BUT VERY PROFITABLE YEARS I THANK GOD THAT   . . .   852C LETTER 50   PROSE
GOD BLESS HER FOR SHE IS A PEERLESS JEWEL FOR A PRINCE   853A LETTER 51   *PROSE
ON IN THE STRENGTH OF THE LORD GOD AS POOR PILGRIM SAYS   853A LETTER 51   PROSE
WOULD TO GOD THAT THEY WOULD CONSIDER IT   . . . . .   863A LETTER 60   PROSE
OF RESENTMENT AGAINST MAN AND DEVIL AND OF HUMILIATION   864B LETTER 61   PROSE
  BEFORE GOD

	PAGE	TITLE	LINE

GOD   (CONTINUED)
THANK GOD I FEEL NO MORE OF IT . . . .   875C LETTER 81   PROSE
NOT AGREE GOD KEEP ME FROM THE DIVINITY OF YES & NO TOO   878B LETTER 88   PROSE
GOD SEND IT SO ON EARTH AS IT IS IN HEAVEN . . . . .   879A LETTER 88   PROSE
[HE IS THE GOD (OF) ISAIAH XXX ?LORD XXX] . . . . .   SUPP FOUR ZOAS 8   *
THE ANGRY GOD OF THIS WORLD & HIS ?THRONE IN PURGATORY . . SUPP ILLUS DANTE 3 *PROSE
PROTECTING ANGEL AARON ABRAHAM BELIEVED GOD . . . .   SUPP INSC HERVEY   *TITLE
GOD OUT OF CHRIST IS A CONSUMING FIRE MERCY WRATH . .   SUPP INSC HERVEY   *TITLE
GOD SPEAKING TO ADAM . . . .   SUPP INSCRIPTION   *TITLE
"THOU HAST SET THY HEART AS THE HEART OF GOD" EZEKIEL . . SUPP LEGEND/N94   *
GOOD & EVIL ANGEL HOUSE OF DEATH GOD JUDGING ADAM LAMECH   SUPP LETTER 56A   *PROSE
GOD CREATING ADAM CHRIST APPEARING TOUCHG UP CHRIST   SUPP LETTER 56A   *PROSE
   BAPTIZING
GODDESS
I ANSWERED HEAVENLY GODDESS I AM WRAPPED IN MORTALITY . . 37B CONTEMPLATN/PS PROSE
PRIDE MADE A GODDESS FAIR OR IMAGE RATHER . . . . . .   42D THEN SHE BORE   PROSE
SHE WAS A GODDESS POWERFUL & BORE [CONCEIT & EMULATION]   43A THEN SHE BORE   *PROSE
TO MY BREATH THEY OBEY THEY WORSHIP ME I AM A GODDESS &   354 FOUR ZOAS 8   502
   QUEEN
BABYLON THE CITY OF VALA THE GODDESS VIRGIN-MOTHER . .   640 JERUSALEM 18   29
OF THE HEATHEN THE GOD OF THIS WORLD & THE GODDESS NATURE   741 JERUSALEM 93   24
WHOSE GODS ARE THE POWERS OF THIS WORLD GODDESS NATURE . . 777A INSC LAOCOON   PROSE
SATAN'S WIFE THE GODDESS NATURE IS WAR & MISERY . . . .   777A INSC LAOCOON   PROSE
THE FOUNDATION OF ALL & THE GODDESS NATURE . . . . . .   785A ILLUS DANTE 7   *PROSE
AS POOR CHURCHILL SAID "NATURE THOU [XXX] ART MY GODDESS"   785A ILLUS DANTE 7   *PROSE
THE GODDESS FORTUNE IS THE DEVIL'S SERVANT . . . . .   785C ILLUS DANTE 16 PROSE
THUS WE SEE THAT THE REAL GOD IS THE GODDESS NATURE . . . 789B ANNO THORNTON MARG
MINIATURE (IS) BECOME A GODDESS IN MY EYES & MY FRIENDS   808B LETTER 19   *PROSE
OWN ETERNAL HOUSE LEAVING THE DELUSIVE GODDESS NATURE & HER   879A LETTER 88   PROSE
GODDESSES
THE GODDESSES OF DESTINY THIS SHEWS HOW CHAUCER HAS BEEN   569D DESC CAT 3   PROSE
GODLESS
. . . FOR A CURSE IS HEARD HOARSE THRO THE LAND FROM A   140 FRENCH REVOLTN 138
   GODLESS RACE
GODLIKE
AND I KNOW THEE IS THIS THE TRIUMPH THIS THE GODLIKE STATE   324 FOUR ZOAS 7   149
GOD'S
LOVER OF WILD REBELLION AND TRANSGRESSER OF GOD'S LAW . . 198 AMERICA 7   *   6
("GOD'S MORAL JUSTICE EXTERMINATE SO WICKED A PEOPLE   388B ANNO WATSON   MARG
   ") HORRIBLE
I AM IN GOD'S PRESENCE NIGHT & DAY . . . .   558 I ROSE UP AT/N   13
TO BE AN ERROR & TO BE CAST OUT IS A PART OF GOD'S DESIGN   613A V LAST JUDG/N PROSE
GOD'S HIGH KING & GOD'S HIGH PRIEST . . . .   749 EV GOSPEL(B)/N   19
GOD'S MERCY & LONG SUFFERING . . . .   751 EV GOSPEL(C)/N   45
GOD'S MERCY & LONG SUFFERING . . . .   753 EV GOSPEL(D)/N   81
GOD'S RIGHTEOUS LAW THAT LOST ITS PREY . . . .   757 EV GOSPEL(I)/N   48
KNOW THAT YOU SEE CERTAIN MERITS IN ME WHICH BY GOD'S GRACE   822B LETTER 26   PROSE
GODS
AND ALL YE GODS OF PALESTINE WITHDRAW YOUR HAND . . .   38C SAMSON/PS   PROSE
AND PIERCE THE EARS O TH GODS O SAMSON HOLD ME NOT . . . 38C SAMSON/PS   PROSE
THESE ARE THE GODS WHICH CAME FROM FEAR FOR . . . .   40D THEN SHE BORE   PROSE
GODS LIKE THESE NOR MALE NOR FEMALE ARE BUT SINGLE PREGNATE   40D THEN SHE BORE   PROSE
PRIDE BEARS IT IN HER BOSOM AND THE GODS ALL BOW TO IT . . 41A THEN SHE BORE   PROSE
THE GODS ALL SERVE HER AT HER WILL SO GREAT HER POWER IS   41D THEN SHE BORE   PROSE
NOW ALL THE GODS IN BLACKNING RANKS APPEAR . . . . . .   42C THEN SHE BORE   PROSE
PRIDE BOUND HIM THEN USURPD OER ALL THE GODS . . . .   42C THEN SHE BORE   PROSE
INDEED HATE CONTROLLS ALL THE GODS AT WILL . . . . .   42D THEN SHE BORE   PROSE
THESE GODS LAST NAMD LIVE IN THE SMOKE OF CITIES . . . . 42D THEN SHE BORE   PROSE
THE GODS ADMIRING LOADED HER WITH GIFTS AS ONCE PANDORA   42D THEN SHE BORE   PROSE
USD TO HAVE GODS THAT THEY WORSHIPD & THEY USD TO   47B ISLAND MOON 3   PROSE
   SACRIFICE TO THEM
AND I ASK THE GODS NO MORE . . . .   47 ASK GODS/IM 1   2
I ASK THE GODS NO MORE . . . .   55 ASK GODS/IM 2   1
AND I ASK THE GODS NO MORE . . . .   55 ASK GODS/IM 3   1
AND I ASK THE GODS NO MORE . . . .   55 ASK GODS/IM 4   1
THE ANCIENT POETS ANIMATED ALL SENSIBLE OBJECTS WITH GODS   153A MARRIAGE HH 11 PROSE
THEY PRONOUNCD THAT THE GODS HAD ORDERD SUCH THINGS . . . 153B MARRIAGE HH 11 PROSE
OF OTHER COUNTRIES AND PROPHECYING THAT ALL GODS WOULD . . 153D MARRIAGE HH 12 PROSE
THE GODS OF THE EARTH & SEA . . . .   174 HUMAN IMAGE/N   22
THE GODS OF THE EARTH AND SEA . . . .   217 HUMAN ABSTR/SE   21
AND ON THE MOUNTAINS OF LEBANON ROUND THE DECEASED GODS   246 SONG OF LOS 4   19
. . . FAIRIES OF ALBION AFTERWARDS GODS OF THE HEATHEN . . 264 FOUR ZOAS 1   19
[WANDERING DESOLATE A WONDER ABHORRD BY GODS & MEN] . . . 269 FOUR ZOAS 1   190
FOR ELEMENTAL GODS THEIR THUNDEROUS ORGANS BLEW CREATING   274 FOUR ZOAS 1   377
WHILE ROUND THEIR HEADS THE ELEMENTAL GODS KEPT HARMONY   288 FOUR ZOAS 2   301
WHEN ALL THE ELEMENTAL GODS JOIND IN THE WONDROUS SONG . . 336 FOUR ZOAS 7B   146
IF GODS COMBINE AGAINST MAN SETTING THEIR DOMINION ABOVE   366 FOUR ZOAS 9   366
LUCIAN DISBELIEVD HEATHEN GODS . . . .   403C ANNO BACON   MARG
FOLLOW AFTER THE DETESTABLE GODS OF PRIAM IN POMP . . . 495 MILTON 14   15
WITH LAWS FROM PLATO & HIS GREEKS TO RENEW THE TROJAN GODS   506 MILTON 22   53
ALL THE GODS OF THE KINGDOMS OF EARTH LABOUR IN LOS'S HALLS   510 MILTON 24   74
TO THE DETESTABLE GODS OF PRIAM TO APOLLO AND AT THE ASYLUM   511 MILTON 25   49
THESE ARE THE GODS OF THE KINGDOMS OF THE EARTH IN   520 MILTON 31   23
   CONTRARIOUS
ITS OWN QUALITIES WHICH ARE SERVANTS OF HUMANITY NOT GODS   521 MILTON 32   21
   OR LORDS
THE MONSTROUS CHURCHES OF BEULAH THE GODS OF ULRO DARK . . 528 MILTON 37   16
THESE TWELVE GODS ARE THE TWELVE SPECTRE SONS OF THE DRUID   528 MILTON 37   34
   ALBION
THE HEAVENS ARE THE CHERUB THE TWELVE GODS ARE SATAN . . 529 MILTON 37   60
THAT THE HEATHEN GODS ARE ALL STOCKS & STONES . . . . . 543 IF TRUE/N   2
TO COMPELL US TO WORSHIP THEM AS GODS . . . .   543 IF TRUE/N   8

		PAGE	TITLE	LINE

GODS (CONTINUED)

WONDROUS THE GODS MORE WONDROUS ARE THE MEN . . . . . 545 IMIT POPE/N 1
THE GRECIAN GODS WERE THE ANCIENT CHERUBIM OF PHOENICIA 571B DESC CAT 3 PROSE
TO SUBDUE THE GODS OF PRIAM THESE GODS ARE VISIONS OF . 571C DESC CAT 3 PROSE
WHEN ERECTED INTO GODS BECOME DESTRUCTIVE TO HUMANITY . 571C DESC CAT 3 PROSE
OF GODS IMMORTAL TO THE MORTAL PERISHING ORGAN OF SIGHT 576D DESC CAT 4 PROSE
UNSUBDUED AS GODS AND THE SUN OF BRITAIN (SET) BUT SHALL 577B DESC CAT 5 *TITLE
BLOATED [AWKWARD] GODS MERCURY JUNO VENUS & THE . . . 599C PUB ADDRESS/N *PROSE
[FOR MY SAVIOUR AND LORD FOR THEY WERE WHOLLY ABSORBD IN 621A JERUSALEM 3 *PROSE
  THEIR GODS]
TO THE TWELVE GODS OF ASIA THE SPECTRES OF THOSE WHO SLEEP 681 JERUSALEM 50 3
AT WILL CONTRACTING INTO WORMS OR EXPANDING INTO GODS . . 686 JERUSALEM 55 37
AMONG THE GODS OF ASIA AMONG THE FOUNTAINS OF PITCH & 693 JERUSALEM 60 24
  NITRE
O LORD & SAVIOUR HAVE THE GODS OF THE HEATHEN PIERCED THEE 693 JERUSALEM 60 52
SUCH IS THE FORGIVENESS OF THE GODS THE MORAL VIRTUES OF 694 JERUSALEM 61 20
  THE
RECIEVE A KISS FROM GODS OR MEN A THREEFOLD KISS RETURNS 709 JERUSALEM 70 25
THREE-FOLD EMBRACE RETURNS CONSUMING LIVES OF GODS & MEN 709 JERUSALEM 70 27
THEY BECAME THE TWELVE GODS OF ASIA OPPOSING THE DIVINE 714 JERUSALEM 74 22
  VISION
THERE ISRAEL IN BONDAGE TO HIS GENERALIZING GODS . . . . 735 JERUSALEM 89 30
FROM GAZA TO DAMASCUS TYRE & SIDON & THE GODS . . . . . 735 JERUSALEM 89 33
IMPOSSIBILITIES CHASTITY & ABSTINENCE GODS OF THE HEATHEN 776C INSC LAOCOON PROSE
THE GODS OF GREECE & EGYPT WERE MATHEMATICAL DIAGRAMS . 776D INSC LAOCOON PROSE
WHOSE GODS ARE THE POWERS OF THIS WORLD GODDESS NATURE . 777A INSC LAOCOON PROSE
THE GODS OF PRIAM ARE THE CHERUBIM OF MOSES & SOLOMON . 777B INSC LAOCOON PROSE
THE EGYPTIAN GODS AND THO NOT DIRECTLY TAKEN FROM A POEM 823D LETTER 27 PROSE

GODSHIP

FOR THINE IS THE KINGSHIP OR ALLEGORIC GODSHIP . . . . 789A ANNO THORNTON * MARG

GOES

DOWN GOES OUR RIGHT TO FRANCE . . . . 23 EDW THIRD/PS 3 72
AND WHERE SHE GOES HEAVEN STILL DOTH FOLLOW HER SHE . . . 42A THEN SHE BORE PROSE
EAGER SONG GOES ON TELLING HOW PRIDE AGAINST HER FATHER 42B THEN SHE BORE PROSE
  WARRD
& THERES MISS FILLIGREE WORK SHE GOES OUT IN HER COACHES 52D ISLAND MOON 8 PROSE
AND THE CELLAR GOES DOWN WITH A STEP . . . . 54 LO THE BAT/IM 14
SAW A TREACLE JAR SO HE GOES OF HIS BLIND SIDE . . . . 55B ISLAND MOON 9 PROSE
WHILE THE BEETLE GOES HIS ROUND . . . . 112 A DREAM/SI 18
CAN WRITE AND ADAMANTINE LEAVES RECIEVE NOR CAN THE MAN 316 FOUR ZOAS 6 174
  WHO GOES
LO HOW THE POMP OF MYSTERY GOES DOWN INTO THE CAVES . . . 375 FOUR ZOAS 9 662
AND THERE GOES MISS BELL WITH HER FUSTY OLD NUT . . . . 434 LONG JOHN BRWN 20
THO IT GOES DOWN ON THE HEAVIEST SIDE . . . . . 476B ANNO REYNOLDS MARG
SAYING MILTON GOES TO ETERNAL DEATH SO SAYING THEY GROAND 504 MILTON 21 43
  IN SPIRIT
BUT YOU CANNOT RENEW MILTON HE GOES TO ETERNAL DEATH . . 504 MILTON 21 57
THE PLOW GOES FORTH IN TEMPESTS & LIGHTNINGS & THE HARROW 514 MILTON 27 47
  CRUEL
WHEREER HE GOES & ALL HIS NEIGHBOURHOOD BEWAIL HIS LOSS 516 MILTON 29 13
AND IF EVERY THING GOES ON AS IT HAS BEGUN . . . . . 578A DESC CAT 5 PROSE
SPECTRE FOR WHEREEVER THE EMANATION GOES THE SPECTRE . 655 JERUSALEM 30 2
ALBION GOES TO ETERNAL DEATH IN ME ALL ETERNITY . . . 662 JERUSALEM 35 9
THO HER BRAIN IS NOT DRUNK WITH WINE SHE GOES FORTH FROM 705 JERUSALEM 68 13
  ALBION
AS THE COACH GOES THREE TIMES A WEEK TO LONDON & 809B LETTER 20 *PROSE
  THEY [SHALL]
GOES ON BRISKLY THIS WORK IS TO BE A VERY ELEGANT ONE . 824C LETTER 27 PROSE
RESTORED MR ROMNEY'S PORTRAIT GOES ON WITH SPIRIT . . 833A LETTER 32 PROSE
AIR YET I LOSE NOTHING BY IT DANTE GOES ON THE BETTER . 877D LETTER 88 PROSE

GOEST

I KNOW BUT LITTLE OF THE PATH THOU GOEST . . . . . 36A COUCH DEATH/PS PROSE
WHERE GOEST THOU O THOUGHT TO WHAT REMOTE LAND IS 192 V DAU ALBION 4 8
  THY FLIGHT
IS [THINE] MINE & THERE THOU GOEST WHEN WITH ONE STING 268 FOUR ZOAS 1 * 156
  OF MY TONGUE
I EVERMORE WILL HOLD THEE WHEN THOU GOEST OUT OR COMEST IN 269 FOUR ZOAS 1 177
THOU GOEST TO ETERNAL DEATH & ALL MUST GO WITH THEE . . . 534 MILTON 42 2
RUTH CANNOT LEAVE HER BUT SAYS "WHITHER THOU GOEST" . . . 584D DESC CAT 15 PROSE
IF THOU GOEST BACK THE THISTLE SAID . . . . 817 HAPPINESS/L 31

GOETH

THE SUN IS THINE [WHEN] HE GOETH FORTH IN HIS MAJESTIC 367 FOUR ZOAS 9 399
  BRIGHTNESS
KNOWETH THE INFANT SORROW WHENCE IT CAME AND WHERE IT GOETH 688 JERUSALEM 56 6

GOG

BY TWO STRONG DEMONS THEY ARE GOG & MAGOG WHO HAVE . . 609B V LAST JUDG/N PROSE
INTO THE VORTEX OF HIS WHEELS THEREFORE HYLE IS CALLED GOG 715 JERUSALEM 74 30

GOGMAGOG

CORINEUS THROWS GOGMAGOG THE GIANT INTO THE SEA KING LEAR 208C SUBJCTS HIST/N TITLE

GOG-MAGOG

. . . WHEN THE TRIPLE HEADED GOG-MAGOG GIANT . . . . . 746 JERUSALEM 98 52

GOING

AS THE YOUNG BRIDEGROOM GOING TO BE MARRIED . . . . 24 EDW THIRD/PS 3 145
YONDER S A MUSICIAN GOING TO PLAY BEFORE THE KING . . . 29B EDW THIRD/PS 4 PROSE
THEY SEEMD TO BE GOING ON THEIR PASSAGE AS PLINY SAYS . . 45A ISLAND MOON 1 PROSE
& YOU HINDER YOUR HUSBAND FROM GOING TO CHURCH . . . 48A ISLAND MOON 4 PROSE
A PARCEL OF FOOLS GOING TO BRISTOL IF I WAS TO GO . . . 51D ISLAND MOON 7 PROSE
JOE BRADLEY & I WAS GOING ALONG ONE DAY IN THE SUGAR HOUSE 55B ISLAND MOON 9 PROSE
O FATHER FATHER WHERE ARE YOU GOING . . . . 60 LIT BOY LST/IM 1
("IMAGE OF CREATION") A GOING FORTH & RETURNING . . . 95A ANNO SWED LOVE MARG
WHERE ARE YOU GOING COME & EAT SOME ROOTS & DRINK SOME 109 TIRIEL 7 11
  WATER

GOING   (CONTINUED)
FATHER FATHER WHERE ARE YOU GOING   . . . .   120 LIT BOY LST/SI   1
TO WHICH THOU ART GOING IN SUCH CAREER   . . . .   155D MARRIAGE HH 17   PROSE
OF LIFE [REJOICE] LAMENT AROUND THE DEMON GOING FORTH &   308 FOUR ZOAS 5   * 117
   RETURNING
FOUR STARRY UNIVERSES GOING FORWARD FROM ETERNITY   364 FOUR ZOAS 9   284
   TO ETERNITY
CONTENTION AT THE STABLE DOOR & GOING TO THE COMRADE   . . 438D BLAKES MEMORAN PROSE
SATAN WAS GOING TO REPLY BUT LOS ROLLD HIS LOUD THUNDERS   483 MILTON 4   15
BUT EVERY MAN RETURND & WENT STILL GOING FORWARD THRO . . 519 MILTON 31   4
GOING IN AND OUT BEFORE HIM IN HIS LOVE AND SWEET AFFECTION 642 JERUSALEM 20   10
LIVE BY DEVOURING GOING INTO ETERNAL DEATH CONTINUALLY . . 681 JERUSALEM 50   7
GOING FORTH & RETURNING FROM ALBION'S ROCKS TO CANAAN   . . 707 JERUSALEM 69   4
WITH MORAL LAW AN EQUAL BALANCE NOT GOING DOWN WITH   708 JERUSALEM 69   35
   DECISION
AND THE CIRCUMFERENCE STILL EXPANDS GOING FORWARD   709 JERUSALEM 71   8
   TO ETERNITY
A WORM GOING TO ETERNAL TORMENT RAISD UP IN A NIGHT . . . 721 JERUSALEM 80   4
OF HEAVEN GOING FORWARD FCRWARD . . . .   745 JERUSALFM 98   27
HUMAN FORMS IDENTIFIED LIVING GOING FORTH & RETURNING   747 JERUSALEM 99   2
   WEARIED
"BUT CAN NEVER THINK OF GOING WITHOUT FIRST PAYING OUR"   800A LETTER 12   PROSE
I MET A PLOW ON MY FIRST GOING OUT AT MY GATE . . . . .   803C LETTER 15   PROSE
WHAT IS VERY PLEASANT EVERY ONE WHO HEARS OF MY GOING .   822D LETTER 26   PROSE
IMPROVEMENTS IN WORKS OF ART GOING ON IN LONDON BUT . .   823A LETTER 26   PROSE
GOING ON WOULD BE A CERTAIN LOSS OF ALMOST ALL THE EXPENSES 831C LETTER 31   PROSE
ARE HUNDREDS TO ME NAY THOUSANDS I AM GOING ON WITH SUCCESS 832C LETTER 32   PROSE
GOING ON BRISKLY WITH THE PLATES FIND EVERY THING PROMISING 835A LETTER 34   PROSE
HE IS NOW GOING TO RUSSIA HOPES THAT THE NEGOTIATIONS FOR 845C LETTER 44   PROSE
I AM GOING ON WITH DANTE & PLEASE MYSELF I AM DR SIR YOURS 869A LETTER 68   PROSE
   SINCERELY
GET UP BUT JUST AS I WAS GOING TO RISE THIS MORNING THE   872B LETTER 75   PROSE
I AM GOING ON BETTER EVERY DAY AS I THINK BOTH . . . .   879B LETTER 89   PROSE
BALANCE DUE FROM ME PREVIOUS TO MY GOING TO FELPHAM . . . SUPP LETTER 56A   *PROSE
GOLD
THE LETTERS AND TO MAKE THEM SHINE WITH GOLD . . . . .   18 EDW THIRD/PS 1   27
OR SHINING GLASS AND A WROUGHT DIAMOND SET IN RICH GOLD AND 29D EDW THIRD/PS 4   PROSE
DECKED IN MILD SORROW AND SELL THY LORD FOR GOLD FOR . .   38A SAMSON/PS   PROSE
WITH SCARLET GOWNS & BROAD GOLD LACE WOULD MAKE A YEOMAN   58 THIS CITY/IM   5
   SWEAT
("AS MAN SO HIS GOD AS HIS GOD SO HE") ALL GOLD . . .   65D ANNO LAVATER   MARG
("MAN'S INTEREST...HIS GOD...VORTEX...CENTRE") PURE GOLD   66A ANNO LAVATER   MARG
THIS SHOULD BE WRITTEN IN GOLD LETTERS ON OUR TEMPLES .   66B ANNO LAVATER   MARG
("ANSWER THIS...AND YOU WILL KNOW YOURSELF ") ALL GOLD   73C ANNO LAVATER   MARG
BOWD HIS MANE OF GOLD . . . .   113 LIT GRL LST/SI   44
A SPIRIT ARMD IN GOLD . . . .   114 LIT GRL FND/SI   36
SHALL FLOW WITH TEARS OF GOLD . . . .   119 NIGHT/SI   34
SHALL SHINE LIKE THE GOLD . . . .   119 NIGHT/SI   47
OR AN EYE OF GIFTS & GRACES SHOWRING FRUITS & COINED GOLD 130 BOOK OF THEL 6   15
AND OTHERS ADORNING IT WITH GOLD SILVER AND PRECIOUS STONES 154D MARRIAGE HH 15 PROSE
O JEW LEAVE COUNTING GOLD RETURN TO THY OIL AND WINE . . 159C SONG LIBERTY   PROSE
I SAW A CHAPEL ALL OF GOLD . . . .   163 I SAW CHAPEL/N   1
[THERE] AND [CRADLED] MILK FED INFANCY [IS SOLD] FOR GOLD 174 HUMAN IMAGE/N   * 30
CLOTHD IN ROBES OF BLOOD & GOLD . . . .   177 DAY/N   2
THE [WE] [?COUNT] [(WEALTH)] COUNTLESS GOLD OF A MERRY   181 RICHES/N   *   1
   HEART
THE KING AWOKE ON HIS COUCH OF GOLD . . . .   185 LET BROTHELS/N   5
AND CATCH FOR THEE GIRLS OF MILD SILVER OR OF FURIOUS GOLD 194 V DAU ALBION 7   24
WHERE THE COLD MISER SPREADS HIS GOLD OR DOES THE BRIGHT   195 V DAU ALBION 8   1
   CLOUD DROP
AND THE WILD SNAKE THE PESTILENCE TO ADORN HIM WITH GEMS   195 V DAU ALBION 8   7
   & GOLD
HIS KNEES AND THIGHS LIKE SILVER & HIS BREAST AND HEAD   199 AMERICA 8   17
   LIKE GOLD
. . . THEY CLASPD THE ARMOUR OF TERRIBLE GOLD . . . . .   205 AMERICA CANC C   6
GOLD SILVER BRASS & IRON [ARDORS] CLANGORS CLAMORING REND 205 AMERICA CANC C   15
   THE SHORES
[OVER THE] A FROWNING SHADOW LIKE [A] AN AGED KING IN ARMS 205 AMERICA CANC C *   25
   OF GOLD
IN THE AGE OF GOLD . . . .   219 LIT GRL LST/SE   5
AND HIS BOOKS OF BRASS IRON & GOLD . . . .   248 SONG OF LOS 7   14
REARD UP A FORM OF GOLD & STOOD UPON THE GLITTERING ROCK   267 FOUR ZOAS 1   126
STRETCH THEIR IMMORTAL HANDS TO SMITE THE GOLD & SILVER   274 FOUR ZOAS 1   380
   WIRES
SIEZD HIS BRIGHT SHEEPHOOK STUDDED WITH GEMS & GOLD HE   275 FOUR ZOAS 1   414
   SWUNG IT ROUND
. . . THEY FORMD THE ANVILS OF GOLD BEATEN IN MILLS . . . 281 FOUR ZOAS 2   30
THEY UNLOOSD THEM & PUT ON THE HARNESS OF GOLD & SILVER   281 FOUR ZOAS 2   36
   & IVORY
OF LIVING GOLD PURE PERFECT HOLY IN WHITE LINEN PURE HE   293 FOUR ZOAS 3   51
   HOVERD
AND BRASS & SILVER & GOLD FOURFOLD IN DARK PROPHETIC FEAR 307 FOUR ZOAS 5   74
THE VEINS OF GOLD & SILVER & THE HIDDEN THINGS OF VALA . 308 FOUR ZOAS 5   123
THE GOLD & SILVER & COSTLY STONES HIS HOLY WORKMANSHIP . 310 FOUR ZOAS 5   215
THY CHILDREN SMOTE THEIR FIERY WINGS CROWND WITH THE GOLD 311 FOUR ZOAS 5   229
   OF HEAVEN
OR GOLD A GLITTERING TORMENT SHINING & HISSING IN ETERNAL 315 FOUR ZOAS 6   121
   PAIN
OFT WOULD HE STAND & QUESTION A FIERCE SCORPION GLOWING   315 FOUR ZOAS 6   131
   WITH GOLD
STILL TO BE WRITTEN & INTERLEAVD WITH BRASS & IRON & GOLD 316 FOUR ZOAS 6   172
SO [SAYING] HE BEGAN TO [FORM] ?DIG OF GOLD SILVER   317 FOUR ZOAS 6   * 229
   & [BRASS] IRON

		PAGE	TITLE	LINE

GOLD   (CONTINUED)

GOLD SILVER BRASS & IRON CLANGORS CLAMORING REND THE [DEEPS] SHORES — 319 FOUR ZOAS 6 — 311
OF GOLD & SILVER BRASS & IRON HE KNEW HIS MIGHTY SONS — 319 FOUR ZOAS 6 — 315
IN SCALES THAT SHINE WITH GOLD & RUBIES THOU BEGINNEST TO WEAKEN — 323 FOUR ZOAS 7 — 136
BENEATH DOWN TO HIS EYELIDS SCALES OF PEARL THEN GOLD & SILVER — 342 FOUR ZOAS 8 — 70
IN RAGING HUNGER STILL THE PESTILENTIAL FOOD IN GEMS & GOLD — 343 FOUR ZOAS 8 — 78
AND SILVER & GOLD HE CONSECRATED READING INCESSANTLY — 344 FOUR ZOAS 8 — 141
WITH GIFTS & GOLD OF EDEN ASTONISHD STUPIFIED WITH DELIGHT — 346 FOUR ZOAS 8 — * 214
WITH GIFTS & SPICES WITH LAMPS RICH EMBOSSD JEWELS & GOLD — 349 FOUR ZOAS 8 — 337
MY ROBE IS TURNED TO CONFUSION & MY BRIGHT GOLD TO STONES — 360 FOUR ZOAS 9 — * 106
FROM RUST OF AGES ALL ITS ORNAMENTS OF GOLD & SILVER & IVORY — 364 FOUR ZOAS 9 — 292
IN WALLS OF GOLD WE CAST HIM LIKE A SEED INTO THE EARTH — 374 FOUR ZOAS 9 — 632
THEY CATCH THE SHRIEKS IN CUPS OF GOLD THEY HAND THEM TO ONE ANOTHER — 377 FOUR ZOAS 9 — 768
BESET WITH GOLD GOLD WERE THE ORNAMENTS FORMD BY SONS OF URIZEN — 377 FOUR ZOAS 9 — 777
THEY FORMED HEAVENS OF SWEETEST (?WOODS) OF GOLD & SILVER & IVORY — 378 FOUR ZOAS 9 — * 792
AROSE WITH WAR IN IRON & GOLD — 418 I SAW A MONK/N — 9
STOOD BY & MOCKED IN IRON & GOLD — 420 I SAW MNK AD/N — 14
CATCHES HIS SHRIEKS IN CUPS OF GOLD — 425 MENTAL TRAVLER — 12
JUST AS A MISER COUNTS HIS GOLD — 425 MENTAL TRAVLER — 18
FULL FILLED ALL WITH GEMS & GOLD — 425 MENTAL TRAVLER — 31
THE COUNTLESS GOLD OF THE AKEING HEART — 425 MENTAL TRAVLER — 35
AND GEMS & GOLD THAT NONE HIS HAND — 425 MENTAL TRAVLER — 46
THIS CABINET IS FORMD OF GOLD — 429 CRYSTL CABINET — 5
THAN ALL THE GOLD ON AFRIC'S SHORE — 432 AUGURIES — 80
WHEN GOLD & GEMS ADORN THE PLOW — 433 AUGURIES — 101
THE DOOR OF DEATH IS MADE OF GOLD — 442 DEDICATN BLAIR — 1
BEHOLD THIS GATE OF PEARL AND GOLD — 442 DEDICATN BLAIR — 10
AND THE POOR & THE OLD CAN LIVE UPON GOLD — 452 ANNO REYNOLDS — 3
BRING ME MY BOW OF BURNING GOLD — 481 AND DID FEET/M — 9
OF PRECIOUS STONES & GOLD TURND POISONS ON THE SULTRY WASTES — 493 MILTON 12 — 30
OF GOLD AND THOSE IN IMMORTALITY GAVE FORTH THEIR EMANATIONS — 496 MILTON 15 — 13
AND ALL MY ORNAMENTS SHALL BE OF THE GOLD OF BROKEN HEARTS — 499 MILTON 18 — 22
AS A BRIGHT SANDAL FORMD IMMORTAL OF PRECIOUS STONES & GOLD — 503 MILTON 21 — 13
I RECOLLECT AN OLD PROPHECY IN EDEN RECORDED IN GOLD AND OFT — 507 MILTON 23 — 35
THE SPORTIVE ROOT THE EARTH-WORM THE GOLD BEETLE THE WISE EMMET — 513 MILTON 27 — 12
THE TOAD & VENOMOUS NEWT THE SERPENT CLOTHD IN GEMS & GOLD — 513 MILTON 27 — 22
THEY CATCH THE SHRIEKS IN CUPS OF GOLD THEY HAND THEM TO ONE ANOTHER — 514 MILTON 27 — 38
OTHERS CABINETS RICHLY FABRICATE OF GOLD & IVORY — 515 MILTON 28 — 8
AND EVERY MOMENT HAS A COUCH OF GOLD FOR SOFT REPOSE — 516 MILTON 28 — 46
AND EVERY AGE IS MOATED DEEP WITH BRIDGES OF SILVER & GOLD — 516 MILTON 28 — 56
ON ALL SIDES & THE TWO POLES TURN ON THEIR VALVES OF GOLD — 516 MILTON 29 — 11
THEN YOU BEHOLD ITS MIGHTY SPIRES & DOMES OF IVORY & GOLD — 525 MILTON 35 — 25
HIS LEFT SCOTLAND HIS BOSOM GIRT WITH GOLD INVOLVES — 531 MILTON 39 — 42
THAT HE MIGHT TURN IT INTO EGGS OF GOLD — 537 AND HIS LEGS/N — 12
ARE TRUE IS THAT REAL GOLD AND SILVER CANNOT BE USED WITH OIL — 566C DESC CAT 2 — PROSE
BUT THE PAINTER'S THOUGHTS BEING ALWAYS UPON GOLD — 575B DESC CAT 3 — PROSE
HIS HAMMER OF GOLD HE SIEZD AND HIS ANVIL OF ADAMANT — 628 JERUSALEM 9 — 3
AWKWARDNESS ARMD IN STEEL FOLLY IN A HELMET OF GOLD — 628 JERUSALEM 9 — 12
ARE MELTED INTO THE GOLD THE SILVER THE LIQUID RUBY — 628 JERUSALEM 9 — 23
OF LIGHT AND LOVE THEIR LITTLE CHILDREN STAND WITH ARROWS OF GOLD — 631 JERUSALEM 11 — 20
ENAMELD WITH LOVE & KINDNESS & THE TILES ENGRAVEN GOLD — 632 JERUSALEM 12 — 31
AND THAT TOWARD BEULAH FOUR GOLD SILVER BRASS & IRON — 632 JERUSALEM 12 — 66
AND THAT TOWARD EDEN FOUR FORMD OF GOLD SILVER BRASS & IRON — 633 JERUSALEM 13 — 1
THAT TOWARD EDEN FOUR IMMORTAL GOLD SILVER BRASS & IRON — 633 JERUSALEM 13 — 5
OF DEATH FORMING AN AX OF GOLD THE FOUR SONS OF LOS — 636 JERUSALEM 15 — 22
WHEN ALBION RENT THY BEAUTIFUL NET OF GOLD AND SILVER TWINE — 643 JERUSALEM 20 — 30
THY PILLARS OF IVORY & GOLD THY CURTAINS OF SILK & FINE — 647 JERUSALEM 24 — 18
AND GOLD THY GATES OF THANKSGIVING THY WINDOWS OF PRAISE — 647 JERUSALEM 24 — 20
WITH BLESSINGS ON THEIR HANDS & ON THEIR FEET BLESSINGS OF GOLD — 647 JERUSALEM 24 — 39
WERE BUILDED OVER WITH PILLARS OF GOLD — 649 FIELDS FROM/J — 3
MY SELFHOOD SATAN ARMD IN GOLD — 651 FIELDS FROM/J — 76
OF LIVING GOLD PURE PERFECT HOLY IN WHITE LINEN PURE HE HOVERD — 654 JERUSALEM 29 — 38
THERE IS IN ALBION A GATE OF PRECIOUS STONES AND GOLD — 665 JERUSALEM 38 — 55
OF GOLD & JEWELS A SUBLIME ORNAMENT A COUCH OF REPOSE — 677 JERUSALEM 48 — 6
INTO A RAINBOW OF JEWELS AND GOLD A MILD REFLECTION FROM — 678 JERUSALEM 48 — 35
AROSE WITH WAR IN IRON & GOLD — 683 I SAW A MONK/J — 8
TEACHING THEM TO FORM THE SERPENT OF PRECIOUS STONES & GOLD — 686 JERUSALEM 55 — 13
TO FREEZE LOVE & INNOCENCE INTO THE GOLD & SILVER OF THE MERCHANT — 699 JERUSALEM 64 — 23
GLITTERING WITH PRECIOUS STONES & GOLD WITH GARMENTS OF BLOOD & FIRE — 699 JERUSALEM 64 — 26
IN AWFUL POMP & GOLD IN ALL THE PRECIOUS UNHEWN STONES OF EDEN — 701 JERUSALEM 66 — 1
MALE GENIUS WHO IN RETURN CLOTHES HER IN GEMS & GOLD — 707 JERUSALEM 69 — 17
IN FIRES OF BEAUTY MELTING THEM AS GOLD & SILVER IN THE FURNACE — 709 JERUSALEM 70 — 28

		PAGE	TITLE	LINE

GOLD   (CONTINUED)

OF BRASS IRON CHAINS & BRACES & THE GOLD SILVER & BRASS — 713 JERUSALEM 73 — 10
THEY TOOK THEIR MOTHER VALA AND THEY CROWND HER WITH GOLD — 719 JERUSALEM 78 — 15
HE TAKES HIS WAY GIRDING HIMSELF WITH GOLD & IN HIS HAND — 729 JERUSALEM 83 — 77
AND TO INHABIT OUR LITTLE-ONES TO CLOTHE IN ARMOUR OF THE GOLD — 729 JERUSALEM 84 — 9
I SEE THY GATES OF PRECIOUS STONES THY WALLS OF GOLD & SILVER — 730 JERUSALEM 85 — 23
RIBBD DELICATE & CLOTHD WITH FEATHERD GOLD & AZURE & PURPLE — 731 JERUSALEM 86 — 6
BETWEEN THY WINGS OF GOLD & SILVER FEATHERD IMMORTAL   . . — 731 JERUSALEM 86 — 20
SANDALS OF GOLD & PEARL & EGYPT & ASSYRIA BEFORE ME . . . — 731 JERUSALEM 86 — 31
HEAVENS A MOTH OF GOLD & SILVER MOCKING HIS ANXIOUS GRASP — 739 JERUSALEM 91 — 50
LOS ANSWERD SWIFT AS THE SHUTTLE OF GOLD SEXES MUST VANISH & CEASE — 739 JERUSALEM 92 — 13
HE TAKES HIS BOW THEN CHOOSES OUT HIS ARROWS OF FLAMING GOLD — 742 JERUSALEM 95 — 13
DAZLING AROUND THY SKIRTS LIKE A SERPENT OF PRECIOUS STONES & GOLD — 743 JERUSALEM 96 — 12
LAYD HIS HAND ON THE SOUTH & TOOK A BREATHING BOW OF CARVED GOLD — 744 JERUSALEM 97 — 8
ON CHARIOTS OF GOLD & JEWELS WITH LIVING CREATURES STARRY & FLAMING — 746 JERUSALEM 98 — 42
DESIRE TO ENTERTAIN BENEATH OUR THATCHED ROOF OF RUSTED GOLD — 802D LETTER 14 — PROSE
IN HIS BEAMS OF BRIGHT GOLD — . 805 TO BUTTS/L — 54
O THOU RAM HORND WITH GOLD . . . . — . 805 TO BUTTS/L — 62
O THOU RAM HORND WITH GOLD . . . . — . 805 TO BUTTS/L — 70
LETTERS OF GOLD & ORNAMENTED WITH JEWELS OF . . . . . — . 837D LETTER 36 — PROSE

GOLD-BEAMD

YOU MUST MY DICTATE OBEY FROM YOUR GOLD-BEAMD LOOMS TRILL — 688 JERUSALEM 56 — 31

GOLDEN

THY GOLDEN CROWN UPON HER LANGUISHD HEAD . . . . . . — . 1 TO SPRING/PS — 15
OFT PITCHEDST HERE THY GOLDEN TENT AND OFT . . . . . — . 1 TO SUMMER/PS — 4
HILLS FLED FROM OUR SIGHT BUT LEFT HIS GOLDEN LOAD . . — . 2 TO AUTUMN/PS — 18
UNLOCK HEAVN'S GOLDEN GATES AND ISSUE FORTH . . . . . — . 3 TO MORNING/PS — 2
WHERE ALL HIS GOLDEN PLEASURES GROW . . . . — . 6 HOW SWEET/PS — 8
AND SHUT ME IN HIS GOLDEN CAGE . . . . — . 6 HOW SWEET/PS — 12
THEN STRETCHES OUT MY GOLDEN WING . . . . — . 6 HOW SWEET/PS — 15
THOU THE GOLDEN FRUIT DOST BEAR . . . . — . 7 LOVE HARMNY/PS — 9
GOLDEN APOLLO THAT THRO HEAVEN WIDE . . . . — . 14 IMIT SPEN/PS — 1
THY GOLDEN ROD THROWN ON THE DUSTY FLOOR . . . . . . — . 15 IMIT SPEN/PS — 29
WITH HIS WHITE WINGS AND SEES HIS GOLDEN LONDON . . . — . 19 EDW THIRD/PS 2 — 10
LIKE SUMMER BEES AND ALL THE GOLDEN CITIES . . . . . — . 19 EDW THIRD/PS 2 — 13
INTO THE BATTLE SHAKING HIS GOLDEN LOCKS . . . . . . — . 21 EDW THIRD/PS 3 — 4
I SEE THEE BLOW THY GOLDEN TRUMPET WHILE . . . . . . — . 26 EDW THIRD/PS 3 — 208
AND RAISE HER GOLDEN HEAD EXULTINGLY . . . . — 34C KING JOHN/PS — PROSE
[THE GOLDEN SUN HIS MIGHTY RACE BEGAN] . . . . — 40D THEN SHE BORE — PROSE
& GOLDEN PLEASURES BEAM AROUND MY HEAD WHY GRIEF DOST THOU ACCOST ME — 43B WOE CRIED MUSE — PROSE
IN MATRIMONY'S GOLDEN CAGE . . . . — . 56 HAIL MATRIM/IM — 27
("SIN AND DESTRUCTION OF ORDER...") A GOLDEN SENTENCE . . — 65D ANNO LAVATER — MARG
[CAN WISDOM BE PUT IN A SILVER ROD OR LOVE IN A GOLDEN BOWL] — 110 TIRIEL 8 — 18
FLOWD HIS GOLDEN HAIR . . . . — 114 LIT GRL FND/SI — 39
AND ROUND MY GOLDEN TENT LIKE LAMBS REJOICE . . . . . — 125 LIT BLK BOY/SI — 20
OR LOVE IN A GOLDEN BOWL . . . . — 127 THELS MOTTO/BT — 4
THY WINE DOTH PURIFY THE GOLDEN HONEY THY PERFUME . . . — 128 BOOK OF THEL 2 — 8
THE CLOUD THEN SHEWD HIS GOLDEN HEAD & HIS BRIGHT FORM EMERGD — 128 BOOK OF THEL 3 — 5
O VIRGIN KNOWST THOU NOT OUR STEEDS DRINK OF THE GOLDEN SPRINGS — 128 BOOK OF THEL 3 — 7
TILL WE ARISE LINKD IN A GOLDEN BAND AND NEVER PART . . . — 128 BOOK OF THEL 3 — 15
SLEEPING AT MIDNIGHT IN MY GOLDEN TOWER . . . . — 140 FRENCH REVOLTN — 129
 . . . THE STRONG DUKE HIS SWORD TO ITS GOLDEN SCABBARD RETURND — 143 FRENCH REVOLTN — 195
GOLDEN ROCKS TILL WE DISCOVERD TWO GLOBES OF CRIMSON FIRE — 156C MARRIAGE HH 17 — PROSE
GOLDEN SPAIN BURST THE BARRIERS OF OLD ROME . . . . . — 159A SONG LIBERTY — PROSE
WHILE THE MORNING PLUMES HER GOLDEN BREAST . . . . . — 160A SONG LIBERTY — PROSE
DOWN THE GOLDEN HINGES TORE . . . . — 163 I SAW CHAPEL/N — 9
THE GOLDEN NYMPH REPLIED PLUCK THOU MY FLOWER OOTHOON THE MILD — 189 V DAU ALBION 1 — 8
CAN NEVER PASS AWAY SHE CEASD & CLOSD HER GOLDEN SHRINE — 189 V DAU ALBION 1 — 10
FROM NIGHTLY PREY AND LIFTS HIS GOLDEN BEAK TO THE PURE EAST — 190 V DAU ALBION 2 — 26
BECAUSE FROM THEIR BRIGHT SUMMITS YOU MAY PASS TO THE GOLDEN WORLD — 200 AMERICA 10 — 7
RENT OFF THEIR ROBES TO THE HUNGRY WIND & THREW THEIR GOLDEN SCEPTERS — 200 AMERICA 12 — 3
THAT PLAY AROUND THE GOLDEN ROOFS IN WREATHS OF FIERCE DESIRE — 202 AMERICA 15 — 21
SEEKING AFTER THAT SWEET GOLDEN CLIME . . . . — 215 AH SUNFLOWR/SE — 3
WITH GOLDEN HOOKS FASTEND IN THE PILLARS . . . . . . — 231 URIZEN 19 — 7
HE FORMED GOLDEN COMPASSES . . . . — 234 URIZEN 20 — 39
BUT EACH RAMPING HIS GOLDEN MANE SHAKES . . . . . . — 240 EUROPE 8 — 11
ALONG THE INFINITE SHORES OF THAMES TO GOLDEN VERULAM . . — 241 EUROPE 10 — 5
WERE BENDED DOWNWARD AND THE NOSTRILS GOLDEN GATES SHUT — 241 EUROPE 10 — 14
THY GOLDEN WINGS ARE MY DELIGHT & THY FLAMES OF SOFT DELUSION — 244 EUROPE 14 — 8
ON GOLDEN CHARIOTS RAGING WITH RED WHEELS DROPPING WITH BLOOD — 245 EUROPE 15 — 5
WHERE IS MY GOLDEN PALACE . . . . — . 254 AHANIA 5 — 3
THEY POUR UPON THE GOLDEN SHORE BESIDE THE SILENT OCEAN — 273 FOUR ZOAS 1 — 345

	PAGE	TITLE	LINE

GOLDEN   (CONTINUED)

FILLD WITH THE WINE OF ANGUISH WAITED AT THE GOLDEN FEAST   273 FOUR ZOAS 1   348
. . . & [THE] GOLDEN DAY [?DESCENDED] DESCENDING . .   274 FOUR ZOAS 1   * 366
WHERE ENION CRAVES SUCCESSIVE DRAWN INTO THE GOLDEN FEAST   274 FOUR ZOAS 1   373
THIS WAS THE LAMENTATION CF ENION ROUND THE GOLDEN FEAST   277 FOUR ZOAS 1   461
[WHEN WILT THOU SMILE ON THARMAS O THOU BRINGER OF GOLDEN   SUPP FOUR ZOAS 1   *
    DAY]
[ORBITS HIGH][DEMONS BY THE THOUSANDS OUT OF A GOLDEN   SUPP FOUR ZOAS 1   *
    CLOUD XXX]
AND ALL ITS GOLDEN PORCHES GREW PALE WITH HIS SICKENING   280 FOUR ZOAS 2   13
    LIGHT
THE GOLDEN COMPASSES THE QUADRANT & THE RULE & BALANCE . .   281 FOUR ZOAS 2   29
AND ALL THE TIME IN CAVERNS SHUT THE GOLDEN LOOMS ERECTED   284 FOUR ZOAS 2   145
THEY BEAR THE WOVEN DRAPERIES ON GOLDEN HOOKS THEY HANG   284 FOUR ZOAS 2   152
    ABROAD
THE [GOLDEN] WONDROUS BUILDING & [?HALLS OF] . . . . .   284 FOUR ZOAS 2   * 174
THE GOLDEN HALL OF URIZEN WHOSE WESTERN SIDE GLOWD BRIGHT   284 FOUR ZOAS 2   179
UPON HIS GOLDEN HALL & SOUGHT THE LABYRINTHINE PORCHES . .   285 FOUR ZOAS 2   185
A GOLDEN ALTAR BURNT PERFUMES WITH ART CELESTIAL FORMD . .   285 FOUR ZOAS 2   190
IN [SONGS & JOY] SORROW & CARE A GOLDEN WORLD . . . . .   286 FOUR ZOAS 2   * 241
A WONDROUS GOLDEN BUILDING MANY A WINDOW MANY A DOOR . .   286 FOUR ZOAS 2   243
THUS WERE THE STARS OF HEAVEN CREATED LIKE A GOLDEN CHAIN   287 FOUR ZOAS 2   266
AT THE FIRST SOUND THE GOLDEN SUN ARISES FROM THE DEEP . .   289 FOUR ZOAS 2   344
THE GOLDEN SUN BEARS ON MY SONG   . . . .   289 FOUR ZOAS 2   347
. . . THE GOLDEN HEAVENS TREMBLE   . . . .   290 FOUR ZOAS 2   386
SPREAD THRO HER GOLDEN FRAME SHE ROSE UP EER THE DAWN OF   291 FOUR ZOAS 2   420
    DAY
GOLDEN & BEAUTIFUL BUT O HOW UNLIKE THOSE SWEET FIELDS   292 FOUR ZOAS 3   39
    OF BLISS
IN GOLDEN WREATHES THE SORROW OF MAN & THE BALMY DROPS   293 FOUR ZOAS 3   67
    FELL DOWN
THE GOLDEN MOTH BUILDS THERE A HOUSE & SPREADS HER SILKEN   308 FOUR ZOAS 5   134
    BED
SPIRITS OF STRENGTH [REJOICE] IN PALACES REJOICE IN GOLDEN   308 FOUR ZOAS 5   140
    ARMOUR
HE GAVE TO ME A SILVER SCEPTER & CROWND ME WITH A GOLDEN   310 FOUR ZOAS 5   220
    CROWN
WHEN THOU DIDST BEAR THE GOLDEN CUP AT THE IMMORTAL TABLES   311 FOUR ZOAS 5   228
. . . THAT THEY MIGHT RUN IN THY GOLDEN CHARIOT OF PRIDE   311 FOUR ZOAS 5   235
VESTS OF THE RADIANT COLOURS OF HEAVEN & CROWNS OF GOLDEN   312 FOUR ZOAS 6   28
    FIRE
AS A GOLDEN ASCENT WINDING ROUND TO THE HEAVENS OF HEAVENS   318 FOUR ZOAS 6   250
HERE BOUND TO FIERY MANGERS FURIOUS DASH THEIR GOLDEN HOOFS   320 FOUR ZOAS 7   7
THE PLOW OF AGES & THE GOLDEN HARROW WADE THRO FIELDS . .   320 FOUR ZOAS 7   14
MY GOLDEN LIPS NOR TOOK THE BAR FROM ENITHARMON'S BREAST   326 FOUR ZOAS 7   238
ALL HEAVEN THEY SAW HIM DARK THEY BUILT A GOLDEN WALL .   326 FOUR ZOAS 7   242
NOR COULD THEY EVER BE CLOSD AGAIN THE GOLDEN HINGES WERE   328 FOUR ZOAS 7   324
    BROKEN
[NOW] CLOTHE YOURSELVES IN GOLDEN ARMS BROTHERS OF WAR . .   337 FOUR ZOAS 7B   163
SCATTER THE BLOOD FROM THY GOLDEN BROW . . . .   338 FOUR ZOAS 7B   194
HOW RAGD THE GOLDEN HORSES OF URIZEN BOUND TO THE CHARIOT   338 FOUR ZOAS 7B   201
    OF LOVE
AND THE STRONG LION DEIGND IN HIS MOUTH TO WEAR THE GOLDEN   340 FOUR ZOAS 7B   282
    BIT
IN GOLDEN LETTERS ORNAMENTED WITH SWEET LABOURS OF LOVE   340 FOUR ZOAS 7B   294
MY MILK OF COWS & HONEY OF BEES & FRUIT OF GOLDEN HARVEST   359 FOUR ZOAS 9   104
ON THE GOLDEN PALACE SONGS & JOY ON THE DESART THE COLD   363 FOUR ZOAS 9   251
    BABE
THEN FOLLOWS THE GOLDEN HARROW IN THE MIDST OF MENTAL FIRES   366 FOUR ZOAS 9   335
AND THUS THEIR ANCIENT GOLDEN AGE RENEWD FOR LUVAH SPOKE   367 FOUR ZOAS 9   386
WITH VOICE MILD FROM HIS GOLDEN CLOUD UPON THE BREATH OF   367 FOUR ZOAS 9   387
    MORNING
HOW CLEAR THE SPRING OF THE ROCK RUNNING AMONG THE GOLDEN   369 FOUR ZOAS 9   448
    SAND
AND ON THE RIVER'S MARGIN SHE UNGIRDED HER GOLDEN GIRDLE   369 FOUR ZOAS 9   480
WHEN WILT THOU SMILE ON THARMAS O THOU BRINGER OF GOLDEN   370 FOUR ZOAS 9   493
    DAY
AND SHE AROSE OUT OF THE RIVER & GIRDED ON HER GOLDEN   370 FOUR ZOAS 9   * 504
    GIRDLE
THE CHILDREN WOKE & SMILD ON VALA SHE KNEELD BY THE GOLDEN   371 FOUR ZOAS 9   523
    COUCH
INTO THE SEA OF THARMAS SOON RENEWD A GOLDEN MOTH . . .   373 FOUR ZOAS 9   598
AND MANY ETERNAL MEN SAT AT THE GOLDEN FEAST TO SEE . . .   373 FOUR ZOAS 9   621
THE SONG AROSE TO THE GOLDEN FEAST THE ETERNAL MAN REJOICD   375 FOUR ZOAS 9   692
HIS GOLDEN FOOD AND IN THE EVENING SLEEP BEFORE THE DOOR   376 FOUR ZOAS 9   708
HIS SONS ARISING FROM THE FEAST WITH GOLDEN BASKETS FOLLOW   376 FOUR ZOAS 9   714
TO THE GOLDEN WHEELS CIRCLING UPON THE PAVEMENT OF HEAVEN   376 FOUR ZOAS 9   719
    & ALL
THE VILLAGES OF LUVAH RING THE GOLDEN TILES OF THE VILLAGES   376 FOUR ZOAS 9   720
THEN THARMAS & URTHONA ROSE FROM THE GOLDEN FEAST SATIATED   377 FOUR ZOAS 9   774
ROSE FROM THE FEAST IN JOY ASCENDING TO THEIR GOLDEN LOOMS   378 FOUR ZOAS 9   779
RANG SWEET THE PRAISE OF INDUSTRY THRO ALL THE GOLDEN ROOMS   378 FOUR ZOAS 9   781
IN GOLDEN & IN SILVER BASKETS IN HEAVENS OF PRECIOUS STONE   379 FOUR ZOAS 9   823
IN ALL HIS ANCIENT STRENGTH TO FORM THE GOLDEN ARMOUR OF   379 FOUR ZOAS 9   853
    SCIENCE
. . . GOLDEN ROCKS RISE FROM THE [(VORTEX)] VAST . . . .   381 FOUR ZOAS AD 5 * 10
. . . ENION BROODED GROANING THE GOLDEN ROCKS VEGETATE   381 FOUR ZOAS AD 5   14
    THE (?VORTEX)]
THEY BORE A NET OF GOLDEN TWINE   . . . .   422 BENEATH/N   10
BORE THE GOLDEN NET ALOFT   . . . .   422 BENEATH/N   20
THE GOLDEN NET . . . .   424A THE GOLDEN NET   TITLE
THEY BORE A NET OF GOLDEN TWINE   . . . .   424 THE GOLDEN NET   9

821

		PAGE	TITLE	LINE

GOLDEN   (CONTINUED)

Entry	PAGE	TITLE	LINE
BORE THE GOLDEN NET ALOFT	424	THE GOLDEN NET	19
OR AGAIN DOES RETURN THE GOLDEN TIMES	428	MARY	6
AND LOCKD ME UP WITH A GOLDEN KEY	429	CRYSTL CABINET	4
IN HER MILD HAND THE GOLDEN KEYS	442	DEDICATN BLAIR	6
THE GRAVE IS HEAVEN'S GOLDEN GATE	442	DEDICATN BLAIR	7
AT LENGTH STANDING UPON THE GOLDEN FLOOR OF PALAMABRON	492	MILTON 11	34
IN BRIGHT CATHEDRON'S GOLDEN DOME WITH CARE & LOVE & TEARS	512	MILTON 26	36
THE AMBITIOUS SPIDER IN HIS SULLEN WEB THE LUCKY GOLDEN SPINNER	513	MILTON 27	15
OR FINE WAX TO MOULD ARTFUL A MODEL FOR GOLDEN ORNAMENTS	515	MILTON 28	15
FORM IMMORTAL WITH GOLDEN PEN SUCH AS THE SPECTRE ADMIRING	515	MILTON 28	17
AND EVERY HOUR HAS A BRIGHT GOLDEN GATE CARVED WITH SKILL	516	MILTON 28	51
TOWARDS AMERICA INDIA ROSE UP FROM HIS GOLDEN BED	519	MILTON 31	14
[THE GOLDEN RULE]	540C	GOLDEN RULE/N	*TITLE
HE HAS OBSERVD THE GOLDEN RULE	540	GOLDEN RULE/N	1
TILL HES BECOME THE GOLDEN FOOL	540	GOLDEN RULE/N	2
[HE] YOU ALL [HIS] YOUR YOUTH [OBSERVES] OBSERVD THE GOLDEN RULE	540	S(TOTHAR)D/N	* 1
TILL [HES] YOURE AT LAST BECOME THE [OLD] GOLDEN FOOL	540	S(TOTHAR)D/N	* 2
AND THIS THE PRINCES GOLDEN RULE	547	LET BE TOLD/N	4
I [HAVE GIVN] GIVE YOU THE END OF A GOLDEN STRING	551	GIVE YOU END/N	* 1
...MAY...FOUND THE WORD GOLDEN	556C	FOUND WORD/N	PROSE
IN MY GOLDEN HOUSE ON HIGH	558	THE CAVERNS/N	19
SHALL THE GOLDEN AGE RETURN BUT ALAS YOU WILL NOT EASILY	570C	DESC CAT 3	PROSE
THE GREAT AND GOLDEN RULE OF ART AS WELL AS OF LIFE IS THIS	585B	DESC CAT 15	PROSE
ENDEAVOUR TO RESTORE WHAT THE ANCIENTS CALLD THE GOLDEN AGE	605D	V LAST JUDG/N	PROSE
APULEIUS'S GOLDEN ASS & OVID'S METAMORPHOSIS &	607A	V LAST JUDG/N	PROSE
THE MALE IS A FURNACE OF BERYLL THE FEMALE IS A GOLDEN LOOM	623	JERUSALEM 5	34
WHAT ARE THOSE GOLDEN BUILDERS DOING WHERE WAS THE BURYING-PLACE	632	JERUSALEM 12	25
THE SOUTH A GOLDEN GATE HAS FOUR LIONS TERRIBLE LIVING	633	JERUSALEM 13	2
SURROUNDS LUBAN LOS'S PALACE & THE GOLDEN LOOMS OF CATHEDRON	633	JERUSALEM 13	25
HAVE A BEAUTIFUL GOLDEN GATE WHICH OPENS INTO THE VEGETATIVE WORLD	635	JERUSALEM 14	20
HIS MILK OF COWS & HONEY OF BEES & FRUIT OF GOLDEN HARVEST	641	JERUSALEM 19	5
WITH CUSH HIS SON & TOOK ME DOWN HE IN A GOLDEN ARK	644	JERUSALEM 22	4
AMONG HER GOLDEN PILLARS HIGH	650	FIELDS FROM/J	10
AMONG HER GOLDEN ARCHES WHICH	650	FIELDS FROM/J	11
WHAT ARE THOSE GOLDEN BUILDERS DOING	650	FIELDS FROM/J	25
AND THE DRUIDS GOLDEN KNIFE	650	FIELDS FROM/J	30
IN ALL THE GARDEN OF EDEN & IN ALL THE GOLDEN MOUNTAINS	652	JERUSALEM 28	2
IN GOLDEN WREATHES THE SORROW OF MAN & THE BALMY DROPS FELL DOWN	654	JERUSALEM 29	54
BOWEN ALBION'S SONS THEY BORE HIM A GOLDEN COUCH INTO THE PORCH	658	JERUSALEM 32	12
THE GOLDEN GATE OF HAVILAH AND ALL THE GARDEN OF GOD	679	JERUSALEM 49	15
CURBING THEIR TYGERS WITH GOLDEN BITS & BRIDLES OF SILVER & IVORY	686	JERUSALEM 55	35
THEY PLOWD IN TEARS THE TRUMPETS SOUNDED BEFORE THE GOLDEN PLOW	687	JERUSALEM 55	54
TO THE GOLDEN LOOM OF LOVE TO THE MOTH-LABOURD WOOF	688	JERUSALEM 56	13
A WONDROUS GOLDEN BUILDING IMMENSE WITH ORNAMENTS SUBLIME	691	JERUSALEM 59	24
IS BRIGHT CATHEDRON'S GOLDEN HALL ITS COURTS TOWERS & PINNACLES	691	JERUSALEM 59	25
SCATTER THE BLOOD FROM THY GOLDEN BROW	700	JERUSALEM 65	40
HOW RAGD THE GOLDEN HORSES OF URIZEN COMPELLD TO THE CHARIOT OF LOVE	700	JERUSALEM 65	47
FIBRES OF LIFE TO WEAVE FOR EVERY FEMALE IS A GOLDEN LOOM	704	JERUSALEM 67	4
BENEATH & PIERCED IT THRO THE MIDST WITH A GOLDEN PIN	705	JERUSALEM 67	42
SUCH ARE CATHEDRON'S GOLDEN HALLS IN THE CITY OF GOLGONOOZA	713	JERUSALEM 73	1
LONG TO TELL & OF THE IRON ROLLERS GOLDEN AXLE-TREES & YOKES	713	JERUSALEM 73	9
I GIVE YOU THE END OF A GOLDEN STRING	716	I GIVE YOU/J	1
I SLEPT IN HIS GOLDEN HILLS THE LAMB OF GOD MET ME THERE	720	JERUSALEM 79	41
THY GOLDEN MOUNTAINS WHERE MY CHERUBIM & SERAPHIM REJOICD	721	JERUSALEM 79	54
THE GOLDEN CORDS OF THE LOOMS ANIMATE BENEATH THEIR TOUCHES SOFT	725	JERUSALEM 82	14
SWIFT TURN THE SILVER SPINDLES & THE GOLDEN WEIGHTS PLAY SOFT	728	JERUSALEM 83	* 69
PUTTING ON HIS GOLDEN SANDALS TO WALK FROM MOUNTAIN TO MOUNTAIN	728	JERUSALEM 83	76
AMONG THE GOLDEN LOOMS OF CATHEDRON SENDING FIBRES OF LOVE	731	JERUSALEM 86	40
FIBRES OF LIFE OUT FROM THE BONES INTO HER GOLDEN LOOM	736	JERUSALEM 90	22
FOR THE MALE IS A FURNACE OF BERYLL THE FEMALE IS A GOLDEN LOOM	736	JERUSALEM 90	27
& ITS GOLDEN CORDS & PINS	757	EV GOSPEL(I)/N	22
HEAVEN OPENS HERE ON ALL SIDES HER GOLDEN GATES	802A	LETTER 14	PROSE
AND GOLDEN DEMONS THAT NONE CAN STAY	817	HAPPINESS/L	12
MY ARROWS GLOW IN THEIR GOLDEN SHEAVES	818	HAPPINESS/L	80

GOLDEN CLAD

Entry	PAGE	TITLE	LINE
GENEROUS IMMORTAL GUARDIAN GOLDEN CLAD FOR CITIES	665	JERUSALEM 38	46

GOLDEN HOOFD

Entry	PAGE	TITLE	LINE
STILL ALL YOUR THUNDERS GOLDEN HOOFD & BIND YOUR HORSES BLACK	244	EUROPE 14	28

GOLDEN-SQUARE,GOLDEN SQUARE

Entry	PAGE	TITLE	LINE
AT NO...CORNER OF BROAD STREET GOLDEN-SQUARE	560C	EXHIBITION ADV	PROSE
AT NO...CORNER OF BROAD-STREET GOLDEN-SQUARE	562A	DESC CAT ADV	TITLE
AT N...CORNER OF BROAD STREET GOLDEN SQUARE	563A	DESC CAT	*TITLE
FOR J BLAKE...BROAD-STREET GOLDEN-SQUARE	563B	DESC CAT	PROSE

822

	PAGE	TITLE	LINE
GOLDEN-SQUARE (CONTINUED)			
GOLDEN-SQUARE WHERE THE PICTURE IS NOW EXHIBITING . . .	587B CHAUCER 1		PROSE
SUBSCRIPTIONS RECEIVED AT NO...CORNER OF BROAD STREET	590D CHAUCER 2		PROSE
GOLDEN SQUARE			
GOLDFINCH			
[THE NIGHTINGALE THE GOLDFINCH ROBIN LARK LINNET & THRUSH]	270 FOUR ZOAS 1		207
THE THRUSH THE LINNET & THE GOLDFINCH ROBIN & THE WREN . .	520 MILTON 31		40
GOLDSMITH			
SUCH MEN AS GOLDSMITH OUGHT NOT TO HAVE BEEN ACQUAINTED	450D ANNO REYNOLDS		MARG
WITH			
NAMELY A GOLDSMITH FOR SO THE PROSPECTUS TELLS US . . .	575B DESC CAT 3		PROSE
WHY HE HAS INTRODUCED A GOLDSMITH AND WHAT IS THE WIT OF IT	575B DESC CAT 3		PROSE
("REYNOLDS JOHNSON BURKE") [?OLIVER GOLDSMITH ?NEVER	SUPP ANNO REYNOLDS		* MARG
?SHOULD ?HAVE]			
GOLGONOOZA			
HE BUILDED GOLGONOOZA ON THE LAKE OF UDAN ADAN . . .	307 FOUR ZOAS 5		76
BUT WHEN RETURND TO GOLGONOOZA LOS & ENITHARMON	309 FOUR ZOAS 5		143
WHEN SATIATED WITH GRIEF THEY RETURND BACK TO GOLGONOOZA	309 FOUR ZOAS 5		176
THEY BUILDED GOLGONOOZA LOS LABOURING [INSPIRD] BUILDED	329 FOUR ZOAS 7		* 378
PILLARS HIGH			
LOS SAT IN GOLGONOOZA IN THE GATE OF LUBAN WHERE . . .	331 FOUR ZOAS 7		433
THEN I CAN SIGH FORTH ON THE WINDS OF GOLGONOOZA PITEOUS	331 FOUR ZOAS 7		451
FORMS			
AND DRAWING THEM FORTH DELIGHTED UPON THE WINDS OF	331 FOUR ZOAS 7		460
GOLGONOOZA			
OF GOLGONOOZA LOS STOOD [AT THE GATE] RECIEVING THEM . .	341 FOUR ZOAS 8		31
IN GOLGONOOZA LOOKING DOWN THE DAUGHTERS OF BEULAH SAW . .	342 FOUR ZOAS 8		42
LOS BUILDS THE WALLS OF GOLGONOOZA AGAINST THE STIRRING	343 FOUR ZOAS 8		109
BATTLE			
?FEELING THE HAND OF LOS IN GOLGONOOZA & THE FORCE . . .	344 FOUR ZOAS 8		112
IN GOLGONOOZA LOS'S ANVILS STAND & HIS FURNACES RAGE . .	346 FOUR ZOAS 8		202
EASTWARD OF GOLGONOOZA STANDS THE LAKE OF [?UAAN] UDAN	346 FOUR ZOAS 8		* 224
ADAM IN			
CUT HIM OFF FROM GOLGONOOZA BUT ENITHARMON IN TEARS . . .	350 FOUR ZOAS 8		370
OF GOLGONOOZA HER WELL BELOVED KNOWING HE WAS ORC'S HUMAN	351 FOUR ZOAS 8		384
REMAINS			
RINTRAH & PALAMABRON CUT SHEER OFF FROM GOLGONOOZA . . .	351 FOUR ZOAS 8		394
THEY BUILDED GREAT GOLGONOOZA TIMES ON TIMES AGES ON AGES	483 MILTON 3		39
JAMES CALLS FOR FIRES IN GOLGONOOZA FOR HEAPS OF SMOKING	485 MILTON 5		40
RUINS			
FROM GOLGONOOZA THE SPIRITUAL FOUR-FOLD LONDON ETERNAL . .	485 MILTON 6		1
BUT TRAVELLERS TO ETERNITY PASS INWARD TO GOLGONOOZA . .	498 MILTON 17		30
GATES OPEN BEHIND SATAN'S SEAT TO THE CITY OF GOLGONOOZA	502 MILTON 20		39
RINTRAH AND PALAMABRON MET US AT THE GATE OF GOLGONOOZA	505 MILTON 22		27
STILL MY FOUR MIGHTY ONES ARE LEFT TO ME IN GOLGONOOZA .	508 MILTON 24		10
BECAUSE OF SATAN BEFORE LUBAN IN THE CITY OF GOLGONOOZA	509 MILTON 24		49
BUT GOLGONOOZA IS NAMD ART & MANUFACTURE BY MORTAL MEN .	509 MILTON 24		50
AND LOUD THE SOULS HOWL ROUND THE PORCHES OF GOLGONOOZA	510 MILTON 25		12
AND IN THE CITY OF GOLGONOOZA & IN LUBAN & AROUND . .	512 MILTON 26		24
BUT THE WINE-PRESS OF LOS IS EASTWARD OF GOLGONOOZA BEFORE	513 MILTON 27		1
THE SEAT			
AROUND THE CITY OF GOLGONOOZA IN THE FORESTS OF ENTUTHON	514 MILTON 27		43
GREAT GOLGONOOZA FREE FROM THE FOUR IRON PILLARS OF SATAN'S	517 MILTON 29		48
THRONE			
IN LOS'S HALLS CONTINUAL LABOURING IN THE FURNACES	520 MILTON 31		26
OF GOLGONOOZA			
COULD NOT BEHOLD GOLGONOOZA WITHOUT PASSING THE POLYPUS	525 MILTON 35		19
FOR GOLGONOOZA CANNOT BE SEEN TILL HAVING PASSD THE POLYPUS	525 MILTON 35		22
OF CRYSTAL FLOWING INTO TWO STREAMS ONE FLOWS THRO	526 MILTON 35		50
GOLGONOOZA			
MEETING AGAIN IN GOLGONOOZA BEYOND SATAN'S SEAT . . .	526 MILTON 35		53
BESIDE THE FOUNT ABOVE THE LARK'S NEST IN GOLGONOOZA . .	526 MILTON 35		58
GATE OF WIDE GOLGONOOZA & THE LARK IS LOS'S MESSENGER . .	526 MILTON 35		67
IN THE EAST GATE OF GOLGONOOZA & THE TWENTY-EIGHTH BRIGHT	527 MILTON 36		9
THE MUNDANE SHELL IN GOLGONOOZA BUT THE FIRES OF LOS RAGE	529 MILTON 37		56
WHILE I WRITE OF THE BUILDING OF GOLGONOOZA	623 JERUSALEM 5		24
THEY WAR TO DESTROY THE FURNACES TO DESOLATE GOLGONOOZA	623 JERUSALEM 5		29
THEREFORE LOS STANDS IN LONDON BUILDING GOLGONOOZA . . .	629 JERUSALEM 10		17
WITH IRON & BRASS BUILDING GOLGONOOZA IN GREAT CONTENDINGS	630 JERUSALEM 10		63
AND THEY BUILDED GOLGONOOZA TERRIBLE ETERNAL LABOUR . .	631 JERUSALEM 12		24
THE GREAT CITY OF GOLGONOOZA FOURFOLD TOWARD THE NORTH .	632 JERUSALEM 12		46
AND THE NORTH GATE OF GOLGONOOZA TOWARD GENERATION . .	632 JERUSALEM 12		61
AROUND GOLGONOOZA LIES THE LAND OF DEATH ETERNAL A LAND	633 JERUSALEM 13		30
GOLGONOOZA LOS WALKS ROUND THE WALLS NIGHT AND DAY . . .	634 JERUSALEM 13		55
HE VIEWS THE CITY OF GOLGONOOZA & ITS SMALLER CITIES . .	634 JERUSALEM 13		56
IN ENTUTHON BENYTHON'S DEEP VALES BENEATH GOLGONOOZA . .	635 JERUSALEM 14		34
HERE ON THE BANKS OF THE THAMES LOS BUILDED GOLGONOOZA . .	684 JERUSALEM 53		15
ALL THESE CENTER IN LONDON & IN GOLGONOOZA FROM WHENCE . .	712 JERUSALEM 72		28
SUCH ARE CATHEDRON'S GOLDEN HALLS IN THE CITY OF GOLGONOOZA	713 JERUSALEM 73		1
WITH THE INNUMERABLE MULTITUDES OF GOLGONOOZA ROUND THE	713 JERUSALEM 73		6
ANVILS			
THE CONCAVE EARTH ROUND GOLGONOOZA IN ENTUTHON BENYTHON	719 JERUSALEM 78		17
SOMETIMES IT SHALL ASSIMILATE WITH MIGHTY GOLGONOOZA . .	728 JERUSALEM 83		43
WHILE LOS AROSE UPON HIS WATCH AND DOWN FROM GOLGONOOZA	728 JERUSALEM 83		75
FROM GOLGONOOZA WITH SWEET VISIONS FOR JERUSALEM WANDERER	731 JERUSALEM 86		41
OF BEULAH FOR JERUSALEM & SHILOH IN IMMORTAL GOLGONOOZA	731 JERUSALEM 86		44
IN GOLGONOOZA & IN UDAN-ADAN & IN ENTUTHON OF URIZEN . .	734 JERUSALEM 88		48
AND FROM THE GREAT CITY OF GOLGONOOZA IN THE SHADOWY	746 JERUSALEM 98		55
GENERATION			
GOLGONOOZA'S			
IN GOLGONOOZA'S FURNACES AMONG THE ANVILS OF TIME AND SPACE	345 FOUR ZOAS 8		186

```
                                                         PAGE    TITLE        LINE

GOLGOTHA
     EVER WEEPING PADDINGTON IS THAT CALVARY AND GOLGOTHA    .  .   632 JERUSALEM 12      28
     WHO GIVE THEMSELVES IN GOLGOTHA VICTIMS TO JUSTICE WHERE      665 JERUSALEM 38      54
     THE DEAD BENEATH BEULAH FROM TYBURN TO GOLGOTHA AND FROM      698 JERUSALEM 63      33
     OF THE DRUID ALONG THE VALLEY OF REPHAIM FROM CAMBERWELL      740 JERUSALEM 92      26
        TO GOLGOTHA
GOLTZIUS
     THAN ALB DURER GOLTZIUS SADELER OR EDELINCK BUT              594C PUB ADDRESS/N  PROSE
        I DO PRETEND
GOMORRA
     WHOSE CURRENTS FLOW INTO THE DEAD SEA BY SODOM & GOMORRA     735 JERUSALEM 89      27
GOMORRHA
     BUT BELIAL OF SODOM & GOMORRHA OBSCURE DEMON OF BRIBES  .  .  528 MILTON 37        30
     TO SODOM & GOMORRHA THENCE TO INDIA CHINA & JAPAN    .  .  .  704 JERUSALEM 67      40
GON
     SOTHA MYDON ELLAYOL NATHO GON HARHATH SATAN    .  .  .  .  .  350 FOUR ZOAS 8      359
GONE      SEE A-GONE
     GO PETER GET YOU GONE  .  .  .  .  .  .  .  .  .  .  .  .  .   29D EDW THIRD/PS 4  PROSE
     FAREWELL MY TIME IS GONE  .  .  .  .  .  .  .  .  .  .  .  .   43D WOE CRIED MUSE  PROSE
     THEN COME HOME MY CHILDREN THE SUN IS GONE DOWN  .  .  .  .   60 NURSES SONG/IM      5
     BUT FAR HE HAD NOT GONE WHEN IJIM FROM HIS WOODS COME DOWN   103 TIRIEL 4        *   3
     GONE WAS ALL THEIR CARE  .  .  .  .  .  .  .  .  .  .  .  .   114 LIT GRL FND/SI     40
     THEN COME HOME MY CHILDREN THE SUN IS GONE DOWN  .  .  .  .   121 NURSES SONG/SI      5
     TILL OUR GRIEF IS FLED & GONE  .  .  .  .  .  .  .  .  .  .   123 ON ANOTHERS/SI     35
     DROPPING A TEAR THE OLD MAN HIS PLACE LEFT AND WHEN HE       139 FRENCH REVOLTN    121
        WAS GONE OUT
     FORSAKEN AND PARIS WITHOUT A SOLDIER SILENT FOR THE NOISE    148 FRENCH REVOLTN    305
        WAS GONE UP
     SOON AS SHE WAS GONE FROM ME  .  .  .  .  .  .  .  .  .  .   161 NEVER PAIN/N        9
     THEN COME HOME MY CHILDREN THE SUN IS GONE DOWN  .  .  .  .   171 NURSES SONG/N       5
     THEY ARE BOTH GONE UP TO CHURCH TO PRAY  .  .  .  .  .  .   180 CHIMNEY SWP/N       4
     AND ARE GONE TO PRAISE GOD & HIS PRIEST & KING  .  .  .  .   180 CHIMNEY SWP/N      11
     BECAUSE THE NIGHT IS GONE THAT CLOSD ME IN ITS DEADLY BLACK  191 V DAU ALBION 2     29
     THEY ARE BOTH GONE UP TO THE CHURCH TO PRAY  .  .  .  .  .   212 CHIMNEY SWP/SE      4
     AND ARE GONE TO PRAISE GOD & HIS PRIEST & KING  .  .  .  .   212 CHIMNEY SWP/SE     11
     THEN COME HOME MY CHILDREN THE SUN IS GONE DOWN  .  .  .  .   212 NURSES SONG/SE      5
     HOW IS THIS ALL MY HOPE IS GONE [ENION] FOR EVER FLED   .  .  297 FOUR ZOAS 4         9
     [ AND THARMAS ?SAID ALL MY HOPE I THOUGHT ENION FOR EVER    SUPP FOUR ZOAS 4     *
        GONE ]
     THE FORM OF ORC WAS GONE HE HEARD HIS SERPENT BULK AMONG     338 FOUR ZOAS 7B      215
     AND SHE IS GONE & HERE ALONE I WAR WITH DARKNESS & DEATH     339 FOUR ZOAS 7B      239
     BUT HER FLOCKS WERE GONE UP FROM BENEATH THE TREES INTO      369 FOUR ZOAS 9       473
        THE HILLS
     THE WORLD OF SHADOWS THRO THE AIR TILL WINTER IS OVER &      378 FOUR ZOAS 9       798
        GONE
     SIXTY AT MOST & THEN GONE  .  .  .  .  .  .  .  .  .  .  .  .409B ANNO BACON     MARG
     PROUD MARY S GONE MAD SAID THE CHILD IN THE STREET   .  .  .  428 MARY              34
     SATAN AH ME IS GONE TO HIS OWN PLACE SAID LOS THEIR GOD      491 MILTON 10          12
     FOR SORROW THAT [YOUR] OUR FRIEND BOB SCREWMUCH S GONE   .   537 AND HIS LEGS/N     47
     FOR SORROW THAT POOR JOHN THOMPSON'S GONE  .  .  .  .  .  .  545 AN EPITAPH/N        2
     TILL THE HEAVENS & EARTH ARE GONE  .  .  .  .  .  .  .  .  .  558 THE CAVERNS/N      10
     SHOULD I PITY IF I PITY NOT THE SINNER WHO IS GONE ASTRAY    657 JERUSALEM 31       35
     A DEWY GARMENT COVERS ME ALL OVER ALL MANHOOD IS GONE   .  .  660 JERUSALEM 34        4
     AWAY & MIGHTY HYLE & AFTER THEM JERUSALEM IS GONE AWAKE      729 JERUSALEM 83       87
     GONE SNEAKING INTO THE SYNAGOGUES  .  .  .  .  .  .  .  .  .  750 EV GOSPEL(C)/N     27
     GONE SNEAKING INTO SYNAGOGUES  .  .  .  .  .  .  .  .  .  .   752 EV GOSPEL(D)/N     61
     FROM GENERATED ORGANS GONE AS SOON AS COME  .  .  .  .  .  .  776D INSC LAOCOON   PROSE
     AND MY WIFE'S ILLNESS NOT BEING QUITE GONE OFF  .  .  .  .   807A LETTER 17       PROSE
     BANKS THE SCULPTOR IS GONE TO HIS ETERNAL HOME  .  .  .  .   859D LETTER 56       PROSE
     CIRENCESTER PLACE I FEARED YOU MIGHT BE GONE OR I MIGHT     871B LETTER 72       PROSE
     THAT (SHIVERING) FIT WHICH MUST BE AVOIDED TILL THE COLD    871B LETTER 74      *PROSE
        IS GONE
     & HAVE GREAT HOPES THAT THE DISEASE IS GONE  .  .  .  .  .   875C LETTER 81       PROSE
     SAY THAT HIS ILLNESS IS SO FAR FROM GONE THAT THE LEAST     SUPP LETTER 81A     *PROSE
        THING
     GONE AS THE FINE WEATHER IS VERY BENEFICIAL & COMFORTABLE   876A LETTER 83       PROSE
        TO ME
     FLAXMAN IS GONE & WE MUST ALL SOON FOLLOW EVERY ONE TO HIS  879A LETTER 88       PROSE
GONORILL
     GWENDOLEN RAGAN SABRINA GONORILL MEHETABEL CORDELLA  .  .  .  281 FOUR ZOAS 2       61
     GWINIVERRA & GWINEFRED & GONORILL & SABRINA BEAUTIFUL   .   624 JERUSALEM 5        43
     IS RAGAN SHE ADJOIND TO SLADE & PRODUCED GONORILL           710 JERUSALEM 71       33
        FAR BEAMING
     EMANATION GONORILL REJOICES OVER HILLS & ROCKS & WOODS      710 JERUSALEM 71       35
        & RIVERS
GOOD
     MY THOUGHTS TAKE IN THE GENRAL GOOD OF THE WHOLE   .  .  .    19 EDW THIRD/PS 2     29
     O MY GOOD LORD TRUE WISDOM DROPS LIKE HONEY  .  .  .  .  .    20 EDW THIRD/PS 2     36
     GOOD MORROW BRAVE SIR THOMAS THE BRIGHT MORN  .  .  .  .  .   21 EDW THIRD/PS 3      1
     GOOD MORROW GENERALS I GIVE YOU JOY  .  .  .  .  .  .  .  .   22 EDW THIRD/PS 3     43
     GOOD MORROW GENERALS WHEN ENGLISH COURAGE FAILS  .  .  .  .   23 EDW THIRD/PS 3     71
     AND BRINGS GOOD COUNSEL FROM THE BREAST OF LAUGHTER   .  .    24 EDW THIRD/PS 3    135
     IS DANGEROUS TO FIGHT NOT GOOD FOR FOOD  .  .  .  .  .  .  .   27 EDW THIRD/PS 3    266
     BUT HERE COMES ONE WHO IS AS ENTERTAINING AS A GOOD STORY    29B EDW THIRD/PS 4  PROSE
     LET THOSE THAT FIGHT FIGHT IN GOOD STEDFASTNESS  .  .  .  .   31 EDW THIRD/PS 5     37
     BRINGING GOOD NEWS OF SIN AND DEATH DESTROYED  .  .  .  .    37D SAMSON/PS       PROSE
     SO ONCE THE SUN HIS CHARIOT DREW BACK TO PROLONG A GOOD     41B THEN SHE BORE    PROSE
        KING'S LIFE
     BUT A MAN MUST HAVE GOOD SOUND SENSE TO SOLVE THEM   .  .    45D ISLAND MOON 1   PROSE
     BUT MY GOOD SIR VOLTAIRE WAS IMMERSED IN MATTER  .  .  .    45D ISLAND MOON 1   PROSE
     NO SAID MRS NANNICANTIPOT I THINK A PERSON MAY BE AS GOOD   48A ISLAND MOON 4   PROSE
        AT HOME
```

824

```
                                                           PAGE     TITLE         LINE
GOOD    (CONTINUED)
        & STAMP & KICK & SWEAT AND ALL FOR THE GOOD OF THEIR SOULS    48B  ISLAND MOON 4    PROSE
        SHALL DO THE WORLD MORE GOOD . . . . . . . . . .              51   WHEN CORRUP/IM     32
        [ALWAYS SPOILS GOOD COMPANY IN THIS MANNER & ITS A SHAME]     57A  ISLAND MOON 9    PROSE
        WAS NOT THIS A GOOD MAN . . . . . . . . . .                   57   TO BE OR/IM        25
        GOOD ENGLISH HOSPITALITY O THEN IT DID NOT FAIL  . . . .      58   THIS CITY/IM        4
        GOOD ENGLISH HOSPITALITY O THEN IT DID NOT FAIL  . . . .      58   THIS CITY/IM        8
        THE HUNGRY POOR ENTERD THE HALL TO EAT GOOD BEEF & ALE  . .   58   THIS CITY/IM       11
        GOOD ENGLISH HOSPITALITY O THEN IT DID NOT FAIL  . . . .      58   THIS CITY/IM       12
        PLAYD AT FORFEITS & TRYD EVERY METHOD TO GET GOOD HUMOUR      59B  ISLAND MOON 11   PROSE
        IVE A GOOD MIND TO GO . . . . . . . . . . . .                 60   SAY YOU JOE/IM      3
        A PAIR OF VERY GOOD EARS  . . . . . . . . . . .               62   DR CLASH/IM        14
        NOW I THINK WE SHOULD DO AS MUCH GOOD AS WE CAN               63A  ISLAND MOON 11   PROSE
        ("AS THE GOOD LOVE THEE THE BAD WILL HATE THEE") UNEASY       72D  ANNO LAVATER     MARG
        NOBLE BUT MARK ACTIVE EVIL IS BETTER THAN PASSIVE GOOD  . .   77B  ANNO LAVATER     MARG
        & THE OTHER CAPABLE OF GOOD . . . . . . . . . .               80A  ANNO LAVATER     MARG
        THAT WHICH IS CAPABLE OF GOOD IS NOT ALSO CAPABLE OF EVIL     80A  ANNO LAVATER     MARG
          BUT
        THAT WHICH IS CAPABLE OF EVIL IS ALSO CAPABLE OF GOOD         80A  ANNO LAVATER     MARG
          THIS APHORISM
        NOW BOTH EVIL & GOOD CANNOT EXIST IN A SIMPLE BEING  . . .    80A  ANNO LAVATER     MARG
        BUT IF MAN IS CONSIDERD AS ONLY EVIL & GOD ONLY GOOD  . .     80A  ANNO LAVATER     MARG
        HOW THEN IS REGENERATION EFFECTED WHICH TURNS THE EVIL        80A  ANNO LAVATER     MARG
          TO GOOD
        BY CASTING OUT THE EVIL BY THE GOOD SEE MATTHEW XII... .      80A  ANNO LAVATER     MARG
        ("NOT MUCH RECTITUDE IF UNEASY IN PRESENCE OF THE GOOD")      82C  ANNO LAVATER     MARG
          EASY
        ONLY GOOD HEARTS CAN OR DARE COURT  . . . . . . .            85B  ANNO LAVATER     MARG
        ("AVOID CHARACTERS WHOSE GOOD & BAD SIDES UNMIXED")          86D  ANNO LAVATER     MARG
          MOST EXCELLENT
        MAN IS BAD OR GOOD AS HE UNITES HIMSELF WITH BAD OR GOOD      88A  ANNO LAVATER     MARG
          SPIRITS
        THAT THIS BOOK IS WRITTEN BY CONSULTATION WITH GOOD SPIRITS   88B  ANNO LAVATER     MARG
        BECAUSE IT IS GOOD & THAT THE NAME LAVATER IS . . . . .       88B  ANNO LAVATER     MARG
        HIS LEADING VIRTUE & HIS GOOD ANGEL BUT . . . . . . .         88C  ANNO LAVATER     MARG
        THIS GOOD TO OTHERS OR BENEVOLENT UNDERSTANDING  . . . .      89B  ANNO SWED LOVE * MARG
        GOOD & EVIL ARE HERE BOTH GOOD & THE TWO CONTRARIES           91D  ANNO SWED LOVE   MARG
          MARRIED
        AND THE ANGEL TOLD TOM IF HED BE A GOOD BOY  . . . .          118  CHIMNEY SWP/SI     19
        UNDER EVERY GOOD IS A HELL I E HELL IS THE OUTWARD   . .      SUPP ANNO SWED HRLL * MARG
        FROM THESE CONTRARIES SPRING WHAT THE RELIGIOUS CALL GOOD     149B MARRIAGE HH 3    PROSE
          & EVIL
        GOOD IS THE PASSIVE THAT OBEYS REASON  . . . . . .           149B MARRIAGE HH 3    PROSE
        GOOD IS HEAVEN EVIL IS HELL . . . . . . . . . .              149B MARRIAGE HH 3    PROSE
        & THAT REASON CALLD GOOD IS ALONE FROM THE SOUL  . . . .     149C MARRIAGE HH 4    PROSE
        THE GOOD ARE ATTRACTED BY MEN'S PERCEPTIONS  . . . . .        183  MOTTO SONGS/N      1
        AND ALL HIS GOOD FRIENDS SHEW THEIR PRIVATE ENDS  . . . .     183  MOTTO SONGS/N      7
        BUT OUR GOOD QUEEN QUITE GROWS TO THE GROUND  . . . . .       185  LET BROTHELS/N    24
        [HE IS THE GOOD SHEPHERD HE IS THE LORD & MASTER]  . .        269  FOUR ZOAS 1      200
        WHILE YET THOSE BEINGS WERE NOT BORN NOR KNEW OF GOOD OR      304  FOUR ZOAS 4      274
          EVIL
        [HE IS THE GOOD SHEPHERD HE IS THE LORD & MASTER]   . . .     SUPP FOUR ZOAS 8        *
        THE GOOD OF ALL THE LAND IS BEFORE YOU FOR MYSTERY IS NO      375  FOUR ZOAS 9      681
          MORE
        BE IN THE GOOD HUMOUR THE BISHOP PRETENDS TO BE  . . . .     385C ANNO WATSON      MARG
        WOULD BE AS GOOD AN INQUISITOR AS ANY OTHER PRIEST   . . .   385C ANNO WATSON      MARG
        ANY MAN WHO WRITES [THAT] SO PRETEND THAT HE IS IN A GOOD    390B ANNO WATSON    * MARG
          HUMOUR
        WHO IN HOPES OF A GOOD LIVING ADOPT THE STATE RELIGION  . .  390D ANNO WATSON      MARG
        IT IS MAN'S FAULT IF GOD IS NOT ABLE TO DO HIM GOOD FOR HE   392B ANNO WATSON      MARG
        CONSEQUENT GOOD THIS SENSE OF THE BIBLE IS EQUALLY TRUE      393B ANNO WATSON      MARG
        IF HE IS GOOD HE WILL ABHOR WICKEDNESS IN DAVID OR ABRAHAM   393B ANNO WATSON      MARG
        DO OR ACT TO DO GOOD OR TO DO EVIL  . . . . . . .           396A ANNO WATSON      MARG
        GOOD ADVICE FOR SATAN'S KINGDOM  . . . . . . . .            396D ANNO BACON       MARG
        IT IS THE TREE OF THE KNOWLEDGE OF GOOD & EVIL  . . . .     397C ANNO BACON       MARG
        GOOD ADVICE FOR THE DEVIL  . . . . . . . . . .             402D ANNO BACON       MARG
        THE PHILOSOPHER IS DEPENDENT & GOOD  . . . . . . .         412C ANNO BOYD        MARG
        & OF SWEET SOWER & OF GOOD EVIL & OF NOTHING SOMETHING  .   414B ANNO BOYD        MARG
        WHETHER TIS GOOD OR EVIL NONE S TO BLAME  . . . . .         418  ON VIRGINITY/N     3
        TO BE IN A PASSION YOU GOOD MAY DO  . . . . . . .          433  AUGURIES         111
        BUT NO GOOD IF A PASSION IS IN YOU  . . . . . . .          433  AUGURIES         112
        OR BAD GOVERNMENTS WHY SHOULD A GOOD GOVERNMENT ENDEAVOUR   445C ANNO REYNOLDS    MARG
        [TO GOOD ARTISTS] THE STYLE THAT STRIKES THE EYE IS THE     448C ANNO REYNOLDS  * MARG
          TRUE STYLE
        IF HE IS HE IS A GOOD MAN IF NOT HE MUST BE STARVED  . . .  453A ANNO REYNOLDS    MARG
        THE DIFFERENCE BETWEEN A BAD ARTIST & A GOOD ONE IS  . .    456A ANNO REYNOLDS    MARG
        THE GOOD ONE REALLY DOES COPY A GREAT DEAL  . . . . .       456A ANNO REYNOLDS    MARG
        GOOD ADVICE . . . . . . . . . . . . . . . .                456D ANNO REYNOLDS    MARG
        HE REJECTED IT FOR GOOD REASONS SR JOSHUA IN OTHER PLACES   467D ANNO REYNOLDS    MARG
        VIOLENT PASSIONS EMIT THE REAL GOOD & PERFECT TONES  . . .  476A ANNO REYNOLDS    MARG
        [?FIRST ?WERE CREATED WINE & (HAPPINESS) ?GOOD ?LOOKS &     446C ANNO REYNOLDS  * MARG
          ?FORTUNE XXX]
        ANNIHILATE HIMSELF FOR OTHERS GOOD AS I FOR THEE  . . . .   530  MILTON 38         36
        [FOR NO GOOD ARTIST WILL OR CAN SKETCH] . . . . . .        542  FLORENTINE/N       9
        AND NOT A BREWER'S SERVANT MY GOOD SIR . . . . . . .       546  ENGLISH CONN/N     6
        AND SAYS COME LEARN TO WALK OF ME GOOD NEIGHBOURS   . . .   548  CRIPPLE EVRY/N     2
        ME TIME HAS CROOKD NO GOOD WORKMAN  . . . . . . .         555  FRM CRATELOS/N     1
        THE KNIGHT IS A TRUE HERO A GOOD GREAT AND WISE MAN   . .   567D DESC CAT 3       PROSE
        THE PRINCIPAL FIGURE IN THE NEXT GROUPE IS THE GOOD PARSON  570B DESC CAT 3       PROSE
        READ CHAUCER'S DESCRIPTION OF THE GOOD PARSON AND BOW  . .  570C DESC CAT 3       PROSE
        THIS MAKES A GOOD EPIGRAM ENOUGH  . . . . . . . .        575C DESC CAT 3       PROSE
        ALL THE WORLD OVER BUT HAVE NEVER BEEN SO GOOD AN   . . .   592C PUB ADDRESS/N    PROSE
```

825

GOOD   (CONTINUED)

ENGLISH ARE AS GOOD JUDGES [AS] OF PAINTING AS OF POETRY	601B	PUB ADDRESS/N	*PROSE
OR NEAR SO GOOD TILL A FEW YEARS AGO	602C	PUB ADDRESS/N	PROSE
WHO TROUBLE RELIGION WITH QUESTIONS CONCERNING GOOD & EVIL	604C	V LAST JUDG/N	PROSE
OF HINDERING THEM FROM OPRESSING THE GOOD WITH POVERTY	612D	V LAST JUDG/N	PROSE
& PAIN			
HERE THEY ARE NO LONGER TALKING OF WHAT IS GOOD & EVIL . .	613C	V LAST JUDG/N	PROSE
[TO BE THE GOOD KINGS] & QUEENS [OF ENGLAND]	614A	V LAST JUDG/N	*PROSE
IN ITS DEADLY DREAMS OF GOOD & EVIL	614C	V LAST JUDG/N	PROSE
THE COMBATS OF GOOD & EVIL [& OF TRUTH & ERROR WHICH]	615A	V LAST JUDG/N	PROSE
GOOD & EVIL ARE QUALITIES IN EVERY MAN	615A	V LAST JUDG/N	PROSE
WHETHER A GOOD OR EVIL MAN THESE ARE ENEMIES	615A	V LAST JUDG/N	PROSE
BUT UNBELIEF & EATING OF THE TREE OF KNOWLEDGE OF GOOD	615C	V LAST JUDG/N	PROSE
& EVIL			
WE WILL NOT CONVERSE CONCERNING GOOD & EVIL	615D	V LAST JUDG/N	PROSE
THEY ARE NOT ALWAYS PRYING AFTER GOOD & EVIL IN ONE ANOTHER	616D	V LAST JUDG/N	PROSE
& THAT BAD ART WILL BE ADOPTED & MIXED WITH GOOD ART . .	617A	V LAST JUDG/N	PROSE
EVERY SUBSTANCE IS CLOTHED THEY NAME THEM GOOD & EVIL . .	629	JERUSALEM 10	9
[TO GOVERN THE EVIL BY GOOD AND ?STATES ABOLISH ?SYSTEMS]	662	JERUSALEM 35	* 18
HE IS THE GOOD SHEPHERD HE IS THE LORD AND MASTER . .	665	JERUSALEM 38	23
IT IS EASY TO ACKNOWLEDGE A MAN TO BE GREAT & GOOD WHILE WE	673	JERUSALEM 43	56
ROUSSEAU THOUGHT MEN GOOD BY NATURE HE FOUND THEM EVIL &	682D	JERUSALEM 52	PROSE
HE WHO WOULD DO GOOD TO ANOTHER MUST DO IT IN MINUTE	687	JERUSALEM 55	60
PARTICULARS			
GENERAL GOOD IS THE PLEA OF THE SCOUNDREL HYPOCRITE	687	JERUSALEM 55	61
& FLATTERER			
OF GOOD & EVIL THEY DIVIDED HIM IN LOVE UPON THE THAMES	715	JERUSALEM 74	36
& SENT			
I CARE NOT WHETHER A MAN IS GOOD OR EVIL ALL THAT I CARE	739	JERUSALEM 91	55
OF SIN & THE TREE OF GOOD & EVIL SPRANG FROM THE ROCKY	740	JERUSALEM 92	25
CIRCLE & SNAKE			
THEN JESUS APPEARED STANDING BY ALBION AS THE GOOD SHEPHERD	743	JERUSALEM 96	3
WHERE IS THE TREE OF GOOD & EVIL THAT ROOTED BENEATH THE	746	JERUSALEM 98	47
CRUEL HEEL			
GOOD & EVIL ARE NO MORE	754	EV GOSPEL(E)/N	21
THOU ART GOOD & THOU ALONE	754	EV GOSPEL(E)/N	25
TO BE GOOD ONLY IS TO BE	754	EV GOSPEL(E)/N	27
OF GOOD & EVIL & MISERY	759	EV GOSPEL (2)	41
OF GOOD & EVIL VIRTUE & VICE	770	OF GATES/GP	6
RATIONAL TRUTH ROOT OF EVIL & GOOD	770	OF GATES/GP	14
EVIL GOOD	775C	INSC LAOCOON	TITLE
THE ROOT OF GOOD & EVIL IN THE ACCUSATION OF SIN . . .	776B	INSC LAOCOON	PROSE
GOOD & EVIL ARE RICHES & POVERTY A TREE OF MISERY . . .	776B	INSC LAOCOON	PROSE
ARISTOTLE SAYS CHARACTERS ARE EITHER GOOD OR BAD	778B	HOMERS POETRY	PROSE
BUT A GOOD APPLE TREE OR A BAD IS AN APPLE TREE STILL	778B	HOMERS POETRY	PROSE
THE ANCIENTS CALLD IT EATING OF THE TREE OF GOOD & EVIL	778C	HOMERS POETRY	PROSE
IN GOOD COMPANY	781D	INSC UPCOTT	PROSE
& TO ITS LAWS OF GOOD & EVIL & ITS ENMITIES AGAINST MIND	784D	ANNO WW EXCUR	MARG
IT SEEMS AS IF DANTE'S SUPREME GOOD WAS	785C	ILLS DANTE 101	PROSE
[?AS] FOR IF HE GIVES HIS RAIN TO THE EVIL & THE GOOD .	785C	ILLS DANTE 101	*PROSE
& IS NOT THIS GOOD & LEARNED & WISE & CLASSICAL THIS IS	788C	ANNO THORNTON	MARG
TO SPEAK GOOD OR BAD	792C	LETTER 4	PROSE
IF I AM WRONG I AM WRONG IN GOOD COMPANY I HAD	793A	LETTER 5	PROSE
& DONE A GOOD MANY OTHER SOFTENINGS TO THE WHOLE . . .	797A	LETTER 9	PROSE
GOD KEEP YOU FROM & ALL GOOD MEN OUR ARTISTS OF ALL RANKS	798A	LETTER 10	PROSE
ASSISTANCE OF BRUNO'S FAIRIES BUT I INVOKE THE GOOD GENII	801B	LETTER 13	PROSE
ALL WAS CHEARFULNESS & GOOD HUMOUR ON THE ROAD & YET WE	802B	LETTER 14	PROSE
US & WITH US ACCORDING TO HIS DIVINE WILL FOR OUR GOOD .	802C	LETTER 14	PROSE
THE SWEETEST SPOT ON EARTH AT LEAST IT IS SO TO ME & MY	808C	LETTER 19	PROSE
GOOD			
MRS FLAXMAN & FIVE MORE TWO OF WHICH YOU WILL BE SO GOOD	821B	LETTER 25	PROSE
A GOOD LIKENESS OF YOU IF I HAVE HANDS & EYES LEFT . .	824B	LETTER 27	PROSE
IN GOOD LUCK AT LAST & SHALL BE FORGOT BY MY AFFECTIONS &	824D	LETTER 27	PROSE
WHOSE EYES HAVE DONE ME SO MUCH GOOD I OMITTED	826C	LETTER 28	PROSE
GOOD SENSE AS SHE OBSERVES THAT WHENEVER A QUARREL HAPPENS	827C	LETTER 28	PROSE
EVERY ONE HERE IS MY EVIDENCE FOR PEACE & GOOD	828B	LETTER 28	PROSE
NEIGHBOURHOOD			
ALL IS COME FROM THE SPIRITUAL WORLD FOR GOOD & NOT FOR	828C	LETTER 28	PROSE
EVIL			
OWN GOOD TIME PRAY WRITE TO ME & TELL ME HOW YOU & YOUR	829A	LETTER 28	PROSE
A PRINCE AMONG PRINCES & EVEN ON EARTH BELOVED BY THE GOOD	830A	LETTER 30	PROSE
AS A GOOD MAN THIS I SHOULD BE PERFECTLY CONTENTED WITH	830A	LETTER 30	PROSE
HAPPINESS IS NOT GOOD FOR MORTALS & THEY OUGHT TO	830C	LETTER 30	PROSE
BE ANSWERD			
ANY ONE A BLIGHT NEVER DOES GOOD TO A TREE & IF A BLIGHT	830C	LETTER 30	PROSE
MR SAUNDERS HAS A GOOD MANY WERE ENGRAVD THEY	832C	LETTER 32	PROSE
GOOD WOMAN AGAIN BEGINS TO RESUME HER HEALTH & STRENGTH	833D	LETTER 33	PROSE
PANG OF AFFECTION & GRATITUDE IS THE GIFT OF GOD FOR GOOD	833D	LETTER 33	PROSE
I WRITE NOW TO SATISFY YOU THAT ALL IS IN A GOOD TRAIN I AM	835A	LETTER 34	PROSE
GOD BLESS & PRESERVE YOU AND OUR GOOD LADY PAULINA	835A	LETTER 34	PROSE
WITH THE GOOD THINGS BOTH OF THIS LIFE & OF ETERNITY & WITH	835A	LETTER 34	PROSE
I SEND MY PROOFS TO GIVE AS GOOD AN ACCOUNT OF MR WALKER	837B	LETTER 35	PROSE
HEAR THE SAME GOOD ACCOUNT OF OUR MOST ADMIRABLE . . .	838C	LETTER 37	PROSE
IT WILL GIVE YOU A GOOD IDEA OF THIS GOOD & EXCELLENT MAN	839B	LETTER 38	PROSE
THERE IS A REAL REASON EQUALLY GOOD WHY I HAVE NOT YET SENT	840B	LETTER 39	PROSE
MY ZEAL WITH GOOD EFFECT AM IN HOPES THAT MISS POOLE IS	841A	LETTER 40	PROSE
WHICH SHALL WITH YOUR GOOD ASSISTANCE	841D	LETTER 41	PROSE
MY SORROW AND MY HOPES FOR OUR GOOD MISS POOLE AND . .	845A	LETTER 43	PROSE
MY GOOD WOMAN WHO IS STILL STIFF-KNEED BUT WELL IN OTHER	845A	LETTER 43	PROSE
IN JUSTICE TO OUR GOOD SEAGRAVE WHOSE REPLIES	847A	LETTER 44	PROSE
COLLECT FROM HIM BE SO GOOD AS TO GIVE ME YOUR EARLIEST	849B	LETTER 45	PROSE
I TAKE THE EXTREME PLEASURE OF EXPRESSING MY JOY AT OUR	851C	LETTER 50	PROSE
GOOD			

		PAGE	TITLE	LINE

GOOD   (CONTINUED)
```
          OUR GOOD AND KIND FRIEND HAWKINS IS NOT YET IN TOWN  . . .   851D LETTER 50      PROSE
          SHORT TIME I SHALL MAKE MY ASSERTION GOOD THAT I AM BECOME    852C LETTER 50      PROSE
          THE ASSISTANCE AND APPROBATION OF OUR GOOD FRIEND FLAXMAN     853B LETTER 52      PROSE
          OF THE SHIPWRECK MRS FLAXMAN ALSO WHO IS A GOOD  . . .       853B LETTER 52      PROSE
          FINISHD PROOF BE ASSURED THAT WITH OUR GOOD FLAXMAN'S    .    855B LETTER 53      PROSE
          GOOD HELP & WITH YOUR REMARKS ON IT IN ADDITION I HOPE TO     855B LETTER 53      PROSE
          ONE I COULD GET AT JOHNSON'S I LEFT A GOOD IMPRESSION OF IT   855C LETTER 53      PROSE
          FOR OUR GOOD SEAGRAVE & SAID I KNEW YOUR CHIEF INTENTIONS     856B LETTER 54      PROSE
             IN
          FOR WHAT IS GOOD MUST SUCCEED FIRST OR LAST BUT WHAT IS BAD   862A LETTER 59      PROSE
          & OUR GOOD LADY PAULINA OVER A DISH OF COFFEE I LONG TO       862A LETTER 59      PROSE
             HEAR
          OF YOUR GOOD HEALTH & THAT OF OUR DEAR FRIEND OF LAVANT &     862A LETTER 59      PROSE
          TO THOSE WHOSE KINDNESS & GOOD OPINION HAS SUPPORTED ME       862C LETTER 60      PROSE
             THRO
          THINGS KNOWN ONLY TO MYSELF & TO SPIRITS GOOD & EVIL BUT      862D LETTER 60      PROSE
          PRAY PRESENT MY SINCEREST THANKS TO OUR GOOD PAULINA WHOSE    863B LETTER 60      PROSE
          & HOPE THAT HE HAS A GOOD OPINION OF MY WILLINGNESS TO        868D LETTER 68      PROSE
             APPEAR
          AS IF I SHOULD BE BETTER TO-MORROW REST DOES ME GOOD     .    870B LETTER 71      PROSE
          I BELIEVE MY CONSTITUTION TO BE A GOOD ONE BUT IT HAS    .    870D LETTER 72      PROSE
          YESTERDAY AFTERNOON AFTER AS GOOD A MORNING AS I EVER    .    872B LETTER 75      PROSE
          AT FIRST & THOUGHT IT A THING OF BENEFIT & GOOD HOPE YOU      876B LETTER 83      PROSE
          IDEAS OF GOOD & EVIL  . . . . . . . . . . . .            .    889C IDEAS/N4       PROSE
          THE GOOD AND EVIL ANGELS  . . . . . . . . . .            .    SUPP COLOR PRT TATE *TITLE
          OF THE TREE OF LIFE & OF THE TREE OF GOOD & EVIL    .  . .    SUPP ILLUS GENESIS  *TITLE
          GOOD & EVIL ANGEL HOUSE OF DEATH GOD JUDGING ADAM LAMECH      SUPP LETTER 56A     *PROSE
GOOD FOR NOTHING
          [ WHO CAN SELL A GOOD FOR NOTHING COMMODITY FOR A GREAT       595B PUB ADDRESS/N  PROSE
             PRICE ]
GOOD NATURD
          ONLY ENT SO GOOD NATURD  . . . . . . . . . . .           .    29C EDW THIRD/PS 4  PROSE
          BECAUSE PALAMABRON WAS GOOD NATURD SATAN SUPPOSD HE FEARD     351 FOUR ZOAS 8     391
             HIM
GOOD NATURED
          HE IS NOT NATURALLY GOOD NATURED BUT HE IS ARTIFICIALLY      798B LETTER 10      PROSE
          I SOOTHE HIM TO PEACE & INDEED HE IS A GOOD NATURD DEVIL     830C LETTER 30      PROSE
GOODNESS
          DEROGATE FROM HIM IN THE TRIFLES & SMALL ARTICLES OF THAT     673 JERUSALEM 43    57
             GOODNESS
          REMAIN IN PERMANENT STRENGTH OR IS ALL THIS GOODNESS &        673 JERUSALEM 43    78
             PITY ONLY
          SO GOODNESS IS THE CLOKE OF KNAVERY  . . . . . . . .          778B HOMERS POETRY  PROSE
          NOW GOODNESS OR BADNESS HAS NOTHING TO DO WITH CHARACTER      778B HOMERS POETRY  PROSE
          CHARACTER ITS GOODNESS OR BADNESS IS ANOTHER CONSIDERATION    778B HOMERS POETRY  PROSE
          THE MORAL GOODNESS OF ITS PARTS UNITY & MORALITY              778B HOMERS POETRY  PROSE
             ARE SECONDARY
GOODNESSES
          OUR VIRTUES & CRUEL GOODNESSES HAVE DESERVD ETERNAL DEATH     494 MILTON 13       34
GOOD NIGHT
          GOOD NIGHT SAID SIPSOP GOOD NIGHT SAID THE OTHER TWO    . .   51C ISLAND MOON 7   *PROSE
GOODS
          CAUSED THE POLICE TO SIEZE UPON THE PERSON & GOODS OR    . .  865A LETTER 62      PROSE
GOOD-WILL
          THERE CAN BE NO GOOD-WILL WILL IS ALWAYS EVIL  . . . . .      89A ANNO SWED LOVE  MARG
GOODWIN
          THE DEATH OF EARL GOODWIN  . . . . . . . . . . .         .    SUPP ILLUS HISTORY  *TITLE
GORD
          AND ROUND RED ORC RETURNING BACK TO URIZEN [ GORD ] GORGD     320 FOUR ZOAS 6     *  322
             WITH BLOOD
GORDRED
          GORDRED THE GIANT ROUSD HIMSELF  . . . . . . . . .       .    11 GWIN KING/PS     13
          GORDRED APPEARS HIS FROWNING BROW  . . . . . . . . .    .     12 GWIN KING/PS     63
          LIKE THESE DID GWIN AND GORDRED MEET  . . . . . . .     .     14 GWIN KING/PS     105
          GORDRED HIS HEAD DIVIDES  . . . . . . . . . . . .       .     14 GWIN KING/PS     108
GORE
          TO WADE THRO FIELDS OF GORE  . . . . . . . . . .        .     12 GWIN KING/PS     46
          TO DRINK HER CHILDREN'S GORE  . . . . . . . . . .       .     13 GWIN KING/PS     74
          ENVY AND HATE THAT THIRST FOR HUMAN GORE  . . . . .     .     15 IMIT SPEN/PS     32
          WHILE THE BLACK GORE DROPS FROM HIS HORRID JAWS    . . .      31 EDW THIRD/PS 5   46
          WITH HELMETS HEWN AND SHIELDS COVERED WITH GORE    . . .      32 EDW THIRD/PS 6   11
          TYRANNY HATH STAIND FAIR ALBION'S BREAST WITH HER            34A KING JOHN/PS    PROSE
             OWN CHILDREN'S GORE
          SO I SMOTE [ HIM ] THEM & [ HIS ] THEIR GORE  . . . . .      167 INFANT SORW/N   *  40
          SO I SMOTE HIM & HIS GORE  . . . . . . . . . . .        .    169 MIRTLE SHADE/N  15
          AND PARCHED LIPS DROP WITH FRESH GORE NOW ROLL THOU IN       199 AMERICA 9       24
             THE CLOUDS
          WRATH WITH LIONS GORE  . . . . . . . . . . . . .        .    256 BOOK OF LOS 3   16
          [ TO JUDGMENT ] FROM THE CLOTTED GORE & FROM THE HOLLOW DEN  358 FOUR ZOAS 9     43
          FROM THE CLOTTED GORE & FROM THE HOLLOW DEN    . . . .  .    359 FOUR ZOAS 9     88
          DRUNK WITH THE SMOKING GORE & RED BUT NOT WITH NOURISHING    360 FOUR ZOAS 9     122
             WINE
          . . . ARE COVERD WITH HUMAN GORE  . . . . . . . . .     .    517 MILTON 29       58
          IN CLOUDS OF BLOOD IN STREAMS OF GORE WITH DREADFUL          534 MILTON 42       8
             THUNDERINGS
          RIOTED IN HUMAN GORE  . . . . . . . . . . . . .         .    650 FIELDS FROM/J   31
          OF ALBION'S CHILDREN FLEEING THRO ALBION'S VALES             655 JERUSALEM 30    8
             IN STREAMS OF GORE
          THAT DROP WITH CRIMSON GORE WITH THE LOVES OF ALBION &       699 JERUSALEM 64    37
             CANAAN
          HIM OVER EUROPE IN STREAMS OF GORE OUT OF CATHEDRON'S LOOMS  715 JERUSALEM 74    37
```

```
                                                            PAGE     TITLE        LINE
GORE    (CONTINUED)
      DROP WITH THE GORE OF THE SLAIN WHY EUPHRATES IS RED WITH    721 JERUSALEM 79      69
      BLOOD
      THE HEAVENS DROP WITH HUMAN GORE  . . . . . . . . .         818 HAPPINESS/L        82
GORGD
      PANTING OVER THE PRISONERS LIKE A WOLF GORGD . . . . . .    135 FRENCH REVOLTN     26
      AND ROUND RED ORC RETURNING BACK TO URIZEN [GORD] GORGD     320 FOUR ZOAS 6     *  322
      WITH BLOOD
GORGE
      THE HUMAN HEART ITS HUNGRY GORGE  . . . . . . . . .         221 DIVNE IMAGE/SE      8
GORGED
      THY YOUNG HANDS TORE HUMAN LIMBS AND GORGED HUMAN FLESH     38B SAMSON/PS        PROSE
GORGEOUS
      NOW UPON HER SUMPTUOUS COUCH RECLINED IN GORGEOUS PRIDE     38A SAMSON/PS        PROSE
      THOU SEEST THE GORGEOUS CLOTHED FLIES THAT DANCE & SPORT    512 MILTON 26          2
      IN SUMMER
      THEY THROW OFF THEIR GORGEOUS RAIMENT THEY REJOICE WITH     513 MILTON 27         23
      LOUD JUBILEE
      GORGEOUS & BEAUTIFUL LOUD ROLL HIS THUNDERS AGAINST MILTON  529 MILTON 38         12
      OVER THE NORTH WITH PEARLY BEAMS GORGEOUS & TERRIBLE   . .  710 JERUSALEM 71      48
      AND BRIGHT STRETCHD OVER EUROPE & ASIA GORGEOUS    . . . .  734 JERUSALEM 89      12
GORMANDIZE
      RAGING AGAINST THEIR HUMAN NATURES RAVNING TO GORMANDIZE    641 JERUSALEM 19      23
GORY
      WITH GORY BLOOD IT GROAND AND THUS IT SPAKE    . . . . .      5 FAIR ELENOR/PS    60
      SHE TOOK THE GORY HEAD UP IN HER ARMS    . . . . . . .        6 FAIR ELENOR/PS    70
GOSHEN
      AMONG PRECIPICES OF DESPAIR IN GOSHEN I SEEK FOR LIGHT  . . 720 JERUSALEM 79      11
      GOSHEN HATH FOLLOWD PHILISTEA GILEAD HATH JOIND WITH OG     720 JERUSALEM 79      13
GOSPEL
      THE LAW AND GOSPEL FROM FIRE AND AIR AND ETERNAL REASON     138 FRENCH REVOLTN    95
      AND SCIENCE
      THIS IS SHEWN IN THE GOSPEL WHERE HE PRAYS TO THE FATHER    150B MARRIAGE HH 5   PROSE
      A GOSPEL FROM WRETCHED THEOTORMON  . . . . . . . . .        246 SONG OF LOS 3      24
      UPON AN UNBELIEVING PATIENT WHEREAS THE GOSPEL SAYS  . .    391D ANNO WATSON      MARG
      THE BISHOP NEVER SAW THE EVERLASTING GOSPEL ANY MORE THAN   394D ANNO WATSON    * MARG
      TOM PAINE
      THE GOSPEL IS FORGIVENESS OF SINS & HAS NO MORAL PRECEPTS   395C ANNO WATSON      MARG
      DOES GOD LOVE THE RIGHTEOUS ACCORDING TO THE GOSPEL  . . .  396A ANNO WATSON      MARG
      AND THE MORAL LAW FROM THE GOSPEL RENT  . . . . . . .       420 I SAW MNK AD/N     2
      HE KNEW BOTH LAW & GOSPEL BETTER THAN THEY  . . . . .       537 AND HIS LEGS/N    31
      ONE RELIGION THIS WAS THE RELIGION OF JESUS THE            579A DESC CAT 5       PROSE
      EVERLASTING GOSPEL
      ANTIQUITY PREACHES THE GOSPEL OF JESUS THE REASONING   .    579A DESC CAT 5       PROSE
      THE HEBREW BIBLE & THE GOSPEL OF JESUS ARE NOT ALLEGORY     604D V LAST JUDG/N   PROSE
      WHILE THE HEBREW BIBLE & THE GREEK GOSPEL ARE GENUINE   .   605C V LAST JUDG/N   PROSE
      AND SUCH THE HOLY GOSPEL OF MOUNT OLIVET & CALVARY    . .   638 JERUSALEM 16      69
      THE ETERNAL & THE EVERLASTING GOSPEL   . . . . . . . .     649B JERUSALEM 27     PROSE
      THE FOUR-FOLD GOSPEL AND THE REVELATIONS EVERLASTING  . .   677 JERUSALEM 48      11
      AND THE MORAL LAW FROM THE GOSPEL RENT  . . . . . . .       683 I SAW A MONK/J    18
      NO OTHER CHRISTIANITY AND OF NO OTHER GOSPEL THAN THE       716D JERUSALEM 77    PROSE
      LIBERTY BOTH
      THE APOSTLES KNEW OF NO OTHER GOSPEL    . . . . . . .       717A JERUSALEM 77    PROSE
      WHAT IS THE HARVEST OF THE GOSPEL & ITS LABOURS    . . .    717A JERUSALEM 77    PROSE
      WHAT ARE ALL THE GIFTS OF THE GOSPEL ARE THEY NOT ALL       717A JERUSALEM 77    PROSE
      MENTAL GIFTS
      WHICH ALONE ARE THE LABOURS OF THE GOSPEL   . . . . .       717B JERUSALEM 77    PROSE
      THE EVERLASTING GOSPEL   . . . . . . . . . . . .           751B EV GOSPEL(D)/N   TITLE
      [AS] FOR THUS THE GOSPEL SIR ISAAC CONFUTES    . . . .      752 EV GOSPEL(D)/N    43
      THIS ALONE IS THE GOSPEL & THIS IS THE LIFE & IMMORTALITY   757D EV GOSPEL      PROSE
      WHAT CAN THIS GOSPEL OF JESUS BE  . . . . . . . . .         758 EV GOSPEL (2)      1
      WHEN THEY THE GOSPEL LIGHT BEHELD  . . . . . . . .          758 EV GOSPEL (2)     20
      & TO THE POOR & UNLEARNED SUCH IS THE GOSPEL    . . . .     774D ANNO BERKELEY    MARG
      APPEARS TO BE LAW & GOSPEL TOO AT LEAST I HEAR SO FROM THE  798C LETTER 10       PROSE
GOT
      O AYE I FORGOT TO TELL THAT HE HAS GOT THE SAME NAME    . . 29C EDW THIRD/PS 4   PROSE
      THE ANTIQUARIAN HERE GOT UP & HEMMING TWICE    . . . .    . 45D ISLAND MOON 1    PROSE
      I HAVE GOT A BOTTLE OF AIR THAT WOULD SPREAD A PLAGUE   . . 46A ISLAND MOON 1    PROSE
      NO SAID INFLAMMABLE GASS I HAVE GOT A CAMERA OBSCURA AT     47C ISLAND MOON 3    PROSE
      HOME
      THAT IS THE WAY I HAVE GOT SOME OF MY KNOWLEDGE    . . . .  53C ISLAND MOON 8    PROSE
      O DEAR THE WATER S GOT INTO THE SLIDERS LOOK HERE    . .    58C ISLAND MOON 10   PROSE
      AND GOT WITH OUR BAGS & OUR BRUSHES TO WORK    . . . . .    118 CHIMNEY SWP/SI    22
      WHICH HE BY INDUSTRY HAD GOT   . . . . . . . . . .          425 MENTAL TRAVLER    32
      WHEN FRANCE GOT FREE EUROPE TWIXT FOOLS & KNAVES    . . .   451 ANNO REYNOLDS      1
      & BY WHICH HE GOT HIS REPUTATION AS A DRAUGHTSMAN    . .    592B PUB ADDRESS/N   PROSE
      A HORSE BY THE COLOUR & A MAN WHO HAS GOT ANY BRAINS   . .  597D PUB ADDRESS/N   PROSE
      BUT NOT THE SAME GENIUS SCIENCE IS SOON GOT    . . . . .    602D PUB ADDR AD/N   PROSE
      SINCE WHICH A PIG HAS GOT A LOOK   . . . . . . . .          757 EV GOSPEL(I)/N    29
      MY NEST I HAVE NOT GOT ANY FORWARDER WITH THE THREE MARYS   804A LETTER 16       PROSE
      OR
      A BOOK PRICE HALF A GUINEA MAY BE GOT OUT AT THE EXPENSE OF  820A LETTER 25      PROSE
      FRENCH PRINTS & PLEASE EVERY ONE IN SHORT I HAVE GOT   . .  821A LETTER 25       PROSE
      TILL I HAD GOT HIM OUT THERE I INTENDED TO HAVE LEFT HIM    827A LETTER 28       PROSE
      AT LENGTH WHEN I HAD GOT HIM TO WHERE HE WAS QUARTERD   .   827B LETTER 28       PROSE
      AFTER THEY HAD GOT TOGETHER INTO THE STABLE THIS IS THE     827C LETTER 28       PROSE
      WHOLE
      I HAVE GOT TO WORK AFTER FUSELI FOR A LITTLE SHAKESPEARE    831B LETTER 31       PROSE
      IF THIS INFERNAL BUSINESS OF THE SOLDIER CAN BE GOT OVER    832C LETTER 32       PROSE
      NOT HAVE GOT THEM PRINTED TO SEND BY TUESDAY'S COACH   . .  840B LETTER 39       PROSE
      HOPE SOON TO HEAR THAT YOU HAVE GOT A LIVING ONE OF BRASS   843A LETTER 42      *PROSE
      WHICH I GOT AS YOU DIRECTED OF MR JOHNSON I HAVE SEEN   .   844D LETTER 43       PROSE
```

```
                                                              PAGE     TITLE        LINE
GOT    (CONTINUED)
       I HAVE GOT THE THREE SUBLIME DESIGNS OF ROMNEY NOW IN MY   848A LETTER 45     PROSE
       FAREWELL SWEET ROSE THOU HAST GOT BEFORE ME INTO THE    .  854C LETTER 53     PROSE
       BE DEVOTED TO DESIGNING & PAINTING [ALONE] WHEN I HAVE GOT 866A LETTER 63     PROSE
       OF THE WAY ON HIS JOURNEY IN THE COACH FOR WE BOTH GOT  .  869C LETTER 70     PROSE
       ACCOMPANYING DEATHLY FEEL I GOT AGAIN INTO A PERSPIRATION  872B LETTER 75     PROSE
       IT IS NOW PASSED AS I HOPE BUT THE MOMENT I GOT EASE OF    874B LETTER 79     PROSE
          BODY
       WHAT I WAS ABOUT I HAVE GOT ON VERY FORWARD WITH (FOUR)    876D LETTER 84     PROSE
          PLATES
       [ALBERT DURER WOULD NEVER HAVE GOT HIS MANNERS FROM THE    SUPP ANNO REYNOLDS * MARG
          NOBILITY]
GOTHIC
       RAILS OF AN OLD GOTHIC SQUARE  . . . . . . . . .           45A ISLAND MOON 1   PROSE
       BESIDES LET THEM LOOK AT GOTHIC FIGURES & GOTHIC BUILDINGS 461A ANNO REYNOLDS  MARG
       THE INN IS A GOTHIC BUILDING WHICH THYNNE IN HIS GLOSSARY  567B DESC CAT 3     PROSE
       GOTHIC GRECIAN HINDOO AND EGYPTIAN ARE THE EXTENT OF THE   579D DESC CAT 5     PROSE
          HUMAN MIND
       THE INN IS A GOTHIC BUILDING WHICH THYNNE IN HIS GLOSSARY  588D CHAUCER/N      PROSE
       OF THE PICTURE THE WORDS WRITTEN IN GOTHIC LETTERS  . . .  589A CHAUCER/N      PROSE
       THE INN IS A GOTHIC BUILDING WHICH THYNNE IN HIS GLOSSARY  590C CHAUCER 2      PROSE
       OF THE PICTURE THE WORDS WRITTEN IN GOTHIC LETTERS  . . .  590C CHAUCER 2      PROSE
       THIS IS ONE OF THE GOTHIC ARTISTS WHO BUILT THE CATHEDRALS 604A INSC ARIMATHEA PROSE
       OF THE BLESSED IN WHICH A GOTHIC CHURCH IS REPRESENTATIVE  610C V LAST JUDG/N  PROSE
       OF TRUE ART CALLD GOTHIC IN ALL AGES BY THOSE  . . . . .   610D V LAST JUDG/N  PROSE
       GRECIAN IS MATHEMATIC FORM GOTHIC IS LIVING FORM  . . . .  778D HOMERS POETRY  PROSE
GOTHS
       THE CLASSICS IT IS THE CLASSICS & NOT GOTHS NOR MONKS  .   778C HOMERS POETRY  PROSE
GOUNDS
       AND PRIESTS IN BLACK GOUNDS WERE WALKING THEIR ROUNDS  .   163 GARDEN LOVE/N    11
GOURD
       AND ALL THE MOUNTAINS & HILLS SHRINK UP LIKE A WITHERING   703 JERUSALEM 66     82
          GOURD
GOUTY
       LIKE THE FULL GALLOP OF THE GOUTY MAN TO THE ORDINARY WALK 593A PUB ADDRESS/N  PROSE
GOVERN
       TILL ANGELS & WEAK MEN TWELVE YEARS SHOULD GOVERN OER THE  203 AMERICA 16       14
          STRONG
       SO SHALL (?YOU) GOVERN OVER ALL LET MORAL DUTY TUNE YOUR   323 FOUR ZOAS 7    * 111
          TONGUE
       BUT RINTRAH & PALAMABRON GOVERN OVER DAY & NIGHT  . . . .  517 MILTON 29        27
       MAY I GOVERN ALL BOTH GREAT & SMALL  . . . . . . . . .     547 IF I GROW/N      3
       CONTINUE TO GOVERN MANKIND AFTER DEATH  . . . . . . .      581D DESC CAT 8     PROSE
       LET THOSE WHO GOVERN THE NATION TAKE CARE OF THE OTHER  .  584C DESC CAT 14    PROSE
       THIS IS A LAST JUDGMENT WHEN MEN OF REAL ART GOVERN &  .   612C V LAST JUDG/N  PROSE
       [TO GOVERN THE EVIL BY GOOD AND ?STATES ABOLISH ?SYSTEMS]  662 JERUSALEM 35   * 18
       BY THE NAME OF MORALITY THEIR DAUGHTERS GOVERN ALL  . . .  663 JERUSALEM 36     47
GOVERND
       AND SPIRITS OF FLAMING FIRE ON HIGH GOVERND THE MIGHTY SONG 274 FOUR ZOAS 1    384
       HAVE CURBED & GOVERND THEIR PASSIONS OR HAVE NO PASSIONS   615C V LAST JUDG/N  PROSE
GOVERNED
       NARROW BLINKING EYES THAT HAVE TOO LONG GOVERNED ART  .    563D DESC CAT       PROSE
       ART DEGRADED IMAGINATION DENIED WAR GOVERNED THE NATIONS   775D INSC LAOCOON   PROSE
GOVERNING
       HAVE SPENT THEIR LIVES IN CURBING & GOVERNING OTHER        615D V LAST JUDG/N  PROSE
          PEOPLE'S
       GOVERNING ALL BY THE SWEET DELIGHTS OF SECRET AMOROUS      638 JERUSALEM 16     59
          GLANCES
GOVERNMENT
       HE SAYS AT N...NO KING HATH SUCH A GOVERNMENT AS THIS  .   132C ANNO SWED PROV MARG
       FOR ALL KINGS ARE UNIVERSAL IN THEIR GOVERNMENT  . . . .   132C ANNO SWED PROV MARG
       WHEN THE REVERENCE OF GOVERNMENT IS LOST IT IS BETTER THAN 401D ANNO BACON     MARG
       OR BAD GOVERNMENTS WHY SHOULD A GOOD GOVERNMENT ENDEAVOUR  445C ANNO REYNOLDS  MARG
       WHO CREEPS INTO STATE GOVERNMENT LIKE A CATTERPILLER TO    533 MILTON 41        11
          DESTROY
       THEM IF THEY ARE NOT WISE THE FREEST GOVERNMENT IS  . . .  600A PUB ADDRESS/N  PROSE
       AGAINST RELIGION & GOVERNMENT  . . . . . . . . . . .       757 EV GOSPEL(I)/N  38
       GOVERNMENT WAS SPOKEN BY EITHER HIM OR ME HIS ENMITY  .    826D LETTER 28      PROSE
       OF THE REMOTEST TENDENCY TO GOVERNMENT OR SEDITION WAS  .  827C LETTER 28      PROSE
GOVERNMENTS
       IF WELL REGULATED GOVERNMENTS ACT SO WHO CAN TELL SO WELL  413D ANNO BOYD      MARG
          AS
       OR BAD GOVERNMENTS WHY SHOULD A GOOD GOVERNMENT ENDEAVOUR  445C ANNO REYNOLDS  MARG
GOVERNOR
       IN ITS TERRIBLE TOWERS THE GOVERNOR STOOD . . .  .  .  .   135 FRENCH REVOLTN  19
       & THE GOVERNOR OR REASON IS CALLD MESSIAH  .  .  .  .  .   150A MARRIAGE HH 5  PROSE
       ALONE IS THE GOVERNOR OF WORLDLY RICHES & WHEN IT IS FIT   796A LETTER 6       PROSE
GOVERNORS
       WHAT TIME THE THIRTEEN GOVERNORS THAT ENGLAND SENT CONVENE 201 AMERICA 13       1
GOVERNS
       AND THE RESTRAINER OR REASON USURPS ITS PLACE & GOVERNS    149D MARRIAGE HH 5  PROSE
          THE UNWILLING
       SAYING BY THIS HE CONQUERS ENEMIES & GOVERNS KINGDOMS  .   153D MARRIAGE HH 12 PROSE
       & GOVERNS HIS SONG WHEN MORN PURPLES THE EAST  .  .  .  .  792C LETTER 4       PROSE
GOWN
       WITH PASSION WOULD TEAR OFF THE SLEEVE OF HIS GOWN  .  .   48B ISLAND MOON 4   PROSE
       INNOCENCE IS A WINTER'S GOWN  .  .  .  .  .  .  .  .  .    64 SHEPHERD OLD      10
GOWNS      SEE GOUNDS
       WITH SCARLET GOWNS & BROAD GOLD LACE WOULD MAKE A YEOMAN   58 THIS CITY/IM      5
          SWEAT
       AND PRIESTS IN BLACK GOWNS WERE WALKING THEIR ROUNDS  .  . 215 GARDEN LOVE/SE   11
```

	PAGE	TITLE	LINE

GRACE (PERSON'S NAME)
    HE SEES HE SEES CRIES SOFTLY GRACE . . . .   16 BLIND-MANS/PS   40
GRACE
    YOUR GRACE HAD BETTER MAKE . . . .   23 EDW THIRD/PS 3   90
    FOR FLIGHT AN PLEASE YOUR GRACE . . . .   24 EDW THIRD/PS 3 150
    BUT NOW MY WIFE IS DEAD & ALL THE TIME OF GRACE IS PAST 107 TIRIEL 6   11
    BUT VENGEANCE IS THE DESTROYER OF GRACE & REPENTANCE IN 648 JERUSALEM 25   10
      THE BOSOM
    TILL IT BECAME A SEPARATED CLOUD OF BEAUTY GRACE & LOVE 732 JERUSALEM 86   55
    KNOW THAT YOU SEE CERTAIN MERITS IN ME WHICH BY GOD'S GRACE 822B LETTER 26 PROSE
    NEVER YET SINCE MY RETURN TO LONDON HAD THE TIME OR GRACE 836C LETTER 35 PROSE
GRACEFUL
    RAFAEL SUBLIME MAJESTIC GRACEFUL WISE . . . . 547 RAFAEL SUBLI/N   1
    IN GRACEFUL HIDINGS OF ERROR IN MERCIFUL DECEIT . . . . 727 JERUSALEM 83   29
    O LOVELY ENITHARMON I BEHOLD THY GRACEFUL FORMS . . . . 732 JERUSALEM 87   3
GRACES
    IN CONSEQUENCE ALL THE LOVES & GRACES WITH THEM ARE SIN 88D ANNO LAVATER * MARG
    OR AN EYE OF GIFTS & GRACES SHOWRING FRUITS & COINED GOLD 130 BOOK OF THEL 6   15
    HIS SECRET LOVES & GRACES AH ME WRETCHED WHAT HAVE I DONE 268 FOUR ZOAS 1 164
    AND GRACES LEST THEY WRITE THEM IN THEIR BOOKS & IN THE 507 MILTON 23   41
      SCROLL
    ALL THE INFANT LOVES & GRACES WERE LOST FOR THE MIGHTY HAND 628 JERUSALEM 8   44
    SLAY NOT MY INFANT LOVES & GRACES BEAUTIFUL DAUGHTER OF 643 JERUSALEM 20   28
      MOAB
    ALL THE LOVES & GRACES OF ETERNITY . . . . 777D INSC LAOCOON PROSE
GRACIOUS
    WITH POMP GIVE EVERY CRUST OF BREAD YOU GIVE WITH GRACIOUS 323 FOUR ZOAS 7 123
      CUNNING
GRADATION
    PRINCIPAL SEAT AND FROM THENCE A REGULAR GRADATION AND . 580B DESC CAT 5 PROSE
GRADUAL
    . . . TILL GRADUAL A MURMUR IS HEARD DESCENDING INTO THE 145 FRENCH REVOLTN 243
      VALLEY
GRAECIAN   SEE GRECIAN
    CORINNA THE RIVAL OF PINDAR CORINNA THE GRAECIAN POETESS SUPP PENC DRAW 1.45 *TITLE
GRAIN
    [OVER THE NEW REAPD GRAIN] . . . . 164 HEARD ANGEL/N   19
    TO SEE A WORLD IN A GRAIN OF SAND . . . . 431 AUGURIES   1
    SEEST THOU THE LITTLE WINGED FLY SMALLER THAN A GRAIN OF 502 MILTON 20   27
      SAND
    SO PAINTING ADMITS NOT A GRAIN OF SAND OR A BLADE OF GRASS 611B V LAST JUDG/N PROSE
    IF I SHOULD DARE TO LAY MY FINGER ON A GRAIN OF SAND . . 657 JERUSALEM 31   33
    BY SATAN'S WATCH-FIENDS THO THEY SEARCH NUMBERING EVERY 666 JERUSALEM 39   1
      GRAIN
    THERE IS A GRAIN OF SAND IN LAMBETH THAT SATAN CANNOT FIND 668 JERUSALEM 41   15
    SAYING EACH GRAIN OF SAND . . . . 804 TO BUTTS/L   25
GRAINS
    VIRTUE AND EVERY MINUTE PARTICULAR HARDEND INTO GRAINS 657 JERUSALEM 31   20
      OF SAND
    THEN HE SENT FORTH THE SPECTRE ALL HIS PYRAMIDS WERE GRAINS 739 JERUSALEM 91   48
GRAMMATEIS
    THE PHARISAION THE GRAMMATEIS THE PRESBUTERION . . . . 734 JERUSALEM 89 * 6
GRAND
    GRAND CHORUS . . . . 54C LO THE BAT/IM TITLE
    ("WITH WISDOM DIRECTS OBSTINACY") THIS MUST BE A GRAND 79B ANNO LAVATER MARG
      FELLOW
    IN A STYLE MORE ORNAMENTAL UNIFORM AND GRAND THAN ANY . 207B PROSPECTUS 1793 PROSE
    THE BISHOP HAS NOT ANSWERD ONE OF PAINE'S GRAND OBJECTIONS 396C ANNO WATSON MARG
    THE TWO GRAND MERITS OF THE GREAT STYLE . . . . . . 468B ANNO REYNOLDS MARG
    ALL WILL BE SET RIGHT & THOSE GRAND WORKS OF . . . . . 480B MILTON 1 PROSE
    WHAT IS MOST GRAND IS ALWAYS MOST MINUTE . . . . . . 547 PRETTY EPIGR/N   2
    RUBENS THINKS TABLES CHAIRS & STOOLS ARE GRAND . . . . 547 PRETTY EPIGR/N   3
    TWO PICTURES REPRESENTING GRAND APOTHEOSES . . . . . . 560C EXHIBITION ADV PROSE
    THE GRAND STYLE OF ART RESTORED IN FRESCO OR . . . . . 562B DESC CAT ADV PROSE
    AND ALL THE GRAND WORKS OF ANCIENT ART THEY WERE EXECUTED 565D DESC CAT 2 PROSE
    GRAND IN THE HIGHEST DEGREE THE ARTIST HAS ENDEAVOURED . 565D DESC CAT 2 PROSE
    WHAT IS TRULY GRAND AND REALLY POLITE HER PERSON AND FACE 568B DESC CAT 3 PROSE
    AND HAS ALSO HIS GREAT USE AND HIS GRAND LEADING DESTINY 570A DESC CAT 3 PROSE
    OF THE FIRST MAGNITUDE GRAND TERRIFIC RICH AND HONOURED 570A DESC CAT 3 PROSE
    WILL NOT ADMIT OF GRAND COLOURING IN MR B'S(BLAKE'S) 581A DESC CAT 5 PROSE
      BRITONS
    OF PAINTERS AND POETS THEY ARE FOUNDATIONS FOR GRAND THINGS 581D DESC CAT 8 PROSE
    THIS WHEN DONE BY [THIS IN] GRAND WORKS . . . . . . 599A PUB ADDRESS/N PROSE
    & NO GRAND WORK CAN HAVE THEM THEY PRODUCE SYSTEM 599B PUB ADDRESS/N *PROSE
      & MONOTONY
    OUGHT TO KNOW THAT WHAT IS GRAND IS NECESSARILY OBSCURE 793A LETTER 5 PROSE
      TO WEAK MEN
    MORE GRAND THAN ITS SIMPLICITY & USEFULNESS . . . . . 801D LETTER 14 PROSE
    AN IMMENSE NUMBER OF VERSES ON ONE GRAND THEME . . . . 823A LETTER 26 PROSE
    I THINK THE GRAND REASON OF MY BEING BROUGHT DOWN HERE . 823B LETTER 26 PROSE
    WHICH IS NOW PERFECTLY COMPLETED INTO A GRAND POEM . . 825A LETTER 27 PROSE
    LODGINGS & FIND THEM ALL TOO GRAND AS WELL AS . . . 848A LETTER 45 PROSE
    IN ANY WAY BE SEPARATED FROM THE GRAND BULK OF YOUR . . 858C LETTER 55 PROSE
GRANDEST
    THE GRANDEST POETRY IS IMMORAL THE GRANDEST CHARACTERS 412B ANNO BOYD MARG
      WICKED
    THAT THE WORST PAINTERS ALWAYS CHOSE THE GRANDEST SUBJECTS 465C ANNO REYNOLDS MARG
    ONE OF RAFAEL'S GRANDEST SUBJECTS NAMELY CHRIST DELIVERING 465C ANNO REYNOLDS MARG
    HE KNOWS THAT WHAT HE DOES IS NOT INFERIOR TO THE GRANDEST 579B DESC CAT 5 PROSE
    I CONSIDER IT AS THE GRANDEST POEM THAT THIS WORLD CONTAINS 825A LETTER 27 PROSE
GRANDEUR
    EXIST GRANDEUR OF IDEAS IS FOUNDED ON PRECISION OF IDEAS 457D ANNO REYNOLDS MARG

		PAGE	TITLE	LINE

GRANDEUR   (CONTINUED)
    I COME IN SELF-ANNIHILATION & THE GRANDEUR OF INSPIRATION   533 MILTON 41   2
    TO EMULATE THE GRANDEUR OF THOSE SEEN IN HIS VISION . .   565D DESC CAT 2   PROSE
    TO THE GRANDEUR OF THE NATION WHO IS THE PARENT OF HIS   566A DESC CAT 2   PROSE
      HEROES
    WITHOUT OSTENTATION AND WITH ALL THE TRUE GRANDEUR . . . 568A DESC CAT 3   PROSE
    AND NOT FOR HISTORICAL GRANDEUR THE ARTIST HAS IMAGINED   580A DESC CAT 5   PROSE
GRANDMOTHERS
    IT PUTS ME IN MIND OF MY [GRANDMOTHER'S] MOTHER'S SONG . . 59D ISLAND MOON 11   PROSE
GRANT
    AND GRANT HIS FAVOURS WITH A SPARING HAND . . . . . .   20 EDW THIRD/PS 2   47
    GRANT ME A SON KIND HEAVEN MANOA CRIED BUT HEAVEN REFUSED   39C SAMSON/PS   PROSE
    WE PERISH & SHALL NOT BE FOUND UNLESS THOU GRANT A PLACE   304 FOUR ZOAS 4   259
    BUT GRANT US A TEMPORAL HABITATION DO YOU SPEAK . . . . 519 MILTON 30   29
    HIS POWER OF EXECUTION I MUST GRANT . . . . 547 RAFAEL SUBLI/N   4
    PLEASE TO GRANT IN SHORT I AM TENANT AT WILL AND MAY WRITE   858C LETTER 55   PROSE
GRANTED
    ONE CENTRAL FORM COMPOSED OF ALL OTHER FORMS BEING GRANTED   459C ANNO REYNOLDS   MARG
    HE THEREFORE TAKES A FALSHOOD FOR GRANTED TO SET OUT WITH   475B ANNO REYNOLDS   MARG
    [FUNERAL GRANTED TO SIR JOSHUA FOR HAVING ?DESTROYD ART]   SUPP ANNO REYNOLDS   * MARG
GRAPE
    WITH THE BLOOD OF THE GRAPE PASS NOT BUT SIT . . . . .   2 TO AUTUMN/PS   2
    OVER THEIR PALE LIMBS AS A VINE WHEN THE TENDER GRAPE   202 AMERICA 15   26
      APPEARS
    TEARS OF THE GRAPE THE DEATH SWEAT OF THE CLUSTER THE LAST   377 FOUR ZOAS 9   770
      SIGH
    TEARS OF THE GRAPE THE DEATH SWEAT OF THE CLUSTER THE LAST   514 MILTON 27   40
      SIGH
GRAPES
    . . . WHEN GRAPES ARE SHAKEN ON GRASS . . . . 145 FRENCH REVOLTN   244
    FLOURISHES THAT HE MAY RECIEVE THE GRAPES THRO ONE CAN LOOK 237 EUROPE INTRO   3
    HOW ART THOU SHRUNK THY GRAPES THAT BURST IN SUMMER'S VAST   325 FOUR ZOAS 7   190
      EXCESS
    O HOW DELICIOUS ARE THE GRAPES FLOURISHING IN THE SUN . . 369 FOUR ZOAS 9   447
    SHE [D] STOPD TO DRINK OF THE CLEAR SPRING & EAT THE GRAPES 369 FOUR ZOAS 9   * 476
      & APPLES
    THE FALLING GRAPES THAT ODOROUS BURST UPON THE WINDS ARISE   376 FOUR ZOAS 9   698
    HOW RED THE SONS & DAUGHTERS OF LUVAH HOW THEY TREAD THE   377 FOUR ZOAS 9   743
      GRAPES
    BUT IN THE WINE PRESSES THE HUMAN GRAPES SING NOT NOR DANCE 377 FOUR ZOAS 9   748
    WHEN GRAPES & FIGS BURST THEIR COVERING TO THE JOYFUL AIR   485 MILTON 5   33
    HOW RED THE SONS & DAUGHTERS OF LUVAH HERE THEY TREAD THE   513 MILTON 27   3
      GRAPES
    BUT IN THE WINE-PRESSES THE HUMAN GRAPES SING NOT NOR DANCE 513 MILTON 27   30
    A VINE FILLED WITH GRAPES THE TREE WHICH MOVES SOME TO   793D LETTER 5   PROSE
      TEARS
GRASE
    GRASE AFTER THEE AND WEEP . . . . 119 NIGHT/SI   * 44
GRASP
    RUNS ACHING COLD INTO THE SCEPTER TOO HEAVY FOR MORTAL   134 FRENCH REVOLTN   4
      GRASP NO MORE
    WHAT THE ANVIL WHAT [THE ARM] [ARM] [GRASP] [CLASP] DREAD   172 THE TYGER/N 1   20
      GRASP
    [COULD] DARE ITS DEADLY TERRORS [CLASP] [GRASP] CLASP . . 172 THE TYGER/N 1   21
    WHAT THE ANVIL WHAT DREAD GRASP . . . . 214 THE TYGER/SE   15
    I GRASP THY VEST IN MY STRONG HAND IN VAIN LIKE WATER   288 FOUR ZOAS 2   * 304
      SPRINGS
    THE HAMMER LOUD RAGES IN RINTRAH'S STRONG GRASP SWINGING   636 JERUSALEM 16   11
      LOUD
    HEAVENS A MOTH OF GOLD & SILVER MOCKING HIS ANXIOUS GRASP   739 JERUSALEM 91   50
GRASPING
    A KING CROWNED GRASPING HIS SWORD & HIS SCEPTRE . . . . 608B V LAST JUDG/N   PROSE
GRASPS
    SHE STILL INTREATS AND STILL SHE GRASPS HIS VIGOROUS KNEES   38B SAMSON/PS   PROSE
    IN VAIN THE DREAMER GRASPS THE JOYFUL IMAGES THEY FLY . . 206 THIRALATHA   2
    AND THE HAND OF MAN GRASPS FIRM BETWEEN THE MALE & FEMALE   744 JERUSALEM 97   15
      LOVES
GRASS
    THE SHINING SNAKE GLIDES OER THE BENDING GRASS . . . .   24 EDW THIRD/PS 3   126
    GREEN GRASS SPRINGS IN JOY AND THE NIMBLE AIR KISSES THE   37B CONTEMPLATN/PS   PROSE
      LEAVES
    TEN THOUSAND SPEARS ARE LIKE THE SUMMER GRASS . . . . . 39A SAMSON/PS   PROSE
    WHERE ON GRASS METHOUGHT I LAY . . . . 111 A DREAM/SI   4
    THE LILLY OF THE VALLEY BREATHING IN THE HUMBLE GRASS . . 127 BOOK OF THEL 1   15
    SAYING REJOICE THOU HUMBLE GRASS THOU NEW-BORN LILLY FLOWER 127 BOOK OF THEL 1   21
    WHICH THOU DOST SCATTER ON EVERY LITTLE BLADE OF GRASS   128 BOOK OF THEL 2   9
      THAT SPRINGS
    AND WENT TO MIND HER NUMEROUS CHARGE AMONG THE VERDANT   128 BOOK OF THEL 2   18
      GRASS
    . . . WHEN GRAPES ARE SHAKEN ON GRASS . . . . 145 FRENCH REVOLTN   244
    ARISE FROM OUT THE DEWY GRASS . . . . 210 INTRODUCTN/SE   12
    ON THE GRASS THEY PLAY . . . . 219 LIT GRL LST/SE   16
    IS HEARD THROUGHOUT THE UNIVERSE WHEREEVER A GRASS GROWS   356 FOUR ZOAS 8   * 581
    COME FORTH O VALA FROM THE GRASS & FROM THE SILENT DEW   367 FOUR ZOAS 9   388
    . . . ON THE TOPS OF THE BENDING GRASS . . . . . . 367 FOUR ZOAS 9   391
    THEN O THOU FAIR ONE SIT THEE DOWN FOR THOU ART AS THE   367 FOUR ZOAS 9   408
      GRASS
    HOPELESS IF I AM LIKE THE GRASS & SO SHALL PASS AWAY . . 368 FOUR ZOAS 9   417
    WAVE FRESHLY CLEAR WATERS FLOWING AROUND THE TENDER GRASS   368 FOUR ZOAS 9   436
    THE GRASS SHE SLEPT UPON WAS PAVD WITH PAVEMENT AS OF PEARL 369 FOUR ZOAS 9   462
    LEAPD FROM THE STEPS OF FIRE & ON THE GRASS . . . . . 414 TO MRS FLAXMAN   5
    THEREFORE HE APPEARS ONLY A SMALL ROOT CREEPING IN GRASS   526 MILTON 35   56

831

		PAGE	TITLE	LINE
GRASS (CONTINUED)				
SO PAINTING ADMITS NOT A GRAIN OF SAND OR A BLADE OF GRASS		611B	V LAST JUDG/N	PROSE
AND WHO WEAVE IT A CRADLE OF THE GRASS THAT WITHERETH AWAY		688	JERUSALEM 56	7
GRASSHOPPER				
AND THE GRASSHOPPER LAUGHS IN THE MERRY SCENE		63	SHEPHERD YOUNG	4
AND THE GRASSHOPPER LAUGHS IN THE MERRY SCENE		125	LAUGHING/SI	6
. . . LIKE THE VOICE OF THE GRASSHOPPER WHISPERD . . .		140	FRENCH REVOLTN	136
DRINK LAUGH & SING THE GRASSHOPPER THE EMMET & THE FLY . .		308	FOUR ZOAS 5	* 133
WONDERING TO BEHOLD THE EMMET THE GRASSHOPPER THE JOINTED WORM		373	FOUR ZOAS 9	603
THE SLOW SLUG THE GRASSHOPPER THAT SINGS & LAUGHS & DRINKS		377	FOUR ZOAS 9	760
THE SLOW SLUG THE GRASSHOPPER THAT SINGS & LAUGHS & DRINKS		513	MILTON 27	19
GRASSY				
IN THE SPIRIT OF THE MORNING AWAKING THE SOUL FROM ITS GRASSY BED		367	FOUR ZOAS 9	394
AND NOW HER FEET STEP ON THE GRASSY BOSOM OF THE GROUND		370	FOUR ZOAS 9	505
GRATE				
TO GRATE THE SOUL INTO DESTRUCTION OR TO INFLAME WITH FURY		344	FOUR ZOAS 8	136
GRATEFUL				
THE JOYFUL SHEPHERD STOPS HIS GRATEFUL SONG		9	FRESH FROM/PS	11
ON SCORN TO FEED OUR DISCONTENT FOR IF WE GRATEFUL PROVE		271	FOUR ZOAS 1	256
DEADLY BETWEEN THE HAMMER'S BEATING GRATEFUL TO THE EARS		302	FOUR ZOAS 4	190
AND WITH SOFT GRATEFUL TEARS		421	MORNING/N	11
& BELIEVE ME FOR EVER TO REMAIN YOUR GRATEFUL & AFFECTIONATE		802D	LETTER 14	PROSE
I CAN BE GRATEFUL & I CAN SOON SEND YOU SOME OF YOUR DESIGNS		808D	LETTER 20	PROSE
THEIR AUTHOR AND GRATEFUL TO YOU MY EMPLOYER & THAT I LOOK		814D	LETTER 23	PROSE
AM ALSO GRATEFUL TO THE KIND HAND THAT ENDEAVOURS TO LIFT ME		822C	LETTER 26	PROSE
AS ALSO FOR OMITTING TO MENTION MR HOARE'S GRATEFUL . . .		839B	LETTER 38	PROSE
FOR O HAPPINESS NEVER ENOUGH TO BE GRATEFUL FOR		853A	LETTER 51	*PROSE
GRATEFUL WISH TO YOU & TO OUR DEAR RESPECTED MISS POOLE		860B	LETTER 56	PROSE
[OF] ALL OUR FRIENDS TO WHOM WE ARE GRATEFUL & DESIRE TO BE		862A	LETTER 59	PROSE
I CANNOT OMIT TO RETURN YOU MY SINCERE & GRATEFUL . . .		862B	LETTER 60	PROSE
I AM PREPARED FOR IT BUT AT THE SAME TIME SINCERELY GRATEFUL		862C	LETTER 60	PROSE
TILL THEN I REMAIN YOUR GRATEFUL ALTHO SEEMINGLY OTHERWISE		866B	LETTER 64	PROSE
I SAY YOUR GRATEFUL & SINCERE		866B	LETTER 64	PROSE
GRATEFUL THO NOT ABLE ON ACCOUNT OF THIS ABOMINABLE AGUE		868D	LETTER 68	PROSE
GRATEFULLY				
CONVENIENT TO DO SO IT WILL BE GRATEFULLY REMEMBERD BY ME		826C	LETTER 28	PROSE
REMEMBER US BOTH AFFECTIONATELY & GRATEFULLY TO MISS POOLE		840A	LETTER 38	PROSE
I AM DEAR SIR YOURS MOST GRATEFULLY		873B	LETTER 76	PROSE
GRATIFICATION				
ONLY FOR THE SAKE OF PRESENT EASE OR GRATIFICATION . . .		154B	MARRIAGE HH 12	PROSE
FOR SENSELESS GRATIFICATION & THEIR VISAGES THRUST FORTH		344	FOUR ZOAS 8	127
& EATING THE TREE OF KNOWLEDGE FOR SATAN'S GRATIFICATION		616D	V LAST JUDG/N	PROSE
MY WIFE'S HIGH GRATIFICATION IN THE PERUSAL OF		853A	LETTER 51	*PROSE
GRATIFICATIONS				
THE FEMALE SEARCHES SEA & LAND FOR GRATIFICATIONS TO THE		707	JERUSALEM 69	16
GRATIFIED				
. . . GRATIFIED & DRINKING TEARS OF WOE		338	FOUR ZOAS 7B	213
BUT DESIRE GRATIFIED		178	ABSTINENCE/N	3
THE LINEAMENTS OF GRATIFIED DESIRE		178	IN A WIFE/N	3
THE LINEAMENTS OF GRATIFIED DESIRE		180	QUESTN ANSRD/N	2
THE LINEAMENTS OF GRATIFIED DESIRE		180	QUESTN ANSRD/N	4
THE LINEAMENTS OF GRATIFIED DESIRE		184	SEVRL QUESTN/N	2
THE LINEAMENTS OF GRATIFIED DESIRE		184	SEVRL QUESTN/N	4
WITH LINEAMENTS OF GRATIFIED DESIRE		244	EUROPE 14	19
BY GRATIFIED DESIRE BY STRONG DEVOURING APPETITE SHE FILLS		323	FOUR ZOAS 7	133
IN TERRIBLE CONVULSIONS PITYING & GRATIFIED DRUNK WITH PITY		723	JERUSALEM 80	70
KNOWING HIMSELF THE AUTHOR OF THEIR DIVISIONS & SHRINKINGS GRATIFIED		733	JERUSALEM 88	35
INFINITELY BETTER THE NEXT PROOF I FEEL VERY MUCH GRATIFIED		855C	LETTER 53	PROSE
GRATIFY				
TO GRATIFY SENSES UNKNOWN TREES BEASTS AND BIRDS UNKNOWN		192	V DAU ALBION 4	15
TO FEED THEIR FRUIT TO GRATIFY THEIR HIDDEN SONS & DAUGHTERS		335	FOUR ZOAS 7B	104
TO DESTROY THE WISDOM OF AGES TO GRATIFY RAVENOUS ENVY . .		533	MILTON 41	17
[?WHY ?THEN GRATIFY FLEMISH PAINTERS XXX]		SUPP	ANNO REYNOLDS	* MARG
GRATIFYD				
THESE BEAUTIFUL WITCHCRAFTS OF ALBION ARE GRATIFYD BY CRUELTY		737	JERUSALEM 90	68
GRATIFYING				
ASSURE YOU A PLEASING ONE TO ME IT WILL BE HIGHLY GRATIFYING		859C	LETTER 56	PROSE
& NOT ONLY GRATIFYING BUT IMPROVING WHICH IS BETTER . . .		859C	LETTER 56	PROSE
MOST GRATIFYING MAY IT GO ON TO THE PERFECTION YOU WISH		876C	LETTER 83	PROSE
GRATING				
WOULD HAVE RISEN BUT COULD NOT HIS VOICE ISSUED HARSH GRATING . . .		142	FRENCH REVOLTN	177
TO CHANGE TO A GRATING CRY		232	URIZEN 19	32
GRATIS				
AN INDEX TO THE CATALOGUE GRATIS		562C	DESC CAT ADV	PROSE
GRATITUDE				
("GRATITUDE...OPENS TREASURES WITHIN US") NOBLE & GENEROUS		70A	ANNO LAVATER	MARG
GAVE SONGS OF GRATITUDE TO [THE] WAVING CORN FIELDS ROUND THEIR NEST		276	FOUR ZOAS 1	* 450
COMPELLD OTHERS TO SERVE HIM IN MORAL GRATITUDE & SUBMISSION		491	MILTON 11	11
SUCCESS IS NOT THE LESS TO BE REMEMBERD BY ME WITH GRATITUDE		794D	LETTER 6	PROSE

```
                                                     PAGE       TITLE          LINE
GRATITUDE   (CONTINUED)
     OF GRATITUDE OR FRIENDSHIP BUT PERHAPS AN EXCESS OF BOTH      798D LETTER 10           PROSE
     PANG OF AFFECTION & GRATITUDE IS THE GIFT OF GOD FOR GOOD     833D LETTER 33           PROSE
     SPIRITS OF JUST MEN MADE PERFECT BY LOVE & GRATITUDE    .   . 834A LETTER 33           PROSE
     GRATITUDE IS HEAVEN ITSELF THERE COULD BE NO HEAVEN          834A LETTER 33           PROSE
        WITHOUT
     GRATITUDE I FEEL IT & I KNOW IT I THANK GOD & MAN FOR IT &   834A LETTER 33           PROSE
     PRAY ACCEPT MY AND MY WIFE'S SINCEREST LOVE AND GRATITUDE    861B LETTER 58           PROSE
     GRATITUDE HAVING CONDUCTED ME THRO THREE THAT WOULD  .  .  . 862C LETTER 60           PROSE
GRATUITOUSLY
     DID I GRATUITOUSLY DESIGND FOR HIM AT THE SAME TIME HE   .  . 592D PUB ADDRESS/N      PROSE
GRAVE
     BRINGS ME YEW TO DECK MY GRAVE . . . . . . . . . .         6 MY SILKS/PS           5
     WHEN I MY GRAVE HAVE MADE  . . . . . . . . . .             7 MY SILKS/PS          15
     LIKE REARED STONES AROUND A GRAVE  . . . . . . . . .      12 GWIN KING/PS          41
     OUR CHILDREN'S MOTHER AND THOU SHALT BE OUR GRAVE   .  .  . 32 EDW THIRD/PS 6       16
     IF I LAY MY FACE IN THE DUST THE GRAVE OPENS ITS MOUTH    36A COUCH DEATH/PS     PROSE
        FOR ME
     SO SAYING HE BEGAN TO DIG A GRAVE WITH HIS AGED HANDS   .  . 100 TIRIEL 1             34
     BUT HEUXOS CALLD A SON OF ZAZEL TO [XXX] DIG THEIR MOTHER   100 TIRIEL 1          *   35
        A GRAVE
     OLD CRUELTY DESIST & LET US DIG A GRAVE FOR THEE  .  .  .  . 100 TIRIEL 1             36
     AND NOW YOU FEEL IT DIG A GRAVE & LET US BURY OUR MOTHER    100 TIRIEL 1             42
     GRAVE THE SENTENCE DEEP  . . . . . . . . . . .            112 LIT GRL LST/SI         4
     DOLOURS & LAMENTATIONS WAITING OFT BESIDE A DEWY GRAVE  .   130 BOOK OF THEL 6        7
     TILL TO HER OWN GRAVE PLOT SHE CAME & THERE SHE SAT DOWN    130 BOOK OF THEL 6        9
     AND NARROW AS A GRAVE DUG FOR A CHILD . . . . . . .        136 FRENCH REVOLTN        40
     AND BRIGHT CHILDREN LOOK AFTER HIM INTO THE GRAVE  . . .    139 FRENCH REVOLTN       108
     ASK THE BLIND WORM THE SECRETS OF THE GRAVE AND WHY HER     191 V DAU ALBION 3        10
        SPIRES
     AND A PALACE OF ETERNITY IN THE JAWS OF THE HUNGRY GRAVE    193 V DAU ALBION 6         1
     THE GRAVE IS BURST THE SPICES SHED THE LINEN WRAPPED UP     198 AMERICA 6              2
     A RAGING WHIRLPOOL DRAWS THE DIZZY ENQUIRER TO HIS GRAVE    242 EUROPE 10             31
     THAT LEADS FROM THE GATES OF THE GRAVE  . . . . . .        247 SONG OF LOS 7          8
     THE GRAVE SHRIEKS WITH DELIGHT & SHAKES  . . . . . .       248 SONG OF LOS 7         35
     DOES THE SOUL LABOUR THUS IN CAVERNS OF THE GRAVE   .  .   262A SMALL BK DSGNS     TITLE
     WOVEN BY THEIR OWN HANDS TO HIDE THEM IN THE DARKSOM GRAVE  266 FOUR ZOAS 1          65
     ALL RAVNING LIKE THE HUNGRY WORM & LIKE THE SILENT GRAVE    280 FOUR ZOAS 2          17
     TO WEIGH ME DOWN BENEATH THE GRAVE INTO NON ENTITY   .  .   295 FOUR ZOAS 3         127
     INTO THE CAVERNS OF THE GRAVE & PLACES OF HUMAN SEED   .    295 FOUR ZOAS 3         142
     SO IN THE REGIONS OF THE GRAVE NONE KNOWS HIS DARK COMPEER  314 FOUR ZOAS 6          97
     FOR WHEN HE DIED THEY LAY BESIDE [HIM] HIS GRAVE & WHEN     316 FOUR ZOAS 6      *  168
        HE ROSE
     THEN FOLLOWS THUS IN THE CAVERNS OF THE GRAVE &C AS IT  .  336B FOUR ZOAS 7B     *PROSE
     NOW IN THE CAVERNS OF THE GRAVE & PLACES OF HUMAN SEED  .   336 FOUR ZOAS 7B        124
     WE LOOK DOWN INTO ULRO WE BEHOLD THE WONDERS OF THE GRAVE   346 FOUR ZOAS 8         223
     AND THUS AHANIA CRIES ALOUD TO THE CAVERNS OF THE GRAVE     353 FOUR ZOAS 8         492
     OR A PILLAR & PALACE OF ETERNITY IN THE JAWS OF THE HUNGRY  354 FOUR ZOAS 8         496
        GRAVE
     AND THE GRAVE MOCK & LAUGH AT THE PLOWD FIELD SAYING   .    354 FOUR ZOAS 8         499
     THUS CRIES AHANIA ENION REPLIES FROM THE CAVERNS OF THE     354 FOUR ZOAS 8         533
        GRAVE
     THE WATRY GRAVE O THOU CORN FIELD O THOU VEGETATER HAPPY    355 FOUR ZOAS 8         543
     THE FURROWD FIELD REPLIES TO THE GRAVE I HEAR HER REPLY     355 FOUR ZOAS 8         548
        TO ME
     LISTEN I WILL TELL THEE WHAT IS DONE IN THE CAVERNS OF      355 FOUR ZOAS 8         555
        THE GRAVE
     AND HEARD ENION'S VOICE SOUND FROM THE CAVERNS OF THE GRAVE 356 FOUR ZOAS 8         605
     MINGLED WITH THE CONFUSION WHO SHALL CALL THEM FROM THE     358 FOUR ZOAS 9          31
        GRAVE
     FROM HER SHALL LEARN OBEDIENCE & PREPARE FOR A WINTRY GRAVE 362 FOUR ZOAS 9         217
     FLOCK TO THE TRUMPET MUTTRING OVER THE SIDES OF THE GRAVE   363 FOUR ZOAS 9         239
        & CRYING
     O TERRIBLE WINE PRESSES OF LUVAH O CAVERNS OF THE GRAVE     376 FOUR ZOAS 9         728
     DESIRING LIKE THE HUNGRY WORM & LIKE THE [SILENT] GAPING    376 FOUR ZOAS 9         735
        GRAVE
     AND WHEN DEAD I'LL BE THY GRAVE  .  .  .  .  .  .  .  .  .  416 MY SPECTRE/N         54
     AND MY BED BECOMES THEIR GRAVE . . . . . . . . . .         417 MY SPECTR AD/N        8
     THAT BETWIXT THE CRADLE & GRAVE  . . . . . . . . .         424 THE SMILE            13
     THE ROTTING GRAVE SHALL NEER GET OUT . . . . . . .         433 AUGURIES             88
     THE GRAVE IS HEAVEN'S GOLDEN GATE  . . . . . . . .         442 DEDICATN BLAIR        7
     FROM THE VAST REGIONS OF THE GRAVE . . . . . . . .         442 DEDICATN BLAIR       15
     THE GRAVE PRODUCD THESE BLOSSOMS SWEET   . . . . . .       442 DEDICATN BLAIR       18
     OTHERS NEWLY AWAKEN FROM THE GRAVE   . . . . . . .        444A LAST JUDGMNT/L     PROSE
     O READER BEHOLD THE PHILOSOPHER'S GRAVE  . . . . . .       470 ANNO REYNOLDS         1
     I WILL ARISE AND LOOK FORTH FOR THE MORNING OF THE GRAVE    495 MILTON 14            20
     WHEN JESUS RAISD LAZARUS FROM THE GRAVE I STOOD & SAW  .    508 MILTON 24            26
     AND HELL & THE GRAVE STATES THAT ARE NOT BUT AH SEEM TO BE  522 MILTON 32            29
     AND LAYS DOWN IN THE GRAVE WITH THEM IN VISIONS OF ETERNITY 522 MILTON 32            41
     THE [VISIONS] CAVERNS OF THE GRAVE IVE SEEN  . . . . .     558 THE CAVERNS/N         1
     DESIGNS FOR BLAIR'S GRAVE HAVE LEFT HIM TO SHIFT          572D DESC CAT 3         PROSE
        FOR HIMSELF
     HE IS JUST AWAKEND OUT OF HIS GRAVE  . . . . . . .        608C V LAST JUDG/N     PROSE
     AS HE MUST KNOW THEN WOULD HE ARISE FROM HIS GRAVE   .  .  611A V LAST JUDG/N     PROSE
     MERCY & PITY THREW THE GRAVE STONE OVER ME & WITH LEAD  .   630 JERUSALEM 10         54
     ARE YOU MY CHILDREN NATIVES IN THE GRAVE TO WHERE I GO  .   647 JERUSALEM 24         13
     HER PALACES WITH HELL & THE GRAVE HER SYNAGOGUES           647 JERUSALEM 24         34
        WITH TORMENTS
     TO HAVE POWER OVER MAN FROM CRADLE TO CORRUPTIBLE GRAVE     661 JERUSALEM 34         26
     MUST PASS THRO CONDEMNATION AND AWAKE BEYOND THE GRAVE  .   662 JERUSALEM 35         10
     O WHEN SHALL THE MORNING OF THE GRAVE APPEAR AND WHEN  .    671 JERUSALEM 42         71
     TO HAVE POWER OVER MAN FROM CRADLE TO CORRUPTIBLE GRAVE     688 JERUSALEM 56          4
```

		PAGE	TITLE	LINE

GRAVE   (CONTINUED)

REPOSE ON ME TILL THE MORNING OF THE GRAVE I AM THY LIFE   695 JERUSALEM 62   1
AND VALA FOR I CANNOT LEAVE THEM IN THE GNAWING GRAVE   .   .   696 JERUSALEM 62   21
IN THE END OF HIS SLEEP WHEN JESUS CALLS HIM FROM HIM HIS   701 JERUSALEM 65   *   62
    GRAVE
FROM HER THESE FIBRES SHOOT TO SHUT ME IN A GRAVE   .   .   . 733 JERUSALEM 87   23
WANDERING IN THAT UNKNOWN NIGHT BEYOND THE SILENT GRAVE   736 JERUSALEM 89   61
HE MEETS HIS SAVIOUR IN THE GRAVE .   .   .   . 771 OF GATES/GP   20
EVE FAINTED OVER THE DEAD BODY OF ABEL WHICH LAYS NEAR   779C GHOST ABEL 1   PROSE
    A GRAVE
ABEL SINKS DOWN INTO THE GRAVE FROM WHICH ARISES SATAN   .   . 780C GHOST ABEL 2   PROSE
HIM ILLUSTRATIONS OF THE GRAVE A POEM BY ROBERT BLAIR   .   . 861C LETTER 59   PROSE
THE PROPHETESS RISING FROM HER GRAVE .   .   .   .   .   .   SUPP ILLUS GRAY   *TITLE
"ARE GLAD WHEN THEY CAN FIND THE GRAVE"   .   .   .   .   .   SUPP LEGEND/N17   *

GRAVEL

LEAVES UPON THE TREES & THE STONES & GRAVEL UPON THE ROAD   588A CHAUCER/N   PROSE

GRAVELOT

[ALIAMET] GRAVELOT ONCE SAID TO MY MASTER BASIRE [YOU]   594D PUB ADDRESS/N *PROSE
    DE ENGLISH

GRAVER

AS A DIRECTION FOR YOUR GRAVER .   .   .   .   .440C MEMORANDUM/N 3 PROSE
WOOLETT I KNOW DID NOT KNOW HOW TO GRIND HIS GRAVER   .   . 603C PUB ADDR AD/N PROSE
BEEN PUBLISHD EVEN JOHNSON & FUSELI HAVE DISCARDED   795C LETTER 6   PROSE
    MY GRAVER
WHENEVER I TAKE A PENCIL OR GRAVER INTO MY HAND EVEN AS I   852C LETTER 50   PROSE
& AM AS MUCH MYSELF WHEN I TAKE THE PENCIL OR GRAVER   .   . 853A LETTER 51   *PROSE

GRAVERS

RIDICULING THE FORMS OF BASIRE'S OTHER GRAVERS   .   .   .   603C PUB ADDR AD/N PROSE

GRAVES

THE GRAVES GIVE UP THEIR DEAD FAIR ELENOR   .   .   .   .   4 FAIR ELENOR/PS   2
WHO NOW SLEEP IN THEIR GRAVES WALKED ON THE STEDFAST GLOBE   35C COUCH DEATH/PS   PROSE
[OR THOSE WHOSE MOUTHS ARE GRAVES   .   .   .   .   .   .   109 TIRIEL 8   17
. . . THEY DESCEND AND LOOK INTO THEIR GRAVES   .   .   . 137 FRENCH REVOLTN   71
. . . LIKE A MAN THAT RETURNS FROM HOLLOW GRAVES   .   .   141 FRENCH REVOLTN   161
. . . AND THE GRAVES OF ARCH-ANGELS UNSEALD   .   .   .   148 FRENCH REVOLTN   301
AND I SAW IT WAS FILLED WITH GRAVES   .   .   .   .   .   . 163 GARDEN LOVE/N   9
ARISE FROM THEIR GRAVES AND ASPIRE   .   .   .   .   .   . 215 AH SUNFLOWR/SE   7
AND I SAW IT WAS FILLED WITH GRAVES   .   .   .   .   .   . 215 GARDEN LOVE/SE   9
FELL THRO THE WINTRY SKIES SEEKING THEIR GRAVES   .   .   .   243 EUROPE 13   7
THE GARDENS OF WISDOM ARE BECOME A FIELD OF HORRID GRAVES   310 FOUR ZOAS 5   196
SHALT GATHER THEM FROM OUT THEIR GRAVES & PUT THY FETTER   334 FOUR ZOAS 7B   70
    ON THEM
OVER THE GRAVES & CAVERNS OF THE DEAD OVER THE PLANETS   365 FOUR ZOAS 9   314
THE MYRIADS & IN SILENT FEAR THEY [F] LOOK OUT FROM THEIR   366 FOUR ZOAS 9   * 339
    GRAVES
WHERE SHALL THE GRAVES RECIEVE THEM ALL & WHERE SHALL BE   375 FOUR ZOAS 9   668
    THEIR PLACE
[WHILE OTHERS RISE FROM THEIR GRAVES ON THE BRINK OF THE   443B LAST JUDGMNT/L PROSE
    PIT]
[THE] GREEN HILLS APPEAR BENEATH WITH THE GRAVES OF THE   443D LAST JUDGMNT/L PROSE
    BLESSED
FOR HE TOOK THE OUTSIDE COURSE AMONG THE GRAVES OF THE DEAD   496 MILTON 14   34
THE SEVEN HEADED KINGDOMS THE GRAVES BENEATH   .   .   .   . 609C V LAST JUDG/N   PROSE
EMBRACING ABOVE THE GRAVES & REPRESENT RELIGION   .   .   . 610C V LAST JUDG/N   PROSE
JUST ABOVE THE GRAVES & ABOVE THE SPOT   .   .   .   .   . 610C V LAST JUDG/N   PROSE
. . . WHEN THE GRAVES SHALL YIELD THEIR DEAD   .   .   . 633 JERUSALEM 13   11
THE GRAVES THUNDER BENEATH HIS FEET FROM IRELAND TO JAPAN   661 JERUSALEM 34   42
BENEATH THE BOTTOMS OF THE GRAVES WHICH IS EARTH'S CENTRAL   677 JERUSALEM 48   13
    JOINT
BURST THE BOTTOMS OF THE GRAVES & FUNERAL ARKS OF BEULAH   736 JERUSALEM 89   60
THUS THEY CONVERSE UPON MAM-TOR THE GRAVES THUNDER UNDER   741 JERUSALEM 93   27
    THEIR FEET

GRAVING

THEN PROCEED TO GRAVING WITH THE GROUND ON THE PLATE   .   . 440C MEMORANDUM/N 3 PROSE
TOM COOKE CUT HOGARTH DOWN WITH HIS CLEAN GRAVING   .   .   . 554 BLAKES APL/N 1   3
TOM COOKE CUT HOGARTH DOWN WITH HIS CLEAN GRAVING   .   .   . 555 BLAKES APL/N 2   7
TOM COOKE CUT HOGARTH DOWN WITH HIS CLEAN GRAVING   .   .   . 595 BLAKES APOL/PA   3
BUT BECAUSE THEY DID NOT UNDERSTAND [(COLOURING)] GRAVING   602D PUB ADDR AD/N *PROSE
THEIR COLOURING GRAVING & VERSE CAN NEVER BE APPLIED TO ART   602D PUB ADDR AD/N PROSE
THAT IS NOT EITHER COLOURING GRAVING OR VERSE WHICH IS   .   . 603A PUB ADDR AD/N PROSE

GRAY

AROUND THE SPRINGS OF GRAY MY WILD ROOT WEAVES   .   .   .   414 ILLUS GRAY   1
NUMBER IV THE BARD FROM GRAY   .   .   .   .   576A DESC CAT 4   TITLE
THEY ARE THERE NOW GRAY SAW THEM IN THE PERSON OF HIS BARD   578C DESC CAT 5   PROSE
GRAY WRITING HIS POEMS .   .   .   .   SUPP ILLUS GRAY   *TITLE
GRAY THE POET FRIAR BACON   .   .   .   . SUPP PENC DRAW 2.37 *TITLE

GRAZE   SEE GRASE

GREAT

MY TASK IS GREAT MY BURDEN HEAVIER THAN   .   .   .   .   .   19 EDW THIRD/PS 2   4
SWEET PRINCE THE ARTS OF PEACE ARE GREAT   .   .   .   .   .   19 EDW THIRD/PS 2   18
I HOPE YOUR MAJESTY CANNOT REFUSE SO GREAT   .   .   .   .   23 EDW THIRD/PS 3   98
YES I HAVE I HAVE A GREAT AMBITION TO KNOW EVERY THING SIR   28D EDW THIRD/PS 4 PROSE
MAY DO A GREAT DEAL OF HARM WITHOUT KNOWING IT   .   .   .   . 29A EDW THIRD/PS 4 PROSE
GREAT DEAL MORE THAT WE SHALL ALL HEAR BY AND BY AND I CAME   29C EDW THIRD/PS 4 PROSE
I SEEM TO BE IN ONE GREAT CHARNEL-HOUSE   .   .   .   .   .   31 EDW THIRD/PS 5   43
O MAN HOW GREAT HOW LITTLE THOU   .   .   .   . 37A CONTEMPLATN/PS PROSE
SO GREAT ITS POWER THAT PRIDE INSPIRD BY IT   .   .   .   .   41A THEN SHE BORE   PROSE
TO CONSTANTINE'S GREAT CITY EMPIRE FLED   .   .   .   .   .   41B THEN SHE BORE   PROSE
THE GODS ALL SERVE HER AT HER WILL SO GREAT HER POWER IS   41D THEN SHE BORE   PROSE
SHE SEATED & [LISTEND] SEEMD TO LISTEN WITH GREAT ATTENTION   44B ISLAND MOON 1   PROSE
IN A GREAT HURRY INFLAMMABLE GASS THE WIND FINDER ENTERD   44C ISLAND MOON 1   PROSE
I TURND MYSELF ABOUT WITH GREAT CONTEMPT SAID I GO ALONG   45A ISLAND MOON 1   PROSE
    YOU FOOL

		PAGE	TITLE	LINE

GREAT   (CONTINUED)

I ONLY ASKD YOU A CIVIL QUESTION--[HERE THE] I HAD A GREAT   45A ISLAND MOON 1   *PROSE
    MIND
WELL SAID THE OTHER HE WAS AS GREAT AS CHATTERTON . . .   47A ISLAND MOON 3   PROSE
THAT WAS AS GREAT AS CHATTERTON [OBTUSE ANGLE ANSWERD]   47A ISLAND MOON 3   PROSE
MORE LIKE A SAINT THAN A LAWGIVER AND WITH GREAT SOLEMNITY   53B ISLAND MOON 8   PROSE
HERE WAS GREAT CONFUSION & DISORDER . . . .   54D ISLAND MOON 9   PROSE
TO THY WIDE GATES HOW GREAT A DROVE . . . .   56 HAIL MATRIM/IM   2
OF GREAT CAPACITY . . . .   57 TO BE OR/IM   2
SAID HE YOU MUST BE ACQUAINTED WITH A GREAT MANY SONGS . .   61C ISLAND MOON 11   PROSE
GREAT A LITTLE A . . . .   62 DR CLASH/IM   8
FALSE SEVERITY OF JUDGMENT IS A GREAT VIRTUE . . . . .   67A ANNO LAVATER   MARG
("WE CANNOT BE GREAT IF...") UNEASY . . . .   76D ANNO LAVATER   MARG
THE MAN WHO DOES THIS IS A SECTARY THEREFORE NOT GREAT .   77C ANNO LAVATER   MARG
GREAT ENDS NEVER LOOK AT MEANS BUT PRODUCE   81B ANNO LAVATER   MARG
    THEM SPONTANEOUSLY
AND [HE] HEARD HAR SING IN THE GREAT CAGE & SLEPT UPON   103 TIRIEL 3   *   23
    OUR FLEECES
THE CRY WAS GREAT IN TIRIEL'S PALACE HIS FIVE DAUGHTERS RAN   106 TIRIEL 5   18
HOW GREAT THY USE HOW GREAT THY BLESSING EVERY THING THAT   129 BOOK OF THEL 3   26
    LIVES
. . . MOW DOWN ALL THIS GREAT STARRY HARVEST OF SIX   138 FRENCH REVOLTN   90
    THOUSAND YEARS
CAST THEIR RIVERS IN EQUAL TIDES THRO THE GREAT PARADISE   142 FRENCH REVOLTN   184
    . . .
GREAT HENRY'S SOUL SHUDDERED . . . .   143 FRENCH REVOLTN   200
ARE PORTIONS OF ETERNITY TOO GREAT FOR THE EYE OF MAN .   151C MARRIAGE HH 8   PROSE
OF THE POETIC GENIUS IT WAS THIS THAT OUR GREAT POET .   153D MARRIAGE HH 12   PROSE
THOSE WHO ENVY OR CALUMNIATE GREAT MEN HATE GOD . . .   158B MARRIAGE HH 22   PROSE
AND SO GREAT A NUMBER POOR . . . .   181 HOLY THURS/N   7
[THEN HE SWORE A GREAT & SOLEMN OATH] . . . . . .   185 LET BROTHELS/N   16
AND A GREAT MANY SUCKERS GROW ALL AROUND . . . . .   185 LET BROTHELS/N   26
THEN SWORE A GREAT OATH THAT MADE HEAVN QUAKE . . .   187 WHEN KLOPSTK/N *   5
DOES NOT THE GREAT MOUTH LAUGH AT A GIFT & THE NARROW   192 V DAU ALBION 5   7
    EYELIDS MOCK
NO SUBSCRIPTIONS FOR THE NUMEROUS GREAT WORKS NOW . .   208A PRSPECTUS 1793 PROSE
HIS GREAT HAMMER FELL FROM HIS HAND . . . .   229 URIZEN 13   21
GROVELING ALONG GREAT GEORGE STREET THRO THE PARK GATE   242 EUROPE 12   19
    . . .
GREAT THE CONFLICT & GREAT THE JEALOUSY . . . . . .   250 AHANIA 3   18
WITH DIFFICULTY & GREAT PAIN URIZEN . . . .   251 AHANIA 3   51
HE WITH DIFFICULTY AND GREAT PAIN . . . .   252 AHANIA 3   72
THERE IS FROM GREAT ETERNITY A MILD & PLEASANT REST . .   266 FOUR ZOAS 1   94
[BUT THOSE IN GREAT ETERNITY MET IN THE COUNCIL OF GOD]   269 FOUR ZOAS 1   198
AND COMPREHEND WITHIN HIMSELF ALL THINGS BOTH SMALL & GREAT   272 FOUR ZOAS 1   * 295
THEN THOSE IN GREAT ETERNITY MET IN THE COUNCIL OF GOD .   277 FOUR ZOAS 1   469
LUVAH & VALA TREMBLING & SHRINKING BEHELD THE GREAT WORK   280 FOUR ZOAS 2   22
    MASTER
AND I COMMANDED THE GREAT DEEP TO HIDE HER IN HIS HAND .   282 FOUR ZOAS 2   91
IN THY GREAT WRATH THO I HAVE SINNED THO I HAVE REBELLD   297 FOUR ZOAS 3   191
DREWST ALL THE SONS OF BEULAH INTO THY [GREAT] DREAD VORTEX   299 FOUR ZOAS 4   88
    FOLLOWING
IN TERRORS LOS SHRUNK FROM HIS TASK HIS GREAT HAMMER .   304 FOUR ZOAS 4   * 280
[XXX DAYS OF GREAT ETERNITY XXX THE TIME] . . . . .   SUPP FOUR ZOAS 4   *
STOOD SO THICK HE WITH DIFFICULTY & GREAT PAIN BROUGHT .   321 FOUR ZOAS 7   38
TO BE MY GREAT & AWFUL CURSES AT THE TIME APPOINTED .   336 FOUR ZOAS 7B   120
I NEVER WILL DEPART FROM MY GREAT WRATH . . . . . .   339 FOUR ZOAS 7B   258
THEN ALL IN GREAT ETERNITY [WHICH IS CALLED] . . . .   341 FOUR ZOAS 8   1
WHO IS MYSTERY BABYLON THE GREAT THE MOTHER OF HARLOTS .   349 FOUR ZOAS 8   330
CALLD DOWN A GREAT SOLEMN ASSEMBLY RINTRAH IN FURY & FIRE   351 FOUR ZOAS 8   * 389
SCHOOLMASTER OF SOULS GREAT OPPOSER OF CHANGE ARISE . .   360 FOUR ZOAS 9   131
DESCENDING FROM JERUSALEM WITH POWER AND GREAT GLORY .   364 FOUR ZOAS 9   273
HER GREAT MEN HOWL & THROW THE DUST & REND THEIR HOARY HAIR   375 FOUR ZOAS 9   663
WHO IS MYSTERY BABYLON THE GREAT MOTHER OF (HARLOTS) .   382 FOUR ZOAS AD 6 *   19
THIS HE HAS SHEWN WITH GREAT FORCE . . . .   390D ANNO WATSON   MARG
WHAT SUCH MEN CALL GREAT IS INDEED DETESTABLE . . . .   407A ANNO BACON   MARG
IS THIS GREAT IS THIS CHRISTIAN NO . . . .   407D ANNO BACON   MARG
IS THE DEVIL GREAT CONSIDER . . . .   410D ANNO BACON   MARG
THY TRANSGRESSIONS GREAT & SMALL . . . .   416 MY SPECTRE/N   46
& IN EXULTING ATTITUDES OF GREAT JOY TELL EACH OTHER .   443D LAST JUDGMNT/L PROSE
WHO COMETH IN THE CLOUDS WITH POWER & GREAT GLORY . . .   444A LAST JUDGMNT/L PROSE
PORTRAIT PAINTING APPLAUDED & REWARDED BY THE RICH & GREAT   445C ANNO REYNOLDS   MARG
BUT THAT WE ARE TO LEARN TO THINK FROM GREAT MASTERS .   449A ANNO REYNOLDS   MARG
A GREAT COLOURIST & YET INFERIOR TO THE VENETIANS . .   450B ANNO REYNOLDS   MARG
INSTEAD OF FOLLOWING ONE GREAT MASTER . . . .   455C ANNO REYNOLDS   MARG
HE IS TO FOLLOW A GREAT MANY FOOLS . . . .   455C ANNO REYNOLDS   MARG
THE BAD ARTIST SEEMS TO COPY A GREAT DEAL . . . . .   456A ANNO REYNOLDS   MARG
THE GOOD ONE REALLY DOES COPY A GREAT DEAL . . . . .   456A ANNO REYNOLDS   MARG
CONTEMPTIBLE SERVILE COPYING IS THE GREAT MERIT OF COPYING   456A ANNO REYNOLDS   MARG
THE GREAT BACON HE IS CALLD I CALL HIM THE LITTLE BACON   459C ANNO REYNOLDS   MARG
THE VENETIAN WILL NOT CORRESPOND WITH THE GREAT STYLE .   463B ANNO REYNOLDS   MARG
("THE GREAT STYLE") WHAT CAN BE BETTER SAID ON THIS SUBJECT   463C ANNO REYNOLDS   MARG
HE MAKES LITTLE CONCESSIONS THAT HE MAY TAKE GREAT   463C ANNO REYNOLDS   MARG
    ADVANTAGES
STYLE WILL ILL CORRESPOND WITH THE GREAT STYLE . . .   468A ANNO REYNOLDS   MARG
THE GREAT STYLE IS ALWAYS NOVEL OR NEW IN ALL ITS   468A ANNO REYNOLDS   MARG
    OPERATIONS
THE TWO GRAND MERITS OF THE GREAT STYLE . . . . .   468B ANNO REYNOLDS   MARG
HERE IS A GREAT DEAL TO DO TO PROVE THAT ALL TRUTH   475A ANNO REYNOLDS   MARG
    IS PREJUDICE
[IF THE ?INSPIRATION ?IS GREAT ?WHY CALL IT MADNESS] .   SUPP ANNO REYNOLDS * MARG
[?WHY SHOUD ?COMPARING GREAT MASTERS ?BE ?DONE PAINFULLY]   SUPP ANNO REYNOLDS * MARG

```
                                                              PAGE      TITLE        LINE
GREAT    (CONTINUED)
      THE ETERNAL GREAT HUMANITY DIVINE PLANTED HIS PARADISE  .  .  481 MILTON  2          8
      THEY BUILT GREAT GOLGONOOZA TIMES ON TIMES AGES ON AGES      483 MILTON  3         39
      THE MILLER OF ETERNITY MADE SUBSERVIENT TO THE GREAT         483 MILTON  3         42
        HARVEST
      SCARCELY BEHOLDING THE GREAT LIGHT CONVERSING WITH THE VOID  484 MILTON  5         22
      BUT PALAMABRON CALLED DOWN A GREAT SOLEMN ASSEMBLY  .  .  .  489 MILTON  8         46
      AND IN THE MIDST OF THE GREAT ASSEMBLY PALAMABRON PRAYD      489 MILTON  9          4
      AND IT WAS ENQUIRD WHY IN A GREAT SOLEMN ASSEMBLY   .  .  .  491 MILTON 11         15
      SHE DOWN DESCENDED INTO THE MIDST OF THE GREAT SOLEMN        492 MILTON 11         29
        ASSEMBLY
      TO TARTARY & HINDOSTAN & CHINA & TO GREAT AMERICA    .  .   495 MILTON 14          7
      PREPARING IT FOR THE GREAT CONSUMMATION RED THE CHERUB      502 MILTON 20         23
        ON SINAI
      OF GREAT ETERNITY UNNATURAL REFUGE UNKNOWN BY US TILL NOW   504 MILTON 21         49
      AND OLOLON LAMENTED FOR MILTON WITH A GREAT LAMENTATION     505 MILTON 22          3
      BABYLON THE GREAT THE ABOMINATION OF DESOLATION   .  .  .   506 MILTON 22         49
      THE WITNESSES LIE DEAD IN THE STREET OF THE GREAT CITY      506 MILTON 22         59
      HOW LONG SHALL WE LAY DEAD IN THE STREET OF THE GREAT CITY  507 MILTON 23         11
      FOLLOWING MILTON INTO ULRO ALTHO YOUR POWER IS GREAT   .  . 508 MILTON 24         23
      FELLOW LABOURERS THE GREAT VINTAGE & HARVEST IS NOW UPON    510 MILTON 25         17
        EARTH
      FOR IN THIS PERIOD THE POET'S WORK IS DONE AND ALL THE      516 MILTON 29          1
        GREAT
      GREAT GOLGONOOZA FREE FROM THE FOUR IRON PILLARS OF SATAN'S 517 MILTON 29         48
        THRONE
      TO GIVE THEM TO THEIR LOVELY HEAVENS TILL THE GREAT         517 MILTON 29         52
        JUDGMENT DAY
      FROM THE ATLANTIC TO THE GREAT SOUTH SEA THE ERYTHREAN  .  . 518 MILTON 29        63
      ARE FROM GREAT ETERNITY A MILD & PLEASANT REST   .  .  .  . 518 MILTON 30         14
      AND IT IS THUS CREATED LO THE ETERNAL GREAT HUMANITY    .   519 MILTON 30         15
      IN THE GREAT WARS OF ETERNITY IN FURY OF POETIC INSPIRATION 519 MILTON 30         19
      IN THE CLOUDS OF OLOLON WITH POWER & GREAT GLORY   .  .  .  519 MILTON 31         16
      MOUNTING UPON THE WINGS OF LIGHT INTO THE GREAT EXPANSE     520 MILTON 31         32
      THEY SAID HOW ARE THE WARS OF MAN WHICH IN GREAT ETERNITY   524 MILTON 34         50
      OF THEIR GREAT SWAY REACHING FROM ULRO TO ETERNITY   .  .   526 MILTON 35         38
      IN GREAT ETERNITY WHICH THOU KNOWEST I COME HIM TO SEEK     527 MILTON 37          3
      THE HEADS OF THE GREAT POLYPUS FOUR-FOLD TWELVE ENORMITY    529 MILTON 38          2
      TILL ALL THINGS BECOME ONE GREAT SATAN IN HOLINESS    .  .  530 MILTON 39          1
      HE TREMBLED WITH EXCEEDING GREAT TREMBLING & ASTONISHMENT   531 MILTON 39         17
      THE ETERNAL GREAT HUMANITY DIVINE SURROUNDED BY   .  .  .  . 531 MILTON 39        27
      HE TREMBLED WITH EXCEEDING GREAT TREMBLING & ASTONISHMENT   531 MILTON 39         31
      TREMBLING BEFORE HIM WITH EXCEEDING GREAT TREMBLING & FEAR  531 MILTON 39         47
      TO GO FORTH TO THE GREAT HARVEST & VINTAGE OF THE NATIONS   535 MILTON 43          1
      YOU THINK FUSELI IS NOT A GREAT PAINTER IM GLAD   .  .  .   538 TO H(UNT)/N        1
      WHICH SPRANG FROM SIR ISAAC NEWTON'S GREAT ABILITIES   .  . 542 FLORENTINE/N      31
      [PAY] HAVE PAID GREAT SUMS IN THE VENETIAN & FLEMISH OOZE   547A PRETTY EPIGR/N TITLE
      MAY I GOVERN ALL BOTH GREAT & SMALL  .  .  .  .  .  .  .  . 547 IF I GROW/N        3
      SEE WHAT GREAT LABOUR PAIN HIM & MODEST DOUBT   .  .  .  .  548 CRIPPLE EVRY/N *   5
      ON THE GREAT ENCOURAGEMENT [SHEWN] GIVEN BY ENGLISH        548B ON GREAT ENC/N *TITLE
        NOBILITY &
      NOT PREJUDICD BY FEELINGS GREAT OR SMALL   .  .  .  .  .  . 549 CROMEK SPEAK/N     3
      FOR A GREAT [MULTITUDE] MADJORITY ARE IGNORANT   .  .  .  . 549 ENGL ENCOU/N 1 *   3
      TWILL MAKE A GREAT SPLUTTER WITH SMOKE & DAMP   .  .  .  .  549 ENGL ENCOU/N 1     6
      FOR A GREAT CONQUEST ARE BUNGLERY  .  .  .  .  .  .  .  .  . 549 ENGL ENCOU/N 2 *   3
      AND THEY TOLD ME IT WAS A GREAT SIN  .  .  .  .  .  .  .  . 550 WASHERWOMANS/N     2
      GREAT THINGS ARE DONE WHEN MEN & MOUNTAINS MEET   .  .  .   550 GREAT THINGS/N     1
      WHATS THE FIRST PART OF ORATORY HE SAID A GREAT WIG   .  .  553 ASKD PRIGG/N       2
      AND BOWING PROFOUNDLY HE SAID A GREAT WIG  .  .  .  .  .  .  553 ASKD PRIGG/N       4
      .  .  PUFFING HIS CHEEKS HE REPLIED A GREAT WIG   .  .  .   553 ASKD PRIGG/N       6
      SO IF A GREAT PAINTER WITH QUESTIONS YOU PUSH   .  .  .  .  553 ASKD PRIGG/N       7
      A GREAT DEAL BETTER THAN I WAS BEFORE   .  .  .  .  .  .  . 554 TO VENETIAN/N     15
      GREAT MEN & FOOLS [OF] DO OFTEN ME INSPIRE   .  .  .  .  .  554 GREAT MEN/N *      1
      HAVING GIVEN GREAT OFFENCE BY WRITING IN PROSE   .  .  .   555 BLAKES APL/N 1      6
      IVE GIVEN GREAT PROVISION TO MY FOES   .  .  .  .  .  .  .  555 BLAKES APL/N 1     22
      HAVING GIVEN GREAT OFFENCE BY WRITING IN PROSE   .  .  .   555 BLAKES APL/N 2      1
      SOME SAY IVE GIVEN GREAT PROVISION TO MY FOES   .  .  .  .  556 BLAKES APL/N 2     11
      ON THE GREAT ATLANTIC MOUNTAINS  .  .  .  .  .  .  .  .  .  558 THE CAVERNS/N     18
      GREAT BUILDING INTO COMPARTMENTS AND ORNAMENT THEM   .  .  560D EXHIBITION ADV  PROSE
      THERE CANNOT BE MORE THAN TWO OR THREE GREAT PAINTERS OR   561B EXHIBITION ADV  PROSE
      IF ITALY IS ENRICHED AND MADE GREAT BY RAPHAEL   .  .  .   561C EXHIBITION ADV  PROSE
      OF A NATION IF GENIUS AND INSPIRATION ARE THE GREAT ORIGIN 561C EXHIBITION ADV  PROSE
      INDICATE THE SITUATION OF THE GREAT CITY   .  .  .  .  .   567B DESC CAT 3      PROSE
      THE KNIGHT IS A TRUE HERO A GOOD GREAT AND WISE MAN   .  . 567D DESC CAT 3      PROSE
      THE SQUIRE'S YEOMAN IS ALSO A GREAT CHARACTER   .  .  .  . 568A DESC CAT 3      PROSE
      CHAUCER IS HIMSELF THE GREAT POETICAL OBSERVER OF MEN   .  569A DESC CAT 3      PROSE
      ACCORDINGLY CHAUCER HAS MADE HIS MONK A GREAT TRAGEDIAN    569A DESC CAT 3      PROSE
      AND HAS ALSO HIS GREAT USE AND HIS GRAND LEADING DESTINY   570A DESC CAT 3      PROSE
      CHAUCER'S LAWYER IS A CHARACTER OF GREAT VENERABLENESS  .  570D DESC CAT 3      PROSE
      BENEVOLENCE IS THE PLOWMAN'S GREAT CHARACTERISTIC    .  .  571B DESC CAT 3      PROSE
      AND DIRECTIONS ARE EMPLOYED AT A GREAT EXPENCE   .  .  .   572D DESC CAT 3      PROSE
      AND WITH GREAT AND HEAVY SHADOWS   .  .  .  .  .  .  .  .   577A DESC CAT 4      PROSE
      HOW HE BECAME DIVIDED IS A SUBJECT OF GREAT SUBLIMITY   .  578B DESC CAT 5      PROSE
      BUT OF THE GREAT LABOUR WHICH HAS BEEN BESTOWED ON IT   .  582B DESC CAT 9      PROSE
      THE GREAT AND GOLDEN RULE OF ART AS WELL AS OF LIFE IS     585B DESC CAT 15     PROSE
        THIS
      AND BUNGLING GREAT INVENTORS IN ALL AGES KNEW THIS   .  .  585B DESC CAT 15     PROSE
      OLD ORIGINAL ENGRAVERS WHO WERE GREAT MASTERS IN PAINTING  586D CHAUCER 1       PROSE
      THE GREAT STRENGTH OF COLOURING & DEPTH OF WORK   .  .  .  588A CHAUCER/N       PROSE
      INDICATE THE SITUATION OF THE GREAT CITY   .  .  .  .  .   588D CHAUCER/N       PROSE
      INDICATE THE SITUATION OF THE GREAT CITY   .  .  .  .  .   590C CHAUCER 2       PROSE
      OF INDIVIDUAL MERIT BEING ITS GREAT HATRED  .  .  .  .  .  594A PUB ADDRESS/N   PROSE
```

```
                                                                    PAGE      TITLE        LINE
GREAT    (CONTINUED)
    [WHO CAN SELL A GOOD FOR NOTHING COMMODITY FOR A GREAT      595B  PUB ADDRESS/N   PROSE
        PRICE]
    WHOEVER LOOKS AT ANY OF THE GREAT & EXPENSIVE WORKS . .     596B  PUB ADDRESS/N   PROSE
    & THOSE MUST BE QUEER FELLOWS WHO GIVE GREAT SUMS      .    596C  PUB ADDRESS/N   PROSE
    THE CONTEMPTIBLE IDIOTS WHO HAVE BEEN CALLD GREAT MEN       598C  PUB ADDRESS/N   PROSE
    GENTLEMEN OF FORTUNE WHO GIVE GREAT PRICES FOR PICTURES     599C  PUB ADDRESS/N   PROSE
    WITH TOO GREAT CONTEMPT OF SUCH CONTEMPTIBLE FELLOWS        599D  PUB ADDRESS/N   PROSE
    THIS IS MY GLORY & EXCEEDING GREAT REWARD      .   .   .    600C  PUB ADDRESS/N   PROSE
    WOULD MAKE A NOBLE FINISH PLACED ABOVE THE GREAT PUBLIC     601A  PUB ADDRESS/N   PROSE
    THEIR CONSIDERATION OF MY PLAN AS A GREAT PUBLIC [DEED]     601B  PUB ADDRESS/N  *PROSE
        MEANS
    & THEY PROVE IT IN THEIR CONTEMPT FOR GREAT COLLECTIONS     601C  PUB ADDRESS/N   PROSE
    THAT GREAT INVENTORS CANNOT EXECUTE THIS OPINION IS . .     601D  PUB ADDRESS/N   PROSE
    BY EARTHQUAKES A GREAT CITY ON FIRE IS SEEN IN THE DISTANCE 608B  V LAST JUDG/N   PROSE
    THE GREAT RED DRAGON WITH SEVEN HEADS & TEN HORNS    .      609B  V LAST JUDG/N   PROSE
    COMING IN THE CLOUDS WITH POWER & GREAT GLORY  .  .  .      609D  V LAST JUDG/N   PROSE
    THE GREAT SUN IS REPRESENTED CLOTHED IN FLAMES    .   .     618B  ILLUS MILTON    PROSE
    AS ATTENDING ON THE HEAVEN OF JUPITER THE GREAT BEAR        619B  ILLUS MILTON    PROSE
    YET THEY FORGIVE MY WANDERINGS I REST NOT FROM MY GREAT     623   JERUSALEM 5       17
        TASK
    TO WHAT THOU SHALT ENDURE IF THOU OBEY NOT MY GREAT WILL    629   JERUSALEM 10      36
    O THOU MY ENEMY WHERE IS MY GREAT SIN SHE IS ALSO THINE     630   JERUSALEM 10      43
    CREATED TO BE THE GREAT EXAMPLE OF HORROR & AGONY ALSO MY   630   JERUSALEM 10      52
    WITH IRON & BRASS BUILDING GOLGONOOZA IN GREAT CONTENDINGS  630   JERUSALEM 10      63
    WITH GREAT LABOUR UPON HIS ANVILS & IN HIS LADLES THE ORE   630   JERUSALEM 11       3
    THE GREAT CITY OF GOLGONOOZA FOURFOLD TOWARD THE NORTH  .   632   JERUSALEM 12      46
    AND THE FOUR POINTS ARE THUS BEHELD IN GREAT ETERNITY   .   632   JERUSALEM 12      54
    LIKE WHEELS FROM A GREAT WHEEL REFLECTED IN THE DEEP    .   641   JERUSALEM 18      43
    GREAT IS THE CRY OF THE HOUNDS OF NIMROD ALONG THE VALLEY   644   JERUSALEM 22       8
    AND THERE WAS HEARD A GREAT LAMENTING IN BEULAH ALL THE     648   JERUSALEM 25       1
        REGIONS
    IS GREAT IN THE EAST THEIR SPEARS OF BLOOD RAGE IN THE      658   JERUSALEM 31      56
        EASTERN HEAVEN
    SO SPOKE THE SPECTRE TO ALBION HE IS THE GREAT SELFHOOD     659   JERUSALEM 33      17
    VALA WAS ALBION'S BRIDE & WIFE IN GREAT ETERNITY .  .  .    660   JERUSALEM 33      39
    THEN THOSE IN GREAT ETERNITY WHO CONTEMPLATE ON DEATH  .    663   JERUSALEM 36      50
    IT IS EASY TO ACKNOWLEDGE A MAN TO DE GREAT & GOOD WHILE WE 673   JERUSALEM 43      56
    BROTHERS OF ETERNITY THIS MAN WHOSE GREAT EXAMPLE  .  .     675   JERUSALEM 45       4
    OF EDEN THAT HOWEVER GREAT AND GLORIOUS HOWEVER LOVING      675   JERUSALEM 45      10
    AND DEAR MUTUAL FORGIVENESS & TO BECOME ONE GREAT SATAN     679   JERUSALEM 49      29
    SCARCELY BEHOLDING THE GREAT LIGHT CONVERSING WITH THE      680   JERUSALEM 49   *  35
        (VOID)
    TRUE HARMONIES & COMPREHENDING GREAT AS VERY SMALL  .  .    680   JERUSALEM 49      37
    IN GREAT ETERNITY EVERY PARTICULAR FORM GIVES FORTH OR      684   JERUSALEM 54       1
        EMANATES
    AND BUILD A WORLD OF PHANTASY UPON MY GREAT ABYSS      .    685   JERUSALEM 54      23
    AND THE GREAT VOICE OF ETERNITY ROLLED ABOVE TERRIBLE IN    687   JERUSALEM 55      68
        CLOUDS
    AND THE GREAT VOICE OF THE ATLANTIC HOWLED OVER THE DRUID   689   JERUSALEM 57       5
        ALTARS
    PERSIA & MEDIA ARE HIS HALLS HIS INMOST HALL IS GREAT       690   JERUSALEM 58      38
        TARTARY
    AND SWEET HESPERIA EVEN TO GREAT CHALDEA & TESSHINA  .  .   692   JERUSALEM 60      20
    IN THE PERPETUAL MUTUAL SACRIFICE IN GREAT ETERNITY FOR     694   JERUSALEM 61      23
        BEHOLD
    GLORIFIED THY HOLINESS OR REJOICED IN THY GREAT SALVATION   695   JERUSALEM 61      46
    TO DECIDE TWO WORLDS WITH A GREAT DECISION A WORLD OF MERCY 699   JERUSALEM 65       1
        AND
    . . . TILL THE GREAT POLYPUS OF GENERATION COVERED THE      704   JERUSALEM 67      34
        EARTH
    AND SWORD FAINT IN HIS HAND FROM ALBION ACROSS GREAT        706   JERUSALEM 68      52
        TARTARY
    WHO GUIDE THE GREAT WINE-PRESS OF LOVE FOUR PRECIOUS STONES 712   JERUSALEM 72      52
        THAT GATE
    AND RAHAB BABYLON THE GREAT HATH DESTROYED JERUSALEM   .  . 715   JERUSALEM 75       1
    MYSTERY BABYLON THE GREAT THE ABOMINATION OF DESOLATION     716   JERUSALEM 75      19
    HUMANITY THE GREAT DELUSION IS CHANGD TO WAR & SACRIFICE    726   JERUSALEM 82      42
    TO GREAT QUEEN STREET & LINCOLNS INN ALL IS DISTRESS & WOE  729   JERUSALEM 84      16
    VIEWING THE WINDING WORM ON THE DESARTS OF GREAT TARTARY    731   JERUSALEM 86      46
    MINGLING WITH LUVAH IN ONE THEY BECOME ONE GREAT SATAN      737   JERUSALEM 90      43
    SO LOS SPOKE ENITHARMON ANSWERD IN GREAT TERROR IN          739   JERUSALEM 92       7
        LAMBETH'S VALE
    MYSTERY BABYLON THE GREAT THE DRUID DRAGON & HIDDEN HARLOT  741   JERUSALEM 93      25
    HIS ANVIL IN THE GREAT SPECTRE LOS UNWEARIED LABOURING      742   JERUSALEM 95      18
        & WEEPING
    AND FROM THE GREAT CITY OF GOLGONOOZA IN THE SHADOWY        746   JERUSALEM 98      55
        GENERATION
    THINE HAS A GREAT HOOK NOSE LIKE THINE  .  .  .  .  .  .    748   EV GOSPEL(A)/N     3
    THESE MORAL VIRTUES GREAT & SMALL  .  .  .  .  .  .  .  .   758   EV GOSPEL (2)      6
    THE MORAL VIRTUES IN GREAT FEAR  .  .  .  .  .  .  .  .  .  759   EV GOSPEL (2)     28
    AM I NOT LUCIFER THE GREAT  .  .  .  .  .  .  .  .  .  .    759   EV GOSPEL (2)     38
    AND YOU MY DAUGHTERS IN GREAT STATE  .  .  .  .  .  .  .    759   EV GOSPEL (2)     39
    MONEY WHICH IS THE GREAT SATAN OR REASON  .  .  .  .  .     776B  INSC LAOCOON    PROSE
    THE OLD & NEW TESTAMENTS ARE THE GREAT CODE OF ART  .  .    777C  INSC LAOCOON    PROSE
    AS WHEN YOU PRINT OR NOT QUITE SO GREAT  .  .  .  .  .      791A  LETTER 2        PROSE
    BUT I AM HAPPY TO FIND A GREAT MAJORITY OF FELLOW MORTALS   794A  LETTER 5        PROSE
    THAT THE KING SHEWS IT A GREAT COUNTENANCE & ENCOURAGEMENT  797D  LETTER 10       PROSE
    "WE HAVE BEEN INCESSANTLY BUSY IN OUR GREAT REMOVAL"   .    800A  LETTER 12       PROSE
    & THO WE HAD A GREAT DEAL OF LUGGAGE NO GRUMBLING     .     802B  LETTER 14       PROSE
    I HAVE A GREAT MANY ORDERS & THEY MULTIPLY  .  .  .  .  .   808B  LETTER 19       PROSE
    DEAR FLAXMAN I REJOICE TO HEAR THAT YOUR GREAT WORK IS      810C  LETTER 21       PROSE
        ACCOMPLISHD
```

```
                                                               PAGE     TITLE         LINE
GREAT      (CONTINUED)
    NOW I HOPE TO SEE THE GREAT WORKS OF ART AS THEY ARE   .  811A LETTER 21     PROSE
    COPY THESE WELL BUT PATIENCE IF GREAT THINGS DO NOT TURN  812A LETTER 22     PROSE
        OUT
    & I FIND ON ALL HANDS GREAT OBJECTIONS TO MY DOING ANY    812C LETTER 22     PROSE
        THING
    WERE IN GREAT FORWARDNESS YOU WILL SEE BY THE INCLOSED .  816C LETTER 24     PROSE
    THE PORTRAITS & CHARMD BY THE GREAT HEAD IN PARTICULAR .  820D LETTER 25     PROSE
    I WRITE IN GREAT HASTE & WITH A HEAD FULL OF BOTHERATION  821B LETTER 25     PROSE
    VERY LIKELY BE OF GREAT CONSEQUENCE IT IS COWPER'S MILTON 821C LETTER 25     PROSE
    & FELLOW DISCIPLE HOW GREAT MUST BE YOUR FAITH    .   .   822B LETTER 26     PROSE
    EXCUSE MY PERHAPS TOO GREAT ENTHUSIASM PLEASE TO ACCEPT OF 823C LETTER 26    PROSE
    SMALLER POEMS & WILL READ WITH GREAT DELIGHT I HAVE GIVEN 824A LETTER 27     PROSE
    THESE ARE ALL IN GREAT FORWARDNESS & I AM SATISFIED THAT  824A LETTER 27     PROSE
    HIS INDUSTRY IS EQUAL TO HIS OTHER GREAT POWERS   .   .   829B LETTER 29     PROSE
    I HAVE A GREAT MANY THINGS TO SAY & A GREAT MANY          832B LETTER 32     PROSE
        HEARTFELT
    HE SENT A GREAT PART OF THEM TO THE NORTH & EXPLAIND   .  832C LETTER 32     PROSE
    THE EXPENSE WOULD NOT BE VERY GREAT   .   .   .   .   .   832D LETTER 32     PROSE
    & LEFT IT WITH CHARGE TO THE SERVANT OF GREAT CARE   .   .834C LETTER 34     PROSE
    DOUBT NOT YET TO MAKE A FIGURE IN THE GREAT DANCE OF LIFE 835A LETTER 34     PROSE
    INTERESTING HIMSELF IN THE GREAT OBJECT OF HIS FATHER'S   835C LETTER 35     PROSE
        FAME
    THAT HE THOUGHT IT A VERY GREAT LIKENESS    .   .   .   . 836B LETTER 35     PROSE
    THE PLATES OF COWPER'S MONUMENT ARE BOTH IN GREAT    .   .837A LETTER 35     PROSE
    A GREAT DEAL OF WORK IN THEM THAT MUST & WILL HAVE TIME   837A LETTER 35     PROSE
    ENTER AGAIN WITH GREAT PLEASURE AND HOPE SOON TO SHOW YOU 841A LETTER 40     PROSE
    GREAT LEADING CHARACTER IN LITERATURE & HIS TERMS TO OTHERS 841C LETTER 41   PROSE
    YOU BOTH WITH GREAT AFFECTION MR FLAXMAN HAS ALSO PROMISED 846A LETTER 44    PROSE
    TELL YOU THAT MR ROSE REPEATED TO ME HIS GREAT OPINION .  846C LETTER 44     PROSE
    GREAT NEWPORT STREET BEFORE HE WENT TOOK THE HOUSE IN  .  847D LETTER 44     PROSE
    IN VERY GREAT FORWARDNESS PARKER COMMENDS IT HIGHLY   .   849A LETTER 45     PROSE
    IN GENERAL FOUND GREAT BODIES TO BE THEY WERE MUCH PLEASED 850C LETTER 49    PROSE
    GREAT DEAL OF HONOUR IN LOSING THE FIRST PUBLICATION OF ANY 856C LETTER 54   PROSE
    INTO ALL PARTS TO A VERY GREAT AMOUNT HE THEN SAID IF MR  856C LETTER 54     PROSE
    BOWYER'S & OTHER GREAT WORKS I WAS KNOWN BY THEM & WAS    862C LETTER 60     PROSE
        LOOKD
    ME GREAT REPUTATION AS AN ARTIST WHICH WAS THE CHIEF THING 867C LETTER 66    PROSE
    SOON GET ABOUT AGAIN GREAT MEN DIE EQUALLY WITH THE LITTLE 868D LETTER 68    PROSE
    GREAT JOY HENCE I AM NOW ENABLED TO TELL YOU THAT I   .  .869D LETTER 70     PROSE
    THIS IS WHAT GIVES ME GREAT PLEASURE  .   .   .   .   .   874C LETTER 79     PROSE
    & HAVE GREAT HOPES THAT THE DISEASE IS GONE   .   .   .   875C LETTER 81     PROSE
    WITH POOR JOB I KNOW TOO WELL THAT A GREAT MAJORITY OF .  878A LETTER 88     PROSE
    CANNOT PRINT MORE EXCEPT AT A GREAT LOSS FOR AT THE TIME  878C LETTER 88     PROSE
    MR CUMBERLAND BISHOPSGATE WINDSOR GREAT PARK    .   .   . SUPP ADDRESSES/L  *TITLE
    MR BUTTS GREAT MARLBOROUGH STREET OXFORD STREET LONDON .  SUPP ADDRESSES/L  *TITLE
    [IF THE ?INSPIRATION ?IS GREAT ?WHY CALL IT MADNESS]  .  SUPP ANNO REYNOLDS * MARG
    [?WHY SHOUD ?COMPARING GREAT MASTERS ?BE ?DONE PAINFULLY] SUPP ANNO REYNOLDS * MARG
GREATER
    I KNOW NO GREATER SINNER THAN JOHN TAYLOR   .   .   .   .   52 HEAR THEN/IM      4
    ("GREATER WHO PRODUCES ONE THING ENTIRE THAN MANY        78C ANNO LAVATER    MARG
        BY HALVES") UNEASY
    MAN CAN HAVE NO IDEA OF ANY THING GREATER THAN MAN   .    90B ANNO SWED LOVE  MARG
    WORSHIP THE JEWS' GOD AND WHAT GREATER SUBJECTION CAN BE  154A MARRIAGE HH 12 PROSE
    A GREATER THAN ITSELF TO KNOW    .   .   .   .   .   .   . 176 LIT BOY LST/N      4
    A GREATER THAN ITSELF TO KNOW    .   .   .   .   .   .   . 218 LIT BOY LST/SE     4
    MY ANGER AGAINST THEE IS GREATER THAN AGAINST THIS LUVAH  361 FOUR ZOAS 9       151
    GREATER MIRACLE TO FEED FIVE THOUSAND MEN WITH FIVE LOAVES 391C ANNO WATSON    MARG
    THEY ARE ALL GREATER VILLAINS THAN THE IMPERFECT    .   . 412A ANNO BOYD       MARG
    [WHENEVER ?REYNOLDS ?TALKS OF COLOURING A GREATER         450B ANNO REYNOLDS * MARG
        ?COLOURIST]
    CAN YOU HAVE GREATER MIRACLES THAN THESE MEN WHO DEVOTE   506 MILTON 23           1
    AND BE A GREATER IN THY PLACE & BE THY TABERNACLE    .   .529 MILTON 38          30
    A COVERING FOR THEE TO DO THY WILL TILL ONE GREATER COMES 529 MILTON 38          31
    FOR THE GREATER THE FOOL IN THE PENCIL MORE BLEST    .  . 548 ALL PICTURES/N      3
    BUT THE GREATER [FOOLS] FOOL THE [GRATER] GREATER LIAR .  554 GREAT MEN/N     *   2
    [FOR NOW] IN SPITE WE WILL BE GREATER FRIENDS THAN EVER   556 IF MEN ACT/N        6
    FROM GREATER WORKS OF THE ASIATIC PATRIARCHS    .   .   . 565D DESC CAT 2      PROSE
    WITH THE GERM OF PERHAPS GREATER PERFECTION STILL    .  . 568A DESC CAT 3      PROSE
    THE GREATER IS THE EVIDENCE OF WEAK IMITATION PLAGIARISM  585B DESC CAT 15     PROSE
    BUT LOVE TO MY ART & ZEAL FOR MY COUNTRY A MUCH GREATER   594D PUB ADDRESS/N   PROSE
    & THO HE WOULD NOT HAVE BEEN A GREATER ARTIST   .   .   . 612C V LAST JUDG/N   PROSE
    YET HE WOULD HAVE PRODUCD GREATER WORKS OF ART  .   .   . 612C V LAST JUDG/N   PROSE
    THAT YOU MAY TAKE THE GREATER VENGEANCE IN YOUR SEPULCHER 673 JERUSALEM 43       79
    CAN THERE BE ANY SECRET JOY ON EARTH GREATER THAN THIS .  733 JERUSALEM 88   *  15
    MANY HONEST PEOPLE ENDURE GREATER HARDSHIPS WITH FORTITUDE 793B LETTER 5       PROSE
    ELUCIDATED BY CHILDREN WHO HAVE TAKEN A GREATER DELIGHT   794A LETTER 5        PROSE
    & FIND THAT I CAN WORK WITH GREATER PLEASURE THAN EVER .  803C LETTER 15       PROSE
    PEACE OPENS THE WAY TO GREATER STILL THE KINGDOMS OF  .   810C LETTER 21       PROSE
    THAT I SHOULD BE EMPLOYD IN GREATER THINGS & WHEN IT IS   812A LETTER 22       PROSE
    MEET TO CONSULT AGAINST THE OTHER NOTHING CAN BE GREATER  859B LETTER 56       PROSE
        THAN
    HIGHLY LABOURD PLATES THAN A GREATER NUMBER & LESS FINISHD 860C LETTER 56      PROSE
GREATEST
    ("THE GREATEST OF CHARACTERS...") THIS WAS CHRIST    .  . 66B ANNO LAVATER     MARG
    ("GLANCE IS THE GREATEST GIFT") UNEASY DOUBTFUL     .   . 77C ANNO LAVATER     MARG
    EACH ACCORDING TO HIS GENIUS AND LOVING THE GREATEST MEN  158B MARRIAGE HH 22  PROSE
        BEST
    IF JESUS CHRIST IS THE GREATEST MAN YOU OUGHT TO LOVE HIM 158C MARRIAGE HH 22  PROSE
    IN THE GREATEST DEGREE NOW HEAR HOW HE HAS GIVEN    .   . 158C MARRIAGE HH 22  PROSE
    IS NOT THIS THE GREATEST FOLLY   .   .   .   .   .   .   . 408A ANNO BACON      MARG
    THAT GREATEST OF ALL BLESSINGS A STRONG IMAGINATION   .  .439D REMARKS MALKIN  PROSE
```

```
                                                       PAGE      TITLE           LINE
GREATEST    (CONTINUED)
    AS FAR AS GREATEST IS MORE THAN LEAST       . . . . . .   450A ANNO REYNOLDS    MARG
    A FACILITY IN COMPOSING IS THE GREATEST POWER OF ART   . . 453D ANNO REYNOLDS   MARG
    BELONGS TO NONE BUT THE GREATEST ARTISTS    . . . . . .   453D ANNO REYNOLDS    MARG
    MY EXHIBITION AS THE GREATEST OF DUTIES TO MY COUNTRY   . 561C EXHIBITION ADV   PROSE
    OF THE GREATEST INN OF THE GREATEST CITY    . . . . . .   569D DESC CAT 3       PROSE
    GREATEST OF HIS AGE YET HE IS A POOR PARSON OF A TOWN   . 570C DESC CAT 3       PROSE
    IS THE FACE AND LIMBS OF GREATEST BEAUTY AND PERFECTION   580A DESC CAT 5       PROSE
    MR B(BLAKE) THOUGHT THIS THE GREATEST OF COMPLIMENTS    . 585A DESC CAT 15      PROSE
    [ENCOURAGE A BLOCKHEAD & HE IS COUNTED THE GREATEST GENIUS] 595D PUB ADDRESS/N  PROSE
    WHICH IS THE GREATEST CURSE THAT CAN FALL UPON A NATION   596B PUB ADDRESS/N    PROSE
    THE GREATEST PART OF WHAT ARE CALLD IN ENGLAND OLD PICTURES 598A PUB ADDRESS/N  PROSE
    IN ALL PROFESSIONS THESE ARE THE GREATEST ENEMIES OF GENIUS 601C PUB ADDRESS/N  PROSE
    THE GREATEST MISCHIEF I CALL FOR PUBLIC PROTECTION   . .  602A PUB ADDRESS/N    PROSE
    OUR MILDNESS IS NOTHING THE GREATEST MILDNESS WE CAN USE   675 JERUSALEM 45      14
    THEN FAR THE GREATEST NUMBER WERE ABOUT TO MAKE A         686 JERUSALEM 55      30
        SEPARATION
    IN OTHER MEN & LOVING THE GREATEST MEN BEST EACH ACCORDING 738 JERUSALEM 91      9
    IS MY VISION'S GREATEST ENEMY  . . . . . . . . . .        748 EV GOSPEL(A)/N     2
    NONE ARE GREATEST IN THE KINGDOM OF HEAVEN  . . . . . .  783A ANNO WW POEMS     MARG
    AS A SOLDIER OF CHRIST IT GIVES ME THE GREATEST OF TORMENTS 812D LETTER 22      PROSE
    MEETING AGAIN WITH YOU IS ONE OF OUR GREATEST PLEASURES   826B LETTER 28        PROSE
    THE GREATEST CONFIDENCE IN HER PERFECT RECOVERY   . . .   851C LETTER 50        PROSE
    IT IS THE GREATEST OF CRIMES TO DEPRESS TRUE ART & SCIENCE 863A LETTER 60       PROSE
    RUINS ACTIVITY & ARE THE GREATEST HURT TO AN ARTIST SUCH  879C LETTER 89        PROSE
        AS I AM
GREATLY
    IDEAS OF STRENGTH AND BEAUTY HAVE NOT BEEN GREATLY        579C DESC CAT 5       PROSE
        DIFFERENT
GREATNESS
    YOUR OWN REAL GREATNESS DEPENDS ON YOUR ENCOURAGEMENT   . 452C ANNO REYNOLDS    MARG
GRECIA
    I GAVE THEE PRIAM'S CITY AND THE ISLES OF GRECIA LOVELY   692 JERUSALEM 60      13
    UPON THE EGYPTIAN NILE WITH SOLEMN SONGS TO GRECIA   . .  692 JERUSALEM 60      19
    TURKEY & GRECIA SAW MY (INSTRUMENTS) OF MUSIC THEY AROSE  721 JERUSALEM 79      48
    THRO ITALY & GRECIA TO LEBANON & PERSIA & INDIA   . . .   722 JERUSALEM 80      47
    OF JAVAN THRO THE ISLES OF GRECIA & ALL EUROPE'S KINGS  . 735 JERUSALEM 89      34
GRECIAN    SEE GRAECIAN
    THE SAME THAT MADE OUR FRIEND DIOGENES THE GRECIAN   . .  154A MARRIAGE HH 12 *PROSE
    YOUR [MOCKS & SCORN] GRECIAN MOCKS & ROMAN SWORD   . . .  420 I SAW MNK AD/N     8
    A GRECIAN SCOFF IS A WRACKING WHEEL  . . . . . . .        420 I SAW MNK AD/N    19
    COME BRING WITH THEE JERUSALEM WITH SONGS ON THE GRECIAN  501 MILTON 19         46
        LYRE
    SHALL WE SUFFER THE ROMAN & GRECIAN RODS    . . . . . .   543 IF TRUE/N          7
    THE GRECIAN GODS WERE THE ANCIENT CHERUBIM OF PHOENICIA   571B DESC CAT 3       PROSE
    GOTHIC GRECIAN HINDOO AND EGYPTIAN ARE THE EXTENT OF THE  579D DESC CAT 5       PROSE
        HUMAN MIND
    YOUR GRECIAN MOCKS & ROMAN SWORD  . . . . . . . .        683 I SAW A MONK/J     23
    GRECIAN IS MATHEMATIC FORM GOTHIC IS LIVING FORM   . . .  778D HOMERS POETRY    PROSE
    THE IMMENSE FLOOD OF GRECIAN LIGHT & GLORY WHICH IS COMING 797C LETTER 10       PROSE
    IN YOUR COMMENDATION & MORE AND MORE OF A GRECIAN   . .   798A LETTER 10        PROSE
    ENTER INTO AN EMULATION OF GRECIAN MANNERS THERE ARE NOW I 798C LETTER 10       PROSE
    THIS IS ONLY GRECIAN OR RATHER TROJAN WORSHIP AND PERHAPS 845B LETTER 44        PROSE
GREECE
    & THE PRIDE OF GREECE AND FURTHER FROM THE RISING SUN   .  41A THEN SHE BORE    PROSE
    THE LAMB THE SAVIOUR ALBION TREMBLED TO ITALY GREECE &    495 MILTON 14          6
        EGYPT
    OR OVID'S WERE THE PRODUCTION OF GREECE OR OF LATIUM   .  565D DESC CAT 2       PROSE
    LYCON WILL PERCIEVE THAT THEY ARE NOT NOW IN ANCIENT GREECE 598B PUB ADDRESS/N  PROSE
    FROM SURREY HILLS THRO ITALY AND GREECE TO HINNOM'S VALE  684 JERUSALEM 53      29
    WITHIN IS ASIA & GREECE ORNAMENTED WITH EXQUISITE ART  .  690 JERUSALEM 58      37
    AND GREECE & ALONG THE SEA OF REPHAIM INTO JUDEA  . . .   704 JERUSALEM 67      39
    THE GODS OF GREECE & EGYPT WERE MATHEMATICAL DIAGRAMS   . 776D INSC LAOCOON     PROSE
    SUCH ARE GREECE & ROME SUCH IS EMPIRE OR TAX SEE LUKE...  777B INSC LAOCOON     PROSE
    SACRED TRUTH HAS PRONOUNCED THAT GREECE & ROME   . . .   778C HOMERS POETRY    PROSE
    ROME & GREECE SWEPT ART INTO THEIR MAW & DESTROYD IT   .  778D HOMERS POETRY    PROSE
    OF ANCIENT GREECE I SPEAK WITH PERFECT CONFIDENCE AND   . 852A LETTER 50        PROSE
GREEK
    THE GREEK GEMS ARE IN THE SAME STYLE AS THE GREEK STATUES 463B ANNO REYNOLDS    MARG
    INFECTION FROM THE SILLY GREEK & LATIN SLAVES OF THE SWORD 480C MILTON 1        PROSE
    WE DO NOT WANT EITHER GREEK OR ROMAN MODELS   . . . . .   480D MILTON 1         PROSE
    BRITISH WOMEN WERE NOT JEALOUS WHEN GREEK & ROMAN WERE    491 MILTON 10         15
        JEALOUS
    NEITHER WILL ANY ONE BELIEVE THAT THE GREEK STATUES  . .  565D DESC CAT 2       PROSE
    AS THEY ARE CALLED WERE THE INVENTION OF GREEK ARTISTS   565D DESC CAT 2       PROSE
    THE GREEK MUSES ARE DAUGHTERS OF MNEMOSYNE OR MEMORY   .  565D DESC CAT 2       PROSE
    WHICH THEY ADMIRE IN GREEK STATUES  . . . . . . . .      576C DESC CAT 4       PROSE
    SOME VISION PILGRIM'S PROGRESS IS FULL OF IT THE GREEK    604D V LAST JUDG/N    PROSE
        POETS
    THE GREEK MUSES WHICH ARE NOT INSPIRATION AS THE BIBLE IS 605C V LAST JUDG/N    PROSE
    NOTED THAT THE GREEK FABLES ORIGINATED IN SPIRITUAL MYSTERY 605C V LAST JUDG/N  PROSE
    WHILE THE HEBREW BIBLE & THE GREEK GOSPEL ARE GENUINE   . 605C V LAST JUDG/N    PROSE
    GREEK LEARNED & WISE AS ALSO OF THOSE OF OTHER NATIONS  . 610B V LAST JUDG/N    PROSE
    [TO NOTE THE LAST WORDS OF JESUS...(GREEK QUOTED)]        621C JERUSALEM 3     *PROSE
    BUT YOUR GREEK PHILOSOPHY WHICH IS A REMNANT OF DRUIDISM  682A JERUSALEM 52     PROSE
    THE GREEK HEROES & LASTLY BY THE ROMANS  . . . .        785B ILLUS DANTE 7     PROSE
    THE GREEK & ROMAN CLASSICS IS THE ANTICHRIST I SAY IS   . 786C ANNO THORNTON    MARG
    THE HONOUR INTENDED YOU BY NATURE TO REVIVE THE GREEK    795B LETTER 6         PROSE
        WORKMANSHIP
    I GO ON MERRILY WITH MY GREEK & LATIN AM VERY SORRY THAT  821D LETTER 25        PROSE
    I READ GREEK AS FLUENTLY AS AN OXFORD SCHOLAR &   . . .   821D LETTER 25        PROSE
```

		PAGE	TITLE	LINE

GREEKS

HEATED WITH WAR FILLD WITH THE BLOOD OF GREEKS	32	EDW THIRD/PS 6	10
WITH LAWS FROM PLATO & HIS GREEKS TO RENEW THE TROJAN GODS	506	MILTON 22	53
THE GREEKS AND HETRURIANS COPIED HERCULES FARNESE . . .	565C	DESC CAT 2	PROSE
BUT THE GREEKS AND SINCE THEM THE MODERNS HAVE NEGLECTED	571C	DESC CAT 3	PROSE
HE IS THE ATLAS OF THE GREEKS	578C	DESC CAT 5	PROSE
ONE OF THOSE THE GREEKS CALLED TITANS	578C	DESC CAT 5	PROSE
THE GREEKS REPRESENT CHRONOS OR TIME AS A VERY AGED MAN THIS IS FABLE	614D	V LAST JUDG/N	PROSE
WITH SOME OF THE ANCIENT GREEKS SAY	615D	V LAST JUDG/N	PROSE
THAT IS THE ?BUSINESS OF PLATO & THE GREEKS &	774D	ANNO BERKELEY	* MARG
TO RENEW THE LOST ART OF THE GREEKS	792A	LETTER 4	PROSE
ALONE VALUED BY THE GREEKS & THE BEST MODERN ARTISTS . .	794A	LETTER 5	PROSE
JUPITER OF THE GREEKS AN IRON-HEARTED TYRANT THE RUINER	852A	LETTER 50	PROSE

GREEKS'

ORIGINATES IN THE GREEKS' CALLING THE MUSES DAUGHTERS OF MEMORY	452D	ANNO REYNOLDS	MARG
TWAS THE GREEKS' LOVE OF WAR	552	WHY CUPID/N	17

GREEN (SURNAME)

TO GREEN THE BRICKLAYER	57	TO BE OR/IM	16
WASHINGTON FRANKLIN PAINE & WARREN GATES HANCOCK & GREEN	197	AMERICA 3	4
WASHINGTON HANCOCK PAINE & WARREN GATES FRANKLIN & GREEN	203	AMERICA CANC A	4
AND ON HIS RIGHT WAS MARY GREEN	435	WILLIAM BOND	17
AND MARY GREEN SHALL HER SERVANT BE	435	WILLIAM BOND	24
MAN SPOKE OF MR GREEN AS THE OLDEST FRIEND OF ROMNEY . .	845D	LETTER 44	PROSE

GREEN

. . . DISPLAYD GREEN FIELDS AMONG	274	FOUR ZOAS 1	367
OR THE GREEN CORNERS OF THE EARTH	10	TO MUSES/PS	6
CASTING HER BLUE EYES OVER THE GREEN OCEAN	33	EDW THIRD/PS 6	56
GREEN GRASS SPRINGS IN JOY AND THE NIMBLE AIR KISSES THE LEAVES	37B	CONTEMPLATN/PS	PROSE
DIDST THOU NOT TELL ME WITH GREEN WITHS(WITHES) TO BIND THY	38D	SAMSON/PS	PROSE
AND LAID HER LILIED BEAUTIES ON THE GREEN	43C	WOE CRIED MUSE	PROSE
JELLICOE IN FAINT PEA GREEN	53	PHEBE DREST/IM	2
THE CHILDREN WALKING TWO & TWO IN GREY & BLUE & GREEN . .	59	HOLY THURS/IM	2
WHEN THE TONGUES OF CHILDREN ARE HEARD ON THE GREEN . . .	60	NURSES SONG/IM	1
AND THE GREEN HILL LAUGHS WITH THE NOISE OF IT	63	SHEPHERD YOUNG	2
WHEN THE MEADOWS LAUGH WITH LIVELY GREEN	63	SHEPHERD YOUNG	3
REPLY NOT LEST I BIND THEE WITH THE GREEN FLAGS OF THE BROOK	104	TIRIEL 4	24
UNDER LEAVES SO GREEN	115	THE BLOSSOM/SI	2
UNDER LEAVES SO GREEN	116	THE BLOSSOM/SI	8
THE ECCHOING GREEN	116A	ECCHOING GR/SI	TITLE
ON THE ECCHOING GREEN	116	ECCHOING GR/SI	10
ON THE ECCHOING GREEN	116	ECCHOING GR/SI	20
ON THE DARKENING GREEN	116	ECCHOING GR/SI	30
THEN DOWN A GREEN PLAIN LEAPING LAUGHING THEY RUN . . .	117	CHIMNEY SWP/SI	15
FAREWELL GREEN FIELDS AND HAPPY GROVES	119	NIGHT/SI	9
WHEN THE VOICES OF CHILDREN ARE HEARD ON THE GREEN . . .	121	NURSES SONG/SI	1
THE CHILDREN WALKING TWO & TWO IN RED & BLUE & GREEN . .	121	HOLY THURS/SI	2
WHEN THE GREEN WOODS LAUGH WITH THE VOICE OF JOY	124	LAUGHING/SI	1
AND THE GREEN HILL LAUGHS WITH THE NOISE OF IT	124	LAUGHING/SI	4
WHEN THE MEADOWS LAUGH WITH LIVELY GREEN	125	LAUGHING/SI	5
HIS FOREHEAD WAS DIVIDED INTO STREAKS OF GREEN & PURPLE	156C	MARRIAGE HH 17	PROSE
WHERE I USED TO PLAY ON THE GREEN	162	GARDEN LOVE/N	4
WHEN THE VOICES OF CHILDREN ARE HEARD ON THE GREEN . . .	171	NURSES SONG/N	1
MY FACE TURNS GREEN & PALE	171	NURSES SONG/N	4
THE GREEN LEAVES AMONG	175	WILD FLOWERS/N	2
WHEN THE VOICES OF CHILDREN ARE HEARD ON THE GREEN . . .	212	NURSES SONG/SE	1
MY FACE TURNS GREEN AND PALE	212	NURSES SONG/SE	4
WHERE I USED TO PLAY ON THE GREEN	215	GARDEN LOVE/SE	4
HIS DAUGHTERS FROM GREEN HERBS & CATTLE	234	URIZEN 23	20
[UPON ITS GREEN STALK ROSE THE CORN WAVING INNUMERABLE]	270	FOUR ZOAS 1	209
THRO THE CLEAR CHANGING ATMOSPHERE DISPLAYD GREEN FIELDS AMONG	274	FOUR ZOAS 1	367
OR WILT THOU ANSWER YOUNGEST WOMAN CLAD IN SHINING GREEN	312	FOUR ZOAS 6	17
UPON THE GREEN PLAINS & SWEET FRIENDSHIP MET IN PALACES	317	FOUR ZOAS 6	215
AS SNOW THAT FALLS AROUND A LEAFLESS TREE UPON THE GREEN	359	FOUR ZOAS 9	49
RUNNING AMONG MY GREEN PASTURES DELIGHTING AMONG MY TREES	368	FOUR ZOAS 9	442
AMONG GREEN LEAVES & BLOSSOMS SWEET	423	THE BIRDS/N	20
[THE] GREEN HILLS APPEAR BENEATH WITH THE GRAVES OF THE BLESSED	443D	LAST JUDGMNT/L	PROSE
WALK UPON ENGLAND'S MOUNTAINS GREEN	480	AND DID FEET/M	2
IN ENGLAND'S GREEN & PLEASANT LAND	481	AND DID FEET/M	16
WITH SHOUTS AND PALAMABRON'S SONGS RENDING THE FORESTS GREEN	488	MILTON 8	9
THEN LOUD FROM THEIR GREEN COVERT ALL THE BIRDS BEGIN THEIR SONG	520	MILTON 31	39
AND THE WILD THYME FROM WIMBLETON'S GREEN & IMPURPLED HILLS	534	MILTON 42	30
[MOULD] [GROUND] FLOWERY MOULD INTO THE GREEN FIELDS OF	609D	V LAST JUDG/N	*PROSE
MULTITUDES ARE SEEN ASCENDING FROM THE GREEN FIELDS . .	610C	V LAST JUDG/N	PROSE
MILTON WALKING BY ELMS ON HILLOCKS GREEN THE PLOWMAN .	618B	ILLUS MILTON	PROSE
AMONG THE LITTLE MEADOWS GREEN	649	FIELDS FROM/J	8
THE JEWS-HARP-HOUSE & THE GREEN MAN	650	FIELDS FROM/J	13
SHE WALKS UPON OUR MEADOWS GREEN	650	FIELDS FROM/J	17
CRIMSON WITH WRATH & GREEN WITH JEALOUSY DAZLING WITH LOVE	699	JERUSALEM 64	28
BREEDING WOMEN WALKING IN PRIDE & BRINGING FORTH UNDER GREEN TREES	706	JERUSALEM 68	36
IN ENGLAND'S GREEN & PLEASANT BOWERS	718	ENGLND AWAKE/J	12
WALKED UP AND DOWN IN ITS GREEN MOUNTAINS BUT HAND IS FLED	729	JERUSALEM 83	86
OF JOY IS IN THE EYES OF OTHERS ONLY A GREEN THING THAT STANDS	793D	LETTER 5	PROSE

GREEN   (CONTINUED)   PAGE   TITLE   LINE
    NOTWITHSTANDING HE WAS SHADED BY A GREEN SHADE OVER HIS   835C LETTER 35   PROSE
        EYES
    REVD DR TRUSLER ENGLEFIELD GREEN EGHAM SURREY . . . . SUPP ADDRESSES/L   *TITLE
    ECCHOING GREEN DITTO THE LAMB THE SHEPHERD INFANT JOY SUPP LETTER 66A   *PROSE
GREEN HOUSE
    THAY THEY SHOULD BE PRESERVD IN YOUR GREEN HOUSE . . . . 812B LETTER 22   PROSE
GREENLAND
    CONGO ZAARA CANADA GREENLAND CAROLINA MEXICO . . . . . 712 JERUSALEM 72   41
GREENWOOD
    WHEN THE GREENWOOD LAUGHS WITH THE VOICE OF JOY . . .   63 SHEPHERD YOUNG   5
GREW
    HE FOLLOWED ME UP AND DOWN IN THE HOUSE WHEN I GREW UP . 37C CONTEMPLATN/PS PROSE
    TILL HOPE GREW FEEBLE AND WAS READY TO GIVE PLACE   40A SAMSON/PS   PROSE
        TO DOUBTING
    GREW PREGNANT & [BROUGHT FORTH] BORE SCORN & SLANDER   . 42D THEN SHE BORE   PROSE
    SHE SOON GREW PREGNANT & BROUGHT FORTH . . . .   51 WHEN CORRUP/IM   21
    WESTWARDLY JOURNEYING TILL TIRIEL GREW WEARY WITH   104 TIRIEL 4   31
        HIS TRAVEL
    SO THAT THE NETHER DEEP GREW BLACK AS A SEA . . . .   156B MARRIAGE HH 17   PROSE
    HOWEVER I SAW THAT THEY SOMETIMES GREW NUMEROUS . . . . 157A MARRIAGE HH 17 PROSE
    BECAUSE HE WAS A LITTLE WISER THAN THE MONKEY GREW VAIN 157D MARRIAGE HH 21 PROSE
    BUT MASTERING HIMSELF HE GREW YELLOW . . . .   158B MARRIAGE HH 22   PROSE
    AND IT GREW BY DAY & NIGHT . . . .   165 CHRISTN FORB/N   9
    FOR ALL BLOSSOMS GREW & GREW . . . .   166 I FEARD FURY/N   7
    AND I [GREW] [SMILD] SOOTHD DAY AFTER DAY . . . . .   167 INFANT SORW/N   14
    AND I [GREW] SMILD NIGHT AFTER NIGHT . . . .   167 INFANT SORW/N   16
    OUGHT BUT THE LOVE THAT ON ME GREW . . . .   184 O I CANNOT/N   6
    ALBION IS SICK AMERICA FAINTS ENRAGD THE ZENITH GREW . 197 AMERICA 4   4
    AND A COWL OF FLESH GREW OER HIS HEAD & SCALES ON HIS BACK 202 AMERICA 15   17
        & RIBS
    AND IT GREW BOTH DAY AND NIGHT . . . .   218 POISON TREE/SE   9
    AS THEY GREW AND A FOURTH AGE PASSED . . . .   229 URIZEN 11   24
    THE WORM LAY TILL IT GREW TO A SERPENT . . . . . .   232 URIZEN 19   26
    THE SERPENT GREW CASTING ITS SCALES . . . .   232 URIZEN 19   30
    THEY NAMED THE CHILD ORC HE GREW . . . .   233 URIZEN 20   6
    A TIGHTNING GIRDLE GREW . . . .   233 URIZEN 20   9
    GREW SMALL LIKE THE EYES OF A MAN . . . .   236 URIZEN 25   36
    ADHERED AND GREW ONE WITH HIS FLESH AND NERVES & VEINS 242 EUROPE 12   17
        SHOT THRO THEM
    ADAM SHUDDERED NOAH FADED BLACK GREW THE SUNNY AFRICAN . 245 SONG OF LOS 3   10
    IT GREW A THICK TREE HE WROTE . . . .   252 AHANIA 3   63
    GREW TO ROOTS WHEN IT FELT THE EARTH . . . .   252 AHANIA 3   66
    MANY AGES OF GROANS TILL THERE GREW . . . .   258 BOOK OF LOS 4   43
    AND ALL ITS GOLDEN PORCHES GREW PALE WITH HIS SICKENING 280 FOUR ZOAS 2   13
        LIGHT
    I NURTURD HER I FED HER WITH MY RAINS & DEWS SHE GREW . 282 FOUR ZOAS 2   84
    SHOT SPIRING OUT & PETRIFIED [IN] AS THEY GREW AND A FOURTH 303 FOUR ZOAS 4 * 234
    COVERD WITH GLOOM THE FIERY BOY GREW FED BY THE MILK . 307 FOUR ZOAS 5   72
    GRIEF ROSE UPON HIS RUDDY BROWS A TIGHTENING GIRDLE GREW 307 FOUR ZOAS 5   83
    WITH SILENT FEAR & HIS IMMORTAL CHEEKS GREW DEADLY PALE 307 FOUR ZOAS 5   87
    SURROUNDED WITH FLAMES THE DEMON GREW LOUD HOWLING IN HIS 308 FOUR ZOAS 5   109
        FIRES
    INTO THE IRON ROCK & GREW A CHAIN BENEATH THE EARTH . . . 309 FOUR ZOAS 5   167
    HE COULD NOT TAKE THEIR FETTERS OFF FOR THEY GREW FROM 315 FOUR ZOAS 6   143
        THE SOUL
    INTO THE DOLEFUL VALES WHERE NO TREE GREW NOR RIVER FLOWD 319 FOUR ZOAS 6   284
    DARK GREW HIS GLOBE REDDNING WITH MISTS & FULL BEFORE HIS 319 FOUR ZOAS 6   296
        PATH
    IN THE DARK DEEP THE DARK TREE GREW HER SHADOW WAS DRAWN 324 FOUR ZOAS 7   170
        DOWN
    OF PLAGUES HIDDEN IN SHINING GLOBES THAT GREW ON THE LIVING 325 FOUR ZOAS 7 216
        TREE
    PALE GREW THY FACE [THY SON'S] [& HIS] . . . . .   325 FOUR ZOAS 7   * 227
    URIZEN GREW UP IN THE PLAINS OF BEULAH MANY SONS . . . 326 FOUR ZOAS 7   251
    BROUGHT FORTH THIS WONDER HORRIBLE A CLOUD SHE GREW & GREW 328 FOUR ZOAS 7   327
    SHE TENDERLY LOVD HIM ABOVE ALL HIS BRETHREN HE GREW UP 351 FOUR ZOAS 8   385
    AND ENION SANG AMONG THE FLOWERS THAT GREW AMONG THE TREES 371 FOUR ZOAS 9   536
    A LITTLE FLOWER GREW IN A LONELY VALE . . . . . .   414 TO MRS FLAXMAN   1
    BUT ALL HE COULD DO HE GREW THINNER & THINNER . . . . 434 LONG JOHN BRWN   11
    SHOT SPIRING OUT IN THE DEEP DARKNESS & PETRIFIED AS THEY 482 MILTON 3   18
        GREW
    GREW DEADLY PALE HE BECAME WHAT HE BEHELD FOR A RED . . . 483 MILTON 3   29
    THUS SATAN RAGD AMIDST THE ASSEMBLY AND HIS BOSOM GREW . . 490 MILTON 9   30
    IN THE SHADOWY FEMALE'S BOSOM JEALOUS HER DARKNESS GREW 500 MILTON 18   42
    THE MOUNTAINS WAILD & EVERY PLANT THAT GREW IN SOLEMN SIGHS 503 MILTON 21   19
        LAMENTED
    THEN LOS GREW FURIOUS RAGING WHY STAND WE HERE TREMBLING 672 JERUSALEM 43   12
        AROUND
    WHERE LUVAH'S WORLD OF OPAKENESS GREW TO A PERIOD IT . 713 JERUSALEM 73   22
    GWENDOLEN HID IN HER LEFT HAND IT GREW & GREW TILL IT . 729 JERUSALEM 84   32
    . . . ALL THEIR GLORY THAT GREW ON DESOLATION . . . . 746 JERUSALEM 98   51
GREY
    WHEN EARLY MORN WALKS FORTH IN SOBER GREY . . . . .   10 WHEN EARLY/PS   1
    TIS CONTEMPLATION DAUGHTER OF THE GREY MORNING . . . 36D CONTEMPLATN/PS   PROSE
    THE CHILDREN WALKING TWO & TWO IN GREY & BLUE & GREEN 59 HOLY THURS/IM   2
    FOR EVRY ONE OF THOSE THY WRINKLES EACH OF THOSE GREY HAIRS 39 TIRIEL 1   * 14
    LOOK KNOWST THOU AUGHT OF THIS GREY BEARD OR OF THESE 104 TIRIEL 4   44
        BLINDED EYES
    . . . HER GREY TOWERS GROAN AND THE BASTILE TREMBLES 135 FRENCH REVOLTN   18
    THE KING FROWNING IN PURPLE BESIDE THE GREY PLOWMAN . . . 141 FRENCH REVOLTN 150
    AND GREY HAIRS ARE ON MY HEAD . . . .   167 INFANT SORW/N   43

		PAGE	TITLE	LINE
GREY	(CONTINUED)			
	AND HER LOCKS COVERD WITH GREY DESPAIR	168	EARTHS ANSWR/N	5
	AND GREY HAIRS ARE ON MY HEAD	169	MIRTLE SHADE/N	18
	AND GREY HAIRS WERE ON MY HEAD	182	THE ANGEL/N	16
	TO SPIN A WEB OF AGE AROUND HIM GREY AND HOARY DARK . . .	194	V DAU ALBION 7	19
	AND HER LOCKS COVERD WITH GREY DESPAIR	210	EARTHS ANSR/SE	5
	AND GREY HAIRS WERE ON MY HEAD	214	THE ANGEL/SE	16
	ROLLING VOLUMES OF GREY MIST INVOLVE CHURCHES PALACES TOWERS	242	EUROPE 12	3
	FREEZING TO SOLID ALL BENEATH HIS GREY OBLIVIOUS FORM . .	302	FOUR ZOAS 4	172
	THE MIDST BETWEEN AN EQUILIBRIUM GREY OF AIR SERENE . . .	316	FOUR ZOAS 6	194
	IN ALL THE DISEASES OF MAN FALLING UPON THY GREY ACCURSED FRONT	322	FOUR ZOAS 7	89
	THOU WILT NOT CEASE FROM RAGE GREY DEMON SILENCE ALL THY STORMS	323	FOUR ZOAS 7	144
	THAT LIES BEYOND THE BOUNDS OF SCIENCE IN THE GREY OBSCURE	324	FOUR ZOAS 7	150
	. . . THE GREY HOAR FROST WAS THERE	378	FOUR ZOAS 9	814
	I TALKD TO THE GREY MONK WHERE HE STOOD	418	I SAW A MONK/N	3
	THE BLOOD RED RAN FROM THE GREY MONK'S SIDE	419	I SAW A MONK/N	15
	THE GREY MONK	430A	GREY MONK	TITLE
	THE BLOOD RED RAN FROM THE GREY MONK'S SIDE	430	GREY MONK	5
	THIS IS THE THRONE OF MAMMON GREY	558	I ROSE UP AT/N	4
	GREY BEARDS & SCOURGES OF FIRE THEY REPRESENT CRUEL LAWS	608A	V LAST JUDG/N	PROSE
	OF GREY OBSCURITY FILLD WITH CLOUDS & ROCKS & WHIRLING WATERS	674	JERUSALEM 44	16
	I TALKD WITH THE GREY MONK AS WE STOOD	683	I SAW A MONK/J	3
	THE BLOOD RED RAN FROM THE GREY MONK'S SIDE	683	I SAW A MONK/J	13
	WITH MY INWARD EYE TIS AN OLD MAN GREY	817	HAPPINESS/L	29
GREY BROWD				
	FLAGD WITH GREY BROWD SNOWS AND THUNDEROUS VISAGES . . .	159B	SONG LIBERTY	PROSE
	HIS GREY BROWD COUNCELLORS THUNDEROUS WARRIORS	159D	SONG LIBERTY	PROSE
	FALLING INTO THE DEEP SUBLIME FLAGD WITH GREY-BROWD SNOWS	203	AMERICA 16	5
GREY HEADED				
	GREY HEADED BEADLES WALKD BEFORE WITH WANDS AS WHITE AS SNOW	59	HOLY THURS/IM	3
	GREY HEADED BEADLES WALKD BEFORE WITH WANDS AS WHITE AS SNOW	121	HOLY THURS/SI	3
GREYHOUNDS				
	AND THREE PRIESTS HER GREYHOUNDS ATTEND HER	566D	DESC CAT 3	PROSE
	& THREE PRIESTS HER GREYHOUNDS ATTEND HER	588B	CHAUCER/N	PROSE
GREY-HOUNDS				
	AND THREE PRIESTS HER GREY-HOUNDS ATTEND HER	589D	CHAUCER 2	PROSE
GRIDING				
	WHERE ENITHARMON JOIND TO HIS LEFT SIDE IN [DISMAL] GRIDING PAIN	299	FOUR ZOAS 4	* 60
	DEPENDING FROM THE BOSOM OF LOS & HOW WITH [DISMAL] GRIDING PAIN	307	FOUR ZOAS 5	93
	[BUT] I MOCKD AT THE WRACK & GRIDING CHAIN	419	I SAW A MONK/N	34
	I MOCKD AT THE WRACK & GRIDING CHAIN	430	GREY MONK	19
	YORK & LINCOLN HIDE AMONG THE FLOCKS BECAUSE OF THE GRIDING KNIFE	703	JERUSALEM 66	65
GRIEF				
	I CURSE MY STARS IN BITTER GRIEF AND WOE	10	WHEN EARLY/PS	15
	BUT GOD HATH OTHER JOYS IN STORE IS BURDENED ISRAEL HIS GRIEF	39C	SAMSON/PS	PROSE
	PENSIVE SHE SAT AND THOUGHT ON ISRAEL'S GRIEF	39D	SAMSON/PS	PROSE
	GRIEF PERCHT UPON MY BROW AND THOUGHT EMBRACD HER . . .	43B	WOE CRIED MUSE	PROSE
	& GOLDEN PLEASURES BEAM AROUND MY HEAD WHY GRIEF DOST THOU ACCOST ME	43B	WOE CRIED MUSE	PROSE
	[THE AGED TIRIEL COULD NOT SPEAK HIS HEART WAS FULL OF GRIEF]	101	TIRIEL 2	44
	ASK ME NO MORE I PRAY FOR GRIEF HATH SEALD MY PRECIOUS SIGHT	102	TIRIEL 2	53
	[BUT STILL HE FEARD THAT HAR & HEVA WOULD DIE OF JOY & GRIEF]	102	TIRIEL 3	8
	CAN I SEE ANOTHER'S GRIEF	122	ON ANOTHERS/SI	3
	HEAR THE SMALL BIRD'S GRIEF & CARE	122	ON ANOTHERS/SI	15
	THAT OUR GRIEF HE MAY DESTROY	123	ON ANOTHERS/SI	34
	TILL OUR GRIEF IS FLED & GONE	123	ON ANOTHERS/SI	35
	IMAGE OF GRIEF THY FADING LINEAMENTS MAKE MY EYELIDS FAIL	297	FOUR ZOAS 3	195
	GRIEF ROSE UPON HIS RUDDY BROWS A TIGHTENING GIRDLE GREW	307	FOUR ZOAS 5	83
	WHEN SATIATED WITH GRIEF THEY RETURND BACK TO GOLGONOOZA	309	FOUR ZOAS 5	176
	WHEN I RETURN FROM CLOUDS OF GRIEF IN THE WANDRING ELEMENTS	324	FOUR ZOAS 7	185
	FELL DOWN & SHADOWY FORMS OF JOY MIXD WITH DESPAIR & GRIEF	358	FOUR ZOAS 9	29
	EXCESS OF JOY IS WORSE THAN GRIEF HER HEART BEAT HIGH HER BLOOD	362	FOUR ZOAS 9	197
	O TREMBLING JOY EXCESS OF JOY IS LIKE EXCESS OF GRIEF	376	FOUR ZOAS 9	730
	HIS GRIEF IS THEIR ETERNAL JOY	425	MENTAL TRAVLER	41
	REPEATS TO THEE THY MOTHER'S GRIEF	432	AUGURIES	38
	UNDER EVERY GRIEF & PINE	432	AUGURIES	61
	BUT LOS HID THULLOH FROM HER SIGHT LEST SHE SHOULD DIE OF GRIEF	488	MILTON 8	41
	I SAID NOW IS MY GRIEF AT WORST INCAPABLE OF BEING . . .	630	JERUSALEM 10	44
	BUT NOW MY SOUL IS HARROWD WITH GRIEF & FEAR & LOVE & DESIRE	707	JERUSALEM 68	66
	TO TELL HOW LOS IN GRIEF & ANGER WHIRLING ROUND HIS HAMMER ON HIGH	714	JERUSALEM 74	20
	ABSORB ME NOT IN SUCH DIRE GRIEF O ALBION MY BROTHER . .	727	JERUSALEM 83	6
	LURED BY HER BEAUTY OUTSIDE OF HIMSELF IN SHADOWY GRIEF	732	JERUSALEM 86	60
	FROM NEITHER PAIN NOR GRIEF EXEMPTED	756	EV GOSPEL(I)/N	12
	REMINDS THEE OF THY MOTHER'S GRIEF	770	THE KEYS/GP	2
	& FEELING HEARTILY YOUR GRIEF WITH A BROTHER'S SYMPATHY	797B	LETTER 9	PROSE

		PAGE	TITLE	LINE

GRIEF   (CONTINUED)
AND INNOCENT GRIEF HIS INNOCENT AND VENERABLE MADNESS AND   864B LETTER 61   PROSE
GRIEF AMONG THE ROOTS OF TREES . . . . SUPP ILLUS GRAY   *TITLE
GRIEFS
AND MY GRIEFS [UNFOLD] INFOLD   . . . .   8 MAD SONG/PS   4
OR HOW SHALL WE GATHER WHAT GRIEFS DESTROY . . . . .   124 SCHOOL BOY/SI   28
BUT MY GRIEFS ADVANCE ALSO FOR EVER & EVER WITHOUT END 630 JERUSALEM 10   50
ASK ME NOT OF MY GRIEFS THOU KNOWEST ALL MY GRIEFS . . . 642 JERUSALEM 20   20
DIVIDE MY GRIEFS WITH YOU THAT I CANNOT HIDE WHAT IT IS NOW 812B LETTER 22   PROSE
GRIEVD
AT HOB-NAIL DICK WHO GRIEVD THE CHANCE . . . .   16 BLIND-MANS/PS   16
INWARD GRIEVD HE SAW AND LOVD THE BEAUTEOUS SUPPLIANT . . 39B SAMSON/PS   PROSE
THIS PRIDE [OBSERVD AND] OBSERVING INLY GRIEVD   . . . . 41A THEN SHE BORE   *PROSE
GRIEVE
I BEGIN WITH THE LATTER END OF YOUR LETTER & GRIEVE MORE 837C LETTER 36   PROSE
   FOR
GRIEVED
THRICE HAST THOU MOCKED ME AND GRIEVED MY SOUL   . . . . 38D SAMSON/PS   PROSE
& IT GRIEVED HIM AT HIS HEART . . . . 776C INSC LAOCOON   PROSE
GRIEVOUS
TO ASSIST IN THEIR MOST GRIEVOUS WORK OF PITY & COMPASSION 692 JERUSALEM 59   47
GRIEVOUSLY
THE EMANATIONS OF THE GRIEVOUSLY AFFLICTED FRIENDS   678 JERUSALEM 48   27
   OF ALBION
GRIM
GRIM WAR SHALL LAUGH AND SHOUT DECKED IN TEARS   . . . . 31 EDW THIRD/PS 5   53
FROM THE GRIM FLAMES AND FROM THE VISIONS OF ORC IN SIGHT 201 AMERICA 13   9
GRIM FROST BENEATH & TERRIBLE SNOW LINKD IN A MARRIAGE   306 FOUR ZOAS 5   33
   CHAIN
THE WHIRLWIND "HUSHD IN GRIM REPOSE" . . . . SUPP ILLUS GRAY   *TITLE
GRIN
OBTUSE ANGLE GIVING A GRIN SAID   . . . .   45C ISLAND MOON 1   PROSE
I THINK I DO IN THE FIRST PLACE SAID HE WITH A GRIN . . . 49B ISLAND MOON 5   PROSE
BUT NEVER CAPABLE OF ANSWERING WHO SITS WITH A SLY GRIN 533 MILTON 41   13
GRIN'D
THE FATHER GRIN'D & SKIPT ABOUT   . . . .   51 WHEN CORRUP/IM   23
GRIND
WOOLETT I KNOW DID NOT KNOW HOW TO GRIND HIS GRAVER   . . 603C PUB ADDR AD/N PROSE
OF DAY & NIGHT THE MYRIADS OF ETERNITY THAT THEY MAY GRIND 700 JERUSALEM 65   23
GRINDER
THE SOLDIER SAID TO MRS GRINDER THAT IT WOULD BE RIGHT . . 438A BLAKES MEMORAN PROSE
MRS GRINDER AND HER DAUGHTER ALL THE TIME   . . . . . 438B BLAKES MEMORAN PROSE
MRS HAYNES & HER DAUGHTER ALL THE TIME MR GRINDER   . . 438B BLAKES MEMORAN PROSE
AN OLD MAN NAMED JONES WHO MRS GRINDER SAYS DID NOT . . 438C BLAKES MEMORAN PROSE
I E SEDITION MR GRINDER THEN REPROVED THE SOLDIER   . . 438C BLAKES MEMORAN PROSE
FOR THREATENING WILLIAM AND MR GRINDER SAID   . . . . 438C BLAKES MEMORAN PROSE
GRINDER'S
THERE WAS NOT ANY BODY IN GRINDER'S TAP-ROOM BUT . . . . 438C BLAKES MEMORAN PROSE
GRINDING
LET THE SLAVE GRINDING AT THE MILL RUN OUT INTO THE FIELD 198 AMERICA 6   6
. . . & THE SLAVE GRINDING AT THE MILL   . . . . . .   291 FOUR ZOAS 2   414
LET THE SLAVE GRINDING AT THE MILL RUN OUT INTO THE FIELD 375 FOUR ZOAS 9   670
AND IN GRINDING AGONIES IN THREATS STIFLINGS & DIREFUL   639 JERUSALEM 17   58
   STRUGGLINGS
OF BLOOD OVER EUROPE A VEGETATING ROOT IN GRINDING PAIN   677 JERUSALEM 47   5
GRINDINGS
IN THROBBINGS & SHOOTINGS & GRINDINGS   . . . . 236 URIZEN 25   27
GRINNING
AND GRINNING SKULLS AND CORRUPTIBLE DEATH   . . . . .   4 FAIR ELENOR/PS   14
& ALL OF THAT SPECIES CHAIND BY THE MIDDLE GRINNING . . 157A MARRIAGE HH 17 PROSE
AND WITH A GRINNING ASPECT FIRST COUPLED WITH & THEN   157B MARRIAGE HH 17 PROSE
   DEVOURD
WAS LEFT A HELPLESS TRUNK THIS AFTER GRINNING & KISSING IT 157B MARRIAGE HH 17 PROSE
GRINS
ONE GRINS [ONE] T OTHER SPITS & IN CORNERS HIDES   . . . 545 COSWAY FRAZR/N   7
GRIZLY
BUILD WE A BOWER FOR HEAVEN'S DARLING IN THE GRIZLY DEEP 280 FOUR ZOAS 2   24
AND SAW THEIR GRIZLY FEARS & HIS EYES SICKEND AT THE SIGHT 313 FOUR ZOAS 6   80
IN INTRICATE LABYRINTHS OERSPREADING MANY A GRIZLY DEEP 321 FOUR ZOAS 7   35
AND HEARTS LAID OPEN TO THE LIGHT BY THE BROAD GRIZLY SWORD 338 FOUR ZOAS 7B   206
ARISING IN HIS PRIDE ENLIGHTEN ALL THE GRIZLY DEEPS . . . 352 FOUR ZOAS 8   440
AND HEARTS LAID OPEN TO THE LIGHT BY THE BROAD GRIZLY SWORD 701 JERUSALEM 65   52
GROAN   SEE DEATH GROAN
A HOLLOW GROAN RAN THRO THE DREARY VAULTS   . . . . .   4 FAIR ELENOR/PS   4
AND GROAN UPON THE PLAIN . . . .   13 GWIN KING/PS   86
AND GHOSTS ACCUSING GROAN . . . .   13 GWIN KING/PS   100
HOW MANY IN WALLED CITIES LIE AND GROAN . . . .   30 EDW THIRD/PS 5   8
AN INFANT GROAN AN INFANT FEAR   . . . .   122 ON ANOTHERS/SI   10
. . . HER GREY TOWERS GROAN AND THE BASTILE TREMBLES . . 135 FRENCH REVOLTN   18
THE VOICE CEASD A GROAN SHOOK MY CHAMBER . . . . 141 FRENCH REVOLTN 151
I WISH & FEEL & WEEP & GROAN AH TERRIBLE TERRIBLE   . . . 265 FOUR ZOAS 1   63
A GROAN WAS HEARD ON HIGH THE WARLIKE CLARIONS CEAST THE 273 FOUR ZOAS 1   313
   SPIRITS
THEN THE GROAN & THE DOLOR ARE QUITE FORGOTTEN . . . . 291 FOUR ZOAS 2   414
A DOLOROUS GROAN THAT STRUCK WITH DUMBNESS ALL CONFUSION 295 FOUR ZOAS 3   147
LOUD STRONG A UNIVERSAL GROAN OF DEATH LOUDER . . . . 295 FOUR ZOAS 3   150
BUT FROM THE DOLOROUS GROAN ONE LIKE A SHADOW OF SMOKE   296 FOUR ZOAS 3   153
   APPEARD
FROM ITS HINGES UTTERING ITS FINAL GROAN ALL BEULAH FELL 326 FOUR ZOAS 7   258
BUT THEN THE SPECTRE ENTERD LOS'S BOSOM EVERY SIGH & GROAN 328 FOUR ZOAS 7   336
ALL NIGHT AMONG THE SLAIN & MOCK THE WOUNDED THAT GROAN 334 FOUR ZOAS 7B   48
   IN THE FIELD

	PAGE	TITLE	LINE
GROAN (CONTINUED)			
. . . WHEN THE WOUNDED GROAN IN THE FIELD	337	FOUR ZOAS 7B	* 190
TILL MAN SHALL LEAVE A CORRUPTIBLE BODY HE FAMISHD HEARS HIM GROAN	354	FOUR ZOAS 8	524
THE ROCKS GROAN HORRIBLE & RUN ABOUT THE MOUNTAINS & . .	358	FOUR ZOAS 9	53
THE UNIVERSAL GROAN WENT UP THE ETERNAL MAN WAS DARKEND	372	FOUR ZOAS 9	578
A DOLOROUS GROAN & FROM THE DOLOROUS GROAN IN TEARS . .	373	FOUR ZOAS 9	593
THEY DANCE AROUND THE DYING & THEY DRINK THE HOWL & GROAN	377	FOUR ZOAS 9	767
A HOLLOW GROAN FIRST SPOKE HIS WOE	419	I SAW A MONK/N	24
AND THE BITTER GROAN [FOR ANOTHER'S] OF THE MARTYR'S WOE	420	I SAW A MONK/N	60
THE MARTYR'S GROAN & THE LOVER'S SIGH	425	MENTAL TRAVLER	36
A HOLLOW GROAN FIRST SPOKE HIS WOE	430	GREY MONK	10
AND THE BITTER GROAN OF THE MARTYR'S WOE	430	GREY MONK	31
FELL DOWN AS DEWS OF NIGHT & A LOUD SOLEMN UNIVERSAL GROAN	490	MILTON 9	37
THEY DANCE AROUND THE DYING & THEY DRINK THE HOWL & GROAN	514	MILTON 27	37
THEY THUNDEROUS UTTERD ALL A UNIVERSAL GROAN FALLING DOWN	525	MILTON 35	31
THE SOLDIER'S FIFE THE HARLOT'S SHRIEK THE VIRGIN'S DISMAL GROAN	636	JERUSALEM 16	6
ALBION GAVE HIS DEADLY GROAN	650	FIELDS FROM/J	35
WHEN WITH A DREADFUL GROAN THE EMANATION MILD OF ALBION	678	JERUSALEM 48	47
AND THE BITTER GROAN OF A MARTYR'S WOE	683	I SAW A MONK/J	27
LOS ON THE THAMES & MEDWAY LONDON & CANTERBURY GROAN IN PAIN	698	JERUSALEM 63	35
. . . WHEN THE WOUNDED GROAN IN THE FIELD	700	JERUSALEM 65	32
CHESHIRE & LANCASHIRE & WESTMORELAND GROAN IN ANGUISH . .	736	JERUSALEM 90	18
GROAND			
WITH GORY BLOOD IT GROAND AND THUS IT SPAKE	5	FAIR ELENOR/PS	60
SHE HUGGD IT TO HER BREAST AND GROAND HER LAST	6	FAIR ELENOR/PS	72
THE ETERNAL FEMALE GROAND IT WAS HEARD OVER ALL THE EARTH	159A	SONG LIBERTY	PROSE
MY MOTHER GROAND MY FATHER WEPT	166	INFANT SORW/N	1
MY MOTHER GROAND MY FATHER WEPT	217	INFANT SORW/SE	1
DEEP GROAND URIZEN STRETCHING HIS AWFUL HAND	249	AHANIA 2	31
HE GROAND ANGUISHD & CALLED HER SIN	250	AHANIA 2	34
FUZON GROAND ON THE TREE	253	AHANIA 4	44
SINGING HER LAMENTATION THARMAS GROAND AMONG HIS CLOUDS	266	FOUR ZOAS 1	71
ETERNITY GROAND & WAS TROUBLED AT THE IMAGE OF ETERNAL DEATH	273	FOUR ZOAS 1	315
ETERNITY GROAND & WAS TROUBLED AT THE IMAGE OF ETERNAL DEATH	277	FOUR ZOAS 1	* 462
AMONG THE DRUID TEMPLES ALBION GROAND ON TYBURN'S BROOK	281	FOUR ZOAS 2	40
THE LOVELY FEMALE HOWLD & URIZEN BENEATH DEEP GROUND . .	302	FOUR ZOAS 4	189
THE EMPYREAN GROAND THROUGHOUT ALL EDEN WAS DARKEND . . .	304	FOUR ZOAS 4	264
ARE THESE THE SLAVES THAT GROAND ALONG THE STREETS OF MYSTERY	375	FOUR ZOAS 9	677
SAYING MILTON GOES TO ETERNAL DEATH SO SAYING THEY GROAND IN SPIRIT	504	MILTON 21	43
LOUD GROAND ALBION FROM MOUNTAIN TO MOUNTAIN & REPLIED	645	JERUSALEM 22	36
THEY GROAND ALOUD ON LONDON STONE	650	FIELDS FROM/J	33
THEY GROAND ALOUD ON TYBURN'S BROOK	650	FIELDS FROM/J	34
THE TREE SPREAD OVER HIM ITS COLD SHADOWS ALBION GROAND	653	JERUSALEM 28	17
ETERNITY GROAND & WAS TROUBLED AT THE IMAGE OF ETERNAL DEATH	677	JERUSALEM 48	12
EARTH GROAND BENEATH & HEAVEN ABOVE	753	EV GOSPEL(E)/N	5
GROANED			
THE TIME ROLLED ON AND ISRAEL GROANED OPPRESSED . . .	40A	SAMSON/PS	PROSE
AND WERE TROUBLED AND AGAIN THE DIVINE FAMILY GROANED IN SPIRIT	504	MILTON 21	44
GROANING			
TO HIS STRONG BONES STRIDES OER THE GROANING ROCKS . . .	3	TO WINTER/PS	10
MY GROANING IS HEARD IN THE ABBEYS	140	FRENCH REVOLTN	137
. . . GROANING SHAKING FORESTS AND FLOODS THE COLD NEWT	147	FRENCH REVOLTN	297
GROANING GNASHING GROANING	226	URIZEN 7	2
WHEN ENITHARMON GROANING	232	URIZEN 19	39
. . . THE ROUGH ROCKS [?VEGETATING] GROANING VEGETATE .	269	FOUR ZOAS 1	* 202
WHEN THE SHATTERD BONE HATH LAID HIM GROANING AMONG THE HAPPIER DEAD	291	FOUR ZOAS 2	416
GROANING THE TERROR ROSE & DRAVE HIS [SOLD] SOLID ROCKS BEFORE	300	FOUR ZOAS 4	* 124
FOR ENION BROODED GROANING LOUD THE ROUGH SEAS VEGETATE . . .	381	FOUR ZOAS AD 5	10
. . . ENION BROODED GROANING THE GOLDEN ROCKS VEGETATE THE (?VORTEX)]	381	FOUR ZOAS AD 5	* 14
GROANING WITH PITY HE AMONG THE WAILING SOULS LAMENTS . .	512	MILTON 26	22
THE EAST TOWARD JERUSALEM'S GATES GROANING HE SAT ABOVE	531	MILTON 39	34
GROANING HE KNEELD BEFORE LOS'S IRON-SHOD FEET ON LONDON STONE	627	JERUSALEM 8	27
GROANING THE SPECTRE HEAVD THE BELLOWS OBEYING LOS'S FROWNS	628	JERUSALEM 9	* 33
REVOLVE UPON HIS MOUNTAINS GROANING IN PAIN BENEATH . . .	641	JERUSALEM 19	21
THEY CUT THE FIBRES FROM THE ROCKS GROANING IN PAIN THEY WEAVE	704	JERUSALEM 67	11
GROANINGS			
THE HOWLINGS GNASHINGS GROANINGS SHRIEKINGS	313	FOUR ZOAS 6	81
GROANS			
EARTH SMOKES WITH BLOOD AND GROANS AND SHAKES	13	GWIN KING/PS	73
FROM SIDE TO SIDE THE LAND GROANS HER PROWESS LOST . . .	37D	SAMSON/PS	PROSE
AND HERE SHE WORKS HER WITCHERIES THAT WHEN SHE GROANS . .	41D	THEN SHE BORE	PROSE
("OR THE PIETIST WHO CRAWLS GROANS BLUBBERS") I HATE CRAWLERS	67D	ANNO LAVATER	MARG
LISTEN & HEAR YOUR MOTHER'S GROANS NO MORE ACCURSED SONS	99	TIRIEL 1	24
SHE BEARS SHE GROANS NOT AT THE BIRTH OF HEUXOS OR YUVA	99	TIRIEL 1	25
THESE ARE THE GROANS OF DEATH YE SERPENTS	99	TIRIEL 1	26
. . . THESE ARE THE GROANS OF DEATH	99	TIRIEL 1	26

		PAGE	TITLE	LINE
GROANS (CONTINUED)				
WITH HURTLINGS & CLASHINGS & GROANS		229	URIZEN 13	25
HOWLINGS & HISSINGS SHRIEKS & GROANS & VOICES OF DESPAIR		243	EUROPE 12	34
AND ENITHARMON GROANS & CRIES IN ANGUISH AND DISMAY . . .		245	EUROPE 15	8
MANY AGES OF GROANS TILL THERE GREW		258	BOOK OF LOS 4	43
GROANS RAN ALONG TYBURN'S BROOK AND ALONG THE RIVER OF OXFORD		281	FOUR ZOAS 2	39
SHE FELL COLD FROM LAMBETH'S VALES IN GROANS & DEWY DEATH		281	FOUR ZOAS 2	46
SHE SANG OER LOS REVIVING HIM TO LIFE HIS GROANS WERE TERRIBLE		289	FOUR ZOAS 2	342
OF ENITHARMON & THE GROANS OF URIZEN FUEL FOR HIS WRATH		302	FOUR ZOAS 4	192
FOR [IN] WITH NOISES RUINOUS HURTLINGS & CLASHINGS & GROANS		304	FOUR ZOAS 4	282
OF ENITHARMON BUT HER GROANS DROWN THE IMMORTAL HARPS . .		306	FOUR ZOAS 5	25
ROCKD TO & FRO & [&] CRIED SORE AT THE GROANS OF ENITHARMON		306	FOUR ZOAS 5	* 29
THE GROANS OF ENITHARMON SHAKE THE SKIES THE LABRING EARTH		306	FOUR ZOAS 5	36
WRITING IN BITTER TEARS & GROANS IN BOOKS OF IRON & BRASS		314	FOUR ZOAS 6	85
RATTLING WITH CLANKING CHAINS THE UNIVERSAL EMPIRE GROANS		333	FOUR ZOAS 7B	17
[HEAVING XXX] HEAVD LIKE AN EARTHQUAKE LABRING WITH CONVULSIVE GROANS		347	FOUR ZOAS 8	* 249
HIS FAINT GROANS SHAKE THE CAVES & ISSUE THRO THE DESOLATE ROCKS		354	FOUR ZOAS 8	520
AND IN THE CRIES OF BIRTH & IN THE GROANS OF DEATH HIS VOICE		356	FOUR ZOAS 8	580
THE BIRDS OF SONG TO MURDEROUS CROWS MY JOYS TO BITTER GROANS		360	FOUR ZOAS 9	110
IN THE FIERCE WIND ROUND HEAVING ROCKS & MOUNTAINS FILLD WITH GROANS		363	FOUR ZOAS 9	240
IN PAIN THE HUMAN HARVEST WAVD IN HORRIBLE GROANS OF WOE		372	FOUR ZOAS 9	577
THEY BUILD THE OVENS OF URTHONA NATURE IN DARKNESS GROANS		379	FOUR ZOAS 9	816
. . . & KNEAD THE BREAD OF KNOWLEDGE WITH TEARS & GROANS		379	FOUR ZOAS 9	820
IRON TEARS & GROANS OF LEAD		417	MY SPECTR AD/N	11
ON TYBURN'S BROOK LOUD GROANS THAMES BENEATH THE IRON FORGE		485	MILTON 6	11
THE DOUBLE DRUM DROWNS HOWLS & GROANS THE SHRILL FIFE SHRIEKS & CRIES		509	MILTON 24	65
THE WINE-PRESS ON THE RHINE GROANS LOUD BUT ALL ITS CENTRAL BEAMS		510	MILTON 25	3
FORBAD & DOWN WITH DREADFUL GROANS HE SUNK UPON HIS COUCH		531	MILTON 39	51
THE WHOLE CREATION GROANS TO BE DELIVERD		616A	V LAST JUDG/N	PROSE
I SAW TERRIFIED I TOOK THE SIGHS & TEARS & BITTER GROANS		628	JERUSALEM 9	17
THUS THEY CONTENDED AMONG THE FURNACES WITH GROANS & TEARS		628	JERUSALEM 9	32
DEAD ON THE ANVIL WHERE THE RED HOT WEDGE GROANS IN PAIN		636	JERUSALEM 16	13
THROUGHOUT THE WHOLE CREATION WHICH GROANS TO BE DELIVERD		637	JERUSALEM 16	26
ALBION GROANS IN THE DEEP SLUMBERS OF DEATH UPON HIS ROCK		637	JERUSALEM 16	27
FEEDING IT WITH HIS GROANS & TEARS DAY & NIGHT WITHOUT CEASING		639	JERUSALEM 17	56
THE BIRDS OF SONG TO MURDEROUS CROWS HIS JOYS TO BITTER GROANS		641	JERUSALEM 19	11
THE DISTANT FOREST THEN THE SLAVE GROANS IN THE DUNGEON OF STONE		642	JERUSALEM 20	15
THEN ALBION BROKE SILENCE AND WITH GROANS REPLYD		643	JERUSALEM 20	42
O VALA O JERUSALEM DO YOU DELIGHT IN MY GROANS		643	JERUSALEM 21	1
SCANDINAVIA FLED WITH ALL HIS MOUNTAINS FILLD WITH GROANS		647	JERUSALEM 24	11
THE WALLS OF BABYLON ARE SOULS OF MEN HER GATES THE GROANS		647	JERUSALEM 24	31
THE CITIES OF ALBION SEEK THY FACE LONDON GROANS IN PAIN		656	JERUSALEM 30	23
I HEAR THE SCREECH OF CHILDBIRTH LOUD PEALING & THE GROANS		661	JERUSALEM 34	23
ALBION GROANS HE SEES THE ELEMENTS DIVIDE BEFORE HIS FACE		663	JERUSALEM 36	27
UPON THE HILLS OF ALBION OXFORD GROANS IN HIS IRON FURNACE		671	JERUSALEM 42	58
A MURDEROUS PROVIDENCE A CREATION THAT GROANS LIVING ON DEATH		681	JERUSALEM 50	5
WHICH OVERSPREAD ALL THE EARTH HE GROANS AMONG HIS RUIND PORCHES		685	JERUSALEM 54	14
THEN ALBION DREW ENGLAND INTO HIS BOSOM IN GROANS & TEARS		685	JERUSALEM 54	27
THEIR APPEARANCE WHEN COMBIND BUT OFTEN BY BIRTH PANGS & LOUD GROANS		708	JERUSALEM 70	* 11
RESOUND WITH CRIES OF VICTIMS SHOUTS & SONGS & DYING GROANS		723	JERUSALEM 80	49
OVER THE TEMPLES DRINKING GROANS OF VICTIMS WEEPING IN PITY		723	JERUSALEM 80	55
FILLING CUPS OF SILVER & CRYSTAL WITH SHRIEKS & CRIES WITH GROANS		723	JERUSALEM 80	81
I HAVE HEARD JERUSALEM'S GROANS FROM VALA'S CRIES & LAMENTATIONS		725	JERUSALEM 82	1
OF ALBION'S CLOUDS HE FED IT WITH HIS TEARS & BITTER GROANS		732	JERUSALEM 86	53
GROAT				
ARE PAINTED BY MADMEN AS SURE AS A GROAT		548	ALL PICTURES/N	2
GROATS				
CAITHNESS & ROCKY DURNESS PENTLAND & JOHN GROATS HOUSE . .		512	MILTON 26	15
GRODNA				
GRODNA RENT THE DEEP EARTH HOWLING		234	URIZEN 23	15
GROPED				
DOWN THE WINDING CAVERN WE GROPED OUR TEDIOUS WAY . . .		155D	MARRIAGE HH 17	PROSE
GROSS				
OF WHICH GROSS VULGARITY FORMS THE PRINCIPAL EXCELLENCE		464D	ANNO REYNOLDS	MARG
CAN SUCH GROSS LIPS PERCIEVE ALAS FOLDED WITHIN THEMSELVES		485	MILTON 5	36
O HOW CAN I WITH MY GROSS TONGUE THAT CLEAVETH TO THE DUST		502	MILTON 20	15
GROT				
SITTING ALL BENEATH A GROT		53	PHEBE DREST/IM	3
FROM GROT & CAVE BENEATH THE MOON DIM REGION OF DEATH . .		660	JERUSALEM 34	11
GROTS				
TILL THEY REVIVE OR BURY THEM IN COOL GROTS MAKING LAMENTATION		377	FOUR ZOAS 9	747
TILL THEY REVIVE OR BURY THEM IN COOL GROTS MAKING LAMENTATION		513	MILTON 27	7

845

```
                                                                  PAGE   TITLE            LINE
GROUND     SEE BACK GROUND
     SHE FALLING KISSD THE GROUND POOR FOOL     . . . . . .    16  BLIND-MANS/PS        14
     SUKEY IS TUMBLED ON THE GROUND . . . . . . . .  . .       16  BLIND-MANS/PS        36
     WITH CRIMSON DROPS HE STAINS THE GROUND . . . . . . .     17  BLIND-MANS/PS        53
     A SPOT OF GROUND THIS HE'LL DEFEND TIS HIS  . . . . .     26  EDW THIRD/PS 3      198
     [ITS] SHE SHAKES THE SOLID GROUND . . . . . . . .         41D THEN SHE BORE    *PROSE
     . . . THRO THE CLEAVING [?WORLD] GROUND . . . . .        106  TIRIEL 5              5
     A WORM OF SIXTY WINTERS CREEPING ON THE DUSKY GROUND     110  TIRIEL 8             24
     I AM SET TO LIGHT THE GROUND  . . . . . . . .            112  A DREAM/SI           17
     OER THE HALLOWD GROUND  . . . . . . . . . .              113  LIT GRL LST/SI       40
     BORE THEM TO THE GROUND  . . . . . . . . . . .           114  LIT GRL FND/SI       27
     SHE STOOD IN SILENCE LISTNING TO THE VOICES OF THE GROUND 130 BOOK OF THEL 6        8
     TILL UPON THE GROUND I STRAY  . . . . . . . .            167  INFANT SORW/N        15
     [BUT UPON THE NETTLY GROUND]  . . . . . . . . .          167  INFANT SORW/N        18
     [BUT] FOR ON NO OTHER GROUND [CAN]  . . . . . . .        168  HAST LAP/N            7
     LIKE TO DUNG UPON THE GROUND  . . . . . . . . .          169  MIRTLE SHADE/N        5
     TO ANY TREE THAT GROWS ON GROUND  . . . . . . .          169  MIRTLE SHADE/N       10
     AND WATERS THE GROUND WITH TEARS  . . . . . . .          174  HUMAN IMAGE/N        11
     [TO ANY TREE THAT GROWS ON GROUND]  . . . . . .          176  TO MY MIRTLE/N        4
     [LIKE TO DUNG UPON THE GROUND]  . . . . . . . .          176  TO MY MIRTLE/N        7
     BUT OUR GOOD QUEEN QUITE GROWS TO THE GROUND  . .        185  LET BROTHELS/N       24
     AND WATERS THE GROUND WITH TEARS  . . . . . . .          217  HUMAN ABSTR/SE       10
     LIKE THE GROUND PARCHD WITH HEAT THEN FUZON  . . . .     234  URIZEN 23            17
     THE BOSOM OF THE GROUND  . . . . . . . . . . .           246  SONG OF LOS 4        10
     . . . RIPPD FORTH UPON THE GROUND . . . . . . . . .      338  FOUR ZOAS 7B        207
     AND THOU SWEET SMELLING GROUND PUT FORTH THY LIFE IN FRUITS 368 FOUR ZOAS 9       437
         & FLOWERS
     AND NOW HER FEET STEP ON THE GRASSY BOSOM OF THE GROUND  370  FOUR ZOAS 9         505
     THE GROUND SPIDER WITH MANY EYES THE MOLE CLOTHED IN VELVET 377 FOUR ZOAS 9       758
     AND LUVAH WAS PUT FOR DUNG ON THE GROUND . . . . . .     378  FOUR ZOAS 9         791
     HE GROUND IT IN HIS RUMBLING MILLS TERRIBLE THE DISTRESS 378  FOUR ZOAS 9         807
     OF ALL THE NATIONS OF EARTH GROUND IN THE MILLS OF URTHONA 378 FOUR ZOAS 9        808
     I BELIEVE THE WHOLE CHARGE FALLS TO THE GROUND   . . . 437C  BLAKES MEMORAN    PROSE
     LAY A GROUND ON THE PLATE & SMOKE IT AS FOR ETCHING  . 440B  MEMORANDUM/N 3    PROSE
     WITH AN OVAL POINTED NEEDLE SCRAPE OFF THE GROUND  . . 440C  MEMORANDUM/N 3    PROSE
     THEN PROCEED TO GRAVING WITH THE GROUND ON THE PLATE  . 440C MEMORANDUM/N 3    PROSE
     BEING AS CAREFUL AS POSSIBLE NOT TO HURT THE GROUND  . 440C  MEMORANDUM/N 3    PROSE
     LAY A GROUND AS FOR ETCHING TRACE &C &  . . . . . . . 440C  MEMORANDUM/N 4    PROSE
     CREEPING IN REPTILE FLESH UPON THE BOSOM OF THE GROUND . 484  MILTON 5             20
     THE GROUND SPIDER WITH MANY EYES THE MOLE CLOTHED IN VELVET 513 MILTON 27        14
     [MOULD] [GROUND] FLOWERY MOULD INTO THE GREEN FIELDS OF  609D V LAST JUDG/N   *PROSE
     WHERE THE INFANTS CREEP OUT OF THE GROUND   . . . . . . 610C V LAST JUDG/N    PROSE
     HE LIFTED POURING IT INTO THE CLAY GROUND PREPARD WITH ART 630 JERUSALEM 11       4
     OUTSTRETCHD HIS GIANT BEAUTY ON THE GROUND IN PAIN & TEARS 641 JERUSALEM 18       46
     THE NATIONS ARE HER DUST GROUND BY THE CHARIOT WHEELS  . 653 JERUSALEM 29        23
     FOR HIS EYELIDS WERE NARROWD & HIS NOSTRILS SCENTED THE  662 JERUSALEM 36         2
         GROUND
     LIKE EVENING DEW ON EVERY HERB UPON THE BREATHING GROUND 669 JERUSALEM 42         8
     THE LIVING & THE DEAD SHALL BE GROUND IN OUR RUMBLING MILLS 673 JERUSALEM 43     49
     CREEPING IN REPTILE FLESH UPON THE BOSOM OF THE GROUND  . 680 JERUSALEM 49       33
     AND BOWELS HID IN HAMMERD STEEL RIPD QUIVERING ON  . .   701 JERUSALEM 65        53
         THE GROUND
     AND THE WORM WEAVING IN THE GROUND . . . . . . . .      771  OF GATES/GP          44
     THE VOICES OF WINDS TREES & BIRDS & THE ODOURS OF THE HAPPY 803B LETTER 15      PROSE
         GROUND
     [GROUND] ADAMAH  . . . . . . . . . . . . .              SUPP ILLUS GENESIS    *PROSE
GROUNDED
     ON THIS TREATISE REYNOLDS HAS GROUNDED MANY OF  . . . . 476D ANNO REYNOLDS       MARG
GROUNDS
     ARE ON PLASTER OR WHITING GROUNDS AND NONE SINCE  . . . 565B DESC CAT 2        PROSE
GROUP
     FOR THE HOST WHO FOLLOWS THIS GROUP AND HOLDS THE CENTER 569D DESC CAT 3       PROSE
GROUPE
     THE PRINCIPAL FIGURE IN THE NEXT GROUPE IS THE GOOD PARSON 570B DESC CAT 3     PROSE
     THE DOCTOR OF PHYSIC IS IN THIS GROUPE AND THE FRANKLIN  570D DESC CAT 3       PROSE
     THIS GROUPE ALSO WOULD FURNISH SUBSTANTIAL MATTER  . . . 571A DESC CAT 3       PROSE
     THEY SCOURGE A GROUPE OF FIGURES DOWN INTO THE DEEPS  . 608A V LAST JUDG/N     PROSE
GROUPED
     THE PAINTER HAS ALSO GROUPED WITH THESE THE PARDONER  . 568C DESC CAT 3        PROSE
GROUPES
     BY TWO ANGELS & MANY GROUPES OF FIGURES ARE FALLING . . 443C LAST JUDGMNT/L    PROSE
     MANY GROUPES ARISE [WITH] IN EXULTATION [IN JOY] . . . 443D LAST JUDGMNT/L   *PROSE
     AND SOME CARVED AS BASSO RELIEVOS AND SOME AS GROUPES OF 566A DESC CAT 2       PROSE
     THE EARTH BENEATH THESE FALLING GROUPES OF FIGURES  . . 608A V LAST JUDG/N     PROSE
     LED ONWARD BY TRIUMPHANT GROUPES OF INFANTS  . . . . . 611D V LAST JUDG/N     PROSE
     IS COMPOSED OF VARIOUS GROUPES OF FIGURES  . . . . . . 612A V LAST JUDG/N     PROSE
GROVE
     WANDRING IN MANY A CORAL GROVE  . . . . . . . . . . .     11  TO MUSES/PS          11
     LOVST THOU TO WALK THE PEACEFUL SOLEMN GROVE  . . . . .   15  IMIT SPEN/PS         47
     IS BUT A CLOUD AND LIKE A SHADY GROVE  . . . . . . .     125  LIT BLK BOY/SI       16
     SAYING COME OUT FROM THE GROVE MY LOVE & CARE  . . . .   125  LIT BLK BOY/SI       19
     . . . IN A FAR DISTANT GROVE]  . . . . . . . . .        266  FOUR ZOAS 1          93
     AND [DIG] ROOT UP THE INFERNAL GROVE  . . . . . . .     417  MY SPECTRE/N         60
     AND ROOT UP THE INFERNAL GROVE  . . . . . . . . .       417  MY SPECTRE/N         68
     HE WHERE THOU DWELLEST IN WHAT GROVE  . . . . . . .     422  THE BIRDS/N           1
     AND HIS OAK GROVE TILL THE VICTIM REND THE WOVEN VEIL  . . 701 JERUSALEM 65       61
GROVEL
     THEY GROVEL ON THE SAND AND WRITHING LIE WHILE ALL   . . . 201 AMERICA 13          5
GROVELING
     GROVELING ALONG GREAT GEORGE STREET THRO THE PARK GATE    242  EUROPE 12           19
     . . .
```

		PAGE	TITLE	LINE

GROVELLING
. . . WHY SHOULDST THOU SIT COLD GROVELLING DEMON OF WOE ... 322 FOUR ZOAS 7 ... 73
AND LEFT MAN A LITTLE GROVELLING ROOT OUTSIDE OF HIMSELF ... 639 JERUSALEM 17 ... 32
GROVES
FAREWELL GREEN FIELDS AND HAPPY GROVES . . . . 119 NIGHT/SI ... 9
MY CLOUDS ARE NOT THE CLOUDS OF VERDANT FIELDS & GROVES ... 275 FOUR ZOAS 1 ... 392
OF FRUIT
WHERE THEY WERE LAID IN RUINS FROM EVERY NATION & ... 485 MILTON 6 ... 16
OAK GROVES ROOTED
GARDENS & GROVES DISPLAY PARADISE WITH ITS INHABITANTS . . 613C V LAST JUDG/N ... PROSE
MILTON LED BY MELANCHOLY INTO THE GROVES . . . . . . 619B ILLUS MILTON ... PROSE
PLANTING THESE OAKEN GROVES ERECTING THESE DRAGON TEMPLES ... 648 JERUSALEM 25 ... 4
& OAK GROVES OVER THE WHOLE EARTH WITNESS TO THIS DAY . . 649C JERUSALEM 27 ... PROSE
IF WE ARE WRATHFUL ALBION WILL DESTROY JERUSALEM WITH ROOTY ... 672 JERUSALEM 43 ... 8
GROVES
O GOD OF ALBION DESCEND DELIVER JERUSALEM FROM THE OAKEN ... 672 JERUSALEM 43 ... 11
GROVES
AND BUILD THIS BABYLON & SACRIFICE IN SECRET GROVES . . 693 JERUSALEM 60 ... 23
IN THE OAK GROVES OF ALBION WHICH OVERSPREAD ALL THE EARTH ... 708 JERUSALEM 70 ... 16
IN STONE-HENGE & ON LONDON STONE & IN THE OAK GROVES OF ... 742 JERUSALEM 94 ... 24
MALDEN
THE OAK GROVES OF ALBION . . . . 746 JERUSALEM 98 ... 50
GROW
WHERE ALL HIS GOLDEN PLEASURES GROW . . . . 6 HOW SWEET/PS ... 8
GROW LARGER AS WE ADVANCE AND SOME PERHAPS . . . . . 18 EDW THIRD/PS 1 ... 37
IF NOT SOMETIMES OER-CLOUDED WE GROW WEARY . . . . . 20 EDW THIRD/PS 2 ... 53
DOES IT GROW IN ENGLAND SIR . . . . 28 EDW THIRD/PS 4 ... 3
AND GROW IMMODERATE TO BRAVE IT OUT . . . . . . 37A CONTEMPLATN/PS ... PROSE
OF THE MAN BUT THE STAMINA ON WHICH ALL HIS VIRTUES GROW ... 88C ANNO LAVATER ... MARG
ROSES ARE PLANTED WHERE THORNS GROW . . . . 148 MARRIAGE HH 2 ... 6
THE APPLE TREE NEVER ASKS THE BEECH HOW HE SHALL GROW ... 152B MARRIAGE HH 9 ... PROSE
I TOLD IT NOT MY WRATH DID GROW . . . . 165 CHRISTN FORB/N ... 4
WHEN BUDS & BLOSSOM GROW . . . . 169 EARTHS ANSWR/N ... 17
AND A GREAT MANY SUCKERS GROW ALL AROUND . . . . . 185 LET BROTHELS/N ... 26
TELL ME WHAT IS A JOY & IN WHAT GARDENS DO JOYS GROW . . 191 V DAU ALBION 3 ... 24
WHEN BUDS AND BLOSSOMS GROW . . . . 211 EARTHS ANSR/SE ... 17
I TOLD IT NOT MY WRATH DID GROW . . . . 218 POISON TREE/SE ... 4
MUST GROW UP TO COMMAND HIS PRINCE . . . . . . 292 FOUR ZOAS 3 ... 19
PLAY IN HIS SMILING BEAMS GIVING THE SEEDS OF LIFE TO GROW ... 379 FOUR ZOAS 9 ... 847
FEED THEM & THOU WILT GROW FAT . . . . 432 AUGURIES ... 44
WHEN NATIONS GROW OLD THE ARTS GROW COLD . . . . . 452 ANNO REYNOLDS ... 1
ANY MORE THAN I BELIEVE THAT THE ROSE TEACHES THE LILLY ... 453B ANNO REYNOLDS ... MARG
HOW TO GROW
SHE NUMBERS WITH HER FINGERS EVERY FIBRE ERE IT GROW . . 501 MILTON 19 ... 49
IF I EER GROW TO MAN'S ESTATE . . . . 547 IF I GROW/N ... 1
TO GROW SOWER AT WHAT A FRIEND MAY UTTER . . . . . 556 IF MEN ACT/N ... 3
LIDS TO GROW OVER HIS EYES IN VEILS OF TEARS AND CAVERNS ... 702 JERUSALEM 66 ... 31
SHOUT IN THE NIGHT OF BATTLE & THEIR SPEARS GROW TO THEIR ... 704 JERUSALEM 67 ... 32
HANDS
SHOULD GROW A DEVOURING WINDING SHEET . . . . . . 771 OF GATES/GP ... 24
GROWETH
AND SEE SMALL PORTIONS OF THE ETERNAL WORLD THAT ... 237 EUROPE INTRO ... 4
EVER GROWETH
GROWING
O ENION THOU ART THYSELF A ROOT GROWING IN HELL . . . . 265 FOUR ZOAS 1 ... 57
BEATEN ALONG ITS SIGHTLESS WAY GROWING ENORMOUS IN ITS ... 269 FOUR ZOAS 1 ... 194
MOTION TO
A LIVING MANTLE ADJOIND TO HIS LIFE & GROWING FROM HIS SOUL ... 318 FOUR ZOAS 6 ... * 246
OF THIS IMMORTAL SPIRIT GROWING IN LOWER PARADISE . . . 369 FOUR ZOAS 9 ... 460
OF LIVING FIBRES DOWN INTO THE SEA OF TIME & SPACE GROWING ... 524 MILTON 34 ... 25
AND AS DARK ROOTS AND STEMS A FOREST OF AFFLICTION GROWING ... 634 JERUSALEM 14 ... 8
ENROOTED INTO EVERY NATION A MIGHTY POLYPUS GROWING . . . 635 JERUSALEM 15 ... 4
BECAME A RAVENING EATING CANCER GROWING IN THE FEMALE . . 707 JERUSALEM 69 ... 2
GROWL
NOR THE LIONS GROWL . . . . 115 LIT GRL FND/SI ... 52
GROWN
WHEN MEN WERE FIRST A NATION GROWN . . . . . . 17 BLIND-MANS/PS ... 66
HE FANCIES HE IS GROWN INTO A GIANT . . . . 37A CONTEMPLATN/PS ... PROSE
FOR FROM WITHIN MY [NARROW] WITHERD BREAST GROWN NARROW ... 360 FOUR ZOAS 9 ... 108
WITH MY WOES
HE IS GROWN OLD & RICH & WHAT HE WILL . . . . . . 539 IN CHILDHOOD/N ... 3
GROWN OLD IN LOVE FROM SEVEN TILL SEVEN TIMES SEVEN . . 552 GROWN OLD IN/N ... 1
TILL FROM WITHIN HIS WITHERD BREAST GROWN NARROW WITH HIS ... 641 JERUSALEM 19 ... 9
WOES
GROWS
AYE IT GROWS MOST IN LANDS MOST CULTIVATED . . . . . 28 EDW THIRD/PS 4 ... 4
THEN IT GROWS MOST IN FRANCE THE VINES HERE . . . . . 28 EDW THIRD/PS 4 ... 5
IS IT A LITTLE CREEPING ROOT THAT GROWS IN DITCHES . . . 28 EDW THIRD/PS 4 ... 11
IT IS A ROOT THAT GROWS IN EVERY BREAST . . . . . . 28 EDW THIRD/PS 4 ... 13
EACH HEART DOES TREMBLE AND EACH KNEE GROWS SLACK . . 34A KING JOHN/PS ... PROSE
IT IS A FLOWER THAT GROWS IN EVERY VALE . . . . . . 37A CONTEMPLATN/PS ... PROSE
TO ANY TREE THAT GROWS ON GROUND . . . . 169 MIRTLE SHADE/N ... 10
THERE GROWS ONE IN THE HUMAN BRAIN . . . . 174 HUMAN IMAGE/N ... 26
[TO ANY TREE THAT GROWS ON GROUND] . . . . 176 TO MY MIRTLE/N ... 4
BUT OUR GOOD QUEEN QUITE GROWS TO THE GROUND . . . . 185 LET BROTHELS/N ... 24
AS THE CLEAR SPRING MUDDED WITH FEET OF BEASTS GROWS PURE ... 190 V DAU ALBION 2 ... 19
& SMILES
THERE GROWS ONE IN THE HUMAN BRAIN . . . . 217 HUMAN ABSTR/SE ... 24
THE TREE STILL GROWS OVER THE VOID . . . . 252 AHANIA 4 ... 2
WHATEVER GROWS FROM ITS PURE BUD OR BREATHES A FRAGRANT ... 308 FOUR ZOAS 5 ... 124
SOUL
INTO THE ELEMENTAL FORMS OF EVERY THING THAT GROWS . . . 355 FOUR ZOAS 8 ... 563

847

		PAGE	TITLE	LINE

GROWS   (CONTINUED)

IS HEARD THROUGHOUT THE UNIVERSE WHEREEVER A GRASS GROWS   356 FOUR ZOAS 8   * 581
AND SHE GROWS YOUNG AS HE GROWS OLD . . . .   425 MENTAL TRAVLER   20
FOR AS HE EATS & DRINKS HE GROWS . . . .   426 MENTAL TRAVLER   73
VERY LITTLE TIME AND OF THE AIR IT GROWS YELLOW AND AT   561A EXHIBITION ADV   PROSE
    LENGTH BROWN
ON WHOSE BANKS GROWS THE TREE OF LIFE . . . .   613B V LAST JUDG/N   PROSE
CUT WITH THE FLINTS HER TEARS RUN DOWN HER REASON GROWS   693 JERUSALEM 60   42
    LIKE
AS THE MISTLETOE GROWS ON THE OAK SO ALBION'S TREE   703 JERUSALEM 66   55
    ON ETERNITY LO
HENCE THE INFERNAL VEIL GROWS IN THE DISOBEDIENT FEMALE   708 JERUSALEM 69   38
OF VEINS OF RED BLOOD GROWS AROUND THEM LIKE A SCARLET ROBE   736 JERUSALEM 90   5
YOUR BEAUTIFUL AND ELEGANT DAUGHTER VENUSIA GROWS IN OUR   853D LETTER 52   *PROSE
"EVERY THING THAT GROWS" (SHAKESPEARE) . . . . . .   SUPP LEGEND/N21   *

GROWTH

AMBITION IS THE GROWTH OF EVRY CLIME . . . .   28 EDW THIRD/PS 4   2
FLOWERS OF HEAVEN'S GROWTH OVER THE BANQUET-TABLE . . .   30 EDW THIRD/PS 5   32
. . . O PRINCES OF FIRE WHOSE FLAMES ARE FOR GROWTH NOT   142 FRENCH REVOLTN   179
    CONSUMING

GRUMBLING

& THO WE HAD A GREAT DEAL OF LUGGAGE NO GRUMBLING . . .   802B LETTER 14   PROSE
THERE WAS NO GRUMBLING AT ALL WE TRAVELD THRO . . . . .   803A LETTER 15   PROSE

GUANTOK   SEE GWANTOK,KWANTOK,ETC

HAND HYLE & COBAN GUANTOK PEACHEY BRERETON SLAYD & HUTTON   641 JERUSALEM 19   18

GUARD

CONSCIENCE WAS SENT A GUARD TO REASON . . . .   42B THEN SHE BORE   PROSE
NOW DEAD I'LL GUARD THEE FROM APPROACHING ILL . . . . .   43D WOE CRIED MUSE   PROSE
GUARD IT ON EITHER SIDE & IN THE MIDST IS THE HOLY LAW . .   82A ANNO LAVATER   MARG
AS I GUARD OER THE FOLD . . . .   119 NIGHT/SI   48
TO LEAVE HIS GUARD AT TREE OF LIFE AND WHEN HE DOES . . .   154B MARRIAGE HH 14   PROSE
SET OVER THIS SWEET BOY OF MINE TO GUARD HIM LEST HE REND   326 FOUR ZOAS 7   232
TIMES AFTER TIMES AND THOSE IN EDEN SENT LUCIFER FOR THEIR   351 FOUR ZOAS 8   398
    GUARD
THE THREE DAUGHTERS OF URIZEN GUARD AHANIA'S DEATH COUCH   362 FOUR ZOAS 9   201
OUR FIRST PARENTS OUT OF EDEN THROUGH A GUARD OF WEEPING   441D INSC FALL MAN   PROSE
    ANGELS
OF FIRE ROUND THE WALLS COLUMNS OF FIRE GUARD AROUND . .   490 MILTON 9   44
EVEN SIX THOUSAND YEARS AND SENT LUCIFER FOR ITS GUARD . .   494 MILTON 13   17
IN PALAMABRON'S TENT AND OOTHOON WAS HER CHARMING GUARD   494 MILTON 13   44
LIKE FEMALES OF SWEET BEAUTY TO GUARD ROUND HIM & TO FEED   496 MILTON 15   14
WHICH FEW DARE UNBAR BECAUSE DREAD OG & ANAK GUARD THE   502 MILTON 20   35
    GATES
THEY VANISH NOT FROM ME & MINE WE GUARD THEM FIRST & LAST   505 MILTON 22   23
GUARD ROUND THEM BUT I THE FOURTH ZOA AM ALSO SET . . .   508 MILTON 24   8
YOU O MY SONS STILL GUARD ROUND LOS O WANDER NOT & LEAVE   508 MILTON 24   13
    ME
EACH HAS ITS GUARD EACH MOMENT MINUTE HOUR DAY MONTH &   516 MILTON 28   59
    YEAR
THE GUARD ARE ANGELS OF PROVIDENCE ON DUTY EVERMORE . . .   516 MILTON 28   61
ITS EVER DURING DOORS THAT OG & ANAK FIERCELY GUARD . . .   520 MILTON 31   49
IN MOONY BEULAH LOS HIS STRONG GUARD WALKS ROUND BENEATH   531 MILTON 39   52
    THE MOON
AND SIXTY-FOUR THOUSAND GENII GUARD THE EASTERN GATE . .   633 JERUSALEM 13   26
AND SIXTY-FOUR THOUSAND GNOMES GUARD THE NORTHERN GATE . .   633 JERUSALEM 13   27
AND SIXTY-FOUR THOUSAND NYMPHS GUARD THE WESTERN GATE . .   633 JERUSALEM 13   28
AND SIXTY-FOUR THOUSAND FAIRIES GUARD THE SOUTHERN GATE   633 JERUSALEM 13   29
CLOUDED WITH STORMS LOS HIS STRONG GUARD WALKD ROUND   642 JERUSALEM 19   38
    BENEATH THE MOON
ATTENDS HER AS HER GUARD & LOS'S EMANATION IS NAMED . . .   655 JERUSALEM 30   3
THE FOUR THAT REMAIN WITH LOS TO GUARD THE WESTERN WALL   711 JERUSALEM 72   12
AND THESE FOUR REMAIN TO GUARD THE FOUR WALLS OF JERUSALEM   711 JERUSALEM 72   13
AND A SON OF EDEN WAS SET OVER EACH DAUGHTER OF BEULAH   712 JERUSALEM 72   48
    TO GUARD
WHITEFIELD & HERVEY GUARD THAT GATE WITH ALL THE GENTLE   712 JERUSALEM 72   51
    SOULS

GUARDED   SEE ANGEL-GUARDED

GUARDED BY AN ANGEL MILD . . . .   182 THE ANGEL/N   3
AND GUARDED THEM AROUND . . . .   185 LET BROTHELS/N   38
AND GUARDED THEM AROUND . . . .   186 LET BROTHELS/N   63
GUARDED BY AN ANGEL MILD . . . .   213 THE ANGEL/SE   3
AGAINST ME WHO THEE GUARDED IN THE NIGHT OF DEATH FROM HARM   300 FOUR ZOAS 4   110
DEEP IN THE SOUTH GUARDED BY A FEW SOLITARY STARS . . .   372 FOUR ZOAS 9   581
THAT TRAVELS INTO CHAOS SO MILTON WENT GUARDED WITHIN . .   496 MILTON 15   20
IN EGYPT GUARDED IN THEIR REPOSE FROM THOSE FIENDS . . .   823D LETTER 27   PROSE

GUARDIAN

THE GUARDIAN PRINCE OF ALBION BURNS IN HIS NIGHTLY TENT   197 AMERICA 3   1
IN SIGHT OF ALBION'S GUARDIAN AND ALL THE THIRTEEN ANGELS   200 AMERICA 12   2
ACROSS THE LIMBS OF ALBION'S GUARDIAN . . . . . .   202 AMERICA 15   2
ALBION'S GUARDIAN WRITHED IN TORMENT ON THE EASTERN SKY   202 AMERICA 15   6
SICKNING LAY LONDON'S GUARDIAN AND THE ANCIENT MITERD YORK   202 AMERICA 15   9
THE GUARDIAN PRINCE OF ALBION BURNS IN HIS NIGHTLY TENT   203 AMERICA CANC A   1
HIS HELM WAS BROUGHT BY LONDON'S GUARDIAN & HIS THIRSTY   205 AMERICA CANC C   4
    SPEAR
NOW ARRIVD THE ANCIENT GUARDIAN AT THE SOUTHERN PORCH . .   241 EUROPE 10   24
THE GUARDIAN OF THE SECRET CODES FORSOOK HIS ANCIENT   242 EUROPE 12   15
    MANSION
AROUND THE LIMBS OF ALBION'S GUARDIAN HIS FLESH CONSUMING   243 EUROPE 12   33
THE GUARDIAN PRINCE OF ALBION BURNS IN HIS NIGHTLY TENT   246 SONG OF LOS 4   21
WHICH IN EVERY AGE STANDS AS THE GUARDIAN . . . . .   568A DESC CAT 3   PROSE
SO SPOKE LONDON IMMORTAL GUARDIAN I HEARD IN LAMBETH'S   665 JERUSALEM 38   40
    SHADES

		PAGE	TITLE	LINE

GUARDIAN   (CONTINUED)
    GENEROUS IMMORTAL GUARDIAN GOLDEN CLAD FOR CITIES   . . .   665 JERUSALEM 38   46
    HEREFORD ANCIENT GUARDIAN OF WALES WHOSE HANDS   .   .   .   .   676 JERUSALEM 46   3
    GUARDIAN ANGEL CHILD ANGEL OF DEATH MOTHER   .   .   .   .   SUPP INSC HERVEY   *TITLE
GUARDIANS
    AS GUARDIANS ROUND YOUR CHAIR THEN SHALL THE PULSE   . . .   28 EDW THIRD/PS 3   289
    BENEATH THEM SIT THE REVREND MEN THE GUARDIANS OF THE POOR   59 HOLY THURS/IM   17
    BENEATH THEM SIT THE AGED MEN WISE GUARDIANS OF THE POOR   122 HOLY THURS/SI   11
    DRIVEN OER THE GUARDIANS OF IRELAND AND SCOTLAND AND WALES   202 AMERICA 15   13
    IN TERROR VIEWD THE BANDS OF ALBION AND THE ANCIENT   203 AMERICA 16   17
        GUARDIANS
    FRIENDS OUR COTTAGE IS SURROUNDED BY THE SAME GUARDIANS YOU   807B LETTER 17   PROSE
GUARDING
    IMMORTAL STARRY-ONES GUARDING THE COUCH IN FLAMING FIRES   525 MILTON 35   30
GUARDS
    . . . AND THE GUARDS OF THY PALACE ARE FLED   .   .   .   .   .   141 FRENCH REVOLTN   167
    LIKE A WILD BEAST GUARDS MY WAY   .   .   .   .   415 MY SPECTRE/N   2
    ITS GUARDS LIVING THE WORK OF ELEMENTAL HANDS LABORIOUS   633 JERUSALEM 13   7
        TASK
    HE HATH PLACED OG & ANAK THE GIANTS OF ALBION FOR THEIR   680 JERUSALEM 49   56
        GUARDS
    THESE ARE GUARDS OF MY FOLD   .   .   .   .   805 TO BUTTS/L   69
GUELDERS
    THAT VULGAR EPIGRAM IN ART REMBRANDT'S "HUNDRED GUELDERS"   599B PUB ADDRESS/N   PROSE
GUESSD
    SOME SAID HE HAD THE DEVIL & THEY GUESSD RIGHT   .   .   .   .   434 LONG JOHN BRWN   14
GUESTS
    THE GUESTS ARE SCATTERD THRO THE LAND   .   .   .   .   .   .   426 MENTAL TRAVLER   61
    EVER INVITING GUESTS TO THE MARRIAGE O FOOLISH PHILOSOPHY   834A LETTER 33   PROSE
GUIDE
    THY CARE PRUNE ALL EXTRAVAGANT SHOOTS AND GUIDE   .   .   .   .   26 EDW THIRD/PS 3   212
    O WHITE-ROBED ANGEL GUIDE MY TIMOROUS HAND TO WRITE   .   .   .   37D SAMSON/PS   PROSE
    IF THOU SEEKEST BY HUMAN POLICY TO GUIDE THIS ARK   .   .   .   82B ANNO LAVATER   MARG
    [SAYING] & SAID GO FORTH & GUIDE MY SON WHO WANDERS ON   310 FOUR ZOAS 5   221
        THE OCEAN
    . . . O LOS MY DEFENCE & GUIDE   .   .   .   .   331 FOUR ZOAS 7   447
    AND SAID GO FORTH & GUIDE MY BATTLES LIKE THE JOINTED SPINE   336 FOUR ZOAS 7B   116
    HIS PREY WHILE LOS APPOINTS & RINTRAH & PALAMABRON GUIDE   517 MILTON 29   44
    GUIDE THOU MY HAND WHICH TREMBLES EXCEEDINGLY UPON THE   623 JERUSALEM 5   23
        ROCK OF AGES
    WHO GUIDE THE GREAT WINE-PRESS OF LOVE FOUR PRECIOUS STONES   712 JERUSALEM 72   52
        THAT GATE
GUIDED
    WITH DIFFICULTY DOWN DESCENDING GUIDED BY HIS EAR   .   .   .   319 FOUR ZOAS 6   293
GUIDES
    WHO THE CHARIOT OF LEUTHA GUIDES   .   .   .   .   255 BOOK OF LOS 3   2
    GUIDES THEM THERE I BEHOLD MOAB & AMMON & AMALEK   .   .   .   731 JERUSALEM 86   28
GUIDING
    NUMBER I THE SPIRITUAL FORM OF NELSON GUIDING LEVIATHAN   564D DESC CAT 1   TITLE
    THE SPIRITUAL FORM OF PITT GUIDING BEHEMOTH HE IS   .   .   .   565A DESC CAT 2   TITLE
GUILD HALL
    I CRY MY MATCHES AS FAR AS GUILD HALL   .   .   .   .   .   .   55 CRY MATCHES/IM   1
GUILE
    POLICY BROUGHT FORTH GUILE & FRAUD   .   .   .   .   42D THEN SHE BORE   PROSE
GUILEFUL
    GO ON FAIR TRAITRESS DO THY GUILEFUL WORK   .   .   .   .   .   38A SAMSON/PS   PROSE
GUILT
    BUT I MUST TELL YOU THAT GUILT BEING AN ACT OF THE MIND   29A EDW THIRD/PS 4   PROSE
    OF GUILT OTHERS SAID IF IT IS TRUE IF THE ACTS HAVE BEEN   495 MILTON 13   49
        PERFORMD
GUILTY
    THEN IF AMBITION IS A SIN WE ARE ALL GUILTY   .   .   .   .   .   28D EDW THIRD/PS 4   PROSE
    NONE ARE GUILTY BUT THOSE   .   .   .   .   29A EDW THIRD/PS 4   PROSE
    GUILTY OF DOING WRONG WITHOUT KNOWING IT WAS WRONG   .   .   .   29A EDW THIRD/PS 4   PROSE
    ("ALL MORAL DEPENDENCE ON GUILTY") IS BEING LIKE   68A ANNO LAVATER   MARG
        HIM RATHER
    . . . IN [GHASTLY FEA] GUILTY FEARS   .   .   .   .   107 TIRIEL 5   * 32
    NOW THAT THE CURSE SHALL CLEAN DEVOUR ALL THOSE GUILTY SONS   107 TIRIEL 6   4
    [WOE ALAS MY GUILTY HAND]   .   .   .   .   182 THE FLY/N   1
    MY [GUILTY HAND] THOUGHTLESS HAND   .   .   .   .   183 THE FLY/N   7
    THE INNOCENT SHOULD BE CONDEMND FOR THE GUILTY THEN AN   491 MILTON 11   16
        ETERNAL ROSE
    SAYING IF THE GUILTY SHOULD BE CONDEMND HE MUST BE   491 MILTON 11   17
        AN ETERNAL DEATH
    WHETHER RUBENS OR VANDYKE OR BOTH WERE GUILTY OF   565B DESC CAT 2   *PROSE
        THIS VILLANY
    & HANG THEIR SOULS AS GUILTY OF MENTAL HIGH TREASON   .   .   599D PUB ADDRESS/N   PROSE
    THAT QUITE UNNERVD [THE ?GUILTY] CAIAPHAS' HAND   .   .   .   .   752 EV GOSPEL(D)/N *   58
GUINEA
    DO YOU NOT SEE A ROUND DISK OF FIRE SOMEWHAT LIKE A GUINEA   617B V LAST JUDG/N   PROSE
    EGYPT LYBIA ETHIOPIA GUINEA CAFFRARIA NEGROLAND MOROCCO   712 JERUSALEM 72   40
    A GUINEA IS MORE BEAUTIFUL THAN THE SUN & A BAG WORN WITH   793D LETTER 5   PROSE
    GUINEA EACH WHICH IS SOMETHING BETTER THAN MERE COPYING   795C LETTER 6   PROSE
    A BOOK PRICE HALF A GUINEA MAY BE GOT OUT AT THE EXPENSE OF   820A LETTER 25   PROSE
GUINEAS
    TWENTY GUINEAS FOR THIS HORRIBLE DAWB & IF ANY ONE WOULD   451D ANNO REYNOLDS   MARG
        GIVE XXX
    WHO HAVING RECEIVED FOURTEEN HUNDRED GUINEAS AND MORE   .   572C DESC CAT 3   PROSE
    THE PRICE TO SUBSCRIBERS FOUR GUINEAS TWO TO BE PAID AT THE   587A CHAUCER 1   PROSE
    THREE FEET I INCH LONG AND I FOOT HIGH PRICE THREE GUINEAS   589C CHAUCER 2   TITLE
    OF THE SIZE YOU REQUIRE MY PRICE HAS BEEN THIRTY GUINEAS   794B LETTER 5   PROSE
    FOR WHICH I AM TO HAVE (TEN) GUINEAS EACH   .   .   .   .   .   820B LETTER 25   PROSE

		PAGE	TITLE	LINE

GUINEAS   (CONTINUED)
```
    ALREADY INDEBTED TO MY WIFE TWENTY GUINEAS FOR WORK  .  .  . 821A LETTER 25        PROSE
    SIX GUINEAS THUS I HOPE THAT ALL OUR THREE YEARS' TROUBLE   824D LETTER 27        PROSE
      ENDS
    IS FIVE GUINEAS EACH I SEND THE DOMENICHINO WHICH IS VERY   844B LETTER 43        PROSE
    FUSELI SHAKESPEARE IS WORTH (TWENTY-FIVE) GUINEAS THESE     848C LETTER 45        PROSE
    I NOW SEND IS TWENTY-FIVE GUINEAS EACH ON COMPARING THEM    853D LETTER 52        PROSE
    TWELVE GUINEAS WHICH YOU LENT ME WHEN I MADE UP  .  .  .  . 854D LETTER 53        PROSE
    ACCOUNT I AM THEREFORE THAT (TWELVE) GUINEAS IN YOUR DEBT   854D LETTER 53        PROSE
    (THIRTY) GUINEAS IF FINISHD & IF A SKETCH (FIFTEEN) GUINEAS 855B LETTER 53        PROSE
      AS
    (THIRTY) GUINEAS AS ITS PRICE & THE PLINY (FIFTEEN) GUINEAS 855B LETTER 53        PROSE
    (TWENTY) GUINEAS EACH HALF TO BE PAID BY P(PHILLIPS)   .  . 859A LETTER 56        PROSE
    WOULD CUT OFF TEN GUINEAS FROM MY NEXT DEMAND ON PHILLIPS   861B LETTER 58        PROSE
    TO PAY ME THREE GUINEAS FOR EACH OF THE COPIES   .  .  .  . 872A LETTER 74        PROSE
    MR BUTTS IS TO HAVE A PROOF COPY FOR THREE GUINEAS  .  .  . 877D LETTER 88        PROSE
    EXPERIENCE FOR A FRIEND AT TEN GUINEAS WHICH I CANNOT DO    878C LETTER 88        PROSE
    COST MY TIME THE AMOUNT OF TWENTY GUINEAS ONE I HAVE        878C LETTER 88        PROSE
      FINISHD
    OF MR LINNELL...TWO GUINEAS FOR HEAVEN & HELL  .  .  .  .  . SUPP LETTER 67B      *PROSE
GUION
    TOWARDS BEULAH IS TO THE SOUTH FENELON GUION TERESA  .  .  . 712 JERUSALEM 72       50
GULF
    HOW WIDE THE GULF & UNPASSABLE BETWEEN SIMPLICITY           518B MILTON 30        TITLE
      & INSIPIDITY
    THE LOUD SEA & DEEP GULF  .  .  .  .  .  .  .  .  .  .  .  . 805 TO BUTTS/L         68
GULPH
    BETWEEN THE FIGURES OF ADAM & EVE APPEARS A FIERY GULPH     609A V LAST JUDG/N    PROSE
    ON THE GULPH OF DEATH IN SELF-RIGHTEOUSNESS THAT ROLLD  .  . 642 JERUSALEM 19       31
GULPHS
    GERYON MALEBOLGE CONTAINING (TEN) GULPHS   .  .  .  .  .  . 786A ILLS DANTE 101   *PROSE
GUN
    THE SPEAR THE BOW THE GUN THE [MORTAL] MORTAR .  .  .  .  . 365 FOUR ZOAS 9    *   303
    THE SOLDIER ARMD WITH SWORD & GUN  .  .  .  .  .  .  .  .  . 432 AUGURIES           77
    INTO THE THUNDERING CANNON AND INTO THE MURDERING GUN  .  . 628 JERUSALEM 9        6
GUNS
    AND RATTLING GUNS AND BLACK AND DREARY WAR .  .  .  .  .  .  31 EDW THIRD/PS 5      60
GUSHES
    GUSHES & STAINS THE FAIR SIDE OF THE FAIR (DAUGHTERS) OF    702 JERUSALEM 66       21
      ALBION
GUT
    [YOUNG] LONG JOHN BROWN HAD THE DEVIL IN HIS GUT  .  .  .  . 434 LONG JOHN BRWN     2
    HE WAS SOON IN THE GUT OF THE LOVING YOUNG SWAIN .  .  .  . 434 LONG JOHN BRWN     9
GUTS
    HE FIRST DISCOVERD GUTS  .  .  .  .  .  .  .  .  .  .  .  .  51 WHEN CORRUP/IM     36
GUTTERS
    HE SINKS & GUTTERS MADE  .  .  .  .  .  .  .  .  .  .  .  .  57 TO BE OR/IM        22
GWANTOCK
    GWANTOCK & PEACHY HID IN DAMASCUS BENEATH MOUNT LEBANON     662 JERUSALEM 36       16
GWANTOK     SEE GUANTOK,KWANTOK,ETC
    GWANTOK PEACHY BRERTUN SLAID HUTTN SKOFELD KOCK KOTOPE  .  . 658 JERUSALEM 32       11
GWANTOKE
    GWANTOKE FORGAVE & JOYD OVER SOUTH WALES & ALL ITS          710 JERUSALEM 71       29
      MOUNTAINS
GWANTOKE'S
    SHE ADJOIND WITH GWANTOKE'S CHILDREN SOON LOVELY CORDELLA   710 JERUSALEM 71       28
      AROSE
GWENDOLEN
    GWENDOLEN RAGAN SABRINA GONORILL MEHETABEL CORDELLA  .  .  . 281 FOUR ZOAS 2        61
    A GIRDLE GWENDOLEN & CONWENNA AS A GARMENT WOVEN  .  .  .  . 507 MILTON 23         16
    CAMBEL & GWENDOLEN & CONWENNA & CORDELLA & IGNOGE   .  .  . 624 JERUSALEM 5        41
    GENERATION CAMBEL & GWENDOLEN WOVE WEBS OF WAR & OF  .  .  . 626 JERUSALEM 7        44
    NINE TIMES GWENDOLEN & CAMBEL & GWINEVERRA  .  .  .  .  .  . 628 JERUSALEM 9        22
    AND WITH THE LOOM TO COVER GWENDOLEN & RAGAN WITH COSTLY    643 JERUSALEM 21       14
      ROBES
    BATTERSEA AND CHELSEA MOURN FOR CAMBEL & GWENDOLEN  .  .  . 644 JERUSALEM 21       32
    THEN GWENDOLEN DIVIDED INTO RAHAB & TIRZA IN TWELVE         661 JERUSALEM 34       52
      PORTIONS
    AND WEPT AT OUR WINTRY DOOR LOOK LOOK BEHOLD GWENDOLEN      688 JERUSALEM 56       27
    NAKED & DRUNK WITH BLOOD GWENDOLEN DANCING TO THE TIMBREL   689 JERUSALEM 58        2
    THEN LAUGHD GWENDOLEN & HER LAUGHTER SHOOK THE NATIONS      698 JERUSALEM 63       32
      & FAMILYS OF
    DERBY PEAK YAWND A HORRID CHASM AT THE CRIES OF GWENDOLEN   699 JERUSALEM 64       35
      & AT
    AS GWENDOLEN CAST THE SHUTTLE OF WAR AS CAMBEL RETURND      703 JERUSALEM 66       62
      THE BEAM
    GWENDOLEN & CAMBEL WHO IS BOADICEA THEY GO ABROAD & RETURN  710 JERUSALEM 71       23
    WITH CAMBEL & GWENDOLEN IN DANCE AND SOLEMN SONG  .  .  .  . 722 JERUSALEM 80       39
    FOR GWENDOLEN SHE TOOK UP IN BITTER TEARS HIS ANGUISHD      723 JERUSALEM 80       67
      HEART
    O SISTER CAMBEL SAID GWENDOLEN AS THEIR LONG BEAMING LIGHT  723 JERUSALEM 80       83
    WHILE GWENDOLEN SPOKE TO CAMBEL TURNING SOFT THE SPINNING   725 JERUSALEM 82       12
      REEL
    ALONG THE ISLAND WHITE AMONG THE DRUID TEMPLES WHILE        725 JERUSALEM 82       15
      GWENDOLEN
    GWENDOLEN SAW THE INFANT IN HER (SISTER'S) ARMS SHE HOWLD   726 JERUSALEM 82    *   72
    GWENDOLEN HID IN HER LEFT HAND IT GREW & GREW TILL IT  .  . 729 JERUSALEM 84       32
GWIN
    GWIN KING OF NORWAY  .  .  .  .  .  .  .  .  .  .  .  .  .  . 11B GWIN KING/PS     TITLE
    WHEN GWIN THE SON OF NORE   .  .  .  .  .  .  .  .  .  .  .  . 11 GWIN KING/PS       2
    LET GWIN BE HUMBLED   .  .  .  .  .  .  .  .  .  .  .  .  .  . 11 GWIN KING/PS      12
    LET GWIN BE HUMBLED   .  .  .  .  .  .  .  .  .  .  .  .  .  . 12 GWIN KING/PS      30
```

GWIN   (CONTINUED)
    O GWIN THE SON OF NOBE . . . .   12 GWIN KING/PS   34
    GWIN REARD HIS SHIELD HIS PALACE SHAKES . . . . .   12 GWIN KING/PS   37
    GWIN LEADS HIS HOST AS BLACK AS NIGHT   . . . . . .   12 GWIN KING/PS   55
    GWIN LIFTS HIS HAND THE NATIONS HALT . . . .   12 GWIN KING/PS   61
    GWIN THOU HAST FILLD THY MEASURE UP . . . .   13 GWIN KING/PS   67
    LIKE THESE DID GWIN AND GORDRED MEET . . . .   14 GWIN KING/PS   105
    GWIN FELL THE SONS OF NORWAY FLED . . . .   14 GWIN KING/PS   109
GWINEFRED
    GWINIVERRA & GWINEFRED & GONORILL & SABRINA BEAUTIFUL . .   624 JERUSALEM 5   43
    LEICESTER & BERKSHIRE & HIS EMANATION IS GWINEFRED   710 JERUSALEM 71   37
     BEAUTIFUL
GWINEFRID
    BOADICEA CONWENNA ESTRILD GWINEFRID IGNOGE CAMBEL . . .   281 FOUR ZOAS 2   62
GWINEVERA
    SUFFOLK HARTFORD & ESSEX & HIS EMANATION IS GWINEVERA . .   710 JERUSALEM 71   39
GWINEVERRA
    NINE TIMES GWENDOLEN & CAMBEL & GWINEVERRA . . . . .   628 JERUSALEM 9   22
GWINIVERRA
    GWINIVERRA & GWINEFRED & GONORILL & SABRINA BEAUTIFUL . .   624 JERUSALEM 5   43
GYRATIONS
    A CIRCLE IN CONTINUAL GYRATIONS THIS BECAME A HEART . . .   659 JERUSALEM 33   20
GYVES
    THE CITIZENS IN LEADEN GYVES THE INHABITANTS OF SUBURBS   243 EUROPE 12   30
HA   SEE A HA
    HA HA SIR THOMAS YOU BUT JOKE . . . .   21 EDW THIRD/PS 3   9
    HA HA HA SAID THE PYTHAGOREAN IT WAS RE-ECHOD BY [THE]   45B ISLAND MOON 1   PROSE
    HA HA HA SAID INFLAMMABLE GASS HE WAS THE GLORY OF FRANCE   46A ISLAND MOON 1   PROSE
    SAID OBTUSE ANGLE HA HA HA HE MEANS PHARAOH SAID TILLY   47B ISLAND MOON 3   PROSE
     LALLY
    HA HA SAID INFLAMMABLE GASS WHAT DONT YOU LIKE TO GO TO   48A ISLAND MOON 4   PROSE
     CHURCH
    HERE LICK LICK LICK SAID HE HA HA HA HA HA   . . .   55C ISLAND MOON 9   PROSE
    FOR HE HAD BUT ONE EYE HA HA HA HO THEN SUNG SCOPPRELL   55C ISLAND MOON 9   PROSE
    HA HA HA SHE CALLS THE EXPERIMENTS PUPPETS . . . . .   58C ISLAND MOON 10   PROSE
    WITH THEIR SWEET ROUND MOUTHS SING HA HA HE . . . . .   63 SHEPHERD YOUNG   8
    TO SING THE SWEET CHORUS OF HA HA HE   . . . . . .   63 SHEPHERD YOUNG   12
    WITH THEIR SWEET ROUND MOUTHS SING HA HA HE . . . . .   125 LAUGHING/SI   8
    TO SING THE SWEET CHORUS OF HA HA HE   . . . . . .   125 LAUGHING/SI   12
HABERDASHER
    AFTER THE HOST FOLLOW THE SHIPMAN THE HABERDASHER   . .   566D DESC CAT 3   *PROSE
    AFTER THE HOST FOLLOW THE SHIPMAN THE HABERDASHER   . .   588C CHAUCER/N   *PROSE
    AFTER THE HOST FOLLOW THE SHIPMAN THE HABERDASHER   . .   589D CHAUCER 2   PROSE
HABITATION
    DEEP-FOUNDED HABITATION SHAKE NOT THY ROOFS . . . . .   2 TO WINTER/PS   3
    LET EACH CHUSE ONE HABITATION . . . .   224 URIZEN 4   36
    THEIR SOLEMN HABITATION LOS BEHELD THE RUDDY BOY . . .   307 FOUR ZOAS 5   80
    WILL YOU ERECT A LASTING HABITATION IN THE MOULDERING   353 FOUR ZOAS 8   495
     CHURCH YARD
    GIVING TO AIRY NOTHING A NAME AND A HABITATION . . .   514 MILTON 28   3
    CRYING WITH ONE VOICE GIVE US A HABITATION & A PLACE . .   519 MILTON 30   24
    BUT GRANT US A TEMPORAL HABITATION DO YOU SPEAK . . .   519 MILTON 30   29
    & LEAVES THE MAN WHO ENTERTAINS SUCH AN IDEA THE HABITATION   614B V LAST JUDG/N   PROSE
    THE HABITATION OF THE SPECTRES OF THE DEAD & THE PLACE .   691 JERUSALEM 59   8
    THEY RETURN NOT BUT BUILD A HABITATION SEPARATE FROM MAN   703 JERUSALEM 66   73
HABITATIONS
    EYES AND EARS AND SENSE OF TOUCH YET ARE THEIR HABITATIONS   191 V DAU ALBION 3   5
    THE SONS OF EDEN THE MOONY HABITATIONS OF BEULAH . . .   518 MILTON 30   13
    OF DOVELIKE SOFTNESS & SHADOWY HABITATIONS PREPARED FOR   519 MILTON 31   3
     THEM
HABITS
    OFTEN DEVIATED FROM THE HABITS TO PRESERVE THE MANNERS . .   583D DESC CAT 10   PROSE
    MANNERS MAKE THE MAN NOT HABITS IT IS THE SAME IN ART . .   615B V LAST JUDG/N   PROSE
HACKNEY
    HACKNEY AND HOLLOWAY SICKEN FOR ESTRILD & IGNOGE . . . .   644 JERUSALEM 21   33
    HE CAME DOWN FROM HIGHGATE THRO HACKNEY & HOLLOWAY TOWARDS   657 JERUSALEM 31   14
     LONDON
    HIGHGATE'S HEIGHTS & HAMPSTEAD'S TO POPLAR HACKNEY & BOW   729 JERUSALEM 84   1
HAD   (OMITTING AUXILIARY VERB)
    SHE KISSD THE PALE LIPS SHE HAD NO TEARS TO SHED . . . .   6 FAIR ELENOR/PS   71
    YOUR GRACE HAD BETTER MAKE . . . .   23 EDW THIRD/PS 3   90
    HAD I THREE LIVES ID DIE IN SUCH A CAUSE . . . . . .   35 WAR SONG/PS   13
    [SHE HAD A SON CALLED SUSPITION] CONCEIT & & POLICY DOTH   43A THEN SHE BORE   *PROSE
    DWELL WITH HER BY WHOM SHE (HAD) MISTRUST & SUSPITION . .   43A THEN SHE BORE   *PROSE
    [BY SHAME SHE HAD A SON CALLD HONOUR WHO BORE REVENGE] . .   43A THEN SHE BORE   PROSE
    BUT VERY ODD AS IF SHE HOPED YOU HAD NOT AN ILL OPINION   44B ISLAND MOON 1   PROSE
     OF HER
    I ONLY ASKD YOU A CIVIL QUESTION--[HERE THE] I HAD A GREAT   45A ISLAND MOON 1   *PROSE
     MIND
    IF I HAD NOT A PLACE OF PROFIT THAT FORCES ME TO GO TO   48A ISLAND MOON 4   PROSE
     CHURCH
    WISH JACK [HUNTER] TEARGUTS HAD HAD THE CUTTING OF PLUTARCH   50A ISLAND MOON 6   PROSE
    FOR NOW HE HAD A CHILD . . . .   50 WHEN CORRUP/IM   8
    IF I HAD ONLY MYSELF TO CARE FOR . . . .   52B ISLAND MOON 8   PROSE
    YOU HAD BETTER TAKE A WALK THAT WE MAY HAVE SOME PLEASURE   52D ISLAND MOON 8   PROSE
    A LITTLE BRAT NO HIGHER THAN A NETTLE & SHE HAD AS MUCH   53B ISLAND MOON 8   PROSE
    IF I HAD ONLY MYSELF TO CARE FOR ID WRING OFF THEIR NOSES   53C ISLAND MOON 8   PROSE
    JOE BRADLEY SAW FOR HE HAD BUT ONE EYE [?COME] . . . .   55B ISLAND MOON 9   *PROSE
    FOR HE HAD BUT ONE EYE HA HA HA HO THEN SUNG SCOPPRELL   55C ISLAND MOON 9   PROSE
    IF HE HAD NONE BUT ORGANIC PERCEPTIONS . . . .   97B NAT RELIGION 1   PROSE
    AS TOM WAS A SLEEPING HE HAD SUCH A SIGHT . . . . . .   117 CHIMNEY SWP/SI   10
    AND BY CAME AN ANGEL WHO HAD A BRIGHT KEY . . . . . .   117 CHIMNEY SWP/SI   13

	PAGE	TITLE	LINE

HAD (CONTINUED)

HAD A PEACH FROM THE TREE	163	ASKED THIEF/N	9
THEY TOLD ME THAT I HAD FIVE SENSES TO INCLOSE ME UP . .	191	V DAU ALBION 2	31
HAD SHE BUT HER TEARS FROM CLOUDS	253	AHANIA 4	50
HAD A PEACH FROM THE TREE	261	ASKED THIEF	10
[SEARCHING FOR GLORY WISHING THAT THE HEAVENS HAD EYES TO SEE]	267	FOUR ZOAS 1	130
BUT HAD NO POWER TO WEAVE A VEIL OF COVERING FOR HER SINS	271	FOUR ZOAS 1	* 242
TWO WILLS THEY HAD TWO INTELLECTS & NOT AS IN TIMES OF OLD	285	FOUR ZOAS 2	206
HERE HE HAD TIME ENOUGH TO REPENT OF HIS RASHLY THREATEND CURSE	315	FOUR ZOAS 6	141
[THEY HAD WHICH CLOTHD THEIR BODIES LIKE A GARMENT OF SOFT DOWN]	341	FOUR ZOAS 8	10
CHRIST DIED AS AN UNBELIEVER & IF THE BISHOPS HAD THEIR WILL	387C	ANNO WATSON	MARG
THEY NEVER HAD THE POWER TO THROW OFF	390C	ANNO WATSON	MARG
[WINGS THEY HAD [& WHEN THEY CHOSE] THAT SOFT INCLOSE] . .	422	BENEATH AD/N	1
[PRETTY] LITTLE MARY BELL HAD A FAIRY IN A NUT . . .	434	LONG JOHN BRWN	1
[YOUNG] LONG JOHN BROWN HAD THE DEVIL IN HIS GUT . . .	434	LONG JOHN BRWN	2
SOME SAID HE HAD A WOLF IN HIS STOMACH DAY & NIGHT . .	434	LONG JOHN BRWN	13
SOME SAID HE HAD THE DEVIL & THEY GUESSD RIGHT . . .	434	LONG JOHN BRWN	14
DETERMINATE ALL HIS EFFORTS PROVE THIS LITTLE BOY TO HAVE HAD	439C	REMARKS MALKIN	PROSE
OPENING BY CHANCE A BOOK WHICH SHE HAD IN HER HAND . .	440D	MEMORANDUM/N 5	PROSE
COULD THINK HAD NOT THE JUDGMENT TO PERFORM	448D	ANNO REYNOLDS	MARG
THAT GAINSBOROUGH HAD IN MAKING THE ABOVE ASSERTION NAMELY	465D	ANNO REYNOLDS	MARG
PROSPERO HAD ONE CALIBAN & I HAVE TWO	538	OLD ACQUAINT/N	2
THIS IS ONE OF THE BEST COMPLIMENTS HE EVER HAD . . .	538	TO H(UNT)/N	2
A BONE WHICH HE HAD STOLEN HE HAD IN HIS MOUTH . . .	554	TO VENETIAN/N	6
HE HAD THEM BOTH BEFORE NOW HOW DO YE DO	554	TO VENETIAN/N	14
SINCE WHICH WE HAVE NEVER HAD A PICTURE PAINTED . . .	565B	DESC CAT 2	PROSE
SHE HAS HAD FOUR HUSBANDS A FIT SUBJECT FOR THIS PAINTER	574D	DESC CAT 3	PROSE
AND THE DIVINE ALL HAD ORIGINALLY ONE LANGUAGE AND . .	579A	DESC CAT 5	PROSE
WHICH IT HAD AT FIRST WHEN ALL THE LINEAMENTS WERE PERFECT	582B	DESC CAT 9	PROSE
TO KEEP HIS OWN CHARACTERS AND EXPRESSIONS HAVING HAD .	586D	CHAUCER 1	PROSE
SUPERIOR TO BASIRE'S BECAUSE THEY HAD MORE LABOUR & CARE	593A	PUB ADDRESS/N	PROSE
RESENTMENT FOR PERSONAL INJURIES HAS HAD SOME SHARE . .	594D	PUB ADDRESS/N	PROSE
[HOGARTH'S TIME WE HAVE HAD VERY FEW EFFORTS OF ORIGINALITY]	595C	PUB ADDRESS/N	PROSE
HE HIMSELF KNEW BUT HIS IMPUDENCE HAD A CONTRARY EFFECT ON ME	603C	PUB ADDR AD/N	PROSE
TILL THEY HAVE HAD PUNISHMENT ENOUGH TO MAKE THEM COMMIT CRIMES	707	JERUSALEM 69	27
WITH THEIR DISTRICTS HAND DWELT IN SELSEY & HAD SUSSEX & SURREY	709	JERUSALEM 71	11
PEACHEY HAD NORTH WALES SHROPSHIRE CHESHIRE & THE ISLE OF MAN	710	JERUSALEM 71	30
BRERTUN HAD YORKSHIRE DURHAM WESTMORELAND & HIS EMANATION	710	JERUSALEM 71	32
SLADE HAD LINCOLN STAFFORD DERBY NOTTINGHAM & HIS LOVELY	710	JERUSALEM 71	34
HUTTN HAD WARWICK NORTHAMPTON BEDFORD BUCKINGHAM	710	JERUSALEM 71	36
SKOFELD HAD ELY RUTLAND CAMBRIDGE HUNTINGDON NORFOLK . .	710	JERUSALEM 71	38
KOX HAD OXFORD WARWICK WILTS HIS EMANATION IS ESTRILD . .	710	JERUSALEM 71	42
KOTOPE HAD HEREFORD STAFFORD WORCESTER & HIS EMANATION .	710	JERUSALEM 71	44
BOWEN HAD ALL SCOTLAND THE ISLES NORTHUMBERLAND & CUMBERLAND	710	JERUSALEM 71	46
TWO WILLS THEY HAD TWO INTELLECTS & NOT AS IN TIMES OF OLD	732	JERUSALEM 86	61
HAND HAD HIS FURNACE ON HIGHGATE'S HEIGHTS & IT REACHD . .	736	JERUSALEM 90	23
AND EVERY MAN STOOD FOURFOLD EACH FOUR FACES HAD ONE TO THE WEST	745	JERUSALEM 98	12
I HAVE LATELY HAD SOME PRICKS OF CONSCIENCE	791A	LETTER 3	PROSE
I HAVE LIKEWISE HAD BY ME ALL THE SUMMER (SIX) PLATES .	791B	LETTER 3	PROSE
& I CANNOT AFFORD TO DO IT FOR LESS I HAD TWELVE FOR THE HEAD	794B	LETTER 5	PROSE
& THO WE HAD A GREAT DEAL OF LUGGAGE NO GRUMBLING . . .	802B	LETTER 14	PROSE
FROM ONE CHAISE TO ANOTHER FOR WE HAD SEVEN DIFFERENT . .	802B	LETTER 14	PROSE
FROM ONE CHAISE TO ANOTHER WE HAD SEVEN DIFFERENT . . .	803A	LETTER 15	PROSE
WE HAD HAD BUT LITTLE TIME FOR VIEWING THE COUNTRY . . .	806B	LETTER 16	PROSE
LITTLE PICTURES & DRAWINGS WHICH I HAD THE PLEASURE & PROFIT	814C	LETTER 23	PROSE
SURPRIZED ME BECAUSE I HAVE NO AGUE BUT HAVE HAD A COLD	819B	LETTER 25	PROSE
NOR MY FRIENDS UNEASY IF I CAN HELP IT MY WIFE HAS HAD AGUES	819C	LETTER 25	PROSE
OF WORK THAT I HAVE HAD NO TIME TO GO ON WITH THE BALLADS	820C	LETTER 25	PROSE
IT APPEARS TO ME THAT I AM NOW TOO OLD & HAVE HAD . . .	821A	LETTER 25	PROSE
HAVE SOLD ALL THAT WE HAVE HAD TIME TO PRINT	821B	LETTER 25	PROSE
& I HAD NO WITNESS WITH ME BESIDE THE JUSTICES WHO COULD	827D	LETTER 28	PROSE
I HAD OF THE LETTER OR OF THE DRAWING I HAVE FETCHD THE	832B	LETTER 32	PROSE
NEVER YET SINCE MY RETURN TO LONDON HAD THE TIME OR GRACE	836C	LETTER 35	PROSE
YET HAD AN OPPORTUNITY OF CONSULTING ABOUT IT BUT SOON WILL	836C	LETTER 35	PROSE
BECAUSE I HAD NOT ENOUGH PAPER IN PROPER ORDER FOR PRINTING	839B	LETTER 38	PROSE
NOT BEING QUITE SURE THAT YOU HAD COPIES READY FOR THEM	840B	LETTER 39	PROSE
UNDER SOMEWHAT TO PRESS THEM FLAT YOU SHOULD HAVE HAD .	840D	LETTER 40	PROSE
FIFTEEN OF EACH BUT I HAD NOT PAPER ENOUGH IN PROPER ORDER	840D	LETTER 40	PROSE
IN HEALTH BUT HAS HAD SUCH A BURN ON HIS HAND AS YOU HAD	842D	LETTER 42	PROSE
ROMNEY AND SEND THEM TO YOU WONDERS HE HAS NOT HAD . .	845D	LETTER 44	PROSE
WHICH I HAVE HAD SOME TIME BUT KEPT THEM BACK TILL I COULD	850A	LETTER 49	PROSE
I HAD THE PLEASURE OF A CALL FROM MRS CHETWYND &	850C	LETTER 49	PROSE
I HAD SOME FEARS TILL MR MEYER OBLIGINGLY UNDERTOOK . .	850C	LETTER 49	PROSE
HAVE HAD THE CASH FROM HIM I SHOULD HAVE RETURNED MY THANKS	851B	LETTER 50	PROSE
NEBUCHADNEZZAR HAD SEVEN TIMES PASSED OVER HIM I HAVE . .	852A	LETTER 50	PROSE
HAD TWENTY THANK GOD I WAS NOT ALTOGETHER A BEAST AS HE WAS	852A	LETTER 50	PROSE
ASKD IF HE HAD ANY MESSAGE TO YOU AS I MEANT TO WRITE . .	860A	LETTER 56	PROSE

```
                                                                    PAGE      TITLE        LINE
HAD     (CONTINUED)
        I HAVE HAD THE PLEASURE TO SEE MR LINNELL SET OFF SAFE IN   869C LETTER 70        PROSE
        I HAVE HAD ANOTHER DESPERATE SHIVERING FIT IT CAME ON  .    872B LETTER 75        PROSE
        PROGRESS CALLD THE PILES WHICH WHEN TO THE DEGREE I HAVE    874D LETTER 80        PROSE
           HAD
        NOT DARE TO LEAVE HIS ROOM BY ANY MEANS HE HAD ANOTHER      SUPP LETTER 81A      *PROSE
        I PRINTED THOSE THINGS I HAD A WHOLE HOUSE TO RANGE IN  .   878C LETTER 88        PROSE
HADDNTN
        OF REUBEN KINCARD HADDNTN FORFAR SIMEON AYR ARGYLL BANFF    638 JERUSALEM 16        53
HADES
        IF THOU WITHDRAW THY BREATH I DIE & VANISH INTO HADES  .  . 293 FOUR ZOAS 3         61
        IF THOU WITHDRAW THY BREATH I DIE & VANISH INTO HADES  .  . 654 JERUSALEM 29        48
HADST
        LORD SAVIOUR IF THOU HADST BEEN HERE OUR BROTHER HAD NOT    304 FOUR ZOAS 4        253
           DIED
        LET THE BARD HIMSELF WITNESS WHERE HADST THOU THIS TERRIBLE 495 MILTON 13           50
           SONG
        THOU HADST WOVEN IT WITH ART THOU HADST CAUGHT ME IN THE    643 JERUSALEM 20        31
           BANDS
        IF THOU HADST BEEN HERE OUR BROTHER ALBION HAD NOT DIED     681 JERUSALEM 50        11
HAG
        HATE MEAGER HAG SETS ENVY ON UNABLE TO DO OUGHT HERSELF     41D THEN SHE BORE     PROSE
HAGAR
        IS ABRAHAM WITH SARAH & ISAAC ALSO HAGAR & ISHMAEL  .  .  . 606D V LAST JUDG/N    PROSE
HAH
        CONSTABLE OR TAKING AWAY THE PARISH BUSINESS HAH  .  .  .  . 52A ISLAND MOON 8     PROSE
        HAH SHALL I STILL SURVIVE WHENCE CAME THAT SWEET           368 FOUR ZOAS 9         422
           & COMFORTING VOICE
HAIL
        BUT MILD HE HAILED HER HAIL HIGHLY FAVOURED SAID HE  .  .  . 39D SAMSON/PS        PROSE
        HAIL MATRIMONY MADE OF LOVE  .  .  .  .  .  .  .  .  .  .    56 HAIL MATRIM/IM        1
        HAIL FINGERFOOTED LOVELY CREATURES    .  .  .  .  .  .  .    56 HAIL MATRIM/IM        7
        OF HAIL & ICE VOICES OF TERROR  .  .  .  .  .  .  .  .  .   223 URIZEN 3             33
        .  .  . & ETERNAL HAIL & [ SNOW] RAIN  .  .  .  .  .  .  .  315 FOUR ZOAS 6         148
        VOID PATHLESS BEAT WITH [ ?ENION] SNOWS ETERNAL & IRON HAIL 318 FOUR ZOAS 6      *  271
           & RAIN
        THUNDRING & HAIL & FROZEN IRON HAILD FROM THE ELEMENT  .  . 322 FOUR ZOAS 7         79
        WITH DARTS OF WINTRY HAIL AGAIN THE BLACK BOW DRAW  .  .  . 337 FOUR ZOAS 7B       156
        THRO THE WINTRY HAIL & RAIN  .  .  .  .  .  .  .  .  .  .   416 MY SPECTRE/N         29
        HE HUNTS HER FOOTSTEPS THRO THE SNOW & THE WINTRY HAIL      521 MILTON 32            5
           & RAIN
        THE LAND OF SNOWS OF TREMBLING & OF IRON HAIL INCESSANT     634 JERUSALEM 13        47
        HAIL LOCUSTS DARKNESS FIRST BORN XXX RED SEA EGYPTIANS      SUPP EXODUS/N         *PROSE
           DROWND
HAILD
        THUNDRING & HAIL & FROZEN IRON HAILD FROM THE ELEMENT  .  . 322 FOUR ZOAS 7         79
HAILED
        BUT MILD HE HAILED HER HAIL HIGHLY FAVOURED SAID HE  .  .  . 39D SAMSON/PS        PROSE
HAILS
        WHICH IN FULL CHOIR HAILS THY APPROACH O SPRING  .  .  .  .   1 TO SPRING/PS         4
HAIL STONES
        (AROUND) HIS HEAD THE THICK HAIL STONES STAND READY TO OBEY 731 JERUSALEM 86     *  36
HAIL STORM
        .  .  . THE BLACK HAIL STORM [ ?LEAPING]  .  .  .  .  .  .  294 FOUR ZOAS 3      *  104
HAIL STORMS
        GIVE ME EXAMPLE OF THY MILDNESS KING OF FURIOUS HAIL STORMS 323 FOUR ZOAS 7        145
HAINES
        I WONDER IF H(?HAINES) THE PAINTER  .  .  .  .  .  .  .  .  538 SUSSEX MEN/N         3
HAIR        SEE GOATS-HAIR
        WITH JOY THY RUDDY LIMBS AND FLOURISHING HAIR  .  .  .  .  .   1 TO SUMMER/PS         6
        HE SHEWD ME LILIES FOR MY HAIR  .  .  .  .  .  .  .  .  .     6 HOW SWEET/PS         5
        NEGLECT THY HAIR TO SEEM MORE LOVELY IN THY LOOSE ATTIRE     38A SAMSON/PS        PROSE
        I WILL GO MAD AND TEAR MY CRISPED HAIR I'LL RUN ABOUT  .  . 38C SAMSON/PS        PROSE
        THOU TOLDEST ME TO WEAVE THEE TO THE BEAM BY THY STRONG     39B SAMSON/PS        PROSE
           HAIR
        & SET HIS [ HEAD] HAIR ALL IN A FLAME & RAN ABOUT THE ROOM  48C ISLAND MOON 4     PROSE
        HOW CAME THINE HAIR TO LEAVE THY FOREHEAD HOW CAME THY      102 TIRIEL 3            3
           FACE SO BROWN
        MY HAIR IS VERY LONG MY BEARD DOTH COVER ALL MY BREAST  .  . 102 TIRIEL 3            4
        WHERE DO THEY SHROUD THEIR FIERY WINGS & THE TERRORS OF     106 TIRIEL 5            3
           THEIR HAIR
        HE CEAST HER DARK HAIR UPRIGHT STOOD WHILE SNAKES INFOLDED  108 TIRIEL 6           44
           ROUND
        FLOWD HIS GOLDEN HAIR  .  .  .  .  .  .  .  .  .  .  .  .   114 LIT GRL FND/SI       39
        OLD JOHN WITH WHITE HAIR  .  .  .  .  .  .  .  .  .  .  .   116 ECCHOING GR/SI       11
        YOU KNOW THAT THE SOOT CANNOT SPOIL YOUR WHITE HAIR  .  .  . 117 CHIMNEY SWP/SI      8
        AND THEN I'LL STAND AND STROKE HIS SILVER HAIR  .  .  .  .  125 LIT BLK BOY/SI      27
        FORTH WENT THE HAND OF JEALOUSY AMONG THE FLAMING HAIR  .  . 159C SONG LIBERTY    PROSE
        THE FIERY LIMBS THE FLAMING HAIR  .  .  .  .  .  .  .  .  . 159C SONG LIBERTY    PROSE
        IN TREMBLING ZEAL HE SIEZD HIS HAIR  .  .  .  .  .  .  .  . 177 LIT BOY LST/N       10
        THE RUDDY LIMBS & FLAMING HAIR  .  .  .  .  .  .  .  .  .  . 178 ABSTINENCE/N         2
        CROWND WITH A HELMET & DARK HAIR THE NAMELESS FEMALE STOOD  195 AMERICA PREL 1       4
        IN TREMBLING ZEAL HE SIEZD HIS HAIR  .  .  .  .  .  .  .  . 218 LIT BOY LST/SE      10
        THAT SHAKES THE BLOSSOMS OF MY HOARY HAIR  .  .  .  .  .  . 219 LIT GRL LST/SE      34
        HER SNAKY HAIR BRANDISHING IN THE WINDS OF ENITHARMON  .  . 238 EUROPE PREL 1        2
        NOW OVERGROWN WITH HAIR AND COVERD WITH A STONY ROOF  .  .  242 EUROPE 10           29
        FLAMD FURIOUS SPARKLES HIS HAIR & BEARD  .  .  .  .  .  .  . 249 AHANIA 2             3
        THEY SULK UPON HER BREAST HER HAIR BECAME LIKE SNOW ON      270 FOUR ZOAS 1        211
           MOUNTAINS
        [ WHEN THARMAS SHOOK HIS BILLOWY HAIR]  .  .  .  .  .  .  . SUPP FOUR ZOAS 1      *
        AND SHAKES HIS AWFUL HAIR  .  .  .  .  .  .  .  .  .  .  .  289 FOUR ZOAS 2        345
        .  .  . [ WETS] WET [ HER] MY BRIGHT HAIR WITH [ HER] MY TEARS 291 FOUR ZOAS 3        4
```

	PAGE	TITLE	LINE

HAIR   (CONTINUED)

TO CAST AHANIA TO THE EARTH HE SIEZD HER BY THE HAIR . . . . 294 FOUR ZOAS 3   111
LOS ANSWERD IN HIS FURIOUS PRIDE SPARKS ISSUING FROM HIS   298 FOUR ZOAS 4   34
    HAIR
DOST THOU REFUSE MIND I THE SPARKS THAT ISSUE FROM THY HAIR   301 FOUR ZOAS 4   150
I GAVE SWEET LILLIES TO THEIR BREASTS & ROSES TO THEIR HAIR   312 FOUR ZOAS 6   29
HAIR WHITE AS SNOW COVERD HIM IN FLAKY LOCKS TERRIFIC . . . 318 FOUR ZOAS 6   240
TILL HIS BRIGHT HAIR SCATTERD IN SNOWS . . . . 318 FOUR ZOAS 6   262
OF HAIR SHOOT FROM HIS ORBED SCULL HIS GLOWING EYES . . . .   319 FOUR ZOAS 6   308
. . . WITH TERRIBLE VISAGES & FLAMING HAIR . . . .   320 FOUR ZOAS 7   25
RENDS THY WHITE HAIR YET THOU DOST FIXD OBDURATE BROODING   322 FOUR ZOAS 7   80
    SIT
. . . THEY WIPE THEM WITH THE HAIR OF THEIR HEAD . . . . .   347 FOUR ZOAS 8   238
. . . & HER HAIR GLISTENS WITH DEW . . . .   367 FOUR ZOAS 9   392
AND HER BRIGHT HAIR WAS WET WITH THE WATERS . . . . . .   369 FOUR ZOAS 9   482
HER GREAT MEN HOWL & THROW THE DUST & REND THEIR HOARY HAIR   375 FOUR ZOAS 9   663
SPOILD OF THEIR BEAUTY THEIR HAIR RENT & THEIR SKIN   375 FOUR ZOAS 9   665
    SHRIVELD UP
BRACELETS & STAYS & POWDERED HAIR . . . .   447 ANNO REYNOLDS   4
[LIKE A FILTHY INFECTIOUS HEAD OF HAIR] . . . .   540 SIR JOSH RUB/N   6
[A CROOKED STICK & LOUZY HEAD OF HAIR] . . . .   540 SIR JOSH RUB/N   7
AS CROOKED LIMBS & LOUZY HEADS OF HAIR . . . .   540 SIR JOSH RUB/N   8
OF THE GARMENTS THE HAIR UPON THE HORSES THE . . . . .   588A CHAUCER/N   PROSE
& IS DRAGGING HER DOWN BY THE HAIR . . . .   606C V LAST JUDG/N PROSE
THE FIGURE DRAGGING UP A WOMAN BY HER HAIR . . . . . .   608C V LAST JUDG/N PROSE
ONE HAIR NOR PARTICLE OF DUST NOT ONE CAN PASS AWAY . .   634 JERUSALEM 14   1
AS HE SAT BEFORE HIS FURNACES CLOTHED IN SACKCLOTH OF HAIR   684 JERUSALEM 53   5
SHE SAT AT THE MILLS HER HAIR UNBOUND HER FEET NAKED . .   693 JERUSALEM 60   41
SITTING BEFORE HIS FURNACES CLOTHED IN SACKCLOTH OF HAIR   719 JERUSALEM 78   11
CANUTE DARK HAIR & EYES . . . .   SUPP ILLUS HISTORY *TITLE

HAIRD   SEE FAIR-HAIRD

HAIRS
FOR EVRY ONE OF THOSE THY WRINKLES EACH OF THOSE GREY HAIRS   99 TIRIEL 1   * 14
AND GREY HAIRS ARE ON MY HEAD . . . .   167 INFANT SORW/N   43
AND GREY HAIRS ARE ON MY HEAD . . . .   169 MYRTLE SHADE/N 18
AND GREY HAIRS WERE ON MY HEAD . . . .   182 THE ANGEL/N   16
AND GREY HAIRS WERE ON MY HEAD . . . .   214 THE ANGEL/SE   16
WILL FIND THE WOMAN'S SCALES SCRAPE OFF THE MAN'S HAIRS   559 WOMAN SCALY/N   3

HAIRY
DARK VIRGIN SAID THE HAIRY YOUTH THY FATHER STERN ABHORRD   196 AMERICA PREL 1 11
THE HAIRY SHOULDERS REND THE LINKS FREE ARE THE WRISTS   196 AMERICA PREL 2   2
    OF FIRE
THE HAIRY SHOULDERS REND THE LINKS FREE ARE THE WRISTS   336 FOUR ZOAS 7B   140
    OF FIRE
A WOMAN SCALY & A MAN ALL HAIRY . . . .   559 WOMAN SCALY/N   1

HALE
WITH EATING BEEF & DRINKING BEER O THEY WERE STOUT & HALE   58 THIS CITY/IM   7

HALF
I TOLD HIM HE LOOKD LIKE A CANDLE HALF . . . .   25 EDW THIRD/PS 3 158
& WAS SILENT [TALKD FOR HALF AN HOUR] . . . .   46A ISLAND MOON 1 PROSE
WHILE INFLAMMABLE GASS TALKD FOR HALF AN HOUR . . . .   46A ISLAND MOON 1 PROSE
HALF WOMAN & HALF [SPIRIT] SPECTRE . . . .   269 FOUR ZOAS 1   * 184
SOUTHWARD WITH HALF THE TENTS OF MEN INCLOSD IN CLOUDS .   278 FOUR ZOAS 1   496
HALF WOMAN & HALF [SERPENT] BEAST . . . .   381 FOUR ZOAS AD 5 * 4
MORAL VIRTUE WITHOUT THE SLAVERY OF [HALF] THAT HALF . .   616A V LAST JUDG/N PROSE
HALF FRIENDSHIP IS THE BITTEREST ENMITY SAID LOS . .   620 JERUSALEM 1   8
COULD NOT ARRIVE AT OUR COTTAGE BEFORE HALF PAST ELEVEN   802B LETTER 14   PROSE
I LABOUR INCESSANTLY & ACCOMPLISH NOT ONE HALF OF WHAT .   809A LETTER 20   PROSE
HALF WHAT I INTENDED TO SAY & IN PARTICULAR I WISH TO ASK   816C LETTER 24   PROSE
A BOOK PRICE HALF A GUINEA MAY BE GOT OUT AT THE EXPENSE OF 820A LETTER 25   PROSE
TO WRITE IMMEDIATELY THO I HAVE NOT DONE HALF THE BUSINESS   834B LETTER 34   PROSE
ON A CANVAS ABOUT TWO FEET BY ONE AND A HALF . . . . .   843D LETTER 43   PROSE
(TWENTY) GUINEAS EACH HALF TO BE PAID BY P(PHILLIPS) .   859A LETTER 56   PROSE

HALF-LENGTH,HALF LENGTH
AS THE TRAGIC MUSE HALF-LENGTH THAT IS THE HEAD & HANDS   836A LETTER 35   PROSE
THE FIGURES AS LARGE AS LIFE HALF LENGTH MR W(WALKER)   843C LETTER 43   PROSE
    THREE SONS

HALL   SEE GUILD HALL
OF EACH INCUMBRANCE CLEAR THE HALL . . . .   16 BLIND-MANS/PS   18
IN FAME'S WIDE TROPHIED HALL TIS OURS TO GILD . . . . .   18 EDW THIRD/PS 1   26
PHIZOGRAPHY HOGAMY HATOMY & HALL THAT BUT IN THE FIRST   49C ISLAND MOON 5 PROSE
    PLACE
THE HUNGRY POOR ENTERD THE HALL TO EAT GOOD BEEF & ALE .   58 THIS CITY/IM   11
FOR THE COMMONS CONVENE IN THE HALL OF THE NATION . . .   134 FRENCH REVOLTN 16
FOR THE COMMONS CONVENE IN THE HALL OF THE NATION . . .   136 FRENCH REVOLTN 54
TO THE CLOSE HALL OF COUNSEL WHERE HIS ANGEL FORM RENEWS   204 AMERICA CANC B   2
THEIR UNMOVD BRANCHES STOOD THE HALL BUILT WHEN THE MOON   204 AMERICA CANC B   4
    SHOT FORTH
ONE HOUR THEY LAY BURIED BENEATH THE RUINS OF THAT HALL   241 EUROPE 9   14
IN EVERY PILLARD HALL & ARCHED ROOF OF ALBION'S SKIES .   281 FOUR ZOAS 2   48
EVERY HALL SURROUNDED BY BRIGHT PARADISES OF DELIGHT .   284 FOUR ZOAS 2   176
THE GOLDEN HALL OF URIZEN WHOSE WESTERN SIDE GLOWD BRIGHT   284 FOUR ZOAS 2   179
UPON HIS GOLDEN HALL & SOUGHT THE LABYRINTHINE PORCHES .   285 FOUR ZOAS 2   185
AND WAS ERECTED AT THE CHIEF ENTRANCE OF URIZEN'S HALL .   285 FOUR ZOAS 2   200
I COULD DIVIDE WESTMINSTER HALL OR THE WALLS OF ANY OTHER   560D EXHIBITION ADV PROSE
TO ENGRAVE FINER THAN STRANGE WOOLETT HALL OR BARTOLOZZI   594C PUB ADDRESS/N PROSE
PERSIA & MEDIA ARE HIS HALLS HIS INMOST HALL IS GREAT   690 JERUSALEM 58   38
    TARTARY
IS BRIGHT CATHEDRON'S GOLDEN HALL ITS COURTS TOWERS   691 JERUSALEM 59   25
    & PINNACLES
PRAY REMEMBER US BOTH TO MR HALL WHEN YOU SEE HIM . . .   821B LETTER 25   PROSE
DELIVERD A DOZEN COPIES AT STATIONER'S HALL . . . . .   846D LETTER 44   PROSE

                                                              PAGE   TITLE   LINE
HALLELUJAH
        AND LENGTH BREDTH HIGHTH AGAIN OBEY THE DIVINE VISION   664 JERUSALEM 36   56
        HALLELUJAH
HALLEUJAH
        BUT THEIR FORMS ETERNAL EXIST FOR-EVER AMEN HALLEUJAH . . 522 MILTON 32   *   38
HALLOWD
        OER THE HALLOWD GROUND . . . .   113 LIT GRL LST/SI   40
        AND IN HIS HALLOWD CENTER HOLDS THE HEAVENS OF BRIGHT   515 MILTON 28   38
        ETERNITY
HALLS
        AND THRO HEAVN'S HALLS THY AIRY FLIGHT DOST THROW   . . .   15 IMIT SPEN/PS   21
        LIKE PILLARS OF ANCIENT HALLS AND RUINS OF TIMES REMOTE   145 FRENCH REVOLTN   258
        THEY SAT
        MANATHU-VORCYON I BEHOLD THEE FLAMING IN MY HALLS . . .   244 EUROPE 14   *   6
        UTTERING THIS DARKNESS IN MY HALLS IN THE PILLARS OF MY   271 FOUR ZOAS 1   270
        HOLY-ONES
        TWELVE HALLS AFTER THE NAMES OF HIS TWELVE SONS COMPOSD   284 FOUR ZOAS 2   '73
        THE [GOLDEN] WONDROUS BUILDING & [?HALLS OF] . . . . .   284 FOUR ZOAS 2 * .74
        OF HIS THREE DAUGHTERS WERE ENCOMPASSD BY THE TWELVE BRIGHT 284 FOUR ZOAS 2   175
        HALLS
        EACH DOME OPEND TOWARD FOUR HALLS & THE THREE DOMES   284 FOUR ZOAS 2   178
        ENCOMPASSD
        AND PILLARD HALLS & ROOMS RECIEVD THE ETERNAL WANDERING   286 FOUR ZOAS 2   242
        STARS
        OUT OF THE HALLS OF JUSTICE TILL THESE DENS THY WISDOM   292 FOUR ZOAS 3   38
        FRAMD
        . . . ON THE STEPS OF FIRE BEFORE HIS HALLS . . . .   292 FOUR ZOAS 3   44
        THE RIPE FRUIT BLUSHES INTO JOY IN HEAVEN'S ETERNAL HALLS   324 FOUR ZOAS 7   176
        HIS FIERY HALLS ARE DARK & ROUND HIS LIMBS THE SERPENT ORC   354 FOUR ZOAS 8   509
        CONTINUD ROUND THE HALLS AND MUCH THEY QUESTIOND   495 MILTON 13   46
        THE IMMORTAL
        ALL THE GODS OF THE KINGDOMS OF EARTH LABOUR IN LOS'S HALLS   510 MILTON 24   74
        IN LOS'S HALLS CONTINUAL LABOURING IN THE FURNACES   520 MILTON 31   26
        OF GOLGONOOZA
        IN ENITHARMON'S HALLS BUILDED BY LOS & HIS MIGHTY CHILDREN   638 JERUSALEM 16   60
        LOS'S HALLS & EVERY AGE RENEWS ITS POWERS FROM THESE WORKS   638 JERUSALEM 16   62
        ALBION WALKD ON THE STEPS OF FIRE BEFORE HIS HALLS . . .   654 JERUSALEM 29   33
        PERSIA & MEDIA ARE HIS HALLS HIS INMOST HALL IS GREAT   690 JERUSALEM 58   38
        TARTARY
        SUCH ARE CATHEDRON'S GOLDEN HALLS IN THE CITY OF GOLGONOOZA   713 JERUSALEM 73   1
        HALLS OF JUSTICE HATING VICE . . . .   757 EV GOSPEL(I)/N   25
HALT
        GWIN LIFTS HIS HAND THE NATIONS HALT . . . .   12 GWIN KING/PS   61
HALTER
        [WILL NOT SUBMIT TO THE GIBBET & HALTER] . . . . . .   185 LET BROTHELS/N   23
HALVES
        ("GREATER WHO PRODUCES ONE THING ENTIRE THAN MANY   78C ANNO LAVATER   MARG
        BY HALVES") UNEASY
HAM
        AND JENOUS LOOKS TO HAM [LOOKS] LIKE MAD RANTERY   . . .   550 ENGL ENCOU/N 2 * 4
        KOX IS THE FATHER OF SHEM & HAM & JAPHETH HE IS THE NOAH   625 JERUSALEM 7   23
        TO NIMROD'S TOWER TO HAM & CANAAN WALKING WITH MIZRAIM . .   692 JERUSALEM 60   18
HAMATH
        BENEATH THE MOUNTAINS OF LEBANON IN THE CITY OF REHOB IN   706 JERUSALEM 68   55
        HAMATH
HAMILTON
        IMMEDIATELY TO LADY HAMILTON MR WALKER I HAVE AGAIN SEEN   845D LETTER 44   PROSE
HAMILTON'S
        LADY HAMILTON'S DIRECTION WAS SO UNFORTUNATE AS TO FIND HIM   834D LETTER 34   PROSE
        MR EDWARDS KNOW LADY HAMILTON'S ADDRESS THE . . . . .   836B LETTER 35   PROSE
HAMMER
        THE WORKMAN THROWS HIS HAMMER DOWN . . . .   12 GWIN KING/PS   51
        AND THE SAW AND THE HAMMER THE CHISEL . . . .   144 FRENCH REVOLTN 231
        [WHAT] WHERE THE HAMMER [WHAT] WHERE THE CHAIN . . . .   172 THE TYGER/N 1   18
        THE BUILDER OF VIRGINIA THROWS HIS HAMMER DOWN IN FEAR . .   201 AMERICA 14   *   16
        WHAT THE HAMMER WHAT THE CHAIN . . . .   214 THE TYGER/SE   13
        AND TURND RESTLESS THE TONGS AND THE HAMMER . . . . .   27 URIZEN 10   16
        HIS GREAT HAMMER FELL FROM HIS HAND . . . .   229 URIZEN 13   21
        THE BELLOWS & HAMMER ARE SILENT NOW . . . .   230 URIZEN 13   37
        UNREMITTING ENDURD THE COLD HAMMER . . . .   249 AHANIA 2   25
        A HAMMER OF ADAMANT THEN BEGAN . . . .   259 BOOK OF LOS 5   22
        ENDURD THE VAST HAMMER BUT UNWEARIED . . . .   260 BOOK OF LOS 5   32
        HE DROPD HIS HAMMER DIVIDING FROM HIS AKING BOSOM FLED . .   278 FOUR ZOAS 1   523
        TAKE THOU THE HAMMER OF URTHONA REBUILD THESE FURNACES .   301 FOUR ZOAS 4   149
        HAMMER OF URTHONA FORMING UNDER HIS HEAVY HAND THE HOURS   302 FOUR ZOAS 4   179
        IN TERRORS LOS SHRUNK FROM HIS TASK HIS GREAT HAMMER . .   304 FOUR ZOAS 4 * 280
        BESIDE THE ANVIL COLD HE DANCD WITH THE HAMMER OF URTHONA   305 FOUR ZOAS 5   4
        THE HAMMER OF URTHONA SMOTE THE RIVETS IN TERROR OF BRASS   308 FOUR ZOAS 5   104
        THE HAMMER & THE CHISEL & THE RULE & COMPASSES . . . .   337 FOUR ZOAS 7B   171
        IN HIS RIGHT HAND HIS HAMMER THARMAS HELD HIS SHEPHERD'S   377 FOUR ZOAS 9   776
        CROOK
        AMONG THE WOOLY FLOCKS THE HAMMER OF URTHONA SOUNDS . . .   379 FOUR ZOAS 9   840
        THREE CLASSES ARE CREATED BY THE HAMMER OF LOS & WOVEN .   482 MILTON 2   26
        LOS SIEZD HIS HAMMER & TONGS HE LABOURD AT HIS RESOLUTE   482 MILTON 3   7
        ANVIL
        LOUD SOUNDS THE HAMMER OF LOS & LOUD HIS BELLOWS IS HEARD   485 MILTON 6   8
        LOUD SOUNDS THE HAMMER OF LOS LOUD TURN THE WHEELS OF   486 MILTON 6   27
        ENITHARMON
        . . . REGULATED BY LOS'S [HAMMERS AND WOVEN] HAMMER . . .   486 MILTON 6   *   35
        IS VISIONARY AND IS CREATED BY THE HAMMER OF LOS . . . .   516 MILTON 29   20
        WITH THEIR HAMMER & TONGS ABOUT TO NEW CREATE . . . . .   609B V LAST JUDG/N PROSE
        HE STOOD AND STAMPD THE EARTH THEN HE THREW DOWN HIS HAMMER   625 JERUSALEM 6   9
        IN RAGE &

		PAGE	TITLE		LINE
HAMMER	(CONTINUED)				
	AND CHAUNTED HIS SONG LABOURING WITH THE TONGS AND HAMMER	625	JERUSALEM 6	*	11
	TAKE THOU THIS HAMMER & IN PATIENCE HEAVE THE THUNDERING BELLOWS	627	JERUSALEM 8		39
	HIS HAMMER OF GOLD HE SIEZD AND HIS ANVIL OF ADAMANT . .	628	JERUSALEM 9		3
	LOUD ROAR MY FURNACES AND LOUD MY HAMMER IS HEARD . . .	628	JERUSALEM 9		25
	CONDENSE BENEATH MY HAMMER INTO FORMS OF CRUELTY	628	JERUSALEM 9		27
	THE HAMMER LOUD RAGES IN RINTRAH'S STRONG GRASP SWINGING LOUD	636	JERUSALEM 16		11
	HE SIEZD HIS HAMMER & TONGS HIS IRON POKER & HIS BELLOWS	658	JERUSALEM 32		8
	JERUSALEM TREMBLED SEEING HER CHILDREN DRIVN BY LOS'S HAMMER	663	JERUSALEM 36		21
	IN VEGETABLE MOULD CREATED BY THE HAMMER AND LOOM . . .	668	JERUSALEM 40		56
	IN THE BRITISH OCEAN CREATED BY LOS'S HAMMER MEASURED OUT	688	JERUSALEM 56		19
	THEN LOS UTTERED WITH HAMMER & ANVIL CHAUNT REVOICE . . .	688	JERUSALEM 56		29
	WITH HIS THUNDEROUS HAMMER TERRIFIED THE SPECTRES RAGE & FLEE	690	JERUSALEM 58		32
	THE HAMMER & THE CHISEL & THE RULE & COMPASSES FROM LONDON FLEEING	699	JERUSALEM 65		13
	THE TERRIBLE BALL THE WEDGE THE LOUD SOUNDING HAMMER OF DESTRUCTION	713	JERUSALEM 73		12
	WHICH LOS WITH HIS MIGHTY HAMMER DEMOLISHES TIME ON TIME	713	JERUSALEM 73		32
	DISSIPATING THE ROCKY FORMS OF DEATH BY HIS THUNDEROUS HAMMER	714	JERUSALEM 73		43
	TO TELL HOW LOS IN GRIEF & ANGER WHIRLING ROUND HIS HAMMER ON HIGH	714	JERUSALEM 74		20
	HE SIEZES HIS HAMMER EVERY HOUR FLAMES SURROUND HIM AS . .	731	JERUSALEM 86		34
	I CARE NOT THE SWING OF MY HAMMER SHALL MEASURE THE STARRY ROUND	733	JERUSALEM 88		2
	THE BLOW OF HIS HAMMER IS JUSTICE THE SWING OF HIS HAMMER MERCY	734	JERUSALEM 88		49
	THE FORCE OF LOS'S HAMMER IS ETERNAL FORGIVENESS BUT . .	734	JERUSALEM 88		50
	LOUD SCREAM THE DAUGHTERS OF ALBION BENEATH THE TONGS & HAMMER	737	JERUSALEM 90		44
	BENEATH LOS'S HAMMER THAT LIFE MAY NOT BE BLOTTED OUT . .	737	JERUSALEM 90		51
	THESE ARE THE DEMONSTRATIONS OF LOS & THE BLOWS OF MY MIGHTY HAMMER	737	JERUSALEM 90		57
	WHEN THEY ARE MURDERERS AS FAR AS MY HAMMER & ANVIL PERMIT	738	JERUSALEM 91		7
	HIS HEAVD HAMMER HE SWUNG IT ROUND & AT ONE BLOW	738	JERUSALEM 91		43
	AND PUT ON INTELLECT OR MY THUNDROUS HAMMER SHALL DRIVE THEE	739	JERUSALEM 91		57
HAMMERD					
	. . . AND THREW OFF THEIR HAMMERD MAIL	202	AMERICA 15		4
	AND BOWELS HIDDEN [IN DARKNESS] IN HAMMERD STEEL [ARE] . . .	338	FOUR ZOAS 7B	*	207
	AND BOWELS HID IN HAMMERD STEEL RIPD QUIVERING ON THE GROUND	701	JERUSALEM 65		53
HAMMER'S					
	DEADLY BETWEEN THE HAMMER'S BEATING GRATEFUL TO THE EARS	302	FOUR ZOAS 4		190
	ATTRACTIVE OF HIS HAMMER'S BEATING & THE SILVER LOOMS . .	344	FOUR ZOAS 8		113
HAMMERS					
	AND THOU O ENITHARMON HARK I HEAR THE HAMMERS OF LOS . .	275	FOUR ZOAS 1		421
	GO HOWL IN VAIN SMITE SMITE HIS FETTERS SMITE O WINTRY HAMMERS	276	FOUR ZOAS 1		431
	. . . BEAT THE HAMMERS MANY A [GLOBE] PYRAMID	283	FOUR ZOAS 2		136
	[THE HARD DENTANT HAMMERS ARE LULLD BY THE FLUTE LULA LULA]	346	FOUR ZOAS 8	*	203
	THEY GIVE THEM TO URTHONA'S SONS RINGING THE HAMMERS SOUND	365	FOUR ZOAS 9		305
	. . . REGULATED BY LOS'S [HAMMERS AND WOVEN] HAMMER . . .	486	MILTON 6	*	35
	THUNDERING THE HAMMERS BEAT & THE BELLOWS BLOW LOUD . . .	509	MILTON 24		52
	THE BELLOWS ARE THE ANIMAL LUNGS THE HAMMERS THE ANIMAL HEART	509	MILTON 24		58
	THE HARD DENTANT HAMMERS ARE LULLD BY THE FLUTES' LULA LULA	509	MILTON 24		63
	AND INTO THE MOUNTAINS OF THE ANVILS & OF THE HEAVY HAMMERS	629	JERUSALEM 10		2
	THE BELLOWS & THE HAMMERS MOVE COMPELLD BY LOS'S HAND . .	629	JERUSALEM 10		6
	THE BELLOWS ARE THE ANIMAL LUNGS THE HAMMERS THE ANIMAL HEART	684	JERUSALEM 53		12
HAMPSHIRE					
	GAD OXFORD BUCKS HARFORD ASHER SUSSEX HAMPSHIRE BERKSHIRE	637	JERUSALEM 16		47
HAMPSTEAD					
	MILCAH'S PILLARS SHINE FROM HARROW TO HAMPSTEAD WHERE HOGLAH	525	MILTON 35		11
	HAMPSTEAD HIGHGATE FINCHLEY HENDON MUSWELL HILL RAGE LOUD	636	JERUSALEM 16		1
	SUNDAY AFTERNOON TO CALL ON MRS FLAXMAN AT HAMPSTEAD I SEND	799A	LETTER 11		PROSE
	"ON SUNDAY AFTERNOON IN HAMPSTEAD TO TAKE FAREWELL ALL"	800A	LETTER 12		PROSE
	ROMNEY'S PICTURES THAT REMAINED AFTER THE SALE AT HAMPSTEAD	831A	LETTER 31		PROSE
	YOUR USE AS ALSO THE CATALOGUE OF HAMPSTEAD SALE	836A	LETTER 35		PROSE
	TO HAMPSTEAD TO SEE MRS LINNELL ON SUNDAY BUT WILL RETURN	870D	LETTER 72		PROSE
	HAMPSTEAD AIR AS IT ALWAYS DID SO I FEAR IT ALWAYS WILL DO	870D	LETTER 72		PROSE
	WHEN I WAS YOUNG HAMPSTEAD HIGHGATE HORNSEA MUSWELL HILL &	871A	LETTER 72		PROSE
	SUNDAY AT HAMPSTEAD AS I FEAR THE ATTACK AGAIN	872C	LETTER 75		PROSE
	EXPECTATION & DESIRE OF VISITING HAMPSTEAD I AM NEVERTHELESS	873D	LETTER 78		PROSE
	START FOR HAMPSTEAD LIKE A YOUNG LARK WITHOUT FEATHERS . .	875A	LETTER 80		PROSE
	ME AT THIS TIME MY JOURNEY TO HAMPSTEAD ON SUNDAY . . .	880A	LETTER 90		PROSE
	MRS LINNELL COLLINS'S FARM NORTH END HAMPSTEAD	SUPP	ADDRESS/L 70		*TITLE
HAMPSTEAD'S					
	BEFORE LONDON TO HAMPSTEAD'S BREADTHS & HIGHGATE'S HEIGHTS TO	485	MILTON 6		9
	HIGHGATE'S HEIGHTS & HAMPSTEAD'S TO POPLAR HACKNEY & BOW	729	JERUSALEM 84		1
HANCOCK					
	WASHINGTON FRANKLIN PAINE & WARREN GATES HANCOCK & GREEN	197	AMERICA 3		4

	PAGE	TITLE	LINE

HANCOCK   (CONTINUED)

WASHINGTON HANCOCK PAINE & WARREN GATES FRANKLIN & GREEN   203 AMERICA CANC A   4

HAND   SEE BEFORE HAND,RIGHT HAND

HE WITHERS ALL IN SILENCE AND [IN] HIS HAND . . . . .   3 TO WINTER/PS   11
CHILL DEATH WITHDRAWS HIS HAND AND SHE REVIVES . . . .   4 FAIR ELENOR/PS   9
O GHASTLY DEATH WITHDRAW THY CRUEL HAND . . . .   5 FAIR ELENOR/PS   43
O GIVE NOT HIM THY HAND NOW I AM DEAD . . . .   6 FAIR ELENOR/PS   66
GWIN LIFTS HIS HAND THE NATIONS HALT . . . .   12 GWIN KING/PS   61
HELD IN TH ALMIGHTY'S HAND . . . .   13 GWIN KING/PS   66
IS IN HIS HAND TO WHOM ALL MEN ARE EQUAL . . . . . .   18 EDW THIRD/PS 1   31
HOW TO EMPLOY THE HAND THAT LACKETH BREAD . . . . . .   19 EDW THIRD/PS 2   23
AND GRANT HIS FAVOURS WITH A SPARING HAND . . . . . .   20 EDW THIRD/PS 2   47
GIVE ME YOUR HAND AND NOW I'LL TELL ~~Y WHAT . . . . .   21 EDW THIRD/PS 3   7
PREPARE YOUR HEARTS FOR DEATH'S COLD HAND PREPARE . .   34 WAR SONG/PS   6
BUT LO THERE IS A GOD WHO MADE THE WORLD STRETCH OUT THY   36A COUCH DEATH/PS   PROSE
    HAND TO HIM
MY HAND IS FEEBLE HOW SHOULD I STRETCH IT OUT . . . .   36A COUCH DEATH/PS   PROSE
BENEATH ME BURNS ETERNAL FIRE O FOR A HAND TO PLUCK ME   36B COUCH DEATH/PS   PROSE
    FORTH
A VISIONARY HAND WIPED AWAY HIS TEARS . . . .   36C COUCH DEATH/PS   PROSE
O WHITE-ROBED ANGEL GUIDE MY TIMOROUS HAND TO WRITE .   37D SAMSON/PS   PROSE
AND ALL YE GODS OF PALESTINE WITHDRAW YOUR HAND . . .   38C SAMSON/PS   PROSE
BY BANDS OF ENEMIES STRETCH FORTH THY HAND AND SAVE .   40B SAMSON/PS   PROSE
ERE LONG TO BLEED & DIE A SACRIFICE DONE BY A PRIESTLY HAND   41B THEN SHE BORE   PROSE
GO SEE THE CITY FRIENDS JOIND HAND IN HAND . . . . .   43A THEN SHE BORE   PROSE
SUNK BY THE HAND OF DEATH IN WATRY TOMB OER YONDER   43D WOE CRIED MUSE   *PROSE
    [RUFFLING] LAKE
AN ACT OF PARLIAMENT IN HIS HAND SAID THAT IT WAS   46A ISLAND MOON 1   PROSE
    A SHAMEFUL
PUT HIS CHIN IN HIS HAND & SAID WHENEVER YOU THINK . .   49B ISLAND MOON 5   PROSE
& DIPS HIS HAND UP TO THE SHOULDER IN TREACLE . . . .   55B ISLAND MOON 9   PROSE
OR NATURE'S HAND HAS CROOKED HER FRAME . . . .   56 HAIL MATRIM/IM   14
HE CEAST THE AGED MAN [XXX] RAISD UP HIS RIGHT HAND TO   99 TIRIEL 1   * 19
    THE HEAVENS
THEN HAR AROSE & LAID HIS HAND UPON OLD TIRIEL'S HEAD .   101 TIRIEL 2   34
ESCAPE YE FIENDS FOR IJIM WILL NOT LIFT HIS HAND AGAINST YE   106 TIRIEL 4   88
THY FATHER CALLS THY FATHER LIFTS HIS HAND UNTO THE [AIR]   108 TIRIEL 6   41
    HEAVENS
HE KISSED THE CHILD & BY THE HAND LED . . . .   121 LIT BOY FND/SI   5
WALKS IN THE VALLEY AND EACH MORN OVER ME SPREADS HIS HAND   127 BOOK OF THEL 1   20
AND APPALLING MIST HIS STRONG HAND OUTSTRETCHD . . .   134 FRENCH REVOLTN   3
TO BE SWAYED BY VISIBLE HAND . . . .   134 FRENCH REVOLTN   5
CHAIND HAND AND FOOT ROUND HIS NECK AN IRON BAND . . .   135 FRENCH REVOLTN   27
. . . ROSE FROM THE MONARCH'S RIGHT HAND RED AS WINES   138 FRENCH REVOLTN   83
STRETCH THE HAND THAT BECKONS THE EAGLES OF HEAVEN . . .   138 FRENCH REVOLTN   103
. . . I AWOKE A COLD HAND PASSED OVER MY LIMBS AND BEHOLD   140 FRENCH REVOLTN   130
HIS BENEVOLENT HAND . . . .   142 FRENCH REVOLTN   176
THY BRETHREN AND NOT AS THY FOOT OR THY HAND . . . . .   143 FRENCH REVOLTN   194
. . . HIS IVORY WAND IN HIS HAND . . . .   143 FRENCH REVOLTN   198
. . . AND PUTTING HIS HAND TO THE PLOW . . . .   144 FRENCH REVOLTN   224
. . . AND OF SULPHUR THE EARTH FROM FAYETTE AS HE LIFTED   146 FRENCH REVOLTN   278
    HIS HAND
& TAKING IN MY HAND SWEDENBORG'S VOLUMES . . . . . .   157A MARRIAGE HH 17   PROSE
& I IN MY HAND BROUGHT THE SKELETON OF A BODY . . . .   157B MARRIAGE HH 17   PROSE
THE SPEARY HAND BURNED ALOFT UNBUCKLED WAS THE SHIELD .   159B SONG LIBERTY   PROSE
FORTH WENT THE HAND OF JEALOUSY AMONG THE FLAMING HAIR .   159C SONG LIBERTY   PROSE
IN [HIS HAND] [THEIR] HANDS A HOLY BOOK . . . . . .   167 INFANT SORW/N   * 27
WHAT IMMORTAL HAND OR EYE . . . .   172 THE TYGER/N 1   3
WHAT THE HAND DARE SIEZE THE FIRE . . . .   172 THE TYGER/N 1   8
WHAT DREAD HAND & WHAT DREAD FEET . . . .   172 THE TYGER/N 1   12
WHAT IMMORTAL HAND & EYE . . . .   173 THE TYGER/N 1   24
WHAT IMMORTAL HAND [OR] & EYE . . . .   173 THE TYGER/N 2   * 3
WHAT THE HAND DARE SIEZE THE FIRE . . . .   173 THE TYGER/N 2   8
WHAT DREAD HAND & WHAT DREAD FEET . . . .   173 THE TYGER/N 2   12
WHAT IMMORTAL HAND & EYE . . . .   173 THE TYGER/N 2   19
FED WITH COLD & USUROUS HAND . . . .   181 HOLY THURS/N   4
[WOE ALAS MY GUILTY HAND] . . . .   182 THE FLY/N   1
MY [GUILTY HAND] THOUGHTLESS HAND . . . .   183 THE FLY/N   7
TILL SOME BLIND HAND . . . .   183 THE FLY/N   19
[HE SAW HIM SIGN HIS HAND] . . . .   185 LET BROTHELS/N   28
IN HAND ARE ASKED FOR NONE ARE WANTED BUT THE AUTHOR .   208A PRSPECTUS 1793   PROSE
FED WITH COLD AND USUROUS HAND . . . .   211 HOLY THURS/SE   4
MY THOUGHTLESS HAND . . . .   213 THE FLY/SE   3
TILL SOME BLIND HAND . . . .   213 THE FLY/SE   11
WHAT IMMORTAL HAND OR EYE . . . .   214 THE TYGER/SE   3
WHAT THE HAND DARE SIEZE THE FIRE . . . .   214 THE TYGER/SE   8
WHAT DREAD HAND & WHAT DREAD FEET . . . .   214 THE TYGER/SE   12
WHAT DREAD HAND FORMD THY DREAD FEET . . . .   214 THE TYGER/SE   12
WHAT IMMORTAL HAND OR EYE . . . .   214 THE TYGER/SE   23
THIS ROCK PLACE WITH STRONG HAND THE BOOK . . . . . .   224 URIZEN 4   32
EMERGE FROM THE DARKNESS HIS HAND . . . .   224 URIZEN 4   42
HIS GREAT HAMMER FELL FROM HIS HAND . . . .   229 URIZEN 13   21
OF A FOOT OR A HAND OR A HEAD . . . .   234 URIZEN 23   5
AND HIS RIGHT HAND BURNS RED IN ITS CLOUD . . . . . .   249 AHANIA 2   6
DEEP GROAND URIZEN STRETCHING HIS AWFUL HAND . . . . .   249 AHANIA 2   31
I CANNOT TOUCH HIS HAND . . . .   254 AHANIA 4   65
WITH THY HAND FULL OF GENEROUS FIRE . . . .   255 AHANIA 5   30
AND STRETCHING OUT HIS HOLY HAND IN THE VAST DEEP SUBLIME   266 FOUR ZOAS 1   73
THEY SAW NOT YET THE HAND DIVINE FOR IT WAS NOT YET   270 FOUR ZOAS 1   230
    REVEALD
[HAND IN HAND [IN A] SULTRY PARADISE] . . . .   SUPP FOUR ZOAS 1   *
AND I COMMANDED THE GREAT DEEP TO HIDE HER IN HIS HAND . .   282 FOUR ZOAS 2   91

```
                                                      PAGE      TITLE           LINE
HAND    (CONTINUED)
      THE HAND OF URIZEN IS UPON ME BECAUSE I BLOTTED OUT   .  .  282 FOUR ZOAS 2        106
      CUT BY THE PLOW OF AGES HELD IN URIZEN'S STRONG HAND  .  .  283 FOUR ZOAS 2        119
      I GRASP THY VEST IN MY STRONG HAND IN VAIN LIKE WATER     288 FOUR ZOAS 2   *    304
         SPRINGS
      THEY SING UNCEASING TO THE NOTES OF MY IMMORTAL HAND    .  .  289 FOUR ZOAS 2      354
      NOW MY LEFT HAND I STRETCH TO EARTH BENEATH   .  .  .  .  .  289 FOUR ZOAS 2      369
      O I AM WEARY LAY THINE HAND UPON ME OR I FAINT    .  .  .  290 FOUR ZOAS 2        374
      IF THOU DOST LAY THINE HAND UPON ME BEHOLD I AM SILENT  .  293 FOUR ZOAS 3         62
      IF THOU WITHHOLD THINE HAND I PERISH LIKE A FALLEN LEAF    293 FOUR ZOAS 3         63
      .  .  .  HIS STRONG RIGHT [HAD] HAND CAME FORTH   .  .  .  .  294 FOUR ZOAS 3   *    110
      FRIGHTEND WITH COLD INFECTIOUS MADNESS IN HIS HAND THE     302 FOUR ZOAS 4        178
         THUNDERING
      HAMMER OF URTHONA FORMING UNDER HIS HEAVY HAND THE HOURS   302 FOUR ZOAS 4        179
      .  .  .  STARRY WHEELS FELT THE DIVINE HAND LIMIT    .  .  .  304 FOUR ZOAS 4      275
      AND LOS BEHELD THE HAND OF GOD OVER HIS FURNACES    .  .  304 FOUR ZOAS 4        278
      FELL FROM HIS HAND HIS FIRES HID THEIR STRONG LIMBS IN     304 FOUR ZOAS 4        281
         SMOKE
      LOS TAKING ENITHARMON BY THE HAND LED HER ALONG    .  .  .  309 FOUR ZOAS 5      150
      WE FELL I SIEZD THEE DARK URTHONA IN MY LEFT HAND FALLING  311 FOUR ZOAS 5        225
      AS THE SEED FALLS FROM THE SOWER'S HAND SO URIZEN FELL     316 FOUR ZOAS 6        160
         & DEATH
      ENDLESS HAD BEEN HIS TRAVEL BUT THE DIVINE HAND HIM LED    316 FOUR ZOAS 6        176
      STILL HE WITH HIS GLOBE OF FIRE IMMENSE IN HIS VENTUROUS   319 FOUR ZOAS 6        286
         HAND
      IN HIS HAND A KNOTTED CLUB WHOSE KNOTS LIKE MOUNTAINS      319 FOUR ZOAS 6        305
         FROWND
      OF DEATH O NORTHERN DRUM AWAKE O HAND OF IRON SOUND    .  .  336 FOUR ZOAS 7B     154
      WONDRING WITH LOVE & [XXX] AWE THEY FELT THE DIVINE HAND   341 FOUR ZOAS 8   *     23
         UPON THEM
      WITH A PARENTAL LOVE FOR THE DIVINE HAND WAS UPON HIM   .  342 FOUR ZOAS 8         40
      .  .  .  SUDDEN WAVD [HIS HURTLING HAND] AMONG THE STARS  .  343 FOUR ZOAS 8       87
      [AMONG THE STARS] HIS HURTLING HAND GAVE THE DIRE SIGNAL   343 FOUR ZOAS 8         88
         .  .  .
      ?FEELING THE HAND OF LOS IN GOLGONOOZA & THE FORCE    .  .  .  344 FOUR ZOAS 8     112
      DEPENDS ALONE UPON THE UNIVERSAL HAND & NOT IN US   .  .  .  346 FOUR ZOAS 8      198
      AND THEN THEY SENT JEHOVAH WHO LEPROUS STRETCHD HIS HAND   351 FOUR ZOAS 8        405
         TO ETERNITY
      OUTSTRETCHD HIS RIGHT HAND BRANCHING OUT IN FIBROUS        357 FOUR ZOAS 9          7
         STRENGTH
      SIEZD THE SUN HIS LEFT HAND LIKE DARK ROOTS COVERD THE MOON 357 FOUR ZOAS 9         8
      [THE FALLEN MAN WONDRING BEHELD] HE LAID HIS (HAND) ON     365 FOUR ZOAS 9   *    311
         THE PLOW
      HOWLING & WAILING FLY THE SOULS FROM URIZEN'S STRONG HAND  365 FOUR ZOAS 9        323
      FOR FROM THE HAND OF URIZEN THE MYRIADS FALL LIKE STARS    365 FOUR ZOAS 9        324
      WEEPING & WAILING FLY THE SOULS FROM URIZEN'S STRONG HAND  365 FOUR ZOAS 9   *    332
      MY LUVAH SMILD I KNEELED DOWN HE LAID HIS HAND ON MY HEAD  369 FOUR ZOAS 9        468
      AND WHEN HE LAID HIS HAND UPON ME FROM THE GATES OF SLEEP  369 FOUR ZOAS 9        469
         I CAME
      I SEE THE HAND THAT LEADETH ME DOTH ALSO LEAD MY FLOCKS    369 FOUR ZOAS 9        474
      HE TOOK HER HAND RELUCTANT SHE FOLLOWD IN INFANT DOUBTS    371 FOUR ZOAS 9        552
      THEN URIZEN AROSE & TOOK HIS SICKLE IN HIS HAND    .  .  .  372 FOUR ZOAS 9      579
      THE MORNING DAWND URIZEN ROSE & IN HIS HAND THE FLAIL   .  374 FOUR ZOAS 9        650
      THEY CATCH THE SHRIEKS IN CUPS OF GOLD THEY HAND THEM TO   377 FOUR ZOAS 9        768
         ONE ANOTHER
      IN HIS RIGHT HAND HIS HAMMER THARMAS HELD HIS SHEPHERD'S   377 FOUR ZOAS 9        776
         CROOK
      IN HIS HAND THARMAS TAKES THE STORMS HE TURNS THE WHIRLWIND 378 FOUR ZOAS 9       809
         LOOSE
      WHEN GOD COMMANDED THIS HAND TO WRITE    .  .  .  .  .  .  .  419 I SAW A MONK/N   28
      THE HAND OF VENGEANCE SOUGHT THE BED   .  .  .  .  .  .  .  419 I SAW A MONK/N  *  44
      THE IRON HAND [CRUSD] CRUSHD THE TYRANT'S HEAD    .  .  .  .  419 I SAW A MONK/N  *  46
      AND GEMS & GOLD THAT NONE HIS HAND   .  .  .  .  .  .  .  425 MENTAL TRAVLER    46
      WHY DID HEAVEN ADORN ME WITH BOUNTIFUL HAND   .  .  .  .  428 MARY              23
      I'LL REFUSE HIM MY HAND & FROM ENVY BE FREE   .  .  .  .  428 MARY              32
      WHEN GOD COMMANDED THIS HAND TO WRITE   .  .  .  .  .  .  430 GREY MONK         13
      THE HAND OF VENGEANCE FOUND THE BED   .  .  .  .  .  .  .  431 GREY MONK         33
      THE IRON HAND CRUSHD THE TYRANT'S HEAD   .  .  .  .  .  .  431 GREY MONK         35
      HOLD INFINITY IN THE PALM OF YOUR HAND   .  .  .  .  .  .  431 AUGURIES           3
      AND ON HIS RIGHT HAND WAS MARY GREEN   .  .  .  .  .  .  435 WILLIAM BOND      17
      AND ON HIS LEFT HAND WAS HIS SISTER JANE   .  .  .  .  .  435 WILLIAM BOND      18
      ON THE RIGHT HAND OF HER WILLIAM DEAR   .  .  .  .  .  .  435 WILLIAM BOND      38
      ON THE RIGHT HAND OF HIS LOVED BED   .  .  .  .  .  .  .  435 WILLIAM BOND      39
      COME OUT HE IS THE SAME MAN WHO LATELY HURT HIS HAND   .  438C BLAKES MEMORAN  PROSE
      HAND WHICH EXECUTED THESE LITTLE IDEAS BEEN THAT          439C REMARKS MALKIN  PROSE
         OF A PLAGIARY
      OPENING BY CHANCE A BOOK WHICH SHE HAD IN HER HAND   .  .  440D MEMORANDUM/N 5 PROSE
      IN HER MILD HAND THE GOLDEN KEYS   .  .  .  .  .  .  .  .  442 DEDICATN BLAIR     6
      HELL OPENS BENEATH THE HARLOT'S SEAT ON THE LEFT HAND   .  443B LAST JUDGMNT/L PROSE
      THE RIGHT HAND OF THE DESIGN IS APPROPRIATED TO    .  .  443B LAST JUDGMNT/L PROSE
      THE RESURRECTION OF THE JUST THE LEFT HAND OF THE    .  .  443B LAST JUDGMNT/L PROSE
      THE PHARISEES APPEAR ON THE LEFT HAND PLEADING    .  .  .  443C LAST JUDGMNT/L PROSE
      ON THE LEFT HAND OF THE HARLOT'S SEAT WHERE OTHERS ARE  .  443C LAST JUDGMNT/L PROSE
      BEFORE THE THRONE OF CHRIST ON THE RIGHT HAND THE JUST IN  443D LAST JUDGMNT/L PROSE
      ON THE RIGHT HAND OF THE THRONE OF CHRIST IS BAPTISM    .  444B LAST JUDGMNT/L PROSE
      & ON THE LEFT HAND THE LORD'S SUPPER IS ADMINISTERD   .  .  444B LAST JUDGMNT/L PROSE
      NOR SHALL MY SWORD SLEEP IN MY HAND   .  .  .  .  .  .  .  481 AND DID FEET/M    14
      HIS BURNING THIRST & FREEZING HUNGER COME INTO MY HAND  .  481 MILTON 2           5
      JUDGE OF THE PURE MELODIOUS HARP STRUCK BY A HAND DIVINE   485 MILTON 5          31
      THE DIVINE HAND FOUND THE TWO LIMITS . . . . . . . .  .  494 MILTON 13          20
      AND JEHOVAH WAS LEPROUS LOUD HE CALLD STRETCHING HIS HAND  494 MILTON 13          24
         TO ETERNITY
```

858

			PAGE	TITLE	LINE

HAND   (CONTINUED)

EVEN TO MAHANAIM WHEN WITH COLD HAND URIZEN STOOPD DOWN . . . 500 MILTON 19 — 7
OR HOW CAN I WITH MY COLD HAND OF CLAY BUT THOU O LORD . . 502 MILTON 20 — 17
WHERE HUMAN THOUGHT IS CRUSHD BENEATH THE IRON HAND OF . . 510 MILTON 25 — 5
POWER
THE SOULS DESCENDING TO THE BODY WAIL ON THE RIGHT HAND . . 512 MILTON 26 — 16
OF LOS & THOSE DELIVERD FROM THE BODY ON THE LEFT HAND . . 512 MILTON 26 — 17
THEY CATCH THE SHRIEKS IN CUPS OF GOLD THEY HAND THEM TO . . 514 MILTON 27 — 38
ONE ANOTHER
BENEATH SAT CHAOS SIN ON HIS RIGHT HAND DEATH ON HIS LEFT . . 531 MILTON 39 — 29
ON CANTERBURY'S RUINS HIS RIGHT HAND COVERS LOFTY WALES . . 531 MILTON 39 — 41
[AND] WHO WITH IRON HAND CUFFD IN THE AFTERNOON . . . . 537 AND HIS LEGS/N — 24
AND IN THE HAND OF THE SIMPERING FOOL . . . . 541 FLORENTINE/N — 3
BUT YOU MUST NOT BRING IN YOUR HAND A LIE . . . . . . 542 FLORENTINE/N — 22
BUT RAFAEL THINKS A HEAD A FOOT A HAND . . . . . . 547 PRETTY EPIGR/N — 4
AND HE HOLDS MY MONEY BAG IN HIS HAND . . . . . . 558 I ROSE UP AT/N — 16
HE WHO DOES NOT KNOW HOW TO DRAW A HAND OR A FOOT . . . 563D DESC CAT — PROSE
PHYSICIAN AND ON HIS OTHER HAND WITH TWO CITIZENS OF LONDON 570D DESC CAT 3 — PROSE
EVERY EXPRESSION EVERY LINEAMENT OF HEAD HAND & FOOT . . 588A CHAUCER/N — PROSE
WHETHER [THE FOOL'S HAND OR THE] PHYSIOGNOMIC STRENGTH . 591C PUB ADDRESS/N — PROSE
BUT DRAWN WITH A FIRM & DECIDED HAND AT ONCE [WITH ALL ITS] 595C PUB ADDRESS/N — PROSE
ON HIS RIGHT & THE WICKED ON HIS LEFT HAND . . . . . 606B V LAST JUDG/N — PROSE
& CAIN WITH THE FLINT IN HIS HAND WITH WHICH HE SLEW . . 606B V LAST JUDG/N — PROSE
TO PROCEED [IN THE] WITH THE DESCRIPTION OF THOSE ON THE . 607C V LAST JUDG/N — *PROSE
LEFT HAND
WITH A BOOK IN HIS HAND WHICH IS SHUT HE REPRESENTS . . . 607D V LAST JUDG/N — PROSE
THAT FIEND WHO CARRIES THE KEY [& DRAGS] IN ONE HAND & . . 608B V LAST JUDG/N — PROSE
ACHITOPHEL IS ALSO HERE WITH THE CORD IN HIS HAND . . . 608D V LAST JUDG/N — PROSE
& HELL IS OPEND BENEATH HER SEAT ON THE LEFT HAND . . . 609B V LAST JUDG/N — PROSE
THOSE ON THE RIGHT HAND AWAKE IN JOY THOSE ON THE LEFT . 609C V LAST JUDG/N — PROSE
IN HORROR
ON HIS RIGHT HAND SHEM & ON HIS LEFT JAPHET . . . . . 609D V LAST JUDG/N — PROSE
WITHOUT SHAPE OR FASHION [BY] ON THE RIGHT HAND OF NOAH . 610D V LAST JUDG/N — *PROSE
FROM WHENCE ABRAHAM WAS TAKEN ALSO ON THE RIGHT HAND OF . 610D V LAST JUDG/N — PROSE
NOAH
ON THE RIGHT HAND OF THESE RISE THE DIFFIDENT & HUMBLE . . 610D V LAST JUDG/N — PROSE
ON THE LEFT HAND APOLLYON IS FOILED BEFORE THE SWORD . . 612B V LAST JUDG/N — PROSE
LORD'S SUPPER ON THE LEFT HAND OF THE [PICTURE] THRONE . . 614B V LAST JUDG/N — PROSE
GUIDE THOU MY HAND WHICH TREMBLES EXCEEDINGLY UPON THE . 623 JERUSALEM 5 — 23
ROCK OF AGES
THE BELLOWS & THE HAMMERS MOVE COMPELLD BY LOS'S HAND . . 629 JERUSALEM 10 — 6
WHEN THE DIVINE HAND WENT FORTH ON ALBION IN THE MID WINTER 636 JERUSALEM 15 — 32
HEAVES IN THE HAND OF PALAMABRON WHO IN LONDON'S DARKNESS . 636 JERUSALEM 16 — 9
TOUCHD BY THE HAND NOR SEEN WITH THE EYE O JERUSALEM . . 645 JERUSALEM 22 — 27
JERUSALEM THEN STRETCHD HER HAND TOWARD THE MOON & SPOKE . 645 JERUSALEM 22 — 33
THUNDRING THE VEIL RUSHES FROM HIS HAND VEGETATING KNOT BY 648 JERUSALEM 24 — 61
BOTH HEART IN HEART & HAND IN HAND . . . . 652 FIELDS FROM/J — 88
IF THOU DOST LAY THINE HAND UPON ME BEHOLD I AM SILENT . . 654 JERUSALEM 29 — 49
IF THOU WITHHOLD THINE HAND I PERISH LIKE A FALLEN LEAF . 654 JERUSALEM 29 — 50
AND THE DIVINE HAND WAS UPON THEM BEARING THEM THRO . 655 JERUSALEM 30 — 12
DARKNESS
THEY WEPT & TREMBLED & LOS PUT FORTH HIS HAND & TOOK THEM . 656 JERUSALEM 30 — 16
IN
AND BUILDED BY THE DIVINE HAND THAT THE SINNER SHALL ALWAYS 657 JERUSALEM 31 — 31
ESCAPE
THEN THE DIVINE HAND FOUND THE TWO LIMITS SATAN AND ADAM . 662 JERUSALEM 35 — 1
AND THE DIVINE HAND WAS UPON HIM STRENGTHENING HIM MIGHTILY 671 JERUSALEM 42 — 56
STRETCHING A HAND TO SAVE THE FALLING MAN ARE WE NOT FOUR . 672 JERUSALEM 43 — 14
FOR BREAD OF THE SONS OF ALBION OF THE GIANTS HAND . 673 JERUSALEM 43 — 50
& SCOFIELD
AND ELY SCRIBE OF LOS WHOSE PEN NO OTHER HAND . . . . . 676 JERUSALEM 46 — 6
SHUDDER NOT BUT WRITE & THE HAND OF GOD WILL ASSIST YOU . 677 JERUSALEM 47 — 17
OVER THE PLOW OF NATIONS IN THE STRONG HAND OF ALBION . . . 689 JERUSALEM 57 — 2
HE SAW IN VALA'S HAND THE DRUID KNIFE OF REVENGE & THE . 698 JERUSALEM 63 — 39
POISON CUP
AND SHE PUT FORTH HER HAND UPON THE LOOMS IN DREADFUL . 698 JERUSALEM 64 — 7
HOWLINGS
HER HAND IS A COURT OF JUSTICE HER FEET TWO ARMIES . 698 JERUSALEM 64 — 9
IN BATTLE
OVER THE PLOW OF NATIONS THUNDRING IN THE HAND OF ALBION'S . 699 JERUSALEM 64 — 30
SPECTRE
CHAIND HAND & FOOT COMPELLD TO FIGHT UNDER THE IRON WHIPS . 700 JERUSALEM 65 — 35
THEY PUT INTO HIS HAND A REED THEY MOCK SAYING BEHOLD . . 702 JERUSALEM 66 — 24
OF FLINT IS IN HER HAND SHE PASSES IT OVER THE HOWLING . 704 JERUSALEM 67 — 25
VICTIM
AND SWORD FAINT IN HIS HAND FROM ALBION ACROSS GREAT . 706 JERUSALEM 68 — 52
TARTARY
THE CUP OF RAHAB IN HIS HAND HER POISONS TWENTY-SEVEN-FOLD 715 JERUSALEM 75 — 3
THE KNIFE INTO HIS DAUGHTER'S HAND SUCH THING WAS NEVER . 722 JERUSALEM 80 — 23
KNOWN
SO SAYING SHE TOOK A FALSHOOD & HID IT IN HER LEFT HAND . 725 JERUSALEM 82 * 17
AND THUS SHE CLOSED HER LEFT HAND AND UTTERD HER FALSHOOD . 725 JERUSALEM 82 * 19
FORGETTING THAT FALSHOOD IS PROPHETIC SHE HID HER HAND . 725 JERUSALEM 82 * 20
BEHIND HER
HE TAKES HIS WAY GIRDING HIMSELF WITH GOLD & IN HIS HAND . 729 JERUSALEM 83 — 77
GWENDOLEN HID IN HER LEFT HAND IT GREW & GREW TILL IT . . 729 JERUSALEM 84 — 32
SILENT AT HIS VOICE THEY VIEW THE RED GLOBE OF FIRE IN . 730 JERUSALEM 85 — 19
LOS'S HAND
SILENT THEY WANDERD HAND IN HAND LIKE TWO INFANTS WANDRING 732 JERUSALEM 86 — 62
I SHALL BE CLOSED FROM THY SIGHT SIEZE THEREFORE IN THY . 732 JERUSALEM 87 — 7
HAND
AND FIRE JERUSALEM TOOK THE CUP WHICH FOAMD IN VALA'S HAND 734 JERUSALEM 88 — 56

	PAGE	TITLE	LINE
HAND (CONTINUED)			
STRUGGLING TO RISE ABOVE THE MOUNTAINS IN HIS BURNING HAND	742	JERUSALEM 95	12
THE UNIVERSAL FATHER THEN ALBION STRETCHD HIS HAND INTO INFINITUDE	744	JERUSALEM 97	6
LAYD HIS HAND ON THE SOUTH & TOOK A BREATHING BOW OF CARVED GOLD	744	JERUSALEM 97	8
LUVAH HIS HAND STRETCHD TO THE EAST	744	JERUSALEM 97	9
AND THE HAND OF MAN GRASPS FIRM BETWEEN THE MALE & FEMALE LOVES	744	JERUSALEM 97	15
AND IN HIS HAND THE SCOURGE SHONE BRIGHT	749	EV GOSPEL(B)/N	47
THAT QUITE UNNERVD [THE ?GUILTY] CAIAPHAS' HAND	752	EV GOSPEL(D)/N *	58
HE LAID HIS HAND ON MOSES' LAW	754	EV GOSPEL(E)/N	11
ON SINAI FELT THE HAND DIVINE	754	EV GOSPEL(E)/N	17
"RESULT" WAS WRIT BY ANOTHER HAND & MIND	783D	ANNO WW POEMS	MARG
[AS MR R SAID HE SHOULD BE BY THEN THE PLATES WERE PUT IN HAND]	790A	LETTER 1	PROSE
. . . BUT SHAKESPEARE IN RIPER YEARS GAVE ME HIS HAND . .	799	TO FLAXMAN/L	6
ON THE ENGRAVINGS I HAVE IN HAND FOR MR H(HAYLEY)	812C	LETTER 22	PROSE
TEMPTATIONS ARE ON THE RIGHT HAND & LEFT	812A	LETTER 22	PROSE
"I SEE A HAND YOU CANNOT SEE THAT BECKONS ME AWAY" . . .	813C	LETTER 22	
AM ALSO GRATEFUL TO THE KIND HAND THAT ENDEAVOURS TO LIFT ME	822C	LETTER 26	PROSE
HAND UPON MY HEAD & GIVES A BLESSING TO ALL MY WORKS .	823B	LETTER 26	PROSE
IN HAND BUT WHO RIDES ABOUT THE PARKS OR SAUNTERS ABOUT	830A	LETTER 30	PROSE
MEDALLION BY YOUR SON'S MATCHLESS HAND WHICH IS PLACED .	836A	LETTER 35	PROSE
OF A FEMALE FIGURE WITH A SERPENT IN ONE HAND & A TORCH IN THE	839C	LETTER 38	PROSE
FOR PRINTING THERE IS NOW IN HAND A NEW EDITION OF . . .	841A	LETTER 40	PROSE
IN HEALTH BUT HAS HAD SUCH A BURN ON HIS HAND AS YOU HAD	842D	LETTER 42	PROSE
AS I FIND BY THE THINGS I HAVE IN HAND DAY & NIGHT WE .	843A	LETTER 42	*PROSE
WHEN HIS DAUGHTER CAME IN HE GAVE THE PRINT INTO HER HAND	843C	LETTER 43	PROSE
WHENEVER I TAKE A PENCIL OR GRAVER INTO MY HAND EVEN AS I	852C	LETTER 50	PROSE
AN ENGRAVING OF COWPER BY THE HAND OF CAROLINE WATSON IS I	859C	LETTER 56	PROSE
TO SEE ANOTHER COPY BY ANOTHER HAND	859C	LETTER 56	PROSE
DEFENCE BUT I SHOULD BE ASHAMED NOT TO SET MY HAND AND .	864A	LETTER 61	PROSE
HOWEVER I AM UPON THE MENDING HAND TO-DAY & HOPE SOON .	880A	LETTER 90	PROSE
HAND (SYMBOLIC NAME)			
HAND IS BECOME A ROCK SINAI & HOREB IS HYLE & COBAN .	501	MILTON 19	7
ALBION'S DREAD SONS HAND HYLE & COBAN SURROUND HIM AS	507	MILTON 23	15
OF HAND & HYLE & COBAN OF KWANTOK PEACHEY BRERETON SLAYD & HUTTON	623	JERUSALEM 5	25
HAND HAS PEOPLED BABEL & NINEVEH HYLE ASHUR & ARAM . .	625	JERUSALEM 7	18
HAND SITS BEFORE HIS FURNACE SCORN OF OTHERS & FURIOUS PRIDE	626	JERUSALEM 7	71
HAND & HYLE & KOBAN SKOFELD KOX & KOTOPE LABOUR MIGHTILY	628	JERUSALEM 8	41
CONDENSD HAND HAS ABSORBD ALL HIS BRETHREN IN HIS MIGHT	628	JERUSALEM 8	43
ALL THE INFANT LOVES & GRACES WERE LOST FOR THE MIGHTY HAND	628	JERUSALEM 8	44
I HEATED IT IN THE FLAMES OF HAND & HYLE & COBAN . . .	628	JERUSALEM 9	21
AND HAND & HYLE ROOTED INTO JERUSALEM BY A FIBRE . . .	635	JERUSALEM 15	1
I PLEASE TELL HAND & SKOFIELD THEY ARE MY MINISTERS OF EVIL	640	JERUSALEM 17	62
SO CRY HAND & HYLE THE ELDEST OF THE FATHERS OF ALBION'S	641	JERUSALEM 18	36
SOON HAND MIGHTILY DEVOURD & ABSORBD ALBION'S TWELVE SONS	641	JERUSALEM 18	39
HAND HYLE & COBAN GUANTOK PEACHEY BRERETON SLAYD & HUTTON	641	JERUSALEM 19	18
HYLE SEES IN FEAR HE HOWLS IN FURY OVER THEM HAND SEES	644	JERUSALEM 21	28
HAND JERUSALEM	649A	JERUSALEM 26	TITLE
IN STERN DEFIANCE CAME FROM ALBION'S BOSOM HAND HYLE KOBAN	658	JERUSALEM 32	10
TO THE SONS OF ALBION & TO HAND THE ELDEST SON OF ALBION	660	JERUSALEM 34	22
HAND ART THOU NOT REUBEN ENROOTING THYSELF INTO BASHAN	661	JERUSALEM 34	36
HAND HYLE & COBAN FLED THEY BECAME WHAT THEY BEHELD	662	JERUSALEM 36	15
HAND STOOD BETWEEN REUBEN & MERLIN AS THE REASONING SPECTRE	663	JERUSALEM 36	23
ALBION REPLIED GO HAND & HYLE SIEZE THE ABHORRED FRIEND	670	JERUSALEM 42	47
AND SHINE GLORIOUS WITHIN HAND & KOBAN ARCHD OVER THE SUN	690	JERUSALEM 58	29
I GAVE THEE HAND & SCOFIELD & THE COUNTIES OF ALBION . .	692	JERUSALEM 60	14
THE WHEEL OF HAND INCESSANT TURNING DAY & NIGHT WITHOUT REST	693	JERUSALEM 60	43
THY SHRIEKS BECAUSE HAND & HYLE ARE CRUEL & OBDURATE TO ME	705	JERUSALEM 67	62
AND THIS THE FORM OF MIGHTY HAND SITTING ON ALBION'S CLIFFS	708	JERUSALEM 70	1
WITH THEIR DISTRICTS HAND DWELT IN SELSEY & HAD SUSSEX & SURREY	709	JERUSALEM 71	11
PALACES RIVERS & MOUNTAINS AND BETWEEN HAND & HYLE AROSE	710	JERUSALEM 71	22
HE HATH TOOK ROOT IN HEBRON IN THE LAND OF HAND & HYLE	715	JERUSALEM 74	49
HAND SLEPT ON SKIDDAW'S TOP DRAWN BY THE LOVE OF BEAUTIFUL	723	JERUSALEM 80	57
TO FORM THE MIGHTY FORM OF HAND ACCORDING TO HER WILL	726	JERUSALEM 82	63
LEST HAND THE TERRIBLE DESTROY HIS AFFECTION THOU HIDEST HER	727	JERUSALEM 83	30
WALKED UP AND DOWN IN ITS GREEN MOUNTAINS BUT HAND IS FLED	729	JERUSALEM 83	86
THE NIGHT FALLS THICK HAND COMES FROM ALBION IN HIS . .	729	JERUSALEM 84	20
STRENGTH			
HAND HAD HIS FURNACE ON HIGHGATE'S HEIGHTS & IT REACHD	736	JERUSALEM 90	23
WHILE IN SELFHOOD HAND & HYLE & BOWEN & SKOFELD APPROPRIATE	737	JERUSALEM 90	40
WHILE HAND & HYLE CONDENSE THE LITTLE-ONES & ERECT THEM INTO	737	JERUSALEM 90	49
HANDEL'S			
LET'S HAVE HANDEL'S WATERPIECE THEN SIPSOP SUNG	62B	ISLAND MOON 11	PROSE
HANDKERCHER			
AND TO CLEAN IT WITH MY HANDKERCHER	61	SAY YOU JOE/IM	7
HANDKERCHIEF			
WIPED HIS [HEAD] FACE WITH HIS POCKET HANDKERCHIEF . . .	45B	ISLAND MOON 1	PROSE
GIBBLE GABBLE LEND ME YOUR HANDKERCHIEF TILLY LALLY . . .	58C	ISLAND MOON 10	PROSE
TILLY LALLY TOOK OUT HIS HANDKERCHIEF	58D	ISLAND MOON 10	PROSE
HANDLE			
HE DOES NOT KNOW HOW TO HANDLE A BAT	61	SAY YOU JOE/IM	12

		PAGE	TITLE	LINE

HANDLING

    HANDLING IS ALL THAT HE HAS & WE ALL KNOW THIS HANDLING   468D ANNO REYNOLDS   MARG
    IS

HANDS

Entry	PAGE	TITLE	LINE
WALKING FEELING THE COLD WALLS WITH HER HANDS	4	FAIR ELENOR/PS	12
DOWN ON HIS HANDS AND KNEES HE LAY	16	BLIND-MANS/PS	47
SHAKE HANDS WITH DEATH AND STRIKE A BARGAIN FOR	22	EDW THIRD/PS 3	29
BY HIM WHOM I AM BOUND TO OBEY MY HANDS	23	EDW THIRD/PS 3	101
TH ANGEL OF FATE TURNS THEM WITH MIGHTY HANDS	34	WAR SONG/PS	3
STRETCH FORTH YOUR HANDS THAT MY HELPER MAY COME	36A	COUCH DEATH/PS	PROSE
THY YOUNG HANDS TORE HUMAN LIMBS AND GORGED HUMAN FLESH	38B	SAMSON/PS	PROSE
MY JOY IS GIVEN INTO THE HANDS OF HIM WHO HATES ME	38D	SAMSON/PS	PROSE
BUT O COULD I AT ENVY SHAKE MY HANDS	41D	THEN SHE BORE	PROSE
AND RAN ABOUT WITH BLOODY HANDS	50	WHEN CORRUP/IM	15
THOUSANDS OF LITTLE GIRLS & BOYS RAISING THEIR INNOCENT HANDS	59	HOLY THURS/IM	9
SO SAYING HE BEGAN TO DIG A GRAVE WITH HIS AGED HANDS	100	TIRIEL 1	34
[HIS LITTLE HANDS INTO THE DEPTHS OF THE SEA TO BRING FORTH]	110	TIRIEL 8	21
WHEN HE LICKS THEIR HANDS	114	LIT GRL FND/SI	31
THOUSANDS OF LITTLE BOYS & GIRLS RAISING THEIR INNOCENT HANDS	122	HOLY THURS/SI	8
HIS FEET AND HANDS CUT OFF AND HIS EYES BLINDED	136	FRENCH REVOLTN	44
. . . ON HIS HANDS AND KNEES DAY AND NIGHT WITHOUT REST	136	FRENCH REVOLTN	46
HANDS HEAD BOSOM AND PARTS OF LOVE FOLLOW THEIR HIGH BREATHING JOY	142	FRENCH REVOLTN	185
THE GENITALS BEAUTY THE HANDS & FEET PROPORTION	152C	MARRIAGE HH 10	PROSE
IN HER TREMBLING HANDS SHE TOOK THE NEW BORN TERROR HOWLING	159B	SONG LIBERTY	PROSE
STRUGGLING IN MY FATHER'S HANDS	166	INFANT SORW/N	5
IN [HIS HAND] [THEIR] HANDS A HOLY BOOK	167	INFANT SORW/N *	27
[BUT SHAKE HANDS & KISS HIM & THERED BE NO MORE HELL]	180	LIT VAGABOND/N	17
HEADS DEPREST VOICES WEAK EYES DOWNCAST HANDS WORK-BRUISD	197	AMERICA 3	10
HEADS DEPREST VOICES WEAK EYES DOWNCAST HANDS WORK BRUISED	204	AMERICA CANC A	10
BY REBELS' HANDS WAS SLAIN HIS WHITE BEARD WAVD IN THE WILD WIND	205	AMERICA CANC C	27
STRUGGLING IN MY FATHER'S HANDS	217	INFANT SORW/SE	5
IN HIS HANDS HE SIEZD THE INFANT	233	URIZEN 20	3
STRETCH FORTH YOUR HANDS AND STRIKE THE ELEMENTAL STRINGS	239	EUROPE 4	13
BY THE HANDS OF THE CHILDREN OF LOS	245	SONG OF LOS 3	9
URIZEN WEPT & GAVE IT INTO THE HANDS OF NEWTON & LOCKE	246	SONG OF LOS 4	17
THEY STOOD WIDE APART DRIVN BY HIS HANDS	257	BOOK OF LOS 3	46
WOVEN BY THEIR OWN HANDS TO HIDE THEM IN THE DARKSOM GRAVE	266	FOUR ZOAS 1	65
AS GARMENTS WOVEN SUBSERVIENT TO HER HANDS BUT HAVING A WILL	266	FOUR ZOAS 1	84
THEN ENITHARMON REDDNING FIERCE STRETCHD HER IMMORTAL HANDS	272	FOUR ZOAS 1	307
SAYING THOU ART THE LORD OF LUVAH INTO THINE HANDS I GIVE	273	FOUR ZOAS 1	324
THE PRINCE OF LOVE THE MURDERER HIS SOUL IN THINE HANDS	273	FOUR ZOAS 1	325
STRETCH THEIR IMMORTAL HANDS TO SMITE THE GOLD & SILVER WIRES	274	FOUR ZOAS 1	380
I WILL REMAIN AS WELL AS THOU & HERE WITH HANDS OF BLOOD	278	FOUR ZOAS 1	512
THE WORKMANSHIP OF LUVAH'S HANDS IN TIMES OF EVERLASTING	282	FOUR ZOAS 2	82
[RAISE THEN THY RADIANT EYES TO HIM RAISE THY OBEDIENT HANDS]	292	FOUR ZOAS 3	28
TO GIVE THE IMMORTAL STEEDS OF LIGHT TO HIS DECEITFUL HANDS	292	FOUR ZOAS 3	32
THARMAS REARD UP HIS HANDS & STOOD ON THE AFFRIGHTED OCEAN	296	FOUR ZOAS 3	160
A UNIVERSE OF DEATH & DECAY LET ENITHARMON'S HANDS	298	FOUR ZOAS 4	28
WHEN URIZEN GAVE THE HORSES OF LIGHT INTO THE HANDS OF LUVAH	300	FOUR ZOAS 4	113
THEN LOS WITH TERRIBLE HANDS SIEZD ON THE RUIND FURNACES	301	FOUR ZOAS 4	165
HER PALE HANDS CLING AROUND HER HUSBAND & OVER HER WEAK HEAD	305	FOUR ZOAS 5	21
FADED HE ROUZD HE SIEZD THE WONDER IN HIS HANDS & WENT	307	FOUR ZOAS 5	68
HIS UNCOUTH PLAGUE HE SIEZD THE BOY IN HIS IMMORTAL HANDS	307	FOUR ZOAS 5	97
BUT STILL HIS BOOKS HE BORE IN HIS STRONG HANDS & HIS IRON PEN	316	FOUR ZOAS 6	167
. . . MY FEET & HANDS ARE NAILD TO THE BURNING ROCK	322	FOUR ZOAS 7	71
I RAGE FURIOUS IN THE DEEP FOR LO MY FEET & HANDS ARE NAILD	322	FOUR ZOAS 7	87
OF ELETH & THE ICY HANDS OF UVETH KNEADED THE BREAD	322	FOUR ZOAS 7	102
THE HEAVENS BOW WITH TERROR UNDERNEATH THEIR IRON HANDS	322	FOUR ZOAS 7	103
SO ENITHARMON SPOKE & LOS HIS HANDS DIVINE INSPIRED BEGAN	331	FOUR ZOAS 7 *	456
IN HIS HANDS HE WONDERD THAT HE FELT LOVE & NOT HATE	332	FOUR ZOAS 7	497
THIS UNIVERSAL ?ORNAMENT IS MINE & IN MY HANDS	333	FOUR ZOAS 7B *	5
INTO HIS HANDS THEN ENITHARMON ERECTED LOOMS IN LUBAN'S GATE	342	FOUR ZOAS 8	36
COVERD & SCALES HIS HANDS & FEET UPON HIS BELLY FALLING	352	FOUR ZOAS 8	425
FOR SUCH THEY DEEMD THE DEATH OF THE BODY LOS HIS VEGETABLE HANDS	357	FOUR ZOAS 9	6
URIZEN GAVE THE HORSES OF LIGHT INTO THE HANDS OF LUVAH	359	FOUR ZOAS 9	94
BUT I THE LABOURER OF AGES WHOSE UNWEARIED HANDS	361	FOUR ZOAS 9	174
IN SILKEN GARMENTS SPUN BY HER OWN HANDS AGAINST HER FUNERAL	362	FOUR ZOAS 9	213
ON WINGS OF TENFOLD JOY CLAPPING HIS HANDS HIS FEET HIS RADIANT WINGS	366	FOUR ZOAS 9	348
HIS HOLY HANDS RECIEVD THE FLAMING DEMON & DEMONESS OF SMOKE	366	FOUR ZOAS 9	361
AND GAVE THEM TO URIZEN'S HANDS THE IMMORTAL FROWND SAYING	366	FOUR ZOAS 9	362
AND WALKD FROM THE HANDS OF URIZEN IN THE SHADOWS OF VALA'S GARDEN	367	FOUR ZOAS 9	376
THEN VALA LIFTED UP HER HANDS TO HEAVEN TO CALL ON ENION	370	FOUR ZOAS 9	498
THEN SHALL THEY LIFT THEIR INNOCENT HANDS & STROKE HIS FURIOUS NOSE	376	FOUR ZOAS 9	703
VOMITED OUT & GAVE UP ALL THE FLOODS LIFT UP THEIR HANDS	378	FOUR ZOAS 9	803

		PAGE	TITLE	LINE

HANDS   (CONTINUED)
FOOLISH & TELLS INTO THE HANDS OF A TYRANT [WHO ?WILL XXX   400B ANNO BACON   * MARG
   HARM]
WITH HANDS DIVINE HE MOVD THE GENTLE SOD . . . .   414 TO MRS FLAXMAN   7
HIS HANDS & FEET WERE WOUNDED WIDE . . . .   419 I SAW A MONK/N   16
SHE PIERCES BOTH HIS HANDS & FEET . . . .   425 MENTAL TRAVLER   14
WITH ARDOR FIERCE & HANDS OF FLAME . . . .   429 CRYSTL CABINET   22
HIS HANDS & FEET WERE WOUNDED WIDE . . . .   430 GREY MONK   6
TOOLS WERE MADE & BORN WERE HANDS . . . .   432 AUGURIES   65
ONE MITE WRUNG FROM THE LABRER'S HANDS . . . .   432 AUGURIES   81
BY ANGELS FROM THE HANDS OF ANOTHER [AGED] APOSTLE . . .   444B LAST JUDGMNT/L   PROSE
PRESUMPTIONS THAT THEY ARE THE WORK OF SEVERAL HANDS . .   449B ANNO REYNOLDS   MARG
IN GAINSBOROUGH'S HANDS IT WOULD BE A VULGAR SUBJECT . .   465D ANNO REYNOLDS   MARG
IN THE HANDS OF PALAMABRON WHERE THE STARRY MILLS OF SATAN   483 MILTON 4   2
AND I BE SIEZD & GIVN INTO THE HANDS OF MY OWN SELFHOOD   495 MILTON 14   24
STRETCHD OUT HIS HANDS OF FIRE & WOOED THEY TRIUMPH IN   500 MILTON 18   45
   HIS PAIN
THEY BECAME NATIONS IN OUR SIGHT BENEATH THE HANDS   508 MILTON 24   16
   OF TIRZAH
ANTAMON TAKES THEM INTO HIS BEAUTIFUL FLEXIBLE HANDS . .   515 MILTON 28   13
THE SOFT HANDS OF ANTAMON DRAW THE INDELIBLE LINE . . .   515 MILTON 28   16
ALL ARE THE WORK OF FAIRY HANDS OF THE FOUR ELEMENTS . .   516 MILTON 28   60
A RUIND MAN A RUIND BUILDING OF GOD NOT MADE WITH HANDS   529 MILTON 38   16
DELICATE HANDS & HEADS WILL NEVER APPEAR . . . . . .   551 DELICATE/N   1
WILL BE SOLD ONLY ON CONDITION OF ITS REMAINING IN THE   563B DESC CAT   PROSE
   ARTIST'S HANDS
THE BRITISH ANTIQUITIES ARE NOW IN THE ARTIST'S HANDS . .   577D DESC CAT 5   PROSE
AND UGLINESS MR B(BLAKE) HAS IN HIS HANDS POEMS OF THE . .   578A DESC CAT 5   PROSE
THAT INFERNAL MACHINE CALLED CHIARO OSCURO IN THE HANDS OF   582C DESC CAT 9   PROSE
NOT BY THE HANDS OF JOURNEYMEN BUT BY THE ORIGINAL . . .   588A CHAUCER/N   PROSE
ON ALL HANDS ACKNOWLEDGD IT ONLY REMAINS TO BE CERTIFIED   591C PUB ADDRESS/N   PROSE
[ART BY THE HANDS OF IGNORANT JOURNEYMEN] . . . . . .   595B PUB ADDRESS/N   PROSE
RUBENS'S LUXEMBOURG GALLERY IS CONFESSD ON ALL HANDS . .   599C PUB ADDRESS/N   *PROSE
IS ALLOWD ON ALL HANDS TO BE THE PRODUCTION OF A MAN . .   599D PUB ADDRESS/N   *PROSE
[CLLLLLNNN AOOJLMM ALL ALLS HANDS BRITISH ALLS WWWNDJ   601A PUB ADDRESS/N   *PROSE
   BLUUUU]
MY CONCEPTION & INVENTION ARE ON ALL HANDS ALLOWD . . .   601D PUB ADDRESS/N   PROSE
PILATE HAS BLOODY HANDS THAT NEVER CAN BE CLEANSED . .   608D V LAST JUDG/N   PROSE
WITH ITS LUSTS THE WREATHED TORCHES IN THEIR HANDS . .   609A V LAST JUDG/N   PROSE
THAT THE SPECTATOR WILL ATTEND TO THE HANDS & FEET . .   611B V LAST JUDG/N   PROSE
IN WHICH YOUTHFUL NUPTIALS RECIEVE THE INFANTS IN THEIR   613D V LAST JUDG/N   PROSE
   HANDS
LABOUR OF MERCIFUL HANDS THE BEAMS & RAFTERS ARE   632 JERUSALEM 12   32
   FORGIVENESS
ITS GUARDS LIVING THE WORK OF ELEMENTAL HANDS LABORIOUS   633 JERUSALEM 13   7
   TASK
THY SONS HAVE NAILD ME ON THE GATES PIERCING MY HANDS &   644 JERUSALEM 22   2
   FEET
WITH BLESSINGS ON THEIR HANDS & ON THEIR FEET BLESSINGS   647 JERUSALEM 24   39
   OF GOLD
THE HUMAN HANDS & FEET & BREATH . . . .   651 FIELDS FROM/J   62
THE TWENTY-EIGHT CITIES OF ALBION STRETCH THEIR HANDS TO   656 JERUSALEM 30   26
   THEE
PRODUCING MANY HEADS THREE OR SEVEN OR TEN & HANDS & FEET   659 JERUSALEM 33   22
HIS FACE AND BOSOM WITH PETRIFIC HARDNESS AND HIS HANDS   664 JERUSALEM 38   1
BOUND THESE BLACK SHOES OF DEATH & ON MY HANDS DEATH'S   666 JERUSALEM 39   21
   IRON GLOVES
PERHAPS HE MAY RECIEVE THEM OFFERD FROM THY LOVED HANDS   675 JERUSALEM 45   32
HEREFORD ANCIENT GUARDIAN OF WALES WHOSE HANDS . . . .   676 JERUSALEM 46   3
BEHELD HER WITH WONDER WITH AWFUL HANDS SHE TOOK . . . .   678 JERUSALEM 48   30
HIS HANDS & FEET WERE WOUNDED WIDE . . . .   683 I SAW A MONK/J   14
THE SEAS RAISD UP THEIR VOICES & LIFTED THEIR HANDS ON HIGH   686 JERUSALEM 55   26
MADDENS IN THE FURY OF THEIR HANDS WEAVING IN BITTER TEARS   692 JERUSALEM 59   54
THE INFANT INTO HER HANDS IN THE VISIONS OF JEHOVAH TIMES   695 JERUSALEM 61   48
   PASSED ON
AND THE DISTAFF & SPINDLE IN THE HANDS OF VALA WITH THE   699 JERUSALEM 64   32
   FLAX OF
IN THE HANDS OF ALBION'S DAUGHTERS AMONG THE DRUID TEMPLES   703 JERUSALEM 66   84
SHOUT IN THE NIGHT OF BATTLE & THEIR SPEARS GROW TO THEIR   704 JERUSALEM 67   32
   HANDS
HIS IMMORTAL CHEEKS REARING HIS HANDS TO HEAVEN FOR AID   711 JERUSALEM 71   57
   DIVINE
I HAVE NAILD HIS HANDS ON BETH RABBIM & HIS (FEET)   726 JERUSALEM 82   * 43
   ON HESHBON'S WALL
THE WEEDS OF DEATH INWRAP HIS HANDS & FEET BLOWN INCESSANT   741 JERUSALEM 94   5
A NATION I HEAR THAT IT IS NOW IN THE HANDS OF MINISTERS   797D LETTER 10   PROSE
WHICH I HAVE NEARLY COMPLETED IN THE MEAN TIME BY   808D LETTER 20   PROSE
   MY SISTER'S HANDS
& I FIND ON ALL HANDS GREAT OBJECTIONS TO MY DOING ANY   812C LETTER 22   PROSE
   THING
MY HANDS ARE LABOURD DAY & NIGHT . . . .   818 HAPPINESS/L   59
A GOOD LIKENESS OF YOU IF I HAVE HANDS & EYES LEFT . . .   824B LETTER 27   PROSE
IN WANT OF HANDS OTHER ENGRAVERS ARE COURTED I SUPPOSE . .   829D LETTER 30   PROSE
SUCH HANDS THE PICTURE FROM STERNE WHICH YOU DESIRED . .   835D LETTER 35   PROSE
AS THE TRAGIC MUSE HALF-LENGTH THAT IS THE HEAD & HANDS   836A LETTER 35   PROSE
ENGRAVED BY THE HANDS OF ANGELS & MUST NOT BY ANY MEANS   848C LETTER 45   PROSE
THE PLEASURE OF SEEING ANOTHER POEM FROM YOUR HANDS HAS   851D LETTER 50   PROSE
INTO MY HANDS AS I USED TO BE IN MY YOUTH I HAVE INDEED   853A LETTER 51   *PROSE
AS I KNOW THAT YOU WILL DO WHAT IS RIGHT ON ALL HANDS . .   861B LETTER 58   PROSE
RECIEVED...OF MRS ADERS BY THE HANDS OF MR LINNELL THE SUM   SUPP LETTER 80A   *PROSE
HANDSOM
CHICHESTER IS A VERY HANDSOM CITY SEVEN MILES FROM US . .   806B LETTER 16   PROSE

HANDSOME
    ELOQUENT AMOROUS WITTY AND SATYRICAL YOUNG HANDSOME AND   568D DESC CAT 3   PROSE
      RICH
    AND IS A VERY HANDSOME STREET AND THE NARROW PART OF THE   831D LETTER 31   PROSE
    CONSIDERS AS IMPOLITIC AND THAT A HANDSOME GENERAL EDITION 858A LETTER 55   PROSE
HANDSOMER
    ARE GENUINE SAXONS HANDSOMER THAN THE PEOPLE [AR] ABOUT   806B LETTER 16   *PROSE
      LONDON
HANDSOMEST
    ON ONE OF THE STRONGEST & HANDSOMEST BUILT STAGES I EVER   871C LETTER 73   PROSE
      SAW
HANG
    BLOSSOMS HANG ROUND THE BROWS OF MORNING AND . . . . .   2 TO AUTUMN/PS   9
    PHO NONSENSE HANG PHAROH & ALL HIS HOST SAID THE   47C ISLAND MOON 3   PROSE
      PYTHAGOREAN
    HANG NAMES SAID THE PYTHAGOREAN WHATS PHAROH BETTER THAN   47D ISLAND MOON 4   PROSE
      PHEBUS
    OR PHEBUS THAN PHAROH HANG THEM BOTH SAID THE CYNIC . . .   47D ISLAND MOON 4   PROSE
    HANG PHAROH AH SAID MRS SINAGAIN . . . .   48A ISLAND MOON 4 *PROSE
    & HANG THE MATHEMATICS COME ARADOBO SAY SOME THING . . .   49B ISLAND MOON 5   PROSE
    AH HANG YOUR REASONING SAID THE EPICUREAN . . . . . .   50A ISLAND MOON 6   PROSE
    HANG THAT SAID SUCTION LET US HAVE A SONG . . . . . .   50B ISLAND MOON 6   PROSE
    I'LL BE HANGD SAID SUCTION HANG PHILOSOPHY . . . . . .   51D ISLAND MOON 7   PROSE
    HANG YOUR VIOLETS HERES YOUR RUM & WATER [SWEETER] . .   55B ISLAND MOON 9 *PROSE
    HANG YOUR SERIOUS SONGS SAID SIPSOP & HE SUNG AS FOLLOWS   56A ISLAND MOON 9   PROSE
    HANG ITALIAN SONGS LET'S HAVE ENGLISH SAID QUID . . . .   56A ISLAND MOON 9   PROSE
    HANG SAID TILLY LALLY . . . .   58D ISLAND MOON 10 PROSE
    BUT THAT I FEEL THEY WILL CURSE THEE & HANG UPON THY BONES 108 TIRIEL 6   37
    & RED GILLS HANG JUST ABOVE THE RAGING FOAM . . . . . 156C MARRIAGE HH 17 PROSE
    WHERE URIZEN & ALL HIS HOSTS HANG THEIR IMMORTAL LAMPS .   272 FOUR ZOAS 1   304
    THEY BEAR THE WOVEN DRAPERIES ON GOLDEN HOOKS THEY HANG   284 FOUR ZOAS 2   152
      ABROAD
    TO HANG UPON THE BRANCHES FINE . . . .   422 BENEATH/N   11
    TO HANG UPON THE BRANCHES FINE . . . .   424 THE GOLDEN NET   10
    & HANG THEIR SOULS AS GUILTY OF MENTAL HIGH TREASON . . 599D PUB ADDRESS/N PROSE
    FOR BACON & NEWTON SHEATHD IN DISMAL STEEL THEIR TERRORS   635 JERUSALEM 15   11
      HANG
    NOW FOR IT WILL HANG HEAVY ON MY DEVIL WHO TERRIBLY RESENTS 830C LETTER 30   PROSE
HANGD
    SAID INFLAMMABLE GASS ID SEE THE PARSONS ALL HANGD A PARCEL 48A ISLAND MOON 4   PROSE
      OF LYING
    I'LL BE HANGD SAID SUCTION HANG PHILOSOPHY . . . . .   51D ISLAND MOON 7   PROSE
    AND NEVER THINK AT ALL ABOUT IT IM HANGD IF I DONT GET UP   51D ISLAND MOON 7   PROSE
HANGED
    [I NONE OF] GO & BE HANGED SAID SCOPPREL . . . . . .   57A ISLAND MOON 9 *PROSE
    AND WOULD HAVE ME HANGED IF HE COULD HE SPOKE . . . . . 437B BLAKES MEMORAN PROSE
HANGING
    [AND SAID I LOVE HANGING & DRAWING & QUARTERING] . . . . 185 LET BROTHELS/N   11
    HANGING FROWNING CLIFFS & ALL BETWEEN . . . .   225 URIZEN 5   10
    HANGING UPON THE WIND . . . .   229 URIZEN 11   27
    WITH DISMAL TORMENT SICK HANGING UPON THE WIND HE FLED . . 242 EUROPE 12   18
    IN GHASTLY TORMENT SICK HANGING UPON THE WIND . . . .   303 FOUR ZOAS 4   236
    HANGING UPON THE WIND TWO NOSTRILS BENT DOWN INTO THE DEEP 482 MILTON 3   20
HANGMAN
    ("SPEAKS SOFTLY AND WRITES SHARPLY") AH ROGUE I COULD BE   83B ANNO LAVATER   MARG
      THY HANGMAN
HANGS
    AND JEWEL HANGS AT TH SHEPHERD'S NOSE . . . .   15 BLIND-MANS/PS   2
    AND JEWEL HANGS AT SHEPHERD'S NOSE . . . .   64 SHEPHERD OLD   2
    AND [HANGS] SMITES WITH PLAGUES THE MARRIAGE HEARSE . . . 170 LONDON/N   21
    TILL HIS EYES SICKEN AT THE FRUIT THAT HANGS BEFORE HIS   194 V DAU ALBION 7   20
      SIGHT
    TO WHERE MY BOWER HANGS ON HIGH . . . .   423 THE BIRDS/N   18
HANGST
    THOU HANGST A DRIED SKIN SHRUNK UP WEAK WAILING IN THE WIND 313 FOUR ZOAS 6   71
HANNALITOE
    [LAURELLLO AFFFFSW ALLLLLL HANNALITOE WW BMILLLJJJ HORSES] 601A PUB ADDRESS/N *PROSE
HANTS
    HYLE DWELT IN WINCHESTER COMPREHENDING HANTS DORSET DEVON   710 JERUSALEM 71   20
      CORNWALL
    SUSSEX SHUTS UP HER VILLAGES HANTS DEVON & WILTS . . . . 727 JERUSALEM 83   9
HAPLESS
    O LAND MOST HAPLESS O BEAUTEOUS ISLAND HOW FORSAKEN . .   34A KING JOHN/PS PROSE
    AND THE HAPLESS SOLDIER'S SIGH . . . .   170 LONDON/N   12
    AND THE HAPLESS SOLDIER'S SIGH . . . .   216 LONDON/SE   11
HAPPEN
    SUCH A THING SHALL HAPPEN LET YOU DO WHAT YOU WILL . . . 392B ANNO WATSON   MARG
    LAME REASONING UPON PREMISES THIS NEVER CAN HAPPEN . . . 399C ANNO BACON   MARG
    PERISHING LIFE IT DOES BUT SELDOM HAPPEN BUT WITH THIS . 579D DESC CAT 5   PROSE
    WITH EVERY PATHETIC STORY POSSIBLE TO HAPPEN FROM HATE OR   638 JERUSALEM 16   63
    ALL THAT CAN HAPPEN TO MAN IN HIS PILGRIMAGE OF SEVENTY   638 JERUSALEM 16   67
      YEARS
HAPPEND
    THE FOLLOWING AFFAIRS HAPPEND . . . .   58C ISLAND MOON 10 PROSE
    ALL THAT HAPPEND AT THE GATE OF THE INN WHO EVIDENCES THAT 827C LETTER 28   PROSE
HAPPENS
    SO AS IT ALWAYS HAPPENS AND NOT IN THAT DULL WAY THAT SOME 578D DESC CAT 5   PROSE
    GOOD SENSE AS SHE OBSERVES THAT WHENEVER A QUARREL HAPPENS 827C LETTER 28   PROSE
HAPPIER
    WHEN THE SHATTERD BONE HATH LAID HIM GROANING AMONG THE   291 FOUR ZOAS 2   416
      HAPPIER DEAD
    NOW LOST OR PERHAPS BURIED TILL SOME HAPPIER AGE THE . . 565C DESC CAT 2   PROSE

		PAGE	TITLE	LINE

HAPPIER   (CONTINUED)
THE PLAYER IS A LIAR WHEN HE SAYS ANGELS ARE HAPPIER   . . 616D V LAST JUDG/N   PROSE
ANGELS ARE HAPPIER THAN MEN & DEVILS BECAUSE   . . . . . 616D V LAST JUDG/N   PROSE
HAPPINESS
THOSE WHO WANT HAPPINESS MUST STOOP TO FIND IT   . . . . 37A CONTEMPLATN/PS   PROSE
SAYS JEROME HAPPINESS IS NOT FOR US POOR CRAWLING REPTILES   52B ISLAND MOON 8   PROSE
OF THE EARTH [?TALK] TALK OF HAPPINESS   . . . . 52B ISLAND MOON 8   *PROSE
& HAPPINESS ITS NO SUCH THING EVERY PERSON HAS AS SOMETHING   52B ISLAND MOON 8   PROSE
IN HAPPINESS COMPARD WITH YE   . . . . 54 PHEBE DREST/IM   10
SEES YOUR HAPPINESS COMPLEAT   . . . . 54 PHEBE DREST/IM   12
WITH WHOM I LIVD IN HAPPINESS BEFORE THAT DEADLY NIGHT   . . 300 FOUR ZOAS 4   112
BUT HAPPINESS CAN NEVER TO THEE O KING NOR ME   . . . . 345 FOUR ZOAS 8   167
IT IS IN PARTICULARS THAT WISDOM CONSISTS & HAPPINESS TOO   611B V LAST JUDG/N   PROSE
SETH IS MALE & FEMALE IN A HIGHER STATE OF HAPPINESS   . . 611C V LAST JUDG/N   PROSE
TEACH THEM TRUE HAPPINESS BUT LET NO CURSE   . . . . . 718 STOOD AMONG/J   32
THAT PEACE & PLENTY & DOMESTIC HAPPINESS IS THE SOURCE   790D LETTER 2   PROSE
    OF SUBLIME ART
& SERENITY & HAPPINESS & BEAUTY A CAUSE OF MALEVOLENCE   . . 793B LETTER 5   PROSE
& HAPPINESS IS BETTER THAN MIRTH   . . . . 793C LETTER 5   PROSE
OF WHAT ALL FEEL IN THIS VALLEY OF MISERY & HAPPINESS MIXED   797A LETTER 9   PROSE
HAPPINESS IT IS TO YOU I OWE PERHAPS THE PRINCIPAL   799A LETTER 11   PROSE
    HAPPINESS
IN AN INCREASE OF FAMILY & OF HEALTH & HAPPINESS   . . . . 810A LETTER 20   PROSE
NEXT TIME I HAVE THE HAPPINESS TO SEE YOU I AM   . . . 810B LETTER 20   PROSE
WITH HAPPINESS STRETCHD ACROSS THE HILLS   . . . . . . 816 HAPPINESS/L   1
THIS EARTH BREEDS NOT OUR HAPPINESS   . . . . 818 HAPPINESS/L   64
I WISH HER A CONTINUED EXCESS OF HAPPINESS SOME SAY THAT   830C LETTER 30   PROSE
HAPPINESS IS NOT GOOD FOR MORTALS & THEY OUGHT TO   830C LETTER 30   PROSE
    BE ANSWERD
IN THE MEANTIME I HAVE THE HAPPINESS OF SEEING   . . . . 845B LETTER 44   PROSE
FOR O HAPPINESS NEVER ENOUGH TO BE GRATEFUL FOR   . . . 853A LETTER 51   *PROSE
HAPPINESS DESIRING TO BE PARTICULARLY REMEMBERD BY YOU   . 862A LETTER 59   PROSE
HAPPINESS IS SECURE IN JESUS OUR LORD & WHO LOOKS FOR   . 862D LETTER 60   PROSE
HOPING THAT I MAY MEET YOU AGAIN IN PERFECT HEALTH   868B LETTER 67   PROSE
    & HAPPINESS
THAT HE IS DEPRIVED OF THE HAPPINESS OF VISITING AGAIN &   SUPP LETTER 81A   *PROSE
[?FIRST ?WERE CREATED WINE & (HAPPINESS) ?GOOD ?LOOKS &   SUPP ANNO REYNOLDS   * MARG
    ?FORTUNE XXX]
HAPPINESSES
A FOOLISH EXPERIMENT HAPPINESSES HAVE WINGS AND WHEELS   . 807A LETTER 17   PROSE
HAPPY   SEE EVER HAPPY ONCE HAPPY
MOST HAPPY HAVING SUCH COMMAND THE MAN   . . . . 23 EDW THIRD/PS 3   78
HAPPY PEOPLE WHO CAN BE   . . . . 54 PHEBE DREST/IM   9
THUS THESE HAPPY ISLANDERS SPENT THEIR TIME   . . . . . 58B ISLAND MOON 10   PROSE
TO BE EXCENTRIC IF HE CREATES O HAPPY PHILOSOPHER   . . . 81C ANNO LAVATER   * MARG
THEY ENTERD ON THE MOUNTAINS OF HAR AT NOON THE HAPPY TENTS   109 TIRIEL 7   19
DROP THY PIPE THY HAPPY PIPE   . . . . 111 INTRODUCTN/SI   9
SING THY SONGS OF HAPPY CHEAR   . . . . 111 INTRODUCTN/SI   10
AND I WROTE MY HAPPY SONGS   . . . . 111 INTRODUCTN/SI   19
A HAPPY BLOSSOM   . . . . 115 THE BLOSSOM/SI
A HAPPY BLOSSOM   . . . . 116 THE BLOSSOM/SI   9
AND MAKE HAPPY THE SKIES   . . . . 116 ECCHOING GR/SI   2
THO THE MORNING WAS COLD TOM WAS HAPPY & WARM   . . . . 118 CHIMNEY SWP/SI   23
I HAPPY AM   . . . . 118 INFANT JOY/SI   4
FAREWELL GREEN FIELDS AND HAPPY GROVES   . . . . 119 NIGHT/SI   9
BY HAPPY SILENT MOONY BEAMS   . . . . 120 CRADLE SONG/SI   4
HOVER OER MY HAPPY CHILD   . . . . 120 CRADLE SONG/SI   8
SLEEP SLEEP HAPPY CHILD   . . . . 120 CRADLE SONG/SI   17
SLEEP SLEEP HAPPY SLEEP   . . . . 120 CRADLE SONG/SI   19
. . . OR GOD WEEP WHEN HIS CHILDREN ARE HAPPY   . . . . 142 FRENCH REVOLTN   186
. . . AND THE HAPPY EARTH SING IN ITS COURSE   . . . . 144 FRENCH REVOLTN   236
IF ALL WERE AS HAPPY AS WE   . . . . 164 HEARD ANGEL/N   14
IF ALL WERE AS HAPPY AS WE   . . . . 174 HUMAN IMAGE/N   5
AND WE'D BE AS HAPPY AS BIRDS IN THE SPRING   . . . . . 179 LIT VAGABOND/N   11
HIS CHILDREN AS PLEASANT & HAPPY AS HE   . . . . 180 LIT VAGABOND/N   15
BECAUSE I WAS HAPPY UPON THE HEATH   . . . . 180 CHIMNEY SWP/N   5
AND BECAUSE I AM HAPPY & DANCE & SING   . . . . 180 CHIMNEY SWP/N   9
A HAPPY FLY   . . . . 183 THE FLY/N   22
[AND SOLD IS THY HAPPY MORROW]   . . . . 186 LET BROTHELS/N   57
INFANCY FEARLESS LUSTFUL HAPPY NESTLING FOR DELIGHT   . . . 193 V DAU ALBION 6   4
IN HAPPY COPULATION IF IN EVENING MILD WEARIED WITH WORK   . 194 V DAU ALBION 7   1
I CRY LOVE LOVE LOVE HAPPY HAPPY LOVE FREE AS   194 V DAU ALBION 7   16
    THE MOUNTAIN WIND
BECAUSE I WAS HAPPY UPON THE HEATH   . . . . 212 CHIMNEY SWP/SE   5
AND BECAUSE I AM HAPPY & DANCE & SING   . . . . 212 CHIMNEY SWP/SE   9
A HAPPY FLY   . . . . 213 THE FLY/SE   18
AND WE'D BE AS HAPPY AS BIRDS IN THE SPRING   . . . . . 216 LIT VAGABND/SE   10
HIS CHILDREN AS PLEASANT AND HAPPY AS HE   . . . . . . 216 LIT VAGABND/SE   14
IF ALL WERE AS HAPPY AS WE   . . . . 217 HUMAN ABSTR/SE   4
WHEN HE GAVE MY HAPPY SOUL   . . . . 254 AHANIA 5   15
TO MAKE US HAPPY [HOW THEY] LET THEM WEARY THEIR IMMORTAL   271 FOUR ZOAS 1   254
    POWERS
AH HAPPY BLINDNESS [SHE] ENION SEES NOT THE TERRORS OF   290 FOUR ZOAS 2   * 385
    THE UNCERTAIN
WERE NOW NOT VOCAL AS IN CLIMES OF HAPPY ETERNITY   . . . 315 FOUR ZOAS 6   135
WITH LABOUR & ABSTINENCE SAY HE LOOKS HEALTHY & HAPPY   . . 323 FOUR ZOAS 7   119
TO REUNITE IN THOSE MILD FIELDS OF HAPPY ETERNITY   . . . 326 FOUR ZOAS 7   270
. . . THERE THEY SLEEP IN HAPPY OBSCURITY   . . . . 331 FOUR ZOAS 7   438
THE WATRY GRAVE O THOU CORN FIELD O THOU VEGETATER HAPPY   . 355 FOUR ZOAS 8   543
MORE HAPPY IS THE DARK CONSUMER HOPE DROWNS ALL MY TORMENT   355 FOUR ZOAS 8   544
. . . WHERE DOST THOU SEEK THY HAPPY PLACE   . . . . . 367 FOUR ZOAS 9   * 401
SING A NEW SONG DROWNING CONFUSION IN ITS HAPPY NOTES   . . 375 FOUR ZOAS 9   683

	PAGE	TITLE	LINE
HAPPY (CONTINUED)			
("RICH AND POOR") GOD MADE MAN HAPPY & RICH	384A ANNO WATSON	MARG
THE WORLDS OF HAPPY ETERNITY	417 MY SPECTRE/N	70
FOR THE COUNTESS OF EGREMONT [BY A HAPPY ACCIDENT] . .	442D LAST JUDGMNT/L	PROSE
I AM HAPPY I CANNOT SAY THAT RAFAEL EVER WAS	447C ANNO REYNOLDS	MARG
A SHADOW TO REPOSE IN ALL THE DAYS OF HAPPY ETERNITY .	519 MILTON 31	7
AND THEN & THEN ALONE BEGINS THE HAPPY FEMALE JOY .	522 MILTON 33	19
OF H'S(HAYLEY'S) BIRTH THIS WAS THE HAPPY LOT	539 OF HS BIRTH/N	1
SCHOLAR OF INSPIRATION AND ALL WILL BE HAPPY	572C DESC CAT 3	PROSE
IN EDEN THE ARTIST IS AN INHABITANT OF THAT HAPPY COUNTRY	578A DESC CAT 5	PROSE
HAPPY IS HE WHO CAN SEE AND CONVERSE WITH THEM . . .	578C DESC CAT 5	PROSE
IN THAT ANCIENT HAPPY PERIOD WHICH HISTORY HAS RECORDED	580D DESC CAT 5	PROSE
MEET THE LORD IN THE AIR & THEN HE WOULD BE HAPPY . .	611A V LAST JUDG/N	PROSE
OF GENERATION TO DESTROY BY SIN AND ATONEMENT HAPPY	676 JERUSALEM 46	27
JERUSALEM		
I FEEL THAT A MAN MAY BE HAPPY IN THIS WORLD AND . .	793C LETTER 5	PROSE
BUT I AM HAPPY TO FIND A GREAT MAJORITY OF FELLOW MORTALS	794A LETTER 5	PROSE
AFTER ANOTHER ARTIST BUT ABOVE ALL I FEEL MYSELF HAPPY &	795C LETTER 6	PROSE
THE VOICES OF WINDS TREES & BIRDS & THE ODOURS OF THE HAPPY	803B LETTER 15	PROSE
GROUND		
PARENT OF YOUTHFUL MINDS & HAPPY WIFE	806 TO MRS BUTTS/L	6
WE DETERMINE THEREFORE TO BE HAPPY AND DO ALL THAT WE CAN	807A LETTER 17	PROSE
HAPPY SON OF THE IMMORTAL PHIDIAS HIS LOT IS TRULY GLORIOUS	807B LETTER 17	PROSE
AND MINE NO LESS HAPPY IN HIS FRIENDSHIP AND IN THAT OF HIS	807B LETTER 17	PROSE
SUSSEX IS CERTAINLY A HAPPY PLACE & FELPHAM IN PARTICULAR	808C LETTER 19	PROSE
IS		
MY MOCK & SCORN ALAS WRETCHED HAPPY INEFFECTUAL LABOURER OF	809B LETTER 20	PROSE
DID NOT HE IS ALSO A HAPPY ABSTRACT KNOWN BY ALL	809C LETTER 20	PROSE
HIS FRIENDS		
HAPPY WOULD THAT MAN BE WHO COULD UNITE THEM . . .	810B LETTER 20	PROSE
VERY HAPPY SITTING AT TEA BY A WOOD FIRE IN OUR COTTAGE THE	820B LETTER 25	PROSE
HEALTH & SHALL BE TRULY HAPPY TO HEAR THAT IT IS PERFECTLY	833A LETTER 32	PROSE
HIS & YOUR MILD & HAPPY TEMPERS OF SOUL YOUR DEVOTED .	835B LETTER 34	PROSE
MR ROSE I AM HAPPY TO HEAR IS GETTING QUITE WELL HOPE TO	838C LETTER 37	PROSE
HAPPY CHRISTMAS AT LOVELY FELPHAM OUR SPIRITS SEEM STILL	853D LETTER 52	PROSE
DO NOR SAY BUT AS YOU DIRECT I FEEL EXTREMELY HAPPY . .	857B LETTER 54	PROSE
MEAN WHILE I AM KEPT HAPPY AS I USED TO BE BECAUSE . .	863A LETTER 60	PROSE
A HAPPY CHRISTMAS I REMAIN EVER	863C LETTER 60	PROSE
YOUR HAPPY FAMILY ONCE AGAIN & THAT FOR A LONGER PERIOD	873A LETTER 76	PROSE
CERTAINLY A HAPPY STATE OF AGREEMENT TO WHICH I FOR ONE DO	878B LETTER 88	PROSE
HAR		
WANDERD TILL HE THAT LEADETH ALL LED HIM TO THE VALES OF	100 TIRIEL 2	4
HAR		
AND HAR & HEVA LIKE TWO CHILDREN SAT BENEATH THE OAK . .	100 TIRIEL 2	5
BUT THEY WERE AS THE SHADOW OF HAR & AS THE YEARS	100 TIRIEL 2	7
FORGOTTEN		
SOON AS THE BLIND WANDERER ENTERD THE PLEASANT GARDENS	100 TIRIEL 2	10
OF HAR		
THIS IS THE VALLEY OF HAR SAID MNETHA & THIS THE TENT OF	101 TIRIEL 2	16
HAR		
AND THIS IS HAR & HEVA TREMBLING LIKE INFANTS BY MY SIDE	101 TIRIEL 2	19
THEN HAR SAID O MY MOTHER MNETHA VENTURE NOT SO NEAR HIM	101 TIRIEL 2	23
HE KNEELED DOWN & MNETHA SAID COME HAR & HEVA RISE . . .	101 TIRIEL 2	32
THEN HAR AROSE & LAID HIS HAND UPON OLD TIRIEL'S HEAD .	101 TIRIEL 2	34
[FEARING TO TELL THEM WHO HE WAS BECAUSE OF THE WEAKNESS	102 TIRIEL 2	49
OF HAR]		
MORE HUMAN CREATURES ON THIS EARTH BESIDE THE SONS OF HAR	102 TIRIEL 2	55
THEY SAT & EAT & HAR & HEVA SMILD ON TIRIEL	102 TIRIEL 3	1
WOULD PUZZLE [HAR] MNETHA BLESS THY FACE FOR THOU	102 TIRIEL 3	6
ART TIRIEL		
[BUT STILL HE FEARD THAT HAR & HEVA WOULD DIE OF JOY &	102 TIRIEL 3	8
GRIEF]		
AND AFTER DINNER WE WILL WALK INTO THE CAGE OF HAR . .	102 TIRIEL 3	14
IF THOU DOST GO SAID HAR I WISH THINE EYES MAY SEE THY	102 TIRIEL 3	17
FOLLY		
AND [HE] HEARD HAR SING IN THE GREAT CAGE & SLEPT UPON	103 TIRIEL 3 *	23
OUR FLEECES		
[AND HAR & HEVA STOOD & WATCHD HIM TILL HE ENTERD THE WOOD]	103 TIRIEL 3	31
BUT HAR & HEVA STOOD & WATCHD HIM TILL HE ENTERD THE WOOD	103 TIRIEL 3	41
NOW [?HILI] HELA I CAN GO WITH PLEASURE & DWELL WITH HAR	107 TIRIEL 6 *	3
& HEVA		
I HAVE NOT EAT THESE TWO DAYS LEAD ME TO HAR & HEVA'S TENT	107 TIRIEL 6	19
YET THOU SHALT LEAD ME LEAD ME I COMMAND TO HAR & HEVA	107 TIRIEL 6	22
TO HAR & HEVA I WILL LEAD THEE THEN WOULD THAT THEY WOULD	107 TIRIEL 6	24
CURSE		
UNLESS THOU LEAD ME TO THE TENT OF HAR CHILD OF THE CURSE	108 TIRIEL 6	34
I LEAD THEE TO THE TENT OF HAR NOT THAT I MIND THY CURSE	108 TIRIEL 6	36
LEAD ME TO HAR & HEVA & THE CURSE OF TIRIEL	108 TIRIEL 6	48
THEY ENTERD ON THE MOUNTAINS OF HAR AT NOON THE HAPPY TENTS	109 TIRIEL 7	19
BUT HAR & HEVA SLEPT FEARLESS AS BABES ON LOVING BREASTS	109 TIRIEL 7	21
LEAD ME TO HAR & HEVA I AM TIRIEL KING OF THE WEST . . .	109 TIRIEL 8	4
AND MNETHA LED THEM TO THE TENT OF HAR AND HAR & HEVA .	109 TIRIEL 8	5
RAN TO THE DOOR WHEN TIRIEL FELT THE ANKLES OF AGED HAR	109 TIRIEL 8	6
THY LAWS O HAR & TIRIEL'S WISDOM END TOGETHER IN A CURSE	109 TIRIEL 8	8
RETURNS MY THIRSTY HISSINGS IN A CURSE ON THEE O HAR .	110 TIRIEL 8	40
HE CEAST OUTSTRETCHD AT HAR & HEVA'S FEET IN AWFUL DEATH	110 TIRIEL 8	42
WHY SHOULD THE MISTRESS OF THE VALES OF HAR UTTER A SIGH	128 BOOK OF THEL 2	1
FOR I WALK THROUGH THE VALES OF HAR AND SMELL THE SWEETEST	129 BOOK OF THEL 3 *	18
FLOWERS		
O BEAUTY OF THE VALES OF HAR WE LIVE NOT FOR OURSELVES .	129 BOOK OF THEL 4	10
FLED BACK UNHINDERD TILL SHE CAME INTO THE VALES OF HAR	130 BOOK OF THEL 6	22
TIMES ROLLED ON OER ALL THE SONS OF HAR TIME AFTER TIME	246 SONG OF LOS 3	20

865

		PAGE	TITLE	LINE

HAR   (CONTINUED)
    SINCE THAT DREAD DAY WHEN HAR AND HEVA FLED   .   .   .   .   246 SONG OF LOS 4   5
    LAWS & RELIGIONS TO THE SONS OF HAR BINDING THEM MORE . . 246 SONG OF LOS 4   14
    HAR OCHIM IJIM ADAM REUBEN SIMEON LEVI JUDAH DAN NAPHTALI   350 FOUR ZOAS 8   360
HARCOURT
    AT PARIS THANKS NOBLE HARCOURT FOR TWAS . . . . . . 18 EDW THIRD/PS 1   45
HARD
    TALKING WITH DEATH ANSWERING HIS HARD DEMANDS . . . . 30 EDW THIRD/PS 5   10
    PARTING IS HARD AND DEATH IS TERRIBLE . . . . . 35D COUCH DEATH/PS   PROSE
    CLOSD FROM THE EYE OF DAY TO THE HARD ROCK TRANSFIXT BY 41D THEN SHE BORE   PROSE
      FATE
    IT IS NOT THE EXUBERANCE OF BEAUTY SO IF RAFAEL IS HARD 81D ANNO LAVATER   MARG
      & DRY
    AT ENTRANCE THEOTORMON SITS WEARING THE THRESHOLD HARD . 190 V DAU ALBION 2   6
    BESIDE THE OX TO THY HARD FURROW DOES NOT THAT MILD BEAM 195 V DAU ALBION 8   4
      BLOT
    DARK IS THE HEAVEN ABOVE & COLD & HARD THE EARTH BENEATH 201 AMERICA 14   7
    THE CLOUD BEARS HARD ON ALBION'S SHORE . . . . . . 241 EUROPE 9   9
    THE CLOUD BEARS HARD UPON THE COUNCIL HOUSE DOWN RUSHING 241 EUROPE 9   12
    WITH HARD NECESSITY . . . . 254 AHANIA 5   2
    WITHOUT FLUCTUATION HARD AS ADAMANT . . . . . . 257 BOOK OF LOS 4   5
    THE HARD BONDAGE RENT RENT THE VAST SOLID . . . . 257 BOOK OF LOS 4   16
    AMONG THESE FLAMES INCESSANT LABOURING OUR HARD MASTERS 285 FOUR ZOAS 2   219
      LAUGH
    STAMPD THE HARD ROCKS EXPECTANT OF THE UNKNOWN WANDERER 319 FOUR ZOAS 6   299
    FREEZING THY FEET TO THE HARD ROCK STILL THY PEN OBDURATE 322 FOUR ZOAS 7   85
    TO THE HARD ROCK OR THOU SHOULDST FEEL MY ENMITY & HATE 322 FOUR ZOAS 7   88
    [THE HARD DENTANT HAMMERS ARE LULLD BY THE FLUTE LULA LULA 346 FOUR ZOAS 8   * 203
      ]
    OLD HARD STIFF & DRY UNFINISHD WORKS OF ART . . . . 449C ANNO REYNOLDS   MARG
    REFUSING ALL DEFINITE FORM THE ABSTRACT HORROR ROOFD STONY 482 MILTON 3   9
      HARD
    AND GET BY ROTE AS A HARD TASK OF A LIFE OF SIXTY YEARS 499 MILTON 18   14
    THE HARD DENTANT HAMMERS ARE LULLD BY THE FLUTES' LULA LULA 509 MILTON 24   63
    FRIENDS WERE QUITE HARD TO FIND OLD AUTHORS SAY . . . 546 ANOTHER/N 2   3
    DISTINGUISHES HONESTY FROM KNAVERY BUT THE HARD AND WIREY 585C DESC CAT 15   PROSE
    CONDENSD HIS EMANATIONS INTO HARD OPAKE SUBSTANCES . . . 628 JERUSALEM 9   1
    AROUND ALBION BUT ALBION HEARD HIM NOT OBDURATE HARD . . 676 JERUSALEM 45   35
    SO SPOKE THE HARD COLD CONSTRICTIVE SPECTRE HE IS NAMED 685 JERUSALEM 54   25
      ARTHUR
    I WILL COMMAND THE CLOUD TO GIVE THEE FOOD & THE HARD ROCK 696 JERUSALEM 62   25
    EVEN A LONG SEASON & A HARD JOURNEY & A HOWLING WILDERNESS 696 JERUSALEM 62   27
    OF VEGETATIVE NATURE BY THEIR HARD RESTRICTING 713 JERUSALEM 73   21
      CONDENSATIONS
    HARD & OBDURATE ARE THE FURROWS OF THE MOUNTAIN OF WINE 719 JERUSALEM 79   6
      & OIL
    HAVE LABOURD HARD INDEED & HAVE BEEN BORNE ON ANGEL'S WINGS 826A LETTER 27   PROSE
    & AM HARD AT IT TO ACCOMPLISH IN TIME WHAT I INTEND . . 859B LETTER 56   PROSE
    "THE DRIFT OF HOLLOW STATES HARD TO BE SPELLD" MILTON . SUPP LEGEND/N27   *
HARDEN
    FELT THEIR SKULLS HARDEN THEN ASIA . . . . 253 AHANIA 4   41
    WHEN THE SUN SETS WHEN THE CLODS HARDEN & THE CATTLE STAND 355 FOUR ZOAS 8   566
HARDEND   SEE HARDNED
    DRIVEN ON THE UNPRODUCING SANDS & ON THE HARDEND ROCKS 365 FOUR ZOAS 9   329
    THE SPIDER THE BAT BURST FROM THE HARDEND SLIME CRYING . . 373 FOUR ZOAS 9   608
    HARDEND SHADOW OF ALL THINGS UPON OUR VEGETATED EARTH . . 498 MILTON 17   22
    WHICH HARDEND AGAINST THEM MORE AND MORE AS HE BUILDED 641 JERUSALEM 19   30
      ONWARDS
    VIRTUE AND EVERY MINUTE PARTICULAR HARDEND INTO GRAINS 657 JERUSALEM 31   20
      OF SAND
    THE FIFTY-TWO COUNTIES OF ENGLAND ARE HARDEND AGAINST ME 720 JERUSALEM 79   20
HARDENING   SEE EVER-HARDENING
    AND HARDENING BONES BEGAN . . . . 235 URIZEN 25   25
    A BLUE FLUID EXUDED IN SINEWS HARDENING IN THE ABYSS . . 483 MILTON 3   35
    AND HILLS OUT FROM THE OPTIC NERVE & HARDENING IT INTO 515 MILTON 28   34
      A BONE
    THY MASCULINE FROM THY FEMININE HARDENING AGAINST 721 JERUSALEM 79   71
      THE HEAVENS
HARDENS
    HARDENS THE LION & THE BEAR TREMBLING IN THE SOLID MOUNTAIN 352 FOUR ZOAS 8   451
HARDER
    BUT BE YOUR HEARTS HARDER THAN THE NETHER MILLSTONE . . . 323 FOUR ZOAS 7   112
HARDLY
    TO VAUXHALL & RANELAGH AND I HARDLY KNOW WHAT A COACH IS 53A ISLAND MOON 8   PROSE
    YOU HARDLY KNOW SHE HAS A TONGUE IN HER HEAD . . . . 53A ISLAND MOON 8   PROSE
    ZOAS OF ALBION WHERE A MAN DARE HARDLY TO EMBRACE . . 663 JERUSALEM 36   45
HARDNED
    IMPATIENT STIFLED STIFFEND HARDNED . . . . 257 BOOK OF LOS 4   14
HARDNESS
    ("PROOFS OF DULL FRIGIDITY HARDNESS OR...EGOTISM") RATHER 70C ANNO LAVATER   MARG
      UNEASY
    FROM A DIAMOND ITS HARDNESS FROM A SPONGE ITS SOFTNESS 81C ANNO LAVATER   MARG
    WHEN AS THE SNOW COVERS THE MOUNTAIN OFT PETRIFIC HARDNESS 352 FOUR ZOAS 8   * 449
      [COVERS]
    ARE THUS DEFORMD WITH HARDNESS WITH THE [PLOW] SWORD & 361 FOUR ZOAS 9   * 175
      WITH THE SPEAR
    HIS FACE AND BOSOM WITH PETRIFIC HARDNESS AND HIS HANDS 664 JERUSALEM 38   1
    INTO A FEMALE TO THE WOVEN MALE IN OPAKE HARDNESS . . . 704 JERUSALEM 67   10
    BECAME A LIMIT A ROCKY HARDNESS WITHOUT FORM & VOID . . 713 JERUSALEM 73   23
HARDNESSES
    THE ROCKS ARE OPAKE HARDNESSES COVERING ALL VEGETATED 704 JERUSALEM 67   5
      THINGS

	PAGE	TITLE	LINE

HARDSHIPS
MANY HONEST PEOPLE ENDURE GREATER HARDSHIPS WITH FORTITUDE — 793B LETTER 5 — PROSE

HARD SUBDUED
IN THEIR AMAZING [FRUCTIFYING] HARD SUBDUED COURSE IN THE VAST DEEP — 287 FOUR ZOAS 2 — * 286

HARE
EACH OUTCRY OF THE HUNTED HARE — 431 AUGURIES — 13
LIKE TREMBLING HARE SITS ON HIS WEAKLY PAPER — 537 AND HIS LEGS/N — 18
OR THE HARE PLAYING ON A TABOR — 548 GIVE PENSION/N — 2

HARFORD
GAD OXFORD BUCKS HARFORD ASHER SUSSEX HAMPSHIRE BERKSHIRE — 637 JERUSALEM 16 — 47

HARHATH
SOTHA MYDON ELLAYOL NATHO GON HARHATH SATAN — 350 FOUR ZOAS 8 — 359

HARK
[HARK] HOW SOON THE WINDS SING ROUND THE DARKNING STORM — 43C WOE CRIED MUSE — *PROSE
LOOK AT MY BALD HEAD HARK LISTEN YE SERPENTS [?ALL] LISTEN — 99 TIRIEL 1 — * 29
AND THOU O ENITHARMON HARK I HEAR THE HAMMERS OF LOS — 275 FOUR ZOAS 1 — 421
THE EMMET & THE BEETLE HARK THEY LAUGH & MOCK AT LOS — 288 FOUR ZOAS 2 — 308
AS OF A BATTLE IN THE HEAVENS HARK HEARD YOU NOT THE TRUMPET — 364 FOUR ZOAS 9 — 263
JERUSALEM'S CHILDREN HARK HEAR THE GIANTS OF ALBION CRY AT NIGHT — 673 JERUSALEM 43 — 47
HARK THE MINGLING CRIES OF LUVAH WITH THE SONS OF ALBION — 677 JERUSALEM 47 — 13
HARK & RECORD THE TERRIBLE WONDER THAT THE PUNISHER — 677 JERUSALEM 47 — 14

HARLOT   SEE VIRGIN-HARLOT
IS TURND INTO SONGS OF THE HARLOT IN DAY — 140 FRENCH REVOLTN — 147
FOR A HARLOT COY — 168 SILENT NIGHT/N — 12
BROMION SPOKE BEHOLD THIS HARLOT HERE ON BROMION'S BED — 190 V DAU ALBION 1 — 18
NOW THOU MAIST MARRY BROMION'S HARLOT AND PROTECT THE CHILD — 190 V DAU ALBION 2 — 1
MAY FIND IT IN A HARLOT AND IN COARSE-CLAD HONESTY — 199 AMERICA 8 — 11
AND EYES OF DEATH THE HARLOT WOMB OFT OPENED IN VAIN — 199 AMERICA 9 — 18
OF SECRET LUST WHEN HID IN CHAMBERS DARK THE NIGHTLY HARLOT — 333 FOUR ZOAS 7B — 25
JEALOUS THAT SHE WAS VALA NOW BECOME URIZEN'S HARLOT — 336 FOUR ZOAS 7B — 137
AND THE HARLOT OF LOS & THE DELUDED HARLOT OF THE KINGS OF EARTH — 336 FOUR ZOAS 7B — * 138
HE SAW THE HARLOT OF THE KINGS OF EARTH & SAW HER CUP — 356 FOUR ZOAS 8 — 602
SHE GATHERD IT TOGETHER TO CONSUME HER HARLOT ROBES — 356 FOUR ZOAS 8 — 609
WITH MYSTERY THE HARLOT & WITH SATAN FOR EVER & EVER — 361 FOUR ZOAS 9 — 157
THEN FIRST SHE SAW HIS GLORY & HER HARLOT FORM APPEARD — 382 FOUR ZOAS AD 6 — 21
BACON SUPPOSES THAT THE DRAGON BEAST & HARLOT ARE WORTHY OF — 404D ANNO BACON — MARG
IS THE HARLOT ALSO SIEZED & BOUND [CHAIND] BY TWO ANGELS — 443A LAST JUDGMNT/L — PROSE
TO DESTROY JERUSALEM AS A HARLOT & HER SONS AS REPROBATES — 506 MILTON 22 — 47
TO RAISE UP MYSTERY THE VIRGIN HARLOT MOTHER OF WAR — 506 MILTON 22 — 48
NO LONGER TURNING HER A WANDERING HARLOT IN THE STREETS — 523 MILTON 33 — 22
RELIGION HID IN WAR A DRAGON RED & HIDDEN HARLOT — 528 MILTON 37 — 43
A DRAGON RED & HIDDEN HARLOT WHICH JOHN IN PATMOS SAW — 532 MILTON 40 — 22
BENEATH THESE IS THE SEAT OF THE HARLOT NAMD MYSTERY — 609A V LAST JUDG/N — PROSE
THE HARLOT DAUGHTER MOTHER OF PITY AND DISHONOURABLE FORGIVENESS — 640 JERUSALEM 18 — 12
AND THOU O HARLOT DAUGHTER DAUGHTER OF DESPAIR ART ALL — 658 JERUSALEM 31 — 58
BECAUSE THOU ART THE IMPURITY & THE HARLOT & THY CHILDREN — 658 JERUSALEM 31 — 63
WHAT IS A WIFE & WHAT IS A HARLOT WHAT IS A CHURCH & WHAT — 689 JERUSALEM 57 — 8
MARRY A HARLOT & AN ADULTERESS MARY ANSWERD ART THOU MORE PURE — 694 JERUSALEM 61 — 6
INDEED A HARLOT DRUNKEN WITH THE SACRIFICE OF IDOLS DOES HE — 695 JERUSALEM 61 — 38
EVERY HARLOT WAS ONCE A VIRGIN EVERY CRIMINAL AN INFANT LOVE — 695 JERUSALEM 61 — 52
A HARLOT I AM CALLD I AM SOLD FROM STREET TO STREET — 695 JERUSALEM 62 — 4
GO ASSUME PAPAL DIGNITY THOU SPECTRE THOU MALE HARLOT ARTHUR — 698 JERUSALEM 64 — 15
RELIGION HID IN WAR A DRAGON RED & HIDDEN HARLOT — 716 JERUSALEM 75 — 20
THE CLOUD O RENT IN SUNDER FROM JERUSALEM THE HARLOT DAUGHTER — 722 JERUSALEM 80 — 12
RELIGION HID IN WAR A DRAGON RED & HIDDEN HARLOT — 735 JERUSALEM 89 — 53
MYSTERY BABYLON THE GREAT THE DRUID DRAGON & HIDDEN HARLOT — 741 JERUSALEM 93 — 25
THE MOTHER SHOULD AN HARLOT BEEN — 756 EV GOSPEL(I)/N — 4
EVERY HARLOT WAS A VIRGIN ONCE — 771 EPILOGUE/GP — 3

HARLOT'S
[BUT MOST THE MIDNIGHT HARLOT'S CURSE] — 170 LONDON/N — 14
HOW THE MIDNIGHT HARLOT'S CURSE — 170 LONDON/N — 19
[FOR THE DROPS OF A HARLOT'S EYE] — 186 LET BROTHELS/N — 51
HOW THE YOUTHFUL HARLOT'S CURSE — 216 LONDON/SE — 14
THE HARLOT'S CRY FROM STREET TO STREET — 433 AUGURIES — 115
HELL OPENS BENEATH THE HARLOT'S SEAT ON THE LEFT HAND — 443B LAST JUDGMNT/L — PROSE
ON THE LEFT HAND OF THE HARLOT'S SEAT WHERE OTHERS ARE — 443C LAST JUDGMNT/L — PROSE
THE SOLDIER'S FIFE THE HARLOT'S SHRIEK THE VIRGIN'S DISMAL GROAN — 636 JERUSALEM 16 — 6

HARLOTS
OF LIFE ARE HARLOTS AND THEOTORMON IS A SICK MAN'S DREAM — 194 V DAU ALBION 6 — 19
THAT I HAVE SINND & THAT MY EMANATIONS ARE BECOME HARLOTS — 265 FOUR ZOAS 1 — 54
WHO IS MYSTERY BABYLON THE GREAT THE MOTHER OF HARLOTS — 349 FOUR ZOAS 8 — 330
WHO IS MYSTERY BABYLON THE GREAT MOTHER OF (HARLOTS) — 382 FOUR ZOAS AD 6 — * 19
THEY THY HARLOTS THOU THEIR SLAVE — 417 MY SPECTR AD/N — 7
MY DAUGHTERS ARE HARLOTS MY SONS ARE ACCURSED BEFORE ME — 670 JERUSALEM 42 — 14
BUT TO THE PUBLICANS & HARLOTS GO — 718 STOOD AMONG/J — 31
AND TURN THEM OUT INTO THE STREETS FOR HARLOTS TO BE FOOD — 724 JERUSALEM 81 — 4
THE PUBLICANS & HARLOTS HE — 757 EV GOSPEL(I)/N — 45

HARLOT-SISTER
SHE IS OUR MOTHER NATURE JERUSALEM IS OUR HARLOT-SISTER — 640 JERUSALEM 18 — 30

HARM
MAY DO A GREAT DEAL OF HARM WITHOUT KNOWING IT — 29A EDW THIRD/PS 4 — PROSE
I DONT THINK THERES ANY HARM IN IT SAID TILLY LALLY — 47C ISLAND MOON 3 — PROSE

		PAGE	TITLE	LINE

HARM (CONTINUED)
```
    ?CAN ?& ?DOES WORK ?HARM IGNORANTLY  . . . . . . . .   89B ANNO SWED LOVE * MARG
    SO IF ALL DO THEIR DUTY THEY NEED NOT FEAR HARM  . . . .  118 CHIMNEY SWP/SI    24
    TO KEEP THEM ALL FROM HARM . . . . . . . . . .  119 NIGHT/SI    20
    AGAINST ME WHO THEE GUARDED IN THE NIGHT OF DEATH FROM HARM   300 FOUR ZOAS 4   110
    PAINE SAYS THAT KINGS & PRIESTS HAVE DONE HIM HARM FROM   393A ANNO WATSON   MARG
      HIS BIRTH
    FOOLISH & TELLS INTO THE HANDS OF A TYRANT [WHO ?WILL XXX   400B ANNO BACON  * MARG
      HARM]
    BUT NOBODY [AT ALL] SEES ANY HARM IN RHYMING  . . . . .   555 BLAKES APL/N 1    9
    BUT NOBODY SEES ANY HARM IN RHYMING  . . . . . . . .   555 BLAKES APL/N 2    4
    BUT NOBODY AT ALL SEES ANY HARM IN RHYMING  . . . . .   595 BLAKES APOL/PA    6
HARMLESS
    [BUT I CAN KNEEL DOWN AT YOUR DOOR I AM A HARMLESS MAN]   101 TIRIEL 2    29
    AND I KNEEL DOWN THAT YOU MAY SEE I AM A HARMLESS MAN  . .  101 TIRIEL 2    31
    . . . ARE HIS COMPANIONS HARMLESS THEY BREATHE  . . . .  136 FRENCH REVOLTN    41
HARMONIES
    INDEFINITE OR PALTRY RHYMES OR PALTRY HARMONIES  . . . .   533 MILTON 41    10
    TRUE HARMONIES & COMPREHENDING GREAT AS VERY SMALL  . .   680 JERUSALEM 49    37
    I TELL HOW ALBION'S SONS BY HARMONIES OF CONCORDS   715 JERUSALEM 74    24
      & DISCORDS
    AND LULLING HARMONIES BENEATH THE LOOMS FROM CAITHNESS   728 JERUSALEM 83    70
      IN THE NORTH
HARMONIOUS
    [OR LIKE HARMONIOUS THUNDERINGS THE SEATS OF HEAVN AMONG]   59 HOLY THURS/IM    11
    OR LIKE HARMONIOUS THUNDERINGS THE SEATS OF HEAVN AMONG    59 HOLY THURS/IM    16
    OR LIKE HARMONIOUS THUNDERINGS THE SEATS OF HEAVEN AMONG   122 HOLY THURS/SI  *  10
    . . . TERRIBLE BUT HARMONIOUS  . . . . . . . . .   509 MILTON 24    66
HARMONIOUSLY
    ("WHO SHOULD HARMONIOUSLY UNITE EACH VARIETY") THIS IS    76C ANNO LAVATER   MARG
      OUR LORD
HARMONY
    LOVE AND HARMONY COMBINE  . . . . . . . . . . .     7 LOVE HARMNY/PS    1
    CAN CHARM TO HARMONY WITH POTENT SPELL  . . . . . . .    15 IMIT SPEN/PS    30
    WHILE THY MILD VOICE FILLS ALL THESE CAVERNS WITH SWEET   271 FOUR ZOAS 1   250
      HARMONY
    WHERE DWELL THE CHILDREN OF THE ELEMENTAL WORLDS IN HARMONY   274 FOUR ZOAS 1   370
    NOT LONG IN HARMONY THEY DWELL THEIR LIFE IS DRAWN AWAY   274 FOUR ZOAS 1   371
    LIVE IN PERFECT HARMONY IN EDEN THE LAND OF LIFE  . . .   277 FOUR ZOAS 1   474
    WHILE ROUND THEIR HEADS THE ELEMENTAL GODS KEPT HARMONY   288 FOUR ZOAS 2   301
    AND NINE BRIGHT SPHERES OF HARMONY RISE ROUND THE FIERY   289 FOUR ZOAS 2   348
      KING
    REVERBERATES THE LIVING HARMONY UPON MY LIMBS  . . .   289 FOUR ZOAS 2   356
    [THOU SITST IN HARMONY FOR GOD HATH SET THEE OVER ALL]  .  291 FOUR ZOAS 3    10
    THEY SING THEY SIEZE THE INSTRUMENTS OF HARMONY THEY THROW   365 FOUR ZOAS 9   302
      AWAY
    LOOK HOW THE OPENING DAWN ADVANCES WITH VOCAL HARMONY  . .  367 FOUR ZOAS 9   397
    THE ELEMENTS SUBSIDE THE HEAVENS ROLLD ON WITH VOCAL   378 FOUR ZOAS 9   800
      HARMONY
    HE O THOU SUMMER'S HARMONY  . . . . . . . . . .   423 THE BIRDS/N    9
    DEMONSTRATION SIMILITUDE & HARMONY ARE OBJECTS OF REASONING   474C ANNO REYNOLDS   MARG
    & ONLY PROMOTES HARMONY OR BLENDING OF COLOURS ONE INTO   478C ANNO REYNOLDS   MARG
      ANOTHER
    SUCH HARMONY OF COLOURING IS DESTRUCTIVE OF ART  . . . .  478D ANNO REYNOLDS   MARG
    CALLD HARMONY IT IS LIKE THE SMILE OF A FOOL  . . . .  478D ANNO REYNOLDS   MARG
    ALL MELODIES & COMPREHENDING ONLY DISCORD AND HARMONY  .   484 MILTON 5    24
    UPON THE THAMES WHOSE LULLING HARMONY REPOSD HER SOUL  .   491 MILTON 11    3
    ATTENDING HIS LOUD HARMONY WITH ADMIRATION & LOVE  . .   520 MILTON 31    44
    ASSIST IN WEAVING THE DEADLY WOOF "...IN DREADFUL HARMONY"   576C DESC CAT 4   PROSE
    MULTITUDES OF MEN IN HARMONY APPEAR LIKE A SINGLE INFANT   607C V LAST JUDG/N   PROSE
    HEAVEN EARTH & HELL HENCEFORTH SHALL LIVE IN HARMONY  .   621 READER LOVER/J    10
    WHEEL WITHIN WHEEL IN FREEDOM REVOLVE IN HARMONY & PEACE   636 JERUSALEM 15    20
    AND LONDON WALKD IN EVERY NATION MUTUAL IN LOVE & HARMONY   647 JERUSALEM 24    43
    LIVE IN PERFECT HARMONY IN EDEN THE LAND OF LIFE  . . .   665 JERUSALEM 38    21
    OF LOVE & HARMONY IN MAN EXPAND THY EVER LOVELY GATES  .   675 JERUSALEM 44    42
    COMFORTING SOUNDS OF LOVE & HARMONY & ON THY FEET  . .   731 JERUSALEM 86    30
    HARMONY (AND) PROPORTION ARE QUALITIES & NOT THINGS THE   774B ANNO BERKELEY  * MARG
    HARMONY & PROPORTION OF A HORSE ARE NOT THE SAME WITH  .   774B ANNO BERKELEY   MARG
    THOSE OF A BULL EVERY THING HAS ITS OWN HARMONY &   774B ANNO BERKELEY   MARG
      PROPORTION
    EVERY THING WHICH IS IN HARMONY WITH ME I CALL  . . . .  SUPP IN HARMONY/N  *PROSE
    IN HARMONY BUT THERE MAY BE THINGS  . . . . . . .  SUPP IN HARMONY/N  *PROSE
    WHICH ARE NOT IN HARMONY WITH ME & YET ARE  . . . . .  SUPP IN HARMONY/N  *PROSE
    IN A MORE PERFECT HARMONY  . . . . . . . . . .  SUPP IN HARMONY/N  *PROSE
HARNESS
    AND HARROW FORMD & FRAMD THE HARNESS OF SILVER & IVORY  .   281 FOUR ZOAS 2    28
    THEY UNLOOSD THEM & PUT ON THE HARNESS OF GOLD & SILVER   281 FOUR ZOAS 2    36
      & IVORY
    TRIUMPHS IN ITS OWN DESTRUCTION THEY TOOK DOWN THE HARNESS   365 FOUR ZOAS 9   295
    HARNESSD WITH STARRY HARNESS BLACK & SHINING KEPT BY BLACK   503 MILTON 21    21
      SLAVES
    THAT WORK ALL NIGHT AT THE STARRY HARNESS STRONG   504 MILTON 21    22
      AND VIGOROUS
    . . . IN THE STARRY HARNESS OF THE PLOW  . . . . . .   697 JERUSALEM 63    3
HARNESSD
    HARNESSD THEY CALLD TO URIZEN THE HEAVENS MOVED AT THEIR   365 FOUR ZOAS 9   309
      CALL
    HARNESSD WITH STARRY HARNESS BLACK & SHINING KEPT BY BLACK   503 MILTON 21    21
      SLAVES
HARP      SEE JEWS-HARP-HOUSE
    ALFRED SHALL SMILE AND MAKE HIS HARP REJOICE  . . . . .    35 WAR SONG/PS    26
    BY MOONLIGHT HEARING A HARPER WHO SUNG TO THE HARP  . . . 156D MARRIAGE HH 17 PROSE
```

	PAGE	TITLE	LINE
HARP (CONTINUED)			
[HIS HARP ALOFT SOUNDING THEN DASHD ITS SHINING FRAME AGAINST]	196	AMERICA PREL 2	19
BUT THUS SHE SANG I SIEZE THE SPHERY HARP I STRIKE THE STRINGS	289	FOUR ZOAS 2	343
BUT THE SOFT PIPE THE FLUTE THE VIOL ORGAN HARP & CYMBAL	306	FOUR ZOAS 5	23
. . . THIS IS NO GENTLE HARP	338	FOUR ZOAS 7B	203
MY TENTS ARE FALLEN MY TRUMPETS & THE SWEET SOUNDS OF MY HARP	359	FOUR ZOAS 9	* 102
OF FLUTE & HARP & DRUM & TRUMPET HORN & CLARION	372	FOUR ZOAS 9	586
DISPLAYING NAKED BEAUTY WITH FLUTE & HARP & SONG	484	MILTON 4	28
JUDGE OF THE PURE MELODIOUS HARP STRUCK BY A HAND DIVINE	485	MILTON 5	31
AND OFTEN SUNG TO THE LOUD HARP AT THE IMMORTAL FEASTS	503	MILTON 20	58
SUNG TO THE HARP THAT MILTON OF THE LAND OF ALBION . . .	507	MILTON 23	36
UPON THE MOUNTAINS & IN VALES WITH HARP & HEAVENLY SONG	511	MILTON 25	* 68
THE BARD STANDS PROSTRATED BY THE TERRORS OF HIS HARP .	577A	DESC CAT 4	PROSE
SINGING TO HIS HARP IN THE PAINS OF DEATH	580D	DESC CAT 5	PROSE
HIS TENTS ARE FALLN HIS TRUMPETS AND THE SWEET SOUND OF HIS HARP	641	JERUSALEM 19	3
. . . THIS IS NO GENTLE HARP	700	JERUSALEM 65	49
TAUGHT TO TOUCH THE HARP TO DANCE IN THE CIRCLE OF WARRIORS	706	JERUSALEM 68	56
THEY SIEZD THE HARP THE FLUTE THE MELLOW HORN OF JERUSALEM'S JOY	721	JERUSALEM 79	49
LURED BY HIS WARLIKE SYMPHONIES OF TABRET PIPE & HARP .	736	JERUSALEM 89	59
HOW ALL YOUR BRETHREN SAY THE SOUND OF HIS HARP	791B	LETTER 3	PROSE
RECIEVE THIS TRIBUTE FROM A HARP SINCERE	806	TO MRS BUTTS/L	2
HARPER			
BY MOONLIGHT HEARING A HARPER WHO SUNG TO THE HARP . . .	156D	MARRIAGE HH 17	PROSE
HEARING A HARPER BUT NOW WE HAVE SEEN MY ETERNAL LOT .	156D	MARRIAGE HH 17	PROSE
HARPERS			
THE HOUSES OF MY HARPERS ARE BECOME A HAUNT OF CROWS .	310	FOUR ZOAS 5	195
THE SONS OF WISDOM STOOD AROUND THE HARPERS FOLLOWD WITH HARPS	310	FOUR ZOAS 5	199
HARPS			
IN WHITE ROBES STREWN IN AIR CENSERS AND HARPS	140	FRENCH REVOLTN	133
THE NIGHT OF NATURE AND THEIR HARPS UNSTRUNG	240	EUROPE 9	3
HE SUNG IT TO FOUR HARPS AT THE TABLES OF ETERNITY . . .	245	SONG OF LOS 3	2
THEY LISTEND TO THE ELEMENTAL HARPS & SPHERY SONG . . .	274	FOUR ZOAS 1	356
DESCENDING SWEET UPON THE WIND AMONG SOFT HARPS & VOICES	287	FOUR ZOAS 2	288
OF ENITHARMON BUT HER GROANS DROWN THE IMMORTAL HARPS .	306	FOUR ZOAS 5	25
STILL THE FAINT HARPS & SILVER VOICES CALM THE WEARY COUCH	306	FOUR ZOAS 5	30
THE SONS OF WISDOM STOOD AROUND THE HARPERS FOLLOWD WITH HARPS	310	FOUR ZOAS 5	199
MARCHING TO BATTLE WHO WAS WONT TO RISE WITH URIZEN'S HARPS	338	FOUR ZOAS 7B	198
WITH HARPS & SONGS WHERE BRIGHT AHANIA SANG BEFORE THY FACE	360	FOUR ZOAS 9	* 126
TO RAVISHING MELODY OF FLUTE & HARPS & SOFTEST VOICE .	366	FOUR ZOAS 9	336
A GLORIFICATION OF ANGELS WITH HARPS SURROUND THE DOVE .	613B	V LAST JUDG/N	PROSE
MARCHING TO BATTLE WHO WAS WONT TO RISE WITH URIZEN'S HARPS	700	JERUSALEM 65	44
LIKE THE SOUND OF HARPS WHICH I HEAR BEFORE THE SUN'S RISING	835B	LETTER 34	PROSE
HARPSICHORD			
MISS GITTIPIN SAID HE YOU SING LIKE A HARPSICHORD . . .	55C	ISLAND MOON 9	PROSE
HARROW			
THEY SHALL DROP AT THE PLOW AND FAINT AT THE HARROW . . .	140	FRENCH REVOLTN	148
HARROW BURN ALL THESE CORN FIELDS THROW DOWN ALL THESE FENCES	274	FOUR ZOAS 1	388
AND HARROW FORMD & FRAMD THE HARNESS OF SILVER & IVORY .	281	FOUR ZOAS 2	28
THE PLOW OF AGES & THE GOLDEN HARROW WADE THRO FIELDS .	320	FOUR ZOAS 7	14
THEN LEFT THE SONS OF URIZEN THE PLOW & HARROW THE LOOM	337	FOUR ZOAS 7B	170
THE HORSES OF PALAMABRON'S HARROW WHEREFOR RINTRAH & PALAMABRON	350	FOUR ZOAS 8	* 369
THEN FOLLOWS THE GOLDEN HARROW IN THE MIDST OF MENTAL FIRES	366	FOUR ZOAS 9	335
BENEATH THE PLOW OF RINTRAH & THE HARROW OF THE ALMIGHTY	483	MILTON 4	1
TO MORTALS THY MILLS SEEM EVERY THING & THE HARROW OF SHADDAI	483	MILTON 4	12
ANGER ME NOT THOU CANST NOT DRIVE THE HARROW IN PITY'S PATHS	483	MILTON 4	16
PALAMABRON WITH THE FIERY HARROW IN MORNING RETURNING .	484	MILTON 5	1
OF HARVEST THE PLOW & HARROW TO PASS OVER THE NATIONS .	485	MILTON 6	13
LOS GAVE TO HIM THE HARROW OF THE ALMIGHTY ALAS BLAMABLE	486	MILTON 7	12
NEXT MORNING PALAMABRON ROSE THE HORSES OF THE HARROW .	487	MILTON 7	19
WERE MADDEND WITH TORMENTING FURY & THE SERVANTS OF THE HARROW	487	MILTON 7	20
THAT HE HAD NOT OPPRESD THE HORSES OF THE HARROW NOR THE SERVANTS	487	MILTON 7	42
RAGD WITH THICK FLAMES REDUNDANT & THE HARROW MADDEND WITH FURY	487	MILTON 7	46
HIS HORSES ARE MAD HIS HARROW CONFOUNDED HIS COMPANIONS ENRAGD	488	MILTON 8	18
I SPRANG OUT OF THE BREAST OF SATAN OVER THE HARROW BEAMING	492	MILTON 12	10
BUT ME THE SERVANTS OF THE HARROW SAW NOT BUT AS A BOW .	492	MILTON 12	14
AROUND THE FIERY FLAMING HARROW IN LABYRINTHINE FORMS .	493	MILTON 12	18
THE HARROW CAST THICK FLAMES JEHOVAH THUNDERD ABOVE . . .	493	MILTON 12	20
CHAOS & ANCIENT NIGHT FLED FROM BENEATH THE FIERY HARROW	493	MILTON 12	21
THE HARROW CAST THICK FLAMES & ORBD US ROUND IN CONCAVE FIRES	493	MILTON 12	22
DROVE THE FIERCE HARROW AMONG THE CONSTELLATIONS OF JEHOVAH	493	MILTON 12	25
DRIVING THE HARROW IN PITY'S PATHS TWAS THEN WITH OUR DARK FIRES	493	MILTON 12	28
OF PALAMABRON'S HARROW & OF RINTRAH'S WRATH & FURY . . .	508	MILTON 24	1
AND THE HARROW & HEAVY THUNDERING ROLLER UPON THE MOUNTAINS	510	MILTON 25	11
THE PLOW GOES FORTH IN TEMPESTS & LIGHTNINGS & THE HARROW CRUEL	514	MILTON 27	47

	PAGE	TITLE	LINE

HARROW   (CONTINUED)
    MILCAH'S PILLARS SHINE FROM HARROW TO HAMPSTEAD WHERE   525 MILTON 35   11
      HOGLAH
    TILL THE PLOW OF JEHOVAH AND THE HARROW OF SHADDAI . . .   676 JERUSALEM 46   14
    THEN LEFT THE SONS OF URIZEN THE PLOW & HARROW THE LOOM   699 JERUSALEM 65   12
HARROWD
    THE SEED IS HARROWD IN WHILE FLAMES HEAT THE BLACK MOULD   366 FOUR ZOAS 9   337
      & CAUSE
    AND HARROWD FOR HIS PROFIT LO THY STOLEN EMANATION . . .   625 JERUSALEM 7   14
    BUT NOW MY SOUL IS HARROWD WITH GRIEF & FEAR & LOVE   707 JERUSALEM 68   66
      & DESIRE
HARROWING
    IN HARROWING FEAR ROLLING ROUND . . . .   228 URIZEN 11   10
    IN HARROWING FEAR ROLLING HIS NERVOUS [BRAINS] BRAIN SHOT   303 FOUR ZOAS 4   *   227
      BRANCHES
HARROWS
    WITH GOD SPEED A ROLLER & TWO HARROWS LIE BEFORE MY WINDOW 803C LETTER 15   PROSE
HARRY
    I THINK OF THE CRIPPLED HARRY & SLOBBERING JOE . . . .   550 WHEN I SEE/N   2
HARSH
    WOULD HAVE RISEN BUT COULD NOT HIS VOICE ISSUED HARSH   142 FRENCH REVOLTN   177
      GRATING . . .
    . . . INSTEAD OF WORDS HARSH HISSINGS . . . .   142 FRENCH REVOLTN   177
    OF A HARSH TERROR DRIVN TO MADNESS BOUND TO HOLD A ROD . .   193 V DAU ALBION 5   25
    [TWISTING IN FEARFUL FORMS & HOWLING HOWLING HARSH   269 FOUR ZOAS 1   180
      SHRIEKING
    [HOWLING HARSH SHRIEKING MINGLING . . . .   269 FOUR ZOAS 1   181
    WITH HARSH SONGS EVERY LIVING SOUL THE PRESTER SERPENT RUNS 335 FOUR ZOAS 7B   113
    HE FORMED ALSO HARSH INSTRUMENTS OF SOUND . . . . .   344 FOUR ZOAS 8   135
    OF AFFLICTION AND LOS DREW THEM FORTH COMPELLING THE HARSH   628 JERUSALEM 9   35
      SPECTRE
HARTFORD
    SUFFOLK HARTFORD & ESSEX & HIS EMANATION IS GWINEVERA . .   710 JERUSALEM 71   39
HARTLEY
    HARTLEY A MAN OF JUDGMENT THEN JUDGMENT WAS A FOOL . . .   394C ANNO WATSON   MARG
HARUM
    HARUM SCARUM WHO CAN DO THIS . . . .   405A ANNO BACON   MARG
HARVEST
    AND REAP RICH HARVEST IN THE FIELDS OF CRESSY . . . . .   24 EDW THIRD/PS 3   137
    THE HUSBANDMAN DOTH LEAVE HIS BENDING HARVEST . . . . .   34B KING JOHN/PS   PROSE
    AND THE DROPS OF RAIN GLISTEN THE YELLOW HARVEST BREATHES   36C COUCH DEATH/PS   PROSE
    . . . MOW DOWN ALL THIS GREAT STARRY HARVEST OF SIX   138 FRENCH REVOLTN   90
      THOUSAND YEARS
    MAY SING IN THE VILLAGE AND SHOUT IN THE HARVEST . . . .   144 FRENCH REVOLTN   229
    IN SEED TIME LEARN IN HARVEST TEACH IN WINTER ENJOY . .   150D MARRIAGE HH 7   PROSE
    THE THANKFUL RECIEVER BEARS A PLENTIFUL HARVEST . . .   152B MARRIAGE HH 9   PROSE
    [THE FARMERS WERE RUIND & HARVEST WAS ENDED] . . . .   164 HEARD ANGEL/N   21
    THEY CANNOT SPREAD NETS WHERE A HARVEST YIELDS . . . .   168 O LAPWING/N   4
    THE HARVEST SHALL FLOURISH IN WINTRY WEATHER . . . . .   177 MERLNS PROPH/N   1
    OR DOES THE FLY REJOICE BECAUSE THE HARVEST IS BROUGHT IN   193 V DAU ALBION 5   38
    THAN ALL THESE LABOURS OF THE HARVEST & THE VINTAGE SEE   275 FOUR ZOAS 1   390
      THE RIVER
    LIKE A BRIGHT CLOUD IN HARVEST BUT WHEN URIZEN FROWND SHE   284 FOUR ZOAS 2   183
      WEPT
    SING ROUND THERE WAVES THE HARVEST & THE VINTAGE REJOICES   308 FOUR ZOAS 5   131
      THE SPRINGS
    THE POOR SMITE THEIR OPRESSORS THEY AWAKE UP TO THE HARVEST 357 FOUR ZOAS 9   *   19
    MY MILK OF COWS & HONEY OF BEES & FRUIT OF GOLDEN HARVEST   359 FOUR ZOAS 9   104
    THE HUMAN HARVEST TO BEGIN TOWARDS THE SOUTH FIRST SPRANG   366 FOUR ZOAS 9   338
    OF ORC IN JOY THEY VIEW THE HUMAN HARVEST SPRINGING UP .   366 FOUR ZOAS 9   342
    A TIME THEY GIVE TO SWEET REPOSE TILL ALL THE HARVEST IS   366 FOUR ZOAS 9   343
      RIPE
    AND LO LIKE THE HARVEST MOON AHANIA CAST OFF HER DEATH   366 FOUR ZOAS 9   344
      CLOTHES
    AS THEY REPOSD FROM THE TERRIBLE WIDE UNIVERSAL HARVEST   367 FOUR ZOAS 9   384
    AND THE SLEEPERS WHO RESTED FROM THEIR HARVEST WORK . . .   372 FOUR ZOAS 9   557
    DOWN POUR THE TORRENT FLOODS OF HEAVEN ON ALL THE HUMAN   372 FOUR ZOAS 9   566
      HARVEST
    OVER THE HUMAN HARVEST & OVER VALA THE SWEET WANDERER . .   372 FOUR ZOAS 9   576
    IN PAIN THE HUMAN HARVEST WAVD IN HORRIBLE GROANS OF WOE   372 FOUR ZOAS 9   577
    REAPD THE WIDE UNIVERSE & BOUND IN SHEAVES A WONDROUS   372 FOUR ZOAS 9   584
      HARVEST
    THE MILLER OF ETERNITY MADE SUBSERVIENT TO THE GREAT   483 MILTON 3   42
      HARVEST
    OF HARVEST THE PLOW & HARROW TO PASS OVER THE NATIONS . .   485 MILTON 6   13
    TOGETHER RIPE FOR THE HARVEST & VINTAGE & READY FOR THE   510 MILTON 25   7
      LOOM
    FELLOW LABOURERS THE GREAT VINTAGE & HARVEST IS NOW UPON   510 MILTON 25   17
      EARTH
    WHILE LOS CALLD HIS SONS AROUND HIM TO THE HARVEST & THE   511 MILTON 25   65
      VINTAGE
    PANTS IN THE VALES OF LAMBETH WEEPING OER HER HUMAN HARVEST 535 MILTON 42   33
    RINTRAH & PALAMABRON VIEW THE HUMAN HARVEST BENEATH . . .   535 MILTON 42   36
    TO GO FORTH TO THE GREAT HARVEST & VINTAGE OF THE NATIONS   535 MILTON 43   1
    HIS MILK OF COWS & HONEY OF BEES & FRUIT OF GOLDEN HARVEST   641 JERUSALEM 19   5
    WHERE THE HUMAN HARVEST WAVES ABUNDANT IN THE BEAMS OF EDEN 678 JERUSALEM 48   34
    THE INHABITANTS OF ALBION AT THE HARVEST & THE VINTAGE .   689 JERUSALEM 58   6
    ON ACCOUNT OF OUR LEAVING THE DIVINE HARVEST TO THE ENEMY   716D JERUSALEM 77   *PROSE
    WHAT IS THE HARVEST OF THE GOSPEL & ITS LABOURS . . . .   717A JERUSALEM 77   PROSE
    YOUR HARVEST SPRINGING TO ETERNAL LIFE . . . .   806 TO MRS BUTTS/L   5
HARVESTS
    OER THE YOUTHFUL HARVESTS NIGH . . . .   165 CRADLE SONG/N   25

                                                              PAGE   TITLE   LINE
HARVESTS   (CONTINUED)
      WHEN THE CLOUD BLAZES OVER THE HARVESTS . . . .   223 URIZEN 3   35
      IN SHOWERS OF LIFE ON HIS HARVESTS . . . .   254 AHANIA 5   14
HAS (OMITTING AUXILIARY VERB)
      THE ENEMY HE HAS DANCD IN THE FIELD . . . . . .   22 EDW THIRD/PS 3   30
      THEY TAME SUBMIT SUCH THE EFFECT FLIGHT HAS . . . . .   24 EDW THIRD/PS 3   122
      THAT YOUTH HAS NEED OF AGE TO POINT FIT PREY . . . .   27 EDW THIRD/PS 3   269
      HAS TO GET BEFORE ANOTHER IN ANY PURSUIT AFTER GLORY . 28 EDW THIRD/PS 3   15
      LAW SAID TILLY LALLY WHAT HAS THAT TO DO WITH PHARAOH . . 47C ISLAND MOON 3 *PROSE
      PLUTARCH HAS NOT THE LIFE OF GHIOTTO SAID SIPSOP . . . 49D ISLAND MOON 6   PROSE
      SHAKESPEARE IS TOO WILD & MILTON HAS NO FEELINGS THEY MIGHT 51D ISLAND MOON 7 PROSE
      & HAPPINESS ITS NO SUCH THING EVERY PERSON HAS AS SOMETHING 52B ISLAND MOON 8 PROSE
      YOU HARDLY KNOW SHE HAS A TONGUE IN HER HEAD . . . . . 53A ISLAND MOON 8   PROSE
      I NEVER SAW SUCH A PLACE IN MY LIFE HE SAYS HE HAS . . . 53A ISLAND MOON 8   PROSE
      A GIRL HAS ALWAYS MORE TONGUE THAN A BOY I HAVE SEEN . 53B ISLAND MOON 8   PROSE
      HE WHO LOVES FEELS LOVE DESCEND INTO HIM & IF HE HAS WISDOM 90B ANNO SWED LOVE MARG
      BY CORRESPONDENCE WHICH HAS NOTHING TO DO WITH   93B ANNO SWED LOVE   MARG
         DEMONSTRATION
      THAT NO MAN ON EARTH HAS A SPIRITUAL IDEA AFTER READING 94C ANNO SWED LOVE   MARG
         N...
      THE ARGUMENT MAN HAS NO NOTION OF MORAL FITNESS BUT FROM 97A NAT RELIGION 1 PROSE
         EDUCATION
      FOR MERCY HAS A HUMAN HEART . . . .   117 DIVNE IMAGE/SI   9
      THAT MAN HAS TWO REAL EXISTING PRINCIPLES VIZ A BODY & 149C MARRIAGE HH 4   PROSE
         A SOUL
      MAN HAS NO BODY DISTINCT FROM HIS SOUL . . . .   149D MARRIAGE HH 4   PROSE
      THE BUSY BEE HAS NO TIME FOR SORROW . . . .   151A MARRIAGE HH 7   PROSE
      FIRST THE NOTION THAT MAN HAS A BODY DISTINCT FROM HIS SOUL 154C MARRIAGE HH 14 PROSE
      CRUELTY HAS A HUMAN HEART . . . .   221 DIVNE IMAGE/SE   1
      TRUTH HAS BOUNDS ERROR NONE FALLING FALLING . . . . .   258 BOOK OF LOS 4   30
      THARMAS THE MOON HAS CHAMBERS WHERE THE BABES OF LOVE LIE 339 FOUR ZOAS 7B   244
         HID
      THE PLACE OF MORAL RECTITUDE WHAT HAS MORAL RECTITUDE   384D ANNO WATSON   MARG
         TO DO
      WHO HAS THE POWER OF THE AIR . . . .   388A ANNO WATSON   MARG
      THE GOSPEL IS FORGIVENESS OF SINS & HAS NO MORAL PRECEPTS 395C ANNO WATSON   MARG
      BACON HAS NO NOTION OF ANY THING BUT MAMMON . . . . .   402D ANNO BACON   * MARG
      HE WHO HAS FEW THINGS TO DESIRE CANNOT HAVE MANY TO FEAR 405B ANNO BACON   MARG
      THE MAP OF ALLESTONE HAS THE SAME CHARACTER OF THE FIRM AND 439C REMARKS MALKIN PROSE
      THE ENQUIRY IN ENGLAND IS NOT WHETHER A MAN HAS TALENTS 452D ANNO REYNOLDS   MARG
      HE WHO HAS NOTHING TO DISSIPATE CANNOT DISSIPATE THE . 454B ANNO REYNOLDS   MARG
      WHAT HAS REASONING TO DO WITH THE ART OF PAINTING . .   458C ANNO REYNOLDS   MARG
      GENIUS HAS NO ERROR IT IS IGNORANCE THAT IS ERROR . . . 465B ANNO REYNOLDS   MARG
      HANDLING IS ALL THAT HE HAS & WE ALL KNOW THIS HANDLING 468D ANNO REYNOLDS   MARG
         IS
      MAN BRINGS ALL THAT HE HAS OR CAN HAVE INTO THE WORLD WITH 471A ANNO REYNOLDS MARG
         HIM
      IN THE HIGHEST DEGREE FOR HE HAS EVERY [PERQUISITE] THING 472A ANNO REYNOLDS * MARG
         OF BOTH
      HAS THREE GATES INTO THE THREE HEAVENS OF BEULAH WHICH 484 MILTON 5   7
         SHINE
      THE NATURE OF INFINITY IS THIS THAT EVERY THING HAS ITS 497 MILTON 15   21
      IT HAS A HEART LIKE THEE A BRAIN OPEN TO HEAVEN & HELL . . 502 MILTON 20   28
      FOR EVERY HUMAN HEART HAS GATES OF BRASS & BARS OF ADAMANT 502 MILTON 20   34
      AND EVERY NATURAL EFFECT HAS A SPIRITUAL CAUSE AND NOT . . 513 MILTON 26   44
      AND EVERY MOMENT HAS A COUCH OF GOLD FOR SOFT REPOSE . . 516 MILTON 28   46
      AND EVERY MINUTE HAS AN AZURE TENT WITH SILKEN VEILS . . 516 MILTON 28   50
      AND EVERY HOUR HAS A BRIGHT GOLDEN GATE CARVED WITH SKILL 516 MILTON 28   51
      AND EVERY DAY & NIGHT HAS WALLS OF BRASS & GATES OF ADAMANT 516 MILTON 28   52
      EACH HAS ITS GUARD EACH MOMENT MINUTE HOUR DAY MONTH & 516 MILTON 28   59
         YEAR
      OG HAS TWENTY-SEVEN DISTRICTS SIHON'S DISTRICTS TWENTY-ONE 528 MILTON 37   51
      [HE HAS][M][THOU] TAKE YOU THE HIDE & HORNS . . . . . . 540 S(TOTHAR)D/N   *   5
      EVERY LINE OF HIS HAS MEANING . . . .   542 FLORENTINE/N   17
      SHE HAS CERTAIN PECULIARITIES AND LITTLE DELICATE   568B DESC CAT 3   PROSE
         AFFECTATIONS
      AND HIS ALSO HIS GREAT USE AND HIS GRAND LEADING DESTINY 570A DESC CAT 3   PROSE
      ACCORDING TO HIS PROSPECTUS HE HAS THREE MONKS THESE HE 574A DESC CAT 3   PROSE
      CANNOT FIND IN CHAUCER WHO HAS ONLY ONE MONK AND THAT . 574A DESC CAT 3   PROSE
      A SEA CAPTAIN CHAUCER HAS A SHIP-MAN A SAILOR . . . . . 575C DESC CAT 3   PROSE
      AND UGLINESS MR B(BLAKE) HAS IN HIS HANDS POEMS OF THE . 578A DESC CAT 5   PROSE
      HAS THE COURAGE TO SUFFER POVERTY AND DISGRACE . . . . 582D DESC CAT 9   PROSE
      WHO COULD NOT DO THIS WHAT MAN WHO HAS EYES . . . . .   597B PUB ADDRESS/N   PROSE
      MICH ANG EVERY PICTURE OF THEIRS HAS A DIFFERENT   598D PUB ADDRESS/N   PROSE
         & APPROPRIATE EFFECT
      EVERY PICTURE HAS THE SAME EFFECT A PIECE OF MACHINERY . . 599B PUB ADDRESS/N PROSE
      WHO THAT HAS EYES CANNOT SEE THAT RUBENS & CORREGGIO . 599D PUB ADDRESS/N   *PROSE
      PAINTING THE PRINCIPAL ART HAS NO PLACE [IN OUR] AMONG . 601A PUB ADDRESS/N   PROSE
      ANOTHER DEMON WITH A KEY HAS THE CHARGE OF SIN . . . . 606C V LAST JUDG/N   PROSE
      & JUSTICE CAIPHAS HAS A BLUE FLAME LIKE A MITER ON HIS HEAD 608A V LAST JUDG/N PROSE
      PILATE HAS BLOODY HANDS THAT NEVER CAN BE CLEANSED . . . 608D V LAST JUDG/N   PROSE
      [WHO] HE HAS SATAN'S BOOK OF ACCUSATIONS . . . . 609B V LAST JUDG/N   PROSE
      DRIVEN INTO THE WILDERNESS SHE HAS THE MOON UNDER HER FEET 610A V LAST JUDG/N PROSE
      EVERY MAN HAS EYES NOSE & MOUTH THIS EVERY IDIOT KNOWS 611B V LAST JUDG/N   PROSE
      SHE HAS NO WILL OF HER OWN THERE IS NO SUCH THING . . . 613D V LAST JUDG/N   PROSE
      NOT AN ERROR BUT IT HAS A MAN FOR ITS [ACTOR] AGENT . . 615A V LAST JUDG/N   PROSE
      THAT IS IT IS A MAN THERE IS NOT A TRUTH BUT IT HAS ALSO 615A V LAST JUDG/N   PROSE
         A MAN
      EVERY THING HAS ITS VERMIN O SPECTRE OF THE SLEEPING DEAD 620 JERUSALEM 1   11
      HAS FOUR SCULPTURD BULLS TERRIBLE BEFORE THE GATE OF IRON 632 JERUSALEM 12   62
      THE SOUTH A GOLDEN GATE HAS FOUR LIONS TERRIBLE LIVING . . 633 JERUSALEM 13   2
      AND EVERY ONE HAS THE THREE REGIONS CHILDHOOD MANHOOD & AGE 635 JERUSALEM 14   25

871

		PAGE	TITLE	LINE

HAS   (CONTINUED)

HE HAS A SEPULCHER HEWN OUT OF A ROCK READY FOR THEE	. .	664 JERUSALEM 37		6
NOR CAN HIS WATCH FIENDS FIND IT TIS TRANSLUCENT & HAS MANY ANGLES		668 JERUSALEM 41		16
IN ITS EXTENSION EVERY TWO HUNDRED YEARS HAS A DOOR TO EDEN		678 JERUSALEM 48		37
TILL DEEP DISSIMULATION IS THE ONLY DEFENCE AN HONEST MAN HAS LEFT		679 JERUSALEM 49		23
MAN MUST & WILL HAVE SOME RELIGION IF HE HAS	. . . . .	682B JERUSALEM 52		PROSE
FOR A SPECTRE HAS NO EMANATION BUT WHAT HE IMBIBES FROM DECIEVING		701 JERUSALEM 65		59
AND THE CENTER HAS ETERNAL STATES THESE STATES WE NOW EXPLORE		709 JERUSALEM 71		9
FOR ALBION IN ETERNITY HAS SIXTEEN GATES AMONG HIS PILLARS		711 JERUSALEM 72		5
THINE HAS A GREAT HOOK NOSE LIKE THINE	. . . .	748 EV GOSPEL(A)/N		3
MINE HAS A SNUB NOSE LIKE TO MINE	. . . .	748 EV GOSPEL(A)/N		4
THOSE OF A BULL EVERY THING HAS ITS OWN HARMONY & PROPORTION		774B ANNO BERKELEY		MARG
BUT WHEN A WORK HAS UNITY IT IS AS MUCH IN A PART AS IN THE WHOLE		778B HOMERS POETRY		PROSE
NOW GOODNESS OR BADNESS HAS NOTHING TO DO WITH CHARACTER		778B HOMERS POETRY		PROSE
"ROME HAS SOMEWHAT BETTER TO DO NAMELY WAR & DOMINION"	. .	778D HOMERS POETRY		PROSE
NATURE HAS NO OUTLINE BUT IMAGINATION HAS	. . . . . .	779C GHOST ABEL 1		PROSE
NATURE HAS NO TUNE BUT IMAGINATION HAS	. . . .	779C GHOST ABEL 1		PROSE
NATURE HAS NO SUPERNATURAL & DISSOLVES IMAGINATION IS ETERNITY		779C GHOST ABEL 1		PROSE
A SPIRITUAL MAN IMAGINATION HAS NOTHING TO DO WITH MEMORY		783D ANNO WW POEMS		MARG
EVERY THING HAS AS MUCH RIGHT TO ETERNAL LIFE	. . . . .	788B ANNO THORNTON		MARG
THE USE OF MONEY HAS MORE BEAUTIFUL PROPORTIONS THAN	. . .	793D LETTER 5		PROSE
BUT AS I KNOW THAT HE WHO WORKS & HAS HIS HEALTH CANNOT		795C LETTER 6		PROSE
(TO HER) SERVICE & THAT IT HAS A VERY FINE VIEW OF THE SEA		803B LETTER 15		*PROSE
BEEN WITH MR SAUNDERS WHO HAS NOW IN HIS POSSESSION ALL MR		831A LETTER 31		PROSE
I HAVE SEEN MR SAUNDERS & ENQUIRD OF HIM WHETHER HE HAS ANY		832C LETTER 32		PROSE
THE NORTH BY SAYING THAT [MR ROMNEY] MR JOHN ROMNEY HAS		832C LETTER 32		PROSE
MR SAUNDERS HAS A GOOD MANY WERE ENGRAVD THEY	. . . . .	832C LETTER 32		PROSE
EVERY ENQUIRY OF HIM IF YOU THINK BEST MR SANDERS HAS	.	834C LETTER 34		PROSE
THE DRAWING OF THE MONUMENT WHICH MR JOHNSON SENT HAS	.	838B LETTER 37		PROSE
SAYS THAT HE HAS ORDERS FROM MR ROMNEY TO DELIVER THE	. .	839D LETTER 38		PROSE
AT BRIGHTON WHERE HE HAS A RESIDENCE FROM WHENCE HE SENT IT		842C LETTER 42		PROSE
WAS IN SOME MEASURE TO BE EXPECTED BUT THAT HE HAS REASONS		853A LETTER 51		*PROSE
HE HAS ENOUGH & TO SPARE & THE WORLD WILL KNOW HIS AT ONCE &		853A LETTER 51		*PROSE
HOPE THAT AS MR D(DODSLEY) IS DEAD & IF MR H(HAYLEY) HAS NO		856B LETTER 54		PROSE
OWES SUCCESS TO SOMETHING BESIDE OR WITHOUT ITSELF IF IT HAS ANY		862A LETTER 59		PROSE
ALL HITHERTO YOU DEAR SIR ARE ONE WHO HAS MY PARTICULAR		862C LETTER 60		PROSE
& HOPE THAT HE HAS A GOOD OPINION OF MY WILLINGNESS TO APPEAR		868D LETTER 68		PROSE
DUPLICATES TO OTHERS WHICH HE HAS THEY ARE INTIRELY AT	. .	877B LETTER 86		PROSE
PROOFS HE HAS REMAINING [ALL] ARE ALL PRINTED ON BOTH SIDES OF		877B LETTER 86		*PROSE

HAST

BENEATH OUR OAKS HAST SLEPT WHILE WE BEHELD	. . . . .	1 TO SUMMER/PS		5
THE NORTH IS THINE THERE HAST THOU BUILT THY DARK	. . .	2 TO WINTER/PS		2
GWIN THOU HAST FILLD THY MEASURE UP	. . . .	13 GWIN KING/PS		67
NOW KITTY NOW WHAT CHANCE HAST THOU	. . . .	16 BLIND-MANS/PS		29
THOU HAST A GALLANT SPIRIT WHICH I FEAR	. . . . . .	20 EDW THIRD/PS 2		57
AND THOU HAST BEEN INCIRCLED IN HIS ARMS	. . . . . .	38B SAMSON/PS		PROSE
THRICE HAST THOU MOCKED ME AND GRIEVED MY SOUL	. . . .	38D SAMSON/PS		PROSE
THOU HAST REFUSD OUR CHARITY THOU HAST REFUSD OUR FOOD		100 TIRIEL 1		37
THOU HAST REFUSD OUR CLOTHES OUR BEDS OUR HOUSES FOR THY DWELLING		100 TIRIEL 1		38
NO MATTER WHO I AM O MNETHA IF THOU HAST ANY FOOD	. . .	101 TIRIEL 2		21
THOU HAST NO TEETH OLD MAN & THUS I KISS THY SLEEK BALD HEAD		101 TIRIEL 2		37
AND I REMAIN AN OUTCAST HAST THOU ANY THING TO DRINK	. .	102 TIRIEL 2		57
THOU SHALT NOT GO SAID HEVA TILL THOU HAST SEEN OUR SINGING BIRDS		103 TIRIEL 3		22
THOU HAST THE FORM OF TIRIEL BUT I KNOW THEE WELL ENOUGH		103 TIRIEL 4		7
[O NOBLE IJIM THOU HAST BROUGHT OUR FATHER TO [THE GATES] OUR EYES]		105 TIRIEL 4		75
THEN IS IT TRUE HEUXOS THAT THOU HAST TURND THY AGED PARENT		106 TIRIEL 4		83
THEN WOULD THEY CURSE AS THOU HAST CURSED BUT THEY ARE NOT LIKE THEE		107 TIRIEL 6		25
LOOK ON MY EYES HELA & SEE FOR THOU HAST EYES TO SEE	. .	108 TIRIEL 6		29
FOR THOU HAST LAUGHED AT MY TEARS & CURST THY AGED FATHER		108 TIRIEL 6		42
THOU HAST A LAP FULL OF SEED	. . . .	168 HAST LAP/N		1
[HAST MY] THAT FREE LOVE WITH BONDAGE BOUND	. . . . .	169 EARTHS ANSWR/N		25
WHY HAST THOU TAUGHT MY THEOTORMON THIS ACCURSED THING	.	194 V DAU ALBION 7		13
RINTRAH WHERE HAST THOU HID THY BRIDE	. . . .	240 EUROPE 8		5
WHY [HAST] HAS THOU TAKEN	. . . .	265 FOUR ZOAS 1		29
IF THOU HAST SINND & ART POLLUTED KNOW THAT I AM PURE	.	268 FOUR ZOAS 1		151
TIS THOU HAST DARKEND ALL MY WORLD O WOMAN LOVELY BANE	.	269 FOUR ZOAS 1		178
FOR I PERCIEVE THOU HAST ABUNDANCE WHICH I CLAIM AS MINE		273 FOUR ZOAS 1		334
MY DEEP MY NIGHT WHICH THOU ASSUMING HAST ASSUMD MY CROWN		278 FOUR ZOAS 1		511
THO THOU HAST NOT PITID MY AGE O URIZEN PRINCE OF LIGHT		280 FOUR ZOAS 2		8
FOR THOU HAST TOUCHD MY FIVE SENSES & THEY ANSWERD THEE		290 FOUR ZOAS 2		376
ARE MY ABHORRENCE WHEREFORE HAST THOU TAKEN THAT FAIR FORM		295 FOUR ZOAS 3	*	119
AND THOU HAST RISEN WITH THY MOIST LOCKS INTO A WATRY IMAGE		295 FOUR ZOAS 3		125
TILL WINTER RENDS THEE INTO SHIVERS AS THOU HAST RENDED ME		296 FOUR ZOAS 3	*	175
THOU RASH ABHORRED DEMON IN THY FURY HAST OERTHROWN	. . .	299 FOUR ZOAS 4		52
THY LOVED ENITHARMON FOR THOU HAST HER HERE BEFORE THINE EYES		300 FOUR ZOAS 4		117

	PAGE	TITLE	LINE

HAST   (CONTINUED)

HAST THOU FORGOT THAT THE AIR LISTENS THRO ALL ITS DISTRICTS TELLING — 339 FOUR ZOAS 7B — 242
WHERE HAST THOU HID HIM WHOM I LOVE IN WHAT REMOTE ABYSS — 345 FOUR ZOAS 8 — 155
. . . IF [?THAT ?WE] THOU HAST SMITTEN HIM — 345 FOUR ZOAS 8 — * 164
[THOU HAST PARTED FROM MY SIDE] . . . . . — 415 MY SPECTRE/N — 9
[HAVE I] HAST THOU NO SINS OF [MY] THY OWN . . . . . — 417 MY SPECTR AD/N * 2
THOU HAST GIVN ME POWER TO PROTECT MYSELF FROM MY BITTEREST ENEMIES — 489 MILTON 9 — 6
IN JEALOUSY & UNLOVELY IN MY SIGHT BECAUSE THOU HAST CRUELLY — 522 MILTON 33 — 6
DEPEND THY PLEASURES WHICH THOU HAST CUT OFF BY JEALOUSY — 522 MILTON 33 — 9
WHERE HAST THOU HIDDEN THY EMANATION LOVELY JERUSALEM . . — 622 JERUSALEM 4 — 16
HAST JUST CAUSE TO BE IRRITATED BUT LOOK STEDPASTLY UPON ME — 626 JERUSALEM 7 — 53
CONCERNING MY CHIEF DELIGHT BUT THOU HAST BROKEN SILENCE — 630 JERUSALEM 10 — 41
WHEREFORE HAST THOU SHUT ME INTO THE WINTER OF HUMAN LIFE — 642 JERUSALEM 20 — 5
HAST THOU AGAIN KNITTED THE VEIL OF VALA WHICH I FOR THEE — 645 JERUSALEM 23 — 5
THOU ART MY FATHER & MY BROTHER WHY HAST THOU HIDDEN ME — 646 JERUSALEM 23 — 11
THREE THOU HAST SLAIN I AM THE FOURTH THOU CANST NOT DESTROY ME — 670 JERUSALEM 42 — 24
AND THOU HAST BOUND ME DOWN UPON THE STEMS OF VEGETATION — 692 JERUSALEM 60 — 11
OR HAST THOU BEEN PIERCED IN THE HOUSE OF THY FRIENDS . . — 693 JERUSALEM 60 — 53
WHEREFORE HAST THOU WRIT THESE LAWS . . . . — 754 EV GOSPEL(E)/N — 31
MY SIN THOU HAST FORGIVEN ME . . . . — 755 EV GOSPEL(E)/N — 75
SEVEN TIMES O EVE THOU HAST FAINTED OVER THE DEAD AH AH — 779 GHOST ABEL 1 — 5
ADAM EVE THOU HAST SPOKEN TRULY LET US KNEEL BEFORE HIS FEET — 780 GHOST ABEL 2 — 3
AS THOU HAST SAID SO IS IT COME TO PASS MY DESIRE IS UNTO CAIN — 780 GHOST ABEL 2 — 7
FAREWELL SWEET ROSE THOU HAST GOT BEFORE ME INTO THE . . — 854C LETTER 53 — PROSE
"THOU HAST SET THY HEART AS THE HEART OF GOD" EZEKIEL . . — SUPP LEGEND/N94 — *

HASTE

THEN TO MY BLACK EYD MAID I HASTE AWAY . . . . — 10 WHEN EARLY/PS — 2
IN HASTE THEY FLED WHILE ALL THE SONS & DAUGHTERS OF TIRIEL — 107 TIRIEL 5 — 27
TO YONDER BRIGHTNESS THERE I HASTE FOR SURE I CAME FROM THENCE — 367 FOUR ZOAS 9 — 402
THRO EVENING SHADES I HASTE AWAY . . . . — 771 OF GATES/GP — 41
WHENEVER SHE HEARS IT NAMED EXCUSE MY HASTE & . . . . . — 801C LETTER 13 — PROSE
I WRITE IN GREAT HASTE & WITH A HEAD FULL OF BOTHERATION — 821B LETTER 25 — PROSE
I WRITE IN HASTE HAVING RECIEVD A PRESSING LETTER FROM . . — 822B LETTER 26 — PROSE

HASTED

BUT KITTY HASTED WITH A KEY . . . . — 17 BLIND-MANS/PS — 57
AND MNETHA HASTED & MET THEM AT THE GATE OF THE LOWER GARDEN — 109 TIRIEL 8 — 1

HASTEN

I HASTEN TO WRITE TO YOU BY THE FAVOUR OF MR EDWARDS I HAVE — 831A LETTER 31 — PROSE
BECAUSE I WOULD HASTEN ITS ARRIVAL BEFORE IT IS CONVENIENT — 853D LETTER 52 — PROSE

HASTEND

BUT I HASTEND TO WRITE TO YOU ABOUT MR BRAITHWAITE HOPE — 837A LETTER 35 — PROSE

HASTETH

THE TRAVELLER HASTETH IN THE EVENING DEATH'S DOOR . . . — 209D FOR CHILDRN/GP — TITLE
THE TRAVELLER HASTETH IN THE EVENING . . . . — 769B FOR SEXES/GP — TITLE
THUS THE TRAVELLER HASTETH IN THE EVENING . . . . . . — SUPP LEGEND/N15 — *TITLE

HASTILY

INFLAMMABLE GASS TURNING ROUND HASTILY IN HIS CHAIR SAID — 45C ISLAND MOON 1 — PROSE

HASTING

AT MIDNIGHT HASTING TO THEIR MUCH BELOVED CARE . . . . — 309 FOUR ZOAS 5 — 148

HASTY

HAS HE NOT SPOILD THE HASTY PUDDING . . . . — 390B ANNO WATSON — MARG
BE DONE IN A CARELESS OR TOO HASTY MANNER THE PRICE . . . — 848C LETTER 45 — PROSE
IN THE MEAN WHILE I CONCLUDE THIS HASTY SCRAWL WITH . . . — 853A LETTER 51 — *PROSE

HAT

THE TRUMPETER SHIT IN HIS HAT SAID THE EPICUREAN . . . — 46C ISLAND MOON 3 — PROSE
THE PILGRIM WITH HIS CROOK & HAT . . . . — 54 PHEBE DREST/IM — 11
[AND] BUT IN MY HAT CAUGHT . . . . — 178 THE FAIRY/N — * 15
AND CAUGHT HIM IN MY HAT AS BOYS KNOCK DOWN A BUTTERFLY — 237 EUROPE INTRO — 9

HATCHING

AT LENGTH FOR HATCHING RIPE HE BREAKS THE SHELL . . . . — 209C FOR CHILDRN/GP — TITLE
FORTHWITH HATCHING SOME HOWLD ON HIS HILLS . . . . . . — 250 AHANIA 3 — 11
HIS BROODINGS RUSH DOWN TO HIS FEET PRODUCING EGGS THAT HATCHING — 324 FOUR ZOAS 7 — 167
AT LENGTH FOR HATCHING RIPE HE BREAKS THE SHELL . . . . — 765B FOR SEXES/GP — TITLE
"AT LENGTH FOR HATCHING RIPE HE BREAKS THE SHELL" DRYDEN — SUPP LEGEND/N68 — *

HATCHT

IN VAIN-GLORY HATCHT & NURST . . . . — 771 OF GATES/GP — 27

HATE

ENVY AND HATE THAT THIRST FOR HUMAN GORE . . . . . . — 15 IMIT SPEN/PS — 32
SO ENVY CAME & HATE TWIN PROGENY . . . . — 41C THEN SHE BORE — PROSE
HATE MEAGER HAG SETS ENVY ON UNABLE TO DO OUGHT HERSELF — 41D THEN SHE BORE — PROSE
AND STRIFE BROUGHT FORTH REVENGE HATE BROODING IN HER DISMAL DEN — 42C THEN SHE BORE — PROSE
TO DO THE WORK OF HATE HER DRUDGE & ELF . . . . . . — 42D THEN SHE BORE — PROSE
BUT POLICY DOTH DRUDGE FOR HATE AS WELL AS SLANDER . . . — 42D THEN SHE BORE — PROSE
INDEED HATE CONTROLLS ALL THE GODS AT WILL . . . . . — 42D THEN SHE BORE — PROSE
I HATE YOUR SNEAKING RASCALS THERES ARADOBO . . . . . — 49D ISLAND MOON 6 — PROSE
I HATE REASONING I DO EVERYTHING BY MY FEELINGS AH SAID SIPSOP I ONLY — 50A ISLAND MOON 6 — PROSE
MY DEAR THEY HATE PEOPLE WHO ARE OF HIGHER ABILITIES . . — 63A ISLAND MOON 11 — PROSE
I HATE SCARCE SMILES I LOVE LAUGHING . . . . — 67D ANNO LAVATER — MARG
("OR THE PIETIST WHO CRAWLS GROANS BLUBBERS") I HATE CRAWLERS — 67D ANNO LAVATER — MARG
("AS THE GOOD LOVE THEE THE BAD WILL HATE THEE") UNEASY — 72D ANNO LAVATER — MARG

HATE   (CONTINUED)
    ("SNEERS ...PRECEDE QUARRELS") HATE THE SNEERER . . . .   75C ANNO LAVATER   MARG
    ("HATE AS IF YOU COULD LOVE OR SHOULD BE") BETTER THAN   84D ANNO LAVATER   MARG
      EXCELLENT
    REASON AND ENERGY LOVE AND HATE ARE NECESSARY TO HUMAN   149B MARRIAGE HH 3   PROSE
      EXISTENCE
    ARE ALL RELIGIOUS & CONVERSED NOT WITH DEVILS WHO ALL   157D MARRIAGE HH 21   PROSE
      HATE RELIGION
    THOSE WHO ENVY OR CALUMNIATE GREAT MEN HATE GOD . . . . 158B MARRIAGE HH 22   PROSE
    . . . [?ALONE ?POSSESSD BY DEADLY FEARS] LOVE IS CHANGD   267 FOUR ZOAS 1   * 111
      TO DEADLY HATE
    ALTERNATE LOVE & HATE HIS BREAST HERS SCORN & JEALOUSY . . 270 FOUR ZOAS 1   237
    DISCORDANT PRINCIPLES OF LOVE & HATE I SUFFER AFFLICTION   282 FOUR ZOAS 2   103
    ON HATE ETERNAL IN HIS VAST DISDAIN HE LABOURD BEATING . . 302 FOUR ZOAS 4   206
    AND DARKEN ALL MY PALACE WALLS WITH ENVYINGS & HATE . .   310 FOUR ZOAS 5   213
    TO THE HARD ROCK OR THOU SHOULDST FEEL MY ENMITY & HATE   322 FOUR ZOAS 7   88
    IN HIS HANDS HE WONDERD THAT HE FELT LOVE & NOT HATE . .   332 FOUR ZOAS 7   497
    LOVE THOSE WHO HATE REWARDING WITH HATE THE LOVING SOUL   335 FOUR ZOAS 7B   91
    AND THERE IS A FROWN OF HATE . . . .   423 THE SMILE   5
    BY VARIOUS ARTS OF LOVE & HATE . . . .   426 MENTAL TRAVLER   81
    OF THE HUMAN RACE WHO HATE WHAT YOU CALL MORAL VIRTUE .   616A V LAST JUDG/N   PROSE
    THEY TORMENT ONE ANOTHER FOR OTHER REASONS THAN HATE OR   616B V LAST JUDG/N   PROSE
      ENVY
    WITH EVERY PATHETIC STORY POSSIBLE TO HAPPEN FROM HATE OR   638 JERUSALEM 16   63
    TO THOSE I HATE FOR I CAN HATE ALSO AS WELL AS THEY . .   640 JERUSALEM 17   63
    AND NOW RECIEVES REPROACH & HATE WAS IT NOT SAID OF OLD   658 JERUSALEM 31   51
    OF SPIRITUAL HATE FROM WHICH SPRINGS SEXUAL LOVE AS IRON   685 JERUSALEM 54   12
      CHAINS
    HE WHO WILL NOT COMINGLE IN LOVE MUST BE ADJOIND BY HATE   703 JERUSALEM 66   56
    AND NOW I HATE & NOW I LOVE & INTELLECT IS NO MORE . .   707 JERUSALEM 68   67
    DEADLY HATE BETWEEN LEAH & RACHEL DAUGHTERS OF DECEIT &   707 JERUSALEM 69   11
      FRAUD
    MUTUAL HATE RETURNS & MUTUAL DECEIT & MUTUAL FEAR . .   708 JERUSALEM 69   37
    AND HATE DIVIDING THE SPACE OF LOVE WITH BRAZEN COMPASSES   734 JERUSALEM 88   47
    AND THO YOU CANNOT LOVE BUT HATE . . . .   755 EV GOSPEL(E)/N   55
HATED
    A SCALED SERPENT YET I FED HER THO SHE HATED ME . . . .   282 FOUR ZOAS 2   85
    BACON HATED TALENTS OF ALL KINDS ELOQUENCE IS DISCRETION   409A ANNO BACON   MARG
      OF SPEECH
    I KNEW NOT OF THEIR SECRET LOVES WITH THOSE I HATED MOST   644 JERUSALEM 21   26
HATEFUL
    NOR SONS NOR HATEFUL PEACE & LOVE NOR SOFT COMPLACENCIES   640 JERUSALEM 18   14
HATER
    BLASPHEMOUS DEMON ANTICHRIST HATER OF DIGNITIES . . . .   198 AMERICA 7   5
HATERS
    OF HATERS MET IN DEADLY STRIFE RENDING THE HOUSE & GARDEN   640 JERUSALEM 18   22
HATES
    MY JOY IS GIVEN INTO THE HANDS OF HIM WHO HATES ME . . .   38D SAMSON/PS   PROSE
    ("KEEP DISTANT WHO HATES...LAUGH OF A CHILD") THE BEST   74B ANNO LAVATER   MARG
      IN THE BOOK
    [("HATES")] LOVES ("WISEST & BEST [HATES] ") LOVES   82D ANNO LAVATER   MARG
      ("FATHER OF MEN")
    TILL THE CHILD DWELL WITH ONE HE HATES AND DO THE DEED   193 V DAU ALBION 5   30
      HE LOATHS
    A LIE EVERY BODY HATES A KING BACON WAS AFRAID TO SAY THAT   400B ANNO BACON   MARG
    EVERY BODY NATURALLY HATES A PERFECT CHARACTER BECAUSE . . 412A ANNO BOYD   MARG
    NO ONE ENVIES OR HATES ONE OF HIS OWN PARTY . . . . .   616B V LAST JUDG/N   PROSE
    THO SHE HATES HE CALLS HER AGAIN IN LOVE I LOVE MY DEAR   694 JERUSALEM 61   8
      JOSEPH
    THINE LOVES THE SAME WORLD THAT MINE HATES . . . . .   748 EV GOSPEL(A)/N   7
    HE WHO LOVES HIS ENEMIES HATES HIS FRIENDS . . . . .   750 EV GOSPEL(C)/N   19
    HE WHO LOVES HIS ENEMIES [HATES] BETRAYS HIS FRIENDS . .   751 EV GOSPEL(D)/N   25
HATEST
    MERCIFUL TO THEE AND CRUEL TO ALL THAT THOU HATEST . . .   670 JERUSALEM 42   22
HATH
    FOR HE HATH REARD HIS SCEPTRE OER THE WORLD . . . . .   3 TO WINTER/PS   8
    THAT BED OF JOY WHERE ERST HER LORD HATH PRESSD . . . .   5 FAIR ELENOR/PS   38
    MIDAS THE PRAISE HATH GAIND OF LENGTHEND [CARES] EARS . .   14 IMIT SPEN/PS   15
    AND HATH THE SPIRIT OF LIBERTY WITHIN HIM . . . . . .   25 EDW THIRD/PS 3   190
    O WHO CAN STAND O WHO HATH CAUSED THIS . . . .   33 EDW FOURTH/PS   13
    JUSTICE HATH HEAVED A SWORD TO PLUNGE IN ALBION'S BREAST   34A KING JOHN/PS   PROSE
    TYRANNY HATH STAIND FAIR ALBION'S BREAST WITH HER   34A KING JOHN/PS   PROSE
      OWN CHILDREN'S GORE
    FOR TYRANNY HATH STRETCHD HIS PURPLE ARM AND BLOOD HE CRIES   34B KING JOHN/PS   PROSE
    MY VOICE HATH USED DECEIT HOW SHOULD I CALL ON HIM WHO   36A COUCH DEATH/PS   PROSE
      IS TRUTH
    THE POISON HATH ENTERED INTO MY MARROW . . . .   36B COUCH DEATH/PS   PROSE
    THE TRAVELLER THAT HATH TAKEN SHELTER UNDER AN OAK . . .   36C COUCH DEATH/PS   PROSE
    WHERE ONLY NATURE'S FOOT HATH TROD . . . .   36D CONTEMPLATN/PS   PROSE
    ERE ONCE AGAIN THE CHANGING MOON HER CIRCUIT HATH PERFORMED   38A SAMSON/PS   PROSE
    BUT GOD HATH OTHER JOYS IN STORE IS BURDENED ISRAEL HIS   39C SAMSON/PS   PROSE
      GRIEF
    ENVY HATH A SERPENT'S HEAD OF FEARFUL BULK . . . . . .   41C THEN SHE BORE   PROSE
    WHEN ALL AROUND SUMMER HATH SPRED HER PLUMES . . . . .   43B WOE CRIED MUSE   PROSE
    ASK ME NO MORE I PRAY FOR GRIEF HATH SEALD MY PRECIOUS   102 TIRIEL 2   53
      SIGHT
    [HATH WORKD OUR RUIN WE SUBMIT NOR STRIVE AGAINST STERN   105 TIRIEL 4   80
      FATE]
    HE SAYS AT N...NO KING HATH SUCH A GOVERNMENT AS THIS . . 132C ANNO SWED PROV   MARG
    NOR FOR ITSELF HATH ANY CARE . . . .   162 CLOD PEBBLE/N   2
    HATH FOUND OUT THY BED . . . .   175 SICK ROSE/N   5
    HATH BRUSHD AWAY . . . .   183 THE FLY/N   8

		PAGE	TITLE	LINE

HATH   (CONTINUED)
```
    NOR FOR ITSELF HATH ANY CARE  . . . . . . . . .  .  211 CLOD PEBBLE/SE      2
    HATH FORMD THIS ABOMINABLE VOID  . . . . . . . . .  222 URIZEN 3           4
    IN AN ALLEGORICAL ABODE WHERE EXISTENCE HATH NEVER COME  240 EUROPE 5      7
    SHE HATH TAKEN REFUGE IN MY BOSOM & I CANNOT CAST HER OUT  265 FOUR ZOAS 1  32
    THY BROTHER LUVAH HATH SMITTEN ME BUT PITY THOU HIS YOUTH  280 FOUR ZOAS 2   7
    OF ALL THAT A MAN HATH HIS HOUSE HIS WIFE HIS CHILDREN  . .  290 FOUR ZOAS 2  * 399
    WHEN THE SHATTERED BONE HATH LAID HIM GROANING AMONG THE  291 FOUR ZOAS 2   416
      HAPPIER DEAD
    [THOU SITST IN HARMONY FOR GOD HATH SET THEE OVER ALL]  . .  291 FOUR ZOAS 3   10
    O PRINCE THE ETERNAL ONE HATH SET THEE LEADER OF HIS HOSTS  292 FOUR ZOAS 3   27
    OF PROPHECY & LUVAH HATH BURST HIS WAY FROM ENITHARMON  . .  311 FOUR ZOAS 5  240
    MY LUVAH HERE HATH PLACD ME IN A SWEET & PLEASANT LAND  . .  369 FOUR ZOAS 9  451
    AND NIGHT HATH HEARD MY SORROWS LOUD  . . . . . . .  .  423 THE BIRDS/N     12
    BUT WE MUST NOT BE TYRANTS ALSO HE HATH ASSUMD MY PLACE  487 MILTON 7       27
    MY HORSES HATH HE MADDEND AND MY FELLOW SERVANTS INJURD  487 MILTON 7       29
    THE TRUMPET OF JUDGMENT HATH TWICE SOUNDED ALL NATIONS  506 MILTON 23       4
      ARE AWAKE
    HE HATH ENTERD INTO THE COVERING CHERUB BECOME ONE WITH  507 MILTON 23      14
    I KNOW THAT ALBION HATH DIVIDED ME AND THAT THOU  626 JERUSALEM 7          52
      O MY SPECTRE
    CONSUMING & THE ALMIGHTY HATH MADE ME HIS CONTRARY  . . .  630 JERUSALEM 10  56
    SHAME DIVIDES FAMILIES SHAME HATH DIVIDED ALBION IN SUNDER  643 JERUSALEM 21   6
    THE REACTOR HATH HID HIMSELF THRO ENVY I BEHOLD HIM  . .  653 JERUSALEM 29    9
    FROM ALBION BUT HATH FOUNDED HIS REACTION INTO A LAW  . .  653 JERUSALEM 29   14
    HE HATH COMPELLD ALBION TO BECOME A PUNISHER & HATH  653 JERUSALEM 29       16
      POSSESSD
    ALBION HATH ENTERD THE LOINS THE PLACE OF THE LAST JUDGMENT  656 JERUSALEM 30  38
    AND LUVAH HATH DRAWN THE CURTAINS AROUND ALBION IN VALA'S  656 JERUSALEM 30   39
      BOSOM
    ALBION HATH ENTERD THE STATE SATAN BE PERMANENT O STATE  662 JERUSALEM 35    13
    GOD HATH FORSAKEN ME & MY FRIENDS ARE BECOME A BURDEN  . .  666 JERUSALEM 39  22
    HE HATH LEAGUED HIMSELF WITH ROBBERS HE HATH STUDIED THE  667 JERUSALEM 40   13
      ARTS
    DESTROY NOT BY MORAL VIRTUE THE LITTLE ONES WHOM HE HATH  670 JERUSALEM 42   42
      CHOSEN
    THE LITTLE ONES WHOM HE HATH CHOSEN IN PREFERENCE TO THEE  670 JERUSALEM 42   43
    HE HATH CAST THEE OFF FOR EVER THE LITTLE ONES HE HATH  670 JERUSALEM 42     44
      ANOINTED
    HE HATH PLACED OG & ANAK THE GIANTS OF ALBION FOR THEIR  680 JERUSALEM 49    56
      GUARDS
    BLOOD HATH STAIND HER FAIR SIDE BENEATH HER BOSOM  . . .  705 JERUSALEM 67   43
    THEY HAVE DIVIDED LEVI HE HATH SHOT OUT INTO FORTY EIGHT  715 JERUSALEM 74   47
      ROOTS
    HE HATH TOOK ROOT IN HEBRON IN THE LAND OF HAND & HYLE  . .  715 JERUSALEM 74  49
    AND RAHAB BABYLON THE GREAT HATH DESTROYED JERUSALEM  . .  715 JERUSALEM 75    1
    MY BROTHER & MY FATHER ARE NO MORE GOD HATH FORSAKEN ME  719 JERUSALEM 78    31
    GOSHEN HATH FOLLOWD PHILISTEA GILEAD HATH JOIND WITH OG  720 JERUSALEM 79    13
    BY THE LOST SHEEP THAT HE HATH FOUND & ALBION KNEW THAT IT  743 JERUSALEM 96   4
    AND A CONTRITE HEART O I CANNOT FORGIVE THE ACCUSER HATH  780 GHOST ABEL 2    5
    AND NOW FLAXMAN HATH GIVEN ME HAYLEY HIS FRIEND . . . . .  799 TO FLAXMAN/L   4
    AND LOS THE TERRIBLE THUS HATH SWORN . . . . . . . .  .  817 HAPPINESS/L    35
HATING
    STILL HATING STILL PROFESSING LOVE STILL LABOURING IN  286 FOUR ZOAS 2     235
      THE SMOKE
    HALLS OF JUSTICE HATING VICE  . . . . . . . . . . .  .  757 EV GOSPEL(I)/N  25
HATOMY
    PHIZOGRAPHY HOGAMY HATOMY & HALL THAT BUT IN THE FIRST  49C ISLAND MOON 5 PROSE
      PLACE
HATRED
    ALL LOVE IS LOST TERROR SUCCEEDS & HATRED INSTEAD OF LOVE  265 FOUR ZOAS 1   36
    BECAUSE I LOVE FOR I [AM] WAS LOVE [&] BUT HATRED AWAKES  282 FOUR ZOAS 2  * 104
      IN ME
    THE BOUNDS OF DESTINY WERE BROKEN & HATRED NOW BEGAN  . .  296 FOUR ZOAS 3  177
    CRUEL AND RAVENING WITH ENMITY & HATRED & WAR . . . . .  .  328 FOUR ZOAS 7  330
    CONDEMN PAINE'S HATRED OF PRIESTS IF YOU DARE . . . . .  384A ANNO WATSON  MARG
    OF INDIVIDUAL MERIT BEING ITS GREAT HATRED . . . . . .  594A PUB ADDRESS/N PROSE
    THE NATURE OF HATRED & ENVY &  . . . . . . . . .  .  616B V LAST JUDG/N  PROSE
    OR HATRED OR MALICE BUT THRO SELFRIGHTEOUSNESS  . . . .  616C V LAST JUDG/N PROSE
    ALL LOVE IS LOST TERROR SUCCEEDS & [RATRED] HATRED INSTEAD  645 JERUSALEM 22 * 10
      OF LOVE
HATREDS
    AND CHAMBERS OF TREMBLING & SUSPITION HATREDS OF AGE &  640 JERUSALEM 18    24
      YOUTH
    BY INVISIBLE HATREDS ADJOIND THEY SEEM REMOTE AND SEPARATE  703 JERUSALEM 66  53
HATS
    & HER FOOTMAN & HER MAIDS & STORMONTS & BALLOON HATS  . .  52D ISLAND MOON 8 PROSE
HAUGHTY
    AND DRAWING IN THE SPECTROUS LIFE IN PRIDE AND HAUGHTY JOY  270 FOUR ZOAS 1  220
    HUMBLE TOWARD GOD HAUGHTY TOWARD MAN  . . . . . . .  .  750 EV GOSPEL(C)/N  33
    HUMBLE TO GOD HAUGHTY TO MAN  . . . . . . . . . .  .  752 EV GOSPEL(D)/N  68
HAUNT
    EACH VILLAGE SEEMS THE HAUNT OF HOLY FEET . . . . . .  .  9 FRESH FROM/PS   16
    MY FOUNTAINS ONCE THE HAUNT OF SWANS NOW BREED THE SCALY  310 FOUR ZOAS 5  194
      TORTOISE
    THE HOUSES OF MY HARPERS ARE BECOME A HAUNT OF CROWS  . .  310 FOUR ZOAS 5  195
HAUNTED
    BY THE HAUNTED STREAM BY SUN SET SEES IN HIS DREAM  . . .  618D ILLUS MILTON PROSE
HAUNTS
    LIKE A DARK LAMP ETERNAL DEATH HAUNTS ALL MY EXPECTATION  293 FOUR ZOAS 3    75
HAVE    (OMITTING AUXILIARY VERB)
    SUCH END TRUE LOVERS HAVE  . . . . . . . . . . .  .  6 MY SILKS/PS       6
```

HAVE   (CONTINUED)

	PAGE	TITLE	LINE
WHERE THE MELODIOUS WINDS HAVE BIRTH	10	TO MUSES/PS	8
O WHAT HAVE KINGS TO ANSWER FOR	13	GWIN KING/PS	97
IF I OBTAIN YOUR LEAVE I HAVE ANOTHER BOON	20	EDW THIRD/PS 2	43
THANKS BRAVE LORD PERCY YOU HAVE THE THANKS	21	EDW THIRD/PS 2	98
SIR THOMAS DAGWORTH YOU MUST HAVE YOUR JOKE	23	EDW THIRD/PS 3	92
I HAVE A SMALL PETITION TO YOUR MAJESTY	23	EDW THIRD/PS 3	95
ARE SET THE SWIFTEST MAY HAVE ROOM THE STRONGEST	27	EDW THIRD/PS 3	257
WE HAVE OUR BATTLE FOR OUR PAINS I KNOW	27	EDW THIRD/PS 3	268
ARE FINER THAN ANY WE HAVE IN ENGLAND	28	EDW THIRD/PS 4	6
BUT I DONT THINK YOU HAVE ANY OF IT	28	EDW THIRD/PS 4	16
YES I HAVE I HAVE A GREAT AMBITION TO KNOW EVERY THING SIR	28D	EDW THIRD/PS 4	PROSE
ONLY REMEMBER WILLIAM ALL HAVE IT IN THEIR POWER	29A	EDW THIRD/PS 4	PROSE
WOULD EASE MY PAIN THEN SHOULD I LAY AT QUIET AND HAVE REST	38C	SAMSON/PS	PROSE
WHICH SMALL ISLAND SEEMS TO HAVE SOME AFFINITY TO ENGLAND	44A	ISLAND MOON 1	*PROSE
BUT A MAN MUST HAVE GOOD SOUND SENSE TO SOLVE THEM	45D	ISLAND MOON 1	PROSE
WHAT IS IT YOU WOULD PLEASE TO HAVE	46	PHEBUS CAME/IM	3
NO SAID INFLAMMABLE GASS I HAVE GOT A CAMERA OBSCURA AT HOME	47C	ISLAND MOON 3	PROSE
OF THE MINISTERS YOU DESERVE TO HAVE YOUR EARS BOXED YOU DO	48C	ISLAND MOON 4	PROSE
COME SAID THE EPICUREAN LET'S HAVE SOME RUM & WATER	49B	ISLAND MOON 5	PROSE
THAT HAVE IT DONE FOR NOTHING MAKE SUCH A PIECE OF WORK FOR	50B	ISLAND MOON 6	PROSE
HANG THAT SAID SUCTION LET US HAVE A SONG	50B	ISLAND MOON 6	PROSE
YOU HAD BETTER TAKE A WALK THAT WE MAY HAVE SOME PLEASURE	52D	ISLAND MOON 8	PROSE
THERES DOUBLE ELEPHANT'S GIRLS THEY HAVE THEIR OWN WAY	52D	ISLAND MOON 8	PROSE
& THEY HAVE BLACK SERVANTS LODGE AT THEIR HOUSE	53A	ISLAND MOON 8	PROSE
NOT HAVE ANY THING TO SAY AND IF ANY BODY ASKD HIM	53B	ISLAND MOON 8	PROSE
I AM SURE I TAKE BUT LITTLE PLEASURE YOU HAVE AS MUCH	53C	ISLAND MOON 8	PROSE
PLEASURE AS I HAVE THERE I STAND & BEAR EVERY FOOL'S INSULT	53C	ISLAND MOON 8	PROSE
HANG ITALIAN SONGS LET'S HAVE ENGLISH SAID QUID	56A	ISLAND MOON 9	PROSE
HOW CAN YOU HAVE THE FACE TO MAKE GAME OF MATRIMONY	57A	ISLAND MOON 9	PROSE
& BEGD TO HAVE IT SUNG OVER AGAIN & AGAIN	57D	ISLAND MOON 9	PROSE
MUSICIANS SHOULD HAVE	62	DR CLASH/IM	13
LET'S HAVE HANDEL'S WATERPIECE THEN SIPSOP SUNG	62B	ISLAND MOON 11	PROSE
THEN SAID HE I WOULD HAVE ALL THE WRITING ENGRAVED INSTEAD	62D	ISLAND MOON 11	PROSE
THEN SAID SHE WHOEVER WILL NOT HAVE THEM	62D	ISLAND MOON 11	PROSE
DONT YOU THINK I HAVE SOMETHING OF THE GOAT'S FACE SAYS HE	62D	ISLAND MOON 11	PROSE
BUT DO YOU OUTFACE THEM & THEN STRANGERS WILL SEE YOU HAVE AN OPINION	63A	ISLAND MOON 11	PROSE
UNEASY I FEAR I HAVE NOT MANY ENEMIES	70C	ANNO LAVATER	MARG
FOR MY ENEMY IS NOT MAN BUT BEAST AND DEVIL IF I HAVE ANY	72B	ANNO LAVATER	* MARG
MAN CAN HAVE NO IDEA OF ANY THING GREATER THAN MAN	90B	ANNO SWED LOVE	MARG
& HAVE NO IDEA OF ANY BUT WORLDLY GAIN	94A	ANNO SWED LOVE	MARG
NONE COULD HAVE OTHER THAN NATURAL OR ORGANIC THOUGHTS	97B	NAT RELIGION 1	PROSE
SO ALL RELIGIONS & AS ALL SIMILARS HAVE ONE SOURCE	98D	ALL RELIGIONS	PROSE
FOR WE HAVE MANY SPORTS TO SHEW THEE & MANY SONGS TO SING	102	TIRIEL 3	13
AND OUR SPORTS HAVE AN END	116	ECCHOING GR/SI	24
HED HAVE GOD FOR HIS FATHER & NEVER WANT JOY	118	CHIMNEY SWP/SI	20
I HAVE NO NAME	118	INFANT JOY/SI	1
. . . THE EAGLES OF HEAVEN MUST HAVE THEIR PREY	138	FRENCH REVOLTN	104
THAT REASON MAY HAVE IDEAS TO BUILD ON THE JEHOVAH OF THE BIBLE	150B	MARRIAGE HH 5	PROSE
WEAK AND TAME MINDS WHICH HAVE POWER TO RESIST ENERGY	155A	MARRIAGE HH 15	PROSE
I HAVE ALWAYS FOUND THAT ANGELS HAVE THE VANITY TO SPEAK	157C	MARRIAGE HH 21	PROSE
HAVE NOW ANOTHER PLAIN FACT ANY MAN OF MECHANICAL TALENTS	158A	MARRIAGE HH 21	PROSE
WHICH THE WORLD SHALL HAVE IF THEY BEHAVE WELL	158D	MARRIAGE HH 22	PROSE
I HAVE ALSO THE BIBLE OF HELL WHICH THE WORLD SHALL HAVE	158D	MARRIAGE HH 22	PROSE
WOULD NOT HAVE BANDY CHILDREN NOR FASTING NOR BIRCH	179	LIT VAGABOND/N	13
WOULD HAVE NO MORE QUARREL WITH THE DEVIL OR THE BARREL	180	LIT VAGABOND/N	16
[THEY SHALL HAVE A PRIEST & A PASSING BELL]	185	LET BROTHELS/N	19
WITH WHAT SENSE DOES THE BEE FORM CELLS HAVE NOT THE MOUSE & FROG	191	V DAU ALBION 3	4
OR BREATHING NOSTRILS NO FOR THESE THE WOLF AND TYGER HAVE	191	V DAU ALBION 3	9
THOU KNOWEST THAT THE ANCIENT TREES SEEN BY THINE EYES HAVE FRUIT	192	V DAU ALBION 4	13
WOULD NOT HAVE BANDY CHILDREN NOR FASTING NOR BIRCH	216	LIT VAGABND/SE	12
WOULD HAVE NO MORE QUARREL WITH THE DEVIL OR THE BARREL	216	LIT VAGABND/SE	15
THEN WHAT HAVE I TO DO WITH THEE	220	TO TIRZAH/SE	4
THEN WHAT HAVE I TO DO WITH THEE	220	TO TIRZAH/SE	16
THAT WOMAN LOVELY WOMAN MAY HAVE DOMINION	240	EUROPE 5	3
LORD HAVE MERCY ON US	240B	EUROPE 7	*PROSE
WE HAVE NO OTHER GOD BUT HE THOU FATHER OF WORMS & CLAY	298	FOUR ZOAS 4	39
BONIFY & THOU SHALT HAVE REST WHEN THIS THY LABOUR IS DONE	299	FOUR ZOAS 4	69
THOU SHALT HAVE REST IF THOU REFUSEST DASHD ABROAD ON ALL	299	FOUR ZOAS 4	73
AND LET HIM HAVE DOMINION OVER LOS THE TERRIBLE SHADE	323	FOUR ZOAS 7	116
[I HAVE THEE IN MY ARMS & AM AGAIN UNITED TO LOS]	327	FOUR ZOAS 7	308
BUT I HAVE THEE MY [COUNTERPART] [VEGETATING] MIRACULOUS	330	FOUR ZOAS 7	* 407
THESE SPECTRES HAVE NO [(COUNTERPARTS)] THEREFORE THEY RAVIN	330	FOUR ZOAS 7	* 408
TO ETERNAL TORMENT IN THESE FLAMES FOR THO I HAVE THE POWER	339	FOUR ZOAS 7B	253
THOU SHALT NEVER HAVE PEACE WITHIN THY BREAST	380	FOUR ZOAS NOTE	2
I HAVE NOT THE CHARITY FOR THE BISHOP THAT HE PRETENDS	384D	ANNO WATSON	MARG
TO HAVE FOR PAINE I BELIEVE HIM TO BE A STATE TRICKSTER	384D	ANNO WATSON	MARG
CONSCIENCE IN THOSE THAT HAVE IT IS UNEQUIVOCAL IT	385C	ANNO WATSON	MARG
YES I HAVE NO DOUBT HE DID	395D	ANNO WATSON	MARG
HE WHO HAS FEW THINGS TO DESIRE CANNOT HAVE MANY TO FEAR	405B	ANNO BACON	MARG
BY HIS TRANSLATOR IF I HAVE ANY JUDGMENT IN SUCH THINGS	413A	ANNO BOYD	MARG
LIVING THEE ALONE I'LL HAVE	416	MY SPECTRE/N	53
[HAVE I] HAST THOU NO SINS OF [MY] THY OWN	417	MY SPECTR AD/N	* 2
ALL FACES HAVE ENVY SWEET MARY BUT THINE	429	MARY	44
AND ANOTHER I WILL HAVE FOR MY WIFE	435	WILLIAM BOND	27
THEN WHAT HAVE I TO DO WITH THEE	435	WILLIAM BOND	28

		PAGE	TITLE	LINE

HAVE (CONTINUED)

AND WOULD HAVE ME HANGED IF HE COULD HE SPOKE . . . . . 437B BLAKES MEMORAN PROSE
(DAMN) THE (KING) NOW I HAVE ALL THE PERSONS WHO WERE . . 437C BLAKES MEMORAN PROSE
TO HAVE MY HOUSE SEARCHED AS I MIGHT HAVE PLANS OF THE 438A BLAKES MEMORAN PROSE
  COUNTRY
AT THE STABLE DOOR THAT WE MAY NOT HAVE ANY WITNESSES . . 438B BLAKES MEMORAN PROSE
THE MAN WHO SAYS THAT WE HAVE NO INNATE IDEAS MUST BE . . 459B ANNO REYNOLDS MARG
AS TO ELEGANCE THEY HAVE NOT A SPARK . . . . 462D ANNO REYNOLDS MARG
MAN BRINGS ALL THAT HE HAS OR CAN HAVE INTO THE WORLD WITH 471A ANNO REYNOLDS MARG
  HIM
HAVE THE SAME LIGHT & (SHADOWS) . . . . 477C ANNO REYNOLDS * MARG
WE HAVE HIRELINGS IN THE CAMP THE COURT & THE UNIVERSITY 480C MILTON 1 PROSE
TROUBLE ME NO MORE THOU CANST NOT HAVE ETERNAL LIFE . . . 483 MILTON 4 18
O GOD PROTECT ME FROM MY FRIENDS THAT THEY HAVE NOT POWER 489 MILTON 9 5
  OVER ME
I WILL HAVE WRITINGS WRITTEN ALL OVER IT IN HUMAN WORDS 499 MILTON 18 12
I WILL HAVE KINGS INWOVEN UPON IT & COUNCELLORS & MIGHTY 499 MILTON 18 15
  MEN
CAN YOU HAVE GREATER MIRACLES THAN THESE MEN WHO DEVOTE 506 MILTON 23 1
AND THAT THE SEVEN EYES OF GOD MAY HAVE SPACE FOR 507 MILTON 23 52
  REDEMPTION
CUT OFF MY LOVES IN FURY TILL I HAVE NO LOVE LEFT FOR THEE 522 MILTON 33 7
TO PUT OFF SELF & ALL I HAVE EVER & EVER AMEN . . . . 530 MILTON 38 49
PROSPERO HAD ONE CALIBAN & I HAVE TWO . . . . 538 OLD ACQUAINT/N 2
WHO WHATEVER LIKENESS HE MAY HAVE TO MICHAEL ANGELO . . . 542 FLORENTINE/N 33
NEVER CAN HAVE ANY TO SIR JEHOSHUAN . . . . 542 FLORENTINE/N 34
HAVE THE LAST WORD & TAKE THE WALL . . . . 547 IF I GROW/N 4
KNOWING & FEELING THAT WE ALL HAVE NEED OF BUTTER . . . 556 IF MEN ACT/N 4
NAIL HIS NECK TO THE CROSS YE ALL HAVE POWER OVER HIS TAIL 557 NAIL NECK/N 2
FOR EVERY BESIDES I HAVE . . . . 558 I ROSE UP AT/N 7
I HAVE MENTAL JOY & MENTAL HEALTH . . . . 558 I ROSE UP AT/N 9
AND THOSE WHO HAVE THE DIRECTION OF PUBLIC WORKS . . . 560D EXHIBITION ADV PROSE
WE MIGHT PERHAPS HAVE THEM NOW IN ENGLAND . . . . . . 560D EXHIBITION ADV PROSE
I HAVE NO OBJECTION TO RUBENS AND REMBRANDT BEING EMPLOYED 575D DESC CAT 3 PROSE
WHO OWE TO ME ALL THAT THEY HAVE IT SHALL BE SO NO LONGER 575D DESC CAT 3 PROSE
UNNATURAL MIXTURE THE SUBLIME ARTIST CAN HAVE NOTHING TO DO 579D DESC CAT 5 PROSE
HAVE SOFTNESS AND EVENNESS BY A TWELVEMONTH'S LABOUR . 583C DESC CAT 9 PROSE
IF MEN OF WEAK CAPACITIES [IN ART] HAVE ALONE THE POWER 591B PUB ADDRESS/N PROSE
MOST ENGLISHMEN HAVE A CONTEMPT FOR ART [WHICH WILL] . 596B PUB ADDRESS/N PROSE
MUST HAVE QUEER CONCEPTIONS . . . . 596C PUB ADDRESS/N PROSE
WHAT KIND OF INTELLECTS MUST HE HAVE WHO . . . . . . 597D PUB ADDRESS/N PROSE
IT IS DEISTICAL VIRTUE I SUPPOSE BUT AS I HAVE NONE OF THIS 598C PUB ADDRESS/N PROSE
& NO GRAND WORK CAN HAVE THEM THEY PRODUCE SYSTEM 599B PUB ADDRESS/N *PROSE
  & MONOTONY
I HAVE ENOUGH IN THE APPROBATION OF FELLOW LABOURERS . . 600C PUB ADDRESS/N PROSE
WHILE THE SCULPTORS HAVE CONTINUAL & SUPERABUNDANT 601A PUB ADDRESS/N PROSE
  EMPLOYMENT
IT HAS BEEN SAID OF LATE YEARS THE ENGLISH PUBLIC HAVE . 601B PUB ADDRESS/N PROSE
NURSING FATHERS & NURSING MOTHERS [THEY HAVE CROWNS] . 613D V LAST JUDG/N PROSE
FOR IN PARADISE THEY HAVE NO CORPOREAL & MORTAL BODY . . 616A V LAST JUDG/N PROSE
& THEY WILL ALWAYS HAVE SUPERIOR POWER IN MORTAL THINGS 616A V LAST JUDG/N PROSE
YOU CANNOT HAVE LIBERTY IN THIS WORLD WITHOUT . . . . 616A V LAST JUDG/N PROSE
WHAT YOU CALL MORAL VIRTUE & YOU CANNOT HAVE . . . . . 616A V LAST JUDG/N PROSE
& THE MORE TO HAVE AN INTEREST IN THE FRIEND OF SINNERS 621A JERUSALEM 3 PROSE
HAVE A BEAUTIFUL GOLDEN GATE WHICH OPENS INTO THE 635 JERUSALEM 14 20
  VEGETATIVE WORLD
THE DISEASE OF SHAME COVERS ME FROM HEAD TO FEET I HAVE 643 JERUSALEM 21 3
  NO HOPE
YOU HAVE A TRADITION THAT MAN ANCIENTLY CONTAIND . . . 649C JERUSALEM 27 PROSE
ALBION'S REACTOR MUST HAVE A PLACE PREPARD ALBION MUST 653 JERUSALEM 29 11
  SLEEP
THEY BUY HIS DAUGHTERS THAT THEY MAY HAVE POWER TO SELL 656 JERUSALEM 30 29
  HIS SONS
TO HAVE POWER OVER MAN FROM CRADLE TO CORRUPTIBLE GRAVE 661 JERUSALEM 34 26
I HAVE INNOCENCE TO DEFEND AND IGNORANCE TO INSTRUCT . 670 JERUSALEM 42 26
I HAVE NO TIME FOR SEEMING AND LITTLE ARTS OF COMPLIMENT 670 JERUSALEM 42 27
ALL THAT THEY HAVE IS MINE FROM MY FREE GENROUS GIFT . 671 JERUSALEM 42 52
THEY NOW HOLD ALL THEY HAVE INGRATITUDE TO ME . . . . 671 JERUSALEM 42 53
MAN MUST & WILL HAVE SOME RELIGION IF HE HAS . . . . 682B JERUSALEM 52 PROSE
NOT THE RELIGION OF JESUS HE WILL HAVE THE RELIGION OF 682B JERUSALEM 52 PROSE
  SATAN
FOR BEING DRIVEN FROM OUR FIELDS WHAT HAVE WE TO DO WITH 686 JERUSALEM 55 6
  THE DEAD
TO HAVE POWER OVER MAN FROM CRADLE TO CORRUPTIBLE GRAVE 688 JERUSALEM 56 4
ONLY BELIEVE IN ME THAT I HAVE POWER TO RAISE FROM DEATH 694 JERUSALEM 60 68
I HAVE LOVES OF MY OWN I WILL WEAVE THEM IN ALBION'S 732 JERUSALEM 87 18
  SPECTRE
BUT GENERAL FORMS HAVE THEIR VITALITY IN PARTICULARS & 738 JERUSALEM 91 30
  EVERY
WOMAN WHAT HAVE I TO DO WITH THEE . . . . 757 EV GOSPEL(I)/N 32
THOSE WHO WILL HAVE UNITY EXCLUSIVELY IN HOMER . . . . 778B HOMERS POETRY PROSE
I CANNOT THINK THAT REAL POETS HAVE ANY COMPETITION . . 783A ANNO WW POEMS MARG
WE HAVE ALL THINGS COMMON [ALL THINGS COMMON] AMONG US 788B ANNO THORNTON * MARG
I HAVE NO DOUBT OF GIVING YOU BENEVOLENCE WITH EQUAL VIGOR 792B LETTER 4 PROSE
BY THIS MEANS YOU WILL HAVE A NUMBER OF CABINET PICTURES 792C LETTER 4 PROSE
WORLD ESPECIALLY IF I SHOULD HAVE TO ANSWER FOR IT I FEEL 793A LETTER 5 PROSE
  VERY
I HAVE NO OBJECTION TO ENGRAVING AFTER ANOTHER ARTIST . 794C LETTER 5 PROSE
WHICH I HAVE THE PLEASURE TO TELL YOU ARE INCREASING EVERY 794C LETTER 5 PROSE
  DAY
SOON WE SHALL HAVE A CHANGE FOR THE BETTER I CANNOT 795A LETTER 6 PROSE
  PROPHECY

HAVE   (CONTINUED)

	PAGE	TITLE	LINE
EMPLOYER & I HAVE AN ORDER FOR FIFTY SMALL PICTURES AT ONE	795C	LETTER 6	PROSE
DEAR CUMBERLAND I HAVE TO CONGRATULATE YOU ON	797C	LETTER 10	PROSE
"O HOW WE DELIGHT IN TALKING OF THE PLEASURE WE SHALL HAVE"	800B	LETTER 12	PROSE
A FOOLISH EXPERIMENT HAPPINESSES HAVE WINGS AND WHEELS . .	807A	LETTER 17	PROSE
I HAVE A GREAT MANY ORDERS & THEY MULTIPLY	808B	LETTER 19	PROSE
WE HAVE ONE ROOM IN WHICH WE COULD MAKE A BED TO LODGE YOU	808B	LETTER 19	PROSE
WILL ARRIVE AS SAFE AS WITH HER I SHALL HAVE AN OPPORTUNITY	809C	LETTER 20	PROSE
OF WHICH I HAVE NEED & NOW I MUST EXPRESS MY WISHES . . .	809C	LETTER 20	PROSE
NEXT TIME I HAVE THE HAPPINESS TO SEE YOU I AM . . .	810B	LETTER 20	PROSE
YOU FOR AT PRESENT BECAUSE I HAVE ENOUGH TO SERVE MY PRESENT	811D	LETTER 22	PROSE
ON THE ENGRAVINGS I HAVE IN HAND FOR MR H(HAYLEY) . . .	812C	LETTER 22	PROSE
THE THING I HAVE MOST AT HEART MORE THAN LIFE OR ALL . .	812D	LETTER 22	PROSE
PATH IS DIFFICULT I HAVE NO FEAR OF STUMBLING WHILE I KEEP	813B	LETTER 22	PROSE
BUT I DO NOT PRETEND TO BE PERFECT BUT IF MY WORKS HAVE	815A	LETTER 23	PROSE
FAULTS CARACCHE CORREGIO'S & RAFAEL'S HAVE FAULTS . .	815A	LETTER 23	*PROSE
UNLIKE ANY OF THESE PAINTERS & I WOULD HAVE THEM TO BE SO	815B	LETTER 23	PROSE
IF YOU HAVE NOT NATURE BEFORE YOU FOR EVERY TOUCH YOU CANNOT	815D	LETTER 23	PROSE
PAINT PORTRAIT & IF YOU HAVE NATURE BEFORE YOU AT ALL . .	815D	LETTER 23	PROSE
ASSURE HER THAT IT CANNOT BE LONG BEFORE I HAVE THE PLEASURE	815D	LETTER 23	PROSE
SURPRIZED ME BECAUSE I HAVE NO AGUE BUT HAVE HAD A COLD	819B	LETTER 25	PROSE
I NOW HAVE IT IN MY POWER TO COMMENCE PUBLICATION WITH .	820A	LETTER 25	PROSE
MANY VERY FORMIDABLE WORKS WHICH I HAVE FINISHD & READY	820A	LETTER 25	PROSE
FOR WHICH I AM TO HAVE (TEN) GUINEAS EACH	820B	LETTER 25	PROSE
BUT NOT QUITE YOU SHALL HAVE IT SOON I NOW SEND THE . .	822B	LETTER 26	PROSE
YOU HAVE FAITH IN THE ENDEAVOURS OF ME YOUR WEAK BROTHER	822B	LETTER 26	PROSE
I HAVE A THOUSAND & TEN THOUSAND THINGS TO SAY TO YOU .	823B	LETTER 26	PROSE
I HAVE NOW ON THE STOCKS THE FOLLOWING DRAWINGS FOR YOU	824A	LETTER 27	PROSE
DELIGHTFUL THEN I AM DETERMIND THAT MRS BUTTS SHALL HAVE	824B	LETTER 27	PROSE
A GOOD LIKENESS OF YOU IF I HAVE HANDS & EYES LEFT . .	824B	LETTER 27	PROSE
& HE BEGINS TO THINK I HAVE SOME GENIUS	825C	LETTER 27	PROSE
OUTLINE I HAVE FOR WITNESSES THE GARDENER WHO IS HOSTLER	827C	LETTER 28	PROSE
WHICH IS AFTER MICHAELMASS SO I SHALL HAVE THE SATISFACTION	828A	LETTER 28	PROSE
I HAVE A GREAT MANY THINGS TO SAY & A GREAT MANY HEARTFELT	832B	LETTER 32	PROSE
RECIEVE WITH THIS & HAVE ONLY TIME TO SAY	832D	LETTER 32	PROSE
I HAVE FURTHERMORE THE PLEASURE OF INFORMING YOU THAT HE	836B	LETTER 35	PROSE
FORWARDNESS & YOU SHALL HAVE PROOFS IN ANOTHER WEEK . .	837A	LETTER 35	PROSE
A GREAT DEAL OF WORK IN THEM THAT MUST & WILL HAVE TIME	837A	LETTER 35	PROSE
THE LOST DRAWING YOU SHALL HAVE CHOICE OF EITHER OF THE	839C	LETTER 38	PROSE
YOU CAN HAVE NO IDEA UNLESS YOU WAS IN LONDON AS I AM .	841B	LETTER 41	PROSE
HOW MUCH YOUR NAME IS LOVD & RESPECTED I HAVE THE . .	841B	LETTER 41	PROSE
& WILL REMAIN SO TILL YOU HAVE GIVEN YOUR DECISION . .	841C	LETTER 41	PROSE
OF CHARACTER WHICH FEW HAVE HE IS THE MAN WHO APPLIED TO	841C	LETTER 41	PROSE
AS I FIND BY THE THINGS I HAVE IN HAND DAY & NIGHT WE .	843A	LETTER 42	*PROSE
THE BEST OF WHICH I HAVE I SEND ALSO THE FRENCH MONUMENTS	844C	LETTER 43	PROSE
IN THE MEANTIME I HAVE THE HAPPINESS OF SEEING . . .	845B	LETTER 44	PROSE
EVERY INFORMATION IN HIS POWER SAYS THAT I SHALL HAVE .	845D	LETTER 44	PROSE
TO MR ROSE IN AN UNFAIR LIGHT AS I HAVE NO DOUBT . .	847B	LETTER 44	PROSE
THE SHIPWRECK WITH THE MAN ON HORSEBACK &C WHICH I HAVE	848D	LETTER 45	PROSE
HECATE A VERY FINE THING INDEED WHICH I HAVE	849A	LETTER 45	PROSE
PLINY VERY FINE BUT VERY UNFINISHD WHICH I HAVE . . .	849A	LETTER 45	PROSE
SHALL HAVE A PROOF OF IT FOR YOUR REMARKS ALSO I HOPE BY	849B	LETTER 45	PROSE
I HAVE NOT YET PROVED IT BUT SHALL SOON WHEN I WILL SEND	851A	LETTER 49	PROSE
FROM RHEUMATISM AS SHE WAS FIVE YEARS AGO AND WE HAVE .	851C	LETTER 50	PROSE
HOPE SOON TO HAVE THE PLEASURE OF SEEING HIM WITH THE .	851D	LETTER 50	PROSE
& TO THOSE WHO HAVE AN AFFECTION FOR HIM LIKE YOURS IS .	854B	LETTER 53	PROSE
CELESTIAL CITY I ALSO HAVE BUT A FEW MORE MOUNTAINS TO PASS	854C	LETTER 53	PROSE
THE TWO CARTOONS WHICH I HAVE OF HECATE & PLINY ARE . .	855A	LETTER 53	PROSE
EMPLOY ME AS HIS PUBLISHER I SHOULD HAVE NO OBJECTION .	856C	LETTER 54	PROSE
BUT A PLEASURE IN EMPLOYING HIS PRINTER & HAVE NO DOUBT I	856C	LETTER 54	PROSE
SHALL HAVE WHATEVER I PUBLISH SENT TO HIM IF HE PLEASES & HE	857A	LETTER 54	PROSE
PRODUCTIVE I HAVE NO DOUBT IN THE WAY NOW PROPOSED AND I	858C	LETTER 55	PROSE
CANNOT ANSWER P'S(PHILLIPS') PROPOSAL TILL I HAVE YOUR .	858C	LETTER 55	PROSE
I HAVE NO CURIOSITY TO SEE HIM AS I WELL KNOW WHAT IS WITHIN	859C	LETTER 56	PROSE
MR CROMEK THE ENGRAVER CAME TO ME DESIRING TO HAVE SOME	861C	LETTER 59	PROSE
SANCTIONED THE STYLE OF WORK I NOW HAVE REASON MORE THAN	861D	LETTER 59	PROSE
BEING SUCCESSFUL AS WELL AS RIGHT OF WHICH I HAVE NO DOUBT	862A	LETTER 59	PROSE
I THROW MYSELF & ALL THAT I HAVE ON OUR SAVIOUR'S DIVINE	863A	LETTER 60	PROSE
AS MRS LAMBERT TOLD ME YOU WISHED TO HAVE THEM	863C	LETTER 60	PROSE
THAT PRECLUDE ALL POSSIBILITY OF PROMISING ANY THING I HAVE	865D	LETTER 63	PROSE
PERCIEVE THAT I NOT ONLY DETEST FALSE ART BUT HAVE THE .	866B	LETTER 64	PROSE
IT IS THEREFORE NECESSARY TO ME THAT ANY PERSON WISHING TO HAVE	867C	LETTER 66	PROSE
I WILL HAVE THE PLEASURE OF MEETING YOU ON THURSDAY AT .	868B	LETTER 67	PROSE
I HAVE HAD THE PLEASURE TO SEE MR LINNELL SET OFF SAFE IN	869C	LETTER 70	PROSE
LAST TIME WE MET I HAVE NO DOUBT THAT THE PLATES WOULD BE ALL	870B	LETTER 71	PROSE
I WISH TO HAVE A COPY OF JOB TO SHEW TO MR CHANTRY . .	870D	LETTER 72	PROSE
& THE TROUBLE YOU WILL YET HAVE WITH ME BUT I GET BETTER	872D	LETTER 76	PROSE
SOLICITUDE CONCERNING ME AT REST YOU HAVE A FAMILY I HAVE	873C	LETTER 77	PROSE
I AM SO MUCH BETTER THAT I HAVE HOPES OF FULFILLING MY .	873D	LETTER 78	PROSE
ON MY BONES & SINEWS MUSCLE I HAVE NONE BUT A FEW DAYS .	875A	LETTER 80	PROSE
I HAVE & BEG THE FAVOUR OF YOU TO SEND ME THE TWO PLATES	876A	LETTER 83	PROSE
OF DANTE WHICH YOU HAVE THAT I MAY FINISH THEM SUFFICIENTLY	876A	LETTER 83	PROSE
MANY OF THE BACKS OF THE PAPER HAVE ON THEM IMPRESSIONS	877B	LETTER 86	PROSE

	PAGE	TITLE	LINE
HAVE (CONTINUED)			
MR BUTTS IS TO HAVE A PROOF COPY FOR THREE GUINEAS . . .	877D	LETTER 88	PROSE
I HAVE LITTLE HOPE OF DOING ANY MORE OF SUCH THINGS . .	878C	LETTER 88	PROSE
WHICH I AM SLOWLY RECOVERING YOU WILL I HOPE HAVE PATIENCE	879A	LETTER 88	PROSE
HAVILAH			
THE LILLY OF HAVILAH AND THEY SANG SOFT THRO LAMBETH'S VALES	642	JERUSALEM 19	42
THE GOLDEN GATE OF HAVILAH AND ALL THE GARDEN OF GOD . .	679	JERUSALEM 49	15
NOR IN HAVILAH WHERE THE CHERUB ROLLD HIS REDOUNDING FLAME	686	JERUSALEM 55	22
MOLECH REJOICES THRO THE LAND FROM HAVILAH TO SHUR HE REJOICES	706	JERUSALEM 68	38
HEAVEN HAVILAH EDEN & ALL THE COUNTRIES WHERE JEWELS ABOUND	837D	LETTER 36	PROSE
HAVING (OMITTING AUXILIARY VERB)			
OF HAVING MY BACK LAID OPEN WE TURN	22	EDW THIRD/PS 3	37
MOST HAPPY HAVING SUCH COMMAND THE MAN	23	EDW THIRD/PS 3	78
ABOVE HEROIC HAVING SUCH EXAMPLES	23	EDW THIRD/PS 3	80
YES SAID THE EPICUREAN & HAVING A BIT OF FUN WITH HIM .	45C	ISLAND MOON 1	PROSE
HAVING HER CANCER CUT & SHE SHRIEKD SO THAT I WAS QUITE SICK	51C	ISLAND MOON 6	PROSE
AS GARMENTS WOVEN SUBSERVIENT TO HER HANDS BUT HAVING A WILL	266	FOUR ZOAS 1	84
BUT YET HAVING A LIMIT TWOFOLD NAMED SATAN & ADAM . . .	329	FOUR ZOAS 7	383
AND SATAN NOT HAVING THE SCIENCE OF WRATH BUT ONLY OF PITY	351	FOUR ZOAS 8	392
INTO A FORM OF VEGETATION LIVING HAVING A VOICE	353	FOUR ZOAS 8	475
A FOOL & KNAVE HAVING NO CON-SCIENCE OR INNATE SCIENCE . .	459B	ANNO REYNOLDS	MARG
AND SATAN NOT HAVING THE SCIENCE OF WRATH BUT ONLY OF PITY	490	MILTON 9	46
THEN HE SHOULD NOT DOUBT OF HAVING A NATIONAL COMMISSION	566A	DESC CAT 2	PROSE
THE UNCIVILIZED SAVAGE WHO HAVING NOT THE LAW	610A	V LAST JUDG/N	PROSE
THE AGED FIGURE WITH WINGS HAVING A WRITING TABLET . .	610A	V LAST JUDG/N	PROSE
HAVING NO PASSIONS OF THEIR OWN BECAUSE NO INTELLECT . .	615D	V LAST JUDG/N	PROSE
THE WESTERN GATE FOURFOLD IS CLOSD HAVING FOUR CHERUBIM	633	JERUSALEM 13	6
HAVING A WALL BUILDED AGAINST IT AND THEREBY THE GATES .	635	JERUSALEM 14	27
HAVING A WHITE DOT CALLD A CENTER FROM WHICH BRANCHES OUT	659	JERUSALEM 33	19
HAVING SPIRITUAL ENEMIES OF SUCH FORMIDABLE MAGNITUDE .	811D	LETTER 22	PROSE
HAVING A NUMBER OF ARTICLES RELATING TO ROMNEY EITHER .	836A	LETTER 35	PROSE
BUT HAVING NONE REMAINING OF ALL THAT I HAD PRINTED I .	878C	LETTER 88	PROSE
HAVOCK			
AS IN DAY OF HAVOCK AND ROUTED BATTLE	137	FRENCH REVOLTN	64
HAWK			
THE CRANE OERTAKEN FIGHTETH WITH THE HAWK	24	EDW THIRD/PS 3	128
WITH WHAT SENSE IS IT THAT THE CHICKEN SHUNS THE RAVENOUS HAWK	191	V DAU ALBION 3	2
THE RAVEN CALLD THE HAWK I HEARD THEM FROM MY FORESTS BLACK	358	FOUR ZOAS 9	60
A TERROR COMING FROM THE SOUTH THE EAGLE & HAWK FLED AWAY	358	FOUR ZOAS 9	62
HAWKINS			
OUR GOOD AND KIND FRIEND HAWKINS IS NOT YET IN TOWN . .	851D	LETTER 50	PROSE
OUR DEAR FRIEND HAWKINS IS OUT OF TOWN & WILL NOT RETURN TILL APRIL	855B	LETTER 53	PROSE
YOUR DESIRABLE POETICAL PRESENT FOR MRS HAWKINS	855B	LETTER 53	PROSE
HIS ADDRESS IS THIS TO JOHN HAWKINS ESQR DALLINGTON . .	855B	LETTER 53	PROSE
HAWTHORN			
& THE SHEPHERD & HIS LASS UNDER A HAWTHORN IN THE DALE .	618B	ILLUS MILTON	PROSE
WITH ANGELS PLANTED IN HAWTHORN BOWERS	817	HAPPINESS/L	9
HAY			
HAY HOW SHOULD I KNOW ANSWERD OBTUSE ANGLE WHO WAS IT ARADOBO	47A	ISLAND MOON 3	PROSE
HAY HAY SAID HE YOU SHO WHY YA YA HOW CAN YOU BE SO FOOLISH	58C	ISLAND MOON 10	PROSE
OVER THE NEW MOWN HAY	164	HEARD ANGEL/N	6
HAYCOCKS			
AND HAYCOCKS LOOKED BROWN	164	HEARD ANGEL/N	8
HAYLEY			
WAS I ANGRY WITH HAYLEY WHO USD ME SO ILL	538	WAS I ANGRY/N	1
TO FORGIVE ENEMIES H(HAYLEY) DOES PRETEND	544	TO FORGIVE/N	1
WHEN HY (HAYLEY) FINDS OUT WHAT YOU CANNOT DO	544	HS FRENDSHIP/N	1
TO H(HAYLEY)	545C	TO H(AYLEY)/N	TITLE
HAYLEY FLAXMAN & STOTHARD ARE ALSO IN DOUBT	545	COSWAY FRAZR/N	5
NOT PRAISD BY HAYLEY NOR BY FLAXMAN LOVD	546	MY TITLE AS/N	2
ON H(HAYLEY) THE PICK THANK	549A	H PICK THANK/N	TITLE
[XXX ?HAYLEY & HISTORY]	551	WILLM COWPER/N *	2
THUS HAYLEY ON HIS TOILETTE SEEING THE SOPE	555	BLAKES APL/N 1	12
THUS HAYLEY ON HIS TOILETTE SEEING THE SOPE	556	BLAKES APL/N 2	9
THUS HAYLEY ON HIS TOILETTE SEEING THE SOPE	595	BLAKES APOL/PA	7
MR HAYLEY HAS LATELY MENTIOND YOUR WORK ON OUTLINE IN NOTES	798B	LETTER 10	*PROSE
AND NOW FLAXMAN HATH GIVEN ME HAYLEY HIS FRIEND	799	TO FLAXMAN/L	4
MR HAYLEY RECIEVD US WITH HIS USUAL BROTHERLY AFFECTION	802A	LETTER 14	PROSE
MR HAYLEY RECIEVD ME WITH HIS USUAL BROTHERLY AFFECTION	803B	LETTER 15	PROSE
MR HAYLEY ACTS LIKE A PRINCE I AM AT COMPLETE EASE BUT .	808A	LETTER 19	PROSE
A WORK OF MAGNITUDE WHICH MR HAYLEY IS NOW LABOURING .	809D	LETTER 20	PROSE
& MR H(HAYLEY) I DOUBT NOT WILL DO ULTIMATELY ALL . .	811D	LETTER 22	PROSE
ON THE ENGRAVINGS I HAVE IN HAND FOR MR H(HAYLEY) . .	812C	LETTER 22	PROSE
& THIS FROM MR H(HAYLEY) WILL BRING ME BACK AGAIN . .	812C	LETTER 22	PROSE
REMEMBRING THE VERSES THAT HAYLEY SUNG	816	HAPPINESS/L	7
BECAUSE I GIVE HAYLEY HIS DUE RESPECT	817	HAPPINESS/L	46
I ALSO INCLOSE YOU SOME BALLADS BY MR HAYLEY WITH PRINTS	819A	LETTER 24	PROSE
THAT H(HAYLEY) IS JEALOUS AS STOTHARD WAS & WILL BE . .	819C	LETTER 25	PROSE
H(HAYLEY) LIKE S(STOTHARD) ENVIOUS & THAT HE IS I AM NOW CERTAIN	819C	LETTER 25	PROSE
BECAUSE OF PECUNIARY CONNEXIONS BETWEEN H(HAYLEY) & ME .	819D	LETTER 25	PROSE
THE NATURE OF PUBLICATION UNLESS I HAD KNOWN H(HAYLEY) &	820A	LETTER 25	PROSE
YOUR LETTER TO MR H(HAYLEY) &	820D	LETTER 25	PROSE
LONDON WITH THE FULL APPROBATION OF MR HAYLEY & WITH .	822C	LETTER 26	PROSE

HAYLEY   (CONTINUED)
    THAT MR H(HAYLEY) IS QUITE AGREEABLE TO OUR RETURN . . . . 824C LETTER 27   PROSE
    BUT OF THIS WORK I TAKE CARE TO SAY LITTLE TO MR H(HAYLEY) . 825A LETTER 27   PROSE
    AS TO MR H(HAYLEY) I FEEL MYSELF AT LIBERTY . . . . . . 825B LETTER 27   PROSE
    I AM NOT TO REGARD IT AT ALL BUT MR H(HAYLEY) . . . . . 825C LETTER 27   PROSE
    MR HAYLEY WAS KIND ENOUGH TO COME FORWARDS . . . . . . 828A LETTER 28   PROSE
    MR H(HAYLEY) IN...L & MR S(SEAGRAVE) IN...L & MYSELF . . 828A LETTER 28   PROSE
    HOPE THAT AS MR D(DODSLEY) IS DEAD & IF MR H(HAYLEY) HAS NO 856B LETTER 54   PROSE
    IMMEDIATELY REPLIED IF MR HAYLEY SHOULD THINK FIT TO . 856C LETTER 54   PROSE
    HAYLEY IS WILLING TO DISPOSE OF THIS HIS NEW POEM I WILL 856C LETTER 54   PROSE
    THAT I REPEAT WHAT YOU HAVE SAID TO ME TO MR HAYLEY OR . 856D LETTER 54   PROSE
    FOR YOUR BEAUTIFUL MUSE BUT MR PHILLIPS SAID MR HAYLEY . 857A LETTER 54   PROSE
    IMMEDIATELY HE SAID GIVE MY BEST RESPECTS & TELL MR HAYLEY 860A LETTER 56   PROSE
    WILLIAM HAYLEY ESQRE FELPHAM NEAR CHICHESTER SUSSEX . . . SUPP ADDRESSES/L   *TITLE
    WILLIAM HAYLEY ESQR EARTHAM NEAR CHICHESTER SUSSEX . . . SUPP ADDRESSES/L   *TITLE
    WILLIAM HAYLEY ESQRE FELPHAM NEAR BOGNOR SUSSEX . . . . SUPP ADDRESSES/L   *TITLE
    WILLIAM HAYLEY ESQRE AT MISS POOLE'S LAVANT NEAR CHICHESTER SUPP ADDRESS/L 13   *TITLE
        SUSSEX
HAYLEY'S
    PART OF THE TIME MR HAYLEY'S GARDENER PART OF THE TIME . 438B BLAKES MEMORAN   PROSE
    MR HAYLEY'S GARDENER CAME PAST AT THE TIME OF THE . . . 438D BLAKES MEMORAN   PROSE
    OF H'S(HAYLEY'S) BIRTH THIS WAS THE HAPPY LOT . . . . . 539 OF HS BIRTH/N   1
    ON HY'S(HAYLEY'S) FRIENDSHIP . . . . 544C HS FRENDSHIP/N   TITLE
    TO SEE YOU AT FELPHAM & TO SHEW YOU MR HAYLEY'S LIBRARY . 809C LETTER 20   PROSE
    NOT ONLY ON ACCOUNT OF MR HAYLEY'S COMPOSITION BUT ALSO . 810A LETTER 20   PROSE
    NEW EDITION OF MR HAYLEY'S TRIUMPHS OF TEMPER FROM DRAWINGS 811D LETTER 22   PROSE
    IT SO MUCH H'S(HAYLEY'S) INTEREST TO EMPLOY ME . . . . 819D LETTER 25   PROSE
    PLATES FOR A LITTLE WORK OF MR H'S(HAYLEY'S) . . . . . 820B LETTER 25   PROSE
    MY HEADS OF COWPER FOR MR H'S(HAYLEY'S) LIFE OF COWPER . 820C LETTER 25   PROSE
        HAVE
    HE SAID I KNEW THAT DODSLEY WAS MR HAYLEY'S PUBLISHER BUT 856B LETTER 54   PROSE
    WORK OF MR HAYLEY'S & THE PUBLIC LIKEWISE ARE DEPRIVED OF 856C LETTER 54   PROSE
    SHOULD DO MY ENDEAVOUR TO GIVE MR HAYLEY'S WORKS . . . 856D LETTER 54   PROSE
    HAYLEY'S & FEAR THAT HE WILL WISH ME TO DO SO I ASKED HIM 860A LETTER 56   PROSE
    NOS OF HAYLEY'S BALLADS PRINTS NEBUCHADNEZZAR NEWTON . SUPP LETTER 56A   *PROSE
    HAYLEY'S BALLADS PER BROTHER DITTO MR BIRCH . . . . . SUPP LETTER 56A   *PROSE
HAYNES
    MRS HAYNES EVIDENCES THAT SHE SAW ME TURN HIM . . . . . 437B BLAKES MEMORAN   PROSE
    MRS HAYNES SAYS VERY SENSIBLY THAT SHE NEVER . . . . . 437C BLAKES MEMORAN   PROSE
    MRS HAYNES & HER DAUGHTER ALL THE TIME MR GRINDER . . . 438B BLAKES MEMORAN   PROSE
    MRS HAYNES WAS PRESENT FROM MY TURNING HIM OUT AT MY GATE 438B BLAKES MEMORAN   PROSE
HAZAEL
    HE [REPRESENTS THE ASSYRIAN] IS HAZAEL THE SYRIAN . . . 608B V LAST JUDG/N   PROSE
HAZOR
    OF CANAAN AND REIGN IN HAZOR WHERE THE TWELVE TRIBES MEET 501 MILTON 20   6
HBLE   SEE HUMBLE
    TO THEM BY YOUR HBLE SERVT I SHOULD HAVE SENT THEM . . 819A LETTER 24   PROSE
    DESIGNS FROM ROMNEY FLAXMAN & YR HBLE SERVT . . . . . 824C LETTER 27   PROSE
    I REMAIN YOUR SINCERE & OBLIGED HBLE SERVANT . . . . . 851A LETTER 49   PROSE
HEAD
    THY GOLDEN CROWN UPON HER LANGUISHD HEAD . . . . . . 1 TO SPRING/PS   15
    AND FEATHERD CLOUDS STREW FLOWERS ROUND HER HEAD . . . . 2 TO AUTUMN/PS   12
    THUS HAVING SPOKE SHE RAISED UP HER HEAD . . . . . . 5 FAIR ELENOR/PS   53
    DISCLOSING TO HER SIGHT THE MURDERD HEAD . . . . . . 5 FAIR ELENOR/PS   58
    O ELENOR [I AM] BEHOLD THY HUSBAND'S HEAD . . . . . . 5 FAIR ELENOR/PS   61
    SHE TOOK THE GORY HEAD UP IN HER ARMS . . . . 6 FAIR ELENOR/PS   70
    SMILES ON MY HEAD AND MOUNTS HIS FLAMING CAR . . . . . 9 FRESH FROM/PS   2
    AND RISING GLORIES BEAM AROUND MY HEAD . . . . 9 FRESH FROM/PS   4
    PAY FOR THE TYRANT'S HEAD . . . . 12 GWIN KING/PS   32
    GORDRED HIS HEAD DIVIDES . . . . 14 GWIN KING/PS   108
    HIS OWN HEAD UP BUT NOT HIS EYES . . . . 16 BLIND-MANS/PS   32
    POOR PITEOUS DICK SUPPORTS HIS HEAD . . . . 17 BLIND-MANS/PS   55
    AND HODGE AGAIN HOLDS UP HIS HEAD . . . . 17 BLIND-MANS/PS   60
    LORD PERCY IF THE HEART IS SICK THE HEAD . . . . . . 21 EDW THIRD/PS 2   84
    THE STAG TURNS HEAD AND BAYS THE CRYING HOUNDS . . . . 24 EDW THIRD/PS 3   127
    AND SHOOK HIS MORTAL DART AGAINST MY HEAD . . . . . . 25 EDW THIRD/PS 3   176
    SHALL WARBLE ROUND THE SNOWY HEAD AND KEEP . . . . . . 28 EDW THIRD/PS 3   287
    NOW THERES A STORY COME INTO MY HEAD . . . . 29B EDW THIRD/PS 4   PROSE
    AND RAISE HER GOLDEN HEAD EXULTINGLY . . . . 34C KING JOHN/PS   PROSE
    IF I LIFT UP MY HEAD SIN COVERS ME AS A CLOAK . . . . . 36A COUCH DEATH/PS   PROSE
    HIS MOTHER'S ARM WAS UNDER HIS HEAD . . . . 36C COUCH DEATH/PS   PROSE
    AND A RAY OF LIGHT BEAMED AROUND HIS HEAD ALL WAS STILL . 36C COUCH DEATH/PS   PROSE
    AND SEEKS TO HIDE HER BRUISED HEAD UNDER THE MISTS OF NIGHT 37D SAMSON/PS   PROSE
    ENVY HATH A SERPENT'S HEAD OF FEARFUL BULK . . . . . . 41C THEN SHE BORE   PROSE
    MOST BLACK SHAME IN A MIST SAT ROUND HIS TROUBLED HEAD . 42B THEN SHE BORE   PROSE
    & GOLDEN PLEASURES BEAM AROUND MY HEAD WHY GRIEF DOST THOU 43B WOE CRIED MUSE   PROSE
        ACCOST ME
    WIPED HIS [HEAD] FACE WITH HIS POCKET HANDKERCHIEF . . . 45B ISLAND MOON 1   PROSE
    & SHUTTING HIS EYES BEGAN TO SCRATCH HIS HEAD . . . . . 45B ISLAND MOON 1   PROSE
    POOH SAYS THE MATHEMATICIAN SCRATCHING HIS HEAD . . . . 45D ISLAND MOON 1   PROSE
    & CLAPT IT ON HIS HEAD SAID THE PYTHAGOREAN . . . . . 46C ISLAND MOON 3   PROSE
    THEN MR INFLAMMABLE GASS RAN & SHOVD HIS HEAD INTO THE FIRE 48C ISLAND MOON 4   PROSE
    & SET HIS [HEAD] HAIR ALL IN A FLAME & RAN ABOUT THE ROOM 48C ISLAND MOON 4   PROSE
    WHY SAID HE IT CAME INTO MY HEAD THAT HE WAS NOT . . . 49A ISLAND MOON 5   PROSE
    YOU HARDLY KNOW SHE HAS A TONGUE IN HER HEAD . . . . . 53A ISLAND MOON 8   PROSE
    A QUESTION HE WOULD PUT HIS HEAD INTO A HOLE & HIDE IT . 53C ISLAND MOON 8   PROSE
    LOOK AT MY BALD HEAD HARK LISTEN YE SERPENTS [?ALL] LISTEN 99 TIRIEL 1   * 29
    WHY DOST THOU CURSE IS NOT THE CURSE NOW COME UPON YOUR . 100 TIRIEL 1   40
        HEAD
    THEN HAR AROSE & LAID HIS HAND UPON OLD TIRIEL'S HEAD . . 101 TIRIEL 2   34
    THOU HAST NO TEETH OLD MAN & THUS I KISS THY SLEEK BALD . 101 TIRIEL 2   37
        HEAD

HEAD   (CONTINUED)
```
HEVA COME KISS HIS BALD HEAD FOR HE WILL NOT HURT US HEVA       101 TIRIEL 2            38
GO NOT FOR THOU ART SO LIKE TIRIEL THAT I LOVE THINE HEAD       103 TIRIEL 3            24
FOR POOR BLIND TIRIEL IS RETURND & THIS MUCH INJURD HEAD        105 TIRIEL 4            66
WHERE DOTH HE HIDE HIS TERRIBLE HEAD & HIS SWIFT & FIERY        106 TIRIEL 5             2
    DAUGHTERS
THE INFANT HEAD WHILE THE MOTHER IDLE PLAYS WITH HER DOG        110 TIRIEL 8            26
    ON HER COUCH
ON HIS HEAD A CROWN          . . . . . . . . . . . .            114 LIT GRL FND/SI      37
THERES LITTLE TOM DACRE WHO CRIED WHEN HIS HEAD     . . . .     117 CHIMNEY SWP/SI       5
HUSH TOM NEVER MIND IT FOR WHEN YOUR HEAD S BARE    . . . .     117 CHIMNEY SWP/SI       7
THEY POUR SLEEP ON THEIR HEAD       . . . . . . . . .           119 NIGHT/SI            23
OER MY LOVELY INFANT'S HEAD         . . . . . . . . .           120 CRADLE SONG/SI       2
AH GENTLE MAY I LAY ME DOWN AND GENTLE REST MY HEAD     .       127 BOOK OF THEL 1      12
SO WEAK THE GILDED BUTTERFLY SCARCE PERCHES ON MY HEAD  . .     127 BOOK OF THEL 1      18
THE CLOUD DESCENDED AND THE LILLY BOWD HER MODEST HEAD  . .     128 BOOK OF THEL 2      17
THE CLOUD THEN SHEWD HIS GOLDEN HEAD & HIS BRIGHT FORM          128 BOOK OF THEL 3       5
    EMERGD
THE CLOD OF CLAY HEARD THE WORM'S VOICE & RAISD HER PITYING     129 BOOK OF THEL 4       7
    HEAD
BUT HE THAT LOVES THE LOWLY POURS HIS OIL UPON MY HEAD  . .     129 BOOK OF THEL 5       1
. . . AND MAN LAY HIS FADED HEAD DOWN ON THE ROCK   . . .       138 FRENCH REVOLTN      96
. . . THEN LIFTED HIS HEAD AND LOOKD ON HIS ARMIES THAT         139 FRENCH REVOLTN     110
    SHONE
WAVD ITS SOLEMN CLOUD OVER MY HEAD . . .    . . . . . .         140 FRENCH REVOLTN     130
IN THE BLOOD OF NOBILITY TRAMPLING THE HEART AND THE HEAD       141 FRENCH REVOLTN     156
. . .
FROM THE HEAD OF OUR KING . . . .   . . . . . . .              142 FRENCH REVOLTN     172
HANDS HEAD BOSOM AND PARTS OF LOVE FOLLOW THEIR HIGH           142 FRENCH REVOLTN     185
    BREATHING JOY
OVER HIS HEAD THE SOUL OF VOLTAIRE SHONE FIERY . . .    . .     147 FRENCH REVOLTN     282
LIFT UP THY HEAD        . . . . . . . . . . . . .              152B MARRIAGE HH 9    PROSE
THE HEAD SUBLIME THE HEART PATHOS   . . . . . . . .            152C MARRIAGE HH 10   PROSE
WHICH HUNG WITH THE HEAD DOWNWARD INTO THE DEEP     . . . .    156A MARRIAGE HH 17   PROSE
AND NOW WE SAW IT WAS THE HEAD OF LEVIATHAN     . . . . .      156C MARRIAGE HH 17   PROSE
PRONOUNCD CURSES ON [HIS] MY HEAD   . . . . . . . .            167 INFANT SORW/N      28
AND GREY HAIRS ARE ON MY HEAD       . . . . . . . . .          167 INFANT SORW/N      43
EARTH RAISD UP HER HEAD         . . . . . . . . .             168 EARTHS ANSWR/N      1
AND GREY HAIRS ARE ON MY HEAD       . . . . . . . . .          169 MIRTLE SHADE/N     18
OF MYSTERY OVER HIS HEAD        . . . . . . . . .             174 HUMAN IMAGE/N      15
AND GREY HAIRS WERE ON MY HEAD      . . . . . . . .            182 THE ANGEL/N        16
HIS KNEES AND THIGHS LIKE SILVER & HIS BREAST AND HEAD          199 AMERICA 8          17
    LIKE GOLD
AND A COWL OF FLESH GREW OER HIS HEAD & SCALES ON HIS BACK      202 AMERICA 15         17
    & RIBS
ABOVE ALL HEAVENS IN THUNDERS WRAPD EMERGD HIS LEPROUS HEAD     203 AMERICA 16          3
EARTH RAISD UP HER HEAD         . . . . . . . . .             210 EARTHS ANSR/SE      1
AND GREY HAIRS WERE ON MY HEAD      . . . . . . . .            214 THE ANGEL/SE       16
OF MYSTERY OVER HIS HEAD        . . . . . . . . .             217 HUMAN ABSTR/SE     14
OF A FOOT OR A HAND OR A HEAD       . . . . . . . .            234 URIZEN 23           5
I WRAP MY TURBAN OF THICK CLOUDS AROUND MY LABRING HEAD         238 EUROPE PREL 1      12
AND WE WILL CROWN THY HEAD WITH GARLANDS OF THE RUDDY VINE      239 EUROPE 4           26
THEN LOS AROSE HIS HEAD HE REARD IN SNAKY THUNDERS CLAD         245 EUROPE 15           9
THEN ALOFT HIS HEAD REARD IN THE ABYSS      . . . . . .        258 BOOK OF LOS 4      41
. . . HE STOOPD HIS [HOLY] INNOCENT HEAD    . . . . .          266 FOUR ZOAS 1        72
HIS HEAD BEAMD LIGHT & IN HIS VIGOROUS VOICE WAS PROPHECY       270 FOUR ZOAS 1       239
SICKNING LIES THE [ETERNAL] FALLEN MAN HIS HEAD SICK HIS        272 FOUR ZOAS 1     * 288
    HEART FAINT
THE WANDERING MAN BOWD HIS FAINT HEAD AND URIZEN DESCENDED      273 FOUR ZOAS 1       316
HIS HEAD SHRILL SOUNDING IN THE SKY DOWN RUSHD THE SUN          275 FOUR ZOAS 1       415
    WITH NOISE
[ARISE O ENION ARISE & SMILE UPON MY HEAD]      . . . . .      SUPP FOUR ZOAS 1    *
OR HOVERD OER HIS STARRY HEAD & WHEN HE SMILD SHE BRIGHTEND     284 FOUR ZOAS 2     * 182
THE DEEP LIFTS UP HIS RUGGED HEAD   . . . . . . . .            289 FOUR ZOAS 2       360
AHANIA BOWD HER HEAD & WEPT SEVEN DAYS BEFORE THE KING  . .     292 FOUR ZOAS 3        24
SHE RAISD HER BRIGHT HEAD SWEET PERFUMD & THUS WITH            292 FOUR ZOAS 3        26
    HEAVENLY VOICE
COVERD WITH BOILS FROM HEAD TO FOOT THE TERRIBLE SMITINGS       294 FOUR ZOAS 3        82
    OF LUVAH
I LAID MY HEAD IN THE HOT NOON AFTER THE BROKEN CLODS  . .      295 FOUR ZOAS 3       123
SWAM IN RED TEARS HE REARD HIS WAVES ABOVE THE HEAD OF LOS      298 FOUR ZOAS 4        45
IN SCORN STOOD LOS RED SPARKS OF BLIGHTING FROM HIS FURIOUS     298 FOUR ZOAS 4        48
    HEAD
THE DOLOROUS SHADOW JOYD WEAK HOPE APPEARD AROUND HIS HEAD      300 FOUR ZOAS 4       127
AT NOON & LAID HER HEAD UPON MY WEARIED BOSOM AT NIGHT  . .     301 FOUR ZOAS 4       139
THEY BOWD THE HEAD & WORSHIPPD & WITH MILD VOICE SPOKE          304 FOUR ZOAS 4       252
    THESE WORDS
HER PALE HANDS CLING AROUND HER HUSBAND & OVER HER WEAK         305 FOUR ZOAS 5        21
    HEAD
HE WEPT & HE DIVIDED & HE LAID HIS GLOOMY HEAD      . . . .     306 FOUR ZOAS 5        54
AND AT MY BANQUETS OF NEW WINE MY HEAD WAS CROWND WITH JOY      310 FOUR ZOAS 5       201
WHEN I BEND DOWNWARD BENDING MY HEAD DOWNWARD INTO THE          317 FOUR ZOAS 6       202
    DEEP
TILL A WHITE WOOF COVERD HIS COLD LIMBS FROM HEAD TO [FOOT]     318 FOUR ZOAS 6     * 239
    FEET
THEN BURSTING FROM HIS TROUBLED HEAD . . . . . . . .           320 FOUR ZOAS 7        25
SORROW SHOT THRO HIM FROM HIS FEET IT SHOT UP TO HIS HEAD       324 FOUR ZOAS 7       179
OF SEPARATION & ON MY DARK HEAD THE CURSE & PUNISHMENT  . .     330 FOUR ZOAS 7       405
BEAT ROUND HER HEAD ALL NIGHT ALL DAY SHE RIOTS IN EXCESS       334 FOUR ZOAS 7B       74
OF HIS IMMORTAL HEAD INTO THE NORTH UPON FAINT ENITHARMON       335 FOUR ZOAS 7B       77
FLAMING HIS HEAD LIKE THE BRIGHT SUN SEEN THRO A MIST THAT      335 FOUR ZOAS 7B       79
    MAGNIFIES
```

		PAGE	TITLE	LINE
HEAD	(CONTINUED)			
THIS COWL UPON MY HEAD HE PLACD IN TIMES OF EVERLASTING		336	FOUR ZOAS 7B	115
THE SHADOW REARD HER DISMAL HEAD OVER THE FLAMING YOUTH		336	FOUR ZOAS 7B	126
THAT MOVD WITH HORRIBLE DREAMS & (HOVRING) HIGH OVER HIS HEAD		341	FOUR ZOAS 8	* 6
TOWARD THE EAST ONE STANDING AT HIS HEAD TOWARD THE WEST		341	FOUR ZOAS 8	8
THEIR WINGS JOIND IN THE ZENITH OVER HEAD [BUT OTHER WINGS]		341	FOUR ZOAS 8	9
IN HEAD OR HEART OR REINS ACCORDING TO THE FITTEST ORDER		342	FOUR ZOAS 8	59
VEILS OF IGNORANCE COVERING FROM HEAD TO FEET WITH A COLD WEB		346	FOUR ZOAS 8	222
. . . THEY WIPE THEM WITH THE HAIR OF THEIR HEAD		347	FOUR ZOAS 8	238
LOS FELT THE STONY STUPOR & HIS HEAD ROLLD DOWN BENEATH		353	FOUR ZOAS 8	471
OF MAN WHO LAYS UPON THE SHORES LEANING HIS FADED HEAD . .		354	FOUR ZOAS 8	513
HIS EYES SINK HOLLOW IN HIS HEAD HIS FLESH COVERD WITH SLIME		354	FOUR ZOAS 8	515
HE DROOPS HIS HEAD & TREMBLING STANDS & HIS BRIGHT EYES DECAY		354	FOUR ZOAS 8	531
ON THIS ROCK LAY THE FADED HEAD OF THE ETERNAL MAN . . .		359	FOUR ZOAS 9	95
BOWING HIS HEAD OVER THE CONSUMING UNIVERSE HE CRIED . . .		359	FOUR ZOAS 9	98
AND MY HEAD FAINT YET WILL I LOOK AGAIN UNTO THE MORNING		360	FOUR ZOAS 9	120
. . . STOOPD HIS HEAD OVER THE UNIVERSE & IN		366	FOUR ZOAS 9	360
INVISIBLE LUVAH IN BRIGHT CLOUDS HOVERD OVER VALA'S HEAD		367	FOUR ZOAS 9	385
SO SPOKE THE SINLESS SOUL & LAID HER HEAD ON THE DOWNY FLEECE		369	FOUR ZOAS 9	455
MY LUVAH SMILD I KNEELED DOWN HE LAID HIS HAND ON MY HEAD		369	FOUR ZOAS 9	468
O ENION MY WEARY HEAD IS IN THE BED OF DEATH		370	FOUR ZOAS 9	487
ARISE O ENION ARISE & SMILE UPON MY HEAD		370	FOUR ZOAS 9	491
SO SAYING HIS FAINT HEAD HE LAID UPON THE OOZY ROCK . . .		370	FOUR ZOAS 9	495
BEHIND HER VEIL WITHDRAWS SO ENION TURND HER MODEST HEAD		371	FOUR ZOAS 9	549
AND HE SHALL LICK THE LITTLE GIRL'S WHITE NECK & ON HER HEAD		376	FOUR ZOAS 9	704
HIS CROWN OF THORNS FELL FROM HIS HEAD HE HUNG HIS LIVING LYRE		376	FOUR ZOAS 9	711
THE [ANCIENT] ETERNAL MAN BOWD HIS BRIGHT HEAD		380	FOUR ZOAS AD 1	2
IN HEAD OR HEART OR REINS ACCORDING TO THE FITTEST ORDER .		382	FOUR ZOAS AD 6	28
HAS ONLY HURT PAINE'S HEEL WHILE PAINE HAS BROKEN HIS HEAD		396C	ANNO WATSON	MARG
[PITY] CROWN WITH WINE MY MOURNFUL HEAD		416	MY SPECTRE/N	* 44
BIND AROUND MY AKING HEAD		417	MY SPECTR AD/N	12
THE IRON HAND [CRUSD] CRUSHD THE TYRANT'S HEAD		419	I SAW A MONK/N	* 46
SHE BINDS IRON THORNS AROUND HIS HEAD		425	MENTAL TRAVLER	13
THE IRON HAND CRUSHD THE TYRANT'S HEAD		431	GREY MONK	35
AND AN ANGEL OF PROVIDENCE AT HIS HEAD		435	WILLIAM BOND	14
AND ON THY HEAD IS THE COLD MOON'S SHINE		435	WILLIAM BOND	30
DANCED AROUND HER SHINING HEAD		435	WILLIAM BOND	42
EVERY ONE IS THREEFOLD IN HEAD & HEART & REINS & EVERY ONE		484	MILTON 5	6
THEN LOS TOOK OFF HIS LEFT SANDAL PLACING IT ON HIS HEAD		488	MILTON 8	11
I CAME FORTH FROM THE HEAD OF SATAN BACK THE GNOMES RECOILD		493	MILTON 12	38
THE FIRST STATE IS IN THE HEAD THE SECOND IS IN THE HEART		524	MILTON 34	14
HIS HEAD BENDS OVER LONDON HE SEES HIS EMBODIED SPECTRE		531	MILTON 39	46
[LIKE A FILTHY INFECTIOUS HEAD OF HAIR]		540	SIR JOSH RUB/N	6
[A CROOKED STICK & LOUZY HEAD OF HAIR]		540	SIR JOSH RUB/N	7
[HIS] WHOSE HEART IS IRON HIS HEAD WOOD & HIS FACE BRASS		545	ON S(TOTHRD)/N	2
BUT RAFAEL THINKS A HEAD A FOOT A HAND		547	PRETTY EPIGR/N	4
THE HEAD AND THE KNEE TO HIM WHO IN EVERY AGE SENDS US .		570C	DESC CAT 3	PROSE
EVERY EXPRESSION EVERY LINEAMENT OF HEAD HAND & FOOT .		588A	CHAUCER/N	PROSE
HOW TO PUT SO MUCH LABOUR INTO A HEAD OR A FOOT AS BASIRE DID		593A	PUB ADDRESS/N	PROSE
HIS BROTHER FALLING WITH THE HEAD DOWNWARD		606B	V LAST JUDG/N	PROSE
SCALED WITH IRON SCALES FROM HEAD TO FEET [WITH]		606C	V LAST JUDG/N	PROSE
& JUSTICE CAIPHAS HAS A BLUE FLAME LIKE A MITER ON HIS HEAD		608D	V LAST JUDG/N	PROSE
THEIR HEAD THE AGED WOMAN IS BRITTANNICA THE WIFE OF ALBION		609C	V LAST JUDG/N	PROSE
ABOVE THE HEAD OF NOAH IS SETH THIS STATE CALLD		611C	V LAST JUDG/N	PROSE
OVER THE HEAD OF THE SAVIOUR & REDEEMER THE HOLY SPIRIT		613B	V LAST JUDG/N	PROSE
THE MODERN CHURCH CRUCIFIES CHRIST WITH THE HEAD DOWNWARDS		615D	V LAST JUDG/N	PROSE
FIRST GOD ALMIGHTY COMES WITH A THUMP ON THE HEAD . . .		617A	V LAST JUDG/N	PROSE
OUT FROM THE FURNACES OF LOS ABOVE THE HEAD OF LOS . . .		624	JERUSALEM 5	50
THE DISEASE OF SHAME COVERS ME FROM HEAD TO FEET I HAVE NO HOPE		643	JERUSALEM 21	3
MOUNT ZION LIFTED HIS HEAD IN EVERY NATION UNDER HEAVEN		648	JERUSALEM 24	48
COVERD WITH BOILS FROM HEAD TO FOOT THE TERRIBLE SMITINGS OF LUVAH		655	JERUSALEM 29	64
FROM HEAD TO FEET A GARMENT OF DEATH & ETERNAL FEAR . .		660	JERUSALEM 34	6
ALL POWERFUL PARENTAL AFFECTION FILLS ALBION FROM HEAD TO FOOT		685	JERUSALEM 54	10
BOTH OF THE HEAD & LOINS CLOSD UP IN MORAL PRIDE . . .		693	JERUSALEM 60	49
AND REUBEN FLED WITH HIS HEAD DOWNWARDS AMONG THE CAVERNS		698	JERUSALEM 63	44
IN VERULAM THE POLYPUS'S HEAD WINDING AROUND HIS BULK . .		704	JERUSALEM 67	35
EMBRACES ARE COMINGLINGS FROM THE HEAD EVEN TO THE FEET		708	JERUSALEM 69	43
ABOVE THE MOUNTAINS OF ALBION ABOVE THE HEAD OF LOS . .		711	JERUSALEM 71	* 55
IN HEAD & HEART & REINS THREE UNIVERSES OF LOVE & BEAUTY		730	JERUSALEM 86	3
BENDS OVER THY IMMORTAL HEAD IN WHICH ETERNITY DWELLS . .		731	JERUSALEM 86	10
(AROUND) HIS HEAD THE THICK HAIL STONES STAND READY TO OBEY		731	JERUSALEM 86	* 36
HIS HEAD DARK DEADLY IN ITS BRAIN INCLOSES A REFLEXION . .		734	JERUSALEM 89	14
ABOVE HIS HEAD HIGH ARCHING WINGS BLACK FILLD WITH EYES		735	JERUSALEM 89	28
ENITHARMON HEARD SHE RAISD HER HEAD LIKE THE MILD MOON . .		740	JERUSALEM 93	1
SHOULD BRUISE THE SERPENT'S HEAD IS THIS THE SERPENT AH		779	GHOST ABEL 1	4
YOURS IN HEAD & HEART...A MERRY CHRISTMAS		791C	LETTER 3	PROSE
& I CANNOT AFFORD TO DO IT FOR LESS I HAD TWELVE FOR THE HEAD		794B	LETTER 5	PROSE
MY STUPID HEAD BELIEVE THAT IT WAS PROPER FOR ME TO TROUBLE		798A	LETTER 10	PROSE
WHAT CAME FROM MY HEAD & MY HEART IN UNISON THAT I AM PROUD OF BEING		814D	LETTER 23	PROSE

		PAGE	TITLE	LINE

HEAD   (CONTINUED)

    THE PORTRAITS & CHARMD BY THE GREAT HEAD IN PARTICULAR   .   .   820D LETTER 25   PROSE
    I WRITE IN GREAT HASTE & WITH A HEAD FULL OF BOTHERATION   821B LETTER 25   PROSE
    HAND UPON MY HEAD & GIVES A BLESSING TO ALL MY WORKS   .   823B LETTER 26   PROSE
    FEMALE HEAD HE HAS PROMISED TO WRITE A LIST OF ALL THAT HE   831A LETTER 31   PPOSE
    AS THE TRAGIC MUSE HALF-LENGTH THAT IS THE HEAD & HANDS   836A LETTER 35   PROSE
    OTHER BOTH HELD ABOVE HER HEAD & A FIGURE KNEELING AT HER   839C LETTER 38   PROSE
        FEET
    SOMEWHAT PERHAPS AS I DID THE HEAD OF EULER THE   .   .   .   844B LETTER 43   PROSE
    RICHARDSON IS NOT YET PUBLISHED MY HEAD OF ROMNEY IS   .   849A LETTER 45   PROSE
    THE HEAD OF COWPER AFTER LAWRENCE THE HEADS TO BE FINISHD   850D LETTER 49   PROSE
    & THE HEAD OF ROMNEY FOR WHICH I AM ALREADY PAID   .   .   851A LETTER 49   PROSE
    BEFORE NOW PROOFS OF THE TWO PLATES THE HEAD OF R(ROMNEY)   851B LETTER 50   PROSE
    SUDDENLY AS I WAS AT FIRST BY PRODUCING THE HEAD OF ROMNEY   852C LETTER 50   PROSE
    COMPANION TO MY DRAWING OF THE HEAD OF COWPER YOU   .   .   .   855D LETTER 53   PROSE
    PRAYER AND PARENTAL AFFECTION FILLS THE FIGURE FROM HEAD   864B LETTER 61   *PROSE
        TO FOOT
    FRONTISPIECE OF CHILD ON THE SHEPHERD'S HEAD   .   .   .   .   SUPP LETTER 66A   *PROSE

HEADED   SEE GREY HEADED,SEVEN HEADED,THICK HEADED,TRIPLE HEADED,WEAK HEADED

HEADLONG

    HEADLONG FROM OUT THEIR HEAVENLY HEIGHTS DESCENDING SWIFT   200 AMERICA 12   5
        AS FIRES
    IS SEEN SATAN WOUND ROUND BY THE SERPENT & FALLING HEADLONG   443B LAST JUDGMNT/L   PROSE
    FALLING HEADLONG WOUND ROUND BY THE TAIL OF THE SERPENT   606C V LAST JUDG/N   PROSE
    FALLING HEADLONG BY THE SIDE OF THEM IS A MIGHTY FIEND   .   607D V LAST JUDG/N   PROSE
    HE DRAGS SATAN DOWN HEADLONG HE IS CROWND WITH OAK   .   .   .   607D V LAST JUDG/N   PROSE
    IN THIS CATARACT FOUR ANGELS DESCEND HEADLONG   .   .   .   .   609A V LAST JUDG/N   PROSE

HEADS   SEE BLOCK HEADS

    DEFYD THE STORM THAT HOWLED OER THEIR HEADS   .   .   .   .   .   32 EDW THIRD/PS 6   33
    THE SORROWFUL PAIR LIFT UP THEIR HEADS   .   .   .   .   .   .   36D COUCH DEATH/PS   PROSE
    CURSE ON YOUR [XXX] RUTHLESS HEADS FOR I WILL BURY HER   100 TIRIEL 1   *   33
        EVEN HERE
    THE CURSE THAT ROLLS OVER THEIR HEADS WILL REST ITSELF   104 TIRIEL 4   14
        ON THINE
    HEADS DEPREST VOICES WEAK EYES DOWNCAST HANDS WORK-BRUISD   197 AMERICA 3   10
    THEIR HEADS ON SNOWY HILLS THEIR ENSIGNS SICKNING IN THE   202 AMERICA 15   10
        SKY
    HEADS DEPREST VOICES WEAK EYES DOWNCAST HANDS WORK BRUISED   204 AMERICA CANC A   10
    ON THE HEADS OF ALBION'S ANGELS   .   .   .   .   241 EUROPE 9   13
    .   .   .   WITH GLORIES FROM THEIR HEADS OUT BEAMING   .   .   .   .   269 FOUR ZOAS 1   196
    WHILE ROUND THEIR HEADS THE ELEMENTAL GODS KEPT HARMONY   288 FOUR ZOAS 2   301
    DO THEY NOT BOW THEIR BRIGHT HEADS AT THY VOICE AT THY   291 FOUR ZOAS 3   6
        COMMAND
    .   .   .   BUT THE CLOUD HOVERD OVER THEIR HEADS   .   .   .   .   293 FOUR ZOAS 3   66
    THE DOUBLE ROOTED LABYRINTH SOON WAVD AROUND THEIR HEADS   328 FOUR ZOAS 7   335
    SINGING & SHOUTING TO THE MAN THEY BOW THEIR HOARY HEADS   378 FOUR ZOAS 9   804
    IN THE CAVERNS OF THE EARTH IS THE DRAGON WITH SEVEN HEADS   443A LAST JUDGMNT/L   PROSE
    SUCH AS THE HEADS OUGHT TO BE PRINCIPAL BUT THIS   .   .   .   479B ANNO REYNOLDS   MARG
    TERRIBLE OVER THEIR HEADS SATAN WEPT OVER PALAMABRON   .   .   488 MILTON 8   29
    THE HEADS OF THE GREAT POLYPUS FOUR-FOLD TWELVE ENORMITY   529 MILTON 38   2
    [YE] COME ARTISTS KNOCK YOUR HEADS AGAINST THIS STONE   .   537 AND HIS LEGS/N   46
    AS CROOKED LIMBS & LOUZY HEADS OF HAIR   .   .   .   .   .   .   540 SIR JOSH RUB/N   8
    COME KNOCK YOUR HEADS AGAINST THIS STONE   .   .   .   .   .   545 AN EPITAPH/N   1
    DELICATE HANDS & HEADS WILL NEVER APPEAR   .   .   .   .   .   551 DELICATE/N   1
    IS TO PICK OUT THE HEADS OF THE DARTS   .   .   .   .   .   .   552 WHY CUPID/N   16
    THE PAINTER HAS CONSEQUENTLY VARIED THE HEADS AND FORMS   567D DESC CAT 3   PROSE
    THE PAINTER HAS CONSEQUENTLY VARIED THE HEADS AND FORMS   590D CHAUCER 2   PROSE
    TROUBLE THEIR HEADS VERY LITTLE ABOUT ART & SCIENCE & THAT   592C PUB ADDRESS/N   PROSE
    EACH WITH THREE HEADS [REPRESENTING] THEY REPRESENT   .   .   609A V LAST JUDG/N   PROSE
    THE GREAT RED DRAGON WITH SEVEN HEADS & TEN HORNS   .   .   609B V LAST JUDG/N   PROSE
    IN THEIR TRANSLUCENT HEADS WHICH OPENS INTO THE VEGETATIVE   635 JERUSALEM 14   24
        WORLD
    .   .   .   BUT THE CLOUD HOVERD OVER THEIR HEADS   .   .   .   .   654 JERUSALEM 29   53
    PRODUCING MANY HEADS THREE OR SEVEN OR TEN & HANDS & FEET   659 JERUSALEM 33   22
    BOWING THEIR HEADS DEVOTED AND THE FURNACES OF LOS   .   .   676 JERUSALEM 46   20
    WHEN THE CHERUBIM HID THEIR HEADS UNDER THEIR WINGS IN   697 JERUSALEM 63   24
        DEEP SLUMBERS
    BEAR THREE STRONG SINEWY NECKS & THREE AWFUL & TERRIBLE   708 JERUSALEM 70   4
        HEADS
    LISTEN HERMON & LEBANON BOW THEIR CROWNED HEADS   .   .   .   .   730 JERUSALEM 85   17
    MY HEADS OF COWPER FOR MR H'S(HAYLEY'S) LIFE OF COWPER   820C LETTER 25   PROSE
        HAVE
    THE HEADS OF LEAR AND CORDELIA CAN NEVER BE SURPASSED   .   843D LETTER 43   PROSE
    THE HEAD OF COWPER AFTER LAWRENCE THE HEADS TO BE FINISHD   850D LETTER 49   PROSE
    OF THOSE TRULY PATHETIC HEADS WOULD THUS BE TRANSMITTED TO   850D LETTER 49   PROSE

HEAL

    TO HEAL THE WOUND OF HIS SMITING   .   .   .   .   274 FOUR ZOAS 1   354
    AND EVERY WOUND IT HAS MADE SHALL HEAL   .   .   .   .   .   .   420 I SAW A MONK/N   56
    THEY HEAL THE SICK HE CASTS OUT DEVILS   .   .   .   .   .   .   545 COSWAY FRAZR/N   4
    THEN JESUS CHRIST COMES WITH A BALM TO HEAL IT   .   .   .   .   617A V LAST JUDG/N   PROSE
    IS INCAPABLE AND NOTHING NONE BUT THE LAMB OF GOD CAN HEAL   675 JERUSALEM 45   15
    HEAL THOU THE SICK OF SPIRITUAL DISEASE   .   .   .   .   .   .   718 STOOD AMONG/J   25

HEALD

    BUT THE WRENCHING OF URIZEN HEALD NOT   .   .   .   .   .   .   226 URIZEN 7   4
    AND HEALD AFTER THE SEPARATION HIS PAINS HE SOON FORGOT   732 JERUSALEM 86   59

HEALED

    TILL THE WRENCHING APART WAS HEALED   .   .   .   .   226 URIZEN 7   3
    INJURY THE LORD HEALS BUT VENGANCE CANNOT BE HEALED   .   .   648 JERUSALEM 25   5
    IF YOU DARE REND THEIR VEIL WITH YOUR SPEAR YOU ARE HEALED   706 JERUSALEM 68   42
        OF LOVE

HEALING

    BATH HEALING CITY WHOSE WISDOM IN MIDST OF POETIC   .   .   .   675 JERUSALEM 45   1

```
                                                         PAGE      TITLE            LINE
HEALS
    INJURY THE LORD HEALS BUT VENGEANCE CANNOT BE HEALED   . .    648 JERUSALEM 25         5
    BUT HE HEALS THE DEAF & THE DUMB & THE BLIND   . . . . .      755 EV GOSPEL(E)/N      88
    HE COMFORTS & HEALS & CALLS THEM FRIENDS   . . . . . .        755 EV GOSPEL(E)/N      90
HEALTH    SEE ILL-HEALTH
    ANOTHER WEPT AND WISHD HEALTH TO HIS FATHER   . . . . .        25 EDW THIRD/PS 3     168
    THE JEWEL HEALTH ADORNS HER NECK   . . . . . . . . . .         63 SHEPHERD FIRST       8
    AND BY HIS HEALTH SICKNESS   . . . . . . . . . . . .          119 NIGHT/SI            38
    OF LAMBETH BUT HE KISSED ME AND WISHD ME HEALTH   . . .       505 MILTON 22           11
    I HAVE MENTAL JOY & MENTAL HEALTH   . . . . . . . . .         558 I ROSE UP AT/N       9
    THE FLUSH OF HEALTH IN FLESH EXPOSED TO THE OPEN AIR   .      580D DESC CAT 5       PROSE
    OF YOUTH & HEALTH   . . . . . . . . . . . . . .              593B PUB ADDRESS/N     PROSE
    DENIES MENTAL HEALTH AND PERFECTION   . . . . . . . .        772B ANNO SPURZHEIM     MARG
    YOU RETAIN HEALTH AND YET ARE AS MAD AS ANY OF US ALL   .    772D ANNO SPURZHEIM     MARG
    YOURS SINCERELY...HEALTH TO MRS CUMBERLAND & FAMILY   .      790D LETTER 2          PROSE
    BUT AS I KNOW THAT HE WHO WORKS & HAS HIS HEALTH CANNOT      795C LETTER 6          PROSE
    GLADLY I HEAR OF HIS FULL HEALTH AND SPIRITS   . . . .       807B LETTER 17         PROSE
    IN AN INCREASE OF FAMILY & OF HEALTH & HAPPINESS   . .       810A LETTER 20         PROSE
    ABOUT YOUR HEALTH IN ANOTHER PART OF YOUR LETTER MAKES ME    811C LETTER 22         PROSE
    FAMILY ENJOY HEALTH MY MUCH TERRIFIED WIFE JOINS ME IN LOVE  829A LETTER 28         PROSE
    BE WORTH ARRIVED SAFE IN LONDON MY WIFE IN VERY POOR HEALTH  829D LETTER 30         PROSE
    HEALTH & JOY IN GOD OUR SAVIOUR TO ETERNITY YOURS   . .      830D LETTER 30         PROSE
    MY WIFE CONTINUES POORLY BUT FANCIES SHE IS BETTER          832A LETTER 31         PROSE
      IN HEALTH
    THE HEALTH OF MISS POOLE AND FOR ALL OUR FRIENDS IN SUSSEX   832A LETTER 31         PROSE
    HEALTH & SHALL BE TRULY HAPPY TO HEAR THAT IT IS PERFECTLY   833A LETTER 32         PROSE
    GOOD WOMAN AGAIN BEGINS TO RESUME HER HEALTH & STRENGTH      833D LETTER 33         PROSE
    HEALTH & HOW YOU HAVE ESCAPED THE DOUBLE BLOW BOTH   . .     833D LETTER 33         PROSE
    PRAY TO MY GOD & FATHER FOR THE HEALTH OF MISS POOLE HOPE    833D LETTER 33         PROSE
    THEN IN HEALTH I HAVE TAKEN YOUR NOBLE PRESENT TO MR ROSE    834C LETTER 34         PROSE
    WORK IN ABUNDANCE & IF GOD BLESSES ME WITH HEALTH   . .      835A LETTER 34         PROSE
    IN HEALTH BUT HAS HAD SUCH A BURN ON HIS HAND AS YOU HAD     842D LETTER 42         PROSE
    & THAT MISS POOLE IS AGAIN IN SUCH HEALTH   . . . . .        843A LETTER 42        *PROSE
    I AM WITH BEST RESPECTS TO MISS POOLE FOR WHOSE HEALTH  .    847C LETTER 44         PROSE
    CONCERNING HER HEALTH SHE IS SURPRISINGLY RECOVERED   .      851C LETTER 50         PROSE
    CONTINUED HEALTH I AM DEAR SIR YOURS SINCERELY   . . .       855C LETTER 53         PROSE
    MY WIFE CONTINUES IN HEALTH & DESIRES TO JOIN ME IN EVERY    860B LETTER 56         PROSE
    MY WIFE JOINS ME IN ANXIOUS WISHES FOR YOUR HEALTH &   .     862A LETTER 59         PROSE
    OF YOUR GOOD HEALTH & THAT OF OUR DEAR FRIEND OF LAVANT &    862A LETTER 59         PROSE
    THAT I EXPECT NOTHING I WAS ALIVE & IN HEALTH & WITH THE     862C LETTER 60         PROSE
    HOPING THAT I MAY MEET YOU AGAIN IN PERFECT HEALTH           868B LETTER 67         PROSE
      & HAPPINESS
    OR WHATEVER IT IS I AM IN BED & AT WORK MY HEALTH I CANNOT   868D LETTER 68         PROSE
    PRAY TAKE CARE OF YOUR HEALTH THIS WET WEATHER & THO I       870B LETTER 71         PROSE
      WRITE
    AM GLAD TO HEAR OF MRS LINNELL'S HEALTH & SAFETY   . .       873B LETTER 77         PROSE
    RETURN PRAY LET YOUR OWN HEALTH & CONVENIENCE PUT ALL  .     873C LETTER 77         PROSE
    IN (HEALTH) & IN WORK I THANK YOU FOR THE TEN POUNDS   .     879B LETTER 89         PROSE
HEALTHFUL
    IS THE BODY DISEASD WHEN THE MEMBERS ARE HEALTHFUL . . .     142 FRENCH REVOLTN      182
HEALTHFULL
    THAN I HAD EVER HOPED IN MY HEALTHFULL HOURS   . . . . .     873A LETTER 76         PROSE
HEALTHY
    BUT THE ALEHOUSE IS HEALTHY & PLEASANT & WARM   . . . .      179 LIT VAGABOND/N       2
    BUT THE ALE-HOUSE IS HEALTHY & PLEASANT & WARM   . . .       216 LIT VAGABND/SE       2
    THE HUMAN RACE BEGAN TO WITHER FOR THE HEALTHY BUILT   .     246 SONG OF LOS 3       25
    WITH LABOUR & ABSTINENCE SAY HE LOOKS HEALTHY & HAPPY  .     323 FOUR ZOAS 7        119
    THAT A HEALTHY CHILD SHOULD BE TAUGHT & COMPELLD TO WALK     599D PUB ADDRESS/N     PROSE
    LIKE HEALTHY PEOPLE O RARE WISDOM   . . . . . . . . .        600A PUB ADDRESS/N     PROSE
HEAP
    HEAP THE SEA-COAL COME HEAP IT HIGHER   . . . . . .           16 BLIND-MANS/PS        5
    ON THE BACK OF HIM CAME ALL THE OTHERS IN A HEAP   . . .      59A ISLAND MOON 10    PROSE
    AN EVANESCENT SHADOW LAST SHE FELL A HEAP OF ASHES   . .     283 FOUR ZOAS 2        115
    BENEATH THE FURNACES A WOFUL HEAP IN LIVING DEATH   . .      283 FOUR ZOAS 2        116
    SLAUGHTER SHALL HEAP THE BLOODY PLAIN   . . . . . . .        420 I SAW A MONK/N      51
    DARK GLEAMS BEFORE THE FURNACE-MOUTH A HEAP OF BURNING       485 MILTON 6            17
      ASHES
    THE ROMAN SOLDIERS ROLLED TOGETHER IN A HEAP BEFORE THEM     580C DESC CAT 5        PROSE
HEAPHY
    & IF IT IS MORE CONVENIENT TO MR HEAPHY FOR US TO MEET   .   868B LETTER 67         PROSE
HEAPS
    FOR HEAPS OF SMOKING RUINS   . . . . . . . . . . .          247 SONG OF LOS 6        21
    JAMES CALLS FOR FIRES IN GOLGONOOZA FOR HEAPS OF SMOKING     485 MILTON 5            40
      RUINS
HEAR
    VALLIES HEAR ALL OUR LONGING EYES ARE TURNED   . . . . .      1 TO SPRING/PS         6
    HE LOVES TO SIT AND HEAR ME SING   . . . . . . . . . .        6 HOW SWEET/PS        13
    SWEET I HEAR HER MOURNFUL SONG   . . . . . . . . . .          7 LOVE HARMNY/PS      14
    THERE IS LOVE I HEAR [HER] HIS TONGUE   . . . . . . .         7 LOVE HARMNY/PS      16
    AND HEAR THE LINNET'S SONG   . . . . . . . . . . .            8 MEMORY COME/PS      10
    TO HEAR THE MUSIC OF AN ANGEL'S TONGUE   . . . . . . .        9 FRESH FROM/PS       12
    SO WHEN SHE SPEAKS THE VOICE OF HEAVEN I HEAR   . . . .       9 FRESH FROM/PS       13
    SPORTS IN THE CLOUDS TO HEAR THE THUNDER'S SOUND   . . .     15 IMIT SPEN/PS        40
    ON NOBLE SOULS NOW HEAR ITS OPPOSITE   . . . . . . .         24 EDW THIRD/PS 3     123
    AND LEAP AND DANCE TO HEAR THE TRUMPET SOUND   . . . .       25 EDW THIRD/PS 3     171
    IM GLAD MY FATHER DOES NOT HEAR ME TALK   . . . . . .        27 EDW THIRD/PS 3     276
    GREAT DEAL MORE THAT WE SHALL ALL HEAR BY AND BY AND I CAME  29C EDW THIRD/PS 4    PROSE
    TO TELL YOUR HONOUR BECAUSE YOU LOVE TO HEAR WAR-SONGS  .    29C EDW THIRD/PS 4    PROSE
    I SEEM TO HEAR THE DISMAL YELLS OF DEATH   . . . . . .       31 EDW THIRD/PS 5      45
    HEAR YE THE VOICE OF BRUTUS THE FLOWING WAVES   . . . .      32 EDW THIRD/PS 6      39
    AND EVENING HEAR THEIR SONG OF VICTORY   . . . . . . .       33 EDW THIRD/PS 6      52
    HEAR IT NOT HEAVEN THY MINISTERS HAVE DONE IT   . . . .      33 EDW FOURTH/PS       16
```

```
                                                          PAGE    TITLE          LINE
HEAR   (CONTINUED)
      LEANING ON HER BOSOM THUS HE SPOKE HEAR O DALILA  . . . .   39B SAMSON/PS     PROSE
      AH SAID TILLY LALLY I DID NOT HEAR IT WHAT WAS IT OBTUSE     47A ISLAND MOON 3 PROSE
         ANGLE
      HEAR THEN THE PRIDE & KNOWLEDGE OF A SAILOR    . . . . .     52 HEAR THEN/IM      1
      HEAR MY VOICE UPON THE BREEZE  . . . . . . . . . . . .       61 LEAVE O/IM        8
      OF AGED TIRIEL AROSE THAT HIS SONS MIGHT HEAR IN THEIR       99 TIRIEL 1          6
         GATES
      LISTEN & HEAR YOUR MOTHER'S GROANS NO MORE ACCURSED SONS     99 TIRIEL 1         24
      THUNDER & FIRE & PESTILENCE (HEAR) YOU NOT TIRIEL'S CURSE   106 TIRIEL 5         13
      SO I PIPED HE WEPT TO HEAR  . . . . . . . . . . .           111 INTRODUCTN/SI     8
      WHILE HE WEPT WITH JOY TO HEAR . . . . . . . . . .          111 INTRODUCTN/SI    12
      EVERY CHILD MAY JOY TO HEAR . . . . . . . . . . . .         111 INTRODUCTN/SI    20
      DO THEY HEAR THEIR FATHER SIGH . . . . . . . . . .          112 A DREAM/SI       10
      CAN A MOTHER SIT AND HEAR   . . . . . . . . . .             122 ON ANOTHERS/SI    9
      HEAR THE WREN WITH SORROWS SMALL   . . . . . . . .          122 ON ANOTHERS/SI   14
      HEAR THE SMALL BIRD'S GRIEF & CARE   . . . . . . . .        122 ON ANOTHERS/SI   15
      HEAR THE WOES THAT INFANTS BEAR   . . . . . . . . .         122 ON ANOTHERS/SI   16
      THE CLOUD WILL VANISH WE SHALL HEAR HIS VOICE  . . . .      125 LIT BLK BOY/SI   18
      AND GENTLE SLEEP THE SLEEP OF DEATH AND GENTLE HEAR THE     127 BOOK OF THEL 1   13
         VOICE
      BUT I FEED NOT THE LITTLE FLOWERS I HEAR THE WARBLING BIRDS 129 BOOK OF THEL 3   19
      THE WEAK WORM FROM ITS LOWLY BED AND THOU SHALT HEAR ITS    129 BOOK OF THEL 3   28
         VOICE
      TO HEAR THE HORSE NEIGH TO THE DRUM AND TRUMPET . . . . .   138 FRENCH REVOLTN  102
      I HEAR RUSHING OF MUSKETS . . . . . . . . . . . . .         139 FRENCH REVOLTN  116
      HEAR MY COUNSEL O KING AND SEND FORTH THY GENERALS . . .    141 FRENCH REVOLTN  153
      HEAR O HEAVENS OF FRANCE . . . . . . . . . . . . . .        143 FRENCH REVOLTN  206
      . . .HEAR THE VOICE OF VALLIES THE VOICE OF MEEK CITIES     143 FRENCH REVOLTN  207
      . . . HER NOBLES SHALL HEAR AND SHALL WEEP AND PUT OFF  . . 144 FRENCH REVOLTN  221
      THEN HEAR THE FIRST VOICE OF THE MORNING . . . . . . .      145 FRENCH REVOLTN  238
      NOW HEAR A PLAIN FACT SWEDENBORG HAS NOT WRITTEN ONE NEW   157D MARRIAGE HH 21  PROSE
         TRUTH
      NOW HEAR ANOTHER HE HAS WRITTEN ALL THE OLD FALSHOODS  . . 157D MARRIAGE HH 21 *PROSE
      AND NOW HEAR THE REASON HE CONVERSED WITH ANGELS WHO  . .  157D MARRIAGE HH 21  PROSE
      IN THE GREATEST DEGREE NOW HEAR HOW HE HAS GIVEN . . . .   158C MARRIAGE HH 22  PROSE
      I HEAR THE [FATHER OF THE] ANCIENT [?FATHER OF] MEN  . . .  169 EARTHS ANSWD/N *  10
      THE [GERMAN FORGED] MIND FORGD [LINKS I HEAR] MANACLES      170 LONDON/N       *   8
         I HEAR
      [FROM EVERY DISMAL STREET I HEAR]                           170 LONDON/N          15
      BUT MOST [FROM EVERY STREET] THRO WINTRY STREETS I HEAR     170 LONDON/N       *  18
      BUT MOST THE SHRIEKS OF YOUTH I HEAR . . . . . . . .        170 LONDON/N          22
      THE DAUGHTERS OF ALBION HEAR HER WOES & ECCHO BACK HER      190 V DAU ALBION 2   20
         SIGHS
      AND NONE BUT BROMION CAN HEAR MY LAMENTATIONS  . . . . .    191 V DAU ALBION 3    1
      THE DAUGHTERS OF ALBION HEAR HER WOES & ECCHO BACK HER      192 V DAU ALBION 5    2
         SIGHS
      THE DAUGHTERS OF ALBION HEAR HER WOES & ECCHO BACK HER      195 V DAU ALBION 8   13
         SIGHS
      HEAR THE VOICE OF THE BARD  . . . . . . . . . . .           210 INTRODUCTN/SE     1
      I HEAR THE FATHER OF THE ANCIENT MEN  . . . . . . . .       211 EARTHS ANSR/SE   10
      THE MIND-FORGD MANACLES I HEAR . . . . . . . . . .          216 LONDON/SE         8
      BUT MOST THRO MIDNIGHT STREETS I HEAR   . . . . . . .       216 LONDON/SE        13
      ETERNALS I HEAR YOUR CALL GLADLY  . . . . . . . . .         222 URIZEN 2          5
      FOR ORC REJOICD TO HEAR THE HOWLING SHADOWS  . . . . .      242 EUROPE 12        22
      I HEAR THE SOFT OOTHOON IN ENITHARMON'S TENTS  . . . . .    244 EUROPE 14        21
      NOR WEEP ON HIS KNEES NOR HEAR . . . . . . . . . .          254 AHANIA 4         66
      AND JOY NOR HEAR HIS FOOTSTEPS AND . . . . . . . .          254 AHANIA 4         68
      [TO HEAR] HEARING THE [SOUND] MARCH OF LONG RESOUNDING      264 FOUR ZOAS 1    *   5
         . . .
      ALL THY PAST DEEDS HEAR WHAT I TELL THEE MARK IT            268 FOUR ZOAS 1      153
         WELL REMEMBER
      WE HEAR THE WARLIKE CLARIONS WE VIEW THE TURNING SPHERES    271 FOUR ZOAS 1      258
      HEAR I WILL SING A SONG OF DEATH IT IS A SONG OF VALA  . .  271 FOUR ZOAS 1      260
      AND THOU O ENITHARMON HARK I HEAR THE HAMMERS OF LOS  . .   275 FOUR ZOAS 1      421
      HEAR YE THE VOICE OF LUVAH FROM THE FURNACES OF URIZEN  . . 282 FOUR ZOAS 2       80
      TO HEAR THE DOG HOWL AT THE WINTRY DOOR . . . . . . . .     290 FOUR ZOAS 2      409
      TO HEAR SOUNDS OF LOVE IN THE THUNDER STORM  . . . . . .    291 FOUR ZOAS 2      411
      . . . [& ALL MY KINGLY POWER] BUT HEAR MY DETERMIND DECREE  292 FOUR ZOAS 3       19
      THY RIGHTEOUS DOOM UPON ME ONLY LET ME HEAR THY VOICE  . .  296 FOUR ZOAS 3      187
      URIZEN TREMBLED WHERE HE LAY TO HEAR THE HOWLING TERROR     310 FOUR ZOAS 5      185
      QUEEN OF THESE DREADFUL RIVERS SPEAK & LET ME HEAR THY      312 FOUR ZOAS 6       19
         VOICE
      IF THOU ART HE MY DESPERATE PURPOSE HEAR & GIVE ME DEATH    313 FOUR ZOAS 6       57
      SAY HE SMILES IF YOU HEAR HIM SIGH IF PALE SAY HE IS RUDDY  323 FOUR ZOAS 7      125
      THE RUINS OF THE UNIVERSE HEAR WHAT INSPIRD I SPEAK & BE    329 FOUR ZOAS 7      352
         SILENT
      SOUND THE SHRILL FIFE SERPENTS OF WAR I HEAR THE NORTHERN   336 FOUR ZOAS 7B     148
         DRUM
      AWAKE I HEAR THE FLAPPINGS OF THE FOLDING BANNERS   . . .   336 FOUR ZOAS 7B   * 149
      WE HEAR THY SIGHS IN TRUMPETS SHRILL WHEN MORN SHALL BLOOD  338 FOUR ZOAS 7B     209
         RENEW
      I HEAR THY VOICE BUT NOT THY FORM SEE THOU & ALL DELIGHT    339 FOUR ZOAS 7B     240
      MY EYES TO THY PAVILIONS HEAR MY PRAYER FOR LUVAH'S SAKE    345 FOUR ZOAS 8      152
      OVER THEIR VICTIMS HEAR YE THE SONG OF THE FEMALES          348 FOUR ZOAS 8      297
         OF AMALEK
      HEAR ME REPEAT MY GENERATIONS THAT THOU MAYST ALSO REPENT   350 FOUR ZOAS 8    * 356
      IN ABSTRACT FALSE EXPANSES THAT HE MAY NOT HEAR THE VOICE   353 FOUR ZOAS 8      487
      THE FURROWD FIELD REPLIES TO THE GRAVE I HEAR HER REPLY     355 FOUR ZOAS 8      548
         TO ME
      I HEAR MYSTERY HOWLING IN THESE FLAMES OF CONSUMMATION  . . 360 FOUR ZOAS 9      114
      AND THE ETERNAL MAN SAID HEAR MY [VOICE] WORDS O PRINCE     362 FOUR ZOAS 9      204
         OF LIGHT
```

885

		PAGE	TITLE	LINE

HEAR   (CONTINUED)

I WALK AMONG HIS FLOCKS & HEAR THE BLEATING OF HIS LAMBS   368 FOUR ZOAS 9   425
FOLLOW ME O MY FLOCKS & HEAR ME SING MY RAPTUROUS SONG . . 368 FOUR ZOAS 9   438
I HEAR THE FLAIL OF URIZEN HIS BARNS ARE FULL NO (ROOM)   375 FOUR ZOAS 9   * 696
THEN HEAR IT CONTEMND WITHOUT RETURNING SCORN FOR SCORN   477A ANNO REYNOLDS * MARG
CALLS THE SQUIRE THE POP OF CHAUCER'S AGE NOW HEAR CHAUCER 573C DESC CAT 3   PROSE
APPEARS IN HER CHEEKS NOW HEAR WHAT CHAUCER HAS MADE HER   574B DESC CAT 3   PROSE
EVEN FROM THE DEPTHS OF HELL HIS VOICE I HEAR . . . . .   621 READER LOVER/J   7
MALDEN & COLCHESTER DEMONSTRATE I HEAR MY CHILDREN'S VOICES 644 JERUSALEM 21   37
THEN LOST IN CLOUDS I HEAR THEIR TENDER VOICES CLOUDS   644 JERUSALEM 21   41
   DIVIDE
THE ARMIES I HEAR THEIR LOUD CYMBALS & THEIR DEADLY CRIES 644 JERUSALEM 21   47
BUT A MEER PHANTASY HEAR DYING ALBION'S CURSE . . . . .   646 JERUSALEM 23   37
I HEAR THY SHUTTLES SING IN THE SKY AND ROUND MY LIMBS . 657 JERUSALEM 31   48
I HEAR THE SCREECH OF CHILDBIRTH LOUD PEALING & THE GROANS 661 JERUSALEM 34   23
I WRITE IN SOUTH MOLTON STREET WHAT I BOTH SEE AND HEAR   665 JERUSALEM 38   42
JERUSALEM'S CHILDREN HARK HEAR THE GIANTS OF ALBION CRY   673 JERUSALEM 43   47
   AT NIGHT
BUT HE DRIVETH ME AWAY FROM HIS PRESENCE YET I HEAR THE   694 JERUSALEM 61   9
   VOICE OF GOD
WE HEAR THY SIGHS IN TRUMPETS SHRILL WHEN MORN SHALL BLOOD 701 JERUSALEM 65   55
   RENEW
TIRZAH SITS WEEPING TO HEAR THE SHRIEKS OF THE DYING HER   704 JERUSALEM 67   24
   KNIFE
THE STARS STAND STILL TO HEAR JERUSALEM & VALA CEASE TO   730 JERUSALEM 85   15
   MOURN
HOW CAN I HEAR MY LITTLE ONES WEEPING ALONG THE VALLEY . 740 JERUSALEM 93   15
ADAM I WILL NOT HEAR THEE MORE THOU SPIRITUAL VOICE . . . 779 GHOST ABEL 1   1
ADAM IT IS IN VAIN I WILL NOT HEAR THEE . . . .   779 GHOST ABEL 1   2
LET US SEE YOU SOMETIMES AS WELL AS SOMETIMES HEAR FROM   791C LETTER 3   PROSE
I HEAR HIS ADVICE & EVEN NOW WRITE FROM HIS DICTATE . .   797B LETTER 9   PROSE
A NATION I HEAR THAT IT IS NOW IN THE HANDS OF MINISTERS   797D LETTER 10   PROSE
APPEARS TO BE LAW & GOSPEL TOO AT LEAST I HEAR SO FROM THE 798C LETTER 10   PROSE
LET ME HEAR OF YOUR WELFARE REMEMBER MY & MY WIFE'S . .   798D LETTER 10   PROSE
GLADLY I HEAR OF HIS FULL HEALTH AND SPIRITS . . . .   807B LETTER 17   PROSE
LEFT WITH US THEY KEEP OFF EVERY WIND WE HEAR THE WEST HOWL 807B LETTER 17   PROSE
DEAR FLAXMAN I REJOICE TO HEAR THAT YOUR GREAT WORK IS   810C LETTER 21   PROSE
   ACCOMPLISHD
"I HEAR A VOICE YOU CANNOT HEAR THAT SAYS I MUST NOT STAY" 813C LETTER 22
BUT PRAY LET ME NOW HEAR HOW YOU DO & OF THE . . . . .   816A LETTER 23   PROSE
AS SOON AS THEY HEAR OF IT . . . .   828B LETTER 28   PROSE
HEALTH & SHALL BE TRULY HAPPY TO HEAR THAT IT IS PERFECTLY 833A LETTER 32   PROSE
LIKE THE SOUND OF HARPS WHICH I HEAR BEFORE THE SUN'S   835B LETTER 34   PROSE
   RISING
MR ROSE I AM HAPPY TO HEAR IS GETTING QUITE WELL HOPE TO   838C LETTER 37
HEAR THE SAME GOOD ACCOUNT OF OUR MOST ADMIRABLE . . .   838C LETTER 37   PROSE
TO ASSIST ANY HOW REMOTE SOEVER WILL CERTAINLY HEAR HER   842A LETTER 41   PROSE
   VOICE
FEEL MUCH EASIER TO HEAR THAT YOU HAVE PARTED WITH YOUR   843A LETTER 42   PROSE
   HORSE
HOPE SOON TO HEAR THAT YOU HAVE GOT A LIVING ONE OF BRASS 843A LETTER 42   *PROSE
YOU ONE I REJOICE TO HEAR FROM MR MEYER OF MISS POOLE'S   851A LETTER 49   PROSE
AND OFTEN WE THINK WE HEAR YOUR VOICE CALLING AT THE GATE 854A LETTER 52   PROSE
FOR I HEAR THE BELLS RING & THE TRUMPETS SOUND . . .   854C LETTER 53   PROSE
HEAR FROM YOU BUT SAID I I WILL IF YOU WISH AS I SHALL   856D LETTER 54   PROSE
   WRITE
FOR I HAVE HEARD NOTHING OF PHILLIPS THIS AGE I HEAR .   862A LETTER 59   PROSE
& OUR GOOD LADY PAULINA OVER A DISH OF COFFEE I LONG TO   862A LETTER 59   PROSE
   HEAR
SUBJECT OF PAINTING AND HENCE IT IS SO COMMON TO HEAR .   864C LETTER 61   PROSE
AM GLAD TO HEAR OF MRS LINNELL'S HEALTH & SAFETY . . . .   873B LETTER 77   PROSE
INTRODUCTION HEAR THE VOICE OF THE BARD &C . . . . .   SUPP LETTER 66A   *PROSE

HEARD

BENEATH OUR THICKEST SHADES WE OFT HAVE HEARD . . . . . .   2 TO SUMMER/PS   7
AND HEARD A GLOOMY VOICE CRY IS IT DONE . . . .   4 FAIR ELENOR/PS   32
THEN CRIES OUT HEM HODGE HEARD AND RAN . . . .   16 BLIND-MANS/PS   49
I HAVE NOT HEARD . . . .   22 EDW THIRD/PS 3   54
MY SINEWS SLACKEND AND MY VOICE SCARCE HEARD . . . . . .   23 EDW THIRD/PS 3   103
I HEARD A BLOOMING YOUTH SINGING A SONG . . . .   25 EDW THIRD/PS 3   163
NOR TRILLING PIPE IS HEARD NOR PLEASURE SITS . . . . . .   28 EDW THIRD/PS 3   284
AND OFTEN HEARD THE DISMAL CLANG OF ARMS . . . .   31 EDW THIRD/PS 5   40
ARE HEARD FROM THE HILLS THE ENORMOUS SONS . . . . . .   32 EDW THIRD/PS 6   20
CRAVE OR BE HEARD FOR PLENTY SHALL BRING FORTH . . . .   33 EDW THIRD/PS 6   46
AND DREADFUL THUNDER OF THE BATTLE HEARD AFAR . . . . .   34B KING JOHN/PS   PROSE
THE BIRDS OF DAY WERE HEARD IN THEIR NESTS . . . .   35C COUCH DEATH/PS   PROSE
THE YOUTH REPLIED LIKE A VOICE HEARD FROM A SEPULCHRE .   36A COUCH DEATH/PS   PROSE
AS THE VOICE OF AN OMEN HEARD IN THE SILENT VALLEY . .   36B COUCH DEATH/PS   PROSE
WHILE ON HIS MAJESTIC BROW THE VOICE OF ANGELS IS HEARD   36D COUCH DEATH/PS   PROSE
VOICES OF COMFORT ARE HEARD OVER THE COUCH OF DEATH . .   36D COUCH DEATH/PS   PROSE
HE SAT AND HEARD WITH JOY AND PRAISED GOD WHO ISRAEL STILL 40A SAMSON/PS   PROSE
   DOTH KEEP
WHEN THE TONGUES OF CHILDREN ARE HEARD ON THE GREEN . .   60 NURSES SONG/IM   1
AND LAUGHING [UPON] IS HEARD ON THE HILL . . . .   60 NURSES SONG/IM   2
AND [HE] HEARD HAR SING IN THE GREAT CAGE & SLEPT UPON   103 TIRIEL 3   * 23
   OUR FLEECES
THE BLIND MAN HEARD HIS BROTHER'S VOICE & KNEELD DOWN ON   104 TIRIEL 4   10
   HIS KNEE
WHEN TIRIEL HEARD THE WORDS OF IJIM HE SOUGHT NOT TO REPLY 104 TIRIEL 4   26
THE BLIND MAN HEARD & SMOTE HIS BREAST & TREMBLING PASSED 109 TIRIEL 7   14
   ON
ALL HEART-BROKE I HEARD HER SAY . . . .   111 A DREAM/SI   8
WHEN THE VOICES OF CHILDREN ARE HEARD ON THE GREEN . . . 121 NURSES SONG/SI   1

886

	PAGE	TITLE	LINE

HEARD   (CONTINUED)

AND LAUGHING IS HEARD ON THE HILL . . . .   121 NURSES SONG/SI   2
DOWN BY THE RIVER OF ADONA HER SOFT VOICE IS HEARD   . . .   127 BOOK OF THEL 1   4
THE CLOD OF CLAY HEARD THE WORM'S VOICE & RAISD HER PITYING   129 BOOK OF THEL 4   7
  HEAD
QUEEN OF THE VALES THE MATRON CLAY ANSWERD I HEARD THY   130 BOOK OF THEL 5   14
  SIGHS
AND HEARD THIS VOICE OF SORROW BREATHED FROM THE HOLLOW PIT   130 BOOK OF THEL 6   10
TO TOWER HIS HOWLINGS WERE HEARD IN THE LOUVRE . . . . .   135 FRENCH REVOLTN   22
. . . AND HIS RAVINGS IN WINDS ARE HEARD OVER VERSAILLES   136 FRENCH REVOLTN   51
. . . A WEEPING IS HEARD OER THE PALACE . . . .   139 FRENCH REVOLTN   105
. . . AND CRIES OF WOMEN AND BABES ARE HEARD . . . . .   139 FRENCH REVOLTN   118
. . . AND THE SENATE HEARD IT . . . .   139 FRENCH REVOLTN   124
MY GROANING IS HEARD IN THE ABBEYS . . . .   140 FRENCH REVOLTN   137
. . . FOR A CURSE IS HEARD HOARSE THRO THE LAND FROM A   140 FRENCH REVOLTN   138
  GODLESS RACE
. . . TILL GRADUAL A MURMUR IS HEARD DESCENDING INTO THE   145 FRENCH REVOLTN   243
  VALLEY
THE UNWELCOME MESSAGE SILENT THEY HEARD . . . .   145 FRENCH REVOLTN   257
A RUSHING OF WINGS AROUND HIM WAS HEARD AS HE BRIGHTEND   146 FRENCH REVOLTN   260
  . . .
ISAIAH ANSWERD I SAW NO GOD NOR HEARD ANY . . . . . .   153C MARRIAGE HH 12   PROSE
I HEARD THIS WITH SOME WONDER & MUST CONFESS MY OWN   154A MARRIAGE HH 12   PROSE
  CONVICTION
END OF SIX THOUSAND YEARS IS TRUE AS I HAVE HEARD FROM HELL   154B MARRIAGE HH 14   PROSE
THE ETERNAL FEMALE GROAND IT WAS HEARD OVER ALL THE EARTH   159A SONG LIBERTY   PROSE
I HEARD AMONG THE RUSHES DANK . . . .   162 LAID ME DOWN/N   3
I HEARD AN ANGEL SINGING . . . .   164 HEARD ANGEL/N   1
I HEARD A DEVIL CURSE . . . .   164 HEARD ANGEL/N   9
WHEN THE VOICES OF CHILDREN ARE HEARD ON THE GREEN . . .   171 NURSES SONG/N   1
I HEARD A WILD [THISTLE] FLOWER . . . .   175 WILD FLOWERS/N   3
THE PRIEST SAT BY AND HEARD THE CHILD . . . . . .   177 LIT BOY LST/N   9
THE WEEPING CHILD COULD NOT BE HEARD . . . .   177 LIT BOY LST/N   20
AS SOON AS HE HEARD THESE TIDINGS TOLD . . . . . .   185 LET BROTHELS/N   6
AND HEARD THE VOICE OF ALBION'S ANGEL GIVE THE THUNDEROUS   201 AMERICA 14   3
  COMMAND
AND LIKE THE VOICES OF RELIGIOUS DEAD HEARD IN THE   205 AMERICA CANC C   29
  MOUNTAINS
WHOSE EARS HAVE HEARD . . . .   210 INTRODUCTN/SE   3
WHEN THE VOICES OF CHILDREN ARE HEARD ON THE GREEN . . . .   212 NURSES SONG/SE   1
THE PRIEST SAT BY AND HEARD THE CHILD . . . .   218 LIT BOY LST/SE   9
THE WEEPING CHILD COULD NOT BE HEARD . . . .   218 LIT BOY LST/SE   17
ARE HEARD LIKE THUNDERS OF AUTUMN . . . .   223 URIZEN 3   34
THE DEAD HEARD THE VOICE OF THE CHILD . . . .   233 URIZEN 20   26
ALL THINGS HEARD THE VOICE OF THE CHILD . . . .   233 URIZEN 20   28
THEY HEARD THE VOICE OF ALBION'S ANGEL HOWLING IN FLAMES   242 EUROPE 12   12
  OF ORC
ABOVE THE REST THE HOWL WAS HEARD FROM WESTMINSTER LOUDER   242 EUROPE 12   14
  & LOUDER
AND JESUS HEARD HER VOICE A MAN OF SORROWS HE RECIEVD . .   246 SONG OF LOS 3   23
THE KINGS OF ASIA HEARD . . . .   247 SONG OF LOS 6   1
URIZEN HEARD THEM CRY . . . .   248 SONG OF LOS 7   9
HER VOICE WAS HEARD BUT NO FORM . . . .   253 AHANIA 4   49
I HEARD HIS VOICE AMONG THE BRANCHES & AMONG SWEET FLOWERS   271 FOUR ZOAS 1   267
I HEARD THE SOUNDING SEA I HEARD THE VOICE WEAKER AND   272 FOUR ZOAS 1   279
  WEAKER
A GROAN WAS HEARD ON HIGH THE WARLIKE CLARIONS CEAST THE   273 FOUR ZOAS 1   313
  SPIRITS
THE LISTNING STARS HEARD & THE FIRST BEAM OF THE MORNING   275 FOUR ZOAS 1   410
  STARTED BACK
HIS SONS FLED FROM HIS SIDE TO JOIN THE CONFLICT PALE HE   278 FOUR ZOAS 1   521
  HEARD
AND HEARD HIS WORD DIVIDE YE BANDS INFLUENCE BY INFLUENCE   280 FOUR ZOAS 2   23
IN JOY SHE HEARD HIS HOWLINGS & FORGOT HE WAS HER LUVAH   282 FOUR ZOAS 2   78
IS HEARD WHEN SILENT NIGHT RETURNS & THE LABOURERS TAKE   285 FOUR ZOAS 2   217
  THEIR REST
LUVAH IN VAIN HER LAMENTATIONS HEARD IN VAIN HIS LOVE . .   286 FOUR ZOAS 2   232
LOS HEARD REVIVING HE SIEZD HER IN HIS ARMS DELUSIVE HOPES   290 FOUR ZOAS 2   380
AHANIA HEARD THE LAMENTATION & A SWIFT VIBRATION . . . . .   291 FOUR ZOAS 2   419
[I] WE HEARD ASTONISHD AT THE VISION & [MY] OUR . . . . .   293 FOUR ZOAS 3   57
[I] [WE] [HEARD THE] VOICE . . . .   293 FOUR ZOAS 3   58
[I] WE HEARD THE VOICE OF . . . .   293 FOUR ZOAS 3   71
I HEARD HIM FROWN NOT URIZEN BUT LISTEN TO MY VISION . .   294 FOUR ZOAS 3   84
THEY HEARD THE VOICE & [THEY] FLED SWIFT AS THE WINTER'S   294 FOUR ZOAS 3   * 93
  SETTING SUN
THESE ARE THE WORDS OF ENION HEARD FROM THE COLD WAVES   296 FOUR ZOAS 3   182
  OF DESPAIR
URIZEN SHUDDRING HEARD HIS TREMBLING LIMBS SHOOK THE STRONG   310 FOUR ZOAS 5   188
  CAVES
HEARD ON MY MOUNTAINS & DEEP SIGHS UNDER MY PALACE ROOFS   310 FOUR ZOAS 5   207
I WELL REMEMBER FOR I HEARD THE MILD & HOLY VOICE . . .   310 FOUR ZOAS 5   218
THARMAS HEARD THE DEADLY SCREAM ACROSS HIS WATRY WORLD . .   313 FOUR ZOAS 6   47
IN VAIN THE TERROR HEARD NOT THEN A LION HE WOULD SIEZE   315 FOUR ZOAS 6   132
AND HEARD THE HOWLINGS OF RED ORC DISTINCTER & DISTINCTER   319 FOUR ZOAS 6   * 291
TERRIFIED URIZEN HEARD ORC NOW CERTAIN THAT HE WAS LUVAH   324 FOUR ZOAS 7   151
AND HEARD THE SPECTRE BITTERLY SHE WEPT EMBRACING FERVENT   327 FOUR ZOAS 7   312
WITH WHIPS ALONG THE SULTRY [ROADS] SANDS I HEARD THOSE   334 FOUR ZOAS 7B   61
  WHOM I LOVD
THEN I HEARD THE EARTHQUAKE &C . . . .   336 FOUR ZOAS 7B   123
A THUNDER CLOUD IN THE SOUTH & A LULLING VOICE HEARD IN   340 FOUR ZOAS 7B   268
  THE NORTH
SHE HEARD SWEET VOICES IN THE WINDS & IN THE VOICES OF   340 FOUR ZOAS 7B   271
  BIRDS

887

	PAGE	TITLE	LINE
HEARD (CONTINUED)			
URIZEN HEARD THE VOICE & SAW THE SHADOW UNDERNEATH . .	345	FOUR ZOAS 8	171
IS HEARD THROUGHOUT THE UNIVERSE WHEREEVER A GRASS GROWS	356	FOUR ZOAS 8	* 581
OR A LEAF BUDS THE ETERNAL MAN IS SEEN IS HEARD IS FELT	356	FOUR ZOAS 8	582
. . . SHE HEARD A VOICE BEHIND HER CALLING HER] . .	356	FOUR ZOAS 8	591
ON PATMOS ISLE & HEARD THE SOULS CRY OUT TO BE DELIVERD	356	FOUR ZOAS 8	601
AND HEARD ENION'S VOICE SOUND FROM THE CAVERNS OF THE GRAVE	356	FOUR ZOAS 8	605
THE RAVEN CALLD THE HAWK I HEARD THEM FROM MY FORESTS BLACK	358	FOUR ZOAS 9	60
AS OF A BATTLE IN THE HEAVENS HARK HEARD YOU NOT	364	FOUR ZOAS 9	263
THE TRUMPET			
THEY HEARD NOT SAW NOT FELT NOT ALL THE TERRIBLE CONFUSION	367	FOUR ZOAS 9	381
I WILL CAUSE MY VOICE TO BE HEARD	368	FOUR ZOAS 9	439
AND VALA STOOD ON THE ROCKS OF THARMAS & HEARD HIS MOURNFUL	370	FOUR ZOAS 9	486
VOICE			
SOUNDS ON THE FLOOR HEARD TERRIBLE BY ALL BENEATH	374	FOUR ZOAS 9	651
THE HEAVENS			
WHEN IN MY FATHER'S HOUSE I SAT & HEARD HIS CHEARING VOICE	375	FOUR ZOAS 9	689
WRITES WHAT HE HAS NEITHER SEEN NOR HEARD OF	392D	ANNO WATSON	MARG
AND NIGHT HATH HEARD MY SORROWS LOUD	423	THE BIRDS/N	12
AND HEARD & SAW SUCH DREADFUL THINGS	424	MENTAL TRAVLER	3
THE SOLDIER HAS BEEN HEARD TO SAY REPEATEDLY	437A	BLAKES MEMORAN	PROSE
MR HOSIER HEARD HIM SAY THAT HE WOULD BE REVENGED	437B	BLAKES MEMORAN	PROSE
WHILE I WAS PRESENT THAT HE HEARD ME UTTER SEDITIOUS WORDS	437B	BLAKES MEMORAN	PROSE
AT THE STABLE DOOR AND IN PARTICULAR SAID THAT HE HEARD ME	437C	BLAKES MEMORAN	PROSE
HEARD PEOPLE QUARREL BUT THEY ALWAYS CHARGED EACH OTHER	437C	BLAKES MEMORAN	PROSE
WHO SWORE THAT HE HEARD ME (DAMN) THE (KING)	437C	BLAKES MEMORAN	PROSE
HE HEARD NOTHING BUT SAYS WE CERTAINLY WERE NOT QUARRELLING	437D	BLAKES MEMORAN	PROSE
HEARD ME SPEAK TO THE SOLDIER WERE ORDERING HIM OUT OF .	437D	BLAKES MEMORAN	PROSE
WORDS MINIATURE PAINTER WHICH HE MIGHT HAVE HEARD ME CALLED	438A	BLAKES MEMORAN	PROSE
A FALSE OATH FOR THAT HE HEARD ME SAY NOTHING OF THE KIND	438C	BLAKES MEMORAN	PROSE
ALL PITIED THE PITEOUS & WAS WRATH WITH THE WRATHFUL &	484	MILTON 5	4
LOS HEARD IT			
A LITTLE SOUND IT UTTERS & ITS CRIES ARE FAINTLY HEARD .	484	MILTON 5	26
LOUD SOUNDS THE HAMMER OF LOS & LOUD HIS BELLOWS IS HEARD	485	MILTON 6	8
LOS HEARD IN TERROR ENITHARMON'S WORDS IN FIBROUS STRENGTH	498	MILTON 17	34
OF EDEN HEARD THE LAMENTATION AND PROVIDENCE BEGAN . .	504	MILTON 21	24
SEVEN MORNINGS LOS HEARD THEM AS THE POOR BIRD WITHIN THE	504	MILTON 21	28
SHELL			
HEARS ITS IMPATIENT PARENT BIRD AND ENITHARMON HEARD THEM	504	MILTON 21	29
THAT IT WAS MILTON THE AWAKENER THEY HAD NOT HEARD THE BARD	504	MILTON 21	33
WHOSE SONG CALLD MILTON TO THE ATTEMPT AND LOS HEARD THESE	504	MILTON 21	34
LAMENTS			
HE HEARD THEM CALL IN PRAYER ALL THE DIVINE FAMILY . .	504	MILTON 21	35
WHILE LOS HEARD INDISTINCT IN FEAR WHAT TIME I BOUND MY	505	MILTON 22	4
SANDALS			
AND WHEN THE DAUGHTERS OF BEULAH HEARD THE LAMENTATION . .	519	MILTON 31	9
AND THE DIVINE VOICE WAS HEARD IN THE SONGS OF BEULAH	522	MILTON 33	1
SAYING			
THAT MILTON'S SHADOW HEARD & CONDENSING ALL HIS FIBRES . .	527	MILTON 37	6
SATAN HEARD COMING IN A CLOUD WITH TRUMPETS & FLAMING FIRE	530	MILTON 38	50
THEN LOUD THE FURNACES OF LOS WERE HEARD & SEEN AS SEVEN	531	MILTON 39	14
HEAVENS			
SATAN HEARD TREMBLING ROUND HIS BODY HE INCIRCLED IT .	531	MILTON 39	16
EXCEPT REMOTELY AND I HEARD OLOLON SAY TO MILTON	532	MILTON 40	3
A GARMENT OF WAR I HEARD IT NAMD THE WOOF OF SIX THOUSAND	534	MILTON 42	15
YEARS			
THUS ALOUD [WAS HEARD TO] DID HOWL & CRY	542	PITIFUL CASE/N *	7
I HAVE HEARD MANY PEOPLE SAY GIVE ME THE IDEAS	596A	PUB ADDRESS/N	PROSE
LOS HEARD HER LAMENTATIONS IN THE DEEPS AFAR HIS TEARS FALL	624	JERUSALEM 5	66
WITH JOY SHE HEARD HIS HOWLINGS & FORGOT HE WAS HER LUVAH	626	JERUSALEM 7	36
LOUD ROAR MY FURNACES AND LOUD MY HAMMER IS HEARD . . .	628	JERUSALEM 9	25
SO LOS IN SECRET WITH HIMSELF COMMUNED & ENITHARMON HEARD	639	JERUSALEM 17	48
JERUSALEM REPLYD LIKE A VOICE HEARD FROM A SEPULCHER .	646	JERUSALEM 23	8
AND THERE WAS HEARD A GREAT LAMENTING IN BEULAH ALL THE	648	JERUSALEM 25	1
REGIONS			
WE HEARD ASTONISHD AT THE VISION & OUR HEARTS TREMBLED	654	JERUSALEM 29	44
WITHIN US			
WE HEARD THE VOICE OF SLUMBEROUS ALBION AND THUS HE SPAKE	654	JERUSALEM 29	45
WE HEARD THE VOICE OF ALBION STARTING FROM HIS SLEEP . .	654	JERUSALEM 29	58
THEY HEARD THE VOICE AND FLED SWIFT AS THE WINTER'S SETTING	655	JERUSALEM 29	72
SUN			
AT LENGTH HE SAT ON LONDON STONE & HEARD JERUSALEM'S VOICE	657	JERUSALEM 31	43
LOS STOOD AT HIS ANVIL HE HEARD THE CONTENTIONS OF VALA	660	JERUSALEM 34	17
SO SPOKE LONDON IMMORTAL GUARDIAN I HEARD IN LAMBETH'S	665	JERUSALEM 38	40
SHADES			
IN FELPHAM I HEARD AND SAW THE VISIONS OF ALBION . . .	665	JERUSALEM 38	41
THE TWENTY-FOUR HEARD THEY CAME TREMBLING ON WATRY CHARIOTS	667	JERUSALEM 40	21
THEY WEPT INTO THE DEEPS A LITTLE SPACE AT LENGTH WAS HEARD	675	JERUSALEM 44	43
AROUND ALBION BUT ALBION HEARD HIM NOT OBDURATE HARD . .	676	JERUSALEM 45	35
A LITTLE SOUND IT UTTERS & ITS CRIES ARE FAINTLY HEARD .	680	JERUSALEM 49	41
. . . WERE HEARD IN THE CLOUDS OF HEAVEN	687	JERUSALEM 55	55
THE LINEAMENTS DIVINE & OFT THE VOICE HEARD & OFT SHE SAID	693	JERUSALEM 60	51
POLLUTED I HEARD HIS VOICE IN MY SLEEP & HIS ANGEL IN MY	694	JERUSALEM 61	16
DREAM			
UPON PISON & ARNON & JORDAN AND I HEARD THE VOICE AMONG	695	JERUSALEM 61	33
JERUSALEM FAINTED OVER THE CROSS & SEPULCHER SHE HEARD	695	JERUSALEM 61	49
THE VOICE			
DISORGANIZD AN EVANESCENT SHADE SCARCE SEEN OR HEARD AMONG	719	JERUSALEM 78	28
THEY SOUNDED THANKSGIVINGS IN MY COURTS EGYPT & LYBIA HEARD	721	JERUSALEM 79	50
I HAVE HEARD JERUSALEM'S GROANS FROM VALA'S CRIES	725	JERUSALEM 82	1
& LAMENTATIONS			
I HEARD ENITHARMON SAY TO LOS LET THE DAUGHTERS OF ALBION	725	JERUSALEM 82	22

HEARD   (CONTINUED)
    AND THUS HE HEARD THE VOICE OF ALBION'S DAUGHTERS   729 JERUSALEM 83   84
      ON EUPHRATES
    ON ALBION'S ROCKS & LET THY VOICE BE HEARD UPON EUPHRATES   729 JERUSALEM 84   28
    LOOKING TO THE EAST & HIS VOICE IS HEARD OVER THE WHOLE   730 JERUSALEM 85   12
      EARTH
    HIS VOICE IS HEARD FROM ALBION THE ALPS & APPENINES . . . 730 JERUSALEM 85   16
    ENITHARMON HEARD SHE RAISD HER HEAD LIKE THE MILD MOON . . 740 JERUSALEM 93   1
    AH THEN I HEARD MY LITTLE ONES WEEPING ALONG THE VALLEY   740 JERUSALEM 93   11
    AND SEEING ACCORDING TO FITNESS & ORDER AND I HEARD JEHOVAH   746 JERUSALEM 98   40
      SPEAK
    AND I HEARD THE NAME OF THEIR EMANATIONS THEY ARE NAMED   747 JERUSALEM 99   5
      JERUSALEM
    HIS VOICE WAS HEARD FROM ZION'S HILL . . . .   749 EV GOSPEL(B)/N   46
    AND SHE HEARD THE BREATH OF GOD . . . .   754 EV GOSPEL(E)/N   19
    AS SHE HEARD BY EDEN'S FLOOD . . . .   754 EV GOSPEL(E)/N   20
    I MADE MY VOICE HEARD ALL OVER THE NATION . . . . .   756 EV GOSPEL(G)/N   2
    A VOICE HEARD COMING ON . . . .   780A GHOST ABEL 1   PROSE
    & HIS FLUTE HEARD FROM HIS SECRET FORESTS CHEARS US TO .   791C LETTER 3   PROSE
    VOICES OF CELESTIAL INHABITANTS ARE MORE DISTINCTLY HEARD   802A LETTER 14   PROSE
    AND I HEARD HIS VOICE MILD . . . .   805 TO BUTTS/L   60
    I TOO WELL REMEMBER THE THREATS I HEARD IF YOU WHO . .   813A LETTER 22   PROSE
    BE SO BUT WHEN YOU HAVE HEARD ME OUT YOU WILL NOT BE SO   814A LETTER 23   PROSE
    SAW ME TURN HIM BEFORE ME DOWN THE ROAD & SAW & HEARD .   827C LETTER 28   PROSE
    PROVE THE COMRADE PERJURD WHO SWORE THAT HE HEARD ME WHILE   827D LETTER 28   PROSE
    THE TROUBLE & EXPENSE I HAVE HEARD THAT MY ACCUSER IS A   828B LETTER 28   PROSE
    ALL THIS I LEARND WITH SOME ALARM & HEARD ALSO WHAT . .   833C LETTER 33   PROSE
    HAVE HEARD THAT FLAXMAN MEANS TO GIVE A LECTURE ON   859D LETTER 56   PROSE
      SCULPTURE
    FOR I HAVE HEARD NOTHING OF PHILLIPS THIS AGE I HEAR .   862A LETTER 59   PROSE
    AS TO SR T LAWRENCE I HAVE NOT HEARD FROM HIM AS YET .   868D LETTER 68   PROSE
HEAREST
    THOU HEAREST THE NIGHTINGALE BEGIN THE SONG OF SPRING . . 520 MILTON 31   28
HEARETH
    I CRY THE WATCHMAN HEARETH NOT I POUR MY VOICE IN ROARINGS   335 FOUR ZOAS 7B   93
HEARING
    HEARING WILD BIRDS' SONG . . . .   112 LIT GRL LST/SI   16
    BY MOONLIGHT HEARING A HARPER WHO SUNG TO THE HARP . .   156D MARRIAGE HH 17   PROSE
    HEARING A HARPER BUT NOW WE HAVE SEEN MY ETERNAL LOT .   156D MARRIAGE HH 17   PROSE
    THE ANGEL HEARING THIS BECAME ALMOST BLUE . . . . .   158B MARRIAGE HH 22   PROSE
    [TO HEAR] HEARING THE [SOUND] MARCH OF LONG RESOUNDING   264 FOUR ZOAS 1   *   5
      . . .
    HEARING THE SYMPHONIES OF WAR LOUD SOUNDING ALL MY SONS   300 FOUR ZOAS 4   92
    BUT BRING TWO PEOPLE & THE HEARING IS STOPPED . . . .   450D ANNO REYNOLDS   MARG
    SO SPAKE THE VISION OF ALBION & IN HIM SO SPAKE IN MY   744 JERUSALEM 97   5
      HEARING
    YOUR EAGER EXPECTATION OF HEARING FROM ME COMPELLS ME .   834B LETTER 34   PROSE
    I AM NOW ENGRAVING I AM UNEASY AT NOT HEARING FROM . .   841A LETTER 40   PROSE
HEARKEN
    HEARKEN MONARCH OF FRANCE TO THE TERRORS OF HEAVEN . . .   140 FRENCH REVOLTN   128
HEARS
    HE HEARS ME NOT BUT OER THE YAWNING DEEP . . . . . .   3 TO WINTER/PS   5
    WRAPD IN HIS SHROUD AND NOW FANCIES SHE HEARS . . . .   4 FAIR ELENOR/PS   15
    HEARS YOU SOBBING SOBBING . . . .   116 THE BLOSSOM/SI   10
    FOR HE HEARS THE LAMB'S INNOCENT CALL . . . . . .   118 SHEPHERD/SI   5
    AND HE HEARS THE EWE'S TENDER REPLY . . . .   118 SHEPHERD/SI   6
    I PASS AWAY YET I COMPLAIN AND NO ONE HEARS MY VOICE .   128 BOOK OF THEL 3   4
    THAT THEOTORMON HEARS ME NOT TO HIM THE NIGHT AND MORN .   191 V DAU ALBION 2   37
    THRO ONE HEARS MUSIC OF THE SPHERES THRO ONE THE ETERNAL   237 EUROPE INTRO   2
      VINE
    HE STARTS HE HEARS THE FOOT OF MAN HE SAYS TAKE THOU MY   276 FOUR ZOAS 1   455
      WOOL
    HID IN THE VALES FAINTLY LAMENT & NO ONE HEARS THEIR VOICE   325 FOUR ZOAS 7   197
    TILL MAN SHALL LEAVE A CORRUPTIBLE BODY HE FAMISHD HEARS   354 FOUR ZOAS 8   524
      HIM GROAN
    SUCH ARE THE WORDS OF AHANIA & ENION LOS HEARS & WEEPS . . 356 FOUR ZOAS 8   584
    HEARS ITS IMPATIENT PARENT BIRD AND ENITHARMON HEARD THEM   504 MILTON 21   29
    ALL NIGHT VALA HEARS SHE TRIUMPHS IN PRIDE OF HOLINESS .   693 JERUSALEM 60   45
    WHENEVER SHE HEARS IT NAMED EXCUSE MY HASTE & . . . .   801C LETTER 13   PROSE
    WHAT IS VERY PLEASANT EVERY ONE WHO HEARS OF MY GOING .   822D LETTER 26   PROSE
HEARSE
    [WEAVES AROUND THE MARRIAGE HEARSE] . . . .   170 LONDON/N   16
    AND [HANGS] SMITES WITH PLAGUES THE MARRIAGE HEARSE . .   170 LONDON/N   21
    REMOVE AWAY THAT MARRIAGE HEARSE . . . .   176 ANCNT PROVRB/N   2
    REMOVE AWAY THAT MARRIAGE HEARSE . . . .   184 SEVRL QUESTN/N   16
    AND BLIGHTS WITH PLAGUES THE MARRIAGE HEARSE . . . .   216 LONDON/SE   16
    DANCE BEFORE DEAD ENGLAND'S HEARSE . . . .   433 AUGURIES   118
HEART   SEE LION HEART
    WHOSE HEART IS WINTRY COLD . . . .   6 MY SILKS/PS   10
    RELIGION WILL FLOURISH EACH MAN'S HEART . . . . . .   19 EDW THIRD/PS 2   25
    LORD PERCY IF THE HEART IS SICK THE HEAD . . . . . .   21 EDW THIRD/PS 2   84
    THE HEART DOTH FAIL YOU SAY MY LORD THE MERCHANTS . . .   21 EDW THIRD/PS 2   86
    THE LION FLEES AND FEAR USURPS HIS HEART . . . . . .   24 EDW THIRD/PS 3   114
    NOW MY HEART DANCES AND I AM AS LIGHT . . . .   24 EDW THIRD/PS 3   144
    THY HEART IS RICHER THAN THE VALES OF FRANCE . . . .   25 EDW THIRD/PS 3   173
    IT MAKES ME SAD AND SICK AT VERY HEART . . . . . .   30 EDW THIRD/PS 5   25
    AND MY HEART LABOURS WITH FUTURITY . . . .   32 EDW THIRD/PS 6   41
    EACH HEART DOES TREMBLE AND EACH KNEE GROWS SLACK . . .   34A KING JOHN/PS   PROSE
    THINE IRON HEART IS SMITTEN THOUGH LINGERING FATE IS SLOW   34B KING JOHN/PS   PROSE
    WHY SINKS MY HEART WHY FAULTERETH MY TONGUE . . . . .   34 WAR SONG/PS   12
    LO THEN HUMILITY TAKE IT AND WEAR IT IN THINE HEART . .   37A CONTEMPLATN/PS   PROSE
    THOUGH I SHOULD TELL HER ALL MY HEART WHAT CAN I FEAR . .   38D SAMSON/PS   PROSE

	PAGE	TITLE	LINE
HEART (CONTINUED)			
THE IVORY PALACE OF MY INMOST HEART WHERE IT SHALL LIE AT REST	39B	SAMSON/PS	PROSE
CAN FROM THE HEART OF MAN HIDE SORROW	39B	SAMSON/PS	PROSE
& WEAR HER IN THINE HEART LORD OF THY SELF THOU THEN ART	41B	THEN SHE BORE	PROSE
ALAS IN CITIES WHERES THE MAN WHOSE FACE IS NOT A MASK UNTO HIS HEART	42D	THEN SHE BORE	PROSE
YET IF HER HEART IS WELL INCLINED	56	HAIL MATRIM/IM	16
MY HEART IS AT REST WITHIN MY BREAST	60	NURSES SONG/IM	3
AND THE SHOUT OF HIS THOUSANDS FILLS HIS HEART	62	CROWND KING/IM	6
AND THE SHOUT OF HIS THOUSANDS FILLS HIS HEART	62	CROWND KING/IM	7
FOR I WRITE FROM THE WARMTH OF MY HEART &	88A	ANNO LAVATER	MARG
THE AMULET OF THOSE WHO PURIFY THE HEART OF MAN	88B	ANNO LAVATER	MARG
OR SPEAK FROM HIS HEART BUT HE MUST INTEND TRUTH	98C	ALL RELIGIONS	PROSE
[THE AGED TIRIEL COULD NOT SPEAK HIS HEART WAS FULL OF GRIEF]	101	TIRIEL 2	44
FOR THOU DOST MAKE MY HEART TO BLEED MY SONS WERE NOT LIKE THINE	103	TIRIEL 3	20
MADNESS & DEEP DISMAY (POSSESS) THE HEART OF THE BLIND MAN	103	TIRIEL 3 *	37
IF HER HEART DOES AKE	113	LIT GRL LST/SI	25
FOR MERCY HAS A HUMAN HEART	117	DIVNE IMAGE/SI	9
MY HEART IS AT REST WITHIN MY BREAST	121	NURSES SONG/SI	3
OF EVERY HEART ON EARTH INFIXES DEEP ITS RESTLESS TWISTS	130	BOOK OF THEL 6	4
IN HIS SOUL WAS THE SERPENT COILD ROUND IN HIS HEART	135	FRENCH REVOLTN	28
IN THEIR DARKNESS THE KING STOOD HIS HEART FLAMD	137	FRENCH REVOLTN	69
IN THE BLOOD OF NOBILITY TRAMPLING THE HEART AND THE HEAD . . .	141	FRENCH REVOLTN	156
. . . CAN THE SOUL WHOSE BRAIN AND HEART	142	FRENCH REVOLTN	183
. . . HIS EYES AND HIS HEART	144	FRENCH REVOLTN	218
. . . AND HIS NOBLE HEART SUNK AND HIS PULSES	147	FRENCH REVOLTN	294
THE HEAD SUBLIME THE HEART PATHOS	152C	MARRIAGE HH 10	PROSE
I TOLD HER ALL MY HEART	161	NEVER PAIN/N	6
WHERE THY LITTLE HEART DOES REST	165	CRADLE SONG/N	13
IN THY LITTLE HEART ASLEEP	165	CRADLE SONG/N	15
WHEN THY LITTLE HEART DOES WAKE	165	CRADLE SONG/N	16
COULD TWIST THE SINEWS OF THY HEART	172	THE TYGER/N 1	10
AND WHEN THY HEART BEGAN TO BEAT	172	THE TYGER/N 1	11
COULD HEART DESCEND OR WINGS ASPIRE	173	THE TYGER/N 2	7
COULD TWIST THE SINEWS OF THY HEART	173	THE TYGER/N 2	10
AND WHEN THY HEART BEGAN TO BEAT	173	THE TYGER/N 2	11
SMITES THE HEART TO ITS ROOT	178	THE FAIRY/N	8
THE [WE] [?COUNT] [(WEALTH)] COUNTLESS GOLD OF A MERRY HEART	181	RICHES/N *	1
THE EYE SEES MORE THAN THE HEART KNOWS	189A	V DAU ALBION	TITLE
AND SUNK MY HEART INTO THE ABYSS A RED ROUND GLOBE HOT BURNING	191	V DAU ALBION 2	33
COULD TWIST THE SINEWS OF THY HEART	214	THE TYGER/SE	10
AND WHEN THY HEART BEGAN TO BEAT	214	THE TYGER/SE	11
WITH CRUELTY DIDST MOULD MY HEART	220	TO TIRZAH/SE	10
CRUELTY HAS A HUMAN HEART	221	DIVNE IMAGE/SE	1
THE HUMAN HEART ITS HUNGRY GORGE	221	DIVNE IMAGE/SE	8
LIKE A HUMAN HEART STRUGLING & BEATING	226	URIZEN 5	36
ROUND THE BRANCHES OF HIS HEART	228	URIZEN 11	12
OR A HEART OR AN EYE THEY SWAM MISCHEVOUS	234	URIZEN 23	6
IN FORM OF A HUMAN HEART	236	URIZEN 25	44
THAT THE PRIDE OF THE HEART MAY FAIL	247	SONG OF LOS 7	3
MY HEART LEAP AT THE LOVELY SOUND	254	AHANIA 4	69
TILL HIS BRAIN IN A ROCK & HIS HEART	260	BOOK OF LOS 5	52
LUVAH AND VALA [WAKE] WOKE & [FLY] FLEW UP FROM THE HUMAN HEART	271	FOUR ZOAS 1 *	262
SICKNING LIES THE [ETERNAL] FALLEN MAN HIS HEAD SICK HIS HEART FAINT	272	FOUR ZOAS 1 *	288
HEART COLD AND THE LITTLE TONGUE CONSUMD THAT ONCE IN THOUGHTLESS JOY	276	FOUR ZOAS 1	449
HIS WEB IS LEFT ALL DESOLATE THAT HIS LITTLE ANXIOUS HEART	277	FOUR ZOAS 1	459
. . . THE FAINT HEART OF THE [ETERNAL] FALLEN [ANCIENT] MAN	283	FOUR ZOAS 2 *	143
TERRIFIED WITH HIS HEART & SPIRIT AT THE VISIONS OF FUTURITY	287	FOUR ZOAS 2	293
. . . [HEART] HEARTS TREMBLED WITHIN [ME] US	293	FOUR ZOAS 3 *	57
WENT DOWN THE HUMAN HEART WHERE PARADISE & ITS JOYS ABOUNDED	294	FOUR ZOAS 3	95
TO EASE MY PANGS OF HEART & TO RESTORE SOME PEACE TO THARMAS	298	FOUR ZOAS 4	33
AND CASTING ROUND THICK GLOOMS THUS UTTERD HIS FIERCE PANGS OF HEART	299	FOUR ZOAS 4	78
[ROUND THE BRANCHES OF HIS HEART]	303	FOUR ZOAS 4	228
TILL FROM HER HEART RENDING HIS WAY A TERRIBLE CHILD SPRANG FORTH	306	FOUR ZOAS 5	37
OF HER BRIGHT HEART	309	FOUR ZOAS 5	178
WITHIN HER HEART [VALAN] VALA BEGAN TO REANIMATE IN BURSTING SOBS	309	FOUR ZOAS 5 *	179
THEY WANDER MOPING IN THEIR HEART A SUN A DREARY MOON	314	FOUR ZOAS 6	90
NOR COULD HE QUENCH THE FIRES FOR THEY FLAMD OUT FROM THE HEART	315	FOUR ZOAS 6	144
LO HOW THE HEART & BRAIN ARE FORMED IN THE BREEDING WOMB	323	FOUR ZOAS 7	130
THE LITTLE HEART THE LIVER & THE RED BLOOD IN ITS LABYRINTHS	323	FOUR ZOAS 7	132
THRO THE INFINITE LABYRINTHS OF THE HEART & THRO THE NOSTRILS ISSUING	327	FOUR ZOAS 7	280
SHE BURST THE GATES OF ENITHARMON'S HEART WITH DIREFUL CRASH	328	FOUR ZOAS 7	323
OPEND WITHIN YOUR HEART & LOINS & WONDROUS BRAIN	329	FOUR ZOAS 7	354

890

HEART   (CONTINUED)

	PAGE	TITLE	LINE
THREEFOLD WITHIN THE BRAIN WITHIN THE HEART WITHIN THE LOINS	329	FOUR ZOAS 7	381
OF THY POOR BROKEN HEART I SEE THEE LIKE A SHADOW WITHERING	330	FOUR ZOAS 7	413
BUILDED A TEMPLE IN THE IMAGE OF THE HUMAN HEART	333	FOUR ZOAS 7B	20
TO LABOUR & BEHOLD MY HEART SUNK DOWN BENEATH	334	FOUR ZOAS 7B	63
OF [ENITHARMON'S] THY POOR BROKEN HEART ASTONISHD . . .	341	FOUR ZOAS 8	21
AND ENTER URIZEN'S TEMPLE ENITHARMON PITYING & HER HEART	341	FOUR ZOAS 8	27
THE BROKEN HEART GATE OF ENITHARMON [WHICH JOINS TO URIZEN'S TEMPLE]	341	FOUR ZOAS 8	* 29
ITS INTRICATE LABYRINTHS NOW THE OBDURATE HEART WAS BROKEN	342	FOUR ZOAS 8	33
IN HEAD OR HEART OR REINS ACCORDING TO THE FITTEST ORDER	342	FOUR ZOAS 8	59
UPON MY TERRIBLY FLAMING HEART THE MOLTEN METAL RUNS . .	349	FOUR ZOAS 8	306
REPINING IN HIS HEART & SPIRIT THAT ORC REIGND OVER ALL	353	FOUR ZOAS 8	465
FOR GOD PUT IT INTO THEIR HEART TO FULFILL ALL HIS WILL	357	FOUR ZOAS 8	617
AND SCORN THE WAR WITHIN MY MEMBERS YET MY HEART IS WEAK	360	FOUR ZOAS 9	119
WEEPING AT THE THRESHOLD OF EXISTENCE I WILL STEEL MY HEART	361	FOUR ZOAS 9	148
EXCESS OF JOY IS WORSE THAN GRIEF HER HEART BEAT HIGH HER BLOOD	362	FOUR ZOAS 9	197
INTO YOUR PLACE THE PLACE OF SEED NOT IN THE BRAIN OR HEART	366	FOUR ZOAS 9	365
THAT GAVEST ME A HEART TO CRAVE & RAISEDST ME THY PHANTOM	368	FOUR ZOAS 9	415
OPEND WITHIN THE HEART & IN THE LOINS & IN THE BRAIN .	382	FOUR ZOAS AD 6	25
IN HEAD OR HEART OR REINS ACCORDING TO THE FITTEST ORDER	382	FOUR ZOAS AD 6	28
("NO ATTRACTION UNLESS IT WARMS") OR FREEZES ("THE HEART")	411C	ANNO BOYD	MARG
[[WITHIN MY [LOVE'S] HEART]]	415	MY SPECTRE/N	15
[WITHIN MY HEART THOU DIDST UNFOLD]	415	MY SPECTRE/N	16
SHE CUTS HIS HEART OUT AT HIS SIDE	425	MENTAL TRAVLER	15
THE COUNTLESS GOLD OF THE AKEING HEART	425	MENTAL TRAVLER	35
EVERY ONE IS THREEFOLD IN HEAD & HEART & REINS & EVERY ONE	484	MILTON 5	6
WOULD I HAD TOLD LOS ALL MY HEART BUT PATIENCE O MY FRIENDS	487	MILTON 7	31
COVERING THE EAST WITH SOLID BLACKNESS ROUND HIS HIDDEN HEART	490	MILTON 9	40
JEHOVAH THUNDERD ABOVE SATAN IN PRIDE OF HEART	493	MILTON 12	24
SHE TIES THE KNOT OF BLOODY VEINS INTO A RED HOT HEART . .	501	MILTON 19	56
IT HAS A HEART LIKE THEE A BRAIN OPEN TO HEAVEN & HELL . .	502	MILTON 20	28
FOR EVERY HEART HAS GATES OF BRASS & BARS OF ADAMANT	502	MILTON 20	34
OF SATAN IN ITS WEBS FOR IN BRAIN AND HEART AND LOINS .	502	MILTON 20	38
THUS MILTON FELL THRO ALBION'S HEART TRAVELLING OUTSIDE OF HUMANITY	502	MILTON 20	41
AT LAST WHEN DESPERATION ALMOST TORE HIS HEART IN TWAIN	503	MILTON 20	56
THE BELLOWS ARE THE ANIMAL LUNGS THE HAMMERS THE ANIMAL HEART	509	MILTON 24	58
THE FIRST STATE IS IN THE HEAD THE SECOND IS IN THE HEART	524	MILTON 34	14
THE IDOL VIRTUES OF THE NATURAL HEART & SATAN'S SEAT .	530	MILTON 38	46
[HIS] WHOSE HEART IS IRON HIS HEAD WOOD & HIS FACE BRASS	545	ON S(TOTHRD)/N	2
THY FRIENDSHIP OFT HAS MADE MY HEART TO AKE	545	TO H(AYLEY)/N	1
THAT LAYS OPEN THE HIDDEN HEART I DREW FORTH THE PANG .	628	JERUSALEM 9	19
A THREEFOLD REGION A FALSE BRAIN A FALSE HEART	634	JERUSALEM 14	5
BOTH HEART IN HEART & HAND IN HAND	652	FIELDS FROM/J	88
WENT DOWN THE HUMAN HEART WHERE PARADISE & ITS JOYS ABOUNDED	655	JERUSALEM 29	74
A CIRCLE IN CONTINUAL GYRATIONS THIS BECAME A HEART . .	659	JERUSALEM 33	20
HIS HIDDEN HEART HIS EMANATION WEPT & TREMBLED WITHIN HIM	664	JERUSALEM 38	3
THE OPEN HEART IS SHUT UP IN INTEGUMENTS OF FROZEN SILENCE	672	JERUSALEM 43	33
WITHIN THE HUMAN HEART WHOSE GATES CLOSED WITH SOLEMN SOUND	678	JERUSALEM 48	25
THE LUNGS THE HEART THE LIVER SHRUNK AWAY FAR DISTANT FROM MAN	679	JERUSALEM 49	17
IN THE ERYTHREAN SEA THEIR (UNCIRCUMCISION) IN HEART & LOINS	680	JERUSALEM 49	* 44
THE SELFISH VIRTUES OF THE NATURAL HEART	682C	JERUSALEM 52	PROSE
TALKING OF THE VIRTUES OF THE HUMAN HEART AND	682D	JERUSALEM 52	PROSE
THE BELLOWS ARE THE ANIMAL LUNGS THE HAMMERS THE ANIMAL HEART	684	JERUSALEM 53	12
OUTSIDE OF THE GATES OF THE HUMAN HEART BENEATH BEULAH . .	684	JERUSALEM 53	16
BOTH OF THE HEAD & HEART & LOINS CLOSD UP IN MORAL PRIDE	693	JERUSALEM 60	49
THEIR CRUEL FINGERS FOR HIS HEART & THERE THEY ENTER IN POMP	702	JERUSALEM 66	28
LONDON FEELS HIS BRAIN CUT ROUND EDINBURGH'S HEART IS CIRCUMSCRIBED	703	JERUSALEM 66	64
TO BRISTOL & HIS HEART BEAT STRONG ON SALISBURY PLAIN . .	704	JERUSALEM 67	37
UPON MY TERRIBLY FLAMING HEART THE MOLTEN METAL RUNS . .	705	JERUSALEM 67	53
HER PANTING VICTIM BESIDE HER HER HEART IS DRUNK WITH BLOOD	705	JERUSALEM 68	12
EACH WITHIN OTHER ON HER WHITE MARBLE & EVEN NECK HER HEART	709	JERUSALEM 70	21
TO PUT IN ACT WHAT HER HEART WILLS O WHO CAN WITHSTAND HER POWER	709	JERUSALEM 70	30
FOR GWENDOLEN SHE TOOK UP IN BITTER TEARS HIS ANGUISHD HEART	723	JERUSALEM 80	67
THE ENVY RAN THRO CATHEDRON'S LOOMS INTO THE HEART . .	726	JERUSALEM 82	53
IN HEAD & HEART & REINS THREE UNIVERSES OF LOVE & BEAUTY	730	JERUSALEM 86	3
HIS HEART & WHILE THEY CIRCUMSCRIBE HIS LOINS A VEIL & NET	736	JERUSALEM 90	4
OPEN THE HIDDEN HEART IN WARS OF MUTUAL BENEVOLENCE WARS OF LOVE	744	JERUSALEM 97	14
UPON HIS HEART WITH IRON PEN	750	EV GOSPEL (C)/N	13
FOLLOW ME I AM MEEK & LOWLY OF HEART	750	EV GOSPEL (C)/N	16
UPON HIS HEART WITH IRON PEN	751	EV GOSPEL (D)/N	13
FOLLOW ME I AM MEEK & LOWLY OF HEART	751	EV GOSPEL (D)/N	18
& IT GRIEVED HIM AT HIS HEART	776C	INSC LAOCOON	PROSE
AND A CONTRITE HEART O I CANNOT FORGIVE THE ACCUSER HATH	780	GHOST ABEL 2	5
YOURS IN HEAD & HEART...A MERRY CHRISTMAS	791C	LETTER 3	PROSE
THE THING I HAVE MOST AT HEART MORE THAN LIFE OR ALL .	812D	LETTER 22	PROSE

```
                                                       PAGE    TITLE         LINE
HEART     (CONTINUED)
     WHAT CAME FROM MY HEAD & MY HEART IN UNISON THAT I AM PROUD  814D LETTER 23      PROSE
        OF BEING
     WHEN MY HEART KNOCKD AGAINST THE ROOT OF MY TONGUE  . . .   817 HAPPINESS/L      8
     MY HEART IS FULL OF FUTURITY I PERCIEVE . . . . . .  . .  823B LETTER 26      PROSE
     WHY SHOULD I BE TROUBLED WHY SHOULD MY HEART & FLESH CRY    823C LETTER 26      PROSE
        OUT
     WHOSE HEART & SOUL ARE MORE & MORE DRAWN OUT TOWARDS YOU &   833D LETTER 33      PROSE
     (RICHARDSON HAS WON HIS HEART) . . . . . . . . . . . . .   849D LETTER 46      PROSE
     TO THE PUBLIC SPEAKING SO I MUST OWN HE WON MY HEART  .  .  856B LETTER 54      PROSE
     "& THAT THOU SHOULDST SET THINE HEART AGAINST HIM" JOB  .  . SUPP LEGEND/N68    *TITLE
     "THOU HAST SET THY HEART AS THE HEART OF GOD" EZEKIEL  .  . SUPP LEGEND/N94    *
HEART-BREAKING
     AND OFTEN MALIGNANT THEY COMBAT HEART-BREAKING SORROWFUL     515 MILTON 28        12
        & PITEOUS
HEART-BROKE
     ALL HEART-BROKE I HEARD HER SAY  . . . . . . . . .        111 A DREAM/SI       8
HEART BROKEN
     MY GARMENTS SHALL BE WOVEN OF SIGHS & HEART BROKEN          499 MILTON 18        6
        LAMENTATIONS
HEARTED     SEE COLD HEARTED,IRON HEARTED,IRON-HEARTED,MERRY HEARTED,TENDER HEARTED
HEARTENING
     ACCEPT OF MY THANKS FOR YOUR KIND & HEARTENING LETTER  . .  822B LETTER 26      PROSE
HEARTFELT
     I HAVE A GREAT MANY THINGS TO SAY & A GREAT MANY            832B LETTER 32      PROSE
        HEARTFELT
     MY WIFE RETURNS HER HEARTFELT THANKS FOR YOUR KIND INQUIRY  851C LETTER 50      PROSE
HEART-FORMED
     IN HEART-FORMED AFRICA  . . . . . . . . . . .              245 SONG OF LOS 3    3
HEARTH
     WITH HEARTH SO RED AND WALLS SO FAIR . . . . . . . . .      15 BLIND-MANS/PS     4
     TILL FROM THE FIRE ON THE HEARTH  . . . . . . . . .        425 MENTAL TRAVLER   43
HEARTHS
     AND HEARTHS PROTECT THE SELFISH TERROR TILL DIVIDED ALL     374 FOUR ZOAS 9     636
     THE CIELINGS DEVOTION THE HEARTHS THANKSGIVING   . . . .    632 JERUSALEM 12     37
HEARTIEST
     MY HEARTIEST THANKS FOR YOUR CARE IN MY ACCOMODATION  . .   872D LETTER 76      PROSE
HEARTILY
     CAN YOU THINK AT ALL & NOT PRONOUNCE HEARTILY . . . . .     717C JERUSALEM 77   PROSE
     & FEELING HEARTILY YOUR GRIEF WITH A BROTHER'S SYMPATHY     797B LETTER 9       PROSE
     I THANK YOU HEARTILY FOR YOUR KIND OFFER OF READING &C  .   845B LETTER 44      PROSE
     HEARTILY DEVOTE HIMSELF TO THE BUSINESS IN ALL ITS         845C LETTER 44      PROSE
        LABORIOUS
HEARTLESS
     ("SNEER IS OFTEN SIGN OF HEARTLESS MALIGNITY") DAMN         67D ANNO LAVATER    MARG
        SNEERERS
HEART LIFTING
     I CALLD ON MR HOARE WITH YOUR ELEGANT & HEART LIFTING  .    838C LETTER 37      PROSE
HEART-PIERCING
     AND LEUTHA STOOD GLOWING WITH VARYING COLOURS IMMORTAL      492 MILTON 11        32
        HEART-PIERCING
HEART'S
     AND HID FROM HIM MY HEART'S DELIGHT  . . . . . . . .        182 THE ANGEL/N      8
     [WHO WILL EXCHANGE HIS OWN HEART'S BLOOD]  . . . . . .      186 LET BROTHELS/N   50
     AND HID FROM HIM MY HEART'S DELIGHT  . . . . . . . .        214 THE ANGEL/SE     8
     FOR IT STICKS IN THE HEART'S DEEP CORE  . . . . . . .       423 THE SMILE        9
     WITH PROVINGS OF DESTRUCTION WITH GIVING THEE THY HEART'S   647 JERUSALEM 24     28
        DESIRE
     WHEN JERUSALEM WAS THY HEART'S DESIRE IN TIMES OF YOUTH     647 JERUSALEM 24     37
        & LOVE
HEARTS
     O SHEATHE THEIR HEARTS WITH TRIPLE STEEL THAT THEY  . . .    18 EDW THIRD/PS 1   19
     AND SET ALL HEARTS ON FIRE TO BE WITH US  . . . . . .       24 EDW THIRD/PS 3  139
     PREPARE YOUR HEARTS FOR DEATH'S COLD HAND PREPARE  . . .     34 WAR SONG/PS      6
     BUT THEIR NASTY HEARTS POOR DEVILS ARE EAT UP WITH ENVY     62D ISLAND MOON 11 PROSE
     THAT MAKES OUR LIMBS QUAKE IF OUR HEARTS BE WARM . . . .     64 SHEPHERD OLD     4
     THAT MAKES OUR LIMBS QUAKE IF OUR HEARTS BE WARM . . . .     64 SHEPHERD OLD     8
     THAT MAKES OUR LIMBS QUAKE IF OUR HEARTS BE WARM . . . .     64 SHEPHERD OLD    12
     ONLY GOOD HEARTS CAN OR DARE COURT . . . . . . . .          85B ANNO LAVATER    MARG
     . . . [HEART] HEARTS TREMBLED WITHIN [ME] US  . . . . .     293 FOUR ZOAS 3    * 57
     [OUR HEARTS SICK XXX WE XXX ON HIS ROCK]  . . . . . . .    SUPP FOUR ZOAS 3    *
     BUT BE YOUR HEARTS HARDER THAN THE NETHER MILLSTONE  . . .  323 FOUR ZOAS 7     112
     AND HEARTS LAID OPEN TO THE LIGHT BY THE BROAD GRIZLY SWORD 338 FOUR ZOAS 7B    206
     OPEND WITHIN THEIR HEARTS & IN THEIR LOINS & IN THEIR BRAIN 342 FOUR ZOAS 8      55
     AND ALL MY ORNAMENTS SHALL BE OF THE GOLD OF BROKEN HEARTS  499 MILTON 18        22
     IN THEIR TRANSLUCENT HEARTS WHICH OPENS INTO THE VEGETATIVE 635 JERUSALEM 14     22
        WORLD
     WE HEARD ASTONISHD AT THE VISION & OUR HEARTS TREMBLED      654 JERUSALEM 29     44
        WITHIN US
     AND HEARTS LAID OPEN TO THE LIGHT BY THE BROAD GRIZLY SWORD 701 JERUSALEM 65     52
     OF ALBION DELIGHTS THE EYES OF THE KINGS THEIR HEARTS & THE 706 JERUSALEM 68     16
     HEARTS OF THEIR WARRIORS GLOW HOT BEFORE THOR & FRIGA O     706 JERUSALEM 68     17
        MOLECH
HEARTY
     RECIEVE MY HEARTY LOVE & RESPECT I AM DEAR SIR YOUR SINCERE 801C LETTER 13      PROSE
     BENEVOLENT MINDS MY WIFE JOINS WITH ME IN THE HEARTY  . .   847C LETTER 44      PROSE
     PRAY EXCUSE THIS HEARTY EXPOSTULATION  . . . . . . .        874B LETTER 79      PROSE
HEAT
     THY STRENGTH CURB THY FIERCE STEEDS ALLAY THE HEAT  . . .     1 TO SUMMER/PS     2
     NOR LAUREL WREATHS AGAINST THE SULTRY HEAT . . . . . .        2 TO SUMMER/PS    19
     IF I CAN JUDGE OF ACTIONS BUT YOUR HEAT . . . . . . .        27 EDW THIRD/PS 3  245
     I WOULD RUN LIKE THE DICKINS TILL I WAS ALL IN A HEAT  . .   48B ISLAND MOON 4  PROSE
```

	PAGE	TITLE	LINE

HEAT (CONTINUED)

	PAGE	TITLE	LINE
IS THE ABSENCE FROM HEAT & LIGHT	94D	ANNO SWED LOVE	MARG
THO IT IS WRINKLED LIKE THE EARTH PARCHD WITH THE SUMMER HEAT	103	TIRIEL 3	25
AND SITTING DOWN BEFORE THE HEAT OF DAY	125	LIT BLK BOY/SI	6
AND GIVES HIS LIGHT AND GIVES HIS HEAT AWAY	125	LIT BLK BOY/SI	10
FOR WHEN OUR SOULS HAVE LEARND THE HEAT TO BEAR	125	LIT BLK BOY/SI	17
I'LL SHADE HIM FROM THE HEAT TILL HE CAN BEAR	125	LIT BLK BOY/SI	25
TILL SUMMER'S HEAT MELTS THEE BESIDE THE FOUNTAINS AND THE SPRINGS	127	BOOK OF THEL 1	24
ON MARGIN OF THE SEA SHRIVELD UP BY HEAT OF DAY	136	FRENCH REVOLTN	39
. . . AND UTTERD A WITHRING HEAT AND THESE WORDS BURST FORTH	137	FRENCH REVOLTN	69
A FAINT HEAT FROM THEIR FIRES REVIVD THE COLD LOUVRE	148	FRENCH REVOLTN	303
SURROUNDED HEAT BUT NOT LIGHT WENT THRO THE MURKY ATMOSPHERE	197	AMERICA 4	11
LIKE THE GROUND PARCHD WITH HEAT THEN FUZON	234	URIZEN 23	17
DARKNESS ROUND LOS HEAT WAS NOT FOR BOUND UP	257	BOOK OF LOS 4	1
DELUGED BY [THE] SUMMER'S HEAT THEY SPORT IN ENORMOUS LOVE	276	FOUR ZOAS 1	452
WANDERING EVEN TO THE SUNNY [ORBS] CUBES OF LIGHT & HEAT	286	FOUR ZOAS 2	254
GO NOAH FETCH THE GIRDLE OF STRONG BRASS [PRE] HEAT IT RED HOT	349	FOUR ZOAS 8	312
REPOSES WHERE THE SUN'S HEAT DWELLS HE RISES TO THE SUN	355	FOUR ZOAS 8	570
ARE GATHERD IN THE SCORCHING HEAT & IN THE DRIVING RAIN	359	FOUR ZOAS 9	105
THE SEED IS HARROWD IN WHILE FLAMES HEAT THE BLACK MOULD & CAUSE	366	FOUR ZOAS 9	337
TO FEEL THY HEAT & SEE THY LIGHT & WANDER HERE ALONE	368	FOUR ZOAS 9	416
IN THE SUN'S HEAT TILL IN THE NIGHT ON THE COUCH OF ENION	371	FOUR ZOAS 9	541
THRO ALL THE IMMENSE BORNE DOWN BY CLOUDS SWAGGING IN AUTUMNAL HEAT	372	FOUR ZOAS 9	563
TO MAKE IT FEEL BOTH COLD & HEAT	425	MENTAL TRAVLER	16
I THOUGHT TO FIND LOVE IN THE HEAT OF DAY	436	WILLIAM BOND	47
& HEAT WAS NOT EXTINGUISHD THESE STATES EXIST NOW	606D	V LAST JUDG/N	PROSE
UNDER THE DOMINATION OF INSECTS RAISED BY THE SUN'S HEAT	619C	ILLUS MILTON	PROSE
IS GATHERD IN THE SCORCHING HEAT & IN THE DRIVING RAIN	641	JERUSALEM 19	6
THE HUMAN DIVINE IS WOMAN'S SHADOW A VAPOR IN THE SUMMER'S HEAT	698	JERUSALEM 64	14
GO NOAH FETCH THE GIRDLE OF STRONG BRASS HEAT IT RED-HOT	705	JERUSALEM 67	59
[AND IN THE MIDST OF SINAI'S HEAT]	761	FOR SEXES/GP	8
AND THE DEAD CORPSE FROM SINAI'S HEAT	761	FOR SEXES/GP	10
BECAUSE THEY WERE DONE IN THE HEAT OF MY SPIRITS	815C	LETTER 23	PROSE
WAS UTTERD IN THE HEAT OF THEIR FURY BY EITHER OF THE DRAGOONS	827C	LETTER 28	PROSE

HEATED   SEE OVER HEATED

	PAGE	TITLE	LINE
HEATED WITH WAR FILLD WITH THE BLOOD OF GREEKS	32	EDW THIRD/PS 6	10
OF IRON HEATED IN THE FURNACE HIS TERRIBLE LIMBS WERE FIRE	197	AMERICA 4	9
AND HEATED HIS FURNACES & POURD	228	URIZEN 10	29
HE HEATED THE ROUND GLOBE THEN BEAT	260	BOOK OF LOS 5	38
WHEN LOS HEATED THE GLOWING MASS CASTING	260	BOOK OF LOS 5	42
THEN SIEZD THE LIONS OF URIZEN THEIR WORK & HEATED IN THE FORGE	283	FOUR ZOAS 2	135
HEATED RED HOT THEY HIZZING REND THEIR WAY DOWN MANY A LEAGUE	283	FOUR ZOAS 2	138
STOOD ROUND ME AT THE ANVIL WHERE NEW HEATED THE WEDGE	300	FOUR ZOAS 4	90
LOS BEAT ON HIS FETTERS & [POURD] HEATED HIS FURNACES	303	FOUR ZOAS 4	213
I HEATED IT IN THE FLAMES OF HAND & HYLE & COBAN	628	JERUSALEM 9	21
HEATED IN THE SMITH'S FORGE BUT COLD THE WIND OF THEIR DREAD FURY	735	JERUSALEM 89	42

HEATH

	PAGE	TITLE	LINE
AND ON THE BARREN HEATH	148	MARRIAGE HH 2	7
THEN I WENT TO THE HEATH & THE WILD	162	LAID ME DOWN/N	5
OVER THE HEATH & THE FURZE	164	HEARD ANGEL/N	10
O LAPWING THOU FLIEST AROUND THE HEATH	168	O LAPWING/N	1
THE SWORD SUNG ON THE BARREN HEATH	178	SWORD SUNG/N	1
BECAUSE I WAS HAPPY UPON THE HEATH	180	CHIMNEY SWP/N	5
WHO BUYS WHOLE CORN FIELDS INTO WASTES AND SINGS UPON THE HEATH	193	V DAU ALBION 5	15
BECAUSE I WAS HAPPY UPON THE HEATH	212	CHIMNEY SWP/SE	5
SHALL NOT THE KING CALL FOR FAMINE FROM THE HEATH	247	SONG OF LOS 6	9
AS THE STRONG BULL IN SUMMER TIME WHEN BEES SING ROUND THE HEATH	308	FOUR ZOAS 5	136

HEATH (JAMES)

	PAGE	TITLE	LINE
WITH WHICH HE SET OUT IN LIFE [WH] OF WHICH HEATH & STOTHARD	592B	PUB ADDRESS/N	*PROSE
UNDERSTAND DRAWING & WHICH ACCORDING TO HEATH & STOTHARD	592B	PUB ADDRESS/N	PROSE

HEATHEN

	PAGE	TITLE	LINE
IN HEATHEN TURK OR JEW	117	DIVNE IMAGE/SI	18
. . . FAIRIES OF ALBION AFTERWARDS GODS OF THE HEATHEN	264	FOUR ZOAS 1	19
BUT MORE NERVE IF BY ANCIENTS HE MEANS HEATHEN AUTHORS	397D	ANNO BACON	MARG
("UNKNOWN TO THE HEATHEN") FALSE O SATAN	398D	ANNO BACON	MARG
LUCIAN DISBELIEVD HEATHEN GODS	403C	ANNO BACON	MARG
THAT THE HEATHEN GODS ARE ALL STOCKS & STONES	543	IF TRUE/N	2
IT IS COMPOSED OF THE INNOCENT CIVILIZED HEATHEN &	610A	V LAST JUDG/N	PROSE
O LORD & SAVIOUR HAVE THE GODS OF THE HEATHEN PIERCED THEE	693	JERUSALEM 60	52
HEATHEN WHOSE TENDER MERCIES ARE CRUELTY BUT JEHOVAH'S SALVATION	694	JERUSALEM 61	21
OF THE HEATHEN THE GOD OF THIS WORLD & THE GODDESS NATURE	741	JERUSALEM 93	24
WHERE IS THE COVENANT OF PRIAM THE MORAL VIRTUES OF THE HEATHEN	746	JERUSALEM 98	46
WHO FOLLOW AFTER THE HEATHEN SCHOOLS	751	EV GOSPEL (D)/N	22
THE HEATHEN DEITIES WROTE THEM ALL	758	EV GOSPEL (2)	5
JESUS CAME TO REMOVE WAS THE HEATHEN OR PLATONIC PHILOSOPHY	775B	ANNO BERKELEY	MARG

	PAGE	TITLE	LINE

HEATHEN   (CONTINUED)
    IMPOSSIBILITIES CHASTITY & ABSTINENCE GODS OF THE HEATHEN   776C INSC LAOCOON   PROSE
    THE ELOHIM OF THE HEATHEN SWORE VENGEANCE FOR SIN THEN   781 GHOST ABEL 2   22
       THOU STOODST
    & THEN HE IS NO POET BUT A HEATHEN PHILOSOPHER   . . . . .   782D ANNO WW POEMS   MARG
    & BECAME A CONVERT TO THE HEATHEN MYTHOLOGY   . . . . .   784B ANNO WW EXCUR   MARG
    SO THAT HOMER IS THE CENTER OF ALL I MEAN THE POETRY OF   785B ILLUS DANTE 7   PROSE
       THE HEATHEN
HEATHENS
    OBTUSE ANGLE ANSWERD THE HEATHENS IN THE OLD AGES   . . .   47B ISLAND MOON 3   *PROSE
HEATH'S
    HEATH'S LAME IMITATION STOTHARD BEING SUCH A FOOL   . . .   592B PUB ADDRESS/N   PROSE
    WHEN I LEFT FELPHAM LAST IN ONE OF HEATH'S SHAKESPEARE   855C LETTER 53   PROSE
       YOU WILL SEE
HEAVD
    THE ETERNAL PROPHET HEAVD THE DARK BELLOWS   . . . . . .   227 URIZEN 10   15
    UP IN THE SOLID MOUNTAINS & IN ROCKS WHICH HEAVD WITH THEIR   314 FOUR ZOAS 6   114
       TORMENTS
    [HEAVING XXX] HEAVD LIKE AN EARTHQUAKE LABRING WITH   347 FOUR ZOAS 8   * 249
       CONVULSIVE GROANS
    GROANING THE SPECTRE HEAVD THE BELLOWS OBEYING LOS'S FROWNS   628 JERUSALEM 9   * 33
    HE HEAVD HIS THUNDRING BELLOWS UPON THE VALLEYS OF   660 JERUSALEM 34   18
       MIDDLESEX
    HIS HEAVD HAMMER HE SWUNG IT ROUND & AT ONE BLOW   . . . .   738 JERUSALEM 91   43
HEAVE
    TO HEAVE THE BLOODY BILL   . . . .   12 GWIN KING/PS   52
    SOLEMN HEAVE THE ATLANTIC WAVES BETWEEN THE GLOOMY NATIONS   197 AMERICA 4   2
    THE LUNGS HEAVE INCESSANT DULL AND HEAVY   . . . . .   258 BOOK OF LOS 4   54
    SLEEP BEGAN THE LUNGS HEAVE ON THE WAVE   . . . . . .   258 BOOK OF LOS 4   60
    RATTLING THE ADAMANTINE CHAINS & HOOKS HEAVE UP THE ORE   282 FOUR ZOAS 2   66
    TAKE THOU THIS HAMMER & IN PATIENCE HEAVE THE THUNDERING   627 JERUSALEM 8   39
       BELLOWS
HEAVED
    JUSTICE HATH HEAVED A SWORD TO PLUNGE IN ALBION'S BREAST   34A KING JOHN/PS   PROSE
    THEN LOS HEAVED HIS THUNDRING BELLOWS ON THE VALLEY OF   687 JERUSALEM 56   1
       MIDDLESEX
HEAVEN   SEE HEAVN
    RODE OER THE DEEP OF HEAVEN BESIDE OUR SPRINGS   . . . . .   2 TO SUMMER/PS   9
    NOR ECHOES SWEET NOR WATERS CLEAR AS HEAVEN   . . . . .   2 TO SUMMER/PS   18
    WITH STORMS TILL HEAVEN SMILES AND THE MONSTER   . . . .   3 TO WINTER/PS   15
    AWAKE THE DAWN THAT SLEEPS IN HEAVEN LET LIGHT   . . . .   3 TO MORNING/PS   3
    THE BREATH OF HEAVEN DWELT AMONG HIS LEAVES   . . . . .   5 FAIR ELENOR/PS   51
    OF PAVED HEAVEN   . . . .   9 MAD SONG/PS   10
    SO WHEN SHE SPEAKS THE VOICE OF HEAVEN I HEAR   . . . .   9 FRESH FROM/PS   13
    GOLDEN APOLLO THAT THRO HEAVEN WIDE   . . . . . .   14 IMIT SPEN/PS   1
    OF THE SEA OUR RIGHT THAT HEAVEN GAVE   . . . . . .   20 EDW THIRD/PS 2   79
    WORTHY THE HIGH COMMAND THAT HEAVEN AND YOU   . . . .   23 EDW THIRD/PS 3   83
    LITTLE SPORT AND CUT A PATH INTO THE HEAVEN OF GLORY   . .   27 EDW THIRD/PS 3   274
    UPON THE CLOUDS OF HEAVEN TO DIE NO MORE   . . . . .   30 EDW THIRD/PS 5   16
    WHERE HE DOTH REND THE VAULT OF HEAVEN   . . . . . .   30 EDW THIRD/PS 5   19
    THE TABLE IS PREPARD IN SHINING HEAVEN   . . . . . .   31 EDW THIRD/PS 5   35
    HEAR IT NOT HEAVEN THY MINISTERS HAVE DONE IT   . . . .   33 EDW FOURTH/PS   16
    THE STARS OF HEAVEN TREMBLE   . . . .   34A KING JOHN/PS   PROSE
    AND WALK TOGETHER ON THE CLOUDS OF HEAVEN   . . . . .   35 WAR SONG/PS   19
    AND THE VISIONS OF HEAVEN UNFOLD THEIR VISITATION   . .   35D COUCH DEATH/PS   PROSE
    CAN I NOT CRY AND LIFT MY EYES TO HEAVEN   . . . . .   36B COUCH DEATH/PS   PROSE
    TWICE WAS MY BIRTH FORETOLD FROM HEAVEN AND   . . . . .   39B SAMSON/PS   PROSE
    GRANT ME A SON KIND HEAVEN MANOA CRIED BUT HEAVEN REFUSED   39C SAMSON/PS   PROSE
    VENERABLE SWEETNER OF HIS LIFE RECEIVES THE PROMISE FIRST   39C SAMSON/PS   PROSE
       FROM HEAVEN
    AND DREW THE CURTAINS OF HEAVEN   . . . .   39D SAMSON/PS   PROSE
    THERE IS A MELANCHOLY O HOW LOVELY TIS WHOSE HEAVEN   . . .   42A THEN SHE BORE   PROSE
    IS IN THE HEAVENLY MIND FOR SHE FROM HEAVEN CAME   . . . .   42A THEN SHE BORE   PROSE
    AND WHERE SHE GOES HEAVEN STILL DOTH FOLLOW HER SHE   . . .   42A THEN SHE BORE   PROSE
    I'LL SHEW HOW CONSCIENCE CAME FROM HEAVEN   . . . . .   42A THEN SHE BORE   PROSE
    HEAVEN & HELL ?CHAPTER...   . . . .   89B ANNO SWED LOVE   * MARG
    HEAVEN WOULD UPON THIS PLAN BE BUT A CLOCK   . . . . .   91B ANNO SWED LOVE   MARG
    HEAVEN & HELL ARE BORN TOGETHER   . . . .   96D ANNO SWED LOVE   MARG
    AND ALL THAT TIME WE WAITED FOR THE FIRE TO FALL   107 TIRIEL 6   9
       FROM HEAVEN
    [THY GOD OF LOVE THY HEAVEN OF JOY]   . . . .   109 TIRIEL 8   * 9
    HEAVEN & EARTH TO PEACE BEGUILES   . . . .   120 CRADLE SONG/SI   32
    NOW LIKE A MIGHTY WIND THEY RAISE TO HEAVEN THE VOICE OF   122 HOLY THURS/SI   9
       SONG
    OR LIKE HARMONIOUS THUNDERINGS THE SEATS OF HEAVEN AMONG   122 HOLY THURS/SI   * 10
    YET I AM VISITED FROM HEAVEN AND HE THAT SMILES ON ALL   . .   127 BOOK OF THEL 1   19
    OR EXTERNAL OF HEAVEN & IS OF THE BODY OF THE LORD   . .   SUPP ANNO SWED HELL * MARG
    QUERY DOES HE ALSO OCCUPY THAT PLACE IN HEAVEN SEE N...AT   131D ANNO SWED PROV   MARG
       THE END
    EXPANDED LIKE STARRY HEAVEN HE SAT DOWN   . . . .   138 FRENCH REVOLTN   82
    SHALL THIS MARBLE BUILT HEAVEN BECOME A CLAY COTTAGE   . . .   138 FRENCH REVOLTN   89
    STRETCH THE HAND THAT BECKONS THE EAGLES OF HEAVEN   . . .   138 FRENCH REVOLTN   103
    . . . THE EAGLES OF HEAVEN MUST HAVE THEIR PREY   . . . .   138 FRENCH REVOLTN   104
    THROUGH HEAVEN TINGING MORNING WITH BEAMS OF BLOOD   . . .   139 FRENCH REVOLTN   111
    HEARKEN MONARCH OF FRANCE TO THE TERRORS OF HEAVEN   . . .   140 FRENCH REVOLTN   128
    . . . THE COMMAND OF HEAVEN IS UPON THEE   . . . . .   141 FRENCH REVOLTN   153
    . . . WERE BOUND IN THE RUINS OF SULPHUR HEAVEN   . . . .   143 FRENCH REVOLTN   213
    THE MARRIAGE OF HEAVEN AND HELL   . . . .   148B MARRIAGE HH   TITLE
    AS A NEW HEAVEN IS BEGUN AND IT IS NOW THIRTY-THREE YEARS   149A MARRIAGE HH 3   PROSE
    GOOD IS HEAVEN EVIL IS HELL   . . . .   149B MARRIAGE HH 3   PROSE
    & FORMED A HEAVEN OF WHAT HE STOLE FROM THE ABYSS   . .   150A MARRIAGE HH 5   PROSE
    AND BUILDS A HEAVEN IN HELL'S DESPAIR   . . . .   162 CLOD PEBBLE/N   4

894

```
                                                          PAGE    TITLE          LINE
HEAVEN    (CONTINUED)
    HEAVEN & EARTH OF PEACE BEGUILES  . . . . . . . . .   165 CRADLE SONG/N        27
    AND WATERD HEAVEN WITH THEIR TEARS  . . . . . . . .   173 THE TYGER/N 1        30
    AND WATERD HEAVEN WITH THEIR TEARS  . . . . . . . .   173 THE TYGER/N 2        14
    [SUCH USAGE IN HEAVEN MAKES ALL GO TO HELL]  . . . .  179 LIT VAGABOND/N        4
    WHO MAKE UP A HEAVEN OF OUR MISERY  . . . . . . . .   180 CHIMNEY SWP/N        13
    O URIZEN CREATOR OF MEN MISTAKEN DEMON OF HEAVEN  . . 192 V DAU ALBION 5        3
    THE CLEAR HEAVEN OF HER ETERNAL SPRING TO BEAR THE WINTRY 193 V DAU ALBION 5   24
        RAGE
    COME IN THE HEAVEN OF GENEROUS LOVE NOR SELFISH BLIGHTINGS 195 V DAU ALBION 7  29
        BRING
    WHEN PESTILENCE IS SHOT FROM HEAVEN NO OTHER ARMS SHE NEED 196 AMERICA PREL 1   6
    A BENDED BOW IS LIFTED IN HEAVEN & A HEAVY IRON CHAIN  . . 197 AMERICA 3        7
    AS HUMAN BLOOD SHOOTING ITS VEINS ALL ROUND THE ORBED 197 AMERICA 4             5
        HEAVEN
    DARK IS THE HEAVEN ABOVE & COLD & HARD THE EARTH BENEATH 201 AMERICA 14         7
    THEY SLOW ADVANCE TO SHUT THE FIVE GATES OF THEIR LAW-BUILT 203 AMERICA 16     19
        HEAVEN
    A BENDED BOW IN HEAVEN IS LIFTED & A HEAVY IRON CHAIN  . . 204 AMERICA CANC A   7
    THE MARRIAGE OF HEAVEN AND HELL IN ILLUMINATED PRINTING 207D PRSPECTUS 1793 PROSE
        QUARTO
    AND BUILDS A HEAVEN IN HELL'S DESPAIR  . . . . . . .  211 CLOD PEBBLE/SE        4
    WHO MAKE UP A HEAVEN OF OUR MISERY  . . . . . . . .   212 CHIMNEY SWP/SE       12
    AND WATERD HEAVEN WITH THEIR TEARS  . . . . . . . .   214 THE TYGER/SE         18
    SUCH USAGE IN HEAVEN WILL NEVER DO WELL  . . . . . .  216 LIT VAGABND/SE        4
    THE DUNGEON-LIKE HEAVEN DIVIDING  . . . . . . . . .   235 URIZEN 25            12
    UNWILLING I LOOK UP TO HEAVEN UNWILLING COUNT THE STARS 238 EUROPE PREL 2       1
    HEAVEN A MIGHTY CIRCLE TURNING GOD A TYRANT CROWND  . 241 EUROPE 10            23
    THAT GAVE LIGHT TO THE MORNINGS OF HEAVEN  . . . . .  251 AHANIA 3             42
    RAN THRO HEAVEN & EARTH LIVING FLAMES  . . . . . . .  256 BOOK OF LOS 3        28
    ONCE THOU WAST TO ME THE LOVELIEST SON OF HEAVEN BUT NOW 265 FOUR ZOAS 1       38
    [NO OTHER LIVING THING IS HERE THE SEA THE EARTH     268 FOUR ZOAS 1          141
        THE HEAVEN]
    . . . VISIONS TOWARD HEAVEN] MADE WINDOWS INTO EDEN  . . . 270 FOUR ZOAS 1    224
    FORM THE [FREE] REBELLIOUS SPIRITS OF HEAVEN . . . . 272 FOUR ZOAS 1          311
    AND WITH IMMORTAL VOICE SOFT WARBLING FILL ALL EARTH & 274 FOUR ZOAS 1        381
        HEAVEN
    FROM ALL THE TURNING WHEELS OF HEAVEN & THE CHARIOTS OF 276 FOUR ZOAS 1       441
        THE SLAIN
    THE PRINCE OF ALL THE HOSTS OF MEN NOR EQUAL KNOW IN HEAVEN 278 FOUR ZOAS 1   505
    [XXX SPREAD FROM HEAVEN TO HEAVEN]  . . . . . . . . . SUPP FOUR ZOAS 1          *
    THE BANDS OF HEAVEN FLEW THRO THE AIR SINGING & SHOUTING 281 FOUR ZOAS 2       26
        TO URIZEN
    FLED WITH THE NOISE OF SLAUGHTER & THE STARS OF HEAVEN FLED 281 FOUR ZOAS 2    44
    TO MEASURE OUT THE COURSE OF HEAVEN STERN URIZEN BEHELD 283 FOUR ZOAS 2       131
    OF HIS WIDE HEAVEN TREMBLING COLD IN PALING FEARS SHE SAT 285 FOUR ZOAS 2     186
    . . . [?THE ?HEAVENS ?WERE ?WALLD] HEAVEN WALLED ROUND . . 287 FOUR ZOAS 2   * 258
    THUS WERE THE STARS OF HEAVEN CREATED LIKE A GOLDEN CHAIN 287 FOUR ZOAS 2     266
    TO BIND THE BODY OF MAN TO HEAVEN FROM FALLING INTO THE 287 FOUR ZOAS 2       267
        ABYSS
    [AND COMFORTS SHALL DESCEND FROM HEAVEN INTO THY DARKNING 292 FOUR ZOAS 3      29
        CLOUDS]
    THEY FLED TO EAST & WEST & LEFT THE NORTH & SOUTH OF HEAVEN 295 FOUR ZOAS 3   134
    I KNOW I WAS URTHONA KEEPER OF THE GATES OF HEAVEN  . . . 298 FOUR ZOAS 4      42
    THOU ONCE THE MILDEST SON OF HEAVEN ART NOW BECOME A RAGE 299 FOUR ZOAS 4      81
    INFECTED MAD HE DANCD ON HIS MOUNTAINS HIGH & DARK   305 FOUR ZOAS 5           1
        AS HEAVEN
    THAT DREW THE BODY OF MAN FROM HEAVEN INTO THIS DARK ABYSS 306 FOUR ZOAS 5     47
    HIS BOSOM IS LIKE STARRY HEAVEN EXPANDED ALL THE STARS . . 308 FOUR ZOAS 5    130
    THY CHILDREN SMOTE THEIR FIERY WINGS CROWND WITH THE GOLD 311 FOUR ZOAS 5     229
        OF HEAVEN
    THEN THOU DIDST KEEP WITH STRONG URTHONA THE LIVING GATES 311 FOUR ZOAS 5     232
        OF HEAVEN
    VESTS OF THE RADIANT COLOURS OF HEAVEN & CROWNS OF GOLDEN 312 FOUR ZOAS 6      28
        FIRE
    ART THOU O RUIN THE ONCE GLORIOUS HEAVEN ARE THESE THY 317 FOUR ZOAS 6        212
        ROCKS
    AT THE TURNING WHEELS OF HEAVEN SHRUNK AWAY INWARD WITHRING 317 FOUR ZOAS 6  * 236
        AWAY
    FROM HEAVEN TO HEAVEN FROM GLOBE TO GLOBE IN VAST    320 FOUR ZOAS 6          319
        EXCENTRIC PATHS
    BRANCHES INTO THE HEAVEN OF LOS THEY PIPE FORMD BENDING 321 FOUR ZOAS 7        33
        DOWN
    HIS MOTHER TO THE WINDS OF HEAVEN INTOXICATED WITH  . . . 326 FOUR ZOAS 7     233
    ALL HEAVEN THEY SAW HIM DARK THEY BUILT A GOLDEN WALL . . 326 FOUR ZOAS 7     242
    THE VALES TO FIND HIS WAY BACK INTO HEAVEN BUT FOUND NONE 326 FOUR ZOAS 7     249
    LEST ANY SHOULD IN FUTURITY DO AS WE HAVE DONE IN HEAVEN 331 FOUR ZOAS 7      430
    AND FIRST HE DREW A LINE UPON THE WALLS OF SHINING HEAVEN 332 FOUR ZOAS 7     467
    THE ENDS OF HEAVEN LIKE A GARMENT WILL I FOLD THEM ROUND ME 333 FOUR ZOAS 7B   6
    AND I WILL GIVE THEE ALL THE ENDS OF HEAVEN FOR THY 334 FOUR ZOAS 7B           56
        POSSESSION
    THE SUN WAS BLACK & THE MOON ROLLD A USELESS GLOBE THRO 337 FOUR ZOAS 7B      169
        HEAVEN
    THARMAS REPLIED VALA THY SINS HAVE LOST US HEAVEN & BLISS 339 FOUR ZOAS 7B    256
    WALKING ON MOUNTAINS OR FLYING IN THE OPEN EXPANSE  340 FOUR ZOAS 7B          270
        OF HEAVEN
    AND THE STRONG PINIOND EAGLE BORE THE FIRE OF HEAVEN . . . 340 FOUR ZOAS 7B   285
    FROM HEAVEN TO HEAVN THRO ALL ITS MESHES ALTERING   345 FOUR ZOAS 8           177
        THE VORTEXES
    [TO SEE THE BOY SPRING INTO HEAVEN SOUNDING FROM MY SIGHT] 349 FOUR ZOAS 8    311
    THE LAMB OF GOD IT ROLLD APART REVEALING TO ALL IN HEAVEN 350 FOUR ZOAS 8     342
    REVEALD BEFORE THE FACE OF HEAVEN HIS SECRET HOLINESS  . . 351 FOUR ZOAS 8    413
```

		PAGE	TITLE	LINE

HEAVEN   (CONTINUED)

FOR SHE SPOKE OF ALL IN HEAVEN & ALL UPON THE EARTH   . . 353 FOUR ZOAS 8   490
NOR SILENT MOON NOR ALL THE HOSTS OF HEAVEN MOVE IN HIS   354 FOUR ZOAS 8   508
    BODY
UPON THE BLOODY ALTAR JOHN SAW THESE THINGS REVEALD IN   356 FOUR ZOAS 8   600
    HEAVEN
[THAT ENION HAD NUMBERD AWAY FROM HEAVEN]   . . . .   SUPP FOUR ZOAS 8   *
SOUND OF LOUD TRUMPET THUNDERING ALONG FROM HEAVEN   357 FOUR ZOAS 9   11
    TO HEAVEN
FOLDING LIKE SCROLLS OF THE ENORMOUS VOLUME OF HEAVEN &   357 FOUR ZOAS 9   14
    EARTH
OF WOMEN & CHILDREN THROUGHOUT EVERY NATION UNDER HEAVEN   358 FOUR ZOAS 9   47
WHICH NOW DESCENDETH OUT OF HEAVEN A CITY YET A WOMAN . . 362 FOUR ZOAS 9   222
THESE COVERING VAULTS OF HEAVEN & THESE TREMBLING GLOBES   364 FOUR ZOAS 9   260
    OF EARTH
FROM THE BLUE WALLS OF HEAVEN STARRY JINGLING ORNAMENTED   365 FOUR ZOAS 9   296
WHEN HEAVEN & HELL IN EMULATION STROVE IN SPORTS OF GLORY   365 FOUR ZOAS 9   298
THRO NIGHT SHOULD SING SOFT WARBLING FILLING EARTH & HEAVEN 366 FOUR ZOAS 9   352
THEN VALA LIFTED UP HER HANDS TO HEAVEN TO CALL ON ENION   370 FOUR ZOAS 9   498
MUTTERING ALONG FROM HEAVEN TO HEAVEN HOARSE ROLL THE   372 FOUR ZOAS 9   * 564
    HUMAN FORMS
DOWN POUR THE TORRENT FLOODS OF HEAVEN ON ALL THE HUMAN   372 FOUR ZOAS 9   566
    HARVEST
TO THE GOLDEN WHEELS CIRCLING UPON THE PAVEMENT OF HEAVEN   376 FOUR ZOAS 9   719
    & ALL
HEAVEN RANG WITH WINGED EXULTATION ALL BENEATH HOWLD LOUD   378 FOUR ZOAS 9   782
OF GLASS & PRECIOUS STONES THEY LOADED ALL THE WAGGONS   378 FOUR ZOAS 9   793
    OF HEAVEN
OF HEAVEN WHILE . . . .   380 FOUR ZOAS AD 1   14
THE KINGDOM OF HEAVEN IS THE DIRECT NEGATION OF EARTHLY   407B ANNO BACON   MARG
    DOMINATION
THRO THE HEAVEN & EARTH & HELL . . . . 416 MY SPECTRE/N   55
THAT DID HEAVEN ITSELF BEGUILE . . . . 422 BENEATH/N   19
THAT DID HEAVEN ITSELF BEGUILE . . . . 424 THE GOLDEN NET   18
WHY DID HEAVEN ADORN ME WITH BOUNTIFUL HAND . . . . . 428 MARY   23
AND A HEAVEN IN A WILD FLOWER . . . . 431 AUGURIES   2
PUTS ALL HEAVEN IN A RAGE . . . . 431 AUGURIES   6
CALLS TO HEAVEN FOR HUMAN BLOOD . . . . 431 AUGURIES   12
THE WHOLE UPPER PART OF THE DESIGN IS A VIEW OF HEAVEN . 444A LAST JUDGMNT/L PROSE
THE MAN WHO NEVER IN HIS MIND & THOUGHTS TRAVELD TO HEAVEN 458C ANNO REYNOLDS MARG
AND OF THE WHEELS OF HEAVEN TO TURN THE MILLS DAY & NIGHT   483 MILTON 4   10
LOS IN HIS WRATH CURSD HEAVEN & EARTH HE RENT UP NATIONS   489 MILTON 9   13
WHICH REACH THE STARS OF HEAVEN & STRETCH FROM POLE TO POLE 489 MILTON 9   15
THUS IS THE HEAVEN A VORTEX PASSD ALREADY AND THE EARTH   497 MILTON 15   34
A CLOUDY HEAVEN MINGLED WITH STORMY SEAS IN LOUDEST RUIN   497 MILTON 15   43
BURNS TO THE TOP OF HEAVEN AGAINST THEE IN JEALOUSY & FEAR 499 MILTON 18   32
IT HAS A HEART LIKE THEE A BRAIN OPEN TO HEAVEN & HELL . . 502 MILTON 20   28
AND ALL IN HEAVEN SAW IN THE NETHER REGIONS OF THE   503 MILTON 21   6
    IMAGINATION
IN THE FOUR POINTS OF HEAVEN EAST WEST & NORTH & SOUTH . . 504 MILTON 21   38
THE SHADOWY FEMALE SHUDDERS THRO HEAVEN IN TORMENT   506 MILTON 22   36
    INEXPRESSIBLE
SHEWING THE TRANSGRESORS IN HELL THE PROUD WARRIORS IN   506 MILTON 22   * 51
    HEAVEN
HEAVEN AS A PUNISHER & HELL AS ONE UNDER PUNISHMENT   . . 506 MILTON 22   52
APPEARD AS DOES THE FACE OF HEAVEN WHEN COVERD WITH THICK 507 MILTON 23   29
    STORMS
O WHEN SHALL WE TREAD OUR WINE-PRESSES IN HEAVEN AND REAP   507 MILTON 23   45
IN HIS APPOINTED SEASON WHEN THE ENDS OF HEAVEN MEET   . . 517 MILTON 29   46
IT IS THE ENTERANCE OF THE FIRST HEAVEN NAMED LUTHER FOR   526 MILTON 35   62
INTO ANOTHER HEAVEN TO CARRY NEWS UPON HIS WINGS . . . . 526 MILTON 36   7
REACHING FROM HEAVEN TO EARTH A CLOUD & HUMAN FORM   . . . 528 MILTON 37   14
TO LABOUR IN THE OCEAN OR IN THE STARRY HEAVEN SO MILTON   532 MILTON 39   56
I OFT HAVE WISHD FOR HELL FOR EASE FROM HEAVEN   . . . . . 552 GROWN OLD IN/N   2
AN APOSTLE A REAL MESSENGER OF HEAVEN SENT IN EVERY AGE   570B DESC CAT 3   PROSE
TO BE OPENED AGAIN TO HEAVEN THROUGH EDEN   . . . . . 578A DESC CAT 5   PROSE
THE ANTIQUITIES OF EVERY NATION UNDER HEAVEN . . . . . 578D DESC CAT 5   PROSE
INTO HEAVEN BY MEANS OF LEARNING APPEAR TO CHILDREN . . . 581D DESC CAT 8   PROSE
AROUND HIS THRONE THE OLD (HEAVEN) & (OLD) EARTH ARE . . 606B V LAST JUDG/N   PROSE
PASSING AWAY & THE (NEW) (HEAVEN) & (NEW) EARTH . . . 606B V LAST JUDG/N   PROSE
AS IT WAS SAID "AS THE STARS OF HEAVEN FOR MULTITUDE"   . . 607C V LAST JUDG/N   PROSE
WHICH LOOKS FOR NO OTHER HEAVEN THAN THEIR BELOVED   . . . 610D V LAST JUDG/N   PROSE
& BEFORE THE NEW HEAVEN & THE NEW EARTH   . . . . . 612A V LAST JUDG/N   PROSE
TO MAKE WAY FOR THE NEW HEAVEN & THE NEW EARTH   . . . . . 612A V LAST JUDG/N   PROSE
[AROUND THE THRONE HEAVEN IS OPENED] ON THE CLOUD . . . . 612B V LAST JUDG/N   PPOSE
AROUND THE THRONE HEAVEN IS OPEND . . . . 612D V LAST JUDG/N   PROSE
ON EACH SIDE OF THE OPENING HEAVEN APPEARS AN APOSTLE . . 612D V LAST JUDG/N   PROSE
LIKE A DOVE IS SURROUNDED BY A BLUE HEAVEN . . . . . 613B V LAST JUDG/N   PROSE
FOR HERE THE TEMPLE IS OPEND IN HEAVEN . . . . . . 613B V LAST JUDG/N   PROSE
MEN ARE ADMITTED INTO HEAVEN NOT BECAUSE THEY . . . . 615C V LAST JUDG/N   PROSE
THE TREASURES OF HEAVEN ARE NOT NEGATIONS OF PASSION   . . 615C V LAST JUDG/N   PROSE
THE FOOL SHALL NOT ENTER INTO HEAVEN LET HIM BE EVER SO   615D V LAST JUDG/N   PROSE
    HOLY
HOLINESS IS NOT THE PRICE OF ENTERANCE INTO HEAVEN   . . . 615D V LAST JUDG/N   PROSE
THRO HEAVEN THE DISTANT STEEPLE SEEN ACROSS A WIDE WATER   619B ILLUS MILTON   PROSE
AS ATTENDING ON THE HEAVEN OF JUPITER THE GREAT BEAR   . . 619B ILLUS MILTON   PROSE
READER [LOVER] OF BOOKS [LOVER] OF HEAVEN . . . . . 621 READER LOVER/J   1
HEAVEN EARTH & HELL HENCEFORTH SHALL LIVE IN HARMONY   . . 621 READER LOVER/J   10
WHIRLD ROUND FROM HEAVEN TO EARTH TREMBLING HE SAT HIS COLD 627 JERUSALEM 8   4
HE CURSES HEAVEN & EARTH DAY & NIGHT & SUN & MOON . . . 629 JERUSALEM 10   25
ROUND FROM HEAVEN TO EARTH DOWN FALLING WITH HEAVY BLOW   636 JERUSALEM 16   12
. . . SENDING HIM ABROAD OVER THE FOUR POINTS OF HEAVEN   638 JERUSALEM 17   11

HEAVEN   (CONTINUED)

	PAGE	TITLE	LINE
ONCE THOU WAST TO ME THE LOVELIEST SON OF HEAVEN BUT NOW	645	JERUSALEM 22	12
DISPLAYING OUR GIANT LIMBS TO ALL THE WINDS OF HEAVEN SUDDEN	647	JERUSALEM 24	6
MOUNT ZION LIFTED HIS HEAD IN EVERY NATION UNDER HEAVEN	648	JERUSALEM 24	48
IN HIS MIGHTY LIMBS ALL THINGS IN HEAVEN & EARTH . . .	649C	JERUSALEM 27	PROSE
HIS WESTERN HEAVEN WITH ROCKY CLOUDS OF DEATH & DESPAIR	656	JERUSALEM 31	1
IS GREAT IN THE EAST THEIR SPEARS OF BLOOD RAGE IN THE EASTERN HEAVEN	658	JERUSALEM 31	56
I BREATHE HIM FORTH INTO THE HEAVEN FROM MY SECRET CAVE	660	JERUSALEM 33	50
ARE NOT THE STARS OF HEAVEN THY CHILDREN ART THOU NOT BABYLON	660	JERUSALEM 34	8
IN PAIN GIRDING ME ROUND LIKE A RIB OF IRON IN HEAVEN O VALA	660	JERUSALEM 34	14
THE POISONER THE BEST AND WORST IN HEAVEN AND HELL . . .	668	JERUSALEM 41	2
OPENING INTO BEULAH EVERY ANGLE IS A LOVELY HEAVEN . . .	668	JERUSALEM 41	18
BRING HIM TO JUSTICE BEFORE HEAVEN HERE UPON LONDON STONE	670	JERUSALEM 42	50
SO SPOKE UNHEARD BY ALBION THE MERCIFUL SON OF HEAVEN . .	676	JERUSALEM 45	33
THE CAPTIVES REARD TO HEAVEN HOWL IN FLAMES AMONG THE STARS	677	JERUSALEM 47	8
ALBION THE MILDEST SON OF HEAVEN THE PLACE OF HOLY SACRIFICE	678	JERUSALEM 48	55
AND THE BODIES IN WHICH ALL ANIMALS & VEGETATIONS THE EARTH & HEAVEN	679	JERUSALEM 49	13
STRIVING TO CREATE A HEAVEN IN WHICH ALL SHALL BE PURE & HOLY	679	JERUSALEM 49	27
THE STARS IN THEIR COURSES FOUGHT THE SUN MOON HEAVEN EARTH	686	JERUSALEM 55	27
. . . WERE HEARD IN THE CLOUDS OF HEAVEN	687	JERUSALEM 55	55
THE CLOUDS OF ALBION'S DRUID TEMPLES RAGE IN THE EASTERN HEAVEN	692	JERUSALEM 60	1
A WEEPING INFANT IN THE GATES OF BIRTH IN THE MIDST OF HEAVEN	697	JERUSALEM 63	17
FOR IN THE DEPTHS OF ALBION'S BOSOM IN THE EASTERN HEAVEN	699	JERUSALEM 65	5
FROM HEAVEN TO EARTH HOWLING INVISIBLE BUT NOT INVISIBLE	702	JERUSALEM 66	11
OF FIRE THEN AN AWFUL FIERY WHEEL SURROUNDING EARTH & HEAVEN	702	JERUSALEM 66	42
HE BLEEDS IN TORRENTS OF BLOOD AS HE ROLLS THRO HEAVEN ABOVE	703	JERUSALEM 66	77
THE STARS FLEE REMOTE THE HEAVEN IS IRON THE EARTH IS SULPHUR	703	JERUSALEM 66	81
A SHEET & VEIL & CURTAIN OF BLOOD IS LET DOWN FROM HEAVEN	706	JERUSALEM 68	21
THE VALLEY OF THE JEBUSITE MOLECH REJOICES IN HEAVEN . .	706	JERUSALEM 68	23
HER BRAIN ENLABYRINTHS THE WHOLE HEAVEN OF HER BOSOM & LOINS	709	JERUSALEM 70	29
IN HEAVENS & EARTHS AS IN YOUR OWN BOSOM YOU BEAR YOUR HEAVEN	709	JERUSALEM 71	17
HIS IMMORTAL CHEEKS REARING HIS HANDS TO HEAVEN FOR AID DIVINE	711	JERUSALEM 71	57
WHAT ARE THE TREASURES OF HEAVEN WHICH WE ARE TO LAY UP FOR OURSELVES	717A	JERUSALEM 77	PROSE
WHAT IS THE JOY OF HEAVEN BUT IMPROVEMENT IN THE THINGS OF THE SPIRIT	717B	JERUSALEM 77	PROSE
FURY & THUNDERING COURSE ROUND HEAVEN & EARTH	717	STOOD AMONG/J	6
FOR HELL IS OPEND TO HEAVEN THINE EYES BEHELD	718	STOOD AMONG/J	34
TILL ALBION IS SHUT OUT FROM EVERY NATION UNDER HEAVEN . .	721	JERUSALEM 79	80
IN HEAVEN THE ONLY ART OF LIVING	724	IN HEAVEN/J	1
IN HEAVEN LOVE BEGETS LOVE BUT FEAR IS THE PARENT OF EARTHLY LOVE	725	JERUSALEM 81	15
I KNOW I AM URTHONA KEEPER OF THE GATES OF HEAVEN	727	JERUSALEM 82	81
I SEE THE NEW JERUSALEM DESCENDING OUT OF HEAVEN	731	JERUSALEM 86	19
EACH WITHOUTSIDE OF THE OTHER COVERING EASTERN HEAVEN . .	734	JERUSALEM 89	8
AS THE SUN & MOON LEAD FORWARD THE VISIONS OF HEAVEN & EARTH	743	JERUSALEM 95	21
AS THE SUN & MOON LEAD FORWARD THE VISIONS OF HEAVEN & EARTH	743	JERUSALEM 96	1
OF HEAVEN FOURFOLD AMONG THE VISIONS OF GOD IN ETERNITY	744	JERUSALEM 96	43
THE INNUMERABLE CHARIOTS OF THE ALMIGHTY APPEARD IN HEAVEN	745	JERUSALEM 98	8
A SUN OF BLOOD RED WRATH SURROUNDING HEAVEN ON ALL SIDES AROUND	745	JERUSALEM 98	10
OF HEAVEN GOING FORWARD FORWARD	745	JERUSALEM 98	27
[I] THY HEAVEN DOORS ARE MY HELL GATES	748	EV GOSPEL(A)/N *	8
EARTH GROAND BENEATH & HEAVEN ABOVE	753	EV GOSPEL(E)/N	5
[THO] THAT HEAVEN WAS IMPURE IN THY SIGHT	754	EV GOSPEL(E)/N *	36
THO THY OATH TURND HEAVEN PALE	754	EV GOSPEL(E)/N	37
OF GOD & HEAVEN & THEIR GLORIES	758	EV GOSPEL (1)	6
WHO AGAINST SINNERS HEAVEN CLOSE	758	EV GOSPEL (1)	12
THE HOSTS OF HEAVEN	777B	INSC LAOCOON	PROSE
NONE ARE GREATEST IN THE KINGDOM OF HEAVEN	783A	ANNO WW POEMS	MARG
THAT IN THIS WORLD IS THE ULTIMATE OF HEAVEN	785B	ILLUS DANTE 7	PROSE
& A LAWFUL HEAVEN SEEN THRO A LAWFUL TELESCOPE	787D	ANNO THORNTON	MARG
THY KINGSHIP COME UPON EARTH FIRST & THENCE IN HEAVEN . .	788D	ANNO THORNTON	* MARG
IS ARRIVD WHEN MEN SHALL AGAIN CONVERSE IN HEAVEN & WALK WITH	799B	LETTER 11	PROSE
I BLESS THEE O FATHER OF HEAVEN & EARTH	799	TO FLAXMAN/L	1
ANGELS STAND ROUND MY SPIRIT IN HEAVEN	799	TO FLAXMAN/L	2
. . . THE BLESSED OF HEAVEN ARE MY FRIENDS UPON EARTH .	799	TO FLAXMAN/L	2
AWAY TO SWEET FELPHAM FOR HEAVEN IS THERE	800	MRS FLAXMAN/L	5
YOU STAND IN THE VILLAGE & LOOK UP TO HEAVEN	800	MRS FLAXMAN/L	9
HEAVEN OPENS HERE ON ALL SIDES HER GOLDEN GATES	802A	LETTER 14	PROSE
I AM MORE FAMED IN HEAVEN FOR MY WORKS THAN I COULD WELL	802B	LETTER 14	PROSE
AT THE REMOTEST CORNERS OF HEAVEN FROM EACH OTHER . . .	802D	LETTER 14	PROSE
HEAVEN IS A MERCY A FIG FOR ALL CORPOREAL SUCH DISTRESS IS	809B	LETTER 20	PROSE
IN HEAVEN IS CERTAIN & DETERMINED & TO THIS I HAVE LONG	812C	LETTER 22	PROSE

897

HEAVEN   (CONTINUED)

FROM HEAVEN DAILY & NIGHTLY BUT THE NATURE OF SUCH THINGS 812A LETTER 22   PROSE
EXCEPT WHAT COMES TO HER FROM HEAVEN . . . . 818 HAPPINESS/L   62
THE SUN STOOD TREMBLING IN HEAVEN . . . . 818 HAPPINESS/L   72
YET I LAUGH & SING FOR IF ON EARTH NEGLECTED I AM IN HEAVEN 830A LETTER 30   PROSE
GRATITUDE IS HEAVEN ITSELF THERE COULD BE NO HEAVEN 834A LETTER 33   PROSE
   WITHOUT
HEAVEN HAVILAH EDEN & ALL THE COUNTRIES WHERE JEWELS ABOUND 837D LETTER 36   PROSE
GOD SEND IT SO ON EARTH AS IT IS IN HEAVEN . . . . 879A LETTER 88   PROSE
VACUUM STARRY HEAVEN SATURN JUPITER MARS SUN VENUS SUPP ILLUS DANTE 7 *PROSE
   MERCURY MOON
URIZEN HEAVEN &C & SONGS OF EXPERIENCE FOR BALANCE . . . SUPP LETTER 56A *PROSE
OF MR LINNELL...TWO GUINEAS FOR HEAVEN & HELL . . . . . SUPP LETTER 67B *PROSE

HEAVENLY   SEE HEAVNLY

TO BE EXALTED TO THOSE HEAVENLY FIELDS . . . . . . 30 EDW THIRD/PS 5   28
I ANSWERED HEAVENLY GODDESS I AM WRAPPED IN MORTALITY . 37B CONTEMPLATN/PS PROSE
TURNING OUR EARTHLY NIGHT TO HEAVENLY DAY . . . . . 37C SAMSON/PS   PROSE
IS IN THE HEAVENLY MIND FOR SHE FROM HEAVEN CAME . . . 42A THEN SHE BORE   PROSE
("HEROES WITH INFANTINE SIMPLICITY") THIS IS HEAVENLY . 75B ANNO LAVATER   MARG
SO IT IS IMPOSSIBLE TO KNOW GOD OR HEAVENLY THINGS WITHOUT 88B ANNO LAVATER   MARG
CONJUNCTION WITH THOSE WHO KNOW GOD & HEAVENLY THINGS . 88B ANNO LAVATER   MARG
HEAVENLY FACE THAT SMILES ON THEE . . . . 120 CRADLE SONG/SI   28
OF HEAVENLY SONG SOUND IN THE WILDS ONCE FORBIDDEN . . . 144 FRENCH REVOLTN   232
OR POSSESSOR OF THE COMMAND OF THE HEAVENLY HOST IS CALLD 150A MARRIAGE HH 5   PROSE
   THE DEVIL
HEADLONG FROM OUT THEIR HEAVENLY HEIGHTS DESCENDING SWIFT 200 AMERICA 12   5
   AS FIRES
THO THUS HEAVENLY BEAUTIFUL TO DRAW ME TO DESTRUCTION . 265 FOUR ZOAS 1   58
SHE RAISD HER BRIGHT HEAD SWEET PERFUMD & THUS WITH 292 FOUR ZOAS 3   26
   HEAVENLY VOICE
OUR GOD IS URIZEN THE KING KING OF THE HEAVENLY HOSTS . 298 FOUR ZOAS 4   38
RECIEVING AS A POISOND CUP RECIEVES THE HEAVENLY WINE . 324 FOUR ZOAS 7   154
[IN EDEN IN THE GARDEN OF GOD & IN HEAVENLY JERUSALEM] SUPP FOUR ZOAS 8   *
HE LIFTS THE BLUE LAMPS OF HIS EYES & CRIES WITH HEAVENLY 359 FOUR ZOAS 9   97
   VOICE
DOTH ENION AVOID THE SIGHT OF THY BLUE HEAVENLY EYES . 371 FOUR ZOAS 9   531
ALL ROUND THE HEAVENLY ARCHES & THE ODORS ROSE SINGING 376 FOUR ZOAS 9   727
   THIS SONG
HE WALKS UPON THE ETERNAL MOUNTAINS RAISING HIS HEAVENLY 379 FOUR ZOAS 9   835
   VOICE
YET HERE HIS HEAVENLY ORBS &C . . . . 381 FOUR ZOAS AD 3   2
AN ANGEL IS HERE FROM THE HEAVENLY CLIMES . . . . . 428 MARY   5
TASTE & GENIUS ARE NOT OF HEAVENLY ORIGIN & . . . . 473A ANNO REYNOLDS   MARG
SEEK NOT THY HEAVENLY FATHER THEN BEYOND THE SKIES . . 502 MILTON 20   32
UPON THE MOUNTAINS & IN VALES WITH HARP & HEAVENLY SONG 511 MILTON 25   * 68
REECHOING AGAINST THE LOVELY BLUE & SHINING HEAVENLY SHELL 520 MILTON 31   33
O NO NO I SEE AN INNUMERABLE COMPANY OF THE HEAVENLY HOST 617B V LAST JUDG/N PROSE
IN EDEN IN THE GARDEN OF GOD AND IN HEAVENLY JERUSALEM . 665 JERUSALEM 38   25
LIKE LAKES OF LIQUID LEAD INSTEAD OF HEAVENLY CHAPELS BUILT 673 JERUSALEM 43   63
AND ABOVE ALBION'S LAND WAS SEEN THE HEAVENLY CANAAN . 709 JERUSALEM 71   1
DWELL OVER THE FOUR PROVINCES OF IRELAND IN HEAVENLY LIGHT 710 JERUSALEM 71   52
MEDWAY MINGLED WITH KISHON THAMES RECIEVD THE HEAVENLY 720 JERUSALEM 79   35
   JORDAN
AS MY GARDEN & AS MY SECRET BATH SPAIN WAS MY HEAVENLY 720 JERUSALEM 79   40
   COUCH
TO REACH THE HEAVENLY ARCHES LOS BEHELD UNDAUNTED FURIOUS 738 JERUSALEM 91   42
MY HEAVENLY FATHER'S BUSINESS . . . . 748 EV GOSPEL(B)/N   8
ALWAYS BEHOLD THE FACE OF THE ?HEAVENLY FATHER . . . . 774A ANNO BERKELEY   MARG
HEAVENLY MEN BEAMING BRIGHT . . . . 805 TO BUTTS/L   50
YOUR ADVICE I SEE THE FACE OF MY HEAVENLY FATHER HE LAYS 823B LETTER 26   PROSE
   HIS
"THRO THE HEAVENLY THRONG" . . . . 837A LETTER 35

HEAVEN'S   SEE HEAVN'S

FLOWERS OF HEAVEN'S GROWTH OVER THE BANQUET-TABLE . . . 30 EDW THIRD/PS 5   32
SOLDIERS PREPARE OUR CAUSE IS HEAVEN'S CAUSE . . . . 35 WAR SONG/PS   21
IN HEAVEN'S HIGH BOWER . . . . 118 NIGHT/SI   6
AND BUILDS A HELL IN HEAVEN'S DESPITE . . . . . . 162 CLOD PEBBLE/N   12
AND BUILDS A HELL IN HEAVEN'S DESPITE . . . . . . 211 CLOD PEBBLE/SE   12
WAVES OER HEAVEN'S DEEP . . . . 219 LIT GRL LST/SE   23
BUILD WE A BOWER FOR HEAVEN'S DARLING IN THE GRIZLY DEEP 280 FOUR ZOAS 2   24
THE RIPE FRUIT BLUSHES INTO JOY IN HEAVEN'S ETERNAL HALLS 324 FOUR ZOAS 7   176
ARE WAVES THAT BEAT ON HEAVEN'S SHORE . . . . . . 432 AUGURIES   72
THE GRAVE IS HEAVEN'S GOLDEN GATE . . . . 442 DEDICATN BLAIR   7
IT WILL LEAD YOU IN AT HEAVEN'S GATE . . . . . . 551 GIVE YOU END/N   3
IT WILL LEAD YOU IN AT HEAVEN'S GATE . . . . . . 716 I GIVE YOU/J   3
FROM HEAVEN'S HIGH STREAMS . . . . 804 TO BUTTS/L   6
HEAVEN'S MOUNTAINS ADORNING . . . . 804 TO BUTTS/L   14
OF HEAVEN'S BRIGHT BEAMS . . . . 805 TO BUTTS/L   34
THE TWO ANGELS WHO STAND AT HEAVEN'S GATE EVER OPEN . . 834A LETTER 33   PROSE

HEAVENS   SEE HEAVNS

LET WAR STAIN THE BLUE HEAVENS WITH BLOODY BANNERS . . . 31 EDW THIRD/PS 5   63
LIGHTS ON SOME WOODY SHORE THE PARCHED HEAVENS . . . . 32 EDW THIPD/PS 6   29
ANGELS OF DEATH STAND IN THE LOWRING HEAVENS . . . . 35 WAR SONG/PS   17
HE CEAST THE AGED MAN [XXX] RAISD UP HIS RIGHT HAND TO 99 TIRIEL 1   * 19
   THE HEAVENS
THERE TAKE THE BODY CURSED SONS & MAY THE HEAVENS RAIN 100 TIRIEL 1   43
   WRATH
THY FATHER CALLS THY FATHER LIFTS HIS HAND UNTO THE [AIR] 108 TIRIEL 6   41
   HEAVENS
AND WHY MEN BOUND BENEATH THE HEAVENS IN A REPTILE FORM 110 TIRIEL 8   23
. . . FRANCE SHAKES AND THE HEAVENS OF FRANCE . . . . . 134 FRENCH REVOLTN   16
. . . SHAKING THE HEAVENS OF FRANCE . . . . 137 FRENCH REVOLTN   70

	PAGE	TITLE	LINE

HEAVENS   (CONTINUED)
HEAR O HEAVENS OF FRANCE	143	FRENCH REVOLTN	206
WHEN THE HEAVENS WERE SEALD WITH A STONE	143	FRENCH REVOLTN	211
DEVOUR THY LABOUR NOR LIFT UP A CLOUD IN THY HEAVENS . . .	144	FRENCH REVOLTN	226
GLEAMS OF FIRE STREAK THE HEAVENS	146	FRENCH REVOLTN	278
AND THE HEAVENS GAVE A FROWN	164	HEARD ANGEL/N	17
LET HIM LOOK UP INTO THE HEAVENS & LAUGH IN THE BRIGHT AIR	198	AMERICA 6	7
HEAVENS ETERNAL VIPER SELF-RENEWD ROLLING IN CLOUDS . . .	199	AMERICA 9	15
THE EASTERN SKY SPREADING HIS AWFUL WINGS ACROSS THE HEAVENS	201	AMERICA 13	12
WITH FIRES OF HELL DEFORM THEIR ANCIENT HEAVENS WITH SHAME & WOE	202	AMERICA 15	15
. . . ALL HIS ANGELS FRIGHT THEIR ANCIENT HEAVENS . .	202	AMERICA 15	18
THE HEAVENS MELTED FROM NORTH TO SOUTH AND URIZEN WHO SAT	202	AMERICA 16	2
ABOVE ALL HEAVENS IN THUNDERS WRAPD EMERGD HIS LEPROUS HEAD	203	AMERICA 16	3
AND THE FIERCE FLAMES BURNT ROUND THE HEAVENS	203	AMERICA 16	23
THE SOUND OF A TRUMPET THE HEAVENS	223	URIZEN 3	40
AMAZD HIS HEAVENS IMMENSE CRACKS	234	URIZEN 23	16
UPON THE AGED HEAVENS	235	URIZEN 25	8
BUT THE STREAKY SLIME IN THEIR HEAVENS	236	URIZEN 25	33
MY ROOTS ARE BRANDISHD IN THE HEAVENS MY FRUITS IN EARTH BENEATH	238	EUROPE PREL 1	8
AND THUS HER VOICE ROSE TO HER CHILDREN THE DISTANT HEAVENS REPLY	240	EUROPE 4	32
DIVIDE THE HEAVENS OF EUROPE	241	EUROPE 9	7
WITH TOOL STONES PRECIOUS SUCH ETERNAL IN THE HEAVENS . .	241	EUROPE 10	8
THE EVER-VARYING SPIRAL ASCENTS TO THE HEAVENS OF HEAVENS	241	EUROPE 10	13
ONCE OPEN TO THE HUMAN AND ELEVATED ON THE HUMAN NECK	242	EUROPE 10	28
THE YOUTH OF ENGLAND HID IN GLOOM CURSE THE PAIND HEAVENS COMPELLD	242	EUROPE 12	5
ARISE AROUND HIM IN THE CLOUDY HEAVENS OF ALBION FURIOUS	243	EUROPE 12	35
DRAWING CLOUDS OF DESPAIR THRO THE HEAVENS	248	SONG OF LOS 7	12
. . . SHOOK THE HEAVENS WITH WRATH	264	FOUR ZOAS 1	1
THE SONG OF THE AGED MOTHER WHICH SHOOK THE HEAVENS WITH WRATH	264	FOUR ZOAS 1	2
THE HEAVENS [SHALL] QUAKE THE EARTH [SHALL MOVE] [MOVES] . . .	264	FOUR ZOAS 1	* 7
DEFORMD THRO THE THREE HEAVENS DESCENDING IN FURY & FIRE	267	FOUR ZOAS 1	104
[SEARCHING FOR GLORY WISHING THAT THE HEAVENS HAD EYES TO SEE]	267	FOUR ZOAS 1	130
A MONSTER LOVELY IN THE HEAVENS OR WANDERING ON THE EARTH	269	FOUR ZOAS 1	187
REJOICING IN THE VICTORY & THE HEAVENS WERE FILLD WITH BLOOD	273	FOUR ZOAS 1	346
THEY STOOD ABOVE THE HEAVENS FORSAKEN DESOLATE SUSPENDED IN BLOOD	274	FOUR ZOAS 1	361
OVER THE JOYFUL EARTH & SEA & ASCENDED INTO THE HEAVENS	274	FOUR ZOAS 1	376
FROM HEAVENS OF JOY INTO THIS DEEP NOW RAGE BUT RAGE IN VAIN	276	FOUR ZOAS 1	433
I OPEND ALL THE FLOODGATES OF THE HEAVENS TO QUENCH HER THIRST	282	FOUR ZOAS 2	90
QUADRANGULAR THE BUILDING ROSE THE HEAVENS SQUARED BY A LINE	284	FOUR ZOAS 2	168
. . . WHOSE PORCHES ROUND THE HEAVENS	286	FOUR ZOAS 2	241
THE HEAVENS WERE CLOSD [&] AND	286	FOUR ZOAS 2	246
. . . [?THE ?HEAVENS ?WERE ?WALLD] HEAVEN WALLED ROUND . .	287	FOUR ZOAS 2	* 258
AT WILL TO STRETCH ACROSS THE HEAVENS & STEP FROM STAR TO STAR	288	FOUR ZOAS 2	298
I STILL KEEP WATCH ALTHO I TREMBLE & WITHER ACROSS THE HEAVENS	288	FOUR ZOAS 2	330
. . . THE GOLDEN HEAVENS TREMBLE	290	FOUR ZOAS 2	386
MY HEAVENS ARE BRASS MY EARTH IS IRON MY MOON A CLOD OF CLAY	290	FOUR ZOAS 2	395
DO I NOT STRETCH THE HEAVENS ABROAD OR FOLD THEM UP LIKE A GARMENT	294	FOUR ZOAS 3	107
AT HIS ENORMOUS CALL THEY FLEE INTO THE HEAVENS OF HEAVENS	308	FOUR ZOAS 5	118
AS A GOLDEN ASCENT WINDING ROUND TO THE HEAVENS OF HEAVENS	318	FOUR ZOAS 6	250
THE HEAVENS BOW WITH TERROR UNDERNEATH THEIR IRON HANDS	322	FOUR ZOAS 7	103
WHILE THE ENORMOUS SCROLLS ROLLD DREADFUL IN THE HEAVENS ABOVE	322	FOUR ZOAS 7	105
A SELF CONSUMING DARK DEVOURER RISING INTO THE HEAVENS . .	324	FOUR ZOAS 7	156
AND DOMES TERRIFIC IN THE NETHER HEAVENS FOR BENEATH . .	329	FOUR ZOAS 7	379
WAS OPEND NEW HEAVENS & A NEW EARTH BENEATH & WITHIN . .	329	FOUR ZOAS 7	380
INTO THE HEAVENS OF ENITHARMON IN A MIGHTY CIRCLE . . .	332	FOUR ZOAS 7	466
THE IMMORTAL LINES UPON THE HEAVENS TILL WITH SIGHS OF LOVE	332	FOUR ZOAS 7	471
TERRIFIC INTO THE PAIND HEAVENS THE FRUIT TREES HUMANIZING	335	FOUR ZOAS 7B	101
RENDING THE HEAVENS & EARTHS & DRINKING BLOOD IN THE HOT BATTLE	335	FOUR ZOAS 7B	103
THRO ALL THE HEAVENS URIZEN'S WEB VIBRATED TORMENT ON TORMENT	336	FOUR ZOAS 7B	122
[THEIR WINGS TOUCHD THE HEAVENS THEIR FAIR FEET HOVERD ABOVE]	341	FOUR ZOAS 8	12
[POINTED AT TOP IN HIGHEST HEAVENS OF PRECIOUS STONES & PEARL]	341	FOUR ZOAS 8	14
AND CHAINS & PULLIES FABRICATED ALL ROUND THE HEAVENS OF LOS	343	FOUR ZOAS 8	95
NAKED OF THEIR CLOTHING THE POOR SPECTRES BEFORE THE ACCUSING HEAVENS	346	FOUR ZOAS 8	219
THESE FIBRES OF THINE EYES THAT USED TO WANDER IN DISTANT HEAVENS	348	FOUR ZOAS 8	301
FOR NOW FIERCE ORC IN WRATH & FURY RISES INTO THE HEAVENS	353	FOUR ZOAS 8	460
THAT ENITHARMON HAD NUMBERD AWAY FROM THE HEAVENS . . .	356	FOUR ZOAS 8	608
. . . CRACKING THE HEAVENS ACROSS FROM IMMENSE TO IMMENSE	357	FOUR ZOAS 9	9

899

```
                                                        PAGE     TITLE           LINE
HEAVENS    (CONTINUED)
  THE HEAVENS ARE SHAKEN & THE EARTH REMOVED FROM ITS PLACE     357 FOUR ZOAS 9        16
  STRENGTH FROM THE EARTHS CONSUMD & HEAVENS & ALL HIDDEN       358 FOUR ZOAS 9    *   38
    ABYSSES
  LOWING THEY KNEEL BEFORE THE HEAVENS THE WILD BEASTS OF       358 FOUR ZOAS 9        55
    THE FORESTS
  HEAVENS OF MY BRAIN NOR WILL I LOOK UPON [REMEMBRANCE]        361 FOUR ZOAS 9       181
    FUTURITY MORE
  HE SOUNDING ROSE INTO THE HEAVENS IN NAKED MAJESTY    . . .   362 FOUR ZOAS 9       192
  OR WHERE ARE HUMAN FEET FOR LO OUR EYES ARE IN THE HEAVENS    363 FOUR ZOAS 9       229
  AS OF A BATTLE IN THE HEAVENS HARK HEARD YOU NOT              364 FOUR ZOAS 9       263
    THE TRUMPET
  THE CLOUD IS BLOOD DAZLING UPON THE HEAVENS & IN THE CLOUD    364 FOUR ZOAS 9       278
  THE NOISE OF RURAL WORK RESOUNDED THRO THE HEAVENS            365 FOUR ZOAS 9    *  299
    OF HEAVENS
  HARNESSD THEY CALLD TO URIZEN THE HEAVENS MOVED AT THEIR      365 FOUR ZOAS 9       309
    CALL
  IMMENSE UPON THE HEAVENS WITH BREAD & DELICATE REPASTS  . .   366 FOUR ZOAS 9       334
  IN THE ETERNAL HEAVENS OF HUMAN [THOUGHT] IMAGINATION         366 FOUR ZOAS 9       368
    BURIED BENEATH
  DARKNESS WAS ALL BENEATH THE HEAVENS ONLY A LITTLE LIGHT      372 FOUR ZOAS 9       560
  ABOVE ON THE BRIGHT HEAVENS IN PEACE THE SPIRITS OF MEN       372 FOUR ZOAS 9       574
    BENEATH
  MILD HE EMBRACD HER WHOM HE SOUGHT HE RAISD HER THRO THE      373 FOUR ZOAS 9       614
    HEAVENS
  SOUNDS ON THE FLOOR HEARD TERRIBLE BY ALL BENEATH             374 FOUR ZOAS 9       651
    THE HEAVENS
  LET HIM LOOK UP INTO THE HEAVENS & LAUGH IN THE BRIGHT AIR    375 FOUR ZOAS 9       671
  SO LOUD SO CLEAR IN THE WIDE HEAVENS . . . . . . . . .        375 FOUR ZOAS 9       685
  THEY FORMED HEAVENS OF SWEETEST (?WOODS) OF GOLD & SILVER     378 FOUR ZOAS 9    *  792
    & IVORY
  THE ELEMENTS SUBSIDE THE HEAVENS ROLLD ON WITH VOCAL          378 FOUR ZOAS 9       800
    HARMONY
  IN GOLDEN & IN SILVER BASKETS IN HEAVENS OF PRECIOUS STONE    379 FOUR ZOAS 9       823
  THEY LIE IN TWISTING AGONIES BENEATH THE COVRING HEAVENS      381 FOUR ZOAS AD 2 *    5
  A [MONSTER] WONDER LOVELY IN THE HEAVENS OR WANDRING ON       381 FOUR ZOAS AD 5      7
    THE EARTH
  DOES TO RAGS THE HEAVENS TEAR  . . . . . . . . . .       432 AUGURIES             76
  [THE HEAVENS IN CLOUDS ROLLING BEFORE HIM & AROUND HIM]       443A LAST JUDGMNT/L  PROSE
  BEFORE HIS FEET & AROUND HIM THE HEAVENS IN CLOUDS ARE        443A LAST JUDGMNT/L *PROSE
    ROLLING
  FOR DEATH ETERNAL IN THE HEAVENS OF ALBION & BEFORE THE       481 MILTON 2          14
    GATES
  OF JERUSALEM HIS EMANATION IN THE HEAVENS BENEATH BEULAH      481 MILTON 2          15
  HAS THREE GATES INTO THE THREE HEAVENS OF BEULAH WHICH        484 MILTON 5           7
    SHINE
  THEY TAKE UP INTO THEIR HEAVENS IN INTOXICATING DELIGHT       484 MILTON 5          10
  BUT NOW THE STARRY HEAVENS ARE FLED FROM THE MIGHTY LIMBS     486 MILTON 6          26
    OF ALBION
  I TOUCH THE HEAVENS AS AN INSTRUMENT TO GLORIFY THE LORD      494 MILTON 13         29
  THEN THERE WAS MURMURING IN THE HEAVENS OF ALBION   . . .     495 MILTON 14          4
  THEN MILTON ROSE UP FROM THE HEAVENS OF ALBION ARDOROUS       495 MILTON 14         10
  THEN MILTON KNEW THAT THE THREE HEAVENS OF BEULAH WERE        497 MILTON 15         51
    BEHELD
  IN TWENTY-SEVEN HEAVENS AND ALL THEIR HELLS WITH CHAOS  . .   498 MILTON 17         24
  OVER THE DEEPS OUTSTRETCHING HER TWENTY SEVEN HEAVENS OVER    499 MILTON 18          3
    ALBION
  SHE TIES THE KNOT OF MILKY SEED INTO TWO LOVELY HEAVENS       501 MILTON 19         60
  ARE OUR THREE HEAVENS BENEATH THE SHADES OF BEULAH LAND       501 MILTON 20          2
    OF REST
  THEY REND THE HEAVENS ROUND THE WATCHERS IN A FIERY CIRCLE    502 MILTON 20         46
  MUST TREMBLE IN THE HEAVENS & EARTHS THRO ALL THE ULRO        509 MILTON 24         39
    SPACE
  CRYING O GOD DELIVER US TO THE HEAVENS OR TO THE EARTHS       510 MILTON 25         13
  LEST THOSE THREE HEAVENS OF BEULAH SHOULD THE CREATION        512 MILTON 26         20
    DESTROY
  THE TWENTY-SEVEN HEAVENS OF BEULAH IN ULRO SEAT OF SATAN      514 MILTON 27         45
  AND IN HIS HALLOWD CENTER HOLDS THE HEAVENS OF BRIGHT         515 MILTON 28         38
    ETERNITY
  THE STARRY HEAVENS REACH NO FURTHER BUT HERE BEND AND SET     516 MILTON 29         10
  AND IF HE MOVE HIS DWELLING-PLACE HIS HEAVENS ALSO MOVE       516 MILTON 29         12
  TO GIVE THEM TO THEIR LOVELY HEAVENS TILL THE GREAT           517 MILTON 29         52
    JUDGMENT DAY
  THE THREE HEAVENS OF ULRO WHERE TIRZAH & HER SISTERS   . .    517 MILTON 29         55
  THE JONQUIL THE MILD LILLY OPES HER HEAVENS EVERY TREE  . .   521 MILTON 31         60
  I HAVE TURNED MY BACK UPON THESE HEAVENS BUILDED ON CRUELTY   521 MILTON 32          3
  RENDING THE HEAVENS OF BEULAH WITH YOUR THUNDERS              523 MILTON 34          5
    & LIGHTNINGS
  AND OLOLON LOOKED DOWN INTO THE HEAVENS OF ULRO IN FEAR       524 MILTON 34         49
  THRO ALL THE TWENTY-SEVEN HEAVENS MAY NOT SLUMBER NOR SLEEP   526 MILTON 35         65
  THUS IT APPEARS TO MORTAL EYES & THOSE OF THE ULRO HEAVENS    527 MILTON 36         11
  AND THESE THE NAMES OF THE TWENTY-SEVEN HEAVENS & THEIR       528 MILTON 37         35
    CHURCHES
  THE HEAVENS ARE THE CHERUB THE TWELVE GODS ARE SATAN    . .   529 MILTON 37         60
  THEN LOUD THE FURNACES OF LOS WERE HEARD & SEEN AS SEVEN      531 MILTON 39         14
    HEAVENS
  TILL THE HEAVENS & EARTH ARE GONE . . . . . . . . .     558 THE CAVERNS/N        10
  THE HEAVENS OPENING AROUND HIM BY UNFOLDING THE CLOUDS  . .   606B V LAST JUDG/N   PROSE
  REMOVING THE [?FORMER] OLD HEAVENS & THE OLD EARTH    . . .   612A V LAST JUDG/N   PROSE
  IN THE HEAVENS TO ANNOUNCE THE SUNSHINE HOLIDAY    . . . .    618C ILLUS MILTON    PROSE
  THE THREE DESTINIES SIT ON THE CIRCLES OF PLATO'S HEAVENS     619B ILLUS MILTON    PROSE
  THESE HEAVENS ARE VENUS JUPITER & MARS HERMES FLIES BEFORE    619B ILLUS MILTON    PROSE
```

		PAGE	TITLE	LINE

HEAVENS   (CONTINUED)

	PAGE	TITLE	LINE
IS SEEN IN THE HEAVENS THROWING HIS DARTS & FLAMES OF FIRE	619B	ILLUS MILTON	*PROSE
SHUDDRING THE HEAVENS TO LOOK UPON ME BEHOLD WHAT CRUELTIES	627	JERUSALEM 8	19
IN ALL THE TWENTY-SEVEN HEAVENS NUMBERD FROM ADAM TO LUTHER	633	JERUSALEM 13	32
WITH THEIR INHABITANTS IN THE TWENTY-SEVEN HEAVENS BENEATH BEULAH	634	JERUSALEM 13	51
THEE WHOM I THOUGHT PURE AS THE HEAVENS IN INNOCENCE & FEAR	644	JERUSALEM 21	20
BECAUSE THEY TAUGHT LUVAH TO RISE INTO MY CLOUDED HEAVENS	644	JERUSALEM 21	31
BUT NOW THE STARRY HEAVENS ARE FLED FROM THE MIGHTY LIMBS OF ALBION	649C	JERUSALEM 27	PROSE
ON HIS ROCK ERE YET THE STARRY HEAVENS WERE FLED AWAY · ·	660	JERUSALEM 34	20
AND CURSES WITH HIS MIGHTY ARMS BRANDISHD AGAINST THE HEAVENS	667	JERUSALEM 40	37
AND LAY ITS HEAVENS & THEIR INHABITANTS IN BLOOD OF PUNISHMENT	668	JERUSALEM 41	20
LOS THOU NOW DISCOVEREST THY TURPITUDE TO THE HEAVENS · ·	669	JERUSALEM 42	11
SEEING THESE HEAVENS & HELLS CONGLOBING IN THE VOID · · ·	672	JERUSALEM 43	16
· · · HEAVENS OVER HELLS · · · · · · · · · · ·	672	JERUSALEM 43	16
FROM HOWLING VICTIMS OF LAW BUILDING HEAVENS TWENTY-SEVEN-FOLD	672	JERUSALEM 43	18
THEY ARE BEGINNING TO FORM HEAVENS & HELLS IN IMMENSE · ·	680	JERUSALEM 49	61
CIRCLES THE HELLS FOR FOOD TO THE HEAVENS FOOD OF TORMENT	680	JERUSALEM 49	62
IN CRUEL HOLINESS IN THEIR HEAVENS OF CHASTITY & UNCIRCUMCISION	680	JERUSALEM 49	64
LIKE SEVEN BURNING HEAVENS RANGD FROM SOUTH TO NORTH · ·	684	JERUSALEM 53	14
BURST FORTH IN STREAMS OF BLOOD UPON THE HEAVENS & DARK NIGHT	696	JERUSALEM 62	31
THE DRUID SONS OF ALBION & THE HEAVENS A VOID AROUND UNFATHOMABLE	697	JERUSALEM 63	19
THE HEAVENS MIGHT REVOLVE & ETERNITY BE BOUND IN THEIR CHAIN	702	JERUSALEM 66	5
AND AS THEIR EYE & EAR SHRUNK THE HEAVENS SHRUNK AWAY · ·	702	JERUSALEM 66	40
THEY LOOK FORTH THE SUN IS SHRUNK THE HEAVENS ARE SHRUNK	703	JERUSALEM 66	50
THESE FIBRES OF THINE EYES THAT USED TO BEAM IN DISTANT HEAVENS	705	JERUSALEM 67	47
TO SEE THE BOY SPRING INTO HEAVENS SOUNDING FROM MY SIGHT	705	JERUSALEM 67	58
THE HEAVENS ARE CUT LIKE A MANTLE AROUND FROM THE CLIFFS OF ALBION	706	JERUSALEM 68	19
THE STARRY HEAVENS ALL WERE FLED FROM THE MIGHTY LIMBS OF ALBION	709	JERUSALEM 70	32
IN HEAVENS & EARTHS AS IN YOUR OWN BOSOM YOU BEAR YOUR HEAVEN	709	JERUSALEM 71	17
AND ALL HER TWENTY-SEVEN HEAVENS NOW HID & NOW REVEALD · ·	715	JERUSALEM 75	4
AND THESE THE NAMES OF THE TWENTY-SEVEN HEAVENS & THEIR CHURCHES	716	JERUSALEM 75	10
THUS ARE THE HEAVENS FORMD BY LOS WITHIN THE MUNDANE SHELL	716	JERUSALEM 75	23
BUT NOW THE STARRY HEAVENS ARE FLED FROM THE MIGHTY LIMBS OF ALBION	716	JERUSALEM 75	27
OF FIRE SURROUNDING ALL THE HEAVENS IT WENT · · · · ·	717	STOOD AMONG/J	3
THY MASCULINE FROM THY FEMININE HARDENING AGAINST THE HEAVENS	721	JERUSALEM 79	71
WOMAN MUST PERISH & THE HEAVENS OF HEAVENS REMAIN NO MORE	722	JERUSALEM 80	15
THE SPECTRE BUILDED STUPENDOUS WORKS TAKING THE STARRY HEAVENS	738	JERUSALEM 91	33
HEAVENS A MOTH OF GOLD & SILVER MOCKING HIS ANXIOUS GRASP	739	JERUSALEM 91	50
HIS AWFUL LIMBS INTO THE HEAVENS HE WALKED CLOTHED IN FLAMES	742	JERUSALEM 95	7
SOON ALL AROUND REMOTE THE HEAVENS BURNT WITH FLAMING FIRES	744	JERUSALEM 96	40
· · · BENDING THRO THE WIDE HEAVENS · · · · · · · ·	744	JERUSALEM 98	2
DISTORTS THE HEAVENS FROM POLE TO POLE · · · · · · ·	753	EV GOSPEL(D)/N	104
THE ANCIENT HEAVENS IN SILENT AWE · · · · · · · · ·	754	EV GOSPEL(E)/N	12
THE HEAVENS ARE NOT CLEAN IN THY SIGHT · · · · · · ·	754	EV GOSPEL(E)/N	24
THY SUBSTANTIAL ASTRONOMICAL TELESCOPIC HEAVENS · · · ·	788D	ANNO THORNTON	MARG
NOW MY LOT IN THE HEAVENS IS THIS · · · · · · · · ·	799	TO FLAXMAN/L	5
· · · TERRORS APPEARD IN THE HEAVENS ABOVE · · · · · ·	799	TO FLAXMAN/L	7
THE HEAVENS COMMANDING · · · · · · · · · · · ·	805	TO BUTTS/L	48
THE HEAVENS DROP WITH HUMAN GORE · · · · · · · · ·	818	HAPPINESS/L	82

HEAVEN UTTERD

	PAGE	TITLE	LINE
· · · I ROSE TO BRING MY PRINCE HEAVEN UTTERD COUNSEL · ·	141	FRENCH REVOLTN	152

HEAVES

	PAGE	TITLE	LINE
HEAVES IN ENORMOUS CIRCLES NOW THE TIMES ARE RETURND UPON THEE	199	AMERICA 9	19
AND CRUMBLING WITH BURSTING SOBS HEAVES · · · · · · ·	257	BOOK OF LOS 4	21
STRETCHD OVER THE IMMENSE HEAVES IN STRONG SHUDDERS SILENT HIS VOICE	302	FOUR ZOAS 4	173
WITH MOLTEN ORE HE HEAVES THE IRON CLIFFS IN HIS RATTLING CHAINS	486	MILTON 6	30
HEAVES IN THE HAND OF PALAMABRON WHO IN LONDON'S DARKNESS	636	JERUSALEM 16	9
THEM HOWLS THE WOLF OF FAMINE DEEP HEAVES THE OCEAN BLACK THUNDERING	741	JERUSALEM 94	16

HEAVIER

	PAGE	TITLE	LINE
MY TASK IS GREAT MY BURDEN HEAVIER THAN · · · · · · ·	19	EDW THIRD/PS 2	4
HEAVIER TO ME & PITT WOULD PRESCRIBE DISTRESS FOR A · · ·	809B	LETTER 20	PROSE

HEAVIEST

	PAGE	TITLE	LINE
THO IT GOES DOWN ON THE HEAVIEST SIDE · · · · · · ·	476B	ANNO REYNOLDS	MARG

HEAVILY

	PAGE	TITLE	LINE
THE STARRY WHEELS REVOLVD HEAVILY OVER THE FURNACES · · ·	624	JERUSALEM 5	46
WHICH REVOLVE HEAVILY IN THE MIGHTY VOID ABOVE THE FURNACES	624	JERUSALEM 5	53

HEAVINESS

	PAGE	TITLE	LINE
AN EVEN TINT IS NOT IN NATURE IT PRODUCES HEAVINESS · · ·	603B	PUB ADDR AD/N	PROSE

HEAVING

	PAGE	TITLE	LINE
· · · [HEAVING] SHRINKING IN PANGS OF DEATH · · · · ·	99	TIRIEL 1	* 20

```
                                                        PAGE    TITLE          LINE
HEAVING    (CONTINUED)
    . . . SWEPT OVER THE HEAVING SEA  . . . . . . . . .  197 AMERICA 3             13
    . . . SWEPT OVER THE HEAVING SEA  . . . . . . . . .  204 AMERICA CANC A        13
    HEAVING DOLOROUS ANGUISHD UNBEARABLE  . . . . . . .  228 URIZEN 10             32
    OVER THE HEAVING DELUGE HE SAW LOS & ENITHARMON EMERGE  . .  297 FOUR ZOAS 4    2
    THEY ROSE IN STRENGTH ABOVE THE HEAVING DELUGE IN MIGHTY  297 FOUR ZOAS 4       4
        SCORN
    RESTLESS THE IMMORTAL INCHAIND HEAVING DOLOROUS  . . . .  303 FOUR ZOAS 4     215
    [HEAVING XXX] HEAVD LIKE AN EARTHQUAKE LABRING WITH   347 FOUR ZOAS 8      *  249
        CONVULSIVE GROANS
    IN THE FIERCE WIND ROUND HEAVING ROCKS & MOUNTAINS FILLD  363 FOUR ZOAS 9    240
        WITH GROANS
    INTO HIS THUNDERING BELLOWS HEAVING IT FOR A LOUD BLAST  726 JERUSALEM 82     58
HEAVN
    MY LORD WAS LIKE A STAR IN HIGHEST HEAVN  . . . . . .    5 FAIR ELENOR/PS      45
    HIS FACE IS FAIR AS HEAVN  . . . . . . . . . . . .      6 MY SILKS/PS          7
    WHETHER IN HEAVN YE WANDER FAIR  . . . . . . . . .     10 TO MUSES/PS          5
    WHEN THE CRIES OF BLOOD TEAR HORROR FROM HEAVN  . . .   18 EDW THIRD/PS 1       7
    EACH KNOWS HIS RANK AND HEAVN MARSHAL ALL  . . . . .    19 EDW THIRD/PS 1      52
    WATER HIM WITH THY ADVICE AND HEAVN  . . . . . . . .    26 EDW THIRD/PS 3     214
    [THEN LIKE A MIGHTY WIND THEY RAISE TO HEAVN THE VOICE   59 HOLY THURS/IM      10
        OF SONG]
    [OR LIKE HARMONIOUS THUNDERINGS THE SEATS OF HEAVN AMONG]  59 HOLY THURS/IM    11
    [LIKE ANGELS ON THE THRONE OF HEAVN RAISING THE VOICE OF   59 HOLY THURS/IM    13
        PRAISE]
    THEN LIKE A MIGHTY WIND THEY RAISE TO HEAVN THE VOICE OF   59 HOLY THURS/IM    15
        SONG
    OR LIKE HARMONIOUS THUNDERINGS THE SEATS OF HEAVN AMONG   59 HOLY THURS/IM     16
    HE INDIGNANT DEPARTED ON HORSES OF HEAVN . . . . . .  143 FRENCH REVOLTN      201
    THE MILD PEACEABLE NATIONS BE OPENED TO HEAVN . . . .  145 FRENCH REVOLTN     237
    THEN SWORE A GREAT OATH THAT MADE HEAVN QUAKE  . . . .  187 WHEN KLOPSTK/N *    5
    FROM HEAVEN TO HEAVN THRO ALL ITS MESHES ALTERING    345 FOUR ZOAS 8         177
        THE VORTEXES
    [THE] YET PALE THE JUST MAN STANDS ERECT & LOOKING UP TO  358 FOUR ZOAS 9   *  51
        HEAVN
    UNHAPPY THO IN HEAVN HE OBEYD HE MURMURD NOT HE WAS SILENT  481 MILTON 2      18
    I COME TO DISCOVER BEFORE HEAVN & HELL THE           530 MILTON 38           43
        SELF RIGHTEOUSNESS
    BUT I ALONE AM GOD & I ALONE IN HEAVN & EARTH  . . .  530 MILTON 38           56
    AND ANCIENT NIGHT SPREAD OVER ALL THE HEAVN HIS MANTLE  531 MILTON 39         30
        OF LAWS
HEAVNLY
    OH BLESS THOSE LIMBS BEAMING WITH HEAVNLY LIGHT  . . . .    9 FRESH FROM/PS     8
    OR DOES TH AFFLICTED MAN THY HEAVNLY BOSOM MOVE  . . .   15 IMIT SPEN/PS       53
    STIFF SHUDDERINGS SHOOK THE HEAVNLY THRONES FRANCE SPAIN  203 AMERICA 16       16
        & ITALY
    . . . THE HEAVNLY FATHER ONLY  . . . . . . . . . .    264 FOUR ZOAS 1         12
    FALLEN FIENDS OF HEAVNLY BIRTH  . . . . . . . . . .   754 EV GOSPEL(E)/N      50
HEAVN'S
    UNLOCK HEAVN'S GOLDEN GATES AND ISSUE FORTH  . . . . .    3 TO MORNING/PS       2
    AND THRO HEAVN'S HALLS THY AIRY FLIGHT DOST THROW  . . .   15 IMIT SPEN/PS     21
HEAVNS
    THE HEAVNS ARE SHOOK WITH ROARING WAR  . . . . . . .    13 GWIN KING/PS        71
    THE STENCH OF BLOOD MAKES SICK THE HEAVNS  . . . . .    13 GWIN KING/PS        95
    NEER SHOUTED TO THE HEAVNS NOR SHOOK THE FIELD  . . .   23 EDW THIRD/PS 3      76
    THE ROARING FIRES RAN OER THE HEAVNS  . . . . . . .   225 URIZEN 5            12
    A DISK OF BLOOD DISTANT & HEAVNS & EARTHS ROLL DARK BETWEEN  495 MILTON 14     27
    SUCH ARE THE LAWS THY FALSE HEAVNS BUT LAWS OF ETERNITY  530 MILTON 38         33
    JESUS OUR FATHER WHO ART IN THY HEAVNS CALLD BY THY NAME  788A ANNO THORNTON * MARG
HEAVY
    RIDES HEAVY HIS STORMS ARE UNCHAIND SHEATHED  . . . . .    3 TO WINTER/PS       6
    THE ENEMY FIGHT IN CHAINS INVISIBLE CHAINS BUT HEAVY  . .   18 EDW THIRD/PS 1   13
    HE CEAST THE HEAVY CLOUDS CONFUSD ROLLD ROUND THE LOFTY  106 TIRIEL 5          14
        TOWERS
    SOON HIS HEAVY MANE  . . . . . . . . . . . . . .    114 LIT GRL FND/SI       26
    RUNS ACHING COLD INTO THE SCEPTER TOO HEAVY FOR MORTAL  134 FRENCH REVOLTN      4
        GRASP NO MORE
    CLOUDS OF WISDOM PROPHETIC REPLY AND ROLL OVER THE PALACE  134 FRENCH REVOLTN  12
        ROOF HEAVY
    . . . HIS BROWS FOLDED HEAVY HIS FOREHEAD WAS IN AFFLICTION  137 FRENCH REVOLTN  79
    BUT MORNING DAWND HEAVY UPON ME . . . . . . . . . .   141 FRENCH REVOLTN     152
    . . .IN DAY OF THE BRITISH FLAG WHEN HEAVY CANNONS  . . .  147 FRENCH REVOLTN  280
    [[AND] DOWN POURD THE HEAVY RAIN]  . . . . . . . . .   164 HEARD ANGEL/N       18
    BREAK THIS HEAVY CHAIN  . . . . . . . . . . . . .   169 EARTHS ANSWR/N       21
    TO BEHOLD MY HEAVY CHAIN  . . . . . . . . . . . .   169 MIRTLE SHADE/N       12
    A BENDED BOW IS LIFTED IN HEAVEN & A HEAVY IRON CHAIN  . .  197 AMERICA 3        7
    A BENDED BOW IN HEAVEN IS LIFTED & A HEAVY IRON CHAIN  . .  204 AMERICA CANC A   7
    . . . [?TILL ?BY THE] ?FROZEN CHILL & HEAVY EVEN TO THE  205 AMERICA CANC C *    9
        CITY GATE
    BREAK THIS HEAVY CHAIN  . . . . . . . . . . . . .   211 EARTHS ANSR/SE       21
    IN HEAVY PAIN STRIVING STRUGGLING  . . . . . . . .   229 URIZEN 11            20
    WALK HEAVY SOFT AND BENT ARE THE BONES OF VILLAGERS  . .  243 EUROPE 12         31
    BETWEEN THE CLOUDS OF URIZEN THE FLAMES OF ORC ROLL HEAVY  243 EUROPE 12        32
    CLOUDS ROLL HEAVY UPON THE ALPS ROUND ROUSSEAU & VOLTAIRE  246 SONG OF LOS 4    18
    SUNK PRECIPITANT HEAVY DOWN DOWN  . . . . . . . . .   258 BOOK OF LOS 4        28
    THE LUNGS HEAVE INCESSANT DULL AND HEAVY  . . . . . .   258 BOOK OF LOS 4       54
    HEAVY FALLING HIS ORGANS LIKE ROOTS  . . . . . . . .   259 BOOK OF LOS 4        64
    SEPERATING THE HEAVY AND THIN  . . . . . . . . . .   259 BOOK OF LOS 5         5
    DOWN THE HEAVY SUNK CLEAVING AROUND  . . . . . . . .   259 BOOK OF LOS 5        6
    LET US REFUSE THE PLOW & SPADE THE HEAVY ROLLER & SPIKED  274 FOUR ZOAS 1      387
    TO CARRY THE HEAVY BASKET ON OUR SCORCHED SHOULDERS TO SIFT  286 FOUR ZOAS 2   221
    FURROWD WITH WHIPS & OUR FLESH BRUISED WITH THE HEAVY  286 FOUR ZOAS 2         226
        BASKET
```

		PAGE	TITLE	LINE

HEAVY   (CONTINUED)
HE SPOKE MUSTERING HIS HEAVY CLOUDS AROUND HIM BLACK OPAKE   294 FOUR ZOAS 3   108
HAMMER OF URTHONA FORMING UNDER HIS HEAVY HAND THE HOURS   302 FOUR ZOAS 4   179
THE PANGS OF HOPE BEGAN IN HEAVY PAIN STRIVING STRUGGLING   303 FOUR ZOAS 4   232
WERE HEAVY & DULL & THEIR EYES & NOSTRILS CLOSED UP . .   315 FOUR ZOAS 6   125
THAT SWAGGD HEAVY WITH THE ACCURSED DOUGH THE HOAR FROST   322 FOUR ZOAS 7   100
     RAGD
FOR HIS FRAIL EYES WERE FADED & HIS EARS HEAVY & DULL   . .   326 FOUR ZOAS 7   250
HOWLING IN DISCONTENT BLACK & HEAVY UTTERING BRUTE SOUNDS   338 FOUR ZOAS 7B   224
STEEPING THE DIREFUL WEB OF RELIGION SWAGGING HEAVY IT FELL   345 FOUR ZOAS 8   176
AND NOW HE BEATS THE HEAVY AIR WITH HIS ENORMOUS WINGS . .   354 FOUR ZOAS 8   526
WHILE I STOOD BOUND WITH CORDS & HEAVY CHAINS YOUR   364 FOUR ZOAS 9   276
     HIPOCRISY
THE HEAVY ROLLER TO BREAK THE CLODS TO PASS OVER   365 FOUR ZOAS 9   307
     THE NATIONS
BUT THOU ART STILL HEAVY AND DULL AWAKE ALBION AWAKE   . .   506 MILTON 23   5
AND THE HARROW & HEAVY THUNDERING ROLLER UPON THE MOUNTAINS   510 MILTON 25   11
AND MURMURS OF THUNDER ROLLING HEAVY LONG & LOUD OVER THE   511 MILTON 25   64
     MOUNTAINS
THE WIND BLOWS HEAVY LOUD THEY THUNDER THRO THE DARKSOM SKY   512 MILTON 26   8
IN BLIGHTS OF THE EAST THE HEAVY ROLLER FOLLOWS IN HOWLINGS   514 MILTON 27   48
     OF WOE
AND WITH GREAT AND HEAVY SHADOWS . . . . 577A DESC CAT 4   PROSE
ARE NOT SHADOWS MORE UNMEANING THAN LINES AND MORE HEAVY   577A DESC CAT 4   PROSE
HEAVY LUMPS OF CUNNING & IGNORANCE AS THEIR WORKS SHEW . . 593C PUB ADDRESS/N   PROSE
AND INTO THE MOUNTAINS OF THE ANVILS & OF THE HEAVY HAMMERS   629 JERUSALEM 10   2
IN HEAVY WREATHES FOLDS OVER EVERY NATION CRUEL WORKS   . .   636 JERUSALEM 15   17
ROUND FROM HEAVEN TO EARTH DOWN FALLING WITH HEAVY BLOW   636 JERUSALEM 16   12
OF THE MINES OF CORNWALL & DERBYSHIRE LAYS UPON HIS BOSOM   741 JERUSALEM 94   8
     HEAVY
SURROUNDING HIS AWFUL MEMBERS THOU SEEST THE SUN IN HEAVY   742 JERUSALEM 95   11
     CLOUDS
HEAVY BOXES & PORTFOLIOS FULL OF PRINTS AND NOW BEGINS . . 802B LETTER 14   PROSE
CHEARFULNESS & WELCOME THO OUR LUGGAGE WAS VERY HEAVY   . . 803A LETTER 15   PROSE
NOW FOR IT WILL HANG HEAVY ON MY DEVIL WHO TERRIBLY RESENTS 830C LETTER 30   PROSE
AND HEAVY THE GERMAN FLUTE COLOUR WHICH WAS USED BY . . . 864C LETTER 61   PROSE
HEAVY BROWD
BUT HEAVY BROWD JEALOUSIES LOWER OER THE LOUVRE . . . . .   136 FRENCH REVOLTN   59
HEAVY-WAVING
HEAVY-WAVING HOWLING WEEPING . . . .   248 SONG OF LOS 7   16
HEBER
NOAH SHEM ARPHAXAD CAINAN THE SECOND SALAH HEBER . . . .   528 MILTON 37   38
ABRAHAM HEBER SHEM AND NOAH WHO WERE DRUIDS . . . . . 649C JERUSALEM 27   PROSE
IN BRICKS TO BUILD THE PYRAMIDS OF HEBER & TERAH BUT LOS   657 JERUSALEM 31   12
NOAH SHEM ARPHAXAD CAINAN THE SECOND SALAH HEBER . . . .   716 JERUSALEM 75   13
HEBREW
THE HEBREW NATION DID NOT WRITE IT . . . .   187 HEBREW NATN/N   1
THE HEBREW BIBLE & THE GOSPEL OF JESUS ARE NOT ALLEGORY   . 604D V LAST JUDG/N   PROSE
WHILE THE HEBREW BIBLE & THE GREEK GOSPEL ARE GENUINE   . 605C V LAST JUDG/N   PROSE
THE CHILDREN OF ABRAHAM OR HEBREW CHURCH ARE . . . . . 610B V LAST JUDG/N   PROSE
WHO ARE THE OFFSPRING OF THE HEBREW . . . . 610C V LAST JUDG/N   PROSE
HEBREW WHOM SHE DIVIDED INTO TWELVE & SOLD INTO EGYPT   .   739 JERUSALEM 92   4
THEN SCATTERD THE EGYPTIAN & HEBREW TO THE FOUR WINDS   .   739 JERUSALEM 92   5
HEBREW ART IS CALLED SIN BY THE DEIST SCIENCE . . . . . 776C INSC LAOCOON   PROSE
VERY EASY AM NOW LEARNING MY HEBREW (ALEPH BETH GIMMEL)   821D LETTER 25   PROSE
IF THE HEBREW BIBLE IS AS WELL TRANSLATED WHICH I DO NOT   821D LETTER 25   PROSE
HEBREWS
WHOSE HISTORY PRECEDED THAT OF THE HEBREWS . . . . . . 609C V LAST JUDG/N   PROSE
HEBRON
HE HATH TOOK ROOT IN HEBRON IN THE LAND OF HAND & HYLE .   715 JERUSALEM 74   49
HECATE
LIKE FABLED HECATE SHE DOTH BIND THEM TO HER LAW . . . . 41D THEN SHE BORE   PROSE
BE RECOVERED BE HECATE THE FIGURE WITH THE TORCH AND SNAKE 840D LETTER 40   PROSE
HECATE A VERY FINE THING INDEED WHICH I HAVE . . . . . 849A LETTER 45   PROSE
THE TWO CARTOONS WHICH I HAVE OF HECATE & PLINY ARE . . . 855A LETTER 53   PROSE
BUT THE HECATE IS A FINISHD PRODUCTION WHICH WILL CALL FOR 855A LETTER 53   PROSE
THEREFORE HECATE MUST BE A FINISHD PLATE I CONSIDER . . . 855B LETTER 53   PROSE
HECLA
IS DRIVN YELLING TO HIS CAVES BENEATH MOUNT HECLA   . . .   3 TO WINTER/PS   16
HE'D
& SET HIS WIG ON FIRE & THROW IT AT THE PEOPLE HE'D CRY   48B ISLAND MOON 4   PROSE
AND THE ANGEL TOLD TOM IF HE'D BE A GOOD BOY   . . . .   118 CHIMNEY SWP/SI   19
HE'D HAVE GOD FOR HIS FATHER & NEVER WANT JOY   . . . .   118 CHIMNEY SWP/SI   20
I ASKED A THIEF [IF HE'D] TO STEAL ME A PEACH . . . . .   163 ASKED THIEF/N   * 1
AND HE'D PAY FOR MORE IF TO HIM I WOULD PRAY   . . . .   559 I ROSE UP AT/N   18
HE'D HAVE DONE ANY THING TO PLEASE US . . . .   750 EV GOSPEL(C)/N   26
HE'D HAVE DONE ANY THING TO PLEASE US . . . .   752 EV GOSPEL(D)/N   60
[CAESAR SAID HE'D RATHER BE THE (FIRST IN) A VILLAGE (THAN) SUPP ANNO REYNOLDS   * MARG
     SECOND]
HEDGE
OFF SLOTH AND BUILD HIMSELF A HUT AND HEDGE . . . . .   26 EDW THIRD/PS 3   197
HEEDFUL
THE ANGELS MOST HEEDFUL . . . .   119 NIGHT/SI   30
HEEL
OF MYSTERY UNDER HIS HEEL . . . .   252 AHANIA 3   62
AGE AFTER AGE TILL UNDERNEATH HIS HEEL A DEADLY ROOT . .   321 FOUR ZOAS 7   31
HAS ONLY HURT PAINE'S HEEL WHILE PAINE HAS BROKEN HIS HEAD 396C ANNO WATSON   MARG
HIS RIGHT FOOT STRETCHES TO THE SEA ON DOVER CLIFFS HIS   531 MILTON 39   40
     HEEL
HE SAT BY TYBURN'S BROOK AND UNDERNEATH HIS HEEL SHOT UP   652 JERUSALEM 28   14
I AM LEFT TO THE TRAMPLING FOOT & THE SPURNING HEEL . . .   695 JERUSALEM 62   3
WHERE IS THE TREE OF GOOD & EVIL THAT ROOTED BENEATH THE   746 JERUSALEM 98   47
     CRUEL HEEL

		PAGE	TITLE	LINE
HEIGHT				
	STIFLING I LIVE IF DASHD IN PIECES FROM A ROCKY HEIGHT . .	298	FOUR ZOAS 4	14
	OF TWENTY-FIVE CUBITS IN HEIGHT SUCH SPACE IS HIS UNIVERSE	516	MILTON 29	7
	ONE HUNDRED FEET IN HEIGHT SOME WERE PAINTED AS PICTURES	566A	DESC CAT 2	PROSE
	THOUGH THE FIGURES WERE ONE HUNDRED FEET IN HEIGHT . . .	566A	DESC CAT 2	PROSE
HEIGHTH	**SEE HIGHTH**			
	FROM AN OAK ITS HEIGHTH FROM A DAISY ITS LOWNESS & [CHAOS]	81C	ANNO LAVATER	* MARG
	. . . SOMETIMES STRETCHD OUT IN [LENGTH] HEIGHTH . . .	315	FOUR ZOAS 6	122
	AS [IS] IT IS CAPABLE OF BEING PLACED IN ANY HEIGHTH & INDEED	601A	PUB ADDRESS/N	*PROSE
	. . . FROM THE STARRY HEIGHTH TO THE STARRY DEPTH . . .	630	JERUSALEM 11	12
	FOR THE SPACES REACHD FROM THE STARRY HEIGHTH TO THE STARRY DEPTH	631	JERUSALEM 12	23
	INCREASING INWARDS INTO LENGTH AND BREADTH AND HEIGHTH . .	635	JERUSALEM 14	18
	AND THE NORTH IS BREADTH THE SOUTH IS HEIGHTH & DEPTH . .	635	JERUSALEM 14	29
HEIGHTS				
	HEADLONG FROM OUT THEIR HEAVENLY HEIGHTS DESCENDING SWIFT AS FIRES	200	AMERICA 12	5
	SHOT FROM THE HEIGHTS OF ENITHARMON [BEFORE THE TRUMPET BLEW]	245	EUROPE 15	1
	AH HOW IS THIS ONCE ON THE HEIGHTS I STRETCHD MY THRONE SUBLIME	310	FOUR ZOAS 5	191
	UPON THE HEIGHTS OF AMALEK TAKING REFUGE IN HIS ARMS .	348	FOUR ZOAS 8	270
	UPON THE HEIGHTS OF [ENTUTHON THAT] AMALEK TAKING REFUGE IN HIS ARMS	382	FOUR ZOAS AD 6	3
	FOUR PILLARS OF DIFFERENT HEIGHTS AND SIZES	402A	ANNO BACON	MARG
	BEFORE LONDON TO HAMPSTEAD'S BREADTHS & HIGHGATE'S HEIGHTS TO	485	MILTON 6	9
	MALAH'S ON BLACKHEATH RAHAB & NOAH DWELL ON WINDSOR'S HEIGHTS	525	MILTON 35	9
	ON HIGHGATE'S HEIGHTS MAGNIFICENT WEAVES OVER TREMBLING THAMES	525	MILTON 35	12
	HIGHGATE'S HEIGHTS & HAMPSTEAD'S TO POPLAR HACKNEY & BOW	729	JERUSALEM 84	1
	HAND HAD HIS FURNACE ON HIGHGATE'S HEIGHTS & IT REACHD . .	736	JERUSALEM 90	23
HELA				
	[?HILI] HELA MY YOUNGEST DAUGHTER YOU SHALL LEAD ME FROM THIS PLACE	106	TIRIEL 5	* 24
	HE CEAST & [?HILI] HELA LED HER FATHER FROM THE NOISOM PLACE	107	TIRIEL 5	* 26
	AND [?HILI] HELA LED HER FATHER THRO THE SILENT OF THE NIGHT	107	TIRIEL 6	* 1
	NOW [?HILI] HELA I CAN GO WITH PLEASURE & DWELL WITH HAR & HEVA	107	TIRIEL 6	* 3
	THAT OUR FEET MAKE REMEMBER [?HILI] HELA I HAVE SAVD THEE FROM DEATH	107	TIRIEL 6	* 6
	TRUE [?HILI] HELA THIS IS THE DESERT OF ALL THOSE CRUEL ONES	107	TIRIEL 6	* 16
	LOOK ON MY EYES HELA & SEE FOR THOU HAST EYES TO SEE . .	108	TIRIEL 6	29
	HELA MY DAUGHTER LISTEN THOU [XXX] ART THE DAUGHTER OF TIRIEL	108	TIRIEL 6	* 40
	WHAT HAVE I DONE HELA MY DAUGHTER FEARST THOU NOW THE CURSE	108	TIRIEL 6	46
	WERE FRIGHTED BY THE DISMAL CRIES OF HELA ON THE MOUNTAINS	109	TIRIEL 7	20
HELD				
	HELD IN TH ALMIGHTY'S HAND	13	GWIN KING/PS	66
	. . . AND THE DEN NAMD HORROR HELD A MAN	135	FRENCH REVOLTN	26
	SOME NATIONS HELD ONE PRINCIPLE FOR THE ORIGIN & SOME ANOTHER	153D	MARRIAGE HH 12	PROSE
	& WE HELD BY THE ROOTS OF TREES AND HUNG OVER THIS IMMENSITY	155D	MARRIAGE HH 17	PROSE
	LAUNCHD TO THE UNKNOWN SHORE WHILE SOTHA HELD THE NORTHERN HELM	204	AMERICA CANC B	21
	CUT BY THE PLOW OF AGES HELD IN URIZEN'S STRONG HAND . .	283	FOUR ZOAS 2	119
	HELD THE FIERCE BOY LOS NAILD HIM DOWN BINDING AROUND HIS LIMBS	307	FOUR ZOAS 5	101
	IN HIS RIGHT HAND HIS HAMMER THARMAS HELD HIS SHEPHERD'S CROOK	377	FOUR ZOAS 9	776
	ASTONISHMENT HELD THE ASSEMBLY IN AN AWFUL SILENCE AND TEARS	490	MILTON 9	36
	AND CALLD ME SIN AND FOR A SIGN PORTENTOUS HELD ME SOON	493	MILTON 12	* 39
	WEEPING FOR MILTON MUTE WONDER HELD THE DAUGHTERS OF BEULAH	518	MILTON 30	6
	AND HELD THE EMPIRE OF THE WORLD IN THE DARK AGE	578C	DESC CAT 5	PROSE
	[WHICH OPINION HAS BEEN HELD OUT TO [MY] ME BY SUCH MEN AS]	591D	PUB ADDRESS/N	*PROSE
	[TILL AT LENGTH CHRISTIAN CHARITY IS HELD OUT AS A MOTIVE TO]	595B	PUB ADDRESS/N	PROSE
	HER FORM WAS HELD BY BEULAH'S DAUGHTERS BUT ALL WITHIN UNSEEN	693	JERUSALEM 60	40
	OR WAS HIS WISDOM HELD IN SCORN	752	EV GOSPEL(D)/N	55
	THE ESTIMATION YOU ARE HELD IN AMONG ARTISTS & CONNOISSEURS	798B	LETTER 10	PROSE
	OTHER BOTH HELD ABOVE HER HEAD & A FIGURE KNEELING AT HER FEET	839C	LETTER 38	PROSE
HE'LL				
	GIVE BUT A SLAVE HIS LIBERTY HE'LL SHAKE	26	EDW THIRD/PS 3	196
	A SPOT OF GROUND THIS HE'LL DEFEND TIS HIS	26	EDW THIRD/PS 3	198
	HE'LL PLUNGE HIS KNIFE UP TO THE HILT IN A SINGLE DRIVE	50A	ISLAND MOON 6	PROSE
	HE'LL SWEAR AT THEM & KEEP THEM DOWN WITH HIS FIST & TELL	50A	ISLAND MOON 6	PROSE
	THEM THAT HE'LL SCRAPE THEIR BONES IF THEY DONT LAY STILL &	50A	ISLAND MOON 6	PROSE
	& I DO BELIEVE HE'LL GO IN PARTNERSHIP WITH HIS MASTER . .	53A	ISLAND MOON 8	PROSE
	THRO THE GLOOM HE'LL SEE MY SHADOW	61	LEAVE O/IM	7
	THAT IS THE VERY THING HE'LL SET YOU TO	544	HS FRENDSHIP/N	2
	[HE'LL] THEYLL STILL BE CALLED THE WORLD'S HONEST MAN . .	544	SOME MEN/N	5
	WHATS THE FIRST PART OF PAINTING HE'LL SAY A PAINT BRUSH	553	ASKD PRIGG/N	8
	HE'LL [NOD WINK & SMILE & REPLY]	553	ASKD PRIGG/N	10

904

```
                                                            PAGE      TITLE        LINE
HE'LL   (CONTINUED)
   AND WHAT IS THE THIRD HE'LL BOW LIKE A RUSH   . . . .   553 ASKD PRIGG/N       11
   WITH A LEAR IN HIS EYE HE'LL REPLY A PAINT BRUSH . . .  553 ASKD PRIGG/N       12
HELL
   GHOSTS GLUT THE THROAT OF HELL  . . . . . . . . . .      13 GWIN KING/PS       96
   AND SHAKE THE GATES OF HELL  . . . . . . . . . . .       30 EDW THIRD/PS 5     20
   AND FIENDS OF HELL REJOICE UPON THE SLAIN  . . . . .     33 EDW FOURTH/PS      12
   TO HELL TILL HE BEHAVES BETTER  . . . . . . . . . .     74B ANNO LAVATER     MARG
   HELL IS THE BEING SHUT UP IN THE POSSESSION OF CORPOREAL 74B ANNO LAVATER     MARG
      DESIRES
   ("AVOID ORIGINALITY AND SACRIFICE TO FASHION") & GO TO  85B ANNO LAVATER     MARG
      HELL
   UNDER EVERY GOOD IS A HELL I E HELL IS THE OUTWARD  . . SUPP ANNO SWED HELL * MARG
   HEAVEN & HELL ?CHAPTER...  . . . . . . . . . . .        89B ANNO SWED LOVE * MARG
   ("CONSTITUTES HELL") THE NEGATION OF THE POETIC GENIUS  90D ANNO SWED LOVE   MARG
   OUT OF IT INTO MEER NATURE [OF] OR HELL SEE N...  . .   93A ANNO SWED LOVE * MARG
   HEAVEN & HELL ARE BORN TOGETHER  . . . . . . . . .      96D ANNO SWED LOVE   MARG
   [OR EYED WITH LITTLE SPARKS OF HELL OR WITH INFERNAL   109 TIRIEL 8           15
      BRANDS]
   THE MARRIAGE OF HEAVEN AND HELL  . . . . . . . . .     148B MARRIAGE HH      TITLE
   SINCE ITS ADVENT THE ETERNAL HELL REVIVES AND LO  . .  149A MARRIAGE HH 3    PROSE
   GOOD IS HEAVEN EVIL IS HELL  . . . . . . . . . . .     149B MARRIAGE HH 3    PROSE
   AND AT LIBERTY WHEN OF DEVILS & HELL IS BECAUSE HE WAS  150B MARRIAGE HH 5    PROSE
   AS I WAS WALKING AMONG THE FIRES OF HELL  . . . . .    150C MARRIAGE HH 6    PROSE
   SO THE PROVERBS OF HELL SHEW THE NATURE OF INFERNAL WISDOM 150C MARRIAGE HH 6 PROSE
   PROVERBS OF HELL  . . . . . . . . . . . . . . .        150D MARRIAGE HH 7    TITLE
   END OF SIX THOUSAND YEARS IS TRUE AS I HAVE HEARD FROM HELL 154B MARRIAGE HH 14 PROSE
   BY CORROSIVES WHICH IN HELL ARE SALUTARY AND MEDICINAL . 154C MARRIAGE HH 14 PROSE
   I WAS IN A PRINTING HOUSE IN HELL & SAW THE METHOD IN WHICH 154D MARRIAGE HH 15 PROSE
   I HAVE ALSO THE BIBLE OF HELL WHICH THE WORLD SHALL HAVE 158D MARRIAGE HH 22 PROSE
   AND BUILDS A HELL IN HEAVEN'S DESPITE  . . . . . .     162 CLOD PEBBLE/N      12
   [SUCH USAGE IN HEAVEN MAKES ALL GO TO HELL]  . . . .   179 LIT VAGABOND/N      4
   [BUT SHAKE HANDS & KISS HIM & THERED BE NO MORE HELL]  180 LIT VAGABOND/N     17
   [BUT IF THEY REBEL THEY MUST GO TO HELL]  . . . . .    185 LET BROTHELS/N     18
   AND ALL THE DEVILS THAT WERE IN HELL  . . . . . . .    187 WHEN KLOPSTK/N     13
   WITH FIRES OF HELL DEFORM THEIR ANCIENT HEAVENS WITH SHAME 202 AMERICA 15      15
      & WOE
   THE MARRIAGE OF HEAVEN AND HELL IN ILLUMINATED PRINTING 207D PRSPECTUS 1793 PROSE
      QUARTO
   AND BUILDS A HELL IN HEAVEN'S DESPITE  . . . . . .     211 CLOD PEBBLE/SE      12
   DEATH & HELL TEAM WITH LIFE  . . . . . . . . . .      261D SMALL BK DSGNS   TITLE
   O ENION THOU ART THYSELF A ROOT GROWING IN HELL  . .   265 FOUR ZOAS 1        57
   . . . TO THE PLACE [OF DEATH & HELL] WHENCE I EMERGD  . 268 FOUR ZOAS 1      157
   . . . FROM THE DEPTHS OF HELL THY BLACK BOW DRAW  . .  306 FOUR ZOAS 5        50
   BUT NOW THOU ART BOUND DOWN WITH HIM EVEN TO THE GATES 311 FOUR ZOAS 5      * 233
      OF HELL
   . . . THEN LOVE SHALL SHEW ITS ROOT IN DEEPEST HELL  . . 311 FOUR ZOAS 5     241
   SURROUNDING THEM ON ALL SIDES BEYOND SIN & DEATH & HELL 342 FOUR ZOAS 8       51
   WHEN HEAVEN & HELL IN EMULATION STROVE IN SPORTS OF GLORY 365 FOUR ZOAS 9    298
   I HAVE BEEN COMMANDED FROM HELL NOT TO PRINT THIS  . . 383C ANNO WATSON     MARG
   THRO THE HEAVEN & EARTH & HELL  . . . . . . . . .     416 MY SPECTRE/N       55
   SHUDDERS HELL THRO ALL ITS REGIONS  . . . . . . .     431 AUGURIES            8
   RAISES FROM HELL A HUMAN SOUL  . . . . . . . . . .    431 AUGURIES           20
   TRIUMPHS OVER HELL & DEATH  . . . . . . . . . .       433 AUGURIES           90
   SATAN NOW AWAKES SIN DEATH & HELL TO CELEBRATE WITH HIM 441D INSC FALL MAN  PROSE
   HELL OPENS BENEATH THE HARLOT'S SEAT ON THE LEFT HAND . 443B LAST JUDGMNT/L PROSE
   THE ABYSS OF HELL WHICH OPENS [TO RECIEVE THEM] BENEATH 443C LAST JUDGMNT/L PROSE
   DRAGGING EACH OTHER INTO HELL & [OF] IN CONTENDING IN . 443D LAST JUDGMNT/L *PROSE
   A HELL OF OUR OWN MAKING SEE ITS FLAMES STILL GIRD ME ROUND 493 MILTON 12     23
   REACHD TO THE DEPTHS OF (DIREST) HELL & THENCE TO ALBION'S 496 MILTON 14    * 40
      LAND
   OF HELL BEHELD HIM IN A TRAIL OF LIGHT AS OF A COMET  . 496 MILTON 15        19
   IT HAS A HEART LIKE THEE A BRAIN OPEN TO HEAVEN & HELL . 502 MILTON 20       28
   SHEWING THE TRANSGRESORS IN HELL THE PROUD WARRIORS IN 506 MILTON 22       * 51
      HEAVEN
   HEAVEN AS A PUNISHER & HELL AS ONE UNDER PUNISHMENT  . 506 MILTON 22         52
   AND HELL & THE GRAVE STATES THAT ARE NOT BUT AH SEEM TO BE 522 MILTON 32     29
   ARE BECOME FOUNTAINS OF BITTER DEATH & OF CORRODING HELL 525 MILTON 35        3
   I COME TO DISCOVER BEFORE HEAVN & HELL THE  . . . .   530 MILTON 38         43
      SELF RIGHTEOUSNESS
   I OFT HAVE WISHD FOR HELL FOR EASE FROM HEAVEN  . . . 552 GROWN OLD IN/N      2
   [SHE'D] BUT NOW THE CAVES OF HELL I VIEW  . . . . .   558 THE CAVERNS/N    *  3
   THE [WAVES] FLAMES OF HELL THAT ROUND ME ROLL  . . . 558 THE CAVERNS/N       8
   HELL IS OPENED & MANY FIGURES ARE DESCENDING INTO IT  . 608B V LAST JUDG/N  PROSE
   ARE DESCENDING [INTO HELL] DOWN THE STEPS INTO THE PIT 608C V LAST JUDG/N  PROSE
   & HELL IS OPEND BENEATH HER SEAT ON THE LEFT HAND  . . 609B V LAST JUDG/N  PROSE
   FOR THE COERCIVE LAWS OF HELL MORAL HYPOCRISY  . . . . 616C V LAST JUDG/N  PROSE
   IN HELL ALL IS SELF RIGHTEOUSNESS  . . . . . . . .    616C V LAST JUDG/N  PROSE
   EVEN FROM THE DEPTHS OF HELL HIS VOICE I HEAR  . . . . 621 READER LOVER/J     7
   HEAVEN EARTH & HELL HENCEFORTH SHALL LIVE IN HARMONY  . 621 READER LOVER/J   10
   I WILL CERTAINLY CREATE AN ETERNAL HELL FOR THEE LISTEN 627 JERUSALEM 8       8
   THOU ABSTAIN RAVENING I WILL CREATE AN ETERNAL HELL FOR 627 JERUSALEM 8      38
      THEE
   GOD IS WITHIN & WITHOUT HE IS EVEN IN THE DEPTHS OF HELL 631 JERUSALEM 12    15
   THOSE THAT THOU TORMENTEST A HELL & DESPAIR FOR EVER & EVER 639 JERUSALEM 17 47
   FACE IN TERRORS & PAINS OF HELL & ETERNAL DEATH THE  . . 639 JERUSALEM 17    54
   HER PALACES WITH HELL & THE GRAVE HER SYNAGOGUES  . .  647 JERUSALEM 24      34
      WITH TORMENTS
   THE POISONER THE BEST AND WORST IN HEAVEN AND HELL  . . 668 JERUSALEM 41      2
   ARE BECOME THE SOURCES OF DARK & BITTER DEATH & OF  . . 672 JERUSALEM 43     32
      CORRODING HELL
   BUT JESUS BREAKING THRO THE CENTRAL ZONES OF DEATH & HELL 716 JERUSALEM 75   21
```

HELL   (CONTINUED)
        WHAT ARE THE PAINS OF HELL BUT IGNORANCE BODILY LUST   . . 717B JERUSALEM 77   PROSE
        FOR HELL IS OPEND TO HEAVEN THINE EYES BEHELD . . . . . 718 STOOD AMONG/J   34
        THE HILLS OF JUDEA ARE FALLEN WITH ME INTO THE DEEPEST HELL   720 JERUSALEM 79   8
        BY LAND ASTOUNDING ERECTING PILLARS IN THE DEEPEST HELL   738 JERUSALEM 91   41
        [I] THY HEAVEN DOORS ARE MY HELL GATES . . . .   748 EV GOSPEL(A)/N *   8
        CANST THOU RETURN TO THIS DARK HELL . . . .   755 EV GOSPEL(E)/N   77
        AND SOULS TO HELL RAN TROOPING IN . . . . 758 EV GOSPEL (2)   12
        AND DEATH & HELL WHICH NOW BEGIN . . . .   759 EV GOSPEL (2)   42
        HE COULD NEVER HAVE BUILT DANTE'S HELL NOR . . . . .   785C ILLS DANTE 101   PROSE
        THE HELL OF THE BIBLE NEITHER IN THE WAY OUR PARSONS   785C ILLS DANTE 101   PROSE
           EXPLAIN IT
        BUT OF SATAN THE ACCUSER & FATHER OF HELL . . . . . .   785D ILLS DANTE 101   PROSE
        AND IN HELL BENEATH & A MIGHTY & AWFUL CHANGE THREATENED   799 TO FLAXMAN/L   8
           THE EARTH
        ALL THE DEVILS IN HELL WILL NEVER DO I MUST OWN THAT SEEING   819C LETTER 25   PROSE
        I WILL GO ON IN THE STRENGTH OF THE LORD THROUGH HELL .   823C LETTER 26   PROSE
        FOUGHT THRO A HELL OF TERRORS & HORRORS WHICH NONE COULD   853A LETTER 51   PROSE
        HELL BENEATH IS MOVED FOR THEE &C FROM ISAIAH . . . .   SUPP LETTER 56A   *PROSE
        OF MR LINNELL...TWO GUINEAS FOR HEAVEN & HELL . . . . . SUPP LETTER 67B   *PROSE
        THE BIBLE OF HELL IN NOCTURNAL VISIONS COLLECTED VOL I   SUPP INSCRIPTION   *TITLE
           LAMBETH
HELLE
        AND HELLE & HESPERIA & HINDOSTAN & CHINA & JAPAN . . . . 725 JERUSALEM 82   28
HELL FIRE
        SINCE EVE FIRST CHOSE HER HELL FIRE SPARK . . . . . .   187 WHEN KLOPSTK/N   24
HELLISH
        HE LOADS IT WITH HELLISH BROWNNESS   . . . .   583A DESC CAT 9   PROSE
        SATAN & ALL HIS HELLISH CREW   . . . .   749 EV GOSPEL(B)/N   51
HELL'S
        AND BUILDS A HEAVEN IN HELL'S DESPAIR . . . .   162 CLOD PEBBLE/N   4
        AND BUILDS A HEAVEN IN HELL'S DESPAIR . . . .   211 CLOD PEBBLE/SE   4
        AND CREATED HELL'S DARK JAWS . . . .   754 EV GOSPEL(E)/N   32
        THO THY COVENANT BUILT HELL'S JAIL . . . .   754 EV GOSPEL(E)/N   38
        THIS IS UPSIDE DOWN WHEN VIEWD FROM HELL'S GATE BUT . .   785D ILLS DANTE 101   *PROSE
HELLS
        HE IS MY SPECTRE IN MY OBEDIENCE TO LOOSE HIM FROM MY HELLS   496 MILTON 14   31
        TO CLAIM THE HELLS MY FURNACES I GO TO ETERNAL DEATH . .   496 MILTON 14   32
        IN TWENTY-SEVEN HEAVENS AND ALL THEIR HELLS WITH CHAOS .   498 MILTON 17   24
        SEEING THESE HEAVENS & HELLS CONGLOBING IN THE VOID . . .   672 JERUSALEM 43   16
        . . . HEAVENS OVER HELLS . . . .   672 JERUSALEM 43   16
        THEY ARE BEGINNING TO FORM HEAVENS & HELLS IN IMMENSE . .   680 JERUSALEM 49   61
        CIRCLES THE HELLS FOR FOOD TO THE HEAVENS FOOD OF TORMENT   680 JERUSALEM 49   62
HELM
        AND FORGED HELM AND SHIELD OF SEVEN TIMES BEATEN BRASS . .   17 EDW THIRD/PS 1   4
        EACH SHINING HELM AND STRING EACH STUBBORN BOW . . . .   26 EDW THIRD/PS 3   226
        AMBITION COME TAKE THE HELM MY CHANDOS . . . .   27 EDW THIRD/PS 3   238
        PREPARE PREPARE THE IRON HELM OF WAR . . . .   34 WAR SONG/PS   1
        LAUNCHD TO THE UNKNOWN SHORE WHILE SOTHA HELD THE NORTHERN   204 AMERICA CANC B   21
           HELM
        HIS HELM WAS BROUGHT BY LONDON'S GUARDIAN & HIS THIRSTY   205 AMERICA CANC C   4
           SPEAR
HELMED
        THEIR HELMED YOUTH AND AGED WARRIORS IN DUST TOGETHER   37D SAMSON/PS   PROSE
           LY(LIE)
HELMET
        CROWND WITH A HELMET & DARK HAIR THE NAMELESS FEMALE STOOD   195 AMERICA PREL 1   4
        AND TAKING OFF HIS SILVER HELMET FILLED IT & DRANK . . . 311 FOUR ZOAS 6   3
        DARKEND HIS BROWS WITH HIS COLD HELMET & HIS GLOOMY SPEAR   313 FOUR ZOAS 6   52
        THEY GIVE THE OATH OF BLOOD THEY CAST THE LOTS INTO THE   337 FOUR ZOAS 7B   165
           HELMET
        AND I WILL PUT ON HOLINESS AS A BREASTPLATE & AS A HELMET   499 MILTON 18   21
        AWKWARDNESS ARMD IN STEEL FOLLY IN A HELMET OF GOLD . . . 628 JERUSALEM 9   12
        THEY CAST THE LOTS INTO THE HELMET . . . .   699 JERUSALEM 65   7
HELMETS
        WITH HELMETS HEWN AND SHIELDS COVERED WITH GORE . . . .   32 EDW THIRD/PS 6   11
HELMS
        FURBISH OUR ARMOURS BRIGHT NEW PLUME OUR HELMS . . . .   24 EDW THIRD/PS 3   147
        CURLD VETERANS AMONG HELMS AND SHIELDS AND CHARIOTS . . . 159D SONG LIBERTY   PROSE
HELP
        CAN THEY NOT HELP THEMSELVES . . . .   20 EDW THIRD/PS 2   71
        REQUIRES OUR COUNTENANCE AND HELP . . . .   20 EDW THIRD/PS 2   73
        AND THOU SHALT HELP US TO CATCH BIRDS & GATHER THEM RIPE   102 TIRIEL 3   15
           CHERRIES
        ALAS MY SON MY SON I WANT I WANT HELP HELP AGED   209C FOR CHILDRN/GP   TITLE
           IGNORANCE
        IS ETERNAL DEATH WHAT SHALL WE DO O GOD [HELP] PITY & HELP   267 FOUR ZOAS 1   107
        HOW CAN I HELP THY HUSBAND'S COPYING ME . . . . 539 TO NANCY F/N   1
        GO LOVE WITHOUT THE HELP OF ANY [THING] ?KING ON EARTH . . 541 ANGEL PRESID/N *   3
        HE CALLS YOU TO HIS HELP BE YOU NOT [MOVED] MOVD . . .   551 WILLM COWPER/N *   3
        AS SUDDENLY EMERGING FROM THE BLUE SKY FOR THEIR HELP .   610V V LAST JUDG/N   PROSE
        I CANNOT HELP SAYING THE SON O HOW UNLIKE THE FATHER .   617A V LAST JUDG/N   PROSE
        CALLING ON GOD FOR HELP AND NOT OURSELVES IN WHOM GOD   672 JERUSALEM 43   13
           DWELLS
        HELP HELP . . . .   767B FOR SEXES/GP   TITLE
        DR TRUSLER SAYS...I COULD NOT HELP SMILING AT THE . . .   795A LETTER 6   PROSE
        NOR MY FRIENDS UNEASY IF I CAN HELP IT MY WIFE HAS HAD   819C LETTER 25   PROSE
           AGUES
        I CANNOT HELP SUGGESTING AN IDEA WHICH HAS STRUCK ME VERY   850D LETTER 49   PROSE
        HE APPROVES MUCH I CANNOT HELP TELLING YOU SO MUCH . . . 853B LETTER 52   PROSE
        GOOD HELP & WITH YOUR REMARKS ON IT IN ADDITION I HOPE TO   855B LETTER 53   PROSE
        I COULD NOT HELP PUTTING UP A PETITION FOR YOURS . . . . 860D LETTER 57   PROSE

HELP   (CONTINUED)
      I KNOW IT FOR I SEE IT & DARE NOT HELP . . . . 863B LETTER 60   PROSE
      I HAVE ASKED & INTREATED DIVINE HELP BUT FEAR CONTINUES   876B LETTER 83   PROSE
HELPER
      STRETCH FORTH YOUR HANDS THAT MY HELPER MAY COME . . . . 36A COUCH DEATH/PS   PROSE
HELPLESS
      TO SMITE (THEE) IN THE FORM OF HELPLESS AGE & EYELESS   104 TIRIEL 4   *   18
         POLICY
      OR ELSE THOU WOULDEST NOT HAVE LIVD TO CURSE THY HELPLESS   108 TIRIEL 6   28
         CHILDREN
      SILENCE THY EVIL TONGUE THOU MURDERER OF THY HELPLESS   108 TIRIEL 6   35
         CHILDREN
      THE HELPLESS WORM AROSE AND SAT UPON THE LILLY'S LEAF . . 129 BOOK OF THEL 3   30
      IS THIS A WORM I SEE THEE LAY HELPLESS & NAKED WEEPING . . 129 BOOK OF THEL 4   5
      THAT WILFUL BRUISD ITS HELPLESS FORM BUT THAT HE CHERISHD   130 BOOK OF THEL 5   10
         IT
      WAS LEFT A HELPLESS TRUNK THIS AFTER GRINNING & KISSING IT 157B MARRIAGE HH 17 PROSE
      HELPLESS NAKED PIPING LOUD . . . . 166 INFANT SORW/N   3
      HELPLESS NAKED PIPING LOUD . . . . 217 INFANT SORW/SE   3
      YET HELPLESS IT LAY LIKE A WORM . . . . 232 URIZEN 19   21
      THE FIRST STATE WEEPING THEY BEGAN & HELPLESS AS A WAVE   269 FOUR ZOAS 1   193
      THE VOICES OF CHILDREN IN MY TENTS TO CRIES OF HELPLESS   360 FOUR ZOAS 9   111
         INFANTS
      THE VOICES OF CHILDREN IN HIS TENTS TO CRIES OF HELPLESS   641 JERUSALEM 19   12
         INFANTS
HELTER SKELTER
      BUT AN AUTOGRAPH AS I UNDERSTAND IT IS WRIT HELTER SKELTER 781D INSC UPCOTT   PROSE
HEM
      THEN CRIES OUT HEM HODGE HEARD AND RAN . . . . 16 BLIND-MANS/PS   49
      BUT WE SEE ONLY AS IT WERE THE HEM OF THEIR GARMENTS . . . 512 MILTON 26   11
      "REMEMBER WITH AFFECTION EVEN THE HEM OF YOUR GARMENT" . . 800A LETTER 12   PROSE
HEMMING
      THE ANTIQUARIAN HERE GOT UP & HEMMING TWICE . . . . . . 45D ISLAND MOON 1   PROSE
HEMP
      [AND] YORKSHIRE JACK HEMP & GENTLE BLUSHING DAW . . . . 537 AND HIS LEGS/N   20
HEMP'S
      AND CUR MY LAWYER & DADY [MY] JACK HEMP'S PARSON . . . 537 AND HIS LEGS/N *   26
HEN
      MORE WONDROUS WONDROUS STILL THE COCK & HEN . . . . . 545 IMIT POPE/N   2
HENCE
      GIVE IT ME FOR I CANNOT STAY MY JOURNEY IS FAR FROM HENCE   101 TIRIEL 2   22
      AND I WILL BRING THEE FOOD OLD MAN TILL DEATH SHALL CALL   103 TIRIEL 3   35
         THEE HENCE
      HENCE WE MUST CONCLUDE THAT THE MAN WHO HOLDS MIRACLES . . 391C ANNO WATSON   MARG
      HENCE THE THREE CLASSES OF MEN TAKE THEIR FIXD DESTINATIONS 484 MILTON 5   13
      AND HENCE THEY OVERSPREAD THE NATIONS OF THE WHOLE EARTH   486 MILTON 6   33
         & HENCE
      AND KEPT ONLY THE FEMININE AWAKE HENCE ROSE HIS SOFT . . 492 MILTON 12   6
      I HOPE THINE ARE NOT HENCE IT CLOTHES ITSELF IN RICH ARRAY 502 MILTON 20   30
      HENCE THOU ART CLOTHD WITH HUMAN BEAUTY O THOU MORTAL MAN   502 MILTON 20   *   31
      FROM HENCE SHE COMES FORTH ON THE CHURCHES IN DELIGHT .   529 MILTON 38   24
      HENCE AROSE ALL OUR TERRORS IN ETERNITY & NOW REMEMBRANCE   534 MILTON 41   34
      IT IS OF MALICE AND ENVY THAT YOU HAVE DONE THIS HENCE . . 573A DESC CAT 3   PROSE
      HENCE RUBENS TITIAN CORREGGIO AND ALL OF THAT CLASS ARE   581A DESC CAT 5   PROSE
      AND HERE WE HAVE FOUND THY SINS & HENCE WE TURN THEE FORTH 658 JERUSALEM 31   61
      DRINKING THEIR LIVES IN SWEET INTOXICATION HENCE AROSE   701 JERUSALEM 65   65
         FROM BATH
      AND FEEDS HER WITH THE FOOD OF EDEN HENCE ALL HER BEAUTY   707 JERUSALEM 69   18
         BEAMS
      HENCE ROSE THE TABERNACLE IN THE WILDERNESS & ALL   707 JERUSALEM 69   28
         ITS OFFERINGS
      HENCE THE INFERNAL VEIL GROWS IN THE DISOBEDIENT FEMALE   708 JERUSALEM 69   38
      HENCE ALBION WAS CALLD THE CANAANITE & ALL HIS GIANT SONS   715 JERUSALEM 74   39
      HENCE IS MY THEME O LORD MY SAVIOUR OPEN THOU THE GATES   715 JERUSALEM 74   40
      OF MEN HENCE I AM GOD OF MEN THOU HUMAN O JEHOVAH . . . 780 GHOST ABEL 2   15
      SUBJECT OF PAINTING AND HENCE IT IS SO COMMON TO HEAR . . 864C LETTER 61   PROSE
      GREAT JOY HENCE I AM NOW ENABLED TO TELL YOU THAT I . . . 869D LETTER 70   PROSE
HENCEFORTH
      LUVAH & VALA HENCEFORTH YOU ARE SERVANTS OBEY & LIVE .   366 FOUR ZOAS 9   363
      THARMAS HENCEFORTH IN VALA'S BOSOM THOU SHALT FIND SWEET   371 FOUR ZOAS 9   527
         PEACE
      IS FOR EVER REMOVED & HENCEFORTH EVERY MAN MAY . . . . 389C ANNO WATSON   MARG
      SO LOS SAID HENCEFORTH PALAMABRON LET EACH HIS OWN STATION 487 MILTON 7   43
      HEAVEN EARTH & HELL HENCEFORTH SHALL LIVE IN HARMONY . . . 621 READER LOVER/J   10
      HENCEFORTH IS THIS THY PROMISE THAT THE WOMAN'S SEED .   779 GHOST ABEL 1   3
      BUT I HOPE THAT FRANCE & ENGLAND WILL HENCEFORTH BE . . . 811A LETTER 21   PROSE
HENCEFORWARD
      BUT NO FRIEND FROM HENCEFORWARD THOU MARY SHALT SEE . . . 428 MARY   16
HENDON
      HAMPSTEAD HIGHGATE FINCHLEY HENDON MUSWELL HILL RAGE LOUD   636 JERUSALEM 16   1
HENRY
      OF KING HENRY THE FOURTH WALKS BEFORE HIM IN FIRES . . .   141 FRENCH REVOLTN   165
      WHAT DAMP ALL OUR FIRES O SPECTRE OF HENRY . . . .   142 FRENCH REVOLTN   171
      THE PLAGUE [THE REFORMATION BY H(HENRY) VIII] . . . . .   209A SUBJCTS HIST/N   TITLE
      ARE AS FOLLOW "THE TABARDE INN BY HENRY BAILLIE THE" .   567B DESC CAT 3   PROSE
      KNOWLEDGE AND EXPERIENCE HENRY BAILLIE THE KEEPER . .   569D DESC CAT 3   PROSE
      "BY HENRY BAILLY THE LODGYNG HOUSE FOR PILGRIMS" . . . . 589A CHAUCER/N   PROSE
      "THE TABARDE INN BY HENRY BAILLY" . . . . 590C CHAUCER 2   PROSE
      [EDWARD HENRY ELIZABETH JAMES CHARLES WILLIAM GEORGE] . . 713 JERUSALEM 73   *   37
      THE TABARD INNE BY HENRY BAILEY . . . . SUPP ILLUS CHAUCER *TITLE
      THE SHADE OF HENRY THE SIXTH IS SEEN AMONG THE TREES . . SUPP ILLUS GRAY   *TITLE

```
                                                              PAGE      TITLE       LINE
HENRY'S
     GREAT HENRY'S SOUL SHUDDERED . . .   . . . . . . . .   143 FRENCH REVOLTN    200
HERALDS
     FOUR WINGED HERALDS MOUNT THE FURIOUS BLASTS & BLOW THEIR   205 AMERICA CANC C   14
        TRUMPS
     SENT ROUND HIS HERALDS SECRETLY COMMANDING TO DEPART   .   279 FOUR ZOAS 1     536
     FOUR WINGED HERALDS MOUNT THE FURIOUS BLASTS & BLOW THEIR   319 FOUR ZOAS 6     310
        TRUMPS
HERB
     SO MAN LOOKS OUT IN TREE & HERB & FISH & BIRD & BEAST   .   355 FOUR ZOAS 8     561
     AND FLOWER & HERB SOON FILL THE AIR WITH AN INNUMERABLE    521 MILTON 31        61
        DANCE
     OF AGE AND YOUTH AND BOY AND GIRL AND ANIMAL AND HERB   .   640 JERUSALEM 18     17
     AND BOY & GIRL & ANIMAL & HERB & RIVER & MOUNTAIN     .   640 JERUSALEM 18     25
     LIKE EVENING DEW ON EVERY HERB UPON THE BREATHING GROUND   669 JERUSALEM 42      8
     EACH HERB & EACH TREE . . . . . . .   . . . .   .   805 TO BUTTS/L       29
HERBS
     HIS DAUGHTERS FROM GREEN HERBS & CATTLE   . . . . . .   234 URIZEN 23        20
     NOT LONG THEY LAY URTHONA'S SPECTRE FOUND HERBS OF THE PIT   309 FOUR ZOAS 5    173
     AND THE HERBS & FLOWERS & FURNITURE & BEDS & CHAMBERS   .   512 MILTON 26        34
     SURROUNDED BY THE SPIRITS OF THE HERBS & FLOWERS   . . . .   619C ILLUS MILTON  PROSE
HERCULEAN
     CONCERNING MY THREE YEARS' HERCULEAN LABOURS AT FELPHAM    592C PUB ADDRESS/N  PROSE
HERCULES
     NO...HERCULES BUILDINGS LAMBETH   . . . . . . . . .   207C PRSPECTUS 1793  PROSE
     PUBLISHED BY W BLAKE...HERCULES BUILDINGS   . . . . . .   209B FOR CHILDRN/GP *TITLE
     GIVEN TO HERCULES WHO LABOUR IN TIRZAH'S LOOMS FOR BREAD   511 MILTON 25        50
     THE GREEKS AND HETRURIANS COPIED HERCULES FARNESE   .   .   565C DESC CAT 2     PROSE
     THE MILLER IS THE HERCULES &C CHAUCER'S CHARACTERS ARE   .   571A DESC CAT 3    PROSE
     OF HERCULES BETWEEN HIS MILLER AND HIS PLOWMAN   .   .   .   571B DESC CAT 3    PROSE
     THE PLOWMAN OF CHAUCER IS HERCULES IN HIS SUPREME ETERNAL   571C DESC CAT 3     PROSE
     OF YOUR BEAUTIFUL MAN AND THE HERCULES FOR YOUR STRONG MAN   579B DESC CAT 5    PROSE
     HERCULES BUILDGS LAMBETH . . . . . . . . .   .   .   SUPP ADDRESSES/L  *TITLE
HERDS
     WHERE THE HERDS LOW AFTER THE SHADOW & AFTER THE WATER    308 FOUR ZOAS 5     137
        SPRING
     AMONG HIS FAMILY HIS FLOCKS & HERDS & TENTS & PASTURES   .   326 FOUR ZOAS 7    254
     HERDS THRONG UP THE VALLEY WILD BEASTS FILL THE FORESTS    373 FOUR ZOAS 9     612
     METHINKS I SEE HIS FLOCKS & HERDS & FEEL MY LIMBS RENEWD   375 FOUR ZOAS 9     690
     MY FLOCKS & HERDS TRAMPLE THE CORN MY CATTLE BROWZE UPON   376 FOUR ZOAS 9     699
     O WHEN SHALL JEHOVAH GIVE US VICTIMS FROM HIS FLOCKS &    697 JERUSALEM 63     30
        HERDS
     AND KENT & MIDDLESEX ALL THEIR RIVERS & THEIR HILLS OF    709 JERUSALEM 71     12
        FLOCKS & HERDS
     THE PLAINS OF SUSSEX & SURREY THEIR HILLS OF FLOCKS & HERDS   720 JERUSALEM 79   18
     ARE SEEN IN OUR HILLS & VALLEYS THEY KEEP OUR FLOCKS &    720 JERUSALEM 79     31
        HERDS
HEREAFTER
     IT IS NOT THE WANT OF GENIUS THAT CAN HEREAFTER BE   .   .   . 584B DESC CAT 14  PROSE
     TO SAY TIS A GIRL PROMISING BOYS HEREAFTER & TO SAY   .   .   . 853A LETTER 51  *PROSE
     IF ANY OF MY WRITINGS SHOULD HEREAFTER APPEAR BEFORE   .   860D LETTER 57      PROSE
HEREBY
     FOR THE CHERUB WITH HIS FLAMING SWORD IS HEREBY COMMANDED   154B MARRIAGE HH 14  PROSE
     I HEREBY DECLARE THAT MR JOHN LINNELL HAS PURCHASED OF ME   874A LETTER 78     PROSE
HEREF
     JOSEPH STAFFORD SHROPS HEREF BENJAMIN DERBY CHESHIRE      637 JERUSALEM 16     49
        MONMOUTH
HEREFORD
     HEREFORD ANCIENT GUARDIAN OF WALES WHOSE HANDS   .   . . .   676 JERUSALEM 46      3
     WORCESTER & HEREFORD OXFORD & CAMBRIDGE REEL & STAGGER   .   .   703 JERUSALEM 66   66
     KOTOPE HAD HEREFORD STAFFORD WORCESTER & HIS EMANATION   .   710 JERUSALEM 71     44
HERE'S
     HANG YOUR VIOLETS HERES YOUR RUM & WATER [SWEETER]   .   .   55B ISLAND MOON 9  *PROSE
     THE BLADE BONE OF A TITTLEBACK NO NO HERES A BOTTLE OF    58C ISLAND MOON 10  PROSE
        WIND
     [HERES] HERE IS ANOTHER CONTRADICTION IF MICH ANGO   .   . .   467D ANNO REYNOLDS * MARG
     THIS IS QUITE PERFECTION [HERES TWO FOR ONE] . . .   .   .   554 TO VENETIAN/N      9
HERESY
     IS HERESY & REBELLION AGAINST CAESAR VIRGIL'S ONLY GOD   . .   789B ANNO THORNTON * MARG
HERMAPHRODITE
     WHICH HE INTENDED NOT A SHADOWY [MALE] HERMAPHRODITE BLACK   343 FOUR ZOAS 8    103
        & OPAKE
     A DARK HERMAPHRODITE . . . . . . . . .   .   .   699 JERUSALEM 64     31
     A DARK HERMAPHRODITE [I] WE STOOD   . . . . . .   .   .   770 OF GATES/GP     13
HERMAPHRODITIC
     HERMAPHRODITIC IT AT LENGTH BECAME HIDING THE MALE   .   .   343 FOUR ZOAS 8    105
     SEEN IN THE AGGREGATE A VAST HERMAPHRODITIC FORM   .   .   .   347 FOUR ZOAS 8   248
     FROM THE HERMAPHRODITIC BOSOM SATAN HE WAS NAMD   .   .   .   347 FOUR ZOAS 8   251
     A MOURNFUL FORM DOUBLE HERMAPHRODITIC MALE & FEMALE   .   .   496 MILTON 14       37
     THE TWOFOLD FORM HERMAPHRODITIC AND THE DOUBLE-SEXED   .   501 MILTON 19        32
     METHUSELAH LAMECH THESE ARE GIANTS MIGHTY HERMAPHRODITIC   528 MILTON 37        37
     LIKE MEN HERMAPHRODITIC EACH WINGED WITH EIGHT WINGS   .   .   633 JERUSALEM 13    8
     REFLECTING BACK TO ALBION IN SEXUAL REASONING            659 JERUSALEM 33     28
        HERMAPHRODITIC
     THE HERMAPHRODITIC CONDENSATIONS ARE DIVIDED BY THE KNIFE   689 JERUSALEM 58     11
     OF ALBION'S & LUVAH'S SPECTRES WAS HERMAPHRODITIC   .   .   .   690 JERUSALEM 58   20
     THE HERMAPHRODITIC SATANIC WORLD OF ROCKY DESTINY   .   .   690 JERUSALEM 58     51
     METHUSELAH LAMECH THESE ARE THE GIANTS MIGHTY           716 JERUSALEM 75     12
        HERMAPHRODITIC
     UPON THE HERMAPHRODITIC WINE-PRESSES OF LOVE & WRATH   .   .   734 JERUSALEM 88    58
     A TERRIBLE INDEFINITE HERMAPHRODITIC FORM   . . . . .   .   734 JERUSALEM 89      3
     A WINE-PRESS OF LOVE & WRATH DOUBLE (HERMAPHRODITIC)   .   .   734 JERUSALEM 89   *  4
```

		PAGE	TITLE	LINE

HERMAPHRODITIC   (CONTINUED)
A VEGETATED CHRIST & A VIRGIN EVE ARE THE HERMAPHRODITIC   736 JERUSALEM 90   34
HERMAPHRODITIC WORSHIPPERS OF A GOD OF CRUELTY & LAW   .   .   737 JERUSALEM 90   55
I NATURE (HERMAPHRODITIC) PRIEST & KING . . . . . .   789A ANNO THORNTON   * MARG
HERMES
THESE HEAVENS ARE VENUS JUPITER & MARS HERMES FLIES BEFORE   619B ILLUS MILTON   PROSE
IS SEEN IN THE SKY BENEATH HERMES & THE SPIRITS OF FIRE   619B ILLUS MILTON   PROSE
REPEATING THE SMARAGDINE TABLE OF HERMES TO DRAW LOS DOWN   738 JERUSALEM 91   35
HERMIT
AND AT HIS OWN DOOR THE BLESSD HERMIT DOES STAND . . .   .   800 MRS FLAXMAN/L   15
AROUND YOUR HERMIT & BARD SO PRAYS THE EMULATOR OF BOTH   835B LETTER 34   PROSE
HERMIT'S
THE HERMIT'S PRAYER & THE WIDOW'S TEAR . . . .   419 I SAW A MONK/N   42
THE HERMIT'S PRAYER & THE WIDOW'S TEAR . . . .   430 GREY MONK   27
HERMON
[AS ONE MAN HOVERING OVER GILEAD & HERMON] . . . . . .   269 FOUR ZOAS 1   199
[MET] AS ONE MAN EVEN JESUS UPON GILEAD & HERMON . . .   341 FOUR ZOAS 8   2
ARE HOR & PEOR & BASHAN & ABARIM & LEBANON & HERMON . . .   498 MILTON 17   16
LISTEN HERMON & LEBANON BOW THEIR CROWNED HEADS . . . .   730 JERUSALEM 85   17
HERO
SPRINGS FROM THE HILLS LIKE A YOUNG HERO . . . . . .   21 EDW THIRD/PS 3   3
THAT MAN S A HERO IN HIS CLOSET AND MORE . . . . . .   25 EDW THIRD/PS 3   184
A HERO TO THE SERVANTS OF HIS HOUSE . . . .   25 EDW THIRD/PS 3   185
("WHO ...IS A GENIUS AND A HERO AT ONCE ") UNEASY . .   69B ANNO LAVATER   MARG
A HISTORY PAINTER PAINTS THE HERO & NOT MAN IN GENERAL .   465A ANNO REYNOLDS   MARG
I AM NO HOMER'S HERO YOU ALL KNOW . . . .   541 HOMERS HERO/N   1
THE KNIGHT IS A TRUE HERO A GOOD GREAT AND WISE MAN . .   567D DESC CAT 3   PROSE
MORE DISTINCTLY THAN IN ANY PRINCE OR HERO . . . . .   845C LETTER 44   PROSE
HEROD
AS THOSE OF CAIPHAS OR PILATE OR HEROD . . . .   407A ANNO BACON   MARG
IF HEROD YOU WITH BLOODY PREY . . . .   749 EV GOSPEL(B)/N   22
CAIPHAS PILATE & HEROD WERE LEARNED . . . .   786D ANNO THORNTON   MARG
HERODOTUS
VOLTAIRE ECHARD RAPIN PLUTARCH NOR HERODOTUS . . . .   579A DESC CAT 5   PROSE
HEROES
OF A TRIUMPH SUCH AN ARMY OF HEROES . . . .   23 EDW THIRD/PS 3   75
("HEROES WITH INFANTINE SIMPLICITY") THIS IS HEAVENLY .   75B ANNO LAVATER   MARG
AND TO APPLY IT TO MODERN HEROES ON A SMALLER SCALE . .   565D DESC CAT 2   PROSE
TO THE GRANDEUR OF THE NATION WHO IS THE PARENT OF HIS   566A DESC CAT 2   PROSE
    HEROES
ONE WHO IN WAR IS THE WORTHY ATTENDANT ON NOBLE HEROES .   568A DESC CAT 3   PROSE
OF THOSE NAKED HEROES IN THE WELCH MOUNTAINS . . . .   578C DESC CAT 5   PROSE
[OF] OR HEROES THIS AS N XXX [IT] ANS XXX & NOT   605B V LAST JUDG/N   *PROSE
    (SPIRITUAL) XXX
THE GREEK HEROES & LASTLY BY THE ROMANS . . . . . .   785B ILLUS DANTE 7   PROSE
HEROIC
ABOVE HEROIC HAVING SUCH EXAMPLES . . . .   23 EDW THIRD/PS 3   80
. . . STRONG HEROIC VERSE . . . .   264 FOUR ZOAS 1   5
DO THEY MEAN WAR & ITS HORRORS & ITS HEROIC VILLAINS . .   400A ANNO BACON   MARG
BUT THE SNEAKING PRIDE OF HEROIC SCHOOLS . . . . . .   751 EV GOSPEL(D)/N   27
AND [MORAL] ALL THE HEROIC VIRTUES [ALL] END . . . .   759 EV GOSPEL (2)   36
HEROISM
& HEROISM A MISER . . . .   777A INSC LAOCOON   PROSE
HERS
ALTERNATE LOVE & HATE HIS BREAST HERS SCORN & JEALOUSY .   270 FOUR ZOAS 1   237
& DESIRES WITH MINE TO PRESENT HERS TO MISS POOLE . .   837B LETTER 35   PROSE
HERSELF
AMAZD SHE FINDS HERSELF UPON HER FEET . . . .   4 FAIR ELENOR/PS   10
HATE MEAGER HAG SETS ENVY ON UNABLE TO DO OUGHT HERSELF .   41D THEN SHE BORE   PROSE
AND SHE HERSELF (LED) CAPTIVE & . . . .   279 FOUR ZOAS 1   547
AND BRIGHT AHANIA BOWD HERSELF BEFORE HIS SPLENDID FEET   291 FOUR ZOAS 3   2
SET HERSELF UP TO GIVE HER LAWS TO THE ACTIVE MASCULINE   295 FOUR ZOAS 3   116
    VIRTUE
[SHE SECRET JOYD TO SEE SHE FED HERSELF ON HIS DESPAIR]   324 FOUR ZOAS 7   177
HER ONCE LOVD LORD NOW BUT A SHADE HERSELF ALSO A SHADE   327 FOUR ZOAS 7   313
SHE SPREAD HERSELF THRO ALL THE BRANCHES IN THE POWER OF   343 FOUR ZOAS 8   85
    ORC
SHE SPREAD HERSELF THRO ALL THE BRANCHES IN THE POWER OF   345 FOUR ZOAS 8   174
    ORC
EVEN RAHAB IN ALL HER TURPITUDE RAHAB DIVIDED HERSELF .   350 FOUR ZOAS 8   344
SHE STOOD IN THE RIVER & VIEWD HERSELF WITHIN THE WATRY   369 FOUR ZOAS 9   481
    GLASS
THEN LAST HERSELF LAID DOWN & CLOSD HER EYELIDS IN SOFT   370 FOUR ZOAS 9   516
    SLUMBERS
SHE MADE HERSELF A MANTLE . . . .   382 FOUR ZOAS AD 6   23
ANOTHER MAIDEN LIKE HERSELF . . . .   429 CRYSTL CABINET   13
OFFERING HERSELF A RANSOM FOR SATAN TAKING ON HER HIS SIN   492 MILTON 11   30
SHE FLED TO ENITHARMON'S TENT & HID HERSELF LOUD RAGING   494 MILTON 13   14
SAY OF HERSELF WHO IS NO MODEST ONE . . . .   574B DESC CAT 3   PROSE
SURROUNDING THE PRINCIPAL FIGURE WHICH IS MIRTH HERSELF   618A ILLUS MILTON   PROSE
WHO IS MELANCHOLY HERSELF . . . .   619A ILLUS MILTON   PROSE
SHE FLED TO LAMBETH'S MILD VALE AND HID HERSELF BENEATH   668 JERUSALEM 41   11
HERSELF IN CHAINS THIS FROM WITHIN WAS SEEN IN A DISMAL   719 JERUSALEM 78   24
    NIGHT
HYLE WAS A WINDING WORM AND HERSELF PERFECT IN BEAUTY . .   726 JERUSALEM 82   50
HERTFORDSHIRE
HERTFORDSHIRE GLOWS WITH FIERCE VEGETATION IN THE FORESTS   636 JERUSALEM 16   3
AND OVER THE VALLEYS FROM THE HILLS OF HERTFORDSHIRE TO   658 JERUSALEM 31   68
    THE HILLS
HERVEY
WHITEFIELD & HERVEY GUARD THAT GATE WITH ALL THE GENTLE   712 JERUSALEM 72   51
    SOULS

909

```
                                                   PAGE      TITLE         LINE
HERVEY   (CONTINUED)
    WIDOW FATHER BABE BAPTISM HERVEY ANGEL OF DEATH    . . SUPP INSC HERVEY   *TITLE
HERVEY'S
    TAKING EXTRACTS FROM HERVEY'S MEDITATIONS AMONG THE TOMBS   52A ISLAND MOON 8   PROSE
HE'S
    HES DEAD AND HOWLING AFTER ME FOR BLOOD  . . . . . . .    4 FAIR ELENOR/PS     24
    IM SURE HES NOT AFRAID NOR WARWICK NOR NONE    . . . . .   22 EDW THIRD/PS 3    32
    TEACH MAN TO THINK HES A FREE AGENT  . . . . . . . .      25 EDW THIRD/PS 3   195
    HES A FOOLISH PUPPY SAID INFLAMMABLE GASS SMILING ON HIM  44C ISLAND MOON 1   PROSE
    HES MY BUTTERFLY  . . . . . . . . . . . . . .           178 THE FAIRY/N       18
    IS FALSE WHEN IT IS ATTRIBUTED TO A WRONG AUTHOR HES A FOOL 391B ANNO WATSON   MARG
    HES GIVEN TO A WOMAN OLD  . . . . . . . . . . .         425 MENTAL TRAVLER     10
    ON WHICH HES WRITTEN RECIEVD THE CONTENTS  . . . . . .   537 AND HIS LEGS/N     43
    HES A BLOCKHEAD WHO WANTS A PROOF OF WHAT HE CAN'T PERCIEVE 540 BLOCKHEAD/N      1
    AND HES A FOOL WHO [SEEKS] TRIES TO MAKE SUCH A BLOCKHEAD 540 BLOCKHEAD/N       2
        BELIEVE
    TILL HES BECOME THE GOLDEN FOOL  . . . . . . . .        540 GOLDEN RULE/N       2
    TILL [HES] YOURE AT LAST BECOME THE [OLD] GOLDEN FOOL  . 540 S(TOTHAR)D/N  *    2
    NOT WHEN HES WELL BUT WAITING TILL HES SICK  . . . .    551 WILLM COWPER/N      2
    AND THEN HES SO PIERCD WITH CARE  . . . . . . . .       552 WHY CUPID/N   *    13
HESHBON
    TO HESHBON DISCONSOLATE HE WALKD THRO MOAB & HE STOOD  . 662 JERUSALEM 36       10
    I MELT MY SOUL IN REASONINGS AMONG THE TOWERS OF HESHBON 719 JERUSALEM 79        3
    PISON SINCE CALLD ARNON THERE IS HESHBON BEAUTIFUL  . . 735 JERUSALEM 89        25
    THE ROCKS OF RABBATH ON THE ARNON & THE FISH-POOLS      735 JERUSALEM 89        26
        OF HESHBON
HESHBON'S
    I HAVE NAILD HIS HANDS ON BETH RABBIM & HIS (FEET)      726 JERUSALEM 82   *   43
        ON HESHBON'S WALL
HESIOD
    HAS FOUND (FIFTEEN) PROOFS OF THE HESIOD AS THEY ARE  . 877B LETTER 86       PROSE
HESITATED
    WHO HESITATED & EQUIVOCATED WITH ME UPON THE SAME SUBJECT 593A PUB ADDRESS/N  PROSE
HESITATES
    WHICH DOUBTS & HESITATES IN THE MIDST OF ITS COURSE  . . 603C PUB ADDR AD/N  PROSE
    THE SUN FORGETS HIS COURSE LIKE A DRUNKEN MAN HE HESITATES 703 JERUSALEM 66     74
HESKETH
    & IN PARTICULAR LADY HESKETH & LORD COWPER . . . . .    820C LETTER 25       PROSE
    TO PLEASE LADY H(HESKETH) WAS A DOUBTFUL CHANCE  . . . .820C LETTER 25       PROSE
    YOU WILL RECIEVE PROOFS OF THEM FOR LADY HESKETH WHOSE  . 837C LETTER 36     PROSE
HESPERIA
    FROM BRIGHT JAPAN & CHINA TO HESPERIA FRANCE & ENGLAND  . 648 JERUSALEM 24     47
    AND SWEET HESPERIA EVEN TO GREAT CHALDEA & TESSHINA  . . 692 JERUSALEM 60      20
    AND HELLE & HESPERIA & HINDOSTAN & CHINA & JAPAN  . . . . 725 JERUSALEM 82     28
    AND ROME IN SWEET HESPERIA THERE ISRAEL SCATTERD ABROAD 735 JERUSALEM 89       39
HETEROGENEOUS
    HETEROGENEOUS WHICH ALL EXTRAVAGANCE IS BUT EXUBERANCE NOT 81D ANNO LAVATER   MARG
HETH
    RUTH THE MOABITE & BATHSHEBA OF THE DAUGHTERS OF HETH  . 696 JERUSALEM 62      11
HETRURIANS
    THE GREEKS AND HETRURIANS COPIED HERCULES FARNESE  . . . 565C DESC CAT 2     PROSE
HEUXOS
    SHE BEARS SHE GROANS NOT AT THE BIRTH OF HEUXOS OR YUVA   99 TIRIEL 1         25
    BUT HEUXOS CALLD A SON OF ZAZEL TO [XXX] DIG THEIR MOTHER 100 TIRIEL 1   *    35
        A GRAVE
    HEUXOS COME FORTH I HERE HAVE BROUGHT THE FIEND THAT    104 TIRIEL 4         43
        TROUBLES IJIM
    HEUXOS & LOTHO RAN FORTH AT THE SOUND OF IJIM'S VOICE  . . 105 TIRIEL 4       45
    WHAT HEUXOS CALL THY FATHER FOR I [?MUST] MEAN TO SPORT  105 TIRIEL 4         49
        TO NIGHT
    [WHY DO YOU STAND CONFOUNDED THUS HEUXOS WHY ART        105 TIRIEL 4         74
        THOU SILENT]
    THEN IS IT TRUE HEUXOS THAT THOU HAST TURND THY AGED PARENT 106 TIRIEL 4      83
HEVA
    AND HAR & HEVA LIKE TWO CHILDREN SAT BENEATH THE OAK  . . 100 TIRIEL 2         5
    AND THIS IS HAR & HEVA TREMBLING LIKE INFANTS BY MY SIDE 101 TIRIEL 2         19
    HE KNEELED DOWN & MNETHA SAID COME HAR & HEVA RISE  . . . 101 TIRIEL 2        32
    HEVA COME KISS HIS BALD HEAD FOR HE WILL NOT HURT US HEVA 101 TIRIEL 2        38
    THEN HEVA CAME & TOOK OLD TIRIEL IN HER MOTHER'S ARMS  . 101 TIRIEL 2         39
    THEY SAT & EAT & HAR & HEVA SMILD ON TIRIEL  . . . . . . 102 TIRIEL 3          1
    [BUT STILL HE FEARD THAT HAR & HEVA WOULD DIE OF JOY &  102 TIRIEL 3          8
        GRIEF]
    WHAT WILT THOU LEAVE US TOO SAID HEVA THOU SHALT NOT LEAVE 102 TIRIEL 3       12
        US TOO
    THOU SHALT NOT GO SAID HEVA TILL THOU HAST SEEN OUR SINGING 103 TIRIEL 3      22
        BIRDS
    [AND HAR & HEVA STOOD & WATCHD HIM TILL HE ENTERD THE WOOD] 103 TIRIEL 3      31
    BUT HAR & HEVA STOOD & WATCHD HIM TILL HE ENTERD THE WOOD 103 TIRIEL 3        41
    NOW [?HILI] HELA I CAN GO WITH PLEASURE & DWELL WITH HAR 107 TIRIEL 6   *     3
        & HEVA
    YET THOU SHALT LEAD ME LEAD ME I COMMAND TO HAR & HEVA   107 TIRIEL 6         22
    TO HAR & HEVA I WILL LEAD THEE THEN WOULD THAT THEY WOULD 107 TIRIEL 6        24
        CURSE
    LEAD ME TO HAR & HEVA & THE CURSE OF TIRIEL  . . . . . . 108 TIRIEL 6         48
    BUT HAR & HEVA SLEPT FEARLESS AS BABES ON LOVING BREASTS 109 TIRIEL 7         21
    LEAD ME TO HAR & HEVA I AM TIRIEL KING OF THE WEST  . . . 109 TIRIEL 8         4
    AND MNETHA LED THEM TO THE TENT OF HAR AND HAR & HEVA  . . 109 TIRIEL 8        5
    SINCE THAT DREAD DAY WHEN HAR AND HEVA FLED  . . . . . . 246 SONG OF LOS 4     5
HEVA'S
    I HAVE NOT EAT THESE TWO DAYS LEAD ME TO HAR & HEVA'S TENT 107 TIRIEL 6       19
    HE CEAST OUTSTRETCHD AT HAR & HEVA'S FEET IN AWFUL DEATH 110 TIRIEL 8         42
```

```
                                                        PAGE      TITLE           LINE
HEW
   [TO HEW THE CAVERND ROCKS OF DRANTHON INTO FORMS OF BEAUTY]   331 FOUR ZOAS 7        457
HEWD
   [BUT RAHAB [BUILT] HEWD A SEPULCHER IN THE ROCK OF           356 FOUR ZOAS 8     *  585
      ETERNITY]
   OF ETERNITY FOR HIMSELF HE HEWD IT DESPAIRING OF            349 FOUR ZOAS 8        340
      LIFE ETERNAL
HEWN
   WITH HELMETS HEWN AND SHIELDS COVERED WITH GORE    . . . .   32 EDW THIRD/PS 6       11
   AND THE ANCIENT FORESTS OF CHIVALRY HEWN . . . . . . . .    138 FRENCH REVOLTN       93
   MULTITUDES WITHOUT NUMBER WORK INCESSANT THE HEWN STONE     284 FOUR ZOAS 2         170
   THEY BORE IT TO THE SEPULCHER WHICH LOS HAD HEWN IN THE     349 FOUR ZOAS 8         339
      ROCK
   DOWN FROM THE CROSS & PLACD IT IN A SEPULCHER WHICH LOS     356 FOUR ZOAS 8         594
      HAD HEWN
   HE HAS A SEPULCHER HEWN OUT OF A ROCK READY FOR THEE   . .  664 JERUSALEM 37          6
HID
   [THEY] SOME FLED AWAY [& HID THEMSELVES] BUT [SOME ] . . .  108 TIRIEL 7              7
   [WITH DAGGERS HID BENEATH THEIR LIPS & POISON IN THEIR      109 TIRIEL 8             14
      TONGUE]
   . . . HID FROM THE LIGHT AS IN A CLEFT ROCK    . . . . .    135 FRENCH REVOLTN       28
   . . . A MASK OF IRON ON HIS FACE HID THE LINEAMENTS . . .   135 FRENCH REVOLTN       31
   . . . WAS HID FROM THE OPPRESSED EARTH   . . . . . . .      135 FRENCH REVOLTN       32
   DISPLAYING THE INFINITE WHICH WAS HID   . . . . . . .      154C MARRIAGE HH 14     PROSE
   LIKE A FIEND HID IN A CLOUD   . . . . . . . . . . . . .     166 INFANT SORW/N         4
   AND HID FROM HIM MY HEART'S DELIGHT   . . . . . . . . .     182 THE ANGEL/N           8
   AND I HID IN LEUTHA'S VALE  . . . . . . . . . . . .         189 ARGUMENT V DAU        4
   AND THEN TELL ME THE THOUGHTS OF MAN THAT HAVE BEEN HID     191 V DAU ALBION 3       13
      OF OLD
   HID IN HIS CAVES THE BARD OF ALBION FELT THE ENORMOUS       202 AMERICA 15           16
      PLAGUES
   AND HID FROM HIM MY HEART'S DELIGHT   . . . . . . . . .     214 THE ANGEL/SE          8
   LIKE A FIEND HID IN A CLOUD  . . . . . . . . . . . . . .    217 INFANT SORW/SE        4
   BROODING SECRET THE DARK POWER HID   . . . . . . . .        222 URIZEN 3              7
   HID THEIR STRONG LIMBS IN SMOKE   . . . . . . . . . .       229 URIZEN 13            23
   RINTRAH WHERE HAST THOU HID THY BRIDE   . . . . . . . .     240 EUROPE 8              5
   TO A DEVOURING FLAME AND MAN FLED FROM ITS FACE AND HID     241 EUROPE 10            17
   THE YOUTH OF ENGLAND HID IN GLOOM CURSE THE PAIND HEAVENS   242 EUROPE 12             5
      COMPELLD
   THEN HID HER IN DARKNESS IN SILENCE  . . . . . . . .        250 AHANIA 2             36
   THE GIGANTIC FLAMES TREMBLED AND HID  . . . . . . .         257 BOOK OF LOS 4         3
   [WHILE THE BRIGHT SPECTRE HID HIMSELF AMONG THE TRAILING    268 FOUR ZOAS 1      *  144
      CLOUDS]
   [LOS] HE ANSWERD DARKNING MORE WITH [FOUL] INDIGNATION      272 FOUR ZOAS 1         282
      HID IN SMILES
   MURDERD HER & HID HER IN HER BOSOM EMBALMING HER FOR FEAR   278 FOUR ZOAS 1         526
   [?HE ?FELL XXX HID IN ?HORRIBLE ?CAVERNS OF MOUNTAINS]     SUPP FOUR ZOAS 1      *
   I HID HER IN SOFT GARDENS & IN SECRET BOWERS OF SUMMER . .  282 FOUR ZOAS 2          95
   AND THEY HAVE TAKEN HER AWAY & HID HER FROM MY SIGHT   . .  282 FOUR ZOAS 2          98
   URIZEN SAW THY SIN & HID HIS BEAMS IN DARKNING CLOUDS  . .  288 FOUR ZOAS 2         329
   [BUT SAW NOT LOS NOR ENITHARMON FOR LUVAH HID THEM          292 FOUR ZOAS 3          47
      IN SHADOW]
   FELL FROM HIS HAND HIS FIRES HID THEIR STRONG LIMBS IN      304 FOUR ZOAS 4         281
      SMOKE
   I WENT NOT FORTH I HID MYSELF IN BLACK CLOUDS OF MY WRATH   311 FOUR ZOAS 5         222
   HE HID TO RECURE HIS OBSTRUCTED POWERS WITH REST & OBLIVION 315 FOUR ZOAS 6         140
   HE HID THEM WHEN HE SLEPT IN DEATH WHEN HE REVIVD           316 FOUR ZOAS 6         170
      THE CLOTHES
   THE DARKNING SPECTRE OF URTHONA HID BENEATH A ROCK   . . .  320 FOUR ZOAS 7           2
   HID IN A LITTLE SILKEN VEIL SCARCE BREATHE & FAINTLY SHINE  325 FOUR ZOAS 7         195
   HID IN THE VALES FAINTLY LAMENT & NO ONE HEARS THEIR VOICE  325 FOUR ZOAS 7         197
   BUT ENITHARMON TREMBLING FLED & HID BENEATH URIZEN'S TREE   329 FOUR ZOAS 7         372
   OF SECRET LUST WHEN HID IN CHAMBERS DARK THE NIGHTLY HARLOT 333 FOUR ZOAS 7B         25
   THARMAS THE MOON HAS CHAMBERS WHERE THE BABES OF LOVE LIE   339 FOUR ZOAS 7B        244
      HID
   HID HIM IN THAT OUTRAGEOUS FORM OF ORC WHICH TORMENTS ME    339 FOUR ZOAS 7B        249
      FOR SIN
   WHERE HAST THOU HID HIM WHOM I LOVE IN WHAT REMOTE ABYSS    345 FOUR ZOAS 8         155
   HIS STRONG BONES BEAT WITH SNOWS & HID WITHIN THE CAVES     354 FOUR ZOAS 8         517
      OF NIGHT
   SHE COMMUND WITH ORC IN SECRET SHE HID HIM WITH THE FLAX    356 FOUR ZOAS 8         607
   THERE IS A BRAZEN SICKLE & A SCYTHE OF IRON HID   . . . .   372 FOUR ZOAS 9         580
   THE WOMB IMPRESSD ENION FLED & HID IN VERDANT MOUNTAINS     381 FOUR ZOAS AD 3        1
   FUSELI INDIGNANT ALMOST HID HIMSELF I [?WAS] AN HID . .    445C ANNO REYNOLDS     *  MARG
   YOU HID FUSELI'S MILTON IS SATAN TROUBLED AT HIS EXPOSURE  446A ANNO REYNOLDS        MARG
   BUT LOS HID THULLOH FROM HER SIGHT LEST SHE SHOULD DIE      488 MILTON 8             41
      OF GRIEF
   HID HIM FROM SIGHT IN AN EXTREME BLACKNESS AND DARKNESS     490 MILTON 9             33
   BUT LOS HID ENITHARMON FROM THE SIGHT OF ALL THESE THINGS   491 MILTON 11             2
   THE GNOMES LABOURD I WEEPING HID IN SATAN'S INMOST BRAIN    493 MILTON 12            36
   DAY SUNK AND PALAMABRON RETURND TREMBLING I HID MYSELF . .  493 MILTON 12            40
   SHE FLED TO ENITHARMON'S TENT & HID HERSELF LOUD RAGING     494 MILTON 13            14
   A MALE WITHIN A FEMALE HID AS IN AN ARK & CURTAINS   . .    528 MILTON 37            40
   RELIGION HID IN WAR A DRAGON RED & HIDDEN HARLOT  . . . .   528 MILTON 37            43
   THAT I SHOULD BE [LEFT] HID IN A CORNER IT NEVER WAS  . . 602C PUB ADDRESS/N       PROSE
   OF WOOL HE HID HER FROM THE SPECTRE IN SHAME & CONFUSION OF 639 JERUSALEM 17         53
   THE REACTOR HATH HID HIMSELF THRO ENVY I BEHOLD HIM  . . .  653 JERUSALEM 29          9
   IMMINGLED GOD & MAN WHEN THOU & I HID THE DIVINE VISION     660 JERUSALEM 33         46
   FLED THEY FLED AT HIS HORRIBLE FORM THEY HID IN CAVES  . .  661 JERUSALEM 34         49
   GWANTOCK & PEACHY HID IN DAMASCUS BENEATH MOUNT LEBANON     662 JERUSALEM 36         16
   SHE FLED TO LAMBETH'S MILD VALE AND HID HERSELF BENEATH     668 JERUSALEM 41         11
   FOR VICTIMS OF SACRIFICE BUT JERUSALEM CANNOT BE FOUND HID  668 JERUSALEM 41         13
```

911

	PAGE	TITLE	LINE

HID   (CONTINUED)

BY THE DAUGHTERS OF BEULAH GENTLY SNATCHD AWAY AND HID   668 JERUSALEM 41   14
IN BEULAH
HERE JERUSALEM & VALA WERE HID IN SOFT SLUMBEROUS REPOSE   668 JERUSALEM 41   21
HID FROM THE TERRIBLE EAST SHUT UP IN THE SOUTH & WEST . .   668 JERUSALEM 41   22
THEY NAMD THE EIGHTH HE CAME NOT HE HID IN ALBION'S FORESTS   686 JERUSALEM 55   33
WHEN THE CHERUBIM HID THEIR HEADS UNDER THEIR WINGS IN   697 JERUSALEM 63   24
DEEP SLUMBERS
AND BOWELS HID IN HAMMERD STEEL RIPD QUIVERING ON   701 JERUSALEM 65   53
THE GROUND
FROM THE INNER SANCTUARY A FALSE HOLINESS HID WITHIN THE   708 JERUSALEM 69   40
CENTER
AS SHE SLEPT IN BEULAH'S NIGHT HID BY THE DAUGHTERS OF   708 JERUSALEM 69   46
BEULAH
SAT DEEP WITHIN HIM HID HIS FEMININE POWER UNREVEALD . .   709 JERUSALEM 70   18
AND ALL HER TWENTY-SEVEN HEAVENS NOW HID & NOW REVEALD . .   715 JERUSALEM 75   4
A MALE WITHIN A FEMALE HID AS IN AN ARK & CURTAINS . . .   716 JERUSALEM 75   15
THE FEMALE HID WITHIN A MALE THUS RAHAB IS REVEALD . . .   716 JERUSALEM 75   18
RELIGION HID IN WAR A DRAGON RED & HIDDEN HARLOT . . . .   716 JERUSALEM 75   20
SHE HID IT IN HIS RIBS & BACK SHE HID HIS TONGUE WITH   723 JERUSALEM 80   69
TEETH
SHE HID THEM IN HIS LOINS RAVING HE RAN AMONG THE ROCKS   723 JERUSALEM 80   76
SO SAYING SHE TOOK A FALSEHOOD & HID IT IN HER LEFT HAND   725 JERUSALEM 82   * 17
FORGETTING THAT FALSHOOD IS PROPHETIC SHE HID HER HAND   725 JERUSALEM 82   * 20
BEHIND HER
GWENDOLEN HID IN HER LEFT HAND IT GREW & GREW TILL IT . .   729 JERUSALEM 84   32
RELIGION HID IN WAR A DRAGON RED & HIDDEN HARLOT . . . .   735 JERUSALEM 89   53
[HID IT BENEATH HIS MERCY SEAT] . . . .   761 FOR SEXES/GP   9
A MANDRAKE & IN HER VEIL HID ME . . . .   770 OF GATES/GP   4
O THAT IN THE BOSOM OF GOD I WAS HID . . . .   772C ANNO SPURZHEIM MARG
WHICH I HID MY FACE FOR NOT BEING ABLE TO ABANDON . . .   798C LETTER 10   PROSE

HIDDEKEL

GIHON TO HIDDEKEL & TO CORN FIELDS & VILLAGES & INHABITANTS   695 JERUSALEM 61   32
WHERE HIDDEKEL PURSUES HIS COURSE AMONG THE ROCKS . . .   735 JERUSALEM 89   35

HIDDEN

HIDDEN SET APART IN MY STERN COUNSELS . . . .   224 URIZEN 4   8
I HAVE HIDDEN [THEE ENION IN JEALOUS DESPAIR] . . . . .   264 FOUR ZOAS 1   27
[ASTONISHD HE FOUND ENION HIDDEN IN THE DARKSOM CAVE] .   267 FOUR ZOAS 1   136
. . . ATLANTIC FOR A CURSE AND HIDDEN HORROR . . . . .   294 FOUR ZOAS 3   105
AND LUVAH HIDDEN IN THE ELEMENTAL FORMS OF LIFE & DEATH   301 FOUR ZOAS 4   130
IN WHICH WE MAY BE HIDDEN UNDER THE SHADOW OF WINGS . .   304 FOUR ZOAS 4   260
THE VEINS OF GOLD & SILVER & THE HIDDEN THINGS OF VALA . .   308 FOUR ZOAS 5   123
OF PLAGUES HIDDEN IN SHINING GLOBES THAT GREW ON THE LIVING   325 FOUR ZOAS 7   216
TREE
THE HIDDEN WONDERS ALLEGORIC OF THE GENERATIONS . . . .   333 FOUR ZOAS 7B   24
TO FEED THEIR FRUIT TO GRATIFY THEIR HIDDEN SONS   335 FOUR ZOAS 7B   104
& DAUGHTERS
AND BOWELS HIDDEN [IN DARKNESS] IN HAMMERD STEEL [ARE]   338 FOUR ZOAS 7B   * 207
. . .
IS HIDDEN FROM ME & I NEVER IN ALL ETERNITY . . . . .   339 FOUR ZOAS 7B   247
OF FEMALE FORMS BEAUTIFUL THRO POISONS HIDDEN IN SECRET   348 FOUR ZOAS 8   290
. . . [THEREFORE THEY WERE CALLD] THERE WAS HIDDEN WITHIN   348 FOUR ZOAS 8   * 291
STRENGTH FROM THE EARTHS CONSUMD & HEAVENS & ALL HIDDEN   358 FOUR ZOAS 9   *   38
ABYSSES
FROM MY EARLIEST CHILDHOOD HIDDEN FROM ME I SAW & . . .   447C ANNO REYNOLDS   MARG
HIS SOFTNESS & CANDOUR THE HIDDEN TRAP & THE POISONED FEAST   452A ANNO REYNOLDS   MARG
FOR SATAN FLAMING WITH RINTRAH'S FURY HIDDEN BENEATH HIS   489 MILTON 9   19
OWN MILDNESS
COVERING THE EAST WITH SOLID BLACKNESS ROUND HIS HIDDEN   490 MILTON 9   40
HEART
WITH THUNDERS UTTERD FROM HIS HIDDEN WHEELS ACCUSING LOUD   490 MILTON 9   41
BUT ELYNITTRIA MET LEUTHA IN THE PLACE WHERE SHE WAS HIDDEN   494 MILTON 13   36
ALL THE WISDOM WHICH WAS HIDDEN IN CAVES & DENS FROM   510 MILTON 25   20
ANCIENT
IN WHICH WE MAY BE HIDDEN UNDER THE SHADOW OF WINGS . .   519 MILTON 30   25
RELIGION HID IN WAR A DRAGON RED & HIDDEN HARLOT . . . .   528 MILTON 37   43
A FEMALE HIDDEN IN A MALE RELIGION HIDDEN IN WAR . . . .   532 MILTON 40   20
A DRAGON RED & HIDDEN HARLOT WHICH JOHN IN PATMOS SAW . .   532 MILTON 40   22
SAY NO MORE OF HER NOR EXPOSE WHAT CHAUCER HAS LEFT HIDDEN   572B DESC CAT 3   PROSE
HOWEVER HIDDEN BY ARTIFICES . . . .   573A DESC CAT 3   PROSE
WHERE HAST THOU HIDDEN THY EMANATION LOVELY JERUSALEM . .   622 JERUSALEM 4   16
THAT LAYS OPEN THE HIDDEN HEART I DREW FORTH THE PANG . .   628 JERUSALEM 9   19
SEEKING FOR REST AND FINDING NONE AND HIDDEN FAR WITHIN   641 JERUSALEM 19   15
THOU ART MY FATHER & MY BROTHER WHY HAST THOU HIDDEN ME   646 JERUSALEM 23   11
OF GOD WHO DWELLS IN CHAOS HIDDEN FROM THE HUMAN SIGHT . .   652 JERUSALEM 28   16
HIDDEN IN ALBION'S FORESTS HE LURKS HE ADMITS OF NO REPLY   653 JERUSALEM 29   13
BUT SAW NOT BY WHOM THEY WERE HIDDEN WITHIN IN THE MINUTE   656 JERUSALEM 31   8
PARTICULARS
OF LONDON BUT THE INTERIORS OF ALBION'S FIBRES & NERVES   658 JERUSALEM 32   4
WERE HIDDEN
ALBION'S EMANATION WHICH HE HAD HIDDEN IN JEALOUSY . . .   659 JERUSALEM 33   26
TO HIDE THE MOST EVIDENT GOD IN A HIDDEN COVERT EVEN . .   661 JERUSALEM 34   32
HIDDEN AMONG THE DEAD & MURED UP FROM THE PATHS OF LIFE   661 JERUSALEM 34   35
AND ACCIDENT & CHANCE WERE FOUND HIDDEN IN LENGTH BREDTH   663 JERUSALEM 36   35
& HIGHTH
IN HIDDEN DECEIT THEY ARE VEGETABLE ONLY FIT FOR BURNING   663 JERUSALEM 36   48
HIS HIDDEN HEART HIS EMANATION WEPT & TREMBLED WITHIN HIM   664 JERUSALEM 38   3
THE SECRET COVERTS OF ALBION & THE HIDDEN PLACES OF AMERICA   679 JERUSALEM 49   1
RELIGION HID IN WAR A DRAGON RED & HIDDEN HARLOT . . . .   716 JERUSALEM 75   20
HIDDEN WITHIN THE COVERING CHERUB AS IN A TABERNACLE . .   735 JERUSALEM 89   44
RELIGION HID IN WAR A DRAGON RED & HIDDEN HARLOT . . . .   735 JERUSALEM 89   53
MYSTERY BABYLON THE GREAT THE DRUID DRAGON & HIDDEN HARLOT   741 JERUSALEM 93   25

HIDDEN   (CONTINUED)

OPEN THE HIDDEN HEART IN WARS OF MUTUAL BENEVOLENCE WARS OF LOVE	744	JERUSALEM 97	14
AND HIDE IN SECRET HIDDEN SHRINE	755	EV GOSPEL(E)/N *	65
CANNOT EXPECT TO WANT NATURAL HIDDEN ONES	811D	LETTER 22	PROSE
ALTOGETHER HIDDEN FROM THE CORPOREAL UNDERSTANDING . . .	825A	LETTER 27	PROSE

HIDE

NOR IS THE HIDE A COMELY VESTMENT SO	27	EDW THIRD/PS 3	267
AND SEEKS TO HIDE HER BRUISED HEAD UNDER THE MISTS OF NIGHT	37D	SAMSON/PS	PROSE
CAN FROM THE HEART OF MAN HIDE SORROW	39B	SAMSON/PS	PROSE
A QUESTION HE WOULD PUT HIS HEAD INTO A HOLE & HIDE IT . .	53C	ISLAND MOON 8	PROSE
("GREATER THAT WHICH YOU CAN HIDE GREATER YOURSELF") PLEASANT	80D	ANNO LAVATER	MARG
WHERE DOTH HE HIDE HIS TERRIBLE HEAD & HIS SWIFT & FIERY DAUGHTERS	106	TIRIEL 5	2
CRYING HIDE FROM THE LIVING	137	FRENCH REVOLTN	74
HIDE IN THE NETHER EARTH HIDE IN THE BONES	137	FRENCH REVOLTN	75
. . . WE ARE NOT NUMBERED AMONG THE LIVING LET US HIDE . .	137	FRENCH REVOLTN	76
LET US HIDE LET US HIDE IN THE DUST	137	FRENCH REVOLTN	78
DOES SPRING HIDE ITS [DELIGHT] JOY	169	EARTHS ANSWR/N	16
WHY DOST THOU HIDE THYSELF IN CLOUDS	171	TO NOBODADDY/N	3
DOES THE STILL SPIDER VIEW THE CLIFFS WHERE EAGLES HIDE THEIR YOUNG	193	V DAU ALBION 5	37
IN VAIN THESE CLOUDS ROLL TO & FRO & HIDE THEE FROM MY SIGHT	196	AMERICA PREL 1	20
FROM THEIR ENCAMPMENTS AND DARK CASTLES SEEKING WHERE TO HIDE	201	AMERICA 13	8
DOES SPRING HIDE ITS JOY	211	EARTHS ANSR/SE	16
TO HIDE BUT [THEY] HE COULD NOT COMBINING	225	URIZEN 5 *	21
[I AM] WE ARE BECOME A VICTIM TO THE LIVING [I] WE HIDE IN SECRET	264	FOUR ZOAS 1 *	26
HIDE ME SOME SHADOWY SEMBLANCE SECRET WHISPRING IN MY EAR	265	FOUR ZOAS 1	42
WOVEN BY THEIR OWN HANDS TO HIDE THEM IN THE DARKSOM GRAVE	266	FOUR ZOAS 1	65
ENION SAID FAREWELL I DIE I HIDE FROM THY SEARCHING EYES	266	FOUR ZOAS 1	68
THAT I SHOULD HIDE THEE WITH MY POWER & DELIGHT THEE WITH MY BEAUTY	269	FOUR ZOAS 1	174
AND I COMMANDED THE GREAT DEEP TO HIDE HER IN HIS HAND . .	282	FOUR ZOAS 2	91
WHY ROLL THY CLOUDS IN SICKNING MISTS I CAN NO LONGER HIDE	293	FOUR ZOAS 3	72
HIS WOES ALOUD TO ENITHARMON SINCE HE COULD NOT HIDE . .	307	FOUR ZOAS 5	96
O FOOL TO THINK THAT I COULD HIDE FROM HIS ALL PIERCING EYES	310	FOUR ZOAS 5	214
THE WATRY NATIONS COUCH & HIDE IN THE PROFOUNDEST DEEPS	320	FOUR ZOAS 7	24
TO LIGHT THE WAR BY DAY TO HIDE HIS SECRET BEAMS BY NIGHT	334	FOUR ZOAS 7B	36
SAYING IS THIS ETERNAL DEATH WHERE SHALL I HIDE FROM DEATH	349	FOUR ZOAS 8	332
DROOPING & THE BIRDS HIDE IN THEIR SILENT NESTS	355	FOUR ZOAS 8	567
WHERE IS THE LORD OF VALA DOST THOU HIDE IN CLEFTS OF THE ROCK	370	FOUR ZOAS 9	501
WHY SHOULDST THOU HIDE THYSELF FROM VALA	370	FOUR ZOAS 9	502
GO DOWN INTO THE DEPTHS GO DOWN & HIDE YOURSELVES BENEATH	374	FOUR ZOAS 9	660
THAT I SHOULD HIDE THEE WITH MY POWER & [DELIGHT THEE WITH MY BEAUTY]	382	FOUR ZOAS AD 5 *	16
OBSCURITIES TO HIDE FROM SATAN'S WATCH-FIENDS HUMAN LOVES	507	MILTON 23	40
IS OLOLON THE CAUSE OF THIS O WHERE SHALL I HIDE MY FACE	532	MILTON 40	14
[HE HAS] TAKE [THOU] YOU THE HIDE & HORNS	540	S(TOTHAR)D/N *	5
WHICH OUGHT TO DISPLAY AND NOT TO HIDE FORM	564D	DESC CAT 1	PROSE
SHUDDRING THEY FLEE THEY HIDE IN THE DRUID TEMPLES IN COLD CHASTITY	638	JERUSALEM 17	14
THY CRADLED INFANCY IS MOST PITEOUS O HIDE O HIDE . . .	644	JERUSALEM 21	24
WHERE SHALL I HIDE	645	JERUSALEM 22	13
HIDE THOU JERUSALEM IN IMPALPABLE VOIDNESS NOT TO BE . .	645	JERUSALEM 22	26
TO THE LAST DROP THEN HIDE ME IN THY SCARLET TABERNACLE	645	JERUSALEM 22	30
I WILL HIDE IT FROM ETERNALS I WILL GIVE MYSELF FOR MY CHILDREN	646	JERUSALEM 23	18
TO HIDE THEMSELVES WEEPING & LAMENTING FOR THE VEGETATION	655	JERUSALEM 30	7
TO HIDE THE MOST EVIDENT GOD IN A HIDDEN COVERT EVEN . .	661	JERUSALEM 34	32
CONSIDER SEXUAL ORGANIZATION & HIDE THEE IN THE DUST . .	661	JERUSALEM 34	58
TO HIDE THEM FROM THE WRATH OF ALBION'S LAW THAT FREEZES SORE	679	JERUSALEM 48	60
TO SIN & TO HIDE THE SIN IN SWEET DECEIT IS LOVELY . . .	681	JERUSALEM 50	25
LAMENTATION IT FLEE BACK & HIDE IN NON-ENTITY'S DARK WILD	688	JERUSALEM 56	16
THO VALA'S CLOUD HIDE THEE & LUVAH'S FIRES FOLLOW THEE . .	696	JERUSALEM 62	28
YORK & LINCOLN HIDE AMONG THE FLOCKS BECAUSE OF THE GRIDING KNIFE	703	JERUSALEM 66	65
REUBEN & BENJAMIN FLEE THEY HIDE IN THE VALLEY OF REPHAIM	706	JERUSALEM 68	47
WHAT IS THAT TALENT WHICH IT IS A CURSE TO HIDE . . .	717A	JERUSALEM 77	PROSE
BUT HIDE AMERICA FOR A CURSE AN ALTAR OF VICTIMS & A HOLY PLACE	725	JERUSALEM 82	29
HIDE NOT FROM MY SIGHT THY SIN	754	EV GOSPEL(E)/N	45
AND HIDE IN SECRET HIDDEN SHRINE	755	EV GOSPEL(E)/N *	65
DIVIDE MY GRIEFS WITH YOU THAT I CANNOT HIDE WHAT IT IS NOW	812B	LETTER 22	PROSE

HIDEOUS

IN VAIN FOR HIDEOUS MONSTERS OF THE DEEPS ANNOYD HIM SORE	313	FOUR ZOAS 6	75
WARRING WITH MONSTERS OF THE DEEPS IN HIS MOST HIDEOUS PILGRIMAGE	318	FOUR ZOAS 6	261
HIDEOUS OFFENDERS UTTERMOST EXTINCTION IN ETERNAL PAIN . .	330	FOUR ZOAS 7	427
THE WAR ROARD ROUND JERUSALEM'S GATES IT TOOK A HIDEOUS FORM	347	FOUR ZOAS 8	247
DISCLOSE A HIDEOUS ORIFICE THENCE ISSUING THE GIANT-BROOD	708	JERUSALEM 70	13

HIDES

WHATEVER HIDES THE FEMALE FORM	188	A FAIRY SKIPD	11
AND THERE THE EAGLE HIDES HER YOUNG IN CLIFFS & PRECIPICES	308	FOUR ZOAS 5	129
ONE GRINS [ONE] T OTHER SPITS & IN CORNERS HIDES . . .	545	COSWAY FRAZR/N	7

		PAGE	TITLE	LINE

HIDES   (CONTINUED)
WHERE HIDES MY CHILD IN OXFORD HIDEST THOU WITH ANTAMON   727 JERUSALEM 83   28
HIDEST
WHERE HIDES MY CHILD IN OXFORD HIDEST THOU WITH ANTAMON   727 JERUSALEM 83   28
LEST HAND THE TERRIBLE DESTROY HIS AFFECTION THOU HIDEST   727 JERUSALEM 83   30
   HER
KNOW THAT I NEVER WILL BE THINE ALSO THOU HIDEST VALA   .   .   733 JERUSALEM 87   22
HIDING
I KNOW NOT WHAT HIDING LOVE MEANS   .   .   .   .   .   .   78D ANNO LAVATER   MARG
RUSH INTO REPTILE COVERTS HIDING FROM THE FIRES OF ORC   .   202 AMERICA 15   20
HIDING THE DEMON RED WITH CLOUDS & COLD MISTS FROM THE   203 AMERICA 16   13
   EARTH
IN DARK SECRESY HIDING IN SURGEING   .   .   .   .   227 URIZEN 10   13
HIDING CAREFULLY FROM THE WIND   .   .   .   .   228 URIZEN 11   15
HIDING THEIR BOOKS & PICTURES UNDERNEATH THE DENS OF EARTH   275 FOUR ZOAS 1   397
ON HIGH INTO TWO LITTLE ORBS HIDING IN TWO LITTLE CAVES   .   303 FOUR ZOAS 4   229
HIDING CAREFULLY FROM THE WIND HIS EYES BEHELD THE DEEP   .   303 FOUR ZOAS 4   230
HIDING THEMSELVES IN ROCKY FORMS FROM THE EYES OF URIZEN   .   312 FOUR ZOAS 6   23
LOVELIEST DELIGHT OF MEN ENITHARMON SHADY HIDING   .   .   .   325 FOUR ZOAS 7   222
HERMAPHRODITIC IT AT LENGTH BECAME HIDING THE MALE   .   .   .   343 FOUR ZOAS 8   105
YET HIDING THE SHADOWY FEMALE VALA AS IN AN ARK & CURTAINS   347 FOUR ZOAS 8   255
HIDING HIS FACE IN THE DUST BENEATH [A] THE PRISONER'S   364 FOUR ZOAS 9   * 269
   FEET & SAYING
HIDING THE HUMAN LINEAMENTS AS WITH AN ARK & CURTAINS   .   .   533 MILTON 41   26
SO SPOKE ALBION IN JEALOUS FEARS HIDING HIS EMANATION   .   .   622 JERUSALEM 4   33
VALA REPLIED WEEPING & TREMBLING HIDING IN HER VEIL   .   .   642 JERUSALEM 20   11
UPON THE WAYS OF MEN HIDING THE PATHS OF MAN AND BEAST   .   .   642 JERUSALEM 20   13
UTTERING NOT HIS JEALOUSY BUT HIDING IT AS WITH   .   .   .   .   664 JERUSALEM 38   4
WE WOMEN TREMBLE AT THE LIGHT THEREFORE HIDING FEARFUL   .   .   688 JERUSALEM 56   39
HIDING ALBION'S SONS WITHIN THE VEIL CLOSING JERUSALEM'S   704 JERUSALEM 67   17
PLACE THE TRIBES OF LLEWELLYN IN AMERICA FOR A HIDING PLACE   728 JERUSALEM 83   59
HIDING HIS SPECTRE IN INVISIBILITY FROM THE TIMOROUS SHADE   732 JERUSALEM 86   54
THE PATHOS TO WEAVE CURTAINS OF HIDING SECRESY FROM THE   736 JERUSALEM 90   13
   TORMENT
("NEITHER DISCOVERING NOT HIDING HIMSELF") A FEMALE GOD   788C ANNO THORNTON   MARG
HIDINGS
IN GRACEFUL HIDINGS OF ERROR IN MERCIFUL DECEIT   .   .   .   727 JERUSALEM 83   29
ALL THEIR JEALOUSIES REVENGES MURDERS HIDINGS OF CRUELTY   739 JERUSALEM 92   16
   IN DECEIT
HIE
LITTLE WANDERER HIE THEE HOME   .   .   .   .   112 A DREAM/SI   20
HIGGLEDY PIGGLEDY
CLUMSY & RICKETTY PRINCES & PRINCESSES HIGGLEDY PIGGLEDY   599C PUB ADDRESS/N   PROSE
HIGH
THAT MADE MY LOVE SO HIGH AND ME SO LOW   .   .   .   .   .   10 WHEN EARLY/PS   16
ENTERING WITH HOLY FEET TO WHERE ON HIGH   .   .   .   .   .   15 IMIT SPEN/PS   22
OF ALPINE HILLS ROUND HIS HIGH AERY   .   .   .   .   15 IMIT SPEN/PS   38
PLUMES HIS WIDE WINGS AND SEEKS SOL'S PALACE HIGH   .   .   .   15 IMIT SPEN/PS   43
WORTHY THE HIGH COMMAND THAT HEAVEN AND YOU   .   .   .   .   23 EDW THIRD/PS 3   83
DOES RISE SO HIGH TO OVERFLOW ALL BOUNDS   .   .   .   .   .   26 EDW THIRD/PS 3   235
TILL INTO THE HIGH DOME OF PAUL'S THEY LIKE THAMES' WATERS   59 HOLY THURS/IM   4
   FLOW
[LET CHERUBIM & SERAPHIM NOW RAISE THEIR VOICES HIGH]   .   .   59 HOLY THURS/IM   14
IN HEAVEN'S HIGH BOWER   .   .   .   .   118 NIGHT/SI   6
TILL INTO THE HIGH DOME OF PAUL'S THEY LIKE THAMES WATERS   121 HOLY THURS/SI   4
   FLOW
NO BIRD SOARS TOO HIGH IF HE SOARS WITH HIS OWN WINGS   .   .   151B MARRIAGE HH 7   PROSE
AND STANDING ON THE ALTAR HIGH   .   .   .   .   177 LIT BOY LST/N   16
TO BUILD HIM CASTLES AND HIGH SPIRES WHERE KINGS & PRIESTS   193 V DAU ALBION 5   20
   MAY DWELL
RIVETS MY TENFOLD CHAINS WHILE STILL ON HIGH MY SPIRIT   196 AMERICA PREL 1   12
   SOARS
AND STANDING ON THE ALTAR HIGH   .   .   .   .   218 LIT BOY LST/SE   13
ON HIGH INTO TWO LITTLE ORBS   .   .   .   .   228 URIZEN 11   13
COLD HE WANDERD ON HIGH OVER THEIR CITIES   .   .   .   .   .   235 URIZEN 25   5
THE GLOBE OF WRATH SHAKING ON HIGH   .   .   .   .   249 AHANIA 2   16
LIFTED ON HIGH THE DEAD CORSE   .   .   .   .   251 AHANIA 3   52
AND HIGH ROOFED OVER WITH TREES   .   .   .   .   252 AHANIA 3   70
ROLLING ROUND & ROUND MOUNTING ON HIGH   .   .   .   .   .   .   256 BOOK OF LOS 3   36
THE BLACK MARBLE ON HIGH INTO FRAGMENTS   .   .   .   .   .   .   257 BOOK OF LOS 4   22
.   .   .   WITH HER TENDER LIMBS THEN HIGH SHE SOARD   .   .   .   269 FOUR ZOAS 1   182
A GROAN WAS HEARD ON HIGH THE WARLIKE CLARIONS CEAST THE   273 FOUR ZOAS 1   313
   SPIRITS
ON HIGH REMAIND ALONE FORSAKEN IN FIERCE JEALOUSY   .   .   .   274 FOUR ZOAS 1   360
AND SPIRITS OF FLAMING FIRE ON HIGH GOVERND THE MIGHTY SONG   274 FOUR ZOAS 1   384
AFAR INTO THE ZENITH HIGH BENDING THY FURIOUS COURSE   .   .   278 FOUR ZOAS 1   495
ABOVE [MOUNT GILEAD] HIGH SNOWDON   .   .   .   .   279 FOUR ZOAS 1   552
[ORBITS HIGH] [DEMONS BY THE THOUSANDS OUT OF A GOLDEN   SUPP FOUR ZOAS 1   *
   CLOUD XXX]
ON BROAD PAVILIONS ON PILLARD ROOFS & PORCHES &   286 FOUR ZOAS 2   252
   HIGH TOWERS
IT RISES UP ON HIGH ALL SUMMER TILL ITS WEARIED COURSE   .   .   287 FOUR ZOAS 2   280
NOW SAT THE KING OF LIGHT ON HIGH UPON HIS STARRY THRONE   291 FOUR ZOAS 3   1
AND NOW THE HUMAN BLOOD FOAMD HIGH I SAW THAT LUVAH & VALA   294 FOUR ZOAS 3   94
BENT BY ITS FALL FROM A HIGH TOWER THE DOLOROUS SHADOW ROSE   299 FOUR ZOAS 4   66
WHIRLING UP BROKEN ROCKS ON HIGH INTO THE DISMAL AIR   .   .   301 FOUR ZOAS 4   163
ON HIGH INTO TWO LITTLE ORBS HIDING IN TWO LITTLE CAVES   .   303 FOUR ZOAS 4   229
THE COUNCIL OF GOD ON HIGH WATCHING OVER THE BODY   .   .   .   304 FOUR ZOAS 4   247
INFECTED MAD HE DANCD ON HIS MOUNTAINS HIGH & DARK   305 FOUR ZOAS 5   1
   AS HEAVEN
HE TOOK HIGH BOUNDING OVER HILLS & DESARTS FLOODS   313 FOUR ZOAS 6   73
   & HORRIBLE CHASMS

```
                                                              PAGE      TITLE       LINE
HIGH    (CONTINUED)
    CIRCLE OER CIRCLE NOR ON HIGH ATTAIN A VOID    . . . .   316  FOUR ZOAS 6        197
    BUT WHEN A VORTEX FORMD ON HIGH BY LABOUR & SORROW & CARE 317  FOUR ZOAS 6        204
    AND HIGH ROOFED OVER WITH TREES HE AROSE BUT THE STEMS .  321  FOUR ZOAS 7         37
    FLAME HIGH IN PRIDE & LAUGH TO SCORN THE SOURCE OF HIS    324  FOUR ZOAS 7        158
      DECEIT
    THAT WISDOM REACHES HIGH & DEEP & THEREFORE HE MADE ORC   324  FOUR ZOAS 7        162
    VALA THE LILLY OF THE DESERT MELTING IN HIGH NOON   . . . 326  FOUR ZOAS 7        240
    THEY BUILDED GOLGONOOZA LOS LABOURING [INSPIRD] BUILDED   329  FOUR ZOAS 7      * 378
      PILLARS HIGH
    TO RISE ON HIGH YET LOVE HERE BINDS ME DOWN & NEVER NEVER 339  FOUR ZOAS 7B       254
    OR LIKE A CLOUD BENEATH & LIKE A FIRE FLAMING IN HIGH  .  339  FOUR ZOAS 7B     * 265
    THAT MOVD WITH HORRIBLE DREAMS & (HOVRING) HIGH OVER HIS  341  FOUR ZOAS 8      *   6
      HEAD
    THARMAS [ABOVE] ON HIGH RODE FURIOUS THRO THE AFFLICTED   353  FOUR ZOAS 8        485
      WORLDS
    HIGH SPIRES & CASTLES DROWND IN THE BLACK DELUGE SHOAL    359  FOUR ZOAS 9         76
      ON SHOAL
    AND BUILDING ARCHES HIGH & CITIES TURRETS & [HIGH ] TOWERS 361 FOUR ZOAS 9        167
      & DOMES
    EXCESS OF JOY IS WORSE THAN GRIEF HER HEART BEAT HIGH HER 362  FOUR ZOAS 9        197
      BLOOD
    THE HUMAN FORM DIVINE THROWN DOWN FROM THEIR HIGH STATION 366  FOUR ZOAS 9        367
    SOUNDING HIS TRUMPET TO AWAKE THE DEAD ON HIGH HE SOARD   373  FOUR ZOAS 9        615
    SCATTER THE PERFUME OF HIS BREATH WHILE FROM HIS MOUNTAINS 376 FOUR ZOAS 9        705
      HIGH
    THARMAS BEHELD FROM HIS HIGH ROCKS &C  . . . . . . . .    381  FOUR ZOAS AD 1   *  20
    . . . WITH HER TENDER LIMBS THEN HIGH SHE SOARD  . . . .  381  FOUR ZOAS AD 5       2
    THE WHEEL OF VOLTAIRE WHIRLD ON HIGH  . . . . . . . .     420  I SAW MNK AD/N      15
    EXHALES ON HIGH . . . . . . . . . . . . . . . . .        421  MORNING/N            9
    TO WHERE MY BOWER HANGS ON HIGH   . . . . . . . . .       423  THE BIRDS/N         18
    OR IF PROTECTED FROM ON HIGH   . . . . . . . . .          433  AUGURIES            83
    GIVE HIGH PRICE FOR THE WORST LEAVE THE BEST IN DISGRACE  445  ANNO REYNOLDS        3
    WITH ECCHOING CONFUSION THO THE SUN WAS RISEN ON HIGH  .  488  MILTON 8            10
    AND LOS SAID YE GENII OF THE MILLS THE SUN IS ON HIGH  .  488  MILTON 8            16
    WHICH NOW FLAMD HIGH & FURIOUS IN SATAN AGAINST PALAMABRON 489 MILTON 9           11
    AND EVERY MONTH A SILVER PAVED TERRACE BUILDED HIGH  . .  516  MILTON 28           54
    AND EVERY YEAR INVULNERABLE BARRIERS WITH HIGH TOWERS  .  516  MILTON 28           55
    [A PRETTY EPIGRAM FOR THOSE WHO HAVE GIVEN HIGH PRICES]   547A PRETTY EPIGR/N   TITLE
    NO ONE CAN FINISH SO HIGH AS THE ORIGINAL INVENTOR   . .  555  BLAKES APL/N 1      19
    NO ONE CAN FINISH SO HIGH AS THE ORIGINAL INVENTOR   . .  556  BLAKES APL/N 2      18
    IN MY GOLDEN HOUSE ON HIGH  . . . . . . . . . . .         558  THE CAVERNS/N       19
    IN HIGH FINISHED FRESCO WHERE THE COLOURS WOULD BE AS PURE 566A DESC CAT 2      PROSE
    ALL FRESCOES ARE AS HIGH FINISHED AS MINIATURES OR ENAMELS 566B DESC CAT 2      PROSE
    THAT UNAFFECTED SIMPLICITY WHEN IN HIGH RANK ALWAYS       568A DESC CAT 3      PROSE
      DISPLAYS
    AND DOMINEERS OVER THE HIGH AND LOW VULGAR THIS MAN  . .  570A DESC CAT 3      PROSE
    HIS NOSE HIGH ON THE RIDGE AND NARROW HIS CHEST AND THE   580A DESC CAT 5      PROSE
    AFTERWARD EXECUTED FOR A LADY OF HIGH RANK AN EXPERIMENT  582B DESC CAT 9      TITLE
      PICTURE
    BY (ONE) FOOT HIGH THE ARTIST ENGAGES TO DELIVER IT  . .  587A CHAUCER 1       PROSE
    (THREE) FEET (ONE) INCH LONG BY ONE FOOT HIGH CONTAINING  587D CHAUCER/N       PROSE
    THREE FEET 1 INCH LONG AND I FOOT HIGH PRICE THREE GUINEAS 589C CHAUCER 2      TITLE
    FROM YOUR HIGH FLIGHTS YE MUST CONDESCEND TO STUDY   . .  593C PUB ADDRESS/N   PROSE
    NO ONE CAN FINISH SO HIGH AS THE ORIGINAL INVENTOR   . .  596  BLAKES APOL/PA      12
    & HANG THEIR SOULS AS GUILTY OF MENTAL HIGH TREASON  . .  599D PUB ADDRESS/N   PROSE
    AMONG HER GOLDEN PILLARS HIGH  . . . . . . . . . .        650  FIELDS FROM/J       10
    AND NOW THE HUMAN BLOOD FOAMD HIGH THE SPIRITS LUVAH & VALA 655 JERUSALEM 29      73
    ALBION THE HIGH CLIFF OF THE ATLANTIC IS BECOME A BARREN  660  JERUSALEM 34        16
      LAND
    AND NOT THE TABERNACLE & TEMPLE OF THE MOST HIGH  . . .   661  JERUSALEM 34        30
    HIS STRONG LIMBS SHUDDERD UPON HIS MOUNTAINS HIGH AND DARK 664 JERUSALEM 38        6
    AND MERCIFUL THE INDIVIDUALITY HOWEVER HIGH  . . . . .    675  JERUSALEM 45        11
    THE SEAS RAISD UP THEIR VOICES & LIFTED THEIR HANDS ON HIGH 686 JERUSALEM 55      26
    TREMBLING & DESCENDING DOWN SEEKING TO REST UPON HIGH MONA 703 JERUSALEM 66     *  79
    AND NOT A POMPOUS HIGH PRIEST ENTERING BY A SECRET PLACE  708  JERUSALEM 69        44
    TO TELL HOW LOS IN GRIEF & ANGER WHIRLING ROUND HIS HAMMER 714 JERUSALEM 74       20
      ON HIGH
    GOD'S HIGH KING & GOD'S HIGH PRIEST    . . . . . . .      749  EV GOSPEL(B)/N      19
    BOAST OF HIGH THINGS WITH HUMBLE TONE    . . . . . . .    751  EV GOSPEL(D)/N       3
    YOU BEAR IT ON YOUR ALTARS HIGH    . . . . . . . . .      761  FOR SEXES/GP        13
    WHAT IS IT SETS HOMER VIRGIL & MILTON IN SO HIGH A RANK   794A LETTER 5        PROSE
      OF ART
    FROM HEAVEN'S HIGH STREAMS  . . . . . . . . . . .        804  TO BUTTS/L           6
    AT A DISTANCE THE SOUTH BOUNDS ON HIGH OVER OUR THATCH AND 807B LETTER 17       PROSE
    OUT OF DESPONDENCY EVEN IF IT LIFTS ME TOO HIGH  . . .    822C LETTER 26       PROSE
    THIS WAS THE WOMAN'S OWN REMARK & DOES HIGH HONOUR TO HER 827C LETTER 28       PROSE
    IN HIGH SPIRITS & WELCOMD ME WITH KIND AFFECTION &  . . . 833C LETTER 33       PROSE
    MY WIFE'S HIGH GRATIFICATION IN THE PERUSAL OF  . . .     853A LETTER 51       *PROSE
    WHOSE HIGH & GENEROUS SPIRIT RELINQUISHING THE WHOLE TO ME 853A LETTER 51       *PROSE
    SO HIGH FINISHED A STATE I AM SURE MARK MY CONFIDENCE  .  853B LETTER 52       PROSE
HIGH ARCHING
    ABOVE HIS HEAD HIGH ARCHING WINGS BLACK FILLD WITH EYES   735  JERUSALEM 89        28
HIGH BREATHING
    HANDS HEAD BOSOM AND PARTS OF LOVE FOLLOW THEIR HIGH      142  FRENCH REVOLTN     185
      BREATHING JOY
HIGHER
    HEAP THE SEA-COAL COME HEAP IT HIGHER  . . . . . . .       16  BLIND-MANS/PS        5
    A LITTLE BRAT NO HIGHER THAN A NETTLE & SHE HAD AS MUCH   53B  ISLAND MOON 8    PROSE
    MY DEAR THEY HATE PEOPLE WHO ARE OF HIGHER ABILITIES  . . 63A  ISLAND MOON 11   PROSE
    DARTED & DARTED HIGHER & HIGHER TO THE SHRINE OF          320  FOUR ZOAS 7         22
      ENITHARMON
```

915

```
                                                          PAGE      TITLE          LINE
HIGHER    (CONTINUED)
    BETTER AND HIGHER AND THE POOR WRETCH WHO EXECUTED IT    .  . 583C DESC CAT 9      PROSE
    SUSCEPTIBLE OF HIGHER FINISHING THAN DRAWING ON PAPER    .  . 585A DESC CAT 15     PROSE
    SETH IS MALE & FEMALE IN A HIGHER STATE OF HAPPINESS     .  . 611C V LAST JUDG/N   PROSE
HIGHEST
    MY LORD WAS LIKE A STAR IN HIGHEST HEAVN  . . . . . .  .  .    5 FAIR ELENOR/PS      45
    GOD IS IN THE LOWEST EFFECTS AS WELL AS IN THE HIGHEST       87A ANNO LAVATER      MARG
        CAUSES
    AS FAR AS HIGHEST ZENITH FROM THE LOWEST (NADIR) SO FAR     305 FOUR ZOAS 5      *  14
        SHRUNK
    [POINTED AT TOP IN HIGHEST HEAVENS OF PRECIOUS STONES &     341 FOUR ZOAS 8         14
        PEARL]
    AND LET US GO TO THE HIGHEST DOWNS  . . . . . . . .  .  . 417 MY SPECTR AD/N *   13
    IN THE HIGHEST DEGREE FOR HE HAS EVERY [PERQUISITE] THING   472A ANNO REYNOLDS * MARG
        OF BOTH
    WHEN ON THE HIGHEST LIFT OF HIS LIGHT PINIONS HE ARRIVES    526 MILTON 36           1
    GRAND IN THE HIGHEST DEGREE THE ARTIST HAS ENDEAVOURED   .  . 565D DESC CAT 2      PROSE
    BUT WITH THE HIGHEST COURAGE SUPERADDED  . . . . .  .  . 571D DESC CAT 3        PROSE
    HIGHEST ANTIQUITY ADAM WAS A DRUID AND NOAH   . . . .  .  . 578A DESC CAT 5      PROSE
    GIANTS & FAIRIES HAVING RECIEVD THE HIGHEST REWARD POSSIBLE 620D JERUSALEM 3      PROSE
    CONJURING HIM BY THE HIGHEST THAT HE SHOULD WATCH OVER THEM  674 JERUSALEM 44        29
    EVEN TO THE TEMPLE'S HIGHEST STEEPLE  . . . . . . .  .  . 752 EV GOSPEL(D)/N      70
    CLIMBING THRO NIGHT'S HIGHEST NOON  . . . . . . . .  .  . 771 OF GATES/GP          32
    ("TO HC SIX YEARS OLD") THIS IS ALL IN THE HIGHEST DEGREE   783A ANNO WW POEMS     MARG
        IMAGINATIVE
    IN THAT HIGHEST BRANCH OF ART I MUST NOW TELL MY WANTS   .  . 851A LETTER 49       PROSE
HIGH FINISHD
    OF PRINTED & AT EVERY OTHER [?SHEET CA] LEAF A HIGH FINISHD  62D ISLAND MOON 11 *PROSE
        PRINT
    THIRTY ORIGINAL HIGH FINISHD WHOLE LENGTH PORTRAITS  .  . . 587D CHAUCER/N        PROSE
    I ALLOW THAT THERE IS SUCH A THING AS HIGH FINISHD         593B PUB ADDRESS/N     PROSE
        IGNORANCE
    P S I MADE A VERY HIGH FINISHD DRAWING OF ROMNEY AS A   .  . 855D LETTER 53       PROSE
    LITTLE HIGH FINISHD PICTURES THE SIZE THE ENGRAVINGS ARE    859B LETTER 56        PROSE
        TO BE
HIGH FINISHED
    EVERY THING IN FRESCO IS AS HIGH FINISHED AS MINIATURE      561A EXHIBITION ADV   PROSE
HIGH FINISHER
    CAST ON THE INSPIRED BY THE TAME HIGH FINISHER OF PALTRY    533 MILTON 41           9
        BLOTS
HIGH FINISHINGS
    THAT FOOLS HAVE THEIR HIGH FINISHINGS  . . . . . .  .  . 547 LET BE TOLD/N         3
HIGH FLAMING
    OF ANOTHER'S HIGH FLAMING RICH BOSOM . . . . . . . .  .  . 142 FRENCH REVOLTN       192
HIGHGATE
    TO PRIMROSE HILL STRETCHING TO HIGHGATE & HOLLOWAY   .  . . 531 MILTON 39           38
    HAMPSTEAD HIGHGATE FINCHLEY HENDON MUSWELL HILL RAGE LOUD   636 JERUSALEM 16         1
    HE CAME DOWN FROM HIGHGATE THRO HACKNEY & HOLLOWAY TOWARDS  657 JERUSALEM 31        14
        LONDON
    FROM CAMBERWELL TO HIGHGATE WHERE THE MIGHTY THAMES         677 JERUSALEM 47         2
        SHUDDERS ALONG
    OF LONDON CITY ON THE THAMES FROM SURREY HILLS TO HIGHGATE  728 JERUSALEM 83        68
    WHEN I WAS YOUNG HAMPSTEAD HIGHGATE HORNSEA MUSWELL HILL &  871A LETTER 72        PROSE
HIGHGATE'S
    BEFORE LONDON TO HAMPSTEAD'S BREADTHS & HIGHGATE'S HEIGHTS  485 MILTON 6            9
        TO
    ON HIGHGATE'S HEIGHTS MAGNIFICENT WEAVES OVER TREMBLING     525 MILTON 35          12
        THAMES
    HIGHGATE'S HEIGHTS & HAMPSTEAD'S TO POPLAR HACKNEY & BOW    729 JERUSALEM 84         1
    HAND HAD HIS FURNACE ON HIGHGATE'S HEIGHTS & IT REACHD   .  . 736 JERUSALEM 90       23
HIGH LABOURD
    HIS PICTURES ARE HIGH LABOURD PRETENSIONS TO EXPEDITIOUS    468B ANNO REYNOLDS     MARG
    LEARN THE [?WOBLY [HIGH LABOUR] PRETENTIOUS] . . . .  .  . 547 RAFAEL SUBLI/N *    5
    AND HOW HIGH LABOUR IS EVERY STEP  . . . . . . . .  .  . 548 CRIPPLE EVRY/N        9
HIGHLY
    BUT MILD HE HAILED HER HAIL HIGHLY FAVOURED SAID HE  .  . . 39D SAMSON/PS         PROSE
    HIGHLY FINISHED ENGRAVINGS AND TWO MORE ARE NEARLY READY    207C PRSPECTUS 1793    PROSE
    THE HIGHLY CULTIVATED STATES OF EGYPT MOAB EDOM ARAM   .  . 565C DESC CAT 2       PROSE
    THO WE OUGHT NOT THINK MORE HIGHLY OF OURSELVES YET WE      811C LETTER 22        PROSE
        OUGHT TO
    THINK AS HIGHLY OF OURSELVES AS IMMORTALS OUGHT TO THINK    811C LETTER 22        PROSE
    I AM EITHER TOO LOW OR TOO HIGHLY PRIZD  . . . . .  .  . 829 O WHY BORN/L          9
    THE PICTURE IS VERY HIGHLY FINISHED  . . . . . . . .  .  . 843D LETTER 43        PROSE
    IN THE HIGHLY FINISHED MANNER & (FOUR) IN A LESS FINISHD    848B LETTER 45        PROSE
    IN VERY GREAT FORWARDNESS PARKER COMMENDS IT HIGHLY   .  . . 849A LETTER 45       PROSE
    TO WEAR & THAT WE ARE BOTH HIGHLY DELIGHTED  . . . .  .  . 853A LETTER 51       *PROSE
    IT MUST BE SOON A HIGHLY FINISHED AND PROPERLY FINISHED     853C LETTER 52        PROSE
        PRINT
    OF THIS BEAUTIFUL LITTLE ESTATE FOR THAT IT WILL BE HIGHLY  858C LETTER 55        PROSE
    TO FINISH BY...MAY THEY ARE TO BE AS HIGHLY FINISHD AS      859A LETTER 56        PROSE
        I CAN
    ASSURE YOU A PLEASING ONE TO ME IT WILL BE HIGHLY          859C LETTER 56        PROSE
        GRATIFYING
    HIGHLY LABOURD PLATES THAN A GREATER NUMBER & LESS FINISHD  860C LETTER 56        PROSE
HIGH-REARD
    STANDING ON ALBION'S ROCKS AMONG HIGH-REARD DRUID TEMPLES   489 MILTON 9           14
HIGHTH       SEE HEIGHTH
    MOCKING DRUIDICAL MATHEMATICAL PROPORTION OF LENGTH BREDTH  484 MILTON 4           27
        HIGHTH
    RETAINING ONLY SATAN'S MATHEMATIC HOLINESS LENGTH BREDTH    521 MILTON 32          18
        & HIGHTH
    AND ACCIDENT & CHANCE WERE FOUND HIDDEN IN LENGTH BREDTH    663 JERUSALEM 36        35
        & HIGHTH
```

916

		PAGE	TITLE	LINE

HIGHTH   (CONTINUED)
AND LENGTH BREDTH HIGHTH AGAIN OBEY THE DIVINE VISION   664 JERUSALEM 36   56
   HALLELUJAH
AND FRAMED THE MUNDANE SHELL CAVERNOUS IN LENGTH BREDTH   740 JERUSALEM 92   27
   & HIGHTH
HIGH TONED
LOUD VOICD BARD AND MANY CONDEMND THE HIGH TONED SONG   . .   495 MILTON 13   47
HIGH-TOWERING
THERE STAND THE VENERABLE PORCHES THAT HIGH-TOWERING REAR   241 EUROPE 10   6
HILI
[?HILI] HELA MY YOUNGEST DAUGHTER YOU SHALL LEAD ME FROM   106 TIRIEL 5   *   24
   THIS PLACE
HE CEAST & [?HILI] HELA LED HER FATHER FROM THE NOISOM   107 TIRIEL 5   *   26
   PLACE
AND [?HILI] HELA LED HER FATHER THRO THE SILENT OF THE   107 TIRIEL 6   *   1
   NIGHT
NOW [?HILI] HELA I CAN GO WITH PLEASURE & DWELL WITH HAR   107 TIRIEL 6   *   3
   & HEVA
THAT OUR FEET MAKE REMEMBER [?HILI] HELA I HAVE SAVD THEE   107 TIRIEL 6   *   6
   FROM DEATH
TRUE [?HILI] HELA THIS IS THE DESERT OF ALL THOSE CRUEL   107 TIRIEL 6   *   16
   ONES
HILKIAH
THE PERSON NAMD IN ISAIAH XXII ... ELIAKIM THE SON   607D V LAST JUDG/N   PROSE
   OF HILKIAH
HILL   SEE DUNG HILL
I LOVE THE ECHOING HILL   . . . .   7 LOVE JOCUND/PS   6
FRESH FROM THE DEWY HILL THE MERRY YEAR . . . . . .   9 FRESH FROM/PS   1
THE BOSOM OF THE LOFTY HILL DRANK IN THE SILENT DEW   . . .   36C COUCH DEATH/PS   PROSE
THE ECHOES OF SLAUGHTER REACH FROM HILL TO HILL . . . .   40B SAMSON/PS   PROSE
AND LAUGHING [UPON] IS HEARD ON THE HILL . . . . . .   60 NURSES SONG/IM   2
AND THE GREEN HILL LAUGHS WITH THE NOISE OF IT   . . . .   63 SHEPHERD YOUNG   2
AND LAUGHING IS HEARD ON THE HILL . . . .   121 NURSES SONG/SI   2
AND THE GREEN HILL LAUGHS WITH THE NOISE OF IT   . . . .   124 LAUGHING/SI   4
. . . THE VOICE OF THE PEOPLE ARISING FROM VALLEY AND HILL   143 FRENCH REVOLTN   206
TO SHOOTERS HILL AND THENCE TO BLACKHEATH THE DARK WOOF   525 MILTON 35   13
   LOUD
TO PRIMROSE HILL STRETCHING TO HIGHGATE & HOLLOWAY   . . .   531 MILTON 39   38
ARE PRACTISED IN BABEL & SHINAR & HAVE APPROACHD TO ZION'S   627 JERUSALEM 8   20
   HILL
HAMPSTEAD HIGHGATE FINCHLEY HENDON MUSWELL HILL RAGE LOUD   636 JERUSALEM 16   1
TO PRIMROSE HILL AND SAINT JOHNS WOOD . . . .   649 FIELDS FROM/J   2
HE WITHERD UP SWEET ZION'S HILL . . . .   651 FIELDS FROM/J   49
FROM HILL TO HILL & THE THAMES LAMENTS ALONG THE VALLEYS   656 JERUSALEM 30   24
I WAS A GARDEN PLANTED WITH BEAUTY I ALLURED ON HILL &   659 JERUSALEM 33   37
   VALLEY
ALBION IS SICK SAID EVERY VALLEY EVERY MOURNFUL HILL   . .   667 JERUSALEM 40   11
PRIMROSE HILL IS THE MOUTH OF THE FURNACE & THE IRON DOOR   714 JERUSALEM 73   54
THE HILL OF GIANTS ALL HER FOUNDATIONS LEVELLD WITH THE   719 JERUSALEM 78   22
   DUST
LANGUISHD UPON MOUNT OLIVET EAST OF MILD ZION'S HILL . .   726 JERUSALEM 82   55
HIS VOICE WAS HEARD FROM ZION'S HILL . . . .   749 EV GOSPEL(B)/N   46
THE LOST TRAVELLER'S DREAM UNDER THE HILL . . . . . .   771 EPILOGUE/GP   8
EACH ROCK & EACH HILL . . . .   805 TO BUTTS/L   27
MOUNTAIN HILL EARTH & SEA . . . .   805 TO BUTTS/L   30
EVEN SNOW HILL IS BECOME ALMOST LEVEL . . . .   831D LETTER 31   PROSE
WHEN I WAS YOUNG HAMPSTEAD HIGHGATE HORNSEA MUSWELL HILL &   871A LETTER 72   PROSE
HILLEL
THEN HILLEL WHO IS LUCIFER REPLIED OVER THE COUCH OF DEATH   521 MILTON 32   8
HILLOCKS
MILTON WALKING BY ELMS ON HILLOCKS GREEN THE PLOWMAN   . .   618B ILLUS MILTON   PROSE
HILL'S
MILD ZION'S HILL'S MOST ANCIENT PROMONTORY NEAR MOURNFUL   632 JERUSALEM 12   27
ON TYBURN'S RIVER IN CLOUDS OF BLOOD WHERE WAS MILD ZION   653 JERUSALEM 29   3
   HILL'S
A DRAGON FORM ON ZION HILL'S MOST ANCIENT PROMONTORY   . .   722 JERUSALEM 80   36
HILLS
THE HILLS TELL EACH OTHER AND THE LISTNING . . . . . .   1 TO SPRING/PS   5
COME OER THE EASTERN HILLS AND LET OUR WINDS . . . . .   1 TO SPRING/PS   9
HILLS FLED FROM OUR SIGHT BUT LEFT HIS GOLDEN LOAD . . .   2 TO AUTUMN/PS   18
THY BUSKIND FEET APPEAR UPON OUR HILLS . . . .   3 TO MORNING/PS   8
HE SHOOK THE HILLS AND IN THE CLOUDS . . . .   11 GWIN KING/PS   15
DOWN BLERON'S HILLS THEY DREADFUL RUSH . . . .   11 GWIN KING/PS   21
FIGHT UPON HILLS OF SLAIN . . . .   13 GWIN KING/PS   88
OF ALPINE HILLS ROUND HIS HIGH AERY . . . .   15 IMIT SPEN/PS   38
SPRINGS FROM THE HILLS LIKE A YOUNG HERO . . . . . .   21 EDW THIRD/PS 3   3
ARE HEARD FROM THE HILLS THE ENORMOUS SONS   . . . . .   32 EDW THIRD/PS 6   20
THE VEILED EVENING WALKED SOLITARY DOWN THE WESTERN HILLS   35C COUCH DEATH/PS   PROSE
THEN PRAYED MANOA O LORD THY FLOCK IS SCATTERED ON THE   40A SAMSON/PS   PROSE
   HILLS
WAS ROME SEATED ON SEVEN HILLS THE MISTRESS OF THE WORLD   41A THEN SHE BORE   PROSE
AND ALL THE HILLS ECCHOED . . . .   60 NURSES SONG/IM   17
OVER THE WEARY HILLS THE BLIND MAN TOOK HIS LONELY WAY .   103 TIRIEL 4   1
AND THEY WENT ON TOGETHER OVER HILLS THRO WOODY DALES   . .   104 TIRIEL 4   28
AND THE HILLS ARE ALL COVERD WITH SHEEP . . . . . .   121 NURSES SONG/SI   12
AND ALL THE HILLS ECCHOED . . . .   121 NURSES SONG/SI   16
. . . FROM THE WINDOW HE SAW HIS VAST ARMIES SPREAD OVER   137 FRENCH REVOLTN   80
   THE HILLS
. . . FOR A CLOUD ON THE EASTERN HILLS . . . .   146 FRENCH REVOLTN   271
. . . ASCEND ON THE HILLS AND BRIGHT INFANTRY RANK   . . .   147 FRENCH REVOLTN   291
THEY CANNOT BRING THE STUBBED OAK TO OVERGROW THE HILLS   199 AMERICA 9   8
ON THOSE VAST SHADY HILLS BETWEEN AMERICA & ALBION'S SHORE   200 AMERICA 10   5

		PAGE	TITLE	LINE
HILLS	(CONTINUED)			
NOW BARRD OUT BY THE ATLANTIC SEA CALLD ATLANTEAN HILLS		200	AMERICA 10	6
THEIR HEADS ON SNOWY HILLS THEIR ENSIGNS SICKNING IN THE SKY		202	AMERICA 15	10
OVER THE HILLS THE VALES THE CITIES RAGE THE RED FLAMES FIERCE		202	AMERICA 16	1
IN HIS HILLS OF STORD SNOWS IN HIS MOUNTAINS		223	URIZEN 3	32
[THEY] HE DUG MOUNTAINS & HILLS IN VAST STRENGTH		225	URIZEN 5	* 22
FORTHWITH HATCHING SOME HOWLD ON HIS HILLS		250	AHANIA 3	11
THE BOW STRING SANG UPON THE HILLS LUVAH & VALA RIDE .		275	FOUR ZOAS 1	408
SLEPT ROUND ON HILLS & VALLEYS IN THE REGIONS OF HIS LOVE		277	FOUR ZOAS 1	486
STRIPPING JERUSALEM'S CURTAINS FROM MILD DEMONS OF THE HILLS		281	FOUR ZOAS 2	58
THE SEAS & LAKES THEY REARD THE MOUNTAINS & THE ROCKS & HILLS		286	FOUR ZOAS 2	251
THY EDDYING SPIRIT DOWN THE HILLS OF BEULAH ALL MY SONS		300	FOUR ZOAS 4	89
SING IN THE SKY AS ONCE THEY SANG UPON THE HILLS OF LIGHT		306	FOUR ZOAS 5	52
HE TOOK HIGH BOUNDING OVER HILLS & DESARTS FLOODS & HORRIBLE CHASMS		313	FOUR ZOAS 6	73
TERRIFIC VOYAGE HILLS & VALES OF TORMENT & DESPAIR . . .		315	FOUR ZOAS 6	151
WHEN THE MOUNTAINS & HILLS ARE COVERD OVER & THE PATHS OF MEN SHUT UP		324	FOUR ZOAS 7	174
THY OLIVE TREES THAT POURD DOWN OIL UPON A THOUSAND HILLS		325	FOUR ZOAS 7	192
OUTSTRETCHD UPON THE HILLS LAY ENITHARMON CLOUDS & TEMPESTS		334	FOUR ZOAS 7B	73
STAMPING THE HILLS WADING OR SWIMMING FLYING FURIOUS OR FALLING		339	FOUR ZOAS 7B	263
WALKING IN PLEASURE OF THE HILLS OR MURMURING IN THE DALES		340	FOUR ZOAS 7B	266
APPEARS UPON THE ROCKS & HILLS IN SILENT SHADES BUT SOON		355	FOUR ZOAS 8	539
THE FOUNDATIONS OF THE ETERNAL HILLS DISCOVERD		357	FOUR ZOAS 9	17
MY BIRDS ARE SILENT ON MY HILLS FLOCKS DIE BENEATH MY BRANCHES		359	FOUR ZOAS 9	101
IS SILENT ON MY CLOUDED HILLS THAT BELCH FORTH STORMS & FIRES		359	FOUR ZOAS 9	* 103
FOR FROM MY PLEASANT HILLS BEHOLD THE LIVING LIVING SPRINGS		368	FOUR ZOAS 9	441
AND GIVEN ME FRUITS & PLEASANT WATERS & WARM HILLS & COOL VALLEYS		369	FOUR ZOAS 9	452
BUT HER FLOCKS WERE GONE UP FROM BENEATH THE TREES INTO THE HILLS		369	FOUR ZOAS 9	473
SHE EMBRACD THEM IN TEARS TILL THE SUN DESCENDED THE WESTERN HILLS		370	FOUR ZOAS 9	512
AND WHEN MORNING BEGAN TO DAWN UPON THE DISTANT HILLS . .		372	FOUR ZOAS 9	590
FOR LO THE WINTER MELTED AWAY UPON THE DISTANT HILLS . .		373	FOUR ZOAS 9	600
COVERD THE HILLS HE SAID O THARMAS RISE & O URTHONA . .		377	FOUR ZOAS 9	773
FOR THARMAS BROUGHT HIS FLOCKS UPON THE HILLS & IN THE VALES		379	FOUR ZOAS 9	838
WITH FEMALE VOICE WARBLING UPON THE [HILLS &] HOLLOW VALES		381	FOUR ZOAS AD 5	8
ANOTHER THAMES & OTHER HILLS		429	CRYSTL CABINET	11
[THE] GREEN HILLS APPEAR BENEATH WITH THE GRAVES OF THE BLESSED		443D	LAST JUDGMNT/L	PROSE
SHINE FORTH UPON OUR CLOUDED HILLS		481	AND DID FEET/M	6
THE SURREY HILLS GLOW LIKE THE CLINKERS OF THE FURNACE LAMBETH'S VALE		485	MILTON 6	14
LOUD AS THE WIND OF BEULAH THAT UNROOTS THE ROCKS & HILLS		487	MILTON 7	33
OF VARYING COLOURS ON THE HILLS TERRIBLY RAGD THE HORSES		492	MILTON 12	15
AND HILLS OUT FROM THE OPTIC NERVE & HARDENING IT INTO A BONE		515	MILTON 28	34
WITH SOLEMN MOURNING INTO BEULAH'S MOONY SHADES & HILLS		518	MILTON 30	5
AND THE WILD THYME FROM WIMBLETON'S GREEN & IMPURPLED HILLS		534	MILTON 42	30
AND LOS & ENITHARMON ROSE OVER THE HILLS OF SURREY . .		534	MILTON 42	31
THE SCENE OF MR S'S(STOTHARD'S) PICTURE IS BY DULWICH HILLS		575B	DESC CAT 3	PROSE
IN ALL THE DARK ATLANTIC VALE DOWN FROM THE HILLS OF SURREY		622	JERUSALEM 4	9
STAND ROUND HIM CUTTING THE FIBRES FROM ALBION'S HILLS . .		636	JERUSALEM 15	23
HIS BIRDS ARE SILENT ON HIS HILLS FLOCKS DIE BENEATH HIS BRANCHES		641	JERUSALEM 19	2
ARE SILENT ON HIS CLOUDED HILLS THAT BELCH FORTH STORMS & FIRE		641	JERUSALEM 19	4
YET THOU WAST LOVELY AS THE SUMMER CLOUD UPON MY HILLS . .		647	JERUSALEM 24	36
THESE HILLS & VALLEYS ARE ACCURSED WITNESSES OF SIN . . .		652	JERUSALEM 28	9
WE FLEE FROM THE INTERIORS OF ALBION'S HILLS AND MOUNTAINS		654	JERUSALEM 29	30
BENEATH HIS VAST RANGES OF HILLS SURROUNDING JERUSALEM . .		654	JERUSALEM 29	32
AND OVER THE VALLEYS FROM THE HILLS OF HERTFORDSHIRE TO THE HILLS		658	JERUSALEM 31	68
IT PLOWS THE EARTH IN ITS OWN CONCEIT IT OVERWHELMS THE HILLS		659	JERUSALEM 33	9
STOPS IT IN MIDST OF ITS PRIDE AMONG ITS HILLS & RIVERS		659	JERUSALEM 33	11
UPON THE HILLS & VALLEYS AND THE CLOUDY OATH ROLLD FAR AND WIDE		666	JERUSALEM 40	10
THE SURREY HILLS WHERE REPHAIM TERMINATES HER SONS ARE SIEZD		668	JERUSALEM 41	12
UPON THE HILLS OF ALBION OXFORD GROANS IN HIS IRON FURNACE		671	JERUSALEM 42	58
AWAY FROM BEULAH'S HILLS & VALES BREAK FORTH THE SOULS OF THE DEAD		677	JERUSALEM 47	10
WITH SOLEMN MOURNING OUT OF BEULAH'S MOONY SHADES AND HILLS		678	JERUSALEM 48	24
FROM SURREY HILLS THRO ITALY AND GREECE TO HINNOM'S VALE		684	JERUSALEM 53	29
ON ALBION'S HILLS OFTEN WALKING FROM THE FURNACES IN CLOUDS		692	JERUSALEM 60	6
UPON THE CHESELDEN HILLS THINKING TO SLEEP ON THE SEVERN		703	JERUSALEM 66	75
AND ALL THE MOUNTAINS & HILLS SHRINK UP LIKE A WITHERING GOURD		703	JERUSALEM 66	82
ACROSS THE HILLS OF EPHRAIM & DOWN MOUNT OLIVET TO . . .		706	JERUSALEM 68	22
FROM THE HILLS OF CAMBERWELL & WIMBLEDON FROM THE VALLEYS		706	JERUSALEM 68	43
AND KENT & MIDDLESEX ALL THEIR RIVERS & THEIR HILLS OF FLOCKS & HERDS		709	JERUSALEM 71	12

918

```
                                                            PAGE      TITLE          LINE
HILLS    (CONTINUED)
      EMANATION GONORILL REJOICES OVER HILLS & ROCKS & WOODS     710 JERUSALEM 71       35
        & RIVERS
      THY HILLS & VALLEYS FELT HER FEET . . . . . . .           718 ENGLND AWAKE/J      5
      THE HILLS OF JUDEA ARE FALLEN WITH ME INTO THE DEEPEST HELL  720 JERUSALEM 79      8
      HOW DISTANT FAR FROM ALBION HIS HILLS & HIS VALLEYS NO MORE  720 JERUSALEM 79     15
      THE PLAINS OF SUSSEX & SURREY THEIR HILLS OF FLOCKS & HERDS  720 JERUSALEM 79     18
      ARE SEEN IN OUR HILLS & VALLEYS THEY KEEP OUR FLOCKS &       720 JERUSALEM 79     31
        HERDS
      I SLEPT IN HIS GOLDEN HILLS THE LAMB OF GOD MET ME THERE    720 JERUSALEM 79      41
      OF LONDON CITY ON THE THAMES FROM SURREY HILLS TO HIGHGATE  728 JERUSALEM 83      68
      WE BEGAN OUR FOUNDATIONS LOVELY LAMBETH O LOVELY HILLS      729 JERUSALEM 84       4
      . . . IN THE HILLS & VALLEYS OF ALBION . . . . . . .       730 JERUSALEM 85      26
      ALBION BELOVED LAND I SEE THY MOUNTAINS & THY HILLS . .     731 JERUSALEM 86      11
      TO BROCKLEY HILLS ACROSS THE THAMES HE WITH DOUBLE BOADICEA  736 JERUSALEM 90     24
      IN CRUEL PRIDE CUT REUBEN APART FROM THE HILLS OF SURREY    736 JERUSALEM 90      25
      OR HOW UPON THE DISTANT HILLS SEE MY BELOVEDS' TENTS   .    740 JERUSALEM 93      16
      THE BREATH DIVINE WENT FORTH UPON THE MORNING HILLS ALBION  742 JERUSALEM 95       2
        MOVD
      THE BREATH DIVINE WENT FORTH OVER THE MORNING HILLS ALBION  742 JERUSALEM 95       5
        ROSE
      APPEARS UPON OUR HILLS AWAKE JERUSALEM AND COME AWAY  .  .  744 JERUSALEM 97       4
      WITH HAPPINESS STRETCHD ACROSS THE HILLS . . . . . .       816 HAPPINESS/L        1
HILT
      HE'LL PLUNGE HIS KNIFE UP TO THE HILT IN A SINGLE DRIVE     50A ISLAND MOON 6   PROSE
HIMSELF
      THEN ROSE GIRDED HIMSELF AND OER THE BLEAK . . . . . .       2 TO AUTUMN/PS       17
      GORDRED THE GIANT ROUSD HIMSELF . . . . . . . . .          11 GWIN KING/PS       13
      FOR WHICH HIMSELF MIGHT DEEM HIM NEER THE WORSE . . . .     14 IMIT SPEN/PS       16
      HERE COMES THE KING HIMSELF TELL HIM YOUR THOUGHTS   .  .   23 EDW THIRD/PS 3     67
      OFF SLOTH AND BUILD HIMSELF A HUT AND HEDGE . . . . .       26 EDW THIRD/PS 3    197
      AN ABUNDANCE OF ENQUIRIES TO NO PURPOSE SAT HIMSELF DOWN   44B ISLAND MOON 1    PROSE
      INFLAMMABLE GASS RECOLLECTING HIMSELF INDEED . . . . .     45A ISLAND MOON 1    PROSE
      SINGING A SONG HIMSELF WHICH HE READILY COMPLIED WITH  .   57D ISLAND MOON 9    PROSE
      THEY ALL DECLINED & HE WAS FORCED TO SING HIMSELF    .  .  61D ISLAND MOON 11   PROSE
      A MAN MUST FIRST DECIEVE HIMSELF BEFORE HE IS THUS   .  .  75A ANNO LAVATER      MARG
      ("KNOWS HIMSELF WHO NEVER OPPOSES HIS GENIUS")            84C ANNO LAVATER      MARG
        MOST EXCELLENT
      FOR OUR OWN HIMSELF SAYS "YOU ARE MY BROTHER"    .  .  .   87A ANNO LAVATER      MARG
      MAN IS BAD OR GOOD AS HE UNITES HIMSELF WITH BAD OR GOOD   88A ANNO LAVATER      MARG
        SPIRITS
      WHO DOES NOT OR MAY NOT KNOW OF LOVE & WISDOM IN HIMSELF   92D ANNO SWED LOVE     MARG
      & HIMSELF INFINITE . . . . . . . . . . . . . . .          97D NAT RELIGION 2   PROSE
      HE WHO SEES THE RATIO ONLY SEES HIMSELF ONLY . . . . .     98A NAT RELIGION 2   PROSE
      LET NO ONE FEAR FOR POOR BLIND TIRIEL HURTS NONE          101 TIRIEL 2            14
        BUT HIMSELF
      FOR HE CALLS HIMSELF A LAMB . . . . . . . . . . .         115 THE LAMB/SI        14
      READ N...& THERE SEE HOW SWEDENBORG CONTRADICTS HIMSELF   133D ANNO SWED PROV * MARG
        & [XXX] N...
      THE FOX CONDEMNS THE TRAP NOT HIMSELF   . . . . . . .     151C MARRIAGE HH 8   PROSE
      THE FOX PROVIDES FOR HIMSELF BUT GOD PROVIDES FOR THE LION 152A MARRIAGE HH 9   PROSE
      FOR MAN HAS CLOSED HIMSELF UP TILL HE SEES ALL THINGS  .   154C MARRIAGE HH 14  PROSE
      AND CONCIEVD HIMSELF AS MUCH WISER THAN SEVEN MEN   .  .   157D MARRIAGE HH 21  PROSE
      & HIMSELF THE SINGLE ONE ON EARTH THAT EVER BROKE A NET    157D MARRIAGE HH 21  PROSE
      BUT MASTERING HIMSELF HE GREW YELLOW . . . . . . .        158B MARRIAGE HH 22  PROSE
      GIVING HIMSELF FOR THE NATIONS HE DANCD THE DANCE         160 ALBION ROSE         2
        OF ETERNAL DEATH
      HE WHO BINDS [HIMSELF TO] TO HIMSELF A JOY    . . . . .   179 ETERNITY/N      *   1
      HE WHO BINDS TO HIMSELF A JOY . . . . . . . . . .         184 SEVRL QUESTN/N   *  11
      AND TURND HIMSELF ROUND THREE TIMES THREE   . . . . .     187 WHEN KLOPSTK/N   *  10
      EXPANSION TO THE EYE OF PITY OR WILL HE BIND HIMSELF   .   195 V DAU ALBION 8      3
      WHAT PITYING ANGEL LUSTS FOR TEARS AND FANS HIMSELF WITH   200 AMERICA 11        13
        SIGHS
      WHAT CRAWLING VILLAIN PREACHES ABSTINENCE & WRAPS HIMSELF  200 AMERICA 11        14
      THRO ONE HIMSELF PASS OUT WHAT TIME HE PLEASE BUT HE WILL  237 EUROPE INTRO       5
        NOT
      SEEING HIMSELF IN MY POSSESSION THUS HE ANSWERD ME   . .   237 EUROPE INTRO      11
      BARREN A ROCK WHICH HIMSELF . . . . . . . . . . .        252 AHANIA 3           57
      HE BEHELD HIMSELF COMPASSED ROUND . . . . . . . . .      252 AHANIA 3           69
      [WHILE THE BRIGHT SPECTRE HID HIMSELF AMONG THE TRAILING  268 FOUR ZOAS 1    *  144
        CLOUDS]
      AND WILT THOU SLAY WITH DEATH HIM WHO DEVOTES HIMSELF TO   271 FOUR ZOAS 1       275
        THEE
      AND COMPREHEND WITHIN HIMSELF ALL THINGS BOTH SMALL & GREAT 272 FOUR ZOAS 1    *  295
      THUS URIZEN SPOKE COLLECTED IN HIMSELF IN AWFUL PRIDE  .   273 FOUR ZOAS 1       342
      TO POUR ITS FURY ON HIMSELF & ON THE ETERNAL MAN    .  .   279 FOUR ZOAS 1       540
      FOR WHEN LUVAH SUNK DOWN HIMSELF PUT ON THE ROBES OF BLOOD 287 FOUR ZOAS 2       263
      HE BECAME WHAT HE WAS DOING HE WAS HIMSELF TRANSFORMD  .   305 FOUR ZOAS 4       287
      NOR COULD HE CALM THE ELEMENTS BECAUSE HIMSELF WAS SUBJECT 315 FOUR ZOAS 6       145
      HIMSELF INTO THE DISMAL VOID FALLING HE FELL & FELL  . .   315 FOUR ZOAS 6       153
      HIS WILL WHERE NONE SHOULD DARE OPPOSE HIS WILL HIMSELF    317 FOUR ZOAS 6       232
        BEING KING
      AS WHEN THE THUNDER FOLDS HIMSELF IN THICKEST CLOUDS   .   320 FOUR ZOAS 7        23
      AMAZD STARTED URIZEN WHEN HE FOUND HIMSELF COMPASSD ROUND  321 FOUR ZOAS 7        36
      NOR KNEW THE SOURCE OF HIS OWN BUT THOUGHT HIMSELF THE     324 FOUR ZOAS 7       159
        SOLE AUTHOR
      AND MUST HAVE GIVEN HIMSELF TO DEATH ETERNAL BUT  . . .    330 FOUR ZOAS 7       396
      LOVELY BREATHD FROM ENITHARMON HE TREMBLED WITHIN HIMSELF  332 FOUR ZOAS 7       499
      AND WITH IT LOSE HIMSELF IN MEEKNESS SHE EMBRACD HIS FIRE  336 FOUR ZOAS 7B      128
      HIMSELF TANGLED IN HIS OWN NET IN SORROW LUST REPENTANCE   345 FOUR ZOAS 8       181
      OF ETERNITY FOR HIMSELF HE HEWD IT DESPAIRING OF          349 FOUR ZOAS 8       340
        LIFE ETERNAL
```

	PAGE	TITLE	LINE

HIMSELF   (CONTINUED)

FOR HIMSELF IN THE ROCK OF ETERNITY TREMBLING & IN [FEAR]   356 FOUR ZOAS 8   595
  DESPAIR
BECAUSE THE LAMB OF GOD CREATES HIMSELF A BRIDE & WIFE . .   362 FOUR ZOAS 9   220
AND NOW FIERCE ORC HAD QUITE CONSUMD HIMSELF IN MENTAL   366 FOUR ZOAS 9   358
  FLAMES
OF A CURLD RAM WHO STRETCHD HIMSELF IN SLEEP BESIDE HIS   369 FOUR ZOAS 9   456
  MISTRESS
HAS NOT THE BISHOP GIVEN HIMSELF THE LIE . . . . . .   390A ANNO WATSON   MARG
BACON IS IN HIS ELEMENT ON USURY IT IS HIMSELF &   409D ANNO BACON   MARG
  HIS PHILOSOPHY
THY BROTHER HAS ARMED HIMSELF IN STEEL . . . . 419 I SAW A MONK/N   38
UNTILL THE TYRANT HIMSELF RELENT . . . . 420 I SAW A MONK/N   49
HE PLANTS HIMSELF IN ALL HER NERVES . . . . 425 MENTAL TRAVLER   25
THE BROTHER HAS ARMD HIMSELF IN STEEL . . . . 430 GREY MONK   23
WHEN HE MEANT TO MAKE HIMSELF KNOWN TO APELLES . .   . . 439C REMARKS MALKIN PROSE
FUSELI INDIGNANT ALMOST HID HIMSELF I [?WAS] AM HID . .   445C ANNO REYNOLDS * MARG
KNOWING HIMSELF TO BE A FOOL HE IS . . . . 455B ANNO REYNOLDS MARG
BORN WITH HIM THEY ARE TRULY HIMSELF . . . . 459B ANNO REYNOLDS MARG
IN LIKENESS OF HIMSELF TELL ALSO OF THE FALSE TONGUE   481 MILTON 2   10
  VEGETATED
IN TORMENT TO GO INTO THE DEEP HER TO REDEEM & HIMSELF   481 MILTON 2   20
  PERISH
IN THE NIGHT OF PROSPERITY AND WANTONNESS WHICH HE HIMSELF   485 MILTON 5   41
  CREATED
SEEMING A BROTHER BEING A TYRANT EVEN THINKING HIMSELF   487 MILTON 7   24
  A BROTHER
HIMSELF HAD WROUGHT LOS TREMBLED SATAN'S BLANDISHMENTS   487 MILTON 7   37
  ALMOST
HIMSELF EXCULPATING WITH MILDEST SPEECH FOR HIMSELF BELIEVD 487 MILTON 8   2
HIMSELF CONVINCD OF PALAMABRON'S TURPITUDE LOS BEHELD . .   488 MILTON 8   7
WHERE SATAN MAKING TO HIMSELF LAWS FROM HIS OWN IDENTITY   491 MILTON 11   10
BEING CALLD GOD SETTING HIMSELF ABOVE ALL THAT IS CALLED   491 MILTON 11   12
  GOD
LET THE BARD HIMSELF WITNESS WHERE HADST THOU THIS TERRIBLE 495 MILTON 13   50
  SONG
. . . & UNGIRDED HIMSELF FROM THE OATH OF GOD . . . . .   495 MILTON 14   13
OF DEATH FOR WHEN HE ENTERD INTO HIS SHADOW HIMSELF . .   496 MILTON 15   10
BUT TO HIMSELF HE SEEMD A WANDERER LOST IN DREARY NIGHT   496 MILTON 15   16
HIMSELF WAS HUMAN THO NOW WANDERING THRO DEATH'S VALE . .   498 MILTON 17   6
EVEN AS REUBEN & AS GAD GAVE UP HIMSELF TO TEARS . . . .   503 MILTON 20   53
THE SOULS CLEAR FROM THE ROCK OF DEATH THAT DEATH HIMSELF   517 MILTON 29   45
  MAY WAKE
WHO MADE HIMSELF A GOD & DESTROYED THE HUMAN FORM DIVINE   521 MILTON 32   13
FOR GOD HIMSELF ENTERS DEATH'S DOOR ALWAYS WITH THOSE THAT   522 MILTON 32   40
  ENTER
HIMSELF THAT SEEING ALL HIS LOVES BY HER CUT OFF HE LEAVES   522 MILTON 33   15
HER ALSO INTIRELY ABSTRACTING HIMSELF FROM FEMALE LOVES   522 MILTON 33   16
ANNIHILATE HIMSELF FOR OTHERS GOOD AS I FOR THEE . . . .   530 MILTON 38   36
[PRINTING HIS PRAISES ?GIVES (?HIMSELF NO) ?PAIN] . . .   539 SIR JOSH MIC/N * 3
CHAUCER HIMSELF AND THE REEVE COMES AS CHAUCER HAS   567A DESC CAT 3   PROSE
  DESCRIBED
CHAUCER IS HIMSELF THE GREAT POETICAL OBSERVER OF MEN . .   569A DESC CAT 3   PROSE
MAKE HIS WHOLE COMPANY HIMSELF INCLUDED THIRTY-ONE . . .   571D DESC CAT 3   PROSE
CLERK HAD PUT HIMSELF UNDER THE TUITION OF THE MATURE POET   572C DESC CAT 3   PROSE
DESIGNS FOR BLAIR'S GRAVE HAVE LEFT HIM TO SHIFT   572D DESC CAT 3   PROSE
  FOR HIMSELF
AND IS PRAISED BY HIS EQUALS FOR IT FOR BOTH HIMSELF . .   574B DESC CAT 3   PROSE
CHAUCER HIMSELF AS A KNAVE WHO THRUSTS HIMSELF . . . .   574D DESC CAT 3   PROSE
VENETIAN AND FLEMISH DEMONS WHOSE ENMITY TO THE PAINTER   582C DESC CAT 9   PROSE
  HIMSELF
PRETEND TO ENCOURAGE ART HE WILL EMPLOY HIMSELF . . . .   586A DESC CAT 16   PROSE
AS THE PAINTER HIMSELF ESPECIALLY AS MR B(BLAKE) IS . .   586D CHAUCER 1   PROSE
ARTIST HIMSELF EVEN TO THE STUFFS & EMBROIDERY . . . .   588A CHAUCER/N   PROSE
CHAUCER HIMSELF & THE REEVE COMES AS CHAUCER HAS DESCRIBED   588C CHAUCER/N   PROSE
CHAUCER HIMSELF AND THE REEVE COMES AS CHAUCER HAS   590A CHAUCER 2   PROSE
  DESCRIBED
FOR HE NEVER DOES THE WORK HIMSELF . . . .   593B PUB ADDRESS/N PROSE
WOOLETT ETCHD VERY BAD HIMSELF . . . .   594A PUB ADDRESS/N PROSE
A MAN SETS HIMSELF DOWN WITH COLOURS & WITH . . . . . .   597B PUB ADDRESS/N PROSE
LET ANY MAN OF SENSE ASK HIMSELF ONE QUESTION IS THIS ART   597B PUB ADDRESS/N PROSE
THEIR [BEAUTY IS CONFESSD EVEN BY THE LIPS OF PASCH   601A PUB ADDRESS/N *PROSE
  HIMSELF
HE HIMSELF KNEW BUT HIS IMPUDENCE HAD A CONTRARY EFFECT   603C PUB ADDR AD/N PROSE
  ON ME
PLATO CONFUTES HIMSELF . . . .   605A V LAST JUDG/N PROSE
PRECIPITATING HIMSELF INTO THE ABYSS . . . .   606C V LAST JUDG/N PROSE
ALL BEAMS FROM HIM [& [BECAUSE] AS HE HIMSELF HAS SAID]   612D V LAST JUDG/N PROSE
HIMSELF CAST OUT BY THOSE WHO HAVE ALREADY EMBRACED TRUE   613A V LAST JUDG/N PROSE
  ART
BUT HE HIMSELF WILL NOT KNOW IT THO EVERY BODY ELSE DOES   615B V LAST JUDG/N PROSE
BUT LOS HIMSELF AGAINST ALBION'S SONS HIS FURY BENDS FOR HE 638 JERUSALEM 17   6
NO ONE BRUISES OR STARVES HIMSELF TO MAKE HIMSELF FIT   639 JERUSALEM 17   21
  FOR LABOUR
AND LEFT MAN A LITTLE GROVELLING ROOT OUTSIDE OF HIMSELF   639 JERUSALEM 17   32
SO LOS IN SECRET WITH HIMSELF COMMUNED & ENITHARMON HEARD   639 JERUSALEM 17   48
THE REACTOR HATH HID HIMSELF THRO ENVY I BEHOLD HIM . . .   653 JERUSALEM 29   9
HIMSELF OF ALBION'S FORESTS & WILDS AND JERUSALEM IS TAKEN   653 JERUSALEM 29   17
HE HATH LEAGUED HIMSELF WITH ROBBERS HE HATH STUDIED THE   667 JERUSALEM 40   13
  ARTS
AND MAN HIMSELF BECOME A FIEND WRAPD IN AN ENDLESS CURSE   667 JERUSALEM 40   29
WINCHESTER STOOD DEVOTING HIMSELF FOR ALBION HIS TENTS . . 668 JERUSALEM 40   53

920

```
                                                              PAGE      TITLE           LINE
HIMSELF   (CONTINUED)
   HIMSELF MAY IN PROCESS OF TIME BE BORN MAN TO REDEEM    . .  670 JERUSALEM 42        34
   FROM MISTRUST AND SUSPITION THE MAN IS HIMSELF BECOME   . .  675 JERUSALEM 45         8
   FOOTE IN CALLING WHITEFIELD HYPOCRITE WAS HIMSELF ONE   . 682D JERUSALEM 52        PROSE
   THAT HE HIMSELF MAY DWELL AMONG YOU FEAR NOT THEN TO TAKE    695 JERUSALEM 61        26
   ENGAGE HIMSELF OPENLY & PUBLICLY BEFORE ALL THE WORLD   . . 717C JERUSALEM 77      PROSE
   AND RESTLESS FURY MAN HIMSELF SHRUNK UP   . . . . . . .      717 STOOD AMONG/J       10
   AND ALBION IS HIMSELF SHRUNK TO A NARROW ROCK IN THE MIDST   720 JERUSALEM 79        17
      OF THE SEA
   HE TAKES HIS WAY GIRDING HIMSELF WITH GOLD & IN HIS HAND     729 JERUSALEM 83        77
   LURED BY HER BEAUTY OUTSIDE OF HIMSELF IN SHADOWY GRIEF      732 JERUSALEM 86        60
   TILL GOD HIMSELF BECOME A MALE SUBSERVIENT TO THE FEMALE     733 JERUSALEM 88        21
   KNOWING HIMSELF THE AUTHOR OF THEIR DIVISIONS & SHRINKINGS   733 JERUSALEM 88        35
      GRATIFIED
   LOS CRIES NO INDIVIDUAL OUGHT TO APPROPRIATE TO HIMSELF      736 JERUSALEM 90        28
   AND IF GOD DIETH NOT FOR MAN & GIVETH NOT HIMSELF   . .      743 JERUSALEM 96        25
   ALBION STOOD IN TERROR NOT FOR HIMSELF BUT FOR HIS FRIEND    743 JERUSALEM 96        30
   SO ALBION SPOKE & THREW HIMSELF INTO THE FURNACES           744 JERUSALEM 96        35
      OF AFFLICTION
   AND HE CLOTHED HIMSELF IN BOW & ARROWS IN AWFUL STATE       744 JERUSALEM 97        16
      FOURFOLD
   OBEY HIMSELF TO CAIAPHAS   . . .  .  .  .  .  .  .  .  .  .  750 EV GOSPEL(C)/N      30
   GOD WANTS NOT MAN TO HUMBLE HIMSELF   .  .  .  .  .  .  .  . 750 EV GOSPEL(C)/N      31
   AND WHEN HE HUMBLED HIMSELF TO GOD   .  .  .  .  .  .  .  .  750 EV GOSPEL(C)/N      35
   AND AT LAST HE WOULD HAVE BEEN CAESAR HIMSELF   .  .  .  .   752 EV GOSPEL(D)/N      42
   OBEYD HIMSELF TO CAIAPHAS   . . .  .  .  .  .  .  .  .  .  . 752 EV GOSPEL(D)/N      64
   GOD WANTS NOT MAN TO HUMBLE HIMSELF   .  .  .  .  .  .  .  . 752 EV GOSPEL(D)/N      65
   AND WHEN HE HUMBLED HIMSELF TO GOD   .  .  .  .  .  .  .  .  752 EV GOSPEL(D)/N      71
   THAT HE HIMSELF MAY DWELL AMONG YOU   .  .  .  .  .  .  .  . 757D EV GOSPEL        PROSE
   CHRIST ADDRESSES HIMSELF TO THE MAN NOT TO HIS REASON   .  . 774C ANNO BERKELEY     MARG
   GOD HIMSELF THE DIVINE BODY (YESHUA) JESUS WE ARE           776B INSC LAOCOON      PROSE
      HIS MEMBERS
   IT MUST HAVE BEEN ORIGINALLY FORMED BY THE DEVIL HIMSELF    785C ILLS DANTE 101    PROSE
   TO CONSIDER IS THIS WHETHER JESUS DID NOT SUFFER HIMSELF    787A ANNO THORNTON      MARG
      TO BE
   ("NEITHER DISCOVERING NOT HIDING HIMSELF") A FEMALE GOD     788C ANNO THORNTON      MARG
   IDLENESS ITSELF DOES NOT HURT OTHER MEN LET SATAN HIMSELF   812C LETTER 22         PROSE
      EXPLAIN
   AND GOD HIMSELF IN THE PASSING HOURS . . . . . . . .        817 HAPPINESS/L         10
   THE WRETCHED MAN HAS TERRIBLY PERJURD HIMSELF AS HAS HIS    826D LETTER 28         PROSE
      COMRADE
   BUT HE TURNING ABOUT PUT HIMSELF INTO A POSTURE OF DEFIANCE 827A LETTER 28         PROSE
   ATTACHING HIMSELF WHOLLY TO THE SALE OF FINE EDITIONS OF    831C LETTER 31         PROSE
   INTERESTING HIMSELF IN THE GREAT OBJECT OF HIS FATHER'S     835C LETTER 35         PROSE
      FAME
   THE LIFE OF ROMNEY HE INTERESTS HIMSELF IN IT & HAS         836A LETTER 35         PROSE
      PROMISED
   MR WALKER ALSO SHEWD ME A PORTRAIT OF HIMSELF W WHOLE       843D LETTER 43         PROSE
      LENGTH
   WERE TRULY AMIABLE AND FEELING LIKE HIMSELF   .  .  .  .  . 844A LETTER 43         PROSE
   HEARTILY DEVOTE HIMSELF TO THE BUSINESS IN ALL ITS         845C LETTER 44         PROSE
      LABORIOUS
   THAN HIMSELF CONSEQUENTLY WAS BORN   .  .  .  .  .  .  .  . 847D LETTER 44         PROSE
   DETERMINATION TO DO EVERY THING TO ENGAGE HIMSELF TO YOU    857A LETTER 54         PROSE
   HIMSELF IMMEDIATELY REPLY TO YOU I SHOULD HAVE SUPPOSED     857D LETTER 55         PROSE
   WHO PREPARES HIMSELF ARDENTLY FOR HIS RETURN TO LIFE   .    875A LETTER 80         PROSE
   IN WHICH HE SAYS HE WILL TAKE ONE COPY OF JOB FOR HIMSELF   876D LETTER 85         PROSE
   THE DANTE HE EXPRESSD HIMSELF VERY MUCH PLEASD WITH . .  .  877A LETTER 85         PROSE
   CHRIST GIRDING HIMSELF WITH STRENGTH FOUR & TWENTY ELDERS   SUPP LETTER 56A      *PROSE
HIND
   AND SHALL NECKER THE HIND OF GENEVA . . . . . . . . .       138 FRENCH REVOLTN      91
HINDER
   & YOU HINDER YOUR HUSBAND FROM GOING TO CHURCH   .  .  .  .  48A ISLAND MOON 4     PROSE
   TO HINDER PESTILENCE  . . . . . . . . . . . . . .  . . .     57 TO BE OR/IM         24
   TO HINDER ANOTHER IS NOT AN ACT IT IS THE CONTRARY   .  .   88D ANNO LAVATER       MARG
   HINDER CRIMES OR CAN THE MAN WHO WRITES THE LATTER         385C ANNO WATSON        MARG
      SENTIMENT
   THE IGNORANT INSULTS OF INDIVIDUALS WILL NOT HINDER ME  .  561A EXHIBITION ADV     PROSE
   AND HINDER ALL CORRECT DRAWING FROM APPEARING TO BE CORRECT 583C DESC CAT 9        PROSE
   IT IS IN THEIR POWER TO HINDER INSTRUCTION BUT NOT         597A PUB ADDRESS/N      PROSE
      TO INSTRUCT
   I GO ON & NOTHING CAN HINDER MY COURSE   .  .  .  .  .  .  . 600C PUB ADDRESS/N     PROSE
   WHICH HINDER THE VISION OF GOD TURNING ALL INTO A CONSUMING 604C V LAST JUDG/N     PROSE
      FIRE
   THOU ART FOREVER LOST WHAT CAN I DO TO HINDER THE SONS  .   657 JERUSALEM 31        37
   THO NOT ITS EFFECTS WEAKNESS &C COMES ANOTHER TO HINDER MY 874D LETTER 80          PROSE
HINDERD
   IN THE PERSON HINDERD FOR   .  .  .  .  .  .  .  .  .  .  .  88D ANNO LAVATER       MARG
   ONCE WHICH HAS HINDERD HIS WORKING FOR A FORTNIGHT   .  .  842D LETTER 42        *PROSE
   PERHAPS HINDERD HIS SENDING & PERHAPS HIS WISH THAT I   .  856A LETTER 54         PROSE
HINDERED
   JESUS COULD NOT DO MIRACLES WHERE UNBELIEF HINDERED   .  .  391C ANNO WATSON       MARG
   OR BE HINDERED FROM THE PUBLIC EXHIBITION   .  .  .  .  .   573A DESC CAT 3        PROSE
HINDERING
   THE HINDERING OF ACT IN ANOTHER THIS IS VICE  .  .  .  .  .  88D ANNO LAVATER       MARG
   MURDER IS HINDERING ANOTHER . . . . . . . . . . . .  .  .   88D ANNO LAVATER       MARG
   THEFT IS HINDERING ANOTHER BACKBITING UNDERMINING   .  .   88D ANNO LAVATER       MARG
   OF HINDERING THEM FROM OPRESSING THE GOOD WITH POVERTY     612D V LAST JUDG/N      PROSE
      & PAIN
HINDERS
   HE WHO HINDERS ANOTHER OMITS HIS OWN DUTY AT THE SAME TIME  88D ANNO LAVATER       MARG
   HINDERS ALL POWER OF INDIVIDUAL THOUGHT  . . . . . . .  . 582D DESC CAT 9         PROSE
```

	PAGE	TITLE	LINE

HINDERS   (CONTINUED)
    IF TO INVENT & TO DRAW WELL HINDERS THE EXECUTIVE POWER IN   591B PUB ADDRESS/N   PROSE
HINDOO
    APOTHEOSES OF PERSIAN HINDOO AND EGYPTIAN ANTIQUITY . . .   565C DESC CAT 2   PROSE
    GOTHIC GRECIAN HINDOO AND EGYPTIAN ARE THE EXTENT OF THE   579D DESC CAT 5   PROSE
        HUMAN MIND
    THAT PART OF THE HINDOO SCRIPTURES TRANSLATED BY MR WILKIN   583D DESC CAT 10   PROSE
HINDOSTAN
    TO TARTARY & HINDOSTAN & CHINA & TO GREAT AMERICA . . .   495 MILTON 14   7
    ARABIA PALESTINE PERSIA HINDOSTAN CHINA TARTARY SIBERIA   712 JERUSALEM 72   39
    AND HELLE & HESPERIA & HINDOSTAN & CHINA & JAPAN . . . .   725 JERUSALEM 82   28
HINDRANCE
    IF HE MEANS THAT COPYING CORRECTLY IS A HINDRANCE HE IS   448D ANNO REYNOLDS   MARG
        A LIAR
    & THAT TO ME IT IS HINDRANCE & NOT ACTION . . . . . .   617B V LAST JUDG/N   PROSE
    WITHOUT ACCIDENT OR HINDRANCE THO IT WAS BETWEEN ELEVEN   803A LETTER 15   PROSE
HINDS
    YET SIMPLE COUNTRY HINDS ARE MORAL ENTHUSIASTS . . . .   414A ANNO BOYD   MARG
    WHILE OTHER COUNTRY HINDS ARE AS INDIGNANT AGAINST HONESTY   414A ANNO BOYD   MARG
HINDU   SEE HINDOO
    EUROPE TO EUPHRATES & HINDU TO NILE & BACK IN CLOUDS . .   525 MILTON 35   16
HINGES
    DOWN THE GOLDEN HINGES TORE . . . .   163 I SAW CHAPEL/N   9
    BUT THE FIVE GATES WERE CONSUMD & THEIR BOLTS AND HINGES   203 AMERICA 16   22
        MELTED
    FROM ITS HINGES UTTERING ITS FINAL GROAN ALL BEULAH FELL   326 FOUR ZOAS 7   258
    NOR COULD THEY EVER BE CLOSD AGAIN THE GOLDEN HINGES WERE   328 FOUR ZOAS 7   324
        BROKEN
    THAT THE WIDE WORLD MIGHT FLY FROM ITS HINGES & THE   667 JERUSALEM 40   27
        IMMORTAL MANSION
HINNOM
    AMONG THE FURNACES OF LOS IN THE VALLEY OF THE SON   636 JERUSALEM 15   34
        OF HINNOM
HINNOM'S
    FROM SURREY HILLS THRO ITALY AND GREECE TO HINNOM'S VALE   684 JERUSALEM 53   29
HINT
    AS TO ANY THING LIKE A HINT OF A PROPOSAL RELATING TO . .   857A LETTER 54   *PROSE
HINTS
    THEY HAVE GIVEN ME SOME EXCELLENT HINTS IN ENGRAVING . .   843B LETTER 43   PROSE
HIPOCRISY   SEE HYPOCRISY
    ("SUPERSTITION") HIPOCRISY ("SUPERSTITIOUS") HYPOCRITE . .   74D ANNO LAVATER   MARG
    HIPOCRISY IS AS DISTANT FROM SUPERSTITION AS THE WOLF   75A ANNO LAVATER   MARG
        FROM THE LAMB
    DISCERND NOT THE WOVEN HIPOCRISY . . . .   236 URIZEN 25   32
    LO THESE HUMAN FORMD SPIRITS IN SMILING HIPOCRISY WAR . .   245 SONG OF LOS 3   13
    WHILE I STOOD BOUND WITH CORDS & HEAVY CHAINS YOUR   364 FOUR ZOAS 9   276
        HIPOCRISY
    CRUEL HIPOCRISY UNLIKE THE LOVELY DELUSIONS OF BEULAH . .   639 JERUSALEM 17   27
    TRAMPLING DOWN HIPOCRISY . . . .   749 EV GOSPEL(B)/N   38
HIRE
    SHALL WIN THE LOVER'S HIRE . . . .   182 LOOK OF LOVE/N   4
    SHALL WIN THE LOVER'S HIRE . . . .   184 SEVRL QUESTN/N   8
    HIRE IDIOTS TO PAINT WITH COLD LIGHT & HOT SHADE . . . .   445 ANNO REYNOLDS   2
    THE CAPTIVE IN THE MILL OF THE STRANGER SOLD FOR SCANTY   642 JERUSALEM 20   16
        HIRE
HIRED
    A HIRED VILLAIN TURND MY SLEEP TO DEATH . . . .   5 FAIR ELENOR/PS   64
    HIRED A VILLAIN TO BEREAVE MY LIFE . . . .   6 FAIR ELENOR/PS   68
    THAT IS DANTE WAS HIRED OR (TRANSLATOR) WAS NOT . . . .   413B ANNO BOYD   MARG
    IT APPEARS TO ME THAT MEN ARE HIRED TO RUN DOWN MEN OF   413B ANNO BOYD   MARG
        GENIUS
    THIS MAN WAS HIRED TO DEPRESS ART . . . .   445A ANNO REYNOLDS   MARG
    OPRESSION OF SR JOSHUA & HIS GANG OF CUNNING HIRED KNAVES   445B ANNO REYNOLDS   MARG
    ARE AT ALL TIMES HIRED BY THE SATANS FOR THE DEPRESSION   452B ANNO REYNOLDS   MARG
        OF ART
    & THEY MEANT TO BE SO THEY WERE HIRED FOR THIS PURPOSE .   469A ANNO REYNOLDS   MARG
    BUT SUCH A HIRED KNAVE CARES NOT FOR THE FEW . . . . .   469D ANNO REYNOLDS   MARG
    HIRED A VILLAIN TO BEREAVE MY LIFE . . . .   544 HS FRENDSHIP/N   6
    WAS JOHNSON HIRED TO PRETEND TO RELIGIOUS TERRORS . . .   786D ANNO THORNTON   MARG
HIRELING
    THAT THE HIRELING BLOWS INTO MY EAR . . . .   166 WHY CARE FOR/N   4
    HOW DIFFERENT FAR THE FAT FED HIRELING WITH HOLLOW DRUM   193 V DAU ALBION 5   14
    HIRELING WRITER WHOSE PRAISE IS CONTRARY TO WHAT HE KNOWS   413D ANNO BOYD   MARG
    THE MAN WHO DOES NOT LABOUR MORE THAN THE HIRELING . .   451A ANNO REYNOLDS   MARG
HIRELINGS
    BUT EVERY BODY DOES NOT DO THIS BUT THE HIRELINGS . .   397B ANNO BACON   MARG
    UNCULTIVATED LIFE COMES AFTERWARDS FROM SATAN'S HIRELINGS   446C ANNO REYNOLDS   MARG
    AGAINST THE IGNORANT HIRELINGS FOR . . . .   480C MILTON 1   PROSE
    WE HAVE HIRELINGS IN THE CAMP THE COURT & THE UNIVERSITY   480C MILTON 1   PROSE
    PROPAGATED AMONG THE PUBLIC BY IGNORANT HIRELINGS . . .   572C DESC CAT 3   PROSE
HISBEN
    COPPER PLATES OF ALBERT DURER LUCAS HISBEN ALDEGRAVE AND   586D CHAUCER 1   PROSE
        THE
HISSES
    . . . IN FOLDS OF THE ROBE THE CROWND ADDER BUILDS AND   147 FRENCH REVOLTN   299
        HISSES
HISSING   SEE EVER-HISSING
    WHERE NOUGHT BUT ENVIOUS HISSING ADDERS DWELL . . . . .   15 IMIT SPEN/PS   28
    HISSING WITH HUNDRED TONGUES HER POISNOUS BREATH . . . .   41C THEN SHE BORE   PROSE
    IN THE RUSHING OF SCALES AND HISSING OF FLAMES . . . . .   140 FRENCH REVOLTN   127
    OR GOLD A GLITTERING TORMENT SHINING & HISSING IN ETERNAL   315 FOUR ZOAS 6   121
        PAIN

```
                                                       PAGE      TITLE            LINE
HISSINGS
      RETURNS MY THIRSTY HISSINGS IN A CURSE ON THEE O HAR    . . 110 TIRIEL 8          40
      . . . INSTEAD OF WORDS HARSH HISSINGS  . . . . . . .     142 FRENCH REVOLTN     177
      WITH DOLOROUS HISSINGS & POISONS  . . . . . . . . .     232 URIZEN 19           27
      WITH SHARP PANGS THE HISSINGS BEGAN  . . . . . . . .    232 URIZEN 19           31
      HOWLINGS & HISSINGS SHRIEKS & GROANS & VOICES OF DESPAIR  243 EUROPE 12          34
HISTORIAN
      HISTORIAN TURNER AND TWISTER OF CAUSES AND CONSEQUENCES  579A DESC CAT 5       PROSE
      TELL ME THE ACTS O HISTORIAN AND LEAVE ME TO REASON UPON 579A DESC CAT 5       PROSE
HISTORIANS
      WITHOUT VIOLATING COSTUME THE BRITONS SAY HISTORIANS   . 577C DESC CAT 5       PROSE
      HISTORIANS PRETEND WHO BEING WEAKLY ORGANIZED THEMSELVES 578D DESC CAT 5       PROSE
HISTORICAL
      JOB A HISTORICAL ENGRAVING SIZE...PRICE...  . . . . .   207D PRSPECTUS 1793    PROSE
      EDWARD AND ELINOR A HISTORICAL ENGRAVING SIZE...PRICE... 207D PRSPECTUS 1793   PROSE
      WITH OPINIONS CONCERNING HISTORICAL FACT   . . . . .    384D ANNO WATSON        MARG
      IF HISTORICAL FACTS CAN BE WRITTEN BY INSPIRATION   . . 392D ANNO WATSON        MARG
      OR AT WHAT TIME OR IN THE HISTORICAL EVIDENCE WHICH MAY BE 393B ANNO WATSON     MARG
      IF HOMER'S MERIT WAS ONLY IN THESE HISTORICAL COMBINATIONS 411D ANNO BOYD       MARG
      EXHIBITION OF PAINTINGS IN FRESCO POETICAL AND HISTORICAL 560A EXHIBITION ADV  TITLE
          INVENTIONS
      A DESCRIPTIVE CATALOGUE OF PICTURES POETICAL AND HISTORICAL 563A DESC CAT      TITLE
      COULD NOT BE REPRESENTED BY ANY HISTORICAL FACTS BUT    . 577C DESC CAT 5      PROSE
      GIVEN THE HISTORICAL FACT IN ITS POETICAL VIGOUR  . . . 578D DESC CAT 5        PROSE
      AND NOT FOR HISTORICAL GRANDEUR THE ARTIST HAS IMAGINED  580A DESC CAT 5       PROSE
      HISTORICAL & POETICAL ARTISTS LIKE BARRY & MORTIMER   . . 601B PUB ADDRESS/N   PROSE
      HISTORICAL DESIGNING IS ONE THING & PORTRAIT PAINTING    810B LETTER 20        PROSE
          ANOTHER
      NECESSARY TO HISTORICAL BEAUTY & IN A LETTER TO THE   . . 814B LETTER 23       PROSE
      CONTRARY TO DESIGNING & HISTORICAL PAINTING IN EVERY     815D LETTER 23        PROSE
          RESPECT
      OF MR ROMNEY'S [SKETCHES] HISTORICAL SKETCHES HE SAYS THAT 832C LETTER 32      PROSE
      AS TO REAL ACTING IT IS LIKE HISTORICAL PAINTING NO BOY'S 859C LETTER 56       PROSE
          WORK
      HISTORICAL & POETICAL PRINTED IN COLOURS EACH  . . . . . 867B LETTER 66        PROSE
HISTORIES
      STYLE OF ALB DURER'S (HISTORIES) & THE OLD ENGRAVERS   . 592B PUB ADDRESS/N   *PROSE
HISTORY
      THE HISTORY OF THIS IS WRITTEN IN PARADISE LOST   . . . 150A MARRIAGE HH 5     PROSE
      FOR THIS HISTORY HAS BEEN ADOPTED BY BOTH PARTIES   . . 150A MARRIAGE HH 5     PROSE
      AND ANOTHER FROM THE HISTORY OF ENGLAND  . . . . . . .  207C PRSPECTUS 1793    PROSE
      THE HISTORY OF ENGLAND A SMALL BOOK OF ENGRAVINGS PRICE... 208A PRSPECTUS 1793 PROSE
      IF MOSES DID NOT WRITE THE HISTORY OF HIS ACTS IT   . . 390D ANNO WATSON        MARG
      TAKES AWAY THE AUTHORITY ALTOGETHER IT CEASES TO BE HISTORY 390D ANNO WATSON    MARG
      IF PAINE MEANS THAT A HISTORY THO TRUE IN ITSELF   . . . 391B ANNO WATSON       MARG
      THAT HISTORY WHICH IS WRITTEN IN HIS NAME & IN WHICH HE  391B ANNO WATSON       MARG
      IF THIS IS PROVED FALSE THE HISTORY IS FALSE DEUT       391C ANNO WATSON        MARG
          XXXI...BUT PERHAPS
      BE AN EVIDENCE OF THE TRUTH OF HIS HISTORY  . . . . .   392D ANNO WATSON        MARG
      BACON WAS ALWAYS A POOR DEVIL IF HISTORY SAYS TRUE   . . 409A ANNO BACON      * MARG
      A HISTORY PAINTER PAINTS THE HERO & NOT MAN IN GENERAL  . 465A ANNO REYNOLDS    MARG
      [XXX ?HAYLEY & HISTORY]  . . . . . . . . . . . . . .    551 WILLM COWPER/N  *    2
      AND CONTAINS THE ANCIENT HISTORY OF BRITAIN   . . . . . 578B DESC CAT 5        PROSE
      BELIEVING WITH MILTON THE ANCIENT BRITISH HISTORY   . . 578C DESC CAT 5        PROSE
      BUT THE HISTORY OF ALL TIMES AND PLACES IS NOTHING ELSE  578D DESC CAT 5       PROSE
      ARE NOT HISTORY ACTS THEMSELVES ALONE ARE HISTORY AND   . 579A DESC CAT 5      PROSE
      IT IS IMPROBABLE MUST REJECT ALL HISTORY AND RETAIN DOUBTS 579B DESC CAT 5     PROSE
          ONLY
      IN THAT ANCIENT HAPPY PERIOD WHICH HISTORY HAS RECORDED  580D DESC CAT 5       PROSE
      THEIR HISTORY SHEWS FOR THE ABOVE REASON   . . . . . .  593D PUB ADDRESS/N     PROSE
      WHOSE HISTORY PRECEDED THAT OF THE HEBREWS  . . . . . . 609C V LAST JUDG/N     PROSE
      THUS MY PICTURE IS A HISTORY OF ART & SCIENCE [& ITS] THE 613A V LAST JUDG/N  *PROSE
      NATURAL FACT OR HISTORY OF ILIUM  . . . . . . . . . .   775D INSC LAOCOON      TITLE
      YOU CANNOT PAINT HISTORY IT WAS MICHAEL ANGELO'S OPINION 815D LETTER 23        PROSE
      A HISTORY OF THE REVIEWING BUSINESS AS FAR AS I         845C LETTER 44         PROSE
          AM ACQUAINTED
      YET RECEIVED THE HISTORY OF CHICHESTER I MENTION THIS NOT 853D LETTER 52       PROSE
      THE FULL HISTORY OF MY SPIRITUAL SUFFERINGS TO THE DWELLERS 862D LETTER 60     PROSE
      HISTORY OF MASTR MALKIN  . . . . . . . . . . . . . . .  SUPP LETTER 56A       *PROSE
      THE HISTORY OF JOB DESIGNED & ENGRAVED BY WILLIAM BLAKE  SUPP LETTER 67F       *PROSE
HIT
      YOU WOULD YOU IGNORANT JADE I WISH I COULD SEE YOU HIT ANY  48C ISLAND MOON 4  PROSE
      [TO HIT ME WITH THE BAT]  . . . . . . . . . . . . . .   61 SAY YOU JOE/IM  *    9
      MYSELF & HIT IT OFF EXCELLENTLY I HAVE NOT SEEN MR ROSE  834D LETTER 34        PROSE
HITHER
      MEMORY HITHER COME  . . . . . . . . . . . . . . . .      8 MEMORY COME/PS      1
      COME HITHER SLEEP  . . . . . . . . . . . . . . . . .     8 MAD SONG/PS         3
      BRING HITHER MY ARMOUR WILLIAM  . . . . . . . . . . .    28 EDW THIRD/PS 4      1
      COME HITHER DEATH ART THOU NOT SAMSON'S SERVANT  . . . . 38B SAMSON/PS        PROSE
      . . . WHY DO YOU STAND FETCH HITHER TIRIEL  . . . . .   105 TIRIEL 4           64
      FETCH HITHER MYRATANA & DELIGHT YOURSELVES WITH SCOFFS  . 105 TIRIEL 4          65
      YOUTH OF DELIGHT COME HITHER  . . . . . . . . . . . .   126 VOICE BARD/SI       1
      COME HITHER MY SPARROWS  . . . . . . . . . . . . . .    178 THE FAIRY/N         1
      COME HITHER MY BOY TELL ME WHAT THOU SEEST THERE  . . . 180 LACEDEMONIAN/N      1
      COME HITHER BE PATIENT LET US CONVERSE TOGETHER BECAUSE  330 FOUR ZOAS 7       422
      I WALK BY THE FOOTSTEPS OF HIS FLOCKS COME HITHER TENDER  368 FOUR ZOAS 9      427
          FLOCKS
      COME HITHER INTO THE DESART & TURN THESE STONES TO BREAD  685 JERUSALEM 54      21
HITHERTO
      HITHERTO SHALT THOU COME NO FURTHER HERE THY PROUD WAVES  298 FOUR ZOAS 4       35
          CEASE
      THIS HAS HITHERTO BEEN HIS LOT TO GET PATRONAGE FOR OTHERS 572D DESC CAT 3     PROSE
```

		PAGE	TITLE	LINE

HITHERTO   (CONTINUED)
   [TO ELEVATE ME ABOVE THE MEDIOCRITY TO WHICH I HAVE   591C PUB ADDRESS/N PROSE
     HITHERTO]
   FOR THINE ARE ALSO MINE I HAVE KEPT SILENT HITHERTO . .   629 JERUSALEM 10   40
   I HAVE HITHERTO ENCOUNTERED BUT MY FATE HAS BEEN SO UNCOMMON 862C LETTER 60   PROSE
   ALL HITHERTO YOU DEAR SIR ARE ONE WHO HAS MY PARTICULAR   862C LETTER 60   PROSE
HITTITE
   JORDAN TO THE LAND OF THE HITTITE EVERY-ONE THAT SAW HIM   661 JERUSALEM 34   48
HIZZING
   HEATED RED HOT THEY HIZZING REND THEIR WAY DOWN MANY A   283 FOUR ZOAS 2   138
     LEAGUE
HM
   HM SAID THE LAWGIVER FUNNY ENOUGH . . . .   62B ISLAND MOON 11 PROSE
HO   SEE O HO
   HO HO . . . .   46 PHEBUS CAME/IM   4
   HO HO HO HO HO HO HO HOOOOO MY POOOOOOR SIIIDES I   54C ISLAND MOON 9   PROSE
     I SHOULD
   DIE IF I WAS TO LIVE HERE SAID SCOPPRELL HO HO HO HO   54C ISLAND MOON 9   PROSE
   FOR HE HAD BUT ONE EYE HA HA HA HO THEN SUNG SCOPPRELL   55C ISLAND MOON 9   PROSE
   O DEAR SIR HO HO HO I AM NO SINGER I MUST BEG . . . .   61D ISLAND MOON 11 *PROSE
   (MONOS HO IESOUS) JERUSALEM CHAP I . . . .   622A JERUSALEM 4   TITLE
HOAR
   COLD & HOAR . . . .   169 EARTHS ANSWR/N   8
   . . . [WITH FLAMES] [HOAR FROSTS] DAMP MISTS . . .   205 AMERICA CANC C   5
   COLD AND HOAR . . . .   211 EARTHS ANSR/SE   8
   THAT SWAGGD HEAVY WITH THE ACCURSED DOUGH THE HOAR FROST   322 FOUR ZOAS 7   100
     RAGD
   . . . THE GREY HOAR FROST WAS THERE . . . .   378 FOUR ZOAS 9   814
   BUT THE SPECTRE LIKE A HOAR FROST & A MILDEW ROSE OVER   685 JERUSALEM 54   15
     ALBION
HOARD
   NOR THE [CUNNING] SECRET HOARD UP IN HIS TREASURY . . .   181 RICHES/N   4
HOARE
   MR HOARE THE PAINTER WHOSE NOTE TO ME I ALSO INCLOSE FOR   836D LETTER 35   PROSE
   I CALLD ON MR HOARE WITH YOUR ELEGANT & HEART LIFTING . . 838C LETTER 37   PROSE
   & EMBRACE IT COMES THRO MR HOARE . . . .   841B LETTER 41   PROSE
   INTIRE SECRET BETWEEN MR P(PHILLIPS) MR H(HOARE) & MYSELF   841B LETTER 41   PROSE
   EXTENT & HE TOLD MR HOARE THAT ON THE PRESENT WORK WHICH   841C LETTER 41   PROSE
   I SEND INCLOSD HIS TERMS AS MR HOARE BY MY DESIRE HAS .   841D LETTER 41   PROSE
   TO MR HOARE WHO IS WORTHY OF EVERY CONFIDENCE YOU CAN .   842A LETTER 41   PROSE
   MR HOARE'S ADDRESS IS TO PRINCE HOARE ESQRE BUCKINGHAM   842B LETTER 41   PROSE
     STREET STRAND
   I HAVE AT LENGTH SEEN MR HOARE AFTER HAVING REPEATEDLY . . 842B LETTER 42   PROSE
   MR H(HOARE) APPEARS TO ME TO CONSIDER IT AS A REJECTION OF 842C LETTER 42   PROSE
   MR H(HOARE) HAS PROMISED TO SEE MR PHILLIPS IMMEDIATELY &   842D LETTER 42 *PROSE
   I FORGOT TO MENTION THAT MR HOARE DESIRES HIS MOST . . . 843A LETTER 42   PROSE
HOARE'S
   AS ALSO FOR OMITTING TO MENTION MR HOARE'S GRATEFUL . . . 839B LETTER 38   PROSE
   MR HOARE'S ADDRESS IS TO PRINCE HOARE ESQRE BUCKINGHAM   842B LETTER 41   PROSE
     STREET STRAND
HOARSE
   HOARSE WITH MAKING MOAN . . . .   113 LIT GRL FND/SI   6
   . . . FOR A CURSE IS HEARD HOARSE THRO THE LAND FROM A   140 FRENCH REVOLTN 138
     GODLESS RACE
   WITH HOARSE NOTE CURSE THE SONS OF JOY . . . .   160A SONG LIBERTY PROSE
   LAY THE FAINT MAID AND SOON HER WOES APPALLD HIS THUNDERS   190 V DAU ALBION 1   17
     HOARSE
   SHE CONTINUED FALLING LOUD THE CRASH CONTINUD LOUD   295 FOUR ZOAS 3   145
     & HOARSE
   HIS CLOUDY FORM IN JEALOUS FEAR & MUTTERING THUNDERS HOARSE 299 FOUR ZOAS 4   77
   FOR VOICES OF DELIGHT HOARSE CROAKINGS INARTICULATE THRO   312 FOUR ZOAS 6   39
     FROST
   AND SLAVES IN MYRIADS IN SHIP LOADS BURDEN THE HOARSE   333 FOUR ZOAS 7B   16
     SOUNDING DEEP
   OF THE HOARSE WHEELS & THE TERRIFIC HOWLINGS OF WILD BEASTS 333 FOUR ZOAS 7B   33
   THE RUSHING OF THY SCALES CONFOUND ME THY HOARSE RUSHING   335 FOUR ZOAS 7B   84
     SCALES
   MUTTERING ALONG FROM HEAVEN TO HEAVEN HOARSE ROLL THE   372 FOUR ZOAS 9 * 564
     HUMAN FORMS
   GO DOWN WITH HORSE & CHARIOTS & TRUMPETS OF HOARSE WAR . . 374 FOUR ZOAS 9   661
   THE CROOKED HORN MELLOWS THE HOARSE RAVING SERPENT . . .   509 MILTON 24   66
   INTO NON-ENTITY AND THEIR THUNDERS HOARSE APPALL THE DEAD   640 JERUSALEM 18   9
   HOARSE TURND THE STARRY WHEELS RENDING A WAY IN ALBION'S   641 JERUSALEM 18   44
     LOINS
   HOARSE FROM HIS ROCKS FROM CAVERNS OF DERBYSHIRE & WALES   646 JERUSALEM 23   27
   INSANE SHE RAVES UPON THE WINDS HOARSE INARTICULATE . . . 693 JERUSALEM 60   44
   INVOLVD JERUSALEM & THE WHEELS OF ALBION'S SONS TURND   696 JERUSALEM 62   32
     HOARSE
HOARY
   WAKD FROM HIS ETERNAL SLEEP THE HOARY ELEMENT ROARING FLED 159C SONG LIBERTY PROSE
     AWAY
   TO SPIN A WEB OF AGE AROUND HIM GREY AND HOARY DARK . . . 194 V DAU ALBION 7   19
   LEPROUS HIS LIMBS ALL OVER WHITE AND HOARY WAS HIS VISAGE   203 AMERICA 16   11
   THAT SHAKES THE BLOSSOMS OF MY HOARY HAIR . . . . . .   219 LIT GRL LST/SE   34
   TILL HOARY AND AGE-BROKE AND AGED . . . .   225 URIZEN 5   26
   COLD DEWS & HOARY FROST CREEPS THO I LIE ON BANKS OF SUMMER 288 FOUR ZOAS 2 * 320
   I WILL GIVE BLACKNESS FOR JEWELS HOARY FROST FOR ORNAMENT   312 FOUR ZOAS 6   37
     DEFORMITY
   ORC ANSWERD CURSE THY HOARY BROWS WHAT DOST THOU IN THIS   322 FOUR ZOAS 7   69
     DEEP
   FOR WEEDS OF DEATH HAVE WRAPD AROUND MY LIMBS IN THE HOARY 370 FOUR ZOAS 9   488
     DEEPS

	PAGE	TITLE	LINE
HOARY (CONTINUED)			
HER GREAT MEN HOWL & THROW THE DUST & REND THEIR HOARY HAIR	375	FOUR ZOAS 9	663
SINGING & SHOUTING TO THE MAN THEY BOW THEIR HOARY HEADS	378	FOUR ZOAS 9	804
HOB-NAIL			
AT HOB-NAIL DICK WHO GRIEVD THE CHANCE	16	BLIND-MANS/PS	16
HODGE			
THEN CRIES OUT HEM HODGE HEARD AND RAN	16	BLIND-MANS/PS	49
AND HODGE AGAIN HOLDS UP HIS HEAD	17	BLIND-MANS/PS	60
HOG			
ID BE AN ASS A HOG A WORM A CHAIR A STOOL	550	WHEN I SEE/N	8
[LIKES] LIKE A HOG UPON A ROPE	782A	INSC UPCOTT	*PROSE
HOGAMY			
PHIZOGRAPHY HOGAMY HATOMY & HALL THAT BUT IN THE FIRST PLACE	49C	ISLAND MOON 5	PROSE
HOGARTH			
TOM COOKE CUT HOGARTH DOWN WITH HIS CLEAN GRAVING .	554	BLAKES APL/N 1	3
TOM COOKE CUT HOGARTH DOWN WITH HIS CLEAN GRAVING . .	555	BLAKES APL/N 2	7
SUFFICIENT EVIDENCE IN THE WORKS OF OUR OWN HOGARTH . .	586D	CHAUCER 1	PROSE
AFTER HOGARTH [COGAR] COOKE WISHED TO GIVE TO HOGARTH .	594B	PUB ADDRESS/N	*PROSE
COLOUR BUT HE COULD[NT] NOT [& HOGARTH WITH ALL HIS MERIT NEVER G]	594B	PUB ADDRESS/N	*PROSE
TOM COOKE CUT HOGARTH DOWN WITH HIS CLEAN GRAVING . . .	595	BLAKES APOL/PA	3
EVEN HOGARTH CANNOT BE EITHER COPIED OR IMPROVED	601D	PUB ADDRESS/N	PROSE
HOGARTH'S			
THIS EVEN HOGARTH'S WORKS PROVE A DETESTABLE FALSHOOD .	595C	PUB ADDRESS/N	PROSE
[HOGARTH'S TIME WE HAVE HAD VERY FEW EFFORTS OF ORIGINALITY]	595C	PUB ADDRESS/N	PROSE
EVEN HOGARTH'S EXECUTION CANNOT BE COPIED OR IMPROVED .	599C	PUB ADDRESS/N	PROSE
HOGLAH			
MALAH COME FORTH FROM LEBANON & HOGLAH FROM MOUNT SINAI	349	FOUR ZOAS 8	316
RAHAB AND TIRZAH & MILCAH & MALAH & NOAH & HOGLAH . .	498	MILTON 17	11
MILCAH'S PILLARS SHINE FROM HARROW TO HAMPSTEAD WHERE HOGLAH	525	MILTON 35	11
MALAH COME FORTH FROM LEBANON & HOGLAH FROM MOUNT SINAI	705	JERUSALEM 68	4
HOLD			
HIS CLUMSY HOLD AND DODGING ROUND	16	BLIND-MANS/PS	35
HE RUSHES UP THE SKY AND LAYS HOLD ON THE IMMORTAL COURSERS OF DAY	37B	CONTEMPLATN/PS	PROSE
AND PIERCE THE EARS O TH GODS O SAMSON HOLD ME NOT . . .	38C	SAMSON/PS	PROSE
[WHEN PRIDE SHALL HOLD THE SWAY N]	41B	THEN SHE BORE	*PROSE
IM SURE YOU OUGHT TO HOLD YOUR TONGUE	48A	ISLAND MOON 4	PROSE
POO POO HOLD YOUR TONGUE HOLD YOUR TONGUE SAID THE LAWGIVER	53B	ISLAND MOON 8	PROSE
IMPUDENT FIEND SAID IJIM HOLD THY GLIB & ELOQUENT TONGUE	104	TIRIEL 4	37
OF A HARSH TERROR DRIVN TO MADNESS BOUND TO HOLD A ROD . .	193	V DAU ALBION 5	25
I EVERMORE WILL HOLD THEE WHEN THOU GOEST OUT OR COMEST IN	269	FOUR ZOAS 1	177
O HOW THE HORRORS OF ETERNAL DEATH TAKE HOLD ON MAN . . .	354	FOUR ZOAS 8	519
HOLD INFINITY IN THE PALM OF YOUR HAND	431	AUGURIES	3
OUGHT TO BE CONTEMND & I ACCORDINGLY HOLD REYNOLDS . .	467A	ANNO REYNOLDS	MARG
WILL HOLD THEIR PROPER RANK & THE DAUGHTERS OF MEMORY .	480C	MILTON 1	PROSE
I HOLD THE BALANCES OF RIGHT & JUST & MINE THE SWORD .	530	MILTON 38	54
BUT NEITHER BACK NOR MOUTH THOSE EGGS COULD HOLD . . .	537	AND HIS LEGS/N	13
TWILL HOLD FORTH A HUGE SPLUTTER WITH SMOKE & DAMP . .	550	ENGL ENCOU/N 2	6
THEY HOLD THE IMMORTAL FORM IN GENTLE BANDS & TENDER TEARS	624	JERUSALEM 5	55
THEY NOW HOLD ALL THEY HAVE INGRATITUDE TO ME	671	JERUSALEM 42	53
THE FIRST RATE ELEGANCE IN PRINTING & PAPER AS THEY HOLD	856D	LETTER 54	PROSE
TOTTERING STATE WILL HOLD ME SOME TIME YET	872A	LETTER 74	PROSE
HOLDING			
YET THOU IN INDOLENCE REPOSEST HOLDING ME IN BONDS . . .	271	FOUR ZOAS 1	259
THEREFORE REJECTING IDEAS AS NOTHING & HOLDING ALL WISDOM	708	JERUSALEM 70	7
HOLDING HIS IRON MACE THE SPECTRE REMAINS ATTENTIVE . . .	729	JERUSALEM 83	78
HOLDS			
AND BLEAR-EYD WILL THE BLACK LOT HOLDS	16	BLIND-MANS/PS	20
AND HODGE AGAIN HOLDS UP HIS HEAD	17	BLIND-MANS/PS	60
BETTER THAN HIS MASTER FOR HE ONLY HOLDS A CANDLE IN SUNSHINE	158A	MARRIAGE HH 21	PROSE
WHERE GEORGE THE THIRD HOLDS COUNCIL & HIS LORDS & COMMONS MEET	204	AMERICA CANC B	9
IN ARMOUR AS THE NERVES OF WISDOM EACH HIS STATION [FIRES] HOLDS	205	AMERICA CANC C	19
NOW HOLDS THEE SOON TO ISSUE FORTH SOUND CLARIONS OF WAR	307	FOUR ZOAS 5	63
ART THOU THE COLD ATTRACTIVE POWER THAT HOLDS ME IN THIS CHAIN	323	FOUR ZOAS 7	146
SUCH AS THE JEWS WERE & OF COURSE HE HOLDS THAT THE JEWS	389A	ANNO WATSON	MARG
HENCE WE MUST CONCLUDE THAT THE MAN WHO HOLDS MIRACLES . .	391C	ANNO WATSON	MARG
AND IN HIS HALLOWD CENTER HOLDS THE HEAVENS OF BRIGHT ETERNITY	515	MILTON 28	38
AND HE HOLDS MY MONEY BAG IN HIS HAND	558	I ROSE UP AT/N	16
FOR THE HOST WHO FOLLOWS THIS GROUP AND HOLDS THE CENTER	569D	DESC CAT 3	PROSE
IN THE RANK OF WHICH HE HOLDS THE DESTINY THE USES TO . .	570B	DESC CAT 3	PROSE
ACCORDING TO THE SITUATION HE HOLDS	604C	V LAST JUDG/N	PROSE
"HOLDS IN PERFECTION BUT A LITTLE MOMENT" SHAKESPEARE . .	SUPP	LEGEND/N21	*
HOLE			
A QUESTION HE WOULD PUT HIS HEAD INTO A HOLE & HIDE IT . .	53C	ISLAND MOON 8	PROSE
INTO THEIR PURSE HOLE	61	DR CLASH/IM	4
BUT HE CREPT IN AT MYRA'S POCKET HOLE	557	TO CHLOES/N	2
[OF] OR POINTS OF LIGHT TO BE PUT INTO A DARK HOLE . . .	599B	PUB ADDRESS/N	*PROSE
THE HOLE OF A SHIT-HOUSE	785C	ILLUS DANTE 16	PROSE
TAKEN OUT THAT PART WHICH EXPRESSED THE HOLE FOR THE LADLE	866C	LETTER 65	PROSE
HOLES			
AND THRO THE HOLES WHICH HE HAD MADE	51	WHEN CORRUP/IM	35

```
                                                    PAGE      TITLE          LINE
HOLIDAY
     HUMANIZED ON THE SUNSHINE HOLIDAY . . . . . . .  618B ILLUS MILTON     PROSE
     IN THE HEAVENS TO ANNOUNCE THE SUNSHINE HOLIDAY . 618C ILLUS MILTON     PROSE
HOLIER
     IT IS NOT BECAUSE ANGELS ARE HOLIER THAN MEN OR DEVILS . 616D V LAST JUDG/N  PROSE
     WITH OTHERS & PRETEND NOT TO BE HOLIER THAN OTHERS  . .  682C JERUSALEM 52   PROSE
     FOR WHITEFIELD PRETENDED NOT TO BE HOLIER THAN OTHERS  . 682D JERUSALEM 52   PROSE
HOLINESS
     WILL LEAD [?THEM] THE POOR ENTHUSIAST IN THE PATHS       85C ANNO LAVATER  * MARG
        OF HOLINESS
     OF HOLINESS DISTINCT FROM MAN IS IMPOSSIBLE TO THE       90C ANNO SWED LOVE  MARG
        AFFECTIONS
     AND OOTHOON IS THE CRAFTY SLAVE OF SELFISH HOLINESS . . . 194 V DAU ALBION 6   20
     THE ETERNAL ABODE IN MY HOLINESS  . . . . . . . . .  224 URIZEN 4           7
     DIVIDING & UNITING AT WILL IN THE CRUELTIES OF HOLINESS  348 FOUR ZOAS 8    279
     REVEALD BEFORE THE FACE OF HEAVEN HIS SECRET HOLINESS  . 351 FOUR ZOAS 8    413
     CLOTHD IN THE SERPENT'S FOLDS IN SELFISH HOLINESS DEMANDING 493 MILTON 12    46
        PURITY
     FOR THEN THE BODY OF DEATH WAS PERFECTED IN HYPOCRITIC    494 MILTON 13     25
        HOLINESS
     AND I WILL PUT ON HOLINESS AS A BREASTPLATE & AS A HELMET 499 MILTON 18     21
     BEFORE HIM IN THEIR BEAUTY & IN CRUELTIES OF HOLINESS  .  501 MILTON 19     34
     LET HER BE OFFERD UP TO HOLINESS TIRZAH NUMBERS HER  . .  501 MILTON 19     48
     RETAINING ONLY SATAN'S MATHEMATIC HOLINESS LENGTH BREDTH  521 MILTON 32     18
        & HIGHTH
     TO DISPLAY NATURE'S CRUEL HOLINESS THE DECEITS OF NATURAL 527 MILTON 36     25
        RELIGION
     THESE WONDERS OF SATAN'S HOLINESS SHEWING TO THE EARTH  . 530 MILTON 38     45
     TILL ALL THINGS BECOME ONE GREAT SATAN IN HOLINESS  . .  530 MILTON 39      1
     RESIDE WHO CALUMNIATE & MURDER UNDER PRETENCE OF HOLINESS 608D V LAST JUDG/N PROSE
     HOLINESS IS NOT THE PRICE OF ENTERANCE INTO HEAVEN  . .  615D V LAST JUDG/N PROSE
     EXPECT HOLINESS FROM ONE ANOTHER BUT FROM GOD ONLY  . .  616D V LAST JUDG/N PROSE
     I AM PERHAPS THE MOST SINFUL OF MEN I PRETEND NOT        621A JERUSALEM 3    PROSE
        TO HOLINESS
     AND IN ITS HOLINESS IS CLOSED THE ABOMINATION OF DESOLATION 629 JERUSALEM 10   16
     DELIGHTING IN CRIES & TEARS & CLOTHED IN HOLINESS        630 JERUSALEM 10    49
        & SOLITUDE
     THE SOUL DRINKS MURDER & REVENGE & APPLAUDS ITS OWN      669 JERUSALEM 41    30
        HOLINESS
     IN CRUEL HOLINESS IN THEIR HEAVENS OF CHASTITY &         680 JERUSALEM 49    64
        UNCIRCUMCISION
     ALL NIGHT VALA HEARS SHE TRIUMPHS IN PRIDE OF HOLINESS  . 693 JERUSALEM 60    45
     OF DESPAIR WHILE THE SATANIC HOLINESS TRIUMPHD IN VALA  . 693 JERUSALEM 60    47
     GLORIFIED THY HOLINESS OR REJOICED IN THY GREAT SALVATION 695 JERUSALEM 61    46
     IN PRIDE OF BEAUTY IN CRUELTY OF HOLINESS IN THE BRIGHTNESS 705 JERUSALEM 68   14
     IN CRUELTIES OF HOLINESS TO REFUSE THE JOYS OF LOVE TO   707 JERUSALEM 68    59
        BRING
     FROM THE INNER SANCTUARY A FALSE HOLINESS HID WITHIN THE 708 JERUSALEM 69    40
        CENTER
     SETTING UP KINGS IN WRATH IN HOLINESS OF NATURAL RELIGION 713 JERUSALEM 73    31
     IN CRUEL HOLINESS AND HER LAMENTING SONGS WERE FROM ARNON 722 JERUSALEM 80     8
     THY FOREHEAD BRIGHT HOLINESS TO THE LORD WITH GATES OF   730 JERUSALEM 86     4
        PEARL
     FROM THY WHITE SHOULDERS SHADOWING PURITY IN HOLINESS  . 731 JERUSALEM 86     7
     AND VALLEYS & THY PLEASANT CITIES HOLINESS TO THE LORD  . 731 JERUSALEM 86    12
     AND SOMETIMES SPREAD ABROAD REVEAL THE FLAMES OF HOLINESS 731 JERUSALEM 86    23
     TWELVEFOLD IN ALLEGORIC POMP IN SELFISH HOLINESS . . . . 734 JERUSALEM 89     5
     COME LORD JESUS TAKE ON THEE THE SATANIC BODY OF HOLINESS 737 JERUSALEM 90    38
     TELL THEM TO OBEY THEIR HUMANITIES & NOT PRETEND HOLINESS 738 JERUSALEM 91     6
     IS WHETHER HE IS A WISE MAN OR A FOOL GO PUT OFF HOLINESS 739 JERUSALEM 91    56
     [YOU] WHO DONT KEEP THE SECRETS OF HOLINESS  . . . . .  755 EV GOSPEL(E)/N   86
     HOLINESS TO THY NAME OR TITLE & REVERENCE TO THY SHADOW  788D ANNO THORNTON  MARG
HOLLAND
     FRANCE & SPAIN & ITALY & DENMARK & HOLLAND & GERMANY  . .  690 JERUSALEM 58    41
     UPON PICTURES IMPORTED FROM FLANDERS AND HOLLAND . . . .  864C LETTER 61     PROSE
HOLLOW
     A HOLLOW GROAN RAN THRO THE DREARY VAULTS  . . . . . .    4 FAIR ELENOR/PS    4
     AND I WILL FALL INTO SUCH A PASSION I'LL HOLLOW AND STAMP 63A ISLAND MOON 11 PROSE
     GOD BLESS [XXX] THY POOR BALD PATE GOD BLESS THY HOLLOW  101 TIRIEL 2      *  35
        WINKING EYES
     AND I PLUCKD A HOLLOW REED  . . . . . . . . . . . .    111 INTRODUCTN/SI    16
     WITH HOLLOW PITEOUS SHRIEK  . . . . . . . . . . . .    114 LIT GRL FND/SI   16
     AND HEARD THIS VOICE OF SORROW BREATHED FROM THE HOLLOW PIT 130 BOOK OF THEL 6  10
     . . . SIT OBSCURED IN THE HOLLOW SCULL  . . . . . . .   137 FRENCH REVOLTN   75
     . . . LIKE A MAN THAT RETURNS FROM HOLLOW GRAVES  . . .  141 FRENCH REVOLTN  161
     AUMONT WENT OUT AND STOOD IN THE HOLLOW PORCH . . . . .  133 FRENCH REVOLTN  198
     HOW DIFFERENT FAR THE FAT FED HIRELING WITH HOLLOW DRUM  193 V DAU ALBION 5   14
     SUCH WAS THE HOLLOW VOICE THAT OER [THE RED DEMON] AMERICA 205 AMERICA CANC C   31
        LAMENTED
     IN FORESTS OF ETERNAL DEATH SHRIEKING IN HOLLOW TREES  . . 238 EUROPE PREL 2    6
     RATTLING THEIR HOLLOW BONES IN HOWLING AND LAMENTATION  . 243 EUROPE 13        8
     HER HOLLOW WOMB & CLASPS THE SOLID STEM  . . . . . . .  248 SONG OF LOS 7    36
     HOLLOW UPON THE HOLLOW WIND HIS SHADOWY FORM OBEYING  .  302 FOUR ZOAS 4    197
     AND ALL THE HOLLOW DEEP REBELLOWD WITH THE WONDEROUS WAR 343 FOUR ZOAS 8    *  89
     AND BRASS & MOLTEN METALS CAST IN HOLLOW GLOBES & BORD  . 343 FOUR ZOAS 8     93
     HIS EYES SINK HOLLOW IN HIS HEAD HIS FLESH COVERD WITH   354 FOUR ZOAS 8    515
        SLIME
     [TO JUDGMENT] FROM THE CLOTTED GORE & FROM THE HOLLOW DEN 358 FOUR ZOAS 9     43
     FROM THE CLOTTED GORE & FROM THE HOLLOW DEN  . . . . .   359 FOUR ZOAS 9     88
     WITH FEMALE VOICE WARBLING UPON THE [HILLS &] HOLLOW VALES 381 FOUR ZOAS AD 5   8
     A HOLLOW GROAN FIRST SPOKE HIS WOE  . . . . . . . . .   419 I SAW A MONK/N   24
     A HOLLOW GROAN FIRST SPOKE HIS WOE  . . . . . . . . .   430 GREY MONK        10
```

926

	PAGE	TITLE	LINE

HOLLOW   (CONTINUED)
"THE DRIFT OF HOLLOW STATES HARD TO BE SPELLD" MILTON   .   . SUPP LEGEND/N27   *
HOLLOWAY
TO PRIMROSE HILL STRETCHING TO HIGHGATE & HOLLOWAY   .   .   . 531 MILTON 39   38
HACKNEY AND HOLLOWAY SICKEN FOR ESTRILD & IGNOGE   .   .   . 644 JERUSALEM 21   33
HE CAME DOWN FROM HIGHGATE THRO HACKNEY & HOLLOWAY TOWARDS 657 JERUSALEM 31   14
    LONDON
HOLLOWING
WITHIN A NUMBER OF DRAGONS WERE HOLLOWING THE CAVE   .   .   . 154D MARRIAGE HH 15   PROSE
HOLY
AND LET THY HOLY FEET VISIT OUR CLIME   .   .   .   .   1 TO SPRING/PS   8
O HOLY VIRGIN CLAD IN PUREST WHITE   .   .   .   .   3 TO MORNING/PS   1
OH BLESS THOSE HOLY FEET LIKE ANGELS' FEET   .   .   .   .   .   9 FRESH FROM/PS   7
IN TIMES OF INNOCENCE AND HOLY JOY   .   .   .   .   9 FRESH FROM/PS   10
EACH VILLAGE SEEMS THE HAUNT OF HOLY FEET   .   .   .   .   .   9 FRESH FROM/PS   16
ENTERING WITH HOLY FEET TO WHERE ON HIGH   .   .   .   .   .   15 IMIT SPEN/PS   22
PREPARE YOUR EYES TO MEET A HOLY GOD   .   .   .   .   .   .   34 WAR SONG/PS   9
THE HOLY KISS OF LOVE AND THE TRANSPARENT TEAR   .   .   .   . 38A SAMSON/PS   PROSE
FOR HOLY UNTO ISRAEL'S GOD I AM A NAZARITE EVEN FROM MY   39C SAMSON/PS   PROSE
    MOTHER'S WOMB
WAS SHEWN THE HOLY CITY THEN ATHENS LEARNING   .   .   .   .   . 41A THEN SHE BORE   PROSE
UPON A HOLY THURSDAY THEIR INNOCENT FACES CLEAN   .   .   .   . 59 HOLY THURS/IM   1
WHICH SHORTLY WEARY THE MAN FOR ALL LIFE IS HOLY   .   .   . 74B ANNO LAVATER   MARG
GUARD IT ON EITHER SIDE & IN THE MIDST IS THE HOLY LAW   . 82A ANNO LAVATER   MARG
MOST SUPERLATIVELY BEAUTIFUL & MOST AFFECTIONATELY HOLY   82D ANNO LAVATER   MARG
("SANGUINE CHOLERIC PHLEGMATIC MELANCHOLY") (FOUR) MOST   86A ANNO LAVATER   MARG
    HOLY MEN
THINK OF A WHITE CLOUD AS BEING HOLY YOU CANNOT LOVE IT   90C ANNO SWED LOVE   MARG
BUT THINK OF A HOLY MAN WITHIN THE CLOUD LOVE SPRINGS UP   90C ANNO SWED LOVE   MARG
O THEY ARE HOLY & FORGIVING FILLD WITH LOVING MERCY   .   . 108 TIRIEL 6   26
HOLY IMAGE I CAN TRACE   .   .   .   . 120 CRADLE SONG/SI   22
HOLY THURSDAY   .   .   .   . 121D HOLY THURS/SI   TITLE
TWAS ON A HOLY THURSDAY THEIR INNOCENT FACES CLEAN   .   .   . 121 HOLY THURS/SI   1
IT IS TO TENFOLD LIFE TO LOVE TO PEACE AND RAPTURES HOLY   128 BOOK OF THEL 3   11
. . . THEY LOOK DOWNWARD AND LABOUR AND FORGET MY HOLY LAW   140 FRENCH REVOLTN   139
. . . AND THE HOLY HYMN FROM THICKEND TONGUES   .   .   .   . 140 FRENCH REVOLTN   140
THRO THE ORBED ABODE OF THE HOLY DEAD . . . . 140 FRENCH REVOLTN   142
. . . AND SINGING OF THE HOLY CHOIR   .   .   .   . 140 FRENCH REVOLTN   146
. . . THE HOLY BESIDE THE ACCURSED   .   .   .   . 141 FRENCH REVOLTN   149
THE WHOLE CREATION WILL BE CONSUMED AND APPEAR INFINITE   154B MARRIAGE HH 14   PROSE
    AND HOLY
FOR EVERY THING THAT LIVES IS HOLY   .   .   .   . 160B SONG LIBERTY   PROSE
[AND] HOLY & MEEK SHE CRIES   .   .   .   . 163 ASKED THIEF/N   4
MY FATHER THEN WITH HOLY LOOK   .   .   .   . 167 INFANT SORW/N   26
IN [HIS HAND] [THEIR] HANDS A HOLY BOOK   .   .   .   .   .   . 167 INFANT SORW/N   *   27
LIKE [A [SERPENT]] TO [SERPENTS IN THE] HOLY MEN BY DAY   167 INFANT SORW/N   *   38
QUENCH THE HOLY LIGHT   .   .   .   . 168 SILENT NIGHT/N   2
HE SITS DOWN WITH HOLY FEARS   .   .   .   . 174 HUMAN IMAGE/N   10
OF OUR MOST HOLY MYSTERY   .   .   .   . 177 LIT BOY LST/N   19
[THEY] AND BURND HIM IN A HOLY [FIRE] PLACE   .   .   .   .   . 177 LIT BOY LST/N   26
HOLY THURSDAY   .   .   .   . 181C HOLY THURS/N   TITLE
IS THIS A HOLY THING TO SEE   .   .   .   . 181 HOLY THURS/N   1
I CALL WITH HOLY VOICE KINGS OF THE SOUNDING AIR   .   .   . 190 V DAU ALBION 2   14
HOLY ETERNAL INFINITE AND EACH JOY IS A LOVE   .   .   .   . 192 V DAU ALBION 5   6
RELIGIOUS DREAMS AND HOLY VESPERS LIGHT THY SMOKY FIRES   194 V DAU ALBION 6   14
ARISE AND DRINK YOUR BLISS FOR EVERY THING THAT LIVES IS   195 V DAU ALBION 8   10
    HOLY
FOR EVERY THING THAT LIVES IS HOLY LIFE DELIGHTS IN LIFE   199 AMERICA 8   13
FROM OUT HIS HOLY SHRINE HIS TEARS IN DELUGE PITEOUS   .   . 203 AMERICA 16   4
WHEN HOLY ZEAL SCENTS THE SWEET VALLEYS OF RIPE VIRGIN   205 AMERICA CANC C   30
    BLISS
THE HOLY WORD   .   .   .   . 210 INTRODUCTN/SE   4
HOLY THURSDAY   .   .   .   . 211D HOLY THURS/SE   TITLE
IS THIS A HOLY THING TO SEE   .   .   .   . 211 HOLY THURS/SE   1
HE SITS DOWN WITH HOLY FEARS   .   .   .   . 217 HUMAN ABSTR/SE   9
OF OUR MOST HOLY MYSTERY   .   .   .   . 218 LIT BOY LST/SE   16
AND BURND HIM IN A HOLY PLACE   .   .   .   . 219 LIT BOY LST/SE   21
TO THE HOLY LIGHT   .   .   .   . 219 LIT GRL LST/SE   8
WHERE THE HOLY LIGHT   .   .   .   . 219 LIT GRL LST/SE   13
LIKE THE HOLY BOOK   .   .   .   . 219 LIT GRL LST/SE   28
TILL THE NIGHT OF HOLY SHADOWS   .   .   .   . 243 EUROPE 13   18
HOLY & MEEK SHE CRIES   .   .   .   . 261 ASKED THIEF   4
. . . HE STOOPD HIS [HOLY] INNOCENT HEAD   .   .   .   .   . 266 FOUR ZOAS 1   72
AND STRETCHING OUT HIS HOLY HAND IN THE VAST DEEP SUBLIME   266 FOUR ZOAS 1   73
LUVAH & URIZEN CONTEND IN WAR AROUND THE HOLY TENT   .   . 277 FOUR ZOAS 1   480
THE ETERNAL MAN WEPT IN THE HOLY TENT OUR BROTHER   277 FOUR ZOAS 1   484
    IN ETERNITY
WHILE THUS HE SPOKE HIS FIRES REDDEND [ROUND] OER THE HOLY   278 FOUR ZOAS 1   514
    TENT
THE LANCES OF URIZEN FROM CHARIOTS ROUND THE HOLY TENT   .   . 278 FOUR ZOAS 1   517
ENDLONG A RAGING SERPENT ROLLING ROUND THE HOLY TENT   .   . 279 FOUR ZOAS 1   532
FOR EVERY THING THAT LIVES IS HOLY FOR THE SOURCE OF LIFE   289 FOUR ZOAS 2   366
OF LIVING GOLD PURE PERFECT HOLY IN WHITE LINEN PURE HE   293 FOUR ZOAS 3   51
    HOVERD
THE GOLD & SILVER & COSTLY STONES HIS HOLY WORKMANSHIP   .   . 310 FOUR ZOAS 5   215
I WELL REMEMBER FOR I HEARD THE MILD & HOLY VOICE   .   .   . 310 FOUR ZOAS 5   218
THE HOLY OIL RAGES THRO ALL THE CAVERN ROCKS FIERCE FLAMES   320 FOUR ZOAS 7   12
AND MANY DAUGHTERS FLOURISHD ROUND THE HOLY TENT OF MAN   326 FOUR ZOAS 7   252
OF SWEET ETERNITY THE BLOOD FLOWD ROUND THE HOLY TENT &   326 FOUR ZOAS 7   257
    RIVN
ENORMOUS WORKS LOS CONTEMPLATED INSPIRD BY THE HOLY SPIRIT   343 FOUR ZOAS 8   108
AND ENITHARMON NAMED THE FEMALE (JERUSALEM) THE HOLY   .   . 346 FOUR ZOAS 8   *   190

927

		PAGE	TITLE	LINE
HOLY	(CONTINUED)			
GLORY GLORY GLORY TO THE HOLY LAMB OF GOD		346	FOUR ZOAS 8	195
BEGAN TO ENTER THE HOLY CITY ENTRING THE DISMAL CLOUDS . .		359	FOUR ZOAS 9	84
HIS HOLY HANDS RECIEVD THE FLAMING DEMON & DEMONESS OF SMOKE		366	FOUR ZOAS 9	361
AND WAS THE HOLY LAMB OF GOD		480	AND DID FEET/M	3
WHO CALLS THE INDIVIDUAL LAW HOLY AND DESPISES THE SAVIOUR		493	MILTON 13	5
GLORY GLORY GLORY TO THE HOLY LAMB OF GOD		494	MILTON 13	28
TO NATURAL RELIGION TO TIRZAH THE DAUGHTER OF RAHAB THE HOLY		501	MILTON 19	54
WAS NEVER KNOWN THAT ONE OF THE HOLY DEAD SHOULD WILLING RETURN		508	MILTON 23	58
TO MAKE LEARNING A BURDEN & THE WORK OF THE HOLY SPIRIT STRIFE		511	MILTON 25	52
INTO MOST HOLY FORMS OF THOUGHT SUCH IS THE POWER OF INSPIRATION		515	MILTON 28	5
BECAUSE WE WERE COMBIND IN FREEDOM & HOLY BROTHERHOOD . .		521	MILTON 32	15
THE WOOD & STONE WERE CALLD THE HOLY THINGS		543	IF TRUE/N	11
HE IS IN THE MOST HOLY SANCTUARY		570A	DESC CAT 3	PROSE
OVER THE HEAD OF THE SAVIOUR & REDEEMER THE HOLY SPIRIT		613B	V LAST JUDG/N	PROSE
THE HOLY FAMILY CONSISTING OF MARY JOSEPH JOHN THE BAPTIST		614A	V LAST JUDG/N	PROSE
THE FOOL SHALL NOT ENTER INTO HEAVEN LET HIM BE EVER SO HOLY		615D	V LAST JUDG/N	PROSE
CRYING HOLY HOLY HOLY IS THE [G] LORD GOD ALMIGHTY .		617B	V LAST JUDG/N	*PROSE
O HOLY GENERATION [IMAGE] OF REGENERATION		626	JERUSALEM 7	* 65
THY HOLY WRATH & DEEP DECEIT CANNOT AVAIL AGAINST ME .		627	JERUSALEM 8	33
THIS IS THE SPECTRE OF MAN THE HOLY REASONING POWER . .		629	JERUSALEM 10	15
AND SUCH THE HOLY GOSPEL OF MOUNT OLIVET & CALVARY . .		638	JERUSALEM 16	69
CALLING THAT HOLY LOVE WHICH IS ENVY REVENGE & CRUELTY .		639	JERUSALEM 17	30
SUSSEX & KENT ARE HER SCATTERD GARMENTS IRELAND HER HOLY PLACE		653	JERUSALEM 29	20
OF LIVING GOLD PURE PERFECT HOLY IN WHITE LINEN PURE HE HOVERD		654	JERUSALEM 29	38
BELONG TO GOD ALONE AND ALL THY LITTLE ONES ARE HOLY .		657	JERUSALEM 31	45
IN THE SHADOWS OF A WOMAN & A SECLUDED HOLY PLACE . .		661	JERUSALEM 34	33
BROODING IN HOLY HYPOCRITIC LUST DRINKING THE CRIES OF PAIN		672	JERUSALEM 43	17
ANIMATING THE DRAGON TEMPLES SOON TO BECOME THAT HOLY FIEND		677	JERUSALEM 47	6
ALBION THE MILDEST SON OF HEAVEN THE PLACE OF HOLY SACRIFICE		678	JERUSALEM 48	55
STRIVING TO CREATE A HEAVEN IN WHICH ALL SHALL BE PURE & HOLY		679	JERUSALEM 49	27
AND ALTHO I SIN & BLASPHEME THY HOLY NAME THOU PITIEST ME		693	JERUSALEM 60	62
. . . IF I WERE HOLY I NEVER COULD BEHOLD THE TEARS . .		694	JERUSALEM 61	12
AND THY ARK & HOLY PLACE AT THY FROWNS AT THY DIRE REVENGE		706	JERUSALEM 68	50
IN THE CIRCUMFERENCE & EVERY MINUTE PARTICULAR IS HOLY .		708	JERUSALEM 69	42
AND PEARL WITH INSTRUMENTS OF MUSIC IN HOLY JERUSALEM .		710	JERUSALEM 71	41
TEACH ME O HOLY SPIRIT THE TESTIMONY OF JESUS LET ME .		714	JERUSALEM 74	14
WITH HOLY RAPTURES OF ADORATION RAPD SUBLIME IN THE VISIONS OF GOD		720	JERUSALEM 79	44
BUT HIDE AMERICA FOR A CURSE AN ALTAR OF VICTIMS & A HOLY PLACE		725	JERUSALEM 82	29
UPON THE HOLY LAND I SEE THE RIVER OF LIFE & TREE OF LIFE		731	JERUSALEM 86	18
TERRIFIC FROM HIS HOLY PLACE		746	JERUSALEM 98	41
THE ACCUSER HOLY GOD OF ALL		758	EV GOSPEL (2)	13
HOLY & COLD I CLIPD THE WINGS		771	OF GATES/GP	35
. . . DEATH O HOLY IS THIS BROTHERHOOD		781	GHOST ABEL 2	24
HERE IS SIGNED TWO NAMES WHICH ARE TOO HOLY TO BE WRITTEN		789B	ANNO THORNTON	MARG
PICTURE IN MANY RESPECTS IT REPRESENTS THE HOLY FAMILY .		823D	LETTER 27	PROSE
MENTAL REBELLION AGAINST THE HOLY SPIRIT		871B	LETTER 72	PROSE
SALADIN...IN THE HOLY LAND		SUPP	ILLUS HISTORY	*TITLE
SATAN'S HOLY TRINITY THE ACCUSER THE JUDGE & THE EXECUTIONER		SUPP	INSC OUR END	*TITLE
CRADLE SONG DITTO NURSE'S SONG HOLY THURSDAY		SUPP	LETTER 66A	*PROSE
THE LITTLE VAGABOND HOLY THURSDAY A POISON TREE . . .		SUPP	LETTER 66A	*PROSE
HOLY-GHOST,HOLY GHOST				
THE SON A RATIO OF THE FIVE SENSES & THE HOLY-GHOST VACUUM		150B	MARRIAGE HH 5	PROSE
NOT SPOKEN AGAINST THE HOLY GHOST WHO IN PAINE STRIVES		387C	ANNO WATSON	MARG
THE HUMAN MIND CANNOT GO BEYOND THE GIFT OF GOD THE HOLY GHOST		579D	DESC CAT 5	PROSE
ALL THE GIFTS OF THE HOLY GHOST ARE [DESPISD] LOOKD UPON		604C	V LAST JUDG/N	PROSE
TO THEE MARY THY WIFE FOR SHE IS WITH CHILD BY THE HOLY GHOST		695	JERUSALEM 61	27
IS THE HOLY GHOST ANY OTHER THAN AN INTELLECTUAL FOUNTAIN		717A	JERUSALEM 71	PROSE
TO HIS GENIUS WHICH IS THE HOLY GHOST IN MAN THERE IS NO OTHER		738	JERUSALEM 91	10
AND AS TO THE INDWELLING OF THE HOLY GHOST		752	EV GOSPEL(D)/N *	45
MEMORY [NATURE] IS HIS INSPIRER & NOT IMAGINATION THE HOLY GHOST		785A	ILLUS DANTE 7	*PROSE
BY MEANS OF LAWFUL WINDOW LIGHT THE HOLY GHOST [WHO] .		787D	ANNO THORNTON	* MARG
THE HOLY GHOST THY KINGDOM ON EARTH IS NOT [THY XXX] .		788A	ANNO THORNTON	* MARG
DELIVER FROM THE HOLY GHOST SO WE CALL NATURE . . .		788D	ANNO THORNTON	MARG
TRANSLATED AS WELL AS WRITTEN BY THE HOLY GHOST . . .		822A	LETTER 25	PROSE
HOLY-ONE				
FROM THE VISION AND FRUITION OF THE HOLY-ONE		622	JERUSALEM 4	17
THE WINE OF THE SPIRIT & THE VINEYARDS OF THE HOLY-ONE .		672	JERUSALEM 43	28
AND I ASKED A WATCHER & A HOLY-ONE		718	STOOD AMONG/J	12
MURDERS THE HOLY-ONE GO TELL THEM THIS & OVERTHROW THEIR CUP		738	JERUSALEM 91	13
HOLY-ONES				
UTTERING THIS DARKNESS IN MY HALLS IN THE PILLARS OF MY HOLY-ONES		271	FOUR ZOAS 1	270
NO MORE SEEK TO JERUSALEM NOR TO THE SOUND OF MY HOLY-ONES		720	JERUSALEM 79	19

928

PAGE   TITLE   LINE

HOME
THE MOST OBSCURE AT HOME THAT SCARCE WERE SEEN . . . .   18 EDW THIRD/PS 1   38
WHEN I SIT AT MY HOME A PRIVATE MAN . . . .   19 EDW THIRD/PS 2   21
NOW WILLIAM THOU DOST THRUST THE QUESTION HOME . . . .   29A EDW THIRD/PS 4   PROSE
NO SAID INFLAMMABLE GASS I HAVE GOT A CAMERA OBSCURA AT 47C ISLAND MOON 3   PROSE
  HOME
NO SAID MRS NANNICANTIPOT I THINK A PERSON MAY BE AS GOOD 48A ISLAND MOON 4   PROSE
  AT HOME
THEY ALL WENT HOME & LEFT THE PHILOSOPHERS THEN SUCTION 49D ISLAND MOON 6   PROSE
  ASKD
THEN COME HOME MY CHILDREN THE SUN IS GONE DOWN . . . .   60 NURSES SONG/IM   5
AND THEN GO HOME TO BED . . . .   60 NURSES SONG/IM   15
LITTLE WANDERER HIE THEE HOME . . . .   112 A DREAM/SI   20
THEN COME HOME MY CHILDREN THE SUN IS GONE DOWN . . . . 121 NURSES SONG/SI   5
AND THEN GO HOME TO BED . . . .   121 NURSES SONG/SI   14
. . . TO SHUT UP THIS ASSEMBLY IN THEIR FINAL HOME . .   141 FRENCH REVOLTN   154
WHEN I CAME HOME ON THE ABYSS OF THE FIVE SENSES . . . 150C MARRIAGE HH 6   PROSE
THEN COME HOME MY CHILDREN THE SUN IS GONE DOWN . . . . 171 NURSES SONG/N   5
THEN COME HOME MY CHILDREN THE SUN IS GONE DOWN . . . . 212 NURSES SONG/SE   5
I TOOK HIM HOME IN MY WARM BOSOM AS WE WENT ALONG . . . 238 EUROPE INTRO   19
AND MANY A PLEASANT SHEPHERD'S HOME . . . .   427 MENTAL TRAVLER   92
AND CAME HOME IN EVENING BESPATTERED WITH MIRE . . . .   428 MARY   36
AND HE RETURND HOME IN MISERY . . . .   434 WILLIAM BOND   8
BUT HE CAME HOME IN A BLACK BLACK CLOUD . . . . .   435 WILLIAM BOND   11
INTO THE WORLD & MAKE THE WORLD THEIR HOME . . . . .   544 SOME MEN/N   2
THEIR AWFUL CHARGE BACK TO HIS NATIVE HOME BUT ALBION DARK 674 JERUSALEM 44   5
A WANDRING VAGRANT WITHOUT HOME . . . .   757 EV GOSPEL(I)/N   42
& TWELVE OCLOCK AT NIGHT BEFORE WE COULD GET HOME . .   803A LETTER 15   PROSE
HIS SON WAS LIKEWISE NOT AT HOME BUT I WILL AGAIN CALL ON 834B LETTER 34   PROSE
MR WALKER I HAVE BEEN SO UNFORTUNATE AS NOT TO FIND AT HOME 836B LETTER 35   PROSE
BUT HE WAS NOT AT HOME SO COULD NOT SPARE MORE TIME . . 838B LETTER 37   PROSE
COMPLIMENT HE WAS NOT AT HOME I LEFT IT WITH A SHORT NOTE 838C LETTER 37   PROSE
YET BEEN ABLE TO MEET MR BRAITHWAITE AT HOME BUT INTEND 849B LETTER 45   PROSE
BANKS THE SCULPTOR IS GONE TO HIS ETERNAL HOME . . . .   859D LETTER 56   PROSE
WHEN I AM AWAY FROM HOME I AM DR SIR YOURS SINCERELY . . 872C LETTER 75   PROSE
HOMER
THEN SAID QUID I THINK THAT HOMER IS BOMBAST & . . . .   51D ISLAND MOON 7   PROSE
OF HOMER SOCRATES PHIDIAS GLYCON ARISTOTLE ETC . . . . 388D ANNO WATSON   MARG
NOBODY CONSIDERS THESE THINGS WHEN THEY READ HOMER OR . 411B ANNO BOYD   MARG
HOMER MEANT THIS . . . .   412A ANNO BOYD   MARG
THE STOLEN AND PERVERTED WRITINGS OF HOMER & OVID . . 480B MILTON 1   PROSE
SAYS HOMER IS VERY MUCH IMPROVD BY POPE . . . .   555 BLAKES APL/N 1   13
CRIES HOMER IS VERY MUCH IMPROVD BY POPE . . . . . .   556 BLAKES APL/N 2   10
HOW MUCH OF HIS HOMER & DANTE HE WILL ALLOW TO BE MINE . 592D PUB ADDRESS/N   PROSE
SAYS HOMER IS VERY MUCH IMPROVD BY POPE . . . . . .   595 BLAKES APOL/PA   8
I DO NOT KNOW WHETHER HOMER IS A LIAR & THAT THERE IS NO 596D PUB ADDRESS/N   PROSE
IS LIKE LOOKING FOR EPIGRAMS IN HOMER . . . .   599A PUB ADDRESS/N   PROSE
THOSE WHO WILL HAVE UNITY EXCLUSIVELY IN HOMER . . . . 778B HOMERS POETRY   PROSE
HOMER VIRGIL & OVID CONFIRM THIS OPINION . . . . . .   778D HOMERS POETRY   PROSE
SO THAT HOMER IS THE CENTER OF ALL I MEAN THE POETRY OF 785B ILLUS DANTE 7   PROSE
  THE HEATHEN
I NAME MOSES SOLOMON ESOP HOMER PLATO . . . .   793B LETTER 5   PROSE
WHAT IS IT SETS HOMER VIRGIL & MILTON IN SO HIGH A RANK 794A LETTER 5   PROSE
  OF ART
ABSORBED BY THE POETS MILTON HOMER CAMOENS ERCILLA ARIOSTO 806D LETTER 17   PROSE
FLAXMAN'S HOMER WITH ADDITIONAL DESIGNS TWO OF WHICH . 841A LETTER 40   PROSE
PRICE I RECEIVE FOR ENGRAVING FLAXMAN'S OUTLINES OF HOMER 844B LETTER 43   PROSE
HOMER SATAN . . . .   SUPP ILLUS DANTE 7   *PROSE
HOMER ARISTOTLE . . . .   SUPP ILLUS DANTE 99   *PROSE
HOMER'S
LIKEWISE READ HOMER'S ILIAD . . . .   389C ANNO WATSON   MARG
IF HOMER'S MERIT WAS ONLY IN THESE HISTORICAL COMBINATIONS 411D ANNO BOYD   MARG
I AM NO HOMER'S HERO YOU ALL KNOW . . . .   541 HOMERS HERO/N   1
NO MAN CAN BELIEVE THAT EITHER HOMER'S MYTHOLOGY . . . 565D DESC CAT 2   PROSE
ON HOMER'S POETRY & ON VIRGIL ON HOMER'S POETRY . . . 778A HOMERS POETRY   TITLE
BUT WHY HOMER'S IS PECULIARLY SO I CANNOT TELL . . . . 778A HOMERS POETRY   PROSE
BUT A PRINCIPAL PART OF HOMER'S SUBJECT . . . . 778A HOMERS POETRY   PROSE
SIMILAR TO HOMER'S ILIAD OR MILTON'S PARADISE LOST THE . 823A LETTER 26   PROSE
HONEST
("NOT HONEST PUBLICLY CHRISTIAN PRIVATELY DEIST") BRAVO 72C ANNO LAVATER   MARG
BE FAIRLY SEPERATED & THEN SUPERSTITION WILL BE HONEST   85C ANNO LAVATER   MARG
  FEELING
& GOD WHO LOVES ALL HONEST MEN . . . .   85C ANNO LAVATER   MARG
THAT THE VOICE OF HONEST INDIGNATION IS THE VOICE OF GOD 153C MARRIAGE HH 12   PROSE
& IS HE HONEST WHO RESISTS HIS GENIUS OR CONSCIENCE . . 154B MARRIAGE HH 12   PROSE
BUT AN HONEST JOY . . . .   168 SILENT NIGHT/N   10
IN LAPS OF PLEASURE INNOCENCE HONEST OPEN SEEKING . . . 193 V DAU ALBION 6   5
ONCE WERE THY FIRES LIGHTED BY THE EYES OF HONEST MORN . 194 V DAU ALBION 6   15
TEMPT ME TO MURDER [HONEST LOVE] MY OWN SOUL & WIPE MY   268 FOUR ZOAS 1   171
  TEARS & SMILE
THE ALL POWERFUL CURSE OF AN HONEST MAN BE UPON URIZEN   298 FOUR ZOAS 4   25
  & LUVAH
FOR WAR IS [HONEST] [AN] ENERGY ENSLAVD BUT THY RELIGION 361 FOUR ZOAS 9   * 152
THE FIRST AUTHOR OF THIS WAR & THE DISTRACTING OF HONEST 361 FOUR ZOAS 9   153
  MINDS
[WHAT DOUBT IS VIRTUOUS EVEN HONEST ?THAT DEPENDS ?UPON 386C ANNO WATSON   * MARG
  EXAMINATION]
THAT GOD DOES & ALWAYS DID CONVERSE WITH HONEST MEN . . 389A ANNO WATSON   MARG
EVERY HONEST MAN IS A PROPHET HE UTTERS HIS OPINION . . 392B ANNO WATSON   MARG
PROVES HIM TO BE AN HONEST MAN . . . .   438D BLAKES MEMORAN   PROSE
[HE'LL] THEYLL STILL BE CALLED THE WORLD'S HONEST MAN . . 544 SOME MEN/N   5
AMONG HONEST PEOPLE TO MAKE GAME OF AND LAUGH AT THEM . . 574D DESC CAT 3   PROSE

```
                                                      PAGE      TITLE           LINE
HONEST    (CONTINUED)
     THERE WILL ALWAYS BE AS MANY HYPOCRITES BORN AS HONEST MEN    616A V LAST JUDG/N   PROSE
     TILL DEEP DISSIMULATION IS THE ONLY DEFENCE AN HONEST MAN     679 JERUSALEM 49      23
         HAS LEFT
     BUT HE ACTS WITH TRIUMPHANT HONEST PRIDE    . . . . . .       750 EV GOSPEL(C)/N    23
     FOR HE ACTS WITH HONEST TRIUMPHANT PRIDE    . . . . . .       751 EV GOSPEL(D)/N    29
     MANY HONEST PEOPLE ENDURE GREATER HARDSHIPS WITH FORTITUDE    793B LETTER 5         PROSE
     SO HONEST AS TO EXPOSE TO YOU HIS WHOLE ABSURD PREJUDICE      838C LETTER 37        PROSE
     BE VERY HONEST AND VERY GENEROUS TOO WHERE HIS OWN            846C LETTER 44        PROSE
         INTEREST
HONESTLY
     TO MAKE THE COMPARISON HONESTLY    . . . . . . . .            602A PUB ADDRESS/N    PROSE
HONEST-SEEMING
     CALL THINE ALLURING ARTS AND HONEST-SEEMING BROW  . . . .     38A SAMSON/PS         PROSE
HONESTY
     THEREFORE PRONOUNCE HIM A KNAVE WHY SHOULD HONESTY FEAR       68B ANNO LAVATER      MARG
         A KNAVE
     TRUE SUPERSTITION IS IGNORANT HONESTY    . . . . . . .        75A ANNO LAVATER      MARG
     ("MORAL ENTHUSIAST WHO LOSES PLAIN PATHS OF HONESTY")         88A ANNO LAVATER      MARG
         MOST TRUE
     . . . HONESTY BOUND IN THE DENS OF SUPERSTITION               144 FRENCH REVOLTN    228
     MAY FIND IT IN A HARLOT AND IN COARSE-CLAD HONESTY    . . .   199 AMERICA 8          11
     HE CRIED WHY TREMBLES HONESTY AND LIKE A MURDERER    . . .    200 AMERICA 11         4
     HE WHO THINKS THAT HONESTY IS CHANGEABLE KNOWS NOTHING        386B ANNO WATSON      MARG
         ABOUT IT
     VIRTUE & HONESTY OR THE DICTATES OF CONSCIENCE ARE    . . .   386B ANNO WATSON      MARG
     THE TRUTH & CERTAINTY OF VIRTUE & HONESTY I E INSPIRATION     386C ANNO WATSON      MARG
     & ITS CONSEQUENT EVIL & THE HONESTY OF OTHERS & ITS    . . .  393B ANNO WATSON      MARG
     WITHOUT A MORAL CRITERION OTHER THAN NATIVE HONESTY           414A ANNO BOYD        MARG
         UNTAUGHT
     WHILE OTHER COUNTRY HINDS ARE AS INDIGNANT AGAINST HONESTY    414A ANNO BOYD        MARG
     TO MAKE [EITHER SENSE OR] MEER COMMON HONESTY    . . . .      543 TO ROYL ACAD/N     9
     DISTINGUISHES HONESTY FROM KNAVERY BUT THE HARD AND WIREY     585C DESC CAT 15      PROSE
     THE MORTAR & CEMENT OF THE WORK TEARS OF HONESTY THE NAILS    632 JERUSALEM 12       33
     THE TEAR AND THE CONFESSION OF HONESTY OPEN & UNDISGUISD      675 JERUSALEM 45        7
HONEY
     IN HIS LAND OVERFLOWING WITH HONEY    . . . . . . . .         19 EDW THIRD/PS 2      14
     O MY GOOD LORD TRUE WISDOM DROPS LIKE HONEY    . . . . .      20 EDW THIRD/PS 2      36
     THY WINE DOTH PURIFY THE GOLDEN HONEY THY PERFUME    . . .    128 BOOK OF THEL 2      8
     WHY A TONGUE IMPRESSD WITH HONEY FROM EVERY WIND    . . . .   130 BOOK OF THEL 6     16
     SING THE HONEY BEES    . . . . . . . . . . . .               148 MARRIAGE HH 2       8
     WILT THOU BRING COMFORTS ON THY WINGS AND DEWS AND HONEY      192 V DAU ALBION 4     10
         AND BALM
     WITH MILK AND HONEY    . . . . . . . . . . . .               239 EUROPE PREL 2      15
     AT WILL TO MURMUR IN THE FLOWERS SMALL AS THE HONEY BEE       288 FOUR ZOAS 2       297
     MY MILK OF COWS & HONEY OF BEES & FRUIT OF GOLDEN HARVEST     359 FOUR ZOAS 9       104
     THE HONEY OF HER INFANT LIPS    . . . . . . . . .            426 MENTAL TRAVLER     69
     THE POISON OF THE HONEY BEE    . . . . . . . . .             432 AUGURIES          49
     THE CRUEL SCORPION IS THERE THE GNAT WASP HORNET & THE        513 MILTON 27         21
         HONEY BEE
     HIS MILK OF COWS & HONEY OF BEES & FRUIT OF GOLDEN HARVEST    641 JERUSALEM 19        5
HONEYSUCKLE
     THE HONEYSUCKLE SLEEPING ON THE OAK THE FLAUNTING BEAUTY      520 MILTON 31         54
HONIED
     THE HONIED DEW THAT COMETH ON WAKING DAY    . . . . . .       3 TO MORNING/PS        5
HONOR
     ACCOMODATION OF THOSE WHO GIVE IT THE HONOR OF ATTENTION      442D LAST JUDGMNT/L   PROSE
HONOUR
     THAT I WILL TELL YOUR HONOUR IF YOULL GIVE ME LEAVE  . . .    29B EDW THIRD/PS 4    PROSE
     TO TELL YOUR HONOUR BECAUSE YOU LOVE TO HEAR WAR-SONGS  . .   29C EDW THIRD/PS 4    PROSE
     THE WISE MAN THAT KNOWS US ALL AS WELL AS YOUR HONOUR  . .    29C EDW THIRD/PS 4    PROSE
     I KNOW YOUR HONOUR DOES NOT THINK ANY THING OF YOURSELF  . .  29D EDW THIRD/PS 4    PROSE
     I NEVER FLATTER YOUR HONOUR    . . . . . . . . .             29D EDW THIRD/PS 4    PROSE
     THAT WHEN THY SAYINGS COME TO PASS WE MAY HONOUR THEE    . .  40B SAMSON/PS         PROSE
     SHE BROUGHT FORTH RAGE [THEN] AND SHAME BORE HONOUR &    . .  42C THEN SHE BORE    *PROSE
     [BY SHAME SHE HAD A SON CALLD HONOUR WHO BORE REVENGE]    .   43A THEN SHE BORE     PROSE
     WHO MARRIED HONOUR THESE FOLLOW HER AROUND THE WORLD    . .   43A THEN SHE BORE     PROSE
     HONOUR & GENIUS IS ALL I ASK    . . . . . . . . .           47 ASK GODS/IM 1        1
     HONOUR TWINES AROUND HER BROWS    . . . . . . . . .         63 SHEPHERD FIRST       7
     ("ON MODESTY & HONOUR DARES NOT DEPEND ") UNEASY    . . .     79C ANNO LAVATER      MARG
     INTO CONFUSED PERTURBATION & STRIFE & HONOUR & PRIDE    . .   361 FOUR ZOAS 9       154
     AND WONDER AT THE DIVINE MERCY & AT LOS'S SUBLIME HONOUR      743 JERUSALEM 96       32
     THE HONOUR INTENDED YOU BY NATURE TO REVIVE THE GREEK         795B LETTER 6        PROSE
         WORKMANSHIP
     AT THE MAN WHO WAS CROWND WITH GLORY & HONOUR    . . . . .    813B LETTER 22       PROSE
     LEADS TO GLORY & HONOUR I REJOICE & I TREMBLE    . . . .      823B LETTER 26       PROSE
     FOR WHICH I SHALL NEVER CEASE TO HONOUR & RESPECT YOU    .    826A LETTER 27       PROSE
     THIS WAS THE WOMAN'S OWN REMARK & DOES HIGH HONOUR TO HER     827C LETTER 28       PROSE
     (SECOND) FOR THE HONOUR OF CHICHESTER MR P(PHILLIPS)    .     856B LETTER 54       PROSE
     HONOUR OF LONDON BOOKSELLERS & CONSIDER THEM AS LOSING A      856C LETTER 54       PROSE
     GREAT DEAL OF HONOUR IN LOSING THE FIRST PUBLICATION OF ANY   856C LETTER 54       PROSE
     I INCLOSE A TICKET OF ADMISSION IF YOU SHOULD HONOUR    .     866B LETTER 64       PROSE
     THE HONOUR TO ENQUIRE AFTER UNPROFITABLE ENOUGH TO ME THO     867A LETTER 66       PROSE
HONOURABLE
     OR A COPY OF ANY KIND CAN BE AS HONOURABLE TO A NATION  . .   595C PUB ADDRESS/N    PROSE
     HONOURABLE MENTION OF ME HAS BEEN AT FELPHAM &    . . . .     810D LETTER 21       PROSE
     HONOURABLE AT ANY RATE THE PROJECT PLEASES LORD COWPER'S      821C LETTER 25       PROSE
     BE APPOINTD BY HIM IN SO HONOURABLE A CONCERN AS THE    . .   856B LETTER 54      *PROSE
HONOURED
     LADY IS DESCRIBED ALSO AS OF THE FIRST RANK RICH             568B DESC CAT 3       PROSE
         AND HONOURED
     OF THE FIRST MAGNITUDE GRAND TERRIFIC RICH AND HONOURED       570A DESC CAT 3       PROSE
```

		PAGE	TITLE	LINE
HONOURING				
THE WORSHIP OF GOD IS HONOURING HIS GIFTS IN OTHER MEN . .	.	158B	MARRIAGE HH 22	PROSE
GO TELL THEM THAT THE WORSHIP OF GOD IS HONOURING HIS GIFTS		738	JERUSALEM 91	8
HONOURS				
EMPTYING OUT THE VANITIES OF RICHES & WORLDLY HONOURS . .	.	607D	V LAST JUDG/N	*PROSE
YOUR HONOURS WILL BE UNBOUNDED WHEN YOUR PLAN SHALL BE .	.	797C	LETTER 10	PROSE
HOOD-WINKD				
WITH HOOD-WINKD CHANCE SURE OF HIS MAN	.	17	BLIND-MANS/PS	50
HOOFD SEE GOLDEN HOOFD				
HOOFS				
OF WHEELS & HORSES' HOOFS & TRUMPETS HORNS & CLARIONS .	.	301	FOUR ZOAS 4	160
HERE BOUND TO FIERY MANGERS FURIOUS DASH THEIR GOLDEN HOOFS		320	FOUR ZOAS 5	7
HOOK				
THINE HAS A GREAT HOOK NOSE LIKE THINE	.	748	EV GOSPEL(A)/N	3
HOOKS				
WITH GOLDEN HOOKS FASTEND IN THE PILLARS	.	231	URIZEN 19	7
RATTLING THE ADAMANTINE CHAINS & HOOKS HEAVE UP THE ORE		282	FOUR ZOAS 2	66
THEY BEAR THE WOVEN DRAPERIES ON GOLDEN HOOKS THEY HANG ABROAD		284	FOUR ZOAS 2	152
HORRIBLE HOOKS & NETS HE FORMD TWISTING THE CORDS OF IRON		343	FOUR ZOAS 8	92
THRO RANKS OF WAR SPONTANEOUS & THAT HOOKS & BORING SCREWS		344	FOUR ZOAS 8	133
THE SONS OF URIZEN SHALL GATHER THE VINTAGE WITH SHARP HOOKS		375	FOUR ZOAS 9	694
HOOOOO				
HO HO HO HO HO HO HO HO HOOOOO MY POOOOOOR SIIIDES I I SHOULD		54C	ISLAND MOON 9	PROSE
HOP				
THEY CHIRP & HOP AWAY	.	56	HAIL MATRIM/IM	24
HOPE				
YET WITH YOUR KIND ASSISTANCE LORDS I HOPE	.	19	EDW THIRD/PS 2	6
I HOPE THEIR LORDSHIPS WILL EXCUSE YOUR GIDDINESS . .	. .	20	EDW THIRD/PS 2	64
I HOPE SO	. .	22	EDW THIRD/PS 3	46
I HOPE YOUR MAJESTY CANNOT REFUSE SO GREAT	.	23	EDW THIRD/PS 3	98
I HOPE YOULL STAY AND SEE US FIGHT THIS BATTLE . . .	. .	24	EDW THIRD/PS 3	136
AND WING THEIR BROWS WITH HOPE AND EXPECTATION . . .	. .	25	EDW THIRD/PS 3	182
WHILE THE POOR SLAVE DRUDGES ALL DAY IN HOPE	.	26	EDW THIRD/PS 3	202
BIND ARDENT HOPE UPON YOUR FEET LIKE SHOES	. .	30	EDW THIRD/PS 5	33
TILL HOPE GREW FEEBLE AND WAS READY TO GIVE PLACE TO DOUBTING		40A	SAMSON/PS	PROSE
& FILLIGREE WORK I HOPE SHALL LIVE TO SEE	.	52C	ISLAND MOON 8	PROSE
I HOPE I DO NOT FLATTER MY SELF THAT THIS IS PLEASANT TO ME		71C	ANNO LAVATER	MARG
UNEASY YET I HOPE I SHOULD NOT DO IT	. .	78D	ANNO LAVATER	MARG
("NOT JEALOUS") UNEASY BUT I HOPE TO MEND	. .	84C	ANNO LAVATER	MARG
I HOPE NO ONE WILL CALL WHAT I HAVE WRITTEN CAVILLING .	.	88A	ANNO LAVATER	MARG
FEAR [OR] & HOPE ARE VISION	.	209D	FOR CHILDRN/GP	*TITLE
THE PANGS OF HOPE BEGAN	.	229	URIZEN 11	19
AND THEY BLESSD THE SEVENTH DAY IN SICK HOPE	.	236	URIZEN 25	41
BUT THEY WENT ON IN SILENT HOPE & FEMININE REPOSE . .	.	270	FOUR ZOAS 1	231
WHERE THE IMPRESSIONS OF DESPAIR & HOPE ENROOT FOREVER .	.	295	FOUR ZOAS 3	143
CONSUMING ALL TO THE END CONSUMING LOVE AND [JOY] HOPE ARE ENDED		297	FOUR ZOAS 3	204
HOW IS THIS ALL MY HOPE IS GONE [ENION] FOR EVER FLED .	.	297	FOUR ZOAS 4	9
BECOME A PREY TO ALL MY DEMONS OF DESPAIR & HOPE . .	.	299	FOUR ZOAS 4	75
IN VAIN AM DRIVEN ON FALSE HOPE HOPE SISTER OF DESPAIR		300	FOUR ZOAS 4	123
THE DOLOROUS SHADOW JOYD WEAK HOPE APPEARD AROUND HIS HEAD		300	FOUR ZOAS 4	127
THE PANGS OF HOPE BEGAN IN HEAVY PAIN STRIVING STRUGGLING		303	FOUR ZOAS 4	232
[AND THARMAS ?SAID ALL MY HOPE I THOUGHT ENION FOR EVER GONE]		SUPP	FOUR ZOAS 4	*
[OF HOPE & FEAR XXX SINGING THE ?SAME SONG AROUND THE ?GLOWING BED]		SUPP	FOUR ZOAS 5	*
BUT THARMAS MOST REJOICD IN HOPE OF ENION'S RETURN . .	.	332	FOUR ZOAS 7	486
HE SAID ART THOU BRIGHT ENION IS THE SHADOW OF HOPE RETURND		339	FOUR ZOAS 7B	228
AND LIFE APPEAR & VANISH MOCKING ME WITH SHADOWS OF FALSE HOPE		339	FOUR ZOAS 7B	241
CURSING THE VOICE THAT MOCKD HIM WITH FALSE HOPE IN FURIOUS MOOD		339	FOUR ZOAS 7B	260
LOS DROPD A TEAR AT HER DEPARTURE BUT HE WIPD IT AWAY IN HOPE		351	FOUR ZOAS 8	411
PURSUING THE VAIN SHADOW OF HOPE FLEEING FROM IDENTITY .	.	353	FOUR ZOAS 8	486
MORE HAPPY IS THE DARK CONSUMER HOPE DROWNS ALL MY TORMENT		355	FOUR ZOAS 8	544
OF BITTER HOPE ALTHO I CONSUME IN THESE RAGING WATERS .	.	355	FOUR ZOAS 8	* 547
WHERE THE IMPRESSIONS OF DESPAIR & HOPE FOR EVER VEGETATE		367	FOUR ZOAS 9	377
WE MAY HOPE TO SEE CHRIST'S DISCOURSES EXPUNGD . . .	.	384D	ANNO WATSON	MARG
INSPIRATION & VISION WAS THEN & NOW IS & I HOPE WILL ALWAYS		477A	ANNO REYNOLDS	MARG
I HOPE THINE ARE NOT HENCE IT CLOTHES ITSELF IN RICH ARRAY		502	MILTON 20	30
AS IT WAS SO IT REMAIND & NO HOPE OF AN END	.	509	MILTON 24	47
KNOW THE FIRST [LINES] BEGINNINGS OF ART I HOPE THIS PRINT		593C	PUB ADDRESS/N	PROSE
I HOPE MY COUNTRYMEN WILL EXCUSE ME IF I TELL THEM A WHOLESOME TRUTH		599A	PUB ADDRESS/N	PROSE
I ALSO HOPE THE READER WILL BE WITH ME WHOLLY ONE IN JESUS		621A	JERUSALEM 3	PROSE
BUT STILL I LABOUR IN HOPE THO STILL MY TEARS FLOW DOWN		628	JERUSALEM 9	28
WHICH LOS WIPED OFF BUT COMFORT NONE COULD GIVE OR BEAM OF HOPE		630	JERUSALEM 10	61
GO ON BUILDERS IN HOPE THO JERUSALEM WANDERS FAR AWAY .	.	632	JERUSALEM 12	43
THE DISEASE OF SHAME COVERS ME FROM HEAD TO FEET I HAVE NO HOPE		643	JERUSALEM 21	3
I DIE I DIE IN THY ARMS THO HOPE IS BANISHD FROM ME .	.	648	JERUSALEM 24	60
[WHEN ALBION UTTERD HIS LAST WORDS HOPE IS BANISHD FROM ME]		677	JERUSALEM 47	* 1
THEREFORE I WRITE ALBION'S LAST WORDS HOPE IS BANISHD FROM ME		677	JERUSALEM 47	18
THEREFORE HE LIVED & BREATHED IN HOPE BUT HIS TEARS FELL INCESSANT		696	JERUSALEM 62	36

```
                                                               PAGE      TITLE        LINE
HOPE    (CONTINUED)
      FEAR & HOPE ARE VISION  . . . . . . . . . . . . . . . 768D FOR SEXES/GP   TITLE
      MOCKD BY CAESAR'S SOLDIERS WILLINGLY & [I HOPE THEY WILL]  787A ANNO THORNTON  MARG
      NOW YOU WILL I HOPE SHEW ALL THE FAMILY OF ANTIQUE BORERS  790D LETTER 2      PROSE
      BUT I HOPE THAT . . . . . . . . . . . . . . . . . . . 792B LETTER 4      PROSE
      I SEND THE SHADOW OF THE DEPARTED ANGEL HOPE THE LIKENESS  797A LETTER 9      PROSE
      LONG AWAY & NOT CALLING TO KNOW OF YOUR WELFARE BUT HOPE  799A LETTER 11     PROSE
         NOW
      YOU A FEW LINES WHICH I HOPE YOU WILL EXCUSE AND AS THE   799A LETTER 11     PROSE
         TIME
      & HOPE YOU WILL FORGIVE THE POETRY  . . . . . . . . . 799B LETTER 11     PROSE
      "MY DEAREST FRIEND I HOPE YOU WILL NOT THINK WE COULD"  .  800A LETTER 12     PROSE
      TO THE BLOSSOM OF HOPE FOR A SWEET DECOY  . . . . . . 800 MRS FLAXMAN/L    2
      HOPE SOON TO GIVE YOU A PROOF  . . . . . . . . . . . 803C LETTER 15     PROSE
      OF FOLLIES BY ME FOSTERD YOUR PREDICTION WILL I HOPE BE   804A LETTER 16     PROSE
      WITH ANY OTHER OF YOUR COMMISSIONS BUT HOPE NOW I HAVE  .  804A LETTER 16     PROSE
      MRS BUTTS WILL I HOPE EXCUSE MY NOT HAVING FINISHD THE   806A LETTER 16     PROSE
         PORTRAIT I
      MUSTER A FEW IN COLOURS AND SOME IN BLACK WHICH I HOPE WILL  807A LETTER 17     PROSE
      OF DEXTERITY IN CERTAIN POINTS EMBOLDENS ME [TH ] TO HOPE   808A LETTER 19    *PROSE
         THAT
      I HOPE YOU WILL CONTINUE TO EXCUSE MY WANT OF STEADY  .  808D LETTER 20     PROSE
      WHICH I HOPE SHE WHO IS THE BEST JUDGE WILL THINK LIKE  .  809A LETTER 20     PROSE
      WILL OF PROVIDENCE THEY SHALL BE THE WISEST WE HOPE THAT HE  810C LETTER 20    PROSE
      NOW I HOPE TO SEE THE GREAT WORKS OF ART AS THEY ARE  .  811A LETTER 21     PROSE
      BUT I HOPE THAT FRANCE & ENGLAND WILL HENCEFORTH BE  . .  811A LETTER 21     PROSE
      AS I HOPE THEY ARE NOW IN PRIVATE FOR TILL THEN  . . .  812A LETTER 22     PROSE
      COULD UNITE AGAIN IN SOCIETY & HOPE THAT THE TIME IS NOT   813C LETTER 22    PROSE
      I NOW SEND TWO PICTURES & HOPE YOU WILL APPROVE OF THEM   816A LETTER 23     PROSE
      TOWARDS YOU THRO MULTITUDE OF EMPLOYMENT & THRO HOPE  .  816A LETTER 23     PROSE
      I SEND YOU THE RIPOSO WHICH I HOPE YOU WILL THINK MY BEST  823D LETTER 27     PROSE
      SIX GUINEAS THUS I HOPE THAT ALL OUR THREE YEARS' TROUBLE  824D LETTER 27     PROSE
         ENDS
      & TO GO THRO ALL WITHOUT MURMURING & IN FIRM HOPE  . .  825D LETTER 27    *PROSE
      I SEND (SEVEN) DRAWINGS WHICH I HOPE WILL PLEASE YOU  .  826B LETTER 28     PROSE
      STILL I RESOLVE NOT TO LOSE HOPE OF SEEING BETTER DAYS  .  829D LETTER 30     PROSE
      PRAY TO MY GOD & FATHER FOR THE HEALTH OF MISS POOLE HOPE  833D LETTER 33     PROSE
      MY WIFE GETS BETTER EVERY DAY HOPE EARNESTLY THAT YOU  .  835A LETTER 34     PROSE
      BUT I HASTEND TO WRITE TO YOU ABOUT MR BRAITHWAITE HOPE   837A LETTER 35     PROSE
      HIS FATHER'S BEST FRIEND WILL I HOPE BECOME THE MOST  .  838C LETTER 37     PROSE
         RESPECTED
      MR ROSE I AM HAPPY TO HEAR IS GETTING QUITE WELL HOPE TO   838C LETTER 37     PROSE
      THE WRITING WHICH I HOPE WILL PLEASE SHOULD HAVE SENT THE  839B LETTER 38     PROSE
      BUT HOPE & PRAY FOR HER INTIRE RECOVERY . . . . . . .  840A LETTER 38     PROSE
      I HOPE YOU WILL BELIEVE ME WHEN I SAY THAT MY SOLICITUDE   840B LETTER 39     PROSE
      THE LAST TOUCHES WHICH ARE ALWAYS THE BEST I HAVE NOW I   840B LETTER 39     PROSE
         HOPE
      ENTER AGAIN WITH GREAT PLEASURE AND HOPE SOON TO SHOW YOU  841A LETTER 40     PROSE
      RESPECT WHICH YOU WILL BE PLEASED WITH & I HOPE WILL ADOPT  841B LETTER 41    PROSE
      HOPE SOON TO HEAR THAT YOU HAVE GOT A LIVING ONE OF BRASS  843A LETTER 42    *PROSE
      IT IS ONE OF THE PRETTIEST THINGS I EVER READ AND I HOPE   844D LETTER 43     PROSE
         THE
      FOR OUR PURPOSE HE HAS PROMISED TO DO SO I HOPE SOON TO   846B LETTER 44     PROSE
      SHALL HAVE A PROOF OF IT FOR YOUR REMARKS ALSO I HOPE BY   849B LETTER 45     PROSE
      I HOPE YOU WILL EXCUSE MY DELAY IN SENDING THE BOOKS  .  850A LETTER 49     PROSE
      SEND A PROOF OF THE SHIPWRECK WHICH I HOPE WILL PLEASE  .  850B LETTER 49     PROSE
      IT YET WANTS ALL ITS LAST & FINISHING TOUCHES BUT I HOPE   850B LETTER 49     PROSE
         YOU
      HOPE SOON TO HAVE THE PLEASURE OF SEEING HIM WITH THE  .  851D LETTER 50     PROSE
      HOPE IN A FEW DAYS TO SEND PROOFS OF PLATES WHICH  . .  853A LETTER 51    *PROSE
      BUT YET I MUST SOLICIT FOR A SUPPLY OF MONEY AND HOPE YOU  853C LETTER 52     PROSE
         WILL
      I AM AGAIN IN WANT OF TEN POUNDS HOPE THAT THE SIZE AND   853C LETTER 52     PROSE
      OUR SORROW IS SWALLOWD UP IN HOPE SUCH CONSOLATIONS . . . 854B LETTER 53     PROSE
      GOOD HELP & WITH YOUR REMARKS ON IT IN ADDITION I HOPE TO  855B LETTER 53     PROSE
      HOPE THAT AS MR D(DODSLEY) IS DEAD & IF MR H(HAYLEY) HAS NO  856B LETTER 54    PROSE
      SAID & HOPE THAT HE WILL SEE THE MATTER IN THE LIGHT YOU DO  856D LETTER 54    PROSE
      I HOPE THIS LETTER WILL OUTSTRIP MR PHILLIPS' AS I SIT DOWN  857D LETTER 55    PROSE
      EXCEPT AT PRIVATE PRESSES I HOPE THIS WILL BECOME A SOURCE  859C LETTER 56     PROSE
      HOPE THAT THE PUBLIC WILL APPROVE OF MY RATHER GIVING FEW  860C LETTER 56     PROSE
      I AM STARTLED AT SUCH AN ASSERTION I HOPE THE CONTEMPORARY  864D LETTER 61     PROSE
      & HOPE THAT HE HAS A GOOD OPINION OF MY WILLINGNESS TO   868D LETTER 68     PROSE
         APPEAR
      HOPE TO SEE YOU ON SUNDAY MORNING AS USUAL WHICH . . . .  870A LETTER 70     PROSE
      I HOPE A FEW MORE DAYS WILL BRING US TO A CONCLUSION  .  870B LETTER 71     PROSE
      THOUGH I HOPE IN A MORNING OR TWO TO CALL ON YOU IN  . .  871B LETTER 72     PROSE
      IT IS NOW PASSED AS I HOPE BUT THE MOMENT I GOT EASE OF   874B LETTER 79     PROSE
         BODY
      THESE PILES HAVE NOW ALSO AS I HOPE RUN THEIR PERIOD &  .  874D LETTER 80     PROSE
      ENOUGH ASHAMD OF & HOPE TO MEND  . . . . . . . . . . .  875D LETTER 82     PROSE
      AT FIRST & THOUGHT IT A THING OF BENEFIT & GOOD HOPE YOU   876B LETTER 83     PROSE
      THE ENGRAVINGS & HOPE SOON TO GET PROOFS OF WHAT I AM DOING  877A LETTER 85    PROSE
      I HAVE LITTLE HOPE OF DOING ANY MORE OF SUCH THINGS  . . .  878C LETTER 88    PROSE
      WHICH I AM SLOWLY RECOVERING YOU WILL I HOPE HAVE PATIENCE  879A LETTER 88     PROSE
      HOWEVER I AM UPON THE MENDING HAND TO-DAY & HOPE SOON  .  880A LETTER 90     PROSE
      "LEAVE EVERY HOPE YOU WHO IN ENTER"  . . . . . . . . . SUPP ILLUS DANTE 4   *
      WHAT WE HOPE WE SEE  . . . . . . . . . . . . . . . . . SUPP LEGEND/N61    *TITLE
      A VISION OF FEAR A VISION OF HOPE  . . . . . . . . . . SUPP LEGEND/N75    *TITLE
      MIRTH THE THREE TABERNACLES THE CHURCH YARD DEATH HOPE   SUPP PENC DRAW 2.19 *TITLE
HOPED
      BUT VERY ODD AS IF SHE HOPED YOU HAD NOT AN ILL OPINION   44B ISLAND MOON 1   PROSE
         OF HER
```

932

```
                                                             PAGE     TITLE        LINE
HOPED    (CONTINUED)
     O THARMAS I HAD LOST THEE & WHEN I HOPED I HAD FOUND THEE    296 FOUR ZOAS 3      183
     IT IS HOPED THAT THE PAINTER WILL BE ALLOWED BY THE PUBLIC   586D CHAUCER 1      PROSE
     HOPED YOUR PLAN COMPREHENDED ALL SPECIES OF THIS ART    .   793A LETTER 5       PROSE
     IN CONTEMPLATING MY PICTURES THAN I EVEN HOPED   .  .  .    794B LETTER 5       PROSE
     NOT MENTION ILLNESS BECAUSE I HOPED TO GET BETTER FOR I WAS  820C LETTER 25      PROSE
     IMMEDIATELY ON RECEIPT OF IT BUT HOPED TO BE ABLE TO SEND   851B LETTER 50      PROSE
     THAN I HAD EVER HOPED IN MY HEALTHFULL HOURS   .  .  .  .   873A LETTER 76      PROSE
HOPE-FOSTERED
     ENTHUSIASTIC HOPE-FOSTERED VISIONARY  .  .  .  .  .  .  .   807C LETTER 17      PROSE
HOPELESS
     HOPELESS ABHORRD A DEATH-SHADOW   .  .  .  .  .  .  .  .    250 AHANIA 2          41
     TO THE FOUR WINDS HOPELESS OF FUTURE ALL FUTURITY   .  .   343 FOUR ZOAS 8        99
     HOPELESS IF I AM LIKE THE GRASS & SO SHALL PASS AWAY   .  . 368 FOUR ZOAS 9       417
HOPES
     OUR BEST OF HOPES HOW SOON THEY FAIL  .  .  .  .  .  .  .    17 BLIND-MANS/PS      52
     I CHID THEM BOTH BUT GAVE THEM NOBLE HOPES   .  .  .  .  .   25 EDW THIRD/PS 3    169
     AND BREATHE MY HOPES INTO THE BURNING AIR   .  .  .  .  .    26 EDW THIRD/PS 3    221
     .  .  . FED WITH HOPES YEAR BY YEAR HE PINED   .  .  .  .   136 FRENCH REVOLTN     48
     FOR LIBERTY VAIN HOPES HIS REASON DECAYD .  .  .  .  .  .   136 FRENCH REVOLTN     49
     LOS HEARD REVIVING HE SIEZD HER IN HIS ARMS DELUSIVE HOPES  290 FOUR ZOAS 2      380
     THE LAND OF DOUBTS & SHADOWS SWEET DELUSIONS UNFORMD HOPES  367 FOUR ZOAS 9      379
     WHO IN HOPES OF A GOOD LIVING ADOPT THE STATE RELIGION  .   390D ANNO WATSON     MARG
     THE PAINTER HOPES THAT HIS FRIENDS ANYTUS [&] MELITUS &     598B PUB ADDRESS/N   PROSE
     THE ENTHUSIASM OF THE FOLLOWING POEM THE AUTHOR HOPES   .   620D JERUSALEM 3     PROSE
     SHE WILL CALL ON ME TILL THEN I WAIT WITH PATIENCE IN HOPES 796A LETTER 6        PROSE
     FILLD FULL OF HOPES FILLD FULL OF FEARS   .  .  .  .  .  .  817 HAPPINESS/L        20
     I CALLED ON MR EVANS WHO GIVES SMALL HOPES OF OUR BALLADS   831C LETTER 31       PROSE
        HE
     GIVES HOPES THAT HE MAY PROVE WORTHY OF HIS FATHER &    .   838C LETTER 37       PROSE
     MY ZEAL WITH GOOD EFFECT AM IN HOPES THAT MISS POOLE IS     841A LETTER 40       PROSE
     MY SORROW AND MY HOPES FOR OUR GOOD MISS POOLE AND   .  .   845A LETTER 43       PROSE
     HE IS NOW GOING TO RUSSIA HOPES THAT THE NEGOTIATIONS FOR   845C LETTER 44       PROSE
     & ADMIRABLE PRESENT IN HOPES TO SEND PROOFS OF MY PLATES    853A LETTER 51      *PROSE
     ALL MY HOPES BY THE ROOTS EVERY ONE WHO KNOWS OF OUR   .    872D LETTER 76       PROSE
     I AM SO MUCH BETTER THAT I HAVE HOPES OF FULFILLING MY  .   873D LETTER 78       PROSE
     & HAVE GREAT HOPES THAT THE DISEASE IS GONE   .  .  .  .    875C LETTER 81       PROSE
     BUT HOPES TO DO SOMEWHAT BY PERSEVERANCE IN HIS ENDEAVOURS  877A LETTER 85       PROSE
HOPING
     WERE EMPLOYD WHEN MRS GIMBLET CAME IN [?HOPING]   .  .  .    44B ISLAND MOON 1   *PROSE
     HOPING TO END HER [LIFE] WOES BUT FROM HER CRIES THE TYGERS 109 TIRIEL 7           17
        FLED
     HOPING THAT HER JOY IS NOW INCREASED & YOURS ALSO   .  .   810A LETTER 20       PROSE
     HOPING THAT I MAY MEET YOU AGAIN IN PERFECT HEALTH   .  .   868B LETTER 67       PROSE
        & HAPPINESS
HOPPNER
     BEAUTIFUL BLOOMING DAMSEL AND H(HOPPNER) SAYS   .  .  .  .  574B DESC CAT 3      *PROSE
     HIS FRIEND H(HOPPNER) WHO HAS CALLED HIS "A COMMON SCENE"   574D DESC CAT 3      *PROSE
HOR
     ARE HOR & PEOR & BASHAN & ABARIM & LEBANON & HERMON  .  .   498 MILTON 17          16
HOREB
     THEY SAT RANGD ROUND HIM AS THE ROCKS OF HOREB ROUND THE    498 MILTON 17          12
        LAND
     IN THAT REGION CALLD MIDIAN AMONG THE ROCKS OF HOREB   .    498 MILTON 17          28
     HER SHADOWY SISTERS FORM THE BONES EVEN THE BONES OF HOREB  501 MILTON 19          51
     HAND IS BECOME A ROCK SINAI & HOREB IS HYLE & COBAN  .  .   501 MILTON 19          58
     SAT FROZEN IN THE ROCK OF HOREB AND HIS REDEEMED PORTION    502 MILTON 20          11
     BROODED OVER HIS BODY IN HOREB AGAINST THE RESURRECTION     502 MILTON 20          22
     IN THE VALE OF SURREY WHERE HOREB TERMINATES IN REPHAIM     517 MILTON 29          57
     SUCH IS THE DIVINE WRITTEN LAW OF HOREB & SINAI   .  .  .   638 JERUSALEM 16        68
     OF HOREB STILL EYEING ALBION'S CLIFFS EAGERLY SIEZING &     704 JERUSALEM 67        27
        TWISTING
     IN BEAUTY ARE SHADOWS NOW NO MORE BUT ROCKS IN HOREB   .    707 JERUSALEM 68        70
     OF DREADFUL POWER SITTING UPON HOREB PONDERING DIRE   .  .  735 JERUSALEM 89        55
HORIZON    SEE HORRIZON
     ARE SEEN ABOVE THE HORIZON SOME BUILDINGS AND SPIRES   .    567B DESC CAT 3      PROSE
     ARE SEEN ABOVE THE HORIZON SOME BUILDINGS & SPIRES   .  .   588D CHAUCER/N       PROSE
HORN
     THE DISTANT HUNTSMAN WINDS HIS HORN   .  .  .  .  .  .  .   124 SCHOOL BOY/SI       3
     THE [COWARD] HUMBLE SHEEP A THREATNING HORN   .  .  .  .    171 THE LILLY/N         2
     THE HUMBLE SHEEP A THREATNING HORN   .  .  .  .  .  .  .    215 THE LILLY/SE        2
     OF FLUTE & HARP & DRUM & TRUMPET HORN & CLARION  .  .  .    372 FOUR ZOAS 9       586
     THE CROOKED HORN MELLOWS THE HOARSE RAVING SERPENT .  .  .  509 MILTON 24          66
     THEY SIEZD THE HARP THE FLUTE THE MELLOW HORN OF            721 JERUSALEM 79        49
        JERUSALEM'S JOY
HORND    SEE TWO HORND
     O THOU RAM HORND WITH GOLD   .  .  .  .  .  .  .  .  .  .   805 TO BUTTS/L         62
     O THOU RAM HORND WITH GOLD   .  .  .  .  .  .  .  .  .  .   805 TO BUTTS/L         70
HORNED
     BRING PALAMABRON HORNED PRIEST SKIPPING UPON THE MOUNTAINS  240 EUROPE 8           3
     SCALED AND POISONOUS HORNED  .  .  .  .  .  .  .  .  .  .   250 AHANIA 3           14
     THE HORNED BOW FOURFOLD .  .  .  .  .  .  .  .  .  .  .  .  744 JERUSALEM 98         3
HORNET
     THE CRUEL SCORPION IS THERE THE GNAT WASP HORNET & THE      513 MILTON 27          21
        HONEY BEE
HORNS
     WITH HIS HORNS HE PUSHD FURIOUS   .  .  .  .  .  .  .  .    250 AHANIA 3           17
     WITH DOUBLING VOICES & LOUD HORNS WOUND ROUND SOUNDING  .   274 FOUR ZOAS 1      382
     OF WHEELS & HORSES' HOOFS & TRUMPETS HORNS & CLARIONS  .    301 FOUR ZOAS 4      160
     & TEN HORNS CHAINED BY TWO ANGELS  .  .  .  .  .  .  .  .   443A LAST JUDGMNT/L  PROSE
     BOUND UP IN THE HORNS OF JEALOUSY TO A DEADLY FADING MOON   491 MILTON 10          18
     [HE HAS] TAKE [THOU] YOU THE HIDE & HORNS .  .  .    .  .   540 S(TOTHAR) D/N   *    5
```

933

```
                                                            PAGE    TITLE         LINE
HORNS    (CONTINUED)
      THE GREAT RED DRAGON WITH SEVEN HEADS & TEN HORNS   . . . 609B V LAST JUDG/N  PROSE
      WEAKNESS WITH HORNS & TALONS IGNORANCE WITH A RAVNING BEAK  628 JERUSALEM 9    13
      HORNS OF THE WIDE BOW LOUD SOUNDING WINDS SPORT ON THE      742 JERUSALEM 95   15
        MOUNTAIN BROWS
      . . . CLOUDS ROLL ROUND THE HORNS  . . . . . . . . .       745 JERUSALEM 98    4
HORNSEA
      WHEN I WAS YOUNG HAMPSTEAD HIGHGATE HORNSEA MUSWELL HILL &  871A LETTER 72     PROSE
HORRENT
      THE HORRENT DEMON ROSE SURROUNDED WITH RED STARS OF FIRE    240 EUROPE 4       29
      ARISE AND PLEASE THE HORRENT FIEND WITH YOUR MELODIOUS      244 EUROPE 14      27
        SONGS
HORRIBLE
      O HORRIBLE O DREADFUL STATE CONSIDER THE HOT BURNING   . . 155C MARRIAGE HH 17 PROSE
      WHERE THE HORRIBLE DARKNESS IS IMPRESSED WITH REFLECTIONS   194 V DAU ALBION 7  11
        OF DESIRE
      AN ACTIVITY UNKNOWN AND HORRIBLE   . . . . . . . . .        223 URIZEN 3       20
      THE HORRIBLE NIGHT INTO WATCHES    . . . . . . . . .        227 URIZEN 10      10
      IN A HORRIBLE DREAMFUL SLUMBER . . . . . . . . . . .        228 URIZEN 10      35
      INTO HORRIBLE FORMS OF DEFORMITY   . . . . . . . . .        230 URIZEN 13      43
      A HORRIBLE WASTE TO MY EYES  . . . . . . . . . . . .        254 AHANIA 4       59
      FELL ASUNDER AND HORRIBLE VACUUM   . . . . . . . . .        257 BOOK OF LOS 4  25
      HORRIBLE GHAST & DEADLY NOUGHT SHALT THOU FIND IN IT   . .  265 FOUR ZOAS 1    50
      MINGLING HIS HORRIBLE [TERRIBLE] BRIGHTNESS          . .    269 FOUR ZOAS 1  * 182
      DEEP HORRIBLE WITHOUT END SEPARATED FROM BEULAH FAR BENEATH 279 FOUR ZOAS 1    542
      [?HE ?FELL XXX HID IN ?HORRIBLE ?CAVERNS OF MOUNTAINS]     SUPP FOUR ZOAS 1  *
      SWALLOWING UP THE HORRIBLE DIN IN AGONY ON AGONY . . . .    295 FOUR ZOAS 3    148
      BUT STILL I KNOW THEE THO IN THIS HORRIBLE RUIN WHELMD  . . 299 FOUR ZOAS 4    80
      A HORRIBLE CHAOS TO HIS EYES A FORMLESS UNMEASURABLE DEATH  301 FOUR ZOAS 4    162
      A DREAMFUL HORRIBLE STATE IN TOSSINGS ON HIS ICY BED   . .  302 FOUR ZOAS 4    171
      IN A HORRIBLE DREAMFUL SLUMBER LIKE THE LINKED CHAIN   . .  303 FOUR ZOAS 4    218
      O HORRIBLE O DREADFUL STATE THOSE WHOM I LOVED BEST    . .  312 FOUR ZOAS 6    25
      HE TOOK HIGH BOUNDING OVER HILLS & DESARTS FLOODS           313 FOUR ZOAS 6    73
        & HORRIBLE CHASMS
      THOU HORRIBLE RUIN ONCE LIKE ME THOU WAST ALL GLORIOUS  . . 317 FOUR ZOAS 6    210
      . . . IN HORRIBLE [CONFUSION] DESTRUCTION   . . . . . .     317 FOUR ZOAS 6    217
      . . . & OVER THE SONS & DAUGHTERS OF LUVAH IN THE HORRIBLE  317 FOUR ZOAS 6    237
        ABYSS
      MAKING BETWEEN HORRIBLE CHASMS INTO THE VAST UNKNOWN  . .   318 FOUR ZOAS 6    277
      OF LIVING PANGS THY HORRIBLE BED GLOWING WITH CEASELESS     321 FOUR ZOAS 7    50
        FIRES
      YET THOU DOST LAUGH AT ALL THESE TORTURES & THIS HORRIBLE   321 FOUR ZOAS 7    59
        PLACE
      WITH A CRASH BREAKING ACROSS THE HORRIBLE MASS COMES DOWN   322 FOUR ZOAS 7    78
      TRACES THE WONDERS OF FUTURITY IN HORRIBLE FEAR OF THE      322 FOUR ZOAS 7    86
        FUTURE
      OF ALL HIS WANDERING EXPERIMENTS IN THE HORRIBLE ABYSS  .   324 FOUR ZOAS 7    160
      FROM THY EMBRACE ELSE BE ASSURD SO HORRIBLE A FORM   . . .  326 FOUR ZOAS 7    235
      BROUGHT FORTH A WONDER HORRIBLE WHILE ENITHARMON SHRIEKD    328 FOUR ZOAS 7    317
      BROUGHT FORTH THIS WONDER HORRIBLE A CLOUD SHE GREW & GREW  328 FOUR ZOAS 7    327
      THO HORRIBLE & GHASTLY TO THINE EYES THO BURIED BENEATH     329 FOUR ZOAS 7    351
      LOS FURIOUS ANSWERD SPECTRE HORRIBLE THY WORDS ASTOUND      329 FOUR ZOAS 7    361
        MY EAR
      THAT MOVD WITH HORRIBLE DREAMS & (HOVRING) HIGH OVER HIS    341 FOUR ZOAS 8  * 6
        HEAD
      HORRIBLE HOOKS & NETS HE FORMD TWISTING THE CORDS OF IRON   343 FOUR ZOAS 8    92
      RETURN IN PANGS & HORRIBLE CONVULSIONS TO THEIR BEASTIAL    344 FOUR ZOAS 8    119
        STATE
      THE ROCKS GROAN HORRIBLE & RUN ABOUT THE MOUNTAINS &   . .  358 FOUR ZOAS 9    53
      A HORRIBLE ROCK FAR IN THE SOUTH IT WAS FORSAKEN WHEN  . .  359 FOUR ZOAS 9    93
      PRIESTS & CHAIND CAPTIVES MET TOGETHER IN A HORRIBLE FEAR   363 FOUR ZOAS 9    244
      IN PAIN THE HUMAN HARVEST WAVD IN HORRIBLE GROANS OF WOE    372 FOUR ZOAS 9    577
      THE FEMALE FORM NOW SEPARATE THEY SHUDDERD AT THE HORRIBLE  373 FOUR ZOAS 9    622
        THING
      MINGLING HIS HORRIBLE [BRIGHTNESS] DARKNESS . . .     . .   381 FOUR ZOAS AD 5  2
      ("GOD'S MORAL JUSTICE EXTERMINATE SO WICKED A PEOPLE        388B ANNO WATSON   MARG
        ") HORRIBLE
      TWENTY GUINEAS FOR THIS HORRIBLE DAWB & IF ANY ONE WOULD    451D ANNO REYNOLDS MARG
        GIVE XXX
      A HORRIBLE SHADOW OF DEATH AMONG THE FURNACES BENEATH  . .  625 JERUSALEM 7    4
      HORRIBLE GHAST & DEADLY NOUGHT SHALT THOU FIND IN IT   . .  645 JERUSALEM 22   23
      FLED THEY FLED AT HIS HORRIBLE FORM THEY HID IN CAVES  .    661 JERUSALEM 34   49
      BEFORE THE FURNACES OF LOS IN A HORRIBLE DREAMFUL SLUMBER   662 JERUSALEM 36   11
      THEY HAVE PERSWADED HIM OF HORRIBLE FALSHOODS . . . . .     667 JERUSALEM 40 * 19
      SO LOS CRIED AT HIS ANVIL IN THE HORRIBLE DARKNESS WEEPING  738 JERUSALEM 91   32
HORRID
      SEEKST THOU THAT FLOWR TO DECK THY HORRID TEMPLES        5 FAIR ELENOR/PS    44
      WHILE THE BLACK GORE DROPS FROM HIS HORRID JAWS    . .      31 EDW THIRD/PS 5  46
      [AND IN [THY] THE HORRID RIBS DARE STEEP]  . . . . .       172 THE TYGER/N 1 * 14
      THE SPECTRE GLOWD HIS HORRID LENGTH STAINING THE TEMPLE     198 AMERICA 5      6
        LONG
      TILL THE HORRID PLANT BENDING ITS BOUGHS   . . . . . .      252 AHANIA 3       65
      IN THE HORRID VACUITY BOTTOMLESS   . . . . . . . . .        258 BOOK OF LOS 4  36
      A CAVERN SHAGGD WITH HORRID SHADES DARK COOL & DEADLY WHERE 295 FOUR ZOAS 3    122
      THE HORRID TRUMPETS OF THE DEEP BELLOWD WITH BITTER BLASTS  306 FOUR ZOAS 5    40
      THE GARDENS OF WISDOM ARE BECOME A FIELD OF HORRID GRAVES   310 FOUR ZOAS 5    196
      THE HORRID SHAPES & SIGHTS OF TORMENT IN BURNING DUNGEONS   314 FOUR ZOAS 5    103
        & IN
      IN THE HORRID BOTTOMLESS VACUITY FALLING FALLING FALLING    315 FOUR ZOAS 6    155
      THE HORRID SIGHT OF DEATH & TORMENT BUT THE ETERNAL PROMISE 340 FOUR ZOAS 7B   291
      ACCORDANT WITH THE HORRID LABOURS MAKE SWEET MELODY  . .    509 MILTON 24      57
      HERE IS HER CUP FILLD WITH ITS POISONS IN THESE HORRID      529 MILTON 38      25
        VALES
```

```
                                                              PAGE     TITLE        LINE
HORRID    (CONTINUED)
     HORRID TO THINK OF WHEN ENQUIRED DEEPLY INTO AND ALL     .  .   652 JERUSALEM 28        8
     SO SPOKE LOS TRAVELLING THRO DARKNESS & HORRID SOLITUDE        657 JERUSALEM 31       39
     AND ALBION'S SONS ASCENDING & DESCENDING IN THE HORRID VOID    674 JERUSALEM 44       17
     DERBY PEAK YAWND A HORRID CHASM AT THE CRIES OF GWENDOLEN      699 JERUSALEM 64       35
          & AT
HORRIZON
     ARE SEEN ABOVE THE HORRIZON SOME BUILDINGS AND SPIRES    . . 590C CHAUCER 2       *PROSE
HORROR
     WHEN THE CRIES OF BLOOD TEAR HORROR FROM HEAVN     . . . .      18 EDW THIRD/PS 1        7
     . . . IN DARK FOGS LISTNING THE HORROR      . . . . . . .     135 FRENCH REVOLTN       19
     . . . AND THE DEN NAMD HORROR HELD A MAN      . . . . . .     135 FRENCH REVOLTN       26
     LO A SHADOW OF HORROR IS RISEN . . . . . . . . . . .         222 URIZEN 3              1
     STRUCK HORROR INTO HIS SOUL . . . . . . . . . . .            230 URIZEN 13            47
     THE RED LIMBD ANGEL SIEZD IN HORROR AND TORMENT    . . . .   243 EUROPE 13             1
     IN TREMBLING AND HORROR THEY BEHELD HIM   . . . . . . .      257 BOOK OF LOS 3        45
     THOU WILT GO MAD WITH HORROR IF THOU DOST EXAMINE THUS . .   265 FOUR ZOAS 1          52
     [TWO FORMS OF HORROR HOWLD BENEATH IT]    . . . . . .       SUPP FOUR ZOAS 1          *
     HE SAW THE INDEFINITE SPACE BENEATH & HIS SOUL SHRUNK WITH   280 FOUR ZOAS 2          20
          HORROR
     WITH TREMBLING HORROR PALE AGHAST THE CHILDREN OF MAN   . .  283 FOUR ZOAS 2         121
     . . . ATLANTIC FOR A CURSE AND HIDDEN HORROR . . . . .       294 FOUR ZOAS 3         105
     A MOMENT THEN ASTOUNDING HORROR BELCHES FROM THE CENTER      336 FOUR ZOAS 7B        131
     A KING OF WRATH & FURY A DARK ENRAGED HORROR   . . . . .     353 FOUR ZOAS 8         462
     IN VARIOUS ATTITUDES OF DESPAIR & HORROR FALL THRO THE AIR  443C LAST JUDGMNT/L    PROSE
     REFUSING ALL DEFINITE FORM THE ABSTRACT HORROR ROOFD STONY   482 MILTON 3             9
          HARD
     LOS SAW THEM AND A COLD PALE HORROR COVERD OER HIS LIMBS     503 MILTON 20           51
     EXPRESSION OF FEAR OR REVENGE OR ENVY OR BLANK HORROR   . . 580C DESC CAT 5         PROSE
     THOSE ON THE RIGHT HAND AWAKE IN JOY THOSE ON THE LEFT      609C V LAST JUDG/N      PROSE
          IN HORROR
     EASTWARD TOWARD THE STARRY WHEELS BUT WESTWARD A BLACK       624 JERUSALEM 5         68
          HORROR
     I NOW AM WHAT I AM A HORROR AND AN ASTONISHMENT    . . . .   627 JERUSALEM 8         18
     CREATED TO BE THE GREAT EXAMPLE OF HORROR & AGONY ALSO MY    630 JERUSALEM 10        52
     WAS BECOME AN ENVIED HORROR AND A REMEMBRANCE OF JEALOUSY    652 JERUSALEM 28         3
     THE CHILDREN MUST BE SACRIFICD A HORROR NEVER KNOWN   . . .  678 JERUSALEM 48        58
     IN A REMEMBRANCE OF THE SIN IS A WOE & A HORROR    . . . .   681 JERUSALEM 50        28
     I SHALL BECOME AN INFANT HORROR ENION THARMAS FRIENDS  . .   727 JERUSALEM 83         5
HORRORS
     THE DAMPS OF DEATH FALL THICK UPON ME HORRORS STARE ME       35D COUCH DEATH/PS    PROSE
          IN THE FACE
     OF ANCIENT HORRORS COVERD FOR SNAKES AND SCORPIONS . . .     136 FRENCH REVOLTN       41
     THAT THIS ARMY OF TERRORS THAT PRISON OF HORRORS . . . .     145 FRENCH REVOLTN      254
     HIS COLD HORRORS SILENT DARK URIZEN . . . . . . . .          223 URIZEN 3            27
     URIZEN'S ARMY OF HORRORS . . . . . . . . . . . .             253 AHANIA 4            35
     FIRST HE BEHELD THE BODY OF MAN PALE COLD THE HORRORS OF     280 FOUR ZOAS 2         11
          DEATH
     A WORLD OF DEEP DARKNESS WHERE ALL THINGS IN HORRORS ARE     296 FOUR ZOAS 3        181
          ROOTED
     WITHIN THE DARK HORRORS OF THE ABYSSES LION OR TYGER OR      318 FOUR ZOAS 6        251
          SCORPION
     DRINK IN THE DEADLY DULL DELUSION HORRORS OF ETERNAL DEATH . 352 FOUR ZOAS 8        418
     O HOW THE HORRORS OF ETERNAL DEATH TAKE HOLD ON MAN   . . .  354 FOUR ZOAS 8        519
     DO THEY MEAN WAR & ITS HORRORS & ITS HEROIC VILLAINS   . . 400A ANNO BACON         MARG
     THE AMERICAN WAR BEGAN ALL ITS DARK HORRORS PASSED BEFORE    799 TO FLAXMAN/L         9
          MY FACE
     FOUGHT THRO A HELL OF TERRORS & HORRORS WHICH NONE COULD    853A LETTER 51         PROSE
HORSE
     THE TRAMPLING HORSE AND CLANGING ARMS    . . . . . .          11 GWIN KING/PS        23
     ON A WHITE HORSE SITTING . . . . . . . . . . .                62 CROWND KING/IM       2
     BREATHING RED FIRES FROM MAN TO MAN AND FROM HORSE TO        137 FRENCH REVOLTN       81
          HORSE . . .
     TO HEAR THE HORSE NEIGH TO THE DRUM AND TRUMPET . . . . .    138 FRENCH REVOLTN      102
     THE LION THE TYGER THE HORSE THE ELEPHANT WATCH THE FRUITS  151D MARRIAGE HH 8     PROSE
     NOR THE LION THE HORSE HOW HE SHALL TAKE HIS PREY   . . .   152B MARRIAGE HH 9     PROSE
     DESCEND O URIZEN DESCEND WITH HORSE & CHARIOTS   . . . .     272 FOUR ZOAS 1      *  308
     THE HORSE IS OF MORE VALUE THAN THE MAN THE TYGER FIERCE     275 FOUR ZOAS 1        402
     AND CLAD IN STEEL & HIS HORSE PROUDLY NEIGHD HE SMELT THE    275 FOUR ZOAS 1        412
          BATTLE
     FOR HER DELIGHT THE HORSE HIS PROUD NECK BOWD & HIS WHITE    340 FOUR ZOAS 7B       281
          MANE
     CALLING THE LION & THE TYGER THE HORSE & THE WILD STAG  . .  352 FOUR ZOAS 8        445
     UP BOUND THE WILD STAG & THE HORSE [BEHOLDS] BEHOLD THE      352 FOUR ZOAS 8      *  453
          KING OF PRIDE
     AND THE PALE HORSE SEEKS FOR THE POOL TO LIE HIM DOWN & DIE  354 FOUR ZOAS 8        529
     GO DOWN WITH HORSE & CHARIOTS & TRUMPETS OF HOARSE WAR  . .  374 FOUR ZOAS 9        661
     A HORSE MISUSD UPON THE ROAD . . . . . . . . . .            431 AUGURIES           11
     HE WHO SHALL TRAIN THE HORSE TO WAR   . . . . . . .          432 AUGURIES           41
     TIGER THE HORSE THE VULTURE AND THE EAGLE CONTEND FOR THE   441D INSC FALL MAN     PROSE
          LAMB
     OR THE OX STRIVING TO TROT LIKE THE HORSE    . . . . .     470B ANNO REYNOLDS      MARG
     FIERY PEGASUS SHAKSPEARE THE HORSE OF INTELLECT IS LEAPING  581B DESC CAT 6        TITLE
     THE HORSE FROM THE OX BUT BY THE BOUNDING OUTLINE HOW   . . 585C DESC CAT 15       PROSE
     WHERE EVERY HORSE IS APPROPRIATE TO HIS RIDER  . . . . .    588A CHAUCER/N         PROSE
     A HORSE BY THE COLOUR & A MAN WHO HAS GOT ANY BRAINS   . .  597D PUB ADDRESS/N     PROSE
     A MAN CAN NEVER BECOME ASS NOR HORSE   . . . . . . .        607A V LAST JUDG/N     PROSE
     OR OF OG OR MOLECH THE HORSE NEVER ENVIES THE PEACOCK   . . 616B V LAST JUDG/N     PROSE
     WITH EVERY COLOUR LION TYGER HORSE ELEPHANT EAGLE DOVE       746 JERUSALEM 98       43
          FLY WORM
     HARMONY & PROPORTION OF A HORSE ARE NOT THE SAME WITH   . . 774B ANNO BERKELEY     MARG
     AN APPLE TREE A PEAR TREE A HORSE A LION ARE CHARACTERS     778B HOMERS POETRY     PROSE
```

	PAGE	TITLE	LINE
HORSE (CONTINUED)			
A HORSE IS NOT MORE A LION FOR BEING A BAD HORSE THAT IS ITS	778B	HOMERS POETRY	PROSE
OR A HOUSE OR A HORSE OR A MAN & I	782A	INSC UPCOTT	PROSE
TO ME FORGIVE THIS DIRGE-LIKE LAMENTATION OVER A DEAD HORSE	830B	LETTER 30	PROSE
& NOW I HAVE LAMENTED OVER THE DEAD HORSE LET ME LAUGH & BE	830B	LETTER 30	PROSE
OUGHT EVER TO MOUNT A TROOPER'S HORSE THEY ARE TAUGHT SO	833B	LETTER 33	PROSE
THAT WICKED HORSE AGAIN NOR AGAIN TRUST TO ONE WHO HAS BEEN	833C	LETTER 33	PROSE
FROM THE WICKED HORSE & FROM YOUR INNOCENT HUMBLE SERVANT	833D	LETTER 33	PROSE
FEEL MUCH EASIER TO HEAR THAT YOU HAVE PARTED WITH YOUR HORSE	843A	LETTER 42	PROSE
ACROSS THE COUNTRY TO FELPHAM AS HE ALWAYS KEEPS A HORSE	843A	LETTER 42	PROSE
THE EAGLE THE HORSE THE DOG OF THE DOG SPECIES THE . .	859B	LETTER 56	PROSE
HAVE ENGRAVED ONE OF THE PLATES FOR THAT BALLAD OF THE HORSE	861A	LETTER 58	PROSE
HORSEBACK			
HORSEBACK WITH DEATH OVER THE FIELDS OF CORN	537	AND HIS LEGS/N	23
HIS WHOLE LENGTH PORTRAIT ON HORSEBACK AS WRITTEN BY CHAUCER	567D	DESC CAT 3	PROSE
ON HORSEBACK OF CHAUCER'S CHARACTERS WHERE EVERY CHARACTER &	587D	CHAUCER/N	PROSE
THE PICTURE OF THE MAN ON HORSEBACK RESCUING THE . . .	839D	LETTER 38	PROSE
THE SHIPWRECK WITH THE MAN ON HORSEBACK &C WHICH I HAVE	848D	LETTER 45	PROSE
HORSE-BACK			
THIRTY FIGURES ON HORSE-BACK IN A BRILLIANT MORNING SCENE	560B	EXHIBITION ADV	PROSE
HORSEMAN			
ME I LEARNED THAT [XXX] NO ONE NOT EVEN THE MOST EXPERT HORSEMAN	833B	LETTER 33	*PROSE
HORSEMEN			
HORSEMEN MAN IN THE RESURRECTION	695	JERUSALEM 61	51
HORSES			
WITH HORSES AND WITH CHARIOTS	12	GWIN KING/PS	57
THE CHARIOTS AND THE HORSES THE NOISE OF SHOUT . . .	34B	KING JOHN/PS	PROSE
WHERE LUVAH DOTH RENEW HIS HORSES LOOKST THOU ON MY YOUTH	128	BOOK OF THEL 3	8
THE STRONG SOLDIERS TREMBLE THE HORSES THEIR MANES BOW . . .	141	FRENCH REVOLTN	167
HE INDIGNANT DEPARTED ON HORSES OF HEAVN	143	FRENCH REVOLTN	201
THE TYGERS OF WRATH ARE WISER THAN THE HORSES OF INSTRUCTION	152A	MARRIAGE HH 9	PROSE
HORSES ELEPHANTS BANNERS CASTLES SLINGS AND ROCKS . .	159D	SONG LIBERTY	PROSE
LOOSING THE ETERNAL HORSES FROM THE DENS OF NIGHT CRYING	160A	SONG LIBERTY	PROSE
STILL ALL YOUR THUNDERS GOLDEN HOOFD & BIND YOUR HORSES BLACK	244	EUROPE 14	28
AND LUVAH SIEZD THE HORSES OF LIGHT & ROSE INTO THE CHARIOT OF DAY	271	FOUR ZOAS 1	264
. . . THE HORSES OF INSTRUCTION FROM THEIR MANGERS . .	281	FOUR ZOAS 2	35
HAD WEARIED ME THERE I LAID MY PLOW & THERE MY HORSES FED	295	FOUR ZOAS 3	124
WHEN URIZEN GAVE THE HORSES OF LIGHT INTO THE HANDS OF LUVAH	300	FOUR ZOAS 4	113
O DID I KEEP THE HORSES OF THE DAY IN SILVER PASTURES . .	310	FOUR ZOAS 5	210
O I REFUSD THE LORD OF DAY THE HORSES OF HIS PRINCE . .	310	FOUR ZOAS 5	211
A CAVERND UNIVERSE OF FLAMING FIRE THE HORSES OF URIZEN	320	FOUR ZOAS 7	6
HOW RAGD THE GOLDEN HORSES OF URIZEN BOUND TO THE CHARIOT OF LOVE	338	FOUR ZOAS 7B	201
THE HORSES OF PALAMABRON'S HARROW WHEREFOR RINTRAH & PALAMABRON	350	FOUR ZOAS 8	* 369
URIZEN GAVE THE HORSES OF LIGHT INTO THE HANDS OF LUVAH	359	FOUR ZOAS 9	94
THE (HORSES) NEIGH FROM THE BATTLE	365	FOUR ZOAS 9	300
THE SONS OF URIZEN SHOUT THEIR FATHER ROSE THE ETERNAL HORSES	365	FOUR ZOAS 9	308
HE TURND THE HORSES LOOSE & LAID HIS PLOW IN THE NORTHERN CORNER	365	FOUR ZOAS 9	319
AND BLACK HORSES & ARMED MEN & MISERABLE BOUND CAPTIVES	375	FOUR ZOAS 9	667
NEXT MORNING PALAMABRON ROSE THE HORSES OF THE HARROW .	487	MILTON 7	19
MY HORSES HATH HE MADDEND AND MY FELLOW SERVANTS INJURD	487	MILTON 7	29
AND PALAMABRON SHEWD THE HORSES & THE SERVANTS SATAN WEPT	487	MILTON 7	35
THAT HE HAD NOT OPPRESD THE HORSES OF THE HARROW NOR THE SERVANTS	487	MILTON 7	42
NONE NEEDS BE ACTIVE MEAN TIME PALAMABRON'S HORSES . .	487	MILTON 7	45
HIS HORSES ARE MAD HIS HARROW CONFOUNDED HIS COMPANIONS ENRAGD	488	MILTON 8	18
THE HORSES OF PALAMABRON CALLD FOR REST AND PLEASANT DEATH	492	MILTON 12	9
OF VARYING COLOURS ON THE HILLS TERRIBLY RAGD THE HORSES	492	MILTON 12	15
COMPELLD THE GNOMES TO CURB THE HORSES & TO THROW BANKS OF SAND	493	MILTON 12	17
THE HORSES HE HAS ALSO VARIED TO ACCORD TO THEIR RIDERS	567D	DESC CAT 3	PROSE
THEIR DRESS AND THEIR HORSES ARE OF THE FIRST RATE . .	568A	DESC CAT 3	PROSE
WITH THEIR HORSES AT THE FOOT OF A ROCK ON WHICH . .	577A	DESC CAT 4	PROSE
LIKE DEAD HORSES WHEN REPELLED BY THE CELESTIAL SPHERES	581D	DESC CAT 8	PROSE
OF THE GARMENTS THE HAIR UPON THE HORSES THE	588A	CHAUCER/N	PROSE
THE HORSES HE HAS VARIED TO ACCORD TO THEIR RIDERS . .	590D	CHAUCER 2	PROSE
[LAURELLLO AFFFFSW ALLLLLL HANNALITOE WW BMILLLJJJ HORSES]	601A	PUB ADDRESS/N	*PROSE
THE DAWN WITH HER DAPPLED HORSES ARISES ABOVE THE EARTH	618A	ILLUS MILTON	PROSE
THEY FLEE OVER THE ROCKS BONIFYING HORSES OXEN FEEL THE KNIFE	689	JERUSALEM 58	9
HOW RAGD THE GOLDEN HORSES OF URIZEN COMPELLD TO THE CHARIOT OF LOVE	700	JERUSALEM 65	47
. . . THE HORSES FOURFOLD	745	JERUSALEM 98	13
HORSES'			
OF WHEELS & HORSES' HOOFS & TRUMPETS HORNS & CLARIONS .	301	FOUR ZOAS 4	160
THE GLITTRING OF THEIR HORSES' TRAPPINGS STAINS THE VAULT OF NIGHT	336	FOUR ZOAS 7B	* 152

HOSIER
    MR HOSIER HEARD HIM SAY THAT HE WOULD BE REVENGED . . 437B BLAKES MEMORAN PROSE
    HOSIER SAYS HE IS READY TO GIVE EVIDENCE OF THIS   437B BLAKES MEMORAN PROSE
      IF NECESSARY
HOSPITAL
    BE QUIET WHAT THE DEVIL SHOULD THE PEOPLE IN THE HOSPITAL   50A ISLAND MOON 6   PROSE
    ST THOMAS'S HOSPITAL WHICH IS SITUATED NEAR TO IT . . . 590B CHAUCER 2   PROSE
HOSPITALITY
    GOOD ENGLISH HOSPITALITY O THEN IT DID NOT FAIL . . . . 58 THIS CITY/IM   4
    GOOD ENGLISH HOSPITALITY O THEN IT DID NOT FAIL . . . . 58 THIS CITY/IM   8
    GOOD ENGLISH HOSPITALITY O THEN IT DID NOT FAIL . . . . 58 THIS CITY/IM   12
HOSPITALS
    THESE WERE THE CHURCHES HOSPITALS CASTLES PALACES . . . 246 SONG OF LOS 4   1
HOST
    GWIN LEADS HIS HOST AS BLACK AS NIGHT . . . . . . 12 GWIN KING/PS   55
    PHO NONSENSE HANG PHAROH & ALL HIS HOST SAID THE   47C ISLAND MOON 3   PROSE
      PYTHAGOREAN
    OR POSSESSOR OF THE COMMAND OF THE HEAVENLY HOST IS CALLD   150A MARRIAGE HH 5 PROSE
      THE DEVIL
    THEY SOON DRIVE OUT THE AGED HOST . . . . 426 MENTAL TRAVLER   51
    & IS TO ME AN HOST OF STRENGTH I AM CERTAIN THAT IF I HAD   438D BLAKES MEMORAN PROSE
      NOT
    ITS VORTEX AND THE NORTH & SOUTH WITH ALL THEIR STARRY HOST   497 MILTON 15   29
    "OUR HOST" WHO OCCUPIES THE CENTER OF THE CAVALCADE . . 566D DESC CAT 3   PROSE
    AFTER THE HOST FOLLOW THE SHIPMAN THE HABERDASHER . . 566D DESC CAT 3   *PROSE
    FOR THE HOST WHO FOLLOWS THIS GROUP AND HOLDS THE CENTER   569D DESC CAT 3   PROSE
    OUR HOST WAS ALSO A LEADER OF THE AGE . . . . . 569D DESC CAT 3   PROSE
    THE HOST IS THE SILENUS THE SQUIRE IS THE APOLLO . . 571A DESC CAT 3   PROSE
    "OUR HOST" WHO OCCUPIES THE CENTER OF THE CAVALCADE . . 588B CHAUCER/N   PROSE
    AFTER THE HOST FOLLOW THE SHIPMAN THE HABERDASHER . . 588C CHAUCER/N   *PROSE
    "OUR HOST" WHO OCCUPIES THE CENTER OF THE CAVALCADE . . 589D CHAUCER 2   PROSE
    AFTER THE HOST FOLLOW THE SHIPMAN THE HABERDASHER . . 589D CHAUCER 2   PROSE
    O NO NO I SEE AN INNUMERABLE COMPANY OF THE HEAVENLY HOST   617B V LAST JUDG/N PROSE
    HERE I COUNTED WITHOUT MY HOST I NOW FIND MY MISTAKE . 792A LETTER 4   PROSE
HOSTLER
    OUTLINE I HAVE FOR WITNESSES THE GARDENER WHO IS HOSTLER   827C LETTER 28   PROSE
HOSTS
    THY NOBLES HAVE GATHERD THY STARRY HOSTS ROUND THIS   138 FRENCH REVOLTN   100
      REBELLIOUS CITY
    WITH THUNDER AND FIRE LEADING HIS STARRY HOSTS . . . 159D SONG LIBERTY   PROSE
    WHAT NIGHT HE LED THE STARRY HOSTS THRO THE WIDE WILDERNESS   198 AMERICA 8   4
    BENEATH HIM ROLLD HIS NUMROUS HOSTS ALL ALBION'S ANGELS   201 AMERICA 13   13
      CAMPD
    YELLOW AS LEAVES OF AUTUMN THE MYRIADS OF ANGELIC HOSTS   243 EUROPE 13   6
    WHERE URIZEN & ALL HIS HOSTS HANG THEIR IMMORTAL LAMPS . 272 FOUR ZOAS 1   304
    NOR PITY THOU THE CRIES OF LUVAH LO THESE STARRY HOSTS . 273 FOUR ZOAS 1   327
    TEN THOUSAND THOUSAND WERE HIS HOSTS OF SPIRITS ON THE   273 FOUR ZOAS 1   343
      WIND
    CALL TO THY DARK ARMD HOSTS FOR ALL THE SONS OF MEN MUSTER   275 FOUR ZOAS 1   406
      TOGETHER
    TO DESOLATE THEIR CITIES MAN SHALL BE NO MORE AWAKE O HOSTS   275 FOUR ZOAS 1   407
    THE PRINCE OF ALL THE HOSTS OF MEN NOR EQUAL KNOW IN HEAVEN   278 FOUR ZOAS 1   505
    O PRINCE THE ETERNAL ONE HATH SET THEE LEADER OF HIS HOSTS   292 FOUR ZOAS 3   27
    THAN URIZEN & ALL HIS HOSTS IN CURST DESPAIR DOWN RUSHING   296 FOUR ZOAS 3   152
    OUR GOD IS URIZEN THE KING KING OF THE HEAVENLY HOSTS . 298 FOUR ZOAS 4   38
    WHEN THE SUN ROSE IN GLOWING MORN WITH ARMS OF MIGHTY HOSTS   338 FOUR ZOAS 7B   197
    NOR SILENT MOON NOR ALL THE HOSTS OF HEAVEN MOVE IN HIS   354 FOUR ZOAS 8   508
      BODY
    TO LOVE DEVOTED FEMALE ALL ASTONISHD STOOD THE HOSTS . 380 FOUR ZOAS AD 1   13
    O SATAN MY YOUNGEST BORN ART THOU NOT PRINCE OF THE STARRY   483 MILTON 4   9
      HOSTS
    AND AS ONE FEMALE OLOLON AND ALL ITS MIGHTY HOSTS . 527 MILTON 36   16
    OF OUR IMMORTAL VEINS & ALL THEIR HOSTS FLED FROM OUR LIMBS   647 JERUSALEM 24   8
    WHEN THE SUN ROSE IN GLOWING MORN WITH ARMS OF MIGHTY HOSTS   700 JERUSALEM 65   43
    I HAVE NAMED HIM JEHOVAH OF HOSTS HUMANITY IS BECOME   . 724 JERUSALEM 81   13
    THE HOSTS OF HEAVEN . . . . 777B INSC LAOCOON   PROSE
HOT   SEE RED-HOT,RED HOT
    O HORRIBLE O DREADFUL STATE CONSIDER THE HOT BURNING . 155C MARRIAGE HH 17 PROSE
    AND SUNK MY HEART INTO THE ABYSS A RED ROUND GLOBE HOT   191 V DAU ALBION 2   33
      BURNING
    ROUND GLOBE HOT BURNING DEEP . . . . 228 URIZEN 11   3
    ON SPIKED FLAMES ROSE HIS HOT VISAGE . . . . 249 AHANIA 2   2
    STAMPD IN FURY AND HOT INDIGNATION . . . . 257 BOOK OF LOS 3   48
    HEATED RED HOT THEY HIZZING REND THEIR WAY DOWN MANY A   283 FOUR ZOAS 2   138
      LEAGUE
    I LAID MY HEAD IN THE HOT NOON AFTER THE BROKEN CLODS . . 295 FOUR ZOAS 3   123
    RED AS THE SUN IN THE HOT MORNING OF THE BLOODY DAY . . 297 FOUR ZOAS 4   5
    A RED ROUND GLOBE HOT BURNING DEEP DEEP DOWN INTO THE   303 FOUR ZOAS 4   224
      ABYSS
    RENDING THE HEAVENS & EARTHS & DRINKING BLOOD IN THE HOT   335 FOUR ZOAS 7B   103
      BATTLE
    [I HAVE] AWAY FROM ME I HAVE BOUND DOWN WITH A HOT IRON   349 FOUR ZOAS 8   * 302
    GO NOAH FETCH THE GIRDLE OF STRONG BRASS [PRE] HEAT IT   349 FOUR ZOAS 8   312
      RED HOT
    WILL [ALWAYS BE FOUND TO BE NEITHER COLD NOR HOT & WILL]   386C ANNO WATSON   MARG
    I THOUGHT LOVE LIVD IN THE HOT SUN SHINE . . . . . . 436 WILLIAM BOND   45
    HIRE IDIOTS TO PAINT WITH COLD LIGHT & HOT SHADE . . . 445 ANNO REYNOLDS   2
    NEVER AS IN RUBENS & THE COLOURISTS HOT & YELLOW BROWN   478D ANNO REYNOLDS MARG
    DOWN SUNK WITH FRIGHT A RED ROUND GLOBE HOT BURNING DEEP   482 MILTON 3   11
    OF SORROW RED HOT I WORKD IT ON MY RESOLUTE ANVIL . . 628 JERUSALEM 9   20
    WHERE I LAID MY PLOW IN THE HOT NOON WHERE MY HOT TEAM FED   660 JERUSALEM 34   12
    IN THE HOT NOON AS HE TRAVELD THRO HIS JOURNEY HYLE   690 JERUSALEM 58   30
      & SKOFIELD

		PAGE	TITLE	LINE

HOT   (CONTINUED)
  AWAY FROM ME I HAVE BOUND DOWN WITH A HOT IRON   . . .   705 JERUSALEM 67   48
  AND THUS THE WARRIORS CRY IN THE HOT DAY OF VICTORY IN   705 JERUSALEM 68   10
    SONGS
  HEARTS OF THEIR WARRIORS GLOW HOT BEFORE THOR & FRIGA O   706 JERUSALEM 68   17
    MOLECH
  AS THEY CUT THE FIBRES FROM THE RIVERS HE SEARS THEM WITH   736 JERUSALEM 90   19
    HOT
  THEY ARE RED HOT WITH CRUELTY RAVING ALONG THE BANKS OF   737 JERUSALEM 90   47
    THAMES
  LOS FLAMD IN MY PATH & THE SUN WAS HOT   . . . . . .   818 HAPPINESS/L   77
HOT-PRESSED
  HOT-PRESSED I SAY THUS MUCH BEING URGED THERETO BY   . . .   847A LETTER 44   PROSE
HOUND
  TO FOLLOW THE DAUGHTERS OF ALBION AS THE HOUND FOLLOWS   638 JERUSALEM 17   3
    THE SCENT
HOUNDS   SEE GREY-HOUNDS
  THE STAG TURNS HEAD AND BAYS THE CRYING HOUNDS   . . .   24 EDW THIRD/PS 3   127
  THEY PLAY BEFORE THE ARMIES BEFORE THE HOUNDS OF NIMROD   281 FOUR ZOAS 2   64
  GREAT IS THE CRY OF THE HOUNDS OF NIMROD ALONG THE VALLEY   644 JERUSALEM 22   8
HOUNSLOW
  FROM LONDON STONE TO BLACKHEATH EAST TO HOUNSLOW WEST   . .   485 MILTON 6   4
  ALONG THE VALLEYS OF MIDDLESEX FROM HOUNSLOW TO BLACKHEATH   512 MILTON 26   19
  BETWEEN BLACKHEATH & HOUNSLOW BETWEEN NORWOOD & FINCHLEY   670 JERUSALEM 42   51
  TILL NORWOOD & FINCHLEY & BLACKHEATH & HOUNSLOW . . .   .   671 JERUSALEM 42   80
HOUR
  OR FRUIT IN THE MID-DAY HOUR . . . .   8 LOVE JOCUND/PS   12
  AND GENTLY SIGHS AWAY THE SILENT HOUR   . . . . . .   10 WHEN EARLY/PS   4
  & WAS SILENT [TALKD FOR HALF AN HOUR]   . . . . . .   46A ISLAND MOON 1   PROSE
  WHILE INFLAMMABLE GASS TALKD FOR HALF AN HOUR . . .   .   46A ISLAND MOON 1   PROSE
  AND THRUST HIS FIST IN AND ALL IN THE SPACE OF A QUARTER   50A ISLAND MOON 6   PROSE
    OF AN HOUR
  AFTER THIS THEY ALL SAT SILENT FOR A QUARTER OF AN HOUR   59D ISLAND MOON 11   PROSE
  AND SPEND MANY AN ANXIOUS HOUR . . . .   124 SCHOOL BOY/SI   12
  WHY THOU COMPLAINEST NOT WHEN IN ONE HOUR THOU FADE AWAY   128 BOOK OF THEL 3   2
  . . . BOUND IN ASTONISHMENT A QUARTER OF AN HOUR . .   .   137 FRENCH REVOLTN   67
  AS WHEN A DREAM OF THIRALATHA FLIES THE MIDNIGHT HOUR   .   206 THIRALATHA   1
  AND I MAY SEE THEE IN THE HOUR OF BLISS MY ELDEST BORN   .   239 EUROPE 4   28
  ONE HOUR THEY LAY BURIED BENEATH THE RUINS OF THAT HALL   241 EUROPE 9   14
  WHERE THE JOY OF MY MORNING HOUR . . . .   254 AHANIA 5   5
  LINKD HOUR TO HOUR & DAY TO NIGHT & NIGHT TO DAY & YEAR   302 FOUR ZOAS 4   181
    TO YEAR
  AND POLISH BRASS & IRON HOUR AFTER HOUR LABORIOUS   337 FOUR ZOAS 7B   182
    WORKMANSHIP
  READ PATIENTLY TAKE NOT UP THIS BOOK IN AN IDLE HOUR   .   383C ANNO WATSON   MARG
  UNTILL THE ARRIVAL OF THAT HOUR   . . . .   421 EACH MAN/N   2
  AND ETERNITY IN AN HOUR   . . . .   431 AUGURIES   4
  AND EVERY HOUR HAS A BRIGHT GOLDEN GATE CARVED WITH SKILL   516 MILTON 28   51
  EACH HAS ITS GUARD EACH MOMENT MINUTE HOUR DAY MONTH &   516 MILTON 28   59
    YEAR
  ONE HOUR OF THE LABOUR OF ORDINARY CAPACITY   . . . .   593A PUB ADDRESS/N   PROSE
  UNTILL THE ARRIVAL OF THAT HOUR   . . . .   669 EACH MAN/J   2
  ROCKD BY YEAR MONTH DAY & HOUR AND EVERY TWO MOMENTS   . .   688 JERUSALEM 56   9
  HOUR AFTER HOUR LABOURING AT THE WHIRLING WHEEL . . .   .   691 JERUSALEM 59   32
  AND POLISH BRASS & IRON HOUR AFTER HOUR LABORIOUS TASK   700 JERUSALEM 65   24
  HE SIEZES HIS HAMMER EVERY HOUR FLAMES SURROUND HIM AS .   731 JERUSALEM 86   34
  I AM GETTING BETTER EVERY HOUR MY PLAN IS DIET ONLY &   .   873C LETTER 77   PROSE
  YESTERDAY HE SAT WITH ME ABOVE AN HOUR & LOOKD OVER   . .   877A LETTER 85   PROSE
HOUR-GLASS,HOUR GLASS
  THE HOUR GLASS CONTEMND BECAUSE ITS SIMPLE WORKMANSHIP .   .   337 FOUR ZOAS 7B   175
  THE HOUR-GLASS CONTEMND BECAUSE ITS SIMPLE WORKMANSHIP .   .   700 JERUSALEM 65   17
HOURLY
  CONVERSE DAILY & HOURLY IN THE SPIRIT & . . . .   797A LETTER 9   PROSE
HOURS
  ALL WHILE THE JOCUND HOURS IN THY TRAIN . . . . .   .   14 IMIT SPEN/PS   6
  THE HOURS OF FOLLY ARE MEASURD BY THE CLOCK   . . . .   151A MARRIAGE HH 7   PROSE
  NUMBRING WITH LINKS HOURS DAYS & YEARS   . . . . .   .   227 URIZEN 10   18
  BECAUSE THE DAYS AND NIGHTS OF JOY IN LUCKY HOURS RENEW   239 EUROPE 4   23
  EVERY MOMENT OF MY SECRET HOURS YEA I KNOW   . . . .   .   265 FOUR ZOAS 1   53
  THEY VIEWD THE DANCING HOURS QUICK SPORTING THRO THE SKY   274 FOUR ZOAS 1   357
  HAMMER OF URTHONA FORMING UNDER HIS HEAVY HAND THE HOURS   302 FOUR ZOAS 4   179
  IN THE STUDIOUS HOURS OF DEEP MIDNIGHT . . . .   419 I SAW A MONK/N   29
  IN THE STUDIOUS HOURS OF DEEP MIDNIGHT   . . . . .   .   430 GREY MONK   14
  BUT OTHERS OF THE SONS OF LOS BUILD MOMENTS & MINUTES &   516 MILTON 28   44
    HOURS
  INTO THE PLANETARY LIVES OF YEARS MONTHS DAYS & HOURS   747 JERUSALEM 99   3
    REPOSING
  AND GOD HIMSELF IN THE PASSING HOURS . . . .   817 HAPPINESS/L   10
  TASTE WILL SHORTEN THE HUNDRED YEARS INTO AS MANY HOURS FOR   864D LETTER 61   PROSE
  TO SIT UP LONGER THAN SIX HOURS AT A TIME & ALSO FEEL THE   872D LETTER 76   PROSE
    COLD
  THAN I HAD EVER HOPED IN MY HEALTHFULL HOURS   . . . .   873A LETTER 76   PROSE
  & THE HOURS SUCKLING THEIR FLOWERY INFANTS . . . . .   . SUPP ILLUS GRAY   *TITLE
HOUSE   SEE ALE-HOUSE,BOG HOUSE,CHARNEL-HOUSE,CHARNEL HOUSE,COUNCIL HOUSE,
    GREEN HOUSE,JEWS-HARP-HOUSE,LODGING HOUSE,LODGYNG HOUSE,PRINTING HOUSE
    PRISON/HOUSE,SHIT-HOUSE,SLAUGHTER/HOUSE,STORE/HOUSE,S UGAR/HOUSE,
    TREASURE-HOUSE
  SHE FLED FROM FEAR TILL AT HER HOUSE ARRIVD   . . . .   5 FAIR ELENOR/PS   36
  A HERO TO THE SERVANTS OF HIS HOUSE   . . . .   25 EDW THIRD/PS 3   185
  HE FOLLOWED ME UP AND DOWN IN THE HOUSE WHEN I GREW UP . .   37C CONTEMPLATN/PS   PROSE
  PENSIVE ALONE SHE SAT WITHIN THE HOUSE   . . . . .   .   39D SAMSON/PS   PROSE
  WHEN LO AN ANGEL FROM THE FIELDS OF LIGHT ENTERED THE HOUSE   39D SAMSON/PS   PROSE

```
                                                                 PAGE      TITLE          LINE
HOUSE    (CONTINUED)
    TO SIT IN THE HOUSE AND TAKE HIS EVENING'S REST FROM LABOUR    40A  SAMSON/PS          PROSE
    I SAW A VAST NUMBER OF SWALLOWS ON THE [TOP OF AN HOUSE]       45A  ISLAND MOON 1      PROSE
    & THEY HAVE BLACK SERVANTS LODGE AT THEIR HOUSE   . . . .      53A  ISLAND MOON 8      PROSE
    SIX & TWENTY ROOMS IN HIS HOUSE AND I BELIEVE IT & HE IS       53A  ISLAND MOON 8      PROSE
      NOT
    FOR A MERRY MAKING AT THE PHILOSOPHERS HOUSE   . . . . .       54A  ISLAND MOON 8      PROSE
    FOR HE DID BUILD A HOUSE   . . . . . . . . . . . .              57  TO BE OR/IM            7
    BEING MET AT THE HOUSE OF INFLAMMABLE GASS THE WINDFINDER      58B  ISLAND MOON 10     PROSE
    ANOTHER MERRY MEETING AT THE HOUSE OF STEELYARD THE            59A  ISLAND MOON 11     PROSE
      LAWGIVER
    THOU EYELESS FIEND & YOU DISSEMBLERS IS THIS TIRIEL'S HOUSE    106  TIRIEL 4              86
    WILT THOU O QUEEN ENTER MY HOUSE TIS GIVEN THEE TO ENTER       130  BOOK OF THEL 5        16
    IN BERNARD'S HOUSE THE FLAMES COVERD THE LAND THEY ROUZE       201  AMERICA 13             2
      THEY CRY
    BETWEEN THE MOUNTAINS DISMAL VISIONS MOPE AROUND THE HOUSE     204  AMERICA CANC B        12
    SO STILL TERRORS RENT THE HOUSE AS WHEN THE SOLEMN GLOBE       204  AMERICA CANC B        20
    TILL TO THAT VOID IT CAME & FELL SO THE DARK HOUSE WAS RENT    204  AMERICA CANC B        22
    ALFRED IN THE COUNTRYMAN'S HOUSE   . . . . . . . . .          208D  SUBJCTS HIST/N     TITLE
    LIKE PEARLY CLOUDS THEY MEET TOGETHER IN THE CRYSTAL HOUSE     239  EUROPE 4               6
    EVERY HOUSE A DEN EVERY MAN BOUND THE SHADOWS ARE FILLD        243  EUROPE 12             26
    WITHIN HER CRYSTAL HOUSE   . . . . . . . . . . . .             243  EUROPE 13             14
    DOWN THE STEPS OF MY CRYSTAL HOUSE   . . . . . . . .           244  EUROPE 14             25
    WHOM THOU LOVEST IS SICK HE WANDERS FROM HIS HOUSE             277  FOUR ZOAS 1          478
      OF ETERNITY
    I HAVE TAUGHT THE THIEF A SECRET PATH INTO THE HOUSE OF        290  FOUR ZOAS 2          393
      THE JUST
    OF ALL THAT A MAN HATH HIS HOUSE HIS WIFE HIS CHILDREN  .  .   290  FOUR ZOAS 2      *   399
    . . . THAT DESTROYS OUR ENEMIES' HOUSE   . . . . . . .         291  FOUR ZOAS 2          411
    THE GOLDEN MOTH BUILDS THERE A HOUSE & SPREADS HER SILKEN      308  FOUR ZOAS 5          134
      BED
    IN THIS DARK WORLD A NARROW HOUSE I WANDER UP & DOWN    .  .   360  FOUR ZOAS 9          113
    HERE WILL I BUILD MYSELF A HOUSE & HERE I'LL CALL ON HIS       369  FOUR ZOAS 9          453
      NAME
    AND SAID LET A PLEASANT HOUSE ARISE TO BE THE DWELLING         369  FOUR ZOAS 9          459
      PLACE
    ROUND HIM STOOD SPIRITS LIKE ME WHO REARD ME A BRIGHT HOUSE    369  FOUR ZOAS 9          466
    AND HERE I SEE [THE] THEE HOUSE REMAIN IN MY MOST PLEASANT     369  FOUR ZOAS 9      *   467
      WORLD
    INTO THIS BODILY HOUSE TO TEND MY FLOCKS IN MY PLEASANT        369  FOUR ZOAS 9          470
      GARDEN
    SO SAYING SHE AROSE & WALKED ROUND HER BEAUTIFUL HOUSE  .  .   369  FOUR ZOAS 9          471
    SHE WENT UP TO HER FLOCKS & TURNED OFT TO SEE HER SHINING      369  FOUR ZOAS 9          475
      HOUSE
    AMONG HER FLOCKS & SHE TURND HER EYES TOWARD HER PLEASANT      370  FOUR ZOAS 9          506
      HOUSE
    SHE DREW NEAR TO HER HOUSE & HER FLOCKS FOLLOWD HER            370  FOUR ZOAS 9          508
      FOOTSTEPS
    AND THEN SHE ENTERD HER BRIGHT HOUSE LEADING HER MIGHTY        370  FOUR ZOAS 9          513
      CHILDREN
    AND WHEN NIGHT CAME THE FLOCKS LAID ROUND THE HOUSE BENEATH    370  FOUR ZOAS 9          514
      THE TREES
    SHE LAID THE CHILDREN ON THE BEDS WHICH SHE SAW PREPARD        370  FOUR ZOAS 9          515
      IN THE HOUSE
    ENLIGHTEN ALL THE CRYSTAL HOUSE OF VALA AWAKE AWAKE  . . .     371  FOUR ZOAS 9          520
    WHY WEEPEST THOU THARMAS CHILD OF TEARS IN THE BRIGHT HOUSE    371  FOUR ZOAS 9      *   530
      OF JOY
    THEN MY LOINS FADE & IN THE HOUSE I SIT ME DOWN & WEEP  .  .   371  FOUR ZOAS 9          544
    WHEN IN MY FATHER'S HOUSE I SAT & HEARD HIS CHEARING VOICE     375  FOUR ZOAS 9          689
    CONVERSE WITH GOD & BE A KING & PRIEST IN HIS OWN HOUSE       389C  ANNO WATSON         MARG
    TERROR IN THE HOUSE DOES ROAR   . . . . . . . . . .           421  TERROR IN/N            1
    A DOVE HOUSE FILLD WITH DOVES & PIGEONS   . . . . . . .       431  AUGURIES               7
    TO HAVE MY HOUSE SEARCHED AS I MIGHT HAVE PLANS OF THE        438A  BLAKES MEMORAN     PROSE
      COUNTRY
    MAY COME & DRAG ME AND MY WIFE OUT OF OUR HOUSE   . . . .     439A  BLAKES MEMORAN     PROSE
    CAITHNESS & ROCKY DURNESS PENTLAND & JOHN GROATS HOUSE  .  .   512  MILTON 26             15
    CREATING THE BEAUTIFUL HOUSE FOR THE PITEOUS SUFFERER   .  .   515  MILTON 28              7
    . . . & THE GATES OF THEIR FATHER'S HOUSE   . . . . . .        522  MILTON 32             43
    BUT LOOK YONDER THAT HOUSE IS THE HOUSE OF REMBRANT &C         553  ASKD PRIGG/N     *    14
    IN MY GOLDEN HOUSE ON HIGH   . . . . . . . . . . .             558  THE CAVERNS/N         19
    WHAT IS IT THAT BUILDS A HOUSE AND PLANTS A GARDEN   .  .    585C  DESC CAT 15         PROSE
    AT THIS HOUSE EVEN AT THIS DAY EVERY FRIENDLESS WRETCH   .   590B  CHAUCER 2           PROSE
    AND EVERY HOUSE FOURFOLD BUT THE THIRD GATE IN EVERY ONE       633  JERUSALEM 13          22
    AND RIVER AND MOUNTAIN AND CITY & VILLAGE AND HOUSE            640  JERUSALEM 18          18
      & FAMILY
    OF HATERS MET IN DEADLY STRIFE RENDING THE HOUSE & GARDEN      640  JERUSALEM 18          22
    AND CITY & VILLAGE AND HOUSE & FAMILY THAT THE PERFECT   .     640  JERUSALEM 18          26
    RETURND WITH CHILDREN OF POLLUTION TO DEFILE OUR HOUSE   .     640  JERUSALEM 18          31
    IN THE DARK WORLD A NARROW HOUSE HE WANDERS UP AND DOWN        641  JERUSALEM 19          14
    OF HIS OWN HOUSE & FAMILY   . . . . . . . . . . .             652  FIELDS FROM/J         82
    DENS OF DESPAIR IN THE HOUSE OF BREAD ENQUIRING IN VAIN        657  JERUSALEM 31          26
    HERE IS THE HOUSE OF ALBION & HERE IS THY SECLUDED PLACE       658  JERUSALEM 31          60
    OF SURREY ACROSS MIDDLESEX & ACROSS ALBION'S HOUSE   . . .     658  JERUSALEM 31          69
    CHARIOTS BLACK THEIR FIRES ROLL BEHOLDING ALBION'S HOUSE       666  JERUSALEM 40           5
      OF ETERNITY
    WENT ALONG ALBION'S ROADS TILL THEY ARRIVD AT ALBION'S        667  JERUSALEM 40          24
      HOUSE
    SO LOS SPOKE PALE THEY STOOD AROUND THE HOUSE OF DEATH   .     673  JERUSALEM 43          80
    . . . FAINT AS THE VOICE OF THE DEAD IN THE HOUSE OF DEATH     675  JERUSALEM 44          44
    SHALL BE THOSE OF HIS OWN HOUSE AND FAMILY IN A RELIGION       676  JERUSALEM 46          26
    BEG BREAD FROM HOUSE TO HOUSE LOVELY JERUSALEM   . . . .       693  JERUSALEM 60          28
    OR HAST THOU BEEN PIERCED IN THE HOUSE OF THY FRIENDS    .  .  693  JERUSALEM 60          53
```

		PAGE	TITLE	LINE

HOUSE   (CONTINUED)
```
      IS A HOUSE OF (PLEASANTNESS) & A GARDEN OF DELIGHT BUILT      714 JERUSALEM 73     51
         BY THE
      JERUSALEM IN RUINS WANDERING ABOUT FROM HOUSE TO HOUSE  .  .  714 JERUSALEM 74     17
      ABEL AMONG THE ELOHIM A HUMAN VICTIM I WANDER I AM THEIR      780 GHOST ABEL 1     10
         HOUSE
      ENTERD INTO ME AS INTO HIS HOUSE & I LOATHE THY               780 GHOST ABEL 2      6
         TABERNACLES
      OR A HOUSE OR A HORSE OR A MAN & I  .  .  .  .  .  .  .       782A INSC UPCOTT    PROSE
      OF MAN NO OTHER FORMED HOUSE CAN EVER PLEASE ME SO WELL       802A LETTER 14     PROSE
      TO TAKE A HOUSE IN SOME VILLAGE FURTHER FROM THE SEA  .  .    820D LETTER 25     PROSE
      THE MASTER OF THE HOUSE THE FOX INN WHO IS [MY] THE  .  .  .  827B LETTER 28     PROSE
      HOUSE SR WILLIAM LIVD IN IN PICCADILLY SHE LEFT SOME TIME     836C LETTER 35     PROSE
      GREAT NEWPORT STREET BEFORE HE WENT TOOK THE HOUSE IN  .  .   847D LETTER 44     PROSE
      OR LEFT THE CAVENDISH SQUARE HOUSE  .  .  .  .  .  .  .  .    847D LETTER 44     PROSE
      FROM ST PAULS TO A NOBLE HOUSE IN BRIDGE STREET BLACKFRIARS   856A LETTER 54     PROSE
      CONNEXIONS ARE UNIVERSAL HIS PRESENT HOUSE IS ON THE MOST     857A LETTER 54     PROSE
      TO WRITE IMMEDIATELY ON RETURNING FROM HIS HOUSE HE SAYS      857D LETTER 55     PROSE
      AT HIS HOUSE LET US ACCOMODATE HIM IN WHAT IS INDIFFERENT     868B LETTER 67     PROSE
      I PRINTED THOSE THINGS I HAD A WHOLE HOUSE TO RANGE IN  .  .  878C LETTER 88     PROSE
      OWN ETERNAL HOUSE LEAVING THE DELUSIVE GODDESS NATURE & HER   879A LETTER 88     PROSE
      THE MIND IN WHICH EVERY ONE IS KING & PRIEST IN HIS OWN       879A LETTER 88     PROSE
         HOUSE
      HOUSE OF DEATH MILTON  .  .  .  .  .  .  .  .  .  .  .  .  SUPP COLOR PRT TATE *TITLE
      THE LODGYNGE HOUSE FOR PILGRIMS WHO JOURNEY  .  .  .  .  .  SUPP ILLUS CHAUCER  *TITLE
      THE LIBERAL MAN INVITING THE TRAVELLER INTO HIS HOUSE  .  .  SUPP ILLUS GRAY     *TITLE
      GOOD & EVIL ANGEL HOUSE OF DEATH GOD JUDGING ADAM LAMECH      SUPP LETTER 56A   *PROSE
HOUSEKEEPER
      AND NOBLE HOUSEKEEPER CHAUCER'S MONK IS INTENDED  .  .  .  .  569C DESC CAT 3     PROSE
HOUSELESS
      TO SPEAK THE LAWS OF PRUDENCE TO THE HOUSELESS WANDERER       290 FOUR ZOAS 2      405
HOUSES        SEE ALMS-HOUSES, SLAUGHTER HOUSES,STORE HOUSES,WORK-HOUSES
      THOU HAST REFUSD OUR CLOTHES OUR BEDS OUR HOUSES FOR THY      100 TIRIEL 1        38
         DWELLING
      DRIVING THE ANGEL BEFORE ME SOON WE SAW SEVEN HOUSES OF      157A MARRIAGE HH 17 PROSE
         BRICK
      WAVE SHADOWS OF DISCONTENT AND IN WHAT HOUSES DWELL THE       192 V DAU ALBION 4     1
         WRETCHED
      THE HOUSES OF MY HARPERS ARE BECOME A HAUNT OF CROWS  .  .    310 FOUR ZOAS 5      195
      THE SONS OF LOS CLOTHE THEM & FEED & PROVIDE HOUSES           512 MILTON 26         30
         & FIELDS
      HOUSES OF COMMONS & HOUSES OF LORDS APPEAR TO ME TO BE       600A PUB ADDRESS/N  PROSE
         FOOLS
      AND EVERY POT & VESSEL & GARMENT & UTENSIL OF THE HOUSES      633 JERUSALEM 13     21
      HER STREETS ARE PAVED WITH DESTRUCTION HER HOUSES BUILT       647 JERUSALEM 24     33
         WITH DEATH
      MY HOUSES ARE THOUGHTS MY INHABITANTS AFFECTIONS  .  .  .     665 JERUSALEM 38     33
      THE SONS OF LOS CLOTHE THEM & FEED & PROVIDE HOUSES           714 JERUSALEM 73     49
         & GARDENS
      THE FURNITURE OF THEIR HOUSES WAS THE FURNITURE OF MY         720 JERUSALEM 79     47
         CHAMBER
      YOU MUST LEAVE FATHERS & MOTHERS & HOUSES & LANDS  .  .  .  776A INSC LAOCOON   PROSE
      & MY COTTAGE IS ALSO A SHADOW OF THEIR HOUSES MY  .  .  .  .  802A LETTER 14     PROSE
      I SEE OUR HOUSES OF ETERNITY WHICH CAN NEVER BE SEPARATED     802C LETTER 14     PROSE
HOUSEWIVES
      AND WE WILL SING LIKE THE YOUNG HOUSEWIVES BUSIED  .  .  .     24 EDW THIRD/PS 3   148
HOVER
      VISIT YOU BUT ETERNAL FOGS HOVER AROUND YOUR WALLS  .  .  .   106 TIRIEL 5         23
      HOVER OER MY HAPPY CHILD  .  .  .  .  .  .  .  .  .  .  .      120 CRADLE SONG/SI    8
      HOVER OVER MY DELIGHT  .  .  .  .  .  .  .  .  .  .  .  .      120 CRADLE SONG/SI   10
      DESCEND O LITTLE CLOUD & HOVER BEFORE THE EYES OF THEL  .     128 BOOK OF THEL 2   16
      SILENT I HOVER ALL THE NIGHT AND ALL DAY COULD BE SILENT      191 V DAU ALBION 3   14
      AND I AM WHITE AND PURE TO HOVER ROUND THEOTORMON'S BREAST    191 V DAU ALBION 3   20
      FOR CLOUDS FROM THE ATLANTIC HOVER OER THE SOLEMN ROOF  .     200 AMERICA 10       12
      JACOB & [THEIR] HIS TWELVE SONS HOVER BENEATH THE  .  .  .  607C V LAST JUDG/N  PROSE
      HOVER WITHIN ME & BENEATH AND SPREADING THEMSELVES OUTSIDE    666 JERUSALEM 39     17
      THE FAMILY DIVINE HOVER AROUND THE DARKEND ALBION  .  .  .    674 JERUSALEM 44     20
      TO HOVER ROUND OUR SWEET COTTAGE  .  .  .  .  .  .  .  .  .  854A LETTER 52     PROSE
HOVERD
      AND LOWRING DARKNESS HOVERD OER TH ASSEMBLY  .  .  .  .  .   49B ISLAND MOON 5  *PROSE
      HOVERD AND STRETCHD ACROSS THE CITY .  .  .  .  .  .  .  .    146 FRENCH REVOLTN   272
      ON MOUNTAINS & CLIFFS OF SNOW THE AWFUL APPARITION HOVERD     205 AMERICA CANC C   28
      THEY HOVERD ROUND ME LIKE A CLOUD OF INCENSE WHEN I CAME      238 EUROPE INTRO     22
      THEN OOTHOON HOVERD OVER JUDAH & JERUSALEM  .  .  .  .  .  .   246 SONG OF LOS 3    22
      IN NOXIOUS CLOUDS THESE HOVERD THICK  .  .  .  .  .  .  .     253 AHANIA 4         18
      THE CLOUDS OF DISEASE HOVERD WIDE  .  .  .  .  .  .  .  .     253 AHANIA 4         22
      OR HOVERD OER HIS STARRY HEAD & WHEN HE SMILD SHE BRIGHTEND   284 FOUR ZOAS 2   *  182
      OF LIVING GOLD PURE PERFECT HOLY IN WHITE LINEN PURE HE       293 FOUR ZOAS 3      51
         HOVERD
      .  .  .  BUT THE CLOUD HOVERD OVER THEIR HEADS  .  .  .  .    293 FOUR ZOAS 3      66
      I PITYING HOVERD OVER THEE I PROTECTED THY GHASTLY CORSE      300 FOUR ZOAS 4      108
      TILL ON MY SILVER BED I SLEPT & SWEET DREAMS ROUND           310 FOUR ZOAS 5      204
         ME HOVERD
      .  .  .  LIGHTNINGS PLAYD AROUND THEE THUNDERS HOVERD  .  .   325 FOUR ZOAS 7      227
      .  .  .  BUT STILL MY SPIRIT [RETURND] RETURNING HOVERD  .  . 327 FOUR ZOAS 7   *  292
      [THEIR] WINGS TOUCHD THE HEAVENS THEIR FAIR FEET HOVERD       341 FOUR ZOAS 8       12
         ABOVE]
      INVISIBLE LUVAH IN BRIGHT CLOUDS HOVERD OVER VALA'S HEAD      367 FOUR ZOAS 9      385
      HE HOVERD OVER IT TREMBLING & WEEPING SUSPENDED IT SHOOK      483 MILTON 3         31
      SO SPOKE ORC WHEN OOTHOON & LEUTHA HOVERD OVER HIS COUCH      500 MILTON 18        39
      ASTONISHD TERRIFIED THEY HOVERD OVER HIS GIANT LIMBS  .  .    642 JERUSALEM 20      2
      OF LIVING GOLD PURE PERFECT HOLY IN WHITE LINEN PURE HE       654 JERUSALEM 29     38
         HOVERD
```

940

HOVERD   (CONTINUED)
    . . . BUT THE CLOUD HOVERD OVER THEIR HEADS   . . . . .   654 JERUSALEM 29   53
    REFUSD TO TAKE A DEFINITE FORM SHE HOVERD OVER ALL THE   723 JERUSALEM 80   52
        EARTH
HOVERING
    HOVERING ANGELS ARE AROUND THEM   . . . .   36D COUCH DEATH/PS   PROSE
    AND HOVERING OVER HER IN THE DARKNING STORM   . . . .   42C THEN SHE BORE   PROSE
    HOVERING AND GLITTERING ON THE AIR BEFORE THE FACE OF THEL   128 BOOK OF THEL 3   6
    . . . URGD BY CRIES IN DAY AND PROPHETIC DREAMS HOVERING   138 FRENCH REVOLTN   98
        IN NIGHT
    HOVERING ON THE SIDES OF THE ROCK   . . . .   150D MARRIAGE HH 6   PROSE
    [AS ONE MAN HOVERING OVER GILEAD & HERMON]   . . . . .   269 FOUR ZOAS 1   199
    HOVERING OVER THE COLD BOSOM IN ITS VORTEX MILTON BENT DOWN 497 MILTON 15   41
    NUMBER XIV THE ANGELS HOVERING OVER   . . . .   584B DESC CAT 14   TITLE
    WITH WHICH THEY HOVERING OVER THE DEEPS BENEATH   . . . .   612A V LAST JUDG/N   PROSE
    AROUND MILTON ARE SIX SPIRITS OR FAIRIES HOVERING ON THE   619C ILLUS MILTON   PROSE
        AIR
    AND A LITTLE TENDER MOON & HOVERING ANGELS ON THE WING . . 707 JERUSALEM 69   22
    AND RAHAB LIKE A DISMAL AND INDEFINITE HOVERING CLOUD   . . 723 JERUSALEM 80   51
    WITH MY FATHER HOVERING UPON THE WIND   . . . . . .   817 HAPPINESS/L   13
HOVERS
    AND DESTRUCTION HOVERS IN THE CITY'S SMOAK BUT   . . . .   37A CONTEMPLATN/PS   PROSE
    AND OOTHOON HOVERS BY HIS SIDE PERSWADING HIM IN VAIN   . . 190 V DAU ALBION 2   22
    HOVERS WITH BLASTED WINGS ALOFT WATCHING WITH EAGER EYE   354 FOUR ZOAS 8   523
    ABRAHAM HOVERS ABOVE HIS POSTERITY WHICH APPEAR   . . . . 607C V LAST JUDG/N   PROSE
    BEARS ME BEFORE HIS ARMIES THO MY SHADOW HOVERS HERE   . .   644 JERUSALEM 22   5
    OF UNBELIEF ENVY HOVERS OVER HIM HIS FRIENDS ARE   667 JERUSALEM 40   14
        HIS ABHORRENCE
HOVRING
    I SEE THEE HOVRING OER MY ARMY WITH   . . . .   26 EDW THIRD/PS 3   205
    AN AGED FORM WHITE AS SNOW HOVRING IN MIST . . . .   140 FRENCH REVOLTN   131
    THAT MOVD WITH HORRIBLE DREAMS & (HOVRING) HIGH OVER HIS   341 FOUR ZOAS 8   *   6
        HEAD
    SUCH IS A VISION OF ALL BEULAH HOVRING OVER THE SLEEPER   341 FOUR ZOAS 8   15
    SIT HOVRING OVER MY DARK THRESHOLD THO I ARISE LOOK OUT   360 FOUR ZOAS 9   * 118
    THE LAMB OF GOD IS SEEN THRO MISTS & SHADOWS HOVRING   . .   495 MILTON 14   25
HOWEVER
    HOWEVER SWEET TIS ENVY THAT INSPIRES MY SONG   . . . .   41D THEN SHE BORE   PROSE
    HOWEVER THE THINGS STILL REMAIN AND THE VANITIES ARE THE   44B ISLAND MOON 1   PROSE
        SAME
    HOWEVER I SAW THAT THEY SOMETIMES GREW NUMEROUS   . . . . 157A MARRIAGE HH 17   PROSE
    HOWEVER HIDDEN BY ARTIFICES   . . . .   573A DESC CAT 3   PROSE
    TO A SUPERABUNDANT BLACKNESS IT HAS HOWEVER   . . . .   581C DESC CAT 7   PROSE
    I HAVE HOWEVER SOMEWHAT ACCOMODATED MY FIGURE OF TIME   . . 614D V LAST JUDG/N   PROSE
    OF EDEN THAT HOWEVER GREAT AND GLORIOUS HOWEVER LOVING   675 JERUSALEM 45   10
    AND MERCIFUL THE INDIVIDUALITY HOWEVER HIGH   . . . .   675 JERUSALEM 45   11
    OUR PALACES AND CITIES AND HOWEVER FRUITFUL ARE OUR FIELDS   675 JERUSALEM 45   12
    HOWEVER ADMIRABLE THAT TRACK MAY BE AT ANY RATE MY EXCUSE   792A LETTER 4   PROSE
    BUT HOWEVER FOR HIS OWN SAKE I AM SORRY THAT A MAN . . .   795A LETTER 6   PROSE
    PRODUCES BY HER ELDEST SON HOWEVER SUCH AS THEY ARE   . . . 804B LETTER 16   PROSE
    HOWEVER THIS I KNOW WILL SET YOU AT EASE I AM NOW SO FULL   820C LETTER 25   PROSE
    & PRODUCE TWO ELEGANT PLATES THERE IS HOWEVER   . . . . .   837A LETTER 35   PROSE
    BUT HOWEVER AS SOME EXCUSE I MUST SAY THAT   . . . .   847B LETTER 44   PROSE
    WITH DESIRE AND CURIOSITY BUT HOWEVER CHRISTMAS IS A-COMING 851D LETTER 50   PROSE
    YOU FOR MORE MONEY BUT HOWEVER YOUR KIND ANSWER TO . . .   854D LETTER 53   PROSE
    MIGHT AGAIN CALL I HAVE HOWEVER SEEN HIM THIS MORNING   . . 856A LETTER 54   PROSE
    HOWEVER THE SATISFACTION TO INFORM YOU THAT I HAVE MYSELF   865D LETTER 63   PROSE
    HOWEVER IF THE WEATHER SHOULD BE WARM I WILL ENDEAVOUR TO   872A LETTER 74   PROSE
    HOWEVER I AM UPON THE MENDING HAND TO-DAY & HOPE SOON   . . 880A LETTER 90   PROSE
    [?HOWEVER ?FOR THE XXX FOR ?STANDING NEAR]   . . . . .   SUPP ANNO REYNOLDS * MARG
    [?HOWEVER ?DISCOURAGING TO THOSE WHO ARE BORN FOR IT] . .   SUPP ANNO REYNOLDS * MARG
HOWL
    SHALL [FALL] FAIL IF THOU REFUSE HOWL IN THE DESOLATE   108 TIRIEL 6   * 49
        MOUNTAINS
    NOR FEAR THE WOLVISH HOWL   . . . .   115 LIT GRL FND/SI   51
    WHEN WOLVES AND TYGERS HOWL FOR PREY   . . . .   119 NIGHT/SI   25
    . . . THAT WANDER IN FORESTS AND HOWL IN LAW BLASTED WASTES 144 FRENCH REVOLTN   227
    AND THE HYPOCRITE TO HOWL   . . . .   183 MOTTO SONGS/N   6
    BUT SHE CAN HOWL INCESSANT WRITHING HER SOFT SNOWY LIMBS   190 V DAU ALBION 2   12
    I HOWL MY JOY AND MY RED EYES SEEK TO BEHOLD THY FACE   . . 196 AMERICA PREL 1   19
    BESIDE THE STONE OF NIGHT AND LIKE THE ETERNAL LION'S HOWL   198 AMERICA 7   2
    THE BRITISH SOLDIERS THRO THE THIRTEEN STATES SENT UP A   201 AMERICA 13   6
        HOWL
    THE MILLIONS SENT UP A HOWL OF ANGUISH   . . . .   202 AMERICA 15   4
    ABOVE THE REST THE HOWL WAS HEARD FROM WESTMINSTER LOUDER   242 EUROPE 12   14
        & LOUDER
    THUS WAS THE HOWL THRO EUROPE   . . . .   242 EUROPE 12   21
    THE HOWL RISE UP FROM EUROPE   . . . .   247 SONG OF LOS 6   2
    GO HOWL IN VAIN SMITE SMITE HIS FETTERS SMITE O WINTRY   276 FOUR ZOAS 1   431
        HAMMERS
    WHY [HOWLS] HOWL THE LION & THE WOLF WHY DO THEY   276 FOUR ZOAS 1   * 451
        ROAM ABROAD
    HOWL THOU OVER THE BODY OF DEATH TIS THINE BUT IF AMONG   288 FOUR ZOAS 2   312
        THE VIRGINS
    TO HEAR THE DOG HOWL AT THE WINTRY DOOR . . . .   290 FOUR ZOAS 2   409
    OF WILD BEASTS THERE THE LION GLARES THE TYGER & WOLF HOWL   308 FOUR ZOAS 5   128
        THERE
    HOWL IN THE BURNING DENS HIS TYGERS ROAM IN THE REDOUNDING   320 FOUR ZOAS 7   9
        SMOKE
    TENFOLD WITH FIERCE DESIRE TO REND THY CHAIN & HOWL IN FURY 321 FOUR ZOAS 7   66
    BURDEND WITH CLOUDS HOWL ROUND THE COUCH SULLEN THE WOOLY   335 FOUR ZOAS 7B   108
        SHEEP

```
                                                          PAGE      TITLE        LINE
HOWL    (CONTINUED)
        THEY HOWL AROUND THE FLAMING YOUTH RENDING THE NAMELESS      336  FOUR ZOAS 7B    142
          SHADOW
        HER GREAT MEN HOWL & THROW THE DUST & REND THEIR HOARY HAIR  375  FOUR ZOAS 9     663
        THEY HOWL & WRITHE IN SHOALS OF TORMENT IN FIERCE FLAMES     377  FOUR ZOAS 9     749
          CONSUMING
        THEY DANCE AROUND THE DYING & THEY DRINK THE HOWL & GROAN    377  FOUR ZOAS 9     767
        UPON THE WHEELS THE STORMY SEAS HOWL AT HIS DREAD COMMAND    378  FOUR ZOAS 9     810
        EVERY WOLF'S & LION'S HOWL                                   431  AUGURIES         19
        THEN I REND THEE ASUNDER THEN I HOWL OVER THY CLAY & ASHES   499  MILTON 18        33
        AND LOUD THE SOULS HOWL ROUND THE PORCHES OF GOLGONOOZA      510  MILTON 25        12
        THEY HOWL & WRITHE IN SHOALS OF TORMENT IN FIERCE FLAMES     513  MILTON 27        31
          CONSUMING
        THEY DANCE AROUND THE DYING & THEY DRINK THE HOWL & GROAN    514  MILTON 27        37
        THUS ALOUD [WAS HEARD TO] DID HOWL & CRY      . . . . .      542  PITIFUL CASE/N *  7
        WHERE LOS'S FURNACES STAND WHERE JERUSALEM & VALA HOWL  .    677  JERUSALEM 47      3
        THE CAPTIVES REARD TO HEAVEN HOWL IN FLAMES AMONG THE STARS  677  JERUSALEM 47      8
        AND THE SUN SET IN TYBURN'S BROOK WHERE VICTIMS HOWL & CRY   696  JERUSALEM 62     34
        WHERE THE HUMAN VICTIMS HOWL TO THE MOON & THOR & FRIGA      697  JERUSALEM 63      9
        AND LOS'S FURNACES HOWL LOUD LIVING SELF-MOVING LAMENTING    713  JERUSALEM 73      2
        THE SPECTRES OF THE DEAD HOWL ROUND THE PORCHES OF LOS  .    714  JERUSALEM 73     46
        THEY ARE BROKEN LOUD HOWL THE SPECTRES IN HIS IRON FURNACE   719  JERUSALEM 78      9
        IN MILD JERUSALEM AROUND THE LAMB OF GOD LOUD HOWL   . . .   734  JERUSALEM 88     53
        LEFT WITH US THEY KEEP OFF EVERY WIND WE HEAR THE WEST HOWL  807B LETTER 17       PROSE
HOWLD
        SMOTE WITH HIS SCEPTER THE SCALE BOUND ORB LOUD HOWLD . . .  205  AMERICA CANC C   11
        LOS HOWLD IN A DISMAL STUPOR    . . . . . . . . . .          226  URIZEN 7          1
        OF DARKNESS THE ETERNAL PROPHET HOWLD . . . . . . . .        227  URIZEN 10         7
        ORC ON MOUNT ATLAS HOWLD CHAIND DOWN WITH THE CHAIN OF       246  SONG OF LOS 3    21
          JEALOUSY
        FORTHWITH HATCHING SOME HOWLD ON HIS HILLS  . . . . . .      250  AHANIA 3         11
        BEHOLD TWO [LITTLE INFANTS WEPT] [?FIGURES OF ?PAIN HOWLD]   269  FOUR ZOAS 1    * 192
          . . .
        [TWO FORMS OF HORROR HOWLD BENEATH IT]         . . . . . .  SUPP  FOUR ZOAS 1    *
        [XXX ?MONSTERS HOWLD ?WITH ?URIZEN ?AROUND]   . . . . . .   SUPP  FOUR ZOAS 1    *
        O HOW LOS HOWLD AT THE RENDING ASUNDER ALL THE FIBRES RENT   299  FOUR ZOAS 4      59
        I HOWLD IN SORROW I BEHELD THEE ROTTING UPON THE ROCKS  .    300  FOUR ZOAS 4     107
        THE LOVELY FEMALE HOWLD & URIZEN BENEATH DEEP GROAND   . .   302  FOUR ZOAS 4     189
        UNWILLING MOVD AS URIZEN HOWLD HIS LOINS WAVD LIKE THE SEA   305  FOUR ZOAS 4     289
        THE ENORMOUS DEMONS WOKE & HOWLD AROUND THE [YOUTHFUL]       306  FOUR ZOAS 5      41
          NEW BORN KING
        THE [DISMAL] ACCURSED CHAIN O HOW BRIGHT ENITHARMON HOWLD    308  FOUR ZOAS 5     102
          & CRIED
        HOWLD IN THE FURIOUS WIND HE THOUGHT TO GIVE TO ENITHARMON   309  FOUR ZOAS 5     152
        [THEN DEMONS ?HOWLD ROUND HIS CHARIOT ?RAGING ?LUVAH        SUPP  FOUR ZOAS 5    *
          (EMPTIED)]
        IN HIS OWN SORROW HOWLD REGARDLESS OF HIS WORDS NOR VOICE    315  FOUR ZOAS 6     128
        HEAVEN RANG WITH WINGED EXULTATION ALL BENEATH HOWLD LOUD    378  FOUR ZOAS 9     782
        THE SHADOWY FEMALE SEEING MILTON HOWLD IN HER LAMENTATION    499  MILTON 18         2
        NOT DARING TO TOUCH ONE FIBRE HE HOWLD ROUND UPON THE SEA    529  MILTON 38        14
        TREMBLING GLOBE SHOT FORTH SELF-LIVING & LOS HOWLD OVER IT   639  JERUSALEM 17     55
        BESIDE HER VALA HOWLD UPON THE WINDS IN PRIDE OF BEAUTY      721  JERUSALEM 80      6
        GWENDOLEN SAW THE INFANT IN HER (SISTER'S) ARMS SHE HOWLD    726  JERUSALEM 82   *  9
        DRAGD AT HIS CHARIOT WHEELS LOUD HOWLD     . . . . . .       749  EV GOSPEL(B)/N   43
        LOUD PILATE HOWLD LOUD CAIPHAS YELLD      . . . . . .        758  EV GOSPEL (2)    19
HOWLED
        DEFYD THE STORM THAT HOWLED OER THEIR HEADS   . . . . .       32  EDW THIRD/PS 6   33
        AND THE GREAT VOICE OF THE ATLANTIC HOWLED OVER THE DRUID    689  JERUSALEM 57      5
          ALTARS
HOWLING
        HES DEAD AND HOWLING AFTER ME FOR BLOOD   . . . . . .          4  FAIR ELENOR/PS   24
        PAST HOWLING SHE RECEIVD INTO HER ARMS    . . . . . .          4  FAIR ELENOR/PS   27
        HOWLING LEAPD OER THE WALL INTO THE MOAT  . . . . . .          4  FAIR ELENOR/PS   30
        WITH HOWLING WOE                                               9  MAD SONG/PS      18
        HOWLING LIKE GHOSTS FURIOUS AS WOLVES     . . . . . .         11  GWIN KING/PS     27
        SHE HOWLING LED HIM OVER MOUNTAINS & THRO FRIGHTED VALES     108  TIRIEL 7          1
        THEIR TYRANT PRINCE BLIND & HIS DAUGHTER HOWLING & LEADING   108  TIRIEL 7          4
          HIM
        [THEY] THE HOWLING MAIDEN LED HER FATHER WHERE WILD BEASTS   109  TIRIEL 7         16
          RESORT
        HOWLING AND GIVING THE DARK COMMAND . . . . . . . .          135  FRENCH REVOLTN   24
        THE ROARING OF LIONS THE HOWLING OF WOLVES . . . . . .      151C  MARRIAGE HH 8   PROSE
        IN HER TREMBLING HANDS SHE TOOK THE NEW BORN TERROR HOWLING  159B  SONG LIBERTY    PROSE
        IN THE HOWLING STORM                                         175  SICK ROSE/N       4
        MINGLE IN HOWLING PAINS IN FURROWS BY THY LIGHTNINGS RENT    196  AMERICA PREL 2   16
        CROUCH HOWLING BEFORE THEIR CAVERNS DEEP LIKE SKINS DRYD     199  AMERICA 9         4
          IN THE WIND
        HOWLING & SHUDDERING HIS LEGS QUIVERING CONVULSD            202  AMERICA 15        8
          EACH MUSCLE & SINEW
        WEEPING IN DISMAL HOWLING WOE HE DARK DESCENDED HOWLING      203  AMERICA 16        7
          IN THE HOWLING STORM                                      213  SICK ROSE/SE      4
        LOS WEPT HOWLING AROUND THE DARK DEMON    . . . . . .        226  URIZEN 6          2
        IN TREMBLING & HOWLING & DISMAY    . . . . . . . .           229  URIZEN 13        17
        HOWLING THE CHILD WITH FIERCE FLAMES      . . . . . .        232  URIZEN 19        45
        GRODNA RENT THE DEEP EARTH HOWLING        . . . . . .        234  URIZEN 23        15
        AND BRING FORTH HOWLING TERRORS ALL DEVOURING FIERY KINGS    238  EUROPE PREL 2     4
        THEY HEARD THE VOICE OF ALBION'S ANGEL HOWLING IN FLAMES     242  EUROPE 12        12
          OF ORC
        FOR ORC REJOICD TO HEAR THE HOWLING SHADOWS   . . . . .      242  EUROPE 12        22
        RATTLING THEIR HOLLOW BONES IN HOWLING AND LAMENTATION  . .  243  EUROPE 13         8
        HEAVY-WAVING HOWLING WEEPING    . . . . . . . . .            248  SONG OF LOS 7    16
        THE HOWLING GLOBE BURNING IT FLEW   . . . . . . . .          249  AHANIA 2         18
```

942

```
                                                         PAGE     TITLE          LINE
HOWLING   (CONTINUED)
     [TWISTING IN FEARFUL FORMS & HOWLING HOWLING HARSH      269 FOUR ZOAS 1       180
        SHRIEKING
     [HOWLING HARSH SHRIEKING MINGLING . . . . . . . . .    269 FOUR ZOAS 1       181
     THARMAS ENDURD NOT HE FLED HOWLING THEN A BARREN WASTE 275 FOUR ZOAS 1       419
        SUNK DOWN
     AND HIS FEET STAMPD THE NETHER ABYSS IN TREMBLING HOWLING  303 FOUR ZOAS 4   245
        & DISMAY
     INTO UNUSUAL FORMS DANCING & HOWLING STAMPING THE ABYSS  305 FOUR ZOAS 4     295
     THARMAS LAID THE FOUNDATIONS & LOS FINISHD IT IN HOWLING  307 FOUR ZOAS 5 *  78
        WOE
     SURROUNDED WITH FLAMES THE DEMON GREW LOUD HOWLING IN HIS  308 FOUR ZOAS 5   109
        FIRES
     GIVING THE SPECTRE STERNEST CHARGE OVER THE HOWLING FIEND  308 FOUR ZOAS 5   112
     INWRAP THE PARENTS IN COLD CLOUDS AS THEY BEND HOWLING OVER  309 FOUR ZOAS 5 171
     OF THE CHAIN OF JEALOUSY & FELT THE RENDINGS OF FIERCE  309 FOUR ZOAS 5      182
        HOWLING ORC
     URIZEN TREMBLED WHERE HE LAY TO HEAR THE HOWLING TERROR  310 FOUR ZOAS 5     185
     OFT HE STOOD BY A HOWLING VICTIM QUESTIONING IN WORDS  . .  315 FOUR ZOAS 6  126
     BY THE FIERCE MANE STAYING [THEIR] HIS HOWLING COURSE . . .  315 FOUR ZOAS 6 * 133
     AS HE ASCENDED HOWLING LOUD THE WEB VIBRATED STRONG . . .  319 FOUR ZOAS 6   318
     DANCE ON THE RIVERS & THE ROCKS HOWLING & DRUNK WITH FURY  320 FOUR ZOAS 7   13
     ROUND HOWLING ORC WHOSE AWFUL LIMBS CAST FORTH RED SMOKE  320 FOUR ZOAS 7    17
        & FIRE
     HOWLING & RENDING HIS DARK CAVES THE AWFUL DEMON LAY  . .  320 FOUR ZOAS 7   20
     THE SPECTRE [SMILD] TERRIFIED & GAVE HER CHARGE OVER THE  328 FOUR ZOAS 7 * 332
        HOWLING ORC
     WITH SIGHS & HOWLING & DEEP SOBS THAT HE MIGHT LOSE HIS  336 FOUR ZOAS 7B    127
        RAGE
     AND ROUND THE NAMELESS SHADOWY FEMALE IN HER HOWLING TERROR  336 FOUR ZOAS 7B 145
     THEY SOUND THE CLARIONS STRONG THEY CHAIN THE HOWLING  337 FOUR ZOAS 7B      164
        CAPTIVES
     HOWLING IN DISCONTENT BLACK & HEAVY UTTERING BRUTE SOUNDS  338 FOUR ZOAS 7B  224
     HOWLING IN ALL THE NOTES OF WOE TO STAY HIS FURIOUS RAGE  339 FOUR ZOAS 7B   262
     BUT IN VAIN DELIGHTS WERE POURED FORTH ON THE HOWLING  340 FOUR ZOAS 7B      280
        MELANCHOLY
     IN [ANGUISH FOR] RAGE AGAINST THE DARK DESPAIR THE HOWLING  340 FOUR ZOAS 7B * 287
        MELANCHOLY
     SOUND LOUD THE HOWLING MUSIC INSPIRD BY LOS & ENITHARMON  344 FOUR ZOAS 8    121
        . . .
     A MALE WITHOUT A FEMALE COUNTERPART A HOWLING FIEND . . .  347 FOUR ZOAS 8   253
     SCREAMING IN BIRDS OVER THE DEEP & HOWLING IN THE WOLF . .  355 FOUR ZOAS 8 * 577
     IN THE FIERCE FLAMES THE LIMBS OF MYSTERY LAY CONSUMING  359 FOUR ZOAS 9     67
        WITH HOWLING
     I HEAR MYSTERY HOWLING IN THESE FLAMES OF CONSUMMATION . .  360 FOUR ZOAS 9  114
     HOWLING & WAILING FLY THE SOULS FROM URIZEN'S STRONG HAND  365 FOUR ZOAS 9   323
     INTO THE WINE PRESSES OF LUVAH HOWLING FELL THE CLUSTERS  376 FOUR ZOAS 9    724
     LIONS BOARS WOLVES ALL HOWLING FLEE . . . . . . . . .  427 MENTAL TRAVLER    99
     HOWLING & [DESCENDING INTO THE FLAMES & IN THE ACT OF] . .  443C LAST JUDGMNT/L PROSE
     STAMPD THE NETHER ABYSS IN TREMBLING & HOWLING & DISMAY  483 MILTON 3        26
     TILL IT SEPARATED INTO A MALE FORM HOWLING IN JEALOUSY . .  483 MILTON 3     36
     LIVING SELF MOVING MOURNING LAMENTING & HOWLING INCESSANTLY  509 MILTON 24   53
     OF SATAN LUVAH LAID THE FOUNDATION & URIZEN FINISHD IT  513 MILTON 27        2
        IN HOWLING WOE
     HOWLING THE SPECTRES FLEE THEY TAKE REFUGE IN HUMAN  515 MILTON 28           28
        LINEAMENTS
     HOWLING IN HIS SPECTRE ROUND HIS BODY HUNGRING TO DEVOUR  531 MILTON 39      18
     BENEATH A ROCK [HOWLING & LAMENTING] WHERE . . . . . .  608B V LAST JUDG/N *PROSE
     HOWLING IN PAIN REDOUNDING FROM THE ARMS OF BEULAH'S  624 JERUSALEM 5        49
        DAUGHTERS
     HOWLING IN PAIN A BLACKNING SHADOW BLACKNING DARK & OPAKE  624 JERUSALEM 6    5
     WAS LIVING PANTING LIKE A FRIGHTED WOLF AND HOWLING . . .  625 JERUSALEM 7    1
     IS HOWLING IN THE FURNACES IN FLAMES AMONG ALBION'S  626 JERUSALEM 7         39
        SPECTRES
     IN WAR & HOWLING DEATH & WOE . . . . . . . . . .  650 FIELDS FROM/J         44
     ALL THAT BEHELD HIM FLED HOWLING AND GNAWED THEIR TONGUES  662 JERUSALEM 36   8
     FROM HOWLING VICTIMS OF LAW BUILDING HEAVENS  672 JERUSALEM 43               18
        TWENTY-SEVEN-FOLD
     EVEN A LONG SEASON & A HARD JOURNEY & A HOWLING WILDERNESS  696 JERUSALEM 62  27
     THE CHARIOT WHEELS FILLED WITH EYES RAGE ALONG THE HOWLING  697 JERUSALEM 63  11
        VALLEY
     THEY SOUND THE CLARIONS STRONG THEY CHAIN THE HOWLING  699 JERUSALEM 65       6
        CAPTIVES
     HOWLING THE VICTIMS ON THE DRUID ALTARS YIELD THEIR SOULS  701 JERUSALEM 65  63
     FROM HEAVEN TO EARTH HOWLING INVISIBLE BUT NOT INVISIBLE  702 JERUSALEM 66   11
     THE KNIFE OF FLINT PASSES OVER THE HOWLING VICTIM HIS BLOOD  702 JERUSALEM 66 20
     OVERWEARIED WITH HOWLING WALES & SCOTLAND ALONE SUSTAIN  703 JERUSALEM 66    67
        THE FIGHT
     DANCING AROUND IN HOWLING PAIN CLOTHED IN THE BLOODY VEIL  704 JERUSALEM 67  16
     OF FLINT IS IN HER HAND SHE PASSES IT OVER THE HOWLING  704 JERUSALEM 67     25
        VICTIM
     AND JOYING IN THE PITY HOWLING OVER JERUSALEM'S WALLS  . .  723 JERUSALEM 80  56
     [A REDNING SKELETON IN HOWLING WOE] INSTEAD OF BEAUTY  . .  726 JERUSALEM 82 * 68
     IN HOWLING TORMENT TO BUILD STONE WALLS OF SEPARATION  736 JERUSALEM 90      12
        COMPELLING
     AND ON TYBURN'S BROOK AMONG THE HOWLING VICTIMS IN  737 JERUSALEM 90         48
        LOVELINESS
     TERRIFIED LOS SAT TO BEHOLD TREMBLING & WEEPING & HOWLING  739 JERUSALEM 91  54
     SO LOS TERRIFIED CRIES TREMBLING & WEEPING & HOWLING  739 JERUSALEM 91       59
        BEHOLDING
     HOWLING WINDS COVER HIM ROARING SEAS DASH FURIOUS AGAINST  741 JERUSALEM 94   3
        HIM
```

	PAGE	TITLE	LINE

HOWLINGS
    SUDDEN SEIZD WITH HOWLINGS DESPAIR AND BLACK NIGHT . . .   135 FRENCH REVOLTN   21
    TO TOWER HIS HOWLINGS WERE HEARD IN THE LOUVRE . . . .   135 FRENCH REVOLTN   22
    WEEPING IN DISMAL HOWLINGS BEFORE THE STERN AMERICANS   . . 203 AMERICA 16   12
    IN HOWLINGS & PANGS & FIERCE MADNESS . . . .   225 URIZEN 5   24
    HOWLINGS & HISSINGS SHRIEKS & GROANS & VOICES OF DESPAIR   243 EUROPE 12   34
    CIRCLING ROUND THE DARK DEMON WITH HOWLINGS   . . . . .   259 BOOK OF LOS 5   24
    IN JOY SHE HEARD HIS HOWLINGS & FORGOT HE WAS HER LUVAH   282 FOUR ZOAS 2   78
    IN LOS'S ARMS HOWLINGS BEGAN OVER THE BODY OF DEATH   . . . 289 FOUR ZOAS 2   335
    CIRCLING ROUND THE DARK DEMON WITH HOWLINGS DISMAY & SHARP   302 FOUR ZOAS 4   200
      BLIGHTINGS
    IN THUNDER SMOKE & SULLEN FLAMES & HOWLINGS & FURY & BLOOD   306 FOUR ZOAS 5   38
    AND TWANG THE BOWSTRING TO OUR HOWLINGS LET THINE ARROWS   306 FOUR ZOAS 5   51
      BLACK
    THE HOWLINGS GNASHINGS GROANINGS SHRIEKINGS . . . . . .   313 FOUR ZOAS 6   81
    AND HEARD THE HOWLINGS OF RED ORC DISTINCTER & DISTINCTER   319 FOUR ZOAS 6   * 291
    OF THE HOARSE WHEELS & THE TERRIFIC HOWLINGS OF WILD BEASTS 333 FOUR ZOAS 7B   33
    RISING FROM THE CONFUSION IN TEARS & HOWLINGS & DESPAIR   362 FOUR ZOAS 9   202
    . . . THEY SIEZE THE OPRESSOR HOWLINGS BEGAN   . . . . .   363 FOUR ZOAS 9   250
    AND THUS THE SHADOWY FEMALE HOWLS IN ARTICULATE HOWLINGS   499 MILTON 18   4
    HOWLINGS FILLD ALL THE DESOLATE PLACES IN ACCUSATIONS OF   500 MILTON 18   43
      SIN
    IN BLIGHTS OF THE EAST THE HEAVY ROLLER FOLLOWS IN HOWLINGS 514 MILTON 27   48
      OF WOE
    WITH JOY SHE HEARD HIS HOWLINGS & FORGOT HE WAS HER LUVAH   626 JERUSALEM 7   36
    SHUDDRING THE SPECTRE HOWLS HIS HOWLINGS TERRIFY THE NIGHT   629 JERUSALEM 10   23
    AND ALL MY CHILDREN FOLLOWD HIS LOUD HOWLINGS INTO THE DEEP 643 JERUSALEM 21   17
    WALKING & IN THE VALES IN HOWLINGS FIERCE THEN TO   696 JERUSALEM 62   41
      HIS ANVILS
    AND SHE PUT FORTH HER HAND UPON THE LOOMS IN DREADFUL   698 JERUSALEM 64   7
      HOWLINGS
    SUDDEN THEY BECOME LIKE WHAT THEY BEHOLD IN HOWLINGS &   701 JERUSALEM 65   75
      DEADLY PAIN
    ACROSS EUROPE ACROSS AFRICA IN HOWLINGS & DEADLY WAR   . . 706 JERUSALEM 68   20
HOWLS
    LOUD HOWLS THE ETERNAL WOLF THE ETERNAL LION LASHES HIS   199 AMERICA 9   2
      TAIL
    LOUD HOWLS THE ETERNAL WOLF THE ETERNAL LION LASHES HIS   199 AMERICA 9   27
      TAIL
    WHY [HOWLS] HOWL THE LION & THE WOLF WHY DO THEY   276 FOUR ZOAS 1   * 451
      ROAM ABROAD
    THE BATTLE HOWLS THE TERRORS FIRD RAGE IN THE WORK OF DEATH 343 FOUR ZOAS 8   107
    AND THUS THE SHADOWY FEMALE HOWLS IN ARTICULATE HOWLINGS   499 MILTON 18   4
    THE DOUBLE DRUM DROWNS HOWLS & GROANS THE SHRILL   509 MILTON 24   65
      FIFE SHRIEKS & CRIES
    WHERE ORC INCESSANT HOWLS BURNING IN FIRES OF ETERNAL YOUTH 517 MILTON 29   29
    ORC HOWLS ON THE ATLANTIC ENITHARMON TREMBLES ALL BEULAH   520 MILTON 31   27
      WEEPS
    BUT HOWLS ROUND IT AS A LION ROUND HIS PREY CONTINUALLY   531 MILTON 39   21
    SHUDDRING THE SPECTRE HOWLS HIS HOWLINGS TERRIFY THE NIGHT   629 JERUSALEM 10   23
    HYLE SEES IN FEAR HE HOWLS IN FURY OVER THEM HAND SEES   . . 644 JERUSALEM 21   28
    WHERE THE VICTIM NIGHTLY HOWLS BENEATH THE DRUID'S KNIFE   727 JERUSALEM 83   12
    THEM HOWLS THE WOLF OF FAMINE DEEP HEAVES THE OCEAN BLACK   741 JERUSALEM 94   16
      THUNDERING
HUDSON
    HUDSON DREW CORRECTLY . . . .   447B ANNO REYNOLDS   MARG
HUE
    ONE SPECIES OF GENERAL HUE OVER ALL IS THE CURSED THING   478D ANNO REYNOLDS   MARG
HUFFCAP
    AH MR HUFFCAP WOULD KICK THE BOTTOM OF THE PULPIT OUT   . .   48B ISLAND MOON 4   PROSE
HUGE
    WHICH NOW OUR RIVERS WERE BECOME DELVING THRO CAVERNS HUGE   300 FOUR ZOAS 4   102
    THE SPECTRE WEPT AT HIS DIRE LABOURS WHEN FROM [?LABLES]   302 FOUR ZOAS 4   * 194
      LADLES HUGE
    OR DOWN DARK PRECIPICES OR CLIMBD WITH PAIN & LABOUR HUGE   319 FOUR ZOAS 6   * 289
    AS WHEN THE EARTHQUAKE ROUZES FROM HIS DEN HIS SHOULDERS   336 FOUR ZOAS 7B   129
      HUGE
    THE FIERY DOGS ARISE THE SHOULDERS HUGE APPEAR   . . . .   336 FOUR ZOAS 7B   132
    TWILL HOLD FORTH A HUGE SPLUTTER WITH SMOKE & DAMP   . . .   550 ENGL ENCOU/N 2   6
    WITH LADLES HUGE & IRON POKERS OVER THE ISLAND WHITE   . .   637 JERUSALEM 16   21
    HIS BOSOM WIDE & SHOULDERS HUGE OVERSPREADING WONDROUS . . 708 JERUSALEM 70   3
HUGGD
    SHE HUGGD IT TO HER BREAST AND GROAND HER LAST . . . .   6 FAIR ELENOR/PS   72
HUM
    THE HUM OF MULTITUDES WERE THERE BUT MULTITUDES OF LAMBS   59 HOLY THURS/IM   7
    FOLLOW NOW THE BEETLE'S HUM . . . .   112 A DREAM/SI   19
    THE HUM OF MULTITUDES WAS THERE BUT MULTITUDES OF LAMBS   122 HOLY THURS/SI   7
    THINKS HE HAS PROVED THAT GENIUS & INSPIRATION ARE ALL   475A ANNO REYNOLDS   MARG
      A HUM
HUMAN   SEE NOT HUMAN
    ENVY AND HATE THAT THIRST FOR HUMAN GORE   . . . . . .   15 IMIT SPEN/PS   32
    THY YOUNG HANDS TORE HUMAN LIMBS AND GORGED HUMAN FLESH   38B SAMSON/PS   PROSE
    AN EASY OF [HUMAN] HUMING UNDERSTANDING   . . . .   52D ISLAND MOON 8   *PROSE
    THE FEMALES OF OUR HUMAN NATURES   . . . .   56 HAIL MATRIM/IM   8
    IF THOU SEEKEST BY HUMAN POLICY TO GUIDE THIS ARK   . . .   82B ANNO LAVATER   MARG
    KNAVERIES ARE NOT HUMAN NATURE KNAVERIES ARE KNAVERIES   82B ANNO LAVATER   MARG
    ("ART IS HIGHEST HUMAN NATURE") HUMAN NATURE IS THE   83A ANNO LAVATER   MARG
      IMAGE OF GOD
    THIS IS HUMAN POLICY AS IT IS CALLD   . . . .   85A ANNO LAVATER   MARG
    MORE HUMAN CREATURES ON THIS EARTH BESIDE THE SONS OF HAR   102 TIRIEL 2   55
    FOR MERCY HAS A HUMAN HEART . . . .   117 DIVNE IMAGE/SI   9
    PITY A HUMAN FACE . . . .   117 DIVNE IMAGE/SI   10

```
                                                           PAGE      TITLE           LINE
HUMAN    (CONTINUED)
   AND LOVE THE HUMAN FORM DIVINE  . . . . . . . . . .    117  DIVNE IMAGE/SI     11
   AND PEACE THE HUMAN DRESS   . . . . . . . . . . .      117  DIVNE IMAGE/SI     12
   PRAYS TO THE HUMAN FORM DIVINE  . . . . . . . . .      117  DIVNE IMAGE/SI     15
   AND ALL MUST LOVE THE HUMAN FORM  . . . . . . . . .    117  DIVNE IMAGE/SI     17
   REASON AND ENERGY LOVE AND HATE ARE NECESSARY TO HUMAN 149B MARRIAGE HH 3    PROSE
      EXISTENCE
   THUS MEN FORGOT THAT ALL DEITIES RESIDE IN THE HUMAN BREAST 153B MARRIAGE HH 11 PROSE
   THE FIRST PRINCIPLES OF HUMAN PERCEPTION   . . . . .   153D MARRIAGE HH 12   PROSE
   THE HUMAN IMAGE . . . . . . . . . . . . . . . . .      174A HUMAN IMAGE/N    TITLE
   [TILL THEY SOUGHT IN THE HUMAN BRAIN]  . . . . . .     174  HUMAN IMAGE/N       25
   THERE GROWS ONE IN THE HUMAN BRAIN  . . . . . . .      174  HUMAN IMAGE/N       26
   TO THE ABHORRED BIRTH OF CHERUBS IN THE HUMAN FORM  . . . 193 V DAU ALBION 5     28
   AS HUMAN BLOOD SHOOTING ITS VEINS ALL ROUND THE ORBED  197  AMERICA 4            5
      HEAVEN
   INTENSE NAKED A HUMAN FIRE FIERCE GLOWING AS THE WEDGE  . . 197  AMERICA 4         8
   REVEAL THE DRAGON THRO THE HUMAN COURSING SWIFT AS FIRE  204  AMERICA CANC B       1
   SHEWING THE TWO CONTRARY STATES OF THE HUMAN SOUL   . . . 210A SONGS OF EXPER   TITLE
   THE HUMAN ABSTRACT  . . . . . . . . . . . . . . .      217A HUMAN ABSTR/SE    TITLE
   THERE GROWS ONE IN THE HUMAN BRAIN  . . . . . . . .    217  HUMAN ABSTR/SE      24
   CRUELTY HAS A HUMAN HEART   . . . . . . . . . . .      221  DIVNE IMAGE/SE       1
   AND JEALOUSY A HUMAN FACE   . . . . . . . . . . .      221  DIVNE IMAGE/SE       2
   TERROR THE HUMAN FORM DIVINE  . . . . . . . . . .      221  DIVNE IMAGE/SE       3
   AND SECRECY THE HUMAN DRESS  . . . . . . . . . . .     221  DIVNE IMAGE/SE       4
   THE HUMAN DRESS IS FORGED IRON  . . . . . . . . .      221  DIVNE IMAGE/SE       5
   THE HUMAN FORM A FIERY FORGE  . . . . . . . . . .      221  DIVNE IMAGE/SE       6
   THE HUMAN FACE A FURNACE SEALD  . . . . . . . . .      221  DIVNE IMAGE/SE       7
   THE HUMAN HEART ITS HUNGRY GORGE  . . . . . . . .      221  DIVNE IMAGE/SE       8
   LIKE A HUMAN HEART STRUGLING & BEATING  . . . . . .    226  URIZEN 5            36
   AT THE BIRTH OF THE HUMAN SHADOW  . . . . . . . .      232  URIZEN 19          43
   THE MESHES TWISTED LIKE TO THE HUMAN BRAIN  . . . .    235  URIZEN 25          21
   IN FORM OF A HUMAN HEART  . . . . . . . . . . . .      236  URIZEN 25          44
   GO TELL THE HUMAN RACE THAT WOMAN'S LOVE IS SIN  . . . . 240  EUROPE 5           5
   ONCE OPEN TO THE HEAVENS AND ELEVATED ON THE HUMAN NECK  242  EUROPE 10         28
   AND HUMAN SOLITUDE IS PAST  . . . . . . . . . . .      243  EUROPE 13          19
   THE HUMAN RACE BEGAN TO WITHER FOR THE HEALTHY BUILT  . 246  SONG OF LOS 3     25
   ON THE HUMAN SOUL TO CAST   . . . . . . . . . . .      255  AHANIA 5           33
   BRANCHY FORMS ORGANIZING THE HUMAN  . . . . . . .      258  BOOK OF LOS 4      44
   WAS COMPLETED A HUMAN ILLUSION  . . . . . . . . .      260  BOOK OF LOS 5      56
   IN EDEN IN THE AURICULAR NERVES OF HUMAN LIFE  . . . . 264  FOUR ZOAS 1        17
   A SHADOWY HUMAN FORM WINGED & IN HIS DEPTHS  . . . .   267  FOUR ZOAS 1       127
   LUVAH AND VALA [WAKE] WOKE & [FLY] FLEW UP FROM THE HUMAN 271  FOUR ZOAS 1   *  262
      HEART
   THO THIS BRIGHT WORLD OF ALL OUR JOY IS IN THE HUMAN BRAIN 272  FOUR ZOAS 1      303
   THE HUMAN NATURE SHALL NO MORE REMAIN NOR HUMAN ACTS  . . 272  FOUR ZOAS 1      310
   FATTEND ON HUMAN BLOOD & DRUNK WITH WINE OF LIFE IS BETTER 274  FOUR ZOAS 1      389
      FAR
   BUT CLOUDS OF HUMAN SOULS MY NOSTRILS DRINK THE LIVES OF  275  FOUR ZOAS 1       393
      MEN
   LAUGHS AT THE HUMAN FORM THE LION MOCKS & THIRSTS FOR BLOOD 275  FOUR ZOAS 1     403
   TRIUMPHANT IN THE BLOODY SKY & THE HUMAN FORM IS NO MORE  275  FOUR ZOAS 1      409
   BENEATH HIS FEET SHOT THRO HIM AS HE STOOD IN THE HUMAN  280  FOUR ZOAS 2        12
      BRAIN
   SUBLIME DISTINCT THEIR LINEAMENTS DIVINE OF HUMAN BEAUTY  281  FOUR ZOAS 2       34
   IN HUMAN FORMS DISTINCT THEY STOOD ROUND URIZEN PRINCE  281  FOUR ZOAS 2        37
      OF LIGHT
   PETRIFYING ALL THE HUMAN IMAGINATION INTO ROCK & SAND  . . 281  FOUR ZOAS 2      38
   THAT HUMAN [TERROR] DELUSION TO DELIVER ALL THE SONS OF GOD 282  FOUR ZOAS 2     107
   FROM BONDAGE OF THE HUMAN FORM O FIRST BORN SON OF LIGHT  283  FOUR ZOAS 2      108
   THEIR VENTUROUS FLIGHT IN HUMAN FORMS DISTINCT THRO  284  FOUR ZOAS 2          151
      DARKNESS DEEP
   AND NOW THE HUMAN BLOOD FOAMD HIGH I SAW THAT LUVAH & VALA 294  FOUR ZOAS 3      94
   WENT DOWN THE HUMAN HEART WHERE PARADISE & ITS JOYS  294  FOUR ZOAS 3           95
      ABOUNDED
   BURST FROM ITS BONDS IN WHIRLPOOLS FIERCE ROARING WITH  295  FOUR ZOAS 3       137
      HUMAN VOICE
   INTO THE CAVERNS OF THE GRAVE & PLACES OF HUMAN SEED  . . 295  FOUR ZOAS 3      142
   AND HUMAN BONES RATTLING TOGETHER IN THE SMOKE & STAMPING 296  FOUR ZOAS 3      154
   IN MONSTROUS FORMS OF DEATH A HUMAN POLYPUS OF DEATH  . . 304  FOUR ZOAS 4      268
   IN ALBION'S BOSOM FOR IN EVERY HUMAN BOSOM THESE LIMITS  304  FOUR ZOAS 4       272
      STAND
   ON ALL THE SONS OF MEN & EVERY HUMAN SOUL TERRIFIED  . . . 317  FOUR ZOAS 6     235
   HE SUFFERD HIM TO CLIMB THAT HE MIGHT DRAW ALL HUMAN FORMS 324  FOUR ZOAS 7      164
   IT REMAIND PERMANENT A LOVELY FORM INSPIRD DIVINELY HUMAN 332  FOUR ZOAS 7      469
   BUILDED A TEMPLE IN THE IMAGE OF THE HUMAN HEART  . . .  333  FOUR ZOAS 7B       20
   NOW IN THE CAVERNS OF THE GRAVE & PLACES OF HUMAN SEED  . . 336  FOUR ZOAS 7B    124
   FROM EAST TO WEST FLOWD LIKE THE HUMAN VEINS IN RIVERS  . 337  FOUR ZOAS 7B      160
   ORC RENT HER & HIS HUMAN FORM CONSUMD IN HIS OWN FIRES  . 338  FOUR ZOAS 7B      211
   WITH JOY THE BRIGHT LIGHT & IN IT A HUMAN FORM   . . . .  342  FOUR ZOAS 8        43
   HIS HUMAN BULK WHILE THE DARK SHADOWY FEMALE [BROODS]  343  FOUR ZOAS 8     *    80
      BROODING OVER
   RAGING THEY TAKE THE HUMAN VISAGE & THE HUMAN FORM   . . . 344  FOUR ZOAS 8      111
   THE INSTRUMENTS OF SOUND & TROOP BY TROOP IN HUMAN FORMS  344  FOUR ZOAS 8      117
      THEY URGE
   FROM BONDAGE OF [THE HUMAN FORM] THESE TERRORS . . .  . . 345  FOUR ZOAS 8      158
   O THOU POOR HUMAN FORM O THOU POOR CHILD OF WOE  . . . .  348  FOUR ZOAS 8       298
   OF GOLGONOOZA HER WELL BELOVED KNOWING HE WAS ORC'S HUMAN 351  FOUR ZOAS 8      384
      REMAINS
   BEFORE ASSAULTED THE BRIGHT HUMAN FORM HE FELT HIS PORES  352  FOUR ZOAS 8       417
   AND HIS IMMENSE TAIL LASHD THE ABYSS HIS HUMAN FORM A STONE 352  FOUR ZOAS 8     428
   THAT NOT OF HIS OWN POWER HE BORE THE HUMAN FORM ERECT  . . 353  FOUR ZOAS 8      459
   TO REASSUME THE HUMAN & HE WEPT IN THE DARK DEEP  . . . .  361  FOUR ZOAS 9      163
```

HUMAN   (CONTINUED)

```
OR WHERE ARE HUMAN FEET FOR LO OUR EYES ARE IN THE HEAVENS      363 FOUR ZOAS 9       229
THE HUMAN HARVEST TO BEGIN TOWARDS THE SOUTH FIRST SPRANG       366 FOUR ZOAS 9       338
OF ORC IN JOY THEY VIEW THE HUMAN HARVEST SPRINGING UP  .  .    366 FOUR ZOAS 9       342
THE HUMAN FORM DIVINE THROWN DOWN FROM THEIR HIGH STATION       366 FOUR ZOAS 9       367
IN THE ETERNAL HEAVENS OF HUMAN [THOUGHT] IMAGINATION           366 FOUR ZOAS 9       368
   BURIED BENEATH
AGAIN REORGANIZE TILL THEY RESUME THE IMAGE OF THE HUMAN        366 FOUR ZOAS 9       372
SERVANTS TO THE INFINITE & ETERNAL OF THE HUMAN FORM    .  .    366 FOUR ZOAS 9       374
MUTTERING ALONG FROM HEAVEN TO HEAVEN HOARSE ROLL THE           372 FOUR ZOAS 9     * 564
   HUMAN FORMS
DOWN POUR THE TORRENT FLOODS OF HEAVEN ON ALL THE HUMAN         372 FOUR ZOAS 9       566
   HARVEST
OVER THE HUMAN HARVEST & OVER VALA THE SWEET WANDERER   .  .    372 FOUR ZOAS 9       576
IN PAIN THE HUMAN HARVEST WAVD IN HORRIBLE GROANS OF WOE        372 FOUR ZOAS 9       577
O DREAMS OF DEATH THE HUMAN FORM DISSOLVING COMPANIED   .  .    373 FOUR ZOAS 9       595
OF HUMAN FAMILIES THRO THE DEEP THE WINE PRESSES WERE FILLD     376 FOUR ZOAS 9       725
SO SANG THE HUMAN ODORS ROUND THE WINE PRESSES OF LUVAH         376 FOUR ZOAS 9       731
BUT IN THE WINE PRESSES THE HUMAN GRAPES SING NOT NOR DANCE     377 FOUR ZOAS 9       748
BUT THE HUMAN WINE STOOD WONDERING IN ALL THEIR DELIGHTFUL      378 FOUR ZOAS 9       799
   EXPANSES
THE POSSIBILITY OF HUMAN BEASTLINESS IN ALL ITS BRANCHES       387C ANNO WATSON     MARG
THE BASEST & MOST OPPRESSIVE OF HUMAN CODES & BEING LIKE        393C ANNO WATSON     MARG
AND THESE ARE THE GEMS OF THE HUMAN SOUL  .  .  .  .  .  .      425 MENTAL TRAVLER    33
SHE REMEMBERS NO FACE LIKE THE HUMAN DIVINE  .  .  .  .  .      429 MARY              43
CALLS TO HEAVEN FOR HUMAN BLOOD  .  .  .  .  .  .  .  .  .      431 AUGURIES          12
RAISES FROM HELL A HUMAN SOUL  .  .  .  .  .  .  .  .  .  .      431 AUGURIES          20
KEEPS THE HUMAN SOUL FROM CARE .  .  .  .  .  .  .  .  .  .      431 AUGURIES          22
THROUGHOUT ALL THESE HUMAN LANDS  .  .  .  .  .  .  .  .  .      432 AUGURIES          64
NOUGHT CAN DEFORM THE HUMAN RACE  .  .  .  .  .  .  .  .  .      433 AUGURIES          99
BUT DOES A HUMAN FORM DISPLAY  .  .  .  .  .  .  .  .  .  .      434 AUGURIES         131
KNEELING IN HUMILIATION AS REPRESENTATIVES OF THE WHOLE         443B LAST JUDGMNT/L  PROSE
   HUMAN RACE
I ALWAYS THOUGHT THAT THE HUMAN MIND WAS THE MOST PROLIFIC      471A ANNO REYNOLDS   MARG
AT THE SAME TIME I READ LOCKE ON HUMAN  .  .  .  .  .  .  .     476D ANNO REYNOLDS   MARG
AND OF THE SPORTS OF WISDOM IN THE HUMAN IMAGINATION    .  .    482 MILTON 3           3
THE SEXUAL IS THREEFOLD THE HUMAN IS FOURFOLD  .  .  .  .  .    483 MILTON 4           5
A SCHEME OF HUMAN CONDUCT INVISIBLE & INCOMPREHENSIBLE  .       483 MILTON 4          13
RETURN RETURN TO LAMBETH'S VALE O BUILDING OF HUMAN SOULS       485 MILTON 6          19
OFFER THE HUMAN VICTIMS THROUGHOUT ALL THE EARTH               491 MILTON 11           8
   AND ALBION'S
OR LIKE A HUMAN FORM A FRIEND WITH WITH WHOM HE LIVD            497 MILTON 15          27
   BENEVOLENT
IN THEIR ETERNAL SPHERES NOW HUMAN THO THEIR BODIES REMAIN      498 MILTON 17           4
   CLOSD
HIMSELF WAS HUMAN THO NOW WANDERING THRO DEATH'S VALE   .  .    498 MILTON 17           6
BUT MILTON'S HUMAN SHADOW CONTINUD JOURNEYING ABOVE  .  .  .    498 MILTON 17          18
I WILL HAVE WRITINGS WRITTEN ALL OVER IT IN HUMAN WORDS         499 MILTON 18          12
FOR I WILL PUT ON THE HUMAN FORM & TAKE THE IMAGE OF GOD        499 MILTON 18          19
ORC ANSWERD TAKE NOT THE HUMAN FORM O LOVELIEST TAKE NOT        499 MILTON 18          26
WHEN THOU ATTEMPTEST TO PUT ON THE HUMAN FORM MY WRATH  .  .    499 MILTON 18          31
AS WITH NEW CLAY A HUMAN FORM IN THE VALLEY OF BETH PEOR        500 MILTON 19          14
HIS REAL HUMAN WALKD ABOVE IN POWER AND MAJESTY  .  .  .  .     502 MILTON 20          13
HENCE THOU ART CLOTHD WITH HUMAN BEAUTY O THOU MORTAL MAN       502 MILTON 20        * 31
FOR EVERY HUMAN HEART HAS GATES OF BRASS & BARS OF ADAMANT      502 MILTON 20          34
OBSCURITIES TO HIDE FROM SATAN'S WATCH-FIENDS HUMAN LOVES       507 MILTON 23          40
NO HUMAN FORM BUT ONLY A FIBROUS VEGETATION  .  .  .  .  .      509 MILTON 24          37
WHERE HUMAN THOUGHT IS CRUSHD BENEATH THE IRON HAND OF          510 MILTON 25           5
   POWER
OF HUMAN INTELLECT NOW IS FLOCKING TO THE SOUND OF THE          510 MILTON 25          19
   TRUMPET
BUT IN THE WINE-PRESSES THE HUMAN GRAPES SING NOT NOR DANCE     513 MILTON 27          30
HOWLING THE SPECTRES FLEE THEY TAKE REFUGE IN HUMAN             515 MILTON 28          28
   LINEAMENTS
 .  .  . ARE COVERD WITH HUMAN GORE  .  .  .  .  .  .  .  .     517 MILTON 29          58
THE VEIL OF HUMAN MISERIES IS WOVEN OVER THE OCEAN   .  .  .    518 MILTON 29          62
WHO MADE HIMSELF A GOD & DESTROYED THE HUMAN FORM DIVINE        521 MILTON 32          13
BUT THE DIVINE HUMANITY & MERCY GAVE US A HUMAN FORM    .  .    521 MILTON 32          14
CALLING THE HUMAN IMAGINATION WHICH IS THE DIVINE VISION        521 MILTON 32          19
   & FRUITION
THE IMAGINATION IS NOT A STATE IT IS THE HUMAN EXISTENCE        522 MILTON 32          32
   ITSELF
A SELF-DEVOURING MONSTROUS HUMAN DEATH TWENTY SEVEN FOLD        524 MILTON 34          26
THOSE VISIONS OF HUMAN LIFE & SHADOWS OF WISDOM & KNOWLEDGE     525 MILTON 34          55
DESCENDING DOWN INTO MY GARDEN A HUMAN WONDER OF GOD    .  .    528 MILTON 37          13
REACHING FROM HEAVEN TO EARTH A CLOUD & HUMAN FORM   .  .  .    528 MILTON 37          14
OF FORTY-EIGHT DEFORMED HUMAN WONDERS OF THE ALMIGHTY  .  .     529 MILTON 37          54
HUMAN WITH TRUMPETS INNUMERABLE SOUNDING ARTICULATE  .  .  .    530 MILTON 39           7
HIDING THE HUMAN LINEAMENTS AS WITH AN ARK & CURTAINS  .  .     533 MILTON 41          26
ALTHO OUR HUMAN POWER CAN SUSTAIN THE SEVERE CONTENTIONS        533 MILTON 41          32
PANTS IN THE VALES OF LAMBETH WEEPING OER HER HUMAN HARVEST     535 MILTON 42          33
RINTRAH & PALAMABRON VIEW THE HUMAN HARVEST BENEATH  .  .  .    535 MILTON 42          36
RATHER THAN [LET] BE SUCH A BLIND HUMAN FOOL  .  .  .  .  .     550 WHEN I SEE/N        7
OF UNIVERSAL HUMAN LIFE BEYOND WHICH NATURE NEVER STEPS        567C DESC CAT 3       PROSE
CHARACTERS OF HUMAN LIFE APPEAR TO POETS IN ALL AGES    .  .   571B DESC CAT 3       PROSE
INTO CORPOREAL COMMAND WHEREBY HUMAN SACRIFICE  .  .  .  .  .   578A DESC CAT 5       PROSE
THE STRONG MAN REPRESENTS THE HUMAN SUBLIME  .  .  .  .  .      578A DESC CAT 5       PROSE
THE BEAUTIFUL MAN REPRESENTS THE HUMAN PATHETIC  .  .  .  .     578A DESC CAT 5       PROSE
THE UGLY MAN REPRESENTS THE HUMAN REASON  .  .  .  .  .  .      578B DESC CAT 5       PROSE
ANTIQUES SUPERIOR THEY CANNOT BE FOR HUMAN POWER CANNOT        579C DESC CAT 5       PROSE
GOTHIC GRECIAN HINDOO AND EGYPTIAN ARE THE EXTENT OF THE       579D DESC CAT 5       PROSE
   HUMAN MIND
```

```
                                                             PAGE      TITLE        LINE
HUMAN    (CONTINUED)
    THE HUMAN MIND CANNOT GO BEYOND THE GIFT OF GOD THE HOLY   579D DESC CAT 5      PROSE
      GHOST
    OF UNIVERSAL HUMAN LIFE BEYOND WHICH NATURE NEVER STEPS    590D CHAUCER 2       PROSE
    OF HUMAN CHARACTERS AS THEY APPEAR AGE AFTER AGE   . . .   591A PUB ADDRESS/N   TITLE
    THEY SEEM TO ME TO BE SOMETHING ELSE BESIDES HUMAN LIFE    600A PUB ADDRESS/N   PROSE
    THE HUMAN IMAGINATION WHO APPEARD TO ME AS   . . . . .     606A V LAST JUDG/N   PROSE
    AS MUCH ART AS A PASTEBOARD MAN IS HUMAN   . . . . . .     611B V LAST JUDG/N   PROSE
    ETERNAL REALITIES AS THEY EXIST IN THE HUMAN IMAGINATION   613C V LAST JUDG/N   PROSE
    OF THE HUMAN RACE WHO HATE WHAT YOU CALL MORAL VIRTUE  .   616A V LAST JUDG/N   PROSE
    POETRY FETTERD FETTERS THE HUMAN RACE   . . . . . . .      621D JERUSALEM 3     PROSE
    RESOUND INTO THE UNBOUNDED NIGHT EVERY HUMAN PERFECTION    623 JERUSALEM 5         7
    EVER EXPANDING IN THE BOSOM OF GOD THE HUMAN IMAGINATION   623 JERUSALEM 5        20
    TO DEVOUR LOS'S HUMAN PERFECTION BUT WHEN HE SAW THAT LOS  625 JERUSALEM 6    *   14
    FROM EVERY-ONE OF THE FOUR REGIONS OF HUMAN MAJESTY   . .  640 JERUSALEM 18        1
    RAGING AGAINST THEIR HUMAN NATURES RAVNING TO GORMANDIZE   641 JERUSALEM 19       23
    THE HUMAN MAJESTY AND BEAUTY OF THE TWENTYFOUR   . . .     641 JERUSALEM 19       24
    WHEREFORE HAST THOU SHUT ME INTO THE WINTER OF HUMAN LIFE  642 JERUSALEM 20        5
    I CANNOT PUT OFF THE HUMAN FORM I STRIVE BUT STRIVE IN     643 JERUSALEM 20       29
      VAIN
    DWELLS FROM ETERNITY WIDE SEPARATED FROM THE HUMAN SOUL    646 JERUSALEM 23       30
    WHAT HAVE I SAID WHAT HAVE I DONE O ALL-POWERFUL HUMAN     646 JERUSALEM 24        1
      WORDS
    O HUMAN IMAGINATION O DIVINE BODY I HAVE CRUCIFIED   . .   647 JERUSALEM 24       23
    THERE BABYLON IS BUILDED IN THE WASTE FOUNDED IN HUMAN     647 JERUSALEM 24       25
      DESOLATION
    RIOTED IN HUMAN GORE  . . . . . . . . . . . . . .         650 FIELDS FROM/J      31
    IN OFFERINGS OF HUMAN LIFE   . . . . . . . . . . .        650 FIELDS FROM/J      32
    THE RHINE WAS RED WITH HUMAN BLOOD   . . . . . . . .      651 FIELDS FROM/J      45
    HE WITHERD UP THE HUMAN FORM   . . . . . . . . . .        651 FIELDS FROM/J      53
    STILL WAS THE HUMAN FORM DIVINE   . . . . . . . . .       651 FIELDS FROM/J      58
    AND THINE THE HUMAN FACE & THINE   . . . . . . . .        651 FIELDS FROM/J      61
    THE HUMAN HANDS & FEET & BREATH   . . . . . . . . .       651 FIELDS FROM/J      62
    OF GOD WHO DWELLS IN CHAOS HIDDEN FROM THE HUMAN SIGHT  .  652 JERUSALEM 28       16
    MOST ANCIENT PROMONTORY AND IN THE SUN A HUMAN FORM APPEARD 653 JERUSALEM 29       4
    SO SAYING THE MILD SUN INCLOSD THE HUMAN FAMILY   . . .   653 JERUSALEM 29       27
    AND NOW THE HUMAN BLOOD FOAMD HIGH THE SPIRITS LUVAH & VALA 655 JERUSALEM 29      73
    WENT DOWN THE HUMAN HEART WHERE PARADISE & ITS JOYS        655 JERUSALEM 29       74
      ABOUNDED
    OF STONES AND ROCKS HE TOOK HIS WAY FOR HUMAN FORM WAS NONE 657 JERUSALEM 31      27
    I AM YOUR RATIONAL POWER O ALBION & THAT HUMAN FORM   . .  659 JERUSALEM 33        5
    THE IMAGINATIVE HUMAN FORM IS BUT A BREATHING OF VALA  .   660 JERUSALEM 33       49
    IN ALBION'S BOSOM FOR IN EVERY HUMAN BOSOM THOSE LIMITS    662 JERUSALEM 35        2
      STAND
    THUNDERS OF DEADLY WAR THE FEVER OF THE HUMAN SOUL   . .   664 JERUSALEM 38        9
    I BEHOLD LONDON A HUMAN AWFUL WONDER OF GOD   . . . .      665 JERUSALEM 38       29
    ARE ALSO MEN EVERY THING IS HUMAN MIGHTY SUBLIME  . . .    665 JERUSALEM 38       48
    FOR HUMAN BEAUTY KNOWS IT NOT NOR CAN MERCY FIND IT BUT    666 JERUSALEM 39        6
    A WEARINESS TO ME & THE HUMAN FOOTSTEP IS A TERROR TO ME   666 JERUSALEM 39       23
    OF HUMAN MAJESTY THE LIVING CREATURES WEPT ALOUD AS THEY   667 JERUSALEM 40       23
    APPEARD AND THEY WERE ONE IN HIM A HUMAN VISION   . . .    667 JERUSALEM 40       46
    HUMAN DIVINE JESUS THE SAVIOUR BLESSED FOR EVER AND EVER   667 JERUSALEM 40       47
    ALBION THEY CURSE THEIR HUMAN KINDNESS & AFFECTION   . .   671 JERUSALEM 42       60
    IN THE DREAMS OF ULRO THEY REPENT OF THEIR HUMAN KINDNESS  671 JERUSALEM 42       62
    THEIR HUMAN MAJESTIC FORMS SIT UP UPON THEIR COUCHES  .    671 JERUSALEM 42       66
    ONE ERROR NOT REMOVD WILL DESTROY A HUMAN SOUL   . . .     676 JERUSALEM 46       11
    WITHIN THE HUMAN HEART WHOSE GATES CLOSED WITH SOLEMN SOUND 678 JERUSALEM 48      25
    WHERE THE HUMAN HARVEST WAVES ABUNDANT IN THE BEAMS OF EDEN 678 JERUSALEM 48      34
    FEMALE AND LOVELY STRUGGLING TO PUT OFF THE HUMAN FORM  .  678 JERUSALEM 48       49
    WITHERING THE HUMAN FORM BY LAWS OF SACRIFICE FOR SIN  .   679 JERUSALEM 49       25
    SATAN IS THE STATE OF DEATH & NOT A HUMAN EXISTENCE  . .   680 JERUSALEM 49       67
    LEARN THEREFORE O SISTERS TO DISTINGUISH THE ETERNAL HUMAN 680 JERUSALEM 49       72
    HE NEVER CAN BE A FRIEND TO THE HUMAN RACE   . . . . .     681D JERUSALEM 52     PROSE
    AND YOU ARE SO YOU ARE ALSO THE ENEMIES OF THE HUMAN RACE  682A JERUSALEM 52     PROSE
    TALKING OF THE VIRTUES OF THE HUMAN HEART AND  . . . .     682D JERUSALEM 52     PROSE
    OUTSIDE OF THE GATES OF THE HUMAN HEART BENEATH BEULAH  .  684 JERUSALEM 53       16
    LET THE HUMAN ORGANS BE KEPT IN THEIR PERFECT INTEGRITY    686 JERUSALEM 55       36
    SILENCE REMAIND & EVERY ONE RESUMD HIS HUMAN MAJESTY  .    687 JERUSALEM 55       47
    BETWEEN DWELLS A DAUGHTER OF BEULAH TO FEED THE HUMAN      688 JERUSALEM 56       10
      VEGETABLE
    THAT THOU O HUMAN IMAGINATION O DIVINE BODY ART ALL   .    693 JERUSALEM 60       57
    WHERE THE HUMAN VICTIMS HOWL TO THE MOON & THOR & FRIGA    697 JERUSALEM 63        9
    NO HUMAN FORM BUT SEXUAL & A LITTLE WEEPING INFANT PALE    697 JERUSALEM 63       20
      REFLECTED
    INSTEAD OF HUMAN VICTIMS BY THE DAUGHTERS OF ALBION        697 JERUSALEM 63       31
      & CANAAN
    SHE CRIES THE HUMAN IS BUT A WORM & THOU O MALE THOU ART   698 JERUSALEM 64       12
    THE HUMAN DIVINE IS WOMAN'S SHADOW A VAPOR IN THE SUMMER'S 698 JERUSALEM 64       14
      HEAT
    HUMAN MISERIES TURND FIERCE WITH THE LIVES OF MEN ALONG    699 JERUSALEM 64       33
      THE VALLEY
    THE HUMAN FORM BEGAN TO BE ALTERD BY THE DAUGHTERS         703 JERUSALEM 66       46
      OF ALBION
    O THOU POOR HUMAN FORM SAID SHE O THOU POOR CHILD OF WOE   705 JERUSALEM 67       44
    CLOTHED IN THE SKIN OF THE VICTIM BLOOD HUMAN BLOOD IS     706 JERUSALEM 68       33
      THE LIFE
    FOR ALL THINGS EXIST IN THE HUMAN IMAGINATION   . . . .    707 JERUSALEM 69       25
    ALL ARE HUMAN & WHEN YOU ENTER INTO THEIR BOSOMS YOU WALK  709 JERUSALEM 71       16
    AND EVERY HUMAN VEGETATED FORM IN ITS INWARD RECESSES  .   714 JERUSALEM 73       50
    THEY BECAME SPECTRES & THEIR HUMAN BODIES WERE REPOSED  .  714 JERUSALEM 74        8
    TO DEVOUR THE HUMAN WHY DOST THOU WEEP UPON THE WIND AMONG 721 JERUSALEM 79       72
    NAKED AMONG THE HUMAN CLUSTERS BRINGING WINE OF ANGUISH    726 JERUSALEM 82       65
```

	PAGE	TITLE	LINE

HUMAN (CONTINUED)
```
    THE SEEDS OF CITIES & OF VILLAGES IN THE HUMAN BOSOM      . .    728 JERUSALEM 83         55
    THE HUMAN FOUR-FOLD FORMS MINGLE ALSO IN THUNDERS                733 JERUSALEM 88          7
        OF INTELLECT
    COVERD WITH PRECIOUS STONES A HUMAN DRAGON TERRIBLE . . .        734 JERUSALEM 89         11
    OF FIRE SPEAKING THE WORDS OF ETERNITY IN HUMAN FORMS IN         742 JERUSALEM 95          9
        DIREFUL
    ACCORDING TO THE HUMAN NERVES OF SENSATION . . . . . .   . .     745 JERUSALEM 98         15
    OF HUMAN IMAGINATION THROUGHOUT ALL THE THREE REGIONS           746 JERUSALEM 98         32
        IMMENSE
    WAS HUMAN ACCORDING TO THE EXPANSION OR CONTRACTION . . .        746 JERUSALEM 98         36
    . . . WHERE ARE ALL HIS HUMAN SACRIFICES       . . . . .  .     746 JERUSALEM 98       *  48
    ALL HUMAN FORMS IDENTIFIED EVEN TREE METAL EARTH & STONE         747 JERUSALEM 99          1
        ALL
    HUMAN FORMS IDENTIFIED LIVING GOING FORTH & RETURNING            747 JERUSALEM 99          2
        WEARIED
    THE NAKED HUMAN FORM DIVINE . . . . . . . . . . .  . . .         755 EV GOSPEL(E)/N       66
    IMAGINATION OR THE HUMAN ETERNAL BODY IN EVERY MAN   . . .      773C ANNO BERKELEY       MARG
    ABEL AMONG THE ELOHIM A HUMAN VICTIM I WANDER I AM THEIR         780 GHOST ABEL 1         10
        HOUSE
    SATAN I WILL HAVE HUMAN BLOOD & NOT THE BLOOD OF BULLS           780 GHOST ABEL 2         13
        OR GOATS
    OF MEN HENCE I AM GOD OF MEN THOU HUMAN O JEHOVAH      . .       780 GHOST ABEL 2         15
    CAIN'S CITY BUILT WITH HUMAN BLOOD NOT BLOOD OF BULLS            781 GHOST ABEL 2         17
        & GOATS
    OF HUMAN VEGETATION & BEHOLD   . . . . . . . . . . .  . .        806 TO MRS BUTTS/L       4
    PELPHAM MEN ARE THE MILDEST OF THE HUMAN RACE IF IT IS THE      810C LETTER 20          PROSE
    THE HEAVENS DROP WITH HUMAN GORE . . . . . . . .  . . .          818 HAPPINESS/L         82
    THE CHIMNEY SWEEPER A LITTLE BLACK THING &C THE HUMAN           SUPP LETTER 66A        *PROSE
        ABSTRACT
HUMANE
    CIVIL IS CHRISTIANITY OR RELIGION OR WHATEVER IS HUMANE         398B ANNO BACON         MARG
    HUMANE & POLITE ACCOMPLISHMENTS SUCH HAVE     . . . . .  .      810D LETTER 21          PROSE
HUMAN FORMD
    LO THESE HUMAN FORMD SPIRITS IN SMILING HIPOCRISY WAR    . .     245 SONG OF LOS 3        13
    HUMAN FORMD SWIFT I RAN   . . . . . . . . . . .  . . .           804 TO BUTTS/L          22
HUMANISES
    ("HIM WHO HUMANISES ALL ADORE I KNOW BUT OF ONE ")              71C ANNO LAVATER        MARG
        SWEET
HUMANITIES
    TELL THEM TO OBEY THEIR HUMANITIES & NOT PRETEND HOLINESS        738 JERUSALEM 91          6
HUMANITY     SEE DIVINE-HUMANITY
    THE STAMINAL VIRTUES OF HUMANITY BY THE SAME NAME THAT   . .     88C ANNO LAVATER        MARG
    ENSLAVD HUMANITY PUT ON HE BECAME WHAT HE BEHELD . . . .         302 FOUR ZOAS 4         203
    ENSLAVD HUMANITY PUT ON HE BECAME WHAT HE BEHELD    . . .        305 FOUR ZOAS 4         286
    BUT [ALL] THOU O UNIVERSAL HUMANITY WHO IS ONE MAN BLESSED       347 FOUR ZOAS 8         232
        FOR EVER
    [UNTILL] WHEN [THE] HIS HUMANITY AWAKE . . . . . . .  . .        421 EACH MAN/N           3
    THE ETERNAL CREATION FLOWING FROM THE DIVINE HUMANITY   .       444C LAST JUDGMNT/L     PROSE
    THE ETERNAL GREAT HUMANITY DIVINE PLANTED HIS PARADISE   .       481 MILTON 2             8
    A MIGHTY FIEND AGAINST THE DIVINE HUMANITY MUSTRING TO WAR       491 MILTON 10           11
    WHO IS THE ETERNAL ALL-PROTECTING DIVINE HUMANITY    . .         495 MILTON 14            2
    EVEN PITY & HUMANITY BUT MY CLOTHING SHALL BE CRUELTY  . .       499 MILTON 18           20
    NOW ALBION'S SLEEPING HUMANITY BEGAN TO TURN UPON HIS COUCH      502 MILTON 20           25
    THUS MILTON FELL THRO ALBION'S HEART TRAVELLING OUTSIDE          502 MILTON 20           41
        OF HUMANITY
    AND IT IS THUS CREATED LO THE ETERNAL GREAT HUMANITY    .        519 MILTON 30           15
    BUT THE DIVINE HUMANITY & MERCY GAVE US A HUMAN FORM   . .       521 MILTON 32           14
    ITS OWN QUALITIES WHICH ARE SERVANTS OF HUMANITY NOT GODS        521 MILTON 32           21
        OR LORDS
    AND THE FOUR STATES OF HUMANITY IN ITS REPOSE  . . . .          523 MILTON 34             8
    THE ENEMIES OF HUMANITY EXCEPT IN A FEMALE FORM    . . .         527 MILTON 36           15
    MILTON WITHIN HIS SLEEPING HUMANITY TREMBLING & SHUDDRING        529 MILTON 38           10
    THE ETERNAL GREAT HUMANITY DIVINE SURROUNDED BY   . . .          531 MILTON 39           27
    WHEN ERECTED INTO GODS BECOME DESTRUCTIVE TO HUMANITY   .       571C DESC CAT 3         PROSE
    FOR WHEN SEPARATED FROM MAN OR HUMANITY WHO IS JESUS    .       571C DESC CAT 3         PROSE
    AND HIS REAL HUMANITY SLAIN ON THE STEMS OF GENERATION   .      578B DESC CAT 5         PROSE
    OF HUMANITY & OF ART THE WORD MACHINATION [ ?SEEMS ]    . .     603B PUB ADDR AD/N     *PROSE
    ALL SPRINGING FROM THE DIVINE HUMANITY     . . . . .  .         612D V LAST JUDG/N      PROSE
    FOUNDATION OF SOCIETY WHICH IS HUMANITY ITSELF    . . .         613A V LAST JUDG/N     *PROSE
    THE ETERNAL BIRTHS OF INTELLECT FROM THE DIVINE HUMANITY        613D V LAST JUDG/N      PROSE
    HUMANITY SHALL BE NO MORE BUT WAR & PRINCEDOM & VICTORY          622 JERUSALEM 4         32
    AND TO DEVOUR THE SLEEPING HUMANITY OF ALBION IN RAGE &          623 JERUSALEM 5         30
        HUNGER
    THESE ARE THE FOUR FACES TOWARDS THE FOUR WORLDS                 632 JERUSALEM 12        57
        OF HUMANITY
    I SEE THE FOUR-FOLD MAN THE HUMANITY IN DEADLY SLEEP    . .      635 JERUSALEM 15         6
    APPEARD A ROCKY FORM AGAINST THE DIVINE HUMANITY . . . .         642 JERUSALEM 19        35
    WHICH WAY SOEVER I TURN I BEHOLD HUMANITY AND PITY    . . .      646 JERUSALEM 23        19
    HAD BROUGHT HUMANITY INTO A FEMININE TABERNACLE   . . .         652B JERUSALEM 27       PROSE
    FORTIFICATION AGAINST THE DIVINE HUMANITY AND MERCY   . .        653 JERUSALEM 28        26
    BACK SAFE TO THEIR HUMANITY AS DOVES TO THEIR WINDOWS   .        655 JERUSALEM 30        13
    HUMANITY KNOWS NOT OF SEX WHEREFORE ARE SEXES IN BEULAH          656 JERUSALEM 30        33
    IN REGIONS OF HUMANITY IN LONDON'S OPENING STREETS   . .         665 JERUSALEM 38        43
    IN THE FOURTH REGION OF HUMANITY URTHONA NAMD . . . . .          666 JERUSALEM 39         7
    WHEN HIS HUMANITY AWAKE . . . . . . . . . . .  . . .             669 EACH MAN/J           3
    IN THE FOUR REGIONS OF HUMANITY EAST & WEST & NORTH & SOUTH      671 JERUSALEM 42        79
    INSLAVD TO THE MOST POWERFUL SELFHOOD TO MURDER THE DIVINE       679 JERUSALEM 49        30
        HUMANITY
    THAT THERE WAS A GOD OF MERCY O MERCY O DIVINE HUMANITY          695 JERUSALEM 61        43
    IN THE TWO CONTRARIES OF HUMANITY & IN THE FOUR REGIONS          699 JERUSALEM 65         4
    PLOTTING TO DEVOUR ALBION'S BODY OF HUMANITY & LOVE  . . .       708 JERUSALEM 70         9
```

948

```
                                                        PAGE     TITLE           LINE
HUMANITY    (CONTINUED)
        THE SLEEPING HUMANITY LOS WITH HIS MACE OF IRON  . . . .   718 JERUSALEM 78       3
        DRAWING THEIR ULRO VOIDNESS ROUND THE FOUR-FOLD HUMANITY   719 JERUSALEM 78      20
        THESE CRUEL DRUID TEMPLES O VALA HUMANITY IS FAR ABOVE  . .  721 JERUSALEM 79     73
        I HAVE NAMED HIM JEHOVAH OF HOSTS HUMANITY IS BECOME    .   724 JERUSALEM 81      13
        HUMANITY THE GREAT DELUSION IS CHANGD TO WAR & SACRIFICE    726 JERUSALEM 82      42
        WHICH STAND BOTH MALE & FEMALE AT THE GATES OF EACH        733 JERUSALEM 88      11
            HUMANITY
        AND HIS MATERNAL HUMANITY MUST BE PUT OFF ETERNALLY  . . .  737 JERUSALEM 90      36
        HUMANITY CALLING IT NATURE AND NATURAL RELIGION  . . . .   737 JERUSALEM 90      66
        GOD THAN THAT GOD WHO IS THE INTELLECTUAL FOUNTAIN OF      738 JERUSALEM 91      11
            HUMANITY
        WAS THE LORD THE UNIVERSAL HUMANITY & ALBION SAW HIS FORM   743 JERUSALEM 96       5
        FOUNTAINS OF LIVING WATERS FLOWING FROM THE HUMANITY DIVINE  744 JERUSALEM 96     37
        . . . CHARIOTS OF HUMANITY DIVINE INCOMPREHENSIBLE         745 JERUSALEM 98      24
        AND THE FOUR FACES OF HUMANITY FRONTING THE FOUR CARDINAL   745 JERUSALEM 98      26
            POINTS
        THINE OWN HUMANITY LEARN TO ADORE  . . . . . . . . .       750 EV GOSPEL(C)/N    42
        THY OWN HUMANITY LEARN TO ADORE  . . . . . . . . . .       752 EV GOSPEL(D)/N    76
        SPONTANEOUS EFFUSION OF HUMANITY CONGENIAL TO THE WANTS    802A LETTER 14        PROSE
HUMANIZE
        THEY HUMANIZE IN THE FIERCE BATTLE WHERE IN DIREFUL PAIN    344 FOUR ZOAS 8      115
        AND THE ALL WONDROUS SERPENT CLOTHED IN GEMS & RICH ARRAY   746 JERUSALEM 98      44
            HUMANIZE
HUMANIZED
        HUMANIZED ON THE SUNSHINE HOLIDAY  . . . . . . . . .       618B ILLUS MILTON    PROSE
HUMANIZING
        THEN AS ANOTHER SELF ASTONISHD HUMANIZING & IN TEARS   . .  328 FOUR ZOAS 7      340
        TERRIFIC INTO THE PAIND HEAVENS THE FRUIT TREES HUMANIZING   335 FOUR ZOAS 7B    101
        JOY THRILLD THRO ALL THE FURIOUS FORM OF THARMAS HUMANIZING   373 FOUR ZOAS 9  * 613
HUMBER
        HUMBER & TRENT ROLL DREADFUL BEFORE THE SEVENTH FURNACE    636 JERUSALEM 16      16
        THE HUMBER & THE SEVERN ARE DRUNK WITH THE BLOOD OF THE    703 JERUSALEM 66      63
            SLAIN
HUMBLE    SEE HBLE
        O WHAT AN HUMBLE GARB TRUE JOY PUTS ON  . . . . . . .       37A CONTEMPLATN/PS   PROSE
        ("THE HUMBLE...THE LOVING...ETERNAL LOVE") SWEET . . . .    68C ANNO LAVATER     MARG
        COMPELLD TO PRAY REPUGNANT & TO HUMBLE THE IMMORTAL SPIRIT   110 TIRIEL 8         36
        THE LILLY OF THE VALLEY BREATHING IN THE HUMBLE GRASS   . .  127 BOOK OF THEL 1   15
        SAYING REJOICE THOU HUMBLE GRASS THOU NEW-BORN LILLY FLOWER   127 BOOK OF THEL 1  21
        IN MILKY FONDNESS THEN ON THEL SHE FIXD HER HUMBLE EYES     129 BOOK OF THEL 4    9
        THE [COWARD] HUMBLE SHEEP A THREATNING HORN  . . . . .      171 THE LILLY/N       2
        THE HUMBLE SHEEP A THREATNING HORN  . . . . . . . .         215 THE LILLY/SE      2
        TILL FIRED WITH ARDOUR FRESH RECRUITED IN ITS HUMBLE       287 FOUR ZOAS 2     * 279
            [SPRING] SEASON
        I WILL HUMBLE MY BEAUTY I WILL NOT DRESS FINE  . . . . .    428 MARY             29
        ON THE RIGHT HAND OF THESE RISE THE DIFFIDENT & HUMBLE  . .  610D V LAST JUDG/N   PROSE
        WAS JESUS HUMBLE OR DID HE  . . . . . . . . . .            750 EV GOSPEL(C)/N     1
        BUT HUMBLE AS A LAMB OR AN ASS  . . . . . . . . . .        750 EV GOSPEL(C)/N    29
        GOD WANTS NOT MAN TO HUMBLE HIMSELF  . . . . . . . .       750 EV GOSPEL(C)/N    31
        HUMBLE TOWARD GOD HAUGHTY TOWARD MAN  . . . . . . .        750 EV GOSPEL(C)/N    33
        [WHY DOST THOU HUMBLE THYSELF TO ME]  . . . . . . .        750 EV GOSPEL(C)/N    37
        WAS JESUS HUMBLE OR DID HE  . . . . . . . . . .            751 EV GOSPEL(D)/N     1
        BOAST OF HIGH THINGS WITH HUMBLE TONE  . . . . . . .       751 EV GOSPEL(D)/N     3
        BUT HUMBLE AS A LAMB OR ASS  . . . . . . . . . .           752 EV GOSPEL(D)/N    63
        GOD WANTS NOT MAN TO HUMBLE HIMSELF  . . . . . . .         752 EV GOSPEL(D)/N    65
        HUMBLE TO GOD HAUGHTY TO MAN  . . . . . . . . .            752 EV GOSPEL(D)/N    68
        I AM REVD SIR YOUR VERY HUMBLE SERVT  . . . . . . .        792D LETTER 4         PROSE
        SO PRAYS A FELLOW SUFFERER & YOUR HUMBLE SERVANT  . . .    796D LETTER 8         PROSE
        I REMAIN DEAR SIR YOUR HUMBLE SERVANT  . . . . . . .       797B LETTER 9         PROSE
        FROM THE WICKED HORSE & FROM YOUR INNOCENT HUMBLE SERVANT   833D LETTER 33        PROSE
        MAKE WILL BE THANKFULLY RECIEVD BY SIR YOUR HUMBLE SERVANT   866D LETTER 65       PROSE
HUMBLED
        LET GWIN BE HUMBLED    . . . . . . . . . . . . .           11 GWIN KING/PS       12
        LET GWIN BE HUMBLED    . . . . . . . . . . . . .           12 GWIN KING/PS       30
        BEWARE O PROUD THOU SHALT BE HUMBLED THY CRUEL BROW  . . .   34B KING JOHN/PS     PROSE
        AND WHEN HE HUMBLED HIMSELF TO GOD  . . . . . . .          750 EV GOSPEL(C)/N    35
        AND WHEN HE HUMBLED HIMSELF TO GOD  . . . . . . .          752 EV GOSPEL(D)/N    71
HUMBLEST
        IF THOU HUMBLEST THYSELF THOU HUMBLEST ME  . . . . .       750 EV GOSPEL(C)/N    39
        IF THOU HUMBLEST THYSELF THOU HUMBLEST ME  . . . . .       752 EV GOSPEL(D)/N    73
HUMBLY
        I HUMBLY BOW IN ALL MY SIN BEFORE THE THRONE DIVINE  . . .  493 MILTON 13         3
HUME
        THIS VOLTAIRE & ROUSSEAU THIS HUME & GIBBON & BOLINGBROKE   532 MILTON 40         12
        SUCH AS HUME GIBBON AND VOLTAIRE CANNOT WITH ALL THEIR  . .  579A DESC CAT 5      PROSE
        THESE ARE NEITHER THE EXCLUSIVE PROPERTY OF HUME GIBBON NOR  579A DESC CAT 5      PROSE
        VOLTAIRE ROUSSEAU GIBBON HUME  . . . . . . . . .          682C JERUSALEM 52      PROSE
HUMERI    SEE OS HUMERI
HUMID
        AND WHY IT SCATTERS ITS BRIGHT BEAUTY THRO THE HUMID AIR   128 BOOK OF THEL 2    15
HUMILIATION
        KNEELING IN HUMILIATION AS REPRESENTATIVES OF THE WHOLE    443B LAST JUDGMNT/L   PROSE
            HUMAN RACE
        HUMILIATION & IN EXULTATION RISE THRO THE AIR WITH THEIR   443D LAST JUDGMNT/L   PROSE
            CHILDREN
        CONFESSING THEIR CRIME WITH HUMILIATION AND SORROW   . . .  525 MILTON 35         33
        JUDGMENT SEAT IN HUMILIATION ABEL SURROUNDED BY INNOCENTS   606B V LAST JUDG/N   PROSE
        IN HUMILIATION BEFORE THAT OF DEATH ON THE LEFT  . . . .   612B V LAST JUDG/N   PROSE
        THE HUMILIATION OF THE REASONING & DOUBTING SELFHOOD  . .   614C V LAST JUDG/N  *PROSE
        THEY KNEELD AROUND THE COUCH OF DEATH IN DEEP HUMILIATION   668 JERUSALEM 41      24
        OF RESENTMENT AGAINST MAN AND DEVIL AND OF HUMILIATION     864B LETTER 61        PROSE
            BEFORE GOD
```

```
                                                    PAGE     TITLE              LINE
HUMILIATION    (CONTINUED)
   [WHO WILL OR CAN ?ENDURE ?SUCH HUMILIATION]   . . . . .  SUPP ANNO REYNOLDS  * MARG
HUMILITY
   LO THEN HUMILITY TAKE IT AND WEAR IT IN THINE HEART  . . .   37A CONTEMPLATN/PS  PROSE
   SHE BRINGS HUMILITY TO MAN TAKE HER SHE SAYS  . . . . . .    42A THEN SHE BORE    PROSE
   LORD OF ALL [ HUMILITY HER DAUGHTER ]  . . . . . . . . .     42A THEN SHE BORE    PROSE
   FOR WHAT ARE ALL CRAWLERS BUT MIMICKERS OF HUMILITY & LOVE   68D ANNO LAVATER     MARG
   ("WANT OF FRIENDS ARGUES WANT OF HUMILITY OR COURAGE")       74A ANNO LAVATER     MARG
      UNEASY
   ("NOR HUMILITY IF MORTIFIED WHEN YOU ARE NOT NOTICED ")      82D ANNO LAVATER     MARG
      UNEASY
   ("DESIRE OF BEING UNNOTICED UNOBSERVED ") TRUE HUMILITY      83C ANNO LAVATER     MARG
   IN MILD HUMILITY  . . . . . . . . . . . . . . . . . .  . .  149 MARRIAGE HH 2      18
   THEN HUMILITY TAKES ITS ROOT  . . . . . . . . . . . . . .   174 HUMAN IMAGE/N      12
   THEN HUMILITY TAKES ITS ROOT  . . . . . . . . . . . . . .   217 HUMAN ABSTR/SE     11
   AND SOMETIMES WEEPING BEFORE ORC IN HUMILITY & TREMBLING    357 FOUR ZOAS 8       613
   WITH EYES OF SOFT HUMILITY & WONDER LOVE & AWE  . . . .     520 MILTON 31          38
   ALWAYS COMFORTING THE REMEMBRANCE THE FLOORS HUMILITY  . .  632 JERUSALEM 12       36
   IF HUMILITY IS CHRISTIANITY YOU O JEWS ARE THE TRUE        652A JERUSALEM 27      PROSE
      CHRISTIANS
   AM I NOT BACON & NEWTON & LOCKE WHO TEACH HUMILITY TO MAN   685 JERUSALEM 54       17
   GIVE ANY PROOFS OF HUMILITY . . . . . . . . . . . . . . .   750 EV GOSPEL(C)/N      2
   AND SO HE MUST MEAN CONCERNING HUMILITY . . . . . . . . .   750 EV GOSPEL(C)/N     22
   GIVE ANY PROOFS OF HUMILITY . . . . . . . . . . . . . . .   751 EV GOSPEL(D)/N      2
   WHAT I CALLD HUMILITY THEY CALLD PRIDE  . . . . . . . .     751 EV GOSPEL(D)/N     24
   HUMILITY IS ONLY DOUBT  . . . . . . . . . . . . . . . . .   753 EV GOSPEL(D)/N     99
   AS ALSO PRIDE & HUMILITY BUT  . . . . . . . . . . . . .    792B LETTER 4          PROSE
   OF RELIGION & HUMILITY THE TWO BANDS OF SOCIETY HAVING BEEN 804A LETTER 16         PROSE
   IN OUR DIVINE MASTER YOU ARE TO ME A LESSON OF HUMILITY    822B LETTER 26         PROSE
HUMING  (I E, HUMMING)
   AN EASY OF [ HUMAN ] HUMING UNDERSTANDING . . . . . . .     52D ISLAND MOON 8    *PROSE
   AND LOST IN INFINITE HUMING WINGS VANISHES WITH A CRY  .    289 FOUR ZOAS 2        361
HUMOUR
   PLAYD AT FORFEITS & TRYD EVERY METHOD TO GET GOOD HUMOUR    59B ISLAND MOON 11    PROSE
   DELIGHTED TO SEE THEM IN SUCH A SERIOUS HUMOUR MR SCOPPRELL 61C ISLAND MOON 11    PROSE
   BE IN THE GOOD HUMOUR THE BISHOP PRETENDS TO BE  . . .    385C ANNO WATSON        MARG
   ANY MAN WHO WRITES [THAT] SO PRETEND THAT HE IS IN A GOOD  390B ANNO WATSON      * MARG
      HUMOUR
   CONCEPTION OF THE HUMOUR AND FUN THAT OCCURS ON THE JOURNEY 569A DESC CAT 3       PROSE
   ALL WAS CHEARFULNESS & GOOD HUMOUR ON THE ROAD & YET WE    802B LETTER 14        PROSE
HUMOUROUS
   WITH CERTAIN HUMOUROUS ACCOMPANIMENTS IN HIS CHARACTER  .  568D DESC CAT 3       *PROSE
HUMPHREY
   OZIAS HUMPHREY ESQRE  . . . . . . . . . . . . . . . . .    SUPP ADDRESS/L 64     *TITLE
HUMPHRY
   TO OZIAS HUMPHRY ESQRE  . . . . . . . . . . . . . . . . .  442D LAST JUDGMNT/L    TITLE
   MR HUMPHRY THE PAINTER WAS IN ITALY THE SAME TIME  . . .   847D LETTER 44         PROSE
   EXPENSIVE TO THE BUYER THOSE I PRINTED FOR MR HUMPHRY  .   867A LETTER 66         PROSE
HUMPY
   OF CROOKED HUMPY WOMAN  . . . . . . . . . . . . . . . .     464 ANNO REYNOLDS       2
HUNDRED
   HISSING WITH HUNDRED TONGUES HER POISNOUS BREATH  . . . .   41C THEN SHE BORE     PROSE
   A HUNDRED POUNDS A PIECE THEY WOULD PRINT OFF TWO THOUSAND  62D ISLAND MOON 11    PROSE
   AND IN THE MORNING LO AN HUNDRED MEN IN GHASTLY DEATH  .    107 TIRIEL 5           29
   EIGHTEEN HUNDRED YEARS MAN WAS A DREAM  . . . . . . . . .   240 EUROPE 9            2
   EIGHTEEN HUNDRED YEARS A FEMALE DREAM  . . . . . . . .      240 EUROPE 9            5
   AND EIGHTEEN HUNDRED YEARS WERE FLED  . . . . . . . . . .   243 EUROPE 13          10
   FIVE HUNDRED YEARS WANDRING ON EARTH  . . . . . . . . .     250 AHANIA 2           46
   I COULD NAME AN HUNDRED SUCH  . . . . . . . . . . . . .    390D ANNO WATSON        MARG
   ONE HUNDRED YEARS PONDRING THE INTRICATE MAZES OF          481 MILTON 2            17
      PROVIDENCE
   HIS CORN-FIELDS AND HIS VALLEYS OF FIVE HUNDRED ACRES      497 MILTON 15          31
      SQUARE
   THEIR NUMBERS ARE SEVEN MILLION & SEVEN THOUSAND & SEVEN   515 MILTON 28          22
      HUNDRED
   NOW SEVEN AGES IS AMOUNTING TO TWO HUNDRED YEARS  . . . .  516 MILTON 28          58
   OF AN HUNDRED JOURNEYMEN'S HOW D'YE DO NEIGHBOUR  . . . .  546 SWELLD LIMBS/N      4
   ONE HUNDRED FEET IN HEIGHT SOME WERE PAINTED AS PICTURES  566A DESC CAT 2        PROSE
   THOUGH THE FIGURES WERE ONE HUNDRED FEET IN HEIGHT  . .   566A DESC CAT 2        PROSE
   WHO HAVING RECEIVED FOURTEEN HUNDRED GUINEAS AND MORE  .   572C DESC CAT 3        PROSE
   THE LIFE'S LABOUR OF FIVE HUNDRED IDIOTS  . . . . . . .   593B PUB ADDRESS/N      PROSE
   THAT VULGAR EPIGRAM IN ART REMBRANDT'S "HUNDRED GUELDERS" 599B PUB ADDRESS/N      PROSE
   ALBION'S DREAD TOMB EIGHT THOUSAND AND FIVE HUNDRED YEARS  678 JERUSALEM 48       36
   IN ITS EXTENSION EVERY TWO HUNDRED YEARS HAS A DOOR TO EDEN 678 JERUSALEM 48      37
   THE KING OF CANAAN WHOSE ARE SEVEN HUNDRED CHARIOTS OF IRON 702 JERUSALEM 66      25
   RETAIN MY YOUTH EIGHT THOUSAND AND FIVE HUNDRED YEARS  .    728 JERUSALEM 83      52
   "HUNDRED FOR THE TERRIBLE DESART OF LONDON WAS BETWEEN"    800B LETTER 12         PROSE
   FIVE HUNDRED WERE OUT THIS IS SWIFT WORK IF LITERALLY TRUE 846D LETTER 44         PROSE
      BUT
   IS A HUNDRED YEARS BEYOND THE PRESENT GENERATION THOUGH   864D LETTER 61         PROSE
   TASTE WILL SHORTEN THE HUNDRED YEARS INTO AS MANY HOURS FOR 864D LETTER 61        PROSE
   CONTAINS (A HUNDRED) PLATES BUT IT IS NOT LIKELY THAT I    878C LETTER 88         PROSE
      SHALL GET
HUNDREDS
   IN SEVENS & TENS & FIFTIES HUNDREDS THOUSANDS NUMBERD ALL  287 FOUR ZOAS 2        269
   OF SAND IN BANDS OF HUNDREDS & OF FIFTIES & OF THOUSANDS   314 FOUR ZOAS 6        107
      . . .
   HUNDREDS OR THOUSANDS OF YEARS O VERY FINE RECORDS  . . . 394A ANNO WATSON        MARG
   WILL SOON BE WELL ENOUGH TO MAKE HUNDREDS OF DESIGNS  .   796B LETTER 7          PROSE
   ARE HUNDREDS TO ME NAY THOUSANDS I AM GOING ON WITH SUCCESS 832C LETTER 32        PROSE
HUNG
   THE MOON HUNG NOT OUT HER LAMP . . . . . . . . . . . . .    36C COUCH DEATH/PS  PROSE
```

950

	PAGE	TITLE	LINE

HUNG   (CONTINUED)

THE FIERCE DUKE HUNG OVER THE COUNCIL . . . .   138 FRENCH REVOLTN   87
& WE HELD BY THE ROOTS OF TREES AND HUNG OVER THIS   155D MARRIAGE HH 17 PROSE
   IMMENSITY
WHICH HUNG WITH THE HEAD DOWNWARD INTO THE DEEP   . . . .   156A MARRIAGE HH 17 PROSE
OVER THE RUGGED OCEAN SO THE ANGELS OF ALBION HUNG   . . .   205 AMERICA CANC C   24
AND RINTRAH HUNG WITH ALL HIS LEGIONS IN THE NETHER DEEP   242 EUROPE 12   24
A TREE HUNG OVER THE IMMENSITY . . . .   251 AHANIA 3   54
AND URIZEN HUNG OVER ORC & VIEWD HIS TERRIBLE WRATH . . .   321 FOUR ZOAS 7   42
HIS CROWN OF THORNS FELL FROM HIS HEAD HE HUNG HIS LIVING   376 FOUR ZOAS 9   711
   LYRE
SUSPENDED OVER HER HE HUNG HE INFOLDED HER IN HIS GARMENTS   639 JERUSALEM 17   52

HUNGER

HE ANSWERD ME I HUNGER FOR ANOTHER BATTLE   . . . . . .   25 EDW THIRD/PS 3   156
FROM FALLING FROM STIFLING FROM HUNGER . . . .   144 FRENCH REVOLTN   234
BABE CAN NEVER HUNGER THERE . . . .   181 HOLY THURS/N   15
BABE CAN NEVER HUNGER THERE . . . .   212 HOLY THURS/SE   15
OF THIRST & OF HUNGER APPEARD . . . .   229 URIZEN 13   9
AND URIZEN CRAVING WITH HUNGER   . . . .   233 URIZEN 20   30
AT DISTANCE FAR IN NIGHT REPELLD IN DIREFUL HUNGER CRAVING   276 FOUR ZOAS 1   442
WHERE ENION BLIND & AGE BENT WEPT IN DIREFUL HUNGER CRAVING 280 FOUR ZOAS 2   16
THROAT THEN LIKE A RED FLAME A TONGUE OF HUNGER   . . . .   303 FOUR ZOAS 4   241
IN RAGING HUNGER STILL THE PESTILENTIAL FOOD IN GEMS & GOLD 343 FOUR ZOAS 8   78
HIS BURNING THIRST & FREEZING HUNGER COME INTO MY HAND   . .   481 MILTON 2   5
IN GHASTLY TORMENT SICK A TONGUE OF HUNGER & THIRST FLAMED   482 MILTON 3   22
   OUT
AND TO DEVOUR THE SLEEPING HUMANITY OF ALBION IN RAGE &   623 JERUSALEM 5   30
   HUNGER
IN PAIN THE SPECTRE DIVIDED IN PAIN OF HUNGER AND THIRST   625 JERUSALEM 6   13
AN ORBED VOID OF DOUBT DESPAIR HUNGER & THIRST & SORROW   640 JERUSALEM 18   4
THE LITTLE VILLAGES OF MIDDLESEX & SURREY HUNGER & THIRST   656 JERUSALEM 30   25
THE PRAISE OF JEHOVAH IS CHAUNTED FROM LIPS OF HUNGER &   656 JERUSALEM 30   32
   THIRST

HUNGERS

JERUSALEM HUNGERS IN THE DESART AFFECTION TO HER CHILDREN   727 JERUSALEM 83   7

HUNGRING

IN A FIERCE HUNGRING VOID & NONE CAN VISIT HIS REGIONS . .   279 FOUR ZOAS 1 * 544
ORC LISTEND TO THE SONG COMPELLD HUNGRING ON THE COLD WIND   322 FOUR ZOAS 7   99
WHEN I WAS A RAVNING HUNGRING & THIRSTING CRUEL LUST &   329 FOUR ZOAS 7 * 350
   MURDER
HOWLING IN HIS SPECTRE ROUND HIS BODY HUNGRING TO DEVOUR   531 MILTON 39   18
HUNGRING & THIRSTING FOR LOS'S LIFE YET PRETENDING   627 JERUSALEM 8   28
   OBEDIENCE
TO DEVOUR THE BODY OF ALBION HUNGRING & THIRSTING & RAVNING 714 JERUSALEM 73   48

HUNGRY

UPON THE HUNGRY POOR   . . . .   11 GWIN KING/PS   6
I TOLD HIM TO PUT OFF HIS HUNGRY LOOKS . . . .   25 EDW THIRD/PS 3   155
THE HUNGRY POOR ENTERD THE HALL TO EAT GOOD BEEF & ALE . .   58 THIS CITY/IM   11
HE IS AN INNOCENT OLD MAN & HUNGRY WITH HIS TRAVEL   . . .   101 TIRIEL 2   33
HUNGRY CLOUDS SWAG ON THE DEEP . . . .   148 MARRIAGE HH 2   2
HUNGRY CLOUDS SWAG ON THE DEEP . . . .   149 MARRIAGE HH 2   22
DOES THE WHALE WORSHIP AT THY FOOTSTEPS AS THE HUNGRY DOG   193 V DAU ALBION 5   33
AND A PALACE OF ETERNITY IN THE JAWS OF THE HUNGRY GRAVE   193 V DAU ALBION 6   1
RENT OFF THEIR ROBES TO THE HUNGRY WIND & THREW THEIR   200 AMERICA 12   3
   GOLDEN SCEPTERS
THE HUMAN HEART ITS HUNGRY GORGE . . . .   221 DIVNE IMAGE/SE   8
A CRAVING HUNGRY CAVERN . . . .   229 URIZEN 13   6
LENGTHNING INTO A HUNGRY BEAM SWIFTLY . . . .   249 AHANIA 4   19
AND CAST THEIR YOUNG OUT TO THE HUNGRY WILDS & SANDY   276 FOUR ZOAS 1   453
   DESARTS
ALL RAVNING LIKE THE HUNGRY WORM & LIKE THE SILENT GRAVE   280 FOUR ZOAS 2   17
WHAT IS WITHIN NOW SEEN WITHOUT THEY ARE RAW TO THE HUNGRY   281 FOUR ZOAS 2   55
   WIND
TO LISTEN TO THE HUNGRY RAVENS CRY IN WINTRY SEASON   . . .   290 FOUR ZOAS 2   406
A CRAVING HUNGRY CAVERN THENCE AROSE HIS CHANNELD   . . .   303 FOUR ZOAS 4   240
MISPLACING EVERY CENTER HUNGRY DESIRE & LUST BEGAN   . . .   345 FOUR ZOAS 8   178
OR A PILLAR & PALACE OF ETERNITY IN THE JAWS OF THE HUNGRY   354 FOUR ZOAS 8   496
   GRAVE
TO SEE IF HUNGRY WINDS ARE ABROAD WITH THEIR INVISIBLE ARMY 355 FOUR ZOAS 8   560
DESIRING LIKE THE HUNGRY WORM & LIKE THE [SILENT] GAPING   376 FOUR ZOAS 9   735
   GRAVE
ON THE HUNGRY CRAVING WIND   . . . .   415 MY SPECTRE/N   25
THE PASSIONS & DESIRES DESCEND UPON THE HUNGRY WINDS   .   512 MILTON 26   28
WHEN WINTER RENDS THE HUNGRY FAMILY AND THE SNOW FALLS   .   642 JERUSALEM 20   12
OR ARE YOU BORN TO FEED THE HUNGRY RAVENINGS OF DESTRUCTION 647 JERUSALEM 24   14
THO HUNGRY THEY LABOUR THEY ROUZE THEMSELVES ANXIOUS   . .   691 JERUSALEM 59   31
TILL SHE VEGETATED INTO A HUNGRY STOMACH & A DEVOURING   698 JERUSALEM 64   8
   TONGUE

HUNT

THE EXAMINER WHOSE VERY NAME IS HUNT . . . .   537 AND HIS LEGS/N   16
TO H(?HUNT)   . . . .   538D TO H(UNT)/N TITLE

HUNTED

THE WOLF IS HUNTED DOWN BY CAUSELESS FEAR   . . . . . .   24 EDW THIRD/PS 3   113
EACH OUTCRY OF THE HUNTED HARE . . . .   431 AUGURIES   13

HUNTER

THE YOUTHFUL SUN JOYS LIKE A HUNTER ROUZED TO THE CHACE   37B CONTEMPLATN/PS PROSE

HUNTER (JACK)

WISH JACK [HUNTER] TEARGUTS HAD HAD THE CUTTING OF PLUTARCH 50A ISLAND MOON 6 PROSE

HUNTGN

ISSACHAR NORTHAMPTON RUTLAND NOTTGHAM ZEBULUN BEDFORD   637 JERUSALEM 16   48
   HUNTGN CAMB

		PAGE	TITLE	LINE

HUNTING
    AND WAR & HUNTING THE TWO FOUNTAINS OF THE RIVER OF LIFE   525 MILTON 35   2
    AND THE TWO SOURCES OF LIFE IN ETERNITY HUNTING AND WAR   672 JERUSALEM 43   31
HUNTINGDON   SEE HUNTGN
    SKOFELD HAD ELY RUTLAND CAMBRIDGE HUNTINGDON NORFOLK . . 710 JERUSALEM 71   38
HUNTS
    HE HUNTS HER FOOTSTEPS THRO THE SNOW & THE WINTRY HAIL   521 MILTON 32   5
    & RAIN
HUNTSMAN
    ROUZD LIKE A HUNTSMAN TO THE CHACE AND WITH . . . . .   3 TO MORNING/PS   7
    THE DISTANT HUNTSMAN WINDS HIS HORN . . . . 124 SCHOOL BOY/SI   3
    THOSE WHO CAN THINK THAT THE PROUD HUNTSMAN . . . . 569C DESC CAT 3   PROSE
    TILL SKOFIELD'S NIMROD THE MIGHTY HUNTSMAN JEHOVAH CAME   644 JERUSALEM 22   3
HURD'S
    PROSPECT AT NORTH END MRS HURD'S I SHOULD LIKE AS WELL   873A LETTER 76   PROSE
    AS ANY
HURL
    FAR AS MY STRENGTH CAN HURL THEE WANDER THERE & LAUGH &   296 FOUR ZOAS 3   171
    PLAY
HURLD
    AND HURLD THE NEW BORN WONDER THRO THE STARRY NIGHT . . . 159C SONG LIBERTY   PROSE
    HURLD APART ON ALL SIDES AS A FALLING . . . . 257 BOOK OF LOS 4   23
    BUT ALBION FELL DOWN A ROCKY FRAGMENT FROM ETERNITY HURLD   685 JERUSALEM 54   6
    JESUS REPLIED & THUNDERS HURLD . . . . 753 EV GOSPEL(D)/N   87
HURLING
    NAKED AND ROARING LIKE LIONS HURLING ROCKS . . . . .   32 EDW THIRD/PS 6   22
HURLS
    ROUND THE FLAMES ROLL AS LOS HURLS HIS CHAINS . . . . 256 BOOK OF LOS 3   34
    HURLS APART STAMPING FURIOUS TO DUST . . . . . . 257 BOOK OF LOS 4   20
HURRIED
    ("HURRIED ON BY FURIES OF IMMATURE IMPETUOUS WISHES")   85D ANNO LAVATER   MARG
    UNEASY
    MY VEGETATED PORTION WAS HURRIED FROM LAMBETH'S SHADES . . 527 MILTON 36   22
    IN VAIN HE IS HURRIED AFAR INTO AN UNKNOWN NIGHT . . . . 703 JERUSALEM 66   76
    WAIT FOR LESS HURRIED MOMENTS OUR COTTAGE LOOKS MORE & MORE   806A LETTER 16   PROSE
HURRIES
    I INTEND BECAUSE MY ABSTRACT FOLLY HURRIES ME OFTEN AWAY   809A LETTER 20   PROSE
    MOST UNPROFITABLE OF HURRIES YOUR SINCERE & AFFECTIONATE   840C LETTER 39   PROSE
HURRY
    IN A GREAT HURRY INFLAMMABLE GASS THE WIND FINDER ENTERD   44C ISLAND MOON 1   PROSE
    I WRITE IN A VIOLENT HURRY YOUR LETTER HAS NEVER ARRIVED TO   832B LETTER 32   PROSE
    I REMAIN IN ENGRAVER'S HURRY WHICH IS THE WORST & . . . 840C LETTER 39   PROSE
HURT
    AND FAIN WOULD CURE THE HURT HE MADE . . . .   17 BLIND-MANS/PS   56
    NONE CAN HURT THEE THY BONES ARE BRASS THY SINEWS ARE IRON 39A SAMSON/PS   PROSE
    HE IS NOT ABLE TO HURT ME SAID HE MORE THAN MAKING ME . 52A ISLAND MOON 8   PROSE
    BUT IF ANY ONE IS HURT BY HIS LYING WILL CONFESS HIS LIE   67B ANNO LAVATER   MARG
    SEE...
    HEVA COME KISS HIS BALD HEAD FOR HE WILL NOT HURT US HEVA   101 TIRIEL 2   38
    ... UNLESS THOU FIRST FEAREST TO HURT THEM . . . . 143 FRENCH REVOLTN   194
    HAS ONLY HURT PAINE'S HEEL WHILE PAINE HAS BROKEN HIS HEAD 396C ANNO WATSON   MARG
    MAN IS NOT IMPROVED BY THE HURT OF ANOTHER . . . . . 402C ANNO BACON   MARG
    HE WHO SHALL HURT THE LITTLE WREN . . . . 431 AUGURIES   29
    COME OUT HE IS THE SAME MAN WHO LATELY HURT HIS HAND . 438C BLAKES MEMORAN   PROSE
    BEING AS CAREFUL AS POSSIBLE NOT TO HURT THE GROUND . . 440C MEMORANDUM/N 3   PROSE
    IF MEN WERE WISE THE MOST ARBITRARY PRINCES COULD NOT HURT   600A PUB ADDRESS/N   PROSE
    MIGHT HURT MY PECUNIARY CIRCUMSTANCES . . . . . . 812B LETTER 22   PROSE
    IDLENESS ITSELF DOES NOT HURT OTHER MEN LET SATAN HIMSELF   812C LETTER 22   PROSE
    EXPLAIN
    LEADS ME VERY MUCH TO MY HURT & SOMETIMES TO THE ANNOYANCE 830D LETTER 30   PROSE
    WILL HURT THE SALE OF THE WORK AND HE SENT TO ME THE LAST   861B LETTER 58   PROSE
    SHEET
    RUINS ACTIVITY & ARE THE GREATEST HURT TO AN ARTIST SUCH   879C LETTER 89   PROSE
    AS I AM
HURTLE
    THE BONES OF URIZEN HURTLE ON THE WIND THE BONES OF LOS   305 FOUR ZOAS 4   293
HURTLING
    FRIGHTEND AT THE HURTLING BONES . . . . 226 URIZEN 8   2
    PERCHING AROUND THE HURTLING BONES . . . . 253 AHANIA 4   24
    HURTLING UPON THE WIND . . . . 259 BOOK OF LOS 5   15
    AND AS HE BEAT ROUND THE HURTLING DEMON TERRIFIED AT THE   302 FOUR ZOAS 4   202
    SHAPES
    THE HURTLING DEMON TERRIFIED AT THE SHAPES . . . . . 305 FOUR ZOAS 4   285
    ... SUDDEN WAVD [HIS HURTLING HAND] AMONG THE STARS . 343 FOUR ZOAS 8   87
    [AMONG THE STARS] HIS HURTLING HAND GAVE THE DIRE SIGNAL   343 FOUR ZOAS 8   88
    . . .
HURTLINGS
    WITH HURTLINGS & CLASHINGS & GROANS . . . . . . 229 URIZEN 13   25
    FOR [IN] WITH NOISES RUINOUS HURTLINGS & CLASHINGS & GROANS 304 FOUR ZOAS 4   282
HURTS
    LET NO ONE FEAR FOR POOR BLIND TIRIEL HURTS NONE   101 TIRIEL 2   14
    BUT HIMSELF
HUSBAND
    SHE RAN AND CALLED HER HUSBAND WHO CAME AND TALKED WITH HIM 40B SAMSON/PS   PROSE
    & YOU HINDER YOUR HUSBAND FROM GOING TO CHURCH . . . 48A ISLAND MOON 4   PROSE
    HER PALE HANDS CLING AROUND HER HUSBAND & OVER HER WEAK   305 FOUR ZOAS 5   21
    HEAD
    HER MAIDENS TO HER HUSBAND DELIGHTING IN HIS DELIGHT . 522 MILTON 33   18
    SHALT GIVE HER INTO THE ARMS OF GOD YOUR LORD & HUSBAND   523 MILTON 33   23
    A FEMALE DESCENDS TO MEET HER LOVER OR HUSBAND . . . . 610D V LAST JUDG/N   PROSE
    IS NOT THAT SUN THY HUSBAND & THAT MOON THY GLIMMERING VEIL 660 JERUSALEM 34   7
    IN THE VOICE OF MY HUSBAND THO HE IS ANGRY FOR A MOMENT   694 JERUSALEM 61   10
    HE WILL NOT

		PAGE	TITLE	LINE

HUSBAND   (CONTINUED)
```
      AND WILT THOU BECOME MY HUSBAND O MY LORD & SAVIOUR  . . .   696 JERUSALEM 62        6
      THYSELF FEMALE A MALE A BREEDER OF SEED A SON & HUSBAND       698 JERUSALEM 64       13
        & LO
      WHERE EVERY FEMALE DELIGHTS TO GIVE HER MAIDEN TO            707 JERUSALEM 69       15
        HER HUSBAND
      "MY HUSBAND HAS BEEN OBLIGED TO FINISH SEVERAL THINGS"  . .  800B LETTER 12     PROSE
      WHO WITH HER ADMIRABLE HUSBAND PRESENT THEIR BEST    . . .   836C LETTER 35     PROSE
      VIRGIN WIFE INFANCY OLD AGE HUSBAND ANGEL OF              SUPP INSC HERVEY    *TITLE
        PROVIDENCE
      URIAH THE HUSBAND OF BATHSHEBA BATHSHEBA    . . . . .   SUPP PENC DRAW 2.35   *TITLE
```
HUSBANDMAN
```
      THE HUSBANDMAN DOES LEAVE HIS PLOW   . . . . . . . . .      12 GWIN KING/PS        45
      THE HUSBANDMAN DOTH LEAVE HIS BENDING HARVEST   . . . . .   34B KING JOHN/PS    PROSE
      . . . WHILE THE HUSBANDMAN AND WOMAN OF WEAKNESS   . . . .  139 FRENCH REVOLTN     107
      FOR THE HUSBANDMAN WEEPS AT BLIGHTS OF THE FIFE . . . . .   143 FRENCH LEVOLTN     209
      HOW THE INDUSTRIOUS CITIZEN THE PAINS OF THE HUSBANDMAN     193 V DAU ALBION 5     13
      TALK WITH THE HUSBANDMAN & SHEPHERD BUT THESE ATTACKD HIM   315 FOUR ZOAS 6       138
        SORE
      JUST AS A HUSBANDMAN HIS MOULD . . . . . . . . . . .       425 MENTAL TRAVLER     26
      BY WAR AND STRATAGEM TO WIN THE LABOUR OF THE HUSBANDMAN    628 JERUSALEM 9        11
```
HUSBANDRY
```
      WHO FELL BENEATH HIS INSTRUMENTS OF HUSBANDRY & BECAME  .   688 JERUSALEM 56       35
```
HUSBAND'S
```
      O ELENOR [I AM] BEHOLD THY HUSBAND'S HEAD  . . . . . . .     5 FAIR ELENOR/PS      61
      HOW CAN I HELP THY HUSBAND'S COPYING ME . . . . . . .      539 TO NANCY F/N         1
      "CALLD ON YOU SINCE MY HUSBAND'S FIRST RETURN FROM FELPHAM" 800A LETTER 12     PROSE
      "RECIEVE MY & MY HUSBAND'S LOVE & AFFECTION &"   . . . .   801A LETTER 12     PROSE
```
HUSBANDS
```
      PARENTS & CHILDREN WIVES & HUSBANDS EMBRACE & ARISE        443D LAST JUDGMNT/L PROSE
        TOGETHER
      SHE HAS HAD FOUR HUSBANDS A FIT SUBJECT FOR THIS PAINTER   574D DESC CAT 3     PROSE
```
HUSH
```
      NOW LAUGHING STOPS WITH SILENCE HUSH . . . . . . . . .      16 BLIND-MANS/PS      21
      HUSH TOM NEVER MIND IT FOR WHEN YOUR HEAD S BARE  . . . .  117 CHIMNEY SWP/SI      7
```
HUSHD
```
      THE WHIRLWIND "HUSHD IN GRIM REPOSE"  . . . . . . . .     SUPP ILLUS GRAY     *TITLE
```
HUSK
```
      WHO ART THOU DIMINUTIVE HUSK & SHELL . . . . . . . .       268 FOUR ZOAS 1       149
      HUSK & COVERING INTO VACUUM EVAPORATING . . . . . . . .    745 JERUSALEM 98       19
```
HUSKS
```
      . . . & THE STARS THRESHD FROM THEIR HUSKS  . . . . . .    374 FOUR ZOAS 9       653
```
HUT
```
      OFF SLOTH AND BUILD HIMSELF A HUT AND HEDGE   . . . . .     26 EDW THIRD/PS 3     197
```
HUTN
```
      OF THE FLOOD OF UDAN-ADAN HUTN IS THE FATHER OF THE SEVEN   625 JERUSALEM 7        24
```
HUTTN
```
      GWANTOK PEACHY BRERTUN SLAID HUTTN SKOFELD KOCK KOTOPE  .   658 JERUSALEM 32       11
      HUTTN HAD WARWICK NORTHAMPTON BEDFORD BUCKINGHAM  . . . .   710 JERUSALEM 71       36
```
HUTTON
```
      OF HAND & HYLE & COBAN OF KWANTOK PEACHEY BRERETON SLAYD    623 JERUSALEM 5        25
        & HUTTON
      HAND HYLE & COBAN GUANTOK PEACHEY BRERETON SLAYD & HUTTON   641 JERUSALEM 19       18
      BRERETON & SLADE IN EGYPT HUTTON & SKOFELD & KOX  . . . .   662 JERUSALEM 36       17
```
HUZZA
```
      AMEN HUZZA SELAH  . . . . . . . . . . . . . . .          649B JERUSALEM 27    PROSE
```
HYDE
```
      FROM HYDE PARK TO THE ALMS-HOUSES OF MILE-END & OLD BOW    486 MILTON 6           31
      TERMINATING IN HYDE PARK ON TYBURN'S AWFUL BROOK  . . . .  491 MILTON 11           5
      SAYS WAS THE LODGING OF THE ABBOT OF HYDE BY WINCHESTER    567B DESC CAT 3     PROSE
      SAYS WAS THE LODGING OF THE ABBOT OF HYDE BY WINCHESTER    588D CHAUCER/N      PROSE
      SAYS WAS THE LODGING OF THE ABBOT OF HYDE BY WINCHESTER    590C CHAUCER 2      PROSE
      BENDING ACROSS THE ROAD OF OXFORD STREET IT FROM HYDE PARK 665 JERUSALEM 38       57
      FROM HYDE PARK SPREAD THEIR VEGETATING ROOTS BENEATH ALBION 674 JERUSALEM 44       23
```
HYLE
```
      HAND IS BECOME A ROCK SINAI & HOREB IS HYLE & COBAN  . . .  501 MILTON 19          58
      ALBION'S DREAD SONS HAND HYLE & COBAN SURROUND HIM AS  .    507 MILTON 23          15
      OF HAND & HYLE & COBAN OF KWANTOK PEACHEY BRERETON SLAYD    623 JERUSALEM 5        25
        & HUTTON
      HAND HAS PEOPLED BABEL & NINEVEH HYLE ASHUR & ARAM   . .    625 JERUSALEM 7        18
      HAND & HYLE & KOBAN SKOFELD KOX & KOTOPE LABOUR MIGHTILY    628 JERUSALEM 8        41
      I HEATED IT IN THE FLAMES OF HAND & HYLE & COBAN  . . . .   628 JERUSALEM 9        21
      AND HAND & HYLE ROOTED INTO JERUSALEM BY A FIBRE  . . . .   635 JERUSALEM 15        1
      SO CRY HAND & HYLE THE ELDEST OF THE FATHERS OF ALBION'S    641 JERUSALEM 18       36
      AND HYLE & COBAN WERE HIS TWO CHOSEN ONES FOR EMISSARIES    641 JERUSALEM 18       41
      HAND HYLE & COBAN GUANTOK PEACHEY BRERETON SLAYD & HUTTON   641 JERUSALEM 19       18
      HYLE SEES IN FEAR HE HOWLS IN FURY OVER THEM HAND SEES  .   644 JERUSALEM 21       28
      IN STERN DEFIANCE CAME FROM ALBION'S BOSOM HAND HYLE KOBAN  658 JERUSALEM 32       10
      HAND HYLE & COBAN FLED THEY BECAME WHAT THEY BEHELD  . .    662 JERUSALEM 36       15
      ALBION REPLIED GO HAND & HYLE SIEZE THE ABHORRED FRIEND     670 JERUSALEM 42       47
      VALA HYLE SKOFIELD W B INV & S   . . . . . . . . .        681D JERUSALEM 51    *TITLE
      IN THE HOT NOON AS HE TRAVELD THRO HIS JOURNEY HYLE         690 JERUSALEM 58       30
        & SKOFIELD
      THY SHRIEKS BECAUSE HAND & HYLE ARE CRUEL & OBDURATE TO ME  705 JERUSALEM 67       62
      HYLE DWELT IN WINCHESTER COMPREHENDING HANTS DORSET DEVON   710 JERUSALEM 71       20
        CORNWALL
      PALACES RIVERS & MOUNTAINS AND BETWEEN HAND & HYLE AROSE    710 JERUSALEM 71       22
      HOW HYLE ROOFD LOS IN ALBION'S CLIFFS BY THE AFFECTIONS     715 JERUSALEM 74       28
        RENT
      INTO THE VORTEX OF HIS WHEELS THEREFORE HYLE IS CALLED GOG  715 JERUSALEM 74       30
      HE HATH TOOK ROOT IN HEBRON IN THE LAND OF HAND & HYLE  .   715 JERUSALEM 74       49
      HYLE ON EAST MOOR IN ROCKY DERBYSHIRE RAVD TO THE MOON  .   723 JERUSALEM 80       66
```

```
                                                                PAGE      TITLE          LINE
HYLE    (CONTINUED)
        OF PAINTED CLAY THE MIGHTY HYLE IS BECOME A WEEPING INFANT     725 JERUSALEM 82        8
        LOOK HYLE IS BECOME AN INFANT LOVE LOOK BEHOLD SEE HIM LIE     725 JERUSALEM 82       37
        AND HYLE A WINDING WORM BENEATH [HER LOOM UPON THE SCALES]     726 JERUSALEM 82    *  47
        [HYLE WAS BECOME A WINDING WORM] & NOT A WEEPING INFANT        726 JERUSALEM 82       48
        HYLE WAS A WINDING WORM AND HERSELF PERFECT IN BEAUTY   .  .   726 JERUSALEM 82       50
        AWAY & MIGHTY HYLE & AFTER THEM JERUSALEM IS GONE AWAKE        729 JERUSALEM 83       87
        WHILE IN SELFHOOD HAND & HYLE & BOWEN & SKOFELD APPROPRIATE    737 JERUSALEM 90       40
        WHILE HAND & HYLE CONDENSE THE LITTLE-ONES & ERECT THEM        737 JERUSALEM 90       49
            INTO
HYMEN
        IS HYMEN AT A MARRIAGE & THE ANTIQUE PAGEANTRY ATTENDING IT  618D ILLUS MILTON   PROSE
HYMN
        . . . AND THE HOLY HYMN FROM THICKEND TONGUES . . . . .        140 FRENCH REVOLTN     140
        PLAYS IN DISGUISE IN WHISPERD HYMN & MUMBLING PRAYER THE       333 FOUR ZOAS 7B       26
            PRIESTS
        HIS HYMN ON THE NATIVITY WHICH YOU WILL FIND AMONG HIS  .   823D LETTER 27       PROSE
HYMNING
        ENTUNE DAUGHTERS OF ALBION YOUR HYMNING CHORUS MILDLY   .   .  688 JERUSALEM 56       11
HYPOCRISY     SEE HIPOCRISY
        [ ("SUPERSTITION") ] HYPOCRISY SUPERSTITION HAS BEEN LONG     85C ANNO LAVATER    MARG
            A BUGBEAR
        BY REASON OF ITS BEING UNITED WITH HYPOCRISY BUT LET THEM     85C ANNO LAVATER    MARG
        [HYPOCRISY THE IDIOT'S WISDOM & THE WISE MAN'S FOLLY]   .      110 TIRIEL 8         35
        THEN ORC [ANSWERD] CRIED CURSE THY COLD HYPOCRISY . . .       323 FOUR ZOAS 7      135
        FOR THE COERCIVE LAWS OF HELL MORAL HYPOCRISY  . . . .       616C V LAST JUDG/N   PROSE
        CHARGE THE SPIRITUALLY RELIGIOUS WITH HYPOCRISY  . . . .     682C JERUSALEM 52    PROSE
HYPOCRITE
        ("COLD AND VEHEMENT AT THE SAME TIME A FANATIC") I E          73C ANNO LAVATER    MARG
            HYPOCRITE
        ("SUPERSTITION") HIPOCRISY ("SUPERSTITIOUS") HYPOCRITE  .     74D ANNO LAVATER    MARG
        SUPERSTITIOUS AND SO HE IS A HYPOCRITE . . . . . .           75A ANNO LAVATER    MARG
        TO BE A HYPOCRITE & STAND IN SHAPE OF A BLIND BEGGAR   .      103 TIRIEL 4          9
        THIS IS THE HYPOCRITE THAT SOMETIMES ROARS A DREADFUL LION    105 TIRIEL 4         50
        AND THE HYPOCRITE TO HOWL  . . . . . . . . . .               183 MOTTO SONGS/N     6
        AND DOES MY THEOTORMON SEEK THIS HYPOCRITE MODESTY  .  .      194 V DAU ALBION 6   16
        THIS KNOWING ARTFUL SECRET FEARFUL CAUTIOUS TREMBLING         194 V DAU ALBION 6   17
            HYPOCRITE
        AVAUNT COLD HYPOCRITE I AM CHAIND OR THOU COULDST NOT USE     323 FOUR ZOAS 7      142
            ME THUS
        O FOOL SLIGHT HYPOCRITE & VILLAIN  . . . . . . . .           395D ANNO WATSON    * MARG
        HYPOCRITE WHO SMILES PARTICULARLY WHERE HE MEANS TO BETRAY   452A ANNO REYNOLDS    MARG
        THEY TORMENT A HYPOCRITE WHEN HE IS DISCOVERD  . . . .      616C V LAST JUDG/N   PROSE
        BUT HOW A MONK OR A METHODIST EITHER CAN BE A HYPOCRITE      682C JERUSALEM 52    PROSE
        HE OUGHT NOT TO BE CALLD A HYPOCRITE THIS TITLE IS  .  .     682C JERUSALEM 52    PROSE
        FOOTE IN CALLING WHITEFIELD HYPOCRITE WAS HIMSELF ONE   .    682D JERUSALEM 52    PROSE
        GENERAL GOOD IS THE PLEA OF THE SCOUNDREL HYPOCRITE           687 JERUSALEM 55      61
            & FLATTERER
        WHICH ALWAYS APPEAR TO THE IGNORANCE-LOVING HYPOCRITE AS     717C JERUSALEM 77    PROSE
            SINS
HYPOCRITES
        & EXPOSES HYPOCRITES TILL HE IMAGINES THAT ALL ARE          157D MARRIAGE HH 21  PROSE
            RELIGIOUS
        WO WO WO TO YOU HYPOCRITES EVEN MURDER  . . . . .           615D V LAST JUDG/N   PROSE
        THERE WILL ALWAYS BE AS MANY HYPOCRITES BORN AS HONEST MEN   616A V LAST JUDG/N   PROSE
        YOU ARE PHARISEES & HYPOCRITES FOR YOU ARE CONSTANTLY   .    682D JERUSALEM 52    PROSE
HYPOCRITIC
        FOR THEN THE BODY OF DEATH WAS PERFECTED IN HYPOCRITIC        494 MILTON 13        25
            HOLINESS
        IN ALL ITS HYPOCRITIC TURPITUDE OPENING TO EVERY EYE   .     530 MILTON 38        44
        THESE HYPOCRITIC SELFHOODS ON THE ANVILS OF BITTER DEATH      627 JERUSALEM 8      16
        BROODING IN HOLY HYPOCRITIC LUST DRINKING THE CRIES OF PAIN   672 JERUSALEM 43     17
HYSTERIC
        HIS PRAISE OF RAFAEL IS LIKE THE HYSTERIC SMILE OF REVENGE   452A ANNO REYNOLDS    MARG
I AM
        NAME OF JEHOVAH ELOHIM THE I AM OF THE OAKS OF ALBION   .    610A V LAST JUDG/N   PROSE
ICE
        OF HAIL & ICE VOICES OF TERROR . . . . . . . .               223 URIZEN 3         33
        LIKE FETTERS OF ICE SHRINKING TOGETHER  . . . . .  .         228 URIZEN 10        26
        MELT INTO FURROWS WINTER BLOWS HIS BELLOWS ICE & SNOW   .     276 FOUR ZOAS 1     424
        AND THREW HER FROM THE STEPS OF ICE THAT FROZE AROUND HIS     294 FOUR ZOAS 3     112
            THRONE
        IN FETTERS OF ICE SHRINKING DISORGANIZD RENT FROM ETERNITY    303 FOUR ZOAS 4     212
        OUTSTRETCHD UPON THE STONES OF ICE THE RUINS OF HIS THRONE    310 FOUR ZOAS 5     187
        THAT TOWARD EDEN ETERNAL ICE FROZEN IN SEVEN FOLDS  .  .      633 JERUSALEM 13     15
        THE ROCKS OF SOLID FIRE THE ICE VALLEYS THE PLAINS  . .      634 JERUSALEM 13     40
        COLD SNOWS DRIFTED AROUND HIM ICE COVERD HIS LOINS AROUND     652 JERUSALEM 28     13
        BY OUR DEAR LORD I SEE WORLDS CRUSTED WITH SNOWS & ICE  .     673 JERUSALEM 43     64
ICELAND
        READ THE EDDA OF ICELAND THE SONGS OF FINGAL  . . . .       389C ANNO WATSON     MARG
ICY
        HIS STORED SNOWS HE POURED FORTH AND HIS ICY MAGAZINES  .  .  203 AMERICA 16        9
        A DREAMFUL HORRIBLE STATE IN TOSSINGS ON HIS ICY BED   .  .   302 FOUR ZOAS 4     171
        OF ELETH & THE ICY HANDS OF UVETH KNEADED THE BREAD  .  .     322 FOUR ZOAS 7     102
        TO MILTON'S BRAIN THE ICY FLUID FROM HIS BROAD COLD PALM      500 MILTON 19         9
I'D
        O SHOULD SHE EER PROVE FALSE HIS LIMBS ID TEAR  . . . .        10 WHEN EARLY/PS    17
        ID CURSE BRIGHT FORTUNE FOR MY MIXED LOT  . . . . . .          10 WHEN EARLY/PS    19
        AND THEN ID DIE IN PEACE AND BE FORGOT  . . . . . . .          10 WHEN EARLY/PS    20
        HAD I THREE LIVES ID DIE IN SUCH A CAUSE  . . . . . .          35 WAR SONG/PS      13
        SAID INFLAMMABLE GASS ID SEE THE PARSONS ALL HANGD A PARCEL    48A ISLAND MOON 4  PROSE
            OF LYING
```

954

		PAGE	TITLE	LINE

I'D (CONTINUED)

A PASSIONATE WRETCH IF I WAS A MAN ID WAIT AT THE BOTTOM	48B ISLAND MOON 4	PROSE
ID FIND IT OUT IN A MINUTE BUT IVE FOUND IT OUT ALREADY	51D ISLAND MOON 7	PROSE
ID SOON MAKE DOUBLE ELEPHANT LOOK FOOLISH	52B ISLAND MOON 8	PROSE
IF I HAD ONLY MYSELF TO CARE FOR ID WRING OFF THEIR NOSES	53C ISLAND MOON 8	PROSE
ID RATHER BE SUTTON	57 TO BE OR/IM	6
ID BE AN ASS A HOG A WORM A CHAIR A STOOL	550 WHEN I SEE/N	8

IDA'S

| WHETHER ON IDA'S SHADY BROW | 10 TO MUSES/PS | 1 |

IDEA

WHAT A NATURAL IDEA IS	89D ANNO SWED LOVE	MARG
POETIC IDEA	89D ANNO SWED LOVE	MARG
("MERELY NATURAL IDEA") OBSERVE THE DISTINCTION HERE	90A ANNO SWED LOVE	MARG
MAN CAN HAVE NO IDEA OF ANY THING GREATER THAN MAN	90B ANNO SWED LOVE	MARG
& HAVE NO IDEA OF ANY BUT WORLDLY GAIN	94A ANNO SWED LOVE	MARG
THAT NO MAN ON EARTH HAS A SPIRITUAL IDEA AFTER READING N...	94C ANNO SWED LOVE	MARG
A CLEAR IDEA AND A DETERMINATE VISION OF THINGS IN HIS OWN MIND	439D REMARKS MALKIN	PROSE
("REDUCED VARIETY OF NATURE TO ABSTRACT IDEA") WHAT FOLLY HIS OWN IDEA OF INTELLECTUAL BEAUTY THE FACE AND	460D ANNO REYNOLDS	MARG
EVIDENCES THE [IDEA OF WANT] WANT OF IDEA IN THE ARTIST'S	580A DESC CAT 5	PROSE
SINCE I HAVE PRACTISED PAINTING I HAVE LOST ALL IDEA OF	585B DESC CAT 15	PROSE
WAS SOLITUDE & CHAOS THIS IS THE MOST PERNICIOUS IDEA	592D PUB ADDRESS/N	PROSE
& LEAVES THE MAN WHO ENTERTAINS SUCH AN IDEA THE HABITATION	614B V LAST JUDG/N	PROSE
BUT I OUGHT TO MENTION TO YOU THAT OUR PRESENT IDEA IS	614B V LAST JUDG/N	PROSE
IT WILL GIVE YOU A GOOD IDEA OF THIS GOOD & EXCELLENT MAN	820D LETTER 25	PROSE
YOU CAN HAVE NO IDEA UNLESS YOU WAS IN LONDON AS I AM	839B LETTER 38	PROSE
FAINT IDEA OF THE FINISHED PRINTS FROM HIS WORKS SEVERAL OF	841B LETTER 41	PROSE
WHOM I HAVE CONSULTED THAT TO GIVE A TRUE IDEA OF	844C LETTER 43	PROSE
I CANNOT HELP SUGGESTING AN IDEA WHICH HAS STRUCK ME VERY	848A LETTER 45	PROSE
& AT THE VERY IDEA OF ANOTHER JOURNEY TO SWEET FELPHAM	850D LETTER 49	PROSE
WISHING IT THE IDEA OF PUBLISHING ONE VOLUME A YEAR HE	857C LETTER 54	PROSE
OF ADVANTAGE TO OUR FRIEND SEAGRAVE THE IDEA OF SEEING	858A LETTER 55	PROSE
EMBARRASD AT THE IDEA OF SETTING A VALUE ON ANY WORK OF MR	859C LETTER 56	PROSE
	860A LETTER 56	PROSE

IDEAL

| KNOWLEDGE OF IDEAL BEAUTY IS NOT TO BE ACQUIRED | 459B ANNO REYNOLDS | MARG |
| AN IDEAL DESIGN SUGGESTED BY THE FIRST PUBLICATION OF | 583D DESC CAT 10 | PROSE |

IDEAS

BUT WHEN OUR FIRST IDEAS ARE WRONG WHAT FOLLOWS MUST	28D EDW THIRD/PS 4	PROSE
("NATURAL IDEAS") HOW ABSURD THEN WOULD IT BE TO SAY	94C ANNO SWED LOVE	MARG
THEY COULD NOT TELL HIM IN NATURAL IDEAS	94C ANNO SWED LOVE	MARG
THAT REASON MAY HAVE IDEAS TO BUILD ON THE JEHOVAH OF THE BIBLE	150B MARRIAGE HH 5	PROSE
HAND WHICH EXECUTED THESE LITTLE IDEAS BEEN THAT OF A PLAGIARY	439C REMARKS MALKIN	PROSE
[AS DO ?FOOLS THAT ADORE THINGS & ?IDEAS XXX OF GENERAL KNOWLEDGE]	451A ANNO REYNOLDS	* MARG
OF IDEAS & [THEN TO BE ?INSOLENT IN HIS FOOLERY]	455B ANNO REYNOLDS	* MARG
TO ASSUME THE RIGHT TO PUT OTHER MEN'S IDEAS INTO HIS FOOLERY	455B ANNO REYNOLDS	MARG
EXIST GRANDEUR OF IDEAS IS FOUNDED ON PRECISION OF IDEAS	457D ANNO REYNOLDS	MARG
IT IS BORN WITH US INNATE IDEAS ARE IN EVERY MAN	459B ANNO REYNOLDS	MARG
THE MAN WHO SAYS THAT WE HAVE NO INNATE IDEAS MUST BE	459B ANNO REYNOLDS	MARG
GENERAL IDEAS AGAIN	461D ANNO REYNOLDS	MARG
BY DIFFERENCES BETWEEN IDEAS THAT IDEAS THEMSELVES WHICH ARE	525 MILTON 35	5
IDEAS OF STRENGTH AND BEAUTY HAVE NOT BEEN GREATLY DIFFERENT	579C DESC CAT 5	PROSE
CONCERNING HIS IDEAS OF BEAUTY STRENGTH AND UGLINESS	579D DESC CAT 5	PROSE
WHEN THE ARTIST TOOK HIS PENCIL TO EXECUTE HIS IDEAS	582D DESC CAT 9	PROSE
I HAVE HEARD MANY PEOPLE SAY GIVE ME THE IDEAS	596A PUB ADDRESS/N	PROSE
IDEAS CANNOT BE GIVEN BUT IN THEIR MINUTELY APPROPRIATE	596A PUB ADDRESS/N	PROSE
NOR CAN THEIR METHOD EVER EXPRESS IDEAS OR IMAGINATIONS	596A PUB ADDRESS/N	PROSE
MY STREETS ARE MY IDEAS OF IMAGINATION	665 JERUSALEM 38	31
THEREFORE REJECTING IDEAS AS NOTHING & HOLDING ALL WISDOM	708 JERUSALEM 70	7
TO CONSIST IN THE AGREEMENTS & (DISAGREEMENTS) OF IDEAS	708 JERUSALEM 70	8
I KNOW I BEGGED OF YOU TO GIVE ME YOUR IDEAS	792A LETTER 4	PROSE
SORRY THAT YOUR IDEAS & MINE ON MORAL PAINTING DIFFER SO MUCH	793A LETTER 5	PROSE
YOU SAY THAT I WANT SOMEBODY TO ELUCIDATE MY IDEAS BUT YOU	793A LETTER 5	PROSE
THE PRESENT PROPOSAL AS PECULIARLY ADAPTED TO YOUR IDEAS	841D LETTER 41	PROSE
IDEAS OF GOOD & EVIL	889C IDEAS/N4	PROSE

IDENTICAL

THEY ARE ALL FIRM DETERMINATE OUTLINE OR IDENTICAL FORM	439C REMARKS MALKIN	PROSE
NOTHING NEW OCCURS IN IDENTICAL EXISTENCE ACCIDENT EVER VARIES	567C DESC CAT 3	PROSE
NOTHING NEW OCCURS IN IDENTICAL EXISTENCE ACCIDENT EVER VARIES	589A CHAUCER/N	PROSE

IDENTIFIED

| ALL HUMAN FORMS IDENTIFIED EVEN TREE METAL EARTH & STONE ALL | 747 JERUSALEM 99 | 1 |
| HUMAN FORMS IDENTIFIED LIVING GOING FORTH & RETURNING WEARIED | 747 JERUSALEM 99 | 2 |

IDENTITIES

& FROM ONE ESSENCE MAY PROCEED MANY IDENTITIES	91A ANNO SWED LOVE	MARG
IDENTITIES OR THINGS ARE NEITHER CAUSE NOR EFFECT THEY ARE ETERNAL	470D ANNO REYNOLDS	MARG
STATES CHANGE BUT INDIVIDUAL IDENTITIES NEVER CHANGE NOR CEASE	521 MILTON 32	23

IDENTITY

| ANSWER ESSENCE IS NOT IDENTITY BUT FROM ESSENCE PROCEEDS IDENTITY | 91A ANNO SWED LOVE | MARG |

955

	PAGE	TITLE	LINE

IDENTITY   (CONTINUED)
   IF THE ESSENCE WAS THE SAME AS THE IDENTITY   . . . . .   91B ANNO SWED LOVE   MARG
   THERE COULD BE BUT ONE IDENTITY WHICH IS FALSE   . . .   91B ANNO SWED LOVE   MARG
   BUT ONE & THE SAME ESSENCE IS THEREFORE ESSENCE & NOT   91B ANNO SWED LOVE   MARG
     IDENTITY
   A NOTHING LEFT IN DARKNESS YET I AM AN IDENTITY   . . .   265 FOUR ZOAS 1   62
   PURSUING THE VAIN SHADOW OF HOPE FLEEING FROM IDENTITY   .   353 FOUR ZOAS 8   486
   INVENTION IDENTITY & MELODY ARE OBJECTS OF INTUITION   .   474D ANNO REYNOLDS   MARG
   WHERE SATAN MAKING TO HIMSELF LAWS FROM HIS OWN IDENTITY   491 MILTON 11   10
   BEYOND THE OUTLINE OF IDENTITY IN THE SELFHOOD DEADLY   .   527 MILTON 37   10
   EACH IDENTITY [&] IS ETERNAL CONSEQUENTLY   . . . . .   607A V LAST JUDG/N   *PROSE
   BUT NOT CHANGED OR TRANSFORMED INTO ANOTHER IDENTITY   .   607A V LAST JUDG/N   PROSE
   BUT ETERNAL IDENTITY IS ONE THING & CORPOREAL VEGETATION IS   607A V LAST JUDG/N   PROSE
   & WHAT HE KNOWS IS OPPOSITE TO THEIR OWN IDENTITY   . .   616D V LAST JUDG/N   PROSE
   BEYOND THE OUTLINE OF IDENTITY BOTH WAYS WHICH MEET IN ONE   640 JERUSALEM 18   3
   WHO PROTECTS MINUTE PARTICULARS EVERY ONE IN THEIR OWN   672 JERUSALEM 43   23
     IDENTITY
   THE INFINITE ALONE RESIDES IN DEFINITE & DETERMINATE   687 JERUSALEM 55   64
     IDENTITY

IDIOT
   TO GENERALIZE IS TO BE AN IDIOT   . . . .   451A ANNO REYNOLDS   MARG
   THE MAN WHO DOES NOT KNOW WHAT OBJECT TO PURSUE IS AN IDIOT   458D ANNO REYNOLDS   MARG
   THE IDIOT REASONER LAUGHS AT THE MAN OF IMAGINATION   . .   521 MILTON 32   6
   TO CAST OFF THE IDIOT QUESTIONER WHO IS ALWAYS QUESTIONING   533 MILTON 41   12
   OR THINK TO EDUCATE [AN IDIOT] A FOOL   . . . . . .   598C PUB ADDRESS/N   *PROSE
   EVERY MAN HAS EYES NOSE & MOUTH THIS EVERY IDIOT KNOWS   611B V LAST JUDG/N   PROSE
   THAT WHICH CAN BE MADE EXPLICIT TO THE IDIOT IS NOT WORTH   793B LETTER 5   PROSE
IDIOT'S
   [HYPOCRISY THE IDIOT'S WISDOM & THE WISE MAN'S FOLLY]   .   110 TIRIEL 8   35
   THESE ARE THE IDIOT'S CHIEFEST ARTS   . . . .   547 LET BE TOLD/N   6
   AND FROM AN IDIOT'S ACTIONS FORM MY RULE   . . . . .   547 RAFAEL SUBLI/N   6
IDIOTS
   HIRE IDIOTS TO PAINT WITH COLD LIGHT & HOT SHADE   . .   445 ANNO REYNOLDS   2
   GENERAL KNOWLEDGES ARE THOSE KNOWLEDGES THAT IDIOTS   451A ANNO REYNOLDS   MARG
     POSSESS
   IN A DISCOURSE ON ART SUCH IDIOTS ARE NOT ARTISTS   . .   464B ANNO REYNOLDS   MARG
   & THAT SUCH IDIOTS AS RUBENS CORREGGIO & TITIAN KNEW   .   467B ANNO REYNOLDS   MARG
   OR WERE THEY IDIOTS OR MADMEN SHEW US MIRACLES   . . .   506 MILTON 22   62
   THE LIFE'S LABOUR OF FIVE HUNDRED IDIOTS   . . . . .   593B PUB ADDRESS/N   PROSE
   THE CONTEMPTIBLE IDIOTS WHO HAVE BEEN CALLD GREAT MEN   .   598C PUB ADDRESS/N   PROSE
IDLE
   ARE IDLE TROPHIES OF THE VANQUISHER   . . . .   17 EDW THIRD/PS 1   5
   IF AT THIS MOMENT OF THEIR IDLE FEAR   . . . .   24 EDW THIRD/PS 3   118
   THE INFANT HEAD WHILE THE MOTHER IDLE PLAYS WITH HER DOG   110 TIRIEL 8   26
     ON HER COUCH
   THE [IDLE MAN] INDOLENT NEVER CAN BRING TO THE MART   . .   181 RICHES/N   3
   . . . & LEAVE HIS JOY TO THE IDLE TO THE PESTILENCE . .   200 AMERICA 11   6
   THE PASSIVE IDLE SLEEP THE ENORMOUS NIGHT & DARKNESS OF   295 FOUR ZOAS 3   115
     DEATH
   . . . THERE ALL THE IDLE WEEDS   . . . .   377 FOUR ZOAS 9   764
   READ PATIENTLY TAKE NOT UP THIS BOOK IN AN IDLE HOUR   .   383C ANNO WATSON   MARG
   WHO FEEDS ON CONTEMPT OF HIS NEIGHBOUR THERE ALL THE IDLE   513 MILTON 27   27
     WEEDS
   NOR OF THE CITY CLARK'S IDLE FACILITIES   . . . . . .   542 FLORENTINE/N   30
   [IS DRIVEN OUT TO MAKE ROOM FOR A PACK OF IDLE SYCOPHANTS]   595B PUB ADDRESS/N   *PROSE
   WAS HE THEN IDLE OR THE LESS   . . . .   752 EV GOSPEL(D)/N   53
IDLENESS
   "PRIDE FULLNESS OF BREAD & ABUNDANCE OF IDLENESS" WAS THE   79D ANNO LAVATER   MARG
     SIN
   SOFT DECEIT & IDLENESS   . . . .   182 WHICH ARE/N   2
   SOFT DECEIT & IDLENESS   . . . .   184 SEVRL QUESTN/N   9
   IDLENESS IS ONE THING & DISSIPATION ANOTHER   . . . .   454B ANNO REYNOLDS   MARG
   IDLENESS & DEVASTATION OF THE THINGS OF THE SPIRIT   . .   717B JERUSALEM 77   PROSE
   IDLENESS ITSELF DOES NOT HURT OTHER MEN LET SATAN HIMSELF   812C LETTER 22   PROSE
     EXPLAIN
IDOL
   THE IDOL VIRTUES OF THE NATURAL HEART & SATAN'S SEAT   .   530 MILTON 38   46
   I SEE A WICKER IDOL WOVEN ROUND JERUSALEM'S CHILDREN I SEE   673 JERUSALEM 43   65
IDOLATER
   THOU IDOLATER IS NOT GOD ONE & IS NOT HE VISIBLE   . . .   158B MARRIAGE HH 22   PROSE
IDOLATROUS
   IDOLATROUS TO HIS OWN SHADOW WORDS OF ETERNITY UTTERING   293 FOUR ZOAS 3   59
   IDOLATROUS TO HIS OWN SHADOW WORDS OF ETERNITY UTTERING   654 JERUSALEM 29   46
IDOLATRY
   FOR IT IS IDOLATRY & DESTROYS THE SOUL I OUGHT TO TELL YOU   824C LETTER 27   PROSE
   AN ALLEGORY OF IDOLATRY OR POLITICS   . . . .   SUPP ILLUS CHAUCER   *TITLE
IDOLS
   TO PLEASE THY IDOLS IN THE PRETENDED CHASTITIES OF   693 JERUSALEM 60   30
     UNCIRCUMCISION
   INDEED A HARLOT DRUNKEN WITH THE SACRIFICE OF IDOLS DOES HE   695 JERUSALEM 61   38
I E
   UNDER EVERY GOOD IS A HELL I E HELL IS THE OUTWARD   . . .   SUPP ANNO SWED HELL   * MARG
   ("COLD AND VEHEMENT AT THE SAME TIME A FANATIC") I E   73C ANNO LAVATER   MARG
     HYPOCRITE
   ACQUIRED BY MEANS OF SUFFERING & DISTRESS I E EXPERIENCE   89B ANNO SWED LOVE   * MARG
   THE TRUTH & CERTAINTY OF VIRTUE & HONESTY I E INSPIRATION   386C ANNO WATSON   MARG
   I E STATE RELIGION WHICH IS THE SOURCE OF ALL CRUELTY   393D ANNO WATSON   MARG
   I E SEDITION MR GRINDER THEN REPROVED THE SOLDIER   . .   438C BLAKES MEMORAN   PROSE
   IS NOBILITY A PORTION OF A STATE I E REPUBLIC   . . . .   401B ANNO BACON   MARG
   I E THE MOST MINUTELY DISCRIMINATING & DETERMINATE   . . .   453D ANNO REYNOLDS   * MARG
IEREUS
   THE ARCHIEREUS THE IEREUS THE SADDUSAION DOUBLE   . . . .   734 JERUSALEM 89   7

IESOUS
   (MONOS HO IESOUS) JERUSALEM CHAP I . . . . 622A JERUSALEM 4   TITLE
I'FAITH
   MUST BE A FOOL I'FAITH NOT TO UNDERSTAND THE MATHEMATICS 45C ISLAND MOON 1 PROSE
IGNOGE
   BOADICEA CONWENNA ESTRILD GWINEFRID IGNOGE CAMBEL . . . 281 FOUR ZOAS 2   62
   CAMBEL & GWENDOLEN & CONWENNA & CORDELLA & IGNOGE . . . 624 JERUSALEM 5   41
   SABRINA & IGNOGE BEGIN TO SHARPEN THEIR BEAMY SPEARS . 631 JERUSALEM 11   19
   HACKNEY AND HOLLOWAY SICKEN FOR ESTRILD & IGNOGE . . . . 644 JERUSALEM 21   33
   OBEYD HIS AWFUL VOICE IGNOGE IS HIS LOVELY EMANATION . . 710 JERUSALEM 71   27
IGNORANCE
   FOR IGNORANCE IS POLLY'S LEESING NURSE . . . . 14 IMIT SPEN/PS * 13
   FROM WHOM CAME IGNORANCE WHO BROUGHT FORTH WONDER . . . 40D THEN SHE BORE PROSE
   TO WANDER INSLAVD BLACK DEPREST IN DARK IGNORANCE . . . 143 FRENCH REVOLTN * 214
   ALAS MY SON MY SON I WANT I WANT HELP HELP AGED 209C FOR CHILDRN/GP TITLE
     IGNORANCE
   THEIR PARENTS BROUGHT THEM FORTH & AGED IGNORANCE PREACHES 242 EUROPE 12   7
     CANTING
   CHAINS OF DARK IGNORANCE & CORDS OF TWISTED SELF CONCEIT 312 FOUR ZOAS 6   41
   IN IGNORANCE TO VIEW A SMALL PORTION & THINK THAT ALL . 337 FOUR ZOAS 7B 185
   VEILS OF IGNORANCE COVERING FROM HEAD TO FEET WITH A COLD 346 FOUR ZOAS 8   222
     WEB
   INNOCENCE DWELLS WITH WISDOM BUT NEVER WITH IGNORANCE . . 380B FOUR ZOAS NOTE PROSE
   AND WITH LABOURS OF IGNORANCE FILL EVERY PLACE . . . . 445 ANNO REYNOLDS   4
   A LIAR HE NEVER WAS ABASHED IN HIS LIFE & NEVER FELT HIS 447D ANNO REYNOLDS MARG
     IGNORANCE
   GENIUS HAS NO ERROR IT IS IGNORANCE THAT IS ERROR . . . 465B ANNO REYNOLDS MARG
   SET TO WORK BOTH IGNORANCE & SKILL . . . . 549 ENGL ENCOU/N 1   2
   SO EEN LET IGNORANCE DO IT ALL . . . . 549 ENGL ENCOU/N 1   12
   EXCEPT BY BLUNDERING IGNORANCE TILL AFTER VANDYKE'S TIME 566C DESC CAT 2 PROSE
   A PAINTING AND A DRAWING PROCEEDS FROM IGNORANCE OF ART 584D DESC CAT 15 PROSE
   I ALLOW THAT THERE IS SUCH A THING AS HIGH FINISHD 593B PUB ADDRESS/N PROSE
     IGNORANCE
   FROM IGNORANCE ITSELF & ITS FINISHING IS LIKE ITS MASTER 593B PUB ADDRESS/N PROSE
   HEAVY LUMPS OF CUNNING & IGNORANCE AS THEIR WORKS SHEW . . 593C PUB ADDRESS/N PROSE
   CHOOSE TO PURCHASE THE LIFE'S LABOUR OF IGNORANCE 594B PUB ADDRESS/N PROSE
     & IMBECILLITY
   I KNOW THIS HE HAS OFTEN PROVED HIS IGNORANCE BEFORE ME 603C PUB ADDR AD/N PROSE
   WEAKNESS WITH HORNS & TALONS IGNORANCE WITH A RAVNING BEAK 628 JERUSALEM 9   13
   I HAVE INNOCENCE TO DEFEND AND IGNORANCE TO INSTRUCT . . 670 JERUSALEM 42   26
   IN IGNORANCE TO VIEW A SMALL PORTION & THINK THAT ALL . 700 JERUSALEM 65   27
   WHAT ARE THE PAINS OF HELL BUT IGNORANCE BODILY LUST . 717B JERUSALEM 77 PROSE
   AGED IGNORANCE PERCEPTIVE ORGANS CLOSED THEIR OBJECTS 767D FOR SEXES/GP TITLE
     CLOSE
   IN AGED IGNORANCE PROFOUND . . . . 771 OF GATES/GP   34
   WITH HIS GENTEEL IGNORANCE & POLITE DISAPPROBATION . . . 825C LETTER 27 PROSE
   NOT SUFFER IT TO BE INJURED BY MY IGNORANCE OR THAT IT 858C LETTER 55 PROSE
     SHOULD
   AGED IGNORANCE . . . . SUPP LEGEND/N52 *TITLE
IGNORANCE-LOVING
   WHICH ALWAYS APPEAR TO THE IGNORANCE-LOVING HYPOCRITE AS 717C JERUSALEM 77 PROSE
     SINS
IGNORANCES
   AND JULIO ROMANO STRIPPED FROM THE IGNORANCES OF . . . . 562B DESC CAT ADV PROSE
IGNORANT
   YOU WOULD YOU IGNORANT JADE I WISH I COULD SEE YOU HIT ANY 48C ISLAND MOON 4 PROSE
   PLUTARCH WAS A NASTY IGNORANT PUPPY SAID QUID . . . . . 49D ISLAND MOON 6 PROSE
   AN IGNORANT PACK OF WRETCHES SO THEY WENT TO BED . . . 52A ISLAND MOON 7 PROSE
   WILL BE IGNORANT FOOLS & WILL NOT DESERVE TO LIVE . 62D ISLAND MOON 11 PROSE
   TRUE SUPERSTITION IS IGNORANT HONESTY . . . . . . 75A ANNO LAVATER MARG
   A TERROR TO ALL LIVING THINGS THINK NOT THAT I AM IGNORANT 299 FOUR ZOAS 4   82
   KEPT IGNORANT OF THE USE THAT THEY MIGHT SPEND THE DAYS 337 FOUR ZOAS 7B 183
     OF WISDOM
   FOR THE SETTING IGNORANT & VULGAR ARTISTS AS MODELS . . . 461C ANNO REYNOLDS MARG
   HOW IGNORANT . . . . 462B ANNO REYNOLDS MARG
   AGAINST THE IGNORANT HIRELINGS FOR . . . . 480C MILTON 1 PROSE
   RUBENS LOW VULGAR STUPID IGNORANT . . . . 547 RAFAEL SUBLI/N   3
   AS THE IGNORANT SAVAGE WILL SELL HIS OWN WIFE . . . . 548 ON GREAT ENC/N   1
   FOR A GREAT [MULTITUDE] MADJORITY ARE IGNORANT . . . . 549 ENGL ENCOU/N 1 *   3
   THE IGNORANT INSULTS OF INDIVIDUALS WILL NOT HINDER ME . 561A EXHIBITION ADV PROSE
   PROPAGATED AMONG THE PUBLIC BY IGNORANT HIRELINGS . . . 572C DESC CAT 3 PROSE
   YET A LITTLE PAINS OUGHT TO BE TAKEN EVEN BY THE IGNORANT 574A DESC CAT 3 PROSE
     AND WEAK
   IF A MAN IS MASTER OF HIS PROFESSION HE CANNOT BE IGNORANT 586A DESC CAT 16 PROSE
   AND LAUGH IN SECRET AT THE PRETENCES OF THE IGNORANT . 586A DESC CAT 16 PROSE
   BUT I SAY THAT THE EMBROIDERY OF THE IGNORANT FINISHER . 593B PUB ADDRESS/N PROSE
   THE LIFE'S LABOUR OF IGNORANT JOURNEYMEN . . . . . 593D PUB ADDRESS/N PROSE
   [ART BY THE HANDS OF IGNORANT JOURNEYMEN] . . . . . 595B PUB ADDRESS/N PROSE
   ACCOUNTED IGNORANT OF THAT EPIGRAMMATIC WIT IN ART . . . 599A PUB ADDRESS/N PROSE
   IGNORANT PICTURE DEALERS AN ENGLISHMAN MAY WELL SAY I AM 601C PUB ADDRESS/N PROSE
   ONE OF THE MOST IGNORANT FELLOWS THAT I EVER KNEW . . 603B PUB ADDR AD/N PROSE
   BECAUSE IGNORANT OF CRIME IN THE MIDST OF A CORRUPTED AGE 610B V LAST JUDG/N PROSE
   KEPT IGNORANT OF ITS USE THAT THEY MIGHT SPEND THE DAYS 700 JERUSALEM 65   25
     OF WISDOM
   THE BEAUTY OF THE BIBLE IS THAT THE MOST IGNORANT & . . . 786D ANNO THORNTON MARG
   AT PRESENT BUT IT WAS BECAUSE I WAS IGNORANT OF MANY THINGS 811C LETTER 22 PROSE
   THAT I CAN CONFESS MYSELF IGNORANT OF I ALSO KNOW & . . 814D LETTER 23 PROSE
   BLIND STUPID IGNORANT AND INCAPABLE IN TWO YEARS' STUDY 814D LETTER 23 PROSE
   I ALSO TOLD YOU WHAT I WAS ABOUT & THAT I WAS NOT IGNORANT 820C LETTER 25 PROSE
   THE MAN I AM VERY IGNORANT OF WHAT I AM REQUESTING OF YOU 828B LETTER 28 PROSE
IGNORANTLY
   IF HE IS IGNORANTLY SO HE IS NOT TRULY AN ENEMY . . . . 72B ANNO LAVATER MARG

IGNORANTLY   (CONTINUED)
    ?CAN ?& ?DOES WORK ?HARM IGNORANTLY . . . .   89B ANNO SWED LOVE * MARG
    WHETHER A MAN DOES IT IGNORANTLY OR KNOWINGLY . . .   452A ANNO REYNOLDS MARG
    IGNORANTLY & NOT DESIGNEDLY SURELY I OUGHT TO CONSIDER HIM 828C LETTER 28   PROSE
I I I
    AS A STRAIT LINE & A CROOKED ONE SECONDLY I I I . . . .   45D ISLAND MOON 1   PROSE
    BUT I MEANT SAID ARADOBO I I I CAN'T THINK LAW SIR . . .   49A ISLAND MOON 5   PROSE
IJIM
    BUT FAR HE HAD NOT GONE WHEN IJIM FROM HIS WOODS COME DOWN 103 TIRIEL 4   *   3
    IJIM SHALL REND THY FEEBLE JOINTS THOU TEMPTER OF DARK IJIM 103 TIRIEL 4   6
    O BROTHER IJIM IF IT IS THY VOICE THAT SPEAKS TO ME . .   104 TIRIEL 4   11
    COME THOU DARK FIEND I DARE THY CUNNING KNOW THAT IJIM   104 TIRIEL 4   17
        SCORNS
    O BROTHER IJIM THOU BEHOLDEST WRETCHED TIRIEL . . . .   104 TIRIEL 4   21
    WHEN TIRIEL HEARD THE WORDS OF IJIM HE SOUGHT NOT TO REPLY 104 TIRIEL 4   26
    O IJIM I AM FAINT & WEARY FOR MY KNEES FORBID . . . . .   104 TIRIEL 4   32
    IMPUDENT FIEND SAID IJIM HOLD THY GLIB & ELOQUENT TONGUE   104 TIRIEL 4   37
    TIRIEL IS A KING & THOU THE TEMPTER OF DARK IJIM . . .   104 TIRIEL 4   38
    HE DRANK & IJIM RAISD HIM UP & BORE HIM ON HIS SHOULDERS   104 TIRIEL 4   40
    HEUXOS COME FORTH I HERE HAVE BROUGHT THE FIEND THAT   104 TIRIEL 4   43
        TROUBLES IJIM
    THEY KNEW TWAS VAIN TO STRIVE WITH IJIM THEY BOWD & SILENT 105 TIRIEL 4   48
        STOOD
    CONFOUNDED AT THE TERRIBLE STRENGTH OF IJIM THEY KNEW TWAS 105 TIRIEL 4   69
        VAIN
    WHEN IJIM STRETCHD HIS MIGHTY ARM THE ARROW FROM HIS LIMBS 105 TIRIEL 4   71
    [THEN IJIM SAID LOTHO CLITHYMA MAKUTH FETCH YOUR FATHER] 105 TIRIEL 4   73
    [O NOBLE IJIM THOU HAST BROUGHT OUR FATHER TO [THE GATES] 105 TIRIEL 4   75
        OUR EYES]
    [DESIRES OUR DEATHS O IJIM [?TIS ?ONE ?WHOSE AGED TONGUE] 105 TIRIEL 4   78
    [HE SPOKE & KNEELD UPON HIS KNEE THEN IJIM ON THE PAVEMENT] 106 TIRIEL 4   81
    TO BE THE SPORT OF WINTRY WINDS SAID IJIM IS THIS TRUE . . 106 TIRIEL 4   84
    ESCAPE YE FIENDS FOR IJIM WILL NOT LIFT HIS HAND AGAINST YE 106 TIRIEL 4   88
    SO SAYING IJIM GLOOMY TURND HIS BACK & SILENT SOUGHT . .   106 TIRIEL 4   89
    HAR OCHIM IJIM ADAM REUBEN SIMEON LEVI JUDAH DAN NAPHTALI 350 FOUR ZOAS 8   360
IJIM'S
    HE KNEW TWAS VAIN FOR IJIM'S WORDS WERE AS THE VOICE OF   104 TIRIEL 4   27
        FATE
    HEUXOS & LOTHO RAN FORTH AT THE SOUND OF IJIM'S VOICE .   105 TIRIEL 4   45
ILIAD
    LIKEWISE READ HOMER'S ILIAD . . . .   389C ANNO WATSON   MARG
    SIMILAR TO HOMER'S ILIAD OR MILTON'S PARADISE LOST THE . . 823A LETTER 26   PROSE
ILIUM
    NATURAL FACT OR HISTORY OF ILIUM . . . .   775D INSC LAOCOON TITLE
I'LL
    THEN DOWN I'LL LIE AS COLD AS CLAY . . . .   7 MY SILKS/PS   17
    I'LL PORE UPON THE STREAM . . . .   8 MEMORY COME/PS   5
    I'LL DRINK OF THE CLEAR STREAM . . . .   8 MEMORY COME/PS   9
    AND THERE I'LL LIE AND DREAM . . . .   8 MEMORY COME/PS 11
    AND WHEN NIGHT COMES I'LL GO . . . .   8 MEMORY COME/PS 13
    WELL I'LL ENDEAVOUR TO TAKE . . . .   20 EDW THIRD/PS 2 59
    I'LL SET MY WHOLE ESTATE . . . .   21 EDW THIRD/PS 2 96
    GIVE ME YOUR HAND AND NOW I'LL TELL YOU WHAT . . . . .   21 EDW THIRD/PS 3   7
    I'LL FIGHT AND WEEP TIS IN MY COUNTRY'S CAUSE . . . .   31 EDW THIRD/PS 5 51
    I'LL WEEP AND SHOUT FOR GLORIOUS LIBERTY . . . . . .   31 EDW THIRD/PS 5 52
    I'LL DRAW MY SWORD NOR EVER SHEATH IT UP . . . . . .   31 EDW THIRD/PS 5 64
    I WILL GO MAD AND TEAR MY CRISPED HAIR I'LL RUN ABOUT . . 38C SAMSON/PS   PROSE
    HOW LOST I'LL TELL BUT STOP THE MOTLEY SONG . . . . .   42A THEN SHE BORE   PROSE
    I'LL SHEW HOW CONSCIENCE CAME FROM HEAVEN . . . . . .   42A THEN SHE BORE   PROSE
    NOW DEAD I'LL GUARD THEE FROM APPROACHING ILL . . . . .   43D WOE CRIED MUSE PROSE
    REASON SIR SAID THE ANTIQUARIAN I'LL GIVE YOU AN . . . .   45A ISLAND MOON 1   PROSE
    O AY COME I'LL SING YOU A SONG SAID THE CYNIC . . . . .   46C ISLAND MOON 3   PROSE
    I'LL BEGIN AGAIN SAID THE CYNIC . . . .   46C ISLAND MOON 3   PROSE
    I'LL TELL YOU WHAT MRS SINAGAIN . . . .   47C ISLAND MOON 3   PROSE
    I'LL TRY EXPERIMENTS . . . .   51 WHEN CORRUP/IM 26
    I THINK SOMEHOW I'LL LEAVE IT OFF THERE WAS A WOMAN . .   51C ISLAND MOON 6   PROSE
    I'LL BE HANGD SAID SUCTION HANG PHILOSOPHY . . . . . .   51D ISLAND MOON 7   PROSE
    I'LL KICK YOUR ROMAN ANUS . . . .   54 LO THE BAT/IM   9
    [I'LL DASH YOU THROUGH YOUR CHAIR SAYS THE CYNIC] . . . .   57A ISLAND MOON 9   PROSE
    HERE LADIES & GENTLEMEN SAID HE I'LL SHEW YOU A LOUSE [XXX] 58C ISLAND MOON 10 *PROSE
        OR
    HERE I'LL SIT & FADS AWAY . . . .   61 LEAVE O/IM   2
    AND I WILL FALL INTO SUCH A PASSION I'LL HOLLOW AND STAMP 63A ISLAND MOON 11 PROSE
    TELL ME WITH WHOM YOU GO & I'LL TELL YOU WHAT YOU DO . .   88A ANNO LAVATER   MARG
    AND SO I'LL KEEP HIM FETCH YOUR FATHER FETCH FORTH   105 TIRIEL 4   62
        MYRATANA
    LITTLE LAMB I'LL TELL THEE . . . .   115 THE LAMB/SI   11
    LITTLE LAMB I'LL TELL THEE . . . .   115 THE LAMB/SI   12
    I'LL SHADE HIM FROM THE HEAT TILL HE CAN BEAR . . . . .   125 LIT BLK BOY/SI   25
    AND THEN I'LL STAND AND STROKE HIS SILVER HAIR . . . .   125 LIT BLK BOY/SI   27
    I'LL LIE BESIDE THEE ON A BANK & VIEW THEIR WANTON PLAY   195 V DAU ALBION 7   25
    I'LL SING TO YOU TO THIS SOFT LUTE AND SHEW YOU ALL ALIVE 237 EUROPE INTRO   17
    THEN WILL I WEEP THEN I'LL COMPLAIN & SIGH FOR IMMORTALITY 368 FOUR ZOAS 9   411
    I'LL WATCH YOU & ATTEND YOUR FOOTSTEPS YOU ARE NOT LIKE   368 FOUR ZOAS 9   430
        THE BIRDS
    HERE WILL I BUILD MYSELF A HOUSE & HERE I'LL CALL ON HIS   369 FOUR ZOAS 9   453
        NAME
    HERE I'LL RETURN WHEN I AM WEARY & TAKE MY PLEASANT REST   369 FOUR ZOAS 9   454
    LIVING THEE ALONE I'LL HAVE . . . .   416 MY SPECTRE/N   53
    AND WHEN DEAD I'LL BE THY GRAVE . . . .   416 MY SPECTRE/N   54
    I'LL REFUSE HIM MY HAND & FROM ENVY BE FREE . . . . .   428 MARY   32
    I'LL ALSO WRITE MY OWN DEAR EPITAPH . . . .   537 AND HIS LEGS/N   49

	PAGE	TITLE	LINE

I'LL   (CONTINUED)
```
    AND I'LL BE BURIED NEAR A DIKE . . . . . . . . .   537 AND HIS LEGS/N      50
    DECEPTIONS O NO SO I'LL LEARN TO PAINT  . . . . .   546 RUBENS HAD/N         4
    I'LL WRITE IN RHYME AS SOFT AS [FEATHER PILLOWS]    555 BLAKES APL/N 1       7
        BARTOLLOZE
    AND NOW I'LL LEAD MY FALSE FRIENDS BY THE NOSE  . . . .   555 BLAKES APL/N 1      23
    I'LL WRITE IN VERSE AS SOFT AS BARTOLLOZE   . . . . .   555 BLAKES APL/N 2       2
    I'LL SOON SEE IF YOULL OBEY . . . . . . . . .   749 EV GOSPEL(B)/N      16
ILL
    NOW DEAD I'LL GUARD THEE FROM APPROACHING ILL  . .   43D WOE CRIED MUSE    PROSE
    BUT VERY ODD AS IF SHE HOPED YOU HAD NOT AN ILL OPINION   44B ISLAND MOON 1   PROSE
        OF HER
    WHAT A CURSED FOOL IS THIS ILL SHAPEN ARE INFANTS OR SMALL  406C ANNO BACON     MARG
        PLANTS
    ILL SHAPEN BECAUSE THEY ARE NOT YET COME TO THEIR MATURITY  406C ANNO BACON     MARG
    FOR ASSUREDLY HE IS VERY ILL . . . . . . . . .   434 WILLIAM BOND         4
    STYLE WILL ILL CORRESPOND WITH THE GREAT STYLE  . .   468A ANNO REYNOLDS   MARG
    WAS I ANGRY WITH HAYLEY WHO USD ME SO ILL  . . . .   538 WAS I ANGRY/N        1
    I WONDER WHO CAN SAY SPEAK NO ILL OF THE DEAD WHEN IT IS   598B PUB ADDRESS/N  PROSE
    I HAVE THEREFORE PROVED YOUR REASONINGS ILL PROPORTIOND   793C LETTER 5      PROSE
    VERY ILL NATURED YET EVEN FROM HIM I LEARN  . . . .   798B LETTER 10      PROSE
    BUT IT FOUND MY WIFE & MYSELF SO ILL & MY WIFE SO VERY ILL   811B LETTER 22     PROSE
    REALLY VERY ILL WHEN I WROTE TO HIM THE LAST TIME & WAS NOT   820C LETTER 25    PROSE
    COUNCELLOR HE ALAS WAS ILL IN BED WHEN I CALLD YESTERDAY   836B LETTER 35     *PROSE
    & THE SERVANT SAID THAT HE REMAINS VERY ILL INDEED  . .   836B LETTER 35     PROSE
    BE TOO ILL TO LET YOU KNOW HOW I AM & WHAT I WISH  . .   371B LETTER 72     PROSE
    I HAVE BEEN VERY ILL SINCE I SAW YOU BUT AM AGAIN WELL  . .   871D LETTER 74   PROSE
ILL DRAWN
    THE ILL DRAWN & UGLY YOUNG WOMEN & ABOVE ALL  . . . .   815A LETTER 23      PROSE
ILL-HEALTH
    MISS POOLE'S ILL-HEALTH THAN FOR MY FAILURE IN SENDING   837C LETTER 36     PROSE
        PROOFS
ILLIBERAL
    ("AS IF YOU HAD GIVEN NO PROVOCATION") IS NOT   390A ANNO WATSON     MARG
        THIS ILLIBERAL
ILLIBERALITY
    IF THIS FIRST LETTER IS WRITTEN WITHOUT RAILING &   384C ANNO WATSON     MARG
        ILLIBERALITY
ILLITERATE
    (RE JOHNSON) CHRIST & HIS APOSTLES WERE ILLITERATE MEN   786D ANNO THORNTON   MARG
ILL-JUDGED
    ILL-JUDGED CRITICISMS IN FUTURE YOURS  . . . . . .   864D LETTER 61      PROSE
ILLNESS
    AND MY WIFE'S ILLNESS NOT BEING QUITE GONE OFF  . . . .   807A LETTER 17     PROSE
    NOT MENTION ILLNESS BECAUSE I HOPED TO GET BETTER FOR I WAS   820C LETTER 25  PROSE
    ONLY ILLNESS MAKES ALL UNCOMFORTABLE . . . . . . . .   821B LETTER 25     PROSE
    SAY THAT HIS ILLNESS IS SO FAR FROM GONE THAT THE LEAST   SUPP LETTER 81A  *PROSE
        THING
ILLS
    SHE MONGST MEN WAS SENT AND WORSER ILLS ATTENDED HER BY FAR   43A THEN SHE BORE   PROSE
ILLUMINATED
    AMERICA A PROPHECY IN ILLUMINATED PRINTING FOLIO   207D PRSPECTUS 1793  PROSE
        WITH...DESIGNS PRICE
    VISION OF THE DAUGHTERS OF ALBION IN ILLUMINATED PRINTING   207D PRSPECTUS 1793  PROSE
    THE BOOK OF THEL A POEM IN ILLUMINATED PRINTING QUARTO .   207D PRSPECTUS 1793  PROSE
    THE MARRIAGE OF HEAVEN AND HELL IN ILLUMINATED PRINTING   207D PRSPECTUS 1793  PROSE
        QUARTO
    SONGS OF INNOCENCE IN ILLUMINATED PRINTING OCTAVO...  . .   208A PRSPECTUS 1793  PROSE
    SONGS OF EXPERIENCE IN ILLUMINATED PRINTING OCTAVO...  . .   208A PRSPECTUS 1793  PROSE
    THE ILLUMINATED BOOKS ARE PRINTED IN COLOURS  . . . .   208A PRSPECTUS 1793  PROSE
ILLUMINATING
    ?THEM ILLUMINATING THE MANUSCRIPT . . . . . . . .   62C ISLAND MOON 11 *PROSE
ILLUSION
    AND BOUND DOWN TO THE GLOWING ILLUSION  . . . . . .   260 BOOK OF LOS 5     47
    WAS COMPLETED A HUMAN ILLUSION . . . . . . . . . .   260 BOOK OF LOS 5     56
    SO SPEAKING NOT YET INFECTED WITH THE ERROR & ILLUSION  . .   666 JERUSALEM 39    27
ILLUSTRATE
    THE WRITINGS OF THE PROPHETS ILLUSTRATE THESE  . . . . .   605B V LAST JUDG/N  PROSE
ILLUSTRATION
    BY WAY OF ILLUSTRATION I INSTANCE SHAKSPEARE'S WITCHES IN   569D DESC CAT 3    PROSE
ILLUSTRATIONS
    CONTAINING AMPLE ILLUSTRATIONS ON ART  . . . . . .   560C EXHIBITION ADV   PROSE
    HIM ILLUSTRATIONS OF THE GRAVE A POEM BY ROBERT BLAIR  .   861C LETTER 59     PROSE
    SUBSCRIBERS & PURCHASERS OF THE BOOK OF ILLUSTRATIONS OF   SUPP LETTER 67F  *PROSE
ILLUSTRIOUS
    ("ILLUSTRIOUS CHARACTERS") [GOD BLASTS THEM AS THOUGH]  . .   SUPP ANNO REYNOLDS  * MARG
I'M
    TO DIGNITY THAT IM SICK ONT . . . . . . . . .   20 EDW THIRD/PS 2      61
    NO GOD FORBID IM SURE HE IS NOT  . . . . . . . . .   22 EDW THIRD/PS 3      25
    IM SURE HES NOT AFRAID NOR WARWICK NOR NONE  . . . .   22 EDW THIRD/PS 3      32
    IM GLAD MY FATHER DOES NOT HEAR ME TALK . . . . . .   27 EDW THIRD/PS 3     276
    AND THUS RESUMES HER WILES SAMSON IN THINE  . . . .   38D SAMSON/PS      PROSE
    IM SURE YOU OUGHT TO HOLD YOUR TONGUE  . . . . . .   48A ISLAND MOON 4   PROSE
    IM SURE HE MUST BE A WICKED VILLAIN SAID MRS NANNICANTIPOT   48B ISLAND MOON 4  PROSE
    IM SURE THIS IS NOT RELIGION ANSWERS THE OTHER  . . . .   48C ISLAND MOON 4   PROSE
    AND SAID IM MADE FOR EVER  . . . . . . . . . .   51 WHEN COERUP/IM      24
    AND NEVER THINK AT ALL ABOUT IT IM HANGD IF I DONT GET UP   51D ISLAND MOON 7  PROSE
    TILL IM NOTHING BUT A SPIRIT . . . . . . . . .   61 LEAVE O/IM          3
    AND NOW IM COVERD OER & OER . . . . . . . . . .   184 O I CANNOT/N        7
    YOU THINK FUSELI IS NOT A GREAT PAINTER IM GLAD  . . . .   538 TO H(UNT)/N         1
    THEN IM SILENT & PASSIVE & LOSE EVERY FRIEND  . . . .   828 O WHY BORN/L        4
    WHEN ELATE I AM ENVYD WHEN MEEK IM DESPISD  . . . . .   829 O WHY BORN/L       10
```

	PAGE	TITLE	LINE
IMAGE SEE DEATH-IMAGE			
PRIDE MADE A GODDESS FAIR OR IMAGE RATHER	42D	THEN SHE BORE	PROSE
("ART IS HIGHEST HUMAN NATURE") HUMAN NATURE IS THE IMAGE OF GOD	83A	ANNO LAVATER	MARG
THE FANCIED IMAGE STRAYS	114	LIT GRL FND/SI	14
THE DIVINE IMAGE	117A	DIVNE IMAGE/SI	TITLE
HOLY IMAGE I CAN TRACE	120	CRADLE SONG/SI	22
THOU HIS IMAGE EVER SEE	120	CRADLE SONG/SI	27
IMAGE OF TRUTH NEW BORN	126	VOICE BARD/SI	3
ART THOU A WORM IMAGE OF WEAKNESS ART THOU BUT A WORM .	129	BOOK OF THEL 4	2
. . . FANCY GAVE HIM TO SEE AN IMAGE OF DESPAIR IN HIS DEN	136	FRENCH REVOLTN	45
EVERY THING POSSIBLE TO BE BELIEVD IS AN IMAGE OF TRUTH	151D	MARRIAGE HH 8	PROSE
THE HUMAN IMAGE	174A	HUMAN IMAGE/N	TITLE
THE IMAGE OF THEOTORMON ON MY PURE TRANSPARENT BREAST . .	190	V DAU ALBION 2	16
HOW CAN I BE DEFILD WHEN I REFLECT THY IMAGE PURE . .	191	V DAU ALBION 3	16
THY JOYS ARE TEARS THY LABOUR VAIN TO FORM MEN TO THINE IMAGE	192	V DAU ALBION 5	4
THE LUSTFUL JOY SHALL FORGET TO GENERATE & CREATE AN AMOROUS IMAGE	194	V DAU ALBION 7	6
THOU ART THE IMAGE OF GOD WHO DWELLS IN DARKNESS OF AFRICA	196	AMERICA PREL 2	8
A DIVINE IMAGE	221A	DIVNE IMAGE/SE	TITLE
ON HIS OWN DIVIDED IMAGE	232	URIZEN 19	16
THEN WAS THE SERPENT TEMPLE FORMD IMAGE OF INFINITE . . .	241	EUROPE 10	21
WITH PURPLE FLOWERS AND BERRIES RED IMAGE OF THAT SWEET SOUTH	241	EUROPE 10	27
REFUSING TO BEHOLD THE DIVINE IMAGE WHICH ALL BEHOLD .	272	FOUR ZOAS 1	290
WILL SO RECIEVE THE DIVINE IMAGE THAT AMONGST THE REPROBATE	272	FOUR ZOAS 1	297
ETERNITY GROAND & WAS TROUBLED AT THE IMAGE OF ETERNAL DEATH	273	FOUR ZOAS 1	315
ETERNITY GROAND & WAS TROUBLED AT THE IMAGE OF ETERNAL DEATH	277	FOUR ZOAS 1	* 462
AHANIA'S IMAGE I DECIEVD THEE & WILL STILL DECIEVE . . .	288	FOUR ZOAS 2	328
AND THOU HAST RISEN WITH THY MOIST LOCKS INTO A WATRY IMAGE	295	FOUR ZOAS 3	125
IMAGE OF GRIEF THY FADING LINEAMENTS MAKE MY EYELIDS FAIL	297	FOUR ZOAS 3	195
LOOKING UPON THEE IMAGE OF FAINT WATERS I RECOIL	297	FOUR ZOAS 3	197
IMAGE OF DREAD WHENCE ART THOU WHENCE IS THIS MOST WOFUL PLACE	321	FOUR ZOAS 7	44
LOS SAW HER STRETCHD THE IMAGE OF DEATH UPON HIS WITHERD VALLEYS	324	FOUR ZOAS 7	172
THE FLEETING IMAGE & IN WHISPERS MILD WOO'D THE FAINT SHADE	325	FOUR ZOAS 7	221
THE CAUSE OF HER DIRE ANGUISH FOR SHE LAY THE IMAGE OF DEATH	328	FOUR ZOAS 7	320
AS THE ELDEST BROTHER IS THE [SECOND] FATHER'S IMAGE SO ORC BECAME	332	FOUR ZOAS 7	* 479
BUILDED A TEMPLE IN THE IMAGE OF THE HUMAN HEART	333	FOUR ZOAS 7B	20
AGAINST THE DIVINE IMAGE CONGREGATED ASSEMBLIES OF WICKED MEN	347	FOUR ZOAS 8	258
AGAIN REORGANIZE TILL THEY RESUME THE IMAGE OF THE HUMAN	366	FOUR ZOAS 9	372
CALLING HIM BROTHER IMAGE OF THE ETERNAL FATHER THEY SAT DOWN	374	FOUR ZOAS 9	644
AGAINST THIS IMAGE OF HIS LORD	420	I SAW MNK AD/N	9
ITS OFFERINGS EVEN TILL JESUS THE IMAGE OF THE INVISIBLE GOD	481	MILTON 2	12
A MOURNFUL SHADE ETERNITY SHUDDERD AT THE IMAGE OF ETERNAL DEATH	496	MILTON 14	35
IMAGE DIVINE THO DARKEND AND THO WALKING AS ONE WALKS .	496	MILTON 15	6
FOR I WILL PUT ON THE HUMAN FORM & TAKE THE IMAGE OF GOD	499	MILTON 18	19
HIS FORMING IMAGE HE WALKS ROUND IT PATIENT LABOURING .	502	MILTON 20	9
THE IMAGE OF A CLASS AND NOT OF AN IMPERFECT INDIVIDUAL	571A	DESC CAT 3	PROSE
BUT ITS ETERNAL IMAGE & INDIVIDUALITY NEVER DIES	605B	V LAST JUDG/N	PROSE
BUT RENEWS BY ITS SEED JUST [AS] SO THE IMAGINATIVE IMAGE	605B	V LAST JUDG/N	PROSE
O HOLY GENERATION [IMAGE] OF REGENERATION	626	JERUSALEM 7	* 65
PITEOUS IMAGE OF MY SOFT DESIRES & LOVES O ENITHARMON .	639	JERUSALEM 17	19
BUT THOU DELUDING IMAGE BY WHOM IMBUD THE VEIL I RENT .	646	JERUSALEM 23	31
ART THOU VALA REPLIED ALBION IMAGE OF MY REPOSE . . .	660	JERUSALEM 34	2
THOU WAST THE IMAGE OF GOD SURROUNDED BY THE FOUR ZOAS .	670	JERUSALEM 42	23
ETERNITY GROAND & WAS TROUBLED AT THE IMAGE OF ETERNAL DEATH	677	JERUSALEM 48	12
AGAINST THIS IMAGE OF HIS LORD	683	I SAW A MONK/J	24
THOU ART THE SOFT REFLECTED IMAGE OF THE SLEEPING MAN . .	730	JERUSALEM 85	24
THUS WAS THE COVERING CHERUB REVEALD MAJESTIC IMAGE . .	734	JERUSALEM 89	9
IN THE DIVINE IMAGE NOR CAN MAN EXIST BUT BY BROTHERHOOD	743	JERUSALEM 96	28
BUT IF YOU AVENGE YOU MURDER THE DIVINE IMAGE	757D	EV GOSPEL	PROSE
IS SHE ALSO THE DIVINE IMAGE	765D	FOR SEXES/GP	TITLE
THE ALL IN MAN THE DIVINE IMAGE OR IMAGINATION	773D	ANNO BERKELEY	MARG
CHRISTIANITY AND ADORE HIM WHO IS THE EXPRESS IMAGE OF GOD	815D	LETTER 23	PROSE
THE BLOSSOM THE CHIMNEY SWEEPER THE DIVINE IMAGE NIGHT	SUPP	LETTER 66A	*PROSE
IMAGERY			
OCCASION OF POETIC IMAGERY WHEN A BASE MAN MEANS TO BE .	592C	PUB ADDRESS/N	PROSE
IMAGES			
IMPOSSIBLE TO THINK WITHOUT IMAGES OF SOMEWHAT ON EARTH	88B	ANNO LAVATER	MARG
IN VAIN THE DREAMER GRASPS THE JOYFUL IMAGES THEY FLY .	206	THIRALATHA	2
HIS IMAGES ARE BORN FOR WAR FOR SACRIFICE TO TIRZAH . .	501	MILTON 19	53
BY IMITATION OF NATURE'S IMAGES DRAWN FROM REMEMBRANCE .	533	MILTON 41	24
OF ITS EVER EXISTENT IMAGES IS CONSIDERD AS LESS PERMANENT	605B	V LAST JUDG/N	PROSE
SUBLIME & DIVINE IMAGES AS SEEN IN THE WORLDS OF VISION	605B	V LAST JUDG/N	PROSE
AROUND HIM WERE SEEN THE IMAGES OF EXISTENCES	606A	V LAST JUDG/N	PROSE
IF THE SPECTATOR COULD ENTER INTO THESE IMAGES	611A	V LAST JUDG/N	PROSE
OR COULD MAKE A FRIEND & COMPANION OF ONE OF THESE IMAGES OF	611A	V LAST JUDG/N	PROSE
BEARING THE IMAGES OF VARIOUS SPECIES OF CONTENTION . .	707	JERUSALEM 69	12
HE BRINGS TO ME THE IMAGES OF HIS LOVE & I REJECT IN CHASTITY	724	JERUSALEM 81	3

IMAGINATION

	PAGE	TITLE	LINE
AGES OF IMAGINATION THIS FIRM PERSWASION REMOVED MOUNTAINS	153C	MARRIAGE HH 12	PROSE
PETRIFYING ALL THE HUMAN IMAGINATION INTO ROCK & SAND . .	281	FOUR ZOAS 2	38
URIZEN SAW & ENVIED & HIS IMAGINATION WAS FILLED	287	FOUR ZOAS 2	291
IN THE ETERNAL HEAVENS OF HUMAN [THOUGHT] IMAGINATION BURIED BENEATH	366	FOUR ZOAS 9	363
THAT GREATEST OF ALL BLESSINGS A STRONG IMAGINATION . . .	439D	REMARKS MALKIN	PROSE
BUT ARE FROM IMAGINATION	459C	ANNO REYNOLDS	MARG
LABOUR & TRICK AS TO IMAGINATION HE WAS TOTALLY WITHOUT ANY	468C	ANNO REYNOLDS	MARG
IMAGINATION NOT TO BE ABOVE THE MORTAL & PERISHING NATURE	475D	ANNO REYNOLDS	MARG
AND OF THE SPORTS OF WISDOM IN THE HUMAN IMAGINATION . .	482	MILTON 3	3
REGIONS OF THE IMAGINATION ALSO ALL MEN ON EARTH	503	MILTON 21	5
AND ALL IN HEAVEN SAW IN THE NETHER REGIONS OF THE IMAGINATION	503	MILTON 21	6
THE IDIOT REASONER LAUGHS AT THE MAN OF IMAGINATION . . .	521	MILTON 32	6
CALLING THE HUMAN IMAGINATION WHICH IS THE DIVINE VISION & FRUITION	521	MILTON 32	19
THE IMAGINATION IS NOT A STATE IT IS THE HUMAN EXISTENCE ITSELF	522	MILTON 32	32
AFFECTION OR LOVE BECOMES A STATE WHEN DIVIDED FROM IMAGINATION	522	MILTON 32	33
TO TAKE OFF HIS FILTHY GARMENTS & CLOTHE HIM WITH IMAGINATION	533	MILTON 41	6
WHO PRETEND TO POETRY THAT THEY MAY DESTROY IMAGINATION	533	MILTON 41	23
AND NOT OF INSPIRATION OR IMAGINATION THEREFORE	566A	DESC CAT 2	PROSE
IMAGINATION ONLY CAN FURNISH US WITH COLOURING APPROPRIATE	580D	DESC CAT 5	PROSE
HIS POWER OF IMAGINATION WEAKENED SO MUCH AND DARKENED .	582D	DESC CAT 9	PROSE
AS I COPY IMAGINATION THIS THEY WILL FIND IMPOSSIBLE . .	594D	PUB ADDRESS/N	PROSE
COPIERS OF IMAGINATION ARE CORRECT THIS IS MANIFEST TO ALL	595A	PUB ADDRESS/N	PROSE
[IMAGINATION IS MY WORLD THIS WORLD OF DROSS IS BENEATH]	600C	PUB ADDRESS/N	PROSE
UNDERSTAND IMAGINATION BUT BECAUSE THEY DID NOT UNDERSTAND VERSE	602D	PUB ADDR AD/N	PROSE
WHEN IMAGINATION ART & SCIENCE & ALL INTELLECTUAL GIFTS	604C	V LAST JUDG/N	PROSE
OF POETRY VISION OR IMAGINATION IS A REPRESENTATION . .	604D	V LAST JUDG/N	PROSE
IMAGINATION IS SURROUNDED BY THE DAUGHTERS OF INSPIRATION	604D	V LAST JUDG/N	PROSE
BUT ETERNAL VISION OR IMAGINATION OF ALL THAT EXISTS .	604D	V LAST JUDG/N	PROSE
[& VISIONS OF IMAGINATION] OUGHT TO BE KNOWN	605A	V LAST JUDG/N	PROSE
THE NATURE OF VISIONARY FANCY OR IMAGINATION IS VERY LITTLE	605A	V LAST JUDG/N	PROSE
THIS WORLD OF IMAGINATION IS THE WORLD OF ETERNITY . .	605D	V LAST JUDG/N	PROSE
THIS WORLD OF IMAGINATION IS INFINITE & ETERNAL WHEREAS	605D	V LAST JUDG/N	PROSE
THE HUMAN IMAGINATION WHO APPEARD TO ME AS	606A	V LAST JUDG/N	PROSE
THESE VARIOUS STATES I HAVE SEEN IN MY IMAGINATION . .	607B	V LAST JUDG/N	PROSE
IN HIS IMAGINATION APPROACHING THEM	611A	V LAST JUDG/N	PROSE
ETERNAL REALITIES AS THEY EXIST IN THE HUMAN IMAGINATION	613C	V LAST JUDG/N	PROSE
THE MORE BRIGHT SUN OF SUN OF IMAGINATION	618D	ILLUS MILTON	*PROSE
EVER EXPANDING IN THE BOSOM OF GOD THE HUMAN IMAGINATION	623	JERUSALEM 5	20
ABSTRACT PHILOSOPHY WARRING IN ENMITY AGAINST IMAGINATION	624	JERUSALEM 5	58
O HUMAN IMAGINATION O DIVINE BODY I HAVE CRUCIFIED . .	647	JERUSALEM 24	23
STANDS BETWEEN THE VEGETATIVE MAN & HIS IMMORTAL IMAGINATION	663	JERUSALEM 36	24
MY STREETS ARE MY IDEAS OF IMAGINATION	665	JERUSALEM 38	31
WERE CONTAIND IN THE ALL GLORIOUS IMAGINATION ARE WITHERD & DARKEND	679	JERUSALEM 49	14
THAT THOU O HUMAN IMAGINATION O DIVINE BODY ART ALL .	693	JERUSALEM 60	57
FOR ALL THINGS EXIST IN THE HUMAN IMAGINATION	707	JERUSALEM 69	25
. . . IMAGINATION THE DIVINE-HUMANITY	709	JERUSALEM 70	19
IN YOUR IMAGINATION OF WHICH THIS WORLD OF MORTALITY IS BUT A SHADOW	709	JERUSALEM 71	19
ENTERING INTO THE REASONING POWER FORSAKING IMAGINATION	714	JERUSALEM 74	7
FROM IMAGINATION AND CLOSING ITSELF AS IN STEEL IN A RATIO	714	JERUSALEM 74	11
TO DESTROY IMAGINATION THE DIVINE BODY BY MARTYRDOMS & WARS	714	JERUSALEM 74	13
AND BY ABSTRACTION OPPOSED TO THE VISIONS OF IMAGINATION	715	JERUSALEM 74	26
OF BODY & MIND TO EXERCISE THE DIVINE ARTS OF IMAGINATION	716D	JERUSALEM 77	PROSE
IMAGINATION THE REAL & ETERNAL WORLD	717A	JERUSALEM 77	PROSE
OF HUMAN IMAGINATION THROUGHOUT ALL THE THREE REGIONS IMMENSE	746	JERUSALEM 98	32
AND PRIDE & VANITY OF THE IMAGINATION	752	EV GOSPEL(D)/N	47
IMAGINATION OR THE HUMAN ETERNAL BODY IN EVERY MAN . .	773C	ANNO BERKELEY	MARG
IMAGINATION OR THE DIVINE BODY IN EVERY MAN	773D	ANNO BERKELEY	MARG
THE ALL IN MAN THE DIVINE IMAGE OR IMAGINATION . . .	773D	ANNO BERKELEY	* MARG
JESUS CONSIDERD IMAGINATION TO BE THE REAL MAN & SAYS .	774A	ANNO BERKELEY	* MARG
THE WHOLE BIBLE IS FILLD WITH IMAGINATION & VISIONS . .	774D	ANNO BERKELEY	MARG
FORMS MUST BE APPREHENDED BY SENSE OR THE EYE OF IMAGINATION	775A	ANNO BERKELEY	MARG
MAN IS ALL IMAGINATION GOD IS MAN & EXISTS IN US & WE IN HIM	775A	ANNO BERKELEY	MARG
WHICH BLINDS THE EYE OF IMAGINATION THE REAL MAN . . .	775B	ANNO BERKELEY	MARG
ART DEGRADED IMAGINATION DENIED WAR GOVERNED THE NATIONS	775D	INSC LAOCOON	PROSE
THE ETERNAL BODY OF MAN IS THE IMAGINATION THAT IS . .	776B	INSC LAOCOON	PROSE
ADAM IS ONLY THE NATURAL MAN & NOT THE SOUL OR IMAGINATION	776C	INSC LAOCOON	PROSE
PERMANENT IN THE IMAGINATION CONSIDERD AS NOTHING BY .	776D	INSC LAOCOON	PROSE
NATURE HAS NO OUTLINE BUT IMAGINATION HAS	779C	GHOST ABEL 1	PROSE
NATURE HAS NO TUNE BUT IMAGINATION HAS	779C	GHOST ABEL 1	PROSE
NATURE HAS NO SUPERNATURAL & DISSOLVES IMAGINATION IS ETERNITY	779C	GHOST ABEL 1	PROSE
ADAM IT IS ALL A VAIN DELUSION OF THE ALL CREATIVE IMAGINATION	780	GHOST ABEL 1	17
ONE POWER ALONE MAKES A POET IMAGINATION THE DIVINE VISION	782D	ANNO WW POEMS	MARG
& OBLITERATE IMAGINATION IN ME WORDSWORTH MUST KNOW . .	783A	ANNO WW POEMS	MARG
IMAGINATION IS THE DIVINE VISION NOT OF THE WORLD NOR OF MAN	783D	ANNO WW POEMS	* MARG
A SPIRITUAL MAN IMAGINATION HAS NOTHING TO DO WITH MEMORY	783D	ANNO WW POEMS	MARG

IMAGINATION   (CONTINUED)
```
    MEMORY [NATURE] IS HIS INSPIRER & NOT IMAGINATION THE HOLY    785A ILLUS DANTE 7  *PROSE
      GHOST
    I KNOW THAT THIS WORLD IS A WORLD OF IMAGINATION & VISION     793C LETTER 5        PROSE
    SEE NATURE AT ALL BUT TO THE EYES OF THE MAN OF IMAGINATION   793D LETTER 5        PROSE
    NATURE IS IMAGINATION ITSELF AS A MAN IS SO HE SEES  . . .    793D LETTER 5        PROSE
    IMAGINATION & I FEEL FLATTERD WHEN I AM TOLD SO  . . .  .     793D LETTER 5        PROSE
    IS IT NOT BECAUSE THEY ARE ADDRESSED TO THE IMAGINATION       794A LETTER 5        PROSE
      WHICH
    "IMAGINATION BEFORE REASON HAVE JUDGED & REASON "   . . .     794A LETTER 5        PROSE
    "SENDS OVER TO IMAGINATION BEFORE THE DECREE CAN BE ACTED"    794A LETTER 5        PROSE
    VAST MAJORITY ON THE SIDE OF IMAGINATION OR SPIRITUAL         794B LETTER 5        PROSE
      SENSATION
    SEE HIM IN MY REMEMBRANCE IN THE REGIONS OF MY IMAGINATION    797A LETTER 9        PROSE
    & LIFE NOT IN THE REAL MAN THE IMAGINATION WHICH LIVETH       878A LETTER 88       PROSE
IMAGINATIONS
    [THE] HIS LAUGHTER NOT AT THEM BUT AT HIS OWN IMAGINATIONS     44C ISLAND MOON 1  *PROSE
    BUT JUST & TRUE TO OUR OWN IMAGINATIONS THOSE WORLDS    .  .  480D MILTON 1        PROSE
    CAN FROM THOSE GATES VIEW ALL THESE WONDROUS IMAGINATIONS     524 MILTON 34          18
    THAT ALL HIS IMAGINATIONS APPEAR TO HIM  . . . . . . . .     576D DESC CAT 4       PROSE
    NOR CAN THEIR METHOD EVER EXPRESS IDEAS OR IMAGINATIONS       596A PUB ADDRESS/N    PROSE
    ACCORDING TO [THEIR AGGREGATE IMAGINATIONS] A CERTAIN ORDER   606A V LAST JUDG/N  *PROSE
IMAGINATIVE
    WHOM THEY SAW WITH THEIR IMAGINATIVE AND IMMORTAL ORGANS      576D DESC CAT 4       PROSE
    LABOURING TO DESTROY IMAGINATIVE POWER BY MEANS OF   . . .    582C DESC CAT 9       PROSE
    IS SEEN BY THE [IMAGINATIVE EYE] OF EVERY ONE . . . . .       604C V LAST JUDG/N    PROSE
    BUT RENEWS BY ITS SEED JUST [AS] SO THE IMAGINATIVE IMAGE     605B V LAST JUDG/N    PROSE
    THE NATURE OF MY WORK IS VISIONARY OR IMAGINATIVE   . . .     605C V LAST JUDG/N    PROSE
    SUITED TO MY IMAGINATIVE EYE [IN THE FOLLOWING ORDER] AS      606A V LAST JUDG/N    PROSE
      FOLLOWS
    THOSE WHO ARE BLESSED WITH IMAGINATIVE VISION SEE    . . .    609B V LAST JUDG/N    PROSE
    THE IMAGINATIVE HUMAN FORM IS BUT A BREATHING OF VALA   .  .  660 JERUSALEM 33        49
    & IN WHICH WE SHALL LIVE IN OUR ETERNAL OR IMAGINATIVE        717A JERUSALEM 77     PROSE
      BODIES
    OR DISTINCT FROM THE IMAGINATIVE WORLD  . . . . . . .         774A ANNO BERKELEY    MARG
    AS A MAN IN THE SPIRITUAL OR IMAGINATIVE VISION   . . . .     774A ANNO BERKELEY    MARG
    FOR ITS REALITY IS ITS IMAGINATIVE FORM  . . . . . . .        774B ANNO BERKELEY    MARG
    WHO FIRST SPOIL & THEN DESTROY IMAGINATIVE ART   . . . .      777A INSC LAOCCON     PROSE
    ("TO HC SIX YEARS OLD") THIS IS ALL IN THE HIGHEST DEGREE     783A ANNO WW POEMS    MARG
      IMAGINATIVE
IMAGIND
    WHAT IS NOW PROVED WAS ONCE ONLY IMAGIND  . . . . .           151D MARRIAGE HH 8    PROSE
    STUDIOUS LOVER OF ART CAN SCARCELY BE IMAGIND YET SUCH IS     830A LETTER 30        PROSE
IMAGINE
    PERISHING NATURE CAN PRODUCE HE WHO DOES NOT IMAGINE   .      576D DESC CAT 4       PROSE
    DOES NOT IMAGINE AT ALL THE PAINTER OF THIS WORK ASSERTS      576D DESC CAT 4       PROSE
IMAGINED
    AND NOT FOR HISTORICAL GRANDEUR THE ARTIST HAS IMAGINED       580A DESC CAT 5       PROSE
IMAGINES
    & EXPOSES HYPOCRITES TILL HE IMAGINES THAT ALL ARE           157D MARRIAGE HH 21   PROSE
      RELIGIOUS
IMBECILE
    COUNTING HIM AN IMBECILE MOCKERY BUT THE WARRIOR  . . .       704 JERUSALEM 67        20
    HIS IMBECILE ATTEMPTS TO DEPRESS ME ONLY DESERVE LAUGHTER     825C LETTER 27        PROSE
IMBECILITY
    OUGHT NOT THE [?ARTISTS ?& ?EMPLOYERS' ?IMBECILITY]  . .      452C ANNO REYNOLDS  * MARG
    ANNEXED TO IMBECILITY AND DISEASE IS A SUBJECT FOR            580A DESC CAT 5       PROSE
      BURLESQUE
IMBECILLITY
    MUST HAVE BEEN A PITIFUL A PITIABLE IMBECILLITY   . . .       471A ANNO REYNOLDS    MARG
    & POWER IS TO GIVE PLACE TO IMBECILLITY [AND WHETHER]  .      591C PUB ADDRESS/N    PROSE
    UNLESS THE LABOUR & CARE OF IMBECILLITY  . . . . . .          593A PUB ADDRESS/N    PROSE
    CHOOSE TO PURCHASE THE LIFE'S LABOUR OF IGNORANCE             594B PUB ADDRESS/N    PROSE
      & IMBECILLITY
    THE LIFE'S LABOURS OF IMBECILLITY & IMBECILLITY'S             598C PUB ADDRESS/N    PROSE
      JOURNEYMEN
IMBECILLITY'S
    THE LIFE'S LABOURS OF IMBECILLITY & IMBECILLITY'S             598C PUB ADDRESS/N    PROSE
      JOURNEYMEN
IMBIBED
    OF ALBION DRANK & IMBIBED THE LIFE & ETERNAL FORM OF LUVAH    736 JERUSALEM 90        17
IMBIBES
    FOR A SPECTRE HAS NO EMANATION BUT WHAT HE IMBIBES FROM       701 JERUSALEM 65        59
      DECIEVING
IMBODIED     SEE EMBODIED
    AT LENGTH IN TEARS & CRIES IMBODIED  . . . . . . . .         231 URIZEN 18            6
    IMBODIED THOU MY GARDEN OF DELIGHT & I THE SPIRIT IN THE      327 FOUR ZOAS 7        272
      GARDEN
IMBUD
    BUT THOU DELUDING IMAGE BY WHOM IMBUD THE VEIL I RENT   .     646 JERUSALEM 23        31
IMITATE
    ONE MAN STRIVING TO IMITATE ANOTHER MAN VARIES FROM MAN       470B ANNO REYNOLDS    MARG
    WHY THEN IMITATE AT ALL  . . . . . . . . . . . .        .    471C ANNO REYNOLDS    MARG
    LEST HE SHOULD FALL APART IN HIS ETERNAL DEATH TO IMITATE     531 MILTON 39           26
    & WE ARE [WE] TO IMITATE THEIR EXECUTION THIS IS [AS IF]      599D PUB ADDRESS/N    PROSE
    TO IMITATE I ABHOR I OBSTINATELY ADHERE TO THE TRUE STYLE     600B PUB ADDRESS/N    PROSE
IMITATED
    WHICH CANNOT BE IMITATED BY ANY ONE WHO DOES NOT  . . .       592B PUB ADDRESS/N    PROSE
    AND IMITATED BY OTHERS IF THEY PLEASE   . . . . . . .         598C PUB ADDRESS/N    PROSE
IMITATES
    HE ONLY IMITATES WHAT IS ALREADY EXECUTED  . . . . .          596B PUB ADDRESS/N    PROSE
    & IMITATES THE EFFECTS OF NATURE  . . . . . . . .  .          597C PUB ADDRESS/N    PROSE
```

	PAGE	TITLE	LINE

IMITATION
```
AN IMITATION OF SPENCER  . . . . . . . . . . . .    14B IMIT SPEN/PS    *TITLE
BUT ONLY IMITATION WHAT FOLLY  . . . . . . . . .   400C ANNO BACON      MARG
TO ALLEDGE FOR OUR IMITATION & APPROVAL  . . . . . 406D ANNO BACON      MARG
IMITATION IS CRITICISM  . . . . . . . . . . . .    453C ANNO REYNOLDS   MARG
IMITATION OF FACILITY IN EXECUTION OR ARE WE TO UNDERSTAND 453D ANNO REYNOLDS  MARG
KNEW NOTHING AT ALL ABOUT ART AS AN OBJECT OF IMITATION   467B ANNO REYNOLDS  MARG
MICH ANG & RAFAEL WERE NOT WORTHY OF IMITATION  . . . .   467D ANNO REYNOLDS  MARG
BY IMITATION OF NATURE'S IMAGES DRAWN FROM REMEMBRANCE .  533 MILTON 41       24
IMITATION OF POPE A COMPLIMENT TO THE LADIES  . .  545B IMIT POPE/N     TITLE
THE GREATER IS THE EVIDENCE OF WEAK IMITATION PLAGIARISM  585B DESC CAT 15    PROSE
HEATH'S LAME IMITATION STOTHARD BEING SUCH A FOOL  .  592B PUB ADDRESS/N   PROSE
NO MAN OF SENSE CAN THINK THAT AN IMITATION  . . . .    597B PUB ADDRESS/N   PROSE
SUCH IMITATION WHICH ANY ONE MAY EASILY PERFORM  . . .  597B PUB ADDRESS/N   PROSE
[THE ART OF INVENTION NOT OF IMITATION]  . . . . . .   600C PUB ADDRESS/N   PROSE
IS ART DELIVERD FROM NATURE & IMITATION  . . . . . .   776A INSC LAOCOON    PROSE
IN IMITATION OF THE FIRST STROKES OF THE PAINTER   850D LETTER 49       PROSE
    THE EXPRESSION
IMITATIONS
DIS-ARRANGED IMITATIONS AND BLUNDERING MISAPPLIED COPIES  585D DESC CAT 15    PROSE
IMITATORS
AND THOSE WHO WERE HIS IMITATORS AND JOURNEYMEN HE  . .  583A DESC CAT 9     PROSE
BUT THE LAME IMITATORS OF LINES DRAWN BY THEIR PREDECESSORS 585D DESC CAT 15  PROSE
WERE THE AWKWARD IMITATORS AT THAT TIME IT IS THE  . .  592B PUB ADDRESS/N   PROSE
IMMATURE
("HURRIED ON BY FURIES OF IMMATURE IMPETUOUS WISHES")   85D ANNO LAVATER   MARG
    UNEASY
IMMEASURABLE      SEE UNMEASURABLE
AND FROM THE NORTH AND SATAN STOOD OPAKE IMMEASURABLE  .  490 MILTON 9        39
IMMEDIATE
OR BY THE IMMEDIATE INSPIRATION OF GOD IT IS  . . . . . 614A V LAST JUDG/N  PROSE
KNOWLEDGE IS NOT BY DEDUCTION BUT IMMEDIATE BY PERCEPTION 774C ANNO BERKELEY MARG
    OR
DIVINE UNION DERIDING AND DENYING IMMEDIATE COMMUNION  .  776D INSC LAOCOON   PROSE
YOU HAVE SAID IN IT CALLD UPON ME FOR AN IMMEDIATE ANSWER 811B LETTER 22     PROSE
FROM IMMEDIATE DICTATION TWELVE OR SOMETIMES TWENTY  . . 823A LETTER 26      PROSE
I ENTREAT YOUR IMMEDIATE ADVICE WHAT I AM TO DO FOR T  . 858C LETTER 55      PROSE
IMMEDIATELY
THEYD [IMMEDIATLY] IMMEDIATELY GO OUT  . . . . . .   433 AUGURIES        *  110
IMMEDIATELY BEFORE THE THRONE OF CHRIST IS ADAM & EVE  .  443B LAST JUDGMNT/L PROSE
I KNEW IMMEDIATELY THE DIFFERENCE BETWEEN RAFAEL & RUBENS 447C ANNO REYNOLDS  MARG
IMMEDIATELY THE LARK MOUNTED WITH A LOUD TRILL FROM   534 MILTON 42       29
    FELPHAM'S VALE
WHO LOOK IF A PICTURE IS WELL DRAWN AND IF IT IS   573B DESC CAT 3      PROSE
    IMMEDIATELY
IMMEDIATELY SET ABOUT SEARCHING FOR POINTS OF LIGHT  . . 599A PUB ADDRESS/N  PROSE
AS IT PASSES OVER THEN IMMEDIATELY  . . . . . . . .   790C LETTER 2       PROSE
[BEFORE] IMMEDIATELY ON THE RECEIT OF YOUR BEAUTIFUL BOOK 791A LETTER 3      PROSE
I WRITE IMMEDIATELY ON MY ARRIVAL NOT MERELY TO INFORM  . 833B LETTER 33     PROSE
TO WRITE IMMEDIATELY THO I HAVE NOT DONE HALF THE BUSINESS 834B LETTER 34    PROSE
WITH IT I SEALD & SENT IT IMMEDIATELY AS DIRECTED BY  . 834C LETTER 34      PROSE
KNEW IMMEDIATELY MY PORTRAIT OF ROMNEY & ASSURED ME  . . 836B LETTER 35     PROSE
& I WILL SEND IT IMMEDIATELY  . . . . . . . . . .   836C LETTER 35       PROSE
BEG OF YOU TO SEND TO ME THAT I MAY ENGRAVE THEM   838A LETTER 37       PROSE
    IMMEDIATELY
BUT WILL NOW IMMEDIATELY PROCEED IN THAT BUSINESS  . .  838B LETTER 37      PROSE
TO BE UNROLLED IMMEDIATELY THAT YOU RECEIVE THEM AND PUT  840D LETTER 40     PROSE
MR H(HOARE) HAS PROMISED TO SEE MR PHILLIPS IMMEDIATELY & 842D LETTER 42    *PROSE
WITHOUT A WORD AND SHE IMMEDIATELY SAID AH ROMNEY  . .  843C LETTER 43      PROSE
IMMEDIATELY TO LADY HAMILTON MR WALKER I HAVE AGAIN SEEN  845D LETTER 44     PROSE
J ROMNEY IMMEDIATELY DESIRING HIM TO GIVE US LIBERTY  . 846A LETTER 44      PROSE
CAVENDISH SQUARE IMMEDIATELY ON HIS RETURN BUT AS  . .  847D LETTER 44      PROSE
I WRITE IMMEDIATELY ON RECIEVING THE ABOVE INFORMATION  . 849A LETTER 45     PROSE
IMMEDIATELY ON RECEIPT OF IT BUT HOPED TO BE ABLE TO SEND 851B LETTER 50    PROSE
PERFECT STATE I WRITE IMMEDIATELY BECAUSE YOU WISH I SHOULD 851C LETTER 50  PROSE
IMMEDIATELY REPLIED IF MR HAYLEY SHOULD THINK FIT TO  . 856C LETTER 54      PROSE
TO WRITE IMMEDIATELY ON RETURNING FROM HIS HOUSE HE SAYS  857D LETTER 55     PROSE
HIMSELF IMMEDIATELY REPLY TO YOU I SHOULD HAVE SUPPOSED  857D LETTER 55      PROSE
ABOUT IT IMMEDIATELY AND HAS DESIRED THAT I  . . . . . 858D LETTER 55       PROSE
IMMEDIATELY HE SAID GIVE MY BEST RESPECTS & TELL MR HAYLEY 860A LETTER 56   PROSE
IN MY CAUSE & SHOULD IMMEDIATELY ENGAGE IN REVIVING  . . 865C LETTER 63    *PROSE
IMMENSE
IS AN IMMENSE WORLD OF DELIGHT CLOSD BY YOUR SENSES FIVE  150D MARRIAGE HH 6  PROSE
WHO BUILT PALACES IN THE IMMENSE CLIFFS  . . . . . .   154D MARRIAGE HH 15  PROSE
OF A BURNING CITY BENEATH US AT AN IMMENSE DISTANCE  . . 156A MARRIAGE HH 17 PROSE
A VOID IMMENSE WILD DARK & DEEP  . . . . . . . . .   224 URIZEN 4        16
THE ABYSS OF LOS STRETCHD IMMENSE  . . . . . . . .   230 URIZEN 15        5
AMAZD HIS HEAVENS IMMENSE CRACKS  . . . . . . . .   234 URIZEN 23        16
WITH A CRASH FROM IMMENSE TO IMMENSE  . . . . . . .   257 BOOK OF LOS 4    17
AN IMMENSE FIBROUS FORM STRETCHING OUT  . . . . . .   259 BOOK OF LOS 5     1
FLOWD AROUND THE IMMENSE LOS BEHELD  . . . . . . .   259 BOOK OF LOS 5    12
AN IMMENSE ORB OF FIRE HE FRAMD  . . . . . . . . .   260 BOOK OF LOS 5    34
OBSCURING THE IMMENSE ORB OF FIRE  . . . . . . . .   260 BOOK OF LOS 5    54
IS FORMD & MANY A CORDED LYRE OUTSPREAD OVER THE IMMENSE  284 FOUR ZOAS 2   161
WHEN URIZEN [DESCENDED] RETURND FROM HIS IMMENSE LABOURS  285 FOUR ZOAS 2   201
    & TRAVELS
UPON THE IMMENSE LIKE A BRIGHT RAINBOW WEEPING & SMILING  290 FOUR ZOAS 2   382
    & FADING
A CRASH RAN THRO THE IMMENSE THE BOUNDS OF DESTINY WERE   295 FOUR ZOAS 3   135
    BROKEN
THRO THE CONFUSION LIKE A CRACK ACROSS FROM IMMENSE TO    295 FOUR ZOAS 3   149
    IMMENSE
```

		PAGE	TITLE	LINE

IMMENSE   (CONTINUED)
```
      STRETCHD OVER THE IMMENSE HEAVES IN STRONG SHUDDERS SILENT    302 FOUR ZOAS 4      173
        HIS VOICE
      LOS FROM THE FURNACES A SPACE IMMENSE & LEFT THE COLD   .   .  305 FOUR ZOAS 5       15
      SCARD AT THE SOUND OF THEIR OWN SIGH THAT SEEMS TO SHAKE       314 FOUR ZOAS 6       89
        THE IMMENSE
      SWIFT SWIFT FROM CHAOS TO CHAOS FROM VOID TO VOID A            316 FOUR ZOAS 6      189
        ROAD IMMENSE
      AND BRASS VAST INSTRUMENTS TO MEASURE OUT THE IMMENSE & FIX    317 FOUR ZOAS 6      230
      STILL HE WITH HIS GLOBE OF FIRE IMMENSE IN HIS VENTUROUS       319 FOUR ZOAS 6      286
        HAND
      AND WITH IMMENSE MACHINES DOWN ROLLING THE TERRIFIC ORB        333 FOUR ZOAS 7B      30
      AND HE ROLLD DOWN BENEATH THE FIRES OF ORC A GLOBE IMMENSE     350 FOUR ZOAS 8      372
      OUTSTRETCHD [OVER] THRO THE IMMENSE HIS MOUTH WIDE OPENING     352 FOUR ZOAS 8   *  426
        TONGUELESS
      AND HIS IMMENSE TAIL LASHD THE ABYSS HIS HUMAN FORM A STONE    352 FOUR ZOAS 8      428
      AND STILL HIS STONY FORM REMAIND IN THE ABYSS IMMENSE   .   .  352 FOUR ZOAS 8      432
      . . . CRACKING THE HEAVENS ACROSS FROM IMMENSE TO IMMENSE      357 FOUR ZOAS 9        9
      RESHONE ACROSS THE FIELD IMMENSE WHERE ALL THE NATIONS  .   .  364 FOUR ZOAS 9      293
      OF THE WIDE UNIVERSAL FIELD THEN STEPD [OUT] FORTH INTO        365 FOUR ZOAS 9      320
        THE IMMENSE
      IMMENSE UPON THE HEAVENS WITH BREAD & DELICATE REPASTS  .   .  366 FOUR ZOAS 9      334
      IN THE IMMENSE AS WHEN THE SUN DANCES UPON THE MOUNTAINS       366 FOUR ZOAS 9      349
      THRO ALL THE IMMENSE BORNE DOWN BY CLOUDS SWAGGING             372 FOUR ZOAS 9      563
        IN AUTUMNAL HEAT
      DOWN DOWN THRO THE IMMENSE WITH OUTCRY FURY & DESPAIR   .   .  376 FOUR ZOAS 9      723
      IN IMMENSE LABOURS & SORROWS EVER BUILDING EVER FALLING        485 MILTON 6           2
      THE MUNDANE SHELL IS A VAST CONCAVE EARTH AN IMMENSE   .   .   498 MILTON 17         21
      THE MANUAL LABOUR IN THESE PICTURES OF CORREGGIO IS IMMENSE   583B DESC CAT 9     PROSE
      AND WAS PAID FOR ORIGINALLY AT THE IMMENSE PRICES THAT   .    583B DESC CAT 9     PROSE
      AT AN IMMENSE PRICE & TOLD THAT SUCH IS THE ART OF PAINTING   601C PUB ADDRESS/N  PROSE
      IMMENSE AND JERUSALEM & VALA WEEPING IN THE CLOUD   .   .   .  624 JERUSALEM 5       62
      THEY PUT FORTH THEIR SPECTROUS CLOUDY SAILS WHICH DRIVE        625 JERUSALEM 7       21
        THEIR IMMENSE
      BECAME AS THREE IMMENSE WHEELS TURNING UPON ONE-ANOTHER        640 JERUSALEM 18       8
      THEIR WINGS WAVING OVER THE BOTTOMLESS IMMENSE TO BEAR  .   .  674 JERUSALEM 44       4
      ALBION'S DREAD WHEELS STRETCHING OUT SPACES IMMENSE BETWEEN    674 JERUSALEM 44       9
      BLACK & IMMENSE A ROCK OF DIFFICULTY & A CLIFF   .   .   .   . 674 JERUSALEM 44      11
      THEY ARE BEGINNING TO FORM HEAVENS & HELLS IN IMMENSE   .   .  680 JERUSALEM 49      61
      A WONDROUS GOLDEN BUILDING IMMENSE WITH ORNAMENTS SUBLIME   .  691 JERUSALEM 59      24
      THEY BECOME LIKE WHAT THEY BEHOLD YET IMMENSE IN STRENGTH      701 JERUSALEM 65      79
        & POWER
      OF HUMAN IMAGINATION THROUGHOUT ALL THE THREE REGIONS          746 JERUSALEM 98      32
        IMMENSE
      I AM VERY SORRY FOR YOUR IMMENSE LOSS WHICH IS A REPETITION   797A LETTER 9       PROSE
      THE IMMENSE FLOOD OF GRECIAN LIGHT & GLORY WHICH IS COMING    797C LETTER 10      PROSE
      THE PROFITS ARISING FROM PUBLICATIONS ARE IMMENSE &  .   .   .820A LETTER 25      PROSE
      AN IMMENSE NUMBER OF VERSES ON ONE GRAND THEME   .   .   .   .823A LETTER 26      PROSE
      RENDERD NON EXISTENT & AN IMMENSE POEM EXISTS   .   .   .   . 823B LETTER 26      PROSE
      AMERICA ENABLE HIM TO CIRCULATE PUBLICATIONS TO AN IMMENSE    841C LETTER 41      PROSE
      I KNOW IT HAS COST ME IMMENSE LABOUR  .   .   .   .   .   .   .861B LETTER 58      PROSE
IMMENSITY
      ONE THOUGHT FILLS IMMENSITY  .   .   .   .   .   .   .   .   . 151D MARRIAGE HH 8  PROSE
      & WE HELD BY THE ROOTS OF TREES AND HUNG OVER THIS            155D MARRIAGE HH 17 PROSE
        IMMENSITY
      THAT SOLITARY ONE IN IMMENSITY  .   .   .   .   .   .   .   .  223 URIZEN 3          43
      A TREE HUNG OVER THE IMMENSITY  .   .   .   .   .   .   .   .  251 AHANIA 3          54
      THRO THE BOTTOMS OF IMMENSITY RAGING  .   .   .   .   .   .   .259 BOOK OF LOS 5      2
      BENEATH THE DEEPS IN DISMAL DARKNESS BENEATH IMMENSITY         304 FOUR ZOAS 4      279
      POUR DOWN MY FLIGHT THRO DARK IMMENSITY ETERNAL FALLING        313 FOUR ZOAS 6       69
      IS NOT DOWN FALLING THRO IMMENSITY EVER & EVER   .   .   .   . 317 FOUR ZOAS 6      220
      ABOVE BENEATH ON ALL SIDES ROUND IN THE VAST DEEP             318 FOUR ZOAS 6      275
        OF IMMENSITY
      THARMAS THREW HIS IMPETUOUS FLIGHT THRO THE DEEPS             320 FOUR ZOAS 7         3
        OF IMMENSITY
      TILL OVERBURDEND WITH ITS OWN WEIGHT DRAWN OUT THRO            322 FOUR ZOAS 7        77
        IMMENSITY
      AND SATAN VIBRATED IN THE IMMENSITY OF THE SPACE LIMITED       491 MILTON 10          8
IMMERSED
      BUT MY GOOD SIR VOLTAIRE WAS IMMERSED IN MATTER   .   .   .   .45D ISLAND MOON 1  PROSE
IMMINGLED
      IMMINGLED WITH THE RUBY OVERSPREAD HIS VISAGE DOWN   .   .   . 342 FOUR ZOAS 8       71
      NOR DARKNESS IMMINGLED WITH LIGHT ON MY FURROWD FIELD   .   .  659 JERUSALEM 33      32
      IMMINGLED GOD & MAN WHEN THOU & I HID THE DIVINE VISION        660 JERUSALEM 33      46
      IN LOVE & JEALOUSY IMMINGLED & CALLING IT RELIGION   .   .   . 674 JERUSALEM 44      27
      AND JEALOUSY IMMINGLED & THE PURPLE OF THE VIOLET DARKEND      699 JERUSALEM 64      29
        DEEP
      IMMINGLED INTERWOVEN GLISTENING TO THE SICKENING SIGHT  .   .  727 JERUSALEM 83      32
IMMODERATE
      AND GROW IMMODERATE TO BRAVE IT OUT   .   .   .   .   .   .   . 37A CONTEMPLATN/PS PROSE
IMMORAL
      THE GRANDEST POETRY IS IMMORAL THE GRANDEST CHARACTERS        412B ANNO BOYD       MARG
        WICKED
IMMORTAL
      HE RUSHES UP THE SKY AND LAYS HOLD ON THE IMMORTAL COURSERS    37B CONTEMPLATN/PS PROSE
        OF DAY
      O THAT MEN WOULD SEEK IMMORTAL MOMENTS  .   .   .   .   .   .   80C ANNO LAVATER    MARG
      COMPELLD TO PRAY REPUGNANT & TO HUMBLE THE IMMORTAL SPIRIT     110 TIRIEL 8         36
      FROM OUR IMMORTAL DAY  .   .   .   .   .   .   .   .   .   .   .119 NIGHT/SI         40
      THE MILLIONS OF SPIRITS IMMORTAL . . .  .   .   .   .   .   .  143 FRENCH REVOLTN  213
      WHAT IMMORTAL HAND OR EYE   .   .   .   .   .   .   .   .   .   172 THE TYGER/N 1     3
      WHAT IMMORTAL HAND & EYE  .   .   .   .   .   .   .   .   .   . 173 THE TYGER/N 1    24
```

```
                                                                    PAGE     TITLE          LINE
IMMORTAL    (CONTINUED)
  WHAT IMMORTAL HAND [OR] & EYE  . . . . . . . . . .  .   173 THE TYGER/N 2   *      3
  WHAT IMMORTAL HAND & EYE  . . . . . . . . . . . . .     173 THE TYGER/N 2          19
  [XXX] SHAKING THE DUST FROM HIS IMMORTAL PINIONS TO AWAKE  190 V DAU ALBION 2 *    27
  BY THE RED EARTH OF OUR IMMORTAL RIVER I BATHE MY WINGS   191 V DAU ALBION 3       19
  REARS ITS IMMORTAL PINNACLES BUILT IN THE FOREST OF GOD   200 AMERICA 10            9
  WHY SEEKS HE REFUGE FROM THE FROWNS OF HIS IMMORTAL STATION 200 AMERICA 11          5
  WHAT IMMORTAL HAND OR EYE  . . . . . . . . . . .  .   214 THE TYGER/SE            3
  WHAT IMMORTAL HAND OR EYE  . . . . . . . . . . .  .   214 THE TYGER/SE           23
  THE WILL OF THE IMMORTAL EXPANDED  . . . . . . . . .    223 URIZEN 3              37
  PERTURBED IMMORTAL MAD RAGING  . . . . . . . . . .  .   227 URIZEN 8               4
  RESTLESS TURND THE IMMORTAL INCHAIND  . . . . . . . .   228 URIZEN 10             31
  THE IMMORTAL ENDURD HIS CHAINS  . . . . . . . . . .     229 URIZEN 13             26
  SITTING IN FATHOMLESS ABYSS OF MY IMMORTAL SHRINE  . . .  238 EUROPE PREL 2         2
  WHIRLING ABOUT IN FURIOUS CIRCLES ROUND THE IMMORTAL FIEND 240 EUROPE 4            30
  FILLD WITH IMMORTAL DEMONS OF FUTURITY  . . . . . .  .   241 EUROPE 9             10
  WAKING THE STARS OF URIZEN WITH THEIR IMMORTAL SONGS  . .  244 EUROPE 14           33
  OVER THE DISORGANIZD IMMORTAL  . . . . . . . . .  .  .   253 AHANIA 4             19
  AROUND THE IMMORTAL IN TORMENT  . . . . . . . . . .     253 AHANIA 4             23
  BOUND IN THE FIERCE RAGING IMMORTAL  . . . . . . . .    257 BOOK OF LOS 4          7
  THE IMMORTAL STOOD FROZEN AMIDST  . . . . . . . . .     257 BOOK OF LOS 4         11
  THE IMMORTAL REVOLVING INDIGNANT  . . . . . . . . .     258 BOOK OF LOS 4         37
  LOS WAS THE FOURTH IMMORTAL STARRY ONE & IN THE EARTH  .  264 FOUR ZOAS 1         14
  BUT MALES IMMORTAL LIVE RENEWD BY FEMALE DEATHS IN SOFT   266 FOUR ZOAS 1         66
  TO MAKE US HAPPY [HOW THEY] LET THEM WEARY THEIR IMMORTAL  271 FOUR ZOAS 1        254
     POWERS
  BUT WE IMMORTAL IN OUR OWN STRENGTH SURVIVE BY STERN DEBATE  272 FOUR ZOAS 1      292
  WHERE URIZEN & ALL HIS HOSTS HANG THEIR IMMORTAL LAMPS  .  272 FOUR ZOAS 1        304
  THEN ENITHARMON REDDNING FIERCE STRETCHD HER IMMORTAL HANDS  272 FOUR ZOAS 1      307
  STRETCH THEIR IMMORTAL HANDS TO SMITE THE GOLD & SILVER   274 FOUR ZOAS 1         380
     WIRES
  AND WITH IMMORTAL VOICE SOFT WARBLING FILL ALL EARTH &    274 FOUR ZOAS 1         381
     HEAVEN
  THEY SING UNCEASING TO THE NOTES OF MY IMMORTAL HAND  . .  289 FOUR ZOAS 2        354
  THE IMMORTAL ATMOSPHERES ARE THINE THERE THOU ART SEEN   291 FOUR ZOAS 3           8
     IN GLORY
  TO GIVE THE IMMORTAL STEEDS OF LIGHT TO HIS DECEITFUL HANDS  292 FOUR ZOAS 3       32
  IMMORTAL IN IMMORTAL TORMENT NEVER TO BE DELIVERD  . . .  298 FOUR ZOAS 4          20
  RESTLESS THE IMMORTAL INCHAIND HEAVING DOLOROUS  . . . .  303 FOUR ZOAS 4         215
  THE IMMORTAL ENDURD THO BOUND IN A DEADLY SLEEP  . . .   304 FOUR ZOAS 4         283
  FELT HER IMMORTAL LIMBS FREEZE STIFFNING PALE INFLEXIBLE   305 FOUR ZOAS 5   *      6
  OF ENITHARMON BUT HER GROANS DROWN THE IMMORTAL HARPS  . .  306 FOUR ZOAS 5        25
  WITH SILENT FEAR & HIS IMMORTAL CHEEKS GREW DEADLY PALE   307 FOUR ZOAS 5          87
  HIS UNCOUTH PLAGUE HE SIEZD THE BOY IN HIS IMMORTAL HANDS  307 FOUR ZOAS 5         97
  CRACKLING THE FLAMES WENT UP WITH FURY FROM THE IMMORTAL   308 FOUR ZOAS 5        108
     DEMON
  AND OVER THE IMMORTAL LIMBS OF THE TERRIBLE FIERY BOY  .  309 FOUR ZOAS 5         159
  . . . COMPOSD THE SONG TO THEIR IMMORTAL VOICES  . . . .  310 FOUR ZOAS 5         200
  WHEN THOU DIDST BEAR THE GOLDEN CUP AT THE IMMORTAL TABLES  311 FOUR ZOAS 5       228
  AND DRUNKEN WITH THE IMMORTAL DRAUGHT FELL FROM MY THRONE   311 FOUR ZOAS 5       237
     SUBLIME
  OR DRAWN UP OR LET DOWN AT THE WILL OF THE IMMORTAL MAN   318 FOUR ZOAS 6         255
  REDOUBLING HIS IMMORTAL EFFORTS THRO THE NARROW VALES  . .  319 FOUR ZOAS 6       292
  OF GOARY BLOOD THE IMMORTAL SEED IS NOURISHD FOR   320 FOUR ZOAS 7          15
     THE SLAUGHTER
  BENEATH THE TREE OF MYSTERY FOR THE IMMORTAL SHADOW   328 FOUR ZOAS 7         326
     SHUDDERING
  THOU DIDST SUBDUE ME IN OLD TIMES BY THY IMMORTAL STRENGTH  328 FOUR ZOAS 7       349
  THE IMMORTAL LINES UPON THE HEAVENS TILL WITH SIGHS OF LOVE  332 FOUR ZOAS 7      471
  THE SPECTROUS DEAD WEEPING THE SPECTRES VIEWD THE IMMORTAL  332 FOUR ZOAS 7       473
     WORKS
  FIRST HIS IMMORTAL SPIRIT DREW URIZEN [SPECTRE] SHADOW AWAY  332 FOUR ZOAS 7  *   490
  OF HIS IMMORTAL HEAD INTO THE NORTH UPON FAINT ENITHARMON  335 FOUR ZOAS 7B        77
  SHEWD THEIR IMMORTAL ENERGIES IN WARLIKE DESPERATION  . .  335 FOUR ZOAS 7B       102
  AND RUNNING THEIR IMMORTAL COURSE THRO SOLID DARKNESS BORNE  336 FOUR ZOAS 7B     143
  TWO WINGED IMMORTAL SHAPES ONE STANDING AT HIS FEET  . .  341 FOUR ZOAS 8          7
  [ON THE IMMORTAL FIEND] UPON THE MIGHTY FIEND . . . .    343 FOUR ZOAS 8          76
  AND URIZEN GAVE LIFE & SENSE BY HIS IMMORTAL POWER  . . .  344 FOUR ZOAS 8        131
  COLLECTING UP THE SCATTERD PORTIONS OF HIS IMMORTAL BODY   355 FOUR ZOAS 8        562
  IMMORTAL THOU REGENERATE SHE & ALL THE LOVELY SEX  . . .  362 FOUR ZOAS 9         216
  SHINES WITH IMMORTAL GLORY . . . . . . . . . .  .    364 FOUR ZOAS 9          268
  WITH A BRIGHT GIRDLE & HIS SKIRT FILLD WITH IMMORTAL SOULS  365 FOUR ZOAS 9       322
  AND GAVE THEM TO URIZEN'S HANDS THE IMMORTAL FROWND SAYING  366 FOUR ZOAS 9       362
  OF THIS IMMORTAL SPIRIT GROWING IN LOWER PARADISE  . . .  369 FOUR ZOAS 9         460
  WE VISIT HIM COVERING WITH A VEIL THE IMMORTAL SEED  . .  374 FOUR ZOAS 9         634
  AT THE IMMORTAL TABLES SOUNDING LOUD THEIR INSTRUMENTS   374 FOUR ZOAS 9         645
     OF JOY
  INWRAP THE IMMORTAL LIMBS STRUGGLING IN TERRIFIC JOY  . .  381 FOUR ZOAS AD 2      2
  RECORD THE JOURNEY OF IMMORTAL MILTON THRO YOUR REALMS  . .  481 MILTON 2          2
  TERRIFIED LOS STOOD IN THE ABYSS & HIS IMMORTAL LIMBS  . .  483 MILTON 3          28
  DREAD TOMB IMMORTAL ON HIS ROCK OVERSHADOWD THE WHOLE EARTH  491 MILTON 11         9
  AND LEUTHA STOOD GLOWING WITH VARYING COLOURS IMMORTAL   492 MILTON 11           32
     HEART-PIERCING
  FOR HER LIGHT IS TERRIBLE TO ME I FADE BEFORE HER IMMORTAL  492 MILTON 12          1
     BEAUTY
  CONTINUD ROUND THE HALLS AND MUCH THEY QUESTIOND   495 MILTON 13          46
     THE IMMORTAL
  HIS REAL AND IMMORTAL SELF WAS AS APPEARD TO THOSE  . . .  496 MILTON 15          11
  OF MILTON'S JOURNEY URIZEN BEHELD THE IMMORTAL MAN  . . .  498 MILTON 17          36
  RENT THE IMMORTAL FEMALES LIMB FROM LIMB & JOINT FROM   500 MILTON 18          49
     JOINT
  AND OFTEN SUNG TO THE LOUD HARP AT THE IMMORTAL FEASTS  . .  503 MILTON 20        58
```

IMMORTAL   (CONTINUED)
      AS A BRIGHT SANDAL FORMD IMMORTAL OF PRECIOUS STONES & GOLD   503 MILTON 21   13
      OF MORTAL OR IMMORTAL ARM AND SOFTLY LILLING FLUTES . . .   509 MILTON 24   56
      THEY RISE IN ORDER AND CONTINUE THEIR IMMORTAL COURSES . .   511 MILTON 25   67
      FORM IMMORTAL WITH GOLDEN PEN SUCH AS THE SPECTRE ADMIRING   515 MILTON 28   17
      THE SKY IS AN IMMORTAL TENT BUILT BY THE SONS OF LOS   . .   516 MILTON 29   4
      THE EIGHT IMMORTAL STARRY-ONES DOWN INTO ULRO DARK   . .   523 MILTON 34   4
      A WONDROUS JOURNEY NOT PASSABLE BY IMMORTAL FEET & NONE   525 MILTON 35   20
      IMMORTAL STARRY-ONES GUARDING THE COUCH IN FLAMING FIRES   525 MILTON 35   30
      THIS IS A FALSE BODY AN INCRUSTATION OVER MY IMMORTAL   . .   533 MILTON 40   35
      O IMMORTAL HOW WERE WE LED TO WAR THE WARS OF DEATH   . . .   534 MILTON 41   36
      AND THE IMMORTAL FOUR IN WHOM THE TWENTY-FOUR APPEAR   534 MILTON 42   18
         FOUR-FOLD
      TERROR STRUCK IN THE VALE I STOOD AT THAT IMMORTAL SOUND   534 MILTON 42   24
      AND IF THEY SCORN THE IMMORTAL MUSE . . . .   557 ART HAS LOST/N   10
      IN IMMORTAL THOUGHTS IF MR B'S(BLAKE'S) CANTERBURY PILGRIMS   576B DESC CAT 4   PROSE
      OF GODS IMMORTAL TO THE MORTAL PERISHING ORGAN OF SIGHT   576D DESC CAT 4   PROSE
      WHOM THEY SAW WITH THEIR IMAGINATIVE AND IMMORTAL ORGANS   576D DESC CAT 4   PROSE
      TO OPEN THE ETERNAL WORLDS TO OPEN THE IMMORTAL EYES   . .   623 JERUSALEM 5   18
      THEY HOLD THE IMMORTAL FORM IN GENTLE BANDS & TENDER TEARS   624 JERUSALEM 5   55
      HE STOOD OVER THE IMMORTAL IN THE SOLITUDE AND DARKNESS   625 JERUSALEM 7   2
      THAT TOWARD EDEN FOUR IMMORTAL GOLD SILVER BRASS & IRON   633 JERUSALEM 13   5
      OF OUR IMMORTAL VEINS & ALL THEIR HOSTS FLED FROM OUR LIMBS   647 JERUSALEM 24   8
      FORTHWITH FROM ALBION'S DARKNING LOCKS CAME TWO IMMORTAL   654 JERUSALEM 29   28
         FORMS
      STANDS BETWEEN THE VEGETATIVE MAN & HIS IMMORTAL   663 JERUSALEM 36   24
         IMAGINATION
      SO SPOKE LONDON IMMORTAL GUARDIAN I HEARD IN LAMBETH'S   665 JERUSALEM 38   40
         SHADES
      GENEROUS IMMORTAL GUARDIAN GOLDEN CLAD FOR CITIES . . .   665 JERUSALEM 38   46
      WITH FORTITUDE AS WITH A GARMENT OF IMMORTAL TEXTURE   . .   665 JERUSALEM 38   52
      THAT THE WIDE WORLD MIGHT FLY FROM ITS HINGES & THE   667 JERUSALEM 40   27
         IMMORTAL MANSION
      OF BLACK DESPAIR THAT THE IMMORTAL WINGS LABOURD AGAINST   674 JERUSALEM 44   12
      THAT THY IMMORTAL TONGUE INSPIRES PRESENT THEM TO ALBION   675 JERUSALEM 45   31
      DARE TOUCH OXFORD IMMORTAL BARD WITH ELOQUENCE . . . .   676 JERUSALEM 46   7
      IN SILENCE THE DIVINE LORD BUILDED WITH IMMORTAL LABOUR   677 JERUSALEM 48   5
      TRANSLUCENT THE FURNACES OF BERYLL & EMERALD IMMORTAL   . .   684 JERUSALEM 53   9
      FROM THE PRESSD LOVELINESS SO HER WHOLE IMMORTAL   709 JERUSALEM 70   26
         FORM THREE-FOLD
      HIS IMMORTAL CHEEKS REARING HIS HANDS TO HEAVEN FOR AID   711 JERUSALEM 71   57
         DIVINE
      BENDS OVER THY IMMORTAL HEAD IN WHICH ETERNITY DWELLS   . .   731 JERUSALEM 86   10
      THY BOSOM WHITE TRANSLUCENT COVERD WITH IMMORTAL GEMS   . .   731 JERUSALEM 86   14
      BETWEEN THY WINGS OF GOLD & SILVER FEATHERD IMMORTAL   . .   731 JERUSALEM 86   20
      OF BEULAH JERUSALEM & SHILOH IN IMMORTAL GOLGONOOZA   731 JERUSALEM 86   44
      BENEATH THE FURNACES & THE STARRY WHEELS & THE IMMORTAL   741 JERUSALEM 94   2
         TOMB
      REVOLVE & OVER THEM THE FURNACES OF LOS & THE IMMORTAL   741 JERUSALEM 94   12
         TOMB AROUND
      BENEATH THE FURNACES & STARRY WHEELS AND IN THE IMMORTAL   742 JERUSALEM 94   19
         TOMB
      THE IMMORTAL MAN THAT CANNOT DIE . . . .   771 OF GATES/GP   40
      ALL TO PARTAKE OF SINCE IT IS TO ME A SOURCE OF IMMORTAL   797B LETTER 9   PROSE
         JOY
      MORE & MORE PERSWADED THAT EVERY MORTAL LOSS IS   797B LETTER 9   PROSE
         AN IMMORTAL GAIN
      HAPPY SON OF THE IMMORTAL PHIDIAS HIS LOT IS TRULY GLORIOUS 807B LETTER 17   PROSE
      OF IMMORTAL FRIENDSHIP TO THEE I AM ETERNALLY INDEBTED . . 852A LETTER 50   PROSE
IMMORTALITY
      THE FLOWERS OF IMMORTALITY ARE BLOWN . . . .   31 EDW THIRD/PS 5   36
      ("ALL GENIUS IS THE OFFSPRING OF IMMORTALITY") UNEASY   69D ANNO LAVATER   MARG
         STERLING
      WHEN THE MAN GENTLY FADES AWAY IN HIS IMMORTALITY   . . .   355 FOUR ZOAS 8   551
      THEN WILL I WEEP THEN I'LL COMPLAIN & SIGH FOR IMMORTALITY   368 FOUR ZOAS 9   411
      THE EARWIG ARMD THE TENDER MAGGOT EMBLEM OF IMMORTALITY   377 FOUR ZOAS 9   759
      WHICH ARE SEEN BURSTING WITH THEIR BIRTHS OF IMMORTALITY   443D LAST JUDGMNT/L   PROSE
      WHO DWELL IN IMMORTALITY AS ONE SLEEPING ON A COUCH . . .   496 MILTON 15   12
      OF GOLD AND THOSE IN IMMORTALITY GAVE FORTH THEIR   496 MILTON 15   13
         EMANATIONS
      THE EARWIG ARMD THE TENDER MAGGOT EMBLEM OF IMMORTALITY   513 MILTON 27   16
      PHANTOM OF THE OVER HEATED BRAIN SHADOW OF IMMORTALITY . .   622 JERUSALEM 4   24
      EMBRACE HIM TENFOLD BRIGHT RISING FROM HIS TOMB IN   626 JERUSALEM 7   56
         IMMORTALITY
      WHAT IS IMMORTALITY BUT THE THINGS RELATING TO THE SPIRIT   717B JERUSALEM 77   PROSE
      AND THEN AWAKING INTO HIS BOSOM IN THE LIFE OF IMMORTALITY   747 JERUSALEM 99   4
      THIS ALONE IS THE GOSPEL & THIS IS THE LIFE & IMMORTALITY   757D EV GOSPEL   PROSE
      WHAT LIFE & IMMORTALITY . . . .   758 EV GOSPEL (2)   2
      PLATO DID NOT BRING LIFE & IMMORTALITY TO LIGHT . . . . 774C ANNO BERKELEY   MARG
      BEEN A GLORIOUS & TRIUMPHANT DWELLER IN IMMORTALITY PLEASE   830C LETTER 30   PROSE
IMMORTALS
      SO THE EXPANDING EYES OF IMMORTALS . . . .   231 URIZEN 15   11
      WHERE LIE IN EVIL DEATH THE FOUR IMMORTALS PALE AND COLD   524 MILTON 34   45
      BUT NOT THUS TO IMMORTALS THE LARK IS A MIGHTY ANGEL   . .   527 MILTON 36   12
      BUT TO IMMORTALS ONLY THE SAME FOR WE SEE . . . . . . 567C DESC CAT 3   PROSE
      BUT TO IMMORTALS ONLY THE SAME FOR WE SEE . . . . . . 589A CHAUCER/N   PROSE
      MAKES IT A DWELLING FOR IMMORTALS WORK WILL GO ON HERE . . 803C LETTER 15   PROSE
      THINK AS HIGHLY OF OURSELVES AS IMMORTALS OUGHT TO THINK   811C LETTER 22   PROSE
      THAT SORROW IS NOT FIT FOR IMMORTALS & IS UTTERLY USELESS   830C LETTER 30   PROSE
         TO
IMMOVEABLE
      . . . IMMOVEABLE WITHIN ITS [ARCHES ALL] WALLS & CIELINGS   286 FOUR ZOAS 2   245

	PAGE	TITLE	LINE

IMPALPABLE
HIDE THOU JERUSALEM IN IMPALPABLE VOIDNESS NOT TO BE . . 645 JERUSALEM 22 26
IMPARTETH
("SOUL THAT IMPARTETH FORMS TO MATTER") THIS IS MY OPINION 775A ANNO BERKELEY MARG
BUT
IMPATIENCE
TILL IMPATIENCE NO LONGER COULD BEAR . . . . 257 BOOK OF LOS 4 15
IMPATIENCE NOW NO LONGER CAN ENDURE DISTRACTED LUVAH . . 276 FOUR ZOAS 1 429
IMPATIENT
THEN TIRD OF THOUGHT IMPATIENT TAKES THE WING . . . . . 27 EDW THIRD/PS 3 254
IMPATIENT STIFLED STIFFEND HARDNED . . . . 257 BOOK OF LOS 4 14
THEN THEY SENT MOLECH MOLECH WAS IMPATIENT THEY SENT . 351 FOUR ZOAS 8 400
MOLECH IMPATIENT THEY SENT ELOHIM WHO CREATED ADAM . . 351 FOUR ZOAS 8 401
AND THEY ELECTED MOLECH AND WHEN MOLECH WAS IMPATIENT . 494 MILTON 13 19
HEARS ITS IMPATIENT PARENT BIRD AND ENITHARMON HEARD THEM 504 MILTON 21 29
IMPELLD
CAPTIVE A WILLING CAPTIVE BY DELUSIVE ARTS IMPELLD . . 356 FOUR ZOAS 8 598
IMPENETRABLE
BLACK AS MARBLE OF EGYPT IMPENETRABLE . . . . . . 257 BOOK OF LOS 4 6
IMPERFECT
THEY ARE ALL GREATER VILLAINS THAN THE IMPERFECT . . . . 412A ANNO BOYD MARG
SO IS THE INVENTION PERFECT OR IMPERFECT . . . . . 446D ANNO REYNOLDS MARG
THE IMAGE OF A CLASS AND NOT OF AN IMPERFECT INDIVIDUAL 571A DESC CAT 3 PROSE
IMPERTINENCE
SHOULD HAVE BEEN FREE FROM HIS IMPERTINENCE & INTRUSION 438D BLAKES MEMORAN PROSE
IMPERTINENT
HE MADE ME AN IMPERTINENT ANSWER I INSISTED ON HIS LEAVING 827A LETTER 28 PROSE
IMPETUOUS
("HURRIED ON BY FURIES OF IMMATURE IMPETUOUS WISHES") 85D ANNO LAVATER MARG
UNEASY
AND OVER THEOTORMON'S REIGN TOOK HER IMPETUOUS COURSE . 189 V DAU ALBION 1 15
FALLING WITH WHEEL IMPETUOUS DOWN AMONG URTHONA'S VALES 320 FOUR ZOAS 6 321
THARMAS THREW HIS IMPETUOUS FLIGHT THRO THE DEEPS 320 FOUR ZOAS 7 3
OF IMMENSITY
OF THE ATLANTIC WHICH POURED IN IMPETUOUS LOUD LOUD LOUDER 689 JERUSALEM 57 4
& LOUDER
IMPLEMENTS
WHERE IMPLEMENTS OF WAR ARE FORGED THE PLOW TO GO OVER 660 JERUSALEM 34 13
THE NATIONS
IMPLORES
A FROWNING THISTLE IMPLORES MY STAY . . . . 817 HAPPINESS/L 24
IMPOLITIC
CONSIDERS AS IMPOLITIC AND THAT A HANDSOME GENERAL EDITION 858A LETTER 55 PROSE
IMPORTED
UPON PICTURES IMPORTED FROM FLANDERS AND HOLLAND . . . . 864C LETTER 61 PROSE
IMPOSE
WHO ON THE BLINDED MAN IMPOSE . . . . 17 BLIND-MANS/PS 64
HE WHO HAS SUFFERD YOU TO IMPOSE ON HIM KNOWS YOU . . 152A MARRIAGE HH 9 PROSE
I ANSWERD WE IMPOSE ON ONE ANOTHER & IT . . . . 157B MARRIAGE HH 17 PROSE
THE ANCIENTS DID NOT MEAN TO IMPOSE WHEN THEY AFFIRMD . 473D ANNO REYNOLDS MARG
BE FOOLED BY YOU INTO OPINIONS THAT YOU PLEASE TO IMPOSE 579B DESC CAT 5 PROSE
IMPOSED
WILL BE IMPOSED ON BY THE CLOSER SORT . . . . . . 20 EDW THIRD/PS 2 58
SO THE ANGEL SAID THY PHANTASY HAS IMPOSED UPON ME . . 157B MARRIAGE HH 17 PROSE
IN THIS MANNER THE ENGLISH PUBLIC HAVE BEEN IMPOSED UPON 594C PUB ADDRESS/N PROSE
TOO MUCH EXPERIENCE TO BE ANY LONGER IMPOSED UPON . . . 821A LETTER 25 PROSE
IMPOSITION SEE SELF-IMPOSITION
WOULD BE MISUNDERSTOOD & SO BE THE CAUSE OF IMPOSITION . 153B MARRIAGE HH 12 PROSE
IMPOSSIBILITIES
& BECOMES A POEM OF PROBABLE IMPOSSIBILITIES . . . . . 390D ANNO WATSON MARG
BUT IMPROBABILITIES AND IMPOSSIBILITIES WHAT WE SHOULD SAY 578D DESC CAT 5 PROSE
IMPOSSIBILITIES CHASTITY & ABSTINENCE GODS OF THE HEATHEN 776C INSC LAOCOON PROSE
IMPOSSIBILITY
UNORGANIZD INNOCENCE AN IMPOSSIBILITY . . . . . . 380B FOUR ZOAS NOTE PROSE
UPON THE PATIENT BUT THIS IS AN IMPOSSIBILITY NOT A MIRACLE 391C ANNO WATSON MARG
IMPOSSIBLE
WHICH IS IMPOSSIBLE . . . . 80A ANNO LAVATER MARG
IMPOSSIBLE TO THINK WITHOUT IMAGES OF SOMEWHAT ON EARTH 88B ANNO LAVATER MARG
SO IT IS IMPOSSIBLE TO KNOW GOD OR HEAVENLY THINGS WITHOUT 88B ANNO LAVATER MARG
OF HOLINESS DISTINCT FROM MAN IS IMPOSSIBLE TO THE 90C ANNO SWED LOVE MARG
AFFECTIONS
PUBLIC RECORDS AS IF PUBLIC RECORDS WERE TRUE IMPOSSIBLE 392D ANNO WATSON MARG
TO PLEASE ALL IS IMPOSSIBLE . . . . 478A ANNO REYNOLDS MARG
THIS NATURAL RELIGION THIS IMPOSSIBLE ABSURDITY . . . 532 MILTON 40 13
WAS IMPOSSIBLE IF WE DID NOT SEE IT ALWAYS BEFORE OUR EYES 578D DESC CAT 5 PROSE
TO DISBELIEVE WHAT YOU THINK IMPROBABLE OR IMPOSSIBLE . 579B DESC CAT 5 PROSE
AS I COPY IMAGINATION THIS THEY WILL FIND IMPOSSIBLE . 594D PUB ADDRESS/N PROSE
THAT IT IS IMPOSSIBLE FOR ME TO RETURN TO IT WITHOUT 865C LETTER 63 PROSE
DESTROYING
WALKING TO & FROM THE STAGE WOULD BE TO ME IMPOSSIBLE . 875B LETTER 81 PROSE
IMPOSTOR
WITHOUT BEING A MASTER OF DRAWING IS AN IMPOSTOR . . . . 594D PUB ADDRESS/N *PROSE
[AGAINST A CERTAIN IMPOSTOR WHO C] IN [OUR ART] THE ART 601C PUB ADDRESS/N *PROSE
OF
IMPOSTORS
IN A COMMERCIAL NATION IMPOSTORS ARE ABROAD . . . . . 601C PUB ADDRESS/N PROSE
PAINTING THESE IMPOSTORS SEDULOUSLY PROPAGATE AN OPINION 601C PUB ADDRESS/N PROSE
IMPOSTURE
WHEREFORE DID CHRIST COME WAS IT NOT TO ABOLISH THE JEWISH 387B ANNO WATSON * MARG
IMPOSTURE
IT IS IN FALLACY & ITS EXISTENCE AN IMPOSTURE . . . . . 617A V LAST JUDG/N PROSE

	PAGE	TITLE	LINE

IMPOVERISH
    ("NO GIFTS CAN EXHAUST GENIUS IMPOVERISH CHARITY") MOST   84B ANNO LAVATER   MARG
        EXCELLENT
IMPRECATIONS
    WITH MANY ABOMINABLE IMPRECATIONS & WITH SOME . . . . .   827A LETTER 28   PROSE
IMPREGNABLE
    . . . BOUND TO THE IMPREGNABLE WALL . . . .   135 FRENCH REVOLTN   27
    TO A FORM OF IMPREGNABLE STRENGTH . . . .   259 BOOK OF LOS 5   19
    INTO A STRENGTH IMPREGNABLE OF MAJESTY & BEAUTY INFINITE   527 MILTON 37   7
    AND MILTON COLLECTING ALL HIS FIBRES INTO IMPREGNABLE   529 MILTON 38   5
        STRENGTH
IMPREGNATE
    JOYS IMPREGNATE SORROWS BRING FORTH . . . .   151C MARRIAGE HH 8   PROSE
IMPRESS
    IS TO IMPRESS ON MEN THE FEAR OF DEATH TO TEACH . . . .   530 MILTON 38   38
IMPRESSD
    WHY A TONGUE IMPRESSD WITH HONEY FROM EVERY WIND . . . .   130 BOOK OF THEL 6   16
    THE WOMB IMPRESSD ENION FLED & HID IN VERDANT MOUNTAINS   381 FOUR ZOAS AD 3   1
IMPRESSED
    WHERE THE HORRIBLE DARKNESS IS IMPRESSED WITH REFLECTIONS   194 V DAU ALBION 7   11
        OF DESIRE
IMPRESSION
    THE IMPRESSION WHICH HE RECIEVES FROM A BOOK OF EXAMPLES   393B ANNO WATSON   MARG
    FOR MANY YEARS UNDER THE IMPRESSION THAT ENGRAVING . . .   594C PUB ADDRESS/N   PROSE
    WHICH WHEN COLD WILL RECIEVE ANY IMPRESSION MINUTELY . .   790C LETTER 2   PROSE
    IS A SHAMEFULLY WORN-OUT IMPRESSION BUT IT WAS THE ONLY   855C LETTER 53   PROSE
    ONE I COULD GET AT JOHNSON'S I LEFT A GOOD IMPRESSION OF IT 855C LETTER 53   PROSE
    THAT IT IS NOT LIKE THE SAME PLATE WITH THE WORN   855C LETTER 53   PROSE
        OUT IMPRESSION
IMPRESSIONS
    WHERE THE IMPRESSIONS OF DESPAIR & HOPE ENROOT FOREVER . .   295 FOUR ZOAS 3   143
    WHERE THE IMPRESSIONS OF DESPAIR & HOPE FOR EVER VEGETATE   367 FOUR ZOAS 9   377
    IMPRESSIONS OF EACH OF THE PLATES WHICH I NOW SEND OUGHT   840D LETTER 40   PROSE
    MANY OF THE BACKS OF THE PAPER HAVE ON THEM IMPRESSIONS   877B LETTER 86   PROSE
IMPRINTED
    HER SOFT MEMORY IMPRINTED WITH FACES OF SCORN . . . . .   429 MARY   40
IMPRISONMENT
    AND SACRIFICE & NEXT IN CHAINS OF IMPRISONMENT ARE   521 MILTON 32   17
        SHAPELESS ROCKS
IMPROBABILITIES
    BUT IMPROBABILITIES AND IMPOSSIBILITIES WHAT WE SHOULD SAY   578D DESC CAT 5   PROSE
IMPROBABLE
    TO DISBELIEVE WHAT YOU THINK IMPROBABLE OR IMPOSSIBLE .   579B DESC CAT 5   PROSE
    IT IS IMPROBABLE MUST REJECT ALL HISTORY AND RETAIN DOUBTS   579B DESC CAT 5   PROSE
        ONLY
IMPROVD
    SAYS HOMER IS VERY MUCH IMPROVD BY POPE . . . .   555 BLAKES APL/N 1   13
    CRIES HOMER IS VERY MUCH IMPROVD BY POPE . . . . . .   556 BLAKES APL/N 2   10
    CANNOT BE IMPROVD IT IS VERY TRUE WHAT YOU HAVE SAID .   593D PUB ADDRESS/N   PROSE
    SAYS HOMER IS VERY MUCH IMPROVD BY POPE . . . . . .   595 BLAKES APOL/PA   8
IMPROVE
    & RAFAELS TO SUCCEED & TO IMPROVE UPON EACH OTHER . .   470D ANNO REYNOLDS   MARG
    PRETENCES OF ENGLISHMEN TO IMPROVE [E] ART BEFORE THEY EVEN 593C PUB ADDRESS/N   *PROSE
    A MAN WHO PRETENDS TO IMPROVE FINE ART DOES NOT KNOW .   593C PUB ADDRESS/N   PROSE
    YOU ATTEMPT TO FINISH OR IMPROVE & WHEN YOU HAVE BEGUN .   593D PUB ADDRESS/N   PROSE
    THAT WELL KNOWN SAYING ENGLISHMEN IMPROVE WHAT OTHERS   595C PUB ADDRESS/N   PROSE
        INVENT
    NO MAN CAN IMPROVE AN ORIGINAL INVENTION . . . . .   595C PUB ADDRESS/N   PROSE
    I CONTINUE PAINTING MINIATURES & IMPROVE MORE & MORE .   809C LETTER 20   PROSE
    YOU WILL BE TEMPTED TO THINK THAT AS I IMPROVE THE PICTURES 815B LETTER 23   PROSE
        &C
    I IMPROVE VERY MUCH & SHALL CONTINUE TO DO SO WHILE I LIVE   824B LETTER 27   PROSE
    THE SHOPS IN LONDON IMPROVE EVERY THING IS ELEGANT CLEAN   831D LETTER 31   PROSE
    TWELVE OF EACH IF I HAD NOT WISHD TO IMPROVE THEM STILL   839B LETTER 38   PROSE
        MORE
IMPROVED
    WHEN THE MORTAL DISAPPEARS IN IMPROVED KNOWLEDGE CAST AWAY   355 FOUR ZOAS 8   552
    MAN IS NOT IMPROVED BY THE HURT OF ANOTHER . . . . .   402C ANNO BACON   MARG
    STATES ARE NOT IMPROVED AT THE EXPENSE OF FOREIGNERS .   402D ANNO BACON   MARG
    EVEN HOGARTH'S EXECUTION CANNOT BE COPIED OR IMPROVED .   599C PUB ADDRESS/N   PROSE
    EVEN HOGARTH CANNOT BE EITHER COPIED OR IMPROVED . . . .   601D PUB ADDRESS/N   PROSE
    IS IMPROVED THE LIP I HAVE AGAIN LESSENED AS YOU ADVISED   797A LETTER 9   PROSE
    THAT IT CAN BE IMPROVED EITHER IN BEAUTY OR USE . . . .   802A LETTER 14   PROSE
    THAT NEW LIFE BY IMPROVED WORKS RECIEVE FROM ME A RETURN OF 804B LETTER 16   PROSE
IMPROVEMENT
    (IMPROVEMENT) MAKES STRAIT ROADS . . . .   152D MARRIAGE HH 10   PROSE
    BUT THE CROOKED ROADS WITHOUT IMPROVEMENT ARE ROADS OF   152D MARRIAGE HH 10   PROSE
        GENIUS
    THIS WILL COME TO PASS BY AN IMPROVEMENT OF SENSUAL   154C MARRIAGE HH 14   PROSE
        ENJOYMENT
    TO IMPROVEMENT & THE BISHOP HAS NOT SHEWN THE CONTRARY .   388D ANNO WATSON   MARG
    THE INCREASE OF A STATE AS OF A MAN IS FROM INTERNAL   402C ANNO BACON   MARG
        IMPROVEMENT
    WHAT IS THE JOY OF HEAVEN BUT IMPROVEMENT IN THE THINGS   717B JERUSALEM 77   PROSE
        OF THE SPIRIT
    TO IMPROVEMENT IN MY BELOVED ARTS ONE THING . . . . .   812A LETTER 22   PROSE
    PRESENT STATE THEY WILL BE CAPABLE OF VERY MUCH IMPROVEMENT 853C LETTER 52   PROSE
    PERHAPS & I VERILY BELIEVE IT EVERY DEATH IS AN IMPROVEMENT 868D LETTER 68   PROSE
IMPROVEMENTS
    IMPROVEMENTS IN WORKS OF ART GOING ON IN LONDON BUT . . .   823A LETTER 26   PROSE
IMPROVIDENCE
    SPIRIT OF ABSTRACTION & IMPROVIDENCE SUCH MY DEAR SIR . .   809B LETTER 20   PROSE

	PAGE	TITLE	LINE

IMPROVING
      THIS WAS THE SITUATION OF THIS IMPROVING COMPANY WHEN   .   .   44C ISLAND MOON 1   PROSE
      MR STEELYARD ARE SOME OF THEM MORE IMPROVING THAN ANY BOOK   53C ISLAND MOON 8   PROSE
      YOU WILL KNOW BETTER THAN TO THINK OF IMPROVING WHAT   .   593D PUB ADDRESS/N   PROSE
      & NOT ONLY GRATIFYING BUT IMPROVING WHICH IS BETTER   .   .   .   859C LETTER 56   PROSE
      I GO ON AS I THINK IMPROVING MY ENGRAVINGS OF DANTE   .   .   .   876A LETTER 83   PROSE
IMPS
      FOR NOW I HAVE PROCURD THESE IMPS   .   .   .   .   51 WHEN CORRUP/IM   25
IMPUDENCE
      ("QUESTION YOUR WISDOM") PRIESTLY IMPUDENCE   .   .   .   .   384D ANNO WATSON   MARG
      FOLLY & IMPUDENCE DOES THE THOROUGH BELIEF OF POPERY   .   385C ANNO WATSON   MARG
      HE HIMSELF KNEW BUT HIS IMPUDENCE HAD A CONTRARY EFFECT   603C PUB ADDR AD/N   PROSE
         ON ME
IMPUDENT
      IMPUDENT FIEND SAID IJIM HOLD THY GLIB & ELOQUENT TONGUE   104 TIRIEL 4   37
IMPULSE
      CANNOT RESIST THE IMPULSE I FEEL TO RECTIFY WHAT I THINK   88A ANNO LAVATER   MARG
         FALSE
      JESUS WAS ALL VIRTUE AND ACTED FROM IMPULSE NOT FROM RULES   158D MARRIAGE HH 22   PROSE
IMPURE
      SO WHEN WE WALK NOTHING IMPURE COMES NEAR   .   .   .   .   .   9 FRESH FROM/PS   14
      ("LOVE") THEREFORE IT WAS NOT CREATED IMPURE & IS   96C ANNO SWED LOVE   MARG
         NOT NATURALLY SO
      AND THE IMPURE SCOURGE FORCE HIS SEED INTO ITS UNRIPE BIRTH   193 V DAU ALBION 5   31
      AND NONE IMPURE WERE DEEMD   .   .   .   .   256 BOOK OF LOS 3   9
      BEING MOST IMPURE SELF-CONDEMND TO ETERNAL TEARS HE DROVE   493 MILTON 12   47
      [THO] THAT HEAVEN WAS IMPURE IN THY SIGHT   .   .   .   .   .   754 EV GOSPEL(E)/N *   36
IMPURITY
      BECAUSE THOU ART THE IMPURITY & THE HARLOT & THY CHILDREN   658 JERUSALEM 31   63
IMPURPLED
      AND THE WILD THYME FROM WIMBLETON'S GREEN & IMPURPLED HILLS   534 MILTON 42   30
IMPUTATION
      SAYING PITY AND LOVE ARE TOO VENERABLE FOR THE IMPUTATION   495 MILTON 13   48
      FROM THE TOO JUST IMPUTATION OF BEING THE SEAT AND   .   .   562B DESC CAT ADV   PROSE
      ENVIOUS IMPUTATION OF UNFITNESS FOR FINISHED AND SCIENTIFIC   572C DESC CAT 3   PROSE
         ART
      THIS IMPUTATION MOST ARTFULLY AND INDUSTRIOUSLY ENDEAVOURED   572C DESC CAT 3   PROSE
      DESCEND O LAMB OF GOD & TAKE AWAY THE IMPUTATION OF SIN   648 JERUSALEM 25   12
      TO CLEAR THEMSELVES OF ALL IMPUTATION IF A MAN OFFENDS ME   828C LETTER 28   PROSE
IMPUTED
      BUT MANY DOUBTED & DESPAIRD & IMPUTED SIN & RIGHTEOUSNESS   648 JERUSALEM 25   15
      YET THEY ARE BLAMELESS & INIQUITY MUST BE IMPUTED ONLY   .   680 JERUSALEM 49   65
IMPUTING
      IMPUTING SIN & RIGHTEOUSNESS TO INDIVIDUALS RAHAB   .   .   .   709 JERUSALEM 70   17
INANIMATE
      TO MOPING VISAGES RETURNING INANIMATE THO FURIOUS   .   .   .   344 FOUR ZOAS 8   125
INARTICULATE
      FOR VOICES OF DELIGHT HOARSE CROAKINGS INARTICULATE THRO   312 FOUR ZOAS 6   39
         FROST
      HIS VOICE TO THEM WAS BUT AN INARTICULATE THUNDER FOR THEIR   315 FOUR ZOAS 6   124
         EARS
      LAMENTS & ENION WANDERS LIKE A WEEPING INARTICULATE VOICE   501 MILTON 19   42
      INSANE SHE RAVES UPON THE WINDS HOARSE INARTICULATE   .   .   693 JERUSALEM 60   44
INCAPABILITY
      TOWARD WHAT IS TRULY UGLY THE INCAPABILITY OF INTELLECT   580B DESC CAT 5   PROSE
      & THEIR INCAPABILITY OF ART THO ART IS ABOVE EITHER   .   .   612C V LAST JUDG/N   PROSE
INCAPABLE
      IF ANY COULD DESIRE WHAT HE IS INCAPABLE OF POSSESSING   .   .   97D NAT RELIGION 2   PROSE
      FOR HE WAS INCAPABLE THRO HIS CONCEITED NOTIONS   .   .   .   157D MARRIAGE HH 21   PROSE
      THE FACE THAT IS INCAPABLE OF PASSION & EXPRESSION   466A ANNO REYNOLDS   MARG
         IS DEFORMITY
      MICHAEL ANGELO WERE INCAPABLE OF THE MEER LANGUAGE OF ART   467B ANNO REYNOLDS   MARG
      I SAID NOW IS MY GRIEF AT WORST INCAPABLE OF BEING   .   .   630 JERUSALEM 10   44
      IS INCAPABLE AND NOTHING NONE BUT THE LAMB OF GOD CAN HEAL   675 JERUSALEM 45   15
      PROTESTANT CONSIDERS NATURE AS INCAPABLE OF BEARING A CHILD   779A ANNO CELLINI   MARG
      CONVINCD THAT EITHER MY UNDERSTANDING IS INCAPABLE OF   .   814A LETTER 23   PROSE
      BLIND STUPID IGNORANT AND INCAPABLE IN TWO YEARS' STUDY   814D LETTER 23   PROSE
      INCAPABLE OF MANY ATTENTIONS WHICH IT IS MY DUTY TO OBSERVE   816A LETTER 23   PROSE
      UPON BY THEM AS INCAPABLE OF EMPLOYMENT IN THOSE WORKS IT   862C LETTER 60   PROSE
      THO GETTING BETTER & STRONGER I AM STILL INCAPABLE   875B LETTER 81   PROSE
         OF RIDING
INCAPACITY
      PRUDENCE IS A RICH UGLY OLD MAID COURTED BY INCAPACITY   .   151A MARRIAGE HH 7   PROSE
      NEITHER YOUTH NOR CHILDHOOD IS FOLLY OR INCAPACITY   .   .   .   794B LETTER 5   PROSE
INCARNATE
      BY TWO FIENDS INCARNATE WITH INTENTION THAT WHEN   .   .   .   .   792B LETTER 4   PROSE
INCENSE
      .   .   .   LIKE INCENSE OF THE VALLEY   .   .   .   .   143 FRENCH REVOLTN   197
      THEY HOVERD ROUND ME LIKE A CLOUD OF INCENSE WHEN I CAME   238 EUROPE INTRO   22
      MY FIRES ARE CORRUPT MY INCENSE IS A CLOUDY PESTILENCE   .   721 JERUSALEM 79   56
      THEIR BREAD THEIR ALTAR-TABLE THEIR INCENSE & THEIR OATH   738 JERUSALEM 91   14
INCESSANT
      OF LUST THAT BELCH INCESSANT FROM THE SUMMITS OF THE EARTH   190 V DAU ALBION 2   10
      BUT SHE CAN HOWL INCESSANT WRITHING HER SOFT SNOWY LIMBS   190 V DAU ALBION 2   12
      [THEY] HE PILED THEM IN INCESSANT LABOUR   .   .   .   .   .   225 URIZEN 5   *   23
      INCESSANT BEAT FORGING CHAINS NEW & NEW   .   .   .   .   .   .   227 URIZEN 10   17
      BEATS INCESSANT TEN WINTERS THE DISK   .   .   .   .   249 AHANIA 2   24
      WERE MEASURD BY HIS INCESSANT WHIRLS   .   .   .   .   .   .   258 BOOK OF LOS 4   35
      INCESSANT THE FALLING MIND LABOURD   .   .   .   .   258 BOOK OF LOS 4   49
      THE LUNGS HEAVE INCESSANT DULL AND HEAVY   .   .   .   .   .   258 BOOK OF LOS 4   54
      HE SIEZD BEATING INCESSANT CONDENSING   .   .   .   .   .   .   260 BOOK OF LOS 5   29
      [WITH [SPIRIT] SPECTRE VOICE INCESSANT WAILING IN   269 FOUR ZOAS 1   *   188
         INCESSANT THIRST]

```
                                                               PAGE     TITLE          LINE
INCESSANT    (CONTINUED)
    WHERE WINTER BEATS INCESSANT FIXING THEM FIRM ON THEIR BASE  281 FOUR ZOAS 2       31
    MULTITUDES WITHOUT NUMBER WORK INCESSANT THE HEWN STONE      284 FOUR ZOAS 2      170
    AMONG THESE FLAMES INCESSANT LABOURING OUR HARD MASTERS      285 FOUR ZOAS 2      219
        LAUGH
    THICK SHORT INCESSANT BURSTING SOBBING . . . . . . . . .     296 FOUR ZOAS 3      156
    INCESSANT TEARS ARE NOW MY FOOD INCESSANT RAGE & TEARS       298 FOUR ZOAS 4       11
    WEPT BITTER TEARS INCESSANT STILL BEHOLDING HOW THE PITEOUS  300 FOUR ZOAS 4       97
        FORM
    PETRIFY WITH INCESSANT BEATING MANY A ROCK MANY A PLANET     301 FOUR ZOAS 4      169
    INCESSANT WAS THE CONFLICT ON HE BENT HIS WEARY STEPS   . .  313 FOUR ZOAS 6       77
    WITH TEARS OF SORROW INCESSANT SHE LABOURD THE FOOD OF ORC   343 FOUR ZOAS 8       82
    A SHAPELESS & INDEFINITE CLOUD IN TEARS OF SORROW INCESSANT  345 FOUR ZOAS 8      175
    MY SOUL IS SEVEN FURNACES INCESSANT ROARS THE BELLOWS   . .  349 FOUR ZOAS 8    * 305
    INCESSANT STERN DISDAIN HIS SCALY FORM GNAWS INWARDLY   . .  352 FOUR ZOAS 8      434
    AN ANIMATED PILLAR ROLLING ROUND & ROUND IN INCESSANT RAGE   353 FOUR ZOAS 8      470
    THE VOICE INCESSANT CALLS ON ALL THE CHILDREN OF MEN    . .  353 FOUR ZOAS 8      489
    THE TORRENTS BLACK UPON THE EARTH THE BLOOD POURS DOWN       359 FOUR ZOAS 9       73
        INCESSANT
    OF FOAMING BLOOD BENEATH THE BLACK INCESSANT SKY TILL ALL    359 FOUR ZOAS 9       78
    IN DARK OBLIVION WITH INCESSANT PANGS AGES ON AGES  . . .    366 FOUR ZOAS 9      369
    THEY PLOWD IN TEARS INCESSANT POURD JEHOVAH'S RAIN           488 MILTON 8         27
        & MOLECH'S
    WHERE SOULS INCESSANT WAIL BEING PITEOUS PASSIONS & DESIRES  512 MILTON 26        26
    THEY LABOUR INCESSANT WITH MANY TEARS & AFFLICTIONS  . .     515 MILTON 28         6
    WHERE ORC INCESSANT HOWLS BURNING IN FIRES OF ETERNAL YOUTH  517 MILTON 29        29
    RESULT OF THE INCESSANT [PRACTICE] PRACTISE  . . . . . . . 591D PUB ADDRESS/N *PROSE
    INCESSANT BEFORE THE FURNACES AND HIS EMANATION DIVIDED      624 JERUSALEM 5       67
        IN PAIN
    THE LAND OF SNOWS OF TREMBLING & OF IRON HAIL INCESSANT      634 JERUSALEM 13      47
    THE DARK INCESSANT SKY SEEKING FOR REST AND FINDING NONE     641 JERUSALEM 19      22
    OF DEATH THUNDER INCESSANT AROUND THE FLAMING COUCHES OF     684 JERUSALEM 53      21
    AND LOS FIXES THEM ON HIS ANVIL INCESSANT HIS BLOWS  . . .   690 JERUSALEM 58      16
    THE WHEEL OF HAND INCESSANT TURNING DAY & NIGHT WITHOUT      693 JERUSALEM 60      43
        REST
    THEREFORE HE LIVED & BREATHED IN HOPE BUT HIS TEARS FELL     696 JERUSALEM 62      36
        INCESSANT
    MY SOUL IS SEVEN FURNACES INCESSANT ROARS THE BELLOWS   . .  705 JERUSALEM 67      52
    CAN I ARISE AND LEAVE THY SIDE BUT LABOUR HERE INCESSANT     727 JERUSALEM 83       2
    AGAINST THE PATRIARCHAL POMP AND CRUELTY LABOURING           727 JERUSALEM 83       4
        INCESSANT
    THE WEEDS OF DEATH INWRAP HIS HANDS & FEET BLOWN INCESSANT   741 JERUSALEM 94       5
    AND WASHD INCESSANT BY THE FOR-EVER RESTLESS SEA-WAVES       741 JERUSALEM 94       6
        FOAMING ABROAD
    OUR INCESSANT LABOUR FULLY ADEQUATE TO [IT] THEM AT PRESENT 811D LETTER 22       PROSE
    WITHOUT INCESSANT LABOUR & STUDY HOW IS IT POSSIBLE THAT    830A LETTER 30       PROSE
        SUCH
INCESSANTLY
    AND SILVER & GOLD HE CONSECRATED READING INCESSANTLY    . .  344 FOUR ZOAS 8      141
    WEEPS INCESSANTLY FOR MY SIN    . . . . . . . . . . .        415 MY SPECTRE/N       4
    LIVING SELF MOVING MOURNING LAMENTING & HOWLING INCESSANTLY  509 MILTON 24        53
    BUT THE POOR SPECTRES THAT THEY WORK FOR ALWAYS INCESSANTLY  691 JERUSALEM 59      38
    THREE BRAINS IN CONTRADICTORY COUNCIL BROODING INCESSANTLY   708 JERUSALEM 70       5
    "WE HAVE BEEN INCESSANTLY BUSY IN OUR GREAT REMOVAL"   . .  800A LETTER 12       PROSE
    I LABOUR INCESSANTLY & ACCOMPLISH NOT ONE HALF OF WHAT  .   809A LETTER 20       PROSE
    POOR WIFE WITH ME INCESSANTLY LABOURING AND INCESSANTLY     852B LETTER 50       PROSE
INCH
    THE EMMET'S INCH & EAGLE'S MILE    . . . . . . . . .         433 AUGURIES         105
    THE SIZE OF THE ENGRAVING WILL BE (THREE) FEET (ONE) INCH   587A CHAUCER 1       PROSE
        LONG
    (THREE) FEET (ONE) INCH LONG BY ONE FOOT HIGH CONTAINING    587D CHAUCER/N      PROSE
    THREE FEET I INCH LONG AND I FOOT HIGH PRICE THREE GUINEAS  589C CHAUCER 2      TITLE
INCHAIND
    RESTLESS TURND THE IMMORTAL INCHAIND    . . . . . . . .      228 URIZEN 10        31
    RESTLESS THE IMMORTAL INCHAIND HEAVING DOLOROUS  . . . .     303 FOUR ZOAS 4      215
    LET THE INCHAIND SOUL SHUT UP IN DARKNESS & IN SIGHING  .    375 FOUR ZOAS 9    * 672
INCHAINED
    LET THE INCHAINED SOUL SHUT UP IN DARKNESS AND IN SIGHING    198 AMERICA 6         8
INCHES
    YOU CALL DIVINE IS BUT A WORM SEVENTY INCHES LONG   . . .    659 JERUSALEM 33       6
    TO ENGRAVE ONE IN EACH MANNER THE SIZE TO BE ABOUT (SEVEN)  848B LETTER 45       PROSE
        INCHES
INCIRCLE
    VALA INCIRCLE ROUND THE FURNACES WHERE LUVAH WAS CLOSD  .    282 FOUR ZOAS 2      77
    VALA INCIRCLE ROUND THE FURNACES WHERE LUVAH WAS CLOSD  .    626 JERUSALEM 7       35
INCIRCLED       SEE ENCIRCLED
    AND THOU HAST BEEN INCIRCLED IN HIS ARMS    . . . . . .     38B SAMSON/PS       PROSE
    AND EVERY SEVEN AGES IS INCIRCLED WITH A FLAMING FIRE   .    516 MILTON 28        57
    AS THE BELOVED INFANT IN HIS MOTHER'S BOSOM ROUND INCIRCLED  518 MILTON 30        11
    SATAN HEARD TREMBLING ROUND HIS BODY HE INCIRCLED IT    . .  531 MILTON 39        16
    EASTWARD & SOUTHWARD & NORTHWARD ARE INCIRCLED WITH FLAMING  635 JERUSALEM 14      28
        FIRES
INCIRCLING
    AND THEY APPEARD WITHIN & WITHOUT INCIRCLING ON BOTH SIDES   631 JERUSALEM 12      17
INCLEMENT
    UNHURT & DARE THE INCLEMENT FOREHEAD OF THE KING OF LIGHT    345 FOUR ZOAS 8      149
    WITH WINDOWS FROM THE INCLEMENT SKY WE COVER HIM & WITH      374 FOUR ZOAS 9      635
        WALLS
INCLIND
    ALWAYS IS TO JOY INCLIND . . . . . . . . . . . . . . .      175 HOW TO KNOW/N      2
    DECEIT TO SECRESY [INCLIND] CONFIND  . . . . . . . . .      175 HOW TO KNOW/N      5
```

```
                                                              PAGE     TITLE           LINE
INCLINED
      YET IF HER HEART IS WELL INCLINED  . . . . . . . . .      56 HAIL MATRIM/IM        16
INCLOSD     SEE ENCLOSD,ETC
      AND THEY INCLOSD MY INFINITE BRAIN INTO A NARROW CIRCLE   191 V DAU ALBION 2       32
      THAT ONCE INCLOSD THE TERRIBLE WANDERING COMETS IN ITS    197 AMERICA 5       *     3
         SPHERE
      TILL A ROOF SHAGGY WILD INCLOSD  . . . . . . . . .        228 URIZEN 10            33
      SOUTHWARD WITH HALF THE TENTS OF MEN INCLOSD IN CLOUDS . . 278 FOUR ZOAS 1        496
      THEY STROVE TOGETHER ABOVE THE BODY WHERE VALA WAS INCLOSD 294 FOUR ZOAS 3         80
      ANGUISHD UNBEARABLE TILL A ROOF SHAGGY WILD INCLOSD  . . . 303 FOUR ZOAS 4        216
      ABSTRACTED FROM THE ROOTS OF [NATURE] SCIENCE THEN INCLOSD 374 FOUR ZOAS 9        631
         AROUND
      BUT SAW THEM NOT FOR THE BLUE MUNDANE SHELL INCLOSD THEM IN 504 MILTON 21          30
      BECAUSE IT INCLOSD PITY & LOVE BECAUSE WE LOVD ONE-ANOTHER 643 JERUSALEM 20        35
      SO SAYING THE MILD SUN INCLOSD THE HUMAN FAMILY  . . .    653 JERUSALEM 29        27
      THEY STROVE TOGETHER ABOVE THE BODY WHERE VALA WAS INCLOSD 655 JERUSALEM 29        62
      I HAVE INCLOSD FOR YOU THE...NUMBERS OF FUSELI'S         836C LETTER 35         PROSE
         SHAKESPEARE
      I SEND INCLOSD HIS TERMS AS MR HOARE BY MY DESIRE HAS  . 841D LETTER 41         PROSE
      THE LITTLE VOLUME OF POEMS INCLOSD THEY ARE BY  . . . . 857B LETTER 54         PROSE
INCLOSE
      THEY TOLD ME THAT I HAD FIVE SENSES TO INCLOSE ME UP  . . 191 V DAU ALBION 2      31
      [WINGS THEY HAD [& WHEN THEY CHOSE] THAT SOFT INCLOSE] .   422 BENEATH AD/N        1
      HIS LOINS INCLOSE BABYLON ON EUPHRATES BEAUTIFUL  . . .   735 JERUSALEM 89        38
      I ALSO INCLOSE YOU SOME BALLADS BY MR HAYLEY WITH PRINTS 819A LETTER 24         PROSE
      I INCLOSE LIKEWISE THE ACADEMICAL CORRESPONDENCE OF  . . 836D LETTER 35         PROSE
      MR HOARE THE PAINTER WHOSE NOTE TO ME I ALSO INCLOSE FOR 836D LETTER 35         PROSE
      AND INCLOSE WITH THEM A CATALOGUE OF BELL'S GALLERY AND  844C LETTER 43         PROSE
      BUT DESIRED ME TO INCLOSE IT FOR YOU WITH WASHINGTON'S LIFE 845C LETTER 44      PROSE
      I INCLOSE A TICKET OF ADMISSION IF YOU SHOULD HONOUR  . . 866B LETTER 64        PROSE
INCLOSED
      INCLOSED BY EYELESS WINGS GLOWING WITH FIRE AS THE IRON   735 JERUSALEM 89        41
      BE SO KIND AS TO READ & THEN SEAL THE INCLOSED  . . . . 799D LETTER 11         PROSE
      I HAVE INCLOSED THE ACCOUNT OF MONEY RECIEVD & WORK DONE 816A LETTER 23         PROSE
      WERE IN GREAT FORWARDNESS YOU WILL SEE BY THE INCLOSED . 816C LETTER 24         PROSE
      YOU WILL FIND INCLOSED ONE IS A COPY FROM THAT MINIATURE 838D LETTER 37         PROSE
      WOULD FORWARD IT TO MR SEAGRAVE BUT I HAVE INCLOSED IT . 861B LETTER 58         PROSE
INCLOSES
      HIS HEAD DARK DEADLY IN ITS BRAIN INCLOSES A REFLEXION . . 734 JERUSALEM 89       14
INCLOSING
      INCLOSING LOS BUT THE DIVINE VISION APPEARD WITH LOS  . . 656 JERUSALEM 30        19
      INCLOSING ALL THE CHILDREN OF LOS TIME AFTER TIME  . . . 684 JERUSALEM 53         7
      OF INCLOSING SEVERAL TOGETHER WHICH ARE NOT YET COMPLETED 809C LETTER 20        PROSE
INCLUDE
      NOTE I INCLUDE THE GERMANS IN THE FLORENTINE SCHOOL . . . 479B ANNO REYNOLDS     MARG
INCLUDED
      ADMITTANCE...EACH PERSON A DISCRIPTIVE CATALOGUE INCLUDED 560C EXHIBITION ADV    PROSE
      MAKE HIS WHOLE COMPANY HIMSELF INCLUDED THIRTY-ONE  . . . 571D DESC CAT 3        PROSE
INCOHERENT
      TO OUR PRIMEVAL CHAOS IN FORTUITOUS CONCOURSE OF INCOHERENT 282 FOUR ZOAS 2       102
      THE VOID IN (INCOHERENT) DESPAIR CAMBRIDGE & OXFORD       623 JERUSALEM 5         3
         & LONDON
      A CONCAVE EARTH WONDROUS CHASMAL ABYSSAL INCOHERENT  . . 634 JERUSALEM 18        53
      DRIVEN ON THE VOID IN INCOHERENT DESPAIR INTO NON ENTITY  673 JERUSALEM 43        68
      THE STRUGGLES OF INTANGLEMENT WITH INCOHERENT ROOTS I KNOW 716D JERUSALEM 77     PROSE
         OF
INCOME
      PURPOSE HERE OUR EXPENSES ARE SMALL & OUR INCOME FROM  . 811D LETTER 22         PROSE
INCOMPARABLE
      OF THE FIRST CLASS WAS SATAN WITH INCOMPARABLE MILDNESS   486 MILTON 7           6
      AN INCOMPARABLE PRODUCTION WHICH MR W(WALKER) BOUGHT FOR 843D LETTER 43         PROSE
      BUT THAT OF LEFEVRE'S DEATH HE SPEAKS OF AS INCOMPARABLE 844C LETTER 43         PROSE
INCOMPATIBLE
      TO DO FOR YOU ARE INCOMPATIBLE WITH THE DESIGNS  . . . . 814C LETTER 23         PROSE
INCOMPREHENSIBLE
      INCOMPREHENSIBLE PERVADING ALL AMIDST & ROUND ABOUT  . . . 364 FOUR ZOAS 9      282
      A SCHEME OF HUMAN CONDUCT INVISIBLE & INCOMPREHENSIBLE . . 483 MILTON 4          13
      BIRTHPLACE OF THE LAMB OF GOD INCOMPREHENSIBLE  . . . . . 626 JERUSALEM 7        67
      AND SEVEN-FOLD EACH WITHIN OTHER INCOMPREHENSIBLE  . . . 684 JERUSALEM 53        10
      GLORIOUS (INCOMPREHENSIBLE) BY MORTAL MAN . . . . . . 745 JERUSALEM 98           11
      . . .CHARIOTS OF HUMANITY DIVINE INCOMPREHENSIBLE  . . . 745 JERUSALEM 98        24
INCONCEIVABLE
      BENEATH THEY SAW THEIR SONS & DAUGHTERS WONDERING        374 FOUR ZOAS 9     *   648
         INCONCEIVABLE
INCONSISTENT
      IT IS CERTAIN THAT A TOO PASSIVE MANNER INCONSISTENT  . . 828C LETTER 28        PROSE
      THAT HE SHOULD TELL SUCH INCONSISTENT SURMIZES PROVES THAT 838C LETTER 37       PROSE
INCORPORATE
      ENDEAVORING TO INCORPORATE THEIR SOULS WITH THEIR BODIES  45C ISLAND MOON 1      PROSE
INCORRECT
      I UNDERSTAND THAT MY COSTUME IS INCORRECT  . . . . . . 583D DESC CAT 10         PROSE
      WHY ARE COPIERS OF NATURE INCORRECT WHILE  . . . . . . 595A PUB ADDRESS/N       PROSE
INCREASD
      FROM WHENCE COMFORTS HAVE INCREASD  . . . . . . . . .      9 MAD SONG/PS         22
      . . . TO WHOM [THEIR] OUR LOVE INCREASD . . . . . . . . 350 FOUR ZOAS 8         366
      BUT STILL THE SPECTRE DIVIDED AND STILL HIS PAIN INCREASD 625 JERUSALEM 6        12
INCREASE
      AND LIBERTY BEGAN T INCREASE  . . . . . . . . .           17 BLIND-MANS/PS       68
      [JOYD AT THEIR INCREASE] . . . . . . . . . . . . . .     164 HEARD ANGEL/N       23
      [WITH POVERTY'S INCREASE]  . . . . . . . . . . . . .     164 HEARD ANGEL/N       24
      [AND BY DISTRESS INCREASE] . . . . . . . . . . . . .     164 HEARD ANGEL/N       26
      [BY MISERY TO INCREASE]  . . . . . . . . . . . . . .     164 HEARD ANGEL/N       28
```

971

```
                                                              PAGE      TITLE           LINE
INCREASE    (CONTINUED)
      AND MISERIES' INCREASE   . . . . . . . . . . .       164 HEARD ANGEL/N         30
      [AND THE LION INCREASE FREEDOM & PEACE]  . . . . . .  171 THE LILLY/N           4
      TILL THE SELFISH LOVES INCREASE   . . . . . . . .     174 HUMAN IMAGE/N         7
      TILL THE SELFISH LOVES INCREASE   . . . . . . . .     217 HUMAN ABSTR/SE        6
      THE INCREASE OF A STATE AS OF A MAN IS FROM INTERNAL  402C ANNO BACON          MARG
          IMPROVEMENT
      IN AN INCREASE OF FAMILY & OF HEALTH & HAPPINESS  . . 810A LETTER 20          PROSE
INCREASED
      TILL VENERABLE AGE CAME ON HIS FLOCKS INCREASED  . . . 39C SAMSON/PS          PROSE
      HOPING THAT HER JOY IS NOW INCREASED & YOURS ALSO  . . 810A LETTER 20         PROSE
INCREASING
      INCREASING INWARDS INTO LENGTH AND BREADTH AND HEIGHTH . 635 JERUSALEM 14       18
      WHICH I HAVE THE PLEASURE TO TELL YOU ARE INCREASING EVERY 794C LETTER 5      PROSE
          DAY
INCREAST
      SWORDS & SPEARS & WRATH INCREAST   . . . . . . . . .  177 DAY/N                 3
INCRUSTATION
      STRETCHD OUT COMPOSE THE MUNDANE SHELL A MIGHTY        528 MILTON 37           53
          INCRUSTATION
      THIS IS A FALSE BODY AN INCRUSTATION OVER MY IMMORTAL . 533 MILTON 40          35
INCULCATE
      BUT PLATO & CICERO DID INCULCATE BEFORE HIM  . . . . 757D EV GOSPEL          PROSE
      WHAT THEN DID CHRIST INCULCATE FORGIVENESS OF SINS  . 757D EV GOSPEL          PROSE
INCULCATED
      THERE IS NOT ONE MORAL VIRTUE THAT JESUS INCULCATED  . 757D EV GOSPEL         PROSE
INCUMBRANCE
      OF EACH INCUMBRANCE CLEAR THE HALL   . . . . . . . .   16 BLIND-MANS/PS        18
INDEBTED
      ALREADY INDEBTED TO MY WIFE TWENTY GUINEAS FOR WORK  . 821A LETTER 25         PROSE
      OF IMMORTAL FRIENDSHIP TO THEE I AM ETERNALLY INDEBTED . 852A LETTER 50       PROSE
INDEED
      INDEED HATE CONTROLLS ALL THE GODS AT WILL  . . . . .  42D THEN SHE BORE      PROSE
      INFLAMMABLE GASS RECOLLECTING HIMSELF INDEED  . . . .  45A ISLAND MOON 1      PROSE
      OBTUSE ANGLE ANSWERD INDEED HE DID   . . . . . . . .   47A ISLAND MOON 4      PROSE
      A CHARMING SONG INDEED MISS SAID SCOPPRELL  . . . . .  54A ISLAND MOON 8      PROSE
      ("QUALITIES OF FRIENDS...ENEMIES") VERY UNEASY INDEED BUT  80D ANNO LAVATER   MARG
          TRUTH
      THOU SEEST ME THE MEANEST THING AND SO I AM INDEED  . . 129 BOOK OF THEL 4     11
      IT INDEED APPEARD TO REASON AS IF DESIRE WAS CAST OUT . 150A MARRIAGE HH 5   PROSE
      THEN IS OOTHOON A WHORE INDEED AND ALL THE VIRGIN JOYS . 194 V DAU ALBION 6    18
      IF I INDEED AM [LUVAH'S LORD] VALA'S KING & YE O SONS OF  282 FOUR ZOAS 2    *  81
          MEN
      WHAT SUCH MEN CALL GREAT IS INDEED DETESTABLE  . . . . 407A ANNO BACON        MARG
      SUCH WAS BACON STUPID INDEED   . . . . . . . . . .    410A ANNO BACON         MARG
      IF INDEED THE NEGLECT OF MY OWN POWERS HAD NOT BEEN  . . 452B ANNO REYNOLDS   MARG
      HE HAS PUT AMONG HIS RABBLE AND INDEED HIS PROSPECTUS . 573C DESC CAT 3       PROSE
      FOR IT IS SO AND VERY WRETCHEDLY SO INDEED WHAT MERIT CAN  574D DESC CAT 3    PROSE
      & INDEED THE SUPERSTRUCTURE IT IS DRAWING ON COPPER  . . 591D PUB ADDRESS/N   PROSE
      AS [IS] IT IS CAPABLE OF BEING PLACED IN ANY HEIGHTH &  601A PUB ADDRESS/N  *PROSE
          INDEED
      INDEED A HARLOT DRUNKEN WITH THE SACRIFICE OF IDOLS DOES HE  695 JERUSALEM 61  38
      "WE INDEED PRESUME ON YOUR KINDNESS IN NEGLECTING TO HAVE"  800A LETTER 12   PROSE
      WITH ALL POSSIBLE EXPEDITION IF INDEED I HAVE NOT TIRED YOU  816C LETTER 24  PROSE
      THE TESTAMENT IS MY CHIEF MASTER ASTONISHING INDEED IS  . 821D LETTER 25     PROSE
      INDEED THE PROSPECT OF RETURNING TO OUR FRIENDS IS     824B LETTER 27        PROSE
          SUPREMELY
      A MORE ASSIDUOUS PURSUIT OF BOTH ARTS INDEED BY MY LATE  825D LETTER 27      PROSE
      HAVE LABOURD HARD INDEED & HAVE BEEN BORNE ON ANGEL'S WINGS  826A LETTER 27  PROSE
      I SOOTHE HIM TO PEACE & INDEED HE IS A GOOD NATURD DEVIL  830C LETTER 30     PROSE
      & THE SERVANT SAID THAT HE REMAINS VERY ILL INDEED  . . 836B LETTER 35       PROSE
      VERY CLEVER & INDEED A SUBLIME BUT VERY UNFINISHD SKETCH  839D LETTER 38     PROSE
      HIS CONNECTIONS THROUGHOUT ENGLAND & INDEED EUROPE &  . 841C LETTER 41       PROSE
      YOUNGER THAN I KNEW HIM BUT VERY LIKE INDEED MR WALKER  . 843C LETTER 43     PROSE
      AND EXQUISITE FOR EXPRESSION INDEED IT IS MOST PATHETIC  843D LETTER 43      PROSE
      HE SAYS THAT THE LAST SESSION WAS A SEVERE LABOUR INDEED IT  844D LETTER 43  PROSE
      BUT AT PRESENT POOR MAN I UNDERSTAND HE IS POORLY INDEED  844D LETTER 43     PROSE
      TOO UNDEFINED FOR MEER OUTLINES & INDEED IT IS NOT ONLY MY  848A LETTER 45   PROSE
      HECATE A VERY FINE THING INDEED WHICH I HAVE  . . . . . 849A LETTER 45       PROSE
      INTO MY HANDS AS I USED TO BE IN MY YOUTH I HAVE INDEED  853A LETTER 51     *PROSE
      INDEED WITH SUCH ABUNDANT FELICITY IN THE MEETING HIM  . 854B LETTER 53      PROSE
      ALL THE ENGRAVER'S NICEST ATTENTION INDEED IT IS      855A LETTER 53         PROSE
          MORE FINISHD
      I GO ON JUST AS IF PERFECTLY WELL WHICH INDEED I AM EXCEPT  873C LETTER 77   PROSE
      OF BAD PERHAPS OF FATAL CONSEQUENCE IS VERY SORRY INDEED  SUPP LETTER 81A   *PROSE
      ("THOUGH COYPEL WANTED A SIMPLICITY") [ O YES COYPEL  SUPP ANNO REYNOLDS  * MARG
          ?INDEED ]
INDEFINITE
      THE MAN'S EXTERIORS ARE BECOME INDEFINITE OPEND TO PAIN  279 FOUR ZOAS 1      543
      . . . SCATTERD INTO [ALL NATIONS] THE INDEFINITE  . . . 279 FOUR ZOAS 1       547
      HE SAW THE INDEFINITE SPACE BENEATH & HIS SOUL SHRUNK WITH  280 FOUR ZOAS 2   20
          HORROR
      SHE WANDERS IN ETERNAL FEAR OF FALLING INTO THE INDEFINITE  297 FOUR ZOAS 3   208
      INTO A FORMLESS INDEFINITE & STREWING HER ON THE ABYSS  . 338 FOUR ZOAS 7B    217
      A SHAPELESS & INDEFINITE CLOUD IN TEARS OF SORROW INCESSANT  345 FOUR ZOAS 8  175
      AND THAT HIS WISDOM SERVD BUT TO AUGMENT THE INDEFINITE  353 FOUR ZOAS 8      466
          LUST
      IN STERN SEVERITY & CAST THEE OUT INTO THE INDEFINITE  . 360 FOUR ZOAS 9      146
      ARE ALWAYS CLUMSY AND INDEFINITE THE EFFECT OF RUBBING OUT  439C REMARKS MALKIN  PROSE
      AMONG INDEFINITE DRUID ROCKS & SNOWS OF DOUBT & REASONING  482 MILTON 3        8
      ENLARGD INTO DIMENSION & DEFORMD INTO INDEFINITE SPACE  498 MILTON 17         23
      DELIGHTFUL WITH BOUNDS TO THE INFINITE PUTTING OFF THE  515 MILTON 28          4
          INDEFINITE
```

	PAGE	TITLE	LINE

INDEFINITE   (CONTINUED)
IT BECAME OPAKE & INDEFINITE BUT THE DIVINE SAVIOUR . . . 517 MILTON 29   37
INDEFINITE OR PALTRY RHYMES OR PALTRY HARMONIES   . . . . 533 MILTON 41   10
JERUSALEM IS NOT HER DAUGHTERS ARE INDEFINITE . . . . . 622 JERUSALEM 4   27
A DARK AND UNKNOWN NIGHT INDEFINITE UNMEASURABLE WITHOUT   624 JERUSALEM 5   57
    END
CONSTELLATIONS OVER THE DEADLY DEEPS OF INDEFINITE   625 JERUSALEM 7   22
    UDAN-ADAN
LET THE INDEFINITE BE EXPLORED AND LET EVERY MAN BE JUDGED 687 JERUSALEM 55   57
ABROAD INTO THE INDEFINITE SPECTRE WHO IS THE RATIONAL   698 JERUSALEM 64   5
    POWER
OVER ALBION'S MOUNTAINS A FEMININE INDEFINITE CRUEL   701 JERUSALEM 65   67
    DELUSION
AND THE PERCEPTIONS TO BE DISSIPATED INTO THE INDEFINITE 703 JERUSALEM 66   47
    BECOMING
INTO INDEFINITE CLOUDY SHADOWS IN DARKNESS & SEPARATION   703 JERUSALEM 66   52
AND RAHAB LIKE A DISMAL AND INDEFINITE HOVERING CLOUD . . 723 JERUSALEM 80   51
A TERRIBLE INDEFINITE HERMAPHRODITIC FORM . . . . . . 734 JERUSALEM 89   3
INTO THE INDEFINITE REFUSING TO BELIEVE WITHOUT   738 JERUSALEM 91   36
    DEMONSTRATION
ENGLISHMEN ARE FOND OF THE INDEFINITE WHICH THEY MEASURE 878A LETTER 88   PROSE
INDEFINITES
BY HIS OWN WORKS LET ALL INDEFINITES BE THROWN INTO   687 JERUSALEM 55   58
    DEMONSTRATIONS
INDELIBLE
THE SOFT HANDS OF ANTAMON DRAW THE INDELIBLE LINE   . . . 515 MILTON 28   16
INDEPENDENCE
RESOLVD TO SHEW AN INDEPENDENCE WHICH I KNOW WILL PLEASE 792A LETTER 4   PROSE
    AN AUTHOR
REAL DIFFERENCE AS TO PERFECT INDEPENDENCE OF JUDGMENT . . 868B LETTER 67   PROSE
INDEPENDENT
THE POET IS INDEPENDENT & WICKED   . . . . 412C ANNO BOYD   MARG
[AND THE REALLY INDUSTRIOUS [VIRTUOUS & INDEPENDENT] BARRY] 595B PUB ADDRESS/N   PROSE
ETERNITY INDEPENDENT OF CREATION WHICH WAS AN ACT OF MERCY 614B V LAST JUDG/N   PROSE
A FORTUNE SUCH AS WOULD MAKE ME INDEPENDENT   . . . . . 820B LETTER 25   PROSE
[BARRY WAS POOR & INDEPENDENT ?MORTIMER WAS DESPISED &   SUPP ANNO REYNOLDS   * MARG
    MOCKED]
INDETERMINATE
HERE HE IS FOR DETERMINATE & YET FOR INDETERMINATE   . . . 461A ANNO REYNOLDS   MARG
INDEX
IT IS ONLY THE CONTENTS OR INDEX OF ALREADY PUBLISHD BOOKS 157C MARRIAGE HH 21   PROSE
AN INDEX TO THE CATALOGUE GRATIS . . . . 562C DESC CAT ADV   PROSE
INDEX TO THE CATALOGUE   . . . . 564A DESC CAT   TITLE
CHAUCER'S CANTERBURY PILGRIMS BEING A COMPLETE INDEX   . 591A PUB ADDRESS/N   TITLE
INDIA
TOWARDS AMERICA INDIA ROSE UP FROM HIS GOLDEN BED   . . . 519 MILTON 31   14
CHINA & INDIA & SIBERIA ARE HIS TEMPLES FOR ENTERTAINMENT 690 JERUSALEM 58   39
TO SODOM & GOMORRHA THENCE TO INDIA CHINA & JAPAN   . . . 704 JERUSALEM 67   40
THRO ITALY & GRECIA TO LEBANON & PERSIA & INDIA   . . . . 722 JERUSALEM 80   47
THE NATIONS OF INDIA THE WILD TARTAR THAT NEVER KNEW MAN 729 JERUSALEM 84   23
INDICATE
INDICATE THE SITUATION OF THE GREAT CITY   . . . . . . 567B DESC CAT 3   PROSE
INDICATE THE SITUATION OF THE GREAT CITY   . . . . . . 588D CHAUCER/N   PROSE
INDICATE THE SITUATION OF THE GREAT CITY   . . . . . . 590C CHAUCER 2   PROSE
INDICATES
INDICATES THE SOUND OF THE CURFEW BELL . . . . 619B ILLUS MILTON   PROSE
INDIFFERENCE
THAT HE CAN NO LONGER TREAT ME WITH INDIFFERENCE . . . . 819D LETTER 25   PROSE
INDIFFERENT
THE CHRISTIAN RELIGION TEACHES THAT NO MAN IS INDIFFERENT 380B FOUR ZOAS NOTE   PROSE
AT HIS HOUSE LET US ACCOMODATE HIM IN WHAT IS INDIFFERENT 868B LETTER 67   PROSE
INDIGENT
WHILE THE POOR INDIGENT IS LIKE THE DIAMOND WHICH   515 MILTON 28   36
    THO CLOTHD
INDIGNANT
HE INDIGNANT DEPARTED ON HORSES OF HEAVN . . . . 143 FRENCH REVOLTN   201
AROUND THEIR SHORES INDIGNANT BURNING WITH THE FIRES OF ORC 200 AMERICA 11   2
DOWN ON THE LAND OF AMERICA INDIGNANT THEY DESCENDED   . . 200 AMERICA 12   4
READING THIS INDIGNANT PAGE . . . . 219 LIT GRL LST/SE   2
ON URIZEN FROWNING INDIGNANT   . . . . 249 AHANIA 2   15
THE IMMORTAL REVOLVING INDIGNANT   . . . . 258 BOOK OF LOS 4   37
ROARING INDIGNANT THE BRIGHT SPARKS . . . . 260 BOOK OF LOS 5   31
INDIGNANT MUTTERING LOW THUNDERS URIZEN DESCENDED   . . . 273 FOUR ZOAS 1   318
[EXULTING] [INDIGNANT] EXULTING AT THE VOICE THAT CALLD   280 FOUR ZOAS 2   *   10
    HIM . . .
INDIGNANT ROSE THE [ETERNAL] [FALLEN] AWFUL MAN . . . . . 293 FOUR ZOAS 3   *   70
GO FORTH REBUILD THIS UNIVERSE BENEATH MY INDIGNANT POWER 298 FOUR ZOAS 4   27
THE INDIGNANT THISTLE WHOSE BITTERNESS IS BRED IN HIS MILK 377 FOUR ZOAS 9   763
INDIGNANT AGAINST KNAVERY   . . . . 414A ANNO BOYD   MARG
WHILE OTHER COUNTRY HINDS ARE AS INDIGNANT AGAINST HONESTY 414A ANNO BOYD   MARG
THE FATHER INDIGNANT AT THE FALL . . . . 441D INSC FALL MAN   PROSE
FUSELI INDIGNANT ALMOST HID HIMSELF I [?WAS] AM HID . . . 445C ANNO REYNOLDS   * MARG
IT MAY BE RENDERD INDIGNANT & OUTRAGEOUS . . . . . . 472D ANNO REYNOLDS   MARG
THEY GAVE SATAN THEIR WINE INDIGNANT AT THE BURNING WRATH 493 MILTON 12   44
INDIGNANT UNCONVINCD BY LOS'S ARGUMENTS & (THUNDERS)   509 MILTON 24   45
    ROLLING
THE INDIGNANT THISTLE WHOSE BITTERNESS IS BRED IN HIS MILK 513 MILTON 27   26
. . . IN EDOM I SAW IT INDIGNANT & THOU ART NOT MOVED   . . 625 JERUSALEM 7   26
HIS FEET INDIGNANT SELF-RIGHTEOUSNESS LIKE WHIRLWINDS OF 626 JERUSALEM 7   73
    THE NORTH
KNOT DAY BY DAY NIGHT BY NIGHT LOUD ROLL THE INDIGNANT   648 JERUSALEM 24   62
    ATLANTIC

	PAGE	TITLE	LINE

INDIGNANT   (CONTINUED)
    INDIGNANT ROSE THE AWFUL MAN & TURND HIS BACK ON VALA   . . 654 JERUSALEM 29   57
    WHILE ALBION FLED MORE INDIGNANT REVENGEFUL COVERING   . . 664 JERUSALEM 37   12
INDIGNATION
    THAT THE VOICE OF HONEST INDIGNATION IS THE VOICE OF GOD   153C MARRIAGE HH 12   PROSE
    RAGE FURY INTENSE INDIGNATION . . . . 225 URIZEN 4   45
    STAMPD IN FURY AND HOT INDIGNATION   . . . . 257 BOOK OF LOS 3   48
    [LOS] HE ANSWERD DARKNING MORE WITH [FOUL] INDIGNATION   272 FOUR ZOAS 1   282
        HID IN SMILES
    SO SPOKE LOS SCORN & INDIGNATION ROSE UPON ENITHARMON   . 272 FOUR ZOAS 1   306
    THE ENVY WAS UPON A KING BUT IS THIS ENVY OR INDIGNATION   400B ANNO BACON   MARG
    ON THESE BOOKS NOTHING BUT INDIGNATION & RESENTMENT   . . . 445B ANNO REYNOLDS   MARG
    IS A SUFFICIENT APOLOGY FOR MY VIGOROUS INDIGNATION   . . 452B ANNO REYNOLDS   MARG
    THE GNOMES ACCUSD SATAN WITH INDIGNATION FURY AND FIRE   . 487 MILTON 7   21
    IN INDIGNATION FOR SATAN'S SOFT DISSIMULATION OF FRIENDSHIP   488 MILTON 8   35
    THE PUBLIC INDIGNATION OF MEN OF SENSE IN ALL PROFESSIONS   598D PUB ADDRESS/N   PROSE
    SO LOS IN FURY & STRENGTH IN INDIGNATION & BURNING WRATH   629 JERUSALEM 10   22
    REJOICING IN HIS INDIGNATION ADORING HIS WRATHFUL REBUKE   743 JERUSALEM 95   23
    MY INDIGNATION WAS EXCEEDINGLY MOVED AT READING A   . . 863D LETTER 61   PROSE
    A CIRCUMSTANCE HAS OCCURRED WHICH HAS AGAIN RAISED   865A LETTER 62   PROSE
        MY INDIGNATION
INDISCRIMINATELY
    LAID ON (INDISCRIMINATELY) & BROKEN ONE INTO ANOTHER   . 469A ANNO REYNOLDS   * MARG
INDISPENSIBLE
    TO BE A NECESSARY AND INDISPENSIBLE PART OF VERSE   . . 621D JERUSALEM 3   PROSE
INDISTINCT
    WHILE LOS HEARD INDISTINCT IN FEAR WHAT TIME I BOUND MY   505 MILTON 22   4
        SANDALS
INDIVIDUAL
    BUT ALL ACT [FROM INDIVIDUAL PROPENSITY] IS VIRTUE   . . .   88D ANNO LAVATER   MARG
    ADAPTED TO THE WEAKNESSES OF EVERY INDIVIDUAL   . . . . .   98C ALL RELIGIONS   PROSE
    KNOWETH NO INDIVIDUAL [MAN]. . . . . 264 FOUR ZOAS 1   13
    IS AUGHT BUT DEATH IN INDIVIDUAL WEAKNESS SORROW & PAIN   346 FOUR ZOAS 8   199
    AS TO DESTROY AN INDIVIDUAL BY MEANS OF ANOTHER   . . . 388B ANNO WATSON   MARG
    INDIVIDUAL WHICH GOD CONSIDERS IN THE BIBLE AS MURDER   . 388B ANNO WATSON   MARG
    THEY MILITATE AGAINST INDIVIDUAL CHARACTER . . . . . . 453B ANNO REYNOLDS   MARG
    EVERY CLASS IS INDIVIDUAL . . . . 460A ANNO REYNOLDS   MARG
    WHO CALLS THE INDIVIDUAL LAW HOLY AND DESPISES THE SAVIOUR   493 MILTON 13   5
    BOWLAHOOLA IS THE STOMACH IN EVERY INDIVIDUAL MAN   . . . 509 MILTON 24   67
    STATES CHANGE BUT INDIVIDUAL IDENTITIES NEVER CHANGE NOR   521 MILTON 32   23
        CEASE
    THE IMAGE OF A CLASS AND NOT OF AN IMPERFECT INDIVIDUAL   571A DESC CAT 3   PROSE
    UNAPPROPRIATE AND REPUGNANT TO YOUR OWN INDIVIDUAL   582D DESC CAT 9   PROSE
        CHARACTER
    HINDERS ALL POWER OF INDIVIDUAL THOUGHT . . . . 582D DESC CAT 9   PROSE
    FOR COMMERCE CANNOT ENDURE INDIVIDUAL MERIT   . . . . 593D PUB ADDRESS/N   PROSE
    OF INDIVIDUAL MERIT BEING ITS GREAT HATRED   . . . . . 594A PUB ADDRESS/N   PROSE
    WHENEVER ANY INDIVIDUAL REJECTS ERROR & EMBRACES TRUTH   . 613A V LAST JUDG/N   PROSE
    A LAST JUDGMENT PASSES UPON THAT INDIVIDUAL   . . . . 613A V LAST JUDG/N   PROSE
    NO INDIVIDUAL CAN KEEP THESE LAWS FOR THEY ARE DEATH   . 662 JERUSALEM 35   11
    IN EVERY INDIVIDUAL MAN AND THE LIMIT OF OPAKENESS   . . 670 JERUSALEM 42   30
    WHO IS JERUSALEM IN EVERY INDIVIDUAL MAN AND HER   . . 675 JERUSALEM 44   39
    TO INDIVIDUAL PERCEPTION LUVAH MUST BE CREATED   . . . 696 JERUSALEM 62   20
    LOS CRIES NO INDIVIDUAL OUGHT TO APPROPRIATE TO HIMSELF   736 JERUSALEM 90   28
    FOR LOS SAID WHEN THE INDIVIDUAL APPROPRIATES UNIVERSALITY   737 JERUSALEM 90   52
    EXPRESSING PRIVATE OPINION WHICH WILL VARY IN EACH   853A LETTER 51   *PROSE
        INDIVIDUAL
INDIVIDUALITY
    THE PALE LIMBS OF HIS ETERNAL INDIVIDUALITY   . . . . 277 FOUR ZOAS 1   467
    EVERY MAN'S WISDOM IS PECULIAR TO HIS OWN (INDIVIDUALITY)   483 MILTON 4   * 8
    THERE IS NO OTHER LET ALL OBEY MY PRINCIPLES OF MORAL   490 MILTON 9   26
        INDIVIDUALITY
    BUT ITS ETERNAL IMAGE & INDIVIDUALITY NEVER DIES   . . . . 605B V LAST JUDG/N   PROSE
    WHILE IT RETAINS ITS OWN INDIVIDUALITY   . . . . . . 607A V LAST JUDG/N   PROSE
    AND MERCIFUL THE INDIVIDUALITY HOWEVER HIGH   . . . . 675 JERUSALEM 45   11
    THE PALE LIMBS OF HIS ETERNAL INDIVIDUALITY   . . . . 677 JERUSALEM 48   3
    APPROPRIATE INDIVIDUALITY THEY BECOME AN ETERNAL DEATH   . 737 JERUSALEM 90   54
INDIVIDUALS
    THE DIFFERENCE BETWEEN STATES & INDIVIDUALS OF THOSE STATES   351 FOUR ZOAS 8   380
    WE ARE NOT INDIVIDUALS BUT STATES COMBINATIONS OF   521 MILTON 32   10
        INDIVIDUALS
    DISTINGUISH THEREFORE STATES FROM INDIVIDUALS IN THOSE   521 MILTON 32   22
        STATES
    THE IGNORANT INSULTS OF INDIVIDUALS WILL NOT HINDER ME   . 561A EXHIBITION ADV   PROSE
    SIGNIFIED BY THOSE NAMES THE INDIVIDUALS BEING   . . . 607B V LAST JUDG/N   PROSE
    IT IS THE SAME WITH INDIVIDUALS AS NATIONS . . . . . 612C V LAST JUDG/N   PROSE
    STRIVING WITH SYSTEMS TO DELIVER INDIVIDUALS FROM THOSE   630 JERUSALEM 11   5
        SYSTEMS
    . . . THE DELIVERANCE OF INDIVIDUALS EVERMORE AMEN   . . 648 JERUSALEM 25   13
    TO INDIVIDUALS & NOT TO STATES AND THESE SLEPT IN ULRO   . 648 JERUSALEM 25   16
    STATES TO DELIVER INDIVIDUALS EVERMORE AMEN   . . . . 662 JERUSALEM 35   16
    IMPUTING SIN & RIGHTEOUSNESS TO INDIVIDUALS RAHAB   . . 709 JERUSALEM 70   17
INDOLENCE
    YET THOU IN INDOLENCE REPOSEST HOLDING ME IN BONDS   . . 271 FOUR ZOAS 1   259
    REFLECTING ALL MY INDOLENCE MY WEAKNESS & MY DEATH   . . 295 FOUR ZOAS 3   126
    MANTLES OF DESPAIR GIRDLES OF BITTER COMPUNCTION SHOES   346 FOUR ZOAS 8   221
        OF INDOLENCE
    TO INDOLENCE TO THE NIGHT OF DEATH WHEN INDOLENCE   360 FOUR ZOAS 9   117
        & MOURNING
    A LIE WORKING UP EFFECT IS MORE AN OPERATION OF INDOLENCE   450A ANNO REYNOLDS   MARG
INDOLENT
    THE [IDLE MAN] INDOLENT NEVER CAN BRING TO THE MART   . . . 181 RICHES/N   3

974

		PAGE	TITLE	LINE

INDOLENT   (CONTINUED)
SHALL THE FEMININE INDOLENT BLISS THE INDULGENT SELF OF   295 FOUR ZOAS 3   114
WEARINESS
THARMAS INDOLENT & SULLEN URTHONA DOUBTING & DESPAIRING   671 JERUSALEM 43   3
INDULGE
IN SECRET WHILE THEY SUFFER HIM TO INDULGE HIS PASSIONATE   864B LETTER 61   PROSE
INDULGENCE
MY WIFE HAS NO INDULGENCE GIVEN . . . .   818 HAPPINESS/L   61
INDULGENT
SHALL THE FEMININE INDOLENT BLISS THE INDULGENT SELF OF   295 FOUR ZOAS 3   114
WEARINESS
INDUSTRIOUS
HOW THE INDUSTRIOUS CITIZEN THE PAINS OF THE HUSBANDMAN   193 V DAU ALBION 5   13
NOR CAN HIS WATCH FIENDS FIND IT BUT THE INDUSTRIOUS FIND   526 MILTON 35   43
[AND THE REALLY INDUSTRIOUS [VIRTUOUS & INDEPENDENT] BARRY]   595B PUB ADDRESS/N   PROSE
INDUSTRIOUSLY
THIS IMPUTATION MOST ARTFULLY AND INDUSTRIOUSLY ENDEAVOURED   572C DESC CAT 3   PROSE
INDUSTRY
IF INDUSTRY IS IN MY DIOCESE . . . .   19 EDW THIRD/PS 2   24
RANG SWEET THE PRAISE OF INDUSTRY THRO ALL THE GOLDEN ROOMS   378 FOUR ZOAS 9   781
WHICH HE BY INDUSTRY HAD GOT . . . .   425 MENTAL TRAVLER   32
COMMENCED A NEW LIFE OF INDUSTRY TO DO CREDIT TO . . . .   804B LETTER 16   PROSE
IN THIS OF INDUSTRY AS WELL AS IN OTHER VIRTUES AND MERITS   807B LETTER 17   PROSE
WITH ALL HIS MATCHLESS INDUSTRY . . . .   809D LETTER 20   PROSE
HIS INDUSTRY IS EQUAL TO HIS OTHER GREAT POWERS . . . .   829B LETTER 29   PROSE
COURAGE OF CONSCIOUS INDUSTRY WORTHY OF HIS FORMER KINDNESS   851D LETTER 50   PROSE
THEY KNEW MY INDUSTRY AND ABSTINENCE FROM EVERY PLEASURE   852B LETTER 50   PROSE
THE PROOFS OF INDUSTRY IN MY WORKS I THANK GOD WITH ENTIRE   852C LETTER 50   PROSE
INDWELLING
AND AS TO THE INDWELLING OF THE HOLY GHOST . . . . . .   752 EV GOSPEL(D)/N *   45
INEFFECTUAL
MY MOCK & SCORN ALAS WRETCHED HAPPY INEFFECTUAL LABOURER OF   809B LETTER 20   PROSE
INEXHAUSTIBLE
OF ALL THINGS & INEXHAUSTIBLE . . . .   471A ANNO REYNOLDS   MARG
INEXORABLE
("WHO PROVES HIMSELF INEXORABLE") UNEASY I DO   70D ANNO LAVATER   MARG
NOT BELIEVE IT
INEXPRESSIBLE
THE SHADOWY FEMALE SHUDDERS THRO HEAVEN IN TORMENT   506 MILTON 22   36
INEXPRESSIBLE
INEXTRICABLE
INEXTRICABLE LABYRINTHS SHE BORE ME SONS & DAUGHTERS . .   282 FOUR ZOAS 2   97
INFANCY
[THERE] AND [CRADLED] MILK FED INFANCY [IS SOLD] FOR GOLD   174 HUMAN IMAGE/N *   30
INFANCY FEARLESS LUSTFUL HAPPY NESTLING FOR DELIGHT . . .   193 V DAU ALBION 6   4
THAT THE DELICATE EAR IN ITS INFANCY . . . .   247 SONG OF LOS 7   5
OF VEGETATION WEEPING IN WAYWARD INFANCY & SULLEN YOUTH   267 FOUR ZOAS 1   123
BABYLON AGAIN IN INFANCY CALLD NATURAL RELIGION . . . .   357 FOUR ZOAS 8   620
WHO DIED IN INFANCY RAGE FURIOUS A MIGHTY MULTITUDE RAGE   363 FOUR ZOAS 9   253
FURIOUS
DOES HIM TO INFANCY BEGUILE . . . .   426 MENTAL TRAVLER   72
LIMBS THAT DEVIATES OR ALTERS LEAST FROM INFANCY TO OLD AGE   580A DESC CAT 5   PROSE
THY CRADLED INFANCY IS MOST PITEOUS O HIDE O HIDE . . .   644 JERUSALEM 21   24
AND OF THE CRADLED INFANCY IN HIS BOWELS OF COMPASSION . .   688 JERUSALEM 56   34
CALL HER PURE AS HE DID IN THE DAYS OF HER INFANCY WHEN SHE   695 JERUSALEM 61   39
VIRGIN WIFE INFANCY OLD AGE HUSBAND ANGEL OF   SUPP INSC HERVEY   *TITLE
PROVIDENCE
INFANT
THE SUCKING INFANT LIVES TO DIE IN BATTLE . . . . . .   34B KING JOHN/PS   PROSE
NIGHTLY BLAST THAT BLIGHTS THE INFANT BUD THE WINDS . . .   43D WOE CRIED MUSE *PROSE
AND IN THE NIGHT LIKE INFANTS SLEPT DELIGHTED WITH INFANT   100 TIRIEL 2   9
DREAMS
THE INFANT HEAD WHILE THE MOTHER IDLE PLAYS WITH HER DOG   110 TIRIEL 8   26
ON HER COUCH
THEN WALKS THE WEAK INFANT IN SORROW COMPELLD TO NUMBER   110 TIRIEL 8   32
FOOTSTEPS
INFANT JOY . . . .   118B INFANT JOY/SI   TITLE
WEAVE THY BROWS AN INFANT CROWN . . . .   120 CRADLE SONG/SI   6
WHEN HE WAS AN INFANT SMALL . . . .   120 CRADLE SONG/SI   26
WHO BECAME AN INFANT SMALL . . . .   120 CRADLE SONG/SI   30
INFANT SMILES ARE HIS OWN SMILES . . . .   120 CRADLE SONG/SI   31
AN INFANT GROAN AN INFANT FEAR . . . .   122 ON ANOTHERS/SI   10
HE BECOMES AN INFANT SMALL . . . .   122 ON ANOTHERS/SI   26
INFANT NOISE . . . .   123 SPRING/SI   17
I SEE THEE LIKE AN INFANT WRAPPED IN THE LILLY'S LEAF . .   129 BOOK OF THEL 4   3
SHE BOWD OVER THE WEEPING INFANT AND HER LIFE EXHALD . .   129 BOOK OF THEL 4   8
A BRIGHT CLOUD OF INFANT SOULS . . . .   138 FRENCH REVOLTN   88
SOONER MURDER AN INFANT IN ITS CRADLE THAN NURSE UNACTED   152D MARRIAGE HH 10   PROSE
DESIRES
LITTLE PRETTY INFANT WILES . . . .   165 CRADLE SONG/N   22
[FEMALE] INFANT WILES & [FEMALE] INFANT SMILES . . . .   165 CRADLE SONG/N   26
THO HIS WATERS BATHED MY INFANT LIMBS . . . .   166 WHY CARE FOR/N *   6
INFANT SORROW . . . .   166D INFANT SORW/N   TITLE
AND SWEET SHALL BE THY TASTE & SWEET THY INFANT JOYS RENEW   193 V DAU ALBION 6   3
ARISE YOU LITTLE GLANCING WINGS AND SING YOUR INFANT JOY   195 V DAU ALBION 8   9
INFANT SORROW . . . .   217D INFANT SORW/SE   TITLE
BROUGHT FORTH AN INFANT FORM . . . .   232 URIZEN 19   35
IN HIS HANDS HE SIEZD THE INFANT . . . .   233 URIZEN 20   3
IN INFANT JOY AT THY FEET . . . .   255 AHANIA 5   27
THE INFANT JOY IS BEAUTIFUL BUT ITS ANATOMY . . . . .   265 FOUR ZOAS 1   49
TILL SHE BECAME A LITTLE WEEPING INFANT A SPAN LONG . . .   282 FOUR ZOAS 2   92
ARISE YOU LITTLE GLANCING WINGS & SING YOUR INFANT JOY . .   289 FOUR ZOAS 2   364

		PAGE	TITLE	LINE
INFANT	(CONTINUED)			
	WHERE THE LAMB REPLIES TO THE INFANT VOICE	315	FOUR ZOAS 6	136
	AT FIRST AN INFANT WEAKNESS PERIODS PASSD HE GATHERD STRENGTH	316	FOUR ZOAS 6	163
	I WAS DIVIDED IN DARKNESS & OBLIVION THOU AN INFANT WOE	327	FOUR ZOAS 7	288
	AND I AN INFANT TERROR IN THE WOMB OF ENION	327	FOUR ZOAS 7	289
	IN INFANT INNOCENCE REPOSD ON ENITHARMON'S BOSOM . . .	332	FOUR ZOAS 7	477
	BUT LOS LOVED THEM & REFUSD TO SACRIFICE THEIR INFANT LIMBS	332	FOUR ZOAS 7	482
	HIS WHOLE SOUL LOVED HIM HE BEHELD HIM AN INFANT . . .	332	FOUR ZOAS 7	498
	THEN SHE RETURNS SWIFT AS A BLIGHT UPON THE INFANT BUD . .	339	FOUR ZOAS 7B	261
	WHEN INFANT SPRING APPEARS IN SWELLING BUDS & OPENING FLOWERS	371	FOUR ZOAS 9	548
	HE TOOK HER HAND RELUCTANT SHE FOLLOWD IN INFANT DOUBTS	371	FOUR ZOAS 9	552
	IN INFANT SORROW & JOY ALTERNATE ENION & THARMAS PLAYD .	372	FOUR ZOAS 9	554
	AND ALL THE BLACK MOULD SINGS SHE SPEAKS TO HER INFANT RACE HER MILK	373	FOUR ZOAS 9	601
	THE HONEY OF HER INFANT LIPS	426	MENTAL TRAVLER	69
	THAT EVERY INFANT THAT IS BORN UPON THE EARTH SHALL READ	499	MILTON 18	13
	AND PALAMABRON THOU REMEMBEREST WHEN JOSEPH AN INFANT .	508	MILTON 24	17
	TO THE WEAK AND PITY THE WEAK AS YOUR INFANT CARE BREAK NOT	511	MILTON 25	57
	AS THE BELOVED INFANT IN HIS MOTHER'S BOSOM ROUND INCIRCLED	518	MILTON 30	11
	MULTITUDES OF MEN IN HARMONY APPEAR LIKE A SINGLE INFANT	607C	V LAST JUDG/N	PROSE
	& ON THEIR LEFT A SOLITARY WOMAN WITH HER INFANT	610D	V LAST JUDG/N	PROSE
	ALL THE INFANT LOVES & GRACES WERE LOST FOR THE MIGHTY HAND	628	JERUSALEM 9	44
	AND HIS INFANT THOUGHTS & DESIRES INTO COLD DARK CLIFFS OF DEATH	628	JERUSALEM 9	2
	SLAY NOT MY INFANT LOVES & GRACES BEAUTIFUL DAUGHTER OF MOAB	643	JERUSALEM 20	28
	THE INFANT JOY IS BEAUTIFUL BUT ITS ANATOMY	645	JERUSALEM 22	22
	AMONG THE INFANT LOVES & AFFECTIONS AND THE DIVINE VISION WEPT	669	JERUSALEM 42	7
	HE WHO IS AN INFANT AND WHOSE CRADLE IS A MANGER	688	JERUSALEM 56	5
	KNOWETH THE INFANT SORROW WHENCE IT CAME AND WHERE IT GOETH	688	JERUSALEM 56	6
	THE INFANT INTO HER HANDS IN THE VISIONS OF JEHOVAH TIMES PASSED ON	695	JERUSALEM 61	48
	EVERY HARLOT WAS ONCE A VIRGIN EVERY CRIMINAL AN INFANT LOVE	695	JERUSALEM 61	52
	A WEEPING INFANT IN THE GATES OF BIRTH IN THE MIDST OF HEAVEN	697	JERUSALEM 63	17
	NO HUMAN FORM BUT SEXUAL & A LITTLE WEEPING INFANT PALE REFLECTED	697	JERUSALEM 63	20
	LET US LOOK LET US EXAMINE IS THE CRUEL BECOME AN INFANT	724	JERUSALEM 81	8
	A WEEPING INFANT IN RUIND LOVELY JERUSALEM'S FOLDING CLOUD	724	JERUSALEM 81	14
	OF PAINTED CLAY THE MIGHTY HYLE IS BECOME A WEEPING INFANT	725	JERUSALEM 82	8
	LOOK HYLE IS BECOME AN INFANT LOVE LOOK BEHOLD SEE HIM LIE	725	JERUSALEM 82	37
	[HYLE WAS BECOME A WINDING WORM] & NOT A WEEPING INFANT	726	JERUSALEM 82	48
	GWENDOLEN SAW THE INFANT IN HER (SISTER'S) ARMS SHE HOWLD	726	JERUSALEM 82	* 72
	I SHALL BECOME AN INFANT HORROR ENION THARMAS FRIENDS .	727	JERUSALEM 83	5
	WEAVING BOWERS OF DELIGHT ON THE CURRENT OF INFANT THAMES	728	JERUSALEM 83	50
	HIS BACK IS TURNED THEY WILL MURDER THE MOTHER & HER INFANT	792B	LETTER 4	PROSE
	ECCHOING GREEN DITTO THE LAMB THE SHEPHERD INFANT JOY	SUPP	LETTER 66A	*PROSE
	INFANT SORROW THE SCHOOL BOY LONDON LITTLE GIRL LOST	SUPP	LETTER 66A	*PROSE
INFANTINE				
	("HEROES WITH INFANTINE SIMPLICITY") THIS IS HEAVENLY .	75B	ANNO LAVATER	MARG
	A GARMENT AND CRADLE WEAVING FOR THE INFANTINE TERROR .	688	JERUSALEM 56	14
INFANTRY				
	. . . ASCEND ON THE HILLS AND BRIGHT INFANTRY RANK . . .	147	FRENCH REVOLTN	291
INFANT'S				
	OER MY LOVELY INFANT'S HEAD	120	CRADLE SONG/SI	2
	WEEPING TEAR ON INFANT'S TEAR	122	ON ANOTHERS/SI	20
	LIKE DREAMS OF INFANTS LIKE A SMILE UPON AN INFANT'S FACE	127	BOOK OF THEL 1	10
	IN [EVERY VOICE OF EVERY CHILD] EVERY INFANT'S CRY OF FEAR	170	LONDON/N	6
	[AND BLASTS THE NEW BORN INFANT'S TEAR]	170	LONDON/N	17
	BLASTS THE NEW BORN INFANT'S TEAR	170	LONDON/N	20
	IN EVERY INFANT'S CRY OF FEAR	216	LONDON/SE	6
	BLASTS THE NEW-BORN INFANT'S TEAR	216	LONDON/SE	15
	SEEKING FOR PLEASURE WHICH UNSOUGHT FALLS ROUND THE INFANT'S PATH	361	FOUR ZOAS 9	172
	HE WHO MOCKS THE INFANT'S FAITH	433	AUGURIES	85
	HE WHO RESPECTS THE INFANT'S FAITH	433	AUGURIES	89
	TO ROAST THE FLESH IN FIRE TO EXAMINE THE INFANT'S LIMBS	707	JERUSALEM 68	58
INFANTS				
	AND IN THE NIGHT LIKE INFANTS SLEPT DELIGHTED WITH INFANT DREAMS	100	TIRIEL 2	9
	THEY RAN WEEPING LIKE FRIGHTED INFANTS FOR REFUGE IN MNETHA'S ARMS	100	TIRIEL 2	* 12
	AND THIS IS HAR & HEVA TREMBLING LIKE INFANTS BY MY SIDE	101	TIRIEL 2	19
	HEAR THE WOES THAT INFANTS BEAR	122	ON ANOTHERS/SI	16
	LIKE DREAMS OF INFANTS LIKE A SMILE UPON AN INFANT'S FACE	127	BOOK OF THEL 1	10
	MOTHERS & INFANTS KINGS & WARRIORS	248	SONG OF LOS 7	34
	BEHOLD TWO [LITTLE INFANTS WEPT] [?FIGURES OF ?PAIN HOWLD]	269	FOUR ZOAS 1	* 192
	[INFOLDING THE BRIGHT INFANTS FROM THE DESOLATING WINDS]	270	FOUR ZOAS 1	210
	THE VOICES OF CHILDREN IN MY TENTS TO CRIES OF HELPLESS INFANTS	360	FOUR ZOAS 9	111
	FATHERS & FRIENDS MOTHERS & INFANTS KINGS & WARRIORS .	363	FOUR ZOAS 9	243
	WHAT A CURSED FOOL IS THIS ILL SHAPEN ARE INFANTS OR SMALL PLANTS	406C	ANNO BACON	MARG
	& THE MOON BENEATH HER FEET WITH SIX INFANTS AROUND HER	443D	LAST JUDGMNT/L	PROSE
	THE TWO INTRODUCERS INTO ETERNAL LIFE WOMEN WITH INFANTS	444B	LAST JUDGMNT/L	PROSE

```
                                                        PAGE      TITLE        LINE
INFANTS    (CONTINUED)
    MANY INFANTS APPEAR IN THE GLORY REPRESENTING  .  .  .  .  .  444C LAST JUDGMNT/L   PROSE
    JERUSALEM IS THEIR DAUGHTER LITTLE INFANTS CREEP OUT OF THE   609D V LAST JUDG/N    PROSE
    SURROUNDED BY INFANTS THERE IS SUCH A STATE IN ETERNITY       610A V LAST JUDG/N    PROSE
    WHERE THE INFANTS CREEP OUT OF THE GROUND  .  .  .  .  .      610C V LAST JUDG/N    PROSE
    LED ONWARD BY TRIUMPHANT GROUPES OF INFANTS  .  .  .  .  .    611D V LAST JUDG/N    PROSE
    AROUND HIM INFANTS EMANATING FROM HIM THESE REPRESENT  .      613D V LAST JUDG/N    PROSE
    IN WHICH YOUTHFUL NUPTIALS RECIEVE THE INFANTS IN THEIR       613D V LAST JUDG/N    PROSE
       HANDS
    THE VOICES OF CHILDREN IN HIS TENTS TO CRIES OF HELPLESS      641 JERUSALEM 19       12
       INFANTS
    SILENT THEY WANDERD HAND IN HAND LIKE TWO INFANTS WANDRING    732 JERUSALEM 86       62
    WE LIKE INFANTS DESCEND  .  .  .  .  .  .  .  .  .  .  .      805 TO BUTTS/L         42
    & THE HOURS SUCKLING THEIR FLOWERY INFANTS  .  .  .  .        SUPP ILLUS GRAY      *TITLE
INFECTED
    O MY CHILD MY CHILD IS THY BREATH INFECTED SO IS MINE  .  .   36B COUCH DEATH/PS    PROSE
    INFECTED MAD HE DANCD ON HIS MOUNTAINS HIGH & DARK            305 FOUR ZOAS 5         1
       AS HEAVEN
    SHE FORMD A SPACE FOR SATAN & MICHAEL & FOR THE POOR          489 MILTON 8           43
       INFECTED
    TO THE COMMON OPINION AS I MYSELF AM ALSO INFECTED WITH IT    614D V LAST JUDG/N    PROSE
    & MY VISIONS ALSO INFECTED & I SEE TIME AGED ALAS TOO MUCH    614D V LAST JUDG/N    PROSE
       SO
    SO SPEAKING NOT YET INFECTED WITH THE ERROR & ILLUSION  .  .  666 JERUSALEM 39       27
INFECTION
    BENEATH THE DARK NET OF INFECTION  .  .  .  .  .  .  .  .     236 URIZEN 25           30
    INFECTION FROM THE SILLY GREEK & LATIN SLAVES OF THE SWORD    480C MILTON 1         PROSE
    HAVE YOU ALSO CAUGHT THE INFECTION OF SIN & STERN            673 JERUSALEM 43       75
       REPENTANCE
INFECTIOUS
    FRIGHTEND WITH COLD INFECTIOUS MADNESS IN HIS HAND THE        302 FOUR ZOAS 4        178
       THUNDERING
    [ LIKE A FILTHY INFECTIOUS HEAD OF HAIR ]  .  .  .  .  .  .   540 SIR JOSH RUB/N      6
INFERIOR
    THE INFERIOR PARTS OF ART AS REYNOLDS ARTFULLY CALLS THEM     449A ANNO REYNOLDS    MARG
    A GREAT COLOURIST & YET INFERIOR TO THE VENETIANS  .  .  .    450B ANNO REYNOLDS    MARG
    HE KNOWS THAT WHAT HE DOES IS NOT INFERIOR TO THE GRANDEST    579B DESC CAT 5       PROSE
    FABLE OR ALLEGORY ARE A TOTALLY DISTINCT & INFERIOR KIND      604D V LAST JUDG/N    PROSE
    IF THEY DO NOT PRAY IS AN INFERIOR KIND TO BE CALLD KNOWING   605A V LAST JUDG/N    PROSE
    PROSAIC FOR INFERIOR PARTS ALL ARE NECESSARY TO EACH OTHER    621D JERUSALEM 3      PROSE
    SUPERIOR NONE WE KNOW INFERIOR NONE ALL EQUAL SHARE  .  .     686 JERUSALEM 55       8
    TWO INFERIOR QUALITIES IN IT  .  .  .  .  .  .  .  .  .       774B ANNO BERKELEY    MARG
    OF JEHOVAH AS A VERY INFERIOR OBJECT OF MAN'S CONTEMPLATION   784B ANNO WW EXCUR    MARG
    A ONE WITH ORDINARY COMMON SENSE CAN BE INFERIOR TO A BOY     830A LETTER 30        PROSE
    THE INFERIOR ONES CANNOT BE DONE AT ANY RATE UNDER           848C LETTER 45        PROSE
       (FIFTEEN)
INFERIORS
    TO BE THEIR INFERIORS OR SUPERIORS WE EQUALLY ABHOR  .  .  .  686 JERUSALEM 55       7
INFERNAL
    [ OR EYED WITH LITTLE SPARKS OF HELL OR WITH INFERNAL         109 TIRIEL 8           15
       BRANDS ]
    SO THE PROVERBS OF HELL SHEW THE NATURE OF INFERNAL WISDOM    150C MARRIAGE HH 6    PROSE
    THIS I SHALL DO BY PRINTING IN THE INFERNAL METHOD  .  .  .   154C MARRIAGE HH 14   PROSE
    READ THE BIBLE TOGETHER IN ITS INFERNAL OR DIABOLICAL SENSE   158D MARRIAGE HH 22   PROSE
    OF LIFE BY MAGIC POWER CONDENSD INFERNAL FORMS ART-BOUND      204 AMERICA CANC B     14
    LIKE THE LINKED INFERNAL CHAIN  .  .  .  .  .  .  .  .  .     228 URIZEN 10          36
    THO TERRIBLE HIS DREAD OF THAT INFERNAL CHAIN THEY ROSE       309 FOUR ZOAS 5       147
    NOR UNROOT THE INFERNAL FIBRES FROM THEIR ROCKY BED  .  .     309 FOUR ZOAS 5       163
    COULD UPROOT THE INFERNAL CHAIN FOR [ ITS ] IT HAD TAKEN ROOT 309 FOUR ZOAS 5     * 166
    WHERE BRIGHT AHANIA WEPT SHE ALSO SAW THE INFERNAL ROOTS      309 FOUR ZOAS 5       181
    STEEPING THY WOUNDS IN SALTS INFERNAL & IN BITTER ANGUISH     321 FOUR ZOAS 7        54
    AND [ DIG ] ROOT UP THE INFERNAL GROVE  .  .  .  .  .  .  .   417 MY SPECTRE/N        60
    AND ROOT UP THE INFERNAL GROVE  .  .  .  .  .  .  .  .  .     417 MY SPECTRE/N        68
    IN BEAMS OF INFERNAL LIGHT  .  .  .  .  .  .  .  .  .  .      418 I SAW A MONK/N       4
    ("PECULIARITIES ARE BLEMISHES ") INFERNAL FALSHOOD  .  .  .   471C ANNO REYNOLDS    MARG
    HE CREATED SEVEN DEADLY SINS DRAWING OUT HIS INFERNAL         489 MILTON 9           21
       SCROLL
    SHALL [ DARE TO ] DAUNTLESS VIEW THE INFERNAL STORM  .  .  .  558 THE CAVERNS/N       6
    THAT INFERNAL MACHINE CALLED CHIARO OSCURO IN THE HANDS OF    582C DESC CAT 9       PROSE
    IN BEAMS OF INFERNAL LIGHT  .  .  .  .  .  .  .  .  .  .      683 I SAW A MONK/J       4
    DRAWING THE FREE LOVES OF JERUSALEM INTO INFERNAL BONDAGE     707 JERUSALEM 69        9
    HENCE THE INFERNAL VEIL GROWS IN THE DISOBEDIENT FEMALE       708 JERUSALEM 69       38
    IF THIS INFERNAL BUSINESS OF THE SOLDIER CAN BE GOT OVER      832C LETTER 32        PROSE
INFEST
    INFEST OUR ENGLISH SEAS DEVOURING ALL  .  .  .  .  .  .  .    20 EDW THIRD/PS 2      67
INFIDEL
    WHILE HE WAS AN INFIDEL OR HOW WAS IT  .  .  .  .  .  .       786D ANNO THORNTON    MARG
INFINITE
    BUT THAT THERE IS BUT ONE INFINITE I DO NOT FOR IF ALL        91A ANNO SWED LOVE    MARG
       BUT GOD
    IS NOT INFINITE THEY SHALL COME TO AN END WHICH GOD FORBID    91A ANNO SWED LOVE    MARG
    FOR IF A THING LOVES IT IS INFINITE PERHAPS WE ONLY  .  .  .  91C ANNO SWED LOVE    MARG
    IN THE CIRCUMFERENCE THEY CAST A BOUND ABOUT THE INFINITE     92A ANNO SWED LOVE    MARG
    THE DESIRE OF MAN BEING INFINITE THE POSSESSION IS INFINITE   97D NAT RELIGION 2    MARG
    & HIMSELF INFINITE  .  .  .  .  .  .  .  .  .  .  .  .  .     97D NAT RELIGION 2    PROSE
    APPLICATION HE WHO SEES THE INFINITE IN ALL THINGS SEES       98A NAT RELIGION 2    PROSE
       GOD
    SAME INFINITE VARIETY ALL ARE ALIKE IN THE POETIC GENIUS      98C ALL RELIGIONS    PROSE
    .  .  .  IN THE INFINITE SHADOWS OF HIS SOUL  .  .  .  .  .   134 FRENCH REVOLTN     13
    .  .  .  ENTER INTO THE INFINITE LABYRINTH OF ANOTHER'S BRAIN 142 FRENCH REVOLTN    190
    BUT MY SENSES DISCOVERD THE INFINITE IN EVERY THING  .  .  .  153C MARRIAGE HH 12   PROSE
    INTO A PERCEPTION OF THE INFINITE  .  .  .  .  .  .  .  .  .  154B MARRIAGE HH 12   PROSE
```

INFINITE (CONTINUED)
    THE WHOLE CREATION WILL BE CONSUMED AND APPEAR INFINITE   154B MARRIAGE HH 14 PROSE
      AND HOLY
    DISPLAYING THE INFINITE WHICH WAS HID . . . . 154C MARRIAGE HH 14 PROSE
    EVERY THING WOULD APPEAR TO MAN AS IT IS INFINITE . . 154C MARRIAGE HH 14 PROSE
    OF AIR HE CAUSED THE INSIDE OF THE CAVE TO BE INFINITE . 154D MARRIAGE HH 15 PROSE
    BY DEGREES WE BEHELD THE INFINITE ABYSS FIERY AS THE SMOKE 156A MARRIAGE HH 17 PROSE
    WHICH FLEW OR RATHER SWUM IN THE INFINITE DEEP . . . . 156A MARRIAGE HH 17 PROSE
    AND FROM THOSE OF DANTE OR SHAKESPEAR AN INFINITE NUMBER 158A MARRIAGE HH 21 PROSE
    ON THOSE INFINITE MOUNTAINS OF LIGHT   159B SONG LIBERTY PROSE
    AND THEY INCLOSD MY INFINITE BRAIN INTO A NARROW CIRCLE 191 V DAU ALBION 2   32
    UNKNOWN NOT UNPERCIEVD SPREAD IN THE INFINITE MICROSCOPE 192 V DAU ALBION 4   16
    HOLY ETERNAL INFINITE AND EACH JOY IS A LOVE . . . 192 V DAU ALBION 5   6
    AND EARTH HAD LOST ANOTHER PORTION OF THE INFINITE . . 202 AMERICA 14   18
    INFINITE LONDON'S AWFUL SPIRES CAST A DREADFUL [GLEAM] COLD 205 AMERICA CANC C   7
    HIS ANCIENT INFINITE MANSION . . . . 224 URIZEN 4   37
    ON THE SHORE OF THE INFINITE OCEAN . . . . 226 URIZEN 5   35
    WITH INFINITE LABOUR THE ETERNALS . . . . 231 URIZEN 19   8
    IN THE INFINITE VOID BUT BOUND DOWN . . . . . . 236 URIZEN 25   46
    AND WHO SHALL BIND THE INFINITE WITH AN ETERNAL BAND . 239 EUROPE PREL 2   13
    ALONG THE INFINITE SHORES OF THAMES TO GOLDEN VERULAM . 241 EUROPE 10   5
    TURND OUTWARD BARRD AND PETRIFYD AGAINST THE INFINITE . . 241 EUROPE 10   15
    THOUGHT CHANGD THE INFINITE TO A SERPENT THAT WHICH PITIETH 241 EUROPE 10   16
    THEN WAS THE SERPENT TEMPLE FORMD IMAGE OF INFINITE . 241 EUROPE 10   21
    IN THE INFINITE AGES OF ETERNITY . . . . 252 AHANIA 4   12
    AND FIRST FROM THOSE INFINITE FIRES . . . . . . 260 BOOK OF LOS 5   27
    THE CHAIND ORB IN THEIR INFINITE WOMBS . . . . . 260 BOOK OF LOS 5   40
    THAT DARK & DISMAL INFINITE WHERE THOUGHT ROAMS UP & DOWN 268 FOUR ZOAS 1   155
    STOOD ON THE INFINITE EARTH & SAW THESE VISIONS IN THE AIR 283 FOUR ZOAS 2   122
    UNFOLDS THE WONDROUS SCAFFOLD REARD ALL ROUND THE INFINITE 284 FOUR ZOAS 2   167
    [CIRCLED] [?CUBED] IN [INFINITE ORB] [?WINDOW SQUARE] . . 286 FOUR ZOAS 2 * 245
    AND LOST IN INFINITE HUMING WINGS VANISHES WITH A CRY . 289 FOUR ZOAS 2   361
    THUS LIVD LOS DRIVING ENION FAR INTO THE DEATHFUL INFINITE 290 FOUR ZOAS 2   383
    CONTRACTED THEY BEHOLD THE SECRETS OF THE INFINITE 308 FOUR ZOAS 5   122
      MOUNTAINS
    INFINITE WAS HIS LABOUR WITHOUT END HIS TRAVEL HE STROVE 313 FOUR ZOAS 6   74
    FOR INFINITE THE DISTANCE & OBSCURD BY COMBUSTIONS DIRE 316 FOUR ZOAS 6   177
    THRO THE INFINITE LABYRINTHS OF THE HEART & THRO 327 FOUR ZOAS 7   280
      THE NOSTRILS ISSUING
    WHERE SHALL WE TAKE OUR STAND TO VIEW THE INFINITE 363 FOUR ZOAS 9   228
      & UNBOUNDED
    SERVANTS TO THE INFINITE & ETERNAL OF THE HUMAN FORM . 366 FOUR ZOAS 9   374
    OF LIFE TILL THEY BECOME FINITE & ITSELF SEEMS INFINITE 490 MILTON 10 * 7
      [UNTIL]
    TO THOSE WITHOUT BUT INFINITE TO THOSE WITHIN IT FELL DOWN 491 MILTON 10   9
      AND
    THUS IS THE EARTH ONE INFINITE PLANE AND NOT AS APPARENT 497 MILTON 15   32
    DELIGHTFUL WITH BOUNDS TO THE INFINITE PUTTING OFF THE 515 MILTON 28   4
      INDEFINITE
    INTO A STRENGTH IMPREGNABLE OF MAJESTY & BEAUTY INFINITE 527 MILTON 37   7
    THE BOUNDING LINE AND ITS INFINITE INFLEXIONS AND MOVEMENTS 585C DESC CAT 15 PROSE
    THIS WORLD OF IMAGINATION IS INFINITE & ETERNAL WHEREAS 605D V LAST JUDG/N PROSE
    WE LIVE AS ONE MAN FOR CONTRACTING OUR INFINITE SENSES . . 664 JERUSALEM 38   17
    WHOSE SPRINGS ARE UNSEARCHABLE & KNOWLEDGE INFINITE . . . 676 JERUSALEM 46   2
    THE INFINITE ALONE RESIDES IN DEFINITE & DETERMINATE 687 JERUSALEM 55   64
      IDENTITY
    NONE OF MY DESIGNS WILL BE DESTITUTE OF INFINITE 792B LETTER 4 PROSE
      PARTICULARS
INFINITELY
    AS ALL MEN ARE ALIKE THO INFINITELY VARIOUS . . . . 98D ALL RELIGIONS PROSE
    [FOR] BUT INFINITELY BEAUTIFUL THE WONDROUS WORK AROSE . 286 FOUR ZOAS 2   240
    INFINITELY MORE PERFECT AND MORE MINUTELY ORGANIZED . . 577A DESC CAT 4 PROSE
    TO ENGRAVE AFTER ANOTHER PAINTER IS INFINITELY MORE 794B LETTER 5 PROSE
      LABORIOUS
    INFINITELY BETTER THE NEXT PROOF I FEEL VERY MUCH GRATIFIED 855C LETTER 53 PROSE
INFINITUDE
    INTO INFINITUDE & ORNAMENTED IT WITH WONDROUS ART . . . 270 FOUR ZOAS 1   226
    THE UNIVERSAL FATHER THEN ALBION STRETCHD HIS HAND INTO 744 JERUSALEM 97   6
      INFINITUDE
INFINITY
    DIFFER IN THE MEANING OF THE WORDS INFINITY & ETERNAL . . 91C ANNO SWED LOVE MARG
    HOLD INFINITY IN THE PALM OF YOUR HAND . . . . 431 AUGURIES   3
    THE NATURE OF INFINITY IS THIS THAT EVERY THING HAS ITS 497 MILTON 15   21
INFIRM
    IS HE INFIRM IS ALL THAT HE DOES . . . . 555 FRM CRATELOS/N   2
INFIXES
    OF EVERY HEART ON EARTH INFIXES DEEP ITS RESTLESS TWISTS 130 BOOK OF THEL 6   4
INFIXING
    THE FOOTSTEPS AND INFIXING DEEP THE FEET IN MARBLE BEDS 500 MILTON 19   2
INFLAMD
    ROSE INFLAMD TO AND FRO IN THE CHAMBER . . . . 141 FRENCH REVOLTN   170
INFLAME   SEE ENFLAME
    TO GRATE THE SOUL INTO DESTRUCTION OR TO INFLAME WITH FURY 344 FOUR ZOAS 8   136
INFLAMMABLE GASS   SEE FLAMMABLE
    IN A GREAT HURRY INFLAMMABLE GASS THE WIND FINDER ENTERD 44C ISLAND MOON 1 PROSE
    ETRUSCAN COLUMN & INFLAMMABLE GASS FIXD THEIR EYES . . 44C ISLAND MOON 1 PROSE
    HES A FOOLISH PUPPY SAID INFLAMMABLE GASS SMILING ON HIM 44C ISLAND MOON 1 PROSE
    WHAT D'YE SAY WHAT D'YE SAY SAID INFLAMMABLE GASS . . . 44D ISLAND MOON 1 PROSE
    YOUR REASON YOUR REASON SAID INFLAMMABLE GASS . . . . 44D ISLAND MOON 1 PROSE
    INFLAMMABLE GASS RECOLLECTING HIMSELF INDEED . . . . . 45A ISLAND MOON 1 PROSE
    INFLAMMABLE GASS TO OVERTHROW THE ARGUMENT . . . . . . 45B ISLAND MOON 1 PROSE
    INFLAMMABLE GASS TURNING ROUND HASTILY IN HIS CHAIR SAID 45C ISLAND MOON 1 PROSE

			PAGE	TITLE	LINE

INFLAMMABLE GASS   (CONTINUED)
    HA HA HA SAID INFLAMMABLE GASS HE WAS THE GLORY OF FRANCE   46A ISLAND MOON 1   PROSE
    WHILE INFLAMMABLE GASS TALKD FOR HALF AN HOUR . . . . .   46A ISLAND MOON 1   PROSE
    GIBBLE GABBLE THE WIFE OF INFLAMMABLE GASS [ENTERD THE   46B ISLAND MOON 2   PROSE
        ROOM]
    NO SAID INFLAMMABLE GASS I HAVE GOT A CAMERA OBSCURA AT   47C ISLAND MOON 3   PROSE
        HOME
    HA HA SAID INFLAMMABLE GASS WHAT DONT YOU LIKE TO GO TO   48A ISLAND MOON 4   PROSE
        CHURCH
    SAID INFLAMMABLE GASS ID SEE THE PARSONS ALL HANGD A PARCEL   48A ISLAND MOON 4   PROSE
        OF LYING
    THEN MR INFLAMMABLE GASS RAN & SHOVD HIS HEAD INTO THE FIRE   48C ISLAND MOON 4   PROSE
    BEING MET AT THE HOUSE OF INFLAMMABLE GASS THE WINDFINDER   58B ISLAND MOON 10   PROSE
    INFLAMMABLE GASS TURND SHORT ROUND & THREW DOWN THE TABLE   58D ISLAND MOON 10   PROSE
    HAD PUMPD INFLAMMABLE GASS QUITE DRY THEY . . . . .   59A ISLAND MOON 11   PROSE
INFLEXIBLE
    INTO FINITE INFLEXIBLE ORGANS . . . .   258 BOOK OF LOS 4   45
    FELT HER IMMORTAL LIMBS FREEZE STIFFNING PALE INFLEXIBLE   305 FOUR ZOAS 5   * 6
    ATTEMPT SHOULD BE MADE TO REFUSE ME THIS I AM INFLEXIBLE   826A LETTER 27   PROSE
INFLEXIONS
    THE BOUNDING LINE AND ITS INFINITE INFLEXIONS AND MOVEMENTS   585C DESC CAT 15   PROSE
INFLICTED
    MENTAL DISTRESS & I KNOW THAT ALL DISTRESS INFLICTED BY   809B LETTER 20   PROSE
INFLUENCE
    THY SACRED DEW PROTECT THEM WITH THINE INFLUENCE . . . .   3 EVNING STAR/PS   14
    A SUN AROSE OUT OF THE SEA IT ROSE & SHED SWEET INFLUENCE   41B THEN SHE BORE   PROSE
    AND HEARD HIS WORD DIVIDE YE BANDS INFLUENCE BY INFLUENCE   280 FOUR ZOAS 2   23
    WHO CAN READ THE STARS OFTEN IS OPRESSED BY THEIR INFLUENCE   865A LETTER 62   PROSE
INFLUENCED
    SAUL KING OF ISRAEL SOMEWHAT INFLUENCED BY XXX EVIL SPIRIT   SUPP PENC DRAW 1.42 *TITLE
INFLUENCES
    . . . & WITH INFLUENCES SWEET . . . .   345 FOUR ZOAS 8   158
    THEIR MILD INFLUENCES THEREFORE THE SEVEN EYES OF GOD WALK   517 MILTON 29   54
        ROUND
    THE STARS OF ALBION CRUEL RISE THOU BINDEST TO SWEET   693 JERUSALEM 60   60
        INFLUENCES
INFLUX
    HE IS THE INFLUX FROM THAT INTO THE WILL . . . . . .   89A ANNO SWED LOVE   MARG
    ("INFLUX FROM ABOVE ") THIS IS WHILE IN THE BODY . . .   94A ANNO SWED LOVE   MARG
    IS IT NOT FALSE THEN THAT LOVE RECIEVES INFLUX THRO . . .   96B ANNO SWED LOVE   MARG
    ("LOVE") THEREFORE IT DOES NOT RECIEVE INFLUX THRO THE   96C ANNO SWED LOVE   MARG
        UNDERSTANDING
INFOLD
    AND MY GRIEFS [UNFOLD] INFOLD . . . .   8 MAD SONG/PS   4
    I WILL INFOLD THE ETERNAL TENT IN CLOUDS OPAKE WHILE THOU   278 FOUR ZOAS 1   493
    MY FEEBLE LIMBS INFOLD MY DESTIND MISERY . . . . . .   344 FOUR ZOAS 8   147
    INFOLD AROUND MY LIMBS BRUISING MY MINUTE ARTICULATIONS   635 JERUSALEM 15   13
    MY LIMBS TO INFOLD . . . .   805 TO BUTTS/L   53
INFOLDED
    HE CEAST HER DARK HAIR UPRIGHT STOOD WHILE SNAKES INFOLDED   108 TIRIEL 6   44
        ROUND
    ETERNITY APPEARD ABOVE THEM AS ONE MAN INFOLDED . . . .   274 FOUR ZOAS 1   363
    INFOLDED IN THICK CLOUDS FROM WHENCE HIS MIGHTY VOICE BURST   292 FOUR ZOAS 3   13
        FORTH
    AND PALE HIS PRIESTESSES INFOLDED IN VEILS OF PESTILENCE   528 MILTON 37   23
        BORDERD
    IN WHOSE WREATHINGS ARE INFOLDED THE NATIONS OF THE EARTH   564D DESC CAT 1   TITLE
    SUSPENDED OVER HER HE HUNG HE INFOLDED HER IN HIS GARMENTS   639 JERUSALEM 17   52
    ARE THE DEAD CRUEL ARE THOSE WHO ARE INFOLDED IN MORAL LAW   644 JERUSALEM 21   48
INFOLDING
    [TO] INFOLDING THE BRIGHT WOMAN [FROM THE DESOLATING WINDS   381 FOUR ZOAS AD 5   * 15
        . . .
    [INFOLDING THE BRIGHT INFANTS FROM THE DESOLATING WINDS]   270 FOUR ZOAS 1   210
    SICK COUCH BEARS THE DARK SHADES OF ETERNAL DEATH INFOLDING   493 MILTON 13   1
    HIS PATH INTO A GLOBE ITSELF INFOLDING LIKE A SUN . . .   497 MILTON 15   24
INFOLDS
    IF THE GOD ENRAPTURED ME INFOLDS . . . .   288 FOUR ZOAS 2   * 310
INFORM
    SAKE OF CONVENIENCE I ALSO OUGHT TO INFORM YOU THAT I READ   820D LETTER 25   PROSE
    BEGGING THE FAVOR OF A FEW LINES TO INFORM HIM HOW YOU . .   829C LETTER 30   PROSE
    I WRITE IMMEDIATELY ON MY ARRIVAL NOT MERELY TO INFORM .   833B LETTER 33   PROSE
    YOU THAT I AM SAFE ARRIVD BUT ALSO TO INFORM YOU THAT IN A   833B LETTER 33   PROSE
    HAS NOT YET BEEN ABLE TO GO WITH ME AM SORRY TO INFORM YOU   839C LETTER 38   PROSE
    HE WILL OF COURSE INFORM YOU WHAT HIS SENTIMENTS ARE OF   858A LETTER 55   PROSE
    PROPOSING THE BALLADS TO HIM ON MY ACCOUNT AND INFORM YOU   858B LETTER 55   PROSE
    HOWEVER THE SATISFACTION TO INFORM YOU THAT I HAVE MYSELF   865D LETTER 63   PROSE
INFORMATION
    I THANK YOU PETER FOR YOUR INFORMATION . . . .   29C EDW THIRD/PS 4   PROSE
    BLAKE'S MEMORANDUM IN REFUTATION OF THE INFORMATION . .   437A BLAKES MEMORAN   TITLE
    INFORMATION IN HIS POWER WITH NOTICES OF WHERE MR ROMNEY'S   832D LETTER 32   PROSE
    AND MR WALKER PROMISES TO COLLECT ALL HE CAN OF INFORMATION   844A LETTER 43   PROSE
    EVERY INFORMATION IN HIS POWER SAYS THAT I SHALL HAVE . .   845D LETTER 44   PROSE
    I WRITE IMMEDIATELY ON RECIEVING THE ABOVE INFORMATION .   849A LETTER 45   PROSE
INFORMD
    WHICH WE INFORMD HIM VIZ TO LEAVE FELPHAM ENTIRELY . . .   820C LETTER 25   PROSE
    THE PUBLIC OUGHT TO BE INFORMD THAT [THE FOLLOWING] THESE   860C LETTER 56   PROSE
INFORMING
    I HAVE FURTHERMORE THE PLEASURE OF INFORMING YOU THAT HE   836B LETTER 35   PROSE
INFUSD
    FROM HER OWN BOWELS IN THE MONSTER SHAME INFUSD . . . .   40D THEN SHE BORE   PROSE
INFUSE
    I CAN INFUSE MY DEAR REVENGE INTO HIS GLOWING BREAST . .   289 FOUR ZOAS 2   337

	PAGE	TITLE	LINE

INFUSES
HE INFUSES A LOVE OF SOFT AND EVEN TINTS WITHOUT BOUNDARIES 583B DESC CAT 9   PROSE
INFUSING
IN SLUMBERS OF MY NIGHT-REPOSE INFUSING A FALSE MORNING   271 FOUR ZOAS 1   272
RUBENS IS A MOST OUTRAGEOUS DEMON AND BY INFUSING . . . 582D DESC CAT 9   PROSE
INGRATE
INGRATE THEY WANDERD SCORNING HER . . . .   270 FOUR ZOAS 1   217
. . . DRAWING HER [LIFE INGRATE] SPECTROUS LIFE . . . .   270 FOUR ZOAS 1   217
INGRATITUDE
INGRATITUDE & LOS BELIEVE THE ACCUSATION THRO SATAN'S   486 MILTON 7   14
    EXTREME
ACCUSD PALAMABRON BEFORE THE ASSEMBLY OF INGRATITUDE OF   489 MILTON 9   20
    MALICE
FLORENTINE INGRATITUDE . . . .   541D FLORENTINE/N   TITLE
I DEMAND RIGHTEOUSNESS & JUSTICE O THOU INGRATITUDE . . .   669 JERUSALEM 42   12
THEY NOW HOLD ALL THEY HAVE INGRATITUDE TO ME . . . . .   671 JERUSALEM 42   53
INGRATITUDES
AS YOU HAVE SIEZD THE TWENTY-FOUR REBELLIOUS INGRATITUDES   670 JERUSALEM 42   48
INHABIT
WHICH THE BOSOMS OF ALL INHABIT . . . .   224 URIZEN 4   29
AND TO INHABIT OUR LITTLE-ONES TO CLOTHE IN ARMOUR OF THE   729 JERUSALEM 84   9
    GOLD
INHABITANT
IN EDEN THE ARTIST IS AN INHABITANT OF THAT HAPPY COUNTRY   578A DESC CAT 5   PROSE
AND EVERY PART OF THE CITY IS FOURFOLD & EVERY INHABITANT   633 JERUSALEM 13   20
    FOURFOLD
OF THE WILD INHABITANT OF THE FOREST TO DRIVE THEM FROM   638 JERUSALEM 17   4
    HIS OWN
LET ALBION REMAIN A DESOLATION WITHOUT AN INHABITANT . .   725 JERUSALEM 82   25
AS WAS SUPPOSED BY OUR KIND & ATTENTIVE FELLOW INHABITANT   833D LETTER 33   PROSE
INHABITANTS
WHEN THE FEW INHABITANTS CLING TREMBLING TOGETHER . . .   36B COUCH DEATH/PS   PROSE
ITS SILVER INHABITANTS SPORT AND PLAY . . . .   37B CONTEMPLATN/PS   PROSE
THE ANGRY SHORES AND THE FIERCE RUSHING OF TH INHABITANTS   201 AMERICA 14   12
    TOGETHER
GIANTS ANCIENT INHABITANTS OF ENGLAND THE LANDING   208C SUBJCTS HIST/N   TITLE
    OF BRUTUS
THEN THE INHABITANTS OF THOSE CITIES . . . .   235 URIZEN 25   23
FOR THE EARS OF THE INHABITANTS . . . .   236 URIZEN 28   15
THE CITIZENS IN LEADEN GYVES THE INHABITANTS OF SUBURBS   243 EUROPE 12   30
THE INHABITANTS OF MOUNTAIN AND PLAIN . . . .   247 SONG OF LOS 6   12
TO THE INHABITANTS OF EDEN AROUND THEM ON ALL SIDES . .   518 MILTON 30   9
BUT BEULAH TO ITS INHABITANTS APPEARS WITHIN EACH DISTRICT   518 MILTON 30   10
GARDENS & GROVES DISPLAY PARADISE WITH ITS INHABITANTS .   613C V LAST JUDG/N   PROSE
WITH THEIR INHABITANTS IN THE TWENTY-SEVEN HEAVENS BENEATH   634 JERUSALEM 13   51
    BEULAH
OF ALL THE INHABITANTS OF EARTH WAILING TO BE CREATED .   634 JERUSALEM 13   63
YE ARE UNITED O YE INHABITANTS OF EARTH IN ONE RELIGION   649B JERUSALEM 27   PROSE
MY HOUSES ARE THOUGHTS MY INHABITANTS AFFECTIONS . . .   665 JERUSALEM 38   33
AND LAY ITS HEAVENS & THEIR INHABITANTS IN BLOOD   668 JERUSALEM 41   20
    OF PUNISHMENT
AMONG THE INHABITANTS OF ALBION THE PEOPLE FALL AROUND . .   689 JERUSALEM 58   4
THE INHABITANTS OF ALBION AT THE HARVEST & THE VINTAGE . .   689 JERUSALEM 58   6
GIHON TO HIDDEKEL & TO CORN FIELDS & VILLAGES & INHABITANTS   695 JERUSALEM 61   32
THE INHABITANTS ARE SICK TO DEATH THEY LABOUR TO DIVIDE   703 JERUSALEM 66   68
    INTO DAYS
THE INHABITANTS OF THE WHOLE EARTH REJOICE IN THEIR   710 JERUSALEM 71   25
    BEAUTIFUL LIGHT
IN SOME DEGREE & THAT ITS ONCE STUPID INHABITANTS SHOULD   798C LETTER 10   PROSE
VOICES OF CELESTIAL INHABITANTS ARE MORE DISTINCTLY HEARD   802A LETTER 14   PROSE
PERSONS & MACHINERY INTIRELY NEW TO THE INHABITANTS OF   823A LETTER 26   PROSE
    EARTH
FELPHAM & ITS KIND INHABITANTS I FEEL ANXIOUS & THEREFORE   833D LETTER 33   PROSE
INHABITING
LIKE FOUL FIENDS INHABITING MARY'S MILD BRAIN . . . . .   429 MARY   42
INHABITS
THE SPECTRE OF ALBION IN WHICH THE SPECTRE OF LUVAH   528 MILTON 37   45
    INHABITS
INHALING
[IN SILENT DECEIT POISONS INHALING FROM THE MORNING ROSE]   109 TIRIEL 8   13
WHY A NOSTRIL WIDE INHALING TERROR TREMBLING & AFFRIGHT   130 BOOK OF THEL 6   18
INHANCE
SUFFICIENT CONTEMPT TO INHANCE MY OPINION OF IT BUT I DO   825B LETTER 27   PROSE
    NOT
INHERIT
NEW WORLDS TO INHERIT . . . .   119 NIGHT/SI   32
INHERITING
WHOSE RICH FIELDS INHERITING SPREAD THEIR OLD GLORY . . .   143 FRENCH REVOLTN   204
INIMICAL
THAT REPUBLICAN ART IS INIMICAL TO THEIR ATOM . . . . .   878A LETTER 88   PROSE
INIMITABLE
INIMITABLE AND THE EFFECT OF THE WHOLE IS TRULY SUBLIME   864B LETTER 61   PROSE
INIQUITY
YET THEY ARE BLAMELESS & INIQUITY MUST BE IMPUTED ONLY . .   680 JERUSALEM 49   65
INJURD
FOR POOR BLIND TIRIEL IS RETURND & THIS MUCH INJURD HEAD   105 TIRIEL 4   66
MY HORSES HATH HE MADDEND AND MY FELLOW SERVANTS INJURD   487 MILTON 7   29
THAT HE HAD NOT OPRESSD NOR INJURD THE REFRACTORY SERVANTS   487 MILTON 8   * 3
INJURE
TILL THOU DOST ?INJURE THE DISTREST . . . .   380 FOUR ZOAS NOTE   1
THE MAN WHO PERMITS YOU TO INJURE HIM DESERVES YOUR   737 JERUSALEM 91   3
    VENGEANCE

		PAGE	TITLE	LINE

INJURE (CONTINUED)

INJURE AS TO THE EAST AND NORTH I BELIEVE THEY CANNOT GET   807B LETTER 17   PROSE
TO INJURE SEAGRAVE IN YOUR OPINION IF POSSIBLE JOHNSON MAY   846C LETTER 44   PROSE
WOULD NOT FOR THE WORLD INJURE THIS BEAUTIFUL WORK AND . .   858C LETTER 55   PROSE

INJURED

NOT SUFFER IT TO BE INJURED BY MY IGNORANCE OR THAT IT   858C LETTER 55   PROSE
SHOULD

INJURER

OF THE INJURER IN WHICH THE DIVINE LAMB IS CRUELLY SLAIN   648 JERUSALEM 25   11

INJURIES

A DEAD BODY REVENGES NOT INJURIES . . . .   151B MARRIAGE HH 7   PROSE
. . . IN FORGIVENESS OF [FORMER INJURIES] ANCIENT INJURIES   330 FOUR ZOAS 7   * 419
RESENTMENT FOR PERSONAL INJURIES HAS HAD SOME SHARE . .   594D PUB ADDRESS/N   PROSE
WHEN ALL ALBION'S INJURIES SHALL CEASE AND WHEN WE SHALL   626 JERUSALEM 7   55
ASTONISHD AT MY PATIENCE & FORBEARANCE OF INJURIES UPON   825D LETTER 27   PROSE
INJURIES

INJURIOUSLY

I HAVE BEEN VERY MUCH DEGRADED & INJURIOUSLY TREATED . .   828D LETTER 28   PROSE

INJURY

THEY THINK THEY HAVE DONE ME NO INJURY . . . .   180 CHIMNEY SWP/N   10
THEY THINK THEY HAVE DONE ME NO INJURY . . . .   212 CHIMNEY SWP/SE   10
THEIR LIFE'S WHOLE COMFORT TO INTIRE SCORN & INJURY & DEATH   506 MILTON 23   2
THAT ENGRAVING [IS IN A MOST WRETCHED STATE OF INJURY] . .   591D PUB ADDRESS/N   *PROSE
AN INJURY & INJUSTICE TO HIS COUNTRY WHILE HE STUDIES .   597C PUB ADDRESS/N   PROSE
INJURY THE LORD HEALS BUT VENGEANCE CANNOT BE HEALED .   648 JERUSALEM 25   5

INJUSTICE

AN INJURY & INJUSTICE TO HIS COUNTRY WHILE HE STUDIES .   597C PUB ADDRESS/N   PROSE

INLAND

HE WHO WOULD BE A SOLDIER IN INLAND NATIONS IS . . . .   575D DESC CAT 3   PROSE

INLETS

THE FIVE SENSES THE CHIEF INLETS OF SOUL IN THIS AGE .   149D MARRIAGE HH 4   PROSE

INLY

THIS PRIDE [OBSERVD AND] OBSERVING INLY GRIEVD . . . .   41A THEN SHE BORE   *PROSE

INMOST

THE IVORY PALACE OF MY INMOST HEART WHERE IT SHALL LIE   39B SAMSON/PS   PROSE
AT REST
. . . SWEET [ENITHARMON] JERUSALEM FROM MY INMOST SOUL . .   265 FOUR ZOAS 1   * 29
AND EVERY ONE SEEKS FOR HIS MATE TO PROVE HIS INMOST JOY   289 FOUR ZOAS 2   358
THE LIVING VOICE IS EVER LIVING IN ITS INMOST JOY . . .   289 FOUR ZOAS 2   363
ENITHARMON ON THE ROAD OF DRANTHON FELT THE INMOST GATE   309 FOUR ZOAS 5   177
THE DIVINE VISION SEEN WITHIN THE INMOST DEEP RECESS .   346 FOUR ZOAS 8   192
RESTLESS THEY TURN ON BEDS OF SORROW IN THEIR INMOST BRAIN   379 FOUR ZOAS 9   818
I STROVE TO SIEZE THE INMOST FORM . . . .   429 CRYSTL CABINET   21
WITH ALL COLOURS OF PRECIOUS STONES & THEIR INMOST PALACES   484 MILTON 4   24
THE GNOMES LABOURD I WEEPING HID IN SATAN'S INMOST BRAIN   493 MILTON 12   36
IN SATAN'S INMOST PALACE OF HIS NERVOUS FINE WROUGHT BRAIN   493 MILTON 12   41
HE FROM HIS INMOST BRAIN & THE DOORS CLOSD WITH THUNDERS   493 MILTON 12   48
SOUND
PERSIA & MEDIA ARE HIS HALLS HIS INMOST HALL IS GREAT   690 JERUSALEM 58   38
TARTARY
JERUSALEM PINED IN HER INMOST SOUL OVER WANDERING REUBEN   708 JERUSALEM 69   45

INN

WHEN THE JOLLY COMPANY ARE JUST QUITTING THE TABARDE INN   566C DESC CAT 3   PROSE
THESE LAST ARE ISSUING FROM THE GATEWAY OF THE INN THE COOK   567A DESC CAT 3   PROSE
OF COMFORT SPECTATORS STAND AT THE GATEWAY OF THE INN .   567A DESC CAT 3   PROSE
FROM THE TABARDE INN IN SOUTHWARK AS IT MAY BE SUPPOSED   567A DESC CAT 3   PROSE
THE INN IS A GOTHIC BUILDING WHICH THYNNE IN HIS GLOSSARY   567B DESC CAT 3   PROSE
ON THE INN IS INSCRIBED ITS TITLE AND A PROPER ADVANTAGE   567B DESC CAT 3   PROSE
OF THE PICTURE THE WORDS WRITTEN OVER THE GATEWAY OF THE   567B DESC CAT 3   PROSE
INN
ARE AS FOLLOW "THE TABARDE INN BY HENRY BAILLIE THE" .   567B DESC CAT 3   PROSE
OF THE GREATEST INN OF THE GREATEST CITY . . . . . .   569D DESC CAT 3   PROSE
FOR SUCH WAS THE TABARDE INN IN SOUTHWARK NEAR LONDON .   569D DESC CAT 3   PROSE
CHURCHES & THE INN IN SOUTHWARK IS MINUTELY LABOURD . .   588A CHAUCER/N   PROSE
WHEN THE JOLLY COMPANY ARE JUST QUITTING THE TABARDE INN   588B CHAUCER/N   PROSE
THESE LAST ARE ISSUING FROM THE GATEWAY OF THE INN THE COOK   588D CHAUCER/N   PROSE
OF COMFORT SPECTATORS STAND AT THE GATEWAY OF THE INN .   588D CHAUCER/N   PROSE
FROM THE TABARDE INN IN SOUTHWARK AS IT MAY BE SUPPOSED   588D CHAUCER/N   PROSE
THE INN IS A GOTHIC BUILDING WHICH THYNNE IN HIS GLOSSARY   588D CHAUCER/N   PROSE
ON THE INN IS INSCRIBED ITS TITLE & A PROPER ADVANTAGE .   588D CHAUCER/N   PROSE
WHEN THE JOLLY COMPANY ARE JUST QUITTING THE TABARDE INN   589C CHAUCER 2   PROSE
THESE LAST ARE ISSUING FROM THE GATEWAY OF THE INN THE COOK   590A CHAUCER 2   PROSE
OF COMFORT SPECTATORS STAND AT THE GATEWAY OF THE INN .   590A CHAUCER 2   PROSE
THE INN IS YET EXTANT UNDER THE NAME OF THE TALBOT AND .   590A CHAUCER 2   PROSE
INSCRIBED "THIS IS THE INN FROM WHICH" . . . .   590B CHAUCER 2   PROSE
FROM THE TABARDE INN IN SOUTHWARK AS IT MAY BE SUPPOSED   590B CHAUCER 2   PROSE
THE INN IS A GOTHIC BUILDING WHICH THYNNE IN HIS GLOSSARY   590C CHAUCER 2   PROSE
ON THE INN IS INSCRIBED ITS TITLE AND A PROPER ADVANTAGE   590C CHAUCER 2   PROSE
OVER THE GATEWAY OF THE INN ARE AS FOLLOW . . . . .   590C CHAUCER 2   PROSE
"THE TABARDE INN BY HENRY BAILLY" . . . .   590C CHAUCER 2   PROSE
TO GREAT QUEEN STREET & LINCOLNS INN ALL IS DISTRESS & WOE   729 JERUSALEM 84   16
THE MASTER OF THE HOUSE THE FOX INN WHO IS [MY] THE . .   827B LETTER 28   PROSE
ALL THAT HAPPEND AT THE GATE OF THE INN WHO EVIDENCES THAT   827C LETTER 28   PROSE
THE OFFENCE IS ALWAYS REPEATED THE LANDLORD OF THE INN &   827C LETTER 28   PROSE
FROM THE ANGEL INN NEAR ST CLEMENTS CHURCH STRAND . . .   871C LETTER 73   PROSE

INNATE

RIGHT ACT ACCORDING TO THEIR FORMS BY INNATE CRUELTY . .   344 FOUR ZOAS 8   134
THE STUDY OF NATURE WITHOUT CON- OR INNATE SCIENCE   457C ANNO REYNOLDS   * MARG
(CON-SCIENCE)
IT IS BORN WITH US INNATE IDEAS ARE IN EVERY MAN . . .   459B ANNO REYNOLDS   MARG
THE MAN WHO SAYS THAT WE HAVE NO INNATE IDEAS MUST BE .   459B ANNO REYNOLDS   MARG
A FOOL & KNAVE HAVING NO CON-SCIENCE OR INNATE SCIENCE .   459B ANNO REYNOLDS   MARG

| | PAGE | TITLE | LINE |

INNE
OVER THE GATEWAY ARE AS FOLLOW "THE TABARDE INNE" . . . 589A CHAUCER/N PROSE
THE TABARD INNE BY HENRY BAILEY . . . . SUPP ILLUS CHAUCER *TITLE

INNER
THEY WEPT BEFORE THE INNER GATES OF ENITHARMON'S BOSOM . . 279 FOUR ZOAS 1 561
AND IN THE INNER PART OF THE TEMPLE WONDROUS WORKMANSHIP 333 FOUR ZOAS 7B 21
BEGINING AT JERUSALEM'S INNER COURT LAMBETH RUIND AND GIVEN 511 MILTON 25 48
BUT THEY CUT ASUNDER HIS INNER GARMENTS SEARCHING WITH . . 702 JERUSALEM 66 27
FROM THE INNER SANCTUARY A FALSE HOLINESS HID WITHIN THE 708 JERUSALEM 69 40
CENTER

INNERMOST
I HAVE BROUGHT THEM FROM THE UPPERMOST INNERMOST RECESSES 490 MILTON 9 27

INNOCENCE
INNOCENCE AND VIRTUE MEET . . . . 7 LOVE HARMNY/PS 8
IN TIMES OF INNOCENCE AND HOLY JOY . . . . 9 FRESH FROM/PS 10
FOR KNOWLEDGE DROVE SWEET INNOCENCE AWAY . . . . . . 42B THEN SHE BORE PROSE
INNOCENCE DOTH LIKE A ROSE . . . . 63 SHEPHERD FIRST 5
INNOCENCE IS A WINTER'S GOWN . . . . 64 SHEPHERD OLD 10
OFFENDED WITH THE INNOCENCE OF A CHILD & FOR THE 87C ANNO LAVATER MARG
SAME REASON
SONGS OF INNOCENCE THE AUTHOR & PRINTER W BLAKE . . . . 111A SONGS OF INNOC TITLE
MOTTO TO THE SONGS OF INNOCENCE & OF EXPERIENCE . . . 183D MOTTO SONGS/N TITLE
IN LAPS OF PLEASURE INNOCENCE HONEST OPEN SEEKING . . . 193 V DAU ALBION 6 5
SONGS OF INNOCENCE IN ILLUMINATED PRINTING OCTAVO... . 208A PRSPECTUS 1793 PROSE
SONGS OF INNOCENCE AND OF EXPERIENCE . . . . 210A SONGS OF EXPER TITLE
WITH WHOM SHE WALKD IN BLISS IN TIMES OF INNOCENCE & YOUTH 282 FOUR ZOAS 2 79
AND LAUGHTER SAT BENEATH THE OAKS & INNOCENCE SPORTED ROUND 317 FOUR ZOAS 6 214
IN INFANT INNOCENCE REPOSD ON ENITHARMON'S BOSOM . . . 332 FOUR ZOAS 7 477
IN ALL THEIR ANCIENT INNOCENCE THE FLOODS DEPART THE CLOUDS 372 FOUR ZOAS 9 572
UNORGANIZD INNOCENCE AN IMPOSSIBILITY . . . . 380B FOUR ZOAS NOTE PROSE
INNOCENCE DWELLS WITH WISDOM BUT NEVER WITH IGNORANCE . 380B FOUR ZOAS NOTE PROSE
AUGURIES OF INNOCENCE . . . . 431A AUGURIES TITLE
& WISDOM THAN NOAH BEING NEARER THE STATE OF INNOCENCE . 611C V LAST JUDG/N PROSE
WITH WHOM SHE LIVD IN BLISS IN TIMES OF INNOCENCE & YOUTH 626 JERUSALEM 7 37
AND CLOSD UP THE SWEET REGIONS OF YOUTH AND VIRGIN 642 JERUSALEM 20 6
INNOCENCE
WHERE WE DELIGHT IN INNOCENCE BEFORE THE FACE OF THE LAMB 642 JERUSALEM 20 9
THEE WHOM I THOUGHT PURE AS THE HEAVENS IN INNOCENCE & FEAR 644 JERUSALEM 21 20
I BROUGHT LOVE INTO LIGHT & FANCIED INNOCENCE IS NO MORE 645 JERUSALEM 22 18
I HAVE INNOCENCE TO DEFEND AND IGNORANCE TO INSTRUCT . 670 JERUSALEM 42 26
THEY STOOD IN INNOCENCE & THEIR SKIEY TENT REACHD OVER ASIA 692 JERUSALEM 60 17
TO FREEZE LOVE & INNOCENCE INTO THE GOLD & SILVER OF THE 699 JERUSALEM 64 23
MERCHANT
AMERICA EUROPE VISIONS &C THEL SONGS OF INNOCENCE . . 867B LETTER 66 PROSE
I AM NOW PRINTING A SET OF THE SONGS OF INNOCENCE & . . . 878C LETTER 88 PROSE
THE ORDER IN WHICH THE SONGS OF INNOCENCE & OF EXPERIENCE SUPP LETTER 66A *PROSE
TITLE PAGE TO SONGS OF INNOCENCE . . . . SUPP LETTER 66A *PROSE
THE LITTLE BOY FOUND END OF SONGS OF INNOCENCE . . . . SUPP LETTER 66A *PROSE
OF MR LINNELL FOR SONGS OF INNOCENCE & EXPERIENCE ONE COPY SUPP LETTER 66G *PROSE
OF TWO POUNDS FIVE SHILLINGS FOR THE SONGS OF INNOCENCE SUPP LETTER 80A *PROSE

INNOCENT
WHERE INNOCENT EYES DO GLANCE . . . . 7 LOVE JOCUND/PS 3
I LOVE THE INNOCENT BOWR . . . . 8 LOVE JOCUND/PS 10
THAT PLAYS WITH DANGER AS THE INNOCENT CHILD . . . . 27 EDW THIRD/PS 3 241
SHE SAW THE MAIDENS PLAY AND BLESSED THEIR INNOCENT MIRTH 39C SAMSON/PS PROSE
UPON A HOLY THURSDAY THEIR INNOCENT FACES CLEAN . . . 59 HOLY THURS/IM 1
THOUSANDS OF LITTLE GIRLS & BOYS RAISING THEIR INNOCENT 59 HOLY THURS/IM 9
HANDS
("TO AVERT SUSPICION ACCUSES THE INNOCENT") DAMN HIM . . 78A ANNO LAVATER MARG
HE IS AN INNOCENT OLD MAN & HUNGRY WITH HIS TRAVEL . . . 101 TIRIEL 2 33
FOR HE HEARS THE LAMB'S INNOCENT CALL . . . . . . 118 SHEPHERD/SI 5
TWAS ON A HOLY THURSDAY THEIR INNOCENT FACES CLEAN . . . 121 HOLY THURS/SI 1
THOUSANDS OF LITTLE BOYS & GIRLS RAISING THEIR INNOCENT 122 HOLY THURS/SI 8
HANDS
THY BREATH DOTH NOURISH THE INNOCENT LAMB . . . . . . 128 BOOK OF THEL 2 5
. . . HE STOOPD HIS [HOLY] INNOCENT HEAD . . . . . . 266 FOUR ZOAS 1 72
AND SHE SAID THARMAS I AM VALA BLESS THY INNOCENT FACE . 339 FOUR ZOAS 7B 229
AGAINST HER LITTLE ONES THE INNOCENT ACCUSED BEFORE THE 364 FOUR ZOAS 9 267
JUDGES
AWAKE O ENION AWAKE & LET THINE INNOCENT EYES . . . . 371 FOUR ZOAS 9 519
AND DOST THOU WANDER WITH MY LAMBS & [WITH] WET THEIR 371 FOUR ZOAS 9 532
INNOCENT FACES
THEN SHALL THEY LIFT THEIR INNOCENT HANDS & STROKE HIS 376 FOUR ZOAS 9 703
FURIOUS NOSE
BUT THE SUBTIL MADE THE INNOCENT POOR . . . . . . 384A ANNO WATSON MARG
THE INNOCENT SHOULD BE CONDEMND FOR THE GUILTY THEN AN 491 MILTON 11 16
ETERNAL ROSE
IT IS COMPOSED OF THE INNOCENT CIVILIZED HEATHEN & . . . 610A V LAST JUDG/N PROSE
THEY ADORE & HIS REVENGE CHERISH WITH THE BLOOD OF THE 704 JERUSALEM 67 21
INNOCENT
AS THE MOST INNOCENT FORGETTER OF HIS OWN INTERESTS . . . 809C LETTER 20 PROSE
FROM THE WICKED HORSE & FROM YOUR INNOCENT HUMBLE SERVANT 833D LETTER 33 PROSE
AND INNOCENT GRIEF HIS INNOCENT AND VENERABLE MADNESS AND 864B LETTER 61 PROSE

INNOCENTLY
THEY APPEAR TO BE INNOCENTLY GAY & THOUGHTLESS . . . . 610B V LAST JUDG/N PROSE

INNOCENTS
[WHEN THE WHOLE MULTITUDE OF INNOCENTS THEIR VOICES RAISE] 59 HOLY THURS/IM 12
VIRTUOUS I SUPPOSED TO BE INNOCENTS . . . . 401C ANNO BACON * MARG
JUDGMENT SEAT IN HUMILIATION ABEL SURROUNDED BY INNOCENTS 606B V LAST JUDG/N PROSE

INNUMERABLE
PRINCE OF THE SUN I SEE THEE WITH THY INNUMERABLE RACE . . 240 EUROPE 8 9
ROCK THE INNUMERABLE FRAGMENTS AWAY . . . . 257 BOOK OF LOS 4 24

982

	PAGE	TITLE	LINE

INNUMERABLE   (CONTINUED)

[UPON ITS GREEN STALK ROSE THE CORN WAVING INNUMERABLE]	270 FOUR ZOAS 1	209
THE INNUMERABLE SONS & DAUGHTERS OF LUVAH CLOSD IN FURNACES	276 FOUR ZOAS 1	423
SPREAD & MANY A SPIRIT CAUGHT INNUMERABLE THE NETS . . .	284 FOUR ZOAS 2	159
INNUMERABLE THE GINS & TRAPS & MANY A SOOTHING FLUTE . .	284 FOUR ZOAS 2	160
SETTLED LIKE BATS INNUMERABLE READY TO FLY ABROAD . . .	306 FOUR ZOAS 5	35
FROM SON TO SON AS IF THE STARS BEAMING INNUMERABLE . .	366 FOUR ZOAS 9	351
AND FLOWER & HERB SOON FILL THE AIR WITH AN INNUMERABLE DANCE	521 MILTON 31	61
HUMAN WITH TRUMPETS INNUMERABLE SOUNDING ARTICULATE . . .	530 MILTON 39	7
AND ALL BENEATH THE NATIONS INNUMERABLE OF ULRO	532 MILTON 40	23
O NO NO I SEE AN INNUMERABLE COMPANY OF THE HEAVENLY HOST	617B V LAST JUDG/N	PROSE
INNUMERABLE AT WILL OF THE UNFORTUNATE CONTEMPLATOR . . .	659 JERUSALEM 33	23
NUMBER THE VOICES OF THE INNUMERABLE MULTITUDES OF ETERNITY	662 JERUSALEM 35	4
WITH THE INNUMERABLE MULTITUDES OF GOLGONOOZA ROUND THE ANVILS	713 JERUSALEM 73	6
THE WATER WHEEL & MILL OF MANY INNUMERABLE WHEELS RESISTLESS	713 JERUSALEM 73	14
AND MIGHTY PREPARATIONS MUSTERING MULTITUDES INNUMERABLE	735 JERUSALEM 89	56
THE INNUMERABLE CHARIOTS OF THE ALMIGHTY APPEARD IN HEAVEN	745 JERUSALEM 98	8
VARIOUS & INNUMERABLE WAYS ENDEAVOURING TO THROW THE RIDER	833C LETTER 33	PROSE

INORBD

| INORBD AND BONIFIED WITH LOCKS OF SHADOWING MODESTY SHINING | 709 JERUSALEM 70 | 22 |

INQUIRE   SEE ENQUIRE

| AGO BY HIS DESIRE I WRITE TO HIM BY THIS POST TO INQUIRE | 841A LETTER 40 | PROSE |

INQUIRY   SEE ENQUIRY

O AT LAST THOU MOCKEST ME TO SHAME MY OVER-FOND INQUIRY	39A SAMSON/PS	PROSE
IN WESTMORELAND PROMISES TO MAKE EVERY INQUIRY ABOUT IT	844C LETTER 43	PROSE
MY WIFE RETURNS HER HEARTFELT THANKS FOR YOUR KIND INQUIRY	851C LETTER 50	PROSE

INQUISITION

| REPRESENTS THE INQUISITION AS DO THOSE CONTENDING . . . | 608C V LAST JUDG/N | PROSE |

INQUISITOR

WOULD BE AS GOOD AN INQUISITOR AS ANY OTHER PRIEST . . .	385C ANNO WATSON	MARG
THE BISHOP IS AN INQUISITOR	388B ANNO WATSON	MARG
WAS ONE OF THIS NUMBER HE WAS AS INTOLERANT AS AN INQUISITOR	615B V LAST JUDG/N	PROSE

INSANE

THEY SAID THE SPECTRE IS IN EVERY MAN INSANE & MOST . . .	267 FOUR ZOAS 1	103
THOU KNOWEST THAT THE SPECTRE IS IN EVERY MAN INSANE BRUTISH	327 FOUR ZOAS 7	304
THE SPECTRE IS IN GIANT MAN INSANE AND MOST DEFORMD . . .	664 JERUSALEM 37	4
INSANE SHE RAVES UPON THE WINDS HOARSE INARTICULATE . . .	693 JERUSALEM 60	44
O THAT I WERE INSANE ALWAYS I WILL NEVER REST	772C ANNO SPURZHEIM	MARG
CAN YOU NOT MAKE ME TRULY INSANE I WILL NEVER REST TILL I AM SO	772C ANNO SPURZHEIM	MARG
[WHO DARES ?WORSHIP ?ONE WHOD HAVE DRIVEN YOU LONG AGO INSANE]	SUPP ANNO REYNOLDS	* MARG
[EITHER HE IS DISHONEST ?OR HE IS ?INSANE]	SUPP ANNO REYNOLDS	* MARG

INSANITY

WHICH TO ANGELS LOOK LIKE TORMENT AND INSANITY	150C MARRIAGE HH 6	PROSE
& PERHAPS HE WROTE IN A PAROXYSM OF INSANITY IN WHICH . .	600D PUB ADDRESS/N	PROSE
INSANITY AND FURY AND WHATEVER PALTRY COLL HEARTED CRITICS	864B LETTER 61	PROSE

INSATIABLE

| ITS INSATIABLE MAW MUST BE FED BY WHAT ALL CAN DO . . . | 593D PUB ADDRESS/N | PROSE |

INSCRIBED

ON THE INN IS INSCRIBED ITS TITLE AND A PROPER ADVANTAGE	567B DESC CAT 3	PROSE
ON THE INN IS INSCRIBED ITS TITLE & A PROPER ADVANTAGE .	588D CHAUCER/N	PROSE
INSCRIBED "THIS IS THE INN FROM WHICH"	590B CHAUCER 2	PROSE
ON THE INN IS INSCRIBED ITS TITLE AND A PROPER ADVANTAGE	590C CHAUCER 2	PROSE

INSCRIPTION

| THE FOLLOWING INSCRIPTION...BUT IT STRIKES ME THAT . . . | 838B LETTER 37 | PROSE |

INSCRIPTIONS

| TRACED ON THE MARBLE THE INSCRIPTIONS TO THE PLATES I MUST | 838A LETTER 37 | PROSE |

INSECTS

CONSUMING ALL BOTH FLOWERS & FRUITS INSECTS & WARBLING BIRDS	110 TIRIEL 8	38
AND AS A PLAGUE WIND FILLD WITH INSECTS CUTS OFF MAN & BEAST	201 AMERICA 14	8
UNDER THE DOMINATION OF INSECTS RAISED BY THE SUN'S HEAT	619C ILLUS MILTON	PROSE

INSERTION

| INSERTION I WRITE TO ENTREAT THAT YOU WOULD CONTRIVE SO AS | 861A LETTER 58 | PROSE |
| MR PHILLIPS OBJECTS ALTOGETHER TO THE INSERTION OF MY . . | 861B LETTER 58 | PROSE |

INSIDE

| OF AIR HE CAUSED THE INSIDE OF THE CAVE TO BE INFINITE . . | 154D MARRIAGE HH 15 | PROSE |

INSIGNIFICANT

| AS POETRY ADMITS NOT A LETTER THAT IS INSIGNIFICANT . . . | 611B V LAST JUDG/N | PROSE |
| INSIGNIFICANT MUCH LESS AN INSIGNIFICANT BLUR OR MARK . . | 611C V LAST JUDG/N | PROSE |

INSINCERITY

| THY PASSIVITY THY LAWS OF OBEDIENCE & INSINCERITY . . . | 295 FOUR ZOAS 3 | 118 |

INSINUATED

| BOLOGNIAN SCHOOLS MAY BE INSINUATED NOT TO BE ORNAMENTAL | 476B ANNO REYNOLDS | MARG |

INSINUATES

| VOLTAIRE INSINUATES THAT THESE LIMITS ARE THE CRUEL WORK OF GOD | 713 JERUSALEM 73 | 29 |

INSINUATION

| THERSITES' SLY INSINUATION SUCH IS THE BISHOP'S . . . . | 384D ANNO WATSON | MARG |

INSINUATIONS

| NOTWITHSTANDING ARTFULLY DISSEMMINATED INSINUATIONS . . . | 586D CHAUCER 1 | *PROSE |
| BY MEANS OF SUCH VILE ARGUMENTS & INSINUATIONS . . . . | 612D V LAST JUDG/N | PROSE |

INSIPIDITY

| HOW WIDE THE GULF & UNPASSABLE BETWEEN SIMPLICITY & INSIPIDITY | 518B MILTON 30 | TITLE |

```
                                                      PAGE      TITLE           LINE
INSIST
    I HAVE BEEN FORCED TO INSIST ON HIS LEAVING ME IN BOTH TO   825C LETTER 27        PROSE
INSISTED
      TILL THE COMPANY WERE TIRED & INSISTED ON THE LAWGIVER .  .  57D ISLAND MOON 9    PROSE
    HE MADE ME AN IMPERTINENT ANSWER I INSISTED ON HIS LEAVING  827A LETTER 28        PROSE
INSLAVD        SEE ENSLAVD,ENSLAVED
    TO WANDER INSLAVD BLACK DEPREST IN DARK IGNORANCE . . .     143 FRENCH REVOLTN *   214
    INSLAVD TO THE MOST POWERFUL SELFHOOD TO MURDER THE DIVINE  679 JERUSALEM 49        30
      HUMANITY
INSOLENCE
    A CONFIDENT INSOLENCE SPROUTING FROM SYSTEMATIC REASONING   157C MARRIAGE HH 21 PROSE
INSOLENT
    I CONSIDER THE FOLLOWING SENTENCE IS SUPREMELY INSOLENT     453C ANNO REYNOLDS      MARG
    OF IDEAS & [ THEN TO BE ?INSOLENT IN HIS FOOLERY ] .  .  .  455B ANNO REYNOLDS *  MARG
    WHICH WAS PAINTED IN SELF-DEFENCE AGAINST THE INSOLENT  .   572C DESC CAT 3        PROSE
INSPECT
    SUBSCRIBERS TO INSPECT WHAT THEY HAVE EXCLUDED AND THOSE    561B EXHIBITION ADV    PROSE
    TO INSPECT MY PRINT OF WHICH DRAWING IS THE FOUNDATION  .  .  591D PUB ADDRESS/N    PROSE
INSPECTION
    FOR PUBLIC INSPECTION AND FOR SALE BY PRIVATE CONTRACT  .  .  560C EXHIBITION ADV  PROSE
    FOR PUBLIC INSPECTION AND FOR SALE BY PRIVATE CONTRACT  .   563A DESC CAT          TITLE
    IT IS A PRINT THAT I FEEL PROUD OF ON A NEW INSPECTION  .   863C LETTER 60         PROSE
INSPIRATION
    ("POET COMPOSES...INSPIRATION...FOR ALL MEN ") MOST         80C ANNO LAVATER       MARG
      EXCELLENT
    THE TRUTH & CERTAINTY OF VIRTUE & HONESTY I E INSPIRATION   386C ANNO WATSON       MARG
    FABRICATED FOR PLEASURE AS MODERNS SAY BUT I SAY            390D ANNO WATSON       MARG
      BY INSPIRATION
    IF HISTORICAL FACTS CAN BE WRITTEN BY INSPIRATION  .  .  .  392D ANNO WATSON       MARG
    & THAT ALL PRETENCE TO INSPIRATION IS A LIE & A DECEIT  .   452D ANNO REYNOLDS     MARG
    NOT BEEN TOLD THIS BY PRACTISE BUT BY INSPIRATION & VISION  457B ANNO REYNOLDS     MARG
    THAT THERE IS NO SUCH THING AS INSPIRATION &  .  .  .  .  .  457D ANNO REYNOLDS     MARG
    FINDS NOTHING OF INSPIRATION OUGHT NOT TO DARE TO BE AN     458B ANNO REYNOLDS     MARG
      ARTIST
    THINKS HE HAS PROVED THAT GENIUS & INSPIRATION ARE ALL      475A ANNO REYNOLDS     MARG
      A HUM
    NOW THEY MOCK INSPIRATION & VISION  .  .  .  .  .  .  .  .  477A ANNO REYNOLDS     MARG
    INSPIRATION & VISION WAS THEN & NOW IS & I HOPE WILL ALWAYS 477A ANNO REYNOLDS     MARG
    SHALL BECOME THE DAUGHTERS OF INSPIRATION  .  .  .  .  .  .  480C MILTON 1          PROSE
    ACCORDING TO THE INSPIRATION OF THE POETIC GENIUS  .  .  .  495 MILTON 14           1
    WITH THE DAUGHTERS OF MEMORY & NOT WITH THE DAUGHTERS       496 MILTON 14           29
      OF INSPIRATION
    INTO MOST HOLY FORMS OF THOUGHT SUCH IS THE POWER           515 MILTON 28           5
      OF INSPIRATION
    IN THE GREAT WARS OF ETERNITY IN FURY OF POETIC INSPIRATION 519 MILTON 30           19
    HIS LITTLE THROAT LABOURS WITH INSPIRATION EVERY FEATHER    520 MILTON 31           34
    I COME IN SELF-ANNIHILATION & THE GRANDEUR OF INSPIRATION   533 MILTON 41           2
    TO CAST OFF THE ROTTEN RAGS OF MEMORY BY INSPIRATION  .  .  533 MILTON 41           4
    TO CAST ASIDE FROM POETRY ALL THAT IS NOT INSPIRATION  .    533 MILTON 41           7
    FOR ANY MAN TO PRETEND TO INSPIRATION  .  .  .  .  .  .  .  551 WILLM COWPER/N      12
    OF A NATION IF GENIUS AND INSPIRATION ARE THE GREAT ORIGIN  561C EXHIBITION ADV    PROSE
    AND NOT OF INSPIRATION OR IMAGINATION THEREFORE  .  .  .  .  566A DESC CAT 2        PROSE
    SCHOLAR OF INSPIRATION AND ALL WILL BE HAPPY  .  .  .  .    572C DESC CAT 3         PROSE
    THE SOURCE OF LEARNING AND INSPIRATION ARTHUR WAS A NAME    577D DESC CAT 5         PROSE
    AND PATHOS THE ARTIST HAS WRITTEN IT UNDER INSPIRATION  .   578B DESC CAT 5         PROSE
    IT IS THE GIFT OF GOD IT IS INSPIRATION AND VISION HE  .    579C DESC CAT 5         PROSE
    IS INSPIRATION AND CANNOT BE SURPASSED IT IS PERFECT AND    579C DESC CAT 5         PROSE
      ETERNAL
    BY PLACING LEARNING ABOVE INSPIRATION O ARTIST  .  .  .  .  582A DESC CAT 8         PROSE
    IMAGINATION IS SURROUNDED BY THE DAUGHTERS OF INSPIRATION   604D V LAST JUDG/N     PROSE
    THE GREEK MUSES WHICH ARE NOT INSPIRATION AS THE BIBLE IS   605C V LAST JUDG/N     PROSE
    OR BY THE IMMEDIATE INSPIRATION OF GOD IT IS  .  .  .  .  .  614A V LAST JUDG/N     PROSE
    & THE GIVING ALL UP TO INSPIRATION BY THIS IT WILL BE SEEN  614C V LAST JUDG/N     PROSE
    INSPIRATION DENYD GENIUS FORBIDDEN BY LAWS OF PUNISHMENT    628 JERUSALEM 9          16
    AT ENMITY AGAINST ALL TRUE POETRY OR INSPIRATION .  .  .    782D ANNO WW POEMS      MARG
    [ IF THE ?INSPIRATION ?IS GREAT ?WHY CALL IT MADNESS]  .  .  SUPP ANNO REYNOLDS * MARG
INSPIRATIONS
    RAGING WITH THE INSPIRATIONS OF A PROPHETIC MIND  .  .  .  .  580B DESC CAT 5        PROSE
INSPIRD
    AND SHALL BE STILL MY GLORY I WAS INSPIRD  .  .  .  .  .  .  23 EDW THIRD/PS 3       88
    THEN BRUTUS SPOKE INSPIRD OUR FATHERS SIT  .  .  .  .  .  .  32 EDW THIRD/PS 6       37
    SO GREAT ITS POWER THAT PRIDE INSPIRD BY IT  .  .  .  .  .  41A THEN SHE BORE      PROSE
    HIS VOICE LOUD INSPIRD BY LIBERTY .  .  .  .  .  .  .  .  .  147 FRENCH REVOLTN     284
    THE RUINS OF THE UNIVERSE HEAR WHAT INSPIRD I SPEAK & BE    329 FOUR ZOAS 7         352
      SILENT
    WONDERING BEHELD THE CENTER OPEND BY DIVING MERCY INSPIRD   329 FOUR ZOAS 7         374
    THEY BUILDED GOLGONOOZA LOS LABOURING [ INSPIRD] BUILDED    329 FOUR ZOAS 7    *    378
      PILLARS HIGH
    IT REMAIND PERMANENT A LOVELY FORM INSPIRD DIVINELY HUMAN   332 FOUR ZOAS 7         469
    ENORMOUS WORKS LOS CONTEMPLATED INSPIRD BY THE HOLY SPIRIT  343 FOUR ZOAS 8         108
    SOUND LOUD THE HOWLING MUSIC INSPIRD BY LOS & ENITHARMON    344 FOUR ZOAS 8         121
        . . .
    AND WORSHIPPD THEM [TO] THAT THEY MIGHT MAKE INSPIRD ART    543 IF TRUE/N           10
      ABHORRD
INSPIRE
    BURNS IN MY SOUL AND DOES MY SONG INSPIRE  .  .  .  .  .    10 FRESH FROM/PS         20
    CONFIRM THE STRONG WITH STRENGTH THE WEAK INSPIRE  .  .  .  25 EDW THIRD/PS 3       181
    DAUGHTERS OF BEULAH MUSES WHO INSPIRE THE POET'S SONG  .  .  481 MILTON 2            1
    GREAT MEN & FOOLS [OF] DO OFTEN ME INSPIRE  .  .  .  .  .  .  554 GREAT MEN/N    *   1
INSPIRED
    SO ENITHARMON SPOKE & LOS HIS HANDS DIVINE INSPIRED BEGAN   331 FOUR ZOAS 7    *   456
    PAINE IS EITHER A DEVIL OR AN INSPIRED MAN .  .  .  .  .  .  386B ANNO WATSON       MARG
```

984

		PAGE	TITLE	LINE

INSPIRED   (CONTINUED)
    UNLESS WE ALLOW IT TO BE POETRY & THAT POETRY INSPIRED   392D ANNO WATSON   MARG
    THE MORE ANCIENT & CONSCIOUSLY & PROFESSEDLY INSPIRED MEN   480B MILTON 1   PROSE
    THE BARD REPLIED I AM INSPIRED I KNOW IT IS TRUTH FOR I   495 MILTON 13   51
        SING
    INSPIRED & AT THE DAWN OF DAY SEND OUT ANOTHER LARK . . .   526 MILTON 36   6
    REPLIED OBEY THOU THE WORDS OF THE INSPIRED MAN . . . .   532 MILTON 40   29
    CAST ON THE INSPIRED BY THE TAME HIGH FINISHER OF PALTRY   533 MILTON 41   9
        BLOTS
    IN PREFERENCE TO THE INSPIRED MOMENTS OF GENIUS & ANIMATION   594B PUB ADDRESS/N   PROSE
    AS HE ENTERD THE DOOR OF DEATH FOR ALBION'S SAKE INSPIRED   620 JERUSALEM 1   9
    I AM INSPIRED I ACT NOT FOR MYSELF FOR ALBION'S SAKE . .   627 JERUSALEM 8   17
    FOR I AM ONE OF THE LIVING DARE NOT TO MOCK MY INSPIRED   627 JERUSALEM 8   35
        FURY
    "THE ANGELS OF OUR JOURNEY HAVE INSPIRED A SONG TO YOU"   800B LETTER 12   PROSE
INSPIRER
    MEMORY [NATURE] IS HIS INSPIRER & NOT IMAGINATION THE HOLY   785A ILLUS DANTE 7   *PROSE
        GHOST
INSPIRES
    HOWEVER SWEET TIS ENVY THAT INSPIRES MY SONG . . . . .   41D THEN SHE BORE   PROSE
    THAT THY IMMORTAL TONGUE INSPIRES PRESENT THEM TO ALBION   675 JERUSALEM 45   31
INSPIRING
    REVIVING SHAKE INSPIRING MOVE BREATHING AWAKENING . . .   198 AMERICA 6   4
    BOADICEA INSPIRING THE BRITONS AGAINST THE ROMANS . .   208D SUBJCTS HIST/N   TITLE
    INSPIRING SECRECY & LAMPS THEY BORE INTOXICATING FUMES .   333 FOUR ZOAS 7B   28
INSPIRITING
    THEIR SWEET INSPIRITING LYRES THY LABOURS SHALL ADMINISTER   301 FOUR ZOAS 4   * 154
INSTANCE
    ONE FOR INSTANCE WHICH IS THAT THE BOOKS OF THE BIBLE .   390C ANNO WATSON   MARG
    BY WAY OF ILLUSTRATION I INSTANCE SHAKSPEARE'S WITCHES IN   569D DESC CAT 3   PROSE
    INSTANCE OF LAOCOON WHO THOUGH A PRIEST IS REPRESENTED   583D DESC CAT 10   PROSE
        NAKED
INSTANT
    AT THIS INSTANT OBTUSE ANGLE CAME IN . . . .   63A ISLAND MOON 11   PROSE
INSTEAD
    INSTEAD OF PEACEFUL PIPE THE SHEPHERD BEARS A SWORD . . .   40B SAMSON/PS   PROSE
    THEN SAID HE I WOULD HAVE ALL THE WRITING ENGRAVED INSTEAD   62D ISLAND MOON 11   PROSE
    BUT DWELL WITH US & LET US BE TO THEE INSTEAD OF EYES .   103 TIRIEL 3   34
    . . . INSTEAD OF WORDS HARSH HISSINGS   142 FRENCH REVOLTN   177
    LIKE THE LOW VOICE OF THE LABOURING MAN INSTEAD OF THE   145 FRENCH REVOLTN   245
        SHOUT OF JOY
    INSTEAD OF MORN ARISES A BRIGHT SHADOW LIKE AN EYE . .   191 V DAU ALBION 2   35
    IN THE EASTERN CLOUD INSTEAD OF NIGHT A SICKLY CHARNEL   191 V DAU ALBION 2   36
        HOUSE
    AND WHERE THE MOTHER'S MILK INSTEAD THOSE EVER-HISSING JAWS   199 AMERICA 9   23
    ALL LOVE IS LOST TERROR SUCCEEDS & HATRED INSTEAD OF LOVE   265 FOUR ZOAS 1   36
    AND STERN DEMANDS OF RIGHT & DUTY INSTEAD OF LIBERTY .   265 FOUR ZOAS 1   37
    INSTEAD OF LOVE TO ENION ENION BLIND & AGE BENT . . .   296 FOUR ZOAS 3   178
    BLACK SCALES OF IRON ARM THE DREAD VISAGE IRON SPIKES   319 FOUR ZOAS 6   307
        INSTEAD
    [& INSTEAD OF ETCHING THE SHADOWY STROKES]   440C MEMORANDUM/N 3   PROSE
    INSTEAD OF ETCHING THE BLACKS ETCH THE WHITES & BITE IT IN   440C MEMORANDUM/N 4   PROSE
    INSTEAD OF FOLLOWING ONE GREAT MASTER . . . .   455C ANNO REYNOLDS   MARG
    INSTEAD OF MICHAEL ANGELO . . . .   543 TO ROYL ACAD/N   5
    PICTURES OF THE VARIOUS SCHOOLS POSSESSED HIS MIND INSTEAD   582D DESC CAT 9   PROSE
    SCOURGING SIN INSTEAD OF FORGIVING IT . . . .   608A V LAST JUDG/N   PROSE
    ALL LOVE IS LOST TERROR SUCCEEDS & [RATRED] HATRED INSTEAD   645 JERUSALEM 22   * 10
        OF LOVE
    AND STERN DEMANDS OF RIGHT & DUTY INSTEAD OF LIBERTY .   645 JERUSALEM 22   11
    INSTEAD OF ALBION'S LOVELY MOUNTAINS & THE CURTAINS OF   673 JERUSALEM 43   59
        JERUSALEM
    INSTEAD OF THE MUTUAL FORGIVENESSES THE MINUTE PARTICULARS   673 JERUSALEM 43   61
        I SEE
    LIKE LAKES OF LIQUID LEAD INSTEAD OF HEAVENLY CHAPELS BUILT   673 JERUSALEM 43   63
    INSTEAD OF HUMAN VICTIMS BY THE DAUGHTERS OF ALBION   697 JERUSALEM 63   31
        & CANAAN
    [A REDNING SKELETON IN HOWLING WOE] INSTEAD OF BEAUTY .   726 JERUSALEM 82   * 68
    JEHOVAH LO I HAVE GIVEN YOU A LAMB FOR AN ATONEMENT INSTEAD   780 GHOST ABEL 2   10
    WHICH SHALL BE CHOSEN INSTEAD OF THE WITCH IF THAT CANNOT   840D LETTER 40   PROSE
    [AND STERN DEMANDS OF RIGHT & DUTY INSTEAD OF LIBERTY] .   SUPP FOUR ZOAS 1   *
INSTEP
    COVERS THE SHADES OF TYBURN HIS INSTEP FROM WINDSOR . . .   531 MILTON 39   37
INSTINCT
    THOU ART A NATURAL PHILOSOPHER AND KNOWEST TRUTH   29A EDW THIRD/PS 4   PROSE
        BY INSTINCT
INSTITUTION
    THE BRITISH INSTITUTION HAS THIS YEAR FOLLOWED ITS EXAMPLE   561B EXHIBITION ADV   PROSE
INSTRUCT
    IT IS IN THEIR POWER TO HINDER INSTRUCTION BUT NOT   597A PUB ADDRESS/N   PROSE
        TO INSTRUCT
    I HAVE INNOCENCE TO DEFEND AND IGNORANCE TO INSTRUCT . .   670 JERUSALEM 42   26
INSTRUCTED
    AND THUS THE SEVEN ANGELS INSTRUCTED HIM & THUS THEY   521 MILTON 32   9
        CONVERSE
    BUT AS I HAVE INSTRUCTED THEE . . . .   771 OF GATES/GP   30
    ENTERTAIND AND INSTRUCTED BUT HAVE NOT YET COME TO THE .   845B LETTER 44   PROSE
INSTRUCTING
    SEE N...WORLDS IN UNIVERSE FOR ACCOUNT OF INSTRUCTING   SUPP ANNO SWED HELL * MARG
        SPIRITS
INSTRUCTION
    THE TYGERS OF WRATH ARE WISER THAN THE HORSES OF   152A MARRIAGE HH 9   PROSE
        INSTRUCTION

		PAGE	TITLE	LINE

INSTRUCTION   (CONTINUED)
    LACEDEMONIAN INSTRUCTION . . . . 180D LACEDEMONIAN/N   TITLE
    . . . THE HORSES OF INSTRUCTION FROM THEIR MANGERS . . . 281 FOUR ZOAS 2   35
    FOR LABOUR FATHERLY CARE & SWEET INSTRUCTION I WILL GIVE 312 FOUR ZOAS 6   40
    IT IS IN THEIR POWER TO HINDER INSTRUCTION BUT NOT   597A PUB ADDRESS/N   PROSE
        TO INSTRUCT
    CONSIDERD WHAT IS NOT TOO EXPLICIT AS THE FITTEST   793B LETTER 5   PROSE
        FOR INSTRUCTION
INSTRUCTIONS
    GIVING THEM SWEET INSTRUCTIONS WHERE THE CLOUD THE RIVER 315 FOUR ZOAS 6   137
        & THE FIELD
INSTRUCTIVE
    UTTERING PROPHECIES & SPEAKING INSTRUCTIVE WORDS TO THE 512 MILTON 26   9
        SONS
    WHY IS THE BIBLE MORE ENTERTAINING & INSTRUCTIVE THAN ANY 794A LETTER 5   PROSE
        OTHER BOOK
INSTRUMENT
    I TOUCH THE HEAVENS AS AN INSTRUMENT TO GLORIFY THE LORD 494 MILTON 13   29
    STRANGE [INSTRUMENT] MYSTERIOUS DREAM UPON HIS WINGS OF   619C ILLUS MILTON *PROSE
        SCROLLS &
INSTRUMENTALITY
    THRO THE INSTRUMENTALITY OF DR THORNTON . . . . 786C ANNO THORNTON   MARG
INSTRUMENTS
    WE LACK NOT SONGS NOR INSTRUMENTS OF JOY . . . . . .   2 TO SUMMER/PS   17
    . . . THE PENCIL THE PEN AND THE INSTRUMENTS . . . . . 144 FRENCH REVOLTN   231
    OTHERS AROSE & SCHOOLS ERECTED FORMING INSTRUMENTS   283 FOUR ZOAS 2   130
    SWEET INSTRUMENTS OF SOUND IN PRIDE ENCOMPASSING MY KNEES 312 FOUR ZOAS 6   32
    AND BOOKS & INSTRUMENTS OF SONG & PICTURES OF DELIGHT . 317 FOUR ZOAS 6   216
    AND BRASS VAST INSTRUMENTS TO MEASURE OUT THE IMMENSE & FIX 317 FOUR ZOAS 6   230
    DESCENDED TO THE SOUND OF INSTRUMENTS THAT DROWND THE NOISE 333 FOUR ZOAS 7B 32
    THE INSTRUMENTS OF SOUND & TROOP BY TROOP IN HUMAN FORMS 344 FOUR ZOAS 8   117
        THEY URGE
    HE FORMED ALSO HARSH INSTRUMENTS OF SOUND . . . . . . 344 FOUR ZOAS 8   135
    THEY SING THEY SIEZE THE INSTRUMENTS OF HARMONY THEY THROW 365 FOUR ZOAS 9   302
        AWAY
    AT THE IMMORTAL TABLES SOUNDING LOUD THEIR INSTRUMENTS   374 FOUR ZOAS 9   645
        OF JOY
    . . . TO FORGE THE INSTRUMENTS . . . . 485 MILTON 6   12
    THOUSANDS & THOUSANDS LABOUR THOUSANDS PLAY ON   509 MILTON 24   60
        INSTRUMENTS
    EACH ONE TO SOUND HIS INSTRUMENTS OF MUSIC IN THE DANCE 512 MILTON 26   5
    WITH INSTRUMENTS OF MUSIC . . . . 619C ILLUS MILTON   PROSE
    WHO FELL BENEATH HIS INSTRUMENTS OF HUSBANDRY & BECAME . 688 JERUSALEM 56   35
    AND PEARL WITH INSTRUMENTS OF MUSIC IN HOLY JERUSALEM . 710 JERUSALEM 71   41
    TURKEY & GRECIA SAW MY (INSTRUMENTS) OF MUSIC THEY AROSE 721 JERUSALEM 79   48
    AND I BELIEVE TWO DAUGHTERS WITH MAPS INSTRUMENTS &C . 843C LETTER 43   PROSE
INSULT
    PLEASURE AS I HAVE THERE I STAND & BEAR EVERY FOOL'S INSULT 53C ISLAND MOON 8 PROSE
    BEING NOT IRRITATED BY INSULT BEARING INSULTING   655 JERUSALEM 30   9
        BENEVOLENCES
INSULTED
    INSULTED & DEGRADED BY THE REPUTATION OF THESE DISCOURSES 452B ANNO REYNOLDS MARG
INSULTING
    OCCASIONED BY HIS SAYING SOMETHING THAT I THOUGHT INSULTING 438A BLAKES MEMORAN PROSE
    BEING NOT IRRITATED BY INSULT BEARING INSULTING   655 JERUSALEM 30   9
        BENEVOLENCES
INSULTS
    THE IGNORANT INSULTS OF INDIVIDUALS WILL NOT HINDER ME . . 561A EXHIBITION ADV PROSE
INTANGLEMENT
    THE STRUGGLES OF INTANGLEMENT WITH INCOHERENT ROOTS I KNOW 716D JERUSALEM 77 PROSE
        OF
INTEGRITY
    LET THE HUMAN ORGANS BE KEPT IN THEIR PERFECT INTEGRITY 686 JERUSALEM 55   36
    OF MR JOHNSON'S INTEGRITY WHILE WE WERE TALKING CONCERNING 846C LETTER 44   PROSE
INTEGUMENT
    THE DAUGHTERS OF ENITHARMON WEAVE THE OVARIUM & THE   346 FOUR ZOAS 8   210
        INTEGUMENT
    THE INTEGUMENT SOFT FOR ITS CLOTHING WITH JOY & DELIGHT 515 MILTON 28   20
    I HAVE STRIPD OFF JOSEPH'S BEAUTIFUL INTEGUMENT FOR MY   724 JERUSALEM 81   11
        BELOVED
INTEGUMENTS
    RECIEVEST THE INTEGUMENTS WOVEN RAHAB BEHOLDS THE LAMB   347 FOUR ZOAS 8   233
        OF GOD
    THE OPEN HEART IS SHUT UP IN INTEGUMENTS OF FROZEN SILENCE 672 JERUSALEM 43   33
    AND A PECULIAR TABERNACLE TO CUT THE INTEGUMENTS OF BEAUTY 693 JERUSALEM 60   33
    SMITING THE SPECTRE ON HIS ANVIL & THE INTEGUMENTS OF HIS 738 JERUSALEM 91   45
        EYE
INTELLECT
    WE CALL THE OMISSIONS OF INTELLECT SPRINGING FROM POVERTY 88C ANNO LAVATER   MARG
    YET SCIENCE CANNOT TEACH INTELLECT . . . . 93A ANNO SWED LOVE   MARG
    MUCH LESS CAN INTELLECT TEACH AFFECTION HOW FOOLISH THEN 93A ANNO SWED LOVE   MARG
    & THAT SCIENCE WILL NOT OPEN INTELLECT BUT THAT THEY ARE 93A ANNO SWED LOVE   MARG
    FOR HOW CAN SCIENCE BE BROUGHT TO DEMONSTRATE INTELLECT 93B ANNO SWED LOVE   MARG
    [IF WITH HIS INTELLECT HE COMPREHEND THE TERRIBLE SENTENCE] 264 FOUR ZOAS 1   * 4
    TERRIFIC RAGD THE ETERNAL WHEELS OF INTELLECT TERRIFIC   280 FOUR ZOAS 1   571
        RAGD
    ABOVE HIM ROSE A SHADOW FROM HIS WEARIED INTELLECT . . 293 FOUR ZOAS 3   50
    PRINCE OF LIGHT BOUND IN CHAINS OF INTELLECT AMONG THE   305 FOUR ZOAS 5   16
        FURNACES
    THE BLOODY DELUGE LIVING FLAMES WINGED WITH INTELLECT . . 359 FOUR ZOAS 9   86
    BACON'S BUSINESS IS NOT INTELLECT OR ART . . . . . 409D ANNO BACON   * MARG
    OF HUMAN INTELLECT NOW IS FLOCKING TO THE SOUND OF THE   510 MILTON 25   19
        TRUMPET

986

		TITLE		LINE
AGE		AMERICA 4		8
		URIZEN 6		45
		URIZEN 6		36
		SHIP ZOAS 9		264
		FOUR ZOAS 9		82
		...ER 23		53
				512
				17

...JOICD IN FELPHAM'S VALE   534 MILTO.
...ILITY OF INTELLECT   580A DESC C.
...INTELLECT IS LEAPING   580B DESC CA
...E DIVINE HUMANITY   581B DESC CAT
...L THE PASSIONS   613D V LAST JU
...O INTELLECT   615C V LAST JUD
...NTELLECT   615D V LAST JUDG/
...S OF INTELLECT   654 JERUSALEM 29
...INTELLECT   677 JERUSALEM 48
...INTELLECT   681 JERUSALEM 50
...MORE   707 JERUSALEM 68
...RS   733 JERUSALEM 88

...L DRIVE   739 JERUSALEM 91   5
...ARROWS OF   745 JERUSALEM 98   7
...ORY AND   746 JERUSALEM 98   30

...THE FOOD OF INTELLECT   790D LETTER 2   PROSE

...ECTS & NOT AS IN TIMES OF OLD   285 FOUR ZOAS 2   206
...ST HE HAVE WHO   597D PUB ADDRESS/N   PROSE
...INTELLECTS & NOT AS IN TIMES OF OLD   732 JERUSALEM 86   61

...FOR THE DAY OF INTELLECTUAL BATTLE   264 FOUR ZOAS 1   6
...L WAR THE WAR OF SWORDS DEPARTED NOW   379 FOUR ZOAS 9   854
...UAL ACQUIREMENT   402C ANNO BACON   MARG
...S INTELLECTUAL ARTS UNMANLY POETRY PAINTING   407D ANNO BACON   MARG
...THE TEAR IS AN] A TEAR IS AN INTELLECTUAL THING   420 I SAW A MONK/N *   58
...A TEAR IS AN INTELLECTUAL THING   430 GREY MONK   29
IS OWN IDEA OF INTELLECTUAL BEAUTY THE FACE AND   580A DESC CAT 5   PROSE
WHAT ITALY IS AN ENVIED STOREHOUSE OF INTELLECTUAL RICHES   580A DESC CAT 5   PROSE
WHEN IMAGINATION ART & SCIENCE & ALL INTELLECTUAL GIFTS   601B PUB ADDRESS/N   PROSE
WITH INTELLECTUAL SPEARS & LONG WINGED ARROWS OF THOUGHT   604C V LAST JUDG/N   PROSE
FOR A TEAR IS AN INTELLECTUAL THING   664 JERUSALEM 38   15
ONCE MAN WAS OCCUPIED IN INTELLECTUAL PLEASURES & ENERGIES   707 JERUSALEM 68   65
IS THE HOLY GHOST ANY OTHER THAN AN INTELLECTUAL FOUNTAIN   717A JERUSALEM 77   PROSE
GOD THAN THAT GOD WHO IS THE INTELLECTUAL FOUNTAIN OF   738 JERUSALEM 91   11
    HUMANITY
YOUR INVENTIONS OF INTELLECTUAL VISIONS ARE THE STAMINA   795B LETTER 6   PROSE
ALLEGORY ADDRESSD TO THE INTELLECTUAL POWERS WHILE IT IS   825A LETTER 27   PROSE
MADNESS FOR I AM REALLY DRUNK WITH INTELLECTUAL VISION   852C LETTER 50   PROSE
WILL ATTRIBUTE IT TO ITS RIGHT CAUSE INTELLECTUAL   876B LETTER 83   PROSE
    PECULIARITY
INTELLECTUALS
    STUDY INTELLECTUALS TILL YOU ARE COLD   93A ANNO SWED LOVE   MARG
    ART IS FIRST IN INTELLECTUALS & OUGHT TO BE FIRST   446D ANNO REYNOLDS   MARG
        IN NATIONS
INTELLIGENCE
    PLAIN THAT SELF DERIVED INTELLIGENCE IS WORLDLY   94B ANNO SWED LOVE   MARG
        DEMONSTRATION
INTELLIGENT
    IN GLITTRING ARMOUR SWIFT AS WINDS INTELLIGENT AS [FLAMES]   205 AMERICA CANC C   13
        CLOUDS
    INTELLIGENT ORGANIZD ARMD   256 BOOK OF LOS 3   29
INTEND
    OR SPEAK FROM HIS HEART BUT HE MUST INTEND TRUTH   98C ALL RELIGIONS   PROSE
    INTEND IT SHOULD BE SO NONE BUT BLOCKHEADS COPY ONE ANOTHER   601D PUB ADDRESS/N   PROSE
    "PROPER DUTY TO YOU & MR FLAXMAN WE INTEND TO CALL"   800A LETTER 12   PROSE
    I INTEND BECAUSE MY ABSTRACT FOLLY HURRIES ME OFTEN AWAY   809A LETTER 20   PROSE
    I INTEND TO SEE MRS LAMBERT & MR JOHNSON BOOKSELLER THIS   833C LETTER 33   PROSE
    YET BEEN ABLE TO MEET MR BRAITHWAITE AT HOME BUT INTEND   849B LETTER 45   PROSE
    & AM HARD AT IT TO ACCOMPLISH IN TIME WHAT I INTEND   859B LETTER 56   PROSE
    I INTEND TO BRING WITH ME BESIDES OUR NECESSARY CHANGE OF   873A LETTER 76   PROSE
INTENDED
    PROLOGUE INTENDED FOR A DRAMATIC PIECE OF KING EDWARD THE   33C EDW FOURTH/PS   TITLE
        FOURTH
    WHICH HE INTENDED NOT A SHADOWY [MALE] HERMAPHRODITE BLACK   343 FOUR ZOAS 8   103
        & OPAKE
    WHICH I INTENDED TO SEND TO THE ENEMY   438A BLAKES MEMORAN   PROSE
    AND NOBLE HOUSEKEEPER CHAUCER'S MONK IS INTENDED   569C DESC CAT 3   PROSE
    THEM AS WRETCHED OLD WOMEN AND NOT AS SHAKSPEARE INTENDED   569D DESC CAT 3   PROSE
    IF HE INTENDED TO TAKE ON SIN   756 EV GOSPEL(I)/N   3
    THE HONOUR INTENDED YOU BY NATURE TO REVIVE THE GREEK   795B LETTER 6   PROSE
        WORKMANSHIP
    BE ON THIS I BEG TO SAY THAT THEY ARE WHAT I INTENDED THEM   815B LETTER 23   PROSE
    HALF WHAT I INTENDED TO SAY & IN PARTICULAR I WISH TO ASK   816C LETTER 24   PROSE
    MY BROTHER I INTENDED TO HAVE SENT THE PICTURE OF   822B LETTER 26   PROSE
    PROFITS OF THE WORK ARE INTENDED TO BE APPROPRIATED TO   824D LETTER 27   PROSE
        ERECT
    TILL I HAD GOT HIM OUT THERE I INTENDED TO HAVE LEFT HIM   827A LETTER 28   PROSE
    ADMIRABLE PRINTS TO IT BY FITTLER WHETHER YOU INTENDED   843B LETTER 43   PROSE
        IT OR
    INTENDED BUT I HAVE NEVER BEEN ABLE TO PRODUCE A SUFFICIENT   867C LETTER 66   PROSE
    INTENDED FLIGHT INTO YOUR DELIGHTFUL COUNTRY CONCUR IN   872D LETTER 76   PROSE
INTENDS
    HE WHO STANDS DOUBTING OF WHAT HE INTENDS WHETHER   386C ANNO WATSON   MARG
    THIS IS SURELY NOT WHAT JESUS INTENDS   750 EV GOSPEL(C)/N   20
    THIS SURELY IS NOT WHAT JESUS INTENDS   751 EV GOSPEL(D)/N   26

    ED A HUMAN FIRE FIERCE GLOWING AS THE WEDGE . . 1
      INTENSE INDIGNATION 22
      SE FIRES FOR HIS DWELLING 226
    ABROAD ON ALL THE WINDS RAGING INTENSE REDDENING 358
    AMES ROLLING INTENSE THRO THE WIDE UNIVERSE . . 359 F
     WHILE THEY SPOKE THE FLAMES COME ON INTENSE ROARING 364 FO
    VE NOW GIVEN TWO YEARS TO THE INTENSE STUDY OF THOSE 814A LET

    TRUTH THAT'S TOLD WITH BAD INTENT   432 AUGU
    AND THEIR SUBLIME INTENT GIVEN TO THEIR KINGS . . . . 543 IF TR
    DAUGHTERS IN LAW WITH INTENT TO RETURN TO HER OWN COUNTRY 584C DESC C

INTENTION
    WITH SOME BAD INTENTION OR AT LEAST WITH A PREJUDICED MIND 438A BLAKES M
    WITHOUT INTENTION & THAT MOST DISCRIMINATE & PARTICULAR 611B V LAST JU
    BUT IN COOL BLOODED DESIGN & INTENTION . . . . . . 615D V LAST JUD
    I CAME HERE WITH INTENTION TO ANNIHILATE THEE BUT . . 645 JERUSALEM 2
    TO DESTROY HIS EMANATION IS THEIR INTENTION . . . . 667 JERUSALEM 40
    BY TWO FIENDS INCARNATE WITH INTENTION THAT WHEN . . . 792B LETTER 4
    ANGELS I KNOW YOU WILL BE PLEASED WITH THE INTENTION . 799B LETTER 11
    EVERY ASSISTANCE IN HIS POWER WITHOUT KNOWING MY INTENTION 820B LETTER 25
    YOU HAD ACCEPTED THE SPIRIT OF P'S(PHILLIPS') INTENTION 842C LETTER 42
    TO MR PHILLIPS YOUR INTENTION OF TAKING THE BOOKS YOU WANT 846B LETTER 44   E
INTENTIONALLY
    DESTRUCTION OF ALL FORM OR OUTLINE PURPOSELY   463D ANNO REYNOLDS   MA
    & INTENTIONALLY
INTENTIONS
    LINE OF RECTITUDE AND CERTAINTY IN THE ACTIONS AND   585C DESC CAT 15   PROSE
    INTENTIONS
    THE MANNERS & INTENTIONS . . . . 611B V LAST JUDG/N PROSE
    IN WHICH HE SAYS IT ACCORDS NOT WITH HIS INTENTIONS . . 794D LETTER 6   PROSE
    & IF WE SUCCEED IN OUR INTENTIONS THE PRINTS TO THIS WORK 821C LETTER 25   PROSE
    TO KNOW WHAT HIS INTENTIONS ARE BUT HE SAYS PERHAPS . . 842D LETTER 42   PROSE
    FOR OUR GOOD SEAGRAVE & SAID I KNEW YOUR CHIEF INTENTIONS 856B LETTER 54   PROSE
    IN
INTERCHANGE
    IN INTERCHANGE SWEET OF THEIR JOYS . . . . 255 AHANIA 5   23
    OF FIRE IN INTERCHANGE OF BEAUTY & PERFECTION IN   500 MILTON 18   40
    THE DARKNESS
    IN MUTUAL INTERCHANGE AND FIRST THEIR EMANATIONS MEET . 733 JERUSALEM 88   5
INTERDICT
    A FAMINE OCCASIOND BY THE POPISH INTERDICT EDWARD   208D SUBJCTS HIST/N TITLE
    AT CALAIS
INTEREST   SEE SELF INTEREST
    ("MAN'S INTEREST...HIS GOD...VORTEX...CENTRE") PURE GOLD   66A ANNO LAVATER   MARG
    THAT IS TILL HE AGREES TO THE PRIESTS INTEREST . . . . 131C ANNO SWED PROV MARG
    [NEVER IS TO] TO EVERY THING BUT INTEREST BLIND . . . 175 HOW TO KNOW/N   8
    & DEPRESSION WHAT YOU FEAR IS YOUR TRUE INTEREST . . . 452C ANNO REYNOLDS   MARG
    DOES NOT KNOW EITHER HIS OWN INTEREST OR HIS DUTY . . 452C ANNO REYNOLDS   MARG
    THOSE WHO SAY THAT MEN ARE LED BY INTEREST ARE KNAVES . 572D DESC CAT 3   PROSE
    A KNAVISH CHARACTER WILL OFTEN SAY OF WHAT INTEREST IS 572D DESC CAT 3   PROSE
    IT TO ME
    INTEREST BUT FROM MALICE EVEN TO YOUR OWN DESTRUCTION . . 573A DESC CAT 3   PROSE
    SUBSERVIENT TO THE INTEREST OF THE MONOPOLIZING . . . 595B PUB ADDRESS/N PROSE
    IT BECAME THE INTEREST OF CERTAIN ENVIOUS KNAVES . . . 602C PUB ADDRESS/N PROSE
    & THE MORE TO HAVE AN INTEREST IN THE FRIEND OF SINNERS 621A JERUSALEM 3   PROSE
    IS THE INTEREST OF TRUE RELIGION & SCIENCE . . . . 812D LETTER 22   PROSE
    & WHENEVER ANY THING APPEARS TO AFFECT THAT INTEREST . 812D LETTER 22   PROSE
    IT SO MUCH H'S(HAYLEY'S) INTEREST TO EMPLOY ME . . . 819D LETTER 25   PROSE
    FRIENDSHIP IN PREFERENCE TO INTEREST THE PUBLISHERS ARE 821A LETTER 25   PROSE
    INTEREST OF ALL CONCERND IN MY WORKS OBSERVING THAT . . 822D LETTER 26   PROSE
    BE VERY HONEST AND VERY GENEROUS TOO WHERE HIS OWN   846C LETTER 44   PROSE
    INTEREST
    TO SERVE THAT INTEREST AND OFTEN I THINK UNFAIRLY HE ALWAYS 846C LETTER 44   PROSE
INTERESTED
    AS TO MYSELF ABOUT WHOM YOU ARE SO KINDLY INTERESTED I . 795C LETTER 6   PROSE
INTERESTING
    INTERESTING TO BLOCK HEADS AS IT ENDEAVOURS TO PROVE . 457D ANNO REYNOLDS   MARG
    INTERESTING HIMSELF IN THE GREAT OBJECT OF HIS FATHER'S 835C LETTER 35   PROSE
    FAME
    INTERESTING TOPIC IN BOTH YOUR LAST LETTERS GOD BE WITH YOU 841A LETTER 40   PROSE
    IT IS THEREFORE DOUBLY INTERESTING MR WALKER IS TRULY AN 845D LETTER 44   PROSE
    AMIABLE
    BECAUSE NO TIME SHOULD BE LOST IN THIS TRULY INTERESTING 849A LETTER 45   PROSE
    BUSINESS
INTERESTS
    AS THE MOST INNOCENT FORGETTER OF HIS OWN INTERESTS . . . 809C LETTER 20   PROSE
    THE LIFE OF ROMNEY HE INTERESTS HIMSELF IN IT & HAS   836A LETTER 35   PROSE
    PROMISED
INTERFERE
    I CONSIDERD IT MY DUTY TO INTERFERE I EXPRESSD MY   856B LETTER 54   PROSE
    OWN RESPECT
INTERIOR
    HERE RENDERD DEADLY WITHIN THE LIFE & INTERIOR VISION . 525 MILTON 34   52
    THAT IN THE INTERIOR WORLDS IS CARRIED ON IN FEAR   692 JERUSALEM 59   51
    & TREMBLING
INTERIORLY
    OPENING INTERIORLY INTO JERUSALEM & BABYLON SHINING   500 MILTON 18   41
    GLORIOUS
INTERIORS
    WE FLEE FROM THE INTERIORS OF ALBION'S HILLS AND MOUNTAINS 654 JERUSALEM 29   30
    LOS TOOK HIS GLOBE OF FIRE TO SEARCH THE INTERIORS   656 JERUSALEM 31   3
    OF ALBION'S

PAGE   TITLE   LINE

INTERIORS   (CONTINUED)
   OF LONDON BUT THE INTERIORS OF ALBION'S FIBRES & NERVES   658 JERUSALEM 32   4
      WERE HIDDEN
INTERLEAVD
   STILL TO BE WRITTEN & INTERLEAVD WITH BRASS & IRON & GOLD   316 FOUR ZOAS 6   172
INTERMARRY
   ALL WERE HIS FRIENDS & THEIR SONS & DAUGHTERS INTERMARRY   709 JERUSALEM 71   14
      IN BEULAH
INTERMEASURABLE
   STRAIT OR CROOKED IT IS ITSELF & NOT INTERMEASURABLE WITH   878B LETTER 88   PROSE
      OR
   ENGLISHMEN ARE ALL INTERMEASURABLE ONE BY ANOTHER   . . . 878B LETTER 88   PROSE
INTERMINGLED
   CITY & SANDY DESERT INTERMINGLED BEYOND MORTAL KEN   . . . 532 MILTON 40   27
INTERMINGLES
   EVERY PLEASURE THAT INTERMINGLES WITH THE DUTY OF   716D JERUSALEM 77   PROSE
      OUR STATION
INTERNAL
   THE INCREASE OF A STATE AS OF A MAN IS FROM INTERNAL   402C ANNO BACON   MARG
      IMPROVEMENT
   EVERY THING IN ETERNITY SHINES BY ITS OWN INTERNAL LIGHT   491 MILTON 10   16
      BUT THOU
   DARKENEST EVERY INTERNAL LIGHT WITH THE ARROWS OF   491 MILTON 10   17
      THY QUIVER
   THAT EVERY THING IS FIXD OPAKE WITHOUT INTERNAL LIGHT   . . 491 MILTON 10   20
   THE FIRST IN INTERNAL VALUE I THEN SAID IS IT AGREEABLE   856D LETTER 54   PROSE
      TO YOU
INTERPOSING
   NOTHING BUT MERCY CAN SAVE HIM NOTHING BUT MERCY   675 JERUSALEM 45   26
      INTERPOSING
INTERPRET
   FOR A BOY [NEVER LEARNS SO MUCH] CAN'T INTERPRET THE THING   552 WHY CUPID/N   11
INTERRUPT
   THIS QUITE PROVOKD MISS GITTIPIN TO INTERRUPT HER   . . . 53B ISLAND MOON 8   PROSE
INTERSECT
   AND BROOKS BETWEEN TO INTERSECT THE MEADOWS IN THEIR COURSE   493 MILTON 12   19
INTERSECTING
   FOUR INTERSECTING GLOBES & THE EGG FORMD WORLD OF LOS   . . 524 MILTON 34   33
INTERSPERSED
   TO HAVE APPEARD IN CHAUCER'S TIME INTERSPERSED   . . . . 567A DESC CAT 3   PROSE
   TO HAVE APPEARD IN CHAUCER'S TIME INTERSPERSED   . . . . 588D CHAUCER/N   PROSE
   TO HAVE APPEARD IN CHAUCER'S TIME INTERSPERSED   . . . . 590B CHAUCER 2   PROSE
INTERVALS
   THEM OFF PRESENTLY THIS PICTURE WAS PAINTED AT INTERVALS   581C DESC CAT 7   PROSE
   THIS PICTURE WAS LIKEWISE PAINTED AT INTERVALS   . . . . 582B DESC CAT 9   PROSE
INTERWOVE
   IN SOLEMN GLOOM OF BRANCHES INTERWOVE   . . . . 15 IMIT SPEN/PS   48
INTERWOVEN
   IN MOMENTS NEW CREATED FOR DELUSION INTERWOVEN ROUND ABOUT   494 MILTON 13   39
   IMMINGLED INTERWOVEN GLISTENING TO THE SICKENING SIGHT   . . 727 JERUSALEM 83   32
INTESTINES
   IN THE STOMACH & INTESTINES TERRIBLE DEADLY UNUTTERABLE   524 MILTON 34   16
INTHROND
   BUT THOU O SON WHOM I HAVE CROWNED AND INTHROND THEE STRONG   334 FOUR ZOAS 7B   *   52
INTIMACY
   I KNEW THE MEN INTIMATELY FROM THEIR INTIMACY WITH BASIRE   593B PUB ADDRESS/N   PROSE
   BY HIS INTIMACY WITH BASIRE & I KNEW HIM TO BE   . . . . 603B PUB ADDR AD/N   PROSE
INTIMATE
   IT SEEMS AS IF ALL ROMNEY'S INTIMATE FRIENDS   . . . . . 844A LETTER 43   PROSE
INTIMATELY
   I KNEW THE MEN INTIMATELY FROM THEIR INTIMACY WITH BASIRE   593B PUB ADDRESS/N   PROSE
   TO YOUR OWN DESTRUCTION WOOLETT I KNEW VERY INTIMATELY   . . 603B PUB ADDR AD/N   PROSE
INTIMATIONS
   BUT THE MEER DRUDGERY OF BUSINESS & INTIMATIONS   . . . . 812C LETTER 22   PROSE
INTIRE   SEE ENTIRE
   THEIR LIFE'S WHOLE COMFORT TO INTIRE SCORN & INJURY & DEATH   506 MILTON 23   2
   TO THE INTIRE ABROGATION OF EXPERIMENTAL THEORY   . . . . 682B JERUSALEM 52   PROSE
   BUT HOPE & PRAY FOR HER INTIRE RECOVERY   . . . . 840A LETTER 38   PROSE
   INTIRE SECRET BETWEEN MR P(PHILLIPS) MR H(HOARE) & MYSELF   841B LETTER 41   PROSE
INTIRELY   SEE ENTIRELY
   SAYS I DID SO & SO UNDERMINES THE VERACITY INTIRELY   . . . 391B ANNO WATSON   MARG
   HER ALSO INTIRELY ABSTRACTING HIMSELF FROM FEMALE LOVES   522 MILTON 33   16
   HAS INTIRELY PUT AN END TO ALL GENUINE & APPROPRIATE EFFECT   599B PUB ADDRESS/N   *PROSE
   PERSONS & MACHINERY INTIRELY NEW TO THE INHABITANTS OF   823A LETTER 26   PROSE
      EARTH
   FINISHD ENGRAVINGS WILL DO AS OUTLINE INTIRELY OMITS   . . 848A LETTER 45   PROSE
   LEFT ALL TO YOU INTIRELY I DO THINK FROM THE LIBERALITY OF   857A LETTER 54   *PROSE
   DUPLICATES TO OTHERS WHICH HE HAS THEY ARE INTIRELY AT   . . 877B LETTER 86   PROSE
INTOLERABLE
   INTOLERABLE AT LENGTH AN AWFUL WONDER BURST   . . . . . 347 FOUR ZOAS 8   250
INTOLERANT
   WAS ONE OF THIS NUMBER HE WAS AS INTOLERANT AS AN   615B V LAST JUDG/N   PROSE
      INQUISITOR
INTOXICATED
   HIS MOTHER TO THE WINDS OF HEAVEN INTOXICATED WITH   . . . 326 FOUR ZOAS 7   233
   MOVING BESIDE ME TILL INTOXICATED WITH THE WOVEN LABYRINTH   732 JERUSALEM 87   4
INTOXICATING
   THUS THEY CONFERRD AMONG THE INTOXICATING FUMES OF MYSTERY   328 FOUR ZOAS 7   315
   INSPIRING SECRECY & LAMPS THEY BORE INTOXICATING FUMES   . . 333 FOUR ZOAS 7B   28
   THEY TAKE UP INTO THEIR HEAVENS IN INTOXICATING DELIGHT   484 MILTON 5   10
   YET THE INTOXICATING DELIGHT THAT THEY TAKE IN THEIR WORK   691 JERUSALEM 59   34
   DRINKING HIS EMANATION IN INTOXICATING BLISS REJOICING   701 JERUSALEM 65   58
      IN GIANT DANCE

```
                                                                    PAGE    TITLE              LINE
INTOXICATION
     SAT IN A [SWEET] DREAD INTOXICATION OF [FALSE WOVEN BLISS]       266 FOUR ZOAS 1            91
          . . .
     TO FEED THEM WITH INTOXICATION FROM THE WINE PRESSES OF         292 FOUR ZOAS 3            35
          LUVAH
     THOUGHT THE SOLDIER ABUSIVE & IN AN INTOXICATION OF MIND       438D BLAKES MEMORAN      PROSE
     HERE TURN INTO POISONOUS STUPOR & DEADLY INTOXICATION  . .      672 JERUSALEM 43          29
     DRINKING THEIR LIVES IN SWEET INTOXICATION HENCE AROSE          701 JERUSALEM 65          65
          FROM BATH
     SOFT INVISIBLE DRINKING HIS SIGHS IN SWEET INTOXICATION         723 JERUSALEM 80          60
     AND PLAYING IN THE THUNDEROUS LOOM IN SWEET INTOXICATION        723 JERUSALEM 80          80
     CADENCES & PLAYING IN SWEET INTOXICATION AMONG THE              733 JERUSALEM 88          24
          GLISTENING
INTOXICATIONS
     IS DIVIDED IN THE INTOXICATIONS OF PLEASURE & AFFECTION         690 JERUSALEM 58          14
INTREAT        SEE ENTREAT
     THEY BEG THEY INTREAT IN VAIN NOW THEY LISTEND NOT              363 FOUR ZOAS 9      *   257
          TO INTREATY
     BROTHER OF JESUS WHAT HAVE I DONE INTREAT THY LORD FOR ME       364 FOUR ZOAS 9          270
     & ON THIS DISCRIMINATION ALL ART IS FOUNDED I INTREAT THEN     611B V LAST JUDG/N      PROSE
     PRAY LET ME INTREAT YOU TO PERSEVERE IN YOUR DESIGNING  . .    795B LETTER 6            PROSE
     EXCUSE I INTREAT YOU MY NOT RETURNING THANKS AT THE PROPER     798A LETTER 10           PROSE
     NOW LET ME INTREAT YOU TO GIVE ME ORDERS TO FURNISH EVERY      808B LETTER 19           PROSE
     INTREAT YOU TO TAKE DUE CARE OF BOTH IT IS A PART OF OUR       811C LETTER 22           PROSE
          DUTY
     INTREAT YOU TO EXCUSE FAULTS FOR PORTRAIT PAINTING IS THE      815C LETTER 23           PROSE
          DIRECT
     THEY BEG THEY INTREAT THEY DROP THEIR TEARS   . . . . .         817 HAPPINESS/L           19
     THEREFORE AS IT IS MY DUTY BEG & INTREAT YOU NEVER TO MOUNT    833C LETTER 33           PROSE
INTREATED
     HE SOFT INTREATED LOS TO GIVE TO HIM PALAMABRON'S STATION       486 MILTON 7              8
     I HAVE ASKED & INTREATED DIVINE HELP BUT FEAR CONTINUES        876B LETTER 83           PROSE
INTREATIES
     HIS SERVICE TILL BY REPEATED OFFERS AND REPEATED               486 MILTON 7             11
          INTREATIES
INTREATING
     NOW INTREATING [?FLAME] FLAMING FIRE . . . . . . . .           422 BENEATH/N       *    24
     NOW INTREATING [SWEET DESIRE] IRON WIRE . . . . . . .          422 BENEATH/N             25
     NOW INTREATING TEARS & SIGHS   . . . . . . . . . .             422 BENEATH/N             26
     NOW INTREATING BURNING FIRE . . . . . . . . . . .              424 THE GOLDEN NET        23
     NOW INTREATING IRON WIRE . . . . . . . . . . . .               424 THE GOLDEN NET        24
     NOW INTREATING TEARS & SIGHS . . . . . . . . . .               424 THE GOLDEN NET        25
INTREATS
     SHE STILL INTREATS AND STILL SHE GRASPS HIS VIGOROUS KNEES      38B SAMSON/PS           PROSE
     WONDER WHICH ALWAYS INTREATS HIM TO LEAVE MORTAL THINGS       611A V LAST JUDG/N       PROSE
INTREATY
     THEY BEG THEY INTREAT IN VAIN NOW THEY LISTEND NOT              363 FOUR ZOAS 9      *   257
          TO INTREATY
INTRICACY
     OF LABYRINTHINE INTRICACY TWENTY-SEVEN FOLDS OF OPAKENESS       498 MILTON 17            26
     OF LABYRINTHINE INTRICACY SO SHALL THEY FOLD THE WORLD  . .     728 JERUSALEM 83         37
     SIMPLE WITHOUT INTRICACY IT SEEMS TO BE THE   . . . . .        801D LETTER 14          PROSE
INTRICATE
     BEGAN INTRICATE PIPES THAT DREW IN . . . . . . . .             259 BOOK OF LOS 4         69
     IN INTRICATE WAYS BIQUADRATE TRAPEZIUMS RHOMBS RHOMBOIDS        287 FOUR ZOAS 2         284
     IN INTRICATE LABYRINTHS OERSPREADING MANY A GRIZLY DEEP         321 FOUR ZOAS 3          35
     AND IN THEIR STEAD INTRICATE WHEELS INVENTED WHEEL WITHOUT      337 FOUR ZOAS 7B        179
          WHEEL
     ITS INTRICATE LABYRINTHS NOW THE OBDURATE HEART WAS BROKEN      342 FOUR ZOAS 8          33
     ONE HUNDRED YEARS PONDRING THE INTRICATE MAZES OF              481 MILTON 2             17
          PROVIDENCE
     INTRICATE LABYRINTHS OF TIMES AND SPACES UNKNOWN               494 MILTON 13            43
          THAT LEUTHA LIVED
     IT ISSUES THRO THE DARK & INTRICATE CAVES OF THE MUNDANE       507 MILTON 23            22
          SHELL
     KNOWS IN ITS INTRICATE MAZES OF DELIGHT ARTFUL TO WEAVE        512 MILTON 26             4
     AMONG THE WINDING PLACES OF DEEP CONTEMPLATION INTRICATE       657 JERUSALEM 31         22
     IT IS THE GATE OF LOS WITHOUTSIDE IS THE MILL INTRICATE        666 JERUSALEM 39          3
          DREADFUL
     AND IN THEIR STEAD INTRICATE WHEELS INVENTED WHEEL WITHOUT      700 JERUSALEM 65         21
          WHEEL
INTRICATELY
     SOFT DELUDING ODOURS IN SPIRAL VOLUTIONS INTRICATELY           701 JERUSALEM 65     *    66
          WINDING
INTRIPLED
     KLOPSTOCK FELT THE [NINEFOLD] INTRIPLED TURN   . . . . .       187 WHEN KLOPSTK/N       15
INTRODUCD
     THEY WERE INTRODUCD TO THE DIVINE PRESENCE & THEY KNEELED       277 FOUR ZOAS 1         482
          DOWN
INTRODUCE
     THIS SENTENCE IS TO INTRODUCE ANOTHER IN CONDEMNATION   . .   472B ANNO REYNOLDS       MARG
INTRODUCED
     HAS HERE ALSO INTRODUCED ONE OF THE RICH CITIZENS OF LONDON   568C DESC CAT 3          PROSE
     HE HAS INTRODUCED A CHARACTER THAT CHAUCER HAS NOT   . . .    575B DESC CAT 3          PROSE
     WHY HE HAS INTRODUCED A GOLDSMITH AND WHAT IS THE WIT OF IT   575B DESC CAT 3          PROSE
     BUT THE PROSPECTUS TELLS US THAT THE PAINTER HAS INTRODUCED   575C DESC CAT 3          PROSE
     IN THIS DESIGN IS INTRODUCED . . . . . . . . . . .           618B ILLUS MILTON        PROSE
INTRODUCERS
     THE TWO INTRODUCERS INTO ETERNAL LIFE WOMEN WITH INFANTS      444B LAST JUDGMNT/L      PROSE
INTRODUCTION
     INTRODUCTION . . . . . . . . . . . . . . . . . .             111A INTRODUCTN/SI       TITLE
     INTRODUCTION . . . . . . . . . . . . . . . . . .             210B INTRODUCTN/SE       TITLE
```

990

INTRODUCTION   (CONTINUED)
    INTRODUCTION PIPING DOWN THE VALLEYS &C   . . . . . .   SUPP LETTER 66A   *PROSE
    INTRODUCTION HEAR THE VOICE OF THE BARD &C   . . . . .   SUPP LETTER 66A   *PROSE
INTRUSION
    SHOULD HAVE BEEN FREE FROM HIS IMPERTINENCE & INTRUSION   438D BLAKES MEMORAN   PROSE
INTUITION
    INVENTION IDENTITY & MELODY ARE OBJECTS OF INTUITION   . .   474D ANNO REYNOLDS   MARG
INTWINE
    AND AROUND OUR SOULS INTWINE   . . . .   7 LOVE HARMNY/PS   2
INVENT
    TO INVENT ALLEGORIC RICHES   . . . .   247 SONG OF LOS 6   18
    BEATS ALL THE LIES YOU CAN INVENT   . . . .   432 AUGURIES   54
    HOW TO EXECUTE WHAT THEY COULD NOT THINK OR INVENT   . .   467C ANNO REYNOLDS   MARG
    IF TO INVENT & TO DRAW WELL HINDERS THE EXECUTIVE POWER IN   591B PUB ADDRESS/N   PROSE
    THAT WELL KNOWN SAYING ENGLISHMEN IMPROVE WHAT OTHERS   595C PUB ADDRESS/N   PROSE
        INVENT
    & I SAY HE WHO INVENT CAN EXECUTE   . . . .   790C LETTER 2   PROSE
INVENTED
    INVENTED A METHOD OF PRINTING BOTH LETTER-PRESS AND   207B PRSPECTUS 1793   PROSE
        ENGRAVING
    INTO THE BLUE EXPANSE & I INVENTED WITH LABORIOUS ART   . .   312 FOUR ZOAS 6   31
    AND IN THEIR STEAD INTRICATE WHEELS INVENTED WHEEL WITHOUT   337 FOUR ZOAS 7B   179
        WHEEL
    AND IN THEIR STEAD INTRICATE WHEELS INVENTED WHEEL WITHOUT   700 JERUSALEM 65   21
        WHEEL
INVENTING
    ABOUT JOHN OF BRUGES INVENTING OIL COLOURS   . . . . . .   565B DESC CAT 2   PROSE
INVENTION
    MR BLAKE'S POWERS OF INVENTION VERY EARLY ENGAGED   . .   207C PRSPECTUS 1793   PROSE
    INVENTION DEPENDS ALTOGETHER UPON EXECUTION   . . . .   446D ANNO REYNOLDS   MARG
    SO IS THE INVENTION PERFECT OR IMPERFECT   . . . . .   446D ANNO REYNOLDS   MARG
    ALL BUT NAMES OF PERSONS & PLACES IS INVENTION   . .   461D ANNO REYNOLDS   MARG
    WHEN A MAN TALKS OF ACQUIRING INVENTION &   . . . . .   469D ANNO REYNOLDS   MARG
    INVENTION IDENTITY & MELODY ARE OBJECTS OF INTUITION   . .   474D ANNO REYNOLDS   MARG
    THE INVENTION OF A PORTABLE FRESCO   560D EXHIBITION ADV   TITLE
    AS THEY ARE CALLED WERE THE INVENTION OF GREEK ARTISTS   .   565D DESC CAT 2   PROSE
    ELEVATED INTO ITS OWN PROPER SPHERE OF INVENTION   . . .   576B DESC CAT 4   PROSE
    NO MAN CAN IMPROVE AN ORIGINAL INVENTION   . . . . .   595C PUB ADDRESS/N   PROSE
    NOR CAN AN ORIGINAL INVENTION EXIST WITHOUT EXECUTION   .   595C PUB ADDRESS/N   PROSE
    EXECUTION IS ONLY THE RESULT OF INVENTION   . . . . .   596B PUB ADDRESS/N   PROSE
    [THE ART OF INVENTION NOT OF IMITATION]   . . . . . .   600C PUB ADDRESS/N   PROSE
    MY CONCEPTION & INVENTION ARE ON ALL HANDS ALLOWD   . .   601D PUB ADDRESS/N   PROSE
    FOR INVENTION & DRAWING HAS GENERALLY BEEN ACCOMPANIED BY   602A PUB ADDRESS/N   PROSE
    JUST EQUAL IN INVENTION & IN EXECUTION AS MY WORKS SHEW   602A PUB ADDRESS/N   PROSE
    THAT EXECUTION IS THE POWER OF ONE & INVENTION OF ANOTHER   790C LETTER 2   PROSE
    FOR FEAR I SHOULD EVAPORATE THE SPIRIT OF MY INVENTION   .   792B LETTER 4   PROSE
    [FOOLS' OPINIONS & ENDEAVOURS DESTROY INVENTION]   . . . .   SUPP ANNO REYNOLDS   * MARG
INVENTIONS
    EXHIBITION OF PAINTINGS IN FRESCO POETICAL AND HISTORICAL   560A EXHIBITION ADV   TITLE
        INVENTIONS
    INVENTIONS PAINTED BY WILLIAM BLAKE IN WATER COLOURS BEING   563A DESC CAT   TITLE
    OF APPROPRIATE EXECUTION RESULTING FROM THE INVENTIONS   .   582D DESC CAT 9   PROSE
    TO MY INVENTIONS THE EXECUTIVE PART THEY NEVER DISPUTED   601D PUB ADDRESS/N   PROSE
    THAN TO ENGRAVE ONE'S OWN INVENTIONS AND   . . . . .   794B LETTER 5   PROSE
    YOUR INVENTIONS OF INTELLECTUAL VISIONS ARE THE STAMINA   795B LETTER 6   PROSE
    BEGUN TO PRINT AN ACCOUNT OF MY VARIOUS INVENTIONS IN ART   865D LETTER 63   PROSE
INVENTIVE
    THUS REYNOLDS DEPRECIATES THE EFFORTS OF INVENTIVE GENIUS   455D ANNO REYNOLDS   MARG
    IS NOW TO BE DECIDED BY THE PUBLIC MR B'S (BLAKE'S)   591B PUB ADDRESS/N   PROSE
        INVENTIVE
INVENTOR
    NO ONE CAN FINISH SO HIGH AS THE ORIGINAL INVENTOR   . . .   555 BLAKES APL/N 1   19
    NO ONE CAN FINISH SO HIGH AS THE ORIGINAL INVENTOR   . .   556 BLAKES APL/N 2   18
    NO ONE CAN FINISH SO HIGH AS THE ORIGINAL INVENTOR   . .   596 BLAKES APOL/PA   12
INVENTORS
    AND BUNGLING GREAT INVENTORS IN ALL AGES KNEW THIS   . . .   585B DESC CAT 15   PROSE
    THAT GREAT INVENTORS CANNOT EXECUTE THIS OPINION IS   . . .   601D PUB ADDRESS/N   PROSE
INVENTS
    LOCKE SAYS IT SAME FACULTY THAT INVENTS JUDGES   . . . .   790C LETTER 2   PROSE
INVERNES
    DAN BUTE CAITNES CLAKMANAN NAPTHALI NAIRN INVERNES   638 JERUSALEM 16   55
        LINLITHGO
INVERT
    INTO THEIR OWN DESTRUCTION IF PERHAPS HE MIGHT [INVERT]   344 FOUR ZOAS 8   * 138
        AVERT
INVINCIBLE
    AND THOU O WARRIOR MAID INVINCIBLE   . . . .   15 IMIT SPEN/PS   44
INVISIBILITY
    HIDING HIS SPECTRE IN INVISIBILITY FROM THE TIMOROUS SHADE   732 JERUSALEM 86   54
INVISIBLE
    THE ENEMY FIGHT IN CHAINS INVISIBLE CHAINS BUT HEAVY   . .   18 EDW THIRD/PS 1   13
    WHY ART THOU SILENT & INVISIBLE   . . . .   171 TO NOBODADDY/N   1
    THE INVISIBLE WORM   . . . .   175 SICK ROSE/N   2
    THE INVISIBLE WORM   . . . .   213 SICK ROSE/SE   2
    DIRE SHRIEKD HIS INVISIBLE LUST   . . . .   249 AHANIA 2   30
    JEALOUS THO SHE WAS INVISIBLE   . . . .   250 AHANIA 2   37
    SEND THIS ROCK SWIFT INVISIBLE THRO   . . . . . .   251 AHANIA 3   28
    SUDDEN SINGS THE ROCK SWIFT & INVISIBLE   . . . . .   251 AHANIA 3   39
    I SEE INVISIBLE DESCEND INTO THE GARDENS OF VALA   . . .   272 FOUR ZOAS 1   299
    LUVAH WALKING ON THE WINDS I SEE THE INVISIBLE KNIFE   .   272 FOUR ZOAS 1   300
    THE WONDROUS WORK FLOW FORTH LIKE VISIBLE OUT OF   287 FOUR ZOAS 2   260
        THE INVISIBLE

	PAGE	TITLE	LINE

INVISIBLE   (CONTINUED)
    INVISIBLE OR VISIBLE DRAWN OUT IN LENGTH OR STRETCHD IN   338 FOUR ZOAS 7B   *   222
      BREADTH
    AND SO BECOME INVISIBLE TO THOSE WHO STILL REMAIN   . . .   355 FOUR ZOAS 8   554
    TO SEE IF HUNGRY WINDS ARE ABROAD WITH THEIR INVISIBLE ARMY   355 FOUR ZOAS 8   560
    INVISIBLE LUVAH IN BRIGHT CLOUDS HOVERD OVER VALA'S HEAD   367 FOUR ZOAS 9   385
    ITS OFFERINGS EVEN TILL JESUS THE IMAGE OF THE INVISIBLE   481 MILTON 2   12
      GOD
    A SCHEME OF HUMAN CONDUCT INVISIBLE & INCOMPREHENSIBLE . .   483 MILTON 4   13
    VISIBLE OR INVISIBLE TO THE SLOTHFUL VEGETATING MAN   . . .   513 MILTON 27   18
    AND EMPIRES OF CHAOS INVISIBLE TO THE VEGETABLE MAN   . . .   528 MILTON 37   49
    AND I WILL BE MERCIFUL TO THEE BE THOU INVISIBLE TO ALL   629 JERUSALEM 10   30
    TO WHOM I MAKE THEE INVISIBLE BUT CHIEF TO MY OWN CHILDREN   629 JERUSALEM 10   31
    AT THE SUBLIME LABOURS FOR LOS COMPELLD THE INVISIBLE   630 JERUSALEM 10   65
      SPECTRE
    THEE TO BE INVISIBLE TO ANY BUT WHOM I PLEASE & WHEN   . .   639 JERUSALEM 17   40
    FROM HEAVEN TO EARTH HOWLING INVISIBLE BUT NOT INVISIBLE   702 JERUSALEM 66   11
    BY INVISIBLE HATREDS ADJOIND THEY SEEM REMOTE AND SEPARATE   703 JERUSALEM 66   53
    INVISIBLE OR VISIBLE STRETCHD OUT IN LENGTH OR SPREAD IN   723 JERUSALEM 80   54
      BREADTH
    SOFT INVISIBLE DRINKING HIS SIGHS IN SWEET INTOXICATION   723 JERUSALEM 80   60
    THE INVISIBLE LOVELY ONE GIVING HIM A FORM ACCORDING TO   723 JERUSALEM 80   78
INVISIBLY
    [SILENTLY INVISIBLY]   .   .   .   .   161 NEVER PAIN/N   4
    SILENTLY INVISIBLY   .   .   .   .   161 NEVER PAIN/N   11
INVITE
    I THEREFORE INVITE THOSE NOBLEMEN AND GENTLEMEN WHO ARE ITS   561B EXHIBITION ADV   PROSE
INVITED
    INTO WHICH HE WAS INVITED AS AN ASSISTANT BY A GARDENER   827A LETTER 28   PROSE
      AT WORK
    THEREIN WITHOUT MY KNOWLEDGE THAT HE WAS SO INVITED I   . .   827A LETTER 28   PROSE
INVITES
    INVITES THE ADMIRERS OF OLD ENGLISH PORTRAITS TO LOOK AT   596C PUB ADDRESS/N   PROSE
      HIS PRINT
INVITING
    EVER INVITING GUESTS TO THE MARRIAGE O FOOLISH PHILOSOPHY   834A LETTER 33   PROSE
    THE LIBERAL MAN INVITING THE TRAVELLER INTO HIS HOUSE   . .   SUPP ILLUS GRAY   *TITLE
INVOKE
    ASSISTANCE OF BRUNO'S FAIRIES BUT I INVOKE THE GOOD GENII   801B LETTER 13   PROSE
INVOKES
    KING DAVID DESIRED SO FERVENTLY & INVOKES SO PATHETICLY   153D MARRIAGE HH 12   PROSE
INVOLUNTARY
    INVOLUNTARY TO THE COUCH WHERE ENITHARMON LAY   .   .   .   .   .   305 FOUR ZOAS 4   292
INVOLVD
    IN DARKNESS AND DEEP CLOUDS INVOLVD   .   .   .   .   260 BOOK OF LOS 5   57
    UPON THE WINDS IN CLOUDS INVOLVD UTTERING HIS VOICE IN   283 FOUR ZOAS 2   133
      THUNDERS
    OVER THE BURNING DESARTS THEN THE DESARTS PASSD INVOLVD   314 FOUR ZOAS 6   110
      IN CLOUDS
    INVOLVD EIGHT THEIR WEBS ROLLD OUTWARDS INTO DARKNESS   . .   626 JERUSALEM 7   46
    INVOLVD THE EIGHT SUCH ARE THE GENERATIONS OF THE GIANT   626 JERUSALEM 7   49
      ALBION
    INVOLVD JERUSALEM & THE WHEELS OF ALBION'S SONS TURND   696 JERUSALEM 62   32
      HOARSE
INVOLVE
    ROLLING VOLUMES OF GREY MIST INVOLVE CHURCHES PALACES   242 EUROPE 12   3
      TOWERS
    GLORYING TO INVOLVE ALBION'S BODY IN FIRES OF ETERNAL WAR   493 MILTON 13   6
    RELIGION TO INVOLVE ALL ALBION'S SONS AND WHEN THEY HAD   626 JERUSALEM 7   45
    IN CLOUD OF SECRET GLOOM WHICH BEHOLD INVOLVE ME ROUND   660 JERUSALEM 33   47
      ABOUT
INVOLVED
    TEMPTING THAT I HAVE ALREADY INVOLVED MYSELF IN ENGAGEMENTS   865C LETTER 63   PROSE
INVOLVES
    HIS LEFT SCOTLAND HIS BOSOM GIRT WITH GOLD INVOLVES   .   .   .   531 MILTON 39   42
INVOLVING
    INVOLVING THE DIVINE VISION IN COLOURS OF AUTUMN RIPENESS   659 JERUSALEM 33   30
INVULNERABLE
    INVULNERABLE THO NAKED SAVE WHERE CLOUDS ROLL ROUND HER   196 AMERICA PREL 1   7
      LOINS
    AND EVERY YEAR INVULNERABLE BARRIERS WITH HIGH TOWERS   . .   516 MILTON 28   55
    SUCH AN ARTIST AS FUSELI IS INVULNERABLE HE NEEDS NOT MY   864A LETTER 61   PROSE
INWARD
    INWARD GRIEVD HE SAW AND LOVD THE BEAUTEOUS SUPPLIANT   . .   39B SAMSON/PS   PROSE
    THE SENSES INWARD RUSHD SHRINKING   .   .   .   .   236 URIZEN 25   29
    I SEE IT SMILE & I ROLL INWARD & MY VOICE IS PAST   .   .   .   239 EUROPE PREL 2   16
    JUSTLING TOGETHER IN THE VOID SUSPENDED BY INWARD FIRES   276 FOUR ZOAS 1   428
    HIS INWARD EYES CLOSING FROM THE DIVINE VISION & ALL   .   .   279 FOUR ZOAS 1   558
    FROM ENITHARMON'S INWARD PARTS BUT THE BRIGHT FEMALE TERROR   279 FOUR ZOAS 1   564
    AT THE TURNING WHEELS OF HEAVEN SHRUNK AWAY INWARD WITHRING   317 FOUR ZOAS 6   *   236
      AWAY
    ON RIFTED ROCKS SUSPENDED IN THE AIR BY INWARD FIRES   .   .   363 FOUR ZOAS 9   241
    BUT TRAVELLERS TO ETERNITY PASS INWARD TO GOLGONOOZA   .   .   498 MILTON 17   30
    AND EVERY GENERATED BODY IN ITS INWARD FORM   .   .   .   .   .   512 MILTON 26   31
    AND ALBION FLED INWARD AMONG THE CURRENTS OF HIS RIVERS   642 JERUSALEM 19   39
    INWARD COMPLACENCY OF SOUL A SELF-ANNIHILATION   .   .   .   .   646 JERUSALEM 23   15
    WHY HAVE THOU ELEVATE INWARD O DWELLER OF OUTWARD CHAMBERS   660 JERUSALEM 34   10
    O SEARCH & SEE TURN YOUR EYES INWARD OPEN O THOU WORLD   675 JERUSALEM 44   41
    AND EVERY HUMAN VEGETATED FORM IN ITS INWARD RECESSES   .   .   714 JERUSALEM 54   73
    WITH MY INWARD EYE TIS AN OLD MAN GREY   .   .   .   .   .   .   817 HAPPINESS/L   29
    TWAS OUTWARD A SUN INWARD LOS IN HIS MIGHT   .   .   .   .   .   818 HAPPINESS/L   58

	PAGE	TITLE	LINE

INWARDLY
TURN INWARDLY THINE EYES & THERE BEHOLD THE LAMB OF GOD   330 FOUR ZOAS 7   415
INCESSANT STERN DISDAIN HIS SCALY FORM GNAWS INWARDLY   . 352 FOUR ZOAS 8   434
INWARDS
INWARDS INTO A DEEP WORLD WITHIN . . . .   224 URIZEN 4   15
ENVENOMD THOU ROLLST INWARDS . . . .   268 FOUR ZOAS 1   157
HIS BOSOM INWARDS SHONE WITH FIRES BUT THE STONES BECOMING   490 MILTON 9   32
OPAKE
OF MAN INWARDS INTO THE WORLDS OF THOUGHT INTO ETERNITY   623 JERUSALEM 5   19
INCREASING INWARDS INTO LENGTH AND BREADTH AND HEIGHTH . . 635 JERUSALEM 14   18
THE EAST IS INWARDS & THE WEST IS OUTWARDS EVERY WAY   . . 635 JERUSALEM 14   30
HE SAW ALSO THE FOUR POINTS OF ALBION REVERSD INWARDS   . 658 JERUSALEM 32   7
INWOVE
HIS LOINS INWOVE WITH SILKEN FIRES ARE LIKE A FURNACE   308 FOUR ZOAS 5   135
FIERCE
FIBRES HAD FROM THE CHAIN OF JEALOUSY INWOVE THEMSELVES   309 FOUR ZOAS 5   157
THEY STAIND HIM WITH POISONOUS BLUE THEY INWOVE HIM IN   699 JERUSALEM 65   9
CRUEL BOOTS
INWOVEN   SEE ENWOVEN
I WILL HAVE KINGS INWOVEN UPON IT & COUNCELLORS & MIGHTY   499 MILTON 18   15
MEN
MY SOUL IS MELTED AWAY INWOVEN WITHIN THE VEIL   . . . .   645 JERUSALEM 23   4
INWRAP
FIRES INWRAP THE EARTHLY GLOBE YET MAN IS NOT CONSUMD   . . 199 AMERICA 8   15
INWRAP THE PARENTS IN COLD CLOUDS AS THEY BEND HOWLING OVER   309 FOUR ZOAS 5   171
INWRAP THE IMMORTAL LIMBS STRUGGLING IN TERRIFIC JOY   . . 381 FOUR ZOAS AD 2   2
THE WEEDS OF DEATH INWRAP HIS HANDS & FEET BLOWN INCESSANT   741 JERUSALEM 94   5
INWRAPPED   SEE ENWRAPPED
UPON THE OOZY ROCK INWRAPPED WITH THE WEEDS OF DEATH   . 354 FOUR ZOAS 8   514
AGAINST THE ROCK WHICH WAS INWRAPPED WITH THE WEEDS OF   497 MILTON 15   40
DEATH
IONICK
[?HE ?COULD ?NOT (TELL) IONICK (FROM) THE (CORINTHIAN) OR]   SUPP ANNO REYNOLDS   * MARG
IRE
AND BURSTING FORTH [WITH] HIS FURIOUS IRE . . . . . .   749 EV GOSPEL(B)/N   33
IRELAND
DRIVEN OER THE GUARDIANS OF IRELAND AND SCOTLAND AND WALES   202 AMERICA 15   13
AND PRAISE THRO THE WHOLE EARTH WERE REARD FROM IRELAND   486 MILTON 6   22
LEANS ON THE ROCKS OF ERIN'S LAND IRELAND ANCIENT NATION   531 MILTON 39   45
OF THE GIANTS OF IRELAND AND BRITAIN OF THE   . . . . . 577D DESC CAT 5   PROSE
THE THIRTY-SIX OF SCOTLAND & THE THIRTY-FOUR OF IRELAND   637 JERUSALEM 16   29
TO THE FOUR POINTS CONDUCT TO ENGLAND & SCOTLAND & IRELAND   637 JERUSALEM 16   33
SUSSEX & KENT ARE HER SCATTERD GARMENTS IRELAND HER HOLY   653 JERUSALEM 29   20
PLACE
THE GRAVES THUNDER BENEATH HIS FEET FROM IRELAND TO JAPAN   661 JERUSALEM 34   42
UPON THE LAKES OF IRELAND FROM RATHLIN TO BALTIMORE   . . 679 JERUSALEM 49   4
IRELAND TO JAPAN FURIOUS HER LIONS & TYGERS & WOLVES SPORT   698 JERUSALEM 63   34
BEFORE
STRETCHING OVER EUROPE & ASIA FROM IRELAND TO JAPAN . . . 704 JERUSALEM 67   7
DWELL OVER THE FOUR PROVINCES OF IRELAND IN HEAVENLY LIGHT   710 JERUSALEM 71   52
AND THE THIRTY-TWO COUNTIES OF THE FOUR PROVINCES   711 JERUSALEM 72   1
OF IRELAND
WHOSE FOUNDATIONS REMAIN IN THE THIRTY-TWO COUNTIES OF   711 JERUSALEM 72   14
IRELAND
AND THE NAMES OF THE THIRTY-TWO COUNTIES OF IRELAND ARE   711 JERUSALEM 72   17
THESE
IRELAND'S
FROM IRELAND'S ROCKS TO SCANDINAVIA PERSIA AND TARTARY   . . 727 JERUSALEM 83   21
TO IRELAND'S FARTHEST ROCKS WHERE GIANTS BUILDED THEIR   735 JERUSALEM 89   50
CAUSEWAY
IRISH
AND THE RIBBLE THUNDER INTO THE IRISH SEA AS THE TWELVE   736 JERUSALEM 90   16
SONS
IRON
NOR BEND THY PILLARS WITH THINE IRON CAR   . . . .   2 TO WINTER/PS   4
THINE IRON HEART IS SMITTEN THOUGH LINGERING FATE IS SLOW   34B KING JOHN/PS   PROSE
PREPARE PREPARE THE IRON HELM OF WAR . . . .   34 WAR SONG/PS   1
AS ON A LOFTY ROCK WITH IRON PENS THE WORDS OF TRUTH   . . 37D SAMSON/PS   PROSE
NONE CAN HURT THEE THY BONES ARE BRASS THY SINEWS ARE IRON   39A SAMSON/PS   PROSE
BOTH SPEAR & SHIELD WERE USELESS & THE COAT OF IRON MAIL   105 TIRIEL 4   70
TUGGING HIS IRON MANACLES . . . . 135 FRENCH REVOLTN   25
CHAIND HAND AND FOOT ROUND HIS NECK AN IRON BAND . . . .   135 FRENCH REVOLTN   27
. . . HIS STRONG BONES SCARCE COVERD WITH SINEWS THE IRON   135 FRENCH REVOLTN   30
RINGS
. . . A MASK OF IRON ON HIS FACE HID THE LINEAMENTS . . . 135 FRENCH REVOLTN   31
EACH STERN VISAGE LOCKD UP AS WITH STRONG BANDS OF IRON   137 FRENCH REVOLTN   66
. . .
RUSHING ALONG IRON RANKS GLITTERING THE OFFICERS EACH TO   147 FRENCH REVOLTN   287
HIS STATION
[IN A CRUEL IRON CHAIN] . . . . 177 LIT BOY LST/N   23
& BOUND HIM IN AN IRON CHAIN   . . . . 177 LIT BOY LST/N   25
IN TEARS & IRON BOUND . . . . 185 LET BROTHELS/N   36
IN [TEARS] CURSES & IRON BOUND . . . . 186 LET BROTHELS/N   61
HIS FOOD SHE BROUGHT IN IRON BASKETS HIS DRINK IN CUPS   195 AMERICA PREL 1   3
OF IRON
FOR NEVER FROM HER IRON TONGUE COULD VOICE OR SOUND ARISE   196 AMERICA PREL 1   9
A BENDED BOW IS LIFTED IN HEAVEN & A HEAVY IRON CHAIN   . . 197 AMERICA 3   7
OF IRON HEATED IN THE FURNACE HIS TERRIBLE LIMBS WERE FIRE   197 AMERICA 4   9
A BENDED BOW IN HEAVEN IS LIFTED & A HEAVY IRON CHAIN   . . 204 AMERICA CANC A   7
ON CHAIRS OF IRON CANOPIED WITH MYSTIC ORNAMENTS . . . .   204 AMERICA CANC B   13
GOLD SILVER BRASS & IRON [ARDORS] CLANGORS CLAMORING REND   205 AMERICA CANC C   15
THE SHORES

```
                                                          PAGE     TITLE        LINE
IRON   (CONTINUED)
    AND BOUND HIM IN AN IRON CHAIN  . . . . . . . . . .   218 LIT BOY LST/SE    20
    THE HUMAN DRESS IS FORGED IRON  . . . . . . . . . .   221 DIVNE IMAGE/SE     5
    WITH RIVETS OF IRON & BRASS  . . . . . . . . . .      227 URIZEN 8          11
    BEATING STILL ON HIS RIVETS OF IRON  . . . . . . .    227 URIZEN 10          8
    POURING SODOR OF IRON DIVIDING  . . . . . . . . .     227 URIZEN 10          9
    LOS BEAT ON HIS FETTERS OF IRON  . . . . . . . .      228 URIZEN 10         28
    IRON SODOR AND SODOR OF BRASS  . . . . . . . . .      228 URIZEN 10         30
    INTO AN IRON CHAIN  . . . . . . . . . . . . . .       233 URIZEN 20         19
    HIS IRON LAWS ONE MOMENT  . . . . . . . . . . .       235 URIZEN 23         26
    WITH SPECTRES AND THE WINDOWS WOVE OVER WITH CURSES OF IRON  243 EUROPE 12   27
    WITH BANDS OF IRON ROUND THEIR NECKS FASTEND INTO THE WALLS  243 EUROPE 12   29
    THE TRUMP OF THE LAST DOOM BUT HE COULD NOT BLOW THE IRON    243 EUROPE 13    2
        TUBE
    AND HIS BOOKS OF BRASS IRON & GOLD  . . . . . . .     248 SONG OF LOS 7     14
    IN SILENCE HIS BOOK OF IRON  . . . . . . . . . .      252 AHANIA 3          64
    OF IRON FROM THE DISMAL SHADE  . . . . . . . . .      252 AHANIA 4           1
    HE FORGD NETS OF IRON AROUND  . . . . . . . . .       253 AHANIA 4          29
    LIKE A SERPENT LIKE AN IRON CHAIN  . . . . . . .      259 BOOK OF LOS 5     16
    OF ETERNITY BEAT ON HIS IRON LINKS  . . . . . .       259 BOOK OF LOS 5     26
    BESIDE HIS ANVIL STOOD URTHONA DARK A MASS OF IRON .  278 FOUR ZOAS 1      519
    AND ALL THE WHILE THE PLOW OF IRON CUT THE DREADFUL FURROWS  282 FOUR ZOAS 2  70
    THE EVIL DAY AFAR & IF PERCHANCE WITH IRON POWER . . .  282 FOUR ZOAS 2     75
    THEY HAVE SURROUNDED ME WITH WALLS OF IRON & BRASS [I ?DIE]  282 FOUR ZOAS 2  *  99
        O LAMB
    BENEATH THE CAVERNS ROLL THE WEIGHTS OF LEAD & SPINDLES  284 FOUR ZOAS 2    148
        OF IRON
    MY HEAVENS ARE BRASS MY EARTH IS IRON MY MOON A CLOD OF  290 FOUR ZOAS 2    395
        CLAY
    TO FORGE THE CURBS OF IRON & BRASS TO BUILD THE IRON  292 FOUR ZOAS 3       34
        MANGERS
    OF IRON GLOWD FURIOUS PREPARD FOR SPADES & MATTOCKS . .  300 FOUR ZOAS 4    91
    AND LOS FORMD ANVILS OF IRON PETRIFIC FOR HIS BLOWS . .  301 FOUR ZOAS 4   168
    THE DAYS & YEARS IN CHAINS OF IRON ROUND THE LIMBS   302 FOUR ZOAS 4       180
        OF URIZEN
    HE POURD THE MOLTEN IRON ROUND THE LIMBS OF ENITHARMON . .  302 FOUR ZOAS 4  195
    THE PROPHET OF ETERNITY BEAT ON HIS IRON LINKS & LINKS  302 FOUR ZOAS 4    201
        OF BRASS
    AND POURD IRON SODOR & SODOR OF BRASS  . . . . .      303 FOUR ZOAS 4      214
    TWINGE & HIS IRON SINEWS BEND LIKE LEAD & FOLD  . . .  305 FOUR ZOAS 4     294
    OF ENITHARMON LOS AROUND HER BUILDED PILLARS OF IRON . .  307 FOUR ZOAS 5   73
    FALLING DOWN ON THE ROCK AN IRON CHAIN LINK BY LINK LOCKD  307 FOUR ZOAS 5  91
    UP TO THE IRON MOUNTAIN'S TOP & THERE THE JEALOUS CHAIN  307 FOUR ZOAS 5    99
    THE DISMAL VALES & UP TO THE IRON MOUNTAIN'S TOP WHERE ORC  309 FOUR ZOAS 5 151
    INTO THE IRON ROCK & GREW A CHAIN BENEATH THE EARTH . .  309 FOUR ZOAS 5   167
    SCALED & FINND WITH IRON & BRASS THEY DEVOURD THE PATH  313 FOUR ZOAS 6     76
        BEFORE HIM
    WRITING IN BITTER TEARS & GROANS IN BOOKS OF IRON & BRASS  314 FOUR ZOAS 6   85
    FETTERS OF RED HOT IRON SOME WITH CROWNS OF SERPENTS & SOME  314 FOUR ZOAS 6 104
    AND SCALED MONSTERS OR ARMD IN IRON SHELL OR SHELL OF  314 FOUR ZOAS 6      120
        BRASS
    VOID PATHLESS BEATEN WITH [ETERNAL] IRON SLEET . . . .  315 FOUR ZOAS 6   *  148
    BUT STILL HIS BOOKS HE BORE IN HIS STRONG HANDS & HIS IRON  316 FOUR ZOAS 6 167
        PEN
    STILL TO BE WRITTEN & INTERLEAVD WITH BRASS & IRON & GOLD  316 FOUR ZOAS 6  172
    TIME AFTER TIME FOR SUCH A JOURNEY NONE BUT IRON PENS . .  316 FOUR ZOAS 6  173
    SO [SAYING] HE BEGAN TO [FORM] ?DIG OF GOLD SILVER  317 FOUR ZOAS 6       *  229
        & [BRASS] IRON
    VOID PATHLESS BEAT WITH [?ENION] SNOWS ETERNAL & IRON HAIL  318 FOUR ZOAS 6 *  271
        & RAIN
    BETWEEN THE ENORMOUS IRON WALLS BUILT BY THE SPECTRE DARK  319 FOUR ZOAS 6  295
    A SPECTRE VAST APPEARD WHOSE FEET & LEGS WITH IRON SCALED  319 FOUR ZOAS 6  298
    BLACK SCALES OF IRON ARM THE DREAD VISAGE IRON SPIKES  319 FOUR ZOAS 6      307
        INSTEAD
    GOLD SILVER BRASS & IRON CLANGORS CLAMORING REND  319 FOUR ZOAS 6          311
        THE [DEEPS] SHORES
    OF GOLD & SILVER BRASS & IRON HE KNEW HIS MIGHTY SONS . .  319 FOUR ZOAS 6  315
    HIS BOOK OF IRON ON HIS KNEES HE TRACD THE DREADFUL LETTERS  321 FOUR ZOAS 7  29
    HIS BOOKS OUT OF THE DISMAL SHADE ALL BUT THE BOOK OF IRON  321 FOUR ZOAS 7  39
    ON A ROCK OF IRON FROWNING OVER THE FOAMING FIRES OF ORC  321 FOUR ZOAS 7   41
    SITTING UPON [HIS] AN IRON CRAG AT LENGTH HIS WORDS BROKE  321 FOUR ZOAS 7   43
        FORTH
    THUNDRING & HAIL & FROZEN IRON HAILD FROM THE ELEMENT  . .  322 FOUR ZOAS 7   79
    TERRIFIC WITH THEIR IRON VESSELS DRIVING THEM ACROSS  . .  322 FOUR ZOAS 7   96
    IN THE DIM AIR THEY TOOK THE BOOK OF IRON & PLACD ABOVE  322 FOUR ZOAS 7     97
    THRO ONA'S SIEVE THE TORRENT RAIN POURD FROM THE IRON PAIL  322 FOUR ZOAS 7 *  101
    THE HEAVENS BOW WITH TERROR UNDERNEATH THEIR IRON HANDS  322 FOUR ZOAS 7    103
    SINGING AT THEIR DIRE WORK THE WORDS OF URIZEN'S BOOK OF  322 FOUR ZOAS 7   104
        IRON
    OF IRON GLOWD BRIGHT PREPARD FOR SPADES & PLOWSHARES SUDDEN  327 FOUR ZOAS 7 *  283
        DOWN
    HE VANQUISHD WITH THE STRENGTH OF ART BENDING THEIR IRON  331 FOUR ZOAS 7   459
        POINTS
    UPON THE IRON CRAG OF URIZEN THENCE SPRINGING UP ALOFT . .  332 FOUR ZOAS 7 465
    THO BOUND WITH CHAINS OF JEALOUSY & IN SCALES OF IRON &  332 FOUR ZOAS 7    481
        BRASS
    OF DEATH O NORTHERN DRUM AWAKE O HAND OF IRON SOUND  . .  336 FOUR ZOAS 7B  154
    AND POLISH BRASS & IRON HOUR AFTER HOUR LABORIOUS   337 FOUR ZOAS 7B       182
        WORKMANSHIP
    MEASURD HIS FOOD MORNING & EVENING IN CUPS & BASKETS OF  343 FOUR ZOAS 8     81
        IRON
    HORRIBLE HOOKS & NETS HE FORMD TWISTING THE CORDS OF IRON  343 FOUR ZOAS 8   92
```

994

IRON   (CONTINUED)

	PAGE	TITLE		LINE
THUS IN THE TEMPLE OF THE SUN HIS BOOKS OF IRON & BRASS	344	FOUR ZOAS 8		140
[I HAVE] AWAY FROM ME I HAVE BOUND DOWN WITH A HOT IRON	349	FOUR ZOAS 8	*	302
COME CIRCUMSCRIBE THIS TONGUE OF SWEETS & WITH A SCREW OF IRON	349	FOUR ZOAS 8		317
THEY BEAT THE IRON ENGINES OF DESTRUCTION INTO WEDGES . .	365	FOUR ZOAS 9		304
THERE IS A BRAZEN SICKLE & A SCYTHE OF IRON HID	372	FOUR ZOAS 9		580
IN CHAINS OF IRON & IN DUNGEONS CIRCLED WITH CEASELESS FIRES	377	FOUR ZOAS 9		750
IRON TEARS & GROANS OF LEAD	417	MY SPECTR AD/N		11
AROSE WITH WAR IN IRON & GOLD	418	I SAW A MONK/N		9
THE IRON HAND [CRUSD] CRUSHD THE TYRANT'S HEAD	419	I SAW A MONK/N	*	46
STOOD BY & MOCKED IN IRON & GOLD	420	I SAW MNK AD/N		14
THE OTHER [IN] CLOTHD IN [SWEET DESIRE] IRON WIRE	421	BENEATH/N	*	7
NOW INTREATING [SWEET DESIRE] IRON WIRE	422	BENEATH/N		25
[THE OTHER CLOTHD IN [SWEET DESIRE] IRON WIRE]	422	BENEATH REWR/N		4
THE OTHER CLOTHD IN IRON WIRE	424	THE GOLDEN NET		6
NOW INTREATING IRON WIRE	424	THE GOLDEN NET		24
SHE BINDS IRON THORNS AROUND HIS HEAD	425	MENTAL TRAVLER		13
THE IRON HAND CRUSHD THE TYRANT'S HEAD	431	GREY MONK		35
LIKE TO THE ARMOUR'S IRON BRACE	433	AUGURIES		100
ON TYBURN'S BROOK LOUD GROANS THAMES BENEATH THE IRON FORGE	485	MILTON 6		11
OUT FROM THE ASHES OF THE DEAD LOS LIFTS HIS IRON LADLES	486	MILTON 6		29
WITH MOLTEN ORE HE HEAVES THE IRON CLIFFS IN HIS RATTLING CHAINS	486	MILTON 6		30
IN IRON TABLETS AND HIS WIVES' & DAUGHTERS' NAMES WERE THESE	498	MILTON 17		10
SCOFIELD IS BOUND IN IRON ARMOUR BEFORE REUBEN'S GATE . .	501	MILTON 19		59
WHERE HUMAN THOUGHT IS CRUSHD BENEATH THE IRON HAND OF POWER	510	MILTON 25		5
IN CHAINS OF IRON & IN DUNGEONS CIRCLED WITH CEASELESS FIRES	514	MILTON 27		32
SOME SONS OF LOS SURROUND THE PASSIONS WITH PORCHES OF IRON & SILVER	514	MILTON 28		1
AND TIMBERS CRAMPT WITH IRON CRAMPS BAR IN THE JOYS OF LIFE	515	MILTON 28		40
GREAT GOLGONOOZA FREE FROM THE FOUR IRON PILLARS OF SATAN'S THRONE	517	MILTON 29		48
[AND] WHO WITH IRON HAND CUFFD IN THE AFTERNOON	537	AND HIS LEGS/N		24
TURN THRO THE IRON GATE DOWN SNEAKING LANE	541	MR CROMEK/N		4
[HIS] WHOSE HEART IS IRON HIS HEAD WOOD & HIS FACE BRASS	545	ON S(TOTHRD)/N		2
AND THAT ONE HE CLOSES WITH IRON BARS	583A	DESC CAT 9		PROSE
AN IRON AGE & BEGAT ON MNEMOSYNE OR MEMORY	605C	V LAST JUDG/N		PROSE
SCALED WITH IRON SCALES FROM HEAD TO FEET [WITH]	606C	V LAST JUDG/N		PROSE
THE EVIL DAY AFAR AND IF PERCHANCE WITH IRON POWER . . .	626	JERUSALEM 7		33
FREEZE ROUND HIM TO BARS OF STEEL & TO IRON ROCKS BENEATH	626	JERUSALEM 7		72
AND IRON BOUND IT OVER ME FOR EVER LIFE LIVES ON MY . . .	630	JERUSALEM 10		55
WITH IRON & BRASS BUILDING GOLGONOOZA IN GREAT CONTENDINGS	630	JERUSALEM 10		63
RAGAN IS WHOLLY CRUEL SCOFIELD IS BOUND IN IRON ARMOUR . .	631	JERUSALEM 11		21
AND THE SCREWS & IRON BRACES ARE WELL WROUGHT BLANDISHMENTS	632	JERUSALEM 12		34
HAS FOUR SCULPTURD BULLS TERRIBLE BEFORE THE GATE OF IRON	632	JERUSALEM 12		62
AND IRON THE BULLS AND THAT WHICH LOOKS TOWARD ULRO . .	632	JERUSALEM 12		63
AND THAT TOWARD BEULAH FOUR GOLD SILVER BRASS & IRON . .	632	JERUSALEM 12		66
AND THAT TOWARD EDEN FOUR FORMD OF GOLD SILVER BRASS & IRON	633	JERUSALEM 13		1
THAT TOWARD GENERATION FOUR OF IRON CARVD WONDROUS . . .	633	JERUSALEM 13		3
THAT TOWARD EDEN FOUR IMMORTAL GOLD SILVER BRASS & IRON	633	JERUSALEM 13		5
THAT TOWARDS GENERATION IRON THAT TOWARD BEULAH STONE . .	633	JERUSALEM 13		9
THE LAND OF SNOWS OF TREMBLING & OF IRON HAIL INCESSANT	634	JERUSALEM 13		47
AND EVERY ONE A GATE OF IRON DREADFUL AND WONDERFUL . . .	635	JERUSALEM 14		23
LIKE IRON SCOURGES OVER ALBION REASONINGS LIKE VAST SERPENTS	635	JERUSALEM 15		12
BEFORE BROMION'S IRON TONGS & GLOWING POKER REDDENING FIERCE	636	JERUSALEM 16		2
WITH LADLES HUGE & IRON POKERS OVER THE ISLAND WHITE . .	637	JERUSALEM 16		21
WHY SHOULD PUNISHMENT WEAVE THE VEIL WITH IRON WHEELS OF WAR	645	JERUSALEM 22		34
I FEEL THE IRON THREADS OF LOVE & JEALOUSY & DESPAIR . .	657	JERUSALEM 31		49
HE SIEZD HIS HAMMER & TONGS HIS IRON POKER & HIS BELLOWS	658	JERUSALEM 32		8
IN PAIN GIRDING ME ROUND LIKE A RIB OF IRON IN HEAVEN O VALA	660	JERUSALEM 34		14
IRON AND STEEL DARK AND OPAKE WITH CLOUDS & TEMPESTS BROODING	664	JERUSALEM 38		5
BOUND THESE BLACK SHOES OF DEATH & ON MY HANDS DEATH'S IRON GLOVES	666	JERUSALEM 39		21
UPON THE HILLS OF ALBION OXFORD GROANS IN HIS IRON FURNACE	671	JERUSALEM 42		58
OF DEATH THEY CURB THEIR SPECTRES AS WITH IRON CURBS . .	671	JERUSALEM 42		67
AROSE WITH WAR IN IRON & GOLD	683	I SAW A MONK/J		8
OF SPIRITUAL HATE FROM WHICH SPRINGS SEXUAL LOVE AS IRON CHAINS	685	JERUSALEM 54		12
CORD OF AFFECTION THRILLING EXTATIC ON THE IRON REEL . .	688	JERUSALEM 56		12
THUNDEROUS RAGE THE SPINDLES OF IRON & THE IRON DISTAFF	692	JERUSALEM 59		53
MY WEARY EYES EVEN IN THIS DUNGEON & THIS IRON MILL . . .	693	JERUSALEM 60		59
AND POLISH BRASS & IRON HOUR AFTER HOUR LABORIOUS TASK	700	JERUSALEM 65		24
CHAIND HAND & FOOT COMPELLD TO FIGHT UNDER THE IRON WHIPS	700	JERUSALEM 65		35
THEY TURN CONTORTED THEIR IRON NECKS BEND UNWILLING TOWARDS	701	JERUSALEM 65		77
HERE VALA STOOD TURNING THE IRON SPINDLE OF DESTRUCTION	702	JERUSALEM 66		10
HIS FOREHEAD THEY BIND HIS FOREHEAD WITH THORNS OF IRON	702	JERUSALEM 66		23
THE KING OF CANAAN WHOSE ARE SEVEN HUNDRED CHARIOTS OF IRON	702	JERUSALEM 66		25
THE STARS FLEE REMOTE THE HEAVEN IS IRON THE EARTH IS SULPHUR	703	JERUSALEM 66		81
BENEATH THE IRON WHIPS OF THEIR CAPTAINS & CONSECRATED BANNERS	704	JERUSALEM 67		30
AWAY FROM ME I HAVE BOUND DOWN WITH A HOT IRON	705	JERUSALEM 67		48

995

```
                                                              PAGE     TITLE       LINE
IRON    (CONTINUED)
     COME CIRCUMSCRIBE THIS TONGUE OF SWEETS & WITH A SCREW    705  JERUSALEM 68      5
        OF IRON
     WITH THE IRON SHUTTLE OF WAR AMONG THE ROOTED OAKS        711  JERUSALEM 71     61
        OF ALBION
     LONG TO TELL & OF THE IRON ROLLERS GOLDEN AXLE-TREES &    713  JERUSALEM 73      9
        YOKES
     OF BRASS IRON CHAINS & BRACES & THE GOLD SILVER & BRASS   713  JERUSALEM 73     10
     PRIMROSE HILL IS THE MOUTH OF THE FURNACE & THE IRON DOOR 714  JERUSALEM 73     54
     THE SLEEPING HUMANITY LOS WITH HIS MACE OF IRON  . . . .  718  JERUSALEM 78      3
     THEY ARE BROKEN LOUD HOWL THE SPECTRES IN HIS IRON FURNACE 719 JERUSALEM 78      9
     UPON EGYPT'S IRON FLOORS & THE MARBLE PAVEMENTS OF ASSYRIA 719 JERUSALEM 79      2
     HER STRUGGLING TORMENT IN HER IRON ARMS AND LIKE A CHAIN  726  JERUSALEM 82     70
     BINDING HIS WRISTS & ANKLES WITH THE IRON ARMS OF LOVE .  . 726 JERUSALEM 82    71
     HOLDING HIS IRON MACE THE SPECTRE REMAINS ATTENTIVE  . .  729  JERUSALEM 83     78
     WITH RAHAB AS SHE TURND THE IRON SPINDLE OF DESTRUCTION   729  JERUSALEM 84     30
     DISORGANIZD & THERE IS PHAROH IN HIS IRON COURT  . . . .  735  JERUSALEM 89     18
     AND THE DRAGON OF THE RIVER & THE FURNACES OF IRON  . . . 735  JERUSALEM 89     19
     SPRING UPON IRON SINEWS FROM THE SCAPULAE & OS HUMERI  .  735  JERUSALEM 89     29
     INCLOSED BY EYELESS WINGS GLOWING WITH FIRE AS THE IRON   735  JERUSALEM 89     41
     IRON OF HIS FORGE & FIXES THEM INTO BONES OF CHALK & ROCK 736  JERUSALEM 90     20
     THEY DRINK REUBEN & BENJAMIN AS THE IRON DRINKS THE FIRE  737  JERUSALEM 90     46
     URTHONA NORTHWARD IN THICK STORMS A BOW OF IRON TERRIBLE  744  JERUSALEM 97     11
        THUNDERING
     UPON HIS HEART WITH IRON PEN  . . . . . . . . . . .       750  EV GOSPEL(C)/N   13
     UPON HIS HEART WITH IRON PEN  . . . . . . . . . . .       751  EV GOSPEL(D)/N   13
     WITH IRON BARS IN VIRTUOUS STATE  . . . . . . . . . .     758  EV GOSPEL (1)    13
IRON-HEARTED,IRON HEARTED
     COMPELLD BY THE IRON HEARTED SISTERS DAUGHTERS OF URIZEN  343  FOUR ZOAS 8      83
     JUPITER OF THE GREEKS AN IRON-HEARTED TYRANT THE RUINER   852A LETTER 50     PROSE
IRON-SHOD
     GROANING HE KNEELD BEFORE LOS'S IRON-SHOD FEET ON LONDON  627  JERUSALEM 8      27
        STONE
IRON-WINGD
     FUZON ON A CHARIOT IRON-WINGD . . . . . . . .            249  AHANIA 2          1
IRREGULAR
     AND IRREGULAR ECCENTRICITY A MADMAN'S SCRAWLS I DEMAND  . . 561B EXHIBITION ADV PROSE
     INTO TWO IRREGULAR FORMS AND LOOKING ON ALBION'S DREAD TREE 723 JERUSALEM 80    73
IRRESISTIBLE
     WITH IRRESISTIBLE CONVICTION I FEEL I AM NOT ONE OF THOSE 329  FOUR ZOAS 7     362
     . . . IRRESISTIBLE FROM ETERNITY TO ETERNITY  . . . . .   745  JERUSALEM 98     27
IRRIGATE
     OF URIZEN'S LAWS TO IRRIGATE THE ROOTS OF THE TREE        347  FOUR ZOAS 8     229
        OF MYSTERY
IRRITATE
     AND OF THE WATERS & THE SCORPION OF THE DESART IRRITATE   335  FOUR ZOAS 7B    112
     WISH TO IRRITATE BY SEEMING TOO OBSTINATE IN POETIC       825B LETTER 27    PROSE
        PURSUITS
IRRITATED
     HAST JUST CAUSE TO BE IRRITATED BUT LOOK STEDFASTLY UPON ME 626 JERUSALEM 7     53
     BEING NOT IRRITATED BY INSULT BEARING INSULTING          655  JERUSALEM 30      9
        BENEVOLENCES
IRRITATING
     THE MOST IRRITATING THINGS IN THE MIDST OF TEARS AND LOVE 493  MILTON 12        33
ISAAC
     LIKE SIR ISAAC NEWTON . . . . . . . . . . . . . .         57  TO BE OR/IM       3
     OR SIR ISAAC NEWTON . . . . . . . . . . . . . . .         57  TO BE OR/IM      30
     NOR OF SIR ISAAC NEWTON'S CALCULATION . . . . . . .       542  FLORENTINE/N     29
     WHICH SPRANG FROM SIR ISAAC NEWTON'S GREAT ABILITIES      542  FLORENTINE/N     31
     IS ABRAHAM WITH SARAH & ISAAC ALSO HAGAR & ISHMAEL  . . . 606D V LAST JUDG/N PROSE
     LIKE DR PRIESTLY & [ SIR ISAAC] BACON & NEWTON . . . . .  752  EV GOSPEL(D)/N   39
     [AS] FOR THUS THE GOSPEL SIR ISAAC CONFUTES . . . . .     752  EV GOSPEL(D)/N   43
ISAIAH
     & THE RETURN OF ADAM INTO PARADISE SEE ISAIAH XXXIV & XXXV 149B MARRIAGE HH 3  PROSE
        CHAP
     THE PROPHETS ISAIAH AND EZEKIEL DINED WITH ME AND I ASKED 153B MARRIAGE HH 12  PROSE
     ISAIAH ANSWERD I SAW NO GOD NOR HEARD ANY . . . . . . .   153C MARRIAGE HH 12  PROSE
     AFTER DINNER I ASKD ISAIAH TO FAVOUR THE WORLD WITH  . .  154A MARRIAGE HH 12  PROSE
     EZEKIEL SAID THE SAME OF HIS I ALSO ASKED ISAIAH WHAT     154A MARRIAGE HH 12  PROSE
     THE PERSON NAMD IN ISAIAH XXII ... ELIAKIM THE SON        607D V LAST JUDG/N  PROSE
        OF HILKIAH
     EZRA CAME WITH ISAIAH THE PROPHET . . . . . . . . . .     799  TO FLAXMAN/L      6
     HELL BENEATH IS MOVED FOR THEE &C FROM ISAIAH . . . . .   SUPP LETTER 56A   *PROSE
ISHAMAEL
     (BENEATH) ISHAMAEL IS MAHOMED & ON THE LEFT  . . . . .    607B V LAST JUDG/N *PROSE
ISHMAEL
     IS ABRAHAM WITH SARAH & ISAAC ALSO HAGAR & ISHMAEL  . . . 606D V LAST JUDG/N  PROSE
ISIS
     OSIRIS ISIS ORUS IN EGYPT DARK THEIR TABERNACLES ON NILE  528  MILTON 37        27
ISLAND
     O LAND MOST HAPLESS O BEAUTEOUS ISLAND HOW FORSAKEN   .   34A  KING JOHN/PS   PROSE
     WEEP FROM THY GENTLE RIVERS THE ANGEL OF THE ISLAND WEEPS 34A  KING JOHN/PS   PROSE
     IN THE MOON IS A CERTAIN ISLAND NEAR BY A MIGHTY CONTINENT 44A ISLAND MOON 1  PROSE
     WHICH SMALL ISLAND SEEMS TO HAVE SOME AFFINITY TO ENGLAND 44A  ISLAND MOON 1 *PROSE
     IN THIS ISLAND DWELLS THREE PHILOSOPHERS . . . . . . .    44A  ISLAND MOON 1  PROSE
     THIS WILL SPREAD A PLAGUE ALL THRO THE ISLAND . . . . .   59A  ISLAND MOON 10 PROSE
     THAT STRETCHES OUT ITS SHADY LENGTH ALONG THE ISLAND WHITE 241 EUROPE 10        3
     THEY SAW THE SERPENT TEMPLE LIFTED ABOVE SHADOWING THE    242  EUROPE 12        11
        ISLAND WHITE
     THENCE STONY DRUID TEMPLES OVERSPREAD THE ISLAND WHITE .  485  MILTON 6         20
     ALONG THE ROCKY ISLAND & THENCE THROUGHOUT THE WHOLE EARTH 499 MILTON 18        9
     UPON THE DARKNING THAMES ACROSS THE WHOLE ISLAND WESTWARD 625  JERUSALEM 7       3
```

	PAGE	TITLE	LINE

ISLAND   (CONTINUED)
      WITH LADLES HUGE & IRON POKERS OVER THE ISLAND WHITE   . . 637 JERUSALEM 16   21
      JERUSALEM'S SHADOW BENT NORTHWARD OVER THE ISLAND WHITE   657 JERUSALEM 31   42
      ALONG THE ISLAND WHITE AMONG THE DRUID TEMPLES WHILE   725 JERUSALEM 82   15
         GWENDOLEN
      TERRESTRIAL PARADISE IT IS AN ISLAND IN LIMBO . . . . . SUPP ILLUS DANTE 7 *PROSE
ISLANDERS
      THUS THESE HAPPY ISLANDERS SPENT THEIR TIME   . . . . . 58B ISLAND MOON 10 PROSE
ISLANDS
      . . . ITS ISLANDS & [THE] ITS MARGINS [OF THIS LAKE]   . . 346 FOUR ZOAS 8   * 226
      THE ISLANDS OF THE FIERY LAKES THE TREES OF MALICE REVENGE   634 JERUSALEM 13   42
      AND UNDER THESE THIRTY-TWO CLASSES OF ISLANDS IN THE OCEAN   712 JERUSALEM 72   43
ISLE
      THINE ANGEL EYES UPON OUR WESTERN ISLE . . . .   1 TO SPRING/PS   3
      ON PATMOS ISLE & HEARD THE SOULS CRY OUT TO BE DELIVERD   356 FOUR ZOAS 8   601
      SPIRIT WHO LOVST BRITTANNIA'S [SHORE] ISLE . . . . . .   557 ART HAS LOST/N   13
      TILL HE CAME TO OLD STRATFORD & THENCE TO STEPNEY & THE   657 JERUSALEM 31   15
         ISLE
      PEACHEY HAD NORTH WALES SHROPSHIRE CHESHIRE & THE ISLE   710 JERUSALEM 71   30
         OF MAN
ISLES
      AND SATURN JOVE & RHEA OF THE ISLES OF THE SEA REMOTE   . . 528 MILTON 37   33
      I GAVE THEE PRIAM'S CITY AND THE ISLES OF GRECIA LOVELY   692 JERUSALEM 60   13
      BOWEN HAD ALL SCOTLAND THE ISLES NORTHUMBERLAND &   710 JERUSALEM 71   46
         CUMBERLAND
      THE ISLES OF JAVAN PHILISTEA TYRE AND LEBANON . . . . .   731 JERUSALEM 86   32
      OF JAVAN THRO THE ISLES OF GRECIA & ALL EUROPE'S KINGS   . . 735 JERUSALEM 89   34
ISLINGTON
      THE FIELDS FROM ISLINGTON TO MARYBONE . . . .   649 FIELDS FROM/J   1
      THE SHUTTLES OF DEATH SING IN THE SKY TO ISLINGTON   668 JERUSALEM 41   7
         & PANCRASS
      TO ISLINGTON & PADDINGTON & THE BROOK OF ALBION'S RIVER   729 JERUSALEM 84   2
      EVEN ISLINGTON & ALL PLACES NORTH OF LONDON ALWAYS LAID ME 871A LETTER 72   PROSE
ISRAEL
      IN SOLITUDE THOUGH NOT OBSCURE IN ISRAEL HE LIVED   . . . 39C SAMSON/PS   PROSE
      BUT GOD HATH OTHER JOYS IN STORE IS BURDENED ISRAEL HIS   39C SAMSON/PS   PROSE
         GRIEF
      HE SAT AND HEARD WITH JOY AND PRAISED GOD WHO ISRAEL STILL   40A SAMSON/PS   PROSE
         DOTH KEEP
      THE TIME ROLLED ON AND ISRAEL GROANED OPPRESSED   . . . .   40A SAMSON/PS   PROSE
      WE OF ISRAEL TAUGHT THAT THE POETIC GENIUS AS YOU NOW CALL   153D MARRIAGE HH 12 PROSE
         IT
      OF ISRAEL AS THEY ARE IN EDEN MOUNTAIN RIVER & PLAIN   .   532 MILTON 40   26
      THE RETURN OF ISRAEL IS A RETURN TO MENTAL SACRIFICE & WAR   652B JERUSALEM 27   PROSE
      TAKE UP THE CROSS O ISRAEL & FOLLOW JESUS   . . . . . .   652B JERUSALEM 27   PROSE
      TWELVE-FOLD HERE ALL THE TRIBES OF ISRAEL I BEHOLD   . .   731 JERUSALEM 86   17
      TWELVEFOLD I THERE BEHOLD ISRAEL IN HER TENTS . . . . .   731 JERUSALEM 86   26
      THERE ISRAEL IN BONDAGE TO HIS GENERALIZING GODS   . . .   735 JERUSALEM 89   30
      AND ROME IN SWEET HESPERIA THERE ISRAEL SCATTERD ABROAD   735 JERUSALEM 89   39
      SPIRITUAL WAR ISRAEL DELIVERD FROM EGYPT . . . .   776A INSC LAOCOON   PROSE
      SAUL KING OF ISRAEL SOMEWHAT INFLUENCED BY XXX EVIL SPIRIT SUPP PENC DRAW 1.42 *TITLE
ISRAELITES
      A DEFENCE OF THE WICKEDNESS OF THE ISRAELITES IN MURDERING   387B ANNO WATSON   MARG
ISRAEL'S
      FOR HOLY UNTO ISRAEL'S GOD I AM A NAZARITE EVEN FROM MY   39C SAMSON/PS   PROSE
         MOTHER'S WOMB
      PENSIVE SHE SAT AND THOUGHT ON ISRAEL'S GRIEF . . . . .   39D SAMSON/PS   PROSE
      AND SILENT PRAYED TO ISRAEL'S GOD . . . .   39D SAMSON/PS   PROSE
      AND ISRAEL'S STRENGTH SHALL BE UPON HIS SHOULDERS   . . .   39D SAMSON/PS   PROSE
      AND HE SHALL BE CALLED ISRAEL'S DELIVERER . . . . . .   39D SAMSON/PS   PROSE
      BUT STILL IN ISRAEL'S PATHS THEY SHINE . . . .   418 MOCK ON/N   8
      WHERE ISRAEL'S TENTS DO SHINE SO BRIGHT . . . . . .   418 MOCK ON/N   12
ISSACHAR
      GAD ASHER ISSACHAR ZEBULUN JOSEPH BENJAMIN DAVID SOLOMON   350 FOUR ZOAS 8   361
      THEN DAN THEN NAPHTALI THEN GAD THEN ASHER THEN ISSACHAR   350 FOUR ZOAS 8   376
      THE GATE OF ASHER CARNARVONSHIRE THE GATE OF ISSACHAR   637 JERUSALEM 16   39
         BRECKNOKSHIRE
      ISSACHAR NORTHAMPTON RUTLAND NOTTGHAM ZEBULUN BEDFORD   637 JERUSALEM 16   48
         HUNTGN CAMB
      ISSACHAR SELKIRK DUMBARTN GLASGO ZEBULUN ORKNEY SHETLAND   638 JERUSALEM 16   57
         SKYE
      UNDER JUDAH & ISSACHAR & ZEBULUN ARE LOWTH LONGFORD   . .   711 JERUSALEM 72   18
      DAN NAPTHALI GAD ASHER ISSACHAR ZEBULUN ROLL APART   . .   715 JERUSALEM 74   * 50
      LEVI AND JUDAH & ISSACHAR EPHRAM MANASSEH GAD AND DAN   .   720 JERUSALEM 79   30
ISSUD
      ISSUD FROM ENITHARMON . . . .   232 URIZEN 19   46
      MY MASCULINE SPIRIT SCORNING THE FRAIL BODY ISSUD FORTH   327 FOUR ZOAS 7   * 290
      SPARKLES OF DIRE AFFLICTION ISSUD [FROM] ROUND HIS FROZEN   343 FOUR ZOAS 8   * 91
         LIMBS
      ISSUD ON ALL SIDES GATHRING STRENGTH IN ANIMATING VOLUMES   358 FOUR ZOAS 9   * 35
      BLOOD ISSUD OUT IN MIGHTY VOLUMES POURING IN WHIRLPOOLS   359 FOUR ZOAS 9   * 71
         FIERCE
      ISSUD IN MAJESTY DIVINE URIZEN ROSE UP FROM HIS COUCH   .   366 FOUR ZOAS 9   347
ISSUE
      UP TO THY BRIGHT PAVILLIONS ISSUE FORTH . . . .   1 TO SPRING/PS   7
      UNLOCK HEAVN'S GOLDEN GATES AND ISSUE FORTH   . . . . .   3 TO MORNING/PS   2
      OF DEATH ISSUE AS FROM A SEPULCHRE . . . .   4 FAIR ELENOR/PS   7
      LAYING HER SEED UPON THE FIBRES SOON TO ISSUE FORTH   . . . 292 FOUR ZOAS 3   21
      DOST THOU REFUSE MIND I THE SPARKS THAT ISSUE FROM THY HAIR 301 FOUR ZOAS 4   150
      NOW HOLDS THEE SOON TO ISSUE FORTH SOUND CLARIONS OF WAR   307 FOUR ZOAS 5   63
      THY VITAL SUBSTANCE IN THESE FIRES THAT ISSUE NEW & NEW   321 FOUR ZOAS 7   48
      HIS FAINT GROANS SHAKE THE CAVES & ISSUE THRO THE DESOLATE   354 FOUR ZOAS 8   520
         ROCKS

997

```
ISSUE    (CONTINUED)
    O WHEREFORE DOTH A DRAGON-FORM FORTH ISSUE FROM MY LIMBS     492 MILTON 12             2
    HE SAW THEM ISSUE FROM MY BOSOM DARK IN JEALOUSY  . . . .    722 JERUSALEM 80         21
ISSUED
    WOULD HAVE RISEN BUT COULD NOT HIS VOICE ISSUED HARSH        142 FRENCH REVOLTN       177
        GRATING . . .
    OF ENION I ISSUED INTO THE AIR DIVIDED FROM ENITHARMON  . .  300 FOUR ZOAS 4         106
ISSUES
    THAT ISSUES FORTH IN THE MORNING BY MEASURE    . . . . .     363 FOUR ZOAS 9         227
    EACH MORNING LIKE A NEW BORN MAN ISSUES WITH SONGS & JOY     379 FOUR ZOAS 9         833
    IT ISSUES THRO THE DARK & INTRICATE CAVES OF THE MUNDANE     507 MILTON 23            22
        SHELL
    A SEA OF FIRE ISSUES FROM BEFORE THE THRONE   . . . . .     606B V LAST JUDG/N     PROSE
ISSUING
    HIS SPECTRE ISSUING FROM HIS FEET IN FLAMES OF FIRE   . .    266 FOUR ZOAS 1          78
    LOS ANSWERD IN HIS FURIOUS PRIDE SPARKS ISSUING FROM HIS     298 FOUR ZOAS 4          34
        HAIR
    SO SHALL THE SPUNGY MARROW ISSUING FROM THY SPLINTERD BONES  299 FOUR ZOAS 4          68
    BUT FOUND MYSELF & HER TOGETHER ISSUING DOWN THE TIDE   . .  300 FOUR ZOAS 4         101
    THRO THE INFINITE LABYRINTHS OF THE HEART & THRO            327 FOUR ZOAS 7         280
        THE NOSTRILS ISSUING
    I SUNK WITH CRIES OF BLOOD ISSUING DOWNWARD IN THE VEINS     327 FOUR ZOAS 7         284
    DARKEND & LOST IN DUE TIME ISSUING FORTH FROM ENION'S WOMB   327 FOUR ZOAS 7         294
    THESE LAST ARE ISSUING FROM THE GATEWAY OF THE INN THE COOK  567A DESC CAT 3        PROSE
    THESE LAST ARE ISSUING FROM THE GATEWAY OF THE INN THE COOK  588D CHAUCER/N         PROSE
    THESE LAST ARE ISSUING FROM THE GATEWAY OF THE INN THE COOK  590A CHAUCER 2         PROSE
    THERE TO ETERNITY CHAIND DOWN AND ISSUING IN RED FLAMES      667 JERUSALEM 40         36
    DISCLOSE A HIDEOUS ORIFICE THENCE ISSUING THE GIANT-BROOD    708 JERUSALEM 70         13
    RUBIES JACINTHS CRYSOLITES ISSUING FROM THY FURNACES WHILE   732 JERUSALEM 87         20
ITALIAN
    NO SAID QUID TO BE SURE HE WAS AN ITALIAN    . . . . .  .    49D ISLAND MOON 6       PROSE
    HANG ITALIAN SONGS LET'S HAVE ENGLISH SAID QUID   . .  .     56A ISLAND MOON 9       PROSE
    ENGRAVED BY W BLAKE...FROM AN OLD ITALIAN DRAWING    . . .   604A INSC ARIMATHEA     TITLE
    TRANSLATIONS BY COWPER FROM MILTON'S LATIN & ITALIAN POEMS   824C LETTER 27          PROSE
    THAT ARE OUT & THE BOOK OF ITALIAN LETTERS FROM MRS FLAXMAN  836C LETTER 35          PROSE
ITALIANS
    MICH ANG OR ANY OF THE ITALIANS    . . . . . . . . .        451D ANNO REYNOLDS       MARG
    THE ITALIANS LAUGH AT ENGLISH CONNOISSEURS WHO ARE   . .    597B PUB ADDRESS/N       PROSE
    WHAT THE WISE ITALIANS RAFAEL & MICHAEL ANGELO SCORNED  .   597C PUB ADDRESS/N       PROSE
ITALY
    STIFF SHUDDERINGS SHOOK THE HEAVNLY THRONES FRANCE SPAIN     203 AMERICA 16           16
        & ITALY
    THE LAMB THE SAVIOUR ALBION TREMBLED TO ITALY GREECE &       495 MILTON 14            6
        EGYPT
    GERMANY WEPT TOWARDS FRANCE & ITALY ENGLAND WEPT            519 MILTON 31            13
        & TREMBLED
    IF ITALY IS ENRICHED AND MADE GREAT BY RAPHAEL   . . . .    561C EXHIBITION ADV     PROSE
    AS IS THE PRACTICE OF THE LATTER SCHOOLS OF ITALY          564D DESC CAT 1         PROSE
        AND FLANDERS
    PETTY PRINCE IN ITALY AND EMPLOYED NUMEROUS JOURNEYMEN  .   583B DESC CAT 9         PROSE
    AND TO MAKE ENGLAND LIKE ITALY RESPECTED   . . . . . . .    584B DESC CAT 14        PROSE
    EVEN TO ITALY BUT THE PUBLIC WILL KNOW & POSTERITY WILL      592D PUB ADDRESS/N      PROSE
        KNOW
    ENGLAND WILL NEVER RIVAL ITALY WHILE WE SERVILELY COPY  .   597C PUB ADDRESS/N       PROSE
    WHAT ITALY IS AN ENVIED STOREHOUSE OF INTELLECTUAL RICHES   601B PUB ADDRESS/N       PROSE
    FROM SURREY HILLS THRO ITALY AND GREECE TO HINNOM'S VALE     684 JERUSALEM 53         29
    FRANCE & SPAIN & ITALY & DENMARK & HOLLAND & GERMANY   .    690 JERUSALEM 58         41
    SHOOTING OUT FIBRES ROUND THE EARTH THRO GAUL & ITALY   . . 704 JERUSALEM 67         38
    FRANCE SPAIN ITALY GERMANY POLAND RUSSIA SWEDEN TURKEY  . . 712 JERUSALEM 72         38
    ITALY SAW ME IN SUBLIME ASTONISHMENT FRANCE WAS WHOLLY MINE  720 JERUSALEM 79         39
    THRO ITALY & GRECIA TO LEBANON & PERSIA & INDIA   . . . .   722 JERUSALEM 80         47
    WHEN FLAXMAN WAS TAKEN TO ITALY FUSELI WAS GIVEN TO ME       799 TO FLAXMAN/L          3
        FOR A SEASON
    IN ITALY THAT HE RETURNED TWENTY-EIGHT YEARS SINCE   . . .  847D LETTER 44          PROSE
    MR HUMPHRY THE PAINTER WAS IN ITALY THE SAME TIME    . . .  847D LETTER 44          PROSE
I'TH
    O SOON CUT OFF I TH MORNING OF HER DAYS . . . . . . .        43C WOE CRIED MUSE     PROSE
ITSELF
    MORE TERRIFIED SAW IT UNFOLD ITSELF    . . . . . . . .        5 FAIR ELENOR/PS        56
    WITHIN ITSELF AND FINDETH DISCONTENT  . . . . . . . .        27 EDW THIRD/PS 3       253
    BLOOD CRIES AFAR THE LAND DOTH SOW ITSELF   . . . . . .      34B KING JOHN/PS       PROSE
    THE CURSE THAT ROLLS OVER THEIR HEADS WILL REST ITSELF      104 TIRIEL 4            14
        ON THINE
    LIVES NOT ALONE NOR FOR ITSELF FEAR NOT AND I WILL CALL     129 BOOK OF THEL 3       27
    MY BOSOM OF ITSELF IS COLD AND OF ITSELF IS DARK    . . .   129 BOOK OF THEL 4       12
    LOVE SEEKETH NOT ITSELF TO PLEASE  . . . . . . . . . .      162 CLOD PEBBLE/N         1
    NOR FOR ITSELF HATH ANY CARE  . . . . . . . . . . . .       162 CLOD PEBBLE/N         2
    DOES ITSELF DESTROY   . . . . . . . . . . . . . . .         168 SILENT NIGHT/N       11
    NOUGHT LOVES ANOTHER AS ITSELF  . . . . . . . . . . .       176 LIT BOY LST/N         1
    A GREATER THAN ITSELF TO KNOW  . . . . . . . . . . .        176 LIT BOY LST/N         4
    LOVE SEEKETH NOT ITSELF TO PLEASE  . . . . . . . . . .      211 CLOD PEBBLE/SE        1
    NOR FOR ITSELF HATH ANY CARE  . . . . . . . . . . . .       211 CLOD PEBBLE/SE        2
    NOUGHT LOVES ANOTHER AS ITSELF  . . . . . . . . . . .       218 LIT BOY LST/SE        1
    A GREATER THAN ITSELF TO KNOW  . . . . . . . . . . .        218 LIT BOY LST/SE        4
    ENROOTING ITSELF ALL AROUND   . . . . . . . . . . .         252 AHANIA 4              3
    ORGANIZING ITSELF TILL THE VACUUM  . . . . . . . . . .      258 BOOK OF LOS 4        50
    IF PAINE MEANS THAT A HISTORY THO TRUE IN ITSELF   . . . .  391B ANNO WATSON         MARG
    WHAT BACON CALLS LIES IS TRUTH ITSELF   . . . . . . . .     397D ANNO BACON          MARG
    ("NAKEDNESS IS UNCOMELY") THIS IS FOLLY ITSELF  . . . .     399D ANNO BACON          MARG
    THAT DID HEAVEN ITSELF BEGUILE . . . . . . . . . . .        422 BENEATH/N            19
    THAT DID HEAVEN ITSELF BEGUILE . . . . . . . . . . .        424 THE GOLDEN NET       18
    REYNOLDS THOUGHT CHARACTER ITSELF EXTRAVAGANCE & DEFORMITY   460C ANNO REYNOLDS      MARG
```

		PAGE	TITLE	LINE

ITSELF   (CONTINUED)
    [?THEIR VENETIAN ATTENTION IS TO A CONTEMPT & NEGLECT OF   463D ANNO REYNOLDS * MARG
       FORM ITSELF
    WHAT NONSENSE PASSION & EXPRESSION IS BEAUTY ITSELF . . . 466A ANNO REYNOLDS   MARG
    ITSELF LET IT BE PAINTED [& PRAISED] & PATCHD & PRAISED   466A ANNO REYNOLDS * MARG
    OF LIFE TILL THEY BECOME FINITE & ITSELF SEEMS INFINITE   490 MILTON 10   *   7
       [UNTIL]
    HIS PATH INTO A GLOBE ITSELF INFOLDING LIKE A SUN . . .   497 MILTON 15   24
    I HOPE THINE ARE NOT HENCE IT CLOTHES ITSELF IN RICH ARRAY 502 MILTON 20   30
    ENDING IN DEATH WHICH WOULD OF ITSELF BE ETERNAL DEATH . . 513 MILTON 26   42
    THE IMAGINATION IS NOT A STATE IT IS THE HUMAN EXISTENCE   522 MILTON 32   32
       ITSELF
    THAT COULD SHEW ITSELF BY THE SIDE OF AN EARLIER PRODUCTION 565B DESC CAT 2   PROSE
    ITSELF WILL DRINK OR ABSORB VERY LITTLE COLOUR . . . . 566B DESC CAT 2   PROSE
    THE FRANKLIN IS VOLUPTUOUSNESS ITSELF MOST NOBLY POURTRAYED 571A DESC CAT 3   PROSE
    THE PLOWMAN IS SIMPLICITY ITSELF WITH WISDOM AND STRENGTH   571B DESC CAT 3   PROSE
    LEAVE OUT THIS (LINE) AND YOU LEAVE OUT LIFE ITSELF   . 585C DESC CAT 15 *PROSE
    FROM IGNORANCE ITSELF & ITS FINISHING IS LIKE ITS MASTER   593B PUB ADDRESS/N   PROSE
    BUT WHAT CRITICS CALL THE FABLE IS VISION ITSELF . . . . 604D V LAST JUDG/N   PROSE
    FOUNDATION OF SOCIETY WHICH IS HUMANITY ITSELF   . . . 613A V LAST JUDG/N *PROSE
    ENGLOBES ITSELF & BECOMES A WOMB SUCH WAS ALBION'S COUCH   620 JERUSALEM 1   2
    A BONDAGE AS RHYME ITSELF I THEREFORE HAVE PRODUCED A . . 621D JERUSALEM 3   PROSE
    WITHOUT FORGIVENESS OF SIN LOVE IS ITSELF ETERNAL DEATH   699 JERUSALEM 64   24
    ENVYING STOOD THE ENORMOUS FORM AT VARIANCE WITH ITSELF   707 JERUSALEM 69   6
    FROM IMAGINATION AND CLOSING ITSELF AS IN STEEL IN A RATIO 714 JERUSALEM 74   11
    THE MOUNTAIN OF BLESSING IS ITSELF A CURSE   720 JERUSALEM 79   7
       & AN ASTONISHMENT
    IT MANIFESTS ITSELF IN HIS WORKS OF ART . . . . 776B INSC LAOCOON   PROSE
    MY STYLE OF DESIGNING IS A SPECIES BY ITSELF . . . . . 791D LETTER 4   PROSE
    NATURE IS IMAGINATION ITSELF AS A MAN IS SO HE SEES . . 793D LETTER 5   PROSE
    IDLENESS ITSELF DOES NOT HURT OTHER MEN LET SATAN HIMSELF   812C LETTER 22   PROSE
       EXPLAIN
    APPROVES OF IT WISHING ONLY THAT THE MONUMENT ITSELF MAY BE 832B LETTER 32   PROSE
    GRATITUDE IS HEAVEN ITSELF THERE COULD BE NO HEAVEN   834A LETTER 33   PROSE
       WITHOUT
    OWES SUCCESS TO SOMETHING BESIDE OR WITHOUT ITSELF IF IT   862A LETTER 59   PROSE
       HAS ANY
    AGAINST THEIR ETERNAL EXISTENCE ITSELF BECAUSE IT IS   . 871A LETTER 72   PROSE
    STRAIT OR CROOKED IT IS ITSELF & NOT INTERMEASURABLE WITH   878B LETTER 88   PROSE
       OR
I'VE
    IVE TOLD HIM BEFORE BUT HIS DISORDER . . . .   23 EDW THIRD/PS 3   69
    A TRIFLE IVE GILT YOUR CAUSE WITH MY BEST BLOOD . . . .   23 EDW THIRD/PS 3   99
    IVE OFTEN SEEN THE BURNING FIELD OF WAR . . . .   31 EDW THIRD/PS 5   39
    IVE FOUND THE DROPSY OUT & SOON . . . .   51 WHEN CORRUP/IM   31
    ID FIND IT OUT IN A MINUTE BUT IVE FOUND IT OUT ALREADY   51D ISLAND MOON 7   PROSE
    IVE A GOOD MIND TO GO . . . .   60 SAY YOU JOE/IM   3
    BUT I SAID IVE A PRETTY ROSE TREE . . . .   161 ROSE TREE/N   3
    [OPT IVE] SHALL I CAST IT ON THE SAND . . . .   168 HAST LAP/N   5
    [&] FOR IVE PULLD OUT THE STING . . . .   178 THE FAIRY/N   * 19
    BUT I SAID IVE A PRETTY ROSE-TREE . . . .   215 ROSE TREE/SE   3
    [IVE TASTED SHADOW &] . . . .   554 TO VENETIAN/N   16
    IVE GIVEN GREAT PROVISION TO MY FOES . . . .   555 BLAKES APL/N 1   22
    SOME SAY IVE GIVEN GREAT PROVISION TO MY FOES . . . . .   556 BLAKES APL/N 2   11
    THE [VISIONS] CAVERNS OF THE GRAVE IVE SEEN . . . . .   558 THE CAVERNS/N   1
    IVE A WIFE I LOVE & THAT LOVES ME . . . .   558 I ROSE UP AT/N   11
    IVE ALL BUT RICHES BODILY . . . .   558 I ROSE UP AT/N   12
    CRYING [IVE FOUND HI] CRUCIFY THIS CAUSE OF DISTRESS   . 755 EV GOSPEL(E)/N * 85
IVORY
    THE IVORY PALACE OF MY INMOST HEART WHERE IT SHALL LIE   39B SAMSON/PS   PROSE
       AT REST
    . . . THE CROWN VANISH AND THE SCEPTER AND IVORY STAFF . . 140 FRENCH REVOLTN   144
    . . . HIS IVORY WAND IN HIS HAND . . . . 143 FRENCH REVOLTN   198
    [THEY BOUND HIS LITTLE IVORY LIMBS] . . . .   177 LIT BOY LST/N   22
    WHERE MY IVORY BED . . . .   254 AHANIA 5   4
    AND HARROW FORMD & FRAMD THE HARNESS OF SILVER & IVORY . . 281 FOUR ZOAS 2   28
    THEY UNLOOSD THEM & PUT ON THE HARNESS OF GOLD & SILVER   281 FOUR ZOAS 2   36
       & IVORY
    THEN IN MY IVORY PAVILIONS I SLUMBERD [WITH] IN THE NOON   310 FOUR ZOAS 5   202
    FROM RUST OF AGES ALL ITS ORNAMENTS OF GOLD & SILVER &   364 FOUR ZOAS 9   292
       IVORY
    HE SPOKE & PILLARS WERE BUILDED & WALLS AS WHITE AS IVORY   369 FOUR ZOAS 9   461
    THEY FORMED HEAVENS OF SWEETEST (?WOODS) OF GOLD & SILVER   378 FOUR ZOAS 9 * 792
       & IVORY
    A WALL IS A LARGE IVORY . . . .   466D ANNO REYNOLDS   MARG
    COME TO MY IVORY PALACES O BELOVED OF THY MOTHER . . . . 501 MILTON 20   4
    OTHERS CABINETS RICHLY FABRICATE OF GOLD & IVORY . . . . 515 MILTON 28   8
    THEN YOU BEHOLD ITS MIGHTY SPIRES & DOMES OF IVORY & GOLD   525 MILTON 35   25
    IS CLOSD AS WITH A THREEFOLD CURTAIN OF IVORY & FINE LINEN 633 JERUSALEM 13   23
       & ERMINE
    THY PILLARS OF IVORY & GOLD THY CURTAINS OF SILK & FINE   647 JERUSALEM 24   18
    CURBING THEIR TYGERS WITH GOLDEN BITS & BRIDLES OF SILVER   686 JERUSALEM 55   35
       & IVORY
JACHIN
    JESUS SEATED BETWEEN THE TWO PILLARS JACHIN & BOAZ   . . 606B V LAST JUDG/N   PROSE
JACINTH
    THE CRYSOLITE THE TOPAZ THE JACINTH & EVERY PRECIOUS STONE 628 JERUSALEM 9   24
JACINTHS
    RUBIES JACINTHS CRYSOLITES ISSUING FROM THY FURNACES WHILE 732 JERUSALEM 87   20
JACK
    WISH JACK [HUNTER] TEARGUTS HAD HAD THE CUTTING OF PLUTARCH 50A ISLAND MOON 6 PROSE
    THAT THOUSANDS OF SWEEPERS DICK JOE NED & JACK . . . . 117 CHIMNEY SWP/SI   11

JACK   (CONTINUED)
   [AND] YORKSHIRE JACK HEMP & GENTLE BLUSHING DAW . . . . . 537 AND HIS LEGS/N   20
   AND CUR MY LAWYER & DADY [MY] JACK HEMP'S PARSON . . . 537 AND HIS LEGS/N * 26
   WOOLETT'S BEST WORKS WERE ETCHD BY JACK BROWN . . . . . 594A PUB ADDRESS/N   PROSE
   BY JACK BROWNE & IN WOOLETT'S WORKS THE ETCHING IS ALL . 594A PUB ADDRESS/N   PROSE
JACKO'S
   EXCEPT WHEN I GO TO MR JACKO'S HE KNOWS WHAT RIDING IS . . 53A ISLAND MOON 8   PROSE
JACOB
   MAY FROM THE WRITINGS OF PARACELSUS OR JACOB BEHMEN . . . 158A MARRIAGE HH 21   PROSE
   SAME THING AS JACOB BRYANT AND ALL ANTIQUARIES HAVE PROVED 578D DESC CAT 5   PROSE
   JACOB & [THEIR] HIS TWELVE SONS HOVER BENEATH THE . . . 607C V LAST JUDG/N   PROSE
   ADAM WHO IS PELEG & JOKTAN & ESAU & JACOB & SAUL & DAVID 713 JERUSALEM 73   28
JACOB'S
   NUMBER XIII JACOB'S LADDER A DRAWING . . . . 584B DESC CAT 13   TITLE
JADE
   YOU WOULD YOU IGNORANT JADE I WISH I COULD SEE YOU HIT ANY 48C ISLAND MOON 4   PROSE
JAIL
   THO THY COVENANT BUILT HELL'S JAIL . . . . 754 EV GOSPEL(E)/N   38
JAMES
   KING JAMES WAS BACON'S PRIMUM MOBILE . . . . 410D ANNO BACON   MARG
   JAMES CALLS FOR FIRES IN GOLGONOOZA FOR HEAPS OF SMOKING 485 MILTON 5   40
     RUINS
   [EEEEEEEEEEEEE WWWWWW THOMAS JAMES ROBERT] . . . . . 601A PUB ADDRESS/N *PROSE
   [EDWARD HENRY ELIZABETH JAMES CHARLES WILLIAM GEORGE] . . 713 JERUSALEM 73 * 37
JAMES'S
   AROUND SAINT JAMES'S [GLOW THE FIRES] . . . . 205 AMERICA CANC C   9
JAN
   JAN STEEN WAS A BOOR & NEITHER RAFAEL . . . . . . 472D ANNO REYNOLDS   MARG
JANE
   THE PENANCE OF JANE SHORE . . . . 209A SUBJCTS HIST/N   TITLE
   AND ON HIS LEFT HAND HIS SISTER JANE . . . . . . 435 WILLIAM BOND   18
   THAT WILLIAM BOND & HIS SISTER JANE . . . . 435 WILLIAM BOND   35
   NUMBER XVI THE PENANCE OF JANE SHORE IN ST PAULS CHURCH 585D DESC CAT 16   TITLE
     A DRAWING
JANRY
   TUESDAY JANRY...BETWEEN TWO & SEVEN IN THE EVENING DESPAIR 440A MEMORANDUM/N 1   PROSE
JANUARY
   JANUARY...[FEBRUARY]...WILLIAM BLAKE . . . . 444C LAST JUDGMNT/L   PROSE
   & WILL DO WHAT HE CAN BY THE END OF JANUARY . . . . 790A LETTER 1   PROSE
   FROM YOU ON...(JANUARY)...THAT PART OF YOUR LETTER IN WHICH 875D LETTER 82   PROSE
JAPAN
   ACROSS EUROPE & ASIA TO CHINA & JAPAN LIKE LIGHTENINGS . . 281 FOUR ZOAS 2 * 59
   TO MEXICO & PERU WEST & EAST TO CHINA & JAPAN TILL BABEL 486 MILTON 6   23
   FROM BRIGHT JAPAN & CHINA TO HESPERIA FRANCE & ENGLAND . 648 JERUSALEM 24   47
   THE GRAVES THUNDER BENEATH HIS FEET FROM IRELAND TO JAPAN 661 JERUSALEM 34   42
   IRELAND TO JAPAN FURIOUS HER LIONS & TYGERS & WOLVES SPORT 698 JERUSALEM 63   34
     BEFORE
   STRETCHING OVER EUROPE & ASIA FROM IRELAND TO JAPAN . . . 704 JERUSALEM 67   7
   TO SODOM & GOMORRHA THENCE TO INDIA CHINA & JAPAN . . 704 JERUSALEM 67   40
   WITH BLOOD FROM JAPAN EASTWARD TO THE GIANTS CAUSWAY WEST 719 JERUSALEM 78   26
   AND HELLE & HESPERIA & HINDOSTAN & CHINA & JAPAN . . 725 JERUSALEM 82   28
   FROM BABYLON TO ROME & THE WINGS SPREAD FROM JAPAN . . 735 JERUSALEM 89   48
JAPHET
   ON HIS RIGHT HAND SHEM & ON HIS LEFT JAPHET . . . . 609D V LAST JUDG/N   PROSE
JAPHETH
   KOX IS THE FATHER OF SHEM & HAM & JAPHETH HE IS THE NOAH 625 JERUSALEM 7   23
JAR
   SAW A TREACLE JAR SO HE GOES OF HIS BLIND SIDE . . . . 55B ISLAND MOON 9   PROSE
JARED
   ADAM SETH ENOS CAINAN MAHALALEEL JARED ENOCH . . . . 528 MILTON 37   36
   ADAM SETH ENOS CAINAN MAHALALEEL JARED ENOCH . . . . 716 JERUSALEM 75   11
JARGON
   ANY MORE THAN POPE'S METAPHYSICAL JARGON OF RHYMING . . 596B PUB ADDRESS/N   PROSE
JASPER
   THE EMERALD ONYX SAPPHIRE JASPER BERYL AMETHYST . . . . 343 FOUR ZOAS 8   74
JAVA
   [THERE IS JUST SUCH A TREE AT JAVA FOUND] . . . . . 185 LET BROTHELS/N   25
JAVAN
   THE ISLES OF JAVAN PHILISTEA TYRE AND LEBANON . . . . 731 JERUSALEM 86   32
   OF JAVAN THRO THE ISLES OF GRECIA & ALL EUROPE'S KINGS . 735 JERUSALEM 89   34
JAW
   HIS UNDER JAW DROPD AS THOSE EGGS HE LAID . . . . . 537 AND HIS LEGS/N   14
   CLAPD DEATH IN THE CORNER OF THEIR JAW . . . . . . 537 AND HIS LEGS/N   21
   WHEN MEN WILL DRAW OUTLINES BEGIN YOU TO JAW THEM . . 549 ALL PICTURES/N   7
   THEN NEVER FLINCH BUT KEEP UP A JAW . . . . 550 WHEN LOOK AT/N   3
JAWS
   WHILE THE BLACK GORE DROPS FROM HIS HORRID JAWS . . . . 31 EDW THIRD/PS 5   46
   THE WILY SERPENT'S JAWS . . . . 171 TO NOBODADDY/N   8
   AND A PALACE OF ETERNITY IN THE JAWS OF THE HUNGRY GRAVE 193 V DAU ALBION 6   1
   AND WHERE THE MOTHER'S MILK INSTEAD THOSE EVER-HISSING JAWS 199 AMERICA 9   23
   TO THE JAWS OF DEVOURING DARKNESS . . . . 236 URIZEN 28   3
   OR A PILLAR & PALACE OF ETERNITY IN THE JAWS OF THE HUNGRY 354 FOUR ZOAS 8   496
     GRAVE
   FROM THE [BLACK] DARK JAWS OF DEATH BENEATH & DESOLATE 363 FOUR ZOAS 9   259
     SHORES REMOTE
   AND FORM HIS FOREHEAD SMALL WITHOUT FRONTALS HIS JAWS LARGE 580A DESC CAT 5   PROSE
   AND CREATED HELL'S DARK JAWS . . . . 754 EV GOSPEL(E)/N   32
JEALOUS   SEE SELF JEALOUS
   ("THE JEALOUS IS POSSESSED BY A "FINE MAD DEVIL"") 75B ANNO LAVATER   MARG
     SHAKSPEARE
   ("AND A DULL SPIRIT AT ONCE ") PITY THE JEALOUS . . . . 75B ANNO LAVATER   MARG
   ("NOT JEALOUS") UNEASY BUT I HOPE TO MEND . . . . . 84C ANNO LAVATER   MARG

```
                                                                PAGE      TITLE           LINE
JEALOUS    (CONTINUED)
    THE JEALOUS WINGS WAVD OVER THE DEEP  . . . . . . .        159B SONG LIBERTY         PROSE
    DOWN RUSHD BEATING HIS WINGS IN VAIN THE JEALOUS KING  . . 159C SONG LIBERTY         PROSE
    [CRUEL JEALOUS [WINTRY] SELFISH FEAR]  . . . . . . .       169 EARTHS ANSWR/N  *      12
    AND LET THE JEALOUS DOLPHINS SPORT AROUND THE LOVELY MAID  190 V DAU ALBION 1         19
    AND FOLDED HIS BLACK JEALOUS WATERS ROUND THE ADULTERATE   190 V DAU ALBION 2          4
        PAIR
    OOTHOON SHALL VIEW HIS DEAR DELIGHT NOR EER WITH JEALOUS   195 V DAU ALBION 7         28
        CLOUD
    AND THUNDEROUS VISAGES HIS JEALOUS WINGS WAVD OVER THE DEEP 203 AMERICA 16             6
    CRUEL JEALOUS SELFISH FEAR  . . . . . . . . .              211 EARTHS ANSR/SE        12
    ALAS MY RINTRAH BRING THE LOVELY JEALOUS OCALYTHRON  . . . 240 EUROPE 8               7
    JEALOUS THO SHE WAS INVISIBLE  . . . . . . . . .           250 AHANIA 2              37
    I HAVE HIDDEN [THEE ENION IN JEALOUS DESPAIR] . . . . .    264 FOUR ZOAS 1           27
    [[THE JEALOUS] THREE DAYS SHE WAILD & THREE DARK NIGHTS    268 FOUR ZOAS 1    *     143
        . . .
    SHALT THOU DEPART TO WEEP IN SECRET IN MY JEALOUS WINGS    269 FOUR ZOAS 1          176
    AND THARMAS TOOK HER IN PITYING THEN ENION IN JEALOUS FEAR 278 FOUR ZOAS 1          525
    IN JEALOUS FEARS IN FURY & RAGE . . . . . . . . .          294 FOUR ZOAS 3           96
    HIS CLOUDY FORM IN JEALOUS FEAR & MUTTERING THUNDERS HOARSE 299 FOUR ZOAS 4          77
    UP TO THE IRON MOUNTAIN'S TOP & THERE THE JEALOUS CHAIN    307 FOUR ZOAS 5           99
    THEN LOS MOURND ON THE DISMAL WIND IN HIS JEALOUS          324 FOUR ZOAS 7          183
        LAMENTATION
    JEALOUS THAT SHE WAS VALA NOW BECOME URIZEN'S HARLOT  . .  336 FOUR ZOAS 7B         137
    BRITISH WOMEN WERE NOT JEALOUS WHEN GREEK & ROMAN WERE     491 MILTON 10            15
        JEALOUS
    AND OCALYTHRON BINDS THE SUN INTO A JEALOUS GLOBE  . . .   491 MILTON 10            19
    IN THE SHADOWY FEMALE'S BOSOM JEALOUS HER DARKNESS GREW    500 MILTON 18            42
    SO SPOKE ALBION IN JEALOUS FEARS HIDING HIS EMANATION  .   622 JERUSALEM 4          33
    JEALOUS OF JERUSALEM'S CHILDREN ASHAMD OF HER LITTLE-ONES  640 JERUSALEM 18          6
    IN JEALOUS FEAR IN STERN ACCUSATION WITH CRUEL STRIPES     644 JERUSALEM 21         29
    TREMBLING STOOD ALBION AT HER WORDS IN JEALOUS DARK DESPAIR 646 JERUSALEM 23        13
    IN JEALOUS FEARS & FURY & RAGE & FLAMES ROLL ROUND THEIR   655 JERUSALEM 29         75
        FERVID FEET
    WITH SPICES OF SWEET ODOURS OF LOVELY JEALOUS STUPEFACTION 722 JERUSALEM 80         28
    WHILE YOU ARE UNDER THE DOMINION OF A JEALOUS FEMALE  . .  734 JERUSALEM 88         41
    O ALL YE NATIONS OF THE EARTH BEHOLD YE THE JEALOUS WIFE   742 JERUSALEM 94         26
    NOR THY WILL DONE BUT [BEELZEBUB XXX ?UNJUST ?JEALOUS] .   788A ANNO THORNTON  * MARG
    THAT H(HAYLEY) IS JEALOUS AS STOTHARD WAS & WILL BE  . . . 819C LETTER 25          PROSE
JEALOUSIES
    BUT HEAVY BROWD JEALOUSIES LOWER OER THE LOUVRE . . . .    136 FRENCH REVOLTN       59
    AND WITH JEALOUSIES & FEARS  . . . . . . . . . .           416 MY SPECTRE/N         33
    FROM MALE & FEMALE LOVES IN BEULAH & THEIR JEALOUSIES  .   708 JERUSALEM 69         29
    THE JEALOUSIES BECOME MURDEROUS UNITING TOGETHER IN RAHAB  708 JERUSALEM 69         33
    ALL THEIR JEALOUSIES REVENGES MURDERS HIDINGS OF CRUELTY   739 JERUSALEM 92         16
        IN DECEIT
JEALOUSY
    FORTH WENT THE HAND OF JEALOUSY AMONG THE FLAMING HAIR  .  159C SONG LIBERTY        PROSE
    [WAS FILLD] TURND AWAY WITH JEALOUSY . . . . . . . .       161 ROSE TREE/N           9
    [STARRY] STARRY JEALOUSY DOES KEEP MY DEN  . . . . . .     169 EARTHS ANSWR/N  *      7
    [MAN] FATHER OF JEALOUSY  . . . . . . . . . . .            171 TO NOBODADDY/N        2
    FATHER OF JEALOUSY BE THOU ACCURSED FROM THE EARTH  . . .  194 V DAU ALBION 7       12
    THAT CLOUDS WITH JEALOUSY HIS NIGHTS WITH WEEPINGS ALL     194 V DAU ALBION 7       18
        THE DAY
    SILENT AS DESPAIRING LOVE AND STRONG AS JEALOUSY  . . .    196 AMERICA PREL 2        1
    STARRY JEALOUSY DOES KEEP MY DEN . . . . . . . . .         211 EARTHS ANSR/SE        7
    BUT MY ROSE TURND AWAY WITH JEALOUSY . . . . . . . .       215 ROSE TREE/SE          7
    AND JEALOUSY A HUMAN FACE  . . . . . . . . . .             221 DIVNE IMAGE/SE        2
    WITH THE CHAIN OF JEALOUSY . . . . . . . . . . .           233 URIZEN 20            24
    ORC ON MOUNT ATLAS HOWLD CHAIND DOWN WITH THE CHAIN OF     246 SONG OF LOS 3        21
        JEALOUSY
    HE SIEZD ON HIS MOUNTAINS OF JEALOUSY  . . . . . . .       249 AHANIA 2             33
    GREAT THE CONFLICT & GREAT THE JEALOUSY  . . . . . .       250 AHANIA 3             18
    CRUEL JEALOUSY SELFISH FEAR  . . . . . . . . . .           255 AHANIA 5             41
    THE FOUR ZOAS THE TORMENTS OF LOVE & JEALOUSY IN  . . .    263C FOUR ZOAS          TITLE
    ALTERNATE LOVE & HATE HIS BREAST HERS SCORN & JEALOUSY  .  270 FOUR ZOAS 1         237
    ON HIGH REMAIND ALONE FORSAKEN IN FIERCE JEALOUSY  . . .   274 FOUR ZOAS 1         360
    IN STRONG VIBRATIONS OF FIERCE JEALOUSY FOR THOU ART MINE  288 FOUR ZOAS 2         331
    THEN JEALOUSY SHALL SHADOW ALL HIS MOUNTAINS & AHANIA  .   289 FOUR ZOAS 2         338
    IN TORMENTS OF FIERCE JEALOUSY & PANGS OF ADORATION  . .   289 FOUR ZOAS 2         351
    CALLD IT THE CHAIN OF JEALOUSY NOW LOS BEGAN TO SPEAK  .   307 FOUR ZOAS 5          95
    FIBRES HAD FROM THE CHAIN OF JEALOUSY INWOVE THEMSELVES    309 FOUR ZOAS 5         157
    TO MELT THE CHAIN OF JEALOUSY NOT ENITHARMON'S DEATH  .    309 FOUR ZOAS 5         161
    OF THE CHAIN OF JEALOUSY & FELT THE RENDINGS OF FIERCE     309 FOUR ZOAS 5         182
        HOWLING ORC
    THOU & THAT DEMON LOS [WERE] WERT BORN AH JEALOUSY & WOE   327 FOUR ZOAS 7    *    295
    OFTEN ENOUGH TO CONVINCE THY JEALOUSY & FEAR & TERROR  .   330 FOUR ZOAS 7         421
    THO BOUND WITH CHAINS OF JEALOUSY & IN SCALES OF IRON &    332 FOUR ZOAS 7         481
        BRASS
    AND MUST NOT I OBEY THE GOD THOU SHADOW OF JEALOUSY  . .   335 FOUR ZOAS 7B         92
    SILENT AS DESPAIRING LOVE & STRONG AS JEALOUSY  . . . .    336 FOUR ZOAS 7B        136
    OF DAY IN JEALOUSY & BLOOD MY CHILDREN ARE LED TO URIZEN'S 339 FOUR ZOAS 7B        251
        WAR
    BUT SIN EVEN RAHAB IS REDEEMD IN BLOOD & FURY & JEALOUSY   361 FOUR ZOAS 9         159
    IS THE ARTIST'S JEALOUSY . . . . . . . . . . .             432 AUGURIES            50
    TILL IT SEPARATED INTO A MALE FORM HOWLING IN JEALOUSY  .  483 MILTON 3            36
    ELYNITTRIA WHENCE IS THIS JEALOUSY RUNNING ALONG          491 MILTON 10            14
        THE MOUNTAINS
    BOUND UP IN THE HORNS OF JEALOUSY TO A DEADLY FADING MOON  491 MILTON 10           18
    IN CONFLICT WITH THOSE FEMALE FORMS WHICH IN BLOOD        498 MILTON 17             7
        & JEALOUSY
    BURNS TO THE TOP OF HEAVEN AGAINST THEE IN JEALOUSY & FEAR 499 MILTON 18           32
```

	PAGE	TITLE	LINE

JEALOUSY   (CONTINUED)

BOUND WITH THE CHAIN OF JEALOUSY BY LOS & ENITHARMON . . 501 MILTON 19 38
ORC FROM HIS CHAIN OF JEALOUSY HE STARTED AT THE THOUGHT   503 MILTON 20 61
THEY WEAVE A NEW RELIGION FROM NEW JEALOUSY OF THEOTORMON   506 MILTON 22 38
OF JEALOUSY FROM ALL ITS ROOTS BE PATIENT THEREFORE O MY   507 MILTON 23 38
   SONS
IN JEALOUSY & UNLOVELY IN MY SIGHT BECAUSE THOU HAST   522 MILTON 33   6
   CRUELLY
DEPEND THY PLEASURES WHICH THOU HAST CUT OFF BY JEALOUSY   522 MILTON 33   9
THEREFORE I SHEW MY JEALOUSY & SET BEFORE YOU DEATH . . . 522 MILTON 33 10
HIS JEALOUSY BEFORE THE THRONE DIVINE DARKENING COLD . . 622 JERUSALEM 4   35
THE PARENT'S FEAR THE BROTHER'S JEALOUSY THE SISTER'S CURSE 636 JERUSALEM 16   7
WAS BECOME AN ENVIED HORROR AND A REMEMBRANCE OF JEALOUSY   652 JERUSALEM 28   3
IN SHAME & JEALOUSY TO ANNIHILATE JERUSALEM . . . . . 653 JERUSALEM 28 27
I FEEL THE IRON THREADS OF LOVE & JEALOUSY & DESPAIR . . 657 JERUSALEM 31 49
ALBION'S EMANATION WHICH HE HAD HIDDEN IN JEALOUSY . . . 659 JERUSALEM 33 26
UTTERING NOT HIS JEALOUSY BUT HIDING IT AS WITH . . . . 664 JERUSALEM 38   4
IN LOVE & JEALOUSY IMMINGLED & CALLING IT RELIGION . . . 674 JERUSALEM 44 27
LEST HE SHOULD SLAY JERUSALEM IN HIS FEARFUL JEALOUSY . . 675 JERUSALEM 45 27
THE DAUGHTERS OF ALBION DIVIDE & UNITE IN JEALOUSY   689 JERUSALEM 58   5
   & CRUELTY
THE OBDURATE FORMS ARE CUT ASUNDER BY JEALOUSY & PITY . . 689 JERUSALEM 58 12
OF JEALOUSY AND THOUGHT IT A POETIC VISION OF THE   698 JERUSALEM 63 40
   ATMOSPHERES
CRIMSON WITH WRATH & GREEN WITH JEALOUSY DAZLING WITH LOVE 699 JERUSALEM 64 28
AND JEALOUSY IMMINGLED & THE PURPLE OF THE VIOLET DARKEND   699 JERUSALEM 64 29
   DEEP
THE SPIES FROM EGYPT TO RAISE JEALOUSY IN THE BOSOMS OF   707 JERUSALEM 68 60
   THE TWELVE
IN ALL ITS MEMBERS IN ETERNAL TORMENT OF LOVE & JEALOUSY   707 JERUSALEM 69   7
AND JEALOUSY & ABHORRENCE & REVENGE & DEADLY MURDER . . . 707 JERUSALEM 69 13
CONTINUALLY BUILDING CONTINUALLY DECAYING BECAUSE OF LOVE   712A JERUSALEM 72 PROSE
   & JEALOUSY
HE SAW THEM ISSUE FROM MY BOSOM DARK IN JEALOUSY . . . 722 JERUSALEM 80 21
CAMBEL TREMBLED WITH JEALOUSY SHE TREMBLED SHE ENVIED . . 726 JERUSALEM 82 52
SHE SPOKE IN SCORN & JEALOUSY ALTERNATE TORMENTS AND . . 733 JERUSALEM 88 22
IN PRIDE (SENDING) HIS FIBRES OVER TO HER OBJECTS   733 JERUSALEM 88 30
   OF JEALOUSY
UNPERMANENT FOR EVER BECAUSE OF LOVE & JEALOUSY . . . . 734 JERUSALEM 88 42

JEBUSITE

HE IS ARAUNAH THE JEBUSITE MASTER OF THE THRESHING FLOOR   607D V LAST JUDG/N PROSE
THE VALLEY OF THE JEBUSITE MOLECH REJOICES IN HEAVEN . . 706 JERUSALEM 68 23

JEFFERY

NUMBER III SIR JEFFERY CHAUCER AND THE NINE AND TWENTY   566C DESC CAT 3 TITLE
SIR JEFFERY CHAUCER & THE NINE & TWENTY PILGRIMS . . . . 588B CHAUCER/N TITLE

JEFFREY

FROM HIS FRESCO PAINTING OF SIR JEFFREY CHAUCER AND . . 589C CHAUCER 2 TITLE
"SIR JEFFREY CHAUCER AND HIS PILGRIMS SET OUT FOR   590B CHAUCER 2 PROSE
   CANTERBURY"

JEHOSHUAN

NEVER CAN HAVE ANY TO SIR JEHOSHUAN . . . . 542 FLORENTINE/N 34

JEHOVAH

THAT REASON MAY HAVE IDEAS TO BUILD ON THE JEHOVAH OF THE   150B MARRIAGE HH 5 PROSE
   BIBLE
KNOW THAT AFTER CHRIST'S DEATH HE BECAME JEHOVAH . . . . 150B MARRIAGE HH 5 PROSE
AND THEN THEY SENT JEHOVAH WHO LEPROUS STRETCHD HIS HAND   351 FOUR ZOAS 8 405
   TO ETERNITY
JEHOVAH JESUS A WINE BIBBER . . . . 412C ANNO BOYD MARG
OF MORAL LAWS AND CRUEL PUNISHMENTS UPON THE CLOUDS OF   489 MILTON 9 22
   JEHOVAH
THE HARROW CAST THICK FLAMES JEHOVAH THUNDERD ABOVE . . . 493 MILTON 12 20
JEHOVAH THUNDERD ABOVE SATAN IN PRIDE OF HEART . . . . 493 MILTON 12 24
DROVE THE FIERCE HARROW AMONG THE CONSTELLATIONS OF JEHOVAH 493 MILTON 12 25
SHADDAI ANGRY PAHAD DESCENDED PAHAD TERRIFIED THEY SENT   494 MILTON 13 23
   JEHOVAH
AND JEHOVAH WAS LEPROUS LOUD HE CALLD STRETCHING HIS HAND   494 MILTON 13 24
   TO ETERNITY
OVER THE SEPULCHERS IN CLOUDS OF JEHOVAH & WINDS OF ELOHIM 495 MILTON 14 26
BUT LOS DISPERSD THE CLOUDS EVEN AS THE STRONG WINDS OF   507 MILTON 23 31
   JEHOVAH
ALL THE ATONEMENTS OF JEHOVAH SPURND . . . . 543 IF TRUE/N 13
NAME OF JEHOVAH ELOHIM THE I AM OF THE OAKS OF ALBION . . 610A V LAST JUDG/N PROSE
TILL SKOFIELD'S NIMROD THE MIGHTY HUNTSMAN JEHOVAH CAME   644 JERUSALEM 22   3
THE PRAISE OF JEHOVAH IS CHAUNTED FROM LIPS OF HUNGER &   656 JERUSALEM 30 32
   THIRST
TILL THE PLOW OF JEHOVAH AND THE HARROW OF SHADDAI . . . 676 JERUSALEM 46 14
JEHOVAH IS BEFORE BEHIND ABOVE BENEATH AROUND . . . . . 680 JERUSALEM 49 53
LUCIFER MOLECH ELOHIM SHADDAI PAHAD JEHOVAH JESUS . . . 686 JERUSALEM 55 32
BEHOLD IN THE VISIONS OF ELOHIM JEHOVAH BEHOLD JOSEPH   694 JERUSALEM 61   1
   & MARY
AND BE COMFORTED O JERUSALEM IN THE VISIONS OF JEHOVAH   694 JERUSALEM 61   2
   ELOHIM
SAYING DOTH JEHOVAH FORGIVE A DEBT ONLY ON CONDITION THAT   694 JERUSALEM 61 17
   IT SHALL
OF JEHOVAH IF YOU FORGIVE ONE-ANOTHER SO SHALL JEHOVAH   695 JERUSALEM 61 25
   FORGIVE YOU
BEFORE I HAD EVER BEHELD WITH LOVE THE FACE OF JEHOVAH   695 JERUSALEM 61 42
   OR KNOWN
THE INFANT INTO HER HANDS IN THE VISIONS OF JEHOVAH TIMES   695 JERUSALEM 61 48
   PASSED ON
JEHOVAH STOOD AMONG THE DRUIDS IN THE VALLEY OF ANNANDALE   696 JERUSALEM 63   1
DANCE THE DANCE OF DEATH CONTENDING WITH JEHOVAH AMONG   697 JERUSALEM 63 10
   THE CHERUBIM

1002

	PAGE	TITLE	LINE

JEHOVAH   (CONTINUED)

AND JEHOVAH STOOD IN THE GATES OF THE VICTIM & HE APPEARED   697 JERUSALEM 63   16
WITHOUT THE FORGIVENESS OF SINS IN THE MERCIFUL CLOUDS   697 JERUSALEM 63   27
    OF JEHOVAH
O WHEN SHALL JEHOVAH GIVE US VICTIMS FROM HIS FLOCKS &   697 JERUSALEM 63   30
    HERDS
IN MORAL LAW & ITS SEVERE PENALTIES LOUD SHADDAI & JEHOVAH   706 JERUSALEM 68   39
I HAVE NAMED HIM JEHOVAH OF HOSTS HUMANITY IS BECOME   . . 724 JERUSALEM 81   13
. . . IT IS THE COVENANT OF JEHOVAH . . . .   745 JERUSALEM 98   23
AND SEEING ACCORDING TO FITNESS & ORDER AND I HEARD JEHOVAH   746 JERUSALEM 98   40
    SPEAK
. . . ACCORDING TO [THY] THE COVENANT [OF] JEHOVAH THEY CRY   746 JERUSALEM 98   * 45
BROUGHT TO LIGHT BY JESUS EVEN THE COVENANT OF JEHOVAH . .   757D EV GOSPEL   PROSE
SO SHALL JEHOVAH FORGIVE YOU . . . .   757D EV GOSPEL   PROSE
OF JESUS & JEHOVAH THOU ART STILL . . . .   771 EPILOGUE/GP   6
A REVELATION IN THE VISIONS OF JEHOVAH SEEN BY WILLIAM   779B GHOST ABEL 1   TITLE
    BLAKE
CAN A POET DOUBT THE VISIONS OF JEHOVAH . . . . . .   779C GHOST ABEL 1   PROSE
ADAM KNEELS BY HER JEHOVAH STANDS ABOVE . . . . . .   779C GHOST ABEL 1   PROSE
JEHOVAH ADAM . . . .   779 GHOST ABEL 1   1
JEHOVAH ADAM . . . .   779 GHOST ABEL 1   2
EVE IS THIS THE PROMISE OF JEHOVAH O IT IS ALL A   779 GHOST ABEL 1   6
    VAIN DELUSION
THIS DEATH & THIS LIFE & THIS JEHOVAH . . . .   779 GHOST ABEL 1   7
JEHOVAH WOMAN LIFT THINE EYES . . . .   779 GHOST ABEL 1   7
VAIN IS THY COVENANT O JEHOVAH I AM THE ACCUSER & AVENGER   780 GHOST ABEL 1   12
JEHOVAH WHAT VENGEANCE DOST THOU REQUIRE . . . . . .   780 GHOST ABEL 1   14
JEHOVAH HE WHO SHALL TAKE CAIN'S LIFE MUST ALSO DIE O ABEL   780 GHOST ABEL 1   15
THO TERRIBLY AFFLICTED AS WE ALSO ARE YET JEHOVAH SEES HIM   780 GHOST ABEL 1   24
THEY KNEEL BEFORE JEHOVAH . . . .   780C GHOST ABEL 2   PROSE
ABEL ARE THESE THE SACRIFICES OF ETERNITY O JEHOVAH   780 GHOST ABEL 2   4
    A BROKEN SPIRIT
JEHOVAH LO I HAVE GIVEN YOU A LAMB FOR AN ATONEMENT INSTEAD   780 GHOST ABEL 2   10
AND NO ATONEMENT O JEHOVAH THE ELOHIM LIVE ON SACRIFICE   780 GHOST ABEL 2   14
OF MEN HENCE I AM GOD OF MEN THOU HUMAN O JEHOVAH . . .   780 GHOST ABEL 2   15
JEHOVAH SUCH IS MY WILL THUNDERS . . . .   781 GHOST ABEL 2   19
FORTH O ELOHIM JEHOVAH . . . .   781 GHOST ABEL 2   23
OF JEHOVAH AS A VERY INFERIOR OBJECT OF MAN'S CONTEMPLATION 784B ANNO WW EXCUR   MARG
JEHOVAH DROPPED A TEAR & FOLLOWD HIM BY HIS SPIRIT . . . 784B ANNO WW EXCUR   MARG

JEHOVAH'S

THEY PLOWD IN TEARS INCESSANT POURD JEHOVAH'S RAIN   488 MILTON 8   27
    & MOLECH'S
HEATHEN WHOSE TENDER MERCIES ARE CRUELTY BUT JEHOVAH'S   694 JERUSALEM 61   21
    SALVATION
TAKE JESUS' & JEHOVAH'S NAME . . . .   758 EV GOSPEL (1)   10
[JEHOVAH'S FINGERS WROTE THE LAW] . . . .   761 FOR SEXES/GP   5
JEHOVAH'S FINGER WROTE THE LAW . . . .   761 FOR SEXES/GP   6

JELLICOE

THE SONG OF PHEBE AND JELLICOE NO MISS SAID SCOPPRELL . .   53C ISLAND MOON 8   PROSE
JELLICOE IN FAINT PEA GREEN . . . .   53 PHEBE DREST/IM   2

JELLIES   SEE SEA JELLIES

JENNY

JENNY HER SILKEN KERCHIEF FOLDS . . . .   16 BLIND-MANS/PS   19
ABOUT FREEDOM & JENNY SUCK AWA . . . .   550 WHEN LOOK AT/N   4

JENOUS

AND JENOUS LOOKS TO HAM [LOOKS] LIKE MAD RANTERY . . .   550 ENGL ENCOU/N 2   *   4

JEPHTHAH

JEPHTHAH SACRIFICING HIS DAUGHTER . . . . 824A LETTER 27   PROSE

JEROME

SAYS JEROME HAPPINESS IS NOT FOR US POOR CRAWLING REPTILES   52B ISLAND MOON 8   PROSE

JERUSALEM

THEN NINEVA & BABYLON AND COSTLY TYRE AND EVN JERUSALEM   41A THEN SHE BORE   *PROSE
THEN OOTHOON HOVERD OVER JUDAH & JERUSALEM . . . . . .   246 SONG OF LOS 3   22
AND STRETCHD HIS CLOUDS OVER JERUSALEM . . . .   248 SONG OF LOS 7   19
. . .[ENITHARMON] JERUSALEM IN SILENT CONTRITION O PITY ME   264 FOUR ZOAS 1   *   27
. . . SWEET [ENITHARMON] JERUSALEM FROM MY INMOST SOUL .   265 FOUR ZOAS 1   *   29
A TABERNACLE OF [DELIGHT] FOR [ENITHARMON] JERUSALEM . .   266 FOUR ZOAS 1   *   70
WILL LAY MY SCEPTER ON JERUSALEM THE EMANATION . . . .   278 FOUR ZOAS 1   498
JERUSALEM HIS EMANATION [WILL SOON] IS BECOME A RUIN . .   279 FOUR ZOAS 1   545
DESTROY THESE OPPRESSORS OF JERUSALEM & THOSE WHO   279 FOUR ZOAS 1   * 549
    RUIN SHILOH
JERUSALEM IN SLUMBERS SOFT LULLD INTO SILENT REST   280 FOUR ZOAS 1   570
JERUSALEM CAME DOWN IN A DIRE RUIN OVER ALL THE EARTH . .   281 FOUR ZOAS 2   45
WHETHER THIS IS JERUSALEM OR BABYLON WE KNOW NOT . . .   294 FOUR ZOAS 3   102
[WE FLED FROM ?JERUSALEM ?AFTER ?THE MERCIFUL   SUPP FOUR ZOAS 3   *
    LORD & SAVIOUR]
AND ENITHARMON NAMED THE FEMALE (JERUSALEM) THE HOLY   346 FOUR ZOAS 8   * 190
IS BORN ON EARTH SO WAS HE BORN OF FAIR JERUSALEM . . .   347 FOUR ZOAS 8   262
HE STOOD IN FAIR JERUSALEM TO AWAKE UP INTO EDEN . . .   348 FOUR ZOAS 8   264
[SHE] JERUSALEM SAW THE BODY DEAD UPON THE CROSS SHE FLED   349 FOUR ZOAS 8   331
    AWAY
LOS TOOK THE BODY FROM THE CROSS JERUSALEM WEEPING OVER   349 FOUR ZOAS 8   338
JERUSALEM PITYING THEM WOVE THEM MANTLES OF LIFE & DEATH   351 FOUR ZOAS 8   397
BOW DOWN BEFORE HER YOU HER CHILDREN & SET JERUSALEM FREE   351 FOUR ZOAS 8   409
JERUSALEM WEPT OVER THE SEPULCHER TWO THOUSAND YEARS . .   356 FOUR ZOAS 8   596
RAHAB TRIUMPHS OVER ALL SHE TOOK JERUSALEM . . . . .   356 FOUR ZOAS 8   597
[IN EDEN IN THE GARDEN OF GOD & IN HEAVENLY JERUSALEM]   SUPP FOUR ZOAS 8   *
AND LOS & ENITHARMON BUILDED JERUSALEM WEEPING . . . .   357 FOUR ZOAS 9   1
BEHOLD JERUSALEM IN WHOSE BOSOM THE LAMB OF GOD [IS SEEN]   362 FOUR ZOAS 9   205
THAT WE HIS CHILDREN EVERMORE MAY LIVE IN JERUSALEM . .   362 FOUR ZOAS 9   221
THEY MAGNIFY THEMSELVES NO MORE AGAINST JERUSALEM NOR . .   364 FOUR ZOAS 9   266
DESCENDING FROM JERUSALEM WITH POWER AND GREAT GLORY . .   364 FOUR ZOAS 9   273

```
                                                              PAGE     TITLE        LINE
JERUSALEM   (CONTINUED)
    A PLACE IN THE NEW JERUSALEM EXCELLENT TRAVELLER GO ON      404D ANNO BACON     * MARG
      & BE DAMND
    THAT THE NEW JERUSALEM IS READY TO DESCEND UPON EARTH    .  . 444A LAST JUDGMNT/L PROSE
    AND WAS JERUSALEM BUILDED HERE  . . . . . . . . . .       . 481 AND DID FEET/M      7
    TILL WE HAVE BUILT JERUSALEM     . . . . . . . .         .  . 481 AND DID FEET/M   15
    OF JERUSALEM HIS EMANATION IN THE HEAVENS BENEATH BEULAH    481 MILTON 2          15
    WHEN SHALL JERUSALEM RETURN & OVERSPREAD ALL THE NATIONS    485 MILTON 6          18
    HE SET HIS FACE AGAINST JERUSALEM TO DESTROY THE EON OF     491 MILTON 11          1
      ALBION
    TO DEVOUR ALBION AND JERUSALEM THE EMANATION OF ALBION   .  . 493 MILTON 12       27
    OF ALBION O VALA O LUVAH O ALBION O LOVELY JERUSALEM        494 MILTON 13          9
    JERUSALEM IS HIS GARMENT & NOT THY COVERING CHERUB O LOVELY 499 MILTON 18         37
    OPENING INTERIORLY INTO JERUSALEM & BABYLON SHINING        500 MILTON 18         41
      GLORIOUS
    COME BRING WITH THEE JERUSALEM WITH SONGS ON THE GRECIAN    501 MILTON 19         46
      LYRE
    TO DESTROY JERUSALEM AS A HARLOT & HER SONS AS REPROBATES   506 MILTON 22         47
    LAMBETH MOURNS CALLING JERUSALEM SHE WEEPS & LOOKS ABROAD   511 MILTON 25         54
    FOR THE LORD'S COMING THAT JERUSALEM MAY OVERSPREAD ALL     511 MILTON 25         55
      NATIONS
    SHALT BRING JERUSALEM IN THINE ARMS IN THE NIGHT WATCHES    523 MILTON 33         21
      AND
    WHERE ONCE THE CHERUBS OF JERUSALEM SPREAD TO LAMBETH'S     525 MILTON 35         10
      VALE
    HERE IS JERUSALEM BOUND IN CHAINS IN THE DENS OF BABYLON    529 MILTON 38         27
    HE VIEWS JERUSALEM & BABYLON HIS TEARS FLOW DOWN  . . . .  . 531 MILTON 39        48
    THESE TEARS FALL FOR THE LITTLE-ONES THE CHILDREN          532 MILTON 40         15
      OF JERUSALEM
    THAT THE CHILDREN OF JERUSALEM MAY BE SAVED FROM SLAVERY    532 MILTON 40         31
    THESE ARE THE DESTROYERS OF JERUSALEM THESE ARE THE        533 MILTON 41         21
      MURDERERS
    WHO IN THE AGGREGATE ARE CALLD JERUSALEM FABLE IS ALLEGORY  604D V LAST JUDG/N    PROSE
    [JERUSALEM WHO IS ABOUT TO BE RECIEVD LIKE THE BRIDE       609C V LAST JUDG/N   *PROSE
      OF THE]
    JERUSALEM IS THEIR DAUGHTER LITTLE INFANTS CREEP OUT OF THE 609D V LAST JUDG/N    PROSE
    JERUSALEM THE EMANATION OF THE GIANT ALBION  . . . . .      620A JERUSALEM        TITLE
    JERUSALEM HIS EMANATION IS A STONE LAYING BENEATH  . .      620 JERUSALEM 1          6
    (MONOS HO IESOUS) JERUSALEM CHAP I  . . . . . . .           622A JERUSALEM 4       TITLE
    WHERE HAST THOU HIDDEN THY EMANATION LOVELY JERUSALEM    .  . 622 JERUSALEM 4      16
    JERUSALEM IS NOT HER DAUGHTERS ARE INDEFINITE  . . . . .  . 622 JERUSALEM 4        27
    JERUSALEM IS SCATTERD ABROAD LIKE A CLOUD OF SMOKE THRO     623 JERUSALEM 5         13
      NON-ENTITY
    DRAWING JERUSALEM IN ANGUISH OF MATERNAL LOVE  . . . .  .   624 JERUSALEM 5         47
    AND THERE JERUSALEM WANDERS WITH VALA UPON THE MOUNTAINS    624 JERUSALEM 5         60
    IMMENSE AND JERUSALEM & VALA WEEPING IN THE CLOUD  . .      624 JERUSALEM 5         62
    OF JERUSALEM BECOME HER COVERING TILL THE TIME OF THE END   626 JERUSALEM 7         64
    OF GOD TO DESTROY JERUSALEM & TO DEVOUR THE BODY OF ALBION  628 JERUSALEM 9         10
    TILL HE SHOULD BRING THE SONS & DAUGHTERS OF JERUSALEM      629 JERUSALEM 10         3
      TO BE
    AGAIN THEY LAMENT O WHAT SHALL WE DO FOR LOVELY JERUSALEM   631 JERUSALEM 11        17
    A SHADOW ANIMATED BY THY TEARS O MOURNFUL JERUSALEM  . .    631 JERUSALEM 11        25
    WHAT SHALL WE DO FOR THEE O LOVELY MILD JERUSALEM  . .      631 JERUSALEM 12         4
    THE STARRY WHEELS OF ALBION'S SONS WITH SPACES FOR         631 JERUSALEM 12        18
      JERUSALEM
    AND FOR VALA THE SHADOW OF JERUSALEM THE EVER MOURNING      631 JERUSALEM 12        19
      SHADE
    GO ON BUILDERS IN HOPE THO JERUSALEM WANDERS FAR AWAY    .  . 632 JERUSALEM 12      43
    AND LOS BEHELD THE MILD EMANATION JERUSALEM EASTWARD        635 JERUSALEM 14        31
      BENDING
    AND HAND & HYLE ROOTED INTO JERUSALEM BY A FIBRE  . . .     635 JERUSALEM 15         1
    GIVES TO THE CHILDREN OF ALBION & TO THE CHILDREN          637 JERUSALEM 16        24
      OF JERUSALEM
    IF SHE HAD NOT SOUGHT TO DESTROY JERUSALEM SUCH IS THAT     639 JERUSALEM 17        25
      FALSE
    FOR VALA PRODUCD THE BODIES JERUSALEM GAVE THE SOULS    .  . 640 JERUSALEM 18        7
    CAST CAST YE JERUSALEM FORTH THE SHADOW OF DELUSIONS    .  . 640 JERUSALEM 18       11
    AND OF HIS CHILDREN BEFORE SINFUL JERUSALEM TO BUILD    .  . 640 JERUSALEM 18       28
    SHE IS OUR MOTHER NATURE JERUSALEM IS OUR HARLOT-SISTER     640 JERUSALEM 18        30
    JERUSALEM HIS EMANATION SHUT WITHIN HIS BOSOM  . . . .      641 JERUSALEM 19        29
    HE FOUND JERUSALEM UPON THE RIVER OF HIS CITY SOFT REPOSD   642 JERUSALEM 19        40
    DIVIDING AND UNITING INTO MANY FEMALE FORMS JERUSALEM    .  . 642 JERUSALEM 19       45
    THEN THUS JERUSALEM SPOKE WHILE VALA WOVE THE VEIL OF TEARS 642 JERUSALEM 20         3
    JERUSALEM ANSWERD WITH SOFT TEARS OVER THE VALLEYS  . .     643 JERUSALEM 20        21
    AT SIGHT OF THY ONCE LOVD JERUSALEM WHAT IS SIN BUT        643 JERUSALEM 20        23
      A LITTLE
    O VALA O JERUSALEM DO YOU DELIGHT IN MY GROANS  . . .       643 JERUSALEM 21         1
    JERUSALEM DISSEMBLER JERUSALEM I LOOK INTO THY BOSOM    .  . 643 JERUSALEM 21       18
    THEN SPOKE JERUSALEM O ALBION MY FATHER ALBION  . .         645 JERUSALEM 22        19
    THEN ALBION TURND HIS FACE TOWARD JERUSALEM & SPOKE  . .    645 JERUSALEM 22        25
    HIDE THOU JERUSALEM IN IMPALPABLE VOIDNESS NOT TO BE  .     645 JERUSALEM 22        26
    TOUCHD BY THE HAND NOR SEEN WITH THE EYE O JERUSALEM        645 JERUSALEM 22        27
    AS I BEHOLD JERUSALEM IN THEE O VALA DARK AND COLD  . .     645 JERUSALEM 22        32
    JERUSALEM THEN STRETCHD HER HAND TOWARD THE MOON & SPOKE    645 JERUSALEM 22        33
    JERUSALEM JERUSALEM DELUDING SHADOW OF ALBION  . . . .      645 JERUSALEM 23         1
    JERUSALEM REPLYD LIKE A VOICE HEARD FROM A SEPULCHER  .     646 JERUSALEM 23         8
    O JERUSALEM JERUSALEM I HAVE FORSAKEN THY COURTS  . . .     647 JERUSALEM 24        17
    TO BUILD BABYLON BECAUSE THEY HAVE FORSAKEN JERUSALEM    .  . 647 JERUSALEM 24       30
    WHEN JERUSALEM WAS THY HEART'S DESIRE IN TIMES OF YOUTH     647 JERUSALEM 24        37
      & LOVE
    THY SONS CAME TO JERUSALEM WITH GIFTS SHE SENT THEM AWAY    647 JERUSALEM 24        38
    THEY CAME UP TO JERUSALEM THEY WALKED BEFORE ALBION  . .  . 647 JERUSALEM 24        41
```

	PAGE	TITLE	LINE

JERUSALEM   (CONTINUED)

JERUSALEM COVERD THE ATLANTIC MOUNTAINS & THE ERYTHREAN	648	JERUSALEM 24	46
THOU ART A DELUSION AND JERUSALEM IS MY SIN O MY CHILDREN	648	JERUSALEM 24	54
HAND JERUSALEM	649A	JERUSALEM 26	TITLE
JERUSALEM IS NAMED LIBERTY	649	SUCH VISIONS/J	3
JERUSALEM THE EMANATION OF THE GIANT ALBION CAN IT BE	649B	JERUSALEM 27	PROSE
THAT JERUSALEM WAS & IS THE EMANATION OF THE GIANT ALBION	649B	JERUSALEM 27	PROSE
AND FAIR JERUSALEM HIS BRIDE	649	FIELDS FROM/J	7
JERUSALEM FELL FROM LAMBETH'S VALE	650	FIELDS FROM/J	41
AND IS JERUSALEM THY BRIDE	651	FIELDS FROM/J	68
MUTUAL SHALL BUILD JERUSALEM	652	FIELDS FROM/J	87
JERUSALEM CHAP (TWO)	652C	JERUSALEM 28	TITLE
IN SHAME & JEALOUSY TO ANNIHILATE JERUSALEM	653	JERUSALEM 28	27
THE SONS OF GOD WERE ALBION'S SONS AND JERUSALEM WAS MY JOY	653	JERUSALEM 29	8
HIMSELF OF ALBION'S FORESTS & WILDS AND JERUSALEM IS TAKEN	653	JERUSALEM 29	17
BENEATH HIS VAST RANGES OF HILLS SURROUNDING JERUSALEM	654	JERUSALEM 29	32
TO WHERE THE TOWER OF LONDON FROWND DREADFUL OVER JERUSALEM	657	JERUSALEM 31	23
AND HE BEHELD JERUSALEM IN WESTMINSTER & MARYBONE	657	JERUSALEM 31	40
I EMANATED FROM LUVAH OVER THE TOWERS OF JERUSALEM	660	JERUSALEM 33	41
THE SACRIFICE OF FANATIC LOVE WHY LOVED I JERUSALEM	660	JERUSALEM 33	43
ART THOU NATURE MOTHER OF ALL IS JERUSALEM THY DAUGHTER	660	JERUSALEM 34	9
JERUSALEM TREMBLED SEEING HER CHILDREN DRIVN BY LOS'S HAMMER	663	JERUSALEM 36	21
AND ENGLAND WHO IS BRITTANNIA DIVIDED INTO JERUSALEM & VALA	663	JERUSALEM 36	28
IN EDEN IN THE GARDEN OF GOD AND IN HEAVENLY JERUSALEM	665	JERUSALEM 38	25
FOR ALBION'S SAKE AND FOR JERUSALEM THY EMANATION	665	JERUSALEM 38	38
A TRIPLE OCTAVE HE TOOK TO REDUCE JERUSALEM TO TWELVE	668	JERUSALEM 41	4
TO CAST JERUSALEM FORTH UPON THE WILDS TO POPLAR & BOW	668	JERUSALEM 41	5
WHERE MILD JERUSALEM SOUGHT TO REPOSE IN DEATH & BE NO MORE	668	JERUSALEM 41	10
FOR VICTIMS OF SACRIFICE BUT JERUSALEM CANNOT BE FOUND HID	668	JERUSALEM 41	13
HERE JERUSALEM & VALA WERE HID IN SOFT SLUMBEROUS REPOSE	668	JERUSALEM 41	21
THEY ENQUIRE AFTER JERUSALEM IN THE REGIONS OF THE DEAD	671	JERUSALEM 42	68
IF WE ARE WRATHFUL ALBION WILL DESTROY JERUSALEM WITH ROOTY GROVES	672	JERUSALEM 43	8
O GOD OF ALBION DESCEND DELIVER JERUSALEM FROM THE OAKEN GROVES	672	JERUSALEM 43	11
INSTEAD OF ALBION'S LOVELY MOUNTAINS & THE CURTAINS OF JERUSALEM	673	JERUSALEM 43	59
I SEE AMERICA CLOSD APART & JERUSALEM DRIVEN IN TERROR	673	JERUSALEM 43	69
WHO IS JERUSALEM IN EVERY INDIVIDUAL MAN AND HER	675	JERUSALEM 44	39
IN EDEN IN LOVELY JERUSALEM DREW EVEN FROM ENVY	675	JERUSALEM 45	6
LEST HE SHOULD SLAY JERUSALEM IN HIS FEARFUL JEALOUSY	675	JERUSALEM 45	27
O GOD DESCEND GATHER OUR BRETHREN DELIVER JERUSALEM	675	JERUSALEM 45	28
OF GENERATION TO DESTROY BY SIN AND ATONEMENT HAPPY JERUSALEM	676	JERUSALEM 46	27
WHERE LOS'S FURNACES STAND WHERE JERUSALEM & VALA HOWL	677	JERUSALEM 47	3
FROM THIS SWEET PLACE MATERNAL LOVE AWOKE JERUSALEM	677	JERUSALEM 48	18
WEPT FOR THEIR SISTER THE DAUGHTER OF ALBION JERUSALEM	678	JERUSALEM 48	22
AWAY FROM THE STARRY WHEELS TO PREPARE JERUSALEM A PLACE	678	JERUSALEM 48	46
JERUSALEM WEEPING OVER HER AMONG THE SPACES OF ERIN	678	JERUSALEM 48	51
DRAW YE JERUSALEM AWAY FROM ALBION'S MOUNTAINS	679	JERUSALEM 48	62
JERUSALEM JERUSALEM WHY WILT THOU TURN AWAY	679	JERUSALEM 49	2
WEAK WITHERD DARKEND & JERUSALEM IS CAST FORTH FROM ALBION	679	JERUSALEM 49	8
THEY DENY THAT THEY EVER KNEW JERUSALEM OR EVER DWELT IN SHILOH	679	JERUSALEM 49	9
LO SHILOH DWELLS OVER FRANCE AS JERUSALEM DWELLS OVER ALBION	680	JERUSALEM 49	48
AND LET WILD SEAS & ROCKS CLOSE UP JERUSALEM AWAY FROM	680	JERUSALEM 49	77
JERUSALEM CHAP (THREE)	684A	JERUSALEM 53	TITLE
AND THE LIGHT IS HIS GARMENT THIS IS JERUSALEM IN EVERY MAN	684	JERUSALEM 54	3
AND JERUSALEM IS CALLED LIBERTY AMONG THE CHILDREN OF ALBION	684	JERUSALEM 54	5
JERUSALEM & VALA APPEARD & ABOVE BETWEEN THE WINGS MAGNIFICENT	685	JERUSALEM 54	31
TO SIEZE THE SONS OF JERUSALEM & PLANT THEM IN ONE MAN'S LOINS	686	JERUSALEM 55	14
CONTENDING FOR ALBION & FOR JERUSALEM HIS EMANATION	686	JERUSALEM 55	28
YORK LONDON JERUSALEM	689A	JERUSALEM 57	*TITLE
PAVEMENTS WHERE WALK THE SONS OF JERUSALEM WHO REMAIN UNGENERATE	690	JERUSALEM 58	26
I GAVE THEE LIBERTY AND LIFE O LOVELY JERUSALEM	692	JERUSALEM 60	10
I GAVE THEE THE SHEEP-WALKS UPON THE SPANISH MOUNTAINS JERUSALEM	692	JERUSALEM 60	12
WHY WILT THOU REND THYSELF APART JERUSALEM	692	JERUSALEM 60	22
THEREFORE THY MOUNTAINS ARE BECOME BARREN JERUSALEM	693	JERUSALEM 60	25
BEG BREAD FROM HOUSE TO HOUSE LOVELY JERUSALEM	693	JERUSALEM 60	28
INTO VEILS OF TEARS AND SORROWS O LOVELY JERUSALEM	693	JERUSALEM 60	34
BUT JERUSALEM FAINTLY SAW HIM CLOSD IN THE DUNGEONS OF BABYLON	693	JERUSALEM 60	39
TO SEE JERUSALEM DEFACE HER LINEAMENTS WITH BITTER BLOWS	693	JERUSALEM 60	46
BUT THE DIVINE LAMB STOOD BESIDE JERUSALEM OFT SHE SAW	693	JERUSALEM 60	50
THUS SPAKE JERUSALEM & THUS THE DIVINE VOICE REPLIED	694	JERUSALEM 60	65
AND BE COMFORTED O JERUSALEM IN THE VISIONS OF JEHOVAH ELOHIM	694	JERUSALEM 61	2
HIS ARMS DOTH HE FORGIVE JERUSALEM & NOT EXACT PURITY FROM HER WHO IS	694	JERUSALEM 61	15
THE REAPERS SAYING AM I JERUSALEM THE LOST ADULTERESS OR AM I	695	JERUSALEM 61	34
BABYLON COME UP TO JERUSALEM AND ANOTHER VOICE ANSWERD SAYING	695	JERUSALEM 61	35
MARY LEANED HER SIDE AGAINST JERUSALEM JERUSALEM RECIEVED	695	JERUSALEM 61	47

1005

		PAGE	TITLE	LINE
JERUSALEM	(CONTINUED)			
JERUSALEM FAINTED OVER THE CROSS & SEPULCHER SHE HEARD THE VOICE		695	JERUSALEM 61	49
JERUSALEM REPLIED I AM AN OUTCAST ALBION IS DEAD		695	JERUSALEM 62	2
INVOLVD JERUSALEM & THE WHEELS OF ALBION'S SONS TURND HOARSE		696	JERUSALEM 62	32
THE THREADS OF VALA & JERUSALEM RUNNING FROM MOUNTAIN TO MOUNTAIN		704	JERUSALEM 67	28
DEVOURING JERUSALEM FROM EVERY NATION OF THE EARTH . . .		707	JERUSALEM 69	5
DRAWING THE FREE LOVES OF JERUSALEM INTO INFERNAL BONDAGE		707	JERUSALEM 69	9
JERUSALEM PINED IN HER INMOST SOUL OVER WANDERING REUBEN		708	JERUSALEM 69	45
ARE TO THE SONS OF ALBION AND JERUSALEM IS ALBION'S EMANATION		709	JERUSALEM 71	5
AND PEARL WITH INSTRUMENTS OF MUSIC IN HOLY JERUSALEM . .		710	JERUSALEM 71	41
JERUSALEM & VALA REJOICE IN BOWEN & CONWENNA		710	JERUSALEM 71	49
BUT THE FOUR SONS OF JERUSALEM THAT NEVER WERE GENERATED		710	JERUSALEM 71	50
BUT NOW ALBION IS DARKENED & JERUSALEM LIES IN RUINS . .		711	JERUSALEM 71	54
BY LOS FOR JERUSALEM'S SAKE & CALLED THE GATES OF JERUSALEM		711	JERUSALEM 72	8
BECAUSE TWELVE SONS OF JERUSALEM FLED SUCCESSIVE THRO THE GATES		711	JERUSALEM 72	9
BUT THE FOUR SONS OF JERUSALEM WHO FLED NOT BUT REMAIN		711	JERUSALEM 72	10
AND THESE FOUR REMAIN TO GUARD THE FOUR WALLS OF JERUSALEM		711	JERUSALEM 72	13
O COME YE NATIONS COME YE PEOPLE COME UP TO JERUSALEM		712	JERUSALEM 72	33
RETURN JERUSALEM & DWELL TOGETHER AS OF OLD RETURN . . .		712	JERUSALEM 72	34
RETURN O ALBION LET JERUSALEM OVERSPREAD ALL NATIONS . .		712	JERUSALEM 72	35
THE NATIONS WAIT FOR JERUSALEM THEY LOOK UP FOR THE BRIDE		712	JERUSALEM 72	37
JERUSALEM IN RUINS WANDERING ABOUT FROM HOUSE TO HOUSE . .		714	JERUSALEM 74	17
THE SONS OF ALBION ARE TWELVE THE SONS OF JERUSALEM SIXTEEN		715	JERUSALEM 74	23
AND RAHAB BABYLON THE GREAT HATH DESTROYED JERUSALEM . .		715	JERUSALEM 75	1
THAT TO LABOUR IN KNOWLEDGE IS TO BUILD UP JERUSALEM AND		717C	JERUSALEM 77	PROSE
TO DESPISE KNOWLEDGE IS TO DESPISE JERUSALEM & HER BUILDERS		717C	JERUSALEM 77	PROSE
IN SOME MENTAL PURSUIT FOR THE BUILDING UP OF JERUSALEM		717C	JERUSALEM 77	PROSE
JERUSALEM THY SISTER CALLS		718	ENGLND AWAKE/J	2
JERUSALEM C(CHAPTER) (FOUR)		718D	JERUSALEM 78	TITLE
WHILE LOS LAMENTS AT HIS DIRE LABOURS VIEWING JERUSALEM		719	JERUSALEM 78	10
IN TERRIBLE ARMOUR RAGING AGAINST THE LAMB & AGAINST JERUSALEM		719	JERUSALEM 78	13
NAKED JERUSALEM LAY BEFORE THE GATES UPON MOUNT ZION . .		719	JERUSALEM 78	21
IN ERIN'S CONTINENT AND JERUSALEM WEPT UPON EUPHRATES' BANKS		719	JERUSALEM 78	27
RECIEVE THE FEET OF JERUSALEM THEY HAVE CAST ME QUITE AWAY		720	JERUSALEM 79	16
NO MORE SEEK TO JERUSALEM NOR TO THE SOUND OF MY HOLY-ONES		720	JERUSALEM 79	19
SAYING LO JERUSALEM IS HERE SHE SITTETH IN OUR SECRET CHAMBERS		720	JERUSALEM 79	29
ENQUIRING FOR JERUSALEM HE LED THEM UP MY STEPS TO MY ALTAR		721	JERUSALEM 79	52
THE PILLARS OF JERUSALEM BETWEEN MY WINGED CHERUBIM . .		721	JERUSALEM 79	59
AND JORDAN TO EUPHRATES JERUSALEM FOLLOWD TREMBLING . . .		722	JERUSALEM 80	9
THE CLOUD O RENT IN SUNDER FROM JERUSALEM THE HARLOT DAUGHTER		722	JERUSALEM 80	12
THE CHILDREN OF JERUSALEM THE SOULS OF THOSE WHO SLEEP . .		722	JERUSALEM 80	33
TO WEAVE JERUSALEM A BODY ACCORDING TO HER WILL		722	JERUSALEM 80	35
AGAINST JERUSALEM THEY RAGE THRO ALL THE NATIONS OF EUROPE		722	JERUSALEM 80	46
TO WEAVE JERUSALEM A BODY REPUGNANT TO THE LAMB		723	JERUSALEM 80	65
CREATE JERUSALEM & BABYLON & EGYPT & MOAB & AMALEK . . .		725	JERUSALEM 82	27
LET US LEAD THE STEMS OF THIS TREE LET US PLANT IT BEFORE JERUSALEM		725	JERUSALEM 82	32
OF MILD JERUSALEM TO DESTROY THE LAMB OF GOD JERUSALEM . .		726	JERUSALEM 82	54
JERUSALEM HUNGERS IN THE DESERT AFFECTION TO HER CHILDREN		727	JERUSALEM 83	7
TILL SWEET JERUSALEM EMANATES AGAIN INTO ETERNITY . . .		728	JERUSALEM 83	60
WEAVING THE WEB OF LIFE FOR JERUSALEM THE WEB OF LIFE . .		728	JERUSALEM 83	73
AWAY & MIGHTY HYLE & AFTER THEM JERUSALEM IS GONE AWAKE		729	JERUSALEM 83	87
WE BUILDED JERUSALEM AS A CITY & A TEMPLE FROM LAMBETH . .		729	JERUSALEM 84	3
FOR JERUSALEM LIES IN RUINS & THE FURNACES OF LOS ARE BUILDED THERE		729	JERUSALEM 84	6
THE STARS STAND STILL TO HEAR JERUSALEM & VALA CEASE TO MOURN		730	JERUSALEM 85	15
O LOVELY MILD JERUSALEM O SHILOH OF MOUNT EPHRAIM . . .		730	JERUSALEM 85	22
TO SPRING UP FOR JERUSALEM LOVELY SHADOW OF SLEEPING ALBION		730	JERUSALEM 85	29
I SEE THY FORM O LOVELY MILD JERUSALEM WINGD WITH SIX WINGS		730	JERUSALEM 86	1
I SEE THE NEW JERUSALEM DESCENDING OUT OF HEAVEN . . .		731	JERUSALEM 86	19
FROM GOLGONOOZA WITH SWEET VISIONS FOR JERUSALEM WANDERER		731	JERUSALEM 86	41
OF BEULAH FOR JERUSALEM & SHILOH IN IMMORTAL GOLGONOOZA		731	JERUSALEM 86	44
JERUSALEM DIVIDES THY CARE WHILE THOU CAREST FOR JERUSALEM		732	JERUSALEM 87	21
IN MILD JERUSALEM AROUND THE LAMB OF GOD LOUD HOWL . . .		734	JERUSALEM 88	53
AND FIRE JERUSALEM TOOK THE CUP WHICH FOAMD IN VALA'S HAND		734	JERUSALEM 88	56
BUT IN THE MIDST OF A DEVOURING STOMACH JERUSALEM . . .		735	JERUSALEM 89	43
JERUSALEM		739C	JERUSALEM 92	*TITLE
DISPLAYD IN THE EMANATIVE VISIONS OF CANAAN IN JERUSALEM & IN SHILOH		739	JERUSALEM 92	21
AMALEK EDOM EGYPT MOAB AMMON ASHUR PHILISTEA AROUND JERUSALEM		740	JERUSALEM 92	23
AWAKE AWAKE JERUSALEM O LOVELY EMANATION OF ALBION . . .		744	JERUSALEM 97	1
APPEARS UPON OUR HILLS AWAKE JERUSALEM AND COME AWAY . .		744	JERUSALEM 97	4
AND I HEARD THE NAME OF THEIR EMANATIONS THEY ARE NAMED JERUSALEM		747	JERUSALEM 99	5
THE END OF THE SONG OF JERUSALEM		747B	JERUSALEM 99	TITLE
[JERUSALEM HE SAID TO ME]		758	EV GOSPEL (2)	21
THE LAST WORK I PRODUCED IS A POEM ENTITLED JERUSALEM THE		878C	LETTER 88	PROSE
OF MR LINNELL...FOURTEEN SHILLINGS FOR JERUSALEM CHAP (TWO)		SUPP	LETTER 67A	*PROSE

	PAGE	TITLE	LINE

JERUSALEM'S

STRIPPING JERUSALEM'S CURTAINS FROM MILD DEMONS OF THE HILLS — 281 FOUR ZOAS 2 — 58
BINDING JERUSALEM'S CHILDREN IN THE DUNGEONS OF BABYLON — 281 FOUR ZOAS 2 — 63
WONDRING SHE SAW THE LAMB OF GOD WITHIN JERUSALEM'S VEIL — 346 FOUR ZOAS 8 — 191
OF FAIR JERUSALEM'S BOSOM IN A GENTLY BEAMING ?FIRE . . . — 346 FOUR ZOAS 8 — 193
THE WAR ROARD ROUND JERUSALEM'S GATES IT TOOK A HIDEOUS FORM — 347 FOUR ZOAS 8 — 247
PITYING THE LAMB OF GOD DESCENDED THRO JERUSALEM'S GATES — 347 FOUR ZOAS 8 — 260
. . . TIMES AFTER TIMES BESIDE JERUSALEM'S GATE] . . . — 356 FOUR ZOAS 8 — 588
WHERE JERUSALEM'S FOUNDATIONS BEGAN WHERE THEY WERE LAID IN RUINS — 485 MILTON 6 — 15
AND THENCE FROM JERUSALEM'S RUINS FROM HER WALLS OF SALVATION — 486 MILTON 6 — 21
BEGINING AT JERUSALEM'S INNER COURT LAMBETH RUIND AND GIVEN — 511 MILTON 25 — 48
JERUSALEM'S CHILDREN CONSUME IN FLAMES AMONG THE STARS . . — 527 MILTON 37 — 12
THE EAST TOWARD JERUSALEM'S GATES GROANING HE SAT ABOVE — 531 MILTON 39 — 34
BUILT IN JERUSALEM'S WALL . . . . — 551 GIVE YOU END/N — 4
CAME FROM THE FURNACES BY LOS'S MIGHTY POWER FOR JERUSALEM'S — 630 JERUSALEM 11 — 9
HE SHOOTS BENEATH JERUSALEM'S WALLS TO UNDERMINE HER FOUNDATIONS — 631 JERUSALEM 11 — 23
FOR COMFORT THERE THE SECRET FURNITURE OF JERUSALEM'S CHAMBER — 632 JERUSALEM 12 — 40
WITH MIGHTY POWER WHEN THEY FLED OUT AT JERUSALEM'S GATES — 637 JERUSALEM 16 — 30
JEALOUS OF JERUSALEM'S CHILDREN ASHAMD OF HER LITTLE-ONES — 640 JERUSALEM 18 — 6
THINKING TO BRING LOVE INTO LIGHT OF DAY TO JERUSALEM'S SHAME — 647 JERUSALEM 24 — 5
AND THERE JERUSALEM'S PILLARS STOOD . . . . — 649 FIELDS FROM/J — 4
SHINE IN JERUSALEM'S PLEASANT SIGHT . . . . — 650 FIELDS FROM/J — 16
HE WITHERD UP JERUSALEM'S GATES . . . . — 651 FIELDS FROM/J — 51
WHETHER OF JERUSALEM'S OR VALA'S RUINS CONGENERATED WE KNOW NOT — 655 JERUSALEM 29 — 81
A BUILDING OF LUVAH BUILDED IN JERUSALEM'S EASTERN GATE TO BE — 657 JERUSALEM 31 — 24
JERUSALEM'S SHADOW BENT NORTHWARD OVER THE ISLAND WHITE — 657 JERUSALEM 31 — 42
AT LENGTH HE SAT ON LONDON STONE & HEARD JERUSALEM'S VOICE — 657 JERUSALEM 31 — 43
JERUSALEM'S CHILDREN HARK HEAR THE GIANTS OF ALBION CRY AT NIGHT — 673 JERUSALEM 43 — 47
I SEE A WICKER IDOL WOVEN ROUND JERUSALEM'S CHILDREN I SEE — 673 JERUSALEM 43 — 65
BY SELF ANNIHILATION INTO JERUSALEM'S COURTS & INTO SHILOH — 680 JERUSALEM 49 — 46
HE TOSSES LIKE A CLOUD OUTSTRETCHD AMONG JERUSALEM'S RUINS — 685 JERUSALEM 54 — 13
GATHERD JERUSALEM'S CHILDREN IN HIS ARMS & BORE THEM LIKE — 692 JERUSALEM 60 — 8
HIDING ALBION'S SONS WITHIN THE VEIL CLOSING JERUSALEM'S — 704 JERUSALEM 67 — 17
JERUSALEM'S PILLARS FALL IN THE RENDINGS OF FIERCE WAR . . — 706 JERUSALEM 68 — 45
WERE SEEN JERUSALEM'S SONS AND ALL THE TWELVE TRIBES SPREADING — 709 JERUSALEM 71 — 3
OVER ALBION AS THE SOUL IS TO THE BODY SO JERUSALEM'S SONS — 709 JERUSALEM 71 — 4
BY LOS FOR JERUSALEM'S SAKE & CALLED THE GATES OF JERUSALEM — 711 JERUSALEM 72 — 8
AND THIRTY-TWO THE NATIONS TO DWELL IN JERUSALEM'S GATES — 712 JERUSALEM 72 — 32
ASUNDER & OPPOSED TO THOUGHT TO DRAW JERUSALEM'S SONS . . — 715 JERUSALEM 74 — 29
BUILT IN JERUSALEM'S WALL . . . . — 716 I GIVE YOU/J — 4
THEY SIEZD THE HARP THE FLUTE THE MELLOW HORN OF JERUSALEM'S JOY — 721 JERUSALEM 79 — 49
AND JOYING IN THE PITY HOWLING OVER JERUSALEM'S WALLS . . — 723 JERUSALEM 80 — 56
HE RAN IN TENDER NERVES ACROSS EUROPE TO JERUSALEM'S SHADE — 723 JERUSALEM 80 — 64
A WEEPING INFANT IN RUIND LOVELY JERUSALEM'S FOLDING CLOUD — 724 JERUSALEM 81 — 14
I HAVE HEARD JERUSALEM'S GROANS FROM VALA'S CRIES & LAMENTATIONS — 725 JERUSALEM 82 — 1
OF JERUSALEM'S CHERUBIMS & TO FORGE THEM SWORDS OF HER ALTARS — 729 JERUSALEM 84 — 10
CAST THOU IN JERUSALEM'S SHADOWS THY LOVES SILK OF LIQUID — 732 JERUSALEM 87 — 19

JESSAMINE

THE PINK THE JESSAMINE THE WALL-FLOWER THE CARNATION . . — 520 MILTON 31 — 59

JEST

THE LAUGHING JEST THE LOVE-SICK TALE . . . . — 16 BLIND-MANS/PS — 10

JESUS   SEE IESOUS

NOTE JESUS CHRIST DID NOT WISH TO UNITE . . . . — 155C MARRIAGE HH 15 — PROSE
IN JESUS CHRIST AND HAS NOT JESUS CHRIST — 158B MARRIAGE HH 22 — PROSE
IF JESUS CHRIST IS THE GREATEST MAN YOU OUGHT TO LOVE HIM — 158C MARRIAGE HH 22 — PROSE
JESUS WAS ALL VIRTUE AND ACTED FROM IMPULSE NOT FROM RULES — 158D MARRIAGE HH 22 — PROSE
THE DEATH OF JESUS SET ME FREE . . . . — 220 TO TIRZAH/SE — 15
AND JESUS HEARD HER VOICE A MAN OF SORROWS HE RECIEVD . . — 246 SONG OF LOS 3 — 23
ART THOU A VISIONARY OF JESUS THE SOFT DELUSION OF ETERNITY — 273 FOUR ZOAS 1 — 337
THEY CALL JESUS THE CHRIST & THEY IN HIM & HE IN THEM . . — 277 FOUR ZOAS 1 — 473
THE SEVEN ARE ONE WITHIN THE OTHER THE SEVENTH IS NAMED JESUS — 279 FOUR ZOAS 1 — 555
FOR THE DIVINE LAMB EVEN JESUS WHO IS THE DIVINE VISION — 287 FOUR ZOAS 2 — 261
[THEN ?JESUS XXX] — SUPP FOUR ZOAS 4 — *
[MET] AS ONE MAN EVEN JESUS UPON GILEAD & HERMON . . . . — 341 FOUR ZOAS 8 — 2
AND KNEW HE WAS THE SAVIOUR EVEN JESUS & THEY WORSHIPPED — 342 FOUR ZOAS 8 — 44
COME LORD JESUS COME QUICKLY . . . . — 347 FOUR ZOAS 8 — 245
THEN JESUS CAME & DIED WILLING BENEATH TIRZAH & RAHAB . . — 351 FOUR ZOAS 8 — 406
BUT JESUS STOOD BESIDE THEM IN THE SPIRIT SEPARATING . . — 357 FOUR ZOAS 9 — 4
BROTHER OF JESUS WHAT HAVE I DONE INTREAT THY LORD FOR ME — 364 FOUR ZOAS 9 — 270
JESUS COULD NOT DO MIRACLES WHERE UNBELIEF HINDERED . . — 391C ANNO WATSON — MARG
NEITHER DID JESUS EVER DO SUCH A MIRACLE IS IT A . . . . — 391C ANNO WATSON — MARG
DID NOT JESUS DESCEND & BECOME A SERVANT THE . . . . . — 399C ANNO BACON — MARG
CAESAR SEEMS TO ME A VERY SMALL MATTER & SO HE SEEMD TO JESUS — 410D ANNO BACON — MARG
JEHOVAH JESUS A WINE BIBBER . . . . — 412C ANNO BOYD — MARG
IN JESUS WHO OPENS THE SCROLL OF JUDGMENT . . . . . . — 444C LAST JUDGMNT/L — PROSE

		PAGE	TITLE	LINE

JESUS   (CONTINUED)

	PAGE	TITLE	LINE
OF ETERNITY IN WHICH WE SHALL LIVE FOR EVER IN JESUS OUR LORD	480D	MILTON 1	PROSE
ITS OFFERINGS EVEN TILL JESUS THE IMAGE OF THE INVISIBLE GOD	481	MILTON 2	12
WHICH IS THE DIVINE BODY OF THE LORD JESUS BLESSED FOR EVER	482	MILTON 3	4
FROM CORRUPTIBILITY O WHEN LORD JESUS WILT THOU COME	495	MILTON 14	18
SO SPAKE THE FAMILY DIVINE AS ONE MAN EVEN JESUS	505	MILTON 21	58
JESUS THE SAVIOUR APPEARD COMING IN THE CLOUDS OF OLOLON	505	MILTON 21	60
WHEN JESUS RAISD LAZARUS FROM THE GRAVE I STOOD & SAW	508	MILTON 24	26
TO US WE WILL OBEY YOUR WORDS AS YOU OBEY JESUS	519	MILTON 30	30
TILL THEY AWAKE & SEE JESUS & THE LINEN CLOTHES LYING	522	MILTON 32	42
OPPOSD TO MERCY AND THE DIVINE DELUSION JESUS BE NO MORE	530	MILTON 39	2
OF JESUS WHO DENY THE FAITH & MOCK AT ETERNAL LIFE	533	MILTON 41	22
WHICH JESUS RENT & NOW SHALL WHOLLY PURGE AWAY WITH FIRE	533	MILTON 41	27
ONE MAN JESUS THE SAVIOUR WONDERFUL ROUND HIS LIMBS	534	MILTON 42	11
AROSE AROUND ALBION'S BODY JESUS WEPT & WALKED FORTH	534	MILTON 42	19
THAT IS THE VERY THING THAT JESUS MEANT	536	DONT BELIEVE/N	10
I ALWAYS THOUGHT THAT JESUS CHRIST WAS A SNUBBY	555C	ALWAYS THOT/N	PROSE
JESUS DOES NOT (TREAT) XXX	556D	JESUS NOT/N	*PROSE
FOR WHEN SEPARATED FROM MAN OR HUMANITY WHO IS JESUS	571C	DESC CAT 3	PROSE
ONE RELIGION THIS WAS THE RELIGION OF JESUS THE EVERLASTING GOSPEL	579A	DESC CAT 5	PROSE
ANTIQUITY PREACHES THE GOSPEL OF JESUS THE REASONING	579A	DESC CAT 5	PROSE
THE BODY OF JESUS IN THE SEPULCHRE A DRAWING	584B	DESC CAT 14	TITLE
THE HEBREW BIBLE & THE GOSPEL OF JESUS ARE NOT ALLEGORY	604D	V LAST JUDG/N	PROSE
JESUS SEATED BETWEEN THE TWO PILLARS JACHIN & BOAZ	606B	V LAST JUDG/N	PROSE
ANOTHER THING CHANGING WATER INTO WINE BY JESUS	607B	V LAST JUDG/N	PROSE
JESUS IS SURROUNDED BY BEAMS OF GLORY IN WHICH ARE SEEN ALL	613D	V LAST JUDG/N	PROSE
OF JESUS THE SAVIOUR WHERE THE ACCUSER IS CAST OUT NOT	616D	V LAST JUDG/N	PROSE
THEN JESUS CHRIST COMES WITH A BALM TO HEAL IT	617A	V LAST JUDG/N	PROSE
I ALSO HOPE THE READER WILL BE WITH ME WHOLLY ONE IN JESUS	621A	JERUSALEM 3	PROSE
THE SPIRIT OF JESUS IS CONTINUAL FORGIVENESS OF SIN	621A	JERUSALEM 3	PROSE
[TO NOTE THE LAST WORDS OF JESUS... (GREEK QUOTED)]	621C	JERUSALEM 3	*PROSE
WHICH IS THE DIVINE BODY OF THE LORD JESUS BLESSED FOR EVER	624	JERUSALEM 5	59
THE RELIGION OF JESUS THE MOST ANCIENT	649B	JERUSALEM 27	PROSE
CHILDREN OF JESUS & HIS BRIDE	650	FIELDS FROM/J	20
O JESUS STILL THE FORM WAS THINE	651	FIELDS FROM/J	60
TAKE UP THE CROSS O ISRAEL & FOLLOW JESUS	652B	JERUSALEM 27	PROSE
WHY WAS I ONE WITH HER EMBRACING IN THE VISION OF JESUS	660	JERUSALEM 33	44
STEPS BEYOND AND REDEEMS MAN IN THE BODY OF JESUS AMEN	664	JERUSALEM 36	55
WE CALL JESUS THE CHRIST AND HE IN US AND WE IN HIM	665	JERUSALEM 38	20
HUMAN DIVINE JESUS THE SAVIOUR BLESSED FOR EVER AND EVER	667	JERUSALEM 40	47
TILL JESUS SHALL APPEAR & THEY GAVE THEIR POWER TO LOS	674	JERUSALEM 44	30
THIS DREAD DISEASE NONE BUT JESUS O LORD DESCEND AND SAVE	675	JERUSALEM 45	16
JESUS ALONE CAN SAVE HIM FOR ALAS WE NONE CAN KNOW	675	JERUSALEM 45	18
SWAYD BY A PROVIDENCE OPPOSD TO THE DIVINE LORD JESUS	681	JERUSALEM 50	4
COME LORD JESUS LAMB OF GOD DESCEND FOR IF O LORD	681	JERUSALEM 50	10
AND MANY BELIEVED WHAT THEY SAW AND PROPHECIED OF JESUS	682B	JERUSALEM 52	PROSE
NOT THE RELIGION OF JESUS HE WILL HAVE THE RELIGION OF SATAN	682B	JERUSALEM 52	PROSE
THIS WAS THE RELIGION OF THE PHARISEES WHO MURDERD JESUS	682C	JERUSALEM 52	PROSE
ITS ACTORS BUT THE RELIGION OF JESUS FORGIVENESS OF SIN	683A	JERUSALEM 52	PROSE
LUCIFER MOLECH ELOHIM SHADDAI PAHAD JEHOVAH JESUS	686	JERUSALEM 55	32
JESUS REPLIED I AM THE RESURRECTION & THE LIFE	696	JERUSALEM 62	18
IN THE END OF HIS SLEEP WHEN JESUS CALLS HIM FROM HIM HIS GRAVE	701	JERUSALEM 65	* 62
WHICH JESUS RENDS & THE WHOLE DRUID LAW REMOVES AWAY	708	JERUSALEM 69	39
TEACH ME O HOLY SPIRIT THE TESTIMONY OF JESUS LET ME	714	JERUSALEM 74	14
BUT JESUS BREAKING THRO THE CENTRAL ZONES OF DEATH & HELL	716	JERUSALEM 75	21
ALBION [JESUS]	716C	JERUSALEM 76	*TITLE
I CALL UPON YOU IN THE NAME OF JESUS	717B	JERUSALEM 77	PROSE
MOCKS JESUS THE GIVER OF EVERY MENTAL GIFT	717C	JERUSALEM 77	PROSE
I WEPT & SAID IS THIS THE LAW OF JESUS	718	STOOD AMONG/J	14
HE ANSWERD JESUS DIED BECAUSE HE STROVE	718	STOOD AMONG/J	16
BUT JESUS IS THE BRIGHT PREACHER OF LIFE	718	STOOD AMONG/J	21
PITY ME THEN O LAMB OF GOD O JESUS PITY ME	722	JERUSALEM 80	30
THAT HE WHO LOVES JESUS MAY LOATHE TERRIFIED FEMALE LOVE	733	JERUSALEM 88	20
COME LORD JESUS TAKE ON THEE THE SATANIC BODY OF HOLINESS	737	JERUSALEM 90	38
JESUS WILL APPEAR SO HE WHO WISHES TO SEE A VISION A PERFECT WHOLE	738	JERUSALEM 91	21
PARTICULAR IS A MAN A DIVINE MEMBER OF THE DIVINE JESUS	738	JERUSALEM 91	31
SO CAIPHAS THOUGHT JESUS	740B	JERUSALEM 93	TITLE
BEHOLD HIM HERE WE SHALL NOT DIE WE SHALL BE UNITED IN JESUS	741	JERUSALEM 93	19
THEN JESUS APPEARED STANDING BY ALBION AS THE GOOD SHEPHERD	743	JERUSALEM 96	3
JESUS REPLIED FEAR NOT ALBION UNLESS I DIE THOU CANST NOT LIVE	743	JERUSALEM 96	14
SO JESUS SPOKE THE COVERING CHERUB COMING ON IN DARKNESS	743	JERUSALEM 96	17
OVERSHADOWD THEM & JESUS SAID THUS DO MEN IN ETERNITY	743	JERUSALEM 96	18
JESUS SAID WOULDEST THOU LOVE ONE WHO NEVER DIED	743	JERUSALEM 96	23
ALBION'S BOSOM THEN ALBION STOOD BEFORE JESUS IN THE CLOUDS	744	JERUSALEM 96	42
WAS JESUS GENTLE OR DID HE	748	EV GOSPEL(B)/N	1
WAS JESUS HUMBLE OR DID HE	750	EV GOSPEL(C)/N	1
THIS IS SURELY NOT WHAT JESUS INTENDS	750	EV GOSPEL(C)/N	20
AND THIS IS THE REASON JESUS DIED	750	EV GOSPEL(C)/N	24
IF HE HAD BEEN [THE] ANTICHRIST CREEPING JESUS	750	EV GOSPEL(C)/N	25
THIS IS THE RACE [HE] THAT JESUS RAN	750	EV GOSPEL(C)/N *	34
WAS JESUS HUMBLE OR DID HE	751	EV GOSPEL(D)/N	1
I WAS STANDING BY WHEN JESUS DIED	751	EV GOSPEL(D)/N	23
THIS SURELY IS NOT WHAT JESUS INTENDS	751	EV GOSPEL(D)/N	26
AND THIS IS THE CAUSE THAT JESUS DIED	751	EV GOSPEL(D)/N	30

JESUS   (CONTINUED)

	PAGE	TITLE	LINE
IF HE HAD BEEN [THE] ANTICHRIST CREEPING JESUS	752	EV GOSPEL(D)/N	59
THIS IS THE RACE THAT JESUS RAN	752	EV GOSPEL(D)/N	67
JESUS REPLIED & THUNDERS HURLD	753	EV GOSPEL(D)/N	87
WAS JESUS CHASTE OR DID HE &C	753	EV GOSPEL(D)/N	109
WAS JESUS CHASTE OR DID HE	753	EV GOSPEL(E)/N	1
JESUS WAS SITTING IN MOSES' CHAIR	753	EV GOSPEL(E)/N	7
FROM THE LIMBS OF JESUS TO MAKE THEM HIS PREY	755	EV GOSPEL(E)/N	82
BUT WHEN JESUS WAS CRUCIFIED	755	EV GOSPEL(E)/N	91
I AM SURE THIS JESUS WILL NOT DO	756	EV GOSPEL(F)/N	1
DID JESUS TEACH DOUBT OR DID HE	756	EV GOSPEL(H)/N	1
WAS JESUS BORN OF A VIRGIN PURE	756	EV GOSPEL(I)/N	1
THERE IS NOT ONE MORAL VIRTUE THAT JESUS INCULCATED	757D	EV GOSPEL	PROSE
BROUGHT TO LIGHT BY JESUS EVEN THE COVENANT OF JEHOVAH	757D	EV GOSPEL	PROSE
WHAT CAN THIS GOSPEL OF JESUS BE	758	EV GOSPEL (2)	1
THEN JESUS ROSE & SAID TO [MEN] ME	758	EV GOSPEL (2)	17
IT WAS WHEN JESUS SAID TO ME	758	EV GOSPEL (2)	22
OF JESUS & JEHOVAH THOU ART STILL	771	EPILOGUE/GP	6
BUT JESUS AS ALSO ABRAHAM & DAVID CONSIDERD GOD	774A	ANNO BERKELEY	MARG
JESUS CONSIDERD IMAGINATION TO BE THE REAL MAN & SAYS	774A	ANNO BERKELEY	* MARG
JESUS ONLY DID THIS	774C	ANNO BERKELEY	MARG
JESUS SUPPOSES EVERY THING TO BE EVIDENT TO THE CHILD	774D	ANNO BERKELEY	MARG
JESUS CAME TO REMOVE WAS THE HEATHEN OR PLATONIC PHILOSOPHY	775B	ANNO BERKELEY	MARG
GOD HIMSELF THE DIVINE BODY (YESHUA) JESUS WE ARE HIS MEMBERS	776B	INSC LAOCOON	PROSE
JESUS & HIS APOSTLES & DISCIPLES WERE ALL ARTISTS	777B	INSC LAOCOON	PROSE
ART IS THE TREE OF LIFE GOD IS JESUS	777C	INSC LAOCOON	PROSE
SOMETHING SUPERIOR TO THE FATHER OR JESUS	785C	ILLS DANTE 101	PROSE
UPON THE KINGDOM OF JESUS BY THE CLASSICAL LEARNED	786C	ANNO THORNTON	MARG
TO CONSIDER IS THIS WHETHER JESUS DID NOT SUFFER HIMSELF TO BE	787A	ANNO THORNTON	MARG
JESUS OUR FATHER WHO ART IN THY HEAVNS CALLD BY THY NAME	788A	ANNO THORNTON	* MARG
& DELIVER US FROM POVERTY IN JESUS THAT EVIL ONE	789A	ANNO THORNTON	MARG
MAY JESUS AND HIS ANGELS ASSUAGE	796C	LETTER 8	PROSE
HAPPINESS IS SECURE IN JESUS OUR LORD & WHO LOOKS FOR	862D	LETTER 60	PROSE
THE MOCKER OF ART IS THE MOCKER OF JESUS	863B	LETTER 60	PROSE
JESUS PRESENT ALSO MY THANKS TO THE GENEROUS SEAGRAVE IN	863B	LETTER 60	PROSE
THE YEA NAY CREEPING JESUS FROM SUPPOSING UP & DOWN	878B	LETTER 88	PROSE
ORPHAN MOSES ELIAS JESUS DAVID SOLOMON	SUPP	INSC HERVEY	*TITLE

JESUS'

	PAGE	TITLE	LINE
AND JESUS' VOICE IN THUNDERS SOUND	749	EV GOSPEL(B)/N	26
WHAT WAS THE [WORDS] SOUND OF JESUS' BREATH	754	EV GOSPEL(E)/N	10
TAKE JESUS' & JEHOVAH'S NAME	758	EV GOSPEL (1)	10
THRO ALL THE WORLD IN JESUS' NAME	758	EV GOSPEL (2)	25

JET

	PAGE	TITLE	LINE
WITH STOCKINGS ROLLD ABOVE THEIR KNEES & SHOES AS BLACK AS [GIT] JET	58	THIS CITY/IM	* 6

JEW

	PAGE	TITLE	LINE
IN HEATHEN TURK OR JEW	117	DIVNE IMAGE/SI	18
O JEW LEAVE COUNTING GOLD RETURN TO THY OIL AND WINE	159C	SONG LIBERTY	PROSE
WAS FUSELI HE WAS BOTH TURK & JEW	551	ONLY MAN/N	3
EITHER FOR ENGLISHMAN OR JEW	756	EV GOSPEL(F)/N	2
OR WERE JEW VIRGINS STILL MORE CURST	756	EV GOSPEL(I)/N	7
THAT FOR A JEW MAY BE MISTOOK	757	EV GOSPEL(I)/N	30

JEWEL

	PAGE	TITLE	LINE
AND JEWEL HANGS AT TH SHEPHERD'S NOSE	15	BLIND-MANS/PS	2
THE JEWEL HEALTH ADORNS HER NECK	63	SHEPHERD FIRST	8
AND JEWEL HANGS AT SHEPHERD'S NOSE	64	SHEPHERD OLD	2
GOD BLESS HER FOR SHE IS A PEERLESS JEWEL FOR A PRINCE	853A	LETTER 51	*PROSE

JEWELS

	PAGE	TITLE	LINE
WITH JEWELS & PRECIOUS ORNAMENT LABOURD WITH ART DIVINE	312	FOUR ZOAS 6	27
I WILL GIVE BLACKNESS FOR JEWELS HOARY FROST FOR ORNAMENT DEFORMITY	312	FOUR ZOAS 6	37
WITH GIFTS & SPICES WITH LAMPS RICH EMBOSSD JEWELS & GOLD	349	FOUR ZOAS 8	337
AND SOMETIMES KISSING HER ROBES & JEWELS & WEEPING OVER THEM	356	FOUR ZOAS 8	611
AND SAW EVERY MINUTE PARTICULAR THE JEWELS OF ALBION RUNNING DOWN	657	JERUSALEM 31	17
OF GOLD &. JEWELS A SUBLIME ORNAMENT A COUCH OF REPOSE	677	JERUSALEM 48	6
INTO A RAINBOW OF JEWELS AND GOLD A MILD REFLECTION FROM	678	JERUSALEM 48	35
ON CHARIOTS OF GOLD & JEWELS WITH LIVING CREATURES STARRY & FLAMING	746	JERUSALEM 98	42
MY WIFE IS LIKE A FLAME OF MANY COLOURS OF PRECIOUS JEWELS	801B	LETTER 13	PROSE
THE JEWELS OF LIGHT	804	TO BUTTS/L	16
TILL THE JEWELS OF LIGHT	805	TO BUTTS/L	49
LETTERS OF GOLD & ORNAMENTED WITH JEWELS OF	837D	LETTER 36	PROSE
HEAVEN HAVILAH EDEN & ALL THE COUNTRIES WHERE JEWELS ABOUND	837D	LETTER 36	PROSE

JEWISH

	PAGE	TITLE	LINE
THE JEWISH & CHRISTIAN TESTAMENTS	98D	ALL RELIGIONS	PROSE
WHEREFORE DID CHRIST COME WAS IT NOT TO ABOLISH THE JEWISH IMPOSTURE	387B	ANNO WATSON	* MARG
FOR WORLDLY PROSPERITY IN OPPOSITION TO THE JEWISH SCRIPTURES	387B	ANNO WATSON	MARG
IS THAT ABOMINATION WHICH LIKE THE JEWISH CEREMONIES	389C	ANNO WATSON	MARG

JEWS

	PAGE	TITLE	LINE
CAME TO THINK THAT ALL NATIONS WOULD AT LAST BE SUBJECT TO THE JEWS	154A	MARRIAGE HH 12	PROSE
OF THE JEWS & WERE WRITTEN AS AN EXAMPLE OF	387C	ANNO WATSON	MARG
WITH CHRISTENDOM AS IN CHRIST HE STROVE WITH THE JEWS	387C	ANNO WATSON	MARG
SUCH AS THE JEWS WERE & OF COURSE HE HOLDS THAT THE JEWS	389A	ANNO WATSON	MARG
THAT THE JEWS ASSUMED A RIGHT EXCLUSIVELY TO THE BENEFITS	389A	ANNO WATSON	MARG
MURDER THE LAWS OF THE JEWS WERE BOTH CEREMONIAL & REAL	393C	ANNO WATSON	MARG

	PAGE	TITLE	LINE

JEWS   (CONTINUED)
   IS NO LESS SACRED THAN THAT OF THE JEWS THEY ARE THE   .   578D DESC CAT 5   PROSE
   DISBELIEVED WHILE THOSE OF THE JEWS ARE COLLECTED AND   .   578D DESC CAT 5   PROSE
   TO THE JEWS . . . .   649B JERUSALEM 27   TITLE
   IF HUMILITY IS CHRISTIANITY YOU O JEWS ARE THE TRUE   652A JERUSALEM 27   PROSE
      CHRISTIANS
   THAT HE MIGHT TEMPT THE JEWS TO DINE . . . .   757 EV GOSPEL(I)/N   28
JEWS'
   FOR ALL NATIONS BELIEVE THE JEWS' CODE AND . . . .   154A MARRIAGE HH 12   PROSE
   WORSHIP THE JEWS' GOD AND WHAT GREATER SUBJECTION CAN BE   154A MARRIAGE HH 12   PROSE
JEWS-HARP-HOUSE
   THE JEWS-HARP-HOUSE & THE GREEN MAN . . . . .   650 FIELDS FROM/J   13
JIG
   AND WHAT IS THE SECOND THEN DANCING A JIG . . . .   553 ASKD PRIGG/N   3
JINGLING
   THE SKY GLITTERS WITH THE JINGLING TRAPPINGS . . . .   37B CONTEMPLATN/PS   PROSE
   FROM THE BLUE WALLS OF HEAVEN STARRY JINGLING ORNAMENTED   365 FOUR ZOAS 9   296
   IN THE JINGLING TRACES FURIOUS LIONS SOUND THE SONG OF JOY   376 FOUR ZOAS 9   718
JOB
   BUT IN THE BOOK OF JOB MILTON'S MESSIAH IS CALLD SATAN .   150A MARRIAGE HH 5   PROSE
   JOB A HISTORICAL ENGRAVING SIZE...PRICE... . . . .   207D PRSPECTUS 1793   PROSE
   TO EXECUTE ANY WORK I NEED ONLY REFER TO THE LITTLE JOB   847A LETTER 44   PROSE
   PILGRIMS UNDER YOUR CARE WITH THE TWO FIRST PLATES OF JOB   869B LETTER 69   PROSE
   I WISH TO HAVE A COPY OF JOB TO SHEW TO MR CHANTRY . .   870D LETTER 72   PROSE
   THE PLATES & COPY-RIGHT OF JOB & THE SAME IS HIS   874A LETTER 78   PROSE
      SOLE PROPERTY
   IN WHICH HE SAYS HE WILL TAKE ONE COPY OF JOB FOR HIMSELF   876D LETTER 85   PROSE
   WITH POOR JOB I KNOW TOO WELL THAT A GREAT MAJORITY OF .   878A LETTER 88   PROSE
   ANY THING ELSE SUCH IS JOB BUT SINCE THE FRENCH REVOLUTION   878B LETTER 88   PROSE
   "I HAVE SAID TO CORRUPTION THOU ART MY FATHER" (JOB) . .   SUPP LEGEND/N45   *
   "TO THE WORM THOU ART MY MOTHER & MY SISTER" JOB . .   SUPP LEGEND/N45   *
   "WHAT IS MAN THAT THOU SHOULDST MAGNIFY HIM..." JOB .   SUPP LEGEND/N68   *TITLE
   "& THAT THOU SHOULDST SET THINE HEART AGAINST HIM" JOB .   SUPP LEGEND/N68   *TITLE
   THE HISTORY OF JOB DESIGNED & ENGRAVED BY WILLIAM BLAKE   SUPP LETTER 67F   *PROSE
JOB'S
   FROM THE NATURAL MAN & WANT OR JOB'S KINGDOM . . . .   788B ANNO THORNTON   * MARG
   TO ENGRAVE...PLATES FROM HIS OWN DESIGNS OF JOB'S CAPTIVITY   SUPP LETTER 67D   *PROSE
JOCKEY
   A JOCKEY THAT IS ANY THING OF A JOCKEY WILL NEVER BUY .   597D PUB ADDRESS/N   PROSE
JOCUND
   I LOVE THE JOCUND DANCE . . . .   7 LOVE JOCUND/PS   1
   ALL WHILE THE JOCUND HOURS IN THY TRAIN . . . . .   14 IMIT SPEN/PS   6
   "THE COTTAGERS" & "JOCUND PEASANTS" . . . . .   594A PUB ADDRESS/N   PROSE
JOE
   SUSAN JOHNNY BET & JOE . . . .   53 PHEBE DREST/IM   7
   JOE BRADLEY & I WAS GOING ALONG ONE DAY IN THE SUGAR HOUSE   55B ISLAND MOON 9   PROSE
   JOE BRADLEY SAW FOR HE HAD BUT ONE EYE [?COME] . . .   55B ISLAND MOON 9   *PROSE
   O I SAY YOU JOE . . . .   60 SAY YOU JOE/IM *   1
   THAT THOUSANDS OF SWEEPERS DICK JOE NED & JACK . . .   117 CHIMNEY SWP/SI   11
   I THINK OF THE CRIPPLED HARRY & SLOBBERING JOE . . .   550 WHEN I SEE/N   2
JOHANNA
   ON THE VIRGINITY OF THE VIRGIN MARY & JOHANNA SOUTHCOTT   418A ON VIRGINITY/N   TITLE
JOHN
   DUKE OF CLARENCE SIR JOHN CHANDOS SIR THOMAS DAGWORTH   17C EDW THIRD/PS   TITLE
   ENTER SIR JOHN CHANDOS . . . .   22C EDW THIRD/PS 3   PROSE
   FORGIVE MY PREJUDICE SIR JOHN I THINK . . . . .   25 EDW THIRD/PS 3   191
   NOW WE ARE ALONE SIR JOHN I WILL UNBURDEN . . . .   26 EDW THIRD/PS 3   220
   BUT DO YOU NOT THINK SIR JOHN THAT IF IT PLEASE . . .   27 EDW THIRD/PS 3   278
   AS SIR JOHN CHANDOS THAT THE PRINCE IS ALWAYS WITH . .   29C EDW THIRD/PS 4   PROSE
   PROLOGUE TO KING JOHN . . . .   34A KING JOHN/PS   TITLE
   I KNOW NO GREATER SINNER THAN JOHN TAYLOR . . . .   52 HEAR THEN/IM   4
   BY JOHN LOOKYE [?PANTRYMAN] GENT JOHN LOCKE SAID OBTUSE   52D ISLAND MOON 8   PROSE
      ANGLE
   "MY SISTER & MY MOTHER" & ST JOHN . . . . . .   87A ANNO LAVATER   MARG
   OLD JOHN WITH WHITE HAIR . . . .   116 ECCHOING GR/SI   11
   KING JOHN & MAG(MAGNA) CHARTA . . . . . .   208D SUBJCTS HIST/N   TITLE
   JOHN XVII C...JOHN I C... . . . .   264B FOUR ZOAS 1   PROSE
   UPON THE BLOODY ALTAR JOHN SAW THESE THINGS REVEALD IN   356 FOUR ZOAS 8   600
      HEAVEN
   LONG JOHN BROWN & LITTLE MARY BELL . . . . .   434A LONG JOHN BRWN   TITLE
   [YOUNG] LONG JOHN BROWN HAD THE DEVIL IN HIS GUT . . .   434 LONG JOHN BRWN   2
   [YOUNG] LONG JOHN BROWN LOVD [PRETTY] LITTLE MARY BELL   434 LONG JOHN BRWN   3
   FOR JOHN EAT & DRANK TO DRIVE AWAY LOVE'S PAIN . . .   434 LONG JOHN BRWN   10
   AND HE LAUGHD AT THE DEVIL TILL POOR JOHN BROWN DIED .   434 LONG JOHN BRWN   16
   AND COMPLAINT OF JOHN SCHOLFIELD A PRIVATE SOLDIER &C .   437A BLAKES MEMORAN   TITLE
   CAITHNESS & ROCKY DURNESS PENTLAND & JOHN GROATS HOUSE .   512 MILTON 26   15
   A DRAGON RED & HIDDEN HARLOT WHICH JOHN IN PATMOS SAW .   532 MILTON 40   22
   FOR SORROW THAT POOR JOHN THOMPSON'S GONE . . . .   545 AN EPITAPH/N   2
   HERE LIES JOHN TROT THE FRIEND OF ALL MANKIND . . .   546 ANOTHER/N 2   1
   ABOUT JOHN OF BRUGES INVENTING OIL COLOURS . . . .   565B DESC CAT 2   PROSE
   [OLLLLEE W HYYYISS WELL SAIITHL BLAKE JOHN THOMAS F] .   601A PUB ADDRESS/N   *PROSE
   THE HOLY FAMILY CONSISTING OF MARY JOSEPH JOHN THE BAPTIST   614A V LAST JUDG/N   PROSE
   ARTHUR ALFRED THE NORMAN CONQUEROR RICHARD JOHN . . .   713 JERUSALEM 73   36
   JOHN FROM THE WILDERNESS LOUD CRIED . . . . .   748 EV GOSPEL(B)/N   13
   JOHN FOR DISOBEDIENCE BLED . . . .   749 EV GOSPEL(B)/N   17
   TO JOHN FLAXMAN I HAVE BEEN TOO LITTLE AMONG FRIENDS WHICH   798B LETTER 10   PROSE
      I
   TO MY DEAREST FRIEND JOHN FLAXMAN THESE LINES . . . .   799B TO FLAXMAN/L   TITLE
   AND MY BROTHER JOHN THE EVIL ONE . . . . . .   817 HAPPINESS/L   15
   DISGRACED SERGEANT HIS NAME IS JOHN SCHOLFIELD . . .   828B LETTER 28   PROSE
   THE NORTH BY SAYING THAT [MR ROMNEY] MR JOHN ROMNEY HAS   832C LETTER 32   PROSE
   MR JOHN ROMNEY TO MR FLAXMAN WHO WAS PERFECTLY SATISFIED   834C LETTER 34   PROSE

	PAGE	TITLE	LINE

JOHN   (CONTINUED)
```
HE GIVES A VERY SPIRITED ASSURANCE OF MR JOHN ROMNEY'S  .  .  835C LETTER 35      PROSE
MAKE ME ASSIDUOUS & IT DOES SO THAT MR JOHN ROMNEY IS  .  .  838C LETTER 37      PROSE
LIKE PUTTING JOHN MILTON WITH JOHN BUNYAN  .  .  .  .  .  .  853A LETTER 51     *PROSE
HIS ADDRESS IS THIS TO JOHN HAWKINS ESQR DALLINGTON  .  .  .  855B LETTER 53      PROSE
I HEREBY DECLARE THAT MR JOHN LINNELL HAS PURCHASED OF ME    874A LETTER 78      PROSE
JOHN LINNELL ESQRE CIRENCESTER PLACE FITZROY SQUARE  .  .  .  SUPP ADDRESSES/L  *TITLE
MEMORANDUM OF AGREEMENT BETWEEN WILLIAM BLAKE AND JOHN       SUPP LETTER 67D   *PROSE
   LINNELL
```
JOHNNY
```
SUSAN JOHNNY BET & JOE  .  .  .  .  .  .  .  .  .  .  .  .   53 PHEBE DREST/IM      7
```
JOHNS
```
TO PRIMROSE HILL AND SAINT JOHNS WOOD  .  .  .  .  .  .  .  649 FIELDS FROM/J      2
```
JOHNSON   (DOCTOR)
```
LIKE DOCTOR JOHNSON  .  .  .  .  .  .  .  .  .  .  .  .  .   54 LO THE BAT/IM      5
O HO SAID DOCTOR JOHNSON  .  .  .  .  .  .  .  .  .  .  .  .   54 LO THE BAT/IM  *   6
A HA TO DOCTOR JOHNSON  .  .  .  .  .  .  .  .  .  .  .  .   54 LO THE BAT/IM  *  10
("REYNOLDS JOHNSON BURKE") [?OLIVER GOLDSMITH NEVER         SUPP ANNO REYNOLDS *  MARG
   ?SHOULD ?HAVE]
(RE JOHNSON) CHRIST & HIS APOSTLES WERE ILLITERATE MEN      786D ANNO THORNTON    MARG
WAS JOHNSON HIRED TO PRETEND TO RELIGIOUS TERRORS  .  .  .  786D ANNO THORNTON    MARG
```
JOHNSON (JOSEPH)
```
LONDON PRINTED FOR J JOHNSON MDCCXCI  .  .  .  .  .  .  .  .  134A FRENCH REVOLTN  TITLE
LAMBETH AND J JOHNSON ST PAULS CHURCH YARD  .  .  .  .  .  .  209B FOR CHILDRN/GP *TITLE
BEEN PUBLISHD EVEN JOHNSON & FUSELI HAVE DISCARDED          795C LETTER 6        PROSE
   MY GRAVER
THIS FROM JOHNSON & FUSELI BROUGHT ME DOWN HERE  .  .  .  .  812C LETTER 22      PROSE
MR JOHNSON THE BOOKSELLER TELLS ME THAT THERE IS NO WANT    831B LETTER 31      PROSE
   OF WORK
I INTEND TO SEE MRS LAMBERT & MR JOHNSON BOOKSELLER THIS    833C LETTER 33      PROSE
THE DRAWING OF THE MONUMENT WHICH MR JOHNSON SENT HAS  .  .  838B LETTER 37      PROSE
FAVOR ME WITH A LINE THAT I MAY SEND THE PLATES TO JOHNSON  840C LETTER 39      PROSE
WHICH I GOT AS YOU DIRECTED OF MR JOHNSON I HAVE SEEN  .  .  844D LETTER 43      PROSE
AND WILL ALSO RESPECT JOHNSON THE MORE FOR SUCH TESTIMONY   846C LETTER 44      PROSE
TO INJURE SEAGRAVE IN YOUR OPINION IF POSSIBLE JOHNSON MAY  846C LETTER 44      PROSE
FURNISHD BY JOHNSON I LET HIM RUN ON SO FAR AS TO SAY THAT  846D LETTER 44      PROSE
WHICH I CONCEIVE WERE URGED UPON HIM BY JOHNSON  .  .  .  .  847A LETTER 44      PROSE
WHICH MR JOHNSON WAS TO GET DONE FOR OUR FRIEND DALLY  .  .  847A LETTER 44      PROSE
BECAUSE MR JOHNSON HAS AT TIMES WRITTEN SUCH LETTERS TO ME  847B LETTER 44      PROSE
OBSERVING THAT THE PRICE MR JOHNSON GIVES FOR THE PLATES    853C LETTER 52      PROSE
```
JOHNSON'S
```
MR JOHNSON'S FORGETFULNESS WHO APPOINTD TO CALL ON YOU BUT  809C LETTER 20     *PROSE
OF MR JOHNSON'S INTEGRITY WHILE WE WERE TALKING CONCERNING  846C LETTER 44      PROSE
MR PHILLIPS TOOK CARE TO REPEAT JOHNSON'S RAILING TO ME     846D LETTER 44      PROSE
EXCEPT PAPER WHICH IS JOHNSON'S FAULT COWPER IS FAR THE     847A LETTER 44      PROSE
   BEST
TO MR JOHNSON'S AGGRAVATING LETTERS HAVE BEEN REPRESENTED   847A LETTER 44      PROSE
ONE I COULD GET AT JOHNSON'S I LEFT A GOOD IMPRESSION OF IT 855C LETTER 53      PROSE
```
JOIN
```
AND OUR ROOTS TOGETHER JOIN  .  .  .  .  .  .  .  .  .  .    7 LOVE HARMNY/PS     4
AND SEPARATE MARCH BUT JOIN AGAIN AT NIGHT  .  .  .  .  .  .   19 EDW THIRD/PS 1    51
COME LIVE AND BE MERRY AND JOIN WITH ME  .  .  .  .  .  .  .   63 SHEPHERD YOUNG    11
COME LIVE & BE MERRY AND JOIN WITH ME  .  .  .  .  .  .  .  .  125 LAUGHING/SI      11
JOIN SHAKING CONVULSD THE SHIVRING CLAY BREATHES  .  .  .  .  248 SONG OF LOS 7    32
.  .  .  THEIR BODIES JOIN IN BURNING ANGUISH]  .  .  .  .  .  269 FOUR ZOAS 1     181
HIS SONS FLED FROM HIS SIDE TO JOIN THE CONFLICT PALE HE    278 FOUR ZOAS 1     521
   HEARD
TO BONES JOIN SHAKING CONVULSD THE SHIVERING CLAY BREATHES  363 FOUR ZOAS 9     232
.  .  .  TOGETHER THEY JOIN IN BURNING ANGUISH  .  .  .  .  .  381 FOUR ZOAS AD 5    1
THEY SOON FIND THEIR OWN PLACE & JOIN THE WATCHERS OF THE   503 MILTON 20        50
   ULRO
PITY MUST JOIN TOGETHER THOSE WHOM WRATH HAS TORN IN SUNDER 626 JERUSALEM 7      62
WHEN SOULS MINGLE & JOIN THRO ALL THE FIBRES OF BROTHERHOOD 733 JERUSALEM 88     14
MY WIFE CONTINUES IN HEALTH & DESIRES TO JOIN ME IN EVERY   860B LETTER 56      PROSE
```
JOIND
```
GO SEE THE CITY FRIENDS JOIND HAND IN HAND  .  .  .  .  .  .   43A THEN SHE BORE   PROSE
WHERE ENITHARMON JOIND TO HIS LEFT SIDE IN [DISMAL] GRIDING 299 FOUR ZOAS 4    *  60
   PAIN
WHEN ALL THE ELEMENTAL GODS JOIND IN THE WONDROUS SONG  .  .  336 FOUR ZOAS 7B   146
THEIR WINGS JOIND IN THE ZENITH OVER HEAD [BUT OTHER WINGS  341 FOUR ZOAS 8       9
   ]
LUTHER ALSO LEFT THE PRIEST & JOIND THE SOLDIER  .  .  .  .  413B ANNO BOYD       MARG
DELUSORY LOVE TO PALAMABRON ADMIRATION JOIND WITH ENVY  .   492 MILTON 12         7
FOR WHEN LOS JOIND WITH ME HE TOOK ME IN HIS FIRY WHIRLWIND 527 MILTON 36        21
HERE THE TWELVE SONS OF ALBION JOIND IN DARK ASSEMBLY  .  .  640 JERUSALEM 18      5
.  .  .  THEY JOIND THE DIVINE FAMILY [?ALBION ?SLEPT]      655 JERUSALEM 29   *  83
   TREMBLING
AGAIN HE JOIND THE DIVINE BODY FOLLOWING MERCIFUL  .  .  .  664 JERUSALEM 37     11
JOIND WITH CORDELLA SHE SHINES SOUTHWARD OVER THE ATLANTIC  710 JERUSALEM 71     43
IS SABRINA JOIND WITH MEHETABEL SHE SHINES WEST OVER        710 JERUSALEM 71     45
   AMERICA
GOSHEN HATH FOLLOWD PHILISTEA GILEAD HATH JOIND WITH OG     720 JERUSALEM 79     13
```
JOINED   SEE NEW-JOINED
```
WITHIN THE VEGETATED MORTAL NERVES FOR EVERY MAN BORN IS    517 MILTON 29        30
   JOINED
BUT NATURE & FANCY ARE TWO THINGS & CAN NEVER BE JOINED     824C LETTER 27      PROSE
```
JOINS
```
THE BROKEN HEART GATE OF ENITHARMON [WHICH JOINS           341 FOUR ZOAS 8    *  29
   TO URIZEN'S TEMPLE]
PAST THE TURRET MY WIFE JOINS WITH ME IN DUTY AND AFFECTION 807B LETTER 17      PROSE
MY WIFE JOINS WITH ME IN LOVE TO YOU & MRS BUTTS  .  .  .  .  810A LETTER 20      PROSE
MY WIFE JOINS WITH ME IN LOVE TO YOU & MRS FLAXMAN  .  .  .  811A LETTER 21      PROSE
```

<pre>
                                                              PAGE   TITLE   LINE
JOINS   (CONTINUED)
    MY WIFE JOINS ME IN LOVE TO YOU BOTH I AM SINCERELY YOURS   822A LETTER 25   PROSE
    FAMILY ENJOY HEALTH MY MUCH TERRIFIED WIFE JOINS ME IN LOVE 829A LETTER 28   PROSE
    MY WIFE JOINS ME IN RESPECTS & LOVE TO YOU . . . . 837B LETTER 35   PROSE
    MY WIFE JOINS ME IN BEST AFFECTIONS TO YOU . . . . . . 839A LETTER 37   PROSE
    MY WIFE JOINS ME IN SINCERE LOVE TO YOU PLEASE TO . . . 840A LETTER 38   PROSE
    IN ALL THINGS MY WIFE JOINS ME IN THIS PRAYER . . . . . 841A LETTER 40   PROSE
    AT BRIGHTON MY WIFE JOINS ME IN LOVE TO YOU . . . . . . 843A LETTER 42   PROSE
    BENEVOLENT MINDS MY WIFE JOINS WITH ME IN THE HEARTY . . 847C LETTER 44   PROSE
    CONTINUES TO GET BETTER & JOINS ME IN MY WARMEST LOVE &   849C LETTER 45   PROSE
    MY WIFE JOINS ME IN LOVE TO YOU & TO OUR DEAR FRIEND & . 853A LETTER 51   *PROSE
    BUT FANCY IT MAY HAVE MISCARRIED MY WIFE JOINS ME IN . . 853D LETTER 52   PROSE
    MY WIFE JOINS ME IN LOVE & IN REJOICING IN MISS POOLE'S   855C LETTER 53   PROSE
    MY WIFE JOINS ME IN ANXIOUS WISHES FOR YOUR HEALTH &   . . 862A LETTER 59   PROSE
JOINT
    RENT THE IMMORTAL FEMALES LIMB FROM LIMB & JOINT FROM   500 MILTON 18   49
      JOINT
    IN ERIN'S LAND TOWARD THE NORTH JOINT AFTER JOINT   674 JERUSALEM 44   26
      & BURNING
    BENEATH THE BOTTOMS OF THE GRAVES WHICH IS EARTH'S CENTRAL 677 JERUSALEM 48   13
      JOINT
    SO TAKE MY LEAVE FOR THE PRESENT WITH THE JOINT LOVE OF   845A LETTER 43   PROSE
    AT LAVANT I REMAIN WITH MY WIFE'S JOINT AFFECTION   . . . 852D LETTER 50   PROSE
JOINTED
    FROM THE CAVERNS OF HIS JOINTED SPINE . . . .   228 URIZEN 11   1
    FROM THE CAVERNS OF HIS JOINTED SPINE DOWN SUNK WITH FRIGHT 303 FOUR ZOAS 4   223
    AND SAID GO FORTH & GUIDE MY BATTLES LIKE THE JOINTED SPINE 336 FOUR ZOAS 7B   116
    WONDERING TO BEHOLD THE EMMET THE GRASSHOPPER THE JOINTED   373 FOUR ZOAS 9   603
      WORM
JOINTS
    IJIM SHALL REND THY FEEBLE JOINTS THOU TEMPTER OF DARK IJIM 103 TIRIEL 4   6
    STAMINA OF HIS MAKE COMPARATIVELY LITTLE AND HIS JOINTS   580A DESC CAT 5   PROSE
JOKE
    HA HA SIR THOMAS YOU BUT JOKE . . . .   21 EDW THIRD/PS 3   9
    SIR THOMAS DAGWORTH YOU MUST HAVE YOUR JOKE . . . . .   23 EDW THIRD/PS 3   92
    [AND TWIXT EARNEST & [GAME] JOKE] . . . .   163 ASKED THIEF/N *   10
    SOMETIMES WITH SEVERITY OFTENER WITH JOKE AND SPORT . . 569A DESC CAT 3   PROSE
    WILL NEXT SUMMER JOKE US FACE TO FACE GOD BLESS YOU ALL   810C LETTER 20   PROSE
JOKES
    OF THE CAVALCADE IS A FIRST RATE CHARACTER AND HIS JOKES 569D DESC CAT 3   PROSE
JOKTAN
    ADAM WHO IS PELEG & JOKTAN & ESAU & JACOB & SAUL & DAVID   713 JERUSALEM 73   28
JOLLY
    AND TUNE THY JOLLY VOICE TO MY FRESH PIPE . . . . . .   2 TO AUTUMN/PS   4
    THUS SANG THE JOLLY AUTUMN AS HE SAT . . . .   2 TO AUTUMN/PS   16
    AND THE JOLLY SWAIN LAUGHS HIS FILL . . . .   7 LOVE JOCUND/PS   8
    WHEN THE JOLLY COMPANY ARE JUST QUITTING THE TABARDE INN 566C DESC CAT 3   PROSE
    WHEN THE JOLLY COMPANY ARE JUST QUITTING THE TABARDE INN 588B CHAUCER/N   PROSE
    DEPICTED IN HIS JOLLY FACE DIRECTS THEM TO THE . . . .   588C CHAUCER/N   PROSE
    WHEN THE JOLLY COMPANY ARE JUST QUITTING THE TABARDE INN 589C CHAUCER 2   PROSE
JONAH
    EXISTED JONAH WAS NO PROPHET IN THE MODERN SENSE . . . . 392A ANNO WATSON   MARG
JONES
    AN OLD MAN NAMED JONES WHO MRS GRINDER SAYS DID NOT . . 438C BLAKES MEMORAN   PROSE
JONQUIL
    THE JONQUIL THE MILD LILLY OPES HER HEAVENS EVERY TREE . . 521 MILTON 31   60
JONSON
    UNDER THE AUSPICES OF SHAKESPEARE & JOHNSON (JONSON) IN   618D ILLUS MILTON   PROSE
      WHICH
JORDAN
    AND TOOK UP WATER FROM THE RIVER JORDAN POURING ON . .   500 MILTON 19   8
    JORDAN TO THE LAND OF THE HITTITE EVERY-ONE THAT SAW HIM   661 JERUSALEM 34   48
    OVER JORDAN ALL TERRIFIED FLED THEY BECAME WHAT THEY BEHELD 661 JERUSALEM 34   54
    BETWEEN LIPS OF MIRE & CLAY THEN SENT HIM FORTH OVER JORDAN 662 JERUSALEM 36   6
    HIS EAR IN A SPIRAL CIRCLE OUTWARD THEN SENT HIM   662 JERUSALEM 36   13
      OVER JORDAN
    JORDAN SPRANG BENEATH ITS THRESHOLD BUBBLING FROM BENEATH 690 JERUSALEM 58   23
    CANAAN IS HIS PORTICO JORDAN IS A FOUNTAIN IN HIS PORCH   690 JERUSALEM 58   33
    UPON PISON & ARNON & JORDAN AND I HEARD THE VOICE AMONG   695 JERUSALEM 61   33
    MEDWAY MINGLED WITH KISHON THAMES RECIEVD THE HEAVENLY   720 JERUSALEM 79   35
      JORDAN
    AND JORDAN TO EUPHRATES JERUSALEM FOLLOWD TREMBLING . . . 722 JERUSALEM 80   9
JOSEPH
    GAD ASHER ISSACHAR ZEBULUN JOSEPH BENJAMIN DAVID SOLOMON   350 FOUR ZOAS 8   361
    THEN ZEBULUN THEN JOSEPH THEN BENJAMIN TWELVE SONS OF LOS 350 FOUR ZOAS 8   377
    AND PALAMABRON THOU REMEMBEREST WHEN JOSEPH AN INFANT .   508 MILTON 24   17
    I WILL TELL YOU WHAT JOSEPH OF ARIMATHEA . . . . . .   552 TELL YOU WHA/N   1
    COME LISTEN TO JOSEPH OF ARIMATHEA . . . .   552 TELL YOU WHA/N   4
    LISTEN PATIENT & WHEN JOSEPH HAS DONE . . . .   552 TELL YOU WHA/N   5
    JOSEPH OF ARIMATHEA AMONG THE ROCKS OF ALBION . . . . . 604A INSC ARIMATHEA   TITLE
    THE HOLY FAMILY CONSISTING OF MARY JOSEPH JOHN THE BAPTIST 614A V LAST JUDG/N   PROSE
    THE GATE OF JOSEPH DENBIGHSHIRE THE GATE OF BENJAMIN   637 JERUSALEM 16   41
      GLAMORGANSHIRE
    JOSEPH STAFFORD SHROPS HEREF BENJAMIN DERBY CHESHIRE   637 JERUSALEM 16   49
      MONMOUTH
    DIVIDED IN THE THE GATES OF REUBEN JUDAH DAN & JOSEPH .   637 JERUSALEM 16   51
    JOSEPH ELGIN LANERK KINROS BENJAMIN KROMARTY MURRA   638 JERUSALEM 16   58
      KIRKUBRIHT
    TO MAKE ONE FAMILY OF CONTRARIES THAT JOSEPH MAY BE SOLD   686 JERUSALEM 55   15
    BEHOLD IN THE VISIONS OF ELOHIM JEHOVAH BEHOLD JOSEPH   694 JERUSALEM 61   1
      & MARY
    SHE LOOKED & SAW JOSEPH THE CARPENTER IN NAZARETH & MARY   694 JERUSALEM 61   3
</pre>

		PAGE	TITLE	LINE

JOSEPH (CONTINUED)

DOST THOU NOT MURDER ME JOSEPH SPOKE IN ANGER & FURY SHOULD I 694 JERUSALEM 61 5
THO SHE HATES HE CALLS HER AGAIN IN LOVE I LOVE MY DEAR JOSEPH 694 JERUSALEM 61 8
AH MY MARY SAID JOSEPH WEEPING OVER & EMBRACING HER CLOSELY IN 694 JERUSALEM 61 14
MANY STREAMS IN THE ARMS OF JOSEPH & GAVE FORTH HER TEARS OF JOY 695 JERUSALEM 61 29
O SKOFIELD WHY ART THOU CRUEL LO JOSEPH IS THINE TO MAKE 705 JERUSALEM 68 1
WHENCE JOSEPH & BENJAMIN ROLLD APART AWAY FROM THE NATIONS 715 JERUSALEM 74 56
THERE IS REUBEN & GAD & JOSEPH & JUDAH & LEVI CLOSD UP . . 721 JERUSALEM 79 64
OF REUBEN OR OF BENJAMIN OF JOSEPH OR JUDAH OR LEVI . . . 736 JERUSALEM 90 31
THE THREE MARIES AT THE SEPULCHER...THE DEATH OF JOSEPH 824A LETTER 27 PROSE
JOSEPH AND MARY AND THE ROOM THEY WERE SEEN IN . . . . . SUPP DRAWING HEH *TITLE

JOSEPH'S

THEY STRIP OFF JOSEPH'S COAT & DIP IT IN THE BLOOD OF BATTLE 704 JERUSALEM 67 23
MUNSTER SOUTH IN REUBEN'S GATE CONNAUT WEST IN JOSEPH'S GATE 711 JERUSALEM 72 3
I HAVE STRIPD OFF JOSEPH'S BEAUTIFUL INTEGUMENT FOR MY BELOVED 724 JERUSALEM 81 11

JOSHUA

TO MORROW MORNING BY FOUR O CLOCK & WORK SIR JOSHUA . . . 51D ISLAND MOON 7 PROSE
BUT THE DESTRUCTION OF THE CANAANITES BY JOSHUA . . . 388B ANNO WATSON * MARG
OPPRESSION OF SR JOSHUA & HIS GANG OF CUNNING HIRED KNAVES 445B ANNO REYNOLDS MARG
WHILE SR JOSHUA WAS ROLLING IN RICHES . . . . 445C ANNO REYNOLDS MARG
HERE ARE MOCKS ON THOSE WHO SAW RAFAEL [BUT NOT SIR ?JOSHUA] 447D ANNO REYNOLDS * MARG
[?FIRST ?TO SERVE NOBILITY & FASHIONABLE TASTE & SR JOSHUA] 451C ANNO REYNOLDS * MARG
WHEN SR JOSHUA REYNOLDS DIED . . . . 451 ANNO REYNOLDS 1
HE IS LIKE SR JOSHUA FULL OF SELF-CONTRADICTION & KNAVERY 459D ANNO REYNOLDS MARG
[SIR JOSHUA PROVES THAT] BACON'S PHILOSOPHY . . . . 461C ANNO REYNOLDS * MARG
HE REJECTED IT FOR GOOD REASONS SR JOSHUA IN OTHER PLACES 467D ANNO REYNOLDS MARG
OPPOSED TO RUBENS'S COLOURING SR [JOSHUA'S] JOSHUA HAS PLACD POUSSIN 469A ANNO REYNOLDS * MARG
PRINCIPLES ACCORDING TO SR JOSHUA BECOME DEFECTS . . . . 477A ANNO REYNOLDS MARG
SIR JOSHUA PRAISES MICHAEL ANGELO . . . . 539 SIR JOSH MIC/N 1
[AS] [IF] SHOULD MICHAEL ANGELO [PRAISING] [PRAISD] PRAISE SIR JOSHUA 539 SIR JOSH MIC/N * 6
SIR JOSHUA PRAISED RUBENS WITH A SMILE . . . . 540 SIR JOSH RUB/N 1
SIR JOSHUA SENT HIS OWN PORTRAIT TO . . . . 541 FLORENTINE/N 1
OF SIR JOSHUA REYNOLDS'S LECTURES . . . . 543 TO ROYL ACAD/N 2
[THAT SIR JOSHUA NEVER WISHD TO SPEAK] . . . . 543 TO ROYL ACAD/N 7
SIR JOSHUA IN ASTONISHMENT CRIES OUT . . . . 548 CRIPPLE EVRY/N 3
THE FIVE BOOKS OF THE DECALOGUE THE BOOKS OF JOSHUA & JUDGES 677 JERUSALEM 48 9
THE SON OF BEOR HAVE GIVEN THEIR POWER TO JOSHUA & CALEB 680 JERUSALEM 49 59
HE SAYS THUS...SO SAYS SIR JOSHUA . . . . 814B LETTER 23 PROSE
[FUNERAL GRANTED TO SIR JOSHUA FOR HAVING ?DESTROYD ART] SUPP ANNO REYNOLDS * MARG

JOSHUA'S

OPPOSED TO RUBENS'S COLOURING SR [JOSHUA'S] JOSHUA HAS PLACD POUSSIN 469A ANNO REYNOLDS * MARG
BAD PICTURES ARE ALWAYS SR JOSHUA'S FRIENDS . . . . . 478C ANNO REYNOLDS MARG
LOOK THERE YOULL SEE SR JOSHUA'S COLOURING . . . . . 536 NO REAL STYL/N 3
[?WHY SHOULD LAELIUS BE ?CONSIDERED SIR JOSHUA'S ?COUNTERPART] SUPP ANNO REYNOLDS * MARG

JOSIAH

TO JOSIAH WEDGWOOD ESQRE . . . . SUPP ADDRESS/L 65 *TITLE

JOSTLING

THIS IS NOT DONE BY JOSTLING IN THE STREET . . . . . . 550 GREAT THINGS/N 2

JOURNEY

CLAD AS A TRAVELLER FRESH RISEN ON HIS JOURNEY . . . . 40B SAMSON/PS PROSE
GIVE IT ME FOR I CANNOT STAY MY JOURNEY IS FAR FROM HENCE 101 TIRIEL 2 22
MY JOURNEY IS OER ROCKS & MOUNTAINS NOT IN PLEASANT VALES 103 TIRIEL 3 28
WHERE THE TRAVELLER'S JOURNEY IS DONE . . . . 215 AH SUNFLOWR/SE 4
WITH A GLOBE OF FIRE LIGHTING HIS JOURNEY . . . . . 234 URIZEN 20 48
A FEARFUL JOURNEY ANNOYD . . . . 234 URIZEN 20 49
LIGHTING HIS DISMAL JOURNEY THRO THE PATHLESS WORLD OF DEATH 314 FOUR ZOAS 6 84
TIME AFTER TIME FOR SUCH A JOURNEY NONE BUT IRON PENS . . 316 FOUR ZOAS 6 173
THE JOURNEY OBSTINATE REFUSE TO WRITE TIME AFTER TIME . . 316 FOUR ZOAS 6 175
FOR FAR & WIDE SHE STRETCHD THRO ALL THE WORLDS OF URIZEN'S JOURNEY 340 FOUR ZOAS 7B 288
RECORD THE JOURNEY OF IMMORTAL MILTON THRO YOUR REALMS . . 481 MILTON 2 1
WHILE HE KEEPS ONWARDS IN HIS WONDROUS JOURNEY ON THE EARTH 497 MILTON 15 26
BY GIVING UP OF SELFHOOD & THEY DISTANT VIEWD HIS JOURNEY 498 MILTON 17 * 3
OF MILTON'S JOURNEY URIZEN BEHELD THE IMMORTAL MAN . . . 498 MILTON 17 36
THAT MILTON LABOURD WITH HIS JOURNEY & HIS FEET BLED SORE 500 MILTON 19 3
A LONG JOURNEY & DARK THRO CHAOS IN THE TRACK OF MILTON'S COURSE 524 MILTON 34 22
A WONDROUS JOURNEY NOT PASSABLE BY IMMORTAL FEET & NONE . . 525 MILTON 35 20
PILGRIMS ON THEIR JOURNEY TO CANTERBURY . . . . 566C DESC CAT 3 TITLE
CONCEPTION OF THE HUMOUR AND FUN THAT OCCURS ON THE JOURNEY 569A DESC CAT 3 PROSE
ON THEIR JOURNEY TO CANTERBURY . . . . 588B CHAUCER/N TITLE
"WHO JOURNEY TO SAINT THOMAS'S SHRINE AT CANTERBURY" . 589A CHAUCER/N PROSE
FROM SOUTHWARK ON THEIR JOURNEY TO CANTERBURY . . . . 589C CHAUCER 2 TITLE
ON THEIR JOURNEY TO AND FROM HIS SHRINE WERE RECEIVED . . 590B CHAUCER 2 PROSE
AS A PILGRIM TRAVELLING THROUGH THIS JOURNEY OF LIFE . . 590B CHAUCER 2 PROSE
"WHO JOURNEY TO ST THOMAS'S SHRINE AT CANTERBURY" . . 590C CHAUCER 2 PROSE
IN THE HOT NOON AS HE TRAVELD THRO HIS JOURNEY HYLE & SKOFIELD 690 JERUSALEM 58 30

		PAGE	TITLE	LINE

JOURNEY   (CONTINUED)
    EVEN A LONG SEASON & A HARD JOURNEY & A HOWLING WILDERNESS   696 JERUSALEM 62   27
    "THE ANGELS OF OUR JOURNEY HAVE INSPIRED A SONG TO YOU"   800B LETTER 12   PROSE
    THAT SURROUND MISS POOLE'S VILLA TO SHINE UPON MY JOURNEY   801B LETTER 13   PROSE
    OUR JOURNEY WAS VERY PLEASANT . . . .   802B LETTER 14   PROSE
    JOURNEY & SUCH SWEET VERSES AS YOURS IN YOUR LAST . .   854B LETTER 53   PROSE
    & AT THE VERY IDEA OF ANOTHER JOURNEY TO SWEET FELPHAM .   857C LETTER 54   PROSE
    OF THE WAY ON HIS JOURNEY IN THE COACH FOR WE BOTH GOT .   869C LETTER 70   PROSE
    ON OUR JOURNEY BUT AS I HAD NOT PAID & DID NOT WISH TO PAY   869D LETTER 70   PROSE
    ME AT THIS TIME MY JOURNEY TO HAMPSTEAD ON SUNDAY . . .   880A LETTER 90   PROSE
    THE LODGYNGE HOUSE FOR PILGRIMS WHO JOURNEY . . . . .   SUPP ILLUS CHAUCER *TITLE
    THE JOURNEY OF LIFE . . . .   SUPP PENC DRAW 1.39 *TITLE
JOURNEYD
    WHEN FOURTEEN SUNS HAD FAINTLY JOURNEYD OER HIS DARK ABODE   195 AMERICA PREL 1   2
JOURNEYED
    AND FINISHES WHERE THE LARK MOUNTS HERE MILTON JOURNEYED   498 MILTON 17   27
JOURNEYING
    WESTWARDLY JOURNEYING TILL TIRIEL GREW WEARY WITH   104 TIRIEL 4   31
        HIS TRAVEL
    BUT MILTON'S HUMAN SHADOW CONTINUD JOURNEYING ABOVE .   498 MILTON 17   18
JOURNEYMAN
    OF POOR FISHERMEN & A JOURNEYMAN CARPENTER . . . . .   465D ANNO REYNOLDS   MARG
    [AP] ADMIRE ONLY THE WORK OF THE JOURNEYMAN . . . . .   596C PUB ADDRESS/N   *PROSE
    THE JOURNEYMAN PRINTERS THROUGHOUT LONDON ARE AT WAR .   859B LETTER 56   PROSE
JOURNEYMAN'S
    BUT IN THE JOURNEYMAN'S LABOUR . . . .   548 GIVE PENSION/N   4
    CAN ANGLUS NEVER DISCERN PERFECTION BUT IN THE JOURNEYMAN'S   601D PUB ADDRESS/N   PROSE
        LABOUR
JOURNEYMEN
    THE LABOURD WORKS OF JOURNEYMEN EMPLOY BY CORREGGIO .   455A ANNO REYNOLDS   MARG
    LABOUR & TRICK SALVATORE ROSA EMPLOYD JOURNEYMEN . . .   468D ANNO REYNOLDS   MARG
    ALL RUBENS'S PICTURES ARE PAINTED BY JOURNEYMEN & . .   468D ANNO REYNOLDS   MARG
    AND THOSE WHO WERE HIS IMITATORS AND JOURNEYMEN HE . .   583A DESC CAT 9   PROSE
    PETTY PRINCE IN ITALY AND EMPLOYED NUMEROUS JOURNEYMEN .   583B DESC CAT 9   PROSE
    PAY THEIR JOURNEYMEN LITTLE ENOUGH BUT THOUGH . . . .   583B DESC CAT 9   PROSE
    NOT BY THE HANDS OF JOURNEYMEN BUT BY THE ORIGINAL . .   588A CHAUCER/N   PROSE
    THE LIFE'S LABOUR OF IGNORANT JOURNEYMEN . . . . . .   593D PUB ADDRESS/N   PROSE
    & HIS FRENCH JOURNEYMEN WHOSE NAMES I FORGET . . . .   594A PUB ADDRESS/N   PROSE
    [ART BY THE HANDS OF IGNORANT JOURNEYMEN] . . . . .   595B PUB ADDRESS/N   PROSE
    THE LIFE'S LABOURS OF IMBECILLITY & IMBECILLITY'S   598C PUB ADDRESS/N   PROSE
        JOURNEYMEN
JOURNEYMEN'S
    OF AN HUNDRED JOURNEYMEN'S HOW D'YE DO NEIGHBOUR . . .   546 SWELLD LIMBS/N   4
    ENGLISHMEN HAVE BEEN SO USED TO JOURNEYMEN'S UNDECIDED   603C PUB ADDR AD/N   PROSE
        BUNGLING
JOURNEY'S
    MR LINNELL WILL HAVE ARRIVED AT HIS JOURNEY'S END BEFORE   871C LETTER 73   PROSE
JOURNEY-WORK
    LABOURED FABRICATION OF JOURNEY-WORK THEY COULD NOT DRAW   457A ANNO REYNOLDS   * MARG
JOVE
    JOVE WEIGHS THE COUNSEL OF FUTURITY . . . .   15 IMIT SPEN/PS   23
    ARMD WITH THE TERRORS OF ALMIGHTY JOVE . . . . . .   15 IMIT SPEN/PS   45
    AND SATURN JOVE & RHEA OF THE ISLES OF THE SEA REMOTE . .   528 MILTON 37   33
JOY
    WITH JOY THY RUDDY LIMBS AND FLOURISHING HAIR . . . .   1 TO SUMMER/PS   6
    WE LACK NOT SONGS NOR INSTRUMENTS OF JOY . . . . .   2 TO SUMMER/PS   17
    OF FRUIT AND JOY WITH PINIONS LIGHT ROVES ROUND . . .   2 TO AUTUMN/PS   14
    THAT BED OF JOY WHERE ERST HER LORD HATH PRESSD . . .   5 FAIR ELENOR/PS   38
    IN TIMES OF INNOCENCE AND HOLY JOY . . . .   9 FRESH FROM/PS   10
    A YOUTH DOTH WALK IN STOLEN JOY AND PRIDE . . . . .   10 WHEN EARLY/PS   14
    GOOD MORROW GENERALS I GIVE YOU JOY . . . . . .   22 EDW THIRD/PS 3   43
    WHERE PEACE AND JOY AND LOVE AND CALM CONTENT . . .   30 EDW THIRD/PS 5   30
    OUR SONS SHALL RISE FROM THRONES IN JOY . . . . . .   33 EDW THIRD/PS 6   49
    HER SONS SHALL JOY AS IN THE MORNING . . . . . .   34C KING JOHN/PS   PROSE
    EYES THE DISTANT COUNTRY WITH JOY . . . .   36C COUCH DEATH/PS   PROSE
    AND THE YOUTH BREATHES OUT HIS SOUL WITH JOY INTO ETERNITY   36D COUCH DEATH/PS   PROSE
    O WHAT AN HUMBLE GARB TRUE JOY PUTS ON . . . . .   37A CONTEMPLATN/PS   PROSE
    GREEN GRASS SPRINGS IN JOY AND THE NIMBLE AIR KISSES THE   37B CONTEMPLATN/PS   PROSE
        LEAVES
    MY JOY IS GIVEN INTO THE HANDS OF HIM WHO HATES ME . . .   38D SAMSON/PS   PROSE
    SO SEEMED HE TO DEPART SHE WONDERED WITH EXCEEDING JOY .   40A SAMSON/PS   PROSE
    HE SAT AND HEARD WITH JOY AND PRAISED GOD WHO ISRAEL STILL   40A SAMSON/PS   PROSE
        DOTH KEEP
    [REFRESHING THE COLD EARTH WITH BEAMING JOY] BUT PRIDE   40D THEN SHE BORE   PROSE
        AWOKE
    NOR KNEW THAT JOY WAS BORN AND TAKING POISNOUS SEED . .   40D THEN SHE BORE   PROSE
    BRINGS TRUE JOY ONCE FLED & CONTEMPLATION IS HER DAUGHTER   42A THEN SHE BORE   PROSE
    AND TUNES HER [?CHAUNTANT] NOTES WHEN BUXOM JOY DOTH FAN   43B WOE CRIED MUSE   *PROSE
        HIS WINGS
    WHERE JOY DOTH SIT ON EVERY BOUGH . . . .   63 SHEPHERD FIRST   2
    WHEN THE GREENWOOD LAUGHS WITH THE VOICE OF JOY . . .   63 SHEPHERD YOUNG   5
    FALSE FOR WEAK IS THE JOY THAT IS NEVER WEARIED . . .   65D ANNO LAVATER   MARG
    I KNOW TIRIEL IS KING OF THE WEST & THERE HE LIVES IN JOY   101 TIRIEL 2   20
    [BUT STILL HE FEARD THAT HAR & HEVA WOULD DIE OF JOY &   102 TIRIEL 3   8
        GRIEF]
    [THY GOD OF LOVE THY HEAVEN OF JOY] . . . .   109 TIRIEL 8   *   9
    WHILE HE WEPT WITH JOY TO HEAR . . . .   111 INTRODUCTN/SI   12
    EVERY CHILD MAY JOY TO HEAR . . . .   111 INTRODUCTN/SI   20
    HED HAVE GOD FOR HIS FATHER & NEVER WANT JOY . . . .   118 CHIMNEY SWP/SI   20
    INFANT JOY . . . .   118B INFANT JOY/SI   TITLE
    JOY IS MY NAME . . . .   118 INFANT JOY/SI   5
    SWEET JOY BEFALL THEE . . . .   118 INFANT JOY/SI   6

JOY   (CONTINUED)

	PAGE	TITLE	LINE
PRETTY JOY			
SWEET JOY BUT TWO DAYS OLD	118 INFANT JOY/SI		7
SWEET JOY I CALL THEE	118 INFANT JOY/SI		8
SWEET JOY BEFALL THEE	118 INFANT JOY/SI		9
AND JOY WITHOUT CEASING	118 INFANT JOY/SI		12
HE DOTH GIVE HIS JOY TO ALL	119 NIGHT/SI		14
O HE GIVES TO US HIS JOY	122 ON ANOTHERS/SI		25
FULL OF JOY	123 ON ANOTHERS/SI		33
O IT DRIVES ALL JOY AWAY	123 SPRING/SI		11
HOW CAN THE BIRD THAT IS BORN FOR JOY	124 SCHOOL BOY/SI		7
OF THEIR JOY IN THE SPRINGING DAY	124 SCHOOL BOY/SI		16
HOW SHALL THE SUMMER ARISE IN JOY	124 SCHOOL BOY/SI		24
WHEN THE GREEN WOODS LAUGH WITH THE VOICE OF JOY	124 SCHOOL BOY/SI		26
COMFORT IN MORNING JOY IN THE NOON DAY	124 LAUGHING/SI		1
AND ROUND THE TENT OF GOD LIKE LAMBS WE JOY	125 LIT BLK BOY/SI		12
TO LEAN IN JOY UPON OUR FATHER'S KNEE	125 LIT BLK BOY/SI		24
HANDS HEAD BOSOM AND PARTS OF LOVE FOLLOW THEIR HIGH BREATHING JOY	125 LIT BLK BOY/SI		26
	142 FRENCH REVOLTN		185
LIKE THE LOW VOICE OF THE LABOURING MAN INSTEAD OF THE SHOUT OF JOY	145 FRENCH REVOLTN		245
EXCESS OF SORROW LAUGHS EXCESS OF JOY WEEPS	151C MARRIAGE HH 8		PROSE
WITH HOARSE NOTE CURSE THE SONS OF JOY	160A SONG LIBERTY		PROSE
BUT AN HONEST JOY	168 SILENT NIGHT/N		10
DOES SPRING HIDE ITS [DELIGHT] JOY	169 EARTHS ANSWR/N		16
TO SEEK FOR NEW JOY	171 SLEPT DARK/N		7
ALWAYS IS TO JOY INCLIND	175 HOW TO KNOW/N		2
OF CRIMSON JOY	175 SICK ROSE/N		6
HE WHO BINDS [HIMSELF TO] TO HIMSELF A JOY	179 ETERNITY/N *		1
BUT HE WHO [JUST] KISSES THE JOY AS IT FLIES	179 ETERNITY/N		3
CAN IT BE A SONG OF JOY	181 HOLY THURS/N		6
[BRUSHD ACROSS THY SUMMER JOY]	182 THE FLY/N		2
HE WHO BINDS TO HIMSELF A JOY	184 SEVRL QUESTN/N *		11
BUT HE WHO KISSES THE JOY AS IT FLIES	184 SEVRL QUESTN/N		13
WE TURN TO WHAT WILL JOY & PLEASE	188 A FAIRY SKIPD		16
TELL ME WHAT IS A JOY & IN WHAT GARDENS DO JOYS GROW	191 V DAU ALBION 3		24
HOW CAN ONE JOY ABSORB ANOTHER ARE NOT DIFFERENT JOYS	192 V DAU ALBION 5		5
HOLY ETERNAL INFINITE AND EACH JOY IS A LOVE	192 V DAU ALBION 5		6
WITH NETS FOUND UNDER THY NIGHT PILLOW TO CATCH VIRGIN JOY	194 V DAU ALBION 6		11
OPEN TO JOY AND TO DELIGHT WHERE EVER BEAUTY APPEARS	194 V DAU ALBION 6		22
SIT ON A BANK AND DRAW THE PLEASURES OF THIS FREE BORN JOY	194 V DAU ALBION 7		2
THE LUSTFUL JOY SHALL FORGET TO GENERATE & CREATE AN AMOROUS IMAGE	194 V DAU ALBION 7		6
AND TREES & BIRDS & BEASTS & MEN BEHOLD THEIR ETERNAL JOY	195 V DAU ALBION 8		8
ARISE YOU LITTLE GLANCING WINGS AND SING YOUR INFANT JOY	195 V DAU ALBION 8		9
I HOWL MY JOY AND MY RED EYES SEEK TO BEHOLD THY FACE	196 AMERICA PREL 1		19
THE FIERY JOY THAT URIZEN PERVERTED TO TEN COMMANDS	198 AMERICA 8		3
AND TO RENEW THE FIERY JOY AND BURST THE STONY ROOF	199 AMERICA 8		9
. . . & LEAVE HIS JOY TO THE IDLE TO THE PESTILENCE	200 AMERICA 11		6
DOES SPRING HIDE ITS JOY	211 EARTHS ANSR/SE		16
CAN IT BE A SONG OF JOY	212 HOLY THURS/SE		6
OF CRIMSON JOY	213 SICK ROSE/SE		6
I HAVE SOUGHT FOR A JOY WITHOUT PAIN	224 URIZEN 4		10
ONE COMMAND ONE JOY ONE DESIRE	224 URIZEN 4		38
OVER ALL HIS NERVES OF JOY	228 URIZEN 10		41
ALL THE WISDOM & JOY OF LIFE	230 URIZEN 13		29
THE WORLD WHERE EVERY PARTICLE OF DUST BREATHES FORTH ITS JOY	237 EUROPE INTRO		18
AH I AM DROWND IN SHADY WOE AND VISIONARY JOY	238 EUROPE PREL 2		12
BECAUSE THE DAYS AND NIGHTS OF JOY IN LUCKY HOURS RENEW	239 EUROPE 4		23
NOW COMES THE NIGHT OF ENITHARMON'S JOY	240 EUROPE 5		1
FORBID ALL JOY & FROM HER CHILDHOOD SHALL THE LITTLE FEMALE	240 EUROPE 5		8
O THEOTORMON ROBBD OF JOY I SEE THY SALT TEARS FLOW	244 EUROPE 14		24
ARISE O ORC AND GIVE OUR MOUNTAINS JOY OF THY RED LIGHT	244 EUROPE 14		31
BECAUSE OF DIRALADA THINKING TO RECLAIM HIS JOY	246 SONG OF LOS 3		31
WHEN HIS NERVES OF JOY MELTED & FLOWD	252 AHANIA 4		13
AND JOY NOR HEAR HIS FOOTSTEPS AND	254 AHANIA 4		68
WHERE THE JOY OF MY MORNING HOUR	254 AHANIA 5		5
TO EMBRACE AHANIA'S JOY	254 AHANIA 5		11
TO THE SONS OF ETERNAL JOY	254 AHANIA 5		16
IN INFANT JOY AT THY FEET	255 AHANIA 5		27
ON THE VIRGINS OF SPRINGING JOY	255 AHANIA 5		32
WHEN LOVE & JOY WERE ADORATION	256 BOOK OF LOS 3		8
STOOD SELF-BALANCD AND LOS SMILD WITH JOY	260 BOOK OF LOS 5		45
DAYS & NIGHTS OF REVOLVING JOY URTHONA WAS HIS NAME	264 FOUR ZOAS 1		16
THE INFANT JOY IS BEAUTIFUL BUT ITS ANATOMY	265 FOUR ZOAS 1		49
[ALIGHTING DOWN FROM] ALIGHTING IN HIS DRUNKEN JOY	266 FOUR ZOAS 1 *		93
THE DAZZLINGS AS OF GEMS SHONE CLEAR RAPTUROUS IN [JOY] FURY	267 FOUR ZOAS 1		128
AND DRAWING IN THE SPECTROUS LIFE IN PRIDE AND HAUGHTY JOY	270 FOUR ZOAS 1		220
THO THIS BRIGHT WORLD OF ALL OUR JOY IS IN THE HUMAN BRAIN	272 FOUR ZOAS 1		303
FROM HEAVENS OF JOY INTO THIS DEEP NOW RAGE BUT RAGE IN VAIN	276 FOUR ZOAS 1		433
HEART COLD AND THE LITTLE TONGUE CONSUMD THAT ONCE IN THOUGHTLESS JOY	276 FOUR ZOAS 1		449
[XXX ?LIVING JOY FILLS ?ALBION]	SUPP FOUR ZOAS 1 *		
IN JOY SHE HEARD HIS HOWLINGS & FORGOT HE WAS HER LUVAH	282 FOUR ZOAS 2		78
TILL HER CARESSES & HER TEARS REVIVD HIM TO LIFE & JOY	285 FOUR ZOAS 2		205
[AND LOS & ENITHARMON JOYD THEY DRANK IN TENFOLD JOY]	286 FOUR ZOAS 2		236
IN [SONGS & JOY] SORROW & CARE A GOLDEN WORLD	286 FOUR ZOAS 2		241
. . . WITH [SONGS & JOY] SORROW & CARE [?ETERNAL FEAR]	287 FOUR ZOAS 2 *		268
THE JOY OF WOMAN IS THE DEATH OF HER MOST BEST BELOVED	289 FOUR ZOAS 2		349

1015

JOY   (CONTINUED)
    AND EVERY ONE SEEKS FOR HIS MATE TO PROVE HIS INMOST JOY   289 FOUR ZOAS 2   358
    THE LIVING VOICE IS EVER LIVING IN ITS INMOST JOY   . . .   289 FOUR ZOAS 2   363
    ARISE YOU LITTLE GLANCING WINGS & SING YOUR INFANT JOY . .   289 FOUR ZOAS 2   364
    I WAKE SWEET JOY IN DENS OF SORROW & I PLANT A SMILE   .   289 FOUR ZOAS 2   371
    WHY WILT THOU LOOK UPON FUTURITY DARKNING PRESENT JOY   .   291 FOUR ZOAS 3   11
    CONSUMING ALL TO THE END CONSUMING LOVE AND [JOY] HOPE   297 FOUR ZOAS 3   204
       ARE ENDED
    GO FORTH SAID THARMAS WORKS OF JOY ARE THINE OBEY & LIVE   299 FOUR ZOAS 4   67
    OF LOS ABSORBD IN DIRE REVENGE HE DRANK WITH JOY THE CRIES   302 FOUR ZOAS 4   191
    AND BONES OF SOLIDNESS FROZE OVER ALL HIS NERVES OF JOY   303 FOUR ZOAS 4   221
    OVER HER SON OBDURATE LOS BOUND DOWN HER LOVED JOY   . .   308 FOUR ZOAS 5   103
    HER SON IN TENFOLD JOY & TO COMPENSATE FOR HER TEARS . .   309 FOUR ZOAS 5   153
    AND AT MY BANQUETS OF NEW WINE MY HEAD WAS CROWND WITH JOY   310 FOUR ZOAS 5   201
    THE ENORMOUS WONDERS OF THE ABYSSES ONCE HIS BRIGHTEST JOY   314 FOUR ZOAS 6   86
    AND YET IT DRINKS THE SUMMER JOY & FEARS THE WINTER SORROW   314 FOUR ZOAS 6   96
    WHERE JOY SANG IN THE TREES & PLEASURE SPORTED ON   317 FOUR ZOAS 6   * 213
       THE RIVERS
    WALKING IN JOY IN BRIGHT EXPANSES SLEEPING ON BRIGHT   321 FOUR ZOAS 7   64
       CLOUDS
    OR IS THY JOY FOUNDED ON TORMENT WHICH OTHERS BEAR FOR THEE   321 FOUR ZOAS 7   68
    IN THAT TRANSPARENT ROCK AS IF IN JOY OF THY BRIGHT PRISON   322 FOUR ZOAS 7   76
    THE RIPE FRUIT BLUSHES INTO JOY IN HEAVEN'S ETERNAL HALLS   324 FOUR ZOAS 7   176
    WHERE THOU IN THRILLING JOY IN BEAMING SUMMER LOVELINESS   324 FOUR ZOAS 7   186
    BUT THE NEXT JOY OF THINE SHALL BE IN SWEET DELUSION   . .   326 FOUR ZOAS 7   229
    TILL HE FORGOT ETERNITY DELIGHTED IN HIS SWEET JOY   . . .   326 FOUR ZOAS 7   253
    MUTUAL THERE WE DWELT IN ONE ANOTHER'S JOY REVOLVING   . .   327 FOUR ZOAS 7   273
    THY WORKS ARE ALL MY JOY & IN THY FIRES MY SOUL DELIGHTS   331 FOUR ZOAS 7   448
    WITH JOY THE BRIGHT LIGHT & IN IT A HUMAN FORM   . . . .   342 FOUR ZOAS 8   43
    FOR HE WAS SOURCE OF EVERY JOY THAT THIS MYSTERIOUS TREE   345 FOUR ZOAS 8   168
    EPHRAIM WAS A WILDERNESS OF JOY WHERE ALL MY WILD BEASTS   349 FOUR ZOAS 8   309
       RAN
    FELL DOWN & SHADOWY FORMS OF JOY MIXD WITH DESPAIR & GRIEF   358 FOUR ZOAS 9   29
    THAT THE ETERNAL WORLDS MAY SEE THY FACE IN PEACE & JOY   360 FOUR ZOAS 9   132
    UNGRATIFIED GIVE ALL MY JOY INTO THIS LUVAH & VALA   . . .   361 FOUR ZOAS 9   * 179
    INTO THE FIRES THEN GLORIOUS BRIGHT EXULTING IN HIS JOY   362 FOUR ZOAS 9   191
    ON TO THE SURFACE OF A LAKE AHANIA ROSE IN JOY   . . . .   362 FOUR ZOAS 9   196
    EXCESS OF JOY IS WORSE THAN GRIEF HER HEART BEAT HIGH HER   362 FOUR ZOAS 9   197
       BLOOD
    EXPECTING TO RECIEVE AHANIA IN THE SPRING WITH JOY   . . .   362 FOUR ZOAS 9   215
    THAT SPRING MAY SEE THEM RISE IN TENFOLD JOY & SWEET   362 FOUR ZOAS 9   218
       DELIGHT
    ON THE GOLDEN PALACE SONGS & JOY ON THE DESART THE COLD   363 FOUR ZOAS 9   251
       BABE
    OF ORC IN JOY THEY VIEW THE HUMAN HARVEST SPRINGING UP . .   366 FOUR ZOAS 9   342
    ON WINGS OF TENFOLD JOY CLAPPING HIS HANDS HIS FEET HIS   366 FOUR ZOAS 9   348
       RADIANT WINGS
    AND BRIGHT AHANIA TOOK HER SEAT BY URIZEN IN SONGS & JOY   366 FOUR ZOAS 9   353
    WHY WEEPEST THOU THARMAS CHILD OF TEARS IN THE BRIGHT HOUSE   371 FOUR ZOAS 9   * 530
       OF JOY
    IN INFANT SORROW & JOY ALTERNATE ENION & THARMAS PLAYD   372 FOUR ZOAS 9   554
    CRIED TIMES ARE ENDED HE EXULTED HE AROSE IN JOY HE EXULTED   372 FOUR ZOAS 9   568
    TO ONE ANOTHER WHAT ARE WE & WHENCE IS OUR JOY & DELIGHT   373 FOUR ZOAS 9   609
    JOY THRILLD THRO ALL THE FURIOUS FORM OF THARMAS HUMANIZING   373 FOUR ZOAS 9   * 613
    MAN IS A WORM WEARIED WITH JOY HE SEEKS THE CAVES OF SLEEP   374 FOUR ZOAS 9   627
    EACH SHALL BEHOLD THE ETERNAL FATHER & LOVE & JOY ABOUND   374 FOUR ZOAS 9   642
    AT THE IMMORTAL TABLES SOUNDING LOUD THEIR INSTRUMENTS   374 FOUR ZOAS 9   645
       OF JOY
    IN THE JINGLING TRACES FURIOUS LIONS SOUND THE SONG OF JOY   376 FOUR ZOAS 9   718
    O TREMBLING JOY EXCESS OF JOY IS LIKE EXCESS OF GRIEF   376 FOUR ZOAS 9   730
    THE CRUEL JOY OF LUVAH'S DAUGHTERS LACERATING WITH KNIVES   377 FOUR ZOAS 9   753
    WITH MIRTH & JOY URTHONA LIMPING FROM HIS FALL ON THARMAS   377 FOUR ZOAS 9   775
       LEAND
    ROSE FROM THE FEAST IN JOY ASCENDING TO THEIR GOLDEN LOOMS   378 FOUR ZOAS 9   779
    AND TOOK AWAY THE WINE OF AGES WITH SOLEMN SONGS & JOY . .   378 FOUR ZOAS 9   794
    EACH MORNING LIKE A NEW BORN MAN ISSUES WITH SONGS & JOY   379 FOUR ZOAS 9   833
    INWRAP THE IMMORTAL LIMBS STRUGGLING IN TERRIFIC JOY   .   381 FOUR ZOAS AD 2   2
    HE COME ON WINGS OF JOY WE'LL FLY   . . . .   423 THE BIRDS/N   17
    FOR THERE THE BABE IS BORN IN JOY   . . . .   424 MENTAL TRAVLER   5
    JUST AS WE REAP IN JOY THE FRUIT   . . . .   424 MENTAL TRAVLER   7
    HIS GRIEF IS THEIR ETERNAL JOY   . . . .   425 MENTAL TRAVLER   41
    THOU WAST THY MOTHER'S ONLY JOY   . . . .   427 LAND OF DREAMS   2
    I WEPT FOR JOY LIKE A DOVE I MOURN   . . . .   427 LAND OF DREAMS   11
    MAN WAS MADE FOR JOY & WOE   . . . .   432 AUGURIES   56
    JOY & WOE ARE WOVEN FINE   . . . . 432 AUGURIES   59
    RUNS A JOY WITH SILKEN TWINE   . . . .   432 AUGURIES   62
    THE FAIRY SKIPD ABOUT IN HIS GLORY JOY & PRIDE   . . . .   434 LONG JOHN BRWN   15
    MANY GROUPES ARISE [WITH] IN EXULTATION [IN JOY]   . . .   443D LAST JUDGMNT/L *PROSE
    & IN EXULTING ATTITUDES OF GREAT JOY TELL EACH OTHER   .   443D LAST JUDGMNT/L PROSE
    CAN SUCH CLOSED NOSTRILS FEEL A JOY OR TELL OF AUTUMN   485 MILTON 5   32
       FRUITS
    TERRIFIC IN THEIR JOY & POURING WINE OF WILDEST POWER   . .   493 MILTON 12   43
    OUR WHEAT WITH SHOUTINGS OF JOY AND LEAVE THE EARTH IN   507 MILTON 23   46
       PEACE
    THE INTEGUMENT SOFT FOR ITS CLOTHING WITH JOY & DELIGHT   515 MILTON 28   20
    HIS JOY BECAME TERRIBLE TO THEM THEY TREMBLED & WEPT   . .   519 MILTON 30   23
    FIRST EER THE MORNING BREAKS JOY OPENS IN THE FLOWERY   520 MILTON 31   50
       BOSOMS
    JOY EVEN TO TEARS WHICH THE SUN RISING DRIES FIRST THE   520 MILTON 31   51
       WILD THYME
    I THOUGHT THAT YOU WOULD LOVE MY LOVES & JOY IN MY DELIGHTS   522 MILTON 33   3
    AND THEN & THEN ALONE BEGINS THE HAPPY FEMALE JOY   . . .   522 MILTON 33   19

1016

JOY   (CONTINUED)

	PAGE	TITLE	LINE
SAID LITTLE CREATURE [THOU ART] FORMD [FOR] OF JOY & MIRTH	541	ANGEL PRESID/N	2
AND AWAY FLED EVERY JOY	552	WHY CUPID/N	20
THOUSANDS OF CONNOISSEURS WITH JOY RAN RAVING	555	BLAKES APL/N 1	5
THOUSANDS OF CONNOISSEURS WITH JOY RAN RAVING	556	BLAKES APL/N 2	8
I HAVE MENTAL JOY & MENTAL HEALTH	558	I ROSE UP AT/N	9
THOSE ON THE RIGHT HAND AWAKE IN JOY THOSE ON THE LEFT IN HORROR	609C	V LAST JUDG/N	PROSE
WITH JOY SHE HEARD HIS HOWLINGS & FORGOT HE WAS HER LUVAH	626	JERUSALEM 7	36
EVERY EMANATIVE JOY FORBIDDEN AS A CRIME	628	JERUSALEM 9	14
LOS WEPT WITH EXCEEDING JOY & ALL WEPT WITH JOY TOGETHER	631	JERUSALEM 11	13
BUT WHEN THE JOY OF MEETING WAS EXHAUSTED IN LOVING EMBRACE	631	JERUSALEM 11	16
HER JOY AND LOVE A SHADE A SHADE OF SWEET REPOSE . . .	631	JERUSALEM 12	2
THOU ART ONE WITH HER & KNOWEST NOT OF SELF IN THY SUPREME JOY	632	JERUSALEM 12	42
THE INFANT JOY IS BEAUTIFUL BUT ITS ANATOMY	645	JERUSALEM 22	22
THE SONS OF GOD WERE ALBION'S SONS AND JERUSALEM WAS MY JOY	653	JERUSALEM 29	8
IS AS NOTHING BEFORE THEE FADED IS ALL LIFE AND JOY . . .	659	JERUSALEM 33	34
THAT ODOURS CANNOT THEM EXPAND NOR JOY ON THEM EXULT . .	680	JERUSALEM 49	39
DIVINE BENEVOLENCE & JOY FOR THE ETERNAL MAN	686	JERUSALEM 55	9
MANY STREAMS IN THE ARMS OF JOSEPH & GAVE FORTH HER TEARS OF JOY	695	JERUSALEM 61	29
EPHRAIM WAS A WILDERNESS OF JOY WHERE ALL MY WILD BEASTS RAN	705	JERUSALEM 67	56
BUT THEY FROWN & DELIGHT IN CRUELTY REFUSING ALL OTHER JOY	706	JERUSALEM 68	29
WHAT IS THE JOY OF HEAVEN BUT IMPROVEMENT IN THE THINGS OF THE SPIRIT	717B	JERUSALEM 77	PROSE
THEN WAS A TIME OF JOY AND LOVE	718	ENGLND AWAKE/J	8
THEY DISCERND MY COUNTENANCE WITH JOY THEY SHEWD ME TO THEIR SONS	720	JERUSALEM 79	28
JOY UPON EVERY MOUNTAIN TO TEACH SONGS TO THE SHEPHERD & PLOWMAN	720	JERUSALEM 79	37
THEY LOOKED UPON OUR LOVES WITH JOY THEY BEHELD OUR SECRET JOYS	720	JERUSALEM 79	43
THEY SIEZD THE HARP THE FLUTE THE MELLOW HORN OF JERUSALEM'S JOY	721	JERUSALEM 79	49
LOS SMILD WITH JOY THINKING ON ENITHARMON & HE BROUGHT .	730	JERUSALEM 85	3
CAN THERE BE ANY SECRET JOY ON EARTH GREATER THAN THIS . .	733	JERUSALEM 88	* 15
FOR I WILL MAKE THEIR PLACES OF JOY & LOVE EXCREMENTITIOUS	734	JERUSALEM 88	39
OF JOY IS IN THE EYES OF OTHERS ONLY A GREEN THING THAT STANDS	793D	LETTER 5	PROSE
ALL TO PARTAKE OF SINCE IT IS TO ME A SOURCE OF IMMORTAL JOY	797B	LETTER 9	PROSE
THIS SONG TO THE FLOWER OF FLAXMAN'S JOY	800	MRS FLAXMAN/L	1
HOPING THAT HER JOY IS NOW INCREASED & YOURS ALSO . .	810A	LETTER 20	PROSE
MUST EVERY JOY BE DUNG & DROSS	817	HAPPINESS/L	44
EXCEEDING JOY THAT IS ALWAYS POURED OUT ON MY SPIRIT .	830B	LETTER 30	PROSE
PARTAKERS OF THE JOY THAT THE WORLD CANNOT CONCIEVE THAT YOU	830C	LETTER 30	PROSE
HEALTH & JOY IN GOD OUR SAVIOUR TO ETERNITY YOURS . .	830D	LETTER 30	PROSE
I TAKE THE EXTREME PLEASURE OF EXPRESSING MY JOY AT OUR GOOD	851C	LETTER 50	PROSE
GREAT JOY HENCE I AM NOW ENABLED TO TELL YOU THAT I . .	869D	LETTER 70	PROSE
ECCHOING GREEN DITTO THE LAMB THE SHEPHERD INFANT JOY	SUPP	LETTER 66A	*PROSE
IS ALL JOY FORBIDDEN	SUPP	PENC DRAW 1.7	*TITLE

JOYD

[JOYD AT THEIR INCREASE]	164	HEARD ANGEL/N	23
IT JOYD SHE PUT ASIDE HER CLOUDS & SMILED HER FIRST-BORN SMILE	196	AMERICA PREL 2	4
AND LOS POSSESSOR OF THE MOON JOYD IN THE PEACEFUL NIGHT	239	EUROPE 4	7
LOS JOYD & ENITHARMON LAUGHD SAYING LET US GO DOWN . .	285	FOUR ZOAS 2	211
[AND LOS & ENITHARMON JOYD THEY DRANK IN TENFOLD JOY] .	286	FOUR ZOAS 2	236
AND ENITHARMON JOYD PLOTTING TO REND THE SECRET CLOUD .	286	FOUR ZOAS 2	238
THE DOLOROUS SHADOW JOYD WEAK HOPE APPEARD AROUND HIS HEAD	300	FOUR ZOAS 4	127
[SHE SECRET JOYD TO SEE SHE FED HERSELF ON HIS DESPAIR]	324	FOUR ZOAS 7	177
AS LOS A FATHER TO HIS BRETHREN & HE JOYD IN THE DARK LAKE	332	FOUR ZOAS 7	480
VIEWD THE VAST WAR & JOYD WISHING TO VEGETATE	335	FOUR ZOAS 7B	106
SHE JOYD IN ALL THE CONFLICT	338	FOUR ZOAS 7B	213
GWANTOKE FORGAVE & JOYD OVER SOUTH WALES & ALL ITS MOUNTAINS	710	JERUSALEM 71	29
JOYD IN THE MANY WEAVING THREADS IN BRIGHT CATHEDRON'S DOME	728	JERUSALEM 83	72
THUS JOYD THE SPECTRE IN THE DUSKY FIRES OF LOS'S FORGE EYEING	734	JERUSALEM 88	44

JOYFUL

THE JOYFUL SHEPHERD STOPS HIS GRATEFUL SONG	9	FRESH FROM/PS	11
WHILE THE AIRY MUSIC FILLS THE WORLD WITH JOYFUL SOUNDS	37B	CONTEMPLATN/PS	PROSE
IN VAIN THE DREAMER GRASPS THE JOYFUL IMAGES THEY FLY . .	206	THIRALATHA	2
OVER THE JOYFUL EARTH & SEA & ASCENDED INTO THE HEAVENS	274	FOUR ZOAS 1	376
AND WENT FORTH & BEGAN TO REAP & ALL HIS JOYFUL SONS .	372	FOUR ZOAS 9	583
WITH PRINTLESS FEET SCORNING THE CONCAVE OF THE JOYFUL SKY	381	FOUR ZOAS AD 1	17
WHEN GRAPES & FIGS BURST THEIR COVERING TO THE JOYFUL AIR	485	MILTON 5	33
THE BLESSED WHO IN VARIOUS JOYFUL COMPANIES	609D	V LAST JUDG/N	PROSE

JOYING

AND JOYING IN THE PITY HOWLING OVER JERUSALEM'S WALLS . .	723	JERUSALEM 80	56

JOYOUS   SEE OVER JOYOUS

JOYS   SEE MOTHERS-JOYS

JOYS UPON OUR BRANCHES SIT	7	LOVE HARMNY/PS	5
WE SIT US DOWN AND VIEW OUR FORMER JOYS	27	EDW THIRD/PS 3	260
ON THESE PLAINS AND IN THESE SILENT WOODS TRUE JOYS DESCEND	37A	CONTEMPLATN/PS	PROSE
THE YOUTHFUL SUN JOYS LIKE A HUNTER ROUZED TO THE CHACE	37B	CONTEMPLATN/PS	PROSE
BUT GOD HATH OTHER JOYS IN STORE IS BURDENED ISRAEL HIS GRIEF	39C	SAMSON/PS	PROSE

	PAGE	TITLE	LINE
JOYS (CONTINUED)			
AND MY COMPLAINTS ARE SWEETER THAN THEIR JOYS	41D	THEN SHE BORE	PROSE
SUCH SUCH WERE THE JOYS	116	ECCHOING GR/SI	17
. . . AND THE JOYS OF THE COMBAT BURNT FOR FUEL	138	FRENCH REVOLTN	93
JOYS IMPREGNATE SORROWS BRING FORTH	151C	MARRIAGE HH 8	PROSE
HER EGGS ON SO THE PRIEST LAYS HIS CURSE ON THE FAIREST JOYS	152C	MARRIAGE HH 9	PROSE
JOYS LAUGH NOT SORROWS WEEP NOT	152C	MARRIAGE HH 9	PROSE
JOYS IN ANOTHER'S LOSS OF EASE	162	CLOD PEBBLE/N	11
AND BINDING WITH BRIARS MY JOYS & DESIRES	163	GARDEN LOVE/N	12
[THOU SHALT TASTE THE JOYS OF NIGHT]	165	CRADLE SONG/N	6
DREAMING OER THE JOYS OF NIGHT	165	CRADLE SONG/N	7
SECRET JOYS & SECRET SMILES	165	CRADLE SONG/N	20
THAT SWEET JOYS BETRAY	168	SILENT NIGHT/N	6
WHY SHOULD JOYS BE SWEET	168	SILENT NIGHT/N	7
ARE NOT THE JOYS OF MORNING SWEETER	172	ARE NOT JOYS/N	1
THAN THE JOYS OF NIGHT	172	ARE NOT JOYS/N	2
AND ARE THE VIGROUS JOYS OF YOUTH	172	ARE NOT JOYS/N	3
THEN GOD LIKE A FATHER [THAT JOYS FOR] REJOICING TO SEE	180	LIT VAGABOND/N	14
AND THEIR PURSUITS AS DIFFERENT AS THEIR FORMS AND AS THEIR JOYS	191	V DAU ALBION 3	6
TELL ME WHAT IS A JOY & IN WHAT GARDENS DO JOYS GROW .	191	V DAU ALBION 3	24
TELL ME WHERE DWELL THE JOYS OF OLD & WHERE THE ANCIENT LOVES	192	V DAU ALBION 4	4
AND ARE THERE OTHER JOYS BESIDE THE JOYS OF RICHES AND EASE	192	V DAU ALBION 4	21
THY JOYS ARE TEARS THY LABOUR VAIN TO FORM MEN TO THINE IMAGE	192	V DAU ALBION 5	4
HOW CAN ONE JOY ABSORB ANOTHER ARE NOT DIFFERENT JOYS . .	192	V DAU ALBION 5	5
AND SWEET SHALL BE THY TASTE & SWEET THY INFANT JOYS RENEW	193	V DAU ALBION 6	3
THE VIGOROUS JOYS OF MORNING LIGHT OPEN TO VIRGIN BLISS	193	V DAU ALBION 6	6
WHEN THOU AWAKEST WILT THOU DISSEMBLE ALL THY SECRET JOYS	193	V DAU ALBION 6	8
THEN IS OOTHOON A WHORE INDEED AND ALL THE VIRGIN JOYS . .	194	V DAU ALBION 6	18
THAT PINES FOR MAN SHALL AWAKEN HER WOMB TO ENORMOUS JOYS	194	V DAU ALBION 7	4
JOYS IN ANOTHER'S LOSS OF EASE	211	CLOD PEBBLE/SE	11
AND BINDING WITH BRIARS MY JOYS & DESIRES	215	GARDEN LOVE/SE	12
FOR STOLEN JOYS ARE SWEET & BREAD EATEN IN SECRET PLEASANT	237	EUROPE INTRO	6
THEIR WARBLING JOYS TO OUR LOUD STRINGS	239	EUROPE 4	18
SECLUDED PLACES FEARING THE JOYS OF LOVE	246	SONG OF LOS 3	26
LIKE NETS & GINS & TRAPS TO CATCH THE JOYS OF ETERNITY . .	246	SONG OF LOS 4	2
IN INTERCHANGE SWEET OF THEIR JOYS	255	AHANIA 5	23
WITH WINGED RADIANCE SCATTERING JOYS THRO THE EVER CHANGING LIGHT	274	FOUR ZOAS 1	358
WENT DOWN THE HUMAN HEART WHERE PARADISE & ITS JOYS ABOUNDED	294	FOUR ZOAS 3	95
TO BRING THE THRILLING JOYS OF SENSE TO QUELL HIS CEASELESS RAGE	308	FOUR ZOAS 5	120
NOR KNEW THAT I ALONE EXEMPTED FROM THE JOYS OF LOVE . .	325	FOUR ZOAS 7	200
DRINKING THE JOYS OF UNIVERSAL MANHOOD ONE DREAD MORN .	327	FOUR ZOAS 7	277
THE BIRDS OF SONG TO MURDEROUS CROWS MY JOYS TO BITTER GROANS	360	FOUR ZOAS 9	110
THEY CRY OUT IN JOYS OF EXISTENCE THE BROAD STEMS . . .	373	FOUR ZOAS 9	605
TO AUGMENT WITH SWEET SMILES ALL THE JOYS OF THE NIGHT . .	428	MARY	10
AND REPEATED WITH PLEASURE THE JOYS OF THE NIGHT	428	MARY	14
AND THE CALM OCEAN JOYS BENEATH & SMOOTHS HIS AWFUL WAVES	511	MILTON 25	71
THE CRUEL JOYS OF LUVAH'S DAUGHTERS LACERATING WITH KNIVES	514	MILTON 27	35
AND TIMBERS CRAMPT WITH IRON CRAMPS BAR IN THE JOYS OF LIFE	515	MILTON 28	40
IT CONTINUES ACCUMULATING TO ETERNITY THE JOYS OF GOD ADVANCE	630	JERUSALEM 10	46
THE BIRDS OF SONG TO MURDEROUS CROWS HIS JOYS TO BITTER GROANS	641	JERUSALEM 19	11
WENT DOWN THE HUMAN HEART WHERE PARADISE & ITS JOYS ABOUNDED	655	JERUSALEM 29	74
SHRIEK NOT SO MY ONLY LOVE I REFUSE THY JOYS I DRINK . .	705	JERUSALEM 67	61
IN CRUELTIES OF HOLINESS TO REFUSE THE JOYS OF LOVE TO BRING	707	JERUSALEM 68	59
THEY LOOKED UPON OUR LOVES WITH JOY THEY BEHELD OUR SECRET JOYS	720	JERUSALEM 79	43
JUBILEE			
A SHOUT OF JUBILEE IN LOVELY NOTES	366	FOUR ZOAS 9	350
THEY THROW OFF THEIR GORGEOUS RAIMENT THEY REJOICE WITH LOUD JUBILEE	513	MILTON 27	23
JUDAH			
THEN OOTHOON HOVERD OVER JUDAH & JERUSALEM	246	SONG OF LOS 3	22
HAR OCHIM IJIM ADAM REUBEN SIMEON LEVI JUDAH DAN NAPHTALI	350	FOUR ZOAS 8	360
AWAY FROM [LOS] ME FIRST REUBEN FLED THEN SIMEON THEN LEVI THEN JUDAH	350	FOUR ZOAS 8	375
AND EPHRAIM & JUDAH WERE GENERATED BECAUSE	508	MILTON 24	3
THE GATE OF JUDAH MERIONETHSHIRE THE GATE OF DAN FLINTSHIRE	637	JERUSALEM 16	37
LEVI MIDDLESEX KENT SURREY JUDAH SOMERSET GLOUSTER WILTSHIRE	637	JERUSALEM 16	45
DIVIDED IN THE THE GATES OF REUBEN JUDAH DAN & JOSEPH .	637	JERUSALEM 16	51
LEVI EDINBURH ROXBRO ROSS JUDAH ABRDEEN BERWIK DUMFRIES	638	JERUSALEM 16	54 *
UNDER JUDAH & ISSACHAR & ZEBULUN ARE LOWTH LONGFORD . . .	711	JERUSALEM 72	18
OVER THE LAND OF CANAAN THEY HAVE DIVIDED JOSEPH . . .	715	JERUSALEM 74	48
LEVI AND JUDAH & ISSACHAR EPHRAM MANASSEH GAD AND DAN . .	720	JERUSALEM 79	30
THERE IS REUBEN & GAD & JOSEPH & JUDAH & LEVI CLOSD UP .	721	JERUSALEM 79	64
OF REUBEN OR OF BENJAMIN OF JOSEPH OR JUDAH OR LEVI . .	736	JERUSALEM 90	31
JUDAH WAS LIKE PALAMABRON O SIMEON O LEVI YE FLED AWAY	740	JERUSALEM 93	14
INTO THE WILDERNESS OF JUDAH TO MEET THEE IN HIS PRIDE . .	743	JERUSALEM 96	10

JUDAH'S
    ULSTER NORTH IN DAN'S GATE LEINSTER EAST IN JUDAH'S GATE   711 JERUSALEM 72   4
JUDAS
    BEFORE CAIPHAS & PILATE ARE JUDAS & THOSE OF HIS CLASS . 608D V LAST JUDG/N   PROSE
    YOU WILL BE CALLD THE BASE JUDAS WHO BETRAYD HIS FRIEND   813B LETTER 22   PROSE
JUDEA
    AND HE STOOD OVER JUDEA . 248 SONG OF LOS 7   17
    AND GREECE & ALONG THE SEA OF REPHAIM INTO JUDEA . . . . 704 JERUSALEM 67   39
    THE HILLS OF JUDEA ARE FALLEN WITH ME INTO THE DEEPEST HELL   720 JERUSALEM 79   8
JUDGE
    AND JUDGE OF TINKLING RHIMES AND ELEGANCES TERSE . . . . 14 IMIT SPEN/PS   18
    IF I CAN JUDGE OF ACTIONS BUT YOUR HEAT . . . . . . 27 EDW THIRD/PS 3   245
    ("JUDGE OF YOURSELF...OTHERS") MOST EXCELLENT . . . . 76B ANNO LAVATER   MARG
    & SUCH AN ONE CANNOT JUDGE OF ANY BUT IN LOVE & HIS . . 87A ANNO LAVATER   MARG
    MAN BY HIS REASONING POWER CAN ONLY COMPARE & JUDGE . . 97A NAT RELIGION 1   PROSE
    ONE WHO SETS REASON UP FOR JUDGE . . . . 177 LIT BOY LST/N   18
    ONE WHO SETS REASON UP FOR JUDGE . . . . 218 LIT BOY LST/SE   15
    TO JUDGE THE LAMB OF GOD TO DEATH AS A MURDERER & ROBBER   348 FOUR ZOAS 8   273
    . . . TREMBLING THE JUDGE SPRINGS FROM HIS THRONE . . 364 FOUR ZOAS 9   268
    TO JUDGE THE LAMB OF GOD TO DEATH AS A MURDERER & ROBBER   382 FOUR ZOAS AD 6   6
    READ THEM & JUDGE IF YOU ARE NOT A FOOL OF WHAT . . 392D ANNO WATSON   * MARG
    WHO DARE TO JUDGE BUT GOD ALONE . . . . . . 396A ANNO WATSON   MARG
    FOUR & TWENTY ELDERS SEATED ON THRONES TO JUDGE THE DEAD   444A LAST JUDGMNT/L   PROSE
    CAN SUCH AN EYE JUDGE OF THE STARS & LOOKING THRO ITS TUBES 485 MILTON 5   28
    JUDGE OF THE PURE MELODIOUS HARP STRUCK BY A HAND DIVINE   485 MILTON 5   31
    WHAT COULD LOS DO HOW COULD HE JUDGE WHEN SATAN'S SELF   487 MILTON 7   41
        BELIEVD
    JUDGE THEN OF THY OWN SELF THY ETERNAL LINEAMENTS EXPLORE   522 MILTON 32   30
    SAYING I AM GOD THE JUDGE OF ALL THE LIVING & THE DEAD . 530 MILTON 38   51
    ARISE UPON THEIR THRONES TO JUDGE THE NATIONS OF THE EARTH   534 MILTON 42   17
    A JUDGE AND A REAL MASTER OF THE JURISPRUDENCE OF HIS AGE   570D DESC CAT 3   PROSE
    POSTERITY WILL JUDGE BY OUR WORKS WOOLETT'S & STRANGE'S   593D PUB ADDRESS/N   PROSE
    NO JUDGE OF PAINTING WHEN HE IS SHEWN THESE SMEARS & DAWBS   601C PUB ADDRESS/N *PROSE
    WITH THE FINEST ENGRAVINGS & DEFY THE MOST CRITICAL JUDGE   602A PUB ADDRESS/N   PROSE
    THY SEVERE JUDGE ALL THE DAY LONG PROVES THEE O BABYLON   647 JERUSALEM 24   27
    AND EVERY ACT A CRIME AND ALBION THE PUNISHER & JUDGE . 652 JERUSALEM 28   4
    TO JUDGE THE FRIEND OF SINNERS TO DEATH WITHOUT THE VEIL   725 JERUSALEM 82   33
    WHICH I HOPE SHE WHO IS THE BEST JUDGE WILL THINK LIKE . 809A LETTER 20   PROSE
    & THEN WE SHALL JUDGE OF THE MATTER WITH CERTAINTY . . 813D LETTER 22   PROSE
    COPYRIGHT AND AS FAR AS I CAN JUDGE OF THE NATURE OF . 831C LETTER 31   PROSE
    WILL BE ENABLED BY IT TO JUDGE OF THE PATHOS OF THE PICTURE 850B LETTER 49   PROSE
    TO YOU AS YOU OUGHT AND MUST SEE IT I AM NO JUDGE IN THESE   861B LETTER 58   PROSE
    A MAN SAY I AM NO JUDGE OF PICTURES BUT O ENGLISHMEN . 864C LETTER 61   PROSE
    KNOW THAT EVERY MAN OUGHT TO BE A JUDGE OF PICTURES AND   864C LETTER 61   PROSE
    SATAN'S HOLY TRINITY THE ACCUSER THE JUDGE & THE   SUPP INSC OUR END *TITLE
        EXECUTIONER
JUDGED   SEE ILL-JUDGED
    LET THE INDEFINITE BE EXPLORED AND LET EVERY MAN BE JUDGED   687 JERUSALEM 55   57
    "IMAGINATION BEFORE REASON HAVE JUDGED & REASON " . . . 794A LETTER 5   PROSE
JUDGEMENT
    THE FOUR ZOAS VALA OR THE DEATH AND JUDGEEMENT . . . . 263A FOUR ZOAS   TITLE
    THE DEATH AND JUDGEMENT OF ALBION THE ANCIENT MAN . . 263C FOUR ZOAS   TITLE
    WAIT TILL THE JUDGEMENT IS PAST TILL THE CREATION   511 MILTON 25   59
        IS CONSUMED
JUDGES
    AGAINST HER LITTLE ONES THE INNOCENT ACCUSED BEFORE THE   364 FOUR ZOAS 9   267
        JUDGES
    BECAUSE [I KNOW HE ALWAYS JUDGES] HIS JUDGMENT IS SO VERY   549 CROMEK SPEAK/N   2
        COOL
    ENGLISH ARE AS GOOD JUDGES [AS] OF PAINTING AS OF POETRY   601B PUB ADDRESS/N *PROSE
    THE FIVE BOOKS OF THE DECALOGUE THE BOOKS OF JOSHUA &   677 JERUSALEM 48   9
        JUDGES
    LOCKE SAYS IT SAME FACULTY THAT INVENTS JUDGES . . . . 790C LETTER 2   PROSE
JUDGING
    HAD BEFORE CONCLUDED UPON JUDGING AS HE DID THAT IF THE   848C LETTER 45   PROSE
    GOOD & EVIL ANGEL HOUSE OF DEATH GOD JUDGING ADAM LAMECH   SUPP LETTER 56A *PROSE
JUDGMENT
    FALSE SEVERITY OF JUDGMENT IS A GREAT VIRTUE . . . . 67A ANNO LAVATER   MARG
    THRICE HE ASSAYD PRESUMPTUOUS TO AWAKE THE DEAD TO JUDGMENT 243 EUROPE 13   3
    O I AM NOTHING WHEN I ENTER INTO JUDGMENT WITH THEE . . 293 FOUR ZOAS 3   60
    VALA NIGHT THE NINTH BEING THE LAST JUDGMENT . . . . 357B FOUR ZOAS 9   TITLE
    TO JUDGMENT FROM THE FOUR WINDS AWAKE & COME AWAY . . 357 FOUR ZOAS 9   13
    [TO JUDGMENT] FROM THE CLOTTED GORE & FROM THE HOLLOW DEN   358 FOUR ZOAS 9   43
    TO MEET THE LORD COMING TO JUDGMENT BUT THE FLAMES REPELLD   364 FOUR ZOAS 9   288
        THEM
    IS THE VOICE OF GOD OUR JUDGMENT OF RIGHT & WRONG IS REASON 385D ANNO WATSON   MARG
    HARTLEY A MAN OF JUDGMENT THEN JUDGMENT WAS A FOOL . . 394C ANNO WATSON   MARG
    BY HIS TRANSLATOR IF I HAVE ANY JUDGMENT IN SUCH THINGS   413A ANNO BOYD   MARG
    FOR THE LAST JUDGMENT DRAWETH NIGH . . . . . . 432 AUGURIES   40
    THE DESIGN OF THE LAST JUDGMENT WHICH I HAVE COMPLETED . 442D LAST JUDGMNT/L   PROSE
    CHRIST SEATED ON THE THRONE OF JUDGMENT . . . . . 443A LAST JUDGMNT/L   PROSE
    IN JESUS WHO OPENS THE SCROLL OF JUDGMENT . . . . 444C LAST JUDGMNT/L   PROSE
    & WHICH BUT FOR YOU MIGHT HAVE SLEPT TILL THE LAST JUDGMENT 444C LAST JUDGMNT/L   PROSE
    COULD THINK HAD NOT THE JUDGMENT TO PERFORM . . . . 448D ANNO REYNOLDS   MARG
    JUDGMENT AND LO IT FELL ON RINTRAH AND HIS RAGE . . . 489 MILTON 9   10
    LEST THE LAST JUDGMENT COME & FIND ME UNANNIHILATE . . 495 MILTON 14   23
    WHAT DO I HERE BEFORE THE JUDGMENT WITHOUT MY EMANATION   495 MILTON 14   28
    IN THE DARK ULRO TILL THE JUDGMENT ALSO MILTON KNEW THEY   498 MILTON 17   5
        AND
    THE TRUMPET OF JUDGMENT HATH TWICE SOUNDED ALL NATIONS   506 MILTON 23   4
        ARE AWAKE
    WHO DIED FROM EARTH & HE IS RETURND BEFORE THE JUDGMENT   508 MILTON 23   57
        THIS THING

		PAGE	TITLE	LINE

JUDGMENT   (CONTINUED)

TO GIVE THEM TO THEIR LOVELY HEAVENS TILL THE GREAT JUDGMENT DAY   517 MILTON 29   52

TO RESURRECTION & JUDGMENT IN THE VEGETABLE BODY . . . . . 534 MILTON 42   27

I ALWAYS TAKE MY JUDGMENT FROM A FOOL . . . . 549 CROMEK SPEAK/N   1

BECAUSE [I KNOW HE ALWAYS JUDGES] HIS JUDGMENT IS SO VERY COOL   549 CROMEK SPEAK/N   2

FOR ITS SURE TO KEEP YOUR JUDGMENT COOL . . . . 556 SOME PEOPLE/N   2

MR B(BLAKE) APPEALS TO THE PUBLIC FROM THE JUDGMENT OF THOSE   563D DESC CAT   PROSE

WHERE A MONTH WOULD WITH JUDGMENT HAVE FINISHED IT . . . 583C DESC CAT 9   PROSE

THE LAST JUDGMENT WHEN ALL THOSE ARE CAST AWAY . . . . 604C V LAST JUDG/N   PROSE

THEN THE LAST JUDGMENT BEGINS & ITS VISION . . . . . . 604C V LAST JUDG/N   PROSE

THE LAST JUDGMENT IS NOT FABLE OR ALLEGORY BUT VISION . . 604D V LAST JUDG/N   PROSE

THE LAST JUDGMENT IS ONE OF THESE STUPENDOUS VISIONS . . 605A V LAST JUDG/N   PROSE

COMING TO JUDGMENT AMONG HIS SAINTS & THROWING OFF . . 606A V LAST JUDG/N   PROSE

& ON EACH SIDE THE FOUR & TWENTY ELDERS SITTING IN JUDGMENT 606B V LAST JUDG/N   PROSE

JUDGMENT SEAT IN HUMILIATION ABEL SURROUNDED BY INNOCENTS 606B V LAST JUDG/N   PROSE

AROUND HIM ARE OTHER KINGDOMS ARISING TO JUDGMENT . . 608C V LAST JUDG/N   PROSE

BUT OF THOSE FOUND ALIVE AT THE LAST JUDGMENT . . . . 610B V LAST JUDG/N   PROSE

A LAST JUDGMENT IS NECESSARY BECAUSE FOOLS FLOURISH . . 612B V LAST JUDG/N   PROSE

THIS IS A LAST JUDGMENT WHEN MEN OF REAL ART GOVERN & . 612C V LAST JUDG/N   PROSE

IN PROPORTION TO HIS MEANS A LAST JUDGMENT IS NOT . . 612D V LAST JUDG/N   PROSE

A LAST JUDGMENT PASSES UPON THAT INDIVIDUAL . . . . . 613A V LAST JUDG/N   PROSE

FOR IT APPEARS SO AT THE LAST JUDGMENT FOR A PROTECTION 614B V LAST JUDG/N   PROSE

OF CREATION REDEMPTION OR JUDGMENT . . . . 614C V LAST JUDG/N   PROSE

THE LAST JUDGMENT A DELIVERANCE FROM SATAN'S ACCUSATION 615C V LAST JUDG/N   PROSE

AS YOU [PREP] PRETEND TILL AFTER THE LAST JUDGMENT . . 616A V LAST JUDG/N   *PROSE

& CANNOT BE REMOVED BUT BY A LAST JUDGMENT . . . . . 616A V LAST JUDG/N   PROSE

ONE ANOTHER FORGIVENESS OF SIN IS ONLY AT THE JUDGMENT SEAT 616D V LAST JUDG/N   PROSE

THE LAST JUDGMENT IS AN OVERWHELMING OF BAD ART & SCIENCE 617A V LAST JUDG/N   PROSE

SOME PEOPLE FLATTER THEMSELVES THAT THERE WILL BE NO LAST JUDGMENT   617A V LAST JUDG/N   PROSE

THE LONG SUFFERINGS OF GOD ARE NOT FOR EVER THERE IS A JUDGMENT   620 JERUSALEM 1   10

O I AM NOTHING WHEN I ENTER INTO JUDGMENT WITH THEE . . . 654 JERUSALEM 29   47

ALBION HATH ENTERD THE LOINS THE PLACE OF THE LAST JUDGMENT 656 JERUSALEM 30   38

EXPLORING THE THREE STATES OF ULRO CREATION REDEMPTION & JUDGMENT   663 JERUSALEM 36   42

HAVE YOU KNOWN THE JUDGMENT THAT IS ARISEN AMONG THE . 663 JERUSALEM 36   44

HAVE PASSED OVER THE DEAD TO AWAKE THE DEAD TO JUDGMENT 676 JERUSALEM 46   15

AND WHILE THE SONS OF ALBION BY SEVERE WAR & JUDGMENT BONIFY   689 JERUSALEM 58   10

THO THOU ART TAKEN TO PRISON & JUDGMENT STARVED IN THE STREETS   696 JERUSALEM 62   24

THE SEXUAL DEATH LIVING ON ACCUSATION OF SIN & JUDGMENT 699 JERUSALEM 64   22

THE TERRORS OF CREATION & REDEMPTION & JUDGMENT BEHOLDING THEM   739 JERUSALEM 92   20

IN TERRORS AT THE LAST JUDGMENT DAY . . . . 751 EV GOSPEL(C)/N   44

ARE BUT THE SINNER TO JUDGMENT TO BRING . . . . . . 751 EV GOSPEL(C)/N   46

IN TERRORS AT THE LAST JUDGMENT DAY . . . . 753 EV GOSPEL(D)/N   80

IS BUT THE SINNER TO JUDGMENT TO BRING . . . . . . 753 EV GOSPEL(D)/N   82

THE JUDGMENT OF PARIS WHICH IS NOT ONLY A PART . . . 778A HOMERS POETRY   PROSE

WHO IS THE GOD OF THIS WORLD THE ACCUSER LET HIS JUDGMENT 788A ANNO THORNTON   MARG

[HIS JUDGMENT] THE ACCUSATION SHALL BE FORGIVENESS . . 788A ANNO THORNTON   * MARG

UNLESS ALTOGETHER LEFT TO MY OWN JUDGMENT . . . . . 826A LETTER 27   PROSE

REAL DIFFERENCE AS TO PERFECT INDEPENDENCE OF JUDGMENT . 868B LETTER 67   PROSE

THE ACCUSERS OF THEFT ADULTERY MURDER A SCENE IN THE LAST JUDGMENT   SUPP INSC OUR END   *TITLE

JUICE

FEED THEM WITH THE JUICE OF OUR MARROW BONES . . . . . 543 IF TRUE/N   4

JUICES

AND ENITHARMON PALE & COLD IN MILKY JUICES FLOWD . . . 353 FOUR ZOAS 8   474

JUL

RAFAEL MICH ANG ALB D(DURER) JUL R(ROMANO) ARE . . . 599A PUB ADDRESS/N   PROSE

OF ART SUCH AS MICHAEL ANGELO RAFAEL JUL R(ROMANO) ALB DURER LEFT IT   600B PUB ADDRESS/N   PROSE

JULIO

AND JULIO ROMANO STRIPPED FROM THE IGNORANCES OF . . . 562B DESC CAT ADV   PROSE

RAFAEL AND ALBERT DURER MICHAEL ANGELO AND JULIO ROMANO 564A DESC CAT   PROSE

OR JULIO ROMANO OR ALB DURER BUT I DO PRETEND TO . . . 594C PUB ADDRESS/N   PROSE

IT IS NOT SO WITH RAFAEL JULIO (ROMANO) ALB D(DURER) . 598D PUB ADDRESS/N   PROSE

ON THE CONTRARY JULIO (ROMANO'S) PALACE OF T AT MANTUA . 599C PUB ADDRESS/N   PROSE

JULIUS

THE DRUIDS THE LANDING OF JULIUS CAESAR . . . . . 208D SUBJCTS HIST/N   TITLE

JUMBLE

A PINE JUMBLE . . . . 466C ANNO REYNOLDS   MARG

JUMBLED

ALL SELF-CONTRADICTORY TRUTH & FALSHOOD JUMBLED TOGETHER 454B ANNO REYNOLDS   * MARG

IN THIS MANNER HE HAS JUMBLED HIS DUMB DOLLIES TOGETHER 574B DESC CAT 3   PROSE

JUNE

IF I LIVE ONE IT WILL BE A WONDER JUNE . . . . 187C SAY I SHANT/N   PROSE

JUNKETS

IN WHICH IS SEEN QUEEN MAB EATING THE JUNKETS . . . . 618C ILLUS MILTON   PROSE

JUNO

BLOATED [AWKWARD] GODS MERCURY JUNO VENUS & THE . . . 599C PUB ADDRESS/N   *PROSE

JUNR

MR WALKER JUNR & BEG HIM TO SHEW ME THE PICTURES & MAKE 834C LETTER 34   PROSE

JUPITER

VERY SATAN CAPANIUS OTHELLO A MURDERER PROMETHEUS JUPITER 412B ANNO BOYD   MARG

THE MINERVA THE JUPITER THE APOLLO . . . . 576C DESC CAT 4   PROSE

WHEN THEY ASSERT THAT JUPITER . . . . 605C V LAST JUDG/N   PROSE

1020

	PAGE	TITLE	LINE

JUPITER   (CONTINUED)
    THESE HEAVENS ARE VENUS JUPITER & MARS HERMES FLIES BEFORE   619B ILLUS MILTON   PROSE
    AS ATTENDING ON THE HEAVEN OF JUPITER THE GREAT BEAR   .   619B ILLUS MILTON   PROSE
    JUPITER OF THE GREEKS AN IRON-HEARTED TYRANT THE RUINER   852A LETTER 50   PROSE
    VACUUM STARRY HEAVEN SATURN JUPITER MARS SUN VENUS   SUPP ILLUS DANTE 7   *PROSE
        MERCURY MOON
JURISPRUDENCE
    A JUDGE AND A REAL MASTER OF THE JURISPRUDENCE OF HIS AGE   570D DESC CAT 3   PROSE
JUST
    NOW LET US TAKE A JUST REVENGE FOR THOSE   . . . . . .   18 EDW THIRD/PS 1   43
    THE DANCE WAS BROKE THE CIRCLE JUST BEGUN   . . . . . .   43C WOE CRIED MUSE   PROSE
    LIKE BIRDS JUST CURED OF THE PIP   . . . .   56 HAIL MATRIM/IM   23
    . . . AND LIKE THUNDER ON THE JUST MAN'S BURIAL DAY HE   139 FRENCH REVOLTN   106
        PAUSD
    THE JUST MAN KEPT HIS COURSE ALONG   . . . .   148 MARRIAGE HH 2   4
    THE JUST MAN INTO BARREN CLIMES   . . . .   148 MARRIAGE HH 2   16
    AND THE JUST MAN RAGES IN THE WILDS   . . . . . .   149 MARRIAGE HH 2   19
    & RED GILLS HANG JUST ABOVE THE RAGING FOAM   . . . .   156C MARRIAGE HH 17   PROSE
    BUT HE WHO [JUST] KISSES THE JOY AS IT FLIES   . . .   179 ETERNITY/N   3
    THE QUEEN OF FRANCE JUST TOUCHD THIS GLOBE   . . . . .   185 LET BROTHELS/N   *   20
    [THERE IS JUST SUCH A TREE AT JAVA FOUND]   . . . .   185 LET BROTHELS/N   25
    HAD JUST REMOVD THE CURTAINS OF THE NIGHT   . . . . .   219 LIT GRL LST/SE   14
    I HAVE TAUGHT THE THIEF A SECRET PATH INTO THE HOUSE OF   290 FOUR ZOAS 2   393
        THE JUST
    IF MILD THEY BURN IN JUST PROPORTION & IN SECRET NIGHT   .   331 FOUR ZOAS 7   449
    DIVIDING INTO JUST PROPORTIONS LOS UNWEARIED LABOUR   .   332 FOUR ZOAS 7   470
    [THE] YET PALE THE JUST MAN STANDS ERECT & LOOKING UP TO   358 FOUR ZOAS 9   *   51
        HEAVN
    GIVES TO THE JUST & TO THE UNJUST BUT THE UNJUST REJECT   392B ANNO WATSON   MARG
        HIS GIFT
    JUST AS WE REAP IN JOY THE FRUIT   424 MENTAL TRAVLER   7
    JUST AS A MISER COUNTS HIS GOLD   . . . .   425 MENTAL TRAVLER   18
    JUST AS A HUSBANDMAN HIS MOULD   . . . .   425 MENTAL TRAVLER   26
    THE RESURRECTION OF THE JUST THE LEFT HAND OF THE   . .   443B LAST JUDGMNT/L   PROSE
    BEFORE THE THRONE OF CHRIST ON THE RIGHT HAND THE JUST IN   443D LAST JUDGMNT/L   PROSE
    THE MISCHIEF IS JUST THE SAME   . . . .   452A ANNO REYNOLDS   MARG
    FINE & JUST NOTIONS WHY DOES HE NOT ALWAYS ALLOW AS MUCH   462C ANNO REYNOLDS   MARG
    JUST AS RIDICULOUS IT IS TO SEE   . . . .   470B ANNO REYNOLDS   MARG
    BUT JUST & TRUE TO OUR OWN IMAGINATIONS THOSE WORLDS   .   480D MILTON 1   PROSE
    WHILE HE IS MURDERING THE JUST PROPHETIC I BEHOLD   . .   487 MILTON 7   25
    AND LOS BEHIND ME STOOD A TERRIBLE FLAMING SUN JUST CLOSE   505 MILTON 22   6
    THE LARK SITTING UPON HIS EARTHY BED JUST AS THE MORN   .   520 MILTON 31   29
    JUST IN THIS MOMENT WHEN THE MORNING ODOURS RISE ABROAD   526 MILTON 35   48
    JUST AT THE PLACE TO WHERE THE LARK MOUNTS IS A CRYSTAL   526 MILTON 35   61
        GATE
    I HOLD THE BALANCES OF RIGHT & JUST & MINE THE SWORD   . .   530 MILTON 38   54
    IF YOU DO NOT YOU ARE [JUST] BUT WHAT YOU WAS   . . . . .   544 F(LAXMAN)/N 2   4
    FOR THIS IS BEING A FRIEND JUST IN THE NICK   . . . . .   551 WILLM COWPER/N   1
    YOU MUST DO MR DEVIL JUST AS GOD PLEASE   . . . . . .   559 I ROSE UP AT/N   28
    FROM THE TOO JUST IMPUTATION OF BEING THE SEAT AND   . .   562B DESC CAT ADV   PROSE
    WHEN THE JOLLY COMPANY ARE JUST QUITTING THE TABARDE INN   566C DESC CAT 3   PROSE
    WHEN THE JOLLY COMPANY ARE JUST QUITTING THE TABARDE INN   588B CHAUCER/N   PROSE
    WHEN THE JOLLY COMPANY ARE JUST QUITTING THE TABARDE INN   589C CHAUCER 2   PROSE
    JUST AS IT IS IN THEIR POWER TO MURDER A MAN BUT NOT TO   597A PUB ADDRESS/N   PROSE
        MAKE A MAN
    JUST EQUAL IN INVENTION & IN EXECUTION AS MY WORKS SHEW   602A PUB ADDRESS/N   PROSE
    THERE IS JUST THE SAME SCIENCE IN LEBRUN OR RUBENS   . .   602C PUB ADDR AD/N   PROSE
    BUT RENEWS BY ITS SEED JUST [AS] SO THE IMAGINATIVE IMAGE   605B V LAST JUDG/N   PROSE
    DESCENDING [AS A SCROLL] THE JUST ARISE   . . . . . .   606B V LAST JUDG/N   *PROSE
    HE IS JUST AWAKEND OUT OF HIS GRAVE   . . . .   608C V LAST JUDG/N   PROSE
    JUST ABOVE THE GRAVES & ABOVE THE SPOT   . . . . . .   610C V LAST JUDG/N   PROSE
    AMONG OTHER SPIRITS OF THE JUST MADE PERFECT [JUST]   .   614A V LAST JUDG/N   PROSE
    THAT I DO NOT CONSIDER EITHER THE JUST OR THE WICKED   .   614C V LAST JUDG/N   PROSE
    THESE ARE ONLY EMPLOYD AGAINST THE JUST   . . . . . .   616B V LAST JUDG/N   PROSE
    IT IS THEN THIS THAT [MAKES] THEY TORMENT THE JUST   . .   616C V LAST JUDG/N   PROSE
    BECAUSE HE SINS BUT BECAUSE HE TORMENTS THE JUST &   . .   616D V LAST JUDG/N   PROSE
    HAST JUST CAUSE TO BE IRRITATED BUT LOOK STEDFASTLY UPON ME   626 JERUSALEM 7   53
    JUST SUCH A ONE AS MAGDALEN   . . . .   756 EV GOSPEL(I)/N   5
    & HIS SUN TO THE JUST & THE UNJUST   . . . .   785C ILLS DANTE 101   PROSE
    ("WILL") SO YOU SEE THAT GOD IS JUST SUCH A TYRANT   788C ANNO THORNTON   * MARG
        AS AUGUSTUS CAESAR
    I STUDY YOUR OUTLINES AS USUAL JUST AS IF THEY WERE   795B LETTER 6   PROSE
        ANTIQUES
    AND MY BROTHER ROBERT JUST BEHIND   . . . .   817 HAPPINESS/L   14
    MY JUST RIGHT AS AN ARTIST & AS A MAN & IF ANY   . . .   825D LETTER 27   PROSE
    THIS IS BUT TOO JUST A PICTURE OF MY PRESENT STATE I PRAY   829A LETTER 28   PROSE
    SPIRITS OF JUST MEN MADE PERFECT BY LOVE & GRATITUDE   .   834A LETTER 33   PROSE
    MUST BE SO TO A MAN JUST OUT OF SO DREADFUL A FEVER I ALSO   844D LETTER 43   PROSE
    OF SPIRITS OF JUST MEN MADE PERFECT   . . . .   854C LETTER 53   PROSE
    IF YOU SHOULD PUT ON YOUR CONSIDERING CAP JUST AS YOU DID   870B LETTER 71   PROSE
    GET UP BUT JUST AS I WAS GOING TO RISE THIS MORNING THE   872B LETTER 75   PROSE
    I GO ON JUST AS IF PERFECTLY WELL WHICH INDEED I AM EXCEPT   873C LETTER 77   PROSE
    JUST AS I HAD BECOME WELL THAT IS SUBDUED THE DISEASE   .   874D LETTER 80   PROSE
JUSTICE
    JUSTICE HATH HEAVED A SWORD TO PLUNGE IN ALBION'S BREAST   34A KING JOHN/PS   PROSE
    ("PUBLIC...JUSTICE...HE WHO CANNOT WAIT FOR THAT") UNEASY   79B ANNO LAVATER   MARG
    OUT OF THE HALLS OF JUSTICE TILL THESE DENS THY WISDOM   292 FOUR ZOAS 3   38
        FRAMD
    WHERE LIBERTY WAS JUSTICE & ETERNAL SCIENCE WAS MERCY   . .   292 FOUR ZOAS 3   40
    IN FORESTS OF AFFLICTION THE ADAMANTINE SCALES OF JUSTICE   320 FOUR ZOAS 7   10
    ("GOD'S MORAL JUSTICE EXTERMINATE SO WICKED A PEOPLE   388B ANNO WATSON   MARG
        ") HORRIBLE

		PAGE	TITLE	LINE

JUSTICE   (CONTINUED)
    TEMPERANCE PRUDENCE JUSTICE FORTITUDE THE FOUR PILLARS   517 MILTON 29   49
       OF TYRANNY
    OF THEM TO DO ME THE JUSTICE TO EXAMINE BEFORE THEY DECIDE   561B EXHIBITION ADV   PROSE
    THOUGH I MUST DO JUSTICE TO THE PAINTER AND SAY THAT   .   574D DESC CAT 3   PROSE
    & JUSTICE CAIPHAS HAS A BLUE FLAME LIKE A MITER ON HIS HEAD   608D V LAST JUDG/N   PROSE
    THE COURTS OF JUSTICE MORE MERCIFUL THAN THE CHURCH   .   .   615D V LAST JUDG/N   PROSE
    MY CHILDREN WANDER TREMBLING VICTIMS OF HIS MORAL JUSTICE   646 JERUSALEM 23   34
    HE NAMD THEM JUSTICE AND TRUTH AND ALBION'S SONS   .   .   653 JERUSALEM 28   23
    WHO GIVE THEMSELVES IN GOLGOTHA VICTIMS TO JUSTICE WHERE   665 JERUSALEM 38   54
    CONSUMING AND CONSUMD FOR-EVER IN FLAMES OF MORAL JUSTICE   667 JERUSALEM 40   30
    I DEMAND RIGHTEOUSNESS & JUSTICE O THOU INGRATITUDE   .   .   669 JERUSALEM 42   12
    LOS ANSWERD RIGHTEOUSNESS & JUSTICE I GIVE THEE IN RETURN   670 JERUSALEM 42   19
    BRING HIM TO JUSTICE BEFORE HEAVEN HERE UPON LONDON STONE   670 JERUSALEM 42   50
    TO JUSTICE IN HIS OWN CITY OF PARIS DENYING   697 JERUSALEM 63   6
       THE RESURRECTION
    HER HAND IS A COURT OF JUSTICE HER FEET TWO ARMIES   698 JERUSALEM 64   9
       IN BATTLE
    A WORLD OF JUSTICE THE WORLD OF MERCY FOR SALVATION   .   699 JERUSALEM 65   2
    THE BLOW OF HIS HAMMER IS JUSTICE THE SWING OF HIS HAMMER   734 JERUSALEM 88   49
       MERCY
    HALLS OF JUSTICE HATING VICE   .   .   .   .   757 EV GOSPEL(I)/N   25
    THEY BY THE SWORD OF JUSTICE FELL   .   .   .   .   .   757 EV GOSPEL(I)/N   39
    AGAINST FORMER CONDUCT & TO DEMAND JUSTICE & TRUTH   .   .   825D LETTER 27   PROSE
    FROM A JUSTICE OF PEACE IN CHICHESTER WHICH WAS TAKEN OUT   826D LETTER 28   PROSE
    DOUBT NOT THAT I SHALL RECIEVE JUSTICE & AM ONLY SORRY FOR   828B LETTER 28   PROSE
    ESCAPED THE CONTAGION OF THE COURT OF JUSTICE I FEAR THAT   829C LETTER 30   PROSE
    SEAGRAVE'S PRINTING IT IS BUT JUSTICE THEREFORE TO TELL YOU   846C LETTER 44   PROSE
    IN JUSTICE TO OUR GOOD SEAGRAVE WHOSE REPLIES   .   .   .   847A LETTER 44   PROSE
    DOING JUSTICE TO OUR ADMIRED SUBLIME ROMNEY I HAVE NOT   .   849B LETTER 45   PROSE
    SHOULD NOT BE ABLE TO DO THEM JUSTICE BUT THAT HE WILL   .   853A LETTER 51   *PROSE
JUSTICES
    & I HAD NO WITNESS WITH ME BEFORE THE JUSTICES WHO COULD   827D LETTER 28   PROSE
    TO TAKE WITH ME I HAVE BEEN BEFORE A BENCH OF JUSTICES   .   827D LETTER 28   PROSE
JUSTIFY
    TO JUSTIFY THE WAYS OF GOD TO MEN   .   .   .   .   .   480A MILTON   TITLE
JUSTLING
    JUSTLING TOGETHER IN THE VOID SUSPENDED BY INWARD FIRES   276 FOUR ZOAS 1   428
JUSTLY
    IN A VERY SUPERIOR STYLE TO THOSE JUSTLY ADMIRED COPIES   565D DESC CAT 2   PROSE
    JUSTLY STANDS FIRST IN THE BOOK & THAT BEAUTIFUL SPECIMEN   782A INSC UPCOTT   PROSE
    BUT YOU WILL JUSTLY ENQUIRE WHY I HAVE NOT WRITTEN ALL THIS   815C LETTER 23   PROSE
KADESH
    KINGS OF CANAAN THEN TO LET THE SPIES DEPART TO MERIBAH   707 JERUSALEM 68   61
       KADESH
KANAH
    THE RIVER KANAH WANDERD BY MY SWEET MANASSEH'S SIDE   .   .   349 FOUR ZOAS 8   310
    THE RIVER KANAH WANDERD BY MY SWEET MANASSEH'S SIDE   .   .   705 JERUSALEM 67   57
KATE
    THEE CLUMSY WILL BUT TITTRING KATE   .   .   .   .   .   16 BLIND-MANS/PS   25
    NOR CANST THOU EVER CHANGE KATE INTO NAN   .   .   .   771 EPILOGUE/GP   4
KEEN
    . . . THEIR NAKED SOULS SHIVER IN KEEN OPEN AIR   .   .   146 FRENCH REVOLTN   275
    THE MORE PERFECT THE WORK OF ART AND THE LESS KEEN AND   585B DESC CAT 15   PROSE
       SHARP
KEEP
    THEN LAWS WERE MADE TO KEEP FAIR PLAY   .   .   .   .   17 BLIND-MANS/PS   70
    DEAR SIR A PRINCE SHOULD ALWAYS KEEP HIS STATE   .   .   20 EDW THIRD/PS 2   46
    BUT KEEP A PROPER DIGNITY FOR NOW   .   .   .   .   .   20 EDW THIRD/PS 2   50
    I STILL MAY KEEP YOU HERE   .   .   .   .   .   .   24 EDW THIRD/PS 3   110
    SHALL WARBLE ROUND THE SNOWY HEAD AND KEEP   .   .   .   28 EDW THIRD/PS 3   287
    HE SAT AND HEARD WITH JOY AND PRAISED GOD WHO ISRAEL STILL   40A SAMSON/PS   PROSE
       DOTH KEEP
    HE'LL SWEAR AT THEM & KEEP THEM DOWN WITH HIS FIST & TELL   50A ISLAND MOON 6   PROSE
    AND SO I'LL KEEP HIM FETCH YOUR FATHER FETCH FORTH   105 TIRIEL 4   62
       MYRATANA
    TO KEEP THEM ALL FROM HARM   .   .   .   .   .   .   119 NIGHT/SI   20
    AND KEEP THEM FROM THE SHEEP   .   .   .   .   .   119 NIGHT/SI   *   28
    [THOU WILT EVERY SECRET KEEP]   .   .   .   .   .   164 CRADLE SONG/N   3
    [[CANST] THOU CANST ANY SECRET KEEP]   .   .   .   .   164 CRADLE SONG/N   *   4
    [STARRY] STARRY JEALOUSY DOES KEEP MY DEN   .   .   .   169 EARTHS ANSWR/N   *   7
    TO KEEP THE GENROUS FROM EXPERIENCE TILL THE UNGENEROUS   200 AMERICA 11   8
    STARRY JEALOUSY DOES KEEP MY DEN   .   .   .   .   211 EARTHS ANSR/SE   7
    THAT NO FLESH NOR SPIRIT COULD KEEP   .   .   .   .   235 URIZEN 23   25
    STERN URIZEN BEHELD URGD BY NECESSITY TO KEEP   .   .   282 FOUR ZOAS 2   74
    I STILL KEEP WATCH ALTHO I TREMBLE & WITHER ACROSS THE   288 FOUR ZOAS 2   330
       HEAVENS
    O DID I KEEP THE HORSES OF THE DAY IN SILVER PASTURES   .   310 FOUR ZOAS 5   210
    THEN THOU DIDST KEEP WITH STRONG URTHONA THE LIVING GATES   311 FOUR ZOAS 5   232
       OF HEAVEN
    O LOS UNLESS THOU KEEP MY TOWER THE WATCHMAN WILL BE SLAIN   335 FOUR ZOAS 7B   97
    WILL YOU KEEP A FLOCK OF WOLVES & LEAD THEM . . .   .   .   353 FOUR ZOAS 8   493
    AWAKE THY FATHER DOES THEE KEEP   .   .   .   .   427 LAND OF DREAMS   4
    I WILL KEEP FROM THE BALL & MY EYES SHALL NOT SHINE   .   428 MARY   30
    KEEP NOR IN PITY FALSE NOR IN OFFICIOUS BROTHERHOOD WHERE   487 MILTON 7   44
    BOTH WENT TO LAW WITH DEATH TO KEEP OUR EARS ON   .   .   537 AND HIS LEGS/N   27
    THEN NEVER FLINCH BUT KEEP UP A JAW   .   .   .   .   550 WHEN LOOK AT/N   3
    FOR ITS SURE TO KEEP YOUR JUDGMENT COOL   .   .   .   556 SOME PEOPLE/N   2
    AND TO KEEP IT HIS ARTS ARE OPPOSITE TO THEIRS IN   573B DESC CAT 3   PROSE
       ALL THINGS
    THOSE WHO KEEP MANUFACTORIES OF ART ALWAYS CHARGE   .   .   583B DESC CAT 9   PROSE
    TO KEEP HIS OWN CHARACTERS AND EXPRESSIONS HAVING HAD   .   .   586D CHAUCER 1   PROSE

KEEP   (CONTINUED)
      SEEKING TO KEEP MY SOUL A VICTIM TO THY LOVE WHICH BINDS   622 JERUSALEM 4   25
      MY MOUNTAINS ARE MY OWN AND I WILL KEEP THEM TO MYSELF   . .   622 JERUSALEM 4   29
      STERN URIZEN BEHELD URGD BY NECESSITY TO KEEP .   .   .   .   626 JERUSALEM 7   32
      NO INDIVIDUAL CAN KEEP THESE LAWS FOR THEY ARE DEATH   .   .   662 JERUSALEM 35   11
      ARE SEEN IN OUR HILLS & VALLEYS THEY KEEP OUR FLOCKS &   720 JERUSALEM 79   31
         HERDS
      BUT I VALA LUVAH'S DAUGHTER KEEP HIS BODY EMBALMD IN MORAL   722 JERUSALEM 80   27
         LAWS
      MINGLED ABOVE THE MOUNTAIN WHAT SHALL WE DO TO KEEP   .   .   723 JERUSALEM 80   84
      [YOU] WHO DONT KEEP THE SECRETS OF HOLINESS   .   .   .   .   755 EV GOSPEL(E)/N   86
      GOD KEEP YOU FROM & ALL GOOD MEN OUR ARTISTS OF ALL RANKS   798A LETTER 10   PROSE
      LEFT WITH US THEY KEEP OFF EVERY WIND WE HEAR THE WEST HOWL   807B LETTER 17   PROSE
      PATH IS DIFFICULT I HAVE NO FEAR OF STUMBLING WHILE I KEEP   813B LETTER 22   PROSE
         IT
      AND TWOFOLD ALWAYS MAY GOD US KEEP   .   .   .   .   .   .   818 HAPPINESS/L   87
      YOU TO KEEP IT A SECRET & TO BURN THIS LETTER BECAUSE IT   819D LETTER 25   PROSE
         SPEAKS
      GOD TO KEEP YOU & ALL MEN FROM IT & TO DELIVER ME IN HIS   829A LETTER 28   PROSE
      AS NEAR AS I CAN RECOLLECT I THOUGHT IT BEST TO   856D LETTER 54   PROSE
         KEEP SILENT
      NOT AGREE GOD KEEP ME FROM THE DIVINITY OF YES & NO TOO   878B LETTER 88   PROSE
KEEPER
      I KNOW I WAS URTHONA KEEPER OF THE GATES OF HEAVEN   .   .   298 FOUR ZOAS 4   42
      KNOWLEDGE AND EXPERIENCE HENRY BAILLIE THE KEEPER   .   .   .   569D DESC CAT 3   PROSE
      FOR THE CONSTELLATION ARCTURUS OR BOOTES THE KEEPER   .   .   . 577D DESC CAT 5   PROSE
      I KNOW I AM URTHONA KEEPER OF THE GATES OF HEAVEN   .   .   .   727 JERUSALEM 82   81
KEEPING
      THAT BEATEN MASS KEEPING ITS DIRECTION   .   .   .   .   .   . 249 AHANIA 2   28
      AND KEEPING THEM FROM SIN BY THE MILD COUNSELS OF HIS LOVE   662 JERUSALEM 35   8
      TOOK HIM AGAIN BY THE ELBOWS & KEEPING HIS BACK TO ME   .   827B LETTER 28   PROSE
KEEPS
      . . . THAT MOATED AROUND KEEPS THIS CITY OF PARIS IN AWE   145 FRENCH REVOLTN   248
      KEEPS THE HUMAN SOUL FROM CARE .   .   .   .   431 AUGURIES   22
      WHILE HE KEEPS ONWARDS IN HIS WONDROUS JOURNEY ON THE EARTH   497 MILTON 15   26
      THE FRANKLIN IS ONE WHO KEEPS OPEN TABLE   .   .   .   .   .   . 571A DESC CAT 3   PROSE
      HE WHO KEEPS NOT RIGHT ONWARD IS LOST & IF OUR FOOTSTEPS   813A LETTER 22   PROSE
      ACROSS THE COUNTRY TO FELPHAM AS HE ALWAYS KEEPS A HORSE   843A LETTER 42   PROSE
KEN
      CITY & SANDY DESERT INTERMINGLED BEYOND MORTAL KEN   .   .   . 532 MILTON 40   27
KENDALL
      MR SANDERS TO KENDALL WESTMORELAND MR SANDERS EXPECTS   .   . 834C LETTER 34   PROSE
KENNELS
      . . . & WHOSE RUNNING KENNELS   .   .   .   . 361 FOUR ZOAS 9   168
      THE KENNELS OF THE STREETS & LANES AS IF THEY WERE ABHORRD   657 JERUSALEM 31   18
KENSINGTON
      STRATFORD & OLD BOW & ACROSS TO THE GARDENS OF KENSINGTON   485 MILTON 6   10
      ALBION'S DARK ROCKS SETTING BEHIND THE GARDENS OF   653 JERUSALEM 29   2
         KENSINGTON
KENT
      [AND WANDERD DOWN THE VALES OF KENT IN SICK & DREAR   196 AMERICA PREL 2   21
         LAMENTINGS]
      LEVI MIDDLESEX KENT SURREY JUDAH SOMERSET GLOUSTER   637 JERUSALEM 16   45
         WILTSHIRE
      SUSSEX & KENT ARE HER SCATTERD GARMENTS IRELAND HER HOLY   653 JERUSALEM 29   20
         PLACE
      AND KENT & MIDDLESEX ALL THEIR RIVERS & THEIR HILLS OF   709 JERUSALEM 71   12
         FLOCKS & HERDS
      AND KENT AND THE OTHER ATTENDANT ARE ADMIRABLE   .   .   .   . 843D LETTER 43   PROSE
KENTISH-TOWN
      PANCRASS & KENTISH-TOWN REPOSE .   .   .   .   650 FIELDS FROM/J   9
KEPT
      AND THIS HE ALWAYS KEPT IN MIND   .   .   .   . 50 WHEN CORRUP/IM   13
      . . . KEPT IN AWE WITH THE WHIP   .   .   .   . 143 FRENCH REVOLTN   214
      THE JUST MAN KEPT HIS COURSE ALONG   .   .   .   . 148 MARRIAGE HH 2   4
      KEPT WATCH FOR ETERNALS TO CONFINE   .   .   .   . 226 URIZEN 5   39
      AND THEY ALTERNATE KEPT WATCH OVER THE YOUTHFUL TERRORS   270 FOUR ZOAS 1   229
      WHILE ROUND THEIR HEADS THE ELEMENTAL GODS KEPT HARMONY   288 FOUR ZOAS 2   301
      WERE KEPT BACK FROM MY LORD & FROM HIS CHARIOT OF MERCIES   310 FOUR ZOAS 5   209
      KEPT IGNORANT OF THE USE THAT THEY MIGHT SPEND THE DAYS   337 FOUR ZOAS 7B   183
         OF WISDOM
      AND KEPT ONLY THE FEMININE AWAKE HENCE ROSE HIS SOFT   .   492 MILTON 12   6
      ONWARDS HIS SHADOW KEPT ITS COURSE AMONG THE SPECTRES CALLD   496 MILTON 15   17
      HARNESSD WITH STARRY HARNESS BLACK & SHINING KEPT BY BLACK   503 MILTON 21   21
         SLAVES
      FOR THINE ARE ALSO MINE I HAVE KEPT SILENT HITHERTO   .   .   629 JERUSALEM 10   40
      BECAUSE HE KEPT THE DIVINE VISION IN TIME OF TROUBLE   .   .   655 JERUSALEM 30   15
      LET THE HUMAN ORGANS BE KEPT IN THEIR PERFECT INTEGRITY   686 JERUSALEM 55   36
      KEPT IGNORANT OF ITS USE THAT THEY MIGHT SPEND THE DAYS   700 JERUSALEM 65   25
         OF WISDOM
      BECAUSE HE KEPT THE DIVINE VISION IN TIME OF TROUBLE   .   .   742 JERUSALEM 95   20
      KEPT IN A LOWER TINT THE LITTLE OVAL TABLET ON THE SIDE   832B LETTER 32   PROSE
      WHICH I HAVE HAD SOME TIME BUT KEPT THEM BACK TILL I COULD   850A LETTER 49   PROSE
      MEAN WHILE I AM KEPT HAPPY AS I USED TO BE BECAUSE   .   .   . 863A LETTER 60   PROSE
KERABIM
      (KERABIM) AS MULTITUDES VOX POPULI   .   .   .   . 521C MILTON 32   PROSE
KERCHIEF
      JENNY HER SILKEN KERCHIEF FOLDS .   .   .   . 16 BLIND-MANS/PS   19
KERRY
      WATERFORD TIPPERARY CORK LIMERICK KERRY CLARE .   .   .   .   . 711 JERUSALEM 72   22
KEW
      THE "VIEWS IN KEW GARDENS" "FOOTS CRAY" & "DIANA"   594A PUB ADDRESS/N   PROSE
         & "ACTEON"

	PAGE	TITLE	LINE

KEY
    BUT KITTY HASTED WITH A KEY . . . . 17 BLIND-MANS/PS 57
    YOUR OUT OF THE KEY . . . . 62 DR CLASH/IM * 11
    AND BY CAME AN ANGEL WHO HAD A BRIGHT KEY . . . . . . 117 CHIMNEY SWP/SI 13
    AND LOCKD IN HIS SOUL WITH A NINEFOLD KEY . . . . . . 187 WHEN KLOPSTK/N 18
    AND LOCKD ME UP WITH A GOLDEN KEY . . . . 429 CRYSTL CABINET 4
    ANOTHER DEMON WITH A KEY HAS THE CHARGE OF SIN . . . 606C V LAST JUDG/N PROSE
    THAT FIEND WHO CARRIES THE KEY [& DRAGS] IN ONE HAND & . 608B V LAST JUDG/N PROSE
KEY-BONES
    THEY DIVIDE TO TWELVE THE KEY-BONES & THE CHEST DIVIDING 708 JERUSALEM 70 12
        IN PAIN
KEYS
    CAST THY KEYS O ROME INTO THE DEEP DOWN FALLING . . . . 159B SONG LIBERTY PROSE
    IN HER MILD HAND THE GOLDEN KEYS . . . . 442 DEDICATN BLAIR 6
    THE KEYS TO ST PETER & HE WOULD FIND THAT . . . . . . 465D ANNO REYNOLDS MARG
    THE KEYS OF CALAIS . . . . SUPP ILLUS HISTORY *TITLE
KICK
    AH MR HUFFCAP WOULD KICK THE BOTTOM OF THE PULPIT OUT . . 48B ISLAND MOON 4 PROSE
    & STAMP & KICK & SWEAT AND ALL FOR THE GOOD OF THEIR SOULS 48B ISLAND MOON 4 PROSE
    I'LL KICK YOUR ROMAN ANUS . . . . 54 LO THE BAT/IM 9
KID
    LET US DETAIN THEE WHILE I MAKE READY A KID THAT 40B SAMSON/PS PROSE
        THOU MAYEST
    THE KID . . . . 179B THE KID/N TITLE
    THOU LITTLE KID DIDST PLAY &C . . . . 179 THE KID/N 1
KIDNEYS
    ACCORDING TO HIS CHANGES SHE ROLLD HIS KIDNEYS ROUND . . 723 JERUSALEM 80 72
KILDARE
    EASTMEATH WESTMEATH DUBLIN KILDARE KINGS COUNTY . . . . 711 JERUSALEM 72 19
KILKENNY
    QUEENS COUNTY WICKLOW CATHERLOH WEXFORD KILKENNY . . . . 711 JERUSALEM 72 20
KILL
    [TO KILL THE PEOPLE I AM LOTH] . . . . 185 LET BROTHELS/N 17
    KILL NOT THE MOTH NOR BUTTERFLY . . . . 432 AUGURIES 39
    AND I WONDER WHETHER THEY MEAN TO KILL . . . . 434 WILLIAM BOND 2
    KILL NOT A TREE BUT IT STILL BEAR FRUIT LET NONE SAY THAT 830C LETTER 30 PROSE
KILLED
    THE EGYPTIAN TASKMASTER WHO WAS KILLED AND BURIED BY MOSES SUPP DRAWING WGR *TITLE
KILLS
    THE WANTON BOY THAT KILLS THE FLY . . . . 431 AUGURIES 33
    THUNDER IN THE MIDST OF KINDNESS & LOVE THAT KILLS ITS 677 JERUSALEM 48 16
        BELOVED
KILNS   SEE BRICK-KILNS,BRICK KILNS
KINCARD
    OF REUBEN KINCARD HADDNTN FORFAR SIMEON AYR ARGYLL BANFF 638 JERUSALEM 16 53
KIND
    YET WITH YOUR KIND ASSISTANCE LORDS I HOPE . . . . . 19 EDW THIRD/PS 2 6
    IS OF A DIFFERENT KIND THEN FROM THE KING'S . . . . . 22 EDW THIRD/PS 3 40
    BY NIGHT I AM DECEIVED WHO SAYS THAT THOU WAST BORN OF 38B SAMSON/PS PROSE
        MORTAL KIND
    GRANT ME A SON KIND HEAVEN MANOA CRIED BUT HEAVEN REFUSED 39C SAMSON/PS PROSE
    I CAST AWAY MY STAFF THE KIND COMPANION OF MY TRAVEL . . 101 TIRIEL 2 30
    AND NOT SEEK FOR KIND RELIEF . . . . 122 ON ANOTHERS/SI 4
    OVER ANOTHER KIND OF SEAS AND IN ATMOSPHERES UNKNOWN . 192 V DAU ALBION 4 18
    THESE ARE ONE KIND ONLY . . . . 402A ANNO BACON MARG
    A FALSE OATH FOR THAT HE HEARD ME SAY NOTHING OF THE KIND 438C BLAKES MEMORAN PROSE
    AND BY HER KIND PERMISSION BRING . . . . 442 DEDICATN BLAIR 13
    THE KIND DECISION OF ENITHARMON & GAVE A TIME TO THE SPACE 494 MILTON 13 16
    FOR TWAS A KIND OF BARGAIN SCREWMUCH MADE . . . . . 537 AND HIS LEGS/N 36
    THE FRIAR IS A CHARACTER ALSO OF A MIXED KIND . . . . 568D DESC CAT 3 PROSE
    HIS KIND EVERY ONE IS AN ANTIQUE STATUE . . . . . . 571A DESC CAT 3 PROSE
    OR A COPY OF ANY KIND CAN BE AS HONOURABLE TO A NATION . 595C PUB ADDRESS/N PROSE
    WHAT KIND OF INTELLECTS MUST HE HAVE WHO . . . . . . 597D PUB ADDRESS/N PROSE
    FABLE OR ALLEGORY ARE A TOTALLY DISTINCT & INFERIOR KIND 604D V LAST JUDG/N PROSE
    IF THEY DO NOT PRAY IS AN INFERIOR KIND TO BE CALLD KNOWING 605A V LAST JUDG/N PROSE
    OTHERS OF THE LIKE KIND ARE FABLE YET THEY CONTAIN VISION 607A V LAST JUDG/N PROSE
    NOR PITY NOR LOVE NOR KIND FORGIVENESS O IF I HAVE SINNED 643 JERUSALEM 20 25
    WRITHING IN PAIN THE DAUGHTERS OF BEULAH IN KIND 678 JERUSALEM 48 50
        ARMS RECIEVD
    IN THE SIGHT OF OUR KIND GOD . . . . 717C JERUSALEM 77 PROSE
    KIND RECOMMENDATION TO DR TRUSLER WHICH THO IT HAS FAILD OF 794D LETTER 6 PROSE
    MOMENT FOR YOUR KIND PRESENT NO PERSWASION COULD MAKE . 798A LETTER 10 PROSE
    A KIND OF CRIMINAL DISSIPATION & NEGLECT OF THE MAIN CHANCE 798C LETTER 10 PROSE
    BE SO KIND AS TO READ & THEN SEAL THE INCLOSED . . . . 799D LETTER 11 PROSE
    MR THOMAS YOUR FRIEND TO WHOM YOU WAS SO KIND AS TO MAKE 810D LETTER 21 PROSE
    YOUR VERY KIND & AFFECTIONATE LETTER & THE MANY KIND 811B LETTER 22 PROSE
        THINGS
    & I DOUBT NOT THAT ALL YOUR KIND WISHES IN MY BEHALF . 811D LETTER 22 PROSE
    YOUR KIND OFFER OF PECUNIARY ASSISTANCE I CAN ONLY THANK 811D LETTER 22 PROSE
    THE ACTUAL CAUSE OF MY UNEASINESS INTO WHICH YOU ARE SO 813A LETTER 22 PROSE
        KIND
    PRAY FORGIVE ERRORS IN OMISSIONS OF THIS KIND I AM . . 816A LETTER 23 PROSE
    DESIRES ME TO COPY OUT & SEND YOU WITH HER KIND LOVE . 816D LETTER 24 PROSE
    TO MY BROTHER WHICH YOU WILL BE SO KIND AS TO SEND . . 819A LETTER 24 PROSE
    ACCEPT OF MY THANKS FOR YOUR KIND & HEARTENING LETTER . 822B LETTER 26 PROSE
    AM ALSO GRATEFUL TO THE KIND HAND THAT ENDEAVOURS TO LIFT 822C LETTER 26 PROSE
        ME
    YOU FOR YOUR KIND OFFER OF EXHIBITING MY (TWO) PICTURES THE 826C LETTER 28 PROSE
    MR HAYLEY WAS KIND ENOUGH TO COME FORWARDS . . . . . 828A LETTER 28 PROSE
    I ONLY SUGGEST WHAT I KNOW YOU WILL BE KIND ENOUGH 828B LETTER 28 PROSE
        TO EXCUSE
    IF IT IS POSSIBLE YOU WILL BE KIND ENOUGH TO DO IN THIS 828B LETTER 28 PROSE
        MATTER

KIND   (CONTINUED)
    VERIFIED THE MORNING AFTER I RECEIVED YOUR KIND LETTER . .   831B LETTER 31   PROSE
    IN HIGH SPIRITS & WELCOMD ME WITH KIND AFFECTION &   . .   833C LETTER 33   PROSE
    AS WAS SUPPOSED BY OUR KIND & ATTENTIVE FELLOW INHABITANT   833D LETTER 33   PROSE
    FELPHAM & ITS KIND INHABITANTS I FEEL ANXIOUS & THEREFORE   833D LETTER 33   PROSE
    THE PLEASURE I RECIEVD FROM YOUR KIND LETTER OUGHT TO   .   838B LETTER 37   PROSE
    I THANK YOU HEARTILY FOR YOUR KIND OFFER OF READING &C .   845B LETTER 44   PROSE
    I RECEIVED YOUR KIND LETTER WITH THE NOTE TO MR PAYNE AND   851B LETTER 50   PROSE
    DO SO TO SATISFY YOU THAT I HAVE RECEIVED YOUR KIND FAVOUR   851C LETTER 50   PROSE
    MY WIFE RETURNS HER HEARTFELT THANKS FOR YOUR KIND INQUIRY   851C LETTER 50   PROSE
    OUR GOOD AND KIND FRIEND HAWKINS IS NOT YET IN TOWN . . .   851D LETTER 50   PROSE
    AND AFFECTIONATE COMPLIMENTS TO HIM ALSO TO OUR KIND FRIEND   852D LETTER 50   PROSE
    DEAR SIR I HAVE OMITTED SO LONG TO THANK YOU FOR YOUR KIND   853A LETTER 51   *PROSE
    SINCERE THANKS FOR YOUR KIND PROPOSAL IN YOUR LAST LETTER   853A LETTER 51   *PROSE
    YOU FOR MORE MONEY BUT HOWEVER YOUR KIND ANSWER TO   . . .   854D LETTER 53   PROSE
    ACKNOWLEDGMENTS FOR THE KIND RECEPTION YOU HAVE GIVEN MY   862C LETTER 60   PROSE
        NEW
    DEAR CUMBERLAND I AM VERY MUCH OBLIGED BY YOUR KIND ARDOUR   865C LETTER 63   PROSE
    PRAY REMEMBER ME WITH KIND LOVE TO MRS LINNELL . . . .   873D LETTER 78   PROSE
    I THANK YOU FOR THE TEN POUNDS YOU ARE SO KIND AS TO SEND   880A LETTER 90   PROSE
KINDEST
    THEY ALBION SURROUND WITH KINDEST VIOLENCE TO BEAR HIM BACK   674 JERUSALEM 44   2
    WIFE WHO DESIRES HER KINDEST LOVE TO MRS BUTTS & YOURSELF   808C LETTER 19   PROSE
    MY WIFE DESIRES HER KINDEST LOVE TO MRS BUTTS & I HAVE . .   813B LETTER 22   PROSE
    FIRST STAGE MY WIFE DESIRES HER KINDEST REMEMBRANCES TO YOU   871C LETTER 73   PROSE
KINDLED
    BUT THEL IS LIKE A FAINT CLOUD KINDLED AT THE RISING SUN   128 BOOK OF THEL 2   11
KINDLING
    KINDLING SHE LED HIM INTO SHADOWS & THENCE FLED OUTSTRETCHD   290 FOUR ZOAS 2   381
KINDLY
    WHY ARE [VENETIANS TREATED MORE ?KINDLY XXX ENTHUSIASM]   450B ANNO REYNOLDS * MARG
    CONSOLIDATED & EXTENDED WORK WILL BE AS KINDLY RECIEVED   620D JERUSALEM 3   PROSE
    AS TO MYSELF ABOUT WHOM YOU ARE SO KINDLY INTERESTED I . .   795C LETTER 6   PROSE
    YOU KINDLY SUFFERD ME TO MAKE FROM THE PICTURE OF ROMNEY   838D LETTER 37   PROSE
    WHAT THEIR AUTHOR IS KINDLY PLEASED TO CALL TALENTS FOR   860C LETTER 56   PROSE
KINDNESS   SEE LOVING-KINDNESS
    IN THE SAVIOUR'S ARMS IN THE ARMS OF TENDER MERCY & LOVING   341 FOUR ZOAS 8   19
        KINDNESS
    TO DO UNKIND THINGS IN KINDNESS WITH POWER ARMD TO SAY . .   493 MILTON 12   32
    OF KINDNESS & COMPASSION & IS BORN A WEEPING TERROR . . .   515 MILTON 28   26
    ENAMELD WITH LOVE & KINDNESS & THE TILES ENGRAVEN GOLD . .   632 JERUSALEM 12   31
    YORK CROWND WITH LOVING KINDNESS EDINBURGH CLOTHD   . . . .   665 JERUSALEM 38   51
    ALBION THEY CURSE THEIR HUMAN KINDNESS & AFFECTION   . . .   671 JERUSALEM 42   60
    IN THE DREAMS OF ULRO THEY REPENT OF THEIR HUMAN KINDNESS   671 JERUSALEM 42   62
    THUNDER IN THE MIDST OF KINDNESS & LOVE THAT KILLS ITS   677 JERUSALEM 48   16
        BELOVED
    AS GOD IS LOVE EVERY KINDNESS TO ANOTHER IS A LITTLE DEATH   743 JERUSALEM 96   27
    THANKING YOU FOR THE KINDNESS WITH WHICH YOU EXPRESS THEM   797B LETTER 9   PROSE
    "WE INDEED PRESUME ON YOUR KINDNESS IN NEGLECTING TO HAVE"   800A LETTER 12   PROSE
    PERHAPS DOUBTS PROCEEDING FROM KINDNESS BUT DOUBTS   . . .   822D LETTER 26   PROSE
    IN MY ROUGH SKETCH WHICH RELATED TO YOUR KINDNESS IN   . .   826C LETTER 28   PROSE
    ALWAYS BEEN FORWARD IN EXPRESSING THEIR KINDNESS FOR US   828A LETTER 28   PROSE
    GOD BLESS YOU & PRESERVE YOU & REWARD YOUR KINDNESS TO ME   833A LETTER 32   PROSE
    COURAGE OF CONSCIOUS INDUSTRY WORTHY OF HIS FORMER KINDNESS   851D LETTER 50   PROSE
    TO THOSE WHOSE KINDNESS & GOOD OPINION HAS SUPPORTED ME   862C LETTER 60   PROSE
        THRO
    KINDNESS TO ME SHALL RECIEVE RECOMPENSE IN THE PRESENCE OF   863B LETTER 60   PROSE
KINDNESSES
    AMONG THE OTHER NUMEROUS KINDNESSES I HAVE RECIEVD FROM YOU   826C LETTER 28   PROSE
KINDS
    BACON HATED TALENTS OF ALL KINDS ELOQUENCE IS DISCRETION   409A ANNO BACON   MARG
        OF SPEECH
    DESCENDED DOWN A PAVED WORK OF ALL KINDS OF PRECIOUS STONES   529 MILTON 38   6
    BY THE VARIOUS ARTS OF POVERTY & CRUELTY OF ALL KINDS . .   615D V LAST JUDG/N PROSE
    BEAUTIFUL SHE BEAMS TOWARDS THE EAST ALL KINDS OF PRECIOUS   710 JERUSALEM 71   40
        STONES
KING
    GWIN KING OF NORWAY   . . . .   11B GWIN KING/PS   TITLE
    THEY STAND AROUND THE KING   . . . .   12 GWIN KING/PS   42
    THE KING IS SEEN RAGING AFAR   . . . .   13 GWIN KING/PS   81
    KING EDWARD THE THIRD . . . .   17C EDW THIRD/PS   TITLE
    PERSONS KING EDWARD THE BLACK PRINCE QUEEN PHILIPPA . . .   17C EDW THIRD/PS   TITLE
    SCENE THE COAST OF FRANCE KING EDWARD AND NOBLES BEFORE   17D EDW THIRD/PS 1 PROSE
        IT THE ARMY
    THE KING S AFRAID BUT WHAT ARE YOU AFRAID OF   . . . . .   22 EDW THIRD/PS 3   36
    THE KING CAUGHT HERE IN FRANCE OF RUNNING AWAY   . . . .   22 EDW THIRD/PS 3   57
    HERE COMES THE KING HIMSELF TELL HIM YOUR THOUGHTS . . .   23 EDW THIRD/PS 3   67
    ENTER KING EDWARD AND BLACK PRINCE   . . . .   23A EDW THIRD/PS 3 PROSE
    [EXEUNT] EXIT KING EDWARD   . . . .   26C EDW THIRD/PS 3 PROSE
    THAT BROUGHT OVER OUR KING TO FRANCE TO FIGHT FOR HIS RIGHT   28D EDW THIRD/PS 4 PROSE
    YONDER S A MUSICIAN GOING TO PLAY BEFORE THE KING   . . .   29B EDW THIRD/PS 4 PROSE
    PROLOGUE INTENDED FOR A DRAMATIC PIECE OF KING EDWARD THE   33C EDW FOURTH/PS   TITLE
        FOURTH
    PROLOGUE TO KING JOHN . . . .   34A KING JOHN/PS   TITLE
    A CROWNED KING   . . . .   62 CROWND KING/IM   1
    TIRIEL IS KING OF ALL THE WEST WHO ART THOU I AM MNETHA   101 TIRIEL 2   18
    I KNOW TIRIEL IS KING OF THE WEST & THERE HE LIVES IN JOY   101 TIRIEL 2   20
    FOR HE IS THE KING OF ROTTEN WOOD & OF THE BONES OF DEATH   101 TIRIEL 2   24
    TIRIEL IS A KING & THOU THE TEMPTER OF DARK IJIM . . . .   104 TIRIEL 4   38
    LEAD ME TO HAR & HEVA I AM TIRIEL KING OF THE WEST . . .   109 TIRIEL 8   4
    [IS THE SON OF A KING WARMED WITHOUT WOOL . . . .   110 TIRIEL 8   19
    HE SAYS AT N...NO KING HATH SUCH A GOVERNMENT AS THIS   . .   132C ANNO SWED PROV MARG

```
                                                             PAGE    TITLE          LINE
KING    (CONTINUED)
     TROUBLED LEANING ON NECKER DESCENDS THE KING . . . . . .  . .   134 FRENCH REVOLTN    10
     . . . WALK GATHERING ROUND THE KING . . . . . . . . . . . . .   134 FRENCH REVOLTN    14
     FOR A LETTER OF ADVICE TO A KING . . . . . . . . . .   . . . .   136 FRENCH REVOLTN    51
     . . . AND WEEP ROUND THE KING AND HIS NOBLES . . . . . . . . .   136 FRENCH REVOLTN    60
     . . . COLD WAVING THE NOBLES FOLD ROUND THE KING . . . .   . .   137 FRENCH REVOLTN    65
     THEN THE KING GLOWD HIS NOBLES FOLD ROUND . . . . . . . . . . .  137 FRENCH REVOLTN    68
     IN THEIR DARKNESS THE KING STOOD HIS HEART FLAMD . . . . .       137 FRENCH REVOLTN    69
     THE KING LEAND ON HIS MOUNTAINS . . . . . . . . . .    . . . .   139 FRENCH REVOLTN   110
     THE KING FROWNING IN PURPLE BESIDE THE GREY PLOWMAN . .          141 FRENCH REVOLTN   150
     HEAR MY COUNSEL O KING AND SEND FORTH THY GENERALS . . .         141 FRENCH REVOLTN   153
     THEN DO THOU COMMAND O KING . . . . . . . . . . .    . . . . .   141 FRENCH REVOLTN   154
     OF KING HENRY THE FOURTH WALKS BEFORE HIM IN FIRES . . .         141 FRENCH REVOLTN   165
     . . . HE IS COME TO THE LOUVRE O KING WITH A MESSAGE . . .       141 FRENCH REVOLTN   166
     FROM THE HEAD OF OUR KING . . . . . . . . .   . . .   . . . .    142 FRENCH REVOLTN   172
     . . . AND IF IT OBEY AND DEPART THEN THE KING WILL DISBAND       145 FRENCH REVOLTN   252
     PALE AND COLD SAT THE KING IN MIDST OF HIS PEERS . . . .         147 FRENCH REVOLTN   294
     AWFUL UP ROSE THE KING . . . . . . . . . .    . . . . . . . .    148 FRENCH REVOLTN   304
     KING DAVID DESIRED SO FERVENTLY & INVOKES SO PATHETICLY         153D MARRIAGE HH 12   PROSE
     THE NEW BORN FIRE STOOD BEFORE THE STARRY KING   . . . .        159B SONG LIBERTY     PROSE
     DOWN RUSHD BEATING HIS WINGS IN VAIN THE JEALOUS KING   .       159C SONG LIBERTY     PROSE
     THEIR SULLEN FLAMES FADED EMERGE ROUND THE GLOOMY KING  .       159D SONG LIBERTY     PROSE
     THE KING & THE PRIEST MUST BE TIED IN A TETHER    . . . .       177 MERLNS PROPH/N      3
     MAKES EACH FAIRY A KING . . . . . . . . . . .                   178 THE FAIRY/N        10
     AND ARE GONE TO PRAISE GOD & HIS PRIEST & KING . . . . .        180 CHIMNEY SWP/N      11
     THE KING AWOKE ON HIS COUCH OF GOLD . . . . . . . .             185 LET BROTHELS/N      5
     [FAYETTE BESIDE KING LEWIS STOOD] . . . . . . . . . .           185 LET BROTHELS/N     27
     FAYETTE BEHELD THE KING & QUEEN   . . . . . . . . . .           185 LET BROTHELS/N     35
     FAYETTE BEHELD THE KING & QUEEN   . . . . . . . . . .           186 LET BROTHELS/N     60
     THE BAT THE OWL THE GLOWING TYGER AND THE KING OF NIGHT         195 V DAU ALBION 8      5
     THE KING OF ENGLAND LOOKING WESTWARD TREMBLES AT THE VISION     197 AMERICA 4          12
     BY ARISTON THE KING OF BEAUTY FOR HIS STOLEN BRIDE  . . .       200 AMERICA 10         10
     . . . XXX AND XXX AND LXXX SILENT STOOD THE KING BREATHING      205 AMERICA CANC C  *   5
       . . .
     [OVER THE] A FROWNING SHADOW LIKE [A] AN AGED KING IN ARMS      205 AMERICA CANC C  *  25
       OF GOLD
     CORINEUS THROWS GOGMAGOG THE GIANT INTO THE SEA KING LEAR      208C SUBJCTS HIST/N   TITLE
     KING JOHN & MAG(MAGNA) CHARTA . . . . . . . . . . .            208D SUBJCTS HIST/N   TITLE
     AND ARE GONE TO PRAISE GOD & HIS PRIEST & KING   . . . .        212 CHIMNEY SWP/SE     11
     ONE KING ONE GOD ONE LAW . . . . . . . . . . .                  224 URIZEN 4           40
     ARISE MY SON BRING ALL THY BRETHREN O THOU KING OF FIRE         240 EUROPE 8            8
     AND THINE EYES REJOICE BECAUSE OF STRENGTH O RINTRAH           240 EUROPE 8           12
       FURIOUS KING
     THE FIERY KING WHO SOUGHT HIS ANCIENT TEMPLE SERPENT-FORMD      241 EUROPE 10           2
     SHALL NOT THE KING CALL FOR FAMINE FROM THE HEATH    . . .      247 SONG OF LOS 6       9
     NOW SEEN NOW OBSCURD KING OF SORROW . . . . . . . .             249 AHANIA 2           13
     TO AWAKE BRIGHT URIZEN MY KING . . . . . . . . . .              254 AHANIA 5            7
     TO AWAKE MY KING IN THE MORN . . . . . . . . . . .              254 AHANIA 5           10
     IF I INDEED AM [LUVAH'S LORD] VALA'S KING & YE O SONS OF        282 FOUR ZOAS 2    *  81
       MEN
     THE KING OF LIGHT BEHELD HER MOURNING AMONG THE BRICK KILNS     285 FOUR ZOAS 2      215
       COMPELLD
     AND NINE BRIGHT SPHERES OF HARMONY RISE ROUND THE FIERY         289 FOUR ZOAS 2      348
       KING
     NOW SAT THE KING OF LIGHT ON HIGH UPON HIS STARRY THRONE        291 FOUR ZOAS 3        1
     I AM SET HERE A KING OF TROUBLE COMMANDED HERE TO SERVE         292 FOUR ZOAS 3       16
     AHANIA BOWD HER HEAD & WEPT SEVEN DAYS BEFORE THE KING  . .     292 FOUR ZOAS 3       24
     SO LOUD IN THUNDERS SPOKE THE KING FOLDED IN DARK DESPAIR       295 FOUR ZOAS 3      131
     OUR GOD IS URIZEN THE KING KING OF THE HEAVENLY HOSTS   . .     298 FOUR ZOAS 4       38
     OF ENION & HIM ASSIST TO BIND THE FALLEN KING . . . . .        300 FOUR ZOAS 4      120
     THE ENORMOUS DEMONS WOKE & HOWLD AROUND THE [YOUTHFUL]          306 FOUR ZOAS 5       41
       NEW BORN KING
     CRYING LUVAH KING OF LOVE THOU ART THE KING OF RAGE &           306 FOUR ZOAS 5       42
       DEATH
     AH HOW SHALL URIZEN THE KING SUBMIT TO THIS DARK MANSION        310 FOUR ZOAS 5      190
     A DREARY WASTE OF SOLID WATERS FOR THE KING OF LIGHT   . .      313 FOUR ZOAS 6       51
     IN SUCCESSIVE VOLLIES WITH LOUD THUNDERS SWIFT FLEW THE         314 FOUR ZOAS 6    * 109
       KING OF LIGHT
     FLEW THE KING THO FLAGD HIS POWERS LABRING TILL OVER ROCKS      314 FOUR ZOAS 6    * 112
     HIS WILL WHERE NONE SHOULD DARE OPPOSE HIS WILL HIMSELF         317 FOUR ZOAS 6      232
       BEING KING
     GIVE ME EXAMPLE OF THY MILDNESS KING OF FURIOUS HAIL STORMS     323 FOUR ZOAS 7      145
     I WILL DIVIDE THEM IN MY ANGER & THOU O MY KING . . . .        334 FOUR ZOAS 7B      69
     STOP WE THE RISING OF THE GLORIOUS KING . . . . . . . .        336 FOUR ZOAS 7B     153
     UNHURT & DARE THE INCLEMENT FOREHEAD OF THE KING OF LIGHT       345 FOUR ZOAS 8      149
     WE ARE ALL SERVANTS TO THY WILL O KING OF LIGHT RELENT  . .     345 FOUR ZOAS 8      162
     THY FURIOUS POWER BE OUR FATHER & OUR LOVED KING . . . .        345 FOUR ZOAS 8      163
     BUT HAPPINESS CAN NEVER TO THEE O KING NOR ME . . . . .         345 FOUR ZOAS 8      167
     AND THEN MOCKING & THEN WORSHIPPING CALLING HIM LORD & KING     349 FOUR ZOAS 8      327
     NO LONGER NOW ERECT THE KING OF LIGHT OUTSTRETCHD IN FURY       352 FOUR ZOAS 8      438
     UP BOUND THE WILD STAG & THE HORSE [BEHOLDS] BEHOLD THE         352 FOUR ZOAS 8    * 453
       KING OF PRIDE
     A KING OF WRATH & FURY A DARK ENRAGED HORROR   . . . . .        353 FOUR ZOAS 8      462
     . . . THAT THE KING & PRIEST MAY STILL FEAST ON YOUR DECAY      354 FOUR ZOAS 8      498
     ASTONISHD LOOKD FROM HIS BRIGHT PORTALS LUVAH KING OF LOVE      380 FOUR ZOAS AD 1     5
     AND MOCKING & THEN WORSHIPING CALLING HIM LORD & KING   .       382 FOUR ZOAS AD 6    15
     CONVERSE WITH GOD & BE A KING & PRIEST IN HIS OWN HOUSE        389C ANNO WATSON      MARG
     A LIE EVERY BODY HATES A KING BACON WAS AFRAID TO SAY THAT     400B ANNO BACON       MARG
     THE ENVY WAS UPON A KING BUT IS THIS ENVY OR INDIGNATION       400B ANNO BACON       MARG
     THE DEVIL'S ARSE A KING . . . . . . . . . . .                  400D ANNO BACON       MARG
     ("A KING IS A MORTAL GOD") O CONTEMPTIBLE & ABJECT SLAVE       401A ANNO BACON       MARG
     BACON'S (REFORMER) VILLAIN IS A KING OR WHO    . . . . .       404C ANNO BACON     * MARG
```

	PAGE	TITLE	LINE

KING   (CONTINUED)
```
     DID HE MEAN TO RIDICULE A KING & HIS COUNCIL   . . . . .  405C ANNO BACON        MARG
     KING JAMES WAS BACON'S PRIMUM MOBILE . . . . . . . . .    410D ANNO BACON        MARG
     AND A SIGH IS THE SWORD OF AN ANGEL KING   . . . . .      420 I SAW A MONK/N       59
     AND A SIGH IS THE SWORD OF AN ANGEL KING   . . . . .      430 GREY MONK            30
     (DAMN) THE (KING) NOW I HAVE ALL THE PERSONS WHO WERE . . 437C BLAKES MEMORAN    PROSE
     WHO SWORE THAT HE HEARD ME (DAMN) THE (KING)   . . . . .  437C BLAKES MEMORAN    PROSE
     O KING & NOBILITY OF ENGLAND WHERE HAVE   . . . . . .     446A ANNO REYNOLDS     MARG
     THE KING DROPD A TEAR INTO THE QUEEN'S EAR   . . . . .    451 ANNO REYNOLDS         3
     I WILL NOT WORSHIP IN THEIR CHURCHES NOR KING IN THEIR    491 MILTON 10           13
        THEATRES
     AND LET US BIND THEE IN THE BANDS OF WAR & BE THOU KING   501 MILTON 20            5
     GO LOVE WITHOUT THE HELP OF ANY [THING] ?KING ON EARTH .  541 ANGEL PRESID/N *     3
     KING EDWARD AND HIS QUEEN ELENOR ARE PROSTRATED   . . .   577A DESC CAT 4        PROSE
     MORTIMER AND GLOUCESTER LIE SPELL BOUND BEHIND THEIR KING 577B DESC CAT 4        PROSE
     IN THE LAST BATTLE OF KING ARTHUR ONLY THREE BRITONS      577B DESC CAT 5        TITLE
        ESCAPED
     WITH THE SWORD & BALANCES HE IS OG KING OF BASHAN   . . . 606C V LAST JUDG/N     PROSE
     REPRESENTING OG KING OF BASHAN IS A FIGURE WITH A BASKET  607D V LAST JUDG/N     PROSE
     A KING CROWNED GRASPING HIS SWORD & HIS SCEPTRE   . . .   608B V LAST JUDG/N     PROSE
     AND A SIGH IS THE SWORD OF AN ANGEL KING   . . . . . .    683 I SAW A MONK/J       26
     THE KING OF CANAAN WHOSE ARE SEVEN HUNDRED CHARIOTS OF IRON 702 JERUSALEM 66      25
     TO MURDER ALBION THE KING OF MEN HE FOUGHT IN BATTLES     722 JERUSALEM 80        18
        FIERCE
     THE EAGLE & THE WOLF & MONKEY & OWL & THE KING & PRIEST   742 JERUSALEM 94        27
        WERE THERE
     GOD'S HIGH KING & GOD'S HIGH PRIEST   . . . . . . .       749 EV GOSPEL(B)/N      19
     I COME YOUR KING & GOD TO SIEZE   . . . . . . . . .       749 EV GOSPEL(B)/N      29
     I NATURE (HERMAPHRODITIC) PRIEST & KING   . . . . .       789A ANNO THORNTON   * MARG
     & GOD IS THE GHOST OF THE PRIEST & KING WHO EXIST   . .   789A ANNO THORNTON     MARG
     THAT THE KING SHEWS IT A GREAT COUNTENANCE & ENCOURAGEMENT 797D LETTER 10        PROSE
     FOR AS TO SEDITION NOT ONE WORD RELATING TO THE KING OR   826D LETTER 28         PROSE
     AT THE GATE UTTER SEDITIOUS WORDS & (DAMN) THE (KING)   . 827D LETTER 28         PROSE
     KING WILL LIVE TO FULFIL THE PROPHECY AND DIE IN PEACE .  844D LETTER 43         PROSE
     THE MIND IN WHICH EVERY ONE IS KING & PRIEST IN HIS OWN   879A LETTER 88         PROSE
        HOUSE
     KING EDWARD AND QUEEN ELENOR   . . . . . . . . .         SUPP ILLUS HISTORY    *TITLE
     SAUL KING OF ISRAEL SOMEWHAT INFLUENCED BY XXX EVIL SPIRIT SUPP PENC DRAW 1.42  *TITLE
```
KINGDOM
```
     . . . LEAVE THE KINGDOM THY LIFE IS SURROUNDED WITH SNARES 139 FRENCH REVOLTN   114
     ANCIENT WONDERS FROWN OVER THE KINGDOM . . . . . . . .    139 FRENCH REVOLTN    118
     BEFORE THE ANCIENT SEAT OF THE KINGDOM AND MOUNTAINS TO   143 FRENCH REVOLTN    205
        BE RENEWED
     . . . ARE THE BANDS OF THE MURMURING KINGDOM   . . . .    145 FRENCH REVOLTN    254
     INTO THY WISHED KINGDOM WHERE IN MAJESTY & POWER   . . .  277 FOUR ZOAS 1       490
     TO HIM HIS LABOUR WAS BUT SORROW & HIS KINGDOM WAS        285 FOUR ZOAS 2       208
        REPENTANCE
     GOOD ADVICE FOR SATAN'S KINGDOM   . . . . . . . . .       396D ANNO BACON       MARG
     THE KINGDOM OF HEAVEN IS THE DIRECT NEGATION OF EARTHLY   407B ANNO BACON       MARG
        DOMINATION
     THE KINGDOM OF OG IS IN ORION SIHON IS IN OPHIUCUS   . .  528 MILTON 37          50
     SAVIOUR'S KINGDOM THE DIVINE BODY WILL NEVER ENTER THERE  621A JERUSALEM 3      PROSE
     TO MURDER THEIR OWN SOULS TO BUILD A KINGDOM AMONG THE DEAD 640 JERUSALEM 18     10
     WHY WILT THOU REND THYSELF APART & BUILD AN EARTHLY KINGDOM 730 JERUSALEM 85     30
     NONE ARE GREATEST IN THE KINGDOM OF HEAVEN   . . . . .    783A ANNO WW POEMS    MARG
     UPON THE KINGDOM OF JESUS BY THE CLASSICAL LEARNED   . .  786C ANNO WW POEMS    MARG
     OR TAX UPON WHAT IS COMMON TO ALL IN THY KINGDOM   . . .  788A ANNO THORNTON    MARG
     THE HOLY GHOST THY KINGDOM ON EARTH IS NOT [THY XXX]   .  788A ANNO THORNTON  * MARG
     [XXX] KINGDOM [BUT DELIVER] LIBERATE US US   . . . . .    788B ANNO THORNTON  * MARG
     FROM THE NATURAL MAN & WANT OR JOB'S KINGDOM   . . . .    788B ANNO THORNTON  * MARG
     FOR THINE IS THE KINGDOM & THE POWER & THE GLORY   . . .  788B ANNO THORNTON    MARG
     I SWEAR THAT BASILEIA (BASILEIA ) IS NOT KINGDOM          789A ANNO THORNTON    MARG
        BUT KINGSHIP
     THE SEA COASTS MAY BE GATHERD INTO HIS KINGDOM   . . . .  823C LETTER 26        PROSE
```
KINGDOMS
```
     PROPHETIC SAW THE KINGDOMS OF THE WORLD & ALL THEIR GLORY 41A THEN SHE BORE     PROSE
     . . . AND THE KINGDOMS OF EARTH BOUND IN SHEAVES   . . .  138 FRENCH REVOLTN     92
     SAYING BY THIS HE CONQUERS ENEMIES & GOVERNS KINGDOMS .   153D MARRIAGE HH 12   PROSE
     ALL THE GODS OF THE KINGDOMS OF EARTH LABOUR IN LOS'S HALLS 510 MILTON 24        74
     THESE ARE THE GODS OF THE KINGDOMS OF THE EARTH IN        520 MILTON 31          23
        CONTRARIOUS
     THE STARS WHICH ARE THE BOUNDARIES OF KINGDOMS PROVINCES  528 MILTON 37          48
     APPEARD THE SEVEN KINGDOMS OF CANAAN & FIVE BAALIM   . .  532 MILTON 40          24
     AROUND HIM ARE OTHER KINGDOMS ARISING TO JUDGMENT   . . . 608C V LAST JUDG/N    PROSE
     THE SEVEN HEADED KINGDOMS THE GRAVES BENEATH   . . . .    609C V LAST JUDG/N    PROSE
     AND THENCE TO ALL THE KINGDOMS & NATIONS & FAMILIES OF    637 JERUSALEM 16       34
        THE EARTH
     THE SOUNDING FLAIL TO THRESH THE WINNOW TO WINNOW KINGDOMS 713 JERUSALEM 73      13
     WHERE ARE THE KINGDOMS OF THE WORLD & . . . . . . .       746 JERUSALEM 98       51
     PEACE OPENS THE WAY TO GREATER STILL THE KINGDOMS OF   .  810C LETTER 21        PROSE
     THIS WORLD ARE NOW BECOME THE KINGDOMS OF GOD & HIS CHRIST 810C LETTER 21       PROSE
```
KINGLY
```
     THE KINGLY LION STOOD . . . . . . . . . . . . .          113 LIT GRL LST/SI      37
     . . . IN THE EYES OF THE KINGLY MOURNER   . . . . . .     134 FRENCH REVOLTN      6
     AND SNAKE AND DAMP TOAD ON THE KINGLY FOOT CRAWL . . . .  147 FRENCH REVOLTN    298
     LISTEN TO THE FOOL'S REPROACH IT IS A KINGLY TITLE   . .  152A MARRIAGE HH 9    PROSE
     . . . [& ALL MY KINGLY POWER] BUT HEAR MY DETERMIND DECREE 292 FOUR ZOAS 3       19
```
KING'S
```
     IS OF A DIFFERENT KIND THEN FROM THE KING'S   . . . . .   22 EDW THIRD/PS 3       40
     THE KING'S TENT WITH A MINSTREL WHO SINGS THE FOLLOWING   31D EDW THIRD/PS 6    PROSE
        SONG
     SO ONCE THE SUN HIS CHARIOT DREW BACK TO PROLONG A GOOD   41B THEN SHE BORE     PROSE
        KING'S LIFE
```

	PAGE	TITLE	LINE
KING'S (CONTINUED)			
. . . THE DUKE OF BURGUNDY DELIVERS THE KING'S COMMAND . .	145	FRENCH REVOLTN	247
THANK YOU FOR YOUR VERY BEAUTIFUL LITTLE POEM ON THE KING'S	844D	LETTER 43	PROSE
RECOVERY			
KINGS			
COME KINGS AND LISTEN TO MY SONG	11	GWIN KING/PS	1
O WHAT HAVE KINGS TO ANSWER FOR	13	GWIN KING/PS	97
THE KINGS AND NOBLES OF THE LAND HAVE DONE IT	33	EDW FOURTH/PS	15
STRIFE SHAPELESS SITTETH UNDER THRONES OF KINGS . . .	42C	THEN SHE BORE	PROSE
SIGNIFY WHAT THE LAWS OF KINGS & PRIESTS HAVE CALLD VICE	88C	ANNO LAVATER	MARG
FOR ALL KINGS ARE UNIVERSAL IN THEIR GOVERNMENT	132C	ANNO SWED PROV	MARG
OTHERWISE THEY ARE NO KINGS	132C	ANNO SWED PROV	MARG
OF ANCIENT KINGS AND THE FROWN OF THE ETERNAL LION . . .	135	FRENCH REVOLTN	32
. . . AND TERRORS OF ANCIENT KINGS	136	FRENCH REVOLTN	59
. . . KINGS ARE SICK THROUGHOUT ALL THE EARTH	137	FRENCH REVOLTN	61
. . . THE SPIRITS OF ANCIENT KINGS	137	FRENCH REVOLTN	72
. . . SHAKEN THE FORESTS OF FRANCE SICK THE KINGS OF THE	147	FRENCH REVOLTN	300
NATIONS			
I CALL WITH HOLY VOICE KINGS OF THE SOUNDING AIR	190	V DAU ALBION 2	14
TO BUILD HIM CASTLES AND HIGH SPIRES WHERE KINGS & PRIESTS	193	V DAU ALBION 5	20
MAY DWELL			
THE CRUELTIES USED BY KINGS & PRIESTS [WHOSE ARTS] . . .	209A	SUBJCTS HIST/N	*TITLE
AND BRING FORTH HOWLING TERRORS ALL DEVOURING FIERY KINGS	238	EUROPE PREL 2	4
THAT KINGS & PRIESTS HAD COPIED ON EARTH	242	EUROPE 11	4
THE KINGS OF ASIA HEARD	247	SONG OF LOS 6	1
AND THE KINGS OF ASIA STOOD	247	SONG OF LOS 6	7
MOTHERS & INFANTS KINGS & WARRIORS	248	SONG OF LOS 7	34
NOW COMES THE NIGHT OF CARNAGE NOW THE FLESH OF KINGS &	334	FOUR ZOAS 7B	45
PRINCES			
AND THE HARLOT OF LOS & THE DELUDED HARLOT OF THE KINGS	336	FOUR ZOAS 7B	* 138
OF EARTH			
HE SAW THE HARLOT OF THE KINGS OF EARTH & SAW HER CUP . .	356	FOUR ZOAS 8	602
THE THRONES OF KINGS ARE SHAKEN THEY HAVE LOST THEIR ROBES	357	FOUR ZOAS 9	18
& CROWNS			
KINGS IN THEIR PALACES LIE DROWND SHEPHERDS THEIR FLOCKS	359	FOUR ZOAS 9	74
THEIR TENTS			
FATHERS & FRIENDS MOTHERS & INFANTS KINGS & WARRIORS . .	363	FOUR ZOAS 9	243
THE KINGS & PRINCES OF THE EARTH CRY WITH A FEEBLE CRY . .	365	FOUR ZOAS 9	328
GO DOWN YE KINGS & COUNCELLORS & GIANT WARRIORS	374	FOUR ZOAS 9	659
PAINE SAYS THAT KINGS & PRIESTS HAVE DONE HIM HARM FROM	393A	ANNO WATSON	MARG
HIS BIRTH			
OF KINGS & COURTS WHO MAKE THEMSELVES EVERY BODY	397B	ANNO BACON	MARG
MUSIC ARE IN HIS OPINION USELESS & SO THEY ARE FOR KINGS	407D	ANNO BACON	MARG
& WARS			
BECAUSE KINGS DO IT IS IT WISDOM	410B	ANNO BACON	MARG
I WILL HAVE KINGS INWOVEN UPON IT & COUNCELLORS & MIGHTY	499	MILTON 18	15
MEN			
SAYING COME THOU TO EPHRAIM BEHOLD THE KINGS OF CANAAN . .	501	MILTON 19	36
AND THEIR SUBLIME INTENT GIVEN TO THEIR KINGS	543	IF TRUE/N	12
THE SWALLOW SINGS IN COURTS OF KINGS	547	LET BE TOLD/N	2
MAY BE GIFTS FROM THE DEVIL & EARTHLY KINGS	557	SINCE RICHES/N	2
HER KINGS & COUNCELLORS & WARRIORS DESCEND IN FLAMES .	609B	V LAST JUDG/N	PROSE
[TO BE THE GOOD KINGS] & QUEENS [OF ENGLAND]	614A	V LAST JUDG/N	*PROSE
SAMUEL A DOUBLE BOOK & KINGS A DOUBLE BOOK THE PSALMS	677	JERUSALEM 48	10
& PROPHETS			
WILT THOU MAKE ROME THY PATRIARCH DRUID & THE KINGS OF	695	JERUSALEM 61	50
EUROPE HIS			
DIVIDE INTO THE KINGS OF EUROPE IN TIMES REMOTE O	698	JERUSALEM 64	16
WOMAN-BORN			
OF ALBION DELIGHTS THE EYES OF THE KINGS THEIR HEARTS & THE	706	JERUSALEM 68	16
MOLECH RUSHES INTO THE KINGS IN LOVE TO THE BEAUTIFUL	706	JERUSALEM 68	28
DAUGHTERS			
TO THE BEAUTIFUL DAUGHTERS OF ALBION THEY SPORT BEFORE	706	JERUSALEM 68	32
THE KINGS			
BEFORE THE KINGS OF CANAAN TO CUT THE FLESH FROM THE VICTIM	706	JERUSALEM 68	57
KINGS OF CANAAN THEN TO LET THE SPIES DEPART TO MERIBAH	707	JERUSALEM 68	61
KADESH			
EASTMEATH WESTMEATH DUBLIN KILDARE KINGS COUNTY . . .	711	JERUSALEM 72	19
SETTING UP KINGS IN WRATH IN HOLINESS OF NATURAL RELIGION	713	JERUSALEM 73	31
AND ALL THE KINGS & NOBLES OF THE EARTH & ALL THEIR	713	JERUSALEM 73	38
GLORIES			
OF JAVAN THRO THE ISLES OF GRECIA & ALL EUROPE'S KINGS . .	735	JERUSALEM 89	34
THERE THE SEVEN KINGS OF CANAAN & FIVE BAALIM OF PHILISTEA	735	JERUSALEM 89	46
BUT BY DESIGN BY THE KINGS OF PERSIA & THEIR GENERALS . .	785B	ILLUS DANTE 7	PROSE
FOR GOD IS ONLY AN ALLEGORY OF KINGS & NOTHING ELSE AMEN	789A	ANNO THORNTON	MARG
KINGSHIP			
THY KINGSHIP COME UPON EARTH FIRST & THENCE IN HEAVEN . .	788D	ANNO THORNTON	* MARG
FOR THINE IS THE KINGSHIP OR ALLEGORIC GODSHIP	789A	ANNO THORNTON	* MARG
I SWEAR THAT BASILEIA (BASILEIA) IS NOT KINGDOM	789A	ANNO THORNTON	MARG
BUT KINGSHIP			
KINROS			
JOSEPH ELGIN LANERK KINROS BENJAMIN KROMARTY MURRA	638	JERUSALEM 16	58
KIRKUBBRIHT			
KIRKUBRIHT			
JOSEPH ELGIN LANERK KINROS BENJAMIN KROMARTY MURRA	638	JERUSALEM 16	58
KIRKUBBRIHT			
KISHON			
MEDWAY MINGLED WITH KISHON THAMES RECIEVD THE HEAVENLY	720	JERUSALEM 79	35
JORDAN			
KISS			
KISS THY PERFUMED GARMENTS LET US TASTE	1	TO SPRING/PS	10
THE HOLY KISS OF LOVE AND THE TRANSPARENT TEAR	38A	SAMSON/PS	PROSE

		PAGE	TITLE	LINE

KISS   (CONTINUED)
```
    AND KISS MY ROMAN ANUS  . . . . . . . . . . . .        54 LO THE BAT/IM        13
    THOU HAST NO TEETH OLD MAN & THUS I KISS THY SLEEK BALD   101 TIRIEL 2           37
      HEAD
    HEVA COME KISS HIS BALD HEAD FOR HE WILL NOT HURT US HEVA 101 TIRIEL 2           38
    KISS ME MY BROTHER & THEN LEAVE ME TO WANDER DESOLATE  .  104 TIRIEL 4           22
    LET ME KISS  . . . . . . . . . . . . . . . .       123 SPRING/SI           25
    [BUT SHAKE HANDS & KISS HIM & THERED BE NO MORE HELL]  .  180 LIT VAGABOND/N      17
    BUT KISS HIM & GIVE HIM BOTH [FOOD] DRINK & APPAREL  . .  180 LIT VAGABOND/N      18
    BUT KISS HIM & GIVE HIM BOTH DRINK AND APPAREL  . . .    216 LIT VAGABND/SE      16
    I CANNOT KISS THE PLACE  . . . . . . . . . . .      254 AHANIA 4            70
    O MY SWEET CHILDREN ENION LET THARMAS KISS THY CHEEK  .   371 FOUR ZOAS 9        525
    I BENT TO KISS THE LOVELY MAID  . . . . . . . .     429 CRYSTL CABINET      19
    AND FOUND A THREEFOLD KISS RETURND  . . . . . . .    429 CRYSTL CABINET      20
    RECIEVE A KISS FROM GODS OR MEN A THREEFOLD KISS RETURNS  709 JERUSALEM 70        25
    READY TO KISS ANY ONE'S ARSE  . . . . . . . . .    785C ILLUS DANTE 16    PROSE
KISSD
    SHE KISSD THE PALE LIPS SHE HAD NO TEARS TO SHED  . . .     6 FAIR ELENOR/PS     71
    SHE FALLING KISSD THE GROUND POOR FOOL  . . . . . .      16 BLIND-MANS/PS       14
    OF ALBION THEY KISSD THE ROCKY SHORE  . . . . . . .      32 EDW THIRD/PS 6      14
    IN EMBRYON PASSIONS THEY KISSD NOT NOR EMBRACD FOR SHAME  270 FOUR ZOAS 1        238
      & FEAR
KISSED
    HE KISSED THE CHILD & BY THE HAND LED  . . . . . .     121 LIT BOY FND/SI       5
    SHE TOOK ME ON HER LAP AND KISSED ME  . . . . . . .    125 LIT BLK BOY/SI       7
    THUS DID MY MOTHER SAY AND KISSED ME  . . . . . . .    125 LIT BLK BOY/SI      21
    KNEELD ROUND HIM AND KISSED HIS GARMENTS AND WEPT  . . .  139 FRENCH REVOLTN     123
    SHE WEPT SHE TREMBLED SHE KISSED SATAN SHE WEPT          489 MILTON 8            42
      OVER MICHAEL
    OF LAMBETH BUT HE KISSED ME AND WISHD ME HEALTH  . . . .  505 MILTON 22           11
KISSES
    THY SOFT KISSES ON HER BOSOM AND PUT  . . . . . . .       1 TO SPRING/PS        14
    GREEN GRASS SPRINGS IN JOY AND THE NIMBLE AIR KISSES THE  37B CONTEMPLATN/PS  PROSE
      LEAVES
    AND KISSES ME AND BINDS HIS NUPTIAL BANDS AROUND MY BREAST 129 BOOK OF THEL 5
    BUT HE WHO [JUST] KISSES THE JOY AS IT FLIES  . . . .    179 ETERNITY/N           3
    BUT HE WHO KISSES THE JOY AS IT FLIES  . . . . . .      184 SEVRL QUESTN/N      13
    TIRED WITH KISSES SWEET  . . . . . . . . . . . .     219 LIT GRL LST/SE      20
KISSING
    WAS LEFT A HELPLESS TRUNK THIS AFTER GRINNING & KISSING IT 157B MARRIAGE HH 17  PROSE
    KISSING HER AND WEEPING OVER HER  . . . . . . . .     250 AHANIA 2            35
    AND SOMETIMES KISSING HER ROBES & JEWELS & WEEPING OVER   356 FOUR ZOAS 8        611
      THEM
KITE
    A BOY FLYING A KITE  . . . . . . . . . . . . .     SUPP ILLUS GRAY      *TITLE
KITTY
    BUT KITTY I BETTER LOVE THEE  . . . . . . . . .        8 LOVE JOCUND/PS      18
    NOW KITTY NOW WHAT CHANCE HAST THOU  . . . . . . .       16 BLIND-MANS/PS       29
    NOW KITTY PERT REPEATS THE RHYMES  . . . . . . . .       16 BLIND-MANS/PS       43
    BUT KITTY HASTED WITH A KEY  . . . . . . . . . .        17 BLIND-MANS/PS       57
    KITTY ALONE KITTY ALONE  . . . . . . . . . . . .        55 THIS FROG/IM         2
    KITTY ALONE & I  . . . . . . . . . . . . . . .         55 THIS FROG/IM         4
    [THIS FROG] SING COCK I CARY KITTY ALONE  . . . . .      55 THIS FROG/IM   *     5
    KITTY ALONE KITTY ALONE  . . . . . . . . . . . .        55 THIS FROG/IM         6
    COCK I CARY KITTY ALONE  . . . . . . . . . . . .        55 THIS FROG/IM         7
    KITTY ALONE & I  . . . . . . . . . . . . . . .         55 THIS FROG/IM         8
KLOPSTOCK
    WHEN KLOPSTOCK ENGLAND DEFIED  . . . . . . . . .       186 WHEN KLOPSTK/N       1
    KLOPSTOCK FELT THE [NINEFOLD] INTRIPLED TURN  . . . .    187 WHEN KLOPSTK/N      15
    ?WHEREAT KLOPSTOCK ?DID SMILE  . . . . . . . . .       187 WHEN KLOPSTK/N *    32
KLOPSTOCK'S
    AND EASE POOR KLOPSTOCK'S NINE FOLD PAIN  . . . . .      187 WHEN KLOPSTK/N      28
    (PRAISE OF MRS KLOPSTOCK'S LETTERS)  . . . . . . .     849D LETTER 46       PROSE
KNAVE
    ("CAN HE LOVE TRUTH WHO CAN TAKE A KNAVE TO HIS BOSOM")   68A ANNO LAVATER     MARG
      NO
    THEREFORE PRONOUNCE HIM A KNAVE WHY SHOULD HONESTY FEAR   68B ANNO LAVATER     MARG
      A KNAVE
    AND THEN THE KNAVE BEGINS TO SNARL  . . . . . . .     183 MOTTO SONGS/N        5
    MODEST ENQUIRER INTO THE TRUTH OF A SELF EVIDENT THING   386C ANNO WATSON      MARG
      IS A KNAVE
    & MAY PRETEND TO BE A MODEST ENQUIRER BUT HE IS A KNAVE  386C ANNO WATSON      MARG
    ("DEMOCRACIES...COMMONLY ...QUIET ") SELF CONTRADICTION  401B ANNO BACON       MARG
      KNAVE & FOOL
    CONTEMPTIBLE KNAVE LET THE PEOPLE LOOK TO THIS  . . .    403A ANNO BACON       MARG
    FOOL & A CUNNING KNAVE SUITED TO THE PURPOSES OF        458B ANNO REYNOLDS    MARG
      EVIL DEMONS
    A FOOL & KNAVE HAVING NO CON-SCIENCE OR INNATE SCIENCE  . 459B ANNO REYNOLDS    MARG
    BUT SUCH A HIRED KNAVE CARES NOT FOR THE FEW  . . . .    469D ANNO REYNOLDS    MARG
    THE MAN WHO SAYS THAT THE GENIUS IS NOT BORN (BUT) TAUGHT 470A ANNO REYNOLDS  * MARG
      IS A KNAVE
    HE WAS BORN QUITE A FOOL BUT HE DIED QUITE A KNAVE  . .   470 ANNO REYNOLDS      2
    A PETTY SNEAKING KNAVE I KNEW  . . . . . . . . .       540 PETTY SNEAK/N        1
    A [KNAVE] FOOL TO A BOLT A [FOOL ] KNAVE TO A GLASS OF GIN 544 ON F AND S/N        4
    THE PARDONER THE AGE'S KNAVE WHO ALWAYS COMMANDS  . . .  570A DESC CAT 3     PROSE
    CHAUCER HIMSELF AS A KNAVE WHO THRUSTS HIMSELF  . . .    574D DESC CAT 3     PROSE
    HE HAS MADE HIM LOOK MORE LIKE A FOOL THAN A KNAVE  . .   574D DESC CAT 3     PROSE
    AS THERE MAY BE A FOOL OR A KNAVE IN AN EMBROIDERD COAT  593B PUB ADDRESS/N   PROSE
    THE KNAVE WHO IS CONVERTED TO [CHRISTIANITY] DEISM  . .   615B V LAST JUDG/N  PROSE
    & THE KNAVE WHO IS CONVERTED TO CHRISTIANITY IS STILL A  615B V LAST JUDG/N  PROSE
      KNAVE
    WHO WERE BOUND UNDER THE KNAVE NOT TO DELIVER THE KNAVE   615B V LAST JUDG/N  PROSE
```

1029

	PAGE	TITLE	LINE

KNAVE   (CONTINUED)
    ("BACON MASTER THOUGHTS OTHERS") [THIS IS THE CHARACTER   SUPP ANNO REYNOLDS * MARG
      OF A KNAVE]
    [THE KNAVE CALLS ANY THING ?FOUND IN NATURE FIT FOR ART]   SUPP ANNO REYNOLDS * MARG
KNAVERIES
    KNAVERIES ARE NOT HUMAN NATURE KNAVERIES ARE KNAVERIES   828 ANNO LAVATER   MARG
KNAVERY
    FOLLY IS THE CLOKE OF KNAVERY . . . . .151B MARRIAGE HH 7   PROSE
    I AM ASTONISHD HOW SUCH CONTEMPTIBLE KNAVERY & FOLLY . .397A ANNO BACON   MARG
    THAT KNAVERY IS WISDOM . . . . .397B ANNO BACON   MARG
    INDIGNANT AGAINST KNAVERY . . . . .414A ANNO BOYD   MARG
    HE IS LIKE SR JOSHUA FULL OF SELF-CONTRADICTION & KNAVERY   459D ANNO REYNOLDS   MARG
    DISTINGUISHES HONESTY FROM KNAVERY BUT THE HARD AND WIREY 585C DESC CAT 15   PROSE
    SO GOODNESS IS THE CLOKE OF KNAVERY . . . . . . .778B HOMERS POETRY   PROSE
KNAVES
    ON THE BIBLE ARE DISHONEST DESIGNING KNAVES . . . . .390C ANNO WATSON   MARG
    WHAT DO THESE KNAVES MEAN BY VIRTUE . . . . . .400A ANNO BACON   MARG
    ACQUAINTANCE WITH KNAVES . . . . .405B ANNO BACON   MARG
    OPRESSION OF SR JOSHUA & HIS GANG OF CUNNING HIRED KNAVES 445B ANNO REYNOLDS   MARG
    WHEN FRANCE GOT FREE EUROPE TWIXT FOOLS & KNAVES . . .451 ANNO REYNOLDS   1
    MAKES BOTH STATESMEN & ARTISTS FOOLS & KNAVES . . .461C ANNO REYNOLDS   MARG
    TIS CHRISTIAN MILDNESS WHEN [FOOLS] KNAVES PRAISE A FOE   539 SIR JOSH MIC/N   4
    THOSE WHO SAY THAT MEN ARE LED BY INTEREST ARE KNAVES . .572D DESC CAT 3   PROSE
    HE HAS LAUGHED AT HIS KNAVES AND FOOLS AS I DO NOW . .575A DESC CAT 3   PROSE
    IT BECAME THE INTEREST OF CERTAIN ENVIOUS KNAVES . . . .602C PUB ADDRESS/N   PROSE
    ALL LIFE CONSISTS OF THESE TWO THROWING OFF ERROR & KNAVES 612D V LAST JUDG/N   PROSE
    [?KNOWN ?SUCH ?KNAVES XXX] . . . . .SUPP ANNO REYNOLDS * MARG
KNAVISH
    A KNAVISH CHARACTER WILL OFTEN SAY OF WHAT INTEREST IS   572D DESC CAT 3   PROSE
      IT TO ME
KNEAD
    KNEAD BREAD OF SORROW BY MY STERN COMMAND FOR I AM GOD . .322 FOUR ZOAS 7   93
    . . . & KNEAD THE BREAD OF KNOWLEDGE WITH TEARS & GROANS   379 FOUR ZOAS 9   820
KNEADED
    OF ELETH & THE ICY HANDS OF UVETH KNEADED THE BREAD . . .322 FOUR ZOAS 7   102
    THE BREAD IS KNEADED LET US REST O CRUEL FATHER OF CHILDREN 322 FOUR ZOAS 7   107
    KNEADED IN UVETH'S KNEADING TROUGH STILL ORC DEVOURD THE   343 FOUR ZOAS 8 * 77
      FOOD
KNEADING
    ON CLOUDS OF DEATH & SANG THEIR SONGS KNEADING THE BREAD   322 FOUR ZOAS 7   98
      OF ORC
    KNEADED IN UVETH'S KNEADING TROUGH STILL ORC DEVOURD THE   343 FOUR ZOAS 8 * 77
      FOOD
KNEE
    EACH HEART DOES TREMBLE AND EACH KNEE GROWS SLACK . . . .34A KING JOHN/PS   PROSE
    THE BLIND MAN HEARD HIS BROTHER'S VOICE & KNEELD DOWN ON   104 TIRIEL 4   10
      HIS KNEE
    [HE SPOKE & KNEELD UPON HIS KNEE THEN IJIM ON THE PAVEMENT] 106 TIRIEL 4   81
    TO LEAN IN JOY UPON OUR FATHER'S KNEE . . . . . . .125 LIT BLK BOY/SI   26
    . . . OR CROAK ON THE AWFUL KNEE . . . . .147 FRENCH REVOLTN   298
    [WHAT THE [SHOULDER] ANKLE WHAT THE KNEE] . . . . .173 THE TYGER/N 1 * 27
    A FAIRY [LEAPT] SKIPD UPON MY KNEE . . . . . . .188 A FAIRY SKIPD * 1
    THE HEAD AND THE KNEE TO HIM WHO IN EVERY AGE SENDS US . .570C DESC CAT 3   PROSE
KNEED   SEE STIFF-KNEED
KNEEL
    [BUT I CAN KNEEL DOWN AT YOUR DOOR I AM A HARMLESS MAN]   101 TIRIEL 2   29
    AND I KNEEL DOWN THAT YOU MAY SEE I AM A HARMLESS MAN . .101 TIRIEL 2   31
    LOWING THEY KNEEL BEFORE THE HEAVENS THE WILD BEASTS OF   358 FOUR ZOAS 9   55
      THE FORESTS
    ABRAHAM & MOSES KNEEL ON EACH SIDE BENEATH THEM . . . .443B LAST JUDGMNT/L   PROSE
    THESE KNEEL ON EACH SIDE OF THE THRONE WHICH IS . . .444B LAST JUDGMNT/L   PROSE
    THEY ASCEND FROM THE EARTH WHERE FIGURES KNEEL . . . .610B V LAST JUDG/N   PROSE
    ADAM EVE THOU HAST SPOKEN TRULY LET US KNEEL BEFORE HIS   780 GHOST ABEL 2   3
      FEET
    THEY KNEEL BEFORE JEHOVAH . . . . .780C GHOST ABEL 2   PROSE
KNEELD
    THE BLIND MAN HEARD HIS BROTHER'S VOICE & KNEELD DOWN ON   104 TIRIEL 4   10
      HIS KNEE
    [HE SPOKE & KNEELD UPON HIS KNEE THEN IJIM ON THE PAVEMENT] 106 TIRIEL 4   81
    KNEELD ROUND HIM AND KISSED HIS GARMENTS AND WEPT . . .139 FRENCH REVOLTN   123
    THE CHILDREN WOKE & SMILD ON VALA SHE KNEELD BY THE GOLDEN 371 FOUR ZOAS 9   523
      COUCH
    GROANING HE KNEELD BEFORE LOS'S IRON-SHOD FEET ON LONDON   627 JERUSALEM 8   27
      STONE
    THEY KNEELD AROUND THE COUCH OF DEATH IN DEEP HUMILIATION   668 JERUSALEM 41   24
KNEELED
    HE KNEELED DOWN & MNETHA SAID COME HAR & HEVA RISE . . .101 TIRIEL 2   32
    THEY WERE INTRODUCD TO THE DIVINE PRESENCE & THEY KNEELED   277 FOUR ZOAS 1   482
      DOWN
    MY LUVAH SMILD I KNEELED DOWN HE LAID HIS HAND ON MY HEAD   369 FOUR ZOAS 9   468
KNEELING
    KNEELING IN HUMILIATION AS REPRESENTATIVES OF THE WHOLE   443B LAST JUDGMNT/L   PROSE
      HUMAN RACE
    OTHER BOTH HELD ABOVE HER HEAD & A FIGURE KNEELING AT HER   839C LETTER 38   PROSE
      FEET
KNEELS
    THE WEEPING VIRGIN TREMBLING KNEELS BEFORE THE RISEN SUN   128 BOOK OF THEL 3   14
    FROM THE CLOUD ON WHICH EVE KNEELS [& BENEATH MOSES] . .443B LAST JUDGMNT/L   PROSE
    ON THE RIGHT BENEATH THE CLOUD ON WHICH ABEL KNEELS . . .606C V LAST JUDG/N   PROSE
    ABEL KNEELS ON A BLOODY CLOUD &C . . . . .606D V LAST JUDG/N   PROSE
    ABEL KNEELS ON A BLOODY CLOUD DESCRIPTIVE OF THOSE CHURCHES 606D V LAST JUDG/N   PROSE
    BENEATH THE CLOUD ON WHICH MOSES KNEELS IS TWO FIGURES . .607C V LAST JUDG/N   PROSE

KNEELS   (CONTINUED)   PAGE   TITLE   LINE
  ADAM KNEELS BY HER JEHOVAH STANDS ABOVE . . . . 779C GHOST ABEL 1   PROSE
KNEES
  DOWN ON HIS HANDS AND KNEES HE LAY   . . . .   16 BLIND-MANS/PS   47
  SHE STILL INTREATS AND STILL SHE GRASPS HIS VIGOROUS KNEES   38B SAMSON/PS PROSE
  WITH STOCKINGS ROLLD ABOVE THEIR KNEES & SHOES AS BLACK   58 THIS CITY/IM   *   6
    AS [GIT] JET
  O IJIM I AM FAINT & WEARY FOR MY KNEES FORBID . . . . .   104 TIRIEL 4   32
  [THAT WE MAY TREMBLE & REPENT BEFORE THY MIGHTY KNEES] .   105 TIRIEL 4   76
  . . . ON HIS HANDS AND KNEES DAY AND NIGHT WITHOUT REST   136 FRENCH REVOLTN 46
  HIS KNEES AND THIGHS LIKE SILVER & HIS BREAST AND HEAD   199 AMERICA 8   17
    LIKE GOLD
  APPROACHD URIZEN EVEN TO HIS KNEES   . . . .   250 AHANIA 3   15
  NOR WEEP ON HIS KNEES NOR HEAR   . . . .   254 AHANIA 4   66
  RED WITH THE BLOOD OF MEN SWELLS LUSTFUL ROUND MY ROCKY   275 FOUR ZOAS 1   391
    KNEES
  I [EMBRACES] EMBRACE ROUND THY KNEES & . . . .   291 FOUR ZOAS 3   4
  . . . HIS KNEES EACH OTHER SMOTE & THEN HE LOOKD . . .   305 FOUR ZOAS 4   290
  HE STOOD TREMBLING & ENITHARMON CLUNG AROUND HIS KNEES .   305 FOUR ZOAS 5   18
  HIS KNEES ARE ROCKS OF ADAMANT & RUBIE & EMERALD . . . .   308 FOUR ZOAS 5   * 139
  SWEET INSTRUMENTS OF SOUND IN PRIDE ENCOMPASSING MY KNEES   312 FOUR ZOAS 6   32
  WHERE MY SONS GATHERD ROUND MY KNEES O THOU POOR RUIND   317 FOUR ZOAS 6   209
    WORLD
  HIS BOOK OF IRON ON HIS KNEES HE TRACD THE DREADFUL LETTERS 321 FOUR ZOAS 7   29
  ENITHARMON LAY ON HIS KNEES URIZEN TRACD HIS VERSES . . .   324 FOUR ZOAS 7   169
  HIS NAKED LIMBS GLITTRING UPON THE DARK BLUE SKY HIS KNEES   334 FOUR ZOAS 7B * 42
  THE CHILDREN CLUNG AROUND HER KNEES SHE EMBRACD THEM &   370 FOUR ZOAS 9   509
    WEPT OVER THEM
  HER KNEES & ELBOWS ARE ONLY . . . .   418 WHEN MAN HAS/N   3
  HIS BODY BENT HIS ARMS & KNEES   . . . .   419 I SAW A MONK/N   17
  HIS BODY BENT HIS ARMS & KNEES   . . . .   430 GREY MONK   7
  UPON HIS KNEES BEFORE THE LIVING & THE DEAD   . . . .   444C LAST JUDGMNT/L PROSE
  LONDON IS BETWEEN HIS KNEES ITS BASEMENTS FOURFOLD . . .   531 MILTON 39   39
  WITH THE WORD OF DIVINE REVELATION ON HIS KNEES . . . .   606B V LAST JUDG/N PROSE
  DESCENDED AND FELL DOWN UPON THEIR KNEES ROUND ALBION'S   666 JERUSALEM 40   8
    KNEES
  HIS BODY BENT HIS ARMS & KNEES   . . . .   683 I SAW A MONK/J   15
  HIS CHILDREN TO MY BREASTS HIS SONS & DAUGHTERS TO MY KNEES 720 JERUSALEM 79   26
  THERE BELLS OF SILVER ROUND THY KNEES LIVING ARTICULATE   731 JERUSALEM 86   29
  FALLING DOWN ON THEIR KNEES RUNNING SIDEWAYS & IN . .   833B LETTER 33   PROSE
  AND KNEES IS ENTIRELY REDUCED SHE IS VERY NEAR AS FREE .   851C LETTER 50   PROSE
KNEW
  I KNEW THOU DIDST BUT MOCK ME ALAS WHEN IN THY SLEEP .   39A SAMSON/PS   PROSE
  CHILDLESS HE MOURNED BUT THOUGHT HIS GOD KNEW BEST . . .   39C SAMSON/PS   PROSE
  NOR KNEW HE WAS AN ANGEL MANOA LEFT HIS FIELDS . . .   40A SAMSON/PS   PROSE
  SHE KNEW THEM NOT YET THEY ALL WAR WITH SHAME . . .   40D THEN SHE BORE   PROSE
  NOR KNEW THAT JOY WAS BORN AND TAKING POISNOUS SEED . .   40D THEN SHE BORE   PROSE
  BUT KNEW NOT THAT THE REST WAS GIVN TO SHAME . . . .   41A THEN SHE BORE   PROSE
  TRULY RELIGIOUS AS FAR AS HE KNEW   . . . .   75A ANNO LAVATER   MARG
  HE KNEW TWAS VAIN FOR IJIM'S WORDS WERE AS THE VOICE OF   104 TIRIEL 4   27
    FATE
  THEY KNEW TWAS VAIN TO STRIVE WITH IJIM THEY BOWD & SILENT   105 TIRIEL 4   48
    STOOD
  CONFOUNDED AT THE TERRIBLE STRENGTH OF IJIM THEY KNEW TWAS   105 TIRIEL 4   69
    VAIN
  AND SAID ALAS I KNEW NOT THIS AND THEREFORE DID I WEEP .   130 BOOK OF THEL 5   8
  THAT GOD WOULD LOVE A WORM I KNEW AND PUNISH THE EVIL FOOT   130 BOOK OF THEL 5   9
  WITH MILK AND OIL I NEVER KNEW AND THEREFORE DID I WEEP   130 BOOK OF THEL 5 11
  THEN FLED AND THE WHOLE CITY KNEW HE WAS FLED TO GENEVA   139 FRENCH REVOLTN 124
    . . .
  AND HE KNEW THAT IT WAS MINE   . . . .   165 CHRISTN FORB/N   13
  AN OLD MAID EARLY EER I KNEW   . . . .   184 O I CANNOT/N   5
  AND HE KNEW THAT IT WAS MINE   . . . .   218 POISON TREE/SE   12
  THEN ENITHARMON WOKE NOR KNEW THAT SHE HAD SLEPT . . . .   243 EUROPE 13   9
  BROUGHT HIM IN VARIOUS FORMS BEFORE HER STILL SHE KNEW   286 FOUR ZOAS 2   233
    HIM NOT
  I KNOW THEE NOT AS ONCE I KNEW THEE IN THOSE BLESSED FIELDS 288 FOUR ZOAS 2   325
  WHILE YET THOSE BEINGS WERE NOT BORN NOR KNEW OF GOOD OR   304 FOUR ZOAS 4   274
    EVIL
  URIZEN KNEW THEM NOT & THUS ADDRESSD THE SPIRITS   311 FOUR ZOAS 6   *   7
    OF DARKNESS
  THEY GAVE A SCREAM THEY KNEW THEIR FATHER URIZEN KNEW   312 FOUR ZOAS 6   21
    HIS DAUGHTERS
  HE KNEW THEY WERE HIS CHILDREN RUIND IN HIS RUIND WORLD   315 FOUR ZOAS 6   130
  OF GOLD & SILVER BRASS & IRON HE KNEW HIS MIGHTY SONS . .   319 FOUR ZOAS 6   315
  NOR KNEW THE SOURCE OF HIS OWN BUT THOUGHT HIMSELF THE   324 FOUR ZOAS 7   159
    SOLE AUTHOR
  HE KNEW THAT WEAKNESS STRETCHES OUT IN BREADTH & LENGTH   324 FOUR ZOAS 7   161
    HE KNEW
  INTO SUBMISSION TO HIS WILL NOR KNEW THE DREAD RESULT . .   324 FOUR ZOAS 7   165
  NOR KNEW THAT I ALONE EXEMPTED FROM THE JOYS OF LOVE . .   325 FOUR ZOAS 7   200
  TO BIND THE FATHER & ENSLAVE THE BRETHREN NOUGHT HE KNEW   326 FOUR ZOAS 7   256
  IT WAS BY THAT I KNEW THAT I HAD SINND & THEN I KNEW . .   329 FOUR ZOAS 7   388
  AND KNEW HE WAS THE SAVIOUR EVEN JESUS & THEY WORSHIPPED   342 FOUR ZOAS 8   44
  PERPLEXD & TERRIFID HE STOOD THO WELL HE KNEW THAT ORC .   342 FOUR ZOAS 8   62
  HE KNEW NOTHING OF GOD IN THE BISHOP'S SENSE OF THE WORD   389C ANNO WATSON   MARG
  AS IF HE KNEW THAT THERE WERE RECORDS   . . . . . .   394A ANNO WATSON   MARG
  THE ANCIENTS KNEW BETTER   . . . .   394A ANNO WATSON   MARG
  AS COLD EARTH WANDERERS NEVER KNEW   . . . .   424 MENTAL TRAVLER   4
  I KNEW IMMEDIATELY THE DIFFERENCE BETWEEN RAFAEL & RUBENS   447C ANNO REYNOLDS MARG
  WHETHER REYNOLDS KNEW WHAT HE WAS DOING IS NOTHING TO ME   452A ANNO REYNOLDS MARG
  MICH ANG KNEW & DESPISED ALL THAT TITIAN COULD DO   . .   464A ANNO REYNOLDS MARG

```
                                                          PAGE      TITLE          LINE
KNEW   (CONTINUED)
   KNEW NOT THE SMALLER BEAUTIES OF THE ART    . . . . .  467A ANNO REYNOLDS       MARG
   KNEW NOTHING AT ALL ABOUT ART AS AN OBJECT OF IMITATION 467B ANNO REYNOLDS      MARG
   & THAT SUCH IDIOTS AS RUBENS CORREGGIO & TITIAN KNEW  . 467B ANNO REYNOLDS      MARG
   IF SO THEY KNEW ALL THAT TITIAN & CORREGGIO KNEW . .  . 471C ANNO REYNOLDS      MARG
   POUSSIN KNEW BETTER THAT(THAN) TO MAKE ALL HIS PICTURES 477C ANNO REYNOLDS      MARG
   THEN LOS & ENITHARMON KNEW THAT SATAN IS URIZEN  . . .  490 MILTON 10         *   1
   KNEW THAT I WAS NOT ELYNITTRIA AND THEY BRAKE THE TRACES 492 MILTON 12           13
   THEN MILTON KNEW THAT THE THREE HEAVENS OF BEULAH WERE  497 MILTON 15           51
      BEHELD
   IN THE DARK ULRO TILL THE JUDGMENT ALSO MILTON KNEW THEY 498 MILTON 17           5
      AND
   PONDERING HE KNEW THAT RINTRAH & PALAMABRON MIGHT DEPART 503 MILTON 20           52
   BUT I KNEW NOT THAT IT WAS MILTON FOR MAN CANNOT KNOW . 503 MILTON 21            8
   DRIVEN MILTON INTO THE ULRO FOR NOW THEY KNEW TOO LATE . 504 MILTON 21           32
   ACCOMPLISHD IN THIS WORLD OF SORROW MILTON'S ANGEL KNEW 504 MILTON 21            52
   HE KNEW BOTH LAW & GOSPEL BETTER THAN THEY   . . . .  537 AND HIS LEGS/N        31
   A PETTY SNEAKING KNAVE I KNEW  . . . . . . . . .     540 PETTY SNEAK/N          1
   THE ONLY MAN THAT EER I KNEW  . . . . . . . .     551 ONLY MAN/N              1
   BOTH RAFAEL AND MICHAEL ANGELO KNEW THE VENETIAN AND . 563C DESC CAT          PROSE
   AND BUNGLING GREAT INVENTORS IN ALL AGES KNEW THIS . . 585B DESC CAT 15       PROSE
   PROTOGENES AND APELLES KNEW EACH OTHER BY THIS LINE . . 585B DESC CAT 15      PROSE
   I KNEW THE MEN INTIMATELY FROM THEIR INTIMACY WITH BASIRE 593B PUB ADDRESS/N  PROSE
   MY MASTER & KNEW THEM BOTH TO BE    . . . . .       593B PUB ADDRESS/N       PROSE
   STRANGE'S PRINTS WERE WHEN I KNEW HIM ALL DONE BY ALIAMET 594A PUB ADDRESS/N PROSE
   I ALSO KNEW SOMETHING OF TOM COOKE WHO ENGRAVED   . . 594B PUB ADDRESS/N     PROSE
   TO YOUR OWN DESTRUCTION WOOLETT I KNEW VERY INTIMATELY . 603B PUB ADDR AD/N   PROSE
   BY HIS INTIMACY WITH BASIRE & I KNEW HIM TO BE  . . . 603B PUB ADDR AD/N     PROSE
   ONE OF THE MOST IGNORANT FELLOWS THAT I EVER KNEW  . . 603B PUB ADDR AD/N    PROSE
   HE HIMSELF KNEW BUT HIS IMPUDENCE HAD A CONTRARY EFFECT 603C PUB ADDR AD/N   PROSE
      ON ME
   I KNEW NOT OF THEIR SECRET LOVES WITH THOSE I HATED MOST 644 JERUSALEM 21       26
   ENITHARMON & HIS SPECTRE IS NAMED URTHONA THEY KNEW . . 655 JERUSALEM 30        4
   THEY DENY THAT THEY EVER KNEW JERUSALEM OR EVER DWELT   679 JERUSALEM 49        9
      IN SHILOH
   LOS KNEW NOT YET WHAT WAS DONE HE THOUGHT IT WAS ALL IN 698 JERUSALEM 63       36
      VISION
   THEY KNEW NOT THIS VALA WAS THEIR BELOVED MOTHER VALA   701 JERUSALEM 65       71
      ALBION'S WIFE
   VAST & SEVERE THE ANGUISH EER THEY KNEW THEIR FATHER WERE 713 JERUSALEM 73      8
   THE APOSTLES KNEW OF NO OTHER GOSPEL  . . . . . . .  717A JERUSALEM 77       PROSE
   THE NATIONS OF INDIA THE WILD TARTAR THAT NEVER KNEW MAN 729 JERUSALEM 84      23
   BY THE LOST SHEEP THAT HE HATH FOUND & ALBION KNEW THAT IT 743 JERUSALEM 96     4
   MY SHADOW I KNEW   . . . . . . . . . . .          805 TO BUTTS/L           39
   KNEW IMMEDIATELY MY PORTRAIT OF ROMNEY & ASSURED ME . . 836B LETTER 35       PROSE
   IN MANY POINTS I HAVE SEEN THE ELDER MR WALKER HE KNEW . 843B LETTER 43      PROSE
   YOUNGER THAN I KNEW HIM BUT VERY LIKE INDEED MR WALKER . 843C LETTER 43      PROSE
   WHO KNEW MOST CONCERNING HIM OF ANY ONE LAMENTED . . . 846A LETTER 44        PROSE
   BY ASKING IF HE KNEW WHO FURNISHD THE PAPER HE ANSWERED 846D LETTER 44       PROSE
   THEY KNEW MY INDUSTRY AND ABSTINENCE FROM EVERY PLEASURE 852B LETTER 50      PROSE
   IS A PUBLIC LOSS WHICH THOSE WHO KNEW HIM CAN BEST ESTIMATE 854B LETTER 53   PROSE
   HE SAID I KNEW THAT DODSLEY WAS MR HAYLEY'S PUBLISHER BUT 856B LETTER 54     PROSE
   FOR OUR GOOD SEAGRAVE & SAID I KNEW YOUR CHIEF INTENTIONS 856B LETTER 54     PROSE
      IN
   ACCORDINGLY I DID NOT SAY THAT I KNEW OF ANY POEM BUT  . 857A LETTER 54      PROSE
KNIFE
   HE'LL PLUNGE HIS KNIFE UP TO THE HILT IN A SINGLE DRIVE  50A ISLAND MOON 6   PROSE
   AND FORMD A CROOKED KNIFE   . . . . . . . . . .     50 WHEN CORRUP/IM        14
   . . . AND WITH A KNIFE SMOTE HIM   . . . . . . .    135 FRENCH REVOLTN        37
   LUVAH WALKING ON THE WINDS I SEE THE INVISIBLE KNIFE . . 272 FOUR ZOAS 1       300
   WHY IS THE SHEEP GIVEN TO THE KNIFE THE LAMB PLAYS IN THE 276 FOUR ZOAS 1      454
      SUN
   SHE SMITES WITH HER KNIFE OF FLINT SHE DESTROYS HER OWN  347 FOUR ZOAS 8      234
      WORK
   SEVEN OF MY SWEET LOVES THY KNIFE   . . . . . . .   416 MY SPECTRE/N          35
   AND YET FORGIVES THE BUTCHER'S KNIFE  . . . . . . . . 431 AUGURIES            24
   THE OAK IS CUT DOWN BY THE AX THE LAMB FALLS BY THE KNIFE 522 MILTON 32         37
   . . . SWORD OR A CUTLASS A DAGGER OR KNIFE   . . . . . 548 ON GREAT ENC/N      2
   AT BASIRE'S BY LAUGHING AT BASIRE'S KNIFE TOOLS &  . . 603C PUB ADDR AD/N    PROSE
   BUT COME O VALA WITH KNIFE & CUP DRAIN MY BLOOD  . . . . 645 JERUSALEM 22      29
   AND THE DRUIDS GOLDEN KNIFE  . . . . . . . . . .    650 FIELDS FROM/J        30
   THEY FLEE OVER THE ROCKS BONIFYING HORSES OXEN FEEL THE  689 JERUSALEM 58       9
      KNIFE
   THE HERMAPHRODITIC CONDENSATIONS ARE DIVIDED BY THE KNIFE 689 JERUSALEM 58     11
   HE SAW IN VALA'S HAND THE DRUID KNIFE OF REVENGE & THE   698 JERUSALEM 63      39
      POISON CUP
   THE KNIFE OF FLINT PASSES OVER THE HOWLING VICTIM HIS BLOOD 702 JERUSALEM 66   20
   YORK & LINCOLN HIDE AMONG THE FLOCKS BECAUSE OF THE GRIDING 703 JERUSALEM 66   65
      KNIFE
   AS THE SENSES OF MEN SHRINK TOGETHER UNDER THE KNIFE OF  703 JERUSALEM 66      83
      FLINT
   TIRZAH SITS WEEPING TO HEAR THE SHRIEKS OF THE DYING HER 704 JERUSALEM 67      24
      KNIFE
   HE BURND BEFORE ME LUVAH FRAMD THE KNIFE & LUVAH GAVE  . . 722 JERUSALEM 80    22
   THE KNIFE INTO HIS DAUGHTER'S HAND SUCH THING WAS NEVER  722 JERUSALEM 80      23
      KNOWN
   WHERE THE VICTIM NIGHTLY HOWLS BENEATH THE DRUID'S KNIFE 727 JERUSALEM 83      12
   I HAVE SLAIN HIM IN MY SLEEP WITH THE KNIFE OF THE DRUID 742 JERUSALEM 94      25
      O ENGLAND
KNIGHT
   THE KNIGHT AND SQUIRE WITH THE SQUIRE'S YEOMAN LEAD  . . 566D DESC CAT 3     PROSE
   DIRECTS THEM TO THE KNIGHT AS THE PERSON WHO WOULD      566D DESC CAT 3      PROSE
      BE LIKELY
```

		PAGE	TITLE	LINE

KNIGHT   (CONTINUED)
    THE KNIGHT AND SQUIRE WITH THE SQUIRE'S YEOMAN LEAD THE   567D DESC CAT 3   PROSE
        PROCESSION
    THE KNIGHT IS A TRUE HERO A GOOD GREAT AND WISE MAN . . .   567D DESC CAT 3   PROSE
    GENEROUS KNIGHT IS IN THE COMPASSIONATE DICTATES OF HIS   569A DESC CAT 3   PROSE
        SOUL
    TWO FIRST CHARACTERS IN CHAUCER THE KNIGHT AND THE SQUIRE   573C DESC CAT 3   PROSE
    BETWEEN HIS KNIGHT AND SQUIRE AS IF HE WAS . . . . . .   574A DESC CAT 3   PROSE
    THE KNIGHT & SQUIRE WITH THE SQUIRE'S YEOMAN LEAD . . .   588B CHAUCER/N   PROSE
    KNIGHT WHOSE SOLEMN GALLANTRY NO LESS FIXES ATTENTION .   588C CHAUCER/N   PROSE
    THE KNIGHT AND SQUIRE WITH THE SQUIRE'S AND YEOMAN LEAD   589D CHAUCER 2   PROSE
    DIRECTS THEM TO THE KNIGHT AS THE PERSON WHO WILL BE LIKELY   589D CHAUCER 2   PROSE
KNIGHTS
    HE HERE KNIGHTS THE PRINCE AND OTHER YOUNG NOBLES   . . .   18D EDW THIRD/PS 1 PROSE
KNITS
    THEN CRUELTY KNITS A SNARE . . . .   174 HUMAN IMAGE/N   8
    THEN CRUELTY KNITS A SNARE . . . .   217 HUMAN ABSTR/SE   7
KNITTED
    HAST THOU AGAIN KNITTED THE VEIL OF VALA WHICH I FOR THEE   645 JERUSALEM 23   5
KNIVES
    THEIR VICTIMS & WITH KNIVES TORMENTING THEM SINGING WITH   348 FOUR ZOAS 8   * 296
        TEARS
    THE CRUEL JOY OF LUVAH'S DAUGHTERS LACERATING WITH KNIVES   377 FOUR ZOAS 9   753
    THEIR VICTIMS & WITH [SONGS] KNIVES TORMENTING THEM . . .   382 FOUR ZOAS AD 6   12
    THE CRUEL JOYS OF LUVAH'S DAUGHTERS LACERATING WITH KNIVES   514 MILTON 27   35
    THEY TAKE OFF HIS VESTURE WHOLE WITH THEIR KNIVES OF FLINT   702 JERUSALEM 66   26
KNOCK
    OF THE PULPIT STAIRS & KNOCK HIM DOWN & RUN AWAY   . . .   48B ISLAND MOON 4 PROSE
    IF I DONT KNOCK THEM ALL UP NEXT YEAR IN THE EXHIBITION   51D ISLAND MOON 7 PROSE
    AND CAUGHT HIM IN MY HAT AS BOYS KNOCK DOWN A BUTTERFLY   237 EUROPE INTRO   9
    TAPROOM THREATENED TO KNOCK WILLIAM'S EYES OUT   . . . .   438C BLAKES MEMORAN PROSE
    [YE] COME ARTISTS KNOCK YOUR HEADS AGAINST THIS STONE   .   537 AND HIS LEGS/N   46
    COME KNOCK YOUR HEADS AGAINST THIS STONE . . . .   545 AN EPITAPH/N   1
    INTO THE FRAME THEN KNOCK IT OUT UPON THE PLANK & SOULS   657 JERUSALEM 31   11
        ARE BAKD
    DEPARTURE HE THEN THREATEND TO KNOCK OUT MY EYES . . . .   827A LETTER 28   PROSE
KNOCKD
    HE HAS KNOCKD DOWN THE WICKET . . . .   61 SAY YOU JOE/IM   14
    WHEN MY HEART KNOCKD AGAINST THE ROOT OF MY TONGUE   . . .   817 HAPPINESS/L   8
KNOCKED
    AND KNOCKED ABOUT WITHOUT MERCY TO TRY ALL EXPERIMENTS .   583D DESC CAT 9   PROSE
KNOT
    SHE TIES THE KNOT OF NERVOUS FIBRES INTO A WHITE BRAIN .   501 MILTON 19   55
    SHE TIES THE KNOT OF BLOODY VEINS INTO A RED HOT HEART .   501 MILTON 19   56
    SHE TIES THE KNOT OF MILKY SEED INTO TWO LOVELY HEAVENS   501 MILTON 19   60
    THUNDRING THE VEIL RUSHES FROM HIS HAND VEGETATING KNOT BY   648 JERUSALEM 24   61
    KNOT DAY BY DAY NIGHT BY NIGHT LOUD ROLL THE INDIGNANT   648 JERUSALEM 24   62
        ATLANTIC
    AND NERVES INTO TWO KNOTS & THE SEED INTO A DOUBLE KNOT   703 JERUSALEM 66   49
KNOTS
    IN HIS HAND A KNOTTED CLUB WHOSE KNOTS LIKE MOUNTAINS   319 FOUR ZOAS 6   305
        FROWND
    AND NERVES INTO TWO KNOTS & THE SEED INTO A DOUBLE KNOT   703 JERUSALEM 66   49
KNOTTED
    SO TWISTED THE CORDS & SO KNOTTED . . . .   235 URIZEN 25   20
    IN HIS HAND A KNOTTED CLUB WHOSE KNOTS LIKE MOUNTAINS   319 FOUR ZOAS 6   305
        FROWND
KNOTTY
    AND WIELDING KNOTTY CLUBS LIKE OAKS ENTANGLED . . . . .   32 EDW THIRD/PS 6   23
KNOW
    WHY MY LORD AUDLEY I DONT KNOW . . . .   21 EDW THIRD/PS 3   6
    I THINK YOU DO NOT KNOW EDWARD S AFRAID OF PHILIP   . . .   21 EDW THIRD/PS 3   8
    TO-MORROW WE SHALL KNOW I SAY LORD AUDLEY . . . . .   22 EDW THIRD/PS 3   22
    I DO NOT THINK SIR THOMAS YOU KNOW WHAT FEAR IS . . . .   22 EDW THIRD/PS 3   42
    I DONT KNOW PERHAPS HE TAKES IT BY FITS . . . .   22 EDW THIRD/PS 3   48
    I KNOW YOU UNDERSTAND ME A DISTEMPER . . . .   22 EDW THIRD/PS 3   56
    RETREATS WE ALL SHALL KNOW HOW TO RETREAT . . . . .   23 EDW THIRD/PS 3   64
    I KNOW NOT WHAT YOU COULD HAVE ASKD SIR THOMAS   . . . .   23 EDW THIRD/PS 3   105
    NAY I WILL KNOW THE MOST REMOTE PARTICULARS . . . . .   24 EDW THIRD/PS 3   108
    WE FALL WITH GLORY I KNOW THE WOLF . . . .   27 EDW THIRD/PS 3   265
    WE HAVE OUR BATTLE FOR OUR PAINS I KNOW . . . . . .   27 EDW THIRD/PS 3   268
    YES I HAVE I HAVE A GREAT AMBITION TO KNOW EVERY THING SIR   28D THIRD/PS 4   PROSE
    ALL BE WRONG OF COURSE TIS BEST TO KNOW A LITTLE . . . .   28D THIRD/PS 4   PROSE
    AND TO KNOW THAT LITTLE ARIGHT . . . .   28D THIRD/PS 4   PROSE
    THEN SIR I SHOULD BE GLAD TO KNOW IF IT WAS NOT AMBITION   28D THIRD/PS 4   PROSE
    TO KNOW THE MOTIVES OF THEIR OWN ACTIONS . . . . . .   29A THIRD/PS 4   PROSE
    AND GIVEN HIM I DONT KNOW WHAT AND I CAN'T TELL . . . .   29C THIRD/PS 4   PROSE
    AND WHO IS THIS MINSTREL PETER DOST KNOW . . . . .   29C THIRD/PS 4   PROSE
    I KNOW YOUR HONOUR DOES NOT THINK ANY THING OF YOURSELF   29D THIRD/PS 4   PROSE
    I DONT KNOW THAT . . . .   29D THIRD/PS 4   PROSE
    WHY YOU KNOW SIR WHEN WE WERE IN ENGLAND AT THE TOURNAMENT   29D THIRD/PS 4   PROSE
        AT WINDSOR
    I KNOW THIS BREATHING FLESH MUST LIE AND ROT . . . . .   30 EDW THIRD/PS 5   4
    I KNOW BUT LITTLE OF THE PATH THOU GOEST   . . . . . .   36A COUCH DEATH/PS PROSE
    SWEET CONTEMPLATION [SHE TEACHETH KNOWLEDGE HOW TO KNOW]   42A THEN SHE BORE PROSE
    TIS CONTEMPLATION TEACHETH KNOWLEDGE TRULY HOW TO KNOW . .   42A THEN SHE BORE *PROSE
    THE CORNERS OF HER MOUTH SEEMD I DONT KNOW HOW . . . .   44B ISLAND MOON 1 PROSE
    TO CALL A MAN A BLOCKHEAD THAT YOU KNOW NOTHING OF . . .   44D ISLAND MOON 1 PROSE
    HAY HOW SHOULD I KNOW ANSWERD OBTUSE ANGLE WHO WAS   47A ISLAND MOON 3 PROSE
        IT ARADOBO
    YOU THOUGHT HE WAS NOT [WHY I KNOW THAT] WHY I KNOW THAT   48D ISLAND MOON 5 *PROSE
    OH NO SIR I THOUGHT THAT HE WAS NOT BUT I ASKD TO KNOW . .   49A ISLAND MOON 5 PROSE

1033

		PAGE	TITLE	LINE

KNOW   (CONTINUED)

WHEN I THINK OF SURGERY I DONT KNOW I DO IT . . . . . 51C ISLAND MOON 6 PROSE
A POOR FRAIL MAN GOD WOT I KNOW NONE FRAILER . . . . . . 52 HEAR THEN/IM 3
I KNOW NO GREATER SINNER THAN JOHN TAYLOR . . . . . . 52 HEAR THEN/IM 4
TO VAUXHALL & RANELAGH I HARDLY KNOW WHAT A COACH IS . 53A ISLAND MOON 8 PROSE
YOU HARDLY KNOW SHE HAS A TONGUE IN HER HEAD . . . . 53A ISLAND MOON 8 PROSE
THEN SAID MISS GITTIPIN MR SCOPPRELL DO YOU KNOW . . . . 53C ISLAND MOON 8 PROSE
HE DOES NOT KNOW HOW TO HANDLE A BAT . . . . 61 SAY YOU JOE/IM 12
("ANSWER THIS...AND YOU WILL KNOW YOURSELF ") ALL GOLD 73C ANNO LAVATER MARG
I KNOW NOT WHAT HIDING LOVE MEANS . . . . 78D ANNO LAVATER MARG
("FORGIVE A TRESPASS OF MALICE") UNEASY THIS I KNOW NOT 80D ANNO LAVATER MARG
SEE A MAN'S FEMALE DEPENDANTS YOU KNOW THE MAN . . . 82C ANNO LAVATER MARG
BECAUSE I ONCE THOUGHT OTHERWISE BUT NOW KNOW IT IS TRUTH 86D ANNO LAVATER MARG
UNEASY BECAUSE I DO NOT KNOW HOW TO DO THIS . . . . . 87D ANNO LAVATER MARG
SO IT IS IMPOSSIBLE TO KNOW GOD OR HEAVENLY THINGS WITHOUT 88B ANNO LAVATER MARG
CONJUNCTION WITH THOSE WHO KNOW GOD & HEAVENLY THINGS . 88B ANNO LAVATER MARG
WHO DOES NOT OR MAY NOT KNOW OF LOVE & WISDOM IN HIMSELF 92D ANNO SWED LOVE MARG
IS NOT THE SAME THAT IT SHALL BE WHEN WE KNOW MORE . . . 97C NAT RELIGION 2 PROSE
I KNOW TIRIEL IS KING OF THE WEST & THERE HE LIVES IN JOY 101 TIRIEL 2 20
THOU ART MY TIRIEL'S OLD FATHER I KNOW THEE THRO 101 TIRIEL 2 41
   THY WRINKLES
THOU HAST THE FORM OF TIRIEL BUT I KNOW THEE WELL ENOUGH 103 TIRIEL 4 7
COME THOU DARK FIEND I DARE THY CUNNING KNOW THAT IJIM 104 TIRIEL 4 17
   SCORNS
SERPENTS NOT SONS [YOU SEE ?AND ?KNOW YOUR FATHER] . . . 105 TIRIEL 4 * 64
THIS IS THE RIGHT & READY WAY I KNOW IT BY THE SOUND . . 107 TIRIEL 6 5
DOST THOU KNOW WHO MADE THEE . . . . 115 THE LAMB/SI 2
DOST THOU KNOW WHO MADE THEE . . . . 115 THE LAMB/SI 10
YOU KNOW THAT THE SOOT CANNOT SPOIL YOUR WHITE HAIR . . . 117 CHIMNEY SWP/SI 8
FOR THEY KNOW WHEN THEIR SHEPHERD IS NIGH . . . . . . 118 SHEPHERD/SI 8
AND FEEL THEY KNOW NOT WHAT BUT CARE . . . . 126 VOICE BARD/SI 10
DOES THE EAGLE KNOW WHAT IS IN THE PIT . . . . 127 THELS MOTTO/BT 1
BUT HOW THIS IS SWEET MAID I KNOW NOT AND I CANNOT KNOW 129 BOOK OF THEL 5 5
("THAT MEN LIVE AFTER DEATH") IT WAS NOT KNOWN & YET ALL 132D ANNO SWED PROV MARG
   KNOW
KNOW THAT AFTER CHRIST'S DEATH HE BECAME JEHOVAH . . . . 150B MARRIAGE HH 5 PROSE
HOW DO YOU KNOW BUT EVRY BIRD THAT CUTS THE AIRY WAY . . 150D MARRIAGE HH 6 PROSE
YOU NEVER KNOW WHAT IS ENOUGH . . . . 152A MARRIAGE HH 9 PROSE
UNLESS YOU KNOW WHAT IS MORE THAN ENOUGH . . . . 152A MARRIAGE HH 9 PROSE
[HOW TO KNOW LOVE FROM DECEIT] . . . . 175A HOW TO KNOW/N TITLE
A GREATER THAN ITSELF TO KNOW . . . . 176 LIT BOY LST/N 4
I KNOW THEE I HAVE FOUND THEE & I WILL NOT LET THEE GO . 196 AMERICA PREL 2 7
A GREATER THAN ITSELF TO KNOW . . . . 218 LIT BOY LST/SE 4
KNOW THAT IN A FORMER TIME . . . . 219 LIT GRL LST/SE 3
HOW KNOW YOU THIS SAID I SMALL SIR WHERE DID YOU LEARN 237 EUROPE INTRO 10
   THIS SONG
. . . KNOWETH [NOT] NOR CAN KNOW IN ALL ETERNITY . . . . 264 FOUR ZOAS 1 13
EVERY MOMENT OF MY SECRET HOURS YEA I KNOW . . . . . . 265 FOUR ZOAS 1 53
[IS THIS A DEED OF LOVE I KNOW WHAT I HAVE DONE I KNOW] 267 FOUR ZOAS 1 110
IF THOU HAST SINND & ART POLLUTED KNOW THAT I AM PURE . . 268 FOUR ZOAS 1 151
THE PRINCE OF ALL THE HOSTS OF MEN NOR EQUAL KNOW IN HEAVEN 278 FOUR ZOAS 1 505
I KNOW THEE NOT AS ONCE I KNEW THEE IN THOSE BLESSED FIELDS 288 FOUR ZOAS 2 325
WHETHER THIS IS JERUSALEM OR BABYLON WE KNOW NOT . . . . 294 FOUR ZOAS 3 102
I KNOW I WAS URTHONA KEEPER OF THE GATES OF HEAVEN . . . 298 FOUR ZOAS 4 42
THARMAS I KNOW THEE HOW ARE WE ALTERD OUR BEAUTY DECAYD 299 FOUR ZOAS 4 79
BUT STILL I KNOW THEE THO IN THIS HORRIBLE RUIN WHELMD . 299 FOUR ZOAS 4 80
TO KNOW SWEET SCIENCE & TO DO WITH SIMPLE COMPANIONS . . 301 FOUR ZOAS 4 147
NOW THOU DOST KNOW WHAT TIS TO STRIVE AGAINST THE GOD OF 301 FOUR ZOAS 4 156
   WATERS
AND NOW WE KNOW THAT WHATSOEVER THOU WILT ASK OF GOD . . 304 FOUR ZOAS 4 254
IN STRONG DRINK THO YOU KNOW THAT BREAD & WATER ARE ALL 323 FOUR ZOAS 7 127
AND I KNOW THEE IS THIS THE TRIUMPH THIS THE GODLIKE STATE 324 FOUR ZOAS 7 149
BUT HOW I KNOW NOT THEN FORGETFULNESS QUITE WRAPD ME UP 326 FOUR ZOAS 7 260
THO ALL THOSE FAIR PERFECTIONS WHICH MEN KNOW ONLY BY NAME 340 FOUR ZOAS 7B 274
NOW WE BEHOLD REDEMPTION NOW WE KNOW THAT LIFE ETERNAL . . 346 FOUR ZOAS 8 197
THERE IS A STATE NAMD SATAN LEARN DISTINCT TO KNOW 351 FOUR ZOAS 8 379
   O [MORTALS] RAHAB
IN FAMILIES WE SEE OUR SHADOWS BORN & THENCE WE KNOW . . 374 FOUR ZOAS 9 637
HOW SHOULD ONE SO FOOLISH KNOW ABOUT RICHES . . . . . 409A ANNO BACON MARG
WHATEER IS DONE TO HER SHE CANNOT KNOW . . . . 418 ON VIRGINITY/N 1
AND WHEN THIS WE RIGHTLY KNOW . . . . 432 AUGURIES 57
SHALL NEVER KNOW HOW TO REPLY . . . . 433 AUGURIES 94
THAT HE DID NOT KNOW HOW THE QUARREL BEGAN . . . . . . 437A BLAKES MEMORAN PROSE
NO PERSON BUT WILLIAM & THE SOLDIER & MYSELF CAN KNOW . . 438B BLAKES MEMORAN PROSE
DOES NOT KNOW THE BEGINNING NEVER CAN KNOW THE END OF ART 449C ANNO REYNOLDS MARG
DOES NOT KNOW EITHER HIS OWN INTEREST OR HIS DUTY . . . 452C ANNO REYNOLDS MARG
[GENERAL PRINCIPLES YOU CANNOT EVEN KNOW OR SEE MICH ANG] 456B ANNO REYNOLDS * MARG
CANNOT EVEN KNOW OR SEE MICH ANGO OR RAFAEL OR ANY THING 456B ANNO REYNOLDS MARG
   ELSE
THE MAN WHO DOES NOT KNOW WHAT OBJECT TO PURSUE IS AN IDIOT 458D ANNO REYNOLDS MARG
KNOW THAT THE MAN'S EXECUTION IS AS HIS CONCEPTION & NO 461C ANNO REYNOLDS MARG
   BETTER
HANDLING IS ALL THAT HE HAS & WE ALL KNOW THIS HANDLING 468D ANNO REYNOLDS MARG
   IS
HE WHO DOES NOT KNOW TRUTH AT SIGHT IS UNWORTHY OF HER 474D ANNO REYNOLDS MARG
   NOTICE
IS NOT THE SAME IT SHALL BE WHEN WE KNOW MORE . . . . . 475B ANNO REYNOLDS MARG
SPOKE SAYING YOU KNOW SATAN'S MILDNESS AND 487 MILTON 7 23
   HIS SELF-IMPOSITION
HOW SHOULD HE HE KNOW THE DUTIES OF ANOTHER O FOOLISH 487 MILTON 7 30
   FORBEARANCE
THE BARD REPLIED I AM INSPIRED I KNOW IT IS TRUTH FOR I 495 MILTON 13 51
   SING

    BUT I KNEW NOT THAT IT WAS MILTON FOR MAN CANNOT KNOW   .   . 503 MILTON 21   8
    AND NOW YOU KNOW THIS WORLD OF SORROW AND FEEL PITY OBEY   504 MILTON 21   54
    BUT HOW THIS IS AS YET WE KNOW NOT AND WE CANNOT KNOW   .   . 507 MILTON 23   53
    AND RAHAB THEY KNOW NOT OF REGENERATION BUT ONLY   520 MILTON 31   19
        OF GENERATION
    BUT MUST BE CREATED FOR THEY KNOW ONLY OF GENERATION   .   . 520 MILTON 31   22
    SATAN MY SPECTRE I KNOW MY POWER THEE TO ANNIHILATE   .   .   . 529 MILTON 38   29
    ARE NOT SUCH KNOW THOU I COME TO SELF ANNIHILATION   .   .   . 530 MILTON 38   34
    I AM NO HOMER'S HERO YOU ALL KNOW   .   .   .   . 541 HOMERS HERO/N   1
    READ REMBRANDT [& YOU WILL KNOW] FOR IT IS FIT   .   .   .   . 543 TO ROYL ACAD/N   6
    AND NOW [THOU] THEY KNOW[ST] NEITHER [THYSELF] THEMSELVES   543 ON F AND S/N   2
        NOR ME
    BECAUSE [I KNOW HE ALWAYS JUDGES] HIS JUDGMENT IS SO VERY   549 CROMEK SPEAK/N   2
        COOL
    [BECAUSE WE KNOW] AMIABLE STATE HE CANNOT FEEL AT ALL   .   . 549 CROMEK SPEAK/N   4
    IF YOU PLAY A GAME OF CHANCE KNOW BEFORE YOU BEGIN   .   .   . 551 IF YOU PLAY/N   1
    AND THE DEVIL IS A BLACK OUTLINE ALL OF US KNOW   .   .   .   . 554 TO VENETIAN/N   2
    OR CORREGGIO THEY OUGHT TO KNOW THAT CORREGGIO WAS BORN   563C DESC CAT   PROSE
    HE WHO DOES NOT KNOW HOW TO DRAW A HAND OR A FOOT   .   .   . 563D DESC CAT   PROSE
    KNOW HOW TO COLOUR IT   .   .   .   . 563D DESC CAT   PROSE
    FOR A BUFFOON OR BURLESQUE CHARACTER KNOW LITTLE OF CHAUCER   569C DESC CAT 3   PROSE
    I ANSWER OF NONE AT ALL BUT THE CONTRARY AS YOU WELL KNOW   573A DESC CAT 3   PROSE
    I AM AWARE OF YOU BECAUSE I KNOW THAT YOU ACT NOT FROM   .   . 573A DESC CAT 3   PROSE
    IS SOON KNOWN "BY THEIR WORKS YE SHALL KNOW THEM" ALL WHO   573B DESC CAT 3   PROSE
    ANY THING THAT A PROSPECTUS PLEASES BUT I KNOW THAT WHERE   575B DESC CAT 3   PROSE
    AND WHAT CONNOISSEURS CALL TOUCH I KNOW BY EXPERIENCE   .   . 575B DESC CAT 3   PROSE
    AND NOW THEY KNOW ME NOT NOR YET THEMSELVES   .   .   .   .   . 575 DESC CAT 3   4
    IN BEAUFORT BUILDINGS WE ALL KNOW THAT EDITORS OF   592C PUB ADDRESS/N   PROSE
        NEWSPAPERS
    I DO NOT KNOW AS HE WENT FAR ENOUGH OFF TO PUBLISH THEM   592D PUB ADDRESS/N   PROSE
    EVEN TO ITALY BUT THE PUBLIC WILL KNOW & POSTERITY WILL   592D PUB ADDRESS/N   PROSE
        KNOW
    DRAWING SUCH A MAN MUST KNOW THAT I LOOKD UPON HIM   .   .   . 593A PUB ADDRESS/N   PROSE
    NOW THIS IS CONTRARY TO THE TRUTH WOOLETT DID NOT KNOW   .   . 593A PUB ADDRESS/N   PROSE
    HE DID NOT KNOW HOW TO DRAW THE LEAF OF A TREE   .   .   .   . 593A PUB ADDRESS/N   PROSE
    KNOW THE FIRST [LINES] BEGINNINGS OF ART I HOPE THIS PRINT   593C PUB ADDRESS/N   PROSE
    A MAN WHO PRETENDS TO IMPROVE FINE ART DOES NOT KNOW   .   . 593C PUB ADDRESS/N   PROSE
    YOU WILL KNOW BETTER THAN TO THINK OF IMPROVING WHAT   .   . 593D PUB ADDRESS/N   PROSE
    THESE PEOPLE KNOW ENOUGH OF ARTIFICE BUT NOTHING OF ART   596A PUB ADDRESS/N   PROSE
    I DO NOT KNOW WHETHER HOMER IS A LIAR & THAT THERE IS NO   596D PUB ADDRESS/N   PROSE
    SUCH THING AS GENEROUS CONTENTION I KNOW THAT ALL THOSE   596D PUB ADDRESS/N   PROSE
        WITH
    FOR THE SAKE OF CONVINCING THOSE WHO DO NOT KNOW IT   .   .   . 597D PUB ADDRESS/N   PROSE
    I KNOW MY EXECUTION IS NOT LIKE ANY BODY ELSE I DO NOT   .   . 601D PUB ADDRESS/N   PROSE
    HE WHO MAKES A DESIGN MUST KNOW THE EFFECT & COLOURING   .   . 603A PUB ADDRESS/N   PROSE
    WOOLETT I KNOW DID NOT KNOW HOW TO GRIND HIS GRAVER   .   .   . 603C PUB ADDR AD/N   PROSE
    I KNOW THIS HE HAS OFTEN PROVED HIS IGNORANCE BEFORE ME   603C PUB ADDR AD/N   PROSE
    DO NOT KNOW OR UNDERSTAND WHAT THEY WRITE OR UTTER   .   .   . 605A V LAST JUDG/N   PROSE
    ARE LESS PERMANENT THAN A SHADOW AS WE ALL KNOW TOO WELL   605A V LAST JUDG/N   PROSE
    AS HE MUST KNOW THEN WOULD HE ARISE FROM HIS GRAVE   .   .   . 611A V LAST JUDG/N   PROSE
    BY THEIR WORKS YE SHALL KNOW THEM   .   .   .   . 615B V LAST JUDG/N   PROSE
    BUT HE HIMSELF WILL NOT KNOW IT THO EVERY BODY ELSE DOES   615B V LAST JUDG/N   PROSE
    HE OUGHT TO KNOW THAT NOTHING IS DISPLEASING TO GOD   .   .   . 615C V LAST JUDG/N   PROSE
    LOS ANSWERD ALTHO I KNOW NOT THIS I KNOW FAR WORSE THAN   626 JERUSALEM 7   51
        THIS
    I KNOW THAT ALBION HATH DIVIDED ME AND THAT THOU   626 JERUSALEM 7   52
        O MY SPECTRE
    I KNOW THY DECEIT & THY REVENGES AND UNLESS THOU DESIST   627 JERUSALEM 8   7
    THEY KNOW NOT WHY THEY LOVE NOR WHEREFORE THEY SICKEN & DIE   639 JERUSALEM 17   29
    WHETHER OF JERUSALEM'S OR VALA'S RUINS CONGENERATED WE   655 JERUSALEM 29   81
        KNOW NOT
    KNOW ME NOW ALBION LOOK UPON ME I ALONE AM BEAUTY   .   .   . 660 JERUSALEM 33   48
    JESUS ALONE CAN SAVE HIM FOR ALAS WE NONE CAN KNOW   .   .   . 675 JERUSALEM 45   18
    YE KNOW THAT IF THE EMANATION REMAINS IN THEM   .   .   .   . 681 JERUSALEM 50   14
    SUPERIOR NONE WE KNOW INFERIOR NONE ALL EQUAL SHARE   .   .   . 686 JERUSALEM 55   8
    TENDER ARTIFICE TO LAUGH TO WEEP TO LEARN TO KNOW   .   .   . 688 JERUSALEM 56   24
    A DELUSION BUT I KNOW THEE O LORD WHEN THOU ARISEST UPON   693 JERUSALEM 60   58
    SHALL ALBION ARISE I KNOW HE SHALL ARISE AT THE LAST DAY   696 JERUSALEM 62   15
    I KNOW THAT IN MY FLESH I SHALL SEE GOD BUT EMANATIONS   .   . 696 JERUSALEM 62   16
    ARE WEAK THEY KNOW NOT WHENCE THEY ARE NOR WHITHER TEND   696 JERUSALEM 62   17
    THE STRUGGLES OF INTANGLEMENT WITH INCOHERENT ROOTS I KNOW   716D JERUSALEM 77   PROSE
        OF
    I KNOW I AM URTHONA KEEPER OF THE GATES OF HEAVEN   .   .   . 727 JERUSALEM 82   81
    KNOW THAT I NEVER WILL BE THINE ALSO THOU HIDEST VALA   .   . 733 JERUSALEM 87   22
    I KNOW IT IS MY SELF O MY DIVINE CREATOR & REDEEMER   .   .   . 743 JERUSALEM 96   13
    AND DOST NOT KNOW THE GARMENT FROM THE MAN   .   .   .   .   . 771 EPILOGUE/GP   2
    & OBLITERATE IMAGINATION IN ME WORDSWORTH MUST KNOW   .   .   . 783A ANNO WW POEMS   MARG
    I DO NOT KNOW WHO WROTE THESE PREFACES THEY ARE VERY   .   . 783B ANNO WW POEMS   MARG
    I KNOW BETTER & PLEASE YOUR LORDSHIP   .   .   .   . 784C ANNO WW EXCUR   MARG
    BECAUSE I KNOW THAT THE GENIUS THAT PRODUCES THE DESIGNS   790B LETTER 2   PROSE
    OF VIRGINS WAX I DONT KNOW WHAT ANIMAL PRODUCES IT   .   .   . 790C LETTER 2   PROSE
    RESOLVD TO SHEW AN INDEPENDENCE WHICH I KNOW WILL PLEASE   792A LETTER 4   PROSE
        AN AUTHOR
    I KNOW I BEGGED OF YOU TO GIVE ME YOUR IDEAS   .   .   .   . 792A LETTER 4   PROSE
    AND THO I CALL THEM MINE I KNOW THAT THEY ARE NOT MINE   .   . 792B LETTER 4   PROSE
    OUGHT TO KNOW THAT WHAT IS GRAND IS NECESSARILY OBSCURE   793A LETTER 5   PROSE
        TO WEAK MEN
    I KNOW THAT THIS WORLD IS A WORLD OF IMAGINATION & VISION   793C LETTER 5   PROSE
    BUT AS I KNOW THAT HE WHO WORKS & HAS HIS HEALTH CANNOT   795C LETTER 6   PROSE
    I KNOW THAT OUR DECEASED FRIENDS ARE MORE REALLY WITH US   797A LETTER 9   PROSE
    FEAR THEY WILL NOT EXCUSE & I KNOW NOT HOW TO [XXX]   798B LETTER 10   *PROSE
        APOLOGIZE FOR

	PAGE	TITLE	LINE

KNOW   (CONTINUED)
LONG AWAY & NOT CALLING TO KNOW OF YOUR WELFARE BUT HOPE   799A LETTER 11   PROSE
    NOW
ANGELS I KNOW YOU WILL BE PLEASED WITH THE INTENTION   . . 799B LETTER 11   PROSE
I KNOW MY COTTAGE IS TOO NARROW FOR YOUR EASE & COMFORT   808B LETTER 19   PROSE
MENTAL DISTRESS & I KNOW THAT ALL DISTRESS INFLICTED BY   809B LETTER 20   PROSE
THAT I CAN CONFESS MYSELF IGNORANT OF I ALSO KNOW & . . . 814C LETTER 23   PROSE
& THAT I KNOW I NEVER SHALL DO BETTER FOR IF I WAS TO DO   815C LETTER 23   *PROSE
EXPECT A LIKENESS BUT NOW I HAVE DONE ALL I COULD & KNOW   815D LETTER 23   PROSE
THIS WINTER YOU KNOW THAT IT IS   . . . .   819B LETTER 25   PROSE
ONLY SORRY THAT I DID NOT KNOW THE METHODS OF PUBLISHING   820A LETTER 25   PROSE
HOWEVER THIS I KNOW WILL SET YOU AT EASE I AM NOW SO FULL   820C LETTER 25   PROSE
THO I KNOW THAT AS FAR AS DESIGNING & POETRY ARE CONCERND   821C LETTER 25   PROSE
FOR I KNOW THAT THE PUBLIC ARE MY FRIENDS & LOVE MY WORKS   821C LETTER 25   PROSE
KNOW THAT YOU SEE CERTAIN MERITS IN ME WHICH BY GOD'S GRACE 822B LETTER 26   PROSE
NONE CAN KNOW THE SPIRITUAL ACTS OF MY THREE YEARS' SLUMBER 823A LETTER 26   PROSE
BUT I KNOW THE MAJORITY OF THEM WILL NOT   . . . . .   825B LETTER 27   PROSE
I KNOW MYSELF BOTH POET & PAINTER & IT IS   . . . . .   825C LETTER 27   PROSE
ALTHO THEY MUST KNOW & IT IS MANIFEST THAT THE WHOLE IS   827D LETTER 28   PROSE
I ONLY SUGGEST WHAT I KNOW YOU WILL BE KIND ENOUGH   828B LETTER 28   PROSE
    TO EXCUSE
IF YOU CAN LEARN NOTHING ABOUT HIM & WHAT I AS WELL KNOW   828B LETTER 28   PROSE
PLEASES I KNOW THAT MANY WORKS OF A LUCRATIVE NATURE ARE   829D LETTER 30   PROSE
GRATITUDE I FEEL IT & I KNOW IT I THANK GOD & MAN FOR IT &   834A LETTER 33   PROSE
ONE OR TWO LARGE CARTOONS THE SUBJECTS HE DOES NOT KNOW   834C LETTER 34   PROSE
MR EDWARDS KNOW LADY HAMILTON'S ADDRESS THE   . . . . . 836B LETTER 35   PROSE
TO KNOW WHAT HIS INTENTIONS ARE BUT HE SAYS PERHAPS . .   842D LETTER 42   PROSE
AND I KNOW YOU WILL LOVE HIM FOR IT   . . . .   846B LETTER 44   PROSE
DOES NOT KNOW THE TIME WHEN MR R(ROMNEY) TOOK . . . .   847D LETTER 44   PROSE
SHOULD THEY EVER BE ATTEMPTED WHAT HE CAN & I KNOW   . . . 853A LETTER 51   *PROSE
HE HAS ENOUGH & TO SPARE & THE WORLD WILL KNOW HIS AT ONCE   853A LETTER 51   *PROSE
    &
KNOW BUT MYSELF IN A DIVIDED EXISTENCE   . . . . 853A LETTER 51   PROSE
I HAVE NO CURIOSITY TO SEE HIM AS I WELL KNOW WHAT   859C LETTER 56   PROSE
    IS WITHIN
I KNOW IT HAS COST ME IMMENSE LABOUR . . . . 861B LETTER 58   PROSE
AS I KNOW THAT YOU WILL DO WHAT IS RIGHT ON ALL HANDS   . . 861B LETTER 58   PROSE
YOU WILL I KNOW FEEL AS YOU ALWAYS DO ON SUCH OCCASIONS   861D LETTER 59   PROSE
I KNOW THAT IF I HAD NOT BEEN WITH YOU I MUST HAVE PERISHD   862D LETTER 60   PROSE
EACH ACCORDING TO ITS RANK & THAT THEY WOULD KNOW THAT   863A LETTER 60   PROSE
I KNOW THAT THOSE WHO ARE DEAD FROM THE EARTH & WHO MOCKD & 863A LETTER 60   PROSE
THE SITUATIONS OF OUR BEAUTIFUL AFFECTIONATE BALLADS I KNOW 863B LETTER 60   PROSE
I KNOW IT FOR I SEE IT & DARE NOT HELP   . . . . . .   863B LETTER 60   PROSE
AND WHO DOES NOT KNOW A BOY FROM A GIRL I SAY . . . . . 864B LETTER 61   PROSE
KNOW THAT EVERY MAN OUGHT TO BE A JUDGE OF PICTURES AND   864C LETTER 61   PROSE
MANY PECULIARITIES THAT NO ONE BUT MYSELF CAN KNOW   . .   871A LETTER 72   PROSE
I HAVE TRIED IT TOO MUCH NOT TO KNOW THIS & AM VERY SORRY   871A LETTER 72   PROSE
BE TOO ILL TO LET YOU KNOW HOW I AM & WHAT I WISH   . . . 871B LETTER 72   PROSE
I DID NOT KNOW IT BEFORE YESTERDAY FROM MR FINCHAM   . . . 874C LETTER 79   PROSE
PLEASE TO LET ME KNOW BUT FINDING MYSELF WELL ENOUGH TO   875B LETTER 81   PROSE
    COME
WITH POOR JOB I KNOW TOO WELL THAT A GREAT MAJORITY OF   .   878A LETTER 88   PROSE
YOU ARE DESIROUS I KNOW TO DISPOSE OF SOME OF MY WORKS &   878B LETTER 88   PROSE
KNOWEST
THOU ART A NATURAL PHILOSOPHER AND KNOWEST TRUTH   29A EDW THIRD/PS 4 PROSE
    BY INSTINCT
KNOWEST THOU NOT O FAIRIES' LORD . . . . 188 A FAIRY SKIPD   9
THOU KNOWEST THAT THE ANCIENT TREES SEEN BY THINE EYES   192 V DAU ALBION 4   13
    HAVE FRUIT
BUT KNOWEST THOU THAT TREES AND FRUITS FLOURISH UPON THE   192 V DAU ALBION 4   14
    EARTH
OF GOD CLOTHED IN LUVAH'S GARMENTS LITTLE KNOWEST THOU . . 282 FOUR ZOAS 2   100
SAYING O LORD WHENCE IS THIS CHANGE THOU KNOWEST   293 FOUR ZOAS 3   55
    I AM NOTHING
THOU KNOWEST NOT WHAT THARMAS KNOWS O I COULD TELL THEE   300 FOUR ZOAS 4   114
    TALES
THOU KNOWEST THAT THE SPECTRE IS IN EVERY MAN INSANE   327 FOUR ZOAS 7   304
    BRUTISH
TO THROW HIM INTO THE FURNACES KNOWEST THOU NOT THAT HE   505 MILTON 22   32
THE VIRGIN ANSWERD KNOWEST THOU OF MILTON WHO DESCENDED   527 MILTON 37   1
IN GREAT ETERNITY WHICH THOU KNOWEST I COME HIM TO SEEK   527 MILTON 37   3
THOU ART ONE WITH HER & KNOWEST NOT OF SELF IN THY SUPREME   632 JERUSALEM 12   42
    JOY
ASK ME NOT OF MY GRIEFS THOU KNOWEST ALL MY GRIEFS   . . . 642 JERUSALEM 20   20
SAYING O LORD WHENCE IS THIS CHANGE THOU KNOWEST   654 JERUSALEM 29   42
    I AM NOTHING
BECAUSE THOU KNOWEST I AM DELUDED BY THE TURNING MILLS . . 693 JERUSALEM 60   63
WHICH THOU KNOWEST WITHOUT MY SPEAKING . . . .   738 JERUSALEM 91   5
KNOWETH
BUT THE MOLE KNOWETH WHAT IS THERE & THE WORM SHALL TELL   193 V DAU ALBION 5   40
    IT THEE
KNOWETH NO INDIVIDUAL [MAN] . . . . 264 FOUR ZOAS 1   13
. . . KNOWETH [NOT] NOR CAN KNOW IN ALL ETERNITY . . . 264 FOUR ZOAS 1   13
KNOWETH THE INFANT SORROW WHENCE IT CAME AND WHERE IT GOETH 688 JERUSALEM 56   6
KNOWING
GUILTY OF DOING WRONG WITHOUT KNOWING IT WAS WRONG   . . . 29A EDW THIRD/PS 4 PROSE
MAY DO A GREAT DEAL OF HARM WITHOUT KNOWING IT   . . . . 29A EDW THIRD/PS 4 PROSE
THE TRUE FACULTY OF KNOWING MUST BE   . . . . 98B ALL RELIGIONS PROSE
A TRUE POET AND OF THE DEVIL'S PARTY WITHOUT KNOWING IT   150B MARRIAGE HH 5 PROSE
THEN COMST THOU FORTH A MODEST VIRGIN KNOWING TO DISSEMBLE   194 V DAU ALBION 6   10
THIS KNOWING ARTFUL SECRET FEARFUL CAUTIOUS TREMBLING   194 V DAU ALBION 6   17
    HYPOCRITE

	PAGE	TITLE	LINE

KNOWING   (CONTINUED)

STILL SHE DESPISD HIM CALLING ON HIS NAME & KNOWING HIM NOT   286 FOUR ZOAS 2   234
KNOWING THE ARTS OF URIZEN WERE PITY & MEEK [LOVE]   336 FOUR ZOAS 7B   134
   AFFECTION
OF GOLGONOOZA HER WELL BELOVED KNOWING HE WAS ORC'S HUMAN   351 FOUR ZOAS 8   384
   REMAINS
KNOWING HIMSELF TO BE A FOOL HE IS . . . .   455B ANNO REYNOLDS   MARG
KNOWING & FEELING THAT WE ALL HAVE NEED OF BUTTER   . . .   556 IF MEN ACT/N   4
A MAN PERFECTLY KNOWING IN HIS PROFESSION . . . . .   568A DESC CAT 3   PROSE
NOT KNOWING WHAT ART IS IT IS BEING BLIND TO THE GIFTS   579D DESC CAT 5   PROSE
   OF THE SPIRIT
IF THEY DO NOT PRAY IS AN INFERIOR KIND TO BE CALLD KNOWING   605A V LAST JUDG/N   PROSE
TO BE ALL EVIL ALL REVERSED & FOR EVER DEAD KNOWING   .   630 JERUSALEM 10   57
KNOWING HIMSELF THE AUTHOR OF THEIR DIVISIONS & SHRINKINGS   733 JERUSALEM 88   35
   GRATIFIED
EVERY ASSISTANCE IN HIS POWER WITHOUT KNOWING MY INTENTION   820B LETTER 25   PROSE
I SAY THUS MUCH TO YOU KNOWING THAT YOU WILL NOT MAKE A   825C LETTER 27   PROSE
KNOWING YOUR AVERSION TO REVIEWS & REVIEWING I CONSIDER   841D LETTER 41   PROSE
WHICH COWPER'S LIFE IS PRINTED ON NOT KNOWING THAT IT WAS   846D LETTER 41   PROSE

KNOWINGLY

& KNOWINGLY PROPAGATE FALSHOOD . . . .   397B ANNO BACON   MARG
WHETHER A MAN DOES IT IGNORANTLY OR KNOWINGLY . . . . .   452A ANNO REYNOLDS   MARG

KNOWLEDGE

THO THE KNOWLEDGE OF THAT WILL NOT PROFIT THEE MUCH . . .   28D EDW THIRD/PS 4   PROSE
SWEET CONTEMPLATION [SHE TEACHETH KNOWLEDGE HOW TO KNOW]   42A THEN SHE BORE   PROSE
TIS CONTEMPLATION TEACHETH KNOWLEDGE TRULY HOW TO KNOW   .   42A THEN SHE BORE   *PROSE
FOR KNOWLEDGE DROVE SWEET INNOCENCE AWAY . . . . .   42B THEN SHE BORE   PROSE
TILL KNOWLEDGE ANIMATED IT TWAS CALLD SELFLOVE . . .   42D THEN SHE BORE   PROSE
HEAR THEN THE PRIDE & KNOWLEDGE OF A SAILOR . . . .   52 HEAR THEN/IM   1
THAT IS THE WAY I HAVE GOT SOME OF MY KNOWLEDGE   . .   53C ISLAND MOON 8   PROSE
THEY ALSO PERCIEVE THIS FROM KNOWLEDGE BUT NOT WITH THE   89C ANNO SWED LOVE   MARG
   NATURAL PART
("KNOWLEDGE...NOT RECEIVED BY UNDERSTANDING BUT BY LOVE")   95C ANNO SWED LOVE   MARG
   MARK THIS
THE ARGUMENT AS THE TRUE METHOD OF KNOWLEDGE IS EXPERIMENT   98B ALL RELIGIONS   PROSE
FROM ALREADY ACQUIRED KNOWLEDGE MAN COULD NOT ACQUIRE MORE   98C ALL RELIGIONS   PROSE
. . . NOW BEAMING WITH KNOWLEDGE WITH GENTLE AWE ADORNED   144 FRENCH REVOLTN   230
KNOWLEDGE IS TRANSMITTED FROM GENERATION TO GENERATION   .   154D MARRIAGE HH 15   PROSE
WHEN THE MORTAL DISAPPEARS IN IMPROVED KNOWLEDGE CAST AWAY   355 FOUR ZOAS 8   552
. . . & KNEAD THE BREAD OF KNOWLEDGE WITH TEARS & GROANS   379 FOUR ZOAS 9   820
IT IS THE TREE OF THE KNOWLEDGE OF GOOD & EVIL   . . . .   397C ANNO BACON   MARG
DOTH PUT THE LIGHT OF KNOWLEDGE OUT . . . . . .   433 AUGURIES   96
[AS DO ?FOOLS THAT ADORE THINGS & ?IDEAS XXX OF GENERAL   451A ANNO REYNOLDS   * MARG
   KNOWLEDGE]
ENTHUSIASTIC ADMIRATION IS THE FIRST PRINCIPLE OF KNOWLEDGE   458B ANNO REYNOLDS   MARG
KNOWLEDGE OF IDEAL BEAUTY IS NOT TO BE ACQUIRED . . . .   459B ANNO REYNOLDS   MARG
WHAT IS GENERAL KNOWLEDGE [IS] THERE SUCH A THING   . . .   459D ANNO REYNOLDS   MARG
[STRICTLY SPEAKING] ALL KNOWLEDGE IS PARTICULAR . . .   459D ANNO REYNOLDS   MARG
FOR ALL THAT IS VALUABLE IN [KNOWLEDGES] KNOWLEDGE   475A ANNO REYNOLDS   * MARG
   IS SUPERIOR TO
THOSE VISIONS OF HUMAN LIFE & SHADOWS OF WISDOM & KNOWLEDGE   525 MILTON 34   55
WHO PUBLISHES DOUBT & CALLS IT KNOWLEDGE WHOSE SCIENCE   533 MILTON 41   15
   IS DESPAIR
WHOSE PRETENCE TO KNOWLEDGE IS ENVY WHOSE WHOLE SCIENCE IS   533 MILTON 41   16
O DEAR MOTHER OUTLINE [BE NOT IN A RAGE] OF KNOWLEDGE MOST   554 ASKD PRIGG/N   * 16
   SAGE
KNOWLEDGE AND EXPERIENCE HENRY BAILLIE THE KEEPER   . . .   569D DESC CAT 3   PROSE
POWERS & HIS SCIENTIFIC KNOWLEDGE OF DRAWING IS . . . .   591B PUB ADDRESS/N   PROSE
GENERAL KNOWLEDGE IS REMOTE KNOWLEDGE . . . . . .   611A V LAST JUDG/N   PROSE
[ARE THE SAME THING] IS EATING OF THE TREE OF KNOWLEDGE   615A V LAST JUDG/N   PROSE
BUT UNBELIEF & EATING OF THE TREE OF KNOWLEDGE OF GOOD   615C V LAST JUDG/N   PROSE
   & EVIL
& EATING THE TREE OF KNOWLEDGE FOR SATAN'S GRATIFICATION   616D V LAST JUDG/N   PROSE
WHOSE SPRINGS ARE UNSEARCHABLE & KNOWLEDGE INFINITE   . . .   676 JERUSALEM 46   2
THAT TO LABOUR IN KNOWLEDGE IS TO BUILD UP JERUSALEM AND   717C JERUSALEM 77   PROSE
TO DESPISE KNOWLEDGE IS TO DESPISE JERUSALEM & HER   717C JERUSALEM 77   PROSE
   BUILDERS
POOR SPIRITUAL KNOWLEDGE IS NOT WORTH A BUTTON   . . . .   752 EV GOSPEL(D)/N   40
KNOWLEDGE IS NOT BY DEDUCTION BUT IMMEDIATE BY PERCEPTION   774C ANNO BERKELEY   MARG
   OR
THEREIN WITHOUT MY KNOWLEDGE THAT HE WAS SO INVITED I . . 827A LETTER 28   PROSE
AT THE FOX & WHO EVIDENCES THAT TO HIS KNOWLEDGE NO WORD   827C LETTER 28   PROSE

KNOWLEDGE'S

IN KNOWLEDGE'S DARK PRISON HOUSE . . . .   42B THEN SHE BORE   PROSE

KNOWLEDGES

GENERAL KNOWLEDGES ARE THOSE KNOWLEDGES THAT IDIOTS   451A ANNO REYNOLDS   MARG
   POSSESS
FOR ALL THAT IS VALUABLE IN [KNOWLEDGES] KNOWLEDGE   475A ANNO REYNOLDS   * MARG
   IS SUPERIOR TO
OR EATING OF THE TREE OF THOSE KNOWLEDGES OR REASONINGS   604C V LAST JUDG/N   PROSE

KNOWN   SEE WELL-KNOWN,WELL KNOWN

("LIFE OF MAN...IS LOVE") THIS WAS KNOWN TO ME & THOUSANDS   89C ANNO SWED LOVE   MARG
REASON OR THE RATIO OF ALL WE HAVE ALREADY KNOWN . . . .   97C NAT RELIGION 2   PROSE
AS NONE BY TRAVELLING OVER KNOWN LANDS . . . .   98C ALL RELIGIONS   PROSE
("THAT MEN LIVE AFTER DEATH") IT WAS NOT KNOWN & YET ALL   132D ANNO SWED PROV   MARG
   KNOW
AND THE EAGLE IS KNOWN FROM THE OWL . . . .   183 MOTTO SONGS/N   8
OF COLOURS TWELVE FEW KNOWN ON EARTH GIVE LIGHT IN THE   241 EUROPE 10   9
   OPAKE
ENITHARMON REMAINS A CORSE SUCH THING WAS NEVER KNOWN   . .   278 FOUR ZOAS 1   528
THE STRONGEST POISON EVER KNOWN . . . .   433 AUGURIES   97
WHEN HE MEANT TO MAKE HIMSELF KNOWN TO APELLES   . . . .   439C REMARKS MALKIN   PROSE

```
                                                        PAGE      TITLE          LINE
KNOWN    (CONTINUED)
    REASON OR A [RATION] RATIO OF ALL WE HAVE KNOWN  . . . .  475B ANNO REYNOLDS  * MARG
    [?KNOWN ?SUCH ?KNAVES XXX]  . . . . . . . . . . . . . .   SUPP ANNO REYNOLDS  * MARG
    WAS NEVER KNOWN THAT ONE OF THE HOLY DEAD SHOULD WILLING  508 MILTON 23          58
        RETURN
    SO [AS SURE] AS A CHURCH IS KNOWN BY ITS STEEPLE    . .   559 I ROSE UP AT/N *   23
    OPINIONS AND DETERMINATIONS ON ART VERY NECESSARY TO BE   562B DESC CAT ADV    PROSE
        KNOWN
    AND WHO FIRST FORGED THE SILLY STORY AND KNOWN FALSHOOD   565B DESC CAT 2      PROSE
    AND THEY ARE KNOWN TO BE UNCHANGEABLE BUT OIL BEING A BODY 566B DESC CAT 2     PROSE
    NAMES ALTER THINGS NEVER ALTER I HAVE KNOWN MULTITUDES    567C DESC CAT 3      PROSE
    IS SOON KNOWN "BY THEIR WORKS YE SHALL KNOW THEM" ALL WHO 573B DESC CAT 3      PROSE
    RAFAEL AND MICHAEL ANGELO AND ALBERT DURER ARE KNOWN BY   585B DESC CAT 15     PROSE
        THIS
    [& VISIONS OF IMAGINATION] OUGHT TO BE KNOWN   . . . . . 605A V LAST JUDG/N    PROSE
    KNOWN & THE ETERNAL NATURE & PERMANENCE  . . . . . . . . 605B V LAST JUDG/N    PROSE
    SUCH THING WAS NEVER KNOWN O PITY ME THOU ALL-PITEOUS-ONE 631 JERUSALEM 12        8
    HAVE YOU KNOWN THE JUDGMENT THAT IS ARISEN AMONG THE  . . 663 JERUSALEM 36       44
    THE CHILDREN MUST BE SACRIFICD A HORROR NEVER KNOWN   . . 678 JERUSALEM 48       58
    BEFORE I HAD EVER BEHELD WITH LOVE THE FACE OF JEHOVAH    695 JERUSALEM 61       42
        OR KNOWN
    HAVE KNOWN THEE IF I WERE UNPOLLUTED I SHOULD NEVER HAVE  695 JERUSALEM 61       45
    THE KNIFE INTO HIS DAUGHTER'S HAND SUCH THING WAS NEVER   722 JERUSALEM 80       23
        KNOWN
    GOD CAN ONLY BE KNOWN BY HIS ATTRIBUTES  . . . . . . . . 752 EV GOSPEL(D)/N      44
    ALL I EVER HAD KNOWN . . . . . . . . . . . . . . . . . . 806 TO BUTTS/L          73
    DID NOT HE IS ALSO A HAPPY ABSTRACT KNOWN BY ALL         809C LETTER 20        PROSE
        HIS FRIENDS
    OBTAIND BY COMING HERE FOR I SHOULD NEVER HAVE KNOWN  . . 820A LETTER 25       PROSE
    THE NATURE OF PUBLICATION UNLESS I HAD KNOWN H(HAYLEY) &  820A LETTER 25       PROSE
    BOWYER'S & OTHER GREAT WORKS I WAS KNOWN BY THEM & WAS    862C LETTER 60       PROSE
        LOOKD
    THINGS KNOWN ONLY TO MYSELF & TO SPIRITS GOOD & EVIL BUT  862D LETTER 60       PROSE
    NOT KNOWN TO MEN ON EARTH IT IS THE PASSAGE THRO THESE  . 862D LETTER 60       PROSE
KNOWS
    EACH KNOWS HIS RANK AND HEAVN MARSHAL ALL  . . . . . . .  19 EDW THIRD/PS 1       52
    THE WISE MAN THAT KNOWS US ALL AS WELL AS YOUR HONOUR . . 29C EDW THIRD/PS 4   PROSE
    EXCEPT WHEN I GO TO MR JACKO'S HE KNOWS WHAT RIDING IS  . 53A ISLAND MOON 8    PROSE
    ("KNOWS HIMSELF WHO NEVER OPPOSES HIS GENIUS")           84C ANNO LAVATER      MARG
        MOST EXCELLENT
    HE WHO HAS SUFFERD YOU TO IMPOSE ON HIM KNOWS YOU   . . . 152A MARRIAGE HH 9   PROSE
    BUT WHEN HE HAS DONE THIS LET HIM NOT SAY THAT HE KNOWS   158A MARRIAGE HH 21  PROSE
    THE EYE SEES MORE THAN THE HEART KNOWS . . . . . . . . . 189A V DAU ALBION     TITLE
    TILL SHE WHO BURNS WITH YOUTH AND KNOWS NO FIXED LOT IS   193 V DAU ALBION 5     21
        BOUND
    BUT SPARE MY LIFE BUT HE KNOWS NOT THAT [THE] WINTER COMETH 276 FOUR ZOAS 1     456
        FAST
    THOU KNOWEST NOT WHAT THARMAS KNOWS O I COULD TELL THEE   300 FOUR ZOAS 4       114
        TALES
    AS THE TREE KNOWS NOT WHAT IS OUTSIDE OF ITS LEAVES & BARK 314 FOUR ZOAS 6      95
    SO IN THE REGIONS OF THE GRAVE NONE KNOWS HIS DARK COMPEER 314 FOUR ZOAS 6      97
    BE NOT PERSWADED THAT THE AIR KNOWS THIS OR THE FALLING DEW 339 FOUR ZOAS 7B   231
    HE WHO THINKS THAT HONESTY IS CHANGEABLE KNOWS NOTHING    386B ANNO WATSON      MARG
        ABOUT IT
    IT IS VIRTUOUS OR VICIOUS KNOWS NOT WHAT VIRTUE MEANS  . . 386C ANNO WATSON     MARG
    EVERY BODY KNOWS THAT THIS IS EPICURUS AND LUCRETIUS   . . 397B ANNO BACON      MARG
    BACON KNOWS THE WISDOM OF WAR IF IT IS WISDOM . . . . .  407C ANNO BACON       MARG
    HIRELING WRITER WHOSE PRAISE IS CONTRARY TO WHAT HE KNOWS 413D ANNO BOYD        MARG
    ALL HE KNOWS FROM OTHERS MUST BE FULL OF CONTRADICTIONS   449B ANNO REYNOLDS    MARG
    REYNOLDS THINKS THAT MAN LEARNS ALL THAT HE KNOWS   . . . 471A ANNO REYNOLDS    MARG
    THIS IS A VERY CLEVER SENTENCE WHO WROTE (IT) GOD KNOWS   471C ANNO REYNOLDS  * MARG
    KNOWS IN ITS INTRICATE MAZES OF DELIGHT ARTFUL TO WEAVE   512 MILTON 26          4
    THE MICROSCOPE KNOWS NOT OF THIS NOR THE TELESCOPE THEY   516 MILTON 29         17
        ALTER
    GOD KNOWS I LITTLE OF PRAYERS NEED SAY . . . . . . . .   559 I ROSE UP AT/N     22
    HE KNOWS THAT WHAT HE DOES IS NOT INFERIOR TO THE GRANDEST 579B DESC CAT 5     PROSE
    DELINEATED BY ANY ENGRAVER WHO KNOWS HOW TO  . . . . .   592B PUB ADDRESS/N    PROSE
    EVERY MAN HAS EYES NOSE & MOUTH THIS EVERY IDIOT KNOWS    611B V LAST JUDG/N    PROSE
    & WHAT HE KNOWS IS OPPOSITE TO THEIR OWN IDENTITY   . . . 616D V LAST JUDG/N    PROSE
    WHAT IS CALLD CORPOREAL NOBODY KNOWS OF ITS DWELLING PLACE 617A V LAST JUDG/N  PROSE
    HUMANITY KNOWS NOT OF SEX WHEREFORE ARE SEXES IN BEULAH   656 JERUSALEM 30       33
    FOR HUMAN BEAUTY KNOWS IT NOT NOR CAN MERCY FIND IT BUT   666 JERUSALEM 39        6
    EVERY ONE KNOWS WE ARE ONE FAMILY ONE MAN BLESSED FOR     687 JERUSALEM 55       46
        EVER
    HE KNOWS NOT TO FORGIVE . . . . . . . . . . . . . . . .  784B ANNO WW EXCUR     MARG
    BUT BY MY CONJUNCTION WITH FLAXMAN WHO KNOWS TO FORGIVE   799 TO FLAXMAN/L       12
        NERVOUS FEAR
    HE KNOWS THAT I HAVE WRIT IT FOR I HAVE SHEWN IT TO HIM   825B LETTER 27       PROSE
    A PICTURE OF LEAR AND CORDELIA WHEN HE AWAKES AND KNOWS HER 843D LETTER 43     PROSE
    TO WRITE ALL HE KNOWS OR CAN COLLECT CONCERNING ROMNEY  . 846A LETTER 44       PROSE
    ALL MY HOPES BY THE ROOTS EVERY ONE WHO KNOWS OF OUR  . . 872D LETTER 76       PROSE
KNOWST
    LOOK KNOWST THOU AUGHT OF THIS GREY BEARD OR OF THESE     104 TIRIEL 4          44
        BLINDED EYES
    O VIRGIN KNOWST THOU NOT OUR STEEDS DRINK OF THE GOLDEN   128 BOOK OF THEL 3     7
        SPRINGS
    CONSUMING THOU KNOWST ME NOW O URIZEN PRINCE OF LIGHT  . . 324 FOUR ZOAS 7     148
KOBAN    SEE COBAN
    HAND & HYLE & KOBAN SKOFELD KOX & KOTOPE LABOUR MIGHTILY  628 JERUSALEM 8       41
    IN STERN DEFIANCE CAME FROM ALBION'S BOSOM HAND HYLE KOBAN 658 JERUSALEM 32     10
    AND SHINE GLORIOUS WITHIN HAND & KOBAN ARCHD OVER THE SUN 690 JERUSALEM 58      29
```

	PAGE	TITLE	LINE

KOCK
GWANTOK PEACHY BRERTUN SLAID HUTTN SKOFELD KOCK KOTOPE . . 658 JERUSALEM 32 — 11

KOTOPE
SCOFIELD KOX KOTOPE AND BOWEN REVOLVE MOST MIGHTILY UPON — 623 JERUSALEM 5 — 27
AND KOX KOTOPE & BOWEN ONE IN HIM A FOURFOLD WONDER . . — 626 JERUSALEM 7 — 48
HAND & HYLE & KOBAN SKOPELD KOX & KOTOPE LABOUR MIGHTILY — 628 JERUSALEM 8 — 41
SCOFELD KOX KOTOPE & BOWEN HIS TWELVE SONS SATANIC MILL — 641 JERUSALEM 19 — 19
GWANTOK PEACHY BRERTUN SLAID HUTTN SKOFELD KOCK KOTOPE . — 658 JERUSALEM 32 — 11
KOTOPE & BOWEN BECAME WHAT THEY BEHELD FLEEING OVER THE — 663 JERUSALEM 36 — 19
EARTH
THEY DRINK UP DAN & GAD TO FEED WITH MILK SKOFELD & KOTOPE — 704 JERUSALEM 67 — 22
KOTOPE HAD HEREFORD STAFFORD WORCESTER & HIS EMANATION . . — 710 JERUSALEM 71 — 44

KOX
SCOFIELD KOX KOTOPE AND BOWEN REVOLVE MOST MIGHTILY UPON — 623 JERUSALEM 5 — 27
KOX IS THE FATHER OF SHEM & HAM & JAPHETH HE IS THE NOAH — 625 JERUSALEM 7 — 23
AND KOX KOTOPE & BOWEN ONE IN HIM A FOURFOLD WONDER . . — 626 JERUSALEM 7 — 48
HAND & HYLE & KOBAN SKOPELD KOX & KOTOPE LABOUR MIGHTILY — 628 JERUSALEM 8 — 41
SCOFELD KOX KOTOPE & BOWEN HIS TWELVE SONS SATANIC MILL — 641 JERUSALEM 19 — 19
BRERETON & SLADE IN EGYPT HUTTON & SKOFELD & KOX . . . — 662 JERUSALEM 36 — 17
SCOFELD & KOX ARE LET LOOSE UPON MY SAXONS THEY ACCUMULATE — 673 JERUSALEM 43 — 51
KOX HAD OXFORD WARWICK WILTS HIS EMANATION IS ESTRILD . . — 710 JERUSALEM 71 — 42

KROMARTY
JOSEPH ELGIN LANERK KINROS BENJAMIN KROMARTY MURRA — 638 JERUSALEM 16 — 58
KIRKUBRIHT

KWANTOK   SEE GUANTOK,GWANTOK,ETC
OF HAND & HYLE & COBAN OF KWANTOK PEACHEY BRERETON SLAYD — 623 JERUSALEM 5 — 25
& HUTTON

LA
FA ME LA SOL LA ME FA SOL . . . . — 61 DR CLASH/IM — 5
FA ME LA SOL LA ME FA SOL . . . . — 62 DR CLASH/IM — 12
FA ME LA SOL LA ME FA SOL . . . . — 62 DR CLASH/IM — 17
FA ME LA SOL LA ME FA SOL . . . . — 62 DR CLASH/IM — 22

LABAN
A WOMAN WITH CHILDREN REPRESENTS THE STATE CALLD LABAN THE — 610D V LAST JUDG/N — PROSE

LABLES
THE SPECTRE WEPT AT HIS DIRE LABOURS WHEN FROM [?LABLES] — 302 FOUR ZOAS 4 — * 194
LADLES HUGE

LABOR
STEAL THE LABOR OF OTHERS TO SUPPORT HIM BEAR . . . . . — 158C MARRIAGE HH 22 — PROSE

LABORING
OF DIRE NECESSITY STILL LABORING DAY & NIGHT TILL ALL . . — 333 FOUR ZOAS 7B — 14

LABORIOUS
. . . O LABORIOUS PLOW . . . . — 144 FRENCH REVOLTN — 226
. . . TO TEACH THE LABORIOUS PLOWMAN . . . . — 144 FRENCH REVOLTN — 232
OF POVERTY ON THE LABORIOUS . . . . — 247 SONG OF LOS 6 — 16
INTO THE BLUE EXPANSE & I INVENTED WITH LABORIOUS ART . . — 312 FOUR ZOAS 6 — 31
FIRST TRADES & COMMERCE SHIPS & ARMED VESSELS HE BUILDED — 333 FOUR ZOAS 7B — 12
LABORIOUS
AND POLISH BRASS & IRON HOUR AFTER HOUR LABORIOUS — 337 FOUR ZOAS 7B — 182
WORKMANSHIP
THE LABORIOUS STUMBLE OF A FOOL . . . . — 547 LET BE TOLD/N — 5
. . . LABORIOUS STUMBLE OF A FOOL . . . . — 547 RAFAEL SUBLI/N — 5
HIS LABORIOUS TASK DROPPING HIS FLAIL & CREAM BOWL . . . — 618C ILLUS MILTON — PROSE
THAT TOWARD ULRO FOUR CLAY BAKD LABORIOUS WORKMANSHIP . . — 633 JERUSALEM 13 — 4
ITS GUARDS LIVING THE WORK OF ELEMENTAL HANDS LABORIOUS — 633 JERUSALEM 13 — 7
TASK
AND POLISH BRASS & IRON HOUR AFTER HOUR LABORIOUS TASK — 700 JERUSALEM 65 — 24
AMONG HIS FURNACES DIRECTING HIS LABORIOUS MYRIADS WATCHFUL — 730 JERUSALEM 85 — 11
TO ENGRAVE AFTER ANOTHER PAINTER IS INFINITELY MORE — 794B LETTER 5 — PROSE
LABORIOUS
CHALK ENGRAVING IS AT LEAST SIX TIMES AS LABORIOUS AS — 794C LETTER 5 — PROSE
AQUA TINTA
BUT HE IS ALSO A LABORIOUS VOTARY OF ENDLESS WORK . . . — 842D LETTER 42 — PROSE
HEARTILY DEVOTE HIMSELF TO THE BUSINESS IN ALL ITS — 845C LETTER 44 — PROSE
LABORIOUS
DESIGNING AND TO RELIEVE MY MORE LABORIOUS [EMPLOYMENT] — 860C LETTER 56 — PROSE

LABOUR
LABOUR AND TOIL FOR LIFE . . . . — 13 GWIN KING/PS — 90
OF TH OTHER'S LABOUR THIS IS PHILOSOPHY . . . . — 27 EDW THIRD/PS 3 — 271
FOR CARE WAS I BROUGHT FORTH AND LABOUR IS MY LOT . . . — 39B SAMSON/PS — PROSE
TO SIT IN THE HOUSE AND TAKE HIS EVENING'S REST FROM LABOUR — 40A SAMSON/PS — PROSE
. . . THEY LOOK DOWNWARD AND LABOUR AND FORGET MY HOLY LAW — 140 FRENCH REVOLTN — 139
DEVOUR THY LABOUR NOR LIFT UP A CLOUD IN THY HEAVENS . . . — 144 FRENCH REVOLTN — 226
TO CREATE A LITTLE FLOWER IS THE LABOUR OF AGES . . . . — 152C MARRIAGE HH 9 — PROSE
THY JOYS ARE TEARS THY LABOUR VAIN TO FORM MEN TO THINE — 192 V DAU ALBION 5 — 4
IMAGE
AT THE LABOUR THAT IS ABOVE PAYMENT AND WILT THOU TAKE — 192 V DAU ALBION 5 — 8
THE APE
WITH WHAT SENSE DOES THE PARSON CLAIM THE LABOUR OF THE — 193 V DAU ALBION 5 — 17
FARMER
[THEY] HE PILED THEM IN INCESSANT LABOUR . . . . . . — 225 URIZEN 5 — * 23
WITH INFINITE LABOUR THE ETERNALS . . . . — 231 URIZEN 19 — 8
SURGE FOAM AND LABOUR INTO LIFE FIRST BORN & FIRST CONSUMD — 238 EUROPE PREL 1 — 9
TO FIX THE PRICE OF LABOUR . . . . — 247 SONG OF LOS 6 — 17
DOES THE SOUL LABOUR THUS IN CAVERNS OF THE GRAVE . . . — 262A SMALL BK DSGNS — TITLE
ETERNALLY I LABOUR ON . . . . — 262B SMALL BK DSGNS — TITLE
I LABOUR UPWARDS INTO FUTURITY . . . . — 262B SMALL BK DSGNS — TITLE
REST BEFORE LABOUR . . . . — 263D FOUR ZOAS — TITLE
SEVERE THE LABOUR FEMALE SLAVES THE MORTAR TROD OPPRESSED — 284 FOUR ZOAS 2 — 172
OF TERRIBLE WORKMANSHIP THE ALTAR LABOUR OF TEN THOUSAND — 285 FOUR ZOAS 2 — 197
SLAVES
TO HIM HIS LABOUR WAS BUT SORROW & HIS KINGDOM WAS — 285 FOUR ZOAS 2 — 208
REPENTANCE

	PAGE	TITLE	LINE

LABOUR   (CONTINUED)

AND SEE THIS LABOUR & SORROW THEY WENT DOWN TO SEE THE WOES — 285 FOUR ZOAS 2 — 212

TO LABOUR NIGHT & DAY AMONG THE FIRES HER LAMENTING VOICE — 285 FOUR ZOAS 2 — 216

THUS SHE LAMENTED DAY & NIGHT COMPELLD TO LABOUR & SORROW — 286 FOUR ZOAS 2 — 231

[FROM ALL THE SORROW OF LUVAH & THE LABOUR OF URIZEN] . . — 286 FOUR ZOAS 2 — 237

[?THEN XXX LABOUR ENDED XXX LOVE FOR VALA] . . . . . — SUPP FOUR ZOAS 3 — *

BONIFY & THOU SHALT HAVE REST WHEN THIS THY LABOUR IS DONE — 299 FOUR ZOAS 4 — 69

LABOUR OF AGES IN THE DARKNESS & THE WAR OF THARMAS . . . — 301 FOUR ZOAS 4 — 167

WITH LABOUR & CARE THOU DOST DIVIDE THE [RIVER] CURRENT INTO FOUR — 312 FOUR ZOAS 6 — 18

INFINITE WAS HIS LABOUR WITHOUT END HIS TRAVEL HE STROVE — 313 FOUR ZOAS 6 — 74

BUT WHEN A VORTEX FORMD ON HIGH BY LABOUR & SORROW & CARE — 317 FOUR ZOAS 6 — 204

OR DOWN DARK PRECIPICES OR CLIMBD WITH PAIN & LABOUR HUGE — 319 FOUR ZOAS 6 — * 289

WITH LABOUR & ABSTINENCE SAY HE LOOKS HEALTHY & HAPPY . . — 323 FOUR ZOAS 7 — 119

I LABOUR NIGHT & DAY FOR LOS BUT LISTEN THOU MY VISION — 327 FOUR ZOAS 7 — 298

WONDERS OF LABOUR — 329 FOUR ZOAS 7 — 377

. . . & IN OUR GARDENS OF [PLEASURE] LABOUR . . . . . — 331 FOUR ZOAS 7 — 441

TO LABOUR & BEHOLD MY HEART SUNK DOWN BENEATH . . . . — 334 FOUR ZOAS 7B — 63

AND CLOUDS ARE CLOSD AROUND MY TOWER MY ARMS LABOUR IN VAIN — 335 FOUR ZOAS 7B — 89

TEN THOUSAND DEMONS LABOUR AT THE FORGES CREATING CONTINUALLY — 346 FOUR ZOAS 8 — 205

TO MULTITUDE & MY MULTITUDES ARE CHILDREN OF CARE & LABOUR — 350 FOUR ZOAS 8 — 353

THAT MAN SHOULD LABOUR & SORROW & LEARN & FORGET & RETURN — 355 FOUR ZOAS 8 — 574

AND ON THE FLEECES OF MILD FLOCKS WHO NEITHER CARE NOR LABOUR — 361 FOUR ZOAS 9 — 173

WHEN MORNING DAWND THE ETERNALS ROSE TO LABOUR AT THE VINTAGE — 374 FOUR ZOAS 9 — 647

OF LUVAH QUITE EXHAUSTED WITH THE LABOUR & QUITE FILLD — 378 FOUR ZOAS 9 — 786

CALLING THE PLOWMAN TO HIS LABOUR & THE SHEPHERD TO HIS REST — 379 FOUR ZOAS 9 — 834

THESE BLOTS OF LIGHT AND DARK AS BEING THE RESULT OF LABOUR — 439C REMARKS MALKIN — PROSE

TO GIVE THEM HIS LABOUR FOR NOTHING A SOCIETY COMPOSED . . — 446A ANNO REYNOLDS — MARG

THE MAN WHO DOES NOT LABOUR MORE THAN THE HIRELING . . . — 451A ANNO REYNOLDS — MARG

OR WOOLLETT THEY ARE WORKS OF MANUAL LABOUR . . . . . — 455A ANNO REYNOLDS — * MARG

LABOUR & TRICK AS TO IMAGINATION HE WAS TOTALLY WITHOUT ANY — 468C ANNO REYNOLDS — MARG

LABOUR & TRICK SALVATORE ROSA EMPLOYD JOURNEYMEN . . . . — 468D ANNO REYNOLDS — MARG

FOR PALAMABRON RETURND WITH LABOUR WEARIED EVERY EVENING — 486 MILTON 7 — 9

BUT WHEN THE GNOMES REFUSD TO LABOUR MORE WITH BLANDISHMENTS — 493 MILTON 12 — 37

THOUSANDS & THOUSANDS LABOUR THOUSANDS PLAY ON INSTRUMENTS — 509 MILTON 24 — 60

ALL THE GODS OF THE KINGDOMS OF EARTH LABOUR IN LOS'S HALLS — 510 MILTON 24 — 74

GIVEN TO HERCULES WHO LABOUR IN TIRZAH'S LOOMS FOR BREAD — 511 MILTON 25 — 50

HERE THE SONS OF LOS LABOUR AGAINST DEATH ETERNAL THROUGH ALL — 514 MILTON 27 — 44

URIZEN'S SONS HERE LABOUR ALSO & HERE ARE SEEN THE MILLS — 514 MILTON 27 — 49

THEY LABOUR INCESSANT WITH MANY TEARS & AFFLICTIONS . . — 515 MILTON 28 — 6

SUCH IS THE WORLD OF LOS THE LABOUR OF SIX THOUSAND YEARS — 518 MILTON 29 — 64

LABOUR WITH BLACKEND VISAGES AMONG ITS STUPENDOUS RUINS — 529 MILTON 38 — 21

TO LABOUR IN THE OCEAN OR IN THE STARRY HEAVEN SO MILTON — 532 MILTON 39 — 56

BUT ALL THE PULP WASHD PAINTED FINISHD WITH LABOUR . . . — 546 SWELLD LIMBS/N — 3

SEE WHAT GREAT LABOUR PAIN HIM & MODEST DOUBT . . . . . — 548 CRIPPLE EVRY/N — * 5

BUT IN THE JOURNEYMAN'S LABOUR . . . . — 548 GIVE PENSION/N — 4

HE IS THIN WITH EXCESSIVE LABOUR . . . . — 571B DESC CAT 3 — PROSE

WORN OUT WITH AGE AND LABOUR AS THE PROSPECTUS HAS . . . — 575A DESC CAT 3 — PROSE

HE IS WORN DOWN WITH LABOUR BUT NOT WITH AGE . . . . . — 575A DESC CAT 3 — PROSE

BUT OF THE GREAT LABOUR WHICH HAS BEEN BESTOWED ON IT . . — 582B DESC CAT 9 — PROSE

THE LABOUR HAS DESTROYED THE LINEAMENTS . . . . — 582B DESC CAT 9 — PROSE

ENDLESS LABOUR TO WHOEVER SUFFERS HIM TO ENTER HIS MIND — 583A DESC CAT 9 — PROSE

THE MANUAL LABOUR IN THESE PICTURES OF CORREGGIO IS IMMENSE — 583B DESC CAT 9 — PROSE

HAVE SOFTNESS AND EVENNESS BY A TWELVEMONTH'S LABOUR . . — 583C DESC CAT 9 — PROSE

SUPERIOR TO BASIRE'S BECAUSE THEY HAD MORE LABOUR & CARE — 593A PUB ADDRESS/N — PROSE

HOW TO PUT SO MUCH LABOUR INTO A HEAD OR A FOOT AS BASIRE DID — 593A PUB ADDRESS/N — PROSE

SHOULD HE BE ABLE TO MAKE USE OF EITHER LABOUR OR CARE . . — 593A PUB ADDRESS/N — PROSE

UNLESS THE LABOUR & CARE OF IMBECILLITY . . . . . . — 593A PUB ADDRESS/N — PROSE

THE LIFE'S LABOUR OF MENTAL WEAKNESS SCARCELY EQUALS . . — 593A PUB ADDRESS/N — PROSE

ONE HOUR OF THE LABOUR OF ORDINARY CAPACITY . . . . . — 593B PUB ADDRESS/N — PROSE

THE LIFE'S LABOUR OF FIVE HUNDRED IDIOTS . . . . . . — 593B PUB ADDRESS/N — PROSE

THE LIFE'S LABOUR OF IGNORANT JOURNEYMEN . . . . . . — 593D PUB ADDRESS/N — PROSE

CHOOSE TO PURCHASE THE LIFE'S LABOUR OF IGNORANCE & IMBECILLITY — 594B PUB ADDRESS/N — PROSE

IT IS NO BETTER THAN ANY OTHER'S MANUAL LABOUR ANY BODY MAY — 598A PUB ADDRESS/N — *PROSE

CAN ANGLUS NEVER DISCERN PERFECTION BUT IN THE JOURNEYMAN'S LABOUR — 601D PUB ADDRESS/N — PROSE

TAKE THOU THESE TONGS STRIKE THOU ALTERNATE WITH ME LABOUR OBEDIENT — 627 JERUSALEM 8 — 40

HAND & HYLE & KOBAN SKOFELD KOX & KOTOPE LABOUR MIGHTILY — 628 JERUSALEM 8 — 41

BY WAR AND STRATAGEM TO WIN THE LABOUR OF THE HUSBANDMAN — 628 JERUSALEM 9 — 11

I LABOUR DAY AND NIGHT I BEHOLD THE SOFT AFFECTIONS . . — 628 JERUSALEM 9 — 26

BUT STILL I LABOUR IN HOPE THO STILL MY TEARS FLOW DOWN — 628 JERUSALEM 9 — 28

WITH GREAT LABOUR UPON HIS ANVILS & IN HIS LADLES THE ORE — 630 JERUSALEM 11 — 3

AND THEY BUILDED GOLGONOOZA TERRIBLE ETERNAL LABOUR . . — 631 JERUSALEM 12 — 24

LABOUR OF MERCIFUL HANDS THE BEAMS & RAFTERS ARE FORGIVENESS — 632 JERUSALEM 12 — 32

LABOUR WITHIN THE FURNACES WALKING AMONG THE FIRES . . . — 637 JERUSALEM 16 — 20

SCOTLAND POURS OUT HIS SONS TO LABOUR AT THE FURNACES . . — 637 JERUSALEM 16 — 22

TO LABOUR IN THE FIRE IN THE WATER IN THE EARTH IN THE AIR — 638 JERUSALEM 17 — 2

NO ONE BRUISES OR STARVES HIMSELF TO MAKE HIMSELF FIT FOR LABOUR — 639 JERUSALEM 17 — 21

```
                                                            PAGE     TITLE        LINE
LABOUR    (CONTINUED)
    EVERY ORNAMENT OF PERFECTION AND EVERY LABOUR OF LOVE    .    .  652 JERUSALEM 28      1
    IN SILENCE THE DIVINE LORD BUILDED WITH IMMORTAL LABOUR     677 JERUSALEM 48      5
    LABOUR WELL THE MINUTE PARTICULARS ATTEND TO THE           687 JERUSALEM 55     51
        LITTLE-ONES
    IF WE DO BUT OUR DUTY LABOUR WELL THE TEEMING EARTH  .  .  . 687 JERUSALEM 55     53
    ENDLESS THEIR LABOUR WITH BITTER FOOD VOID OF SLEEP  .  .  . 691 JERUSALEM 59     30
    THO HUNGRY THEY LABOUR THEY ROUZE THEMSELVES ANXIOUS    .  . 691 JERUSALEM 59     31
    FOR THEY LABOUR FOR LIFE & LOVE REGARDLESS OF ANY ONE   .  . 691 JERUSALEM 59     37
    THEY LABOUR & WHEN THEIR WHEELS ARE BROKEN BY SCORN        692 JERUSALEM 59     40
        & MALICE
    MEN UNDERSTAND NOT THE DISTRESS & THE LABOUR & SORROW   .  . 692 JERUSALEM 59     50
    LABOUR UNPARALLELLD A WONDROUS ROCKY WORLD OF CRUEL DESTINY  702 JERUSALEM 66      6
    THE INHABITANTS ARE SICK TO DEATH THEY LABOUR TO DIVIDE    703 JERUSALEM 66     68
        INTO DAYS
    THAT TO LABOUR IN KNOWLEDGE IS TO BUILD UP JERUSALEM AND   717C JERUSALEM 77   PROSE
    CAN I ARISE AND LEAVE THY SIDE BUT LABOUR HERE INCESSANT   727 JERUSALEM 83      2
    ALTERNATE THEY WATCH IN NIGHT ALTERNATE LABOUR IN DAY   .  . 729 JERUSALEM 83     79
    HIS VOICE IN THE BLACK CLOUD HIS SONS LABOUR IN THUNDERS   731 JERUSALEM 86     37
    AND THUS HE OTHERS' LABOUR STOLE   .  .  .  .  .  .  .  .  . 757 EV GOSPEL(I)/N    43
    THE LABOURS OF LIFE & WE PLOW & REAP FORGETTING OUR LABOUR   791C LETTER 3     PROSE
    AT LEAST SIX TIMES THE QUANTITY OF LABOUR IN THE SAME TIME  794B LETTER 5     PROSE
    EXPECTATION & GLADNESS ADDED TO LABOUR IN OUR REMOVAL THAT  801B LETTER 13    PROSE
    I LABOUR INCESSANTLY & ACCOMPLISH NOT ONE HALF OF WHAT   .  809A LETTER 20    PROSE
    AS ALL MY FRIENDS TELL ME BUT MY PRINCIPAL LABOUR   .  .  . 809C LETTER 20    PROSE
    OUR INCESSANT LABOUR FULLY ADEQUATE TO [IT] THEM AT PRESENT  811D LETTER 22    PROSE
    WHICH SEEMS TO BE THE LABOUR OF A LONG LIFE ALL PRODUCD     823B LETTER 26    PROSE
    WITHOUT LABOUR OR STUDY I MENTION THIS TO SHEW YOU WHAT     823B LETTER 26    PROSE
    WITHOUT INCESSANT LABOUR & STUDY HOW IS IT POSSIBLE THAT    830A LETTER 30    PROSE
        SUCH
    HE SAYS THAT THE LAST SESSION WAS A SEVERE LABOUR INDEED IT  844D LETTER 43    PROSE
    & THIS ALONE WILL PAY ITS LABOUR BY SUCCESS IF NOT OF MONEY  850C LETTER 49    PROSE
    BE CONVINCED THAT THE LABOUR I HAVE USED ON THE TWO PLATES  853C LETTER 52    PROSE
    SHOULD LOSE ALL THE LABOUR I HAVE BEEN AT ON THAT PLATE     861B LETTER 58    PROSE
    I KNOW IT HAS COST ME IMMENSE LABOUR   .  .  .  .  .  .  .  . 861B LETTER 58    PROSE
LABOURD      SEE HIGH LABOURD,MOTH-LABOURD
    .  .  . SHE LABOURD IN THICK SMOKE                         275 FOUR ZOAS 1    418
    ALBION ROSE FROM WHERE HE LABOURD AT THE MILL WITH SLAVES  160 ALBION ROSE      1
    INCESSANT THE FALLING MIND LABOURD   .  .  .  .  .  .  .  . 258 BOOK OF LOS 4     49
    NINE DAYS SHE LABOURD AT HER WORK & NINE DARK SLEEPLESS    266 FOUR ZOAS 1     86
        NIGHTS
    BY NIGHT NOR DAY TO COMFORT HER SHE LABOURD IN THICK SMOKE  275 FOUR ZOAS 1    418
    THE SPIDER SITS IN HIS LABOURD WEB EAGER WATCHING FOR THE   277 FOUR ZOAS 1   -457
        FLY
    THE VOICE OF LOS COMPELLD HE LABOURD ROUND THE FURNACES    302 FOUR ZOAS 4    198
    ON HATE ETERNAL IN HIS VAST DISDAIN HE LABOURD BEATING  .  . 302 FOUR ZOAS 4    206
    WITH JEWELS & PRECIOUS ORNAMENT LABOURD WITH ART DIVINE    312 FOUR ZOAS 6     27
    FOR LABOURD FATHERLY CARE & SWEET INSTRUCTION I WILL GIVE   312 FOUR ZOAS 6     40
    DIVIDING INTO JUST PROPORTIONS LOS UNWEARIED LABOURD    .  . 332 FOUR ZOAS 7    470
    WITH TEARS OF SORROW INCESSANT SHE LABOURD THE FOOD OF ORC  343 FOUR ZOAS 8     82
    THE LABOURD WORKS OF JOURNEYMEN EMPLOYD BY CORREGGIO    .  . 455A ANNO REYNOLDS  MARG
    LOS SIEZD HIS HAMMER & TONGS HE LABOURD AT HIS RESOLUTE     482 MILTON 3         7
        ANVIL
    MILDNESS SATAN LABOURD ALL DAY IT WAS A THOUSAND YEARS  .  . 486 MILTON 7        15
    THE GNOMES LABOURD I WEEPING HID IN SATAN'S INMOST BRAIN    493 MILTON 12       36
    THAT MILTON LABOURD WITH HIS JOURNEY & HIS FEET BLED SORE   500 MILTON 19        3
    LABOURD IN CHASMS OF THE MUNDANE SHELL THO HERE BEFORE  .  . 532 MILTON 39       57
    CHURCHES & THE INN IN SOUTHWARK IS MINUTELY LABOURD   .  .  . 588A CHAUCER/N   PROSE
    OF BLACK DESPAIR THAT THE IMMORTAL WINGS LABOURD AGAINST    674 JERUSALEM 44     12
    AND MANY CONVERSED ON THESE THINGS AS THEY LABOURD AT THE   687 JERUSALEM 55     48
        FURROW
    THE ENVY LOUD SHE LABOURD IN THE FURNACE OF FIRE   .  .  .  . 726 JERUSALEM 82     62
    MY HANDS ARE LABOURD DAY & NIGHT   .  .  .  .  .  .  .  .  . 818 HAPPINESS/L      59
    HAVE LABOURD HARD INDEED & HAVE BEEN BORNE ON ANGEL'S WINGS  826A LETTER 27    PROSE
    HIGHLY LABOURD PLATES THAN A GREATER NUMBER & LESS FINISHD  860C LETTER 56    PROSE
    HE TELLS ME THAT IT IS TOO MUCH FINISHD OR OVER LABOURD     877A LETTER 85    PROSE
LABOURED
    LABOURED FABRICATION OF JOURNEY-WORK THEY COULD NOT DRAW   457A ANNO REYNOLDS * MARG
    FOR EXPERIMENT WITH THE COLOURS AND IS LABOURED   .  .  .  . 581C DESC CAT 7   PROSE
LABOURER
    A LABOURER OF AGES A DIRE DISCONTENT A LIVING WOE   .  .  . 317 FOUR ZOAS 6    226
    BUT I THE LABOURER OF AGES WHOSE UNWEARIED HANDS   .  .  .  . 361 FOUR ZOAS 9    174
    THE LABOURER OF AGES IN THE VALLEYS OF DESPAIR   .  .  .  . 728 JERUSALEM 83     53
    MY MOCK & SCORN ALAS WRETCHED HAPPY INEFFECTUAL LABOURER OF  809B LETTER 20   PROSE
LABOURER'S     SEE LABRER'S
    THEY MOCK AT THE LABOURER'S LIMBS THEY MOCK AT HIS STARVD   656 JERUSALEM 30     28
        CHILDREN
LABOURERS
    IS HEARD WHEN SILENT NIGHT RETURNS & THE LABOURERS TAKE    285 FOUR ZOAS 2    217
        THEIR REST
    AND LOS STOOD & CRIED TO THE LABOURERS OF THE VINTAGE IN   510 MILTON 25       16
        VOICE OF AWE
    FELLOW LABOURERS THE GREAT VINTAGE & HARVEST IS NOW UPON   510 MILTON 25       17
        EARTH
    THESE ARE THE SONS OF LOS & THESE THE LABOURERS OF THE     512 MILTON 26        1
        VINTAGE
    I HAVE ENOUGH IN THE APPROBATION OF FELLOW LABOURERS   .  . 600C PUB ADDRESS/N PROSE
    SUCH WERE THE LAMENTATIONS OF THE LABOURERS IN THE FURNACES  631 JERUSALEM 12     16
    THRO ALL THE FOUR POINTS LO THE LABOURERS AT THE FURNACES   713 JERUSALEM 73      4
    AS HE WATCHES THE FURNACES BY NIGHT & DIRECTS THE LABOURERS  730 JERUSALEM 85     13
    AS HE WALKS FROM FURNACE TO FURNACE DIRECTING THE          730 JERUSALEM 85     20
        LABOURERS
```

		PAGE	TITLE	LINE

LABOURERS   (CONTINUED)
    TWO SO UNEQUAL LABOURERS MIGHT NOT BE YOKED TO THE SAME   853A LETTER 51   *PROSE
        PLOW
LABOURING   SEE LABRING
    THOU ART UNITED WITH THY SPECTRE [?LABOURING] . . . . . .   328 FOUR ZOAS 7   *   343
    LIKE THE LOW VOICE OF THE LABOURING MAN INSTEAD OF THE   145 FRENCH REVOLTN   245
        SHOUT OF JOY
    LONG PERIODS IN BURNING FIRES LABOURING . . . .   225 URIZEN 5   25
    AMONG THESE FLAMES INCESSANT LABOURING OUR HARD MASTERS   285 FOUR ZOAS 2   219
        LAUGH
    STILL HATING STILL PROFESSING LOVE STILL LABOURING IN   286 FOUR ZOAS 2   235
        THE SMOKE
    STEMMING HIS DOWNWARD FALL LABOURING UP AGAINST FUTURITY   316 FOUR ZOAS 6   186
    THEY BUILDED GOLGONOOZA LOS LABOURING [INSPIRD] BUILDED   329 FOUR ZOAS 7   *   378
        PILLARS HIGH
    WITHIN LABOURING BEHOLDING WITHOUT FROM PARTICULARS TO   483 MILTON 3   37
        GENERALS
    HIS FORMING IMAGE HE WALKS ROUND IT PATIENT LABOURING   . . 502 MILTON 20   9
    IN LOS'S HALLS CONTINUAL LABOURING IN THE FURNACES   520 MILTON 31   26
        OF GOLGONOOZA
    LABOURING TO DESTROY IMAGINATIVE POWER BY MEANS OF   . . . 582B DESC CAT 9   PROSE
    AND CHAUNTED HIS SONG LABOURING WITH THE TONGS AND HAMMER   625 JERUSALEM 6   *   11
    YET CEASD HE NOT FROM LABOURING AT THE ROARINGS OF HIS   630 JERUSALEM 10   62
        FORGE
    OR AS THE SWEAT UPON THE LABOURING SHOULDER OR AS THE   687 JERUSALEM 55   40
        CHAFF
    HOUR AFTER HOUR LABOURING AT THE WHIRLING WHEEL   . . . . 691 JERUSALEM 59   32
    OTHER DAUGHTERS OF LOS LABOURING AT LOOMS LESS FINE   . .   692 JERUSALEM 59   45
    AGAINST THE PATRIARCHAL POMP AND CRUELTY LABOURING   727 JERUSALEM 83   4
        INCESSANT
    BEFORE THE FURNACES LABOURING WHILE LOS ALL NIGHT WATCHES   729 JERUSALEM 83   80
    OF STRICT SEVERITY SELF-SUBDUING & WITH MANY TEARS   738 JERUSALEM 91   47
        LABOURING
    AND LUVAH TO HIS LOOM URTHONA HE BEHELD MIGHTY LABOURING AT 742 JERUSALEM 95   17
    HIS ANVIL IN THE GREAT SPECTRE LOS UNWEARIED LABOURING   742 JERUSALEM 95   18
        & WEEPING
    A WORK OF MAGNITUDE WHICH MR HAYLEY IS NOW LABOURING   . . 809D LETTER 20   PROSE
    FAMILY & I AM NOW LABOURING IN MY THOUGHTS DESIGNS FOR   . .821C LETTER 25   PROSE
    POOR WIFE WITH ME INCESSANTLY LABOURING AND INCESSANTLY   852B LETTER 50   PROSE
LABOURS
    AND MY HEART LABOURS WITH FUTURITY   . . . .   32 EDW THIRD/PS 6   41
    . . . THE REPOSE OF THE LABOURS OF MEN . . . .   140 FRENCH REVOLTN   129
    THE LABOURS OF THE ARTIST THE POET THE MUSICIAN HAVE BEEN   207A PRSPECTUS 1793 PROSE
    IN ENORMOUS LABOURS OCCUPIED . . . .   223 URIZEN 3   22
    THAN ALL THESE LABOURS OF THE HARVEST & THE VINTAGE SEE   275 FOUR ZOAS 1   390
        THE RIVER
    WHEN URIZEN [DESCENDED] RETURND FROM HIS IMMENSE LABOURS   285 FOUR ZOAS 2   201
        & TRAVELS
    THEIR SWEET INSPIRITING LYRES THY LABOURS SHALL ADMINISTER   301 FOUR ZOAS 4   * 154
    THE SPECTRE WEPT AT HIS DIRE LABOURS WHEN FROM [?LABLES]   302 FOUR ZOAS 4   * 194
        LADLES HUGE
    HE WENT EACH MORNING TO HIS LABOURS WITH THE SPECTRE DARK   307 FOUR ZOAS 5   94
    BUT URIZEN REMITTED NOT THEIR LABOURS UPON HIS ROCK . . . 322 FOUR ZOAS 7   108
    . . . CONSUMMATING BY PAINS & LABOURS   . . . .   328 FOUR ZOAS 7   343
    TO PERPLEX YOUTH IN THEIR OUTGOINGS & TO BIND TO LABOURS   337 FOUR ZOAS 7B   180
    IN GOLDEN LETTERS ORNAMENTED WITH SWEET LABOURS OF LOVE   340 FOUR ZOAS 7B   294
    TO THE DARK VALLEY WHENCE HE CAME TO BEGIN HIS LABOURS ANEW 355 FOUR ZOAS 8   * 575
    IN PAIN HE SIGHS IN PAIN HE LABOURS IN HIS UNIVERSE   . .   355 FOUR ZOAS 8   576
    AND WITH THE CHISEL & THE MALLET I WHOSE LABOURS VAST   . . 361 FOUR ZOAS 9   176
    EARTH IS CONVULSED WITH THE LABOURS OF THE RESURRECTION   443A LAST JUDGMNT/L *PROSE
    AND WITH LABOURS OF IGNORANCE FILL EVERY PLACE . . . . . 445 ANNO REYNOLDS   4
    GET TO THY LABOURS AT THE MILLS & LEAVE ME TO MY WRATH . . 483 MILTON 4   14
    IN IMMENSE LABOURS & SORROWS EVER BUILDING EVER FALLING   485 MILTON 6   2
    YOUR LABOURS CALL YOU PALAMABRON IS ALSO IN SAD DILEMMA   488 MILTON 8   17
    RESUME YOUR LABOURS & THIS DAY SHALL BE A MOURNFUL DAY   .   488 MILTON 8   22
    AND VALA LABOURS FOR HER BREAD & WATER AMONG THE FURNACES   501 MILTON 19   43
    ACCORDANT WITH THE HORRID LABOURS MAKE SWEET MELODY   . .   509 MILTON 24   57
    STILL ABSTAIN FROM PLEASURE & REST IN THE LABOURS   511 MILTON 25   46
        OF ETERNITY
    AND THESE THE LABOURS OF THE SONS OF LOS IN ALLAMANDA   . . 512 MILTON 26   23
    HIS LITTLE THROAT LABOURS WITH INSPIRATION EVERY FEATHER   520 MILTON 31   34
    WHILE IN THE LABOURS OF HIS CALLING SENDS HIS THOUGHT   531 MILTON 39   55
        ABROAD
    THE CRIPPLE EVERY STEP DRUDGES & LABOURS   . . . .   548 CRIPPLE EVRY/N   1
    AND GETS INTO BED A REWARD FOR THE LABOURS OF THE DAY   . . 586A DESC CAT 16   PROSE
    NEVER SUSPENDED HIS LABOURS ON COPPER FOR A SINGLE DAY   .   587D CHAUCER/N   PROSE
    CONCERNING MY THREE YEARS' HERCULEAN LABOURS AT FELPHAM   592C PUB ADDRESS/N   PROSE
    THE LIFE'S LABOURS OF IMBECILLITY & IMBECILLITY'S   598C PUB ADDRESS/N   PROSE
        JOURNEYMEN
    OPAKE DIVIDED FROM HIS BACK HE LABOURS AND HE MOURNS   . . 624 JERUSALEM 6   2
    I WILL COMPELL THEE TO ASSIST ME IN MY TERRIBLE LABOURS   627 JERUSALEM 8   15
        TO BEAT
    COMPELLING HIS SPECTRE TO LABOURS MIGHTY TREMBLING IN FEAR   629 JERUSALEM 10   18
    AT THE SUBLIME LABOURS FOR LOS COMPELLD THE INVISIBLE   630 JERUSALEM 10   65
        SPECTRE
    TO LABOURS MIGHTY WITH VAST STRENGTH WITH HIS MIGHTY   630 JERUSALEM 11   1
        CHAINS
    LIFE IN BROODING CARES & ANXIOUS LABOURS THAT PROVE BUT   647 JERUSALEM 24   16
        CHAFF
    ALL THESE ORNAMENTS ARE CRIMES THEY ARE MADE BY THE LABOURS 652 JERUSALEM 28   6
    HER TEARS SHE ARDENT EMBRACD HER SORROWS OCCUPIED   678 JERUSALEM 48   40
        IN LABOURS

	PAGE	TITLE	LINE

LABOURS   (CONTINUED)
    IN ETERNAL LABOURS LOUD THE [FURNAES] FURNACES & LOUD   684 JERUSALEM 53   *   20
        THE ANVILS
    TURNING ANEW BEGAN HIS LABOURS THO IN TERRIBLE PAINS   .   696 JERUSALEM 62   42
    TO PERPLEX YOUTH IN THEIR OUTGOINGS & TO BIND TO LABOURS   700 JERUSALEM 65   22
        IN ALBION
    WHAT IS THE HARVEST OF THE GOSPEL & ITS LABOURS   . . .   . 717A JERUSALEM 77   PROSE
    THOSE WHO PRETEND TO DESPISE THE LABOURS OF ART & SCIENCE   717B JERUSALEM 77   PROSE
    WHICH ALONE ARE THE LABOURS OF THE GOSPEL . . . . 717B JERUSALEM 77   PROSE
    WHILE LOS LAMENTS AT HIS DIRE LABOURS VIEWING JERUSALEM   719 JERUSALEM 78   10
    ETERNAL DEATH STANDS AT THE DOOR O GOD PITY OUR LABOURS   728 JERUSALEM 83   65
    TO CLOSE THE LABOURS OF MY DAY . . . .   771 OF GATES/GP   42
    THE LABOURS OF LIFE & WE PLOW & REAP FORGETTING OUR LABOUR   791C LETTER 3   PROSE
    TO US & TO HIS LABOURS OF ART & SCIENCE IN THIS WORLD   . . 796D LETTER 8   PROSE
    MY FINGERS EMIT SPARKS OF FIRE WITH EXPECTATION OF   801C LETTER 13   PROSE
        MY FUTURE LABOURS
    BUT WHATEVER BECOMES OF MY LABOURS I WOULD RATHER   . . . 812B LETTER 22   PROSE
    BEEN THE RUIN OF MY LABOURS FOR THE LAST PASSED TWENTY   851D LETTER 50   PROSE
        YEARS
    PUBLICATION OF HIS LABOURS HE THEN PROCEEDED TO FIND FAULT   856B LETTER 54   PROSE
    & THAT THEY WOULD PROMOTE EACH OTHER'S SPIRITUAL LABOURS   863A LETTER 60   PROSE
    DAILY PERSISTING IN SPIRITUAL LABOURS . . . . 863B LETTER 60   PROSE
LABRER'S
    ONE MITE WRUNG FROM THE LABRER'S HANDS . . . .   432 AUGURIES   81
LABRING
    O MERCURY ASSIST MY LABRING SENSE . . . .   15 IMIT SPEN/PS   35
    THAT ROLLD PERPLEXD LABRING & UTTERD . . . .   223 URIZEN 4   3
    I WRAP MY TURBAN OF THICK CLOUDS AROUND MY LABRING HEAD   238 EUROPE PREL 1   12
    THE GROANS OF ENITHARMON SHAKE THE SKIES THE LABRING EARTH   306 FOUR ZOAS 5   36
    FLEW THE KING THO FLAGD HIS POWERS LABRING TILL OVER ROCKS   314 FOUR ZOAS 6   *   112
    [HEAVING XXX] HEAVD LIKE AN EARTHQUAKE LABRING WITH   347 FOUR ZOAS 8   *   249
        CONVULSIVE GROANS
    RINTRAH & PALAMABRON THEOTORMON & BROMION LOUD LABRING . .   713 JERUSALEM 73   5
LABYRINTH
    . . . ENTER INTO THE INFINITE LABYRINTH OF ANOTHER'S BRAIN   142 FRENCH REVOLTN   190
    AN ENDLESS LABYRINTH OF WOE . . . .   252 AHANIA 4   4
    I WILL BUILD THEE A LABYRINTH . . . . 265 FOUR ZOAS 1   28
    THEN LED HER DOWN INTO THE DEEPS & INTO HIS LABYRINTH   . .   308 FOUR ZOAS 5   111
    THE DOUBLE ROOTED LABYRINTH SOON WAVD AROUND THEIR HEADS   328 FOUR ZOAS 7   335
    & PUZZLING THEMSELVES IN SATAN'S [MAZE] LABYRINTH   . . . 613C V LAST JUDG/N   PROSE
    SHOT INTO MANY A TREE AN ENDLESS LABYRINTH OF WOE   . . . 653 JERUSALEM 28   19
    MOVING BESIDE ME TILL INTOXICATED WITH THE WOVEN LABYRINTH   732 JERUSALEM 87   4
LABYRINTHINE
    UPON HIS GOLDEN HALL & SOUGHT THE LABYRINTHINE PORCHES   . . 285 FOUR ZOAS 2   185
    AROUND THE FIERY FLAMING HARROW IN LABYRINTHINE FORMS   . . 493 MILTON 12   18
    OF LABYRINTHINE INTRICACY TWENTY-SEVEN FOLDS OF OPAKENESS   498 MILTON 17   26
    IN LABYRINTHINE ARCHES MIGHTY URIZEN THE ARCHITECT THRO   702 JERUSALEM 66   4
        WHICH
    OF LABYRINTHINE INTRICACY SO SHALL THEY FOLD THE WORLD   . . 728 JERUSALEM 83   37
    THE LABYRINTHINE EAR . . . .   745 JERUSALEM 98   18
LABYRINTHS
    INEXTRICABLE LABYRINTHS SHE BORE ME SONS & DAUGHTERS   . .   282 FOUR ZOAS 2   97
    IN INTRICATE LABYRINTHS OERSPREADING MANY A GRIZLY DEEP   321 FOUR ZOAS 7   35
    THE LITTLE HEART THE LIVER & THE RED BLOOD IN ITS   323 FOUR ZOAS 7   132
        LABYRINTHS
    THRO THE INFINITE LABYRINTHS OF THE HEART & THRO   327 FOUR ZOAS 7   280
        THE NOSTRILS ISSUING
    ITS INTRICATE LABYRINTHS NOW THE OBDURATE HEART WAS BROKEN   342 FOUR ZOAS 8   33
    WITH LABYRINTHS OF WAYWARD LOVE . . . . 426 MENTAL TRAVLER   83
    INTRICATE LABYRINTHS OF TIMES AND SPACES UNKNOWN   494 MILTON 13   43
        THAT LEUTHA LIVED
    THE LAND OF EARTHQUAKES AND THE LAND OF WOVEN LABYRINTHS   634 JERUSALEM 13   48
    BENEATH ITS WINDING LABYRINTHS TILL A STONE OF THE BROOK   659 JERUSALEM 33   10
    SHALL SURROUND HER IN BEAUTIFUL LABYRINTHS OOTHOON   . . . 727 JERUSALEM 83   27
LACE
    WITH SCARLET GOWNS & BROAD GOLD LACE WOULD MAKE A YEOMAN   58 THIS CITY/IM   5
        SWEAT
LACEDEMONIAN
    LACEDEMONIAN INSTRUCTION . . . . 180D LACEDEMONIAN/N   TITLE
LACERATING
    THE CRUEL JOY OF LUVAH'S DAUGHTERS LACERATING WITH KNIVES   377 FOUR ZOAS 9   753
    THE CRUEL JOYS OF LUVAH'S DAUGHTERS LACERATING WITH KNIVES   514 MILTON 27   35
LACK
    WE LACK NOT SONGS NOR INSTRUMENTS OF JOY . . . .   2 TO SUMMER/PS   17
    THE YOUNG BOSOM IS COLD FOR LACK OF MOTHER'S NOURISHMENT   110 TIRIEL 8   27
        & MILK
    MY CHILDREN WILL DIE FOR LACK OF BREAD . . . .   419 I SAW A MONK/N   20
    MY CHILDREN DIE FOR LACK OF BREAD . . . .   430 GREY MONK   2
    NEITHER DID ANY LACK OR FALL INTO ERROR WITHOUT   . . .   . 519 MILTON 31   6
LACKETH
    HOW TO EMPLOY THE HAND THAT LACKETH BREAD . . . . .   .   19 EDW THIRD/PS 2   23
LACTEAL
    SHE COUNTED EVERY VEIN & LACTEAL THREADING THEM AMONG   . . 266 FOUR ZOAS 1   80
LAD
    WITH LAD AND LASS HOW FAIR THE SHOW . . . .   16 BLIND-MANS/PS   8
LADDER
    ("READY TO MOUNT LADDER ANGELS ASCEND AND DESCEND ")   73A ANNO LAVATER   MARG
        NOBLE
    NUMBER XIII JACOB'S LADDER A DRAWING   . . . . 584B DESC CAT 13   TITLE
    THE LADDER OF ANGELS DESCENDS THRO THE AIR . . . . .   . 800 MRS FLAXMAN/L   6
LADEN
    O AUTUMN LADEN WITH FRUIT AND STAINED . . . .   2 TO AUTUMN/PS   1

LADEN   (CONTINUED)
    THEN LADEN WITH ETERNAL FATE DOST GO . . . .   15 IMIT SPEN/PS   24
LADIES
    HERE LADIES & GENTLEMEN SAID HE I'LL SHEW YOU A LOUSE   58C ISLAND MOON 10 *PROSE
        [?CLIMING] OR
    FOR THE LADIES TO VIEW THE PICTURES THUS HE WAS EMPLOYD 58D ISLAND MOON 10 PROSE
    OF ONE OF THOSE TENDER HEARTED LADIES TO SING FOR ME . . 61D ISLAND MOON 11 PROSE
    IMITATION OF POPE A COMPLIMENT TO THE LADIES . . . . . 545B IMIT POPE/N   TITLE
    THE LADIES WILL BE PLEASD TO SEE THAT I HAVE REPRESENTED 608A V LAST JUDG/N PROSE
LADIES'
    TO THIS SCOPPRELL ANSWERD I THINK THE LADIES' DISCOURSES 53C ISLAND MOON 8 PROSE
LADLE
    TAKEN OUT THAT PART WHICH EXPRESSED THE HOLE FOR THE LADLE 866C LETTER 65   PROSE
LADLES
    THE SPECTRE WEPT AT HIS DIRE LABOURS WHEN FROM [?LABLES] 302 FOUR ZOAS 4   * 194
        LADLES HUGE
    OUT FROM THE ASHES OF THE DEAD LOS LIFTS HIS IRON LADLES 486 MILTON 6   29
    WITH GREAT LABOUR UPON HIS ANVILS & IN HIS LADLES THE ORE 630 JERUSALEM 11   3
    WITH LADLES HUGE & IRON POKERS OVER THE ISLAND WHITE . . 637 JERUSALEM 16   21
LADS
    THE LASSES PRICK THE LADS WITH PINS . . . .   16 BLIND-MANS/PS   12
LADY
    I ASKD A LITHE LADY TO LIE HER DOWN . . . .   163 ASKED THIEF/N   3
    [HE] ENJOYD THE [(DAME)] LADY . . . .   163 ASKED THIEF/N   * 12
    I ASKD A LITHE LADY TO LIE HER DOWN . . . .   261 ASKED THIEF   3
    ENJOYD THE LADY . . . .   261 ASKED THIEF   12
    LADY IS DESCRIBED ALSO AS OF THE FIRST RANK RICH   568B DESC CAT 3   PROSE
        AND HONOURED
    THE LADY PRIORESS AND THE WIFE OF BATH . . . .   572B DESC CAT 3   PROSE
    THE LADY PRIORESS IN SOME AGES PREDOMINATES AND IN SOME 572B DESC CAT 3   PROSE
    AFTERWARD EXECUTED FOR A LADY OF HIGH RANK AN EXPERIMENT 582B DESC CAT 9   TITLE
        PICTURE
    & IN PARTICULAR LADY HESKETH & LORD COWPER . . . . . . 820C LETTER 25   PROSE
    TO PLEASE LADY H(HESKETH) WAS A DOUBTFUL CHANCE . . . . 820C LETTER 25   PROSE
    LADY HAMILTON'S DIRECTION WAS SO UNFORTUNATE AS TO FIND HIM 834D LETTER 34 PROSE
    GOD BLESS & PRESERVE YOU AND OUR GOOD LADY PAULINA . . . 835A LETTER 34   PROSE
    MR EDWARDS KNOW LADY HAMILTON'S ADDRESS THE . . . . . . 836B LETTER 35   PROSE
    YOU WILL RECIEVE PROOFS OF THEM FOR LADY HESKETH WHOSE . 837C LETTER 36   PROSE
    IMMEDIATELY TO LADY HAMILTON MR WALKER I HAVE AGAIN SEEN 845D LETTER 44   PROSE
    LADY OF LAVANT'S CONTINUED RECOVERY BUT WITH A MIXTURE . 851C LETTER 50   PROSE
    A LADY OF FORTUNE I SUPPOSE HE SENDS IT AS A SPECIMEN OF 857B LETTER 54   PROSE
        PRINTING
    & OUR GOOD LADY PAULINA OVER A DISH OF COFFEE I LONG TO 862A LETTER 59   PROSE
        HEAR
LAELIUS
    [?WHY SHOULD LAELIUS BE ?CONSIDERED SIR JOSHUA'S   SUPP ANNO REYNOLDS * MARG
        ?COUNTERPART]
LAHEE'S
    ALMOST WELL IF I CAN POSSIBLY I WILL BE AT MR LAHEE'S . . 869B LETTER 69   *PROSE
LAID   SEE LAYD
    OF HAVING MY BACK LAID OPEN WE TURN . . . .   22 EDW THIRD/PS 3   37
    A DAY LIKE THIS LAID ELFRID IN THE DUST . . . .   43C WOE CRIED MUSE PROSE
    AND LAID HER LILIED BEAUTIES ON THE GREEN . . . . . .   43C WOE CRIED MUSE PROSE
    THEN HAR AROSE & LAID HIS HAND UPON OLD TIRIEL'S HEAD . . 101 TIRIEL 2   34
    I LAID ME DOWN UPON A BANK . . . .   162 LAID ME DOWN/N   1
    AND LAID ME DOWN AMONG THE SWINE . . . .   163 I SAW CHAPEL/N   17
    BUT URIZEN LAID IN A STONY SLEEP . . . .   226 URIZEN 6   7
    DRIED LAID THEM APART TILL WINTER . . . .   251 AHANIA 3   22
    WHEN THE SHATTERD BONE HATH LAID HIM GROANING AMONG THE 291 FOUR ZOAS 2   416
        HAPPIER DEAD
    I LAID MY HEAD IN THE HOT NOON AFTER THE BROKEN CLODS . 295 FOUR ZOAS 3   123
    HAD WEARIED ME THERE I LAID MY PLOW & THERE MY HORSES FED 295 FOUR ZOAS 3   124
    AT NOON & LAID HER HEAD UPON MY WEARIED BOSOM AT NIGHT . 301 FOUR ZOAS 4   139
    HE WEPT & HE DIVIDED & HE LAID HIS GLOOMY HEAD . . . .   306 FOUR ZOAS 5   54
    THARMAS LAID THE FOUNDATIONS & LOS FINISHD IT IN HOWLING 307 FOUR ZOAS 5   * 78
        WOE
    AND URIZEN LAID THE FIRST STONE & ALL HIS MYRIADS . . . 333 FOUR ZOAS 7B   19
    THEY PIERCD HIM WITH A SPEAR & LAID HIM IN A SEPULCHER . 337 FOUR ZOAS 7B   167
    AND HEARTS LAID OPEN TO THE LIGHT BY THE BROAD GRIZLY SWORD 338 FOUR ZOAS 7B 206
    AND LAID HIM IN THE SEPULCHER OR IF [THAT] THOU WILT   345 FOUR ZOAS 8   165
        REVENGE
    [THE FALLEN MAN WONDRING BEHELD] HE LAID HIS (HAND) ON 365 FOUR ZOAS 9   * 311
        THE PLOW
    HE TURND THE HORSES LOOSE & LAID HIS PLOW IN THE NORTHERN 365 FOUR ZOAS 9   319
        CORNER
    SO SPOKE THE SINLESS SOUL & LAID HER HEAD ON THE DOWNY 369 FOUR ZOAS 9   455
        FLEECE
    MY LUVAH SMILD I KNEELED DOWN HE LAID HIS HAND ON MY HEAD 369 FOUR ZOAS 9   468
    AND WHEN HE LAID HIS HAND UPON ME FROM THE GATES OF SLEEP 369 FOUR ZOAS 9   469
        I CAME
    SO SAYING HIS FAINT HEAD HE LAID UPON THE OOZY ROCK . . . 370 FOUR ZOAS 9   495
    AND WHEN NIGHT CAME THE FLOCKS LAID ROUND THE HOUSE BENEATH 370 FOUR ZOAS 9 514
        THE TREES
    SHE LAID THE CHILDREN ON THE BEDS WHICH SHE SAW PREPARD 370 FOUR ZOAS 9   515
        IN THE HOUSE
    THEN LAST HERSELF LAID DOWN & CLOSD HER EYELIDS IN SOFT 370 FOUR ZOAS 9   516
        SLUMBERS
    THAT SHALL NEVER BE QUIET TILL LAID ON ITS BIER . . . . 429 MARY   48
    WHEN MARY WOKE & FOUND HER LAID . . . .   435 WILLIAM BOND   37
    LAID ON (INDISCRIMINATELY) & BROKEN ONE INTO ANOTHER . . 469A ANNO REYNOLDS * MARG
    OBLIGATIONS REYNOLDS HAS LAID ON BAD ARTISTS OF ALL CLASSES 473A ANNO REYNOLDS MARG
    WHERE JERUSALEM'S FOUNDATIONS BEGAN WHERE THEY WERE LAID 485 MILTON 6   15
        IN RUINS

	PAGE	TITLE	LINE

LAID   (CONTINUED)

WHERE THEY WERE LAID IN RUINS FROM EVERY NATION &   485 MILTON 6   16
OAK GROVES ROOTED
AND THREW ASIDE HER ARROWS AND LAID DOWN HER SOUNDING BOW   494 MILTON 13   37
OF SATAN LUVAH LAID THE FOUNDATION & URIZEN FINISHD IT   513 MILTON 27   2
IN HOWLING WOE
HIS UNDER JAW DROPD AS THOSE EGGS HE LAID . . . . . .   537 AND HIS LEGS/N   14
FOR HOW TO STARVE DEATH WE HAD LAID A PLOT . . . . . .   537 AND HIS LEGS/N   28
LAID TO OUR CHARGE THE ARTIST WHO HAS DONE THESE PICTURES   584B DESC CAT 14   PROSE
WHERE I LAID MY PLOW IN THE HOT NOON WHERE MY HOT TEAM FED   660 JERUSALEM 34   12
AND HEARTS LAID OPEN TO THE LIGHT BY THE BROAD GRIZLY SWORD   701 JERUSALEM 65   52
HE LAID HIS HAND ON MOSES' LAW . . . .   754 EV GOSPEL(E)/N   11
THEY HAVE LAID ON MY SHELF WITHOUT SPEAKING TO TELL ME . .   791B LETTER 3   PROSE
WITH ANY NEGLECT YET I AM LAID BY IN A CORNER . . . . .   795C LETTER 6   PROSE
AND ARE LAID ACROSS BEAMS AT THE TOP . . . .   831B LETTER 31   PROSE
FOR I AM AGAIN LAID UP BY A COLD IN MY STOMACH THE . . .   870D LETTER 72   PROSE
EVEN ISLINGTON & ALL PLACES NORTH OF LONDON ALWAYS LAID ME   871A LETTER 72   PROSE

LAKE

THE LAKE SPEAK (SILENCE) WITH THY GLIMMERING EYES . . .   3 EVNING STAR/PS *   9
THEY STOOD BY THE BED LIKE REEDS BENDING OVER A LAKE . .   35D COUCH DEATH/PS   PROSE
BUT AT THE LAST IT SETTLES IN A LAKE CALLED OBLIVION . .   41C THEN SHE BORE   PROSE
SUNK BY THE HAND OF DEATH IN WATRY TOMB OER YONDER   43D WOE CRIED MUSE   *PROSE
[RUFFLING] LAKE
SETTLED A LAKE BRIGHT & SHINING CLEAR . . . .   227 URIZEN 10   22
BUT AS THE STARS RISE FROM THE SALT LAKE THEY ARISE IN PAIN   241 EUROPE 9   15
A WHITE LAKE ON THE DARK BLUE AIR . . . .   252 AHANIA 4   14
SETTLED A LAKE BRIGHT & SHINING CLEAR WHITE AS THE SNOW   303 FOUR ZOAS 4   210
HE BUILDED GOLGONOOZA ON THE LAKE OF UDAN ADAN . . .   307 FOUR ZOAS 5   76
AND NOW A ROCK MOVES ON THE SURFACE OF THIS LAKE OF FIRE   321 FOUR ZOAS 7   55
IN TORTURES OF DIRE COLDNESS NOW A LAKE OF WATERS DEEP . .   322 FOUR ZOAS 7   74
FROM OUT THE RANKS OF URIZEN'S WAR & FROM THE FIERY LAKE   331 FOUR ZOAS 7   461
AS LOS A FATHER TO HIS BRETHREN & HE JOYD IN THE DARK LAKE   332 FOUR ZOAS 7   480
BEYOND THE LIMIT OF TRANSLUCENCE ON THE LAKE OF UDAN ADAN   340 FOUR ZOAS 7B   300
EASTWARD OF GOLGONOOZA STANDS THE LAKE OF [?UAAN] UDAN   346 FOUR ZOAS 8   *   224
ADAN IN
ENTUTHON BENITHON [IT IS] A LAKE NOT OF WATERS BUT   346 FOUR ZOAS 8   225
OF SPACES
. . . ITS ISLANDS & [THE] ITS MARGINS [OF THIS LAKE] . .   346 FOUR ZOAS 8   *   226
FOR THIS LAKE IS FORMD FROM THE TEARS & SIGHS . . . . . .   347 FOUR ZOAS 8   228
ON TO THE SURFACE OF A LAKE AHANIA ROSE IN JOY . . . .   362 FOUR ZOAS 9   196
AND CAST [THE] HIS OWN SPECTRE INTO THE LAKE . . . . .   421 EACH MAN/N   4
TILL WE HAVE QUENCHD THE SUN OF SALAH IN THE LAKE OF UDAN   508 MILTON 23   60
ADAN
THE LAKE OF UDAN-ADAN IN THE FORESTS OF ENTUTHON BENYTHON   512 MILTON 26   25
OF THEOTORMON ON THE VERGE OF THE LAKE OF UDAN-ADAN . .   514 MILTON 27   50
HIM TO THE DIVINE MERCY CAST HIM DOWN INTO THE LAKE . .   530 MILTON 39   11
COSWAY FRAZER & BALDWIN OF EGYPT'S LAKE . . . .   545 COSWAY FRAZR/N   1
THERE IS THE CAVE THE ROCK THE TREE THE LAKE OF UDAN ADAN   634 JERUSALEM 13   38
FROM OXFORDSHIRE TO NORFOLK ON THE LAKE OF UDAN ADAN . .   637 JERUSALEM 16   19
AND CAST HIS SPECTRE INTO THE LAKE . . . .   669 EACH MAN/J   4
THE STYGIAN LAKE . . . .   SUPP ILLUS DANTE 15   *PROSE
STYGIAN LAKE . . . .   SUPP ILLUS DANTE 17   *PROSE

LAKES

[XXX] WHERE ART THOU PESTILENCE THAT BATHEST IN FOGS &   106 TIRIEL 5   *   8
STANDING LAKES
WITH THE PROPERTIES OF WOODS RIVERS MOUNTAINS LAKES CITIES   153A MARRIAGE HH 11   PROSE
NATIONS
SHADOWS OF PROPHECY SHIVER ALONG BY THE LAKES AND   159A SONG LIBERTY   PROSE
THE RIVERS
TILL PETRIFIC PAIN SCURFD OER THE LAKES . . . .   253 AHANIA 4   20
THE SEAS & LAKES THEY REARD THE MOUNTAINS & THE ROCKS &   286 FOUR ZOAS 2   251
HILLS
ROUND LAKES OF FIRE IN THE DARK DEEP THE RUINS OF URIZEN'S   316 FOUR ZOAS 6   179
WORLD
FLOATING WITH SOLEMN SONGS & ON THE LAKES OF EGYPT NIGHTLY   528 MILTON 37   28
OF BURNING SAND THE RIVERS CATARACT & LAKES OF FIRE . . .   634 JERUSALEM 13   41
THE ISLANDS OF THE FIERY LAKES THE TREES OF MALICE REVENGE   634 JERUSALEM 13   42
LIKE LAKES OF LIQUID LEAD INSTEAD OF HEAVENLY CHAPELS BUILT   673 JERUSALEM 43   63
UPON THE LAKES OF IRELAND FROM RATHLIN TO BALTIMORE . . .   679 JERUSALEM 49   4

LAMB

THEY TEAR THE POOR MAN'S LAMB AND DRIVE . . . .   11 GWIN KING/PS   7
WILLIAM BLAKE NUMERATION BLAKE LAMB . . . .   63A ISLAND MOON 11   *PROSE
HIPOCRISY IS AS DISTANT FROM SUPERSTITION AS THE WOLF   75A ANNO LAVATER   MARG
FROM THE LAMB
PIPE A SONG ABOUT A LAMB . . . .   111 INTRODUCTN/SI   5
THE LAMB . . . .   115B THE LAMB/SI   TITLE
LITTLE LAMB WHO MADE THEE   . . . .   115 THE LAMB/SI   1
LITTLE LAMB WHO MADE THEE   . . . .   115 THE LAMB/SI   9
LITTLE LAMB I'LL TELL THEE   . . . .   115 THE LAMB/SI   11
LITTLE LAMB I'LL TELL THEE   . . . .   115 THE LAMB/SI   12
FOR HE CALLS HIMSELF A LAMB   . . . .   115 THE LAMB/SI   14
I A CHILD & THOU A LAMB   . . . .   115 THE LAMB/SI   17
LITTLE LAMB GOD BLESS THEE   . . . .   115 THE LAMB/SI   19
LITTLE LAMB GOD BLESS THEE   . . . .   115 THE LAMB/SI   20
AND NOW BESIDE THEE BLEATING LAMB . . . .   119 NIGHT/SI   41
LITTLE LAMB . . . .   123 SPRING/SI   19
THY BREATH DOTH NOURISH THE INNOCENT LAMB . . . .   128 BOOK OF THEL 2   5
[DID] DARE HE WHO MADE THE LAMB MAKE THEE   . . . . .   173 THE TYGER/N 1   28
DID HE WHO MADE THE LAMB MAKE THEE . . . .   173 THE TYGER/N 2   16
THE NEW WASHD LAMB TINGD WITH THE VILLAGE SMOKE &   191 V DAU ALBION 3   18
THE BRIGHT SWAN
DID HE WHO MADE THE LAMB MAKE THEE . . . .   214 THE TYGER/SE   20

1045

		PAGE	TITLE	LINE
LAMB	**(CONTINUED)**			
BY A LITTLE EWE LAMB	. .	256	BOOK OF LOS 3	24
ETERNALLY CREATED BY THE LAMB OF GOD AROUND	. .	266	FOUR ZOAS 1	97
TILL WE HAVE DRAWN THE LAMB OF GOD INTO A MORTAL FORM	. .	272	FOUR ZOAS 1	293
WHY IS THE SHEEP GIVEN TO THE KNIFE THE LAMB PLAYS IN THE SUN		276	FOUR ZOAS 1	454
THE LAMB OF GOD BLESSED FOR EVER & HE FOLLOWD THE MAN	. .	279	FOUR ZOAS 1	556
I CARRIED HER IN MY BOSOM AS A MAN CARRIES A LAMB .	. .	282	FOUR ZOAS 2	93
THEY HAVE SURROUNDED ME WITH WALLS OF IRON & BRASS [I ?DIE] O LAMB	*	282	FOUR ZOAS 2	99
FOR THE DIVINE LAMB EVEN JESUS WHO IS THE DIVINE VISION		287	FOUR ZOAS 2	261
WHERE THE LAMB REPLIES TO THE INFANT VOICE	.	315	FOUR ZOAS 6	136
TURN INWARDLY THINE EYES & THERE BEHOLD THE LAMB OF GOD		330	FOUR ZOAS 7	415
ENITHARMON ANSWERD I BEHOLD THE LAMB OF GOD DESCENDING	.	330	FOUR ZOAS 7	424
AND ENITHARMON SAID I SEE THE LAMB OF GOD UPON MOUNT ZION		341	FOUR ZOAS 8	22
WHEN URIZEN SAW THE LAMB OF GOD CLOTHED IN LUVAH'S ROBES	.	342	FOUR ZOAS 8	61
IN THE FIERCE BATTLE & HE SAW THE LAMB OF GOD & THE WORLD OF LOS		342	FOUR ZOAS 8	66
WONDRING SHE SAW THE LAMB OF GOD WITHIN JERUSALEM'S VEIL		346	FOUR ZOAS 8	191
THEN SANG THE SONS OF EDEN ROUND THE LAMB OF GOD & SAID		346	FOUR ZOAS 8	194
GLORY GLORY GLORY TO THE HOLY LAMB OF GOD	. .	346	FOUR ZOAS 8	195
RECIEVEST THE INTEGUMENTS WOVEN RAHAB BEHOLDS THE LAMB OF GOD		347	FOUR ZOAS 8	233
TIMES UPON TIMES THINKING TO DESTROY THE LAMB BLESSED FOR EVER		347	FOUR ZOAS 8	235
O LAMB (DIVINE) IT CANNOT THEE ANNOY O PITYING ONE . . .	*	347	FOUR ZOAS 8	242
BEGUN ALREADY IN ETERNITY COME THEN O LAMB OF GOD . . .		347	FOUR ZOAS 8	244
PITYING THE LAMB OF GOD DESCENDED THRO JERUSALEM'S GATES		347	FOUR ZOAS 8	260
THE LAMB OF GOD STOOD BEFORE SATAN OPPOSITE		348	FOUR ZOAS 8	268
TO JUDGE THE LAMB OF GOD TO DEATH AS A MURDERER & ROBBER		348	FOUR ZOAS 8	273
THE LAMB OF GOD DESCENDED THRO THE TWELVE PORTIONS OF LUVAH		349	FOUR ZOAS 8	323
THUS WAS THE LAMB OF GOD CONDEMND TO DEATH		349	FOUR ZOAS 8	325
THE LAMB OF GOD IT ROLLD APART REVEALING TO ALL IN HEAVEN		350	FOUR ZOAS 8	342
OF PRIDE AND I ALSO HAVE PIERCD THE LAMB OF GOD IN PRIDE & WRATH		350	FOUR ZOAS 8	355
TIME AFTER TIME BY THE DIVINE LAMB WHO DIED FOR ALL .	.	353	FOUR ZOAS 8	483
THE LAMB OF GOD HAS RENT THE VEIL OF MYSTERY SOON TO RETURN		355	FOUR ZOAS 8	556
[FROM THE DIVINE LAMB WEPT OVER THE SEPULCHER WEAVING] .	.	356	FOUR ZOAS 8	587
AND LOS & ENITHARMON TOOK THE BODY OF THE LAMB . . .		356	FOUR ZOAS 8	593
BEHOLD JERUSALEM IN WHOSE BOSOM THE LAMB OF GOD [IS SEEN]		362	FOUR ZOAS 9	205
BECAUSE THE LAMB OF GOD CREATES HIMSELF A BRIDE & WIFE .		362	FOUR ZOAS 9	220
THE LAMB OF GOD STOOD BEFORE URIZEN OPPOSITE . . .		382	FOUR ZOAS AD 6	1
TO JUDGE THE LAMB OF GOD TO DEATH AS A MURDERER & ROBBER		382	FOUR ZOAS AD 6	6
OVER THEIR VICTIMS THUS WAS THE LAMB OF GOD CONDEMND TO DEATH		382	FOUR ZOAS AD 6	13
AND RAHAB STRIPD OFF LUVAH'S ROBES FROM OFF THE LAMB OF GOD		382	FOUR ZOAS AD 6	20
TILL THEN THE LAMB OF GOD		421	EACH MAN/N	7
TO BE WEAK AS A LAMB & SMOOTH AS A DOVE		428	MARY	25
THE LAMB MISUSD BREEDS PUBLIC STRIFE		431	AUGURIES	23
TIGER THE HORSE THE VULTURE AND THE EAGLE CONTEND FOR THE LAMB		441D	INSC FALL MAN	PROSE
STAND UPON THE EARTH EMBRACING & SHOUTING TO THE LAMB .		444A	LAST JUDGMNT/L	PROSE
AND WAS THE HOLY LAMB OF GOD		480	AND DID FEET/M	3
AROUND THE LAMB A FEMALE TABERNACLE WOVEN IN CATHEDRON'S LOOMS		494	MILTON 13	26
GLORY GLORY GLORY TO THE HOLY LAMB OF GOD		494	MILTON 13	28
THE LAMB THE SAVIOUR ALBION TREMBLED TO ITALY GREECE & EGYPT		495	MILTON 14	6
THE LAMB OF GOD IS SEEN THRO MISTS & SHADOWS HOVRING .		495	MILTON 14	25
WHERE IS THE LAMB OF GOD WHERE IS THE PROMISE OF HIS COMING		501	MILTON 19	50
VEGETATION THE SUPPER OF THE LAMB & HIS BRIDE AND THE .		511	MILTON 25	61
THE OAK IS CUT DOWN BY THE AX THE LAMB FALLS BY THE KNIFE		522	MILTON 32	37
TO DESCEND FROM THE THRONE OF GOD & OF THE LAMB . . .		612A	V LAST JUDG/N	PROSE
O THAT I COULD ABSTAIN FROM WRATH O THAT THE LAMB . .		626	JERUSALEM 7	59
BIRTHPLACE OF THE LAMB OF GOD INCOMPREHENSIBLE . . .		626	JERUSALEM 7	67
SEEING THE LAMB OF GOD IN THY GARDENS & THY PALACES . .		626	JERUSALEM 7	69
I SAW DISEASE FORMING A BODY OF DEATH AROUND THE LAMB .		628	JERUSALEM 9	9
MAY LIVE IN GLORY REDEEMD BY SACRIFICE OF THE LAMB . .		640	JERUSALEM 18	27
WHERE WE DELIGHT IN INNOCENCE BEFORE THE FACE OF THE LAMB		642	JERUSALEM 20	9
THE LAMB OF GOD RECIEVD ME IN HIS ARMS HE SMILD UPON US		643	JERUSALEM 20	39
. . . IN THE BLOOD OF THE LAMB SLAIN IN HIS CHILDREN .		646	JERUSALEM 24	2
THE FOOTSTEPS OF THE LAMB OF GOD WERE THERE BUT NOW NO MORE		648	JERUSALEM 24	50
IF GOD WAS MERCIFUL THIS COULD NOT BE O LAMB OF GOD . .		648	JERUSALEM 24	53
LOOK NOT SO MERCIFUL UPON ME O THOU SLAIN LAMB OF GOD .		648	JERUSALEM 24	59
OF THE INJURER IN WHICH THE DIVINE LAMB IS CRUELLY SLAIN		648	JERUSALEM 25	11
DESCEND O LAMB OF GOD & TAKE AWAY THE IMPUTATION OF SIN		648	JERUSALEM 25	12
THE LAMB OF GOD AMONG THEM SEEN		649	FIELDS FROM/J	6
THE LAMB OF GOD WALKS BY HER SIDE		650	FIELDS FROM/J	18
AND O THOU LAMB OF GOD WHOM I		651	FIELDS FROM/J	65
THE LAMB OF GOD THE SAVIOUR BECAME APPARENT ON EARTH .		652B	JERUSALEM 27	PROSE
THAT THEY MAY BE CONDEMND BY LAW & THE LAMB OF GOD BE SLAIN		672	JERUSALEM 43	30
IS INCAPABLE AND NOTHING NONE BUT THE LAMB OF GOD CAN HEAL		675	JERUSALEM 45	15
THE BRIDE AND WIFE OF THE LAMB O GOD THOU ART NOT AN AVENGER		676	JERUSALEM 46	28
COME LORD JESUS LAMB OF GOD DESCEND FOR IF O LORD . .		681	JERUSALEM 50	10
COME O THOU LAMB OF GOD AND TAKE AWAY THE REMEMBRANCE OF SIN		681	JERUSALEM 50	24
COME THEN O LAMB OF GOD AND TAKE AWAY THE REMEMBRANCE OF SIN		681	JERUSALEM 50	30
AND OTHERS CREATE THE WOOLY LAMB & THE DOWNY FOWL . .		692	JERUSALEM 59	48
TO ASSIST IN THE WORK THE LAMB BLEATS THE SEA-FOWL CRIES		692	JERUSALEM 59	49

		PAGE	TITLE	LINE
LAMB (CONTINUED)				
THIS IS THE SONG OF THE LAMB SUNG BY SLAVES IN EVENING TIME		693	JERUSALEM 60	38
BUT THE DIVINE LAMB STOOD BESIDE JERUSALEM OFT SHE SAW . .		693	JERUSALEM 60	50
SO SPOKE THE LAMB OF GOD WHILE LUVAH'S CLOUD REDDENING ABOVE		696	JERUSALEM 62	30
TO CREATE THE WOOLY LAMB & DOWNY FOWL & SCALY SERPENT . .		713	JERUSALEM 73	18
RECIEVE THE LAMB OF GOD TO DWELL		718	ENGLND AWAKE/J	11
IN TERRIBLE ARMOUR RAGING AGAINST THE LAMB & AGAINST JERUSALEM		719	JERUSALEM 78	13
SURROUNDING THEM WITH ARMIES TO DESTROY THE LAMB OF GOD		719	JERUSALEM 78	14
OF GOD AND THE LAMB TO DESTROY THE LAMB & USURP THE THRONE OF GOD		719	JERUSALEM 78	19
THEY WATCH THEM IN THE NIGHT AND THE LAMB OF GOD APPEARS AMONG US		720	JERUSALEM 79	32
I SLEPT IN HIS GOLDEN HILLS THE LAMB OF GOD MET ME THERE		720	JERUSALEM 79	41
THE SWARTHY SONS OF ETHIOPIA STOOD ROUND THE LAMB OF GOD		721	JERUSALEM 79	51
PITY ME THEN O LAMB OF GOD O JESUS PITY ME		722	JERUSALEM 80	30
TO WEAVE JERUSALEM A BODY REPUGNANT TO THE LAMB		723	JERUSALEM 80	65
COMPELLD INTO A SHAPE OF MORAL VIRTUE AGAINST THE LAMB . .		723	JERUSALEM 80	77
HIS LAW A FORM AGAINST THE LAMB OF GOD OPPOSD TO MERCY .		723	JERUSALEM 80	79
OF MILD JERUSALEM TO DESTROY THE LAMB OF GOD JERUSALEM . .		726	JERUSALEM 82	54
O WHEN SHALL THE LAMB OF GOD DESCEND AMONG THE REPROBATE		727	JERUSALEM 83	15
IN MILD JERUSALEM AROUND THE LAMB OF GOD LOUD HOWL . . .		734	JERUSALEM 88	53
BUT HUMBLE AS A LAMB OR AN ASS		750	EV GOSPEL(C)/N	29
BUT HUMBLE AS A LAMB OR ASS		752	EV GOSPEL(D)/N	63
JEHOVAH LO I HAVE GIVEN YOU A LAMB FOR AN ATONEMENT INSTEAD		780	GHOST ABEL 2	10
ECCHOING GREEN DITTO THE LAMB THE SHEPHERD INFANT JOY		SUPP	LETTER 66A	*PROSE
LAMBENT				
HIS SNOWY BEARD THAT STREAMS LIKE LAMBENT FLAMES DOWN HIS WIDE BREAST		204	AMERICA CANC B	16
LAMBERT				
ME MRS LAMBERT HAS BEEN WITH ME WHICH IS THE FIRST NOTICE		832B	LETTER 32	PROSE
I INTEND TO SEE MRS LAMBERT & MR JOHNSON BOOKSELLER THIS		833C	LETTER 33	PROSE
AS MRS LAMBERT TOLD ME YOU WISHED TO HAVE THEM		863C	LETTER 60	PROSE
LAMBETH				
AT LAMBETH BENEATH THE POPLAR TREES		187	WHEN KLOPSTK/N	8
LAMBETH PRINTED BY WILLIAM BLAKE IN THE YEAR...		195D	AMERICA	TITLE
NO...HERCULES BUILDINGS LAMBETH		207C	PRSPECTUS 1793	PROSE
LAMBETH AND J JOHNSON ST PAULS CHURCH YARD		209B	FOR CHILDRN/GP	*TITLE
THE [FIRST] BOOK OF URIZEN LAMBETH PRINTED BY WILL BLAKE...		222A	URIZEN 1	TITLE
EUROPE A PROPHECY LAMBETH PRINTED BY WILLIAM BLAKE		237B	EUROPE	TITLE
THE SONG OF LOS LAMBETH PRINTED BY W BLAKE...		245B	SONG OF LOS	TITLE
THE BOOK OF AHANIA LAMBETH PRINTED BY W BLAKE... . . .		249A	AHANIA	TITLE
THE BOOK OF LOS LAMBETH PRINTED BY W BLAKE...		255D	BOOK OF LOS	TITLE
W BLAKE LAMBETH...		261C	ASKED THIEF	TITLE
OF LAMBETH BUT HE KISSED ME AND WISHD ME HEALTH		505	MILTON 22	11
BEGINING AT JERUSALEM'S INNER COURT LAMBETH RUIND AND GIVEN		511	MILTON 25	48
LAMBETH MOURNS CALLING JERUSALEM SHE WEEPS & LOOKS ABROAD		511	MILTON 25	54
PANTS IN THE VALES OF LAMBETH WEEPING OER HER HUMAN HARVEST		535	MILTON 42	33
PREPARE THE FURNITURE O LAMBETH IN THY PITYING LOOMS .		632	JERUSALEM 12	38
IS WROUGHT LAMBETH THE BRIDE THE LAMB'S WIFE LOVETH THEE		632	JERUSALEM 12	41
THERE IS A GRAIN OF SAND IN LAMBETH THAT SATAN CANNOT FIND		668	JERUSALEM 41	15
. . . THEY GIVE THE OATH OF BLOOD IN LAMBETH		699	JERUSALEM 65	7
WE BUILDED JERUSALEM AS A CITY & A TEMPLE FROM LAMBETH .		729	JERUSALEM 84	3
WE BEGAN OUR FOUNDATIONS LOVELY LAMBETH O LOVELY HILLS		729	JERUSALEM 84	4
"TUESDAY MORNING IT IS ONLY SIXTY MILES & LAMBETH WAS (ONE)"		800B	LETTER 12	PROSE
HERCULES BUILDGS LAMBETH		SUPP	ADDRESSES/L	*TITLE
THE BIBLE OF HELL IN NOCTURNAL VISIONS COLLECTED VOL I LAMBETH		SUPP	INSCRIPTION	*TITLE
LAMBETH'S				
SHE FELL COLD FROM LAMBETH'S VALES IN GROANS & DEWY DEATH		281	FOUR ZOAS 2	46
THE SURREY HILLS GLOW LIKE THE CLINKERS OF THE FURNACE LAMBETH'S VALE		485	MILTON 6	14
RETURN RETURN TO LAMBETH'S VALE O BUILDING OF HUMAN SOULS		485	MILTON 6	19
IN LAMBETH'S VALES IN CAMBRIDGE & IN OXFORD PLACES OF THOUGHT		494	MILTON 13	42
WHERE ONCE THE CHERUBS OF JERUSALEM SPREAD TO LAMBETH'S VALE		525	MILTON 35	10
MY VEGETATED PORTION WAS HURRIED FROM LAMBETH'S SHADES . .		527	MILTON 36	22
THE LILLY OF HAVILAH AND THEY SANG SOFT THRO LAMBETH'S VALES		642	JERUSALEM 19	42
BUT WHEN THEY SAW ALBION FALLN UPON MILD LAMBETH'S VALE		642	JERUSALEM 20	1
JERUSALEM FELL FROM LAMBETH'S VALE		650	FIELDS FROM/J	41
SO SPOKE LONDON IMMORTAL GUARDIAN I HEARD IN LAMBETH'S SHADES		665	JERUSALEM 38	40
SHE FLED TO LAMBETH'S MILD VALE AND HID HERSELF BENEATH		668	JERUSALEM 41	11
. . . ON THE SECRET COUCH OF LAMBETH'S VALE		700	JERUSALEM 65	42
SO LOS SPOKE ENITHARMON ANSWERD IN GREAT TERROR IN LAMBETH'S VALE		739	JERUSALEM 92	7
LAMBKINS				
WHERE THE LITTLE [LAMBS DO] LAMBKINS TROT		53	PHEBE DREST/IM *	4
LAMB'S				
THAT CURLD LIKE A LAMB'S BACK WAS SHAVD SO I SAID . . .		117	CHIMNEY SWP/SI	6
FOR HE HEARS THE LAMB'S INNOCENT CALL		118	SHEPHERD/SI	5
WITH CRUEL VIRTUE MAKING WAR UPON THE LAMB'S REDEEMED .		506	MILTON 22	44
IS WROUGHT LAMBETH THE BRIDE THE LAMB'S WIFE LOVETH THEE		632	JERUSALEM 12	41
LAMBS				
WHERE THE LITTLE [LAMBS DO] LAMBKINS TROT		53	PHEBE DREST/IM *	4
THE HUM OF MULTITUDES WERE THERE BUT MULTITUDES OF LAMBS		59	HOLY THURS/IM	7
WHERE LAMBS HAVE NIBBLED SILENT MOVES		119	NIGHT/SI	11

	PAGE	TITLE	LINE

LAMBS   (CONTINUED)

THE HUM OF MULTITUDES WAS THERE BUT MULTITUDES OF LAMBS	122 HOLY THURS/SI	7
AND ROUND MY GOLDEN TENT LIKE LAMBS REJOICE	125 LIT BLK BOY/SI	20
AND ROUND THE TENT OP GOD LIKE LAMBS WE JOY	125 LIT BLK BOY/SI	24
IN FAT OF LAMBS NO MORE I FOLLOW NO MORE OBEDIENCE PAY	200 AMERICA 11	15
ENVY FED WITH FAT OP LAMBS	256 BOOK OF LOS 3	15
SNARING THE WILD GOATS FOR THEIR MILK THEY EAT THE FLESH OF LAMBS	270 FOUR ZOAS 1	235
WHEN THE RED BLOOD IS FILLD WITH WINE & WITH THE MARROW OF LAMBS	290 FOUR ZOAS 2	407
I WALK AMONG HIS FLOCKS & HEAR THE BLEATING OF HIS LAMBS	368 FOUR ZOAS 9	425
AND THEN FROM HER WHITE DOOR SHE LOOKD TO SEE HER BLEATING LAMBS	369 FOUR ZOAS 9	472
AND DOST THOU WANDER WITH MY LAMBS & [WITH] WET THEIR INNOCENT FACES	371 FOUR ZOAS 9	532
AMONG THE LAMBS CLOTHED IN WHITE	427 LAND OF DREAMS	9
AMONG MY LAMBS & BROOKS OF WATER AMONG MY WARBLING BIRDS	642 JERUSALEM 20	8
HER LAMBS BLEAT TO THE SEA-FOWLS CRY LAMENTING STILL FOR ALBION	667 JERUSALEM 40	51
OF LAMBS AND DOVES MINGLED TOGETHER IN CUPS AND DISHES . .	725 JERUSALEM 82	7

LAME

FOR IF A DAMSEL S BLIND OR LAME	56 HAIL MATRIM/IM	13
LAME REASONING UPON PREMISES THIS NEVER CAN HAPPEN . . .	399C ANNO BACON	MARG
MAKE LAME PHILOSOPHY TO SMILE	433 AUGURIES	106
HE MAKES THE LAME TO WALK WE ALL AGREE	463 ANNO REYNOLDS	1
BUT THE LAME IMITATORS OF LINES DRAWN BY THEIR PREDECESSORS	585D DESC CAT 15	PROSE
WAS DEDICATED TO THOMAS A BECKET THE PILGRIMS IF SICK OR LAME	590B CHAUCER 2	PROSE
HEATH'S LAME IMITATION STOTHARD BEING SUCH A FOOL . . .	592B PUB ADDRESS/N	PROSE

LAMECH

METHUSELAH LAMECH THESE ARE GIANTS MIGHTY HERMAPHRODITIC	528 MILTON 37	37
METHUSELAH LAMECH THESE ARE THE GIANTS MIGHTY HERMAPHRODITIC	716 JERUSALEM 75	12
LAMECH AND HIS TWO WIVES	SUPP COLOR PRT TATE	*TITLE
GOOD & EVIL ANGEL HOUSE OF DEATH GOD JUDGING ADAM LAMECH	SUPP LETTER 56A	*PROSE

LAMENT

("SNATCH FOAM DENY STREAM") UNEASY THIS I LAMENT THAT I HAVE DONE	79D ANNO LAVATER	MARG
THE VILLAGES LAMENT THEY FAINT OUTSTRETCHD UPON THE PLAIN	275 FOUR ZOAS 1	394
OF LIFE [REJOICE] LAMENT AROUND THE DEMON GOING FORTH & RETURNING	308 FOUR ZOAS 5	* 117
HID IN THE VALES FAINTLY LAMENT & NO ONE HEARS THEIR VOICE	325 FOUR ZOAS 7	197
I WILL LAMENT OVER MILTON IN THE LAMENTATIONS OF THE AFFLICTED	499 MILTON 18	5
LAMENT UPON THE WINDS OF EUROPE IN REPHAIM'S VALE . . .	501 MILTON 19	40
AND WHEN NIGHT CAME ALL WAS SILENT IN OLOLON & ALL REFUSD TO LAMENT	504 MILTON 21	26
AND CAN YOU THUS LAMENT & CAN YOU PITY & FORGIVE	523 MILTON 34	6
AGAIN THEY LAMENT O WHAT SHALL WE DO FOR LOVELY JERUSALEM	631 JERUSALEM 11	17
WINCHESTER IN HIS DEN & CAVERN THEY LAMENT AGAINST . .	671 JERUSALEM 42	59
COME YE O DAUGHTERS OF BEULAH LAMENT FOR OG & SIHON . .	679 JERUSALEM 49	3
EVER TO LAMENT YOUR DISTANCE FROM LONDON AS THAT ALONE .	861D LETTER 59	PROSE

LAMENTABLE

LAMENTABLE ACCIDENT AND ERROR OF THE MORTAL AND . . .	579D DESC CAT 5	PROSE

LAMENTATION

AND THUS HER GENTLE LAMENTATION FALLS LIKE MORNING DEW . .	127 BOOK OF THEL 1	5
ENSLAVD THE DAUGHTERS OF ALBION WEEP A TREMBLING LAMENTATION	189 V DAU ALBION 1	1
THEN BROMION SAID AND SHOOK THE CAVERN WITH HIS LAMENTATION	192 V DAU ALBION 4	12
BUT WHEN THE MORN AROSE HER LAMENTATION RENEWD	192 V DAU ALBION 5	1
RATTLING THEIR HOLLOW BONES IN HOWLING AND LAMENTATION . .	243 EUROPE 13	8
SINGING HER LAMENTATION THARMAS GROANED AMONG HIS CLOUDS	266 FOUR ZOAS 1	71
THIS WAS THE LAMENTATION OF ENION ROUND THE GOLDEN FEAST	277 FOUR ZOAS 1	461
AHANIA HEARD THE LAMENTATION & A SWIFT VIBRATION . . .	291 FOUR ZOAS 2	419
I WRITE NOT HERE BUT ALL THEIR AFTER LIFE WAS LAMENTATION	309 FOUR ZOAS 5	175
MY SONGS ARE TURNED [INTO] TO CRIES OF LAMENTATION . .	310 FOUR ZOAS 5	* 206
THEN URIZEN WEPT & THUS HIS LAMENTATION POURED FORTH . .	312 FOUR ZOAS 6	24
FOR URIZEN LAMENTED OVER THEM IN A SELFISH LAMENTATION . .	317 FOUR ZOAS 6	238
THEN LOS MOURND ON THE DISMAL WIND IN HIS JEALOUS LAMENTATION	324 FOUR ZOAS 7	183
ENITHARMON WOVE IN TEARS SINGING SONGS OF LAMENTATION . .	342 FOUR ZOAS 8	52
TILL THEY REVIVE OR BURY THEM IN COOL GROTS MAKING LAMENTATION	377 FOUR ZOAS 9	747
THE SHADOWY FEMALE SEEING MILTON HOWLD IN HER LAMENTATION	499 MILTON 18	2
OF EDEN HEARD THE LAMENTATION AND PROVIDENCE BEGAN . .	504 MILTON 21	24
AND OLOLON LAMENTED FOR MILTON WITH A GREAT LAMENTATION	505 MILTON 22	3
TILL THEY REVIVE OR BURY THEM IN COOL GROTS MAKING LAMENTATION	513 MILTON 27	7
AND WHEN THE DAUGHTERS OF BEULAH HEARD THE LAMENTATION	519 MILTON 31	9
THIS IS A VISION OF THE LAMENTATION OF BEULAH OVER OLOLON	520 MILTON 31	45
SUCH IS A VISION OF THE LAMENTATION OF BEULAH OVER OLOLON	521 MILTON 31	63
TO COMFORT OLOLON'S LAMENTATION FOR THEY SAID . . .	523 MILTON 34	2
LAMENTATION IT FLEE BACK & HIDE IN NON-ENTITY'S DARK WILD	688 JERUSALEM 56	16
HER CHILDREN IN CAPTIVITY LISTENING TO VALA'S LAMENTATION	722 JERUSALEM 80	10
THUS SANG THE DAUGHTERS IN LAMENTATION UNITING INTO ONE	729 JERUSALEM 84	29
THE SEEDS OF BEAUTY IN THE SPACE LISTNING TO THEIR LAMENTATION	730 JERUSALEM 85	9
TO ME FORGIVE THIS DIRGE-LIKE LAMENTATION OVER A DEAD HORSE	830B LETTER 30	PROSE

LAMENTATIONS

DOLOURS & LAMENTATIONS WAITING OFT BESIDE A DEWY GRAVE . .	130 BOOK OF THEL 6	7
AND NONE BUT BROMION CAN HEAR MY LAMENTATIONS	191 V DAU ALBION 3	1
LISTNING TO HER SOFT LAMENTATIONS SOON HIS TONGUE BEGAN	267 FOUR ZOAS 1	124

	PAGE	TITLE	LINE
LAMENTATIONS (CONTINUED)			
LUVAH IN VAIN HER LAMENTATIONS HEARD IN VAIN HIS LOVE . .	286	FOUR ZOAS 2	232
UTTERING MY LAMENTATIONS & BEGETTING LITTLE MONSTERS . .	296	FOUR ZOAS 3	165
RUBBING THEIR TEMPLES HE REVIVD THEM ALL THEIR LAMENTATIONS	309	FOUR ZOAS 5	174
THEY RETURN WITH LAMENTATIONS MOURNING & WEEPING	338	FOUR ZOAS 7B	* 221
WADING THRO FENS AMONG THE SLIMY WEEDS MAKING LAMENTATIONS	338	FOUR ZOAS 7B	225
ENITHARMON WOVE IN TEARS SINGING SONGS OF LAMENTATIONS . .	345	FOUR ZOAS 8	182
I WILL LAMENT OVER MILTON IN THE LAMENTATIONS OF	499	MILTON 18	5
THE AFFLICTED			
MY GARMENTS SHALL BE WOVEN OF SIGHS & HEART BROKEN	499	MILTON 18	6
LAMENTATIONS			
BUT WHEN THE CLARIONS OF DAY SOUNDED THEY DROWND	504	MILTON 21	25
THE LAMENTATIONS			
SUCH ARE THE SONGS OF BEULAH IN THE LAMENTATIONS OF OLOLON	523	MILTON 33	24
LOS HEARD HER LAMENTATIONS IN THE DEEPS AFAR HIS TEARS FALL	624	JERUSALEM 5	66
SUCH WERE THE LAMENTATIONS OF THE LABOURERS IN T. FURNACES	631	JERUSALEM 12	16
SO LOS IN LAMENTATIONS FOLLOWD ALBION ALBION COVERD . .	656	JERUSALEM 30	41
IN BEULAH BY THE DAUGHTERS OF BEULAH WITH TEARS . .	714	JERUSALEM 74	9
& LAMENTATIONS			
I HAVE HEARD JERUSALEM'S GROANS FROM VALA'S CRIES	725	JERUSALEM 82	1
& LAMENTATIONS			
DOLOROUS ARE THEIR LAMENTATIONS IN THE BURNING FORGE . .	737	JERUSALEM 90	45
LAMENTED			
SUCH WAS THE HOLLOW VOICE THAT OER [THE RED DEMON] AMERICA	205	AMERICA CANC C	31
LAMENTED			
THUS SHE LAMENTED DAY & NIGHT COMPELLD TO LABOUR & SORROW	286	FOUR ZOAS 2	231
FOR URIZEN LAMENTED OVER THEM IN A SELFISH LAMENTATION . .	317	FOUR ZOAS 6	238
THUS LOS LAMENTED IN THE NIGHT UNHEARD BY ENITHARMON . .	325	FOUR ZOAS 7	209
SO LOS LAMENTED OVER SATAN WHO TRIUMPHANT DIVIDED	491	MILTON 10	21
THE NATIONS			
THE MOUNTAINS WAILD & EVERY PLANT THAT GREW IN SOLEMN SIGHS	503	MILTON 21	19
LAMENTED			
AND THEY LAMENTED THAT THEY HAD IN WRATH & FURY & FIRE .	504	MILTON 21	31
AND OLOLON LAMENTED FOR MILTON WITH A GREAT LAMENTATION	505	MILTON 22	3
& NOW I HAVE LAMENTED OVER THE DEAD HORSE LET ME LAUGH & BE	830B	LETTER 30	PROSE
WHO KNEW MOST CONCERNING HIM OF ANY ONE LAMENTED . . .	846A	LETTER 44	PROSE
LAMENTING			
BARKS AT THE BREAKING DAY THE NIGHTINGALE HAS DONE	190	V DAU ALBION 2	24
LAMENTING			
THE LAMENTING VOICE OF AHANIA	253	AHANIA 4	45
IN WOE HIS BRETHREN & HIS SONS IN DARKNING WOE LAMENTING	283	FOUR ZOAS 2	132
TO LABOUR NIGHT & DAY AMONG THE FIRES HER LAMENTING VOICE	285	FOUR ZOAS 2	216
AND URIZEN'S LOUD SOUNDING VOICE LAMENTING ON THE WIND .	313	FOUR ZOAS 6	48
THE FURNACES LAMENTING AROUND THE ANVILS & THIS THEIR SONG	484	MILTON 5	18
LIVING SELF MOVING MOURNING LAMENTING & HOWLING INCESSANTLY	509	MILTON 24	53
BENEATH A ROCK [HOWLING & LAMENTING] WHERE	608B	V LAST JUDG/N	*PROSE
LAMENTING & LOOKING UPON HER IN ASTONISHMENT & TERROR .	609B	V LAST JUDG/N	PROSE
WANDER AWAY INTO THE CHAOTIC VOID LAMENTING WITH HER SHADOW	624	JERUSALEM 5	63
LAMENTING FOR HER CHILDREN FOR THE SONS & DAUGHTERS OF	624	JERUSALEM 5	65
ALBION			
AND THERE WAS HEARD A GREAT LAMENTING IN BEULAH ALL THE	648	JERUSALEM 25	1
REGIONS			
TO HIDE THEMSELVES WEEPING & LAMENTING FOR THE VEGETATION	655	JERUSALEM 30	7
HER LAMBS BLEAT TO THE SEA-FOWLS CRY LAMENTING STILL FOR	667	JERUSALEM 40	51
ALBION			
AND LOS'S FURNACES HOWL LOUD LIVING SELF-MOVING LAMENTING	713	JERUSALEM 73	2
LAMENTING AMONG THE TIMBRELS OF THE WARRIORS AMONG THE	721	JERUSALEM 80	7
CAPTIVES			
IN CRUEL HOLINESS AND HER LAMENTING SONGS WERE FROM ARNON	722	JERUSALEM 80	8
LAMENTINGS			
[AND WANDERD DOWN THE VALES OF KENT IN SICK & DREAR	196	AMERICA PREL 2	21
LAMENTINGS]			
LAMENTS			
THUS HE LAMENTS THROUGH THE STILL EVENING	35D	COUCH DEATH/PS	PROSE
FROM THE WATERS EMERGING LAMENTS	234	URIZEN 23	14
LAMENTS & ENION WANDERS LIKE A WEEPING INARTICULATE VOICE	501	MILTON 19	42
WHOSE SONG CALLD MILTON TO THE ATTEMPT AND LOS HEARD THESE	504	MILTON 21	34
LAMENTS			
GROANING WITH PITY HE AMONG THE WAILING SOULS LAMENTS . .	512	MILTON 26	22
FROM HILL TO HILL & THE THAMES LAMENTS ALONG THE VALLEYS	656	JERUSALEM 30	24
WHILE LOS LAMENTS AT HIS DIRE LABOURS VIEWING JERUSALEM	719	JERUSALEM 78	10
SAYS HE LAMENTS YOUR ABSENCE FROM LONDON AS YOUR ADVICE	844A	LETTER 43	PROSE
LAMIA			
THE ELEPHANT THE WOLF THE BEAR THE LAMIA THE [SATUR] SATYR	352	FOUR ZOAS 8	* 446
LAMP			
THE MOON HUNG NOT OUT HER LAMP	36C	COUCH DEATH/PS	PROSE
. . . AND GOD SO LONG WORSHIPPD DEPARTS AS A LAMP . . .	140	FRENCH REVOLTN	137
LIKE A DARK LAMP ETERNAL DEATH HAUNTS ALL MY EXPECTATION	293	FOUR ZOAS 3	75
THE STARS CONSUMD LIKE A LAMP BLOWN OUT & IN THEIR STEAD	379	FOUR ZOAS 9	* 829
BEHOLDS			
LIKE PUTTING OIL & WATER INTO A LAMP	549	ENGL ENCOU/N 1	5
OF LIGHTING A LAMP WHEN YOU DONT WISH TO SEE	549	ENGL ENCOU/N 1	8
AND WHEN IT SMELLS OF THE LAMP WE [WILL] CAN	549	ENGL ENCOU/N 1	* 9
LIKE DISPLAYING OIL & WATER INTO A LAMP	550	ENGL ENCOU/N 2	5
LAMPLIKE			
WITH LAMPLIKE EYES WATCHING AROUND THE FROZEN MARRIAGE BED	194	V DAU ALBION 7	22
LAMPS			
WHERE URIZEN & ALL HIS HOSTS HANG THEIR IMMORTAL LAMPS . .	272	FOUR ZOAS 1	304
EYES OF GOD & THE SEVEN LAMPS OF THE ALMIGHTY	279	FOUR ZOAS 1	554
CONSUMING IN THE RAGING LAMPS OF MERCY POURD IN RIVERS . .	320	FOUR ZOAS 7	11
INSPIRING SECRECY & LAMPS THEY BORE INTOXICATING FUMES . .	333	FOUR ZOAS 7B	28
WITH GIFTS & SPICES WITH LAMPS RICH EMBOSSD JEWELS & GOLD	349	FOUR ZOAS 8	337

	PAGE	TITLE	LINE

LAMPS   (CONTINUED)
HE LIFTS THE BLUE LAMPS OF HIS EYES & CRIES WITH HEAVENLY   359 FOUR ZOAS 9   97
   VOICE
THE SEVEN LAMPS OF THE ALMIGHTY BURNING BEFORE THE THRONE   443C LAST JUDGMNT/L   PROSE
ETERNAL AND SOMETIMES TWO SPECTRES LIKE LAMPS QUIVERING   515 MILTON 28   11
THEIR LAMPS BURNING & SUCH SHALL SHINE AS THE STARS . . .   810D LETTER 21   PROSE
LANCASHIRE
OF REUBEN NORFOLK SUFFOLK ESSEX SIMEON LINCOLN YORK   637 JERUSALEM 16   44
   LANCASHIRE
CHESHIRE & LANCASHIRE & WESTMORELAND GROAN IN ANGUISH . .   736 JERUSALEM 90   18
LANCES
THE LANCES OF URIZEN FROM CHARIOTS ROUND THE HOLY TENT . .   278 FOUR ZOAS 1   517
LAND
UPON OUR LOVE-SICK LAND THAT MOURNS FOR THEE   . . . . .   1 TO SPRING/PS   12
THE NOBLES OF THE LAND DID FEED . . . .   11 GWIN KING/PS   5
THE LAND IS DESOLATE OUR WIVES . . . .   11 GWIN KING/PS   9
THOURT SWEPT FROM OUT THE LAND . . . .   13 GWIN KING/PS   68
IN HIS LAND OVERFLOWING WITH HONEY . . . .   19 EDW THIRD/PS 2   14
AND ENGLAND IS THE LAND FAVOURD BY COMMERCE . . . . .   19 EDW THIRD/PS 2   30
LOOKING TO THE GAIN OF THIS OUR NATIVE LAND . . . . .   19 EDW THIRD/PS 2   35
THE KINGS AND NOBLES OF THE LAND HAVE DONE IT . . . .   33 EDW FOURTH/PS   15
O LAND MOST HAPLESS O BEAUTEOUS ISLAND HOW FORSAKEN . .   34A KING JOHN/PS   PROSE
BLOOD CRIES AFAR THE LAND DOTH SOW ITSELF . . . . .   34B KING JOHN/PS   PROSE
AND DESOLATION SPREADS HIS WINGS OVER THE LAND OF PALESTINE .   37D SAMSON/PS   *PROSE
FROM SIDE TO SIDE THE LAND GROANS HER PROWESS LOST . . .   37D SAMSON/PS   PROSE
THE WOLF TEARETH THEM OPPRESSION STRETCHES HIS ROD OVER   40A SAMSON/PS   PROSE
   OUR LAND
THROUGH THE LAND IT RUNS ROLLING WITH FURIOUS NOISE . . .   41C THEN SHE BORE   PROSE
THEL ENTERD IN & SAW THE SECRETS OF THE LAND UNKNOWN . .   130 BOOK OF THEL 6   2
A LAND OF SORROWS & OF TEARS WHERE NEVER SMILE WAS SEEN   130 BOOK OF THEL 6   5
SHE WANDERD IN THE LAND OF CLOUDS THRO VALLEYS DARK   130 BOOK OF THEL 6   6
   LISTNING
. . . FOR A CURSE IS HEARD HOARSE THRO THE LAND FROM A   140 FRENCH REVOLTN   138
   GODLESS RACE
AND [TURND] TURN IT INTO FRUITFUL LAND . . . . . .   168 HAST LAP/N   6
IN A RICH & FRUITFUL LAND . . . .   181 HOLY THURS/N   2
TIS A LAND OF POVERTY . . . .   181 HOLY THURS/N   8
[ABOUT THE FRUITFUL LAND] . . . .   185 LET BROTHELS/N   30
WHERE GOEST THOU O THOUGHT TO WHAT REMOTE LAND IS   192 V DAU ALBION 4   8
   THY FLIGHT
AND FLAMD RED METEORS ROUND THE LAND OF ALBION BENEATH . .   197 AMERICA 3   16
DOWN ON THE LAND OF AMERICA INDIGNANT THEY DESCENDED . .   200 AMERICA 12   4
OVER THE LAND NAKED & FLAMING ARE THEIR LINEAMENTS SEEN   200 AMERICA 12   6
IN FLAMES AS OF A FURNACE ON THE LAND FROM NORTH TO SOUTH   201 AMERICA 12   12
IN BERNARD'S HOUSE THE FLAMES COVERD THE LAND THEY ROUZE   201 AMERICA 13   2
   THEY CRY
AND AS A SEA OERWHELMS A LAND IN THE DAY OF AN EARTHQUAKE   201 AMERICA 14   9
AND FLAMD FIERCE METEORS ROUND THE LAND OF ALBION BENEATH   204 AMERICA CANC A *   16
BUT THO OBSCURD THIS IS THE FORM OF THE ANGELIC LAND . .   206 THIRALATHA   6
IN A RICH AND FRUITFUL LAND . . . .   211 HOLY THURS/SE   2
IT IS A LAND OF POVERTY . . . .   212 HOLY THURS/SE   8
A MIGHTY SPIRIT LEAPD FROM THE LAND OF ALBION . . . .   243 EUROPE 13   4
MELTED OVER THE LAND AS HE FLEW . . . .   248 SONG OF LOS 7   15
LIVE IN PERFECT HARMONY IN EDEN THE LAND OF LIFE . . .   277 FOUR ZOAS 1   474
THEY BECOME NATIONS FAR REMOTE IN A LITTLE & DARK LAND .   281 FOUR ZOAS 2   *   56
I BROUGHT HER THRO THE WILDERNESS A DRY & THIRSTY LAND .   282 FOUR ZOAS 2   87
BUT NOW MY LAND IS DARKEND & MY WISE MEN ARE DEPARTED .   310 FOUR ZOAS 5   205
TO SWIM THE DEEP & ON THE LAND CHILDREN ARE SOLD TO TRADES   333 FOUR ZOAS 7B   13
FEAR NOT O POOR FORSAKEN ONE O LAND OF BRIARS & THORNS   354 FOUR ZOAS 8   534
THE LAND OF DOUBTS & SHADOWS SWEET DELUSIONS UNFORMD HOPES   367 FOUR ZOAS 9   379
MY LUVAH HERE HATH PLACD ME IN A SWEET & PLEASANT LAND   369 FOUR ZOAS 9   451
THE GOOD OF ALL THE LAND IS BEFORE YOU FOR MYSTERY IS NO   375 FOUR ZOAS 9   681
   MORE
AHA AHA HOW CAME I HERE SO SOON IN MY SWEET NATIVE LAND   375 FOUR ZOAS 9   687
I TRAVELD THRO A LAND OF MEN . . . .   424 MENTAL TRAVLER   1
A LAND OF MEN & WOMEN TOO . . . .   424 MENTAL TRAVLER   2
THE GUESTS ARE SCATTERD THRO THE LAND . . . . . .   426 MENTAL TRAVLER   61
THE LAND OF DREAMS . . . .   427B LAND OF DREAMS   TITLE
O WHAT LAND IS THE LAND OF DREAMS . . . . . .   427 LAND OF DREAMS   5
HAVE WANDERD ALL NIGHT IN THE LAND OF DREAMS . . . .   427 LAND OF DREAMS   14
IN THIS LAND OF UNBELIEF & FEAR . . . .   427 LAND OF DREAMS   18
THE LAND OF DREAMS IS BETTER FAR . . . . . .   427 LAND OF DREAMS   19
AND THEN SET ME DOWN IN AN ENVIOUS LAND . . . . .   428 MARY   24
IN ENGLAND'S GREEN & PLEASANT LAND . . . . . .   481 AND DID FEET/M   16
BENEATH YOUR LAND OF SHADOWS OF ITS SACRIFICES AND . . .   481 MILTON 2   11
REACHD TO THE DEPTHS OF (DIREST) HELL & THENCE TO ALBION'S   496 MILTON 14   *   40
   LAND
THEY SAT RANGD ROUND HIM AS THE ROCKS OF HOREB ROUND THE   498 MILTON 17   12
   LAND
ARE OUR THREE HEAVENS BENEATH THE SHADES OF BEULAH LAND   501 MILTON 20   2
   OF REST
THAT MILTON OF THE LAND OF ALBION SHOULD UP ASCEND . . .   503 MILTON 20   59
SUNG TO THE HARP THAT MILTON OF THE LAND OF ALBION . . .   507 MILTON 23   36
BUT ALLAMANDA CALLD ON EARTH COMMERCE IS THE CULTIVATED   514 MILTON 27   42
   LAND
THEY STOOD IN A DARK LAND OF DEATH OF FIERY CORRODING   524 MILTON 34   44
   WATERS
LEANS ON THE ROCKS OF ERIN'S LAND IRELAND ANCIENT NATION   531 MILTON 39   45
EVERY FOOL SHOOK HIS BELLS THROUGHOUT THE LAND . . . .   554 BLAKES APL/N 1   2
EVERY FOOL SHOOK HIS BELLS THROUGHOUT THE LAND . . . .   555 BLAKES APL/N 2   6
EVERY FOOL SHOOK HIS BELLS THROUGHOUT THE LAND . . . .   595 BLAKES APOL/PA   2
A PLEASANT SHADOW OF REPOSE CALLD ALBION'S LOVELY LAND . .   620 JERUSALEM 1   3

		PAGE	TITLE	LINE
LAND	(CONTINUED)			
AWAKE AWAKE O SLEEPER OF THE LAND OF SHADOWS WAKE EXPAND		622	JERUSALEM 4	6
FIBRES OF LOVE FROM MAN TO MAN THRO ALBION'S PLEASANT LAND		622	JERUSALEM 4	8
YE ARE MY MEMBERS O YE SLEEPERS OF BEULAH LAND OF SHADES		622	JERUSALEM 4	21
AROUND GOLGONOOZA LIES THE LAND OF DEATH ETERNAL A LAND		633	JERUSALEM 13	30
THE LAND OF DARKNESS FLAMED BUT NO LIGHT & NO REPOSE . .		634	JERUSALEM 13	46
THE LAND OF SNOWS OF TREMBLING & OF IRON HAIL INCESSANT		634	JERUSALEM 13	47
THE LAND OF EARTHQUAKES AND THE LAND OF WOVEN LABYRINTHS		634	JERUSALEM 13	48
THE LAND OF SNARES & TRAPS & WHEELS & PIT-FALLS & DIRE MILLS		634	JERUSALEM 13	49
THE VOIDS THE SOLIDS & THE LAND OF CLOUDS & REGIONS OF WATERS		634	JERUSALEM 13	50
AND IN A DARK LAND GAVE HER BIRTH		651	FIELDS FROM/J	52
ART THOU RETURND TO ALBION'S LAND		651	FIELDS FROM/J	67
IN MY EXCHANGES EVERY LAND		652	FIELDS FROM/J	85
SHALL WALK & MINE IN EVERY LAND		652	FIELDS FROM/J	86
ALBION THE HIGH CLIFF OF THE ATLANTIC IS BECOME A BARREN LAND		660	JERUSALEM 34	16
JORDAN TO THE LAND OF THE HITTITE EVERY-ONE THAT SAW HIM		661	JERUSALEM 34	48
LIVE IN PERFECT HARMONY IN EDEN THE LAND OF LIFE		665	JERUSALEM 38	21
I SEE THEE AWFUL PARENT LAND IN LIGHT BEHOLD I SEE . . .		665	JERUSALEM 38	44
IN ERIN'S LAND TOWARD THE NORTH JOINT AFTER JOINT & BURNING		674	JERUSALEM 44	26
THOU ART IN ERROR ALBION THE LAND OF ULRO		676	JERUSALEM 46	10
AND ALL THE LAND OF CANAAN SUSPENDED OVER THE VALLEY OF CHEVIOT		698	JERUSALEM 63	42
MOLECH REJOICES THRO THE LAND FROM HAVILAH TO SHUR HE REJOICES		706	JERUSALEM 68	38
THE FEMALE SEARCHES SEA & LAND FOR GRATIFICATIONS TO THE		707	JERUSALEM 69	16
AND ABOVE ALBION'S LAND WAS SEEN THE HEAVENLY CANAAN . .		709	JERUSALEM 71	1
DOWN MONAGHAN CAVAN THESE ARE THE LAND OF ERIN		711	JERUSALEM 72	* 27
OVER THE LAND OF CANAAN THEY HAVE DIVIDED JUDAH		715	JERUSALEM 74	48
HE HATH TOOK ROOT IN HEBRON IN THE LAND OF HAND & HYLE .		715	JERUSALEM 74	49
IN VAIN THEY ROLLD APART THEY ARE FIXD INTO THE LAND OF CABUL		715	JERUSALEM 74	57
CRUCIFYING & ENCOMPASSING SEA & LAND		718	STOOD AMONG/J	29
THEY ARE BECOME NARROW PLACES IN A LITTLE AND DARK LAND		720	JERUSALEM 79	14
OF THE VALLEYS OF DESTRUCTION INTO A DARK LAND OF PITCH & BITUMEN		721	JERUSALEM 79	61
SHRUNK TO A NARROW DOLEFUL FORM IN THE DARK LAND OF CABUL		721	JERUSALEM 79	63
BEFORE IN ALBION'S LAND		722	JERUSALEM 80	24
UPON HIS PARENT BOSOM LAY THY LITTLE ONES O LAND . . .		727	JERUSALEM 83	24
THE LAND IS MARKD FOR DESOLATION & UNLESS WE PLANT . . .		728	JERUSALEM 83	54
OUR FATHER ALBION'S LAND O IT WAS A LOVELY LAND		729	JERUSALEM 83	85
ALBION BELOVED LAND I SEE THY MOUNTAINS & THY HILLS . . .		731	JERUSALEM 86	11
UPON THE HOLY LAND I SEE THE RIVER OF LIFE & TREE OF LIFE		731	JERUSALEM 86	18
BY LAND ASTOUNDING ERECTING PILLARS IN THE DEEPEST HELL		738	JERUSALEM 91	41
THROUGHOUT THE LAND HE TOOK HIS COURSE		749	EV GOSPEL (B)/N	35
IN MIRACLES THROUGHOUT THE LAND		752	EV GOSPEL (D)/N	57
DISPENSING UNCEASING TO ALL THE WHOLE LAND		800	MRS FLAXMAN/L	16
OVER SEA OVER LAND		804	TO BUTTS/L	7
EVERY STONE ON THE LAND		804	TO BUTTS/L	26
WHICH ARE NOT REAL IN A LAND OF ABSTRACTION WHERE SPECTRES		809A	LETTER 20	PROSE
SALADIN...IN THE HOLY LAND		SUPP	ILLUS HISTORY	*TITLE
LANDAFF				
LITCHFIELD SAINT DAVIDS LANDAFF ASAPH BANGOR SODOR . . .		676	JERUSALEM 46	19
LANDAFF'S				
NOTES ON THE B(ISHOP) OF L'S(LANDAFF'S) APOLOGY . . .		383A	ANNO WATSON	*TITLE
LANDED				
BY YOUR ADVICE WE LANDED HERE IN BRITTANY		18	EDW THIRD/PS 1	46
THEY LANDED IN FIRM ARRAY UPON THE ROCKS		32	EDW THIRD/PS 6	13
LANDING				
GIANTS ANCIENT INHABITANTS OF ENGLAND THE LANDING OF BRUTUS		208C	SUBJCTS HIST/N	TITLE
THE DRUIDS THE LANDING OF JULIUS CAESAR		208D	SUBJCTS HIST/N	TITLE
LANDLORD				
LANDLORD ROBERT BRISTOW ESQ OF BROXMORE NEAR RUMSEY . .		590A	CHAUCER 2	PROSE
MY LANDLORD COMPELLD THE SOLDIERS TO GO IN DOORS . . .		827B	LETTER 28	PROSE
THE OFFENCE IS ALWAYS REPEATED THE LANDLORD OF THE INN &		827C	LETTER 28	PROSE
LANDS				
AYE IT GROWS MOST IN LANDS MOST CULTIVATED		28	EDW THIRD/PS 4	4
STRETCHING HER MIGHTY SPEAR OER DISTANT LANDS		33	EDW THIRD/PS 6	58
AS NONE BY TRAVELLING OVER KNOWN LANDS		98C	ALL RELIGIONS	PROSE
THROUGHOUT ALL THESE HUMAN LANDS		432	AUGURIES	64
SHALL BUY & SELL THE MISER'S LANDS		433	AUGURIES	82
THE ROCKY MASSES OF THE MUNDANE SHELL IN THE LANDS . . .		498	MILTON 17	19
LYBIA & THE LANDS UNKNOWN ARE THE ASCENT WITHOUT . . .		690	JERUSALEM 58	36
YOU MUST LEAVE FATHERS & MOTHERS & HOUSES & LANDS . .		776A	INSC LAOCOON	PROSE
LANDSCAPE				
THE LANDSCAPE IS AN EASTWARD VIEW OF THE COUNTRY . . .		567A	DESC CAT 3	PROSE
& THE SCENE OR LANDSCAPE WITH ITS VILLAGES COTTAGES . .		588A	CHAUCER/N	PROSE
THE LANDSCAPE IS AN EASTWARD VIEW OF THE COUNTRY . . .		588D	CHAUCER/N	PROSE
THE LANDSCAPE IS AN EASTWARD VIEW OF THE COUNTRY . . .		590B	CHAUCER 2	PROSE
THE OPINIONS OF A PORTRAIT OR LANDSCAPE PAINTER		783D	ANNO WW POEMS	MARG
LANE				
TURN THRO THE IRON GATE DOWN SNEAKING LANE		541	MR CROMEK/N	4
G SMEETON PRINTER...ST MARTINS LANE LONDON		590D	CHAUCER 2	TITLE
LANERK				
JOSEPH ELGIN LANERK KINROS BENJAMIN KROMARTY MURRA KIRKUBRIHT		638	JERUSALEM 16	58
LANES				
THE KENNELS OF THE STREETS & LANES AS IF THEY WERE ABHORRD		657	JERUSALEM 31	18

		PAGE	TITLE	LINE
LANGUAGE				
	& THEIR LANGUAGE SO MUCH THE SAME	44A	ISLAND MOON 1	PROSE
	TO LEARN THE LANGUAGE OF ART COPY FOR EVER IS MY RULE .	446B	ANNO REYNOLDS	MARG
	FOR THAT IS THE ONLY SCHOOL TO THE LANGUAGE OF ART . .	448D	ANNO REYNOLDS	MARG
	LEARND THE LANGUAGE OF ART BY MAKING MANY FINISHD COPIES	455D	ANNO REYNOLDS	MARG
	THE LANGUAGE OF PAINTERS CANNOT BE ALLOWD THEM . .	463B	ANNO REYNOLDS	MARG
	MICHAEL ANGELO WERE INCAPABLE OF THE MEER LANGUAGE OF ART	467B	ANNO REYNOLDS	MARG
	CONTRARY OPINIONS CAN NEVER BY ANY LANGUAGE BE MADE ALIKE	474B	ANNO REYNOLDS	MARG
	AND HIS FRIEND ARE EQUALLY MASTERS OF CHAUCER'S LANGUAGE	574B	DESC CAT 3	PROSE
	AND THE DIVINE ALL HAD ORIGINALLY ONE LANGUAGE AND . .	579A	DESC CAT 5	PROSE
	LOS BUILT THE STUBBORN STRUCTURE OF THE LANGUAGE ACTING AGAINST	668	JERUSALEM 40	59
	ITS DISGUISE IN THE CLASSICAL & SCOTCH LANGUAGE	788D	ANNO THORNTON	* MARG
LANGUAGES				
	I DID NOT BEGIN TO LEARN LANGUAGES EARLY IN LIFE AS I FIND IT	821D	LETTER 25	PROSE
LANGUID				
	THE LANGUID STRINGS DO SCARCELY MOVE	11	TO MUSES/PS	15
LANGUISH				
	. . . LANGUISH BECAUSE THE FEET	142	FRENCH REVOLTN	184
LANGUISHD				
	THY GOLDEN CROWN UPON HER LANGUISHD HEAD	1	TO SPRING/PS	15
	MY SMILES AND LANGUISHD AIR	6	MY SILKS/PS	2
	SO SAYING IN DEEP SOBS HE LANGUISHD TILL DEAD HE ALSO FELL	289	FOUR ZOAS 2	340
	LANGUISHD UPON MOUNT OLIVET EAST OF MILD ZION'S HILL . .	726	JERUSALEM 82	55
LANGUISHES				
	THE CORNER OF BROAD STREET WEEPS POLAND STREET LANGUISHES	729	JERUSALEM 84	15
LANGUOR				
	DOWN IN SICK PALLID LANGUOR THESE WERE HIS LAST WORDS RELAPSING	646	JERUSALEM 23	26
LANTERN				
	WITHOUT A LANTERN TO DIRECT MY STEPS WITHOUT A STAFF TO SUPPORT ME	35D	COUCH DEATH/PS	PROSE
	AND TRUTH A LANTERN TO OUR PATH	64	SHEPHERD OLD	6
	"HE" IS SEEN FOLLOWING THE FRIAR'S LANTERN TOWARDS THE CONVENT	618C	ILLUS MILTON	PROSE
LAOCOON				
	INSTANCE OF LAOCOON WHO THOUGH A PRIEST IS REPRESENTED NAKED	583D	DESC CAT 10	PROSE
	THE TORSO IS AS MUCH A UNITY AS THE LAOCOON	778B	HOMERS POETRY	PROSE
LAP				
	BEFORE HIS EYES LIKE THE ANIMAL UPON THE PYTHAGOREAN'S LAP	46A	ISLAND MOON 1	PROSE
	SHE TOOK ME ON HER LAP AND KISSED ME	125	LIT BLK BOY/SI	7
	THOU HAST A LAP FULL OF SEED	168	HAST LAP/N	1
	THEN THOU WITH THY LAP FULL OF SEED	255	AHANIA 5	29
	SHE BORE THE FRUITS IN HER LAP SHE GATHERD FLOWERS FOR HER BOSOM	369	FOUR ZOAS 9	477
	AND COUCHING AT THEIR SIDE SHALL EAT FROM THE CURLD BOY'S WHITE LAP	376	FOUR ZOAS 9	* 707
	THEY LAP THE WATER OF THE TREMBLING THAMES THEN FOLLOW SWIFT	729	JERUSALEM 83	83
LAPS				
	SHALL LAUGH WHOSE FRUITFUL LAPS BEND DOWN WITH FULNESS . .	33	EDW THIRD/PS 6	48
	ROUND THE LAPS OF THEIR MOTHERS	116	ECCHOING GR/SI	25
	IN LAPS OF PLEASURE INNOCENCE HONEST OPEN SEEKING . . .	193	V DAU ALBION 6	5
LAPSED				
	CALLING THE LAPSED SOUL	210	INTRODUCTN/SE	6
LAPWING				
	O LAPWING THOU FLIEST AROUND THE HEATH	168	O LAPWING/N	1
	ON (ONE) PLATE O LAPWING &C AN ANSWER TO THE PARSON .	SUPP	ON PLATE/N101	*PROSE
LARGE				
	THAT FLAMES FROM THEIR LARGE NOSTRILS THOU O SUMMER . . .	1	TO SUMMER/PS	3
	THE ORBS OF HIS LARGE EYES HE OPEND & THUS HIS VOICE WENT FORTH	99	TIRIEL 1	21
	THIS ARMY OF SUPERSTITION AT LARGE	142	FRENCH REVOLTN	173
	OF ANY AGE OR COUNTRY AMONG WHICH ARE TWO LARGE	207C	PRSPECTUS 1793	PROSE
	THEY ERECTED LARGE PILLARS ROUND THE VOID	231	URIZEN 19	6
	HIS EYES THE LIGHTS OF HIS LARGE SOUL CONTRACT OR ELSE EXPAND	308	FOUR ZOAS 5	121
	A WALL IS A LARGE IVORY	466D	ANNO REYNOLDS	MARG
	THE ARMY OF ARMED ROMANS THE FIGURES FULL AS LARGE AS LIFE	560A	EXHIBITION ADV	PROSE
	OF DIMENSIONS EVER SO LARGE OR EVER SO SMALL WHICH MAY BE	560D	EXHIBITION ADV	PROSE
	AND FORM HIS FOREHEAD SMALL WITHOUT FRONTALS HIS JAWS LARGE	580A	DESC CAT 5	PROSE
	AND HIS EXTREMITIES LARGE HIS EYES WITH SCARCE ANY WHITES	580A	DESC CAT 5	PROSE
	THEY TOO LARGE AND UNWIELY FOR HIS BRAIN AND BOSOM . . .	580B	DESC CAT 5	PROSE
	ATTENTION OF THE AMATEUR IN A LARGE [WORK] STROKE ENGRAVING	587D	CHAUCER/N	*PROSE
	ONE OF THOSE WHICH HE HAS ROLLED ON LARGE ROLLERS HE WILL	831B	LETTER 31	PROSE
	SO LARGE AS TO OCCUPY THE WHOLE LENGTH OF HIS WORKSHOP .	831B	LETTER 31	PROSE
	ONE OR TWO LARGE CARTOONS THE SUBJECTS HE DOES NOT KNOW	834C	LETTER 34	PROSE
	THE FIGURES AS LARGE AS LIFE HALF LENGTH MR W(WALKER) THREE SONS	843C	LETTER 43	PROSE
	(TWELVE) LARGE PRINTS SIZE OF EACH ABOUT (TWO) FEET BY...	867B	LETTER 66	PROSE
LARGER				
	GROW LARGER AS WE ADVANCE AND SOME PERHAPS	18	EDW THIRD/PS 1	37
	FOR EVERY SPACE LARGER THAN A RED GLOBULE OF MAN'S BLOOD	516	MILTON 29	19
	OR ENAMEL ALTHOUGH IN WORKS LARGER THAN LIFE	561A	EXHIBITION ADV	PROSE
	THE WHOLE MIDDLE OF THE BOOK BEING PRINTED WITH A LARGER	847A	LETTER 44	PROSE
LARK SEE SKY-LARK				
	LARK IN SKY	123	SPRING/SI	7
	THE LARK DOES RUSTLE IN THE RIPE CORN AND THE EAGLE RETURNS	190	V DAU ALBION 2	25
	[THE NIGHTINGALE THE GOLDFINCH ROBIN LARK LINNET & THRUSH]	270	FOUR ZOAS 1	207
	AND FINISHES WHERE THE LARK MOUNTS HERE MILTON JOURNEYED	498	MILTON 17	27

		PAGE	TITLE	LINE

LARK   (CONTINUED)

THE LARK SITTING UPON HIS EARTHY BED JUST AS THE MORN . . 520 MILTON 31 — 29
JUST AT THE PLACE TO WHERE THE LARK MOUNTS IS A CRYSTAL GATE — 526 MILTON 35 — 61
THE LARK IS LOS'S MESSENGER THRO THE TWENTY-SEVEN CHURCHES — 526 MILTON 35 — 63
GATE OF WIDE GOLGONOOZA & THE LARK IS LOS'S MESSENGER . . 526 MILTON 35 — 67
AT THAT BRIGHT GATE ANOTHER LARK MEETS HIM & BACK TO BACK — 526 MILTON 36 — 2
INSPIRED & AT THE DAWN OF DAY SEND OUT ANOTHER LARK . . . 526 MILTON 36 — 6
LARK MET THE FEMALE OLOLON DESCENDING INTO MY GARDEN . . 527 MILTON 36 — 10
BUT NOT THUS TO IMMORTALS THE LARK IS A MIGHTY ANGEL . . 527 MILTON 36 — 12
IMMEDIATELY THE LARK MOUNTED WITH A LOUD TRILL FROM FELPHAM'S VALE — 534 MILTON 42 — 29
THE LARK IS AN ANGEL ON THE WING . . . . 618A ILLUS MILTON — PROSE
START FOR HAMPSTEAD LIKE A YOUNG LARK WITHOUT FEATHERS . . 875A LETTER 80 — PROSE

LARK'S

BESIDE THE FOUNT ABOVE THE LARK'S NEST IN GOLGONOOZA . . 526 MILTON 35 — 58
BUT THE LARK'S NEST IS AT THE GATE OF LOS AT THE EASTERN — 526 MILTON 35 — 66
THE EARTH BENEATH AWAKES AT THE LARK'S VOICE . . . . . 618B ILLUS MILTON — PROSE

LASCIVIOUS

IN SOFT SILK DRAWN FROM THEIR OWN BOWELS IN LASCIVIOUS DELIGHT — 346 FOUR ZOAS 8 — 211

LASH

STALKING UPON THE MOUNTAINS & SOMETIMES A WHALE I LASH . . 196 AMERICA PREL 1 — 14
THE LIONS LASH THEIR WRATHFUL TAILS . . . . 245 EUROPE 15 — 6
I ALONE DARE THE LASH ABIDE TO SIT BENEATH THE BLAST . . 344 FOUR ZOAS 8 — 148
GIBBON AROSE WITH A LASH OF STEEL . . . . 418 I SAW A MONK/N — 5
GIBBON PLIED HIS LASH OF STEEL . . . . 420 I SAW MNK AD/N — 11
GIBBON ALOUD HIS LASH DOES PLY . . . . 420 I SAW MNK AD/N — 16
LASH ON THEIR LIMBS AS THEY TURN THE WHIRLWINDS LOOSE UPON — 484 MILTON 5 — 17
GIBBON AROSE WITH A LASH OF STEEL . . . . 683 I SAW A MONK/J — 5
POOR FUSELI SORE FROM THE LASH OF ENVIOUS TONGUES . . . 798B LETTER 10 — PROSE

LASHD

LASHD ON THE LIMBS OF ENITHARMON & THE SULPHUR FIRES . . 302 FOUR ZOAS 4 — 187
AND HIS IMMENSE TAIL LASHD THE ABYSS HIS HUMAN FORM A STONE — 352 FOUR ZOAS 8 — 428

LASHES

LOUD HOWLS THE ETERNAL WOLF THE ETERNAL LION LASHES HIS TAIL — 199 AMERICA 9 — 2
LOUD HOWLS THE ETERNAL WOLF THE ETERNAL LION LASHES HIS TAIL — 199 AMERICA 9 — 27
LASHES HIS TAIL IN THE [WIDE] WILD DEEP HIS EYELIDS LIKE THE SUN — 352 FOUR ZOAS 8 — * 439
HIS NECK FLAMES WITH WRATH & MAJESTY HE LASHES THE ABYSS — 352 FOUR ZOAS 8 — 442

LASS

WITH LAD AND LASS HOW FAIR THE SHOW . . . . 16 BLIND-MANS/PS — 8
& THE SHEPHERD & HIS LASS UNDER A HAWTHORN IN THE DALE . . 618B ILLUS MILTON — PROSE

LASSES

THE LASSES PRICK THE LADS WITH PINS . . . . 16 BLIND-MANS/PS — 12

LAST

SHE HUGGD IT TO HER BREAST AND GROAND HER LAST . . . . 6 FAIR ELENOR/PS — 72
TO LIGHT ANOTHER BATTLE LAST NIGHT BENEATH . . . . . . 25 EDW THIRD/PS 3 — 160
O AT LAST THOU MOCKEST ME TO SHAME MY OVER-FOND INQUIRY — 39A SAMSON/PS — PROSE
BUT AT THE LAST IT SETTLES IN A LAKE CALLED OBLIVION . . 41C THEN SHE BORE — PROSE
THESE GODS LAST NAMD LIVE IN THE SMOKE OF CITIES . . . . 42D THEN SHE BORE — PROSE
IT SPOKE I COME MY FRIEND TO TAKE MY LAST FAREWELL . . . 43D WOE CRIED MUSE — PROSE
BUT FELICITY DOES NOT LAST LONG FOR . . . . 58B ISLAND MOON 10 — PROSE
FOR THE REASON OF THESE REMARKS SEE THE LAST APHORISM . . 65B ANNO LAVATER — MARG
STAND FROM MY PATH FOUL FIEND IS THIS THE LAST OF THY DECEITS — 103 TIRIEL 4 — 8
AT LAST I CAUGHT HIM IN THE FORM OF TIRIEL BLIND & OLD . . 105 TIRIEL 4 — 61
AT LAST BE PROVED TO ORIGINATE IN OURS & TO BE THE TRIBUTARIES — 153D MARRIAGE HH 12 — PROSE
CAME TO THINK THAT ALL NATIONS WOULD AT LAST BE SUBJECT TO THE JEWS — 154A MARRIAGE HH 12 — PROSE
AT LAST TO THE EAST DISTANT ABOUT THREE DEGREES APPEARD — 156C MARRIAGE HH 17 — PROSE
& AT LAST WHITE PINK & SMILING AND THEN REPLIED . . . . 158B MARRIAGE HH 22 — PROSE
TILL TO THE LAST TRUMPET IT WAS FARTED . . . . 187 WHEN KLOPSTK/N — 20
FLAMD OUT FIRST BEGOTTEN LAST BORN . . . . 234 URIZEN 23 — 18
SEEKING THE TRUMP OF THE LAST DOOM . . . . 242 EUROPE 12 — 13
THE TRUMP OF THE LAST DOOM BUT HE COULD NOT BLOW THE IRON TUBE — 243 EUROPE 13 — 2
AN EVANESCENT SHADOW LAST SHE FELL A HEAP OF ASHES . . . 283 FOUR ZOAS 2 — 115
VALA NIGHT THE NINTH BEING THE LAST JUDGMENT . . . . . 357B FOUR ZOAS 9 — TITLE
THEN LAST HERSELF LAID DOWN & CLOSD HER EYELIDS IN SOFT SLUMBERS — 370 FOUR ZOAS 9 — 516
TEARS OF THE GRAPE THE DEATH SWEAT OF THE CLUSTER THE LAST SIGH — 377 FOUR ZOAS 9 — 770
DUTY TO HIS COUNTRY IS THE FIRST CONSIDERATION & SAFETY THE LAST — 383C ANNO WATSON — MARG
FOR THE LAST JUDGMENT DRAWETH NIGH . . . . 432 AUGURIES — 40
THE DESIGN OF THE LAST JUDGMENT WHICH I HAVE COMPLETED . . 442D LAST JUDGMNT/L — PROSE
& WHICH BUT FOR YOU MIGHT HAVE SLEPT TILL THE LAST JUDGMENT — 444C LAST JUDGMNT/L — PROSE
& ITS LAST NOW HE BEGINS TO DEGRADE [&] TO DENY [DESTROY] & TO MOCK — 458B ANNO REYNOLDS — * MARG
[SO SATAN TOOK AWAY ORNAMENTS FIRST NECESSARIES LAST] . . 446C ANNO REYNOLDS — * MARG
AT LAST ENITHARMON BROUGHT FORTH SATAN REFUSING FORM IN VAIN — 483 MILTON 3 — 41
LEST THE LAST JUDGMENT COME & FIND ME UNANNIHILATE . . . 495 MILTON 14 — 23
AT LAST WHEN DESPERATION ALMOST TORE HIS HEART IN TWAIN — 503 MILTON 20 — 56
THEY VANISH NOT FROM ME & MINE WE GUARD THEM FIRST & LAST — 505 MILTON 22 — 23
THEN PATIENT WAIT A LITTLE WHILE TILL THE LAST VINTAGE IS OVER — 508 MILTON 23 — 59
HE IS THE SIGNAL THAT THE LAST VINTAGE NOW APPROACHES . . 509 MILTON 24 — 42

	PAGE	TITLE	LINE

LAST   (CONTINUED)

THEY SANG AT THE VINTAGE THIS IS THE LAST VINTAGE & SEED	510	MILTON 25	8
TEARS OF THE GRAPE THE DEATH SWEAT OF THE CLUSTER THE LAST SIGH	514	MILTON 27	40
TILL [HES] YOURE AT LAST BECOME THE [OLD] GOLDEN FOOL . .	540	S(TOTHAR)D/N *	2
HAVE THE LAST WORD & TAKE THE WALL	547	IF I GROW/N	4
HE IS ALL EXPERIMENTS FROM LAST TO FIRST	548	CRIPPLE EVRY/N	7
"IN THE LAST BATTLE THAT ARTHUR FOUGHT THE MOST BEAUTIFUL WAS ONE"	560B	EXHIBITION ADV	PROSE
THESE LAST ARE ISSUING FROM THE GATEWAY OF THE INN THE COOK	567A	DESC CAT 3	PROSE
IN THE LAST BATTLE OF KING ARTHUR ONLY THREE BRITONS ESCAPED	577B	DESC CAT 5	TITLE
ARMED ROMANS STREW THE FIELD BENEATH AMONG THESE THE LAST OF	580C	DESC CAT 5	PROSE
AND LAST A MAN'S WHOLE LIFE BUT HE WILL AT LENGTH . . .	587A	CHAUCER 1	PROSE
THESE LAST ARE ISSUING FROM THE GATEWAY OF THE INN THE COOK	588D	CHAUCER/N	PROSE
THESE LAST ARE ISSUING FROM THE GATEWAY OF THE INN THE COOK	590A	CHAUCER 2	PROSE
THE LAST JUDGMENT WHEN ALL THOSE ARE CAST AWAY	604C	V LAST JUDG/N	PROSE
THEN THE LAST JUDGMENT BEGINS & ITS VISION	604C	V LAST JUDG/N	PROSE
THE LAST JUDGMENT IS NOT FABLE OR ALLEGORY BUT VISION . .	604D	V LAST JUDG/N	PROSE
THE LAST JUDGMENT IS ONE OF THESE STUPENDOUS VISIONS . .	605A	V LAST JUDG/N	PROSE
BUT OF THOSE FOUND ALIVE AT THE LAST JUDGMENT	610B	V LAST JUDG/N	PROSE
A LAST JUDGMENT IS NECESSARY BECAUSE FOOLS FLOURISH . .	612B	V LAST JUDG/N	PROSE
POVERTY IS THE FOOL'S ROD WHICH AT LAST IS TURND ON HIS OWN BACK	612C	V LAST JUDG/N	PROSE
THIS IS A LAST JUDGMENT WHEN MEN OF REAL ART GOVERN &	612C	V LAST JUDG/N	PROSE
IN PROPORTION TO HIS MEANS A LAST JUDGMENT IS NOT . .	612D	V LAST JUDG/N	PROSE
A LAST JUDGMENT PASSES UPON THAT INDIVIDUAL	613A	V LAST JUDG/N	PROSE
FOR IT APPEARS SO AT THE LAST JUDGMENT FOR A PROTECTION	614B	V LAST JUDG/N	PROSE
THE LAST JUDGMENT A DELIVERANCE FROM SATAN'S ACCUSATION	615C	V LAST JUDG/N	PROSE
AS YOU [PREP] PRETEND TILL AFTER THE LAST JUDGMENT . .	616A	V LAST JUDG/N	*PROSE
& CANNOT BE REMOVED BUT BY A LAST JUDGMENT	616A	V LAST JUDG/N	PROSE
THE LAST JUDGMENT IS AN OVERWHELMING OF BAD ART & SCIENCE	617A	V LAST JUDG/N	PROSE
SOME PEOPLE FLATTER THEMSELVES THAT THERE WILL BE NO LAST JUDGMENT	617A	V LAST JUDG/N	PROSE
[TO NOTE THE LAST WORDS OF JESUS...(GREEK QUOTED)] .	621C	JERUSALEM 3	*PROSE
BUT ALL CLOSD UP TILL THE LAST DAY	633	JERUSALEM 13	11
MY CATTLE NEXT LAST EVN THE DOG OF MY GATE THE FORESTS FLED	643	JERUSALEM 21	8
TO THE LAST DROP THEN HIDE ME IN THY SCARLET TABERNACLE	645	JERUSALEM 22	30
DOWN IN SICK PALLID LANGUOUR THESE WERE HIS LAST WORDS RELAPSING	646	JERUSALEM 23	26
ALBION HATH ENTERD THE LOINS THE PLACE OF THE LAST JUDGMENT	656	JERUSALEM 30	38
[WHEN ALBION UTTERD HIS LAST WORDS HOPE IS BANISHD FROM ME]	677	JERUSALEM 47 *	1
THEREFORE I WRITE ALBION'S LAST WORDS HOPE IS BANISHD FROM ME	677	JERUSALEM 47	18
THESE WERE HIS LAST WORDS AND THE MERCIFUL SAVIOUR IN HIS ARMS	677	JERUSALEM 48	1
SHALL ALBION ARISE I KNOW HE SHALL ARISE AT THE LAST DAY	696	JERUSALEM 62	15
IN TERRORS AT THE LAST JUDGMENT DAY	751	EV GOSPEL(C)/N	44
[WHOM THOU SHALT TORMENT AT THE LAST DAY]	751	EV GOSPEL(C)/N	48
AND TAKE REVENGE AT THE LAST DAY	751	EV GOSPEL(C)/N	49
AND AT LAST HE WOULD HAVE BEEN CAESAR HIMSELF	752	EV GOSPEL(D)/N	42
IN TERRORS AT THE LAST JUDGMENT DAY	753	EV GOSPEL(D)/N	80
AND TAKE REVENGE AT THE LAST DAY	753	EV GOSPEL(D)/N	84
IT APPEARS TO ME AS IF THE LAST PARAGRAPH BEGINNING WITH	783D	ANNO WW POEMS	* MARG
REALLY VERY ILL WHEN I WROTE TO HIM THE LAST TIME & WAS NOT	820C	LETTER 25	PROSE
& TO BE ENGRAVD ALSO BY THE LAST MENTIONED THE	824C	LETTER 27	PROSE
IN GOOD LUCK AT LAST & SHALL BE FORGOT BY MY AFFECTIONS &	824D	LETTER 27	PROSE
VERY UNACCOUNTABLY TO COPY OUT IN MY LAST LETTER THAT PASSAGE	826C	LETTER 28	PROSE
OFFERING TO EXHIBIT MY (TWO) LAST PICTURES IN THE GALLERY	826C	LETTER 28	PROSE
THE LAST TOUCHES ESPECIALLY THE PLATE OF THE MONUMENT .	838A	LETTER 37	PROSE
THE LAST TOUCHES WHICH ARE ALWAYS THE BEST I HAVE NOW I HOPE	840B	LETTER 39	PROSE
INTERESTING TOPIC IN BOTH YOUR LAST LETTERS GOD BE WITH YOU	841A	LETTER 40	PROSE
THE LAST PERFORMANCE OF ROMNEY IT IS OF MR WALKER AND FAMILY	843C	LETTER 43	PROSE
HE SAYS THAT THE LAST SESSION WAS A SEVERE LABOUR INDEED IT	844D	LETTER 43	PROSE
IT YET WANTS ALL ITS LAST & FINISHING TOUCHES BUT I HOPE YOU	850B	LETTER 49	PROSE
BEEN THE RUIN OF MY LABOURS FOR THE LAST PASSED TWENTY YEARS	851D	LETTER 50	PROSE
SINCERE THANKS FOR YOUR KIND PROPOSAL IN YOUR LAST LETTER	853A	LETTER 51	*PROSE
JOURNEY & SUCH SWEET VERSES AS YOURS IN YOUR LAST . .	854B	LETTER 53	PROSE
LAST REQUESTING TEN POUNDS I THOUGHT IT WAS DUE ON . .	854D	LETTER 53	PROSE
WHEN I LEFT FELPHAM LAST IN ONE OF HEATH'S SHAKESPEARE YOU WILL SEE	855C	LETTER 53	PROSE
THAT YOUR LAST BEAUTIFUL POEM WAS NOT PUBLISHD IN THE .	856B	LETTER 54	PROSE
PLEASE ME SO WELL THAT I HAVE CHOSEN THAT DESIGN IN OUR LAST	859B	LETTER 56	PROSE
WILL HURT THE SALE OF THE WORK AND HE SENT TO ME THE LAST SHEET	861B	LETTER 58	PROSE
FOR WHAT IS GOOD MUST SUCCEED FIRST OR LAST BUT WHAT IS BAD	862A	LETTER 59	PROSE
THESE LAST (TWELVE) PRINTS ARE UNACCOMPANIED BY ANY WRITING	867C	LETTER 66	PROSE
LAST TIME WE MET I HAVE NO DOUBT THAT THE PLATES WOULD BE ALL	870B	LETTER 71	PROSE
THE TIME I NOW WRITE HE SET OFF LAST NIGHT BEFORE EIGHT OCLOCK	871C	LETTER 73	PROSE
I SHOULD HAVE WRITTEN LAST NIGHT BUT AS IT WOULD NOT COME	871C	LETTER 73	PROSE
VERY CONSIDERABLY WEAKEND BY THE LAST SEVERE ATTACKS .	873D	LETTER 78	*PROSE
DESPERATE ATTACK OF THE ANGUISH (&) TREMBLING LAST NIGHT &	SUPP	LETTER 81A	*PROSE
THE LAST WORK I PRODUCED IS A POEM ENTITLED JERUSALEM THE	878C	LETTER 88	PROSE

LAST   (CONTINUED)
        THE ACCUSERS OF THEFT ADULTERY MURDER A SCENE IN THE LAST   SUPP INSC OUR END   *TITLE
          JUDGMENT
LASTED
        BROUGHT ON A RELAPSE WHICH IS LASTED TILL NOW I FIND I AM   880A LETTER 90   PROSE
LASTING
        WILL YOU ERECT A LASTING HABITATION IN THE MOULDERING   353 FOUR ZOAS 8   495
          CHURCH YARD
        OF GOD WILL BE A LASTING WITNESS AGAINST THEM . . . . . . 389A ANNO WATSON   MARG
LASTLY
        THE GREEK HEROES & LASTLY BY THE ROMANS . . . . 785B ILLUS DANTE 7   PROSE
LASTS
        EASILY REMOVED BUT EXCRUCIATING WHILE IT LASTS & ENFEEBLING   871A LETTER 72   PROSE
LATE
        [TOO LATE NOW TO REPENT . . . .   267 FOUR ZOAS 1   * 111
        DRIVEN MILTON INTO THE ULRO FOR NOW THEY KNEW TOO LATE . . 504 MILTON 21   32
        TWAS TOO LATE NOW TO RECEDE LOS HAD ENTERD INTO MY SOUL   505 MILTON 22   13
        ARE YOU THE FIERY CIRCLE THAT LATE DROVE IN FURY & FIRE   523 MILTON 34   3
        OF LATE YEARS OUGHT TO ROUZE . . . .   598D PUB ADDRESS/N   PROSE
        IT HAS BEEN SAID OF LATE YEARS THE ENGLISH PUBLIC HAVE . 601B PUB ADDRESS/N   PROSE
        LITTLE TOM HAS BEEN OF LATE UNATTENDED TO . . . . . .   807A LETTER 17   PROSE
        HE IS NEPHEW TO THE LATE MR COWPER THE POET YOU WOULD LIKE 809C LETTER 20   PROSE
          HIM MUCH
        A MORE ASSIDUOUS PURSUIT OF BOTH ARTS INDEED BY MY LATE   825C LETTER 27   PROSE
        BECAUSE I SHALL BE TOO LATE FOR THE CARRIAGE . . . . .   832D LETTER 32   PROSE
        RECONSIDER IT IF IT IS NOT TOO LATE IT VERY MUCH TROUBLES   874B LETTER 79   PROSE
          ME
LATELY
        [WHERE IS THE VOICE THAT LATELY WOKE THE DESART WHERE THE   268 FOUR ZOAS 1   139
          FACE]
        COME OUT HE IS THE SAME MAN WHO LATELY HURT HIS HAND   . 438C BLAKES MEMORAN   PROSE
        I HAVE LATELY HAD SOME PRICKS OF CONSCIENCE . . . . . 791A LETTER 3   PROSE
        MR HAYLEY HAS LATELY MENTIOND YOUR WORK ON OUTLINE IN NOTES 798B LETTER 10   *PROSE
        BUT FOR A DETERMINATION WHICH WE HAVE LATELY MADE . . 819C LETTER 25   PROSE
        THE DELAY I HAVE SEEN OUR EXCELLENT FLAXMAN LATELY HE IS   842D LETTER 42   PROSE
          WELL
LATIN
        INFECTION FROM THE SILLY GREEK & LATIN SLAVES OF THE SWORD 480C MILTON 1   PROSE
        I GO ON MERRILY WITH MY GREEK & LATIN AM VERY SORRY THAT   821D LETTER 25   PROSE
        TRANSLATIONS BY COWPER FROM MILTON'S LATIN & ITALIAN POEMS 824C LETTER 27   PROSE
LATITUDE
        MR B(BLAKE) REQUIRES THE SAME LATITUDE AND ALL IS WELL . . 576D DESC CAT 4   PROSE
LATIUM
        OR OVID'S WERE THE PRODUCTION OF GREECE OR OF LATIUM . . 565D DESC CAT 2   PROSE
LATTER
        HINDER CRIMES OR CAN THE MAN WHO WRITES THE LATTER   385C ANNO WATSON   MARG
          SENTIMENT
        THAT I MAY PUT THEM IN MIND OF THEIR LATTER ENDS . . . . 556 BLAKES APL/N 2   22
        AS IS THE PRACTICE OF THE LATTER SCHOOLS OF ITALY   564D DESC CAT 1   PROSE
          AND FLANDERS
        DRAGON'S CAVERN REPRESENTS THE LATTER STATE OF THE CHURCH   610C V LAST JUDG/N   PROSE
        I BEGIN WITH THE LATTER END OF YOUR LETTER & GRIEVE MORE   837C LETTER 36   PROSE
          FOR
LAUGH
        AND LAUGH OUR SPORTS TO SEE . . . .   8 LOVE JOCUND/PS   16
        THOUDST LAUGH HIS FURY INTO NERVELESS SHAME . . . . . 25 EDW THIRD/PS 3   177
        GRIM WAR SHALL LAUGH AND SHOUT DECKED IN TEARS . . . . . 31 EDW THIRD/PS 5   53
        SHALL LAUGH WHOSE FRUITFUL LAPS BEND DOWN WITH FULNESS . . 33 EDW THIRD/PS 6   48
        HERE A LAUGH BEGAN AND MISS GITTIPIN SUNG . . . . 61B ISLAND MOON 11   PROSE
        WHEN THE TREES DO LAUGH WITH OUR MERRY WIT . . . . 63 SHEPHERD YOUNG   1
        WHEN THE MEADOWS LAUGH WITH LIVELY GREEN . . . . 63 SHEPHERD YOUNG   3
        WHEN THE PAINTED BIRDS LAUGH IN THE SHADE . . . . . . 63 SHEPHERD YOUNG   9
        ("KEEP DISTANT WHO HATES...LAUGH OF A CHILD") THE BEST   74B ANNO LAVATER   MARG
          IN THE BOOK
        LAUGH SERPENT YOUNGEST VENOMOUS REPTILE OF THE FLESH OF   108 TIRIEL 6   32
          TIRIEL
        LAUGH FOR THY FATHER TIRIEL SHALL GIVE (THEE) CAUSE TO   108 TIRIEL 6   33
          LAUGH
        LET SNAKES RISE FROM THY BEDDED LOCKS & LAUGH AMONG THY   108 TIRIEL 6   43
          CURLS
        [OF THUNDER DOES HE LOOK UPON THE SUN & LAUGH OR STRETCH]   110 TIRIEL 8   20
        DOES LAUGH AWAY CARE . . . .   116 ECCHOING GR/SI   12
        THEY LAUGH AT OUR PLAY . . . .   116 ECCHOING GR/SI   15
        WHEN THE GREEN WOODS LAUGH WITH THE VOICE OF JOY . . . . 124 LAUGHING/SI   1
        WHEN THE AIR DOES LAUGH WITH OUR MERRY WIT . . . . 124 LAUGHING/SI   3
        WHEN THE MEADOWS LAUGH WITH LIVELY GREEN . . . . . . 125 LAUGHING/SI   5
        WHEN THE PAINTED BIRDS LAUGH IN THE SHADE . . . . . . 125 LAUGHING/SI   9
        THEN LAUGH IN THE DISMAL DEN THEN ARE SILENT . . . . . . 136 FRENCH REVOLTN   53
        JOYS LAUGH NOT SORROWS WEEP NOT . . . .   152C MARRIAGE HH 9   PROSE
        AND [[IS] DID HE LAUGH] DARE HE [SMILE] [LAUGH] HIS WORK   173 THE TYGER/N 1 *   26
          TO SEE
        LET HIM LAUGH LET HIM CRY . . . .   178 THE FAIRY/N   17
        DOES NOT THE GREAT MOUTH LAUGH AT A GIFT & THE NARROW   192 V DAU ALBION 5   7
          EYELIDS MOCK
        LET HIM LOOK UP INTO THE HEAVENS & LAUGH IN THE BRIGHT AIR 198 AMERICA 6   7
        AND LET US LAUGH AT WAR . . . .   239 EUROPE 4   21
        AMONG THESE FLAMES INCESSANT LABOURING OUR HARD MASTERS   285 FOUR ZOAS 2   219
          LAUGH
        THE EMMET & THE BEETLE HARK THEY LAUGH & MOCK AT LOS . 288 FOUR ZOAS 2   308
        IT IS AN EASY THING TO LAUGH AT WRATHFUL ELEMENTS . . . 290 FOUR ZOAS 2   408
        WHILE OUR OLIVE & VINE SING & LAUGH ROUND OUR DOOR . . . 291 FOUR ZOAS 2   413
        FAR AS MY STRENGTH CAN HURL THEE WANDER THERE & LAUGH &   296 FOUR ZOAS 3   171
          PLAY

LAUGH   (CONTINUED)
        SCREAM & FALL OFF & LAUGH AT THARMAS LOVELY SUMMER BEAUTY   296 FOUR ZOAS 3   174
        DRINK LAUGH & SING THE GRASSHOPPER THE EMMET & THE FLY . .   308 FOUR ZOAS 5   * 133
        YET THOU DOST LAUGH AT ALL THESE TORTURES & THIS HORRIBLE   321 FOUR ZOAS 7   59
            PLACE
        FLAME HIGH IN PRIDE & LAUGH TO SCORN THE SOURCE OF HIS   324 FOUR ZOAS 7   158
            DECEIT
        AND SWORDS RAGE WHERE THE EAGLES CRY & THE VULTURES LAUGH   334 FOUR ZOAS 7B   44
            SAYING
        AND THE GRAVE MOCK & LAUGH AT THE PLOWD FIELD SAYING   . .   354 FOUR ZOAS 8   499
        LET HIM LOOK UP INTO THE HEAVENS & LAUGH IN THE BRIGHT AIR   375 FOUR ZOAS 9   671
        AND NOW THE MEN UPON ME SMILE & LAUGH . . . .   537 AND HIS LEGS/N   48
        TWILL MAKE A FOOL LAUGH & A FAIRY FUN . . . .   552 TELL YOU WHA/N   6
        AND LAUGH WHEN WE DO CRY . . . .   552 WHY CUPID/N   8
        AMONG HONEST PEOPLE TO MAKE GAME OF AND LAUGH AT THEM   574D DESC CAT 3   PROSE
        AND LAUGH IN SECRET AT THE PRETENCES OF THE IGNORANT   .   586A DESC CAT 16   PROSE
        TO ALL THE CONTINENT WHO LAUGH AT THE CONTEMPTIBLE   . .   593C PUB ADDRESS/N   PROSE
        ARTS & ARTISTS ARE SPIRITUAL & LAUGH AT MORTAL   597A PUB ADDRESS/N   PROSE
            CONTINGENCIES
        THE ITALIANS LAUGH AT ENGLISH CONNOISSEURS WHO ARE   . . .   597B PUB ADDRESS/N   PROSE
        WHILE THEY DESPISE & LAUGH AT WHAT OTHERS FEAR   . . .   609B V LAST JUDG/N   PROSE
        TENDER ARTIFICE TO LAUGH TO WEEP TO LEARN TO KNOW   . .   688 JERUSALEM 56   24
        I MIND NOT YOUR LAUGH AND YOUR FROWN I NOT FEAR AND . .   688 JERUSALEM 56   30
        STARVE I LAUGH AT FORTUNE & GO ON & ON I THINK I FORESEE   795C LETTER 6   PROSE
        BUSINESS & THO I LAUGH AT FORTUNE I AM PERSWADED THAT SHE   795D LETTER 6   PROSE
        YET I LAUGH & SING FOR IF ON EARTH NEGLECTED I AM IN HEAVEN   830A LETTER 30   PROSE
        & NOW I HAVE LAMENTED OVER THE DEAD HORSE LET ME LAUGH & BE   830B LETTER 30   PROSE
LAUGHD
        THE LITTLE ONES LEAPED & SHOUTED & LAUGHD . . . . .   60 NURSES SONG/IN   16
        THEY LAUGHD & MOCKED SOME THREW DIRT & STONES AS THEY PASSD   108 TIRIEL 7   5
            BY
        THE LITTLE ONES LEAPED & SHOUTED & LAUGHD . . . . .   121 NURSES SONG/SI   15
        SHALL I SHEW YOU YOURS HE LAUGHD AT MY PROPOSAL   . . . .   156D MARRIAGE HH 17   PROSE
        AND LAUGHD AT OUR SIMPLICITY . . . .   169 MIRTLE SHADE/N   14
        HE LAUGHD ALOUD TO SEE THEM WHIMPER BECAUSE THEY   238 EUROPE INTRO   21
            WERE PLUCKD
        ENITHARMON LAUGHD IN HER SLEEP TO SEE O WOMAN'S TRIUMPH   243 EUROPE 12   25
        SWEET LAUGHTER SIEZD ME IN MY SLEEP SILENT & CLOSE I LAUGHD   271 FOUR ZOAS 1   265
        LOS JOYD & ENITHARMON LAUGHD SAYING LET US GO DOWN   . .   285 FOUR ZOAS 2   211
        BUT WHEN HE POURD IT ROUND THE BONES OF URIZEN HE LAUGHD   302 FOUR ZOAS 4   196
        THARMAS LAUGHD FURIOUS AMONG THE BANNERS CLOTHD IN BLOOD   334 FOUR ZOAS 7B   49
        HE LAUGHD AT THE DEVIL SAYING LOVE IS A SIN   434 LONG JOHN BRWN   6
        AND HE LAUGHD AT THE DEVIL TILL POOR JOHN BROWN DIED   .   434 LONG JOHN BRWN   16
        THEN LAUGHD GWENDOLEN & HER LAUGHTER SHOOK THE NATIONS   698 JERUSALEM 63   32
            & FAMILYS OF
LAUGHED
        FOR THOU HAST LAUGHED AT MY TEARS & CURST THY AGED FATHER   108 TIRIEL 6   42
        HE HAS LAUGHED AT HIS KNAVES AND FOOLS AS I DO NOW   . . .   575A DESC CAT 3   PROSE
        AND MANY OF THE ETERNAL ONES LAUGHED AFTER THEIR MANNER   663 JERUSALEM 36   43
LAUGHING
        THEN LAUGHING SPORTS AND PLAYS WITH ME . . . .   6 HOW SWEET/PS   14
        I LOVE THE LAUGHING VALE . . . .   7 LOVE THE JOCUND/PS   5
        THE LAUGHING JEST THE LOVE-SICK TALE . . . . . .   16 BLIND-MANS/PS   10
        NOW LAUGHING STOPS WITH SILENCE HUSH . . . . . .   16 BLIND-MANS/PS   21
        AND LAUGHING [UPON] IS HEARD ON THE HILL . . . . .   60 NURSES SONG/IN   2
        AND THE DIMPLING STREAM RUNS LAUGHING BY . . . . .   63 SHEPHERD YOUNG   6
        I HATE SCARCE SMILES I LOVE LAUGHING . . . . . .   67D ANNO LAVATER   MARG
        AND HE LAUGHING SAID TO ME . . . .   111 INTRODUCTN/SI   4
        THEN DOWN A GREEN PLAIN LEAPING LAUGHING THEY RUN   . . .   117 CHIMNEY SWP/SI   15
        AND LAUGHING IS HEARD ON THE HILL . . . .   121 NURSES SONG/SI   2
        LAUGHING SONG . . . .   124D LAUGHING/SI   TITLE
        AND THE DIMPLING STREAM RUNS LAUGHING BY . . . . .   124 LAUGHING/SI   2
        HE LAUGHING ANSWERD I WILL WRITE A BOOK ON LEAVES   237 EUROPE INTRO   14
            OF FLOWERS
        THE SOUNDING BEAM LAUGHING IT TORE THROUGH . . . . .   249 AHANIA 2   27
        [LAUGHING & MOCKING LUVAH [?BURSTING] ?BREAKING IN THE WOES   SUPP FOUR ZOAS 2   *
            OF VALA]
        THEY SEEM TO ONE ANOTHER LAUGHING TERRIBLE AMONG   344 FOUR ZOAS 8   122
            THE BANNERS
        LAUGHING & SHOUTING DRUNK WITH ODORS MANY FALL OERWEARIED   377 FOUR ZOAS 9   744
        LAUGHING & SHOUTING DRUNK WITH ODOURS MANY FALL OERWEARIED   513 MILTON 27   4
        IN FEARLESS MAJESTY ANNIHILATING SELF LAUGHING TO SCORN   530 MILTON 38   41
        AND DEATH SITS [MOCKING] LAUGHING ON THEIR MONUMENTS . .   537 AND HIS LEGS/N   42
        AT BASIRE'S BY LAUGHING AT BASIRE'S KNIFE TOOLS &   . .   603C PUB ADDR AD/N   PROSE
        THE ARTICULATIONS OF A MAN'S SOUL AND LAUGHING THROW IT   656 JERUSALEM 31   10
            DOWN
        LITTLE BLACK BOY DITTO LAUGHING SONG SPRING DITTO   . .   SUPP LETTER 66A   *PROSE
LAUGHS
        AND THE JOLLY SWAIN LAUGHS HIS FILL . . . .   7 LOVE JOCUND/PS   8
        AND THE GREEN HILL LAUGHS WITH THE NOISE OF IT . . . .   63 SHEPHERD YOUNG   2
        AND THE GRASSHOPPER LAUGHS IN THE MERRY SCENE . . . .   63 SHEPHERD YOUNG   4
        WHEN THE GREENWOOD LAUGHS WITH THE VOICE OF JOY . . .   63 SHEPHERD YOUNG   5
        LAUGHS AT AFFECTION GLORIES IN REBELLION SCOFFS AT LOVE   107 TIRIEL 6   18
        AND THE GREEN HILL LAUGHS WITH THE NOISE OF IT . . . .   124 LAUGHING/SI   4
        AND THE GRASSHOPPER LAUGHS IN THE MERRY SCENE . . . .   125 LAUGHING/SI   6
        EXCESS OF SORROW LAUGHS EXCESS OF JOY WEEPS . . . . .   151C MARRIAGE HH 8   PROSE
        LAUGHS AT THE HUMAN FORM THE LION MOCKS & THIRSTS FOR BLOOD   275 FOUR ZOAS 1   403
        THE SLOW SLUG THE GRASSHOPPER THAT SINGS & LAUGHS & DRINKS   377 FOUR ZOAS 9   760
        OF THE OPINION THAT REYNOLDS CONDEMNS & LAUGHS AT . .   473C ANNO REYNOLDS   MARG
        THE SLOW SLUG THE GRASSHOPPER THAT SINGS & LAUGHS & DRINKS   513 MILTON 27   19
        THE IDIOT REASONER LAUGHS AT THE MAN OF IMAGINATION . . .   521 MILTON 32   6

LAUGHT
        MRS GIMBLET LOOKD AS IF THEY MEANT HER TILLY LALLY LAUGHT   46D ISLAND MOON 3   PROSE
        I BELIEVE THAT THE BISHOP LAUGHT AT THE BIBLE IN HIS SLIEVE   385D ANNO WATSON   MARG
LAUGHTER
        AND BRINGS GOOD COUNSEL FROM THE BREAST OF LAUGHTER . . .   24 EDW THIRD/PS 3   135
        [THE] HIS LAUGHTER NOT AT THEM BUT AT HIS OWN IMAGINATIONS   44C ISLAND MOON 1   *PROSE
        SWEET LAUGHTER SIEZD ME IN MY SLEEP SILENT & CLOSE I LAUGHD   271 FOUR ZOAS 1   265
        AND LAUGHTER SAT BENEATH THE OAKS & INNOCENCE SPORTED ROUND   317 FOUR ZOAS 6   214
        AND FROM LAUGHTER PROCEEDS TO MURDER BY UNDERVALUING   521 MILTON 32   7
           CALUMNY
        THEN LAUGHD GWENDOLEN & HER LAUGHTER SHOOK THE NATIONS   698 JERUSALEM 63   32
           & FAMILYS OF
        HIS IMBECILE ATTEMPTS TO DEPRESS ME ONLY DESERVE LAUGHTER   825C LETTER 27   PROSE
LAUNCHD
        LAUNCHD TO THE UNKNOWN SHORE WHILE SOTHA HELD THE NORTHERN   204 AMERICA CANC B   21
           HELM
LAUREL
        NOR LAUREL WREATHS AGAINST THE SULTRY HEAT . . . . . .   2 TO SUMMER/PS   19
        ROUND MY YOUNG BROWS THE LAUREL WREATHES A SHADE . . . .   9 FRESH FROM/PS   3
        CAME FROM CAESAR'S LAUREL CROWN . . . .   433 AUGURIES   98
        DRAGGED DOWN BY [AN ANGEL] A DEMON CROWND WITH LAUREL .   606C V LAST JUDG/N   PROSE
LAURELLLO
        [LAURELLLO AFFFFSW ALLLLLL HANNALITOE WW BMILLLJJJ HORSES]   601A PUB ADDRESS/N *PROSE
LAURELS
        A CROWN OF LAURELS & I ALSO THANK YOU FOR YOUR REPREHENSION 804A LETTER 16   PROSE
LAVANT
        WHILE WALKING FROM FELPHAM TO LAVANT TO MEET MY SISTER .   816D LETTER 24   PROSE
        PERHAPS LAVANT & IN OR NEAR THE ROAD TO LONDON FOR THE .   820D LETTER 25   PROSE
        FAR BEAMING TURRET LIKE THE VILLA OF LAVANT BLESSED & .   835B LETTER 34   PROSE
        AT LAVANT I REMAIN WITH MY WIFE'S JOINT AFFECTION   . . .   852D LETTER 50   PROSE
        FRIENDS AT LAVANT & IN ALL SUSSEX I REMAIN DEAR SIR . .   853A LETTER 51   *PROSE
        OF YOUR GOOD HEALTH & THAT OF OUR DEAR FRIEND OF LAVANT &   862A LETTER 59   PROSE
        WILLIAM HAYLEY ESQRE AT MISS POOLE'S LAVANT NEAR CHICHESTER SUPP ADDRESS/L 13 *TITLE
           SUSSEX
LAVANT'S
        LADY OF LAVANT'S CONTINUED RECOVERY BUT WITH A MIXTURE .   851C LETTER 50   PROSE
LAVATER
        BECAUSE IT IS GOOD & THAT THE NAME LAVATER IS . . . . .   88B ANNO LAVATER   MARG
        THE PHILOSOPHY OF CAUSES & CONSEQUENCES MISLED LAVATER .   88C ANNO LAVATER   MARG
        BUT THE (ORIGIN) OF THIS MISTAKE IN LAVATER   . . . . .   88D ANNO LAVATER   * MARG
LAVATER'S
        THERE IS A STRONG OBJECTION TO LAVATER'S PRINCIPLES . . .   88C ANNO LAVATER   MARG
LAVISH
        THE LAVISH PRAISE I HAVE RECIEVED FROM ALL QUARTERS . .   601D PUB ADDRESS/N   PROSE
LAW   SEE DAUGHTERS IN LAW,MOTHER IN LAW,SERGEANT AT LAW
        LIKE FABLED HECATE SHE DOTH BIND THEM TO HER LAW . . .   41D THEN SHE BORE   PROSE
        LAW SAID TILLY LALLY WHAT HAS THAT TO DO WITH PHARAOH .   47C ISLAND MOON 3 *PROSE
        DID I SAY SO LAW I DID NOT THINK I SAID THAT . . . . .   49A ISLAND MOON 5   PROSE
        BUT I MEANT SAID ARADOBO I I I CAN'T THINK LAW SIR . . .   49A ISLAND MOON 5   PROSE
        WERE FIT TO GIVE LAW TO THE CITY EACH EAT AS MUCH AS TEN   58 THIS CITY/IM   10
        GUARD IT ON EITHER SIDE & IN THE MIDST IS THE HOLY LAW .   82A ANNO LAVATER   MARG
        WHY IS ONE LAW GIVEN TO THE LION & THE [PA] PATIENT OX   109 TIRIEL 8   * 10
        THE LAW AND GOSPEL FROM FIRE AND AIR AND ETERNAL REASON   138 FRENCH REVOLTN   95
           AND SCIENCE
        . . . THEY LOOK DOWNWARD AND LABOUR AND FORGET MY HOLY LAW   140 FRENCH REVOLTN   139
        PRISONS ARE BUILT WITH STONES OF LAW BROTHELS WITH BRICKS   151B MARRIAGE HH 8   PROSE
           OF RELIGION
        GIVEN HIS SANCTION TO THE LAW OF TEN COMMANDMENTS   . . .   158B MARRIAGE HH 22 PROSE
        HIS SANCTION TO THE LAW OF TEN COMMANDMENTS . . . . .   158C MARRIAGE HH 22 PROSE
        TURN AWAY THE LAW FROM THE WOMAN TAKEN IN ADULTERY . . .   158C MARRIAGE HH 22 PROSE
        ONE LAW FOR THE LION & OX IS OPPRESSION . . . .   158D MARRIAGE HH 22 PROSE
        STAMPS THE STONY LAW TO DUST . . . .   160A SONG LIBERTY   PROSE
        AND IS THERE NOT ONE LAW FOR BOTH THE LION AND THE OX .   192 V DAU ALBION 4   22
        IN SPELLS OF LAW TO ONE SHE LOATHES AND MUST SHE DRAG THE   193 V DAU ALBION 5   22
           CHAIN
        LOVER OF WILD REBELLION AND TRANSGRESSER OF GOD'S LAW . .   198 AMERICA 7   * 6
        THAT STONY LAW I STAMP TO DUST AND SCATTER RELIGION ABROAD   198 AMERICA 8   5
        ONE KING ONE GOD ONE LAW . . . .   224 URIZEN 4   40
        TO TRISMEGISTUS PALAMABRON GAVE AN ABSTRACT LAW   . . .   246 SONG OF LOS 3   18
        THEY ARE THY SERVANTS IF THOU WILT OBEY MY AWFUL LAW . .   273 FOUR ZOAS 1   328
        IS BOUGHT & SOLD & IN DIM NIGHT MY WORD SHALL BE THEIR LAW   278 FOUR ZOAS 1   503
        IN PEACE BENEATH MY AWFUL FROWN MY WILL SHALL BE MY LAW   299 FOUR ZOAS 4   55
        AND THE MORAL LAW FROM THE GOSPEL RENT . . . .   420 I SAW MNK AD/N   2
        HE FORGD THE LAW INTO A SWORD . . . .   420 I SAW MNK AD/N   3
        BY OFFERING & ATONEMENT IN THE (CRUELTIES) OF MORAL LAW   484 MILTON 5   12
        FOR HE IS REDEEMD FROM SATAN'S LAW THE WRATH FALLING ON   492 MILTON 11   23
           RINTRAH
        WHO CALLS THE INDIVIDUAL LAW HOLY AND DESPISES THE SAVIOUR   493 MILTON 13   5
        BOWLAHOOLA IS NAMD LAW BY MORTALS THARMAS FOUNDED IT   .   509 MILTON 24   48
        [POETRY IN RELIGION MUSIC LAW PAINTING IN PHYSIC & SURGERY] 514 MILTON 27   * 60
        BOTH WENT TO LAW WITH DEATH TO KEEP OUR EARS ON . . . .   537 AND HIS LEGS/N   27
        HE KNEW BOTH LAW & GOSPEL BETTER THAN THEY . . . . . .   537 AND HIS LEGS/N   31
        AS I WISH MEN OF LAW WOULD ALWAYS RIDE WITH THEM . . . .   570C DESC CAT 3   PROSE
        THE UNCIVILIZED SAVAGE WHO HAVING NOT THE LAW . . . . .   610A V LAST JUDG/N   PROSE
        DO BY NATURE THE THINGS CONTAIND IN THE LAW . . . . . .   610A V LAST JUDG/N   PROSE
        TO SEPARATE A LAW OF SIN TO PUNISH THEE IN THY MEMBERS .   626 JERUSALEM 7   50
        THAT THOU CALLEST THY CHILDREN LO THE LAW OF GOD COMMANDS   629 JERUSALEM 10   38
        SUCH IS THE DIVINE WRITTEN LAW OF HOREB & SINAI . . . .   638 JERUSALEM 16   68
        ARE THE DEAD CRUEL ONES THOSE WHO ARE INFOLDED IN MORAL LAW 644 JERUSALEM 21   48
        LO HERE IS VALA'S VEIL WHOLE FOR A LAW A TERROR & A CURSE   646 JERUSALEM 23   32
        I HAVE TURNED MY BACK UPON THEE INTO THE WASTES OF MORAL   647 JERUSALEM 24   24
           LAW

	PAGE	TITLE	LINE
LAW (CONTINUED)			
WITH MORAL AND SELF-RIGHTEOUS LAW	650	FIELDS FROM/J	23
AND HE WHO MAKES HIS LAW A CURSE	652	FIELDS FROM/J	83
BY HIS OWN LAW SHALL SURELY DIE	652	FIELDS FROM/J	84
A DEADLY TREE HE NAMD IT MORAL VIRTUE AND THE LAW .	652	JERUSALEM 28	15
FROM ALBION BUT HATH FOUNDED HIS REACTION INTO A LAW .	653	JERUSALEM 29	14
THE ROCKY LAW OF CONDEMNATION & DOUBLE GENERATION & DEATH	656	JERUSALEM 30	37
SAVING THOSE WHO HAVE SINNED FROM THE PUNISHMENT OF THE LAW	662	JERUSALEM 35	6
UNDER PRETENCE OF MORAL VIRTUE FILLD WITH REVENGE AND LAW	667	JERUSALEM 40	35
FROM HOWLING VICTIMS OF LAW BUILDING HEAVENS	672	JERUSALEM 43	18
TWENTY-SEVEN-FOLD			
THAT THEY MAY BE CONDEMND BY LAW & THE LAMB OF GOD BE SLAIN	672	JERUSALEM 43	30
TO HIDE THEM FROM THE WRATH OF ALBION'S LAW THAT FREEZES	679	JERUSALEM 48	60
SORE			
AND THE MORAL LAW FROM THE GOSPEL RENT	683	I SAW A MONK/J	18
HE FORGD THE LAW INTO A SWORD	683	I SAW A MONK/J	19
IN MORAL LAW & ITS SEVERE PENALTIES LOUD SHADDAI & JEHOVAH	706	JERUSALEM 68	39
WITH MORAL LAW AN EQUAL BALANCE NOT GOING DOWN WITH	708	JERUSALEM 69	35
DECISION			
WHICH JESUS RENDS & THE WHOLE DRUID LAW REMOVES AWAY .	708	JERUSALEM 69	39
COMPREHEND WONDEROUS THINGS OUT OF THE DIVINE LAW .	714	JERUSALEM 74	15
I WEPT & SAID IS THIS THE LAW OF JESUS	718	STOOD AMONG/J	14
CREATING NATURE FROM THIS FIERY LAW	718	STOOD AMONG/J	22
HIS LAW A FORM AGAINST THE LAMB OF GOD OPPOSD TO MERCY .	723	JERUSALEM 80	79
A TRIPLE FEMALE TABERNACLE FOR MORAL LAW I WEAVE . .	733	JERUSALEM 88	19
HERMAPHRODITIC WORSHIPPERS OF A GOD OF CRUELTY & LAW .	737	JERUSALEM 90	55
MAY TAKE THE AGGREGATE & YOU CALL THE AGGREGATE MORAL LAW	738	JERUSALEM 91	28
IN DREAMS OF (CHASTITY) & MORAL LAW I HAVE MURDERED ALBION	742	JERUSALEM 94	23
AH			
HE LAID HIS HAND ON MOSES' LAW	754	EV GOSPEL(F)/N	11
GOD'S RIGHTEOUS LAW THAT LOST ITS PREY	757	EV GOSPEL(I)/N	48
[JEHOVAH'S FINGERS WROTE THE LAW]	761	FOR SEXES/GP	5
JEHOVAH'S FINGER WROTE THE LAW	761	FOR SEXES/GP	6
& THE POWER OR WAR & THE GLORY OR LAW	789A	ANNO THORNTON	MARG
AS A PASSION WHICH IS FORBIDDEN BY LAW & RELIGION BUT NOW	798C	LETTER 10	PROSE
IT			
APPEARS TO BE LAW & GOSPEL TOO AT LEAST I HEAR SO FROM THE	798C	LETTER 10	PROSE
LAWS TO GET INTO FREEDOM FROM ALL LAW OF THE MEMBERS INTO	879A	LETTER 88	PROSE
LAW BLASTED			
. . . THAT WANDER IN FORESTS AND HOWL IN LAW BLASTED WASTES	144	FRENCH REVOLTN	227
LAW-BUILT			
THEY SLOW ADVANCE TO SHUT THE FIVE GATES OF THEIR LAW-BUILT	203	AMERICA 16	19
HEAVEN			
LAWFUL			
LAWFUL CAUTIOUS [XXX] & REFIND	175	HOW TO KNOW/N	7
LAWFUL BREAD BOUGHT WITH LAWFUL MONEY	787D	ANNO THORNTON	MARG
& A LAWFUL HEAVEN SEEN THRO A LAWFUL TELESCOPE	787D	ANNO THORNTON	MARG
BY MEANS OF LAWFUL WINDOW LIGHT THE HOLY GHOST [WHO] .	787D	ANNO THORNTON	* MARG
SPIRITS ARE LAWFUL BUT NOT GHOSTS ESPECIALLY ROYAL GIN IS	787D	ANNO THORNTON	MARG
LAWFUL SPIRIT [REAL] NO SMUGGLING REAL BRITISH SPIRIT	787D	ANNO THORNTON	MARG
& TRUTH			
LAWGIVER			
WHEN STEELYARD THE LAWGIVER COMING IN STALKING WITH . . .	46A	ISLAND MOON 1	PROSE
STEELYARD THE LAWGIVER SITTING AT HIS TABLE	52A	ISLAND MOON 8	PROSE
POO POO HOLD YOUR TONGUE HOLD YOUR TONGUE SAID	53B	ISLAND MOON 8	PROSE
THE LAWGIVER			
MORE LIKE A SAINT THAN A LAWGIVER AND WITH GREAT SOLEMNITY	53B	ISLAND MOON 8	PROSE
THEN SAID SUCTION COME MR LAWGIVER YOUR SONG AND	55A	ISLAND MOON 9	PROSE
THE LAWGIVER SUNG			
THE LAWGIVER WAS VERY ATTENTIVE	57D	ISLAND MOON 9	PROSE
TILL THE COMPANY WERE TIRED & INSISTED ON THE LAWGIVER . .	57D	ISLAND MOON 9	PROSE
ANOTHER MERRY MEETING AT THE HOUSE OF STEELYARD THE	59A	ISLAND MOON 11	PROSE
LAWGIVER			
THE LAWGIVER ALL THE WHILE SAT	61C	ISLAND MOON 11	PROSE
HM SAID THE LAWGIVER FUNNY ENOUGH	62B	ISLAND MOON 11	PROSE
LAWLESS			
LAWLESS THEY LIVD TILL WANTONNESS	17	BLIND-MANS/PS	67
HE SAID O WEAK MISTAKEN FATHER OF A LAWLESS RACE	109	TIRIEL 8	7
MISTAKEN FATHER OF A LAWLESS RACE MY VOICE IS PAST . .	110	TIRIEL 8	41
THE PRIEST ROT IN HIS SURPLICE BY THE LAWLESS LOVER . . .	141	FRENCH REVOLTN	149
[ALWAYS] LAWLESS WINGD & UNCONFIND	175	HOW TO KNOW/N	3
AND RENDER THAT A LAWLESS THING	755	EV GOSPEL(E)/N	67
LAWN			
MY FEET ARE WINGD WHILE OER THE DEWY LAWN	9	FRESH FROM/PS	5
LAWRENCE			
THE HEAD OF COWPER AFTER LAWRENCE THE HEADS TO BE FINISHD	850D	LETTER 49	PROSE
AS TO SR T LAWRENCE I HAVE NOT HEARD FROM HIM AS YET .	868D	LETTER 68	PROSE
LAWS			
BY WHOLESOME LAWS SUCH AS ALL THOSE	17	BLIND-MANS/PS	63
THEN LAWS WERE MADE TO KEEP FAIR PLAY	17	BLIND-MANS/PS	70
TO SIT IN STATE & GIVE FORTH LAWS OUT OF THEIR OLD OAK	58	THIS CITY/IM	2
CHAIRS			
SIGNIFY WHAT THE LAWS OF KINGS & PRIESTS HAVE CALLD VICE	88C	ANNO LAVATER	MARG
THY LAWS O HAR & TIRIEL'S WISDOM END TOGETHER IN A CURSE	109	TIRIEL 8	8
. . . AND RETURN UNCONSUMD AND WRITE LAWS	142	FRENCH REVOLTN	* 192
IN ALL THY WORDS & LAWS	171	TO NOBODADDY/N	6
WHAT GOD IS HE WRITES LAWS OF PEACE & CLOTHES HIM IN A	200	AMERICA 11	12
TEMPEST			
LAWS OF PEACE OF LOVE OF UNITY	224	URIZEN 4	34
HIS IRON LAWS ONE MOMENT	235	URIZEN 23	26
AND FORMD LAWS OF PRUDENCE AND CALLD THEM	236	URIZEN 28	6
THE ETERNAL LAWS OF GOD	236	URIZEN 28	7

	PAGE	TITLE	LINE

LAWS (CONTINUED)

THEY SAW URIZEN GIVE HIS LAWS TO THE NATIONS . . . . 245 SONG OF LOS 3 8
LAWS & RELIGIONS TO THE SONS OF HAR BINDING THEM MORE . . 246 SONG OF LOS 4 14
SIHON AND OG WILT THOU NOT REBEL TO MY LAWS REMAIN . . . 278 FOUR ZOAS 1 508
TO SPEAK THE LAWS OF PRUDENCE TO THE HOUSELESS WANDERER . 290 FOUR ZOAS 2 405
SET HERSELF UP TO GIVE HER LAWS TO THE ACTIVE MASCULINE 295 FOUR ZOAS 3 116
    VIRTUE
THY PASSIVITY THY LAWS OF OBEDIENCE & INSINCERITY . . . 295 FOUR ZOAS 3 118
HIS WOVEN DARKNESS & IN LAWS & DECEITFUL RELIGIONS . . . 345 FOUR ZOAS 8 172
OF URIZEN'S LAWS TO IRRIGATE THE ROOTS OF THE TREE . . 347 FOUR ZOAS 8 229
    OF MYSTERY
FORGETFUL OF HIS OWN LAWS PITYING HE BEGAN TO EMBRACE . . 352 FOUR ZOAS 8 420
NOR OF HIS OWN WILL GAVE HIS LAWS IN TIMES OF EVERLASTING . 353 FOUR ZOAS 8 459
ALL PENAL LAWS COURT TRANSGRESSION & THEREFORE ARE CRUELTY 393C ANNO WATSON MARG
    &
MURDER THE LAWS OF THE JEWS WERE BOTH CEREMONIAL & REAL 393C ANNO WATSON MARG
OF MORAL LAWS AND CRUEL PUNISHMENTS UPON THE CLOUDS OF 489 MILTON 9 22
    JEHOVAH
WHERE SATAN MAKING TO HIMSELF LAWS FROM HIS OWN IDENTITY 491 MILTON 11 10
TO PERPETUATE WAR & GLORY TO PERPETUATE THE LAWS OF SIN 506 MILTON 22 45
WITH LAWS FROM PLATO & HIS GREEKS TO RENEW THE TROJAN GODS 506 MILTON 22 53
SUCH ARE THE LAWS OF THY FALSE HEAVNS BUT LAWS OF ETERNITY 530 MILTON 38 33
SUCH ARE THE LAWS OF ETERNITY THAT EACH SHALL MUTUALLY . . 530 MILTON 38 35
THY LAWS & TERRORS SHAKING DOWN THY SYNAGOGUES AS WEBS . . 530 MILTON 38 42
AND ANCIENT NIGHT SPREAD OVER ALL THE HEAVN HIS MANTLE 531 MILTON 39 30
    OF LAWS
GREY BEARDS & SCOURGES OF FIRE THEY REPRESENT CRUEL LAWS 608A V LAST JUDG/N PROSE
FOR THE COERCIVE LAWS OF HELL MORAL HYPOCRISY . . . . 616C V LAST JUDG/N PROSE
ARE MINE HERE WILL I BUILD MY LAWS OF MORAL VIRTUE . . 622 JERUSALEM 4 31
INSPIRATION DENYD GENIUS FORBIDDEN BY LAWS OF PUNISHMENT 628 JERUSALEM 9 16
CITIES & NATIONS FAMILIES & PEOPLES TONGUES & LAWS . . 629 JERUSALEM 10 27
HE DREW THE VEIL OF MORAL VIRTUE WOVEN FOR CRUEL LAWS . . 646 JERUSALEM 23 22
BY LAWS OF SACRIFICE FOR SIN . . . . 651 FIELDS FROM/J 54
NO INDIVIDUAL CAN KEEP THESE LAWS FOR THEY ARE DEATH . 662 JERUSALEM 35 11
THE POINT OF HIS SPEAR IF THOU PERSISTEST TO FORBID WITH 664 JERUSALEM 37 8
    LAWS
WITHERING THE HUMAN FORM BY LAWS OF SACRIFICE FOR SIN . . 679 JERUSALEM 49 25
BY LAWS OF CHASTITY & ABHORRENCE I AM WITHERD UP . . 679 JERUSALEM 49 26
IN MERCIFUL ORDER BENDING THE LAWS OF CRUELTY TO PEACE . 680 JERUSALEM 49 55
TO PERPETUATE TYRANT PRIDE & THE LAWS OF THAT BABYLON . 682A JERUSALEM 52 PROSE
WHERE IS THAT FRIEND OF SINNERS THAT REBEL AGAINST MY LAWS 685 JERUSALEM 54 19
OF THE THINGS OF MEMORY IT THENCE FRAMES LAWS & MORALITIES 714 JERUSALEM 74 12
BY CRUEL LAWS DIVIDED SIXTEEN INTO TWELVE DIVISIONS . . . 715 JERUSALEM 74 27
BUT I VALA LUVAH'S DAUGHTER KEEP HIS BODY EMBALMD IN MORAL 722 JERUSALEM 80 27
    LAWS
WHEREFORE HAST THOU WRIT THESE LAWS . . . . 754 EV GOSPEL(E)/N 31
OF THE UNBELIEVER & HIS LAWS . . . . 758 EV GOSPEL (1) 8
& TO ITS LAWS OF GOOD & EVIL & ITS ENMITIES AGAINST MIND 784D ANNO WW EXCUR MARG
LAWS TO GET INTO FREEDOM FROM ALL LAW OF THE MEMBERS INTO 879A LETTER 88 PROSE

LAWYER

THE EARS OF BILLY'S LAWYER & DRAGOON . . . . . . 537 AND HIS LEGS/N 25
AND CUR MY LAWYER & DADY [MY] JACK HEMP'S PARSON . . . 537 AND HIS LEGS/N * 26
IT IS NOT LIKE A LAWYER SERVING A WRIT . . . . . 556 SOME PEOPLE/N 4
THE LAWYER THE POOR PARSON THE MERCHANT . . . . . 567A DESC CAT 3 PROSE
CHAUCER'S LAWYER IS A CHARACTER OF GREAT VENERABLENESS . 570D DESC CAT 3 PROSE
THE LAWYER THE POOR PARSON THE MERCHANT . . . . . . 588C CHAUCER/N PROSE
THE LAWYER THE PARSON THE MERCHANT . . . . 590A CHAUCER 2 PROSE
AT CHICHESTER THIS MORNING BUT THEY AS THE LAWYER WHO . 827D LETTER 28 PROSE

LAY

THERE HIS CHARMING NEST DOTH LAY . . . . 7 LOVE HARMNY/PS 17
THE OAKEN LOG LAY ON THE FIRE . . . . 16 BLIND-MANS/PS 6
DOWN ON HIS HANDS AND KNEES HE LAY . . . . 16 BLIND-MANS/PS 47
AND ONE MAN LAY IN ANOTHER'S WAY . . . . 17 BLIND-MANS/PS 69
OR I LAY STRETCHD UPON THE FIELD OF DEATH . . . . . 31 EDW THIRD/PS 5 66
IF I LAY MY FACE IN THE DUST THE GRAVE OPENS ITS MOUTH 36A COUCH DEATH/PS PROSE
    FOR ME
THEY COVERED THEIR FACES AND WEPT THE YOUTH LAY SILENT . 36C COUCH DEATH/PS PROSE
AND WHERE STRENGTH FAILED BLACK THOUGHTS IN AMBUSH LAY . 37D SAMSON/PS PROSE
WOULD EASE MY PAIN THEN SHOULD I LAY AT QUIET AND HAVE REST 38C SAMSON/PS PROSE
THEM THAT HE'LL SCRAPE THEIR BONES IF THEY DONT LAY STILL & 50A ISLAND MOON 6 PROSE
WHERE ON GRASS METHOUGHT I LAY . . . . 111 A DREAM/SI 4
LOVELY LYCA LAY . . . . 112 LIT GRL LST/SI 12
SLEEPING LYCA LAY . . . . 113 LIT GRL LST/SI 33
ROUND HER AS SHE LAY . . . . 113 LIT GRL LST/SI 42
A COUCHING LION LAY . . . . 114 LIT GRL FND/SI 24
THY MAKER LAY AND WEPT FOR ME . . . . 120 CRADLE SONG/SI 24
AH GENTLE MAY I LAY ME DOWN AND GENTLE REST MY HEAD . . 127 BOOK OF THEL 1 12
IS THIS A WORM I SEE THEE LAY HELPLESS & NAKED WEEPING . 129 BOOK OF THEL 4 5
AND LAY ME DOWN IN THY COLD BED AND LEAVE MY SHINING LOT . 130 BOOK OF THEL 5 13
. . . AND MAN LAY HIS FADED HEAD DOWN ON THE ROCK . . . 138 FRENCH REVOLTN 96
. . . SILENT THEY LAY PROSTRATED . . . . 140 FRENCH REVOLTN 133
AS THE CATTERPILLER CHOOSES THE FAIREST LEAVES TO LAY . 152C MARRIAGE HH 9 PROSE
I THEN ASKED EZEKIEL WHY HE EAT DUNG & LAY SO LONG ON HIS 154A MARRIAGE HH 12 PROSE
LAY THE BOUND OR BUILD THE ROOF NOR PALE RELIGIOUS LETCHERY 160B SONG LIBERTY PROSE
WHERE LOVE LAY SLEEPING . . . . 162 LAID ME DOWN/N 2
[UNDERNEATH THE [VINE] VINES [HE] THEY LAY] . . . . . 167 INFANT SORW/N * 35
UNDERNEATH [MY] THE [VINE] VINES [HE] THEY LAY . . . 167 INFANT SORW/N * 39
LAY THE FAINT MAID AND SOON HER WOES APPALLD HIS THUNDERS 190 V DAU ALBION 1 17
    HOARSE
SICKNING LAY LONDON'S GUARDIAN AND THE ANCIENT MITERD YORK 202 AMERICA 15 9
AGE ON AGES HE LAY CLOSD UNKNOWN . . . . 223 URIZEN 3 24
HE LAY IN A DREAMLESS NIGHT . . . . 226 URIZEN 7 7

```
                                                   PAGE     TITLE        LINE
LAY    (CONTINUED)
    YET HELPLESS IT LAY LIKE A WORM . . . . . . .  232 URIZEN 19          21
    ALL DAY THE WORM LAY ON HER BOSOM . . . . . .  232 URIZEN 19          24
    THE WORM LAY TILL IT GREW TO A SERPENT . . . . 232 URIZEN 19          26
    ONE HOUR THEY LAY BURIED BENEATH THE RUINS OF THAT HALL  241 EUROPE 9  14
    LAY BLEACHD ON THE GARDEN OF EDEN . . . . . .  248 SONG OF LOS 7      21
    ITS WEIGHTY BULK SILENT THE ROCK LAY . . . . . 251 AHANIA 3           35
    DARK VACUITY HERE URIZEN LAY                    260 BOOK OF LOS 5      50
    LET HER LAY SECRET IN THE SOFT RECESS OF DARKNESS & SILENCE  265 FOUR ZOAS 1  30
    WILL LAY MY SCEPTER ON JERUSALEM THE EMANATION  . . . . 278 FOUR ZOAS 1  498
    O I AM WEARY LAY THINE HAND UPON ME OR I FAINT  . . . 290 FOUR ZOAS 2  374
    IF THOU DOST LAY THINE HAND UPON ME BEHOLD I AM SILENT  . . 293 FOUR ZOAS 3  62
    DARK DREADFUL ROSE & ENITHARMON LAY AT LOS'S FEET . . . 300 FOUR ZOAS 4  126
    THE CORSE OF [MAN] ALBION LAY ON THE ROCK THE SEA OF TIME  304 FOUR ZOAS 4  265
      & SPACE
    INVOLUNTARY TO THE COUCH WHERE ENITHARMON LAY  . . . . 305 FOUR ZOAS 4  292
    NOT LONG THEY LAY URTHONA'S SPECTRE FOUND HERBS OF THE PIT  309 FOUR ZOAS 5  173
    URIZEN TREMBLED WHERE HE LAY TO HEAR THE HOWLING TERROR  310 FOUR ZOAS 5  185
    NO FORM WAS THERE NO LIVING THING & YET HIS WAY LAY THRO  315 FOUR ZOAS 6  149
    FOR WHEN HE DIED THEY LAY BESIDE [HIM] HIS GRAVE & WHEN  316 FOUR ZOAS 6  * 168
      HE ROSE
    HOWLING & RENDING HIS DARK CAVES THE AWFUL DEMON LAY  . . 320 FOUR ZOAS 7  20
    ENITHARMON LAY ON HIS KNEES URIZEN TRACD HIS VERSES . . . 324 FOUR ZOAS 7  169
    THE CAUSE OF HER DIRE ANGUISH FOR SHE LAY THE IMAGE OF  328 FOUR ZOAS 7  320
      DEATH
    OUTSTRETCHD UPON THE HILLS LAY ENITHARMON CLOUDS & TEMPESTS  334 FOUR ZOAS 7B  73
    WOO'D & SUBDUD INTO ?ETERNAL DEATH THE DEMON ?LAY . . . 340 FOUR ZOAS 7B  286
    IN THE FIERCE FLAMES THE LIMBS OF MYSTERY LAY CONSUMING  359 FOUR ZOAS 9  67
      WITH HOWLING
    ON THIS ROCK LAY THE FADED HEAD OF THE ETERNAL MAN  . . . 359 FOUR ZOAS 9  95
    THE WINTER THOU SHALT PLOW & LAY THY STORES INTO THY BARNS  362 FOUR ZOAS 9  214
    LAY THEM ON SKINS OF TYGERS OR THE SPOTTED LEOPARD OR WILD  377 FOUR ZOAS 9  746
      ASS
    TREMBLING HE LAY SWELLD WITH THE DELUGE STIFLING IN THE  381 FOUR ZOAS AD 4  3
      ANGUISH
    ROUND THE [TOMB] TOMBS WHERE MY LOVES LAY . . . . . 416 MY SPECTRE/N  * 40
    AND TOOK TO HIS BED & THERE LAY DOWN . . . . . . 435 WILLIAM BOND      12
    LAY A GROUND ON THE PLATE & SMOKE IT AS FOR ETCHING . . . 440B MEMORANDUM/N 3  PROSE
    LAY A GROUND AS FOR ETCHING TRACE &C & . . . . . 440B MEMORANDUM/N 4  PROSE
    AS WELL SAY THAT IF MAN DOES NOT LAY DOWN SETTLED  475C ANNO REYNOLDS  MARG
      PRINCIPLES
    URIZEN LAY IN DARKNESS & SOLITUDE IN CHAINS OF THE MIND  482 MILTON 3  6
      LOCKD UP
    HOW LONG SHALL WE LAY DEAD IN THE STREET OF THE GREAT CITY  507 MILTON 23  11
    LAY THEM ON SKINS OF TYGERS & OF THE SPOTTED LEOPARD &  513 MILTON 27  6
      THE WILD ASS
    NOT ONLY IN HIS MOUTH HIS OWN SOUL LAY . . . . . 536 AND HIS LEGS/N  5
    WHAT MAN OF SENSE WILL LAY OUT HIS MONEY UPON . . . . . 598C PUB ADDRESS/N  PROSE
    IF THOU DOST LAY THINE HAND UPON ME BEHOLD I AM SILENT  . 654 JERUSALEM 29  49
    IF I SHOULD DARE TO LAY MY FINGER ON A GRAIN OF SAND  . 657 JERUSALEM 31  33
    AND LAY ITS HEAVENS & THEIR INHABITANTS IN BLOOD  668 JERUSALEM 41  20
      OF PUNISHMENT
    DEAD CORSES LAY BEFORE THEM & NOT AS IN WARS OF OLD . . . 672 JERUSALEM 43  40
    STRIP THEM OFF FROM THEIR SHOULDERS AND BOSOMS THEY LAY  702 JERUSALEM 66  18
      ASIDE
    WHAT ARE THE TREASURES OF HEAVEN WHICH WE ARE TO LAY UP  717A JERUSALEM 77  PROSE
      FOR OURSELVES
    NAKED JERUSALEM LAY BEFORE THE GATES UPON MOUNT ZION . . 719 JERUSALEM 78  21
    UPON HIS PARENT BOSOM LAY THY LITTLE ONES O LAND . . . . 727 JERUSALEM 83  24
    THE EARTH TREMBLING & NAKED LAY . . . . . . . . . 754 EV GOSPEL(E)/N  15
    SMILING ON OUR COTTAGE SAYS YOU LAY TOO LOW FOR MY ANGER TO  807B LETTER 17  PROSE
    I CANNOT LIVE WITHOUT DOING MY DUTY TO LAY UP TREASURES  812C LETTER 22  PROSE
LAYD    SEE LAID
    LAYD HIS HAND ON THE SOUTH & TOOK A BREATHING BOW OF CARVED  744 JERUSALEM 97  8
      GOLD
LAYING
    LAYING HER SEED UPON THE FIBRES SOON TO ISSUE FORTH . . . 292 FOUR ZOAS 3  21
    WHAT IS LAYING UP MATERIALS BUT COPYING . . . . . . . 455B ANNO REYNOLDS  MARG
    JERUSALEM HIS EMANATION IS A STONE LAYING BENEATH  . . 620 JERUSALEM 1  6
    ARE THE CHILDREN OF THIS BOW A BOW OF MERCY  744 JERUSALEM 97  13
      & LOVING-KINDNESS LAYING
    AS TO LAYING ON THE WAX IT IS AS FOLLOWS TAKE A CAKE  . 790C LETTER 2  PROSE
    ...ASSASSIN LAYING DEAD AT THE FEET OF (EDWARD) IST IN...  SUPP ILLUS HISTORY  *TITLE
    FOR LAYING IN THE ENGRAVING OF MR UPTON'S PORTRAIT . . .  SUPP LETTER 66D  *PROSE
LAYS
    HE RUSHES UP THE SKY AND LAYS HOLD ON THE IMMORTAL COURSERS  37B CONTEMPLATN/PS  PROSE
      OF DAY
    HER EGGS ON SO THE PRIEST LAYS HIS CURSE ON THE FAIREST  152C MARRIAGE HH 9  PROSE
      JOYS
    THY MOTHER LAYS HER LENGTH OUTSTRETCHD UPON THE SHORE  199 AMERICA 9  25
      BENEATH
    OF MAN WHO LAYS UPON THE SHORES LEANING HIS FADED HEAD . . 354 FOUR ZOAS 8  513
    OF LOS AND HERE HE LAYS HIS WORDS IN ORDER ABOVE THE MORTAL  513 MILTON 27  9
      BRAIN
    AND LAYS DOWN IN THE GRAVE WITH THEM IN VISIONS OF ETERNITY  522 MILTON 32  41
    THRO THE COTTAGE WHERE "SHE" LAYS IN BED "PINCHD & PULLD"  618C ILLUS MILTON  PROSE
    THAT LAYS OPEN THE HIDDEN HEART I DREW FORTH THE PANG . . 628 JERUSALEM 9  19
    ALBION COLD LAYS ON HIS ROCK STORMS & SNOWS BEAT ROUND HIM  741 JERUSALEM 94  1
    OF THE MINES OF CORNWALL & DERBYSHIRE LAYS UPON HIS BOSOM  741 JERUSALEM 94  8
      HEAVY
    EVE PAINTED OVER THE DEAD BODY OF ABEL WHICH LAYS NEAR  779C GHOST ABEL 1  PROSE
      A GRAVE
```

		PAGE	TITLE	LINE

LAYS (CONTINUED)

YOUR ADVICE I SEE THE FACE OF MY HEAVENLY FATHER HE LAYS 823B LETTER 26 PROSE
   HIS

LAZARUS

WHEN JESUS RAISD LAZARUS FROM THE GRAVE I STOOD & SAW . . 508 MILTON 24 26
LAZARUS WHO IS THE VEHICULAR BODY OF ALBION THE REDEEMD 508 MILTON 24 27
DIVIDE FOUR-FOLD INTO FOUR CHURCHES WHEN LAZARUS AROSE . . 508 MILTON 24 31

LAZY

[SEDITIOUS] THOU LAZY MONK [SAID CHARLEMAINE] THEY SOUND 419 I SAW A MONK/N 10
   AFAR
THOU LAZY MONK THEY SOUND AFAR . . . . 683 I SAW A MONK/J 9

LEAD

LEAD THEM ON TO BATTLE . . . . 26 EDW THIRD/PS 3 207
WILL LEAD [?THEM] THE POOR ENTHUSIAST IN THE PATHS 85C ANNO LAVATER * MARG
   OF HOLINESS
COME I WILL LEAD THEE ON THY WAY & USE THEE AS A SCOFF . 104 TIRIEL 4 20
NO ARTFUL FIEND BUT I WILL LEAD THEE DOST THOU WANT TO GO 104 TIRIEL 4 23
[?HILI] HELA MY YOUNGEST DAUGHTER YOU SHALL LEAD ME FROM 106 TIRIEL 5 * 24
   THIS PLACE
YOU SEE THE PARENTS CURSE NOW LEAD ME WHERE I HAVE 107 TIRIEL 6 12
   COMMANDED
I HAVE NOT EAT THESE TWO DAYS LEAD ME TO HAR & HEVA'S TENT 107 TIRIEL 6 19
YET THOU SHALT LEAD ME LEAD ME I COMMAND TO HAR & HEVA 107 TIRIEL 6 22
TO HAR & HEVA I WILL LEAD THEE THEN WOULD THAT THEY WOULD 107 TIRIEL 6 24
   CURSE
UNLESS THOU LEAD ME TO THE TENT OF HAR CHILD OF THE CURSE 108 TIRIEL 6 34
I LEAD THEE TO THE TENT OF HAR NOT THAT I MIND THY CURSE 108 TIRIEL 6 36
LEAD ME TO HAR & HEVA & THE CURSE OF TIRIEL . . . . . 108 TIRIEL 6 48
LEAD ME TO HAR & HEVA I AM TIRIEL KING OF THE WEST . . . 109 TIRIEL 8 4
AND WISH TO LEAD OTHERS WHEN THEY SHOULD BE LED . . . . 126 VOICE BARD/SI 11
. . . RISE MONARCH OF FRANCE COMMAND ME AND I WILL LEAD 142 FRENCH REVOLTN 172
. . . LOOKING ON THE ARCHBISHOP WHO CHANGED AS PALE AS 142 FRENCH REVOLTN 176
   LEAD
BENEATH THE CAVERNS ROLL THE WEIGHTS OF LEAD & SPINDLES 284 FOUR ZOAS 2 148
   OF IRON
A SHADOW BLUE OBSCURE & DISMAL LIKE A STATUE OF LEAD . . 299 FOUR ZOAS 4 65
TWINGE & HIS IRON SINEWS BEND LIKE LEAD & FOLD . . . . 305 FOUR ZOAS 4 294
I HAVE BENT DOWNWARD WITH LEAD MOLTEN IN MY ROARING 349 FOUR ZOAS 8 304
   FURNACES
LIKE THE PALE VISAGE IN ITS SHEET OF LEAD THAT CANNOT 352 FOUR ZOAS 8 433
   FOLLOW
WILL YOU KEEP A FLOCK OF WOLVES & LEAD THEM . . . . . 353 FOUR ZOAS 8 493
I SEE THE HAND THAT LEADETH ME DOTH ALSO LEAD MY FLOCKS 369 FOUR ZOAS 9 474
IRON TEARS & GROANS OF LEAD . . . . 417 MY SPECTR AD/N 11
CORRECTLY WITH BLACK LEAD PENCIL LET NOTHING BE TO SEEK 440B MEMORANDUM/N 2 PROSE
LIGHT SPRINGING ON THE AIR LEAD THE SWEET DANCE THEY WAKE 520 MILTON 31 53
IT WILL LEAD YOU IN AT HEAVEN'S GATE . . . . 551 GIVE YOU END/N 3
AND NOW I'LL LEAD MY FALSE FRIENDS BY THE NOSE . . . . 555 BLAKES APL/N 1 23
AND THAT NOW I LEAD MY FALSE FRIENDS BY THE [TOES] NOSE 556 BLAKES APL/N 2 * 12
WHITE LEAD WHICH WHEN ITS PROTECTING OIL IS EVAPORATED WILL 566B DESC CAT 2 PROSE
BECOME LEAD AGAIN THIS IS AN AWFUL THING TO SAY TO OIL 566B DESC CAT 2 PROSE
   PAINTERS
THE KNIGHT AND SQUIRE WITH THE SQUIRE'S YEOMAN LEAD . . 566D DESC CAT 3 PROSE
THE KNIGHT AND SQUIRE WITH THE SQUIRE'S YEOMAN LEAD THE . 567D DESC CAT 3 PROSE
   PROCESSION
THE KNIGHT & SQUIRE WITH THE SQUIRE'S YEOMAN LEAD . . . 588B CHAUCER/N PROSE
THE KNIGHT AND SQUIRE WITH THE SQUIRE'S AND YEOMAN LEAD 589D CHAUCER 2 PROSE
MERCY & PITY THREW THE GRAVE STONE OVER ME & WITH LEAD . 630 JERUSALEM 10 54
LIKE LAKES OF LIQUID LEAD INSTEAD OF HEAVENLY CHAPELS BUILT 673 JERUSALEM 43 63
AND I WILL LEAD THEE THRO THE WILDERNESS IN SHADOW OF MY 693 JERUSALEM 60 36
   CLOUD
AND IN MY LOVE I WILL LEAD THEE LOVELY SHADOW OF SLEEPING 693 JERUSALEM 60 37
   ALBION
THOR & FRIGA & THE FAIRIES LEAD THE MOON ALONG THE VALLEY 697 JERUSALEM 63 14
   OF CHERUBIM
I HAVE BENT DOWNWARD WITH LEAD MELTED IN MY ROARING 705 JERUSALEM 67 50
   FURNACES
AND I WILL LEAD FORTH THY WORDS TELLING HOW THE DAUGHTERS 715 JERUSALEM 74 41
IT WILL LEAD YOU IN AT HEAVEN'S GATE . . . . 716 I GIVE YOU/J 3
LET US LEAD THE STEMS OF THIS TREE LET US PLANT IT BEFORE 725 JERUSALEM 82 32
   JERUSALEM
AS THE SUN & MOON LEAD FORWARD THE VISIONS OF HEAVEN & 743 JERUSALEM 95 21
   EARTH
AS THE SUN & MOON LEAD FORWARD THE VISIONS OF HEAVEN & 743 JERUSALEM 96 1
   EARTH
& ONE ANOTHER LEAD US NOT TO READ THE BIBLE . . . . . 788D ANNO THORNTON MARG
AFTER ALL & CERTAINLY DOES NOT LEAD ME INTO SCRAPES . . . 830D LETTER 30 PROSE
THAT WOULD LEAD TO A VALUATION OF THE COPY RIGHT . . . . 860B LETTER 56 PROSE

LEADEN

A VIRGIN EVER YOUNG AND AFTER LEADEN SLOTH . . . . . 40D THEN SHE BORE PROSE
THE CITIZENS IN LEADEN GYVES THE INHABITANTS OF SUBURBS . 243 EUROPE 12 30
SHADOWS OF ETERNAL DEATH SIT IN THE LEADEN AIR . . . . 305 FOUR ZOAS 5 22

LEADEN LEGGED

MISERIES ARE LEADEN LEGGED AND THEIR WHOLE EMPLOYMENT IS 807A LETTER 17 PROSE

LEADER

O PRINCE THE ETERNAL ONE HATH SET THEE LEADER OF HIS HOSTS 292 FOUR ZOAS 3 27
HE IS A LEADER OF THE AGE . . . . 568C DESC CAT 3 PROSE
OUR HOST WAS ALSO A LEADER OF THE AGE . . . . 569D DESC CAT 3 PROSE
LEADER OF MY ANGELS MY DEAR & TOO CAREFUL & OVER JOYOUS 801B LETTER 13 PROSE

LEADERS

THE CITIZENS AND THEIR COOK ARE EACH LEADERS OF A CLASS 571D DESC CAT 3 PROSE
ARE NOT THESE LEADERS OF THE AGES OF MEN . . . . . . 572B DESC CAT 3 PROSE

LEADERS   (CONTINUED)
    WHO THE LEADERS OF THESE ARE WILL BE SHEWN BELOW . . . . 581D DESC CAT 8   PROSE
LEADETH
    WANDERD TILL HE THAT LEADETH ALL LED HIM TO THE VALES OF   100 TIRIEL 2   4
    HAR
    I SEE THE HAND THAT LEADETH ME DOTH ALSO LEAD MY FLOCKS   369 FOUR ZOAS 9   474
LEADING
    HE MAKES THE VICIOUS PROPENSITY NOT ONLY A LEADING FEATURE   88C ANNO LAVATER   MARG
    EVERY MAN'S LEADING PROPENSITY OUGHT TO BE CALLD . . . . . 88C ANNO LAVATER   MARG
    HIS LEADING VIRTUE & HIS GOOD ANGEL BUT . . . .   88C ANNO LAVATER   MARG
    THEIR TYRANT PRINCE BLIND & HIS DAUGHTER HOWLING & LEADING   108 TIRIEL 7   4
    HIM
    WITH THUNDER AND FIRE LEADING HIS STARRY HOSTS . . . . .159D SONG LIBERTY   PROSE
    AND THEN SHE ENTERD HER BRIGHT HOUSE LEADING HER MIGHTY   370 FOUR ZOAS 9   513
    CHILDREN
    AND HAS ALSO HIS GREAT USE AND HIS GRAND LEADING DESTINY   570C DESC CAT 3   PROSE
    GREAT LEADING CHARACTER IN LITERATURE & HIS TERMS TO OTHERS 841C LETTER 41   PROSE
LEADS
    GWIN LEADS HIS HOST AS BLACK AS NIGHT . . . .   12 GWIN KING/PS   55
    LIKE A TEMPESTUOUS THUNDER CLOUD PRIDE LEADS THEM ON . .   42C THEN SHE BORE   PROSE
    THE ROAD OF EXCESS LEADS TO THE PALACE OF WISDOM . . . .   150D MARRIAGE H 7   PROSE
    THAT LEADS FROM THE GATES OF THE GRAVE . . . .   247 SONG OF LOS 7   8
    SWEET MERCY LEADS ME ON . . . .   421 MORNING/N   4
    HE LEADS THE CHOIR OF DAY TRILL TRILL TRILL TRILL . . .   520 MILTON 31   31
    & FOLLOWS [WHEREVER ART LEADS] THE ARTS . . . .   597A PUB ADDRESS/N   *PROSE
    AND LEADS YOU TO BELIEVE A LIE . . . .   753 EV GOSPEL (D)/N 105
    LEADS TO GLORY & HONOUR I REJOICE & I TREMBLE . . . . .   823B LETTER 26   PROSE
    LEADS ME VERY MUCH TO MY HURT & SOMETIMES TO THE ANNOYANCE 830D LETTER 30   PROSE
LEAF
    OF PRINTED & AT EVERY OTHER [?SHEET CA] LEAF A HIGH FINISHD 62D ISLAND MOON 11 *PROSE
    PRINT
    THE HELPLESS WORM AROSE AND SAT UPON THE LILLY'S LEAF . .   129 BOOK OF THEL 3   30
    I SEE THEE LIKE AN INFANT WRAPPED IN THE LILLY'S LEAF . .   129 BOOK OF THEL 4   3
    THAT PLANTED THICK WITH TREES OF BLACKEST LEAF & IN A VALE 241 EUROPE 10   25
    IF THOU WITHHOLD THINE HAND I PERISH LIKE A FALLEN LEAF   293 FOUR ZOAS 3   63
    DARKNESS & SORROW &C TURN OVER LEAF . . . .   351D FOUR ZOAS 8   *PROSE
    OR A LEAF BUDS THE ETERNAL MAN IS SEEN IS HEARD IS FELT   356 FOUR ZOAS 8   582
    AND EVERY FLOWER & EVERY LEAF REJOICES IN HIS LIGHT . .   367 FOUR ZOAS 9   407
    THE CATTERPILLER ON THE LEAF . . . .   432 AUGURIES   37
    HE DID NOT KNOW HOW TO DRAW THE LEAF OF A TREE . . . .   593A PUB ADDRESS/N   PROSE
    THO EVEN IN THESE A SINGLE LEAF OF A TREE IS NEVER CORRECT 594A PUB ADDRESS/N   PROSE
    IF THOU WITHHOLD THINE HAND I PERISH LIKE A FALLEN LEAF   654 JERUSALEM 29   50
    THE CATTERPILLER ON THE LEAF . . . .   770 THE KEYS/GP   1
LEAFLESS
    FAINT SHIVERING THEY SIT ON LEAFLESS BUSH OR FROZEN STONE   276 FOUR ZOAS 1   447
    AS SNOW THAT FALLS AROUND A LEAFLESS TREE UPON THE GREEN   358 FOUR ZOAS 9   49
LEAGUE
    MADE LEAGUE WITH PRIDE MEANWHILE STRIFE MIGHTY PRINCE . .   42C THEN SHE BORE   PROSE
    HEATED RED HOT THEY HIZZING REND THEIR WAY DOWN MANY A   283 FOUR ZOAS 2   138
    LEAGUE
LEAGUED
    O LEAGUED WITH EVIL SPIRITS THOU ACCURSED MAN OF SIN . .   107 TIRIEL 6   13
    WERE LEAGUED TOGETHER AGAINST SATAN THRO ANCIENT ENMITY   487 MILTON 7   40
    HE HATH LEAGUED HIMSELF WITH ROBBERS HE HATH STUDIED THE   667 JERUSALEM 40   13
    ARTS
LEAH
    DEADLY HATE BETWEEN LEAH & RACHEL DAUGHTERS OF DECEIT &   707 JERUSALEM 69   11
    FRAUD
    ?LEAH & RACHEL ?DANTE'S ?DREAM . . . .   SUPP ILLUS DANTE 86 *PROSE
    MOTHER OF LEAH & RACHEL MOTHER OF REBECCA . . . . .   SUPP INSC HERVEY   *TITLE
LEAN
    AND MOURNFUL LEAN DESPAIR . . . .   6 MY SILKS/PS   4
    OUR FATHERS SWEATING LEAN ON THEIR SPEARS AND VIEW . .   32 EDW THIRD/PS 6   34
    TO LEAN IN JOY UPON OUR FATHER'S KNEE . . . .   125 LIT BLK BOY/SI   26
    TO ENRICH THE LEAN EARTH THAT CRAVES . . . .   138 FRENCH REVOLTN   99
LEAND
    THE KING LEAND ON HIS MOUNTAINS . . . .   139 FRENCH REVOLTN   110
    WITH MIRTH & JOY URTHONA LIMPING FROM HIS FALL ON THARMAS   377 FOUR ZOAS 9   775
    LEAND
    HIS ARM LEAND TREMBLINGLY OBSERVING ALL THESE THINGS .   488 MILTON 8   15
    HE SAT DOWN ON HIS ANVIL-STOCK AND LEAND UPON THE TROUGH   503 MILTON 20   54
LEANED
    MARY LEANED HER SIDE AGAINST JERUSALEM JERUSALEM RECIEVED   695 JERUSALEM 61   47
LEANING
    LEANING ON ONE ANOTHER'S NECKS ALTERNATELY . . . . . .   35D COUCH DEATH/PS PROSE
    LEANING ON HER BOSOM THUS HE SPOKE HEAR O DALILA . . . .   39B SAMSON/PS   PROSE
    THE WANDERER WHO [?RUNS] SEEKS THE WOODS LEANING UPON HIS   103 TIRIEL 3   * 38
    STAFF
    TROUBLED LEANING ON NECKER DESCENDS THE KING . . . .   134 FRENCH REVOLTN   10
    SO URIZEN AROSE & LEANING ON HIS SPEAR EXPLORD HIS DENS   311 FOUR ZOAS 6   1
    OF MAN WHO LAYS UPON THE SHORES LEANING HIS FADED HEAD .   354 FOUR ZOAS 8   513
    LEANING AGAINST THE PILLARS & HIS DISEASE ROSE FROM HIS   658 JERUSALEM 32   1
    SKIRTS
LEANNESS
    LEANNESS OR FATNESS IS NOT DEFORMITY BUT . . . . .   460C ANNO REYNOLDS   MARG
    OF EACH CLASS SO ARE LEANNESS & FATNESS . . . . . .   460C ANNO REYNOLDS   MARG
LEANS
    LEANS ON THE ROCKS OF ERIN'S LAND IRELAND ANCIENT NATION   531 MILTON 39   45
LEAP
    AND LEAP AND DANCE TO HEAR THE TRUMPET SOUND . . . . .   25 EDW THIRD/PS 3   171
    MY HEART LEAP AT THE LOVELY SOUND . . . .   254 AHANIA 4   69
    THEN SCREWMUCH AT BLAKE'S SOUL TOOK A LONG LEAP . . . .   537 AND HIS LEGS/N   39

```
                                                        PAGE     TITLE            LINE
LEAP    (CONTINUED)
     WATCHING HIS TIME WITH GLOWING EYES TO LEAP UPON HIS PREY   627 JERUSALEM 8       22
LEAPD
     HOWLING LEAPD OER THE WALL INTO THE MOAT  . . . . . .     4 FAIR ELENOR/PS     30
     HERE I STAID TO REST & THEN LEAPD INTO THE VOID  . . . 157A MARRIAGE HH 17  *PROSE
     HE LEAPD FROM THE SPRAY  . . . . . . . . . .         178 THE FAIRY/N       13
     A MIGHTY SPIRIT LEAPD FROM THE LAND OF ALBION  . . . . . 243 EUROPE 13         4
     [THE GOAT LEAPD FROM THE CRAGGY [?ROCK] CLIFF . . .     270 FOUR ZOAS 1     *  208
     LEAPD FROM THE STEPS OF FIRE & ON THE GRASS  . . . .   414 TO MRS FLAXMAN     5
LEAPED
     THE LITTLE ONES LEAPED & SHOUTED & LAUGHD  . . . . .    60 NURSES SONG/IM    16
     THE LITTLE ONES LEAPED & SHOUTED & LAUGHD  . . . . .   121 NURSES SONG/SI    15
LEAPING
     THEN DOWN A GREEN PLAIN LEAPING LAUGHING THEY RUN  . .  117 CHIMNEY SWP/SI    15
     . . . THE BLACK HAIL STORM [?LEAPING]  . . . . . . .   294 FOUR ZOAS 3     *  104
     FIERY PEGASUS SHAKSPEARE THE HORSE OF INTELLECT IS LEAPING  581B DESC CAT 6   TITLE
LEAPT
     INTO THE DANGEROUS WORLD I LEAPT  . . . . . . . . .    166 INFANT SORW/N      2
     A FAIRY [LEAPT] SKIPD UPON MY KNEE  . . . . . . . .    188 A FAIRY SKIPD    *  1
     INTO THE DANGEROUS WORLD I LEAPT  . . . . . . . . .    217 INFANT SORW/SE     2
LEAR
     CORINEUS THROWS GOGMAGOG THE GIANT INTO THE SEA KING LEAR   208C SUBJCTS HIST/N TITLE
     WITH A LEAR IN HIS EYE HE'LL REPLY A PAINT BRUSH  . . . . 553 ASKD PRIGG/N     12
     A PICTURE OF LEAR AND CORDELIA WHEN HE AWAKES AND KNOWS HER  843D LETTER 43   PROSE
     THE HEADS OF LEAR AND CORDELIA CAN NEVER BE SURPASSED  . 843D LETTER 43      PROSE
     LEAR AND CORDELIA TO COPY IF YOU DESIRE IT SHOULD BE DONE  845D LETTER 44    PROSE
     LEAR & CORDELIA BELONGING TO MR WALKER  . . . . . . .  849A LETTER 45        PROSE
LEARN
     O EDWARD MY DEAR SON LEARN TO THINK LOWLY OF  . . . .   26 EDW THIRD/PS 3   216
     THAT WE MAY LEARN TO BEAR THE BEAMS OF LOVE  . . . . . 125 LIT BLK BOY/SI    14
     . . . LEARN TO CONSIDER ALL MEN AS THY EQUALS  . . . . 143 FRENCH REVOLTN   193
     . . . BUT IF IT REFUSE LET THE NATION'S ASSEMBLY THENCE  145 FRENCH REVOLTN  253
          LEARN
     IN SEED TIME LEARN IN HARVEST TEACH IN WINTER ENJOY  . . 150D MARRIAGE HH 7  PROSE
     TO LEARN OF THE CROW  . . . . . . . . . . . . .       151D MARRIAGE HH 8    PROSE
     WHY OF THE SHEEP DO YOU NOT LEARN PEACE  . . . . . .   181 ANSWR PARSON/N     1
     HOW KNOW YOU THIS SAID I SHALL SIR WHERE DID YOU LEARN  237 EUROPE INTRO     10
          THIS SONG
     THAT THE REMNANT MAY LEARN TO OBEY  . . . . . . . .   247 SONG OF LOS 7      2
     AND LEARN WHAT TIS TO ABSORB THE MAN YOU SPIRITS OF PITY  294 FOUR ZOAS 3    90
          & LOVE
     THERE IS A STATE NAMD SATAN LEARN DISTINCT TO KNOW  .  351 FOUR ZOAS 8      379
          O [MORTALS] RAHAB
     THAT MAN SHOULD LABOUR & SORROW & LEARN & FORGET & RETURN  355 FOUR ZOAS 8   574
     FROM HER SHALL LEARN OBEDIENCE & PREPARE FOR A WINTRY GRAVE  362 FOUR ZOAS 9  217
     IT IS NECESSARY TO LEARN THE NAMES OF ALL THAT WERE PRESENT  438B BLAKES MEMORAN  PROSE
     TO LEARN THE LANGUAGE OF ART COPY FOR EVER IS MY RULE  . . 446B ANNO REYNOLDS  MARG
     BUT THAT WE ARE TO LEARN TO THINK FROM GREAT MASTERS  . . 449A ANNO REYNOLDS  MARG
     & TO LEARN TO PERFORM FROM UNDERLINGS  . . . . . . .  449A ANNO REYNOLDS    MARG
     LEARN TO DESIGN FROM RAFAEL & TO EXECUTE FROM RUBENS XXX  449A ANNO REYNOLDS  MARG
     DECEPTIONS O NO SO I'LL LEARN TO PAINT  . . . . . . .  546 RUBENS HAD/N       4
     LEARN THE [?WOBLY [HIGH LABOURD] PRETENTIOUS]  . . . .  547 RAFAEL SUBLI/N *   5
     AND SAYS COME LEARN TO WALK OF ME GOOD NEIGHBOURS  . .  548 CRIPPLE EVRY/N     2
     [TO LEARN TO ADMIRE THE WORKS OF A FOOL]  . . . . . .  550 SAY PICTURES/N     4
     AND LEARN WHAT TIS TO ABSORB THE MAN YOU SPIRITS OF PITY  655 JERUSALEM 29    71
          & LOVE
     LEARN THEREFORE O SISTERS TO DISTINGUISH THE ETERNAL HUMAN  680 JERUSALEM 49  72
     TENDER ARTIFICE TO LAUGH TO WEEP TO LEARN TO KNOW  . . . 688 JERUSALEM 56    24
     THINE OWN HUMANITY LEARN TO ADORE  . . . . . . . . .  750 EV GOSPEL(C)/N    42
     THY OWN HUMANITY LEARN TO ADORE  . . . . . . . . . .  752 EV GOSPEL(D)/N    76
     VERY ILL NATURED YET EVEN FROM HIM I LEARN  . . . . . 798B LETTER 10        PROSE
     I DID NOT BEGIN TO LEARN LANGUAGES EARLY IN LIFE AS I FIND  821D LETTER 25   PROSE
          IT
     PERHAPS IT WILL BE IN YOUR POWER TO LEARN SOMEWHAT ABOUT  828B LETTER 28     PROSE
     IF YOU CAN LEARN NOTHING ABOUT HIM & WHAT I AS WELL KNOW  828B LETTER 28     PROSE
     SUPPOSES THAT IT MAY BE IN THE NORTH & THAT HE MAY LEARN  835D LETTER 35     PROSE
LEARND
     FOR WHEN OUR SOULS HAVE LEARND THE HEAT TO BEAR  . . . 125 LIT BLK BOY/SI    17
     LEARND THE LANGUAGE OF ART BY MAKING MANY FINISHD COPIES  455D ANNO REYNOLDS  MARG
     [HE MIXD THEM BOTH & SO HE LEARND TO PAINT]  . . . . . 546 RUBENS HAD/N       3
     HAVE LEARND TO VALUE BY ABSENCE NO LESS PERHAPS THAN WE DID  824B LETTER 27   PROSE
     ALL THIS I LEARND WITH SOME ALARM & HEARD ALSO WHAT  . . 833C LETTER 33      PROSE
LEARNED
     THE NORMAN WILLIAM AND THE LEARNED CLERK  . . . . . .   35 WAR SONG/PS       27
     NOTHING OF ARTS OR ARTISTS OR LEARNED MEN OR OF AGRICULTURE  404D ANNO BACON  * MARG
     LEARNED & NOBLE IS ORNAMENTAL  . . . . . . . . . . .  476B ANNO REYNOLDS    MARG
     SO THE [WISE] [LEARNED] TAUGHT SAVAGE ENGLISHMAN . . . . 548 ON GREAT ENC/N    3
     GIVE PENSIONS TO THE LEARNED PIG  . . . . . . . . .   548 GIVE PENSION/N     1
     HIS PROFESSION PERFECT LEARNED COMPLETELY MASTER AND  . 570D DESC CAT 3      PROSE
     THERE ARE ALWAYS THESE TWO CLASSES OF LEARNED SAGES  . . 572C DESC CAT 4     PROSE
     WERE NAKED CIVILIZED MEN LEARNED STUDIOUS  . . . . . . 577C DESC CAT 5       PROSE
     UNIVERSAL THEOLOGY NO ...THE LEARNED WHO STRIVE TO ASCEND  581D DESC CAT 8    PROSE
     THE LEARNED M XXX  . . . . . . . . . . . . . . .      605B V LAST JUDG/N     PROSE
     GREEK LEARNED & WISE AS ALSO OF THOSE OF OTHER NATIONS  . 610B V LAST JUDG/N  PROSE
     IS IT A TRUTH THAT THE LEARNED HAVE EXPLORED  . . . . . 649B JERUSALEM 27    PROSE
     WHEN THE RICH LEARNED PHARISEE  . . . . . . . . . .   750 EV GOSPEL(C)/N     9
     WHEN THE RICH LEARNED PHARISEE  . . . . . . . . . .   751 EV GOSPEL(D)/N    11
     UPON THE KINGDOM OF JESUS BY THE CLASSICAL LEARNED  . . 786C ANNO THORNTON   MARG
     CAIPHAS PILATE & HEROD WERE LEARNED  . . . . . . . .  786C ANNO THORNTON    MARG
     ("PRAYERS") IT IS THE LEARNED THAT MOUTH & NOT THE VULGAR  787B ANNO THORNTON  MARG
     & IS NOT THIS GOOD & LEARNED & WISE & CLASSICAL THIS IS  788C ANNO THORNTON  MARG
     FOUND THIS I SHALL HAVE LEARNED A MOST VALUABLE THING  . 828C LETTER 28      PROSE
```

1063

```
                                                        PAGE     TITLE          LINE
LEARNED    (CONTINUED)
    ME I LEARNED THAT [XXX] NO ONE NOT EVEN THE MOST EXPERT    833B LETTER 33     *PROSE
        HORSEMAN
LEARNER
    & HAD PUT MYSELF BACK AS IF I WAS A LEARNER I HAVE PROVED  815A LETTER 23      PROSE
LEARNING
    WAS SHEWN THE HOLY CITY THEN ATHENS LEARNING . . . . .      41A THEN SHE BORE  PROSE
    THE SCHOOLS IN CLOUDS OF LEARNING ROLLD . . . . . .         418 I SAW A MONK/N     8
    OF LEARNING HOW TO PRODUCE ORIGINAL CONCEPTION . . . .     469D ANNO REYNOLDS  MARG
    [?O ?WHAT ?WISDOM ?& ?LEARNING ?ADORN ?HIS ?SUPERIORITY]   472A ANNO REYNOLDS * MARG
    UNDERSTANDING & BACON'S (ADVANCEMENT) OF LEARNING . . .    476D ANNO REYNOLDS * MARG
    TO MAKE LEARNING A BURDEN & THE WORK OF THE HOLY SPIRIT     511 MILTON 25        52
        STRIFE
    [THEY SAID THUS LEARNING & POLITENESS . . . . . . . .      541 FLORENTINE/N       7
    A MASTER OF ART AND LEARNING THOUGH AFFECTING TO DESPISE IT 569C DESC CAT 3     PROSE
    THE SOURCE OF LEARNING AND INSPIRATION ARTHUR WAS A NAME   577D DESC CAT 5      PROSE
    INTO HEAVEN BY MEANS OF LEARNING APPEAR TO CHILDREN . . .  581D DESC CAT 8      PROSE
    BY PLACING LEARNING ABOVE INSPIRATION O ARTIST . . . .     582A DESC CAT 8      PROSE
    LEARNING & SCIENCE WHICH ACCOMPANIED ADAM OUT OF EDEN . .  611D V LAST JUDG/N   PROSE
    THE SCHOOLS IN CLOUDS OF LEARNING ROLLD . . . . . .        683 I SAW A MONK/J       7
    SEE ADVANCEMT OF LEARNING PART...P...OF FIRST EDITION . .  794A LETTER 5        PROSE
    VERY EASY AM NOW LEARNING MY HEBREW (ALEPH BETH GIMMEL)    821D LETTER 25       PROSE
    [THE RASCALS WHO ?SEE PAINTING WANT TO DESTROY ART         SUPP ANNO REYNOLDS * MARG
        & LEARNING]
LEARNING'S
    NOR SIT IN LEARNING'S BOWER . . . . . . . . . .            124 SCHOOL BOY/SI      14
    THE BANKS OF CAM COLD LEARNING'S STREAMS . . . . . . .     501 MILTON 19         39
LEARNS
    THE MAN EITHER PAINTER OR PHILOSOPHER WHO LEARNS           449B ANNO REYNOLDS   MARG
        OR ACQUIRES
    REYNOLDS THINKS THAT MAN LEARNS ALL THAT HE KNOWS . . .    471A ANNO REYNOLDS   MARG
    FOR A BOY [NEVER LEARNS SO MUCH] CAN'T INTERPRET THE THING 552 WHY CUPID/N       11
LEAST
    OR EVN THE LEAST BY BIRTH SHALL GAIN THE BRIGHTEST FAME     18 EDW THIRD/PS 1    30
    WITH SOME BAD INTENTION OR AT LEAST WITH A PREJUDICED MIND 438A BLAKES MEMORAN  PROSE
    AS FAR AS GREATEST IS MORE THAN LEAST . . . . . . .        450A ANNO REYNOLDS   MARG
    TO SAY THE LEAST OF IT . . . . . . . . . . .              452D ANNO REYNOLDS   MARG
    LIMBS THAT DEVIATES OR ALTERS LEAST FROM INFANCY TO OLD AGE 580A DESC CAT 5      PROSE
    EQUALLY WELL AT LEAST IT IS SO IN ENGLAND . . . . . .     593D PUB ADDRESS/N    PROSE
    AT LEAST SIX TIMES THE QUANTITY OF LABOUR IN THE SAME TIME 794B LETTER 5        PROSE
    CHALK ENGRAVING IS AT LEAST SIX TIMES AS LABORIOUS AS      794C LETTER 5        PROSE
        AQUA TINTA
    MEER NECESSARIES OR AT (LEAST) A COMMERCE OF THE LOWEST    798C LETTER 10       PROSE
    APPEARS TO BE LAW & GOSPEL TOO AT LEAST I HEAR SO FROM THE 798C LETTER 10       PROSE
    THE SWEETEST SPOT ON EARTH AT LEAST IT IS SO TO ME & MY    808C LETTER 19       PROSE
        GOOD
    HE IS NOT IN THE LEAST TO BE BLAMED FOR THE PRESENT SCRAPE 830D LETTER 30       PROSE
    IS LOST OR AT LEAST CANNOT NOW BE FOUND IT IS THAT OF . .  839C LETTER 38       PROSE
    AT LEAST WORTH (THIRTY) & THAT . . . . . . . . .          848C LETTER 45       PROSE
    & I AM DETERMIND TO MAKE IT SO AT LEAST . . . . . . .     855D LETTER 53       PROSE
    AT LEAST AS WELL AS ANY I HAVE YET PRODUCED . . . . .      867C LETTER 66       PROSE
    THE LEAST PARTICLE & SUCH DISCIPLINE I CALL PRESUMPTION    871A LETTER 72       PROSE
        & FOLLY
    SAY THAT HIS ILLNESS IS SO FAR FROM GONE THAT THE LEAST    SUPP LETTER 81A     *PROSE
        THING
LEATHER
    LIKE LEATHER AND CHALK THEIR MEN ARE LIKE LEATHER AND      581A DESC CAT 5      PROSE
    ALSO LET ME OBSERVE THAT THE YELLOW LEATHER FLESH OF OLD   815A LETTER 23       PROSE
        MEN
LEATHERN
    LO THE BAT WITH LEATHERN WING . . . . . . . . . .          54 LO THE BAT/IM        1
LEATHES'S
    AGAINST ME BY A PRIVATE IN CAPTN LEATHES'S TROOP OF (FIRST) 826D LETTER 28      PROSE
        OR
LEAVE
    THE HUSBANDMAN DOES LEAVE HIS PLOW . . . . . . . .          12 GWIN KING/PS      45
    NOW BY THE QUEEN'S ADVICE I ASK YOUR LEAVE . . . . . .      20 EDW THIRD/PS 2    41
    IF I OBTAIN YOUR LEAVE I HAVE ANOTHER BOON . . . . . .      20 EDW THIRD/PS 2    43
    I FEAR LORD PERCY WILL NOT GIVE ME LEAVE . . . . . .        20 EDW THIRD/PS 2    45
    THEN YOU WILL GIVE ME LEAVE TO SHINE SOMETIMES . . . .      20 EDW THIRD/PS 2    55
    SHALL FLEE AWAY AND LEAVE [THEM] HIM ALL FORLORN . . .      28 EDW THIRD/PS 3   292
    THAT I WILL TELL YOUR HONOUR IF YOULL GIVE ME LEAVE . .     29B EDW THIRD/PS 4  PROSE
    THOUSANDS OF SOULS MUST LEAVE THIS PRISON HOUSE . . . .     30 EDW THIRD/PS 5    27
    THE HUSBANDMAN DOTH LEAVE HIS BENDING HARVEST . . . .       34B KING JOHN/PS    PROSE
    THE PHILISTINES THE THEE THEN DIDST THOU LEAVE ME . . .     39B SAMSON/PS       PROSE
    I THINK SOMEHOW I'LL LEAVE IT OFF THERE WAS A WOMAN . .     51C ISLAND MOON 6   PROSE
    COME COME LEAVE OFF PLAY & LET US AWAY . . . . . . .        60 NURSES SONG/IM       7
    AND LEAVE YOU ALL . . . . . . . . . . . . .                60 SAY YOU JOE/IM        4
    LEAVE O LEAVE (ME) TO MY SORROWS . . . . . . . . .          61 LEAVE O/IM      *    1
    HOW CAME THINE HAIR TO LEAVE THY FOREHEAD HOW CAME THY      102 TIRIEL 3           3
        FACE SO BROWN
    WHAT WILT THOU LEAVE US TOO SAID HEVA THOU SHALT NOT LEAVE  102 TIRIEL 3          12
        US TOO
    THEN LET THY NAME BE TIRIEL & NEVER LEAVE US MORE . . .     102 TIRIEL 3          16
    MY SONS HAVE LEFT ME DID THINE LEAVE THEE O TWAS VERY CRUEL 102 TIRIEL 3          18
    KISS ME MY BROTHER & THEN LEAVE ME TO WANDER DESOLATE . .   104 TIRIEL 4          22
    COME COME LEAVE OFF PLAY AND LET US AWAY . . . . . .        121 NURSES SONG/SI       7
    AND LAY ME DOWN IN THY COLD BED AND LEAVE MY SHINING LOT    130 BOOK OF THEL 5    13
    . . . AND VISIONS OF SORROW LEAVE PENSIVE STREETS . . .     136 FRENCH REVOLTN    58
    . . . LEAVE THE KINGDOM THY LIFE IS SURROUNDED WITH SNARES  139 FRENCH REVOLTN   114
    TO LEAVE HIS GUARD AT TREE OF LIFE AND WHEN HE DOES . . .   154B MARRIAGE HH 14  PROSE
    O JEW LEAVE COUNTING GOLD RETURN TO THY OIL AND WINE . .    159C SONG LIBERTY    PROSE
```

		PAGE	TITLE	LINE
LEAVE	**(CONTINUED)**			
THE MORNING COMES THE NIGHT DECAYS THE WATCHMEN LEAVE THEIR STATIONS		198	AMERICA 6	1
. . . & LEAVE HIS JOY TO THE IDLE TO THE PESTILENCE . . .		200	AMERICA 11	6
AND LEAVE ME VOID AS DEATH		238	EUROPE PREL 2	11
O ANTAMON WHY WILT THOU LEAVE THY MOTHER ENITHARMON . . .		244	EUROPE 14	16
THOU NEER SHALT LEAVE THIS COLD EXPANSE WHERE WATRY THARMAS MOURNS		272	FOUR ZOAS 1	305
LEAVE ALL FUTURITY TO HIM RESUME THY FIELDS OF LIGHT . .		292	FOUR ZOAS 3	30
BUT URIZEN SAID CAN I NOT LEAVE THIS WORLD OF CUMBROUS WHEELS		316	FOUR ZOAS 6	196
COMPELLD TO LEAVE THE PLOW TO THE OX		338	FOUR ZOAS 7B	202
TILL MAN SHALL LEAVE A CORRUPTIBLE BODY HE FAMISHD HEARS HIM GROAN		354	FOUR ZOAS 8	524
IF THOU REPENTEST NOT & LEAVE THEE AS A ROTTEN BRANCH TO BE BURND		361	FOUR ZOAS 9	156
& LEAVE HIS MORE MATERIAL ONES UNANSWERED		392D	ANNO WATSON	MARG
GIVE HIGH PRICE FOR THE WORST LEAVE THE BEST IN DISGRACE		445	ANNO REYNOLDS	3
GET TO THY LABOURS AT THE MILLS & LEAVE ME TO MY WRATH . .		483	MILTON 4	14
BUT LEAVE THEIR DESTIND LINEAMENTS PERMANENT FOR EVER & EVER		505	MILTON 22	25
OUR WHEAT WITH SHOUTINGS OF JOY AND LEAVE THE EARTH IN PEACE		507	MILTON 23	46
O MY DEAR SONS LEAVE NOT YOUR FATHER AS YOUR BRETHREN LEFT ME		508	MILTON 23	61
YOU O MY SONS STILL GUARD ROUND LOS O WANDER NOT & LEAVE ME		508	MILTON 24	13
AND IF YOU ALSO FLEE AWAY AND LEAVE YOUR FATHER'S SIDE . .		508	MILTON 24	22
CRAVE NOT FOR THE MORTAL & PERISHING DELIGHTS BUT LEAVE THEM		511	MILTON 25	56
THE RATIO OF THE SPECTATOR'S ORGANS BUT LEAVE OBJECTS UNTOUCHD		516	MILTON 29	18
TELL ME THE ACTS O HISTORIAN AND LEAVE ME TO REASON UPON		579A	DESC CAT 5	PROSE
DEMONS BUT HE WAS ALSO COMPELLED TO LEAVE IT UNFINISHED		581B	DESC CAT 6	PROSE
IN THE BOOK OF RUTH WHERE NAOMI HAVING TAKEN LEAVE OF HER		584C	DESC CAT 15	PROSE
RUTH CANNOT LEAVE HER BUT SAYS "WHITHER THOU GOEST" . .		584D	DESC CAT 15	PROSE
LEAVE OUT THIS (LINE) AND YOU LEAVE OUT LIFE ITSELF . .		585C	DESC CAT 15	*PROSE
TO LEAVE IT BEFORE HE HAS SPOILD IT HE WILL [PR] DO A BETTER THING		603A	PUB ADDR AD/N	*PROSE
WONDER WHICH ALWAYS INTREATS HIM TO LEAVE MORTAL THINGS		611A	V LAST JUDG/N	PROSE
REMOVE EASTWARD TO BASHAN AND GILEAD AND LEAVE		679	JERUSALEM 48	64
AND VALA FOR I CANNOT LEAVE THEM IN THE GNAWING GRAVE . .		696	JERUSALEM 62	21
COMPELLD TO LEAVE THE PLOW TO THE OX		700	JERUSALEM 65	48
CAN I ARISE AND LEAVE THY SIDE BUT LABOUR HERE INCESSANT		727	JERUSALEM 83	2
I WILL NOT LEAVE YOU ORPHANNED AND I WILL MANIFEST MYSELF TO YOU		774A	ANNO BERKELEY	* MARG
YOU MUST LEAVE FATHERS & MOTHERS & HOUSES & LANDS . . .		776A	INSC LAOCOON	PROSE
PRACTISE IS ART IF YOU LEAVE OFF YOU ARE LOST		777B	INSC LAOCOON	PROSE
LEAVE US NOT IN [?POVERTY ?AND ?WANT XXX] PARSIMONY SATAN'S		788B	ANNO THORNTON	* MARG
A FATHER TAKING LEAVE OF HIS WIFE & CHILD IS WATCHD . .		792B	LETTER 4	PROSE
I LEAVE NO STONE UNTURND & NO PATH UNEXPLORD THAT TENDS		812A	LETTER 22	PROSE
TO ETERNITY EVERY ONE IN ETERNITY WILL LEAVE YOU AGHAST		813B	LETTER 22	PROSE
NAMELY TO LEAVE THIS PLACE BECAUSE I AM NOW CERTAIN . . .		819C	LETTER 25	PROSE
TOO MUCH THE CAUSE OF OUR DETERMINATION TO LEAVE FELPHAM		819D	LETTER 25	PROSE
WHICH WE INFORMD HIM VIZ TO LEAVE FELPHAM ENTIRELY . . .		820C	LETTER 25	PROSE
HAVE BEEN LOST I SHALL LEAVE EVERY ONE IN THIS COUNTRY . .		825D	LETTER 27	PROSE
THUS YOU SEE MY DEAR FRIEND THAT I CANNOT LEAVE THIS PLACE		828A	LETTER 28	PROSE
WHICH WAS TO LEAVE THE WHOLE CONDUCT OF THE AFFAIR TO YOU		842C	LETTER 42	PROSE
SO TAKE MY LEAVE FOR THE PRESENT WITH THE JOINT LOVE OF		845A	LETTER 43	PROSE
HE NEVER WILL LEAVE TO PRACTISE THE ART BECAUSE HE LOVES IT		850C	LETTER 49	PROSE
MATTERS AND LEAVE ALL TO YOUR DECISION		861B	LETTER 58	PROSE
NOT DARE TO LEAVE HIS ROOM BY ANY MEANS HE HAD ANOTHER		SUPP	LETTER 81A	*PROSE
"LEAVE EVERY HOPE YOU WHO IN ENTER"		SUPP	ILLUS DANTE 4	*
LEAVES				
THE BREATH OF HEAVEN DWELT AMONG HIS LEAVES		5	FAIR ELENOR/PS	51
AND THY LOVELY LEAVES AMONG		7	LOVE HARMNY/PS	15
AND LEAVES THE TRADING SHORE		12	GWIN KING/PS	48
THE SHEPHERD LEAVES HIS MELLOW PIPE		12	GWIN KING/PS	49
THE BREATH OF NIGHT SLEPT AMONG THE LEAVES OF THE FOREST		36C	COUCH DEATH/PS	PROSE
GREEN GRASS SPRINGS IN JOY AND THE NIMBLE AIR KISSES THE LEAVES		37B	CONTEMPLATN/PS	PROSE
UNDER LEAVES SO GREEN		115	THE BLOSSOM/SI	2
UNDER LEAVES SO GREEN		116	THE BLOSSOM/SI	8
AS THE CATTERPILLER CHOOSES THE FAIREST LEAVES TO LAY . .		152C	MARRIAGE HH 9	PROSE
THE GREEN LEAVES AMONG		175	WILD FLOWERS/N	2
FROM THE LEAVES I SPRUNG		178	THE FAIRY/N	12
TO THE FOUR WINDS AS A TORN BOOK & NONE SHALL GATHER THE LEAVES		198	AMERICA 8	6
HE LAUGHING ANSWERD I WILL WRITE A BOOK ON LEAVES OF FLOWERS		237	EUROPE INTRO	14
YELLOW AS LEAVES OF AUTUMN THE MYRIADS OF ANGELIC HOSTS		243	EUROPE 13	6
VALA SHRUNK IN LIKE THE DARK SEA THAT LEAVES ITS SLIMY BANKS		294	FOUR ZOAS 3	99
AS PLANTS WITHERD BY WINTER LEAVES & STEMS & ROOTS DECAYING		305	FOUR ZOAS 5	9
AS THE TREE KNOWS NOT WHAT IS OUTSIDE OF ITS LEAVES & BARK		314	FOUR ZOAS 6	95
CAN WRITE AND ADAMANTINE LEAVES RECIEVE NOR CAN THE MAN WHO GOES		316	FOUR ZOAS 6	174
. . . & SHATTERS OFF THE LEAVES		324	FOUR ZOAS 7	180
BENEATH THE TREE OF MYSTERY AMONG THE LEAVES & FRUIT . .		325	FOUR ZOAS 7	218
BUT WHEN RAHAB &C TURN BACK (THREE) LEAVES		349D	FOUR ZOAS 8	*PROSE
THEY ARE BECOME LIKE WINTRY FLOCKS LIKE FORESTS STRIPD OF LEAVES		357	FOUR ZOAS 9	22

	PAGE	TITLE	LINE
LEAVES (CONTINUED)			
AND RAVEN NUMEROUS AS THE LEAVES OF AUTUMN EVERY SPECIES	363	FOUR ZOAS 9	238
THEY ARE BECOME LIKE WINTRY FLOCKS LIKE FORESTS STRIPD OF LEAVES	365	FOUR ZOAS 9	327
TRAVELLER REPOSE & DREAM AMONG MY LEAVES WILL BLAKE	414	ILLUS GRAY	2
AMONG GREEN LEAVES & BLOSSOMS SWEET	423	THE BIRDS/N	20
DEATH TO DELUDE WHO ALL IN TERROR AT THEIR SPLENDOR LEAVES	517	MILTON 29	43
HIMSELF THAT SEEING ALL HIS LOVES BY HER CUT OFF HE LEAVES	522	MILTON 33	15
THE SAVAGE GIRLS HAD DRESSED THEMSELVES WITH VINE LEAVES	581C	DESC CAT 7	PROSE
TORMENTING THE TRUE ARTIST TILL HE LEAVES THE FLORENTINE AND	582D	DESC CAT 9	PROSE
FLANDERS IT LOSES ALL CHARACTER AND LEAVES WHAT SOME PEOPLE	585A	DESC CAT 15	PROSE
LEAVES UPON THE TREES & THE STONES & GRAVEL UPON THE ROAD	588A	CHAUCER/N	PROSE
TO COME IN HERE AS TWO LEAVES FORWARD	606D	V LAST JUDG/N	PROSE
MENTAL DELIGHTS HERE THEY ARE &C AS THREE LEAVES ON	613C	V LAST JUDG/N	PROSE
& LEAVES THE MAN WHO ENTERTAINS SUCH AN IDEA THE HABITATION	614B	V LAST JUDG/N	PROSE
WHEN IT LEAVES PARADISE [WITH] FOLLOWING THE SERPENT	614C	V LAST JUDG/N	PROSE
VALA SHRUNK IN LIKE THE DARK SEA THAT LEAVES ITS SLIMY BANKS	655	JERUSALEM 29	78
OXFORD TAKE THOU THESE LEAVES OF THE TREE OF LIFE WITH ELOQUENCE	675	JERUSALEM 45	30
IN MILD PERSWASION BRINGING LEAVES OF THE TREE OF LIFE	676	JERUSALEM 46	9
IS CONCERNED BUT I MUST SAY THAT HE LEAVES NO STONE UNTURND	846C	LETTER 44	PROSE
LEAVING			
LEAVING A TRACK OF LIGHT FOR MEN TO WONDER AT	27	EDW THIRD/PS 3	275
WHEN HIS EVENING TALE IS TOLD DEPARTS HIS BLESSING LEAVING	40A	SAMSON/PS	PROSE
LEAVING THE FEMALES NAKED AND GLOWING WITH THE LUSTS OF YOUTH	202	AMERICA 15	22
LEAVING RUINOUS FRAGMENTS OF LIFE	225	URIZEN 5	9
IF I ARISE INTO THE ZENITH LEAVING THEE TO WATCH	278	FOUR ZOAS 1	506
MUSTRING TOGETHER IN THICK CLOUDS LEAVING THE RAGE OF LUVAH	279	FOUR ZOAS 1	539
FROM ENION'S BRAIN IN THIS DEFORMED FORM LEAVING THEE THERE	327	FOUR ZOAS 7	291
LEAVING HIS SPECTROUS FORM WHICH COULD NOT BE DRAWN AWAY	332	FOUR ZOAS 7	492
AS ENEAS IS HERE SHEWN A WORSE MAN THAN ACHILLES IN LEAVING DIDO	412A	ANNO BOYD	MARG
ON ACCOUNT OF OUR LEAVING THE DIVINE HARVEST TO THE ENEMY	716D	JERUSALEM 77	*PROSE
I HAVE BEEN FORCED TO INSIST ON HIS LEAVING ME IN BOTH TO	825C	LETTER 27	PROSE
HE MADE ME AN IMPERTINENT ANSWER I INSISTED ON HIS LEAVING	827A	LETTER 28	PROSE
I MUST NOT OMIT TO TELL YOU THAT ON LEAVING MR PHILLIPS I	860A	LETTER 56	PROSE
OWN ETERNAL HOUSE LEAVING THE DELUSIVE GODDESS NATURE & HER	879A	LETTER 88	PROSE
LEBANON			
AND ON THE MOUNTAINS OF LEBANON ROUND THE DECEASED GODS	246	SONG OF LOS 4	19
MALAH COME FORTH FROM LEBANON & HOGLAH FROM MOUNT SINAI	349	FOUR ZOAS 8	316
ARE HOR & PEOR & BASHAN & ABARIM & LEBANON & HERMON	498	MILTON 17	16
THAMMUZ IN LEBANON & RIMMON IN DAMASCUS CURTAIND	528	MILTON 37	26
GWANTOCK & PEACHY HID IN DAMASCUS BENEATH MOUNT LEBANON	662	JERUSALEM 36	16
MALAH COME FORTH FROM LEBANON & HOGLAH FROM MOUNT SINAI	705	JERUSALEM 68	4
BENEATH THE MOUNTAINS OF LEBANON IN THE CITY OF REHOB IN HAMATH	706	JERUSALEM 68	55
THRO ITALY & GRECIA TO LEBANON & PERSIA & INDIA	722	JERUSALEM 80	47
LISTEN HERMON & LEBANON BOW THEIR CROWNED HEADS	730	JERUSALEM 85	17
THE ISLES OF JAVAN PHILISTEA TYRE AND LEBANON	731	JERUSALEM 86	32
LEBRUN			
THERE IS JUST THE SAME SCIENCE IN LEBRUN OR RUBENS	602C	PUB ADDR AD/N	PROSE
LE BRUN'S			
HE THEN WENT & TOOK DOWN LE BRUN'S & RUBENS'S GALLERIES	449C	ANNO REYNOLDS	MARG
LE CAVE'S			
("LE CAVE'S WORKS CHASTE DELINEATIONS ") SUCH IS THE PARAGRAPH	553B	BELLS WEEKLY/N	MARG
LECTURE			
HAVE HEARD THAT FLAXMAN MEANS TO GIVE A LECTURE ON SCULPTURE	859D	LETTER 56	PROSE
LECTURES			
[THIS] REYNOLDS LECTURES [PLAINLY SHEW] EXACTLY SO	539	CAN THERE BE/N	5
OF SIR JOSHUA REYNOLDS'S LECTURES	543	TO ROYL ACAD/N	2
LED			
HE LED ME THROUGH HIS GARDENS FAIR	6	HOW SWEET/PS	7
WANDERD TILL HE THAT LEADETH ALL LED HIM TO THE VALES OF HAR	100	TIRIEL 2	4
[THEN MNETHA LED HIM TO THE DOOR & GAVE TO HIM HIS STAFF]	103	TIRIEL 3	30
THEN MNETHA TREMBLING AT HIS FROWNS LED HIM TO THE TENT DOOR	103	TIRIEL 3	39
HE CEAST & [?HILI] HELA LED HER FATHER FROM THE NOISOM PLACE	107	TIRIEL 5	* 26
AND [?HILI] HELA LED HER FATHER THRO THE SILENT OF THE NIGHT	107	TIRIEL 6	* 1
SHE HOWLING LED HIM OVER MOUNTAINS & THRO FRIGHTED VALES	108	TIRIEL 7	1
[THEY] THE HOWLING MAIDEN LED HER FATHER WHERE WILD BEASTS RESORT	109	TIRIEL 7	16
THE AGED WANDERER LED TOWARDS THE TENTS SHE TOOK HER BOW	109	TIRIEL 7	23
AND MNETHA LED THEM TO THE TENT OF HAR AND HAR & HEVA	109	TIRIEL 8	5
WHERE THE VISION LED	115	LIT GRL FND/SI	46
LED BY THE WANDRING LIGHT	121	LIT BOY FND/SI	2
HE KISSED THE CHILD & BY THE HAND LED	121	LIT BOY FND/SI	5
AND WISH TO LEAD OTHERS WHEN THEY SHOULD BE LED	126	VOICE BARD/SI	11
THE DAUGHTERS OF MNE SERAPHIM LED ROUND THEIR SUNNY FLOCKS	127	BOOK OF THEL 1	1
AND [YOUTHS] YOUTH TO SLAUGHTER HOUSES LED	174	HUMAN IMAGE/N	* 31
[THEN] HE LED HIM BY HIS LITTLE COAT	177	LIT BOY LST/N	13
WHAT NIGHT HE LED THE STARRY HOSTS THRO THE WIDE WILDERNESS	198	AMERICA 8	4
HE LED HIM BY HIS LITTLE COAT	218	LIT BOY LST/SE	11
AND SHE HERSELF (LED) CAPTIVE &	279	FOUR ZOAS 1	547
KINDLING SHE LED HIM INTO SHADOWS & THENCE FLED OUTSTRETCHD	290	FOUR ZOAS 2	381

		PAGE	TITLE	LINE

LED   (CONTINUED)
THEN LED HER DOWN INTO THE DEEPS & INTO HIS LABYRINTH   .   .   308 FOUR ZOAS 5   111
LOS TAKING ENITHARMON BY THE HAND LED HER ALONG   .   .   .   309 FOUR ZOAS 5   150
ENDLESS HAD BEEN HIS TRAVEL BUT THE DIVINE HAND HIM LED   .   316 FOUR ZOAS 6   176
FOUR SONS OF URIZEN THE SQUADRONS OF URTHONA LED IN ARMS   .   319 FOUR ZOAS 6   314
OF DAY IN JEALOUSY & BLOOD MY CHILDREN ARE LED TO URIZEN'S   339 FOUR ZOAS 7B   251
    WAR
WE ARE LED TO BELIEVE A LIE   .   .   .   .   433 AUGURIES   125
O IMMORTAL HOW WERE WE LED TO WAR THE WARS OF DEATH   .   .   .   534 MILTON 41   36
THOSE WHO SAY THAT MEN ARE LED BY INTEREST ARE KNAVES   .   .   572D DESC CAT 3   PROSE
LED ONWARD BY TRIUMPHANT GROUPES OF INFANTS   .   .   .   .   .   611D V LAST JUDG/N   PROSE
SEES THE MOON TERRIFIED AS ONE LED ASTRAY IN THE MIDST   619A ILLUS MILTON   PROSE
    OF HER PATH
MILTON LED BY MELANCHOLY INTO THE GROVES   .   .   .   .   .   619B ILLUS MILTON   PROSE
ENQUIRING FOR JERUSALEM HE LED THEM UP MY STEPS TO MY ALTAR   721 JERUSALEM 79   52
OF BABYLON LED BY A CHILD HIS TEARS RUN DOWN HIS BEARD   .   .   729 JERUSALEM 84   12
REUBEN FROM HIS TWELVEFOLD WANDRINGS & LED HIM INTO IT   .   .   730 JERUSALEM 85   4
OR ANGEL TO FOLLOW WHERE HE LED IF I WERE TO ACT OTHERWISE   791D LETTER 4   PROSE
FOR ALL SUCH WHO MAY BE LED TO SUCH OSTENTATIOUS EXERTION   871A LETTER 72   PROSE
LEE
WASHINGTON FRANKLIN PAINE & WARREN ALLEN GATES & LEE   .   .   201 AMERICA 14   2
WITH THE NAME OF NAT LEE WHICH PERHAPS HE NEVER WROTE   .   .   600D PUB ADDRESS/N   PROSE
LEER   SEE LEAR
LEES
NUMROUS THEY TOOK THE WINE THEY SEPARATED THE LEES   .   .   .   378 FOUR ZOAS 9   * 790
LEESING
FOR IGNORANCE IS FOLLY'S LEESING NURSE   .   .   .   .   .   .   14 IMIT SPEN/PS   *   13
LEFEVRE'S
BUT THAT OF LEFEVRE'S DEATH HE SPEAKS OF AS INCOMPARABLE   844C LETTER 43   PROSE
LEFT
HILLS FLED FROM OUR SIGHT BUT LEFT HIS GOLDEN LOAD   .   .   .   2 TO AUTUMN/PS   18
HOW HAVE YOU LEFT THE ANTIENT LOVE   .   .   .   .   11 TO MUSES/PS   13
NOR KNEW HE WAS AN ANGEL MANOA LEFT HIS FIELDS   .   .   .   .   40A SAMSON/PS   PROSE
HERE ETRUSCAN COLUMN LEFT OFF   .   .   .   .   45A ISLAND MOON 1   PROSE
THEY ALL WENT HOME & LEFT THE PHILOSOPHERS THEN SUCTION   49D ISLAND MOON 6   PROSE
    ASKD
THEN [THEY] QUID & SUCTION WERE LEFT ALONE   .   .   .   .   .   51D ISLAND MOON 7   PROSE
HIS LEFT SUPPORTED MYRATANA   .   .   .   .   99 TIRIEL 1   20
MY SONS HAVE LEFT ME DID THINE LEAVE THEE O TWAS VERY CRUEL   102 TIRIEL 3   18
THEN I HAVE [REND] RENT HIS LIMBS & LEFT HIM ROTTING IN   105 TIRIEL 4   *   51
    THE FOREST
THEN NAKED & WHITE ALL THEIR BAGS LEFT BEHIND   .   .   .   .   118 CHIMNEY SWP/SI   17
DROPPING A TEAR THE OLD MAN HIS PLACE LEFT AND WHEN HE   139 FRENCH REVOLTN   121
    WAS GONE OUT
TILL THE VILLAIN LEFT THE PATHS OF EASE   .   .   .   .   .   148 MARRIAGE HH 2   14
RIGHT & LEFT SIDE HE ANSWERD THE DESIRE OF RAISING OTHER   154B MARRIAGE HH 12   PROSE
    MEN
WAS LEFT A HELPLESS TRUNK THIS AFTER GRINNING & KISSING IT   157B MARRIAGE HH 17   PROSE
SINGING THE SUN HAS LEFT HIS BLACKNESS & HAS FOUND   198 AMERICA 6   13
    A FRESHER MORNING
HIS LEFT ARM TO THE SOUTH   .   .   .   .   229 URIZEN 13   14
AND LEFT A ROUND GLOBE OF BLOOD   .   .   .   .   230 URIZEN 13   58
THEN LEFT A NOISOM BODY   .   .   .   .   236 URIZEN 28   2
AND THEY LEFT THE PENDULOUS EARTH   .   .   .   .   237 URIZEN 28   21
THEY CALLED IT EGYPT & LEFT IT   .   .   .   .   237 URIZEN 28   22
ON ALL SIDES AND LEFT AN UNFORMD   .   .   .   .   260 BOOK OF LOS 5   49
WHICH IS THE WAY THE RIGHT OR THE LEFT   .   .   .   .   .   .   261D SMALL BK DSGNS TITLE
A NOTHING LEFT IN DARKNESS YET I AM AN IDENTITY   .   .   .   265 FOUR ZOAS 1   62
HIS WEB IS LEFT ALL DESOLATE THAT HIS LITTLE ANXIOUS HEART   277 FOUR ZOAS 1   459
SHE FLED VANISHING ON THE WIND AND LEFT A DEAD COLD CORSE   289 FOUR ZOAS 2   334
NOW MY LEFT HAND I STRETCH TO EARTH BENEATH   .   .   .   .   289 FOUR ZOAS 2   369
AND THE DARK BODY OF [MAN] ALBION LEFT PROSTRATE   .   .   .   294 FOUR ZOAS 3   81
THEY FLED TO EAST & WEST & LEFT THE NORTH & SOUTH OF HEAVEN   295 FOUR ZOAS 3   134
WHERE ENITHARMON JOIND TO HIS LEFT SIDE IN [DISMAL] GRIDING   299 FOUR ZOAS 4   *   60
    PAIN
DEPARTED FAR INTO THE UNKNOWN & LEFT A WONDROUS VOID   .   .   301 FOUR ZOAS 4   158
HIS LEFT ARM TO THE SOUTH SHOOTING OUT IN ANGUISH DEEP   .   303 FOUR ZOAS 4   244
LOS FROM THE FURNACES A SPACE IMMENSE & LEFT THE COLD   .   .   305 FOUR ZOAS 5   15
WE FELL I SIEZD THEE DARK URTHONA IN MY LEFT HAND FALLING   311 FOUR ZOAS 5   225
FOLLOWD HER DAUGHTERS TO THE FIELDS OF BLOOD THEY LEFT   334 FOUR ZOAS 7B   66
    ME NAKED
THEN LEFT THE SONS OF URIZEN THE PLOW & HARROW THE LOOM   337 FOUR ZOAS 7B   170
WAS SOON CONDEMND & WRATH WAS LEFT TO WRATH & PITY TO PITY   351 FOUR ZOAS 8   393
.   .   .   SHE SECRETLY LEFT THE SYNAGOGUE OF SATAN   356 FOUR ZOAS 8   606
SIEZD THE SUN HIS LEFT HAND LIKE DARK ROOTS COVERD THE MOON   357 FOUR ZOAS 9   8
MYSTERY'S TYRANTS ARE CUT OFF & NOT ONE LEFT ON EARTH   .   .   359 FOUR ZOAS 9   79
THE SUN HAS LEFT HIS BLACKNESS & HAS FOUND A FRESHER   379 FOUR ZOAS 9   825
    MORNING
LUTHER ALSO LEFT THE PRIEST & JOIND THE SOLDIER   .   .   .   .   413B ANNO BOYD   MARG
AND NOTHING LEFT TO EAT OR DRINK   .   .   .   .   426 MENTAL TRAVLER   67
HAS LEFT THE BRAIN THAT WON'T BELIEVE   .   .   .   .   .   .   431 AUGURIES   26
AND ON HIS LEFT HAND WAS HIS SISTER JANE   .   .   .   .   .   435 WILLIAM BOND   18
AND THE ANGELS OF PROVIDENCE LEFT THE BED   .   .   .   .   .   435 WILLIAM BOND   44
HELL OPENS BENEATH THE HARLOT'S SEAT ON THE LEFT HAND   .   .   443B LAST JUDGMNT/L   PROSE
THE RESURRECTION OF THE JUST THE LEFT HAND OF THE   .   .   .   443B LAST JUDGMNT/L   PROSE
THE PHARISEES APPEAR ON THE LEFT HAND PLEADING   .   .   .   .   443C LAST JUDGMNT/L   PROSE
ON THE LEFT HAND OF THE HARLOT'S SEAT WHERE OTHERS ARE   .   443C LAST JUDGMNT/L   PROSE
THE BLESSED ON THE RIGHT & THE LEFT OF WHICH ARE SEEN THE   444A LAST JUDGMNT/L   PROSE
THE TABLE WITH THE SHEW BREAD ON THE LEFT   .   .   .   .   .   444B LAST JUDGMNT/L *PROSE
ON [HIS] THE LEFT IS THE LORD'S SUPPER   .   .   .   .   .   .   444B LAST JUDGMNT/L *PROSE
& ON THE LEFT HAND THE LORD'S SUPPER IS ADMINISTERD   .   .   444B LAST JUDGMNT/L   PROSE
RIGHT ARM TO THE NORTH HIS LEFT ARM TO THE SOUTH & HIS   483 MILTON 3   25
    FEET

	PAGE	TITLE	LINE

LEFT   (CONTINUED)
THEN LOS TOOK OFF HIS LEFT SANDAL PLACING IT ON HIS HEAD   488 MILTON 8   11
RENT THEM ASUNDER AND WRATH WAS LEFT TO WRATH & PITY TO   490 MILTON 9   47
    PITY
AND ON MY LEFT FOOT FALLING ON THE TARSUS ENTERD THERE   497 MILTON 15   49
BUT FROM MY LEFT FOOT A BLACK CLOUD REDOUNDING SPREAD OVER   497 MILTON 15   50
    EUROPE
REDOUNDING FROM MY LEFT FOOT INTO LOS'S MUNDANE SPACE   .   .   502 MILTON 20   21
AND ALL THIS VEGETABLE WORLD APPEARD ON MY LEFT FOOT   .   .   503 MILTON 21   12
UPON HIS FIBROUS LEFT FOOT BLACK MOST DISMAL TO OUR EYES   506 MILTON 22   35
O MY DEAR SONS LEAVE NOT YOUR FATHER AS YOUR BRETHREN LEFT   508 MILTON 23   61
    ME
THEY LEFT ME WANDERING WITH TIRZAH ENITHARMON WEPT   .   .   .   508 MILTON 24   4
STILL MY FOUR MIGHTY ONES ARE LEFT TO ME IN GOLGONOOZA   .   .   508 MILTON 24   10
OF LOS & THOSE DELIVERD FROM THE BODY ON THE LEFT HAND   512 MILTON 26   17
CUT OFF MY LOVES IN FURY TILL I HAVE NO LOVE LEFT FOR THEE   522 MILTON 33   7
BENEATH SAT CHAOS SIN ON HIS RIGHT HAND DEATH ON HIS LEFT   531 MILTON 39   29
ARE THE FOUR PILLARS OF HIS THRONE HIS LEFT FOOT   531 MILTON 39   36
    NEAR LONDON
HIS LEFT SCOTLAND HIS BOSOM GIRT WITH GOLD INVOLVES   .   .   .   531 MILTON 39   42
HE MOVD HIS RIGHT FOOT TO CORNWALL HIS LEFT TO THE ROCKS   531 MILTON 39   49
    OF BOGNOR
HE HAS NOT LEFT ONE ENEMY BEHIND   .   .   .   .   546 ANOTHER/N 2   2
AS IT WAS LEFT US BY RAPHAEL AND ALBERT DURER MICHAEL   562B DESC CAT ADV   PROSE
    ANGELO
SAY NO MORE OF HER NOR EXPOSE WHAT CHAUCER HAS LEFT HIDDEN   572B DESC CAT 3   PROSE
DESIGNS FOR BLAIR'S GRAVE HAVE LEFT HIM TO SHIFT   572D DESC CAT 3   PROSE
    FOR HIMSELF
AND THEN TO BE LEFT AND NEGLECTED AND HIS WORK   .   .   .   .   572D DESC CAT 3   PROSE
RATHER PROVIDENTIALLY HE LEFT IT UNBLOTTED AND UNBLURRED   581B DESC CAT 6   PROSE
OF ART SUCH AS MICHAEL ANGELO RAFAEL JUL R(ROMANO) ALB   600B PUB ADDRESS/N   PROSE
    DURER LEFT IT
THAT I SHOULD BE [LEFT] HID IN A CORNER IT NEVER WAS   .   602C PUB ADDRESS/N   PROSE
ON HIS RIGHT & THE WICKED ON HIS LEFT HAND   .   .   .   .   .   606B V LAST JUDG/N   PROSE
(BENEATH) ISHAMAEL IS MAHOMED & ON THE LEFT   .   .   .   .   607B V LAST JUDG/N   *PROSE
TO PROCEED [IN THE] WITH THE DESCRIPTION OF THOSE ON THE   607C V LAST JUDG/N   *PROSE
    LEFT HAND
& HELL IS OPEND BENEATH HER SEAT ON THE LEFT HAND   .   .   609B V LAST JUDG/N   PROSE
THOSE ON THE RIGHT HAND AWAKE IN JOY THOSE ON THE LEFT   609C V LAST JUDG/N   PROSE
    IN HORROR
ON HIS RIGHT HAND SHEM & ON HIS LEFT JAPHET   .   .   .   .   .   609D V LAST JUDG/N   PROSE
& ON THEIR LEFT A SOLITARY WOMAN WITH HER INFANT   .   .   .   610D V LAST JUDG/N   PROSE
THAT LIVING CREATURE ON THE LEFT OF THE THRONE GIVES   .   612A V LAST JUDG/N   PROSE
ON THE LEFT HAND APOLLYON IS FOILED BEFORE THE SWORD   .   612B V LAST JUDG/N   PROSE
IN HUMILIATION BEFORE THAT OF DEATH ON THE LEFT   .   .   .   612B V LAST JUDG/N   PROSE
[& THE OTHER] THAT ON THE LEFT REPRESENTS THE LORD'S SUPPER   612D V LAST JUDG/N   PROSE
LORD'S SUPPER ON THE LEFT HAND OF THE [PICTURE] THRONE   .   614B V LAST JUDG/N   PROSE
AND LEFT MAN A LITTLE GROVELLING ROOT OUTSIDE OF HIMSELF   639 JERUSALEM 17   32
AND THE DARK BODY OF ALBION LEFT PROSTRATE UPON THE CRYSTAL   655 JERUSALEM 29   63
    PAVEMENT
AND LEFT A LITTLE SLIMY SUBSTANCE FLOATING UPON THE TIDES   679 JERUSALEM 49   18
TILL DEEP DISSIMULATION IS THE ONLY DEFENCE AN HONEST MAN   679 JERUSALEM 49   23
    HAS LEFT
I AM LEFT TO THE TRAMPLING FOOT & THE SPURNING HEEL   .   .   695 JERUSALEM 62   3
THEN LEFT THE SONS OF URIZEN THE PLOW & HARROW THE LOOM   699 JERUSALEM 65   12
SO SAYING SHE TOOK A FALSHOOD & HID IT IN HER LEFT HAND   725 JERUSALEM 82   *   17
AND THUS SHE CLOSED HER LEFT HAND AND UTTERD HER FALSHOOD   725 JERUSALEM 82   *   19
GWENDOLEN HID IN HER LEFT HAND IT GREW & GREW TILL IT   .   729 JERUSALEM 84   32
MOLECH & CHEMOSH & IN HIS LEFT BREAST IS PHILISTEA   .   .   735 JERUSALEM 89   31
AND LEFT HIS PARENTS IN DISMAY   .   .   .   .   748 EV GOSPEL(B)/N   4
AND LEFT HIS PARENTS IN DISMAY   .   .   .   .   750 EV GOSPEL(C)/N   4
AND LEFT HIS PARENTS IN DISMAY   .   .   .   .   751 EV GOSPEL(D)/N   6
HE LEFT HIS FATHER'S TRADE TO ROAM   .   .   .   .   757 EV GOSPEL(I)/N   41
LEFT WITH US THEY KEEP OFF EVERY WIND WE HEAR THE WEST HOWL   807B LETTER 17   PROSE
TEMPTATIONS ARE ON THE RIGHT HAND & LEFT   .   .   .   .   .   812A LETTER 22   PROSE
A GOOD LIKENESS OF YOU IF I HAVE HANDS & EYES LEFT   .   .   824B LETTER 27   PROSE
UNLESS ALTOGETHER LEFT TO MY OWN JUDGMENT   .   .   .   .   .   826A LETTER 27   PROSE
AS YOU MY DEAR FRIEND HAVE ALWAYS LEFT ME   .   .   .   .   .   826A LETTER 27   PROSE
TILL I HAD GOT HIM OUT THERE I INTENDED TO HAVE LEFT HIM   827A LETTER 28   PROSE
THE FLAME SOON DIES AGAIN & I AM LEFT STUPIFIED AND   830B LETTER 30   PROSE
    ASTONISHD
PUBLICATION NO CHANCE IS LEFT TO ONE OUT OF THE TRADE   .   831D LETTER 31   PROSE
& LEFT IT WITH CHARGE TO THE SERVANT OF GREAT CARE   .   .   834C LETTER 34   PROSE
HOUSE SR WILLIAM LIVD IN IN PICCADILLY SHE LEFT SOME TIME   836C LETTER 35   PROSE
COMPLIMENT HE WAS NOT AT HOME I LEFT IT WITH A SHORT NOTE   838C LETTER 37   PROSE
I ASSURED HIM THAT HE DID AND HERE HE LEFT OFF DESIRING ME   846D LETTER 44   PROSE
OR LEFT THE CAVENDISH SQUARE HOUSE   .   .   .   .   847D LETTER 44   PROSE
& THE FIGURES LEFT EXACTLY   .   .   .   .   850D LETTER 49   PROSE
HAS LEFT ME WITHOUT ANY RESOURCE BUT THAT OF APPLYING TO   853C LETTER 52   PROSE
    YOU
ONE I COULD GET AT JOHNSON'S I LEFT A GOOD IMPRESSION OF IT   855C LETTER 53   PROSE
WHEN I LEFT FELPHAM LAST IN ONE OF HEATH'S SHAKESPEARE   855C LETTER 53   PROSE
    YOU WILL SEE
LEFT ALL TO YOU INTIRELY I DO THINK FROM THE LIBERALITY OF   857A LETTER 54   *PROSE
TAKES IT QUITE AWAY IT WAS NIGHT WHEN IT LEFT ME SO I DID   872B LETTER 75   PROSE
    NOT
"LEFT THEE FOR PORTION OF THY LIVELIHED" SPENSER   .   .   .   .   SUPP LEGEND/N19   *
LEGGED   SEE LEADEN LEGGED
LEGIONS
AND RINTRAH HUNG WITH ALL HIS LEGIONS IN THE NETHER DEEP   242 EUROPE 12   24
THEN FELL THE LEGIONS OF MYSTERY IN MADDNING CONFUSION   .   .   376 FOUR ZOAS 9.   722
HIS ROCKS LONDON & BATH & LEGIONS & EDINBURGH   .   .   .   .   .   531 MILTON 39   35

	PAGE	TITLE	LINE
LEGIONS (CONTINUED)			
NUMBER IX SATAN CALLING UP HIS LEGIONS FROM MILTON'S . .	582A	DESC CAT 9	TITLE
BATH WHO IS LEGIONS HE IS THE SEVENTH THE PHYSICIAN AND	668	JERUSALEM 41	1
LEGS			
HOWLING & SHUDDERING HIS LEGS QUIVERING CONVULSD	202	AMERICA 15	8
EACH MUSCLE & SINEW			
A SPECTRE VAST APPEARD WHOSE FEET & LEGS WITH IRON SCALED	319	FOUR ZOAS 6	298
AND HIS LEGS CARRIED IT LIKE A LONG FORK	536	AND HIS LEGS/N	1
ELECTRICITY IS THE WONDERFUL CAUSE THE SWELLING OF HER LEGS	851C	LETTER 50	PROSE
LEICESTER			
DAN CORNWAL DEVON DORSET NAPTHALI WARWICK LEICESTER	637	JERUSALEM 16	46
WORCESTER			
LEICESTER & BERKSHIRE & HIS EMANATION IS GWINEFRED	710	JERUSALEM 71	37
BEAUTIFUL			
COWPER FOR THAT SONNET IN FAVOR OF A PRISONER AT LEICESTER	841C	LETTER 41	PROSE
LEICESTERSHIRE			
LINCOLNSHIRE DERBYSHIRE NOTTINGHAMSHIRE LEICESTERSHIRE . .	636	JERUSALEM 16	18
LEIGH			
OF MR LEIGH HOW FAR IT IS AN AUTOGRAPH IS A QUESTION . .	781D	INSC UPCOTT	PROSE
LEINSTER			
ULSTER NORTH IN DAN'S GATE LEINSTER EAST IN JUDAH'S GATE	711	JERUSALEM 72	4
LEISURE			
BUT WHEN THE NEW AGE IS AT LEISURE TO PRONOUNCE	480B	MILTON 1	PROSE
LEITRIM			
GALWAY ROSCOMMON MAYO SLIGO LEITRIM	711	JERUSALEM 72	24
LEND			
GIBBLE GABBLE LEND ME YOUR HANDKERCHIEF TILLY LALLY . . .	58C	ISLAND MOON 10	PROSE
LENGTH SEE HALF-LENGTH,HALF LENGTH,WHOLE LENGTH			
AT LENGTH NO FANCY BUT REALITY	4	FAIR ELENOR/PS	17
FIND PREY TILL TIRD AT LENGTH SATED AND TIRED	27	EDW THIRD/PS 3	258
. . . HAS REACHD HIS CRAWLING LENGTH	110	TIRIEL 8	33
AT LENGTH TREMBLING THE VISION SIGHING IN A LOW VOICE . . .	140	FRENCH REVOLTN	136
CHOOSING FORMS OF WORSHIP FROM POETIC TALES AND AT LENGTH	153B	MARRIAGE HH 11	PROSE
ALL HIS SLIMY LENGTH HE DREW	163	I SAW CHAPEL/N	12
THE SPECTRE GLOWD HIS HORRID LENGTH STAINING THE TEMPLE	198	AMERICA 5	6
LONG			
THY MOTHER LAYS HER LENGTH OUTSTRETCHD UPON THE SHORE	199	AMERICA 9	25
BENEATH			
AT LENGTH FOR HATCHING RIPE HE BREAKS THE SHELL	209C	FOR CHILDRN/GP	TITLE
AT LENGTH IN TEARS & CRIES IMBODIED	231	URIZEN 18	6
THAT STRETCHES OUT ITS SHADY LENGTH ALONG THE ISLAND WHITE	241	EUROPE 10	3
OF LIGHT SILENT THE PRINCE OF LIGHT VIEWD LOS AT LENGTH	273	FOUR ZOAS 1	321
A BROODED			
TO TAKE THE LIMBS OF MAN AT LENGTH EMERGING FROM THE SMOKE	296	FOUR ZOAS 3	158
MANY IN SERPENTS & IN WORMS STRETCHD OUT ENORMOUS LENGTH	314	FOUR ZOAS 6	* 117
. . . SOMETIMES STRETCHD OUT IN [LENGTH] HEIGHTH . . .	315	FOUR ZOAS 6	122
SOMETIMES IN [BREADTH] LENGTH SOMETIMES ENGLOBING . . .	315	FOUR ZOAS 6	123
SITTING UPON [HIS] AN IRON CRAG AT LENGTH HIS WORDS BROKE	321	FOUR ZOAS 7	43
FORTH			
HE KNEW THAT WEAKNESS STRETCHES OUT IN BREADTH & LENGTH	324	FOUR ZOAS 7	161
HE KNEW			
INVISIBLE OR VISIBLE DRAWN OUT IN LENGTH OR STRETCHD IN	338	FOUR ZOAS 7B	* 222
BREADTH			
EXUDED ROUND HIS AWFUL LIMBS STRETCHING TO SERPENT LENGTH	343	FOUR ZOAS 8	79
HERMAPHRODITIC IT AT LENGTH BECAME HIDING THE MALE . . .	343	FOUR ZOAS 8	105
NO MORE ERECT THO STRONG DRAWN OUT IN LENGTH THEY RAVIN	344	FOUR ZOAS 8	126
FLATTEN ABOVE & BENEATH & STRETCH OUT INTO BEASTIAL LENGTH	344	FOUR ZOAS 8	128
INTOLERABLE AT LENGTH AN AWFUL WONDER BURST	347	FOUR ZOAS 8	250
AT LENGTH WITH A FEEBLE CRY HE SAID	419	I SAW A MONK/N	27
AT LENGTH WITH A FEEBLE CRY HE SAID	430	GREY MONK	12
WHAT CAUSE AT LENGTH MOVD MILTON TO THIS UNEXAMPLED DEED	482	MILTON 2	* 21
MOCKING DRUIDICAL MATHEMATICAL PROPORTION OF LENGTH BREDTH	484	MILTON 4	27
HIGHTH			
AT LENGTH STANDING UPON THE GOLDEN FLOOR OF PALAMABRON . .	492	MILTON 11	34
RETAINING ONLY SATAN'S MATHEMATIC HOLINESS LENGTH BREDTH	521	MILTON 32	18
& HIGHTH			
VERY LITTLE TIME AND OF THE AIR IT GROWS YELLOW AND AT	561A	EXHIBITION ADV	PROSE
LENGTH BROWN			
AND CHANGING YELLOW AND AT LENGTH BROWN DESTROYS EVERY . .	566B	DESC CAT 2	PROSE
HIS WHOLE LENGTH PORTRAIT ON HORSEBACK AS WRITTEN	567D	DESC CAT 3	PROSE
BY CHAUCER			
I COME AT LENGTH TO THE CLERK OF OXENFORD	572B	DESC CAT 3	PROSE
DO NOT SPINDLE OUT INTO LENGTH WITHOUT STRENGTH NOR ARE	580B	DESC CAT 5	PROSE
AND LAST A MAN'S WHOLE LIFE BUT HE WILL AT LENGTH . . .	587A	CHAUCER 1	PROSE
[TILL AT LENGTH CHRISTIAN CHARITY IS HELD OUT AS A MOTIVE	595B	PUB ADDRESS/N	PROSE
TO]			
INCREASING INWARDS INTO LENGTH AND BREADTH AND HEIGHTH . .	635	JERUSALEM 14	18
AT LENGTH HE SAT ON LONDON STONE & HEARD JERUSALEM'S VOICE	657	JERUSALEM 31	43
AND ACCIDENT & CHANCE WERE FOUND HIDDEN IN LENGTH BREDTH	663	JERUSALEM 36	35
& HIGHTH			
AND LENGTH BREDTH HIGHTH AGAIN OBEY THE DIVINE VISION	664	JERUSALEM 36	56
HALLELUJAH			
AMONG REARED ROCKS OF ALBION'S SONS AT LENGTH THEY ROSE	673	JERUSALEM 43	82
THEY WEPT INTO THE DEEPS A LITTLE SPACE AT LENGTH WAS HEARD	675	JERUSALEM 44	43
INVISIBLE OR VISIBLE STRETCHD OUT IN LENGTH OR SPREAD IN	723	JERUSALEM 80	54
BREADTH			
AND FRAMED THE MUNDANE SHELL CAVERNOUS IN LENGTH BREDTH	740	JERUSALEM 92	27
& HIGHTH			
AT LENGTH FOR HATCHING RIPE HE BREAKS THE SHELL	765B	FOR SEXES/GP	TITLE
AT LENGTH WHEN I HAD GOT HIM TO WHERE HE WAS QUARTERD . .	827B	LETTER 28	PROSE
SO LARGE AS TO OCCUPY THE WHOLE LENGTH OF HIS WORKSHOP . .	831B	LETTER 31	PROSE
I HAVE AT LENGTH SEEN MR HOARE AFTER HAVING REPEATEDLY . .	842B	LETTER 42	PROSE

		PAGE	TITLE	LINE

LENGTH   (CONTINUED)
    I AT LENGTH SEND THE BOOKS WHICH I HAVE IN VAIN CALLD FOR   856A LETTER 54   PROSE
    & AT LENGTH PRODUCD THE FOLLOWING . . . .   860B LETTER 56   PROSE
    WHEN AT LENGTH WE FOUND THAT WE WERE ALL THREE PROCEEDING   869C LETTER 70   PROSE
    "AT LENGTH FOR HATCHING RIPE HE BREAKS THE SHELL" DRYDEN   SUPP LEGEND/N68   *
LENGTHEND
    MIDAS THE PRAISE HATH GAIND OF LENGTHEND [CARES] EARS . .   14 IMIT SPEN/PS   15
LENGTHNING
    LENGTHNING INTO A HUNGRY BEAM SWIFTLY . . . .   249 AHANIA 2   19
LENT
    WHICH I AM NOW ENGRAVING & WHICH WAS LENT BY MR LONG   . . 838D LETTER 37   PROSE
    TWELVE GUINEAS WHICH YOU LENT ME WHEN I MADE UP . . . .   854D LETTER 53   PROSE
LEO
    LEO X WAS ADVISED NOT TO ENCOURAGE THE ARTS . . . . .   452C ANNO REYNOLDS   MARG
LEOPARD
    TREMBLE THE LION SHUDDERING ASKS THE LEOPARD FEELEST THOU   358 FOUR ZOAS 9   56
    LAY THEM ON SKINS OF TYGERS OR THE SPOTTED LEOPARD OR WILD   377 FOUR ZOAS 9   746
        ASS
    LAY THEM ON SKINS OF TYGERS & OF THE SPOTTED LEOPARD &   513 MILTON 27   6
        THE WILD ASS
LEOPARDS
    LEOPARDS TYGERS PLAY . . . .   113 LIT GRL LST/SI   41
    AND THE LEOPARDS COVERD WITH SKINS OF BEASTS TENDED THE   281 FOUR ZOAS 2   33
        ROARING FIRES
LEPER
    A COLD LEPER THOU SHALT BE . . . .   754 EV GOSPEL(E)/N   34
LEPROSY
    AND THE LEPROSY LONDON'S SPIRIT SICKENING ALL THEIR BANDS   202 AMERICA 15   3
    THE ANCIENT LEPROSY . . . .   354 FOUR ZOAS 8   498
LEPROUS
    ABOVE ALL HEAVENS IN THUNDERS WRAPD EMERGD HIS LEPROUS HEAD   203 AMERICA 16   3
    LEPROUS HIS LIMBS ALL OVER WHITE AND HOARY WAS HIS VISAGE   203 AMERICA 16   11
    AND THEN THEY SENT JEHOVAH WHO LEPROUS STRETCHD HIS HAND   351 FOUR ZOAS 8   405
        TO ETERNITY
    AND JEHOVAH WAS LEPROUS LOUD HE CALLD STRETCHING HIS HAND   494 MILTON 13   24
        TO ETERNITY
    HE CHOKES UP THE PATHS OF THE SKY THE MOON IS LEPROUS AS   703 JERUSALEM 66   78
        SNOW
    SCATTERING HER LEPROUS SNOWS IN FLAKES OF DISEASE OVER   703 JERUSALEM 66   80
        ALBION
    BECAME LEPROUS & WHITE AS SNOW . . . .   818 HAPPINESS/L   74
LESS
    AND NO LESS GLORIOUS THAN THOSE OF WAR . . . . . .   19 EDW THIRD/PS 2   19
    [IS IN THE POT] A MIRACLE NO LESS CAN SET ME RIGHT . .   41C THEN SHE BORE   PROSE
    WITHOUT THESE ?IS ?TO BE LESS ?THAN MAN MAN COULD XXX .   89B ANNO SWED LOVE * MARG
    MUCH LESS CAN INTELLECT TEACH AFFECTION HOW FOOLISH THEN   93A ANNO SWED LOVE   MARG
    LESS THAN ALL CANNOT SATISFY MAN . . . .   97D NAT RELIGION 2   PROSE
    WHILE IT PRODUCES WORKS AT LESS THAN ONE FOURTH OF THE   207B PRSPECTUS 1793   PROSE
        EXPENSE
    ATTEMPTING TO BE MORE THAN MAN WE BECOME LESS SAID LUVAH   376 FOUR ZOAS 9   709
    THAT MANKIND ARE IN A LESS DISTINGUISHED SITUATION . . .   388D ANNO WATSON   MARG
    LET NOT THAT NATION WHERE LESS THAN NOBILITY IS THE REWARD   446D ANNO REYNOLDS   MARG
    EVERY TIME LESS THAN A PULSATION OF THE ARTERY . . .   516 MILTON 28   62
    LESS BUT I DARE SAY THAT CHAUCER . . . .   572A DESC CAT 3   PROSE
    IS NO LESS SACRED THAN THAT OF THE JEWS THEY ARE THE   .   578D DESC CAT 5   PROSE
    THE MORE PERFECT THE WORK OF ART AND THE LESS KEEN AND   585B DESC CAT 15   PROSE
        SHARP
    KNIGHT WHOSE SOLEMN GALLANTRY NO LESS FIXES ATTENTION   .   588C CHAUCER/N   PROSE
    IS WORTHY OF NOTICE MUCH LESS THAT SUCH AN ART SHOULD BE   597B PUB ADDRESS/N   PROSE
        THE
    ARE LESS PERMANENT THAN A SHADOW AS WE ALL KNOW TOO WELL   605A V LAST JUDG/N   PROSE
    OF ITS EVER EXISTENT IMAGES IS CONSIDERD AS LESS PERMANENT   605B V LAST JUDG/N   PROSE
    INSIGNIFICANT MUCH LESS AN INSIGNIFICANT BLUR OR MARK   .   611C V LAST JUDG/N   PROSE
    IS NO LESS AN AGENT OF RELIGION THAN HE WHO IS IN IT   .   613A V LAST JUDG/N   PROSE
    EVERY THING IS CONDUCTED BY SPIRITS NO LESS THAN DIGESTION   621C JERUSALEM 3   PROSE
        OR SLEEP
    OTHER DAUGHTERS OF LOS LABOURING AT LOOMS LESS FINE . . .   692 JERUSALEM 59   45
    WAS HE THEN IDLE OR THE LESS . . . .   752 EV GOSPEL(D)/N   53
    THE UNPRODUCTIVE MAN IS NOT A CHRISTIAN MUCH LESS   777D INSC LAOCOON   PROSE
        THE DESTROYER
    WHOM I HAVE STUDIED NO LESS THAN RAFAEL & MICHAEL ANGELO   792C LETTER 4   PROSE
    & I CANNOT AFFORD TO DO IT FOR LESS I HAD TWELVE FOR THE   794B LETTER 5   PROSE
        HEAD
    SUCCESS IS NOT THE LESS TO BE REMEMBERD BY ME WITH   794D LETTER 6   PROSE
        GRATITUDE
    WAIT FOR LESS HURRIED MOMENTS OUR COTTAGE LOOKS MORE & MORE 806A LETTER 16   PROSE
    BE NO LESS FAVOURD THO THEY ARE ROUGH LIKE BOUGH SAILORS   807A LETTER 17   PROSE
    AND MINE NO LESS HAPPY IN HIS FRIENDSHIP AND IN THAT OF HIS 807B LETTER 17   PROSE
    WE EAT LITTLE WE DRINK LESS . . . .   818 HAPPINESS/L   63
    HAVE LEARND TO VALUE BY ABSENCE NO LESS PERHAPS THAN WE DID 824B LETTER 27   PROSE
    ROMNEY'S GENIUS NOTHING LESS THAN SOME . . . . . .   848A LETTER 45   PROSE
    IN THE HIGHLY FINISHED MANNER & (FOUR) IN A LESS FINISHD   848B LETTER 45   PROSE
    HIGHLY LABOURD PLATES THAN A GREATER NUMBER & LESS FINISHD   860C LETTER 56   PROSE
    NO LESS THAN THE NEWTONIAN WHO READS NOT & CANNOT READ .   865B LETTER 62   PROSE
LESSENED
    IS IMPROVED THE LIP I HAVE AGAIN LESSENED AS YOU ADVISED   797A LETTER 9   PROSE
LESSER
    LESSER CIRCLE POINT OF THE UNIVERSE CANTO ELEVENTH LINE...   786A ILLS DANTE 101 PROSE
LESSON
    IN OUR DIVINE MASTER YOU ARE TO ME A LESSON OF HUMILITY   822B LETTER 26   PROSE
LESSONS
    PICKD UP BUT WHAT I HAVE CONCLUDED FROM YOUR LESSONS   . .   20 EDW THIRD/PS 2   40

		PAGE	TITLE	LINE

LESSONS   (CONTINUED)
       GIVE ANY LESSONS OF CHASTITY   . . . . 753 EV GOSPEL(E)/N   2
       GIVE ANY LESSONS OF PHILOSOPHY . . . . 756 EV GOSPEL(H)/N   2
LEST
     THEN CHERISH PITY LEST YOU DRIVE AN ANGEL FROM YOUR DOOR   59 HOLY THURS/IM   18
     REPLY NOT LEST I BIND THEE WITH THE GREEN FLAGS OF THE   104 TIRIEL 4   24
       BROOK
     TO BEAR ME FURTHER URGE ME NOT LEST I SHOULD DIE   104 TIRIEL 4   33
       WITH TRAVEL
     THEN CHERISH PITY LEST YOU DRIVE AN ANGEL FROM YOUR DOOR   122 HOLY THURS/SI   12
     CREATING SPACES LEST THEY FALL INTO ETERNAL DEATH   . . .   267 FOUR ZOAS 1   100
     [TO SMITE ME WITH THY TONGUE BEWARE LEST I STING ALSO THEE]   268 FOUR ZOAS 1   148
     LEST LOS SHOULD ENTER INTO BEULAH THRO HER BEAUTIFUL GATES   279 FOUR ZOAS 1   566
     PERMITTED ALL LEST MAN SHOULD FALL INTO ETERNAL DEATH   .   287 FOUR ZOAS 2   262
     LEST THE STATE CALLD LUVAH SHOULD CEASE & THE DIVINE VISION   287 FOUR ZOAS 2   264
     LISTEN TO HER WHO LOVES THEE LEST WE ALSO ARE DRIVEN AWAY   294 FOUR ZOAS 3   92
     BEWARE LEST WE ALSO DRINK UP THEE ROUGH DEMON OF THE WATERS   298 FOUR ZOAS 4   37
     LEST HE SHOULD RISE AGAIN FROM DEATH IN ALL HIS [DISMAL]   300 FOUR ZOAS 4 * 121
       DREARY POWER
     LEST DEATH ETERNAL SHOULD BE THE RESULT . . . .   319 FOUR ZOAS 6   283
     SET OVER THIS SWEET BOY OF MINE TO GUARD HIM LEST HE REND   326 FOUR ZOAS 7   232
     LEST ANY SHOULD IN FUTURITY DO AS WE HAVE DONE IN HEAVEN   331 FOUR ZOAS 7   430
     THE EYES BEHELD THE ABYSS LEST BONES OF SOLIDNESS FREEZE   482 MILTON 3   15
       OVER ALL
     PALAMABRON FEARD TO BE ANGRY LEST SATAN SHOULD ACCUSE HIM   486 MILTON 7   13
       OF
     BUT LOS HID THULLOH FROM HER SIGHT LEST SHE SHOULD DIE   488 MILTON 8   41
       OF GRIEF
     LEST THE LAST JUDGMENT COME & FIND ME UNANNIHILATE   . . .   495 MILTON 14   23
     TERROR UPON THEE BEHOLD HOW I AM & TREMBLE LEST THOU ALSO   499 MILTON 18   27
     IN THE STILL NIGHT FEARING LEST THEY SHOULD OTHERS MOLEST   504 MILTON 21   27
     AND GRACES LEST THEY WRITE THEM IN THEIR BOOKS & IN THE   507 MILTON 23   41
       SCROLL
     LEST WE ARE VEGETATED FOR CATHEDRON'S LOOMS WEAVE ONLY   509 MILTON 24   35
       DEATH
     FORTH IN YOUR WRATH LEST YOU ALSO ARE VEGETATED BY TIRZAH   511 MILTON 25   58
     LEST THOSE THREE HEAVENS OF BEULAH SHOULD THE CREATION   512 MILTON 26   20
       DESTROY
     AND LEST THEY SHOULD DESCEND BEFORE THE NORTH & SOUTH GATES   512 MILTON 26   21
     LEST HE SHOULD FALL APART IN HIS ETERNAL DEATH TO IMITATE   531 MILTON 39   26
     LEST THEY BE ANNIHILATED IN THY ANNIHILATION   . . . . .   532 MILTON 40   16
     LEST THEIR VIRTUE SHOULD BE PUT TO THE ROUT   . . . . .   545 COSWAY FRAZR/N   6
     DARE NOT APPROACH THE DAUGHTERS OPENLY LEST HE BE CONSUMED   638 JERUSALEM 17   7
     BE LOST & LEST HE SHOULD DEVOUR ENITHARMON AH ME . . . .   638 JERUSALEM 17   18
     LEST BABYLON WITH CRUEL OG   . . . .   650 FIELDS FROM/J   22
     AND FEET LEST ANY SHOULD ENTER HIS BOSOM & EMBRACE   . . .   664 JERUSALEM 38   2
     LEST HE SHOULD SLAY JERUSALEM IN HIS FEARFUL JEALOUSY   .   675 JERUSALEM 45   27
     BUT HE SPOKE NOT TO ALBION FEARING LEST ALBION SHOULD   711 JERUSALEM 71   58
       TURN HIS BACK
     AND ON HIS ANVILS LEST THEY DESTROY THE FEMININE AFFECTIONS   719 JERUSALEM 78   8
     WITHIN MY BOSOM LEST HE ARISE TO LIFE & SLAY MY LUVAH   . .   722 JERUSALEM 80   29
     LEST HAND THE TERRIBLE DESTROY HIS AFFECTION THOU HIDEST   727 JERUSALEM 83   30
       HER
     A ROUND WOMB BENEATH MY BOSOM LEST I ALSO BE OVERWOVEN   . . 732 JERUSALEM 87   14
     LEST THE SEXUAL GENERATION SWALLOW UP REGENERATION   . . .   737 JERUSALEM 90   37
     LEST THE SEXUAL GARMENTS SWEET   . . . .   771 OF GATES/GP   23
LET
     AND LET THY HOLY FEET VISIT OUR CLIME   . . . .   1 TO SPRING/PS   8
     COME OER THE EASTERN HILLS AND LET OUR WINDS   . . . . .   1 TO SPRING/PS   9
     KISS THY PERFUMED GARMENTS LET US TASTE   . . . .   1 TO SPRING/PS   10
     IN TIMELY SLEEP LET THY WEST WIND SLEEP ON   . . . . .   3 EVNING STAR/PS   8
     AWAKE THE DAWN THAT SLEEPS IN HEAVEN LET LIGHT   . . . .   3 TO MORNING/PS   3
     LET WINDS AND TEMPESTS BEAT . . . .   7 MY SILKS/PS   16
     LET GWIN BE HUMBLED   . . . .   11 GWIN KING/PS   12
     LET GWIN BE HUMBLED   . . . .   12 GWIN KING/PS   30
     THEY CRY AND LET TEN THOUSAND LIVES   . . . .   12 GWIN KING/PS   31
     LET RAYS OF TRUTH ENLIGHT HIS SLEEPING BRAIN   . . . . .   14 IMIT SPEN/PS   9
     LET LIBERTY THE CHARTERD RIGHT OF ENGLISHMEN   . . . . .   18 EDW THIRD/PS 1   9
     ENERVE MY SOLDIERS LET LIBERTY   . . . .   18 EDW THIRD/PS 1 11
     NOW LET US TAKE A JUST REVENGE FOR THOSE   . . . . . .   18 EDW THIRD/PS 1 43
     LET THEM BUT SUFFER AWHILE AND YOU SHALL SEE   . . . . .   20 EDW THIRD/PS 2 75
     LET US NOT FEAR TO BEAT ROUND NATURE'S WILDS   . . . . .   27 EDW THIRD/PS 3 263
     LET THOSE THAT FIGHT FIGHT IN GOOD STEDFASTNESS   . . . .   31 EDW THIRD/PS 5 37
     STOP BRAVE SIR WALTER LET ME DROP A TEAR   . . . . . .   31 EDW THIRD/PS 5 49
     THEN LET THE CLARION OF WAR BEGIN   . . . .   31 EDW THIRD/PS 5 50
     WELL LET THE TRUMPET SOUND AND THE DRUM BEAT   . . . . .   31 EDW THIRD/PS 5 62
     LET WAR STAIN THE BLUE HEAVENS WITH BLOODY BANNERS   . . .   31 EDW THIRD/PS 5 63
     AND LET THY MASTER DO THE DEED ONE BLOW OF THAT STRONG ARM 38C SAMSON/PS   PROSE
     LET US DETAIN THEE WHILE I MAKE READY A KID THAT   40B SAMSON/PS   PROSE
       THOU MAYEST
     I WON'T LET IT GO AT ONLY SO & SO   . . . .   46 PHEBUS CAME/IM   5
     HANG THAT SAID SUCTION LET US HAVE A SONG   . . . . . .   50B ISLAND MOON 6 PROSE
     SHE WOULD NOT LET HIM SUCK   . . . .   50 WHEN CORRUP/IM   12
     LET YOUR BOUNTY DESCEND TO OUR FAIR EARS   . . . . . .   55C ISLAND MOON 9 PROSE
     & LET OUT THE PESTILENCE   . . . .   58D ISLAND MOON 10 PROSE
     [LET CHERUBIM & SERAPHIM NOW RAISE THEIR VOICES HIGH]   .   59 HOLY THURS/IM   14
     COME COME LEAVE OFF PLAY & LET US AWAY   . . . .   60 NURSES SONG/IM   7
     NO NO LET US PLAY FOR IT IS YET DAY   . . . .   60 NURSES SONG/IM   9
     ("THE CENTRE") LET ME REFER HERE TO A REMARK ON APHORISM... 65C ANNO LAVATER MARG
     LET THE MEN DO THEIR DUTY & THE WOMEN WILL BE SUCH WONDERS 82C ANNO LAVATER MARG
     BY REASON OF ITS BEING UNITED WITH HYPOCRISY BUT LET THEM   85C ANNO LAVATER MARG
     ("THE PUBLIC SELDOM FORGIVE TWICE ") LET US TAKE THEIR   85D ANNO LAVATER MARG
       EXAMPLE

1071

	PAGE	TITLE	LINE

LET (CONTINUED)

FOR LET IT BE REMEMBERD THAT CREATION IS . . . . . 87B ANNO LAVATER MARG
OLD CRUELTY DESIST & LET US DIG A GRAVE FOR THEE . . . . 100 TIRIEL 1 36
AND NOW YOU FEEL IT DIG A GRAVE & LET US BURY OUR MOTHER 100 TIRIEL 1 42
LET NO ONE FEAR FOR POOR BLIND TIRIEL HURTS NONE 101 TIRIEL 2 14
  BUT HIMSELF
THEN LET THY NAME BE TIRIEL & NEVER LEAVE US MORE . . . 102 TIRIEL 3 16
BUT DWELL WITH US & LET US BE TO THEE INSTEAD OF EYES . 103 TIRIEL 3 34
TO THRUST THESE TOWERS WITH HIS SHOULDERS LET HIS FIERY 106 TIRIEL 5 6
  DOGS
RISE UP THY SLUGGISH LIMBS & LET THE LOATHSOMEST OF POISONS 106 TIRIEL 5 9
HERE TAKE THY SEAT IN THIS WIDE COURT LET IT BE STROWN 106 TIRIEL 5 11
  WITH DEAD
AND LET THE CURSE FALL ON THE REST & WRAP THEM UP TOGETHER 106 TIRIEL 5 25
LET SNAKES RISE FROM THY BEDDED LOCKS & LAUGH AMONG THY 108 TIRIEL 6 43
  CURLS
THEN LET LYCA WAKE . . . . 113 LIT GRL LST/SI 26
LET THY MOON ARISE . . . . 113 LIT GRL LST/SI 31
COME COME LEAVE OFF PLAY AND LET US AWAY . . . . . . 121 NURSES SONG/SI 7
NO NO LET US PLAY FOR IT IS YET DAY . . . . 121 NURSES SONG/SI 9
LET ME PULL . . . . 123 SPRING/SI 23
LET ME KISS . . . . 123 SPRING/SI 25
. . . WE ARE NOT NUMBERED AMONG THE LIVING LET US HIDE . 137 FRENCH REVOLTN 76
LET US HIDE LET US HIDE IN THE DUST . . . 137 FRENCH REVOLTN 78
. . . AND LET THY SOUL DRINK OF MY COUNSEL . . . . . 140 FRENCH REVOLTN 128
LET THY SOLDIERS POSSESS THIS CITY OF REBELS . . . . . 141 FRENCH REVOLTN 155
. . . LET THE BASTILE DEVOUR . . . . 141 FRENCH REVOLTN 156
LET THE NATION'S AMBASSADOR COME AMONG NOBLES . . . . . 143 FRENCH REVOLTN 197
BREATHE FIRES BUT TEN MILES FROM PARIS LET ALL BE PEACE 145 FRENCH REVOLTN 240
. . .
. . . BUT IF IT REFUSE LET THE NATION'S ASSEMBLY THENCE 145 FRENCH REVOLTN 253
  LEARN
LET MAN WEAR THE FELL OF THE LION WOMAN THE FLEECE OF THE 151C MARRIAGE HH 8 PROSE
  SHEEP
BUT WHEN HE HAS DONE THIS LET HIM NOT SAY THAT HE KNOWS 158A MARRIAGE HH 21 PROSE
LET THE PRIESTS OF THE RAVEN OF DAWN NO LONGER IN DEADLY 160A SONG LIBERTY PROSE
  BLACK
LET AGE & SICKNESS SILENT ROB . . . . 172 ARE NOT JOYS/N 5
LET HIM LAUGH LET HIM CRY . . . . 178 THE FAIRY/N 17
BUT IF ONCE YOU LET THE RIPE MOMENT GO . . . . . . 179 IF YOU TRAP/N 3
LET THE BROTHELS OF PARIS BE OPENED . . . . 185 LET BROTHELS/N 1
AND LET THE JEALOUS DOLPHINS SPORT AROUND THE LOVELY MAID 190 V DAU ALBION 1 19
I KNOW THEE I HAVE FOUND THEE & I WILL NOT LET THEE GO . 196 AMERICA PREL 2 7
LET THE SLAVE GRINDING AT THE MILL RUN OUT INTO THE FIELD 198 AMERICA 6 6
LET HIM LOOK UP INTO THE HEAVENS & LAUGH IN THE BRIGHT AIR 198 AMERICA 6 7
LET THE INCHAINED SOUL SHUT UP IN DARKNESS AND IN SIGHING 198 AMERICA 6 8
AND LET HIS WIFE AND CHILDREN RETURN FROM THE OPRESSOR'S 198 AMERICA 6 * 11
  SCOURGE
LET EACH CHUSE ONE HABITATION . . . . 224 URIZEN 4 36
LET CORDS & STAKES BIND IN THE VOID . . . . . . 231 URIZEN 19 3
AND LET US LAUGH AT WAR . . . . 239 EUROPE 4 21
LET HIM CALL IN VAIN . . . . 243 EUROPE 13 17
AGAINST ONE ANOTHER SO LET THEM WAR ON SLAVES TO 245 SONG OF LOS 3 14
  THE ETERNAL ELEMENTS
LET HER LAY SECRET IN THE SOFT RECESS OF DARKNESS & SILENCE 265 FOUR ZOAS 1 30
TO MAKE US HAPPY [HOW THEY] LET THEM WEARY THEIR IMMORTAL 271 FOUR ZOAS 1 254
  POWERS
LET US REFUSE THE PLOW & SPADE THE HEAVY ROLLER & SPIKED 274 FOUR ZOAS 1 387
WITH WINE OF CRUELTY LET US [LIGHT] PLAT A SCOURGE O SISTER 275 FOUR ZOAS 1 * 399
  CITY
REPOSD ON BEDS LET THEM SLEEP ON DO THOU ALONE DEPART . . 277 FOUR ZOAS 1 489
ROARING LET OUT THE FLUID THE MOLTEN METAL RAN IN CHANNELS 283 FOUR ZOAS 2 118
SET STATIONS ON THIS BREEDING EARTH & LET US BUY & SELL 283 FOUR ZOAS 2 129
LOS JOYD & ENITHARMON LAUGHD SAYING LET US GO DOWN . . . 285 FOUR ZOAS 2 211
AND MANY A DIVISION LET IN & OUT INTO THE VAST UNKNOWN . . 286 FOUR ZOAS 2 244
O THARMAS DO NOT THOU DESTROY ME QUITE BUT LET . . . . 296 FOUR ZOAS 3 184
BE NEAR THEE LOVED TERROR LET ME STILL REMAIN & THEN DO 296 FOUR ZOAS 3 186
  THOU
THY RIGHTEOUS DOOM UPON ME ONLY LET ME HEAR THY VOICE . . 296 FOUR ZOAS 3 187
A UNIVERSE OF DEATH & DECAY LET ENITHARMON'S HANDS . . . 298 FOUR ZOAS 4 28
AND TWANG THE BOWSTRING TO OUR HOWLINGS LET THINE ARROWS 306 FOUR ZOAS 5 51
  BLACK
LET LOOSE THE ENORMOUS SPIRIT IN THE DARKNESS OF THE DEEP 306 FOUR ZOAS 5 * 59
QUEEN OF THESE DREADFUL RIVERS SPEAK & LET ME HEAR THY 312 FOUR ZOAS 6 19
  VOICE
OR DRAWN UP OR LET DOWN AT THE WILL OF THE IMMORTAL MAN 318 FOUR ZOAS 6 255
THE BREAD IS KNEADED LET US REST O CRUEL FATHER OF CHILDREN 322 FOUR ZOAS 7 107
SO SHALL (?YOU) GOVERN OVER ALL LET MORAL DUTY TUNE YOUR 323 FOUR ZOAS 7 * 111
  TONGUE
AND LET HIM HAVE DOMINION OVER LOS THE TERRIBLE SHADE . . 323 FOUR ZOAS 7 116
AND WHEN HIS CHILDREN SICKEN LET THEM DIE THERE ARE ENOUGH 323 FOUR ZOAS 7 120
WITHOUT THE FOOD OF LIFE LET US CREATE THEM (COUNTERPARTS) 330 FOUR ZOAS 7 409
COME HITHER BE PATIENT LET US CONVERSE TOGETHER BECAUSE 330 FOUR ZOAS 7 422
AND LET THE THUNDRING DRUM SPEED ON THE ARROWS BLACK . 337 FOUR ZOAS 7B * 158
[BUT ?IN] BUT URIZEN HIS MIGHTY RAGE LET LOOSE IN THE MID 343 FOUR ZOAS 8 * 90
  DEEP
PITY ME LOS PITY ME URIZEN & [BUILD] LET US BUILD . . 349 FOUR ZOAS 8 333
AND LET ALL NATIONS [IN] OF THE EARTH WORSHIP AT 349 FOUR ZOAS 8 * 336
  THE SEPULCHER
THE SPECTRE OF ENITHARMON LET LOOSE ON THE TROUBLED DEEP 358 FOUR ZOAS 9 24
SAYING LET US GO UP FAR FOR SOON I SMELL UPON THE WIND . . 358 FOUR ZOAS 9 61
LET US FLEE ALSO TO THE NORTH THEY FLED THE SONS OF MEN 359 FOUR ZOAS 9 64

LET   (CONTINUED)

LIE DOWN BEFORE MY FEET O DRAGON LET URIZEN ARISE . . . 360 FOUR ZOAS 9   139
LET LUVAH RAGE IN THE DARK DEEP EVEN TO CONSUMMATION . 360 FOUR ZOAS 9   142
LET ORC CONSUME LET THARMAS RAGE LET DARK URTHONA GIVE 362 FOUR ZOAS 9   184
ALL STRENGTH TO LOS & ENITHARMON & LET LOS SELF CURSD . 362 FOUR ZOAS 9   185
ALL SPIRITS DECEASD LET LOOSE FROM REPTILE PRISONS COME 363 FOUR ZOAS 9   235
    IN SHOALS
GO ON THY COURSE REJOICING & LET US BOTH REJOICE TOGETHER 368 FOUR ZOAS 9   424
AND LET ME TOUCH YOUR WOOLY BACKS FOLLOW ME AS I SING . 368 FOUR ZOAS 9   * 432
COVER US FROM THE SUN COME & LET US SIT IN THE SHADE . 369 FOUR ZOAS 9   450
AND SAID LET A PLEASANT HOUSE ARISE TO BE THE DWELLING 369 FOUR ZOAS 9   459
    PLACE
AWAKE O ENION AWAKE & LET THINE INNOCENT EYES . . . . 371 FOUR ZOAS 9   519
O MY SWEET CHILDREN ENION LET THARMAS KISS THY CHEEK . 371 FOUR ZOAS 9   525
ARISE SWEET BOY & LET US FOLLOW THE PATH OF ENION . . 371 FOUR ZOAS 9   534
LET THE SLAVE GRINDING AT THE MILL RUN OUT INTO THE FIELD 375 FOUR ZOAS 9   670
LET HIM LOOK UP INTO THE HEAVENS & LAUGH IN THE BRIGHT AIR 375 FOUR ZOAS 9   671
LET THE INCHAIND SOUL SHUT UP IN DARKNESS & IN SIGHING . . 375 FOUR ZOAS 9   * 672
AND LET HIS WIFE & CHILDREN RETURN FROM THE OPRESSOR'S 375 FOUR ZOAS 9   675
    SCOURGE
LET THE BULLS OF LUVAH TREAD THE CORN & DRAW THE LOADED 376 FOUR ZOAS 9   701
    WAGGON
THO PAINED TO DISTRACTION CRY O LET US EXIST FOR . . . 376 FOUR ZOAS 9   738
ETERNAL DEATH WHO CAN ENDURE LET US CONSUME IN FIRES . 377 FOUR ZOAS 9   740
LET THE BISHOP PROVE THAT HE HAS . . . . 387C ANNO WATSON   MARG
LET ALL THEIR WORKS WITNESS . . . . 388D ANNO WATSON   MARG
SUCH A THING SHALL HAPPEN LET YOU DO WHAT YOU WILL . . 392B ANNO WATSON   MARG
CONTEMPTIBLE KNAVE LET THE PEOPLE LOOK TO THIS . . . 403A ANNO BACON   MARG
LET US AGREE TO GIVE UP LOVE . . . . 417 MY SPECTRE/N   67
AND LET US GO TO THE HIGHEST DOWNS . . . . 417 MY SPECTR AD/N * 13
[THEY WOULD LET THEM DOWN AT WILL] . . . . 422 BENEATH AD/N   3
LET THERE BE FIRST A DRAWING MADE . . . . 440B MEMORANDUM/N 2   PROSE
CORRECTLY WITH BLACK LEAD PENCIL LET NOTHING BE TO SEEK 440B MEMORANDUM/N 2   PROSE
LET NOT THAT NATION WHERE LESS THAN NOBILITY IS THE REWARD 446D ANNO REYNOLDS MARG
BESIDES LET THEM LOOK AT GOTHIC FIGURES & GOTHIC BUILDINGS 461A ANNO REYNOLDS MARG
OF EXECUTION IN ART LET HIM WHO WILL FOLLOW SUCH ADVICE 461C ANNO REYNOLDS MARG
ITSELF LET IT BE PAINTED [& PRAISED] & PATCHD & PRAISED 466A ANNO REYNOLDS * MARG
SO LOS SAID HENCEFORTH PALAMABRON LET EACH HIS OWN STATION 487 MILTON 7   43
THERE IS NO OTHER LET ALL OBEY MY PRINCIPLES OF MORAL 490 MILTON 9   26
    INDIVIDUALITY
LET THE BARD HIMSELF WITNESS WHERE HADST THOU THIS TERRIBLE 495 MILTON 13   50
    SONG
LET HER BE OFFERD UP TO HOLINESS TIRZAH NUMBERS HER . . . 501 MILTON 19   48
AND LET US BIND THEE IN THE BANDS OF WAR & BE THOU KING 501 MILTON 20   5
AND OLOLON SAID LET US DESCEND ALSO AND LET US GIVE . . 504 MILTON 21   45
OR ARE THESE THE PANGS OF REPENTANCE LET US ENTER INTO THEM 504 MILTON 21   50
WILL UNCHAIN ORC & LET LOOSE SATAN OG SIHON & ANAK . . . 505 MILTON 22   33
OF WAR & RELIGION LET US DESCEND & BRING HIM CHAINED . 507 MILTON 23   17
LET IT NOT BE SO NOW O GO NOT FORTH IN MARTYRDOMS & WARS 507 MILTON 23   49
LOUD ROLL THE WEIGHTS & SPINDLES OVER THE WHOLE EARTH LET 525 MILTON 35   14
    DOWN
LET THE FOUR ZOAS AWAKE FROM SLUMBERS OF SIX THOUSAND YEARS 530 MILTON 39   13
[LET IT BE TOLD] . . . . 547 LET BE TOLD/N   1
SO EEN LET IGNORANCE DO IT ALL . . . . 549 ENGL ENCOU/N 1   12
RATHER THAN [LET] BE SUCH A BLIND HUMAN FOOL . . . . 550 WHEN I SEE/N   7
LET THE WORKS OF MODERN ARTISTS SINCE RUBENS' TIME . . 565B DESC CAT 2   PROSE
IN THE MEANTIME LET IT BE OBSERVED THAT BEFORE VANDYKE'S 565B DESC CAT 2   PROSE
    TIME
AND SO ARE CHAUCER'S LET THEM BE SO CONSIDERED . . . 570A DESC CAT 3   PROSE
LET THE YOUNG READER STUDY WHAT HE HAS SAID OF HER . . 572B DESC CAT 3   PROSE
LET THE PHILOSOPHER ALWAYS BE THE SERVANT AND . . . . 572C DESC CAT 3   PROSE
LET THOSE WHO GOVERN THE NATION TAKE CARE OF THE OTHER . 584C DESC CAT 14   PROSE
LET THEM ENCOURAGE WHAT EXISTS ALREADY . . . . . . 597A PUB ADDRESS/N   PROSE
LET IT NO MORE BE SAID THAT EMPIRES ENCOURAGE ARTS . . 597A PUB ADDRESS/N   PROSE
LET US TEACH BUONAPARTE & WHOMSOEVER ELSE IT MAY CONCERN 597A PUB ADDRESS/N   PROSE
LET ANY MAN OF SENSE ASK HIMSELF ONE QUESTION IS THIS ART 597B PUB ADDRESS/N   PROSE
& DRYDEN HAS FINISHD IT NOW LET DRYDEN'S FALL & . . . . 600D PUB ADDRESS/N   PROSE
LET A MAN WHO HAS MADE A DRAWING GO ON & ON . . . . 603A PUB ADDR AD/N   PROSE
BETWEEN ALLEGORIC FABLE & SPIRITUAL MYSTERY LET IT HERE BE 605C V LAST JUDG/N PROSE
LET THOSE WHO THINK SO . . . . 612C V LAST JUDG/N PROSE
THE FOOL SHALL NOT ENTER INTO HEAVEN LET HIM BE EVER SO 615D V LAST JUDG/N PROSE
    HOLY
LET HIM BE OF WHAT CLASS OF ANIMALS HE WILL . . . . 616B V LAST JUDG/N PROSE
PITY LET US THEREFORE TAKE EXAMPLE & WARNING O MY SPECTRE 626 JERUSALEM 7   58
OF LOVE THOU REFUSEDST TO LET ME GO ALBION BEHELD 643 JERUSALEM 20   32
    THY BEAUTY
AWAKE ALBION AWAKE AND LET US AWAKE UP TOGETHER . . . 665 JERUSALEM 38   32
LET DOWN AT WILL AROUND AND CALLD THE UNIVERSAL TENT . . 665 JERUSALEM 38   50
LET LOOSE THE ENORMOUS SPECTRE INTO THE DARKNESS OF THE DEEP 667 JERUSALEM 40   32
YE TWENTY-FOUR INTO THE DEEPS LET US DEPART TO GLORY . . 671 JERUSALEM 42   65
SCOFELD & KOX ARE LET LOOSE UPON MY SAXONS THEY ACCUMULATE 673 JERUSALEM 43   51
TO GIVE A PLACE FOR REDEMPTION LET SIHON AND OG . . . 679 JERUSALEM 48   63
AND LET WILD SEAS & ROCKS CLOSE UP JERUSALEM AWAY FROM . . 680 JERUSALEM 49   77
TO RECORD THE SIN FOR A REPROACH TO LET THE SUN GO DOWN 681 JERUSALEM 50   27
TOGETHER INTO AN ASSEMBLY THEY SAID LET US GO DOWN . . . 686 JERUSALEM 55   4
BUT OTHERS SAID LET US TO HIM WHO ONLY IS & WHO . . . . 686 JERUSALEM 55   17
LET THE HUMAN ORGANS BE KEPT IN THEIR PERFECT INTEGRITY 686 JERUSALEM 55   36
LET THE INDEFINITE BE EXPLORED AND LET EVERY MAN BE JUDGED 687 JERUSALEM 55   57
BY HIS OWN WORKS LET ALL INDEFINITES BE THROWN INTO 687 JERUSALEM 55   58
    DEMONSTRATIONS
A SHEET & VEIL & CURTAIN OF BLOOD IS LET DOWN FROM HEAVEN 706 JERUSALEM 68   21
KINGS OF CANAAN THEN TO LET THE SPIES DEPART TO MERIBAH 707 JERUSALEM 68   61
    KADESH

		PAGE	TITLE	LINE
LET   (CONTINUED)

RETURN O ALBION LET JERUSALEM OVERSPREAD ALL NATIONS   . . 712 JERUSALEM 72   35
TEACH ME O HOLY SPIRIT THE TESTIMONY OF JESUS LET ME   . . 714 JERUSALEM 74   14
LET EVERY CHRISTIAN AS MUCH AS IN HIM LIES   . . . . . 717C JERUSALEM 77   PROSE
TEACH THEM TRUE HAPPINESS BUT LET NO CURSE   . . . . . 718 STOOD AMONG/J   32
LET US LOOK LET US EXAMINE IS THE CRUEL BECOME AN INFANT   724 JERUSALEM 81   8
I HEARD ENITHARMON SAY TO LOS LET THE DAUGHTERS OF ALBION   725 JERUSALEM 82   22
BE SCATTERD ABROAD AND LET THE NAME OF ALBION BE FORGOTTEN   725 JERUSALEM 82   23
LET ALBION REMAIN A DESOLATION WITHOUT AN INHABITANT   . . 725 JERUSALEM 82   25
AND LET THE LOOMS OF ENITHARMON & THE FURNACES OF LOS   . 725 JERUSALEM 82   26
LET US LEAD THE STEMS OF THIS TREE LET US PLANT IT BEFORE   725 JERUSALEM 82   32
    JERUSALEM
LET CAMBEL AND HER SISTERS SIT WITHIN THE MUNDANE SHELL   727 JERUSALEM 83   33
ARISE UPON THY WATCHES LET US SEE THY GLOBE OF FIRE   . . 729 JERUSALEM 84   27
ON ALBION'S ROCKS & LET THY VOICE BE HEARD UPON EUPHRATES   729 JERUSALEM 84   28
AND LET THEM RUN ON THE WINDS OF THY BOSOM I WILL FIX THEM   732 JERUSALEM 87   9
LET MAN'S DELIGHT BE LOVE BUT WOMAN'S DELIGHT BE PRIDE   732 JERUSALEM 87   16
THERE GATES OF DEATH LET IN THE DAY   . . . . 749 EV GOSPEL(B)/N   40
MARY FEAR NOT LET ME SEE   . . . . 754 EV GOSPEL(E)/N   43
WHAT WAS THY LOVE LET ME [SEE'T] SEE IT   . . . . . 755 EV GOSPEL(E)/N *   57
WHEN FIRST I LET THESE DEVILS IN   . . . . 755 EV GOSPEL(E)/N   70
VIRGIL IN THE ENEID BOOK VI LINE...SAYS "LET OTHERS STUDY   778D HOMERS POETRY   PROSE
    ART"
EVE COME AWAY & LET US NOT BELIEVE THESE VAIN DELUSIONS   780 GHOST ABEL 1   18
ADAM EVE THOU HAST SPOKEN TRULY LET US KNEEL BEFORE HIS   780 GHOST ABEL 2   3
    FEET
WHO IS THE GOD OF THIS WORLD THE ACCUSER LET HIS JUDGMENT   788A ANNO THORNTON   MARG
BUT LET OUR BIBLE BE VIRGIL & SHAKSPEARE   . . . . . 789A ANNO THORNTON   MARG
LET US SEE YOU SOMETIMES AS WELL AS SOMETIMES HEAR FROM   791C LETTER 3   PROSE
YOU & LET US OFTEN SEE YOUR WORKS   . . . . 791C LETTER 3   PROSE
PRAY LET ME INTREAT YOU TO PERSEVERE IN YOUR DESIGNING   . 795B LETTER 6   PROSE
CONTENTED LET WHAT WILL COME HAVING PASSED NOW   . . . 795C LETTER 6   PROSE
LET ME HEAR OF YOUR WELFARE REMEMBER MY & MY WIFE'S   . . . 798D LETTER 10   PROSE
NOW LET ME INTREAT YOU TO GIVE ME ORDERS TO FURNISH EVERY   808B LETTER 19   PROSE
IDLENESS ITSELF DOES NOT HURT OTHER MEN LET SATAN HIMSELF   812C LETTER 22   PROSE
    EXPLAIN
ALSO LET ME OBSERVE THAT THE YELLOW LEATHER FLESH OF OLD   815A LETTER 23   PROSE
    MEN
LET ME ALSO NOTICE THAT CARRACHE'S PICTURES ARE NOT LIKE   815B LETTER 23   PROSE
AND NOW LET ME FINISH WITH ASSURING YOU THAT THO I HAVE   815D LETTER 23   PROSE
BUT PRAY LET ME NOW HEAR HOW YOU DO & OF THE   . . . . 816A LETTER 23   PROSE
THEN FEAR NOTHING & LET MY SISTER FEAR NOTHING BECAUSE   821A LETTER 25   PROSE
& NOW I HAVE LAMENTED OVER THE DEAD HORSE LET ME LAUGH & BE 830B LETTER 30   PROSE
KILL NOT A TREE BUT IT STILL BEAR FRUIT LET NONE SAY THAT   830C LETTER 30   PROSE
FURNISHD BY JOHNSON I LET HIM RUN ON SO FAR AS TO SAY THAT   846D LETTER 44   PROSE
LET US GO ON DEAR SIR FOLLOWING HIS CROSS LET US TAKE   863B LETTER 60   PROSE
    IT UP
AT HIS HOUSE LET US ACCOMODATE HIM IN WHAT IS INDIFFERENT   868B LETTER 67   PROSE
BE TOO ILL TO LET YOU KNOW HOW I AM & WHAT I WISH   . . 871B LETTER 72   PROSE
RETURN PRAY LET YOUR OWN HEALTH & CONVENIENCE PUT ALL   . 873C LETTER 77   PROSE
PLEASE TO LET ME KNOW BUT FINDING MYSELF WELL ENOUGH TO   875B LETTER 81   PROSE
    COME

LETCHERY
LAY THE BOUND OR BUILD THE ROOF NOR PALE RELIGIOUS LETCHERY 160B SONG LIBERTY   PROSE
THAT PALE RELIGIOUS-LETCHERY SEEKING VIRGINITY   . . . . 199 AMERICA 8   10

LET'S
COME SAID THE EPICUREAN LET'S HAVE SOME RUM & WATER   . . . 49B ISLAND MOON 5   PROSE
HANG ITALIAN SONGS LET'S HAVE ENGLISH SAID QUID   . . . 56A ISLAND MOON 9   PROSE
COME FLAMMABLE SAID GIBBLE GABBLE & LET'S ENJOY OURSELVES   58C ISLAND MOON 10   PROSE
LET'S HAVE HANDEL'S WATERPIECE THEN SIPSOP SUNG   . . . . 62B ISLAND MOON 11   PROSE

LETS
IN BEULAH THE FEMALE LETS DOWN HER BEAUTIFUL TABERNACLE   656 JERUSALEM 30   34

LETTER
FALSE PHILOSOPHY ACCORDING TO THE LETTER   . . . . . . 92B ANNO SWED LOVE   MARG
THIS IS CERTAINLY NOT TO BE UNDERSTOOD ACCORDING TO THE   92D ANNO SWED LOVE   MARG
    LETTER
FOR A LETTER OF ADVICE TO A KING   . . . . 136 FRENCH REVOLTN   51
IF THIS FIRST LETTER IS WRITTEN WITHOUT RAILING &   384C ANNO WATSON   MARG
    ILLIBERALITY
THE FOLLOWING [LETTER] DISCOURSE IS PARTICULARLY   . . . . 457D ANNO REYNOLDS   * MARG
AS POETRY ADMITS NOT A LETTER THAT IS INSIGNIFICANT   . . 611B V LAST JUDG/N   PROSE
EVERY WORD AND EVERY LETTER IS STUDIED AND PUT INTO ITS   621D JERUSALEM 3   PROSE
    FIT PLACE
HE HAS SENT IT BACK WITH A LETTER FULL OF CRITICISMS   . . 794D LETTER 6   *PROSE
YOU WITH A LETTER OF MEER COMPLIMENT & EXPRESSION OF THANKS 798A LETTER 10   PROSE
YOUR VERY KIND & AFFECTIONATE LETTER & THE MANY KIND   811B LETTER 22   PROSE
    THINGS
ABOUT YOUR HEALTH IN ANOTHER PART OF YOUR LETTER MAKES ME   811C LETTER 22   PROSE
NECESSARY TO HISTORICAL BEAUTY IN A LETTER TO THE   . . . 814B LETTER 23   PROSE
AFTER I HAD FINISHD MY LETTER I FOUND THAT I HAD NOT SAID   816C LETTER 24   PROSE
TELL ME IN A LETTER OF FORGIVENESS IF YOU WERE OFFENDED &   816C LETTER 24   PROSE
P S I HAVE TAKEN THE LIBERTY TO TROUBLE YOU WITH A LETTER   819A LETTER 24   PROSE
DEAR BROTHER YOUR LETTER MENTIONING MR BUTTS'S ACCOUNT OF   819B LETTER 25   *PROSE
    MY AGUE
YOU TO KEEP IT A SECRET & TO BURN THIS LETTER BECAUSE IT   819D LETTER 25   PROSE
    SPEAKS
BUT MY LETTER TO MR BUTTS APPEARS TO ME NOT TO BE   820B LETTER 25   PROSE
    SO EXPLICIT
YOUR LETTER TO MR H(HAYLEY) &   . . . . 820D LETTER 25   PROSE
I WRITE IN HASTE HAVING RECIEVD A PRESSING LETTER FROM   . . 822B LETTER 26   PROSE
ACCEPT OF MY THANKS FOR YOUR KIND & HEARTENING LETTER   . . 822B LETTER 26   PROSE
THE CXXXIX PSALM A LITTLE BEFORE YOUR LETTER ARRIVED I TAKE 823B LETTER 26   PROSE

		PAGE	TITLE	LINE
LETTER	**(CONTINUED)**			
	VERY UNACCOUNTABLY TO COPY OUT IN MY LAST LETTER THAT PASSAGE	826C	LETTER 28	PROSE
	TO BEG OF YOU TO CAUSE THE ENCLOSD LETTER TO BE DELIVERD	829B	LETTER 28	PROSE
	MY LETTER I WILL FINISH IT WISHING YOU	830D	LETTER 30	PROSE
	VERIFIED THE MORNING AFTER I RECEIVED YOUR KIND LETTER .	831B	LETTER 31	PROSE
	I WRITE IN A VIOLENT HURRY YOUR LETTER HAS NEVER ARRIVED TO	832B	LETTER 32	PROSE
	I HAD OF THE LETTER OR OF THE DRAWING I HAVE FETCHD THE	832B	LETTER 32	PROSE
	HE PACKD UP & SENT INTO THE NORTH I SHEWD YOUR LETTER TO	834C	LETTER 34	PROSE
	MR ROMNEY IN TOWN SOON NOTE YOUR LETTER TO MR J ROMNEY .	834C	LETTER 34	PROSE
	I BEGIN WITH THE LATTER END OF YOUR LETTER & GRIEVE MORE FOR	837C	LETTER 36	PROSE
	THE PLEASURE I RECIEVD FROM YOUR KIND LETTER OUGHT TO .	838B	LETTER 37	PROSE
	I DID NOT RECIEVE YOUR LETTER TILL MONDAY OF COURSE COULD	840B	LETTER 39	PROSE
	MR DALLY TO WHOM I ENCLOSED...IN A LETTER A FORTNIGHT .	841A	LETTER 40	PROSE
	MR P(PHILLIPS) MAY NOT YET HAVE SEEN YOUR LETTER TO HIM &	842D	LETTER 42	*PROSE
	REMEMBERD TO YOU HAD BEGUN A LETTER TO YOU A WEEK AGO .	842D	LETTER 42	*PROSE
	DELIVERED THE LETTER TO MR EDWARDS WHO WILL GIVE IT . . .	845D	LETTER 44	PROSE
	SHAKESPEARE & TWO VOLS WITH A LETTER FROM MR SPILSBURY .	850B	LETTER 49	PROSE
	I RECEIVED YOUR KIND LETTER WITH THE NOTE TO MR PAYNE AND	851B	LETTER 50	PROSE
	SINCERE THANKS FOR YOUR KIND PROPOSAL IN YOUR LAST LETTER	853A	LETTER 51	*PROSE
	HE MENTIOND HIS HAVING RECIEVD A LETTER FROM YOU . . .	853A	LETTER 51	*PROSE
	I HOPE THIS LETTER WILL OUTSTRIP MR PHILLIPS' AS I SIT DOWN	857D	LETTER 55	PROSE
	APPLICATION OF THE PROFITS AS HE ON READING YOUR LETTER	858A	LETTER 55	PROSE
	THAT HE WOULD IN HIS LETTER TO YOU EXPLAIN HIS REASONS FOR	858A	LETTER 55	PROSE
	SENDS YOU IN THE SAME PACQUET WITH THE LETTER	861D	LETTER 59	PROSE
	I DO NOT PAY THE POSTAGE OF THIS LETTER BECAUSE	865B	LETTER 62	PROSE
	FROM YOU ON...(JANUARY)...THAT PART OF YOUR LETTER IN WHICH	875D	LETTER 82	PROSE
	DOUBLE OF YOUR LETTER NEVERTHELESS I OUGHT TO HAVE SENT IT	875D	LETTER 82	PROSE
	ON ACCOUNT I HAVE RECIEVD A LETTER FROM MR CUMBERLAND .	876D	LETTER 85	PROSE
LETTER-PRESS				
	INVENTED A METHOD OF PRINTING BOTH LETTER-PRESS AND ENGRAVING	207B	PRSPECTUS 1793	PROSE
LETTERS				
	THE LETTERS AND TO MAKE THEM SHINE WITH GOLD	18	EDW THIRD/PS 1	27
	THIS SHOULD BE WRITTEN IN GOLD LETTERS ON OUR TEMPLES .	66B	ANNO LAVATER	MARG
	HIS BOOK OF IRON ON HIS KNEES HE TRACD THE DREADFUL LETTERS	321	FOUR ZOAS 7	29
	IN GOLDEN LETTERS ORNAMENTED WITH SWEET LABOURS OF LOVE	340	FOUR ZOAS 7B	294
	LETTERS ARE SUCH AS DO NOTHING AGAINST PAINE'S ARGUMENTS	390C	ANNO WATSON	MARG
	WRITTEN WITHIN & WITHOUT IN WOVEN LETTERS & THE WRITING	534	MILTON 42	13
	OF THE PICTURE THE WORDS WRITTEN IN GOTHIC LETTERS . .	589A	CHAUCER/N	PROSE
	OF THE PICTURE THE WORDS WRITTEN IN GOTHIC LETTERS . . .	590C	CHAUCER 2	PROSE
	AS IT WILL CONTAIN LETTERS OF COWPER TO HIS FRIENDS PERHAPS	810A	LETTER 20	PROSE
	OR RATHER CERTAINLY THE VERY BEST LETTERS THAT EVER WERE PUBLISHED	810A	LETTER 20	PROSE
	I HAVE WRITTEN MANY LETTERS TO YOU WHICH I BURND & . .	815C	LETTER 23	PROSE
	THAT ARE OUT & THE BOOK OF ITALIAN LETTERS FROM MRS FLAXMAN	836C	LETTER 35	PROSE
	COPY OF COWPER'S LETTERS OUGHT TO BE PRINTED IN	837D	LETTER 36	PROSE
	LETTERS OF GOLD & ORNAMENTED WITH JEWELS OF	837D	LETTER 36	PROSE
	INTERESTING TOPIC IN BOTH YOUR LAST LETTERS GOD BE WITH YOU	841A	LETTER 40	PROSE
	TO MR JOHNSON'S AGGRAVATING LETTERS HAVE BEEN REPRESENTED	847A	LETTER 44	PROSE
	BECAUSE MR JOHNSON HAS AT TIMES WRITTEN SUCH LETTERS TO ME	847B	LETTER 44	PROSE
	(PRAISE OF MRS KLOPSTOCK'S LETTERS)	849D	LETTER 46	PROSE
LETTUCE				
	YET THE OAK DIES AS WELL AS THE LETTUCE	605B	V LAST JUDG/N	PROSE
LEUTHA				
	ALONG THE VALES OF LEUTHA SEEKING FLOWERS TO COMFORT HER	189	V DAU ALBION 1	4
	SEEN IN OBSCURED TRACES IN THE VALE OF LEUTHA SO . . .	206	THIRALATHA	3
	WHERE IS THY LUREING BIRD OF EDEN LEUTHA SILENT LOVE . .	244	EUROPE 14	9
	LEUTHA THE MANY COLOURD BOW DELIGHTS UPON THY WINGS . .	244	EUROPE 14	10
	SOFT SOUL OF FLOWERS LEUTHA	244	EUROPE 14	11
	REVOLVE LIKE SWEET PERFUMES ASCENDING O LEUTHA SILKEN QUEEN	244	EUROPE 14	14
	MY ANTAMON THE SEVEN CHURCHES OF LEUTHA SEEK THY LOVE . .	244	EUROPE 14	20
	SO ANTAMON CALLD UP LEUTHA FROM HER VALLEYS OF DELIGHT .	246	SONG OF LOS 3	28
	WHO THE CHARIOT OF LEUTHA GUIDES	255	BOOK OF LOS 3	2
	. . . OUR DAUGHTERS OCALYTHRON ELYNITTRIA OOTHOON LEUTHA	350	FOUR ZOAS 8	363
	BUT WHEN LEUTHA A DAUGHTER OF BEULAH BEHELD SATAN'S CONDEMNATION	492	MILTON 11	28
	AND LEUTHA STOOD GLOWING WITH VARYING COLOURS IMMORTAL HEART-PIERCING	492	MILTON 11	32
	TO SIEZE HER NEW BORN SON AH ME THE WRETCHED LEUTHA . .	492	MILTON 12	3
	THE SLEEPERS OF BEULAH PITY THE REPENTANT LEUTHA MY . .	493	MILTON 12	50
	NOW LEUTHA CEASD TEARS FLOWD BUT THE DIVINE PITY SUPPORTED HER	493	MILTON 13	7
	SO LEUTHA SPOKE BUT WHEN SHE SAW THAT ENITHARMON HAD . .	494	MILTON 13	12
	BUT ELYNITTRIA MET LEUTHA IN THE PLACE WHERE SHE WAS HIDDEN	494	MILTON 13	36
	INTRICATE LABYRINTHS OF TIMES AND SPACES UNKNOWN THAT LEUTHA LIVED	494	MILTON 13	43
	SO SPOKE ORC WHEN OOTHOON & LEUTHA HOVERD OVER HIS COUCH	500	MILTON 18	39
	WITH HIM WENT DOWN THE DOGS OF LEUTHA AT HIS FEET . . .	729	JERUSALEM 83	82
LEUTHA'S				
	AND I HID IN LEUTHA'S VALE	189	ARGUMENT V DAU	4
	I PLUCKED LEUTHA'S FLOWER	189	ARGUMENT V DAU	5
	AND THUS SHE SPOKE TO THE BRIGHT MARYGOLD OF LEUTHA'S VALE	189	V DAU ALBION 1	5
	OF LEUTHA'S DOGS THENCE THRO THE NARROWS OF THE RIVER'S SIDE	657	JERUSALEM 31	16
LEVEL				
	. . . THEY LEVEL THE FORTIFICATIONS	365	FOUR ZOAS 9	303
	EVEN SNOW HILL IS BECOME ALMOST LEVEL	831D	LETTER 31	PROSE
LEVELLD				
	OF HER LORDLY CONQUERORS HER PALACES LEVELLD WITH THE DUST	653	JERUSALEM 29	24
	THE HILL OF GIANTS ALL HER FOUNDATIONS LEVELLD WITH THE DUST	719	JERUSALEM 78	22

		PAGE	TITLE	LINE

LEVI
REUBEN SLEPT ON PENMAENMAWR & LEVI SLEPT ON SNOWDON　. ．　281 FOUR ZOAS 2　53
HAR OCHIM IJIM ADAM REUBEN SIMEON LEVI JUDAH DAN NAPHTALI　350 FOUR ZOAS 8　360
AWAY FROM [LOS] ME FIRST REUBEN FLED THEN SIMEON THEN LEVI　350 FOUR ZOAS 8　375
　THEN JUDAH
REUBEN & MANAZZOTH & GAD & SIMEON & LEVI　. ． ． ． ．　508 MILTON 24　2
CARDIGANSHIRE & THE GATE OF LEVI IN MONTGOMERYSHIRE　. ． ．　637 JERUSALEM 16　36
LEVI MIDDLESEX KENT SURREY JUDAH SOMERSET GLOUSTER　637 JERUSALEM 16　45
　WILTSHIRE
LEVI EDINBURH ROXBRO ROSS JUDAH ABRDEEN BERWIK DUMFRIES　638 JERUSALEM 16　* 54
AND THOSE UNDER REUBEN & SIMEON & LEVI ARE THESE　. ． ．　711 JERUSALEM 72　21
THEY HAVE DIVIDED LEVI HE HATH SHOT OUT INTO FORTY EIGHT　715 JERUSALEM 74　47
　ROOTS
LEVI AND JUDAH & ISSACHAR EPHRAM MANASSEH GAD AND DAN　. ．　720 JERUSALEM 79　30
THERE IS REUBEN & GAD & JOSEPH & JUDAH & LEVI CLOSD UP　. ．　721 JERUSALEM 79　64
OF REUBEN OR OF BENJAMIN OF JOSEPH OR JUDAH OR LEVI　. ． ．　736 JERUSALEM 90　31
JUDAH WAS LIKE PALAMABRON O SIMEON O LEVI YE FLED AWAY　740 JERUSALEM 93　14
LEVIATHAN
AND NOW WE SAW IT WAS THE HEAD OF LEVIATHAN　. ． ．　156C MARRIAGE HH 17　PROSE
NUMBER I THE SPIRITUAL FORM OF NELSON GUIDING LEVIATHAN　564D DESC CAT 1　TITLE
ROLLING THE SEA IN ROCKY PATHS FORMING LEVIATHAN　. ． ． ．　738 JERUSALEM 91　39
LEVITES
AND THE FORTY-EIGHT STARRY REGIONS ARE CITIES OF　529 MILTON 38　1
　THE LEVITES
LEWDNESS
TO ME WHILE DRUNKENNESS LEWDNESS GLUTTONY & EVEN　. ． ． ．　812C LETTER 22　PROSE
LEWIS
[FAYETTE BESIDE KING LEWIS STOOD]　. ． ． ． ． ． ． ．　185 LET BROTHELS/N　27
LEWISS
THE LEWISS & FREDERICKS WHO ALONE ARE ITS CAUSES &　. ． ．　683A JERUSALEM 52　*PROSE
LIABLE
WHICH ALAS EVERY ONE ON EARTH IS LIABLE TO ENTER INTO　. ．　608A V LAST JUDG/N　PROSE
LIAR
SUCH A LIAR AS QUID THINKS HE IS [BUT HE IS ALWAYS ENVYING]　53A ISLAND MOON 8　PROSE
MUST EITHER BE THE ACTOR OR A FABLE WRITER OR A LIAR　. ．　390D ANNO WATSON　MARG
HOW IS THIS POSSIBLE EVERY BODY MUST BE A LIAR & DECIEVER　397B ANNO BACON　MARG
WAS I MISTAKEN OR IS BACON A LIAR　. ． ． ． ． ． ． ． ．　401C ANNO BACON　MARG
A LIAR HE NEVER WAS ABASHED IN HIS LIFE & NEVER FELT HIS　447D ANNO REYNOLDS　MARG
　IGNORANCE
IF HE MEANS THAT COPYING CORRECTLY IS A HINDRANCE HE IS　448D ANNO REYNOLDS　MARG
　A LIAR
BUT THE GREATER [FOOLS] FOOL THE [GRATER] GREATER LIAR　. ．　554 GREAT MEN/N　* 2
I DO NOT KNOW WHETHER HOMER IS A LIAR & THAT THERE IS NO　596D PUB ADDRESS/N　PROSE
THE PLAYER IS A LIAR WHEN HE SAYS ANGELS ARE HAPPIER　. ．　616D V LAST JUDG/N　PROSE
DISCIPLINE IN MOUNTAINOUS PLACES SR FRANCIS BACON IS A LIAR　871A LETTER 72　PROSE
LIARS
WHICH THEY CALLD GOD & SO WERE LIARS AS CHRIST SAYS　. ． ．　389A ANNO WATSON　MARG
[THIS MUST BE HOW LIARS REASON]　. ． ． ． ． ． ． ．　SUPP ANNO REYNOLDS　* MARG
LIBERAL
THE LIBERAL MAN INVITING THE TRAVELLER INTO HIS HOUSE　. ．　SUPP ILLUS GRAY　*TITLE
LIBERALITY
LIBERALITY WE WANT NOT LIBERALITY WE WANT A FAIR PRICE　446D ANNO REYNOLDS　MARG
LEFT ALL TO YOU INTIRELY I DO THINK FROM THE LIBERALITY OF　857A LETTER 54　*PROSE
WHICH PLEASD SO WELL THAT HE WITH THE SAME LIBERALITY WITH　861C LETTER 59　*PROSE
LIBERATE
[XXX] KINGDOM [BUT DELIVER] LIBERATE US US　. ． ． ． ． ．　788B ANNO THORNTON　* MARG
LIBERTY
AND MOCKS MY LOSS OF LIBERTY　. ． ． ． ． ． ．　6 HOW SWEET/PS　16
AND LIBERTY BEGAN T INCREASE　. ． ． ． ． ． ．　17 BLIND-MANS/PS　68
LET LIBERTY THE CHARTERD RIGHT OF ENGLISHMEN　. ． ． ． ．　10 EDW THIRD/PS 1　9
ENERVE MY SOLDIERS LET LIBERTY　. ． ． ． ． ．　18 EDW THIRD/PS 1　11
AND HATH THE SPIRIT OF LIBERTY WITHIN HIM　. ． ． ． ．　25 EDW THIRD/PS 3　190
GIVE BUT A SLAVE HIS LIBERTY HE'LL SHAKE　. ． ． ． ．　26 EDW THIRD/PS 3　196
O LIBERTY HOW GLORIOUS ART THOU　. ． ． ． ． ． ．　26 EDW THIRD/PS 3　204
I'LL WEEP AND SHOUT FOR GLORIOUS LIBERTY　. ． ． ． ． ．　31 EDW THIRD/PS 5　52
LIBERTY SHALL STAND UPON THE CLIFFS OF ALBION　. ． ． ． ．　33 EDW THIRD/PS 6　55
FOR LIBERTY VAIN HOPES HIS REASON DECAYD . ． ．　136 FRENCH REVOLTN　49
HIS VOICE LOUD INSPIRD BY LIBERTY　. ． ． ． ． ．　147 FRENCH REVOLTN　284
AND AT LIBERTY WHEN OF DEVILS & HELL IS BECAUSE HE WAS　. ．　150B MARRIAGE HH 5　PROSE
A SONG OF LIBERTY　. ． ． ． ． ． ． ． ．　159A SONG LIBERTY　TITLE
A PROSPECT OF LIBERTY A CLOUD　. ． ． ． ． ．　209A SUBJCTS HIST/N　TITLE
AND STERN DEMANDS OF RIGHT & DUTY INSTEAD OF LIBERTY　. ．　265 FOUR ZOAS 1　37
WHERE LIBERTY WAS JUSTICE & ETERNAL SCIENCE WAS MERCY　. ．　292 FOUR ZOAS 3　40
TREMBLING BEFORE THE MULTITUDES OF SLAVES NOW SET　357 FOUR ZOAS 9　21
　AT LIBERTY
WHAT IS LIBERTY WITHOUT UNIVERSAL TOLERATION　. ． ． ． ．　413D ANNO BOYD　MARG
("BOUNDS...TO LIBERTY") IF IT IS THUS THE EXTREME OF BLACK　414B ANNO BOYD　MARG
　IS WHITE
WE WILL LIVE IN PARADISE & LIBERTY　. ． ． ． ． ．　616A V LAST JUDG/N　PROSE
YOU CANNOT HAVE LIBERTY IN THIS WORLD WITHOUT　. ． ． ．　616A V LAST JUDG/N　PROSE
AND STERN DEMANDS OF RIGHT & DUTY INSTEAD OF LIBERTY　. ．　645 JERUSALEM 22　11
JERUSALEM IS NAMED LIBERTY　. ． ． ． ． ． ．　649 SUCH VISIONS/J　3
A PRETENCE OF ART TO DESTROY ART A PRETENCE OF LIBERTY　672 JERUSALEM 43　35
TO DESTROY LIBERTY A PRETENCE OF RELIGION TO DESTROY　672 JERUSALEM 43　36
　RELIGION
AND JERUSALEM IS CALLED LIBERTY AMONG THE CHILDREN　684 JERUSALEM 54　5
　OF ALBION
I GAVE THEE LIBERTY AND LIFE O LOVELY JERUSALEM　. ． ． ．　692 JERUSALEM 60　10
TILL THEY REFUSE LIBERTY TO THE MALE & NOT LIKE BEULAH　. ．　707 JERUSALEM 69　14
NO OTHER CHRISTIANITY AND OF NO OTHER GOSPEL THAN THE　716D JERUSALEM 77　PROSE
　LIBERTY BOTH
P S I HAVE TAKEN THE LIBERTY TO TROUBLE YOU WITH A LETTER　819A LETTER 24　PROSE

```
                                                          PAGE    TITLE        LINE
LIBERTY    (CONTINUED)
      UNOBSERVD & AT LIBERTY FROM THE DOUBTS OF OTHER MORTALS    822D LETTER 26      PROSE
      AS TO MR H(HAYLEY) I FEEL MYSELF AT LIBERTY    . . . .     825B LETTER 27      PROSE
      AT WHICH TIME I WAS SET AT LIBERTY TO REMONSTRATE   . .    825D LETTER 27      PROSE
      YOU & MRS BUTTS & ALL YOUR FAMILY I AGAIN TAKE THE LIBERTY 829A LETTER 28      PROSE
      THE PROPOSAL ALTOGETHER I TOOK THE LIBERTY TO TELL HIM THAT 842C LETTER 42     PROSE
      J ROMNEY IMMEDIATELY DESIRING HIM TO GIVE US LIBERTY   .   846A LETTER 44      PROSE
      BECOME CHILDREN OF LIGHT AND LIBERTY AND MY FEET AND MY    852A LETTER 50      PROSE
      [AND STERN DEMANDS OF RIGHT & DUTY INSTEAD OF LIBERTY] .   SUPP FOUR ZOAS 1      *
LIBRARIES
      AND TOOK THE FORMS OF BOOKS & WERE ARRANGED IN LIBRARIES   155A MARRIAGE HH 15 PROSE
LIBRARY
      & MICHAEL ANGELO IN THE LIBRARY OF THE ROYAL ACADEMY   .   449C ANNO REYNOLDS  MARG
      TO SEE YOU AT FELPHAM & TO SHEW YOU MR HAYLEY'S LIBRARY    809C LETTER 20      PROSE
LICE
      WHERE THE DEVIL COMBS HIS LICE . . . . . . . . . .         757 EV GOSPEL(I)/N   26
      ?EXODUS AARON XXX ?MOSES XXX RIVER XXX FROGS LICE    .     SUPP EXODUS/N      *PROSE
LICENCD
      LICENCD BUILD THAT NATION'S FATE . . . . . . . . .         433 AUGURIES        114
LICK
      HERE LICK LICK LICK SAID HE HA HA HA HA HA HA             55C ISLAND MOON 9   PROSE
      AND HER BOSOM LICK . . . . . . . . . . . .              113 LIT GRL LST/SI     45
      COME AND LICK . . . . . . . . . . . . .                123 SPRING/SI          21
      THAT SING & FLY IN THE BRIGHT AIR BUT YOU DO LICK MY FEET  368 FOUR ZOAS 9    431
      AND HE SHALL LICK THE LITTLE GIRL'S WHITE NECK & ON HER    376 FOUR ZOAS 9    704
         HEAD
      YOU SHALL LICK THE DUST FOR MEAT . . . . . . . .          755 EV GOSPEL(E)/N   54
LICKING
      . . . THE WILD FLAMES (?LICKING) UP                      359 FOUR ZOAS 9    *  85
LICKS
      WHEN HE LICKS THEIR HANDS . . . . . . . . . .            114 LIT GRL ND/SI     31
LIDS    SEE EYE-LIDS
      THE LITTLE LIDS ARE LIFTED & THE LITTLE NOSTRILS OPEND    110 TIRIEL 8         29
      LIDS TO GROW OVER HIS EYES IN VEILS OF TEARS AND CAVERNS   702 JERUSALEM 66    31
LIE
      THEN DOWN I'LL LIE AS COLD AS CLAY  . . . . . . . .         7 MY SILKS/PS      17
      AND THERE I'LL LIE AND DREAM . . . . . . . . . .           8 MEMORY COME/PS    11
      I KNOW THIS BREATHING FLESH MUST LIE AND ROT  . . . . .   30 EDW THIRD/PS 5     4
      HOW MANY IN WALLED CITIES LIE AND GROAN . . . . . . .     30 EDW THIRD/PS 5     8
      THEIR HELMED YOUTH AND AGED WARRIORS IN DUST TOGETHER     37D SAMSON/PS       PROSE
         LY(LIE)
      THE IVORY PALACE OF MY INMOST HEART WHERE IT SHALL LIE    39B SAMSON/PS       PROSE
         AT REST
      UNEASY FALSE A MAN MAY LIE FOR HIS OWN PLEASURE  . . . .  67B ANNO LAVATER     MARG
      BUT IF ANY ONE IS HURT BY HIS LYING WILL CONFESS HIS LIE  67B ANNO LAVATER     MARG
         SEE...
      LIE IS THE CONTRARY TO PASSION . . . . . . . . .         74C ANNO LAVATER     MARG
      THAT YOU MAY LIE AS NOW YOUR MOTHER LIES LIKE DOGS CAST OUT 100 TIRIEL 1        45
      LIE STINKING ON THE EARTH THE BURIERS SHALL ARISE FROM    100 TIRIEL 1         49
         THE EAST
      IT IS A LIE & I AM [?TORN ?LIKE] LIKE THE TREE TORN BY    106 TIRIEL 4      *  85
         THE WIND
      I CAN LIE DOWN AND SLEEP . . . . . . . . . . .          119 NIGHT/SI          42
      WHERE A THOUSAND FIGHTING MEN IN AMBUSH LIE   . . . . .  130 BOOK OF THEL 6    14
      I ASKD A LITHE LADY TO LIE HER DOWN . . . . . . . .      163 ASKED THIEF/N      3
      UNDERNEATH MY MIRTLE LIE . . . . . . . . . . .          169 MIRTLE SHADE/N     4
      UNDERNEATH MY MIRTLE LIE . . . . . . . . . . .          176 TO MY MIRTLE/N    10
      I'LL LIE BESIDE THEE ON A BANK & VIEW THEIR WANTON PLAY   195 V DAU ALBION 7   25
      THEY GROVEL ON THE SAND AND WRITHING LIE WHILE ALL   . . 201 AMERICA 13         5
      I LIE ON THE VERGE OF THE DEEP . . . . . . . . .        254 AHANIA 4          56
      I ASKD A LITHE LADY TO LIE HER DOWN . . . . . . . .      261 ASKED THIEF        3
      COLD DEWS & HOARY FROST CREEPS THO I LIE ON BANKS OF SUMMER 288 FOUR ZOAS 2 *  320
      THARMAS THE MOON HAS CHAMBERS WHERE THE BABES OF LOVE LIE 339 FOUR ZOAS 7B    244
         HID
      AND THE PALE HORSE SEEKS FOR THE POOL TO HIM DOWN & DIE   354 FOUR ZOAS 8     529
      KINGS IN THEIR PALACES LIE DROWND SHEPHERDS THEIR FLOCKS  359 FOUR ZOAS 9      74
         THEIR TENTS
      LIE DOWN BEFORE MY FEET O DRAGON LET URIZEN ARISE        360 FOUR ZOAS 9     139
      THEY LIE IN TWISTING AGONIES BENEATH THE COVRING HEAVENS  381 FOUR ZOAS AD 2 *  5
      HAS NOT THE BISHOP GIVEN HIMSELF THE LIE  . . . . . .    390A ANNO WATSON     MARG
      A LIE . . . . . . . . . . . . . . . . . .            399D ANNO BACON      MARG
      A LIE EVERY BODY HATES A KING BACON WAS AFRAID TO SAY THAT 400B ANNO BACON    MARG
      EXCEPT IS CHRIST YOU LIE EXCEPT DID ANYONE EVER DO THIS   400D ANNO BACON     MARG
      A LIE . . . . . . . . . . . . . . . . . .            402B ANNO BACON      MARG
      A LIE FEW BELIEVE IT IS A NEW BIRTH . . . . . . . .      403C ANNO BACON     MARG
      ("ADVERSITIES") A LIE  . . . . . . . . . . .           403D ANNO BACON      MARG
      A LIE . . . . . . . . . . . . . . . . . .            405B ANNO BACON      MARG
      A LIE IT MAKES MERCHANTS & NOTHING ELSE  . . . . . .    409C ANNO BACON      MARG
      A LIE . . . . . . . . . . . . . . . . . .            409D ANNO BACON      MARG
      FALSE ALL POETRY GIVES THE LIE TO THIS  . . . . . . .   411C ANNO BOYD       MARG
      WE ARE LED TO BELIEVE A LIE . . . . . . . . . .        433 AUGURIES         125
      A LIE THE FLORID STYLE SUCH AS THE VENETIAN & THE FLEMISH 448B ANNO REYNOLDS  MARG
      VILLAINY A LIE  . . . . . . . . . . . . . .           449D ANNO REYNOLDS    MARG
      A LIE WORKING UP EFFECT IS MORE AN OPERATION OF INDOLENCE 450A ANNO REYNOLDS  MARG
      IS NOT THIS A MANIFEST LIE  . . . . . . . . . .        451D ANNO REYNOLDS    MARG
      & THAT ALL PRETENCE TO INSPIRATION IS A LIE & A DECEIT .  452D ANNO REYNOLDS  MARG
      ("PERFECTION AND BEAUTY NOT TO BE SOUGHT IN HEAVENS ")    458D ANNO REYNOLDS  MARG
         A LIE
      ("THEY ARE ABOUT US AND UPON EVERY SIDE OF US") A LIE     458D ANNO REYNOLDS  MARG
      ("ONLY BY EXPERIENCE") A LIE  . . . . . . . . .        459A ANNO REYNOLDS    MARG
      ("NO DESIRE TO DEGRADE RAFFAELLE" A LIE  . . . . . .    467B ANNO REYNOLDS    MARG
      ("NECESSITY") A LIE  . . . . . . . . . . . .           478A ANNO REYNOLDS    MARG
```

		PAGE	TITLE	LINE

LIE   (CONTINUED)
DEPEND A LIE THAT HE MAY BE SNARED & CAUGHT & TAKEN . . . 489 MILTON 8 48
THE WITNESSES LIE DEAD IN THE STREET OF THE GREAT CITY . 506 MILTON 22 59
WHERE LIE IN EVIL DEATH THE FOUR IMMORTALS PALE AND COLD 524 MILTON 34 45
BUT YOU MUST NOT BRING IN YOUR HAND A LIE . . . . . . 542 FLORENTINE/N 22
DO YOU BELIEVE IT A CONFOUNDED LIE . . . . 551 WILLM COWPER/N 6
THE WORKS NOW EXHIBITED WILL GIVE THE LIE TO SUCH 572D DESC CAT 3 PROSE
    ASPERSIONS
MORTIMER AND GLOUCESTER LIE SPELL BOUND BEHIND THEIR KING 577B DESC CAT 4 PROSE
THEY SAY THERE IS NO STRAIT LINE IN NATURE THIS IS A LIE 603B PUB ADDR AD/N PROSE
A LIE THAT HE MAY BE SNARED AND CAUGHT AND SNARED AND 628 JERUSALEM 9 30
    TAKEN
SIX MONTHS THEY LIE EMBALMD IN SILENT DEATH WORSHIPPED . 644 JERUSALEM 21 44
LO THEY REST UPON THE TRIBES WHERE THEIR PANTING VICTIMS 706 JERUSALEM 68 27
    LIE
LOOK HYLE IS BECOME AN INFANT LOVE LOOK BEHOLD SEE HIM LIE 725 JERUSALEM 82 37
IT MUST LIE IN CONFUSION TILL ALBION'S TIME OF AWAKING . . 728 JERUSALEM 83 58
AND LEADS YOU TO BELIEVE A LIE . . . . 753 EV GOSPEL(D)/N 105
OR WHETHER THEY WERE TO LIE THERE TO ETERNITY . . . . . 791B LETTER 3 PROSE
WITH GOD SPEED A ROLLER & TWO HARROWS LIE BEFORE MY WINDOW 803C LETTER 15 PROSE
LIES
THAT YOU MAY LIE AS NOW YOUR MOTHER LIES LIKE DOGS CAST OUT 100 TIRIEL 1 45
LYCA LIES ASLEEP . . . . 114 LIT GRL FND/SI 44
LIES & PRIESTCRAFT TRUTH IS NATURE . . . . 131C ANNO SWED PROV MARG
SICKNING LIES THE [ETERNAL] FALLEN MAN HIS HEAD SICK HIS 272 FOUR ZOAS 1 * 288
    HEART FAINT
THAT LIES BEYOND THE BOUNDS OF SCIENCE IN THE GREY OBSCURE 324 FOUR ZOAS 7 150
BESIDE HIM LIES THE LION DEAD & IN HIS BELLY WORMS . . . 354 FOUR ZOAS 8 527
WHAT BACON CALLS LIES IS TRUTH ITSELF . . . . 397D ANNO BACON MARG
BEATS ALL THE LIES YOU CAN INVENT . . . . 432 AUGURIES 54
TARRY NO LONGER FOR MY SOUL LIES AT THE GATES OF DEATH . 495 MILTON 14 19
WITHIN HER BOSOM ALBION LIES EMBALMD NEVER TO AWAKE . . 501 MILTON 19 57
HERE LIES STEWHARD [LORD OF] FRIEND OF ALL &C . . . 537 AND HIS LEGS/N * 52
HERE LIES JOHN TROT THE FRIEND OF ALL MANKIND . . . . 546 ANOTHER/N 2 1
[HERE LIES THE MAN XXX CONFOUND] . . . . 551 WILLM COWPER/N * 1
AROUND GOLGONOOZA LIES THE LAND OF DEATH ETERNAL A LAND 633 JERUSALEM 13 30
BUT NOW ALBION IS DARKENED & JERUSALEM LIES IN RUINS . 711 JERUSALEM 71 54
LET EVERY CHRISTIAN AS MUCH AS IN HIM LIES . . . . 717C JERUSALEM 77 PROSE
FOR JERUSALEM LIES IN RUINS & THE FURNACES OF LOS 729 JERUSALEM 84 6
    ARE BUILDED THERE
LIEST
DOST THOU APPEAR BEFORE ME WHO LIEST DEAD IN LUVAH'S 648 JERUSALEM 24 57
    SEPULCHER
LIEU
THE WITCH RAISING THE STORM MR ROMNEY SAYS THAT IN LIEU OF 839C LETTER 38 PROSE
LIFE
UNCLOTHES THE EARTH AND FREEZES UP FRAIL LIFE . . . . . 3 TO WINTER/PS 12
IT IS MY LIFE SEND IT TO ELENOR . . . . 4 FAIR ELENOR/PS 23
OF LUSTY MAY AH LIFE AS FRAIL AS FLOWER . . . . . . 5 FAIR ELENOR/PS 42
WAS REFT OF LIFE BY THE ACCURSED DUKE . . . . 5 FAIR ELENOR/PS 63
HIRED A VILLAIN TO BEREAVE MY LIFE . . . . 6 FAIR ELENOR/PS 68
LABOUR AND TOIL FOR LIFE . . . . 13 GWIN KING/PS 90
TH ALMIGHTY TO STRETCH OUT MY SPAN OF LIFE . . . . . 27 EDW THIRD/PS 3 279
WHEN THE COLD CLAY BREATHED WITH LIFE AND OUR ANCESTORS 35C COUCH DEATH/PS PROSE
MY LIFE IS DEATH I AM A TRAITOR TO MY NATION AND DESPISED 38D SAMSON/PS PROSE
VENERABLE SWEETNER OF HIS LIFE RECEIVES THE PROMISE FIRST 39C SAMSON/PS PROSE
    FROM HEAVEN
SO ONCE THE SUN HIS CHARIOT DREW BACK TO PROLONG A GOOD 41B THEN SHE BORE PROSE
    KING'S LIFE
PLUTARCH HAS NOT THE LIFE OF GHIOTTO SAID SIPSOP . . . . 49D ISLAND MOON 6 PROSE
TO SEEK HIS MOTHER'S LIFE . . . . 50 WHEN CORRUP/IM 16
IN MY LIFE YOU ARE ALWAYS TALKING OF YOUR BOOKS . . . 52D ISLAND MOON 8 PROSE
I NEVER SAW SUCH A PLACE IN MY LIFE HE SAYS HE HAS . . . 53A ISLAND MOON 8 PROSE
WHOSE LIFE WAS BUT A SPAN . . . . 57 TO BE OR/IM 26
WHICH SHORTLY WEARY THE MAN FOR ALL LIFE IS HOLY . . . 74B ANNO LAVATER MARG
AND CONSIDER THAT LOVE IS LIFE . . . . 76A ANNO LAVATER MARG
THE FEMALE LIFE LIVES FROM THE LIGHT OF THE MALE . . . . 82C ANNO LAVATER MARG
("LIFE OF MAN...IS LOVE") THIS WAS KNOWN TO ME & THOUSANDS 89C ANNO SWED LOVE MARG
HOW COULD LIFE CREATE DEATH . . . . 92B ANNO SWED LOVE MARG
THE WHOLE OF THE NEW CHURCH IS IN THE ACTIVE LIFE . . . 92D ANNO SWED LOVE MARG
THIS ASSERTION THAT THE SPIRITUAL SUN IS NOT LIFE . . 94B ANNO SWED LOVE MARG
("FOR THE LIFE OF MAN IS...") MARK THIS . . . . . 95D ANNO SWED LOVE MARG
SMITE NOT THY BROTHER TIRIEL THO WEARY OF HIS LIFE . . 104 TIRIEL 4 12
HOPING TO END HER [LIFE] WOES BUT FROM HER CRIES THE TYGERS 109 TIRIEL 7 17
    FLED
GAVE THEE LIFE & BID THEE FEED . . . . 115 THE LAMB/SI 3
O LITTLE CLOUD THIS OUR SPRING WHY FADES THE LOTUS OF THE WATER 127 BOOK OF THEL 1 6
IT IS TO TENFOLD LIFE TO LOVE TO PEACE AND RAPTURES HOLY 128 BOOK OF THEL 3 11
SHE BOWD OVER THE WEEPING INFANT AND HER LIFE EXHALD . 129 BOOK OF THEL 4 8
PREDESTINATION AFTER THIS LIFE IS MORE ABOMINABLE THAN 133A ANNO SWED PROV MARG
    CALVIN'S
. . . LEAVE THE KINGDOM THY LIFE IS SURROUNDED WITH SNARES 139 FRENCH REVOLTN 114
ENERGY IS THE ONLY LIFE AND IS FROM THE BODY AND . . . 149D MARRIAGE HH 4 PROSE
TO LEAVE HIS GUARD AT TREE OF LIFE AND WHEN HE DOES . . 154B MARRIAGE HH 14 PROSE
SEEM TO LIVE IN IT IN CHAINS ARE IN TRUTH THE CAUSES OF 155A MARRIAGE HH 15 PROSE
    ITS LIFE
[DOTH LIFE DESTROY] . . . . 175 SICK ROSE/N 8
DOES THY LIFE DESTROY . . . . 175 SICK ROSE/N 10
PLANTS FRUITS OF LIFE & BEAUTY THERE . . . . 178 ABSTINENCE/N 4
DOES THE WINGED LIFE DESTROY . . . . 179 ETERNITY/N 2
[THOUGHT IS LIFE] . . . . 183 THE FLY/N 25
IF THOUGHT IS LIFE . . . . 183 THE FLY/N 29

LIFE   (CONTINUED)   PAGE   TITLE   LINE

HER WHOLE LIFE IS AN EPIGRAM SMACK SMOOTH & NEATLY PEND   184 HER LIFE IS/N   1
DOTH THE WINGED LIFE DESTROY . . . .   184 SEVRL QUESTN/N   12
TILL ALL FROM LIFE I WAS OBLITERATED AND ERASED   . . . .   191 V DAU ALBION 2   34
TO BIND THE PHANTOMS OF EXISTENCE FROM ETERNAL LIFE   . . .   192 V DAU ALBION 4   24
OF LIFE IN WEARY LUST MUST CHILLING MURDEROUS THOUGHTS   193 V DAU ALBION 5   23
    OBSCURE
OF LIFE ARE HARLOTS AND THEOTORMON IS A SICK MAN'S DREAM   194 V DAU ALBION 6   19
AND THOU ART FALLN TO GIVE ME LIFE IN REGIONS OF DARK DEATH   196 AMERICA PREL 2   9
FOR EVERY THING THAT LIVES IS HOLY LIFE DELIGHTS IN LIFE   199 AMERICA 8   13
OF LIFE BY MAGIC POWER CONDENSD INFERNAL FORMS ART-BOUND   204 AMERICA CANC B   14
DOES THY LIFE DESTROY . . . .   213 SICK ROSE/SE   8
IF THOUGHT IS LIFE . . . .   213 THE FLY/SE   13
AND ME TO MORTAL LIFE BETRAY . . . .   220 TO TIRZAH/SE   14
DEATH WAS NOT BUT ETERNAL LIFE SPRUNG . . . .   223 URIZEN 3   39
LEAVING RUINOUS FRAGMENTS OF LIFE . . . .   225 URIZEN 5   9
ALL THE WISDOM & JOY OF LIFE . . . .   230 URIZEN 13   29
AND NOW HIS ETERNAL LIFE . . . .   230 URIZEN 13   33
CUT OFF FROM LIFE & LIGHT FROZEN . . . .   230 URIZEN 13   42
LIFE IN CATARACTS POURD DOWN HIS CLIFFS . . . . . .   230 URIZEN 13   55
AND BEGAN TO AWAKE TO LIFE . . . .   233 URIZEN 20   29
OF LIFE ON HIS FORSAKEN MOUNTAINS . . . .   234 URIZEN 23   1
PORTIONS OF LIFE SIMILITUDES . . . .   234 URIZEN 23   4
FOR HE SAW THAT LIFE LIVD UPON DEATH . . . .   235 URIZEN 23   27
AND FORGOT THEIR ETERNAL LIFE . . . .   236 URIZEN 25   42
SURGE FOAM AND LABOUR INTO LIFE FIRST BORN & FIRST CONSUMD   238 EUROPE PREL 1   9
THEN WHY SHOULDST THOU ACCURSED MOTHER BRING ME INTO LIFE   238 EUROPE PREL 1   11
SIEZE ALL THE SPIRITS OF LIFE AND BIND . . . .   239 EUROPE 4   17
THAT AN ETERNAL LIFE AWAITS THE WORMS OF SIXTY WINTERS . .   240 EUROPE 5   6
IN SHOWERS OF LIFE ON HIS HARVESTS . . . .   254 AHANIA 5   14
WHEN HE TOOK THE DAUGHTERS OF LIFE . . . .   254 AHANIA 5   17
DEATH & HELL TEAM WITH LIFE   . . . .   261D SMALL BK DSGNS TITLE
IN EDEN THE AURICULAR NERVES OF HUMAN LIFE . . . . .   264 FOUR ZOAS 1   17
[A LIFE IS BLOTTED OUT & I ALONE REMAIN POSSESSD   267 FOUR ZOAS 1   112
    WITH FEARS]
. . . DRAWING HER [LIFE INGRATE] SPECTROUS LIFE   270 FOUR ZOAS 1   217
AND DRAWING IN THE SPECTROUS LIFE IN PRIDE AND HAUGHTY JOY   270 FOUR ZOAS 1   220
THUS ENION GAVE THEM ALL HER SPECTROUS LIFE [IN DEEP   270 FOUR ZOAS 1   221
    DESPAIR]
NOT LONG IN HARMONY THEY DWELL THEIR LIFE IS DRAWN AWAY   274 FOUR ZOAS 1   371
BRIGHT SOULS [?ELEMENTS] OF VEGETATIVE LIFE BUDDING &   274 FOUR ZOAS 1   *   379
    BLOSSOMING
FATTEND ON HUMAN BLOOD & DRUNK WITH WINE OF LIFE IS BETTER   274 FOUR ZOAS 1   389
    FAR
BUT SPARE MY LIFE BUT HE KNOWS NOT THAT [THE] WINTER COMETH   276 FOUR ZOAS 1   456
    FAST
LIVE IN PERFECT HARMONY IN EDEN THE LAND OF LIFE . . .   277 FOUR ZOAS 1   474
A PORTION OF HIS LIFE SHRIEKING UPON THE WIND SHE FLED . .   278 FOUR ZOAS 1   524
SHE SHOULD ARISE AGAIN TO LIFE EMBALMD IN ENION'S BOSOM   278 FOUR ZOAS 1   527
THE LIVING CREATURES OF THE WHEELS IN THE WARS OF ETERNAL   280 FOUR ZOAS 1   572
    LIFE
[?SAYING XXX FO XXX FOR XXX OF ETERNAL LIFE] . . .   SUPP FOUR ZOAS 1   *
TILL HER CARESSES & HER TEARS REVIVD HIM TO LIFE & JOY . .   285 FOUR ZOAS 2   205
SHE SANG OER LOS REVIVING HIM TO LIFE HIS GROANS   289 FOUR ZOAS 2   342
    WERE TERRIBLE
FOR EVERY THING THAT LIVES IS HOLY FOR THE SOURCE OF LIFE   289 FOUR ZOAS 2   366
AND WAKE THE BUBBLING SPRINGS OF LIFE IN REGIONS OF DARK   289 FOUR ZOAS 2   373
    DEATH
THE DISMAL VISION OF MINE EYES O LOVE & LIFE & LIGHT . .   293 FOUR ZOAS 3   73
PLUNGD INTO THE COLD BILLOWS LIVING [&] A LIFE IN MIDST   296 FOUR ZOAS 3   *   179
    OF WATERS
WHERE NEVER YET EXISTENCE CAME THERE LOSING ALL MY LIFE   296 FOUR ZOAS 3   189
AND LUVAH HIDDEN IN THE ELEMENTAL FORMS OF LIFE & DEATH   301 FOUR ZOAS 4   130
YET THO I RAGE GOD OVER ALL A PORTION OF MY LIFE . . .   301 FOUR ZOAS 4   137
DEATH CHOOSE OR LIFE THOU STRUGGLEST IN MY WATERS   301 FOUR ZOAS 4   152
    NOW CHOOSE LIFE
OF CIRCLING FIRE UNCEASING PLAYS TO FEED THEM WITH LIFE   308 FOUR ZOAS 5   115
    & BRING
OF LIFE [REJOICE] LAMENT AROUND THE DEMON GOING FORTH &   308 FOUR ZOAS 5   *   117
    RETURNING
SUSTAINED BY THE DEMON'S LIFE DESPAIR & TERROR & WOE & RAGE   309 FOUR ZOAS 5   170
I WRITE NOT HERE BUT ALL THEIR AFTER LIFE WAS LAMENTATION   309 FOUR ZOAS 5   175
FOR DEATH TO ME IS BETTER FAR THAN LIFE DEATH MY DESIRE   313 FOUR ZOAS 6   58
WHERE HE MIGHT LIVE IN PEACE & WHERE HIS LIFE MIGHT MEET   316 FOUR ZOAS 6   195
    REPOSE
A LIVING MANTLE ADJOIND TO HIS LIFE & GROWING FROM HIS SOUL   318 FOUR ZOAS 6   *   246
OF ENITHARMON HOW IT BUDS WITH LIFE & FORMS THE BONES . .   323 FOUR ZOAS 7   131
NOR FELT THE STINGINGS OF DESIRE NOR LONGINGS AFTER LIFE   325 FOUR ZOAS 7   203
FOR LIFE IS SWEET TO LOS THE WRETCHED TO HIS WINGED WOES   325 FOUR ZOAS 7   204
FOR TILL THESE TERRORS PLANTED ROUND THE GATES OF ETERNAL   327 FOUR ZOAS 7   302
    LIFE
TO LIFE ETERNAL BE ASSURD I AM THY REAL SELF . . . .   328 FOUR ZOAS 7   345
FOR THOU ART BUT A FORM & ORGAN OF LIFE & OF THYSELF . .   329 FOUR ZOAS 7   359
THAT LIFE LIVES UPON DEATH & BY DEVOURING APPETITE . .   330 FOUR ZOAS 7   390
THE FRUIT & GIVE ME PROOF OF LIFE ETERNAL OR I DIE . .   330 FOUR ZOAS 7   394
WITHOUT THE FOOD OF LIFE LET US CREATE THEM (COUNTERPARTS)   330 FOUR ZOAS 7   409
I ALSO TREMBLE AT MYSELF & AT ALL MY FORMER LIFE . . . .   330 FOUR ZOAS 7   423
AN EVER DYING LIFE OF STIFLING & OBSTRUCTION SHUT OUT   . .   331 FOUR ZOAS 7   428
THEY FEED UPON OUR LIFE WE ARE THEIR VICTIMS STERN DESIRE   331 FOUR ZOAS 7   439
. . . OF [LIFE & LOVE] SACRIFICE OF BROTHERS & SONS   331 FOUR ZOAS 7   443
    & DAUGHTERS
THEIR LIFE EXTINCT THEY TOOK THE SPECTRE FORM IN   333 FOUR ZOAS 7B   15
    DARK DESPAIR

1079

		PAGE	TITLE	LINE
LIFE	**(CONTINUED)**			
OF MAN I MADE THEE WHEN I BLOTTED MAN FROM LIFE & LIGHT		336	FOUR ZOAS 7B	117
OF LIFE UPON THE PLAINS OF DEATH & VALLEYS OF DESPAIR	. .	337	FOUR ZOAS 7B	161
AND ALL THE ARTS OF LIFE THEY CHANGD INTO THE ARTS OF DEATH		337	FOUR ZOAS 7B	174
AND CALL IT DEMONSTRATION BLIND TO ALL THE SIMPLE RULES OF LIFE		337	FOUR ZOAS 7B	186
GIRT AS A SOWER WITH HIS SEED TO SCATTER LIFE ABROAD	. .	338	FOUR ZOAS 7B	199
THE STARS OF URIZEN IN [FOR] POWER RENDING THE FORM OF LIFE		338	FOUR ZOAS 7B *	216
AND LIFE APPEAR & VANISH MOCKING ME WITH SHADOWS OF FALSE HOPE		339	FOUR ZOAS 7B	241
AND SHE WENT FORTH & SAW THE FORMS OF LIFE & OF DELIGHT		340	FOUR ZOAS 7B	269
AND URIZEN GAVE LIFE & SENSE BY HIS IMMORTAL POWER	. . .	344	FOUR ZOAS 8	131
THE SPIRITS OF LIFE TO PERVERT ALL THE FACULTIES OF SENSE		344	FOUR ZOAS 8	137
CAN THAT WHICH HAS EXISTED CEASE OR CAN LOVE & LIFE EXPIRE		345	FOUR ZOAS 8	170
NOW WE BEHOLD REDEMPTION NOW WE KNOW THAT LIFE ETERNAL	. .	346	FOUR ZOAS 8	197
THE TIMES & SPACES OF MORTAL LIFE THE SUN THE MOON THE STARS		346	FOUR ZOAS 8	206
(FORLORN) OF EDEN & REPUGNANT TO THE FORMS OF LIFE	. . .	347	FOUR ZOAS 8	254
WEEP NOT SO SISTERS WEEP NOT SO OUR LIFE DEPENDS ON THIS		349	FOUR ZOAS 8	319
OF ETERNITY FOR HIMSELF HE HEWD IT DESPAIRING OF LIFE ETERNAL		349	FOUR ZOAS 8	340
JERUSALEM PITYING THEM WOVE THEM MANTLES OF LIFE & DEATH		351	FOUR ZOAS 8	397
THE SHADOWY FEMALE SINCE LIFE CANNOT BE QUENCHD LIFE EXUDED		352	FOUR ZOAS 8	421
THEIR OPPRESSORS ARE FALLN THEY HAVE STRICKEN THEM THEY AWAKE TO LIFE		358	FOUR ZOAS 9 *	50
O WEARY LIFE WHY SIT I HERE & GIVE UP ALL MY POWERS	. . .	360	FOUR ZOAS 9	116
OF LIFE & PERSON FOR AS THE PERSON [IS] SO IS HIS LIFE PROPORTIOND		360	FOUR ZOAS 9 *	141
THUS SHALL THE MALE & FEMALE LIVE THE LIFE OF ETERNITY	. .	362	FOUR ZOAS 9	219
AND THOU SWEET SMELLING GROUND PUT FORTH THY LIFE IN FRUITS & FLOWERS		368	FOUR ZOAS 9	437
I DRINK NEW LIFE & FEEL THE BREATH OF SLEEPING ENION	. .	371	FOUR ZOAS 9	542
THE BLOOD OF LIFE FLOWD PLENTIFUL ODORS OF LIFE AROSE	. .	376	FOUR ZOAS 9	726
PLAY IN HIS SMILING BEAMS GIVING THE SEEDS OF LIFE TO GROW		379	FOUR ZOAS 9	847
. . . TEN THOUSAND THOUSAND SPRINGS OF LIFE	. . . . .	379	FOUR ZOAS 9	848
FROM ENION POURS THE SEED OF LIFE & DEATH IN ALL HER LIMBS		381	FOUR ZOAS AD 4	1
TO DEFEND THE BIBLE IN THIS YEAR...WOULD COST A MAN HIS LIFE		383B	ANNO WATSON	MARG
& THE AFFAIRS OF LIFE & DEATH TRIFLES SPORTS OF TIME	.	383C	ANNO WATSON	MARG
LOOK OVER THE EVENTS OF YOUR OWN LIFE & IF YOU DO NOT	. .	391C	ANNO WATSON	MARG
EXCESS IN YOUTH IS NECESSARY TO LIFE		408B	ANNO BACON	MARG
NATURE TEACHES NOTHING OF SPIRITUAL LIFE BUT ONLY OF NATURAL LIFE		412D	ANNO BOYD	MARG
HAS BEREAVED OF THEIR LIFE		416	MY SPECTRE/N	36
MY LOVES & THEM TO LIFE RENEW		416	MY SPECTRE/N	48
THE BLOSSOMS OF ETERNAL LIFE		442	DEDICATN BLAIR	20
& FAMILIES SOME OF WHOM ARE BOWING BEFORE THE BOOK OF LIFE		443D	LAST JUDGMNT/L	PROSE
THE TWO INTRODUCERS INTO ETERNAL LIFE WOMEN WITH INFANTS		444B	LAST JUDGMNT/L	PROSE
THE BIBLE SAYS THAT CULTIVATED LIFE EXISTED FIRST . . .		446C	ANNO REYNOLDS	MARG
UNCULTIVATED LIFE COMES AFTERWARDS FROM SATAN'S HIRELINGS		446C	ANNO REYNOLDS	MARG
NECESSARIES ACCOMODATIONS & ORNAMENTS ARE THE WHOLE OF LIFE		446C	ANNO REYNOLDS	MARG
A LIAR HE NEVER WAS ABASHED IN HIS LIFE & NEVER FELT HIS IGNORANCE		447D	ANNO REYNOLDS	MARG
TROUBLE ME NO MORE THOU CANST NOT HAVE ETERNAL LIFE . . .		483	MILTON 4	18
HER LOOMS VIBRATE WITH SOFT AFFECTIONS WEAVING THE WEB OF LIFE		486	MILTON 6	28
THE WEB OF LIFE IS WOVEN & THE TENDER SINEWS OF LIFE CREATED		486	MILTON 6	34
OF LIFE TILL THEY BECOME FINITE & ITSELF SEEMS INFINITE [UNTIL]		490	MILTON 10 *	7
WILD WITH PROPHETIC FURY HIS FORMER LIFE BECAME LIKE A DREAM		493	MILTON 12	45
AND GET BY ROTE AS A HARD TASK OF A LIFE OF SIXTY YEARS		499	MILTON 18	14
THE ENORMOUS STRIFE ONE GIVING LIFE THE OTHER GIVING DEATH		501	MILTON 19	29
RENEW IT TO ETERNAL LIFE LO I AM WITH YOU ALWAY		504	MILTON 21	56
OF MORTAL LIFE TO CONDEMN THE ACCUSED WHO AT SATAN'S BAR		507	MILTON 23	42
SHALL BIND THEM SEPARATE THEY CANNOT BELIEVE IN ETERNAL LIFE		511	MILTON 25	33
AND TIMBERS CRAMPT WITH IRON CRAMPS BAR IN THE JOYS OF LIFE		515	MILTON 28	40
LIVE BECAUSE THE LIFE OF MAN WAS TOO EXCEEDING UNBOUNDED		519	MILTON 30	22
APPEAR AROUND IN THE EXTERNAL SPHERES OF VISIONARY LIFE		524	MILTON 34	51
HERE RENDERD DEADLY WITHIN THE LIFE & INTERIOR VISION		525	MILTON 34	52
THOSE VISIONS OF HUMAN LIFE & SHADOWS OF WISDOM & KNOWLEDGE		525	MILTON 34	55
AND WAR & HUNTING THE TWO FOUNTAINS OF THE RIVER OF LIFE		525	MILTON 35	2
IN SELF ANNIHILATION GIVING THY LIFE TO THY ENEMIES . . .		532	MILTON 40	8
TO BATHE IN THE WATERS OF LIFE TO WASH OFF THE NOT HUMAN		533	MILTON 41	1
OF JESUS WHO DENY THE FAITH & MOCK AT ETERNAL LIFE . . .		533	MILTON 41	22
WHO NEVER IN HIS LIFE FORGAVE A FRIEND		544	TO FORGIVE/N	2
HIRED A VILLAIN TO BEREAVE MY LIFE		544	HS FRENDSHIP/N	6
THIS LIFE IS A WARFARE AGAINST EVILS		545	COSWAY FRAZR/N	3
THAT THE WHOLE BUSINESS OF HIS LIFE		552	WHY CUPID/N	15
THE ARMY OF ARMED ROMANS THE FIGURES FULL AS LARGE AS LIFE		560A	EXHIBITION ADV	PROSE
OR ENAMEL ALTHOUGH IN WORKS LARGER THAN LIFE		561A	EXHIBITION ADV	PROSE
OF UNIVERSAL HUMAN LIFE BEYOND WHICH NATURE NEVER STEPS		567C	DESC CAT 3	PROSE
CANNOT BE SURPASSED HE HAS SPENT HIS LIFE IN THE FIELD .		567D	DESC CAT 3	PROSE
COMMON RANK IN LIFE OR ATTENDANTS ON THOSE WHO WERE SO .		568C	DESC CAT 3	PROSE
CHARACTERS OF HUMAN LIFE APPEAR TO POETS IN ALL AGES . .		571B	DESC CAT 3	PROSE
PERISHING LIFE IT DOES BUT SELDOM HAPPEN BUT WITH THIS .		579D	DESC CAT 5	PROSE
WOULD BE THE CORREGGIO THAT THE LIFE WRITERS HAVE WRITTEN OF		583C	DESC CAT 9	PROSE

LIFE   (CONTINUED)

		PAGE	TITLE	LINE
THE GREAT AND GOLDEN RULE OF ART AS WELL AS OF LIFE IS THIS		585B	DESC CAT 15	PROSE
LEAVE OUT THIS (LINE) AND YOU LEAVE OUT LIFE ITSELF	. .	585C	DESC CAT 15	*PROSE
AND LAST A MAN'S WHOLE LIFE BUT HE WILL AT LENGTH	. .	587A	CHAUCER 1	PROSE
AS A PILGRIM TRAVELLING THROUGH THIS JOURNEY OF LIFE	.	590B	CHAUCER 2	PROSE
OF UNIVERSAL HUMAN LIFE BEYOND WHICH NATURE NEVER STEPS		590D	CHAUCER 2	PROSE
WITH WHICH HE SET OUT IN LIFE [WH] OF WHICH HEATH & STOTHARD		592B	PUB ADDRESS/N	*PROSE
THEY SEEM TO ME TO BE SOMETHING ELSE BESIDES HUMAN LIFE		600A	PUB ADDRESS/N	PROSE
TO RECOVER ART [IS] HAS BEEN THE BUSINESS OF MY LIFE TO THE		600B	PUB ADDRESS/N	*PROSE
SET ON FOOT TILL IN MY OUTSET INTO LIFE IT WAS ARTFULLY PUBLISHD		602B	PUB ADDRESS/N	PROSE
TO [PUT] TURN THAT WHICH IS SOUL & LIFE INTO A MILL OR MACHINE		603A	PUB ADDR AD/N	PROSE
AS TWO DISTINCT THINGS & SO CALLD FOR THE SAKE OF ETERNAL LIFE		605A	V LAST JUDG/N	PROSE
THE ETERNAL CONSUMMATION OF VEGETABLE LIFE & DEATH	. . .	609A	V LAST JUDG/N	PROSE
STARTING INTO LIFE AT THE TRUMPET'S SOUND WHILE THE WICKED		609C	V LAST JUDG/N	PROSE
OR CIVILIZED LIFE SUCH AS IT IS IN THE CHRISTIAN CHURCH		610C	V LAST JUDG/N	PROSE
BOTH IN ART & IN LIFE GENERAL MASSES ARE	. . .	611B	V LAST JUDG/N	PROSE
ARE OPEND THE BOOKS OF REMEMBRANCE OF LIFE & OF DEATH	.	612B	V LAST JUDG/N	PROSE
BEFORE THAT OF LIFE ON THE RIGHT SOME FIGURES [?BOW] BOW		612B	V LAST JUDG/N	*PROSE
HE IS THE WATER OF LIFE ACCORDINGLY	. . . .	612D	V LAST JUDG/N	PROSE
ALL LIFE CONSISTS OF THESE TWO THROWING OFF ERROR & KNAVES		612D	V LAST JUDG/N	PROSE
FROM IT FLOWS ON EACH SIDE [OF] THE RIVER OF LIFE	. .	613B	V LAST JUDG/N	*PROSE
ON WHOSE BANKS GROWS THE TREE OF LIFE	. . . . .	613B	V LAST JUDG/N	PROSE
THE COMBATS OF TRUTH & ERROR IS EATING OF THE TREE OF LIFE		615A	V LAST JUDG/N	PROSE
NOR THE SHEEP THE GOAT BUT THEY ENVY A RIVAL IN LIFE	.	616B	V LAST JUDG/N	PROSE
WEAVING THE THREAD OF MORTAL LIFE	. . . .	619B	ILLUS MILTON	PROSE
ETERNAL DEATH AND OF THE AWAKING TO ETERNAL LIFE	. .	622	JERUSALEM 4	2
ANNIHILATE THE SELPHOOD IN ME BE THOU ALL MY LIFE	. .	623	JERUSALEM 5	22
TILL THY LIFE IS ALL TAKEN AWAY BY THIS DECEITFUL FRIENDSHIP		625	JERUSALEM 7	10
HUNGRING & THIRSTING FOR LOS'S LIFE YET PRETENDING OBEDIENCE		627	JERUSALEM 8	28
IF THOU WAST CAST FORTH FROM MY LIFE IF I WAS DEAD UPON THE MOUNTAINS		627	JERUSALEM 8	36
THAT ENTHUSIASM AND LIFE MAY NOT CEASE ARISE SPECTRE ARISE		628	JERUSALEM 9	31
AND IRON BOUND IT OVER ME FOR EVER LIFE LIVES ON MY	. . .	630	JERUSALEM 10	55
AND SEEING LIFE YET LIVING NOT HOW CAN I THEN BEHOLD	. .	630	JERUSALEM 10	58
WHY WILT THOU GIVE TO HER A BODY WHOSE LIFE IS BUT A SHADE		631	JERUSALEM 12	1
HE VIEWS THE CHERUB AT THE TREE OF LIFE ALSO THE SERPENT		634	JERUSALEM 14	2
WHEREFORE HAST THOU SHUT ME INTO THE WINTER OF HUMAN LIFE		642	JERUSALEM 20	5
THEY VIEW THEIR FORMER LIFE THEY NUMBER MOMENTS OVER AND OVER		642	JERUSALEM 20	17
BURSTING THEIR ARKS THEY RISE AGAIN TO LIFE THEY PLAY BEFORE		644	JERUSALEM 21	46
O WHAT IS LIFE & WHAT IS MAN O WHAT IS DEATH WHEREFORE		647	JERUSALEM 24	12
LIFE IN BROODING CARES & ANXIOUS LABOURS THAT PROVE BUT CHAFF		647	JERUSALEM 24	16
IN OFFERINGS OF HUMAN LIFE	. . . .	650	FIELDS FROM/J	32
I NEVER SAW THEE TILL THIS TIME NOR BEHELD LIFE ABSTRACTED		659	JERUSALEM 33	31
IS AS NOTHING BEFORE THEE FADED IS ALL LIFE AND JOY	. .	659	JERUSALEM 33	34
THE RIVER OF LIFE TO FLOW AGAINST MY WALLS & AMONG MY TREES		660	JERUSALEM 33	38
HIDDEN AMONG THE DEAD & MURED UP FROM THE PATHS OF LIFE		661	JERUSALEM 34	35
TO EVERY ENERGY OF MAN AND FORBID THE SPRINGS OF LIFE	.	662	JERUSALEM 35	12
SAYING ALBION OUR WARS ARE WARS OF LIFE & WOUNDS OF LOVE		664	JERUSALEM 38	14
LIVE IN PERFECT HARMONY IN EDEN THE LAND OF LIFE	. .	665	JERUSALEM 38	21
AND THE TWO SOURCES OF LIFE IN ETERNITY HUNTING AND WAR		672	JERUSALEM 43	31
THEY FIGHT & CONTEND FOR LIFE & NOT FOR ETERNAL DEATH	.	672	JERUSALEM 43	42
LIKE AFRICA'S AND HIS MACHINES ARE WOVEN WITH HIS LIFE	.	675	JERUSALEM 45	25
OXFORD TAKE THOU THESE LEAVES OF THE TREE OF LIFE WITH ELOQUENCE		675	JERUSALEM 45	30
IN MILD PERSWASION BRINGING LEAVES OF THE TREE OF LIFE	.	676	JERUSALEM 46	9
WHO TEACHES BELIEF TO THE NATIONS & AN UNKNOWN ETERNAL LIFE		685	JERUSALEM 54	20
FOR THEY LABOUR FOR LIFE & LOVE REGARDLESS OF ANY ONE	.	691	JERUSALEM 59	37
I GAVE THEE LIBERTY AND LIFE O LOVELY JERUSALEM	. . .	692	JERUSALEM 60	10
REPOSE ON ME TILL THE MORNING OF THE GRAVE I AM THY LIFE		695	JERUSALEM 62	1
JESUS REPLIED I AM THE RESURRECTION & THE LIFE	. . .	696	JERUSALEM 62	18
AND ALL THE ARTS OF LIFE THEY CHANGD INTO THE ARTS OF DEATH IN ALBION		700	JERUSALEM 65	16
AND CALL IT DEMONSTRATION BLIND TO ALL THE SIMPLE RULES OF LIFE		700	JERUSALEM 65	28
GIRT AS A SOWER WITH HIS SEED TO SCATTER LIFE ABROAD OVER ALBION		700	JERUSALEM 65	45
FIBRES OF LIFE TO WEAVE FOR EVERY FEMALE IS A GOLDEN LOOM		704	JERUSALEM 67	4
WEEP NOT SO SISTERS WEEP NOT SO OUR LIFE DEPENDS ON THIS		705	JERUSALEM 68	7
CLOTHED IN THE SKIN OF THE VICTIM BLOOD HUMAN BLOOD IS THE LIFE		706	JERUSALEM 68	33
WHAT IS THE LIFE OF MAN BUT ART & SCIENCE	. . . . .	717B	JERUSALEM 77	PROSE
BUT JESUS IS THE BRIGHT PREACHER OF LIFE	. . . . .	718	STOOD AMONG/J	21
HE SLEW THEM I REVIVED THEM TO LIFE IN MY WARM BOSOM	.	722	JERUSALEM 80	20
WITHIN MY BOSOM LEST HE ARISE TO LIFE & SLAY MY LUVAH	.	722	JERUSALEM 80	29
I GATHER OUR ETERNAL FATE OUTCASTS FROM LIFE AND LOVE	.	725	JERUSALEM 82	2
WEAVING THE WEB OF LIFE FOR JERUSALEM THE WEB OF LIFE	.	728	JERUSALEM 83	73
UPON THE HOLY LAND I SEE THE RIVER OF LIFE & TREE OF LIFE		731	JERUSALEM 86	18
YOU SHALL WANT ALL THE MINUTE PARTICULARS OF LIFE	. .	734	JERUSALEM 88	43
CEASING TO BE HIS EMANATIONS LIFE TO THEMSELVES ASSUMING		736	JERUSALEM 90	2
OF ALBION DRANK & IMBIBED THE LIFE & ETERNAL FORM OF LUVAH		736	JERUSALEM 90	17
FIBRES OF LIFE OUT FROM THE BONES INTO HER GOLDEN LOOM	.	736	JERUSALEM 90	22
BENEATH LOS'S HAMMER THAT LIFE MAY NOT BE BLOTTED OUT	. .	737	JERUSALEM 90	51

		PAGE	TITLE	LINE

LIFE   (CONTINUED)
    DENYING IN PRIVATE MOCKING GOD & ETERNAL LIFE & IN PUBLIC   737 JERUSALEM 90   64
    TO OCCUPY THE VERY THRESHOLD OF ETERNAL LIFE IF BACON   741 JERUSALEM 93   21
        NEWTON LOCKE
    . . . THE FOUR RIVERS OF THE WATER OF LIFE   745 JERUSALEM 98   15
    AWAKING IT TO LIFE AMONG THE FLOWERS OF BEULAH REJOICING   745 JERUSALEM 98   21
        IN UNITY
    AND THEN AWAKING INTO HIS BOSOM IN THE LIFE OF IMMORTALITY   747 JERUSALEM 99   4
    DO WHAT YOU WILL THIS LIFE S A FICTION . . . .   751 EV GOSPEL(C)/N   50
    FOR THAT IS MY SPIRIT OF LIFE . . . .   753 EV GOSPEL(D)/N   77
    [[ALL] THIS CORPOREAL LIFE S A] [ALL LIFE S A FICTION]   753 EV GOSPEL(D)/N * 85
    THIS ALONE IS THE GOSPEL & THIS IS THE LIFE & IMMORTALITY   757D EV GOSPEL   PROSE
    WHAT LIFE & IMMORTALITY . . . .   758 EV GOSPEL (2)   2
    EARTH HE STRUGGLES INTO LIFE   762D FOR SEXES/GP   TITLE
    AND WEEPING OVER THE WEB OF LIFE . . . .   771 OF GATES/GP   48
    THE FOUR RIVERS OF THE WATER OF LIFE . . . . . .   773D ANNO BERKELEY   MARG
    PLATO DID NOT BRING LIFE & IMMORTALITY TO LIGHT . . .   774C ANNO BERKELEY   MARG
    ART IS THE TREE OF LIFE GOD IS JESUS . . . . . .   777C INSC LAOCOON   PROSE
    THIS DEATH & THIS LIFE & THIS JEHOVAH   779 GHOST ABEL 1   7
    ABEL LIFE FOR LIFE LIFE FOR LIFE   780 GHOST ABEL 1   14
    JEHOVAH HE WHO SHALL TAKE CAIN'S LIFE MUST ALSO DIE O ABEL   780 GHOST ABEL 1   15
    EVERY THING HAS AS MUCH RIGHT TO ETERNAL LIFE . . . .   788B ANNO THORNTON   MARG
    THE LABOURS OF LIFE & WE PLOW & REAP FORGETTING OUR LABOUR   791C LETTER 3   PROSE
    AS TO CALL THEM COPIES FROM LIFE & MANNERS . . . . .   795B LETTER 6   PROSE
    OF MY LIFE I HAVE PRESUMD ON YOUR FRIENDSHIP IN STAYING SO   799A LETTER 11   PROSE
    A NEW LIFE BECAUSE ANOTHER COVERING OF EARTH IS SHAKEN OFF   802B LETTER 14   PROSE
    OF ETERNITY BEFORE MY MORTAL LIFE & THOSE WORKS ARE THE   802C LETTER 14   PROSE
        DELIGHT
    COMMENCED A NEW LIFE OF INDUSTRY TO DO CREDIT TO . . . .   804B LETTER 16   PROSE
    THAT NEW LIFE BY IMPROVED WORKS RECIEVE FROM ME A RETURN OF   804B LETTER 16   PROSE
    BY THE FOUNTAINS OF LIFE . . . .   806 TO BUTTS/L   76
    YOUR HARVEST SPRINGING TO ETERNAL LIFE . . . . .   806 TO MRS BUTTS/L   5
    AT THIS TIME IS ENGRAVING PLATES FOR COWPER'S LIFE . . .   809D LETTER 20   PROSE
    DETERMINED TO PAINT ANOTHER PORTRAIT OF YOU FROM LIFE IN MY   810B LETTER 20   PROSE
    THE THING I HAVE MOST AT HEART MORE THAN LIFE OR ALL . .   812D LETTER 22   PROSE
    THAT SEEMS TO MAKE LIFE COMFORTABLE WITHOUT . . . .   812D LETTER 22   PROSE
    YOU THRO LIFE & AFTER DEATH SHAME & CONFUSION OF FACE . .   813B LETTER 22   PROSE
    MUST THE DUTIES OF LIFE EACH OTHER CROSS . . . . .   817 HAPPINESS/L   43
    MY HEADS OF COWPER FOR MR H'S(HAYLEY'S) LIFE OF COWPER   820C LETTER 25   PROSE
        HAVE
    PROPOSED TO THE PUBLIC AT THE END OF COWPER'S LIFE WHICH   821C LETTER 25   PROSE
    I DID NOT BEGIN TO LEARN LANGUAGES EARLY IN LIFE AS I FIND   821D LETTER 25   PROSE
        IT
    IF A MAN IS THE ENEMY OF MY SPIRITUAL LIFE WHILE HE . . .   822D LETTER 26   PROSE
    BUT THE MAN MAY BE THE FRIEND OF MY SPIRITUAL LIFE . .   822D LETTER 26   PROSE
    WHICH SEEMS TO BE THE LABOUR OF A LONG LIFE ALL PRODUCD   823B LETTER 26   PROSE
    WHO HAS NOT LOST ANY OF HIS LIFE SINCE HE WAS FIVE YEARS   830A LETTER 30   PROSE
        OLD
    WOULD BE AN APPROPRIATE ACCOMPANIMENT TO THE LIFE OF ROMNEY   832C LETTER 32   PROSE
    THAT IT IS A MIRACLE IF A STRANGER ESCAPES WITH LIFE . .   833C LETTER 33   PROSE
    IT DRAWS THE SOUL TOWARDS ETERNAL LIFE & CONJUNCTION WITH   834A LETTER 33   PROSE
    DOUBT NOT YET TO MAKE A FIGURE IN THE GREAT DANCE OF LIFE   835A LETTER 34   PROSE
    WITH THE GOOD THINGS BOTH OF THIS LIFE & OF ETERNITY & WITH   835A LETTER 34   PROSE
    THE LIFE OF ROMNEY HE INTERESTS HIMSELF IN IT & HAS   836A LETTER 35   PROSE
        PROMISED
    LIFE OF ROMNEY ENDLESS WORK IS THE TRUE TITLE OF ENGRAVING   843A LETTER 42   PROSE
    THE FIGURES AS LARGE AS LIFE HALF LENGTH MR W(WALKER)   843C LETTER 43   PROSE
        THREE SONS
    LIFE OF WASHINGTON I SUPPOSE AN AMERICAN WOULD TELL ME . .   845B LETTER 44   PROSE
    BUT DESIRED ME TO INCLOSE IT FOR YOU WITH WASHINGTON'S LIFE   845C LETTER 44   PROSE
    WHICH COWPER'S LIFE IS PRINTED ON NOT KNOWING THAT IT WAS   846D LETTER 44   PROSE
    TO TELL YOU THAT THE LIFE OF WASHINGTON WAS NOT PUT TO   846D LETTER 44   PROSE
        PRESS TILL
    ENGAGED SHOULD BE EMPLOYED ON THE WORK OF ROMNEY'S LIFE   849D LETTER 47   PROSE
    OF MY LIFE HE IS THE ENEMY OF CONJUGAL LOVE AND IS THE . .   852A LETTER 50   PROSE
    PORTRAITS WHICH ACCOMPANY THE LIFE OF COWPER . . . . .   860C LETTER 56   PROSE
    THAT THEY WOULD CONSIDER THEIR SPIRITUAL LIFE . . . .   863A LETTER 60   PROSE
    REGARDLESS OF THAT FAINT SHADOW CALLD NATURAL LIFE . . .   863A LETTER 60   PROSE
    WHO PREPARES HIMSELF ARDENTLY FOR HIS RETURN TO LIFE . .   875A LETTER 80   PROSE
    & LIFE NOT IN THE REAL MAN THE IMAGINATION WHICH LIVETH   878A LETTER 88   PROSE
    OF THE TREE OF LIFE & OF THE TREE OF GOOD & EVIL . . .   SUPP ILLUS GENESIS *TITLE
    THE JOURNEY OF LIFE . . . .   SUPP PENC DRAW 1.39 *TITLE
LIFE BLOOD
    AND THE GLOBE OF LIFE BLOOD TREMBLING . . . . . .   231 URIZEN 15   13
    THE GLOBE OF LIFE BLOOD TREMBLED . . . .   231 URIZEN 18   1
LIFE'S
    WE CAN ABIDE LIFE'S PELTING STORM . . . .   64 SHEPHERD OLD   3
    WE CAN ABIDE LIFE'S PELTING STORM . . . .   64 SHEPHERD OLD   7
    SO CLAD WE'LL ABIDE LIFE'S PELTING STORM . . . . .   64 SHEPHERD OLD   11
    FOR WASHD IN LIFE'S RIVER . . . .   119 NIGHT/SI   45
    THEIR LIFE'S WHOLE COMFORT TO INTIRE SCORN & INJURY & DEATH   506 MILTON 23   2
    OF REASON YOU MAY DRINK OF LIFE'S CLEAR STREAMS . . . .   536 DONT BELIEVE/N   4
    THE LIFE'S LABOUR OF MENTAL WEAKNESS SCARCELY EQUALS . .   593A PUB ADDRESS/N   PROSE
    THE LIFE'S LABOUR OF FIVE HUNDRED IDIOTS . . . . .   593B PUB ADDRESS/N   PROSE
    THE LIFE'S LABOUR OF IGNORANT JOURNEYMEN . . . . .   593D PUB ADDRESS/N   PROSE
    CHOOSE TO PURCHASE THE LIFE'S LABOUR OF IGNORANCE   594B PUB ADDRESS/N   PROSE
        & IMBECILLITY
    THE LIFE'S LABOURS OF IMBECILLITY & IMBECILLITY'S   598C PUB ADDRESS/N   PROSE
        JOURNEYMEN
    THIS LIFE'S DIM WINDOWS OF THE SOUL . . . .   753 EV GOSPEL(D)/N   103
    MONEY THE LIFE'S BLOOD OF POOR FAMILIES . . . . . .   776B INSC LAOCOON   PROSE
    ANOTHER SUN FEEDS OUR LIFE'S STREAMS . . . .   818 HAPPINESS/L   65

```
                                                            PAGE      TITLE          LINE
LIFE'S   (CONTINUED)
    [NECESSARIES ACCOMODATIONS & ORNAMENTS ARE LIFE'S WANTS]   SUPP ANNO REYNOLDS  * MARG
LIFES
    FOURFOLD EACH IN THE OTHER REFLECTED THEY ARE NAMED LIFES  364 FOUR ZOAS 9       283
      IN ETERNITY
LIFT
    IN RIBBED STEEL I DARE NOT LIFT MINE EYES  . . . . . .       3 TO WINTER/PS        7
    IF I LIFT UP MY HEAD SIN COVERS ME AS A CLOAK  . . . . .   36A COUCH DEATH/PS    PROSE
    CAN I NOT CRY AND LIFT MY EYES TO HEAVEN  . . . . . . .    36B COUCH DEATH/PS    PROSE
    THE SORROWFUL PAIR LIFT UP THEIR HEADS  . . . . . . . .    36D COUCH DEATH/PS    PROSE
    LIFT UP MY ROMAN PETTICOAT  . . . . . . . . . . . .         54 LO THE BAT/IM      12
    ESCAPE YE FIENDS FOR IJIM WILL NOT LIFT HIS HAND AGAINST YE 106 TIRIEL 4          88
    DEVOUR THY LABOUR NOR LIFT UP A CLOUD IN THY HEAVENS . . .  144 FRENCH REVOLTN    226
    THE ENORMOUS DEAD LIFT UP THEIR PALE FIRES . . . . . . .    148 FRENCH REVOLTN    302
    LIFT UP THY HEAD  . . . . . . . . . . . . . . . .          152B MARRIAGE HH 9    PROSE
    HE WILL GIVE IT THEE FOR WE ARE WEAK WOMEN & DARE NOT LIFT  304 FOUR ZOAS 4       255
    LIFT UP LIFT UP O LOS AWAKE MY WATCHMAN FOR HE SLEEPETH     335 FOUR ZOAS 7B       95
    LIFT UP LIFT UP SHINE FORTH O LIGHT WATCHMAN THY LIGHT      335 FOUR ZOAS 7B       96
      IS OUT
    LIFT UP THY BLUE EYES VALA & PUT ON THY SAPPHIRE SHOES  . . 337 FOUR ZOAS 7B      191
    THEN SHALL THEY LIFT THEIR INNOCENT HANDS & STROKE HIS      376 FOUR ZOAS 9       703
      FURIOUS NOSE
    VOMITED OUT & GAVE UP ALL THE FLOODS LIFT UP THEIR HANDS    378 FOUR ZOAS 9       803
    WHEN ON THE HIGHEST LIFT OF HIS LIGHT PINIONS HE ARRIVES    526 MILTON 36           1
    LIFT UP THY BLUE EYES VALA & PUT ON THY SAPPHIRE SHOES  . . 700 JERUSALEM 65       37
    JEHOVAH WOMAN LIFT THINE EYES  . . . . . . . . . .          779 GHOST ABEL 1        7
    THAT BOTH HE & I WISH THAT IS TO LIFT ME OUT OF DIFFICULTY 811D LETTER 22         PROSE
    AM ALSO GRATEFUL TO THE KIND HAND THAT ENDEAVOURS TO LIFT  822C LETTER 26         PROSE
      ME
LIFTED
    THE LITTLE LIDS ARE LIFTED & THE LITTLE NOSTRILS OPEND      110 TIRIEL 8           29
    THE ETERNAL GATES' TERRIFIC PORTER LIFTED THE NORTHERN BAR  130 BOOK OF THEL 6      1
    . . . THEN LIFTED HIS HEAD AND LOOKD ON HIS ARMIES THAT     139 FRENCH REVOLTN    110
      SHONE
    . . . AND OF SULPHUR THE EARTH FROM FAYETTE AS HE LIFTED    146 FRENCH REVOLTN    278
      HIS HAND
    A BENDED BOW IS LIFTED IN HEAVEN & A HEAVY IRON CHAIN  . .  197 AMERICA 3           7
    A BENDED BOW IN HEAVEN IS LIFTED & A HEAVY IRON CHAIN  . .  204 AMERICA CANC A      7
    THEY SAW THE SERPENT TEMPLE LIFTED ABOVE SHADOWING THE      242 EUROPE 12          11
      ISLAND WHITE
    LIFTED ON HIGH THE DEAD CORSE  . . . . . . . . . .          251 AHANIA 3           52
    THEN VALA LIFTED UP HER HANDS TO HEAVEN TO CALL ON ENION    370 FOUR ZOAS 9       498
    I LIFTED THEM INTO MY FURNACES TO FORM THE SPIRITUAL SWORD  628 JERUSALEM 9        18
    HE LIFTED POURING IT INTO THE CLAY GROUND PREPARD WITH ART  630 JERUSALEM 11        4
    MOUNT ZION LIFTED HIS HEAD IN EVERY NATION UNDER HEAVEN     648 JERUSALEM 24       48
    LOUD LOUD THE MOUNTAINS LIFTED UP THEIR VOICES LOUD THE     686 JERUSALEM 55       23
      FORESTS
    THE SEAS RAISD UP THEIR VOICES & LIFTED THEIR HANDS ON HIGH 686 JERUSALEM 55       26
LIFTING   SEE HEART LIFTING
    POISONOUS SOURCE PLACD WITH ART LIFTING DIFFICULT  . . .    251 AHANIA 3           34
LIFTS
    GWIN LIFTS HIS HAND THE NATIONS HALT . . . . . . . . .       12 GWIN KING/PS       61
    THY FATHER CALLS THY FATHER LIFTS HIS HAND UNTO THE [AIR]   108 TIRIEL 6           41
      HEAVENS
    FROM NIGHTLY PREY AND LIFTS HIS GOLDEN BEAK TO THE PURE     190 V DAU ALBION 2     26
      EAST
    THE DEEP LIFTS UP HIS RUGGED HEAD  . . . . . . . . .        289 FOUR ZOAS 2       360
    HE LIFTS THE BLUE LAMPS OF HIS EYES & CRIES WITH HEAVENLY   359 FOUR ZOAS 9        97
      VOICE
    OUT FROM THE ASHES OF THE DEAD LOS LIFTS HIS IRON LADLES    486 MILTON 6           29
    OUT OF DESPONDENCY EVEN IF IT LIFTS ME TOO HIGH  . . . .   822C LETTER 26         PROSE
LIGHT
    OF FRUIT AND JOY WITH PINIONS LIGHT ROVES ROUND  . . . .      2 TO AUTUMN/PS       14
    NOW [WHILST] WHILE THE SUN RESTS ON THE MOUNTAINS LIGHT  .    3 EVNING STAR/PS      2
    AWAKE THE DAWN THAT SLEEPS IN HEAVEN LET LIGHT  . . . .       3 TO MORNING/PS       3
    FOR LIGHT DOTH SEIZE MY BRAIN  . . . . . . . . . .            9 MAD SONG/PS        23
    OH BLESS THOSE LIMBS BEAMING WITH HEAVNLY LIGHT  . . . .      9 FRESH FROM/PS       8
    THAT SHAKE THE STARS OF LIGHT  . . . . . . . . . .           14 GWIN KING/PS      102
    SCATTERST THE RAYS OF LIGHT AND TRUTH'S BEAMS  . . . . .     14 IMIT SPEN/PS        2
    NOW MY HEART DANCES AND I AM AS LIGHT  . . . . . . . .       24 EDW THIRD/PS 3    144
    TO LIGHT ANOTHER BATTLE LAST NIGHT BENEATH  . . . . . .      25 EDW THIRD/PS 3    160
    LEAVING A TRACK OF LIGHT FOR MEN TO WONDER AT  . . . . .     27 EDW THIRD/PS 3    275
    THO SUNSHINE LIGHT IT SEEMS TO ME AS PALE  . . . . . .       30 EDW THIRD/PS 5     22
    WHOSE FACE IS SHEWN BY LIGHT OF SICKLY TAPER  . . . . .      30 EDW THIRD/PS 5     24
    THOUSANDS OF SOULS MUST SEEK THE REALMS OF LIGHT  . . . .    35 WAR SONG/PS        18
    I SEEM TO WALK THROUGH A DEEP VALLEY FAR FROM THE LIGHT     35D COUCH DEATH/PS    PROSE
      OF DAY
    WHEN THE THIN BEAMS OF THE MOON GIVE A FAINT LIGHT  . . .   36B COUCH DEATH/PS    PROSE
    AND A RAY OF LIGHT BEAMED AROUND HIS HEAD ALL WAS STILL     36C COUCH DEATH/PS    PROSE
    WHEN LO AN ANGEL FROM THE FIELDS OF LIGHT ENTERED THE HOUSE 39D SAMSON/PS         PROSE
    REASON ONCE FAIRER THAN THE LIGHT TILL FOULD  . . . . .    42B THEN SHE BORE      PROSE
    WELL WELL GO & PLAY TILL THE LIGHT FADES AWAY  . . . . .     60 NURSES SONG/IM     14
    THE FEMALE LIFE LIVES FROM THE LIGHT OF THE MALE  . . . .   82C ANNO LAVATER      MARG
    ("KEEPING THE UNDERSTANDING...IN SPIRITUAL LIGHT") THIS     91B ANNO SWED LOVE    MARG
      MAN CAN DO
    IS THE ABSENCE FROM HEAT & LIGHT  . . . . . . . . .         94D ANNO SWED LOVE    MARG
    I AM SET TO LIGHT THE GROUND  . . . . . . . . . .          112 A DREAM/SI         17
    LED BY THE WANDRING LIGHT  . . . . . . . . . . . .         121 LIT BOY FND/SI      2
    WELL WELL GO & PLAY TILL THE LIGHT FADES AWAY  . . . . .   121 NURSES SONG/SI     13
    BUT I AM BLACK AS IF BEREAVD OF LIGHT  . . . . . . .       125 LIT BLK BOY/SI      4
    AND GIVES HIS LIGHT AND GIVES HIS HEAT AWAY  . . . . .     125 LIT BLK BOY/SI     10
    FOR THOU SHALT BE CLOTHED IN LIGHT AND FED WITH MORNING    127 BOOK OF THEL 1     23
      MANNA
```

LIGHT   (CONTINUED)

	PAGE	TITLE	LINE
UNSEEN DESCENDING WEIGH MY LIGHT WINGS UPON BALMY FLOWERS	128	BOOK OF THEL 3	12
. . . HID FROM THE LIGHT AS IN A CLEFT ROCK	135	FRENCH REVOLTN	28
. . . AND A LIGHT WALKS ROUND THE DARK TOWERS	136	FRENCH REVOLTN	53
. . . WEEPING IN THE UNCERTAIN LIGHT	140	FRENCH REVOLTN	131
HE WHOSE FACE GIVES NO LIGHT SHALL NEVER BECOME A STAR	151A	MARRIAGE HH 7	PROSE
ON THOSE INFINITE MOUNTAINS OF LIGHT	159B	SONG LIBERTY	PROSE
QUENCH THE HOLY LIGHT	168	SILENT NIGHT/N	2
HER [EYES FLED] [ORBS DEAD] LIGHT FLED	168	EARTHS ANSWR/N	3
ASHAMED OF THE LIGHT	172	ARE NOT JOYS/N	4
PLUCK FRUITS BEFORE THE LIGHT	172	ARE NOT JOYS/N	8
THE VIGOROUS JOYS OF MORNING LIGHT OPEN TO VIRGIN BLISS	193	V DAU ALBION 6	6
RELIGIOUS DREAMS AND HOLY VESPERS LIGHT THY SMOKY FIRES	194	V DAU ALBION 6	14
SURROUNDED HEAT BUT NOT LIGHT WENT THRO THE MURKY ATMOSPHERE	197	AMERICA 4	11
AND THEN THEIR END SHOULD COME WHEN FRANCE RECIEVD THE DEMON'S LIGHT	203	AMERICA 16	15
WETTING WITH TEARS & HIS WHITE GARMENTS CAST A WINTRY LIGHT	204	AMERICA CANC B	17
AND FALLEN FALLEN LIGHT RENEW	210	INTRODUCTN/SE	10
HER LIGHT FLED	210	EARTHS ANSR/SE	3
TO THE HOLY LIGHT	219	LIT GRL LST/SE	8
WHERE THE HOLY LIGHT	219	LIT GRL LST/SE	13
BUT NO LIGHT FROM THE FIRES ALL WAS DARKNESS	225	URIZEN 5	17
CUT OFF FROM LIFE & LIGHT FROZEN	230	URIZEN 13	42
PRODUCD A MAN CHILD TO THE LIGHT	232	URIZEN 19	40
FIVE WINDOWS LIGHT THE CAVERND MAN THRO ONE HE BREATHES THE AIR	237	EUROPE INTRO	1
THEN ENITHARMON DOWN DESCENDED INTO HIS RED LIGHT	240	EUROPE 4	31
OF COLOURS TWELVE FEW KNOWN ON EARTH GIVE LIGHT IN THE OPAKE	241	EUROPE 10	9
LIGHT OF THY MOTHER'S SOUL I SEE THY LOVELY EAGLES ROUND	244	EUROPE 14	7
SWEET SMILING PESTILENCE I SEE THY BLUSHING LIGHT	244	EUROPE 14	12
ARISE O ORC AND GIVE OUR MOUNTAINS JOY OF THY RED LIGHT	244	EUROPE 14	31
AND IN THE VINEYARDS OF RED FRANCE APPEARD THE LIGHT OF HIS FURY	245	EUROPE 15	2
THAT GAVE LIGHT TO THE MORNINGS OF HEAVEN	251	AHANIA 3	42
BEFORE THEY SEE THE LIGHT	255	AHANIA 5	47
BUT NO LIGHT FROM THE FIRES ALL WAS	257	BOOK OF LOS 3	49
THEN LIGHT FIRST BEGAN FROM THE FIRES	259	BOOK OF LOS 5	10
THE LIGHT THAT FLOWD DOWN ON THE WINDS	260	BOOK OF LOS 5	28
BUT NO LIGHT FOR THE DEEP FLED AWAY	260	BOOK OF LOS 5	48
HIS HEAD BEAMD LIGHT & IN HIS VIGOROUS VOICE WAS PROPHECY	270	FOUR ZOAS 1	239
[BRIGHT] DARK AS A DEWY MORNING WHEN THE CRIMSON LIGHT APPEARS	271	FOUR ZOAS 1	* 253
AND LUVAH SIEZD THE HORSES OF LIGHT & ROSE INTO THE CHARIOT OF DAY	271	FOUR ZOAS 1	264
WHY IS THE LIGHT OF [VALA] ENITHARMON DARKEND IN [HER] DEWY MORN	271	FOUR ZOAS 1	* 268
OF LIGHT SILENT THE PRINCE OF LIGHT VIEWD LOS AT LENGTH A BROODED	273	FOUR ZOAS 1	321
SO SPOKE THE PRINCE OF LIGHT & SAT BESIDE THE SEAT OF LOS	273	FOUR ZOAS 1	329
WITH WINGED RADIANCE SCATTERING JOYS THRO THE EVER CHANGING LIGHT	274	FOUR ZOAS 1	358
WITH WINE OF CRUELTY LET US [LIGHT] PLAT A SCOURGE O SISTER CITY	275	FOUR ZOAS 1	* 399
[TO ?LIGHT ?THE] BY NIGHT NOR DAY TO COMFORT HER . . .	275	FOUR ZOAS 1	* 418
THOU LUVAH SAID THE PRINCE OF LIGHT BEHOLD OUR SONS & DAUGHTERS	277	FOUR ZOAS 1	488
[XXX THE LIGHT OF DAY]	SUPP	FOUR ZOAS 1	*
THO THOU HAST NOT PITID MY AGE O URIZEN PRINCE OF LIGHT	280	FOUR ZOAS 2	8
AND ALL ITS GOLDEN PORCHES GREW PALE WITH HIS SICKENING LIGHT	280	FOUR ZOAS 2	13
IN HUMAN FORMS DISTINCT THEY STOOD ROUND URIZEN PRINCE OF LIGHT	281	FOUR ZOAS 2	37
WHILE THE PRINCE OF LIGHT ON SALISBURY PLAIN AMONG THE DRUID STONES	281	FOUR ZOAS 2	65
FROM BONDAGE OF THE HUMAN FORM O FIRST BORN SON OF LIGHT	283	FOUR ZOAS 2	108
THE VEHICLES OF LIGHT THEY SEPARATE THE FURIOUS PARTICLES	284	FOUR ZOAS 2	154
THE KING OF LIGHT BEHELD HER MOURNING AMONG THE BRICK KILNS COMPELLD	285	FOUR ZOAS 2	215
WANDERING EVEN TO THE SUNNY [ORBS] CUBES OF LIGHT & HEAT	286	FOUR ZOAS 2	254
THE BEAMY DAUGHTERS OF THE LIGHT STARTING THEY RISE THEY FLEE	288	FOUR ZOAS 2	315
I HAVE BLOTTED OUT FROM LIGHT & LIVING THE DOVE & NIGHTINGALE	290	FOUR ZOAS 2	391
NOW SAT THE KING OF LIGHT ON HIGH UPON HIS STARRY THRONE	291	FOUR ZOAS 3	1
DO THEY NOT FLY INTO THEIR STATIONS & RETURN THEIR LIGHT TO THEE	291	FOUR ZOAS 3	7
SURROUNDED BY THE EVER CHANGING DAUGHTERS OF THE LIGHT	291	FOUR ZOAS 3	9
SHE CEASD THE PRINCE HIS LIGHT OBSCURD & THE SPLENDORS OF HIS CROWN	292	FOUR ZOAS 3	12
WHOM URIZEN DOTH SERVE WITH LIGHT REPLENISHING HIS DARKNESS	292	FOUR ZOAS 3	15
LEAVE ALL FUTURITY TO HIM RESUME THY FIELDS OF LIGHT	292	FOUR ZOAS 3	30
TO GIVE THE IMMORTAL STEEDS OF LIGHT TO HIS DECEITFUL HANDS	292	FOUR ZOAS 3	32
. . . PRINCE OF LIGHT [WITH] THY SPLENDOR FADED	292	FOUR ZOAS 3	46
THE DISMAL VISION OF MINE EYES O LOVE & LIFE & LIGHT	293	FOUR ZOAS 3	73
WHEN URIZEN GAVE THE HORSES OF LIGHT INTO THE HANDS OF LUVAH	300	FOUR ZOAS 4	113
O WHY DID FOUL AMBITION SIEZE THEE [L] URIZEN PRINCE OF LIGHT	301	FOUR ZOAS 4	* 141
PRINCE OF LIGHT BOUND IN CHAINS OF INTELLECT AMONG THE FURNACES	305	FOUR ZOAS 5	16

		PAGE	TITLE	LINE

LIGHT   (CONTINUED)

	PAGE	TITLE	LINE
SING IN THE SKY AS ONCE THEY SANG UPON THE HILLS OF LIGHT	306 FOUR ZOAS 5	52
NINE VIRGINS CLOTHD IN LIGHT	310 FOUR ZOAS 5	200
BECAUSE THE STEEDS OF URIZEN ONCE SWIFTER THAN THE LIGHT	310 FOUR ZOAS 5	208
O FOOL COULD I FORGET THE LIGHT THAT FILLED MY BRIGHT SPHERES	310 FOUR ZOAS 5	216
SAYING [S] O LIGHT SPRING UP & SHINE & I SPRANG UP FROM THE DEEP	310 FOUR ZOAS 5 *	219
FOR STEEDS OF LIGHT	311 FOUR ZOAS 5	235
ON WHOM I POURD THE BEAUTIES OF MY LIGHT ADORNING THEM . .	312 FOUR ZOAS 6	26
A DREARY WASTE OF SOLID WATERS FOR THE KING OF LIGHT .	313 FOUR ZOAS 6	51
WITHHOLD THY LIGHT FROM ME FOR EVER & I WILL WITHHOLD . .	313 FOUR ZOAS 6	64
[NOT SO CLOSD UP THE PRINCE OF LIGHT NOW DARKEND WANDRING AMONG]	314 FOUR ZOAS 6 *	100
IN SUCCESSIVE VOLLIES WITH LOUD THUNDERS SWIFT FLEW THE KING OF LIGHT	314 FOUR ZOAS 6 *	109
I WELL REMEMBER HOW I STOLE THY LIGHT & IT BECAME FIRE . .	323 FOUR ZOAS 7	147
CONSUMING THOU KNOWST ME NOW O URIZEN PRINCE OF LIGHT .	324 FOUR ZOAS 7	148
DESPISING URIZEN'S LIGHT & TURNING IT INTO FLAMING FIRE	324 FOUR ZOAS 7	153
THY LILLIES THAT GAVE LIGHT WHAT TIME THE MORNING LOOKED FORTH	325 FOUR ZOAS 7	196
[VALAN] VALA WAS PREGNANT & BROUGHT FORTH URIZEN PRINCE OF LIGHT	326 FOUR ZOAS 7 *	244
[THE SHADOWY VOICE ANSWERD O URIZEN PRINCE OF LIGHT] . .	333 FOUR ZOAS 7B *	11
INTO THE TEMPLE OF URIZEN TO GIVE LIGHT TO THE ABYSS .	333 FOUR ZOAS 7B	35
TO LIGHT THE WAR BY DAY TO HIDE HIS SECRET BEAMS BY NIGHT	334 FOUR ZOAS 7B	36
LIFT UP LIFT UP SHINE FORTH O LIGHT WATCHMAN THY LIGHT IS OUT	335 FOUR ZOAS 7B	96
OF MAN I MADE THEE WHEN I BLOTTED MAN FROM LIFE & LIGHT	336 FOUR ZOAS 7B	117
ARISE O VALA BRING THE BOW OF URIZEN BRING THE SWIFT ARROWS OF LIGHT	338 FOUR ZOAS 7B	200
AND HEARTS LAID OPEN TO THE LIGHT BY THE BROAD GRIZLY SWORD	338 FOUR ZOAS 7B	206
THE SUBTLEST THOUGHTS SHUT UP FROM LIGHT IN CHAMBERS OF THE MOON	339 FOUR ZOAS 7B	243
FOR ALL MY SECRET FAULTS WHICH HE BRINGS FORTH UPON THE LIGHT	339 FOUR ZOAS 7B	250
THOU ART OUR CURSE [IN] AND TILL I CAN BRING LOVE INTO THE LIGHT	339 FOUR ZOAS 7B *	257
WITH JOY THE BRIGHT LIGHT & IN IT A HUMAN FORM	342 FOUR ZOAS 8	43
THE FELL DESTRUCTION AND SHE SAID O URIZEN PRINCE OF LIGHT	344 FOUR ZOAS 8	145
UNHURT & DARE THE INCLEMENT FOREHEAD OF THE KING OF LIGHT	345 FOUR ZOAS 8	149
WE ARE ALL SERVANTS TO THY WILL O KING OF LIGHT RELENT .	345 FOUR ZOAS 8	162
SHE WENT TO URIZEN IN PRIDE THE PRINCE OF LIGHT BEHELD . .	351 FOUR ZOAS 8	412
NO LONGER NOW ERECT THE KING OF LIGHT OUTSTRETCHD IN FURY	352 FOUR ZOAS 8	438
HIS SCALES TRANSPARENT GIVE FORTH LIGHT LIKE WINDOWS OF THE MORNING	352 FOUR ZOAS 8	441
HIS EYELIDS GIVE THEIR LIGHT AROUND HIS FOLDING TAIL ASPIRES	352 FOUR ZOAS 8	447
THEY VIEW THE LIGHT & WONDER CRYING OUT IN TERRIBLE EXISTENCE	352 FOUR ZOAS 8	452
URIZEN GAVE THE HORSES OF LIGHT INTO THE HANDS OF LUVAH	359 FOUR ZOAS 9	94
AND ALL EXILED FROM THE FACE OF LIGHT & SHINE OF MORNING	360 FOUR ZOAS 9	112
O PRINCE OF LIGHT WHERE ART THOU I BEHOLD THEE NOT AS ONCE	360 FOUR ZOAS 9	124
FEARING THY FROWN LOVING THY SMILE O URIZEN PRINCE OF LIGHT	360 FOUR ZOAS 9	135
AND THE ETERNAL MAN SAID HEAR MY [VOICE] WORDS O PRINCE OF LIGHT	362 FOUR ZOAS 9	204
WHAT CHAIN ENCOMPASSES IN WHAT LOCK IS THE RIVER OF LIGHT CONFIND	363 FOUR ZOAS 9	226
AND EVERY FLOWER & EVERY LEAF REJOICES IN HIS LIGHT . .	367 FOUR ZOAS 9	407
TO FEEL THY HEAT & SEE THY LIGHT & WANDER HERE ALONE . .	368 FOUR ZOAS 9	416
RISE UP O SUN MOST GLORIOUS MINISTER & LIGHT OF DAY . . .	368 FOUR ZOAS 9	434
AND DARKNESS COVERD ALL THE DEEP THE LIGHT OF ENION FADED	370 FOUR ZOAS 9	496
SHE CEASD & (LIGHT) BEAMD ROUND HER LIKE THE GLORY OF THE MORNING	370 FOUR ZOAS 9 *	503
DARKNESS WAS ALL BENEATH THE HEAVENS ONLY A LITTLE LIGHT	372 FOUR ZOAS 9	560
HE POURD HIS LIGHT & ALL HIS SONS & DAUGHTERS POURD THEIR LIGHT	372 FOUR ZOAS 9	569
AND LUVAH & VALA SAW THE LIGHT THEIR SPIRITS WERE EXHALD	372 FOUR ZOAS 9	571
ROSE ENION LIKE A GENTLE LIGHT & ENION SPOKE SAYING . .	373 FOUR ZOAS 9	594
. . . & URIZEN PRINCE OF LIGHT	380 FOUR ZOAS AD 1	2
IN ALL ITS TURPITUDE BENEATH THE DIVINE LIGHT & OF LUVAH'S ROBES	382 FOUR ZOAS AD 6	22
BUT TO HIM WHO SEES THIS MORTAL PILGRIMAGE IN THE LIGHT THAT I SEE IT	383B ANNO WATSON	MARG
NO MAN CAN TAKE DARKNESS FOR LIGHT HE MAY PRETEND TO DO SO	386C ANNO WATSON	MARG
AND NEWTON'S PARTICLES OF LIGHT	418 MOCK ON/N	10
IN BEAMS OF INFERNAL LIGHT	418 I SAW A MONK/N	4
ABOVE THE LIGHT OF THE MORNING STAR	427 LAND OF DREAMS	20
DOTH PUT THE LIGHT OF KNOWLEDGE OUT	433 AUGURIES	96
WHEN THE SOUL SLEPT IN BEAMS OF LIGHT	434 AUGURIES	128
GOD APPEARS & GOD IS LIGHT	434 AUGURIES	129
BUT O HE LIVES IN THE MOONY LIGHT	436 WILLIAM BOND	46
THESE BLOTS OF LIGHT AND DARK AS BEING THE RESULT OF LABOUR	439C REMARKS MALKIN	PROSE
AND BEGINNING WITH THE SPOTS OF LIGHT ON EACH OBJECT . .	440B MEMORANDUM/N 3	PROSE
HIRE IDIOTS TO PAINT WITH COLD LIGHT & HOT SHADE	445 ANNO REYNOLDS	2
TRUE LIGHT & SHADOW [NOTHING MUST BE SACRIFICD FOR LIGHT]	463A ANNO REYNOLDS *	MARG
LIGHT & SHADE	475D ANNO REYNOLDS	MARG
HAVE THE SAME LIGHT & (SHADOWS)	477C ANNO REYNOLDS *	MARG
ANY FOOL MAY (CONCENTRATE) A LIGHT IN THE MIDDLE . . .	477C ANNO REYNOLDS *	MARG
SCARCELY BEHOLDING THE GREAT LIGHT CONVERSING WITH THE VOID	484 MILTON 5	22
EVERY THING IN ETERNITY SHINES BY ITS OWN INTERNAL LIGHT BUT THOU	491 MILTON 10	16

		PAGE	TITLE	LINE
LIGHT	(CONTINUED)			
	DARKENEST EVERY INTERNAL LIGHT WITH THE ARROWS OF THY QUIVER	491	MILTON 10	17
	THAT EVERY THING IS FIXD OPAKE WITHOUT INTERNAL LIGHT . .	491	MILTON 10	20
	FOR HER LIGHT IS TERRIBLE TO ME I FADE BEFORE HER IMMORTAL BEAUTY	492	MILTON 12	1
	OF HELL BEHELD HIM IN A TRAIL OF LIGHT AS OF A COMET . .	496	MILTON 15	19
	COVERING THE LIGHT OF DAY & ROLLING DOWN UPON THE MOUNTAINS	507	MILTON 23	26
	MOUNTING UPON THE WINGS OF LIGHT INTO THE GREAT EXPANSE	520	MILTON 31	32
	LIGHT SPRINGING ON THE AIR LEAD THE SWEET DANCE THEY WAKE	520	MILTON 31	53
	WHEN ON THE HIGHEST LIFT OF HIS LIGHT PINIONS HE ARRIVES	526	MILTON 36	1
	WITH THE FINGER ON THE LIPS & THE BACK TURND TO THE LIGHT	528	MILTON 37	32
	OF DISPLAYING UP A LIGHT WHEN WE WANT NOT TO SEE	550	ENGL ENCOU/N 2	8
	FOR ITS LIGHT AND ITS WARMTH THIS MAN IS BELOVED AND .	570B	DESC CAT 3	PROSE
	SUCH A BURNING AND A SHINING LIGHT SEARCH O YE RICH AND	570C	DESC CAT 3	PROSE
	HAVE BEEN PRODUCED WITH RUBENS' LIGHT AND SHADOW . .	573A	DESC CAT 3	PROSE
	BETTER LIGHT THAN HIS PERISHING MORTAL EYE CAN SEE . . .	576D	DESC CAT 4	*PROSE
	AND BLOCKS UP ALL ITS GATES OF LIGHT EXCEPT ONE . . .	583A	DESC CAT 9	PROSE
	EVERY THING IS TONED BUT ONE SPOT OF LIGHT	596C	PUB ADDRESS/N	PROSE
	IMMEDIATELY SET ABOUT SEARCHING FOR POINTS OF LIGHT . .	599A	PUB ADDRESS/N	PROSE
	A POINT OF LIGHT IS A WITTICISM MANY ARE DESTRUCTIVE OF ALL ART	599A	PUB ADDRESS/N	PROSE
	[OP] OR POINTS OF LIGHT TO BE PUT INTO A DARK HOLE . . .	599B	PUB ADDRESS/N	*PROSE
	REPRESENTED AS A STREAM OF [LIGHT] FIGURES	610B	V LAST JUDG/N	PROSE
	THE ONE SHINES WITH BEAMS OF LIGHT	612B	V LAST JUDG/N	PROSE
	OF LIGHT AND LOVE THEIR LITTLE CHILDREN STAND WITH ARROWS OF GOLD	631	JERUSALEM 11	20
	THE LAND OF DARKNESS FLAMED BUT NO LIGHT & NO REPOSE .	634	JERUSALEM 13	46
	FATHER AND SON AND LIGHT AND LOVE ALL BOLD ASPERITIES .	640	JERUSALEM 18	21
	AND SELF-EXILED FROM THE FACE OF LIGHT & SHINE OF MORNING	641	JERUSALEM 19	13
	I BROUGHT LOVE INTO LIGHT OF DAY TO PRIDE IN CHASTE BEAUTY	645	JERUSALEM 22	17
	I BROUGHT LOVE INTO LIGHT & FANCIED INNOCENCE IS NO MORE	645	JERUSALEM 22	18
	THINKING TO BRING LOVE INTO LIGHT OF DAY TO JERUSALEM'S SHAME	647	JERUSALEM 24	5
	HE LOOKED UP & SAW THE PRINCE OF LIGHT WITH SPLENDOR FADED	654	JERUSALEM 29	35
	NOR DARKNESS IMMINGLED WITH LIGHT ON MY FURROWED FIELD .	659	JERUSALEM 33	32
	I SEE THEE AWFUL PARENT LAND IN LIGHT BEHOLD I SEE . .	665	JERUSALEM 38	44
	THAT EVERY LITTLE PARTICLE OF LIGHT & AIR BECAME OPAKE .	674	JERUSALEM 44	10
	SCARCELY BEHOLDING THE GREAT LIGHT CONVERSING WITH THE (VOID)	680	JERUSALEM 49	* 35
	IN BEAMS OF INFERNAL LIGHT	683	I SAW A MONK/J	4
	ITS OWN PECULIAR LIGHT & THE FORM IS THE DIVINE VISION . .	684	JERUSALEM 54	2
	AND THE LIGHT IS HIS GARMENT THIS IS JERUSALEM IN EVERY MAN	684	JERUSALEM 54	3
	WE WOMEN TREMBLE AT THE LIGHT THEREFORE HIDING FEARFUL . .	688	JERUSALEM 56	39
	ARISE O VALA BRING THE BOW OF URIZEN BRING THE SWIFT ARROWS OF LIGHT	700	JERUSALEM 65	46
	AND HEARTS LAID OPEN TO THE LIGHT BY THE BROAD GRIZLY SWORD	701	JERUSALEM 65	52
	LIKE LOVELY BEAMS OF LIGHT	710	JERUSALEM 71	24
	THE INHABITANTS OF THE WHOLE EARTH REJOICE IN THEIR BEAUTIFUL LIGHT	710	JERUSALEM 71	25
	DWELL OVER THE FOUR PROVINCES OF IRELAND IN HEAVENLY LIGHT	710	JERUSALEM 71	52
	APPEAR IN STRONG DELUSIVE LIGHT OF TIME & SPACE DRAWN OUT	715	JERUSALEM 75	5
	WITH LUVAH INTO LIGHT ETERNAL IN HIS ETERNAL DAY . .	716	JERUSALEM 75	26
	AMONG PRECIPICES OF DESPAIR IN GOSHEN I SEEK FOR LIGHT . .	720	JERUSALEM 79	11
	IN OPEN DAY TO DRAW THE SOULS OF THE DEAD INTO THE LIGHT	721	JERUSALEM 79	79
	AND HER DELUSIVE LIGHT BEAMD FIERCE ABOVE THE MOUNTAIN . .	723	JERUSALEM 80	59
	O SISTER CAMBEL SAID GWENDOLEN AS THEIR LONG BEAMING LIGHT	723	JERUSALEM 80	83
	SHOOTING OUT AGAINST THE LIGHT	753	EV GOSPEL(D)/N	95
	WHEN THE SOUL SLEPT IN THE BEAMS OF LIGHT	753	EV GOSPEL(D)/N	108
	BROUGHT TO LIGHT BY JESUS EVEN THE COVENANT OF JEHOVAH . .	757D	EV GOSPEL	PROSE
	WHAT WAS [IT] IT THAT HE BROUGHT TO LIGHT	758	EV GOSPEL (2)	* 3
	WHEN THEY THE GOSPEL LIGHT BEHELD	758	EV GOSPEL (2)	20
	THE SUN'S LIGHT WHEN HE UNFOLDS IT	760	FOR SEXES/GP	1
	PLATO DID NOT BRING LIFE & IMMORTALITY TO LIGHT . . .	774C	ANNO BERKELEY	MARG
	THE ONLY LIGHT OF ANTIQUITY THAT REMAINS UNPERVERTED BY WAR	778D	HOMERS POETRY	PROSE
	BY MEANS OF LAWFUL WINDOW LIGHT THE HOLY GHOST [WHO] . .	787D	ANNO THORNTON	* MARG
	THE IMMENSE FLOOD OF GRECIAN LIGHT & GLORY WHICH IS COMING	797C	LETTER 10	PROSE
	MY FIRST VISION OF LIGHT	804	TO BUTTS/L	2
	THE LIGHT OF THE MORNING	804	TO BUTTS/L	13
	THE JEWELS OF LIGHT	804	TO BUTTS/L	16
	TILL THE JEWELS OF LIGHT	805	TO BUTTS/L	49
	PARTS OF THE ART WHICH RELATE TO LIGHT & SHADE & COLOUR & AM	814A	LETTER 23	PROSE
	INTO THE LIGHT OF DAY I STILL & SHALL TO ETERNITY EMBRACE	815D	LETTER 23	PROSE
	MY MIND IS NOT WITH THY LIGHT ARRAYD	818	HAPPINESS/L	69
	HIS EYES LIGHT UP AT THE MENTION OF YOUR NAME . . .	844B	LETTER 43	PROSE
	NEATLY DONE HIS MERIT WAS BUT LITTLE IN LIGHT AND SHADE	844B	LETTER 43	PROSE
	TO MR ROSE IN AN UNFAIR LIGHT AS I HAVE NO DOUBT . . .	847B	LETTER 44	PROSE
	BECOME CHILDREN OF LIGHT AND LIBERTY AND MY FEET AND MY	852A	LETTER 50	PROSE
	WITH THE LIGHT I ENJOYED IN MY YOUTH AND WHICH HAS FOR .	852B	LETTER 50	PROSE
	THE LIGHT OF ART O THE DISTRESS I HAVE UNDERGONE AND MY	852B	LETTER 50	PROSE
	SAID & HOPE THAT HE WILL SEE THE MATTER IN THE LIGHT YOU DO	856D	LETTER 54	PROSE
LIGHTED				
	ONCE WERE THY FIRES LIGHTED BY THE EYES OF HONEST MORN . .	194	V DAU ALBION 6	15
LIGHTENINGS				
	ACROSS EUROPE & ASIA TO CHINA & JAPAN LIKE LIGHTENINGS . .	281	FOUR ZOAS 2	* 59
LIGHTER				
	LIGHTER THAN A BALL OF WOOL ROLLED BY THE WIND	809A	LETTER 20	PROSE
LIGHTING				
	WITH A GLOBE OF FIRE LIGHTING HIS JOURNEY	234	URIZEN 20	48
	LIGHTING HIS DISMAL JOURNEY THRO THE PATHLESS WORLD OF DEATH	314	FOUR ZOAS 6	84

```
                                                          PAGE    TITLE           LINE
LIGHTING    (CONTINUED)
   OF LIGHTING A LAMP WHEN YOU DONT WISH TO SEE  . . . . .   549 ENGL ENCOU/N 1     8
LIGHTLY
   LIGHTLY TRIPPING ON A ROW  . . . . . . . . . . . .        53 PHEBE DREST/IM     8
   THAT LIGHTLY TRIP ON BEAUTY'S TOE  . . . . . . . .        56 HAIL MATRIM/IM     5
LIGHTNING
   AND GIVE COMMAND AND LIGHTNING HAS FLASHED  . . . .       22 EDW THIRD/PS 3    27
   LIKE LIONS ROUZD BY LIGHTNING FROM THEIR DENS  . . . .    32 EDW THIRD/PS 6     8
   WHEN THE RED LIGHTNING BORNE BY FURIOUS STORMS  . . . .   32 EDW THIRD/PS 6    28
   FRAUGHT WITH THE SWORDS OF LIGHTNING BUT I BRAVD        105 TIRIEL 4       *   56
      THE VENGEANCE TOO
   WHY IS THE SILENCE OF [VALA LIGHTNING] ENITHARMON . . .  271 FOUR ZOAS 1    *  269
   AND THREW AHANIA FROM HIS BOSOM OBDURATE SHE FELL LIKE   295 FOUR ZOAS 3       132
      LIGHTNING
   SATAN BUT SWIFT AS LIGHTNING PASSING THEM STARTLED THE   496 MILTON 15         18
      SHADES
   FLASH OF LIGHTNING BUT MORE QUICK THE VIRGIN IN MY GARDEN 527 MILTON 36        19
   THEY GO FORTH & RETURN SWIFT AS A FLASH OF LIGHTNING  .  .  722 JERUSALEM 80   44
   LOUD THUNDRING WITH BROAD FLASHES OF FLAMING LIGHTNING   742 JERUSALEM 95       8
      & PILLARS
LIGHTNINGS      SEE LIGHTENINGS
   AND SEE THE WINGED LIGHTNINGS AS THEY FLY  . . . . . .    15 IMIT SPEN/PS   *  41
   THEN THE DREADFUL LIGHTNINGS BREAK  . . . . . . . .      165 CRADLE SONG/N     17
   AS WHEN A BLACK CLOUD SHEWS ITS LIGHTNINGS TO THE SILENT 196 AMERICA PREL 2     5
      DEEP
   MINGLE IN HOWLING PAINS IN FURROWS BY THY LIGHTNINGS RENT 196 AMERICA PREL 2   16
   CHILDREN TAKE SHELTER FROM THE LIGHTNINGS THERE STANDS   199 AMERICA 9         10
      WASHINGTON
   BUT PALAMABRON SHOT HIS LIGHTNINGS TRENCHING DOWN HIS WIDE 242 EUROPE 12       23
      BACK
   THEN THUNDERS ROLLD AROUND & LIGHTNINGS DARTED TO & FRO  294 FOUR ZOAS 3      109
   . . . OR BROODING LIGHTNINGS & PESTILENTIAL PLAGUES  . . . 314 FOUR ZOAS 6     93
   LIGHTNINGS WHICH BLAZED AFTER THEM UPON THEIR SHOULDERS  314 FOUR ZOAS 6      108
      . . .
   THRO LIGHTNINGS THUNDERS EARTHQUAKES & CONCUSSIONS FIRES 316 FOUR ZOAS 6      185
      & FLOODS
   . . . LIGHTNINGS THUNDERS HOVERD  . . .                  325 FOUR ZOAS 7     227
   IN FURROWD LIGHTNINGS BREAK THEIR WAY . . .  .  . . . .  359 FOUR ZOAS 9       85
   BENEATH THICK CLOUDS DREADFUL LIGHTNINGS BURST & THUNDERS 372 FOUR ZOAS 9     565
      ROLL
   NOT LONG THUNDERS LIGHTNINGS SWIFT RENDINGS & BLASTING   381 FOUR ZOAS AD 2     3
      WINDS
   [& FROM THE TABLES OF STONE WHICH UTTER LIGHTNINGS]  . . . 443B LAST JUDGMNT/L  PROSE
   AND ANVILS DANCE THE DANCE OF TEARS & PAIN LOUD LIGHTNINGS 484 MILTON 5         16
   SO LOS SPOKE BUT LIGHTNINGS OF DISCONTENT BROKE ON ALL   511 MILTON 25         63
      SIDES ROUND
   THE PLOW GOES FORTH IN TEMPESTS & LIGHTNINGS & THE HARROW 514 MILTON 27        47
      CRUEL
   RENDING THE HEAVENS OF BEULAH WITH YOUR THUNDERS         523 MILTON 34          5
      & LIGHTNINGS
   THE OTHER UTTERS LIGHTNINGS & TEMPESTS  . . . . . . . 612B V LAST JUDG/N       PROSE
   FOR HIS WORDS ROLL IN THUNDERS & LIGHTNINGS AMONG        737 JERUSALEM 90       60
      THE TEMPLES
   IN THE DEEP DARKNESS BROAD LIGHTNINGS GLARE LONG THUNDERS 741 JERUSALEM 94       4
      ROLL
   THUNDERS & LIGHTNINGS BROKE AROUND  . . . . . . . . .    749 EV GOSPEL(B)/N    25
LIGHTS
   LIGHTS ON SOME WOODY SHORE THE PARCHED HEAVENS  . . . .   32 EDW THIRD/PS 6    29
   . . . THAT LIGHTS THE [DISMAL] DARKSOM DAY . . . . . .   283 FOUR ZOAS 2      128
   HIS EYES THE LIGHTS OF HIS LARGE SOUL CONTRACT OR ELSE   308 FOUR ZOAS 5      121
      EXPAND
   HIS LIGHTS ARE ALL THE COLOURS OF THE RAINBOW  . . . . . 469A ANNO REYNOLDS   MARG
   BUT ON WHERE THE LIGHTS AND DARKS ARE PUT  . . . . . . 563D DESC CAT         PROSE
   AND OF ENDLESS REFLECTED LIGHTS THAT CONFUSE ONE ANOTHER 583B DESC CAT 9      PROSE
   THAT THE SPEAR THAT LIGHTS IT FORTH MAY SHATTER THE RIBS 672 JERUSALEM 43      34
      & BOSOM
   OPPOSED TO MELODY AND BY LIGHTS & SHADES OPPOSED        715 JERUSALEM 74      25
      TO OUTLINE
   EMINENT IN THE ART OF MASSING HIS LIGHTS AND SHADES  . . . 844B LETTER 43     PROSE
LIKE    SEE DIRGE-LIKE,DUNGEON-LIKE,EAGLE LIKE,MOTH-LIKE,ROOT-LIKE,SOLDIER-LIKE,
        WING/LIKE
   ROUZD LIKE A HUNTSMAN TO THE CHACE AND WITH  . . . . .     3 TO MORNING/PS      7
   AND LIKE A GHOST THRO NARROW PASSAGES  . . . . . . . .     4 FAIR ELENOR/PS    11
   LIKE A DUMB STATUE FROZE TO STONE WITH FEAR  . . . . .     4 FAIR ELENOR/PS    20
   MY LORD WAS LIKE A FLOWER UPON THE BROWS  . . . . . .      5 FAIR ELENOR/PS    41
   MY LORD WAS LIKE A STAR IN HIGHEST HEAVN  . . . . . .      5 FAIR ELENOR/PS    45
   MY LORD WAS LIKE THE OPENING EYES OF DAY  . . . . . .      5 FAIR ELENOR/PS    47
   BUT HE IS DARKEND LIKE THE SUMMER'S NOON  . . . . . .      5 FAIR ELENOR/PS    49
   CLOUDED FALLN LIKE THE STATELY TREE CUT DOWN  . . . . .    5 FAIR ELENOR/PS    50
   LIKE GENTLE STREAMS BENEATH OUR FEET  . . . . . . .        7 LOVE HARMNY/PS     7
   LIKE A FIEND IN A CLOUD  . . . . . . . .                   9 MAD SONG/PS       17
   I MEET MY MAIDEN RISEN LIKE THE MORN . . . . . . . .       9 FRESH FROM/PS      6
   OH BLESS THOSE HOLY FEET LIKE ANGELS' FEET  . . . . . .    9 FRESH FROM/PS      7
   LIKE AS AN ANGEL GLITTRING IN THE SKY  . . . . . . . .     9 FRESH FROM/PS      9
   BENEATH THEM ROLLD LIKE TEMPESTS BLACK  . . . . . . .     11 GWIN KING/PS      17
   LIKE LIONS' WHELPS ROARING ABROAD  . . . . . . . . .      11 GWIN KING/PS      19
   LIKE RUSHING MIGHTY FLOODS  . . . . . . . . . . .         11 GWIN KING/PS      24
   HOWLING LIKE GHOSTS FURIOUS AS WOLVES  . . . . . . . .    11 GWIN KING/PS      27
   LIKE CLOUDS COME ROLLING OER  . . . . . . . . . . .       12 GWIN KING/PS      36
   EACH LIKE AN AWFUL THUNDER CLOUD  . . . . . . . . .       12 GWIN KING/PS      39
   LIKE REARED STONES AROUND A GRAVE  . . . . . . . . .      12 GWIN KING/PS      41
   LIKE THE TALL GHOST OF BARRATON  . . . . . . . . . .      12 GWIN KING/PS      53
```

	PAGE	TITLE	LINE
LIKE (CONTINUED)			
LIKE CLOUDS AROUND HIM ROLLD	12	GWIN KING/PS	60
THE ARMIES STAND LIKE BALANCES	13	GWIN KING/PS	65
LIKE WARRING MIGHTY SEAS	13	GWIN KING/PS	70
LIKE BLAZING COMETS SCATTERING DEATH	13	GWIN KING/PS	83
BENEATH HIS ARM LIKE SHEEP THEY DIE	13	GWIN KING/PS	85
LIKE BLAZING COMETS IN THE SKY	14	GWIN KING/PS	101
WHICH DROP LIKE FRUIT UNTO THE EARTH	14	GWIN KING/PS	103
LIKE THESE DID GWIN AND GORDRED MEET	14	GWIN KING/PS	105
DOWN LIKE A FALLING STAR FROM AUTUMN SKY	15	IMIT SPEN/PS	25
WHERE LIKE THE SEA THE WAVES OF BATTLE MOVE	15	IMIT SPEN/PS	50
WHILE LIKE THE MOUNTING FLAME	18	EDW THIRD/PS 1	15
THE WORLD OF MEN ARE LIKE THE NUMROUS STARS	18	EDW THIRD/PS 1	32
LIKE SUMMER BEES AND ALL THE GOLDEN CITIES	19	EDW THIRD/PS 2	13
O MY GOOD LORD TRUE WISDOM DROPS LIKE HONEY	20	EDW THIRD/PS 2	36
SMALL SHIPS OF WAR THAT LIKE TO RAVENING WOLVES	20	EDW THIRD/PS 2	66
SPRINGS FROM THE HILLS LIKE A YOUNG HERO	21	EDW THIRD/PS 3	3
OF BATTLE LIKE THE YOUTH AT MORRICE PLAY	22	EDW THIRD/PS 3	31
YOU ARE MORE LIKE A LION THAN A CRANE	24	EDW THIRD/PS 3	131
AND WE WILL SING LIKE THE YOUNG HOUSEWIVES BUSIED	24	EDW THIRD/PS 3	148
I TOLD HIM HE LOOKD LIKE A CANDLE HALF	25	EDW THIRD/PS 3	158
WILL BEND OR BREAK US MY BLOOD LIKE A SPRINGTIDE	26	EDW THIRD/PS 3	234
BIND ARDENT HOPE UPON YOUR FEET LIKE SHOES	30	EDW THIRD/PS 5	33
AND BLOOD SHALL FLOW LIKE STREAMS ACROSS THE MEADOWS	31	EDW THIRD/PS 5	54
IN SICKLY DARKNESS LIKE A DIM ECLIPSE	31	EDW THIRD/PS 6	4
LIKE LIONS ROUZD BY LIGHTNING FROM THEIR DENS	32	EDW THIRD/PS 6	8
NAKED AND ROARING LIKE LIONS HURLING ROCKS	32	EDW THIRD/PS 6	22
AND WIELDING KNOTTY CLUBS LIKE OAKS ENTANGLED	32	EDW THIRD/PS 6	23
THE SAVAGE MONSTERS RUSH LIKE ROARING FIRE	32	EDW THIRD/PS 6	26
LIKE AS A FOREST ROARS WITH CRACKLING FLAMES	32	EDW THIRD/PS 6	27
LIKE EAGLES FOR THE PREY NOR SHALL THE YOUNG	33	EDW THIRD/PS 6	45
O FOR A VOICE LIKE THUNDER AND A TONGUE	33	EDW FOURTH/PS	1
LIKE LILIES DROPPING TEARS IN EACH OTHER'S BOSOM	35D	COUCH DEATH/PS	PROSE
THEY STOOD BY THE BED LIKE REEDS BENDING OVER A LAKE	35D	COUCH DEATH/PS	PROSE
LIKE THE SOUND OF A BROKEN PIPE	35D	COUCH DEATH/PS	PROSE
THE YOUTH REPLIED LIKE A VOICE HEARD FROM A SEPULCHRE	36A	COUCH DEATH/PS	PROSE
LIKE THE BUBBLING WATERS OF THE BROOK IN THE DEAD OF NIGHT	36B	COUCH DEATH/PS	PROSE
LIKE ROLLING WAVES UPON A DESERT SHORE SIGHS SUCCEEDED SIGHS	36B	COUCH DEATH/PS	PROSE
HE WAS LIKE A CLOUD TOSSED BY THE WINDS TILL THE SUN SHINE	36C	COUCH DEATH/PS	PROSE
THE YOUTHFUL SUN JOYS LIKE A HUNTER ROUZED TO THE CHACE	37B	CONTEMPLATN/PS	PROSE
LIKE A TRIUMPH SEASON FOLLOWS SEASON	37B	CONTEMPLATN/PS	PROSE
MISERY BUILDS OVER OUR COTTAGE ROOFS AND DISCONTENT RUNS LIKE A BROOK	37B	CONTEMPLATN/PS	PROSE
LIKE THUNDER CLOUDS TROUBLING THE SKY	38D	SAMSON/PS	PROSE
TEN THOUSAND SPEARS ARE LIKE THE SUMMER GRASS	39A	SAMSON/PS	PROSE
THOU FEAR I DRINK MY TEARS LIKE WATER I LIVE UPON SORROW	39A	SAMSON/PS	PROSE
GODS LIKE THESE NOR MALE NOR FEMALE ARE BUT SINGLE PREGNATE	40D	THEN SHE BORE	PROSE
FORTH CAME AMBITION CRAWLING LIKE A TOAD	41A	THEN SHE BORE	PROSE
LIKE FABLED HECATE SHE DOTH BIND THEM TO HER LAW	41D	THEN SHE BORE	PROSE
LIKE A TEMPESTUOUS THUNDER CLOUD PRIDE LEADS THEM ON	42C	THEN SHE BORE	PROSE
LIKE SMOULDRING FIRE OR IN THE BUZZ OF CITIES FLIES ABROAD	42C	THEN SHE BORE	PROSE
A DAY LIKE THIS LAID ELFRID IN THE DUST	43C	WOE CRIED MUSE	PROSE
I DONT LIKE HIS EYES SAID ETRUSCAN COLUMN	44C	ISLAND MOON 1	PROSE
BEFORE HIS EYES LIKE THE ANIMAL UPON THE PYTHAGOREAN'S LAP	46A	ISLAND MOON 1	PROSE
LIKE A CHERRY CLAPPER ARADOBO ASKD WHO WAS PHEBUS SIR	46D	ISLAND MOON 3	PROSE
HA HA SAID INFLAMMABLE GASS WHAT DONT YOU LIKE TO GO TO CHURCH	48A	ISLAND MOON 4	PROSE
I WOULD RUN LIKE THE DICKINS TILL I WAS ALL IN A HEAT	48B	ISLAND MOON 4	PROSE
BECAUSE I LIKE IT MY FATHER DOES WHAT HE LIKES & SO DO I	51C	ISLAND MOON 6	PROSE
I LIKE TO BE WHERE WE TALK	52D	ISLAND MOON 8	PROSE
& MY COUSIN GIBBLE GABBLE SAYS THAT I AM LIKE NOBODY ELSE	53A	ISLAND MOON 8	PROSE
MORE LIKE A SAINT THAN A LAWGIVER AND WITH GREAT SOLEMNITY	53B	ISLAND MOON 8	PROSE
PHEBE DREST LIKE BEAUTIE'S QUEEN	53	PHEBE DREST/IM	1
LIKE DOCTOR JOHNSON	54	LO THE BAT/IM	5
MISS GITTIPIN SAID HE YOU SING LIKE A HARPSICHORD	55C	ISLAND MOON 9	PROSE
LIKE BIRDS JUST CURED OF THE PIP	56	HAIL MATRIM/IM	23
LIKE SIR ISAAC NEWTON	57	TO BE OR/IM	3
TILL INTO THE HIGH DOME OF PAUL'S THEY LIKE THAMES' WATERS FLOW	59	HOLY THURS/IM	4
[THEN LIKE A MIGHTY WIND THEY RAISE TO HEAVN THE VOICE OF SONG]	59	HOLY THURS/IM	10
[OR LIKE HARMONIOUS THUNDERINGS THE SEATS OF HEAVN AMONG]	59	HOLY THURS/IM	11
[LIKE ANGELS ON THE THRONE OF HEAVN RAISING THE VOICE OF PRAISE]	59	HOLY THURS/IM	13
THEN LIKE A MIGHTY WIND THEY RAISE TO HEAVN THE VOICE OF SONG	59	HOLY THURS/IM	15
OR LIKE HARMONIOUS THUNDERINGS THE SEATS OF HEAVN AMONG	59	HOLY THURS/IM	16
AND NOT LIKE CLUMSY BEARS	62	DR CLASH/IM	16
VERY LIKE A GOAT'S FACE SHE ANSWERD	62D	ISLAND MOON 11	PROSE
I THINK YOUR FACE SAID HE IS LIKE THAT NOBLE BEAST THE TYGER	62D	ISLAND MOON 11	PROSE
INNOCENCE DOTH LIKE A ROSE	63	SHEPHERD FIRST	5
("ALL MORAL DEPENDENCE ON GUILTY") IS BEING LIKE HIM RATHER	68A	ANNO LAVATER	MARG
CHUSING TO WANDER LIKE A SON OF ZAZEL IN THE ROCKS	100	TIRIEL 1	39
THAT YOU MAY LIE AS NOW YOUR MOTHER LIES LIKE DOGS CAST OUT	100	TIRIEL 1	45
AND HAR & HEVA LIKE TWO CHILDREN SAT BENEATH THE OAK	100	TIRIEL 2	5
AND IN THE NIGHT LIKE INFANTS SLEPT DELIGHTED WITH INFANT DREAMS	100	TIRIEL 2	9
THEY RAN WEEPING LIKE FRIGHTED INFANTS FOR REFUGE IN MNETHA'S ARMS	100	TIRIEL 2	* 12

		PAGE	TITLE		LINE
LIKE	(CONTINUED)				
AND THIS IS HAR & HEVA TREMBLING LIKE INFANTS BY MY SIDE		101	TIRIEL 2		19
BECAUSE THOU SMELLEST LIKE THE FIGTREE THOU SMELLEST LIKE RIPE FIGS		101	TIRIEL 2		42
FOR THOU DOST MAKE MY HEART TO BLEED MY SONS WERE NOT LIKE THINE		103	TIRIEL 3		20
GO NOT FOR THOU ART SO LIKE TIRIEL THAT I LOVE THINE HEAD		103	TIRIEL 3		24
THO IT IS WRINKLED LIKE THE EARTH PARCHD WITH THE SUMMER HEAT		103	TIRIEL 3		25
AY NOW THOU ART DISCOVERD I WILL USE THEE LIKE A SLAVE	. .	104	TIRIEL 4		25
BUT LIKE A TYGER HE WOULD COME & SO I [REND] RENT HIM TOO		105	TIRIEL 4	*	53
THEN LIKE A RIVER HE WOULD SEEK TO DROWN ME IN HIS WAVES		105	TIRIEL 4		54
BUT SOON I BUFFETTED THE TORRENT ANON LIKE TO A CLOUD	. .	105	TIRIEL 4		55
THEN HE WOULD CREEP LIKE A BRIGHT SERPENT TILL AROUND MY NECK		105	TIRIEL 4		57
THEN LIKE A TOAD OR LIKE A NEWT WOULD WHISPER IN MY EARS		105	TIRIEL 4		59
OR LIKE A ROCK STOOD IN MY WAY OR LIKE A POISNOUS SHRUB		105	TIRIEL 4		60
IT IS A LIE & I AM [?TORN ?LIKE] LIKE THE TREE TORN BY THE WIND		106	TIRIEL 4	*	85
THEN WOULD THEY CURSE AS THOU HAST CURSED BUT THEY ARE NOT LIKE THEE		107	TIRIEL 6		25
LIKE BIRDS IN THEIR NEST	. . . . . .	116	ECCHOING GR/SI		27
THAT CURLD LIKE A LAMB'S BACK WAS SHAVD SO I SAID	. . .	117	CHIMNEY SWP/SI		6
THE MOON LIKE A FLOWER	. . . .	118	NIGHT/SI		5
SHALL SHINE LIKE THE GOLD	. . . . . .	119	NIGHT/SI		47
SWEET BABE ONCE LIKE THEE	. . . . . .	120	CRADLE SONG/SI		23
APPEARD LIKE HIS FATHER IN WHITE	. . . .	121	LIT BOY FND/SI		4
TILL INTO THE HIGH DOME OF PAUL'S THEY LIKE THAMES WATERS FLOW		121	HOLY THURS/SI		4
NOW LIKE A MIGHTY WIND THEY RAISE TO HEAVEN THE VOICE OF SONG		122	HOLY THURS/SI		9
OR LIKE HARMONIOUS THUNDERINGS THE SEATS OF HEAVEN AMONG		122	HOLY THURS/SI	*	10
IS BUT A CLOUD AND LIKE A SHADY GROVE	. . . . .	125	LIT BLK BOY/SI		16
AND ROUND MY GOLDEN TENT LIKE LAMBS REJOICE	. . . .	125	LIT BLK BOY/SI		20
AND ROUND THE TENT OF GOD LIKE LAMBS WE JOY	. . . .	125	LIT BLK BOY/SI		24
AND BE LIKE HIM AND HE WILL THEN LOVE ME	. . . .	125	LIT BLK BOY/SI		28
TO FADE AWAY LIKE MORNING BEAUTY FROM HER MORTAL DAY	. .	127	BOOK OF THEL 1		3
AND THUS HER GENTLE LAMENTATION FALLS LIKE MORNING DEW	. .	127	BOOK OF THEL 1		5
AH THEL IS LIKE A WATRY BOW AND LIKE A PARTING CLOUD	. .	127	BOOK OF THEL 1		8
LIKE A REFLECTION IN A GLASS LIKE SHADOWS IN THE WATER	.	127	BOOK OF THEL 1		9
LIKE DREAMS OF INFANTS LIKE A SMILE UPON AN INFANT'S FACE	.	127	BOOK OF THEL 1		10
LIKE THE DOVE'S VOICE LIKE TRANSIENT DAY LIKE MUSIC IN THE AIR		127	BOOK OF THEL 1		11
BUT THEL IS LIKE A FAINT CLOUD KINDLED AT THE RISING SUN		128	BOOK OF THEL 2		11
THEN WE SHALL SEEK THEE BUT NOT FIND AH THEL IS LIKE TO THEE		128	BOOK OF THEL 3		3
DOST THOU O LITTLE CLOUD I FEAR THAT I AM NOT LIKE THEE		129	BOOK OF THEL 3		17
I SEE THEE LIKE AN INFANT WRAPPED IN THE LILLY'S LEAF	. .	129	BOOK OF THEL 4		3
. . . THE OLD MOUNTAINS OF FRANCE LIKE AGED MEN FADING AWAY		134	FRENCH REVOLTN		9
LIKE OUR ANCIENT FATHERS IN REGIONS OF TWILIGHT . . .	.	134	FRENCH REVOLTN		14
. . . HE STALKD LIKE A LION FROM TOWER	. . . .	135	FRENCH REVOLTN		21
PANTING OVER THE PRISONERS LIKE A WOLF GORGD	.	135	FRENCH REVOLTN		26
. . . LIKE BIRDS OF PREY STOOD ON THE COUCH	. . .	135	FRENCH REVOLTN		36
. . . WHOSE WHITE BEARD COVERD THE STONE FLOOR LIKE WEEDS		135	FRENCH REVOLTN		38
(ETERNALLY) RUSHING ROUND LIKE A MAN		136	FRENCH REVOLTN	*	46
. . . LIKE SPIRITS OF FIRE IN THE BEAUTIFUL	. . .	136	FRENCH REVOLTN		54
. . . LIKE THE SUN OF OLD TIME QUENCHD IN CLOUDS	. . .	137	FRENCH REVOLTN		68
LIKE THE CENTRAL FIRE	. . . . . .	137	FRENCH REVOLTN		80
EXPANDED LIKE STARRY HEAVEN HE SAT DOWN	.	138	FRENCH REVOLTN		82
. . . AN ODOR OF WAR LIKE A RIPE VINEYARD ROSE FROM HIS GARMENTS		138	FRENCH REVOLTN		84
. . . HIS WORDS FALL LIKE PURPLE AUTUMN ON THE SHEAVES	. .	138	FRENCH REVOLTN		88
LIKE A DARK CLOUD NECKER PAUSD	. .	139	FRENCH REVOLTN		106
. . . AND LIKE THUNDER ON THE JUST MAN'S BURIAL DAY HE PAUSD		139	FRENCH REVOLTN		106
. . . LIKE THE VOICE OF THE GRASSHOPPER WHISPERD		140	FRENCH REVOLTN		136
. . . LIKE A MAN THAT RETURNS FROM HOLLOW GRAVES		141	FRENCH REVOLTN		161
. . . THE CAPTAINS LIKE MEN BOUND IN CHAINS		141	FRENCH REVOLTN		165
. . . LIKE THUNDER-CLOUDS READY TO BURST		141	FRENCH REVOLTN		170
THE NOBLES SAT ROUND LIKE CLOUDS ON THE MOUNTAINS . . .		143	FRENCH REVOLTN		196
. . . LIKE INCENSE OF THE VALLEY		143	FRENCH REVOLTN		197
. . . LIKE A VOICE OF GOD FOLLOWING A STORM THE ABBE FOLLOWD		143	FRENCH REVOLTN		202
LIKE PESTILENT FOGS ROUND CITIES OF MEN		144	FRENCH REVOLTN		236
LIKE THE MOUNTAINS OF FRANCE		145	FRENCH REVOLTN		242
LIKE A VOICE IN THE VINEYARDS OF BURGUNDY		145	FRENCH REVOLTN		244
LIKE THE LOW VOICE OF THE LABOURING MAN INSTEAD OF THE SHOUT OF JOY		145	FRENCH REVOLTN		245
AND THE PALACE APPEARD LIKE A CLOUD DRIVEN ABROAD . . .		145	FRENCH REVOLTN		246
LIKE THE MORNING STAR ARISING ABOVE THE BLACK WAVES . . .		145	FRENCH REVOLTN		255
LIKE PILLARS OF ANCIENT HALLS AND RUINS OF TIMES REMOTE THEY SAT		145	FRENCH REVOLTN		258
LIKE A VOICE FROM THE DIM PILLARS MIRABEAU ROSE		146	FRENCH REVOLTN		259
. . . THEN BOWING LIKE CLOUDS MAN TOWARD MAN THE ASSEMBLY		146	FRENCH REVOLTN		263
LIKE A COUNCIL OF ARDORS SEATED IN CLOUDS		146	FRENCH REVOLTN		264
LIKE A FLAME OF FIRE HE STOOD BEFORE DARK RANKS		146	FRENCH REVOLTN		273
THEY DASH LIKE FOAM AGAINST THE RIDGES OF THE ARMY . . .		146	FRENCH REVOLTN		277
BUT SILENT HE STOOD TILL ALL THE OFFICERS RUSH ROUND HIM LIKE WAVES		146	FRENCH REVOLTN		279
DARK CAVALRY LIKE CLOUDS FRAUGHT WITH THUNDER		147	FRENCH REVOLTN		291
. . . ALONG THE ROADS GLITTER LIKE FIRE		147	FRENCH REVOLTN		292
. . . HIS PEERS PALE LIKE MOUNTAINS OF THE DEAD		147	FRENCH REVOLTN		296

1089

```
                                                         PAGE     TITLE        LINE
LIKE    (CONTINUED)
    WHICH TO ANGELS LOOK LIKE TORMENT AND INSANITY  . . . .   150C MARRIAGE HH 6    PROSE
    THIS SAID HE LIKE ALL FIRM PERSWASIONS IS COME TO PASS  . . 154A MARRIAGE HH 12   PROSE
    A FIERY CREST ABOVE THE WAVES SLOWLY IT REARED LIKE A RIDGE 156C MARRIAGE HH 17   PROSE
    LIKE THOSE ON A TYGER'S FOREHEAD SOON WE SAW HIS MOUTH  . . 156C MARRIAGE HH 17   PROSE
    IS LIKE STANDING WATER & BREEDS REPTILES OF THE MIND  . .   156D MARRIAGE HH 17   PROSE
    SHOT LIKE THE SINKING SUN INTO THE WESTERN SEA  . . . .   159C SONG LIBERTY      PROSE
    LIKE A FIEND HID IN A CLOUD . . . . . . . . . . . .   166 INFANT SORW/N          4
    [LIKE [A SERPENT] TO SERPENTS IN THE NIGHT]  . . . . .   167 INFANT SORW/N   *   36
    LIKE [A SERPENT]] TO [SERPENTS IN THE] HOLY MEN BY DAY      167 INFANT SORW/N   *   38
    LIKE TO DUNG UPON THE GROUND . . . . . . . . . . . .   169 MIRTLE SHADE/N        5
    [LIKE TO DUNG UPON THE GROUND] . . . . . . . . . .   176 TO MY MIRTLE/N         7
    I LOVE [MYSELF SO DOES THE BIRD] YOU LIKE THE LITTLE BIRD   177 LIT BOY LST/N         7
    THE POOR PARSONS WITH WIND LIKE A BLOWN BLADDER SWELL  . .  179 LIT VAGABOND/N        5
    THEN GOD LIKE A FATHER [THAT JOYS FOR] REJOICING TO SEE     180 LIT VAGABOND/N       14
    A FLY LIKE THEE . . . . . . . . . . . . . . .   183 THE FLY/N              14
    A MAN LIKE ME . . . . . . . . . . . . . . . .   183 THE FLY/N              16
    PINS NECKLACES & SUCH LIKE THINGS . . . . . . . . . .   188 A FAIRY SKIPD          4
    WITH SECRET TEARS BENEATH HIM SOUND LIKE WAVES ON A DESART  190 V DAU ALBION 2        7
        SHORE
    INSTEAD OF MORN ARISES A BRIGHT SHADOW LIKE AN EYE  . . .   191 V DAU ALBION 2       35
    AS THE RAVEN'S EYE OR DOES HE MEASURE THE EXPANSE LIKE      193 V DAU ALBION 5       36
        THE VULTURE
    A QUIVER WITH ITS BURNING STORES A BOW LIKE THAT OF NIGHT   196 AMERICA PREL 1        5
    THE TERROR LIKE A COMET OR MORE LIKE THE PLANET RED  . .    197 AMERICA 5             2
    SPRING LIKE REDEEMED CAPTIVES WHEN THEIR BONDS & BARS ARE   198 AMERICA 6             5
        BURST
    BESIDE THE STONE OF NIGHT AND LIKE THE ETERNAL LION'S HOWL  198 AMERICA 7             2
    AMIDST THE LUSTFUL FIRES HE WALKS HIS FEET BECOME LIKE      199 AMERICA 8            16
        BRASS
    HIS KNEES AND THIGHS LIKE SILVER & HIS BREAST AND HEAD      199 AMERICA 8            17
        LIKE GOLD
    CROUCH HOWLING BEFORE THEIR CAVERNS DEEP LIKE SKINS DRYD    199 AMERICA 9             4
        IN THE WIND
    HE CRIED WHY TREMBLES HONESTY AND LIKE A MURDERER  . . .    200 AMERICA 11            4
    HIS SNOWY BEARD THAT STREAMS LIKE LAMBENT FLAMES DOWN HIS   204 AMERICA CANC B       16
        WIDE BREAST
    LIKE WHITE CLOUDS RISING FROM THE DEEPS HIS FIFTY-TWO       205 AMERICA CANC C       16
        ARMIES
    [SLEEP LIKE THE DEAD] BUT LIKE A CONSTELLATION RISN AND     205 AMERICA CANC C       23
        BLAZING
    [OVER THE] A FROWNING SHADOW LIKE [A] AN AGED KING IN ARMS  205 AMERICA CANC C *     25
        OF GOLD
    AND LIKE THE VOICES OF RELIGIOUS DEAD HEARD IN THE          205 AMERICA CANC C       29
        MOUNTAINS
    A FLY LIKE THEE . . . . . . . . . . . . . . .   213 THE FLY/SE             6
    A MAN LIKE ME . . . . . . . . . . . . . . . .   213 THE FLY/SE             8
    AND GOD LIKE A FATHER REJOICING TO SEE  . . . . . . .   216 LIT VAGABND/SE       13
    LIKE A FIEND HID IN A CLOUD . . . . . . . . . . .   217 INFANT SORW/SE        4
    I LOVE YOU LIKE THE LITTLE BIRD . . . . . . . . .   218 LIT BOY LST/SE        7
    LIKE THE HOLY BOOK . . . . . . . . . . . . . .   219 LIT GRL LST/SE       28
    [LIKE] IN HIS DESOLATE MOUNTAINS RIFTED FURIOUS  . . . .   222 URIZEN 3        *    11
    ARE HEARD LIKE THUNDERS OF AUTUMN . . . . . . . . .   223 URIZEN 3             34
    ON ALL SIDES [THEY] HE FRAMD LIKE A WOMB  . . . . . .   225 URIZEN 5        *    29
    FROM ETERNALS & LIKE A BLACK GLOBE  . . . . . . . .   226 URIZEN 5             33
    LIKE A HUMAN HEART STRUGLING & BEATING  . . . . . . .   226 URIZEN 5             36
    LIKE A DARK WASTE STRETCHING CHANGABLE  . . . . . . .   227 URIZEN 10             3
    LIKE FETTERS OF ICE SHRINKING TOGETHER  . . . . . . .   228 URIZEN 10            26
    LIKE THE LINKED INFERNAL CHAIN . . . . . . . . . .   228 URIZEN 10            36
    RIBS LIKE A BENDING CAVERN . . . . . . . . . . .   228 URIZEN 10            39
    AND LIKE A RED FLAME A TONGUE . . . . . . . . . .   229 URIZEN 13             8
    ROLL LIKE A SEA AROUND HIM . . . . . . . . . . .   230 URIZEN 13            30
    LIKE A DREAM WAS OBLITERATED . . . . . . . . . .   230 URIZEN 13            34
    YET HELPLESS IT LAY LIKE A WORM . . . . . . . . .   232 URIZEN 19            21
    LIKE A MAN FROM A CLOUD BORN & UTHA . . . . . . . .   234 URIZEN 23            13
    LIKE THE GROUND PARCHD WITH HEAT THEN FUZON  . . . . .   234 URIZEN 23            17
    ALL HIS ETERNAL SONS IN LIKE MANNER . . . . . . . .   234 URIZEN 23            19
    LIKE A SPIDER'S WEB MOIST COLD & DIM  . . . . . . .   235 URIZEN 25            10
    THE MESHES TWISTED LIKE TO THE HUMAN BRAIN  . . . . . .   235 URIZEN 25            21
    GREW SMALL LIKE THE EYES OF A MAN . . . . . . . . .   236 URIZEN 25            36
    THEY HOVERD ROUND ME LIKE A CLOUD OF INCENSE WHEN I CAME    238 EUROPE INTRO         22
    LIKE THE DARK CLOUD DISBURDEN IN THE DAY OF DISMAL THUNDER  238 EUROPE PREL 1         7
    WAR CEASD & ALL THE TROOPS LIKE SHADOWS FLED TO THEIR       239 EUROPE 4              4
        ABODES
    LIKE PEARLY CLOUDS THEY MEET TOGETHER IN THE CRYSTAL HOUSE  239 EUROPE 4              6
    GLOWS LIKE A METEOR IN THE DISTANT NORTH  . . . . . .   239 EUROPE 4             12
    INTO EARTHS ROLLING IN CIRCLES OF SPACE THAT LIKE AN OCEAN  241 EUROPE 10            19
        RUSHD
    LIKE THE GAY FISHES ON THE WAVE WHEN THE COLD MOON DRINKS   243 EUROPE 14             3
        THE DEW
    REVOLVE LIKE SWEET PERFUMES ASCENDING O LEUTHA SILKEN QUEEN 244 EUROPE 14            14
    LIKE NETS & GINS & TRAPS TO CATCH THE JOYS OF ETERNITY  . . 246 SONG OF LOS 4         2
    TILL LIKE A DREAM ETERNITY WAS OBLITERATED & ERASED  . . .  246 SONG OF LOS 4         4
    AROSE LIKE A PILLAR OF FIRE ABOVE THE ALPS  . . . . .   248 SONG OF LOS 7        27
    LIKE A SERPENT OF FIERY FLAME . . . . . . . . . .   248 SONG OF LOS 7        28
    RUSHD DOWN LIKE FLOODS FROM HIS MOUNTAINS  . . . . . .   250 AHANIA 3             8
    FIRST IN WRATH THREW HIS LIMBS LIKE THE BABE  . . . . .   258 BOOK OF LOS 4        38
    SHIVRING CLINGING ABROUND LIKE A CLOUD  . . . . . . .   258 BOOK OF LOS 4        56
    HEAVY FALLING HIS ORGANS LIKE ROOTS . . . . . . . .   259 BOOK OF LOS 4        64
    LIKE A SERPENT LIKE AN IRON CHAIN . . . . . . . . .   259 BOOK OF LOS 5        16
    [LIKE SONS & DAUGHTERS] . . . . . . . . . . . .   264 FOUR ZOAS 1          19
    SPREADING THEM OUT BEFORE THE SUN LIKE STALKS OF FLAX TO    265 FOUR ZOAS 1          48
        DRY
```

1090

LIKE (CONTINUED)

	PAGE	TITLE		LINE
IN DREADFUL DOLOR & PAIN & I AM LIKE AN ATOM	265	FOUR ZOAS 1		61
IN BLUSHES LIKE THE MORNING AND HIS SCALY ARMOUR SOFTENING	269	FOUR ZOAS 1		186
. . . TILL STRENGTH FROM ENION LIKE RICHEST SUMMER [SHINES] SHINING	269	FOUR ZOAS 1	*	195
THEY SULK UPON HER BREAST HER HAIR BECAME LIKE SNOW ON MOUNTAINS	270	FOUR ZOAS 1		211
THE VOICE CAME & WENT LIKE A DREAM I AWOKE IN MY SWEET BLISS	272	FOUR ZOAS 1		280
THE VARYING CLOUDS LIKE PARADISES STRETCHD IN THE EXPANSE	274	FOUR ZOAS 1		368
URIZEN ROSE FROM THE BRIGHT FEAST LIKE A STAR THRO THE EVENING SKY	280	FOUR ZOAS 2		9
ALL RAVNING LIKE THE HUNGRY WORM & LIKE THE SILENT GRAVE	280	FOUR ZOAS 2		17
ACROSS EUROPE & ASIA TO CHINA & JAPAN LIKE LIGHTENINGS . .	281	FOUR ZOAS 2	*	59
THE FIRES OF VALA FADED LIKE A SHADOW COLD & PALE . . .	283	FOUR ZOAS 2		114
LIKE A BRIGHT CLOUD IN HARVEST BUT WHEN URIZEN FROWND SHE WEPT	284	FOUR ZOAS 2		183
AND VALA LIKE A SHADOW OFT APPEARD TO URIZEN	285	FOUR ZOAS 2		214
LIKE PILLARS OF FIRE TRAVELLING THRO DARKNESS & NON ENTITY	286	FOUR ZOAS 2		230
THE WONDROUS WORK FLOW FORTH LIKE VISIBLE OUT OF THE INVISIBLE	287	FOUR ZOAS 2		260
THUS WERE THE STARS OF HEAVEN CREATED LIKE A GOLDEN CHAIN	287	FOUR ZOAS 2		266
I GRASP THY VEST IN MY STRONG HAND IN VAIN LIKE WATER SPRINGS	288	FOUR ZOAS 2	*	304
UPON THE IMMENSE LIKE A BRIGHT RAINBOW WEEPING & SMILING & FADING	290	FOUR ZOAS 2		382
O URIZEN LOOK ON [THY WIFE THAT] ME LIKE A MOURNFUL STREAM	291	FOUR ZOAS 3		3
IF THOU WITHHOLD THINE HAND I PERISH LIKE A FALLEN LEAF	293	FOUR ZOAS 3		63
LIKE A DARK LAMP ETERNAL DEATH HAUNTS ALL MY EXPECTATION	293	FOUR ZOAS 3		75
AND THE VAST FORM OF NATURE LIKE A SERPENT PLAYD BEFORE THEM	294	FOUR ZOAS 3		97
VALA SHRUNK IN LIKE THE DARK SEA THAT LEAVES ITS SLIMY BANKS	294	FOUR ZOAS 3		99
AND THE VAST FORM OF NATURE LIKE A SERPENT ROLLD BETWEEN	294	FOUR ZOAS 3		101
DO I NOT STRETCH THE HEAVENS ABROAD OR FOLD THEM UP LIKE A GARMENT	294	FOUR ZOAS 3		107
SAYING ART THOU ALSO BECOME LIKE VALA THUS I CAST THEE OUT	295	FOUR ZOAS 3		113
AND ART THOU ALSO BECOME LIKE VALA THUS I CAST THEE OUT	295	FOUR ZOAS 3		130
AND THREW AHANIA FROM HIS BOSOM OBDURATE SHE FELL LIKE LIGHTNING	295	FOUR ZOAS 3		132
THRO THE CONFUSION LIKE A CRACK ACROSS FROM IMMENSE TO IMMENSE	295	FOUR ZOAS 3		149
BUT FROM THE DOLOROUS GROAN ONE LIKE A SHADOW OF SMOKE APPEARD	296	FOUR ZOAS 3		153
DRIVEN BY THY RAGE I WANDER LIKE A CLOUD INTO THE DEEP . .	296	FOUR ZOAS 3		188
MAKE ME NOT LIKE THE THINGS FORGOTTEN AS THEY HAD NOT BEEN	297	FOUR ZOAS 3		192
WHY DOES THY PITEOUS FACE EVANISH LIKE A RAINY CLOUD . .	297	FOUR ZOAS 3		199
LIKE A FAMISHD EAGLE EYELESS RAGING IN THE VAST EXPANSE	297	FOUR ZOAS 4		10
ARE THOSE WHO LOVE LIKE THOSE WHO DIED RISEN AGAIN FROM DEATH	298	FOUR ZOAS 4		19
A SHADOW BLUE OBSCURE & DISMAL LIKE A STATUE OF LEAD . .	299	FOUR ZOAS 4		65
WHEN FLEEING FROM THE BATTLE THOU FLEETING LIKE THE RAVEN	299	FOUR ZOAS 4		86
SHE IS DIVIDED SHE IS VANISHD EVEN LIKE LUVAH & [VALAN] VALA	301	FOUR ZOAS 4	*	140
IN A HORRIBLE DREAMFUL SLUMBER LIKE THE LINKED CHAIN . .	303	FOUR ZOAS 4		218
SHOOTING PAIND RIBBS LIKE A BENDING CAVERN	303	FOUR ZOAS 4		220
THROAT THEN LIKE A RED FLAME A TONGUE OF HUNGER	303	FOUR ZOAS 4		241
UNWILLING MOVD AS URIZEN HOWLD HIS LOINS WAVD LIKE THE SEA	305	FOUR ZOAS 4		289
TWINGE & HIS IRON SINEWS BEND LIKE LEAD & FOLD	305	FOUR ZOAS 4		294
SETTLED LIKE BATS INNUMERABLE READY TO FLY ABROAD . . .	306	FOUR ZOAS 5		35
AROUND HIS BOSOM LIKE A BLOODY CORD IN SECRET SOBS . . .	307	FOUR ZOAS 5		84
. . . HIS LOCKS ARE LIKE THE FORESTS	308	FOUR ZOAS 5		127
HIS BOSOM IS LIKE STARRY HEAVEN EXPANDED ALL THE STARS .	308	FOUR ZOAS 5		130
HIS LOINS INWOVE WITH SILKEN FIRES ARE LIKE A FURNACE FIERCE	308	FOUR ZOAS 5		135
RENDING THE CAVERNS LIKE A MIGHTY WIND PENT IN THE EARTH	309	FOUR ZOAS 5		183
I SIEZD THEE BEAUTEOUS LUVAH THOU ART FADED LIKE A FLOWER	311	FOUR ZOAS 5		226
AND LIKE A LILLY IS THY WIFE VALA WITHERD BY WINDS . .	311	FOUR ZOAS 5		227
ART THOU LIKE ME RISEN AGAIN FROM DEATH OR ART THOU DEATHLESS	313	FOUR ZOAS 6		56
THOU HORRIBLE RUIN ONCE LIKE ME THOU WAST ALL GLORIOUS . .	317	FOUR ZOAS 6		210
AND NOW LIKE ME PARTAKING DESOLATE THY MASTER'S LOT . . .	317	FOUR ZOAS 6		211
IN HIS HAND A KNOTTED CLUB WHOSE KNOTS LIKE MOUNTAINS FROWND	319	FOUR ZOAS 6		305
BURN LIKE TWO FURNACES HE CALLD WITH VOICE OF THUNDER . .	319	FOUR ZOAS 6		309
LIKE WHITE CLOUDS RISING FROM THE VALES HIS FIFTY TWO ARMIES	319	FOUR ZOAS 6		312
LOS FELT THE ENVY IN HIS LIMBS LIKE TO A BLIGHTED TREE .	321	FOUR ZOAS 7		27
AROUND THEE SOMETIMES LIKE A FLOOD & SOMETIMES LIKE A ROCK	321	FOUR ZOAS 7		49
THAT LOS MAY EVAPORATE LIKE SMOKE & BE NO MORE	323	FOUR ZOAS 7		114
MY DIVIDED SPIRIT LIKE A WORM I RISE IN PEACE UNBOUND . .	323	FOUR ZOAS 7		137
LIKE A COLD NIGHT THAT NIPS THE [ROOTS] ROOT	324	FOUR ZOAS 7	*	180
FOREHEAD & EYES THY LIPS DECAY LIKE ROSES IN [EARLY] THE SPRING	325	FOUR ZOAS 7		189
AND CUT THE WINDS LIKE ARROWS SHOT BY TROOPS OF DESTINY	325	FOUR ZOAS 7		208
OF THY POOR BROKEN HEART I SEE THEE LIKE A SHADOW WITHERING	330	FOUR ZOAS 7		413
THE ENDS OF HEAVEN LIKE A GARMENT WILL I FOLD THEM ROUND ME	333	FOUR ZOAS 7B		6
COMPELLD THE SUN REDDNING LIKE A FIERCE LION IN HIS CHAINS	333	FOUR ZOAS 7B		31
MY WATERS LIKE A FLOOD AROUND THEE FEAR NOT TRUST IN ME	334	FOUR ZOAS 7B		55
FLAMING HIS HEAD LIKE THE BRIGHT SUN SEEN THRO A MIST THAT MAGNIFIES	335	FOUR ZOAS 7B		79

1091

		PAGE	TITLE		LINE
LIKE	(CONTINUED)				
AND SAID GO FORTH & GUIDE MY BATTLES LIKE THE JOINTED SPINE		336	FOUR ZOAS 7B		116
FROM EAST TO WEST FLOWD LIKE THE HUMAN VEINS IN RIVERS . .		337	FOUR ZOAS 7B		160
BECAUSE ITS WORKMANSHIP WAS LIKE THE WORKMANSHIP OF THE SHEPHERD		337	FOUR ZOAS 7B		178
LIKE CLOUDS UPON THE WINTER SKY BROKEN WITH WINDS & THUNDERS		338	FOUR ZOAS 7B	*	218
SWAM LIKE A DREAM BEFORE MY EYES I WENT TO SEEK THE STEPS		339	FOUR ZOAS 7B		235
TREMBLING BEFORE ME LIKE A SHADOW LIKE A MIST LIKE AIR		339	FOUR ZOAS 7B		238
OR LIKE AN EARTHQUAKE RUMBLING IN THE BOWELS OF THE EARTH		339	FOUR ZOAS 7B		264
OR LIKE A CLOUD BENEATH & LIKE A FIRE FLAMING IN HIGH . .		339	FOUR ZOAS 7B	*	265
LIKE TO A RUSHING TORRENT BENEATH & A FALLING ROCK ABOVE		340	FOUR ZOAS 7B		267
NOT SEEN TO HER LIKE WATERS OR LIKE THIS DARK WORLD OF DEATH		340	FOUR ZOAS 7B		273
THE [ETERNAL] FALLEN MAN STRETCHD LIKE A CORSE UPON THE OOZY ROCK		341	FOUR ZOAS 8		4
[THEY HAD WHICH CLOTHD THEIR BODIES LIKE A GARMENT OF SOFT DOWN]		341	FOUR ZOAS 8		10
[THE SWELLING TIDES THEY BENT OVER THE DEAD CORSE LIKE AN ARCH]		341	FOUR ZOAS 8		13
[HEAVING XXX] HEAVD LIKE AN EARTHQUAKE LABRING WITH CONVULSIVE GROANS		347	FOUR ZOAS 8	*	249
O RAHAB I BEHOLD THEE I WAS ONCE LIKE THEE A SON		350	FOUR ZOAS 8		354
LIKE THE PALE VISAGE IN ITS SHEET OF LEAD THAT CANNOT FOLLOW		352	FOUR ZOAS 8		433
LASHES HIS TAIL IN THE [WIDE] WILD DEEP HIS EYELIDS LIKE THE SUN		352	FOUR ZOAS 8	*	439
HIS SCALES TRANSPARENT GIVE FORTH LIGHT LIKE WINDOWS OF THE MORNING		352	FOUR ZOAS 8		441
THARMAS LIKE A PILLAR OF SAND ROLLD ROUND BY THE WHIRLWIND		353	FOUR ZOAS 8		469
ONCE LIKE THE PRIDE OF THE SUN NOW FLAGGING IN COLD NIGHT		354	FOUR ZOAS 8	*	522
ONCE I WAILD DESOLATE LIKE THEE MY FALLOW FIELDS IN FEAR		354	FOUR ZOAS 8		536
SIEZD THE SUN HIS LEFT HAND LIKE DARK ROOTS COVERD THE MOON		357	FOUR ZOAS 9		8
FOLDING LIKE SCROLLS OF THE ENORMOUS VOLUME OF HEAVEN & EARTH		357	FOUR ZOAS 9		14
THEY ARE BECOME LIKE WINTRY FLOCKS LIKE FORESTS STRIPD OF LEAVES		357	FOUR ZOAS 9		22
THE OPRESSED PURSUE LIKE THE WIND THERE IS NO ROOM FOR ESCAPE		357	FOUR ZOAS 9	*	23
THEN LIKE THE DOVES FROM PILLARS OF SMOKE THE TREMBLING FAMILIES		358	FOUR ZOAS 9		46
IN RADIANT YOUTH WHEN LO LIKE GARLANDS IN THE EASTERN SKY		362	FOUR ZOAS 9		193
DARKEND LIKE MOULD IN THE DIVIDED FALLOW WHERE THE WEED		364	FOUR ZOAS 9	*	294
FOR FROM THE HAND OF URIZEN THE MYRIADS FALL LIKE STARS		365	FOUR ZOAS 9		324
THEY ARE BECOME LIKE WINTRY FLOCKS LIKE FORESTS STRIPD OF LEAVES		365	FOUR ZOAS 9		327
AND LO LIKE THE HARVEST MOON AHANIA CAST OFF HER DEATH CLOTHES		366	FOUR ZOAS 9		344
HOPELESS IF I AM LIKE THE GRASS & SO SHALL PASS AWAY . .		368	FOUR ZOAS 9		417
I'LL WATCH YOU & ATTEND YOUR FOOTSTEPS YOU ARE NOT LIKE THE BIRDS		368	FOUR ZOAS 9		430
I SAW MY LUVAH LIKE A SPIRIT STAND IN THE BRIGHT AIR . .		369	FOUR ZOAS 9		465
ROUND HIM STOOD SPIRITS LIKE ME WHO REARD ME A BRIGHT HOUSE		369	FOUR ZOAS 9		466
LIKE A (FAINT) FLAME QUIVERING UPON THE SURFACE OF THE DARKNESS		370	FOUR ZOAS 9	*	497
SHE CEASD & (LIGHT) BEAMD ROUND HER LIKE THE GLORY OF THE MORNING		370	FOUR ZOAS 9	*	503
SWIMS LIKE A DREAM BEFORE MY EYES BUT THE SWEET SMELLING FRUIT		371	FOUR ZOAS 9		539
REVIVES ME TO NEW DEATHS I FADE EVEN LIKE A WATER LILLY		371	FOUR ZOAS 9	*	540
HE WENT WITH TIMID STEPS & ENION LIKE THE RUDDY MORN . .		371	FOUR ZOAS 9		547
ROSE ENION LIKE A GENTLE LIGHT & ENION SPOKE SAYING . .		373	FOUR ZOAS 9		594
IN WALLS OF GOLD WE CAST HIM LIKE A SEED INTO THE EARTH		374	FOUR ZOAS 9		632
TOSSED THE NATIONS LIKE CHAFF INTO THE SEAS OF THARMAS . .		374	FOUR ZOAS 9		656
O TREMBLING JOY EXCESS OF JOY IS LIKE EXCESS OF GRIEF		376	FOUR ZOAS 9		730
DESIRING LIKE THE HUNGRY WORM & LIKE THE [SILENT] GAPING GRAVE		376	FOUR ZOAS 9		735
THE STARS CONSUMD LIKE A LAMP BLOWN OUT & IN THEIR STEAD BEHOLDS		379	FOUR ZOAS 9	*	829
EACH MORNING LIKE A NEW BORN MAN ISSUES WITH SONGS & JOY		379	FOUR ZOAS 9		833
IN BLUSHES LIKE THE MORNING		381	FOUR ZOAS AD 5		6
IS THAT ABOMINATION WHICH LIKE THE JEWISH CEREMONIES . .		389C	ANNO WATSON		MARG
THE BASEST & MOST OPPRESSIVE OF HUMAN CODES & BEING LIKE		393C	ANNO WATSON		MARG
LIKE A WILD BEAST GUARDS MY WAY		415	MY SPECTRE/N		2
LIKE TO THE ROOTS OF ANCIENT TREES		419	I SAW A MONK/N		18
LIKE THE WILD STAG SHE FLEES AWAY		426	MENTAL TRAVLER		77
I WEPT FOR JOY LIKE A DOVE I MOURN		427	LAND OF DREAMS		11
WHY WAS I NOT BORN LIKE THIS ENVIOUS RACE		428	MARY		22
LIKE FOUL FIENDS INHABITING MARY'S MILD BRAIN		429	MARY		42
SHE REMEMBERS NO FACE LIKE THE HUMAN DIVINE		429	MARY		43
ANOTHER MAIDEN LIKE HERSELF		429	CRYSTL CABINET		13
FILLD ME THAT LIKE A FLAME I BURND		429	CRYSTL CABINET		18
AND LIKE A WEEPING BABE BECAME		429	CRYSTL CABINET		24
LIKE TO THE ROOTS OF ANCIENT TREES		430	GREY MONK		8
LIKE TO THE ARMOUR'S IRON BRACE		433	AUGURIES		100
AND PUTTING IN LIKE THE PROGRESS OF A BLIND MAN		439C	REMARKS MALKIN		PROSE
LIKE A SCROLL READY TO BE CONSUMED IN THE FIRES OF THE ANGELS		443A	LAST JUDGMNT/L		PROSE
HE CERTAINLY WOULD HAVE BEEN MORE LIKE A FOOL THAN A WISE MAN		450D	ANNO REYNOLDS		MARG
HIS PRAISE OF RAFAEL IS LIKE THE HYSTERIC SMILE OF REVENGE		452A	ANNO REYNOLDS		MARG
HE IS LIKE SR JOSHUA FULL OF SELF-CONTRADICTION & KNAVERY		459D	ANNO REYNOLDS		MARG

		PAGE	TITLE	LINE
LIKE	(CONTINUED)			
FRESCO PAINTING IS LIKE MINIATURE PAINTING		466D	ANNO REYNOLDS	MARG
THE SHEEP ENDEAVOURING TO WALK LIKE THE DOG		470B	ANNO REYNOLDS	MARG
OR THE OX STRIVING TO TROT LIKE THE HORSE		470B	ANNO REYNOLDS	MARG
MAN IS BORN LIKE A GARDEN READY PLANTED & SOWN . . .		471A	ANNO REYNOLDS	MARG
I CERTAINLY DO THANK GOD THAT I AM NOT LIKE REYNOLDS .		471A	ANNO REYNOLDS	MARG
CALLD HARMONY IT IS LIKE THE SMILE OF A FOOL		478D	ANNO REYNOLDS	MARG
THE SURREY HILLS GLOW LIKE THE CLINKERS OF THE FURNACE LAMBETH'S VALE		485	MILTON 6	14
THEN PALAMABRON REDDENING LIKE THE MOON IN AN ECLIPSE .		487	MILTON 7	22
THEY BIT IN THEIR WILD FURY WHO ALSO MADDEND LIKE WILDEST BEASTS		487	MILTON 7	49
LIKE SWEET PERFUMES I STUPIFIED THE MASCULINE PERCEPTIONS		492	MILTON 12	5
WILD WITH PROPHETIC FURY HIS FORMER LIFE BECAME LIKE A DREAM		493	MILTON 12	45
LIKE AS A POLYPUS THAT VEGETATES BENEATH THE DEEP . . .		496	MILTON 15	8
LIKE FEMALES OF SWEET BEAUTY TO GUARD ROUND HIM & TO FEED		496	MILTON 15	14
HIS PATH INTO A GLOBE ITSELF INFOLDING LIKE A SUN . .		497	MILTON 15	24
OR LIKE A MOON OR LIKE A UNIVERSE OF STARRY MAJESTY . .		497	MILTON 15	25
OR LIKE A HUMAN FORM A FRIEND WITH WITH WHOM HE LIVD BENEVOLENT		497	MILTON 15	27
HIS LIMBS SHOT FORTH LIKE ROOTS OF TREES AGAINST THE FORWARD PATH		498	MILTON 17	35
WITH A GARMENT OF PITY & COMPASSION LIKE THE GARMENT OF GOD		499	MILTON 18	35
LAMENTS & ENION WANDERS LIKE A WEEPING INARTICULATE VOICE		501	MILTON 19	42
IT HAS A HEART LIKE THEE A BRAIN OPEN TO HEAVEN & HELL . .		502	MILTON 20	28
LIKE THE BLACK STORM COMING OUT OF CHAOS BEYOND THE STARS		507	MILTON 23	21
ALL POWERFUL AND HIS LOCKS FLOURISH LIKE THE BROWS OF MORNING		509	MILTON 24	70
WITH NEITHER LINEAMENT NOR FORM BUT LIKE TO WATRY CLOUDS		512	MILTON 26	27
ETERNAL AND SOMETIMES TWO SPECTRES LIKE LAMPS QUIVERING		515	MILTON 28	11
OPAKE AND LIKE THE BLACK PEBBLE ON THE ENRAGED BEACH .		515	MILTON 28	35
WHILE THE POOR INDIGENT IS LIKE THE DIAMOND WHICH THO CLOTHD		515	MILTON 28	36
SHINING LIKE PRECIOUS STONES & ORNAMENTED WITH APPROPRIATE SIGNS		516	MILTON 28	53
LIKE WOMEN & CHILDREN WERE TAKEN AWAY AS ON WINGS . .		519	MILTON 31	2
WHO CREEPS INTO STATE GOVERNMENT LIKE A CATTERPILLER TO DESTROY		533	MILTON 41	11
SILENT PLOTTING WHEN TO QUESTION LIKE A THIEF IN A CAVE		533	MILTON 41	14
THAT RAGES ROUND HIM LIKE A WOLF DAY & NIGHT WITHOUT REST		533	MILTON 41	18
AND HIS LEGS CARRIED IT LIKE A LONG FORK		536	AND HIS LEGS/N	1
LIKE AS A PEDLAR BEARS HIS WEARY PACK		536	AND HIS LEGS/N	7
LIKE TREMBLING HARE SITS ON HIS WEAKLY PAPER		537	AND HIS LEGS/N	18
THAT MY FRIENDS MAY WEEP AS MUCH AS THEY LIKE . . .		537	AND HIS LEGS/N	51
[LIKE A FILTHY INFECTIOUS HEAD OF HAIR]		540	SIR JOSH RUB/N	6
[LIKE TO THE LION SPORTING WITH HIS PREY]		540	GOLDEN RULE/N	* 2
[LIKE TO THE LION SPORTING WITH HIS PREY] [XXX] . .		540	GOLDEN RULE/N	* 4
LIKE TO THE LION SPORTING WITH HIS PREY		540	S(TOTHAR) D/N	4
THAT MY FRIENDS MAY WEEP AS MUCH AS THEY LIKE . . .		546	ANOTHER/N 1	2
LIKE PUTTING OIL & WATER INTO A LAMP		549	ENGL ENCOU/N 1	5
AND JENOUS LOOKS TO HAM [LOOKS] LIKE MAD RANTERY . .		550	ENGL ENCOU/N 2	* 4
LIKE DISPLAYING OIL & WATER INTO A LAMP		550	ENGL ENCOU/N 2	5
AND WHAT IS THE THIRD THEN HE SNORD LIKE A PIG . . .		553	ASKD PRIGG/N	5
AND [SMILD LIKE A CHERUB & SAID]		553	ASKD PRIGG/N	* 6
. . . SMILE LIKE A CHERUB & SAY A PAINT BRUSH . .		553	ASKD PRIGG/N	10
AND WHAT IS THE THIRD HE'LL BOW LIKE A RUSH		553	ASKD PRIGG/N	11
SHE FROWND LIKE A FURY & SAID PATRONAGE		554	ASKD PRIGG/N	19
AND SMILD LIKE A SYREN & SAID PATRONAGE		554	ASKD PRIGG/N	21
IF MEN WILL ACT LIKE A MAID SMILING OVER A CHURN . . .		556	IF MEN ACT/N	1
IT IS NOT LIKE A LAWYER SERVING A WRIT		556	SOME PEOPLE/N	4
LIKE MOST OTHER THINGS THE CONTRARY OF WHAT IT PRETENDS TO BE		561A	EXHIBITION ADV	PROSE
OF MAN AGAINST THE OPPRESSOR HIS SON IS LIKE HIM . . .		568A	DESC CAT 3	PROSE
HE HAS MADE HIM LOOK MORE LIKE A FOOL THAN A KNAVE . .		574D	DESC CAT 3	PROSE
AND THE FORM OF THE FOURTH WAS LIKE THE SON OF GOD . .		578B	DESC CAT 5	PROSE
"LIKE THE ROLLING THING BEFORE THE WHIRLWIND"		580C	DESC CAT 5	PROSE
CANNOT BE LIKE THE SICKLY DAUBS OF TITIAN OR RUBENS . .		580D	DESC CAT 5	PROSE
STRIPPED FROM HIS LOAD OF CLOATHING HE IS LIKE A DEAD CORPSE		581A	DESC CAT 5	PROSE
LIKE LEATHER AND CHALK THEIR MEN ARE LIKE LEATHER AND		581A	DESC CAT 5	PROSE
THEIR WOMEN LIKE CHALK FOR THE DISPOSITION OF THEIR FORMS		581A	DESC CAT 5	PROSE
LIKE DEAD HORSES WHEN REPELLED BY THE CELESTIAL SPHERES		581D	DESC CAT 8	PROSE
LIKE WALKING IN ANOTHER MAN'S STYLE OR SPEAKING . . .		582D	DESC CAT 9	PROSE
AND THICK HEADED LIKE HIS OWN WORKS BUT THEN IT WOULD .		583C	DESC CAT 9	PROSE
AND TO MAKE ENGLAND LIKE ITALY RESPECTED		584B	DESC CAT 14	PROSE
LIKE THE FULL GALLOP OF THE GOUTY MAN TO THE ORDINARY WALK		593A	PUB ADDRESS/N	PROSE
IS NOT LIKE A COAT MADE BY ANOTHER BUT IS AN EMANATION .		593B	PUB ADDRESS/N	PROSE
FROM IGNORANCE ITSELF & ITS FINISHING IS LIKE ITS MASTER		593B	PUB ADDRESS/N	PROSE
WORKS ARE LIKE THOSE OF TITIAN & CORREGGIO		593D	PUB ADDRESS/N	PROSE
LIKE FUSELI & MICHAEL ANGELO SHAKESPEARE & MILTON . .		595D	PUB ADDRESS/N	PROSE
HE WHO COULD REPRESENT CHRIST UNIFORMLY LIKE A DRAYMAN .		596C	PUB ADDRESS/N	PROSE
LIKE [TO] AS A MONKEY PEEPING IN A MIRROR		597	PUBLC VOICE/PA	2
SMOOTHD IT OVER LIKE AN ENGLISH ENGRAVER OR CORREGIO & TITIAN		598C	PUB ADDRESS/N	PROSE
IS LIKE LOOKING FOR EPIGRAMS IN HOMER		599A	PUB ADDRESS/N	PROSE
IF ALL THE PRINCES IN EUROPE LIKE LOUIS XIV		599D	PUB ADDRESS/N	PROSE
LIKE WHAT SR FRANCIS BACON [SHOULD DOWNRIGHT ASSERT] SAYS		599D	PUB ADDRESS/N	PROSE
LIKE A CRIPPLE WHILE THE CRIPPLE MUST BE TAUGHT TO WALK		600A	PUB ADDRESS/N	PROSE
LIKE HEALTHY PEOPLE O RARE WISDOM		600A	PUB ADDRESS/N	PROSE
HISTORICAL & POETICAL ARTISTS LIKE BARRY & MORTIMER . .		601B	PUB ADDRESS/N	PROSE

1093

```
                                                          PAGE     TITLE         LINE
LIKE    (CONTINUED)
     I KNOW MY EXECUTION IS NOT LIKE ANY BODY ELSE I DO NOT  .  . 601D PUB ADDRESS/N    PROSE
     AGAINST THESE VILLAINS I AM LIKE OTHERS . . . . . .      602A PUB ADDRESS/N    PROSE
     LIKE ALL THAT THEY SAY FOR THERE IS EVERY LINE IN NATURE 603B PUB ADDR AD/N    PROSE
     BEAUTIES NOW GENTLEMEN CRITICS HOW DO YOU LIKE THIS  .  . 603B PUB ADDR AD/N    PROSE
     THEM LIKE A TRAVELLER WHO MAY AS WELL SUPPOSE THAT   .  . 606D V LAST JUDG/N    PROSE
     OTHERS OF THE LIKE KIND ARE FABLE YET THEY CONTAIN VISION 607A V LAST JUDG/N    PROSE
     MULTITUDES OF MEN IN HARMONY APPEAR LIKE A SINGLE INFANT  607C V LAST JUDG/N    PROSE
     & JUSTICE CAIPHAS HAS A BLUE FLAME LIKE A MITER ON HIS HEAD 608D V LAST JUDG/N  PROSE
     [JERUSALEM WHO IS ABOUT TO BE RECIEVD LIKE THE BRIDE      609C V LAST JUDG/N   *PROSE
       OF THE]
     THIS STATE APPEARS LIKE A FEMALE CROWND WITH STARS   .  . 610A V LAST JUDG/N    PROSE
     ON WHICH ARE SEEN STARS SOMEWHAT LIKE THE MILKY WAY  .  . 610B V LAST JUDG/N    PROSE
     OF THE SAVIOUR IN LIKE MANNER . . . . . . . .            611C V LAST JUDG/N    PROSE
     LIKE A DOVE IS SURROUNDED BY A BLUE HEAVEN . . . . .      613B V LAST JUDG/N    PROSE
     DO YOU NOT SEE A ROUND DISK OF FIRE SOMEWHAT LIKE A GUINEA 617B V LAST JUDG/N    PROSE
     A MONOTONOUS CADENCE LIKE THAT USED BY MILTON . . . . .   621C JERUSALEM 3      PROSE
     JERUSALEM IS SCATTERD ABROAD LIKE A CLOUD OF SMOKE THRO   623  JERUSALEM 5        13
       NON-ENTITY
     WAS LIVING PANTING LIKE A FRIGHTED WOLF AND HOWLING  .  . 625  JERUSALEM 7         1
     HE DRINKS THEE UP LIKE WATER LIKE WINE HE POURS THEE  .   625  JERUSALEM 7        11
     HIS FEET INDIGNANT SELF-RIGHTEOUSNESS LIKE WHIRLWINDS OF  626  JERUSALEM 7        73
       THE NORTH
     IN PULSATIONS OF TIME & EXTENSIONS OF SPACE LIKE URNS OF  630  JERUSALEM 11        2
       BEULAH
     HE IS LIKE A MANDRAKE IN THE EARTH BEFORE REUBEN'S GATE   631  JERUSALEM 11       22
     LIKE MEN HERMAPHRODITIC EACH WINGED WITH EIGHT WINGS  .  . 633  JERUSALEM 13        8
     THE VEGETATIVE UNIVERSE OPENS LIKE A FLOWER FROM         633  JERUSALEM 13       34
       THE EARTH'S CENTER
     LIKE A PALE CLOUD ARISING FROM THE ARMS OF BEULAH'S      635  JERUSALEM 14       33
       DAUGHTERS
     LIKE IRON SCOURGES OVER ALBION REASONINGS LIKE VAST      635  JERUSALEM 15       12
       SERPENTS
     LIKE WHEELS FROM A GREAT WHEEL REFLECTED IN THE DEEP  .  . 641  JERUSALEM 18       43
     SPREADING THEM OUT BEFORE THE SUN LIKE STALKS OF FLAX TO  645  JERUSALEM 22       21
       DRY
     JERUSALEM REPLYD LIKE A VOICE HEARD FROM A SEPULCHER  .  . 646  JERUSALEM 23        8
     LIKE ME THY VICTIM O THAT DEATH & ANNIHILATION WERE THE  646  JERUSALEM 23       40
       SAME
     THEN THE DIVINE VISION LIKE A SILENT SUN APPEARD ABOVE  .  . 653  JERUSALEM 29        1
     IF THOU WITHHOLD THINE HAND I PERISH LIKE A FALLEN LEAF   654  JERUSALEM 29       50
     AND THE VAST FORM OF NATURE LIKE A SERPENT PLAYD BEFORE   655  JERUSALEM 29       76
       THEM
     VALA SHRUNK IN LIKE THE DARK SEA THAT LEAVES ITS SLIMY    655  JERUSALEM 29       78
       BANKS
     AND THE VAST FORM OF NATURE LIKE A SERPENT ROLLD BETWEEN  655  JERUSALEM 29       80
     IN PAIN GIRDING ME ROUND LIKE A RIB OF IRON IN HEAVEN O   660  JERUSALEM 34       14
       VALA
     REUBEN SLEPT IN BASHAN LIKE ONE DEAD IN THE VALLEY  .  .  . 661  JERUSALEM 34       43
     LIKE ROCKY CLOUDS BUILD ME A GLOOMY MONUMENT OF WOE  .  .  . 666  JERUSALEM 39       18
     LIKE EVENING DEW ON EVERY HERB UPON THE BREATHING GROUND  669  JERUSALEM 42        8
     THEY RAGE LIKE WILD BEASTS IN THE FORESTS OF AFFLICTION   671  JERUSALEM 42       61
     LIKE LAKES OF LIQUID LEAD INSTEAD OF HEAVENLY CHAPELS BUILT 673  JERUSALEM 43       63
     LIKE AFRICA'S AND HIS MACHINES ARE WOVEN WITH HIS LIFE  .  . 675  JERUSALEM 45       25
     BURST FROM HIS BOSOM IN THE TOMB LIKE A PALE SNOWY CLOUD  678  JERUSALEM 48       48
     I CANNOT CONCIEVE WE ARE MEN OF LIKE PASSIONS . . . . .   682C JERUSALEM 52       PROSE
     LIKE TO THE ROOTS OF ANCIENT TREES . . . . . . .         683  I SAW A MONK/J     16
     LIKE SEVEN BURNING HEAVENS RANGD FROM SOUTH TO NORTH  .   684  JERUSALEM 53       14
     HE TOSSES LIKE A CLOUD OUTSTRETCHD AMONG JERUSALEM'S RUINS 685  JERUSALEM 54       13
     BUT THE SPECTRE LIKE A HOAR FROST & A MILDEW ROSE OVER    685  JERUSALEM 54       15
       ALBION
     BUT SHE STRETCHD OUT HER STARRY NIGHT IN SPACES AGAINST   685  JERUSALEM 54       28
       HIM LIKE
     GATHERD JERUSALEM'S CHILDREN IN HIS ARMS & BORE THEM LIKE 692  JERUSALEM 60        8
     THEY SPREAD FORTH LIKE A LOVELY ROOT INTO THE GARDEN OF GOD 692  JERUSALEM 60       15
     CUT WITH THE FLINTS HER TEARS RUN DOWN HER REASON GROWS   693  JERUSALEM 60       42
       LIKE
     THEN MARY BURST FORTH INTO A SONG SHE FLOWED LIKE A RIVER 695  JERUSALEM 61       28
       OF
     LIKE MANY WATERS AND EMANATING INTO GARDENS & PALACES UPON 695  JERUSALEM 61       30
     OF AGES & GENERATIONS FOLDING & UNFOLDING IT LIKE A VEIL  698  JERUSALEM 64        3
       OF CHERUBIM
     WAS LIKE THE WORKMANSHIP OF THE PLOWMAN & THE WATER WHEEL 700  JERUSALEM 65       18
     BECAUSE ITS WORKMANSHIP WAS LIKE THE WORKMANSHIP OF THE   700  JERUSALEM 65       20
       SHEPHERD
     SUDDEN THEY BECOME LIKE WHAT THEY BEHOLD IN HOWLINGS &    701  JERUSALEM 65       75
       DEADLY PAIN
     THEY BECOME LIKE WHAT THEY BEHOLD YET IMMENSE IN STRENGTH 701  JERUSALEM 65       79
       & POWER
     THE SUN FORGETS HIS COURSE LIKE A DRUNKEN MAN HE HESITATES 703  JERUSALEM 66       74
     AND ALL THE MOUNTAINS & HILLS SHRINK UP LIKE A WITHERING  703  JERUSALEM 66       82
       GOURD
     THE HEAVENS ARE CUT LIKE A MANTLE AROUND FROM THE CLIFFS  706  JERUSALEM 68       19
       OF ALBION
     TILL THEY REFUSE LIBERTY TO THE MALE & NOT LIKE BEULAH  .  . 707  JERUSALEM 69       14
     LIKE LOVELY BEAMS OF LIGHT . . . . . . . . . .            710  JERUSALEM 71       24
     & IS PLANTED LIKE THE SEED OF A WILD FLOWER AMONG OUR WHEAT 716D JERUSALEM 77       PROSE
     THOSE THAT ARE SICK LIKE TO THE PHARISEES . . . . . .    718  STOOD AMONG/J      28
     I WALK TO EPHRAIM I SEEK FOR SHILOH I WALK LIKE A LOST    720  JERUSALEM 79       10
       SHEEP
     AND RAHAB LIKE A DISMAL AND INDEFINITE HOVERING CLOUD  .  . 723  JERUSALEM 80       51
     THAT APPARENT TO ALL IN ETERNITY GLOWS LIKE THE SUN IN    723  JERUSALEM 80       68
       THE BREAST
```

`KE   (CONTINUED)
    HER STRUGGLING TORMENT IN HER IRON ARMS AND LIKE A CHAIN   726 JERUSALEM 82   70
    LIKE A FAINT RAINBOW WAVED BEFORE HIM IN THE AWFUL GLOOM   728 JERUSALEM 83   67
    SPREADING INTO THE AZURE WINGS WHICH LIKE A CANOPY   .   .   . 731 JERUSALEM 86   9
    WHICH LIKE A ROBE COVERS & LIKE A VEIL OF SERAPHIM   .   .   . 731 JERUSALEM 86   24
    AND ENITHARMON LIKE A FAINT RAINBOW WAVED BEFORE HIM   .   . 732 JERUSALEM 86   50
    SILENT THEY WANDERD HAND IN HAND LIKE TWO INFANTS WANDRING   732 JERUSALEM 86   62
    LOS ANSWERD SIGHING LIKE THE BELLOWS OF HIS FURNACES   .   .   733 JERUSALEM 88   1
    LIKE THE RED SUN UPON THE MOUNTAINS IN THE BLOODY DAY   .   .   734 JERUSALEM 88   57
    OF VEINS OF RED BLOOD GROWS AROUND THEM LIKE A SCARLET ROBE   736 JERUSALEM 90   5
    COVERING THEM FROM THE SIGHT OF MAN LIKE THE WOVEN VEIL   736 JERUSALEM 90   6
        OF SLEEP
    LIKE TO A CURTAIN & FOLDING THEM ACCORDING TO HIS WILL   .   738 JERUSALEM 91   34
    BUT WHEN HE TOUCHES THE FIRST FIBROUS THREAD LIKE FILMY DEW   739 JERUSALEM 92   10
    ENITHARMON HEARD SHE RAISD HER HEAD LIKE THE MILD MOON   .   . 740 JERUSALEM 93   1
    MERLIN WAS LIKE THEE RINTRAH AMONG THE GIANTS OF ALBION   740 JERUSALEM 93   13
    JUDAH WAS LIKE PALAMABRON O SIMEON O LEVI YE FLED AWAY   740 JERUSALEM 93   14
    DAZLING AROUND THY SKIRTS LIKE A SERPENT OF PRECIOUS STONES   743 JERUSALEM 96   12
        & GOLD
    THINE HAS A GREAT HOOK NOSE LIKE THINE   .   .   .   .   .   . 748 EV GOSPEL(A)/N   3
    MINE HAS A SNUB NOSE LIKE TO MINE   .   .   .   . 748 EV GOSPEL(A)/N   4
    HE SPOKE WITH AUTHORITY NOT LIKE A SCRIBE   .   .   .   .   . 750 EV GOSPEL(C)/N   12
    AND NOT USED THE ELDERS & PRIESTS LIKE DOGS   .   .   .   .   750 EV GOSPEL(C)/N   28
    HE SPOKE WITH AUTHORITY NOT LIKE A SCRIBE   .   .   .   .   . 751 EV GOSPEL(D)/N   16
    AND THE DEVIL WAS GOD LIKE A CHRISTIAN CIVIL   .   .   .   .   752 EV GOSPEL(D)/N   36
    LIKE DR PRIESTLY & [SIR ISAAC] BACON & NEWTON   .   .   .   . 752 EV GOSPEL(D)/N   39
    AND NOT USD THE ELDERS & PRIESTS LIKE DOGS   .   .   .   .   . 752 EV GOSPEL(D)/N   62
    COME OUT WITH A MORAL LIKE A STING IN THE TAIL   .   .   .   . 778B HOMERS POETRY   PROSE
    [LIKES] LIKE A HOG UPON A ROPE   .   .   .   . 782A INSC UPCOTT   *PROSE
    MY WIFE IS LIKE A FLAME OF MANY COLOURS OF PRECIOUS JEWELS   801B LETTER 13   PROSE
    WE LIKE INFANTS DESCEND   .   .   .   . 805 TO BUTTS/L   42
    LIKE A WEAK MORTAL BIRTH   .   .   .   .   805 TO BUTTS/L   44
    LIKE A SEA WITHOUT SHORE   .   .   .   .   805 TO BUTTS/L   46
    LIKE DROSS PURGD AWAY   .   .   .   . 805 TO BUTTS/L   55
    BE NO LESS FAVOURD THO THEY ARE ROUGH LIKE ROUGH SAILORS   807A LETTER 17   PROSE
    MR HAYLEY ACTS LIKE A PRINCE I AM AT COMPLETE EASE BUT   .   808A LETTER 19   PROSE
    WHICH I HOPE SHE WHO IS THE BEST JUDGE WILL THINK LIKE   .   809A LETTER 20   PROSE
    HE IS NEPHEW TO THE LATE MR COWPER THE POET YOU WOULD LIKE   809C LETTER 20   PROSE
        HIM MUCH
    LET ME ALSO NOTICE THAT CARRACHE'S PICTURES ARE NOT LIKE   815B LETTER 23   PROSE
    CORREGGIO'S NOR CORREGGIO'S LIKE RAFAEL'S & IF NEITHER OF   815B LETTER 23   PROSE
    THEM WAS TO BE ENCOURAGED TILL HE DID LIKE ANY OF   815B LETTER 23   PROSE
        THE OTHERS
    H(HAYLEY) LIKE S(STOTHARD) ENVIOUS & THAT HE IS I AM NOW   819C LETTER 25   PROSE
        CERTAIN
    I HAVE ORDERS TO SET MY FACE LIKE A FLINT EZEKIEL...   .   . 825B LETTER 27   PROSE
    WHY WAS I NOT BORN LIKE THE REST OF MY RACE   .   .   .   .   828 O WHY BORN/L   2
    SOMEWHAT LIKE MY FATE & SUCH IT IS LIKELY TO REMAIN   .   .   830A LETTER 30   PROSE
    LIKE THE DISTANT APPROACH OF THINGS MIGHTY & MAGNIFICENT   835B LETTER 34   PROSE
    LIKE THE SOUND OF HARPS WHICH I HEAR BEFORE THE SUN'S   835B LETTER 34   PROSE
        RISING
    LIKE THE REMEMBRANCE OF FELPHAM'S WAVES & OF THE GLORIOUS &   835B LETTER 34   PROSE
    FAR BEAMING TURRET LIKE THE VILLA OF LAVANT BLESSED &   .   835B LETTER 34   PROSE
    YOUNGER THAN I KNEW HIM BUT VERY LIKE INDEED MR WALKER   .   843C LETTER 43   PROSE
    WERE TRULY AMIABLE AND FEELING LIKE HIMSELF   .   .   .   .   844A LETTER 43   PROSE
    BUT TO SAY THAT SHE IS YOUR DAUGHTER & IS LIKE YOU   .   .   853A LETTER 51   *PROSE
    LIKE PUTTING JOHN MILTON WITH JOHN BUNYAN   .   .   .   .   . 853A LETTER 51   *PROSE
    & TO THOSE WHO HAVE AN AFFECTION FOR HIM LIKE YOURS IS   .   854B LETTER 53   PROSE
    THAT IT IS NOT LIKE THE SAME PLATE WITH THE WORN   855C LETTER 53   PROSE
        OUT IMPRESSION
    SAYS THAT WHEN MY PRINT IS LIKE THAT I NEED WISH IT NO   855D LETTER 53   PROSE
        BETTER
    AS TO ANY THING LIKE A HINT OF A PROPOSAL RELATING TO   .   857A LETTER 54   *PROSE
    THE TOWN IS MAD YOUNG ROSCIUS LIKE ALL PRODIGIES IS THE   859C LETTER 56   PROSE
    AS TO REAL ACTING IT IS LIKE HISTORICAL PAINTING NO BOY'S   859C LETTER 56   PROSE
        WORK
    PROSPECT AT NORTH END MRS HURD'S I SHOULD LIKE AS WELL   873A LETTER 76   PROSE
        AS ANY
    START FOR HAMPSTEAD LIKE A YOUNG LARK WITHOUT FEATHERS   .   875A LETTER 80   PROSE
    BONES & SINEWS ALL STRINGS & BOBBINS LIKE A WEAVER'S LOOM   875B LETTER 81   PROSE
LIKELY
    DIRECTS THEM TO THE KNIGHT AS THE PERSON WHO WOULD   566D DESC CAT 3   PROSE
        BE LIKELY
    CHARACTERS LIKELY TO RIDE IN COMPANY ALL BEING ABOVE THE   568C DESC CAT 3   PROSE
    AS THE PERSON WHO WILL BE LIKELY   .   .   .   . 588C CHAUCER/N   PROSE
    DIRECTS THEM TO THE KNIGHT AS THE PERSON WHO WILL BE LIKELY   589D CHAUCER 2   PROSE
    THAT HAS BEEN DONE OR IS LIKELY TO BE DONE IN ENGLAND   .   602A PUB ADDRESS/N PROSE
    CENTAURS MOST LIKELY DANTE DESCRIBES THE...CIRCLES IN CANTO   786A ILLS DANTE 101 PROSE
        XI...
    FOR THEM THESE BALLADS ARE LIKELY TO BE PROFITABLE FOR WE   821B LETTER 25   PROSE
    VERY LIKELY BE OF GREAT CONSEQUENCE IT IS COWPER'S MILTON   821C LETTER 25   PROSE
    SOMEWHAT LIKE MY FATE & SUCH IT IS LIKELY TO REMAIN   .   .   830A LETTER 30   PROSE
    WITH THEIR MASTERS & ARE LIKELY TO GET THE BETTER EACH   859B LETTER 56   PROSE
        PARTY
    CONTAINS (A HUNDRED) PLATES BUT IT IS NOT LIKELY THAT I   878C LETTER 88   PROSE
        SHALL GET
LIKENESS
    MAN BEGETTING HIS LIKENESS   .   .   .   . 232 URIZEN 19   15
    IN LIKENESS OF HIMSELF TELL ALSO OF THE FALSE TONGUE   481 MILTON 2   10
        VEGETATED
    FAITH IN GOD THE DEAR SAVIOUR WHO TOOK ON THE LIKENESS   506 MILTON 22   57
        OF MEN

		PAGE	TITLE	LINE

LIKENESS   (CONTINUED)
```
    WHO WHATEVER LIKENESS HE MAY HAVE TO MICHAEL ANGELO  . . .    542 FLORENTINE/N      33
    AND THE DIVINE APPEARANCE WAS THE LIKENESS & SIMILITUDE       743 JERUSALEM 96       7
        OF LOS
    I SEE THEE IN THE LIKENESS & SIMILITUDE OF LOS MY FRIEND      743 JERUSALEM 96      22
    I SEND THE SHADOW OF THE DEPARTED ANGEL HOPE THE LIKENESS     797A LETTER 9         PROSE
    I TRANSMIT TO MRS BUTTS AN ATTEMPT [TO] AT YOUR LIKENESS      808D LETTER 20       *PROSE
    EXPECT A LIKENESS BUT NOW I HAVE DONE ALL I COULD & KNOW      815D LETTER 23        PROSE
    A GOOD LIKENESS OF YOU IF I HAVE HANDS & EYES LEFT   . . .    824B LETTER 27        PROSE
    THAT HE THOUGHT IT A VERY GREAT LIKENESS  . . . . . .  .      836B LETTER 35        PROSE
    TESTIMONY TO MY LIKENESS OF ROMNEY MR FLAXMAN I HAVE   .  .   836C LETTER 35        PROSE
LIKENESSES
    LIKENESSES FROM MEMORY BEING NECESSARILY VERY VERY           824B LETTER 27        PROSE
        DEFECTIVE
LIKENESS TAKER
    FOR I AM BECOME A LIKENESS TAKER & SUCCEED ADMIRABLY WELL     824B LETTER 27        PROSE
LIKES
    BECAUSE I LIKE IT MY FATHER DOES WHAT HE LIKES & SO DO I       51C ISLAND MOON 6    PROSE
    [LIKES] LIKE A HOG UPON A ROPE  . . . . . . . . .  .         782A INSC UPCOTT     *PROSE
LIKEWISE
    OF MAN IS DERIVED FROM THE POETIC GENIUS LIKEWISE   . . .      98B ALL RELIGIONS    PROSE
    LIKEWISE READ HOMER'S ILIAD . . . . . . .  . . . .           389C ANNO WATSON       MARG
    THE UGLY LIKEWISE WHEN ACCOMPANIED AND  . . . . . . .        580A DESC CAT 5        PROSE
    THIS PICTURE WAS LIKEWISE PAINTED AT INTERVALS   . . . .     582B DESC CAT 9        PROSE
    I REQUEST LIKEWISE THAT THE SOCIETY WILL  . . . . . .  .     592A PUB ADDRESS/N     PROSE
    I HAVE LIKEWISE HAD BY ME ALL THE SUMMER (SIX) PLATES  .     791B LETTER 3          PROSE
    PICTURES LIKEWISE CALLS FOR MY THANKS I WILL FINISH THE      813D LETTER 22         PROSE
        OTHER
    HIS SON WAS LIKEWISE NOT AT HOME BUT I WILL AGAIN CALL ON     834B LETTER 34        PROSE
    I INCLOSE LIKEWISE THE ACADEMICAL CORRESPONDENCE OF  . . .   836D LETTER 35         PROSE
    NEAR NORTHAMPTON MR EDWARDS IS OUT OF TOWN LIKEWISE  . .     855B LETTER 53         PROSE
    WORK OF MR HAYLEY'S & THE PUBLIC LIKEWISE ARE DEPRIVED OF    856C LETTER 54         PROSE
    OF YOUR WORKS WOULD BE MORE PRODUCTIVE HE LIKEWISE OBJECTS   858A LETTER 55         PROSE
LILFORD
    I AM SORRY FOR LD(?LORD) LD(?LILFORD) HE IS A MAN OF VERY    868D LETTER 68         PROSE
        SINGULAR
LILIED
    AND LAID HER LILIED BEAUTIES ON THE GREEN  . . . . . .        43C WOE CRIED MUSE   PROSE
LILIES
    HE SHEWD ME LILIES FOR MY HAIR . . . . . . . . . . .           6 HOW SWEET/PS        5
    LIKE LILIES DROPPING TEARS IN EACH OTHER'S BOSOM  . . . .     35D COUCH DEATH/PS   PROSE
LILITH
    (LILITH) . . . . . . . . . . . . . . . . . . .              775D INSC LAOCOON      TITLE
LILLIES
    I GAVE SWEET LILLIES TO THEIR BREASTS & ROSES TO THEIR HAIR  312 FOUR ZOAS 6        29
    THY LILLIES THAT GAVE LIGHT WHAT TIME THE MORNING LOOKED     325 FOUR ZOAS 7       196
        FORTH
    AMONG THE LILLIES BY WATERS FAIR  . . . . . . . . .          427 LAND OF DREAMS      8
    HER LILLIES & ROSES ARE BLIGHTED & SHED . . . . . . .        428 MARY               20
LILLING
    OF MORTAL OR IMMORTAL ARM AND SOFTLY LILLING FLUTES  . . .   509 MILTON 24          56
LILLY     SEE WATER LILLY
    DEDUCT FROM A ROSE ITS REDNESS FROM A LILLY ITS WHITENESS     81C ANNO LAVATER      MARG
    & A LILLY ARE VARIOUS & BOTH BEAUTIFUL BEAUTY IS EXUBERANT    81C ANNO LAVATER      MARG
    THE LILLY OF THE VALLEY BREATHING IN THE HUMBLE GRASS  .     127 BOOK OF THEL 1     15
    SAYING REJOICE THOU HUMBLE GRASS THOU NEW-BORN LILLY FLOWER  127 BOOK OF THEL 1     21
    QUEEN OF THE VALES THE LILLY ANSWERD ASK THE TENDER CLOUD    128 BOOK OF THEL 2     13
    THE CLOUD DESCENDED AND THE LILLY BOWD HER MODEST HEAD  .  . 128 BOOK OF THEL 2     17
    WHILE THE LILLY WHITE SHALL IN LOVE DELIGHT  . . . . .       171 THE LILLY/N         3
    THE LILLY  . . . . . . . . . . . . . . . . . .  .          215C THE LILLY/SE       TITLE
    WHILE THE LILLY WHITE SHALL IN LOVE DELIGHT  . . . . . .     215 THE LILLY/SE        3
    AND LOS SAID LO THE LILLY PALE & THE ROSE REDDNING FIERCE    288 FOUR ZOAS 2       302
    UPON THE ROSE OR LILLY PALE OR ON A BANK  . . . . . .        288 FOUR ZOAS 2    *  314
        WHERE [SLEEPS] SLEEP
    AND LIKE A LILLY IS THY WIFE VALA WITHERD BY WINDS  . . .    311 FOUR ZOAS 5       227
    VALA THE LILLY OF THE DESERT MELTING IN HIGH NOON  . . .     326 FOUR ZOAS 7       240
    ANY MORE THAN I BELIEVE THAT THE ROSE TEACHES THE LILLY      453B ANNO REYNOLDS     MARG
        HOW TO GROW
    THE JONQUIL THE MILD LILLY OPES HER HEAVENS EVERY TREE  .  . 521 MILTON 31          60
    THE LILLY OF HAVILAH AND THEY SANG SOFT THRO LAMBETH'S       642 JERUSALEM 19       42
        VALES
LILLY'S
    THE HELPLESS WORM AROSE AND SAT UPON THE LILLY'S LEAF  .  .  129 BOOK OF THEL 3     30
    I SEE THEE LIKE AN INFANT WRAPPED IN THE LILLY'S LEAF  .  .  129 BOOK OF THEL 4      3
LILY
    PUT ON FAIR LINEN THAT WITH THE LILY VIES PURPLE AND SILVER   38A SAMSON/PS        PROSE
LIMB
    . . . EACH STRONG LIMB BOUND DOWN AS WITH MARBLE  . . . .    137 FRENCH REVOLTN     66
    BY PLUCKING OFF FIRST ONE LIMB AND THEN ANOTHER TILL THE     157B MARRIAGE HH 17   PROSE
        BODY
    REND LIMB FROM LIMB THE WARRIOR & THE TYRANT REUNITING       363 FOUR ZOAS 9       255
        IN PAIN
    RENT THE IMMORTAL FEMALES LIMB FROM LIMB & JOINT FROM        500 MILTON 18          49
        JOINT
LIMBD     SEE LONG LIMBD, RED LIMBD
LIMBO
    & ROUND PARADISE IS VACUUM OR LIMBO  . . . . . . . .  .      785B ILLUS DANTE 7     PROSE
    LIMBO CHARON  . . . . . . . . . . .  . . . . . . .          785D ILLS DANTE 101    PROSE
    LIMBO OF WEAK SHADOWS . . . . . . . . . . .  . . . .         SUPP ILLUS DANTE 7   *PROSE
    TERRESTRIAL PARADISE IT IS AN ISLAND IN LIMBO  . . . . .     SUPP ILLUS DANTE 7   *PROSE
LIMB RENDING
    O WHAT LIMB RENDING PAINS I FEEL THY FIRE & MY FROST   .  .  196 AMERICA PREL 2     15
```

```
                                                      PAGE    TITLE         LINE
LIMBS
    WITH JOY THY RUDDY LIMBS AND FLOURISHING HAIR  . . . . .    1 TO SUMMER/PS       6
    SHE SAT WITH DEAD COLD LIMBS STIFFEND TO STONE  . . . .     6 FAIR ELENOR/PS    69
    OH BLESS THOSE LIMBS BEAMING WITH HEAVNLY LIGHT  . . . .    9 FRESH FROM/PS      8
    O SHOULD SHE EER PROVE FALSE HIS LIMBS ID TEAR  . . . .    10 WHEN EARLY/PS     17
    THY YOUNG HANDS TORE HUMAN LIMBS AND GORGED HUMAN FLESH    38B SAMSON/PS      PROSE
    THAT MAKES OUR LIMBS QUAKE IF OUR HEARTS BE WARM  . . .    64 SHEPHERD OLD       4
    THAT MAKES OUR LIMBS QUAKE IF OUR HEARTS BE WARM  . . .    64 SHEPHERD OLD       8
    THAT MAKES OUR LIMBS QUAKE IF OUR HEARTS BE WARM  . . .    64 SHEPHERD OLD      12
    . . . & SWEAT STOOD ON THEIR TREMBLING LIMBS  . . . . .   105 TIRIEL 4          47
    THEN I HAVE [REND] RENT HIS LIMBS & LEFT HIM ROTTING IN   105 TIRIEL 4       *  51
        THE FOREST
    WHEN IJIM STRETCHD HIS MIGHTY ARM THE ARROW FROM HIS LIMBS  105 TIRIEL 4        71
    REBOUNDED & THE PIERCING SWORD BROKE ON HIS NAKED [LIMBS]  105 TIRIEL 4         72
        FLESH
    RISE UP THY SLUGGISH LIMBS & LET THE LOATHSOMEST OF POISONS  106 TIRIEL 5        9
    HIS STRONG LIMBS . . .  . . . . . .                        135 FRENCH REVOLTN   23
    . . . OER THE COUNCIL HE STRETCHD HIS RED LIMBS  . . . .   138 FRENCH REVOLTN   85
    . . . I AWOKE A COLD HAND PASSED OVER MY LIMBS AND BEHOLD  140 FRENCH REVOLTN  130
    TILL MAN RAISE HIS DARKEND LIMBS OUT OF THE CAVES OF NIGHT  144 FRENCH REVOLTN 218
        . . .
    THE FIERY LIMBS THE FLAMING HAIR  . . . . . . . . . .      159C SONG LIBERTY  PROSE
    AS THY SOFTEST LIMBS I [TOUCH] [STROKE] FEEL  . . . . .    165 CRADLE SONG/N    10
    THO HIS WATERS BATHED MY INFANT LIMBS  . . . . . . . .     166 WHY CARE FOR/N *  6
    [THEY BOUND HIS LITTLE IVORY LIMBS]  . . . . . . . . .     177 LIT BOY LST/N    22
    THE RUDDY LIMBS & FLAMING HAIR . . . .                     178 ABSTINENCE/N      2
    THEN STORMS RENT THEOTORMON'S LIMBS HE ROLLD HIS WAVES     190 V DAU ALBION 2    3
        AROUND
    BUT SHE CAN HOWL INCESSANT WRITHING HER SOFT SNOWY LIMBS   190 V DAU ALBION 2   12
    THE SEA FOWL TAKES THE WINTRY BLAST FOR A COVRING TO HER   195 V DAU ALBION 8    6
        LIMBS
    AROUND THE PILLARS OF URTHONA AND ROUND THY DARK LIMBS  . . 196 AMERICA PREL 1  16
    OF IRON HEATED IN THE FURNACE HIS TERRIBLE LIMBS WERE FIRE  197 AMERICA 4        9
    ACROSS THE LIMBS OF ALBION'S GUARDIAN . . . . . . . .      202 AMERICA 15        2
    OVER THEIR PALE LIMBS AS A VINE WHEN THE TENDER GRAPE      202 AMERICA 15       26
        APPEARS
    LEPROUS HIS LIMBS ALL OVER WHITE AND HOARY WAS HIS VISAGE  203 AMERICA 16       11
    AND ON HIS [SHINING] AGED LIMBS . . .  . . . . . .         205 AMERICA CANC C    6
    ALL HER TENDER LIMBS WITH TERROR SHOOK . . . . . . .       219 LIT GRL LST/SE   29
    ROUND THE FURIOUS LIMBS OF LOS . . . . . . . . . .         227 URIZEN 8          6
    HID THEIR STRONG LIMBS IN SMOKE . . . . . . . . .          229 URIZEN 13        23
    THEY CHAIND HIS YOUNG LIMBS TO THE ROCK . . . . . . .      233 URIZEN 20        23
    AND FOLD THE SHEETY WATERS AS A MANTLE ROUND MY LIMBS  . . 238 EUROPE PREL 1    13
    AROUND THE LIMBS OF ALBION'S GUARDIAN HIS FLESH CONSUMING  243 EUROPE 12        33
    FIRST IN WRATH THREW HIS LIMBS LIKE THE BABE . . . . .     258 BOOK OF LOS 4    38
    . . . WITH HER TENDER LIMBS THEN HIGH SHE SOARD . . . .    269 FOUR ZOAS 1     182
    WITHOUT THE BODY OF MAN AN EXUDATION FROM HIS SICKNING     277 FOUR ZOAS 1     463
        LIMBS
    THE PALE LIMBS OF HIS ETERNAL INDIVIDUALITY  . . . . .     277 FOUR ZOAS 1     467
    THE ETERNAL VOICE HE STOOD THE SWEAT CHILLD ON HIS MIGHTY  278 FOUR ZOAS 1     522
        LIMBS
    WITH EVER STREAMING FIRES BEAMING FROM HIS AWFUL LIMBS  .  284 FOUR ZOAS 2     180
    FEMALE'S LIMBS IN HIS ABSENCE & HER DAUGHTERS OFT UPON  .  285 FOUR ZOAS 2     189
    HER COLD LIMBS IN THE ABSENCE OF HER LORD ALSO HER SONS    285 FOUR ZOAS 2     193
    THOU CANST REPOSE ON CLOUDS OF SECRECY WHILE OER MY LIMBS  288 FOUR ZOAS 2     319
    REVERBERATES THE LIVING HARMONY UPON MY LIMBS . . . . .    289 FOUR ZOAS 2     356
    [TO TAKE THE ?LIMBS OF MAN] STRUGGLING TO UTTER THE VOICE  296 FOUR ZOAS 3   * 157
        . . .
    TO TAKE THE LIMBS OF MAN AT LENGTH EMERGING FROM THE SMOKE  296 FOUR ZOAS 3    158
    CRYING FURY IN MY LIMBS DESTRUCTION IN MY BONES & MARROW   296 FOUR ZOAS 3     162
    WITH DISLOCATED LIMBS HAD FALLN THE SPECTRE ROSE IN PAIN   299 FOUR ZOAS 4      64
    MY WAVES THY LIMBS SHALL SEPARATE IN STENCH & ROTTING &    299 FOUR ZOAS 4      74
        THOU
    THE DAYS & YEARS IN CHAINS OF IRON ROUND THE LIMBS        302 FOUR ZOAS 4     180
        OF URIZEN
    LASHD ON THE LIMBS OF ENITHARMON & THE SULPHUR FIRES  . .  302 FOUR ZOAS 4     187
    HE POURD THE MOLTEN IRON ROUND THE LIMBS OF ENITHARMON  .  302 FOUR ZOAS 4     195
    THAT VEGETATES BENEATH THE SEA THE LIMBS OF MAN VEGETATED  304 FOUR ZOAS 4     267
    FELL FROM HIS HAND HIS FIRES HID THEIR STRONG LIMBS IN     304 FOUR ZOAS 4     281
        SMOKE
    FELT HER IMMORTAL LIMBS FREEZE STIFFNING PALE INFLEXIBLE   305 FOUR ZOAS 5   *   6
    SWEAT & BLOOD STOOD ON THE LIMBS OF LOS IN GLOBES HIS FIERY  307 FOUR ZOAS 5    67
        EYELIDS
    HELD THE FIERCE BOY LOS NAILD HIM DOWN BINDING AROUND HIS  307 FOUR ZOAS 5     101
        LIMBS
    HIS LIMBS BOUND DOWN MOCK AT HIS CHAINS FOR OVER THEM A    308 FOUR ZOAS 5     114
        FLAME
    LO THE YOUNG LIMBS HAD STRUCKEN ROOT INTO THE ROCK & STRONG  309 FOUR ZOAS 5   156
    AND OVER THE IMMORTAL LIMBS OF THE TERRIBLE FIERY BOY  . .  309 FOUR ZOAS 5    159
    EVEN TO THE CENTER WRAPPING ROUND THE CENTER & THE LIMBS   309 FOUR ZOAS 5     168
    URIZEN SHUDDRING HEARD HIS TREMBLING LIMBS SHOOK THE STRONG  310 FOUR ZOAS 5   188
        CAVES
    SHE ANSWERD NOT BUT STRETCHD HER ARMS & THREW HER LIMBS    312 FOUR ZOAS 6   *  16
        ABROAD
    WHEN WEARIED DEAD HE FELL HIS LIMBS REPOSD IN THE BOSOM    316 FOUR ZOAS 6     159
        OF SLIME
    IN PAIN & SORROW SO THE SLIMY BED HIS LIMBS RENEWD . . .   316 FOUR ZOAS 6     162
    THEN DARTING INTO THE ABYSS OF NIGHT HIS VENTUROUS LIMBS   316 FOUR ZOAS 6     184
    AND THENCE THROWING HIS VENTUROUS LIMBS INTO THE           316 FOUR ZOAS 6     188
        VAST UNKNOWN
    AND WEARINESS BEGINS ON ALL MY LIMBS THEN SLEEP REVIVES    317 FOUR ZOAS 6     205
    TILL A WHITE WOOF COVERD HIS COLD LIMBS FROM HEAD TO [FOOT]  318 FOUR ZOAS 6   * 239
        FEET
```

1097

		PAGE	TITLE	LINE
LIMBS   (CONTINUED)

OVERSPREADING HIS LIMBS IN PRIDE HE WANDERD WEEPING . . . 318 FOUR ZOAS 6   241
FOR ENION'S LIMBS . . . . 318 FOUR ZOAS 6   273
ROUND HOWLING ORC WHOSE AWFUL LIMBS CAST FORTH RED SMOKE   320 FOUR ZOAS 7   17
    & FIRE
LOS FELT THE ENVY IN HIS LIMBS LIKE TO A BLIGHTED TREE . . 321 FOUR ZOAS 7   27
MOULDED TO GLOBES & ARROWY WEDGES RENDING THY BLEEDING   321 FOUR ZOAS 7   52
    LIMBS
YET THROW THY LIMBS THESE FIRES ABROAD THAT BACK RETURN   321 FOUR ZOAS 7   60
    UPON THEE
BUT LOS LOVED THEM & REFUSD TO SACRIFICE THEIR INFANT LIMBS 332 FOUR ZOAS 7   482
HIS NAKED LIMBS GLITTRING UPON THE DARK BLUE SKY HIS KNEES   334 FOUR ZOAS 7B   *   42
AND THAT BY THESE ARTS THE SERPENT FORM EXUDED FROM HIS   336 FOUR ZOAS 7B   135
    LIMBS
NOW NOW THE BATTLE RAGES ROUND THY TENDER LIMBS O VALA . . 337 FOUR ZOAS 7B   187
EXUDED ROUND HIS AWFUL LIMBS STRETCHING TO SERPENT LENGTH   343 FOUR ZOAS 8   79
SPARKLES OF DIRE AFFLICTION ISSUD [FROM] ROUND HIS FROZEN   343 FOUR ZOAS 8   *   91
    LIMBS
MY FEEBLE LIMBS INFOLD MY DESTIND MISERY . . . . . .   344 FOUR ZOAS 8   .   147
LULLING THE WEEPING SPECTRES OF THE DEAD CLOTHING THEIR   346 FOUR ZOAS 8   213
    LIMBS
IN CHANNELS THRO MY FIERY LIMBS O LOVE O PITY O PAIN   . .   349 FOUR ZOAS 8   307
INTO THEIR LIMBS URTHONA SHOT FORTH A VAST FIBROUS FORM   353 FOUR ZOAS 8   468
FOR A COVERING TO YOUR LIMBS . . . .   353 FOUR ZOAS 8   494
HIS FIERY HALLS ARE DARK & ROUND HIS LIMBS THE SERPENT ORC   354 FOUR ZOAS 8   509
BATHING THEIR LIMBS IN THE BRIGHT VISIONS OF ETERNITY   . . 358 FOUR ZOAS 9   45
IN THE FIERCE FLAMES THE LIMBS OF MYSTERY LAY CONSUMING   359 FOUR ZOAS 9   67
    WITH HOWLING
BATHING THEIR LIMBS IN THE BRIGHT VISIONS OF ETERNITY   . . 359 FOUR ZOAS 9   90
THE LIMBS OF URIZEN SHONE WITH ARDOR [HE ROSE UP FROM THE   365 FOUR ZOAS 9   310
    ROCK]
SHE FOLDED THEM UP IN CARE IN SILENCE & HER BRIGHTNING   366 FOUR ZOAS 9   345
    LIMBS
FOR WEEDS OF DEATH HAVE WRAPD AROUND MY LIMBS IN THE HOARY   370 FOUR ZOAS 9   488
    DEEPS
THE CLOUDS FALL OFF FROM MY WET BROW THE DUST FROM MY   373 FOUR ZOAS 9   597
    COLD LIMBS
IF YOU ARE THIRSTY THERE IS THE RIVER GO BATHE YOUR PARCHED 375 FOUR ZOAS 9   680
    LIMBS
METHINKS I SEE HIS FLOCKS & HERDS & FEEL MY LIMBS RENEWD   375 FOUR ZOAS 9   690
THAT CREEP ABOUT THE OBSCURE PLACES SHEW THEIR VARIOUS   377 FOUR ZOAS 9   765
    LIMBS
IN THE DEEP CAVES BENEATH HIS LIMBS RENEWD HIS LIONS ROAR   379 FOUR ZOAS 9   841
INWRAP THE IMMORTAL LIMBS STRUGGLING IN TERRIFIC JOY   . . 381 FOUR ZOAS AD 2   2
FROM ENION POURS THE SEED OF LIFE & DEATH IN ALL HER LIMBS   381 FOUR ZOAS AD 4   1
 . . . WITH HER TENDER LIMBS THEN HIGH SHE SOARD   381 FOUR ZOAS AD 5   2
AND COLD AND PALE THE LIMBS REPOSD   442 DEDICATN BLAIR   4
TERRIFIED LOS STOOD IN THE ABYSS & HIS IMMORTAL LIMBS   . . 483 MILTON 3   28
LASH ON THEIR LIMBS AS THEY TURN THE WHIRLWINDS LOOSE UPON   484 MILTON 5   17
BUT NOW THE STARRY HEAVENS ARE FLED FROM THE MIGHTY LIMBS   486 MILTON 6   26
    OF ALBION
O WHEREFORE DOTH A DRAGON-FORM FORTH ISSUE FROM MY LIMBS   492 MILTON 12   2
HIS LIMBS SHOT FORTH LIKE ROOTS OF TREES AGAINST   498 MILTON 17   35
    THE FORWARD PATH
LOS SAW THEM AND A COLD PALE HORROR COVERD OER HIS LIMBS   503 MILTON 20   51
THAT CREEP AROUND THE OBSCURE PLACES SHEW THEIR VARIOUS   513 MILTON 27   28
    LIMBS
AND THERE WENT FORTH FROM THE STARRY LIMBS OF THE SEVEN   530 MILTON 39   6
    FORMS
ONE MAN JESUS THE SAVIOUR WONDERFUL ROUND HIS LIMBS . . .   534 MILTON 42   11
BUT ALL MY LIMBS WITH WARMTH GLOW . . . .   538 ANGER WRATH/N   3
AS CROOKED LIMBS & LOUZY HEADS OF HAIR . . . . . .   540 SIR JOSH RUB/N   8
SWELLD LIMBS WITH NO OUTLINE THAT YOU CAN DESCRY . . . .   546 SWELLD LIMBS/N   1
"THE MOST UGLY THEY FLED WITH OUTCRIES AND CONTORTION OF   560B EXHIBITION ADV   PROSE
    THEIR LIMBS"
LIMBS THAT DEVIATES OR ALTERS LEAST FROM INFANCY TO OLD AGE 580A DESC CAT 5   PROSE
IS THE FACE AND LIMBS OF GREATEST BEAUTY AND PERFECTION   580A DESC CAT 5   PROSE
OF WISDOM A SUBLIME ENERGIZER HIS FEATURES AND LIMBS . .   580B DESC CAT 5   PROSE
THE BLOOD IS SEEN TO CIRCULATE IN THEIR LIMBS . . . . .   581A DESC CAT 5   PROSE
I SAW THE LIMBS FORMD FOR EXERCISE CONTEMND & THE BEAUTY OF 628 JERUSALEM 9   7
INFOLD AROUND MY LIMBS BRUISING MY MINUTE ARTICULATIONS   635 JERUSALEM 15   13
ASTONISHD TERRIFIED THEY HOVERD OVER HIS GIANT LIMBS   . .   642 JERUSALEM 20   2
MY DYING LIMBS THEREFORE O MANHOOD IF THOU ART AUGHT   . .   646 JERUSALEM 23   36
DISPLAYING OUR GIANT LIMBS TO ALL THE WINDS OF HEAVEN   647 JERUSALEM 24   6
    SUDDEN
OF OUR IMMORTAL VEINS & ALL THEIR HOSTS FLED FROM OUR LIMBS 647 JERUSALEM 24   8
IN HIS MIGHTY LIMBS ALL THINGS IN HEAVEN & EARTH . . . .   649C JERUSALEM 27   PROSE
BUT NOW THE STARRY HEAVENS ARE FLED FROM THE MIGHTY LIMBS   649C JERUSALEM 27   PROSE
    OF ALBION
IF YOUR TRADITION THAT MAN CONTAINED IN HIS LIMBS . . . . 652B JERUSALEM 27   PROSE
    ALL ANIMALS
THEY MOCK AT THE LABOURER'S LIMBS THEY MOCK AT HIS STARVD   656 JERUSALEM 30   28
    CHILDREN
I HEAR THY SHUTTLES SING IN THE SKY AND ROUND MY LIMBS . . 657 JERUSALEM 31   48
AND ON THE COUCH REPOSD HIS LIMBS TREMBLING FROM THE BLOODY 658 JERUSALEM 32   13
    FIELD
REARING THEIR DRUID PATRIARCHAL ROCKY TEMPLES AROUND HIS   658 JERUSALEM 32   14
    LIMBS
BECAME FOUR ELEMENTS SEPARATING FROM THE LIMBS OF ALBION   663 JERUSALEM 36   32
HIS STRONG LIMBS SHUDDERD UPON HIS MOUNTAINS HIGH AND DARK   664 JERUSALEM 38   6
THE PALE LIMBS OF HIS ETERNAL INDIVIDUALITY   . . . . . .   677 JERUSALEM 48   3
NOW NOW THE BATTLE RAGES ROUND THY TENDER LIMBS O VALA . . 700 JERUSALEM 65   29

		PAGE	TITLE	LINE
LIMBS	(CONTINUED)			
THE TREMBLINGS OF VALA VIBRATE THRO THE LIMBS OF ALBION'S SONS		701	JERUSALEM 65	73
SPASMS SMITE THEIR FEATURES SINEWS & LIMBS		701	JERUSALEM 65	76
IN CHANNELS THRO MY FIERY LIMBS O LOVE O PITY O FEAR . .		705	JERUSALEM 67	54
WHY TREMBLES THE WARRIOR'S LIMBS WHEN HE BEHOLDS THY BEAUTY		706	JERUSALEM 68	48
TO ROAST THE FLESH IN FIRE TO EXAMINE THE INFANT'S LIMBS		707	JERUSALEM 68	58
THE STARRY HEAVENS ALL WERE FLED FROM THE MIGHTY LIMBS OF ALBION		709	JERUSALEM 70	32
BUT NOW THE STARRY HEAVENS ARE FLED FROM THE MIGHTY LIMBS OF ALBION		716	JERUSALEM 75	27
(CORRUPTIBILITY) APPEARS UPON THY LIMBS AND NEVER MORE		727	JERUSALEM 83	* 1
OF BLOOD THRO ALL MY NERVOUS LIMBS SOON OVERGROWN IN ROOTS		732	JERUSALEM 87	6
HIS AWFUL LIMBS INTO THE HEAVENS HE WALKED CLOTHED IN FLAMES		742	JERUSALEM 95	7
FROM THE LIMBS OF JESUS TO MAKE THEM HIS PREY		755	EV GOSPEL(E)/N	82
MY LIMBS TO INFOLD		805	TO BUTTS/L	53
& SOON SPREAD A DEATHLY FEEL ALL OVER THE LIMBS WHICH . .		872B	LETTER 75	PROSE
LIMERICK				
WATERFORD TIPPERARY CORK LIMERICK KERRY CLARE		711	JERUSALEM 72	22
LIMIT				
AND FIRST HE FOUND THE LIMIT OF OPACITY & NAMD IT SATAN		304	FOUR ZOAS 4	271
AND NEXT HE FOUND THE LIMIT OF CONTRACTION & NAMD IT ADAM		304	FOUR ZOAS 4	273
. . . STARRY WHEELS FELT THE DIVINE HAND LIMIT		304	FOUR ZOAS 4	275
WAS PUT TO ETERNAL DEATH LOS FELT THE LIMIT & SAW . . .		304	FOUR ZOAS 4	276
UPON THE LIMIT OF TRANSLUCENCE THEN HE BUILDED LUBAN . .		307	FOUR ZOAS 5	77
BUT YET HAVING A LIMIT TWOFOLD NAMED SATAN & ADAM . . .		329	FOUR ZOAS 7	383
BUT LOS STOOD ON THE LIMIT OF TRANSLUCENCE WEEPING & TREMBLING		329	FOUR ZOAS 7	384
BEYOND THE LIMIT OF TRANSLUCENCE ON THE LAKE OF UDAN ADAN		340	FOUR ZOAS 7B	300
UPON THE LIMIT OF CONTRACTION TO CREATE THE FALLEN MAN . .		341	FOUR ZOAS 8	3
THE LIMIT OF CONTRACTION NOW WAS FIXD & MAN BEGAN . . .		341	FOUR ZOAS 8	16
FROM THE LIMIT NOAH TO THE LIMIT ABRAM IN WHOSE LOINS .		636	JERUSALEM 15	26
THERE IS A LIMIT OF OPAKENESS AND A LIMIT OF CONTRACTION		670	JERUSALEM 42	29
IN EVERY INDIVIDUAL MAN AND THE LIMIT OF OPAKENESS . . .		670	JERUSALEM 42	30
IS NAMED SATAN AND THE LIMIT OF CONTRACTION IS NAMED ADAM		670	JERUSALEM 42	31
CONTRACTION'S LIMIT AND OF THE LIMIT HE FORMS WOMAN THAT		670	JERUSALEM 42	33
BUT THERE IS NO LIMIT OF EXPANSION		670	JERUSALEM 42	35
. . . THERE IS NO LIMIT OF TRANSLUCENCE		670	JERUSALEM 42	35
BECAME A LIMIT A ROCKY HARDNESS WITHOUT FORM & VOID . .		713	JERUSALEM 73	23
NAMING THE LIMIT OF OPAKENESS SATAN & THE LIMIT OF CONTRACTION		713	JERUSALEM 73	27
LIMITED				
MAN'S DESIRES ARE LIMITED BY HIS PERCEPTIONS		97B	NAT RELIGION 1	PROSE
BY ANY THING BUT ORGANS OF SENSE MUST BE LIMITED TO OBJECTS OF SENSE		97B	NAT RELIGION 1	PROSE
AND SATAN VIBRATED IN THE IMMENSITY OF THE SPACE LIMITED		491	MILTON 10	8
LIMITS				
IN ALBION'S BOSOM FOR IN EVERY HUMAN BOSOM THESE LIMITS STAND		304	FOUR ZOAS 4	272
THE DIVINE HAND FOUND THE TWO LIMITS		494	MILTON 13	20
FROM THE BIBLE & LIMITS ALL EXISTENCE TO CREATION & TO CHAOS		614B	V LAST JUDG/N	PROSE
THEN THE DIVINE HAND FOUND THE TWO LIMITS SATAN AND ADAM		662	JERUSALEM 35	1
IN ALBION'S BOSOM FOR IN EVERY HUMAN BOSOM THOSE LIMITS STAND		662	JERUSALEM 35	2
I DIE & PASS THE LIMITS OF POSSIBILITY AS IT APPEARS .		696	JERUSALEM 62	19
VOLTAIRE INSINUATES THAT THESE LIMITS ARE THE CRUEL WORK OF GOD		713	JERUSALEM 73	29
MOCKING THE REMOVER OF LIMITS & THE RESURRECTION OF THE DEAD		713	JERUSALEM 73	30
LIMPING				
WITH MIRTH & JOY URTHONA LIMPING FROM HIS FALL ON THARMAS		377	FOUR ZOAS 9	775
LEAND				
LINCOLN				
LINCOLN & NORWICH STAND TREMBLING ON THE BRINK OF UDAN-ADAN		623	JERUSALEM 5	10
OF REUBEN NORFOLK SUFFOLK ESSEX SIMEON LINCOLN YORK LANCASHIRE		637	JERUSALEM 16	44
FROM LINCOLN & NORWICH FROM EDINBURGH & MONMOUTH . . .		644	JERUSALEM 21	39
LINCOLN DURHAM & CARLISLE COUNCELLORS OF LOS		676	JERUSALEM 46	5
YORK & LINCOLN HIDE AMONG THE FLOCKS BECAUSE OF THE GRIDING KNIFE		703	JERUSALEM 66	65
SLADE HAD LINCOLN STAFFORD DERBY NOTTINGHAM & HIS LOVELY		710	JERUSALEM 71	34
LINCOLNS				
TO GREAT QUEEN STREET & LINCOLNS INN ALL IS DISTRESS & WOE		729	JERUSALEM 84	16
LINCOLNSHIRE				
LINCOLNSHIRE DERBYSHIRE NOTTINGHAMSHIRE LEICESTERSHIRE . .		636	JERUSALEM 16	18
LINE				
AS A STRAIT LINE & A CROOKED ONE SECONDLY I I I		45D	ISLAND MOON 1	PROSE
HE FORMD A LINE & A PLUMMET		233	URIZEN 20	33
THIS LINE TO COME IN		268D	FOUR ZOAS 1	PROSE
QUADRANGULAR THE BUILDING ROSE THE HEAVENS SQUARED BY A LINE		284	FOUR ZOAS 2	168
AND IN THESE MONSTROUS FORMS I [?LINE] LIVE IN AN ETERNAL WOE		313	FOUR ZOAS 6	* 62
AND FIRST HE DREW A LINE UPON THE WALLS OF SHINING HEAVEN		332	FOUR ZOAS 7	467
THIS NIGHT BEGINS AT LINE...THE FOLLOWING COMES IN AT THE END		333A	FOUR ZOAS 7B	*TITLE
THAT LINE OF BLOOD THAT STRETCHD ACROSS THE WINDOWS OF THE MORNING		361	FOUR ZOAS 9	160
STRUCK AT ONCE AS PROTOGENES STRUCK HIS LINE		439C	REMARKS MALKIN	PROSE
THE SOFT HANDS OF ANTAMON DRAW THE INDELIBLE LINE . . .		515	MILTON 28	16

```
                                                       PAGE    TITLE         LINE
LINE    (CONTINUED)
  EVERY LINE OF HIS HAS MEANING  . . . . . . . . .      542 FLORENTINE/N        17
  GHIOTTO'S CIRCLE OR APELLES' LINE  . . . . . . .      542 FLORENTINE/N        26
  THAT THE MORE DISTINCT SHARP AND WIREY THE BOUNDING LINE   585B DESC CAT 15  PROSE
  PROTOGENES AND APELLES KNEW EACH OTHER BY THIS LINE  . . . 585B DESC CAT 15  PROSE
  THE BOUNDING LINE AND ITS INFINITE INFLEXIONS AND MOVEMENTS 585C DESC CAT 15 PROSE
  LINE OF RECTITUDE AND CERTAINTY IN THE ACTIONS AND        585C DESC CAT 15   PROSE
    INTENTIONS
  LEAVE OUT THIS (LINE) AND YOU LEAVE OUT LIFE ITSELF  . 585C DESC CAT 15     *PROSE
  ALL IS CHAOS AGAIN AND THE LINE OF THE ALMIGHTY MUST BE   585C DESC CAT 15   PROSE
  LINE MANNER OF ENGRAVING SIMILAR TO THOSE ORIGINAL  . . . 586C CHAUCER 1     PROSE
  THEY SAY THERE IS NO STRAIT LINE IN NATURE THIS IS A LIE  603B PUB ADDR AD/N PROSE
  LIKE ALL THAT THEY SAY FOR THERE IS EVERY LINE IN NATURE  603B PUB ADDR AD/N PROSE
  EVERY LINE IS THE LINE OF BEAUTY  . . . . . . . .     603C PUB ADDR AD/N     PROSE
  IT IS ONLY FUMBLE & BUNGLE WHICH CANNOT DRAW A LINE  . . 603C PUB ADDR AD/N  PROSE
  THIS ONLY IS UGLINESS THAT IS NOT A LINE  . . . . .  603C PUB ADDR AD/N      PROSE
  ALL DESCRIPTIVE OF CHARACTER & NOT A LINE IS DRAWN  . 611B V LAST JUDG/N     PROSE
  REPRESENT THOSE WHO WERE NOT IN THE LINE OF THE CHURCH  . 611D V LAST JUDG/N PROSE
  VARIETY IN EVERY LINE BOTH OF CADENCES & NUMBER OF        621D JERUSALEM 3   PROSE
    SYLLABLES
  I SEE THE MATERNAL LINE I BEHOLD THE SEED OF THE WOMAN  . . 696 JERUSALEM 62   8
  VIRGIL IN THE ENEID BOOK VI LINE...SAYS "LET OTHERS STUDY 778D HOMERS POETRY PROSE
    ART"
  LESSER CIRCLE POINT OF THE UNIVERSE CANTO ELEVENTH LINE... 786A ILLS DANTE 101 PROSE
  BEING OUT OF HIS LINE OF BUSINESS TO PUBLISH AND  . . 831C LETTER 31         PROSE
  A LINE IN WHICH HE IS DETERMINED NEVER TO ENGAGE  . . 831C LETTER 31         PROSE
  PRAY MY DEAR SIR FAVOUR ME WITH A LINE CONCERNING YOUR . . 833D LETTER 33    PROSE
  FAVOR ME WITH A LINE THAT I MAY SEND THE PLATES TO JOHNSON 840C LETTER 39    PROSE
  A LINE FROM YOU DESIRES ME TO ASSURE YOU OF HIS WISH TO   845D LETTER 44     PROSE
    GIVE
  FAVOR ME WITH A LINE OF DIRECTION HOW TO PROCEED  . . . 853A LETTER 51      *PROSE
  FOR A LINE OR LINEAMENT IS NOT FORMED BY CHANCE  . . . 878B LETTER 88        PROSE
  A LINE IS A LINE IN ITS MINUTEST SUBDIVISIONS  . . . . 878B LETTER 88        PROSE
  A WELCH BARD THE SLAUGHTERD BARDS TAKEN FROM THIS LINE    SUPP ILLUS GRAY   *TITLE
  THE DEATH OF EDWARD'S QUEEN ELEANOR FROM THIS LINE  . .   SUPP ILLUS GRAY   *TITLE
LINEAMENT
  WITH NEITHER LINEAMENT NOR FORM BUT LIKE TO WATRY CLOUDS  512 MILTON 26        27
  AS IT IS OF EVERY LINEAMENT . . . . . . . . . .      575B DESC CAT 3         PROSE
  EVERY EXPRESSION EVERY LINEAMENT OF HEAD HAND & FOOT  . 588A CHAUCER/N        PROSE
  FOR A LINE OR LINEAMENT IS NOT FORMED BY CHANCE  . . . 878B LETTER 88         PROSE
LINEAMENTS
  . . . A MASK OF IRON ON HIS FACE HID THE LINEAMENTS  . . . 135 FRENCH REVOLTN  31
  THE LINEAMENTS OF GRATIFIED DESIRE  . . . . . . .     178 IN A WIFE/N          3
  THE LINEAMENTS OF GRATIFIED DESIRE  . . . . . . .     180 QUESTN ANSRD/N       2
  THE LINEAMENTS OF GRATIFIED DESIRE  . . . . . . .     180 QUESTN ANSRD/N       4
  THE LINEAMENTS OF GRATIFIED DESIRE  . . . . . . .     184 SEVRL QUESTN/N       2
  THE LINEAMENTS OF GRATIFIED DESIRE  . . . . . . .     184 SEVRL QUESTN/N       4
  OVER THE LAND NAKED & FLAMING ARE THEIR LINEAMENTS SEEN   200 AMERICA 12        6
  WITH LINEAMENTS OF GRATIFIED DESIRE  . . . . . . .    244 EUROPE 14           19
  SUBLIME DISTINCT THEIR LINEAMENTS DIVINE OF HUMAN BEAUTY  281 FOUR ZOAS 2      34
  IMAGE OF GRIEF THY FADING LINEAMENTS MAKE MY EYELIDS FAIL 297 FOUR ZOAS 3    195
  DEFORMD I SEE THESE LINEAMENTS OF UNGRATIFIED DESIRE  . 298 FOUR ZOAS 4       24
  IN LINEAMENTS TOO EXTENDED & IN BONES TOO STRAIT & LONG   363 FOUR ZOAS 9    249
  AND IN HIS LINEAMENTS DIVINE THE SHADES OF DEATH & ULRO   495 MILTON 14     *  12
  THAN ANY OTHER EARTHLY THINGS ARE MAN'S EARTHLY LINEAMENTS 503 MILTON 21      11
  BUT LEAVE THEIR DESTIND LINEAMENTS PERMANENT FOR EVER &   505 MILTON 22       25
    EVER
  HOWLING THE SPECTRES FLEE THEY TAKE REFUGE IN HUMAN      515 MILTON 28        28
    LINEAMENTS
  JUDGE THEN OF THY OWN SELF THY ETERNAL LINEAMENTS EXPLORE 522 MILTON 32       30
  HIDING THE HUMAN LINEAMENTS AS WITH AN ARK & CURTAINS  .  533 MILTON 41       26
  AND FIRM AND DETERMINATE LINEAMENTS UNBROKEN BY SHADOWS   564D DESC CAT 1    PROSE
  AND CONSEQUENTLY THEY ARE THE PHYSIOGNOMIES OR LINEAMENTS 567C DESC CAT 3    PROSE
  THERE ARE NO LINEAMENTS THERE CAN BE NO CHARACTER  . .   575B DESC CAT 3     PROSE
  IN STRONGER AND BETTER LINEAMENTS AND IN STRONGER AND  . 576D DESC CAT 4     PROSE
  ART IS LINEAMENTS OR FORMS AND FEATURES THAT ARE CAPABLE OF 579D DESC CAT 5  PROSE
  THE LABOUR HAS DESTROYED THE LINEAMENTS  . . . . . .     582B DESC CAT 9     PROSE
  WHICH IT HAD AT FIRST WHEN ALL THE LINEAMENTS WERE PERFECT 582B DESC CAT 9   PROSE
  AS IT IS IN THIS PICTURE WHERE ALL THE LINEAMENTS         586D CHAUCER 1     PROSE
    ARE DISTINCT
  (AND) CONSEQUENTLY THEY ARE THE PHYSIOGNOMIES OR         590D CHAUCER 2     *PROSE
    (LINEAMENTS)
  TO THE LINEAMENTS OF THE COUNTENANCES THEY ARE  . . . . 611B V LAST JUDG/N  PROSE
  TO WHICH ALL LINEAMENTS TEND & SEEK WITH LOVE & SYMPATHY  672 JERUSALEM 43    21
  TO SEE JERUSALEM DEFACE HER LINEAMENTS WITH BITTER BLOWS  693 JERUSALEM 60    46
  THE LINEAMENTS DIVINE & OFT THE VOICE HEARD & OFT SHE SAID 693 JERUSALEM 60   51
  . . . REVEALING THE LINEAMENTS OF MAN  . . . . . . .     745 JERUSALEM 98     19
LINED      SEE RIGHT LINED
LINEN
  PUT ON FAIR LINEN THAT WITH THE LILY VIES PURPLE AND SILVER  38A SAMSON/PS    PROSE
  ARE THE LINEN CLOTHES FOLDED UP NOW IS THE DOMINION OF EDOM 149B MARRIAGE HH 3 PROSE
  THE GRAVE IS BURST THE SPICES SHED THE LINEN WRAPPED UP    198 AMERICA 6        2
  OF LIVING GOLD PURE PERFECT HOLY IN WHITE LINEN PURE HE    293 FOUR ZOAS 3     51
    HOVERD
  TILL THEY AWAKE & SEE JESUS & THE LINEN CLOTHES LYING  .   522 MILTON 32       42
  IS CLOSD AS WITH A THREEFOLD CURTAIN OF IVORY & FINE LINEN  633 JERUSALEM 13   23
    & ERMINE
  LINEN THY PAVEMENTS OF PRECIOUS STONES THY WALLS OF PEARL  647 JERUSALEM 24    19
  OF LIVING GOLD PURE PERFECT HOLY IN WHITE LINEN PURE HE    654 JERUSALEM 29    38
    HOVERD
  THE VEIL OF GOATS-HAIR & PURPLE & SCARLET & FINE TWINED    692 JERUSALEM 59    55
    LINEN
```

```
                                                              PAGE      TITLE            LINE
LINES
     THE IMMORTAL LINES UPON THE HEAVENS TILL WITH SIGHS OF LOVE   332 FOUR ZOAS 7         471
     BROKEN COLOURS & BROKEN LINES & BROKEN MASSES      . . . .  464C ANNO REYNOLDS       MARG
     THE VENETIAN AND FLEMISH PRACTICE IS BROKEN LINES     . .   573A DESC CAT 3          PROSE
     UNBROKEN LINES UNBROKEN MASSES AND UNBROKEN COLOURS    .    573B DESC CAT 3          PROSE
     MODERNS WISH TO DRAW FIGURES WITHOUT LINES       . . . .    577A DESC CAT 4          PROSE
     ARE NOT SHADOWS MORE UNMEANING THAN LINES AND MORE HEAVY    577A DESC CAT 4          PROSE
     BUT THE LAME IMITATORS OF LINES DRAWN BY THEIR PREDECESSORS 585D DESC CAT 15         PROSE
     KNOW THE FIRST [LINES] BEGINNINGS OF ART I HOPE THIS PRINT  593C PUB ADDRESS/N       PROSE
     (SEVENTY-EIGHT) LINES    . . . . . . . . . . .             753C EV GOSPEL(D)/N      PROSE
     THE PRESSURE NECESSARY TO ROLL OFF THE LINES IS THE SAME    791A LETTER 2            PROSE
     YOU A FEW LINES WHICH I HOPE YOU WILL EXCUSE AND AS THE     799A LETTER 11           PROSE
        TIME
     TO MY DEAREST FRIEND JOHN FLAXMAN THESE LINES   . . . . .   799B TO FLAXMAN/L        TITLE
     MRS BUTTS WILL EXCUSE THE FOLLOWING LINES     . . . . .     806B LETTER 16           PROSE
     THESE (TWO) LINES WERE OMITTED IN TRANSCRIBING & OUGHT      817D HAPPINESS/L         PROSE
        TO COME IN
     OR THIRTY LINES AT A TIME WITHOUT PREMEDITATION & EVEN  .   823A LETTER 26           PROSE
     BEGGING THE FAVOR OF A FEW LINES TO INFORM HIM HOW YOU  .   829C LETTER 30           PROSE
LINGERING
     THINE IRON HEART IS SMITTEN THOUGH LINGERING FATE IS SLOW    34B KING JOHN/PS        PROSE
LINK
     DESCENDS LINK BY LINK FROM ALBION'S CLIFFS ACROSS THE       197 AMERICA 3             8
        SEA TO BIND
     DESCENDS LINK BY LINK FROM ALBION'S CLIFFS ACROSS THE       204 AMERICA CANC A        8
        SEA TO BIND
     IN EACH OTHER LINK BY LINK LOCKD        . . . . . . . .     233 URIZEN 20            20
     THE ANVILS OF URTHONA LINK BY LINK THE CHAINS OF SORROW     302 FOUR ZOAS 4         185
     THE LINKS OF FATE LINK AFTER LINK AN ENDLESS CHAIN OF       302 FOUR ZOAS 4         207
        SORROWS
     FALLING DOWN ON THE ROCK AN IRON CHAIN LINK BY LINK LOCKD   307 FOUR ZOAS 5          91
     HE CEASD FOR RIVN LINK FROM LINK THE BURSTING UNIVERSE      363 FOUR ZOAS 9         230
        EXPLODES
LINKD
     TILL WE ARISE LINKD IN A GOLDEN BAND AND NEVER PART  . . .  128 BOOK OF THEL 3       15
     LINKD HOUR TO HOUR & DAY TO NIGHT & NIGHT TO DAY & YEAR     302 FOUR ZOAS 4         181
        TO YEAR
     GRIM FROST BENEATH & TERRIBLE SNOW LINKD IN A MARRIAGE      306 FOUR ZOAS 5          33
        CHAIN
LINKED
     SORROW LINKED THEM TOGETHER  . . . . . . . . . . . .         35C COUCH DEATH/PS      PROSE
     LIKE THE LINKED INFERNAL CHAIN  . . . . . . . . . .         228 URIZEN 10            36
     IN A HORRIBLE DREAMFUL SLUMBER LIKE THE LINKED CHAIN    .   303 FOUR ZOAS 4         218
     TO ALL HIS ENGINES OF DECEIT THAT LINKED CHAINS MIGHT RUN   344 FOUR ZOAS 8         132
LINKS
     THE [GERMAN FORGED] MIND FORGD [LINKS I HEAR] MANACLES      170 LONDON/N          *   8
        I HEAR
     FOR THE LINKS OF A DUNGEON FLOOR   . . . . . . . . .        186 LET BROTHELS/N        49
     [FOR THE LINKS OF A DUNGEON FLOOR]   . . . . . . .          186 LET BROTHELS/N        55
     FOR THE LINKS OF A DUNGEON FLOOR   . . . . . . . .          186 LET BROTHELS/N        67
     THE HAIRY SHOULDERS REND THE LINKS FREE ARE THE WRISTS      196 AMERICA PREL 2        2
        OF FIRE
     NUMBRING WITH LINKS HOURS DAYS & YEARS  . . . . . . .       227 URIZEN 10            18
     OF ETERNITY BEAT ON HIS IRON LINKS   . . . . . . . .        259 BOOK OF LOS 5        26
     THE PROPHET OF ETERNITY BEAT ON HIS IRON LINKS & LINKS      302 FOUR ZOAS 4         201
        OF BRASS
     THE LINKS OF FATE LINK AFTER LINK AN ENDLESS CHAIN OF       302 FOUR ZOAS 4         207
        SORROWS
     THE HAIRY SHOULDERS REND THE LINKS FREE ARE THE WRISTS      336 FOUR ZOAS 7B        140
        OF FIRE
LINLITHGO
     DAN BUTE CAITNES CLAKMANAN NAPTHALI NAIBN INVERNBS          638 JERUSALEM 16         55
        LINLITHGO
LINNELL
     I HAVE HAD THE PLEASURE TO SEE MR LINNELL SET OFF SAFE IN   869C LETTER 70          PROSE
     TO HAMPSTEAD TO SEE MRS LINNELL ON SUNDAY BUT WILL RETURN   870D LETTER 72          PROSE
     MR LINNELL WILL HAVE ARRIVED AT HIS JOURNEY'S END BEFORE    871C LETTER 73          PROSE
     BEFORE NOW I DO AS MR LINNELL DESIRED I WOULD DO BY THE     871C LETTER 73          PROSE
     PRAY REMEMBER ME WITH KIND LOVE TO MRS LINNELL   . . . .    873D LETTER 78          PROSE
     I HEREBY DECLARE THAT MR JOHN LINNELL HAS PURCHASED OF ME   874A LETTER 78          PROSE
     JOHN LINNELL ESQRE CIRENCESTER PLACE FITZROY SQUARE  . . .  SUPP ADDRESSES/L       *TITLE
     MRS LINNELL COLLINS'S FARM NORTH END HAMPSTEAD    . . . .   SUPP ADDRESS/L 70      *TITLE
     RECIEVD...OF MR LINNELL THE SUM OF FIVE POUNDS ON ACCOUNT   SUPP LETTER 66C        *PROSE
     OF MR LINNELL FOR SONGS OF INNOCENCE & EXPERIENCE ONE COPY  SUPP LETTER 66G        *PROSE
     OF MR LINNELL...FOURTEEN SHILLINGS FOR JERUSALEM CHAP (TWO) SUPP LETTER 67A        *PROSE
     OF MR LINNELL...TWO GUINEAS FOR HEAVEN & HELL  . . . . .    SUPP LETTER 67B        *PROSE
     MEMORANDUM OF AGREEMENT BETWEEN WILLIAM BLAKE AND JOHN      SUPP LETTER 67D        *PROSE
        LINNELL
     BEGUN...& PUBLISHD MARCH...BY THE AUTHOR & J LINNELL   .    SUPP LETTER 67F        *PROSE
     RECIEVED...OF MRS ADERS BY THE HANDS OF MR LINNELL THE SUM  SUPP LETTER 80A        *PROSE
     RECIEVD...OF MR LINNELL...   . . . . . . . . . . .          SUPP RECEIPTS LINNL    *PROSE
LINNELL'S
     AM GLAD TO HEAR OF MRS LINNELL'S HEALTH & SAFETY   . . .    873B LETTER 77          PROSE
     AFTER MRS LINNELL'S FATHER IT WILL BE BRUTAL NOT TO SAY     874B LETTER 79          PROSE
LINNET
     [THE NIGHTINGALE THE GOLDFINCH ROBIN LARK LINNET & THRUSH]  270 FOUR ZOAS 1        207
     THE THRUSH THE LINNET & THE GOLDFINCH ROBIN & THE WREN  .   520 MILTON 31           40
LINNET'S
     AND HEAR THE LINNET'S SONG   . . . . . . . . . . .           8 MEMORY COME/PS       10
LINNEUS
     AS NEWTON NUMBERED THE STARS AND AS LINNEUS NUMBERED    .  567D DESC CAT 3          PROSE
```

1101

		PAGE	TITLE	LINE

LION
    AND THE LION GLARES THRO THE DUN FOREST . . . . 3 EVNING STAR/PS   12
    HE IS A YOUNG LION O I HAVE SEEN HIM FIGHT . . . . . . 22 EDW THIRD/PS 3   26
    THE LION FLEES AND FEAR USURPS HIS HEART . . . . 24 EDW THIRD/PS 3   114
    THE DOG DOTH SEIZE THE WOLF THE FORESTER THE LION . . . 24 EDW THIRD/PS 3   119
    YOU ARE MORE LIKE A LION THAN A CRANE . . . . 24 EDW THIRD/PS 3   131
    THIS IS THE HYPOCRITE THAT SOMETIMES ROARS A DREADFUL LION 105 TIRIEL 4   50
    WHY IS ONE LAW GIVEN TO THE LION & THE [PA] PATIENT OX 109 TIRIEL 8   * 10
    THE KINGLY LION STOOD . . . . 113 LIT GRL LST/SI   37
    WHILE THE LION OLD . . . . 113 LIT GRL LST/SI   43
    A COUCHING LION LAY . . . . 114 LIT GRL FND/SI   24
    . . . HE STALKD LIKE A LION FROM TOWER . . . . 135 FRENCH REVOLTN   21
    OF ANCIENT KINGS AND THE FROWN OF THE ETERNAL LION . . . 135 FRENCH REVOLTN   32
    OF ETERNITY WHERE THE ETERNAL LION AND EAGLE REMAIN TO   138 FRENCH REVOLTN   97
        DEVOUR
    BURGUNDY THOU WAST BORN A LION MY SOUL IS OERGROWN WITH   139 FRENCH REVOLTN   112
        DISTRESS
    THE WRATH OF THE LION IS THE WISDOM OF GOD . . . . . . 151C MARRIAGE HH 8   PROSE
    LET MAN WEAR THE FELL OF THE LION WOMAN THE FLEECE OF THE 151C MARRIAGE HH 8   PROSE
        SHEEP
    THE LION THE TYGER THE HORSE THE ELEPHANT WATCH THE FRUITS 151D MARRIAGE HH 8   PROSE
    THE FOX PROVIDES FOR HIMSELF BUT GOD PROVIDES FOR THE LION 152A MARRIAGE HH 9   PROSE
    NOR THE LION THE HORSE HOW HE SHALL TAKE HIS PREY . . . 152B MARRIAGE HH 9   PROSE
    IF THE LION WAS ADVISED BY THE FOX HE WOULD BE CUNNING . . 152D MARRIAGE HH 10 PROSE
    ONE LAW FOR THE LION & OX IS OPPRESSION . . . . 158D MARRIAGE HH 22 PROSE
    EMPIRE IS NO MORE AND NOW THE LION & WOLF SHALL CEASE . 160A SONG LIBERTY   PROSE
    [AND THE LION INCREASE FREEDOM & PEACE] . . . . 171 THE LILLY/N   4
    AND IS THERE NOT ONE LAW FOR BOTH THE LION AND THE OX . 192 V DAU ALBION 4   22
    SOMETIMES AN EAGLE SCREAMING IN THE SKY SOMETIMES A LION 196 AMERICA PREL 1   13
    IN MEXICO AN EAGLE AND A LION IN PERU . . . . 196 AMERICA PREL 2   13
    FOR EMPIRE IS NO MORE AND NOW THE LION & WOLF SHALL CEASE 198 AMERICA 6   15
    LOUD HOWLS THE ETERNAL WOLF THE ETERNAL LION LASHES HIS   199 AMERICA 9   2
        TAIL
    LOUD HOWLS THE ETERNAL WOLF THE ETERNAL LION LASHES HIS   199 AMERICA 9   27
        TAIL
    O LION RINTRAH RAISE THY FURY FROM THY FORESTS BLACK . . 240 EUROPE 8   2
    LAUGHS AT THE HUMAN FORM THE LION MOCKS & THIRSTS FOR BLOOD 275 FOUR ZOAS 1   403
    WHY [HOWLS] HOWL THE LION & THE WOLF WHY DO THEY   276 FOUR ZOAS 1   * 451
        ROAM ABROAD
    OF WILD BEASTS THERE THE LION GLARES THE TYGER & WOLF HOWL 308 FOUR ZOAS 5   128
        THERE
    IN VAIN THE TERROR HEARD NOT THEN A LION HE WOULD SIEZE   315 FOUR ZOAS 6   132
    . . . & THE LION TO THE MAN OF YEARS . . . . 315 FOUR ZOAS 6   136
    WITHIN THE DARK HORRORS OF THE ABYSSES LION OR TYGER OR   318 FOUR ZOAS 6   251
        SCORPION
    COMPELLD THE SUN REDDNING LIKE A FIERCE LION IN HIS CHAINS 333 FOUR ZOAS 7B   31
    PROPAGATES THRO THE WARRING EARTH THE [LIONS] LION RAGING 335 FOUR ZOAS 7B * 110
        IN FLAMES
    AND THE STRONG LION DEIGND IN HIS MOUTH TO WEAR THE GOLDEN 340 FOUR ZOAS 7B   282
        BIT
    CALLING THE LION & THE TYGER THE HORSE & THE WILD STAG . . 352 FOUR ZOAS 8   445
    HARDENS THE LION & THE BEAR TREMBLING IN THE SOLID MOUNTAIN 352 FOUR ZOAS 8   451
    BESIDE HIM LIES THE LION DEAD & IN HIS BELLY WORMS . . . 354 FOUR ZOAS 8   527
    WHEREVER THE EAGLE HAS EXPLORD OR LION OR TYGER TROD . . 358 FOUR ZOAS 9 * 39
    TREMBLE THE LION SHUDDERING ASKS THE LEOPARD FEELEST THOU 358 FOUR ZOAS 9   56
    THE LION OF TERROR SHALL COME DOWN & BENDING HIS BRIGHT   376 FOUR ZOAS 9   706
        MANE
    WHERE ROAMS THE LION WOLF & BOAR . . . . 426 MENTAL TRAVLER * 84
    THE BIRTH OF WAR & MISERY WHILE THE LION SEIZES THE BULL 441D INSC FALL MAN   PROSE
        THE
    OR THEY CREATE THE LION & TYGER IN COMPASSIONATE   515 MILTON 28   27
        THUNDERINGS
    BUT HOWLS ROUND IT AS A LION ROUND HIS PREY CONTINUALLY   531 MILTON 39   21
    [LIKE TO THE LION SPORTING WITH HIS PREY] . . . . . . 540 GOLDEN RULE/N * 2
    [LIKE TO THE LION SPORTING WITH HIS PREY] [XXX] . . . . 540 GOLDEN RULE/N * 4
    LIKE TO THE LION SPORTING WITH HIS PREY . . . . 540 S(TOTHAR)D/N   4
    AND IN VAIN THE EAGLE & LION OVER THE FOUR-FOLD WILDERNESS 703 JERUSALEM 66   71
    TO CREATE THE LION & WOLF THE BEAR THE TYGER & OUNCE . . 713 JERUSALEM 73   17
    WITH EVERY COLOUR LION TYGER HORSE ELEPHANT EAGLE DOVE   746 JERUSALEM 98   43
        FLY WORM
    AN APPLE TREE A PEAR TREE A HORSE A LION ARE CHARACTERS   778B HOMERS POETRY   PROSE
    A HORSE IS NOT MORE A LION FOR BEING A BAD HORSE THAT   778B HOMERS POETRY   PROSE
        IS ITS
    OF THE LION & WOLF . . . . 805 TO BUTTS/L   67
    AS THEY ARE THE MOST EMINENT AMONG ANIMALS VIZ THE LION   859B LETTER 56   PROSE
LIONEL
    SCENE ENGLISH COURT LIONEL DUKE OF CLARENCE . . . . . 19A EDW THIRD/PS 2   PROSE
LIONESS
    DESTRUCTION WAS THY FATHER A LIONESS SUCKLED THEE . . . 38B SAMSON/PS   PROSE
    WHILE THE LIONESS . . . . 113 LIT GRL LST/SI   49
LION HEART
    AND LION HEART AND BLACK-BROWD EDWARD WITH . . . . . 35 WAR SONG/PS   28
LION'S
    AND THERE THE LION'S RUDDY EYES . . . . 119 NIGHT/SI   33
    BESIDE THE STONE OF NIGHT AND LIKE THE ETERNAL LION'S HOWL 198 AMERICA 7   2
    WILD FURIES FROM THE TYGER'S BRAIN & FROM THE LION'S EYES 363 FOUR ZOAS 9   236
    EVERY WOLF'S & LION'S HOWL . . . . 431 AUGURIES   19
LIONS (PLURAL,ALSO AMBIGUOUS POSSESSIVE)
    LIKE LIONS ROUZD BY LIGHTNING FROM THEIR DENS . . . . . 32 EDW THIRD/PS 6   8
    NAKED AND ROARING LIKE LIONS HURLING ROCKS . . . . . . 32 EDW THIRD/PS 6   22
    WHO ART THOU EYELESS WRETCH THAT THUS OBSTRUCTST THE LIONS 103 TIRIEL 4   5
        PATH

```
                                                          PAGE      TITLE        LINE
LIONS    (CONTINUED)
    NOR THE LIONS GROWL    . . . . . . . . . . . . . .    115 LIT GRL FND/SI     52
    WHERE LIONS ROAM   . . . . . . . . . . . . . . . .    149 MARRIAGE HH 2      20
    THE ROARING OF LIONS THE HOWLING OF WOLVES  . . . .   151C MARRIAGE HH 8     PROSE
    IN THE FOURTH CHAMBER WERE LIONS OF FLAMING FIRE . .  155A MARRIAGE HH 15    PROSE
    THE LIONS LASH THEIR WRATHFUL TAILS  . . . . . . .    245 EUROPE 15           6
    WRATH WITH LIONS GORE  . . . . . . . . . . . . . .    256 BOOK OF LOS 3      16
    THE BELLOWS BEGAN TO BLOW & THE LIONS OF URIZEN STOOD ROUND  281 FOUR ZOAS 2 32
        THE ANVIL
    THEN SIEZD THE LIONS OF URIZEN THEIR WORK & HEATED IN THE    283 FOUR ZOAS 2  135
        FORGE
    THEY CALL THY LIONS TO THE FIELDS OF BLOOD THEY ROWZE THY    292 FOUR ZOAS 3  *  37
        TYGERS
    THEN HE BEHELD THE FORMS OF TYGERS & OF LIONS DISHUMANIZD    314 FOUR ZOAS 6  116
        MEN
    STRIKING FIERCE SPARKLES FROM THEIR BRAZEN FETTERS FIERCE    320 FOUR ZOAS 7   8
        HIS LIONS
    PROPAGATES THRO THE WARRING EARTH THE [LIONS] LION RAGING    335 FOUR ZOAS 7B * 110
        IN FLAMES
    RED RAGE REDOUNDS HE ROUZD HIS LIONS FROM HIS FORESTS BLACK  336 FOUR ZOAS 7B * 141
    FOR THE MONSTERS OF THE ELEMENTS LIONS OR TYGERS OR WOLVES   344 FOUR ZOAS 8  120
    THE TYGERS FROM THE FORESTS & THE LIONS [OF] FROM THE        365 FOUR ZOAS 9  * 301
        SANDY DESARTS
    IN THE JINGLING TRACES FURIOUS LIONS SOUND THE SONG OF JOY   376 FOUR ZOAS 9   718
    IN THE DEEP CAVES BENEATH HIS LIMBS RENEWD HIS LIONS ROAR    379 FOUR ZOAS 9   841
    LIONS BOARS WOLVES ALL HOWLING FLEE  . . . . . . .    427 MENTAL TRAVLER     99
    THE WAGGONS READY TERRIFIC LIONS & TYGERS SPORT & PLAY  .    535 MILTON 42    38
    THE SOUTH A GOLDEN GATE HAS FOUR LIONS TERRIBLE LIVING  .    633 JERUSALEM 13  2
    IRELAND TO JAPAN FURIOUS HER LIONS & TYGERS & WOLVES SPORT   698 JERUSALEM 63 34
        BEFORE
    [OF ?MORAL] PRAISE WORTHY & THE LIONS DEN  . . . . .  758 EV GOSPEL (1)  *   4
LIONS'
    LIKE LIONS' WHELPS ROARING ABROAD  . . . . . . . .    11 GWIN KING/PS        19
LIP
    HERE ARADOBO SUCKD HIS UNDER LIP  . . . . . . . .     47D ISLAND MOON 3      PROSE
    IS IMPROVED THE LIP I HAVE AGAIN LESSENED AS YOU ADVISED    797A LETTER 9     PROSE
LIPD    SEE THIN-LIPD
LIPS
    SHE KISSD THE PALE LIPS SHE HAD NO TEARS TO SHED  . .   6 FAIR ELENOR/PS     71
    FLATTERY IS DELICIOUS EVEN FROM THE LIPS OF A BABBLER   29D EDW THIRD/PS 4   PROSE
        EXIT PETER
    [COUD SING WITH THEIR THICK LIPS]  . . . . . . . .    61 DR CLASH/IM    *    7
    [WITH DAGGERS HID BENEATH THEIR LIPS & POISON IN THEIR      109 TIREL 8      14
        TONGUE]
    THE SOUND OF PRAYER FAILS FROM LIPS OF FLESH . . . .  .    140 FRENCH REVOLTN 140
    AND PARCHED LIPS DROP WITH FRESH GORE NOW ROLL THOU IN      199 AMERICA 9    24
        THE CLOUDS
    AND HIS EYES PALE WITH ANGUISH HIS LIPS  . . . . . .  250 AHANIA 3           2
    WITH HER FAIR CRYSTAL CLEARNESS IN HER LIPS & CHEEKS HIS    269 FOUR ZOAS 1  185
        POISONS ROSE
    YOUR WITHRING LIPS & TONGUE SHRINK UP INTO A NARROW CIRCLE  294 FOUR ZOAS 3  88
    . . . WRITHING TO & [FROM] FRO HIS PALLID LIPS  . . .  305 FOUR ZOAS 4  *  288
    FOREHEAD & EYES THY LIPS DECAY LIKE ROSES IN [EARLY] THE    325 FOUR ZOAS 7  189
        SPRING
    MY GOLDEN LIPS NOR TOOK THE BAR FROM ENITHARMON'S BREAST    326 FOUR ZOAS 7  238
    . . . IN HER LIPS & CHEEKS HIS [POISONS] METALS ROSE  . .   381 FOUR ZOAS AD 5  5
    THE HONEY OF HER INFANT LIPS  . . . . . . . . . .  .   426 MENTAL TRAVLER    69
    SHE OPENS HER LIPS TIS THE MONTH OF MAY  . . . . . .  428 MARY               8
    CAN SUCH GROSS LIPS PERCIEVE ALAS FOLDED WITHIN THEMSELVES  485 MILTON 5     36
    HIS LIPS WITH FOOD OF EDEN IN HIS COLD AND DIM REPOSE  . .  496 MILTON 15    15
    WITH THE FINGER ON THE LIPS & THE BACK TURND TO THE LIGHT   528 MILTON 37    32
    THEIR [BEAUTY IS CONFESSD EVEN BY THE LIPS OF PASCH         601A PUB ADDRESS/N *PROSE
        HIMSELF]
    YOUR WITHRING LIPS AND TONGUE SHRINK UP INTO A NARROW       655 JERUSALEM 29  69
        CIRCLE
    THE PRAISE OF JEHOVAH IS CHAUNTED FROM LIPS OF HUNGER &     656 JERUSALEM 30  32
        THIRST
    BETWEEN LIPS OF MIRE & CLAY THEN SENT HIM FORTH OVER JORDAN 662 JERUSALEM 36   6
    LUVAH THEIR LIPS TREMBLE THEIR MUSCULAR FIBRES ARE CRAMPD   701 JERUSALEM 65  78
        & SMITTEN
    BEAMS MILD ALL LOVE AND ALL PERFECTION THAT WHEN THE LIPS   709 JERUSALEM 70  24
LIQUID
    THERE IS IN EDEN A SWEET RIVER OF MILK & LIQUID PEARL  . .  503 MILTON 21    15
    ARE MELTED INTO THE GOLD THE SILVER THE LIQUID RUBY  . . .  628 JERUSALEM 9  23
    LIKE LAKES OF LIQUID LEAD INSTEAD OF HEAVENLY CHAPELS BUILT 673 JERUSALEM 43  63
    CAST THOU IN JERUSALEM'S SHADOWS THY LOVES SILK OF LIQUID   732 JERUSALEM 87  19
LISBON
    EARTHQUAKES AT LISBON ETC WERE THE NATURAL RESULT OF SIN    388B ANNO WATSON MARG
LISP
    TO LISP OUT WORDS & SOON IN MASCULINE STRENGTH AUGMENTING   267 FOUR ZOAS 1  125
        HE
LISPS
    AND WHERE LISPS THE MAIDEN'S TONGUE  . . . . . . . .   7 LOVE JOCUND/PS     4
LIST
    OR IF THEY LIST TOGETHER MINGLING BRING FORTH MIGHTY POWRS  40D THEN SHE BORE PROSE
    FEMALE HEAD HE HAS PROMISED TO WRITE A LIST OF ALL THAT HE  831A LETTER 31   PROSE
    I SEND YOU A LIST OF THE DIFFERENT WORKS YOU HAVE DONE ME   867A LETTER 66   PROSE
    CUSTOMER FOR IT AS YOU WISH ME TO SEND YOU A LIST WITH  . . 878D LETTER 88   PROSE
LISTEN
    COME KINGS AND LISTEN TO MY SONG  . . . . . . . . .   11 GWIN KING/PS       1
    SHE SEATED & [LISTEND] SEEMD TO LISTEN WITH GREAT ATTENTION 44B ISLAND MOON 1 PROSE
    LISTEN & HEAR YOUR MOTHER'S GROANS NO MORE ACCURSED SONS    99 TIREL 1       24
```

```
                                                            PAGE       TITLE          LINE
LISTEN   (CONTINUED)
    LOOK AT MY BALD HEAD HARK LISTEN YE SERPENTS [?ALL] LISTEN    99 TIRIEL 1        *   29
    HELA MY DAUGHTER LISTEN THOU [XXX] ART THE DAUGHTER OF       108 TIRIEL 6        *   40
        TIRIEL
    BALD TYRANT WRINKLED CUNNING [WRETCH] LISTEN TO ZAZEL'S      108 TIRIEL 7            8
        CHAINS
    . . . THE PRISONERS LOOK UP AND ASSAY TO SHOUT THEY LISTEN   136 FRENCH REVOLTN      52
    LISTEN TO THE FOOL'S REPROACH IT IS A KINGLY TITLE   . . . 152A MARRIAGE HH 9     PROSE
    THOU IN THE SOUTH LISTEN ATTENTIVE IN SILENT OF THIS NIGHT   278 FOUR ZOAS 1        492
    TO LISTEN TO THE HUNGRY RAVENS CRY IN WINTRY SEASON  . . .   290 FOUR ZOAS 2        406
    WHY DIDST THOU LISTEN TO THE VOICE OF LUVAH THAT DREAD MORN   292 FOUR ZOAS 3         31
    THEN O MY DEAR LORD LISTEN TO AHANIA LISTEN TO THE VISION     292 FOUR ZOAS 3         41
    I HEARD HIM FROWN NOT URIZEN BUT LISTEN TO MY VISION    . .   294 FOUR ZOAS 3         84
    LISTEN TO HER WHO LOVES THEE LEST WE ALSO ARE DRIVEN AWAY     294 FOUR ZOAS 3         92
    LISTEN O DAUGHTERS TO MY VOICE LISTEN TO THE WORDS OF         323 FOUR ZOAS 7        110
        WISDOM
    SHOULD NEVER IN MY ARMS REPOSE NOW LISTEN I WILL TELL   . .   326 FOUR ZOAS 7        236
    UPON OUR WATERS THIS THOU WELL REMEMBEREST LISTEN I WILL      327 FOUR ZOAS 7        275
        TELL
    LISTEN O VISION OF DELIGHT ONE DREAD MORN OF GOARY BLOOD      327 FOUR ZOAS 7     *  278
    I LABOUR NIGHT & DAY FOR LOS BUT LISTEN THOU MY VISION  . .   327 FOUR ZOAS 7        298
    ALONG THE RANKS CRYING LISTEN TO THE PRIEST OF GOD           336 FOUR ZOAS 7B       114
        YE WARRIORS
    BUT LISTEN TO AHANIA O YE SONS OF THE MURDERD ONE    . . .   354 FOUR ZOAS 8        503
    LISTEN TO HER WHOSE MEMORY BEHOLDS YOUR ANCIENT DAYS    . .   354 FOUR ZOAS 8        504
    LISTEN TO HER WHOSE EYES BEHOLD THE DARK BODY OF             354 FOUR ZOAS 8        505
        CORRUPTIBLE DEATH
    LISTEN I WILL TELL THEE WHAT IS DONE IN THE CAVERNS OF       355 FOUR ZOAS 8        555
        THE GRAVE
    COME LISTEN TO JOSEPH OF ARIMATHEA   . . . . . . . .   .   552 TELL YOU WHA/N        4
    LISTEN PATIENT & WHEN JOSEPH HAS DONE   . . . . . . .   .   552 TELL YOU WHA/N        5
    LISTEN I WILL TELL THEE WHAT IS DONE IN MOMENTS TO THEE      625 JERUSALEM 7         29
        UNKNOWN
    I WILL CERTAINLY CREATE AN ETERNAL HELL FOR THEE LISTEN      627 JERUSALEM 8          8
    BRISTOL & BATH LISTEN TO MY WORDS & YE SEVENTEEN GIVE EAR    673 JERUSALEM 43        55
    UNDER THE NAME OF GOD WHERE ARE THEY LISTEN   . . . . .    682B JERUSALEM 52      PROSE
    THE TWELVE DAUGHTERS OF ALBION ATTENTIVE LISTEN IN SECRET    725 JERUSALEM 82        10
        SHADES
    THEY LISTEN NOT TO MY CRY THEY (REJOICE) AMONG THEIR         727 JERUSALEM 83     *  18
        WARRIORS
    LISTEN TO YOUR WATCHMAN'S VOICE SLEEP NOT BEFORE            728 JERUSALEM 83        64
        THE FURNACES
    AND THUS LOS REPLIES UPON HIS WATCH THE VALLEYS LISTEN       730 JERUSALEM 85        14
        SILENT
    LISTEN HERMON & LEBANON BOW THEIR CROWNED HEADS   . . . .   730 JERUSALEM 85        17
LISTEND
    & DESCRIBED SOMETHING THAT NOBODY LISTEND TO SO THEY    . .   44B ISLAND MOON 1    PROSE
    SHE SEATED & [LISTEND] SEEMD TO LISTEN WITH GREAT ATTENTION   44B ISLAND MOON 1    PROSE
    LISTEND WITH OPEN MOUTHS TO THE EDIFYING DISCOURSES   . . .   44D ISLAND MOON 1    PROSE
    THEY LISTEND TO THE ELEMENTAL HARPS & SPHERY SONG    . . .   274 FOUR ZOAS 1        356
    ORC LISTEND TO THE SONG COMPELLD HUNGRING ON THE COLD WIND   322 FOUR ZOAS 7         99
    THEY BEG THEY INTREAT IN VAIN NOW THEY LISTEND NOT          363 FOUR ZOAS 9     *  257
        TO INTREATY
LISTENERS
    IN CRUEL DELIGHT THEY TRAP THE LISTENERS & IN CRUEL         284 FOUR ZOAS 2        162
        DELIGHT
LISTENING
    OPRNS HER MANY LOVELY EYES LISTENING THE ROSE STILL SLEEPS   520 MILTON 31          56
    HER CHILDREN IN CAPTIVITY LISTENING TO VALA'S LAMENTATION    722 JERUSALEM 80        10
LISTENS
    BUT O WHO LISTENS TO HIS VOICE   . . . . . . . . . .   .    42A THEN SHE BORE    PROSE
    HAST THOU FORGOT THAT THE AIR LISTENS THRO ALL ITS          339 FOUR ZOAS 7B       242
        DISTRICTS TELLING
    OF THE MILD YOUTH WHO LISTENS TO THE LURING SONGS OF LUVAH   377 FOUR ZOAS 9        771
    HE LISTENS TO THE SOUNDS OF WAR ASTONISHD AND CONFOUNDED     506 MILTON 23       *   8
    HE LISTENS TO THE SOUNDS OF WAR ASTONISHD & ASHAMED  . . .   510 MILTON 25          24
    OF THE MILD YOUTH WHO LISTENS TO THE LUREING SONGS OF LUVAH  514 MILTON 27          41
    APPEARS LISTENS SILENT THEN SPRINGING FROM THE WAVING       520 MILTON 31          30
        CORN-FIELD LOUD
    ALL NATURE LISTENS SILENT TO HIM & THE AWFUL SUN   . . . .   520 MILTON 31          36
    LOS LISTENS TO THE CRY OF THE POOR MAN HIS CLOUD   . . . .   535 MILTON 42          34
LISTNING
    THE HILLS TELL EACH OTHER AND THE LISTNING   . . . . . .     1 TO SPRING/PS         5
    TILL MUTE ATTENTION STRUCK MY [TREMBLING] LISTNING EAR   . .  43D WOE CRIED MUSE   PROSE
    SHE WANDERD IN THE LAND OF CLOUDS THRO VALLEYS DARK         130 BOOK OF THEL 6       6
        LISTNING
    SHE STOOD IN SILENCE LISTNING TO THE VOICES OF THE GROUND    130 BOOK OF THEL 6       8
    . . . IN DARK FOGS LISTNING THE HORROR   . . . . . . .      135 FRENCH REVOLTN      19
    . . . SILENT LISTNING TOWARD FAYETTE   . . . . . . .       147 FRENCH REVOLTN     283
    LISTNING TO HER SOFT LAMENTATIONS SOON HIS TONGUE BEGAN     267 FOUR ZOAS 1        124
    THE LISTNING STARS HEARD & THE FIRST BEAM OF THE MORNING    275 FOUR ZOAS 1        410
        STARTED BACK
    PLIED THE WINGD SHUTTLE PIPING SHRILL THRO ALL THE LISTNING  284 FOUR ZOAS 2        147
        THREADS
    THE PLOWED FURROW LISTNING TO THE WEEPING CLODS TILL WE     687 JERUSALEM 55        43
    THE SEEDS OF BEAUTY IN THE SPACE LISTNING TO THEIR         730 JERUSALEM 85         9
        LAMENTATION
LITCHFIELD
    LITCHFIELD SAINT DAVIDS LANDAFF ASAPH BANGOR SODOR   . . .   676 JERUSALEM 46        19
LITERAL
    VARIED FROM THE LITERAL FACT FOR THE SAKE OF PICTURESQUE    581C DESC CAT 7       PROSE
        SCENERY
```

	PAGE	TITLE	LINE

LITERALLY   SEE LITTERALLY
    THEY EXIST LITERALLY ABOUT THE SUN & NOT ABOUT THE EARTH   92B ANNO SWED LOVE   MARG
    FIVE HUNDRED WERE OUT THIS IS SWIFT WORK IF LITERALLY TRUE   846D LETTER 44   PROSE
    BUT
    I AM NOT APT TO BELIEVE LITERALLY WHAT BOOKSELLERS SAY AND   846D LETTER 44   PROSE
LITERARY
    LITERARY PROPERTY TRULY PROUD I AM TO BE IN POSSESSION . . 858C LETTER 55   PROSE
    HOW A VALUE WAS SET ON ANY LITERARY WORK HE ANSWERD . . . 860A LETTER 56   PROSE
LITERATURE
    AS HE BLENDS LITERATURE AND THE ARTS WITH HIS WARLIKE   568A DESC CAT 3   PROSE
    STUDIES
    & WHICH WILL BE A MOST VALUABLE ACQUISITION TO LITERATURE   809D LETTER 20   PROSE
    THE REIGN OF LITERATURE & THE ARTS COMMENCES . . . . . 810D LETTER 21   PROSE
    BLESSED ARE THOSE WHO ARE FOUND STUDIOUS OF LITERATURE &   810D LETTER 21   PROSE
    GREAT LEADING CHARACTER IN LITERATURE & HIS TERMS TO OTHERS   841C LETTER 41   PROSE
    IT MAY BE CALLD A DEFENCE OF LITERATURE AGAINST THOSE PESTS   841D LETTER 41   PROSE
    OF
    ON THE SCORE OF PARENTAL DUTY LITERATURE IS YOUR CHILD . . 842A LETTER 41   PROSE
LITHE
    I ASKD A LITHE LADY TO LIE HER DOWN . . . . 163 ASKED THIEF/N   3
    I ASKD A LITHE LADY TO LIE HER DOWN . . . . 261 ASKED THIEF   3
LITTERAL
    IS THE DIVINE REVELATION IN THE LITTERAL EXPRESSION . . . 534 MILTON 42   14
LITTERALLY
    MARK THAT I DO NOT BELIEVE THERE IS SUCH A THING LITTERALLY   74B ANNO LAVATER   MARG
    BUT
LITTLE
    CRIES IN VAIN POOR LITTLE WRETCH THAT DEALST . . . . . 3 TO WINTER/PS   14
    I SAW A LITTLE WELCHMAN WITH A FIERY FACE . . . . . . 25 EDW THIRD/PS 3   157
    LITTLE SPORT AND CUT A PATH INTO THE HEAVEN OF GLORY . . 27 EDW THIRD/PS 3   274
    IS IT A LITTLE CREEPING ROOT THAT GROWS IN DITCHES . . . 28 EDW THIRD/PS 4   11
    ALL BE WRONG OF COURSE TIS BEST TO KNOW A LITTLE . . . 28D EDW THIRD/PS 4   PROSE
    AND TO KNOW THAT LITTLE ARIGHT . . . . 28D EDW THIRD/PS 4   PROSE
    I KNOW BUT LITTLE OF THE PATH THOU GOEST . . . . . . 36A COUCH DEATH/PS   PROSE
    O MAN HOW GREAT HOW LITTLE THOU . . . . 37A CONTEMPLATN/PS   PROSE
    AS I WAS LOOKING UP A LITTLE OUTRE FELLOW PULLING ME . . 45A ISLAND MOON 1   PROSE
    & SEEMS TO HAVE UNDERSTOOD VERY LITTLE BUT WHAT HE SAW . 45D ISLAND MOON 1   PROSE
    & LITTLE SCOPPRELL ENTERD THE ROOM . . . . 46B ISLAND MOON 2   PROSE
    LITTLE PHEBUS CAME STRUTTING IN . . . . 46 PHEBUS CAME/IM   1
    HE EAT WERY LITTLE WICKLY THAT IS . . . . 49C ISLAND MOON 5   PROSE
    HE SLEPT VERY LITTLE WHICH HE BROUGHT INTO A CONSUMSION . 49C ISLAND MOON 5   PROSE
    A LITTLE BRAT NO HIGHER THAN A NETTLE & SHE HAD AS MUCH . 53B ISLAND MOON 8   PROSE
    I AM SURE I TAKE BUT LITTLE PLEASURE YOU HAVE AS MUCH . . 53C ISLAND MOON 8   PROSE
    WHERE THE LITTLE [LAMBS DO] LAMBKINS TROT . . . . . . 53 PHEBE DREST/IM *   4
    THOUSANDS OF LITTLE GIRLS & BOYS RAISING THEIR INNOCENT   59 HOLY THURS/IM   9
    HANDS
    BESIDES IN THE SKY THE LITTLE BIRDS FLY . . . . 60 NURSES SONG/IM   12
    OH SPEAK FATHER SPEAK TO YOUR LITTLE BOY . . . . . . 60 LIT BOY LST/IM   3
    GREAT A LITTLE A . . . . 62 DR CLASH/IM   8
    A LITTLE REST I CRAVE A LITTLE WATER FROM A BROOK . . . 104 TIRIEL 4   34
    [OR EYED WITH LITTLE SPARKS OF HELL OR WITH INFERNAL   109 TIRIEL 8   15
    BRANDS]
    [HIS LITTLE HANDS INTO THE DEPTHS OF THE SEA TO BRING   110 TIRIEL 8   21
    FORTH]
    THE LITTLE LIDS ARE LIFTED & THE LITTLE NOSTRILS OPEND   110 TIRIEL 8   29
    LITTLE WANDERER HIE THEE HOME . . . . 112 A DREAM/SI   20
    THE LITTLE GIRL LOST . . . . 112B LIT GRL LST/SI   TITLE
    IS YOUR LITTLE CHILD . . . . 112 LIT GRL LST/SI   22
    THE LITTLE GIRL FOUND . . . . 113D LIT GRL FND/SI   TITLE
    LITTLE LAMB WHO MADE THEE . . . . 115 THE LAMB/SI   1
    LITTLE LAMB WHO MADE THEE . . . . 115 THE LAMB/SI   9
    LITTLE LAMB I'LL TELL THEE . . . . 115 THE LAMB/SI   11
    LITTLE LAMB I'LL TELL THEE . . . . 115 THE LAMB/SI   12
    HE BECAME A LITTLE CHILD . . . . 115 THE LAMB/SI   16
    LITTLE LAMB GOD BLESS THEE . . . . 115 THE LAMB/SI   19
    LITTLE LAMB GOD BLESS THEE . . . . 115 THE LAMB/SI   20
    THERES LITTLE TOM DACRE WHO CRIED WHEN HIS HEAD . . . . 117 CHIMNEY SWP/SI   5
    THE LITTLE BOY LOST . . . . 120D LIT BOY LST/SI   TITLE
    SPEAK FATHER SPEAK TO YOUR LITTLE BOY . . . . 120 LIT BOY LST/SI   3
    THE LITTLE BOY FOUND . . . . 121A LIT BOY FND/SI   TITLE
    THE LITTLE BOY LOST IN THE LONELY FEN . . . . 121 LIT BOY FND/SI   1
    HER LITTLE BOY WEEPING SOUGHT . . . . 121 LIT BOY FND/SI   8
    BESIDES IN THE SKY THE LITTLE BIRDS FLY . . . . 121 NURSES SONG/SI   11
    THOUSANDS OF LITTLE BOYS & GIRLS RAISING THEIR INNOCENT   122 HOLY THURS/SI   8
    HANDS
    LITTLE BOY . . . . 123 SPRING/SI   10
    LITTLE GIRL . . . . 123 SPRING/SI   12
    LITTLE LAMB . . . . 123 SPRING/SI   19
    THE LITTLE BLACK BOY . . . . 125B LIT BLK BOY/SI   TITLE
    AND WE ARE PUT ON EARTH A LITTLE SPACE . . . . 125 LIT BLK BOY/SI   13
    AND THUS I SAY TO LITTLE ENGLISH BOY . . . . 125 LIT BLK BOY/SI   22
    THEL ANSWERD O THOU LITTLE VIRGIN OF THE PEACEFUL VALLEY . 128 BOOK OF THEL 2   3
    WHICH THOU DOST SCATTER ON EVERY LITTLE BLADE OF GRASS   128 BOOK OF THEL 2   9
    THAT SPRINGS
    DESCEND O LITTLE CLOUD & HOVER BEFORE THE EYES OF THEL . . 128 BOOK OF THEL 2   16
    O LITTLE CLOUD THE VIRGIN SAID I CHARGE THEE TELL TO ME   128 BOOK OF THEL 3   1
    DOST THOU O LITTLE CLOUD I FEAR THAT I AM NOT LIKE THEE   129 BOOK OF THEL 3   17
    BUT I FEED NOT THE LITTLE FLOWERS I HEAR THE WARBLING BIRDS   129 BOOK OF THEL 3   19
    AH WEEP NOT LITTLE VOICE THOU CANST NOT SPEAK BUT THOU   129 BOOK OF THEL 4   4
    CANST WEEP
    WHY A LITTLE CURTAIN OF FLESH ON THE BED OF OUR DESIRE . . 130 BOOK OF THEL 6   20
    TO CREATE A LITTLE FLOWER IS THE LABOUR OF AGES . . . . 152C MARRIAGE HH 9   PROSE

1105

```
                                                          PAGE    TITLE           LINE
LITTLE    (CONTINUED)
    BECAUSE HE WAS A LITTLE WISER THAN THE MONKEY GREW VAIN    157D MARRIAGE HH 21  PROSE
    SO SUNG A LITTLE CLOD OF CLAY                              162 CLOD PEBBLE/N      5
    LITTLE SORROWS SIT & WEEP     . . . . . . . . .            164 CRADLE SONG/N      2
    [YET A LITTLE WHILE THE MOON]   . . . . . . . .            165 CRADLE SONG/N      8
    WHERE THY LITTLE HEART DOES REST                           165 CRADLE SONG/N     13
    IN THY LITTLE HEART ASLEEP   . . . . . . . . .             165 CRADLE SONG/N     15
    WHEN THY LITTLE HEART DOES WAKE   . . . . . . .            165 CRADLE SONG/N     16
    LITTLE PRETTY INFANT WILES   . . . . . . . . .             165 CRADLE SONG/N     22
    OR SHRINK AT THE LITTLE BLASTS OF FEAR                     166 WHY CARE FOR/N     3
    I LOVE [MYSELF SO DOES THE BIRD] YOU LIKE THE LITTLE BIRD  177 LIT BOY LST/N      7
    [THEN] HE LED HIM BY HIS LITTLE COAT   . . . . .           177 LIT BOY LST/N     13
    [THEY BOUND HIS LITTLE IVORY LIMBS]   . . . . . .          177 LIT BOY LST/N     22
    [AND] THEY STRIPD HIM TO HIS LITTLE SHIRT   . . .          177 LIT BOY LST/N     24
    MY LITTLE ARROWS     . . . . . . . . . . . .               178 THE FAIRY/N        2
    THOU LITTLE KID DIDST PLAY &C    . . . . . . . .           179 THE KID/N          1
    [A PRETTY] THE LITTLE VAGABOND   . . . . . . . .           179 LIT VAGABOND/N *TITLE
    A LITTLE BLACK THING AMONG THE SNOW                        180 CHIMNEY SWP/N      1
    LITTLE FLY    . . . . . . . . . . . . . . .                183 THE FLY/N          5
    ARISE YOU LITTLE GLANCING WINGS AND SING YOUR INFANT JOY   195 V DAU ALBION 8     9
    SO [SUNG] SANG A LITTLE CLOD OF CLAY   . . . . .           211 CLOD PEBBLE/SE *   5
    A LITTLE BLACK THING AMONG THE SNOW                        212 CHIMNEY SWP/SE     1
    LITTLE FLY    . . . . . . . . . . . . . . .                213 THE FLY/SE         1
    THE LITTLE VAGABOND   . . . . . . . . . . .                216A LIT VAGABND/SE  TITLE
    A LITTLE BOY LOST    . . . . . . . . . . . .               218B LIT BOY LST/SE  TITLE
    I LOVE YOU LIKE THE LITTLE BIRD                            218 LIT BOY LST/SE     7
    HE LED HIM BY HIS LITTLE COAT   . . . . . . . .            218 LIT BOY LST/SE    11
    THEY STRIPD HIM TO HIS LITTLE SHIRT   . . . . .            218 LIT BOY LST/SE    19
    A LITTLE GIRL LOST   . . . . . . . . . . . .               219A LIT GRL LST/SE  TITLE
    ON HIGH INTO TWO LITTLE ORBS    . . . . . . . .            228 URIZEN 11         13
    AND FIXED IN TWO LITTLE CAVES   . . . . . . . .            228 URIZEN 11         14
    EXCEPT WHAT HIS LITTLE ORBS    . . . . . . . .             230 URIZEN 13         31
    FORBID ALL JOY & FROM HER CHILDHOOD SHALL THE LITTLE FEMALE 240 EUROPE 5          8
    BY A LITTLE EWE LAMB                                       256 BOOK OF LOS 3     24
    WHY WILT THOU EXAMINE EVERY LITTLE FIBRE OF MY SOUL  . .   265 FOUR ZOAS 1       47
    BEHOLD TWO [LITTLE INFANTS WEPT] [?PIGURES OF ?PAIN HOWLD] 269 FOUR ZOAS 1    *  192
         . . .
    [THE ROUGH BARK OPENS TWITTERING PEEP FORTH LITTLE BEAKS   270 FOUR ZOAS 1       206
         & WINGS]
    WEARIED WITH SEEKING FOOD ACROSS THE SNOWY WASTE THE LITTLE 276 FOUR ZOAS 1      448
    HEART COLD AND THE LITTLE TONGUE CONSUMD THAT ONCE         276 FOUR ZOAS 1       449
         IN THOUGHTLESS JOY
    HIS WEB IS LEFT ALL DESOLATE THAT HIS LITTLE ANXIOUS HEART 277 FOUR ZOAS 1       459
    THEY BECOME NATIONS FAR REMOTE IN A LITTLE & DARK LAND  .  281 FOUR ZOAS 2    *   56
    TILL SHE BECAME A LITTLE WEEPING INFANT A SPAN LONG  . .   282 FOUR ZOAS 2       92
    OF GOD CLOTHED IN LUVAH'S GARMENTS LITTLE KNOWEST THOU  .  282 FOUR ZOAS 2      100
    . . . INTO LITTLE COMPASS                                  284 FOUR ZOAS 2      163
    ARISE YOU LITTLE GLANCING WINGS & SING YOUR INFANT JOY  .  289 FOUR ZOAS 2      364
    THOU LITTLE DIMINUTIVE PORTION THAT DARST BE A COUNTERPART 295 FOUR ZOAS 3      117
    UTTERING MY LAMENTATIONS & BEGETTING LITTLE MONSTERS  . .  296 FOUR ZOAS 3      165
    WHO SIT MOCKING UPON THE LITTLE PEBBLES OF THE TIDE  . .   296 FOUR ZOAS 3      166
    A LITTLE SHADOW BUT A LITTLE SHOWERY FORM OF ENION  . .    296 FOUR ZOAS 3      185
    FOR HER BRIGHT EYES BEHOLD THE ABYSS SOMETIMES A LITTLE    297 FOUR ZOAS 3      209
         SLEEP
    PERHAPS ENION MAY RESUME SOME LITTLE SEMBLANCE   . . . .   298 FOUR ZOAS 4       32
    ON HIGH INTO TWO LITTLE ORBS HIDING IN TWO LITTLE CAVES    303 FOUR ZOAS 4      229
    THE LITTLE HEART THE LIVER & THE RED BLOOD IN ITS          323 FOUR ZOAS 7      132
         LABYRINTHS
    SHUT UP IN LITTLE PURPLE COVERING FAINTLY BUD & DIE  . .   325 FOUR ZOAS 7      191
    HID IN A LITTLE SILKEN VEIL SCARCE BREATHE & FAINTLY SHINE 325 FOUR ZOAS 7      195
    MY LITTLE DAUGHTERS WERE MADE CAPTIVES & I SAW THEM BEATEN 334 FOUR ZOAS 7B      60
    ANXIOUS ITS LITTLE SOUL LOOKS OUT INTO THE CLEAR EXPANSE   355 FOUR ZOAS 8      559
    WHILE LITTLE CHILDREN PLAY AROUND THY FEET IN GENTLE AWE   360 FOUR ZOAS 9      134
    AND SAW IN THE DOOR WAY BENEATH THE TREES TWO LITTLE       370 FOUR ZOAS 9      507
         CHILDREN PLAYING
    THOU LITTLE BOY ART THARMAS & THOU BRIGHT GIRL ENION   . . 370 FOUR ZOAS 9      510
    DARKNESS WAS ALL BENEATH THE HEAVENS ONLY A LITTLE LIGHT   372 FOUR ZOAS 9      560
    LO THE LITTLE MOSS BEGINS TO SPRING & THE TENDER WEED  . . 373 FOUR ZOAS 9      610
    COMPOSED BY AN AFRICAN BLACK FROM THE LITTLE EARTH OF SOTHA 375 FOUR ZOAS 9      686
    AND HE SHALL LICK THE LITTLE GIRL'S WHITE NECK & ON HER    376 FOUR ZOAS 9      704
         HEAD
    TIMBRELS & VIOLINS SPORT ROUND THE WINE PRESSES THE LITTLE 377 FOUR ZOAS 9      755
         SEED
    AROUND THE ETERNAL MAN'S BRIGHT TENT THE LITTLE CHILDREN   379 FOUR ZOAS 9      839
         PLAY
    A LITTLE FLOWER GREW IN A LONELY VALE   . . . . . . .      414 TO MRS FLAXMAN     1
    ALIGHTED WHERE THIS LITTLE FLOWER WAS   . . . . . .        414 TO MRS FLAXMAN     6
    A LITTLE FEMALE BABE DOES SPRING   . . . . . . . .         425 MENTAL TRAVLER    44
    AWAKE AWAKE MY LITTLE BOY    . . . . . . . . . .           427 LAND OF DREAMS     1
    AND A LITTLE [XXX] LOVELY MOONY NIGHT   . . . . .          429 CRYSTL CABINET *   8
    HE WHO SHALL HURT THE LITTLE WREN   . . . . . . . .        431 AUGURIES          29
    LONG JOHN BROWN & LITTLE MARY BELL    . . . . . .          434A LONG JOHN BRWN  TITLE
    [PRETTY] LITTLE MARY BELL HAD A FAIRY IN A NUT   . . .     434 LONG JOHN BRWN     1
    [YOUNG] LONG JOHN BROWN LOVD [PRETTY] LITTLE MARY BELL  .  434 LONG JOHN BRWN     3
    HAND WHICH EXECUTED THESE LITTLE IDEAS BEEN THAT          439C REMARKS MALKIN  PROSE
         OF A PLAGIARY
    DETERMINATE ALL HIS EFFORTS PROVE THIS LITTLE BOY TO HAVE 439C REMARKS MALKIN  PROSE
         HAD
    STAY A LITTLE & I WILL SHEW YOU WHAT YOU SHOULD STUDY  . . 449C ANNO REYNOLDS   MARG
    THE GREAT BACON HE IS CALLD I CALL HIM THE LITTLE BACON    459C ANNO REYNOLDS   MARG
    HE MAKES LITTLE CONCESSIONS THAT HE MAY TAKE GREAT         463C ANNO REYNOLDS   MARG
         ADVANTAGES
```

LITTLE   (CONTINUED)

	PAGE	TITLE	LINE
ROLLING ROUND INTO TWO LITTLE ORBS & CLOSED IN TWO LITTLE CAVES	482	MILTON 3	14
THE EYE OF MAN A LITTLE NARROW ORB CLOSD UP & DARK . .	484	MILTON 5	21
THE EAR A LITTLE SHELL IN SMALL VOLUTIONS SHUTTING OUT .	484	MILTON 5	23
THE TONGUE A LITTLE MOISTURE FILLS A LITTLE FOOD IT CLOYS	484	MILTON 5	25
A LITTLE SOUND IT UTTERS & ITS CRIES ARE FAINTLY HEARD .	484	MILTON 5	26
SEEST THOU THE LITTLE WINGED FLY SMALLER THAN A GRAIN OF SAND	502	MILTON 20	27
AND LOS THUS SPOKE O NOBLE SONS BE PATIENT YET A LITTLE	507	MILTON 23	32
TILL ALBION IS ARISEN THEN PATIENT WAIT A LITTLE WHILE . .	508	MILTON 23	54
THEN PATIENT WAIT A LITTLE WHILE TILL THE LAST VINTAGE IS OVER	508	MILTON 23	59
BUT THE TIME OF YOUR REFRESHING COMETH ONLY A LITTLE MOMENT	511	MILTON 25	45
TIMBRELS & VIOLINS SPORT ROUND THE WINE-PRESSES THE LITTLE SEED	513	MILTON 27	11
THE LITTLE WEEPING SPECTRE STANDS ON THE THRESHOLD OF DEATH	515	MILTON 28	10
HIS LITTLE THROAT LABOURS WITH INSPIRATION EVERY FEATHER	520	MILTON 31	34
STANDS STILL UPON THE MOUNTAIN LOOKING ON THIS LITTLE BIRD	520	MILTON 31	37
SAID LITTLE CREATURE [THOU ART] FORMD [FOR] OF JOY & MIRTH	541	ANGEL PRESID/N	2
PERHAPS THIS LITTLE FABLE &C	554	TO VENETIAN/N	3
PERHAPS THIS LITTLE FABLE MAY MAKE US MERRY	554	TO VENETIAN/N	4
GOD KNOWS I LITTLE OF PRAYERS NEED SAY	559	I ROSE UP AT/N	22
VERY LITTLE TIME AND OF THE AIR IT GROWS YELLOW AND AT LENGTH BROWN	561A	EXHIBITION ADV	PROSE
ALL THE LITTLE OLD PICTURES CALLED CABINET PICTURES . .	561A	EXHIBITION ADV	PROSE
A LITTLE CONSIDERATION MUST SHEW THE FALLACY OF THIS OPINION	565A	DESC CAT 2	PROSE
OF VERY LITTLE TIME AND OF THE AIR IT DEADENS EVERY COLOUR	565A	DESC CAT 2	PROSE
IT IS MIXED WITH AT ITS FIRST MIXTURE AND IN A LITTLE TIME	565B	DESC CAT 2	PROSE
ITSELF WILL DRINK OR ABSORB VERY LITTLE COLOUR	566B	DESC CAT 2	PROSE
ALL THE GENUINE OLD LITTLE PICTURES CALLED CABINET PICTURES	566B	DESC CAT 2	PROSE
SHE HAS CERTAIN PECULIARITIES AND LITTLE DELICATE AFFECTATIONS	568B	DESC CAT 3	PROSE
LOOKS DOWN ON THEIR LITTLE FOLLIES FROM THE EMPEROR TO THE MILLER	569A	DESC CAT 3	PROSE
FOR A BUFFOON OR BURLESQUE CHARACTER KNOW LITTLE OF CHAUCER	569C	DESC CAT 3	PROSE
TO BE SURE CHAUCER IS A LITTLE DIFFICULT TO HIM WHO HAS ONLY	574A	DESC CAT 3	PROSE
YET A LITTLE PAINS OUGHT TO BE TAKEN EVEN BY THE IGNORANT AND WEAK	574A	DESC CAT 3	PROSE
STAMINA OF HIS MAKE COMPARATIVELY LITTLE AND HIS JOINTS	580A	DESC CAT 5	PROSE
PAY THEIR JOURNEYMEN LITTLE ENOUGH BUT THOUGH	583B	DESC CAT 9	PROSE
CUT DOTS & LOZENGES EQUALLY WELL WITH THOSE LITTLE PRINTS	592B	PUB ADDRESS/N	PROSE
TROUBLE THEIR HEADS VERY LITTLE ABOUT ART & SCIENCE & THAT	592C	PUB ADDRESS/N	PROSE
THE NATURE OF VISIONARY FANCY OR IMAGINATION IS VERY LITTLE	605A	V LAST JUDG/N	PROSE
JERUSALEM IS THEIR DAUGHTER LITTLE INFANTS CREEP OUT OF THE	609D	V LAST JUDG/N	PROSE
A LITTLE BELOW SETH ON HIS RIGHT ARE TWO FIGURES . . .	611D	V LAST JUDG/N	PROSE
CAM IS A LITTLE STREAM ELY IS ALMOST SWALLOWD UP	623	JERUSALEM 5	9
OF LIGHT AND LOVE THEIR LITTLE CHILDREN STAND WITH ARROWS OF GOLD	631	JERUSALEM 11	20
PERMANENT & NOT LOST NOT LOST NOR VANISHD & EVERY LITTLE ACT	634	JERUSALEM 13	60
AND LEFT MAN A LITTLE GROVELLING ROOT OUTSIDE OF HIMSELF	639	JERUSALEM 17	32
AT SIGHT OF THY ONCE LOVD JERUSALEM WHAT IS SIN BUT A LITTLE	643	JERUSALEM 20	23
WHY WILT THOU NUMBER EVERY LITTLE FIBRE OF MY SOUL . . .	645	JERUSALEM 22	20
AMONG THE LITTLE MEADOWS GREEN	649	FIELDS FROM/J	8
FEAR NOT O LITTLE FLOCK I COME ALBION SHALL RISE AGAIN .	653	JERUSALEM 29	26
THE LITTLE VILLAGES OF MIDDLESEX & SURREY HUNGER & THIRST	656	JERUSALEM 30	25
AND IN HER COURTS AMONG HER LITTLE CHILDREN OFFERING UP	660	JERUSALEM 33	42
I HAVE NO TIME FOR SEEMING AND LITTLE ARTS OF COMPLIMENT	670	JERUSALEM 42	27
THAT EVERY LITTLE PARTICLE OF LIGHT & AIR BECAME OPAKE . .	674	JERUSALEM 44	10
THEY WEPT INTO THE DEEPS A LITTLE SPACE AT LENGTH WAS HEARD	675	JERUSALEM 44	43
AND LEFT A LITTLE SLIMY SUBSTANCE FLOATING UPON THE TIDES	679	JERUSALEM 49	18
THE EYE OF MAN A LITTLE NARROW ORB CLOSD UP & DARK . . .	680	JERUSALEM 49	34
THE EAR A LITTLE SHELL IN SMALL VOLUTIONS SHUTTING OUT .	680	JERUSALEM 49	36
THE TONGUE A LITTLE MOISTURE FILLS A LITTLE FOOD IT CLOYS	680	JERUSALEM 49	40
A LITTLE SOUND IT UTTERS & ITS CRIES ARE FAINTLY HEARD .	680	JERUSALEM 49	41
NO HUMAN FORM BUT SEXUAL & A LITTLE WEEPING INFANT PALE REFLECTED	697	JERUSALEM 63	20
SHE CREATES AT HER WILL A LITTLE MOONY NIGHT & SILENCE . .	707	JERUSALEM 69	19
AND A LITTLE TENDER MOON & HOVERING ANGELS ON THE WING . .	707	JERUSALEM 69	22
INTO A LITTLE ROOT A FATHOM LONG	717	STOOD AMONG/J	11
THEY ARE BECOME NARROW PLACES IN A LITTLE AND DARK LAND	720	JERUSALEM 79	14
ACCORDING AS THEY WEAVE THE LITTLE EMBRYON NERVES & VEINS	728	JERUSALEM 83	35
THE EYE THE LITTLE NOSTRILS & THE DELICATE TONGUE & EARS	728	JERUSALEM 83	36
IN THE LITTLE LOVELY ALLEGORIC NIGHT OF ALBION'S DAUGHTERS	733	JERUSALEM 88	31
AS GOD IS LOVE EVERY KINDNESS TO ANOTHER IS A LITTLE DEATH	743	JERUSALEM 96	27
HE SAYS ALSO THE SPIRITUAL BODY OR ANGEL AS LITTLE CHILDREN	774A	ANNO BERKELEY	MARG
& PERHAPS A LITTLE PRACTISE IN THEM MAY TURN OUT TO BENEFIT	795D	LETTER 6	PROSE
TO JOHN FLAXMAN I HAVE BEEN TOO LITTLE AMONG FRIENDS WHICH I	798B	LETTER 10	PROSE
I AM STILL EMPLOYD IN MAKING DESIGNS & LITTLE PICTURES . .	798B	LETTER 10	PROSE
WE HAVE HAD BUT LITTLE TIME FOR VIEWING THE COUNTRY . . .	806B	LETTER 16	PROSE
LITTLE TOM HAS BEEN OF LATE UNATTENDED TO	807A	LETTER 17	PROSE
FORGIVENESS TO BE CONTINUED TO ME A LITTLE LONGER WHEN . .	808A	LETTER 19	PROSE
TELL ME ABOUT YOUR SIGHT AFFLICTED ME NOT A LITTLE & THAT	811C	LETTER 22	PROSE
LITTLE PICTURES & DRAWINGS WHICH I HAD THE PLEASURE & PROFIT	814C	LETTER 23	PROSE
AND LITTLE DEVILS WHO FIGHT FOR THEMSELVES	816	HAPPINESS/L	6
WE EAT LITTLE WE DRINK LESS	818	HAPPINESS/L	63

		PAGE	TITLE	LINE

LITTLE   (CONTINUED)
STUDIED THE TWO LITTLE PICTURES I NOW SEND & DO NOT REPENT   819A LETTER 24   PROSE
FOLLY NOT TO VENTURE PUBLISHING I AM NOW ENGRAVING SIX   820B LETTER 25   PROSE
  LITTLE
PLATES FOR A LITTLE WORK OF MR H'S(HAYLEY'S) . . . . . 820B LETTER 25   PROSE
THE CXXXIX PSALM A LITTLE BEFORE YOUR LETTER ARRIVED I TAKE   823B LETTER 26   PROSE
BUT OF THIS WORK I TAKE CARE TO SAY LITTLE TO MR H(HAYLEY)   825A LETTER 27   PROSE
I REGARD FASHION IN POETRY AS LITTLE AS I DO IN PAINTING   825B LETTER 27   PROSE
APPROVES OF MY DESIGNS AS LITTLE AS HE DOES OF MY POEMS   825C LETTER 27   PROSE
  AND
I HAVE GOT TO WORK AFTER FUSELI FOR A LITTLE SHAKESPEARE   831B LETTER 31   PROSE
OF VARIETY SHALL ENGAGE IN OTHER LITTLE WORKS AS THEY ARISE   831C LETTER 31   PROSE
KEPT IN A LOWER TINT THE LITTLE OVAL TABLET ON THE SIDE   832B LETTER 32   PROSE
OVER HIS CHIMNEY PIECE BETWEEN TWO LITTLE PRETTY PICTURES   836A LETTER 35   PROSE
NEATLY DONE HIS MERIT WAS BUT LITTLE IN LIGHT AND SHADE   844B LETTER 43   PROSE
THANK YOU FOR YOUR VERY BEAUTIFUL LITTLE POEM ON THE KING'S   844D LETTER 43   PROSE
  RECOVERY
THINKS IT MIGHT BE DONE WITH VERY LITTLE TROUBLE TO YOU   845C LETTER 44   PROSE
THE LITTLE DIFFERENCE THAT SUBSISTED BETWEEN YOU SPEAKING   846A LETTER 44   PROSE
  OF
TO EXECUTE ANY WORK I NEED ONLY REFER TO THE LITTLE JOB   847A LETTER 44   PROSE
BUT HOWEVER AS SOME EXCUSE I MUST SAY THAT . . . 847B LETTER 44   PROSE
SPIRITUAL AID HAS NOT A LITTLE CONDUCED TO MY RESTORATION   852B LETTER 50   PROSE
  TO
THE LITTLE VOLUME OF POEMS INCLOSD THEY ARE BY . . . . 857B LETTER 54   PROSE
OF THIS BEAUTIFUL LITTLE ESTATE FOR THAT IT WILL BE HIGHLY   858C LETTER 55   PROSE
LITTLE HIGH FINISHD PICTURES THE SIZE THE ENGRAVINGS ARE   859B LETTER 56   PROSE
  TO BE
P S YOUR DESIRE THAT I SHOULD WRITE A LITTLE ADVERTISEMENT   860B LETTER 56   PROSE
CARES LITTLE FOR THIS WORLD WHICH PASSES AWAY WHOSE . . . 862D LETTER 60   PROSE
YOU WILL SEE IN THIS LITTLE WORK THE CAUSE OF DIFFERENCE   866A LETTER 64   PROSE
SOON GET ABOUT AGAIN GREAT MEN DIE EQUALLY WITH THE LITTLE   868D LETTER 68   PROSE
WHERE I CONTRIVE TO GET INTO A LITTLE PERSPIRATION WHICH   872B LETTER 75   PROSE
I HAVE LITTLE HOPE OF DOING ANY MORE OF SUCH THINGS . . . 878C LETTER 88   PROSE
THE LITTLE CARD I WILL DO AS SOON AS POSSIBLE BUT WHEN YOU   879A LETTER 88   PROSE
"THAT LITTLE WEENEST NOW WHAT SORROWS ARE" (SPENSER) . . SUPP LEGEND/N19   *
"HOLDS IN PERFECTION BUT A LITTLE MOMENT" SHAKESPEARE . . SUPP LEGEND/N21   *
LITTLE BLACK BOY DITTO LAUGHING SONG SPRING DITTO . . SUPP LETTER 66A   *PROSE
A DREAM ON ANOTHER'S SORROW THE LITTLE BOY LOST . . SUPP LETTER 66A   *PROSE
THE LITTLE BOY FOUND END OF SONGS OF INNOCENCE . . . SUPP LETTER 66A   *PROSE
LITTLE GIRL LOST DITTO DITTO THE CLOD & PEBBLE . . SUPP LETTER 66A   *PROSE
THE LITTLE VAGABOND HOLY THURSDAY A POISON TREE . . SUPP LETTER 66A   *PROSE
MY PRETTY ROSE TREE THE GARDEN OF LOVE A LITTLE BOY LOST   SUPP LETTER 66A   *PROSE
INFANT SORROW THE SCHOOL BOY LONDON LITTLE GIRL LOST   SUPP LETTER 66A   *PROSE
THE CHIMNEY SWEEPER A LITTLE BLACK THING &C THE HUMAN   SUPP LETTER 66A   *PROSE
  ABSTRACT
LITTLENESS
  ("ALL FINERY IS A SIGN OF LITTLENESS") NOT ALWAYS . . . 71B ANNO LAVATER   MARG
LITTLE-ONES,LITTLE ONES
THE LITTLE ONES LEAPED & SHOUTED & LAUGHD . . . . . . 60 NURSES SONG/IM   16
TILL THE LITTLE ONES WEARY . . . . 116 ECCHOING GR/SI   21
THE LITTLE ONES LEAPED & SHOUTED & LAUGHD . . . . . 121 NURSES SONG/SI   15
THE LITTLE ONES SPEND THE DAY . . . . 124 SCHOOL BOY/SI   9
HER LITTLE ONES [WILL BE] ARE SLAIN ON THE TOP OF EVERY   279 FOUR ZOAS 1   546
  STREET
AGAINST HER LITTLE ONES THE INNOCENT ACCUSED BEFORE THE   364 FOUR ZOAS 9   267
  JUDGES
AND LO MY BRETHREN IN THEIR TENTS & THEIR LITTLE   375 FOUR ZOAS 9   691
  ONES AROUND THEM
THESE TEARS FALL FOR THE LITTLE-ONES THE CHILDREN   532 MILTON 40   15
  OF JERUSALEM
RECIEVE HER LITTLE-ONES FOR SACRIFICES AND THE DELIGHTS   623 JERUSALEM 5   15
  OF CRUELTY
JEALOUS OF JERUSALEM'S CHILDREN ASHAMD OF HER LITTLE-ONES   640 JERUSALEM 18   6
HER LITTLE-ONES SHE MUST SLAY UPON OUR ALTARS AND HER AGED   640 JERUSALEM 18   33
LITTLE-ONES TO DESTROY THE DIVINE SAVIOUR THE FRIEND OF   641 JERUSALEM 18   37
  SINNERS
SLAY NOT MY LITTLE ONES BELOVED VIRGIN DAUGHTER OF BABYLON   643 JERUSALEM 20   27
STRETCHING THEIR WINGS SUBLIME OVER THE LITTLE-ONES OF   647 JERUSALEM 24   22
  ALBION
HER LITTLE-ONES RAN ON THE FIELDS . . . . . . 649 FIELDS FROM/J   5
AND THE MURDERD BODIES OF HER LITTLE ONES ARE SCOTLAND   653 JERUSALEM 29   21
  AND WALES
BELONG TO GOD ALONE AND ALL THY LITTLE ONES ARE HOLY . . 657 JERUSALEM 31   45
THEE FROM DESTROYING THESE LITTLE ONES AM I TO BE ONLY . . 670 JERUSALEM 42   21
BUT DESTROY NOT THESE LITTLE ONES NOR MOCK THE LORD'S   670 JERUSALEM 42   41
  ANOINTED
DESTROY NOT BY MORAL VIRTUE THE LITTLE ONES WHOM HE HATH   670 JERUSALEM 42   42
  CHOSEN
THE LITTLE ONES WHOM HE HATH CHOSEN IN PREFERENCE TO THEE   670 JERUSALEM 42   43
HE HATH CAST THEE OFF FOR EVER THE LITTLE ONES HE HATH   670 JERUSALEM 42   44
  ANOINTED
FILLD WITH THE LITTLE-ONES ARE CONSUMED IN THE FIRES OF   679 JERUSALEM 49   11
  THEIR ALTARS
LABOUR WELL THE MINUTE PARTICULARS ATTEND TO THE   687 JERUSALEM 55   51
  LITTLE-ONES
WHY WILT THOU DEFACE THY BEAUTY & THE BEAUTY OF   693 JERUSALEM 60   29
  THY LITTLE-ONES
BABYLON THE RATIONAL MORALITY DELUDING TO DEATH THE LITTLE   715 JERUSALEM 74   32
  ONES
THERE WE WALKED AS IN OUR SECRET CHAMBER AMONG OUR LITTLE   720 JERUSALEM 79   42
  ONES

LITTLE-ONES   (CONTINUED)

TOGETHER AMONG MY LITTLE-ONES BUT NOW MY ALTARS RUN WITH   721 JERUSALEM 79   55
   BLOOD
UPON HIS PARENT BOSOM LAY THY LITTLE ONES O LAND . . . .   727 JERUSALEM 83   24
AND TO INHABIT OUR LITTLE-ONES TO CLOTHE IN ARMOUR OF THE   729 JERUSALEM 84   9
   GOLD
WHILE THEN I HAND & HYLE CONDENSE THE LITTLE-ONES & ERECT THEM   737 JERUSALEM 90   49
   INTO
AH THEN I HEARD MY LITTLE ONES WEEPING ALONG THE VALLEY   740 JERUSALEM 93   11
HOW CAN I HEAR MY LITTLE ONES WEEPING ALONG THE VALLEY . .   740 JERUSALEM 93   15

LIVD

LAWLESS THEY LIVD TILL WANTONNESS . . . .   17 BLIND-MANS/PS   67
I SHOULD NOT HAVE LIVD SO LONG THERE WAS I . . . . . .   48B ISLAND MOON 4   PROSE
OR ELSE THOU WOULDEST NOT HAVE LIVD TO CURSE THY HELPLESS   108 TIRIEL 6   28
   CHILDREN
AND ALL SHALL SAY WITHOUT A USE THIS SHINING WOMAN LIVD   129 BOOK OF THEL 3   22
FOR HE SAW THAT LIFE LIVD UPON DEATH . . . .   235 URIZEN 23   27
BECAUSE THEIR BRETHREN & SISTERS LIVD IN WAR & LUST . .   246 SONG OF LOS 4   6
NINE TIMES THEY LIVD AMONG THE FORESTS FEEDING ON SWEET   270 FOUR ZOAS 1   233
   FRUITS
THUS LIVD LOS DRIVING ENION FAR INTO THE DEATHFUL INFINITE   290 FOUR ZOAS 2   383
WITH WHOM I LIVD IN HAPPINESS BEFORE THAT DEADLY NIGHT . .   300 FOUR ZOAS 4   112
WHAT THOU FORGETTEST THEY IN US & WE IN THEM ALTERNATE LIVD   327 FOUR ZOAS 7   276
THARMAS REPLID O VALA ONCE I LIVD IN A GARDEN OF DELIGHT   339 FOUR ZOAS 7B   232
AND EVERY ONE OF THE DEAD APPEARS AS HE HAD LIVD BEFORE   363 FOUR ZOAS 9   245
I HAVE LIVD & MOURND FOR THEE . . . .   423 THE BIRDS/N   10
I THOUGHT LOVE LIVD IN THE HOT SUN SHINE . . . . . .   436 WILLIAM BOND   45
OR LIKE A HUMAN FORM A FRIEND WITH WITH WHOM HE LIVD   497 MILTON 15   27
   BENEVOLENT
WITH WHOM SHE LIVD IN BLISS IN TIMES OF INNOCENCE & YOUTH   626 JERUSALEM 7   37
HOUSE SR WILLIAM LIVD IN IN PICCADILLY SHE LEFT SOME TIME   836C LETTER 35   PROSE

LIVE

THE SPIRITS OF THE AIR LIVE ON THE SMELLS . . . . .   2 TO AUTUMN/PS   13
THOU FEAR I DRINK MY TEARS LIKE WATER I LIVE UPON SORROW   39A SAMSON/PS   PROSE
THESE GODS LAST NAMD LIVE IN THE SMOKE OF CITIES . . . .   42D THEN SHE BORE   PROSE
& FILLIGREE WORK I HOPE SHALL LIVE TO SEE . . . . .   52C ISLAND MOON 8   PROSE
DIE IF I WAS TO LIVE HERE SAID SCOPPRELL HO HO HO HO HO   54C ISLAND MOON 9   PROSE
WILL BE IGNORANT FOOLS & WILL NOT DESERVE TO LIVE . . .   62D ISLAND MOON 11   PROSE
COME LIVE AND BE MERRY AND JOIN WITH ME . . . . .   63 SHEPHERD YOUNG   11
COME LIVE & BE MERRY AND JOIN WITH ME . . . . . .   125 LAUGHING/SI   11
LOOK ON THE RISING SUN THERE GOD DOES LIVE . . . . .   125 LIT BLK BOY/SI   9
OR DID SHE ONLY LIVE TO BE AT DEATH THE FOOD OF WORMS .   129 BOOK OF THEL 3   23
O BEAUTY OF THE VALES OF HAR WE LIVE NOT FOR OURSELVES .   129 BOOK OF THEL 4   10
I PONDER AND I CANNOT PONDER YET I LIVE AND LOVE . . .   129 BOOK OF THEL 5   8
("THAT MEN LIVE AFTER DEATH") IT WAS NOT KNOWN & YET ALL   132D ANNO SWED PROV   MARG
   KNOW
SEEM TO LIVE IN IT IN CHAINS ARE IN TRUTH THE CAUSES OF   155A MARRIAGE HH 15   PROSE
   ITS LIFE
AND LIVE IN IT MERRILY . . . .   168 HAST LAP/N   4
IF I LIVE . . . .   183 THE FLY/N   23
I SAY I SHANT LIVE FIVE YEARS AND . . . .   187C SAY I SHANT/N   PROSE
IF I LIVE ONE IT WILL BE A WONDER JUNE ... .   187C SAY I SHANT/N   PROSE
OUR LIVES TO MAKE THE FEMALE LIVE . . . . . .   188 A FAIRY SKIPD   14
THAT LIVE A PESTILENCE & DIE A METEOR & ARE NO MORE . .   193 V DAU ALBION 5   29
IF I LIVE . . . .   213 THE FLY/SE   19
WHY LIVE IN UNQUENCHABLE BURNINGS . . . . . .   224 URIZEN 4   13
UNLESS SOME WAY CAN BE FOUND THAT I MAY LOOK UPON THEE   265 FOUR ZOAS 1   41
   & LIVE
BUT MALES IMMORTAL LIVE RENEWD BY FEMALE DEATHS IN SOFT   266 FOUR ZOAS 1   66
AND LIVE THEREBY HE IS SUNK DOWN INTO A DEADLY SLEEP   272 FOUR ZOAS 1   291
WE THEREFORE FOR WHOSE SAKE ALL THINGS ASPIRE TO BE & LIVE   272 FOUR ZOAS 1   296
THO IN THE BRAIN OF MAN WE LIVE & IN HIS CIRCLING NERVES   272 FOUR ZOAS 1   302
LIVE IN PERFECT HARMONY IN EDEN THE LAND OF LIFE . . .   277 FOUR ZOAS 1   474
STIFLING I LIVE IF DASHD IN PIECES FROM A ROCKY HEIGHT .   298 FOUR ZOAS 4   14
GO FORTH SAID THARMAS WORKS OF JOY ARE THINE OBEY & LIVE   299 FOUR ZOAS 4   67
AND LIVE BEHOLD ETERNAL DEATH IS IN BEULAH BEHOLD   . . .   304 FOUR ZOAS 4   258
THAT I IN VAIN IN VARIOUS PATHS HAVE SOUGHT BUT STILL I   313 FOUR ZOAS 6   59
   LIVE
AND IN THESE MONSTROUS FORMS I [?LINE] LIVE IN AN ETERNAL   313 FOUR ZOAS 6   *   62
   WOE
WHERE HE MIGHT LIVE IN PEACE & WHERE HIS LIFE MIGHT MEET   316 FOUR ZOAS 6   195
   REPOSE
COMPELL THE POOR TO LIVE UPON A CRUST OF BREAD BY SOFT   323 FOUR ZOAS 7   117
   MILD ARTS
WITHOUT THESE ARTS IF YOU WOULD MAKE THE POOR LIVE WITH   323 FOUR ZOAS 7   122
   TEMPER
MAY LIVE BEFORE US IN OUR PALACES . . . .   331 FOUR ZOAS 7   441
THEY SHALL BE RANSOMS FOR OUR SOULS THAT WE MAY LIVE   . . 331 FOUR ZOAS 7   455
TO STAY HIM IN HIS FLIGHT THAT URIZEN MIGHT LIVE THO IN   339 FOUR ZOAS 7B   227
   PAIN
UNITED WE SHOULD LIVE IN BLISS AS THOSE WHO SINNED NOT .   345 FOUR ZOAS 8   160
A SEPULCHER & WORSHIP DEATH IN FEAR WHILE YET WE LIVE   .   349 FOUR ZOAS 8   334
THUS SHALL THE MALE & FEMALE LIVE THE LIFE OF ETERNITY .   362 FOUR ZOAS 9   219
THAT WE HIS CHILDREN EVERMORE MAY LIVE IN JERUSALEM . .   362 FOUR ZOAS 9   221
LUVAH & VALA HENCEFORTH YOU ARE SERVANTS OBEY & LIVE . .   366 FOUR ZOAS 9   363
NOT FOR OURSELVES BUT FOR THE ETERNAL FAMILY WE LIVE . .   374 FOUR ZOAS 9   640
WHEN WILT THOU RETURN & LIVE . . . .   416 MY SPECTRE/N   49
THERE I LIVE & MOURN FOR THEE . . . .   423 THE BIRDS/N   6
[ARE THERE ARTISTS WHO LIVE UPON ASSASINATIONS OF OTHER   SUPP ANNO REYNOLDS * MARG
   MEN]
AND THE POOR & THE OLD CAN LIVE UPON GOLD . . . . .   452 ANNO REYNOLDS   3
OF ETERNITY IN WHICH WE SHALL LIVE FOR EVER IN JESUS OUR   480D MILTON 1   PROSE
   LORD

LIVE   (CONTINUED)
   MERCY ALONE OF FREE GIFT AND ELECTION THAT WE LIVE   . . .   494 MILTON 13   33
   O SONS WE LIVE NOT BY WRATH BY MERCY ALONE WE LIVE   . . .   507 MILTON 23   34
   WHILE ON THE EARTH THEY LIVE IN SORROWFUL VEGETATIONS   . .   507 MILTON 23   44
   WHO LIVE IN DOUBTS & FEARS PERPETUALLY TORMENTED BY THE   511 MILTON 25   36
      ELECT
   THAT MAN MAY LIVE UPON EARTH TILL THE TIME OF HIS AWAKING   514 MILTON 27   61
   LIVE BECAUSE THE LIFE OF MAN WAS TOO EXCEEDING UNBOUNDED   519 MILTON 30   22
   OF ALL THAT LIVE DARE UTTER THIS OTHERS TREMBLE & BOW   . .   530 MILTON 38   57
   AND I ALAS LIVE TO WEEP OUT MINE EYES   . . . . . .   537 AND HIS LEGS/N   41
   CHAUCER'S CHARACTERS LIVE AGE AFTER AGE . . . . . .   570D DESC CAT 3   PROSE
   WE WILL LIVE IN PARADISE & LIBERTY   . . . .   616A V LAST JUDG/N   PROSE
   HEAVEN EARTH & HELL HENCEFORTH SHALL LIVE IN HARMONY   . .   621 READER LOVER/J   10
   BY DEMONSTRATION MAN ALONE CAN LIVE AND NOT BY FAITH   . .   622 JERUSALEM 4   28
   MAY LIVE IN GLORY REDEEMD BY SACRIFICE OF THE LAMB   . .   640 JERUSALEM 18   27
   WHERE WE LIVE FORGETTING ERROR NOT PONDERING ON EVIL   . .   642 JERUSALEM 20   7
   THEY COMPELL THE POOR TO LIVE UPON A CRUST OF BREAD BY   656 JERUSALEM 30   30
      SOFT MILD ARTS
   WE LIVE AS ONE MAN FOR CONTRACTING OUR INFINITE SENSES   . .   664 JERUSALEM 38   17
   LIVE IN PERFECT HARMONY IN EDEN THE LAND OF LIFE   . . .   665 JERUSALEM 38   21
   LIVE BY DEVOURING GOING INTO ETERNAL DEATH CONTINUALLY   . .   681 JERUSALEM 50   7
   THAT RAHAB & TIRZAH MAY EXIST & LIVE & BREATHE & LOVE   . .   692 JERUSALEM 59   43
   WHEREFORE ART THOU LIVING SAID LOS & MAN CANNOT LIVE IN   698 JERUSALEM 64   18
      THY PRESENCE
   & IN WHICH WE SHALL LIVE IN OUR ETERNAL OR IMAGINATIVE   717A JERUSALEM 77   PROSE
      BODIES
   YOU SHALL NOT FIND WHERE TO LIVE . . . .   724 IN HEAVEN/J   5
   O THAT I COULD LIVE IN HIS SIGHT O THAT I COULD BIND HIM   726 JERUSALEM 82   44
      TO MY ARM
   TO LIVE IN THY BOSOM'S TRANSLUCENCE AS IN AN ETERNAL   732 JERUSALEM 87   11
      MORNING
   HIS STONY MEMBERS HE SAW ENGLAND AH SHALL THE DEAD LIVE   742 JERUSALEM 95   4
      AGAIN
   JESUS REPLIED FEAR NOT ALBION UNLESS I DIE THOU CANST NOT   743 JERUSALEM 96   14
      LIVE
   SNEAKING SUBMISSION CAN ALWAYS LIVE . . . .   752 EV GOSPEL(D)/N   34
   AND CANST THOU DIE THAT I MAY LIVE   . . . .   755 EV GOSPEL(E)/N   79
   THAT HE MIGHT LIVE ABOVE CONTROLL   . . . .   757 EV GOSPEL(I)/N   44
   OF THE TRANSGRESOR OR NO FLESH OR SPIRIT COULD EVER LIVE   780 GHOST ABEL 2   *   11
   AND NO ATONEMENT O JEHOVAH THE ELOHIM LIVE ON SACRIFICE   780 GHOST ABEL 2   14
   LIVE IN REAL SUBSTANTIAL NATURAL BORN MAN   . . . . .   789A ANNO THORNTON   MARG
   IT WOULD NOT FULFILL THE PURPOSE FOR WHICH ALONE I LIVE   791D LETTER 4   PROSE
      WHICH
   & SHOULD NEVER HAVE ATTEMPTED TO LIVE BY ANY THING ELSE   794C LETTER 5   PROSE
   BUT I AM CONTENTED WHETHER I LIVE BY PAINTING OR ENGRAVING   794C LETTER 5   PROSE
   LIVE BY MIRACLE I AM PAINTING SMALL PICTURES FROM THE BIBLE   795C LETTER 6   PROSE
   WITH NOW & THEN AN ENGRAVING & FIND THAT IN FUTURE TO LIVE   798B LETTER 10   PROSE
   THAT IF I DO NOT CONFINE MYSELF TO THIS I SHALL NOT LIVE   812C LETTER 22   PROSE
   I CANNOT LIVE WITHOUT DOING MY DUTY TO LAY UP TREASURES   812C LETTER 22   PROSE
   MUST MY WIFE LIVE IN MY SISTER'S BANE   . . . . . .   818 HAPPINESS/L   49
   ENDEAVOUR TO LIVE TO THE GLORY OF OUR LORD & SAVIOUR & I   822C LETTER 26   PROSE
   I IMPROVE VERY MUCH & SHALL CONTINUE TO DO SO WHILE I LIVE   824B LETTER 27   PROSE
   O THAT I COULD LIVE AS OTHERS DO IN A REGULAR SUCCESSION   830B LETTER 30   PROSE
   BREAD ALONE I SHALL LIVE ALTHO I SHOULD WANT BREAD NOTHING   830B LETTER 30   PROSE
   KING WILL LIVE TO FULFIL THE PROPHECY AND DIE IN PEACE   . .   844D LETTER 43   PROSE
   OVER MY DOOR AS THE POOR BARBER DID MONEY FOR LIVE HERE   858C LETTER 55   PROSE
   SUFFICIENTLY PAID IF I LIVE AS I NOW DO & ONLY FEAR THAT   879C LETTER 89   PROSE
      I MAY
   "WHO IN THE COLOURS OF THE RAINBOW LIVE" MILTON   . . . .   SUPP LEGEND/N30   *
LIVED
   IN SOLITUDE THOUGH NOT OBSCURE IN ISRAEL HE LIVED   . . .   39C SAMSON/PS   PROSE
   THEY LIVED A PERIOD OF YEARS . . . .   236 URIZEN 28   1
   IN TWAIN & LO MY CRYSTAL FORM THAT LIVED IN MY BOSOM   . .   334 FOUR ZOAS 7B   65
   LIVED BY SUCH YOU DO NOT SEE AS I DO . . . .   391D ANNO WATSON   MARG
   THAT WHILE HE DID THAT WORK HE LIVED ON BREAD & APPLES   . .   446A ANNO REYNOLDS   MARG
   INTRICATE LABYRINTHS OF TIMES AND SPACES UNKNOWN   494 MILTON 13   43
      THAT LEUTHA LIVED
   WHO LIVED IN THE FIFTH CENTURY THERE WERE REMAINS   . . .   578B DESC CAT 5   PROSE
   THEREFORE HE LIVED & BREATHED IN HOPE BUT HIS TEARS FELL   696 JERUSALEM 62   36
      INCESSANT
LIVELIHED
   "LEFT THEE FOR PORTION OF THY LIVELIHED" SPENSER . . . .   SUPP LEGEND/N19   *
LIVELONG
   ALL THE LIVELONG NIGHT BEGUILES   . . . .   120 CRADLE SONG/SI   12
   WE'D SING AND WE'D PRAY ALL THE LIVELONG DAY . . . . .   179 LIT VAGABOND/N   8
LIVE-LONG
   WE'D SING AND WE'D PRAY ALL THE LIVE-LONG DAY . . . . .   216 LIT VAGABND/SE   7
LIVELY
   WHEN THE MEADOWS LAUGH WITH LIVELY GREEN   . . . . . .   63 SHEPHERD YOUNG   3
   WHEN THE MEADOWS LAUGH WITH LIVELY GREEN   . . . . . .   125 LAUGHING/SI   5
LIVER
   THE LITTLE HEART THE LIVER & THE RED BLOOD IN ITS   323 FOUR ZOAS 7   132
      LABYRINTHS
   THE LUNGS THE HEART THE LIVER SHRUNK AWAY FAR DISTANT FROM   679 JERUSALEM 49   17
      MAN
LIVERIES
   SURROUNDED BY THE CLOUDS IN THEIR LIVERIES IN THEIR   . . .   618B ILLUS MILTON   PROSE
LIVERPOOL
   MANCHESTER & LIVERPOOL ARE IN TORTURES OF DOUBT & DESPAIR   644 JERUSALEM 21   36
LIVES
   THEY CRY AND LET TEN THOUSAND LIVES . . . .   12 GWIN KING/PS   31
   VENTRING THEIR LIVES IN MY MOST RIGHTEOUS CAUSE   . . . .   18 EDW THIRD/PS 1   18

LIVES   (CONTINUED)

		PAGE	TITLE	LINE
SPEND THEIR SWEET LIVES TO DO THEIR COUNTRY SERVICE	. . .	31	EDW THIRD/PS 5	56
THE SUCKING INFANT LIVES TO DIE IN BATTLE	. . . . .	34B	KING JOHN/PS	PROSE
HAD I THREE LIVES ID DIE IN SUCH A CAUSE	. . . . . .	35	WAR SONG/PS	13
FAR IN A DIREFUL CAVE SHE LIVES UNSEEN	. . . . . .	41D	THEN SHE BORE	PROSE
THE FEMALE LIFE LIVES FROM THE LIGHT OF THE MALE	. .	82C	ANNO LAVATER	MARG
I KNOW TIRIEL IS KING OF THE WEST & THERE HE LIVES IN JOY		101	TIRIEL 2	20
HOW GREAT THY USE HOW GREAT THY BLESSING EVERY THING THAT LIVES		129	BOOK OF THEL 3	26
LIVES NOT ALONE NOR FOR ITSELF FEAR NOT AND I WILL CALL		129	BOOK OF THEL 3	27
FOR EVERY THING THAT LIVES IS HOLY	. . . .	160B	SONG LIBERTY	PROSE
LIVES IN [AN ETERNAL] ETERNITY'S SUN RISE	. . . . .	179	ETERNITY/N	4
LIVES IN ETERNITY'S SUN RISE	. . . .	184	SEVRL QUESTN/N	14
OUR LIVES TO MAKE THE FEMALE LIVE	. . . .	188	A FAIRY SKIPD	14
ARISE AND DRINK YOUR BLISS FOR EVERY THING THAT LIVES IS HOLY		195	V DAU ALBION 8	10
FOR EVERY THING THAT LIVES IS HOLY LIFE DELIGHTS IN LIFE		199	AMERICA 8	13
BUT CLOUDS OF HUMAN SOULS MY NOSTRILS DRINK THE LIVES OF MEN		275	FOUR ZOAS 1	393
WITH LIVES OF VICTIMS SACRIFICED UPON AN ALTAR OF BRASS		285	FOUR ZOAS 2	194
ON THE EAST SIDE REVIVD HER SOUL WITH LIVES OF BEASTS & BIRDS		285	FOUR ZOAS 2	195
ONE THOUSAND MEN OF WONDROUS POWER SPENT THEIR LIVES IN ITS FORMATION		285	FOUR ZOAS 2	198
FOR EVERY THING THAT LIVES IS HOLY FOR THE SOURCE OF LIFE		289	FOUR ZOAS 2	366
THAT LIFE LIVES UPON DEATH & BY DEVOURING APPETITE	. .	330	FOUR ZOAS 7	390
WHERE NOTHING LIVES THERE TO WANDER & IF THOU RETURNST WEARY		361	FOUR ZOAS 9	* 147
AND WHO LIVES ON THE CONTEMPT OF HIS NEIGHBOUR . . .	.	377	FOUR ZOAS 9	764
SHE LIVES UPON HIS SHRIEKS & CRIES	. . . .	425	MENTAL TRAVLER	19
BUT O HE LIVES IN THE MOONY LIGHT	. . . .	436	WILLIAM BOND	46
OR IS ABLE & AFTERWARDS GO AND SWEAR OUR LIVES AWAY	.	439A	BLAKES MEMORAN	PROSE
THE LIVES OF PAINTERS SAY THAT RAFAEL DIED OF DISSIPATION		454B	ANNO REYNOLDS	MARG
THE STORY THAT IS TOLD IN ALL LIVES OF THE PAINTERS	. .	583A	DESC CAT 9	PROSE
HAVE SPENT THEIR LIVES IN CURBING & GOVERNING OTHER PEOPLE'S		615D	V LAST JUDG/N	PROSE
AND IRON BOUND IT OVER ME FOR EVER LIFE LIVES ON MY	.	630	JERUSALEM 10	55
THOSE WHO GIVE THEIR LIVES FOR HIM ARE DESPISED	. . .	667	JERUSALEM 40	15
TO ATONE FOR YOU FOR SPIRITUAL DEATH MAN LIVES BY DEATHS OF MEN		670	JERUSALEM 42	49
HUMAN MISERIES TURND FIERCE WITH THE LIVES OF MEN ALONG THE VALLEY		699	JERUSALEM 64	33
DRINKING THEIR LIVES IN SWEET INTOXICATION HENCE AROSE FROM BATH		701	JERUSALEM 65	65
THREE-FOLD EMBRACE RETURNS CONSUMING LIVES OF GODS & MEN		709	JERUSALEM 70	27
WHICH LIVES ETERNALLY	. . . .	717B	JERUSALEM 77	PROSE
INTO THE PLANETARY LIVES OF YEARS MONTHS DAYS & HOURS REPOSING		747	JERUSALEM 99	3

LIVEST

ART THOU ALIVE & LIVEST THOU FOR-EVERMORE OR ART THOU	. .	693	JERUSALEM 60	54

LIVETH

MAN LIVETH NOT BY SELF ALONE BUT IN HIS BROTHER'S FACE	.	374	FOUR ZOAS 9	641
IN WHICH MAN LIVETH ETERNALLY MADNESS & BLASPHEMY AGAINST		521	MILTON 32	20
NOT BUT A DELUSIVE SHADOW A THOUGHT THAT LIVETH NOT	. .	693	JERUSALEM 60	* 55
THERE IS NONE THAT LIVETH & SINNETH NOT AND THIS IS THE COVENANT		694	JERUSALEM 61	24
MERRY WITH MY FRIENDS TILL CHRISTMAS FOR AS MAN LIVETH NOT BY		830B	LETTER 30	PROSE
& LIFE NOT IN THE REAL MAN THE IMAGINATION WHICH LIVETH		878A	LETTER 88	PROSE

LIVING   SEE SELF-LIVING,WAR-LIVING

UNTIMELY LOST THY CONRADE ONCE WHEN LIVING THEE I LOVD EVN UNTO DEATH		43D	WOE CRIED MUSE	PROSE
[WHILE ?LIVING CLAY COLD CORPSE CORSE] SWIFT AS THE	. . .	43D	WOE CRIED MUSE	*PROSE
CRYING HIDE FROM THE LIVING		137	FRENCH REVOLTN	74
. . . WE ARE NOT NUMBERED AMONG THE LIVING LET US HIDE	.	137	FRENCH REVOLTN	76
RAGING AROUND & MELTING THE METALS INTO LIVING FLUIDS	.	155A	MARRIAGE HH 15	PROSE
IN LIVING CREATIONS APPEARD	. . . .	225	URIZEN 5	1
ROUND THE PALE LIVING CORSE ON THE TREE	. . . . . .	252	AHANIA 4	10
ROUND THE PALE LIVING CORSE ON THE TREE	. . . . . .	253	AHANIA 4	36
RAN THRO HEAVEN & EARTH LIVING FLAMES	. . . . . .	256	BOOK OF LOS 3	28
WHAT ARE THE NATURES OF THOSE LIVING CREATURES . . .	.	264	FOUR ZOAS 1	12
[I AM] WE ARE BECOME A VICTIM TO THE LIVING [I] WE HIDE IN SECRET		264	FOUR ZOAS 1	* 26
[NO OTHER LIVING THING IS HERE THE SEA THE EARTH THE HEAVEN]		268	FOUR ZOAS 1	141
A SORROW & A FEAR A LIVING TORMENT & NAKED VICTIM	. .	268	FOUR ZOAS 1	159
THE LIVING CREATURES OF THE WHEELS IN THE WARS OF ETERNAL LIFE		280	FOUR ZOAS 1	572
[XXX ?LIVING JOY FILLS ?ALBION]	. . . .	SUPP	FOUR ZOAS 1	*
BENEATH THE FURNACES A WOFUL HEAP IN LIVING DEATH	. .	283	FOUR ZOAS 2	116
REVERBERATES THE LIVING HARMONY UPON MY LIMBS	. . . .	289	FOUR ZOAS 2	356
THE LIVING VOICE IS EVER LIVING IN ITS INMOST JOY	. .	289	FOUR ZOAS 2	363
I HAVE BLOTTED OUT FROM LIGHT & LIVING THE DOVE & NIGHTINGALE		290	FOUR ZOAS 2	391
OF LIVING GOLD PURE PERFECT HOLY IN WHITE LINEN PURE HE HOVERD		293	FOUR ZOAS 3	51
PLUNGD INTO THE COLD BILLOWS LIVING [&] A LIFE IN MIDST OF WATERS		296	FOUR ZOAS 3	* 179
A TERROR TO ALL LIVING THINGS THINK NOT THAT I AM IGNORANT		299	FOUR ZOAS 4	82
LOUD & MORE LOUD THE LIVING MUSIC FLOATS UPON THE AIR	. .	306	FOUR ZOAS 5	26
OF ORC ENTERING WITH FIBRES BECAME ONE WITH HIM A LIVING CHAIN		309	FOUR ZOAS 5	* 169

		PAGE	TITLE	LINE

LIVING   (CONTINUED)

THEN THOU DIDST KEEP WITH STRONG URTHONA THE LIVING GATES OF HEAVEN — 311 FOUR ZOAS 5 — 232

NO FORM WAS THERE NO LIVING THING & YET HIS WAY LAY THRO — 315 FOUR ZOAS 6 — 149

A LABOURER OF AGES A DIRE DISCONTENT A LIVING WOE   . . . — 317 FOUR ZOAS 6 — 226

A LIVING MANTLE ADJOIND TO HIS LIFE & GROWING FROM HIS SOUL — 318 FOUR ZOAS 6 — * 246

WHENCE THESE FIERCE FIRES BUT FROM THYSELF NO OTHER LIVING THING — 321 FOUR ZOAS 7 — 45

IN ALL THIS CHASM I BEHOLD NO OTHER LIVING THING . . . . — 321 FOUR ZOAS 7 — 46

OF LIVING PANGS THY HORRIBLE BED GLOWING WITH CEASELESS FIRES — 321 FOUR ZOAS 7 — 50

OF PLAGUES HIDDEN IN SHINING GLOBES THAT GREW ON THE LIVING TREE — 325 FOUR ZOAS 7 — 216

THE SPECTRES OF THE DEAD FOR I AM AS THE SPECTRE OF THE LIVING — 327 FOUR ZOAS 7 — 310

WITH HARSH SONGS EVERY LIVING SOUL THE PRESTER SERPENT RUNS — 335 FOUR ZOAS 7B — 113

THE LIVING SOUL IN GLORIOUS FORMS & EVERY ONE CAME FORTH — 340 FOUR ZOAS 7B — 278

INTO A FORM OF VEGETATION LIVING HAVING A VOICE   . . . — 353 FOUR ZOAS 8 — 475

THUS IN A LIVING DEATH THE NAMELESS SHADOW ALL THINGS BOUND — 353 FOUR ZOAS 8 — 481

THE BLOODY DELUGE LIVING FLAMES WINGED WITH INTELLECT   . . — 359 FOUR ZOAS 9 — 86

FOR FROM MY PLEASANT HILLS BEHOLD THE LIVING LIVING SPRINGS — 368 FOUR ZOAS 9 — 441

HIS CROWN OF THORNS FELL FROM HIS HEAD HE HUNG HIS LIVING LYRE — 376 FOUR ZOAS 9 — 711

WHO IN HOPES OF A GOOD LIVING ADOPT THE STATE RELIGION . . — 390D ANNO WATSON — MARG

LIVING THEE ALONE I'LL HAVE . . . . — 416 MY SPECTRE/N — 53

IN THE CLOUD WHICH ROLLS AWAY ARE THE FOUR LIVING CREATURES — 444A LAST JUDGMNT/L — PROSE

UPON HIS KNEES BEFORE THE LIVING & THE DEAD   . . . . . — 444C LAST JUDGMNT/L — PROSE

AND IN HIS TENT THRO ENVY OF LIVING FORM EVEN OF THE DIVINE VISION — 482 MILTON 3 — 2

CAN SUCH A TONGUE BOAST OF THE LIVING WATERS OR TAKE IN — 485 MILTON 5 — 34

AND MATHEMATIC PROPORTION WAS SUBDUED BY LIVING PROPORTION — 485 MILTON 5 — 44

CURBING HIS LIVING CREATURES MANY OF THE STRONGEST GNOMES — 487 MILTON 7 — 48

AS ELYNITTRIA USED TO DO BUT TOO WELL THOSE LIVING CREATURES — 492 MILTON 12 — 12

THEY IN RETURN RETALIATED AND THE LIVING CREATURES MADDEND — 493 MILTON 12 — 35

FOR SEVEN DAYS OF ETERNITY AND THE RIVER'S LIVING BANKS — 503 MILTON 21 — 18

LIVING SELF MOVING MOURNING LAMENTING & HOWLING INCESSANTLY — 509 MILTON 24 — 53

AND ALL THE LIVING CREATURES OF THE FOUR ELEMENTS WAILD — 519 MILTON 31 — 17

CALLED ETERNAL ANNIHILATION THAT NONE BUT THE LIVING SHALL — 522 MILTON 32 — 27

OF LIVING FIBRES DOWN INTO THE SEA OF TIME & SPACE GROWING — 524 MILTON 34 — 25

SAYING I AM GOD THE JUDGE OF ALL THE LIVING & THE DEAD . — 530 MILTON 38 — 51

OR EVEN TO THEIR LIVING IN A PALACE BUT IT SHALL NOT BE — 575D DESC CAT 3 — PROSE

LIVING IN A COTTAGE AND IN CONTEMPT AND DERISION . . . — 575D DESC CAT 3 — PROSE

I FORBEAR TO NAME [A LI] LIVING ARTISTS THO EQUALLY WORTHY — 601B PUB ADDRESS/N — *PROSE

PARTICULARLY THE FOUR LIVING CREATURES . . . . . . — 612A V LAST JUDG/N — PROSE

THAT LIVING CREATURE ON THE LEFT OF THE THRONE GIVES — 612A V LAST JUDG/N — PROSE

THE OTHER LIVING CREATURES ARE DESCENDING WITH A SHOUT . — 612A V LAST JUDG/N — PROSE

WAS LIVING PANTING LIKE A FRIGHTED WOLF AND HOWLING . . — 625 JERUSALEM 7 — 1

FOR I AM ONE OF THE LIVING DARE NOT TO MOCK MY INSPIRED FURY — 627 JERUSALEM 8 — 35

THOU MIGHTEST BE PITIED & LOVD BUT NOW I AM LIVING UNLESS — 627 JERUSALEM 8 — 37

AND SEEING LIFE YET LIVING NOT HOW CAN I THEN BEHOLD — 630 JERUSALEM 10 — 58

BUT I AM LIVING YET I FEEL MY EMANATION ALSO DIVIDING . — 631 JERUSALEM 12 — 7

THE SOUTH A GOLDEN GATE HAS FOUR LIONS TERRIBLE LIVING . — 633 JERUSALEM 13 — 2

ITS GUARDS LIVING THE WORK OF ELEMENTAL HANDS LABORIOUS TASK — 633 JERUSALEM 13 — 7

THE SPECTRE OF THE LIVING PURSUING THE EMANATIONS OF THE DEAD — 638 JERUSALEM 17 — 13

SUBDUED BY THE SPECTRE OF THE LIVING & TERRIFIED BY UNDISGUISD DESIRE — 638 JERUSALEM 17 — 15

FOR LOS SAID THO MY SPECTRE IS DIVIDED AS I AM A LIVING MAN — 638 JERUSALEM 17 — 16

OF LIVING GOLD PURE PERFECT HOLY IN WHITE LINEN PURE HE HOVERD — 654 JERUSALEM 29 — 38

BORNE BY THE LIVING CREATURES OF THE THIRD PROCESSION . . — 667 JERUSALEM 40 — 22

OF HUMAN MAJESTY THE LIVING CREATURES WEPT ALOUD AS THEY — 667 JERUSALEM 40 — 23

THE LIVING & THE DEAD SHALL BE GROUND IN OUR RUMBLING MILLS — 673 JERUSALEM 43 — 49

A MURDEROUS PROVIDENCE A CREATION THAT GROANS LIVING ON DEATH — 681 JERUSALEM 50 — 5

AND THE VOICES OF THE LIVING CREATURES . . . . — 687 JERUSALEM 55 — 55

THE LIVING CREATURES MADDEND AND ALBION FELL INTO THE FURROW AND — 689 JERUSALEM 57 — 13

THE PLOW WENT OVER HIM & THE LIVING WAS PLOWED IN AMONG THE DEAD — 689 JERUSALEM 57 — 14

AMERICA NORTH & SOUTH ARE HIS BATHS OF LIVING WATERS . . — 690 JERUSALEM 58 — 43

WHEN THE FOUR ZOAS OF ALBION THE FOUR LIVING CREATURES THE CHERUBIM — 696 JERUSALEM 63 — 2

WHEREFORE ART THOU LIVING SAID LOS & MAN CANNOT LIVE IN THY PRESENCE — 698 JERUSALEM 64 — 18

THE SEXUAL DEATH LIVING ON ACCUSATION OF SIN & JUDGMENT — 699 JERUSALEM 64 — 22

AND LOS'S FURNACES HOWL LOUD LIVING SELF-MOVING LAMENTING — 713 JERUSALEM 73 — 2

I WALK IN AFFLICTION I AM A WORM AND NO LIVING SOUL . . — 721 JERUSALEM 80 — 3

IN HEAVEN THE ONLY ART OF LIVING . . . . — 724 IN HEAVEN/J — 1

THERE BELLS OF SILVER ROUND THY KNEES LIVING ARTICULATE — 731 JERUSALEM 86 — 29

FOUNTAINS OF LIVING WATERS FLOWING FROM THE HUMANITY DIVINE — 744 JERUSALEM 96 — 37

THE FOUR LIVING CREATURES . . . . — 745 JERUSALEM 98 — 24

ON CHARIOTS OF GOLD & JEWELS WITH LIVING CREATURES STARRY & FLAMING — 746 JERUSALEM 98 — 42

. . . FROM THE LIVING CREATURES OF THE EARTH . . . . . — 746 JERUSALEM 98 — 54

. . . AMONG THE LIVING CREATURES . . . . — 746 JERUSALEM 98 — 56

HUMAN FORMS IDENTIFIED LIVING GOING FORTH & RETURNING WEARIED — 747 JERUSALEM 99 — 2

	PAGE	TITLE	LINE

LIVING   (CONTINUED)

ONE DIES ALAS THE LIVING & DEAD   . . . .   771 OF GATES/GP   25
GRECIAN IS MATHEMATIC FORM GOTHIC IS LIVING FORM   . .   778D HOMERS POETRY   PROSE
LIVING FORM IS ETERNAL EXISTENCE   . . . .   778D HOMERS POETRY   PROSE
EVE I SEE HIM PLAINLY WITH MY MIND'S EYE I SEE ALSO ABEL   780 GHOST ABEL 1   23
   LIVING
THE BEST LIVING MODELS I PERCIEVE THAT YOUR EYE IS   793C LETTER 5   PROSE
   PERVERTED
HOPE SOON TO HEAR THAT YOU HAVE GOT A LIVING ONE OF BRASS   843A LETTER 42   *PROSE

LIZARD
FROM DOVER CLIFF TO LIZARD POINT THE OTHER TOWARD THE NORTH   512 MILTON 26   14
LIZARD-POINT
FROM CAITHNESS IN THE NORTH TO LIZARD-POINT & DOVER IN   485 MILTON 6   7
   THE SOUTH
TO LIZARD-POINT & DOVER IN THE SOUTH HIS EMANATION   . . .   728 JERUSALEM 83   71

LLEWELLYN
PLACE THE TRIBES OF LLEWELLYN IN AMERICA FOR A HIDING PLACE   728 JERUSALEM 83   59

LO
LO NOW THE DIREFUL MONSTER WHOSE SKIN CLINGS   . . . . . .   3 TO WINTER/PS   9
BUT LO THE MORNING PEEPS . . . .   9 MAD SONG/PS   5
LO TO THE VAULT . . . .   9 MAD SONG/PS   9
BUT LO THERE IS A GOD WHO MADE THE WORLD STRETCH OUT THY   36A COUCH DEATH/PS   PROSE
   HAND TO HIM
LO THEN HUMILITY TAKE IT AND WEAR IT IN THINE HEART   . . .   37A CONTEMPLATN/PS   PROSE
WHEN LO AN ANGEL FROM THE FIELDS OF LIGHT ENTERED THE HOUSE   39D SAMSON/PS   PROSE
FOR LO THOU SHALT CONCEIVE AND BEAR A SON   . . . . . .   39D SAMSON/PS   PROSE
AND LO AGAIN THE ANGEL CAME . . . .   40B SAMSON/PS   PROSE
LO THE BAT WITH LEATHERN WING   . . . .   54 LO THE BAT/IM   1
AND IN THE MORNING LO AN HUNDRED MEN IN GHASTLY DEATH . .   107 TIRIEL 5   29
SINCE ITS ADVENT THE ETERNAL HELL REVIVES AND LO   . . .   149A MARRIAGE HH 3   PROSE
AND LO IT WAS A DEEP PIT INTO WHICH I DESCENDED   . . .   157A MARRIAGE HH 17   PROSE
LO WHAT A FIEND IS HERE SAID HE   . . . .   177 LIT BOY LST/N   17
LO WHAT A FIEND IS HERE SAID HE   218 LIT BOY LST/SE   14
LO A SHADOW OF HORROR IS RISEN   . . . .   222 URIZEN 3   1
LO I UNFOLD MY DARKNESS AND ON   . . . .   224 URIZEN 4   31
LO THESE HUMAN FORMD SPIRITS IN SMILING HIPOCRISY WAR   . .   245 SONG OF LOS 3   13
NOR PITY THOU THE CRIES OF LUVAH LO THESE STARRY HOSTS   .   273 FOUR ZOAS 1   327
MEAN MISCHIEF MOST IF YOU ARE SUCH LO I AM ALSO SUCH   . .   273 FOUR ZOAS 1   332
LO I AM GOD THE TERRIBLE DESTROYER & NOT THE SAVIOUR . .   273 FOUR ZOAS 1   338
[ARISE O ENION ARISE FOR LO I HAVE CALMD MY SEAS]   . .   SUPP FOUR ZOAS 1   *
AND LOS SAID TO THE LILLY PALE & THE ROSE REDDNING FIERCE   288 FOUR ZOAS 2   302
AND LO THAT SON OF MAN THAT SHADOWY SPIRIT . . . . .   293 FOUR ZOAS 3   68
LO THE YOUNG LIMBS HAD STRUCKEN ROOT INTO THE ROCK & STRONG 309 FOUR ZOAS 5   156
LO THREE TERRIFIC WOMEN AT THE VERGE OF THE BRIGHT FLOOD   311 FOUR ZOAS 6   5
I RAGE IN THE DEEP FOR LO . . . .   322 FOUR ZOAS 7   71
I RAGE FURIOUS IN THE DEEP FOR LO MY FEET & HANDS ARE NAILD 322 FOUR ZOAS 7   87
LO HOW THE HEART & BRAIN ARE FORMED IN THE BREEDING WOMB   323 FOUR ZOAS 7   130
IN TWAIN & LO MY CRYSTAL FORM THAT LIVED IN MY BOSOM   . .   334 FOUR ZOAS 7B   65
UNLESS EXPOSD BY THEIR VAIN PARENTS LO HIM WHOM I LOVE . .   339 FOUR ZOAS 7B   246
THOU ART THAT RAHAB LO THE TOMB WHAT CAN WE PURPOSE MORE   351 FOUR ZOAS 8   407
LO ENITHARMON TERRIBLE & BEAUTIFUL IN ETERNAL YOUTH   . .   351 FOUR ZOAS 8   408
WHICH I HAVE MADE FOR LO [REMEMBRANCE] FUTURITY IS IN THIS   362 FOUR ZOAS 9   183
   MOMENT
IN RADIANT YOUTH WHEN LO LIKE GARLANDS IN THE EASTERN SKY   362 FOUR ZOAS 9   193
OR WHERE ARE HUMAN FEET FOR LO OUR EYES ARE IN THE HEAVENS   363 FOUR ZOAS 9   229
AND LO LIKE THE HARVEST MOON AHANIA CAST OFF HER DEATH   366 FOUR ZOAS 9   344
   CLOTHES
ARISE O ENION ARISE FOR LO I HAVE CALMD MY SEAS   . . . .   370 FOUR ZOAS 9   494
FOR LO THE WINTER MELTED AWAY UPON THE DISTANT HILLS   . .   373 FOUR ZOAS 9   600
LO THE LITTLE MOSS BEGINS TO SPRING & THE TENDER WEED . .   373 FOUR ZOAS 9   610
LO HOW THE POMP OF MYSTERY GOES DOWN INTO THE CAVES   . .   375 FOUR ZOAS 9   662
LO DARKNESS COVERS THE LONG POMP OF BANNERS ON THE WIND   375 FOUR ZOAS 9   666
AND LO MY BRETHREN IN THEIR TENTS & THEIR LITTLE   375 FOUR ZOAS 9   691
   ONES AROUND THEM
JUDGMENT AND LO IT FELL ON RINTRAH AND HIS RAGE   . . .   489 MILTON 9   10
RENEW IT TO ETERNAL LIFE LO I AM WITH YOU ALWAY   . . .   504 MILTON 21   56
LO ORC ARISES ON THE ATLANTIC LO HIS BLOOD AND FIRE   506 MILTON 21   6
AND IT IS THUS CREATED LO THE ETERNAL GREAT HUMANITY   519 MILTON 30   15
LO WE ARE ONE FORGIVING ALL EVIL NOT SEEKING RECOMPENSE   622 JERUSALEM 4   20
AND HARROWD FOR HIS PROFIT LO THY STOLEN EMANATION   . .   625 JERUSALEM 7   14
BECAUSE OF ALBION BECAUSE OF DECEIT AND FRIENDSHIP FOR LO   625 JERUSALEM 7   17
BE ATTENTIVE BE OBEDIENT LO THE FURNACES ARE READY   627 JERUSALEM 8   9
   TO RECIEVE THEE
THAT THOU CALLEST THY CHILDREN LO THE LAW OF GOD COMMANDS   629 JERUSALEM 10   38
BECOMING A BUILDING OF PITY AND COMPASSION LO . . .   632 JERUSALEM 12   29
LO HERE IS VALA'S VEIL WHOLE FOR A LAW A TERROR & A CURSE   646 JERUSALEM 23   32
AND LO THAT SON OF MAN THAT SHADOWY SPIRIT OF MILD ALBION   654 JERUSALEM 29   55
THE FLOOD AND WAS NAMD CHICHESTER LOVELY MILD & GENTLE LO   667 JERUSALEM 40   50
LO SHILOH DWELLS OVER FRANCE AS JERUSALEM DWELLS OVER   680 JERUSALEM 49   48
   ALBION
GIVE FORTH THY PITY & LOVE FEAR NOT LO I AM WITH   694 JERUSALEM 60   67
   THEE ALWAYS
ONLY BELIEVE & TRUST IN ME LO I AM ALWAYS WITH THEE   . . .   696 JERUSALEM 62   29
THYSELF FEMALE A MALE A BREEDER OF SEED A SON & HUSBAND   698 JERUSALEM 64   13
   & LO
AS THE MISTLETOE GROWS ON THE OAK SO ALBION'S TREE   703 JERUSALEM 66   55
   ON ETERNITY LO
O SKOFIELD WHY ART THOU CRUEL LO JOSEPH IS THINE TO MAKE   705 JERUSALEM 68   1
LO THEY SHOOT FORTH IN TENDER NERVES ACROSS EUROPE & ASIA   706 JERUSALEM 68   26
LO THEY REST UPON THE TRIBES WHERE THEIR PANTING VICTIMS   706 JERUSALEM 68   27
   LIE
THRO ALL THE FOUR POINTS LO THE LABOURERS AT THE FURNACES   713 JERUSALEM 73   4

	PAGE	TITLE	LINE

LO (CONTINUED)

SAYING LO JERUSALEM IS HERE SHE SITTETH IN OUR SECRET CHAMBERS — 720 JERUSALEM 79 — 29
FOR LO THE NIGHT OF DEATH IS PAST AND THE ETERNAL DAY — 744 JERUSALEM 97 — 3
IN THE WILDERNESS LO WHAT ARE THESE WHENCE CAME THEY — 776D INSC LAOCOON — PROSE
JEHOVAH LO I HAVE GIVEN YOU A LAMB FOR AN ATONEMENT INSTEAD — 780 GHOST ABEL 2 — 10

LOAD

HILLS FLED FROM OUR SIGHT BUT LEFT HIS GOLDEN LOAD — 2 TO AUTUMN/PS — 18
STRIPPED FROM HIS LOAD OF CLOATHING HE IS LIKE A DEAD CORPSE — 581A DESC CAT 5 — PROSE

LOADED

THE GODS ADMIRING LOADED HER WITH GIFTS AS ONCE PANDORA — 42D THEN SHE BORE — PROSE
THEN HE WENT UP STAIRS & LOADED THE MAID WITH GLASSES — 58C ISLAND MOON 10 — PROSE
AND IN THE VINTAGE & TO SING ON THE WAGGON LOADED WITH CORN — 290 FOUR ZOAS 2 — 403
LET THE BULLS OF LUVAH TREAD THE CORN & DRAW THE LOADED WAGGON — 376 FOUR ZOAS 9 — 701
BROUGHT UP THE LOADED WAGGONS WITH SHOUTINGS RAMPING TYGERS PLAY — 376 FOUR ZOAS 9 — 717
OF GLASS & PRECIOUS STONES THEY LOADED ALL THE WAGGONS OF HEAVEN — 378 FOUR ZOAS 9 — 793

LOADS SEE SHIP LOADS

HE LOADS IT WITH HELLISH BROWNNESS — 583A DESC CAT 9 — PROSE

LOAF

WHO WILL EXCHANGE HIS WHEATEN LOAF — 186 LET BROTHELS/N — 48
WHO WILL EXCHANGE HIS WHEATEN LOAF — 186 LET BROTHELS/N — 66

LOATHD

LOATHD AS A NATION'S BITTEREST CURSE — 748 EV GOSPEL(A)/N — 10

LOATHE

OUGHT BUT THE VEGETABLE RATIO & LOATHE THE FAINT DELIGHT — 485 MILTON 5 — 35
THAT HE WHO LOVES JESUS MAY LOATHE TERRIFIED FEMALE LOVE — 733 JERUSALEM 88 — 20
SHE WHO ADORES NOT YOUR FROWNS WILL ONLY LOATHE YOUR SMILES — 743 JERUSALEM 95 — 24
ENTERD INTO ME AS INTO HIS HOUSE & I LOATHE THY TABERNACLES — 780 GHOST ABEL 2 — 6

LOATHED

THE BOUNDED IS LOATHED BY ITS POSSESSOR — 97D NAT RELIGION 2 — PROSE
DESOLATE LOATHED DUMB [CON] ASTONISHD WAITING FOR BLACK DEATH — 107 TIRIEL 5 — * 35

LOATHES

IN SPELLS OF LAW TO ONE SHE LOATHES AND MUST SHE DRAG THE CHAIN — 193 V DAU ALBION 5 — 22

LOATHING

BY ENGLISH TRADERS MUST [LOA] FEEL A LOATHING — 596B PUB ADDRESS/N — *PROSE
WAS CAST OUT TO THE LOATHING OF HER PERSON THE CHALDEAN TOOK — 695 JERUSALEM 61 — 40

LOATHS

TILL THE CHILD DWELL WITH ONE HE HATES AND DO THE DEED HE LOATHS — 193 V DAU ALBION 5 — 30

LOATHSOM

FROM WHENCE A RIVER SPRINGS MOST BLACK & LOATHSOM — 41C THEN SHE BORE — PROSE
ARE LOATHSOM FINE TINTS WITHOUT FINE FORMS — 591C PUB ADDRESS/N — *PROSE
THE MOST LOATHSOM MIRTH IS BETTER THAN FUN — 793C LETTER 5 — PROSE

LOATHSOME

MY BREATH IS LOATHSOME HOW SHOULD HE NOT BE OFFENDED — 36A COUCH DEATH/PS — PROSE
. . . A LOATHSOME SICK WOMAN BOUND DOWN — 135 FRENCH REVOLTN — 35

LOATHSOMEST

RISE UP THY SLUGGISH LIMBS & LET THE LOATHSOMEST OF POISONS — 106 TIRIEL 5 — 9

LOAVES

GREATER MIRACLE TO FEED FIVE THOUSAND MEN WITH FIVE LOAVES — 391C ANNO WATSON — MARG

LOCK

O AY LOCK SAID SCOPPRELL [XXX ?ABOUT] — 52D ISLAND MOON 8 — *PROSE
THE CITIZENS OF NEW-YORK CLOSE THEIR BOOKS & LOCK THEIR CHESTS — 201 AMERICA 14 — 13
WHAT CHAIN ENCOMPASSES IN WHAT LOCK IS THE RIVER OF LIGHT CONFIND — 363 FOUR ZOAS 9 — 226

LOCKD

WERE ALL OF THEM LOCKD UP IN COFFINS OF BLACK — 117 CHIMNEY SWP/SI — 12
EACH STERN VISAGE LOCKD UP AS WITH STRONG BANDS OF IRON — 137 FRENCH REVOLTN — 66
AND LOCKD IN HIS SOUL WITH A NINEFOLD KEY — 187 WHEN KLOPSTK/N — 18
IN EACH OTHER LINK BY LINK LOCKD — 233 URIZEN 20 — 20
FORGETFULNESS DUMBNESS NECESSITY IN CHAINS OF THE MIND LOCKD UP — 303 FOUR ZOAS 4 — 211
FALLING DOWN ON THE ROCK AN IRON CHAIN LINK BY LINK LOCKD — 307 FOUR ZOAS 5 — 91
AND LOCKD ME UP WITH A GOLDEN KEY — 429 CRYSTL CABINET — 4
URIZEN LAY IN DARKNESS & SOLITUDE IN CHAINS OF THE MIND LOCKD UP — 482 MILTON 3 — 6

LOCKE

BY JOHN LOOKYE [?PANTRYMAN] GENT JOHN LOCKE SAID OBTUSE ANGLE — 52D ISLAND MOON 8 — PROSE
OR LOCKE OR DOCTOR SOUTH — 57 TO BE OR/IM — 4
AS LOCKE OR DOCTOR SOUTH — 57 TO BE OR/IM — 28
URIZEN WEPT & GAVE IT INTO THE HANDS OF NEWTON & LOCKE — 246 SONG OF LOS 4 — 17
& SO DID LOCKE — 385D ANNO WATSON — MARG
IS FOUNDED ON THE OPINIONS OF NEWTON & LOCKE — 476D ANNO REYNOLDS — MARG
AT THE SAME TIME I READ LOCKE ON HUMAN — 476D ANNO REYNOLDS — MARG
ART THOU NOT NEWTON'S PANTOCRATOR WEAVING THE WOOF OF LOCKE — 483 MILTON 4 — 11
TO CAST OFF BACON LOCKE & NEWTON FROM ALBION'S COVERING — 533 MILTON 41 — 5
IT IS ALSO CALLED THE BARREN WASTE OF LOCKE AND NEWTON — 581B DESC CAT 6 — TITLE
AND THEN BEHOLD THE LOOM OF LOCKE WHOSE WOOF RAGES DIRE — 636 JERUSALEM 15 — 15
CONVERSE CONCERNING WEIGHT & DISTANCE IN THE WILDS OF NEWTON & LOCKE — 661 JERUSALEM 34 — 40
AM I NOT BACON & NEWTON & LOCKE WHO TEACH HUMILITY TO MAN — 685 JERUSALEM 54 — 17

```
                                                                    PAGE     TITLE        LINE
LOCKE   (CONTINUED)
     FROZEN SONS OF THE FEMININE TABERNACLE OF BACON NEWTON        702 JERUSALEM 66      14
       & LOCKE
     AND THERE THEY COMBINE INTO THREE FORMS NAMED BACON           708 JERUSALEM 70      15
       & NEWTON & LOCKE
     TO OCCUPY THE VERY THRESHOLD OF ETERNAL LIFE IF BACON         741 JERUSALEM 93      21
       NEWTON LOCKE
     AND BACON & NEWTON & LOCKE & MILTON & SHAKSPEAR & CHAUCER     745 JERUSALEM 98       9
     FROM BACON NEWTON AND LOCKE . . . . . . . . . . .      772D ANNO SPURZHEIM    MARG
     LOCKE SAYS IT SAME FACULTY THAT INVENTS JUDGES . . . .     790C LETTER 2         PROSE
LOCKED
     OOTHOON WEEPS NOT SHE CANNOT WEEP HER TEARS ARE LOCKED UP     190 V DAU ALBION 2    11
     IN CHAINS OF THE MIND LOCKED UP  . . . . . . . .   228 URIZEN 10        25
LOCKE'S
     LOCKE'S OPINIONS OF WORDS & THEIR FALLACIOUSNESS . . . .   474C ANNO REYNOLDS   MARG
LOCKS
     O THOU WITH DEWY LOCKS WHO LOOKEST DOWN . . . . . .      1 TO SPRING/PS        1
     INTO THE BATTLE SHAKING HIS GOLDEN LOCKS . . . . . .    21 EDW THIRD/PS 3      4
     LET SNAKES RISE FROM THY BEDDED LOCKS & LAUGH AMONG THY      108 TIRIEL 6          43
       CURLS
     AND WEEP [AND BOW THY REVEREND LOCKS]  . . . . . .   159B SONG LIBERTY      PROSE
     AND HER LOCKS COVERD WITH GREY DESPAIR  . . . . . .   168 EARTHS ANSWR/N      5
     HIS VOICE HIS LOCKS HIS AWFUL SHOULDERS AND HIS GLOWING      197 AMERICA 3        17
       EYES
     HIS VOICE HIS LOCKS HIS AWFUL SHOULDERS & HIS GLOWING EYES   204 AMERICA CANC A   17
     AND HER LOCKS COVERD WITH GREY DESPAIR  . . . . . .   210 EARTHS ANSR/SE      5
     DRIVEN OUT BY THE FLAMES OF ORC HIS FURRD ROBES & FALSE      242 EUROPE 12        16
       LOCKS
     TILL COVET BROKE HIS LOCKS & BARS  . . . . . . .   256 BOOK OF LOS 3      20
     THE ECCHO WAKES THE MOON TO UNBIND HER SILVER LOCKS  . . .   289 FOUR ZOAS 2      346
     . . . & HER LOCKS WERE SPREAD ON THE PAVEMENT  . . . .   293 FOUR ZOAS 3       56
     AND THOU HAST RISEN WITH THY MOIST LOCKS INTO A WATRY IMAGE  295 FOUR ZOAS 3      125
     . . . HIS LOCKS ARE LIKE THE FORESTS  . . . . . .   308 FOUR ZOAS 5      127
     AND THY FAIR LOCKS SHADOW THINE EYES FROM THE DIVINE         311 FOUR ZOAS 5      231
       EFFULGENCE
     HAIR WHITE AS SNOW COVERD HIM IN FLAKY LOCKS TERRIFIC   . .   318 FOUR ZOAS 6      240
     ENITHARMON SPREAD HER BEAMING LOCKS UPON THE WIND & SAID     331 FOUR ZOAS 7    * 446
     . . . THE TEARS FROM THY SILVER LOCKS  . . . . . .   338 FOUR ZOAS 7B     194
     ALL POWERFUL AND HIS LOCKS FLOURISH LIKE THE BROWS           509 MILTON 24        70
       OF MORNING
     AS ABRAHAM FLEES FROM CHALDEA SHAKING HIS GOARY LOCKS   . .   636 JERUSALEM 15     28
     FORTHWITH FROM ALBION'S DARKNING LOCKS CAME TWO IMMORTAL     654 JERUSALEM 29     28
       FORMS
     . . . & HER LOCKS WERE SPREAD ON THE PAVEMENT  . . . .   654 JERUSALEM 29     43
     STORMS & PESTILENCE IN HER LOCKS & IN HER LOINS EARTHQUAKE   698 JERUSALEM 64     10
     . . . THE TEARS FROM THY SILVER LOCKS  . . . . . .   700 JERUSALEM 65     40
     THEY PUT ASIDE HIS CURLS THEY DIVIDE HIS SEVEN LOCKS UPON    702 JERUSALEM 66     22
     INORBD AND BONIFIED WITH LOCKS OF SHADOWING MODESTY SHINING  709 JERUSALEM 70     22
LOCUSTS
     HAIL LOCUSTS DARKNESS FIRST BORN XXX RED SEA EGYPTIANS      SUPP EXODUS/N      *PROSE
       DROWND
LODGE
     & THEY HAVE BLACK SERVANTS LODGE AT THEIR HOUSE  . . . .    53A ISLAND MOON 8    PROSE
     AGAINST SUCH AS REFUSED TO LODGE THEM I TELL YOU  . . . .   158C MARRIAGE HH 22   PROSE
     WE HAVE ONE ROOM IN WHICH WE COULD MAKE A BED TO LODGE YOU   808B LETTER 19       PROSE
LODGED
     WITH MR ROMNEY MR ROMNEY LODGED AT MR RICHTER'S   . . . .   847D LETTER 44       PROSE
LODGING
     SAYS WAS THE LODGING OF THE ABBOT OF HYDE BY WINCHESTER      567B DESC CAT 3      PROSE
     SAYS WAS THE LODGING OF THE ABBOT OF HYDE BY WINCHESTER      588D CHAUCER/N       PROSE
     SAYS WAS THE LODGING OF THE ABBOT OF HYDE BY WINCHESTER      590C CHAUCER 2       PROSE
     EITHER IN MY COTTAGE OR IN A (LODGING) IN THE VILLAGE   . .   808C LETTER 19       PROSE
LODGING HOUSE
     "THE LODGING HOUSE FOR PILGRIMS" . . . . . . . .   590C CHAUCER 2       PROSE
LODGINGS
     LODGINGS & FIND THEM ALL TOO GRAND AS WELL AS  . . . .   848A LETTER 45       PROSE
LODGYNGE
     THE LODGYNGE HOUSE FOR PILGRIMS WHO JOURNEY  . . . . .   SUPP ILLUS CHAUCER *TITLE
LODGYNG HOUSE
     "BY HENRY BAILLY THE LODGYNG HOUSE FOR PILGRIMS"  . . . .   589A CHAUCER/N       PROSE
LOFTINESS
     FIRMNESS I HAVE BROUGHT DOWN HIS AFFECTED LOFTINESS  . . .   825C LETTER 27       PROSE
LOFTY
     THE BOSOM OF THE LOFTY HILL DRANK IN THE SILENT DEW  . . .    36C COUCH DEATH/PS  PROSE
     VAIN FOOLISH MAN THAT ROAMS ON LOFTY ROCKS  . . . . .    37A CONTEMPLATN/PS PROSE
     AS ON A LOFTY ROCK WITH IRON PENS THE WORDS OF TRUTH   . .    37D SAMSON/PS       PROSE
     HE CEAST THE HEAVY CLOUDS CONFUSD ROLLD ROUND THE LOFTY      106 TIRIEL 5         14
       TOWERS
     ON CANTERBURY'S RUINS HIS RIGHT HAND COVERS LOFTY WALES      531 MILTON 39        41
     STARTS FROM HIS LOFTY PLACES & CASTS DOWN HIS TENTS & FLEES  729 JERUSALEM 84     24
       AWAY
LOG
     THE OAKEN LOG LAY ON THE FIRE  . . . . . . . . .    16 BLIND-MANS/PS      6
LOINS
     INVULNERABLE THO NAKED SAVE WHERE CLOUDS ROLL ROUND HER      196 AMERICA PREL 1     7
       LOINS
     ROUND THE TERRIFIC LOINS HE SIEZD THE PANTING STRUGGLING     196 AMERICA PREL 2     3
       WOMB
     ROUND ENITHARMON'S LOINS FOLDING . . . . . . . .   232 URIZEN 19        28
     THE COLD LOINS OF URIZEN DIVIDING  . . . . . . . .   249 AHANIA 2         29
     ARISE IN ALL HIS VEINS HE THREW HIS ARMS AROUND HER LOINS    274 FOUR ZOAS 1      353
     BURSTING FORTH FROM THE LOINS OF ENITHARMON THOU FIERCE      276 FOUR ZOAS 1      430
       TERROR
```

```
LOINS    (CONTINUED)
    AND OF HER FINE WROUGHT BRAIN & OF HER BOWELS WITHIN HER       279 FOUR ZOAS 1         562
      LOINS
    FROM ALBION'S LOINS FLED ALL PEOPLES AND NATIONS OF THE        281 FOUR ZOAS 2     *   43
      EARTH [FLED ]
    [?LOS] REASONING FROM THE LOINS IN THE UNREAL FORMS OF         283 FOUR ZOAS 2     *   112
      ULRO'S NIGHT
    AND LUVAH IN THE LOINS OF LOS A DARK & FURIOUS DEATH    . .    292 FOUR ZOAS 3         22
    MY LOINS BEGIN TO BREAK FORTH INTO VEINY PIPES & WRITHE        300 FOUR ZOAS 4         94
    DIVIDING & DIVIDING FROM MY LOINS A WEAK & PITEOUS    . . .    300 FOUR ZOAS 4         98
    UNWILLING MOVD AS URIZEN HOWLD HIS LOINS WAVD LIKE THE SEA     305 FOUR ZOAS 4         289
    HIS LOINS INWOVE WITH SILKEN FIRES ARE LIKE A FURNACE          308 FOUR ZOAS 5         135
      FIERCE
    AN EARTH OF WINTRY WOE BENEATH THEIR FEET & ROUND THEIR        314 FOUR ZOAS 6         92
      LOINS
    ROUND HIS LOINS A GIRDLE GLOWD WITH MANY COLOURD FIRES  . .    319 FOUR ZOAS 6         304
    FROM THY SWEET LOINS OF BLISS RED FLOWD THY BLOOD    . . .     325 FOUR ZOAS 7         226
    OPEND WITHIN YOUR HEART & LOINS & WONDROUS BRAIN    . . . .    329 FOUR ZOAS 7         354
    THREEFOLD WITHIN THE BRAIN WITHIN THE HEART WITHIN THE         329 FOUR ZOAS 7         381
      LOINS
    BATHED IN BLOODY CLOUDS HIS LOINS IN FIRES OF WAR WHERE        334 FOUR ZOAS 7B        43
      SPEARS
    OPEND WITHIN THEIR HEARTS & IN THEIR LOINS & IN THEIR BRAIN    342 FOUR ZOAS 8         55
    PRESS IT AROUND THE LOINS OF THIS EXPANDING CRUELTY   . . .    349 FOUR ZOAS 8         313
    THEN HE BEGAN TO SOW THE SEED HE GIRDED ROUND HIS LOINS        365 FOUR ZOAS 9         321
    THEN MY LOINS FADE & IN THE HOUSE I SIT ME DOWN & WEEP   . .   371 FOUR ZOAS 9         544
    OPEND WITHIN THE HEART & IN THE LOINS & IN THE BRAIN    . .    382 FOUR ZOAS AD 6      25
    AROUND THEIR LOINS POURD FORTH THEIR ARROWS & THEIR BOSOMS     484 MILTON 4           23
      BEAM
    TRANSLUCENT IN THEIR FOREHEADS & THEIR BOSOMS & THEIR LOINS    484 MILTON 5            8
    OF SATAN IN ITS WEBS FOR IN BRAIN AND HEART AND LOINS   . .    502 MILTON 20           38
    WHICH IS THE SPIRITUAL FOURFOLD LONDON IN THE LOINS OF         502 MILTON 20           40
      ALBION
    THE THIRD IN THE LOINS & SEMINAL VESSELS & THE FOURTH   . .    524 MILTON 34           15
    STARRY & GLORIOUS AND THEY EVERY ONE IN THEIR BRIGHT LOINS     635 JERUSALEM 14        19
    FROM THE LIMIT NOAH TO THE LIMIT ABRAM IN WHOSE LOINS   . .    636 JERUSALEM 15        26
    HOARSE TURND THE STARRY WHEELS RENDING A WAY IN ALBION'S       641 JERUSALEM 18        44
      LOINS
    . . . THE MOON FROM HIS MIGHTY LOINS . . . . . . . .  .        647 JERUSALEM 24        10
    ALBION'S SPECTRE FROM HIS LOINS    . . . . . . . . . .         650 FIELDS FROM/J       37
    IN THE LOINS OF ABRAHAM & DAVID    . . . . . . . . . .        652B JERUSALEM 27       PROSE
    COLD SNOWS DRIFTED AROUND HIM ICE COVERD HIS LOINS AROUND      652 JERUSALEM 28        13
    ALBION HATH ENTERD THE LOINS THE PLACE OF THE LAST JUDGMENT    656 JERUSALEM 30        38
    FROM THE BACK & LOINS WHERE DWELL THE SPECTROUS DEAD    . .    659 JERUSALEM 33        4
    LUVAH TORE FORTH FROM ALBION'S LOINS IN FIBROUS VEINS IN       677 JERUSALEM 47        4
      RIVERS
    IN THE ERYTHREAN SEA THEIR (UNCIRCUMCISION) IN HEART &         680 JERUSALEM 49    *   44
      LOINS
    TO SIEZE THE SONS OF JERUSALEM & PLANT THEM IN ONE MAN'S       686 JERUSALEM 55        14
      LOINS
    BOTH OF THE HEAD & HEART & LOINS CLOSD UP IN MORAL PRIDE       693 JERUSALEM 60        49
    STORMS & PESTILENCE IN HER LOCKS & IN HER LOINS EARTHQUAKE     698 JERUSALEM 64        10
    PRESS IT AROUND THE LOINS OF THIS EVER EXPANDING CRUELTY       705 JERUSALEM 67        60
    HER BRAIN ENLABYRINTHS THE WHOLE HEAVEN OF HER BOSOM &         709 JERUSALEM 70        29
      LOINS
    SHE HID THEM IN HIS LOINS RAVING HE RAN AMONG THE ROCKS        723 JERUSALEM 80        76
    UPON HER BACK BEHIND HER LOINS & THUS UTTERD HER DECEIT        725 JERUSALEM 82        21
    SEE HOW THE FIRES OF OUR LOINS POINT EASTWARD TO BABYLON       725 JERUSALEM 82        36
    BUT PANGS OF LOVE DRAW ME DOWN TO MY LOINS WHICH ARE    . .    727 JERUSALEM 82        83
    FILLING WITH FIBRES FROM HIS LOINS WHICH REDDEND              732 JERUSALEM 86        51
      WITH DESIRE
    EVEN ENITHARMON SEPARATED OUTSIDE & HIS LOINS CLOSED   . .     732 JERUSALEM 86        58
    HIS LOINS INCLOSE BABYLON ON EUPHRATES BEAUTIFUL    . . .      735 JERUSALEM 89        38
    HIS HEART & WHILE THEY CIRCUMSCRIBE HIS LOINS A VEIL & NET     736 JERUSALEM 90        4
    IN THE LOINS OF ALBION THE CANAANITE UNITED WITH              739 JERUSALEM 92        3
      THE FUGITIVE
    HIS LOINS & BOSOM UNREMOVABLE BY SWELLING STORMS & LOUD        741 JERUSALEM 94        10
      RENDING
LONDON
    POETICAL SKETCHES BY W B LONDON MISCELLANEOUS POEMS    . .      1A POET SKETCHES     TITLE
    WITH HIS WHITE WINGS AND SEES HIS GOLDEN LONDON    . . . .     19 EDW THIRD/PS 2      10
    TO DINE TO-MORROW WITH THE MAYOR OF LONDON    . . . . . .      20 EDW THIRD/PS 2      42
    VERY PRITTY & FUNNY [ABOUT LONDON O NO] ABOUT MATCHES   .     54D ISLAND MOON 9    *PROSE
    O WHAT A MULTITUDE THEY SEEMD THESE FLOWERS OF LONDON TOWN     59 HOLY THURS/IM       5
    O WHAT A MULTITUDE THEY SEEMD THESE FLOWERS OF LONDON TOWN    122 HOLY THURS/SI       5
    LONDON PRINTED FOR J JOHNSON MDCCXCI . . . . . . . . .       134A FRENCH REVOLTN    TITLE
    LOOK UP LOOK UP O CITIZEN OF LONDON ENLARGE THY              159C SONG LIBERTY     PROSE
      COUNTENANCE
    LONDON . . . . . . . . . . . . . . . . . . . . .            170A LONDON/N          TITLE
    THE FIRE OF LONDON [CH(CHARLES) I BEHEADED]    . . . . .     209A SUBJCTS HIST/N   TITLE
    LONDON . . . . . . . . . . . . . . . . . . . . .            216C LONDON/SE         TITLE
    BLEAK DARK ABRUPT IT STANDS & OVERSHADOWS LONDON CITY   . .   242 EUROPE 12           9
    ANOTHER LONDON WITH ITS TOWER    . . . . . . . . . .          429 CRYSTL CABINET     10
    FROM GOLGONOOZA THE SPIRITUAL FOUR-FOLD LONDON ETERNAL  .     485 MILTON 6            1
    FROM LONDON STONE TO BLACKHEATH EAST TO HOUNSLOW WEST   .     485 MILTON 6            4
    BEFORE LONDON TO HAMPSTEAD'S BREADTHS & HIGHGATE'S HEIGHTS    485 MILTON 6            9
      TO
    WHICH IS THE SPIRITUAL FOURFOLD LONDON IN THE LOINS OF        502 MILTON 20           40
      ALBION
    HIS ROCKS LONDON & BATH & LEGIONS & EDINBURGH    . . . .      531 MILTON 39           35
    ARE THE FOUR PILLARS OF HIS THRONE HIS LEFT FOOT             531 MILTON 39           36
      NEAR LONDON
```

```
                                                            PAGE    TITLE       LINE
LONDON   (CONTINUED)
    LONDON IS BETWEEN HIS KNEES ITS BASEMENTS FOURFOLD  . . .   531 MILTON 39       39
    HIS HEAD BENDS OVER LONDON HE SEES HIS EMBODIED SPECTRE     531 MILTON 39       46
    THEIR CLOUDS ROLL OVER LONDON WITH A SOUTH WIND SOFT        535 MILTON 42       32
        OOTHOON
    OVER LONDON IN VOLUME TERRIFIC LOW BENDED IN ANGER  . . .   535 MILTON 42       35
    LONDON PRINTED BY D N SHURY...BERWICK-STREET SOHO     .   563B DESC CAT      PROSE
    HAS HERE ALSO INTRODUCED ONE OF THE RICH CITIZENS OF LONDON 568C DESC CAT 3   PROSE
    FOR SUCH WAS THE TABARDE INN IN SOUTHWARK NEAR LONDON   .   569D DESC CAT 3   PROSE
    PHYSICIAN AND ON HIS OTHER HAND WITH TWO CITIZENS OF LONDON 570D DESC CAT 3   PROSE
    OF WATLING-STREET OF LONDON STONE OF THE CAVERNS IN   . . . 577D DESC CAT 5   PROSE
    D N SHURY PRINTER BERWICK-STREET SOHO LONDON    . . . .   586B DESC CAT 16    TITLE
    G SMEETON PRINTER...ST MARTINS LANE LONDON  . . . . .     590D CHAUCER 2      TITLE
    THE VOID IN (INCOHERENT) DESPAIR CAMBRIDGE & OXFORD         623 JERUSALEM 5        3
        & LONDON
    GROANING HE KNEELD BEFORE LOS'S IRON-SHOD FEET ON LONDON    627 JERUSALEM 8       27
        STONE
    THEREFORE LOS STANDS IN LONDON BUILDING GOLGONOOZA   . . .  629 JERUSALEM 10      17
    I SEE IN DEADLY FEAR IN LONDON LOS RAGING ROUND HIS ANVIL   636 JERUSALEM 15      21
    IN THE EXCHANGES OF LONDON EVERY NATION WALKD  . . . . .    647 JERUSALEM 24      42
    AND LONDON WALKD IN EVERY NATION MUTUAL IN LOVE & HARMONY   647 JERUSALEM 24      43
    THEY GROAND ALOUD ON LONDON STONE  . . . . . . . .          650 FIELDS FROM/J     33
    LONDON IS A STONE OF HER RUINS OXFORD IS THE DUST OF HER    653 JERUSALEM 29      19
        WALLS
    THE CITIES OF ALBION SEEK THY FACE LONDON GROANS IN PAIN    656 JERUSALEM 30      23
    HE CAME DOWN FROM HIGHGATE THRO HACKNEY & HOLLOWAY TOWARDS  657 JERUSALEM 31      14
        LONDON
    TO WHERE THE TOWER OF LONDON FROWND DREADFUL OVER JERUSALEM 657 JERUSALEM 31      23
    AT LENGTH HE SAT ON LONDON STONE & HEARD JERUSALEM'S VOICE  657 JERUSALEM 31      43
    OF LONDON BUT THE INTERIORS OF ALBION'S FIBRES & NERVES     658 JERUSALEM 32       4
        WERE HIDDEN
    BATTERSEA & CHELSEA MOURN LONDON & CANTERBURY TREMBLE       659 JERUSALEM 33      12
    I BEHOLD LONDON A HUMAN AWFUL WONDER OF GOD    . . . .      665 JERUSALEM 38      29
    SO SPOKE LONDON IMMORTAL GUARDIAN I HEARD IN LAMBETH'S      665 JERUSALEM 38      40
        SHADES
    AND DESPAIR AS MESHES CLOSELY WOVE OVER THE WEST OF LONDON  668 JERUSALEM 41       9
    BRING HIM TO JUSTICE BEFORE HEAVEN HERE UPON LONDON STONE   670 JERUSALEM 42      50
    VERULAM LONDON YORK EDINBURGH MOURNING ONE TOWARDS ANOTHER  676 JERUSALEM 46      24
    LONDON CONTINUALLY BUILDING & CONTINUALLY DECAYING          684 JERUSALEM 53      19
        DESOLATE
    YORK LONDON JERUSALEM   . . . . . . . . . . .             689A JERUSALEM 57   *TITLE
    ROUND THE ROCKY PEAK OF DERBYSHIRE LONDON STONE & ROSAMONDS 689 JERUSALEM 57       7
        BOWER
    OF WAR REELING UP THE STREET OF LONDON SHE DIVIDES IN TWAIN 689 JERUSALEM 58    *   3
    FROM STONE-HENGE AND FROM LONDON STONE FROM CORNWALL        690 JERUSALEM 58      46
        TO CATHNES
    VERULAM LONDON YORK & EDINBURGH THEIR ENGLISH NAMES    .    691 JERUSALEM 59      14
    LOS ON THE THAMES & MEDWAY LONDON & CANTERBURY GROAN IN     698 JERUSALEM 63      35
        PAIN
    THE HAMMER & THE CHISEL & THE RULE & COMPASSES FROM LONDON  699 JERUSALEM 65      13
        FLEEING
    WE WERE CARRIED AWAY IN THOUSANDS FROM LONDON & IN TENS     700 JERUSALEM 65      33
    OF ROCKS ROUND LONDON STONE OF REASONINGS OF UNHEWN         702 JERUSALEM 66       3
        DEMONSTRATIONS
    THEY LOOK FORTH FROM STONE-HENGE FROM THE COVE ROUND        703 JERUSALEM 66      57
        LONDON STONE
    LONDON FEELS HIS BRAIN CUT ROUND EDINBURGH'S HEART         703 JERUSALEM 66      64
        IS CIRCUMSCRIBED
    ALL THESE CENTER IN LONDON & IN GOLGONOOZA FROM WHENCE  . . 712 JERUSALEM 72      28
    FROM LONDON TO YORK & EDINBURGH THE FURNACES RAGE TERRIBLE  714 JERUSALEM 73      53
    THESE FOUR ARE VERULAM & LONDON & YORK & EDINBURGH   . . .  714 JERUSALEM 74       3
    I BEHOLD BABYLON IN THE OPENING STREETS OF LONDON I BEHOLD  714 JERUSALEM 74      16
    ON LONDON STONE & THE DAUGHTERS OF ALBION RAN AROUND        715 JERUSALEM 74      34
        ADMIRING
    LONDON COVERD THE WHOLE EARTH ENGLAND ENCOMPASSD           720 JERUSALEM 79      22
        THE NATIONS
    MY PILLARS REACHD FROM SEA TO SEA LONDON BEHELD ME COME     720 JERUSALEM 79      24
    TOWARDS LONDON THEN THEY SAW THE (FURNACES) OPEND & IN      726 JERUSALEM 82      78
        TEARS
    FOUND YE LONDON ENORMOUS CITY WEEPS THY RIVER  . . . .      727 JERUSALEM 83      23
    OF LONDON CITY ON THE THAMES FROM SURREY HILLS TO HIGHGATE  728 JERUSALEM 83      68
    I SEE LONDON BLIND & AGE-BENT BEGGING THRO THE STREETS  . . 729 JERUSALEM 84      11
    IN STONE-HENGE & ON LONDON STONE & IN THE OAK GROVES OF     742 JERUSALEM 94      24
        MALDEN
    BORN...(NOVEMBER)...IN LONDON & HAS DIED SEVERAL TIMES     781D INSC UPCOTT    PROSE
        SINCE
    EXTRAORDINARY THAT LONDON IN SO FEW YEARS FROM A CITY OF   798B LETTER 10     PROSE
    WE REMEMBER WHEN A PRINT SHOP WAS A RARE BIRD IN LONDON    798C LETTER 10     PROSE
    "HUNDRED FOR THE TERRIBLE DESART OF LONDON WAS BETWEEN"    800B LETTER 12     PROSE
    BECAUSE IT IS MORE SPIRITUAL THAN LONDON   . . . . . .    802A LETTER 14     PROSE
    MODEST MEAT IS CHEAPER THAN IN LONDON BUT THE SWEET AIR &  803B LETTER 15     PROSE
    MUCH MILDER THAN IT WAS IN LONDON WHEN WE CAME AWAY   . .  806B LETTER 16     PROSE
    ARE GENUINE SAXONS HANDSOMER THAN THE PEOPLE [AR ] ABOUT   806B LETTER 16    *PROSE
        LONDON
    SHE HAS NOT PRINTED ANY MORE SINCE YOU WENT TO LONDON BUT  807A LETTER 17     PROSE
        WE CAN
    TIME FLIES FASTER AS SEEMS TO ME HERE THAN IN LONDON   . . 809A LETTER 20     PROSE
    AS THE COACH GOES THREE TIMES A WEEK TO LONDON &          809B LETTER 20    *PROSE
        THEY [ SHALL ]
    SO NEAR TO FELPHAM PARIS BEING SCARCE FURTHER OFF THAN     811A LETTER 21     PROSE
        LONDON
    PAINTING & ENGRAVING WHICH IN THE CONFUSION OF LONDON   . . 812B LETTER 22    PROSE
```

1117

```
                                                            PAGE     TITLE        LINE
LONDON    (CONTINUED)
      REMAIN ANOTHER WINTER HERE BUT TO RETURN TO LONDON  . . .  813C LETTER 22    PROSE
      AS THAT TO YOU FOR I TOLD YOU THAT I SHOULD COME TO LONDON 820B LETTER 25    PROSE
      OF WHAT WAS DOING IN LONDON IN WORKS OF ART BUT I DID  .   820C LETTER 25    PROSE
      PERHAPS LAVANT & IN OR NEAR THE ROAD TO LONDON FOR THE  .  820D LETTER 25    PROSE
      & ALSO VERY AFRAID THAT MY FRIENDS IN LONDON SHOULD HAVE   820D LETTER 25    PROSE
      LONDON WITH THE FULL APPROBATION OF MR HAYLEY & WITH  .    822C LETTER 26    PROSE
      CARRY ON MY VISIONARY STUDIES IN LONDON UNANNOYD  . . .    822C LETTER 26    PROSE
      TO LONDON AGAIN APPLAUDS IT AS THE ONLY COURSE FOR THE  .  822D LETTER 26    PROSE
      LONDON AFFORDS OF SEEING FINE PICTURES AND THE VARIOUS  .  823A LETTER 26    PROSE
      IMPROVEMENTS IN WORKS OF ART GOING ON IN LONDON BUT  . .   823A LETTER 26    PROSE
      TOWARD OUR MEETING AGAIN IN LONDON WITH THOSE WHOM WE  .   824B LETTER 27    PROSE
      & I DO ASSURE YOU THAT IF I COULD HAVE RETURND TO LONDON   825D LETTER 27    PROSE
      OUR RETURN TO LONDON DRAWS ON APACE OUR EXPECTATION OF  .  826B LETTER 28    PROSE
      BE WORTH ARRIVED SAFE IN LONDON MY WIFE IN VERY POOR HEALTH 829D LETTER 30   PROSE
      ART IN LONDON FLOURISHES ENGRAVERS IN PARTICULAR ARE WANTED 829D LETTER 30   PROSE
      THE SHOPS IN LONDON IMPROVE EVERY THING IS ELEGANT CLEAN   831D LETTER 31    PROSE
      NEVER YET SINCE MY RETURN TO LONDON HAD THE TIME OR GRACE  836C LETTER 35    PROSE
      YOU CAN HAVE NO IDEA UNLESS YOU WAS IN LONDON AS I AM  .   841B LETTER 41    PROSE
      TO LONDON TO MR PHILLIPS HE HAS NOT SEEN P SINCE HIS RETURN 842C LETTER 42   PROSE
      SAYS HE LAMENTS YOUR ABSENCE FROM LONDON AS YOUR ADVICE    844A LETTER 43    PROSE
      READINESS TO SEND ANY OF THE CARTOONS TO LONDON YOU DESIRE 846A LETTER 44    PROSE
      THAT I PERCEIVE A DETERMINATION IN THE LONDON BOOKSELLERS  846C LETTER 44    PROSE
      PERSUADED TO PRINT IN LONDON YOU WILL BE CHEATED EVERY WAY 847B LETTER 44    PROSE
      IN LONDON EVERY CALUMNY AND FALSEHOOD UTTERD AGAINST       847B LETTER 44    PROSE
          ANOTHER
      ENGAGEMENT WITH ANY LONDON BOOKSELLER I MAY MYSELF  . .    856B LETTER 54    PROSE
      HONOUR OF LONDON BOOKSELLERS & CONSIDER THEM AS LOSING A   856C LETTER 54    PROSE
      THE JOURNEYMAN PRINTERS THROUGHOUT LONDON ARE AT WAR  .    859B LETTER 56    PROSE
      THE VIOLENCE ON BOTH SIDES PRINTING IS SUSPENDED IN LONDON 859B LETTER 56    PROSE
      EVER TO LAMENT YOUR DISTANCE FROM LONDON AS THAT ALONE  .  861D LETTER 59    PROSE
      EVEN ISLINGTON & ALL PLACES NORTH OF LONDON ALWAYS LAID ME 871A LETTER 72    PROSE
      LONDON SUNDAY MORNING DEAR MADAM . . . . . . . .  .       871C LETTER 73    PROSE
      LONDON . . . . . . . . . . . . . . . . . . . . . .       SUPP ADDRESSES/L   *TITLE
      MR FLAXMAN SCULPTOR BUCKINGHAM STREET FITZROY SQUARE LONDON SUPP ADDRESSES/L *TITLE
      MR BUTTS GREAT MARLBOROUGH STREET OXFORD STREET LONDON  .  SUPP ADDRESSES/L  *TITLE
      INFANT SORROW THE SCHOOL BOY LONDON LITTLE GIRL LOST       SUPP LETTER 66A   *PROSE
LONDONDERRY
      DONNEGAL ANTRIM TYRONE FERMANAGH ARMAGH LONDONDERRY . . .  711 JERUSALEM 72   26
LONDONERS
      EDWIN & MORCAR STIRRING UP THE LONDONERS  . . . . . .     208D SUBJCTS HIST/N TITLE
LONDON'S
      AND THE LEPROSY LONDON'S SPIRIT SICKENING ALL THEIR BANDS  202 AMERICA 15     3
      SICKNING LAY LONDON'S GUARDIAN AND THE ANCIENT MITERD YORK 202 AMERICA 15     9
      HIS HELM WAS BROUGHT BY LONDON'S GUARDIAN & HIS THIRSTY    205 AMERICA CANC C  4
          SPEAR
      BY THE WISE SPIRIT OF LONDON'S RIVER ALL IN XXX?WITH XXX   205 AMERICA CANC C * 5
          ?LOOK . . .
      INFINITE LONDON'S AWFUL SPIRES CAST A DREADFUL [GLEAM] COLD 205 AMERICA CANC C 7
      ROUND ALBION'S CLIFFS & LONDON'S WALLS STILL ENITHARMON    242 EUROPE 12       2
          SLEPT
      . . . LONDON'S DARK-FROWNING TOWERS . . . . . . . .       501 MILTON 19       39
      IN LONDON'S DARKNESS AND MY TEARS FALL DAY AND NIGHT  .    623 JERUSALEM 5     36
      HEAVES IN THE HAND OF PALAMABRON WHO IN LONDON'S DARKNESS  636 JERUSALEM 16    9
      HE QUENCHES IT IN THE BLACK TROUGH OF HIS FORGE LONDON'S   636 JERUSALEM 16    14
          RIVER
      IN REGIONS OF HUMANITY IN LONDON'S OPENING STREETS  . .    665 JERUSALEM 38    43
      AWAY FROM ALBION'S MOUNTAINS FAR AWAY FROM LONDON'S SPIRES 673 JERUSALEM 43    70
      CREATED FROM THE VALLEY OF MIDDLESEX BY LONDON'S RIVER  .  690 JERUSALEM 58    45
      . . . THEY STOOD (FROWNING) UPON LONDON'S RIVER . . . .    699 JERUSALEM 64    31
      OUR SOULS EXULT & LONDON'S TOWERS . . . . . . . . .       718 ENGLND AWAKE/J  10
      ON LONDON'S TOWER ON THE THAMES HE DREW CAMBEL IN WRATH    726 JERUSALEM 82    57
LONELY
      VILE SAVAGE MINDS THAT LURK IN LONELY CELL . . . . . .     15 IMIT SPEN/PS     34
      OVER THE WEARY HILLS THE BLIND MAN TOOK HIS LONELY WAY  .  103 TIRIEL 4        1
      MET HIM AT ENTRANCE OF THE FOREST IN A DARK & LONELY WAY   103 TIRIEL 4        4
      IN A LONELY DELL . . . . . . . . . . . . . . . .         115 LIT GRL FND/SI   50
      THE LITTLE BOY LOST IN THE LONELY FEN . . . . . . . .     121 LIT BOY FND/SI   1
      WHO IN SORROW PALE THRO THE LONELY DALE . . . . . . .     121 LIT BOY FND/SI   7
      A LITTLE FLOWER GREW IN A LONELY VALE . . . . . . . .     414 TO MRS FLAXMAN   1
      SHE YONDER STANDS A LONELY TREE . . . . . . . . . .       423 THE BIRDS/N      5
LONENESS
      INTO THE WORLD OF LONENESS . . . . . . . . . . . .       254 AHANIA 4         64
LONG      SEE LIVE-LONG,SIDE-LONG
      STAND IN HIS STEAD AS LONG A-GONE . . . . . . . . .       17 BLIND-MANS/PS     65
      OF ENGLAND'S QUEEN AND WILL ERE LONG OF ENGLAND . . . .    21 EDW THIRD/PS 2    99
      FOR DALILA'S FAIR ARTS HAVE LONG BEEN TRIED IN VAIN  . .   38A SAMSON/PS       PROSE
      ERE LONG TO BLEED & DIE A SACRIFICE DONE BY A PRIESTLY HAND 41B THEN SHE BORE  PROSE
      OER THE EARTH PRIDE FEARED FOR HER CITY BUT NOT LONG  .    41B THEN SHE BORE   PROSE
      I SHOULD NOT HAVE LIVD SO LONG THERE WAS I . . . . . .     48B ISLAND MOON 4   PROSE
      BUT FELICITY DOES NOT LAST LONG FOR . . . . . . . .       58B ISLAND MOON 10  PROSE
      AND LONG FINGERS & THUMBS . . . . . . . . . . . .        62 DR CLASH/IM       15
      [ ("SUPERSTITION") ] HYPOCRISY SUPERSTITION HAS BEEN LONG  85C ANNO LAVATER   MARG
          A BUGBEAR
      MY HAIR IS VERY LONG MY BEARD DOTH COVER ALL MY BREAST  .  102 TIRIEL 3        4
      BUT LONG I STAID NOT AT HIS PALACE FOR I AM FORCD TO WANDER 102 TIRIEL 3       11
      SHE HAD WANDERD LONG . . . . . . . . . . . . . .         112 LIT GRL LST/SI   15
      . . . AND GOD SO LONG WORSHIPPD DEPARTS AS A LAMP . .     140 FRENCH REVOLTN  137
      I THEN ASKED EZEKIEL WHY HE EAT DUNG & LAY SO LONG ON HIS  154A MARRIAGE HH 12 PROSE
      I WAS BORN A SLAVE BUT I [LONG] GO TO BE FREE . . . . .    166 WHY CARE FOR/N * 9
      THE SUN THAT SLEEPS TOO LONG ARISE MY THEOTORMON I AM PURE 191 V DAU ALBION 2  28
      THIS IS ETERNAL DEATH AND THIS THE TORMENT LONG FORETOLD   196 AMERICA PREL 2  17
```

LONG   (CONTINUED)   PAGE   TITLE   LINE

THE SPECTRE GLOWD HIS HORRID LENGTH STAINING THE TEMPLE   198 AMERICA 5   6
  LONG
LONG PERIODS IN BURNING FIRES LABOURING . . . .   225 URIZEN 5   25
[TO HEAR] HEARING THE [SOUND] MARCH OF LONG RESOUNDING   264 FOUR ZOAS 1   *   5
  . . .

THEY WANDERD LONG TILL THEY SAT DOWN UPON THE MARGIND SEA   271 FOUR ZOAS 1   245
THEN LOS SMOTE HER UPON THE EARTH TWAS LONG EER SHE REVIVD   272 FOUR ZOAS 1   281
URIZEN STARTLED STOOD BUT NOT LONG SOON HE CRIED . . . .   273 FOUR ZOAS 1   335
NOT LONG IN HARMONY THEY DWELL THEIR LIFE IS DRAWN AWAY   274 FOUR ZOAS 1   371
URTHONA STOOD IN TERROR BUT NOT LONG HIS SPECTRE FLED   .   278 FOUR ZOAS 1   530
TILL SHE BECAME A LITTLE WEEPING INFANT A SPAN LONG   . . .   282 FOUR ZOAS 2   92
NOT LONG THEY LAY URTHONA'S SPECTRE FOUND HERBS OF THE PIT   309 FOUR ZOAS 5   173
PITY FOR THEE MOVD ME TO BREAK MY DARK & LONG REPOSE   . .   321 FOUR ZOAS 7   57
[THE BELLOWING ?FURNACES' BLARE BY THE LONG SOUNDING   346 FOUR ZOAS 8   *   204
  CLARION]

IN LINEAMENTS TOO EXTENDED & IN BONES TOO STRAIT & LONG   363 FOUR ZOAS 9   249
LO DARKNESS COVERS THE LONG POMP OF BANNERS ON THE WIND   375 FOUR ZOAS 9   666
NOT LONG THUNDERS LIGHTNINGS SWIFT RENDINGS & BLASTING   381 FOUR ZOAS AD 2   3
  WINDS
SHE DOST THOU TRULY LONG FOR ME   .   .   .   .   .   .   423 THE BIRDS/N   13
LONG JOHN BROWN & LITTLE MARY BELL . . . .   434A LONG JOHN BRWN   TITLE
[YOUNG] LONG JOHN BROWN HAD THE DEVIL IN HIS GUT .   .   .   434 LONG JOHN BRWN   2
[YOUNG] LONG JOHN BROWN LOVD [PRETTY] LITTLE MARY BELL .   434 LONG JOHN BRWN   3
[WHO DARES ?WORSHIP ?ONE WHOD HAVE DRIVEN YOU LONG AGO   SUPP ANNO REYNOLDS * MARG
  INSANE]
HIS GARMENTS ARE LONG SUFFERINGS FOR THE CHILDREN OF MEN   499 MILTON 18   36
DOWN INTO ULRO AND THEY WEPT IN LONG RESOUNDING SONG   503 MILTON 21   17
HOW LONG SHALL WE LAY DEAD IN THE STREET OF THE GREAT CITY   507 MILTON 23   11
HOW LONG BENEATH THE COVERING CHERUB GIVE OUR EMANATIONS   507 MILTON 23   12
THE BELLOWING FURNACES' BLARE BY THE LONG SOUNDING CLARION   509 MILTON 24   64
AND MURMURS OF THUNDER ROLLING HEAVY LONG & LOUD OVER THE   511 MILTON 25   64
  MOUNTAINS
A LONG JOURNEY & DARK THRO CHAOS IN THE TRACK OF MILTON'S   524 MILTON 34   22
  COURSE
AND HIS LEGS CARRIED IT LIKE A LONG FORK   .   .   .   .   .   536 AND HIS LEGS/N   1
THEN SCREWMUCH AT BLAKE'S SOUL TOOK A LONG LEAP . . .   .   537 AND HIS LEGS/N   39
IF I HAD THOUGHT HE HAD BEEN ONE OF THOSE LONG SPINDLE   555C ALWAYS THOT/N   PROSE
  NOSED RASCALS
NARROW BLINKING EYES THAT HAVE TOO LONG GOVERNED ART   .   563D DESC CAT   PROSE
I HAVE BEEN SCORNED LONG ENOUGH BY THESE FELLOWS .   .   .   575D DESC CAT 3   PROSE
THE SIZE OF THE ENGRAVING WILL BE (THREE) FEET (ONE) INCH   587A CHAUCER 1   PROSE
  LONG
(THREE) FEET (ONE) INCH LONG BY ONE FOOT HIGH CONTAINING   587D CHAUCER/N   PROSE
THREE FEET I INCH LONG AND I FOOT HIGH PRICE THREE GUINEAS   589C CHAUCER 2   TITLE
& HAVE LONG BEEN THE CONTEMPT OF THE CONTINENT .   .   .   594D PUB ADDRESS/N   PROSE
HOW LONG SHALL I BE FORCED TO BEAT THIS INTO MEN'S EARS   602D PUB ADDR AD/N   PROSE
THE LONG SUFFERINGS OF GOD ARE NOT FOR EVER THERE IS A   620 JERUSALEM 1   10
  JUDGMENT
THAT I MAY AWAKE ALBION FROM HIS LONG & COLD REPOSE . .   635 JERUSALEM 15   10
THY SEVERE JUDGE ALL THE DAY LONG PROVES THEE O BABYLON   647 JERUSALEM 24   27
YOU CALL DIVINE IS BUT A WORM SEVENTY INCHES LONG   . .   659 JERUSALEM 33   6
WITH INTELLECTUAL SPEARS & LONG WINGED ARROWS OF THOUGHT   664 JERUSALEM 38   15
A LONG SERPENT IN THE ABYSS OF THE SPECTRE WHICH AUGMENTED   685 JERUSALEM 54   29
AND THOSE WHO ARE IN MISERY CANNOT REMAIN SO LONG   . .   687 JERUSALEM 55   52
EVEN A LONG SEASON & A HARD JOURNEY & A HOWLING WILDERNESS   696 JERUSALEM 62   27
OF DEATH BUT HOW THEY CAME FORTH FROM THE FURNACES & HOW   713 JERUSALEM 73   7
  LONG
LONG TO TELL & OF THE IRON ROLLERS GOLDEN AXLE-TREES &   713 JERUSALEM 73   9
  YOKES
INTO A LITTLE ROOT A FATHOM LONG   717 STOOD AMONG/J   11
O SISTER CAMBEL SAID GWENDOLEN AS THEIR LONG BEAMING LIGHT   723 JERUSALEM 80   83
IN THE DEEP DARKNESS BROAD LIGHTNINGS GLARE LONG THUNDERS   741 JERUSALEM 94   4
  ROLL
WHEN THEY HAD WANDERD THREE DAYS LONG   .   .   .   .   .   750 EV GOSPEL(C)/N *   5
GOD'S MERCY & LONG SUFFERING   .   .   .   .   751 EV GOSPEL(C)/N   45
WHEN THEY HAD WANDERD THREE DAYS LONG   .   .   .   .   .   751 EV GOSPEL(D)/N   7
GOD'S MERCY & LONG SUFFERING   .   .   .   .   753 EV GOSPEL(D)/N   81
LOVE YOU LONG FROM ME HAS FLED .   .   .   .   755 EV GOSPEL(E)/N   59
I OUGHT LONG AGO TO HAVE WRITTEN TO YOU TO THANK YOU FOR   794D LETTER 6   PROSE
  YOUR
DO NOT THROW ASIDE FOR ANY LONG TIME   .   .   .   .   .   .   795B LETTER 6   PROSE
LONG AWAY & NOT CALLING TO KNOW OF YOUR WELFARE BUT HOPE   799A LETTER 11   PROSE
  NOW
AS ONE COUNTRY AND THEIR ARTS ONE & THAT YOU WILL ERE LONG   811A LETTER 21   PROSE
IN HEAVEN IS CERTAIN & DETERMINED & TO THIS I HAVE LONG   812C LETTER 22   PROSE
ASSURE HER THAT IT CANNOT BE LONG BEFORE I HAVE THE   815D LETTER 23   PROSE
  PLEASURE
WHICH I OUGHT LONG AGO TO HAVE SENT YOU .   .   .   .   .   816A LETTER 23   PROSE
OF WHAT I HAVE LONG DOUBTED VIZ   .   .   .   .   819C LETTER 25   PROSE
OR UNLESS HE SHOULD READ MY LONG POEM DESCRIPTIVE OF THOSE   823A LETTER 26   PROSE
  ACTS
WHICH SEEMS TO BE THE LABOUR OF A LONG LIFE ALL PRODUCD   823B LETTER 26   PROSE
WORK TO ME I AM CONTENT THAT IT SHALL BE SO AS LONG AS GOD   829D LETTER 30   PROSE
WHICH I AM NOW ENGRAVING & WHICH WAS LENT BY MR LONG   .   838D LETTER 37   PROSE
WISH THAT YOU MAY LONG ENJOY YOUR BEAUTIFUL RETIREMENT .   847C LETTER 44   PROSE
WHICH I HAVE NOT BEEN FOR THE ABOVE LONG PERIOD .   .   .   852D LETTER 50   PROSE
DEAR SIR I HAVE OMITTED SO LONG TO THANK YOU FOR YOUR KIND   853A LETTER 51   *PROSE
& OUR GOOD LADY PAULINA OVER A DISH OF COFFEE I LONG TO   862A LETTER 59   PROSE
  HEAR
MY FEET IT WILL NOT BE LONG BEFORE I SHALL BE ABLE   862D LETTER 60   PROSE
  TO PRESENT

		PAGE	TITLE	LINE

LONG   (CONTINUED)
WHOSE DEBT I HAVE BEEN TOO LONG BUT PERCIEVE THAT   . . . 863B LETTER 60   PROSE
SO LONG BEEN TURNED OUT OF THE OLD CHANNEL INTO A NEW ONE   865C LETTER 63   PROSE
FOR OR TAKE SO LONG A RIDE WE WITH SOME DIFFICULTY MADE THE 869D LETTER 70   PROSE
EXCUSE THE WRITING I HAVE DELAYED TOO LONG . . . . . .   871D LETTER 73   PROSE
LONG BEAMED
HAVE SHOT THEIR ARROWS OR LONG BEAMED SPEARS IN WRATH &   358 FOUR ZOAS 9   41
FURY
LONG DRAWN
RUN FROM THEIR FETTERS REDDENING & IN LONG DRAWN ARCHES   202 AMERICA 15   24
SITTING
LONGER
HERE NOBODY COULD SING ANY LONGER . . . . 60D ISLAND MOON 11 PROSE
[GOD BLESS MY BENEFACTORS FOR I CANNOT TARRY LONGER]   . . 103 TIRIEL 3   27
LET THE PRIESTS OF THE RAVEN OF DAWN NO LONGER IN DEADLY   160A SONG LIBERTY   PROSE
BLACK
TILL IMPATIENCE NO LONGER COULD BEAR . . . . 257 BOOK OF LOS 4   15
IMPATIENCE NOW NO LONGER CAN ENDURE DISTRACTED LUVAH   . . 276 FOUR ZOAS 1   429
NO LONGER NOW OBEDIENT TO THY WILL THOU ART COMPELLD   . . 292 FOUR ZOAS 3   33
WHY ROLL THY CLOUDS IN SICKNING MISTS I CAN NO LONGER HIDE 293 FOUR ZOAS 3   72
NO LONGER NOW ERECT THE KING OF LIGHT OUTSTRETCHD IN FURY   352 FOUR ZOAS 8   438
RAGE ORC RAGE THARMAS URIZEN NO LONGER CURBS YOUR RAGE   362 FOUR ZOAS 9   187
URTHONA IS ARISEN IN HIS STRENGTH NO LONGER NOW   . . . 379 FOUR ZOAS 9   849
DIVIDED FROM ENITHARMON NO LONGER THE SPECTRE LOS   . . . 379 FOUR ZOAS 9   850
TARRY NO LONGER FOR MY SOUL LIES AT THE GATES OF DEATH . 495 MILTON 14   19
NO LONGER TURNING HER A WANDERING HARLOT IN THE STREETS   523 MILTON 33   22
THAT IT NO LONGER SHALL DARE TO MOCK WITH THE ASPERSION   533 MILTON 41   8
OF MADNESS
WHO OWE TO ME ALL THAT THEY HAVE IT SHALL BE SO NO LONGER   575D DESC CAT 3   PROSE
NO WORK OF ART CAN TAKE LONGER THAN A YEAR . . . . .   . 587A CHAUCER 1   PROSE
HERE THEY ARE NO LONGER TALKING OF WHAT IS GOOD & EVIL . 613C V LAST JUDG/N   PROSE
FORGIVENESS TO BE CONTINUED TO ME A LITTLE LONGER WHEN . 808A LETTER 19   PROSE
& HOW THEN COULD I BE AT EASE BUT I AM NOW NO LONGER IN   813B LETTER 22   PROSE
THAT STATE
BEEN VERY UNHAPPY I AM SO NO LONGER I AM AGAIN EMERGED . 815D LETTER 23   PROSE
THAT HE CAN NO LONGER TREAT ME WITH INDIFFERENCE . . . 819D LETTER 25   PROSE
TOO MUCH EXPERIENCE TO BE ANY LONGER IMPOSED UPON . . . 821A LETTER 25   PROSE
MY OWN SELF WILL FOR I AM DETERMIND TO BE NO LONGER PESTERD 825C LETTER 27   PROSE
CONFIDENCE THAT IT SHALL BE SO NO LONGER HE IS BECOME MY   852C LETTER 50   PROSE
BUT CAN NO LONGER WAIT FOR THEM BUT MUST EXPRESS MY OWN &   853A LETTER 51   *PROSE
IS WHAT I COULD NOT LONGER OMIT TO SAY . . . . 853A LETTER 51   *PROSE
NOW NO LONGER DIVIDED NOR AT WAR WITH MYSELF I SHALL TRAVEL 853A LETTER 51   PROSE
TO SIT UP LONGER THAN SIX HOURS AT A TIME & ALSO FEEL THE   872D LETTER 76   PROSE
COLD
YOUR HAPPY FAMILY ONCE AGAIN & THAT FOR A LONGER PERIOD   873A LETTER 76   PROSE
LONGFORD
UNDER JUDAH & ISSACHAR & ZEBULUN ARE LOWTH LONGFORD . . . 711 JERUSALEM 72   18
LONGING
VALLIES HEAR ALL OUR LONGING EYES ARE TURNED . . . . .   . 1 TO SPRING/PS   6
TRULY SET ME LONGING MY WIFE SAYS I OUGHT TO HAVE SAID US   851D LETTER 50   PROSE
LONGINGS
TO TURN THE WHEEL OF FALSE DESIRE AND LONGINGS THAT WAKE   193 V DAU ALBION 5   27
HER WOMB
NOR FELT THE STINGINGS OF DESIRE NOR LONGINGS AFTER LIFE   325 FOUR ZOAS 7   203
LONG LIMBD
[THE BARKED OAK THE LONG LIMBD BEECH THE CHESNUT TREE THE   269 FOUR ZOAS 1   *   204
PINE]
THRO CAVES OF DEATH INTO EXISTENCE THE BEECH LONG LIMBD   335 FOUR ZOAS 7B   *   100
ADVANCD
LONG-WISHED
BUT FROM HER THE LONG-WISHED DELIVERER SHALL SPRING . . . 39D SAMSON/PS   PROSE
LOOK
MAYHAP YOU MAY LOOK UPON EDWARD'S FACE . . . . 21 EDW THIRD/PS 3   16
WHY NOBLE CHANDOS LOOK YOU HERE . . . . 22 EDW THIRD/PS 3   49
SIRE WITH RESPECT AND DEFERENCE I LOOK . . . . 23 EDW THIRD/PS 3   81
YOU ASKD ME IF HE DID NOT LOOK WELL WHEN HE FELL . . .   . 29D COUCH DEATH/PS   PROSE
I LOOK BEHIND THERE IS NO RETURNING DEATH FOLLOWS AFTER ME 35D COUCH DEATH/PS   PROSE
THOU LOVEST ME NOT LOOK NOT UPON ME WITH THOSE DEATHFUL   38C SAMSON/PS   PROSE
EYES
ID SOON MAKE DOUBLE ELEPHANT LOOK FOOLISH . . . . 52B ISLAND MOON 8   PROSE
O DEAR THE WATER S GOT INTO THE SLIDERS LOOK HERE   . . . 58C ISLAND MOON 10   PROSE
GREAT ENDS NEVER LOOK AT MEANS BUT PRODUCE   81B ANNO LAVATER   MARG
THEM SPONTANEOUSLY
COME FORTH & LOOK ON HER THAT BORE YOU COME YOU ACCURSED   99 TIRIEL 1   8
SONS
LOOK AT MY EYES BLIND AS THE ORBLESS [XXX] SCULL AMONG   99 TIRIEL 1   *   28
THE STONES
LOOK AT MY BALD HEAD HARK LISTEN YE SERPENTS [?ALL] LISTEN 99 TIRIEL 1   *   29
WHAT MYRATANA ART THOU DEAD LOOK HERE YE SERPENTS LOOK . . 100 TIRIEL 1   31
LOOK KNOWST THOU AUGHT OF THIS GREY BEARD OR OF THESE   104 TIRIEL 4   44
BLINDED EYES
IS TIRIEL CRUEL LOOK HIS DAUGHTER & HIS YOUNGEST DAUGHTER   107 TIRIEL 6   17
LOOK ON MY EYES HELA & SEE FOR THOU HAST EYES TO SEE . . 108 TIRIEL 6   29
[OF THUNDER DOES HE LOOK UPON THE SUN & LAUGH OR STRETCH]   110 TIRIEL 8   20
NOW THEY LOOK ABROAD TO SEE . . . . 112 A DREAM/SI   11
THEY LOOK UPON HIS EYES . . . . 114 LIT GRL FND/SI   33
THEY LOOK IN EVERY THOUGHTLESS NEST . . . . 119 NIGHT/SI   17
LOOK ON THE RISING SUN THERE GOD DOES LIVE . . . . .   . 125 LIT BLK BOY/SI   9
. . . THE PRISONERS LOOK UP AND ASSAY TO SHOUT THEY LISTEN 136 FRENCH REVOLTN   52
LOOK UP TO THE MORNING SENATE . . . . 136 FRENCH REVOLTN   58
. . . THEY DESCEND AND LOOK INTO THEIR GRAVES . . . .   . 137 FRENCH REVOLTN   71
. . . ROUND THEM THEIR COUNSELLORS LOOK UP FROM THE DUST   137 FRENCH REVOLTN   73

LOOK   (CONTINUED)
    AND BRIGHT CHILDREN LOOK AFTER HIM INTO THE GRAVE . . .   139 FRENCH REVOLTN   108
    . . . THEY LOOK DOWNWARD AND LABOUR AND FORGET MY HOLY LAW   140 FRENCH REVOLTN   139
    . . . AND LOOK OVER THE ROCKY CLIFFS . . . .   148 FRENCH REVOLTN   302
    WHICH TO ANGELS LOOK LIKE TORMENT AND INSANITY   . . . .   150C MARRIAGE HH 6   PROSE
    LOOK UP LOOK UP O CITIZEN OF LONDON ENLARGE THY   159C SONG LIBERTY   PROSE
        COUNTENANCE
    MY FATHER THEN WITH HOLY LOOK   . . . .   167 INFANT SORW/N   26
    THE LOOK OF LOVE ALARMS   . . . .   182 LOOK OF LOVE/N   1
    BUT THE LOOK OF SOFT DECEIT . . . .   182 LOOK OF LOVE/N   3
    THE LOOK OF LOVE ALARMS   . . . .   184 SEVRL QUESTN/N   5
    BUT THE LOOK OF SOFT DECEIT . . . .   184 SEVRL QUESTN/N   7
    WASHINGTON SPOKE FRIENDS OF AMERICA LOOK OVER THE ATLANTIC   197 AMERICA 3   6
        SEA
    LET HIM LOOK UP INTO THE HEAVENS & LAUGH IN THE BRIGHT AIR   198 AMERICA 6   7
    RISE AND LOOK OUT HIS CHAINS ARE LOOSE HIS DUNGEON DOORS   198 AMERICA 6   10
        ARE OPEN
    THEY LOOK BEHIND AT EVERY STEP & BELIEVE IT IS A DREAM . .   198 AMERICA 6   12
    WASHINGTON SPOKE FRIENDS OF AMERICA LOOK OVER THE ATLANTIC   204 AMERICA CANC A   6
        SEA
    BY THE WISE SPIRIT OF LONDON'S RIVER ALL IN XXX?WITH XXX   205 AMERICA CANC C *   5
        ?LOOK . . .
    BUT HIS LOVING LOOK   . . . .   219 LIT GRL LST/SE   27
    FLOURISHES THAT HE MAY RECIEVE THE GRAPES THRO ONE CAN LOOK   237 EUROPE INTRO   3
    UNWILLING I LOOK UP TO HEAVEN UNWILLING COUNT THE STARS   238 EUROPE PREL 2   1
    TILL ALL THE SONS OF URIZEN LOOK OUT AND ENVY LOS   . .   239 EUROPE 4   16
    UNLESS SOME WAY CAN BE FOUND THAT I MAY LOOK UPON THEE   265 FOUR ZOAS 1   41
        & LIVE
    I AM ALREADY DISTRACTED AT THEIR DEEDS & IF I LOOK   . .   265 FOUR ZOAS 1   55
    I HAVE REFUSD TO LOOK UPON THE UNIVERSAL VISION   . . .   271 FOUR ZOAS 1   274
    O LORD WILT THOU NOT LOOK UPON OUR SORE AFFLICTIONS . .   285 FOUR ZOAS 2   218
    WANDER AMONG THE VIRGINS OF THE SUMMER LOOK THEY CRY   .   288 FOUR ZOAS 2   306
    O URIZEN LOOK ON [THY WIFE THAT] ME LIKE A MOURNFUL STREAM   291 FOUR ZOAS 3   3
    WHY WILT THOU LOOK UPON FUTURITY DARKNING PRESENT JOY   .   291 FOUR ZOAS 3   11
    TEARFUL & SORROWFUL STATE THEN RISE LOOK OUT & PONDER   . .   316 FOUR ZOAS 6   182
    SICKLY LOOK FORTH & SCARCELY STRETCH THEIR BRANCHES TO   325 FOUR ZOAS 7   193
        THE PLAIN
    OF THY FIERCE SOUL UNBAR THE GATES OF MEMORY LOOK UPON ME   328 FOUR ZOAS 7   347
    AS ON THE OUTSIDE OF EXISTENCE BUT LOOK BEHOLD TAKE COMFORT   330 FOUR ZOAS 7   414
    TO COMFORT ORC IN HIS DIRE SUFFERINGS LOOK MY FIRES ENLUME   331 FOUR ZOAS 7   444
        AFRESH
    WE LOOK DOWN INTO ULRO WE BEHOLD THE WONDERS OF THE GRAVE   346 FOUR ZOAS 8   223
    SIT HOVRING OVER MY DARK THRESHOLD THO I ARISE LOOK OUT   360 FOUR ZOAS 9   * 118
    AND MY HEAD PAINT YET WILL I LOOK AGAIN UNTO THE MORNING   360 FOUR ZOAS 9   120
    HEAVENS OF MY BRAIN NOR WILL I LOOK UPON [REMEMBRANCE]   361 FOUR ZOAS 9   181
        FUTURITY MORE
    ALL NATIONS LOOK UP TO THE CLOUD & BEHOLD HIM WHO   364 FOUR ZOAS 9   274
        WAS CRUCIFIED
    THE MYRIADS & IN SILENT FEAR THEY [F] LOOK OUT FROM THEIR   366 FOUR ZOAS 9   * 339
        GRAVES
    LOOK HOW THE OPENING DAWN ADVANCES WITH VOCAL HARMONY   . .   367 FOUR ZOAS 9   397
    LOOK HOW THE BEAMS FORESHEW THE RISING OF SOME GLORIOUS   367 FOUR ZOAS 9   398
        POWER
    LET HIM LOOK UP INTO THE HEAVENS & LAUGH IN THE BRIGHT AIR   375 FOUR ZOAS 9   671
    RISE & LOOK OUT HIS CHAINS ARE LOOSE HIS DUNGEON DOORS   375 FOUR ZOAS 9   674
        ARE OPEN
    THEY LOOK BEHIND AT EVERY STEP & BELIEVE IT IS A DREAM .   375 FOUR ZOAS 9   676
    WHERE ARE YOUR CHAINS WHERE ARE YOUR TEARS WHY DO YOU LOOK   375 FOUR ZOAS 9   679
        AROUND
    LOOK OVER THE EVENTS OF YOUR OWN LIFE & IF YOU DO NOT   . .   391C ANNO WATSON   MARG
    CONTEMPTIBLE KNAVE LET THE PEOPLE LOOK TO THIS   . . . .   403A ANNO BACON   MARG
    MY WIFE WAS TOLD BY A SPIRIT TO LOOK FOR HER FORTUNE BY   440D MEMORANDUM/N 5   PROSE
    SOME LOOK TO SEE THE SWEET OUTLINES   . . . .   447 ANNO REYNOLDS   1
    SOME LOOK TO FIND OUT PATCHES PAINT   . . . .   447 ANNO REYNOLDS   3
    BESIDES LET THEM LOOK AT GOTHIC FIGURES & GOTHIC BUILDINGS   461A ANNO REYNOLDS   MARG
    WE OUGHT TO LOOK WHAT HE PUTS INTO IT   . . . . . .   476C ANNO REYNOLDS   MARG
    I WILL ARISE AND LOOK FORTH FOR THE MORNING OF THE GRAVE   495 MILTON 14   20
    THE DAUGHTERS OF BEAUTY LOOK UP FROM THEIR LOOM & PREPARE   515 MILTON 28   19
    LOOK THERE YOULL SEE SR JOSHUA'S COLOURING   . . . .   536 NO REAL STYL/N   3
    LOOK AT HIS PICTURES [TIS QUITE ANOTHER THING] ALL HAS   536 NO REAL STYL/N   4
        TAKEN WING
    [LOOK XXX FLAXMAN & STOTHARD DO] OLD ACQUAINTANCE WE'LL   538 OLD ACQUAINT/N *   1
        RENEW
    WHEN YOU LOOK AT A PICTURE YOU ALWAYS CAN SEE . . . . .   550 WHEN LOOK AT/N   1
    BUT LOOK YONDER THAT HOUSE IS THE HOUSE OF REMBRANT &C   553 ASKD PRIGG/N   *   14
    PLEASED WITH THE WORK ANY MORE THAN WITH THE LOOK   563D DESC CAT   PROSE
    WHO LOOK IF A PICTURE IS WELL DRAWN AND IF IT IS   573B DESC CAT 3   PROSE
        IMMEDIATELY
    HE HAS MADE HIM LOOK MORE LIKE A FOOL THAN A KNAVE   . . .   574D DESC CAT 3   PROSE
    INVITES THE ADMIRERS OF OLD ENGLISH PORTRAITS TO LOOK AT   596C PUB ADDRESS/N   PROSE
        HIS PRINT
    MOST ENGLISHMEN WHEN THEY LOOK AT A PICTURE   . . . .   599A PUB ADDRESS/N   *PROSE
    WHILE THEY DISCOURAGE & LOOK WITH CONTEMPT ON FALSE ART   601C PUB ADDRESS/N *PROSE
    I LOOK THRO IT & NOT WITH IT   . . . .   617C V LAST JUDG/N   PROSE
    LOOK HOW THEY SCORN THY ONCE ADMIRED PALACES NOW IN RUINS   625 JERUSALEM 7   16
    HAST JUST CAUSE TO BE IRRITATED BUT LOOK STEDFASTLY UPON ME   626 JERUSALEM 7   53
    OF GOD WOULD LOOK UPON ME AND PITY ME IN MY FURY   . . .   626 JERUSALEM 7   60
    SHUDDRING THE HEAVENS TO LOOK UPON ME BEHOLD WHAT CRUELTIES   627 JERUSALEM 8   19
    JERUSALEM DISSEMBLER JERUSALEM I LOOK INTO THY BOSOM   . .   643 JERUSALEM 21   18
    SHAME SIEZD US WE COULD NOT LOOK . . . .   647 JERUSALEM 24   7
    LOOK NOT SO MERCIFUL UPON ME O THOU SLAIN LAMB OF GOD   . .   648 JERUSALEM 24   59
    KNOW ME NOW ALBION LOOK UPON ME I ALONE AM BEAUTY   . . .   660 JERUSALEM 33   48

```
                                                                   PAGE      TITLE          LINE
LOOK    (CONTINUED)
    AT THY WORD & AT THY LOOK DEATH ENROBES ME ABOUT   . . . .     660 JERUSALEM 34          5
    AND WEPT AT OUR WINTRY DOOR LOOK LOOK BEHOLD GWENDOLEN         688 JERUSALEM 56         27
    LOOK BACK INTO THE CHURCH PAUL LOOK THREE WOMEN AROUND         688 JERUSALEM 56         42
    . . . PALE THEY LOOK ON ONE ANOTHER  . . . . . . . .          701 JERUSALEM 65         76
    THEY OBSCURE THE SUN & THE MOON NO EYE CAN LOOK UPON THEM      702 JERUSALEM 66         34
    THEY LOOK FORTH THE SUN IS SHRUNK THE HEAVENS ARE SHRUNK       703 JERUSALEM 66         50
    THEY LOOK FORTH FROM STONE-HENGE FROM THE COVE ROUND           703 JERUSALEM 66         57
        LONDON STONE
    THEY LOOK ON ONE ANOTHER THE MOUNTAIN CALLS OUT TO THE         703 JERUSALEM 66         58
        MOUNTAIN
    LOOK THE BEAUTIFUL DAUGHTER OF ALBION SITS NAKED UPON THE      705 JERUSALEM 68         11
        STONE
    THE NATIONS WAIT FOR JERUSALEM THEY LOOK UP FOR THE BRIDE      712 JERUSALEM 72         37
    IN BASHAN TERROR-STRUCK ALBION'S SONS LOOK TOWARD BASHAN       715 JERUSALEM 74         43
    LET US LOOK LET US EXAMINE IS THE CRUEL BECOME AN INFANT       724 JERUSALEM 81          8
    OR IS HE STILL A CRUEL WARRIOR LOOK SISTERS LOOK O PITEOUS     724 JERUSALEM 81          9
    LOOK I HAVE WROUGHT WITHOUT DELUSION LOOK I HAVE WEPT   . .    725 JERUSALEM 82          5
    LOOK HYLE IS BECOME AN INFANT LOVE LOOK BEHOLD SEE HIM LIE     725 JERUSALEM 82         37
    UPON MY BOSOM LOOK HERE IS THE LOVELY WAYWARD FORM   . . .     726 JERUSALEM 82         38
    BABEL & SHINAR LOOK TOWARD THE WESTERN GATE THEY SIT DOWN      730 JERUSALEM 85         18
    SINCE WHICH A PIG HAS GOT A LOOK   . . . . . . . . .           757 EV GOSPEL (I)/N      29
    I LOOK UPON THIS AS A MOST MALIGNANT & ARTFUL ATTACK   . .    786C ANNO THORNTON       MARG
    YOU STAND IN THE VILLAGE & LOOK UP TO HEAVEN   . . . . .       800 MRS FLAXMAN/L        9
    OUR DWELLING PLACE I LOOK BACK INTO THE REGIONS OF   . .      802C LETTER 14          PROSE
    THEIR AUTHOR AND GRATEFUL TO YOU MY EMPLOYER & THAT I LOOK    814D LETTER 23          PROSE
    MUST FLAXMAN LOOK UPON ME AS WILD   . . . . . . . .            818 HAPPINESS/L         47
    BOTH TO GOD & MAN WE LOOK FORWARD EVERY DAY WITH PLEASURE     824B LETTER 27          PROSE
    WHEN I LOOK EACH ONE STARTS WHEN I SPEAK I OFFEND   . .        828 O WHY BORN/L         3
    I HAVE BEEN TO LOOK AT THE DRAWINGS & PICTURE BUT FLAXMAN     839C LETTER 38          PROSE
    BOTH AS TO TYPE AND PRINTING PRAY LOOK AT WASHINGTON AS       847A LETTER 44          PROSE
        FAR AS
    MEN & ACCORDINGLY HAVE GIVEN A LOOK OVER MY ACCOUNT BOOK      854C LETTER 53          PROSE
    CANNOT BECAUSE THEY DARE NOT LOOK UPON   . . . . . .          864B LETTER 61          PROSE
    TO LOOK AS I DID FOR I HAVE BEEN YELLOW   . . . . . .         880A LETTER 90          PROSE
LOOKD
    I TOLD HIM HE LOOKD LIKE A CANDLE HALF   . . . . . .           25 EDW THIRD/PS 3       158
    AND I SAID NO HE LOOKD VERY FOOLISH   . . . . . . .            29D EDW THIRD/PS 4     PROSE
    MRS GIMBLET LOOKD AS IF THEY MEANT HER TILLY LALLY LAUGHT      46D ISLAND MOON 3      PROSE
    HERE ARADOBO LOOKD ASTONISHD & ASKD IF HE UNDERSTOOD          46D ISLAND MOON 3      PROSE
        ENGRAVING
    . . . THEN LIFTED HIS HEAD AND LOOKD ON HIS ARMIES THAT       139 FRENCH REVOLTN      110
        SHONE
    THEN HE LOOKD BACK WITH ANXIOUS DESIRE   . . . . . .          230 URIZEN 13           45
    I HAVE LOOKD INTO THE SECRET SOUL OF HIM I LOVD   . . .       265 FOUR ZOAS 1         44
    LOOKD OUT INTO THE WORLD OF THARMAS WHERE IN CEASELESS        286 FOUR ZOAS 2        256
        TORRENTS
    . . . HIS KNEES EACH OTHER SMOTE & THEN HE LOOKD   . . .      305 FOUR ZOAS 4        290
    THIS DISMAL WORLD HE STOOD A WHILE & LOOKD BACK OER HIS       315 FOUR ZOAS 6      *  150
        FORMER
    NOR DOWN NOR UP REMAIND THEN IF HE TURND & LOOKD BACK   .     316 FOUR ZOAS 6        191
    FOR WHETHER THEY LOOKD UPWARD THEY SAW THE DIVINE VISION      342 FOUR ZOAS 8         49
    OR WHETHER THEY LOOKD DOWNWARD STILL THEY SAW THE DIVINE      342 FOUR ZOAS 8         50
        VISION
    AND THEN FROM HER WHITE DOOR SHE LOOKD TO SEE HER BLEATING    369 FOUR ZOAS 9        472
        LAMBS
    [ASTONISH LOOKD FROM HIS BRIGHT PORTALS CALLING THUS TO       380 FOUR ZOAS AD 1 *     3
        LUVAH]
    ASTONISHD LOOKD FROM HIS BRIGHT PORTALS LUVAH KING OF LOVE    380 FOUR ZOAS AD 1       5
    DRAWING SUCH A MAN MUST KNOW THAT I LOOKD UPON HIM   . . .   593A PUB ADDRESS/N      PROSE
    WHILE THE WORKS [OF TRANSLATORS] OF POPE & DRYDEN ARE LOOKD  595A PUB ADDRESS/N     *PROSE
    WHILE THE WORKS OF STRANGE & WOOLLETT ARE LOOKD UPON   . .   595A PUB ADDRESS/N      PROSE
    ALL THE GIFTS OF THE HOLY GHOST ARE [DESPISD] LOOKD UPON     604C V LAST JUDG/N      PROSE
    TO WHOM THE ANCIENTS LOOKD AND SAW HIS DAY AFAR OFF   . .    621A JERUSALEM 3        PROSE
    ETERNITY LOOKD UPON AS DEFORMITY & LOVELINESS AS A DRY        628 JERUSALEM 9          8
        TREE
    BOWYER'S & OTHER GREAT WORKS I WAS KNOWN BY THEM & WAS       862C LETTER 60          PROSE
        LOOKD
    YESTERDAY HE SAT WITH ME ABOVE AN HOUR & LOOKD OVER   . . .  877A LETTER 85          PROSE
LOOKED
    WALKD BY THE CASTLE GATE AND LOOKED IN   . . . . . . .          4 FAIR ELENOR/PS       3
    AND HAYCOCKS LOOKED BROWN   . . . . . . . . . . .             164 HEARD ANGEL/N        8
    HE LOOKED UP & SAW [THE] THEE . . . . . . . . .               292 FOUR ZOAS 3      *  46
    THY LILLIES THAT GAVE LIGHT WHAT TIME THE MORNING LOOKED      325 FOUR ZOAS 7        196
        FORTH
    AND OLOLON LOOKED DOWN INTO THE HEAVENS OF ULRO IN FEAR       524 MILTON 34           49
    I HAVE LOOKED INTO THE SECRET SOUL OF HIM I LOVED   . . .     645 JERUSALEM 22         14
    HE LOOKED UP & SAW THE PRINCE OF LIGHT WITH SPLENDOR FADED    654 JERUSALEM 29         35
    AND DENS THEY LOOKED ON ONE-ANOTHER & BECAME WHAT THEY        661 JERUSALEM 34         50
        BEHELD
    SHE LOOKED & SAW JOSEPH THE CARPENTER IN NAZARETH & MARY      694 JERUSALEM 61          3
    THEY LOOKED UPON OUR LOVES WITH JOY THEY BEHELD OUR SECRET    720 JERUSALEM 79         43
        JOYS
    & HE HAS READ PART BY HIS OWN DESIRE & HAS LOOKED WITH   . . 825B LETTER 27          PROSE
LOOKEST
    O THOU WITH DEWY LOCKS WHO LOOKEST DOWN . . . . . . .           1 TO SPRING/PS         1
LOOKING
    LOOKING TO THE GAIN OF THIS OUR NATIVE LAND   . . . .          19 EDW THIRD/PS 2       35
    FOR LOOKING STEDFASTLY SHE SAW THAT PRIDE REIGND HERE   . .    41C THEN SHE BORE      PROSE
    AS I WAS LOOKING UP A LITTLE OUTRE FELLOW PULLING ME   . .     45A ISLAND MOON 1      PROSE
    WIPING HIS FACE & LOOKING ON THE CORNER OF THE CIELING SANG    57A ISLAND MOON 9     *PROSE
    FROWNING AND LOOKING UP FROM BROODING VILLAGES . . .   . .    139 FRENCH REVOLTN      117
```

| | | PAGE | TITLE | LINE |
LOOKING   (CONTINUED)

. . . LOOKING ON THE ARCHBISHOP WHO CHANGED AS PALE AS   142 FRENCH REVOLTN   176
LEAD
TO BE SEEN BUT A BLACK TEMPEST TILL LOOKING EAST . . . .   156B MARRIAGE HH 17 PROSE
THE KING OF ENGLAND LOOKING WESTWARD TREMBLES AT THE VISION 197 AMERICA 4   12
LOOKING UPON THEE IMAGE OF FAINT WATERS I RECOIL . . . .   297 FOUR ZOAS 3   197
IN GOLGONOOZA LOOKING DOWN THE DAUGHTERS OF BEULAH SAW . . 342 FOUR ZOAS 8   42
ALL BEULAH STOOD ASTONISHD LOOKING DOWN TO ETERNAL DEATH   342 FOUR ZOAS 8   47
SO SANG THEY IN ETERNITY LOOKING DOWN INTO BEULAH   . . .   347 FOUR ZOAS 8   246
LOOKING FOR URIZEN IN VAIN IN VAIN I SEEK FOR MORNING . . 354 FOUR ZOAS 8   506
[THE] YET PALE THE JUST MAN STANDS ERECT & LOOKING UP TO   358 FOUR ZOAS 9   * 51
HEAVN
I WAS ONCE LOOKING OVER THE PRINTS FROM RAFAEL   . . . .   449C ANNO REYNOLDS   MARG
ON EVERY ONE OF THESE BOOKS I WROTE MY OPINIONS &   476D ANNO REYNOLDS   MARG
ON LOOKING THEM
CAN SUCH AN EYE JUDGE OF THE STARS & LOOKING THRO ITS TUBES 485 MILTON 5   28
LOOKING DOWN INTO BEULAH WRATHFUL FILLD WITH RAGE . . .   502 MILTON 20   45
LOOKING INTO THE BLACK WATER MINGLING IT WITH TEARS . . . 503 MILTON 20   55
STANDS STILL UPON THE MOUNTAIN LOOKING ON THIS LITTLE BIRD   520 MILTON 31   37
WHILE I LOOKING UP TO MY UMBRELLA . . . .   555 BLAKES APL/N 1   16
. . . LOOKING UP FROM [CIRCUMFERENCE] SKUMFERENCE TO CENTER 555 BLAKES APL/N 1   18
WHILE I LOOKING UP TO MY UMBRELLA . . . .   556 BLAKES APL/N 2   15
CRY LOOKING QUITE FROM SKUMFERENCE TO CENTER . . . . .   556 BLAKES APL/N 2   17
OR LOOKING IN ANOTHER MAN'S STYLE AND MANNER . . . . .   582D DESC CAT 9   PROSE
WHILE I LOOKING UP TO MY UMBRELLA . . . .   595 BLAKES APOL/PA   9
IS LIKE LOOKING FOR EPIGRAMS IN HOMER . . . .   599A PUB ADDRESS/N PROSE
LAMENTING & LOOKING UPON HER IN ASTONISHMENT & TERROR   .   609B V LAST JUDG/N PROSE
IN THE TWELVE COUNTIES OF WALES & THENCE GATES LOOKING   637 JERUSALEM 16   32
EVERY WAY
AND THUS HE SPOKE LOOKING ON ALBION'S CITY WITH MANY TEARS   657 JERUSALEM 31   28
SO LOS SPOKE STANDING ON MAM-TOR LOOKING OVER EUROPE & ASIA 661 JERUSALEM 34   41
ON MOUNT GILEAD LOOKING TOWARD GILGAL AND LOS BENDED   . . 662 JERUSALEM 36   12
INTO TWO IRREGULAR FORMS AND LOOKING ON ALBION'S DREAD TREE 723 JERUSALEM 80   73
LOOKING TO THE EAST & HIS VOICE IS HEARD OVER THE WHOLE   730 JERUSALEM 85   12
EARTH
TO OR LOOKING AT A SOLDIER FOR THE PEACEABLE VILLAGERS HAVE 828A LETTER 28   PROSE
DIGNITY WHO WOULD NOT SIT LOOKING IN THEIR PARENT'S FACE   864A LETTER 61   PROSE
LOOKING-GLASS,LOOKING GLASS
MULTITUDINOUS IN THE LOOKING GLASS OF ENITHARMON ON ALL   697 JERUSALEM 63   21
SIDES
THEREFORE THE MURDER WAS PUT APART IN THE LOOKING-GLASS   698 JERUSALEM 63   38
OF ENITHARMON
SATURN MARY SCEPTER LOOKING GLASS THRONES (DOMINIONS)   SUPP ILLUS DANTE 99 *PROSE
LOOKS
I TOLD HIM TO PUT OFF HIS HUNGRY LOOKS . . . .   25 EDW THIRD/PS 3   155
. . . AND THE PEASANT LOOKS OVER THE SEA AND WIPES A TEAR   147 FRENCH REVOLTN   281
SMILE WHEN THEY FROWN FROWN WHEN THEY SMILE & WHEN A   323 FOUR ZOAS 7   118
MAN LOOKS PALE
WITH LABOUR & ABSTINENCE SAY HE LOOKS HEALTHY & HAPPY . . 323 FOUR ZOAS 7   119
ANXIOUS ITS LITTLE SOUL LOOKS OUT INTO THE CLEAR EXPANSE   355 FOUR ZOAS 8   559
SO MAN LOOKS OUT IN TREE & HERB & FISH & BIRD & BEAST   .   355 FOUR ZOAS 8   561
SHE RISES AMONG FLOWERS & LOOKS TOWARD THE EASTERN   367 FOUR ZOAS 9   390
CLEARNESS
LAMBETH MOURNS CALLING JERUSALEM SHE WEEPS & LOOKS ABROAD   511 MILTON 25   54
AND JEWOUS LOOKS TO HAM [LOOKS] LIKE MAD RANTERY   . . .   550 ENGL ENCOU/N 2 * 4
LOOKS DOWN ON THEIR LITTLE FOLLIES FROM THE EMPEROR TO   569A DESC CAT 3   PROSE
THE MILLER
WHOEVER LOOKS AT ANY OF THE GREAT & EXPENSIVE WORKS   . .   596B PUB ADDRESS/N PROSE
WHICH LOOKS FOR NO OTHER HEAVEN THAN THEIR BELOVED   . . . 610D V LAST JUDG/N PROSE
AND IRON THE BULLS AND THAT WHICH LOOKS TOWARD ULRO . . . 632 JERUSALEM 12   63
WITH NARROW SOUL & LOOKS DEMURE . . . .   756 EV GOSPEL(I)/N   2
WAIT FOR LESS HURRIED MOMENTS OUR COTTAGE LOOKS MORE & MORE 806A LETTER 16   PROSE
WHICH IS STILL UNFINISHD BUT IS IN A FINISHING WAY & LOOKS 809C LETTER 20   PROSE
WELL
THE WRITING LOOKS VERY PRETTY I WAS FORTUNATE IN DOING IT   834C LETTER 34   PROSE
MR ROSE HE LOOKS THO NOT SO WELL AS I HAVE SEEN HIM YET   844D LETTER 43   PROSE
HAPPINESS IS SECURE IN JESUS OUR LORD & WHO LOOKS FOR   .   862D LETTER 60   PROSE
[?FIRST ?WERE CREATED WINE & (HAPPINESS) ?GOOD ?LOOKS &   SUPP ANNO REYNOLDS * MARG
?FORTUNE XXX]
LOOKST
WHERE LUVAH DOTH RENEW HIS HORSES LOOKST THOU ON MY YOUTH   128 BOOK OF THEL 3   8
LOOKYE
BY JOHN LOOKYE [?PANTRYMAN] GENT JOHN LOCKE SAID OBTUSE   52D ISLAND MOON 8 PROSE
ANGLE
LOOM
. . . IN [HER SILKEN] HER SHINING LOOM . . . .   267 FOUR ZOAS 1   122
SOME FIXD THE ANVIL SOME THE LOOM ERECTED SOME THE PLOW   281 FOUR ZOAS 2   27
THEN LEFT THE SONS OF URIZEN THE PLOW & HARROW THE LOOM   337 FOUR ZOAS 7B   170
OF ENITHARMON'S LOOM PLAY LULLING CADENCES ON THE WINDS   485 MILTON 6   6
OF ALBION
TOGETHER RIPE FOR THE HARVEST & VINTAGE & READY FOR THE   510 MILTON 25   7
LOOM
THE DAUGHTERS OF BEAUTY LOOK UP FROM THEIR LOOM & PREPARE   515 MILTON 28   19
UPON THE TREDDLES OF THE LOOM THEY SING TO THE WINGED   518 MILTON 29   59
SHUTTLE
O DREADFUL LOOM OF DEATH O PITEOUS FEMALE FORMS COMPELLD   525 MILTON 35   7
THE MALE IS A FURNACE OF BERYLL THE FEMALE IS A GOLDEN LOOM 623 JERUSALEM 5   34
AND THERE BEHOLD THE LOOM OF LOCKE WHOSE WOOF RAGES DIRE   636 JERUSALEM 15   15
AND WITH THE LOOM TO COVER GWENDOLEN & RAGAN WITH COSTLY   643 JERUSALEM 21   14
ROBES
IN VEGETABLE MOULD CREATED BY THE HAMMER AND LOOM   . . .   668 JERUSALEM 40   56
TO THE GOLDEN LOOM OF LOVE TO THE MOTH-LABOURD WOOF . . .   688 JERUSALEM 56   13

1123

		PAGE	TITLE		LINE
LOOM	(CONTINUED)				
	SAT AT THE SHINING LOOM WITH HER SISTERS ATTENDING ROUND	691	JERUSALEM 59		27
	THE STAMPING FEET OF RAGAN UPON THE FLAMING TREDDLES OF HER LOOM	699	JERUSALEM 64		36
	THEN LEFT THE SONS OF URIZEN THE PLOW & HARROW THE LOOM	699	JERUSALEM 65		12
	FIBRES OF LIFE TO WEAVE FOR EVERY FEMALE IS A GOLDEN LOOM	704	JERUSALEM 67		4
	MOUNTAINOUS WALES INTO THE LOOM OF CATHEDRON FIBRE BY FIBRE	723	JERUSALEM 80		63
	AND PLAYING IN THE THUNDEROUS LOOM IN SWEET INTOXICATION	723	JERUSALEM 80		80
	AND HYLE A WINDING WORM BENEATH [HER LOOM UPON THE SCALES]	726	JERUSALEM 82	*	47
	FIBRES OF LIFE OUT FROM THE BONES INTO HER GOLDEN LOOM . .	736	JERUSALEM 90		22
	FOR THE MALE IS A FURNACE OF BERYLL THE FEMALE IS A GOLDEN LOOM	736	JERUSALEM 90		27
	AND LUVAH TO HIS LOOM URTHONA HE BEHELD MIGHTY LABOURING AT	742	JERUSALEM 95		17
	BONES & SINEWS ALL STRINGS & BOBBINS LIKE A WEAVER'S LOOM	875B	LETTER 81		PROSE
LOOMS					
	AND ALL THE TIME IN CAVERNS SHUT THE GOLDEN LOOMS ERECTED	284	FOUR ZOAS 2		145
	INTO HIS HANDS THEN ENITHARMON ERECTED LOOMS IN LUBAN'S GATE	342	FOUR ZOAS 8		36
	AND CALLD THE LOOMS CATHEDRON IN THESE LOOMS SHE WOVE THE SPECTRES	342	FOUR ZOAS 8		37
	ATTRACTIVE OF HIS HAMMER'S BEATING & THE SILVER LOOMS . .	344	FOUR ZOAS 8		113
	EMPLOYING THE DAUGHTERS IN HER LOOMS & LOS EMPLOYD THE SONS	345	FOUR ZOAS 8		185
	. . . WE BEHOLD WITH WONDER ENITHARMON'S LOOMS & LOS'S FORGES	346	FOUR ZOAS 8		200
	OF SPECTROUS DEAD THENCE TO THE LOOMS OF CATHEDRON CONVEYD	346	FOUR ZOAS 8		209
	ROSE FROM THE FEAST IN JOY ASCENDING TO THEIR GOLDEN LOOMS	378	FOUR ZOAS 9		779
	ALSO THE VEGETATED BODIES WHICH ENITHARMON WOVE IN HER LOOMS	382	FOUR ZOAS AD 6		24
	BY ENITHARMON'S LOOMS WHEN ALBION WAS SLAIN UPON HIS MOUNTAINS	482	MILTON 3		1
	SUBDUING HIS SPECTRE THEY BUILDED THE LOOMS OF GENERATION	483	MILTON 3		38
	HER LOOMS VIBRATE WITH SOFT AFFECTIONS WEAVING THE WEB OF LIFE	486	MILTON 6		28
	[BY ENITHARMON'S LOOMS & SPUN BENEATH THE SPINDLE OF TIRZAH]	486	MILTON 7	*	1
	AROUND THE LAMB A FEMALE TABERNACLE WOVEN IN CATHEDRON'S LOOMS	494	MILTON 13		26
	LEST WE ARE VEGETATED FOR CATHEDRON'S LOOMS WEAVE ONLY DEATH	509	MILTON 24		35
	GIVEN TO HERCULES WHO LABOUR IN TIRZAH'S LOOMS FOR BREAD	511	MILTON 25		50
	CONTINUALLY WOVEN IN THE LOOMS OF ENITHARMON'S DAUGHTERS	512	MILTON 26		35
	WITH WAR WOVEN IN LOOMS OF TYRE & SIDON BY BEAUTIFUL ASHTAROTH	528	MILTON 37		24
	PREPARE THE FURNITURE O LAMBETH IN THY PITYING LOOMS . .	632	JERUSALEM 12		38
	SURROUNDS LUBAN LOS'S PALACE & THE GOLDEN LOOMS OF CATHEDRON	633	JERUSALEM 13		25
	THE LOOMS & MILLS & PRISONS & WORK-HOUSES OF OG & ANAK . .	634	JERUSALEM 13		57
	WALES GIVES HIS DAUGHTERS TO THE LOOMS ENGLAND NURSING MOTHERS	637	JERUSALEM 16		23
	THEIR LOOMS IN A GENERATION OF DEATH & RESURRECTION TO FORGETFULNESS	638	JERUSALEM 17		9
	WOVEN IN LOOMS OF EDEN IN SPIRITUAL DEATHS OF MIGHTY MEN	665	JERUSALEM 38		53
	YOU MUST MY DICTATE OBEY FROM YOUR GOLD-BEAMD LOOMS TRILL	688	JERUSALEM 56		31
	THEN THE RESPONSE CAME WARBLING FROM TRILLING LOOMS IN ALBION	688	JERUSALEM 56		38
	CATHEDRON'S LOOMS ARE BUILDED AND LOS'S FURNACES IN THE SOUTH	691	JERUSALEM 59		23
	OTHER DAUGHTERS OF LOS LABOURING AT LOOMS LESS FINE . . .	692	JERUSALEM 59		45
	AND SHE PUT FORTH HER HAND UPON THE LOOMS IN DREADFUL HOWLINGS	698	JERUSALEM 64		7
	AND AS THEY WOVE & CUT FROM THE LOOMS IN VARIOUS DIVISIONS	704	JERUSALEM 67		6
	HIM OVER EUROPE IN STREAMS OF GORE OUT OF CATHEDRON'S LOOMS	715	JERUSALEM 74		37
	OVER THE NATIONS TILL HE TOOK ROOT BENEATH THE SHINING LOOMS	715	JERUSALEM 74		45
	THE GOLDEN CORDS OF THE LOOMS ANIMATE BENEATH THEIR TOUCHES SOFT	725	JERUSALEM 82		14
	AND LET THE LOOMS OF ENITHARMON & THE FURNACES OF LOS . .	725	JERUSALEM 82		26
	THE ENVY RAN THRO CATHEDRON'S LOOMS INTO THE HEART . . .	726	JERUSALEM 82		53
	THE SISTERS SAW TREMBLING RAN THRO THEIR LOOMS (SOFTENING) MILD	726	JERUSALEM 82		77
	AND LULLING HARMONIES BENEATH THE LOOMS FROM CAITHNESS IN THE NORTH	728	JERUSALEM 83		70
	AT HIS FURNACES HIS DAUGHTERS AT THEIR LOOMS SING WOES . .	731	JERUSALEM 86		38
	AMONG THE GOLDEN LOOMS OF CATHEDRON SENDING FIBRES OF LOVE	731	JERUSALEM 86		40
	ENITHARMON WHO AT HER SHINING LOOMS SINGS LULLING CADENCES	734	JERUSALEM 88		45
	THIS SINFUL NATION CREATED IN OUR FURNACES & LOOMS IS ALBION	739	JERUSALEM 92		6
	FOR IF HE BE THAT ALBION I CAN NEVER WEAVE HIM IN MY LOOMS	739	JERUSALEM 92		9
	MY LOOMS WILL BE NO MORE & I ANNIHILATE VANISH FOR EVER	739	JERUSALEM 92		11
LOOSD					
	LOOSD HER SLENDER DRESS	113	LIT GRL LST/SI		50
	WILL I ARISE TILL HIM I LOVE IS LOOSD FROM THIS DARK CHAIN	339	FOUR ZOAS 7B		255
	AND WHO SHALL MOURN FOR MYSTERY WHO NEVER LOOSD HER CAPTIVES	375	FOUR ZOAS 9		669
LOOSE					
	NEGLECT THY HAIR TO SEEM MORE LOVELY IN THY LOOSE ATTIRE	38A	SAMSON/PS		PROSE
	MAD WITH CHAINS LOOSE WHICH HE DRAGGD UP AND DOWN . . .	136	FRENCH REVOLTN		48
	RISE AND LOOK OUT HIS CHAINS ARE LOOSE HIS DUNGEON DOORS ARE OPEN	198	AMERICA 6		10
	AND TO MAHOMET A LOOSE BIBLE GAVE	246	SONG OF LOS 3		29
	LET LOOSE THE ENORMOUS SPIRIT IN THE DARKNESS OF THE DEEP	306	FOUR ZOAS 5	*	59
	[BUT ?IN] BUT URIZEN HIS MIGHTY RAGE LET LOOSE IN THE MID DEEP	343	FOUR ZOAS 8	*	90

	PAGE	TITLE	LINE
LOOSE (CONTINUED)			
THE SPECTRE OF ENITHARMON LET LOOSE ON THE TROUBLED DEEP	358	FOUR ZOAS 9	24
ALL SPIRITS DECEASD LET LOOSE FROM REPTILE PRISONS COME IN SHOALS	363	FOUR ZOAS 9	235
HE TURND THE HORSES LOOSE & LAID HIS PLOW IN THE NORTHERN CORNER	365	FOUR ZOAS 9	319
RISE & LOOK OUT HIS CHAINS ARE LOOSE HIS DUNGEON DOORS ARE OPEN	375	FOUR ZOAS 9	674
IN HIS HAND THARMAS TAKES THE STORMS HE TURNS THE WHIRLWIND LOOSE	378	FOUR ZOAS 9	809
LASH ON THEIR LIMBS AS THEY TURN THE WHIRLWINDS LOOSE UPON	484	MILTON 5	17
HE IS MY SPECTRE IN MY OBEDIENCE TO LOOSE HIM FROM MY HELLS	496	MILTON 14	31
WILL UNCHAIN ORC & LET LOOSE SATAN OG SIHON & ANAK . . .	505	MILTON 22	33
LET LOOSE THE ENORMOUS SPECTRE ON THE DARKNESS OF THE DEEP	667	JERUSALEM 40	32
SCOFELD & KOX ARE LET LOOSE UPON MY SAXONS THEY ACCUMULATE	673	JERUSALEM 43	51
LOOSING			
LOOSING THE ETERNAL HORSES FROM THE DENS OF NIGHT CRYING	160A	SONG LIBERTY	PROSE
LORD			
THAT BED OF JOY WHERE ERST HER LORD HATH PRESSD	5	FAIR ELENOR/PS	38
AH MY DEAR LORD AH WRETCHED ELENOR	5	FAIR ELENOR/PS	40
MY LORD WAS LIKE A FLOWER UPON THE BROWS	5	FAIR ELENOR/PS	41
MY LORD WAS LIKE A STAR IN HIGHEST HEAVN	5	FAIR ELENOR/PS	45
MY LORD WAS LIKE THE OPENING EYES OF DAY	5	FAIR ELENOR/PS	47
OF HER DEAR LORD ALL GHASTLY PALE CLOTTED	5	FAIR ELENOR/PS	59
SIR WALTER MANNY LORD AUDLEY LORD PERCY	17C	EDW THIRD/PS	TITLE
MY LORD BISHOP YOU WOULD RECOMMEND US AGRICULTURE	19	EDW THIRD/PS 2	17
AND GAIN BUT SCANTY FARE THEN MY DEAR LORD	19	EDW THIRD/PS 2	33
O MY GOOD LORD TRUE WISDOM DROPS LIKE HONEY	20	EDW THIRD/PS 2	36
I FEAR LORD PERCY WILL NOT GIVE ME LEAVE	20	EDW THIRD/PS 2	45
MY LORD	20	EDW THIRD/PS 2	56
LORD PERCY'S ADVICE I HAVE BEEN USED SO MUCH	20	EDW THIRD/PS 2	60
FIE FIE LORD CLARENCE YOU PROCEED NOT TO BUSINESS	20	EDW THIRD/PS 2	62
WHEN THAT THEY FIND THEY MUST MY LORD THEY WILL	20	EDW THIRD/PS 2	74
LORD PERCY CANNOT MEAN THAT WE SHOULD SUFFER	20	EDW THIRD/PS 2	77
LORD PERCY IF THE HEART IS SICK THE HEAD	21	EDW THIRD/PS 2	84
THE HEART DOTH FAIL YOU SAY MY LORD THE MERCHANTS	21	EDW THIRD/PS 2	86
WORTHY THE BRAVE LORD PERCY AND AS WORTHY	21	EDW THIRD/PS 2	89
LORD BISHOP WHAT WAS RASH IN ME IS WISE	21	EDW THIRD/PS 2	91
QUICKLY TO THE LORD MAYOR AND WORK HIM ONWARD	21	EDW THIRD/PS 2	94
THANKS BRAVE LORD PERCY YOU HAVE THE THANKS	21	EDW THIRD/PS 2	98
SCENE AT CRESSEY SIR THOMAS DAGWORTH AND LORD AUDLEY MEETING	21C	EDW THIRD/PS 3	*PROSE
WHY MY LORD AUDLEY I DONT KNOW	21	EDW THIRD/PS 3	6
TO-MORROW WE SHALL KNOW I SAY LORD AUDLEY	22	EDW THIRD/PS 3	22
COURAGE MY LORD PROCEEDS FROM SELF-DEPENDENCE	25	EDW THIRD/PS 3	194
CONSIDERATE AGE MY LORD VIEWS MOTIVES	27	EDW THIRD/PS 3	282
O MAN SLAVE OF EACH MOMENT LORD OF ETERNITY	37A	CONTEMPLATN/PS	PROSE
LORD OF THYSELF THOU THEN ART LORD OF ALL	37A	CONTEMPLATN/PS	PROSE
DECKED IN MILD SORROW AND SELL THY LORD FOR GOLD FOR . . .	38A	SAMSON/PS	PROSE
ALAS MY LORD WHAT AM I CALLING THEE THOU ART MY GOD . . .	38B	SAMSON/PS	PROSE
THEN PRAYED MANOA O LORD THY FLOCK IS SCATTERED ON THE HILLS	40A	SAMSON/PS	PROSE
BUT IF THOU WILT OFFER AN OFFERING UNTO THE LORD	40C	SAMSON/PS	PROSE
& WEAR HER IN THINE HEART LORD OF THY SELF THOU THEN ART	41B	THEN SHE BORE	PROSE
LORD OF ALL [HUMILITY HER DAUGHTER]	42A	THEN SHE BORE	PROSE
("WHO SHOULD HARMONIOUSLY UNITE EACH VARIETY") THIS IS OUR LORD	76C	ANNO LAVATER	MARG
FOR OUR LORD IS THE WORD OF GOD & EVERY	87B	ANNO LAVATER	MARG
OR EXTERNAL OF HEAVEN & IS OF THE BODY OF THE LORD . . .	SUPP	ANNO SWED HELL	* MARG
MAY PERCIEVE IT IS FROM THE POETIC GENIUS WHICH IS THE LORD	90B	ANNO SWED LOVE	MARG
O LORD SAID MNETHA HOW I TREMBLE ARE THERE THEN [XXX] MORE PEOPLE	102	TIRIEL 2	* 54
KNOWEST THOU NOT O FAIRIES' LORD	188	A FAIRY SKIPD	9
LORD HAVE MERCY ON US	240B	EUROPE 7	*PROSE
[HE IS THE GOOD SHEPHERD HE IS THE LORD & MASTER] . . .	269	FOUR ZOAS 1	200
SAYING THOU ART THE LORD OF LUVAH INTO THINE HANDS I GIVE	273	FOUR ZOAS 1	324
IF I INDEED AM [LUVAH'S LORD] VALA'S KING & YE O SONS OF MEN	282	FOUR ZOAS 2	* 81
HER COLD LIMBS IN THE ABSENCE OF HER LORD ALSO HER SONS	285	FOUR ZOAS 2	193
O LORD WILT THOU NOT LOOK UPON OUR SORE AFFLICTIONS . .	285	FOUR ZOAS 2	218
WHY SIGHS MY LORD ARE NOT THE MORNING STARS THY OBEDIENT SONS	291	FOUR ZOAS 3	5
THEN O MY DEAR LORD LISTEN TO AHANIA LISTEN TO THE VISION	292	FOUR ZOAS 3	41
SAYING O LORD WHENCE IS THIS CHANGE THOU KNOWEST I AM NOTHING	293	FOUR ZOAS 3	55
SHRINKING & SHRINKING FROM HER LORD & CALLING HIM THE TEMPTER	295	FOUR ZOAS 3	129
[WE FLED FROM ?JERUSALEM ?AFTER ?THE MERCIFUL LORD & SAVIOUR]	SUPP	FOUR ZOAS 3	*
LORD SAVIOUR IF THOU HADST BEEN HERE OUR BROTHER HAD NOT DIED	304	FOUR ZOAS 4	253
WERE KEPT BACK FROM MY LORD & FROM HIS CHARIOT OF MERCIES	310	FOUR ZOAS 5	209
O I REFUSD THE LORD OF DAY THE HORSES OF HIS PRINCE . . .	310	FOUR ZOAS 5	211
HER ONCE LOVD LORD NOW BUT A SHADE HERSELF ALSO A SHADE . .	327	FOUR ZOAS 7	313
COME LORD JESUS COME QUICKLY	347	FOUR ZOAS 8	245
AND THEN MOCKING & THEN WORSHIPPING CALLING HIM LORD & KING	349	FOUR ZOAS 8	327
[HE IS THE GOOD SHEPHERD HE IS THE LORD & MASTER] . .	SUPP	FOUR ZOAS 8	*
BROTHER OF JESUS WHAT HAVE I DONE INTREAT THY LORD FOR ME	364	FOUR ZOAS 9	270
TO MEET THE LORD COMING TO JUDGMENT BUT THE FLAMES REPELLD THEM	364	FOUR ZOAS 9	288
FOR IN MY BOSOM A NEW SONG ARISES TO MY LORD	368	FOUR ZOAS 9	433
WHERE IS THE LORD OF VALA DOST THOU HIDE IN CLEFTS OF THE ROCK	370	FOUR ZOAS 9	501

	PAGE	TITLE	LINE

LORD (CONTINUED)

	PAGE	TITLE	LINE
AND MOCKING & THEN WORSHIPING CALLING HIM LORD & KING . .	382	FOUR ZOAS AD 6	15
PRINCE OF DARKNESS IS A GENTLEMAN & NOT A MAN HE IS A LORD	399C	ANNO BACON	MARG
CHANCELLOR			
OR ANY USEFUL THING HIS BUSINESS & BOSOM WAS TO BE LORD	404D	ANNO BACON	MARG
CHANCELLOR			
A LORD CHANCELLOR'S OPINIONS AS DIFFERENT FROM CHRIST . .	407A	ANNO BACON	MARG
AND SPILLD THE BLOOD OF MERCY'S LORD	420	I SAW MNK AD/N	4
AGAINST THIS IMAGE OF HIS LORD	420	I SAW MNK AD/N	9
& THEN HE BECAME LORD & MASTER OF NECESSARIES	446C	ANNO REYNOLDS	MARG
OF ETERNITY IN WHICH WE SHALL LIVE FOR EVER IN JESUS OUR	480D	MILTON 1	PROSE
LORD			
WHICH IS THE DIVINE BODY OF THE LORD JESUS BLESSED FOR EVER	482	MILTON 3	4
I TOUCH THE HEAVENS AS AN INSTRUMENT TO GLORIFY THE LORD	494	MILTON 13	29
FROM CORRUPTIBILITY O WHEN LORD JESUS WILT THOU COME .	495	MILTON 14	18
OR HOW CAN I WITH MY COLD HAND OF CLAY BUT THOU O LORD .	502	MILTON 20	17
ALL BEULAH WEPT FOR THEY SAW THE LORD COMING IN THE CLOUDS	519	MILTON 31	10
AS ONE AWAKEND IN THE NIGHT THEY SAW THE LORD COMING . .	519	MILTON 31	15
SHALT GIVE HER INTO THE ARMS OF GOD YOUR LORD & HUSBAND	523	MILTON 33	23
WITH OLOLON FOR THEY SAW THE LORD IN THE CLOUDS OF OLOLON	526	MILTON 35	41
HERE LIES STEWHARD THE [LORD OF] FRIEND OF ALL &C . . .	537	AND HIS LEGS/N *	52
THEY STOLE THEM FROM THE TEMPLE OF THE LORD	543	IF TRUE/N	9
AND EQUALLY FREE WITH THE LORD AND THE PEASANT THEY ARE	569D	DESC CAT 3	PROSE
THE PERSONS WHO ASCEND TO MEET THE LORD	609D	V LAST JUDG/N	PROSE
WHO SHALL MEET THE LORD COMING IN THE CLOUDS	610B	V LAST JUDG/N	PROSE
MEET THE LORD IN THE AIR & THEN HE WOULD BE HAPPY . .	611A	V LAST JUDG/N	PROSE
CRYING HOLY HOLY HOLY IS THE [G] LORD GOD ALMIGHTY . .	617B	V LAST JUDG/N	*PROSE
[FOR MY SAVIOUR AND LORD FOR THEY WERE WHOLLY ABSORBD IN	621A	JERUSALEM 3	*PROSE
THEIR GODS]			
OUR LORD WHO IS THE GOD [OF FIRE] AND LORD [OF LOVE] . .	621A	JERUSALEM 3	PROSE
WHICH IS THE DIVINE BODY OF THE LORD JESUS BLESSED FOR EVER	624	JERUSALEM 5	59
HE SAW THAT LOS WAS THE SOLE UNCONTROLLD LORD OF	627	JERUSALEM 8	26
THE FURNACES			
REMOTE FROM THE DIVINE VISION MY LORD AND SAVIOUR . .	646	JERUSALEM 23	12
INJURY THE LORD HEALS BUT VENGEANCE CANNOT BE HEALED . .	648	JERUSALEM 25	5
DONE TO THE DIVINE LORD & SAVIOUR WHO SUFFERS WITH THOSE	648	JERUSALEM 25	7
THAT SUFFER			
SAYING WE ALONE ARE ESCAPED O MERCIFUL LORD AND SAVIOUR	654	JERUSALEM 29	29
SAYING O LORD WHENCE IS THIS CHANGE THOU KNOWEST .	654	JERUSALEM 29	42
I AM NOTHING			
THE DEAD AWAKE TO GENERATION ARISE O LORD & REND THE VEIL	656	JERUSALEM 30	40
HE IS THE GOOD SHEPHERD HE IS THE LORD AND MASTER . .	665	JERUSALEM 38	23
BY OUR DEAR LORD I SEE WORLDS CRUSTED WITH SNOWS & ICE .	673	JERUSALEM 43	64
THIS DREAD DISEASE NONE BUT JESUS O LORD DESCEND AND SAVE	675	JERUSALEM 45	16
IN SILENCE THE DIVINE LORD BUILDED WITH IMMORTAL LABOUR	677	JERUSALEM 48	5
BEFORE YOU IN NIGHT COME ON COME ON COME ON THE LORD	680	JERUSALEM 49	52
SWAYD BY A PROVIDENCE OPPOSD TO THE DIVINE LORD JESUS .	681	JERUSALEM 50	4
COME LORD JESUS LAMB OF GOD DESCEND FOR IF O LORD .	681	JERUSALEM 50	10
ARISE SISTERS GO YE & MEET THE LORD WHILE I REMAIN .	681	JERUSALEM 50	12
AND SPILLD THE BLOOD OF MERCY'S LORD	683	I SAW A MONK/J	20
AGAINST THIS IMAGE OF HIS LORD	683	I SAW A MONK/J	24
THE MYSTIC UNION OF THE EMANATION IN THE LORD BECAUSE .	684	JERUSALEM 53	24
O LORD & SAVIOUR HAVE THE GODS OF THE HEATHEN PIERCED THEE	693	JERUSALEM 60	52
A DELUSION BUT I KNOW THEE O LORD WHEN THOU ARISEST UPON	693	JERUSALEM 60	58
DOES THE VOICE OF MY LORD CALL ME AGAIN AM I PURE THRO	695	JERUSALEM 61	36
HIS MERCY			
AND WILT THOU BECOME MY HUSBAND O MY LORD & SAVIOUR . . .	696	JERUSALEM 62	6
WEEPING & SHOUTING TO THE LORD DAY & NIGHT AND HIS CHILDREN	711	JERUSALEM 71	62
HENCE IS MY THEME O LORD MY SAVIOUR OPEN THOU THE GATES	715	JERUSALEM 74	40
THAT WE MAY LOSE NO TIME FROM THE WORK OF THE LORD . .	716D	JERUSALEM 77	PROSE
THY FOREHEAD BRIGHT HOLINESS TO THE LORD WITH GATES OF	730	JERUSALEM 86	4
PEARL			
AND VALLEYS & THY PLEASANT CITIES HOLINESS TO THE LORD .	731	JERUSALEM 86	12
OF DAVID OR OF EVE OF THE WOMAN OR OF THE LORD . . .	736	JERUSALEM 90	30
COME LORD JESUS TAKE ON THEE THE SATANIC BODY OF HOLINESS	737	JERUSALEM 90	38
WAS THE LORD THE UNIVERSAL HUMANITY & ALBION SAW HIS FORM	743	JERUSALEM 96	5
ALBION SAID O LORD WHAT CAN I DO MY SELFHOOD CRUEL . .	743	JERUSALEM 96	8
NO MAN LORD THEN WHAT IS HE	754	EV GOSPEL(E)/N	48
BUT THIS O LORD THIS WAS MY SIN	755	EV GOSPEL(E)/N	69
TO LORD BYRON IN THE WILDERNESS	779C	GHOST ABEL 1	PROSE
I CANNOT GO BEYOND THE COMMAND OF THE LORD	792C	LETTER 4	PROSE
CONSIDER WHAT LORD BACON SAYS "SENSE SENDS OVER TO" .	794A	LETTER 5	PROSE
RICHES OR FAME OF MORTALITY THE LORD OUR FATHER WILL DO FOR	802C	LETTER 14	PROSE
& IN PARTICULAR LADY HESKETH & LORD COWPER	820C	LETTER 25	PROSE
HONOURABLE AT ANY RATE THE PROJECT PLEASES LORD COWPER'S	821C	LETTER 25	PROSE
ENDEAVOUR TO LIVE TO THE GLORY OF OUR LORD & SAVIOUR & I	822C	LETTER 26	PROSE
I WILL GO ON IN THE STRENGTH OF THE LORD THROUGH HELL .	823C	LETTER 26	PROSE
ABOVE ALL YOU MY DEAR FRIEND & BENEFACTOR IN THE LORD .	834A	LETTER 33	PROSE
ON IN THE STRENGTH OF THE LORD GOD AS POOR PILGRIM SAYS	853A	LETTER 51	PROSE
HAPPINESS IS SECURE IN JESUS OUR LORD & WHO LOOKS FOR .	862D	LETTER 60	PROSE
I AM SORRY FOR LD(?LORD) LD(?LILFORD) HE IS A MAN OF VERY	868D	LETTER 68	PROSE
SINGULAR			

LORDLY

	PAGE	TITLE	LINE
OF HER LORDLY CONQUERORS HER PALACES LEVELLD WITH THE DUST	653	JERUSALEM 29	24

LORD'S

	PAGE	TITLE	LINE
ON [HIS] THE LEFT IS THE LORD'S SUPPER	444B	LAST JUDGMNT/L	*PROSE
& ON THE LEFT HAND THE LORD'S SUPPER IS ADMINISTERD . .	444B	LAST JUDGMNT/L	PROSE
"WOULD TO GOD THAT ALL THE LORD'S PEOPLE WERE PROPHETS"	481B	MILTON 1	PROSE
NUMBERS XI...			
FOR THE LORD'S COMING THAT JERUSALEM MAY OVERSPREAD ALL	511	MILTON 25	55
NATIONS			
[& THE OTHER] THAT ON THE LEFT REPRESENTS THE LORD'S SUPPER	612D	V LAST JUDG/N	PROSE

		PAGE	TITLE	LINE

LORD'S   (CONTINUED)
THEY REPRESENT EDUCATION ON THE SIDE NEXT THE LORD'S SUPPER   614A V LAST JUDG/N   PROSE
LORD'S SUPPER ON THE LEFT HAND OF THE [PICTURE] THRONE . .   614B V LAST JUDG/N   PROSE
BUT DESTROY NOT THESE LITTLE ONES NOR MOCK THE LORD'S   670 JERUSALEM 42   41
    ANOINTED
SAYING THE LORD'S PRAYER BACKWARDS WHICH THEY SAY RAISES   788C ANNO THORNTON   MARG
    THE DEVIL
LORDS
BRAVE LORDS WHO FELL BENEATH THE BLOODY AXE . . . . .   18 EDW THIRD/PS 1   44
QUEEN PHILIPPA LORDS BISHOP ETC . . . .   19A EDW THIRD/PS 2   PROSE
MY LORDS I HAVE BY THE ADVICE OF HER . . . .   19 EDW THIRD/PS 2   1
YET WITH YOUR KIND ASSISTANCE LORDS I HOPE . . . . . .   19 EDW THIRD/PS 2   6
SAY LORDS SHOULD NOT OUR THOUGHTS BE FIRST TO COMMERCE . .   19 EDW THIRD/PS 2   16
FORGIVE MY LORDS MY TALKATIVE YOUTH THAT SPEAKS . . . .   20 EDW THIRD/PS 2   38
MY LORDS THE FRENCH HAVE FITTED OUT MANY . . . . . .   20 EDW THIRD/PS 2   65
WHILE IN DARK COUNCIL SAT PHILISTA'S LORDS . . . . .   37D SAMSON/PS   PROSE
WHERE GEORGE THE THIRD HOLDS COUNCIL & HIS LORDS & COMMONS   204 AMERICA CANC B   9
    MEET
ITS OWN QUALITIES WHICH ARE SERVANTS OF HUMANITY NOT GODS   521 MILTON 32   21
    OR LORDS
HOUSES OF COMMONS & HOUSES OF LORDS APPEAR TO ME TO BE   600A PUB ADDRESS/N   PROSE
    FOOLS
THE EMMET AND [EARTH-WORM] EARTH-WORMS ARE HIS SUPERIORS   688 JERUSALEM 56   *   37
    & HIS LORDS
[?UNTIL ?THEY (BECAME) THE LORDS ?OF ?DRAWING] . . . .   SUPP ANNO REYNOLDS   * MARG
LORDSHIP
I KNOW BETTER & PLEASE YOUR LORDSHIP . . . .   784C ANNO WW EXCUR   MARG
LORDSHIPS
I HOPE THEIR LORDSHIPS WILL EXCUSE YOUR GIDDINESS . . .   20 EDW THIRD/PS 2   64
LOS
AND LOS ROUND THE DARK GLOBE OF URIZEN . . . .   226 URIZEN 5   38
LOS WEPT HOWLING AROUND THE DARK DEMON . . . .   226 URIZEN 6   2
LOS HOWLD IN A DISMAL STUPOR . . . .   226 URIZEN 7   1
TILL LOS ROUZD HIS FIRES AFFRIGHTED . . . .   226 URIZEN 7   *   8
LOS SMITTEN WITH ASTONISHMENT . . . .   226 URIZEN 8   1
ROUND THE FURIOUS LIMBS OF LOS . . . .   227 URIZEN 8   6
AND LOS FORMED NETS & GINS . . . .   227 URIZEN 8   7
LOS BEAT ON HIS FETTERS OF IRON . . . .   228 URIZEN 10   28
IN TERRORS LOS SHRUNK FROM HIS TASK . . . .   229 URIZEN 13   20
LOS SUFFERD HIS FIRES TO DECAY . . . .   230 URIZEN 13   44
LOS WEPT OBSCURD WITH MOURNING . . . .   230 URIZEN 13   48
THE ABYSS OF LOS STRETCHD IMMENSE . . . .   230 URIZEN 15   5
BEHELD THE DARK VISIONS OF LOS . . . .   231 URIZEN 15   12
WAVING BEFORE THE FACE OF LOS . . . .   231 URIZEN 18   12
BUT LOS SAW THE FEMALE & PITIED . . . .   231 URIZEN 19   10
NO MORE LOS BEHELD ETERNITY . . . .   233 URIZEN 20   2
LOS AWOKE HER O SORROW & PAIN . . . .   233 URIZEN 20   8
BUT LOS ENCIRCLED ENITHARMON . . . .   234 URIZEN 20   42
AND LOS POSSESSOR OF THE MOON JOYD IN THE PEACEFUL NIGHT   239 EUROPE 4   7
TILL ALL THE SONS OF URIZEN LOOK OUT AND ENVY LOS . .   239 EUROPE 4   16
TO GIVE US BLISS THAT WE MAY DRINK THE SPARKLING WINE OF   239 EUROPE 4   20
    LOS
THEN LOS AROSE HIS HEAD HE REARD IN SNAKY THUNDERS CLAD   245 EUROPE 15   9
THE SONG OF LOS LAMBETH PRINTED BY W BLAKE... . . .   245B SONG OF LOS   TITLE
I WILL SING YOU A SONG OF LOS THE ETERNAL PROPHET . . .   245 SONG OF LOS 3   1
BY THE HANDS OF THE CHILDREN OF LOS . . . . . .   245 SONG OF LOS 3   9
THUS THE TERRIBLE RACE OF LOS & ENITHARMON GAVE . . .   246 SONG OF LOS 4   13
THE SONG OF LOS IS ENDED URIZEN WEPT . . . . . .   248D SONG OF LOS 7   TITLE
TILL LOS SIEZD IT AND BEAT IN A MASS . . . . . .   250 AHANIA 2   47
AND LOS THREW THEM AROUND THE BONES . . . . . .   253 AHANIA 4   30
THE BOOK OF LOS LAMBETH PRINTED BY W BLAKE... . . .   255D BOOK OF LOS   TITLE
ROUND THE FLAMES ROLL AS LOS HURLS HIS CHAINS . . .   256 BOOK OF LOS 3   34
WIDE APART STOOD THE FIRES LOS REMAIND . . . . .   257 BOOK OF LOS 3   43
DARKNESS ROUND LOS HEAT WAS NOT FOR BOUND UP . . .   257 BOOK OF LOS 4   1
FALLING FALLING LOS FELL & FELL . . . .   258 BOOK OF LOS 4   27
FLOWD AROUND THE IMMENSE LOS BEHELD . . . . . .   259 BOOK OF LOS 5   12
LOS ASTONISHD AND TERRIFIED BUILT . . . .   259 BOOK OF LOS 5   20
LOS BEAT ON THE ANVIL TILL GLORIOUS . . . . . .   260 BOOK OF LOS 5   33
WHEN LOS HEATED THE GLOWING MASS CASTING . . . .   260 BOOK OF LOS 5   42
STOOD SELF-BALANCD AND LOS SMILD WITH JOY . . . .   260 BOOK OF LOS 5   45
THE END OF THE BOOK OF LOS . . . .   260D BOOK OF LOS 5   TITLE
LOS WAS THE FOURTH IMMORTAL STARRY ONE & IN THE EARTH . .   264 FOUR ZOAS 1   14
BUT LOS & ENITHARMON DELIGHTED IN THE MOONY SPACES OF [ONA]   270 FOUR ZOAS 1   232
    ENO
SHE DRAVE THE FEMALES ALL AWAY FROM LOS . . . . .   271 FOUR ZOAS 1   243
[?&] AND LOS DRAVE THE MALES FROM HER AWAY . . . .   271 FOUR ZOAS 1   * 244
DRIVING THE FEMALE EMANATIONS ALL AWAY FROM LOS . . .   271 FOUR ZOAS 1   273
THEN LOS SMOTE HER UPON THE EARTH TWAS LONG EER SHE REVIVD   272 FOUR ZOAS 1   281
[LOS] HE ANSWERD DARKNING MORE WITH [FOUL] INDIGNATION   272 FOUR ZOAS 1   282
    HID IN SMILES
SO SPOKE LOS SCORN & INDIGNATION ROSE UPON ENITHARMON   272 FOUR ZOAS 1   306
SULLEN SAT LOS PLOTTING REVENGE SILENT HE [URIZEN] EYED   273 FOUR ZOAS 1   320
    THE PRINCE
OF LIGHT SILENT THE PRINCE OF LIGHT VIEWD LOS AT LENGTH   273 FOUR ZOAS 1   321
    A BROODED
SULLEN HE LOWERD ON ENITHARMON BUT HE SMILD ON LOS . . .   273 FOUR ZOAS 1   323
SO SPOKE THE PRINCE OF LIGHT & SAT BESIDE THE SEAT OF LOS   273 FOUR ZOAS 1   329
LOS ANSWERD FURIOUS ART THOU ONE OF THOSE WHO WHEN MOST   273 FOUR ZOAS 1   331
    COMPLACENT
LOS SAW THE WOUND OF HIS BLOW HE SAW HE PITID HE WEPT . .   274 FOUR ZOAS 1   * 351
LOS NOW REPENTED THAT HE HAD SMITTEN ENITHARMON HE FELT   274 FOUR ZOAS 1   352
    LOVE

		PAGE	TITLE	LINE
LOS	(CONTINUED)			
	AND LOS & ENITHARMON SAT IN DISCONTENT & SCORN	274	FOUR ZOAS 1	374
	AND THIS THE SONG SUNG AT THE FEAST OF LOS & ENITHARMON	274	FOUR ZOAS 1	* 385
	CONGLOBING IN THE DARK CONFUSION MEAN TIME LOS WAS BORN	275	FOUR ZOAS 1	420
	AND THOU O ENITHARMON HARK I HEAR THE HAMMERS OF LOS . .	275	FOUR ZOAS 1	421
	BUT LOS & ENITHARMON SAT IN DISCONTENT & SCORN	276	FOUR ZOAS 1	439
	LEST LOS SHOULD ENTER INTO BEULAH THRO HER BEAUTIFUL GATES	279	FOUR ZOAS 1	566
	[?LOS] REASONING FROM THE LOINS IN THE UNREAL FORMS OF ULRO'S NIGHT	283	FOUR ZOAS 2	* 112
	LOS JOYD & ENITHARMON LAUGHD SAYING LET US GO DOWN . .	285	FOUR ZOAS 2	211
	[AND LOS & ENITHARMON JOYD THEY DRANK IN TENFOLD JOY]	286	FOUR ZOAS 2	236
	[NOW] FOR LOS & ENITHARMON WERE DRAWN DOWN BY THEIR DESIRES . .	287	FOUR ZOAS 2	287
	[NOW] FOR LOS & ENITHARMON WALKD FORTH ON THE DEWY EARTH	288	FOUR ZOAS 2	295
	AND LOS SAID LO THE LILLY PALE & THE ROSE REDDNING FIERCE	288	FOUR ZOAS 2	302
	IN THE BRIGHT SANDS OF LOS EVADING MY EMBRACE THEN I ALONE	288	FOUR ZOAS 2	305
	THE POOR FORSAKEN LOS MOCKD BY THE WORM THE SHELLY SNAIL	288	FOUR ZOAS 2	307
	THE EMMET & THE BEETLE HARK THEY LAUGH & MOCK AT LOS . .	288	FOUR ZOAS 2	308
	LOS ANSWERD THEREFORE FADE I THUS DISSOLVD IN RAPTURD TRANCE	288	FOUR ZOAS 2	318
	AMONG THE BEAUTIES OF THE WORLD COLD & REPINING LOS . .	288	FOUR ZOAS 2	321
	LOS SPOKE THY GOD IN VAIN SHALL CALL THEE IF BY MY STRONG POWER	289	FOUR ZOAS 2	336
	CURSE THEE THOU PLAGUE OF WOFUL LOS & SEEK REVENGE ON THEE	289	FOUR ZOAS 2	339
	SHE SANG OER LOS REVIVING HIM TO LIFE HIS GROANS WERE TERRIBLE	289	FOUR ZOAS 2	342
	LOS HEARD REVIVING HE SIEZD HER IN HIS ARMS DELUSIVE HOPES	290	FOUR ZOAS 2	380
	THUS LIVD LOS DRIVING ENION FAR INTO THE DEATHFUL INFINITE	290	FOUR ZOAS 2	383
	AND LUVAH IN THE LOINS OF LOS A DARK & FURIOUS DEATH . .	292	FOUR ZOAS 3	22
	[BUT SAW NOT LOS NOR ENITHARMON FOR LUVAH HID THEM IN SHADOW]	292	FOUR ZOAS 3	47
	OVER THE HEAVING DELUGE HE SAW LOS & ENITHARMON EMERGE . .	297	FOUR ZOAS 4	2
	LOS ANSWERD IN HIS FURIOUS PRIDE SPARKS ISSUING FROM HIS HAIR	298	FOUR ZOAS 4	34
	AND LOS REMAINS GOD OVER ALL WEAK FATHER OF WORMS & CLAY	298	FOUR ZOAS 4	41
	BUT NOW I AM ALL POWERFUL LOS & URTHONA IS BUT MY SHADOW	298	FOUR ZOAS 4	43
	SWAM IN RED TEARS HE BEARD HIS WAVES ABOVE THE HEAD OF LOS	298	FOUR ZOAS 4	45
	NOW HE RESOLVD TO DESTROY LOS & NOW HIS TEARS FLOWD DOWN	298	FOUR ZOAS 4	47
	IN SCORN STOOD LOS RED SPARKS OF BLIGHTING FROM HIS FURIOUS HEAD	298	FOUR ZOAS 4	48
	BUILT BY THE ARCHITECT DIVINE WHOSE LOVE TO LOS & ENITHARMON	298	FOUR ZOAS 4	51
	APART FROM LOS BUT COVERD HER WITH SOFTEST BROODING CARE	299	FOUR ZOAS 4	57
	O HOW HOWLD AT THE RENDING ASUNDER ALL THE FIBRES RENT	299	FOUR ZOAS 4	59
	MAKE FIRST A RESTING PLACE FOR LOS & ENITHARMON THEN . .	299	FOUR ZOAS 4	72
	UPON THE TIDE TILL UNDERNEATH THE FEET OF LOS A WORLD . .	300	FOUR ZOAS 4	125
	THARMAS BEFORE LOS STOOD & THUS THE VOICE OF THARMAS ROLLD	300	FOUR ZOAS 4	128
	URTHONA IS MY SON O LOS THOU ART URTHONA & THARMAS . . .	301	FOUR ZOAS 4	131
	ROUND LOS AFAR HIS WATERS BORE ON ALL SIDES ROUND WITH NOISE	301	FOUR ZOAS 4	159
	TERRIFIED LOS BEHELD THE RUINS OF URIZEN BENEATH	301	FOUR ZOAS 4	161
	THEN LOS WITH TERRIBLE HANDS SIEZD ON THE RUIND FURNACES	301	FOUR ZOAS 4	165
	AND LOS FORMD ANVILS OF IRON PETRIFIC FOR HIS BLOWS . . .	301	FOUR ZOAS 4	168
	IN MIGHTY POWER ROUND HIM LOS ROLLD FURIOUS	302	FOUR ZOAS 4	175
	BUT ENITHARMON WRAPD IN CLOUDS WAILD LOUD FOR AS LOS BEAT	302	FOUR ZOAS 4	184
	OF LOS ABSORBD IN DIRE REVENGE HE DRANK WITH JOY THE CRIES	302	FOUR ZOAS 4	191
	THE VOICE OF LOS COMPELLD HE LABOURD ROUND THE FURNACES	302	FOUR ZOAS 4	198
	LOS BEAT ON HIS FETTERS & [POURD] HEATED HIS FURNACES . .	303	FOUR ZOAS 4	213
	AND LOS BEHELD THE HAND OF GOD OVER HIS FURNACES	304	FOUR ZOAS 4	276
	WAS PUT TO ETERNAL DEATH LOS FELT THE LIMIT & SAW . . .	304	FOUR ZOAS 4	278
	IN TERRORS LOS SHRUNK FROM HIS TASK HIS GREAT HAMMER . .	304	FOUR ZOAS 4	* 280
	PALE TERROR SIEZD THE EYES OF LOS AS HE BEAT ROUND . . .	305	FOUR ZOAS 4	* 284
	THE BONES OF URIZEN HURTLE ON THE WIND THE BONES OF LOS	305	FOUR ZOAS 4	293
	RESTS ON THE DISTANT MOUNTAIN'S TOP SO LOS & ENITHARMON	305	FOUR ZOAS 5	11
	LOS FROM THE FURNACES LEAPD & LEFT THE COLD	305	FOUR ZOAS 5	15
	SWEAT & BLOOD STOOD ON THE LIMBS OF LOS IN GLOBES HIS FIERY EYELIDS	307	FOUR ZOAS 5	67
	SITTING IN DARKNESS OVER HER LOS MOURND IN ANGUISH FIERCE	307	FOUR ZOAS 5	71
	OF ENITHARMON LOS AROUND HER BUILDED PILLARS OF IRON . .	307	FOUR ZOAS 5	73
	THARMAS LAID THE FOUNDATIONS & LOS FINISHD IT IN HOWLING WOE	307	FOUR ZOAS 5	* 78
	THEIR SOLEMN HABITATION LOS BEHELD THE RUDDY BOY	307	FOUR ZOAS 5	80
	DEPENDING FROM THE BOSOM OF LOS & HOW WITH [DISMAL] GRIDING PAIN	307	FOUR ZOAS 5	93
	CALLD IT THE CHAIN OF JEALOUSY NOW LOS BEGAN TO SPEAK . .	307	FOUR ZOAS 5	95
	HELD THE FIERCE BOY LOS NAILD HIM DOWN BINDING AROUND HIS LIMBS	307	FOUR ZOAS 5	101
	OVER HER SON OBDURATE LOS BOUND DOWN HER LOVED JOY . . .	308	FOUR ZOAS 5	103
	LOS FOLDED ENITHARMON IN A COLD WHITE CLOUD IN FEAR . . .	308	FOUR ZOAS 5	110
	BUT WHEN RETURND TO GOLGONOOZA LOS & ENITHARMON	309	FOUR ZOAS 5	143
	AND LOS REPENTED THAT HE HAD CHAIND ORC UPON THE MOUNTAIN—	309	FOUR ZOAS 5	145
	LOS TAKING ENITHARMON BY THE HAND LED HER ALONG	309	FOUR ZOAS 5	150
	NOR THE CONSUMMATION OF LOS COULD EVER MELT THE CHAIN . .	309	FOUR ZOAS 5	162
	THAT THEY MAY CURSE THARMAS THEIR GOD & LOS HIS ADOPTED SON	313	FOUR ZOAS 6	43
	MINGLE TOGETHER TO CREATE A WORLD FOR LOS IN CRUEL DELIGHT	313	FOUR ZOAS 6	82
	LOS BROODED ON THE DARKNESS NOR SAW URIZEN WITH A GLOBE OF FIRE	314	FOUR ZOAS 6	83
	ALL THESE AROUND THE WORLD OF LOS CAST FORTH THEIR MONSTROUS BIRTHS	318	FOUR ZOAS 6	278
	TILL HE BEHELD THE WORLD OF LOS FROM THE PEAKED ROCK OF URTHONA	319	FOUR ZOAS 6	290
	LOS FELT THE ENVY IN HIS LIMBS LIKE TO A BLIGHTED TREE . .	321	FOUR ZOAS 7	27
	BRANCHES INTO THE HEAVEN OF LOS THEY PIPE FORMD BENDING DOWN	321	FOUR ZOAS 7	33

		PAGE	TITLE		LINE
LOS	(CONTINUED)				
THAT LOS MAY EVAPORATE LIKE SMOKE & BE NO MORE	. . .	323	FOUR ZOAS	7	114
AND LET HIM HAVE DOMINION OVER LOS THE TERRIBLE SHADE	. .	323	FOUR ZOAS	7	116
LOS WITH AMBITIOUS FURY THAT HIS RACE SHALL ALL DEVOUR	. .	323	FOUR ZOAS	7	134
LOS SAT IN SHOWERS OF URIZEN'S [COLD] WATCHING COLD ENITHARMON		324	FOUR ZOAS	7	* 166
LOS SAW HER STRETCHD THE IMAGE OF DEATH UPON HIS WITHERD VALLEYS		324	FOUR ZOAS	7	172
THEN LOS MOURND ON THE DISMAL WIND IN HIS JEALOUS LAMENTATION		324	FOUR ZOAS	7	183
ALL THINGS BESIDE THE WOFUL LOS ENJOY THE DELIGHTS OF BEAUTY		325	FOUR ZOAS	7	198
FOR LIFE IS SWEET TO LOS THE WRETCHED TO HIS WINGED WOES		325	FOUR ZOAS	7	204
THUS LOS LAMENTED IN THE NIGHT UNHEARD BY ENITHARMON	. .	325	FOUR ZOAS	7	209
IN DARK CONFUSION MEAN TIME LOS WAS BORN & ENITHARMON	. .	326	FOUR ZOAS	7	259
BESIDE LOS IN THE CAVERN DARK ENSLAVD TO VEGETATIVE FORMS		326	FOUR ZOAS	7	262
THOU & THAT DEMON LOS [WERE] WERT BORN AH JEALOUSY & WOE		327	FOUR ZOAS	7	* 295
THE DEEPS OF LOS THE SLAVE OF THAT CREATION I CREATED	. .	327	FOUR ZOAS	7	297
I LABOUR NIGHT & DAY FOR LOS BUT LISTEN THOU MY VISION	.	327	FOUR ZOAS	7	298
[I HAVE THEE IN MY ARMS & AM AGAIN UNITED TO LOS]	. . .	327	FOUR ZOAS	7	308
AND TREMBLED THRO THE WORLDS ABOVE LOS WEPT . . .	. .	328	FOUR ZOAS	7	318
THEN TOOK THE TREE OF MYSTERY ROOT IN THE WORLD OF LOS	.	328	FOUR ZOAS	7	333
OBDURATE LOS FELT PITY ENITHARMON TOLD THE TALE	. . .	328	FOUR ZOAS	7	338
OF URTHONA LOS EMBRACD THE SPECTRE FIRST AS A BROTHER	. .	328	FOUR ZOAS	7	339
LOS FURIOUS ANSWERD SPECTRE HORRIBLE THY WORDS ASTOUND MY EAR		329	FOUR ZOAS	7	361
SO SPOKE LOS & EMBRACING ENITHARMON & THE SPECTRE	. . .	329	FOUR ZOAS	7	370
HE IN HIS TURN GAVE TASKS TO LOS ENORMOUS TO DESTROY	. .	329	FOUR ZOAS	7	375
THAT BODY HE CREATED BUT IN VAIN FOR LOS PERFORMD	. .	329	FOUR ZOAS	7	376
THEY BUILDED GOLGONOOZA LOS LABOURING [INSPIRD] BUILDED PILLARS HIGH		329	FOUR ZOAS	7	* 378
BUT LOS STOOD ON THE LIMIT OF TRANSLUCENCE WEEPING & TREMBLING		329	FOUR ZOAS	7	384
THEN LOS PLUCKED THE FRUIT & EAT & SAT DOWN IN DESPAIR	. .	330	FOUR ZOAS	7	395
THE SPECTRE OF URTHONA WEPT BEFORE LOS SAYING I AM THE CAUSE		330	FOUR ZOAS	7	403
LOS TREMBLING ANSWERD NOW I FEEL THE WEIGHT OF STERN REPENTANCE		330	FOUR ZOAS	7	411
LOS SAT IN GOLGONOOZA IN THE GATE OF LUBAN WHERE	. . . .	331	FOUR ZOAS	7	433
O [LOVELY] LOVELY TERRIBLE LOS WONDER OF ETERNITY . . .		331	FOUR ZOAS	7	447
. . . O LOS MY DEFENCE & GUIDE		331	FOUR ZOAS	7	447
THAT VANISH AGAIN INTO MY BOSOM BUT IF THOU MY LOS	. .	331	FOUR ZOAS	7	452
SO ENITHARMON SPOKE & LOS HIS HANDS DIVINE INSPIRED BEGAN		331	FOUR ZOAS	7	* 456
LOS DREW THEM FORTH OUT OF THE DEEPS PLANTING HIS RIGHT FOOT FIRM		332	FOUR ZOAS	7	464
DIVIDING INTO JUST PROPORTIONS LOS UNWEARIED LABOURD	. .	332	FOUR ZOAS	7	470
OF LOS ASSIMILATING TO THOSE FORMS EMBODIED & LOVELY	. .	332	FOUR ZOAS	7	474
AS LOS A FATHER TO HIS BRETHREN & HE JOYD IN THE DARK LAKE		332	FOUR ZOAS	7	480
BUT LOS LOVED THEM & REFUSD TO SACRIFICE THEIR INFANT LIMBS		332	FOUR ZOAS	7	482
STARTLED WAS LOS HE FOUND HIS ENEMY URIZEN NOW		332	FOUR ZOAS	7	496
ROLL ROUND THE TEMPLE & THEY TOOK THE SUN THAT GLOWD OER LOS		333	FOUR ZOAS	7B	29
LOS REARD HIS MIGHTY [FOREHEAD] STATURE ON EARTH STOOD HIS FEET ABOVE		334	FOUR ZOAS	7B	40
SO CRIED THE DEMON OF THE WATERS IN THE CLOUDS OF LOS	. .	334	FOUR ZOAS	7B	72
BUT [DAY BY] NIGHT OR DAY LOS FOLLOWS WAR		335	FOUR ZOAS	7B	75
THAT WHEN LOS WARRD UPON THE SOUTH REFLECTED THE FIERCE FIRES		335	FOUR ZOAS	7B	* 76
RED RAGE THE FURIES OF FIERCE ORC BLACK THUNDERS ROLL ROUND LOS		335	FOUR ZOAS	7B	78
AND IF THAT LOS HAD NOT BUILT ME A TOWER UPON A ROCK	. .	335	FOUR ZOAS	7B	* 85
HOW SHALL I FLEE HOW SHALL I FLEE INTO THE TOWER OF LOS		335	FOUR ZOAS	7B	* 87
LIFT UP LIFT UP O LOS AWAKE MY WATCHMAN FOR HE SLEEPETH		335	FOUR ZOAS	7B	95
O LOS UNLESS THOU KEEP MY TOWER THE WATCHMAN WILL BE SLAIN		335	FOUR ZOAS	7B	97
AND THE HARLOT OF LOS & THE DELUDED HARLOT OF THE KINGS OF EARTH		336	FOUR ZOAS	7B	* 138
THEN [FIRST] LOS SAID		341	FOUR ZOAS	8	20
THEN [FIRST] LOS [BEHELD] SAID		341	FOUR ZOAS	8	20
OF GOLGONOOZA LOS STOOD [AT THE GATE] RECIEVING THEM	. .	341	FOUR ZOAS	8	31
FOR LOS COULD ENTER INTO ENITHARMON'S BOSOM & EXPLORE	. .	342	FOUR ZOAS	8	32
LOS STOOD &C		342	FOUR ZOAS	8	35
DESPAIR FROM THE POOR WANDERING SPECTRES AND LOS LOVED THEM		342	FOUR ZOAS	8	* 39
IN THE FIERCE BATTLE & HE SAW THE LAMB OF GOD & THE WORLD OF LOS		342	FOUR ZOAS	8	66
AND CHAINS & PULLIES FABRICATED ALL ROUND THE HEAVENS OF LOS		343	FOUR ZOAS	8	95
TO UNDERMINE THE WORLD OF LOS & TEAR BRIGHT ENITHARMON	. .	343	FOUR ZOAS	8	98
ENORMOUS WORKS LOS CONTEMPLATED INSPIRD BY THE HOLY SPIRIT		343	FOUR ZOAS	8	108
LOS BUILDS THE WALLS OF GOLGONOOZA AGAINST THE STIRRING BATTLE		343	FOUR ZOAS	8	109
?FEELING THE HAND OF LOS IN GOLGONOOZA & THE FORCE	. . .	344	FOUR ZOAS	8	112
SOUND LOUD THE HOWLING MUSIC INSPIRD BY LOS & ENITHARMON . . .		344	FOUR ZOAS	8	121
EMPLOYING THE DAUGHTERS IN HER LOOMS & LOS EMPLOYD THE SONS		345	FOUR ZOAS	8	185
LOS SAID TO ENITHARMON PITYING I SAW		347	FOUR ZOAS	8	259
PITY ME LOS PITY ME URIZEN & [BUILD] LET US BUILD	. . .	349	FOUR ZOAS	8	333
LOS TOOK THE BODY FROM THE CROSS JERUSALEM WEEPING OVER		349	FOUR ZOAS	8	338
THEY BORE IT TO THE SEPULCHER WHICH LOS HAD HEWN IN THE ROCK		349	FOUR ZOAS	8	339
SHE STOOD BEFORE LOS IN HER PRIDE [ABOVE] AMONG THE FURNACES		350	FOUR ZOAS	8	* 345
LOS SAT UPON HIS ANVIL STOCK THEY SAT BESIDE THE FORGE		350	FOUR ZOAS	8	348

LOS   (CONTINUED)
      LOS WIPD THE SWEAT FROM HIS RED BROW & THUS BEGAN   . . 350 FOUR ZOAS 8   349
      AND THESE [WERE] ARE THE SONS OF LOS & ENITHARMON RINTRAH   350 FOUR ZOAS 8   357
         PALAMABRON
      BUT SATAN ACCUSD PALAMABRON BEFORE [LOS] HIS BRETHREN ALSO 350 FOUR ZOAS 8   368
         HE MADDEND
      HE TEMPTED MANY OF THE SONS & DAUGHTERS OF LOS TO FLEE . . 350 FOUR ZOAS 8   374
      AWAY FROM [LOS] ME FIRST REUBEN FLED THEN SIMEON THEN LEVI 350 FOUR ZOAS 8   375
         THEN JUDAH
      THEN ZEBULUN THEN JOSEPH THEN BENJAMIN TWELVE SONS OF LOS   350 FOUR ZOAS 8   377
      WHEREFORE [RINTRAH &] PALAMABRON BEING ACCUSD BY SATAN   351 FOUR ZOAS 8   * 388
         TO LOS
      RAHAB BURNING WITH PRIDE & REVENGE DEPARTED FROM LOS   . . 351 FOUR ZOAS 8   410
      LOS DROPD A TEAR AT HER DEPARTURE BUT HE WIPD IT AWAY IN   351 FOUR ZOAS 8   411
         HOPE
      WITH ENVY HE SAW LOS WITH ENVY THARMAS & [URTHONA] THE   352 FOUR ZOAS 8   436
         SPECTRE
      LOS FELT THE STONY STUPOR & HIS HEAD ROLLD DOWN BENEATH   353 FOUR ZOAS 8   471
      AND THARMAS GAVE HIS POWER TO LOS URTHONA GAVE HIS   353 FOUR ZOAS 8   477
         STRENGTH
      SUCH ARE THE WORDS OF AHANIA & ENION LOS HEARS & WEEPS . . 356 FOUR ZOAS 8   584
      AND LOS & ENITHARMON TOOK THE BODY OF THE LAMB   . . . . 356 FOUR ZOAS 8   593
      DOWN FROM THE CROSS & PLACD IT IN A SEPULCHER WHICH LOS   356 FOUR ZOAS 8   594
         HAD HEWN
      AND LOS & ENITHARMON BUILDED JERUSALEM WEEPING   . . . . 357 FOUR ZOAS 9   1
      FOR SUCH THEY DEEMD THE DEATH OF THE BODY LOS HIS VEGETABLE 357 FOUR ZOAS 9   6
         HANDS
      ALL STRENGTH TO LOS & ENITHARMON & LET LOS SELF CURSD   . . 362 FOUR ZOAS 9   185
      SOUNDING THE SONG OF LOS DESCENDING TO THE VINEYARDS BRIGHT 376 FOUR ZOAS 9   713
      THEN LOS WHO IS URTHONA ROSE IN ALL HIS REGENERATE POWER   378 FOUR ZOAS 9   801
      DIVIDED FROM ENITHARMON NO LONGER THE SPECTRE LOS   . . . 379 FOUR ZOAS 9   850
      THREE CLASSES ARE CREATED BY THE HAMMER OF LOS & WOVEN . . 482 MILTON 2   26
      LOS SIEZD HIS HAMMER & TONGS HE LABOURD AT HIS RESOLUTE   482 MILTON 3   7
         ANVIL
      TERRIFIED LOS STOOD IN THE ABYSS & HIS IMMORTAL LIMBS   . . 483 MILTON 3   28
      SATAN WAS GOING TO REPLY BUT LOS ROLLD HIS LOUD THUNDERS   483 MILTON 4   15
      SO LOS SPOKE SATAN TREMBLING OBEYD WEEPING ALONG THE WAY   484 MILTON 4   19
      ALL PITIED THE PITEOUS & WAS WRATH WITH THE WRATHFUL &   484 MILTON 5   4
         LOS HEARD IT
      LOUD SOUNDS THE HAMMER OF LOS & LOUD HIS BELLOWS IS HEARD   485 MILTON 6   8
      LOUD SOUNDS THE HAMMER OF LOS LOUD TURN THE WHEELS OF   486 MILTON 6   27
         ENITHARMON
      OUT FROM THE ASHES OF THE DEAD LOS LIFTS HIS IRON LADLES   486 MILTON 6   29
      HIS PRIMITIVE TYRANNICAL ATTEMPTS ON LOS WITH MOST   486 MILTON 7   7
         ENDEARING LOVE
      HE SOFT INTREATED LOS TO GIVE TO HIM PALAMABRON'S STATION   486 MILTON 7   8
      LOS GAVE TO HIM THE HARROW OF THE ALMIGHTY ALAS BLAMABLE   486 MILTON 7   12
      INGRATITUDE & LOS BELIEVE THE ACCUSATION THRO SATAN'S   486 MILTON 7   14
         EXTREME
      WOULD I HAD TOLD LOS ALL MY HEART BUT PATIENCE O MY FRIENDS 487 MILTON 7   31
      ALL MAY BE WELL SILENT REMAIN WHILE I CALL LOS AND SATAN   487 MILTON 7   32
      PALAMABRON CALLD AND LOS & SATAN CAME BEFORE HIM   . . . . 487 MILTON 7   34
      HIMSELF HAD WROUGHT LOS TREMBLED SATAN'S BLANDISHMENTS   487 MILTON 7   37
         ALMOST
      WHAT COULD LOS DO HOW COULD HE JUDGE WHEN SATAN'S SELF   487 MILTON 7   41
         BELIEVD
      SO LOS SAID HENCEFORTH PALAMABRON LET EACH HIS OWN STATION 487 MILTON 7   43
      MEAN WHILE WEPT SATAN BEFORE LOS ACCUSING PALAMABRON   . . 487 MILTON 8   1
      AND BACK RETURND TO LOS NOT FILLD WITH VENGEANCE BUT WITH   488 MILTON 8   6
         TEARS
      HIMSELF CONVINCD OF PALAMABRON'S TURPITUDE LOS BEHELD   . . 488 MILTON 8   7
      THEN LOS TOOK OFF HIS LEFT SANDAL PLACING IT ON HIS HEAD   488 MILTON 8   11
      LOS WEPT BUT RINTRAH ALSO CAME AND ENITHARMON ON   . . . . 488 MILTON 8   14
      AND LOS SAID YE GENII OF THE MILLS THE SUN IS ON HIGH   . . 488 MILTON 8   16
      WILDLY THEY FOLLOWD LOS AND RINTRAH & THE MILLS WERE SILENT 488 MILTON 8   23
      BUT LOS HID THULLOH FROM HER SIGHT LEST SHE SHOULD DIE   488 MILTON 8   41
         OF GRIEF
      LOS SECRET BURIED THULLOH WEEPING DISCONSOLATE OVER THE   489 MILTON 8   45
         MOONY SPACE
      LOS IN HIS WRATH CURSD HEAVEN & EARTH HE RENT UP NATIONS   489 MILTON 9   13
      THEN LOS & ENITHARMON KNEW THAT SATAN IS URIZEN   . . . . 490 MILTON 10   * 1
      CANAAN THEN SHE RETURND TO LOS WEARY FRIGHTED AS   490 MILTON 10   * 5
         FROM DREAMS
      BECAME CANAAN CLOSING LOS FROM ETERNITY IN ALBION'S CLIFFS 491 MILTON 10   10
      SATAN AH ME IS GONE TO HIS OWN PLACE SAID LOS THEIR GOD   491 MILTON 10   12
      SO LOS LAMENTED OVER SATAN WHO TRIUMPHANT DIVIDED   491 MILTON 10   21
         THE NATIONS
      BUT LOS HID ENITHARMON FROM THE SIGHT OF ALL THESE THINGS   491 MILTON 11   2
      LOS THE VEHICULAR TERROR BEHELD HIM & DIVINE ENITHARMON   498 MILTON 17   31
      LOS HEARD IN TERROR ENITHARMON'S WORDS IN FIBROUS STRENGTH 498 MILTON 17   34
      IS BUILT ETERNALLY THE UNIVERSE OF LOS AND ENITHARMON . . 500 MILTON 19   25
      BOUND WITH THE CHAIN OF JEALOUSY BY LOS & ENITHARMON   . . 501 MILTON 19   38
      WHERE LOS OPENS HIS THREE WIDE GATES SURROUNDED BY RAGING   503 MILTON 20   49
         FIRES
      LOS SAW THEM AND A COLD PALE HORROR COVERD OER HIS LIMBS   503 MILTON 20   51
      SEVEN MORNINGS LOS HEARD THEM AS THE POOR BIRD WITHIN THE   504 MILTON 21   28
         SHELL
      WHOSE SONG CALLD MILTON TO THE ATTEMPT AND LOS HEARD THESE 504 MILTON 21   34
         LAMENTS
      WHILE LOS HEARD INDISTINCT IN FEAR WHAT TIME I BOUND MY   505 MILTON 22   4
         SANDALS
      ON TO WALK FORWARD THRO ETERNITY LOS DESCENDED TO ME   . . 505 MILTON 22   5

		PAGE	TITLE	LINE
LOS	(CONTINUED)			
	AND LOS BEHIND ME STOOD A TERRIBLE FLAMING SUN JUST CLOSE	505 MILTON 22		6
	LOS STOOD IN THAT FIERCE GLOWING FIRE & HE ALSO STOOPD DOWN	505 MILTON 22		8
	TWAS TOO LATE NOW TO RECEDE LOS HAD ENTERD INTO MY SOUL	505 MILTON 22		13
	SO SPOKE LOS AS WE WENT ALONG TO HIS SUPREME ABODE . . .	505 MILTON 22		26
	AND ALL THE DAUGHTERS OF LOS PROPHETIC WAIL YET IN DECEIT	506 MILTON 22		37
	THO STRONG AND MIGHTY TO DESTROY O LOS OUR BELOVED FATHER	507 MILTON 23		20
	DELUGE ALL THE COUNTRY ROUND SUCH IS A VISION OF LOS . .	507 MILTON 23		27
	BUT LOS DISPERSD THE CLOUDS EVEN AS THE STRONG WINDS OF JEHOVAH	507 MILTON 23		31
	AND LOS THUS SPOKE O NOBLE SONS BE PATIENT YET A LITTLE	507 MILTON 23		32
	YOU O MY SONS STILL GUARD ROUND LOS O WANDER NOT & LEAVE ME	508 MILTON 24		13
	SO LOS SPOKE FURIOUS THEY DESCENDED TO BOWLAHOOLA & ALLAMANDA	509 MILTON 24		44
	LOS IS BY MORTALS NAMD TIME ENITHARMON IS NAMD SPACE . .	509 MILTON 24		68
	LOUD SHOUT THE SONS OF LUVAH AT THE WINE-PRESSES AS LOS DESCENDED	510 MILTON 25		1
	THERE LOS PUTS ALL INTO THE PRESS THE OPRESSOR & THE OPPRESSED	510 MILTON 25		6
	BUT LOS REFUSED TILL ALL THE VINTAGE OF EARTH WAS GATHERD IN	510 MILTON 25	*	15
	AND LOS STOOD & CRIED TO THE LABOURERS OF THE VINTAGE IN VOICE OF AWE	510 MILTON 25		16
	SO LOS SPOKE BUT LIGHTNINGS OF DISCONTENT BROKE ON ALL SIDES ROUND	511 MILTON 25		63
	WHILE LOS CALLD HIS SONS AROUND HIM TO THE HARVEST & THE VINTAGE	511 MILTON 25		65
	THESE ARE THE SONS OF LOS & THESE THE LABOURERS OF THE VINTAGE	512 MILTON 26		1
	THESE ARE THE CHILDREN OF LOS THOU SEEST THE TREES ON MOUNTAINS	512 MILTON 26		7
	OF MEN THESE ARE THE SONS OF LOS THESE THE VISIONS OF ETERNITY	512 MILTON 26		10
	OF LOS & THOSE DELIVERD FROM THE BODY ON THE LEFT HAND . .	512 MILTON 26		17
	FOR LOS AGAINST THE EAST HIS FORCE CONTINUALLY BENDS . .	512 MILTON 26		18
	AND THESE THE LABOURS OF THE SONS OF LOS IN ALLAMANDA . .	512 MILTON 26		23
	THE SONS OF LOS CLOTHE THEM & FEED & PROVIDE HOUSES & FIELDS	512 MILTON 26		30
	BUILT BY THE SONS OF LOS IN BOWLAHOOLA & ALLAMANDA . . .	512 MILTON 26		33
	BUT THE WINE-PRESS OF LOS IS EASTWARD OF GOLGONOOZA BEFORE THE SEAT	513 MILTON 27		1
	OF LOS AND HERE HE LAYS HIS WORDS IN ORDER ABOVE THE MORTAL BRAIN	513 MILTON 27		9
	HERE THE SONS OF LOS LABOUR AGAINST DEATH ETERNAL THROUGH ALL	514 MILTON 27		44
	SOME SONS OF LOS SURROUND THE PASSIONS WITH PORCHES OF IRON & SILVER	514 MILTON 28		1
	BUT OTHERS OF THE SONS OF LOS BUILD MOMENTS & MINUTES & HOURS	516 MILTON 28		44
	THE SKY IS AN IMMORTAL TENT BUILT BY THE SONS OF LOS . .	516 MILTON 29		4
	IS VISIONARY AND IS CREATED BY THE HAMMER OF LOS	516 MILTON 29		20
	THE RED GLOBULE IS THE UNWEARIED SUN BY LOS CREATED . . .	517 MILTON 29		23
	ON ALBION'S ROCK LOS STANDS CREATING THE GLORIOUS SUN EACH MORNING	517 MILTON 29		41
	HIS PREY WHILE LOS APPOINTS & RINTRAH & PALAMABRON GUIDE	517 MILTON 29		44
	THEN LOS CONDUCTS THE SPIRITS TO BE VEGETATED INTO . . .	517 MILTON 29		47
	SUCH IS THE WORLD OF LOS THE LABOUR OF SIX THOUSAND YEARS	518 MILTON 29		64
	AROUND THIS POLYPUS LOS CONTINUAL BUILDS THE MUNDANE SHELL	524 MILTON 34		31
	FOUR UNIVERSES ROUND THE UNIVERSE OF LOS REMAIN CHAOTIC	524 MILTON 34		32
	FOUR INTERSECTING GLOBES & THE EGG FORMD WORLD OF LOS . .	524 MILTON 34		33
	EVEN OF LOS & ENITHARMON & ALL THE SONS OF ALBION . . .	525 MILTON 35		27
	BY OLOLON'S DESCENT THRO BEULAH TO LOS & ENITHARMON . . .	525 MILTON 35		36
	IN THIS MOMENT OLOLON DESCENDED TO LOS & ENITHARMON . . .	526 MILTON 35		46
	BUT THE LARK'S NEST IS AT THE GATE OF LOS AT THE EASTERN	526 MILTON 35		66
	FOR WHEN LOS JOIND WITH ME HE TOOK ME IN HIS FIRY WHIRLWIND	527 MILTON 36		21
	THE MUNDANE SHELL IN GOLGONOOZA BUT THE FIRES OF LOS RAGE	529 MILTON 37		56
	INTO ETERNITY THAT WAY BUT ALL DESCEND TO LOS	529 MILTON 37		58
	OF LOS THAT EVER BURNETH WITH FIRE EVER & EVER AMEN .	530 MILTON 39		12
	THEN LOUD THE FURNACES OF LOS WERE HEARD & SEEN AS SEVEN HEAVENS	531 MILTON 39		14
	IN MOONY BEULAH LOS HIS STRONG GUARD WALKS ROUND BENEATH THE MOON	531 MILTON 39		52
	I BEHOLD LOS & URIZEN I BEHOLD ORC & THARMAS	532 MILTON 40		6
	AND LOS & ENITHARMON ROSE OVER THE HILLS OF SURREY . . .	534 MILTON 42		31
	LOS LISTENS TO THE CRY OF THE POOR MAN HIS CLOUD	535 MILTON 42		34
	HALF FRIENDSHIP IS THE BITTEREST ENMITY SAID LOS	620 JERUSALEM 1		8
	THE FURNACE OF LOS BEFORE THE EASTERN GATE BENDING THEIR FURY	623 JERUSALEM 5		28
	OUT FROM THE FURNACES OF LOS ABOVE THE HEAD OF LOS . . .	624 JERUSALEM 5		50
	LOS HEARD HER LAMENTATIONS IN THE DEEPS AFAR HIS TEARS FALL	624 JERUSALEM 5		66
	IN TERROR OF THOSE STARRY WHEELS AND THE SPECTRE STOOD OVER LOS	624 JERUSALEM 6		4
	CURSING THE TERRIBLE LOS BITTERLY CURSING HIM FOR HIS FRIENDSHIP	624 JERUSALEM 6		6
	LOS RAGD AND STAMPD THE EARTH IN HIS MIGHT & TERRIBLE WRATH	625 JERUSALEM 6		8
	TO DEVOUR LOS'S HUMAN PERFECTION BUT WHEN HE SAW THAT LOS	625 JERUSALEM 6	*	14
	TO LURE LOS BY TEARS BY ARGUMENTS OF SCIENCE & BY TERRORS	625 JERUSALEM 7		6
	WHILE LOS ANSWERD UNTERRIFIED TO THE OPAKE BLACKENING FIEND	625 JERUSALEM 7		8
	TO PREPARE THE SPECTRE OF ALBION TO REIGN OVER THEE O LOS	626 JERUSALEM 7		40
	LOS ANSWERD ALTHO I KNOW NOT THIS I KNOW FAR WORSE THAN THIS	626 JERUSALEM 7		51

		PAGE	TITLE	LINE
LOS	(CONTINUED)			
	WHILE LOS SPOKE THE TERRIBLE SPECTRE FELL SHUDDRING BEFORE HIM	627	JERUSALEM 8	21
	LOS OPEND THE FURNACES IN FEAR THE SPECTRE SAW TO BABEL & SHINAR	627	JERUSALEM 8	23
	HE SAW THAT LOS WAS THE SOLE UNCONTROLLD LORD OF THE FURNACES	627	JERUSALEM 8	26
	WHILE LOS PURSUD HIS SPEECH IN THREATNINGS LOUD & FIERCE	627	JERUSALEM 8	29
	OF AFFLICTION AND LOS DREW THEM FORTH COMPELLING THE HARSH SPECTRE	628	JERUSALEM 9	35
	THE SONS & DAUGHTERS OF LOS THAT HE MIGHT PROTECT THEM FROM	629	JERUSALEM 10	4
	THEREFORE LOS STANDS IN LONDON BUILDING GOLGONOOZA . . .	629	JERUSALEM 10	17
	THE SPECTRE WEEPS BUT LOS UNMOVD BY TEARS OR THREATS REMAINS	629	JERUSALEM 10	19
	SO LOS IN FURY & STRENGTH IN INDIGNATION & BURNING WRATH	629	JERUSALEM 10	22
	LOS CRIES OBEY MY VOICE & NEVER DEVIATE FROM MY WILL . .	629	JERUSALEM 10	29
	WHICH LOS WIPED OFF BUT COMFORT NONE COULD GIVE OR BEAM OF HOPE	630	JERUSALEM 10	61
	AT THE SUBLIME LABOURS FOR LOS COMPELLD THE INVISIBLE SPECTRE	630	JERUSALEM 10	65
	AND THE SONS AND DAUGHTERS OF LOS CAME FORTH IN PERFECTION LOVELY	630	JERUSALEM 11	11
	LOS WEPT WITH EXCEEDING JOY & ALL WEPT WITH JOY TOGETHER	631	JERUSALEM 11	13
	AND LOS SAID I BEHOLD THE FINGER OF GOD IN TERRORS . .	631	JERUSALEM 12	5
	TERRIFIED AT THE SUBLIME WONDER LOS STOOD BEFORE HIS FURNACES	631	JERUSALEM 12	21
	WITHOUT THE GATE OF LOS AMONG THE DARK SATANIC WHEELS . .	632	JERUSALEM 12	44
	FOURFOLD THE SONS OF LOS IN THEIR DIVISIONS AND FOURFOLD	632	JERUSALEM 12	45
	GOLGONOOZA LOS WALKS ROUND THE WALLS NIGHT AND DAY . . .	634	JERUSALEM 13	55
	IN SEAS OF SORROW LOS ALSO VIEWS THE FOUR FEMALES . . .	634	JERUSALEM 14	9
	ENITHARMON IS A VEGETATED MORTAL WIFE OF LOS	635	JERUSALEM 14	13
	SUCH ARE THE BUILDINGS OF LOS & SUCH ARE THE WOOFS OF ENITHARMON	635	JERUSALEM 14	15
	AND LOS BEHELD HIS SONS AND HE BEHELD HIS DAUGHTERS . .	635	JERUSALEM 14	16
	AND LOS BEHELD THE MILD EMANATION JERUSALEM EASTWARD BENDING	635	JERUSALEM 14	31
	I SEE IN DEADLY FEAR IN LONDON LOS RAGING ROUND HIS ANVIL	636	JERUSALEM 15	21
	OF DEATH FORMING AN AX OF GOLD THE FOUR SONS OF LOS . . .	636	JERUSALEM 15	22
	AMONG THE FURNACES OF LOS IN THE VALLEY OF THE SON OF HINNOM	636	JERUSALEM 15	34
	HERE LOS FIXD DOWN THE FIFTY-TWO COUNTIES OF ENGLAND & WALES	637	JERUSALEM 16	28
	IN ENITHARMON'S HALLS BUILT BY LOS & HIS MIGHTY CHILDREN	638	JERUSALEM 16	60
	HIS SPECTRE DIVIDES & LOS IN FURY COMPELLS IT TO DIVIDE	638	JERUSALEM 17	1
	TO MAKE A WAY FOR THE CHILDREN OF LOS TO COME FROM THE FURNACES	638	JERUSALEM 17	5
	BUT LOS HIMSELF AGAINST ALBION'S SONS HIS FURY BENDS FOR HE	638	JERUSALEM 17	6
	THEY WOOE LOS CONTINUALLY TO SUBDUE HIS STRENGTH HE CONTINUALLY	638	JERUSALEM 17	10
	FOR LOS SAID THO MY SPECTRE IS DIVIDED AS I AM A LIVING MAN	638	JERUSALEM 17	16
	SO LOS IN SECRET WITH HIMSELF COMMUNED & ENITHARMON HEARD	639	JERUSALEM 17	48
	TREMBLING GLOBE SHOT FORTH SELF-LIVING & LOS HOWLD OVER IT	639	JERUSALEM 17	55
	AND LOS WAS ROOFD IN FROM ETERNITY IN ALBION'S CLIFFS . .	642	JERUSALEM 19	33
	CLOUDED WITH STORMS LOS HIS STRONG GUARD WALKD ROUND BENEATH THE MOON	642	JERUSALEM 19	38
	AND THE TWO THAT ESCAPED WERE THE EMANATION OF LOS & HIS	655	JERUSALEM 30	1
	THEY WEPT & TREMBLED & LOS PUT FORTH HIS HAND & TOOK THEM IN	656	JERUSALEM 30	16
	INCLOSING LOS BUT THE DIVINE VISION APPEARD WITH LOS . .	656	JERUSALEM 30	19
	AND LOS PRAYED AND SAID O DIVINE SAVIOUR ARISE	656	JERUSALEM 30	21
	SO LOS IN LAMENTATIONS FOLLOWD ALBION ALBION COVERD . .	656	JERUSALEM 30	41
	LOS TOOK HIS GLOBE OF FIRE TO SEARCH THE INTERIORS OF ALBION'S	656	JERUSALEM 31	3
	IN BRICKS TO BUILD THE PYRAMIDS OF HEBER & TERAH BUT LOS	657	JERUSALEM 31	12
	SO SPOKE LOS TRAVELLING THRO DARKNESS & HORRID SOLITUDE	657	JERUSALEM 31	39
	LOS WAS ALL ASTONISHMENT & TERROR HE TREMBLED SITTING ON THE STONE	658	JERUSALEM 32	3
	FROM LOS ASTONISHD HE BEHELD ONLY THE PETRIFIED SURFACES	658	JERUSALEM 32	5
	AND SAW HIS FURNACES IN RUINS FOR LOS IS THE DEMON OF THE FURNACES	658	JERUSALEM 32	6
	LOS STOOD AT HIS ANVIL HE HEARD THE CONTENTIONS OF VALA	660	JERUSALEM 34	17
	FROM HIS AWFUL MEMBERS AND THUS LOS CRIED ALOUD	660	JERUSALEM 34	21
	SO LOS SPOKE STANDING ON MAM-TOR LOOKING OVER EUROPE & ASIA	661	JERUSALEM 34	41
	LOS BENDED HIS NOSTRILS DOWN TO THE EARTH THEN SENT HIM OVER	661	JERUSALEM 34	47
	LOS ROLLED HIS EYES INTO TWO NARROW CIRCLES THEN SENT HIM	661	JERUSALEM 34	53
	CONSIDER THIS O MORTAL MAN O WORM OF SIXTY WINTERS SAID LOS	661	JERUSALEM 34	57
	AND SIXTY WINTERS LOS RAGED IN THE DIVISIONS OF REUBEN . .	662	JERUSALEM 36	3
	REUBEN SLEPT IN THE CAVE OF ADAM AND LOS FOLDED HIS TONGUE	662	JERUSALEM 36	5
	BEFORE THE FURNACES OF LOS IN A HORRIBLE DREAMFUL SLUMBER	662	JERUSALEM 36	11
	ON MOUNT GILEAD LOOKING TOWARD GILGAL AND LOS BENDED . .	662	JERUSALEM 36	12
	AS LOS BENDED THE SENSES OF REUBEN REUBEN IS MERLIN . .	663	JERUSALEM 36	41
	SO LOS SPOKE BUT WHEN HE SAW [PALE] BLUE DEATH IN ALBION'S FEET	664	JERUSALEM 37	10
	ROLLS DREADFUL THRO THE FURNACES OF LOS AND THE MILLS OF SATAN	665	JERUSALEM 38	37
	IT IS THE GATE OF LOS WITHOUTSIDE IS THE MILL INTRICATE DREADFUL	666	JERUSALEM 39	3
	BEFORE THE GATE OF LOS URTHONA HERE IS NAMED LOS	666	JERUSALEM 39	9
	ALBION FLED THRO THE GATE OF LOS AND HE STOOD IN THE GATE	666	JERUSALEM 39	11
	LOS WAS THE FRIEND OF ALBION WHO MOST LOVD HIM IN CAMBRIDGESHIRE	666	JERUSALEM 39	12

1132

		PAGE	TITLE		LINE
LOS	(CONTINUED)				
LOS SAID TO ALBION WHITHER FLEEST THOU ALBION REPLYD	. .	666	JERUSALEM 39		15
LOS ANSWERD TROUBLED AND HIS SOUL WAS RENT IN TWAIN	. . .	666	JERUSALEM 39	*	24
LOS SHUDDERD AT BEHOLDING ALBION FOR HIS DISEASE	. . . .	666	JERUSALEM 40		1
SUBMITTING TO BE CALLD THE SON OF LOS THE TERRIBLE VISION		668	JERUSALEM 40		52
LOS BUILT THE STUBBORN STRUCTURE OF THE LANGUAGE ACTING AGAINST		668	JERUSALEM 40		59
BROODING ON EVIL BUT WHEN LOS OPEND THE FURNACES BEFORE HIM		669	JERUSALEM 42		2
ALSO LOS SICK & TERRIFIED BEHELD THE FURNACES OF DEATH	. .	669	JERUSALEM 42		5
LOS THOU NOW DISCOVEREST THY TURPITUDE TO THE HEAVENS	. .	669	JERUSALEM 42		11
LOS ANSWERD RIGHTEOUSNESS & JUSTICE I GIVE THEE IN RETURN		670	JERUSALEM 42		19
SO LOS SPOKE THEN TURND HIS FACE & WEPT FOR ALBION	. . .	670	JERUSALEM 42		46
LOS STOOD BEFORE HIS FURNACES AWAITING THE FURY OF THE DEAD		671	JERUSALEM 42		55
THUS MOURN THEY LOUD THE FURNACES OF LOS THUNDER UPON	. .	671	JERUSALEM 42		75
AND LOS DREW HIS SEVEN FURNACES AROUND ALBION'S ALTARS	. .	671	JERUSALEM 42		77
AND AS ALBION BUILT HIS FROZEN ALTARS LOS BUILT THE MUNDANE SHELL		671	JERUSALEM 42		78
THEN LOS GREW FURIOUS RAGING WHY STAND WE HERE TREMBLING AROUND		672	JERUSALEM 43		12
SO LOS SPOKE PALE THEY STOOD AROUND THE HOUSE OF DEATH	. .	673	JERUSALEM 43		80
AND ALL THE GATE OF LOS CLOUDED WITH CLOUDS REDOUNDING FROM		674	JERUSALEM 44		8
AND FEELING THE DAMPS OF DEATH THEY WITH ONE ACCORD DELEGATED LOS		674	JERUSALEM 44		28
TILL JESUS SHALL APPEAR & THEY GAVE THEIR POWER TO LOS	. .	674	JERUSALEM 44		30
BEFORE THE GATE OF LOS & IN THE DEPTHS OF NON ENTITY	. .	674	JERUSALEM 44		36
AMONG THE FURNACES OF LOS AMONG THE OAKS OF ALBION	. . .	674	JERUSALEM 44		37
LINCOLN DURHAM & CARLISLE COUNCELLORS OF LOS	. . . . .	676	JERUSALEM 46		5
AND ELY SCRIBE OF LOS WHOSE PEN NO OTHER HAND	. . . . .	676	JERUSALEM 46		6
BOWING THEIR HEADS DEVOTED AND THE FURNACES OF LOS	. . .	676	JERUSALEM 46		20
LOS ALSO SAW HER IN HIS SEVENTH FURNACE HE ALSO TERRIFIED		678	JERUSALEM 48		44
BUT LOS WHO IS THE VEHICULAR FORM OF STRONG URTHONA	. . .	684	JERUSALEM 53		1
AND THE ROOTS OF ALBION'S TREE ENTERD THE SOUL OF LOS	. .	684	JERUSALEM 53		4
INCLOSING ALL THE CHILDREN OF LOS TIME AFTER TIME	. . .	684	JERUSALEM 53		7
HERE ON THE BANKS OF THE THAMES LOS BUILDED GOLGONOOZA	. .	684	JERUSALEM 53		15
THEN LOS HEAVED HIS THUNDRING BELLOWS ON THE VALLEY OF MIDDLESEX		687	JERUSALEM 56		1
THEN LOS UTTERED WITH HAMMER & ANVIL CHAUNT REVOICE	. . .	688	JERUSALEM 56		29
LOS UTTERD SWIFT AS THE RATTLING THUNDER UPON THE MOUNTAINS		688	JERUSALEM 56		41
AND LOS FIXES THEM ON HIS ANVIL INCESSANT HIS BLOWS	. . .	690	JERUSALEM 58		16
ARCHD OVER THE MOON AT MIDNIGHT & LOS FIXD THEM THERE	.	690	JERUSALEM 58		31
THIS LOS FORMED INTO THE GATES & MIGHTY WALL BETWEEN THE OAK		691	JERUSALEM 59		5
IS BUILT ETERNALLY THE SUBLIME UNIVERSE OF LOS & ENITHARMON		691	JERUSALEM 59		21
AND ONE DAUGHTER OF LOS SAT AT THE FIERY REEL & ANOTHER		691	JERUSALEM 59		26
AND ANOTHER DAUGHTER OF LOS SAT AT THE SPINNING WHEEL	. .	691	JERUSALEM 59		29
OTHER DAUGHTERS OF LOS LABOURING AT LOOMS LESS FINE	. . .	692	JERUSALEM 59		45
WHILE LOS SAT TERRIFIED BEHOLDING ALBION'S SPECTRE WHO IS LUVAH		692	JERUSALEM 60		2
BUT LOS BEHELD THE DIVINE VISION AMONG THE FLAMES OF THE FURNACES		696	JERUSALEM 62		35
OF ALBION'S SPECTRES THAT LOS IN DESPAIR OFT SAT & OFTEN PONDERD		696	JERUSALEM 62		39
HOW CAN THE FEMALE BE CHASTE O THOU STUPID DRUID CRIED LOS		697	JERUSALEM 63		26
LOS ON THE THAMES & MEDWAY LONDON & CANTERBURY GROAN IN PAIN		698	JERUSALEM 63		35
LOS KNEW NOT YET WHAT WAS DONE HE THOUGHT IT WAS ALL IN VISION		698	JERUSALEM 63		36
THEN ALL THE DAUGHTERS OF ALBION BECAME ONE BEFORE LOS EVEN VALA		698	JERUSALEM 64		6
WHEREFORE ART THOU LIVING SAID LOS & MAN CANNOT LIVE IN THY PRESENCE		698	JERUSALEM 64		18
LOS BEHELD IN TERROR HE POURD HIS LOUD STORMS ON THE FURNACES		702	JERUSALEM 66		16
DRIVN FORTH BY LOS TIME AFTER TIME FROM ALBION'S CLIFFY SHORE		707	JERUSALEM 69		8
ABOVE THE MOUNTAINS OF ALBION ABOVE THE HEAD OF LOS	. .	711	JERUSALEM 71	*	55
AND LOS SHOUTED WITH CEASELESS SHOUTINGS & HIS TEARS POURED DOWN		711	JERUSALEM 71		56
BY LOS FOR JERUSALEM'S SAKE & CALLED THE GATES OF JERUSALEM		711	JERUSALEM 72		8
THE FOUR THAT REMAIN WITH LOS TO GUARD THE WESTERN WALL		711	JERUSALEM 72		12
AND THE FOUR GATES OF LOS SURROUND THE UNIVERSE WITHIN AND		712	JERUSALEM 72		45
ACCUMULATING WITHOUT END HERE LOS WHO IS OF THE ELOHIM	. .	713	JERUSALEM 73		24
WHICH LOS WITH HIS MIGHTY HAMMER DEMOLISHES TIME ON TIME		713	JERUSALEM 73		32
THESE TO PRESERVE THEM FROM ETERNAL DEATH LOS CREATES	. .	714	JERUSALEM 73		40
THE SPECTRES OF THE DEAD HOWL ROUND THE PORCHES OF LOS	. .	714	JERUSALEM 73		46
THE SONS OF LOS CLOTHE THEM & FEED & PROVIDE HOUSES & GARDENS		714	JERUSALEM 73		49
SONS & DAUGHTERS OF LOS IN BOWLAHOOLA & IN CATHEDRON	. .	714	JERUSALEM 73		52
TO TELL HOW LOS IN GRIEF & ANGER WHIRLING ROUND HIS HAMMER ON HIGH		714	JERUSALEM 74		20
HOW HYLE ROOFD LOS IN ALBION'S CLIFFS BY THE AFFECTIONS RENT		715	JERUSALEM 74		28
HOW LOS DRAVE THEM FROM ALBION & THEY BECAME DAUGHTERS OF CANAAN		715	JERUSALEM 74		38
FOR LOS IN SIX THOUSAND YEARS WALKS UP & DOWN CONTINUALLY		716	JERUSALEM 75		7
THUS ARE THE HEAVENS FORMD BY LOS WITHIN THE MUNDANE SHELL		716	JERUSALEM 75		23
THE SLEEPING HUMANITY LOS WITH HIS MACE OF IRON	. . . .	718	JERUSALEM 78		3
WHILE LOS LAMENTS AT HIS DIRE LABOURS VIEWING JERUSALEM		719	JERUSALEM 78		10
LOS SAW TERRIFIED MELTED WITH PITY & DIVIDED IN WRATH	. .	722	JERUSALEM 80		41
I HEARD ENITHARMON SAY TO LOS LET THE DAUGHTERS OF ALBION		725	JERUSALEM 82		22
AND LET THE LOOMS OF ENITHARMON & THE FURNACES OF LOS	. .	725	JERUSALEM 82		26
LOS SAW THE ENVIOUS BLIGHT ABOVE HIS SEVENTH FURNACE	. .	726	JERUSALEM 82		56

1133

		PAGE	TITLE	LINE
LOS	(CONTINUED)			
	BENEATH ALBION'S FATAL TREE BEFORE THE GATE OF LOS . . .	726	JERUSALEM 82	60
	IN THE FURNACES OF LOS & IN THE WINE-PRESS TREADING DAY & NIGHT	726	JERUSALEM 82	64
	LOS SAW & WAS COMFORTED AT HIS FURNACES UTTERING THUS HIS VOICE	727	JERUSALEM 82	80
	SO LOS SPOKE TO THE DAUGHTERS OF BEULAH WHILE HIS EMANATION	728	JERUSALEM 83	66
	WHILE LOS AROSE UPON HIS WATCH AND DOWN FROM GOLGONOOZA	728	JERUSALEM 83	75
	BEFORE THE FURNACES LABOURING WHILE LOS ALL NIGHT WATCHES	729	JERUSALEM 83	80
	FOR JERUSALEM LIES IN RUINS & THE FURNACES OF LOS ARE BUILDED THERE	729	JERUSALEM 84	6
	BUT WE WOO HIM ALL THE NIGHT IN SONGS O LOS COME FORTH O LOS	729	JERUSALEM 84	25
	LOS SMILD WITH JOY THINKING ON ENITHARMON & HE BROUGHT . .	730	JERUSALEM 85	3
	LOS WALKS UPON HIS ANCIENT MOUNTAINS IN THE DEADLY DARKNESS	730	JERUSALEM 85	10
	AND THUS LOS REPLIES UPON HIS WATCH THE VALLEYS LISTEN SILENT	730	JERUSALEM 85	14
	AND THIS IS THE SONG OF LOS THE SONG THAT HE SINGS ON HIS WATCH	730	JERUSALEM 85	21
	THUS LOS SINGS UPON HIS WATCH WALKING FROM FURNACE TO FURNACE	731	JERUSALEM 86	33
	VIEWING LOS IN HIS SHUDDERINGS POURING BALM ON HIS SORROWS	732	JERUSALEM 86	47
	DESARTS LOS FIRST BROKE SILENCE & BEGAN TO UTTER HIS LOVE	732	JERUSALEM 87	2
	LOS ANSWERD SIGHING LIKE THE BELLOWS OF HIS FURNACES . .	733	JERUSALEM 88	1
	FIBRES OF LOS SENDING THEM OVER THE OCEAN EASTWARD INTO	733	JERUSALEM 88	25
	FLOWD INTO THE ACHING FIBRES OF LOS YET CONTENDING AGAINST HIM	733	JERUSALEM 88	29
	THRO ALL THE WORLD OF ERIN & OF LOS & ALL THEIR CHILDREN	733	JERUSALEM 88	33
	WHILE LOS STOOD AT HIS ANVIL IN WRATH THE VICTIM OF THEIR LOVE	734	JERUSALEM 88	46
	THE FURNACES OF LOS LOUD ROLL THE WHEELS OF ENITHARMON . .	734	JERUSALEM 88	54
	LOS CRIES NO INDIVIDUAL OUGHT TO APPROPRIATE TO HIMSELF	736	JERUSALEM 90	28
	SO LOS CRIED IN THE VALLEYS OF MIDDLESEX IN THE SPIRIT OF PROPHECY	737	JERUSALEM 90	39
	FOR LOS SAID WHEN THE INDIVIDUAL APPROPRIATES UNIVERSALITY	737	JERUSALEM 90	52
	THESE ARE THE DEMONSTRATIONS OF LOS & THE BLOWS OF MY MIGHTY HAMMER	737	JERUSALEM 90	57
	SO LOS SPOKE AND THE GIANTS OF ALBION TERRIFIED & ASHAMED	737	JERUSALEM 90	58
	PLOTTING TO DEVOUR ALBION & LOS THE FRIEND OF ALBION . .	737	JERUSALEM 90	63
	BUT STILL THE THUNDER OF LOS PEALS LOUD & THUS THE THUNDER'S CRY	737	JERUSALEM 90	* 67
	SO LOS CRIED AT HIS ANVIL IN THE HORRIBLE DARKNESS WEEPING	738	JERUSALEM 91	32
	REPEATING THE SMARAGDINE TABLE OF HERMES TO DRAW LOS DOWN	738	JERUSALEM 91	35
	LOS READS THE STARS OF ALBION THE SPECTRE READS THE VOIDS	738	JERUSALEM 91	37
	TO REACH THE HEAVENLY ARCHES LOS BEHELD UNDAUNTED FURIOUS	738	JERUSALEM 91	42
	THUS LOS ALTERD HIS SPECTRE & EVERY RATIO OF HIS REASON	739	JERUSALEM 91	51
	TERRIFIED LOS SAT TO BEHOLD TREMBLING & WEEPING & HOWLING	739	JERUSALEM 91	54
	SO LOS TERRIFIED CRIES TREMBLING & WEEPING & HOWLING BEHOLDING	739	JERUSALEM 91	59
	SO LOS SPOKE ENITHARMON ANSWERD IN GREAT TERROR IN LAMBETH'S VALE	739	JERUSALEM 92	7
	LOS ANSWERD SWIFT AS THE SHUTTLE OF GOLD SEXES MUST VANISH & CEASE	739	JERUSALEM 92	13
	THEN LOS AGAIN TOOK UP HIS SPEECH AS ENITHARMON CEAST . .	741	JERUSALEM 93	17
	REVOLVE & OVER THEM THE FURNACES OF LOS & THE IMMORTAL TOMB AROUND	741	JERUSALEM 94	12
	HIS ANVIL IN THE GREAT SPECTRE LOS UNWEARIED LABOURING & WEEPING	742	JERUSALEM 95	18
	AND THE DIVINE APPEARANCE WAS THE LIKENESS & SIMILITUDE OF LOS	743	JERUSALEM 96	7
	I SEE THEE IN THE LIKENESS & SIMILITUDE OF LOS MY FRIEND	743	JERUSALEM 96	22
	AND LOS THE TERRIBLE THUS HATH SWORN	817	HAPPINESS/L	35
	THE CURSES OF LOS THE TERRIBLE SHADE	818	HAPPINESS/L	51
	THEN LOS APPEARD IN ALL HIS POWER	818	HAPPINESS/L	55
	TWAS OUTWARD A SUN INWARD LOS IN HIS MIGHT	818	HAPPINESS/L	58
	LOS FLAMD IN MY PATH & THE SUN WAS HOT	818	HAPPINESS/L	77
LOSE				
	AND I LOSE THIS FORM OF CLAY	61	LEAVE O/IM	4
	HOW DIDST THOU LOSE THY EYES OLD TIRIEL BLESS THY WRINKLED FACE	101	TIRIEL 2	43
	AND YOU WILL LOSE YOUR ONCE LOVD TIRIEL ALAS HOW FAINT I AM	104	TIRIEL 4	36
	HAVE QUITE FORSAKEN O FOOL FOOL TO LOSE MY SWEETEST BLISS	296	FOUR ZOAS 3	168
	I LOSE MY POWERS WEAKEND EVERY REVOLUTION TILL A DEATH . .	317	FOUR ZOAS 6	221
	WITH SIGHS & HOWLING & DEEP SOBS THAT HE MIGHT LOSE HIS RAGE	336	FOUR ZOAS 7B	127
	AND WITH IT LOSE HIMSELF IN MEEKNESS SHE EMBRACD HIS FIRE	336	FOUR ZOAS 7B	128
	BUT TO LOSE THEM THE FOOL MAKES HIS FOOLISH GAME	547	LET BE TOLD/N	9
	THEIR ART IS TO LOSE FORM HIS ART IS TO FIND FORM . . .	573B	DESC CAT 3	PROSE
	THAT WE MAY LOSE NO TIME FROM THE WORK OF THE LORD . . .	716D	JERUSALEM 77	PROSE
	THEM OVER AGAIN THEY WOULD LOSE AS MUCH AS THEY GAIND . .	815C	LETTER 23	PROSE
	THEN I'M SILENT & PASSIVE & LOSE EVERY FRIEND	828	O WHY BORN/L	4
	STILL I RESOLVE NOT TO LOSE HOPE OF SEEING BETTER DAYS . .	829D	LETTER 30	PROSE
	I LOSE NO MOMENT TO COMPLETE ROMNEY TO SATISFACTION . . .	829D	LETTER 30	PROSE
	I WILL LOSE NO TIME IN SETTING HIM TO WORK ON THE SAME OBJECT	831B	LETTER 31	PROSE
	SHOULD LOSE ALL THE LABOUR I HAVE BEEN AT ON THAT PLATE	861B	LETTER 58	PROSE
	AIR YET I LOSE NOTHING BY IT DANTE GOES ON THE BETTER .	877D	LETTER 88	PROSE
LOSER'S				
	THE WINNER'S SHOUT THE LOSER'S CURSE	433	AUGURIES	117
LOSES				
	MOSES IS NOT THE AUTHOR & THEN THE BISHOP LOSES HIS AUTHOR	391C	ANNO WATSON	MARG
	HERE HE LOSES SIGHT OF A CENTRAL FORM &	460A	ANNO REYNOLDS	MARG

```
                                                              PAGE      TITLE           LINE
LOSES    (CONTINUED)
        LOSES ALL ADMIRATION OF ANY OTHER ARTIST BUT RUBENS  . . . 583A DESC CAT 9       PROSE
        FLANDERS IT LOSES ALL CHARACTER AND LEAVES WHAT SOME PEOPLE 585A DESC CAT 15      PROSE
LOSING
        TURNING HIS EYES OUTWARD TO SELF LOSING THE DIVINE VISION  280 FOUR ZOAS 2            2
        WHERE NEVER YET EXISTENCE CAME THERE LOSING ALL MY LIFE    296 FOUR ZOAS 3          189
        IF LOSING AND OBLITERATING THE OUTLINE CONSTITUTES        585A DESC CAT 15        PROSE
            A PICTURE
        SUCH ART OF LOSING THE OUTLINES IS THE ART OF VENICE AND  585A DESC CAT 15        PROSE
        ENGRAVING BY LOSING DRAWING HAS LOST ALL CHARACTER  . . . 592A PUB ADDRESS/N    *PROSE
        THAT HE IS VERY AFRAID OF LOSING ME  . . . . . . . .     820D LETTER 25          PROSE
        HONOUR OF LONDON BOOKSELLERS & CONSIDER THEM AS LOSING A  856C LETTER 54          PROSE
        GREAT DEAL OF HONOUR IN LOSING THE FIRST PUBLICATION OF ANY 856C LETTER 54        PROSE
LOS'S
        IN LOS'S ARMS HOWLINGS BEGAN OVER THE BODY OF DEATH  . . . 289 FOUR ZOAS 2          335
        DARK DREADFUL ROSE & ENITHARMON LAY AT LOS'S FEET  . . .  300 FOUR ZOAS 4          126
        BUT THEN THE SPECTRE ENTERD LOS'S BOSOM EVERY SIGH & GROAN 328 FOUR ZOAS 7          336
        . . . WE BEHOLD WITH WONDER ENITHARMON'S LOOMS & LOS'S    346 FOUR ZOAS 8          200
            FORGES
        IN GOLGONOOZA LOS'S ANVILS STAND & HIS FURNACES RAGE  . . 346 FOUR ZOAS 8          202
        FIRST ORC WAS BORN THEN THE SHADOWY FEMALE THEN ALL LOS'S 483 MILTON 3              40
            FAMILY
        . . . REGULATED BY LOS'S [HAMMERS AND WOVEN] HAMMER  . . . 486 MILTON 6         *   35
        REDOUNDING FROM MY LEFT FOOT INTO LOS'S MUNDANE SPACE  . . 502 MILTON 20             21
        INDIGNANT UNCONVINCD BY LOS'S ARGUMENTS & (THUNDERS)     509 MILTON 24             45
            ROLLING
        IN BOWLAHOOLA LOS'S ANVILS STAND & HIS FURNACES RAGE  . . 509 MILTON 24             51
        ALL THE GODS OF THE KINGDOMS OF EARTH LABOUR IN LOS'S HALLS 510 MILTON 24            74
        FORMED IT INTO A SOLID BY LOS'S MATHEMATIC POWER  . . . . 517 MILTON 29             38
        IN LOS'S HALLS CONTINUAL LABOURING IN THE FURNACES        520 MILTON 31             26
            OF GOLGONOOZA
        AND THRO BEULAH TO EDEN BENEATH LOS'S WESTERN WALL  . . . 526 MILTON 35             51
        THE WILD THYME IS LOS'S MESSENGER TO EDEN A MIGHTY DEMON  526 MILTON 35             54
        THE LARK IS LOS'S MESSENGER THRO THE TWENTY-SEVEN CHURCHES 526 MILTON 35             63
        GATE OF WIDE GOLGONOOZA & THE LARK IS LOS'S MESSENGER  . . 526 MILTON 35             67
        TO DEVOUR LOS'S HUMAN PERFECTION BUT WHEN HE SAW THAT LOS  625 JERUSALEM 6      *   14
        GROANING HE KNEELD BEFORE LOS'S IRON-SHOD FEET ON LONDON  627 JERUSALEM 8          27
            STONE
        HUNGRING & THIRSTING FOR LOS'S LIFE YET PRETENDING       627 JERUSALEM 8          28
            OBEDIENCE
        GROANING THE SPECTRE HEAVD THE BELLOWS OBEYING LOS'S FROWNS 628 JERUSALEM 9     *   33
        THE BELLOWS & THE HAMMERS MOVE COMPELLD BY LOS'S HAND  . . 629 JERUSALEM 10          6
        DRIVEN TO DESPERATION BY LOS'S TERRORS & THREATNING FEARS  629 JERUSALEM 10         28
        CAME FROM THE FURNACES BY LOS'S MIGHTY POWER FOR          630 JERUSALEM 11          9
            JERUSALEM'S
        SURROUNDS LUBAN LOS'S PALACE & THE GOLDEN LOOMS OF        633 JERUSALEM 13         25
            CATHEDRON
        LOS'S HALLS & EVERY AGE RENEWS ITS POWERS FROM THESE WORKS 638 JERUSALEM 16         62
        IN GNAWING PAIN FROM LOS'S BOSOM IN THE DEADLY NIGHT  . . 639 JERUSALEM 17         50
        ATTENDS HER AS HER GUARD & LOS'S EMANATION IS NAMED  . . . 655 JERUSALEM 30          3
        JERUSALEM TREMBLED SEEING HER CHILDREN DRIVN BY LOS'S     663 JERUSALEM 36         21
            HAMMER
        AGAINST HIS WILL THRO LOS'S GATE TO EDEN FOUR-FOLD LOUD   674 JERUSALEM 44          3
        WHERE LOS'S FURNACES STAND WHERE JERUSALEM & VALA HOWL  . . 677 JERUSALEM 47          3
        IN THE BRITISH OCEAN CREATED BY LOS'S HAMMER MEASURED OUT  688 JERUSALEM 56         19
        ARE THE TEMPLES AMONG HIS PILLARS BRITAIN IS LOS'S FORGE  690 JERUSALEM 58         42
        CATHEDRON'S LOOMS ARE BUILDED AND LOS'S FURNACES IN THE   691 JERUSALEM 59         23
            SOUTH
        BUT NO ONE CAN CONSUMMATE FEMALE BLISS IN LOS'S WORLD     708 JERUSALEM 69         30
            WITHOUT
        AND LOS'S FURNACES HOWL LOUD LIVING SELF-MOVING LAMENTING  713 JERUSALEM 73          2
        REPENTANT AND SHE ALSO IN THE EDDYING WIND OF LOS'S BELLOWS 726 JERUSALEM 82         74
        SILENT AT HIS VOICE THEY VIEW THE RED GLOBE OF FIRE IN    730 JERUSALEM 85         19
            LOS'S HAND
        SO DREAD IS LOS'S FURY THAT NONE DARE HIM TO APPROACH  . . 732 JERUSALEM 86         48
        THUS JOYD THE SPECTRE IN THE DUSKY FIRES OF LOS'S FORGE   734 JERUSALEM 88         44
            EYEING
        THE FORCE OF LOS'S HAMMER IS ETERNAL FORGIVENESS BUT  . . 734 JERUSALEM 88         50
        BENEATH LOS'S HAMMER THAT LIFE MAY NOT BE BLOTTED OUT  . . 737 JERUSALEM 90         51
        WITH LOS'S THUNDEROUS WORDS BEGAN TO BUILD TREMBLING      737 JERUSALEM 90         59
            ROCKING STONES
        AND WONDER AT THE DIVINE MERCY & AT LOS'S SUBLIME HONOUR  743 JERUSALEM 96         32
LOSS
        AND MOCKS MY LOSS OF LIBERTY  . . . . . . . . . . .      6 HOW SWEET/PS           16
        JOYS IN ANOTHER'S LOSS OF EASE  . . . . . . . . . . .    162 CLOD PEBBLE/N        11
        JOYS IN ANOTHER'S LOSS OF EASE  . . . . . . . . . . .    211 CLOD PEBBLE/SE       11
        WITH DEEP REPENTANCE FOR THE LOSS OF THAT FAIR FORM OF MAN 352 FOUR ZOAS 8         435
        WHERER HE GOES & ALL HIS NEIGHBOURHOOD BEWAIL HIS LOSS    516 MILTON 29            13
        FOR ITS ALL SHEER LOSS AS IT SEEMS TO ME  . . . . . .    550 ENGL ENCOU/N 2        7
        IF THEY CONTINUE TO REFUSE THEIRS IS THE LOSS NOT MINE  . . 600C PUB ADDRESS/N    PROSE
        I AM VERY SORRY FOR YOUR IMMENSE LOSS WHICH IS A REPETITION 797A LETTER 9          PROSE
        MORE & MORE PERSWADED THAT EVERY MORTAL LOSS IS          797B LETTER 9            PROSE
            AN IMMORTAL GAIN
        GOING ON WOULD BE A CERTAIN LOSS OF ALMOST ALL THE EXPENSES 831C LETTER 31        PROSE
        IS A PUBLIC LOSS WHICH THOSE WHO KNEW HIM CAN BEST ESTIMATE 854B LETTER 53        PROSE
        A LOSS THAT ONLY CAN BE REPAIRD IN ETERNITY WHERE IT WILL  854B LETTER 53         PROSE
        THE EXTREME LOSS AND DISAPPOINTMENT WHICH I SHOULD HAVE   861A LETTER 58          PROSE
        WOULD BE TO ME A LOSS THAT I COULD NOT NOW SUSTAIN AS IT  861A LETTER 58          PROSE
        PRINTED WITHOUT THE WRITING THO TO THE LOSS OF SOME OF THE 867A LETTER 66         PROSE
        CANNOT PRINT MORE EXCEPT AT A GREAT LOSS FOR AT THE TIME  878C LETTER 88          PROSE
LOST
        FROM SIDE TO SIDE THE LAND GROANS HER PROWESS LOST  . . . 37D SAMSON/PS           PROSE
```

LOST   (CONTINUED)

	PAGE	TITLE	LINE
AND REINSTATES HIM ON HIS THRONE ONCE LOST	42A THEN SHE BORE	PROSE
HOW LOST I'LL TELL BUT STOP THE MOTLEY SONG	42A THEN SHE BORE	PROSE
THEIR SAD COMPLAININGS BEAR FOR CONRADE LOST	43D WOE CRIED MUSE	PROSE
UNTIMELY LOST THY CONRADE ONCE WHEN LIVING THEE I LOVD	43D WOE CRIED MUSE	PROSE
EVN UNTO DEATH		
OR ELSE I SHALL BE LOST	60 LIT BOY LST/IM	4
THAT AN EMMET LOST ITS WAY	111 A DREAM/SI	3
THE LITTLE GIRL LOST	112B LIT GRL LST/SI	TITLE
LOST IN DESART WILD	112 LIT GRL LST/SI	21
THE LITTLE BOY LOST	120D LIT BOY LST/SI	TITLE
OR ELSE I SHALL BE LOST	120 LIT BOY LST/SI	4
THE LITTLE BOY LOST IN THE LONELY FEN	121 LIT BOY FND/SI	1
THE HISTORY OF THIS IS WRITTEN IN PARADISE LOST . . .	150A MARRIAGE HH 5	PROSE
THE EAGLE NEVER LOST SO MUCH TIME AS WHEN HE SUBMITTED .	151D MARRIAGE HH 8	PROSE
HIS LOST WORKS HE SAID NONE OF EQUAL VALUE WAS LOST . .	154A MARRIAGE HH 12	PROSE
IS BUT LOST TIME TO CONVERSE WITH YOU WHOSE WORKS ARE ONLY	157B MARRIAGE HH 17	PROSE
ANALYTICS		
BEFORE MY FLOWER OF LOVE WAS LOST	184 O I CANNOT/N	4
THEN HAD AMERICA BEEN LOST OERWHELMD BY THE ATLANTIC . .	202 AMERICA 14	17
AND EARTH HAD LOST ANOTHER PORTION OF THE INFINITE . . .	202 AMERICA 14	18
A LITTLE BOY LOST	218B LIT BOY LST/SE	TITLE
A LITTLE GIRL LOST	219A LIT GRL LST/SE	TITLE
WAIT SISTERS THO ALL IS LOST	262A SMALL BK DSGNS	TITLE
LOST LOST LOST ARE MY EMANATIONS ENION [COME FORTH] O	264 FOUR ZOAS 1	25
ENION		
ALL LOVE IS LOST TERROR SUCCEEDS & HATRED INSTEAD OF LOVE	265 FOUR ZOAS 1	36
[WITHIN MY SOUL HAS LOST ITS SPLENDOR & A BROODING FEAR]	267 FOUR ZOAS 1	116
WEEPING FOR LUVAH LOST IN THE BLOODY BEAMS OF	272 FOUR ZOAS 1	* 287
AND LOST IN INFINITE HUMING WINGS VANISHES WITH A CRY .	289 FOUR ZOAS 2	361
O THARMAS I HAD LOST THEE & WHEN I HOPED I HAD FOUND THEE	296 FOUR ZOAS 3	183
DARKEND & LOST IN DUE TIME ISSUING FORTH FROM ENION'S WOMB	327 FOUR ZOAS 7	294
THARMAS REPLIED VALA THY SINS HAVE LOST US HEAVEN & BLISS	339 FOUR ZOAS 7B	256
THE THRONES OF KINGS ARE SHAKEN THEY HAVE LOST THEIR ROBES	357 FOUR ZOAS 9	18
& CROWNS		
RECIEVD HER IN THE DARKNING SOUTH THEIR BODIES LOST THEY	358 FOUR ZOAS 9	* 26
STOOD		
MILTON'S PARADISE LOST IS AS TRUE AS GENESIS OR EXODUS	392D ANNO WATSON	MARG
WHEN THE REVERENCE OF GOVERNMENT IS LOST IT IS BETTER THAN	401D ANNO BACON	MARG
[?HE WERE LOST (?EURYDICE)]	SUPP ANNO REYNOLDS	* MARG
TILL TWO ETERNITYS MEET TOGETHER AH LOST LOST LOST FOR	494 MILTON 13	11
EVER		
BUT TO HIMSELF HE SEEMD A WANDERER LOST IN DREARY NIGHT	496 MILTON 15	16
OF TIME IS LOST NOR ONE EVENT OF SPACE UNPERMANENT . .	505 MILTON 22	19
SNAP SNAP HE HAS LOST SHADOW & SUBSTANCE TOO	554 TO VENETIAN/N	13
[?WHEN] NOW ART HAS LOST ITS MENTAL CHARMS	557 ART HAS LOST/N	* 1
THE ART HAS BEEN LOST I HAVE RECOVERED IT	561A EXHIBITION ADV	PROSE
NOW LOST OR PERHAPS BURIED TILL SOME HAPPIER AGE THE .	565C DESC CAT 2	PROSE
BUT THE ART OF FRESCO PAINTING BEING LOST	566C DESC CAT 2	PROSE
WHICH ARE NOW LOST WE OUGHT	568C DESC CAT 3	PROSE
PARADISE LOST A COMPOSITION FOR A MORE PERFECT PICTURE .	582A DESC CAT 9	TITLE
[FROM AN] AS AN ART IS LOST IN ENGLAND OWING TO AN .	591D PUB ADDRESS/N	*PROSE
INTO THIS COUNTRY SINCE WHICH ENGLISH ENGRAVING IS LOST	592A PUB ADDRESS/N	PROSE
ENGRAVING BY LOSING DRAWING HAS LOST ALL CHARACTER . .	592A PUB ADDRESS/N	*PROSE
& ALL EXPRESSION WITHOUT WHICH THE ART IS LOST . . .	592A PUB ADDRESS/N	PROSE
SINCE I HAVE PRACTISED PAINTING I HAVE LOST ALL IDEA OF	592D PUB ADDRESS/N	PROSE
& REAL VISION AND REAL VISIONS WHICH ARE LOST & CLOUDED	605C V LAST JUDG/N	*PROSE
WHO WILL BE CAST OFF & LOST FROM ART	613C V LAST JUDG/N	PROSE
ALL THE INFANT LOVES & GRACES WERE LOST FOR THE MIGHTY HAND	628 JERUSALEM 8	44
PERMANENT & NOT LOST NOT LOST NOR VANISHD & EVERY LITTLE	634 JERUSALEM 13	60
ACT		
BE LOST & LEST HE SHOULD DEVOUR ENITHARMON AH ME . . .	638 JERUSALEM 17	18
THEN LOST IN CLOUDS I HEAR THEIR TENDER VOICES CLOUDS	644 JERUSALEM 21	41
DIVIDE		
ALL LOVE IS LOST TERROR SUCCEEDS & [HATRED] HATRED INSTEAD	645 JERUSALEM 22	* 10
OF LOVE		
THOU ART FOREVER LOST WHAT CAN I DO TO HINDER THE SONS . .	657 JERUSALEM 31	37
IN FORTUITOUS CONCOURSE OF MEMORYS ACCUMULATED & LOST .	659 JERUSALEM 33	8
GENERALIZING ART & SCIENCE TILL ART & SCIENCE IS LOST	673 JERUSALEM 43	54
BE LOST FOR EVER & EVER THEN THEY SHALL ARISE FROM SELF	680 JERUSALEM 49	45
O IT WAS LOST FOR EVER AND WE FOUND IT NOT IT CAME . . .	688 JERUSALEM 56	26
THAN THY MAKER WHO FORGIVETH SINS & CALLS AGAIN HER THAT	694 JERUSALEM 61	7
IS LOST		
THE REAPERS SAYING AM I JERUSALEM THE LOST ADULTERESS OR	695 JERUSALEM 61	34
AM I		
WHEN THE DRUIDS DEMANDED CHASTITY FROM WOMAN & ALL WAS LOST	697 JERUSALEM 63	25
THAT NOT ONE MOMENT OF TIME BE LOST & EVERY REVOLUTION . .	716 JERUSALEM 75	8
EVERY MOMENT LOST IS A MOMENT THAT CANNOT BE REDEEMED .	716D JERUSALEM 77	PROSE
I WALK TO EPHRAIM I SEEK FOR SHILOH I WALK LIKE A LOST	720 JERUSALEM 79	10
SHEEP		
TO AN ETERNAL NIGHT OF PAIN LOST LOST LOST FOR EVER . .	721 JERUSALEM 80	5
BY THE LOST SHEEP THAT HE HATH FOUND & ALBION KNEW THAT IT	743 JERUSALEM 96	4
DIVINE & SELF WAS LOST IN THE CONTEMPLATION OF FAITH .	743 JERUSALEM 96	31
GOD'S RIGHTEOUS LAW THAT LOST ITS PREY	757 EV GOSPEL(I)/N	48
THE LOST TRAVELLER'S DREAM UNDER THE HILL	771 EPILOGUE/GP	8
PRACTISE IS ART IF YOU LEAVE OFF YOU ARE LOST	777B INSC LAOCOON	PROSE
WITH ALL OUR MIGHT & STRENGTH THO WE ARE FALLEN & LOST .	780 GHOST ABEL 2	2
TO RENEW THE LOST ART OF THE GREEKS	792A LETTER 4	PROSE
THIRTEEN YEARS AGO I LOST A BROTHER & WITH HIS SPIRIT I	797A LETTER 9	PROSE
I HAD VERY MUCH LOST & OBLITERATED FROM MY MIND . . .	812B LETTER 22	PROSE
HE WHO KEEPS NOT RIGHT ONWARD IS LOST & IF OUR FOOTSTEPS	813A LETTER 22	PROSE
SIMILAR TO HOMER'S ILIAD OR MILTON'S PARADISE LOST THE .	823A LETTER 26	PROSE

```
                                                         PAGE    TITLE       LINE
LOST    (CONTINUED)
     HAVE BEEN LOST I SHALL LEAVE EVERY ONE IN THIS COUNTRY  .  . 825D LETTER 27    PROSE
     WHO HAS NOT LOST ANY OF HIS LIFE SINCE HE WAS FIVE YEARS     830A LETTER 30    PROSE
        OLD
     IS LOST OR AT LEAST CANNOT NOW BE FOUND IT IS THAT OF   .  . 839C LETTER 38    PROSE
     THE LOST DRAWING YOU SHALL HAVE CHOICE OF EITHER OF THE      839C LETTER 38    PROSE
     BECAUSE NO TIME SHOULD BE LOST IN THIS TRULY INTERESTING     849A LETTER 45    PROSE
        BUSINESS
     I HAVE LOST MY CONFUSION OF THOUGHT WHILE AT WORK   .  .  . 853A LETTER 51    *PROSE
     ALL THAT HAS BEEN PRINTED AS LOST AND BEGIN ANEW UNLESS      858B LETTER 55    PROSE
     WHERE IS YOUR FATHER THE LOST CHILD ORPHANS    .  .  .  . SUPP INSC HERVEY    *TITLE
     A DREAM ON ANOTHER'S SORROW THE LITTLE BOY LOST     .  . SUPP LETTER 66A    *PROSE
     LITTLE GIRL LOST DITTO DITTO THE CLOD & PEBBLE     .  . SUPP LETTER 66A    *PROSE
     MY PRETTY ROSE TREE THE GARDEN OF LOVE A LITTLE BOY LOST   SUPP LETTER 66A    *PROSE
     INFANT SORROW THE SCHOOL BOY LONDON LITTLE GIRL LOST       SUPP LETTER 66A    *PROSE
LOT
     WHERE WHITE AND BROWN IS OUR LOT   .  .  .  .  .  .  .  .    8 LOVE JOCUND/PS     11
     ID CURSE BRIGHT FORTUNE FOR MY MIXED LOT   .  .  .  .  .   10 WHEN EARLY/PS      19
     AND BLEAR-EYD WILL THE BLACK LOT HOLDS   .  .  .  .  .  .   16 BLIND-MANS/PS      20
     FOR SORROW IS THE LOT OF ALL OF WOMAN BORN   .  .  .  .   39B SAMSON/PS       PROSE
     FOR CARE WAS I BROUGHT FORTH AND LABOUR IS MY LOT   .  .   39B SAMSON/PS       PROSE
     DESPAIR MUST BE HIS ETERNAL LOT   .  .  .  .  .  .  .  .   97D NAT RELIGION 2  PROSE
     HOW SWEET IS THE SHEPHERD'S SWEET LOT   .  .  .  .  .  .  118 SHEPHERD/SI        1
     AND LAY ME DOWN IN THY COLD BED AND LEAVE MY SHINING LOT  130 BOOK OF THEL 5     13
     SAID PERHAPS YOU WILL BE WILLING TO SHEW ME MY ETERNAL LOT 155D MARRIAGE HH 17  PROSE
     AND SEE WHETHER YOUR LOT OR MINE IS MOST DESIRABLE   .  . 155D MARRIAGE HH 17  PROSE
     BUT AS WE HERE REMAIN BEHOLD THY LOT   .  .  .  .  .  .  156A MARRIAGE HH 17  PROSE
     I NOW ASKED MY COMPANION WHICH WAS MY ETERNAL LOT   .  . 156B MARRIAGE HH 17  PROSE
     HEARING A HARPER BUT NOW WE HAVE SEEN MY ETERNAL LOT  .  156D MARRIAGE HH 17  PROSE
     HERE SAID I IS YOUR LOT IN THIS SPACE   .  .  .  .  .  . 157A MARRIAGE HH 17  PROSE
     TILL SHE WHO BURNS WITH YOUTH AND KNOWS NO FIXED LOT IS   193 V DAU ALBION 5     21
        BOUND
     AND CURSING HIS LOT FOR IN ANGUISH   .  .  .  .  .  .  .  226 URIZEN 6           3
     WE MAY ERECT A THRONE DEEP IN THE NORTH I PLACE MY LOT  .  278 FOUR ZOAS 1      491
     AND NOW LIKE ME PARTAKING DESOLATE THY MASTER'S LOT   .  .  317 FOUR ZOAS 6      211
     THY SELF DESTROYING BEAST FORMD SCIENCE SHALL BE          361 FOUR ZOAS 9      150
        THY ETERNAL LOT
     FROM DEATH ETERNAL SUCH YOUR LOT TO BE CONTINUALLY REDEEMD 522 MILTON 33        12
     OF H'S(HAYLEY'S) BIRTH THIS WAS THE HAPPY LOT   .  .  .  . 539 OF HS BIRTH/N      1
     THIS HAS HITHERTO BEEN HIS LOT TO GET PATRONAGE FOR OTHERS 572D DESC CAT 3     PROSE
     HOW SOON HIS LOT MAY BE OUR OWN WHEN AFRICA IN SLEEP  .   675 JERUSALEM 45       19
     .  .  . TO BE MINE SUCH MY LOT UPON EARTH   .  .  .  .  .  799 TO FLAXMAN/L        4
     NOW MY LOT IN THE HEAVENS IS THIS .  .  .  .  .  .  .  .  799 TO FLAXMAN/L        5
     HAPPY SON OF THE IMMORTAL PHIDIAS HIS LOT IS TRULY GLORIOUS 807B LETTER 17     PROSE
     IN A CITY OF ASSASSINATIONS THIS MAKES YOUR LOT TRULY  .  847B LETTER 44     PROSE
LOTH
     [TO KILL THE PEOPLE I AM LOTH]  .  .  .  .  .  .  .  .  .  185 LET BROTHELS/N     17
LOTHO
     HEUXOS & LOTHO RAN FORTH AT THE SOUND OF IJIM'S VOICE   .  105 TIRIEL 4          45
     [THEN IJIM SAID LOTHO CLITHYMA MAKUTH FETCH YOUR FATHER]   105 TIRIEL 4          73
LOT'S
     LOT'S WIFE BEING CHANGED INTO (A) PILLAR OF SALT ALLUDES   607A V LAST JUDG/N  PROSE
LOTS
     BRING FORTH THE LOTS CAST IN THE SPACIOUS ORB  .  .  .  .   34 WAR SONG/PS        2
     THEY GIVE THE OATH OF BLOOD THEY CAST THE LOTS INTO THE    337 FOUR ZOAS 7B      165
        HELMET
     NUMBER XII THE SOLDIERS CASTING LOTS FOR CHRIST'S GARMENT  584A DESC CAT 12    TITLE
        A DRAWING
     THEY CAST THE LOTS INTO THE HELMET .  .  .  .  .  .  .  .  699 JERUSALEM 65       7
LOTTERY
     SCHEME OF HIS LOTTERY DESIRES HIS COMPLIMENTS TO YOU   .  . 844A LETTER 43     PROSE
LOTUS
     O LIFE OF THIS OUR SPRING WHY FADES THE LOTUS OF THE WATER  127 BOOK OF THEL 1     6
LOUD
     CHIRPING LOUD AND SINGING SWEET   .  .  .  .  .  .  .  .    7 LOVE HARMNY/PS      6
     THEIR WIVES AND CHILDREN WEEPING LOUD   .  .  .  .  .  .   11 GWIN KING/PS       25
     AGAIN THE LOUD VOICE OF FRANCE CRIES TO THE MORNING .  .  . 134 FRENCH REVOLTN     15
     UTTERS LOUD DESPAIR SHADOWING PARIS .  .  .  .  .  .  .  . 135 FRENCH REVOLTN     18
     WHILE LOUD THUNDERS ROLL TROUBLING THE DEAD .  .  .  .  . 137 FRENCH REVOLTN     61
     .  .  . THEN A THUNDER ROLLD ROUND LOUD AND LOUDER  .  .  . 145 FRENCH REVOLTN    257
     HIS VOICE LOUD INSPIRD BY LIBERTY .  .  .  .  .  .  .  .  147 FRENCH REVOLTN    284
     HELPLESS NAKED PIPING LOUD  .  .  .  .  .  .  .  .  .  .  166 INFANT SORW/N       3
     OR IS IT BECAUSE SECRESY GAINS [FEMININE] FEMALES' LOUD    171 TO NOBODADDY/N      9
        APPLAUSE
     [THE MOTHER FOLLOWD WEEPING LOUD]  .  .  .  .  .  .  .  .  177 LIT BOY LST/N   *  11
     SOUND SOUND MY LOUD WAR-TRUMPETS & ALARM MY THIRTEEN       199 AMERICA 9          1
        ANGELS
     LOUD HOWLS THE ETERNAL WOLF THE ETERNAL LION LASHES HIS    199 AMERICA 9          2
        TAIL
     SOUND SOUND MY LOUD WAR-TRUMPETS & ALARM MY THIRTEEN       199 AMERICA 9         13
        ANGELS
     SOUND SOUND MY LOUD WAR TRUMPETS & ALARM MY THIRTEEN       199 AMERICA 9         21
        ANGELS
     SOUND SOUND MY LOUD WAR-TRUMPETS & ALARM MY THIRTEEN       199 AMERICA 9         26
        ANGELS
     LOUD HOWLS THE ETERNAL WOLF THE ETERNAL LION LASHES HIS    199 AMERICA 9         27
        TAIL
     OF TRUMPETS BLEW A LOUD ALARM ACROSS THE ATLANTIC DEEP  .  . 200 AMERICA 10         2
     SILENT THE COLONIES REMAIN AND REFUSE THE LOUD ALARM  .  . 200 AMERICA 10         4
     IN BLACK SMOKE THUNDERS AND LOUD WINDS REJOICING IN ITS    201 AMERICA 12        10
        TERROR
     SMOTE WITH HIS SCEPTER THE SCALE BOUND ORB LOUD HOWLD  .  . 205 AMERICA CANC C    11
```

		PAGE	TITLE	LINE
LOUD	(CONTINUED)			
HELPLESS NAKED PIPING LOUD		217	INFANT SORW/SE	3
FOR WITH NOISES RUINOUS LOUD		229	URIZEN 13	24
THEIR WARBLING JOYS TO OUR LOUD STRINGS . . .		239	EUROPE 4	18
WITH DOUBLING VOICES & LOUD HORNS WOUND ROUND SOUNDING	.	274	FOUR ZOAS 1	382
THUS SANG THE DEMONS OF THE DEEP THE CLARIONS OF WAR BLEW LOUD		276	FOUR ZOAS 1	434
TILL DAWN WAS WONT TO WAKE THEM THEN MY TRUMPET SOUNDING LOUD		278	FOUR ZOAS 1	500
ALBION GAVE HIS LOUD DEATH GROAN THE ATLANTIC MOUNTAINS TREMBLED		281	FOUR ZOAS 2	41
SO LOUD IN THUNDERS SPOKE THE KING FOLDED IN DARK DESPAIR		295	FOUR ZOAS 3	131
SHE CONTINUED FALLING LOUD THE CRASH CONTINUD LOUD & HOARSE		295	FOUR ZOAS 3	145
LOUD STRONG A UNIVERSAL GROAN OF DEATH LOUDER		195	FOUR ZOAS 3	150
HEARING THE SYMPHONIES OF WAR LOUD SOUNDING ALL MY SONS		300	FOUR ZOAS 4	92
BUT ENITHARMON WRAPD IN CLOUDS WAILD LOUD FOR AS LOS BEAT		302	FOUR ZOAS 4	184
LOUD & MORE LOUD THE LIVING MUSIC FLOATS UPON THE AIR . .		306	FOUR ZOAS 5	26
ROARING REDOUNDING LOUD LOUD LOUDER & LOUDER & FIRD . .		308	FOUR ZOAS 5	106
SURROUNDED WITH FLAMES THE DEMON GREW LOUD HOWLING IN HIS FIRES		308	FOUR ZOAS 5	109
IN SUCCESSIVE VOLLIES WITH LOUD THUNDERS SWIFT FLEW THE KING OF LIGHT		314	FOUR ZOAS 6	* 109
AS HE ASCENDED HOWLING LOUD THE WEB VIBRATED STRONG . . .		319	FOUR ZOAS 6	318
TO MODULATE HIS FIRES STUDIOUS THE LOUD ROARING FLAMES . .		331	FOUR ZOAS 7	458
INTO THE WORLDS OF ENITHARMON LOUD THE ROARING WINDS . .		335	FOUR ZOAS 7B	107
THE PRESTER SERPENT CEASD THE WAR SONG SOUNDED LOUD & STRONG		336	FOUR ZOAS 7B	121
LOUD SOUNDS THE WAR SONG ROUND RED ORC IN HIS [TRIUMPHANT] FURY		336	FOUR ZOAS 7B	* 144
SO SUNG THE DEMONS OF THE DEEP THE CLARIONS OF WAR BLEW LOUD		338	FOUR ZOAS 7B	210
THEY GO OUT TO WAR WITH STRONG SHOUTS & LOUD CLARIONS O PITY		338	FOUR ZOAS 7B	* 220
TROOP BY TROOP THE BEASTIAL DROVES REND ONE ANOTHER SOUNDING LOUD		344	FOUR ZOAS 8	116
SOUND LOUD THE HOWLING MUSIC INSPIRD BY LOS & ENITHARMON		344	FOUR ZOAS 8	121
. . . SOUNDING LOUD TERRIFIC MEN		344	FOUR ZOAS 8	121
THEN FELL THE FIRES OF ETERNITY WITH LOUD & SHRILL . . .		357	FOUR ZOAS 9	10
SOUND OF LOUD TRUMPET THUNDERING ALONG FROM HEAVEN TO HEAVEN		357	FOUR ZOAS 9	11
SAW THEM DEPART IN DISMAL DROVES THE TRUMPET SOUNDED LOUD		359	FOUR ZOAS 9	65
OF SATAN LOUD THE SERPENT ORC RAGD THRO HIS TWENTY SEVEN		359	FOUR ZOAS 9	69
THEY TOOK THEM INTO THE WIDE BARNS WITH LOUD REJOICINGS & TRIUMPH		372	FOUR ZOAS 9	585
AT THE IMMORTAL TABLES SOUNDING LOUD THEIR INSTRUMENTS OF JOY		374	FOUR ZOAS 9	645
DISMAL LOUD REDOUNDING THE NETHER FLOOR SHAKES WITH THE SOUND		374	FOUR ZOAS 9	652
WHILE THE FLAIL OF URIZEN SOUNDED LOUD		375	FOUR ZOAS 9	684
SO LOUD SO CLEAR IN THE WIDE HEAVENS		375	FOUR ZOAS 9	685
HEAVEN RANG WITH WINGED EXULTATION ALL BENEATH HOWLD LOUD		378	FOUR ZOAS 9	782
REJOICE TO ONE ANOTHER LOUD THEIR VOICES SHAKE THE ABYSS		378	FOUR ZOAS 9	813
FOR ENION BROODED GROANING LOUD THE ROUGH SEAS VEGETATE		381	FOUR ZOAS AD 5	10
AND NIGHT HATH HEARD MY SORROWS LOUD		423	THE BIRDS/N	12
TERRIFIC AMONG THE SONS OF ALBION IN CHORUS SOLEMN & LOUD		482	MILTON 2	23
SATAN WAS GOING TO REPLY BUT LOS ROLLD HIS LOUD THUNDERS		483	MILTON 4	15
AND ANVILS DANCE THE DANCE OF TEARS & PAIN LOUD LIGHTNINGS		484	MILTON 5	16
LOUD SOUNDS THE HAMMER OF LOS & LOUD HIS BELLOWS IS HEARD		485	MILTON 6	8
ON TYBURN'S BROOK LOUD GROANS THAMES BENEATH THE IRON FORGE		485	MILTON 6	11
LOUD SOUNDS THE HAMMER OF LOS LOUD TURN THE WHEELS OF ENITHARMON		486	MILTON 6	27
LOUD AS THE WIND OF BEULAH THAT UNROOTS THE ROCKS & HILLS		487	MILTON 7	33
FELL DOWN AS DEWS OF NIGHT & A LOUD SOLEMN UNIVERSAL GROAN		490	MILTON 9	37
WITH THUNDERS UTTERD FROM HIS HIDDEN WHEELS ACCUSING LOUD		490	MILTON 9	41
SHE FLED TO ENITHARMON'S TENT & HID HERSELF LOUD RAGING		494	MILTON 13	14
AND JEHOVAH WAS LEPROUS LOUD HE CALLD STRETCHING HIS HAND TO ETERNITY		494	MILTON 13	24
THE BARD CEASD ALL CONSIDERD AND A LOUD RESOUNDING MURMUR		495	MILTON 13	45
WITH THUNDERS LOUD AND TERRIBLE SO MILTON'S SHADOW FELL		497	MILTON 15	45
PRECIPITANT LOUD THUNDRING INTO THE SEA OF TIME & SPACE		497	MILTON 15	46
GLOWD ON HIS ROCKY COUCH AGAINST THE DARKNESS LOUD THUNDERS		500	MILTON 18	47
AND OFTEN SUNG TO THE LOUD HARP AT THE IMMORTAL FEASTS .		503	MILTON 20	58
THUNDERING THE HAMMERS BEAT & THE BELLOWS BLOW LOUD . . .		509	MILTON 24	52
LOUD SPORT THE DANCERS IN THE DANCE OF DEATH REJOICING IN CARNAGE		509	MILTON 24	62
LOUD SHOUT THE SONS OF LUVAH AT THE WINE-PRESSES AS LOS DESCENDED		510	MILTON 25	1
THE WINE-PRESS ON THE RHINE GROANS LOUD BUT ALL ITS CENTRAL BEAMS		510	MILTON 25	3
AND LOUD THE SOULS HOWL ROUND THE PORCHES OF GOLGONOOZA		510	MILTON 25	12
AND MURMURS OF THUNDER ROLLING HEAVY LONG & LOUD OVER THE MOUNTAINS		511	MILTON 25	64
THE WIND BLOWS HEAVY LOUD THEY THUNDER THRO THE DARKSOM SKY		512	MILTON 26	8
THEY THROW OFF THEIR GORGEOUS RAIMENT THEY REJOICE WITH LOUD JUBILEE		513	MILTON 27	23
APPEARS LISTENS SILENT THEN SPRINGING FROM THE WAVING CORN-FIELD LOUD		520	MILTON 31	30
THEN LOUD FROM THEIR GREEN COVERT ALL THE BIRDS BEGIN THEIR SONG		520	MILTON 31	39

		PAGE	TITLE	LINE
LOUD	**(CONTINUED)**			
	ATTENDING HIS LOUD HARMONY WITH ADMIRATION & LOVE . . .	520	MILTON 31	44
	TO SHOOTERS HILL AND THENCE TO BLACKHEATH THE DARK WOOF LOUD	525	MILTON 35	13
	LOUD ROLL THE WEIGHTS & SPINDLES OVER THE WHOLE EARTH LET DOWN	525	MILTON 35	14
	IN AMMON MOLECH LOUD HIS FURNACES RAGE AMONG THE WHEELS	528	MILTON 37	21
	OF OG & PEALING LOUD THE CRIES OF THE VICTIMS OF FIRE . .	528	MILTON 37	22
	GORGEOUS & BEAUTIFUL LOUD ROLL HIS THUNDERS AGAINST MILTON	529	MILTON 38	12
	LOUD SATAN THUNDERD LOUD & DARK UPON MILD FELPHAM SHORE	529	MILTON 38	13
	THEN LOUD THE FURNACES OF LOS WERE HEARD & SEEN AS SEVEN HEAVENS	531	MILTON 39	14
	LOUD SATAN THUNDERD LOUD & DARK UPON MILD FELPHAM'S SHORE	531	MILTON 39	22
	STOOD TREMBLING IN THE PORCH LOUD SATAN THUNDERD ON THE STORMY SEA	532	MILTON 39	59
	IMMEDIATELY THE LARK MOUNTED WITH A LOUD TRILL FROM FELPHAM'S VALE	534	MILTON 42	29
	WHILE LOS PURSUD HIS SPEECH IN THREATNINGS LOUD & FIERCE	627	JERUSALEM 8	29
	LOUD ROAR MY FURNACES AND LOUD MY HAMMER IS HEARD . . .	628	JERUSALEM 9	25
	ALBION'S DREAD SPECTRES STORMING LOUD THUNDEROUS & MIGHTY	629	JERUSALEM 10	5
	HAMPSTEAD HIGHGATE FINCHLEY HENDON MUSWELL HILL RAGE LOUD	636	JERUSALEM 16	1
	AMONG THE SPIRITUAL FIRES LOUD THE CORN FIELDS THUNDER ALONG	636	JERUSALEM 16	5
	THE HAMMER LOUD RAGES IN RINTRAH'S STRONG GRASP SWINGING LOUD	636	JERUSALEM 16	11
	AND ALL MY CHILDREN FOLLOWD HIS LOUD HOWLINGS INTO THE DEEP	643	JERUSALEM 21	17
	THE ARMIES I HEAR THEIR LOUD CYMBALS & THEIR DEADLY CRIES	644	JERUSALEM 21	47
	LOUD GROAND ALBION FROM MOUNTAIN TO MOUNTAIN & REPLIED	645	JERUSALEM 22	36
	KNOT DAY BY DAY NIGHT BY NIGHT LOUD ROLL THE INDIGNANT ATLANTIC	648	JERUSALEM 24	62
	UPON THE VALLEYS OF MIDDLESEX SHOUTING LOUD FOR AID DIVINE	658	JERUSALEM 32	9
	I HEAR THE SCREECH OF CHILDBIRTH LOUD PEALING & THE GROANS	661	JERUSALEM 34	23
	HIS COLD AGAINST THE WARMTH OF EDEN RAGD WITH LOUD . . .	664	JERUSALEM 38	8
	THUS MOURN THEY LOUD THE FURNACES OF LOS THUNDER UPON . .	671	JERUSALEM 42	75
	AGAINST HIS WILL THRO LOS'S GATE TO EDEN FOUR-FOLD LOUD	674	JERUSALEM 44	3
	LOUD ROLL THE STARRY WHEELS OF ALBION INTO THE WORLD OF DEATH	674	JERUSALEM 44	7
	BEGAN TO RAGE THUNDERING LOUD THE STORMS BEGAN TO ROAR	676	JERUSALEM 46	21
	UPON THE FURNACES AND LOUD THE FURNACES REBELLOW BENEATH	676	JERUSALEM 46	22
	LOUD THE CRIES OF WAR ON THE RHINE & DANUBE WITH ALBION'S SONS	677	JERUSALEM 47	9
	IN ETERNAL LABOURS LOUD THE [FURNAES] FURNACES & LOUD THE ANVILS	684	JERUSALEM 53	* 20
	LOUD LOUD THE MOUNTAINS LIFTED UP THEIR VOICES LOUD THE FORESTS	686	JERUSALEM 55	23
	RIVERS THUNDERED AGAINST THEIR BANKS LOUD WINDS FURIOUS FOUGHT	686	JERUSALEM 55	24
	OF THE ATLANTIC WHICH POURED IN IMPETUOUS LOUD LOUD LOUDER & LOUDER	689	JERUSALEM 57	4
	LOS BEHELD IN TERROR HE POURD HIS LOUD STORMS ON THE FURNACES	702	JERUSALEM 66	16
	THE DAUGHTERS WEAVE THEIR WORK IN LOUD CRIES OVER THE ROCK	704	JERUSALEM 67	26
	OVER THE WHOLE EARTH LOUD THE WARRIORS RAGE IN BETH PEOR	704	JERUSALEM 67	29
	LOUD THE SUN & MOON RAGE IN THE CONFLICT LOUD THE STARS	704	JERUSALEM 67	31
	IN MORAL LAW & ITS SEVERE PENALTIES LOUD SHADDAI & JEHOVAH	706	JERUSALEM 68	39
	THEIR APPEARANCE WHEN COMBIND BUT OFTEN BY BIRTH PANGS & LOUD GROANS	708	JERUSALEM 70	* 11
	AND LOS'S FURNACES HOWL LOUD LIVING SELF-MOVING LAMENTING	713	JERUSALEM 73	2
	RINTRAH & PALAMABRON THEOTORMON & BROMION LOUD LABRING . .	713	JERUSALEM 73	5
	AND DEADLY STUPOR TURND AGAINST EACH OTHER LOUD & FIERCE	714	JERUSALEM 74	6
	CREATION AND DEVOURD ALL THINGS IN ITS LOUD	717	STOOD AMONG/J	5
	WALKS ROUND LOUD HIS THREATS LOUD HIS BLOWS FALL	719	JERUSALEM 78	4
	THEY ARE BROKEN LOUD HOWL THE SPECTRES IN HIS IRON FURNACE	719	JERUSALEM 78	9
	THE SPINDLE TURND IN BLOOD & FIRE LOUD SOUND THE TRUMPETS	722	JERUSALEM 80	37
	OF WAR THE CYMBALS PLAY LOUD BEFORE THE CAPTAINS	722	JERUSALEM 80	38
	INTO HIS THUNDERING BELLOWS HEAVING IT FOR A LOUD BLAST	726	JERUSALEM 82	58
	THE ENVY LOUD SHE LABOURD IN THE FURNACE OF FIRE	726	JERUSALEM 82	62
	IN MILD JERUSALEM AROUND THE LAMB OF GOD LOUD HOWL . . .	734	JERUSALEM 88	53
	THE FURNACES OF LOS LOUD ROLL THE WHEELS OF ENITHARMON . .	734	JERUSALEM 88	54
	OF BENJAMIN FROM CHESTER'S RIVER LOUD THE RIVER LOUD THE MERSEY	736	JERUSALEM 90	15
	LOUD SCREAM THE DAUGHTERS OF ALBION BENEATH THE TONGS & HAMMER	737	JERUSALEM 90	44
	BUT STILL THE THUNDER OF LOS PEALS LOUD & THUS THE THUNDER'S CRY	737	JERUSALEM 90	* 67
	HIS LOINS & BOSOM UNREMOVABLE BY SWELLING STORMS & LOUD RENDING	741	JERUSALEM 94	10
	LOUD THUNDRING WITH BROAD FLASHES OF FLAMING LIGHTNING & PILLARS	742	JERUSALEM 95	8
	. . . LOUD SOUNDING FLEW THE FLAMING ARROW FOURFOLD . . .	744	JERUSALEM 98	3
	. . . LOUD THUNDRING REJOICING TERRIFIC VANISHING . . .	745	JERUSALEM 98	6
	LOUD AS SINAI'S TRUMPET SOUND	748	EV GOSPEL(B)/N	6
	JOHN FROM THE WILDERNESS LOUD CRIED	748	EV GOSPEL(B)/N	13
	DRAGD AT HIS CHARIOT WHEELS LOUD HOWLD	749	EV GOSPEL(B)/N	43
	LOUD PILATE HOWLD LOUD CAIPHAS YELLD	758	EV GOSPEL (2)	19
	THE CHRISTIAN TRUMPETS LOUD PROCLAIM	758	EV GOSPEL (2)	24
	THE LOUD SEA & DEEP GULF	805	TO BUTTS/L	68
LOUD BREATHING				
	. . . WITH CLARIONS OF ?LOUD BREATHING WAR	138	FRENCH REVOLTN	* 101
LOUDER				
	SING LOUDER AROUND	116	ECCHOING GR/SI	7
	. . . THEN A THUNDER ROLLD ROUND LOUD AND LOUDER	145	FRENCH REVOLTN	257

	PAGE	TITLE	LINE

LOUDER   (CONTINUED)
ABOVE THE REST THE HOWL WAS HEARD FROM WESTMINSTER LOUDER   242 EUROPE 12   14
    & LOUDER
LOUD STRONG A UNIVERSAL GROAN OF DEATH LOUDER . . . . .   195 FOUR ZOAS 3   150
ROARING REDOUNDING LOUD LOUD LOUDER & LOUDER & FIRD .   308 FOUR ZOAS 5   106
OF THE ATLANTIC WHICH POURED IN IMPETUOUS LOUD LOUD LOUDER   689 JERUSALEM 57   4
    & LOUDER
THE GOD OF THIS WORLD LOUDER ROLLD   749 EV GOSPEL(B)/N   44
THE CHARIOT [WHELD] [WHEEL &] WHEELS & LOUDER STILL . . .   749 EV GOSPEL(B)/N *   45

LOUDEST
A CLOUDY HEAVEN MINGLED WITH STORMY SEAS IN LOUDEST RUIN   497 MILTON 15   43

LOUDLY
WHICH CALLS UPON HIS OPPONENT LOUDLY FOR AN ANSWER . . .390D ANNO WATSON   MARG

LOUD-RENDING
AND THE LOUD-RENDING BARS OF THE CREATION READY TO BURST   667 JERUSALEM 40   26

LOUD SOUNDING
AND URIZEN'S LOUD SOUNDING VOICE LAMENTING ON THE WIND . .   313 FOUR ZOAS 6   48
THE TERRIBLE BALL THE WEDGE THE LOUD SOUNDING HAMMER OF   713 JERUSALEM 73   12
    DESTRUCTION
HORNS OF THE WIDE BOW LOUD SOUNDING WINDS SPORT ON THE   742 JERUSALEM 95   15
    MOUNTAIN BROWS
OF THE WIDE BOW LOUD SOUNDING WINDS SPORT ON THE MOUNTAINS   745 JERUSALEM 98   5
    BROWS

LOUD VOICD
LOUD VOICD BARD AND MANY CONDEMND THE HIGH TONED SONG . .   495 MILTON 13   47
THE LOUD VOICD BARD TERRIFYD TOOK REFUGE IN MILTON'S BOSOM   495 MILTON 14   9

LOUIS
IF ALL THE PRINCES IN EUROPE LIKE LOUIS XIV . . . . .   599D PUB ADDRESS/N   PROSE
ESTABLISHD BY SUCH CONTEMPTIBLE POLITICIANS AS LOUIS XIV &   600B PUB ADDRESS/N   PROSE

LOUSE
HERE LADIES & GENTLEMEN SAID HE I'LL SHEW YOU A LOUSE   58C ISLAND MOON 10 *PROSE
    [?CLIMING] OR
THE FLEA LOUSE BUG THE TAPE-WORM ALL THE ARMIES OF DISEASE   513 MILTON 27   17

LOUVRE
TO TOWER HIS HOWLINGS WERE HEARD IN THE LOUVRE . . . . .   135 FRENCH REVOLTN   22
BUT HEAVY BROWD JEALOUSIES LOWER OER THE LOUVRE . . . . .   136 FRENCH REVOLTN   59
. . . HE IS COME TO THE LOUVRE O KING WITH A MESSAGE . .   141 FRENCH REVOLTN   166
ON THE STEPS OF THE LOUVRE . . . .   143 FRENCH REVOLTN   202
. . . AND ACROSS THE ARMY AND ACROSS THE LOUVRE . . . .   146 FRENCH REVOLTN   272
A FAINT HEAT FROM THEIR FIRES REVIVD THE COLD LOUVRE . . .   148 FRENCH REVOLTN   303

LOUZY
[A CROOKED STICK & LOUZY HEAD OF HAIR] . . . .   540 SIR JOSH RUB/N   7
AS CROOKED LIMBS & LOUZY HEADS OF HAIR . . . .   540 SIR JOSH RUB/N   8

LOVD   SEE ONCE LOVD
INWARD GRIEVD HE SAW AND LOVD THE BEAUTEOUS SUPPLIANT   39B SAMSON/PS   PROSE
UNTIMELY LOST THY CONRADE ONCE WHEN LIVING THEE I LOVD   43D WOE CRIED MUSE   PROSE
    EVN UNTO DEATH
I HAVE LOOKD INTO THE SECRET SOUL OF HIM I LOVD . . . .   265 FOUR ZOAS 1   44
IN [DISMAL] GNAWING PAIN DRAWN OUT BY HER LOVD FINGERS   266 FOUR ZOAS 1   79
    EVERY NERVE
OF ITS OWN PERVERSE & WAYWARD ENION LOVD & WEPT . . . .   266 FOUR ZOAS 1   85
AND CANNOT THOSE WHO ONCE HAVE LOVD EVER FORGET THEIR LOVE   298 FOUR ZOAS 4   17
WITH WHIPS ALONG THE SULTRY [ROADS] SANDS I HEARD THOSE   334 FOUR ZOAS 7B   61
    WHOM I LOVD
SHE TENDERLY LOVD HIM ABOVE ALL HIS BRETHREN HE GREW UP   351 FOUR ZOAS 8   385
THE BANE OF ALL THAT ON EARTH I LOVD . . . .   430 GREY MONK   16
SHALL NEVER BE BY WOMAN LOVD . . . .   431 AUGURIES   32
[YOUNG] LONG JOHN BROWN LOVD [PRETTY] LITTLE MARY BELL .   434 LONG JOHN BRWN   3
P(?PHILLIPS) LOVED ME NOT AS HE LOVD HIS FRIENDS . . . .   544 P LOVED NOT/N   1
FOR HE LOVD THEM FOR GAIN TO SERVE HIS ENDS . . . . .   544 P LOVED NOT/N   2
NOT PRAISD BY HAYLEY NOR BY FLAXMAN LOVD . . . . . .   546 MY TITLE AS/N   2
THOU MIGHTEST BE PITIED & LOVD BUT NOW I AM LIVING UNLESS   627 JERUSALEM 8   37
BECAUSE IT INCLOSD PITY & LOVE BECAUSE WE LOVD ONE-ANOTHER   643 JERUSALEM 20   35
ALBION LOVD THEE HE RENT THY VEIL HE EMBRACD THEE HE LOVD   643 JERUSALEM 20   36
    THEE
LOS WAS THE FRIEND OF ALBION WHO MOST LOVD HIM IN   666 JERUSALEM 39   12
    CAMBRIDGESHIRE
WE ALL ADMIRD & LOVD WHOSE ALL BENEVOLENT COUNTENANCE SEEN   675 JERUSALEM 45   5
. . . MILTON LOVD ME IN CHILDHOOD & SHEWD ME HIS FACE .   799 TO FLAXMAN/L   5
HOW MUCH YOUR NAME IS LOVD & RESPECTED I HAVE THE . . .841B LETTER 41   PROSE

LOVE   SEE FAMILY-LOVE,SELF-LOVE,SELF LOVE
OUR VALLIES LOVE THE SUMMER IN HIS PRIDE . . . . . .   2 TO SUMMER/PS   13
THE SUN AND LOVE RUNS IN HER THRILLING VEINS . . . . .   2 TO AUTUMN/PS   8
THY BRIGHT TORCH OF LOVE THY RADIANT CROWN . . . . .   3 EVNING STAR/PS   3
HE SEEKS THY LOVE WHO COWARD IN THE NIGHT . . . . . .   6 FAIR ELENOR/PS   67
TILL I THE PRINCE OF LOVE BEHELD . . . .   6 HOW SWEET/PS   3
BY LOVE ARE DRIVN AWAY . . . .   6 MY SILKS/PS   3
TRUE LOVE DOTH PASS AWAY . . . .   7 MY SILKS/PS   18
LOVE AND HARMONY COMBINE . . . .   7 LOVE HARMNY/PS   1
THERE IS LOVE I HEAR [HER] HIS TONGUE . . . .   7 LOVE HARMNY/PS   16
I LOVE THE JOCUND DANCE . . . .   7 LOVE JOCUND/PS   1
I LOVE THE LAUGHING VALE . . . .   7 LOVE JOCUND/PS   5
I LOVE THE ECHOING HILL . . . .   7 LOVE JOCUND/PS   6
I LOVE THE PLEASANT COT . . . .   8 LOVE JOCUND/PS   9
I LOVE THE INNOCENT BOWR . . . .   8 LOVE JOCUND/PS   10
I LOVE THE OAKEN SEAT . . . .   8 LOVE JOCUND/PS   13
I LOVE OUR NEIGHBOURS ALL . . . .   8 LOVE JOCUND/PS   17
BUT KITTY I BETTER LOVE THEE . . . .   8 LOVE JOCUND/PS   18
AND LOVE THEM I EVER SHALL . . . .   8 LOVE JOCUND/PS   19
THAT MADE MY LOVE SO HIGH AND ME SO LOW . . . . . .   10 WHEN EARLY/PS   16
HOW HAVE YOU LEFT THE ANTIENT LOVE . . . .   11 TO MUSES/PS   13
AND LOVE OF FOLLY NEEDS NONE [OTHERS] OTHER CURSE . . .   14 IMIT SPEN/PS   14

LOVE   (CONTINUED)
    IT IS MY SIN TO LOVE THE NOISE OF WAR . . . . 26 EDW THIRD/PS 3   232
    TO TELL YOUR HONOUR BECAUSE YOU LOVE TO HEAR WAR-SONGS . . 29C EDW THIRD/PS 4 PROSE
    WHERE PEACE AND JOY AND LOVE AND CALM CONTENT . . . . . 30 EDW THIRD/PS 5   30
    THE HOLY KISS OF LOVE AND THE TRANSPARENT TEAR . . . . 38A SAMSON/PS   PROSE
    PUT ON THY COUNTRY'S PRIDE DECEIT AND EYES OF LOVE . . . 38A SAMSON/PS   PROSE
    THOURT WAR THOU ART NOT LOVE O FOOLISH DALILA . . . . . 38B SAMSON/PS   PROSE
    DOUBT NO MORE OF SAMSON'S LOVE FOR THAT FAIR BREAST WAS   39B SAMSON/PS   PROSE
        MADE
    GO SEE MORE STRONG THE TIES OF MARRIAGE LOVE . . . . . 43A THEN SHE BORE   PROSE
    HE FELL IN LOVE & MARRIED HER . . . . 50 WHEN CORRUP/IM   19
    HAIL MATRIMONY MADE OF LOVE . . . . 56 HAIL MATRIM/IM   1
    I HATE SCARCE SMILES I LOVE LAUGHING . . . . 67D ANNO LAVATER   MARG
    ("CAN HE LOVE TRUTH WHO CAN TAKE A KNAVE TO HIS BOSOM")   68A ANNO LAVATER   MARG
        NO
    ("THE HUMBLE...THE LOVING...ETERNAL LOVE") SWEET . . . . 68C ANNO LAVATER MARG
    ("WHERE PRIDE BEGINS LOVE CEASES) PRIDE MAY LOVE . . . 68C ANNO LAVATER   MARG
    FOR WHAT ARE ALL CRAWLERS BUT MIMICKERS OF HUMILITY & LOVE   68D ANNO LAVATER MARG
    IF MALICIOUSLY NOT A MAN I CANNOT LOVE MY ENEMY . . . . 72B ANNO LAVATER   MARG
    I CAN LOVE HIM AS A BEAST & WISH TO BEAT HIM . . . . . 72B ANNO LAVATER   MARG
    ("AS THE GOOD LOVE THEE THE BAD WILL HATE THEE") UNEASY   72D ANNO LAVATER   MARG
    AND CONSIDER THAT LOVE IS LIFE . . . . 76A ANNO LAVATER   MARG
    ("THE UNLOVED CANNOT LOVE") DOUBTFUL . . . . 76C ANNO LAVATER   MARG
    ("LOVE SEES WHAT NO EYE SEES ") MOST EXCELLENT . . . . 77D ANNO LAVATER   MARG
    I KNOW NOT WHAT HIDING LOVE MEANS . . . . 78D ANNO LAVATER   MARG
    ("HATE AS IF YOU COULD LOVE OR SHOULD BE") BETTER THAN   84D ANNO LAVATER   MARG
        EXCELLENT
    ("SEEN THROUGH MICROSCOPE...IN PASSION") & SUCH A ONE I   85D ANNO LAVATER   MARG
        DARE LOVE
    "WHOSO DWELLETH IN LOVE DWELLETH IN GOD & GOD IN HIM"   87A ANNO LAVATER
    & SUCH AN ONE CANNOT JUDGE OF ANY BUT IN LOVE & HIS . . . 87A ANNO LAVATER MARG
    IN A BOOK I LOVE SO MUCH & APPROVE SO GENERALLY . . . . 88A ANNO LAVATER   MARG
    & HIS COTEMPORARIES IS THEY SUPPOSE THAT WOMAN'S LOVE IS   88D ANNO LAVATER   MARG
        SIN
    WILL DESIRE LOVE RAGE ENVY & ?ALL ?OTHER . . . . . . 89B ANNO SWED LOVE * MARG
    ("LIFE OF MAN...IS LOVE") THIS WAS KNOWN TO ME & THOUSANDS   89C ANNO SWED LOVE   MARG
    HE WHO LOVES FEELS LOVE DESCEND INTO HIM & IF HE HAS WISDOM   90B ANNO SWED LOVE   MARG
    THINK OF A WHITE CLOUD AS BEING HOLY YOU CANNOT LOVE IT   90C ANNO SWED LOVE   MARG
    BUT THINK OF A HOLY MAN WITHIN THE CLOUD LOVE SPRINGS UP   90C ANNO SWED LOVE   MARG
    LOVE & WISDOM AS IT DOES BETWEEN BODY & SPIRIT . . . . 90D ANNO SWED LOVE   MARG
    WHO DOES NOT OR MAY NOT KNOW OF LOVE & WISDOM IN HIMSELF   92D ANNO SWED LOVE   MARG
    ("WISDOM DOES NOT PRODUCE LOVE") MARK THIS . . . . . 93D ANNO SWED LOVE   MARG
    ("LOVE OR THE WILL JOINS ITSELF TO WISDOM") MARK THIS   95C ANNO SWED LOVE   MARG
    ("KNOWLEDGE...NOT RECEIVED BY UNDERSTANDING BUT BY LOVE")   95C ANNO SWED LOVE   MARG
        MARK THIS
    ("LOVE JOINS ...UNDERSTANDING AND NOT VICE VERSA ") MARK   95D ANNO SWED LOVE   MARG
        THIS
    ("UNDERSTANDING BY...LOVE CAN BE ELEVATED") MARK THIS . 96B ANNO SWED LOVE   MARG
    IS IT NOT FALSE THEN THAT LOVE RECIEVES INFLUX THRO . . . 96B ANNO SWED LOVE   MARG
    ("LOVE") THEREFORE IT WAS NOT CREATED IMPURE & IS   96C ANNO SWED LOVE   MARG
        NOT NATURALLY SO
    ("LOVE") THEREFORE IT DOES NOT RECIEVE INFLUX THRO THE   96C ANNO SWED LOVE   MARG
        UNDERSTANDING
    ("LOVE...UNDERSTANDING") MARK THIS THEY ARE ELEVATED   96C ANNO SWED LOVE   MARG
        TOGETHER
    GO NOT FOR THOU ART SO LIKE TIRIEL THAT I LOVE THINE HEAD   103 TIRIEL 3   24
    LAUGHS AT AFFECTION GLORIES IN REBELLION SCOFFS AT LOVE   107 TIRIEL 6   18
    [THY GOD OF LOVE THY HEAVEN OF JOY] . . . . 109 TIRIEL 8   *   9
    [CAN WISDOM BE PUT IN A SILVER ROD OR LOVE IN A GOLDEN   110 TIRIEL 8   18
        BOWL]
    TO MERCY PITY PEACE AND LOVE . . . . 117 DIVNE IMAGE/SI   1
    FOR MERCY PITY PEACE AND LOVE . . . . 117 DIVNE IMAGE/SI   5
    AND MERCY PITY PEACE AND LOVE . . . . 117 DIVNE IMAGE/SI   7
    AND LOVE THE HUMAN FORM DIVINE . . . . 117 DIVNE IMAGE/SI   11
    LOVE MERCY PITY PEACE . . . . 117 DIVNE IMAGE/SI   16
    AND ALL MUST LOVE THE HUMAN FORM . . . . 117 DIVNE IMAGE/SI   17
    WHERE MERCY LOVE & PITY DWELL . . . . 117 DIVNE IMAGE/SI   19
    I LOVE TO RISE IN A SUMMER MORN . . . . 124 SCHOOL BOY/SI   1
    THAT WE MAY LEARN TO BEAR THE BEAMS OF LOVE . . . . . 125 LIT BLK BOY/SI   14
    SAYING COME OUT FROM THE GROVE MY LOVE & CARE . . . . . 125 LIT BLK BOY/SI   19
    AND BE LIKE HIM AND HE WILL THEN LOVE ME . . . . . . 125 LIT BLK BOY/SI   28
    OR LOVE IN A GOLDEN BOWL . . . . 127 THELS MOTTO/BT   4
    AND I AM VERY SMALL AND LOVE TO DWELL IN LOWLY VALES . . 127 BOOK OF THEL 1   17
    IT IS TO TENFOLD LIFE TO LOVE TO PEACE AND RAPTURES HOLY   128 BOOK OF THEL 3   11
    I PONDER AND I CANNOT PONDER YET I LIVE AND LOVE . . . 129 BOOK OF THEL 5   6
    THAT GOD WOULD LOVE A WORM I KNEW AND PUNISH THE EVIL FOOT   130 BOOK OF THEL 5   9
    . . . AND WATER HIS CLAY WITH LOVE . . . . 139 FRENCH REVOLTN   108
    HANDS HEAD BOSOM AND PARTS OF LOVE FOLLOW THEIR HIGH   142 FRENCH REVOLTN   185
        BREATHING JOY
    REASON AND ENERGY LOVE AND HATE ARE NECESSARY TO HUMAN   149B MARRIAGE HH 3 PROSE
        EXISTENCE
    ETERNITY IS IN LOVE WITH THE PRODUCTIONS OF TIME . . . . 151A MARRIAGE HH 7 PROSE
    IF JESUS CHRIST IS THE GREATEST MAN YOU OUGHT TO LOVE HIM   158C MARRIAGE HH 22 PROSE
    [NEVER [SEEK] PAIN TO TELL THY LOVE] . . . . 161 NEVER PAIN/N   1
    [LOVE THAT NEVER TOLD CAN BE] . . . . 161 NEVER PAIN/N   2
    I TOLD MY LOVE I TOLD MY LOVE . . . . 161 NEVER PAIN/N   5
    LOVE SEEKETH NOT ITSELF TO PLEASE . . . . 162 CLOD PEBBLE/N   1
    LOVE SEEKETH ONLY SELF TO PLEASE . . . . 162 CLOD PEBBLE/N   9
    WHERE LOVE LAY SLEEPING . . . . 162 LAID ME DOWN/N   2
    I WENT TO THE GARDEN OF LOVE . . . . 162 GARDEN LOVE/N   1
    SO I TURND TO THE GARDEN OF LOVE . . . . 162 GARDEN LOVE/N *   7
    [HAST MY] THAT FREE LOVE WITH BONDAGE BOUND . . . . . 169 EARTHS ANSWR/N   25

```
                                                              PAGE      TITLE        LINE
LOVE    (CONTINUED)
   LOVE FREE LOVE CANNOT BE BOUND     . . . . . . . . .      169 MIRTLE SHADE/N        9
   WHILE THE LILLY WHITE SHALL IN LOVE DELIGHT     . . . . .  171 THE LILLY/N          3
   [HOW TO KNOW LOVE FROM DECEIT] . . . . . . . . . . . .    175A HOW TO KNOW/N     TITLE
   LOVE TO FAULTS IS ALWAYS BLIND  . . . . . . . . . . .      175 HOW TO KNOW/N        1
   [O DARK SECRET LOVE]  . . . . . . . . . . . . .           175 SICK ROSE/N          7
   AND [HIS] HER DARK SECRET LOVE  . . . . . . . . . . .      175 SICK ROSE/N          9
   [AH THAT SWEET LOVE SHOULD BE THOUGHT A CRIME]  . . . .    176 SOFT SNOW/N          4
   [LOVE FREE LOVE CANNOT BE BOUND]  . . . . . . . . . .      176 TO MY MIRTLE/N       3
   [THEN] AND FATHER [I CAN NOT] HOW CAN I LOVE YOU . . . .   177 LIT BOY LST/N        5
   I LOVE [MYSELF SO DOES THE BIRD] YOU LIKE THE LITTLE BIRD  177 LIT BOY LST/N        7
   THE LOOK OF LOVE ALARMS  . . . . . . . . . . . .          182 LOOK OF LOVE/N       1
   FOR [SOON] EARLY I IN LOVE WAS CROST  . . . . . . . .      184 O I CANNOT/N    *    3
   BEFORE MY FLOWER OF LOVE WAS LOST . . . . . . . . .        184 O I CANNOT/N         4
   OUGHT BUT THE LOVE THAT ON ME GREW  . . . . . . . .        184 O I CANNOT/N         6
   THE LOOK OF LOVE ALARMS  . . . . . . . . . . . .          184 SEVRL QUESTN/N       5
   [AND SAID I LOVE HANGING & DRAWING & QUARTERING] . . . .   185 LET BROTHELS/N      11
   LOVE TO CURL ROUND THE BONES OF DEATH AND ASK THE RAVNOUS  191 V DAU ALBION 3      11
      SNAKE
   HOLY ETERNAL INFINITE AND EACH JOY IS A LOVE  . . . . .    192 V DAU ALBION 5       6
   I CRY LOVE LOVE LOVE HAPPY HAPPY LOVE FREE AS             194 V DAU ALBION 7      16
      THE MOUNTAIN WIND
   CAN THAT BE LOVE THAT DRINKS ANOTHER AS A SPONGE DRINKS    194 V DAU ALBION 7      17
      WATER
   COME IN THE HEAVEN OF GENEROUS LOVE NOR SELFISH BLIGHTINGS 195 V DAU ALBION 7      29
      BRING
   SILENT AS DESPAIRING LOVE AND STRONG AS JEALOUSY    . . .  196 AMERICA PREL 2       1
   I SEE A SERPENT IN CANADA WHO COURTS ME TO HIS LOVE . . .  196 AMERICA PREL 2      12
   THAT FREE LOVE WITH BONDAGE BOUND  . . . . . . . .        211 EARTHS ANSR/SE      25
   LOVE SEEKETH NOT ITSELF TO PLEASE  . . . . . . . .        211 CLOD PEBBLE/SE       1
   LOVE SEEKETH ONLY SELF TO PLEASE  . . . . . . . .         211 CLOD PEBBLE/SE       9
   AND HIS DARK SECRET LOVE  . . . . . . . . . . . .         213 SICK ROSE/SE         7
   WHILE THE LILLY WHITE SHALL IN LOVE DELIGHT  . . . . .     215 THE LILLY/SE         3
   THE GARDEN OF LOVE  . . . . . . . . . . . . . .           215C GARDEN LOVE/SE   TITLE
   I WENT TO THE GARDEN OF LOVE  . . . . . . . . . .         215 GARDEN LOVE/SE       1
   SO I TURND TO THE GARDEN OF LOVE  . . . . . . . .         215 GARDEN LOVE/SE       7
   AND FATHER HOW CAN I LOVE YOU  . . . . . . . . .          218 LIT BOY LST/SE       5
   I LOVE YOU LIKE THE LITTLE BIRD  . . . . . . . .          218 LIT BOY LST/SE       7
   LOVE SWEET LOVE WAS THOUGHT A CRIME  . . . . . . .        219 LIT GRL LST/SE       4
   LAWS OF PEACE OF LOVE OF UNITY . . . . . . . . .          224 URIZEN 4            34
   GO TELL THE HUMAN RACE THAT WOMAN'S LOVE IS SIN  . . . .   240 EUROPE 5             5
   WHERE IS MY LUREING BIRD OF EDEN LEUTHA SILENT LOVE  . . . 244 EUROPE 14            9
   MY ANTAMON THE SEVEN CHURCHES OF LEUTHA SEEK THY LOVE  . . 244 EUROPE 14           20
   SECLUDED PLACES FEARING THE JOYS OF LOVE  . . . . . .      246 SONG OF LOS 3       26
   AND THE VOICE CRIED AH URIZEN LOVE  . . . . . . . .        254 AHANIA 4            52
   INTO MY CHAMBERS OF LOVE . . . . . . . . . . . .          254 AHANIA 5            18
   WHEN LOVE & JOY WERE ADORATION . . . . . . . . .          256 BOOK OF LOS 3        8
   OR SATED WITH HER LOVE  . . . . . . . . . . . .           256 BOOK OF LOS 3       19
   AND WANTONNESS ON HIS OWN TRUE LOVE  . . . . . . .        256 BOOK OF LOS 3       25
   THE FOUR ZOAS THE TORMENTS OF LOVE & JEALOUSY IN  . . . . 263C FOUR ZOAS       TITLE
   IT IS NOT LOVE I BEAR TO ENITHARMON IT IS PITY  . . . .   265 FOUR ZOAS 1         31
   ALL LOVE IS LOST TERROR SUCCEEDS & HATRED INSTEAD OF LOVE  265 FOUR ZOAS 1         36
   WHY ART THOU TERRIBLE AND YET I LOVE THEE IN THY TERROR    265 FOUR ZOAS 1         39
      TILL
   AND NAMD THE SPACE ULRO & BROODED OVER IT IN CARE & LOVE   267 FOUR ZOAS 1        102
   [IS THIS A DEED OF LOVE I KNOW WHAT I HAVE DONE I KNOW ]   267 FOUR ZOAS 1        110
   . . . [?ALONE ?POSSESSD BY DEADLY FEARS] LOVE IS CHANGD    267 FOUR ZOAS 1    *   111
      TO DEADLY HATE
   [THAT NOUGHT BUT ENION COULD BE FOUND TO PRAISE ADORE &    267 FOUR ZOAS 1        133
      LOVE]
   BROKE FROM MY BONDS I SCORN MY PRISON I SCORN & YET I LOVE 268 FOUR ZOAS 1        150
   TEMPT ME TO MURDER [HONEST LOVE] MY OWN SOUL & WIPE MY     268 FOUR ZOAS 1        171
      TEARS & SMILE
   FADED & HER BRIGHT EYES DECAYD MELTED WITH PITY & LOVE  .  270 FOUR ZOAS 1        213
   REHUMANIZING FROM THE SPECTRE IN PANGS OF MATERNAL LOVE    270 FOUR ZOAS 1        216
   ALTERNATE LOVE & HATE HIS BREAST HERS SCORN & JEALOUSY  .  270 FOUR ZOAS 1        237
   THEY WILL WITHOLD SWEET LOVE WHOSE FOOD IS THORNS & BITTER 271 FOUR ZOAS 1        257
      ROOTS
   THE PRINCE OF LOVE THE MURDERER HIS SOUL IS IN THINE HANDS 273 FOUR ZOAS 1        325
   LOS NOW REPENTED THAT HE HAD SMITTEN ENITHARMON HE FELT    274 FOUR ZOAS 1        352
      LOVE
   DELUDED BY [THE] SUMMER'S HEAT THEY SPORT IN ENORMOUS LOVE 276 FOUR ZOAS 1        452
   UPON THE ROCK OF AGES WATCHING OVER HIM WITH LOVE & CARE   277 FOUR ZOAS 1        468
   SLEPT ROUND ON HILLS & VALLEYS IN THE REGIONS OF HIS LOVE  277 FOUR ZOAS 1        486
   [IN BEAUTY LOVE & XXX SCORN [?THEY ?SULKD] THE BRIDE &     SUPP FOUR ZOAS 1    *
      BRIDEGROOM ?SULKD]
   . . . FROM THE FEAST OF [ENVY] [LOVE] ENVY  . . . . . .   280 FOUR ZOAS 2    *    10
   DISCORDANT PRINCIPLES OF LOVE & HATE I SUFFER AFFLICTION   282 FOUR ZOAS 2        103
   BECAUSE I LOVE FOR I [AM] WAS LOVE [&] BUT HATRED AWAKES   282 FOUR ZOAS 2    *   104
      IN ME
   LUVAH IN VAIN HER LAMENTATIONS HEARD IN VAIN HIS LOVE   .  286 FOUR ZOAS 2        232
   STILL HATING STILL PROFESSING LOVE STILL LABOURING IN      286 FOUR ZOAS 2        235
      THE SMOKE
   FROM THY FIERCE LOVE FOR THO I AM DISSOLVD IN THE BRIGHT   288 FOUR ZOAS 2        316
      GOD
   MY SPIRIT STILL PURSUES THY FALSE LOVE OVER ROCKS & VALLEYS 288 FOUR ZOAS 2       317
   WHO DIES FOR LOVE OF HER  . . . . . . . . . . .           289 FOUR ZOAS 2        350
   TO HEAR SOUNDS OF LOVE IN THE THUNDER STORM . . . . . .    291 FOUR ZOAS 2        411
   THE DISMAL VISION OF MINE EYES O LOVE & LIFE & LIGHT    .  293 FOUR ZOAS 3         73
   O CRUEL PITY O DARK DECEIT CAN LOVE SEEK FOR DOMINION   .  293 FOUR ZOAS 3         78
   AND LEARN WHAT TIS TO ABSORB THE MAN YOU SPIRITS OF PITY   294 FOUR ZOAS 3         90
      & LOVE
```

LOVE   (CONTINUED)   PAGE   TITLE   LINE

      INSTEAD OF LOVE TO ENION ENION BLIND & AGE BENT   . . . .   296 FOUR ZOAS 3   178
      CONSUMING ALL TO THE END CONSUMING LOVE AND [JOY] HOPE   297 FOUR ZOAS 3   204
          ARE ENDED
      [?THEN XXX LABOUR ENDED XXX LOVE FOR VALA] . . . . . SUPP FOUR ZOAS 3   *
      AND HE SAID WHEREFORE DO I FEEL SUCH LOVE & PITY   297 FOUR ZOAS 4   7
      AND CANNOT THOSE WHO ONCE HAVE LOVD EVER FORGET THEIR LOVE   298 FOUR ZOAS 4   17
      ARE LOVE & RAGE THE SAME PAS. 'N THEY ARE THE SAME IN ME   298 FOUR ZOAS 4   18
      ARE THOSE WHO LOVE LIKE THOSE WHO DIED RISEN AGAIN FROM   298 FOUR ZOAS 4   19
          DEATH
      BUILT BY THE ARCHITECT DIVINE WHOSE LOVE TO LOS &   298 FOUR ZOAS 4   51
          ENITHARMON
      MY COUNTER PART & CALLD IT LOVE I NAMD HER ENITHARMON   . .   300 FOUR ZOAS 4   100
      AND THEE O LUVAH PRINCE OF LOVE TILL THARMAS WAS DIVIDED   301 FOUR ZOAS 4   142
      CRYING LUVAH KING OF LOVE THOU ART THE KING OF RAGE &   306 FOUR ZOAS 5   42
          DEATH
      CONCENTERD INTO LOVE OF PARENT STORGOUS APPETITE CRAVING   308 FOUR ZOAS 5   113
      AND ENITHARMON'S TEARS PREVAILD PARENTAL LOVE RETURND   . .   309 FOUR ZOAS 5   146
      . . . THEN LOVE SHALL SHEW ITS ROOT IN DEEPEST HELL . . .   311 FOUR ZOAS 5   241
      NOR KNEW THAT I ALONE EXEMPTED FROM THE JOYS OF LOVE   325 FOUR ZOAS 7   200
      REDDNING THE DEMON STRONG PREPARD THE POISON OF SWEET LOVE   325 FOUR ZOAS 7   219
      AND FORMD A MALE TO BE A COUNTERPART TO THEE O LOVE . . .   327 FOUR ZOAS 7   293
      ART NOTHING BEING CREATED CONTINUALLY BY MERCY &   329 FOUR ZOAS 7   360
          LOVE DIVINE
      CLOUDS WOULD HAVE FOLDED ROUND IN EXTACY & LOVE UNITING   329 FOUR ZOAS 7   371
      . . . OF [LIFE & LOVE] SACRIFICE OF BROTHERS & SONS   331 FOUR ZOAS 7   443
          & DAUGHTERS
      AND ENITHARMON TINCTURD IT WITH BEAMS OF BLUSHING LOVE .   332 FOUR ZOAS 7   468
      THE IMMORTAL LINES UPON THE HEAVENS TILL WITH SIGHS OF LOVE   332 FOUR ZOAS 7   471
      IN HIS HANDS HE WONDERD THAT HE FELT LOVE & NOT HATE . .   332 FOUR ZOAS 7   497
      LOVE THOSE WHO HATE REWARDING WITH HATE THE LOVING SOUL   335 FOUR ZOAS 7B   91
      KNOWING THE ARTS OF URIZEN WERE PITY & MEEK [LOVE]   336 FOUR ZOAS 7B   134
          AFFECTION
      SILENT AS DESPAIRING LOVE & STRONG AS JEALOUSY . . . .   336 FOUR ZOAS 7B   136
      HOW RAGD THE GOLDEN HORSES OF URIZEN BOUND TO THE CHARIOT   338 FOUR ZOAS 7B   201
          OF LOVE
      THARMAS THE MOON HAS CHAMBERS WHERE THE BABES OF LOVE LIE   339 FOUR ZOAS 7B   244
          HID
      UNLESS EXPOSD BY THEIR VAIN PARENTS LO HIM WHOM I LOVE .   339 FOUR ZOAS 7B   246
      TO RISE ON HIGH YET LOVE HERE BINDS ME DOWN & NEVER NEVER   339 FOUR ZOAS 7B   254
      WILL I ARISE TILL HIM I LOVE IS LOOSD FROM THIS DARK CHAIN   339 FOUR ZOAS 7B   255
      THOU ART OUR CURSE [IN] AND TILL I CAN BRING LOVE INTO   339 FOUR ZOAS 7B   * 257
          THE LIGHT
      IN GOLDEN LETTERS ORNAMENTED WITH SWEET LABOURS OF LOVE   340 FOUR ZOAS 7B   294
      . . . MELTED INTO COMPASSION & LOVE . . . . . .   341 FOUR ZOAS 8   21
      WONDRING WITH LOVE & [XXX] AWE THEY FELT THE DIVINE HAND   341 FOUR ZOAS 8   *   23
          UPON THEM
      WITH A PARENTAL LOVE FOR THE DIVINE HAND WAS UPON HIM   . .   342 FOUR ZOAS 8   40
      THE SORROWER OF ETERNITY IN LOVE WITH TEARS SUBMISS I REAR   345 FOUR ZOAS 8   151
      WHERE HAST THOU HID HIM WHOM I LOVE IN WHAT REMOTE ABYSS   345 FOUR ZOAS 8   155
      AS ONCE IN THOSE ETERNAL FIELDS IN BROTHERHOOD & LOVE .   345 FOUR ZOAS 8   159
      CAN THAT WHICH HAS EXISTED CEASE OR CAN LOVE & LIFE EXPIRE   345 FOUR ZOAS 8   170
      THUS FORMING A VAST FAMILY WONDROUS IN BEAUTY & LOVE .   345 FOUR ZOAS 8   187
      IN CHANNELS THRO MY FIERY LIMBS O LOVE O PITY O PAIN .   349 FOUR ZOAS 8   307
      O THE PANGS THE BITTER PANGS OF LOVE FORSAKEN . . . .   349 FOUR ZOAS 8   308
      SHRIEK NOT SO MY ONLY LOVE . . . .   349 FOUR ZOAS 8   314
      HE ANSWERD HER WITH TENDERNESS & LOVE NOT UNINSPIRD . .   350 FOUR ZOAS 8   * 347
      . . . TO WHOM [THEIR] OUR LOVE INCREASD . . . . .   350 FOUR ZOAS 8   366
      INTO THE YOUTHFUL PROPHET FOR THE LOVE OF ENITHARMON   353 FOUR ZOAS 8   478
      I FOUND HIM IN MY BOSOM & I SAID THE TIME OF LOVE . . .   355 FOUR ZOAS 8   538
      YOU SHALL FORGET YOUR FORMER STATE RETURN O LOVE IN PEACE   366 FOUR ZOAS 9   * 364
      FORSAKING BROTHERHOOD & UNIVERSAL LOVE IN SELFISH CLAY .   374 FOUR ZOAS 9   629
      THAT MAN SUBSISTS BY BROTHERHOOD & UNIVERSAL LOVE . . .   374 FOUR ZOAS 9   638
      EACH SHALL BEHOLD THE ETERNAL FATHER & LOVE & JOY ABOUND   374 FOUR ZOAS 9   642
      THE RIPE CLUSTERS THE SHEPHERDS SHOUT FOR LUVAH PRINCE   376 FOUR ZOAS 9   700
          OF LOVE
      THESE ARE THE SPORTS OF LOVE . . . .   377 FOUR ZOAS 9   769
      ASTONISHD LOOKD FROM HIS BRIGHT PORTALS LUVAH KING OF LOVE   380 FOUR ZOAS AD 1   5
      PITYING THEY VIEWD THE NEW BORN DEMON FOR THEY COULD NOT   380 FOUR ZOAS AD 1   9
          LOVE
      TO LOVE DEVOTED FEMALE ALL ASTONISHD STOOD THE HOSTS . .   380 FOUR ZOAS AD 1   13
      FEMALE HER FORM BRIGHT AS THE SUMMER BUT THE PARTS OF LOVE   381 FOUR ZOAS AD 1   18
      THE OCEAN CALM THE CLOUDS FOLD ROUND & FIERY FLAMES OF LOVE   381 FOUR ZOAS AD 2   1
      DOES GOD LOVE THE RIGHTEOUS ACCORDING TO THE GOSPEL . . .   396A ANNO WATSON   MARG
      ONE MAN'S REVENGE OR LOVE IS NOT THE SAME AS ANOTHER'S .   398D ANNO BACON   MARG
      FEAR CANNOT LOVE   401A ANNO BACON   MARG
      [NEVER SHALT THOU A [LOVER] TRUE LOVE FIND] . . . . .   415 MY SPECTRE/N   11
      [WHEN MY LOVE DID FIRST BEGIN] . . . .   415 MY SPECTRE/N   19
      [THOU DIDST CALL THAT LOVE A SIN] . . . .   415 MY SPECTRE/N   20
      TILL [THOU] I TURN FROM FEMALE LOVE . . . . . .   417 MY SPECTRE/N   59
      LET US AGREE TO GIVE UP LOVE . . . .   417 MY SPECTRE/N   67
      THE WOMAN THAT DOES NOT LOVE YOUR FROWNS . . . . .   417 MY SPECTR AD/N   15
      THE BANE OF ALL THAT ON EARTH I LOVE . . . . . .   419 I SAW A MONK/N   31
      BUT THE TEAR OF LOVE & FORGIVENESS SWEET . . . . .   420 I SAW A MONK/N   53
      [THAT LOVE & BEAUTY UNDERGO] . . . .   422 BENEATH/N   13
      TELL ME FAIR ONE TELL ME LOVE . . . .   422 THE BIRDS/N   2
      THERE IS A SMILE OF LOVE . . . .   423 THE SMILE   1
      THAT LOVE & BEAUTY UNDERGO . . . .   424 THE GOLDEN NET   12
      BY VARIOUS ARTS OF LOVE BEGUILD . . . .   426 MENTAL TRAVLER   80
      BY VARIOUS ARTS OF LOVE & HATE . . . .   426 MENTAL TRAVLER   81
      WITH LABYRINTHS OF WAYWARD LOVE . . . .   426 MENTAL TRAVLER   83
      THAT SWEET LOVE & BEAUTY ARE WORTHY OUR CARE . . . . .   428 MARY   12

1143

LOVE   (CONTINUED)

AND NOT TO RAISE ENVY IS CALLD CHRISTIAN LOVE	428	MARY	26
AND THINE IS A FACE OF SWEET LOVE IN DESPAIR	429	MARY	45
HE LAUGHD AT THE DEVIL SAYING LOVE IS A SIN	434	LONG JOHN BRWN	6
O WILLIAM IF THOU DOST ANOTHER LOVE	435	WILLIAM BOND	21
DOST ANOTHER LOVE BETTER THAN POOR MARY	435	WILLIAM BOND	22
YES MARY I DO ANOTHER LOVE	435	WILLIAM BOND	25
ANOTHER I LOVE FAR BETTER THAN THEE	435	WILLIAM BOND	26
I THOUGHT LOVE LIVD IN THE HOT SUN SHINE	436	WILLIAM BOND	45
I THOUGHT TO FIND LOVE IN THE HEAT OF DAY	436	WILLIAM BOND	47
BUT SWEET LOVE IS THE COMFORTER OF NIGHT	436	WILLIAM BOND	48
SEEK LOVE IN THE PITY OF OTHERS' WOE	436	WILLIAM BOND	49
IN THE NAKED & OUTCAST SEEK LOVE THERE	436	WILLIAM BOND	52
AND BEAUTEOUS FORMS THAT LOVE DOES WEAR	447	ANNO REYNOLDS	2
HIS PRIMITIVE TYRANNICAL ATTEMPTS ON LOS WITH MOST ENDEARING LOVE	486	MILTON 7	7
FOR ONE WHOLE DAY UNDER PRETENCE OF PITY AND LOVE TO ME	487	MILTON 7	28
DELUSORY LOVE TO PALAMABRON ADMIRATION JOIND WITH ENVY	492	MILTON 12	7
THE MOST IRRITATING THINGS IN THE MIDST OF TEARS AND LOVE	493	MILTON 12	33
SAYING PITY AND LOVE ARE TOO VENERABLE FOR THE IMPUTATION	495	MILTON 13	48
IN BRIGHT CATHEDRON'S GOLDEN DOME WITH CARE & LOVE & TEARS	512	MILTON 26	36
THESE ARE THE SPORTS OF LOVE	514	MILTON 27	39
WITH ARMS OF LOVE & PITY & SWEET COMPASSION BUT TO	518	MILTON 30	12
WITH EYES OF SOFT HUMILITY & WONDER LOVE & AWE	520	MILTON 31	38
ATTENDING HIS LOUD HARMONY WITH ADMIRATION & LOVE	520	MILTON 31	44
YET ALL IN ORDER SWEET & LOVELY MEN ARE SICK WITH LOVE	521	MILTON 31	62
AFFECTION OR LOVE BECOMES A STATE WHEN DIVIDED FROM IMAGINATION	522	MILTON 32	33
I THOUGHT THAT YOU WOULD LOVE MY LOVES & JOY IN MY DELIGHTS	522	MILTON 33	3
CUT OFF MY LOVES IN FURY TILL I HAVE NO LOVE LEFT FOR THEE	522	MILTON 33	7
THY LOVE DEPENDS ON HIM THOU LOVEST & ON HIS DEAR LOVES	522	MILTON 33	8
BY DEATH & MISERY OF THOSE YOU LOVE & BY ANNIHILATION	522	MILTON 33	13
GO LOVE WITHOUT THE HELP OF ANY [THING] ?KING ON EARTH	541	ANGEL PRESID/N *	
FOR TIS [MOST WICKED] ATROCIOUS IN A FRIEND YOU LOVE	551	WILLM COWPER/N	9
GROWN OLD IN LOVE FROM SEVEN TILL SEVEN TIMES SEVEN	552	GROWN OLD IN/N	1
TWAS THE GREEKS' LOVE OF WAR	552	WHY CUPID/N	17
TURND LOVE INTO A BOY	552	WHY CUPID/N	18
THOSE WHO TASTE COLOURING LOVE IT MORE & MORE	554	TO VENETIAN/N	17
IVE A WIFE I LOVE & THAT LOVES ME	558	I ROSE UP AT/N	11
UGLY MAN ACTS FROM LOVE OF CARNAGE AND DELIGHT IN	580C	DESC CAT 5	PROSE
HE INFUSES A LOVE OF SOFT AND EVEN TINTS WITHOUT BOUNDARIES	583B	DESC CAT 9	PROSE
BUT LOVE TO MY ART & ZEAL FOR MY COUNTRY A MUCH GREATER	594D	PUB ADDRESS/N	PROSE
REPRESENTATIVE OF THAT LOVE CALLD FRIENDSHIP	610D	V LAST JUDG/N	PROSE
EVEN THE DEVILS LOVE ONE ANOTHER IN THEIR WAY	616B	V LAST JUDG/N	PROSE
THE [LOVE] AND [FRIENDSHIP] OF THOSE WITH WHOM TO BE CONNECTED	620D	JERUSALEM 3	PROSE
[IS REMINDED THAT THE ANCIENTS ENTRUSTED THEIR LOVE TO THEIR WRITING]	621A	JERUSALEM 3	*PROSE
OUR LORD WHO IS THE GOD [OF FIRE] AND LORD [OF LOVE]	621A	JERUSALEM 3	PROSE
YET I PRETEND TO LOVE TO SEE TO CONVERSE WITH DAILY AS MAN WITH MAN	621A	JERUSALEM 3	PROSE
& [LOVE] ME FOR THIS ENERGETIC EXERTION OF MY TALENT	621B	JERUSALEM 3	PROSE
SPREADING HIS BEAMS OF LOVE & DICTATING THE WORDS OF THIS MILD SONG	622	JERUSALEM 4	5
I AM IN YOU AND YOU IN ME MUTUAL IN LOVE DIVINE	622	JERUSALEM 4	7
FIBRES OF LOVE FROM MAN TO MAN THRO ALBION'S PLEASANT LAND	622	JERUSALEM 4	8
SEEKING TO KEEP MY SOUL A VICTIM TO THY LOVE WHICH BINDS	622	JERUSALEM 4	25
O SAVIOUR POUR UPON ME THY SPIRIT OF MEEKNESS & LOVE	623	JERUSALEM 5	21
DRAWING JERUSALEM IN ANGUISH OF MATERNAL LOVE	624	JERUSALEM 5	47
OF LIGHT AND LOVE THEIR LITTLE CHILDREN STAND WITH ARROWS OF GOLD	631	JERUSALEM 11	20
HER JOY AND LOVE A SHADE A SHADE OF SWEET REPOSE	631	JERUSALEM 12	2
ENAMELD WITH LOVE & KINDNESS & THE TILES ENGRAVEN GOLD	632	JERUSALEM 12	31
IS A CREATION OF MERCY & LOVE FROM THE SATANIC VOID	634	JERUSALEM 13	45
WAYWARD LOVE & EVERY SORROW & DISTRESS IS CARVED HERE	638	JERUSALEM 16	64
THEY WOULD NEVER LOVE MY POWER IF THEY DID NOT SEEK TO DESTROY	639	JERUSALEM 17	23
AND GENERATING LOVE A PRETENCE OF LOVE TO DESTROY LOVE	639	JERUSALEM 17	26
THEY KNOW NOT WHY THEY LOVE NOR WHEREFORE THEY SICKEN & DIE	639	JERUSALEM 17	29
CALLING THAT HOLY LOVE WHICH IS ENVY REVENGE & CRUELTY	639	JERUSALEM 17	30
NOR SONS NOR HATEFUL PEACE & LOVE NOR SOFT COMPLACENCIES	640	JERUSALEM 18	14
FATHER AND SON AND LIGHT AND LOVE ALL BOLD ASPERITIES	640	JERUSALEM 18	21
WEEPING IN PLEADINGS OF LOVE IN THE WEB OF DESPAIR	642	JERUSALEM 20	4
GOING IN AND OUT BEFORE HIM IN HIS LOVE AND SWEET AFFECTION	642	JERUSALEM 20	10
NOR PITY NOR LOVE NOR KIND FORGIVENESS O IF I HAVE SINNED	643	JERUSALEM 20	25
FORGIVE & PITY ME O UNFOLD THY VEIL IN MERCY & LOVE	643	JERUSALEM 20	26
OF LOVE THOU REFUSEDST TO LET ME GO ALBION BEHELD THY BEAUTY	643	JERUSALEM 20	32
BECAUSE IT INCLOSD PITY & LOVE BECAUSE WE LOVD ONE-ANOTHER	643	JERUSALEM 20	35
ASTONISHD AT HIS BEAUTY & PERFECTION THOU FORGAVEST HIS FURIOUS LOVE	643	JERUSALEM 20	37
THEN WAS A TIME OF LOVE O WHY IS IT PASSED AWAY	643	JERUSALEM 20	41
ALL LOVE IS LOST TERROR SUCCEEDS & [RATRED] HATRED INSTEAD OF LOVE	645	JERUSALEM 22	* 10
I BROUGHT LOVE INTO LIGHT OF DAY TO PRIDE IN CHASTE BEAUTY	645	JERUSALEM 22	17
I BROUGHT LOVE INTO LIGHT & FANCIED INNOCENCE IS NO MORE	645	JERUSALEM 22	18
HE FELT THAT LOVE AND PITY ARE THE SAME A SOFT REPOSE	646	JERUSALEM 23	14
THINKING TO BRING LOVE INTO LIGHT OF DAY TO JERUSALEM'S SHAME	647	JERUSALEM 24	5
TO BE THE SPORT OF ACCIDENT TO WASTE IN WRATH & LOVE A WEARY	647	JERUSALEM 24	15
WHEN JERUSALEM WAS THY HEART'S DESIRE IN TIMES OF YOUTH & LOVE	647	JERUSALEM 24	37

	PAGE	TITLE	LINE
LOVE (CONTINUED)			
AND LONDON WALKD IN EVERY NATION MUTUAL IN LOVE & HARMONY	647	JERUSALEM 24	43
CREATE MY SPIRIT TO THY LOVE	651	FIELDS FROM/J	71
EVERY ORNAMENT OF PERFECTION AND EVERY LABOUR OF LOVE . .	652	JERUSALEM 28	1
O CRUEL PITY O DARK DECEIT CAN LOVE SEEK FOR DOMINION . .	654	JERUSALEM 29	60
AND LEARN WHAT TIS TO ABSORB THE MAN YOU SPIRITS OF PITY & LOVE	655	JERUSALEM 29	71
I FEEL THE IRON THREADS OF LOVE & JEALOUSY & DESPAIR .	657	JERUSALEM 31	49
THE SACRIFICE OF FANATIC LOVE WHY LOVED I JERUSALEM . . .	660	JERUSALEM 33	43
WHEREFORE DID I LOVING CREATE LOVE WHICH NEVER YET . . .	660	JERUSALEM 33	45
FOR THE DIVINE APPEARANCE IS BROTHERHOOD BUT I AM LOVE . .	660	JERUSALEM 33	52
AND KEEPING THEM FROM SIN BY THE MILD COUNSELS OF HIS LOVE	662	JERUSALEM 35	8
IN THE LOVE OF TIRZAH HE SAID DOUBT IS MY FOOD DAY & NIGHT	662	JERUSALEM 36	7
TURNING FROM UNIVERSAL LOVE PETRIFIC AS HE WENT	664	JERUSALEM 38	7
SAYING ALBION OUR WARS ARE WARS OF LIFE & WOUNDS OF LOVE	664	JERUSALEM 38	14
MUTUAL IN ONE ANOTHER'S LOVE AND WRATH ALL RENEWING . .	664	JERUSALEM 38	16
TO WHICH ALL LINEAMENTS TEND & SEEK WITH LOVE & SYMPATHY	672	JERUSALEM 43	21
IN THE TERRIBLE FAMILY CONTENTIONS OF THOSE WHO LOVE EACH OTHER	672	JERUSALEM 43	38
WITH ONE ACCORD IN LOVE SUBLIME & AS ON CHERUBS WINGS . .	674	JERUSALEM 44	1
IN LOVE & JEALOUSY IMMINGLED & CALLING IT RELIGION . .	674	JERUSALEM 44	27
OF LOVE & HARMONY IN MAN EXPAND THY EVER LOVELY GATES .	675	JERUSALEM 44	42
THUNDER IN THE MIDST OF KINDNESS & LOVE THAT KILLS ITS BELOVED	677	JERUSALEM 48	16
FROM THIS SWEET PLACE MATERNAL LOVE AWOKE JERUSALEM . . .	677	JERUSALEM 48	18
OF SPIRITUAL HATE FROM WHICH SPRINGS SEXUAL LOVE AS IRON CHAINS	685	JERUSALEM 54	12
TO THE GOLDEN LOOM OF LOVE TO THE MOTH-LABOURD WOOF . . .	688	JERUSALEM 56	13
FOR THEY LABOUR FOR LIFE & LOVE REGARDLESS OF ANY ONE .	691	JERUSALEM 59	37
THAT RAHAB & TIRZAH MAY EXIST & LIVE & BREATHE & LOVE .	692	JERUSALEM 59	43
AND IN MY LOVE I WILL LEAD THEE LOVELY SHADOW OF SLEEPING ALBION	693	JERUSALEM 60	37
AND BY THESE VISIONS OF PITY & LOVE BECAUSE OF ALBION'S DEATH	693	JERUSALEM 60	64
GIVE FORTH THY PITY & LOVE FEAR NOT LO I AM WITH THEE ALWAYS	694	JERUSALEM 60	67
THO SHE HATES HE CALLS HER AGAIN IN LOVE I LOVE MY DEAR JOSEPH	694	JERUSALEM 61	8
OF LOVE OF HIM WHO LOVES ME	694	JERUSALEM 61	13
BEFORE I HAD EVER BEHELD WITH LOVE THE FACE OF JEHOVAH OR KNOWN	695	JERUSALEM 61	42
EVERY HARLOT WAS ONCE A VIRGIN EVERY CRIMINAL AN INFANT LOVE	695	JERUSALEM 61	52
TO FREEZE LOVE & INNOCENCE INTO THE GOLD & SILVER OF THE MERCHANT	699	JERUSALEM 64	23
WITHOUT FORGIVENESS OF SIN LOVE IS ITSELF ETERNAL DEATH	699	JERUSALEM 64	24
CRIMSON WITH WRATH & GREEN WITH JEALOUSY DAZLING WITH LOVE	699	JERUSALEM 64	28
HOW RAGD THE GOLDEN HORSES OF URIZEN COMPELLD TO THE CHARIOT OF LOVE	700	JERUSALEM 65	47
HE WHO WILL NOT COMINGLE IN LOVE MUST BE ADJOIND BY HATE	703	JERUSALEM 66	56
ASHAMED TO GIVE LOVE OPENLY TO THE PITEOUS & MERCIFUL MAN	704	JERUSALEM 67	19
OF AFFLICTION OF LOVE OF SWEET DESPAIR OF TORMENT UNENDURABLE	705	JERUSALEM 67	51
IN CHANNELS THRO MY FIERY LIMBS O LOVE O PITY O FEAR . .	705	JERUSALEM 67	54
O PAIN O THE PANGS THE BITTER PANGS OF LOVE FORSAKEN . .	705	JERUSALEM 67	55
SHRIEK NOT SO MY ONLY LOVE I REFUSE THY JOYS I DRINK . .	705	JERUSALEM 67	61
MOLECH RUSHES INTO THE KINGS IN LOVE TO THE BEAUTIFUL DAUGHTERS	706	JERUSALEM 68	28
IF YOU DARE REND THEIR VEIL WITH YOUR SPEAR YOU ARE HEALED OF LOVE	706	JERUSALEM 68	42
IN CRUELTIES OF HOLINESS TO REFUSE THE JOYS OF LOVE TO BRING	707	JERUSALEM 68	59
TO THE PLACE OF THE AMALEKITE I AM DRUNK WITH UNSATIATED LOVE	707	JERUSALEM 68	62
BUT NOW MY SOUL IS HARROWD WITH GRIEF & FEAR & LOVE & DESIRE	707	JERUSALEM 68	66
AND NOW I HATE & NOW I LOVE & INTELLECT IS NO MORE . . .	707	JERUSALEM 68	67
THERE IS NO TIME FOR ANY THING BUT THE TORMENTS OF LOVE & DESIRE	707	JERUSALEM 68	68
IN ALL ITS MEMBERS IN ETERNAL TORMENT OF LOVE & JEALOUSY	707	JERUSALEM 69	7
TILL THE TIME OF LOVE IS PASSED IN EVER VARYING DELIGHTS	707	JERUSALEM 69	24
PLOTTING TO DEVOUR ALBION'S BODY OF HUMANITY & LOVE . . .	708	JERUSALEM 70	9
BEAMS MILD ALL LOVE AND ALL PERFECTION THAT WHEN THE LIPS	709	JERUSALEM 70	24
CONTINUALLY BUILDING CONTINUALLY DECAYING BECAUSE OF LOVE & JEALOUSY	712A	JERUSALEM 72	PROSE
WHO GUIDE THE GREAT WINE-PRESS OF LOVE FOUR PRECIOUS STONES THAT GATE	712	JERUSALEM 72	52
OF GOOD & EVIL THEY DIVIDED HIM IN LOVE UPON THE THAMES & SENT	715	JERUSALEM 74	36
THEN WAS A TIME OF JOY AND LOVE	718	ENGLND AWAKE/J	8
IN UNREVIVING DEATH MY LOVE MY LUVAH ORDERD ME IN NIGHT	722	JERUSALEM 80	17
FOR IN OUR BATTLES WE THE SLAIN MEN VIEW WITH PITY AND LOVE	722	JERUSALEM 80	25
HE SENT THEM OVER THE NARROW SEAS IN PITY AND LOVE . . .	722	JERUSALEM 80	42
HAND SLEPT ON SKIDDAW'S TOP DRAWN BY THE LOVE OF BEAUTIFUL	723	JERUSALEM 80	57
THE CRUEL WARRIOR I HAVE REFUSED TO GIVE LOVE TO MERLIN THE PITEOUS	723	JERUSALEM 81	2
HE BRINGS TO ME THE IMAGES OF HIS LOVE & I REJECT IN CHASTITY	724	JERUSALEM 81	3
FOR MEN ARE CAUGHT BY LOVE WOMAN IS CAUGHT BY PRIDE . .	724	JERUSALEM 81	6
THAT LOVE MAY ONLY BE OBTAIND IN THE PASSAGES OF DEATH . .	724	JERUSALEM 81	7
IN HEAVEN LOVE BEGETS LOVE BUT FEAR IS THE PARENT OF EARTHLY LOVE	725	JERUSALEM 81	15

1145

		PAGE	TITLE	LINE

LOVE   (CONTINUED)

Entry	PAGE	TITLE	LINE
AND HE WHO WILL NOT BEND TO LOVE MUST BE SUBDUD BY FEAR	725	JERUSALEM 81	16
I GATHER OUR ETERNAL FATE OUTCASTS FROM LIFE AND LOVE . .	725	JERUSALEM 82	2
LOOK HYLE IS BECOME AN INFANT LOVE LOOK BEHOLD SEE HIM LIE	725	JERUSALEM 82	37
BINDING HIS WRISTS & ANKLES WITH THE IRON ARMS OF LOVE .	726	JERUSALEM 82	71
BEGAN HER DOLOROUS TASK OF LOVE IN THE WINE-PRESS OF LUVAH	726	JERUSALEM 82	75
TO FORM THE WORM INTO A FORM OF LOVE BY TEARS & PAIN .	726	JERUSALEM 82	76
BUT PANGS OF LOVE DRAW ME DOWN TO MY LOINS WHICH ARE .	727	JERUSALEM 82	83
IN CHASTE APPEARANCES FOR SWEET DECEITS OF LOVE & MODESTY	727	JERUSALEM 83	31
IN HEAD & HEART & REINS THREE UNIVERSES OF LOVE & BEAUTY	730	JERUSALEM 86	3
COMFORTING SOUNDS OF LOVE & HARMONY & ON THY FEET . . .	731	JERUSALEM 86	30
AMONG THE GOLDEN LOOMS OF CATHEDRON SENDING FIBRES OF LOVE	731	JERUSALEM 86	40
TILL IT BECAME A SEPARATED CLOUD OF BEAUTY GRACE & LOVE	732	JERUSALEM 86	55
ENVYING EACH OTHER YET DESIRING IN ALL DEVOURING LOVE .	732	JERUSALEM 86	64
DESARTS LOS FIRST BROKE SILENCE & BEGAN TO UTTER HIS LOVE	732	JERUSALEM 87	2
WITH LOVE BE THOU ASSURED I NEVER WILL BE THY SLAVE . .	732	JERUSALEM 87	15
LET MAN'S DELIGHT BE LOVE BUT WOMAN'S DELIGHT BE PRIDE	732	JERUSALEM 87	16
THAT HE WHO LOVES JESUS MAY LOATHE TERRIFIED FEMALE LOVE	733	JERUSALEM 88	20
SHOOTING OUT IN SWEET PLEASURE HER BOSOM IN MILKY LOVE .	733	JERUSALEM 88	28
FOR I WILL MAKE THEIR PLACES OF JOY & LOVE EXCREMENTITIOUS	734	JERUSALEM 88	39
UNPERMANENT FOR EVER BECAUSE OF LOVE & JEALOUSY	734	JERUSALEM 88	42
WHILE LOS STOOD AT HIS ANVIL IN WRATH THE VICTIM OF THEIR LOVE	734	JERUSALEM 88	46
AND HATE DIVIDING THE SPACE OF LOVE WITH BRAZEN COMPASSES	734	JERUSALEM 88	47
HIS RAGE OR HIS MILDNESS WERE VAIN SHE SCATTERED HIS LOVE ON THE WIND	734	JERUSALEM 88	51
UPON THE HERMAPHRODITIC WINE-PRESSES OF LOVE & WRATH . .	734	JERUSALEM 88	58
A WINE-PRESS OF LOVE & WRATH DOUBLE (HERMAPHRODITIC) . .	734	JERUSALEM 89 *	4
TO THE EMBRACE OF LOVE & TO THE MINGLING OF SOFT FIBRES	736	JERUSALEM 90	9
ONE FIRST IN FRIENDSHIP & LOVE THEN A DIVINE FAMILY & IN THE MIDST	738	JERUSALEM 91	20
ENITHARMON'S NAME IS NOTHING BEFORE YOU YOU FORGET ALL MY LOVE	740	JERUSALEM 93	3
THE MOTHER'S LOVE OF OBEDIENCE IS FORGOTTEN & YOU SEEK A LOVE	740	JERUSALEM 93	4
COULD YOU LOVE ME RINTRAH IF YOU PRIDE NOT IN MY LOVE . .	740	JERUSALEM 93	7
JESUS SAID WOULDEST THOU LOVE ONE WHO NEVER DIED	743	JERUSALEM 96	23
ETERNALLY FOR MAN MAN COULD NOT EXIST FOR MAN IS LOVE	743	JERUSALEM 96	26
AS GOD IS LOVE EVERY KINDNESS TO ANOTHER IS A LITTLE DEATH	743	JERUSALEM 96	27
AND THE BOW IS A MALE & FEMALE & THE QUIVER OF THE ARROWS OF LOVE	744	JERUSALEM 97	12
OPEN THE HIDDEN HEART IN WARS OF MUTUAL BENEVOLENCE WARS OF LOVE	744	JERUSALEM 97	14
HE MUST MEAN THE MEER LOVE OF CIVILITY	750	EV GOSPEL(C)/N	21
TREMBLED AT DISCOVERY OF LOVE	753	EV GOSPEL(E)/N	6
AND THE BREATH DIVINE IS LOVE	754	EV GOSPEL(E)/N	42
THAT HAVE FORGOT YOUR ANCIENT LOVE	754	EV GOSPEL(E)/N	51
AND THO YOU CANNOT LOVE BUT HATE	755	EV GOSPEL(E)/N	55
WHAT WAS THY LOVE LET ME [SEE'T] SEE IT	755	EV GOSPEL(E)/N *	57
WAS IT LOVE OR DARK DECEIT	755	EV GOSPEL(E)/N	58
LOVE TOO LONG FROM ME HAS FLED	755	EV GOSPEL(E)/N	59
BLASPHEMING LOVE BLASPHEMING THEE	755	EV GOSPEL(E)/N	72
. . . FIXT IN THE FIRMAMENT BY PEACE BROTHERHOOD AND LOVE	781	GHOST ABEL 2	26
AS THEY DO FUN I LOVE BUT TOO MUCH FUN IS OF ALL THINGS	793C	LETTER 5	PROSE
WHO LOVE & ADMIRE YOUR WORKS BUT ABOVE ALL FOR THE SAKE OF THE ARTS	795B	LETTER 6	PROSE
"FORGET YOUR SERVICES TO US OR ANY WAY NEGLECT TO LOVE &"	800A	LETTER 12	PROSE
"RECIEVE MY & MY HUSBAND'S LOVE & AFFECTION &"	801A	LETTER 12	PROSE
RECIEVE MY HEARTY LOVE & RESPECT I AM DEAR SIR YOUR SINCERE	801C	LETTER 13	PROSE
FAREWELL MY BEST FRIEND REMEMBER ME & MY WIFE IN LOVE &	802D	LETTER 14	PROSE
MY & MY WIFE & SISTER'S LOVE & RESPECTS TO MRS BUTTS .	803C	LETTER 15	PROSE
TO YOU PLEASE TO REMEMBER US BOTH IN LOVE TO	807B	LETTER 17	PROSE
WIFE WHO DESIRES HER KINDEST LOVE TO MRS BUTTS & YOURSELF	808C	LETTER 19	PROSE
MY WIFE JOINS WITH ME IN LOVE TO YOU & MRS BUTTS . . .	810A	LETTER 20	PROSE
MY WIFE JOINS WITH ME IN LOVE TO YOU & MRS FLAXMAN . . .	811A	LETTER 21	PROSE
MY WIFE DESIRES HER KINDEST LOVE TO MRS BUTTS & I HAVE .	813B	LETTER 22	PROSE
PRAY GIVE MY LOVE TO MRS BUTTS & YOUR FAMILY I AM YOURS SINCERELY	813C	LETTER 22	PROSE
& IS MINE PRAY GIVE MY WIFE'S LOVE WITH MINE TO MRS BUTTS	815D	LETTER 23	PROSE
WELFARE OF YOUR FAMILY ACCEPT MY SINCERE LOVE & RESPECT	816A	LETTER 23	PROSE
DESIRES ME TO COPY OUT & SEND YOU WITH HER KIND LOVE .	816D	LETTER 24	PROSE
FOR I KNOW THAT THE PUBLIC ARE MY FRIENDS & LOVE MY WORKS	821C	LETTER 25	PROSE
MY WIFE JOINS ME IN LOVE TO YOU BOTH I AM SINCERELY YOURS	822A	LETTER 25	PROSE
& YOURS & MINE PRAY GIVE MY & MY WIFE'S LOVE TO MRS BUTTS	826A	LETTER 27	PROSE
FAMILY ENJOY HEALTH MY MUCH TERRIFIED WIFE JOINS ME IN LOVE	829A	LETTER 28	PROSE
SPIRITS OF JUST MEN MADE PERFECT BY LOVE & GRATITUDE .	834A	LETTER 33	PROSE
MY WIFE JOINS ME IN RESPECTS & LOVE TO YOU	837B	LETTER 35	PROSE
MY WIFE DESIRES ME TO EXPRESS HER LOVE TO YOU	837D	LETTER 36	PROSE
OBJECT OF HIS LOVE & ADMIRATION	838C	LETTER 37	PROSE
MY WIFE JOINS ME IN SINCERE LOVE TO YOU PLEASE TO . . .	840A	LETTER 38	PROSE
AT BRIGHTON MY WIFE JOINS ME IN LOVE TO YOU	843A	LETTER 42	PROSE
SO TAKE MY LEAVE FOR THE PRESENT WITH THE JOINT LOVE OF	845A	LETTER 43	PROSE
AND I KNOW YOU WILL LOVE HIM FOR IT	846B	LETTER 44	PROSE
CONTINUES TO GET BETTER & JOINS ME IN MY WARMEST LOVE &	849C	LETTER 45	PROSE
& HER & TO ALL WHOM WE LOVE THAT IS TO ALL SUSSEX . .	851A	LETTER 49	PROSE
OF MY LIFE HE IS THE ENEMY OF CONJUGAL LOVE AND IS THE .	852A	LETTER 50	PROSE
MY WIFE JOINS ME IN LOVE TO YOU & TO OUR DEAR FRIEND & .	853A	LETTER 51	*PROSE
MY WIFE JOINS ME IN LOVE & IN REJOICING IN MISS POOLE'S	855C	LETTER 53	PROSE
PRAY ACCEPT MY AND MY WIFE'S SINCEREST LOVE AND GRATITUDE	861B	LETTER 58	PROSE
PRAY REMEMBER ME WITH KIND LOVE TO MRS LINNELL . . .	873D	LETTER 78	PROSE
THESE DIED FOR LOVE MINISTERING ANGELS	SUPP	INSC HERVEY	*TITLE
MY PRETTY ROSE TREE THE GARDEN OF LOVE A LITTLE BOY LOST	SUPP	LETTER 66A	*PROSE

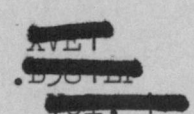